797,885 Books
are available to read at

www.ForgottenBooks.com

Forgotten Books' App
Available for mobile, tablet & eReader

ISBN 978-1-333-82951-3
PIBN 10656642

This book is a reproduction of an important historical work. Forgotten Books uses state-of-the-art technology to digitally reconstruct the work, preserving the original format whilst repairing imperfections present in the aged copy. In rare cases, an imperfection in the original, such as a blemish or missing page, may be replicated in our edition. We do, however, repair the vast majority of imperfections successfully; any imperfections that remain are intentionally left to preserve the state of such historical works.

Forgotten Books is a registered trademark of FB &c Ltd.
Copyright © 2017 FB &c Ltd.
FB &c Ltd, Dalton House, 60 Windsor Avenue, London, SW19 2RR.
Company number 08720141. Registered in England and Wales.

For support please visit www.forgottenbooks.com

1 MONTH OF FREE READING

at

www.ForgottenBooks.com

By purchasing this book you are eligible for one month membership to ForgottenBooks.com, giving you unlimited access to our entire collection of over 700,000 titles via our web site and mobile apps.

To claim your free month visit:
www.forgottenbooks.com/free656642

* Offer is valid for 45 days from date of purchase. Terms and conditions apply.

English
Français
Deutsche
Italiano
Español
Português

www.forgottenbooks.com

Mythology Photography **Fiction** Fishing Christianity **Art** Cooking Essays Buddhism Freemasonry Medicine **Biology** Music **Ancient Egypt** Evolution Carpentry Physics Dance Geology **Mathematics** Fitness Shakespeare **Folklore** Yoga Marketing **Confidence** Immortality Biographies Poetry **Psychology** Witchcraft Electronics Chemistry History **Law** Accounting **Philosophy** Anthropology Alchemy Drama Quantum Mechanics Atheism Sexual Health **Ancient History Entrepreneurship** Languages Sport Paleontology Needlework Islam **Metaphysics** Investment Archaeology Parenting Statistics Criminology **Motivational**

PIONEERS AND PROMINENT MEN OF UTAH

COMPRISING

PHOTOGRAPHS - GENEALOGIES - BIOGRAPHIES

PIONEERS

ARE THOSE MEN AND WOMEN WHO CAME TO UTAH BY WAGON, HAND CART OR AFOOT, BETWEEN JULY 24, 1847, AND DECEMBER 30, 1868, BEFORE THE RAILROAD

PROMINENT MEN

ARE STAKE PRESIDENTS, WARD BISHOPS, GOVERNORS, MEMBERS OF THE BENCH, ETC., WHO CAME TO UTAH AFTER THE COMING OF THE RAILROAD

The Early History
of the Church of Jesus Christ of
Latter-Day Saints

VOLUME 2 OF 2

ILLUSTRATED

By

FRANK ESSHOM

The greatest inheritance of man is a posterity; the greatest inheritance of a posterity is a Christian Ancestry—that these greatest inheritances may live in record, this volume is issued.

SALT LAKE CITY, UTAH
UTAH PIONEERS BOOK PUBLISHING COMPANY
PUBLISHERS
1913

COPYRIGHTED, 1913
BY
UTAH PIONEERS BOOK
PUBLISHING COMPANY

COMPOSITION, ELECTROTYPING, PRINTING
AND BINDING BY THE
W. B. CONKEY COMPANY
HAMMOND, INDIANA

GENEALOGIES AND BIOGRAPHIES

GENEALOGIES AND BIOGRAPHIES

These genealogies are alphabetically arranged, and show, if the information was furnished, who was the oldest member of the family that came to Utah; his father's name and his mother's maiden name; when and where he was born; when he came to Utah; the company he came with; who he married, and when, and where; who the father and mother of the wife or wives were; where they lived, or when they came to Utah; whom the children of the "oldest member" of the family were, when they were born, and who they married—continuing this genealogy with the genealogies of his lineal male descendants (who are subscribers to this history), to any generation that may intervene between the "oldest member" of the family and this date—September, 1913.

BOLD FACED CAPITAL letters indicate the "oldest member" or head of the family.
CAPITAL LETTERS indicate sons, or lineal male descendants.
Where two or more brothers came to Utah, and their father and mother did not come, they will be found in the regular alphabetical order and not in family group.

The abbreviations—b. is for born, m. for married, and d. for died, where used in the family record.
The genealogy of the father of the wife will be found in the regular alphabetical order.
Within the parentheses (—) will be found the names of the parents of the person who precedes the parentheses.

A

ABBOTT, MYRON (son of Stephen Abbott, born Aug. 16, 1804, Providence, Pa., died Oct. 19, 1843, at Nauvoo, and Abigail Smith, born Sept. 11, 1806, Williamson, Ontario Co., N. Y.; married Dec. 1, 1825. She came to Utah October, 1849, and attached to Capt. James Brown's family, settled in Ogden, when there were only six families there). He was born Dec. 1, 1837, Perry, Pike Co., Ill. Came to Utah 1849.
Married Laura Josephine Allen April 25, 1861, Ogden, Utah (daughter of Orville Morgan Allen, born June 9, 1805, in Pike county, Mo., pioneer 1852, died 1893, and Jane Wilson). She was born April 4, 1846, and came to Utah with father. Their children: Myron Alma b. Feb. 15, 1862, m. Mary M. Leavitt; Stephen Orville b. June 9, 1863; Mary Luella b. Dec. 2, 1865, m. Thomas D. Leavitt April 14, 1881; James Smith b. Jan. 23, 1868, m. Chloe E. Robinson Aug. 19, 1892; William Elias b. Oct. 16, 1869, m. Mary Jane Leavitt March 20, 1890; John Austin b. Aug. 12, 1871, m. Chrissie E. Whitney March 12, 1895; Josepha Jane b. April 17, 1873, m. Robert Roberts Nov. 19, 1890; Abigail J. b. Sept. 20, 1875. Family home Ogden, Utah.
Married Emily Malin 1870, Salt Lake City. She was born Sept. 25, 1839, at Angrogne, Piedmont, Italy. Only child: Emily Pauline b. Dec. 24, 1871, m. John Maddock Sept. 21, 1892.
Married Lovisa Leavitt Jan. 1, 1878 (daughter of Lemuel Sturdifont Leavitt, pioneer October, 1849, and Melvina Thompson—married Oct. 15, 1850, Salt Lake City). She was born Oct. 22, 1861, Santa Clara, Utah. Their children: Melvina b. May 14, 1879, m. John Horsley; Mary Isabelle b. Feb. 4, 1881, m. George Woodruff; Ezra Abiel b. July 12, 1882, d. 1897; Sidney Smith b. March 7, 1884, d. 1901; Lemuel Raymond b. Nov. 25, 1885; Thomas Edward b. March 31, 1887; David Arthur b. Sept. 23, 1888; Myron Decatur b. March 4, 1890; Lyman b. April 28, 1892; George Nathan b. March 17, 1894; Israel b. Feb. 20, 1896; Clarence Leon b. Feb. 10, 1898; Laura Josephine b. Sept. 6, 1902. Family home Bunkerville.
Married Emma Knight March 4, 1886, St. George, Utah (daughter of Samuel Knight), who was born Dec. 26, 1863, Santa Clara, Utah. Their child: Samuel b. May 2, 1889. Family home Bunkerville.
Settled at Wilson, Weber county, 1866; moved to Plymouth, Box Elder county, 1870, and to Bunkerville, Nev., 1877. Member of school board and justice of the peace many years. Lieutenant in Utah militia under Brigham Johnston's approach. Member U. S. Marshal Burton's posse at Kingdon Fort, and one of the eight men who took the rolling breastwork into the fort before its surrender, and was later one of Burton's chief witnesses at his murder trial. Bishop's counselor 30 years. Died Sept. 3, 1907.

ABBOTT, MYRON ALMA (son of Myron Abbott and Laura Josephine Allen). Born Feb. 15, 1862, Ogden, Utah.
Married Mary Matilda Leavitt April 14, 1881, St. George, Utah (daughter of Lemuel Sturdifont Leavitt and Betsy Mortinson; latter came to Utah 1862). She was born Nov. 6, 1864, Santa Clara, Utah. Their children: Stephen Perry b. Oct. 21, 1883, m. Clara Ann Etta Poulson July 20, 1905; Edward Lawrence b. Dec. 9, 1886, m. Josephine Bennett Sept. 17, 1909; James Howard b. Oct. 30, 1889; Mary Josepha b. Sept. 27, 1892; William Leon b. April 16, 1895; George Myron b. April 15, 1899; Lemuel Brooks b. March 27, 1902; Thomas Lay b. Aug. 8, 1905. Family home Annabella, Utah.
He is the eighth generation from George and Hannah Chandler Abbott, first settlers of Andover, Mass., 1643. Commissioner Sevier county 1894; justice of the peace 1898; sheriff three terms 1904-10. Engaged in farming, mining, and interested in good horse breeding and the upbuild of his native state.

ABBOTT, WILLIAM (son of Thomas Abbott and Elizabeth Jackson of Irchester, Northamptonshire, Eng.). Born Feb. 22, 1808. Came to Utah Oct. 18, 1865, following Henry Chipman company, which arrived Sept. 15.
Married Charlotte Ellerbone Dec. 10, 1828, Irchester, Eng. (daughter of Joseph Ellerbone and Elizabeth Frear of Irchester). She was born Jan. 6, 1808. Their children: Two girls, twins, d. infants; John, m. Esther Robinson; James, d. aged 21; Ely, m. Emily Bowden; William, d. aged 17; Thomas m. Ellen Routhen; Harriett, d. aged 16; Mary Ann Elizabeth b. Dec. 10, 1843, m. Thomas Cheshire Jan. 7, 1866; Joseph, m. Mary Percival. Family home Irchester, Eng.
Elder; teacher. One of Heber C. Kimball's converts (1840). For years his home was kept open to all in the English mission field, and as a meeting place for converts. Died June 22, 1889, Salt Lake City.

ABEGGLEN, ULRICH (son of Christian Abegglen, born November, 1790, at Gundlischvand, and Margaretha Gertsch, born Feb. 3, 1799, at Lauterbrunnen, both of Canton Bern, Switzerland; latter a pioneer Oct. 29, 1862, William H. Dame company). He was born March 1, 1840, at Gundlischvand. Came to Utah Sept. 13, 1861, a few days preceding arrival of the main company of Sextus E. Johnson (Sept. 24), the last immigrant train of that season.
Married Magdalena Galli 1863 (daughter of Peter Galli and Magdalena Hasler, married at Gundlischvand—pioneers September, 1861). She was born Aug. 23, 1837, and came to Utah in 1860. Their children: John b. Oct. 29, 1864, d. same day; Maria Anna Elizabeth b. June 29, 1866, m. David Robb Dec. 16, 1891; Maria Magdalena b. May 3, 1869, m. John P. Allen Oct. 24, 1895; Alice Priscilla b. June 29, 1871, m. Frank Robb Jan. 20, 1892; Emma Luella b. June 1, 1873, m. Thomas Mathews July 19, 1897; Ulrich Lorenz b. March 18, 1879. Family home Midway, Wasatch county, Utah.
Pioneer Oct. 29, 1864, to Wasatch county. Missionary to Switzerland 1901-04. Assisted in founding of town of Midway 1865.

ABEL ISAAC (son of John Abel of Sheffield, Eng.). Born May 14, 1829, Yorkshire, Eng. Came to Utah October, 1863.
Married Ann Methley Dec. 25, 1849, Yorkshire, Eng. (daughter of Charles Methley and Rebecca Eaton of that shire). She was born June 27, 1824. Their children: Ellen, m. Thomas Steele; Mary Ann, m. Elijah Bourne; Emily, m. William Paxman; Rosa, m. Elijah Bourne; Sarah Ann, and Isaac Cynosuer, died; George Edward, m. Mary Ellen Shelley; Elizabeth, m. Stephen Baker. Family home American Fork, Utah.
Secretary for high priest's quorum. Tax collector. Farmer. Died Dec. 7, 1907.

ABEL, GEORGE EDWARD (son of Isaac Abel and Ann Methley). Born Oct. 27, 1865, American Fork, Utah.
Married Mary Ellen Shelley Nov. 11, 1885, Logan, Utah (daughter of Thomas Shelley and Charlotte Elsmore of England). She was born June 2, 1865. Their children: George Edward b. Aug. 15, 1886, m. Lottie Hunter; Thomas Ammon b. March 1, 1889, m. Frances Brook; Charlotte Ann b. Dec. 30, 1893; Isaac b. Sept. 4, 1896, died; Rosa b. April 13, 1898; Meda Emily b. July 31, 1900; Frances Bray b. Nov. 12, 1902; Methley b. Jan. 20, 1905; Mary Ellen b. Jan. 24, 1908. Family home American Fork, Utah.
High priest; missionary to Samoa 1890-03; bishop's counselor. Farmer.

708 PIONEERS AND PROMINENT MEN OF UTAH

ABPLANALP, PETER (son of Johannes Abplanalp and Katharina Schilt, both of Brienzwyler, Canton Bern, Switzerland). He was born March 2, 1829, Brienzwyler. Came to Utah 1861.
Married Margaretha Eggler in 1856, Brienzwyler, Switzerland (daughter of Johannes Eggler and Margaretha Schilt, immigrants Pikepond, Sullivan county, N. Y. from Switzerland). She was born Feb. 22, 1835, and came to Utah with husband. Their children: Peter, m. Mary Alder; Margaretha b. April 4, 1859, m. Edward Watkins Oct. 28, 1880; Elizabeth b. Aug. 27, 1858, m. Jedediah Wardle; George, m. Amanda Wardle; John, m. Avey Wall; Joseph Sidney, m. Hannah Jenkins; Emily, m. William Workman; Franklin, m. Polly Howard; Heinrich, m. Lillie Ross; William, m. Bessie Jenkins. Family resided Mound City, Midway and Vernal, Utah.
Lieutenant in territorial militia. High priest; bishop of Vernal. Farmer and miner. Died May 28, 1900, Vernal, Utah.

ACORD, ABRAM (son of Zurr Acord and Martha Luster of Germany, later of Ohio, Indiana, and Sidney, Iowa). Born March 22, 1830, in Fremont county, Ohio. Came to Utah 1861, William K. McKissack company.
Married Nancy Frost March 24, 1855, in Atchison county, Mo. (daughter of Samuel Buchanan Frost and Rebecca Forman of the Carolinas, Tennessee and Iowa, pioneers 1861, William K. McKissack company). She was born April 22, 1840, in Hancock county, Ill. Their children: Oliver b. Jan. 29, 1858, m. Electa Webb; Frederick St. Clair b. May 29, 1858, m. Olive Allred; Henry Luster b. May 23, 1861, m. Christina Larsen; Mary Frances b. June 3, 1863, m. Henry Christopher Strate; Jennie b. Dec. 12 1865, m. Joseph Smith Hyde; William Anderson b. March 28, 1868, died; Elizabeth b. Oct. 15, 1870, m. Erastus Beck; Nora b. Feb. 14, 1872, died; Abram Fletcher b. May 5, 1874, m. Millie Seegmiller; James Ernest b. March 23, 1876, m. Edith Judd; Nellie b. July 7, 1879, m. Peter Christian Larsen; Jacob Alonzo b. March 22, 1882, m. Viola Bushy.
Married Maud Mary Robinson March 23, 1874, Salt Lake City (daughter of John Robinson and Emma Lucas of Spring City, Utah, formerly of England, pioneers October, 1856, handcart company). She was born October, 1858. Their children: Celia Jane b. July 3, 1875; Clara m. Levi Tenney; Hetta Maud b. April 30, 1879, m. David Little; John b. July 9, 1881; Ethel m. Andrew Peterson; Ida, died; Minnie and Cora, twins, b. 1892, died; Hugh. Family home Colonia Diaz, Mex.

ADAIR, SAMUEL. Came to Utah in 1848. His children: Jane, m. Charles Searle; Catherine, m. Fred Rugg; Newton, m. Janett; George. m. Elily Tyler; John, m. Jane Hancock. Family lived in "Dixie," Washington county, Utah. Farmer and orchardist. He died in Arizona.

ADAMS, ARZA (son of Joshua Adams and Betsy Chipman of Canada). Born Jan. 22, 1804. Came to Utah in 1848.
Married Sabina Clarke March 23, 1831, Augusta, Can. (daughter of Nathan Clarke and Nancy McCathron of Canada). She was born Sept. 1, 1812. Their children: Nathan b. Feb. 2, 1832, m. Mary Plunkett; Joshua b. Sept. 26, 1833, m. Lydia Thornton; George b. Feb. 16, 1835, m. Sabina Ann b. Feb. 17, 1837, m. Alexander Nicoll; Sidney M. b. May 1, 1839, died; Elizabeth Nancy b. April 30, 1842, died; Theother b. March 4, 1845; Joseph b. Dec. 17, 1846, m. Caroline Hansen; Orpha b. Oct. 23, 1849, m. William S. Robinson.
Married Marrilla Olney in Canada (daughter of David Olney of Canada). She was born June 18, 1833. Their children: John O. m. Mattie Peterson, Alva Barnabas m. Edith Summers; Alvin Francis m. Margaret Christenson; Adeline died; Lucy Ann m. Martin Ambrose; Quincy and Moroni, died. Family home American Fork, Utah.
Married Katherine Cunningham March 7, 1859, Salt Lake City (daughter of James Cunningham and Elizabeth Nicholson, of Fifeshire, Scotland, pioneers November, 1858, Atwood and Willis company). She was born Aug. 17, 1838. Their children: James Arza b. Oct. 19, 1858, died; Elizabeth b. Nov. 26, 1859, m. William Robinson; Charles Franklin b. April 10, 1861, died; Bulah b. June 22, 1862, m. Daniel Rhoades; Agnes b. June 10, 1864, died; Alexander b. Jan. 10, 1866, m. Mina Murdock; Margarette b. Jan. 21, 1868, m. Hiram Mulliner; Phoebe b. Sept. 17, 1870; Mary m. Carl Anderson; Isabelle b. July 30, 1874, m. Joseph Householder; Daniel Erwin b. Oct. 10, 1876, m. Annie Jensen. Family home American Fork, Utah.
High priest; missionary to Canada; ward teacher. Justice of peace. First miller in American Fork. Died April 15, 1889, American Fork, Utah.

ADAMS, DAVID BARCLAY (son of James Adams and Margaret Barclay). Born May 4, 1814, Carron Ironworks, Stirlingshire, Scotland. Came to Utah 1852 from Pennsylvania.
Married Mary Cook in Scotland. She was born Oct. 10, 1811. Their children: James B. Nov. 15, 1835; Adam b. May 1, 1837; Ann b. Dec. 1, 1838; Margaret b. Jun, m. Philo T. Farnsworth; Mary b. Feb. 1, 1843; David Cook b. Aug. 25, 1845, m. Mary Eleanor Armstrong Oct. 12, 1867; Ellen b. May 10, 1848, m. Urban Van Stewart. Family home Beaver, Utah.
Married Lydia Catherine Mann at Council Bluffs, Iowa (daughter of George William Mann and Elizabeth Cook of Beverly, Can.). She was born Jan. 5, 1830. Their children: George William b. July 7. 1850; Gilbert Mann b. Oct. 27, 1852, m. Armelia Allen; Elizabeth b. Sept. 19, 1854. m. John T. Covington; Robert Nelson b. Nov. 19, 1856, m. Margaret Ann Schurz; Alexander F. b. March 15, 1859, m. Martha Naizer; Lydia C. b. April 11, 1861, m. Orson W. Allen, 1883; Lewis b. May 26, 1863, m. Adelaide M. Lewis; Cynthia Jane b. Jan. 12, 1866, m. William H. Heaps; Christina b. April 3, 1868, m. Earnest Griffin; Daniel Cook b. April 23, 1870, m. Almira Larsen; Andrew Patterson b. June 28, 1873, m. Hattie Burr. Family home Adamsville, Utah.
Settled at Beaver, Utah; moved to Adamsville; made bishop of Adamsville March, 1869. Justice of peace. Iron manufacturer. Died Aug. 4, 1891, Escalante, Utah.

ADAMS, DAVID COOK (son of David Barclay Adams and Mary Cook). Born Aug. 25, 1845, near Penn Glendon Ironworks, Southampton, Pa. Came to Utah 1852.
Married Mary Eleanor Armstrong Oct. 12, 1867, Salt Lake City (daughter of John C. Armstrong and Mary Kirkbride—pioneers, A. O. Smoot company). She was born Oct. 22, 1848, Salt Lake City. Their children: Mary Jane b. July 14, 1868, m. Isaac Smith Goodwin; John David b. March 26, 1871, m. Margaret C. Stewart Dec. 30, 1891; Rosa Eleanor b. June 1, 1873, m. William U. Stewart; Lydia Ann b. Aug. 21, 1875, m. Martin Olsen; Ellen S. b. Nov. 20, 1877, m. Andrew Albertus Morris; Josephine b. Oct. 19, 1879; William J. b. Aug. 1, 1882; Joseph A. b. Nov. 29, 1884; Marcia b. March 21, 1886, m. Chester L. Skinner, 1904; Clara Mabel b. Jan. 18, 1889; Leona May b. Sept. 13, 1892, m. Leland W. Dean May 17, 1910. Family home, Teasdale.
Elder; Sunday school superintendent 1883-86.

ADAMS, JOHN DAVID (son of David Cook Adams and Mary Eleanor Armstrong). Born March 26, 1871, Adamsville, Utah.
Married Margaret Caroline Stewart Dec. 30, 1891 (daughter of Urban Van Stewart and Mary Ann Jones), who was born Nov. 26, 1873, Beaver, Utah.

ADAMS, DANIEL C. (son of David Barclay Adams and Lydia Catherine Mann). Born April 23, 1870, Adamsville, Utah.
Married Almira Larsen March 14, 1900, Manti, Utah (daughter of Hans C. Larsen and Maria Sorenson), who was born Oct. 27, 1877. Their children: Daniel Christial b. Dec. 21, 1900; Violet Catherine b. Dec. 25, 1903; Maria Elizabeth b. Dec. 7, 1906; Erma Almira b. Aug. 9, 1909. Family home Teasdale, Utah.
Elder. Constable and school trustee. Farmer.

ADAMS, DAVID (son of John Adams, born 1792 in Lincolnshire, and Sarah Jovis, born in Oxfordshire, Eng.). He was born July 14, 1828, in Buckinghamshire, Eng. Came to Utah Sept. 12, 1857, Jesse B. Martin company.
Married Maria Thetford April 17, 1851 (daughter of Charles Thetford and Fannie Mason), who was born Nov. 26, 1829, and came to Utah with husband. Their children: David Edward b. Nov. 27, 1851, m. Caroline H. Lind Jan. 24, 1876; William Orson b. Jan. 2, 1854, m. Dorothy R. Norton February, 1877; George Mason b. Oct. 1, 1856, m. Martha Devey April 10, 1876; Fanny Maria b. June 2, 1860, m. William T. Monk April 29, 1891; Louise Elizabeth b. Oct. 16, 1863; Earnest Thetford b. Feb. 18, 1866; Albert John b. July 7, 1868, m. Ada Jane Mellor June 2, 1898; Emily Catherine b. Jan. 21, 1871, m. Franklin F. Peay Jan. 15, 1890; Rose b. Oct. 28, 1873, m. Joseph M. Lindsey June 24, 1898; Sarah Amelia b. Aug. 24, 1877. Family resided Salt Lake City and Alpine, Utah.
Seventy; high priest; first counselor in bishopric Alpine ward 1877-93. School trustee 16 years; city councilman two terms; alderman. Assisted in the erection of many public buildings in Alpine stake. Lieutenant in Nauvoo Legion. Died April 11, 1911.

ADAMS, ELIAS (son of Job Adams and Sabra Otis of Vermont). Born Feb. 18, 1792, in Vermont; later moved to Illinois, where Adams county was named in his honor. Came to Utah in 1850.
Married Elvira Curtis 1823. Their children: Mary Ann; Rufus; John Quincy m. Ellen Dolan; Lizaetta; Selecta; Annie M. m. Isaac Shepherd; George W. m. Mary Ann Pilling. Two children died in infancy.
Married Belinda Railey 1837 (daughter of Joseph and Catherine Railey). She was born 1816. Their children: Catherine, m. Richard Pilling; Joseph Samuel, m. Belle Smith; Elias, m. Elizabeth R. Harris and Lettie M. Bennett; Caroline, m. George P. Stoddard; Joshua, m. Sarah Criddle; Malinda J., m. John W. Burton; Hyrum m. Rose Higgs and Annie Penrod. Family home Kaysville, Utah.
Of same distinguished lineage as John Adams, second president of the United States. Served 5 years in the war of 1812 and both his grandfathers were officers in the revolution. Presiding elder of the branch at Mt. Pisgah, Iowa; high priest. Pioneer reservoir builder, as he built the Adams irrigation reservoir at Kaysville (now Layton) in the early '50s. Lived on the old Indian trail crossing the mountains near Kaysville, where the redmen often visited him, prompted through the strong friendships he had formed among them, in the inherent kindness he bestowed upon all alike. Many a suffering traveler, hungry, cold and almost helpless, has partaken of his unbounded hospitality. His posterity number nearly 500. In January, 1886 this rugged pioneer fell from the front porch and sustained internal injuries from which he died Feb. 17 following being within one day of reaching the age of 94.

ADAMS, ELIAS, JR. (son of Elias Adams and Belinda Railey). Born Jan. 2, 1843, Adams county, Ill. Came to Utah 1850.
Married Elizabeth R. Harris Nov. 29, 1863, Kaysville, Utah (daughter of Isaac and Esther Harris; latter a pioneer 1853, settling at Kaysville). She was born Aug. 10, 1845; died May 7, 1888. Their children: Esther Ann b. Sept. 10, 1865, m. Robert Green; Elizabeth Belinda b. April 13, 1868, m. T. W. Sandall; Dennis Elias b. Feb. 21, 1870, m. Priscilla Harris; Ella Rose b. Oct. 29, 1871, m. William A. Dawson; Joshua Isaac b. March 9, 1874, m. Elizabeth Evans; Rufus William b. Jan. 18, 1877, m. Lizzie Dunn; John Hyrum b. July 23, 1879, died; George Winfield b. March 22, 1881; Jabez Samuel b. April 16, 1884, m. Alice Ellison; Catherine Mariah b. Jan. 31, 1887, m. Laurence E. Ellison. Family home Layton, Utah.
Married Lettie May Bennett April 22, 1903 (daughter of John Bennett, pioneer 1852, and Ellen Ellison, pioneer 1853). She was born July 23, 1876, Kaysville, Utah. Their children: Clair John b. Feb. 21, 1904; Clyde Bennett b. July 3, 1905; Ruth Ellen b. Aug. 23, 1908.
High priest; made trips to bring immigrants to Utah 1863 by ox train; chairman building committee Layton meeting house. Sheepman and farmer. Died Aug. 27, 1912, Layton, Utah.

ADAMS, DENNIS ELIAS (son of Elias Adams, Jr., and Elizabeth R. Harris. Born Feb. 21, 1870, at Kaysville, Utah.
Married Priscilla Harris (daughter of Thomas Harris and Mary Anne Payne, both of Thatcher, Utah). Their children: Basil Harris b. July 9, 1891; Earl Dennis b. May 18, 1893; Thomas Elias b. Sept. 21, 1895; Norma b. Oct. 18, 1897; Claud Harris b. Oct. 4, 1898; Ruby Juanita b. Jan. 4, 1901; Therese Pearl b. Sept. 19, 1903; Mamie Priscilla b. Dec. 28, 1905; Lyle Jabez b. May 1, 1907; Wilma b. April 6, 1910; Floyd W. b. Oct. 21, 1912.
Bishop's counselor; supervisor of parents' classwark and member board of Sunday schools in Bear River stake. Box Elder county commissioner six years. Vice president Rocky Mountain States Good Roads Association. Manager Adams Brothers Land Company. Farmer.

ADAMS, JOSHUA (son of Elias Adams and Belinda Railey). Born Dec. 30, 1848, Mt. Pisgah, Iowa. Came to Utah 1850.
Married Sarah Criddle Dec. 29, 1873, Salt Lake City (daughter of John Criddle and Elizabeth Ann Taylor Driggs of Kaysville, Utah). She was born Nov. 8, 1857. Their children: Job b. Sept. 27, 1874, m. Amanda Woolf; Sarah Matilda b. Oct. 4, 1876, m. Richard J. Smith; John b. Oct. 7, 1878, m. Luvenia Bishop; Malinda May b. May 8, 1881, m. Leo Mecham; Amanda Sabra b. Nov. 24, 1884, m. Elijah Clark; Mary Elizabeth b. Nov. 11, 1887, d. Sept. 11, 1890; Lillie Alice b. Jan. 23, 1893, m. Thomas Shomaker; Laura Bell b. Feb. 2, 1896, m. Leo Lewis; Eva Louise b. Nov. 8, 1905. Family home Clifton, Idaho.
High priest; president Y. M. M. I. A. Road overseer eight years; president of Oneida irrigation district four years. Farmer.

ADAMS, HUGH (son of George Adams and Margret Yadem). Born June 4, 1829, Old Craighall, near Musselburgh, Parish of Inveresk, Scotland. Came to Utah Oct. 2, 1854, Daniel Garn company.
Married Margret Webster July 23, 1855 (daughter of James Webster and Margret Anderson), who was born March 24, 1831, and came to Utah 1854, Wm. W. Brewerton company. Their children: Hugh J. b. May 11, 1856, m. Ida Clarkson; Orval W. b. June 19, 1858, m. Marion Nelson; Margret Ann b. June 12, 1860, m. Brigham Benson; George W. b. Sept. 21, 1862, m. Elizabeth Hews.
Married Mary Horlocher July, 1863, Logan, Utah (daughter of Jacob Horlocher and Margret Ackerman), who was born Mar. 17, 1831, Aarau, Canton Aargou, Switzerland. Their children: Wm. Thomas b. June 11, 1864, d. July 15, 1880; Mary Ann b. Aug. 14, 1865, m. David E. Haws; John Quincy b. Dec. 16, 1866, m. Sarah M. Cowley Dec. 16, 1891; Annie B. b. Nov. 8, 1870, m. John M. Barry May, 1891; Albert b. Oct. 9, 1876, d. July 20, 1878.
Married Alice Smith May 20, 1866 (daughter of Ralph P. Smith and Marion Crookston, pioneers 1860, David Cannon company). She was born April 6, 1848, Preston Links, Scotland. Their children: Alice Louisa b. Jan. 8, 1868, d. March 1, 1868; Joseph S. b. Jan. 27, 1869; Elizabeth b. Oct. 8, 1870, m. Joseph Jenson, d. Sept. 20, 1893; Peter b. Apr. 3, 1873, d. April 3, 1873; Agnes b. July 6, 1875, m. Frederick Jacobs; Emma b. July 23, 1877, d. July 23, 1877; Walter S. b. July 17, 1878, m. Carrie Hansen; Thomas S. b. April 29, 1881, m. Luella Norr; James S. b. March 4, 1883, m. Patience Smith; Ellen C. b. Feb. 19, 1885, m. George Maughan.
Settled at Logan, Utah, 1868.

ADAMS, JOHN QUINCY (son of Hugh Adams and Mary Horlocher). Born Dec. 16, 1866, Logan, Utah.
Married Sarah M. Cowley Dec. 16, 1891, Logan, Utah (daughter of Nephi K. Cowley, pioneer 1850, and Unity H. Apperley). She was born Feb. 4, 1870, Logan, Utah. Their children: John Vernon b. Nov. 7, 1892; Sarah Unity b. Feb. 20, 1894, d. Feb. 28, 1894.
Married Armenia Julia Parry Jan. 2, 1895, Logan, Utah (daughter of John Parry and Harriet Roberts, pioneers 1856, Handcart company). She was born Nov. 14, 1862, Salt Lake City. Their children: Armenia b. June 6, 1901; Verena Julia b. Jan. 17, 1903; Harriet Marie b. Oct. 9, 1904.

Elder seventy and high priest; formerly second, then first, counselor to Bishop William Hyde, fifth ward, Logan; chosen and sustained as bishop of same ward 1907; missionary to N. W. states 1898-1900. Member board of trustees State Agricultural College since March 14, 1907; has held many other offices of trust and honor in the community in which he resides.

ADAMS, JAMES (son of James and Mary Adams). Born March, 1799, in New Hampshire. Came to Utah 1852, James Allred company.
Married Betsy Leavitt, who was born 1803, Stansted, Lower Canada, and died 1848, Council Bluffs, Iowa. Their children: Sally b. May 29, 1825, m. Wm. Snow Jan. 11, 1846; Hannah A. b. Jan. 11, 1833, m. Horace S. Eldredge Feb. 2, 1855; John b. March 5, 1836, m. Flavilla Leavitt; Lucy b. Feb. 4, 1839, m. Elias Vanfleet May 10, 1860.
Settled in Centerville, Utah, and died there Feb. 18, 1874.

ADAMS, JAMES (son of George Adams and Margret Yadem). Born March 9, 1831, at Old Craighall, near Musselburgh, Inveresk parish, Scotland. Came to Utah 1852, John M. Wood company.
Married Margaret Japp Moffatt early in 1859 (daughter of Joseph and Elizabeth Moffatt, former a pioneer 1853). She was born Jan. 12, 1830. Their children: James H. b. Nov. 17, 1860, m. Agnes Izatt Adams; Joseph M. b. Nov. 11, 1862, m. Carrie Goodsell; George L. b. May 9, 1865, m. Ellen Smith; Samuel b. Feb. 12, 1867, m. Minnie Goodsell; Isabell b. Sept. 23, 1869, m. George E. Crockett; Jessie Ann b. Aug. 26, 1871, m. Karl Conrad Schaub March 29, 1893. Family home Logan, Utah.
Assisted in building up the Cache valley in all the pioneer activities. Watermaster of the Logan & Richmond Canal Co. Superintendent Logan city waterworks several years. High priest and all subordinate positions, and teacher in Sunday schools many years.

ADAMS, JOHN (son of George Adams and Elizabeth Harriet Winterbourn of Buckleburry, Berkshire, Eng.). Born Aug. 12, 1827, Buckleburry, Eng. Came to Utah Sept. 24, 1862, Homer Duncan company.
Married Jane Merritt July 7, 1850, in Berkshire, Eng. (daughter of John Merritt and Alice Blackney of Cold Ash, Berkshire). She was born Nov. 16, 1822. Their children: Alice b. May 11, 1851, m. James Carter; Henry b. Aug. 22, 1853, m. Charlotte Hyder Evans; Harriet Jane b. June 20, 1868, m. Parley P. Christianson. Family home Nephi, Juab county, Utah.
Married Sarah Albery Montague July 9, 1884, Salt Lake City (daughter of George Albery and Sarah Spiers of Hampshire, Eng.). She was born Nov. 15, 1847, and came to Utah 1884. Their children: George b. May 31, 1885, d. Sept. 3, 1886; Mervin Isaac b. March 27, 1887, m. Luella Foote. Family home Nephi.
High councilor and all minor offices. Carpenter—assisted in building many public and private buildings in Nephi. Died Aug. 24, 1908.

ADAMS, HENRY (son of John Adams and Jane Merritt). Born Aug. 22, 1853, Cold Ash, Eng. Came to Utah 1862.
Married Charlotte Hyder Evans Feb. 21, 1876, Salt Lake City (daughter of William M. Evans and Charlotte Jarrold Hyder of Nephi, pioneers 1850). She was born June 14, 1853. Their children: Henrietta Jane b. Feb. 13, 1877, m. Alfred Orme; Charlotte b. Dec. 29, 1878, m. George E. Howard; Henry Merritt b. March 13, 1881, m. Letitia Cooper; John Winford b. July 28, 1883, m. Ivy Lenoa Freeman; William Lloyd b. April 25, 1885, m. Belva Bird; Alice b. June 4, 1887, d. June 6, 1887; De Gratia b. Sept. 7, 1888, d. Dec. 23, 1901; Walter Clarence b. Nov. 8, 1892, m. Mabel I. Waldram. Family home Nephi, Utah.
Justice of peace, Juab county; coroner; deputy sheriff; county attorney five terms. Lawyer.

ADAMS, ORSON BENNETT. Born March 9, 1815, New York. Came to Utah July 29, 1847, in command of a detachment of the Mormon Battalion, first sergeant Co. C.
Married Susan Smith (daughter of Anthony Smith and Sarah Marman), who was born May 30, 1819, and came to Utah Oct. 2, 1847, Priddy Meeks' section of Jedediah Grant company. Their children: John S. b. May 15, 1864; Jane Averet May 3, 1866, m. Mary E. Adair May 17, 1876; Susan, m. William Hanes.
Married Margret Jane Carter, May —, Parowan, Utah (daughter of Preddy Carter).
Married Dorothy Frost, at Parowan, Utah.

ADAMS, JOHN PAGE (son of Orson B. Adams and Susan Smith). Born May 11, 1844, Macedonia, Ill.
Married Jane Averet May 3, 1866, Washington, Utah (daughter of Elisha Averet and Sarah Witt), who was born in 1851 at Salt Lake City. Their children: Lucinda Jane b. March 26, 1867, m. Mitton Alexander; Sarah Jerusha b. 1869, m. Marion E. Parks; Lucy b. 1870, m. Fred Ward.
Married Mary E. Adair May 17, 1876, Washington Co., Utah (daughter of Thomas J. Adair and Mary Vancil, pioneers 1852, Captain Brown company). She was born April 15, 1858, Washington, Utah. Their children: Ann b. March 1, —, m. Henry Rose 1896; May b. Oct. 27, —, m. Walter Elder

1897; Arminta b. July 23, —, m. J. S. Hallavas 1901; Lilly b. Dec. 23, —, m. J. S. Barnhurst 1899; Ada b. May 25, —, m. Fred Wardrop 1903; Ida b. May 25, —; John Bennet b. Aug. 3, —, m. May E. Tolbut 1905; Rebecca b. June 27, —, m. Comodore Myers 1903; Susannah b. June 7, —, m. Ammon Roberts 1909; Viola b. Feb. 3, —, m. Ernest Lamb 1898; William Alford b. Feb. 5, —, died; James Augustus b. Aug. 3, 1896; Ezram b. Sept. 13, 1901.

ADAMS, SAMUEL (son of John Adams and Sarah Brandley of Baddley Edge, Eng.). Born Aug. 1805. Came to Utah about Sept. 20, 1861, Joseph Young company.
Married Bessie Mountford about 1833 (daughter of William and Hannah Mountford), who was born April 15, 1815. Their children: Samuel b. April 16, 1835; Ann b. April 30, 1837; Thomas b. Dec. 22, 1840; Sarah b. May 12, 1853; Joseph b. May 6, 1845; Hyrum b. Oct. 22, 1846; Emma b. Jan. 27, 1850; Eliza b. June 8, 1852; Lorenzo b. May 10, 1857.

ADAMS, S. F. (son of Samuel Adams, born March 1, 1810, and Phoebe Ferry, born Nov. 11, 1815—both at Raunds, Northamptonshire, Eng.). He was born May 16, 1834, Raunds, Northamptonshire. Came to Utah Oct. 1853, Joseph A. Young company.
Married Sarah Wiggens July, 1855 (daughter of Ebenezer Wiggens and Ellen Wiggens, pioneers, 1852). She was born September, 1836, and died Oct. 6, 1877. Their children: Sarah E. b. May 15, 1856, m. George E. Brower December, 1880; Samuel W. b. Feb. 8, 1858, d. October, 1858; David b. Oct. 5, 1860, d. Aug. 30, 1873; William E. b. April 8, 1862, m. Jessie Scott December, 1895; May b. Aug. 30, 1864, m. M. S. Browning December, 1884; Phoebe b. March 22, 1867, m. Thomas Clark July 3, 1893; Eliza E. b. Sept. 16, 1869, d. March 23, 1895; Catherine b. Nov. 20, 1871, m. John Stander Oct. 17, 1889; Martha R. b. Sept. 27, 1873, m. Joseph Clark September, 1898; Herbert b. Dec. 4, 1875; Robert b. Dec. 4, 1875, m. Eliza Gibson Sept. 12, 1900. Family resided in Ogden up to 1871, then Richmond, Utah.
Married Hannah Eskelson (Allsop) Nov. 28, 1879, Richmond, Utah. (daughter of N. C. Eskelson and Mette Fransin, pioneers 1863, Napika company). She was born Jan. 29, 1849, Urland, Denmark. Their children: Lottie Ametlie b. Nov. 15, 1880, d. Jan. 3, 1894; John Q. b. May 4, 1882, m. Jane Clough Dec. 2, 1908; Nellie May b. July 6, 1885, d. Jan. 7, 1894; Ferry Leroy b. Feb. 8, 1889, m. Cora Parsons Nov. 17, 1908; Vertris I. b. Feb. 15, 1894.
Was in Echo Canyon campaign resisting Johnston's army. From Richmond, in 1888, moved to Riverside, Idaho, near Blackfoot. Commissioner Bingham county, Idaho, 1892-94; trustee Riverside school, 1892-98. Bishop's counselor, 1896-1903.

ADAMS, WILLIAM (son of Charles Adams and Cathrine Mills of Bagley Borough, County Cavan, Ireland. Born Jan. 8, 1822, at Hillsborough, County Down, Ireland. Came to Utah Oct. 27, 1849, George A. Smith company.
Married Mary Ann Leech, October, 1842, at Hillsborough (daughter of Hugh Leech and Ann Jemeson of that place), who was born Oct. 22, 1822. Their children: Charles m. Sarah Ann Davenport; James J.; Anna Cathrine m. Mr. Ward; Hugh Leech m. Juliet Bayless; Margaret m. Morgan Richards; William; Mary Emma m. James Ollerton; Thomas m. Emily M. Caldwell. Family home Parowan, Iron Co., Utah.
Seventy; missionary to Pennsylvania 1870-73; counselor to president of San Juan stake, Utah. City councilman. Farmer, merchant and stockraiser. Died at Bluff City, San Juan county, Utah.

ADAMS, CHARLES (son of William Adams and Mary Ann Leech). Born Sept. 16, 1843, Hillsborough, Ireland. Came to Utah Oct. 27, 1849.
Married Sarah Ann Davenport, March 31, 1863, Parowan, Utah (daughter of Thomas Davenport and Sarah Burrows, of Newbold, Derbyshire, Eng., pioneers November, 1851). She was born Feb. 14, 1847. Their children: Charles D. b. Sept. 28, 1866; Sarah Francella b. Oct. 1, 1868; Thomas D. b. Nov. 15, 1870; Minnie Miriam, b. Feb. 19, 1872; Mary Ann, b. March 23, 1876; William Leech b. Jan. 26, 1879; Joseph Burrows, b. Feb. 4, 1881; Laura Pearl, b. Nov. 20, 1884; Lawrence James b. Oct. 10, 1884. Family home Parowan.
President 69th quorum seventies; bishop's counselor; bishop 17 years; high councilor. Iron county assessor and county commissioner; Parowan city councilman and mayor; member of house of representatives 1892. Farmer, merchant and stockraiser.

ADAMS, THOMAS (son of William Adams and Mary Ann Leech). Born Nov. 4, 1860, at Parowan, Utah.
Married Emily M. Caldwell June 28, 1899, at Salt Lake City (daughter of Isaac J. Caldwell and Eliza Ann Russell of Salt Lake City). She was born Dec. 23, 1869. Only child; Thomas C. b. May 12, 1901. Family home, Salt Lake City.
Missionary to Ireland 1895-97; president conference at Belfast; Sunday school teacher; block teacher; home missionary. Attorney. Died Oct. 11, 1905, at Salt Lake City.

ADAMS, WILLIAM HENRY (son of John Adams and Mary Nash of Dover, Kent, Eng.). Born June 4, 1817, Dover, Eng. Came to Utah Oct. 10, 1848, Willard Richards company.
Married Martha Jennings (daughter of Matthew and Eliva Jennings of Dover, Eng.), who was born July 24, 1808, and died Aug. 17, 1852, Pleasant Grove. Their children: Mary b. 1842; Martha b. 1843; William Henry b. June 26, 1845, m. Melissa J. Caldwell; Eliza b. Oct. 6, 1847, m. George Higgins; John Alma b. Aug. 5, 1850, m. Mary Frampton.
Married Frances Ann Otten 1858, who came to Utah September, 1853, Jacob Gates company. Their children: Alice Maria b. 1859, m. Joseph Whiteley; Annie Jane b. 1861, m. John Newman; Joseph H. b. 1865, m. Colinda Rogers. Families lived at Pleasant Grove, Utah.
One of three first settlers in Pleasant Grove July 19, 1850. Assisted in the erection of the first stone and adobe buildings in Salt Lake City. Stonemason. Died Oct. 6, 1898, Pleasant Grove.

ADAMS, WILLIAM HENRY (son of William Henry Adams and Martha Jennings). Born June 26, 1845, Dover, Kent, Eng. Came to Utah 1848, with parents.
Married Melissa J. Caldwell March 22, 1869, Salt Lake City (daughter of Matthew Caldwell and Barzilla Guymon of Fountain Green, Utah, pioneers Sept. 16, 1850, Aaron Johnson company). She was born April 7, 1851, Spanish Fork, Utah. Their children: Martha Barzilla b. June 13, 1870, m. Martin Lund; Alice Almira b. Oct. 18, 1872, m. Jasper H. Robertson; William Albert b. Dec. 19, 1874, m. Virginia Brann; Delos E. b. Feb. 17, 1877, m. Hannah Peterson; Melissa Jane b. Sept. 4, 1879, m. Orson Despain; Elva Vilate b. March 28, 1882, m. D. W. West; John Matthew b. Oct. 7, 1884, and Guy Wilford b. March 25, 1887, d. 1891; Burton Henry b. May 27, 1889; Byron Lewis b. Aug. 25, 1891, m. Nora Adamson. Family home Fountain Green, Utah.
Personal guard Brigham Young and Orson Hyde. A survivor of the vicissitudes of pioneer days, among which was going for months without bread, subsisting on roots, thistles and segos. Veteran of many Indian fights and incipient Indian disturbances. Missionary to Southern States 1880-81; home missionary three years; ward teacher 40 years; high priest; in superintendency of Fountain Green Sunday school nineteen years. Farmer and brick mason.

ADAMSON, HENRY (son of Andrew Adamson and Margaret Cunningham of Fifeshire, Scotland). Born in 1807, in Fifeshire. Came to Utah in 1864.
Married Margaret Nicholson 1834, Dysart, Fifeshire, (daughter of Alexander Nicholson and Nancy Allen of Sinclairtown and Dysart, Scotland). She was born Nov. 11, 1811. Their children: Andrew m. Lottie ——; Alexander m. Mary Hutchinson; Peter m. Ann Cousins; Nancy Agnes, Ellen, and Nancy Agnes, latter three d. infants; John m. Fanny Fackender; Henry m. Mary ——, m. Martha ——; David m. Elizabeth Ann and Mary Jane Wilkinson; James m. Elizabeth ——.
Block teacher; miner and sheepman. Died January, 1890, at Franklin, Idaho.

ADAMSON, ALEXANDER (son of Henry Adamson and Margaret Nicholson). Born Jan. 27, 1837, at Bosland, Fifeshire, Scotland. Came to Utah Sept. 12, 1861, John Murdock company.
Married Mary Hutchison April 12, 1861, in Fifeshire, Scotland, (daughter of David Hutchison and Jeanette Crookston of Dysart, Scotland, pioneers Sept. 12, 1861). She was born July 25, 1839. Their children: Jeanette b. Aug. 9, 1862, m. James Brown; Margaret b. Feb. 25, 1864, m. E. W. Winn; Henry b. Sept. 26, 1865, m. Minnie Hansen; Mary Jane b. Sept. 7, 1867, m. Heber B. Sycks; Katherine b. May 17, 1869, m. David Hutchison; Alexander b. Dec. 15, 1870, m. Louisa Tillett; David b. Nov. 24, 1872, m. Jessie Myers; Elizabeth Helen b. Nov. 15, 1874, m. Joseph Karren; Peter b. Nov. 9, 1876, m. Blanche Myers; Thomas b. Oct. 26, 1879, m. Pearl Christopherson.
High priest; block teacher. Black Hawk Indian war veteran. Farmer. Pioneer of American Fork and helped make the first canals, dams and wagon roads.

AFFLECK, JOHN (son of Andrew Affleck and Margaret Truitt of Newcastle-on-Tyne, Northumberland, Eng). Born April 21, 1849, at Newcastle-on-Tyne. Came to Utah Sept. 4, 1866, Thomas E. Ricks company.

AHLSTROM, JOHN G. (son of Ola Ahlstrom and Ingerborg Bundenson of Malmo, Sweden). Born Dec. 12, 1850, Malmo, Sweden. Came to Utah September, 1860.
Married Mary Ellen Arthur Nov. 20, 1870, Salt Lake City (daughter of Evan Arthur and Cathrine James of St. John, Utah, pioneers Oct. 13, 1863, Rosel Hyde company). She was born Dec. 28, 1852. Their children: John A. m. Sara Evans; Minnie E. m. Alvin Caldwell; Cathrine Ann, died; William J.; Mary L., m. Charles H. Green; Edna. m. John McIntosh; Ernest E. m. Lena St. Jeor; Elmer H. Family home St. John, Utah.
Bishop of St. John ward, 1898-04; Sunday school supt., 1888-96; school trustee eight years. U. S. mail contractor 18 years. Farmer.

PIONEERS AND PROMINENT MEN OF UTAH   711

AINGE, GEORGE (son of James Ainge of Warwickshire, Eng). Came to Utah in 1856 with Oxteam company.
Married Elizabeth Hoffwood in England (daughter of John and Annie Hoffwood of Worcestershire, Eng.). Their children: George, m. Polly McKee; Elizabeth; Emma, m. John Harris; Hilliary d. aged 15; Mehelia Teresia d. infant; Jongh; Alfred, drowned at age of 8; William d. aged 22. Family home Weisley, Warwickshire, Eng.
Elder. Black Hawk Indian war veteran. Farmer and sheepman. Died at Spanish Fork, Utah.

AINGE, GEORGE (son of George Ainge and Elizabeth Hoffwood). Born Dec. 24, 1836, Worcestershire, Eng. Came to Utah 1856, Benjamin Hodgett ox team company.
Married Polly McKee at Provo, Utah (daughter of Thomas McKee and Percy Sweat of Spanish Fork, Utah; pioneers ox team company). Their children: Polly and George Thomas, d. infants; William; Percy, m. Erie Stewart; Alfred, m. Sadie Arnold; Harriet Lavira, m. Joseph Arnold; John, m. Miss Wilkins; Thomas, m. Amelia Yeager; Joseph and James, d. infants; Charles; Stella. m. William Taylor; Wilma, m. Lloyd Gilroy; Ruby, m. H. Nielsen; Nile.
Elder; ward teacher. Indian war veteran; member territorial militia. Farmer.

AINSWORTH, JAMES (son of Joseph Ainsworth and Mary Huff of Staffordshire, Eng., latter with three children, pioneer 1862). Born Aug. 9, 1851, West Bromwich, Staffordshire, Eng. Came to Utah Oct. 17, 1862, Henry W. Miller company.
Married Emma M. Flygare Jan. 15, 1877, Brigham City, Utah (daughter of Nels and Anna Flygare, pioneers 1862). She was born July 25, 1856. Their children: Mary Ann b. 1878, m. Alden T. Ivie; Maude Ellen b. 1880, m. Ray Ivie; James Albert b. 1885, d. Aug. 9, 1887. Family home Carey, Idaho.
Married Clara Rosetta Johnson July 15, 1909, Logan, Utah (daughter of Daniel Johnson and Catherine Jenson of Logan, pioneers 1854, H. P. Jenson company). She was born 1872, Logan, Utah. Family home Mt. Glenn, Oregon.

AINSWORTH, JOSEPH (son of Joseph Ainsworth and Mary Huff of Staffordshire, Eng.). Born Jan. 22, 1848, Wood Green, Staffordshire, Eng. Came to Utah Oct. 17, 1862, with mother and family, Henry W. Miller company.
Married Hannah Maria Hamson May 15, 1877, Brigham City, Utah (daughter of George F. Hamson, pioneer July 18, 1861, and Belleta Mortenson of Brigham City). She was born Sept. 1, 1859. Their children: Joseph Leon b. May 20, 1878, m. Terressa Maud Howard; Rose Arleta b. Feb. 24, 1881, m. Walter Pyrah; Ruby Melvina b. March 17, 1883; Paul Revere b. June 18, 1887; James Alfred b. Feb. 6, 1891; Millie Jane b. March 2, 1893; John Mellville b. July 1, 1894; Jennie Viola b. Nov. 25, 1895; Roy Vernon b. Jan. 8, 1898; Gladys Marion b. July 23, 1900; Effie Emma b. Oct. 28, 1902. Family resided Blaine Ward, Cassia county, Idaho, and La Grande, Oregon. Called to protect the people of San Pete county during Black Hawk Indian war, and served through the trouble; also member Salt Lake county militia.
Counselor to Bishop G. S. Harris, Blaine Ward, Cassia stake, 1898-07; high councilor Union stake, Le Grande, Oregon. Justice of peace fifteen years, Blaine county, Idaho.

ALBISTON, JOHN (son of John Albiston, born June 3, 1783, Congleton, and Hannah Thacker, born July 10, 1783, both in Chestershire, Eng.). He was born April 4, 1814, at Stockport, Lancashire, Eng. Came to Utah Sept. 5, 1854, Darwin Richardson company.
Married Elizabeth Mellor May 6, 1833, at Saddleworth, Yorkshire, Eng., who was born Feb. 27, 1812, and came to Utah with husband. Their children: James; Hannah; Charles b. April 11, 1839; Martha b. Dec. 9, 1840; John b. Feb. 7, 1842, m. Mary Ann Lee Dec. 3, 1863; Joseph b. July 7, 1844, m. Christina Scow; Elizabeth Ann b. May 11, 1847; Mary Pamelia; Ruth Agnes b. Oct. 17, 1855, m. Joseph Johnson.
President Ashton branch of Manchester conference, as well as Sheffield and Bradford conferences; missionary to England. Assisted in public works at Grantsville and Ogden, Utah.

ALBISTON, JOHN, JR. (son of John Albiston and Elizabeth Mellor). Born Feb. 7, 1842.
Married Mary Ann Lee Dec. 3, 1863, Richmond, Utah (daughter of George Lee and Sarah Peaker, pioneers Sept. 16, 1859, Edward Stevenson company). She was born Jan. 24, 1846. Their children: Sarah Elizabeth b. Sept. 27, 1864, m. Charles Peterson Dec. 21, 1887; Mary Ann b. Oct. 24, 1866; John William b. April 20, 1868; George Heber b. Sept. 29, 1870, m. Anna Smith Oct. 16, 1895; Ruth Emma b. Dec. 24, 1872, m. Gilbert Bright Nov. 16, 1892; Joseph Henry b. Nov. 27, 1874, m. Zina Buckley Aug. 9, 1895; Lorenzo b. May 4, 1877; Lilly May b. May 6, 1878, m. John Gregory Nov. 20, 1895; Hyrum James b. Sept. 3, 1880; Samuel b. Nov. 14, 1882; Nephi b. Aug. 17, 1884; Charles Lee b. May 17, 1886; Stephen m. March 20, 1889; Amy Pearl b. Aug. 19, 1891. Family resided Richmond, Utah, and Franklin, Idaho.
Clerk of teachers' and of high priests' quorums. Member William Head's cavalry company of minutemen; captain first martial band in Idaho.

ALBISTON, JOHN W. (son of John Albiston, Jr., and Mary Ann Lee). Born April 20, 1868.
Engaged in threshing machine and saw mill business.

ALBRAND, WILLIAM JOHN F. (son of Charles F. and Amelia Albrand of Germany). Born August, 1818, in Germany. Came to Utah 1854.
Married Jane Ann Richardson May 4, 1860, Salt Lake City (daughter of Adam Richardson and Mary Thompson of Washing Wells, Durhamshire, Eng.). She was born Aug. 10, 1831. Their children: Mary Amelia, m. Orvil Hatch; William J. E., m. Margerite A. Kent; Jane Ann, m. Parley E. Hatch; Williamminna I. d. infant. Family home Salt Lake City.
Missionary to eastern states; seventy. Gardener. Died Feb., 1905, Salt Lake City, Utah.

ALBRAND, WILLIAM J. E, (son of William John F. Albrand and Jane Ann Richardson). Born Aug. 3, 1865, Salt Lake City, Utah.
Married Margerite A. Kent Sept. 27, 1889, at Logan, Utah (daughter of Adam Kent and Mary Bell of Durhamshire, Eng., pioneers 1863). She was born March 30, 1866. Their children: Ephraim b. Oct. 15, 1890, d. infant; Margerite L. b. April 8, 1892, d. infant; William C. b. Nov. 8, 1893; Edna I. b. Nov. 8, 1896; Earl K. b. Oct. 5, 1901; Mary b. Dec. 10, 1904; Jane Ann b. Aug. 26, 1907. Family home Salt Lake City, Utah.
Missionary to England 1896-98; member 109th quorum seventies; high priest; bishop's counselor. Drayman; contractor.

ALDER, ALFRED. Born May 3, 1824, Wiltshire, Eng. Came to Utah Sept. 23, 1853.
Married Susan Field, who was born Feb. 29, 1832, and came to Utah next day. Their children: Eliza b. Nov. 25, 1849, d. next day; Alfred W. b. March 13, 1851 (d. Jan. 27, 1910), m. Sarah Jensen Jan. 24, 1884; John Field b. Oct. 13, 1852, d. Sept. 5, 1855; Susan M. b. Feb. 31, 1855, died; Theodore D. b. Sept. 17, 1857, m. Alice Pauli; Clara J. b. Dec. 13, 1859, m. Charlie Robins; Elizabeth J. b. May 14, 1862, d. Nov. 16, 1864; Margret A. b. Aug. 10, 1864, m. William Lamont; Agusta U. b. Aug. 27, 1866, m. Hyrum Jensen; Ella S. b. Nov. 2, 1868, m. Byron D. Wilcox; Edgar F. b. Feb. 24, 1871, d. Dec. 12, 1877; Jessie G. b. Sept. 23, 1873, d. Dec. 30, 1889.
Married Mavena Warr Aug., 1882, who was born in England. Only child: Alice A. b. March 19, 1885.
One of first blacksmiths to come to Utah. High councilor in Oneida stake.

ALDER, ALFRED W. (son of Alfred Alder and Susan Field). Born March 13, 1851, St. Louis, Mo.
Married Sarah Jensen Jan. 24, 1884, Salt Lake City, who was born 1864 at Lehi, Utah. Their children: Myrtle S. b. Oct. 26, 1884, m. Ernest E. Dixon Nov. 1, 1905; Reuel J. b. March 17, 1886, m. Ella Zigham; Edgar J. b. Dec. 30, 1888, m. Azula Griffith; Priscilla J. b. Feb. 20, 1891; Alfreda J. b. Nov. 20, 1892; Alfred J. b. Dec. 25, 1894; Susan b. July 20, 1897; Jesse b. May 8, 1899; Orin J. b. June 28, 1902; Alton J. b. Nov. 28, 1904; Aldora J. b. May 25, 1908.
Missionary to Arizona. Blacksmith and farmer.

ALDER, CONRAD. Born July 15, 1824, Schonengrund, Appenzell, Switzerland. Came to Utah Oct. 5, 1860, William Budge handcart company.
Married Annie Elizabeth Merz in Switzerland (daughter of Laurenz Merz and Anna Catharine Ramsauer), who was born April 30, 1830. Their children: Elizabeth, m. Henry Gassman 1887 at Logan; Conrad. m. Julia Annie Theurer.
Died Sept., 1866, Providence, Utah.

ALDER, CONRAD (son of Conrad Alder and Annie E. Merz). Born May 18, 1866, Providence, Utah.
Married Julia Annie Theurer Dec. 11, 1889, Logan, Utah (daughter of Frederick Theurer and Christena Scheuler, former a pioneer Aug. 30, 1860, Jesse E. Murphy company, the latter Sept. 20, 1861, Joseph W. Young company). She was born April 10, 1870, Providence, Utah. Their children: Leon C. b. Sept. 21, 1890, m. Vesta Freelove Campbell March 6, 1912; Rachel Vilate b. Nov. 28, 1892; Frederick Theurer b. March 31, 1895; Idell Christena b. July 11, 1897; May Elizabeth b. May 1, 1900; Preston Denton b. Dec. 18, 1905; Owen Edwin b. May 12, 1909. Family home Providence, Utah.
Member 32d quorum seventies; missionary to Germany 1902-05; assistant Sunday school superintendent twenty years. School trustee two terms; member town board. Farmer and stockraiser.

ALDOUS, ROBERT (son of James Aldous and Mary Ann Page of Huntingdonshire, Eng.). He was born July 17, 1811, Kelsale, Suffolk, Eng. Came to Utah Sept. 14, 1853, Claudius V. Spencer company.
Married Mary Ann Parkin Dec. 24, 1835 (daughter of Luke and Nancy Parkin). She was born Nov. 9, 1814, and came to Utah with husband. Their children: George P. b. Oct. 30, 1836, m. Christiane M. Thurston Dec. 24, 1865; Georgiana M. b. April, 1838, m. Martin Harris; Charles b. April 9, 1840, m. Lucy Drake Nov. 26, 1862; Frederick b.

Nov., 1841, m. Margaret Wilson; Angeline P. b. Dec. 27, 1843, m. Brigham Bingham Dec. 24, 1862; Henry b. 1845, died. Family home Huntsville, Utah.
Worked on some of the first public works in Salt Lake City; also on Ogden tabernacle; superintended the building of three bridges in Ogden canyon when first opened. Carpenter and builder; built first school in Huntsville and was its first superintendent; also built first log house there. Watermaster five years. Seventy; high priest.

ALDOUS, GEORGE P. (son of Robert Aldous and Mary Ann Parkin of Huntingdonshire, Eng.). Born Oct. 30, 1836, Fen Stanton, Eng.
Married Christiana M. Thurston Dec. 24, 1865, Huntsville, Utah (daughter of Evan C. Thurston and Magdelina Christenson). She was born Jan. 13, 1848, Logstor, Aalborg amt., Denmark. Their children: Georgiana b. Nov., 1866, d. infant; Mary Ann b. March 17, 1868, m. William McFarland July 18, 1894; Magdelina C. b. March 16, 1870, m. Hans F. Peterson June 19, 1895; George b. March 20, 1872, m. Ethel Cowan Feb. 6, 1897; Martha E. b. April 22, 1874, m. Edward S. Green June 13, 1900; Johanna b. May 5, 1876, m. Charles C. Bihler Feb. 16, 1904; Robert T. b. April 10, 1878; Clara A. b. June 12, 1880; Joseph H. b. July 23, 1883; Alfred E. b. Nov. 13, 1884; Edward C. b. May, 1887; Mabel E. b. March 29, 1890, m. Philip Slater Oct. 5, 1908. Family home West Weber, Utah.

ALDOUS, CHARLES (son of Robert Aldous and Mary Ann Parkin). Born in Huntingdonshire, Eng., April 9, 1840. Came to Utah 1853.
Married Lucy Drake Nov. 26, 1862, at Lynn, Weber county, Utah (daughter of Daniel N. Drake and Lucinda Johnson of Ohio, pioneers 1849). Their children: Charles N.; Frederick Robert; John L.; Henry; George; Annie; Marie; Therea; Alvin; Mary Ann.
Farmer and horticulturist.

ALEXANDER, ALVAH (son of Jabez Alexander, born Aug. 22, 1754, Marlborough. N. H., and Lois Pool, born Dec. 1, 1758, and married in Acworth). He was born March 12, 1799, Acworth, N. H. Came to Utah Oct. 3, 1852, Capt. Harmon Cutler company.
Married Phoebe Houston, May 9, 1822, who was born June 4, 1804, Acworth, N. H. Their children: Henry Samuel, b. July 12, 1823, m. Mary Marsteller 1845; m. Jane Houston 1848; m. Sarah Miles July 23, 1850; Louisa Pool; Maria; Alvah Jedethan, b. Sept. 21, 1831, m. Elizabeth Soule, March 13, 1854; Orpha Ann. Family home East Mill Creek, Utah. Farmer. Died March 27, 1890.

ALEXANDER, HENRY SAMUEL (son of Alvah Alexander and Phœbe Houston). Born July 12, 1823, in Washington county, Vt. Came to Utah Sept. 1848, Livingston-Kimball company.
Married Mary Marsteller 1845 at Nauvoo, Ill. (her parents were from Virginia). Their children: Charles Marsteller, m. Lovisa Comstock Snyder; Arthur, died. Family home South Mill Creek, Utah.
Married Jane Houston 1848 at Council Bluffs, Iowa (daughter of Samuel Houston of Iowa). Family home Salt Lake City, Utah.
Married Sarah Miles July 23, 1850, Salt Lake City, Utah (daughter of Samuel Miles and Sarah Prudence Marks of Connecticut, pioneers Oct. 28, 1849, Ezra T. Benson company). She was born Dec. 27, 1832. Their children: Henry Miles m. Sarah Jane Ross; Sarah Henrietta m. George Clift; Lelia Naomi m. William Van Wagoner; William, James Monroes and Lillie May, these three died; Clara Prudence m. Edward D. Clyde; Katie Josephine m. Robert Turner; Orpha Luella m. Robert Foreman; George Snyder m. Jane Ann Taylor. Family resided in Heber and Summit county, Utah.
Patriarch. Wasatch county commissioner. Sawmill and lumberman. Died March 6, 1903.

ALEXANDER, CHARLES MARSTELLER (son of Henry Samuel Alexander and Mary Marsteller). Born Nov. 21, 1846, in Lee county, Iowa. Came to Utah with father.
Married Lovisa Comstock Snyder, Dec. 26, 1871, Salt Lake City, Utah (daughter of George G. Snyder and Sarah Hatch, pioneers 1849). She was born Feb. 25, 1854. Their children: Mary Blanche b. Feb. 16, 1873, m. Brigham Murdock; Sarah Luella b. Jan. 21, 1876; Caroline b. Oct. 4, 1879, m. William T. Wooten; Charles Snyder b. June 5, 1881, died; Louis b. July 2, 1883; Mabel b. March 28, 1886, m. Robert Price; Guy Becker b. Oct. 13, 1888; Blaine Marsteller b. Aug. 25, 1895; Nellie b. March 1, 1898 Family home, Heber, Utah.
Elder. Lumberman.

ALEXANDER, ALVAH JEDETHAN (son of Alvah Alexander and Phoebe Houston). Born Sept. 21, 1831, Northfield, Vt. Came to Utah Oct. 3, 1852, Capt. Harmon Cutler company.
Married Elizabeth Soule March 13, 1854 (daughter of Solomon Soule and Lydia Bessee, pioneers Aug. 1853, Independent company). She was born Feb. 6, 1834. Their children: Mary Elizabeth b. Jan. 21, 1855, m. James O'Neil 1875; Phoebe Annette b. Jan. 3, 1857, m. George Bonner 1878; Alvah b. June 11, 1858, m. Dessie Bonner 1880; Adelbert b. July 7, 1860, m. Viola D. Epperson 1885; Ella Gertrude b. Jan. 1, 1863, m. Robert B. Ross 1881; Frederic Soule b. May 16, 1865, d. Jan. 23, 1869; Ada Deanna b. March 6, 1867, m. Thomas E. Bonner 1883; Charles Edwin b. May 4, 1870, m. Lala R. Springer 1891; Henry LeRoy b. July 10, 1872, m. Susie Davis 1893; Florence Mina b. April 15, 1875, d. March 25, 1878; Effie May b. April 6, 1879, m. Everice Bronson 1897. Family resided at Mill Creek and Midvay, Utah.
Asst. and Sunday School Supt., 1873-1900; bishop's counselor, Midway ward 1876-1903. With eldest brother, started first shingle sawmill in Utah 1853; in lumber business 38 years. County selectman eight years; justice of peace two terms; president of town board two terms; school trustee several terms.

ALEXANDER, ALVAH (son of Alvah J. Alexander and Elizabeth Soule). Born June 11, 1858, Lehi, Utah.
Married Dessie Bonner October, 1880, Midway, Utah (daughter of George Bonner and Margaret Edmundston), who was born Jan. 14, 1862, Midway, Utah. Only child: Alvah b. Dec. 15, 1881.
Merchant, stockraiser and ranchman.

ALEXANDER, HORACE MARTIN (son of James Alexander and Frances Ehart of Montgomery county, Va.). Born Feb. 15, 1812, Montgomery county. Came to Utah Oct. 16, 1847, with part of Mormon Battalion from California.
Married Nancy Reader Walker Sept. 14, 1834, Clay county Mo., who was born Dec. 8, 1817. Their children: Frances Evelyn b. Sept. 1, 1836, m. Jesse P. Steele; Nancy Maria b. March 24, 1839, died; Sarah Malinda b. March 5, 1841, m. John Green, later Hans Mortensen; Dionetia Emily b. Oct. 18, 1843, m. Hans Mortensen; Horace Martin b. Jan. 3, 1847, died. Family resided Clay county, Mo., and Nauvoo, Ill.
Married Martha Burwell Feb. 15, 1849, Salt Lake City, who was born March 31, 1830. Their children: James Thornton b. June 24, 1850, m. Emily Johnson and Rebecca Noah; Henry R. b. Nov. 17, 1851; Elizabeth; Masie; Margaret; Ella Amelia, latter five died; Alice Geraldine b. April 26, 1856, m. Joseph Blackett; John Wesley b. Nov. 1858, died; Flora Adelaide b. 1859, m. Thomas Bryon; Jedediah M. b. Nov., 1862, died; Charlotte Almira b. May 11, 1863, m. Frank Gamble; Celestia b. Nov. 27, 1865, m. William Sumption and Max Kless; Celestine m. William Humphries; Hubert and George, died; Mildred m. A. G. Peterson. Family home, Springville, Utah.
Married Catherine Houston Feb. 15, 1849, Salt Lake City (daughter of James Houston), who was born March 12, 1831. Their children: William Denton b. Dec. 4, 1851, m. Helena Coray, and Prudella Allman; Mary Helen b. Jan. 16, 1854, m. Jonathan Harvey; Eliza Fredonia b. March 4, 1856, m. Samuel P. Richards; Franklin D. b. Oct. 31, 1858, m. Naoma Wilson; Heber M. b. Dec. 13, 1860, died; Susan Amelia b. March 27, 1861 (deceased), m. Isaac Roberts; Ophelia Leona b. July 18, 1864, m. John F. Clark; Lucy Jane b. Oct. 29, 1866 (deceased), m. John Collett; Blanch J. b. March 30, 1870, died; Maud b. May 16, 1875, m. E. M. West. Family home Salt Lake City.
Married Julia Owens 1854, Salt Lake City. Their children: Albert b. March 8, 1855; Amasa B. b. May 21, 1856, m. Agness Henry; Frances b. 1858 and Amelia b. 1860, both died. Family home Parowan, Utah.
High priest; missionary to southern states 1875. Capt. Silver Grays, Springville, Utah, 1869; member police force. Salt Lake City 1850-53; Corporal Co. B Mormon Battalion. Contractor and builder; farmer. Died Sept. 18, 1881, Provo, Utah.

ALEXANDER, WILLIAM DENTON (son of Horace Martin Alexander and Catharine Houston). Born Dec. 4, 1851, Salt Lake City.
Married Helena Coray Oct. 10, 1878, Salt Lake City (daughter of Howard Coray and Martha Jane Knowlton), who was born Feb. 1, 1852. Their children: Helena Cora b. July 23, 1879, m. D. Foster Cluff; Maud May b. Dec. 20, 1880, m. Horace Secrest; Ethel b. April 27, 1882, died; William Denton b. June 26, 1884; Don Horace b. April 13, 1887, died; Howard b. March 12, 1892, died; George Louis b. Jan. 1, 1896. Family home Provo, Utah.
Married Prudella Allman May 16, 1906, Salt Lake City (daughter of Thomas Allman and Elmira Phillips, pioneers 1850 and 1861 respectively). She was born Dec. 12, 1865. Their children: Ralph Houston b. April 9, 1907. Family home Provo, Utah.
Missionary to Hawaiian Islands 1878-81. Justice of peace 1888-91; alderman 1888-89; member school board 1904-08. Contractor and builder; horticulturist.

ALEXANDER, ROBERT (son of —— Alexander and Mary McFarland of Lurgan, Ireland). Born 1826, County Tyrone, Ireland. Came to Utah 1852, Captain McGaw company.
Married Mary Melvillie 1846, Lurgan, Ireland (daughter of Henry Melville and Elizabeth Gregg, pioneers 1852, Captain McGaw company). She was born Aug. 13, 1822. Their children: Elizabeth, d. aged 2; Mary, m. Samuel McIntyre; Anna, m. Frank E. Cook. Family home St. Louis, Mo.
Seventy; home missionary. Painter. Died Feb. 20, 1887, twelfth ward, Salt Lake City.

ALFORD, JOHN (son of William Alford and Miss Goldsbrough of Dorsetshire, Eng.). Born July 3, 1826, in Dorsetshire. Came to Utah fall of 1865, with an oxteam company.
Married Margaret Russell Anderson (Ripley) June 10, 1872, Salt Lake City, by Daniel H. Wells (daughter of John Anderson and Jane Russell of Leith, near Edinburgh, Scotland, pioneers 1862). She was born May 26, 1850. Their

children: John W. b. July 2, 1873, m. Ruby Venice Pike; Jeanne Russell b. Sept. 30, 1875, m. Ray F. Brandon; Frances Elizabeth, d. aged 8; William George, d. aged 6; Robert G. Family home Salt Lake City.
Seventy at Salt Lake City; missionary to England 1870-71; high priest. He, with George Goddard, was in the mercantile business; they sold out and he became associated with the Z. C. M. I., where he remained almost to the time of his death, April 11, 1901, Salt Lake City.
Margaret Russell Anderson was the widow of Robert Ripley, whom she married in Scotland. He was lost at sea. Their children: Robert Ripley b. infant; Helene Ripley m. George Noble.

ALFORD, JOHN W. (son of John Alford and Margaret Russell Anderson Ripley). Born July 2, 1873, Salt Lake City.
Married Ruby Venice Pike June 12, 1900, Salt Lake City, by Judge Morrell (daughter of John W. Pike and Amy Tuckfield of England; they came to Utah 1870). She was born Dec. 16, 1876. Only child; Robert Pike b. April 21, 1903.
Was associated for a time with the A. H. Crabbe Company as secretary and director. President, manager and senior member Alford Bros. Company, haberdashers.

ALLEMAN, JOHN (son of John Christopher Alleman and Catherine Heppick of Dauphin Co., Pa.). Born June 28 1808, Middleton, Dauphin county, Pa. Came to Utah 1852.
Married Christean Stentz Dec. 11, 1832, Dauphin Co. (daughter of Michael Stentz and Maria Catharine Winagle—pioneers 1852). She was born Nov. 28, 1811. Their children: Anna Catharine, m. Joseph W. Bissell; Benjamin Jordan, m. Sariah Jane Starr; Susanna, m. Benjamin T. Blanchard; John Henry, m. Zebina Starr; Christean Mary, m. William Sumsion; Daniel Joseph, m. Amanda Elizabeth Starr; Sarah Jane, m. Alma Spafford; Martha Elizabeth, m. Edward L. Whiting; James Hyrum; William David, m. Martha Jane Reynolds. Family home Springville, Utah.

ALLEN, ALBERN (son of Daniel and Clarissa Allen). Born May 22, 1802, Cornwall, Litchfield county, Conn. Came to Utah Oct. 16, 1847, with Mormon Battalion from California.
Married Marcia Allen 1826, Hartwick, N. Y. (daughter of Gideon Allen, born Nov. 2, 1774, Washington, Conn., d. Jan. 10, 1861, at Ogden, Utah, and Rachel Hand, deceased—pioneers Sept. 20, 1848, Brigham Young company). She was born Nov. 6, 1804, Litchfield, Conn., and died Dec. 25, 1866, at Kanarraville, Utah. Their children: Rufus Chester b. Oct. 22, 1827, m. Lavenia H. Yearsley; Alanson David b. May 2, 1829 (d. March 3, 1887), m. Chastina Hadlock; Clarissa Abbie b. June 3, 1831 (d. March 17, 1905), m. Moses S. Clark; Marshall Frederick b. 1834, m. Emma Holmes; Rachel b. 1836, d. 1846; Rebecca b. 1838, d. 1868 Summit county, Utah; Sarah b. 1840, d. 1842 at Nauvoo, Ill.; Sarah Ann b. 1843, d. 1846; Mary Ellen b. Jan. 14, 1850, at Ogden, m. Charles W. Hinchcliff.
Married Mary Ann Hoops (Yearsley) (daughter of George and Albina Hoops). She was born Jan. 4, 1811, West Chester, Pa., and died 1905 at Salt Lake City; came to Utah Sept. 25, 1849, with Heber C. Kimball company. Their child: Marcia b. Nov. 21, 1854, at Ogden, m. Charles E. Layne Feb. 9, 1873.
Married Mary Jane Morris (McCarty) (daughter of Jacob Morris, a pioneer). She was born April 11, 1818, Circleville, Ohio, and died Dec. 4, 1893, at Ogden, Utah. Their children: Albern b. Dec. 2, 1854, at Ogden, m. Elizabeth Evans.
Married Elizabeth Hill (deceased). Their children: Sariah, m. James Wright; Martha, died; a daughter died at Huntsville, Utah; Isada, died; Elizabeth b. July, 1867, m. Harry Kosminski. Families lived at Ogden, Utah.
Missionary; president 33d quorum seventies at Nauvoo, 1846; member Company A Mormon Battalion; settled at Ogden 1849; member high council. Assisted in bringing immigrants to Utah 1857; chosen to preside over the little settlement, Genoa, about 100 miles west of Florence, a supply depot and assembling station for mountain-bound immigrants and future Utah pioneers.

ALLEN, ALANSON DAVID (son of Albern Allen and Marcia Allen). Born May 2, 1829, Delaware county, N. Y. Came to Utah Oct. 27, 1849, George A. Smith company.
Married Chastina Hadlock Nov. 10, 1850, Salt Lake City (daughter of Stephen A. Hadlock and Sally Aulton; latter a pioneer of Sept., 1850, Capt. Everett company). She was born April 2, 1828, and died March 20, 1913. Their children: Emeline Clarissa b. Aug. 26, 1851, m. Erastus Perry Bingham; Albern Alanson b. Dec. 28, 1852, m. Louisa Stowell Dec. 27, 1883; Orin Daniel b. March 18, 1854, m. Anna C. Bendrup; Emily Chastina b. Nov. 30, 1855, m. John Newry; Marinda b. Feb. 15, 1857, m. John Ingles; Esther b. Sept. 27, 1858, m. John Tangreen; Ammon b. April 23, 1860, m. Isabella Hyslop; Hyrum b. Feb. 20, 1862, m. Nancy A. Wilson; Samuel b. Sept. 15, 1863, m. Louisa C. Danielson; Sarah Ann b. Dec. 9, 1865, m. William G. Moyes; Emma Rozina b. Jan. 18, 1868, m. John H. Jorgenson; Mary Vileta b. Jan. 29, 1870, d. Aug. 6, 1901; David Orlo b. April 21, 1872, m. Emma Louisa Berlin; Andrew Stephen b. Feb. 23, 1874, m. Mary Elizabeth Hyslop. Family home Huntsville, Weber county, Utah.
Seventy. Captain Utah militia 1861-66; captain of ten Echo Canyon war. Farmer.

ALLEN, ALBERN ALANSON (son of Alanson David Allen and Chastina Hadlock). Born Dec. 28, 1852, Willard, Box Elder county, Utah.
Married Louisa Stowell Dec. 27, 1883, Salt Lake City, Utah (daughter of Wm. R. R. and Harriet E. Stowell). Their children: Albern Ethan b. Nov. 20, 1884, m. Winifred Oldham Sept. 12, 1906; Josephine b. Aug. 9, 1886, m. Thomas Leroy Pass June, 1909; Daniel Chester b. Feb. 3, 1889; Rachel Chastina b. Nov. 25, 1890; Heber Clawson b. Jan. 15, 1893; Laura Pearl b. Feb. 27, 1900. Family home Huntsville, Weber county, Utah.
Bishop's counselor. Farmer.

ALLEN, ALBERN ETHAN (son of Albern Alanson Allen and Louisa Stowell). Born Nov. 20, 1884.
Married Winifred Oldham Sept. 12, 1906 (daughter of Samuel Oldham), who was born Dec. 27, 1882, Paradise, Utah. Their children: Lucile b. Sept. 25, 1908; Maud b. Jan. 15, 1911. Family home Providence, Utah.
Elder. School teacher.

ALLEN, ALBERN, JR. (son of Albern Allen and Mary Jane Morris (McCarty). Born Dec. 2, 1854, Ogden, Utah.
Married Elizabeth Evans Jan. 5, 1882, Salt Lake City (daughter of Thomas Evans and Margaret Powell). She was born March 27, 1856, Merthyr Tydfil, Glamorganshire, Wales, and died March 10, 1890, at Ogden, Utah. Their children: Thomas Evans b. Nov. 23, 1882, m. Fern Jackman June 14, 1911; Albern Morris b. Sept. 29, 1885, m. Blanche Lansing Nov. 19, 1906; Edward Nelson b. Nov. 18, 1887; Lawrence and Ruby b. Jan. 23, 1899, both d. same day.
Married Annie Catherine Hansen Feb. 19, 1891, Logan, Utah (daughter of Niels Hansen, born May 23, 1845—pioneer 1868, and Christina Jorgensen, born May, 1836, both of Sjelland, Denmark, died Nov. 14, 1885, at Huntsville, Utah). She was born Aug. 11, 1870, Huntsville, Utah. Their children: David Chester b. March 14, 1892; Marie b. Dec. 10, 1893, d. same day; Merrill b. Aug. 20, 1895, d. same day; Laura and Pearl b. July 7, 1897, both d. same day; Ruth b. Dec. 4, 1899, d. Jan. 24, 1900. Family home Ogden, Utah.

ALLEN, ALEXANDER ALMA (son of Ezra Heela Allen, born July 28, 1814, Madrid, St. Lawrence county, N. Y., and Sarah B. Fiske of Potsdam, N. Y.—married Dec. 25, 1837). He was born Sept. 28, 1845, Nauvoo, Ill. Came to Utah Sept. 14, 1852.
Married Maria E. Cowley April 5, 1869 (daughter of Charles Cowley and Ann Kellet), who was born Oct. 24, 1847, and came to Utah 1850. Their children: Eveline b. April 26, 1870, m. David Brown Nov. 28, 1893; Ezra James b. April 9, 1871; Annie E. b. Sept. 9, 1873, m. John A. Larsen Dec. Oct 14, 1891; Maria b. June 27, 1874, m. John P. Chris Poulsen b. 1896; Amaretta b. April 21, 1876, m. Wm. Fifield Nov. 29, 1893; Alexander C. b. Jan. 27, 1880, m. Rachel Chapman Feb. 3, 1904; Amelia A. b. June 26, 1883, m. J. E. Swann May 18, 1904; Alice A. b. Jan. 17, 1885.
Married Elizabeth Clarke April 11, 1878, Salt Lake City (daughter of John H. Clarke and Elizabeth Herler of England). She was born March 18, 1858, Ogden, Utah. Their children: Oliver A. b. Jan. 9, 1879, m. Zena Erickson; Ethan J. b. Oct. 9, 1880, m. Anne Fifield; Ellen E. b. March 4, 1883, m. Wm. Willisen; Royal b. July 13, 1885; Nettie b. Nov. 12, 1887; Iven b. June 24, 1889; Orin Wm. b. Oct. 11, 1892; Luella E. b. Jan. 11, 1896. Family home Weston, Idaho.
High Priest; Bishop; Missionary to Southern states; Sunday School officer and teacher. Policeman; justice of peace.

ALLEN, ANDREW LEE (son of Elijah Allen, born 1763, and Mehitable Hall, both of New Hampshire). He was born April 24, 1791, Limeric Parsonfield, N. H. Came to Utah Aug. 12, 1852, John M. Higbee company.
Married Clarinda Knapp 1826, who was born Aug. 10, 1802, and came to Utah with husband. Their children: Elijah b. Feb. 7, 1826, m. Eliza Ann Bickmore; Lydia b. June 5, 1827; Sophronia b. Nov. 6, 1828, m. Abram Foster; Charles b. Oct. 15, 1830, m. Adelaide Hoops; Andrew b. Aug. 16, 1832, m. Manerva Whittle; James b. Oct. 12, 1833, m. Mary Mathews; Sidney b. Aug. 12, 1835, m. Ann Cooper; Susan b. Dec. 31, 1837, m. John Goaslind; Levi b. April 1, 1842, m. Lavinia Henson; Julia b. June 8, 1844. Family home Provo, Utah.

ALLEN, ELIJAH (son of Andrew Lee Allen and Clarinda Knapp). Born Feb. 7, 1826, Burton, N. Y.
Married Eliza Ann Bickmore (daughter of William and Christina Bickmore), who was born Jan. 29, 1830. Their children: Elijah b. Feb. 24, 1860; William b. April 17, 1854; Eliza Ann b. June 1, 1856, m. Manassah Barnes; James Carson b. March 21, 1858, m. Betsy Lowe March 1, 1883; Andrew b. Dec. 23, 1859, m. Susie Preece; Henry Heber b. March 11, 1862, m. Algena Poulsen; Joseph Smith b. Oct. 20, 1863, m. Phoebe Andersen Dec. 9, 1885. Family home Fort Herriman, Utah.
Served in Co. B, Mormon Battalion.

ALLEN, JOSEPH SMITH (son of Elijah Allen and Eliza Ann Bickmore). Born Oct. 20, 1863, Ft. Herriman, Utah.
Married Phoebe Andersen (daughter of George Andersen, pioneer 1850, and Mary Ann Davis, d. Aug. 19, 1890, Bountiful, Utah). She was born March 5, 1859, Richmond, Utah. Their children: Joseph Merle b. Nov. 10, 1886; Phoebe Mavil b. July 11, 1889; George Q. b. March 5, 1892; Elmo Smith b. Nov. 25, 1893; Elijah Grover b. Feb. 5, 1895; Alice

Erma b. July 11, 1897; Lucile b. July 27, 1900; Grant Andersen b. Feb. 4, 1904; Mary Ina b. Oct. 20, 1909. Family home Coveville, Utah.
Missionary to southern states and at bureau of information, Salt Lake City; first counselor in the bishopric of Coveville, Utah. Justice of the peace; county commissioner, Cache county, Utah.

ALLEN, LEVI (son of Andrew L. Allen and Clarinda Knapp). Born April 1, 1842, at Virginia, Ill.
Married Lavinia S. Henson Dec. 12, 1888, at Logan, Utah (daughter of Alfred Henson and Mary Ann Sewell, both of whom came to Utah by oxteam in 1868). She was born July 23, 1871, at Franklin, Idaho. Their children: Clarinda H. b. Nov. 3, 1889, m. Louis H. Johnson June 19, 1907; Levi H. b. June 15, 1891; Elijah H. b. May 6, 1893; Jas. H. b. April 1, 1895; Lydia H. b. Sept. 11, 1897; Luren H. b. Aug. 6, 1900; Mary H. b. Oct. 9, 1902; Verona H. b. Feb. 10, 1905; Alfred H. b. Dec. 6, 1907; Olive H. b. March 11, 1910. Family home Cove, Utah.
Assisted in building of St. George temple; assistant superintendent of Sunday school; high priest.

ALLEN, DANIEL (son of Daniel Allen and Nancy Stewart of Chautauqua county, N. Y.). Born Dec. 9, 1804, Whitestown, Oneida county, N. Y. Came to Utah Sept. 22, 1849.
Married Mary Ann Morris Oct. 6, 1828, Cayuga county, N. Y. Their children: LeRoy, d. child; Alma, d. aged 14; Mary Ann. m. John Lowry; Diantha, m. William Berry; Eliza, m. George Baum; Daniel, d. infant.
Married Louisa Jane Berry June 22, 1847, Winter Quarters, Neb. (daughter of Jesse Berry and Amelia Shanks of Tennessee and Illinois, pioneers 1849, Samuel Gulley oxteam company). Their children: Cynthia; Orson; Robert; Joseph; Millie; Lydia; Samuel; Artimicia; John. Family home Salt Lake City.
Married Sarah Whitely 1854, Salt Lake Endowment House. Their children: Isaac; David; Harriet; Hyrum; Fred; James; Anna.
Seventy; missionary to "Dixie" 1862. Black Hawk Indian war veteran. Worked on Nauvoo Temple. Tanned first leather in Utah. Shoemaker and tanner; merchant. Died Jan. 15, 1892, Escalante, Utah.

ALLEN, ELIHU M. (son of Elihu M. Allen and Lola Ann Clauson of New York). Born Oct. 5, 1835, Dryden, N. Y. Came to Utah Aug. 8, 1847, John Scott company.
Married Mary Elizabeth Graham 1854 (daughter of James and Mary Graham, of Pennsylvania), who was born Oct. 8, 1836. Came to Utah 1858, Jedediah Grant company.
Their children: Charles M. b. May 29, 1855; Elihu b. Nov. 8, 1857, m. Mary A. Byard Oct. 13, 1880; Mary L. b. Aug. 23, 1860, m. Hyrum B. Pidcock; F. Isadora b. June 21, 1862, m. F. Edward Chatelain 1882; John F. b. Aug. 11, 1864, m. Mary Harmon 1886; George A. b. June 1, 1866, m. Musett Gribbel 1894; Lola B. b. July 1, 1868, m. Alexander Chatelain 1886; Joseph W. b. March 7, 1870, m. Helen Hatten 1894; Eliza E. b. Dec. 24, 1872, m. Thomas Wright 1891; David b. Aug. 14, 1874, m. Pearl Jensen 1893; Thomas J. b. Sept. 3, 1876. Family home Huntsville, Utah.
Farmer. Elder. Died Nov. 25, 1912, Pocatello, Idaho.

ALLEN, IRA (son of Simeon Allen of Franklin, Mass., born March 11, 1779, and Elizabeth Leavens, born July 4, 1774). He was born April 27, 1814, Thompson, Windham county, Conn. Came to Utah Sept., 1860.
Married Calista Bass Nov. 23, 1834 (daughter of Luther Bass). Their children: John Bass b. April 18, 1835, d. same day; Andrew Augustus b. Oct. 1, 1836, m. Sarah A. Cartwright June 14, 1857; Simeon Franklin b. April 3, 1839, m. Boletta Johnson Dec. 5, 1863; Charles Francis b. May 7, 1841, d. May 7, 1841; Elizabeth Marie b. June 6, 1842, m. Thomas Williams March 8, 1860; Emily Louise b. March 15, 1844, m. Thos. Williams Dec. 24, 1864; Joseph Smith b. Oct. 13, 1846, m. Ellen Israelsen May 23, 1868. Families resided Cedar City and Hyrum, Utah.
Married Keziah Bensen Dec. 1, 1852 (daughter of Alva Bensen and Cynthia Vail), who was born March 10, 1825, Hendricks, Ind. Their children: George Clark b. Dec. 11, 1853, m. Martha Hansen May 28, 1877; Albert J. b. April 26, 1855, m. Phenette Williams Feb. 5, 1877; Ethan Ira b. May 13, 1857, d. 1867; David Bensen b. Feb. 20, 1859, m. Waibor Nielsen Jan. 26, 1887; Hyrum Cache b. Oct. 22, 1861, d. 1863; Doctor Jasper b. Feb. 4, 1864, d. 1864; Fredric Ferransen b. Jan. 10, 1866, d. 1870; John Vernon b. May 7, 1868, d. 1876.
Married Cynthia Elizabeth Bensen (daughter of Alva Bensen and Cynthia Vail). Their children: Cynthia Angela b. June 17, 1859, d. 1863; Elam b. Jan. 22, 1862, m. Alma M. Nielsen March 26, 1891; Laura Ann b. May 11, 1864, m. Albert Savage Oct. 8, 1883; Julia Elizabeth b. June 19, 1866, m. Welby Hufaker March 26, 1896; James Cyrus b. Jan. 29, 1869, m. Ellen Nielsen Jan. 6, 1904; Eliza Jane b. June 3, 1871, m. John Rigby Oct. 7, 1889; Charlotte Temple b. Nov. 3, 1873, m. David Nielsen; Lucy Keziah b. May 28, 1876, m. Isaac Quinney Feb. 14, 1907; Thomas Edwin b. May 31, 1879, m. Minie Petersen June 11, 1902.
Pioneer of Hyrum 1860. Ward clerk; ward teacher. Postmaster. Pioneer canal and road builder. Died Dec. 21, 1900.

ALLEN, ANDREW AUGUSTUS (son of Ira Allen and Calista Bass). Born Oct. 1, 1836, Woodstock, Windham county, Conn.
Married Sarah Ann Cartwright, June 14, 1857, Cedar City, Utah (daughter of Thomas Cartwright and Sarah Yates), who was born Jan. 12, 1840, in Lancashire, Eng. Their children: Andrew Augustus b. Aug. 25, 1858, m. Lovisa Hammond April 4, 1889; Calista Ann b. April 23, 1861, d. May 19, 1878; Thomas Ira b. Oct. 1, 1863, m. Minnie Hammond Jan. 6, 1879; George Q. b. Feb. 16, 1866, d. 1872; Sarah Ellen b. May 30, 1868, m. Ezra Peterson Dec. 22, 1887.
Married Rebecca Christine Nielsen April 14, 1887, Logan, Utah (daughter of Hans Enoch Nielsen, pioneer Sept. 29, 1854, James Brown company, and Nancy Margaret Osborn, pioneer 1852). She was born Jan. 24, 1864, Hyrum, Utah. Their children: Lauretta Jane b. June 27, 1888, m. Reuben Hansen June 1, 1911; Margaret Vilate b. Sept. 11, 1890; Glen Nielsen b. July 15, 1892; Esther b. March 18, 1895; Elva Mae b. Aug. 25, 1898; Bessie b. May 13, 1901; Hollis Verne b. July 19, 1905. Family resided Hyrum, Utah.
Sunday school superintendent; high councilor.

ALLEN, ANDREW AUGUSTUS, JR. (son of Andrew Augustus Allen and Sarah Ann Cartwright). Born Aug. 25, 1858, Cedar City.
Married Lovisa Hammond April 4, 1889, Logan, Utah (daughter of Milton Dates Hammond and Lovisa Miller), who was born July 15, 1866, Providence, Utah. Their children: Hazel Lovisa b. Feb. 3, 1891; Sarah Mabel b. May 15, 1894; Milton Andrew b. April 8, 1897; Ethel Morene b. Nov. 25, 1899; Helen Lenore b. Jan. 27, 1904; Lucile b. March 4, 1907. Family home Hyrum, Utah.
Sunday school and ward teacher; pres. Y. M. M. I. A.; missionary to northern states; bishop 2d ward, Hyrum. Has been school trustee, city councilman and mayor of Hyrum.

ALLEN, JOHN R. (son of James Allen, born 1808, Somerset, Pulaski county, Ky., and Nancy Allen, born 1812, same place). He was born Jan. 29, 1841, Wadsborough, Ky. Came to Utah Sept., 1862, independent company.
Married Sarah Janett Leavitt Nov. 2, 1875, who was born April 17, 1855, Centerville, Utah. Their children: Mahala b. Aug. 9, 1876, m. Allen Green Marler Nov. 12, 1895; John Rial b. April 2, 1878, m. Elsie Elizabeth Bright, Sept. 20, 1899; Annie Mabel b. Aug. 22, 1879, m. James Barjeson; Jesse Leavitt b. Nov. 13, 1881; Hyrum b. June 24, 1883, m. Bell Naylor; Sallie Janette b. March 27, 1886, m. Alma Donaldson Nov. 1, 1907; Jennie b. Oct. 8, 1887, m. Bianca Johnston; Delia b. Nov. 28, 1890, m. William Henry Ellis; Glen b. Sept. 17, 1892; Netta b. Oct. 23, 1894, m. Alma Harris; Dovey Dean b. Aug. 22, 1896; Roasel Lou b. Jan. 11, 1903; Emma Jean. Family home Lewiston, Utah.

ALLEN, JOSEPH S. Came to Utah in 1848, oxteam company.
Married Lucy Morley. Their children: Mary, m. Orville S. Cox; Lucy, m. Frederick W. Cox, Jr.; Caroline, m. Isaac Jones; Isaac, m. Harriet Squires; Albert, m. Harriet Fowler; Harriet, m. John Esplin; Simeon, m. Miss Walker; Clara, d. in childhood. Family home North Bend (near Thistle), Utah.
Elder in Zion's camp. Frontiersman of the typical old school. Cooper by trade and followed farming. Died April 25, 1889, at Huntington, Utah.

ALLEN LEWIS (son of Rial Allen of Andrew county, Mo.). Born June 11, 1813, in Kentucky. Came to Utah Aug., 1862, independent oxteam company.
Married Elizabeth Alexander, 1836, in Jackson county, Mo. (daughter of Jonathan Alexander, pioneer Washington county, Utah 1862). She was born March 2, 1819. Their children: Tabitha Jane b. Oct. 7, 1838, m. Woodruff Freeman; Beulah Ann b. May 24, 1840, m. Willis Webb; William b. Sept. 12, 1842, d. infant; Rial b. Feb. 27, 1844, m. Susan Collins; Jonathan Alexander b. Jan. 30, 1846, m. Jane Nelson; Samuel b. Jan. 17, 1848, d. infant; James B. b. Aug. 16, 1850, m. Maria West; Margaret E. b. Jan. 20, 1852, m. Brigham Y. Baird; Sarah Melissa b. May 30, 1854, m. Daniel V. Leroy; Andrew Jackson b. Dec. 20, 1856, m. Sariah E. Pulsipher; Martha Permelia b. May 23, 1858, m. William Marshall; Nancy Esther b. Dec. 9, 1861, m. Isaac E. Black; Mary Ellen b. April 11, 1866, m. Albert Allen. Family resided Washington, and Moccasin spring ranch, near Kanab, Utah.
Ward teacher; seventy; high priest; missionary to Nevada. Farmer. Died Dec., 1883, Orderville, Utah.

ALLEN, ORVILLE MORGAN. Born June 9, 1805, Pike county, Mo. Came to Utah December, 1852, captain of one of the large companies of immigrants to Utah.
Married Jane Wilson 1825. Among their children was Laura Josephine b. April 4, 1846, m. Myron Abbott April 25, 1861, Ogden, Utah.
He was a lineal descendant of Ethan Allen of Revolutionary fame. Joined the L. D. S. church 1838, for which he was disinherited by his father. Once a member of bodyguard of Joseph Smith at Nauvoo. On arrival in Utah,

settled at Springville, later at Spanish Fork, Toquerville, and Kanab, and at latter place he served as probate judge of Kane county. Finally settled at Pima, Ariz., 1880; there he died 1893, aged 68 years. He was the father of fifteen children.

ALLEN, PETER (son of John Allen and Hannah Willis of Cold Ash, Berkshire, Eng.). Born Jan. 5, 1849, Cold Ash, Eng. Came to Utah Sept. 15, 1861, Ira Eldredge company.
Married Ellen Thomas Oct. 10, 1868, Salt Lake City (daughter of Benjamin and Ellen Thomas of Pembrokeshire, South Wales). She was born May 14, 1849. Their children: John David b. Aug. 14, 1869; Mary Ellen b. Dec. 10, 1870, m. Juhn T. Price; Parley Peter b. Jan. 11, 1872, m. Rhoda Ann Beveridge; Anna b. March 11, 1873, m. Howard Messenger; Joseph Franklin b. April 14, 1875, m. Ella Nelson; Hyrum b. March 30, 1877, m. Rose Wright; Moroni b. Nov. 4, 1878, m. Maud Steers Broadbent; Hannah b. May 15, 1882, m. Peter Neil; Benjamin Thomas b. Nov. 25, 1884; Martha Jane b. Aug. 2, 1886. Family resided Laketown, Utah, Star Valley, Wyo., Alberta, Can., La Grande, Ore.
Married Louisa Fisher Nov. 6, 1884, Logan, Utah (daughter of Ulrich and Elizabeth Fisher of Paris, Bear Lake county, Idaho). She was born Oct. 14, 1868. Their children: Louise Elizabeth b. Feb. 23, 1886, m. Dan B. Locke; Lilly May b. Sept. 5, 1887, m. David Beveridge; Henry James b. Sept. 11, 1889, m. Ida May Beveridge; Ezra Clarence b. Oct. 14, 1891, m. Inis McKin; Samuel Ray b. Feb. 6, 1894; Heber b. Dec. 26, 1895; Catharine Edith b. Jan. 3, 1898; Charlotte Irene b. April 22, 1900; Elmer b. Aug. 18, 1905; Elva Fisher b. June 20, 1908. Family home, La Grande, Ore.
Seventy; high priest; missionary to England 1903-04.

ALLEN, RUFUS (son of Gideon Allen and Rachel Hand). Born 1814, in Connecticut. Came to Utah July 24, 1847, Brigham Young company.
Married Mary Phelps, 1860, at Ogden, Utah (daughter of John Phelps and Mary Shaw of Riverdale, Utah). She was born July 1, 1831. Their children: Rachel; Rufus; Elizabeth L.; William b. Jan. 10, 1866, m. Polly Child March 17, 1887; Arlo; Harriet; Alma.
President 76th quorum seventies. Died Dec. 4, 1887, at Riverdale, Utah.

ALLEN, WILLIAM (son of Rufus Allen and Mary Phelps). Born Jan. 10, 1866, Riverdale, Utah.
Married Polly Child March 17, 1887, Logan, Utah (daughter of Myron B. Child and Emaline Elmer of Riverdale, Utah, pioneers 1850). She was born Nov. 13, 1867. Their children: Clara L. b. Feb. 8, 1888, m. Joseph K. Wright; Elnora b. Feb. 1, 1890, m. Arthur Couch; W. Arthur b. July 28, 1892; Mary E. b. March 10, 1894; John D. b. Oct. 24, 1896; Isabel b. Dec. 15, 1898; Gertrude b. April 5, 1901, d. aged 15 months; Myron E. b. Nov. 25, 1903; Herbert R. b. July 7, 1908; Lillian b. Feb. 28, 1910; Lois b. April 1, 1912. Family home Riverdale, Utah.
Elder. County assessor several years. Farmer.

ALLEN, SAMUEL (son of William Allen and Hannah Lord, of Radcliffe, Eng.). Born May 29, 1829, at Radcliffe, Eng. Came to Utah Oct. 14, 1853, Cyrus H. Wheelock company.
Married Harriet Moore 1853 at Salt Lake City (daughter of Peter Moore and Harriet Burgess of Lower Teen, Staffordshire, Eng.). She was born Aug. 13, 1829. Their children: Caroline; Melissa; Martha; Samuel H.; Sarah H.; Mary; Rozella; William. Family home Mt. Pleasant, Utah.
Farmer. Died March 10, 1910, at Mt. Pleasant, Utah.

ALLEN, SAMUEL H. (son of Samuel Allen and Harriet Moore). Born Aug. 15, 1862, Mt. Pleasant, Utah.
Married Ida May Lowry June 8, 1892, Manti, Utah (daughter of John Lowry and Sarah Jane Brown of Manti, Utah,—pioneers sent, 1847, John Brown company). She was born July 30, 1865. Their children: Lowry b. April 3, 1893; Erma b. Nov. 12, 1895; Ruth b. April 3, 1899; Ethel b. April 18, 1901; Olive b. May 11, 1902; Marjorie b. Aug. 26, 1905. Family resided Provo and Salt Lake City, Utah.
Member 124th quorum seventies; missionary to England 1883-85; Sunday school teacher and superintendent, Utah county physician five years; member Mt. Pleasant city council two terms; district school trustee; first principal Mt. Pleasant high school 1887-88. Life patron International Council of Women. Member Utah State Board of Medical Examiners and State Board of Health; surgeon R. G. W. R. R.; gynecologist and surgeon on staff of L. D. S. hospital; resident physician Maryland Maternity hospital at Baltimore 1890-91; state commissioner for the adult blind; member Salt Lake County and State Medical societies; member American Medical association; life member Surgeons' club of Rochester, Minn.; member American Medical association of Vienna, Austria.

ALLMAN, THOMAS (son of John Allman and Catherine Mollart, of Hanley, Staffordshire, Eng.). Born May 30, 1819, Hanley, Eng. Came to Utah Sept. 8, 1850, Aaron Johnson company.
Married Prudence Mills at Hanley, Eng. She died at Nauvoo. Their children: John b. 1840, d. 1846; Ruben b. May 31, 1843, d. 1844.

Married Jane Walker Oct. 5, 1844, Nauvoo, Ill. (daughter of Samuel Walker of Worthington, Staffordshire, Eng.). She was born March 12, 1815. Only child: Emma Jane, m. Samuel Steven Jones. Family home Salt Lake City.
Married Elmira Phillips 1862, American Fork, Utah (daughter of Richard Phillips and Margaret Luker—pioneers Sept. 13, 1861, Milo Andrus company). She was born Oct. 21, 1838. Their children: Mary Ann b. June 26, 1864, m. George Grant Simons; Prudella b. Dec. 12, 1865, m. Warren E. Connant and William D. Alexander; Thomas M. b. April 4, 1867, m. Elizabeth Lloyd and Mary A. Allen; Levi W. b. April 16, 1869, m. Mary Aurora Noble; Clara V. b. March 5, 1871, m. Chas. B. Snyder; Albert b. April 10, 1873, m. Almira Curtis; Jessie M. b. July 24, 1876, m. Burt Brown; Dora b. Oct. 14, 1878, m. Conrad Hansen; Nora b. Oct. 14, 1878, m. James Paul Conroy; Dianthy b. Feb. 8, 1881, died; Samuel b. Oct. 12, 1882, m. Libby Hochstrasser. Family home Provo, Utah.
Member high council, Utah stake, three years; first counselor to bishop of first ward 26 years; counselor to president of high priests' quorum in Utah stake. Provo city councilman. Carpenter, cabinetmaker and builder. Died July 22, 1889, Provo, Utah.

ALLMAN, THOMAS M. (son of Thomas Allman and Elmira Phillips). Born April 4, 1867, Provo, Utah.
Married Elizabeth Lloyd Nov. 28, 1889, Provo, Utah (daughter of William E. Lloyd and Sarah Morgan of Spanish Fork, Utah). She was born March 3, 1871. Only child: Thomas Grant b. Oct. 18, 1890.
Married Mary Alice Allen Dec. 2, 1896, Provo, Utah (daughter of William W. Allen and Eliza Ann Fenn of Nephi, Utah—pioneers 1852). She was born Feb. 13, 1871. Their children: Vernon Allen b. Dec. 25, 1897; Glen Walker b. Aug. 9, 1901; Melba Elmira b. Jan. 21, 1904; Marva Alice b. Sept. 9, 1906; Edna Elizabeth b. May 28, 1911. Family home Provo, Utah.
Carpenter and builder; expert wood carver, taking first prizes for this class of artistic work at the Utah State fair in the years 1900, 1904, 1909, Utah State Art institute in 1910, and Western States fair held at Denver in 1910.

ALLRED, DAVID H. Born in Tennessee in 1825. Came to Utah in 1859.
Married Aurora Brown in Tennessee. She was born in 1827. Their children: William, m. Matilda Christenson; James, m. Maria Black; John, m. Mary Wilson; Mary, m. Louis Austinson; Percy, m. Sene Black; Sarah, m. George L. Bemis.
Farmer. Died at the family home Aug. 26, 1910, Spring City, Utah.

ALLRED, ISAAC (son of John Allred and Mary McCurdy). Born Jan. 27, 1788, Pendleton county, Ga. Came to Utah July 24, 1847, Brigham Young company.
Married Mary Calvert Feb. 14, 1811 (daughter of John Calvert and Mary McGardy of Georgia). She was born March 19, 1793. Their children: Elizabeth b. Jan. 6, 1812; John Calvert b. Oct. 5, 1813, m. Eliza Bates Aug. 22, 1833; Nancy Weasley b. Nov. 9, 1815, m. Asa Earl Feb. 26, 1842; Sarah Lovisa b. Nov. 14, 1817, m. Allen Taylor Sept. 5, 1833; William More b. Dec. 24, 1819, m. Orissa Angelia Bates Jan. 9, 1842; Redden Alexander b. Feb. 21, 1822, m. Julia Ann Bates Dec. 19, 1843; Jedick Newton b. Feb. 11, 1822, m. Lucy Hoyt Nov. 26, 1843; Mary Caroline b. Dec. 9, 1824, m. Joseph Egbert Dec. 6, 1843; James b. Jan. 28, 1827; Paulinus Harvey b. Jan. 21, 1829, m. Malissa Norton; Joseph Anderson b. April 26, 1831, m. Rhoda Palmer; Isaac Morley b. Jan. 2, 1835, m. Charlott Henderson; Sidney Rigdon b. Oct. 23, 1837, m. Lucy Ann Allred May 13, 1860.
Married Matilda Stewart. Only child: Matilda S. b. May 12, 1853, m. John Robinson Dec. 11, 1871.

ALLRED, WILLIAM MORE (son of Isaac Allred and Mary Calvert). Born Dec. 24, 1819, Nashville, Tenn.
Married Orissa Angelia Bates Jan. 9, 1842 (daughter of Cyrus and Lydia Bates, former a pioneer Oct. 1, 1851, James Cummings company). She was born Aug. 17, 1823. Their children: William Lansing b. Oct. 18, 1842, m. Sarah A. Wilkes Jan. 23, 1867; Mary Adaline b. Dec. 20, 1844, m. Mosiah Booth; Byron Harvey b. May 29, 1847, m. Phoebe Irena Cook Oct. 5, 1867; Marvin Adelbert b. Aug. 13, 1849, m. Amanda J. Bird July 17, 1871; Amelia Lorinda b. July 30, 1851; Malvin Hilbert b. Oct. 11, 1853; Medwin Newton b. Feb. 20, 1855, m. Maria J. Stock May 31, 1875; Orissa Angelia b. June 16, 1857, m. William C. Wilhelmson May 31, 1875; Lydia Lavette b. Sept. 23, 1859, m. C. A. Merkley May 24, 1877; Seymour Legrand b. April 15, 1862, m. Claudia Stock June 21, 1883; Nelson Calvert b. Oct. 5, 1865, m. Sarah Miranda Nelson April 12, 1888; Orson Pratt b. Nov. 29, 1867, m. Sarah Jane Rich Nov. 25, 1887.
Married Martha Martindale Feb., 1857 (daughter of William Martindale). Their children: Edgar Martindale b. Feb. 27, 1858, m. Nancy Hunt Nov. 19, 1890; Martha B. b. Nov., 1860.
Sunday school superintendent, St. Charles 24 years, and of Bear Lake stake three years; high priest. Pioneer of Grantsville, Utah, 1856, of St. Charles, Bear Lake Valley, Ida., and of Fairview, Star Valley, Wyo.

ALLRED, WILLIAM LANSING (son of William More Allred and Orissa Angelia Bates). Born Oct. 18, 1842.
Married Sarah A. Wilkes Jan. 23, 1867, St. Charles, Ida. (daughter of William Wilkes, pioneer 1851, James Cum-

mings company). Their children: Sarah Ann, m. William Pugmire; William Lansing; John Wilkes; Elizabeth Uzelle, m. William H. Michaelson; Ernest b. June 16, 1877, m. Orissa Rich. Family home St. Charles, Ida.

ALLRED, REDDEN ALEXANDER (son of Isaac Allred and Mary Calvert). Born Feb. 21, 1822. Married Julia Bates Dec. 21, 1843. Only child: Milford Alexander b. Feb. 17, 1857, m. Elizabeth Johnson Sept. 15, 1879.

ALLRED, MILFORD ALEXANDER (son of Redden Alexander Allred and Julia Bates). Born Feb. 17, 1857, Salt Lake City. Married Elizabeth Johnson Sept. 15, 1879, Ephraim, Utah (daughter of Christopher and Marian Johnson of Risor, Norway). She was born Sept. 23, 1856. Their children: Ida May b. Aug. 15, 1880, d. child; Marian Bell b. May 8, 1883, m. William L. Burton; Milford Lasalle b. May 27, 1885, d. infant; Ella Maud b. Oct. 16, 1886, m. John G. Stoker; Ethelwin b. Jan. 21, 1889, d. child; Arthur J. b. Sept. 11, 1891; Amos Larue b. Sept. 23, 1893; Milton Russel b. Oct. 4, 1896. Family home Salt Lake City. Miner and fireman in copper mine at Bisbee, Ariz. Died there May 20, 1898.

ALLRED, PAULINUS HARVEY (son of Isaac Allred and Mary Calvert). Born Jan. 21, 1829, Farmington. Bedford county, Tenn. Came to Utah July 24, 1847, Brigham Young company. Married Melissa Norton (daughter of David and Elizabeth Norton), who was born in Indiana. Their children: James b. Jan. 10, 1849, m. Kate M. Jones; Isaac H. b. Nov. 22, 1850, m. Ursula Mulliner June 4, 1871; Dilbert b. March 25, 1853, m. Orinda Davis; Melissa b. Dec. 14, 1854, m. Chris Peterson; Paulinus Heber b. March 7, 1857, m. Sarah Jacobs; Orissa b. Nov. 9, 1858, m. Ed. Smith; Alma H. b. March 31, 1861, m. Luella Angel; Joseph H. b. June 6, 1863, d. child. Family home Lehi, Utah. Colonel Nauvoo Legion; seventy; assisted in bringing immigrants to Utah.

ALLRED, ISAAC H. (son of Paulinus Harvey and Melissa Norton Allred). He was born Nov. 22, 1850, Cottonwood, Salt Lake county, Utah. Married Ursula Mulliner June 4, 1871, Lehi, Utah (daughter of Samuel Mulliner, pioneer 1847, and Mary Richardson). She was born Nov. 26, 1854, Salt Lake City. Their children: Paulinus Harvey b. Jan. 17, 1874, m. Salome M. Kunz Aug. 23, 1905; Joseph S. b. June 1, 1878, m. Mary J. Dayley Feb. 26, 1906; Mary U. b. Feb. 12, 1880, m. Ed. Parsons June 10, 1904; Sterling H. b. Oct. 3, 1882, d. Dec. 29, 1911; Lillian A. b. Oct. 1, 1885, m. Robert Stone Jan. 28, 1904; Fannie O. b. Oct. 6, 1888, m. Herbert Adams Jan. 9, 1912; Iona Rose b. March 17, 1891, m. Robert Manning July 24, 1907. High priest; member first bishopric of Riverside, Bingham county, Ida. Lieutenant of scouts during early Indian troubles.

ALLRED, JAMES. Came to Utah 1851. Married Elizabeth Warren, who died 1880. Their children: William Hockley; Morton; Isaac; Lafayette; Reuben Warren, m. Lucy Ann Butler; James Tillman Sanford, m. Paulina Allred; Andrew Jackson, m. Eliza Ivey and Martina Anderson; Hannah; Elizabeth; Nancy; Wiley Payne, m. Sarah Zabriskie, m. Elizabeth Ann Davis, m. Johannah Olsen, m. Caroline Andrea Frederickson. Farmer. Died 1876 Spring City, Utah.

ALLRED, REUBEN WARREN, (son of James Allred and Elizabeth Warren). Born Nov. 18, 1815, Bedford county, Tenn. Came to Utah 1849, Allen Taylor company. Married Lucy Ann Butler, who was born Aug. 6, 1814, and came to Utah with husband. Their children: Nancy Cynthia b. Jan. 20, 1840, m. Joseph S. Black; Thomas Butler b. March 17, 1841, m. Catherine Ann Clay Sept. 26, 1870; Anna Caroline: Lucy Ann, m. Sidney R. Allred; Reuben Warren, m. Clara A. Robinson Dec., 1870; Drucilla E., m. Louis F. Lund; Ephraim L., m. Harriet M. Bronson; Eliza Elvira, m. Reddick R. Allred; John L., m. Sarah Elvira Bardick. Family home Spring City, Utah.

ALLRED, THOMAS BUTLER (son of Reuben Warren Allred and Lucy Ann Butler). Born March 17, 1841. Came to Utah with parents. Married Frances Ann Fretwell Feb. 22, 1864. She died Aug. 15, 1866. Only child: Thomas Butler. Married Catherine A. Clay Sept. 26, 1870. Their children: Kenion Berley b. June 20, 1871, m. Anna E. Hess April 19, 1906; Joseph b. March 3, 1874; Reuben Warren b. Oct. 9, 1875; Martha Catherine b. May 17, 1878, m. Miles Gruner Feb. 22, 1899; Lucy Emmeline b. Aug. 6, 1880, m. William T. Stapley, Feb. 22, 1912; Cynthia Butler b. Nov. 9, 1882; John Ephraim b. Oct. 10, 1884; Clay b. Oct. 7, 1887. Family resided Spring City, Deseret and Hinckley, Utah. Married Hannah Stoddard Barney Dec. 25, 1879. Their children: Angus; Alpin L.; Lloyd. Family home Deseret, Utah. Ward teacher 45 years; seventy. Minute man in early Indian troubles. Made three trips across plains for immigrants. Member city council of Spring City. Worked on Manti temple. Indian war veteran. Died Nov. 27, 1910, Salt Lake City.

ALLRED, WILEY PAYNE (son of James Allred and Elizabeth Warren). Born May 31, 1818, Farmington. Bedford county, Tenn. Came to Utah 1851. Married Sarah Zabriskie June 26, 1836 (daughter of Henry Zabriskie and Ellen Galpin, of Eugene county, Ind.—pioneers 1851). She was born Oct. 8, 1814, Eugene county, Ind., died May 22, 1851, while en route to Utah. Their children: James Henry b. June 17, 1837; Parley Pratt b. July 8, 1839, m. Caroline Anderson; Elizabeth Hannah b. Sept. 27, 1843, m. Sanford Holman; Wiley Payne b. Jan. 19, 1847, m. Emma Anderson; Sarah Eleanor b. June 10, 1850. Family resided Provo and Fountain Green, Utah. Married Elizabeth Ann Davis July 2, 1851. She was born July 15, 1815. Their child: Mary Eliza b. July 31, 1852, m. Andrew Anderson. Family home Fountain Green, Utah. Married Johannah Olsen Oct. 28, 1863, Salt Lake City (daughter of Hans Olsen of Hydleberg, Sweden). She was born Nov. 10, 1835, and came to Utah 1863. Their children: William Alma b. July 28, 1864, m. Nancy Miles; Hulda Deseret b. March 10, 1866, m. Joseph Nielson; Martin b. June 11, 1868, m. Susan Jane Barney; Isaac b. Sept. 7, 1870, m. Johannah Christina Christensen; Reuben, m. April 28, 1874, died; Lena b. Dec. 15, 1875, died; John Taylor b. Nov. 31, 1879. Family home Spring City and Emery, Utah. Married Caroline Andrea Frederickson July 31, 1871, Salt Lake City. She was born Nov. 18, 1841; died Nov. 8, 1873, Fountain Creek, Utah. High priest; bishop in Sevier county 1853. Settled at Provo, moved to San Pete county and from there to Emery. Indian war veteran. Stone cutter. Died March 28, 1912, Emery, Utah.

ALLRED, ISAAC (son of Wiley Payne Allred and Johannah Olsen). He was born Sept. 7, 1870, Fountain Green, Utah. Married Johannah Christina Christensen March 20, 1889, Manti, Utah (daughter of Casper Christensen, born Sept. 6, 1827, Hjorring, Denmark, and Maren Lund, born Aug. 1, 1842, Lyngby Sogn, Denmark. They came to Utah 1875 and located at Spring City). She was born Nov. 22, 1868. Their children: Isaac Marion b. May 16, 1892, d. Oct. 3, 1893; Mary Johannah b. June 25, 1894, m. Edward Lynn Peacock June 28, 1912; Reuben Merrill b. March 12, 1897; Harvey b. June 17, 1900; Senie Theora b. Feb. 21, 1903; James Casper b. Jan. 22, 1906, d. May 18, 1907. Howard W. P. b. July 26, 1908, d. Aug. 8, 1908; Glendon Ludene b. Sept. 14, 1911. Family home Emery, Utah. Member 149th quorum seventies; missionary to Northwestern states 1907-09; presided over elders' quorum; ward teacher; Sunday school teacher fifteen years; member stake high council. President Emery Canal & Reservoir Co.; member Emery city council; health officer; member advisory board Emery Stockraisers' association. Farmer.

ALLRED, JOHN JONES (son of William Allred and Sarah Ann Warren of Bedford county, Tenn.). Born Sept. 1, 1821, Bedford county, Tenn. Came to Utah Aug. 16, 1851, David H. Cannon company. Married Jane Hoops Sept. 4, 1845, who was born Aug. 26, 1827. Their children: Sarah Eliza b. Jan. 16, 1848, m. Harden Whitlock 1863; Rebecca Jane b. Dec. 14, 1851, m. Oliver De Milla, 1863; Mary Elizabeth b. Oct. 10, 1851. Family home Platte county, Mo. Married Mary Young Bridgman Sept. 22, 1852, Smithville. Clay county, Mo. (daughter of Robert Bridgman and Polly Davis of Clay county, Mo., pioneers Sept. 1850, Aaron Johnson company). She was born March 10, 1837. Their children: Alice Virginia b. April 27, 1854, m. Oliver D. Gifford; John Newton b. June 28, 1856, m. Anna B. Campbell; Henry Lafayette b. Jan. 20, 1858, d. Feb. 26, 1866; James H. b. Sept. 22, 1859, d. Feb. 19, 1861; Charles Albert b. Feb. 16, 1861, d. Sept. 6, 1861; Orson Hyde b. May 22, 1863, d. June 10, 1865; Joseph Parley b. Dec. 26, 1864, m. Rozina Brown; Anson L. b. May 6, 1866, d. Aug. 1866; Edward W. b. Oct. 25, 1868, m. Alvreen Lemons; Clara R. b. May 19, 1870, m. James William Adams; Evinda L. b. May 4, 1872, m. Cornelius Workman; Florence O. b. Feb. 13, 1874, m. Moses M. Emmett; Mary Emma b. May 2, 1875, m. Robert D. Jolley; Angnettie b. Aug. 19, 1876, m. Franklin Asay; Willard B. b. Feb. 10, 1878, m. Mary M. Zeller; Polly A. b. March 2, 1880, m. Ira W. Lynn. Family home Washington county, Utah. High priest. Died March 16, 1898.

ALLRED, JOSEPH PARLEY (son of John Jones Allred and Mary Young Bridgman). Born Dec. 26, 1864, Shunesburg, Washington county, Utah. Married Rozina Brown June 13, 1888, St. George, Utah (daughter of Robert H. Brown and Eunice Pectol of Springdale, Washington county, Utah, former a pioneer, 1851, latter, 1850). She was born June 17, 1868. Their children: Joseph Parley b. June 15, 1889; Eunice Sarah b. Aug. 8, 1891; John Alvin b. Dec. 6, 1893; Mary Melissa b. May 28, 1896; Berneta Rozina b. June 21, 1899; Ervin b. Nov. 7, 1901; Chastie Emerine b. Oct. 8, 1904. Family home Orderville, Kane county, Utah.

ALLRED, SILAS LAFAYETTE (son of Lafayette Allred and Marinda M. Knapp). Born at Council Bluffs, 1848. Came to Utah, in 1851, Isaac Allred company. Married Sarah Louisa Turner in 1871 at Provo, Utah (daughter of John Wesley Turner and Sarah Fawcett, pioneers 1847). She was born in 1854. Their children: Nellie

PIONEERS AND PROMINENT MEN OF UTAH

B. m. Chas. W. Tenney; Eugene Scott m. Retta Bowlden; Edna L. m. Ray Packard; John Frank m. Margaret Wood; Charles Henry m. Coset Brown; Fawn m. Francis J. Headquist; Lillian; Bessie m. J. Francis Jones; William m. Ethel Reed; Dott; Zelia; Sadie. Family home Bellevue, Blaine county, Idaho.
Elder. Farmer and stockraiser.

ALLRED, EUGENE SCOTT (son of Silas Lafayette Allred and Sarah Louisa Turner). Born Oct. 27, 1875, Provo, Utah.
Married Retta Bowlden June 1, 1896, Springville, Utah (daughter of Jas. Bowlden of London, Eng., and Ophelia Leona Avery of Springville, Utah). She was born Dec. 8, 1876. Their children: Leone b. Oct. 27, 1897, d. infant; Clarence Eugene b. May 21, 1899; Silas Earl b. March 19, 1901; Harold b. Oct. 3, 1902; Howard b. March 17, 1905; Ralph b. Oct. 5, 1908.
Elder, presiding at Cove Branch, Blaine county, Oneida, and Bellevue, Idaho; superintendent of Sunday school. Early settler in Idaho. Farmer and stock-raiser.

ALLSOP, JOHN (son of Ira Allsop and Lucretia Winn of Manchester, Eng.). Born Sept. 20, 1823, Nottingham, Eng.; came to Utah Oct. 1854.
Married Mary E. Wood Sept. 12, 1854, Rawlins, Wyo. (daughter of Joseph Wood). She was born Jan. 20, 1836, on Isle of Man, Eng. Their children: John Ira b. July 2, 1855, m. Mary E. Tanner; Susannah m. W. C. Ormond; Charles m. Rose Rawsell; Thomas m. Sylvia Pert; Alice m. Palmer Calkins; Elizabeth m. George Hamp; Joseph m. Louisa Egbert; Reuben m. Annie Olsen. Family home Richmond, Utah.
Married Annah Eskelson March 17, 1868, Salt Lake City (daughter of Nels Eskelson). She was born in Denmark. Their children: Sarah b. March 17, 1869, m. Edward Thompson March 18, 1883; Josephine b. July 12, 1870, m. William Frish Sept. 1, 1888; Ezra b. March 12, 1873; George b. Nov. 20, 1875, d. Oct. 26, 1876.

ALLSOP, JOHN IRA (son of John Allsop and Mary E. Wood). Born July 2, 1855.
Married Mary E. Tanner May 8, 1879, Salt Lake City (daughter of George Tanner and Martha Craner of Tooele, Utah, who came to Utah with a handcart company). She was born Nov. 5, 1862. Their children: John b. April 12, 1880, d. Jan. 8, 1889; Evelyn b. June 26, 1883, m. Kepler Sessions Nov. 11, 1903; George b. Feb. 15, 1885, m. Eliza Christenson Oct. 4, 1906; Elizabeth b. Feb. 13, 1887, m. Denzil Poulsen Feb. 28, 1906; William b. Jan. 30, 1889; Alma b. Jan. 30, 1892; Louisa b. Jan. 15, 1894; Chloe b. June 13, 1896, m. John B. Goldsberry, Jan. 30, 1913; Albert b. March 26, 1901. Family resided Richmond, Utah, and Gentile Valley, Idaho; for the past 18 years, Grace, Idaho.

ALSTON, JOSEPH. Came to Utah Oct. 10, 1848, Willard Richards and Amasa M. Lyman's last division of 10 wagons.
Married Margaret Hall of Blackburn, Lancashire, Eng., who came to Utah with husband. Their children: Jane, m. David Ingersoll; Annie, m. Frank Edwards; Susannah A. b. July 23, 1856, m. James T. Chamberlain July 23, 1882; Joseph, Jr., m. Louisa Grant; Margaret Alice b. April 16, 1863 (d. Jan. 30, 1888), m. Alfred Joseph Broderick Dec. 31, 1880; Lydia. Family home American Fork, Utah.
Farmer. Died at American Fork.

ALVORD, THADDEUS. Born Oct. 28, 1781. Came to Utah Oct. 28, 1849.
Married Martha Bromley January, 1801. Seven children were born to them.
Married Sally Wellington. Only child: Charlotte, died.
Married Sally Briggs 1829. Six children were born to them.

ALVORD, JOSEPH B. (son of Thaddeus Alvord). Born Dec. 4, 1830, Waterford, Oakland county, Mich.). Came to Utah Oct. 28, 1849.
Married Lenora Berrett. Only child: Lenora.
Married Sarah E. Mower Nov. 15, 1880. Four children were born to them, among whom was Joseph B., who married Bertha Heidberg.
Settled at North Ogden 1851, and took an active part in the developing of the country, in irrigation and educational lines. Died Jan. 9, 1907, West Weber, Utah.

ALVORD, JOSEPH B. (son of Joseph B. Alvord and Sarah E. Mower). Born Aug. 20, 1883, West Weber, Utah.
Married Bertha Heidberg March 18, 1907, Salt Lake City. Their children: Joseph Byron and Oscar Hilden. Family home. West Weber.
Missionary to Netherlands two years. Farmer.

AMES, IRA (son of Ithamer Ames of Bennington county, Vt.). Born Sept. 22, 1804, in Bennington county, Vt. Came to Utah fall of 1851.
Married Charity Carter Dec. 5, 1826, at Benson, Vt. (daughter of Jabez Carter of Benson). She was born Feb. 25, 1807, and came to Utah with husband. Their children: Clarissa b. Dec. 16, 1827, m. Philip Pugsley Aug., 1866; Rebecca b. 1830, m. Isaiah Huntsman Jan. 16, 1849; Clark; Ira; Daniel d. infant. The family home was Wellsville, Cache Valley, Utah.
Member Wellsville quorum seventies. Shoemaker, tanner, flourmiller, merchant and farmer. Died Jan. 15, 1869, Wellsville, Utah.

ANDERSEN, ANDERS NIELSEN (son of Niels Andersen of Lystrup and Anne Christoffersen of Hyllede, Presto amt. Denmark). Born Oct. 31, 1812. Came to Utah Sept. 27, 1862, John R. Murdock company.
Married Cathrine Sophia Pedersen (daughter of Peder Pedersen and Kjersten Nielsen Hansen), who was born March 27, 1827. Their children: Annie Chrestina b. Nov. 13, 1852, m. Peter Johnson May 9, 1888; Jonathan Nielsen b. Dec. 13, 1865, m. Ellen M. Tingey Nov. 19, 1885.
Married Mette Christena Nielsen Oct. 12, 1878, Salt Lake City (daughter of Niels Pedersen and Annie Rasmussen, who came to Utah Aug. 20, 1883). She was born Dec. 19, 1838, Denmark. Families lived at Brigham City, Utah.
Was a pioneer road builder of Box Elder county. Died Jan. 20, 1899.

ANDERSEN, JONATHAN NIELSEN (son of Anders Nielsen Andersen and Cathrine S. Pedersen). Born Dec. 13, 1865, Brigham City, Utah.
Married Ellen M. Tingey Nov. 19, 1885, Logan. Utah (daughter of Henry Tingey and Maria Page). She was born July 14, 1866, Bountiful, Utah. Their children: Jonathan W. b. Nov. 3, 1887; Ernest Luther b. Jan. 18, 1889; Joseph Lester b. July 27, 1890; James Earl b. Jan. 18, 1892; Ellen Myrtle b. March 2, 1895; David Oswald b. Dec. 5, 1896; Alonzo b. Sept. 17, 1899; Cora Maria b. Feb. 23, 1902; Catherine Lucretia b. Aug. 14, 1903; Amelia Lavern b. March 8, 1912. Family home Brigham City, Utah.
Ward teacher 1882-1912; president Elders Quorum, member religion class board; asst. Sunday school supt.; seventy; high priest.

ANDERSEN, ANDREW (son of Jens Andersen of Denmark). Born 1814, Hvisted, Denmark. Came to Utah Sept. 15, 1859, Robert F. Neslen company.
Married Mary Ann Jespersen (daughter of Niels Jespersen of Denmark), who was born 1816. Their children: Jens b. Jan. 1834, m. Christiana Nielsen; Niels Peter b. Sept. 16, 1836, m. Karen Christina Christensen; Kjirsten Marie b. 1838, m. F. J. Christensen; Andreas b. Sept. 8, 1840, m. Elsie ———; Mary Johanna b. 1842, died; Christian b. June 15, 1844, m. Martha Heap; John b. 1846, died; Louis C. b. May 24, 1849, m. Lena Bertelsen; Jens Antone, died; Jens Christian Antone, d. 1855. Family home Monroe, Utah.
High priest. Early settler Spring City, moved to the Muddy 1865, and to Monroe in 1871. Farmer (deceased).

ANDERSEN, LOUIS CHRISTIAN (son of Andrew Andersen and Mary Ann Jespersen). Born May 24, 1849, Denmark. Came to Utah 1859 with parents.
Married Lena Bertelsen June 17, 1872, Salt Lake City (daughter of Bertel Hansen and Berzette Jensen; latter came to Utah 1868). She was born July 24, 1856, in Denmark. Their children: Louis b. May 15, 1873; Caroline b. May 7, 1876, m. Jacob Barney; Mary b. April 17, 1879, m. Thomas Barney; Nora b. Feb. 25, 1882, m. Christian Nielsen; Andrew b. Nov. 12, 1884, d. 1890; Orvel b. Sept. 9, 1887, m. Rose Sorenson; Agnes b. March 2, 1890, m. Christian Sorenson; June Monroe b. May 14, 1893; Audrey b. April 9, 1896. Family home Monroe, Utah.
Pioneer Sanpete and Sevier counties; helped colonize the Muddy. Elder. Farmer and stockraiser. Died July 13, 1912, Monroe, Utah.

ANDERSEN, CHRISTEN (son of Andrew Andersen of Svenstrup, Soro amt. Denmark). Born Feb. 18, 1796, Copenhagen, Denmark. Came to Utah 1862.
Married Katherine Jensen 1829, Svenstrup, Denmark (daughter of Jens Jensen of Svenstrup—pioneer 1862). She was born 1805. Their children: Andrew b. Nov. 19, 1830, m. Nellie Widenberg Sept., 1860; Jens; Christian; Ingerborg; Dorthea. Family home Svenstrup, Denmark.
Member 67th quorum seventies; high priest; missionary.

ANDERSEN, GEORGE (son of Sern and Maria Andersen of Lystrup, Presto amt, Sjelland, Denmark). Born Nov. 14, 1836, at Lystrup. Came to Utah 1862.
Married Mary Ann Davis Aug. 19, 1860 (daughter of David Davis and Caroline F. Angel). She was born Jan. 11, 1844, Nauvoo, Hancock county, Ill. Their children: George D. b. Sept. 23, 1861, m. Annie Hogan 1887; Caroline F. b. Oct. 31, 1863; Mary Ann b. Dec. 11, 1865, m. David Bench June 19, 1886; Phoebe b. March 5, 1868, m. Joseph Allen Dec. 9, 1885; Sarah Alice b. Jan. 10, 1870, m. Charles C. Harris April 14, 1886. Family home Richmond, Utah.
Married Elva Armina Carson Nov. 11, 1872, Salt Lake City (daughter of George Carson, pioneer 1851, and Elva Rawlins, Oct. 10, 1848, Amasa Lyman company—married July 31, 1833). She was born June 25, 1854, Draper, Salt Lake county, Utah. Their children: William b. June 13, 1873, m. Rachel R. Knapp Sept. 23, 1898; Elva Ann b. June 27, 1875; Joseph Henry b. April 12, 1878; James Alvin b. April 20, 1880, m. May Webb April 21, 1900; George Andrew b. Aug.

PIONEERS AND PROMINENT MEN OF UTAH

29, 1882, m. Lorena Fisher Nov. 7, 1907; Minnetta b. Jan. 12, 1885, m. Ray A. Lewis Aug. 17, 1910; Millie Jennett, b. April 8, 1887; Nellie Armina b. July 26, 1889; Leroy Carson b. Oct. 23, 1891; Florence Elizabeth b. April 16, 1894; John Albert b. Aug. 9, 1896. Family home Richmond, Utah.
Settled in Richmond 1860. Seventy. Farmer and stockraiser.

ANDERSEN, WILLIAM (son of George Andersen and Elva Armina Carson). Born June 13, 1873, Richmond, Utah.
Married Rachel Rozina Knapp Sept. 23, 1896, Logan, Utah (daughter of Silas Knapp and Harriet B. Skidmore), who was born Aug. 16, 1875, Richmond, Utah. Their children: Silas William b. Feb. 28, 1902; George Henry b. Feb. 15, 1904.

ANDERSEN, JAMES MICHAEL (son of Anders Andersen, born Nov. 24, 1815, and Christene Rasmussen, born Sept. 24, 1817, both in Sjelle, Aarhuus amt, Denmark). He was born Jan. 1, 1855, in Aarhuus amt. Came to Utah Sept. 29, 1866, with his elder brother, Rasmus, in the Peter Nebeker company, being then eleven years old.
Married Maria White July 21, 1874 (daughter of John S. White, pioneer July 29, 1847, with part of Mormon Battalion, and Adelaide Everett, pioneer Oct. 2, 1847, Jedediah M. Grant company—married April 5, 1849, Salt Lake City). She was born June 9, 1857, in Farmington, Utah. Their children: John M. m. March 16, 1876, m. Mary Marler June 26, 1899; James H. b. Aug. 19, 1879, m. Laverna Call July 18, 1900; Florence Marie b. June 1, 1881, m. Loran Marler Oct. 11, 1900; Everett b. March 28, 1883, d. Nov. 19, 1884; Effie b. Nov. 29, 1885, m. Wm. A. Bowman Dec. 20, 1905; Laura b. Jan. 25, 1888, m. Joseph Watkins Dec. 20, 1911; Lillian b. Feb. 1, 1892; Emery H. b. July 28, 1894; Bracy b. Oct. 10, 1898, d. Jan. 6, 1899.
Married Susan E. Stephenson Nov. 23, 1887, Logan, Utah (daughter of Francis Marion Stephenson, pioneer 1850, Milo Andrus company, and Sarah Ann Bright, pioneer Oct. 29, 1852, Isaac Stewart company—married Jan. 13, 1864, Richmond, Utah). She was born July 27, 1865, Richmond, Utah. Their children: George Francis b. March 16, 1894; Barbara b. Oct. 6, 1907. Families resided in Lewiston, Cache county, Utah.
Engaged in freighting to various parts of Utah and Idaho; moved to Lewiston 1874; school trustee. President 39th quorum seventies; missionary to Southern states, and barely escaped with his life several times from unreasoning mobs; high priest in Lewiston second ward.

ANDERSEN, JORGEN CHRISTIAN (son of Anders O. Jorgensen and Karen Larsen, of Bromme, Soro amt, Sjelland, Denmark). Born Sept. 25, 1807, Nortrup, Denmark. Came to Utah Oct. 7, 1858, Rosel Kind Homer company.
Married Anne Petersen 1830, Bromme, Denmark. Their children: Karen b. Feb. 4, 1831, m. Niels Christensen 1853; Hans b. Sept. 18, 1833, m. Catherine Sophia Sorensen; Otto b. March 27, 1835, m. Hedevi Mary Petersen.
Married Karen Andersen January, 1856, Bromme, Denmark. Their children: Mary b. Jan., 1856, m. Henry Sorensen; John Christian m. Mary Jane Hvrse; Niels Peter m. Ellen McKinley; Anne Caroline b. Nov., 1865, m. Hyrum Hansen. Family home Teton, Idaho.
Became a member of the 57th quorum seventies in Dec., 1858. Carpenter. Died Oct. 3, 1866, Mendon, Utah.

ANDERSEN, ANDREW (son of Jorgen Christian Andersen and Anne Petersen). Born Sept. 18, 1832, Bromme, Denmark. Came to Utah in 1858.
Married Catherine Sophia Sorensen Nov. 14, 1857, Copenhagen, Denmark (daughter of Neccloi Sorensen and Malinda Olsen, pioneers with R. K. Homer company). She was born May 7, 1831. Only child: Lydia b. Oct. 4, 1858, m. George L. Farrell. Settled at Mendon, Utah, 1859.
Married Sophia Larsen Nov. 13, 1871, Salt Lake City (daughter of Magnus and Mary Larsen, both of Mendon, Utah,—pioneers 1862). She was born Feb. 7, 1853, Denmark. Their children: Catherine Sophia b. April 21, 1873, m. Francis C. Andersen; Andrew Otto b. May 10, 1875, m. Retta Hansen; John Christian b. May 22, 1877, m. Sine Sorensen; Lars Magnus b. Sept. 3, 1879; Ezra Taft b. March 3, 1882; Mary Caroline b. Jan. 14, 1885; George Linel b. Feb. 22, 1887, m. Elizabeth Tholton; William b. July 31, 1889, d. Aug. 1, 1889; Anne Amelia b. Jan. 17, 1891, m. Bruse Pitt; Henry Waldemar b. Jan. 4, 1894. Family home Mendon, Utah.
Member of 57th quorum seventies; first counselor to Bishop Henry Hughes for 14 years; president high priests quorum Hyrum stake ten years. Carpenter.

ANDERSEN, PETER (son of Anders Nielsen and Inger Jacobsen of Gabafluss, Aulum Sogn, Jutland, Denmark). Born Sept. 18, 1834, in Denmark. Came to Utah Sept. 5, 1863, John F. Sanders company.
Married Larssina Thingsgard Nov. 1, 1856, Denmark (daughter of Niels Thingsgard of Holstebro, Ringkjobing amt, Denmark, pioneer 1863, Capt. Sanders company). She was born Sept. 14, 1830. Their children: Neils Andreas b. Aug. 1, 1857, d. Aug. 2, 1857; Carsten Emlil Moller Joseph b. Oct. 9, 1858, d. Sept. 15, 1858; Carsten Emlil Moller Joseph b. Oct. 4, 1859, d. Oct. 8, 1859; Hans Christian Marius b. July 8, 1860, d. Oct. 4, 1863; Niels Andreas b. July 2, 1861, d. Aug., 1861; Juliana Elizabeth b. Oct. 16, 1866, m. Albert West; Nephi b.

Sept. 7, 1869; Inger b. March 8, 1871, m. Lars Jespersen; Rozina Matilda b. April 10, 1873, d. 1875. Family resided Salt Lake and Huntsville, Utah.
Married Carolina Jensen Nov. 4, 1866, Salt Lake City (daughter of Jens Davidsen), who was born Sept. 30, 1843, Gemsing sogn, Denmark. Their children: Peter Albert b. Dec. 29, 1869, m. Jane Langlois; Andeas b. Feb. 21, 1871, m. Elizabeth Margaret Sorenson; Emanalina b. May 20, 1873, m. Wm. Engstrom; Mary b. Feb. 28, 1878, m. Charles Carstensen; John b. July 30, 1880; Dorthea b. July 8, 1882, m. John Stalling; Anna Malena b. Sept. 19, 1884.
Married Birte Crestina Thommasen. Their children: Josephine b. April, 1881, m. Sofus Mollerup; Rozina Matilda b. Sept. 20, 1883, m. Gustaf Peterson; Anna Margaret b. March 1, 1885, m. Julius White; Johanna b. July 1, 1887, m. Erlii Stayly; Niels Albert b. April 8, 1888; Thomas Julius b. Dec. 8, 1890; Peter Marinus b. Sept. 27, 1892, m. Liza Dickerson; Hans Lawrence, b. April 8, 1894; Birte b. June 11, 1896.
Ordained a seventy March 27, 1867, and a high priest March 28, 1908.

ANDERSON, ANDERS (son of Andrew Anderson, born 1790, and Katrine Larsen Anderson, born 1800, both in Hvatlen, Solburga, Sweden). He was born April 25, 1826, in Solburga, Sweden. Came to Utah Sept. 5, 1868, with John F. Sanders company.
Married Anna Jacobson 1854 (daughter of Jacob Swenson, a pioneer 1863, John F. Sanders company, and Cassie Erickson). Only child: Annie Louise b. Oct. 6, 1863, m. Freeman Malin Aug. 1, 1888.

ANDERSON, ANDREAS (son of Andreas Anderson, born 1768, and Maria Larson, born 1777, both of Sweden). He was born March 26, 1817, in Sweden. Came to Utah 1860, with the Verdeburg company.
Married Stena Caisa Nelson (daughter of Andreas Nelson and Sarah Swenson), who was born Nov. 20, 1820, and came to Utah with husband. Only child: Andreas John b. April 26, 1851, m. Malissa Isabel Judd, Jan. 19, 1873.

ANDERSON, ANDREAS JOHN (son of Andreas Anderson and Stena Caisa Nelson). Born April 26, 1851, and came from railroad terminal, Omaha, to Utah 1860, with independent oxteam company.
Married Malissa Isabel Judd Jan. 19, 1873, Salt Lake City (daughter of William R. Judd and Isabel Norton—married March 23, 1854, S. L. City). She was born Jan. 15, 1855, Lehi, Utah. Their children: Stena May b. April 23, 1874, m. Joseph Frederickson; Teresa Bell b. Nov. 11, 1875, m. Frank L. Clark; John Riley b. March 31, 1877, m. Elizabeth Martindale; Andreas Judd b. Nov. 25, 1878, m. Evelyn Erickson; Sarah Edna b. Nov. 7, 1880; Frankie Vilate b. July 28, 1882; Hazel Dell b. March 24, 1884, m. John R. Gibson; Wanda b. Feb. 6, 1886; Wilma Gay b. Oct. 24, 1887, m. Lawrence Gillet; Nellie Lial b. Dec. 5, 1888; Norton Wallace b. Aug. 4, 1891; Walter Scott b. May 15, 1895; Genevieve b. Aug. 31, 1898.
Settled in Grantsville 1860, and is serving his third term as city councilman, bending every effort to keep that town abreast with modern progress. Farmer and stockraiser.

ANDERSON, ANDREW (son of Anders Johanson, born June 29, 1796, Skogardshus Gnarp, Sweden, and Hannah Larson, born Feb. 9, 1792, Almanningstus, Sweden—both of Hickeberg, Sweden). He was born March 29, 1823, Skogardshus Gnarp, Sweden. Came to Utah Aug. 29, 1859, James S. Brown company.
Married Anna Christina Olson May, 1844, Hickeberg, Malmohus, Sweden (daughter of Ola Olson and Christina Skonstrom). She was born May 22, 1822, and came to Utah 1859 with husband. Their children: Christian b. Dec. 18, 1845; Swan b. May 18, 1847, m. Mary Christensen 1873; Lewis b. Oct. 24, 1850, m. Mary A. Crowther Nov. 14, 1870; Andrew b. Sept. 13, 1854, m. Diantha Christensen Jan. 25, 1875; Hannah b. April 13, 1858; Erastus W. b. May 9, 1859, m. Annie E. Bogh Sept. 2, 1880; Joseph b. Sept. 7, 1862, m. Olive Taylor April 17, 1890; Brigham b. Dec. 5, 1863; Anna C. b. May 22, 1866, m. Ole Sorensen Jr. 1885.
Married Martha Olson June 13, 1867, Salt Lake City. She was born April 4, 1843, in Sweden. Their children: Mary A. b. March 23, 1868, m. Wiley P. Allred; Martha C. b. Jan. 10, 1870; Hannah J. b. Jan. 14, 1872, m. J. Oscar Robertson March 5, 1890; Andrew H. b. April 23, 1875, m. Ada M. Carter Oct. 21, 1903; James O. b. June 19, 1878; Alexander b. June 20, 1883; Ida Pernilla b. Aug. 4, 1885, m. Hyrum V. Jorgason Nov. 8, 1905.
Married Mary Eliza Allred Aug. 1, 1870, Salt Lake City (only daughter of Wiley Payne Allred and Elizabeth Ann Davis). She was born July 31, 1852, Provo, Utah. Their children: Wiley P. b. June 1, 1872; Mary E. b. Jan. 29, 1874; Andrew P. b. Jan. 14, 1876; Elizabeth A. b. April 23, 1878; George E. b. Sept. 8, 1880; James S. b. Dec. 19, 1882; Edna L. b. March 26, 1885; Wilson W. b. Jan. 17, 1887. Families resided Moroni and Fountain Greer, Utah.
Pioneer to Moroni, Utah. Indian war veteran. Merchant and farmer.

ANDERSON, LEWIS (son of Andrew Anderson and Anna C. Olson). He was born Oct. 24, 1850, Hickeberg, Sweden.
Married Mary A. Crowther Nov. 14, 1870, Salt Lake City (daughter of Thomas Crowther, pioneer Sept. 10, 1855, Edward Stephenson company, and Sarah Thompson). She

was born May 7, 1851, Tipton, Salopshire, Eng. Their children: Lewis Robert b. March 26, 1872, m. Clara Munk Dec. 11, 1895; Thomas Jefferson b. April 4, 1874, m. Eliza Westenskow Jan. 19, 1898; Etta b. Aug. 18, 1880, m. Peter A. Poulson Jan. 6, 1904; Sarah Jane b. Jan. 14, 1883, m. Erastus Westenskow Oct. 9, 1904; Mary Mabel b. March 3, 1887, m. George B. Taylor Dec. 22, 1909; Joseph Franklin b. May 17, 1890. Family home Manti, Utah.
President South San Pete stake and of Manti temple. Vice-president Manti City savings bank; president Manti Live Stock Co.; president Anderson-Taylor Co., Salt Lake City.

ANDERSON, ANDREW (son of Andrus Nielsen, born 1801, Sjarop, Sweden, and Elna Larson, born May 16, 1811, Klagstorp, Malmohus, Sweden). He was born Nov. 10, 1836, Klagstorp, Sweden. Came to Utah Sept. 12, 1863, John R. Young company.
Married Christeena M. Jensen June 18, 1863 (daughter of Andrew Jensen, born February, 1810, Klastofte, died Nov. 29, 1883, and Catherine Larson, both of Denmark, pioneers 1860). She was born April 21, 1834, and came to Utah with husband. Their children: Andrew C. b. April 23, 1864, m. Sarah Russell Nov. 1882; Louis b. Feb. 2, 1866, m. Harriet Cole Dec. 20, 1887; Ellen C. b. March 21, 1868, m. Lindsay Brady Dec. 31, 1886; Martin b. April 19, 1870, m. Sarah O. Smith April 28, 1897; Joseph b. Aug. 14, 1872, m. Sarah Johnson Dec. 9, 1896; Mary b. Feb. 12, 1875, m. David Smart Dec. 9, 1896; Annie b. May 6, 1877, m. Christan A. Christenson Dec. 20, 1899; Christan b. Oct. 25, 1879, d. May 25, 1881. Family home Union, Salt Lake county, Utah.
Missionary from Sweden to Denmark before coming to Utah, 1859-63; and from Utah to Sweden 1892-94; and again 1897-99. Had charge of immigrant company on return from Sweden.

ANDERSON, ANDREW (son of Mons Arneson and Ingar Marie Olsen of Bolge, Norway). Born Jan. 22, 1836, in Aagaard, Norway. Came to Utah Sept. 7, 1855, Noah T. Guymon company.
Married Alice Brooks, Salt Lake City (daughter of Newton Brooks), who was born Feb. 16, 1835, in Lancashire, Eng. Only child: Hyrum B. Family home College Ward, Cache county, Utah.
Married Johannah Morte Dealey, Salt Lake City (whose father's name was Dealey and mother's Bradley). Their children: Wilford; Nephi; Andrew; all born at the family home Hyrum, Utah.
High priest; seventy—16 years in one quorum. Served in the Echo Canyon campaign and joined in the move south. Road supervisor and all-round pioneer in the early days around Hyrum, working barefooted and subsisting on the most primitive edibles many times when crickets and grasshoppers devoured everything in sight.

ANDERSON, HYRUM B. (son of Andrew Anderson and Alice Brooks). Born in 1873, Hyrum, Utah.
Married Rachel Stanley March 16, 1905, Logan, Utah (daughter of Michael Stanley and Naomi Ann Kemp of Lewiston, Utah). Their children: Bernice b. Aug. 1906; Elgo Hiram b. April, 1909; Cloe Olive b. Dec. 1910. Family home near Hyrum, Utah.
Farmer and stockraiser.

ANDERSON, CHRISTIAN (son of Anders Petersen and Marie Kirstine Amitzbol, of Denmark). Born May 6, 1840, Guldborg, Laaland, Denmark. Came to Utah Sept. 27, 1862, John R. Murdock second church train.
Married Rasmina Johnsen Aug. 6, 1863, Gunnison, Utah (daughter of Anders Johnsen and Johanne Jorgensen of Kippinge, Island of Falster, Denmark). She was born July 21, 1821. Their children: Christian, died; Hannah Maria, m. William C. Cooper.
Married Anna Kirstina Beauregard. Only child: Anna Maria, died.
Married Anna Dorthea Christiansen. Their children: Ester Sophia b. June 26, 1879, m. William A. Huntsman; Nephi Amitzbol b. Nov. 7, 1881, m. Dolores C. Pyper; Mary Dorthea b. Sept. 8, 1883, d. Sept. 18, 1890; Andrew Peter b. April 8, 1885; Joseph Fillmore b. Dec. 2, 1886, m. Maggie Anderson; Ephraim Ditlov b. Sept. 29, 1888, m. Josephine E. Crow; Hyrum Christian b. Jan. 22, 1890, d. infant; James (adopted) b. June 8, 1874, m. Zina Larsen.
Married Hannah Christine Christiansen. Their children: Christine Virginia b. Dec. 18, 1879, m. Charles J. Warren; Christian Henry b. Sept. 13, 1881; Katrine Julia b. July 13, 1883; Sarah May b. May 17, 1885; Elizabeth b. Nov. 2, 1886, d. infant; Karrie Juniette b. June 19, 1888, d. April 24, 1889; Anna Geneva b. March 13, 1890; Zina Olivia b. July 17, 1892; Wilford John b. March 1, 1894; Mabel Filicia b. Feb. 27, 1896; Julius Evan b. July 27, 1899; August Vivian b. Aug. 2, 1901.
Local missionary on Islands of Laaland and Falster, Denmark, 1857, and later at Copenhagen; president in 42d quorum seventies; member high council of Millard stake and its clerk 23 years; president high priests' quorum nine years; bishop of Fillmore ward six years; head teacher of theology of Fillmore Sunday school 30 years. City recorder four years; city councilman six years; justice of peace six years; county recorder four years; county clerk four years; county treasurer two years. Druggist, editor, merchant and farmer.

ANDERSON, NEPHI AMITZBOL (son of Christian Anderson and Anna Dorthea Christiansen). Born Nov. 7, 1881, Fillmore, Utah.
Married Dolores Caroline Pyper Oct. 9, 1907, at Salt Lake City (daughter of Robert A. Pyper and Cordelia Webb of Salt Lake City). She was born Jan. 8, 1881. Their children: Lucile Dolores b. Dec. 3, 1908; Eva Marie b. Dec. 24, 1909. Family home Fillmore, Utah.
Member 42d quorum seventies; missionary to Texas 1899-1902; member high council, Millard stake; president Y. M. M. I. A. County clerk six years; city recorder two years. Real estate agent and farmer.

ANDERSON, GUSTAF (son of Andreas Anderson). Born April 7, 1824, at Kleva, Sweden. Came to Utah 1868 by ox-team with a Scandinavian company.
Married Maria C. Hokenson (daughter of Johannes Hokenson). She was born Jan. 16, 1836. Their children: Anna C. b. Sept. 2, 1858, m. C. C. Wangsgard; A. J. b. Aug. 2, 1860, m. Cynthia Yeamans Dec. 7, 1882; Orson; Mary m. Wm. H. Burrows; Ida m. Joseph L. Peterson; Lottie m. J. A. Newey; Emil, m. Selma ——. Family home Huntsville, Utah.

ANDERSON, A. J. (son of Gustaf Anderson and Maria C. Hokenson). Born Aug. 2, 1860, in Sweden. Came to Utah with parents.
Married Cynthia Yeamans Dec. 7, 1882, Salt Lake City (daughter of Thomas Yeamans and Martha Moore). She was born Sept. 24, 1863, Huntsville, Utah. Their children: Thomas Lester b. June 15, 1885; Mary E. b. March 12, 1887, m. W. Lyle Allred June 15, 1910; Walter G. b. May 13, 1889; Elizabeth b. Sept. 11, 1891; Clifford O. b. Nov. 16, 1893; Eva J. b. April 14, 1895; Vernal b. Feb. 20, 1897; Orabell b. March 19, 1899; Arcet John b. Jan. 29, 1901; Ruth W. b. Feb. 17, 1906. Family home Huntsville, Utah.
School trustee 1885-95; justice of peace. Sunday school superintendent 1892-1909; first counselor to Bishop John Halls, Huntsville, Utah.

ANDERSON, GUSTAVE (son of Anders Anderson, born Dec. 4, 1799, Frisco Dahisland, Sweden, and Kajsa Pearson, born Oct. 12, 1805, Grunsta Parish, Dahisland, Sweden). He was born Jan. 5, 1850, Grunsta Parish, Sweden. Came to Utah Oct. 1, 1862, Capt. Joseph Horne third church train.
Married Emily Jennis Hunter Feb. 22, 1874 (daughter of Edward Hunter and Mary Ann Whitside). She was born Nov. 24, 1854, Kaysville, Utah. Their children: Gustave Edward b. Jan. 11, 1875, m. Vinnie Ann Clark Dec. 5, 1906; William Harvey b. Aug. 28, 1877, m. Lillian H. Anderson Oct. 14, 1903; Mary Jennis b. Dec. 27, 1880; Ethel May b. June 27, 1882, m. S. G. Clark Dec. 10, 1903; Lewis Earl b. Oct. 6, 1885, m. Bertha Shelby Jan. 19, 1911; George Noel b. Jan. 3, 1888; Sarah Vere b. May 30, 1891; Myra Magdalene b. Nov. 12, 1893. Family home Grantsville, Utah.
Missionary to Sweden 1882-84; seventy; high priest; high councilor; Bishop's counselor 1884-1906. City councilman Grantsville 1885-87, alderman 1887-1890, mayor 1898-1899 and again 1902-1903.

ANDERSON, HOGAN (son of Hogan Anderson of Sweden). Born March 23, 1826, in Sweden. Came to Utah Sept. 4, 1859, Geo. Rowley handcart company.
Married Cecelia Swenson Nov. 2, 1863, Mt. Pleasant, Utah (daughter of Larse Swenson and Mary Oleson, of Sweden, pioneers 1863). She was born Feb. 23, 1841. Their children: Emily b. Oct. 26, 1864, m. John Barber; Hogan Oscar b. March 9, 1866, m. Olena Oleson; Hannah b. Nov. 19, 1867, m. Alfred Hanson; Axel b. Nov. 10, 1869, m. Alice Lemmon; William F. b. Nov. 6, 1871, m. Rosette Lemmon; Lewis K. b. Nov. 7, 1873, m. Annie Dibble; Christin b. Oct. 21, 1875, died; Olof E. b. Sept. 25, 1877, m. Rubie Chapman; Salma b. July 11, 1880, m. James R. Thurman; Albert b. Sept. 17, 1882, died; Lambert b. Sept. 17, 1882, died; Lionel b. Jan. 27, 1894, m. Hilda Hoganson. Family resided Mt. Pleasant, Utah, and Salem, Ida.
High priest. Assisted in bringing emigrants to Utah by oxteam in 1863. Miller; farmer. Died Oct. 31, 1892, Salem, Ida.

ANDERSON, AXEL (son of Hogan Anderson and Cecelia Swenson). Born Nov. 10, 1869, Mt. Pleasant, Utah.
Married Alice Lemmon Oct. 24, 1894, Logan, Utah (daughter of William Lemmon and Annie Elisa Homer, of Smithfield, Utah, pioneers 1852). She was born Nov. 12, 1872. Their children: Madeline b. April 19, 1896; Annie b. April 20, 1898; Axel Glenn b. Dec. 9, 1899; George W. b. Aug. 30, 1903; Alice Edna b. March 1, 1905; Mada Artimzie b. Dec. 3, 1908. Family home Warm River, Ida.
Assistant Sunday school superintendent, Salem, Ida; chorister at Warm River ward; ordained a high priest and chosen first counselor to Bishop D. T. Howell of Warm River Nov. 2, 1912. Sawmill man and farmer.

ANDERSON, JAMES (son of Archibald Anderson and Agnes Adamson). Born Oct. 3, 1842, in Lanarkshire, Scotland. Came to Utah Sept. 26, 1856, Daniel D. McArthur handcart company.
Married Hannah M. Cheney Jan. 1, 1866 (daughter of Elam Cheney and Hannah Compton, married 1846, Nauvoo, Ill.,

pioneers 1847, Brigham Young company). She was born Feb. 6, 1849. Their children: James b. Oct. 22, 1866, m. Ada Sanderson Nov. 1886; Hannah A. b. June 8, 1869, m. Walter Hurst April, 1887; Deseret M. b. May 13, 1871, m. L. O. Larsen June 13, 1894; Archibald E. b. March 7, 1872, m. Ida Breckinridge May, 1900; Elam H. b. June 10, 1876, m. Lizzie Peterson April, 1900; Agnes E. b. Jan. 26, 1878, m. George Terry, October, 1900; Sylvia R. b. Oct. 31, 1882, m. Lester Miner September. 1904; John W. b. Dec. 7, 1884, d. March 19, 1891; Lorin A. b. Feb. 6, 1889. Family home Fairview, Utah. High priest. Assisted Bishop Seeley in bringing emigrants to Utah. Indian war veteran in the various troubles with the unruly redskins. Settled at Spanish Fork 1857, moved to Fairview 1860.

ANDERSON, JAMES P. (son of Niels Anderson, born Oct. 30, 1795, Wilkes county, Ga., and Nancy Pace, born March 30, 1801, Clarke county, Ga., married Aug. 9, 1821). He was born Aug. 14, 1826, Nashville, Tenn. Came to Utah Oct. 6, 1851, Capt. Cardon company.
Married Eliza Morton March 10, 1857 (daughter of Joshua Morton and Harriet Schofield, pioneers Nov. 30, 1856, Edward Martin handcart company). She was born 1835. Their children: James M.; Nancy; Milton Thomas; Mary; Harriet.
Seventy. Served in Utah militia.

ANDERSON, MILTON THOMAS (son of James P. Anderson and Eliza Morton). Born Oct. 15, 1861, Beaver, Utah.
Married Ruth Owens, Mantl, San Pete county, Utah (daughter of George Owens and Sarah Valentine). She was born April 16, 1871, in England. Their children: Milton Owen b. March 23, 1899; Rulon b. April 24, 1900; Vernes and Verneice b. Oct. 23, 1902; Aubrey b. Nov. 11, 1905; Sarah b. June 13, 1907; Letha b. May 6, 1909; James A. b. July 5, 1910, d. Oct. 29, 1910.

ANDERSON, JENS (son of Anders Larsen, born June 16, 1765, and Maren Knudsen, both of Orslev, Kloster, Viborg amt, Denmark). He was born Jan. 7, 1821, at Kragerup, Denmark. Came to Utah Oct. 5, 1854, Hans Peter Olsen company.
Married Anna Jorgensen. She was born March 8, 1824, and came to Utah with husband. Their children: Peter b. Dec. 10, 1847, m. Martha Anna Lowell April 4, 1872; Christian b. Feb. 19, 1852, m. Anna Christensen April 17, 1871; Joseph S. b. Oct. 3, 1855, m. Anna M. Nielson Dec. 6, 1875. Family resided Deseret and Oak City, Utah. Followed trade of carpenter.

ANDERSON, JOSEPH S. (son of Jens Anderson and Anna Jorgensen). Born Oct. 3, 1855, Fillmore, Utah.
Married Anna M. Nielson Dec. 6, 1875, Salt Lake City (daughter of Lars and Sidsel Nielson), who was born March 20, 1858. Their children: Ada b. Oct. 8, 1876; Franklin b. Nov. 14, 1877, m. Eliza Hartley April 3, 1902; Sidsel b. Aug. 19, 1880; Joseph Lars b. April 28, 1882, m. Mary E. Stephensen Nov. 7, 1906; Lillian b. Feb. 21, 1884; Albert b. Dec. 16, 1886; John Milo b. Dec. 7, 1888; Louis Elby b. Nov. 16, 1890; Edna b. Sept. 23, 1893; Eva b. Oct. 12, 1896; Estella b. Dec. 7, 1898; Lester b. July 9, 1901. Family home Oak City, Millard county, Utah.
Farmer. School trustee; member irrigation board.

ANDERSON, JENS CHRISTIAN (son of Anders Peterson and Karen Christensen, born 1777, of Denmark). He was born May 6, 1821, Hjorring amt, Denmark. Came to Utah Sept. 13, 1857, Christian Christensen handcart company.
Married Margaret Nielsen April 28, 1849 (daughter of Christian Nielsen and Johanna M. Larsen, latter a pioneer Sept. 13, 1857). She was born June 29, 1830. Their children: Lauritz Peter b. July 28, 1849, m. Nanna Erickson; Anndrear Johanna b. Nov. 14, 1851, m. Jens Munsen; Beietta Christena b. Feb. 18, 1854, m. Tillman Allred; Josephena Brighamina b. March 4, 1856, m. Hans Jensen; Hyrum Smith b. Oct 19, 1858, m. Millie Sorenson; James Christian b. Feb. 27, 1861, m. Annie Parsons Oct. 9, 1888; Heber Christian b. Feb. 9, 1863, m. Theresa Schaugaard; Margarete Fredrica b. Sept. 2, 1866, m. Joseph Y. Jenson; Orson Hyde b. May 28, 1868, m. Hannah Torgersen Oct. 19, 1888; Albertina b. July 21, 1875, m. Parley Anderson May 11, 1898. Family resided Salina, Koosharem and Richfield, Utah.
Married Carolina Jensen Feb., 1858, Salt Lake City (daughter of Jens Jensen, pioneer 1857, Christianson handcart company). She was born April 4, 1835, Denmark. Their children: Anna Mary b. Oct 19, 1858; Caroline b. Jan. 27, 1861; Jenesena b. Jan. 10, 1862, m. Samuel L. Page; Anna Mina b. Feb. 6, 1864, m. Carlos Rasmussen Oct. 11, 1858; Jens Christian Carlos b. Oct. 24, 1866, m. Minnie Turbet; Erastus Snow b. Jan. 23, 1869, m. Mary Jane Norton; Andrew b. April 23, 1871, m. Emma Martinsen May 3, 1899; Swening Christian b. June 19, 1873, m. Beda Erickson May 11, 1896; Diantha Matelde b. Dec. 6, 1875, m. James A. Bagley May 3, 1899; Mary Ellen b. Dec. 15, 1878, m. Jasper Williams. Family home Koosharem, Utah.

ANDERSON, JOHANAS (son of Anders Johansen and Anna Jenson of Wiarp, Sweden). Born Feb. 18, 1823, Wiarp, Sweden. Came to Utah in 1859.
Married Johanna Olson Dec. 18, 1852, in Sweden (daughter of Ola Mortenson and Ingar Bengtson of Jyholt, Sweden).

She was born Sept. 10, 1822, in Jyholt, Sweden. Their children: Anna b. June 11, 1854 (deceased), m. Wm. Hibbard; Olaf b. Nov. 25, 1857, Ida Josephine b. 1860 and Hannah Ida b. Oct. 19, 1861, latter three died; John H. b. Sept. 24, 1864, m. Anna Charlotte Eliason. Family home Logan, Utah. High priest. Died Aug. 1, 1904.

ANDERSON, JOHN HYRUM (son of Johanas Anderson and Johanna Olson). Born Sept. 24, 1864, Logan, Utah.
Married Anna C. Eliason Nov. 18, 1885, Logan, Utah (daughter of Andrew Peter Eliason and Anna Marie Erickson of Logan, Utah). She was born Oct. 11, 1866. Their children: John b. Dec. 3, 1886, m. Coila Montrose; Anna Charlotte b. Jan. 8, 1889, m. J. Ruben Larsen; Jos. Andrew b. March 19, 1891; Ida Geneva b. April 23, 1893; Luella Elizabeth b. Dec. 17, 1894; Hyrum Woodruff b. Dec. 15, 1898; Melvin Eliason b. June 25, 1903; Johanna Marie b. Jan. 20, 1906; Melvin Budge b. Sept. 26, 1909.
Missionary to Sweden; bishop of Mendon and at present time of Logan fourth ward; member of high council of Cache stake. Mayor of Logan. Vice-president First National Bank of Logan. Progressive and widely known business man.

ANDERSON, JOHN (son of Jno. H. Anderson and Anna Charlotte Eliason). Born Dec. 3, 1886, at Logan, Utah.
Married Coila Montrose March 17, 1909, Logan, Utah (daughter of Jno. A. Montrose and Harriet Horsley, of Soda Springs, Ida.) She was born April 29, 1888. Her parents came to Utah Oct. 17, 1862, Capt. Henry W. Miller company. Their children: John Montrose b. Dec. 26, 1909; Coila Luella b. Jan. 24, 1911. Family home Logan, Utah.
Counselor to bishop of River Heights ward, Logan, Utah; missionary to Sweden.

ANDERSON, JOHN. Born 1805 at Leith, Firth of Forth, Scotland. Came to Utah 1863.
Married Jane Russell at Leith, Scotland (daughter of Jeanette Morrison of Denny, Loanhead, Scotland). She was born 1807. Their children: Jessie, m. Mr. Robson; John, d. aged 21; Thomas, m. Marguerite Robertson; James; Helen, m. Simon Greive; David P., m. Annie Smith; Mary Jane, m. David Smelle; Elizabeth, m. Thomas Jackson; Robert R., m. Elizabeth Holland; Marguerite R., m. John Alford; William C. Family home Salt Lake City, Utah.
Missionary in Scotland 23 years; high priest; block teacher; Sunday school teacher; home missionary. Shoemaker. Died about 1888 in Salt Lake City.

ANDERSON, DAVID P. (son of John Anderson and Jane Russell). Born June 18, 1838, at Leith, Scotland. Came to Utah Nov. 9, 1856, James G. Willie handcart company. This company of about 500 persons nearly perished in the early winter storms and for the want of provisions.
Married Annie Smith Oct. 4, 1861, at Salt Lake City (daughter of Thomas and Martha Smith—pioneers 1860, Jesse Murphy company). Their children: David S. b. May 12, 1862, London, Eng. Their children: David S. b. May 12, 1863, m. Annie Simpson; William b. May 11, 1863, m. Agnes Lewis; Robert R. b. Dec. 3, 1864, m. Nettie Latimer; John b. Oct. 9, 1866, m. Adela Arnold; Ernest E., d. aged 26; Edgar, m. Ann Dunn; Roy, m. Clara Brigs; Frank M., d. youth; Arthur D., died; Roscoe S. Family home Salt Lake City, Utah.
High priest; choir leader five years. Contractor and builder.

ANDERSON, LARS (son of Anders and Rangnel Clsen of Furness, Vang, Norway). Born Dec., 1811, Furne s, Norway. Came to Utah 1863.
Married Johanna Larsdatter, at Naes, Hedemarken amt, Norway (daughter of Lars and Johanna Neilsen of Ness, Norway). Their children: Lars; Ricca, m. Albert Balstadt; Julena, m. Neils Peterson; Annette b. July 29, 1847, m. Andrew Peterson; Martha, m. Amasa Tucker. Family home Fairview, Utah.
Elder. Died April 1, 1891, Mesa, Ariz.

ANDERSON, NEILS (son of Anders Olsen and Ane Marie Olsen of Sjeperup, Holbek amt, Denmark). Born July 13, 1834, in Sjeperup. Came to Utah Aug., 1863, William Wallace Cluff company.
Married Anne Kirstine Paulsen June 11, 1858 (daughter of Frederick Paulsen and Anna Katrine Anderson, who came to Utah in 1865). She was born Nov. 26, 1839, and came to Utah in 1862. Their children: Johanna Christina; Nelsena Sophia b. Aug. 31, 1862, m. Lucas B. Howard Jan. 5, 1881; Neils Thorwald b. June 2, 1865; Mary Ann b. Nov. 1, 1867; Emma b. 1870; Sara Julia b. July 31, 1874, m. Albert S. Newman Oct. 10, 1900; Amelia Caroline b. Oct. 8, 1877. Lived at Weston, Richmond, Honeyville, Goshen, South Jordan, and Big Cottonwood, Utah.

ANDERSON, PARLEY (son of Anders Anderson, of Sweden, and Kirsten Torgersen, of Norway). Born July 27, 1866, Christiania, Norway.
Married Albertena Anderson May 11, 1898, Manti, Utah (daughter of Jens Christian Anderson and Margarete Nielsen—pioneers Sept. 13, 1857, Christian Christiansen handcart company). She was born July 21, 1875, Salina, Utah. Their children: Edna Hortense b. Feb. 25, 1899; Hazel b. March 8, 1901; Grace b. Oct. 19, 1902; Cora b. March 10, 1905; Margaret b. May 20, 1907.
Bishop Koosharem ward, Sevier stake, 1904-07.

ANDERSON, PAUL. Born at Dagsdorf, Skone, Sweden. Came to Utah fall 1862, oxteam company.
Married Chastey Hoganson. Their children: Selia, m. William Christianson; Inger, m. Marten Williamson; Mary, m. William Christianson; Christina. m. Levy Holdaway; Annie, died. Family home Dagsdorf, Sweden, and Lake View, Utah.
High priest. Farmer and stockraiser.

ANDERSON, PETER N. Born Feb. 6, 1835, Malmo, Sweden. Came to Utah 1860.
Married Caroline Jepsen, 1859, in Malmo (daughter of Olin Jepsen of Malmo), who was born Feb. 12, 1836. Their children: Josephine, m. Joseph M. Smith; Andrew; Annie, m. Good Rasmussen; Betsy. m. Niel McMullen; John, m. Emma Marten; Olin, m. Nettie Thornton; Caroline, m. George Allen. Family home Hyrum, Utah.
Elder; missionary in Sweden. Carpenter. Died Sept. 29, 1902, Burton, Ida.

ANDERSON, WILLIAM (son of Andrew Anderson and Marie Williams of Denmark). Born March 6, 1818, Karleby, Falster Island, Denmark. Came to Utah Sept. 30, 1853, John Forsgren company.
Married Henrietta Berntzen Nov., 1841, in Falster, Denmark (daughter of Didlen Berntzen and Laurentza Tommerup of Denmark). She was born March 18, 1822. Their children: William C. b. Jan. 20, 1843; Christian b. April 21, 1844, m. Emily A. Pickering; Peter H. b. Sept. 26, 1845, m. Esther Smith; Mary Christine b. June 3, 1849, m. William A. Cox; Frederick b. Feb. 11, 1851, m. Sarah A. Cox; Hannah b. Jan. 1, 1853, m. Jorgen Madsen; Laurentza b. Sept. 12, 1855, m. John Lowry; Henrietta b. Sept. 17, 1865; John b. Sept. 20, 1867. Family home Manti, San Pete county, Utah.
High councilor. Member legislature 1860-62; county selectman 1867-83; probate judge. Died Nov. 14, 1904.

ANDERSON, PETER H. (son of William Anderson and Henrietta Berntzen). Born Sept. 26, 1845, in Denmark.
Married Esther Smith Dec. 1, 1866, Salt Lake City (daughter of Albert Smith and Esther Dutcher), who was born May 9, 1849. Their children: Etta b. Oct. 15, 1867, m. George Crawford; William H. b. March 16, 1869, m. Anna Watt; Hubert b. Aug. 5, 1871, died; Izenna b. Aug. 1, 1873, m. Edward Reid; Alice b. Jan. 5, 1876, m. Stephen Barton; Ross b. April 23, 1879, m. Euphemia Olson; Frank b. Nov. 21, 1882, m. Violet Carleson; Elinor b. June 4, 1885, m. Hal Taylor; Matilda b. June 4, 1888, m. Joseph W. Thompson; Henry b. July 7, 1891.
City councilman and city marshal, Manti, Utah. Farmer and stockraiser. Died July 13, 1903.

ANDERSON, ROSS (son of Peter H. Anderson and Esther Smith). Born April 23, 1879, Manti, Utah.
Married Euphemia Olson Sept. 18, 1901, Manti, Utah (daughter of John Olson and Almira E. Henrie. of Moroni, Utah). She was born Oct. 13, 1879. Their children: John Ross b. May 22, 1903; Elliott Vernon b. June 17, 1906; William Ray b. Dec. 27, 1908. Family home Salt Lake City.
Principal Mayfield schools 1900; professor biology and comparative anatomy, College of Physicians and Surgeons, Baltimore, Md., 1903-04, and graduate same college 1906; established pathological department L. D. S. hospital and was senior of same 1906-09; professor pathology and bacteriology University of Utah 1906-09; established Central Utah hospital, Mt. Pleasant, Utah, 1910, and successfully operated same for two years; surgeon D. & G. R. R.; senior surgeon Judge Mercy hospital, Salt Lake City.

ANDERSON, WILLIAM HOPKINS (son of Robt. S. Anderson, born July 30, 1803, at Washington, Pa., and Dorcas Ann Sims Hopkins, born Oct. 11, 1812, Mount Pleasant, Ohio). He was born Feb. 14, 1835, at Florence, Washington county, Pa. Came to Utah July 16, 1859, Alfred Randall company.
Married Mary Allen Sept. 3, 1861 (daughter of Isaac Allen and Elizabeth C. Wright—pioneers Sept. 16, 1859, Edward Stevenson company). She was born Dec. 13, 1839. Came to Utah Oct., 1859. Their children: William A. b. Sept. 26, 1862, m. Ida Ella McCammon Dec. 24, 1885; Dorcas Elizabeth b. Feb. 16, 1865, d. Aug. 2, 1876; Mary E. b. March 19, 1867, m. Charles Harton, Feb. 14, 1895.
City clerk Wellsville, Utah; postmaster Portage, Boxelder county, 30 years; justice of peace 27 years; notary public eight years. Bishop's counselor three years; tithing clerk four years; school trustee 12 years.

ANDERTON, JAMES (son of John Anderton and Mary Leather of Lancashire, Eng.). Born Dec. 17, 1840, Wigan, Lancashire. Came to Utah Oct. 5, 1864, Isaac Canfield company.
Married Dinah Prestige-Palmer, 1866, on "the Muddy," Nev., who came to Utah in 1863 (daughter of William Prestige of Leamington, Warwickshire, Eng., pioneer Oct. 6, 1863). She was born April 27, 1830. There were no children.
High priest; early settler on "the Muddy"; moved to Salt Lake City and Mill Creek; removed to Sevier county in 1872. Freighted to mining camps of Utah and Nevada for 25 years. Merchant, farmer and fruit grower.

ANDREW, FREDERICK CHADWICK. Born June 14, 1820, Stockport, Lancashire, Eng. Came to Utah 1854.
Married Elizabeth Whittaker July 17, 1842, Stockport, Eng., who was born April 3, 1822, and came to Utah, 1854, with husband. Their children: James W., d. aged 2; John W., m. Eveline Whittaker; Robert W., d. infant; Samuel W. m. Vilate Fulmer; Alice W., d. infant; Joseph F. W., m. Mariam Gibby; Richard S. W. (deceased), m. Elizabeth Croxall; Elizabeth W., died; Fredrick W., d. aged 6 years; Fred W. died. Family home, 7th ward, Salt Lake City.
General blacksmith. Died March 2, 1878, Salt Lake City.

ANDREW, JOHN W. (son of Frederick C. Andrew and Elizabeth Whittaker). Born Aug. 27, 1845, Heywood, Lancashire, Eng. Came to Utah with parents.
Married Eveline Whittaker Nov. 8, 1869, Salt Lake City, Daniel H. Wells officiating (daughter of George Whittaker). She was born Jan. 23, 1851. Their children: John and Fredrick, d. infants; Amy Eveline b. July 8, 1873, m. Everet P. Yawell; Lizzie b. Nov. 26, 1875; Arzella b. Jan. 24, 1879; Alice b. July 18, 1881, m. Richard Williams; Robert E. b. Oct. 19, 1887. Family home, Salt Lake City.
Seventy; high priest. Musician. Died May 14, 1912, Salt Lake City.

ANDREW, SAMUEL WHITTAKER (son of Frederick Chadwick Andrew and Elizabeth Whittaker). Born May 18, 1852, Stockport, Eng. Came to Utah Oct., 1854.
Married Mary Vilate Fullmer Nov. 8. 1875, Salt Lake City (daughter of David Fullmer and Rhoda Ann Marvin, of Northumberland county, Penn.—pioneers 1848). She was born Apr. 26, 1853. Their children: Samuel Fullmer b. Sept. 7, 1876, m. Ida Luella Perry; David Fullmer b. Nov. 11, 1877; Fred Fullmer b. March 28, 1881, m. Mina Marie Therkill; Mary Vilate Fullmer b. May 8, 1883, m. Joseph J. Gardiner; June Fullmer b. April 9, 1885; Richard Marvin Fullmer b. April 14, 1887, died; Rhoda Ethel Fullmer b. Jan. 14, 1891, died; Walter Silas Fullmer b. Oct. 21, 1893; Alice Edna Fullmer b. July 3, 1895. Lived at Salt Lake City; moved to Mapleton 1891, and to Union county, Ore., 1904.
High priest; high councilor. School trustee. Blacksmith and farmer.

ANDREWS, SAMUEL (son of William Andrews of Rome, Floyd county, Ga.). Born Oct., 1907. Came to Utah 1869.
Married Elizabeth Potts in Georgia. Their children: William, m. Elizabeth Smith; Amanda E., m. Henry Hall; Martha P., m. John P. Beesley; James C., and Marietta, died; Lavonia, m. Isaiah Barkdoll Lott; Edna Adaline, m. Jacob Snyder.
Carpenter and farmer (deceased).

ANDRUS, MILO (son of Ruluf Andrus and Azuba Smith, of Essex county, N. Y.). Born March 6, 1814, Hartford, Conn. Came to Utah Sept., 1850, from a mission in England, at the head of his own company.
Married Abigail Jane Daley Feb. 21, 1833, Florence, Ohio (daughter of John Daley of Florence, Ohio—pioneer 1848, Heber C. Kimball company). She was born Jan. 26, 1815. Their children: Mary Jane b. Nov. 15, 1833, m. William D. Hendricks; James b. June 14, 1835, m. Laura Altha Gibson; m. Masomas Luvina Gibson; Sarah Ann b. May 31, 1837; John Daley b. April 22, 1841, m. Catharine Wetherby; Millenium b. Aug. 31, 1845, m. William F. Fisher; Amanda b. Nov. 19, 1847, m. Howard Egan. Family home Florence, Ohio, St. George, Utah, and Oxford, Ida.
Married Adaline Alexander 1852, who was born Jan. 1, 1835, in Weakley county, Tenn. Their children: Laron b. Jan. 27, 1853, m. Rosanna P. Terry; m. Jane Carr; m. Maria Gummersall; Louis b. Aug. 3, 1854; Henrietta; Lavona; Randolph. Family home Holliday, Utah.
Married Lucy Loomis at Salt Lake City. Their children: Luvenia b. Feb. 28, 1854, m. James Miller; m. James McComb; Alma, m. Sarena Gardner; Jacob, d. aged 12; Lucy, d. aged 2; Esmerelda, m. William McKell. Family home Draperville, West Jordan, Utah.
Married Margaret Ann Boyce Feb., 1857, at Big Cottonwood, Utah (daughter of George Boyce of Michigan, pioneer 1847). She was born April 20, 1862, m. James Larsen; Hyrum b. June 17, 1864, m. Jennie Garner; Mansfield b. March 4, 1866, m. Una May Telford; Brigham b. May 28, 1868; Horace b. May 17, 1872, m. Hattie Horner; Margaret A. b. Oct. 24, 1874, m. John Jorgensen; Joseph b. Sept. 15, 1877, m. Maud Gee; Benjamin b. Sept. 15, 1877, m. Miss Rose; Eveline Charlote b. June 26, 1880, m. Orson Brower. Family home Big Cottonwood, Utah.
Missionary 1833-37-44 to Ohio, England and New York; first counselor to President Young; policeman at Nauvoo, Ill., and pres. of a quorum of seventies in 1844; president stake of Zion in St. Louis, Mo., 1855; acting bishop of Cottonwood, 1858; brought several companies of immigrants to Utah; patriarch. Farmer. Died June 19, 1893, at Oxford, Idaho.

ANDRUS, JAMES (son of Milo Andrus and Abigail Jane Daley). Born June 14, 1835, at Florence, Ohio. Came to Utah Sept. 24, 1848, Heber C. Kimball company.
Married Laura Altha Gibson March 11, 1867, at Big Cottonwood, Utah (daughter of George Washington Gibson and Mary Sparks of South Carolina—pioneers of 1847, Capt. Brown company). She was born June 27, 1837. Their chil-

dren: Laura Jane b. Nov. 30, 1857, m. A. F. McDonald, Jr.; James b. July 30, 1860, m. Adelaide Dodge; Mary Luvina b. Feb. 24, 1862; Elizabeth Luella b. Dec. 6, 1863, m. J. M. Gates; Elnora b. Nov. 7, 1865, m. J. M. Macfarlane; Edgar b. Aug. 5, 1868; Milo Washington b. Sept. 7, 1871, m. Mary J. Nixon; Gideon Lafayette, b. March 8, 1874, m. Jane Petty; Thamazine Millennium b. Dec. 1, 1876, m. George R. Lund. Family home St. George, Utah.

Married Manomas Luvina Gibson 1861 at Salt Lake City (daughter of George Washington Gibson and Mary Sparks). Their children: Lottie Luvina b. Aug. 19, 1862; George Judson b. Oct. 17, 1863; Medora b. March 6, 1866; John Edwin b. July 26, 1868; Moses Wilford b. April 7, 1870, m. Orpha Morris; Robert Nathaniel b. March 4, 1873; Alexander Burto b. Feb. 14, 1875, m. Rosilla Brooks; Charles b. March 5, 1878, m. Rosilla Turner; Thomas b. May 26, 1880, m. Lizzie Whitehead; Vilate b. May 14, 1883, m. Nephi J. Wadsworth, Jr.; Ethel b. Oct. 14, 1885, m. George A. Sorenson; Pearl b. Aug. 7, 1897.

Bishop of St. George ward; member high council; missionary. Chairman of county commissioners; representative of first state legislature in Utah. Farmer and stockraiser; merchant and banker.

ANDRUS, LARON A. (son of Milo Andrus and Adaline Alexander). Born Jan. 27, 1853, at Holliday, Utah.

Married Rosanna P. Terry Sept. 16, 1872, at Salt Lake City (daughter of William R. Terry and Mary Phillips); who was born July 7, 1856. Their children: Laron T. b. Dec. 9, 1873, m. Emma E. Toone; Franklin W. b. Feb. 3, 1876, m. Dessie Hogan; Mary Adaline b. June 16, 1878; Rosa May b. Sept. 14, 1879; Cloe T. b. April 18, 1887; Silas T. b. Oct. 28, 1883; Milo T. b. Nov. 4, 1885; Edgar T. b. Oct. 3, 1888; Otto T. b. Feb. 22, 1891.

Married Jane Carr March 23, 1896, Logan, Utah (daughter of Thomas Carr and Mary Thornley). She was born March 23, 1865, at Leyland, Lancashire, Eng.

Married Maria Gummersall (daughter of Jonathan Gummersall, born Sept. 23, 1823, and Hannah Smith, born 1828, both of England). She was born March 26, 1855, West Hartlepool, Durham, Eng.

Bishop's counselor (1884) 20 years; missionary to Great Britain 26 months; asst. supt. of Sunday schools; high priest. Farmer and stock-raiser.

ANDRUS, MANSFIELD (son of Milo Andrus and Margaret Ann Boyce). Born March 4, 1866, at West Jordan, Utah.

Married Una May Telford March 4, 1891, Logan, Utah (daughter of John D. Telford, born March 11, 1824; died Aug. 1883, and Sarah Coltron, both of Richmond, Utah, both pioneers—the latter, 1858). She was born April 29, 1871. Their children: Willbern b. Dec. 7, 1891, m. Clarissia Davenport; Orel b. Dec. 14, 1893; Oneta May b. Feb. 1, 1895; Milo b. Sept. 17, 1897; Adria b. Nov. 10, 1899; George T. b. April 27, 1901; Alton T. b. Aug. 27, 1903; Henry T. b. Dec. 1, 1905; Edith b. April 19, 1908; Viola b. May 29, 1911. Family home Ora, Idaho.

Supt. of Sunday schools at Lodi 1895; member bishopric 1896; ordained bishop 1908. Member committee on Yellowstone tabernacle.

ANGELL, SOLOMON (son of Phoebe Ann Angell of Nauvoo, Ill.). Came to Utah Sept. 20, 1848, Brigham Young company.

Married Eunice C. Young, who came to Utah 1848, Brigham Young company. Their children: Sarah Elizabeth, m. Jefferson Wright; Alma Thurman, m. Charlotte Boyce; John Osborn, m. Ermina Sarah Prudence Cahoon; Albert, m. Thirza Viola Cahoon; George, Wm. Henry and Emma, latter three died; Mary, m. Samuel Lorenzo Ensign. Family home Salt Lake City.

Member 33d quorum seventies. Carpenter and millwright. Died Sept. 20, 1882, Leeds, Utah.

ANGELL, JOHN OSBORN (son of Solomon Angell and Eunice C. Young). Born Jan. 10, 1844, Kirtland, Ohio. Came to Utah Sept. 20, 1848, Brigham Young company.

Married Ermina Sarah Prudence Cahoon at Salt Lake City (daughter of William F. Cahoon and Nancy M. Gibbs, pioneers Sept., 1848). Their children: William Osborn, m. Katherine ———; Solomon, m. Annie Foulks; Eunice Ermina, m. Frederick Burt; Lerona Martisa, died.

Married Sarah Jane Mikesell, Oct. 21, 1872, Salt Lake City (daughter of Hyrum Mikesell and Ann Agnes Scott—pioneers Oct. 15, 1849, Allen Taylor company). Their children: Martha Jane b. Aug. 13, 1873, m. John Daynes; John Osborn b. Dec. 24, 1874, m. Vina Pinney; Mary Caroline b. April 19, 1876, m. Frank Dibble; Ella A. b. Nov. 13, 1877; Hyrum Alma b. March 8, 1879, m. Maud Wright; Ralph b. March 23, 1881; Clara Adella b. Feb. 10, 1883, m. Frank Gilmore; Geo. Enoch b. March 11, 1885, died; Albert A. b. Jan. 17, 1887; Ernest Leroy b. Jan. 29, 1889, died. Family home Salt Lake City.

Member 33d quorum seventies; missionary to Dixie. Carpenter.

ARAVE, NELSON. Born Dec. 20, 1834, in Canada. Came to Utah 1851.

Married Aroline Wadsworth Feb. 18, 1855, Uinta, Weber county, Utah (daughter of Abiah Wadsworth and Eliza Hardy of Uinta county, pioneers Sept. 9, 1851, Abraham Day company). She was born Sept. 16, 1836. Their children: Nelson A. b. Jan. 20, 1856, died; Joseph W. b. June 4, 1857, m. Dora Zucer, April, 1895; William b. Jan. 14, 1860, m. Ida Clark May 12, 1881; David E. b. Dec. 23, 1861, m. Mary A. Fowles Sept. 22, 1886; Frederick b. March 23, 1863, died; Frank b. March 2, 1866, m. Sarah Andrews Nov. 10, 1885; Heber b. Oct. 15, 1868, m. Sarah Boyington Jan. 1, 1888; Elnoria b. Sept. 16, 1871, m. Levi Cox Sept. 22, 1886; Dora b. Oct. 26, 1873, m. Joseph Fowles Aug., 1895; Louis b. July 18, 1876, died; Ada Bell b. Dec. 11, 1879, m. Alma Rigby 1900; Eugene b. Nov. 25, 1882, m. Lillian Simpson 1902. Family home Hooper, Weber county, Utah.

Married Mary Ann Williams Oct. 9, 1865, Salt Lake City (daughter of Daniel Williams and Eliza Ames of South Wales). She was born May 6, 1848, in South Wales. Their children: Eliza M. b. June 24, 1868, m. Christen Hansen Oct. 1, 1890; Daniel W. b. Jan. 9, 1870, m. Susan P. Eastman Dec. 10, 1890; Harriet E. b. Oct. 12, 1873, m. George W. Cantrell 1890; Hyrum b. Aug. 2, 1876, m. Nancy J. Hunt Oct. 11, 1896; James T. b. Oct. 22, 1878, d. Nov. 2, 1896; Janette b. Sept. 16, 1880, m. Wm. E. Stoddard May 10, 1899; Mary Jane b. May 4, 1882, d. Oct., 1885; Josephine b. Nov. 27, 1885, m. John W. Armour Oct. 11, 1905; Nelson b. Dec. 20, 1891, d. Dec. 27, 1891; Parley Gilbert b. June 30, 1893; Arthur Leroy b. April 5, 1896. Family resided Morgan, Hooper and Ogden, Utah; Taylor and Basalt, Idaho.

Ward teacher. Died July 6, 1906.

ARAVE, DAVID E. (son of Nelson Arave and Aroline Wadsworth). Born Dec. 23, 1861, Uinta, Weber county, Utah.

Married Mary A. Fowles Sept. 22, 1886, Logan, Utah (daughter of Joseph Fowles and Mary A. Jones of Hooper, Utah, who came to Utah in 1869). She was born Sept. 20, 1871. Their children: Joseph C. b. Sept. 14, 1891; David E. b. Feb. 2, 1894; Vernal L. b. Nov. 26, 1895; Herschel b. Dec. 6, 1897; Cecil b. Oct. 20, 1901, died; Elgin b. Nov. 3, 1903; Orland b. March 23, 1906; Ellis G. b. March 21, 1909, died; Ariel b. Sept. 29, 1911, died; Zelma (adopted) b. March 29, 1909. Family home, Taylor, Idaho.

Sunday school superintendent; elder; high priest; bishop; ward teacher.

ARCHIBALD, WILLIAM RUSSELL (son of Thomas Archibald and Elizabeth Russell, of Harthill, Scotland). He was born March 16, 1840, in Scotland. Came to Utah Oct. 4, 1863, Thomas E. Ricks company.

Married Elizabeth Halliday 1857, Harthill, Scotland (daughter of Thomas Halliday and Agnes Fuers of Crofthead, Scotland). She was born April 12, 1840. Their children: Thomas H. b. Jan. 4, 1858, m. Aurena V. Tims; Margaret H.; James H.; William R.; Robert; John; Alexander; Andrew; Joseph; Hyrum; Agnes; Christiney; Elizabeth; Mary. Family resided Wellsville and Clarkston, Utah. Pioneer. Died April 7, 1903, at latter place.

ARCHIBALD, THOMAS HALLIDAY (son of William Russell Archibald and Elizabeth Halliday). He was born Jan. 24, 1858, Crofthead, Scotland. Came to Utah 1863, with parents.

Married Amice V. Tims 1884 (daughter of John Tims and Charlotte Marshall of England—pioneers 1854, Levi Richards company). She was born Aug. 20, 1864. Their children: Charlotte b. April 23, 1885, m. Thomas Udy; William R. b. Oct. 1, 1886, m. Kate Moore; Thomas Edward b. July 10, 1888, died; John Frankland b. May 30, 1890, m. Agnes Rudd; Cora b. April 15, 1892, m. Alvin Smith; May b. May 1, 1894; Evan b. Feb. 2, 1897, died; Elizabeth b. April 24, 1898, died; Lavetha b. Sept. 22, 1899; Locius Elwin b. Feb. 12, 1901; Earl b. March 3, 1905. Family home, Plymouth, Utah.

Settled in Wellsville; moved to Clarkston 1876, and to Plymouth 1885.

Bishop Plymouth ward 1891-1912.

ARGENT, JOHN (son of Thomas Argent and Ann Middleditch, both born in 1760, at Glensford, Suffolk, Eng.). He was born March 12, 1804, Foxearth, Essex, Eng. Came to Utah Oct. 17, 1862, Henry W. Miller company.

Married Mary Gridley 1823 (daughter of Daniel Gridley and Elizabeth Sparks), who was born Aug. 8, 1803. Their children: Rosetta b. Aug. 28, 1823, m. Edward Reeves; Hannah b. June 6, 1828, m. William Aylett; Maria b. Oct. 14, 1831, m. William Goodwin; Adelaide b. May 23, 1834, m. Joseph Bannister; Emily b. Feb. 4, 1837, m. James Bateman; Jesse b. March 13, 1840; Seebrey b. Feb. 11, 1843, m. James Jarvis. Family home Orsett, Essex, England.

ARGYLE, JOSEPH (son of Joseph Argyle and Frances Smith of Market, Bosworth, Leicestershire, Eng.). Born Sept. 12, 1818, at Market, Bosworth. Came to Utah Nov. 31, 1856, Capt. Edmund Ellsworth "frozen" handcart company.

Married Jane Finch Dec. 24, 1840 (daughter of William and Rebecca Finch), who was born Feb. 29, 1824, and came to Utah with husband. Their children: Joseph b. Feb. 25, 1842, m. Ellen Taylor Holroyd Sept. 28, 1867; Benjamin, m. Jane Robinson; William; Mary and Fannie, m. John Staniford; Lorenzo, m. Emily E. Manwill Dec. 25, 1876; Priscilla, m. Orlando Warner; Hyrum, m. Aurelia Thomas; Eliza, m. Wilbur Burnham; Ann, m. Jos. M. Thomas; Frank, m. Agnes Cowen; Maria, m. Ely Robinson.

Veteran of many Indian skirmishes. Pulled a handcart from Iowa City to Salt Lake City.

ARGYLE, JOSEPH Jr. (son of Joseph Argyle and Jane Finch). Born Feb. 25, 1842, Birmingham, Eng. Came to Utah in 1856 with father.
Married Ellen Taylor Holroyd Sept. 28, 1867, Salt Lake City, Utah (daughter of Thomas Edward Holroyd and Dinah Williams, pioneers Oct. 1, 1861, Joseph Horne company). She was born March 27, 1851, at Birkenhead, Chestershire, Eng. Their children: Joseph H. b. July 5, 1868, m. Elizabeth Kynaston Nov. 3, 1892; Thomas H. b. Sept. 6, 1870, m. Levania Mann Nov. 17, 1892; Ben. H. b. Dec. 6, 1872, m. Ida May Hogan Dec. 7, 1892; Robert H. b. May 15, 1875, m. Lois Helen Coltrin Nov. 6, 1895; William H. b. Nov. 8, 1877, m. Clara Atkinson Dec. 21, 1899; Jesse H. b. Jan 13, 1880, m. Vida E. McKean June 26, 1907; Mary Ellen b. Sept. 8, 1882, m. John C. Stocks March 23, 1904; Delpha b. April 2, 1885; Adelbert b. April 2, 1885, m. Alta Jolley Jan. 23, 1907; Dinah May b. Oct. 25, 1887, m. Ernest Hansen March 1, 1913; Hazel b. April 17, 1891; Emeline b. March 15, 1893, m. Thomas Roberts Jr. March 5, 1913. Family home Woods Cross, Davis County, Utah.
Black Hawk Indian war veteran, and performed much military service. Was one of the famous "rolling battery" of ten in the Morrisite trouble 1868. Early settler at Bountiful, Utah.

ARGYLE, LORENZO (son of Joseph Argyle and Jane Finch). Born Oct. 26, 1852, at Birmingham, Eng.
Married Emily E. Manwill Dec. 25, 1876, Bountiful, Utah (daughter of John F. Manwill and Emily Brown), who was born April 19, 1856, Payson, Utah. Their children: Rebecca Jane; Eliza E.; Joseph L.; Fannie M.; Alma M.; Melissa; Benjamin; Mary; Olive Ann; Florence; James Leon; Etta Viola; Vergie Izetta, Claud Viron. Family home Lake Shore, Utah county.
Bishop 33 years; Sunday school superintendent four years.

ARMATAGE, SAMUEL (son of Joseph Armatage of Rothwell, Yorkshire, Eng., born Oct. 25, 1811, and Sarah Ann Kitchen, born Dec. 9, 1817, both of Barnsley in Leeds, Yorkshire, Eng). He was born Feb. 6, 1848, Barnsley in Leeds. Came to Utah Oct. 3, 1863, Daniel D. McArthur company.
Married Mary Ann Kennington Nov. 18, 1872, Salt Lake City (daughter of Richard Kennington and Mary Ann Davison, pioneers Sept. 26, 1856, Edmund Ellsworth and Daniel D. McArthur handcart company). She was born May 20, 1854. Their children: Mary Ann b. Oct. 16, 1877; Samuel Richard b. Jan. 28, 1882, m. Zina R. Hayes June 25, 1902.
Sheepman, Rush Valley, Utah; moved to Bear Lake Co., Idaho, 1876. President Y. M. M. I. A.; president deacons' quorum; member 114th quorum of seventy; missionary to England 1902-04.

ARMATAGE, SAMUEL RICHARD (son of Samuel Armatage and Mary Ann Kennington). He was born Jan. 28, 1882, Bennington, Bear Lake Co., Idaho.
Married Zina Ruth Hayes June 25, 1902, Paris, Idaho (daughter of Alma Hayes and Louise Sheffield), who was born July 16, 1883, Georgetown, Idaho. Their children: George Lester b. Jan. 10, 1903; Iola Louise b. July 20, 1905; Wilford Richard b. Nov. 24, 1907; Mary Ruth b. June 1, 1910. Family resided Bennington and Georgetown, Idaho.
Elder and seventy. Lumberman and timberman, assisting in forest reclamation service. Farmer and stockraiser.

ARMSTRONG, JAMES (son of William Armstrong, who died Sept., 1849, St. Louis, Mo., and Agnes Smith Parker). He was born Nov. 24, 1844, Carlisle, Cumberlandshire, Eng. Came to Utah with his mother Oct. 3, 1854, Horace S. Eldredge and Orson Pratt company.
Married Anna K. Olsen Aug. 7, 1871, Salt Lake City (daughter of Peter K. and Anna K. Olsen), who was born Sept. 26, 1852, in Denmark. Their children: William James b. May 11, 1872, d. Jan. 6, 1877; Agness Ann b. June 19, 1874, d. Feb. 22, 1876; Joseph Andrew b. Nov. 1, 1876; Mary Kirstena b. Nov. 12, 1878, d. Dec. 6, 1881; Sarah Virginia b. March 10, 1881; James Arthur b. April 13, 1883; Nancy Helen b. March 9, 1885; Effie Olivia b. April 1, 1887; Anna Grace b. Dec. 20, 1889; Horace Adrain b. Nov. 14, 1891, d. May 16, 1892; Jediah Alif b. Sept. 26, 1893, d. Sept. 19, 1907.
Settled at Ephraim. Black Hawk war veteran. Member city council four terms. Seventy and clerk of 47th quorum of seventies. Furniture dealer; farmer and woolgrower.

ARMSTRONG, THOMAS COLUMBUS (son of Thomas Columbus Armstrong of London, Eng.). Born in London, Eng.
Married Annie Rebecca Curtiss at Salt Lake City (daughter of Joseph Curtiss and Sarah Morrell of London—pioneers 1861, Capt. Harmon company). She was born June, 1842. Their children: Lizzie, m. Henry Robson; Annie, m. Joseph Canton; William F. m. Thomas, died; Nellie, m. Steven Canton; James, m. Mabel Powell; Joseph C., m. Millie T. Christensen; Lula, m. Frank Strickley; Truman. Family home Salt Lake City.
Grain merchant. Died April 27, 1893, Salt Lake City.

ARMSTRONG, JOSEPH COLUMBUS (son of Thomas Columbus Armstrong and Annie Rebecca Curtiss). Born Sept. 17, 1877, Salt Lake City.
Married Millie T. Christensen Nov. 10, 1907, Salt Lake City (daughter of Nels Christensen and Mary Sorenson of Copenhagen, Denmark). She was born July 2, 1886. Their children: Thomas b. June 24, 1909; Harry LeRoy b. Aug. 31, 1910. Family home Salt Lake City.
Organized the Uniform rank Woodmen of the World in California 1896. Police officer four years.

ARMSTRONG, WILLIAM B. (son of John Armstrong of the border between Scotland and England and Elizabeth Tallentyre). He was born March 19, 1841, at Carlisle, Cumberlandshire, Eng. Was baptized in the L. D. S. faith June 28, 1863, and came to Utah June 14, 1876, with the John Woodhouse company of 131 immigrants.
Married Patience Dawson Feb. 22, 1862, Hull, Yorkshire, Eng. (daughter of William Dawson and Jane Dunn of that place). She was born in August, 1837. Their children: William B. m. Mary Kemp; John J., m. Ruth Draper; Robert, m. Matilda Olson; Orson E., m. Angeline Neilsen; Arthur B., d. aged 3; Albert B., m. Priscilla J. Jordan; m. Mary E. Gold; Truman Henry, m. Eliza T. Sessions.
Married Sarah Foster April 19, 1883, at Salt Lake City, Utah (daughter of Christopher Foster and Frances Hazelgrove of Leeds, Eng., who came to Utah in 1881). She was born Aug. 23, 1859. Only child: Christopher F., died in infancy. Family home Salt Lake City.
Missionary to England 1899-1901; high priest; block teacher; seventy. Master mechanic Utah Central R. R. and Utah Southern R. R. 1876-1883. General mechanic. Died Oct. 13. 1904.

ARMSTRONG, WILLIAM B. (son of William B. Armstrong and Patience Dawson). Born Sept. 24, 1863. Came to Utah June, 1876, with his parents.
Married Mary Kemp Jan. 2, 1888, Manti, Utah (daughter of Charles Kemp and Sarah Blackham of Moroni, Utah—pioneers 1855). She was born April 14, 1867, Moroni, Utah. Their children: William B. b. March 1, 1889; Sarah b. Jan. 15, 1891, m. James Mathison; Donna J. b. July 23, 1897; Charles L. b. April 6, 1901; Martha H. b. Aug. 12, 1906. Family home 17th ward, Salt Lake City.

ARMSTRONG, ORSON E. (son of William B. Armstrong and Patience Dawson). Born May 18, 1870; came to Utah with parents.
Married Angeline Neilsen April 16, 1908, at Salt Lake City, Utah (daughter of Neils C. Neilsen and Annie M. Sorenson), who was born April 6, 1872, at Moroni, Utah. Their children: Orson E. b. Feb. 1, 1909; Angeline b. March 4, 1910. Family home Salt Lake City.

ARNOLD, HENRY (son of Henry Arnold and Elizabeth Monk of Hereford, Herefordshire, Eng). Born Feb. 15, 1822, Hereford, Herefordshire. Came to Utah Aug. 28, 1852.
Married Cynthia M. Wilcox Jan. 1, 1869, Salt Lake City (daughter of Walter E. Wilcox and Maria W. Richards of Massachusetts—pioneers October, 1852). She was born July 28, 1846. Their children: Alice Maria, m. Joseph W. Smith; Henrietta Cynthia, m. Samuel Doyle Walker; Walter Mahonri, m. Sarah Ann Potts; Vernon Harcourt d. infancy; Amelia Adelaide, m. Robert Jones; Ethyln, m. Walter G. Saville; Le Roy Albert d. aged 1 year; Sydney C. d. infant; Ellen, m. Elmer E. Erickson. Family home Salt Lake City.
Counselor to Bishops Raleigh, Morris and Watson. Tailor; proprietor Globe bakery. Died in September, 1888, Salt Lake City.

ARTHUR, CHRISTOPHER ABEL (son of Robert Arthur and Mary Abel). Born Sept. 25, 1796, Dorking, Surrey, Eng. Came to Utah Sept. 26, 1853, Claudius V. Spencer company, 12 days later than main company arrived.
Married Ann Jones 1826, who was born 1796. Their children: Joshua b. July 19, 1828, m. Charlotte Evans 1852; Christopher Jones b. March 9, 1832, m. Caroline E. S. Haight Dec. 30, 1854; m. Ann E. Perry Feb. 17, 1875; m. Marion Brown Nov. 22, 1875; m. Jane Condie Jan. 18, 1877; Benjamin Abel b. April 26, 1834, m. Janet Easton Feb. 12, 1863; Mary Ann b. Sept. 26, 1836, m. James Whittaker March 12, 1856. Family resided Cedar City and Beaver, Utah.
Married Maria Groves 1855, Cedar City, Utah.
Followed farming and stock raising.

ARTHUR, CHRISTOPHER JONES (son of Christopher Abel Arthur and Ann Jones). Born March 9, 1832, Abersychan, Monmouthshire, S. W. Came to Utah Sept. 26, 1853, Claudius V. Spencer company.
Married Caroline E. S. Haight Dec. 30, 1854 (daughter of Isaac Chauncey Haight and Ann Eliza Snyder), who was born Dec. 5, 1837. Their children: Eliza Ann H. b. July 7, 1857; Christopher H. b. July 23, 1859; Caroline K. H. b. Aug. 11, 1861, m. William T. Jones Jan. 27, 1882; Joshua H. b. May 27, 1864; Benjamin F. H. b. Sept. 9, 1866; Mary H. b. Oct. 21, 1868; Sarah H. b. Feb. 11, 1871, m. Isaac A. Nelson Jan. 19, 1896. Family home Cedar City, Utah.
Married Ann Elizabeth Perry Feb. 17, 1875, Cedar City, Utah (daughter of George Perry and Susannah Ward, pioneers 1852, Joseph Jepson company). She was born Dec. 1, 1851, St. Louis, Mo.
Married Marion Brown Nov. 22, 1875 (daughter of Robert Brown and Elizabeth Beveridge), who was born July 2, 1844. Family home Cedar City, Utah.
Married Jane Condie Jan. 18, 1877, St. George, Utah

(daughter of George Condie and Mary Hunter), who was born Aug. 10, 1858, Stonerig, Stirlingshire, Scotland. Their children: Sarah Mary Jane C. b. May 13, 1878, m. John T. Bullock Sept. 18, 1900; Caroline E. C. b. Nov. 8, 1880. m. James C. Parry Nov. 9, 1904; Robert Abel C. b. May 12, 1883, m. Florence Sawyer; Jacob C. b. Nov. 21, 1886; Janet C. b. Aug. 8, 1888; Norman Chester b. April 8, 1897. Family home Cedar City.
Drove oxteam from Council Bluffs to Salt Lake City. First settled in Big Cottonwood on the James Huntsman farm. Went to Cedar City 1854. Director of Deseret Iron Company, one of the early infant industries—succumbed 1860. Bishop's counselor 15 years; tithing clerk 42 years; of the stake 20 years; ward recorder 20 years; president 63d quorum high priests; bishop seven years; patriarch since 1893. City councilman 20 years; mayor two years. Aide to Col. W. H. Dame of the Nauvoo legion. Missionary to Sheffield, Eng., conference five months; with "Millennial Star" office 20 months. Successful in all his pursuits. Surveyor.

ARTHUR, BENJAMIN ABEL (son of Christopher Abel Arthur and Ann Jones). Born April 26, 1834, Aberaychan, Monmouthshire, South Wales. Came to Utah Sept. 14, 1853, Claudius V. Spencer company.
Married Janet Easton Feb. 12, 1863 (daughter of Robert Easton), who was born Dec. 7, 1842. Their children: Margaret Ann b. Nov. 12, 1863, m. George Harmon; Mary Jannet b. Sept. 25, 1866, d. May 7, 1866; Benjamin E. b. April 16, 1867, d. Dec. 26, 1905; Elizabeth b. July 2, 1869, d. same day; Laura Jane b. July 25, 1870; Caroline Agnes b. July 7, 1873; Sarah Ellen b. Dec. 21, 1875; Ida b. March 28, 1878; Christopher Robert b. Aug. 16, 1882. Family home Greenville, Beaver county, Utah. He died Feb. 23, 1883; his wife died in December, 1911.

ARTHUR, EVAN (son of John Arthur and Margaret Rowlands of Machynlleth, Montgomeryshire, North Wales). Born Oct. 4, 1806, in Machynlleth. Came to Utah Oct. 13, 1863, Rosel Hyde company.
Married Catherine James (daughter of John James), who was born March 30, 1807. Their children: John; Evan, m. Maria b. Oct. 2, 1846, m. John Wood Sept. 12, 1888; Ada Jane Ellen Walter; Catherine, m. John T. Davis; Margaret, m. Bennett May 15, 1868; Mary Ellen, m. John G. Ahlstrom. Family home St. John, Tooele county, Utah. She was born Jan. 19, 1863, Horton W. Haight company). She was born Jan. vens March 16, 1888; m. Melissa Lewins Aug. 28, 1895; Nina

ARTHUR, EDWARD JAMES (son of Evan Arthur and Catherine James). Born Jan. 1, 1845, Machynlleth, N. W.
Married Catherine Bennett May 15, 1868, Deseret, Utah (daughter of John Bennett and Jane Roberts, pioneers Oct. Mathew Orr; Edward James b. Jan. 1, 1848, m. Catherine Evan G. Morgan; Ann, m. John A. Davis; Elizabeth, m. 16, 1850, Connasky, Flintshire, N. W. Their children: Edward B. b. Aug. 16, 1869, m. Myrtle Eldrige; Catherine E. b. Jan. 22, 1871, m. James Caldwell; Jane E. b. Oct. 15, 1874, m. Walter S. Orr; John B. b. Aug. 29, 1874, m. Hattie Paul; Evan B. b. Aug. 15, 1876, m. Azelia Evan; m. Iantha Richards; Mary Ann b. June 6, 1879, m. M. M. Bush; Margaret b. June 25, 1881, m. Lehi Heneffer; Eleanor b. June 23, 1883; Gwladys May b. Oct. 14, 1885; Emily b. Dec. 27, 1887, m. Williard Bullock; Benjamin Harden b. Dec. 26, 1889, Family home St. John, Utah.
Married Sadie Thomas Benedict Oct. 8, 1907, Salt Lake City.
Justice of peace; Tooele county commissioner; school trustee. Farmer and wool grower.

ASHBY, WILLIAM HARDIN (son of Nathaniel Ashby, born April 15, 1805, at Salem, and Susan Hammond, born Aug. 28, 1808, Marblehead, Mass.). He was born July 16, 1829, Salem, Mass. Came to Utah Sept. 20, 1848, Brigham Young company.
Married Nancy Maria Badger Jan. 14, 1865 (daughter of Rodney Badger and Nancy Garr, married March 9, 1845, Hancock county, Ill.; pioneers Oct. 2, 1847, Jedediah M. Grant company). She was born Feb. 27, 1846. Their children: William Hardin b. April 7, 1867, m. Martha Ann Steb. Nov. 9, 1870, m. Edward A. Wood Nov. 8, 1893; Rodney Badger b. Oct. 26, 1872, m. Jane Marinda Stephenson Sept. 29, 1889; Nathaniel b. Sept. 20, 1874, m. Jane Johnson Nov. 1901; Emma Louisa b. Oct. 9, 1876, m. Simeon T. Stephenson Dec. 15, 1897; Susan b. Dec. 14, 1878, m. John Charles Bennett Sept. 18, 1901; Robert b. Dec. 29, 1880, m. Hannah Cropper June 3, 1903; Mary Edith b. March 23, 1883, m. John H. Stephenson June 13, 1906; Martha Ellen b. Feb. 26, 1885, m. Marion E. Stevens June 2, 1909; Florence b. Jan. 18, 1887; Austin Garr b. Jan. 9, 1889; Clinton b. Oct. 14, 1891. Family home Holden, Utah.

ASHBY, RODNEY BADGER (son of William Hardin Ashby and Nancy Maria Badger). Born Oct. 26, 1872, Holden, Utah.
Married Jane Marinda Stephenson Sept. 29, 1898, Salt Lake City (daughter of Anthony Stephenson, pioneer 1861, and Mary Ann Bennett, pioneer 1860). Their children: Eleanor Jane b. July 16, 1899; Mary Lottie b. Nov. 29, 1901; Ray Badger b. Oct. 18, 1903; Rodney Anthony b. Jan. 20, 1905; Emily Maria b. March 11, 1907; Orrin Thomas b. Aug. 24, 1909; George Marion b. June 30, 1911. Family resided Holden and Leamington, Utah.
Bishop of Leamington ward.

ASHTON, EDWARD (son of Richard Ashtn and Elizabeth Savage of Montgomeryshire. North Wales Born Aug. 21, 1821. In Montgomeryshire. Came to Utah ly, 1852, Daniel Jones company).
Married Jane Treharne Feb. 6, 1854, 'alt Lake City (daughter of William Treharne and Ann ichards of Salt Lake City, pioneers July, 1852, Daniel nes company). She was born April 2, 1828. Their children: Edward T., m. Effie W. Morris; Jedediah William, m. Mary Eliza Salisbury; Brigham Willard. m. Mary Alice Ittit; Elizabeth Ann; Sarah Jane, m. Joseph E. Price; Emma Treharne, m. Albert Richards; George S., m. Leah Fidki Family home Salt Lake City.
Member 2d quorum seventies; teacher and choir leader 20 years at 15th ward Salt Lake City. Cotnected with the O. S. L. R. R. 25 years. Died Feb. 7, 1904, at Salt Lake City.

ASHTON, EDWARD T. (son of Edward Ashton and Jane Treharne). Born July 14, 1855, Salt Lake Ci.
Married Effie Walker Morris April 4, 1878 Salt Lake City (daughter of Elias Morris and Mary L. Walb of Salt Lake City). She was born Jan. 10, 1859. Their chiren: Edward M. b. Jan. 12, 1879, m. Nancy Louise Ashby Badger; Elias C. b. Feb. 16, 1880, m. Rosabell Hall; Marvi O. b. April 1, 1883, m. Rachel Jeremy; Raymond J. b. Jan 23, 1886; Effie b. Jan. 9, 1889. m. Joseph Kjar; Jane b. Arch 24, 1896. Family home Salt Lake City.
Married Cora Lindsay Dec., 1883, Salt Lake ity (daughter of Henry Lindsay of South Carolina, who ame to Utah Aug., 1881). She was born Nov. 7, 1864. Their children: Cora Lindsay; Ina Jane, m. Le Grande Ricards: Henry; Amy; Clifford Ashton; Elmer; Jed; Eva; Mir e; Elizabeth; Norma. Family home Salt Lake City.
Member 2d quorum seventies; missionary Wales 1891-93; bishop of 24th ward of Salt Lake City; conselor in Salt Lake stake. Contractor and builder.

ASHTON, EDWARD M. (son of Edward Trarne Ashton and Effie Walker Morris). Born Jan. 12, 1879, Salt Lake City.
Married Nancy Louise Ashby Badger Oct. 5, 1902, Salt Lake City (daughter of Rodney C. Badger ad Louisa A. Ashby of Salt Lake City and Ogden, Utah). he was born Aug. 30, 1881. Their children: Morris Badge b. Sept. 11, 1903; Virginia Louise b. Sept. 14, 1905; Beatri b. Dec. 31, 1908; Richard Edward b. Jan. 10, 1912.
President T. M. M. I. A., Liberty stake and Sugar ward: bishop 31st ecclesiastical ward. Employed wen 13 years of age in Zion's Savings Bank & Trust Co., a aining position of chief clerk to George M. Cannon, ashier, and remaining there until 19 years of age, when I was called on a mission to Germany, serving 38 month. Embarked in business for himself as a real estate and stck broker in 1902. Later he formed a partnership with Edv E. Jenkins. which partnership has been incorporated un r the firm name of Ashton-Jenkins Company, one of the argest real estate concerns in Salt Lake City.

ASHTON, GEORGE S. (son of Edward Ashton al Jane Treharne). Born July 27, 1870, at Salt Lake City.
Married Leah Fidkin Sept. 27, 1893, at Salt Lake City (daughter of William Fidkin and Alice Crowton f Birmingham. Eng., who came to Utah 1873). She was rn Feb. 17, 1872. Their children: Leah b. June 19, 1894; Jorge W. b. Nov. 1, 1896; Lucile F. b. April 20, 1898; Allen b. May 25, 1900; Emma b. Dec. 16, 1902; William F. b. F. 27, 1905; Melvin A. b. May 8, 1908; Reed b. Sept. 16, 1912. Family home Salt Lake City.
High priest; missionary among the Indians 93-94; 1st counselor in bishopric of 15th ward. Contract.

ASHTON, ROBERT (son of Robert Ashton, bor 1794, Billinge, Lancashire, and Maria Heaton, born 180 Highton, Lancashire, Eng.). He was born March 15, 1827, pholland, Lancashire. Came to Utah Aug. 1855.
Married Sarah Liptrot 1848, who was born y 1849, and died 1855. Their children: Sarah Ann b. Au 1849, m. William John. Family home West Portage, Box Elder county, Utah.
Married Jane Cornish July 2, 1855 (daughter ' William and Elizabeth Cornish of the Isle of Man). he was born Oct. 11, 1831. Their children: Robert Nephi May 1, 1856; Joseph b. Dec. 6, 1857; Maria Elizabeth b. Set 2, 1860, m. Chas. Landon; John William b. Nov. 23, 1862; Syrum b. April 2, 1865, m. Emma Elias Aug. 13, 1888; Iigham b. March 21, 1868; Heber b. Sept. 4, 1870; Thomas rancis b. Jan. 13, 1873. Family home Wellsville and Wes Portage, Utah.
Settled at Cash Fort; moved to Cache valley 18; was in "the move" south in 1858; water master; high pri t. president of elders' quorum two years in absence regular president; moved to Malad valley 1877; home ssionary there three years; supt. of Samaria irrigation pr ct. Has several great-great-grandchildren.

ASHTON, THOMAS. Born Nov. 7, 1813, Parr, Lcashire. Eng. Came to Utah Sept. 27, 1851, Morris Phelps ompany.
Married Mary Howard Nov. 20, 1836, who die Aug. 2, 1849. Five children were born.

Married Sarah E. Mills Sept 25, 1849, who died 1850. They had one child.
Married Arminta Lawrence Feb. 18, 1851, Council Bluffs, Iowa. Eleven children were born.
High priest. Took a very active part in the planning and making of Lehi's first water ditch and one of its water-masters. Active in planning and making the first bridge across Jordan river and in building Lehi's first meeting house. Elected a member of the Lehi city council six time. Wheelwright and carriage builder. Died Jan. 2, 1903, Lehi, Utah.

ASHTON WILLIAM (son of Robert Ashton and Maria Carlisle of Kentucky and Montgomery, Ala., respectively). Born Feb. 9, 1837, in Alabama. Came to Utah 1862, independent company.
Marrie Ellen Elizabeth Croxford Feb. 6, 1865, of Pleasant Grove, Utah (daughter of William Croxford and Ellen Loader of Oxfordshire, Eng.). She was born Dec. 22, 1844, and came to Utah Sept. 26, 1862, James Wareham independent company. Their children: Kate b. Jan. 6, 1867, m. Samuel M. Brow; Leslie b. Feb. 27, 1869, m. Eva Hall; William Stanley b. May 29, 1871, m. Hannah Elizabeth Odekirk; Lynn b. Sept. 19, 1873, m. Annie Evans; m. Elizabeth Marshall; Reece Llellyn April 13, 1876, died; Grace Ellen b. Dec. 3, 1878, m. Dani H. Hillman; Ethelyn b. Jan. 11, 1882; Clarence b. 1886, die; Hazel b. Feb. 3, 1887. Family home at Vernal, Utah.
Ran ferry at Green River, Wyo., 1858-59; carried U. S. mail as pony express; came to and helped found town of Vernal, pt. 1, 1878, and was its first tax assessor; school trustee; studied law; secretary Ashley Co-Op. store for twenty ears. Was devout church member. Died Oct. 15, 1909 at Vernal.

ASHTON WILLIAM STANLEY (son of William Ashton and Ellen Elzabeth Croxford). Born May 29, 1871, Pleasant Grove, Utah.
Marri Hannah Elizabeth Odekirk May 29, 1895, at Vernal aughter of Heber Odekirk and Hannah Brown of Vernal) by James M. Shafer. Their children: Nellie Merle b. June), 1896; Hilda b. Nov. 15, 1900.
Active in church matters. Went to Vernal Nov. 3, 1879; has bee with Ashley Co-op. Store Co. for 21 years as buyer. armer and stockraiser.

ASHWOTH, BENJAMIN. Born in England. Came to Utah 1187.
Marri Eliza Dorsey in England. Their children: Sarah, m. Isaac Chapman; Martha, m. Daniel Brian; Emma, m. John Hill; Tite, m. Charles O'Brien; Reuben; Thomas S., m. Ruby Fsset. Family home Salt Lake City.
Foun yman. Died 1883, at Salt Lake City.

ASHWORTH, THOMAS S. (son of Benjamin Ashworth and Eliza Dsey). Born Oct. 24, 1865, Mill Creek, Utah.
Marri Ruby Basset Jan. 28, 1890, at Salt Lake City (daughter of Charles H. Basset and Mary Knight of Alleganycounty, New York; former came to Utah 1852; latter Sept. 8 1850, Capt. Aaron Johnson company). She was born M r 13, 1871. Their children: Nellie Basset b. Aug. 3, 1891; Evan b. Sept. 4, 1894; Lola b. Nov. 11, 1897; Orpha b. Dec. , 1900; Dorsey b. Jan. 24, 1904; Willes Bassett b. Feb. 1 1906. Family home Salt Lake City.
Elder Piano-tuner.

ASPER GEORGE E. (son of William Asper and Mary Alstrom of Salt Lake City, Utah, pioneers 1860). Born Sept. 1 1875, Salt Lake City.
Marr i Ellen M. Macduff June 29, 1906, at Salt Lake City (daughter of Malcolm Macduff and Jane Lord of Salt Lake Cy, pioneers 1861). She was born May 15, 1873, Salt Lake Cy, Utah. Family home Salt Lake City.

ASTILI ZACHARIAH. Born in 1834, at Birmingham, Eng. Came Utah 1854.
Marri Rosanna Clark Dec. 24, 1869 (daughter of Alfred Clark rd Anna Waterfield, pioneers Sept. 5, 1866, Samuel D. White company—married Jan. 1844, at Derbyshire, Eng.). She was born July 5, 1846. Their children: Zachariah b. Dec. 3 1870; Rosanna b. Sept. 7, 1872; Lizzie b. Oct. 14, 1874, n F. C. Ewing July 21, 1893; Wm. T. b. Dec. 18, 1877, m. An Warren Dec. 28, 1898; Henry b. Sept. 13, 1880, m. Martha Atkinson June 10, 1902. Family home Ogden, Utah.
Marri d Diana Bune June, 1884, Ogden, Utah (daughter of James une), who was born May, 1847, in Holland. Only child s James b. Sept. 1888.
Prominent in civic affairs in Ogden; was engineer of its first v lunteer fire department. Died Oct. 7, 1897.

ASTIL, WILLIAM T. (son of Zachariah Astili and Rosanna Clark) Born Dec. 18, 1877.
Mar d Anna Warren Dec. 28, 1898, Ogden, Utah (daughter Clinton Warren and Frances Wonder), who was born 1877. Their children: Rosa A. b. March 30, 1900; a b. Jan. 6, 1902. Family home Ogden, Utah.
Toffee, seed and commission merchant.

ASTLE, FRANCIS (son of James Astle, born Aug. 5, 1780, and Rachel King, both of Celleston, Derbyshire, Eng.). He was born Feb. 2, 1810, Diseworth, Leicestershire. Came to Utah, Sept. 13, 1861, Joseph Horne company.
Married Felica Raynor March 21, 1836, Derby, Derbyshire, Eng. (daughter of William Raynor and Mary Roland of Hucknall Torkard, Nottinghamshire, Eng., pioneers 1861, Joseph Horne company). She was born May 4, 1814. Their children: Mary; James b. March 8, 1839, died; James b. Nov. 13, 1841; Joseph Charles; John; Francis Thomas. Family home Hyrum, Utah.
High priest. Farmer. Died Dec. 13, 1884, Montpelier, Idaho.

ASTLE, JOHN (son of Francis Astle and Felica Raynor). Born June 16, 1846, Hucknall Torkard, Nottingham, Eng. Came to Utah, Sept. 13, 1861, walking all the way.
Married Isabella Jane Bradshaw Dec. 9, 1866 (daughter of Richard Bradshaw and Elizabeth Simpson, married March, 1843, Manchester, Eng., pioneers Dec. 1, 1856, Martin and Tyler handcart company). She was born March 14, 1846. Their children: Elizabeth F. b. Feb. 4, 1868, m. Alvin S. McCombs Oct. 2, 1889; John F. b. Sept. 21, 1869, m. Lauretta Hepworth Sept. 9, 1891; Richard T. b. Sept. 2, 1871, m. Henrietta Jensen Oct. 24, 1895; Wm. W. b. Sept. 27, 1873, m. Elizabeth A. Shaw Aug. 20, 1902; Rachel J. b. Aug. 30, 1875; Abraham A. b. Aug. 26, 1877; Sarah I. b. Sept. 20, 1879, m. Adolphus A. Call Aug. 9, 1899; Joseph H. b. Aug. 24, 1881, m. Elizabeth E. Price June 13, 1906; Violet E. b. Dec. 17, 1883. Family resided Montpelier, Idaho, and Afton, Wyo.
Married Melvina A. Banks April 3, 1884, Salt Lake City (daughter of Wm. H. Banks, pioneer Aug. 29, 1863, John R. Murdock company, and Margret Armitage). She was born March 21, 1867, Tooele, Utah. Their children: Alma P. b. Oct. 5, 1886, m. Martha C. Dutson Sept. 30, 1909; James R. b. Aug. 28, 1888; John A. b. Jan. 17, 1891; Sylva J. b. Sept. 26, 1892; Ernest B. b. Sept. 22, 1894; Elwood W. b. Jan. 20, 1897; Alex, m. Oct. 26, 1899; Lehi S. b. Jan. 4, 1903; Ruby H. b. April 29, 1908. Family home Afton, Wyo.
Home missionary 20 years; missionary to England; high councilor. Crossed plains three times by oxteam. Assisted Capt. Nebeker, 1866, in bringing immigrants from Missouri river points.

ASTLE, JOHN F. (son of John Astle and Isabella Jane Bradshaw). Born Sept. 21, 1869, Montpelier, Idaho.
Married Lauretta Hepworth Sept. 9, 1891, Logan, Utah (daughter of Edmund Hepworth and Hannah Cowling), who was born Sept. 26, 1874, Oxford, Idaho. Their children: John F., Jr. b. July 13, 1892; Klea L. b. Sept. 9, 1894; Vernon L. b. April 5, 1898; Austanie E. b. Oct. 13, 1899; Clara P. b. March 12, 1901; David E. b. Aug. 12, 1902; Evelyn V. b. Jan. 4, 1904; Doretta A. b. March 17, 1906; Agnes L. b. July 3, 1907; Elva M. b. May 23, 1909; Grace E. b. Feb. 19, 1912. Family home Grover, Wyo.
Missionary to southern and eastern states. One of seven presidents 103d quorum seventies. Bishop's counselor.

ATHAY, JAMES (son of Francis Athay and Jane Haines of Shipham, Eng.). Born Sept. 1, 1830. Came to Utah 1864.
Married Ellen Morris (daughter of William and Mary Morris, pioneers 1863). She was born April 12, 1832. Their children: Henry b. June 25, 1858, m. Ellen Louisa Price, Oct. 2, 1884; William b. Sept. 25, 1859, m. Emma Smith Sept. 22, 1883; Marintha b. July 25, 1861, m. P. Lindsay Sept. 29, 1881; Alice b. Aug. 25, 1863, m. Arthur Budge Sept. 22, 1883. Family home Paris, Idaho.
Married Mary Lindsay Oct. 3, 1887, Logan, Utah (daughter of Wm. Lindsay), who was born Oct. 1862, Kaysville. Only child was a daughter, Agnes.

ATHAY, HENRY (son of James Athay and Ellen Morris). Born June 25, 1858.
Married Ellen Louisa Price Oct. 2, 1884, Logan, Utah. (daughter of Robert Price and Matilda Louisa Kelsey, pioneers Sept. 12, 1861, Milo Andrus company). She was born in Salt Lake City. Their children: Ellen Edna; Matilda Louisa; Henry E.; James Russell. Family home Paris, Idaho.
High priest. Councilman of Paris three terms.

ATKIN, THOMAS (son of John Atkin and Mary Ashley of Barkworth, Lincolnshire, Eng.). Born Feb. 10, 1804, Legsby, Lincolnshire. Came to Utah Sept. 23, 1849, Orson Spencer company.
Married Mary Morley Feb. 13, 1826, Lincolnshire, Eng. (daughter of Thomas Morley and Mary Hole of Lincolnshire.) She was born Feb. 24, 1800. Their children: Eliza b. Jan. 15, 1827, died; George b. Jan. 3, 1828, d. infant; Emily b. Oct. 17, 1830, m. Richard Warburton; Thomas Jr. b. July 7, 1833, m. Mary Ann Maughan May 20, 1856; George b. March 12, 1936, m. Sarah Matilda Utley May 20, 1856; Hannah, d. infant. Family home Tooele, Utah.
First counselor to Bishop Rowberry; missionary to England 1863; high priest. Carpenter and builder; farmer and stockraiser. Died Dec. 16, 1888, Tooele, Utah.

ATKIN, THOMAS (son of Thomas Atkin and Mary Morley). Born July 7, 1833, Louth, Lincolnshire, Eng. Came to Utah 1849.
Married Mary Ann Maughan May 20, 1856 (daughter of

724   PIONEERS AND PROMINENT MEN OF UTAH

(daughter of George Condie and Mary Hunter), who was born Aug. 10, 1858. Stonerig, Stirlingshire, Scotland. Their children: Sarah Mary Jane C. b. May 13, 1878, m. John T. Bullock Sept. 18, 1900; Caroline E. C. b. Nov. 8, 1880, m. James C. Parry Nov. 9, 1904; Robert Abel C. b. May 12, 1883, m. Florence Sawyer; Jacob C. b. Nov. 21, 1886; Janet C. b. Aug. 8, 1888; Norman Chester b. April 8, 1897. Family home Cedar City.
Drove oxteam from Council Bluffs to Salt Lake City. First settled in Big Cottonwood on the James Huntsman farm. Went to Cedar City 1854. Director of Deseret Iron Company, one of the early infant industries—succumbed 1860. Bishop's counselor 15 years; tithing clerk 42 years; of the stake 20 years; ward recorder 20 years; president 63d quorum high priests; bishop seven years; patriarch since 1893. City councilman 20 years; mayor two years. Aide to Col. W. H. Dame of the Nauvoo legion. Missionary to Sheffield, Eng., conference five months; with "Millennial Star" office 20 months. Successful in all his pursuits. Surveyor.

ARTHUR, BENJAMIN ABEL (son of Christopher Abel Arthur and Ann Jones). Born April 25, 1834, Aberaychan, Monmouthshire, South Wales. Came to Utah Sept. 14, 1853, Claudius V. Spencer company.
Married Janet Easton Feb. 12, 1863 (daughter of Robert Easton), who was born Dec. 7, 1842. Their children: Margaret Ann b. Nov. 12, 1863, m. George Harmon; Mary Jannet b. Sept. 25, 1865, d. May 7, 1866; Benjamin E. b. April 16, 1867, d. Dec. 26, 1905; Elizabeth b. July 2, 1869, d. same day; Laura Jane b. July 25, 1870; Caroline Agnes b. July 7, 1873; Sarah Ellen b. Dec. 21, 1875; Ida b. March 28, 1878; Christopher Robert b. Aug. 16, 1882. Family home Greenville, Beaver county, Utah. He died Feb. 23, 1883; his wife died in December, 1911.

ARTHUR, EVAN (son of John Arthur and Margaret Rowlands of Machynlleth, Montgomeryshire, North Wales). Born Oct. 4, 1806, in Machynlleth. Came to Utah Oct. 13, 1863, Rosel Hyde company.
Married Catherine James (daughter of John James), who was born March 30, 1807. Their children: John; Evan, m. Maria b. Oct. 2, 1868, m. John Wood Sept. 12, 1888; Ada Jane Ellen Walter; Catherine, m. John T. Davis; Margaret, m. Bennett May 15, 1868; Mary Ellen, m. John G. Ahlstrom. Family home St. John, Tooele county, Utah.
19, 1863, Horton W. Haight company). She was born Jan. vens March 16, 1888; m. Melissa Leviens Aug. 28, 1895; Nina

ARTHUR, EDWARD JAMES (son of Evan Arthur and Catherine James). Born Jan. 1, 1845, Machynlleth, N. W.
Married Catherine Bennett May 15, 1868, Deseret, N. W. (daughter of John Bennett and Jane Roberts, pioneers Oct. Mathew Orr; Edward James b. Jan. 1, 1845, m. Catherine Evan G. Morgan; Ann, m. John A. Davis; Elizabeth, m. 16, 1850, Goodwincy, Flintshire, N. W. Their children: Edward B. b. Aug. 16, 1869, m. Myrtle Eldridge; Catherine E. b. Jan. 22, 1871, m. James Caldwell; Jane E. b. Oct. 15, 1872, m. Walter S. Orr; John B. b. Aug. 29, 1874, m. Hattie Paul; Evan B. b. Aug. 15, 1876, m. Azelia Evan; m. Iantha Richards; Mary Ann b. June 6. 1879, m. M. L. Bush; Margaret b. June 25, 1881, m. Lehi Heneffler; Eleanor b. June 23, 1883; Gwladys May b. Oct. 14, 1885; Emily b. Dec. 27, 1887, m. Williard Bullock; Benjamin Harden b. Dec. 26, 1889. Family home St. John, Utah.
Married Sadie Thomas Benedict Oct. 8, 1907, Salt Lake City.
Justice of peace; Tooele county commissioner; school trustee. Farmer and wool grower.

ASHBY, WILLIAM HARDIN (son of Nathaniel Ashby, born April 15, 1805, at Salem, and Susan Hammond, born Aug. 28, 1808, Marblehead, Mass.). He was born July 16, 1839, Salem, Mass. Came to Utah Sept. 20, 1848, Brigham Young company.
Married Nancy Maria Badger Jan. 14, 1865 (daughter of Rodney Badger and Nancy Garr, married March 9, 1845, Hancock county, Ill.; pioneers Oct. 2, 1847, Jedediah M. Grant company). She was born Feb. 27, 1846. Their children: William Hardin b. April 7, 1867, m. Martha Ann Stre b. Nov. 9, 1870, m. Edward A. Wood Nov. 8, 1893; Rodney Badger b. Oct. 26, 1872, m. Jane Marinda Stephenson Sept. 29, 1898; Nathaniel b. Sept. 20, 1874, m. Jean Johnson Nov., 1901; Emma Louisa b. Oct. 9, 1876, m. Simeon T. Stephenson Dec. 15, 1897; Susan b. Dec. 14, 1878, m. John Charles Bennett Sept. 18, 1901; Robert b. Dec. 29, 1889, m. Hannah Cropper June 3, 1903; Mary Edith b. March 23, 1883, m. John B. Stephenson June 13, 1906; Martha Ellen b. Feb. 26, 1885, m. Marion R. Stevens June 2, 1909; Florence b. Jan. 18, 1887; Austin Garr b. Jan. 9, 1889; Clinton b. Oct. 14, 1891. Family home Holden, Utah.

ASHBY, RODNEY BADGER (son of William Hardin Ashby and Nancy Maria Badger). Born Oct. 26, 1872, Holden, Utah.
Married Jane Marinda Stephenson Sept. 29, 1898, Salt Lake City (daughter of Anthony Stephenson, pioneer 1861, and Mary Ann Bennett, pioneer 1860). Their children: Eleanor Jane b. July 16, 1899; Mary Lottie b. Nov. 29, 1901; Ray Badger b. Oct. 18, 1903; Rodney Anthony b. Jan. 20, 1905; Emily Maria b. March 11, 1907; Orrin Thomas b. Aug. 24, 1909; George Marion b. June 30, 1911. Family resided Holden and Leamington, Utah.
Bishop of Leamington ward.

ASHTON, EDWARD (son of Richard Ashton and Elizabeth Savage of Montgomeryshire, North Wales). Born Aug. 22, 1821, in Montgomeryshire. Came to Utah July, 1852, Daniel Jones company.
Married Jane Treharne Feb. 6, 1854, Salt Lake City (daughter of William Treharne and Ann Richards of Salt Lake City, pioneers July, 1852, Daniel Jones company). She was born April 2, 1828. Their children: Edward T., m. Effie W. Morris; Jedediah William, m. Mary Eliza Salisbury; Brigham Willard, m. Mary Alice Pettit; Elizabeth Ann; Sarah Jane, m. Joseph E. Price; Emily Treharne, m. Albert Richards; George S., m. Leah Fidkin. Family home Salt Lake City.
Member 2d quorum seventies; teacher and choir leader 20 years at 15th ward Salt Lake City. Connected with the O. S. L. R. R. 25 years. Died Feb. 7, 1904, at Salt Lake City.

ASHTON, EDWARD T. (son of Edward Ashton and Jane Treharne). Born July 14, 1855, Salt Lake City.
Married Effie Walker Morris April 4, 1878, Salt Lake City (daughter of Elias Morris and Mary L. Walker of Salt Lake City). She was born Jan. 10, 1859. Their children: Edward M. b. Jan. 12, 1879, m. Nancy Louise Ashby Badger; Elias C. b. Feb. 16, 1880, m. Rosabell Hall; Marvin O. b. April 8, 1883, m. Rachel Jeremy; Raymond J. b. Jan. 23, 1886; Effie b. Jan. 9, 1889, m. Joseph Kjar; Jane b. March 24, 1896. Family home Salt Lake City.
Married Cora Lindsay Dec., 1883, Salt Lake City (daughter of Henry Lindsay of South Carolina, who came to Utah Aug., 1881). She was born Nov. 7, 1864. Their children: Cora Lindsay; Ina Jane, m. Le Grande Richards: Henry; Amy; Clifford Ashton; Elmer; Jed; Eva; Minnie; Elizabeth; Norma. Family home Salt Lake City.
Member 2d quorum seventies; missionary to Wales 1891-93; bishop of 24th ward of Salt Lake City; counselor in Salt Lake stake. Contractor and builder.

ASHTON, EDWARD M. (son of Edward Treharne Ashton and Effie Walker Morris). Born Jan. 12, 1879, Salt Lake City.
Married Nancy Louise Ashby Badger Oct. 15, 1902, Salt Lake City (daughter of Rodney C. Badger and Louise A. Ashby of Salt Lake City and Ogden, Utah). She was born Aug. 30, 1881. Their children: Morris Badger b. Sept. 13, 1903; Virginia Louise b. Sept. 14, 1905; Beatrice b. Dec. 31, 1908; Richard Edward b. Jan. 10, 1912.
President Y. M. M. I. A., Liberty stake and Sugar ward; bishop 31st ecclesiastical ward. Employed when 13 years of age in Zion's Savings Bank & Trust Co., attaining position of chief clerk to George M. Cannon, cashier, and remaining there until 19 years of age, when he was called on a mission to Germany, serving 38 months. Embarked in business for himself as a real estate and stock broker in 1902. Later he formed a partnership with Edw. E. Jenkins, which partnership has been incorporated under the firm name of Ashton-Jenkins Company, one of the largest real estate concerns in Salt Lake City.

ASHTON, GEORGE S. (son of Edward Ashton and Jane Treharne). Born July 27, 1870, at Salt Lake City.
Married Leah Fidkin Sept. 27, 1893, at Salt Lake City (daughter of William Fidkin and Alice Crowston of Birmingham, Eng., who came to Utah 1873). She was born Feb. 27, 1872. Their children: Leah b. June 19, 1894; George W. b. Nov. 1, 1896; Lucile F. b. April 20, 1898; Aliene b. May 29, 1900; Emma b. Dec. 16, 1902; William F. b. Feb. 27, 1905; Melvin A. b. May 8, 1908; Reed B. Sept. 16, 1912. Family home Salt Lake City.
High priest; missionary among the Indians 1893-94; 1st counselor in bishopric of 15th ward. Contractor.

ASHTON, ROBERT (son of Robert Ashton, born 1794, Billinge, Lancashire, and Maria Heaton, born 1802, Highton, Lancashire, Eng.). He was born March 15, 1827, Upholland, Lancashire. Came to Utah Aug. 1855.
Married Sarah Liptrot 1848, who was born in 1832 and died 1855. Their children: Sarah Ann b. Aug. 1849, m. William John. Family home West Portage, Box Elder county, Utah.
Married Jane Cornish July 2, 1855 (daughter of William and Elizabeth Cornish of the Isle of Man). She was born Oct. 11, 1831. Their children: Robert Nephi b. May 1, 1856; Joseph b. Dec. 5, 1857; Maria Elizabeth b. Sept. 2, 1860, m. Chas. Landon; John William b. Nov. 23, 1862; Hyrum b. April 2, 1865, m. Emma Elias Aug. 18, 1884; Brigham b. March 21, 1868; Heber b. Sept. 4, 1870; Thomas Francis b. Jan. 13, 1873. Family home Wellsville and West Portage, Utah.
Settled at Calls Fort; moved to Cache valley 1857; was in "the move" south in 1858; water master; high priest; president of elders' quorum two years in absence of regular president; moved to Malad valley 1877; home missionary there three years; supt. of Samaria irrigation project. Has several great-great-grandchildren.

ASHTON, THOMAS. Born Nov. 7, 1813, Parr, Lancashire, Eng. Came to Utah Sept. 27, 1851, Morris Phelps company.
Married Mary Howard Nov. 20, 1836, who died Aug. 2, 1849. Five children were born.

Married Sarah E. Mills Sept 25, 1849, who died 1850. They had one child.
Married Arminta Lawrence Feb. 18, 1851, Council Bluffs, Iowa. Eleven children were born.
High priest. Took a very active part in the planning and making of Lehi's first water ditch and one of its water-masters. Active in planning and making the first bridge across Jordan river and in building Lehi's first meeting house. Elected a member of the Lehi city council six times. Wheelwright and carriage builder. Died Jan. 22, 1903, Lehi, Utah.

ASHTON, WILLIAM (son of Robert Ashton and Maria Carlisle of Kentucky and Montgomery, Ala., respectively). Born Feb. 9, 1837, in Alabama. Came to Utah 1862, independent company.
Married Ellen Elizabeth Croxford Feb. 6, 1865, of Pleasant Grove, Utah (daughter of William Croxford and Ellen Loader of Oxfordshire, Eng.). She was born Dec. 22, 1844, and came to Utah Sept. 26, 1862, James Wareham independent company. Their children: Kate b. Jan. 6, 1867, m. Samuel M. Brown; Leslie b. Feb. 27, 1869, m. Eva Hall; William Stanley b. May 29, 1871, m. Hannah Elizabeth Odekirk; Lynn b. Sept. 19, 1873, m. Annie Evans; m. Elizabeth Marshall; Reece Llellyn b. April 13, 1876, died; Grace Ellen b. Dec. 3, 1878, m. Daniel H. Hillman; Ethelyn b. Jan. 11, 1882; Clarence b. 1886, died; Hazel b. Feb. 3, 1887. Family home at Vernal, Utah.
Ran ferry at Green River, Wyo., 1858-59; carried U. S. mail as pony express; came to and helped found town of Vernal Sept. 1, 1878, and was its first tax assessor; school trustee; studied law; secretary Ashley Co-Op. store for twenty years. Was devout church member. Died Oct. 15, 1909, at Vernal.

ASHTON, WILLIAM STANLEY (son of William Ashton and Ellen Elizabeth Croxford). Born May 29, 1871, Pleasant Grove, Utah.
Married Hannah Elizabeth Odekirk May 29, 1895, at Vernal (daughter of Heber Odekirk and Hannah Brown of Vernal), by James M. Shafer. Their children: Nellie Merle b. June 10, 1896; Hilda b. Nov. 15, 1900.
Active in church matters. Went to Vernal Nov. 3, 1879; has been with Ashley Co-op. Store Co. for 21 years as buyer. Farmer and stockraiser.

ASHWORTH, BENJAMIN. Born in England. Came to Utah 1847.
Married Eliza Dorsey in England. Their children: Sarah, m. Isaac Chapman; Martha, m. Daniel Brian; Emma, m. John Hill; Vilate, m. Charles O'Brien; Reuben; Thomas S., m. Ruby Basset. Family home Salt Lake City.
Foundryman. Died 1883, at Salt Lake City.

ASHWORTH, THOMAS S. (son of Benjamin Ashworth and Eliza Dorsey). Born Oct. 24, 1865, Mill Creek, Utah.
Married Ruby Basset Jan. 28, 1890, at Salt Lake City (daughter of Charles H. Basset and Mary Knight of Allegany county, New York; former came to Utah 1852; latter Sept. 8, 1850, Capt. Aaron Johnson company). She was born May 13, 1871. Their children: Mellie Basset b. Aug. 3, 1891; T. Evan b. Sept. 4, 1894; Lola b. Nov. 11, 1897; Orpha b. Dec. 4, 1900; Dorsey b. Jan. 24, 1904; Willes Bassett b. Feb. 14, 1906. Family home Salt Lake City.
Elder. Piano-tuner.

ASPER, GEORGE E. (son of William Asper and Mary Alstrom of Salt Lake City, Utah, pioneers 1860). Born Sept. 13, 1875, Salt Lake City.
Married Ellen M. Macduff June 29, 1906, at Salt Lake City (daughter of Malcolm Macduff and Jane Lord of Salt Lake City, pioneers 1861). She was born May 15, 1873, Salt Lake City, Utah. Family home Salt Lake City.

ASTILL, ZACHARIAH. Born in 1834, at Birmingham, Eng. Came to Utah 1854.
Married Rosanna Clark Dec. 24, 1869 (daughter of Alfred Clark and Anna Waterfield, pioneers Sept. 5, 1866, Samuel D. White company—married Jan. 1844, at Derbyshire, Eng.). She was born July 5, 1846. Their children: Zachariah b. Dec. 31, 1870; Rosanna b. Sept. 7, 1872; Lizzie b. Oct. 1, 1874, m. F. C. Ewing July 31, 1893; Wm. T. b. Dec. 18, 1877, m. Anna Warren Dec. 28, 1898; Henry b. Sept. 13, 1880, m. Sarah Atkinson June 10, 1902. Family home Ogden, Utah.
Married Diana Bune June, 1884, Ogden, Utah (daughter of James Bune), who was born May, 1847, in Holland. Only child was James b. Sept. 1888.
Prominent in civic affairs in Ogden; was engineer of its first volunteer fire department. Died Oct. 7, 1897.

ASTILL, WILLIAM T. (son of Zachariah Astill and Rosanna Clark). Born Dec. 18, 1877.
Married Anna Warren Dec. 28, 1898, Ogden, Utah (daughter of Anton Warren and Frances Wonder), who was born July 6, 1877. Their children: Rosa A. b. March 30, 1900; Willa H. b. Jan. 6, 1902. Family home Ogden, Utah.
Produce, seed and commission merchant.

ASTLE, FRANCIS (son of James Astle, born Aug. 5, 1780, and Rachel King, both of Celleston, Derbyshire, Eng.). He was born Feb. 2, 1810, Diseworth, Leicestershire. Came to Utah, Sept. 13, 1861, Joseph Horne company.
Married Felica Raynor March 21, 1836, Derby, Derbyshire, Eng. (daughter of William Raynor and Mary Roland of Hucknall Torkard, Nottinghamshire, Eng., pioneers 1861, Joseph Horne company). She was born May 4, 1814. Their children: Mary; James b. March 8, 1839, died; James b. Nov. 18, 1841; Joseph Charles; John; Francis Thomas. Family home Hyrum, Utah.
High priest. Farmer. Died Dec. 13, 1884, Montpelier, Idaho.

ASTLE, JOHN (son of Francis Astle and Felica Raynor). Born June 16, 1846, Hucknall Torkard, Nottingham, Eng. Came to Utah, Sept. 13, 1861, walking all the way.
Married Isabella Jane Bradshaw Dec. 9, 1866 (daughter of Richard Bradshaw and Elizabeth Simpson, married March, 1843, Manchester, Eng., pioneers Dec. 1, 1856, Martin and Tyler handcart company). She was born March 14, 1846. Their children: Elizabeth F. b. Feb. 4, 1868, m. Alvin S. McCombs Oct. 2, 1889; John F. b. Sept. 21, 1869, m. Lauretta Hepworth Sept. 9, 1891; Richard T. b. Sept. 2, 1871, m. Henrietta Jensen Oct. 24, 1895; Wm. W. b. Sept. 27, 1873, m. Elizabeth A. Shaw Aug. 20, 1902; Rachel J. b. Aug. 30, 1875; Abraham A. b. Aug. 26, 1877; Sarah L. b. Sept. 20, 1879, m. Adolphus A. Call Aug. 9, 1899; Joseph H. b. Aug. 24, 1881, m. Elizabeth B. Price June 13, 1906; Violet E. b. D c. 17, 1883. Family resided Montpelier, Idaho, and Afton, Wyo.
Married Melvina A. Banks April 3, 1884, Salt Lake City (daughter of Wm. H. Banks, pioneer Aug. 29, 1863, John R. Murdock company, and Margret Armitage). She was born March 21, 1867, Tooele, Utah. Their children: Alma P. b. Oct. 5, 1886, m. Martha C. Dutson Sept. 30, 1909; James R. b. Aug. 28, 1888; John A. b. Jan. 17, 1891; Sylva J. b. Sept. 26, 1892; Ernest B. b. Sept. 22, 1894; Elwood W. b. Jan. 20, 1897; Mary M. b. Oct. 26, 1899; Lehi S. b. Jan. 4, 1903; Ruby H. b. April 29, 1908. Family home Afton, Wyo.
Home missionary 20 years; missionary to England; high councilor. Crossed plains three times by oxteam. Assisted Capt. Nebeker, 1866, in bringing immigrants from Missouri river points.

ASTLE, JOHN F. (son of John Astle and Isabella Jane Bradshaw). Born Sept. 21, 1869, Montpelier, Idaho.
Married Lauretta Hepworth Sept. 9, 1891, Logan, Utah (daughter of Edmund Hepworth and Hannah Cowling), who was born Sept. 26, 1874, Oxford, Idaho. Their children: John F., Jr. b. July 13, 1892; Klea L. b. Sept. 9, 1894; Vernon L. b. April 5, 1898; Austanie E. b. Oct. 19, 1899; Clara P. b. March 12, 1901; David E. b. Aug. 12, 1902; Evelyn V. b. Jan. 4, 1904; Doretta A. b. March 17, 1906; Agnes L. b. July 3, 1907; Elva M. b. May 23, 1909; Grace E. b. Feb. 19, 1912. Family home Grover, Wyo.
Missionary to southern and eastern states. One of seven presidents 103d quorum seventies. Bishop's counselor.

ATHAY, JAMES (son of Francis Athay and Jane Haines of Shipham, Eng.). Born Sept. 1, 1830. Came to Utah 1864.
Married Ellen Morris (daughter of William and Mary Morris, pioneers 1863). She was born April 12, 1832. Their children: Henry b. June 25, 1858, m. Ellen Louisa Price, Oct. 2, 1884; William b. Sept. 25, 1859, m. Emma Smith Sept. 22, 1883; Marintha b. July 25, 1861, m. P. Lindsay Sept. 29, 1881; Alice b. Aug. 25, 1863, m. Arthur Budge Sept. 22, 1883. Family home Paris, Idaho.
Married Mary Lindsay Oct. 3, 1887, Logan, Utah (daughter of Wm. Lindsay), who was born Oct. 1862, Kaysville. Only child was a daughter, Agnes.

ATHAY, HENRY (son of James Athay and Ellen Morris). Born June 25, 1858.
Married Ellen Louisa Price Oct. 2, 1884, Logan, Utah. (daughter of Robert Price and Matilda Louisa Kelsey, pioneers Sept. 12, 1861, Milo Andrus company). She was born in Salt Lake City. Their children: Ellen Edna; Matilda Louisa; Henry E.; James Russell. Family home Paris, Idaho.
High priest. Councilman of Paris three terms.

ATKIN, THOMAS (son of John Atkin and Mary Ashley of Barkworth, Lincolnshire, Eng.). Born Feb. 10, 1804, Legsby, Lincolnshire. Came to Utah Sept. 23, 1849, Orson Spencer company.
Married Mary Morley Feb. 13, 1826, Lincolnshire, Eng. (daughter of Thomas Morley and Mary Hole of Lincolnshire.) She was born Feb. 24, 1800. Their children: Eliza b. Jan. 15, 1827, died; George b. Jan. 3, 1828, d. infant; Emily b. Oct. 17, 1830, m. Richard Warburton; Thomas Jr. b. July 7, 1833, m. Mary Ann Maughan May 20, 1856; George b. March 12, 1936, m. Sarah Matilda Littler May 20, 1856; Hannah, d. infant. Family home Tooele, Utah.
First counselor to Bishop Rowberry; missionary to England 1860-63; high priest. Carpenter and builder; farmer and stockraiser. Died Dec. 16, 1888, Tooele, Utah.

ATKIN, THOMAS (son of Thomas Atkin and Mary Morley). Born July 7, 1833, Louth, Lincolnshire, Eng. Came to Utah 1849.
Married Mary Ann Maughan May 20, 1856 (daughter of

726   PIONEERS AND PROMINENT MEN OF UTAH

Peter Maughan and Ruth Harrison), who was born Jan. 16, 1839. Their children: Thomas M. b. June 7, 1858, m. Shettie Rowberry Sept., 1880; Ruth Eveline b. Nov. 16, 1859, m. John D. Gordon Sept. 10, 1878; Mary Ann b. Dec. 19, 1861, m. Edward Lougy Sept. 9, 1880; Edith b. Oct. 30, 1864, m. Peter Clegg Jan. 1886; Edward B. b. Oct. 30, 1864, m. Nettie Smith; Peter b. May 3, 1872, died; Willard George b. Aug. 25, 1875, m. Clara Isgreen Nov. 16, 1910; William Franklin b. Jan 14, 1878, m. Annie Maud Tate Dec. 9, 1908. Family home Tooele, Utah.
Sunday school supt. Tooele six years; high priest; bishop Tooele ward 24 years; now a patriarch. School trustee; county delegate to Utah state constitutional convention.

ATKIN, GEORGE (son of Thomas Atkin and Mary Morley). Born March 12, 1836, Louth, Lincolnshire, Eng. Came to Utah 1849.
Married Sarah Matilda Utley May 20, 1856, Tooele, Utah (daughter of John Utley and Elizabeth Rutledge, pioneers 1849, Orson Spencer company). She was born Dec. 25, 1840. Their children: George b. Jan. 3, 1858; Mary E. b. March 3, 1860; Emily b. Nov. 18, 1862; L. John b. July 16, 1864; Alice b. April 4, 1866; Sarah M. b. Sept. 6, 1868; Thomas H. b. Oct. 3, 1870; William T. b. June 8, 1872; Mildred b. Sept. 8, 1878. Family home Tooele, Utah.
Married Emma Johnson. Their children: Rebecca; Effie. Seventy; missionary to England 1876-79; supt. Sunday schools 20 years. Marshal; city counselor. Mercantile manager. Died Jan. 2, 1899, Tooele, Utah.

ATKIN, WILLIAM T. (son of George Atkin and Sarah Matilda Utley). Born June 8, 1872, Tooele, Utah.
Married Ada E. Foulger Dec. 21, 1898, Salt Lake City (daughter of Herbert J. Foulger and Eliza Hagel, pioneers Oct. 3, 1863, Daniel D. McArthur company). She was born Jan. 14, 1880. Their children: Wm. George b. Dec. 15, 1899; Ruth b. May 29, 1901; Naomi b. May 10, 1903; Mary b. Jan. 7, 1905; Lois b. Aug. 12, 1907. Family home Salt Lake city.
High priest; pres. 4th quorum elders; supt. 27th ward Sunday school 9 years, and of Ensign Stake Sunday schools. Sales manager Colorado Fuel and Iron company 15 years; manager National Real Estate and Investment company.

ATKIN, WILLIAM (son of William Atkin and Elizabeth Warren of Empingham, Eng.). Born March 27, 1835, in Empingham. Came to Utah Nov. 10, 1859, George Rowley handcart company.
Married Rachael Thompson Dec. 18, 1854, Empingham, Eng. (daughter of Joseph Thompson and Bridget Ann Phillips, both born at Ballymote, County Sligo, Ireland, and lived at Baridan, Eng.). She was born 1837. Their children: Esther Ann. d. 1868; William; Rachael Violet, m. Swen O. Nielson; Joseph Thompson; Henry Thomas; John Peter; George Albert; Heber Charles; Mary; Hyrum; Nettie; Enoch, d. infant.
Alternate high councilor in St. George stake and temple worker. City marshal at St. George. Died May 22, 1890, St. George.

ATKINSON, JAMES WILLIAM (son of William Plummer Atkinson and Rebecca Clipson of Whittlesey, Eng.). Born Jan. 3, 1811. Came to Utah Oct. 4, 1863, Horton D Haight oxtrain, a division of Amasa M. Lyman company.
Married Louisa Crunkhorn Sept. 2, 1846, Jewington, London. Eng. (daughter of John Crunkhorn and Mary Mitchell of Standground, Northamptonshire). She was born June 9, 1821. Their children: James William b. July 26, 1848, m. Mary Handy; Frederick Henry b. Nov. 10, 1851, m. Matilda Adelaide Sperry; Rosa Louisa b. June 23, 1854, m. James J. Call; Jessie Ann b. July 13, 1856, m. James Patton; Fanny Eliza b. Aug. 2, 1862, d. July 27, 1863. Family resided Salt Lake City and Smithfield, Utah, Weston and Franklin, Idaho.

ATKINSON, FREDERICK HENRY (son of James William Atkinson and Louisa Crunkhorn). Born Nov. 10, 1851. Came to Utah 1863.
Married Matilda Adelaide Sperry Jan. 1, 1874, Clifton, Idaho (daughter of John C. Sperry and Matilda Van Luven of Clifton, Idaho). She was born Feb. 18, 1856. Their children: Frederick Henry b. Nov. 28, 1874, m. Amy Gertrude Hendricks; William Charles b. Sept. 1, 1876, d. Nov. 19, 1888; James Alvin b. April 11, 1878, m. Nellie Phillips; John Richard b. Dec. 31, 1880, d. May 9, 1881; Samuel Hyrum b. Feb. 13, 1882, m. Mattie Phillips; Dora Matilda b. Feb. 12, 1884, d. Feb. 23, 1901; Nora Ann b. Dec. 4, 1885; Frank Walter b. May 4, 1890; Earl Joseph b. May 29, 1894; May Alzina b. June 18, 1896; Pearl Eva b. Feb. 5, 1899. Family home Dayton, Idaho. Died Sept. 21, 1901.

ATKINSON, FREDERICK HENRY, Jr. (son of Frederick Henry Atkinson and Matilda Adelaide Sperry). Born Nov. 28, 1874, Clifton, Idaho.
Married Amy Gertrude Hendricks Feb. 20, 1901, Logan, Utah (daughter of William S. Hendricks and Margaret M. Raney of Richmond, Utah). She was born Sept. 4, 1881. Their children: Fenton Frederick b. Nov. 26, 1901; Reed Hendricks b. Jan. 23, 1904; Margaret b. Feb. 20, 1910. Family home Baker City, Ore.

ATKINSON, ALFRED JOHN. Born Dec. 29, 1826, Southwork, Surrey, London, Eng. Came to Utah Oct. 29, 1855, C. A. Harper company.
Married Ann Boting April 27, 1848, London, Eng. Their children: Alfred H.; John William, died; Emily Jane: Emily Ann; Joseph Charles, died; Eleanor; Brigham E.; Elizabeth B.; Miriam A.; Mary M.
Settled at Mendon, Cache county; moved to Clarkston, thence to Newton. Farmer and merchant.

ATKINSON, ALFRED H. (son of Alfred John Atkinson and Ann Boting). Born Feb. 4, 1849, London, Eng. Came to Utah 1855.
Married J. Mathilda Petersen July 10, 1871 (daughter of Johanas Petersen and Anna K. Olsen), who was born Nov. 19, 1852. Their children: Ann Mathilda b. May 13, 1873, m. Lars S. Christensen Nov. 9, 1898; Alfred John b. Dec. 3, 1874, m. Catherine Archibald Sept. 29, 1897; Charles Ezra b. June 30, 1876, m. Ellen Richeson Feb. 24, 1904; Joseph L. b. April 28, 1878, m. Barbara Godfrey Oct. 10, 1906; Lucy A. b. July 25, 1880, m. Isaac Benson Dec. 21, 1898; Clara A. b. July 26, 1882, m. John Larsen Nov., 1901; Lydia E. b. Oct. 7, 1884, m. Harry Camper April 7, 1910; Rose V. b. April 21, 1888, m. Wallace Young Dec. 23, 1910; Heber Delbert b. Jan. 12, 1890, m. Selma Christensen Nov. 15, 1911. Family home Clarkston, Cache county, Utah.
Married Ada E. Pack Oct. 1886, Logan (daughter of Samuel Pack and Maria Holten), who was born June 6, 1886, Northampton, Eng. Their children: Frances Ada b. July 5, 1889, m. Nelse Stender June 1, 1911; Samuel Alfred b. Sept. 19, 1890; William Thomas b. May 29, 1893. Family home Clarkston, Utah.

ATKINSON, WILLIAM (son of Joseph Atkinson and Jane Brown of Sackville, New Brunswick, Can.). Born Sept. 22, 1812, Sackville, St. John, N. B., Can. Came to Utah Sept. 11, 1853, captain in Jesse W. Crosby company.
Married Phebe Campbell (daughter of Isaac Campbell and Ann Wry, pioneers Sept. 11, 1853). She was born Oct. 9, 1809, and came to Utah with husband. Their children: Sariah A. b. Sept. 28, 1834, m. Marriner W. Merrill Nov. 11, 1833; Marriner; Frances E. b. March 11, 1836, m. Ransom Hatch Dec. 18, 1854; Mary J. b. Sept. 23, 1838, m. Edwin Pace May 2, 1856; William N. b. May 2, 1840, m. Selina Knighton Dec. 18, 1861; James I. b. Nov. 28, 1841, m. Hannah P. Brown March 7, 1870; Peter b. 1843, died; John b. 1843; Thomas F. b. July 22, 1844, m. Elizabeth Simmons March 11, 1865; Amos S. b. Nov. 11, 1846, m. Alice Prescott Nov. 23, 1868; Arilla and Aquilla b. 1848, died; Phebe b. Jan. 22, 1849, m. Henry Hales Jan. 15, 1872; Profinda b. 1851, died; Rhoda b. May 3, 1856. Family home Bountiful, Utah.
Married Sarah A. Tingey Nov. 1862, Salt Lake City (daughter of Henry Tingey and Ann Young, pioneers 1852). She was born March 1, 1847, Bedfordshire, Eng. Their children: Henry b. April 10, 1864, m. Mary Ann Prescott Feb. 7, 1884; Olive b. Dec. 6, 1865, m. George H. Muir March 24, 1887; Charles H. b. July 10, 1867, m. Helen M. Ellis March 23, 1892; Mary A. b. June 27, 1869, m. William R. Depple March 19, 1890; John E. b. July 9, 1871; Charlotte E. b. Feb. 22, 1873, m. Walter Hatch Nov. 9, 1892; Joseph H. b. Dec. 8, 1875, m. Mary J. Hales Dec. 23, 1895; Clara b. March 7, 1879, m. William Argyle Dec. 21, 1899.
Missionary to St. John, N. B., Can; first counselor to Bishop John Stoker, Bountiful. Assisted in the erection of many public buildings.

ATKINSON, WILLIAM N. (son of William Atkinson and Phebe Campbell). Born May 2, 1840, Sackville, St. John, New Brunswick, Can. Came to Utah 1853.
Married Selina Knighton Dec. 18, 1861, at Bountiful (daughter of George Knighton and Catherine Wrigley, latter a pioneer 1864), who was born Dec. 13, 1841, Derbyshire, Eng. Their children: Sarah Jane b. Dec. 17, 1863, m. Stephen C. Hatch Oct. 10, 1881; William Henry b. Sept. 17, 1865, m. Hannah Bennett Nov. 4, 1885; Selina b. Oct. 22, 1867; George N. b. Dec. 3, 1870, m. Linda Duncan Nov., 1890; Mary b. Feb. 19, 1873; Melvina b. March 22. 1876; Melvin b. April 24, 1879, m. Mary A. Sweeten Aug. 25, 1899; Oscar b. Jan. 25, 1882, m. Ann Webb Nov. 4, 1903. Family home South Bountiful, Utah.
Assisted immigration to Utah, 1861, with Ira Eldredge company, completing third trip across the plains by oxteam. President Y. M. M. I. A., Bountiful 1890; ward clerk. Assisted in the erection of many public buildings.

ATKINSON, JAMES ISAAC (son of William Atkinson and Phebe Campbell). Born Nov. 28, 1841, New Brunswick, Can. Came to Utah Sept. 13, 1853.
Married Hannah P. Brown March 7, 1870, Salt Lake City (daughter of William Brown, pioneer Sept. 19, 1847, and Elizabeth Andrews). She was born April 10, 1853, Bountiful, Utah. Their children: Minnie M. b. Aug. 27, 1871, m. Henry Moss Dec. 20, 1893; Elizabeth E. b. April 24, 1873, died Jan. 1, 1874; Hannah C. b. Oct. 7, 1875, m. Stephen L. Moyle Oct. 10, 1895; Dora M. b. Dec. 16, 1877; James L. Jr. b. April 22, 1880, m. Anna M. Rudy Oct. 11, 1900; Myrtle J. b. July 14, 1882, m. Ira R. Rudy April 28, 1904; Lawrence G. b. Sept. 10, 1886, m. Myrtle I. Rudy Nov. 16, 1905; Winnie E. b. March 27, 1892, m. Harold M. Whitecar June 22, 1911; Alice L. b. Aug. 22, 1897.
Hauled rock from Granite quarry for building Salt Lake temple 1860-61. Served as lieutenant in Black Hawk war

in Andrew Bigler company from July 1, 1866, to Sept. 1, 1866; Oct. 9, 1911, joined the Grand Army of the Republic. Member board of directors in Deseret Live Stock Co., Woods Cross. Utah. High councilor Davis stake. Farmer; cattle raiser.

ATWOOD, DAN. Born 1788. Came to Utah Oct. 14, 1850, with Wilford Woodruff company.
Married Polly Sawyer Jan. 16, 1812, in Connecticut (daughter of Arsel Sawyer), who was born June 12, 1790. Their children: Warren, m. Harriett Baldwin; John, m. Julia Barrows; Millen, m. Relief Cram, April 20, 1848; Emily, m. William Branch; Miner Grant, m. Mary D. Guild; Samuel, m. Mary Jane Cornwell; Mary, m. Orville Atwood; Fannie, m. Edson Stohl. Family home Salt Lake City.
Teamster; lumberman and builder.

ATWOOD, MINER GRANT (son of Dan Atwood and Polly Sawyer). Born March 18, 1823, Mansfield, Conn. Came to Utah 1850.
Married Mary D. Guild Oct. 6, 1844, Lisbon, Conn. (daughter of William D. Guild and Hannah Morey of Plainfield, Conn.). She was born March 14, 1824, and came to Utah with husband. Their children: Isora. m. John A. Knight; Otis M., died; Millen Dan, m. Sarah Wanlass; Jane, m. Harry Burrows; Mary. m. Moroni Preece; Elnora, m. John Robert Shaw; Alice, died.
Married Rosina Jennett. Their child: Edgar G. Atwood.
Farmer. Died May 10, 1887, Salt Lake City.

ATWOOD, MILLEN DAN (son of Miner Grant Atwood and Mary D. Guild). Born May 16, 1853, Salt Lake City.
Married Sarah Wanlass Oct. 8, 1877, Salt Lake City (daughter of Jackson Wanlass and Jane Bell of Cumberlandshire, Eng., pioneers Oct. 1852. Oxteam company). Their children: Millen William b. July 4, 1878, m. Jennie Stewart; Francis Dan b. June 12, 1882; Lawrence Miner b. March 4, 1886, m. Cora Warnick; John Leslie b. May 26, 1889, m. Hazel Carlisle; Sarah Delilah b. March 15, 1893; Ardena Jane b. March 5, 1897. Resided at Salt Lake City and Pleasant Grove.
First counselor to Bishop C. P. Warnick of Manila ward; high priest and trustee of public schools of Pleasant Grove; marshal. Farmer and stock raiser.

ATWOOD, LAWRENCE MINER (son of Millen Dan Atwood and Sarah Wanlass). Born March 4, 1886, Salt Lake City.
Married Cora Augusta Warnick Sept. 11, 1907, Salt Lake City (daughter of Charles Warnick and Christina Larson of Pleasant Grove), who was born Sept. 14, 1885. Their children: Cora Marval b. July 17, 1908; Grant Lawrence b. Aug. 16, 1912. Family home Pleasant Grove, Utah.
Missionary to Australia 1909-11; teacher in elders' quorum, also Sunday school and Y. M. M. I. A. Farmer; deputy treas. Utah county.

ATWOOD, SIMEON (son of Hezekiah Atwood. born 1786, Hawbrook, Berkshire county, Mass., and Chloe Ann Rawley, born 1790, West Stockbridge, Mass.). Born April 12, 1814, Mendon, Monroe county, N. Y. Came to Utah Oct. 2, 1862, Capt. James B. Brown company.
Married Melissa Turrell Sept. 30, 1834, Pomford, Chautauqua county, N. Y. (daughter of Doctor C. Turrell). She was born May 24, 1819. Their children: Alonzo T. b. Feb. 19, 1837, m. Mary Barber 1860; William b. Jan. 30, 1839, m. Sara Wade; Walter H. b. Jan. 25, 1841, m. Deidamia Stickney, 1863; Charles B. b. Dec. 14, 1843, m. Louise Brown 1863; Doctor T. b. July 28, 1851, m. Mary Palfreyman; Melissa A. b. Nov. 21, 1853, m. Robert Pixton; George N. b. Sept. 16, 1854. Family home South Cottonwood, Utah.

ATWOOD, WALTER HENRY (son of Simeon Atwood and Melissa Turrell). Born Jan. 25, 1841, in Crawford county, Pa.
Married Deidamia Stickney March 26, 1863, Salt Lake City (daughter of Joseph Clark Stickney and Rachel Cram; former afterward married Elizabeth Steward, and they were pioneers Oct. 16, 1862, Isaac A. Canfield company). She was born Feb. 3, 1846, Peterborough, N. H. Their children: Rachel E. b. June 16, 1864, m. Albert Shaw 1879; Abbie R. b. March 27, 1868, m. William E. Bird 1886; Henry C. b. March 31, 1871, m. Carrie E. Lyons 1893; Edward A. b. Dec. 6, 1873, m. Janie Murphy 1896; Alfred W. b. Aug. 2, 1876, m. Emma Anderson 1898; Lucebia D. b. April 14, 1879, m. William C. Wiechert 1900; Walter S. b. Jan. 2, 1882, m. A. Elizabeth Newman 1907. Family home South Cottonwood, Utah.
Married Julia F. Dibble 1865, who was born Feb. 5, 1846. Their children: John F. b. Aug. 12, 1866, m. Vinnie Harmon 1890; Ida B. b. Nov. 1, 1868, m. Fred D. Jaynes 1892.
Missionary to eastern states; conducted one of Brigham Young's sawmills in Cottonwood canyon, supplying lumber for the famous Salt Lake Tabernacle. Pioneer dry-farmer and canal builder, brick manufacturer, conducting a large brickyard for years, and said to have made first brick in Utah; lumber and coal merchant. City councilman of Murray; has built a score of houses there to improve that city, investing many thousands of dollars following that purpose.

AUER, ULRICH (son of Jacob Auer and Elizabeth Deitrich of Senwald, Switzerland). Born July 22, 1840, Eichberg, Switzerland. Came to Utah Aug. 28, 1860, Jessie E. Murphy company.

Married Mary Jane Cutcliff February, 1873, Salt Lake City (daughter of George Cutcliff and Elizabeth Jones of Devonshire, Eng.; latter came to Utah 1870). She was born July 5, 1835, and died June 29, 1908, Salt Lake City. Their children: Mary Jane, m. Lewis Grossen; Louisa, d. 1878. Family home, Pleasant Green.
Married Regula Bodiner Nov. 2, 1910, Salt Lake City (daughter of John Bodiner of Switzerland).
Seventy; missionary to Switzerland and Germany 1896-98; acting teacher Pleasant Green ward; high priest. Farmer and stockraiser.

AUGER, JABEZ. Born 1833, Saffron Waldron, Essex, Eng. Came to Utah 1866.
Married Sarah Ann Cosgrove 1855 (daughter of Matthew Cosgrove and Margaret Dutton), who was born Dec. 14, 1831. Their children: Charles b. March 6, 1857; Elizabeth b. Sept. 26, 1858; Henry b. Jan. 6, 1860; Samuel and Rosa Ann, twins, b. March 7, 1861; Henry Daniel b. June 5, 1863, m. Sarah Ellen Hibbert Dec. 13, 1888; Rosa Jabezina b. Sept. 13, 1866, m. W. H. Croft May, 1884. Family home Centerville, Utah.
Shoemaker; farmer. Died Nov. 23, 1868.

AUGER, HENRY DANIEL (son of Jabez Auger and Sarah Ann Cosgrove). Born June 5, 1863, Stratford, Eng.
Married Sarah Ellen Hibbert Dec. 13, 1888, Logan, Utah (daughter of Benjamin Hibbert, handcart pioneer, and Mary Millar). She was born Dec. 20, 1867, Peterson, Utah. Their children: Jabez Earl b. Sept. 24, 1889; William Henry b. Jan. 1, 1891, m. Alta Jensen March 31, 1910; Ellen May b. May 5, 1893, m. Edward Hebdon Sept. 7, 1910; Leland Lorenzo b. Aug. 2, 1895; Hazel Ann b. Oct. 14, 1898; Cora Emma b. Oct. 3, 1900; Leslie George b. June 1, 1902; Alta Rosa b. Aug. 28, 1904; Thelma Lillian b. Oct. 16, 1911. Family home Glendale, Oneida county, Idaho.
Bishop's counselor 1899-05; assistant Sunday school supt. Glendale ward 12 years. Trustee district No. 38, Oneida county, eight years. Farmer.

AUSTIN, JOHN (son of Joseph Austin, born 1798, and Ann Mills, born 1800, married 1820. Both of Bedfordshire, Eng.). Born Dec. 3, 1827, in Bedfordshire. Came to Utah Aug. 20, 1868, Joseph S. Rawlins company.
Married Emma Grace March 20, 1847, Studham, Bedfordshire, Eng. (daughter of Thomas Grace and Mary Ann Grace), who was born March 20, 1827, and came to Utah with husband. Their children: Harriet b. in 1847, m. John Jacobs; George O. b. Jan. 13, 1849, m. Elizabeth MacFarland; Joseph b. Aug. 8, 1850; Hyrum b. Aug. 8, 1850; Alfred b. Nov. 3, 1851, latter three died; Parley Pratt b. May 28, 1853, m. Charlotte Butt; Heber Charles b. Dec. 20, 1855, m. Deseret Taylor; William b. Jan. 28, 1857, m. Alice Schofield; Sarah b. Jan. 13, 1859, m. Charles Allen; Julia b. April 17, 1860, m. John Brown; Hector b. Sept. 9, 1861, died; Annie Marie b. July 3, 1863, m. Charles Munns; Mark b. Oct. 3, 1864, m. Mania Vaughan; Thomas b. Dec. 27, 1866, m. Mary Thomas; John Ezra b. Feb. 17, 1868, m. Sarah E. Thomas; Luticia b. Nov. 14, 1869, m. Samuel Southwick; Franklin b. Aug., 1871, died. Family home Lehi, Utah.
President high priests' quorum Lehi, Utah; block teacher. Pioneer in irrigation systems.

AUSTIN, GEORGE O. (son of John Austin and Emma Grace). Born Jan. 13, 1849, in England. Came to Utah Sept. 13, 1866, William Henry Chipman company.
Married Elizabeth MacFarland Feb. 26, 1872, Pleasant Grove, Utah (daughter of Andrew MacFarland and Elizabeth Nichol of Scotland). She was born Oct. 16, 1850. Their children: Andrew M. b. March 8, 1873, m. Ida Cox; Elizabeth b. Aug., 1875, m. F. E. McKeage; Emma b. March 20, 1878; Agnes b. Nov. 17, 1880, m. John M. Hayes; George b. April, 1883, died; John M. b. July 23, 1884; Clarence b. March 5, 1887; Edwin N. b. Sept. 20, 1889, m. Vera Smith. Family resided Salt Lake City and Lehi, Utah.
Elder; high councilor. Lehi city councilman; mayor of Lehi two terms; member of legislature two terms. Stock raiser; general agriculture supt. for the Utah-Idaho Sugar Co. 23 years; pres. Austin & Sons Live Stock Co., director of Austin Bros. Association; pres. of Price River Irrigation Co.

AUSTIN, ANDREW M. (son of George O. Austin and Elizabeth MacFarland). Born March 8, 1873, Salt Lake City.
Married Ida Cox June 25, 1896, Lehi, Utah (daughter of Edward Cox and Hannah Ashton of Illinois and England, pioneers 1850). She was born March 6, 1876. Their children: Ida; Sadie; George; Fern; Clarence Ray; Bessie. Family home, Salt Lake City.
Deacon. General manager Austin & Sons Livestock Co.

AUSTIN, HEBER CHARLES (son of John Austin and Emma Grace). Born Dec. 20, 1855, Studham, Bedfordshire, Eng.
Married Deseret Taylor Dec. 31, 1879, Lehi, Utah (daughter of James Whitehead Taylor and Ann Rogers). She was born March 29, 1859, Lehi, Utah. Their children: Daisy May b. May 11, 1881, m. Eli Webb, April, 1903; Raymond b. May 13, 1884; Margaret Ann b. Sept. 12, 1887, m. Alexander Robb Oct. 1906; Victor b. Oct. 30, 1889; Bernice Emma b. Jan. 25, 1891; Mary Alice b. Nov. 27, 1895; Myrtle Ina b. Jan. 27, 1897; Edith Rose b. Aug. 25, 1899; Agatha Bessie b. June 21, 1904.
Farmer; railroad grader and freighter; assistant agriculturist at Utah sugar factory 1891; assisted in building Idaho

Falls sugar factory, agricultural supt. of same 1903; agriculturist for Blackfoot factory 1905; sheep owner; director in Farmers' and Merchants' Bank of Idaho Falls. Missionary 1899; president Norwich conference; high councilor Alpine stake 1901-03; bishop Lincoln ward, Bingham (Idaho) stake 1905; president of Bingham stake 1908.

AUSTIN, MARK (son of John Austin and Emma Grace). Born Oct. 3, 1864, Studham, Bedfordshire, Eng. Married Maria Vaughan March 30, 1887, Logan, Utah (daughter of Michael Vaughan and Jane Maria Brain of Lehi), who was born Jan. 19, 1865. Their children: Hazel b. Sept. 7, 1888; Emma Jane b. Jan. 2, 1891, died; Ruby b. June 4, 1893; Francis Mark b. Feb. 3, 1896; Lillian Millard b. May 5, 1899; Michael John b. May 22, 1901; Robert Roy b. Jan. 25, 1904. Family resided Lehi, Utah, and Sugar City, Idaho.
Bishop of Sugar ward; president of the Fremont stake of Zion. Farmer; sugar factory expert and beet agriculturist.

AUSTIN, THOMAS H. (son of John Austin and Emma Grace). Born Dec. 27, 1866, in England. Came to Utah with parents.
Married Mary E. Thomas Sept. 2, 1887, Lehi, Utah (daughter of Joseph A. Thomas and Mary Lawrence of Beaver, Utah), who was born May 4, 1867. Their children: Reuben b. Aug. 20, 1888; Joseph Lee b. Sept. 29, 1890, died; Flossie b. Oct. 1893; Gilbert b. Oct. 1895; Bazie b. Sept. 1897, died; Thomas Blain b. Feb. 20, 1899; Thalma b. July 6, 1901; Lula b. Aug. 1903; Walden b. Nov. 1905, died; Ruth b. Jan. 6, 1907. Family home, Salt Lake City.
Engaged in sheep and livestock business.

AVERY, JOHN NELSON (son of Hezekiah Avery, born 1809, and Henrietta Nelson, born Aug. 4, both of Pennsylvania). He was born May 2, 1844, in Illinois. Came to Utah 1849, Capt. Allred company.
Married Sarah Josephine Roberts May 26, 1866 (daughter of Sidney Roberts and Sarah Ann Rowell; latter a pioneer 1852). She was born April 1, 1848. Their children: Josephine Euphemia b. June 16, 1867, m. Andrew Hooper; John Alonzo b. Jan. 13, 1869, m. Hattie Bybee; Sarah Amelia (m. William R. Godfrey) and Henrietta Adelia, twins, b. April 13, 1871; Clarence Heber b. Sept. 4, 1873, m. Dorothy Higgins; David Oliver b. Dec. 17, 1875; Etta Lucinda b. May 21, 1877, m. James Francis; Effie b. Dec. 14, 1879, m. Joseph Bell; Noah Elmer b. May 1, 1882; Jesse Eugene b. Oct. 15, 1886, m. Emma Bell; George Marion b. March 29, 1891. Family home Dempsey, Idaho.
Sheriff Millard county 1869-70. Bishop's counselor 1877-78. First lieutenant in Utah army 1867-68.

AYLETT, WILLIAM (son of William Aylett of Hockley, Eng.). Born Jan. 28, 1828, Hockley, Eng. Came to Utah Oct. 1, 1866, Joseph S. Rawlins company.
Married Hannah Argent 1855, Orsett, Essexshire, Eng. (daughter of John Argent and Mary Gridley of Midvale, Utah, pioneers Oct. 17, 1862, Henry W. Miller company). She was born June 6, 1828. Their children: Mary Ann b. March 13, 1856, m. Jasper N. Barr; William b. April 27, 1858, m. Mary Ann Brown July 30, 1857; Jesse b. Nov. 6, 1859, m. Martha Ann Beckstead Aug. 14, 1884; Walter; Jedediah b. March 25, 1863, m. Mary E. Wardle; m. Alice Penrose; Elizabeth; John Argent b. Sept. 28, 1867, m. Martha Ann Egbert April 27, 1889; Heber C. b. April 22, 1870, m. Lenora Sprattling Dec. 22, 1903; Hannah Maria b. July 18, 1875, m. David Egbert. Family home West Jordan.
Farmer. Died Nov. 21, 1902.

AYLETT, WILLIAM JR. (son of William Aylett and Hannah Argent). Born April 27, 1858, Orsett, Eng. Married Mary Ann Brown July 30, 1857, West Jordan, Utah (daughter of Samuel Brown and Catherine Wilbur, Salt Lake City, pioneers Oct., 1858, Rosel Kind Homer company). She was born May 20, 1856. Family home Midvale, Utah.
Stockraiser; merchant; banker.

AYLETT, JOHN A. (son of William Aylett and Hannah Argent). Born Sept. 28, 1867, West Jordan, Utah. Married Martha Ann Egbert April 27, 1889, West Jordan (daughter of John A. Egbert and Emma Crimmit of the same place, pioneers Oct. 16, 1849, Allen Taylor company). She was born March 17, 1869. Their children: Vera Aleta b. April 21, 1890, m. Vincent W. Lawson; John Hollis b. Oct. 28, 1896; Kelvin William b. Dec. 6, 1901; Mattie Lorene b. August 7, 1908. Family home Midvale, Utah.
President Y. M. M. I. A. Jordan stake. Member of city council Midvale. Manager West Jordan Mercantile Co.

AYLETT, HEBER C. (son of William Aylett and Hannah Argent). Born April 22, 1870, West Jordan, Utah.
Married Lenora Sprattling Dec. 22, 1903, West Jordan (daughter of Frank Sprattling and Ellen McClery of the same place). She was born Dec. 3, 1885. Only child: Heber Darrel b. Nov. 20, 1904. Family home Midvale, Utah.
Stockraiser, merchant and banker.

AYRTON, WILLIAM (son of John Ayrton and Isabella Lambert of Skipton, Yorkshire, Eng.). Born Sept. 3, 1825, at Skipton. Came to Utah 1856, Captain Stringham company. Married Elizabeth Davis Aug. 22, 1868, Salt Lake City (daughter of David Davis and Grace Roberts of North Wales); born Aug. 14, 1835. Only child was David James Ayrton (adopted). Family home Salt Lake City, Utah. Landscape gardener.

AYRTON, DAVID JAMES (son of Victor H. James and Annie Thomas). Born Nov. 19, 1870, at San Francisco, Cal. Came to Utah Nov. 20, 1873.

B

BABCOCK, ADOLPHUS (son of Daniel Babcock). Came to Utah 1847, oxteam company.
Married Jerusha Jane Rowley in New York. Their children: Lorenzo, m. Amy Ann Marble; Lucy, m. William Wood; George, m. Molly Easton; Eliza, m. Brigham Young; M. John Groves, m. Dominicus Carter; Parmelia, m. Branch Young; Alburn, m. Mary Conover; m. Hannah King; John, m. Harriet McKee; William Henry b. July 15, 1848, m. Mary Jane Parsons. Family home Spanish Fork, Utah.
Farmer. Died March, 1872.

BABCOCK, LORENZO (son of Adolphus Babcock and Jerusha Jane Rowley). Came to Utah with part of Mormon Battalion, Co. C.
Married Amy Ann Marble, at Nauvoo, Ill. (daughter of Nathaniel Marble and Mary King). She was born Feb. 14, 1826. Their children: George, d. infant; William, m. Louisa Loveland; John, m. Augusta Mary Hansett; Amy Ann, d. infant; Nathaniel, m. Lydia Simmons; Mary Ann, m. James Dickens Fullmer; Joseph, m. Sarah Norton; Jerusha Jane, m. James Bryner. Family resided Gunnison and Vernon, Utah.
Elder; ward teacher. Settlement guard in early Indian troubles. Died in 1906 or 1907, at Mona, Jaub county, Utah.

BABCOCK, WILLIAM HENRY (son of Adolphus Babcock and Jerusha Jane Rowley). Born July 15, 1848, Salt Lake City.
Married Mary Jane Parsons, Dec. 20, 1868, Salt Lake City (daughter of George Parsons and Lydia Rebecca Fisher of Missouri; and later of Spanish Fork, Utah, pioneers 1854). She was born May 10, 1854, in Missouri. Their children: George Oliver b. April 25, 1870, d. aged 5; William Henry b. Oct. 18, 1872, m. Alice Thompson; Alburn P. b. Nov. 24, 1874, m. Anna Raycraft; Mary R. b. Dec. 31, 1876, m. William Henry Davis; Benjamin Franklin b. Feb. 1, 1878, d. aged 23; Lydia Jane b. April 26, 1880, m. Ray Cook; John b. Nov. 24, 1882, d. infant; Lucy Elvina b. Jan. 21, 1883, d. aged 9; Vardis Andrew b. Aug. 1887; Ernest LeRoy Miller (adopted) b. Feb. 11, 1902. Family home, Spring Glen, Utah.
Married Maggie Grove at Salt Lake City (daughter of John Grove of Salt Lake City, a pioneer with oxteam company). Only child born was William.
Elder. Black Hawk Indian war veteran. Farmer.

BABCOCK, GEORGE.
Married Annie Katherine ———. Their children: Lovica, m. John Loveless; Rozilla A., m. Vardis Simmons; George Henry, m. Sadie Reese; Rufus Daniel b. Feb. 20, 1875, m. Marie Madsen. Family home, Spanish Fork, Utah.
Died 1874, at Spanish Fork, Utah.

BABCOCK, RUFUS DANIEL (son of George Babcock and A——— Katherine ———). Born Feb. 20, 1875, Spanish Fork, Utah.
Married Marie Madsen Jan. 1, 1898, at Lake View, Utah (daughter of Peter Madsen and Lena Johnson of Lake View, Utah, pioneers 1856). She was born Dec. 23, 1874. Their children: Lena Katherine b. Sept. 1, 1898; Rufus Stanford b. March 31, 1900; Lynn Sterling b. May 20, 1902; Vesper Ellsworth b. Sept. 24, 1904; Kenneth Hyrum b. June 5, 1907; Iola b. Feb. 5, 1908. Family home, Vineyard, Utah.
Elder; ward teacher. Farmer.

BABBITT, RICHARD (son of Henry William Babbitt and Elizabeth Taylor). Born July 2, 1842. Came to Utah 1850. Married Fidelia Chapman (daughter of Welcome Chapman and Susan Amelia Rigley), who was born Oct. 11, 1849, Winter Quarters, Neb.
Brought the first printing ink to Salt Lake City 1850. Settled in Tooele valley, and assisted in building forts; moved to Cache valley and sawed his building lumber by hand, enduring all the hardships of pioneering that country. After moving near Brigham City, the call for the move south came, and they went to San Pete valley; here they endured many hardships on account of the hostility of the Indians. Went to Manti, then to Spring City, and from here went on a mission to The Muddy, where he stayed two years, and returned to Brigham City; resided here seven years, when he moved to Malad City, Idaho, where he now resides.

BACHMAN, JACOB (son of Hans R. Bachman, born April 3, 1791, and Elizabeth Aerna, born April 10, 1791, both of Switzerland; married Sept. 26, 1824). He was born April 15, 1830, Wiflisburg, Switzerland. Came to Utah Oct. 15, 1863, Samuel D. White company.
Married Elizabeth Sutter of Rozberg, Switzerland. Their children: Mary b. Feb. 21, 1854, died; Frana b. Feb. 23, 1857, m. Henry A. Hill; Jacob b. Oct. 27, 1858; Elizabeth b.

March 14, 1860, m. W. H. Reeder; Emuel b. Aug. 17, 1862, m. Mary Jane Heninger; Rosilla b. Feb. 26, 1864, m. Moroni D. Ferrin March 6, 1889; Bertha b. April 19, 1865, m. A. J. Stallings July 3, 1885; Alma b. Nov., 1866, d. Dec. 25, 1890. Family resided at Lynn and Eden, Weber county, Utah.
Married Anna Hazel Sweller April, 1867, at Salt Lake City (daughter of Anna Sweller), who was born Sept. 29, 1847, Ottenbach, Switzerland. Their children: Joseph b. Feb. 8, 1868, m. Maggie McBride Dec. 8, 1890; Annie b. Aug. 9, 1870, m. William Ingles March 10, 1901; John R. b. Oct. 19, 1875, m. Nellie Fordham Aug. 19, 1900; Emma Josephine b. Dec. 5, 1887. Family home Eden, Utah.
High priest. Farmer.

BACHMAN, EMUEL (son of Jacob Bachman and Elizabeth Sutter). Born Aug. 17, 1862, Bern, Switzerland. Came to Utah a child in arms.
Married Mary Jane Heninger Dec. 1884, at Eden (daughter of Reese T. Heninger and Frances Lowthen), who was born Oct. 3, 1855, and died Nov. 6, 1885. Only child: Emuel, Jr., b. Nov. 1, 1885, m. Esther Colman.
Married Mary Jane Taylor Dec. 1884, at Eden (daughter Joseph Taylor and Jane Lake). No children.
Member Co. A of the Mormon Battalion. Pioneer of Lewisville, Idaho, 1885. Now bishop of Harrisville ward, North Weber stake.

BACHMAN, JOSEPH (son of Jacob Bachman and Anna Hazel Sweller). Born Feb. 8, 1869, Eden, Utah.
Married Margaret H. McBride, Dec. 8, 1890 (daughter of Heber R. McBride, born May 13, 1843, Churchton, Eng., a pioneer Nov. 30, 1856, Edward Martin handcart company, and Elizabeth Ann Burns, born Feb. 17, 1851). She was born March 30, 1871, Eden, Utah. Their children: J. Reel b. Oct. 19, 1895; Malva E. b. April 21, 1898; Comfort M. b. Sept. 2, 1900; Blaine b. Aug. 6, 1902; Velva b. June 30, 1906; Alta b. Nov. 24, 1910.
Counselor 133d quorum seventies; Sunday school officer; teacher Y. M. M. I. A.

BACKHOUSE, JAMES. Came to Utah Sept. 15, 1861, Ira Eldredge company.
Married Jane Williams. She was born in 1824, and died July 24, 1898. Their children: Mary Alice, m. Edwin J. Ward; Jennie; James, m. Charlotte Peterson; John; Eleanor, m. John Slaugh; William. Family home Pleasant Grove, Utah.
High priest. Cotton spinner; farmer. Died June, 1909.

BACKMAN, SAMUEL C. (son of Sven Backman and Ingred Dahlberg). Born Dec. 7, 1835, in Sweden. Came to Utah in July 1878.
Married Anna J. Anderson March 1858, Goteborg, Sweden (daughter of Anders Anderson and Martha Benson of Sweden). She was born May 13, 1830. Their children: Andrew S., m. Johanna Larson; Gustave H., m. Grace Pollard; George S., m. Ophelia Alldredge; Wm. J., m. Edith Gill; Anna W., m. Zeke Billington. Family home, Salt Lake City.
Member seventies; presiding elder of the 15th ward; high priest. Plumber and coppersmith. Made copper towers in temple. Died Jan. 20, 1913, Salt Lake City.

BACKMAN, GUSTAVE H. (son of Samuel C. Backman and Anna J. Anderson). Born May 18, 1864, Goteborg, Sweden. Came to Utah July 3, 1877.
Married Grace Pollard June 25, 1890, Logan, Utah (daughter of Bishop Joseph Pollard and Mary Anne Bailey, of Salt Lake City). She was born Nov. 27, 1867. Their children: Gustave Pollard b. Nov. 11, 1891, m. Annie Davis; LeGrand Pollard b. Dec. 18, 1893; Milton Vaughn b. Sept. 8, 1898; Grace Lucille b. Dec. 31, 1899; Ralph Vernon b. May 4, 1904; Harold Samuel b. June 16, 1907; Edna Louise b. Jan. 2, 1909. Family home, Salt Lake City.
Chorister 16th ward. City recorder. Attorney-at-law.

BACON, CHANCY. Born Oct. 22, 1811, in Madison county, N. Y. Came to Utah July 23, 1852, Robert Richie Independent company.
Married Mary Glazier in April, 1831, who died at LaHarpe, Hancock county, Ill., in Feb. 1878. Her father was a pioneer, settling at Provo. Only child: Francis, m. Jane Loader.
Lived at Pleasant Grove, Utah; died there Aug. 31, 1888.

BACON, FRANCIS (son of Chancy Bacon and Mary Glazier). Born 1832 in Madison county, N. Y. Came to Utah 1852 with father.
Married Jane Loader Feb. 5, 1860. She was born in England. Dec. 7, 1841. Their children: Eliza Jane b. Dec. 7, 1860, m. William Hess, Aug. 10, 1878; Franklin R. b. June 4, 1862, m. Sara Hess 1885; Nelson Ames b. Feb. 6, 1864, d. March 11, 1864h
Married Elizabeth Simpson April 10, 1864, Pleasant Grove, Utah. She was born Oct. 6, 1842, in England. Their children: Chancy b. May 17, 1865, m. Lettie Thompson 1889; Elizabeth b. July 19, 1867, m. Allen Thompson 1888; Lorenzo b. Nov. 26, 1869, m. Lucy Dunn, Nov. 19, 1899; Albert b. July 18, 1873, m. Lottie Smith Oct. 28, 1897; Lawrence b. July 17, 1876; Florence b. Jan. 30, 1881; Leroy b. June 19, 1886. Family resided Pleasant Grove, Utah, and Georgetown, Idaho.
Went to Idaho in 1865, and operated probably the first ferry-boat on Bear river; later moved to California, where he engaged in various enterprises and returned to Utah four years later. Moved to Georgetown, Idaho, in 1876, and has held many positions of honor and trust. Priest; teacher and seventy; school trustee.

BADGER, ORSON P. (son of Ephraim Badger and Harriet Farr; latter native of Vermont). He was born 1835, Waterford, Caledonia county, Vt. Came to Utah 1847.
Married Eliza Jane Gay in 1855. She was born Sept. 27, 1838, Rockingham, Richmond county, N. C. Their children: Orson P. b. Oct. 29, 1857, m. Annis Shaw Sept. 25, 1879; Amanda Jane, m. Thomas Farr; Harriet Ann; Eliza May, m. William Taylor.

BADGER, ORSON P. JR. (son of Orson Badger and Eliza Jane Gay). Born Oct. 29, 1857, Salt Lake City.
Married Annis Shaw, Sept. 25, 1879 (daughter of William Shaw and Diana Chase, pioneers 1848). She was born at Ogden, Utah.

BADGER, RODNEY (son of John Badger and Lydia Chamberlain). Born Feb. 4, 1824, Waterford, Vt. Came to Utah July 24, 1847, Brigham Young company.
Married Nancy Garr March 9, 1845, La Harpe, Hancock county, Ill. (daughter of Fielding Garr and Paulina Turner of Richmond, Ind). She was born Oct. 17, 1822, and came to Utah Oct. 2, 1847, Jedediah M. Grant company. Their children: Nancy Maria, m. William Hardin Ashby; Rodney Carlos, m. Louisa Adeline Ashby Nobles; George William, m. Mary Stevens; Charlotte Louisa. Family home Salt Lake City, Utah.
Sheriff of Salt Lake county; lieutenant territorial militia. He was drowned in the Weber river April 29, 1853, in attempting to save the family of an immigrant whose wagon had capsized in the stream.

BADGER, RODNEY CARLOS (son of Rodney Badger and Nancy Garr). Born Sept. 6, 1848, Salt Lake City, Utah.
Married Louisa Adeline Ashby Nobles Dec. 27, 1877, Salt Lake City (daughter of Joseph Bates Nobles and Susan Hammond Ashby of Salt Lake City, pioneers respectively 1847 and 1848). She was born Nov. 9, 1849. Their children: Carlos Ashby b. Oct. 31, 1878, m. Rosalia Jenkins; Ralph Ashby b. April 8, 1880, m. Julia Peterson; Nancy Louisa Ashby b. Aug. 30, 1881, m. Edward M. Ashton; Elizabeth Ashby b. July 17, 1883; Alice Ashby b. March 3, 1885; Edna Ashby b. April 20, 1887, and Hammond Ashby b. Jan. 18, 1889, latter three died.
Missionary to California 1877; member bishopric 15th ward; Y. M. M. I. A. general board 1875 to 1912; president high priests, Salt Lake stake, 1909 to date. Indian war veteran; connected with Deseret national bank and Badger Bros., brokers.

BADGER, CARLOS ASHBY (son of Rodney Badger and Louisa Adeline Ashby Nobles), born Oct. 31, 1878, at Salt Lake City, Utah.
Married Rosalia Jenkins June 26, 1901, at Salt Lake City, Utah (daughter of Thomas Jenkins and Mahala Elmer of Salt Lake City, Utah, pioneers—the former of 1848, the latter of Oct. 1, 1870). She was born April 20, 1877. Their children: Carlos Jenkins b. April 14, 1902; Ashby Jenkins, b. Oct. 15, 1903; Rosalia b. Feb. 25, 1905; Alice b. March 23, 1907; Elizabeth b. Sept. 22, 1908; Thomas Jenkins b. May 21, 1910; Rodney Jenkins b. July 13, 1912. Family home Salt Lake City, Utah.
Missionary to Colorado 1897-1900; high priest; M. I. A. and stake president; Sunday school assistant superintendent in 4th ward and in Liberty stake. State senator 1909-13; secretary to U. S. Senator Reed Smoot 1904-07. Lawyer, being a graduate of George Washington university, Washington, D. C.

BAGLEY, DANIEL (son of Eli Bagley, born Jan. 7, 1804, in Ohio, and Nancy Ann Belt, born March 21, 1811, in Butler Co., Ohio, married Jan. 15, 1825). He was born Feb. 24, 1829, Decatur county, Ind., and came to Utah 1853, Daniel Miller company.
Married Mary Wood 1845 (daughter of John Wood and Rebecca Belt). She was born March 22, 1833. Came to Utah with her husband. Their children: Margaret Melissa b. Jan. 24, 1852, m. Thomas Flanigan; Cedenia b. Nov. 22, 1854, m. Merrill E. Willis 1870.
Called by Brigham Young on mission to Southern Utah to settle Dixie 1865, and to Arizona by Erastus Snow 1877. Assisted in hauling rock for the foundation of the Salt Lake temple. Went to Echo canyon to resist Johnston's army. Walker and Black Hawk Indian war veteran. Lived in Arizona until 1895, then moved to Springville, Utah, where he died.

BAGNALL, JOSEPH (son of George Bagnall, born Oct. 11, 1805, Wakefield, Yorkshire, Eng., and Ann Rawling). He was born Dec. 27, 1839, Wakefield, Eng. Came to Utah Nov. 9, 1865, Henson Walker company.
Married Sarah Ann Frobisher Dec. 27, 1864 (daughter of Thomas Frobisher and Ann Cookson). Their children: Joseph b. Nov. 22, 1870, m. Hannah Christensen; William H., b. Jan. 22, 1873, m. Lena Christensen.
Settled at Moroni, Utah, December, 1865; stone cutter on St. George temple; moved to Chester, San Pete county, 1876, where he served as school trustee 15 years; first counselor to Bishop Christensen 14 years, and assisted in erecting many buildings for public use.

BAILEY, FRANCIS WILLIAM (son of Francis William Bailey and Eliza Smith of Southampton, Eng.). Born Aug. 6, 1840, at Ferham, Hantshire, Eng. Came to Utah Oct. 17, 1862, Henry Miller company.
Married Annie Eliza Ingram April, 1862, at Southampton, Eng. (daughter of George Ingram and Caroline Tapper of Southampton). She was born Nov. 15, 1833. Their children: Francis Tracy, m. Rachel Whittaker; Mary Harriet, m. George Richmond; Owen A., m. Mary Strong; William Esau, m. Esther Faust; Jacob Ralph, m. Della McKnight; m. Polly Paramore; Samuel Charles, m. Eliza A. Paramore. Family home Salt Lake City, Utah.
Elder. Formerly a sea captain. Followed various occupations in Utah.

BAILEY, FRANCIS TRACY (son of Francis William Bailey and Annie Eliza Ingram). Born April 16, 1863, Peterson, Utah.
Married Rachel Whittaker, Dec. 16, 1885, at Logan, Utah (daughter of Isaac Whittaker and Betsy Gallent of Manchester and Norwich, Eng.). She was born Sept. 23, 1866. Only child: Hazel L. b. June 6, 1890, m. George Anderson. Family home Salt Lake City, Utah.
Seventy; missionary to England 1899 and 1901; president Y. M. M. I. A. of 15th and 24th wards; Sunday school teacher in 16th ward. Special policeman; notary public. Formerly a sailor; railroad brakeman; yardmaster and conductor on all railroads operating in Utah. Later practiced medicine.

BAILEY, JAMES WATSON (son of James Bailey and Mary Ann Tucker of Kanesville, Ill.). He was born Aug. 2, 1850. Came to Utah July, 1851.
Married Nancy Ann Borrson Sept. 19, 1874 (daughter of Niels Henry Borrson and Johanna Nielson). She was born Jan. 7, 1857, at Spanish Fork, Utah. Their children: James Henry b. Dec. 9, 1875, died; Nettie Ann b. June 15, 1877, m. Ferdinand Oleson; Elonora b. May 28, 1879, d. 1892; Elmira b. May 16, 1882, m. Albert Johnson; John Volney b. Sept. 4, 1896. Family home Spring City, Utah, and Basalt, Idaho.
Settled at Fillmore, Millard county; Indian war veteran; moved to San Pete county 1874; ward teacher there 5 years in Spring City; moved to Basalt, Idaho. Farmer.

BAILEY, JOHN (son of William F. Bailey, born 1779, and Sarah Hackett, born 1779, both at Sheepshead, Leicestershire, Eng.). He was born April 28, 1807. Came to Utah Nov. 30, 1856, with Edward Martin handcart company.
Married Jane Allgood, 1837 (daughter of Langley Allgood of Wakefield). She was born July 4, 1810, and came to Utah with husband. Their children: Langley Allgood b. March 27, 1838, m. Sarah Andrews Nov. 17, 1861; John b. Nov. 21, 1840, m. Charlotte Shephard; Thomas b. July 1, 1844, d. Sept. 6, 1858; David b. Jan. 11, 1851, m. Elizabeth Blackham.

BAILEY, LANGLEY ALLGOOD (son of John Bailey and Jane Allgood). Born March 27, 1838, Whitwick, Leicestershire, Eng.
Married Sarah Andrews, Nov. 17, 1861, Nephi, Utah (daughter of William Andrews and Ann Wright, pioneers, July, 1860). She was born Jan. 12, 1845, Packington, Eng. Their children: John Wright Andrews b. Sept. 11, 1862, died; William b. Jan. 29, 1864, m. Kate E. Udall Dec. 10, 1902; Langley Allgood b. April 5, 1866, m. Elva Bigler 1900; Elizabeth Ann b. April 5, 1868, died; Thomas b. Nov. 7, 1869, m. Mary Eleanor Chapman May 31, 1900; Sarah Ann, b. Jan. 15, 1872, m. George A. Allen July 12, 1893; Mary Jane b. April 7, 1874, m. Fred M. Beck, Jan. 17, 1900; Rosey Alice b. July 17, 1876, m. H. Lee Boyer, June 18, 1902; Catherine b. May 7, 1879, m. William Alvin Bowles, Nov. 17, 1910; Henry Andrews b. July 2, 1881, died; George Ernest b. Oct. 4, 1884, died; Bertha b. Oct. 17, 1886.
Married Sarah Emma Warner, April 5, 1883, Salt Lake City (daughter of William H. Warner and Elizabeth Andrews). She was born April 25, 1864, Nephi, Utah, and died Aug. 1, 1904. Their children: William Henry b. Feb. 13, 1888, m. Maggie May Peacock, Aug. 27, 1910; Elizabeth b. April 5, 1892, died; Wilford b. Aug. 20, 1893; Reed Warner b. Jan. 29, 1896; Pearl b. Dec. 8, 1899.
High priest; missionary to England; tithing clerk 21 years; superintendent Sunday schools of Nephi 11 years; superintendent Juab stake Sunday schools 7 years; seventy in 49th quorum; high councilor; school trustee 1877-1879.

BAILEY, JOHN (son of John Bailey and Mary Noon of Mill Lane, Leicestershire, Eng.). Born Jan. 10, 1830, in Leicestershire. Came to Utah Sept. 3, 1852, Abraham O. Smoot company.
Married Elizabeth Milnes June 16, 1849, Bradford, Yorkshire, Eng. (daughter of Edward and Betsey Milnes of Bradford, pioneers 1852, Abraham O. Smoot company). She was born Feb. 11, 1830, and came to Utah with husband. Their children: John H., m. Sophia Ann Needham; Mary Elizabeth. m. Fred Taylor; Martha, m. Heber C. Caine; Sarah Ann, m. Joseph Arthur; William Edward, Charles Albert, and Alfred Milnes—latter three died. Family home Salt Lake City.
Teacher; home missionary; worked on building of Salt Lake Temple. Took part in Echo canyon trouble. Assisted in taking out provisions to belated handcart companies. Settled at Springville 1858 and conducted co-op. store. Died March 24, 1887, Salt Lake City.

BAILEY, JOHN HENRY (son of John Bailey and Elizabeth Milnes). Born Nov. 22, 1850, Bradford, Eng. Came to Utah with parents.
Married Sophia Ann Needham Dec. 9, 1872, Salt Lake City (daughter of John Needham and Sarah Ann Booth of Nauvoo, Ill., pioneers 1850). She was born Nov. 24, 1852. Their children: John Henry b. Jan. 10, 1874, m. Marie Edwards; Arthur N. b. Aug. 23, 1877; Burt N. b. Jan. 19, 1889; Seymour N. b. May 29, 1882, m. Emma Watson; Pearl Sophia b. May 10, 1889, m. H. B. Clawson. Family home Salt Lake City.
Member 124th quorum seventies. Teacher. Helped in building Salt Lake Temple 1865. Merchant since 1865.

BAILEY, JOHN HENRY, JR. (son of John Henry Bailey and Sophia Ann Needham). Born Jan. 10, 1874, Salt Lake City.
Married Marie Edwards at Salt Lake City (daughter of George Edwards and Caffy M. Gardy of England, California, and Kansas). She was born Oct. 29, 1876. Their children: Russel b. July 10, 1902; Harold b. July 20, 1906; Virginia Dorothy b. Aug. 2, 1908. Family home Salt Lake City.
Missionary to England 1898-1900.

BAILEY, JOSEPH M. (son of Henry Bailey and Emelia Read of England). Born Dec. 16, 1842, Buckinghamshire, Eng. Came to Utah Nov. 2, 1864, Warren S. Snow company.
Married Ann M. Folker Dec. 21, 1867, Salt Lake City (daughter of John and Mary Folker, pioneers Sept., 1854, Cummings and Dunn company). She was born July 12, 1849. Their children: Joseph William, b. Feb. 17, 1870, m. Mary Orilla Shaw; Matilda E. b. April 11, 1872, m. Gilbert George Wright. Family home Ogden, Utah. Died there March 7, 1875.

BAILEY, JOSEPH WILLIAM (son of Joseph M. Bailey and Ann M. Folker). He was born Feb. 17, 1870, Plain City, Weber county, Utah.
Married Mary Orilla Shaw March 25, 1891, Ogden, Utah (daughter of John Shaw, born Feb. 17, 1850, in Salt Lake City, and Julia Barker of Ogden, Utah). She was born Aug. 27, 1870. Only child: Ruth Ann b. Nov. 27, 1897. Family home Ogden, where he died Sept. 7, 1912.

BAINBRIDGE, FRED NANCE, came to Utah in 1847.
Married Elizabeth Hendricks in 1847 at Salt Lake City (daughter of Jas. Hendricks and Elizabeth Doris, pioneers 1847). Only child: James Wesley, m. Sarah J. Lewis.

BAINBRIDGE, JAMES WESLEY (son of Fred Nance Bainbridge and Elizabeth Hendricks). Born Oct. 21, 1848, Salt Lake City.
Married Sarah J. Lewis Sept. 7, 1874, Salt Lake City (daughter of Wm. Crawford Lewis and Sarah J. Veach, of Richmond, Lewiston and Bear Lake, Utah). She was born April 9, 1854. Their children: James Wesley b. Oct. 15, 1875, m. Eugenia Strong; Jennie b. Sept. 23, 1877, m. Arthur Gifford; Libbie b. Aug. 2, 1879, m. Fred B. Sommers; Wm. C. b. Jan. 23, 1881, m. Rachel Patterson; Leonard L. b. Nov. 4, 1883; Vesta C. b. May 3, 1891, m. Orrin Robinson; Nettie b. Jan. 3, 1898.

BAIR, JOHN (son of Adam Bair, born March 12, 1785, and Catherine Bowermaster, born Feb. 5, 1765, both of Pennsylvania). He was born Nov. 26, 1810, Somerset, Pa. Came to Utah 1850, ox team company.
Married Lucinda Owen (Tyler), in Ohio (daughter of Abel and Betsy Owen, latter a pioneer). She was born in New York. Their children: Elizabeth, m. William King; Belinda Jane, m. Robert Wall; Amanda, m. George Shaver; Delos, m. Nancy Jane Kent; Dolores, d. infant; Emma b. Feb. 14, 1854, m. Dennis A. Winn; Marion, d. infant; Meriam, m. Jeff Sharp; m. Robert Tartar; m. Jeff Edmundson; m. Jack Doran. Family home Kaysville, Utah.
Married Jerusha Ann Richardson (Card), (daughter of Samuel Richardson). She was born in Massachusetts, and died March 11, 1861. Their children: Joseph b. Oct. 25, 1848, died; Hyrum b. Nov. 16, 1850, m. Mary E. Van Orden Nov. 26, 1871; Francis Adam b. Feb. 28, 1853, m. Jane Brower Feb. 17, 1873; Samuel John b. Dec. 20, 1856, died; George Orton b. Jan. 17, 1858, m. Valeria Richardson 1882. Family home Farmington, Utah.
Built and operated the first ferryboat in Utah on the Bear river, he also built the first saw mill in Davis county. Settled at Richmond 1859. Took part in Echo canyon war. High priest. Indian war veteran. Shoemaker; lawyer; farmer, and stockraiser. Died Oct. 11, 1884.
Lucinda Owen (first wife) was widow of Lumus Tyler. Their children: Lola, m. John Richardson; Louisa, m. Thomas Tidwell.

BAIR, HYRUM (son of John Bair and Jerusha Ann Richardson). Born Nov. 16, 1850, Farmington, Utah.
Married Mary E. Van Orden Nov. 26, 1871, Richmond, Utah (daughter of Peter Edmund Van Orden and Martha Ann Knight), who was born Oct. 30, 1852, Kaysville, Utah. Their children: Hyrum Lester b. Sept. 29, 1872, m. Harriet A. Skidmore June 9, 1897; John Francis b. July 15, 1875, m. Annie Spackman Dec. 5, 1900; George Edmund b. Aug. 29, 1877, m. Maud Hill Jan. 4, 1905; Amelia A. b. Nov. 10, 1879, m. William Sorensen March 4, 1908; Charles Henry b. July 23, 1881, d. Aug. 11, 1881; Mary Ellen b. July 8, 1882, d.

April 20, 1888; Julian Alvin b. March 9, 1885, m. Ida K. Walters Oct. 10, 1906; Clara May b. June 24, 1888, m. Alvin Johnson Nov. 23, 1910; Mattie Maria b. April 14, 1890, m. Ray C. Rich Sept. 20, 1911; Milton Earl b. Oct. 25, 1892; Julia Valeria b. Oct. 15, 1895. Family home Richmond, Utah.

BAIRD, ALEXANDER (son of Robert Baird and Agnes Bell of Glasgow, Scotland). Born Jan. 10, 1832, Paisley, Scotland. Came to Utah Oct. 4, 1863, Thomas E. Ricks company.
Married Sarah DeLacey April 10, 1860, in Boston (daughter of Felix DeLacey of Dublin, Ireland). She was born May 18, 1839. Their children: Agnes and Alexander, died; William DeLacey m. Charlotte M. Keller July 23, 1884; Sarah Theresa, m. Felix Smout; Mary Ellen b. Oct. 28, 1867, m. J. M. Koller, Jr., 1883; Peter, m. Hannah Peterson 1890; Martha, m. Albert Bailey. Family home Brigham City, Utah.
Sheriff and deputy sheriff for twenty years; watchman.

BAIRD, BRIGHAM YOUNG (son of Samuel Baird and Matilda Rutledge of St. Joseph, Mo.). Born Feb. 6, 1846, in Alabama. Came to Utah 1863.
Married Margarett Elizabeth Allen Sept. 26, 1872, Salt Lake City (daughter of Lewis Allen and Elizabeth Alexander of Andrew county, Mo., pioneers Aug. 3, 1862, independent ox-team company). She was born Jan. 20, 1852. Their children: Matilda Elizabeth, m. John H. Harris; Brigham Young, Jr., m. Malvina Parker; Louis; Nellie, m. Charles R. Pugh; Lois, m. Ira Heaton; Samuel; Alma, died; Effa; William Junior. Family home Kanab, Utah.
Bishop's counselor, member high council. Kanab city councilman. Farmer and sheepraiser. Died Nov. 6, 1889.

BAIRD, JAMES HYRUM (son of Samuel Baird and Matilda Rutledge of St. Joseph, Mo.). Born Feb. 5, 1848, Quincy, Ill. Came to Utah 1864, with an oxteam company.
Married Fanny Sessions March 7, 1870, Salt Lake City (daughter of Perrigrine Sessions and Emmerette Loveland, pioneers 1847 and 1850, respectively). She was born Oct. 25, 1855. Their children: Sylvia b. May 4, 1871, died; Hyrum b. April 4, 1873; Perry b. Aug. 6, 1874, died; Minnie b. Feb. 9, 1876, m. Daniel H. Walker; Chloe b. Aug. 10, 1877, m. James A. Lee; Zina b. Jan. 10, 1879, m. John Reed; Asa b. May 24, 1880, m. Winnie Kirkman; Eliza Jane b. Aug. 17, 1881; Walter b. March 10, 1883, m. Amelia Tree; Emmerette b. June 15, 1885, died; Chester b. Nov. 14, 1887, died; Chancy b. Jan. 31, 1890; Clarence b. Jan. 6, 1892; Amelia b. May 21, 1893; Samuel b. Nov. 25, 1894; James Sessions b. June 27, 1897; Joseph Reese b. Aug. 4, 1899.
Married Margaret Ellen Randall July 8, 1880, Salt Lake City, Utah (daughter of Alfred Jason Randall and Margaret Harvey of Ohio, pioneers with an oxteam company). She was born March 31, 1858. Their children: Alice b. July 31, 1881, died; Wilford b. Oct. 17, 1882, m. Gertrude E. Luck; Margaret b. Dec. 6, 1884, m. George Henry Evans; Myron b. Nov. 27, 1886, died; Orrin Randall b. Sept. 27, 1888; Edwin b. Jan. 8, 1892; Matilda b. Oct. 8, 1894, died; Abner Harley b. Sept. 17, 1897; Chestina b. Nov. 14, 1899; Ruby b. March 4, 1902. Families resided at Syracuse, Davis county, Utah.
Seventy; high priest. Crossed plains three times for immigrants. Black Hawk Indian war veteran. School trustee at Centerville, Utah. Blacksmith and farmer. Died Feb. 8, 1910.

BAIRD (BYARD), ROBERT E. (son of James Baird and Elizabeth Erwing of Londonderry, Ireland). Born May 15, 1817, in Londonderry. Came to Utah July 24, 1847, Brigham Young company.
Married Hannah McCullough July 23, 1840 (daughter of John McCullough and Sarah Rogers), who was born Dec. 10, 1817, and came to Utah Sept. 1847. Their children: John b. May 2, 1841, m. Mary Ann Heath 1867; Joseph b. Dec. 1, 1846, died; Ellen b. June 1, 1848, m. William Bishop 1864; Robert b. Dec. 27, 1850, m. Emma J. Taylor, 1875; Hannah b. Sept. 5, 1854, m. Conrad Lyman April 11, 1891. Family home Salt Lake City and Weber county, Utah.
Married Jane Hadley 1857, Salt Lake City (daughter of Richard Hadley and Mary Shooter, pioneers respectively Oct. 3 and Sept. 25, 1855, Richard Ballantyne company). She was born April 8, 1835, in Herefordshire, Eng. Their children: James b. April 25, 1858, m. Charlotte Lund Nov. 4, 1882; Eliza b. May 7, 1860, m. Heber Taylor Jan. 5, 1883; Jane b. March 28, 1862, m. Edward Perkins Oct. 5, 1884; John b. Feb. 17, 1864; Hannah b. Aug. 1, 1866, d. 1868; Hannah Mary b. Nov. 22, 1868, m. Samuel Merrill 1895; Mary b. Feb. 9, 1871, m. Delbert Merrill March 13, 1901; Caroline b. Oct. 23, 1874, m. William Layman April 7, 1894.
Married Mary Hadley 1868, Salt Lake City (daughter of Richard Hadley and Mary Shooter), who was born April 20, 1837, in Herefordshire, Eng. Their children: Mary Ann b. June 2, 1859, m. Elijah Allen 1879; Elizabeth b. Sept. 27, 1860, m. Isaac Wilson 1880; William b. April 7, 1862, m. Sarah E. Hadley 1885; Ellen b. April 20, 1864, m. Cyrus Kennedy 1885; Jannett b. April 16, 1866, m. Isaac Allred Dec. 27, 1886; Robert b. Sept. 27, 1867; Joseph b. May 19, 1869;

m. Margaret Field Nov. 10, 1899; Franklin b. May 5, 1871, m. Zina McBride 1895; Josephine b. July 23, 1874, died. Families resided Lynne Ward, Weber county, Utah.
Justice of peace; city councilman Ogden. President 53rd quorum seventies; president Lynn district.

BAIRD, JOHN (son of Robert E. Baird and Hannah McCullough). Born May 2, 1841, Westchester, Pa.
Married Mary Ann Heath 1867 at Ogden, Utah, who was born in England. Their children: John; Elliott; Alvin, died; Mary Ann, m. James Monroe; Amy, m. Stephen Browning. Family home Soda Springs, Idaho.
Elder; seventy.

BAIRD, JOHN (son of Robert E. Baird and Jane Hadley). Born Feb. 17, 1864, Lynn Ward, Utah.

BAKER, BENJAMIN (son of Thomas Potter Baker and Polly (or Mary) Tanner of Charleston, Montgomery county, N. Y.). Born March 26, 1796, Charleston, N. Y. Came to Utah Oct. 19, 1848, Amasa M. Lyman company.
Married Abigail Kruzen Taylor Feb. 1821, Albion, Oswego county, N. Y. (daughter of Thomas Taylor and Mary Rosina Shoulder of that place). She was born March 28, 1801, and died June 19, 1847. Their children: William Taylor; Mary Rosina, m. Nathan Tanner; Susan Eliza; Edward Orlando; Zarilda Jane, m. Emery Barrus; Chancy Leroy. Family home Montrose, Lee county, Ia. and Grantsville, Utah.

BAKER, BENJAMIN WALTER. He was born Aug. 30, 1830, London, Eng. Came to Utah Sept. 28, 1851, John Brown company.
Married Sarah Ann Woodford 1861 (daughter of Charles Woodford), who was born 1845 in England. Their children: Benjamin Charles, b. Nov. 5, 1862, m. Lucy Evans; Sarah Elizabeth b. Sept. 6, 1864, m. Henry Checketts; James Edward b. Sept. 4, 1866. Family home Slaterville, Utah, and Franklin, Idaho.

BAKER, BENJAMIN CHARLES (son of Benjamin Walter Baker and Sarah Ann Woodford). Born Nov. 5, 1862, Slaterville, Utah.
Married Lucy Evans June 2, 1881, Eagle Rock, Idaho (daughter of John D. Evans and Margaret Haries, who came to Utah 1878). She was born June 13, 1865, in Wales. Their children: Elizabeth Ann b. Oct. 17, 1882, m. J. R. Durant Dec. 17, 1902; Margaret Lucy b. March 20, 1885, m. Charles Lund March 20, 1903; Charles Walter b. Jan. 15, 1887; Zelma b. Jan. 28, 1889, m. James Naylor Oct. 1906; Lucilla b. Jan. 2, 1892, m. Alma Hancock Sept. 2, 1909; Harold E. b. April 20, 1896; John Raynold b. April 7, 1898. Family home Franklin, Idaho.
Second counselor to the president of the Y. M. M. I. A.

BAKER, GEORGE (son of John Baker and Mary Hayes of England). Born 1819 in England. Came to Utah Aug. 27, 1860, Daniel Robinson company.
Married Mary Baker 1840, in England (daughter of Thomas Baker), who was born 1819 and died 1847. Their children: Thomas b. Jan. 21, 1841, m. Martha Ann Larson; Ann b. 1843, m. William Lund; Harriet b. 1845, died.
Married Mary Ann Randall 1848, who was born 1819 in England. Came to Utah 1860. Their children: George b. 1849, died; Merrilda, died; Eliza Jane b. 1855, m. Frederick W. Jones; Mary E. b. 1857, m. William Terry; William Benjamin b. 1862, m. Elizabeth Larson (deceased) and Delia Maudsley.
First counselor to President Bristol (Eng.) branch; president Chanceville (N. J.) branch 1858. Settled at St. George. Died there in 1887.

BAKER, THOMAS (son of George Baker and Mary Baker). Born Jan. 21, 1841. Came to Utah Sept. 7, 1859, Horton D. Haight company.
Married Martha Ann Larson 1866, Salt Lake City (daughter of Lars Larson and Mary Bellows), who was born 1849 at Council Bluffs. Their children: Thomas Henry b. 1866, m. Fedonia Lloyd; George b. 1869, died; Benjami . b. 1872, m. Samantha Mangum; Mary b. 1874 and William b. 1876, died; Alfred b. 1879, m. Mary Chidester; Frederick W. b. 1882, m. Lida Combs; Philip b. 1884, m. Maud Stringham; Martin Alfonzo b. 1886; Reuben b. 1888, died.
Farmer. Settled at St. George 1862; moved to Pine Valley 1867 and to Thurber, Wayne county, 1889. High priest.

BAKER, SIMON (son of Benjamin Baker, born Oct. 26, 1780, Leyden, Mass., and Rebecca Thorn, born May 12, 1786). Born Oct. 18, 1811, at West Winfield, Herkimer county, N. Y. Came to Utah Oct. 2, 1847, Jedediah M. Grant company.
Married Mercy Young Dec. 21, 1829 (daughter of Abiathar Young and Lydia French of Winfield, N. Y.). She was born Jan. 27, 1807. Their children: Jarvis Young b. Nov. 13, 1830, m. Rachel Richards Dec. 25, 1864; Amenzo White b. June 9, 1832, m. Agnes Steele Nov. 19, 1864; Albert Mowry b. Oct. 3, 1833, m. Jane Maria Curtis and Jane Coon; Betsie b. Jan. 24, 1835, m. John Topham; George Washington b. Sept. 9, 1837, m. Agnes Richards Jan. 18, 1861; Joseph b. Aug. 15, 1839, m. Lucy A. Pack; Rebecca b. June 9, 1841, m.

Suellen Marion Johnson July 26, 1862; Mary b. July 3, 1843; Sarah b. July 3, 1843, m. William C. Farnsworth. Family home Salt Lake City.

Married Charlotte Leavitt April 8, 1845 (daughter of Wire Leavitt and Abigail Cole). 'She was born Dec. 5, 1818. Their children: Abigail b. Jan. 7, 1846, m. Thomas Matthews June 17, 1865; Benjamin b. July 6, 1847, m. Margaret A. Rowe; Charlotte b. April 5, 1849, m. William Longstroth; Simon b. Nov. 20, 1850, died; Phoebe b. Aug. 27, 1852, died; Wiear b. July 20, 1854, m. Electa Haws; Samuel Leavitt b. June 26, 1856, m. Annie Leavitt; Hannah b. Dec. 28, 1857, m. William Willie; Jeremiah b. June 18, 1860, m. Mary T. Lemmon. Families resided Salt Lake and Mendon, Cache county, Utah.

Married Elizabeth Staples March 18, 1853 (daughter of James Staples and Sarah Limerick, who were married April 12, 1831, in England). She was born Jan. 8, 1838. Their children: Sarah Ann b. Aug 19, 1854; James Staples b. Aug. 25, 1856, m. Louisa Staples and Elizabeth Cunningham; Elizabeth b. July 8, 1858, m. Spencer D. Shumway Oct. 23, 1877; Maria b. Nov. 8, 1860, m. Merlin T. Stone Jan. 17, 1878; Mercy b. July 15, 1863, died.

Married Ann Staples Feb. 10, 1857, Salt Lake City (daughter of James Staples and Sarah Limerick), who was born April 3, 1832, Cheltenham, Eng. Only child: Henry b. Jan. 2, 1858, m. Isabel Dennet.

Married Amy Walker May 20, 1853 (daughter of David Walker and Ann Bennett); no children.

Said to have made first molasses in Utah. Colonist to Carson Valley, Nev.; served in Echo Canyon war. Died Oct. 22, 1863.

BAKER, ALBERT MOWRY (son of Simon Baker and Mercy Young). Born Oct. 3, 1833, Pomfort, N. Y. Came to Utah 1847 with parents.

Married Jane Maria Curtis Dec. 25, 1854, Salt Lake City (daughter of Charles Curtis and Sarah Wright), who was born Nov. 14, 1835.

Married Jane Coon April 11, 1865, Salt Lake City (daughter of Abraham Coon and Elizabeth Wilson). Their children: Jane Maria, m. Samuel G. Spencer; Albert Mowry, m. Alice Barnes; Sarah Elizabeth; Charles Henry, m. Charlotte L. Ladle; Abraham Coon, m. Lolo Pratt; Laura, m. James P. Jensen; Jesse Simon; Edna.

President 28th quorum seventies; ward teacher; home missionary. Made two trips to Florence, Neb., for immigrants. Went to Carson, Nev., to assist in settling that country. Captain in Utah militia. Justice of peace. Farmer and stockraiser. Died Sept. 3, 1909, Mendon, Utah.

BAKER, GEORGE WASHINGTON (son of Simon Baker and Mercy Young). Born Sept. 9, 1837, Pomfert, N. Y. Came to Utah 1847.

Married Agnes Richards Jan. 18, 1861, Mendon, Cache county, Utah (daughter of John Richards and Agnes Hill, pioneers 1851, Luman Shurtliff company). She was born Nov. 1, 1843, Nauvoo, Ill. Their children: George Washington, Jr. b. Oct. 9, 1862, m. Oralie M. Atwood; Mary Emma b. July 30, 1864, m. Jens Jenson Dec. 18, 1885; Julia b. Aug. 3, 1866, m. F. R. Christensen Aug. 24, 1887; Joseph Albert b. March 30, 1869, m. Alice H. Hinckley July 18, 1904; Lucy Agnes b. June 2, 1871, m. Charles A. Johnson April 27, 1891; John Simon b. June 9, 1873, d. Aug. 10, 1909; Willard b. June 26, 1876, m. Lena E. Foster Feb. 16, 1907; Lyman b. May 17, 1878, m. Edith Lant April 23, 1901; Celestia b. Sept. 1, 1881, m. William Howell Nov. 12, 1903; Olive b. July 18, 1885, m. H. Sumner Hatch June 30, 1909; Seth b. Aug. 11, 1887.

Missionary to Snake Indians 1853-54; served in Echo Canyon war. Went from Salt Lake City to Mendon, Utah. 1860. First mayor of Mendon 1870; also justice of peace.

BAKER, GEORGE WASHINGTON, JR. (son of George Washington Baker and Agnes Richards). Born Oct. 9, 1862, Mendon, Utah.

Married Oralie Melissa Atwood June 24, 1897 (daughter of William Atwood and Sarah Jane Wade), who was born Oct. 7, 1869, Salt Lake City. Their children: George Lowell b. June 3, 1899; Oralie Virginia b. Oct. 9, 1901; Dorothy Aileen b. Sept. 7, 1907.

Physician; president State Medical Society 1902-04; sanitary inspector 1900; graduate Rush Medical College, Chicago.

BAKER, JOSEPH (son of Simon Baker and Mercy Young). Born Aug. 15, 1839, Montrose, Lee county, Iowa.

Married Lucy A. Pack July 10, 1859, Salt Lake City (daughter of John Pack and Lucy Ives, pioneers 1847). She was born June 22, 1837, and died April 16, 1874, Mendon, Utah. Their children: Joseph Linden b. March 22, 1860, d. Jan. 10, 1880; Jesse Merrit b. Nov. 11, 1861, m. Sarah Ann Dowdle; Simon Pack b. Jan. 3, 1864, d. July 9, 1888, m. Sarah J. Bassett; John Rupert b. Nov. 29, 1865, m. Sarah J. Bassett; Lucy Amelia b. Oct. 22, 1867, m. Albert W. Raybould; Charlotte Eleanor b. June 16, 1869, m. David T. Owens; Tamzon Louella b. Feb. 22, 1871, m. Ernest Jennings; Ward Eaton b. Jan. 15, 1873, d. Aug. 10, 1873; George C. b. April 10, 1874, d. same day.

Married Mary Alice Morgan (daughter of Thomas Morgan and Ann Roberts), who was born March 6, 1855, Merthyr Tydfil, South Wales. Their children: Mary Elizabeth b. April 28, 1876, d. Feb. 22, 1877; Thomas Morgan b. March 27, 1877; Albert Marvin b. June 20, 1879; Richard Morgan b. Dec. 24, 1880; Annie Maria b. Oct. 30, 1882; Alice b. March 20, 1884, m. Ferris E. Jones; David M. b. Nov. 2, 1885, m. Gladys B. Crompton July 17, 1911; William Melvin b. March 12, 1887; Alma b. June 12, 1889; Florence Geneva b. March 22, 1891, d. April 16, 1896; Hazel May b. May 30, 1893; Margaret Edna b. Oct. 7, 1895, d. Nov. 25, 1909; Mary Geneva Morris (adopted) b. Sept. 23, 1901. Family home Brigham, Utah.

Settled in Iron county, Utah, 1850; moved to Carson Valley, Nev., shortly afterward, and to Cache valley in 1855. President of elders' quorum. Coroner of Cache county, 1894; justice of peace 16 years.

BAKER, JESSE MERRIT (son of Joseph Baker and Lucy A. Pack). Born Nov. 11, 1861, Mendon, Utah.

Married Sarah Ann Dowdle, Oct. 22, 1885, Logan, Utah (daughter of Robert Hughes Dowdle and Henrietta Messervy, of Franklin, Oneida county, Idaho). She was born June 15, 1863, at Franklin. Their children: Jesse Alvin b. Oct. 18, 1886, d. June 11, 1893; Lucy Ada b. Nov. 29, 1887, m. Henry M. Hodgson Oct. 12, 1910; Laura Henrietta b. Dec. 15, 1889, m. Samuel J. Orin Aug. 16, 1911; Louise May b. Aug. 30, 1891; Mary Lovier b. June 16, 1895; Lorin M. b. March 13, 1897; Doris b. April 5, 1899; Sarah Grace b. April 21, 1901; Harold Ray b. Aug. 9, 1903. Family home Fremont county, Idaho.

Settled in Snake River valley 1884. High priest; bishop's counselor 1884-92; missionary to eastern states 1892-94; president Y. M. M. I. A. 14 years; high councilor. Farmer; merchant.

BAKER, WILLIAM (son of William Baker and Lydia Standing of Sailhurst parish, Sussex, Eng.). Born Dec. 24, 1814, in Sailhurst parish. Came to Utah 1858 in M. L. Shepherd company.

Married Frances Friend Nov. 16, 1844, in Sailhurst parish (daughter of Jesse Friend and Mary Crittenden of that parish). She was born April 15, 1826 (died May 23, 1906), and came to Utah with husband. Their children: Jesse W. b. Aug. 31, 1845, m. Elenor Clark; Geo. b. Jan. 1, 1848, m. Mary A. Evans; Alfred b. Aug. 14, 1851, m. Keturah Lewis; Rhoda C. b. Nov. 1, 1855, m. Lewis Litzel Schwab; Lovina H. b. Feb. 7, 1859; m. Geo. R. Reed; Mary A. F. b. Nov. 28, 1863, m. Abram Wood; Henry F. b. Nov. 20, 1867, m. Amy Walker. Pioneer. Died Dec. 1, 1898.

BAKER, HENRY F. (son of William Baker and Frances Friend). Born Nov. 20, 1867, Minersville, Utah.

Married Amy Walker Dec. 13, 1893, St. George, Utah. Their children: Cecil H. b. Dec. 2, 1895; Alvin b. Jan. 11, 1898; Jesse b. June 15, 1900; Lois M. b. Sept. 3, 1902; Thora b. Oct. 7, 1904, died; Harold b. June 27, 1907; Joseph Delos b. Dec. 23, 1909. Family home Minersville, Utah.

High priest; member of high council; missionary to England 1902-1903; counselor to bishop; afterward bishop; Sunday school superintendent.

BAKER, WILLIAM GEORGE (son of Henry Baker and Jean Rio Griffiths of London, Eng.). Born June 10, 1835, in London. Came to Utah Sept. 28, 1851, John Brown company.

Married Hannah Hayward Nov. 25, 1855 (daughter of William Hayward and Ruth Hughes, pioneers Oct. 9, 1853, Appleton Harmon company). Their children: William George b. Oct. 19, 1856, m. Amanda Jensen; Ruth Jean Rio b. April 17, 1859, m. James C. Peterson; Henry b. May 7, 1861, m. Hannah B. Ramsey; William Hayward b. Aug. 17, 1863, died; Frank Arnold b. Jan. 7, 1866, m. Nettie Spencer; Mary Hannah Hayward b. March 25, 1868, m. Victor E. Bean; Walter b. Feb. 9, 1870, m. Anna Sophia Boyce; John Richard b. April 27, 1872, m. Annie Jensen; Charles Fredrick b. June 21, 1874, died; Elizabeth b. Aug. 23, 1875, m. William Thomas Ogden; Eugene Hayward, b. June 6, 1878, m. Rhoda Cottam; Claude Vincent b. March 20, 1881, m. Lillie Liston; Edward Lester b. Oct. 11, 1883. Family home Richfield, Utah.

Married Nicolina Marie Bertelsen June 1, 1867, Nephi, Utah (daughter of Niels and Marie Bertelsen), who was born Jan. 26, 1845, Aalborg, Denmark. Their children: Mary Ottaminnie b. March 22, 1868, m. Leo A. Bean; William Louis b. Jan. 14, 1870, m. Laura Jones; Nelson b. Oct. 9, 1871, m. Natalia Borg; Lars Arthur b. Jan. 13, 1874, m. Caroline Jensen; Annie Eliza b. Dec. 30, 1875, died; Ida Elizabeth b. March 24, 1878, died; Ralph b. May 12, 1879, m. Mary Ann Toller; Ruth Henrietta b. Oct. 17, 1881, m. Frank K. Seegmiller; Albert James b. Jan. 16, 1883, died Oct. 12, 1887; Hazel Adelia b. June 25, 1887.

School trustee Richfield school district; justice of the peace; county treasurer. Attorney at law.

BAKER, NELSON (son of William George Baker and Nicolina Marie Bertelsen). Born Oct. 9, 1871, Nephi, Utah.

Married Natalia Borg March 31, 1897, Richfield, Utah (daughter of O. F. Borg and Brighamina Nielsen, pioneers respectively of 1864 and 1866). She was born Oct. 6, 1874, Richfield, Utah. Their children: Minnie Ailene b. Jan. 1, 1898; Owen Nelson b. May 29, 1901; Evan William b. March 6, 1903; Elva Natalia b. Dec. 22, 1905; Edward Louis b. Jan. 16, 1908; Anna Marguerette b. March 21, 1911.

Mechanical engineer.

BALL, JOHN PRICE (son of James Ball and Isabel Price, of Coalville, Eng.). Born Oct. 4, 1828, Coalville, Leicestershire, Eng. Came to Utah Oct. 16, 1862, Isaac A. Canfield company.

Married Emma Henderson April 2, 1859 Loughborough,

PIONEERS AND PROMINENT MEN OF UTAH 733

Eng., who was born Jan. 10, 1828, Sheepshead, Leicestershire, Eng. Family home Salt Lake City.
Married Phoebe Birkenhead March 4, 1870, Salt Lake City (daughter of Isaac Birkenhead and Mary Ann Wife of Birmingham, Eng.), who was born Jan. 17, 1852. Their children: Isabel b. Oct. 14, 1872, m. James W. Ure, Jr.; Amy A. b. Nov. 24, 1873, m. Edward H. Davis: John Price, Jr. b. Nov. 3, 1875, died; James H. b. Dec. 30, 1877, m. Sylvia Garff; Isaac B. b. July 17, 1880. m. Rachel Hodgson; Thomas William b. July 6, 1883, m. Rinda Hamlin. Family home Salt Lake City.
Merchant. Died Oct. 16, 1890.

BALL, JAMES H. (son of John Price Ball and Phoebe Birkenhead). Born Dec. 30, 1877, Salt Lake City.
Married Sylvia Garff June 15, 1905, Salt Lake City (daughter of Christian Garff and Augusta Elizabeth Hansen, pioneers 1858), who was born April 30, 1879. Only child: Dorothy b. Dec. 15, 1908.
Lawyer. Served in U. S. army in Philippines during war with Spain.

BALLANTYNE, RICHARD (son of David Ballantyne, born 1748 near Roxburgh, Scotland, and died Dec. 12, 1831, and Ann Bannerman, born 1789 at Dundee, Scotland; married Oct. 28, 1808). Born Aug. 26, 1817, at Earlston, Berwick, Scotland. Came to Utah Sept. 20, 1848, Brigham Young company.
Married Huldah Meriah Clark Feb. 18, 1847 (daughter of Gardner Clark and Delecta Farrer who were married 1813 at Geneseo, N. Y.; the former died 1847 at Winter Quarters, Iowa, and the latter came to Utah 1848). She was born Oct. 26, 1823, and came to Utah with husband. Their children: Richard Alando b. June 1, 1848, m. Mary Ann Stewart Dec. 27, 1875; Delecta Annie Jane b. Nov. 22, 1849, m. Louis F. Moench Feb. 15, 1874; David Henry b. Nov. 16, 1851, d. Aug. 31, 1863; Meriah Cedenia b. June 25, 1856, m. Austin C. Brown Feb. 2, 1874; John Taylor b. Dec. 28, 1857, m. Mahala E. Wilson March 18, 1885; Annie b. July 15, 1860, m. Louis F. Moench; Roseitha b. March 10, 1862, m. Jesse G. Stratford Nov. 23, 1882; Isabella b. Aug. 3, 1864, m. Louis Alvin West Nov. 23, 1882; Joseph b. Feb. 20, 1868, m. Rosannah A. Brown. Family homes Salt Lake City, Nephi, Ogden and Eden, Utah.
Married Mary Pearce Nov. 27, 1855, Salt Lake City (daughter of Edward Pearce and Elizabeth Bennett), who was born Oct. 1, 1828, at Ratcliffe, London, Eng., and came to Utah Sept. 25, 1856, with her husband's company. Their children: Zachariah b. Oct. 31, 1856, m. Martha Ferrin; Mary Elizabeth b. Sept. 7, 1858, m. Willard Farr; Jane Susannah b. Feb. 10, 1861, m. Edward H. Anderson; James Edward b. Nov. 1, 1863, m. Sarah H. Critchlow; Eliza Jane b. June 8, 1866, m. Henry J. Garner; Heber Charles b. Feb. 28, 1867; m. Ada Belnap. Family resided at Salt Lake City, Nephi and Ogden, Utah.
Married Caroline Albertine Sanderson Nov. 7, 1856, at Salt Lake City (daughter of Kanute Alexanderson and Ingebor Christina Larsen), who was born Sept. 19, 1837, at Roken, Norway. Their children: Thomas Henry b. Dec. 12, 1858, m. Martha Carstensen Sept. 6, 1883; Caroline Josephine b. Jan. 30, 1861, m. Marcus Farr; Matilda b. Dec. 30, 1862, d. Sept. 4, 1882; Catherine Mena b. Dec. 29, 1864, d. Nov. 18, 1866; Jedediah b. Nov. 18, 1867, m. Nettie Wilson; Brigham b. Feb. 18, 1871; Laura Elizabeth b. June 23, 1874. Family resided at Salt Lake City, Nephi, Ogden and Eden.
Missionary to Hindoostan, India, 1852, laboring in Calcutta and Madras, and publishing a paper there. Brought a company of immigrants to Utah Sept. 25, 1855. Pioneer to the Salmon river 1857 and returning moved to Nephi, 1857, and to Ogden 1860; located the town of Eden 1866, and there served as bishop until 1871. High councilor 37 years and superintendent Sunday schools of Weber stake. Organized the first Sunday school in the dominant church December, 1849, and therefore is known as "father of the Sunday schools." County commissioner of Weber county 12 years; alderman of Ogden several terms: school trustee. Publisher and editor of "Ogden Junction" 1877. Merchant and farmer.

BALLANTYNE, RICHARD ALANDO (son of Richard Ballantyne and Huldah Meriah Clark). Born June 1, 1848, on the Elkhorn river, Nebraska.
Married Mary Ann Stewart Dec. 27, 1875, Salt Lake City (daughter of Isaac Mitton Stewart and Elizabeth White), who was born March 4, 1858, Draper, Utah. Their children: Mary Delecta b. April 7, 1877, m. Heber Fielding Burton Dec. 14, 1898; Elizabeth Huldah b. Oct. 28, 1879, m. George D. Cardon Sept. 10, 1902; Richard Stewart b. Dec. 25, 1881, m. Ardella Romney Sept. 30, 1909; Alando Bannerman b. July 18, 1884; Leona Bertha b. Sept. 21, 1886, m. Kenneth R. Woolley March 4, 1911; Geneva Alice b. Sept. 14, 1888; Isaac Stewart b. Sept. 21, 1890, d. June 14, 1892; Prescindia Stewart b. Oct. 23, 1892, m. Herbert S. Woolley Sept. 6, 1911; Glenna Marie b. Dec. 25, 1894; Zina Leanore b. June 8, 1897; William Stewart b. Jan. 17, 1900, d. Aug. 16, 1912; Mary Stewart b. May 27, 1902; Ruth b. Nov. 22, 1905. Family homes Ogden, Draper and Logan, Utah.
From 9 to 23 years of age he worked in a store, on the farm and in the canyons for his father. Missionary to the southern states 1879-80; home missionary in Salt Lake stake over two years; high priest: Sunday school superintendent and teacher 30 years; member Sunday school board of Weber stake; bishop's counselor. School trustee at Draper 6 years; commissioner to locate university lands two years; helped build Union and Central Pacific and O. S. L. railroads, also to build the Davis & Weber county, East Jordan & Draper and West Cache county canals. Farmer; bookkeeper.

BALLANTYNE, JOHN T. (son of Richard Ballantyne and Huldha Meriah Clark). Born Dec. 28, 1857, Salt Lake City, Utah.
Married Mahala E. Wilson March 18, 1885, Lehi, Utah (daughter of David Wilson and Rachel P. Loveless of Payson, Utah, pioneers 1850). She was born June 30, 1863. Their children: Effie b. Dec. 21, 1885, m. Releigh Campbell; Ivy b. Feb. 9, 1888, m. Harrison B. Child; John W. b. Jan. 10, 1890; LeRoy T. b. Nov. 16, 1892; David W. b. Dec. 2, 1894; Ozro M. b. November, 1896, d. infant; Orin b. Feb. 12, 1898, d. aged 13 months; Leslie C. b. Jan. 6, 1899; Ezra b. June 29, 1901, d. aged 7 years: Cleone b. Sept. 16, 1904; Eugene and Geneva b. Aug. 23, 1906, the former d. at 2 years of age; Hulda b. April 15, 1909.
Bishop; high priest. Farmer; bookkeeper. Died Dec. 30, 1910, Riverdale, Utah.

BALLANTYNE, THOMAS H. (son of Richard Ballantyne and Caroline Albertine Sanderson). Born Dec. 12, 1858, Nephi, Utah.
Married Martha Carstensen Sept. 6, 1883, Salt Lake City (daughter of Peter C. Carstensen and Karen Petersen). Their children: Thomas C.; Leroy C.; Varsell; Lucille; Juanita; Roy. Family home Ogden, Utah.
President 77th quorum seventies 16 years. Chief of police four years at Ogden; chief deputy U. S. marshal 4 years. Contractor and builder.

BALLANTYNE, JAMES EDWARD (son of Richard Ballantyne and Mary Pearce). Born Nov. 1, 1863, at Ogden, Utah.
Married Sarah H. Critchlow March 3, 1886, Logan, Utah (daughter of Benjamin C. Critchlow and Martha A. Garner of Ogden, pioneers 1851, Henry Walton company). She was born April 16, 1868. Their children: James Leodale b. Jan. 3, 1887; Benjamin Franklin b. July 23, 1888; William Edward b. April 17, 1890; Belva b. Jan. 20, 1897; Dorothy Beatrice b. June 8, 1904. Family home Ogden, Utah.
Missionary to southern states 1892; Sunday school superintendent. Deputy city assessor and collector 2 years. Engaged in real estate, insurance, loans and investments.

BALLARD, WILLIAM (son of Barnett and Mary Ballard of Berkshire, Eng.). Born 1790 in Berkshire, Eng. Came to Utah Sept. 3, 1852, first P. E. fund company conducted by A. O. Smoot.
Married Hannah Russell in England (daughter of George Russell and Hannah Higgelton of Hannington, Hantshire, Eng.). She was born April 9, 1799. Their children: Charles b. Jan. 10, 1821, m. Rebecca Hatton; George b. Dec. 26, 1823; John b. Aug. 18, 1826, m. Sarah Hawkins; Henry b. Jan. 27, 1832, m. Margaret McNeil, m. Emily McNeil. Family home Logan, Utah.
After many years of active work was ordained patriarch.

BALLARD, HENRY (son of William Ballard and Hannah Russell). Born Jan. 27, 1832, Thatcham, Berkshire, Eng. Came to Utah Oct. 16, 1852, Eli B. Kelsey company.
Married Margaret McNeil May 5, 1861 (daughter of Thomas McNeil and Janet Reid of Tranent, Scotland, pioneers 1859, Capt. Wright company). She was born April 14, 1846 Tranent, Haddingtonshire. Their children: Henry William b. Jan. 16, 1863, died; Henry William b. Sept. 20, 1864, m. Elvira Davidson Oct. 2, 1884; Thomas McNeil b. July 8, 1866, m. Phoebe Smith, April 2, 1890; Charles James and Janet M., twins, b. May 15, 1868 and George Albert N. April 9, 1870; latter three died; Melvin Joseph b. Feb. 9, 1873, m. Mattie A. Jones, June 17, 1896; Ellen Phoebe b. Sept. 19, 1875, died; Rebecca Ann b. Feb. 8, 1878, m. Louis S. Gardon June 17, 1896; Lettie May b. Dec. 13, 1881, m. George W. Squires Feb. 22, 1899; Mary Myrtle b. Aug. 21, 1885, m. D. Ray Shurtliff Sept. 3, 1908. Family home Logan, Utah.
Married Emily McNeil Oct. 4, 1867, Salt Lake City (daughter of Thomas McNeil and Janet Reid), who was born June 19, 1847, Tranent, Scotland. Their children: Emily Elizabeth b. Feb. 12, 1870, died; Willard Russell b. Nov. 26, 1872, m. Bessie Griffin June 10, 1896; Franklin Hyrum b. Nov. 28, 1874, m. Sarah Stevens Jan. 8, 1902; Ernest Reid b. Oct. 20, 1876, m. Amanda Miller June 22, 1904; Lydia Jane b. Sept. 9, 1878, m. William H. Griffin June 9, 1897; Jennie Lulu b. Nov. 4, 1880, m. Franklin T. Griffin Dec. 31, 1899; Amy Eugenie b. Jan. 13, 1885, died.
Drove herd of sheep across plains; Echo Canyon campaigner under Porter Rockwell. Hauled first load of logs for the old school house, first load of logs for the tabernacle and first load of sand for the temple at Logan, Utah. Bishop 2d ward 39 years, then ordained patriarch; missionary to England 1887-89 and presided over London conference. Died Feb. 6, 1908.

BALLARD, HENRY WILLIAM (son of Henry Ballard and Margaret McNeil). Born Sept. 20, 1864, Logan, Utah.
Married Elvira Davidson, Oct. 2, 1884, Logan, Utah (daughter of Robert Davidson and Ada Hemingway), who was born Jan. 14, 1866, Logan, Utah. Their children: Ada Elvira b. March 14, 1886, died; Henry William, Jr., b. Dec. 1, 1888, m. Almeda Roundy July 12, 1911; Margaret Elvaretta b. Dec. 28, 1891, m. Edwin Roundy Oct. 18, 1911; Melvin Joseph b. Feb. 9, 1895; Robert Leroy b. Sept. 27, 1897; Leone b. Sept. 3, 1900. Family home Logan and Benson, Utah.
Bishop Benson ward, Cache stake since 1891. Assisted his father in his varied career as pioneer.

PIONEERS AND PROMINENT MEN OF UTAH

BALLE, JENS THOMPSON (son of Thomas Balle and Mary C. Rod, both of Nibe, Denmark). Born Jan. 20, 1819, Nibe, Denmark. Came to Utah Oct. 5, 1854, Hans Peter Olsen company.
Married Ingry Christine Peterson in Denmark (daughter of Peter Peterson, of Basle, Denmark). She was born Aug. 27, 1815. Their children: Louis P., b. 1846, died; Marinus b. Feb. 22, 1848, m. Dianthy Nelson; Christian Thompson b. Nov. 22, 1849, m. Emma E. Thustrup; George P., b. Aug. 1851, m. Christine Anderson. Family resided in Ephraim and Mayfield, Utah.
High priest; bishop fourth ward, Ephraim, Utah, ten years. Died Aug. 1899.

BALLE, CHRISTIAN THOMPSON (son of Jens Thompson Balle and Ingry Christine Peterson). Born Nov. 22, 1849, Aalborg, Denmark.
Married Emma C. Thustrup June 5, 1876, Salt Lake City (daughter of Jens Christian Thustrup and Annie Marie Nielsen, pioneers Sept. 1868). She was born Sept. 15, 1854. Their children: Eugenie Maria b. April 26, 1877, m. James Holt; James Christian b. Jan. 20, 1879, m. Edith Olson; William Andrew b. April 20, 1881, died; Emma Rosalie b. March 24, 1883, m. L. D. Young; Myrtle Eulalie b. April 7, 1885, m. Bertman Behunin; Homer Leroy b. March 14, 1887, died; Evalena b. March 10, 1889, m. Earl Allbruht; Leo Royal b. Dec. 31, 1890; Pearl Ivy b. April 9, 1893; Flossie Bell b. April 14, 1895; Lillian Odessa b. Aug. 22, 1898. Family homes Mayfield and Fremont, Utah.
High priest; bishop Fremont ward, Wayne stake, Utah; elder; seventy; missionary to Denmark Sept. 1886.

BALLS, JOHN (son of William Coats and Betsy Balls, of Chediston, Eng.). Born Oct. 13, 1825, at Chediston. Came to Utah Sept. 2, 1868, Simpson M. Molen company.
Married Sarah Baxter (daughter of John Baxter and Sarah Butcher), who was born Dec. 6, 1826, and came to Utah with husband. Their children: William b. Feb. 14, 1849, m. Mary E. Metcalf Nov. 21, 1870; Mary b. Aug. 9, 1851, m. Chris Leyon, March 1869; John b. Oct. 11, 1853; Sarah b. Sept. 5, 1855, m. Elijah Seamons Feb. 11, 1872; Hannah Elizabeth b. Jan. 4, 1857, m. John Thomas Lyon; Ellen b. Nov. 3, 1859, m. James S. Hancey Oct. 9, 1879; James b. July 4, 1861, m. Lucy F. Thurston Jan. 24, 1884; Eliza b. Sept. 5, 1863, m. Lorenzo Petersen Dec. 14, 1882; Dariel b. April 12, 1865, m. Mary E. Davis; Heber b. Sept. 20, 1867, m. Tomina Nielsen Dec. 15, 1898; Jabez Henry b. Oct. 5, 1871; Charles Herbert b. Sept. 18, 1873, m. Bessie Elwood Jan. 29, 1897. Family home Hyde Park, Utah.
Married Mary Ann Hawks 1879, Salt Lake City.
High priest. Watermaster ten years; sawyer of first frame sawmill in Hyde Park; farmer and stockraiser. Died Oct. 30, 1902.

BALLS, WILLIAM (son of John Balls and Sarah Baxter). Born Feb. 16, 1849, Suffolk, Eng.
Married Mary Ellen Metcalf Nov. 21, 1872, at Hyde Park (daughter of Anthony Metcalf and Mary Reeder, pioneers Oct. 14, 1853, Cyrus H. Wheelock company). She was born March 16, 1856, Hyde Park, Utah. Their children: William Nathaniel b. April 1, 1873, and Sarah Elizabeth b. Nov. 27, 1874, both died; Mary Marietta b. April 28, 1876, m. Reuben A. Perkins Feb. 3, 1897; George David b. May 24, 1878, m. Julia Webber Dec. 19, 1900; Ida May b. May 28, 1880, m. William Hill July, 1898; Florence b. March 31, 1882, m. Riley Harris Dec. 3, 1903; John Alma b. Oct. 6, 1883, m. Ethel Woolf June 7, 1905; Wilford b. Oct. 28, 1885, m. Modda Seamons April 15, 1908; Mabel b. April 26, 1889; Clarence b. Dec. 19, 1890; Clarence b. June 22, 1892, died; Maggie b. Feb. 25, 1894; Lavaught and Levere, twins, b. Nov. 22, 1896, former died; Lyman b. Nov. 4, 1898. Family home Hyde Park, Utah.
High priest and many minor offices. Trustee Logan and Richmond Canal Co. 14 years; trustee Logan, Hyde Park and Smithfield Canal Co. five years. Farmer; stock and sheepraiser.

BALSER, JOHN (son of John Balser and Ann Barson of Liverpool, Eng.). Born July 29, 1823, in Liverpool. Came to Utah Sept. 3, 1852, Abraham O. Smoot company.
Married Emma Evans March 16, 1846, St. Louis, Mo. (daughter of John Evans and Mary Steed of Liverpool, Eng., latter a pioneer Sept. 3, 1852, Capt. A. O. Smoot company). She was born April 18, 1824. Their children: William and Annie died; Rhoda Amelia, and John Watson; Edward d. aged 8; Frederick, died; Emma, m. Frank W. Yearnce; John Lewis, m. Hattie Coon; Luella J., m. John N. Lees; Ellen G. and Mary May, died. Family home Salt Lake City, Utah.
Seventy; block and Sunday school teacher. Manufacturer of tents and awnings; carpenter. Died June 4, 1899, at Salt Lake City, Utah.

BANKS, WILLIAM F. BROOMHEAD (son of Benjamin Broomhead, born 1825, and Sarah Jarvis, born 1825, both of Birmingham, Eng.). He was born June 14, 1851, St. Louis, Mo. Came to Utah 1854.
Married Letitia A. Davis March 13, 1876 (daughter of John T. Davis and Letitia A. George), who was born Nov. 23, 1856. Their children: William G. B. b. Jan. 17, 1878, m. Nancy E. Tolman Oct. 8, 1895; Sarah Letitia b. Sept. 11, 1880, died; J. Elmer b. Sept. 8, 1882, m. E. Mae Smith June 9, 1909; Albert J. b. Dec. 12, 1884, m. Ethel L. Humphreys Oct. 10, 1906; Ben F. b. Oct. 4, 1886, m. Hilva Johnson June 24, 1908; Lureta b. Oct. 24, 1888, m. Joseph H. Tolman Jan. 15, 1908; Mary E. b. June 22, 1891, died; Eva Byrl b. April 22, 1896; Barbara P. b. Sept. 5, 1898, died; Lewis D. b. March 3, 1901. Family homes Spanish Fork and Lake Shore, Utah, and Bancroft, Idaho.
Bishop's counselor 1886-93; assistant Sunday school superintendent, Utah stake; high councilor 1898-92, Bannock stake.

BANKS, WILLIAM G. BROOMHEAD (son of William F. Broomhead Banks and Letitia A. Davis). Born Jan. 17, 1878, Spanish Fork, Utah.
Married Nancy E. Tolman Oct. 8, 1895, Pocatello, Idaho (daughter of Joseph H. Tolman and Adella Woods), who was born Oct. 14, 1878, Ophir, Utah. Their children: Jennie E. b. Oct. 24, 1896; Letitia A. B. Nov. 15, 1898; Elmer G. b. Sept. 15, 1900; William J. b. Jan. 17, 1903. Family home Bancroft, Idaho.
Elder; ward teacher.

BARBER, JOHN (son of James Barber and Louisa Weeds, of Norwich, Eng.). Born May 1821, Norwich, Eng. Came to Utah Nov. 9, 1862, William Miller company.
Married Charlotte Kirby Sept. 22, 1861 (daughter of John Kirby and Charlotte Wright), who was born Nov. 26, 1830, and came to Utah with husband. Their children: John R. b. Dec. 12, 1862, m. Emily Anderson March 28, 1887; Laura b. Feb. 21, 1865, m. Chas. A. Saury Sept. 17, 1886; Charlotte b. May 20, 1867, m. Chas. F. Lutz Sept. 22, 1898; Thomas K. b. May 14, 1890. Family home Logan, Utah.
Married Marie Peterson, July 2, 1885, Logan, Utah, who was born Sept. 24, 1818, at Trunlum, Norway. No issue.
Brickmaker and bricklayer; farmer.

BARBER, JOHN R. (son of John Barber and Charlotte Kirby). Born Dec. 12, 1862, Logan, Utah.
Married Emily Anderson March 28, 1887 (daughter of Hogan Anderson, born March 28, 1826, and Cecelia Swenson, born Feb. 23, 1841, married Nov. 2, 1863). She was born Oct. 26, 1864, Mt. Pleasant, Utah. Their children: Emil Arthur b. March 18, 1885, m. Marie Anna Ronnenkamp Oct. 4, 1911; Emily Lorinda b. Jan. 16, 1888, m. Nicholas N. Newby Oct. 4, 1907; John W. b. Sept. 21, 1889; Ida Mae b. Dec. 24, 1891; Amelia Cecelia b. July 5, 1894; Ellen Vilate b. Sept. 6, 1896; Geo. Hogan b. Oct. 21, 1898; Joseph Wilding b. March 19, 1901; Theodore b. June 19, 1903; Eva Charlotte b. Sept. 6, 1908. Family home Herbert, Idaho.
Teacher, farmer and stockraiser.

BARENTSON, ANDREW MARCUS. Born Jan. 22, 1832, in Denmark. Came to Utah 1861, oxteam company.
Married Mariah Erickson in Denmark. Their children: Susannah, m. Samuel R. Jewkes; Eliza, m. James C. Woodward. Family home Fountain Green, Utah.
Married Patria Yergersen in 1870, at Salt Lake City (daughter of Niels Yergersen of Fountain Green, Utah, came to Utah 1863). Their children: Andrew M., m. Lottie Johnson; Mariah, m. Joshua Coombs; Lena, m. Oliver Johnson; William; Matilda, m. William Sorenson. Family home Fountain Green, Utah.
High priest; counselor in bishopric of Fountain Green. Black Hawk Indian war veteran. Farmer and stockraiser.

BARKER, BYRON (son of Frderick Barker). Born at Watertown, N. Y., Nov. 16, 1842. Came to Utah Oct. 20, 1849, David Moore company.
Married Julia C. Hubbard (daughter of Charles W. Hubbard and Mary Ann Bosworth, pioneers Sept. 24, 1848, Heber C. Kimball company). She was born April 3, 1848. Their children: George b. April 26, 1869; Stella b. Oct. 17, 1870; Emma b. April 24, 1872; Mary Ann b. Oct. 25, 1873; Charles b. Oct. 23, 1875; May b. March 25, 1878; Permella b. Sept. 17, 1880; Violate b. April 30, 1883; Frederick C. b. Sept. 9, 1884; Matilda b. Dec. 30, 1885; Ethel Lvverne b. July 28, 1888; Leo C. b. Jan. 16, 1892.

BARKER. GEORGE BYRON (son of Byron Barker and Julia C. Hubbard). Born April 26, 1869.
Married Emma Stauffer. Their children: Clarence Leroy b. Aug. 12, 1890, m. Ethel Beesley; Raymond b. Jan. 16, 1910.

BARKER, CHARLES. Born March 10, 1823, Birmingham, Eng. Came to Utah Oct. 1861.
Married Fanny Kitchen (daughter of John Kitchen and Betsie Lund), who was born March 10, 1833.

BARKER, CHARLES W. (son of Charles Barker and Fanny Kitchen). Born Jan. 3, 1872, Taylorsville, Utah.
Married Lizzie Duncombe 1890, Ogden, Utah (daughter of David Duncombe and Fanny M. Haynes, pioneers). She was born Sept. 9, 1870. Their children: Frances L. b. Oct. 6, 1891; Gerald b. Jan. 12, 1894; Maude b. Dec. 18, 1896; Walter b. Aug. 30, 1898; Ida b. Feb. 20, 1901; Marie b. Oct. 10, 1904; Milton b. Feb. 2, 1909; Willard b. Dec. 20, 1912. Family home Taylorsville.

PIONEERS AND PROMINENT MEN OF UTAH 735

BARKER, GEORGE (son of William Barker, who died Dec. 15, 1829, and Jane Barker, who died Dec. 4, 1825, both of Shelfanger, Norfolk, Eng.). Born March 1793 at Shelfanger. Came to Utah Oct. 20, 1849, Allen Taylor company.
Married Charlotte Brazeworth May 13, 1813, at Shelfanger, who died July 27, 1813, aged 22 years.
Married Sarah Gerard Dec. 18, 1815, of Diss, Norfolk, who died in 1830 en voyage to America. Their children: Frederick[1] b. Nov. 24, 1816, d. March 3, 1817; Ellis[1] b. Dec. 6, 1818, d. Aug. 22, 1819; James b. June 7, 1820, m. Mary Catherine Malan June 6, 1856; Frederick[2] b. 1822, m. Jane L. Johnson 1852, who died Aug. 20, 1864; m. Mariette Wright July 10, 1865; Ellis[2] d. 1885; Simon b. Oct. 1826, m. Jemima Newey Nov. 4, 1856. Family resided at Shelfanger, Eng.; LeRayville, Jefferson county, N. Y.; Ogden, Utah.
Settled at Brown's Fort, now Ogden, Utah, Oct. 24, 1849, after having lived in every town or camp established by the migrating saints. Died Nov. 21, 1869.

BARKER, JAMES (son of George Barker and Sarah Gerard). Born June 7, 1820, Shelfanger, Norfolk, Eng. Came to Utah 1849 with father.
Married Mary Catherine Malan June 6, 1856, Ogden, Utah (daughter of John Daniel Malan, born Nov. 20, 1804, Piedmont, Italy, died May 6, 1886, Ogden, Utah, and Pauline Combe, born Aug. 6, 1805, Angrogna, Italy, died June 23, 1864, Ogden; married April 28, 1825, in Italy; pioneers to Utah in 1855). She was born July 10, 1829, at Piedmont, Italy. Their children: James John b. July 20, 1858, m. Vincy Rice Stone May 16, 1888; Sarah b. Nov. 4, 1860, m. Jefferson C. Slade 1883; George Ellis b. Nov. 13, 1865, m. Dora Brown; Elfrida Gay b. July 1, 1868, m. Julius A. Farley Nov. 11, 1886; Olla May b. Feb. 20, 1873, m. Moroni H. Thomas Aug. 15, 1906. Family home Ogden.
Was active in the pioneer work of organizing Ogden. Went to California and returned with immigrants 1850-54.

BARKER, JAMES JOHN (son of James Barker and Mary Catherine Malan). Born July 20, 1858, at Ogden.
Married Vincy Rice Stone May 16, 1888, Logan, Utah (daughter of Amos Pease Stone and Minerva Leantine Jones, pioneers). She was born Jan. 16, 1864, Ogden, Utah. Their children: Desmond James b. March 15, 1889; Amos Howard b. Dec. 9, 1891; Minerva Leantine b. July 15, 1894; Ruth Vincy b. Sept. 19, 1896, Ellis Webster b. Jan. 7, 1900; Elwood Ives b. Aug. 13, 1902; Clarence Elliott b. Jan. 3, 1905. Family home Ogden.
Missionary to Tennessee 1896-99; president 98th quorum seventies. Ogden city councilman 1910-11. Farmer, horticulturist and coal dealer.

BARKER, DESMOND JAMES (son of James John Barker and Vincy Rice Stone). Born March 15, 1889, at Ogden.
Missionary to Budapest, Hungary, 1910, where he and his associate, Samuel V. Spry, were pioneer missionaries; member Sunday school board of Ogden stake.

BARKER, SIMON (son of George Barker and Sarah Gerard). Born Oct. 1, 1826, Shelfanger, Eng. Came to Utah in 1849 with father's family.
Married Jemima Newey Nov. 4, 1855, Salt Lake City (daughter of John Newey, pioneer 1855, and Leah Welland, who had died in England). Their children: George Simon, m. Alice Whitney; Clarissa Ann, m. Walker Barlow; Frederick Ellis, m. Cecelia Sharp; Leah May, d. infant; Eveline, m. Charles Willard James. Family home Mound Fort, Ogden.
Member 98th quorum seventies; high priest. Farmer.

BARKER, GEORGE SIMON (son of Simon Barker and Jemima Newey). Born April 20, 1857, at Ogden.
Married Alice Whitney Nov. 3, 1881, Salt Lake City (daughter of William Whitney and Hannah Shingler, of Leek, Staffordshire, Eng.). She was born Dec. 18, 1854. Their children: George Simon, Jr., b. Aug. 27, 1884, m. Florence Emily Dee; Joseph Frederick b. Jan. 19, 1885, m. Rosabelle Cora Dee; Alice Maud b. June 9, 1887; Henry Claud b. Nov. 26, 1889; William Whitney b. Oct. 6, 1892. Family home Ogden.
Member 98th quorum seventies; missionary to West Virginia 1892-95; acted as clerk for the 98th quorum seventies several years. Stenographer and farmer. Died Sept. 2, 1895.

BARKER, GEORGE SIMON, JR. (son of George Simon Barker and Alice Whitney). Born Aug. 27, 1882, Ogden, Utah.
Married Florence Emily Dee Sept. 17, 1908, Salt Lake City (daughter of Thomas Duncombe Dee, of Llanelly, Caermarthenshire, South Wales, and Annie Taylor, of Lofcoegriam, Chestershire, Eng., pioneers 1860). She was born Feb. 12, 1886. Their children: Thomas George b. April 25, 1909; Richard Dee b. Jan. 22, 1912. Family home Ogden, Utah.
Member 98th quorum seventies; missionary to Australia 1901-04; president Y. M. M. I. A. at Mound Fort ward 1904-07; first counselor to Bishop Moroni S. Marriott of Ogden 10th ward. Lawyer.

BARKER, JAMES (son of Fredrick Barker and Ann Blye, both of Norfolk, Eng.). Born April 7, 1827, Diss, Norfolk. Came to Utah Oct. 20, 1849, Allen Taylor company.
Married Polly Emiline Blodgett March 7, 1851, Ogden, Utah (daughter of Newman Greenleaf Blodgett and Sally Mith Utley, pioneers 1850). She was born Dec. 1, 1832, Bath, N. H. Their children: James Hyrum b. March 9, 1852, d. Feb. 10, 1862; Mary Ann b. Dec. 24, 1853, m. William F. Garner; Fredrick G. b. Dec. 23, 1855, d. Dec. 12, 1864; Newman Henry b. Jan. 27, 1858, m. Esther Caroline Chadwick; Sarah Jane b. July 13, 1860, m. Frederick W. Ellis; Sally Ann b. April 20, 1863, m. Charles Edward Clark; Polly Emiline b. Feb. 14, 1865, m. Edward James Davis; Joseph b. Oct. 29, 1867, m. Frances Alice Chadwick; Harriet L. b. June 29, 1870, m. Samuel Shaw; Lyman b. March 15, 1872, m. Harriet Ellen Ward; Horace Alonzo b. April 1, 1875, d. April 3, 1875. Family home North Ogden, Utah.
President elders' quorum; president 76th and 38th quorums seventies; superintendent North Ogden Sunday schools; member bishopric, North Ogden; assisted in bringing immigrants to Utah in 1856.

BARKER, LYMAN (son of James Barker and Polly Emiline Blodgett). Born March 15, 1872.
Married Harriet Ellen Ward Jan. 9, 1901. Their children: Horace Lyman b. Nov. 11, 1901; Harriet Verna b. Dec. 4, 1904; Louis Ward b. Sept. 8, 1907; Mildred b. Nov. 11, 1910.

BARKER, JOHN HENRY HUMPHREY (son of John Humphrey Barker of Welton, Eng., and Annie Delnap of Dublin). Born April 1, 1842, Wandsworth, Surrey, Eng. Came to Utah Oct. 17, 1862, Henry W. Miller company.
Married Susan McDermott June 28, 1862 (daughter of William McDermott and Mary Kimber), who was born May 20, 1843. Their children: John Henry b. Nov. 2, 1863, m. Emily Parson; Annie D. b. Sept. 19, 1865, m. Nahum Curtis; William J. b. Aug. 8, 1867, m. Frances Parson; Fredrick G. b. July 23, 1869, m. Lovina Weston; Eliza G. b. Nov. 12, 1871, m. Ira Bowen; Mary D. b. Feb. 21, 1874, m. William Arnn; Lucy D. b. March 25, 1876, m. G. H. Robinson; Jennie D. b. July 14, 1878, m. William Jensen; Bessie b. March 3, 1881, m. J. H. Weston.
Married Christina M. Benson March 4, 1879, Salt Lake City (daughter of Peter Benson and Kersten Erickson, pioneers 1857). She was born Feb. 22, 1864. Their children: Myrinda b. June 8, 1880, m. John Hansen; Irvin b. July 26, 1885, m. Rena L. Richards; George b. Aug. 22, 1890, m. Estua Weston; Jessie b. Nov. 4, 1892; Susie b. Dec. 6, 1894; Maud b. Aug. 14, 1899; Naomi b. Aug. 14, 1897; Waldo b. Dec. 3, 1901.
Married Johanna Yensen April 9, 1879, Salt Lake City. She was born Dec. 12, 1844. Their children: Henry Y. b. July 8, 1851; Davis Y. b. Jan. 7, 1884. Families lived at Newton, Cache county, Utah.
School teacher 1866-67. Died Feb. 27, 1910.

BARKER, JOHN HENRY (son of John Henry Humphrey Barker and Susan McDermott). Born Nov. 2, 1863, Salt Lake City.
Married Emily Parson Sept. 21, 1887, Logan, Utah (daughter of James Parson and Mary Ann Catt), who was born April 30, 1866, in England. Their children: John Henry b. July 14, 1888; Pearl S. b. May 20, 1891; Frank Harvey b. June 9, 1893; Levon b. Sept. 1, 1896; Rhoda b. March 4, 1899; Stephen b. March 3, 1901; Grace b. May 13, 1903; James W. b. May 15, 1906. Family home Cache Junction, Utah.
Merchant. Postmaster Cache Junction 1891; deputy sheriff in Cache county, and was later elected sheriff.

BARLOW, EDWARD (son of John Barlow and Mary Ann Crompton of Unsworth, Lancashire, Eng.). Born Aug. 14, 1801, at Unsworth. Came to Utah Sept. 13, 1861, Joseph Horne company.
Married Betty Crompton, Prestwich, Eng. (daughter of William Crompton). Their children: Thomas b. June 12, 1823, m. Ann Hulme; William b. March 13, 1826, m. Ann Lees; Ann, m. Charles R. Dana; Sarah, m. Mark Eastwood. Weaver by occupation. Died Nov. 9, 1877.

BARLOW, THOMAS (son of Edward Barlow and Betty Crompton). Born June 13, 1823, Prestwich, Eng.
Married Ann Hulme Nov. 5, 1848, Oldham, Eng. (daughter of George Hulme and Ann Barlow), who was born May 3, 1826. Their children: Walker b. June 9, 1851, m. Clarissa A. Barker; Edward b. July 16, 1854, m. Lizzie Flowers; Elizabeth A. b. Oct. 31, 1856, m. Tobias Furniss; George T. b. July 6, 1858, m. Sarah Coop; Abraham b. May 23, 1861, died. Family resided in England and in Pittsburg, Pa.
Married Eliza Cato 1862 (daughter of Charles Cato and Ann Higbee), who was born Feb. 1, 1831, at Tringe, Eng. Their children: Ann Priscilla b. Oct. 16, 1863, m. John Tillotson; Sarah Emaline b. Dec. 10, 1865; Charles Cato b. Sept. 18, 1867; Joseph Cato b. May 5, 1869; Eliza Alberta b. Sept. 19, 1872, m. Leander Harris.
Weaver, building own looms and his own residences; confectioner and baker. Ward secretary and treasurer Ogden.

BARLOW, WALKER (son of Thomas Barlow and Ann Hulme). Born June 9, 1851, Blakely Lane, Lancastershire, Eng.
Married Clarissa A. Barker Nov. 18, 1876, Ogden, Utah (daughter of Simon Barker and Jemima Newey, pioneers 1849). She was born April 13, 1859. Their children: Anna J. b. Aug. 20, 1877, m. Levi J. Taylor, Jr.; Leah May b. Jan. 9, 1879, m. Christopher H. Burton; George W. b. Dec. 16, 1880; Simon b. Nov. 4, 1882; Alice b. April 20, 1885; John Fredrick b. March 31, 1889; Joseph Willard b. Sept. 9, 1891; Ezra Thomas b. June 4, 1895; Ellis Edward b. Aug. 15, 1899. Family home Ogden, Utah.
Carpenter, farmer and dairyman.

PIONEERS AND PROMINENT MEN OF UTAH

BARLOW, ISRAEL (son of Jonathan Barlow, born June 1, 1769, and Annis Gillett, born 1781, both at Granville, Hampden county, Mass.). He was born Sept. 13, 1806, at Granville. Came to Utah Sept. 23, 1848, Brigham Young company.
Married Elizabeth Haven Feb. 23, 1840 (daughter of John Haven, pioneer Sept. 23, 1848, Brigham Young company, and Elizabeth Howe). She was born Dec. 28, 1811, Holliston, Middlesex county, Mass., and died Dec. 25, 1892, Bountiful, Utah. Their children: James Nathaniel b. May 8, 1841, d. same day; Israel, Jr. b. Sept. 5, 1842, m. Annie Yeates April 26, 1863; Pamela Elizabeth b. Sept. 6, 1844, m. David W. Thompson Sept. 10, 1861; Ianthius Haven, b. May 1, 1846, m. Hannah Wintle Dec. 7, 1867; John Haven b. July 27, 1848, m. Elizabeth Cook Oct. 24, 1868; Mary A. b. Nov. 15, 1850, m. David O. Willey Dec. 7, 1868; Wilford b. Feb. 3, 1854, m. Laura Ann Jackson Jan. 24, 1876; Willard Albert b. Feb. 3, 1854, d. Oct. 28, 1854. Family home Bountiful, Utah.
Married Elizabeth Barton 1844, Nauvoo, Ill. (daughter of Nathan Barton), who was born Sept. 10, 1801, in Pennsylvania, and died Oct. 21, 1874, at Bountiful, Utah.
Married Lucy Heap Dec. 3, 1855, Salt Lake City (daughter of Thomas Heap, pioneer Oct. 24, 1855, Milo Andrus company, and Sarah Waters). She was born Sept. 24, 1836, Litchfield, Staffordshire, Eng., died July 4, 1901, Afton, Wyo. Their children: Truman Heap b. June 13, 1857, d. Feb. 19, 1913, m. Fanny Call Nov. 28, 1878, m. Sarah Call June 29, 1887; Sarah Isabelle b. June 26, 1859, m. Joseph H. Call June 26, 1879; Annis Janet b. Sept. 30, 1860, m. Chester Vinson Call Oct. 28, 1880; Emma Jane b. Aug. 19, 1862, m. Ira Call Oct. 23, 1880; Hyrum Heap b. Aug. 30, 1864, m. Margaret Burton Jan. 2, 1889; Minnie Rette b. Nov. 17, 1865, m. Chester Vinson Call Sept. 5, 1884; Granville b. July 31, 1867, m. Eliza Ann Burningham Dec. 18, 1889; Nathan b. March 26, 1869, m. Dora Matilda Tolman June 24, 1891. Family home Bountiful, Utah.
Married Cordelia Maria Dalrymple May 27, 1865, Salt Lake City (daughter of Luther Dalrymple and Sally Hammond), who was born Oct. 4, 1822, Warren county, N. Y., died March 1906, Lewiston, Utah. Family resided at Bountiful and Logan, Utah.
Seventy; president 6th quorum seventies; patriarch 1882; missionary to England 1853-55; president Birmingham conference; bodyguard to Joseph Smith; member Zion and Kirtland camps. Assisted in bringing immigrants to Utah; pioneer of Bountiful 1849. Pioneer nurseryman and apiarist; farmer and stockraiser. Died Nov. 1, 1883, Bountiful, Utah.

BARLOW, ISRAEL, JR. (son of Israel Barlow and Elizabeth Haven). Born Sept. 5, 1842, Nauvoo, Ill.
Married Annie Yeates April 26, 1863, Salt Lake City (daughter of John Yeates and Mary Ann Ledbury), who was born Aug 8, 1843, and died April 26, 1901. Their children: Israel[3] b. May 17, 1864, m. Joan V. Hjorth Sept. 21, 1892; Annie L. b. Jan. 10, 1866, m. Lamoni Call April 5, 1883; Mary Elizabeth b. Oct. 6, 1867, m. Ernest W. Smedley Nov. 28, 1888; Clara Ellen b. Oct. 10, 1869, died; Pamela b. June 9, 1872, m. James F. Jones Jan. 3, 1895; John Yeates b. March 4, 1874, m. Ida May Critchlow Dec. 16, 1897, who died July 1901, m. Susannah S. Taggart Sept. 24, 1902; Eva Antoinette b. Feb. 28, 1876, m. Charles A. Jensen Dec. 19, 1894; Edmund F. b. June 14, 1879, m. Lucy A. Garrett June 18, 1903; Alice Janet b. June 2, 1881, m. True B. Hatch March 22, 1900; Ianthius Winford b. Jan. 3, 1883, m. Chloe C. McMullin July 26, 1901; Rosa M. b. Nov. 21, 1885, m. Laurence M. Watt March 30, 1903; Jennie Hazel b. Nov. 10, 1887, d. May 12, 1891.
Missionary to Nevada 1870-79; seventy; high priest; patriarch March 19, 1900; president 70th quorum seventies; counselor to Bishop J. H. Grant. Assisted to bring immigrants to Utah. Member Utah militia. Farmer; fruitgrower and stockraiser; pioneer dry farmer.

BARLOW, ISRAEL, III (son of Israel Barlow and Annie Yeates). Born May 17, 1864, Bountiful, Utah.
Married Joan Vilate Hjorth Sept. 21, 1892 (daughter of Peter H. Hjorth, pioneer Sept. 22, 1861, Capt. Samuel A. Woolley company, and Anna Jensen, pioneer Sept. 20, 1868, Peter Nebeker company, married Dec. 7, 1868, Salt Lake City). She was born Dec. 12, 1869, Millville, Utah. Their children: Israel Owen b. Aug. 18, 1906; Newel Hjorth b. May 8, 1908. Family home Bountiful, Utah.
First counselor of 1st quorum elders Davis stake 1884-92; president 74th quorum seventies 1896-1910; assistant Sunday school superintendent of Davis stake 1897-1910; missionary to southern states 1886-88; president Mississippi conference 1887-88; missionary to bureau of information Temple Block 1906-09. School trustee and justice of peace West Bountiful 1892-96; assessor of Davis county 1896-1900. School teacher; farmer and stockraiser.

BARLOW, TRUMAN H. (son of Israel Barlow[1] and Lucy Heap). Born June 12, 1857, Bountiful, Utah.
Married Fanny Call Nov. 28, 1878 (daughter of Anson Call, born May 13, 1810, Fletcher, Franklin county, Vt., and Emma Summers, born Aug. 5, 1828, Worcestershire, Eng.). She was born Aug. 11, 1860. Their children: Truman C. b. Oct. 29, 1879, m. Nellie Rampton; Fanny Pearl b. March 18, 1883; m. Clarence Holbrook; Clarence Anson b. June 29, 1885; m. Silvia Hatch; Myron C. b. Sept. 15, 1887, m. Viola Ford; Klimber C. b. Jan. 14, 1892; Loren C. b. April 8, 1895.
Married Sarah Call June 27, 1887, Salt Lake City (daughter of Anson Call, pioneer July 24, 1847, Brigham Young company, and Emma Summers, pioneer Nov. 9, 1856, James G. Willie handcart company). She was born Dec. 8, 1870.

Their children: Israel Call b. Dec. 6, 1891; Emma b. July 7, 1895; Naomi b. May 23, 1900; Annie b. April 9, 1902; Elmer b. Nov. 15, 1904; Eva b. April 26, 1907; Joel b. March 10, 1910; Woodrow b. Sept. 27, 1912. Family home Bountiful, Utah.
Settler of Chesterfield, Idaho, 1883-92. High priest; member Bountiful bishopric 1903-09; missionary and president Indiana conference 1894. School trustee. Farmer and stockraiser. Died Feb. 19, 1913, at Salt Lake City.

BARLOW, JOHN (son of James and Ann Barlow of England). Born Aug. 3, 1838, Manchester, Eng. Came to Utah 1857, oxteam company.
Married Lunes Barlow July 26, 1875, Salt Lake City (daughter of Oswald Barlow and Mary Jane Oliver of England, pioneers 1852). She was born March 21, 1857. Their children: John b. May 6, 1876, d. Nov. 15, 1891; James Edward b. Dec. 9, 1878, m. Kate Isabel; Mary Ann b. Oct. 8, 1879, d. infant; Emma Jane b. June 17, 1881, m. John R. Jensen; Hyrum b. Jan. 18, 1883, m. Maud Miller; Ephraim b. Sept. 3, 1885; Richard Oliver b. May 11, 1887; Lunes May b. Nov. 4, 1889, m. Charles A. Hansen; Eva Belle b. Jan. 6, 1893. Family resided Cedar Valley and Richfield, Utah.
Elder; ward teacher. Early settler of Cedar Valley and Sevier county. Farmer.

BARLOW, OSWALD (son of James Barlow and Ann Crompton, born Aug. 27, 1805, both of Manchester, Eng.). He was born July 22, 1829, at Manchester. Came to Utah 1852, driving a merchant team overland.
Married Catherine Nightingale (daughter of John Nightingale and Jane Brown, the latter coming to Utah with last handcart company of 1856). She was born March 17, 1827. Came to Utah Oct. 9, 1853, Appleton Harmon company. Their children: James b. Oct. 22, 1849, m. Anne C. S. Carlson Oct. 13, 1878; Oswald F. b. Aug. 11, 1854, m. Dorothy Heath 1877; Willard b. June 12, 1862, m. Elizabeth Luke 1888; Joseph b. 1865, m. Adelaide Angel 1889 (both dead); Heber F. b. 1867, died. Family home Salt Lake City, Utah.
Married Mary Jane Oliver (daughter of William Oliver), who was born 1831. Their children: William H. b. Aug. 6, 1855; Lunes b. March 21, 1857, m. John Barlow Jan. 26, 1875; David H. b. 1860; Albert George b. July 4, 1862; Heber Franklin b. Sept. 6, 1866 (all deceased); Arthur b. Aug. 6, 1871, m. Clara Woodbury.
Settled at St. George, Utah. Mason by occupation.

BARLOW, JAMES (son of Oswald Barlow and Catherine Nightingale). Born Oct. 22, 1849, Manchester, Eng.
Married Anne C. S. Carlson Feb. 13, 1878, St. George, Utah (daughter of Andreas Carlson and Anne Marie Nielsen). She was born July 18, 1860, Asverga, Denmark. Their children: James Oswald b. Jan. 25, 1881; Andrew b. May 21, 1883; Leo Nightingale b. July 6, 1884; Walter Edwin b. April 11, 1886; Heber Chase b. Nov. 10, 1888; Ray b. March 15, 1904; all children now dead. Family home Richfield, Utah.
Farmer and stockraiser.

BARNARD, JAMES S. (parents lived at Clackmannan, Scotland). Born May 15, 1818, Black Row, Clackmannan, Scotland. Came to Utah 1853, David Wilkins company.
Married Jennette Snedden at Airdrie, Lanarkshire, Scotland (daughter of J. Snedden). Their children: Andrew S.; Jennette S. m. John S. Gibson; John S., m. Belle Forsythe; Johan S., m. William Gibson; James S.; Joseph S.; Elizabeth J., d. aged 2; Laura S., Isabelle S., Ellen S., all died except Johan S. Family home Salt Lake City, Utah.
Mining operator. Died in 1856.

BARNES, ALBERT RAYMOND (son of Dr. Francis Barnes, born Oct. 22, 1835, Vergennes, Vt., and Lucinda Raymond, born April 19, 1835, Waverly, N. Y., married 1861). He was born March 18, 1867, Attica, Ind. Came to Utah Nov. 1899.
Married Josephine C. Naisbitt June 22, 1907 (daughter of Henry W. Naisbitt and Elizabeth Irvine, married 1856, Salt Lake City; former a pioneer 1854, the latter 1855). She was born Aug. 4, 1878. Only child: Francis Raymond b. Sept. 26, 1910. Family home Salt Lake City.
Deputy attorney general 1908-09; attorney general 1909-13. Graduated from Ann Arbor law school June 1899.

BARNES, MARK (son of John Barnes and Hannah Woodward of England). Born March 6, 1809, Manchester, Eng. Came to Utah July, 1862.
Married Ann Armstrong in 1831, Edinburgh, Scotland (daughter of Joseph and Elspeth Armstrong of Ireland). She was born Dec. 2, 1811. Their children: Joseph b. Oct. 1, 1833, m. Mary Craig; Mark b. June 1836; Martha b. Dec. 29, 1835, m. William Dyet. Family home Salt Lake City.
Married Maria Bidgood 1890, Salt Lake City (daughter of Abraham Bidgood and Agnes Gillard of England, pioneers Aug. 19, 1868, John R. Murdock company). She was born Feb. 15, 1832.
Missionary to Jersey Islands, England and Scotland 1858; superintendent 11th ward Sunday school 1875. Farmer and expert gardener. Died Aug. 30, 1890.

PIONEERS AND PROMINENT MEN OF UTAH

BARNES, JOSEPH (son of Mark Barnes and Ann Armstrong). Born Oct. 1, 1833, at Kelso, Roxburghshire, Scotland.
Married Mary Craig Oct. 31, 1851, in Scotland (daughter of John Craig and Unity McCune, who came to Utah in 1892). She was born April 8, 1835. Their children: Unity b. Dec. 30, 1853, m. James Brown; Mark b. 1855; Hyrum b. Nov. 11, 1861; Ruth, m. Mr. Ellison; Joseph b. Jan. 26, 1859, m. Rose McDade; Martha b. Oct. 12, 1861, m. Peter Bird; Mary b. June 1868, m. Robert Colman; Elspeth b. July 1874, m. Daniel Kelly. Family home Salt Lake City.
High priest. Died July 12, 1905.

BARNES, WILLIAM (son of Thomas Barnes and Nancy Boardman of Bolton, Lancashire, Eng.). Born June 22, 1853, at Bolton. Came to Utah Sept. 29, 1866, Daniel Thompson company.
Married Margaret Ellen Clegg Dec. 28, 1873, at Heber City, Utah (daughter of Jonathan Clegg and Ellen Wombsley of Heber City, pioneers Nov. 30, 1856, Edward Martin "frozen" handcart company). She was born Nov. 21, 1855. Their children: William Henry, m. Eliza Jordon; Robert b. Sept. 11, 1875, killed at the age of 19; Nancy Ellen b. Nov. 18, 1877, m. William Thompson; Sarah Alice b. Nov. 27, 1879, m. Urich Stribble; Margaret b. 1881, m. Charles Ludlow; Elizabeth b. Oct. 20, 1883, m. George Burt; Sylvia b. Feb. 22, 1885, m. John Owens; Rosella b. Sept. 16, 1887, m. John Phipps; Lenvra b. June 14, 1889, m. William H. Park; Jonathan b. Feb. 26, 1819, drowned at the age of 14; Lillie b. Nov. 22, 1892, m. Frank Phipps; Richard T. b. Aug. 8, 1894; Earl b. July 1, 1896; Charles Brigham b. July 1, 1899.
Elder. Located at Heber City 1866. Coal miner; farmer; quarryman.

BARNETT, GEORGE (son of James Barnett and Ann Berrett of Steeple Ashton, Wiltshire, Eng.). Born May 27, 1828, at Steeple Ashton. Came to Utah Nov. 2, 1864, Warren S. Snow train with part of John M. Kay's party of English immigrants.
Married Mary Ann Mathews at Steeple Ashton (daughter of Robert Mathews of above place, pioneers with George Halliday company). Their children: Lorenzo Alma, m. Mary Wade; Rosena S. E., d. March 3, 1852; Georgena, m. James Roylance; Clara Virtue, m. Joseph Orton; Agnes Sarah A., d. Aug. 6, 1864. Family home Pleasant View, Utah.
Presided over a branch of the church at Steeple Ashton, Eng. 1861-64; elder. Died at Pleasant View, Utah.

BARNEY, CHARLES. Came to Utah Sept. 9, 1852, Bryant Jolley company.
Married Mercy Yeoman. Their children: Luther; Lewis b. 1808, m. Elizabeth Turner; Lucian; Henry; Walter b. 1819, m. Caroline Haws; John; Melinda.
Married Deborah Street. Their children: Emerine m. Benjamin Leland; Betsy, m. Benjamin Leland; Benjamin T., m. Caroline Beard-Tippets; Margaret, m. Joseph Gilbert; Thomas Jefferson, m. Lucinda Box; William, m. Hannah Stoddard; Sarah Jane, m. Joseph S. Black. Family home Spring City, Utah.
First settler at Spanish Fork, where he died Feb. 28, 1866.

BARNEY, LEWIS (son of Charles Barney and Mercy Yeoman). Born Sept. 18, 1808.
Married Elizabeth Turner (daughter of Walter and Lydia Turner), who was born June 8, 1808. Their children: Walter b. 1836, m. Matilda Farr; Sarah, d. infant; James Henry b. Jan. 30, 1840, m. Emily Tolton March 4, 1866; Alma, died; Joseph S. b. 1846, m. Ormanda Oviatt; Orson b. 1852, died. Family resided at Spanish Fork, Spring City and Circle Valley, Utah.
Married Elizabeth Beard in 1852 at Salt Lake City, who came to Utah 1852. Their children: Arthur, m. Miss Strong; Margaret, d. child; Martha, m. Charles Robinson; m. Thomas Briscoe; David; William, d. child; Emeline, m. Albert Thompson. Family home Monroe, Utah.
Hunter in first pioneer company to cross plains; Indian war veteran. Seventy. Died in Colorado.

BARNEY, JAMES HENRY (son of Lewis Barney and Elizabeth Turner). Born Jan. 30, 1840.
Married Emily Tolton (daughter of Edward Tolton and Mary Ann Tomlinson), who was born Nov. 9, 1848, St. Louis, Mo. Their children: Mary Elizabeth b. Oct. 13, 1867, m. John Rogers; Lewis Edward b. Feb. 1, 1869, m. Etta Watts; Margaret b. July 29, 1870, m. Chris Erickson; Henry Victor, m. Margaret Charlesworth; Lydia Ann, m. Alfred Black; Clara Edith, m. Alonzo George; Frank Eugene b. Sept. 6, 1878, m. Mary Rappleye; Frances Emmeline, m. Frank Westbrook; Esther Adeline, m. George Schuyler; Nellie May, m. Will Cushing; Carrie, m. Sterling Hardy; Jennie; Archie. Family resided Spanish Fork, Circle Valley and Kanosh, Utah.
Constable at Circle Valley. Assisted in bringing immigrants to Utah with Abner Lowry Oct. 22, 1866. High priest; president of elders' quorum 12 years.

47

BARNEY, JOSEPH S. (son of Lewis Barney and Elizabeth Turner. Born Dec. 22, 1845, Nauvoo, Ill.
Married Ormanda Oviatt Nov. 4, 1866, Ephraim. Utah (daughter of Henry H. Oviatt and Sally Ray Whitlock of Spring City, Utah, pioneers Sept. 9, 1852, Bryant Jolley company). She was born Oct. 28, 1849. Their children: Elzada b. June 24, 1868, m. Albert Hall; Joseph Orson b. Feb. 19, 1870, m. Elizabeth Prowse; Henry Orville b. June 17, 1872, m. Elnora Prowse; Lawrence b. April 7, 1874, m. Lavina Esther Beal; Clarence Adelbert b. March 23, 1877. m. Elizabeth Anderson; Walter Lewellyn b. April 11, 1879, m. Mary Elizabeth Millgate; Florence Elenor b. Dec. 7, 1881, m. William Johnson; Arnold Earl b. Feb. 12, 1886, m. Esther Allen; Ray b. Aug. 29, 1888, died. Family home Kanosh, Utah.
Indian fighter and war veteran; pony express and mail carrier in Circle Valley, from whence the family was finally driven by Indians in the early days; went to Beaver, where he assisted in repressing many Indian raids. High priest. Constable Kanosh 12 years. Ranchman and farmer.

BARNEY, JOSEPH ORSON (son of Joseph S. Barney and Ormanda Oviatt). Born Feb. 19, 1870, Kanosh, Utah.
Married Elizabeth Jane Prowse Dec. 28, 1894, Chihuahua, Old Mexico (daughter of William Prowse and Louisa Malinda James of Deseret, Utah, and Mexico, pioneers 1849, contingent Mormon battalion). She was born June 17, 1877. Their children: Elzada b. April 28, 1896; Ardith b. Nov. 10, 1898; Wanda b. June 5, 1907. Family resided Mesa, Ariz. and Kanosh, Utah.
High priest. Road supervisor. Assistant Sunday school superintendent; first counselor to Bishop Hitchcock, Clawson, Utah. Farmer.

BARNEY, LAWRENCE (son of Joseph S. Barney and Ormanda Oviatt). He was born April 7, 1874, Kanosh, Utah.
Married Lavina Esther Beal July 21, 1909, Manti, Utah (daughter of Newell Knight Beal and Ada Elvira DeMill). She was born Oct. 8, 1888. Their children: Veda Ray b. June 6, 1910; Marven Lawrence b. May 8, 1912. Family home Ferron, Utah.
Member 149th quorum seventies; missionary to northern states April 17, 1907, to May 21, 1909; president Y. M. M. I. A.; first counselor to stake presidency of Y. M. M. I. A.; ward teacher. Farmer and stockraiser.

BARNEY, WALTER (son of Charles Barney and Mercy Yeoman). Born Jan. 7, 1819, Ohio. Came to Utah 1847, Co. C, Mormon Battalion.
Married Caroline Haws 1849 (daughter of Gilberth Haws, pioneer Sept. 23, 1848, and Hannah Whitcomb). She was born Jan. 27, 1825. Only child: Walter, m. Ann Allred. Family home Provo, Utah.
Married Susan Zabriskie at Provo, Utah (daughter of Henry Zabriskie). Their children: John H. b. March 20, 1859, m. Ellen Jane Siddall; Polly Ann, m. Benjamin Hoops, Charles, m. Lottie La Moyne; William, died; Jane, m. Martin Allred; Minerva, m. Alexander Beckstead. Family resided Ephraim, Mt. Pleasant, Spanish Fork, Fountain Green and Monroe, Utah.
High priest. Pioneer in San Pete and Sevier counties; Indian war veteran.

BARNEY, JOHN HENRY (son of Walter Barney and Susan Zabriskie). Born March 20, 1859, Ephraim, Utah.
Married Ellen Jane Siddall Nov. 14, 1886, Monroe, Utah (daughter of Henry Siddall of England, who came to Utah 1872). She was born Aug. 18, 1868, and died Oct. 2, 1902. Their children: Mary b. Nov. 26, 1887, m. John Richey; Orvin b. Nov. 24, 1889, died; Roy b. May 1, 1895; Byron b. March 25, 1897; Gilbert b. March 27, 1899; Glen b. Dec. 3, 1901, died. Family home Monroe, Utah.
Married Elmina Anderson Sept. 5, 1903, Richfield, Utah (daughter of Christian Anderson and Maria Jensen of Denmark), who was born Jan. 3, 1880. Their children: Clarence b. May 25, 1904; Annie b. March 16, 1906; Zelma b. Nov. 2, 1907; Elva b. Dec. 3, 1909; Eldon J. b. Oct. 20, 1911. Family home Monroe, Utah.
Farmer and stockraiser.

BARNEY, BENJAMIN F. (son of Charles Barney and Deborah [Riffle] Street). Born March 12, 1832, Springfield, Ill. Came to Utah 1852.
Married Caroline Beard-Tippets April 27, 1849, Springfield, Ill. Their children: Benjamin Kimball b. Feb. 12, 1850, and Laura Alice b. Feb. 14, 1852, both died; William Franklin b. Sept. 3, 1856, m. Lovisa Losy; Erastus James b. Oct. 29, 1858, m. Mary Aikens; Wilbur Joseph b. Oct. 19, 1860, died; Charles b. July 14, 1861; Francis Marion b. Sept. 12, 1863, m. Rhoda Shepherd; Alma b. April 6, 1865, m. Annie Davis; Ephraim b. Jan. 30, 1868. Family home Spanish Fork, Utah.
Married Priscilla Shepherd April 8, 1855, Salt Lake City (daughter of Moses and Eliza Shepherd). Their children: Priscilla b. April 3, 1859, m. Carlos L. Hutchings; Benjamin F. b. May 23, 1861, died; Thomas J. b. Feb. 11, 1863, m. Ellen Olive Higgins; m. Mary Anderson; m. Hannah Green; Eldora b. Sept. 23, 1865, m. John Carter; Joseph b. July 13, 1869, m. Etta Higgins; George W. b. April 8, 1870, m. Mahala Yer-Pearson; Evaline b. March 7, 1878, m. Morris Peterson; Ammor b. Nov. 15, 1881, died; Arletta b. Feb. 2, 1882, m. Walter Jensen; Joshua b. Jan. 6, 1884, m. Della Roberts; Moses S.

b. Dec. 19, 1887. Family resided Spanish Fork and Elsinore, Utah.
Married Caroline Nielsen Dec. 7, 1865, Salt Lake City (daughter of James and Boel Nielsen of Denmark). She was born May 28, 1844, Roskilde, Denmark, and came to Utah 1862. Their children; Nancy b. Dec. 4, 1866, d. Dec. 16, 1867; David b. July 13, 1868, m. Hannah Yergensen; Nephi b. Jan. 28, 1870, d. May 12, 1890; Sarah Jane b. March 6, 1872, m. James W. Anderton; Stella b. Oct. 8, 1874, m. John Anderton; Don Carlos Smith b. Sept. 23, 1877, m. Sarah Elenor Roberts; Moroni b. Feb. 11, 1880, m. Elsie Serena King; Elias b. June 19, 1882, m. Mary Jane Greene; Edgar b. April 14, 1884, m. Lillie Huntsman; Lucian b. March 3, 1887, m. Evaline Levi. Resided at Spanish Fork and Elsinore, Utah.
High priest. Indian war veteran. Farmer, fruitgrower and stockraiser. Died Dec. 7, 1904, at Elsinore.

BARNHURST, SAMUEL (son of Joseph Barnhurst and Priscilla Underhill of England). Born Aug. 24, 1827. Came to Utah Aug. 7, 1857, with company bringing Apostles John Taylor and Erastus Snow and other returning missionaries.
Married Anna Marie Jensen Oct. 1857 (daughter of Jens Christian Peterson and Sophia Christensen), who was born Sept. 23, 1833, Denmark and came to Utah Sept. 13, 1857, Christian Christiansen handcart company, traveling part of time with Johnston's invading army. Their children: Anna Mary b. Nov. 18, 1858, m. John Z. Alger April 6, 1877; Mary Anna b. Nov. 18, 1858, m. Niels Ivor P. Clove; Samuel James b. Nov. 1860, m. Laura Ann Hatch Jan. 21, 1886; Priscilla Sophia b. May 6, 1863, m. William R. Riggs Jan. 17, 1886; Jens Christensen b. Aug. 18, 1865, m. Hulda E. Sandin; Julia Anna Marie b. April 15, ——, m. A. W. Huntington; Joseph Erastus b. May 8, ——, m. Lillie Dale Adams.

BARNHURST, SAMUEL JAMES (son of Samuel Barnhurst and Anna Marie Jensen). Born November, 1860.
Married Laura A. Hatch Jan. 21, 1886, St. George, Utah (daughter of Meitliah Hatch of Company C, Mormon Battalion, and Permelia Snider, pioneer Oct. 10, 1849). She was born Sept. 23, 1870. Their children: Samuel H. b. March 5, 1887, m. Ada Workman June 25, 1906; Meltire Hatch b. Feb. 24, 1893; Joseph Hatch b. May 19, 1895; Orson Hatch b. Oct. 1, 1897; Ira Hatch b. Aug. 1, 1903; Laura b. May 16, 1906. Family home Hatch, Garfield county, Utah.
High priest; bishop's counselor 1900-06; superintendent Sunday school 1906-09; first counselor Y. M. M. I. A. 1895-96.

BARRACLOUGH, JOHN (son of John Barraclough and Harriet Jowett). Born July 28, 1854, Bradford, Yorkshire, Eng. Came to Utah Oct. 16, 1869, Joseph Rawson company.
Married Mary Josephine Fish Oct. 9, 1875 (daughter of Joseph Fish and Mary Steele, married March 22, 1859). She was born March 11, 1860. Their children: Harriet May b. Aug. 28, 1886; Ambrose Fish b. Sept. 14, 1889, m. Nancy Griffth April 6, 1910; Edmund Steele b. Feb. 8, 1892. Family home Beaver, Beaver county, Utah.
Deputy clerk second district court twenty-five years.

BARRETT, CLARENCE (son of Michael Barrett and Ellen M. McCallum of Toronto, Canada). Born Feb. 11, 1843.
Married Georgianna Pacific Robbins April 18, 1870, Salt Lake City (daughter of John Rogers Robbins and Phoebe A. Wright, who was born on S. S. Brooklyn, Pacific ocean, on way to California June 16, 1846. Their children: Ellen L. b. Jan. 14, 1871, m. Caleb E. Summerhays; John R. b. Dec. 19, 1872, d. infant; Isabel b. Dec. 6, 1874, m. Joseph P. White; Daisy b. April 21, 1877, d. infant. Family home Salt Lake City, Utah.

BARRUS, EMERY (son of Benjamin Barrus, born April 4, 1784, Richmond, N. H. died 1864, Chautauqua, N. Y., and Betsy Stebbins, born March 21, 1871 in Massachusetts, died July 20, 1828, in New York). He was born April 8, 1809, Chautauqua county, N. Y. Came to Utah Oct. 9, 1853, Appleton Harmon company.
Married Huldah Abigail Nickerson (daughter of Freeman Nickerson, born Feb. 19, 1779, Dennis, Mass., and died Jan. 22, 1847, Chariton Point, Iowa, while on the way to Utah, and Huldah Chapman, born 1780 in Connecticut, came to Utah, 1850, died 1860, Provo, Utah). She was born April 15, 1816, in Pennsylvania. Their children: Lydia b. Oct. 22, 1834, m. Festus Sprague April 1, 1857; Betsy N. b. March 28, 1836, d. Jon. 12, 1839; Benjamin Franklin b. May 30, 1838, m. Lovina Ann Steele Sept. 29, 1861; Emery Freeman b. March 13, 1841, died; Mary Huldah b. April 8, 1843, m. Charles Lailey; Orrin Elezer b. Sept. 14, 1845, m. Catherine Wilson; Emery Alexander b. March 27, 1848, d. Nov. 16, 1858; Ruel Michael b. Nov. 14, 1850, m. Ida Pearl Hunter; Owen Henry b. Dec. 28, 1853, m. Olive Deseret McBride Feb. 18, 1877, m. Mary Ann Hunter Dec. 21, 1892; Sarah Abigail b. April 9, 1856, m. Eleazer Freeman Nickerson; John Nickerson b. June 1, 1858, m. Alice Burton; Eliza Alvira b. Sept. 15, 1860, m. Charles Post.
Married Jane Zerildah Baker (daughter of Benjamin Baker, pioner 1857). She was born Nov. 3, 1841. Their children: Emeline Abigail b. Nov. 30, 1859, m. Henry Tanner; James Baker b. Aug. 7, 1862, m. Charlotte Ann Mathews; William Taylor b. June 1, 1864, m. Matilda McBride; Thomas b. July 20, 1866, and Freeman b. Oct. 12, 1869, died; Chauncey Baker b. Jan. 15, 1872; Catherine Rozena b. Feb. 24, 1877, m. Henry Watson. Family home Grantsville, Utah.
High priest; patriarch. Carpenter; stockraiser; farmer. Seventy. Died Oct. 5, 1899.

BARRUS, BENJAMIN FRANKLIN (son of Emery Barrus and Huldah Abigail Nickerson). Born May 30, 1838, in Cattaraugus county, N. Y. Came to Utah 1853, driving a herd of cattle across the plains.
Married Lovina Ann Steele Sept. 29, 1861 (daughter of Samuel Steele, born July 15, 1822, Plattsburg, Clinton county, N. Y., pioneer 1851, Joshua Grant company, and Elvira Salome Thayer, born Sept. 15, 1826, in New York). She was born Sept. 29, 1844, in Illinois. Their children: Benjamin Franklin b. Aug. 23, 1862, died; Emery Freeman b. Sept. 30, 1865, m. Martha Tolman Sept. 22, 1888; Samuel Leonard b. Jan. 14, 1868, died; Orrin Orland b. May 29, 1870, m. Mary Clark Feb. 4, 1897; Lovina Angelia b. Dec. 30, 1872, m. Ulysses Cline July 26, 1893; Albert Almond b. June 1, 1875, m. Margaret Alice Millward March 4, 1896; Mary Luella b. Nov. 25, 1877, m. George E. Millward March 4, 1896; Aldo Benoni b. Nov. 15, 1879, m. Mabel Robinson Jan. 8, 1902; Elvira Chloena b. Dec. 9, 1881, died; Sylvia Ellen b. Jan. 17, 1886, died; Calvin Cleone b. Oct. 24, 1887, d. Jan. 13, 1891.

BARRUS, RUEL (son of Benjamin Barrus and Betsy Stebbins). Born Aug. 11, 1821, at Villanova, Chautauqua county, N. Y. Came to Utah Oct. 15, 1854, with others of Mormon Battalion.
Married Ellen Martin Aug. 10, 1859 (daughter of Samuel Martin, pioneer Sept. 25, 1855, Richard Ballantyne company, and Priscilla Layton, who died in St. Louis). She was born Sept. 23, 1844. Their children: Ellen P. b. Feb. 12, 1861, m. Charles Schaeffer; Betsy A. b. Nov. 11, 1862; Zeitha A. b. March 28, 1864; Fannie I. b. June 11, 1866, m. William Sanford; Lona b. Aug. 12, 1870, m. Charles Nelson; Ruel M. b. March 14, 1873, m. Angeline Anderson; Darias M. b. April 20, 1876, m. Lizzie Ratcliffe; Royal L. b. June 27, 1879; Essie Glee b. March 13, 1885.
Seventy; second lieutenant Company B, Mormon Battalion; major in Echo Canyon campaign.

BARTCH, GEORGE W. (son of John G. Bartch and Mary Magdelene Steiner of Dushore, Pa.). Born March 15, 1849, Dushore, Pa. Came to Utah March, 1888.
Married Amanda Alice Guild Feb. 16, 1871, Bloomsburg, Pa. daughter of Aaron D. and Sarah A. Guild. of Bloomsburg). She was born April 23, 1847. Their children: Minnie Alice, m. W. H. Child; Rae, m. J. A. Lloyd; Olive Amanda, m. Dwight M. Guillotte. Family home Salt Lake City.
Received the academic degree of M. S. 1871; superintendent public schools at Shenandoah, Pa., 1874-84; practiced law at Bloomsburg, Pa., 1884-86, at Canon City, Colo. 1886-88, and at Salt Lake City 1888-89; probate judge of Salt Lake county 1889-93; associate justice supreme court of Utah territory 1893-95; of state supreme court 1895-1906 chief justice 1899-1900 and 1905-06; resigned Oct. 1, 1906, to resume practice of law at Salt Lake City.

BARTHOLOMEW, DAVIS (son of Joseph Bartholomew, born Dec. 9, 1780, and Elizabeth Jones, both of Tredyffrin, Chester county, Pa.). He was born July 15, 1812, East Whiteland, Chester county, Pa. Came to Utah November, 1852, Warren Snow company.
Married Ruth I. Jones March 27, 1851 (daughter of Merlin Jones and Roxanna Ives, pioneers 1852, Warren Snow company). She was born Nov. 19, 1825. Their children: Henry b. May 9, 1852, m. Clara M. Tuttle; Davis S. b. April 30, 1854, d. Feb. 14, 1884; Josephine b. Aug. 1, 1856, d. Aug. 5, 1857; Merlin J. b. Jan. 17, 1858, m. Mary A. Green Sept. 2, 1891; Serena b. Aug. 5, 1860, m. George W. Stanger; Hannah b. Dec. 22, 1862, d. Jan. 18, 1883; Charlotte B. April 30, 1844, m. George Green Dec. 16, 1891; John E. b. Aug. 20, 1866, d. Oct. 9, 1866; Elizabeth b. Sept. 15, 1867, d. Dec. 7, 1867; Mary A. b. March 31, 1869, m. William H. Green Dec. 16, 1891. Family home Slaterville, Weber county, Utah.

BARTHOLOMEW, HENRY (son of Davis Bartholomew and Ruth I. Jones). Born May 9, 1852, Council Bluffs, Iowa.
Married Clara M. Tuttle Nov. 5, 1902, Salt Lake City (daughter of Newton Tuttle, pioneer 1854, and Emily A. Tuttle, pioneer 1850). She was born Feb. 12, 1865, Bountiful, Utah. Only child: Davis b. June 16, 1905.

BARTHOLOMEW, MERLIN J. (son of Davis Bartholomew and Ruth I. Jones). Born Jan. 17, 1858, Slaterville, Utah.
Married Mary A. Green Sept. 2, 1891, Logan, Utah (daughter of Ammon Green and Almira Mesick, pioneers 1848). She was born March 13, 1871. Their children: Merlin D. b. Oct. 6, 1893, d. Aug. 30, 1894; Almira Ethel b. March 8, 1898; Henry G. b. June 2, 1902; Emily I. b. March 28, 1904; Ella R. b. June 25, 1909.
Missionary to North Carolina 1891 and to Missouri 1906. Farmer.

BARTHOLOMEW, JOSEPH (son of John Bartholomew and Nancy McNant). Born Jan. 16, 1820, at Charleston, Clarke county, Ind. Came to Utah Sept. 14, 1852, Claudius V. Spencer company.
Married Polly Benson Dec. 10, 1843 (daughter of Benja-

min Benson and Kesiah Messinger). She was born Feb. 12, 1816, in New York. Their children: Joseph S. and Hyrum, twins, Aug. 30, 1844, both died; John b. Sept. 11, 1845, m. Eliza R. Metcalf Oct. 11, 1868; Mary Kesiah b. April 29, 1847, m. John E. Metcalf; Joseph b. Jan. 5, 1850, m. Emma Mellor; George Marston, b. Nov. 5, 1851, m. Selina Roper; Elizabeth Almera b. July 25, 1854, m. William Brown; Eliza Elvira b. July 25, 1854, m. James Mellor; William Orange b. Sept. 6, 1856, d. Oct. 24, 1874; James Orson b. Dec. 29, 1858.
Married Electa Benson.
Settled at Springville, Utah; moved to Gunnison, San Pete county, Utah. Veteran of Black Hawk war, Salina canyon and Grass creek Indian engagements.

BARTHOLOMEW, JOHN (son of Joseph Bartholomew and Polly Benson). Born Sept. 11, 1845, Mackinaw, McLean county, Ill. Came to Utah 1852 with parents.
Married Eliza Roxey Metcalf Oct. 11, 1868, Salt Lake City (daughter of England Metcalf and Mary Wasiin, pioneers Sept. 14, 1853, Claudius V. Spencer company). Their children: John Edward b. Nov. 6, 1869, m. Rose H. Breathuarte; Roxey Ellen b. March 30, 1872, m. Joseph Christenson; William b. Jan. 24, 1874, d. Oct. 23, 1878; Sarah Jane b. Sept. 8, 1876, m. A. B. Christenson; Alma b. Oct. 10, 1878, m. Elsie Christenson; Joseph Smith b. Sept. 20, 1880, m. Emma James; Julia b. Nov. 6, 1882, m. Otis V. Ercanbrach; Mary Elizabeth b. June 24, 1885, m. Charles Stewart; Rose b. March 3, 1889, m. T. W. Peterson; Alice b. Aug. 9, 1889, died; Henry Lee b. Oct. 1, 1891.
Bishop Fayette ward 1877-1912. Road supervisor; school trustee. Was a member of one of the constitutional commissions which met to frame the Utah state constitution. Indian war veteran.

BARTLETT, CHARLES CLAYMORE (son of Henry Bartlett and Selucia Davis of Geauga county, Ohio). Born Dec. 26, 1848, in Newberry township, Geauga county Ohio. Came to Utah Oct. 10, 1866, mule train company.
Married Anna Katrina Jensen Sept. 12, 1868, Salt Lake City, Utah (daughter of Jens Christian Jensen and Anna Larsen, of Hjorring amt, Denmark). She was born Nov. 9, 1844, at Mosbjerg, Denmark, and came to Utah Oct. 17, 1866. Their children: Charles Bart b. Aug. 27, 1869, m. Clara Louisa Alice Watt; George Henry b. July 8, 1871, m. Clara Louisa Bingham; Selucia Annie b. Sept. 11, 1873, d. aged 7; Nellie Leonora b. Nov. 3, 1875, m. John Merkley; Randolph b. Feb. 11, 1878, d. aged 3; Ashley b. April 19, 1880, m. Winnie Lydia Billings; Marcus b. Nov. 6, 1883, d. aged 9 mos.; May b. Feb. 11, 1885, m. William Sidney Henderson; Sarah b. Jan. 5, 1887, m. Frederick G. Bingham; Rosa b. Oct. 13, 1889. Family home Vernal, Utah.
High priest; missionary; counselor to Bishop George Freestone about 12 years; acting bishop, Vernal ward, 1894-96; Sunday school superintendent; state clerk 1893-9; counselor in the elders' quorum a number of years; acting teacher 15 years. Pioneer of Vernal. First coun'y clerk, Uinta county, 1880; county superintendent of schools 1882; school trustee for a number of years; school teacher. Superintended the construction of first ward meeting house at Vernal. Farmer; horticulturist; apiarist.

BARTLETT, CHARLES BART (son of Charles Claymore Bartlett and Anna Katrina Jensen). Born Aug. 27, 1869, Mountain Dell, Utah.
Married Margaret Alice Watt Oct. 26, 1899, Salt Lake City (daughter of George D. Watt, Jr. and Elizabeth Micklejohn, of Butte, Mont.), who was born Aug. 28, 1867. Their children: Charles Bart b. July 25, 1900; George Watt b. Nov. 3, 1901. Family home Whiterock, Uinta county, Utah.
Member 97th quorum seventy; missionary to New Zealand, 1892-96 and 1902-05; was president of mission; Sunday school superintendent, Vernal 1905-07; president Vernal quorum of seventy; bishop Vernal ward. Pioneer in the bee industry in Utah; assisted in instituting agricultural college in New Zealand.

BARTON, JOHN (son of William Barton and Elizabeth Winstanley of Winstanley, Lancashire, Eng.). Born Feb. 23, 1806, Winstanley, Eng. Came to Utah Oct. 5, 1862, Ansel P. Harmon company.
Married Elizabeth Bell Sept. 6, 1835, Halzchchurch, near Wigan, Lancashire, Eng. (daughter of William Bell and Margaret Martlew), who was born Dec. 21, 1814. Their children: William Bell, m. Ellen Birchall; James, m. Eliza Barton (William Bell and James were twins); Elizabeth, died; John, m. Sarah Flint; Isaac, m. Agnes E. Parr; Peter, m. Ellen Beazer; Joseph. m. Mary A. Allen; Hyrum, m. Georgeana Crabbe; Bertha, m. William Irvine. Family home, Salt Lake City, Utah.
High priest. Mechanical engineer; farmer. Died Aug. 26, 1874.

BARTON, WILLIAM B. (son of John Barton and Elizabeth Bell). Born July 21, 1836, Wigan, Eng. Came to Utah Sept. 2, 1860, J. D. Ross company.
Married Ellen Birchall March 13, 1860, St. Helens, Lancashire, Eng. (daughter of William Birchall and Esther Middlehurst of St. Helens). She was born March 24, 1836. Their children: William John b. Jan. 2, 1861, m. Uphemia Meredith; Frederick B. b. April 14, 1863, m. Louisa Stenhouse; Frank b. Feb. 2, 1865, m. Rachael Mansell; Eva b. March 18, 1867; Bell b. Dec. 9, 1868; Brigham b. June 21, 1871, m. Jennette James; Faith b. April 14, 1873, d. Sept. 28,

1873; Oscar b. Nov. 19, 1874, d. Sept. 1, 1875; Matilda b. Aug. 23, 1877, m. John W. Whitmore. Family home Salt Lake City.
High priest; missionary to England 1874-76; patriarch; bishops' councelor. Clerk in tithing office, Teasdale's stores, and in water works department. Furniture maker, building contractor. Put up the first flat bed printing press of the Deseret News.

BARTON, ISAAC (son of John Barton and Elizabeth Bell). Born Dec. 11, 1842 in England. Came to Utah 1861.
Married Agnes E. Parr Dec., 1870, Salt Lake City (daughter of John Parr and Barbara McKechnia of Salt Lake City, pioneers 1868). She was born Oct. 1, 1850. Their children: Hattie b. Oct. 14, 1871, died; Isaac Reid, m. Sarah Ethel Armstrong; Agnes McKechnia; Richard A. Shipp; Barbara Bell; Florence W.; Bertha M., died. Family home Salt Lake City.
Bishop of 19th ward, Salt Lake City, 20 years; counselor to president of high priests' quorum. Merchant.

BARTON, JOSEPH (son of John Barton and Elizabeth Bell). Born July 25, 1848, St. Helens, Lancashire, Eng. Came to Utah with father.
Married Mary Ann Allen April 5, 1869, Salt Lake City (daughter of Robert Allen and Leah Harmon, of Salt Lake City; former a pioneer Sept. 1866). She was born Nov. 30, 1852. Their children: May A.; Charles Harmon, m. Millicent Nelson; Clarence Elmer, m. Beatrice Vera; Hattie Josephine; Edna Maud; Roy Allen, m. Minerva Armstrong. Family home Kaysville, Utah.
One of the presidents of the 143d quorum seventies; president 3d quorum elders' of Davis stake several years. County surveyor 21 years; county clerk 14 years; county engineer six years; prosecuting attorney eight years; Kaysville city recorder eight years; city councilman two years; member Utah legislature three terms 1884-86-90; member 1st board of trustees, and 1st superintendent of territorial reform school. Civil engineer; superintendent Sumpter Valley railway.

BARTON, STEPHEN SMITH (son of Sally Penn of Lebanon, Ill.). Born Jan. 3, 1839, Lebanon. Came to Utah 1855.
Married Jane Evans Feb. 5, 1857, Paragonah, Utah (daughter of Abraham and Mary Evans of Merthyr Tydfil, Wales; former died en route to Utah, latter came in 1856, with handcart company). She was born Feb. 9, 1841. Their children: Edward b. Sept. 1857; died; Sally Ann b. Sept. 10, 1858, m. Peter Isaac Olson; Mary Jane b. March 10, 1860, m. John Baker Topham; Emily Frances b. Nov. 9, 1863, m. Seren Olsen; Stephen, died; Julia Elizabeth, m. Leroy McBride; Catherine, died; William Penn, m. Lavina Davenport. Family home Paragonah, Utah.
Married Eliza Smith (daughter of Thomas Smith of Parowan, Utah; pioneer 1852, oxteam company). Their children: John Calvin; Olive Nichols, m. Thomas Edwards; Nora, m. John Rice; Sadie, m. Frank Savage; Stella, m. Mr. Edwards. Family home Paragonah, Utah.
High priest; bishop of Paragonah ward for several years; ward clerk. Justice of peace; school trustee many years. Farmer, carpenter and stockraiser.

BARTON, WILLIAM (son of Elizabeth Walling of Southport, Eng.). Born 1811. Came to Utah Nov. 30, 1856, Edward Martin handcart company.
Married Mary Ann Taylor 1850, Southport, Eng. (daughter of John Taylor and Margaret Baxter of Staffordshire, Eng.). She was born March 1, 1821, Liverpool, Eng., and came to Utah with husband. Their children: Fannie, m. Frederick Lutz; Elizabeth, d. aged 2 years. Family home Salt Lake City.
Pioneer. Died Feb. 8, 1897.

BARTON, WILLIAM KILSHAW. Born March 16, 1826, England. Came to Utah 1852.
Married Malinda Jane ——. Their children: Ethelbert, m. Ada Cook; Walter K., m. Angeline Pettey; Wiloska, d. aged 16. Family home Manti, Utah.
Married Frances Quirt. Their children: Malinda Jane, m. Joseph J. Taylor; Clara, m. George Pettey; James A., m. Lottie Peacock; George Raphael, m. Josephine L. ——; Salena, d. aged 19; Alexander, m. Belle Hall; Sarah Ann, m. Christian Poulsen; Stephen Colonel, m. Alice Anderson. Family home Manti.
Married Ann Cook at Manti (daughter of James Cook and Ann Lane of England, pioneers 1852, Joseph Young company). She was born Nov. 5, 1844. Their children: Alpha; Frances, d. aged 2; Alice Maud, m. William W. Brown; Lily May, m. Frank Hall; Nicholas Hyrum, d. aged 7; Isabel, m. George Edward Bench; Ruth Cook, m. Andrew Madsen; Armina, d. aged 4; Ann, d. infant; Emily Amelia, m. Elden Smith; Ellen Spencer, m. Sydney Frederickson; Edgar, d. infant. Family home Manti, Utah.
Missionary to England; Sunday school superintendent; choir leader. Farmer; merchant. Died in Dec. 1886.

BASCOM, JOEL ALMON (son of Ezekiel Bascom and Sarah Peet of Brooksfield, Madison county, N. Y.). Born March 27, 1832, Brooksfield, N. Y. Came to Utah Aug. 18, 1856, Philemon C. Merrill company.
Married Alice Jane Bell, Dec. 6, 1857, Provo, Utah (daugh-

ter of John Watson Bell and Ann Fish of Newcastle, Northumberland, Eng.; Mrs Bell came across plains alone with her eight children in 1855, a year later than Mr. Bell). She was born April 15, 1840, at Newcastle. Their children: Zina Ann, m. John A. Evans; Ida Jane, m. Elias Wilard Williams, Jr.; Joel Almon, Jr. b. Oct. 22, 1862, m. Elnora Haws, m. Josephine Fredericka Nash: John Watson Bell, m. Rachel Lybbert; Mary Emma, m. John Thomas Kay; Ira Kimball, m. Alice Rasmussen; William, m. May Lock; Charley, m. Alice Gurr; Hannah, Bell, Alice, Lodema, James and Oren d. infants. The family resided at Provo, Mona and Vernal, Utah.
Home missionary; high priest; block and Sunday school teacher. Fought in Black Hawk and Walker Indian wars, and took part in demonstration at Echo Canyon resisting advance of Johnston's army. Was on Provo police force nine years, and constable at Mona three terms.

BASCOM, JOEL ALMON, JR. (son of Joel Almon Bascom and Alice Jane Bell). Born Oct. 22, 1862, Provo, Utah.
Married Elnora Haws Oct. 28, 1885, Logan, Utah (daughter of Albert Haws and Nancy Haws, cousins, of Provo and Vernal, Utah). She was born March 11, 1862, and died April 28, 1903. Their children: Joel Albert, b. 1894, d. at birth; Roland and Almon, twins, b. April 18, 1896; Charles Basil b. April 21, 1903, d. July 27, 1903. Family home Vernal, Utah.
Married Josephine Fredricka Nash Oct. 5, 1904, at Salt Lake City (daughter of Michael O. Nash of Hodland, Norway, and Josephine Fredricka Olsen of Christiania, Norway, now of Salem, Utah county, who came to Utah in 1870). She was born July 2, 1880. Their children: Howard Edwin b. Dec. 10, 1905; William Cecil b. April 22, 1907; Bernard Kimball b. April 7, 1909; Marion Everett b. April 5, 1911; George Ivin b. March 11, 1913. Family home Vernal, Utah.
Elder; ward and block teacher. Made home in Naples ward in Vernal, 1888. Has built irrigation canals, wagon roads and located asphalt mines. Farmer and cattleman.

BASCOM, IRA KIMBALL (son of Joel Almon Bascom and Alice Jane Bell). Born March 26, 1873, Mona, Utah.
Married Alice Rasmussen January 20, 1911, Naples, Utah, Bishop Albert H. Goodrich officiating. She was the daughter of Mads Peter Rasmussen and Mary Rasmussen of Ahigren, Denmark. Family home Naples, Utah. Only child: Preston Shirley b. Oct. 15, 1911.
Missionary to England; ward and Sunday school teacher; seventy. Came to Ashley Valley as a young man and assisted in building the first canals, wagon roads, farms and homes.

BASSETT, CHARLES HENRY (son of Elias Bassett and Matilda Salter of Ossian, Allegany county, N. Y.). Born March 14, 1828, Ossian, N. Y. Came to Utah 1852.
Married Mary Elizabeth Knight March 5, 1853, at Salt Lake City (daughter of Joseph Knight, Jr., and Betsy Coverti, who was born June 16, 1836, in Clay county, Mo. and came to Utah Sept. 12, 1850, Thomas Johnson company. Their children: Mary Ellen b. June 9, 1854, m. L. B. Rodeback; Melvie Amanda b. July 28, 1856, m. Charles Harvey Glines; William Henry b. March 14, 1858, m. Marette Cook; James Lester b. Jan. 25, 1860, d. infant; Ernest Knight b. June 13, 1861, m. Lucy Goodwin; Lutie C. b. July 13, 1868, d. infant; Ruby Rosaltha b. May 13, 1871, m. Thomas S. Ashworth; Roscoe Knight b. May 28, 1874, d. infant; Lute Knight b. April 13, 1879. Family home Salt Lake City, Utah.
Member of 10th quorum seventies and high priest; missionary to Ohio 1854. Went to California 1866 for merchandise; bookkeeper General Tithing office, Salt Lake City, 20 years; merchant. Died Feb. 26, 1907, Salt Lake City.

BASSETT, THOMAS (son of Richard Thomas and Mary Millward of Canton, near Cardiff, South Wales). Born June 7, 1827, Canton, S. W. Came to Utah July 18, 1876.
Married Margaret Edwards Jan. 27, 1851, Cardiff, South Wales (daughter of William Edwards, who came to Utah 1876). She was born Nov. 1, 1827. Their children: William E., m. Catherine Smith: Mary; Rebecca, m. Henry Hughes; Margaret, m. Walter Muir; Thomas E., m. Lucy A. Lutz; Sarah, m. Simon T. Baker. Family resided Mendon, Utah, and Rexburg, Idaho.
High priest. Farmer. Died May 23, 1903, at Rexburg.

BASSETT, THOMAS E. (son of Thomas Bassett and Margaret Edwards). Born Nov. 26, 1862, Canton, S. W. Came to · ah with parents.
 ied Lucy A. Lutz April 14, 1886, Logan, Utah (daughter of Thomas J. Lutz and Mary Merrill, of Smithfield, Utah, pioneers 1854). She was born May 1, 1867. Their children: Elsie May b. Feb. 23, 1887, d. Feb. 23, 1887; Lucy Maud b. July 20, 1891; Margaret Gladys b. Aug. 22, 1894; Mary Merrilla b. Oct. 12, 1899; Thomas Myrthen b. Jan. 25, 1903; Hazel Irene b. Aug. 16, 1904. Family home Rexburg, Idaho.
Member 84th quorum seventies and high priest; missionary to England 1888-90; alternate high councilor; Sunday school superintendent and president of Y. M. M. I. A. of Rexburg for several years; second counselor to President Ricks of Bannock stake, then first counselor and later became president of Fremont stake; settled at Mendon, Utah, July 18, 1876, and served as president of teachers' quorum three years. Moved to where Rexburg now stands in 1883;

there he assisted in making the first canals, wagon roads, and building the first bridges. First school teacher and first postmaster of Rexburg; president Ricks Academy district board 1902. Farmer; dealer in real estate, loans and insurance.

BASTIAN, JACOB (son of Bastian Sorenson and Margen Olesdatter of Copenhagen, Denmark). Born March 14, 1835, at Copenhagen. Came to Utah Sept. 13, 1857, Christian Christiansen handcart company.
Married Gjertro Petersen Aug. 25, 1857, Twindsdock, Eng. (parents lived at Sundbyvester, Isle of Amager, Denmark). She was born July 30, 1834, and died Sept. 21, 1397, Salt Lake City, Utah.
Married Johanne Marie Sander Oct. 27, 1857, Tooele. Utah (daughter of Sander Anderson and Johanne Catrine Hansen of Liedfrost, Veile amt, Denmark, the former d. at North Platte, Neb., Aug. 12, 1867, latter a pioneer Sept. 13, 1857, Christian Christiansen handcart company). She was born July 30, 1835. Their children: Jacob Sander b. Sept. 12, 1858, m. Harriett Ann Taylor; Gearsen Sander b. July 1, 1860, m. Emily S. Paxman: Hanna b. Dec. 15, 1861; Catrine Marie b. Feb. 21, 1863, m. Herman Tegan; Margen Olive b. May 6, 1865, d. Aug. 26, 1866; Karen Melvine b. July 9, 1867, d. Feb. 20, 1892; Emma Johanne b. Feb. 11, 1869, m. Homer Baron; Julie Jacobine b. Jan. 1, 1871, m. Hyrum Bryan; Bastian Soren b. Feb. 5, 1873, m. Lottie Hansen; Ludvig Alminda b. Feb. 26, 1875, m. Nora Harmick. Family resided Lehi, Moroni and Washington, Utah.
Married Christina Hansen Feb. 7, 1861, Moroni, San Pete county, Utah (daughter of Louis Hansen and Caroline Neilsdatter of Moroni, pioneers September, 1859). She was born Oct. 11, 1845. Their children: Laura Christina, m. P. E. Van Orden; Charles J., m. Elia Hartley; Martha K., Hannah S. and Margaret, latter three died; Lewis H., m. E. Pearl Huntsman; Caroline G. and James, d. childhood; Serena A., m. L. E. Farnsworth; J. Wilford, m. Birda Timothy; Roetta C., m. Robert Sainsbury; Christa E., m. Elmer Carling. Family home Washington, Washington county.
Married Metta Maria Sander Oct. 1867, Salt Lake City, Utah (daughter of Sander Anderson and Johanne Catrine Hansen), who was born Jan. 25, 1848. Their children: Sander and Joseph, d. young; Erastus S., m. Orilla Jolley; Hyrum, d. child; Jacobena b. Dec. 1874, d. March, 1889; Mary, m. Arthur L. Crawford; Hans T., m. Lula Robinson; Andrew, b. April 25, 1886, d. Nov. 1893; Neils, m. Ethel Sullivan. Family home, Washington, Utah.
President elders' quorum; member Washington quorum of seventy. Assisted in settling "Dixie" country, 1861. Farmer; carpenter.

BASTIAN, JACOB SANDER (son of Jacob Bastian and Johanne Marie Sander). Born Sept. 12, 1858, Lehi, Utah.
Married Harriett Ann Taylor March 22, 1876, St. George, Utah (daughter of Allen Taylor and Phoebe Roberts of Kaysville, Utah). She was born Oct. 31, 1859, at Kaysville, Their children: Anna Marie b. July 5, 1879, m. M. W. Mansfield; Jacob F. b. Feb. 17, 1881, d. child; Phoebe Harriett b. June 3, 1883, m. F. E. Brown; Johanna Gertrude b. Jan. 3, 1885, m. Ernest Ernesten; Jennie Estella b. Nov. 25, 1887, m. M. L. Mansfield; Catrine Taylor b. July 1, 1890; Amanda Melvina b. March 16, 1893, m. Parley Reese; Georgia Anna b. Aug. 10, 1894; Alma b. Dec. 14, 1896; George Arthur b. May 6, 1898; Dora b. June 25, 1900.
Ordained bishop of Loa, Utah Nov. 6, 1910 and high priest Nov. 24, 1894; missionary to Denmark Jan. 3, 1901 to July 1, 1903. Farmer and stockraiser. Superintended building of Johnson valley reservoir, near Fish lake, Sevier county, Utah.

BASTIAN, GEARSEN S. (son of Jacob Bastian and Johanne Marie Sander). Born July 1, 1860, Moroni, Utah.
Married Emily S. Paxman April 3, 1885, St. George, Utah (daughter of David Paxman and Elizabeth Ann Blundon of Walthamstow, Eng. who came to Utah 1870). She was born Jan. 29, 1861. Their children: Gearsen Marion; Rhoda E.; Julia; Karl; Myrtle; Woodruff; Elmer. Family resided at Washington, Loa and Sigurd, Utah.
Seventy; missionary to Scandinavia 1887; home missionary, Sevier stake; 2d counselor to Willis F. Robison, bishop Loa ward; 2d counselor in presidency of Wayne stake 1893-1903; president of Wayne stake 1906-10. In 1861 he settled with his parents in the "Dixie" country, living at Washington, and took an active part in the upbuilding of that country. Farmer and stockraiser.

BATE, WILLIAM (son of Peter Bate and Margaret Ross). Born May 12, 1846. Came to Utah Sept. 1, 1859, Horton D. Haight company.
Married Hannah Shelly (daughter of William Shelly), who was born in 1848. Their children: W. A. b, February, 1870; Edwin; Samuel, died; Ernest; Jane; John; Edith; Pearl; Amy.
Married Maud Annett Nell (daughter of Phillip Nell and Clara Nokess), who was born in August, 1871. Their children: Edward; Rose; Cora; Earl; Vera; Arnold; Austin; Rulon; Glenn; Otis.

BATE, W. A. (son of William Bate and Hannah Shelly). Born in 1870 at American Fork, Utah.
Married Ida Ann Bills June 7, 1893, Salt Lake City (daughter of G. S. Bills and Ellen G. Holt), who was born in 1876.

PIONEERS AND PROMINENT MEN OF UTAH

Their children: Clyde A. b. March 23, 1894; Ethel Viola b. May 5, 1895; Jesse W. b. Dec. 5, 1896.
Married Harriet E. Green (daughter of Charles Green and Mary Ann Frances), who was born in 1878, American Fork, Utah. No children.
Farmer. Missionary to Ireland and England.

BATEMAN, JOSEPH (son of Thomas Bateman). Born October, 1839, in Lancashire, Eng. Came to Utah about 1850.
Married Mary E. Allen (daughter of D. R. and Eliza Allen). Their children: Estella; Joseph Samuel; Theodore; Mary; Royal; Margaret; David; Ethel; Clara; Stephen; Charles.

BATEMAN, JOSEPH SAMUEL (son of Joseph Bateman and Mary E. Allen). Born Feb. 17, 1864, West Jordan, Utah.
Married Alzina Johnson, Feb. 29, 1888, Logan, Utah (daughter of Peter Johnson and Christina Peterson), who was born Dec. 18, 1868, in Denmark. Their children: Hazel b. April 6, 1889, m. William Dunsdon; Leslie b. Oct. 23, 1891; Miri b. Aug. 5, 1894; Irving b. Jan. 18, 1897; Lola b. July 23, 1900; Earl b. April 20, 1906; Elsie b. April 6, 1909; Joseph b. Dec. 31, 1902. Family resided Alpine and Lehi, Utah.

BATEMAN, JOSEPH (son of Thomas and Betty Bateman of Bolton, Lancashire, Eng. and Nauvoo, Ill.). Born 1806, Bolton, Eng. Came to Utah Sept. 20, 1848, Lorenzo Snow company.
Married Margaret Turner 1826 in England (daughter of John and Mary Turner of Preston, Eng.). She was born July 24, 1804, and came to Utah with husband. Their children: James, m. Hannah Wilson; William, m. Sarah Lavender; Mary, m. Hyrum Bowen; John, died; Margaret b. Jan. 5, 1831, m. Dennis Wilson Winn; Betty, died. Family home Salt Lake City.
Settler Cedar City 1850, and remained there until the time of his death in 1855. He assisted in every way to build up the country around Cedar City. Made the brick for the council house at Salt Lake City.

BATEMAN, THOMAS (son of Thomas Bateman, born 1786, Bolton, Eng., died 1844, Nauvoo, Ill.). He was born Sept. 17, 1808, at Bolton. Came to Utah Sept. 15, 1850, in company with James Pace train.
Married Mary Street Aug. 1829, Manchester Eng., who was born May 12, 1810, in that city. Their children: Harriet b. Nov. 4, 1830; Samuel b. July 1, 1832; Elizabeth b. Feb. 16, 1834; Thomas b. Jan. 27, 1836; Joseph and James Boame b. Dec. 9, 1837; Mary Boame b. Feb. 27, 1840; James Morgan b. March 3, 1842; William Lehi b. Jan. 1, 1844; John b. Feb. 21, 1846; Martha Ann b. Sept. 15, 1847; Margaret b. June 30, 1849.

BATEMAN, WILLIAM LEHI (son of Thomas Bateman and Mary Street). Born Jan. 1, 1844, Lee county, Iowa. Came to Utah with parents.
Married Sophrona Almina Watkins Dec. 26, 1870 (daughter of William Lamphord Watkins and Mary Almina Hammond, pioneers Sept. 11, 1852, advance contingent William Whitehead company). She was born Sept. 5, 1852. Their children: William Lehi b. Oct. 13, 1871, died; Sophrona Almina b. April 1, 1873, m. I. Frank Goff Feb. 22, 1895; Thomas Philip b. April 16, 1875, m. Josephine M. Wilson Sept. 9, 1897; Samuel Alford b. Sept. 13, 1877, m. Ada C. Arnold Oct. 14, 1897; Orlando James b. July 8, 1880, m. Millie M. Sutton Nov. 20, 1901; Joseph Deseret b. Oct. 30, 1882, m. Lenora Bagley Dec. 1, 1903; George Leo b. April 9, 1885, m. Melrhea Cushing March 4, 1908; Laura May b. Dec. 6, 1887, m. George Walter Larson Aug. 1, 1906, d. Sept. 8, 1899; Mary Zilpha b. Nov. 21, 1890, m. Silas L. Brady Aug. 17, 1910; Myrtle Marinda b. Jan. 12, 1894; Loren Eugene b. Jan. 15, 1896; Gladys Veloy b. Dec. 5, 1897. Family home West Jordan, Utah.
Veteran Black Hawk war; 1st counselor Y. M. M. I. A. West Jordan ward; president 12th quorum elders Salt Lake stake.

BATES, CYRUS W. Born 1827 in New York state. Came to Utah 1862 with his own party.
Married Harriet C. Mathews (daughter of Orrin Mathews and Hannah Burr), who was born 1825 and came to Utah with husband. Their children: Ormes Eaton b. Jan. 17, 1848, m. Augusta Eleason 1875; Harriet C. b. Aug. 22, 1855, m. Orson W. Bates; Effie E. b. Dec. 4, 1861, m. R. H. Hunter.

BATES, ORMES EATON (son of Cyrus W. Bates and Harriet C. Mathews). Born Jan. 17, 1848, New York state.
Married Augusta Eleason March 2, 1875, Salt Lake City (daughter of Eric Eleason and Anna Nielsen, pioneers Sept. 12, 1863, John Royal Young company). She was born May 5, 1854, in Sweden. Their children: Ormes Alberto b. Feb. 2, 1876; Augusta Erminda b. Aug. 27, 1878; Cyrus Parley b. Dec. 12, 1881; Fredrick C. b. April 4, 1884; Harriet Birdie b. Dec. 8, 1886, m. Wilford M. Christensen; Alice Myrtle b. June 5, 1889; Effie Lorna b. Feb. 18, 1893. Family home Hyrum, Utah.
High priest. Active in the affairs of his community.

BATES, JOSEPH W. (son of Joseph W. Bates and Mary Ann Harris, of Staffordshire, Eng.). Born Jan. 16, 1827, Dudley, Staffordshire. Came to Utah June, 1849, with part of Mormon battalion.
Married Harriet Billington 1850 (daughter of Joseph Billington and Martha Brown, former a pioneer 1848; latter died at Council Bluffs, Iowa). She was born Nov. 27, 1831, and died May 12, 1909. Their children: Eliza Jane b. Nov. 18, 1852, m. Parley P. Sabin Dec. 11, 1871; [3] Joseph W. b. Oct. 1, 1855, m. Martha A. McEntire Oct. 14, 1877; Hugh F. b. Oct. 13, 1858, d. child; Harriet May b. May 22, 1863, d. child; Edward H. b. Sept. 11, 1865, m. Rowena Huish; Lewis A. b. Dec. 31, 1869, d. aged ten years. Family resided Salt Lake City and Payson, Utah.
Worked as stonecutter on Nauvoo temple 3 years and on Salt Lake temple 7 years. Member 32d and later of 46th quorum seventies; member Mormon battalion. Lieutenant-colonel Black Hawk Indian war 1865-67. Died June 30, 1890.

BATES, JOSEPH W. (son of Joseph W. Bates and Harriet Billington). Born Oct. 1, 1855, Salt Lake City.
Married Martha A. McEntire Oct. 14, 1877, Payson, Utah (daughter of Henry McEntire and Martha Gillispie, who came to Utah 1870). She was born April 1, 1861, in Smith county, Va. Their children: Martha A. b. Nov. 8, 1878, m. William Betts; Harriet M. b. Nov. 16, 1881, m. Joseph L. Francom; [4] Joseph W. b. Sept. 27, 1884, m. Sarah A. Francom; Lewis E. b. April 24, 1887, and Mary W. b. Jan. 26, 1889, died; Charles H. b. March 16, 1891, m. Delia Hiatt Nov. 27, 1912; Irwin E. b. Dec. 31, 1894, died; Susan E. b. Nov. 25, 1896; Lillie V. b. March 15, 1900, died. Family home Payson, Utah.
President elders' quorum of 1st ward, Payson. City Sexton since Jan. 1908.

BATES, [4] JOSEPH WILLIAM (son of [3] Joseph W. Bates and Martha A. McEntire). Born Sept. 27, 1884, Payson, Utah.
Married Sarah L. Francom (daughter of Samuel Francom of Africa, and Emma C. Erlandson, married at Salt Lake City). Their children: Lillie and Ruth. Family home Payson.
Seventy; missionary to Central States June 5, 1911.

BATES, ORMUS E. (son of Cyrus Bates and Lydia Herrington of Wisconsin). Born March 25, 1815, in Wisconsin.
Came to Utah Sept. 1851, William B. Cummings company.
Married Phebe M. Matison 1835 in New York state (daughter of John Matison and Elizabeth Hill of New York, pioneers 1851, William B. Cummings company). She was born Jan. 31, 1817. Their children: Orson P. b. March 3, 1836, m. Ann E. Brower; Erin L. b. May 21, 1838, m. Victoria Brower; Lavirna E. b. Aug. 4, 1840, m. William H. Lee; Mary E. b. Dec. 5, 1842, m. Orlando Gee; Ormus E. b. April 11, 1845, m. Susan E. Tuttle; Orssia M. b. Jan. 8, 1848, m. William A. Critchfield; Arlin H. b. Feb. 14, 1851, m. Luvena Adams; Marintha A. b. March 14, 1853, m. William A. Tolman; Myron H. b. Oct. 18, 1855, m. Charlotte Hilstead. Family home Tooele, Utah.
Married Morilla Spink at Nauvoo, Ill., who came to Utah with husband. Their children: Orville E. b. Oct. 1845, m. Ellen Wakefield; Sarah M. b. June 9, 1847, m. Elijah Read; Angnett, m. Apollus Lamson; Onley; Aretha, m. Joseph Wakefield; Lavina; Lancing; Marion.
Married Matilda Read at Winter Quarters, Neb. Their children: Cyrus b. 1850, m. Adelaid Bates; Lydia b. 1852, m. Enoch Martin; Laronia b. 1854, m. Joseph Godfrey; Julia b. 1856, m. Edward Bird.
Married Ellen Mecham at Salt Lake City (daughter of Joseph Mecham, pioneer). Their children: Armintha, m. W. Pettit; Oliver, m. Luana Kelley; Albert, m. Irene Day; Lillie M., m. F. Fowler. Family home Erda, Utah.
Married Margrette Busenbark at Salt Lake City. Their children: Lucila, m. George Davy; Marcellus; Orin, m. Ruth Larkin; Jane, m. Nephi Wagstaff; Isaac; George, m. Sarah Biveno. Family home Erda, Utah.
Married Sarah Hymas Oct. 10, 1862, at Salt Lake City (daughter of Benjamin Hymas, pioneer 1862). Their children: Loila, m. Homer Wolfe; Earnest, m. Jane Wolfe; Herman; Tena, m. Sterling Williams. Family home Erda, Utah.
Married Sarah Weir in 1863, Salt Lake City (daughter of Samuel Weir of Bristol, Eng., pioneer 1862). She was born 1842, Bristol, Eng. Their children: Celestia b. June 12, 1864, m. Edward Dalton; Annie b. March 23, 1866, m. Horace W. Woolley; Arthur, b. Feb. 14, 1869, m. Ella and Etta Anderson; Almeda b. May 8, 1871, m. Oliver Dukes and R. T. Latey; Helamain, d. infant.
Elder, a pioneer of Tooele county. Miner, farmer and stockraiser. Died Aug. 4, 1873, Rush Valley, Utah.
Sarah Weir Bates (widow Ormus E.) married Edwin Hall July 1877, Tooele, Utah, by whom she had one child, Ella, who married a Mr. Hannahs.

BATH, WILLIAM (son of Simon Bath and Maria Watts of Poulton, Somersetshire, Eng.). He was born in August, 1831, at Poulton. Came to Utah Sept. 1, 1860, John Smith company.
Married Eve Morgan March 31, 1860, Scranton, Pa. (daughter of Daniel Morgan and Mary Todd of Scranton), who was born June 15, 1842. Their children: William H., d. aged 15; Mary E., d. aged 2; Daniel Morgan, m. Rachel

Brooks; Simon R., m. Louie Capson; Alonzo, d. aged 23; Joseph, d. infant.
Married Mary Pierce November, 1873, at Salt Lake City (daughter of Thomas Pierce and Margaret Thomas of Ystrad, Glamorganshire, Wales, latter a pioneer 1862). She was born May 31, 1851. Their children: Mary Isabelle, b. George Gowan; Eve, m. Charles McKeague; Margaret d. aged 4; Sarah Ann, m. William Smith; William Thomas, m. Laura Crabtree; Alfred Edmund, m. Margaret Averett; Emma d. aged 7; Hyrum; Catherine Priscilla d. aged 1 year. Family resided Salt Lake City, Utah.
Elder. Miner; located Buckhorn mine at Ophir, Utah.

BATTY, MILES (son of Joseph Batty and Nancy Barker of Ossett, Yorkshire, Eng.). Born March 2, 1832, at Ossett. Came to Utah 1850, A. O. Smoot merchandise train.
Married Mary Henrietta Mecham July 24, 1864, Salt Lake City (daughter of Ephraim Mecham and Polly Derby of Wallsburg, Utah, pioneers 1852). She was born April 10, 1848. Their children: Miles M. b. June 12, 1865, m. Permelia E. Bigelow; Ephraim A. b. Nov. 29, 1867, m. Polly A. Lamb; Mary E. b. March 27, 1870, m. Frank Bigelow; George L. b. Dec. 1, 1871, m. Frelia Mecham; Charles H. b. May 23, 1874, m. Bertha M. Richens; William W. b. July 13, 1876; Celestia V. b. Nov. 3, 1878, m. Ray Pickup; Emma A. b. Oct. 16, 1886, m. Ezra B. Bussey. Family resided Wanship and Wallsburg, Utah.

BATTY, MILES M. (son of Miles Batty and Mary H. Mecham). Born June 12, 1865, Wanship, Summit county, Utah.
Married Permelia E. Bigelow June 7, 1886, at Wallsburg (daughter of Daniel Bigelow and Permelia Mecham, ox team pioneers). She was born Sept. 25, 1867. Their children: Permelia H. b. June 10, 1887, d. Feb. 22, 1891; Emily V. b. Dec. 9, 1888, m. James A. Freestone; Zina b. Jan. 15, 1890, m. Raymond M. Searle; Adora E. b. Dec. 9, 1891, m. Reuben T. Freestone; May b. Dec. 9, 1893, d. March 22, 1894; Celestia b. April 6, 1895; Marquis I. b. Aug. 30, 1896; Mary B. b. July 21, 1898; Daniel V. b. June 6, 1900; Albert D. b. Jan. 12, 1902; Laura b. Aug. 20, 1904, d. March 21, 1905; Dorothy b. March 6, 1912. Family home Vernal, Utah.
Missionary to England 1907-09; high priest; president Y. M. M. I. A.; bishop's counselor. Constable at Wallsburg four years; once a contractor for supplies for U. S. Government. Farmer.

BAUM, GEORGE (son of John C. Baum, born March 18, 1804, and Hannah Crismon, born Dec. 8, 1808, Brandywine, Chester county, Pa.). He was born Nov. 2, 1829, at Brandywine. Came to Utah Sept. 26, 1850, independent company.
Married Hannah Jane Cloward 1851, Provo, Utah (daughter of Jacob and Hannah Cloward, pioneers 1851). She was born Oct. 12, 1833, and died Nov. 21, 1860. Their children: Jane Elizabeth b. May 14, 1853, d. infant; Mary Jane b. April 25, 1854, m William Wright; Hannah Melissa b. Feb. 4, 1856, m. David Nephi Penrod; Martha Malinda b. May 21, 1860, died.
Married Eliza Ann Allen of Provo, Utah (daughter of Daniel and Eliza Allen), who was born July 5, 1842, and died Jan. 20, 1875. Their children: Eliza Isabell b. Dec. 2, 1863, and George Daniel b. March 7, 1866, died; John William b. April 26, 1868; Owen Abraham b. Jan. 10, 1872; Orson b. Jan. 12, 1875.
Married Sarah Elizabeth Carter Nov. 21, 1875, Provo, Utah (daughter of John F Carter and Sophia Sweet of Oxford county, Maine, pion 1849). She was born Aug. 14, 1851, Manti, Utah. T r children: Clara Elizabeth b. July 24, 1876; Sophia Eldora b. Jan. 24, 1878; Jacob A. b. Nov. 7, 1879; David Wallace b. Feb. 25, 1882; Lafayette b. April 15, 1884; Arthur b. June 21, 1887, and Ernest b. Sept. 27, 1888, died; Elmer b. Oct. 21, 1892. Families resided Provo, Utah.
High priest. Settled at Provo 1850. Freighted from Leavenworth, Kans., to Salt Lake City, 1856, for Y. X. company. Assisted to bring immigrants to Utah. Farmer, merchant and manufacturer.

BAUM, ISAAC (son of John C. Baum and Hannah Crismon). Born April 7, 1832, Uklan township, Chester county, Pa. Came to Utah 1850, independent company.
Married Melissa Sessions May 6, 1856 (daughter of Richard Sessions and Lucretia Hawaii, who was born March 11, 1838. Their children: Louisa Maria b. April 26, 1857, m. Chauncy C. Lee June 27, 1876, d. Oct. 27, 1896; Isaac Richard b. Aug. 17, 1860, m. Gabriella Ivie Feb. 1890; Hannah Araltta b. Dec. 25, 1862, m. William H. Murdock July 25, 1881; John William b. June 3, 1865, m. Maria Hickens; Hannah Lucretia b. May 23, 1867, d. Aug. 25, 1883; Eliza Jane b. Dec. 30, 1869, d. Aug. 17, 1872; Ada May b. June 11, 1872, d. July 15, 1872; Mary Elizabeth b. Aug. 10, 1873, m. David C. Hanks Dec. 6, 1893; Sarah Emeline b. Jan. 3, 1876, m. William G. Welke Dec. 13, 1910; David Alexander b. Oct. 3, 1878, d. Nov. 17, 1879; Rachel Isabel b. Sept. 18, 1880.
Assisted in bringing immigrants to Utah. Indian war veteran. High councilor.

BAUM, JACOB (son of Jacob Baum). Came to Utah 1850, independent company.
Married Agnes Nancy Harris Oct. 12, 1826, who died Sept. 11, 1846, Council Bluffs, Iowa. Their children: Jacob Harris b. Dec. 30, 1830; Jane b. July 2, 1832, m. Elisha Thomas; Elizabeth b. Jan. 27, 1834, m. George A. Bean; Jacob Harris b. May 29, 1836, m. Malinda Cummings; Jeanetta Rachel b. July 17, 1837, m. Alexander Sessions.

BAUM, JACOB HARRIS (son of Jacob Baum and Agnes Nancy Harris). Born May 29, 1836, in Pennsylvania. Came to Utah 1852.
Married Malinda Cummings July 24, 1864, Heber, Utah (daughter of John G. and Rachel Cummings of Gibson county, Tenn., pioneers 1852). She was born April 6, 1840, and died Jan. 31, 1909, Provo, Utah. Their children: Rachel Ann b. May 29, 1865, m. John Gatherum; Thomas J. b. April 12, 1868, and John E. b. Feb. 5, 1869, died; Elizabeth b. March 21, 1871, m. Fred Ferguson; Malinda b. June 18, 1873, m. Mads Jorgensen; Jane b. Sept. 19, 1876; Harmon David b. Dec. 18, 1877, m. Susie Moore; William Harris b. Oct. 8, 1884, m. Grace Ferguson.
Member 45th quorum seventies; special missionary to bring immigrants to Utah; his health was ruined on this trip. Block teacher. Farmer. Died March 21, 1912, Gunnison, Utah.

BAUM, HARMON DAVID (son of Jacob Harris Baum and Malinda Cummings). Born Dec. 18, 1877, Provo, Utah.
Married Susie Moore Dec. 1, 1903, Provo, Utah (daughter of George S. and Agnes Moore, pioneers Sept. 24, 1861, Joseph Young and Ansel Harmon company). She was born March 19, 1877. Their children: Mildred b. Oct. 14, 1904; Altha b. May 8, 1909.
Following his father's activities, he was a farmer.

BAUM, WILLIAM HARRIS (son of Jacob Harris Baum and Malinda Cummings). Born Oct. 8, 1884, Provo, Utah.
Married Grace Ferguson Dec. 12, 1906, Provo, Utah (daughter of John Burkholder Ferguson and Mary Ann Shantey, of Westmoreland county, Pa., and they came to Provo, Utah, March, 1905). She was born Oct. 4, 1886. Their children: William Homer b. Jan. 4, 1908; Alva Grace b. Oct. 25, 1909; Mary Bernice b. Feb. 4, 1911. Family home Provo, Utah.
Elder; ward teacher. Farmer and orchardist.

BAXTER, JOHN ROBB (son of John Baxter, born Jan. 16, 1823, and Jean Robb, born May 23, 1824, both in Aberdeen, Scotland, married June 4, 1844). He was born Feb. 9, 1851, in Aberdeen. Came to Utah Sept 1868, Harvey H. Cluff company.
Married Jannett Jack Nov. 16, 1887 (daughter of William Jack and Jessie Thornton, former came to Utah 1869). She was born Aug. 4, 1861. Their children: John Robb b. Oct. 7, 1888; William Jack b. Sept. 15, 1890; Thomas Gardiner b. Aug. 22, 1892; Jessie b. Dec. 21, 1895; Alma b. Jan. 23, 1896; Jean b. Jan. 13, 1897; Jessie Minerva b. Aug. 1, 1900. Family home Spring City.
Missionary to Great Britain 1880-82; counselor in high priest's quorum. Recorder; justice of peace; city councilman; mayor Spring City one term.

BAXTER, ROBERT WRIGHT (son of John Baxter, born in 1800, and Margaret Wright, born June 11, 1798, both at Donaghadee, County Down, Ireland. He was born Feb. 2, 1819, at Donaghadee. Came to Utah Sept. 25, 1855, Richard Ballantyne company.
Married Isabella Gray Jan. 31, 1845 (daughter of John Gray and Elizabeth McCutcheon, both of whom died in Kilmarnock, Scotland). She was born March 12, 1822, and died June 4, 1847, at Greenock, Scotland. Only child: Isabella b. June 16, 1846, d. infant.
Married Jane Love 1848 at Greenock, Scotland (daughter of Dougall Love and Jane McPhail, the former died in Canada, the latter in Scotland). She was born Dec. 11, 1825, in Argyleshire, Scotland. Their children: Robert b. Nov. 2, 1848, m. Mary Ellen Barnes; Archibald McPhail b. June 18, 1850, d. Aug. 27, 1873; Jane McPhail b. Oct. 30, 1851, m. Francis Gunnell April 5, 1869; Willard Snow b. Nov. 9, 1853, m. Lydia Hopkins; Stephen Golding b. Oct. 17, 1856, m. Ella Wolf Dec. 20, 1893; Jerusha Golding b. Jan. 1, 1859, m. Peter Maughan Feb. 22, 1882; Lilly Lyon b. Sept. 19, 1861, m. Henry Ames Dec. 26, 1878; Margret Wright b. Feb. 17, 1864, m. William H. Maughan Dec. 17, 1885; John Love b. Nov. 1, 1866, m. Susan Brown Dec. 8, 1892. Family home Salt Lake City, Utah.
Married Jane McKimmon Dec. 28, 1856, at Salt Lake City (daughter of Donald McKimmon, who died in Scotland). She was born March 12, 1824, in Argyleshire, Scotland. Only child: John McKimmon b. June 2, 1859, m. Agnes Smith. Family home Salt Lake City, Utah.
Married Marion Stuart Oct. 11, 1868, at Salt Lake City (daughter of Daniel Stuart and Catharine Glen, married about 1849, Kirkliston, Scotland, pioneers 1853). She was born March 3, 1851, at Kirkliston. Their children: Catharine Stuart b. Oct. 20, 1870, m. Charles Nielsen Dec. 29, 1892; Daniel Stuart b. Oct. 25, 1872, and James Stuart b. Oct. 21, 1877, both d. infants. Family home Wellsville, Utah.
Member Nauvoo legion. President 28th quorum seventies; high priest; patriarch; home missionary. Farmer; shoemaker.

PIONEERS AND PROMINENT MEN OF UTAH 743

BAXTER, ZIMRI HAFFORD (son of William Baxter, born Sept. 23, 1784, died 1815, and Rebecca Priest, born June 1796, died Oct. 4, 1861, both of Vassalboro, Kennebec county, Maine). He was born Feb. 14, 1807 at Vassalboro. Came to Utah December, 1849.
Married Eunice Seavey May 2, 1832, Milton, Maine (daughter of Thomas Seavey, born 1749, Scarboro, Maine, died 1819, and Mary Fly, born 1770, and died 1847, in Maine). She was born March 1, 1811. Their children: Benson Edgley b. June 3, 1833; William Franklin b. Sept. 6, 1834; Henry Priest b. Feb. 19, 1836; John b. July 10, 1837; Laura St. Clair b. May 11, 1839; Emily Abigail b. Feb. 20, 1841; Alma b. Dec. 3, 1842; Zimri Seavey b. Aug. 25, 1844; Eunice Seavey b. April 7, 1846, m. Jabez Broadhead; Joseph b. 1847; Charles Albert and Clarice Adelaide b. Aug. 22, 1849, latter m. Daniel Morgan; Roselia b. 1854; Zimri Hafford b. Sept. 1, 1857, m. Wealthea Matilda Higgins.
Married Ann Jackson 1856, Nephi, Utah. Only child: Joseph William, m. Mary Neilsen.
Married Alice Ashworth May 1, 1871, Salt Lake City, who came to Utah 1870, and died March 28, 1877. Their children: Eliza Jane b. Aug. 3, 1872; Philander b. Nov. 19, 1873; Alice Rebecca b. Oct. 5, 1875.
Shortly after coming to Utah, settled at Big Cottonwood; moved to Nephi 1851; built flouring mills at both places, also a grist mill at Big Cottonwood and a nail factory at Nephi; built Nephi tabernacle 1871. Captain of the famous "Silver Greys" of the Nauvoo Legion. Justice of peace and school trustee. Carpenter, joiner and millwright. Died Dec. 10, 1887.

BAXTER, JOSEPH WILLIAM (son of Zimri Hafford Baxter and Ann Jackson). Born April 22, 1859, Nephi, Utah.
Married Mary Neilsen May 22, 1878, Nephi, Utah (daughter of Peter Neilsen and Ana Poulsen of Denmark, who came to Utah September 1874, Christian Larsen company). She was born Sept. 14, 1863. Their children: Joseph William, Jr. b. April 2, 1879; George Henry b. Dec. 21, 1880; Edwin Peter b. May 18, 1883; Franklin Albert b. Oct. 16, 1885; Robert Zimri b. Nov. 3, 1886; Francis Leroy b. Jan. 16, 1890; Mary Beatrice b. July 28, 1892; Ruth Viola b. July 12, 1897; Ruel Allan b. June 5, 1899; Alma Leo and Anna Leone b. July 25, 1903.
Assistant Sunday school superintendent, Big Cottonwood, 1898-99; superintendent Sunday school, Indian Valley, Idaho, 1899-1906. Farmer and fruitgrower.

BAY, JAMES WILLARD. Came to Utah in 1848.
Married Lucinda Sprague. Their children: Mary b. March 16, 1853, m. Richard C. Snow; James Willard b. March 3, 1855, m. Mary LeBaron, Jan. 1, 1871. Family home Junction, Utah. Farmer. Died at Junction.

BEACH, NATHANIEL. Born Dec. 13, 1815, in Massachusetts. Came to Utah 1847.
Married Isabell Adaline Saxton, who was born Feb. 9, 1817, and came to Utah with husband. Their children: Albert Orlando, died; Lyman Smith, m. Mary Jane Sutliff (Cox); Isabell Adaline, m. Oscar Coolidge; Daniel Marion, m. Susan M. Bessy; Mary Ann, died. Family home Manti, Utah.
Indian war veteran. Farmer.

BEACH, LYMAN SMITH (son of Nathaniel Beach and Isabell Adaline Saxton). Born May 7, 1848. Salt Lake City.
Married Mary Jane Sutliff (Cox) Jan. 3, 1870, Salt Lake City (adopted daughter of Edwin Cox), who was born May 3, 1852. Came to Utah with oxteam company. Their children: Lyman LeRoy b. Dec. 23, 1871, died; Isabell b. Nov. 12, 1873, m. Hans Peter Rasmussen, Jr.; Luella Jane b. Sept. 10, 1875, m. Abner Coford; Francis Henry b. Nov. 5, 1877, m. Johannah Maria Anderson; Emily Amelia b. Jan. 10, 1880, m. Vincent Peter Martin; Albert Nathaniel b. Oct. 25, 1882, m. Rowena Taylor; Edwin Marion b. Dec. 23, 1883, m. Edith Marion (Caldwell; Lucy Kate b. Sept. 23, 1886, m. Lawrence Hyatt; William Roscoe b. Oct. 15, 1888, m. Adelaide Hammond; Edna b. Jan. 23, 1892, m. Henry Wilcox; Crystal Jerusha b. Jan. 8, 1896, died. Family resided Manti, Ferron and Molen, Utah.
First and third bishop of Molen ward; counselor to Bishop Rasmussen. Settled at Ferron 1880; assisted in making canals and wagon roads in Emery county and in bringing immigrants to Utah, 1868. Veteran Black Hawk war. Died Sept. 3, 1911, Molen, Utah.

BEACH, FRANCIS HENRY (son of Lyman Smith Beach and Mary Jane Sutliff). Born Nov. 5, 1877, Manti, Utah.
Married Johannah Maria Anderson, March 24, 1903, Molen, Utah (daughter of Andrew H. Anderson and Maria Larson of Denmark). She was born Nov. 17, 1881. Only child: Francis Lyman b. June 5, 1908.
Farmer and sheepraiser.

BEACH, RUFUS (son of John and Sarah Beach of Schoharie county, N. Y.). Came to Utah 1847.
Married Harriet Cordelia Williams (daughter of Daniel R. Williams). Their children: Aaron W. b. Oct. 27, 1847, m. Sarah E. Thomas Nov. 20, 1868. Family home Salt Lake City.

Married Sarah Gibbs. Only child: Kate. Family home Salt Lake City.
Married Nellie Whitehead Nov. 20, 1912.
President 27th quorum seventies 1845.

BEACH, AARON W. (son of Rufus Beach and Harriet Cordelia Williams). Born Oct. 27, 1847, Salt Lake City.
Married Sarah E. Thomas Nov. 20, 1868. Their children: Elizabeth Cordelia b. Dec. 25, 1869; James Ernest b. Dec. 16, 1871; Charles Henry b. Jan. 1, 1873, m. Nellie H. Chase Dec. 28, 1898; Emma Louise b. June 18, 1875, m. William Rounds, Nov. 6, 1895; Aaron Wesley b. Oct. 1877; Rachel b. Sept. 18, 1879, m. William S. Berrett Dec. 28, 1898; Eliza b. Feb. 12, 1881, m. Andrew H. Johnson Oct. 28, 1898; Rufus b. Dec. 17, 1883; Mabel b. Dec. 30, 1886, m. George A. Duncan May 4, 1904; Ruth b. March 20, 1889, m. Lawrence Christensen Jan. 5, 1911; Clara Marie b. Dec. 7, 1892; Harriet Elvira b. May 2, 1895, m. Willis Bray March 11, 1912. Family home Idaho Falls, Idaho.

BEAL, JOHN (son of John Beal, born 1772, and Christina Lewis, born 1760, both of Wells, Somersetshire, Eng., married 1792). He was born July 10, 1801, Wells, Eng. Came to Utah 1849.
Married Ann Deacon 1822 in Cheddar Parish, Somersetshire (daughter of William and Ann Deacon), who was born 1797, and died crossing the plains. Their children: William b. July, 1833, m. Sarah Fowler; Henry b. April 30, 1835, m. Mary Thorpe; John b. Dec. 20, 1836, m. Rosana Avery and Ellen T. Chandler. Family home, Manti, Utah.
Came from England to New York 1822. Active pioneer in San Pete county and one of the founders of Ephraim, Utah. Died 1896.

BEAL, HENRY (son of John Beal and Ann Deacon). Born April 30, 1835, Syracuse, N. Y. Came to Utah 1850.
Married Mary Thorpe July 4, 1854, Ephraim, Utah (daughter of Thomas Thorpe and Ann Storer), who was born May 27, 1827. Their children: Ann (adopted) b. Dec. 28, 1847; Sarah Jane (adopted) b. June 25, 1849; Joseph (adopted) b. Dec. 16, 1851; Ann Eliza b. Sept. 2, 1853, m. Alfred Pehrson; William Henry b. Sept. 23, 1855, died; John Samuel b. June 29, 1857, m. Emma Thursby; George A. b. Sept. 8, 1859, m. Malinda Bean; Henry Thomas b. Oct. 9, 1861, m. Herberta Peterson; David Nelson b. Nov. 15, 1863, m. Martha Hanson; Mary Jemima b. March 13, 1866, m. Martin Isaacson; Emma Rosabell b. Dec. 14, 1868, m. George Klenke. Family home Ephraim, Utah.
Married Anna Christena Byergo March 28, 1863, Salt Lake City (daughter of Andrew Byergo and Anna Christena). She was born Aug. 2, 1844, Füvlum, Denmark. Their children: Mary Ann b. Jan. 26, 1866, m. Christian Foister; Alice b. Jan. 16, 1868, m. Marenus Simonson; Sarah Ann b. March 28, 1872, m. Thorwald Hanson; Thomas Andrew b. July 20, 1874, m. Ida Albertina Peterson; Orson Henry b. Nov. 7, 1876; Elinora Christena b. Feb. 13, 1879, m. Carl A. Mattson; Owen Franklin b. July 12, 1882; Violet Birdilla b. Dec. 3, 1891. Family home Ephraim, Utah.
Married Mary Ann Thompson April 25, 1868, Salt Lake City (daughter of Niels Thompson and Anna Maria Johnson, latter a pioneer 1862, Capt. Murdock company). She was born April 7, 1850, Aarhuus, Denmark. Their children: John William b. March 24, 1871, died; Henry Leroy b. Aug. 12, 1873, m. Zealia Larson; Anna Maria b. Oct. 9, 1875, m. Jacob Hind (died) and Ole Thompson; Mary Matilda b. Jan. 1, 1878, m. Ole Olson; Hyrum Franklin b. April 18, 1880, died; Ellen Christena b. Aug. 2, 1881, m. Robert H. Hardin; Charles; Andrew b. March 27, 1885, died; Martha Mary Ann b. Feb. 15, 1888. Family home, Ephraim, Utah.
Assisted in building the fort, and erected second house, at Ephraim. President first teachers' quorum, and member bishopric; high councilor; member presidency; San Pete stake with President Canute Peterson twenty-five years; ordained patriarch. One of the incorporators Ephraim Co-op store; helped build Climax roller mill; railroad contractor Sanpete Valley R. R. and R. G. W. R. R.; mayor Ephraim 1895. In 1897 assisted Joseph F. Smith, Anthon H. Lund, and William B. Preston to locate the towns of Preston, Lund, Georgetown and White River near Ely, Nev. President of Snow academy; county commissioner; member Utah legislature; Utah delegate to Trans-Mississippi congress at St. Louis.

BEAL, GEORGE A. (son of Henry Beal and Mary Thorpe). Born Sept. 8, 1859, Ephraim, San Pete county, Utah.
Married Melinda Bean Nov. 14, 1878 (daughter of George W. Bean, pioneer 1847, and Emily Haws, pioneer 1850). Their children: Emily Estella b. Oct. 28, 1879, m. Jack Christie; George A. b. Sept. 3, 1881, m. Josephine Nielsen; Clarice M. b. Sept. 14, 1883, m. Bert Tuttle; Leo N. b. Sept. 17, 1885, m. Myrtle Bartlett; Erin T. b. March 9, 1888, m. Elva Johnson; Mary M. b. March 17, 1890; Eldon H. b. May 13, 1893; David C. b. Oct. 22, 1896; Merrill D. b. Nov. 3, 1898; John Raymond b. March 8, 1903. Family resided Ephraim and Richfield, Utah.

BEAL, JOHN (son of John Beal and Ann Deacon). Born Dec. 20, 1836, Syracuse, N. Y. Came to Utah 1849.
Married Rosana Avery 1857, who was born 1832. Their child: John Henry b. 1858. Family home, Ogden, Utah.
Married Lucy Etherington 1860, who was born 1833, in England; died 1867.
Married Ellen T. Chandler Jan. 27, 1871, Salt Lake City (daughter of William and Rachel Chandler), who was born Dec. 28, 1848.

Settled at Manti; moved to Ephraim, Sanpete county, 1856; moved to Ogden, 1857; worked on Salt Lake Temple; assisted in bringing immigrants to Utah. Farmer and stockraiser. One of the founders of Circleville, Utah, 1865.

BEAL, WILLIAM. Came to Utah Sept. 24, 1848, Heber C. Kimball company.
Married Clarissa Allen. Their children: Oscar; Lyman; Franklin, m. Charlotte Hill; John Alma, m. Lavina Esther DeMill and Jemima Pecktol; Harriet, m. Alma Millet; Nancy, m. Ortimus Millet; Eunice, m. Alma Millet.
Settler of Manti, Utah.

BEAL, JOHN ALMA (son of William Beal and Clarissa Allen). Born in October at Parma, Ohio. Came to Utah Sept. 24, 1848, with parents.
Married Lavina Esther DeMill 1860 at Salt Lake City (daughter of Freeborn DeMill and Ann Knight of Manti, Utah, pioneers 1848). She died 1880. Their children; John Alma, died; Ira Allen b. June 13, 1862, m. Silva Funk; Willis, died; Asa, m. Geneva Funk; Newel Knight, m. Ada Elvira DeMill; Emily P., m. Oscar DeMill; Esther Lavina, died; Raynal, m. Annie Keel; Edgar, m. Almeda DeMill, m. Jennie Keel; Cora, m. Henry Peterson. Family home Manti, Utah.
Married Jemima Pecktol in 1880 at Rockville, Utah.
Seventy. Settler of Manti; took active part in protecting it against Indians; assisted to build canals and wagon roads in and around that country. Farmer. Died Jan. 18, 1902, Rockville, Utah.

BEAL, IRA ALLEN (son of John Alma Beal and Lavina Esther DeMill). Born June 13, 1862, at Manti.
Married Silva Funk (Henningsen) Oct. 18, 1888, Manti, Utah (daughter of Daniel Buckley Funk of Ohio and Mary Jane Pecktol of Kentucky, settlers of Manti 1848). She was born Jan. 16, 1862, and was the widow of Christian Henningsen, and their children were: Parley b. Oct. 11, 1883, m. Ora Jensen; Mary b. Oct. 12, 1886, m. Peter Scow. Family resided at Sterling, Utah.
Ira Allen Beal was father of Ira Allen b. July 7, 1889, m. Irene Jensen; Cora Bell b. Aug. 31, 1890, d. infant; Masel b. Feb. 26, 1894; William b. April 25, 1899, died; Milla b. April 25, 1899.
High priest; ward teacher; associated with Y. M. M. I. A. several years. President Emery town board; settler of Emery 1894 and assisted in upbuilding of that county. Blacksmith; photographer; farmer.

BEAL, NEWEL KNIGHT (son of John Alma Beal and Lavina Esther DeMill). Born April 1, 1867, Manti, Utah.
Married Ada Elvira DeMill Jan. 5, 1888, St. George, Utah (daughter of Oliver DeMill and Fadella Wingate of Rockville, Utah). She was born Feb. 14, 1869. Their children: Esther Lavina b. Oct. 8, 1869, m. Lawrence Barney; Fadelia b. Nov. 4, 1871, m. Peter Peterson; Jemima Bell b. Aug. 26, 1892; Lillian b. March 16, 1895; Cyrus b. Jan. 13, 1899; Ada, died; Emily b. Nov. 9, 1903. Family home Ferron, Utah.
President 91st quorum seventies 1903-06; missionary to Arkansas 1898-1900; high priest; bishop Ferron ward 1906; president elders' quorum and president Y. M. M. I. A. at Emery; superintendent Sunday school at Ferron. Farmer and poultryman; apiarist.

BEAN, JAMES (son of James Bean). Born March 3, 1804, Christian county, Ky. Came to Utah Sept. 14, 1848, Daniel Miller company.
Married Elizabeth Lewis July 27, 1824, Lincoln county, Mo. (daughter of John Lewis), who was born Sept. 22, 1803, Lincoln county, Mo. Their children: William; Nancy, m. Thomas Williams; m. John D. Lee; m. Zachariah Decker; Sarah Ann, m. William W. Casper; George Washington, m. Elizabeth Baum; m. Emily Haws; m. Mary Wall; James Addison, m. Harriet Catherine Fausett; Mary Elizabeth, m. Amos W. Haws; Cornelia, died. Family home Provo, Utah.
Bishop's counselor. Farmer and mechanic. Died in June, 1882.

BEAN, GEORGE WASHINGTON (son of James Bean and Elizabeth Lewis). Born April 1, 1831, Wayne county, Ill. Came to Utah Oct. 2, 1847, Jeadiah M. Grant company.
Married Elizabeth Baum Jan. 6, 1853, at Provo (daughter of Jacob Baum and Agnes Harris of Chester county, Pa., pioneers Oct. 1852, Jacob Baum company). She was born Jan. 27, 1834. Their children: Elizabeth Agnes b. Aug. 19, 1854, m. Parley Peterson; George Teancum b. Dec. 26, 1856, m. Celia Hunt; Epaminondas b. June 13, 1859, m. Ina F. Hunt; Anne Alida b. July 28, 1861, m. Paul Von Nordeck; Victor Emanuel b. Feb. 5, 1864, m. Mary Hannah Baker; Marquis LaFayette b. Nov. 4, 1865, m. Annie Horne; Willard Washington b. May 16, 1868, m. Gussie Felt; Flora Diana b. Nov. 14, 1871, m. Joseph L. Horne; Orestes Utah b. Nov. 8, 1873; Junius b. Oct. 17, 1878, died. Family home Provo.
Married Emily Haws Dec. 10, 1856, at Provo (daughter of John Haws and Martha Masters of Wayne county, Ill., pioneers 1850). She was born Feb. 27, 1836. Their children: Malinda b. Jan. 26, 1858, m. George A. Beal: Onias, died; Lola b. Sept. 10, 1861, m. Reuben Farnsworth; Ella b. March 5, 1865, m. A. D. Thurber; Charles L. b. Jan. 29, 1867, m. Mary Jensen; Emily b. July 17, 1869, m. Edward Payne; Burton John b. Dec. 2, 1871, m. Ora Bartlett. Family home Richfield, Utah.
Married Mary Jane Wall Dec. 15, 1856, at Provo (daughter of William Wall and Nancy Haws of Illinois, pioneers Sept. 1850, William Wall company). She was born April 12, 1841. Their children: William James b. March 14, 1858, m. Natalia Outzen; Mary Geneva b. Dec. 15, 1859, m. William Collins; Leo Albert b. Sept 1, 1861, m. Ottaminnie Baker; Nancy Vilate b. April 6, 1864, m. Abram Johnson; Eliza Isabelle b. Dec. 4, 1865, died; Chloe Diantha b. Dec. 4, 1867, m. John E. Eversoll; Malissa b. Feb. 21, 1870, m. S. G. Clark; Virginius b. July 21, 1872, m. Annie Bartlett; Eda Jane b. Sept. 22, 1874, m. John H. Eversoll; Isaac Wall b. Nov. 30, 1876, m. Hattie Bartlett; Jesse Fuller b. Feb. 21, 1878, m. Cecil Gardner; Taylor Jay b. Nov. 5, 1881; Cornelia b, Dec. 11, 1884. Family home Richfield.
Veteran Black Hawk war; pioneers to Sevier valley 1851. Probate judge Provo eight years and Richfield six years; U. S. revenue collector; assessor and collector Utah county; deputy U. S. marshal. Helped establish Mormon fort at Las Vegas, Nev., 1859; assisted to bring back colony of Sacramento valley; first counselor to President Seegmiller, Sevier stake; high priest. Farmer and stockraiser. Died Dec. 9, 1897.

BEAN, LEO ALBERT (son of George Washington Bean and Mary Jane Wall). Born Sept. 1, 1861, Provo, Utah.
Married Ottaminnie Baker Dec. 7, 1887, Logan, Utah (daughter of William G. Baker and Nicolina Marie Bertelsen, pioneers Sept. 28, 1851, John Brown company). She was born March 22, 1868, Nephi, Utah. Their children: Leo Claudius b. April 28, 1889, m. Mary Hall; George Albert b. Feb. 6, 1891; Minnie b. Aug. 22, 1892, died; William Louis b. June 7, 1394; Mary Aileen b. March 1, 1897; Geneva b. May 21, 1899. Family home Richfield, Utah.
Member high council; first counselor to president Y. M. M. I. A.; superintendent Sunday schools; missionary to southern states. City marshal Richfield 1888-91.

BEAN, VIRGINIUS (son of George Washington Bean and Mary Jane Wall). Born July 21, 1872, Provo, Utah.
Married Annie Bartlett May 22, 1895, Salt Lake City (daughter of Henry Bartlett and Illiad McKee of Putnam county, Tenn). She was born Aug. 1, 1876. Their children: Henry Dwight b. March 5, 1896; Virginius Arlie b. April 26, 1897; Byron Jesse b. Jan. 14, 1900; Edwin Bartlett b. Jan. 30, 1904; Virginia b. Feb. 12, 1908. Family home Richfield, Utah.
High priest; missionary to southern and northwestern states 1900-02 and 1907-08, respectively; secretary Sevier stake Sunday schools; president second deacons' quorum; counselor teachers' quorum; bishop Richfield second ward from 1904 to present time. City councilman at Richfield 1912-13; director Sevier Valley Canal Co.; school teacher 1894-1900 at Burrville, Koosharem, Inverury and Escalante, Utah. Farmer.

BEAN, JAMES ADDISON (son of James and Elizabeth Lewis). Born March 11, 1834, Adams county, Ill. Came to Utah Sept. 14, 1848, Daniel Miller company.
Married Harriet Catherine Fausett Feb. 10, 1853, Provo, Utah (daughter of William McGee Fausett and Matilda Butcher, pioneers Sept. 1851, Alexander Stephens company). She was born March 8, 1833. Their children: James William b. Nov. 19, 1853, m. Olive Smoot; Harriet Ann b. May 31, 1855, m. Orson Cluff; Josephine b. Nov. 18, 1857, died; Mary Louisa b. Oct. 3, 1859, m. Thomas C. P. Peterson; Naomi b. Feb. 11, 1863, m. John E. Armitstead; George A. b. Feb. 22, 1861, m. Mary E. Haws; Leonidas H. b. Sept. 15, 1865, m. Elizabeth Buckley; Marcellus b. Nov. 6, 1867, m. Joannah Edman; Frances Matilda b. Sept. 7, 1873, m. Elias A. Gee; Howard b. Oct. 6, 1869, died; Laurence Lafayette b. May 24, 1871, m. Elizabeth Jones; Goldie Fern b. April 14, 1881, m. John William Brown. Family home Provo, Utah.
Member 31st quorum seventies; missionary to Las Vegas, Nev., two years, also to Iowa, Missouri and Illinois, 1876; high priest. School trustee Provo, Utah, and city councilmen two years. Veteran Black Hawk, Timpanogas and Walker Indian wars. Farmer and freighter; manager Utah county stock association 11 years.

BEAN, JAMES WILLIAM (son of James Addison Bean and Harriet Catherine Fausett). Born Nov. 19, 1853, Provo, Utah.
Married Olive Smoot Oct. 18, 1876, Salt Lake City (daughter of Abraham O. Smoot and Diana Eldredge of Provo, pioneers Sept. 1847). She was born Feb. 10, 1860, Salt Lake City. Their children: Luella and Estella, twins, b. Oct. 8, 1877, former d. Oct. 2, 1879; latter d. Oct. 11, 1879; William Cullen b. May 4, 1879, d. July 25, 1880; Diana b. Feb. 7, 1881, m. Roy D. Thatcher; Harriet Virginia b. Nov. 1, 1882; Pauline b. Oct. 9, 1885, d. Aug. 23, 1891; Azua b. Aug. 22, 1887; Margaret b. Dec. 6, 1888; Ross Smoot b. March 17, 1890; Lee Addison b. Aug. 12, 1891; Orea b. June 6, 1894; Ruth b. June 8, 1896; Seth b. Oct. 8, 1897; George Elmer b. April 13, 1899; Joseph Wayne b. Oct. 25, 1900. Family home Provo, Utah.
Married Pauline Emelia Hardy Nov. 19, 1884, Salt Lake City (daughter of Charles Marcus Hardy and Mary Sophia Doldi, pioneers Sept. 28, 1861, Schuttler company). She was born July 7, 1857. Their children: Josephine Olive b. July 28, 1886, m. William Udell Scofield; James Horace b. July 13, 1890; Elife b. April 17, 1892; Charles Sterling b. April 15, 1897; Milo b. Dec. 10, 1898; Marcus Hardy b. Sept. 4, 1901. Family home Provo, Utah.
Missionary to southern states; tithing clerk 25 years; high priest; member of high council of Utah stake. Bookkeeper; accountant; agriculturist.

BEAN, JOSEPH (son of George Bean, born Sept. 14, 1778, and Mary Milner, born Oct. 23, 1777, both of Yorkshire, Eng.). He was born April 18, 1814, at Ulleskelf, near York, Eng. Came to Utah Sept. 16, 1859, Edward Stevenson company.
Married Sarah Beanland (daughter of John Beanland and Elizabeth Crabtree), who was born Sept. 21, 1821, and came to Utah with husband. Their children: George b. Aug. 22, 1842; Mary Elizabeth b. Feb. 16, 1845, m. William C. Murphy; Sarah b. Feb. 11, 1847, m. Henry Coulam; Emma b. Dec. 19, 1848; Eliza b. March 31, 1851, m. Joseph Smith Jan. 18, 1859; Margaret b. June 7, 1853; Esther Siddons b. April 9, 1855; Joseph Hyrum Parley b. March 23, 1857; Joshua Beanland b. Oct. 9, 1858, m. Amy Hulbert Jan. 11, 1882; William Samuel Milner b. Aug. 14, 1861, m. Elizabeth Armstrong; Annie Louisa b. July 28, 1864.
High priest; counselor to Bishop Alexander McRae of the eleventh ward. Trustee of district school board. Black Hawk war veteran.

BEARD, THOMAS (son of Thomas Beard and Ellen E. Clark of Whaley Bridge, Eng.). Born Dec. 14, 1836, at Whaley Bridge. Came to Utah Sept. 24, 1862, Homer Duncan company.
Married Mary Ann Openshaw Simister June 5, 1859, at Whaley Bridge (daughter of John and Amelia Openshaw of New Mills, Eng.). She was born Oct. 1823. Their children: Mary Hannah b. May 29, 1860, m. Thomas Birch; James Thomas b. Nov. 24, 1863, m. Mary Goodworth; Ellen Amelia b. Nov. 23, 1866, d. 1876. Family home Coalville, Summit county, Utah.
Married Mahaleth Abiah Tanner June 27, 1884 (daughter of John Tanner and June Chase of Cottonwood, Salt Lake county). She was born March 30, 1868. Their children: John b. Feb. 26, 1887; Lydia Jane b. July 8, 1890; Lilly Ann b. Dec. 4, 1898; George Thomas b. April 26, 1899; Stephen, died; Susan Ellen, died; Aaron b. July 15, 1902; Mary Ann b. May 16, 1904; Edward Chancy b. Oct. 1, 1905. Family home Coalville.
Opened Wasatch coal mine. Florist and gardener. Organized first Sunday school in Summit county 1863; missionary to England; high priest; president 27th quorum seventies Coalville. City councilman two years; school trustee.

BEATIE, HAMPDEN SIDNEY (son of Josiah N. Beatie and Eleanor Rogers of Virginia). Born Dec. 31, 1826, Washington county, Va. Came to Utah in September, 1849.
Married Marion T. Mumford Jan. 1, 1849, in Missouri (daughter of Edward T. Mumford and Hannah T. Crosby, pioneers Sept. 1849). She was born April 12, 1831, and died Sept. 5, 1904. Their children: H. J., m. Phoebe S. Young; Hannah Eleanor, m. C. B. Hawley, m. Edward Bartliff; H. S., m. Ellen E. Richardson; Josephine E., m. Rulon S. Wells; Mary E. (died), m. Heber M. Wells; Marion M., m. H. G. Whitney; Edward F.; Frank L., m. Mary Clawson; Florence B., m. Guy Thatcher. Family home Salt Lake City.
Seventy. County coroner. Pioneer Carson county, Nev. Lieutenant-colonel in Utah militia. Manager Z. C. M. I. Died Sept. 11, 1887.

BEATIE, W. J. (son of Hampden Sidney Beatie and Marion T. Mumford). Born Jan. 1, 1850, at Salt Lake City.
Married Phoebe L. Young Jan. 7, 1872, Salt Lake City (daughter of Brigham Young and Clarissa Ross of Salt Lake City). She was born Aug. 1, 1854. Their children: Clarissa Marion b. Oct. 21, 1872, died; Josephine Y. b. Sept. 2, 1874, m. Charles L. Burton; Walter J. b. Oct. 23, 1876, d. Oct. 23, 1876; Hazel Y. b. Nov. 27, 1850, m. Edward F. Kimball; Mary T. b. Sept. 23, 1882, d. April 25, 1883; N. R. b. Oct. 26, 1886; Walter Sidney b. June 12, 1888, m Margaret Taylor. Family home Salt Lake City.
Member 7th quorum seventies; missionary to England 1877-79; high priest. National bank examiner.

BEAUREGARD, CHRISTIAN PETER (son of Peter Christensen Beauregard and Maren Nielsen of Viborg amt, Denmark). Born March 18, 1826, Randers, Denmark. Came to Utah Sept. 27, 1862, John R. Murdock company.
Married Anna K. Sorensen April 1, 1848, in Denmark (daughter of Soren Hansen and Sine Anderson), who was born Nov. 25, 1825, and came to Utah with husband. Their children: Peter b. 1848 and Anna b. 1849, d. infants; Jens Peter b. July 9, 1850, m. Elizabeth Tarbuck June 28, 1869; Marinus b. Feb. 5, 1852, m. Amelia Edwards Feb. 2, 1882; Charles Christian b. Sept. 27, 1853, m. Kaire Nicholos May 21, 1874; Stine Westborg b. Jan. d. 1884; Neils b. 1855, d. 1857; Sigurd b. 1857, d. 1857; Neils Jacob b. July 13, 1858, m. Stella McRae Jan. 11, 1883; Augusta Tomine b. Sept. 14, 1860, m. Ted Davis April 22, 1878; Frances Amelia b. May 30, 1862, m. Orson Huntsman Feb. 1, 1883; John b. July 27, 1866, d. Feb. 10, 1869; Christian b. April 6, 1868, d. April 29, 1868.
Married Martha Day Oct. 17, 1884, St. George, Utah (daughter of Richard and Elizabeth Day), who was born Jan. 3, 1858, in England. Their children: Richard Alonzo b. Feb. 9, 1886, m. Mary Warner Dec. 8, 1910; Laura b. March 29, 1887, m. Albert Dearden Dec. 1, 1910; Wilford b. March 29, 1893. Families resided Fillmore, Utah.
Justice of peace 1875-79. President Fillmore Irrigation company. Member high council of Millard stake; patriarch. Blacksmith.

BEAUREGARD, MARINUS (son of Christian Peter Beauregard and Ann K. Sorensen). Born Feb. 5, 1852, Mirah, Denmark. Came to Utah with parents.
Married Amelia Edwards Feb. 2, 1882, Fillmore Utah (daughter of Caleb and Cynthia Edwards), who was born Sep. 3, 1857, Manti, Utah. Their children: Marinus Dennis b. Dec. 21, 1882; Electa b. Nov. 15, 1884, m. Joseph Dennison; Amelia; Amelia Frances L. b. Nov. 13, 1890, m. Clarence Halverson; Dora Irene b. Nov. 5, 1895, d. Aug. 8 1896; Mina Archie b. Sept. 10, 1898; Leah b. Nov. 7, 1900. Family resided Fillmore and Sterling, Utah.
School trustee at Sterling four years. Promoter of Gunnison waterworks 1910-11. City councilman at Gunnison 1910-11. President Gunnison Valley Power company 1911; director Gunnison Valley bank.

BEAUREGARD, MARINUS DENNIS (son of Marinus Beauregard and Amelia Edwards). Born Dec. 21, 1882, Fillmore, Utah.
Missionary to eastern states 1907-09; ward and Sunday school teacher 1909-11; home missionary. City treasurer of Gunnison 1909. President Gunnison Valley Power company.

BECK, JOSEPH ELLISON (son of Antram Beck of Pennsylvania). Came to Utah in 1849.
Married Forsyth. Their children: Lucilda, m. John Snell; Thomas Harrison, m. Mary Dennis; John, m. Polly Jones; Margaret Fannie, m. Richard Murray; Albert, m. Maggie Thomas; Rebecca, m. John Berry. Family home Spanish Fork, Utah.
Seventy. Farmer. Died at Spanish Fork, Utah.

BECKSTEAD, ALEXANDER (son of Francis and Margaret Beckstead of Germany). Born March 18, 1802, Williamsburg, Canada. Came to Utah Sept. 1849, Redden Allred company.
Married Catherine Lince Jan. 25, 1823, Williamsburg, Canada, who was born July 6, 1807. Their children: Margarett Mariah b. Dec. 9, 1823, m. Samuel Egbert 1839; Gordan Silas b. Nov. 25, 1825, m. Barbara Parks 1854, m. Elizabeth Hunsaker 1859; Henry b. Sept. 4, 1827, m. Luseen Bird Bydee June 6, 1849; William b. Sept. 24, 1829, d. July 21, 1830; Harriett V. b. June 17, 1831, m. Abraham Hunsaker; Thomas Wesley b. April 27, 1833, m. Lydia Rose 1853, m. Sarah Easton 1866; Lucy Ann b. March 16, 1835, d. July 21, 1848; Emeline b. April 4, 1837, m. William Andrew Bills July 4, 1852; Sarah E. b. Dec. 31, 1838, m. John W. Winward 1856; Samuel Alexander b. Dec. 25, 1840, m. Araminta C. Allen 1856, d. March 28, 1861; Amanda Jane b. Jan. 3, 1843, d. Sept. 6, 1844; George Washington b. Dec. 3, 1845, d. Dec. 19, 1912, m. Araminta C. Allen; John Alma b. Aug. 9, 1848, m. Sabina Harrison; Mary Ellen b. Aug. 9, 1848, d. same day; Joseph Alonzo b. Dec. 27, 1850, m. Elizabeth Shields.
Married Kesiah Albina Petty Nov. 18, 1854 (daughter of Robert C. and Margarett Petty of Benton county, Tenn.). Their children: Hyrum b. Oct. 27, 1855, m. Myer Robins; Moses W. b. Jan. 27, 1857, m. Lucrice Davis; Aaron b. May 12, 1858, m. Eva Pierce; Fanney Kesiah b. Dec. 5, 1859, m. John J. Williams; Robert b. March 7, 1861, m. Sarah E. Naylor; Margarett A. b. May 26, 1862, m. Joseph Hibbard; Martha Ann b. Jan. 16, 1864, m. Jesse Aylett; Francis Albert b. Jan. 15, 1866, m. Miss Hanser; Ira b. Dec. 26, 1867, m. Jose Conry; Alexander b. Feb. 17, 1870, m. Miss Jackson. Family home West Jordan, Utah.
Married Clarissa Ann Brown Feb. 1856, Salt Lake City. Their children: Eliza b. April 10, 1857, m. Orson Lee; Catherine b. Feb. 16, 1859, m. Mr. Foisy; Viola J. b. 1860; died; Clarissa Ann b. Feb. 1862, died; Heber Alexander b. Aug. 11, 1864; Araminta b. July 4, 1867, died; Susan V. b. Aug. 20, 1869, died.
Settled at West Jordan, 1850, assisted in bringing immigrants to Utah. Veteran Black Hawk war.

BECKSTEAD, HENRY (son of Alexander Beckstead and Catherine Lince). Born Dec. 4, 1827, Morrisburg, Canada.
Married Luseen Bird Bybee June 6, 1849, North Pijon, Mo. (daughter of Byram Bybee and Betsey Bird Lane, pioneers 1852). She was born Feb. 7, 1831. Their children: William Alexander b. Sept. 1, 1852, m. Araminta E. Beckstead, 1872; Henry Byrum b. June 28, 1853, m. Catherine Egbert, March. 1869; Gordon Silas b. July 13, 1854, m. Elzina J. Beckstead Nov. 30, 1874; Betsy Luseen b. April 6, 1856, m. John C. Egbert 1872; Deliah Jane b. April 22, 1858, m. Brigham Sellers 1873. Family resided Uinta, Ogden and South Jordan, Utah.
Married Emily Grace Williams 1857, Salt Lake City (daughter of William Williams, pioneer 1856, handcart company and Bathsheba Burne, who came to Utah 1871). She was born Dec. 23, 1838, Cornwall, Eng. Their children: Emily Bathsheba b. Jan. 31, 1859, m. Alexander Bills; Samuel Henry b. June 14, 1860, m. Mary Ann Howard 1882; Catherine b. Dec. 26, 1862, m. Arthur John Holt; Joseph M. b. Sept. 5, 1864, d. 1865; John Carlos b. Jan. 23, 1868, drowned 1868; Isaac Newton b. Sept. 17, 1868, m. Josephine Ehrngreen (died), m. Florence Hutchings; Jesse Nimrod b. March 12, 1870, m. Mariah Wing, died.
Married Emma Marsden April, 1882, Salt Lake City (daughter of William, pioneer 1854, oxteam company, and Sarah M. Marsden, pioneer Sept. 12, 1861, John R. Murdock company). She was born May, 1845, Yorkshire, Eng. Their children: George Nelson b. Feb. 24, 1866, m. Birdie Palmer; Charles and Alonzo, twins, b. Jan. 17, 1868, d. 1868; John Walter and William Arthur, twins, b. Sept. 3, 1870, d. 1870.

Married Elizabeth Wood April, 1862, Salt Lake City (daughter of James Wood and Mary Bates, pioneers 1856). She was born March 20, 1846, in England. Their children: James b. May 7, 1863, d. 1891; Mary Ann b. Jan. 17, 1867, m. Henry W. Beckstead, 1883; Sarah E. b. Oct. 14, 1869, m. David Shields 1886.
Married Mary Hannah Williams (daughter of Joseph J. Williams and Johanna Tripp, pioneers Aug 20, 1868, Joseph W. Rawlins company). She was born April 2, 1854, in England. Their children: Joseph E. b. Feb. 9, 1872, d. Feb. 22, 1872; John T. b. May 4, 1873, m. Miss Page.
Settled at Farmington 1850, Uinta 1851, and lived at Ogden 1855-61. Sheriff Weber county 1855-58. Participated in Echo Canyon campaign; Indian war veteran. Moved to South Jordan and was a member of the bishopric of that ward 20 years. Died 1888 West Jordan.

BECKSTEAD, HENRY BYRAM (son of Henry Beckstead and Luseen Bird Bybee). Born June 28, 1850, Davis county, Utah.
Married Catherine Mariah Egbert March 1, 1869 (daughter of Samuel Egbert and Margaret M. Beckstead, pioneers 1849, Redden Allred company). She was born Sept. 27, 1850, West Jordan, Utah. Their children: Byram Henry b. April 5, 1870, m. Annie J. Holt Nov. 20, 1889; Samuel William b. June 25, 1872, d. aged 3; Margarett Geneva b. April 2, 1874, m. Samuel E. Holt Aug. 16, 1893; Emanuel Lafayette b. March 13, 1876, m. Nina Editha Beckstead 1897; Perry Wallace b. Oct. 26, 1877, m. Lenora Mackey April 27, 1904; Birdie Luseen b. Oct. 16, 1879, m. Joseph Frederick Palmer Dec. 29, 1898; Luella b. May 5, 1882, m. Thomas A. Newbold Nov. 1901; Ivey Grace b. May 9, 1884, d. April 20, 1895; Rhoda Mariah b. Aug 8, 1887; Daniel Mortimer b. Oct. 10, 1889, d. April 23, 1895; Polly b. May 21, 1891, d. 3 days old; Rosamond b. Dec. 8, 1893, d. June 14, 1901. Family home South Jordan, Utah.
Married Amanda Jane Egbert March 14, 1878 (daughter of Samuel Egbert and Margaret M. Beckstead), who was born Jan. 5, 1857, West Jordan. Their children: Angus Z. b. Dec. 30, 1878, m. Matilda Peterson Aug. 1900; Walter Edgar b. Feb. 28, 1881, m. Geneva Beckstead 1902; Alfred Ray b. March 26, 1884, m. Sarah Weeb April 12, 1905; Ebenezer D. b. July 11, 1886, d. Feb. 19, 1888; Maurice S. b. Aug. 8, 1888 (d. June 27, 1909), m. Alice Blake Oct. 30, 1907; Lulu Mariah b. May 29, 1891, m. John Weeb Nov. 10, 1909; Elmer Byram b. Aug. 24, 1895.
President 95th quorum seventies for 25 years; missionary to southern states 1882-83; Sunday school superintendent eight years; sexton 30 years. Veteran Black Hawk Indian war. Superintendent of South Jordan Canal company 12 years. Home missionary six years; ward missionary 40 years.

BECKSTEAD, GORDON SILAS (son of Henry Beckstead and Luseen Bird Bybee). Born July 13, 1854, East Weber, Utah.
Married Elzina J. Beckstead Nov. 30, 1874, Salt Lake City (daughter of Samuel Alexander Beckstead and Araminta Allen, pioneers Sept. 20, 1849, Allen Taylor division of Brigham Young company). She was born March 7, 1860. Their children: Silas A. b. May 28, 1876, d. Nov. 24, 1879; Alfred E. b. Oct. 25, 1878, died Sept. 12, 1876; Etta F. b. Jan. 20, 1880, m. N. H. Henderson; Gordon O. b. Aug. 7, 1881, m. Hannah Ericksen; Henry A. b. June 16, 1853, m. Sarah M. Bowlden; Eliza O. b. Jan. 10, 1886, m. Hyram Stocking; Araminta L. b. Aug 4, 1889, m. Hyram A. Nordberg; Clarence H. b. April 11, 1892, m. Martha P. Newbold; Lee Allen b. Aug. 5, 1897. Family home South Jordan, Utah.
High priest; president 16th quorum elders Salt Lake Stake 1896; secretary-treasurer and president 95th quorum seventies. Constable 18 years and school trustee 17 years, South Jordan, Utah; member B. Y. university South American exploring expedition 1900, serving as captain. Helped build both South Jordan and Salt Lake canals.

BEDDO, JAMES (son of George Beddo and Jane Meredith of Victoria, South Wales). He was born Jan. 27, 1847, at Victoria. Came to Utah Sept. 3, 1852, Abraham O. Smoot company.
Married Romania Deseret Neel Dec. 6, 1875, Salt Lake City (daughter of John Neel and Clemency Lytton Casper of Ogden, Utah, pioneers Sept. 3, 1855, John Hindley company). She was born March 1, 1857. Their children: James William, m. Jennie Elizabeth Allen; George Raymond, m. Sadie Alice Pearce; Wriley Guy; Dan Meredith; Ira Washington; Romania Alvira; Harvey Neel; Bryan Earl. Family resided Shelton ward, Bingham county, Idaho, and Vernal, Utah.
Member elders' quorum; home missionary Fremont county, Idaho, three months. School trustee in Bingham county, Idaho, 1882-88. Manager Harrison and Great Feeder Canal companies. Bingham county, Idaho, 1890-97. Worked on Salt Lake temple 1867.

BEER, BENJAMIN JAMES BEER (son of Benjamin James Beer of London, Eng.). Born Sept. 21, 1812, London, Eng. Came to Utah Sept. 26, 1856, Edmund Ellsworth and Daniel D. McArthur company, the first to cross the plains with handcarts.
Married Mary Ann Livesey 1863. Salt Lake City (daughter of John Livesey, accidentally killed in St. Louis, Mo., and Mary Elizabeth Gill of Manchester, Eng., pioneer Nov. 21, 1862). She was born Sept. 25, 1846, and came to Utah with mother. Their children: Benjamin John b. Jan. 31, 1865, m. Mary Elizabeth Taylor; William Francis b. Nov. 7, 1866, m. Josephine Luella Taylor. Family home Salt Lake City. Painter and paperhanger. Died 1906.

BEER, WILLIAM FRANCIS (son of Benjamin James Beer and Mary Ann Livesey). Born Nov. 7, 1866, Salt Lake City.
Married Josephine Luella Taylor Sept. 20, 1889 (daughter of Joseph E. Taylor and Louise R. Capener of Salt Lake City). She was born May 31, 1869. Their children: William Francis, Jr., b. March 25, 1896; Vivian Luella b. Dec. 4, 1898; Kenneth Verender b. Dec. 9, 1903. Family home Salt Lake City.
Graduate of medicine in Columbian University, Washington. D. C., 1892; assistant surgeon-general of the state of Utah 1896-1904; associate gynecologist L. D. S. hospital since its organization in 1905; member state and county medical societies, also of American medical association.

BEESLEY, EBENEZER (son of William Sheppard Beesley and Susannah Edwards of England). Born Dec. 14, 1840, Bicester, Oxfordshire, Eng. Came to Utah Sept. 4, 1859, George Rowley handcart company.
Married Sarah Hancock March 26, 1859, Woburn, Buckinghamshire, Eng. (daughter of Henry Hancock and Sarah Ayres, of England, pioneers Sept. 4, 1859, George Rowley company). She was born Jan. 14, 1840. Their children: Ebenezer, m. Emily Jane Cooper; William Henry d. June 18, 1863; Frederick, m. Elizabeth Ellen Solomon; Adelbert, m. Adelaide Pugsley; Ella, m. Ernest E. Ridges; Lorenzo, m. Josephine Hopwood; Alvin Augustus, m. Ruby Pratt; Franklin, m. Mamie Sullivan; Amy Susannah, m. Edwin Lee; Sarah Em., m. William F. Everett. Family home Salt Lake City.
Married Annie F. Buckeridge April 19, 1869, Salt Lake City (daughter of John Buckeridge and Caroline Brunswick of Theil, Buckinghamshire). She was born Aug. 8, 1845. Their children: Truman John, died; Willard George; Frances Caroline, died; Clarissa Alice; Alma Frewin, died; Wilford Angus, m. Emma Frewin. Family home Salt Lake City.
Member 30th quorum seventies; high priest; leader of ward and tabernacle choirs. First president of Beesley Music Company. Shoemaker. Died March 21, 1906, Salt Lake City.

BEESLEY, FREDERICK (son of Ebenezer Beesley and Sarah Hancock). Born Jan. 13, 1864, Salt Lake City.
Married Elizabeth Ellen Solomon Nov. 27, 1885, Logan, Utah (daughter of Alfred Solomon and Ellen Gyde of Salt Lake City, pioneers 1857). She was born May 27, 1864. Their children: Frederick Alfred b. Dec. 25, 1888, m. Mary Hazel Bowman; Elmer Ebenezer b. Feb. 5, 1889; James Gyde b. July 18, 1890, died; Ethel Elizabeth b. June 16, 1892; Mabel Ellen b. June 12, 1894; Blanche b. June 14, 1900; William Noall b. Sept. 18, 1904. Family home Salt Lake City.
President 109th quorum seventies; missionary to Sandwich Islands 1885-89; and 1890-91; assistant Sunday school superintendent 22d ward; president Y. M. M. I. A. Secretary and treasurer Beesley Music Company.

BEESLEY, ADELBERT (son of Ebenezer Beesley and Sarah Hancock). Born Jan. 3, 1866, Salt Lake City.
Married Adelaide Pugsley July 20, 1892, Manti, Utah (daughter of Philip Pugsley and Martha Roach), who was born Jan. 22, 1866, at Salt Lake City, Utah. Their children: Stella b. May 13, 1893; Adelaide, b. May 10, 1894, d. aged 5; Mary b. Sept. 11, 1896, d. infant; Albert P. b. Feb. 11, 1898; Philipp G. b. July 17, 1900, d. aged 14; Lucile b. Sept. 10, 1902; Howard R. b. Nov. 28, 1904; Ardelle b. May 30, 1910. Lived at Salt Lake City, Utah.
Member 30th and 161st and secretary of 109th quorum seventies; missionary to Samoa 1888-91. Theatrical musician many years.

BEESLEY, JOSEPH S. (son of John Beesley, born Nov. 5, 1799, and Mary Miller, born Feb. 13, 1808, both of Lancashire, Eng.). He was born Feb. 23, 1844, near Cedar Grove, Franklin county, Ind. Came to Utah in 1862.
Married Eliza Ann Andrews 1874 (daughter of John Andrews and Elizabeth Wise, pioneers Sept. 1852, Isaac Bullock company). She was born Nov. 26, 1852, Nephi, Utah. Their children: John A. b. Nov. 19, 1875, m. Cloe Thayne, July 22, 1909; Joseph S., Jr. b. Oct. 28, 1878; Mary E. b. Feb. 2, 1880, m. John J. Hunt, July 7, 1908; Emily b. July 20, 1882; Eliza Ann b. Oct. 12, 1883; Sarah Naomi b. Oct. 7, 1885, m. John P. Bowers Feb. 20, 1906; Emer A. b. Nov. 14, 1887; Hannah B. b. Oct. 15, 1889; Charles A. b. Feb. 9, 1891; Margaret Ann b. Dec. 4, 1893; Seymour A. b. Feb. 6, 1895; Arthur A. b. Dec. 2, 1897. Family resided Provo, Utah, and Idaho towns.
Drove oxteams to transport worthy poor from Utah to the Missouri river and back 1864; assisted with his own means to build the Provo temple; moved from Provo to Idaho in 1898, and there assisted to build the first meeting house at Driggs. Was ordained a high priest and member of the high council when the Teton stake was organized. Moved to Rexburg Idaho in 1903.

PIONEERS AND PROMINENT MEN OF UTAH

BEHUNIN, ISAAC. Came to Utah 1847, second oxteam company.
Married Almina Tyler. Their children: Andrew; Almina, m. Amos Stevens; Nancy, m. Nelson Higgins; Mosiah, m. Carolina Hill; Cutler, m. Jane Nay; Hyrum, died. Family resided Richfield and Manti, Utah.
Married (name of second wife unknown). Their children: William, died; Morton; Alma, died.
Veteran Black Hawk war. Farmer and sheepraiser. Died at Ferron, Utah.

BEHUNIN, MOSIAH (son of Isaac Behunin and Almina Tyler). Born 1844, in Illinois. Came to Utah 1847 with parents.
Married Carolina Hill 1867, Salt Lake City (daughter of Isaac Hill and Martha Blazzard), who was born Jan. 16, 1854. Their children: Isaac S. b. Nov. 12, 1870, m. Olive Mintchie; Joseph Henry b. March 24, 1872, m. Mary Zwahlen; Brigham Daniel b. Sept. 13, 1874, m. Mary Jane Biddlecome; David b. Nov. 18, 1876, m. Cornelia Larsen; John b. April 2, 1879, m. Dorcus Ann Biddlecome; Caroline, m. Robert D. Redford; Elizor, m. Hazel Westwood; George A. b. April 2, —, m. Mary Jane Biddlecome; Mary Jane, m. Elbert Wilcox; Cynthia b. Jan. 1, —, m. Charles Blackburn; Robert Peary. Family home Ferron, Utah.
Seventy. Sent to Rabbit valley in 1872, to make peace with the Indians. Farmer and horticulturist. Died April 6, 1908, Ferron, Utah.

BEHUNIN, JOSEPH HENRY (son of Mosiah Behunin and Carolina Hill). Born March 24, 1872, Rockville, Utah.
Married Mary Zwahlen Dec. 31, 1895, Ferron, Utah (daughter of John Zwahlen and Mary Shultiess, of Bern, Switzerland, who came to Utah in 1874). She was born July 31, 1872. Their children: Ida May b. Oct. 22, 1896; Vera b. April 11, 1898; Blanche b. Dec. 29, 1899; Leland b. March 22, 1901; Cecil b. April 12, 1903. Family home Ferron, Utah.
Member 97th quorum seventies; Pres. Y. M. M. I. A.; Sunday school teacher. County horticultural inspector.

BEHUNIN, DAVID (son of Mosiah Behunin and Carolina Hill). Born Nov. 18, 1876, Richfield, Utah.
Married Cornelia Larsen March 9, 1909, Castle Dale, Utah (daughter of Hans Larsen and Anna Maria Christensen of Helsingor, Denmark). She was born Oct. 20, 1888. Only child: David Wendel b. May 12, 1912. Family home Ferron, Utah.
Priest. Moved to Rabbit valley with his father in 1872. Farmer and stockraiser; bookkeeper.

BELCHER, EDWARD EVERETT (son of Joseph Belcher of St. Louis, Mo.). Born July 4, 1835, Boston, Mass. Came to Utah 1852.
Married Elizabeth Jane Perkins Dec. 1863, in Washoe valley, near Nevada City, Nev. (daughter of Wilson Gardner Perkins and Diana Anderson of Grundy county, Mo., pioneers 1848, John D. Lee company). She was born Feb. 11, 1837. Their children: Mary Ida b. Sept. 16, 1864, m. Marriott Lutz; m. Sandy Brown; Luella V. b. Jan. 29, 1869, m. John D. Fackrell; Laura b. July 29, 1871, d. aged 18; Elizabeth S. b. Oct. 7, 1875, m. Carl Bartholomew; Edward Harvey b. Dec. 10, 1877, m. Cora Myrtle Johnson; Clarence Leroy b. Dec. 4, 1882, m. Rozell Halladay.
Elder. First located at Bountiful; went to Randolph, 1870, and to Vernal 1885. Farmer and cattleraiser; paperhanger and painter. Discoverer of Belcher mine in Nevada. Died April 8, 1892.

BELCHER, EDWARD HARVEY (son of Edward Everett Belcher and Elizabeth Jane Perkins). Born Dec. 10, 1877, Randolph, Utah.
Married Cora Myrtle Johnson Dec. 11, 1902, Vernal, Utah (daughter of Lycurgus Johnson and Cora Belle Davis of Vernal). She was born April 21, 1883. Their children: Hilda Ardus b. Sept. 20, 1903; Cora Elizabeth b. Aug. 7, 1905; Edward Warren b. Dec. 23, 1907; Loris Myrtle b. June 11, 1911. Family home Vernal since 1885.
Member 97th quorum seventies and one of its presidents; counselor to Bishops David Bennion, Frederick G. Froerer Bingham and George E. Wilkins of second ward, Vernal; counselor and secretary of stake Y. M. M. I. A. 1899-1909; assistant Sunday school superintendent. Recorder of Vernal City, and its postmaster; assistant cashier of Uinta state ban .

BELL, ALFRED (son of William and Be'sie Bell). Born 1796, in Shelby county, Ill. Came to Utah 1851.
Married Martha Louisa Montgomery (daughter of James Montgomery), who was born April 7, 1807. Their children: William M. b. July 22, 1833, m. Martha Kirstine Benson April 9, 1859; Eli b. Nov. 12, 1834, m. Louisa Ann McClellan Aug. 18, 1858. Family home Lehi, Utah.
Veteran war of 1812. Judge at Lehi 1851-59.

BELL, WILLIAM MILTON (son of Alfred Bell and Martha Louisa Montgomery). Born July 22, 1833, Shelbyville, Ill.
Married Martha Kirstine Benson April 9, 1859, Salt Lake City (daughter of Jeppa Denson, pioneer 1853, and Maren Kirstine Kofoed). She was born Jan. 19, 1837, Bornholm, Denmark. Their children: William Alfred b. April 7, 1860, m. Adeline Roeberry Dec. 25, 1888; Martha Jane b. Nov. 2, 1861, m. Swen H. Jacobs; Marion b. Jan. 17, 1864, m. Oluf S. Anderson Nov. 18, 1885; Eli Jeppa b. March 25, 1866, m. Mary A. Dudley April 5, 1905; Hyrum b. Dec. 24, 1868, m. Amanda Sangreen Sept. 1, 1892; Joseph Robert b. April 20, 1871, m. Mary E. Smith April 30, 1901; Lily Elnora b. Aug. 11, 1873, m. Silas Hinckley; Sarah Rebecca b. Nov. 18, 1871, m. D. Rolla Harris June 9, 1897.
Assisted in bringing immigrants to Utah. Pioneer Cache and Snake River valleys. Carpenter.

BELL, ELI J. (son of William Milton Bell and Martha Kirstine Benson). Born March 25, 1866, Lehi, Utah.
Married Mary Ann Dudley April 5, 1905 (daughter of Hyrum Smith Dudley and Fidelia Sophia Tippets, natives of Utah). She was born June 2, 1877, Alma, Weber county, Utah. Their children: Milton Smith b. March 21, 1906; Lamont Dudley b. Aug. 15, 1907; Cecelia Dudley b. Nov. 1, 1908; Eli b. June 27, 1911; Levon B. and Levere T. (twins) b. April 1, 1913.
Missionary to Norway 1900-02. Farmer; carpenter.

BELL, JOHN WATSON (son of John and Alice Bell of Newcastle, Northumberlandshire, Eng.). Born May 25, 1895, Newcastle, Eng. Came to Utah Oct. 1854, Benjamin Clapp company.
Married Ann Fish October, 1835, Newcastle, Eng. (daughter of Robert and Dorothy Fish of Bedlington, Eng.). She came to Utah Oct. 1855, leaving the Missouri river with two yoke of oxen and one yoke of cows, came across the plains accompanied by her eight children—Anna, m. Henry Reynolds, m. William Lance; Robert, d. infant; Alice Jane b. April 15, 1840, m. Joel Almon Bascom; John Watson, Jr., m. Laura Roberts; Emma Dorothy, m. Ephraim Roberts; Alma; Mary, m. William Baldwin; Sarah, m. William Lance. Family resided Provo and Mona, Utah.
Pioneer of Mona, where he died in 1877. High priest. He was a tailor by occupation.

BELL, THOMAS (son of John Bell of Barford, Norfolk, Eng.). Born July 7, 1825, Norfolk, Eng. Came to Utah 1852.
Married Mahala Elwood Nov. 22, 1854, Salt Lake City, who was born at Spexall, Suffolk, Eng. Their children: John Thomas b. Oct. 4, 1855, m. Lucy Ann Wardle; Mary Jane b. Feb. 18, 1858, died; Herbert Horace b. Feb. 26, 1859, m. Lucy Payne; William James b. May 6, 1867, m. Elizabeth Payne; Thomas Henry b. May 9, 1864, m. Josephine Peterson.
Married Henrietta Euphemia Lundquist Nov. 7, 1865, Salt Lake City, who was born Nov. 2, 1846, Malmo, Sweden. Their children: Mahala Charlotte b. Oct. 5, 1866, m. James William Sylvester; Alice Henriette b. Aug. 19, 1868, m. Ira Miles; Bernard Amiel b. Oct. 4, 1870, m. Fannie Wardle; Emily Johanna b. Nov. 5, 1872, m. Christian Johnson; Charles Theodore b. Sept. 5, 1874, m. Charlotte Doxford; Alverette Matilda b. Oct. 4, 1876, m. Edward Ross; Joseph Alvin b. Oct. 2, 1878; Amoran b. Feb. 2, 1889, died. Family resided at Ephraim, Levan and Elsinore, Utah.
High priest; seventy. Veteran Black Hawk and Walker Indian wars. Justice of peace. Mechanic; farmer. Died April 6, 1906, Elsinore, Utah.

BELL, HERBERT HORACE (son of Thomas Bell and Mahala Elwood). Born Feb. 26, 1859, Ephraim, Utah.
Married Lucy Payne Dec. 5, 1878, St. George, Utah (daughter of Edward Payne and Emma Powell, pioneers Sept. 2, 1864, Joseph S. Rawlins company). She was born March 16, 1858. Their children: Herbert b. Oct. 19, 1879, d. infant; Minnie b. March 16, 1881, d. Sept. 29, 1883; Emma Pearl b. Feb. 18, 1883, m. Peter Hendrickson; Myrtle Elizabeth b. Dec. 10, 1884; Lucy Edna b. Sept. 7, 1886, and Mattie Fern b. Jan. 29, 1888, d. infants; Quintin Clyde b. July 27, 1889; Ivan Earnest b. Oct. 15, 1891; Ivis Madis b. June 29, 1891; Rulon Edward and Rodney Thomas b. June 27, 1896; Iretta b. Sept. 15, 1898; Montez b. Feb. 16, 1901; Jennie La Pearl b. Nov. 7, 1902. Family home Glenwood, Utah.
High priest; seventy; missionary to central states 1884-85; missionary to England 1907-08; bishop of Glenwood ward since 1886. County commissioner of Sevier county 1896-1900; president of Glenwood town board 1895-99; member board of education Sevier school district. Farmer and fruitgrower.

BELLISTON, JAMES THOMAS (son of John Belliston, born March 24, 1796, London, Eng., and Elizabeth Carpenter of London). He was born Feb. 18, 1819, at London. Came to Utah Oct. 6, 1853, Cyrus H. Wheelock company.
Married Louisa Miller Sept. 10, 1838 (daughter of John Miller and Louisa Woolley), who was born March 24, 1819. Their children: Louisa E. b. Sept. 22, 1840; John b. April 9, 1842; William Robert b. Sept. 26, 1843; Thomas b. Dec. 1, 1845, m. Sophia Bardsley April 9, 1868; James Thomas b. Feb. 5, 1848, m. Mary Howard; Louisa Maria b. Sept. 1, 1852; Emily b. Oct. 19, 1855; Joseph Ephraim b. June 10, 1858, m. Ada Read; Sarah b. May 4, 1864, m. Amos A. Allen.
Missionary to Great Britain 1875-76; counselor to president of high priests' quo um.

BELLISTON, THOMAS (son of James Thomas Belliston and Louisa Miller). Born Dec. 1, 1845, Birmingham, Eng.
Married Sophia Bardsley April 9, 1868, Salt Lake City (daughter of George Bardsley and Elizabeth Garside, former

a pioneer Sept. 29, 1866, Daniel Thompson company). She was born June 29, 1848, Ashton-Under-Lyne, Eng. Their children: Thomas W. b. Feb. 4, 1869, m. Elizabeth Foster 1889; George James b. Oct. 15, 1870; John b. Aug. 28, 1872, m. Nellie Lomax; Samuel b. Sept. 2, 1874; Albert Henry b. June 29, 1876, m. Jennie G. Wheeler Oct. 21, 1903; Wilford b. Aug. 18, 1878, m. Lucy M. Warr; Louisa b. Nov. 18, 1880, m. A. Owen Johnson 1908; Lester b. Jan. 14, 1883, m. Triphena Howell; Nellie b. March 23, 1885; Ralph B. b. May 15, 1887, m. Alice Farnsworth; Minnie b. Aug. 16, 1889. Family home Nephi, Utah.

Assisted in bringing immigrants to Utah 1866. President Y. M. M. I. A. 1880; counselor to stake superintendent Y. M. M. I. A. 1881; president 71st quorum seventies 1892; member high council, Juab stake, 1902. School trustee 1899-05; Nephi city councilman 1900-1901; Juab county commissioner 1903-1904.

BELLOWS, JOHN F. (son of James Bellows and Judith Hopper). Born May 24, 1825, in Wayne county, Ill. Came to Utah Oct. 5, 1850, Stephen Markham company.

Married Marilla Plum of Illinois, who came to Utah with her mother 1850, Stephen Markham company. Their children: James Merlin and John Marion, died; Sarah Marilla, m. John Leatham; Judith Abigail, m. Thomas Leatham; Joseph Smith, m. Alice Youd; Hyrum Smith, m. Elizabeth Draper; Charles Henry, m. Jane Huff; Agnes D.; Elizabeth, m. Andrew J. Simmons; Mary Elva (adopted), m. Thomas Holmes. Family resided Payson and Lake Shore, Utah.

Indian war veteran; served under Col. Markham in San Pete county 1853; took part in Echo Canyon trouble. Far , timberman and stockraiser. Died 1894 at Lake Shomer

BELLOWS, HYRUM SMITH (son of John F. Bellows and Marilla Plum). Born Aug. 31, 1860, Payson, Utah.

Married Elizabeth Draper Feb. 18, 1883, Benjamin, Utah (daughter of Thomas Draper and Sarah Ward of Leicestershire, Eng.). She was born Dec. 25, 1862. Their children: Phoebe Elizabeth b. June 9, 1885, m. Thomas Hancock, Jr.; Joseph Hyrum; m. March 8, 1887; Etta May b. April 8, 1889; John Marion b. Nov. 12, 1892; Hazel b. Feb. 3, 1895; Alice Cornelia b. July 8, 1897, died. Family home Lake Shore, Utah.

Teacher; farmer. Died at Spring Glen, Utah.

BELNAP, GILBERT (son of Rosel Belnap, born Jan. 4, 1789, Cayuga county, N. Y., and Jane Richmond of Whitty, Canada, born in Vermont, U. S. A.). He was born Dec. 22, 1821, Hope, New-Castle district, Upper Canada. Came to Utah Sept. 17, 1850, Jonathan Foote company.

Married Adaline Knight Dec. 21, 1845 (daughter of Vinson Knight and Martha McBride, latter a pioneer Sept. 17, 1850). She was born May 4, 1831. Their children: Gilbert Rosel b. Jan. 8, 1847, m. Sarah Jane Cole March 30, 1867; John McBride b. May 11, 1849, d. June 22, 1850, Salt Creek, Mo.; Reuben b. June 14, 1851, m. Lucene V. Hammon Jan. 11, 1870; Joseph b. Jan. 26, 1853, m. Manerva P. Howard April 26, 1875; Martha Jane b. Sept. 17, 1855, m. Levi B. Hammon Jan. 11, 1870; Hyrum b. March 24, 1858, m. Christiana Rasmussen Sept. 20, 1883; Augustus Weber b. March 25, 1860, m. Mary Read April 21, 1886; Volney b. Feb. 17, 1862, d. March 14, 1862; Vinson K. b. June 26, 1863, m. Sarah Emily Hardy Oct. 20, 1886; Amasa b. June 22, 1866, m. Lillian Rose Garner Oct. 20, 1886; Adaline b. Aug. 1, 1868, m. John A. Lowe Nov. 18, 1891; Mary Louisa b. Dec. 11, 1871, m. Joseph H. Lowe Dec. 13, 1889; Lola Almira b. June 5, 1874, m. David William Coolbear Aug. 8, 1900.

Married Henrietta McBride June, 1852, Ogden, Utah. Their children: William James b. Aug. 31, 1853, m. Eliza Ann Watts Dec. 22, 1873; Oliver b. Sept. 20, 1855, m. Margaret Ann Manning Jan. 6, 1881; Francis Marion b. June 5, 1857, m. Lillie Lubena Robinson Dec. 26, 1878; Isadora Estella b. Oct. 31, 1860, m. John F. Stoddard Aug. 14, 1876.

This pioneer left Nauvoo, Ill., Feb. 1846, traveling through the frozen snow to Council Bluffs, Iowa. In 1850 he started for Utah, arriving at Salt Lake City with his wife and one child in a wagon drawn by an ox and a cow. Settled at Ogden in Oct. 1850, and was elected first marshal, and in 1853 appointed city attorney of Ogden. Went with first settlers to the Salmon river (Idaho) mission 1855 and remained until late in 1857, when he joined Lot Smith's command to meet Johnston's army. In March 1858 was sent by Gov. Young to release settlers at Ft. Limhi (on the Salmon river) from the Indians. Attorney Weber county 1861 and again in 1871; revised and compiled Ogden city ordinances, which were published in book form in 1871; sheriff Weber county 1862-70; county assessor and collector 1876-82. Oct. 22, 1853, commissioned by Gov. Young as 1st lieutenant Co. B. Cavalry battalion, Weber military district, President Hooper Irrigation company 1867-8. Presiding elder 17th district. Hooper: bishop Hooper ward May 28, 1877, to Aril 20, 1888. Died Feb. 26, 1899.

BELNAP, GILBERT ROSEL (son of Gilbert Belnap and Adaline Knight). Born Jan. 8, 1847.

Married Sarah Jane Cole March 30, 1867. Their children: Sarah Elizabeth b. Jan. 14, 1870; Adaline b. May 27, 1872; Gilbert Martin b. Nov. 22, 1874, d. July 20, 1875; Rosel Cole b. Jan. 27, 1881; Weltha b. July 27, 1886; Maud b. Oct. 7, 1889.

BELNAP, FRANCIS MARION (son of Gilbert Belnap and Henrietta McBride). Born June 5, 1857.
Married Lillie Lubena Robinson Dec. 26, 1878. Their children: Frances Eugene b. June 20, 1860; Gilbert Ray b. Jan. 11, 1882, d. Feb. 24, 1882; John Marion b. Sept. 1, 1882; Lillis Myrtle b. Jan. 9, 1886; Parley William b. June 2, 1888, d. Feb. 26, 1911; George Ellis b. Feb. 23, 1891; Orson Victor b. Jan. 14, 1893; Voletta b. Sept. 18, 1895; Christel Fern b. July 16, 1896; Laverne b. Feb. 21, 1899; Lorenzo b. July 22, 1902.

BEMIS, GEORGE H. Born Aug. 13, 1826, Bangor, Maine. Came to Utah in 1869.
Married Eleanor Merrick 1853 in Wisconsin, who was born in 1834. Their children: George L., m. Sarah Allred; Austin H., m. Lena Clopenstine; Fred; Frank, died; Kate, m. John Allen; Fanny, m. Richard Turkington; Jessie, m. Benjamin Fox; Sarah, m. Harry Check; Harlon, m. Daisy Meyers. Family home Bingham, Utah.
Miner. Died Aug. 11, 1884.

BEMIS, GEORGE L. (son of George H. Bemis and Eleanor Merrick). Born Nov. 5, 1854, in Wisconsin. Came to Utah in 1869.
Married Sarah Allred Aug. 11, 1878, Spring City, Utah (daughter of David H. Allred and Aurora Brown, of Tennessee, pioneers 1859). She was born May 24, 1856. Only child: George. Family home Salt Lake City.
Mining engineer.

BENCH, WILLIAM. Born in England. Came to Utah 1852, Capt. Wimmer company.
Married Ann Bench at Southampton, Hampshire, Eng. Their children: John L., m. Maria Picknel, m. Lovisa Griffin, m. Clara Bench; William, m. Martena Tatton; George Edward, m. Jane Horton; Mary, m. Frank Wall; Martha, m. George D. Watt.
Married Miss Fowler. Only child: William E., m. Ella Cowley. Families resided Manti, Utah.
Seventy. Indian war veteran. Blacksmith. Died at Manti.

BENCH, GEORGE EDWARD (son of William and Ann Bench). Born March 20, 1842, at Southampton, Eng. Came to Utah 1852 with father.
Married Jane Horton Dec. 19, 1863, Salt Lake City (daughter of Edmund and Maria Horton, of Wanship, Utah). She was born April 18, 1843. Their children: Eliza Jane, m. Aaron D. Squire; Esther Ann; George Edward, m. Isabel Barton; Arthur Frank, m. Alice Hogan; Emma Lillian, m. John Hall; Mary Ann, m. Louis A. Lauber; Ella Maria, m. Frank Cox; Claris Isabel, m. Arthur Larson; Wilford Edmund; Jennie Maud, m. Fred W. Cox, Jr. Family home Manti, Utah.
High priest; missionary to England 1895-97; Sunday school superintendent. City marshal and superintendent water works, Manti. Black Hawk Indian war veteran; served in Echo Canyon war. Farmer.

BENCH, GEORGE EDWARD, JR. (son of George Edward Bench and Jane Horton). Born Oct. 12, 1869, Manti, Utah.
Married Isabel Barton June 3, 1896, at Manti (daughter of William Kilshaw Barton and Ann Cook, of that place, pioneers of 1852, Joseph Young company). She was born Feb. 3, 1875. Their children: Lyle Alpha b. May 13, 1898; Edward Barton b. Nov. 30, 1899; George Kilshaw b. Sept. 10, 1901, d. Jan. 7, 1902; Lola Ann b. March 16, 1904; Wallace K. b. Dec. 26, 1908. Family home Manti, Utah.
Elder. Contractor and builder; dairyman and farmer.

BENEDICT, JOSEPH MOTT (son of Francis Knapp Benedict and Emeline Mott of Freeport, Queens county, Long Island, N. Y.). Born April 29, 1844, North Canaan, Conn. Came to Utah 1870.
Married Sarah Ellen Pierson June 5, 1867, Westfield, N. J. (daughter of William Pierson and Elizabeth Corriell of Westfield, N. J.). She was born May 24, 1846. Their children: Nellie May, d. infant; Frances Bertha, m. Charles S. Cowan; Chauncy Mott b. Dec. 15, 1875, m. Clara Clawson, who died, m. Geneve Ellerbeck. Family home Salt Lake City.
Physician and surgeon. Founder of Salt Lake county medical society and of the Holy Cross hospital of Salt Lake City; first surgeon for D. & R. G. Ry. Died July 24, 1896.

BENEDICT, CHAUNCY MOTT (son of Joseph Mott Benedict and Sarah Ellen Pierson). Born Dec. 15, 1875, Salt Lake City.
Married Clara Clawson Oct. 29, 1901, Salt Lake City (daughter of Spencer Clawson and Nabbie Young of Salt Lake City). She was born Feb. 8, 1903, d. Feb. 10, 1903. Only child: Joseph Clawson b. Feb. 8, 1903, d. Feb. 10, 1903.
Married Geneve Ellerbeck Sept. 28, 1907, Salt Lake City (daughter of Thomas Winton Ellerbeck of Lancashire, and Heneretta Dyer of Devonshire, Eng., pioneers Sept. 1862). She was born Dec. 17, 1877. Their child: Joseph Ellerbeck b. May 26, 1910.
Physician and surgeon. Graduate Cornell university. Member state and county medical societies; member of staff of St. Mark's hospital.

BENNETT, BENJAMIN (son of Benjamin Bennett and Elizabeth Millington). Born 1794, Connah's Quay, Flintshire, North Wales. Came to Utah Oct. 5, 1860, Williams Budge company.
Married Catherine Jones Dec. 31, 1816 (daughter of John Jones), who died when within 100 miles of Salt Lake City. Their children: John b. 1822, m. Jane Roberts; Benjamin, m. Elizabeth Bowen; Jonathan, m. Jane Jones; Catherine, m. Thomas Hewitt; Edward, m. Mary Ann Coppack; Elizabeth, m. John Kenney.
Active in church work. Died at Holden, Utah, Feb. 20, 1880.

BENNETT, JOHN (son of Benjamin Bennett and Catherine Jones). Born Sept. 4, 1822, Flintshire, North Wales. Came to Utah Oct. 15, 1863, Samuel D. White company.
Married Jane Roberts Oct. 27, 1843, at Chester, Eng. (daughter of Edward Roberts and Elizabeth Jones) who was born June 22, 1824, Flintshire, North Wales, and died at Holden, April 17, 1905. Their children: Elizabeth b. Aug. 25, 1844, m. John D. Hunter Oct. 27, 1863; Benjamin b. Jan. 1, 1846, m. Emma Holman Sept. 17, 1869; Edward b. Jan. 3, 1848, m. Elizabeth J. Wood March 2, 1877; Catherine b. June 16, 1850, m. Edward J. Arthur 1868; Samuel b. April 13, 1853, m. Martha Fauhrmaester Jan. 17, 1876; Mary Ann b. June 27, 1855, m. Anthony Stephenson March 9, 1874; Jane, b. March 1, 1857, m. James J. Stephenson Dec. 21, 1877; John b. May 29, 1860, died at sea; Jonathan b. Sept. 17, 1862, m. Marinda Stevens April 21, 1886; William T. b. March 5, 1865, m. Elizabeth J. Sibley Nov. 15, 1883; Emaline b. Jan. 17, 1869, m. Joseph C. Beckstrand Oct. 25, 1893. Family resided Deseret and Holden, Utah.
First settled at Fillmore, Utah; worked at building of dam and fort at Deseret 1863-64, and in building the first telegraph line in Millard county. President elders quorum. Died April 20, 1870.

BENNETT, EDWARD (son of John Bennett and Jane Roberts). Born Jan. 3, 1848, Connah's Quay, Flintshire, North Wales.
Married Elizabeth J. Wood March 2, 1877, St. George, Utah (daughter of Charles Wood and Ann Day, both born in Kent, England, later of Cape Town, South Africa, pioneers Oct. 5, 1860, William Budge company). She was born Aug. 8, 1857, Cape Town, South Africa. Their children: John Charles b. Feb. 16, 1878, m. Susan Ashby; Elizabeth Ann b. May 8, 1880, m. Alfred Ainge; Jane Myrtle b. July 24, 1882; Edward b. Sept. 2, 1884, m. Martha Estella Ashby; Benjamin Samuel b. Dec. 8, 1887; Laverne b. Aug. 23, 1890; Hattie b. May 24, 1892; Gladys b. May 7, 1894; Mark Llewellyn b. Feb. 6, 1896; Jonathan Royal b. Aug. 2, 1898; Emma Fay b. May 1902. Family home Holden, Utah.
Missionary to Great Britain 1887-89; president Manchester conference; counselor in presidency of high priests' quorum of Millard stake. Millard county assessor 1905-07; school trustee. Farmer and stockraiser.

BENNETT, SAMUEL (son of John Bennett and Jane Roberts). Born April 13, 1853, at family home in Flintshire.
Married Martha M. Fauhrmaester Jan. 17, 1876 (daughter of Frederick William Fauhrmaester and Sophia Lindow, pioneers 1860). She was born March 25, 1857, in Iowa. Their children: Jane S., d. young; Mary; Martha E.; Samuel; Josephine; Ida; John; Joseph; Leah; Rachel; Artimesia. Family home Holden, Utah.
Worked on St. George temple; missionary to England 1902-04; bishop's counselor Holden ward. Treasurer and one of first board of directors in founding town of Melville, now Delta, Utah.

BENNETT, DAVID (son of Alma Bennett of Illinois). Came to Utah 1847, captain of an oxteam company.
Married Jennie Lovell. Their children: Laura, m. William Young; Hettie Maud, m. William Beers; Alma, m. Polly Wilcox; Martha Ellen, m. David F. Hamilton; Josephine, died at the age of 3 years; Rodolphus, m. Hannah Allred; Emma, m. James Parker. Family home Springville, Utah.
Seventy; elder. Indian war veteran. Farmer. Died at Springville.

BENNETT, RICHARD. Born Nov. 15, 1842, Birmingham, Eng. Came to Utah 1868.
Married Maria Foster in 1864 (daughter of William and Ann Foster, pioneers 1868). She was born 1844. Their children: John F. b. July 1865, m. Rosetta Elizabeth Wallace Nov. 1898; Jane, m. Joseph C. Sharp; Nellie; William, m. Ethel Farr. Family home Salt Lake City.
Stationary engineer for Taylor Armstrong company 30 years.

BENNETT, JOHN F. (son of Richard Bennett and Maria Foster). Born July 11, 1865, Birmingham, Eng. Came to Utah with parents.
Married Rosetta Elizabeth Wallace Nov. 1897 (daughter of Henry and Ellen Wallace of Salt Lake City, pioneers Oct. 6, 1862, Ansel P. Harmon company). She was born at Salt Lake City. Their children: Wallace b. Nov. 13, 1898; Harold b. Sept. 20, 1900; Elizabeth b. June 24, 1903; Mary b. May 29, 1906; Richard b. March 10, 1911. Family home Salt Lake City.
High priest; member Deseret Sunday school board. President and manager Bennett Glass & Paint company; director of Z. C. M. I., Zion's Savings bank, Utah State National bank, Home Fire Insurance company, and Benefit Building society.

BENNION, JOHN (son of John Bennion and Elizabeth Roberts of Hawarden, Flintshire, Wales). Born 1823 at Hawarden. Came to Utah Oct. 3, 1847, John Taylor company.
Married Esther Wainwright at Liverpool, Eng., in 1842 (daughter of Edward Wainwright and Mary Jones of Liverpool). She came to Utah with husband. Their children: Samuel Roberts b. Nov. 10, 1842, m. Mary Panter and Agnes Thompson; Mary, m. George Calder; Annie d. on the plains; Angeline, m. George M. Spencer; Rachel, m. William Spencer; John Edward, m. Marion McIntyre; Moroni and Elizabeth, died; Marie, m. Angus M. Cannon; Harriet, m. Benjamin Harker and M. F. Cowley; Esther Ann, d. infant.
Married Esther Birch at Salt Lake City, Utah (daughter of John Birch of England). Their children: Enoch, d. aged 16 years; Israel, m. Jeannett Sharp; Harden, m. Vilate K. Nebeker; David, m. Clara Pehrson; Justin, d. infant; Owen b. March 15, 1869, m. Anna Sophia Elg; Willard, d. aged 17 years; Ida, m. John H. Chase; Archie Birch, m. Sadie Squires.
Married Mary Turpin. Their children: Heber, m. Susie Winters; Alfred, m. Eliza Slade; William, m. Mary Wilson; Marcus, m. Lucy Smith; Edwin, m. Mary E. Lindsay; Milton, m. Cora Lindsay; Zina, m. John M. Cannon; John Angus, d. infant. Families resided Taylorsville, Utah.
Farmer and stockraiser. Died in September, 1877.

BENNION, SAMUEL ROBERTS (son of John Bennion and Esther Wainwright). Born Nov. 10, 1842, Nauvoo, Ill. Came to Utah Oct. 3, 1847, John Taylor company.
Married Mary Panter Sept. 1866, at Salt Lake City (daughter of William Panter and Lucy Lowe of Bedfordshire, Eng.). She was born Nov. 6, 1846, and came to Utah Sept. 1, 1860, John Smith company. Their children: Enos b. Jan. 26, 1868, m. Jane Mackay; Nora, m. Thomas W. Dimond; Laura; Edith; Elizabeth; Hattie, died; Mary Esther, m. R. W. Stringfellow; Ethel; Clyde H.
Married Agnes Thompson Aug. 16, 1879, Salt Lake City (daughter of Joseph Thompson of Doncaster, and Ann Grayson of Sheffield, Eng., pioneers 1852). She was born Nov. 2, 1857. Their children: John b. Oct. 21, 1880, m. Mary Goodman; Vilate b. Nov. 7, 1882; Samuel Roberts, Jr. b. Aug. 16, 1884; Cora b. Aug. 17, 1887, died; Ashley b. July 31, 1890. Family home Vernal, Utah.
Missionary to St. Louis and Illinois 1866-67, and to England 1883-85; president Uinta stake 1887-1906; member 7th quorum seventies. President bank of Vernal; president Vernal Milling & Light company.

BENNION, DAVID (son of John Bennion and Esther Birch). Born Feb. 1, 1865, Vernon. Utah.
Married Clara Pehrson Feb. 19, 1891, Logan, Utah (daughter of Peter A. Pehrson and Christina Peterson of Vernon, Utah, pioneers 1853). She was born Jan. 16, 1869. Their children: Merrill b. July 7, 1894; Gladys b. Dec. 4, 1896; Jenness b. May 3, 1899; Edna b. March 12, 1902; Carol b. Aug. 10, 1905; Stanley b. March 10, 1907; Clara Ida b. Aug. 21, 1910.
Missionary to southern states 1887-89; president seventies at Grantsville. Moved to Uinta county, Utah, 1901. Ward clerk Vernal; stake superintendent Y. M. M. I. A.; high councilor; bishop Vernal 2d ward; counselor in presidency of Uinta stake. Mayor of Vernal. Assistant cashier of Vernal bank; president Ashley Lumber company.

BENNION, OWEN (son of John Bennion and Esther Birch). Born March 15, 1869, Long Valley, Lincoln county, Nev.
Married Anna Sophia Elg at Salt Lake City (daughter of Knute August Elg and Johanna Foraline of Vernon, Utah), she was born Nov. 29, 1873, St. John, Utah. Their children: Lois b. Aug. 9, 1893; Hazel b. Jan. 31, 1895; Verna b. Nov. 22, 1897; Birch Forrest b. Jan. 26, 1899; Evan Owen b. Nov. 29, 1901. Family resided Vernon, Taylorsville and Roosevelt, Utah.
High priest; bishop's counselor; ward teacher; president Y. M. M. I. A. at Vernon, Utah. Justice of peace at Vernon. President Dry Gulch Irrigation company; director Roosevelt Mercantile and Roosevelt Realty company. Farmer and stockraiser.

BENSON, EZRA TAFT (son of John Benson and Chloe Taft of Mendon, Worcester county, Mass). Born Feb. 22, 1811, at Mendon, Mass. Came to Utah July 24, 1847, captain second ten, Brigham Young first division, and on Aug. 2 with Porter Rockwell, returned to meet the incoming immigrant trains with mail, and a special letter from President Young. Having performed their mission they returned and on the Big Sandy met the memorable expedition east-bound for Winter Quarters, headed by President Young, and returned east with the caravan. The following year, May 7, 1848, with part of his numerous family he joined the exodus for Utah that left Winter Quarters practically uninhabited.
Married Pamelia Andrus Jan. 1, 1832 (daughter of Jonathan Harvey Andrus and Lucina Parsons, married July 16, 1807). She was born Oct. 21, 1809, and came to Utah in 1848. Their children: Chloe Jane; Adin Parsons; Jonathan; Harvey; Charles Taft; Emma Parsons b. Feb. 28, 1842, m. Bolivar Roberts; Isabella b. March 9, 1846, m. William Goodwin; Charlotte Taft b. July 4, 1851, m. W. S. Narcross.
Married Adeline Brooks Andrus April 27, 1844, Nauvoo, Ill. (daughter of Jonathan Harvey Andrus and Lucina Parsons), who was born March 18, 1813, Windsor, Conn. Came to Utah Oct. 2, 1847. Their children: George Taft b. May 1, 1846, m. Louisa Ballif Dec. 20, 1867; Florence Adeline b. Sept. 17, 1851, d. Dec. 24, 1852; Frank b. Oct. 13, 1853, m. Amanda Ellason.
Married Eliza Perry March 4, 1847, Council Bluffs, Iowa (daughter of John Perry and Grace Ann W. Williams, pioneers July, 1849). She was born March 30, 1829, and came to Utah 1848 with husband. Their children: Alice Eliza b. Aug. 11, 1848, m. James Goodwin Dec. 20, 1867; John Perry b. Sept. 24, 1849, m. Evalina Hales 1870; Malina A. b. Sept. 27, 1851, m. Frederick Goodwin 1874; Orion W. b. Oct. 4, 1853, m. Harriet Williams Oct. 16, 1876; Carrie S. b. May 22, 1860, m. William J. J. Price 1890; Abbie Della b. Oct. 16, 1862, m. Hyrum Thatcher 1884; Grace A. b. Jan. 31, 1867, m. John E. Price 1893.
Married Mary Knight (daughter of James Knight and Maria Wallace, pioneers 1852, Edward Hunter company). She was born Jan. 29, 1829, Worcester, Eng. Their children: Louise, m. Charles Bruce; Heber, died; Moroni b. Nov. 5, 1861; Lorenzo T. b. Aug. 3, 1863, m. Margaret A. Morgan March 29, 1884; Joseph b. July 13, 1865, m. Sigrid L. Larson Sept. 24, 1890; Ida b. April 16, 1867, m. Edward Lewis Dec. 30, 1889; Don Carlos b. Sept. 29, 1869, m. Lillian Hurst April 26, 1899.
Married Elizabeth Golliaher June 5, 1852, Salt Lake City (daughter of William C. Golliaher and Elizabeth Orton), who was born Dec. 30, 1831. Their children: Fred Golliaher b. Jan. 17, 1854, m. Clara J. Rice; Brigham Young b. Dec. 17, 1858, m. Margret Ann Adams; Luella b. Nov. 1860, m. Harvey W. Curtis; William C. b. Nov. 1862, m. Ida M. Mason; Hyrum Smith b. May 3, 1864, m. Nana Rice; Edith b. April 22, 1867, m. William B. Parkinson; Lizzie b. July 9, 1869, m. Evan R. Owen.
Married Mary Larsen Sept. 3, 1866 (daughter of Magnus and Mary Larsen), who was born Dec. 19, 1843. Their children: Walter b. June 17, 1867; Henry T. b. March 19, 1869, m. Selma Lundberg Oct. 4, 1905. Families resided in Salt Lake City and Logan, Utah.
Ordained member high council of the twelve apostles July 16, 1846; president Boston conference 1844-46; missionary in eastern states; missionary to England 1856, and presided over the British mission. In 1864 he, with Apostle Lorenzo Snow, Elders Joseph F. Smith, William W. Cluff and Alma L. Smith were sent on a special mission to the Sandwich Islands to set in order the affairs of the church, which they successfully accomplished, returning in 1865. Took active part in organization of provisional government of Deseret; member house branch of legislature several sessions, 1859-69. Contractor on Central Pacific. Pre-eminently connected with the settlement of Cache valley. Died Sept. 3, 1869, Ogden, Utah.

BENSON, GEORGE TAFT (son of Ezra Taft Benson and Adeline Brooks Andrus). Born May 1, 1846, Garden Grove, Iowa.
Married Louisa Ballif Dec. 20, 1867, Salt Lake City (daughter of Serge Louis Ballif and Elise Lecoultre, pioneers Oct. 28, 1854, Robt. L. Campbell company). She was born Feb. 25, 1850, Lausanne, Switzerland. Their children: Lulu b. March 28, 1869, m. William C. Parkinson Feb. 11, 1887; Ezra Taft b. Aug. 6, 1871, d. Aug. 28, 1871; Elise b. March 10, 1873, m. G. Alfred Alder Oct. 9, 1896; George Taft b. June 24, 1875, m. Sarah Dunkley Oct. 19, 1898; Serge Ballif b. Oct. 2, 1877, m. Linda Nelson Oct. 2, 1893; Adeline b. July 31, 1879, m. Leo Peck Dec. 20, 1900; Florence (twin to Adeline), m. Stanley Jonasson Jan. 17, 1906; William Kennedy b. Feb. 9, 1882, d. Feb. 28, 1882; Frank Taft b. April 23, 1883, m. Elizabeth Eames Jan. 27, 1909; Marie b. July 19, 1885, d. March 6, 1890. Family resided Logan, Utah and Preston, Idaho.
Sunday school superintendent; high councilor; counselor bishopric in Preston and Whitney eight years; bishop of Whitney 20 years. Assessor and collector at Logan nine years. Farmer.

BENSON, BRIGHAM YOUNG (son of Ezra Taft Benson and Elizabeth Golliaher). Born Dec. 17, 1858, Salt Lake City.
Married Margret Ann Adams Dec. 29, 1881, at Logan (daughter of Hugh Adams and Margret Webster, pioneers 1854, Daniel Garn company). She was born June 12, 1860. Their children: Ezra Taft b. Sept. 29, 1882, m. Cynthia Esther Pingree; Afton b. April 7, 1885; Luella b. June 30, 1887; Vance Hugh b. Jan. 18, 1891; Vernon Brigham b. Jan. 18, 1891. Family home Trenton, Cache county, Utah.
Bishop's counselor; president Trenton Clarkson Milling and Elevator company; director West Cache Canal company; director Lewiston state bank; Director Cache county fair association.

BENSON, JEROME (son of Benjamin Benson and Nazia Messenger, former died 1852, in Pottawattamie county, Iowa, latter came to Utah and died at Springville in 1868; they were married Oct. 1795). He was born Nov. 10, ——, in New York. Came to Utah 1852, Ezra T. Benson company.
Married Mary Rhodes Oct. 1830, Lafayette, Tippecanoe county, Ind. (daughter of George and Susan Rhodes of Lafayette, Ind., pioneers 1852, Ezra T. Benson company). She was born 1811. Their children: George, died; Susannah, m. James Vance; Eirvelin, m. Charles C. Olseni; Benjamin, died; Mary, m. John Walton; Louisa, m. Samuel Brown; Amelia, m. Henry Willis; Lovina, m. Paul Van Curen; Jerome Messenger, m. Etta ——; Alma and Alvey, died. Family resided at Springville and Provo, Utah.
Elder. Went to California in 1853. Carpenter and farmer. Died April 17, 1873, San Bernardino, Cal.

BENSON, NELS (son of Nils Benson, born Sept. 1, 1802, in Tunnersja, and Johannah Johansom, born Feb. 18, 1813, Oringe, Halland Lan, Sweden). He was born Aug. 23, 1846, Oringe, Halland Lan, Weenga Sogn. Came to Utah Sept. 30, 1862, Joseph Horne company.
Married Philindia Eldredge Kofford Dec. 18, 1870 (daughter of Paul E. Kofford and Fanny Merrick, pioneers 1853, Capt. Forsgren company). She was born Feb. 18, 1854, Manti, Sanpete county, Utah. Their children: Fanny Philindia b. Feb. 16, 1873, d. May 5, 1879; Johannah Icebindia b. May 6, 1875, m. Karl M. Sorenson Aug. 28, 1895; Nels Ernest b. Jan. 24, 1878, m. Annie Frederickson; John Irven b. Nov. 6, 1882, m. Marsha Strate Oct. 23, 1912.
Married Mary A. A. Works June 26, 1890, Manti, Utah (daughter of James Marks Works, pioneer 1847, and Phoebe Jones, pioneer 1854, David Jones company, married Sept. 22, 1858, Salt Lake City). She was born Sept. 22, 1865, Manti, Utah. Their children: Merrill Lamont b. March 27, 1892; Elden Works b. Feb. 22, 1895, d. Aug. 5, 1895; Ezel Phebe b. Jan. 24, 1897; Nels Rudger b. July 12, 1898; Edwin LeRoy b. April 21, 1900; Ruth Miriam b. March 23, 1902; Ruby Rosilla b. March 23, 1902; Elda Mary b. Nov. 5, 1903; Alma Nelden b. Nov. 6, 1905.
Sunday school teacher 42 years; president Y. M. M. I. A. eight years; missionary to Sweden, departing May 12, 1892; honorably released May 3, arrived home May 28, 1894; one of presidents 80th quorum seventies. Member Spring City council ten years. Black Hawk war veteran. Assisted in making first canals, wagon roads and telegraph lines around Spring City. Miner and farmer.

BENSON, JOHN IRVEN (son of Nels Benson and Philindia Eldredge Kofford). Born Nov. 6, 1882, Spring City, Utah. Married Marsha Strate Oct. 23, 1912. Family home Clear Creek, Utah.
Ward clerk; first counselor M. I. A; Sunday school teacher and assistant superintendent; missionary to Sweden 1909-11. Fireman Utah Fuel company three years.

BENSON, YEPPA. He was born in December, 1795. Came to Utah Oct. 3, 1853.
Married Hannah Hansen. Their children: Minnie b. 1864, m. Christ Lund; Yeppa b. April 1, 1866, m. Catherine Swivel Sept. 25, 1889. Family home Lehi, Utah, where he died Jan. 1, 1872.

BENSON, YEPPA, JR. (son of Yeppa Benson and Hannah Hansen). Born April 1, 1866, Lehi, Utah.
Married Catherine Swivel Sept. 25, 1889, Logan Utah (daughter of Jacob Swivel and Annie E. Marts). who was born April 1, 1866, Providence, Utah. Their children: Edna Catherine b. Dec. 11, 1890; Clarence Yeppa b. Aug. 27, 1892, m. Nettie Bird Feb. 1, 1911; Aaron Conrad b. Dec. 13, 1894; Yetta Elverna b. Feb. 18, 1897; Annie Elizabeth b. April 16, 1899; Florence Swivel b. July 6, 1901; Minnie Swivel b. May 19, 1903; Adelia Swivel b. April 27, 1906; Thelma Christian b. June 15, 1908. Family home Weston, Idaho.
President 142d quorum seventies; missionary to western states; choir leader Chicago branch 1904-05; superintendent Sunday schools, Weston, Idaho; bishop Weston ward.

BENZON, ANDREW BECK (son of Andrew Beck Benson of Copenhagen, Denmark). Born 1835, Copenhagen. Came to Utah Sept. 26, 1862, James Wareham company.
Married Catherine Wickel Feb. 11, 1862, St. Louis, Mo. (daughter of Harmon Wickel and Elizabeth Rickard of Earl township, Lancaster county, Pa., pioneers 1862, James Wareham company). She was born April 25, 1840. Their children: Elenora K., m. Hyrum A. Silver; Andrew B., m. Elizabeth Wilson; Edwin d. aged 4 years; Joseph, m. Guinn Jones; Arthur d. aged 4 years; Minnie, m. William Afflick; Owen, m. Lillian May Dunlap. Family home Salt Lake City, Utah.
High priest; block teacher. Salesman. Died 1895, at Salt Lake City.

BENZON, OWEN (son of Andrew Beck Benzon and Catherine Wickel). Born Jan. 2, 1877, at Salt Lake City, Utan. Married Lillian May Dunlap Feb. 27, 1911, Ogden, Utah (daughter of Eldom Dunlap and Lucy Scott of West Point, Miss.), who was born Feb. 15, 1885.

BERG, OLE H. (son of Hendrik Anderson of Rod Skjeberg, Smaalenene, Fredrikshald, Norway). Born Sept. 12, 1844, at Anerod, Rokke Parish, Norway). Came to Utah Oct. 8, 1866, Andrew Scott company.
Married Anna J. Nielson Dec. 16, 1866 (daughter of Hans Nielsen and Maren Jacobsen of Odense, Denmark, latter a pioneer Nov. 8, 1865, Capt. Atwood company). She was born Oct. 19, 1847, in Odense. Came to Utah 1865, Miner G. Atwood company. Their children: Oliva, m. George A. Nuttall; Anna, m. Enoch Jorgensen; Mary, m. Warren W. Beckstead; Elnora, m. James Prestwich; Christina d. 1894; Henry Ward d. 1900; Alma F. d. 1882; Flora, m. Walter Jenkins; Edna, m. Oscar E. Groshell; Oscar Wyman, m. Josephine Thomas. Family home Provo, Utah.
President 34th quorum seventies; Sunday school teacher 14 years; missionary to Norway 1889-91; high councilor 15 years; bishop 1st ward, Provo, 11 years. City councilman at Provo, and member board of education; Utah county coroner. Contractor and builder 35 years; undertaker and embalmer.

BERGLUND, CARL F. (son of John Berglund, born 1764, and Anna Berglund, both of Calmar Lan, Sweden). He was born May 17, 1825, in Calmar Lan. Came to Utah Oct. 2, 1864, John Smith independent company.
Married Lucia M. Beck (daughter of Jacob S. Beck and Dorthea Christensen). Only child: Oscar B. b. Nov. 17, 1858. Family home Gunnison, Utah.
Farmer and merchant.

BERGLUND, OSCAR B. (son of Carl F. Berglund and Lucia M. Beck). Born Nov. 17, 1858, Frederikshavn, Denmark. Lives at Gunnison, Utah.
Farmer; stock merchant; manager Gunnison co-operative mercantile store.

BERNHISEL, DR. JOHN MILTON (son of Samuel Bernhisel, born Nov. 26, 1769, Perry county, Pa., and Susan Bower, born March 6, 1775). He was born July 23, 1799, Sandy Hill, Pa. Came to Utah Sept. 24, 1848, Heber C. Kimball company.
Married Julia Ann Haight (Van Orden) in 1845 (daughter of Caleb and Keturah Haight, pioneers 1848, Heber C. Kimball company). She was born Oct. 6, 1805. Only child: John Milton, Jr., m. Henrietta Harris. Family home Salt Lake City.
Delegate to Washington in 1849 for admission of Utah as the state of Deseret; Utah's first territorial representative to U. S. congress 1851; first vice president of Z. C. M. I.; selected books for Utah's first library. Personal attache of Joseph Smith, living in his house at the time of assassination.

BERNHISEL, JOHN MILTON (son of John Milton Bernhisel and Julia Ann Haight). Born Dec. 21, 1846, Winter Quarters, Iowa (now Neb.).
Married Henrietta Harris Jan. 3, 1876, Salt Lake City (daughter of Robert Harris and Hannah Maria Eagles, pioneers 1850, Joseph Horne company). She was born Aug. 11, 1854, Kaysville, Davis county, Utah. Their children: *John Milton b. March 2, 1878, m. Ruey Pond June 4, 1902; Estella Maria b. June 26, 1880, m. Milton Oliver Bell June 7, 1906; Janetta b. Jan. 9, 1882, m. Joseph LeRoy Pond June 28, 1905; Sarah Louisa b. Feb. 6, 1885; Everett Clark b. March 29, 1899; Ralph b. July 10, 1891, m. Nellie Hendricks Sept. 13, 1911; Harris Fay b. Oct. 1, 1893. Family home Lewiston, Cache county, Utah.
Representative from Cache county to first Utah state legislature. Veteran Black Hawk war. Justice of peace 1884-90, Lewiston, where he drove the first stake for its permanent settlement.

BERRETT, ALFRED (son of Thomas Berrett and Mary Ann Marks). Born Jan. 13, 1825, Steeple Ashton, Wiltshire, Eng. Came to Utah 1852, Capt Tidwell company.
Married Elizabeth Matthews Sept. 16, 1850 (daughter of Robert and Sarah Matthews). Their children: Alfred A.; Marlon; Mary Ann; Ellen; Sarah; Virtue; Victoria; Hamlet E.
Married Sarah Jane Ray July 20, ——, North Ogden, Utah. Their children: Elizabeth; Bessie; Lena D.; Maud M.; Roletta.

BERRETT, MARLON (son of Alfred Berrett and Elizabeth Matthews). Born Dec. 12, 1855, North Ogden, Utah.
Married Elizabeth Ann Holmes Feb. 2, 1881 (daughter of Henry and Ellen Holmes). Their children: Elizabeth M.; Ellen V.; Alfred W.; Virtue P.; Marlon H.; Hazel M.; Martha M.; Charles R.

BERRETT, ROBERT (son of Robert Berrett, born Nov. 11, 1768, and Eleanor Fryer, born Feb. 1769, both of Steeple Ashton, Wiltshire, Eng., married Dec. 26, 1792). He was born June 23, 1797, at Steeple Ashton. Came to Utah Oct. 28, 1849, George A. Smith company.
Married Sarah Hyet Griffin Aug. 1825 (daughter of Silas Griffin and Ann Perrott of Steeple Ashton, Eng., married Feb. 4, 1803, and died in England). She was born April 30, 1807, and died May 1849. Their children: Rhoda Rebecca b. Jan. 1829, d. 1849; *Leonora d. aged 2; Robert Griffin b. June 23, 1831, m. Sarah Ann Woodhead March 14, 1855; *Leonora b. April 12, 1833, d. aged 1 year; Anne b. May 27, 1835, m. Oliver C. Bess March 1854; Charles Henry b. Dec. 25, 1837, m. Melissa Campbell Dec. 25, 1861, m. Charlotte Jones April 10, 1872; Richard Thomas b. Jan. 4, 1840, m. Mary Ann Nunns Jan. 1, 1860, m. Annie Elizabeth Toone Feb. 14, 1878; *Leonora Hyet b. Sept. 18, 1841, m. Joseph B. Alvord April 1858; Albert Edward b. Feb. 2, 1845, d. May 1897; Samuel Franklin b. March 18, 1848, m. Elizabeth Newby Feb. 10, 1867. Family resided North Ogden, Salt Lake City and Ogden, Utah.

BERRETT, ROBERT GRIFFIN (son of Robert and Sarah Hyet Griffin). Born June 23, 1831, Steeple Ashton, Eng. Came to Utah 1849 with parents.
Married Sarah Ann Woodhead March 14, 1855, North Ogden, Utah (daughter of William Woodhead and Charlotte Spencely of Grimsby, Yorkshire, Eng., pioneers Oct. 24, 1855, Milo Andrus company). She was born Aug. 1, 1835. Their children: Rhoda, m. John Jones; Eleanor, m. Samuel Robinson; Charlotte, m. John W. Gibson; Robert William d. June 15, 1877; Susan B., m. William M. Ellis; Diana Berrett d. Aug. 17, 1867; Chas. Edward, m. Elizabeth Poll; Melissa Berrett d. Jan. 5, 1873; Arthur G. Berrett, m. Ellen

Brown; Edmund R. Berrett, m. Hannah Chugg; Harriet Amelia, m. William T. Spackman. Family home North Ogden, Utah.

Member of 38th quorum seventies; missionary to England and eastern states; president of the 38th quorum seventies; superintendent of North Ogden Sunday school. Justice of the peace and town sexton. Died May 7, 1890.

BERRETT, RICHARD THOMAS (son of Robert Berrett and Sarah Hyet Griffin). Born Jan. 4, 1840, Steeple Ashton, Eng. Came to Utah 1849 with parents.

Married Mary Ann Nunns Jan. 1, 1860 (daughter of Francis and Mary Nunns), who was born Dec. 6, 1839, Leeds, Yorkshire, Eng. Came to Utah Sept. 1859, George Rowley handcart company. Their children: Mary Ann b. Oct. 8, 1860, m. Bryan W. Orton Feb. 14, 1878; Susan b. Dec. 20, 1861, d. Jan. 2, 1862; Sarah b. Nov. 20, 1862, m. Joseph W. Summerhays June 5, 1884; Rose Emily b. Nov. 18, 1864, m. William H. Crandall Dec. 15, 1882; Richard Edward b. Aug. 23, 1867, m. Isabel C. Ford Dec. 22, 1887; George Albert b. May 31, 1869, d. Nov. 16, 1869; Arthur Henry b. March 18, 1871, d. April 7, 1871; Alice b. March 6, 1872, m. Robert Irwin March 10, 1892. Family home North Ogden, Utah.

Married Annie Elizabeth Toone Feb. 14, 1878, Salt Lake City (daughter of Edward Toone and Caroline Jackson, married Sept. 17, 1855, Cardiff, Wales). She was born Nov. 7, 1857, Lambeth, London, Eng. Their children: Emily Louisa b. Dec. 28, 1878, m. John Q. Blaylock Oct. 10, 1899; Albert Edward b. Oct. 28, 1880, d. Aug. 12, 1881; Thomas Francis b. April 13, 1882, m. Harriet L. Brown May 7, 1902; Walter Herbert b. April 6, 1884, m. Charlotte J. Gibson June 21, 1906; Orson Toone b. Aug. 12, 1887, m. Clara Dickson Jan. 29, 1908; Earl Ray b. Aug. 28, 1898; Edna Caroline b. June 1, 1895. Family home North Ogden, Utah.

Territorial militiaman 1855; served in the Echo Canyon campaign. Constable 1873-78, North Ogden; trustee 1868-70. Director Rice Creek Irrigation company four years; watermaster 30 years; assisted in bringing immigrants to Utah.

BERRETT, SAMUEL F. (son of Robert Berrett and Sarah H. Griffin). Born March 18, 1848, Steeple Ashton, Eng. Came to Utah 1849 with parents.

Married Elizabeth D. Newby Feb. 9, 1867, Salt Lake City (daughter of John Newby and Isabella Smurthwaite of Sunderland, Eng.). She was born Dec. 28, 1849. Their children: Samuel John b. Nov. 9, 1867; Edward R. b. Nov. 11, 1869, d. Aug. 19, 1879; Thomas H. b. Feb. 16, 1872, d. Feb. 18, 1872; George Frederick b. June 11, 1873; Franklin C. b. March 12, 1876; William S. b. Sept. 2, 1878; Robert E. b. March 18, 1881; Lewis b. June 21, 1883; S. Isabella b. Oct. 1, 1885; George A. b. June 1888; Oliver T. b. Feb. 21, 1894.

Married Arrilila Minerva Rose May 1871, Salt Lake City (daughter of John Rose and Minerva Peat of Canada, pioneers to Utah). Their children: Albert William b. Sept. 23, 1872; Juletta b. Feb. 27, 1874. Families resided Pleasant View, Weber county, Utah.

High priest; second counselor to Bishop E. W. Wade and president Y. M. M. I. A.. Pleasant View ward; chairman of Old Folks committee twenty years. Justice of peace. Farmer and stockraiser.

BERRY, JOHN WILLIAM (son of Jesse W. Berry, born Jan. 9, 1791, Louisville, Ky., and Armelia Shanks, born Jan. 24, 1804, Nashville, Tenn.). He was born Dec. 17, 1822, in Wilson county, Tenn. Came to Utah in Oct. 1849.

Married Nancy Jane Bass April 5, 1842, who was born June 19, 1828. She refused to come to Utah with him, and they never met again. Only child: Jesse David b. Sept. 25, 1843, d. Oct. 9, 1843.

Married Jane Elizabeth Thomas May 8, 1851, Salt Lake City (daughter of James Thomas and Mary Morrow, pioneers Oct. 2, 1847, Jedediah M. Grant company). She was born Jan. 14, 1831, in Dallas county, Ala. Their children: John M. b. Oct. 11, 1853, m. Maggie C. Condie Sept. 20, 1898; Mary Jane b. Aug. 24, 1855, m. Joseph L. Hales Feb. 21, 1875; William W. b. July 19, 1857, m. Rachel E. Allen Jan. 22, 1879; Nancy A. b. May 8, 1859, m. George Ingram Oct. 8, 1880; James T. b. March 22, 1861, m. Sarah J. Roundy Oct. 8, 1880; Cynthia L. b. Sept. 25, 1862, m. John W. Brown March 12, 1880; Thurza E. b. April 1, 1865, m. John W. Brown April 18, 1886; Robert A. b. May 16, 1867, m. Harriet Allred March 1, 1892; Joseph S. b. March 4, 1869, m. Samantha Parker May 19, 1891; George A. b. June 12, 1873, m. Nora Davis Oct. 8, 1896. Family home Kanarraville, Iron county, Utah.

Married Julia Ardence Hales Dec. 28, 1858 (daughter of Charles and Julia Hales), who was born July 17, 1842.

Bishop's counselor; captain of missionaries returning from Europe 1858. Early settler in southern Utah. Carried express from San Pete to Salt Lake City July 24, 1853, and while so engaged was ambushed and shot by an Indian, and carried the bullet until his death at Kanarraville April 12, 1890.

BERRY, JOHN M. (son of John W. Berry and Jane Elizabeth Thomas). Born Oct. 11, 1853, Spanish Fork, Utah.

Married Maggie C. Condie Sept. 20, 1898, at St. George, Utah (daughter of George Condie and Margaret Achinson), who was born Jan. 7, 1872, Kanosh, Millard county, Utah. Their children: Mary Jane b. March 24, 1900; George Lorin b. Aug. 16, 1902; Margaret Myrtle b. March 29, 1904; Ivie Grace b. Feb. 5, 1907; John Eldon b. July 30, 1911. Family home Benson, Cache county, Utah.

BETTS, JAMES (son of Peter Betts and Eliza Franklin of Sheffield, Eng.). Born Dec. 22, 1845, Sheffield, Eng. Came to Utah 1862.
Married Margaret Powell in South Wales (daughter of John Powell and Elizabeth Harris, pioneers Sept. 26, 1856, Edmund Ellsworth handcart company). She was born March 12, 1848. Their children: Margaret Eliza b. Dec. 28, 1870, m. William J. Taylor; James b. Feb. 7, 1870, d. infant; Mary Elizabeth b. Jan. 4, 1872, m. Colin McMurphy; William b. Jan. 7, 1874, m. Martha A. Bates; John A. b. March 3, 1876, m. Ellen A. Cushing; David S. b. March 2, 1878, m. Iris Reed. Family home Payson, Utah.
Crossed plains for immigrants in 1866 and again in 1869; president of elders' quorum. City marshal Payson 1872-1874.

BETTS, WILLIAM (son of James Betts and Margaret Powell). Born Jan. 7, 1874, Payson, Utah.
Married Martha A. Bates Nov. 6, 1902, Salt Lake City (daughter of Joseph W. Bates and Martha A. McIntyre), who was born Nov. 8, 1878, at Payson. Their children: Martha Lucile b. May 15, 1904; Charles W. b. Dec. 2, 1906; Joseph Byron b. March 17, 1908; Margaret Ida b. Nov. 16, 1910.
Secretary elders' quorum 1901-02.

BEUS, MICHAEL. Born 1811, Piedmont, Italy. Came to Utah Sept. 26, 1855, Edmund Ellsworth handcart company.
Married Marianne Combe, Piedmont, Italy, who was born 1813. Their children: Ann, m. Moses Byrne; James, m. Clarinda Hill; John, m. Margaret Justet; Michael, m. Elizabeth Ladrap; Paul, m. Catherine Combe; L. P., m. Mary Terry; Mary, m. Edward Priest; Magdalene, m. Paul Cardon. Farmer and stockraiser.

BEUS, PAUL (son of Michael Beus and Marianne Combe). Born March 19, 1847, Piedmont, Italy.
Married Catherine Combe Nov. 8, 1883, Salt Lake City (daughter of Peter Combe and Susana Gill of Piedmont, Italy). She was born April 13, 1864. Their children: Michael b. Jan. 11, 1886; J. R. b. Dec. 13, 1886, m. Areta Steward; Cora C. b. March 12, 1888, m. Job Kendall; Lida S. b. June 30, 1890; Edna M. b. Dec. 11, 1891; Zina M. b. Dec. 25, 1893; Julia H. b. Jan. 26, 1896.
Ward teacher 18 years.

BEVAN, JAMES (son of John Bevan and Ann Bairfoot of Herefordshire, Eng.). Born Oct. 19, 1821, in Herefordshire, Eng. Came to Utah July 28, 1847.
Married Mary Shields May 9, 1850, Council Bluffs, Iowa (daughter of John Shields and Primrose Cunningham), who was born Oct. 29, 1827. Their children: John A. b. Feb. 4, 1851, m. Letitia Kelsey; Mary b. Nov. 17, 1852, m. Peter Mahnkin; Primrose b. Jan. 8, 1855, m. Alvin Walters; James F. b. June 7, 1858, died; Heber J. b. March 11, 1860, m. Mariah Little; Joseph b. Feb. 15, 1862, m. Emma Elkington; Margaret b. Aug. 30, 1866, died; Eliza b. Dec. 29, 1864, m. J. P. Skelton; Archibald b. Sept. 8, 1868, m. Cristeena Lundsteen; Violet b. Oct. 8, 1872, m. Abia Johnson. Family home Tooele, Utah.
Married Isabell McPhearson Nov. 3, 1859, Salt Lake City (daughter of Hugh McPhearson and Isabell Sutherland), who was born in Scotland. Their children: Isabell b. Oct. 16, 1860, m. William Elkington; George b. Sept. 4, 1862; Anna E. b. Dec. 11, 1864, m. Thomas Spiers; Hugh, died; Martha b. Feb. 18, 1868, m. John England; Mary b. Feb. 18, 1868, died; Charles, died; Sarah b. Oct. 18, 1872, m. George Bates; Mariah Jane b. Nov. 13, 1876, m. Charles Balshweiler; Amos b. July 13, 1879, m. Nellie Kirk. Family home Tooele, Utah.
Settled in Tooele 1852. Senior president 43d quorum of seventies for many years; member Mormon Battalion and captain of ten in Echo Canyon campaign against Gen. Albert Sidney Johnston's hostile entrance to Utah. Father of 23 children, 71 grandchildren and about 20 great-grandchildren.

BEVAN, JOHN A. (son of James Bevan and Mary Shields). Born Feb. 4, 1851, Council Bluffs, Iowa.
Married Letitia M. Kelsey Nov. 20, 1876, Salt Lake City (daughter of Eli B. Kelsey and Mary Ann Shields). She was born Nov. 14, 1855, Tooele, Utah. Their children: James Earnest b. Sept. 2, 1877, d. 1898; John Alexander b. Nov. 20, 1878, m. Amy Icegreen 1902; Grace b. March 26, 1881; Mary b. April 26, 1883, m. R. W. Brown 1906; Agnes b. April 16, 1889, d. 1892; Eli Edson b. Oct. 26, 1892, m. Sarah Shields 1910; Parley Woodruff b. Jan. 7, 1900, d. 1910.
Missionary to southern states 1883-86 and 1901-02; president 43d quorum seventies ten years. County assessor and commissioner. Member of high council of Tooele stake; first counselor to president of high priests quorum, and worker in the Sunday school for 55 years, and now a resident of Tooele for 62 years. The oldest survivor of a posterity of 430.

BICKINGTON, WILLIAM. Born 1811, Maxstoke, Warwickshire, Eng. Came to Utah 1853.
Married Ann Reeder. Only child: Francis, who died crossing plains. Settler of Marriott, Utah, 1855, where he died November, 1869.

BIDDLE, WILLIAM GANDER (son of Thomas Biddle and Harriet Westley of Walsall, Staffordshire, Eng.). Born Nov. 24, 1832, at Walsall. Came to Utah Oct. 17, 1862, Henry W. Miller company.
Married Elizabeth Heath Oct. 19, 1856, Birmingham. Eng. (daughter of John Egerton Heath and Mary Ann Vale of Birmingham). She was born Feb. 2, 1835. Their children: John T. b. Nov. 7, 1857, m. Emmeline D. Pierce; William A. b. Feb. 20, 1859, m. Ellen Sophrona Ohlson; Amanda b. Nov. 24, 1860, d. Oct. 3, 1862; Emma Jane b. May 11, 1864, d. July 3, 1864; Alice M. b. March 13, 1867, m. Hyrum Ohlson; Albert H. b. Oct. 5, 1869, m. Kate Vanderhoof; George E. b. Jan. 15, 1872, m. Mary Ann Greenwell; Elizabeth A. b. Dec. 7, 1874, m. Charles H. Bird; Ida May b. Dec. 7, 1876, m. William A. Wilton. Family home Ogden, Utah.

BIDDLE, WILLIAM ALFRED (son of William Gander Biddle and Elizabeth Heath). Born Feb. 20, 1859, Walsall, Eng.
Married Ellen Sophrona Ohlson Jan. 4, 1884, Salt Lake City (daughter of Gustave Adolph Ohlson and Lena Larson, pioneers 1860 to Ogden, Utah). She was born March 2, 1861. Their children: Ella Loretta b. Oct. 9, 1884, m. Warren S. Williams; William Ohlson b. March 1, 1886; Ruby Elinor b. Nov. 15, 1887, m. Leland S. Williams.
Married Augusta Amelia Korth March 7, 1890, Salt Lake City, who was born Oct. 15, 1879, Berlin, Germany, and came to Utah Dec. 24, 1893. Their children: Esther Amanda b. Nov. 29, 1902; Elmer Korth b. Nov. 27, 1904; Harold Frederick b. Aug. 31, 1906; Alice Harriet b. March 13, 1910.

BIDWELL, ROBERT WILLIAMS (son of Mary Williams of Cattaraugus county, N. Y.). Came to Utah Sept. 14, 1850, William Foote company.
Married Elizabeth Roe, Farmersville, Cattaraugus county, N. Y. (daughter of William Roe of western New York). She was born Oct. 6, 1805. Their children: Sarah Ann b. July 12, 1830, m. John Mower; Elizabeth, d. infant; Lavern b. July 3, 1833, m. Ransom Hatch; Joseph b. Feb. 2, 1837, m. Hannahette Mower; Emma C. b. March 11, 1839, m. George Mower; William M. and Gazelum G. b. Oct. 10, 1841; Julia b. Aug. 13, 1844, m. Calvin Wheeler. Family resided Bountiful and North Ogden, Utah. Pioneer died Jan. 4, 1851.

BIDWELL, JOSEPH (son of Robert Williams Bidwell and Elizabeth Roe). Born Feb. 2, 1837, in Caldwell county, Mo. Came to Utah 1850 with parents.
Married Hannahette Mower, North Ogden, Utah (daughter of Henry Mower and Mary Amie of Pleasant View, Weber county, Utah, pioneers Sept. 9, 1851, Abraham Day company). She was born Oct. 10, 1841. Their children: Sarah Elizabeth b. May 26, 1858, m. Charles F. Wade; Joseph, Jr., b. Dec. 22, 1860, m. Susan M. Wheeler; George Henry b. July 12, 1864, m. Mary A. Robertson; Amelia Jane b. June 22, 1866, m. James O. Webster. Family home Pleasant View, Utah.
Took active part in Echo canyon trouble. Farmer. Deceased.

BIDWELL, JOSEPH, JR. (son of Joseph Bidwell and Hannahette Mower). Born Dec. 22, 1860, Pleasant View, Utah.
Married Susan Maria Wheeler March 8, 1889, Logan, Utah (daughter of William Wheeler and Martha Leah Howell of Slaterville, Utah, the former came to Utah Sept. 4, 1857, William Walker company, the latter Sept. 13, 1861, Duncan company). She was born Oct. 27, 1862. Their children: Andrew b. March 2, 1890; Nellie Josephine b. June 27, 1891; Babe b. April 28, 1895; Robert Stanley b. July 14, 1897. Family home Pleasant View, Utah.
Missionary to eastern states two years; high priest; bishop's counselor of Pleasant View ward. Justice of peace several terms; school teacher 20 years. Farmer.

BIGELOW, NAHUM. Born in Vermont. Came to Utah Oct. 6, 1850, William Snow oxteam company.
Married Mary Gibbs. Their children: Mary Jane, m. Brigham Young; Hyrum, m. Martha Mecham; Lucy, m. Brigham Young; Asa, m. Julia Ann Cook; Lavina, m. John Witt; Liola, died; Sariah, m. Daniel Cook; Moroni, m. Elvira Mecham; Daniel b. March 18, 1842, m. Parmelia Mecham July 23, 1865; m. Emeline Augusta Stevens April 9, 1882; m. Clara Oestensen May 9, 1887; Joseph, died.
Elder. Farmer, carpenter and joiner. Died Jan. 1851, Farmington, Utah.

BIGELOW, DANIEL (son of Nahum Bigelow and Mary Gibbs). Born March 18, 1842, Camp Creek, Mercer county, Ill. Came to Utah Oct. 6, 1850, William Snow oxteam company.
Married Parmelia Mecham July 23, 1865, Silver Creek, Summit county, Utah (daughter of Ephraim Mecham and Polly Derby of Nauvoo, Ill., pioneers 1852, oxteam company). She was born Sept. 11, 1832. Their children: Daniel Don Louis b. May 22, 1866, m. Annie Boren; Parmelia Emily b. Sept. 25, 1867, m. Marques Batty; William Cecil b. Aug. 27, 1869, d. infant; Polly Adora b. Feb. 18, 1871, m. Frank M. Allred; Emma May b. July 30, 1873, d. aged five; Nephi Boberg (adopted) b. Feb. 10, 1887, m. Amanda Prestwich.
Married Emeline Augusta Stevens April 9, 1882, at Salt Lake City (daughter of William Stevens and Emma Crowden of Somersetshire, Eng., pioneers 1860, oxteam company). She was born Feb. 27, 1856. Their children: Moroni b. Aug.

1, 1883, died; Mary Maria b. Feb. 1, 1884, m. Morgan H. Edwards; Rhoda Rhoana b. Nov. 19, 1885; Parley Percival b. Feb. 26, 1888; Ellen Charlotte b. Dec. 15, 1890, m. Joseph Scadden.

Married Clara Ostensen May 9, 1887, at Salt Lake City (daughter of Peter Ostensen and Caroline Anderson of Norway). She was born March 1, 1864. Their children Lafey Leroy b. May 27, 1888, d. May 15, 1911; Lucy Lavina b. Jan. 21, 1890, m. Lewis Fausett; Hyrum Harold b. July 19, 1893, d. aged two; Clara Caroline b. Dec. 16, 1895; Daniel Dewey b. July 17, 1898; Philip Eddie b. Feb. 26, 1901; Ada Majora b. Jan. 11, 1903; Elza Emer b. Aug. 27, 1905. Family home Wallsburg, Utah.

High priest; missionary to St. George, Utah; stake high councilor; Sunday school superintendent. Justice of the peace. Lumberman, farmer and stockraiser. Resides at Wallsburg.

BIGGS, JOHN (son of Joseph Biggs, born 1786, Kimpton, Herefordshire, Eng., and Mary Shirwood). Born June 7, 1831, at Kimpton. Came to Utah Oct. 25, 1861, A. R. Wright freight train.

Married Martha Lovina Henson Nov. 10, 1861 (daughter of James and Hetty Henson). Only child: Martha Hetty b. Aug. 20, 1862, d. child. Family home Salt Lake City.

Married Jane Theodora Wright June 21, 1869, Salt Lake City (daughter of George Wright and Deborah Ann Haisley, latter a pioneer Sept. 15, 1868, John Gillespie company). She was born 1852, Busby, Scotland. Their children: John W. b. Jan. 26, 1872, m. Bular Brawley; Lorenzo W. b. Feb. 26, 1874, m. Ella Peck; Joseph S. b. Nov. 18, 1876, m. Minerva Olive Allen; Rebecca W. b. Nov. 5, 1877, m. John Oliverson; Margrett W. b. Feb. 10, 1880, m. George Cornish; Della b. April 29, 1881, d. July 13, 1901; Eva W. b. Oct. 26, 1882, m. William Oliverson; Ruby Pearl W. b. Sept. 3, 1884, m. John Hampton; Alma W. b. Oct. 20, 1886; Sophia W. b. May 16, 1889, m. Albert Day Feb. 7, 1912; Phoebe W. b. Dec. 8, 1890, m. Marion Aller April 7, 1909; Lucy W. b. April 15, 1902, m. M. D. Waterson Oct. 9, 1912.

Married Jane R. Ramsbotham Nov. 22, 1870, Salt Lake City (daughter of Henry Ramsbotham and Mather Whitehead, pioneers Oct. 1869). She was born June 23, 1854. Their children: Henry R. b. June 3, 1875, m. Minnie Oldham; Jane Theodora b. Dec. 24, 1876, m. George Jolley; Elizabeth R. b. Jan. 19, 1879, m. William Durant; Alice R. b. June 10, 1881, m. Albert W. Funk; Maud R. b. May 5, 1884, m. John L. Adamson; Mary R. b. Jan. 3, 1890, m. Elmer Handy Oct. 16, 1912; William R. b. June 6, 1896.

BIGLER, ADAM C. (son of Jacob Bigler and Sarah Cunningham of Farmington, Utah). Born Dec. 17, 1828, in Harrison county, W. Va. Came to Utah Oct. 11, 1859, L. G. Rice and J. L. Stoddard company.

Married Sarah Anne Compton (daughter of Allen Compton and Mary Burton, pioneers Oct. 11, 1859). Their children: James Allen, b. June 18, 1855; Mary F. b. Jan. 4, 1857, m. Arthur A. Steed; Marion F. b. Oct. 22, 1859, m. John W. Hess; John A. b. Sept. 14, 1862, m. Lydia Beveridge; Sarah E. b. Aug. 20, 1863, and Mariah L. b. July 12, 1864, died; Robert B. b. Dec. 25, 1866, m. Fannie M. Reed.

Married Isabelle C. Miller, Farmington, Utah (daughter of Daniel A. Miller and Hannah Bigler). Their children: James T. b. Jan. 22, 1868, m. Louisa M. Stevenson; Jacob William b. Aug. 17, 1869; Edward b. Jan. 26, 1871, m. Bertha Pierson; Hannah Isabelle b. Oct. 5, 1872, m. Nephi Wolverton; Laura Elizabeth b. Oct. 19, 1873, m. Willard Archibald; Adam, Jr. b. April 2, 1876, m. Annie Howell; Joseph Arnold b. Nov. 14, 1878; Alvira b. Sept. 28, 1881, m. Fred Sylvester; Stanley Miller b. Sept. 30, 1890. Family home Farmington, Utah.

Road supervisor at Farmington four years; lumber dealer; farmer and stockraiser.

BIGLER, JOHN A. (son of Adam C. Bigler and Sarah Compton). Born Sept. 14, 1862, Farmington, Utah.

Married Lydia Beveridge May 27, 1906, Springville, Utah (daughter of William Beveridge and Lydia Stevenson of Evanston, Wyo.), who was born Sept. 2, 1883. Their children: Lydia b. Aug. 4, 1907, d. infant; Florence C. b. Dec. 6, 1908. Family home Salt Lake City.

Construction foreman.

BIGLER, JACOB G. (son of Mark Bigler, born in Pennsylvania, and Susannah Ogden, born in Maryland). He was born April 4, 1813, Harrison county, W. Va. Came to Utah 1852, Lorenzo Johnson company.

Married Amy Lorett Chase June 13, 1844, Nauvoo, Ill. (daughter of Abner Chase, born April 24, 1784, died March 21, 1829, and Amy Scott, born Oct. 5, 1789, died April 10, 1872, both of Virginia). She was born Nov. 7, 1822. Their children: Jacob, m. Elizabeth Harley; David, m. Eliza Betts; Abner, m. Elizabeth Tranter; Mary Ann, m. Ebenezer Tanner; Mark, m. Madaline Pyper; Amy Lorett, m. James Harvey Mangum; Charles Edwin, m. Mary T. Stephens; Susannah, m. John Robert Goldsbrough; James, m. Maud Whitbeck; Alice, m. Frederick Garrett.

Married Armelia Caroline Mangum Feb. 12, 1852, Kanesville, Iowa (daughter of William Mangum, born Dec. 25, 1811, in St. Clair county, Ala., and Sarah Adair, born Dec. 27, 1813, in Pickens county, Ala., pioneers 1852, Lorenzo Johnson company). Their children: Armelia b. July 17,

12, 1877; Oley b. May 15, 1880, m. Birdie Stagles; William R. b. July 9, 1884, m. Ethel Post; Olive b. Dec. 12, 1886, d. March 25, 1896; Norman S. b. April 10, 1889, m. Mary Miles; Martha J. b. March 17, 1891; Iva Patrenia b. July 25, 1893, d. May 15, 1895.
Married Patrenia Amundson March 1, 1869, Salt Lake City (daughter of Oley and Mary Amundson). Their children: Orson b. Nov. 1, 1874, m. Rosa ——; Samuel b. Jan. 6, 1874, m. Lottie Parry; Homer L. b. Oct. 25, 1876.
Married Annie Eastwood Feb. 6, 1879, Salt Lake City (daughter of John and Sarah Eastwood). Their children: Annie B. b. Jan. 13, 1880, m. Richard Farmer; Sarah R. b. Oct. 27, 1881, m. Lyman Butterfield; William L. b. Aug. 21, 1883; Lorenzo E. b. March 26, 1886, m. Rosa Bills; Heber L. b. May 22, 1888, d. April 1, 1895; Wilford L. b. Nov. 17, 1890; Byron E. b. April 30, 1893, d. April 22, 1895.
Settled on the Little Cottonwood 1849; moved to Provo 1858, and later to Mountain Green. Veteran Echo Canyon war. High priest; president South Jordan branch 1856-77; bishop South Jordan ward 23 years. Taught school at West Jordan two years.

BILLS, GORDON SILAS (son of William Andrew Bills and Emeline Beckstead). Born March 18, 1854, West Jordan, Utah.
Married Ellen G. Holt Sept. 27, 1875, Salt Lake City (daughter of Mathew Holt and Ann Harrison), who was born March 10, 1859, in England. Their children: Ida A. b. Nov. 14, 1876, m. Arthur Bate; Silas W. b. Sept. 25, 1878; Rosa E. b. Dec. 28, 1881; Arthur b. July 14, 1883; Sadie E. b. Aug. 25, 1885, m. Ether Stocking; Edna P. b. April 11, 1888, Hazel b. Jan. 28, 1891, m. Mahonri Butterfield; Edward A. b. June 15, 1893; Harriett L. b. July 5, 1896; Emma b. Oct. 3, 1898.
Married Bertha L. Jensen May 1, 1879, Salt Lake City (daughter of Lars and Maria Jensen). Their children: Ezra b. Dec. 26, 1881, m. Ethel Walker; Raymond b. Jan. 24, 1883, m. Della Crane; Carrie M. b. Sept. 4, 1886, m. Joseph Green; Edith N.; Bertie M. b. June 8, 1888; Elizabeth b. Jan. 24, 1891, m. Alvin Miller; Reynold b. July 9, 1895; Leslie M.
Seventy; president Y. M. M. I. A., South Jordan ward; missionary to southern states 1879-81; 2nd and later 1st counselor to Bishop Orrin P. Miller; bishop of Riverton ward. School trustee; assessor and collector at South Jordan 1875-79.

BING, WILLIAM SHERMAN (son of William Bing of Missouri). Born April 5, 1878, Kirksville, Mo. Came to Utah April, 1894.
Married Bessie Claire Emels May 11, 1899, Salt Lake City (daughter of Harry T. Emels and Mary Grosheil of Cairo, Iowa. Came to Utah Dec. 6, 1891). She was born Nov. 14, 1878. Their children: Harry Emels; William Sherman, died: Virginia. Family resided Salt Lake City, Utah, and Santiago, California.
Proprietor of Salt Lake Stamp company.

BINGHAM, CALVIN (son of Lucius and Lucy Bingham). Born Sept. 27, 1827, Fowler, N. Y. Came to Utah 1854, oxteam company.
Married Elizabeth Thorne (daughter of Ashel Thorne, pioneer 1854). She was born March 25, 1832. Their children: Clarinda b. Sept. 6, 1850, m. Hyrum S. Phelps; Calvin Perry b. Jan. 28, 1852, m. Olive E. Phelps; Mary Elizabeth b. Dec. 25, 1853, m. Hyrum S. Phelps; Lucy Jane b. May 29, 1856, m. Robert Williams; Barbara Ann b. Aug. 25, 1858, m. Robert Williams; Ann Mariah b. June 28, 1862, m. William L. Le Scur; Ashel b. Nov. 20, 1864, d. Sept. 27, 1883; William Augustine b. Aug. 16, 1867, m. Maud Holliday; Lydia Emeline b. Feb. 26, 1870, m. Fred Wood; Orissa Vilate April 29, 1873, d. infant; Alice b. Nov. 20, 1875, m. Rollin Walker.
High priest; bishop. Veteran Echo Canyon war. Blacksmith and farmer. Died May 27, 1883.

BINGHAM, CALVIN PERRY (son of Calvin Bingham and Elizabeth Thorne). Born June 28, 1852, in Pottawattamie county, Iowa. Came to Utah 1854 with parents.
Married Olive E. Phelps Oct. 9, 1872, Salt Lake City (daughter of Morris Phelps and Sarah Thompson of Jackson county, Mo., pioneers 1849, cow and oxteam company). She was born Nov. 24, 1856, Alpine, Utah. Their children: Ina Teressa b. April 13, 1794, d. Oct. 7, 1876; Rhoda Alzina b. Jan. 19, 1876, d. Dec. 27, 1882; Sarah Elizabeth b. July 9, 1879, m. LeRoy Goodrich; Charles Perry b. March 26, 1882, m. Mary Alice Gardner; Hyrum Carl b. Oct. 19, 1884, d. June 6, 1889; Ashel Calvin b. Aug. 7, 1887, m. Grace Casper; Maud Ethel b. May 25, 1890, m. George Pearce; Mary Clarinda b. July 25, 1893; Ralph b. Aug. 16, 1896, d. June 1910; Jedediah G. b. May 16, 1899; Thornton P. b. May 13, 1906. Family resided Montpelier, Idaho, Vernal, Utah, and Mesa City, Ariz.
Sunday school superintendent; high priest; bishop's counselor; bishop; ward teacher. Farmer and horse dealer.

BINGHAM, CHARLES PERRY (son of Calvin Perry Bingham and Olive E. Phelps). Born March 26, 1882, Mesa City, Ariz.
Married Mary Alice Gardner Jan. 3, 1906, Salt Lake City (daughter of Charles Alma Gardner and Martha Timothy, of Wallsburg, Utah). She was born Nov. 2, 1884. Their children: Merl b. Feb. 24, 1907; Charles Leland b. Sept. 13, 1908; Ercil Calvin b. Aug. 14, 1910. Family home Roosevelt, Utah.
Elder; assistant Sunday school superintendent; ward teacher; first assistant in presidency Y. M. M. I. A.; secretary S. S. union board. Farmer.

BINGHAM, ERASTUS (son of Elisha Warner Bingham and Sally Perry). Born March 12, 1798, Concord, Essex county, Vt. Came to Utah Sept. 19, 1847, Daniel Spencer company.
Married Lucinda Gates March 21, 1820 (daughter of Thomas Gates, pioneer Sept. 19, 1847). She was born March 19, 1799, Concord, Vt. Their children: Mary b. April 1, 1820, m. Elijah Norman Freeman, m. Willard Snow, m. Lorin Farr; Sanford b. May 3, 1821, m. Martha Ann Lewis, m. Agnes Fife; Lucinda, m. Loren Hastings; Erastus, Jr. b. Sept. 30, 1822, m. Olive Hovey Freeman, m. Susan Green; Thomas, m. Karen Happuch Holladay; Maria, m. Isaac Newton Goodale; Willard, m. Janet Gates; Edwin, m. Phoebe Jane Burke, m. Amanda Snow; Jacob d. child; Brigham Heber b. Dec. 15, 1841, m. Angeline Therisa Aldous, m. Mary Alice Lomax.

BINGHAM, SANFORD (son of Erastus Bingham and Lucinda Gates). Born May 3, 1821, Concord, Vt. Came to Utah with his father 1847.
Married Martha Ann Lewis July 18, 1847, while crossing plains (daughter of Benjamin Franklin Lewis, massacred at Haun's Mill Oct. 30, 1838, and Joannah Ryon, who died in Nauvoo Jan. 16, 1846). She was born Feb. 20, 1833, and came to Utah with husband. Their children: Sanford Jr. b. Sept. 1, 1848, m. Julia Hall Sept. 19, 1872; Martha Ann b. Jan. 29, 1850, m. Joseph Fife Feb. 16, 1866; Benjamin Franklin b. Sept. 25, 1851, m. Mary E. Jensen Jan. 8, 1885; John b. May 10, 1853, m. Mary Jane Hickenson Oct. 28, 1872; Sophia Cordelia b. Dec. 30, 1854, m. Robert H. Hopkins; William b. Oct. 16, 1856, m. Annie M. Peterson Aug. 9, 1885; Joannah b. Aug. 28, 1858, m. John T. Bybee July 24, 1877; Joseph Smith b. June 23, 1860, m. Annie Annie M. Hansen April 1, 1880; Elisha Erastus b. March 25, 1862, m. Elizabeth L. Walker Nov. 2, 1882; Rebecca Jane b. Nov. 7, 1864, m. Hans Christian Hansen Dec. 21, 1882; Lorin Beason b. Sept. 16, 1866, m. Rose Jenkins June 6, 1894; Lucinda Elizabeth b. Nov. 27, 1868, m. George A. Pincock Oct. 20, 1886. Family home Riverdale, Utah.
Married Agnes Fife Oct. 10, 1863, Salt Lake City (daughter of Adam Fife, pioneer 1857, Capt. Wilkie company, and Ellen Sharp). She was born May 14, 1846, Clackmannan, Scotland. Their children: Martha Agnes b. Aug. 3, 1864, m. Wilson G. Wright March 16, 1888; Adam Aranthon b. Nov. 14, 1865, m. Annie Stratton Nov. 14, 1889; Walter b. April 29, 1867, m. Jessie McDonald Oct. 20, 1886; Ellen b. March 30, 1869, m. Joseph K. Wright Dec. 8, 1886; Mary b. Jan. 5, 1871, m. James H. Cook June 1, 1898; Enoch b. Dec. 12, 1872, m. Alice Tracy July 21, 1893; Margaret b. Oct. 22, 1874; Sanford James b. March 2, 1877, m. Sophia Stratton June 26, 1901; Andrew b. Jan. 19, 1879, m. Adele Child Dec. 7, 1898; Tracy b. Aug. 2, 1882, d. Dec. 26, 1893; Oscar Dec. 13, 1884, drowned Dec. 26, 1893; Norman b. Sept. 18, 1886, m. Ellen Garner Jan. 20, 1909; Maria b. May 31, 1895. Family home Riverdale, Utah.
President Riverdale branch Sept. 1868; bishop Riverdale ward 1868-1902. Assessor and collector; town constable; justice of peace; member town board of trustees; deputy U. S. collector Weber and Box Elder counties 1868-69. Died Nov. 22, 1910.

BINGHAM, BENJAMIN F. (son of Sanford Bingham and Martha Ann Lewis). Born Sept. 25, 1851, Bingham Fort, Utah.
Married Elizabeth Jensen Jan. 8, 1885, Trenton, Utah (daughter of Neils Jensen and Johana Sandberg of Logan, Utah), who was born Nov. 6, 1863. Their children: Benjamin F., Jr. b. Nov. 26, 1885, m. Adelia Lapray; Ed. B. b. July 15, 1888, m. Hazel Cunningham; Murriel b. Oct. 14, 1892; Gilbert b. May 14, 1896; Kenneth b. Feb. 5, 1901; Loyal b. June 17, 1903; Carlton b. March 5, 1907. Family home Trenton, Utah.
Bishop. County commissioner. Farmer and stockraiser.

BINGHAM, BENJAMIN F., JR. (son of Benjamin F. Bingham and Mary Elizabeth Jensen). Born Nov. 26, 1885, Trenton Utah.
Married Adelia Lapray Sept. 26, 1907, Logan, Utah (daughter of David Lapray and Heneretta Hoffman), who was born May 2, 1885. Their children: Wanda b. July 3, 1909; Goldie b. April 11, 1910. Family home, Trenton, Utah.
Missionary to central states 1907-09. Farmer.

BINGHAM, ADAM ARANTHON (son of Sanford Bingham and Agnes Fife). Born Nov. 14, 1865, Riverdale, Utah.
Married Annie Stratton Nov. 14, 1889, Logan, Utah (daughter of Edward Stratton and Adele JoSeules, former a pioneer Sept. 29, 1853, the latter Sept. 15, 1859, Robert F. Neslen company). She was born Jan. 5, 1873, Riverdale, Utah. Their children: Annie Adele b. Jan. 5, 1891, m. Moroni Shipley July 22, 1908; Aranthon Edward b. Feb. 28, 1893; Margaret Lottie b. March 18, 1895; Sophia Madeline b. March 4, 1897; Boneta b. June 5, 1901; Harold Sanford b. Dec. 9, 1903; Leonora b. March 15, 1906; Leland Joseph b. March 31, 1909; George Morzette b. May 26, 1911. Family home Riverdale, Utah.
President Y. M. M. I. A. 1896-97; missionary to Colorado 1898-1900, and presided over West Colorado conference; bishop Riverdale ward 1902-1912.

BINGHAM, ERASTUS (son of Erastus Bingham and Lucinda Gates). Born Sept. 30, 1822, St. Johnsbury, Vt.
Married Olive Hovey Freeman (daughter of Isaac F. and Lydia Freeman), who was born Jan. 8, 1820, Waterford, Vt. Their children: Olive Louise b. Oct. 3, 1844, m. William Walker; Erastus Perry b. March 20, 1846, m. Emeline Chastina Allen Feb. 21, 1870; Lucinda Marie b. June 1,

1848, m. William Foy; Lydia Roxanla b. Jan. 6, 1850, m. George Lish; Isaac Farwell b. Sept. 20, 1852, died; Mary Ann b. Feb. 9, 1854, m. Peter C. Geetesen Aug. 1871; Lorenzo b. Dec. 7, 1856, m. Rebecca Guthrie; Diana b. July 19, 1858, m. William G. Smith Aug. 7, 1876; Ophalla b. Aug. 19, 1860, m. William Foy.

Married Susan Green (daughter of Benjamin P. Green and Lucy Wisdom), who was born Aug. 5, 1839, Halifax, N. S. Their children: Susan Melissa b. Nov. 23, 1856, m. Winslow Farr; Nephi b. April 9, 1858; Lucy Ann b. March 5, 1860, m. Joseph Wheeler; Marintha b. May 26, 1861, m. Stewart Eccles; Eda b. Jan. 21, 1863; Enoch b. March 7, 1864, m. Maria Slater 1883; Daniel (twin to Enoch), m. Eliza Graham; Harriet Adelthe b. Nov. 2, 1865, m. Joseph Wheeler; Erastus Alma b, Sept. 28, 1868, m. Annie Lard Jan. 2, 1888; Violette May b. May 30, 1870, m. John Holt; Benjamin Wisdom b. Jan. 11 1872; Myrtle Adel b. Sept. 2, 1873; Clara Isabel b. Aug. 29, 1876, m. Joseph Woods March 9, 1909; Rozina Diantha b. July 21, 1878, m. James R. McGee; Jacob Moroni b. Nov. 4, 1881, m. Francis Harriet.

Member Company B, Mormon Battalion; major in Echo Canyon campaign; president 38th quorum seventies, Ogden; president 75th quorum seventies, Huntsville, Utah.

BINGHAM, ERASTUS PERRY (son of Erastus Bingham and Olive Hovey Freeman). Born March 20, 1846 La Harpe, Hancock county, Ill.

Married Emeline Chastina Allen Feb. 21, 1871, Salt Lake City (daughter of Alanson David Allen, pioneer Oct. 27, 1849, and Chastina Hadlock, pioneer 1850, Capt. Everett company). She was born Aug. 26, 1851, Ogden, Utah. Their children: Perry Alanson b. April 8, 1871, m. Alvelda Olsen June 1, 1898; Emeline Chastina b. Oct. 14, 1872, m. William A. McBride Jan. 23, 1895; Francis b. July 19, 1874, m. Annie Sophia Hansen March 6, 1898; Albern Allen b. April 14, 1876, m. Pitia J. Poulsen Feb. 1904; Joseph Franklin b. Nov. 23, 1877, m. Harriet Ann Geeder Jan. 8, 1908; Olive Rebecca b. Aug. 20, 1879, m. Alex Wrigley Aug. 15, 1909; Louisa Marinda b. Dec. 10, 1880; William Henry b. April 13, 1882, m. Christiana Michelson Nov. 25, 1907; Mary Lucinda b. Aug. 25, 1883; Thomas Lorenzo b. Feb. 18, 1885, m. Lavina Munson Dec. 18, 1907; Ezra b. Sept. 6, 1886, m. Mary Wood Jan. 8, 1908; Edward Erastus b. March 7, 1888; Clarence b. Nov. 7, 1889; Wilford Levi b. Aug. 14, 1891; Lorin b. Oct. 6, 1893; Leonard b. Oct. 6, 1893; Ceduia b. Aug. 4, 1895; David Moroni b. Aug. 17, 1897; Arnold Hyrum b. June 14, 1899. Family home Huntsville, Utah.

President 75th quorum seventies. School trustee, Huntsville for two terms.

BINGHAM, PERRY ALANSON (son of Erastus Perry Bingham and Emeline Chastina Allen). Born April 8, 1871, Huntsville, Utah.

Married Avelda M. Olsen 1898, Salt Lake City (daughter of Christian Olsen and Andrea M. C. Poulsen, came to Utah 1871). She was born Aug. 23, 1876, Plain City, Utah. Their children: Harvey Perry b. May 4, 1899; Avelda Lucetta b. Sept. 17, 1903; Myrtle Marie b. Aug. 24, 1906.

Counselor in presidency of 6th quorum elders, Weber stake; superintendent Sunday schools, Middleton, Utah.

BINGHAM, THOMAS (son of Erastus Bingham and Lucinda Gates). Born July 19, 1824, Grafton, N. H. Came to Utah July 29, 1847, with contingent of Mormon Battalion, Co. B.

Married Karen Happuch Holladay Sept. 6, 1849, Salt Lake City (daughter of John Holladay and Katherine Higgins of Marion county, Ala., pioneers July 29, 1847, William Crosby company.) She was born May 4, 1830. Their children: Thomas, Jr., b. Aug. 12, 1850, m. Mary Elizabeth Gfroerer; m. Margaret Louisa Gfroerer; Mary b. Sept. 18, 1852, m. Mark M. Hall; m. Phillip Stringham; Lucinda Katherine b. Nov. 3, 1854, m. Charles A. Nye; David Holladay b. Aug. 19, 1857, m. Harriet Perry; Charles C. R. b. June 12, 1860, m. Mary Holden; m. Mary Michelson; Phoebe Karen b. June 4, 1862, m. George W. Hislop; Elzada b. April 21, 1864, d. child; Martha b. Oct 1, 1866, m. Don Carlos Perry; Clara b. Oct. 25, 1868, d. child; Tracy Tyler b. Oct. 24, 1871, d. infant. Family home Ogden, Utah.

Seventy; ordained bishop of Mountain Dell, Tooele county, Utah, Sept. 11, 1881; previously counselor to Bishop F. A. Hammond of Huntsville for many years; Sunday school worker since 1879; missionary to San Bernardino, Cal., March 4, 1851, to May 1855; missionary to Salmon River Indians 1856-58. Selectman when Uinta county was created in 1880 and was elected probate judge at first election, August 1881, and held that office five years. Bingham Canyon was named for him and his brothers, who held claims there 1848-50. Timberman and sawmillman, 1860-77. Died Dec. 31, 1889, Maeser, Utah.

BINGHAM, THOMAS, JR. (son of Thomas Bingham and Karen Happuch Holladay). Born Aug. 12, 1850, Ogden, Utah.

Married Mary Elizabeth Gfroerer June 1, 1874, Salt Lake City (daughter of Frederick G. Gfroerer and Elizabeth Sabin of Pennsylvania, pioneers 1847). She was born Dec. 20, 1854. Their children: Mary Lenora b. June 11, 1875; David Thomas b. March 20, 1877, d. infants; Annie Elizabeth b. Feb. 17, 1879, m. Stephen M. Dudley; George Sanford b. June 23, 1881, m. Janet A. Gerber; Francis Marion b. Oct. 9, 1884, m. Leona Henderson; Mark Moroni b. Dec. 19, 1886; Edna b. June 22, 1889, m. J. Urbin Allred; Edwin b. June 22, 1889, m. Mary M. Wilson; Roseltha b. June 10, 1895.

Married Margaret Louisa Gfroerer Oct. 25, 1875, Salt Lake City (daughter of Frederick G. Gfroerer and Elizabeth Sabin), who was born Dec. 20, 1854. Their children: Clara Louisa b. April 19, 1878, m. George H. Bartlett; Maggie Maria b. Sept. 8, 1880, m. George Victor Billings; Frederick F. b. Nov. 4, 1882, m. Sarah Bartlett; Lester b. Oct. 7, 1885, m. Martha Mae Roberson; Karen b. Aug. 30, 1888, m. William Hacking; Helen Vilate b. May 13, 1891, m. Sanford Dudley. Families resided Maeser, Utah.

BINGHAM, FREDERICK GFROERER (son of Thomas Bingham and Margaret Louisa Gfroerer). Born Nov. 4, 1882, Mountain Dell, Uinta county, Utah.

Married Sarah Bartlett Sept. 19, 1906, Salt Lake City (daughter of Charles Claymore Bartlett and Annie Katrina Jensen of Vernal, Utah, pioneers Oct. 10, 1866, Independent company). She was born Jan. 6, 1887. Their children: Elgia b. June 21, 1907; Merle b. Jan. 12, 1909; Zelda b. Dec. 4, 1910. Family home Vernal, Utah.

Member 77th quorum seventies; missionary to southern states Sept. 24, 1902, to Feb. 5, 1905; ordained high priest Aug. 25, 1907; stake superintendent of Sunday schools July 7, 1906 to Jan. 4, 1908; high councilor 1907-10; bishop of 2d ward, Vernal, Sept. 18, 1910, to Sept. 3, 1911; missionary to Unita Indian reservation. Member of Winder & Bingham Mercantile company, later incorporated as the Acorn Mercantile company, which dealt in general merchandise and machinery. Farmer and stockraiser.

BINGHAM, WILLARD (son of Erastus Bingham and Lucinda Gates). Born Feb. 19, 1830.

Married Janet Gates (daughter of Samuel Gates and Lydia Downer), who was born Jan. 12, 1836. Their children: Flora Janet b. in May, m. Levi J. Taylor; Willard b. Oct. 30, ———, m. Cynthia Melissa Ann Shurtliff; Josephine b. in May, m. Levi J. Taylor; Jedediah Grant b. in Oct., m. Margaret Peterson; Parley Pratt b. Dec. 30, 1859, m. Margaret McFarland Ida b. Feb. 9, ———; Elijah and Elisha Junius b. June 2, ———; Ezra; Erastus La Grand; Lydia; Mariah; Lucinda b. March 13, ———; Zilpha Isador; Nancy Jane; Emmaretta. Family resided Huntsville and Wilson, Utah.

Married Amanda Melvina Snow (daughter of Willard Snow). Their children: Willard Eugene; Melvina; Wilford; Rosetta; Susan; Mary Ellen; Rebecca; Florence Adelaide; Tyler; Isabel.

Married Clara Smith. Their children: Willard S.; Clara; Leroy; Idella; Thomas; Uvada; Hyrum; Viola; Leah; Eldon.

BINGHAM, PARLEY PRATT (son of Willard Bingham and Janet Gates). Born Dec. 30, 1859, Ogden, Utah.

Married Margaret McFarland at Salt Lake City (daughter of James McFarland and Hannah Boyack), who was born March 1, 1860, West Weber, Utah. Their children: Parley Pratt; William M.; George Willard; Samuel Levi; Maggie Mae; Ethel and Edith (twins); Eliza Ellen; Jeddie Archibald; Rosabel; Howard Rulon; Lois Fontella. Family resided Wilson and Smithfield, Utah.

Married Isabel McFarland. Their children: Percy Young; Leone; Ralph M.; Annetta; Wallis James; Lawrence Pratt; Wynona; Norman.

BINGHAM, BRIGHAM HEBER (son of Erastus Bingham and Lucinda Gates). Born Dec. 15, 1841.

Married Angeline Therisa Aldous Dec. 24, 1861 (daughter of Robert Aldous and Mary Ann Parkin, married Dec. 24, 1835, Huntingdon, Eng., pioneers Sept. 14, 1853, Claudius V. Spencer company). She was born Dec. 27, 1844. Their children: Brigham Heber, Jr. b. Dec. 15, 1862, m. Catherine Rozilla Wilson Jan. 17, 1884; Edwin Aldous b. Aug. 31, 1864, m. Geneva Martin Nov. 24, 1885; Angeline Maria b. Sept. 14, 1866, d. age 5 months; Robert b. Dec. 12, 1867, m. Marinda Tracy April 17, 1889; Elijah b. Jan. 25, 1870, m. Mary Francis Fife Oct. 1891; Edna b. March 11, 1872, m. Martin P. Brown Jan. 17, 1894; Joseph b. Sept. 4, 1874, m. Martha C. Mortensen April 4, 1894; Georgianna b. March 8, 1877, m. James Combe Oct. 5, 1905; Mary Ann b. July 15, 1879, m. Claude M. Dee March 1, 1904; Lucinda b. Oct. 27, 1881, d. May, 1891; Erastus A. b. March 17, 1884, m. Hilda Bonerude Feb. 15, 1905. She was born Dec. 10, 1863, Darwin, Lancastershire, Eng. Their children: Ethel Etcle b. March 18, 1887, m. Stephen Farnsworth 1904; John Brigham b. Jan. 12, 1889, m. Pearl Cluff 1910; Minerva Alice b. March 14, 1891; Maude Ellen b. Feb. 24, 1894, m. Eddie Cluff 1910; Dora May b. Feb. 27, 1893; Mary Elizabeth b. Dec. 15, 1900. Families resided Wilson, Weber county, Utah.

Bishop of Wilson ward 1880-90; bishop Mormon colony at Garcia, Mex. Assisted in building first school houses at Lynn and Huntsville. Pioneer to Wilson, Utah, 1869. Director Wilson Irrigation company 14 years.

BINGHAM, BRIGHAM HEBER, JR. (son of Brigham Heber Bingham and Angeline Therisa Aldous). Born Dec. 15, 1862, Lynn, Weber county, Utah.

Married Catherine Rozilla Wilson Jan. 17, 1884, Salt Lake City (daughter of Louis Dunbar Wilson and Catherine Wiggins). She was born Oct. 15, 1863, Ogden, Utah. Their children: Heber Raymond b. Nov. 20, 1884; Clara Rozilla b. March 1, 1887, m. Hyrum Fletcher April 3, 1910; Brigham Albert b. Nov. 2, 1888; Pearl Elva b. Jan. 26, 1891; Annis b. Jan. 8, 1893; Martha May b. May 7, 1895; Verna Catharine b. Dec. 9, 1897; Wallace Dunbar b. July 9, 1902; Hazel b. Nov. 30, 1903; Howard Wilson b. July 21, 1906. Family home Wilson, Utah.

Missionary to Australia 1899-1901; superintendent Wilson Sunday school three years; president Y. M. M. I. A.; one of the seven presidents of 54th quorum seventies. Driven out of Mexico by the rebellion, July 30, 1912.

BINGHAM, EDWIN ALDOUS (son of Brigham Heber Bingham and Angeline Therisia Aldous). Born Aug. 31, 1864. Married Genevra Martin Nov. 24, 1885, Logan, Utah (daughter of John Martin and Sarah Ann Sargent), who was born Aug. 30, 1866. Their children: Genevra b. Sept. 25, 1886, d. Sept. 25, 1886; Edwin Marion b. Oct. 16, 1887, m. Laura Activa Olsen Dec. 8, 1910; Sarah Ann b. Nov. 21, 1889, m. William Eugene Young Nov. 11, 1908; Ella May b. Feb. 12, 1892; Florence b. Feb. 25, 1894; Mabel b. March 7, 1896; John Martin b. April 19, 1898; Dora Angeline b. April 5, 1900; Annetta b. Aug. 1, 1902; Mary Arvilla b. Jan. 28, 1906; Ireta b. July 16, 1908. Family home Wilson, Weber county, Utah.
President Y. M. M. I. A. five years: superintendent Sunday schools; missionary to England 1902-05; member council of 54th quorum seventies; appointed bishop of Wilson ward Oct. 13, 1908. Assisted in building first meeting house at Wilson.

BIRCH, WILLIAM. Born Sept. 2, 1788, Staffordshire, Eng. Came to Utah 1856.
Married Phoebe Craddock, who was born April 13, 1786. Their children: Jane b. Aug. 6, 1812; Susannah b. Aug. 3, 1814; Phoebe b. Jan. 1, 1817; David b. July 24, 1819; William b. April 23, 1822; Richard b. May 25, 1824; James b. March 21, 1828. Family home Staffordshire, Eng.
Married Sarah Ashton in England, who was born 1800, in Staffordshire.

BIRCH, RICHARD (son of William Birch and Phoebe Craddock). Born May 25, 1824, Staffordshire, Eng. Came to Utah 1846.
Married Ellen Harris in England (daughter of William Harris and Ann Davis), who was born Sept. 13, 1821, in Staffordshire. Their children: William Harris b. Nov. 12, 1847, d. infant; James b. Jan. 20, 1850, died; Ellen b. May 26, 1852, m. John Jones; John b. Nov. 22, 1855, died; Jonah b. May 2, 1856, m. Emma McMichael; Robert b. Aug. 25, 1858, m. Margaret McMichael; Richard b. Feb. 21, 1862, m. Malinda Stewart. Family resided in England, St. Louis, Mo., and Salt Lake City.
Married Mary Ann Hale at Salt Lake City, who was born Dec. 23, 1827, in Staffordshire, Eng. Their children: William b. Jan. 16, 1859, m. Nettie Wight; John b. June 30, 1862; Mary Jane b. Nov. 10, 1864, m. William Miller; David b. Aug. 17, 1867, m. Nancy Garn; Elizabeth b. Aug. 17, 1867, m. John Sargent; Samuel b. July 21, 1870, died. Family homes Salt Lake City and Hoytsville, Utah.
Patriarch. Pioneer to Hoytsville, Utah. Farmer.

BIRCH, JONAH (son of Richard Birch and Ellen Harris). Born May 2, 1856, Salt Lake City.
Married Emma McMichael Dec. 12, 1880, Hoytsville, Utah (daughter of Robert McMichael and Elizabeth McMullin, pioneers Sept. 3, 1852, A. O. Smoot company). She was born Sept. 11, 1857, Salt Lake City. Their children: Jonah Don b. Nov. 4, 1881; Robert M. b. Oct. 21, 1883, m. Nellie Williams March 21, 1906; Ellen Elizabeth b. Dec. 30, 1885, m. Claud Abbot Dec. 25, 1906; Emma b. Dec. 5, 1887, m. Noble Farnsworth March 20, 1907; William Richard b. June 8, 1890, m. Belva Johnston July 13, 1910; James Byron b. June 25, 1892; Baby b. April 10, 1897.
Farmer and stockraiser.

BIRCUMSHAW, JOSEPH (son of William Bircumshaw and Hannah Haslet of Nottingham and Derbyshire, Eng.). Born March 7, 1829, Heanor, Derbyshire. Came to Utah Nov. 8, 1865, Miner G. Atwood oxteam train.
Married Rosetta Plackett (daughter of Thomas Plackett and Mary Pheasent of Bresaon, Derbyshire, Eng., pioneers Oct. 10, 1864, Warren S. Snow company). She was born Sept. 12, 1823. Their children: Mary, died; Thomas b. Feb. 1, 1846; Henry b. Oct. 2, 1848, d. May 9, 1908; Mary Ellen b. Aug. 13, 1851, m. Moses Wilkinson Jan. 11, 1869; Joseph Hyrum b. 1853, d. aged 5; John Willard b. Jan. 13, 1856, m. Mary Jane White Oct. 23, 1876; Rosannah b. Jan. 15, 1858; Orson, Lovenia, Emily and Zillah Louisa, all died when children, the last in 1866, being the only one who died in Utah.
Married Naomi Potraer (Simms) of Copenhagen, Denmark, in 1869. There were no children from this marriage.
High priest; elder. Built many houses in Salt Lake City, where he died Oct. 3, 1869.

BIRCUMSHAW, JOHN WILLARD (son of Joseph Bircumshaw and Rosetta Plackett). Born Jan. 13, 1856, Nottingham, Eng. Came to Utah 1865 with parents.
Married Mary Jane White Oct. 23, 1876, Salt Lake City (daughter of James White and Jane Knight of London, Eng., pioneers Sept. 26, 1862, James Wareham company). She was born June 22, 1858. Their children: Laura b. Sept. 27, 1877, m. Ephraim M. Mohlman; Myrtle May b. Aug. 16, 1879, m. William T. Quinn; Joseph b. Nov. 14, 1881, m. Annie O'Brien; Jennie Rosetta b. Nov. 24, 1883, m. William M. Gillette; Willard James b. Sept. 30, 1888; Henry b. Feb. 10, 1891; Albert b. Dec. 15, 1893; Ray b. Aug. 31, 1895; Ruth b. Oct. 7, 1901. Family home Park City, Utah.

BIRD, BENJAMIN. Came to Utah 1850, with Milo Andrus company. His children: James; Richard, m. Laura ———; William, m. Miss Gully; Charles, m. Mary Ann Kenardy.
Farmer. Lived at Provo, Utah. Died there in 1864.

BIRD, CHARLES (son of Benjamin Bird). Born Sept. 19, 1803, Flanders, Morris county, N. J. Came to Utah in 1850.
Married Mary Ann Kenardy of Barrington, Mass., who was born Dec. 7, 1807. Their children: John, m. Sarah ———; Freeman, died; Betsy, m. Norman Blias; m. George Hardy; m. ——— Kimball; Henrietta, m. Charles Shumway; Mauda Sahilia, died; Kelsy; Bradford K., m. Sarah Hill; Eliza, m. Alonzo Merrill; Charles; George; William. Family home Cottonwood, Utah.
Married Sarah Dunston in 1855 at Salt Lake City, who was born in 1828. Their children: Norman; Mary Ann.
President Smith's bodyguard; counselor to Bishop Smoot of Cottonwood ward four years; raised provisions for early settlers. Farmer and merchant; clothier. Died Sept. 29, 1884, Mendon, Utah.

BIRD, BRADFORD K. (son of Charles Bird and Mary Ann Kenardy). Born Jan. 26, 1840, in Adams county, Ill.
Married Sarah Hill Dec. 1, 1868, Mendon, Utah (daughter of John Hill, pioneer 1850). She was born Oct. 9, 1850. Their children: George B. b. Nov. 10, 1869, m. Meda McCurdy; John Albert b. May 11, 1872, died; Margaret Lusina b. Aug. 29, 1873; Charles K. b. July 3, 1876, d. May 31, 1887; Alexander R. b. Oct. 13, 1880. Family home Vernal, Utah.
High priest; superintendent Sunday schools of Naples ward six years. Indian war veteran and took part in Echo Canyon trouble; crossed the plains five times with immigrants. Farmer.

BIRD, CHARLES. Born in New Jersey. Came to Utah in 1855 from Chemung county, N. Y., by oxteam.
Married Amanda Reaves. Their children: Richard; William; Reaves; Charles; Polly; Amanda.
Farmer. Died at Springville, Utah.

BIRD, JAMES (son of Charles Bird and Amanda Reaves). Born 1806 in Pennsylvania. Came to Utah 1852 with Captain Allred oxteam company.
Married Jane Carpenter in 1831, Chemung county, N. Y., who was born in Connecticut 1812 and died May 7, 1892, Lincoln county, Nev. Their children: Taylor Reaves, m. Alice Stokes; Sarah and Amanda, died, the former aged 15; Marybah, m. Lyman Woods; Jasper, m. Ann Starr. Family resided at Provo and St. George, Utah, and in Nevada.
Bishop at Provo. Farmer and stockraiser. Died June 16, 1879, in St. George.

BIRD, TAYLOR REAVES (son of James Bird and Jane Carpenter). Born Feb. 25, 1832, in New York.
Married Alice Stokes Oct. 26, 1862, St. George, Utah (daughter of Joseph Stokes and Alice Clark of England). She was born Jan. 24, 1838, in England. Came to Utah in 1852, oxteam company. Their children: Taylor Reaves, Jr., b. Aug. 24, 1863, d. June 4, 1864; Clarence b. June 7, 1865, m. Charlotte Searle; Alice b. Dec. 17, 1867, m. Albert Johnson; Ida b. June 14, 1870, m. Thomas Johnson; Effie b. May 27, 1872, m. Henry Rhoades; Rhoda b. Jan. 10, 1875, d. Oct. 1, 1876; Eliza Jane b. July 13, 1877, m. Hyrum Taylor; Isabell b. June 29, 1880, d. Nov. 28, 1882. Family resided St. George, Utah, and Clover Valley, Lincoln county, Nev.
Indian war veteran; took part in Echo Canyon trouble. Sheriff of Washington Co., Utah; justice of peace Clover Valley, Nev. Farmer and stockraiser.

BIRD, CLARENCE (son of Taylor Reaves Bird and Alice Stokes). Born June 7, 1865, at St. George, Utah.
Married Charlotte Searle (Murray) July 9, 1903, at Vernal, Utah (daughter of Charles D. Searle and Jane Adair of Payson, Utah, oxteam pioneers). She was then the widow of George Q. Murray, whom she married Feb. 2, 1893, at Vernal, and by whom the children were George Orin Murray b. Nov. 2, 1893; Elsie Jane b. April 1, 1896; Margaret b. Dec. 14, 1897. She was born Oct. 29, 1874. Family home Vernal, Utah.
Farmer; fruitgrower and cattleraiser.

BIRD, JAMES. Born May 18, 1811, London, Eng. Came to Utah November, 1850.
Married Margaret Montgomery. Their children: Edmund b. Aug. 3, 1847, m. Janie Day; Frederick Montgomery b. May 13, 1849, m. Helen George. Family home Salt Lake City. Cabinet maker. Died April 18, 1896.

BIRD, EDMUND (son of James Bird and Margaret Montgomery). Born Aug. 3, 1847, Boston, Mass.
Married Janie Day Nov. 20, 1869, Salt Lake City (daughter of Thomas and Elizabeth Day). She was born in Luton, Eng. Their children: Margaret Anna b. Oct. 15, 1871; Francis M. b. Feb. 27, 1875; Nellie May b. April 15, 1879 [given twice]; Fred Lawrence b. Aug. 5, 1881; *Nellie May b. Feb. 21, 1884; Cora Lue b. May 8, 1885. Family home Kanosh, Utah.
Carpenter and builder.
* [Probably named after child who died.]

BISHOP, FRANCIS M. (son of Delevan D. Bishop and Pamelia Alden of Essex county, N. Y.). Born Aug. 2, 1843, in Essex county, N. Y. Came to Utah August, 1870.
Married Sina Pratt Jan. 24, 1873, Salt Lake City (daughter of Orson Pratt and Della Ann Bishop, pioneers July 22,

1847). She was born Feb. 25, 1850, and died in 1901. Their children: Allie Belle, m. Fred Graham; Bertha, m. Victor Christopherson; Florence, m. Orson Truelson; Alden M. m. Georgia Whitehead; Francis E., died. Family home Salt Lake City.
Married Ella Derr Feb. 25, 1902, Salt Lake City (daughter of William H. Derr and Mary Ellen Rogers of Philadelphia, Pa., pioneers September, 1847). She was born Oct. 26, 1869. Their children: William DeLancy b. Sept. 19, 1903; Miriam b. June 1, 1906; Virginia P. b. Jan. 28, 1908.
Enlisted in Union army July 27, 1861, in 1st Michigan infantry, served five years. Promoted from corporal to sergeant-major, 2d lieutenant and 1st lieutenant. Transferred V. R. C., promoted to captain of Company H, 2d U. S. volunteers. Mustered out Nov. 7, 1865, at Fort Leavenworth, Kas. Member Major Powell's exploring expedition in Colorado Canyon 1871-72. Professor natural science in university of Deseret. He, with David McKenzie and T. E. Bailey, started first free-school in Utah. Member 144th quorum seventies; president elders' quorum in Waterloo. Member board of education; trustee of 7th school district.

BISHOP, WILLIAM (son of John Bishop and Cathrine Evans). Born June 11, 1828, and came to Utah Sept. 25, 1855, Richard Ballantyne company.
Married Harriet Morris (daughter of John Morris and Maria Linney), who was born in 1839. Their children: Harriet Louisa b. July 12, 1864, m. Samuel K. McMurdie Nov. 13, 1882; Cathrine M. b. Dec. 12, 1865; William John b. March 6, 1867; James M. b. Feb. 10, 1869; Maria Jane b. Jan. 22, 1871; Robert M. b. Dec. 15, 1873; Emma M. b. March 6, 1876, m. Joseph Lofthouse Dec. 18, 1897; Mary Ann b. Sept. 18, 1879; Richard b. July 29, 1881, m. Maria Tames Dec. 18, 1907. Family home Paradise, Utah.
High priest; teacher. Participated in the Echo canyon campaign. Watermaster nine years.

BISHOP, WILLIAM H. (son of Sylvanus Bishop, born April 10, 1765, and Rachel Spicer, born July 19, 1775, both at Kinderhook, N. Y.). He was born Sept. 11, 1821, Oswego, N. Y. Came to Utah in 1848.
Married Eliza Pratt (daughter of Namlah Pratt and Elizabeth Roberts), who was born in Vermont. Their children: Mary Elizabeth b. Dec. 18, 1841, m. William Duggins; Vesta Lucetta b. May 15, 1843, m. Edwin Twitchell Feb. 22, 1860; William Sylvanus b. Jan. 25, 1845, and Joseph Franklin b. Dec. 25, 1846, died; Mahonri M. b. Nov. 25, 1848, m. Mary Gibbs; m. Janette Brunson; Penelope b. Sept. 16, 1850, m. Solomon Wixom; Eliza Eldula b. July 28, 1853, m. Henry Hobbison; Nelson Spicer b. Nov. 1, 1855, m. Annie Melville; Heber Lafayette b. Dec. 15, 1857, m. Ella Cahoon; m. Mary Bennett; Savallie b. Dec. 31, 1859, m. Brigham Melville. Family home Pisgah, Morgan county, Ill., previous to 1848.
Married Malinda Case (daughter of Susan Case). Their children: Julia; Artimus; Susan.
Colonel in the Black Hawk Indian war. Settled at Salt Lake City; moved to Provo, then to Fillmore; died there Aug. 10, 1884.

BITNER, BRENEMAN B. (son of Abraham Bitner and Ann Barr, of Illinois). Born Dec. 15, 1837, in Washington county, Pa. Came to Utah in 1849.
Married Mary Benedict in 1864 at Salt Lake City (daughter of Joshua Benedict and Fidelia Mosea, of Connecticut, pioneers, Sept. 12, 1861, Milo Andrus company). She was born Aug. 23, 1846.
Married Martina M. Halseth April 10, 1866, at Salt Lake City (daughter of Peter and Martha Halseth of Christiania, Norway; former came to Utah about 1873). She was born Aug. 18, 1847. Their children: Breneman H. b. June 24, 1867, m. Miriam Butler; Anna b. Feb. 20, 1869, m. George W. Derr; Elizabeth M. b. Nov. 9, 1871, m. Frederick L. Sheets; Luella b. Dec. 7, 1873, m. Nephi L. Taylor; Alice b. March 11, 1875, m. Wallace C. Castleton; Susanna b. June 23, 1877, m. Fredrick L. Morris; Nettie b. Oct. 11, 1879, m. Homer Swartwood; Ardella b. Oct. 4, 1881, m. Benjamin F. Tibby; Florence b. March 4, 1884, d. aged 18; Roy H. b. Sept. 28, 1886, m. Erma Felt; Erma M. b.· Sept. 14, 1888, m. Edward J. Evans; Madeline b. April 15, 1893. Family resided Big Cottonwood, Utah.
Married Sarah A. Osguthorpe Jan. 4, 1869, Salt Lake City (daughter of John Osguthorpe and Lydia Roper of Sheffield, Eng., pioneers fall of 1853, Charles Wilkin company). She was born May 22, 1847. Their children: Mary E. b. Feb. 21, 1870, m. Heber S. Sheets; Milton O. b. Jan. 29, 1872; Lydia b. July 31, 1875, m. William S. Romney; Ada b. June 30, 1880, m. Bryant S. Hinckley; Hoffman H. b. Nov. 14, 1877, m. Nellie Harworth; Chloe b. Nov. 28, 1883, m. Ernest W. Evans; Ella b. May 5, 1887. Family home Salt Lake City, Utah, 17th ward.
One of the seven presidents of seventies; missionary to Pennsylvania and Illinois 1871-72; elder; high priest. Deputy assessor Salt Lake county. Farmer and stockraiser. Died April 10, 1909.

BITTER, TRAUGOTT (son of Gotthard Bitter, born 1802, Schnakainen, East Prussia, Germany, and Luisa Neuman, born 1801). He was born Dec. 2, 1834, Kreuzburg, East Prussia, Germany). Came to Utah Sept. 20, 1861, Joseph Young company.

Married Wilhelmina R. Aust Sept. 25, 1859 (daughter of Gottfried Bernhard Aust and Louisa Charlotte Huebner), who was born June 6, 1836, and came to Utah with husband. Their children: Martha b. Aug. 29, 1860, m. Hyrum Ricks April 1, 1880; William b. Oct. 28, 1862, d. Oct. 15, 1863; Joseph b. Aug. 24, 1864, m. Eliza Erickson March 8, 1888; Amelia b. Nov. 15, 1866; Albert b. Nov. 18, 1868, d. July 27, 1870; George b. Jan. 17, 1871, d. Oct. 22, 1872; Richard Alfred b. July 15, 1873; Willard Rudolph b. March 3, 1876, d. Jan. 5, 1890; Charles b. Jan. 5, 1878, m. Printha E. Facer Oct. 15, 1902. Family home Logan, Utah.
High priest. Carpenter on Salt Lake theater. Moved to St. George in 1862, to Logan in 1864, where he helped build the Logan temple and tabernacle.

BITTER, JOSEPH (son of Traugott Bitter and Wilhelmina R. Aust). Born Aug. 24, 1864, Srit Lake City.
Married Eliza C. Erickson March 8, 1888 (daughter of Michael Erickson and Mary E. Anderson, married April 2, 1861, Malling, Aarhuus amt, Denmark). She was born April 23, 1866. Their children: Martha Elizabeth b. Jan. 6, 1889; Joseph E. b. March 24, 1891; Veda Wilhelmina b. Nov. 7, 1892; William E. b. March 2, 1894; George E. b. Jan. 24, 1896; Vernon E. b. Nov. 29, 1897; Howard E. b. Oct. 4, 1899; Gladys Eliza b. Oct. 23, 1901; Reed E. b. Dec. 27, 1903; Lee E. b. Feb. 12, 1906; Olive b. April 20, 1908; Vera b. June 5, 1911.

BJORK, WILLIAM (son of John Bjork and Catherine Erickson). Born April 6, 1837, Hjo, Sweden. Came to Utah Aug. 19, 1866, John K. Murdock company.
Married Agusta Gustava Anderson Dec. 29, 1868, Salt Lake City (daughter of Anders Nielson and Anna Maja Anderson), who was born Oct. 15, 1836. Only child: Wilhelmina b. Sept. 9, 1869.
Married Eva C. Anderson Aug. 12, 1885, Logan, Utah (daughter of Anders Erickson and Katherina Anderson, of Sweden). She was born March 31, 1852. Their children: Velma b. Jan. 5, 1890; Beatrice b. Oct. 18, 1892. Family home Pleasant Grove, Utah.
Missionary in Sweden six years; high priest. Railroad workman, farmer, stockraiser and fruitgrower.

BLACK, GEORGE DAVID (son of George Black, born 1820 in Mississippi, and Mary McRee, born Oct. 17, 1819). He was born Feb. 18, 1841, Copiah county, Mississippi. Came to Utah July 27, 1847.
Married Mary Hunt Sept. 16, 1862 (daughter of Jefferson Hunt and Celia Mount, pioneers July 27, 1847). She was born July 12, 1845. Their children: Nancy Jane b. Jan. 22, 1863; George David b. Oct. 24, 1864; Charles Jefferson b. Nov. 24, 1866; William Jesse b. March 16, 1868; Harriet Erminie b. April 21, 1871; Joseph Warren b. May 28, 1873; John Franklin b. May 28, 1876; Mary b. March 21, 1878; Grace b. May 20, 1879; Henry Harrison b. May 22, 1881; Celia Margaret b. Nov. 14, 1883; Wallace Edwin b. Dec. 1, 1885; Maud Eline b. Jan. 22, 1889.
Presiding elder Oxford ward, Idaho, 1872-1875; member high council, Bannock stake 1875; superintendent Sunday schools, Wilford, four years. Justice of peace Oxford, Idaho, four years. Lieutenant Utah militia.

BLACK, CHARLES JEFFERSON (son of George David Black and Mary Hunt). Born Nov. 24, 1866, Ogden, Utah.
Married Maloney Pratt Jan. 19, 1891, Wilford, Idaho (daughter of William J. Pratt and Alice Smart). No children.
Married Mary Ann Steers Jan. 22, 1896, Logan, Utah (daughter of Elijah Steers and Elizabeth Candland), who was born Nov. 26, 1873. Their children: Blanche b. Nov. 12, 1896; Gladys b. Sept. 29, 1898; Charles Leslie b. June 18, 1901; Fern b. Jan. 18, 1903; Frank S. b. Jan. 16, 1904; Myrtle b. Jan. 26, 1906; Lucile b. Feb. 10, 1908; Cecil Jefferson b. Nov. 27, 1910.
Bishop's counselor at Wilford 1893-1900, and St. Anthony, Idaho, 1900-1902; ordained bishop of La Grande, Ore., 1907.

BLACK, JOSEPH HENDERSON (son of Thomas Black and Lydia Ann Henderson of Pittsburg, Pa.). Born July 25, 1831, Lawrenceville, Allegheny county, Pa. Came to Utah Nov. 14, 1863.
Married Betsy Ann Snyder (Johnstun) July 30, 1868, Salt Lake City (daughter of Samuel Comstock Snyder and Henrietta Maria Stockwell of Snyderville, Utah, pioneers July 24, 1847, Brigham Young company). She was born July 17, 1830. Their children: Lydia b. Jan. 26, 1871, m. Elisha William Davis; Joseph Alonzo b. April 9, 1874, m. Minnie E. Brannan. Family home Vernal, Utah.
Settled at Snyderville in 1864. Bishop Park city ward; organized the first Sunday school in Uinta county and was superintendent of schools there. Justice of peace. Carpenter and builder; freighter and teamster. Died April 12, 1909, Vernal, Utah.

BLACK, JOSEPH ALONZO (son of Joseph Henderson Black and Betsy Ann Snyder). Born April 9, 1874, Snyderville, Utah.
Married Minnie E. Brannan Oct. 18, 1903, Vernal, Utah (daughter of John M. Brannan of Ireland and Elizabeth Eliason (Rasmussen) of Stavanger, Norway, who came to Utah 1871, married at Wanship, Utah). She was born Nov.

5, 1875. Their children: Veda Lavon b. Sept. 18, 1904; Beulah Deon b. April 2, 1906; Carman Alonzo b. Dec. 23, 1907; Grace b. Nov. 20, 1909, d. aged 14 months; Joseph Henderson b. May 25, 1912.
Seventy; missionary to Southern states 1900-02; assistant Sunday school superintendent; president Y. M. M. I. A. Settled in Ashley valley 1878, with his parents.

BLACK, WILLIAM (son of William Black, born in Belfast, and Mary Gardner of County Antrim, Ireland). Born Aug. 20, 1784, Lisburn, Ireland. Came to Utah Sept. 15, 1850, James Pace company.
Married Jane Johnston July 31, 1822 (daughter of Daniel Johnston and Margaret Chambers, pioneers 1850, James Pace company). She was born June 11, 1801. Their children: George b. May 6, 1823, m. Susan Jacaway; Mary b. April 25, 1825, m. John McDonald; William V. b. Feb. 27, 1832, m. Elmira and Victoria Ayers; Joseph S. b. July 14, 1836, m. Nancy Cynthia Allred Nov. 12, 1855, m. Sarah Jane Barney Nov. 14, 1860, m. Caroline Thompson Feb. 14, 1864, m. Louisa Jane Stocks Feb. 13, 1883. Family home Nauvoo, Ill.
Missionary to England two years; high priest. Soldier in British army 20 years. One of the founders of Spring City 1859. Died Jan. 28, 1873, Rockville, Kane county, Utah.

BLACK, GEORGE (son of William Black and Jane Johnston). Born May 6, 1823, at Lisburn.
Married Susan Jacaway April 6, 1850 (daughter of Mary Ann Jones), who was born Sept. 18, 1835, and came to Utah Sept. 13, 1850, Perrigrine Sessions company. Their children: Mary Ann b. 1852, died; George W. b. May 23, 1854, m. Esther Clarinda King Feb. 15, 1877; Susan b. Jan. 26, 1858, m. A. Woolsey 1876; William b. Nov. 28, 1863, m. Matilda Emily King July, 1887; John Franklin b. Jan. 19, 1866, m. Eliza Rosetta King Jan. 2, 1896; Nephi James b. Feb. 3, 1871, m. Phoebe Lorana Horup May 1, 1892; Melissa b. May 12, 1872, m. W. O. Harvey.
Married Mary Ann Donnelly (daughter of Phil Donnelly and Mary Ann McKowen, former pioneer 1857, William S. Young company). She was born Jan. 26, 1834, Magherafelt, Londonderry, Ireland. Their children: Joseph b. Dec. 12, 1856; Alice J. b. July 7, 1857, m. Edwin R. Rappleye March 1, 1876; Mary Ann b. Nov. 11, 1859, m. Alfred Whitcott Dec. 25, 1883; Lillian b. Jan. 13, 1863; Edward Lenox b. June 6, 1868, m. Pearl A. Kimball Dec. 21, 1898; Lauretta b. June 11, 1871; Birdie b. Aug. 11, 1876, m. Pearl Patrick Nov. 10, 1897.
Moved to Fillmore 1851, and to San Pete county 1855; from here to St. George with first wagons; to Rockville in time of Indian troubles; then to Kanosh, where he died November, 1872. Veteran Black Hawk war.

BLACK, GEORGE, JR. (son of George Black and Susan Jacaway). Born May 23, 1854, Fillmore, Utah.
Married Esther Clarinda King Feb. 15, 1877, St. George, Utah (daughter of Culbert King and Eliza Esther McCullough). She was born Sept. 24, 1858, Fillmore, Utah. Their children: George King b. Jan. 9, 1879, m. Sarah Lucille Snow Oct. 6, 1903; Louisa b. Oct. 3, 1880, d. April 12, 1881; Bertha E. b. Jan. 26, 1882, m. James S. Passey Sept. 2, 1902; Culbert Lorin b. March 8, 1884, d. Jan. 18, 1889; Henry b. March 26, 1886, d. Dec. 30, 1888; John Edward b. March 29, 1888, d. Oct. 6, 1888; Collins R. b. Oct. 19, 1889, d. Sept. 19, 1891; Esther b. March 15, 1894; Susan b. March 23, 1897; Richard Levi b. May 15, 1900, d. April 9, 1901.
Settled at Kingston, Piute county, 1877; moved to Coyote 1879; missionary to Great Britain Sept. 5, 1891-93; second counselor to Bishop Culbert King; first counselor to Bishop C. L. King; bishop of Marion ward since 1908.

BLACK, WILLIAM, JR (son of William Black and Jane Johnston). Born Feb. 27, 1832, at Lisburn.
Married Elmira Ayers 1854, Manti, Utah (daughter of Caleb Ayers, died in Council Bluffs, and Lucinda Haggerty, —latter a pioneer 1853, J. C. Little company). She was born 1834 in New Jersey. Their children: Jane b. 1856, m. Ezra Rappleye; Elmira b. June 25, 1857, m. John Styler; William V. Jr. b. Feb. 8, 1860, m. Anne Rotherham; Lucinda Catherine b. 1861, m. Uriah Curtis; Elizabeth b. Feb. 19, 1863, m. William Broadneld; Annie Eldona b. 1865, m. Uriah Hoyt; Fanny Vrena b. Aug. 24, 1866, m. Alfred Mikesell; Eleanor b. July 17, 1868, m. James Walton; Heber b. Sept. 17, 1870, m. Hattie Simmons. Family home Rockville, Utah.
Married Victoria Ayers April 7, 1856, Salt Lake City (daughter of Caleb Ayers and Lucinda Haggerty), who was born Nov. 8, 1839, in New Jersey. Their children: George Ayers b. March 3, 1861, m. Emily Partridge; Agnes b. Feb. 11, 1863, m. William McLeod; Ira Adelbert b. Feb. 1868; Joseph V. b. Sept. 14, 1872, m. Amelia Jane Cahoon; Clara b. Sept. 27, 1874, m. Frederick G. Warnick; Victoria b. Jan. 27, 1877, m. George M. Christensen; Arthur C. b. Oct. 12, 1878, m. Helen Powell; Marzett b. Jan. 14, 1881, m. Joseph Walton; Marion b. Jan. 14, 1881, m. Stella Damren; Lois b. April 25, 1883, m. James Ewing; William Alonzo b. May 16, 1886, m. Janet Bywater.
Seventy in 18th quorum and president 21st quorum; high priest; presiding elder at Deseret 1877. Assisted in locating Manti and Spring City, being a pioneer to San Pete county. Contractor on D. & R. G. R. R. Veteran Walker and Black Hawk Indian wars. President Deseret Irrigation company; assisted in locating the dams and canals at Abraham, Hinckley, Deseret and Oasis.

BLACK, JOSEPH S. (son of William Black and Jane Johnston). Born July 14, 1836, at Lisburn.
Married Nancy Cynthia Allred Nov. 12, 1855, San Pete, Utah (daughter of Reuben Warren Allred and Lucy Ann Butler, pioneers 1849, Allen Taylor company). She was born Jan. 20, 1840, Nauvoo, Ill. Their children: Nancy Cynthia b. July 21, 1857, m. Andrew Peterson; Joseph S., Jr., b. Feb. 5, 1860, m. Ada Western Jan. 22, 1880; William Reuben b. Sept. 27, 1861, m. Mary Moody April 1884, d. April 18, 1889; m. Lucy Whicker April 14, 1890; George Warren b. May 7, 1864, m. Birdie Robinson Oct. 15, 1895; Thomas B.; Nephi A. b. April 22, 1868, m. Ada Rapplye Dec. 10, 1894; Dennis W. b. Sept. 4, 1870, m. Maggie Barney Dec. 16, 1896; Emma A. b. April 11, 1874, m. William Elder; Pearl Luella b. Feb. 19, 1877, m. Dana Gibbs Feb. 24, 1895; Ida Deseret b. July 28, 1880, m. Minor Aldridge.
Married Sarah Jane Barney Nov. 14, 1860. Their children: Sarah Jane; Emelia; Hannah; Charles Henry b. Feb. 27, 1871, m. Mable A. Warner Dec. 1, 1892; Clorinda Louisa b. Sept. 18, 1873, m. William A. Pratt Sept. 23, 1891; Valentine; Parley Pratt b. Oct 7, 1877, m. Theresa E. Noll April 7, 1904; Ada R. b. Feb. 3, 1880, m. Benjamin Blake, Jr., Oct. 1903; Joseph F. b. Nov. 16, 1883, m. Nellie Baysinger; Camelia Hortense b. Dec. 18, 1887, d. Feb. 26, 1900.
Married Caroline Thompson Feb. 14, 1861 (daughter of Peter P. and Dorothy Thompson, pioneers 1851). She was born October 24, 1843. Their children: Josephine b. March 12, 1863, m. Albert Petty Nov. 28, 1882; Daniel J. b. Oct. 5, 1865, m. Phoebe Amanda Henry Aug. 13, 1884; Diantha b. April 19, 1867, m. Joseph Hansen July 2, 1889; Hannah C. b. Feb. 22, 1869, d. Nov. 22, 1874; Peter T. b. April 15, 1871, m. Isabel Jane Bennett March 15, 1893; Courtenah b. March 18, 1873, m. Colmore Cropper Oct. 24, 1894; Phoebe b. Sept. 12, 1875, m. John W. Reid Oct. 24, 1891; Nellis David b. Dec. 1, 1877, d. April 28, 1900; Dora Maud b. March 11, 1880, m. Ole Johnson Sept. 2, 1904; Lillian Louise b. Jan. 20, 1883, m. Nels Peterson Nov. 21, 1900; Carrie Amanda b. March 1, 1885, m. Peter Jensen Sept. 9, 1908.
Married Louisa Jane Stocks Feb. 13, 1883 (daughter of William and Mary Stocks of England). Their children: Sarah Eliza b. Nov. 3, 1885, m. Harvey Kemp May 14, 1893; Joseph Valentine b. Dec. 24, 1887; Louise Valeria b. April 3, 1889, m. Joseph Alva Young May 1, 1907; Flossie Bartell b. April 22, 1894; Wallace b. Nov. 2, 1890; Roland b. Jan. 27, 1893. Families resided Deseret, Utah.
Seventy; high priest; counselor to Bishop C. G. Larsen; bishop Deseret ward many years. Major Sanpete militia; Spring City selectman. Died Aug. 13, 1910.

BLACK, PETER THOMPSON (son of Joseph S. Black and Caroline Thompson). Born April 5, 1871, Kanosh, Utah.
Married Isabella Jane Bennett March 15, 1893, Manti, Utah (daughter of Joshua Bennett, pioneer Oct. 29, 1852, William H. Dame company, and Isabella Jane Holt, pioneer 1863). She was born Dec. 7, 1873, South Cottonwood, Utah. Their children: Lorin Winford b. April 17, 1894; d. Feb. 21, 1909; Averno Thompson b. April 12, 1896; Edith Lillas b. Jan. 29, 1898; Nels Clayton b. March 24, 1900; Harold J. b. June 23, 1902; Golden Holt b. Jan. 2, 1905; Lucian Paul b. July 18, 1909. Family home Deseret, Utah.
First counselor to Bishop Joseph W. Damron. Justice of peace of Deseret 1904; sheriff of Millard county.

BLACK, WILLIAM V. (son of William V. Black and Almira Ayers). Born Feb. 8, 1860.
Married Annie Rotterham. Their children: William V., Jr., b. Nov. 9, 1889; Charles b. 1891; Elmira; Elizabeth.

BLACK, WILLIAM MORLEY (son of John Black and Mary Kline of Ohio). Born Feb. 11, 1826. Came to Utah July 24, 1849, oxteam company.
Married Margaret Ruth Banks in Illinois (daughter of Nathaniel B. and Barbara Banks of Illinois), who was born Jan. 20, 1829, and came to Utah 1852, oxteam company. Their children: Martin Luther b. Feb. 16, 1848, m. Mary Caroline Lee Aug. 23, 1868; m. Sariah Pulsipher April 14, 1910; Martha Jane, m. George Gale; Mary Elizabeth, died; Olive and William, d. infants; John M., m. Theresa Cox; m. Harriet Spencer; Isaac E., m. Nancy E. Allen; m. Olive H. Olsen; George H., m. Sarah Minerva Washburn. Family resided in Illinois and Ephraim, Utah.
Married Mary Jane Washburn 1850 at Manti, Utah (daughter of Abraham and Tamar Washburn of Manti, pioneers 1848, oxteam company). She was born July 28, 1832. Their children: Tamar Jane, m. John R. Young; Sarah Amelia, m. Lorenzo Zabriskie Young; William Grant, m. Lucretia Maxwell; Benjamin D., m. Annie Porter; m. Susan Palmer; m. Anne Baldwin; Mary Ann and Eva, m. James Palmer; Charles T., m. Mary Stalworthy; Margaret, m. Samuel J. Rowley; Orson. Family home Orderville, Utah.
Married Maria Hansen at Ephraim, Utah (daughter of Andrew and Abalone Hansen of Ephraim, pioneers 1856, oxteam company). Their children: Joseph A., Johanna Fisher; Rachel, m. Warner Porter; William, d. infant; Myrtle, m. James Palmer; Harriet, m. Willard Guyman; Miller S., m. Julia Sherman; David, m. Theda Kartchner; Myrtle, m. Nellie Porter; Abalone, m. Walter Porter. Family resided Ephraim, Beaver and Glendale, Utah.
Married Linette Richardson. She was born 1830. Only child was Daniel, who died in infancy. Family home Ephraim, Utah.
Married Louisa Washburn at Salt Lake City (daughter of Abraham and Clarinda Washburn of Ossining, N. Y., pioneers 1848, oxteam company). Their children: William, d. child; Catherine, d. infant; Calista, m. Robert Peal; Parley P., m. Dorcas Everett; Clara, m. Willis M. Webb; Edward; Lorena; Ella; Jane. Family home Washington, Utah.

760 PIONEERS AND PROMINENT MEN OF UTAH

Married Sarah Marinda Thompson Oct. 1874, Salt Lake City. Their children: Mary Bell, m. James Carroll; Amy Jane, m. Thomas Carroll; William, d. infant; Eliza Roxey, d. child. Family home Glendale, Utah.
Member 81st quorum seventies; high priest; patriarch. Indian war veteran. Miller.

BLACK, MARTIN LUTHER (son of William Morley Black and Margaret Ruth Banks). Born Feb. 16, 1848, in Illinois. Came to Utah 1852, Capt. Wimmer company.
Married Mary Caroline Lee Aug. 22, 1868, Salt Lake City (daughter of John Percival Lee and Eliza Foscue of Lincoln county, Tenn., pioneers 1850, Shadrach Roundy company). She was born Dec. 30, 1850. Their children: Martin Louis b. July 11, 1869, and Ethel b. July 2, 1870, died; Victor Lee b. Jan. 29, 1873; Percy A. b. Nov. 17, 1874, m. Cora Jakeman; May b. May 15, 1876, m. Louis Keith; Edna b. March 3, 1878, m. Chris Neilson; Arthur b. May 11, 1880; Phillip b. Nov. 2, 1890. Family home Huntington, Utah.
Married Sariah Eliza Pulsipher April 14, 1910, Salt Lake City (daughter of Charles Pulsipher and Sariah Robbins, pioneers 1850). She was born March 22, 1863.
President high priests' quorum at Huntington, Utah; ward teacher. Farmer and miller.

BLACK, ISAAC E. (son of William M. Black and Margaret Ruth Banks). Born Dec. 29, 1857, Nephi, Utah.
Married Nancy E. Allen Feb. 22, 1877, St. George, Utah (daughter of Lewis Allen and Elizabeth Alexander of Washington county, Utah, pioneers 1862, oxteam company). She was born Dec. 15, 1861. Their children: James Edwin b. March 11, 1880, m. Sarah Lavina Foote; Elizabeth b. Oct. 16, 1881, d. aged 13; Margaret b. April 11, 1884, m. William Edgar Cox; Allen b. Dec. 25, 1885, d. infant; Alvin b. Oct. 2, 1886, m. Sarah E. Cox; Clarence Andrew b. Jan. 10, 1890, m. Sarah Matilda Biddlecome; Elmer b. Sept. 25, 1893; May b. May 6, 1895; Rial b. Dec. 8, 1897; Nellie b. Aug. 22, 1899; Permelia b. Aug. 29, 1901. Family home Huntington, Utah.
Married Elvina Hansina Olsen Oct. 10, 1885, at St. George (daughter of Christian Wilhelmj Olsen and Anne Johanna Ellersøn of Sweden). She was born May 15, 1868. Their children: Martin Isaac b. Aug. 27, 1885, m. Laura Sherman; Leroy b. Jan. 26, 1888, m. Jeannett Wayman; William Henry b. Oct. 28, 1889, and Fannie b. Sept. 23, 1890, d. infants; Harvey b. Oct. 4, 1891, and Frank Afton b. April 10, 1894, d. in youth; Dora b. June 19, 1896, d. infant; Annie b. March 22, 1898; Glen b. Aug. 19, 1899, d. infant; Walter b. Dec. 24, 1900; Ward b. Aug. 6, 1902; Ellis b. Dec. 21, 1905; Rulon b. Feb. 26, 1907; Marie b. Oct. 25, 1911. Family home Huntington, Utah.
Member 81st quorum seventies: high priest; missionary to Denver 1907; ward teacher. Miller and farmer.

BLACK, ALVIN (son of Isaac E. Black and Nancy E. Allen). Born Oct. 2, 1887, Huntington, Utah.
Married Sarah Elizabeth Cox April 25, 1907, Manti, Utah (daughter of Ellias Cox and Mary E. Sherman of Huntington; pioneers Sept. 24, 1848, Heber C. Kimball company). She was born March 12, 1888. Their children: Claude Elias b. May 8, 1908; Vernon Alvin b. March 9, 1911. Family home Huntington.
Elder. Farmer and miller.

BLACKBURN, ELIAS HICKS (son of Thomas Blackburn and Elizabeth Bone of Bedford county, Pa.). Born Sept. 17, 1827, in Bedford county, Pa. Came to Utah in 1849, Milo Andrus company.
Married Sarah Jane Goff, March 3, 1847, in Pottawattamie county, Iowa (daughter of James and Jane Goff of Iowa, who came to Utah in 1850). Their children: Eliza Platte b. July 22, 1849, m. Lena Busenbark; Sarah Jane b. Feb. 10, 1851, m. Frank Richards; Orson Hyde b. June 3, 1854, m. Hannah Gibbons; Thomas, b. July 18, 1858, m. Juliette Maxfield; Anna Laura b. Aug. 29, 1863, d. infant; James Elisha b. April 29, 1865, m. Delilah Emily Oyler, m. Ada Agnes Fillmore; Alice, b. Sept. 6, 1877, m. George A. Richardson.
Married Nancy Phipps Lane, April 12, 1852, Salt Lake City, who was born July 16, 1833, in Illinois. Their children: William W. b. March 3, 1853, d. at birth; George Albert b. June 23, 1854; Bathsheba b. Sept. 14, 1855, m. C. A. Grundy; David Patten b. March 2, 1857; Mariah Ellen b. Aug. 26, 1858, m. Solomon Walker; Alma Jehu b. June 10, 1860; Lewis Henry b. June 23, 1863, d. child; Mary D. b. Dec. 17, 1864, m. Joseph Fisher; Frank Adelbert b. Aug. 29, 1866, d. child; Emily b. Dec. 4, 1868, m. Monroe McClellan; Heber Charles b. Aug. 27, 1871, m. Niobe Turnbow, m. Louisa Taylor; Luella b. Aug. 16, 1872, m. Edward Goodwin; Parley Pratt b. March 9, 1874, m. Margaret M. Banzo.
Married Elizabeth Hales April 9, 1855, at Salt Lake City. Utah (daughter of John and Elizabeth Hales of California). She was born March 17, 1839, in Michigan. Their children: Brigham b. Jan. 30, 1856; Mary Elizabeth b. March 5, 1858; Harriet Eliza b. March 8, 1860. Family home Provo.
Married Hannah Haws January 1857, at Salt Lake City, Utah (daughter of John and Martha Haws of Illinois). She was born March 15, 1832, in Wayne county, Ill. Their children: Martha Ann b. June 7, 1858, d. in maidenhood; John Ambrose b. July 7, 1864; Warren b. June 17, 1869; Oscar b. Oct. 2, 1871, d. a youth.
Married Virtue Leah Crompton Jan. 30, 1862, at Salt Lake City (daughter of Steven Crompton and Ann Gladman of Norfolk, Eng.). She was born Dec. 21, 1844. Came to Utah in 1860. Their children: Harriet Elizabeth b. April 24, 1864, m. Charles P. Okerlund; Howard Florence b. Dec. 29, 1865, m. Florence Oyler; Eliza May b. Feb. 23, 1868, m. Wilford Pace; William b. Oct. 28, 1871, m. Emily Fordham; Minnie Lillie b. Nov. 4, 1873, m. George McClellan; Ezra b. Aug. 26, 1875, d. at birth; Seth Hicks b. Oct. 18, 1876, m. Millie Nebeker; Joseph C. b. Jan. 29, 1879, m. Mabel Halliday; Nellie b. March 16, 1880, d. at birth; Danial Steven b. Oct. 23, 1880, m. Eva Edwards. Families resided at Minersville, Provo and Loa, Utah.
Missionary to England; first bishop of Provo 1849-1858; bishop of Loa 1880-1889. Pioneer of Provo, Minersville and Loa. Farmer and pioneer doctor. Died April 6, 1908, at Loa.

BLACKBURN, JAMES ELISHA (son of Elias Hicks Blackburn and Sarah Jane Goff). Born April 29, 1865, at Minersville.
Married Delilah Emily Oyler Feb. 28, 1890, at Loa (daughter of Ammon Oyler and Delilah Snyder of Virginia. Came to Utah in 1871). She was born Nov. 17, 1873. Their children: Clara May b. June 5, 1891; Ralph b. Feb. 7, 1893; Alma Lester b. April 11, 1896; Melvin Oyler b. Feb. 18, 1904.
Married Ada Agnes Fillmore Jan. 18, 1905, at Manti, Utah (daughter of Norman Fillmore and Eleanor Searle), who was born Dec. 26, 1881. Their children: Ronald Ellsha b. June 27, 1907; Morris b. Oct. 12, 1910. Family home Richfield, Utah.
Member 36th quorum seventies. Farmer.

BLACKBURN, JEHU (son of Thomas Blackburn and Elizabeth Bone), born in Bedford county, Pa. Came to Utah 1847, Capt. Nebeker company.
Married Julia Ann Jameson about 1846, Winter Quarters, Neb. (daughter of Charles Jameson and Mary Shadrick of Pennsylvania, pioneers 1847, Mormon battalion and Capt. Brown company). Their children: Jehu, Jr., b. March 26, 1848, m. Catherine Rebecca Foy, m. Margarett Evelyn Woolsey; Julia Ann b. Feb. 1, 1850, m. Mathoni L. Burns; Ephraim, died.
Married Susan Jameson at Salt Lake City (daughter of Charles Jameson and Mary Shadrick). Their children: Manassa, died; Clifton, m. Isabel Stoddard; Anthony, m. Mary Ellen Stoddard; Thaddeus, m. Maraby Stoddard; Alonzo, m. Jane Stoddard; Madora, m. John Ramsey; Byron, m. Ida Maxfield; Melissa, m. Albert Stoddard; Scott, m. Minnie Pose.
High priest. Died at Nephi, Utah.

BLACKBURN, JEHU, Jr. (son of Jehu Blackburn and Julia Ann Jameson). Born March 26, 1848, Salt Lake City.
Married Catherine Rebecca Foy Nov. 4, 1866, Minersville, Utah (daughter of Thomas B. Foy and Catherine Fink, pioneers of Washington county). She was born March 28, 1848. Their children: Jehu Thomas, m. Alice Pierce; Ephraim, m. Alice Taylor; Frederick, m. Miss Roberts Catherine Julia, m. William Ladell; Manassa, m. Angeline Taylor; Nellie, m. Henry Robison; William Sheridan, died; Charles Theodore; Adolphus and Theron, died; Leslie.
Married Margarett Evelyn Woolsey at Rabbit Valley, Utah (daughter of Hyrum Woolsey and Lucinda Jameson of Millard county, pioneers July 24, 1847, Brigham Young company). She was born July 25, 1864. Their children: Lucinda Hemmelwright, m. Clifton McClutchy; Joseph m. Millie Bishop; Arthur G. Newberry, m. Hannah Anderson; Dan F. Newberry, m. Katie Morrill.
Elder. Made a trip across the plains for merchandise. Black Hawk Indian war veteran.

BLAIR, HARRISON (son of Michael Blair, born 1795, in Kentucky, and Jane Blair of Adams county, Ill.). He was born May 19, 1819, in Adams county, Ill. Came to Utah in 1857 with a party of those who were called in to anticipate arrival of Johnston's army.
Married Mary Ann McNutt in Adams county (daughter of James McNutt of Kentucky and Elizabeth McNutt of Virginia). She was born Aug. 7, 1833, and died Feb. 2, 1897. Their children: Priscilla Jane, m. Hyrum Bennett North; William Oliver, m. Elizabeth McGhea; Elizabeth, m. Siney Lewis; Michael Harrison, m. Sarah Friar; Mary Allen, m. Victor Reynolds; Ellen, m. Job Baker; Samuel McNutt; George Cannon; Lucy Ann, m. Charles Christensen; David Brinton; Warren Montgomery; John James. Family home Holliday (North Cottonwoody), Utah.
High priest; ward teacher. Came from California at the call of Brigham Young to help build up Salt Lake county and vicinity. Farmer. Died Dec. 28, 1858.

BLAIR, SETH MILLINGTON (son of James Blair and Catherine Jordan, the latter of Tennessee). Born March 15, 1819, Ralls county, Mo. Came to Utah 1850, independent company.
Married Cornelia Jane Espy Dec. 7, 1837, in Tennessee. Their children: Preston; Ellen, m. Edwin Ellsworth; Seth, died.
Married Sarah Maria East Nov. 15, 1855, Salt Lake City (daughter of Edwin W. East and Willmirth Greer of Salt Lake, pioneers 1853, Seth Millington Blair company). She was born Dec. 31, 1840 and died July 3, 1890. Their children: Lehi, died; Mary, m. Logan Gilbert Holdaway; Wallace and Nancy died; Willmirth, m. J. C. White. Family homes Salt Lake City and St. George, Utah. Died March 17, 1875, Logan, Utah.

BLAKE, BENJAMIN FREDERICK (son of Isaac Blake). Born March 12, 1815, in England. Came to Utah 1852.
Married Harriett Hollis 1841 in England, who was born Dec. 11, 1820, and came to Utah with husband. Their children: Mariah, died; Frederick, m. Sarah Hardy, Emily —— and Mary ——; Caroline, m. Warren Hardy; Edward, died; Elizabeth, m. Henry Riding; Emma, m. John Carter; George, died; Benjamin, m. Elizabeth Blake; Jane, m. Eugene Elisha Branch; Harriett, m. Nels Sandberge; Anna Eliza, Henry and Isaac, died.
High priest. Furniture and cabinet maker. Died March 9, 1883.

BLAKE, THOMAS (son of John Blake and Sarah Piper of South Jordan, Utah). Born May 9, 1859, Bridgeport, Dorsetshire, Eng. Came to Utah June 14, 1876, John Woodhouse company.
Married Bettie Platt Sept. 9, 1880, Salt Lake City (daughter of John Platt and Betty Butterworth of Royton, Lancashire, Eng., who came to Utah June 10, 1881, Joseph R. Matthews company). She was born Feb. 20, 1858. Their children: Thomas William b. June 8, 1882; Herbert John b. April 10, 1885; Alice b. Feb. 2, 1887; Amy Floretta b. May 20, 1889; James Platt b. June 6, 1891; Mildred b. Dec. 28, 1895; Bettie Hannah b. June 9, 1898. Family home South Jordan, Utah.
One of seven presidents of 96th quorum seventies; missionary to England 1897-99; high priest; bishop South Jordan ward July 8, 1900, until his death. Engaged in sheep business at South Jordan and farmer. Died Aug. 7, 1911, South Jordan.

BLAKE, WILLIAM (son of William Blake, born Jan. 1806, and Sarah Barrow, born March 1818, at North Molton, Devonshire, Eng.). He was born Aug. 4, 1848, at North Molton, Eng. Came to Utah Oct. 26, 1864, William Hyde company.
Married Mary Lake Oct. 2, 1871 (daughter of William Lake and Emma Court, of Devonshire, Eng., pioneers Sept. 25, 1866, John D. Holladay company). She was born Jan. 6, 1850. Their children: David John b. Sept. 10, 1872; m. Alice Thuesen Jan. 5, 1901; William James b. March 5, 1874, m. Magdelina Andersen Feb. 1899; Sarah Emily b. April 29, 1876, m. William A. Moody June 1899; Isaac Brigham b. April 14, 1877, m. Ella Andersen Oct. 1905; Joseph Lake b. March 9, 1879, m. Vernie Rooker; Mary Jane b. Jan. 11, 1881, m. John Nordstrum; Annie Lake b. Jan. 4, 1884, m. Edward F. Carter May 6, 1903; Samuel Henry b. Oct. 12, 1885, m. Annie Bevan May 1910; James Theophilus b. March 18, 1887, m. Emma Bunnel Dec. 4, 1912; Benjamin b. June 24, 1890; Catherine Ruth b. June 10, 1892; Horace Charles b. Nov. 15, 1894. Family resided Center ward, Wasatch county, Salt Lake City and Provo, Utah.
Assisted in bringing immigrants to Utah 1866-68; high priest; bishop's counselor 1883-93; bishop Center ward, Wasatch stake 1894-98. Moved to Utah county 1898 where he was justice of peace four terms at Vineyard. Went on mission to England Jan. 8, 1913.

BLANCHARD, ASEPH (son of John Blanchard). Born Oct. 3, 1800, Buffalo, N. Y. Came to Utah 1852.
Married Junietta Leonard.
Married Eunice Elizabeth Thompson, Detroit, Mich. (daughter of Thomas Thompson and Charlotte Rice, pioneers 1852, Isaac Bullock company). She was born Jan. 2, 1824, Detroit, Mich. Their children: Alma Moroni b. April 5, 1842, m. Emma Bocock; Jane Elizabeth b. Jan. 22, 1846, m. Simeon Alvord; Ether Enoch b. Aug. 16, 1847, m. Silvia Goff; Junietta Charlotte b. April 2, 1850, m. Calvin Van Luvin; Rozella Francena b. Jan. 14, 1865, m. Arba Lamson. Family home Springville, Utah.
High priest. Veteran Black Hawk war.

BLANCHARD, ALMA MORONI (son of Aseph Blanchard and Eunice Elizabeth Thompson). Born April 5, 1842.
Married Emma Bocock at Salt Lake City, who was born June 23, 1843, in Sheffield, Eng. Their children: Medora, m. C. A. Hickenlooper; Alma Moroni, Jr.. m. Hattie L. Smith; Sarah E., m. Francis Ferrin; Byron, m. Annie McLain. Family home Springville, Utah.

BLANCHARD, ALMA MORONI, JR. (son of Alma Moroni Blanchard and Emma Bocock). He was born Oct. 15, 1869.
Married Hattie L. Smith (daughter of Henry Smith and Lydia Kershaw). Their children: Arlo Merle; Henry D.; Delbert A.; Floyd I.; William A.; Virgil A.; Stella N. Family home Chester, Idaho.
Farmer and stockraiser.

BLASER, FREDRICK (son of Ulrich Blaser and Anna Barbara Mueller of Treub, Canton Bern, Switzerland). Born June 5, 1839, Kunglirch, Canton Bern, Switzerland. Came to Utah May 13, 1883, by rail.
Married Elizabeth Lerch, who was born Nov. 10, 1841, and came to Utah with husband. Their children: Edward b. Sept. 10, 1869, m. Lucina Scott July 12, 1898; Elizabeth b. Aug. 30, 1870, m. Alfred Dorney June 7, 1893; Augustus Fredrick b. Oct. 6, 1871, m. Minnie C. John Aug. 10, 1898; Mary b. June 6, 1873, m. Claude Follick Dec. 7, 1891; John Arnold b. Nov. 22, 1874, m. Anna Sommers Sept. 25, 1903; Henry Lewis b. Aug. 22, 1876, m. Addie McClellan June 6, 1907; Rose Ida b. April 11, 1880, m. Martin Ahlstrom Sept. 30, 1905; Sarah b. Oct. 1, 1885, m. George Williams Sept. 27, 1906.
Married Anna Rohner 1893, who was born Nov. 17, 1857. Only child: Freeda b. April 12, 1899.
Teacher and elder.

BLASER, AUGUSTUS FREDRICK (son of Fredrick Blaser, and Elizabeth Lerch, born Oct. 6, 1871, Valderne, Switzerland. Came to Utah May 12, 1883.
Married Minnie C. John Aug. 10, 1898, Bannock county, Idaho (daughter of Charles John and Elizabeth Williams, pioneers 1862). She was born June 7, 1880, West Portage, Utah. Their children: Fredrick Warren b. April 30, 1899; Minnie Irma b. May 20, 1900; Robert Augustus b. July 20, 1901; Thelma Juanita b. Aug. 18; 1903; Gladys Elizabeth b. May 4, 1905; Dora Mabel b. June 29, 1908; Irwin Ralph b. Oct. 28, 1909. Family home Dempsey, Idaho.
High priest; 1st counselor and successor to Bishop W. McClellan of Dempsey ward, Pocatello stake.

BLISS, NORMAN INGLES (son of Jesse Bliss and Fanny Tuttle, of Hartwick, Otsego county, N. Y.). Born Aug. 19, 1819. Came to Utah Sept. 20, 1848, Brigham Young company.
Married Mary Eliza Cole. Their children: Orley DeWight b. 1840, m. Harriet Few. Family resided Salt Lake City and Dixie, Utah.
Married Betsy Bird. Their children: Mary Ann, m. Thomas Stapley.
Married Sariah Lewis. Their children: Wilford Norman; Lucy; Almeda; Eliza; Frank.
Married Lydia Stout April 30, 1871 (daughter of Allen Joseph Stout and Amanda Melvina Fisk). Their children: Fanny Melvina b. June 15, 1873, m. John R. Terry March 20, 1889; Norman Ingles Jr. b. Jan. 24, 1875, m. Mary Elizabeth Morris Oct. 31, 1895; Lily Cecelia b. Aug. 26, 1877, m. Ozro DeMill Dec. 16, 1893; Sanford b. Nov. 10, 1879, died; Alfred Fisk b. Dec. 15, 1882, m. Mattie Cropper Jan. 1905.
Teamster for President Young while crossing the plains; pioneer to Dixie 1860.

BLISS, NORMAN INGLES, JR. (son of Norman Ingles Bliss and Lydia Stout). Born Jan. 24, 1875, Toquerville, Utah.
Married Mary Elizabeth Morris Oct. 31, 1895, Rockville, Utah (daughter of Daniel M. Morris and Sophia Russell), who was born June 16, 1887. Their children: Clarence b. Oct. 25, 1896; Clark Len b. May 31, 1898; Orin V. b. Feb. 25, 1901; Maitland b. Jan. 1, 1903; Earl Morris b. Nov. 6, 1905.
Married Harriet Theobald April 1, 1908, Salt Lake City (daughter of George Theobald and Naomi Tanner, of Beaver, Utah). She was born March 30, 1887, Washington county, Utah. Their children: Norman Stanley b. Jan. 31, 1909; Mary Zelma b. Jan. 19, 1911.

BLUNCK, HENRY C. (son of Christian Blunck, born Dec. 26, 1851, and Margaretha Schluter, born Dec. 25, 1848, both of Schleswig-Holstein, Germany). He was born Aug. 25, 1877. Came to Utah Oct. 16, 1891, Theodore Bradley company.
Married Hedwig Staub Oct. 2, 1903 (daughter of Wilhelm and Sophia Staub, married 1887, Solothurn, Switzerland; came to Utah 1893). She was born March 9, 1888.
President Herbert independent branch of Fremont stake. Director of Fremont fair association 1910. His father, Christian Blunck, presided over the branch at Kiel, Germany, for many years, and is at present gathering genealogies and preaching the gospel in his native land.

BOARDMAN, ROBERT (son of Robert Boardman and Elizabeth Machin, of Gosberton, Risegate, Lincolnshire, Eng.). He was born March 27, 1822, at Gosberton. Came to Utah Sept. 5, 1866, Samuel D. White company.
Married Mary Green June 18, 1844, at Gosberton (daughter of Thomas Green and Jane Hill, of that place). She was born Dec. 21, 1816. Their children: Fanny, m. Enoch Richens; Robert, m. Elizabeth Ann Strong; Thomas; Hyrum, Alvin Joseph, and Jane Elizabeth, died. Family home Provo, Utah.
High priest; president Staveley (Eng.) branch. Farmer. Died Jan. 9, 1911.

BOARDMAN, ROBERT, JR. (son of Robert Boardman and Mary Green). Born May 22, 1846, Kirton, Lincolnshire, Eng. Came to Utah Oct. 3, 1863, Daniel D. McArthur company.
Married Elizabeth Ann Strong June 13, 1868, Salt Lake City (daughter of John Strong and Agnes Miller, of Kendal, Westmoreland. Eng., pioneers Oct. 24, 1855, Milo Andrus company). She was born July 9, 1849. Their children: Elizabeth Agnes b. Nov. 9, 1868, m. Heber Duke; Robert Miles b. May 6, 1871, m. Sarah F. McKinney; Mary Jane b. Jan. 3, 1875, m. Joseph O. Ward; Hyrum Alvin b. May 15, 1877, m. Mary Emma Halliday; Emma Alice b. Nov. 24, 1879, m. Edward Lowe; Bertha Olly b. Aug. 13, 1882, m. Martin Strebel; John William b. June 16, 1885, m. Josie Cluff; Tella G. b. Nov. 24, 1887, m. Ronda Simmons; Lester b. Feb. 11, 1890, died. Family home Provo, Utah.
High priest. Assisted in hauling stone for the Salt Lake temple 1867. Black Hawk war veteran. Sent to North Platte for immigrants in John G. Holman company 1868. Farmer and fruitgrower.

BODELL, JOSEPH, (son of Henry Bodell, and Jane Elsey, of Nottingham, Eng., former was born Jan. 25, 1816, Breaston, Derbyshire, Eng., and died on the plains while on his way to Utah). He was born June 12, 1840, at Breaston. Came to Utah June 21, 1858.
Married Carrie Marie Jorgensen 1861, Salt Lake City, who was born May 23, 1844, Denmark, and died April 4, 1862, at Salt Lake City. Only child: Carrie Marie b. Feb. 28, 1862, d. Sept. 2, 1862.
Married Emma Jane Farmer at Salt Lake City (daughter of James Farmer and Sarah Trussler, former a pioneer 1856, latter died at Steyning, Sussex, Eng., 1851). She was born July 26, 1843. Their children: Joseph Samuel Henry b. Aug. 23, 1863, m. Sarah L. Howard Oct. 3, 1888; Sarah Jane b. Aug. 27, 1865, d. May 25, 1866; James Fredrick b. July 26, 1866, d. Sept. 19, 1867; Emma Jane b. Nov. 9, 1867, m. J. R. Freeman Feb. 14, 1884; John Trussler b. March 15, 1869, m. Eliza Freeman Sept. 10, 1890, Elizabeth Eliza b. Nov. 14, 1870, m. Daniel Densley March 9, 1888; William Almon b. July 28, 1872, m. Francis R. Tempest Jan. 12, 1899; Agnes Fannie b. July 17, 1874, m. Joseph H. Crump Nov. 20, 1895; Martha Mary Sirinda b. Dec. 23, 1875, m. W. A. Crane Jan. 17, 1897. Family resided Salt Lake City and Herriman, Utah.
Member 20th quorum seventies at Salt Lake City 1861. Choir leader at Herriman prior to 1876. Butcher; farmer. Died Aug. 19, 1876.

BODELL, JOSEPH SAMUEL HENRY (son of Joseph Bodell and Emma Jane Farmer). Born Aug. 23, 1863, Herriman, Utah.
Married Sarah L. Howard Oct. 3, 1888, Logan, Utah (daughter of Samuel L. Howard and Sarah J. Hamilton, of Mill Creek, Utah). She was born Jan. 16, 1870. Their children: Sarah Jane b. Oct. 1, 1889, m. John Slagowski Oct. 20, 1909; Joseph Samuel b. April 6, 1892; Emma Virginia b. Sept. 14, 1893; Mary Myrtle b. July 13, 1895; Marriner Lorenzo b. April 10, 1897, d. May 27, 1903; Eliza Erma b. June 27, 1899; John William b. Dec. 11, 1900; Mildred and Milton b. March 3, 1903; James Alexander b. Dec. 6, 1904; Jesse Moroni b. Oct. 20, 1906, d. Oct. 30, 1906; Elizabeth Fern b. Oct. 21, 1907; Editha Farrel Louvina b. Jan. 14, 1911. Family home Herriman, Utah.
Missionary to England Oct. 1884 to Nov. 1886; superintendent Sunday schools and 2nd counselor to Bishops James S. Crane and Thomas Butterfield, Herriman ward; president Y. M. M. I. A.; choir leader. School trustee; juvenile probation officer. Merchant and farmer.

BOGGS, FRANCIS. Born May 17, 1809, in Belmont county, Ohio. Came to Utah 1847.
Married Eveline Martin, who was born March 23, 1816, Tyler county, West Virginia. Their children: Mary b. April 12, 1843, m. Stephen Chadwick Perry; Eveline; Hyrum; Phoebe Jane; Nancy Orpha. Family home Washington, Utah.
Seventy. Carpenter. Died Jan. 22, 1889.

BOND, JESSE (son of James Bond and Sarah Card, of Huntingford, Gloucestershire, Eng.) He was born Feb. 27, 1832, Huntingford, Eng. Came to Utah Nov. 13, 1855, Isaac Allred company.
Married Sarah Adams Sept. 24, 1861, Provo, Utah (daughter of Samuel and Bessie Adams, of Staffordshire, who came to Utah 1861). She was born May 12, 1843. Their children: William J.; Jane; Franklin, died; Joseph T.; Dora; Minnie; Gertrude; Elaine, died; Lacy. Family home Heber City, Utah.
Went to the Missouri river for immigrants in 1861; on the return trip was appointed captain of ten wagons. Crossed the plains five times with oxteam; has rung the curfew bell for 23 years.
High priest. Town official of Heber. Farmer.

BOND, STEPHEN (son of James Bond and Sarah Card). Born Aug. 20, 1829, Road Somersetshire, Eng.). Came to Utah 1857.
Married Sarah Clark 1860 at Lehi, Utah (daughter of Thomas Clark and Elizabeth Boulton of Gloucester, Eng.), who was born Dec. 8, 1836. Their children: Stephen, m. Emily Sidodoway; William, m. Alice Taylor; Sarah Elizabeth, m. John W. Crook; Alfred Thomas, m. Leila Clift; John, m. Mary Jeffs; Emily, m. John Heber Murdock. Family home Heber, Utah.
Elder; secretary 20th quorum seventies. Cabinet-maker. Died Dec. 28, 1875, Heber City, Utah.

BOND, WILLIAM. Born Feb. 17, 1817, near Manchester, Eng. Came to Utah amidst the storm of Dec. 10-16, 1856, William B. Hodgett company, being assisted into the valley by relief trains sent to rescue.
Married Mary Ann Barker 1837. Their children: six boys and six girls, one of whom, Mary Jane b. Jan. 15, 1850, m. Micah Francis Harris Jan. 15, 1868. Family home Fall River, Mass., Provo, Salt Lake City and Henefer, Utah.
Farmer. Died May 24, 1898, Henefer, Utah.

BONNER, GEORGE (son of George Bonner). Born Jan. 18, 1820, in Ireland. Came to Utah 1857.
Married Margerette Edmiston in Scotland, who was born May 1, 1830, and came to Utah 1858. Their children: Christina, m. Albert Gallatin McCurdy; George, m. Phoebe Alexander; William, m. Eliza Brunson; Robert; Margaret, m. Stephen Shelton; Annie, m. Jesse Nelson; Dessie, m. Alva Alexander; Mary Jane, m. Tipton Epperson; Thomas, m. Ada Alexander.

BONNER, JAMES EVERET (son of Patrick Everet Bonner and Mary Mahoney of Alexander, Fairfax county, Va). He was born April 2, 1823, Douglas, Isle of Man, Eng. Came to Utah 1868.
Married Susan H. Besley Jan. 1859, Alexander, Va. (daughter of Joseph F. Besley of North Carolina, who came to Utah 1870). She was born August, 1821. Their children: Harriet E., m. James Scott; Harry H., d. aged 22. Family home Alexander, Va.
Married Annie Lisle June 1869, Salt Lake City, Bishop Laurence Scanlan officiating (daughter of Joseph Lisle and Martha Marthey of Salt Lake City, pioneers 1861). She was born 1845. Their children: Asie M. b. 1875; Hellerd E., m. Mary F. Scott.
Physician; landscape gardener.

BONNETT, JOHN JAMES (son of John Peter Bonnett and Marietta Malan of Piedmont, Turin, Angrogne, Italy). Born Nov. 25, 1835, at Angrogne, Italy. Came to Utah Oct. 26, 1855, Milo Andrus company.
Married Ann Hughes June 1860, Provo, Utah (daughter of David Hughes and Ann Phillips), who was born March 12, 1840. Their children: David James, m. Fannie Amelia Cluff; Clement, m. Mary Fawcett; John, m. Delia Fitzgerald; Ellis, m. Geneva Craft; Celia, m. William Flemming, m. Isaac McEwan; George, m. Hattie Laycock; Evelin; May, m. Augustif Hofman. Family resided Ogden and Provo. Utah.
Helped build canals in vicinities of Ogden and Provo. Farmer.

BONNETT, DAVID JAMES (son of John James Bonnett and Ann Hughes). Born May 14, 1863, Provo, Utah.
Married Fannie Amelia Cluff Sept. 3, 1885, Logan, Utah (daughter of Samuel Samson Cluff and Francis Amelia Worsley, of Lancashire, Eng., later of Ohio, U. S. A.). She was born March 21, 1865. Their children: Vivien b. June 2, 1889; Murry David b. Jan. 14, 1891; Earl C. and Muriel C. b. Jan. 10, 1893; Harvey Glenn b. Nov. 3, 1897; Aileen b. Nov. 28, 1905. Family home Pleasant View Ward, Provo, Utah.
In charge of grounds of Telluride Power company. Farmer; gardener.

BOOTH, HIRAM EVANS (son of Joseph Booth and Caroline Bishop of Postville, Iowa). Born Oct. 25, 1860, at Postville. Came to Utah Dec. 8, 1888.
Married Lillian B. Redhead May 29, 1889, Postville, Iowa (daughter of George Redhead and Anna Howard).
United States district attorney. Senior member of law firm, Booth, Lee, Badger, Rich and Parke. Treasurer (daily) Herald-Republican Publishing company.

BOOTH, MORRIS ARTEMUS (son of Willis Henry Booth and Susannah Pierce). Born Feb. 26, 1872.
Married Jennie Alvord Oct. 14, 1899, Salt Lake City (daughter of Benjamin T. Alvord and Malinda Crocket), who was born Feb. 26, 1872. Their children: Morris Alvord b. March 12, 1901; Dorris May B. b. May 16, 1904; Muriel Loue b. Dec. 31, 1908.
Engaged in the mercantile business, being connected with the Booth & Pierce Mercantile Company; engaged in the hotel business at Brigham City.

BOOTH, RICHARD THORNTON (son of James Booth and Jane Pilkinton). Born Aug. 21, 1822, Turton, near Bolton, Lancashire, Eng. Came to Utah Sept. 12, 1857, Jesse B. Martin company.
Married Elsie Edge Aug. 21, 1846, Bedford Leigh, Lancashire, Eng. (daughter of John Edge and Sarah Davis). Their children: John Edge; James Davis; Martha Hannah; Sarah Jane; Robert Ebenezer; Margaret Alice; Richard Thornton; Alfred Lewis; Joseph Wilford; Mary May. Family home Alpine, Utah; died there May 28, 1888.

BOOTH, JOHN EDGE (son of Richard Thornton Booth and Elsie Edge). Born June 29, 1847, Bradshaw Gate, Bedford Leigh, Lancashire, Eng. Came to Utah when 10 years of age.
Married Maria Josephine Harvey Oct. 1, 1873 (daughter of Lewis and Lucinda Harvey), who died Oct. 1, 1884. Their children: Josephine Diantha, m. Dr. J. Lloyd Woodruff; Vienna Hortense, m. Earnest Kimball; Hannah Rowena, m. Raymond Ray; Richard Harvey, m. Cordelia Darius.
Married Hannah Billings April 1876 (daughter of George P. and Edith Billings), who died May 23, 1881, leaving no children.

Married Delia Ina Winters June 22, 1887 (daughter of Oscar F. and Mary Ann Winters, pioneers 1852). Their children: James Milton, m. Cora Lewis; Delilah Maria; Elsie Vernessa; Edwin Winters.
Judge fourth judicial court of Utah since 1899.

BOOTH, RICHARD T., JR. (son of Richard T. Booth and Elsie Edge of Lancashire, Eng.). Born Jan. 6, 1862, Alpine, Utah.
Married Elizabeth Ward June 16, 1887, Logan, Utah (daughter of Richard Ward and Alice Davis of Rock Springs, Wyo., who came to Utah 1880). Their children: Leslie Elmer, died; Elizabeth, m. Jerome Beck. Family home Alpine, Utah.
Died while on mission Nov. 23, 1887, Kansas City, Mo. Farmer.

BOOTH, ALFRED LEWIS (son of Richard Thornton Booth and Elsie Edge). Born June 17, 1864, Alpine, Utah.
Married May Ashworth April 12, 1900, Salt Lake City (daughter of William Booth Ashworth of Lancashire, Eng., and Elizabeth Shepherd of San Bernardino, Cal.). She was born Sept. 28, 1874, Beaver, Utah. Their children: Editha b. March 12, 1903; Leona b. Oct. 25, 1905; Herbert and William, d. infants. Family home Provo, Utah.
Instructor mathematical department Brigham Young university 1887-91. Assistant stake Sunday school superintendent 1892-1900; missionary to England 1894-96; president 45th quorum seventies 1900; counselor to Bishops Joseph B. Keeler, Moroni Snow and Edward D. Partridge, 4th ward, Provo, 1900-07, and set apart bishop of that ward Jan. 13, 1907. Justice of peace 1896-98. Member Provo board of education 1898-1902. City attorney 1902-04; city councilman 1904-08 membe state senate 1911-14.

BOOTHE, HENRY (son of Lewis Boothe and Charlotta Windham, of Virginia). Born Sept. 26, 1802, Edgecombe county, N. C. Came to Utah 1851, Capt. Smith company.
Married Susannah Lyster July 4, 1826, in Alabama (daughter of Nathaniel Lyster and Stacy Henley, of Jones county, N. C.). She was born Oct. 4, 1800. Their children: John A. b. Aug. 19, 1831, m. Lydia Ann Sherman Feb. 29, 1864; Lewis N. b. Dec. 3, 1832, m. Mary J. Rees Feb. 26, 1860; Willis H. b. Feb. 3, 1834, m. Susannah Neff Pierce; Emily C. b. Oct. 12, 1836, m. Benjamin Murphy; Darius D. b. Dec. 24, 1838, m. Adelaide Anderson: Amanda C. b. Dec. 29, 1840, m. G. W. Hawkins Aug. 7, 1859; Martha b. May 1, 1843, m. E. Carson.
Married Caroline Anderson who was born Feb. 22, 1814, in Sweden.

BOOTHE, LEWIS NATHANIEL (son of Henry Boothe and Susannah Lyster). Born Dec. 3, 1832, Wilcox county, Ala.
Married Mary Jane Rees Feb. 26, 1860, Brigham City, Utah (daughter of John D. Rees and Mary Morgan, of Cardiff, Wales, pioneer 1852). She was born May 24, 1844, and died Jan. 16, 1879. Their children: Lenora b. Dec. 24, 1860, m. R. L. Bybee June 30, 1881; Arvilla S. b. Sept. 19, 1862, m. Casey P. Bowen July 25, 1879; Lewis H. b. Aug. 14, 1864, d. Sept. 12, 1876; Permilla, b. Nov. 21, 1866, m. G. T. Rogers Aug. 6, 1882; John M. b. Feb. 24, 1869, m. Emily Orme Dec. 22, 1886; Vilate b. Dec. 13, 1871, m. Fred Summerhill June 1891; Geneva R. b. Feb. 11, 1873, d. Sept. 22, 1884; Eva b. April 1875, m. Alonzo Johnson Oct. 9, 1895; Lillian b. March 27, 1877, m. Alma Hunsaker Aug. 15, 1907; Fredrick E. b. Jan. 16, 1879, d. July 5, 1879. Family home Honeyville, Utah.
Married Elizabeth Hunsaker April 26, 1880, Salt Lake City (daughter of Abraham Hunsaker and Eliza Collins, who was born Nov. 17, 1837, in Illinois. Only child: Rose May b. March 9, 1881, m. John Wheatley March 1, 1900.
Settled at Brigham City; moved to Honeyville 1875. Missionary to Southern states Nov. 13, 1877 to March 22, 1879; 1st counselor to Bishop Thomas Wheatley, second counselor to Bishop Hunsaker Sept. 9, 1877, to Jan. 3, 1889. Enlisted in standing army 1858, and served as Indian interpreter and guide under Col. Lyons, U. S. A., in expedition against Indians 1859. Freighter of the early days.

BOOTHE, WILLIS HENRY (son of Henry Boothe and Susannah Lyster). Born Feb. 3, 1834.
Married Susannah Neff Pierce March, 1860, Salt Lake City (daughter of John Neff Pierce, pioneer 1847). She was born 1833 and died 1910. Their children: Willis H. b. 1864, m. Sarah Rich; Amanda b. 1862, m. Evan Morgan; Olive b. 1866, m. William Johnson; John N. b. 1868, m. Telle Wilds; Frank B. b. 1870, m. Jens Stork; M. A. b. 1872, m. Jennie Alvord. Family home Brigham City, Utah.
Farmer and stockraiser.

BOREN, COLEMAN. Came to Utah 1851, oxteam company.
Married Malinda Keller. Their children: William Jasper, m. Lucina Mecham; Joseph, m. Martha Clinger; Susan, m. John Jones; Minerva, m. Peter Wentz; Lorana, m. Charles Gray, m. Amasa Mecham; Coleman Briant, m. Nancy Jane Riggs; Nathan Alma, died; Ephraim, m. Lizzie McAffee. Family home Provo, Utah.
Married Flora Hughes. Their children: Josephine; Henry; Albert; Manassa.
Farmer. Died at Provo, Utah.

BOREN, WILLIAM JASPER (son of Coleman Boren and Malinda Keller). Born at Peoria, Ill. Came to Utah 1851, with parents.
Married Lucina Mecham July 4, 1859, Provo, Utah (daughter of Moses Mecham and Elvira Derby, pioneers 1850, oxteam company). She was born March 12, 1841. Their children: William Jasper, Jr., b. April 11, 1860, m. Temperance Wall Sept. 6, 1883; Samuel b. May 8, 1861, m. Abigail Lamb; Lucina Izora, m. Austir Glenn; Malinda Elvira, d. infant; Moses M., m. Jane Lamb; Lorana, m. James Wall; Annie M., m. Don L. Bigelow; Alma L., died; Ida Viola, m. George Fayette Mecham; Clinton C., m. Polly Mecham; Sarah M., m. Omero C. Merrotti; Wilford Wells, m. Emma Holmberg; Polly May, m. Arthur Snow. Family home Wallsburg, Utah.
Seventy, and counselor to Bishop William M. Wall, Wallsburg ward. Road supervisor; watermaster. Veteran Black Hawk Indian war. Farmer and shinglemaker. Died May 16, 1900.

BOREN, WILLIAM JASPER (son of William Jasper Boren and Lucina Mecham). Born April 11, 1860, Provo, Utah.
Married Temperance Wall Sept. 6, 1883, at Salt Lake City (daughter of William Madison Wall and Elizabeth Penrod, of Illinois). She was born Oct. 8, 1865. Their children: Malinda b. Sept. 19, 1884, m. Alfred Ford, Jr.; William b. Oct. 30, 1886, m. Elva Lamb; Archie b. May 28, 1889, m. Myrtle Daybell; Maud b. July 8, 1892; Ray b. Oct. 9, 1894; Ellis b. Sept. 9, 1896; Polly May b. Aug. 7, 1899; Ethel b. July 5, 1901; Eldwin b. May 30, 1904; Areva b. Aug. 3, 1908. Family home Wallsburg.
Missionary to North Carolina 1901-03; high priest; 2d. and later 1st counselor to Bishop George P. Garff of Wallsburg ward. Constable; road supervisor; deputy road commissioner. Sunday school superintendent. Public school trustee 15 years. Second counselor to president of Y. M. M. I. A. Farmer and stockraiser

BORG, PETER HANSON. He was born March 16, 1805, Sleminge-Scona, Sweden. Came to Utah Sept. 15, 1864, William B. Preston company.
Married Ingre Jensen 1828, Andersloff, Scona, Sweden (daughter of Jens Jensen), who was born Sept. 12, 1812. Their children: Hanse b. Sept. 14, 1831, m. Carna L. Jepson; Lars Peter b. Sept. 3, 1833, m. Marie Christensen; Karna b. March 25, 1836, m. H. C. Hansen; Svend b. July 27, 1838, m. Eva Christina Alff; Hannah b. Sept. 9, 1840, m. Hans Eliason Mortensen; Rasmus b. Dec. 25, 1842, m. Anette Cecilia Nielson; Cathrin b. Sept. 14, 1844, d. Sept. 13, 1857; Ole Peter b. Oct. 19, 1847, m. Brighamina Malvina Nielsen; Ingre b. Nov. 2, 1849, d. June 3, 1857; Jense b. Sept. 26, 1852, m. Sarah Marie Jorgensen. Family home Mt. Pleasant, Utah.
High priest. Harness maker. Died April 12, 1875, Mt. Pleasant, Utah.

BORG, OLE PETER (son of Peter Hanson Borg and Ingre Jensen). Born Oct. 19, 1847, Scona, Sweden.
Married Brighamina Malvina Nielsen May 24, 1869, Salt Lake City (daughter of Hans T. Nielsen and Nicolina Rasmina Espasen, of Denmark, pioneers Oct. 22, 1866, Abner Lowry company). She was born Sept. 22, 1854. Their children: Oliver Henry, b. July 17, 1871, m. Amy Avery; Joseph Edward b. June 1, 1873, m. Sena Beck; Brighamina Natalia b. Oct. 6, 1874, m. Nelson Baker; Annie Mathilda b. Oct. 29, 1875, d. Sept. 27, 1876; Emma Nicolina b. July 24, 1877; Alma Peter b. Feb. 5, 1880, m. Laura Whitehead; James Anton b. Aug. 23, 1881, m. Alverda Christina Mickleson; Zelma Emelia b. Feb. 5, 1884, m. Lorenzo Anderson; Ammon Junius, b. June 10, 1886, d. Sept. 27, 1890; Clarence b. Feb. 5, 1889, d. same day; Eugene b. Feb. 13, 1890; Evan b. June 28, 1894.
Married Fena Nielsen June 1877, Salt Lake City (daughter of Hans T. Nielsen and Nicolina Rasmina Espassen), who was born July 29, 1858. Their children: Charles Emil b. Sept. 24, 1878, d. Sept. 14, 1879; Henrietta Nicolina b. July 8, 1880, m. Adolph Nielsen; Alma Ferdinand b. Feb. 25, 1883, m. Alvira Larson; Hanse Egede b. Nov. 25, 1885, m. Martina Sorenson; Daniel Erastus b. June 17, 1889, m. Mary J. Clapp; Seth Mahonri b. Aug. 16, 1892; Edith Evaline b. May 17, 1896; Edna Durilla b. Jan. 9, 1899. Family home Richfield, Utah.
High priest; president elders' quorum 1890-98. Harness maker. Farmer.

BORUP, PETER (son of Peder and Hannah Peterson of Jutland, Denmark). Born February, 1823, in Jutland. Came to Utah Sept. 12, 1861, John R. Murdock company.
Married Christena Christenson in Denmark (daughter of Christen and Christina Christenson, former a pioneer 1861, John R. Murdock company). She was born 1824. Their children: Carl b. Sept. 29, 1850, m. Caroline Thomas Nov. 3, 1873; Siveren b. Sept. 15, 1853, m. Mary Baker; Loana; Sarah; Peter, Jr. b. Nov. 15, 1869, m. Laura Mattinson; Parley.
Married Mariah Hanson (daughter of Jens Hanson). Their child: Louisa, m. Samuel Morgan.
Settled at Goshen, Utah; moved to Little Colorado River valley, Arizona, and later to Panguitch, Utah. Died Oct. 1878.

BORUP, PETER (son of Peter Borup and Christina Christenson). Born Nov. 15, 1869, Goshen, Utah.
Married Laura Mattinson May 12, 1897, Payson, Utah (daughter of Robert Mattinson and Betsy Burnhope), who was born July 14, 1872, at Payson. Their children: Leta L. b. Dec. 31, 1898; Klea L. b. June 8, 1903; Carl M. b. April 11, 1906; Fern C. b. Aug. 19, 1909. Family resided Goshen, Panguitch and Eureka, Utah.
Missionary to Norway 1906-08; bishop Eureka ward. Member public library board.

BOUCK, JOHN A. Born 1798 in New York state. Came to Utah 1847.
Married Elizabeth Howell 1849 at Salt Lake City, who was born 1831. Their children: John F., m. Mary Mellen; William C., m. Margerite E. Yates; Elizabeth, m. Swen Oleson; Sarah Ann, m. Thomas W. Powell; Louisa, m. J. W. Jenkins; Alexander, m. Elizabeth Jones; Hiram, m. Elizabeth A. Thomas; Mary, m. John Hiller; Heber, m. Amelia J. Tuttle. Family home 16th ward, Salt Lake City.
High priest. Farmer and stockraiser. Died 1884, 16th ward, Salt Lake City.

BOUCK, JOHN F. (son of John A. Bouck and Elizabeth Howell). Born March 11, 1853, Salt Lake City.
Married Mary Mellen July 3, 1877, Salt Lake City (daughter of John Mellen and Jane Ramsden, pioneers), Judge Elias Smith officiating. She was born Sept. 29, 1866. Their children: Mamie b. Oct. 26, 1878, m. John Daniels; Maud b. Jan. 13, 1880, m. Andrew Paul; Louisa b. Feb. 19, 1882, m. Ernest Cook; John Clifton b. March 29, 1884, m. Mona Coon; Hyrum Sidney b. May 30, 1886, m. Cora Staker; Martha Ella b. Aug. 1, 1888, d. aged 13; Gertrude b. Dec. 10, 1893. Family home Pleasant Green, Utah.
Miner; farmer and stockraiser; brick-maker.

BOUCK, WILLIAM C. (son of John Adam Bouck and Elizabeth Howell). Born May 25, 1854, Salt Lake City.
Married Margerite E. Yates Dec. 22, 1881, Salt Lake City (daughter of William Yates and Mary Partington of Upholland, Lancashire, Eng., pioneers 1863). She was born Feb. 17, 1861. Their children: William A. b. Dec. 10, 1882, m. Eva Egbert; Walter O. b. March 11, 1885, m. Vida Egbert; Eugene P. b. April 2, 1887, m. Annie Mortig. Family home 29th ward, Salt Lake City.
Elder. Farmer and freighter.

BOUCK, ALEXANDER (son of John Adam Bouck and Elizabeth Howell). Born April 4, 1861, Salt Lake City.
Married Elizabeth Jones Dec. 16, 1891, Logan, Utah, President Merrill officiating (daughter of William Jones and Sarah Jeffrey of Birmingham, Eng., who came to Utah Nov. 1879). She was born May 12, 1861. Their children: Ruth b. Nov. 7, 1892, m. Frank Duber; Alexander, Jr. b. Feb. 23, 1894. Family home 16th ward, Salt Lake City.
Elder and block teacher. Lumber dealer; stockraiser.

BOUCK, ALEXANDER, JR. (son of Alexander Bouck and Elizabeth Jones). Born Feb. 23, 1894, Salt Lake City.

BOUCK, HIRAM (son of John Adam Bouck and Elizabeth Howell). Born April 6, 1863, Salt Lake City.
Married Elizabeth A. Thomas Dec. 20, 1889, Salt Lake City, Judge Elias Smith officiating (daughter of Thomas Thomas and Mary Reese of North Wales, who came to Utah 1873). She was born April 9, 1870. Their children: Erma b. Jan. 6, 1891, m. Lawrence W. Ridges, m. Gomer C. Roberts; Verna May b. April 8, 1899. Family home 16th ward, Salt Lake City.
Stationary-engineer. Machinist.

BOULTON, THOMAS (son of Martin and Martha Boulton of Burford parish, Shropshire, Eng.). Born Jan. 21, 1825 at Burford. Came to Utah 1860, Martin and Thomas company.
Married Sarah Cook March 26, 1849, Leominster, Eng. (daughter of Thomas Cook and Sarah Harris of Sapy, Worcestershire, Eng.). She was born Oct. 17, 1817. Their children: Mary, died; Martin (d. April 12, 1889), m. Mary Alice Clark; Thomas B., died; Sarah Ann, m. William H. Firth. Family resided Ogden and Provo, Utah.
High priest; president of Whiteburn branch, England. Miller. Died April 29, 1881 at Provo.

BOURNE, THOMAS B. (son of Charles Bourne of Ledbury, Eng.). Born Oct. 26, 1797, at Ledbury. Came to Utah Sept. 26, 1856, Edmund Ellsworth company.
Married Susannah Lane. Their children: Charles b. Nov. 12, 1820, m. Jane Alder 1842; Sarah b. 1822, m. William Fletcher; Elizabeth b. 1824, m. William Thompson; Hannah b. 1828. Family home Ledbury, Eng.
Married Margret Evans, who was born March 24, 1807, in England. Their children: George E. b. July 2, 1830, m. Mary Ann Tayson Sept. 2, 1856; William b. 1832; Mary Ann b. Oct. 6, 1833, m. William Ayland in 1856; Margret b. March 6, 1835, m. Truman Leonard Jan. 6, 1857; James b. Jan. 10, 1838, m. Olive Roberry; Priscilla b. Nov. 13, 1841, m. John W. Moore July 30, 1882; Louise b. March 27, 1843, m. John Paul Aug. 10, 1863; John b. July 17, 1849, m. Mary Jane Stewart July 1865. Family resided at Ledbury, Eng. and moved to Farmington, Utah in 1856.

BOURNE, CHARLES (son of Thomas B. Bourne and Susannah Lane). Born Nov. 12, 1820, Ledbury, Eng.
Married Jane Alder in 1842, at Ledbury (daughter of William Alder and Elizabeth Bevan, the latter a pioneer Sept. 14, 1853, Claudius V. Spencer company). She was born in 1825, at Ledbury. Their children: Lorenzo b. Nov. 30, 1846 and Charles, died; Jane; Hannah Arvilla b. Sept. 24, 1854, m. Ernest Potter and Jacob M. Secrist; Jane E. b. Oct. 3, 1857, m. William H. Stevenson Dec. 12, 1878; Alice Ann b. March 15, 1860, m. John G. Petty 1891; Charles H. b. Feb. 4, 1863, m. Silvia Vanfleet Jan. 12, 1887; John A. b. Sept. 28, 1865, m. Emeline Hess June 1, 1892; William b. Nov. 17, 1867; George A. b. Oct. 7, 1868, m. Annie Lovesy June 23, 1897; Margret b. March 1, 1871. Family home Farmington, Utah.
Contractor and builder. Prominent in church and civil affairs.

BOURNE, JOHN A. (son of Charles Bourne and Jane Alder). Born Sept. 28, 1865, Farmington, Utah.
Married Emeline Hess June 1, 1892, Logan, Utah (daughter of John W. Hess and Julia Peterson, pioneers July 29, 1847, with part of Mormon Battalion). She was born July 22, 1868, at Farmington. No children.

BOWEN, CACEY POTTER (son of Elias Bowen of Vermont, and Cynthia Harrington, of Canada). He was born Dec. 13, 1820, Bennington county, Vt. Came to Utah in 1849.
Married Eleanor McGarey (daughter of Charles M. McGarey and Charlotte Earl), who was born Oct. 19, 1836. Their children: Charlotte Elizabeth b. Feb. 19, 1852, m. William Boatwright; Cynthia Ellen b. Sept. 1, 1854, m. Fred Taylor; Sarah Z. b. Nov. 29, 1856, m. John Boldware; Cacey Potter, Jr. b. Oct. 24, 1858, m. Susannah Avilla Boothe July 25, 1879; Malissa Jane b. Dec. 24, 1860, m. John Standing; Charles McGarey b. Feb. 10, 1863, m. Florence A. Thorp; Lilly May b. April 8, 1865, m. Edwin Barton; Rhoda Bell b. Feb. 22, 1867, m. Dave James; Mary Ann b. Dec. 2, 1870; Louisa b. May 22, 1873; William Orson b. Aug. 4, 1875, d. Nov. 23, 1897; Nellie Myrtle b. March 10, 1877, m. Van Vellett; Edith Ivey b. Sept. 22, 1879, m. Herschel Lyman. Family resided Ogden and Beaver Dam, Utah.
Indian war veteran. Died Jan. 21, 1902.

BOWEN, CACEY POTTER, JR. (son of Cacey Potter Bowen and Eleanor McGarey). Born Oct. 24, 1858, Ogden, Utah.
Married Susannah Avilla Boothe July 25, 1879, Brigham City, Utah (daughter of Lewis N. Boothe and Mary Jane Reese). She was born Sept. 19, 1862, Santa Rosa, Cal. Their children: Cacey Lavon b. July 31, 1880, m. Ethel L. Earl Jan. 1899; Cynthia Eleanor b. Aug. 30, 1882, m. Peter Creeze Sept. 1902; Lewis b. Dec. 7, 1884, m. Mary Anderson Feb. 7, 1906; Avilla May b. Jan. 8, 1886, m. Jedediah Abbott May 7, 1909; Russell b. March 7, 1888, died; Mary Pearl b. Feb. 5, 1891, m. Wilford C. Anderson Sept. 16, 1909; Earl b. March 17, 1893; Clyde b. June 11, 1895; Melitrude b. June 6, 1897; Grant Reese b. Oct. 6, 1899; McMeredith b. May 7, 1902. Family resided at Beaver, Utah and Lyman, Idaho.
Sunday school superintendent 24 years in Beaver ward, Utah; bishop of Lyman ward, Idaho.

BOWEN, DAVID (son of William Bowen, born July 24, 1784, and Jane Evans, born Oct. 3, 1784, both of Llanelly, Brecknockshire, South Wales). He was born Aug. 15, 1823, at Llanelly, and came to Utah in December, 1856, with John A. Hunt company.
Married Jane Foster (daughter of George Foster and Eleanor Parry), who was born June 19, 1820. Their children: William Parry b. July 5, 1845, m. Ruth Jones Feb. 9, 1868; George Foster b. March 20, 1849, m. Mary Elizabeth Miller March 24, 1873; Eleanor Jane b. Dec. 8, 1852, m. William J. Thomas Oct. 3, 1874; John Evans b. July 2, 1855, m. Mary Ann Christmas, Sept. 15, 1879; Lucy Ann; Julia Susannah b. Oct. 26, 1859; David Chalinder b. Jan. 1, 1863, m. Harriet Hopla Jan. 23, 1887.
Settled at Spanish Fork in 1856; blacksmith; farmer and stockraiser; director Co-op, Mercantile company 1868-69. Member, city council. Missionary to Pennsylvania and England 1878-80; high priest. Died Jan. 16, 1910.

BOWEN, GEORGE FOSTER (son of David Bowen and Jane Foster). Born March 20, 1849, Llanelly, Wales.
Married Mary Elizabeth Miller March 24, 1873, Salt Lake City (daughter of James Miller and Margaret Anderson). She was born Sept. 15, 1853, Salt Lake City. Their children: Jane Foster b. Feb. 16, 1874, m. George S. Boyack Nov. 17, 1897; Margaret Ellen b. Aug. 26, 1876, m. John W. Bell Dec. 10, 1902; David Miller b. Nov. 5, 1878, m. Elizabeth Taylor Feb. 14, 1900; George Anderson b. Aug. 30, 1881, m. Madie Warner, May 12, 1905; James Miller b. Oct. 17, 1883, m. Belva A. Gallup Jan. 3, 1905; William Wallace b. March 12, 1886; Mary b. March 29, 1888; Charles Milton b. Oct. 5, 1890; Arthur Washington b. Feb. 22, 1892; John Chalinder b. Dec. 31, 1895.
Settled at Spanish Fork; moved to Lake Shore 1884; returned to Spanish Fork 1890; also lived at Garland for five years. Railroad freighter; director Lake Shore Water company 1885. Farmer and stockraiser. Constable at Spanish Fork 1897-98.

BOWERS, ISAAC (son of James Bowers, born Jan. 27, 1811, and Maria Lay, born Nov. 5, 1811, both of Staffordshire, Eng.). He was born Dec. 6, 1841. Came to Utah Sept. 26, 1856, Edmund Ellsworth company.
Married Elizabeth Youd Dec. 3, 1861, Liverpool, Eng., who was born Feb. 14, 1845. Their children: James I. b. Oct. 4, 1862, m. Rachel B. Boyack; John and Elizabeth Jane (twins) b. Nov. 13, 1864; Hezekiah b. June 10, 1867, m. Emily Simpson Nov. 7, 1893; Jacob T. b. Oct. 26, 1869, m. Sarah J. Roach, March 2, 1892; Emma M. b. Sept. 4, 1872, m. Hyrum Waters Jan. 10, 1894; Mary E. b. March 30, 1875, m. Charles Waters, Dec. 16, 1895; Alfred b. Sept. 4, 1877, m.

Manetta Nielson, Dec. 16, 1908; Ephraim b. May 27, 1880; Chloe b. April 14, 1883, m. Charles Hanks, July 5, 1905; Charles Delbert b. June 3, 1886; Sarah Ellen b. April 1, 1891, m. Delbert Beckstead Dec. 5, 1911.

Assisted to bring immigrants to Utah; settled at Pleasant Grove; moved to Nephi in 1858, to Monroe in 1865, and to Spanish Fork in 1867. Veteran Black Hawk war; delegate to the live stock convention held in St. Louis in 1885.

BOWERS, ISAIAH (son of James Bowers and Maria Lay). Born April 21, 1846, in Staffordshire. Came to Utah Sept. 26, 1856.

Married Harriet A. Hoyt June 6, 1868, Salt Lake City (daughter of Israel Hoyt and Clarissa A. Miller, pioneers 1847). She was born Oct. 16, 1850. Their children: Israel H. b. March 10, 1869; Clarissa A. H. b. Oct. 8, 1871, m. Heber J. Meeks, Dec. 31, 1889; Isaiah Lay b. March 25, 1874, m. Maria Heaton, Nov. 16, 1899; Maria H. b. Oct. 5, 1876, m. Edward Carroll, Nov. 4, 1896; Ella H. b. Sept. 8, 1879, m. John L. Covington Dec. 4, 1896; Jonathan b. Oct. 26, 1882; Lillian H. b. June 5, 1886; Harriet H. b. May 20, 1889, m. B. H. Sornson Oct. 3, 1912. Family home Orderville, Utah.

Married Philinda Amanda Sperry in October, 1884, St. George, Utah (daughter of Charles Sperry and Emily Miller, pioneers of 1847). She was born Nov. 16, 1849, at Salt Lake City. Their children: William S. b. Aug. 13, 1886; Sarah E. b. June 13, 1890; Joy S. b. Oct. 10, 1893. Family home Orderville, Utah.

BOWLDEN, JAMES (son of Richard Bowlden and Mary Rafe of Brixton Surrey, London, Eng.). He was born in 1849. Came to Utah Nov. 4, 1864, Warren S. Snow company.

Married Ophelia Leona Avery in 1872, Springville, Utah (daughter of Thomas Avery and Lydia Harrington of Mills county, Iowa, pioneers). She was born Jan. 3, 1856. Their children: Lydia, m. C. M. Humphrey; Retta, m. E. S. Allred; J. L., m. Martha Clark; Clara, m. J. L. Strang; Ossa, m. J. B. Ferguson; T. Richard; Rulon A. Family home Springville, Utah.

Seventy. Farmer.

BOWLES, EDWARD (son of Isaac Bowles). Born Sept. 23, 1806, Wiltshire, Eng. Came to Utah Nov. 9, 1856, James G. Willie company.

Married Ann Bolton. Their children: Thomas b. Aug. 18, 1836, m. Susannah Washburn Jan. 29, 1859; Enoch b. Nov. 25, 1844, m. Amelia Webb March 27, 1864, m. Siña Kendall Dec. 14, 1887. Family home Nephi, Utah.

Married Amelia ———. Only child: William.

Elder.

BOWLES, THOMAS (son of Edward Bowles and Ann Bolton). He was born Aug. 18, 1836, Wiltshire, Eng.

Married Susannah Washburn Jan. 29, 1859, Manti, Utah (daughter of Abraham and Tamar Washburn), who was born June 4, 1843, Nauvoo, Ill. Their children: Thomas Edward b. Dec. 5, 1860, m. Louisa Bale March 18, 1879; William Abraham b. June 5, 1863, m. Viola Johnson Dec. 27, 1883; Martha Ann b. Aug. 13, 1866, m. George Taylor. Family home Nephi, Utah.

High priest; counselor to David Cazair in the high priest's quorum.

BOWLES, THOMAS EDWARD (son of Thomas Bowles and Susannah Washburn). Born Dec. 5, 1860, Moroni, Utah.

Married Louisa Bale (daughter of Richard Bale and Sarah Miller), who was born Sept. 28, 1864, Whitwick, Leicestershire, Eng. Their children: William Thomas b. May 16, 1882, m. Elizabeth A. Pitman Nov. 13, 1902; Earnest Richard b. Sept. 15, 1891, m. Clarissa E. Hancock Feb. 19, 1907; Samuel Clifford b. Sept. 15, 1891, m. Sarah Campbell, March 6, 1912; Alvin Roy b. Nov. 11, 1898; Arthur Lloyd b. Oct. 10, 1900; Retta Louisa b. June 21, 1904; Sarah Vivian b. Feb. 21, 1907. Family home Nephi, Utah.

BOWLES, SAMUEL CLIFFORD (son of Thomas Edward Bowles and Louisa Bale). Born Sept. 15, 1891, Nephi, Utah.

Married Sarah Campbell March 6, 1912. Family resides near Rigby, Idaho.

BOWTHORPE, WILLIAM (son of Thomas Bowthorpe and Priscilla Pye of Norwich, Norfolkshire, Eng.). Born Sept. 30, 1806, Buff., Eng. Came to Utah Oct. 13, 1853, Levi Kendall and Cyrus Wheelock company.

Married Mary Ann Tuttle Dec. 22, 1835, Norwich, Eng. She was born Dec. 18, 1810. Their children: Virtue Ann, m. Preston Lewis; George, b. child; Hannah Charlotte b. Nov. 4, 1840, m. George Finley Brooks Feb. 13, 1858; Maria Mary Ann, m. George Baker, m. Benjamin Neff; ² William d. aged 12; Phoebe, m. William Taylor; ² William b. June 8, 1851, m. C. Elizabeth Reynolds; Nephi b. April 24, 1855, m. Lynn Reynolds. Family home Cottonwood, Utah.

Seventy; high priest; ward teacher; missionary to England three years. Silk weaver; farmer. Died April 5, 1878, Cottonwood, Utah.

BOWTHORPE, WILLIAM, JR. (son of William Bowthorpe and Mary Ann Tuttle). Born June 8, 1851, Norwich, Eng. Came to Utah with parents.

Married C. Elizabeth Reynolds Feb. 13, 1877, Salt Lake City (daughter of Warren F. Reynolds and Christena McNeal of South Cottonwood, pioneers 1853). She was born April 11, 1858. Their children: Glays C. b. Dec. 22, 1877, m. William J. Baxter; ⁴ William W. b. June 1, 1879, d. infant; Hanmer R. b. March 5, 1881, m. Zina Peterson; Pearl R. b. Dec. 7, 1882, m. Hurst Thompson; Asa R. b. April 7, 1885; Wilford R. b. May 21, 1887, m. Dean Fagg; Nellie E. b. July 10, 1889; Clarence G. b. Sept. 15, 1892; Hazel R. b. March 14, 1895; Ethel May b. July 30, 1897; Geneva R. b. June 28, 1900. Family home Cottonwood, Utah.

Member 128th quorum seventies; missionary to England 1900-02; president seventies; Sunday school teacher; home missionary in Granite stake six years; special missionary in East Mill Creek and Big Cottonwood three years. Road supervisor in Salt Lake county four years. Farmer and stockraiser.

BOYACK, JAMES (son of William Boyack and Catherine Moody of Mains, Forfarshire, Scotland). Born Aug. 25, 1805. Came to Utah Oct. 24, 1855, Milo Andrus company.

Married Elizabeth Mealmaker Nov. 23, 1855, Salt Lake City (daughter of William Mealmaker and Jenet Robertson, of Mains). She was born April 30, 1805. Their children: James, Jr., b. Sept. 14, 1828, m. Margary Waterhouse; Ann b. April 1829, m. James Ririe; Margret b. Sept. 24, 1831, m. Henry Cleveland; Hannah b. March 12, 1835, m. James McFarland; Elizabeth b. April 15, 1838, m. Robert McKell; Mary b. Feb. 23, 1840, m. John Robertson; William M. b. 1841, m. Susan Duncan; Joseph G. b. July 1, 1842, m. Jessie Archibald; Peter F. b. July 1, 1844, m. Rachel Hicks; Robert M. b. March 21, 1847, m. Emily Jane Stoker; David D. (twin of Robert), m. Orilla Brimhall.

Settled at Spanish Forks 1856. Died there Feb. 1, 1888.

BOYACK, JAMES, JR. (son of James Boyack and Elizabeth Mealmaker). Born Sept. 14, 1828, at Mains.

Married Margary Waterhouse Nov. 23, 1855, Salt Lake City (daughter of Thomas Waterhouse and Isabella Donaldson, of Dundee, Scotland). She was born Dec. 10, 1832. Their children: ² James A. b. Sept. 9, 1856, m. Sarah M. Cox Williams; Margary Ann b. June 23, 1858, m. Robert Kinder; Elizabeth M. b. April 4, 1861, m. John D. Evans; Mary Jane b. Sept. 3, 1863, m. William Howells; Jemia E. b. Aug. 21, 1865, m. Richard Smith; Dessa b. Dec. 5, 1867; Isabella b. Dec. 22, 1869, m. Charles H. Peterson; George S. b. July 8, 1872, m. Jane T. Bowen; Ralph B. b. May 9, 1876, m. Sarah E. Morgan. Family home Spanish Fork, Utah.

Died Dec. 19, 1893.

BOYACK, JAMES A. (son of James Boyack and Margary Waterhouse). Born Sept. 9, 1856, Spanish Fork, Utah.

Married Sarah M. Cox Williams April 7, 1881, Salt Lake City (daughter of Samuel Cox and Mary Williams, of England, pioneers Oct. 1864). She was born Feb. 1, 1861. Their adopted children: Ethel b. Dec. 20, 1887; Rosalia b. March 28, 1894. Family home Spanish Fork, Utah.

Missionary 1907-09 to Ohio; superintendent Sunday schools 1893-07; president seventies since 1900.

BOYCE, JOHN (son of Benjamin Boyce and Margaret Hartley of Fredericksburg, Can.). Born Feb. 20, 1814, at Fredericksburg. Came to Utah 1852.

Married Jane Herns June 7, 1835 (daughter of Thomas Herns and Margaret Crank), who was born in Barry, Pike county, Ill. Their children: Thomas; Martha b. March 21, 1836; Benjamin b. Oct. 7, 1839. Family home Kirtland, Ohio.

Married Mary Ann Barzee 1841, at Kirtland (daughter of James W. Barzee and Betsy Whiteham), who was born Nov. 4, 1819. Their children: Chester b. April 2, 1842; Martin Calvin b. April 7, 1844, m. Louisa Marshall early in 1865; John b. May 24, 1846, d. Feb. 2⁸, 1865; David b. Feb. 16, 1848, m. Eliza Handy; Betsy Ann b. Nov. 27, 1851, m. Albert W. Clements; Albert M. b. March 16, 1854, m. Ida M. Herrick Jan. 25, 1886; Joseph Y. b. Oct. 26, 1856, m. Eunice S. Merrick; Elijah b. June 15, 1860, m. Frien Henderson; Elisha b. Feb. 11, 1863. Family resided Smithfield, Utah, and Oxford, Idaho.

High priest; patriarch. Farmer. Died March 31, 1886, at Oxford.

BOYCE, JOSEPH YOUNG (son of John Boyce and Mary Ann Barzee). Born Oct. 26, 1856, Spanish Fork, Utah.

Married Eunice Sophia Merrick March 8, 1876, Richmond, Utah (daughter of D. M. Merrick and Sophia Duffin, pioneers 1852). She was born March 18, 1857, Ogden, Utah. Their children: Joseph Lorenzo b. Feb. 1, 1877, m. July 23, 1880; Nellie Alnora b. Jan. 22, 1879, m. George Helmandolar Oct. 12, 1900; Leander M. b. Sept. 11, 1882, m. Maud Davis Dec. 12, 1905; Ruby b. Sept. 24, 1888; Vesta b. Jan. 15, 1894; Eva b. July 6, 1900, died. Family home Oxford, Idaho.

President Y. M. M. I. A. 1880-89; superintendent Sunday schools 1895-99; president 88th quorum seventies. Farmer and fruit grower.

BOYCE, JOHN (son of Benjamin Boyce, born Dec. 18, 1812, and Susannah Judd, born Feb. 25, 1815, both of Leads county, Canada). He was born Feb. 22, 1842, Madison Island (near Nauvoo), Ill. Came to Utah Oct. 6, 1850, William Snow company.

Married Elizabeth Ann Keat Dec. 18, 1864, (daughter of James Keat and Ann Prodger, former a pioneer 1857). She was born Aug. 8, 1842, and came to Utah Sept. 20, 1861, Joseph Young company. Their children: Lizzie Adell b. Aug. 21, 1869, m. O. N. Despain 1889; John, Jr. b. June 18, 1866, died; Eliza Content b. March 11, 1872, m. John Quist 1898; Ida Lurena b. April 26, 1874, m. Cyrus Winters 1908; Ella

Mehitable b. May 18, 1878, m. George Butler 1896; James b. Nov. 27, 1879, d. Nov. 29, 1879.
Married Ella Eugenia Despain Jan. 30, 1879, Salt Lake City (daughter of Solomon Despain and Ruth Amelia Newell, pioneers 1861, David Cannon company). She was born Aug. 27, 1858, Deans Island, Mississippi county, Ark. Their children: Ira John b. June 16, 1880, m. Pearl Mitchell 1907; Elunie Mildred b. Aug. 25, 1882, m. George Baugh 1905; Benjamin b. March 15, 1884, m. Maud Brown 1905; Verna Maud b. Feb. 5, 1886, m. Benjamin Judd 1902; Mabel Clare b. Feb. 28, 1888; Ella Jean b. April 3, 1890, m. Wallace Clark 1911; Joel Luther b. July 7, 1894; Edith Dora b. June 14, 1896; Daniel b. May 5, 1898; Leona Elizabeth b. Jan. 25, 1901; Laronzo b. June 9, 1903. Family resided Salt Lake City and Granite, Utah.
Assisted to bring immigrants to Utah; bishop's counselor 30 years in Granite ward. Justice of peace two years; Salt Lake county fruit-tree inspector two years.

BOYD, GEORGE ALFRED (son of James B. Boyd and Anne Adams). Born Aug. 1, 1841, Newbury, Berkshire, Eng. Came to Utah 1863, William Godbe company.
Married Isabell Jane Roe in 1867, at Salt Lake City (daughter of James Roe), who was born in 1847. Their children: Eliza N.; Mamie, m. William Brigawan; Priscilla A., m. Arthur Dixon; George A., m. Alice Miller; John W.; Edward, m. Flora Ellis; Albert Levi; Susie, m. August Steiner; James Butler, m. Louise Fitts. Family home Salt Lake City.
Elder. Assisted Capt. Hyde to bring immigrants to Utah. Farmer and fruit-grower.

BOYDEN, CHARLES. Came to Utah Sept. 3, 1860, James D. Ross company.
Married Sarah Korns at Stafford, Staffordshire, Eng. She was born in 1819. Their children: William d. infant; John, m. Jessie Mitchell; Fannie, m. James Whitehead; Mary Ann, m. Josiah Lees; Louisa, m. Oliver R. Ostler.
High priest; missionary to Sandwich Islands four years; Sunday school superintendent. Farmer and stockraiser. Died in 1887, Peterson, Morgan county, Utah.

BOYLE, HENRY G. (son of John Boyle and Jane Taylor, of Virginia). Born March 7, 1824, in Virginia. Came to Utah June 5, 1848.
Married Keziah D. Holliday Sept. 6, 1849, Salt Lake City (daughter of John Holliday and Katherine Higgins, pioneers 1847). She was born in 1833. Their children: William H. b. Feb. 19, 1851, m. Mary Jane Ewell; Sarah Louisa b. Feb. 28, 1853, m. William A. Carter. Family home Weber county, Utah.
Married Elizabeth Ballard Feb. 24, 1859, Payson, Utah. Eight children.
Married Arabella McKinley Sept. 30, 1865, Salt Lake City. Six children.
Married Martha Frances Taylor, Sept. 26, 1889, Salt Lake City. Six children.
Filled 4 missions; first president southern states mission. Died November 1908, in Arizona.

BOYLE, WILLIAM HENRY (son of Henry G. Boyle and Keziah D. Holliday). Born Feb. 19, 1851, Ogden, Utah.
Married Mary Jane Ewell Dec. 24, 1869, Santaquin, Utah (daughter of William Thomas Ewell and Polly Lee). She was born Feb. 5, 1849. Their children: Mary Keziah b. Dec. 13, 1870, m. B. D. Harper; Susah Louisa b. Jan. 30, 1873, m. W. B. Thurman; William H. b. Oct. 19, 1874, m. Minnie Wright; Lydia Ann b. Aug. 11, 1876, m. John F. Harris; Emma Jane b. July 18, 1878, m. George H. Chatwin; James Hollis b. April 15, 1881, m. Olive Palmer; Zachariah Levi b. March 5, 1883, d. April 15, 1883; Leona Pearl b. March 6, 1893. Family home Santaquin, Utah.
Member board of education nine years; member city council.

BOYLE, PETER ADAMS (son of John Boyle of Edinburgh, Scotland). Born Nov. 20, 1827, at Edinburgh. Came to Utah Sept. 3, 1855, John Hindley company.
Married Elizabeth Sinclair Jan. 1, 1846, at Edinburgh, who was born Aug. 4, 1821. Their children: John A., m. Mary Snow; James M.; Robert B.; William W.; A. McLaren. Family home, Ogden.
Member 60th quorum seventies. Engaged in furniture business and lathe turning; cabinet maker. Died Aug. 12, 1880, at Ogden.

BOYNTON, ABRAHAM D. Born March 12, 1815, in Massachusetts. Came to Utah late in 1852.
Married Maria H. Burbank about 1844, Haverhill, Essex county, Mass. (daughter of John Burbank of Haverhill). She was born July 22, 1817. Their children: Charles, d. infant; Joseph H., m. Flora Burges, m. Millie Holbrook; John, d. aged 24; Caroline, m. Benjamin Davis; George, d. aged 6; Shollitta, m. John K. Crosby; Mary E., m. Heber J. Burmingham; Augusta A., m. Nephi Dourdon. Family home Bountiful, Utah.
Member of seventies; ward teacher. Merchant and farmer. Said to have owned the first stove in Bountiful. Died Oct. 1, 1865.

BOYNTON, JOSEPH H. (son of Abraham D. Boynton and Maria H. Burbank). Born Dec. 27, 1850, Haverhill, Mass. Came to Utah with parents.
Married Flora Burges Oct. 10, 1875, Salt Lake City (daughter of Bowers Burges and Elizabeth Brown of Maine, who came to Utah in 1872). She was born April 13, 1861. Their children: Joseph H. b. July 16, 1878, m. Mary J. Brampton; George T. b. April 27, 1880, d. infant; Charles W. b. Dec. 6, 1881, m. Lillie Agett; Hannah J. b. May 24, 1884, m. Frederick Moffitt; Wanda Rilla b. Sept. 18, 1887, m. Orson Agett. Family home Bountiful, Utah.
Married Millie Holbrook Dec. 18, 1890, Bountiful, Utah (daughter of Jonathan Holbrook and Millie Smith of Bountiful), who was born 1868. Their children: Jesse b. Sept. 18, 1891; John R. b. Sept. 17, 1893; Sylvia b. March 8, 1896, m. Henry Kirby; Martha b. March 8, 1898; Frederick b. Dec. 11, 1900; Bessie b. Dec. 10, 1902; Emma b. Jan. 16, 1905.
Member 100th quorum seventies. Farmer and stockraiser.

BRACKEN, JAMES BENNETT (son of Levi Bracken). Born in 1815. Came to Utah 1852.
Married Sarah Head (daughter of Anthony Head), who was born Feb. 29, 1816, and died July 4, 1900. Their children: Martha Ann, m. Cyrus Hancock; James Bennett, m. Marion Whipple; William Albert, m. Clara Burgess; Narvil and Levi, died; Orlando Henry, m. Martha Ann Mathews; Marcellus, m. Jeanette McMurtry; Alzado, m. James Day; Family home Pine Valley, Washington county, Utah.
Pioneer; died at Panguitch, Utah, 1899.

BRACKEN, ORLANDO HENRY (son of James Bennett Bracken and Sarah Head). Born March 9, 1854, Payson, Utah.
Married Martha Ann Mathews Feb. 4, 1879, near Panguitch, Utah (daughter of James Mathews, who died 1871, and Clara Slade, pioneers 1849, Captain Thomas company). She was born March 9, 1860. Their children: Orlando James, b. Nov. 13, 1879, m. Mary Ann Worthin; Daisy Ann, b. Jan. 5, 1881; Clara, b. Aug. 12, 1882, m. Leroy W. Rust; Ethelind, b. Feb. 21, 1884, m. Fred S. Carpenter; Eugene, b. Oct. 5, 1887; George, b. Aug. 8, 1889; Frank, b. June 4, 1890; Guy, b. Sept. 28, 1891; Alice, b. Sept. 8, 1894; Gaild, b. Oct. 5, 1897; Leland H. b. Dec. 20, 1900.
Elder; ward teacher; assistant superintendent of Sunday school. County commissioner 1908-12; deputy sheriff 1 term; school trustee Pine Valley and Vernal, Utah. Engaged in merchandising at Vernal and Roosevelt, Utah; farmer.

BRACKEN, WILLIAM (son of Joshua Bracken and Hannah Bell, emigrants from Northumberlandshire, Eng.). He was born Oct. 26, 1842, Lockport, N. Y. Came to Utah Oct. 11, 1852, James Snow company.
Married Minnie Ahlstrom Dec. 12, 1863 (daughter of Peter Ahlstrom and Inger Godfrey), who was born Nov. 13, 1845. Their children: William, Jr., b. Nov. 13, 1864, m. Elizabeth Russell; Watson A. b. Nov. 1, 1866, m. Jessie Lineback Nov. 25, 1895; Henry b. Jan. 31, 1869; George b. March 3, 1871, m. Agnes Crookston March 13, 1898; Charles b. Sept. 24, 1873, m. Laura Evans April 29, 1899; Minnie b. Aug. 24, 1871, m. William Burton April 6, 1897; Alice b. March 15, 1879; Edna b. April 16, 1881; Ernest b. Aug. 18, 1884, m. Clara Nelson June 17, 1906; Myrtle, m. Clyde Abbott Dec. 21, 1907. Family home Stockton, Utah.
Married Calista Lee March 18, 1888, Toele, Utah (daughter of William Lee and Laverna Bates, married 1855). She was born Nov. 29, 1857, at Tooele. Their children: Estella M. b. Dec. 24, 1889; Ethel C. b. Oct. 15, 1891; Ross J. b. August 26, 1893; Verne b. Oct. 29, 1895; Glen L. b. Dec. 14, 1897; Flora E. b. July 23, 1900. Family home Mercur, Utah.

BRACKEN, WILLIAM, JR. (son of William Bracken and Minnie Ahlstrom). Born Nov. 13, 1864, Stockton, Utah.
Married Elizabeth Russell at Tooele (daughter of William G. Russell and Elizabeth Vickery), who was born March 18, 1862. Their children: Hazel b. Sept. 24, 1886; Nelist b. Oct. 3, 1888; Henry b. Jan. 6, 1890; Alice b. Aug. 23, 1891; Arnold b. May 4, 1892; Lois b. Sept. 9, 1895; Theodore b. June 10, 1897; Claud b. Nov. 16, 1899; Mabel b. Jan. 7, 1901. Family home Stockton.

BRADFORD, LARKIN H. (son of Larkin Bradford and Jane Catherine James of Huntsville, Ala.). Born Jan. 8, 1838, Huntsville, Ala. Came to Utah 1864.
Married Annie Davis Rex July 24, 1865, Salt Lake City (daughter of William Rex and Clara White Davis of Bruton, Somersetshire, Eng., latter a pioneer Sept. 13, 1861, Joseph Horne company). She was born May 28, 1841. Their children: Clara P., m. Robert C. Egbert; Larkin, m. Gertrude Abbott; Cornelia A., d. child; Catherine E., d. infant; Robert B., m. Keziah Williams; Moss D., m. Allie Stonebreaker; Charles L., m. Jane McSparren; Maybelle E., d. infant; Pearl L., m. C. Leroy Cooper; Arlie R.; Finis J. Family home, Salt Lake City.
Elder. Detective. Tinner and pattern maker. Died April 21, 1910, Midvale, Utah.

BRADFORD, PLEASANT SPRAGUE (son of Hial Bradford born April 25, 1808, in Vermont, and Abigal Sprague, born Aug. 14, 1814, in New York state, married Aug. 21, 1830). He was born Feb. 2, 1843, in Hancock county, Ill. Came to Utah Oct. 1, 1847, Edward Hunter company.
Married Jane Jones Oct. 15, 1864 (daughter of Charles

Jones and Mary Ann Weeks, former a pioneer Sept. 3, 1852, A. O. Smoot company, latter of Sept. 1853, Claudius Spencer company, married Sept. 1846, Wellington, Kentshire, Eng.). She was born Jan. 30, 1849. Came to Utah with parents. Their children: Pleasant J. b. Dec. 27, 1866, m. Jane Howard Dec. 13, 1893; Reuben Sprague b. Nov. 26, 1868; Mary Abigal b. July 27, 1870; Hial Lee b. Jan. 27, 1872, m. Jane E. Warner July 1900; Charles Union b. May 24, 1874, m. Isabel Hamilton Feb. 1, 1900; William Livingston b. April 6, 1876; Emma Elizabeth b. Sept. 8, 1877; Delila Jane b. May 28, 1879, m. Roger W. Creer Sept. 25, 1901; Lillian Irene b. Oct. 26, 1881; Sylvester Young b. Dec. 13, 1883; Minnie Othelia b. April 20, 1885, m. Antira J. Amason June, 1907; Ina Geneva b. Feb. 9, 1887, m. David M. Jones Dec. 20, 1909; Mabel LaVern b. March 24, 1890, m. James Beckstrom June, 1908. Family home Spanish Fork, Utah.
Married Dora Hanson 1885, Logan, Utah (daughter of James Hanson and Karen Anderson, latter a pioneer 1854, Capt. Christensen company). She was born 1869, in Spanish Fork. Their children: Frank b. Feb. 4, 1888, m. Myrtle Hales; Pearl Estella b. April 1, 1891, m. Sidney S. Berean 1910; Earnest Leroy b. Sept. 27, 1893; Melvin Ray b. March 7, 1896; Dora Viola b. May 4, 1898; Reva Merlene b. Aug. 30, 1900; Kenneth Miles b. July 25, 1902; Lida Othea b. June 22, 1905.
Assisted in bringing immigrants to Utah. Called to help settle Arizona, where he assisted in building canals and roads, and the building of mills. Seventy. Deceased.

BRADFORD, CHARLES UNION (son of Pleasant Sprague Bradford and Jane Jones). Born May 24, 1874, Spanish Fork, Utah.
Married Isabel Hamilton Feb. 1, 1900, Salt Lake City (daughter of Henry Hamilton, pioneer, oxteam company, died June 16, 1901, and Jennett Johnson, pioneer with handcart company, both born in Scotland). His Their children: Charles Russell b. Nov. 23, 1900; Jennie Fontella b. June 30, 1902; Floyd Henry b. March 19, 1904; William Oral b. July 3, 1906; Harold Sterling b. April 4, 1908. Family home Spanish Fork, Utah, and Shelley, Idaho.
Flour miller twenty years. Constructor of mills and power plants.

BRADFORD, SYLVESTER (son of Hial Bradford and Abigal Sprague). Born Nov. 17, 1839, Switzerland county, Ind. Came to Utah Oct. 1, 1847, Edward Hunter company.
Married Mary Ann Jones Oct. 15, 1864 (daughter of Charles Jones and Mary Ann Weeks). She was born June 15, 1847. Their children: Sylvester b. Sept. 25, 1865; Hial Charles; Rawsel S. b. Dec. 4, 1869, m. Hannah Jex, March 22, 1893; Robert John b. March 22, 1873, m. Mary E. Payzant Feb. 25, 1903; George W. b. April 24, 1875, m. Rachel Shepherd June 23, 1897; Lewis E. D. June 10, 1877; Niel G. b. Oct. 18, 1879, m. Mary Barnes Feb. 10, 1906; Pleasant M.; Eli Alma. Family home Spanish Fork, Utah.
Married Anna Christina Hanson April 7, 1884, Salt Lake City (daughter of James Hanson and Karen Anderson, the latter a pioneer 1854, Capt. Christensen company). She was born Jan. 14, 1863, Spanish Fork, Utah. Their children: Granville b. May 5, 1885; Lester Glenn b. July 26, 1895; James Henry b. July 9, 1897.
Settled in Salt Lake county; moved to Spanish Fork 1864. Missionary to northern states 1881-83; missionary to England 1886-88; president 19th quorum seventies; high priest. Veteran Black Hawk war.

BRADFORD, RAWSEL S. (son of Sylvester Bradford and Mary Ann Jones). Born Dec. 4, 1869, Spanish Fork, Utah.
Married Hannah Jex March 22, 1892, Manti, Utah (daughter of William Jex and Eliza Goodson), who was born Oct. 5, 1867, at Spanish Fork. Their children: Hannah b. Jan. 20, 1893; Mary A. b. Nov. 8, 1895; Eliza G. b. Nov. 6, 1897; Lewis S. b. March 16, 1901; Mildred J. b. Feb. 24, 1903; Alice R. b. Jan. 11, 1905; Rawsel W. b. Feb. 1, 1906; John J. b. Dec. 17, 1910.
Missionary to Hawaiian Islands 1906-09. Farmer and flour miller.

BRADFORD, ROBERT JOHN (son of Sylvester Bradford and Mary Ann Jones). Born March 22, 1873.
Married Mary Eliza Payzant Feb. 25, 1903. Their children: Mary Emma b. Feb. 13, 1904; Robert Louis b. Dec. 30, 1905; Sylvester Allen b. Dec. 9, 1907; Mark Payzant b. July 9, 1910. Family home Spanish Fork, Utah.
Missionary to northern states 1900-02.

BRADLEY, GEORGE W. Born Jan. 15, ——. Came to Utah 1847, Willard Richards oxteam company.
Married Elizabeth Betsy Kroll. Their children: Amanda, m. Daniel Henrie; Abiah, m. Isaac Morley; Jerome, d. aged 21; Louisa, m. Abner Lowry; George W., m. Leonora Reese; Zephaniah, m. Myra Draper; m. Martha Jane Draper; Sylvia d. child.
Married Cynthia Adair. Their children: James, m. Luna Draper; Lucy, m. Anthony Bruno. Families resided Manti, Nephi and Moroni, Utah.
Bishop of Nephi and Moroni. Assisted in building the first ferry boat to carry immigrants across Green river. Appointed probate judge of Juab county Feb. 7, 1852, by Gov. Brigham Young. Farmer. Died Sunday, March 8, 1891, Moroni, Utah.

BRADLEY, AMOS ALMA (son of George W. Bradley and Abiah Richmond of Salem, N. Y.). Born Aug. 10, 1849, Salt Lake City. *[In the preceding genealogy he is given as a part of the family of George W. Bradley and Elizabeth Betsy Kroll.]
Married Leonora Reese July 18, 1869, Salt Lake City (daughter of Thomas Reese and Margret Davis, pioneers Oct. 2, 1856, Edward Bunker handcart company). She was born Aug. 2, 1853. Their children: Amos Alma, Jr., b. Aug. 23, 1869, m. Amelia Christensen Dec. 26, 1887; Anna R. b. July 8, 1871, m. James Jacobson Dec. 3, 1890; Sylvia b. Feb. 25, 1873, m. William Homer June 16, 1891; Lydia Leonora b. Feb. 9, 1875, m. W. R. Young June 19, 1895; Malinda Euphemia b. Feb. 7, 1877, m. Frank B. Ford Oct. 1899; Thomas Jefferson b. Jan. 22, 1879, m. Sarah Ellen Estaugh Aug. 1899; Charles Henry b. Nov. 28, 1880, and Betsy M. b. Sept. 9, 1882, died; Roscoe A. b. Oct. 4, 1889, m. Effie Bates June 4, 1913; Dora b. May 24, 1893, m. Raphel Larson Sept. 1911. Family home Moroni, Utah.
President high priests' quorum, Moroni. One of the active citizens of his community in its development.

BRADLEY, AMOS ALMA, JR. (son of Amos Alma Bradley and Leonora Reese). Born Aug. 23, 1869, Moroni, Utah.
Married Amelia Christensen Dec. 26, 1887, Manti, Utah (daughter of Niels and Christana Christensen, pioneers with Capt. Christiansen company, whose handcart company came Sept. 13, 1857). She was born at Moroni, Utah. Their children: Amos Melvin b. Oct. 7, 1888, m. Hazel McGary Nov. 5, 1909; Nielson b. March 12, 1892, d. Nov. 26, 1893; Reese Victor b. Aug. 31, 1895; Heber Wells b. May 22, 1898; Christana A. b. April 21, 1902; Newel Alma b. April 29, 1907, d. Jan. 3, 1911.

BRAIN, EDWARD (son of Aaron and Hannah Brain of Bath, Somersetshire, Eng., pioneers 1848). Born Aug. 15, 1822. Came to Utah 1864.
Married Mary Ann Johnson Dec. 24, 1869 (daughter of Benjamin Johnson and Charlotte Budd of Salt Lake City, pioneers Aug. 20, 1868, Joseph S. Rawlins company). She was born May 4, 1851, Bedfordshire, Eng. Their children: Mabel R. b. Feb. 14, 1871, m. Brigham A. Seare; Edward B. b. March 15, 1872, d. aged 3; Henry B. b. March 10, 1874, m. Jane Bult; Ebenezer J. b. Dec. 23, 1875, m. Ivy Hayes; Fred B. b. May 27, 1878, m. Beatrice Coleman; Albert G. b. Jan. 13, 1881, m. Irene Crofts; Alice D. b. Feb. 16, 1883, m. Frederick Hust. Family home 20th ward, Salt Lake City. Brickmaker.

BRANCH, WILLIAM HENRY (son of William Henry Branch of Lisbon, Conn.). Born Aug. 9, 1820, Lisbon, Conn. Came to Utah Oct. 14, 1850, Wilford Woodruff company.
Married Emily Cornelia Atwood Nov. 24, 1844, Mansfield, Conn. (daughter of Daniel Atwood and Wilford Woodruff company). She was born March 1, 1819. Their children: Nelson b. Nov. 1845, d. infant; Erving b. Oct. 1847, d. April 1850; [3] William Henry b. Aug. 23, 1851, m. Hephzibah C. Hirst; Eugene Elisha b. Aug. 19, 1854, m. Jane Blake; Emily Cornelia b. Dec. 10, 1855, m. George Brooks; Rozilla Polly b. Nov. 5, 1857, m. Brigham J. Lund; Candice, died. Family resided Salt Lake City, St. George and Price, Utah.
Married Ella Coombs May 9, 1877, St. George, Utah (daughter of Abraham Coombs and Olive Olivia Curtis, latter a pioneer 1860, Ebenezer Hanks company). She was born March 27, 1857, San Bernardino, Cal. Their children: Olive b. Dec. 19, 1878, m. Herbert West Millburn April 22, 1897; Jane b. March 6, 1881, m. Elbert L. Thomas April 12, 1905; Frank b. April 4, 1884, d. Aug. 31, 1907; Arabella b. Dec. 19, 1887, m. Henry A. Pace Sept. 9, 1910; Elia Irene b. June 11, 1890, m. Don Carlos Woodward Aug. 15, 1910.
High priest and ward clerk. Road supervisor; captain of police; sheriff Washington county; watermaster. Bricklayer and plasterer; farmer. Died Sept. 19, 1890, Price, Utah.

BRANCH, WILLIAM HENRY (son of William Henry Branch and Emily Cornelia Atwood). Born August 23, 1851, Salt Lake City.
Married Hephzibah Caroline Hirst May 29, 1879, Salt Lake City (daughter of William Henry Hirst and Hannah Drake, of Thornhill, Yorkshire, Eng., who came to Utah Nov. 7, 1878). She was born May 1, 1856. Their children: Eva b. Dec. 27, 1880, died; Cornelia b. March 12, 1882, m. John David Barber; Eliza Jane b. Dec. 31, 1883, m. John Ellwood Carruth; Hannah May b. May 14, 1885; Emily b. April 18, 1887, m. Lawrence S. Stone; Frances Ruby b. Jun. 17, 1889, m. Leo Knopp Jan. 28, 1913; Earl b. Sept. 17, 1891, died; Olive b. Jan. 15, 1894; William Henry b. Feb. 18, 1896; Karl Hirst b. Sept. 9, 1901. Family resided Salt Lake City, St. George and Coalville, Utah.
Member 21st quorum seventies; missionary to England 1877-80, and to Sandwich Islands 1874-77; high priest; bishop; president T. M. M. A. Deputy sheriff two terms; justice of peace; constable; city marshal; city councilman two terms; deputy United States marshal. Brickmason and plasterer.

BRANCH, EUGENE ELISHA (son of William Henry Branch and Emily Cornelia Atwood). He was born Aug. 19, 1854, Salt Lake City.
Married Jane Blake Jan. 18, 1877, St. George, Utah (daughter of Benjamin Fredrick Blake and Harriett Hollis, both of England, pioneers 1852). She was born Dec. 20, 1857. Their children: Eugene Elisha, Jr., b. Oct. 8, 1877, m. Agnes

768   PIONEERS AND PROMINENT MEN OF UTAH

Winifred Liddell; Rosilla b. June 11, 1879, m. Ebenezer Hunt Thayn; Irvin b. Nov. 28, 1881, m. Anna May Smith; Levi b. Dec. 28, 1884, m. Mary Brace; Ernest b. March 28, 1887; Ezra b. July 12, 1889, m. Vilate Hanson; Ray b. June 24, 1891; Melville b. Jan. 14, 1894; Olive b. April 2, 1896; Effie b. Nov. 2, 1901.
Missionary to northwestern states 1898-1900; bishop Wellington ward 1902-06; ward clerk; Sunday school superintendent; ward teacher. School trustee. Mason. Died Oct. 29, 1906, Wellington, Utah.

BRANCH, EUGENE ELISHA (son of Eugene Elisha Branch and Jane Blake). Born Oct. 8, 1877, St. George, Utah.
Married Agnes Winifred Liddell Sept. 20, 1900, at St. George (daughter of Abraham Liddell of Rutherglen, near Glasgow, Scotland, pioneer Sept. 15, 1868, John Gillespie company, and Lucy Jones of South Wales, pioneer Oct. 26, 1864, William Hyde company). She was born May 5, 1878. Their children: Gladys b. Sept. 8, 1901; Eugene Amos b. Dec. 10, 1904; Melba and Thelma (twins), b. April 11, 1907, latter died.
Member 101st quorum seventies; missionary to southern states 1909-11, and president North Carolina conference; high priest; 1st counselor to Bishop Edgar H. Thayn; 2d counselor to Bishop John W. Hill; Sunday school superintendent eight years; president Y. M. M. I. A., Wellington ward. Treasurer Wellington town board; chairman Wellington school district No. 8. Farmer.

BRANSFORD, JOHN SAMUEL (son of Milford Bard Bransford and Sarah Ellen Cooper, who lived in Plumas county, Cal.). Born Aug. 26, 1856, at Richmond, Miss. Came to Utah February, 1899.
Married Rachel S. Blood July 31, 1878, at Greenville, Cal. (daughter of John Nelson Blood, of same place), who was born Dec. 19, 1857. Their children: Stella, m. Lewis A. Evans; Wallace Milford, m. Louise Grace Emery. Family home Salt Lake City, Utah.
Mayor Salt Lake City 1907-12. Mining operator and capitalist.

BRENCHLEY, RICHARD (son of William Brenchley, born March 11, 1805, Faversham, East Kent, Eng., and Caroline Wellar, of Borden, East Kent). He was born Feb. 22, 1840, at Borden. Came to Utah Oct. 12, 1861, Capt. Horne company.
Married Jane Gray April 15, 1861 (daughter of William Gray and Ann Broadbent), who was born July 8, 1834, and came to Utah with husband. Only child: Harriet Lydia b. Feb. 17, 1862, m. George Spence April 14, 1887.
Married Mary J. Clegg Dec. 26, 1864, Salt Lake City (daughter of Thomas Clegg who died in England 1863, and Ann Massee, pioneer Sept. 25, 1843, Peter Nebeker company). She was born Jan. 18, 1844, Stockport, Eng. Their children: Jane Clegg b. Oct. 17, 1865, m. Thomas Thorpe May 2, 1886; Mary C. b. June 27, 1867, m. Robert Leshman Nov. 10, 1885; Caroline C. b. June 17, 1869, m. Joseph Thorpe Jan. 18, 1891; Richard C. b. June 10, 1871, died; William C. b. Sept. 8, 1873, m. Sarah Murray Jan. 6, 1897; John b. Jan. 3, 1875 m. Cassie Hall Jan. 7, 1903; Thomas b. April 1, 1878, m. Laura Hall Jan. 10, 1900; Joseph C. b. Jan. 21, 1880, m. Florence Memmott April 12, 1905; Alfred C. b. Feb. 26, 1885, died.
Settled at Wellsville. Second counselor in presidency high priests' quorum, Wellsville ward. Watermaster six years.

BRIDGES, HENRY MALLION (son of George Bridges and —— Mallion of Birmingham, Eng.). Born March 22, 1807, at Birmingham. Came to Utah September, 1864.
Married Sarah Louisa Lowe 1824, at Birmingham. She was born Dec. 26, 1804. Their children: Mary Ann, m. Patrick Martin; Susanna J., m. Edwin Taylor; Charles Henry, m. Frances Elizabeth Jones; Thomas Warner. d. child; Sarah Louisa, m. Daniel Agustus Husasy. Family home Birmingham, Eng., and East Mill Creek. Utah.
Active in ward religion work and in the British mission. Tailor. Died Oct. 18, 1882.

BRIDGES, CHARLES HENRY (son of Henry Mallion Bridges and Sarah Louisa Lowe). Born Aug. 9, 1835, at Birmingham. Came to Utah Sept. 26, 1856, Edmund Ellsworth handcart company.
Married Frances Elizabeth Pearson June 20, 1860, Salt Lake City (daughter of Joshua Pearson and Sarah Jefcutt of Stitchford Yardley, Eng., pioneers Sept. 4, 1859, George Rowley handcart company). She was born Sept. 5, 1837. Their children: Marian, m. David Follick: Sarah E., d. child; Charles Henry Jr., m. Mary Nate; Thaddeus, died; Louisa, d. child; Thomas Pearson, m. Elnora V. Kent; Wallace J., died; Grace, m. David A. Lewis; Gertrude, died. Family resided at Salt Lake City, Utah, and Montpelier, Idaho.
Senior president 79th quorum seventies; home missionary. Died Jan. 7, 1913, Montpelier, Idaho.

BRIDWELL, GEORGE M. (son of Thomas Jefferson Bridwell and Sarah J. Little of Augusta, Ga.). Born Oct. 17, 1853, at Augusta. Came to Utah Nov. 22, 1890, William Spry missionary company.
Married Mary E. Tice March 7, 1880, at Augusta (daughter of William J. Tice and Mary E. Garrison of Augusta, who came to Utah Nov. 22, 1890). She was born Oct. 7, 1859. Their children: George T., d. infant; Mary M., m. D. S. Donaldson; Sarah A., d. aged two; Lizzie Belle, m. C. W. Dansie; William Jefferson; George K., m. Nellie Brooks; Lee Roy Watson; Harry Thomas; Lena Ruth; Gordon Alexander; Beulah I., m. Paul Stonewall Jackson. Family home Salt Lake City, Utah.
High priest; home missionary; second counselor to Bishop H. Sperry of 4th ward, Salt Lake City; member high council pioneer stake. Superintendent Salt Lake public school buildings. Contractor.

BRIGGS, GEORGE (son of George Briggs, born Oct. 15, 1858, and Sarah Susannah Blackburn, born April 18, 1859, both of Tupton, Derbyshire, Eng.). He was born Aug. 13, 1883, Lyman, Oneida Co., Idaho.
Married Martha Burns June 22, 1904, Salt Lake City. Their children: Raymond George b. May 3, 1905; Elda Susannah b. Oct. 16, 1909.
Bishop Archer ward, Fremont stake, Idaho.

BRIGGS, JAMES (son of John Briggs, born Feb. 3, 1813, and Ruth Butterworth, born April 23, 1817, both of England). He was born Jan. 4, 1845. Came to Utah Nov. 30, 1856, Edward Martin handcart company.
Married Caroline Clark April 29, 1865, Salt Lake City (daughter of Benjamin Thomas Clark and Ann Schugar, former of Sugar House ward, Utah, pioneer Oct. 14, 1853, Cyrus H. Wheelock company, latter died in England). She was born April 28, 1845, and died March 23, 1909. Their children: John b. Aug. 3, 1866, m. Sarah Elizabeth Gillett Oct. 21, 1884; Ruth Ann b. March 19, 1869, m. James W. Siddoway March 11, 1886; James Lorenzo b. May 3, 1871, m. Mary Naylor June 1896; Benjamin Thomas b. Nov. 12, 1872, m. Charlotte Hawkins Dec. 14, 1898; Caroline Emma b. Nov. 26, 1874, m. George R. Trowbridge April 28, 1897; Clara b. June 11, 1877, m. Roy P. Anderson April 28, 1894; George Albert b. Feb. 14, 1879, m. Eva Blackford Sept. 5, 1906; Joseph Edward b. June 20, 1885, m. Isabella Weir July 30, 1905; Daniel Arthur b. April 7, 1888. Family home Sugar House ward, Salt Lake county.
Seventy; missionary to England 1882-98; president Manchester conference. Veteran Black Hawk Indian war. Died Feb. 15, 1906.

BRIGGS, JOHN (son of James Briggs and Caroline Clark). Born Aug. 3, 1866, Sugar House ward, Salt Lake county.
Married Sarah Elizabeth Gillett Oct. 21, 1884, Salt Lake City (daughter of Carlos N. Gillett and Celestia A. Pendleton), who was born June 11, 1866. Their children: James and Carl B. b. Dec. 11, 1887; Edith and Ethel b. August 1891; Caroline b. Feb. 1894; Benjamin b. Jan. 21, 1896; Ernest b. Dec. 24, 1896; Bessie b. Feb. 1897; George b. April 1907. Family home Teton City, Idaho.
Teton City councilman; school trustee. Blacksmith.

BRIGGS, GEORGE ALBERT (son of James Briggs and Caroline Clark). Born Feb. 14, 1879, Sugar House ward, Salt Lake county.
Married Eva Blackford Sept. 5, 1906, Salt Lake City (daughter of Joseph Blackford and Mary Smith of Oldham, Eng., latter came to Utah Dec. 1, 1901). She was born Dec. 3, 1878. Their children: Mary Caroline b. Sept. 8, 1907; James b. March 26, 1909; Florence b. Oct. 8, 1910. Family home Teton City, Idaho.
Seventy.

BRIGHT, ISAAC PRESTON (son of John Bright, born Dec. 15, 1808, and Susan Pugh, born Nov. 17, 1810, both of Knox county, Tenn.). He was born Oct. 13, 1844, Hancock county, Ill. Came to Utah Sept. 15, 1852, Isaac Stewart company.
Married Mary. Etta Smith Sept. 30, 1866, Oxford, Idaho (daughter of B. B. Smith and Delilah Hyler, pioneers Sept. 10, 1863, William B. Preston company). She was born Sept. 13, 1848. Their children: Mary Florence b. Oct. 7, 1867, m. Moroni H. Stocks Jan. 2, 1890; Clara Ann b. June 6, 1869; Isaac Preston, Jr., b. Feb. 6, 1871, m. Mereida Peart Dec. 17, 1895. Family home Richmond, Utah.
Married Cordelia Brower Feb. 17, 1873, Salt Lake City (daughter of Ariah C. Brower and Margaret Elizabeth Hussey), who was born Dec. 11, 1857, Grantsville, Utah. Their children: John Monroe b. Oct. 13, 1875, m. Amy Johnson March 5, 1902; Cordelia Etta b. Dec. 19, 1877, m. Milo A. Wheeler March 1, 1905; Elsie Elizabeth b. Jan. 17, 1879, m. Riley Allen Sept. 20, 1899; Martha McKinnie b. Nov. 17, 1881, m. Joseph Aller Oct. 2, 1901; Charles Minet b. Sept. 16, 1883, m. Jennie McCarthy; Zaloma b. April 19, 1886, m. Jefferson Stowell Dec. 2, 1904.
Married Martha A. Craghead March 27, 1887, Logan, Utah (daughter of Thomas L. Craghead and Harriet Wilson), who was born Jan. 7, 1846, Oxford, Idaho. Their children: Harriet S. b. Dec. 8, 1887; Elda b. Aug. 18, 1889, m. Austin Smith Dec. 26, 1912; George b. Nov. 25, 1890, m. Marguerite France Nov. 6, 1912; Zorda and Zola, twins, b. July 25, 1897; Sarah Matilda b. Feb. 26, 1900; Nettie b. Oct. 6, 1903.
Settled at Alpine, Utah, in 1852; pioneer to Richmond; moved to Lewiston 1874. Assisted to bring immigrants to Utah.

BRIGHT, ISAAC PRESTON, JR. (son of Isaac Preston Bright and Mary Etta Smith). Born Feb. 6, 1871, Richmond, Utah.
Married Merelda Peart Dec. 17, 1895, at Richmond (daughter of Benjamin Peart and Elizabeth Ashment, former born at Salt Lake City, latter came to Utah Oct. 1868, Simpson Molen company). She was born Dec. 17, 1872, Franklin, Idaho. Their children: Preston Leon b. Sept. 26, 1896; Esse Merelda b. Jan. 6, 1900; Ray Cornelius b. Dec. 28, 1902; Lorin Vernon b. Nov. 25, 1905.

BRIGHT, JOHN (son of John Bright and Susan Pugh). Born March 26, 1849, Pottawattamie county, Iowa. Came to Utah Sept. 15, 1852, in company with elder brother.
Married Phoebe Smith (daughter B. B. Smith and Delilah Hyler), who was born Dec. 28, 1853, and came to Utah with parents. Their children: John Wesley b. Jan. 12, 1873, m. Alice Taggart Oct. 28, 1896; Phoebe Etta b. March 27, 1874, m. Thomas Waddoups Dec. 18, 1890; Alice May b. Dec. 25, 1875, m. Henry Taggart; Sarah Florence b. Oct. 2, 1878, m. Marcus Taggart Nov. 3, 1897; Adah b. Feb. 3, 1881, m. C. B. Wheeler July 11, 1906; Emma b. Aug. 26, 1882; Delilah b. March 16, 1884, m. George Gregory June 11, 1903. Family home Lewiston, Utah.
Veteran Indian wars. Settled at Alpine in 1852; moved to Richmond in 1860, and to Lewiston in 1874. Went across the plains during the summer of 1868 to assist straggling and unfortunate immigrants.

BRIM, ALFRED WALLACE (son of Frederick and Eunice Brim of Madison county, N. Y.). Born Nov. 15, 1815, in Madison county, and came to Utah in 1852.
Married Mary Ann Merrill 1849 in Ohio (daughter of Gilman Merrill and Rebecca Sevier, pioneers of Ogden, Utah). She was born Nov. 23, 1830. Their children: Alfred Gilman b. 1850, m. Agnes Asper; Alonzo Adelbert b. March 10, 1853, m. Mary Jane Cluff; Willard Wallace b. 1855, m. Lillian Monison; Hyrum Fredrick and George Franklin, died; Alice Ann b. Nov. 25, 1862, m. Oluf Henrickson; Evaline Mae b. May 2, 1865, m. J. P. Dean. Family home Coalville, Utah.
One of the first to haul stone for the Salt Lake temple; also one of the first tanners in Utah. Died May 2, 1897.

BRIM, ALONZO ADELBERT (son of Alfred Wallace Brim and Mary Ann Merrill). Born March 10, 1853, Salt Lake City.
Married Mary Jane Cluff Oct. 7, 1877, Salt Lake City (daughter of Benjamin Cluff and Mary Ellen Foster of Provo, Utah). She was born June 25, 1855. Their children: Mary Leone b. July 9, 1878, m. Sidney P. Phillips; Stella Aleane b. March 27, 1880, m. Raymond Rasband; Mildred Alice b. Oct. 9, 1883, m. George W. Smith; Rula Merrill b. Aug. 10, 1886, m. Caleb Pickett; Alonzo Adelbert b. Dec. 26, 1891; Harold Cluff b. April 23, 1893; Walter Wallace b. May 28, 1898. Family home Center Ward, Utah.
Missionary to Sandwich Islands 1883-86; engineer on Church sugar factory in Sandwich Islands; bishop Center ward.

BRIMHALL, GEORGE WASHINGTON (son of Sylvanus Brimhall and Lydia Ann Guiteau). Born Nov. 14, 1814, South Fremont, Oneida county, N. Y. Came to Utah 1849.
Married Lucretia Metcalf. Their children: Rufus; Mary; Sylvanus. Family home Galesburg, Ill.
Married Rachel Ann Mayer Feb. 2, 1852, Salt Lake City (daughter of George Mayer and Ann Yost of Nauvoo, Ill., pioneers Sept. 24, 1848, Heber C. Kimball company). She was born Feb. 9, 1829, Bucyrus, Crawford county, Ohio. Their children: George Henry b. Dec. 9, 1852, m. Elizabeth Wilkins; m. Flora Robertson; Rachel Emma b. May 22, 1854, m. Charles O. Robertson; Emer M. b. Feb. 15, 1856, m. Angeline Davis; Orilla M. b. April 14, 1858, m. David Boysack; Omer M. b. March 9, 1860, m. Sally Reese; Ruth R. b. Jan. 17, 1863; Prudence M. b. Dec. 26, 1865; Ether Record b. March 4, 1868, m. Sophrona Smith; Tryphena M. b. Oct. 24, 1870, m. George P. Garff; Grace M. b. Sept. 5, 1875, m. John M. Calderwood. Family home Spanish Fork, Utah.
Patriarch; assisted in the erection of the Nauvoo temple and in locating the settlement of Parowan. Member of the legislature, representing Iron county; one of the pioneer musicians of Utah. Settled at Ogden; moved to Salt Lake City, thence to Spanish Fork in 1865. Farmer and builder.

BRIMHALL, GEORGE HENRY (son of George Washington Brimhall and Rachel Ann Mayer). Born Dec. 9, 1852, Salt Lake City, Utah.
Married Alsina Elizabeth Wilkins Dec. 28, 1874, Salt Lake City (daughter of George W. Wilkins and Catherine Augusta Lovett, pioneers Oct. 12, 1847). She was born May 7, 1856. Their children: Lucy Jane b. Dec. 13, 1875, m. Jesse William Knight; Alsina Elizabeth b. Dec. 16, 1876, m. Lafayette Hinckley Holbrook; George Washington b. Oct. 25, 1878, m. Hattie Wolfe; Mark Henry b. June 18, 1880, m. Guinevere Smellie; Wells Lovett b. April 26, 1882, m. Fern Smoot; Milton Albert b. Oct. 21, 1883, d. Jan. 8, 1884. Family home Spanish Fork, Utah.
Married Flora Robertson Sept. 11, 1885, Logan, Utah (daughter of James Robertson and Matilda Graham), who was born March 14, 1866. Their children: Dean Robertson b. Dec. 11, 1886; Fay Robertson b. May 16, 1889, m. Julian Moses Cummings; Fawn Robertson b. May 16, 1889, m. Thomas McKay; Burns Robertson b. Jan. 19, 1892; Ruth Afton b. April 8, 1895; Paul Robertson b. June 9, 1898; Alta Robertson b. July 23, 1901; Golden H. b. Aug. 12, 1906; Areo Robertson b. Aug. 3, 1909. Family home Provo, Utah.
One of first graduates of Brigham Young Academy; superintendent Spanish Fork public schools; two terms superintendent Utah county and Provo city schools; president Utah State Teachers' Association and president Brigham Young University, in which he served as a preparatory teacher, director normal school, principal high school, and professor of pedagogy and psychology; member general board of education and board of examiners; stake superintendent Y. M. M. I. A.

BRIMHALL, EMER M. (son of George Washington Brimhall and Rachel Ann Mayer). Born Feb. 15, 1856, Ogden (Mounds Fort), Utah.
Married Angeline Davis (daughter of Peter Davis). Their children: Silas Emer; Peter Harris; Clare, m. George Jensen; Melva; David; Glen; Dell; Allen; Tryphena; Ida, died; Ida Grant Margaret. Family home Spanish Fork, Utah.
Pioneer dry farmer and stockman at Brimhall's ranch, Spanish Fork.

BRINGHURST, SAMUEL (son of Joseph Bringhurst, born Feb. 18, 1790, Philadelphia, Pa., and Elizabeth Evans of Chester county, Pa.). He was born Dec. 21, 1812, at Philadelphia. Came to Utah Oct. 10, 1847, John Taylor company.
Married Eleanor Beitler (daughter of John Beitler), who was born Dec. 25, 1816. Their children: William A. b. Jan. 26, 1839, m. Selinda D. Palmer; Anna b. March 12, 1842, m. Jacob Houtz; Henry L. b. Aug. 13, 1844, d. March 21, 1846; Robert P. b. Nov. 25, 1846, m. Jane Wilson; Samuel b. April 7, 1850; Eleanor b. April 7, 1850; John B. b. June 13, 1854; Mary E. b. June 14, 1854; Louis b. Sept. 24, 1856.
Pioneer; wheelwright and farmer in Salt Lake county.

BRINGHURST, WILLIAM A. (son of Samuel Bringhurst and Eleanor Beitler). Born Jan. 26, 1839, Lionville, Chester county, Pa.
Married Selinda D. Palmer Sept 27, 1862 (daughter of Mifflin Palmer and Catherine Dally, pioneers Sept. 13, 1861, Joseph Horne company). She was born in 1842. Their children: William A. b. Sept. 27, 1863, m. Martha Granger; Howard b. Aug. 14, 1865, m. Lana M. Davis; Eliza B. b. March 14, 1868, m. Conrad M. Kleenman; Mary E. b. Feb. 3, 1870, m. Walter H. Clark; Mufflin M. b. Feb. 26, 1872; Lorenzo b. March 13, 1874, m. Eleanor Woodbury; George R. b. March 3, 1876, m. Lulu Harrison; Franklin P. b. Jan. 17, 1878, m. Edna A. Lamb; Daniel b. Sept. 26, 1880; Henry b. Dec. 17, 1882, m. Melina Hannum. Family resided at Salt Lake city and Toquerville, Utah.
Married Susan A. Steele May 25, 1867 (daughter of John Steele and Catharine Campbell, pioneers with Mormon Battalion). She was born April 28, 1851, Parowan, Utah. Their children: John S. b. July 30, 1868, m. Maran A. Stapley April, 1888; Anna A. b. March 30, 1870, m. John C. Naigie, Jr. March 20, 1887; Joseph A. b. Oct. 10, 1872, m. Adalin N. Hardy, June 16, 1896; Mary E. b. Aug. 21, 1875, m. R. H. Duffin Nov. 29, 1891; Eleanor C. b. Feb. 8, 1878, m. Ben C. Granger Aug. 31, 1898; Mahroni L. b. Sept. 5, 1880; Jesse W. b. June 13, 1883; Laura S. b. Aug. 22, 1885, m. B. F. Duffin Aug. 31, 1909.
Married Mary J. Stapley (daughter of Charles Stapley, born Nov. 28, 1824, Kent, Eng., and Sarah Parkinson, born May 24, 1831, Cambridgeshire, Eng.). She was born Feb. 11, 1865, Toquerville, Utah. Their children: Marisa W. b. Dec. 1, 1886; Vida b. Dec. 8, 1888; Samuel b. Dec. 24, 1892; Vera b. Nov. 3, 1894; Leo b. Jan. 23, 1897; Charles b. Dec. 22, 1899; Arvilla b. May 28, 1902.
Bishop Toquerville ward, St. George stake 1874-1912. Assessor and collector; sheriff and judge in Kane county.

BRINGHURST, WILLIAM (son of Joseph Bringhurst and Elizabeth Evans). Born Nov. 8, 1818, Philadelphia, Pa. Came to Utah Oct. 10, 1847, John Taylor company.
Married Ann Dillworth March 28, 1845, Chester county, Pa.) (daughter of Caleb Dillworth and Eliza Woolerton, the latter a pioneer 1847). She was born Feb. 12, 1821. Their children: Charles Harper b. April 23, 1846, d. Dec. 23, 1846; William Joseph b. Aug. 5, 1848, m. Eliza Taylor; Eliza Jane b. Aug. 14, 1851, m. Amasa L. Hayward; Ann Dillworth b. Aug. 13, 1853, m. John A. Groesbeck; Deseret b. Dec. 25, 1856, m. Milan L. Crandall; Clara Olivia b. July 11, 1858, m. Edward James Hall; John Frank b. Dec. 13, 1861, m. Mahala Harriett Crandall. Family resided Salt Lake City and Springville, Utah.
Married Ellen Wiscombe (daughter of James Wiscombe). Only child: Ferris W. b. June, 1877.
Bishop of Springville. City councilman; member territorial legislature; member board of directors of Brigham Young academy. Director Provo Woolen Mills; merchant, farmer and stockraiser.

BRINGHURST, JOHN FRANK (son of William Bringhurst and Ann Dillworth). Born Dec. 13, 1861, at Springville. Married Mahala Harriett Crandall Oct. 23, 1885, Logan, Utah (daughter of Martin Pardon Crandall and Harriett Tylor). She was born Dec. 12, 1866, at Springville. Their children: John Frank b. Aug. 22, 1886, died; William b. March 14, 1888; Harriett b. April 6, 1890; Norma b. April 29, 1892; Mark Dillworth b. Sept. 26, 1894; Joseph Crandall b. Feb. 24, 1897; Gideon Martin b. Dec. 6, 1899, d. May 20, 1904; Ann Dillworth b. March 21, 1902, d. May 4, 1902; Clara b.

Feb. 15, 1904; Frederick Ralston b. Oct. 1, 1906. Family home Springville.
Bishop of Springville since July 24, 1904. Traveling adjuster for the Consolidated Wagon and Machine co., and manager Spanish Fork branch 4 years; commissioned postmaster of Springville June 23, 1910.

BRINKERHOFF, JAMES. Born May 22, 1816, Sempronius, Cayuga county, N. Y. Came to Utah 1850.
Married Sally Ann Snider Jan. 24, 1830, who was born Oct. 22, 1815, at husband's birthplace, and died Feb. 8, 1895, Thurber, Utah. Only child: George, m. Rosannah V. Cutler. He died March 4, 1875, Glendale, Utah.

BRINKERHOFF, GEORGE (son of James Brinkerhoff and Sally Ann Snider). Born Oct. 29, 1852, Centerville, Davis Co., Utah.
Married Rosannah V. Cutler Nov. 5, 1879, St. George, Utah.
Ordained bishop of Thurber ward June, 1882, and again July 29, 1906; ordained an elder and high priest June, 1882; missionary to eastern states Nov. 22, 1887. Settled at St. George 1862; moved to West Point, on The Muddy, Nev.; returned with that colony to Glendale, and then to Thurber, Utah, in 1879.

BRISCOE, GAMELIEL (son of Bryan Briscoe and Margarette Frieyera). Born Dec. 18, 1818, Preston, Lancastershire, Eng. Came to Utah Aug. 20, 1868, Chester Loveland company.
Married Elizabeth Ellbeck in 1847, Benton, Yorkshire, Eng. (daughter of John Ellbeck and Mary Brockbank of Yorkshire). She was born May 12, 1819. Their children: Mary, d. infant; Mary Ann, d. aged 8; Thomas, m. Martha Barnett; Robert, m. Mr. Morgan; Jane, m. Thomas Tennant; Gameliel, Jr., d. infant; Ellen, m. Thomas Flynn; Eliza, m. William Alexander. Family home Salt Lake city.
Married Matilda Taylor Dec. 12, 1902, Salt Lake City (daughter of John Taylor and Ann Maria Sager of West Bromwich, Staffordshire, Eng., pioneers June 4, 1866). She was born April 15, 1847.
Block teacher. Worked on Salt Lake temple. Farmer and lumberman.

BRITTON, RICHARD (son of Anna Baker of Yorkrhire, Eng.). Born Jan. 23, 1814. Came to Utah Sept. 15, 1851, Capt. Howell company.
Married Elizabeth Lee of Bambre, Oxfordshire, Eng. (daughter of Thomas Lee of Bambre, pioneer 1851, Capt. Devenish company). Their children: Mary Britton, m. James Lovelace; Sarah Amelia, m. John Wootton; Joseph; Caroline, m. George Shelton; Harriet, m. Daniel Leatham; Frederick, m. Charlotte Varney. Family home Salt Lake City.
Married Elizabeth Bayless at Salt Lake City. Only child: Susan, m. David Staples. Family home Salt Lake City.
High priest. Walker Indian war veteran. Jeweler. Died Oct. 4, 1889.

BROADBENT, JOSEPH (son of John Broadbent, born June 21, 1816, and Betty Lees, born May 28, 1817, both of Oldham, Lancashire, Eng.). He was born Aug. 26, 1836, at Oldham. Came to Utah Sept. 4, 1859, George Rowley handcart company.
Married Sarah Dixon (daughter of Semuel Dixon and Hannah Perseful), who was born Sept. 8, 1832. Their children: Joseph Samuel b. Nov. 3, 1863, m. Amanda Tweedie; John James and Edward William b. Jan. 25, 1877, m. Ellen Condor. Family home Lehi, Utah.
Married Elizabeth Greenwood Jan 26, 1889, Logan, Utah (daughter of James Greenwood and Hannah Turner), who was born Oct. 25, 1863, Lancashire, Eng.
Married Sarah Lee April 8, 1897, Salt Lake City (daughter of George Lee and Sarah Peaker, of Sheffield, Eng., pioneers Sept. 16, 1859, Edward Stevenson company). She was born Dec. 25, 1852, in England and came to Utah with her parents.
Settled at Lehi, and served as choir leader and Sunday school teacher for 35 years; member missionaries aid committee nine years. Black Hawk Indian war veteran. Farmer and merchant.

BROADBENT, JOSEPH SAMUEL (son of Joseph Broadbent and Sarah Dixon). Born Nov. 3, 1863, Lehi, Utah.
Married Amanda Tweedie at Logan, Utah (daughter of Christian Frederick Tweedie and Cristena Peterson, pioneers 1857, handcart company). She was born March 11, 1862, American Fork, Utah. Their children: Joseph Leslie b. June 3, 1891; Sylvester Daniel b. June 7, 1893; Hugh William b. Feb. 17, 1899; Nevin Edward b. March 26, 1901.
Married Annie Shaw Jan. 10, 1906 (daughter of Hugh Shaw and Mary Dixon). She was born May 2, 1884. Only child: Harold b. Oct. 28, 1906.
Missionary to England, 1896-98; Sunday school superintendent. Member city council Lehi. Farmer and merchant.

BROADBENT, LEVI (son of John Broadbent and Sarah Colley of Kexly, Lincolnshire, Eng.). Born July 24, 1817. Came to Utah Sept. 6, 1852, Captain Outhouse company.
Married Eliza Code June 15, 1848, at Lincoln, Eng. (daughter of William Code and Mary Revill of Hackthorn, Lincolnshire, Eng.). She was born Oct. 14, 1830. Their children: Louiza, Levi and Charles all died infants. Family home Salt Lake City.
Elder; block teacher. Gardener. Died Dec. 3, 1897.

BROADBENT, THOMAS (son of James Wrigley and Nannie Broadbent of Oldham, Eng., taking his mother's name). Born Dec. 29, 1833, Saddleworth, Yorkshire, Eng. Came to Utah September, 1862.
Married Elizabeth Gleadhill at Oldham (daughter of James Gleadhill and Molly Buckley of Oldham), who was born Jan. 31, 1836, Crompton, Lancashire, Eng. Their children: Lorenzo Daniel b. Dec. 21, 1855, died; Lehi b. Oct. 17, 1856; James Thomas b. Oct. 17, 1858, m. Sarah Allis Jarvis; Alexander George b. Oct. 24, 1860, died; Francis William b. Dec. 23, 1861; Elizabeth Ann b. Aug. 23, 1863. Family resided Manti and Provo, Utah.
Married Mary Jane Nuttall April 11, 1863, Salt Lake City (daughter of Thomas Nuttall and Mary Standring of Rochdale, Eng.). She was born June 21, 1843, Rochdale, Eng. Their children: Mary Elizabeth b. Feb. 26, 1864, m. George Gourley; m. Halbert Davis; George Heber b. Dec. 14, 1865, died; Annie Eliza b. May 14, 1867, m. Lorenzo Huish; Joseph Franklin b. May 1, 1869, m. Retta Passey; David Albert b. May 14, 1871, m. Mima Melissa Murdock; Charles Nuttall b. June 1873, m. Jennie Wood; Geneva Lavina b. June 16, 1875, died; Sylvester b. April 3, 1878, m. Josephine Murdock; Serena b. Nov. 4, 1880, m. Hiram Vance; Leo Moroni b. May 7, 1883, died; Thomas Standring b. Aug. 5, 1885, m. Violet Long. Family home Provo, Utah.
Married Chana Ellen Spainhower Dec. 27, 1877, Salt Lake City (daughter of William and Margarette Spainhower of Stokes county, N. C.). She was born July 26, 1859. Their children: Nannie Ellen b. Oct. 27, 1878, m. James Shaw; Sarah Jane b. July 26, 1880, m. Bert Kingsbury; Nora Alice b. July 22, 1882, m. Benjamin Hart Bullock; John Thomas and William Henry b. July 17, 1885, both died; Margaret Ann b. July 17, 1885, died; Bertha Felicia b. Sept. 19, 1887; Rebecca Melita b. Sept. 12, 1889, died; Chana Elizabeth b. Sept. 21, 1891; Minnie Amelia b. Feb. 17, 1893, died; Florence Adelia b. Nov. 9, 1894; Arthur Marion b. March 4, 1897; Eva Eudora b. March 30, 1899; Marlin Nield b. June 18, 1902. Family home Elsinore, Utah.
High priest; Sunday school superintendent; chorister. Black Hawk Indian war veteran. Farmer and stockraiser. Died Dec. 14, 1901, Santaquin, Utah.

BROADBENT, DAVID ALBERT (son of Thomas Broadbent and Mary Jane Nuttall). Born May 14, 1871, Goshen, Utah.
Married Mima Melissa Murdock May 1, 1901, Manti, Utah (daughter of Joseph R. Murdock and Margarette Wright of Charleston, Utah). She was born Nov. 26, 1879. Their children: Joseph Grant b. May 28, 1902; Vida b. Dec. 21, 1903; Naomi b. Feb. 15, 1906; Leah b. April 1, 1908; Margarette b. Sept. 1, 1909; Dee Albert b. July 9, 1911; Mary b. March 8, 1913. Family home Heber, Utah.
High priest; counselor to Bishop Rasband 7 years; stake superintendent of religion classes; organized first Sunday school in Louisiana. County superintendent public schools; principal Heber schools 6 years.

BROADHEAD, WILLIAM. Born June 28, 1806. Came to Utah Sept. 12, 1853, Daniel A. Miller company.
Married Sarah Golden in England, who was born June 20, 1800. Their children: John, d. infant; John, died; David, m. Harriet Betts; Elizabeth, m. John Denton; William, died; Robert, m. Alice Clegg; Thomas, died; Jabez, m. Eunice Baxter.

BROADHEAD, DAVID (son of William Broadhead and Sarah Golden). Born Oct. 2, 1829, Coventry, Warwickshire, Eng. Came to Utah Oct. 14, 1855, Milo Andrus company.
Married Harriet Betts, Jan. 29, 1850, Coventry (daughter of Joseph Betts and Elizabeth Bennett of Coventry), who was born Feb. 19, 1831, Foleshill, Warwickshire. Their children: Amelia b. 1850, died; Harriet b. Nov. 16, 1853, m. Walter Scott; Julia b. June 9, 1855, m. George B. Hobbs; David B. b. Feb. 17, 1857, m. Melvina Peters; William Golden b. Feb. 8, 1859, m. Louisa Jones; Joseph b. Jan. 31, 1861, m. Ellen Christian Norton; Elijah b. Jan. 29, 1864, d. May 1885; Thomas b. April 4, 1866, m. Mary Broadhead; Rose b. March 30, 1868, m. Oscar Booth; m. D. Parley Austin; Sarah b. June 12, 1870, m. Alfred A. McCune; Hyrum b. March 3, 1873, m. Polly Jennings; Samuel Daken b. April 19, 1876, m. Alice Ann Carter. Family home Nephi, Utah.
One of the presidents 49th quorum seventies; patriarch; high counselor; home missionary. Ribbon weaver; farmer.

BROADHEAD, ROBERT (son of William Broadhead and Sarah Golden). Born June 3, 1836, at Coventry. Came to Utah Sept. 12, 1853.
Married Alice Clegg Jan. 15, 1861, Heber City, Utah (daughter of Jonathan Clegg and Ellen Wolmsley of Lancashire, Eng., pioneers Dec. 18, 1856, Edward Martin handcart company). She was born Oct. 23, 1846. Their children: Sarah, m. James McDonald; Robert, died; Ellen, m. Joshua Sweat; Elizabeth, m. Lewis Sweat; Margaret, m. David M. Ivie; William, m. Edith Murald; m. Susie Carroll; m. Amelia Anderson; Jonathan, d. infant; Elmer, m. Elizabeth McAffie; Mary, m. Thomas Broadhead; Rozilla, m. Joseph

Horricks; Thomas, m. Barbara Ann McAffie; Susie, m. Erick Gabrielson; Jabez, d. infant. Family home Heber City, Utah.
High priest. Pioneer to Heber City, where he has helped to build canals and wagon roads. Farmer.

BROCKBANK, ISAAC (son of Daniel Brockbank and Agnes Morris of Cocks Bank, Preston Patrick, Westmoreland, Eng.). Born May 17, 1805, Underbarrow, Westmoreland, Eng. Came to Utah Sept. 4, 1852, Abraham O. Smoot company.
Married Elizabeth Mainwaring, 1835, Liverpool, Eng. (daughter of Peter Mainwaring and Jane —— of Liverpool, Eng.). She was born in 1812. Their children: Isaac b. July 13, 1837, m. Katherine A. Howard; Elizabeth b. Nov. 8, 1838, m. John Bushnell; Joshua b. May 15, 1848, m. Sarah Ann Jex; Agnes b. 1851, m. Albert K. Thurber; Samuel b. Sept. 15, 1853, m. Mary J. Thomas; Joseph b. Sept. 15, 1859, m. Emma J. McKell; Martha Ann b. Sept. 5, 1861 (d. Jan. 5, 1906), m. Joseph H. Hales, Nov. 16, 1882. Family home Spanish Fork, Utah.
Counselor in bishopric Spanish Fork 1854-55. Died 1878.

BROCKBANK, ISAAC, JR. (son of Isaac Brockbank and Elizabeth Mainwaring). Born July 13, 1837, Liverpool, Eng. Came to Utah with father.
Married Katherine A. Howard June 25, 1860, Salt Lake City (daughter of William Howard and Elizabeth Anderson, of Big Cottonwood, Utah, pioneers 1853, John Hindley company). She was born April 25, 1843. Their children: Daniel E., m. Lutie Young; Elizabeth B., m. Harry G. Meyer; Lucas Thurber, m. Myrtle Mitchener; Katherine, m. Frederick E. Arnold; Lockhart, m. Nina Atwood; Albert; George M., m. Jennie B. Reid. Family home Salt Lake City.
Married Mary Ann Park Jan. 7, 1865, Salt Lake City (daughter of John Park and Louisa Smith of Provo, Utah, pioneers Oct. 10, 1847, John Taylor company). She was born July 17, 1843, in Upper Canada and came to Utah with parents. Their children: John P. b. April 3, 1867, m. Emmen S. Truman; Louisa P. b. June 28, 1869, m. Charles Reynolds; Heber P. b. Nov. 19, 1871, m. Elizabeth Brasher; Mary P. b. March 9, 1873, m. John A. North; Jane P. b. Dec. 12, 1874, d. aged 9; James W. P. b. Dec. 12, 1874, m. Sarah Andrus; Joseph P. b. Dec. 27, 1876, m. Willard Jeral; Taylor P. b. Jan. 31, 1879, m. Sarah LeCheminant; Agnes P. b. Aug. 4, 1881, m. Levi Fuller; Margaret E. P. b. May 10, 1883, d. aged 6; Alma P. b. Feb. 10, 1885. Family home Big Cottonwood, Salt Lake county.
Counselor to bishop eighth ward, Salt Lake City 1871-1890; high priest; associated with presiding bishopric 1871-1887. Salt Lake City councilman 1880-82. Railroad contractor.

BROCKBANK, HEBER P. (son of Isaac Brockbank and Mary Ann Park). Born Nov. 19, 1871.
Married Elizabeth Brasher (daughter of John and Elizabeth Brasher). Their children: Perdita, b. April 1, 1899; Ivy, b. Jan. 22, 1901; Eva, b. Feb. 13, 1906; Della b. Nov. 6, 1910. Family home Huntinton, Emery county, Utah.
Missionary to central states. Farmer and stockman.

BROCKBANK, ALMA P. (son of Isaac Brockbank and Mary Ann Park). Born Feb. 10, 1885, Cottonwood ward.
Elder; block teacher. Farmer; stockraiser; gardener.

BRODERICK, THOMAS BEGSHAW (son of John and Mary Broderick of London, Eng.). Born Dec. 24, 1824. Came to Utah 1855.
Married Elizabeth Hilyard May 5, 1854, Beth Summit. Eng. (daughter of Andrew and Mary Hilyard of Ditchet, Eng.), who was born March 16, 1834, Ditchet, Eng., died May 1, 1871, Salt Lake City. Their children: Thomas, killed in snowslide; Alfred Joseph b. Dec. 21, 1859, m. Margaret Alice Alston, m. Annie Caroline Anderson, m. Hertha Natalie Olsen; John b. Jan. 2, 1862, m. Augusta C. Anderson Jan. 8, 1892; Charles Heber b. Sept. 1864 (d. 1900), m. Clara L. Anderson. Family home Salt Lake City.
Elder. Shoemaker and merchant. Died Sept. 14, 1864.

BRODERICK, ALFRED JOSEPH (son of Thomas Begshaw Broderick and Elizabeth Hilyard). Born Dec. 21, 1859, Salt Lake City.
Married Margaret Alice Alston Dec. 31, 1880, Mayfield, Utah (daughter of Joseph Alston and Margaret Hall of American Fork, Utah, oxteam pioneers. She was born April 16, 1863, and died Jan. 30, 1888. Their children: Jennie Elizabeth b. Oct. 7, 1881, m. Edwin Larson; Alice Leona b. Nov. 4, 1883, d. infant; Alfred Leonard b. Feb. 27, 1886, m. Virgie Searl; Margaret Adelia b. Jan. 22, 1888, d. infant. Family home Mayfield, Utah.
Married Annie Caroline Anderson Nov. 8, 1888, Manti, Utah (daughter of August Anderson, who did not come to Utah and Martina Anderson of Mayfield). She was born July 28, 1870, and died Jan. 4, 1906. Their children: Thomas Alma b. Aug. 11, 1889; Crystal Adelia b. March 19, 1892, m. Alma Jorgensen; Alfred Milton b. Jan. 8, 1894; Wilford W. b. July 16, 1895; Flossie Irene b. May 26, 1898; Lorenzo b. Feb. 21, 1900; Joseph Alston b. Dec. 25, 1901; Anna Bell b. Nov. 1, 1903, d. infant. Family home Emery, Utah.
Married Hertha Natalie Olsen March 31, 1909, Manti, Utah (daughter of Mads Olsen and Gustava Larson of Nygaard, Bon St. Norge, Eidsvold, Norway). She was born Aug. 15, 1885. Their children: Iola Christina b. March 23, 1910; Reuben Arnold b. Oct. 24, 1912. Family home, Emery, Utah.

President 149th and member 91st quorum seventies; high priest; missionary to northern states March 15, 1895, returning May 17, 1897; since Aug. 6, 1910, high councilor Emery stake. Public school trustee; Emery city councilman. President Emery Canal and Reservoir company eight years; manager Emery Farmers' Co-op. Merchant; farmer; apiarist.

BROMLEY, WILLIAM (son of William Bromley and Mary Wells of Dowesby, Lincolnshire, Eng.). Born Sept. 21, 1819, at Dowesby. Came to Utah Sept. 5, 1866, Samuel D. White company.
Married Sarah Bullimore Dec. 21, 1847, at Dowesby (daughter of Joseph Bullimore and Ann Harrison of Gonerby Moor, Lincolnshire, Eng.). She was born Oct. 6, 1816, at Gonerby Moor. Their children: Celestia C., m. Edward Buys March 23, 1867; Joseph W., m. Annie Rasmussen; Melissa Amanda, d. Feb. 5, 1873; Benjamin Jesse, m. Amy Wing 1882. Family home Buysville, Wasatch county, Utah. Missionary to England 1881-83, and to Australia 1888-91; high priest. Farmer. Died Feb. 14, 1908, Heber City, Utah.

BROMLEY, WILLIAM MICHAEL. Born Oct. 13, 1839, Worcestershire, Eng. Came to Utah Nov. 1853, Joseph Reynolds company.
Married Elizabeth Roylance Nov. 10, 1858, Springville, Utah (daughter of John Roylance of Springville), who was born in 1842. Their children: William R.; John R.; Franki; Mary; Elizabeth; Sylvia; Willis; Luella; Archie; Flora. Family resided Springville and American Fork, Utah.
Married Rosena Singleton July 19, 1870, Salt Lake City (daughter of Francis Singleton and Amelia Ann Williams of Portsmouth, Eng., pioneers Nov. 2, 1864, Warren Snow company). She was born April 17, 1852. Their children: Amelia S.; Julia; Mary; Phoebe; Cora Melinda; Jane A.; Louei William F.; Alice.
Married Caroline Whiting 1879, Salt Lake City (daughter of Edward and Elizabeth Whiting of Springville). She was born 1853. Their children: Elizabeth; William.
Married Beulah Chipman March 1885, American Fork, Utah (daughter of Washburn and Margaret Chipman of American Fork). She was born 1862. Their children: Leah; Edna; Washburn.
Missionary to England 1872-73; missionary to New Zealand, and introduced the Gospel to the Maoris 1881-84; bishops' counselor Springville; bishop of American Fork 1884; president high priests' quorum Alpine stake. Marshal and justice of the peace. Colonel in Nauvoo Legion. Bookkeeper. Died April 14, 1911, American Fork, Utah.

BRONSON, WILMER WHARTEN (son of Leman Bronson and Lucy Bras). Born Oct. 20, 1830, in Michigan. Came to Utah 1848.
Married Olivia Andrus, who was born Sept. 27, 1833. Their children: Martha, m. T. B. Hammond; Calista b. Nov. 22, 1859, m. Walter J. Lindsay; Adelaide b. Feb. 7, 1863.
Married Elizabeth Fisher. Their children: Mary, m. George Langlois; Elizabeth b. March 10, 1870, m. Peter M. Jensen; Mary; Leman; Lushen, m. Ruth Taylor; Rosabell, m. Frank Randall; Maud, m. Hyrum Carver.

BROOKS, CHARLES P. (son of Charles Edward Brooks and Adeline Cannon). Born Aug. 21, 1851, Washingtonville, Orange county, N. Y. Came to Utah March 4, 1874.
Married Mellicent A. Godbe Sept. 28, 1876, Salt Lake City (daughter of William Samuel Godbe and Mary Hampton of Salt Lake City, pioneers July 5, 1851, independent company). She died Sept. 27, 1889. Their children: Clara Godbe b. Dec. 6, 1879, m. H. J. Pitts; Miriam b. April 24, 1885; Marjorie b. Sept. 27, 1888, m. Levi J. Riter.
Married Miriam Godbe Dec. 15, 1891 (sister of first wife). No children. Family home Salt Lake City.
County surveyor 1891-92; member board of health 1890-93, and member board of public works 1905-12; special engineer for planning and constructing sewer systems of Salt Lake City. Mining and civil engineer.

BROOKS, GEORGE FINLEY (son of Thomas Philip Brooks and Elizabeth Harper of Ipswich, Eng.). Born Nov. 4, 1833, at Harwich, Essex, Eng. Came to Utah Nov. 30, 1856, Edward Martin handcart company.
Married Hannah Charlotte Bowthorpe Feb. 12, 1858, at Cottonwood, Utah (daughter of William Bowthorpe and Mary Ann Tuttle of Norwich, Norfolk, Eng., pioneers Oct. 3, 1853, Kendall and Wheelock company). She was born Nov. 5, 1840. Their children: George Thomas b. Dec. 18, 1858, d. Jan. 18, 1859; Julia Lucretia b. June 1, 1860, m. Andrew Busby; Daniel Hanmer b. Aug. 21, 1862, d. Feb. 19, 1884; Finly George b. Oct. 24, 1864, m. Annie R. Rumel; Hannah Charlotte b. July 5, 1867; Edmund William b. March 8, 1870, d. Sept. 11, 1871; David Francis b. July 5, 1872, d. Dec. 5, 1876; Major Chandler b. Jan. 2, 1875, d. March 7, 1875; Frederick Bowthorpe b. Feb. 6, 1876, m. Barbara Gurstner; Austin Bowthorpe b. Feb. 2, 1878, m. Charlotte Kellin; Henry Bowthorpe b. July 20, 1880, m. Ada Yard. Family home Salt Lake City, Utah.
One of the presidents of the 8th quorum seventies; high priest; patriarch; member high council; Sunday school teacher; member Nauvoo Legion. Grocer. Died Oct. 27, 1911.

BROOM, JOHN (son of John and Frances Broom of Bristol, Eng.). Born March 22, 1823, Sheffield, Yorkshire, Eng. Came to Utah October, 1851, Alfred Cardon company.
Married Elizabeth Heywood 1845, at Sheffield. Eng., who died 1849 at St. Louis, Mo. Their children: Elizabeth, m. Peter Mellon; Annie, m. Hans Madson.
Married Hester Dunsdon 1850, St. Louis, Mo., who came to Utah with husband. Their children: Sarah Jane, m. George Francis Brown; Emily, d. infant; twins, died.
Member 38th quorum seventies; withdrew from L. D. S. church 1872. Settled at Ogden 1851. Located and named Broom's Bench 1855; built Broom Hotel 1882. Capitalist. Died at Ogden.

BROUGH, GEORGE (son of William Brough and Alice Sokel of New Molton, Yorkshire, Eng.). Born July 1, 1823, at New Molton. Came to Utah Sept. 22, 1852, Joseph Outhouse company.
Married Elizabeth Hudson March 17, 1852 (daughter of Gilbert and Rebecca Hudson), who was born Aug. 29, 1821, and came to Utah with husband. Their children: George W. b. Feb. 8, 1854, m. Jane E. Crawforth Jan. 5, 1874; Moroni b. March 12, 1856, m. Mary Crawforth Nov. 14, 1878; Robert A. b. July 24, 1859, m. Caroline Buhanin Nov. 26, 1885; Elizabeth Ann b. July 18, 1861, m. James A. Allred Nov. 14, 1878. Family home Spring City, Utah.
Married Elizabeth Mace Sept. 12, 1888, Manti, Utah (daughter of George Mace and Elizabeth Frost). She was born April 13, 1824, Stockport, near Manchester, Eng.
Missionary to England 1882; tithing clerk 1863-81. Postmaster 1865-83.

BROUGH, GEORGE W., (son of George Brough and Elizabeth Hudson). Born Feb. 8, 1854, Lehi, Utah.
Married Jane Elizabeth Crawforth Jan. 5, 1874, Salt Lake City (daughter of Charles Crawforth and Martha Moore), who was born June 17, 1855, Mormon Grove, Mo. Their children: Rozina A. b. Jan. 17, 1876, m. Joseph W. Majors Dec. 19, 1894; George A. b. Oct. 3, 1878, m. Edith Anderson Oct. 11, 1899; Raymond G. b. April 30, 1881, m. Edna Allred Jan. 11, 1905; Charles William b. Dec. 2, 1883, m. Ella Woodruff May 16, 1907; Owen L. b. Feb. 22, 1886; Eve D. b. Nov. 29, 1888, m. Amos P. Hansen Nov. 24, 1909; Vera b. June 8, 1893; Oral b. Jan. 12, 1906, died. Family home Spring City, Utah.
City councilman six years. Secretary elders' quorum.

BROWN, ABIA WILLIAM (son of Abia William Brown, born Oct. 18, 1799, Mount Holly, N. J., and Abby Cadwalider, born Jan. 31, 1797, Jefferson county, Ohio). He was born May 5, 1840, Harrisonville, Harrison county, Ohio. Came to Utah Sept. 27, 1861, Sextus F. Johnson company.
Married Emma Susan Sibley Nov. 29, 1869 (daughter of Thomas Henry Sibley and Mary Susan Bowman), who was born May 10, 1851. Their children: Frank Scott b. Sept. 20, 1870, m. Sarah Ella Church; Eva Ann, m. James H. Hartt Oct. 31, 1892; Abia William Lee b. Feb. 24, 1874, m. Rebecca N. Judd May 22, 1896; Abby Emma b. Oct. 31, 1876; Mary Cadwalider b. Oct. 10, 1877, m. William Potter; Thomas Reese b. Jan. 18, 1880; Rex Roland b. March 24, 1882, m. Arletta Esplin Dec. 8, 1910; Lily Lenore b. Feb. 16, 1884, m. Asa W., 1908; Macy b. June 30, 1888, m. Hyram C. Robinson; Verne Orr b. May 3, 1889; Abby b. July 7, 1891; Elice b. Nov. 29, 1891; Marjorie b. Jan. 28, 1894; Jessiel b. May 17, 1896; Benjamin Levi b. July 2, 1897. Family resided Fredonia, Ariz., since 1884.
Married Lucinda A. Stewart Aug. 23, 1882, St. George, Utah (daughter of Levi Stewart and Margery Wilkinson), who was born Jan. 8, 1864, Salt Lake City.
Missionary to England, and presided over Bristol conference 1867-69; president 65th quorum seventies; first counselor to Bishop Thomas P. Jensen; high priest. School teacher. Located present site of Fredonia, Ariz.

BROWN, ALBERT (son of James and Mary Brown of Windsor, Hartford Co., Conn.). Born November, 1807. Came to Utah Sept. 2, 1863, Captain Patterson company.
Married Sarah Campbell 1839, Kirtland, Ohio, who was born in 1820. Their children: Robert, d. infant; Don Carlos; Samuel James, m. Elizabeth E. Solomon; Emma Sarah, m. Alfred Solomon; Francis M., m. Ellen Wanless; Albert; Ellen. Family home, Salt Lake City.
Seventy; high priest; missionary to eastern states two years; patriarch; member "Zion's Camp"; doorkeeper of Nauvoo temple at dedication; member Nauvoo Legion. Carpenter. Died January, 1891, East Mill Creek, Utah.

BROWN, SAMUEL JAMES (son of Albert Brown and Sarah Campbell). Born Feb. 16, 1846, Nauvoo, Ill. Came to Utah Sept. 2, 1863, with father.
Married Elizabeth E. Solomon Jan. 11, 1868, Salt Lake Endowment House, Wilford Woodruff officiating (daughter of William H. Solomon and Elizabeth Drew of Truro, Cornwall, Eng., pioneers Oct. 1860, Captain Murdock company). She was born May 7, 1852. Their children: Samuel J. b. Oct. 23, 1868, d. infant; Albert b. Feb. 18, 1870, m. Emily Willey; Samuel H. b. April 7, 1871, d. aged 9; Elizabeth E. b. Sept. 28, 1873, m. John A. Eardley; Ernest b. Nov. 25, 1874, m. Lucy Shaw; Mary L. b. Jan. 12, 1877, d. aged 4; Amanda D. b. Sept. 9, 1878, m. William T. Edwards;

Ammon S. b. July 16, 1880, m. Francis Barnes; Minnie B. b. Jan. 2, 1883, m. George J. Evans; Alma E. b. Aug. 24, 1884, m. Lucile Evans; Hilda M. b. Oct. 18, 1886; Stella M. b. Dec. 3, 1888; Leonard b. June 8, 1891; Larue b. Sept. 16, 1895.
High priest; second counselor to Bishop Brimley of 5th ward 10 years. Made two trips across the plains. School trustee. Carpenter; contractor and smelter builder.

BROWN, AUSTIN CRAVATH (son of Alfred Brown, born Jan. 17, 1806, Hartland, Niagara county, N. Y., and Eliza Doty, a direct descendant of Edward Doty, who came over on the "Mayflower" 1620. She was born April 29, 1808, in New York —; married in 1848). He was born April 30, 1850, near Council Bluffs, Iowa. Came to Utah Sept. 17, 1850, Jonathan Foote company.
Married Meriah C. Ballantyne, Feb. 2, 1874 (daughter of Richard Ballantyne and Huldah M. Clark, pioneers 1848). She was born June 25, 1856, Salt Lake City. Their children: Austin A.; Meriah, m. Thomas C. Chatland; Inez R.; Eliza; Richard; Helen; Annabel, m. Elbert F. Wilson; Laura Delecta, m. Zachariah Evans; Austin Joseph, m. May Shriver; Leona Ballantyne; Mary Vilate, m. Claud R. Clark; Horace Ballantyne; Zina Ballantyne. Family home Ogden, Utah.
Married Mary Fairbanks, May 8, 1886, Salt Lake City (daughter of John B. Fairbanks and Sarah Van Wagoner, pioneers of 1847). She was born Feb. 18, 1858, Payson, Utah. Only child: Eva May. Family home Payson, Utah.

BROWN, BARTLETT (son of Timothy Brown and Meredith Ward of Westmoreland, N. H., who later were the first settlers of Waterville, Vt., in 1797). Born Nov. 4, 1798, at Waterville. Came to Utah 1849 on way to California, located with family 1854.
Married Joanna Austin Leach (daughter of William B. Leach and Susanna Stevens of Waterville, pioneers Aug. 4, 1854, Bartlett Brown company). She was born Nov. 11, 1812, at Waterville, Vt., and died Feb. 24, 1880, Centerville, Utah. Their children: Amanda, m. Oscar Tyler; Newel Abraham, m. Martha Jane Thomas, m. Sarah P. Thomas, m. Annie Swingewood, m. Rosanah Robinson (Mitchell); Byron Wellman, m. Sarah Stoddard, m. Josephine Clark; Austin Milton, m. Fannie Stephenson; Orin Clinton, m. Mary Thomas; Helen Jeanet, m. Newton Adair; Leveret Wesley, m. Rachel Nagley. High priest. Worked on St. George temple. Farmer. Died 1891, Lehi, Utah.

BROWN, (ABRAM) ABRAHAM (son of Abram Brown, the miller, and Atta Austin, both of Londonderry, Vt.). Born Aug. 31, 1808, Andover, Winsor county, Vt. Came to Utah Oct. 1, 1852, Isaac Bullock company.
Married Harriet Sheldon March 26, 1834, Simmonsville, Vt.) daughter of William Sheldon of Andover, Vt, and Hannah Barker of Langsgrove, N. H.; they died at Kirtland, Ohio, and Rock Island, Ill., respectively). She was born in 1805. Their children: Amanda, m. Oscar Tyler; Newel Abraham, m. Martha Jane Thomas, m. Sarah P. Thomas, m. Annie Swingewood, m. Rosanah Robinson (Mitchell); Byron Wellman, m. Sarah Stoddard, m. Josephine Clark; Austin Milton, m. Fannie Stephenson; Orin Clinton, m. Mary Thomas; Helen Jeanet, m. Newton Adair; Leveret Wesley, m. Rachel Nagley. High priest. Worked on St. George temple. Farmer. Died 1891, Lehi, Utah.

BROWN, NEWEL ABRAHAM (son of Abraham (Abram) Brown and Harriet Sheldon). Born Nov. 19, 1837, Kirtland, Ohio. Came to Utah Oct. 1, 1852, Isaac Bullock company.
Married Martha Jane Thomas Nov. 19, 1862, Lehi, Utah (daughter of Daniel S. Thomas and Martha Jones of Tennessee, pioneers 1849, Capt. Allred company). She was born Jan. 1, 1844, in Hancock county, Ill. (deceased). Their children: Newel Thomas b. Sept. 20, 1863, died; Harriet Martha b. June 11, —, m. George E. Davis; Mary Louisa b. Oct. 13, 1868, m. David Roberts; Celestia b. April 6, 1871, m. Charles Turner, m. Chase Featherstone; John Leveret b. June 24, 1873; Leonora b. June 28, 1874; Agnes b. Nov. 1, 1876; Viola Emeret b. March 27, 1882, died; Virginia, m. J e Keats; Margaret Emma, died. Family home Lehi, Utah.
Married Sarah P. Thomas (daughter of Daniel S. Thomas and Martha P. Jones), who was born 1847, and is now dead. Only child: Sarah Emma.
Married Annie Swingewood May 16, 1906, Salt Lake City (daughter of Thomas Swingewood of Clay Cross, Derbyshire, Eng.). She was born March 4, 1860, and came to Utah May 8, 1902, (deceased). Their children: Timothy Albert b. March 4, 1907; Myra b. Aug. 13, 1908. Family home Lehi, Utah.
Married Rosanah Robinson (Mitchell) Jan. 31, 1912, Salt Lake City (daughter of James Stephenson Robinson and Martha Elizabeth Anderson of Pittsburg, Kan.)
Missionary to England 1891; high priest. Settled at Lehi, 1852. Assisted in bringing immigrants to Utah. Veteran Black Hawk Indian war. Freighter, cattleman and merchant.

BROWN, AUSTIN MILTON (son of Abram Brown and Harriett Shelden). Born Aug. 5, 1841, Kirtland, Ohio. Came to Utah September, 1852, Isaac Bullock company.
Married Fanny Stevenson Oct. 28, 1865, Salt Lake City (daughter of John Stevenson and Mary Vickers of Preston,

Lancashire, Eng., pioneers 1862, Joseph Horne company). She was born Sept. 1, 1848. Their children: John M. b. Oct. 25, 1866, m. Annie E. Taylor; Fanny E. b. Oct. 23, 1871, d. infant; Irene E. b. April 5, 1874, m. James G. Smith; Mary E. b. March 15, 1882, m. William E. Sheriff; Mable V. b. April 15, 1884, m. James B. Cowen; Austin Ira b. Dec. 27, 1887, m. Ruby Fowler. Family home, Salt Lake City.
Treasurer and assistant Sunday school superintendent of Pleasant Green ward; missionary to West Virginia 1896; high priest; block teacher. Constable at Pleasant Green. Crossed the plains nine times. Farmer and stockraiser.

BROWN, BENJAMIN (son of Asa Brown). Born Sept. 30, 1794, Queensbury, N. Y. Came to Utah Sept. 20, 1848, Brigham Young company.
Married Sarah Mumford Sept. 12, 1819 (daughter of Henry Mumford and Sarah Thompson), who was born April 20, 1795. Their children: Lorenzo b. Feb. 2, 1823, m. Frances Crosby, March 24, 1844; Homer b. Aug. 9, 1830, m. Sarah A. Wolf, Oct. 20, 1852. Family home Salt Lake City.
Bishop 4th ward Salt Lake City; missionary to eastern states and to Great Britain.

BROWN, LORENZO (son of Benjamin Brown and Sarah Mumford). Born Feb. 2, 1823, Chautauqua, N. Y.
Married Frances Crosby March 24, 1844, Nauvoo, Ill. (daughter of Joshua Crosby and Hannah Cann, pioneers Sept. 10, 1851). She was born Oct. 21, 1817, in Nova Scotia. Their children: Benjamin b. March 22, 1845; m. Jane Goheen, 1865; Edward Mumford b. Jan. 1, 1849, m. Ella J. Dodge, Oct. 14, 1869; Sarah Hannah b. Aug. 18, 1851, m. George H. Crosby, April 4, 1868; Lorenzo John b. May 20, 1854, m. Nina M. Young, 1872. Family home Salt Lake City.

BROWN, BENJAMIN (son of Lorenzo Brown and Frances Crosby). Born March 22, 1845, Nauvoo, Ill.
Married Jane Goheen 1865. Their children: Jane; Frances; Marian; Eliza; Hannah; Ella; Emma Belle; Benjamin; Cordelia. Family home Pine Valley, Utah.
Member high council St. John's stake; bishop of Nutrioso ward, Arizona. Indian war veteran.

BROWN, EDWARD MUMFORD (son of Lorenzo Brown and Frances Crosby). Born Jan. 1, 1849, Salt Lake City.
Married Ella J. Dodge, Oct. 20, 1869 (daughter of Walter E. Dodge), who died Jan. 21, 1899.
Married Jane E. Lund May 21, 1901 (daughter of Robert C. Lund.)
Mayor St. George two terms; chairman board of commissioners Washington county two terms; first president Washington county Commercial club; member city council, St. George. Indian war veteran.

BROWN, EBENEZER. Born Dec. 6, 1802, and came to Utah July 29, 1847, with part of Mormon Battalion (second sergeant, Co. A).
Married Ann Weaver July 20, 1823, who was born Aug. 5, 1805. Their children: Joseph Guernsey b. Nov. 8, 1824, m. Harriet M. Young Dec. 31, 1851; Harriet b. Feb. 6, 1827, m. Albert Stratton; Norman b. Nov. 6, 1830, m. Annie Smith; John W. b. June 17, 1837, m. Fanny Draper. Family home Draper, Utah.
Married Samantha Pulsipher.

BROWN, JOSEPH GUERNSEY (son of Ebenezer Brown and Ann Weaver). Born Nov. 8, 1824, New York state.
Married Harriet M. Young Dec. 31, 1851, Salt Lake City (daughter of Lorenzo Dow Young, pioneer 1847 and Persis Goodall, pioneer Oct. 13, 1850, James Lake company). She was born July 21, 1834, Kirtland, Ohio. Their children: Homer Achilles b. Oct. 25, 1853; Persis Ann b. Dec. 23, 1855, m. Howard O. Spencer March 22, 1875; Joseph Guernsey, Jr., b. April 17, 1857, m. Clara Little Jan. 10, 1884; Lucy Elizabeth b. April 12, 1859, m. William D. Johnson Jr. March 27, 1877; Angeline b. Jan. 6, 1861, m. W. J. F. McAllister Jan. 23, 1879; Lorenzo Young b. Sept. 19, 1862, m. Elizabeth Haycock Jan. 27, 1885; Ebenezer b. Oct. 10, 1864, m. Clara Little Oct. 17, 1888; Juliatte L. b. Feb. 13, 1869; Feramorz Little b. Feb. 25, 1872; Jennie b. June 9, 1876, m. Lyman E. Stewart Sept. 22, 1896; Williamia b. Dec. 15, 1877.
Married Esther Brown Jan. 18, 1857, Salt Lake City, who was born Nov. 1, 1834, Isle of Man. Their children: Martha Selina b. Dec. 18, 1857; Celestia Ann b. Dec. 3, 1859, m. Joseph L. Smith; Esther E. b. Sept. 16, 1861; Isaac O. b. Sept. 21, 1863, m. Nellie Robinson; Rosannah E. b. Aug. 28, 1865, m. Francis M. Hamblin; Ella More b. Oct. 25, 1868; James Arthur b. June 18, 1871, m. Emily Pugh; Harriet L. b. Aug. 17, 1874, m. R. S. McAllister.
Married Lovina Manhart March 22, 1857, Salt Lake City (daughter of William Manhart, pioneer 1852, Orson Hyde company). She was born Jan. 14, 1838, Canada. Their children: John Franklin b. Oct. 11, 1858, m. Annie Elizabeth Fuller Aug. 22, 1878; Edward M. b. Feb. 10, 1861; Edwin b. July 17, 1862; Delia Jane b. July 25, 1868, m. Benj. Hamlin July 10, 1891; William M. b. April 13, 1870; Alvin Harris b. Jan. 5, 1873; Nellie M. b. July 27, 1875, m. David Robinson Dec. 2, 1893; David James b. Sept. 1, 1878, m. Barbara Mary Houseman Oct. 25, 1908. Families resided Draper and Kanab, Utah.
Pioneers to The Muddy; bishop's counselor, Kanab, Utah.

BROWN, JOHN FRANKLIN (son of Joseph Guernsey Brown and Lovina Manhart). Born Oct. 11, 1858, Draper, Utah.
Married Annie Elizabeth Fuller Aug. 22, 1878, St. George, Utah (daughter of Lucius Hubbard Fuller and Annie Lay), who was born May 26, 1860, Santa Clara, Cal. Their children Lucius Franklin b. Jan. 4, 1880, m. Rosena Kitchen Nov. 23, 1905; Annie Elizabeth b. Jan. 29, 1882; John Hyrum b. Sept. 30, 1884, m. Josephine Finley Sept. 1, 1911; Lovina b. Jan. 8, 1887, m. Erastus Nielson Sept. 1, 1909; Ivy b. March 28, 1889, m. Reese Rogers May 12, 1911; Stanley Horace b. Jan. 21, 1891; Sytha b. March 15, 1894; Harriet Maria b. Aug. 22, 1896; Joseph Guernsey b. April 12, 1899; Feramorz b. Nov. 17, 1902. Family home Kanab, Utah.
Prosecuting attorney of Kane county 8 years, and sheriff; mayor Kanab three terms; trustee two terms; road commissioner.

BROWN, GEORGE WASHINGTON (son of Nathaniel Brown and Avis Hill, of Newburg, Cuyahoga co., Ohio). Born Jan. 25, 1827, Newburg, Ohio: Came to Utah July 24, 1847, Brigham Young company.
Married Amy Elizabeth Hancock Dec. 1851, Salt Lake City (daughter of Levi W. and Clarissa Hancock of Ohio, pioneers July 28, 1847, escorted by Captain Brown's wing of Mormon Battalion). She was born May 14, 1836, and died July 28, 1862, Springville, Utah. Their children: George Washington b. Nov. 13, 1852, died; Isaac Nathaniel b. March 18, 1855, m. Eliza Rocksina Murdock; Brigham John b Sept. 7, 1859, m. Elizabeth Kelley; Sidney Hancock b. July 28, 1862, died. Family resided Salt Lake City and Springville, Utah.
Married Emma Barrows Aug. 16, 1858, Salt Lake City (daughter of Ethan and Lorena Barrows), who was born Oct. 14, 1843, Nauvoo, Ill., and died Dec. 8, 1897, Charleston, Utah. Only child: Ethan Leonard b. June 12, 1859, m. Sarah Elizabeth Hanks. Family home, Charleston, Utah.
High priest. Assisted in bringing immigrants to Utah. Indian war veteran. Helped to settle Springville, Kamas, Payson, Wallsburg, Center Creek and Charleston, Utah. Died Dec. 9, 1906.

BROWN, ISAAC NATHANIEL (son of George Washington Brown and Amy Elizabeth Hancock). Born March 18, 1855, Salt Lake City.
Married Eliza Rocksina Murdock Oct. 14, 1876, Salt Lake City (daughter of Joseph Stacy Murdock, of Hamilton, Madison county, N. Y., pioneer 1847, and Elizabeth Clark of England). She was born Oct. 30, 1857. Their children: Amy Elizabeth b. Nov. 10, 1877, m. Rudolph Korth; Eliza b. Nov. 18, 1879, and Isaac b. Sept. 18, 1881, died; Sarah b. Oct. 22, 1883, m. Francis Cummings; Joseph Stacy b. Aug. 22, 1885, m. Emily J. Gordon; Esther b. April 8, 1887, m. William E. Horner; Ella Maria b. June 16, 1889, m. William Murray; George Washington b. June 20, 1891, m. Mary D. Jones; Avis b. Dec. 8, 1892; John Alma b. Sept. 22, 1901. Family home Charleston, Utah.
Elder. Settled in Provo River Valley in 1860, where he has assisted in making canals and wagon roads and developing the country. Secretary of Sunday schools. Farmer and stockraiser.

BROWN, JAMES (son of James Brown and Polly [Mary] Williams of Roan county, N. C.). Born Sept. 30, 1801, in Roan county, N. C. Came to Utah in charge of invalided and discharged Mormon Battalion soldiers and Mississippi immigrants, arriving at Salt Lake City July 29, 1847, escorted into the city by the men of prominence, to the inspiring strains of martial music. He left Aug. 9 for California to collect his soldiers' pay, and brought back the first $10,000 in gold doubloons to the valley, which was the first money put in circulation by the colonists. This was but few months previous to the first discovery of gold in California by members of the Mormon Battalion.
Married Martha Stephens 1823, in Roan county (daughter of Alexander Stephens of same place), who was born (Oct. 12, 1806, and died April 30, 1840. Their children: John M. b. 1824, m. Ann Foutz; Alexander b. March 3, 1826, m. Amanda McCurtney; Jesse S. b. 1828, m. Caroline Stewart; Nancy b. 1830, m. Eleazer Davis; Daniel b. 1832; James M. b. Nov. 17, 1834, m. Adelaide Exervid; William b. Aug. 21, 1836, m. Mary Bybee; Benjamin F. b. May 9, 1838, m. Susan A. Wright; Moroni b. Sept. 25, 1840, m. Evaline C. Connover.
Married Susan Foutz, Esther Rapier, Sally Wood and Mary Black, who were the mothers of six boys and eleven girls, many of whom have risen to prominence.
Married Cecilia Robella in 1854, while immigration agent at St. Louis, Mo., who came to Utah with him Sept. 29, 1854. Their children: Charles David b. Jan. 23, 1856, m. Sarah Ellen Dixon June 26, 1879; James Frederick b. July 2, 1859, m. Ester Marriott 1884. Family home Ogden, Utah.
Justice of peace; member Ogden city council from 1855 continuously until his death. Member Utah legislature several terms. Founder of Ogden, as he purchased Miles Goodyear claim, a Mexican grant, comprising the land where Ogden, Weber county, now stands, in January, 1848, for $3000 and planted first crops in Weber valley with seed brought from California. Captain Company C, Mormon Battalion. One of the illustrious citizen pioneers of Utah history. Earliest missionary to the Southern states 1842; to British Guiana 1852 but returned unsuccessful to St. Louis, where he remained as immigration agent until 1854. First counselor to President Lorin Farr, and an intimate adviser to those high in authority. Died Sept. 30, 1863, from fatally crushing his arm in a molasses mill, dying from gangrene.

PIONEERS AND PROMINENT MEN OF UTAH

BROWN, JAMES M. (son of James Brown and Martha Stephens). Born Nov. 17, 1834, Brown county, Ill.
Married Adelaide Exervid July 24, 1855, Fort Supply, near Fort Bridger, Wyo. (daughter of Battice and Sally Exervid of Fort Laramie, Neb., pioneers 1847). She was born 1838, at Fort Laramie. Their children: James W. b. June 22, 1856; Moroni F. b. Sept. 23, 1857, m. Lizzie Weaver; Phoebe Adelaide b. May 14, 1859, m. John Shanbutt; Nephi b. Sept. 23, 1866, m. Jane Stephens; Francis A. b. Feb. 26, 1862, m. Emma Weber; Adelbert b. Feb. 27, 1864; Albert b. Nov. 17, 1865, m. Rachel Brown; Hubert b. Sept. 17, 1867; Lewis H. b. Nov. 10, 1869; Martha Z, b. June 7, 1872; Nancy V. b. Jan. 10, 1876. Family home Ogden, Utah.
Married Matilda Hornsby Oct. 8, 1902, Salt Lake City, who was born Nov. 26, 1865, in South Wales.
High councillor Weber stake; Indian missionary at Fort Supply 1857, and Malad Valley.

BROWN, CHARLES DAVID (son of James Brown and Cecilia Robella). Born Jan. 23, 1856, Ogden, Utah.
Married Sarah Ellen Dixon June 26, 1879, Salt Lake City (daughter of William W. Dixon and Sabra Lake, pioneers of 1850). She was born Oct. 1, 1861, Harrisville, Utah. Their children: Cecilia Etta b. May 2, 1880, m. Leroy E. Cowles Nov. 3, 1904; Sabra Alice b. May 21, 1882, m. Joseph E. Storey Feb. 1, 1905; Phebe Pearl b. Jan. 25, 1885, m. Herbert B. Foulger May 31, 1905; William Riley b. Nov. 5, 1888.

BROWN, JAMES POLLY (son of Robert Brown and Margaret Polly of Shelby county, Ky., and Floyd county, Ind.). Born April 22, 1803, in Shelby county, Ky. Came to Utah July 29, 1847, Nelson Higgins company and Captain James Brown's contingent of the Mormon Battalion.
Married Eunice Reesor (daughter of Frederick Reesor and Sarah Castor), who was born in March, 1809, and came to Utah with husband. Their children: William Ferguson, and Frederick both died; Newman b. July 18, 1832, m. Sarah Petty; m. Laura Ann Taylor; Robert m. Eunice Pectol; Sarah Jane b. Oct. 27, 1834, m. John Lowry Nov. 27, 1851; Mary Ann b. Oct. 2, 1841, m. Archie Buchanan; John b. April, 1847, died; Eunice Ann b. March, 1850, m. Peter Monk.
Member Mormon Battalion. Early settler to San Pete county and later moved to St. George. Died 1872, Rockville, Utah.

BROWN, JAMES STEPHENS (son of Daniel Brown and Elizabeth Stephens of Davidson county, N. C.). Born July 4, 1828, in Davidson county. Came to Utah Sept. 28, 1848, with part of Mormon Battalion (member Company D).
Married Lydia Jane Tanner July, 1853, Salt Lake City (daughter of Nathan Tanner and Rachel Winter Smith of Salt Lake county, pioneers Oct. 19, 1848, Amasa M. Lyman company). She was born Jan. 19, 1838, and came to Utah with parents. Their children: Lydia J., m. Homer M. Brown; Rachel E., m. Octavius Fullmer; Emmerette, m. Walter Brown; James T., m. Miriam Little; August and Valentine, d. infants; Zina May, m. John Gerstner.
Married Rebecca Ann McBride at Salt Lake City (daughter of William McBride and Elizabeth Ball Harris, of Salt Lake county, pioneers Sept. 29, 1848, Willard Richards company). She was born Aug. 28, 1838. Their children: Deseret, d. aged 4; Daniel, d. infant; Alvirette, m. Christopher Sproat; Vantile Mack, m. Caroline Christensen; Bertina, m. James Tregeagle; Pauline, m. Thomas Turner; Homer, m. Mattie Moffett; Alphonso, m. Harriette Powell.
Married Eliza Lester Jan. 31, 1863, Salt Lake City (daughter of Thomas Lester and Sarah Cooper of Calverton, Nottinghamshire, Eng.). She was born May 6, 1839. Their children: Leo L. d. infant; Zemania, m. Emma Wolf; Wilford, d. infant; Elando, m. Mary McIlveen; Annie E., m. Ernest E. Jacobs; Frank, m. Winifred Tibbs; Charles L., d. infant; Sarah Emma; Ada, m. Harold Egbert Grant.
Married Elizabeth M. Clegg March 4, 1872 (daughter of Benjamin Clegg and Grace McIntyre of Tooele, Utah). She was born Dec. 8, 1854. Their children: Lillious, d. aged 14; Guardelio, m. Bessie Parry; Mark C., m. Claire Cummings; Benjamin J., m. Alice Galloway; Louetta; Myrtle J., m. Henry W. Latimer. Families resided Salt Lake City.

BROWN, JOHN (son of John Brown and Martha Chapman of Sumner county, Tenn.). Born Oct. 23, 1820, in Tennessee. Came to Utah July 22, 1847, Brigham Young company, captain 13th ten, and with Orson Pratt, was the first of the expeditionary party to gaze on the valley of Great Salt Lake.
Married Elizabeth Crosby May 21, 1844, Nauvoo, Ill. (daughter of John Crosby and Elizabeth Colman of Monroe county, Miss., latter a pioneer Oct. 19, 1848, Amasa M. Lyman company). She was born Dec. 21, 1822. Their children: Samuel, John Crosby (b. 1848) and Amasa Lyman, first three, died; Martha Elizabeth, m. James Orson Bullock; Pauline Eliza; Sarah, m. Joseph S. Staker; Sytha, m. Wilson I. Snyder; William Crosby, m. Ada Johnson; James Lehi, m. Selena Charlotte Curtis; m. Ella Larson; Parilee, m. George S. Hayes. Family resided Salt Lake City, Lehi and Pleasant Grove, Utah.
Married Amy Snyder Feb. 22, 1854 (daughter of Samuel Snyder and Henrietta Maria Stockwell of Salt Lake City). She was born Feb. 24, 1834. Their children: Henrietta, died; Laura Jane, m. Ezra F. Walker; Robert, died; May Ann, m. Albert Delanna Clark; Robert Alexander, died; Minetta Permelia, m. James T. Thorne.
Married Margerett Zimmerman March 3, 1857, Salt Lake City (daughter of George Gotleib Zimmerman and Julia Ann Hoke of Pennsylvania), who was born March 25, 1836. Their children: Julia Ann, died; Harriett Rosan, m. Isaac J. Hayes; Joseph and Josephine, died; Lydia Christina, m. Louis Warren Lund; Margerett, m. William Lehi Hayes; Susan Elizabeth, m. Swen L. Swensen; Amy Cassandra, m. Richard R. Lyman; John Zimmerman, m. Alice Vivia Driggs; Lawrence Hoke, died. Families resided Pleasant Grove, Utah.
In the summer of 1846 he started for Utah in company with William Crosby and Robert Crow company, who later came to Utah with Capt. James Brown's detachment of the Mormon Battalion, with whom the party wintered in Pueblo, where they had expected to join the main body of the pioneers coming to Utah. He and seven others returned to Mississippi upon learning that President Young had not yet left Winter Quarters, and that the exodus from Nauvoo was not yet complete. In April, 1847, he joined Brigham Young's pioneer company bound for Utah, and was the chief hunter of the caravan. He was among the first to assist in the plowing, planting and preliminary irrigating in Salt Lake valley. He was said to have swung the first scythe on the native grasses of Utah that produced the first hay for the famished, travel-worn animals. He was among the first explorers of the several points of the valley which afterward became the sources of water supply, or strategic defense against the Indians. He was foremost in the Indian fight at Battle Creek Canyon December, 1848, and captain of Parley P. Pratt's company that explored southern Utah in the winter of 1849. Early in 1850 he formed the patrol that protected the settlers night and day against the constant incursions of hostile Indians. Later that year he was sent east as traveling agent for the Perpetual Emigration Fund, and spent two years at the different gathering points of Utah-bound immigration, outfitting the different trains for their journey across the plains. In 1852 he was elected to the territorial legislature and commissioned aide-de-camp in the general staff of the Nauvoo Legion with rank of colonel; in 1853 he was again superintendent of immigration with headquarters at New Orleans, transferring over 2,000 European immigrants to river steamboats, and landing at Keokuk, Iowa, where he outfitted them for their trip to Utah. President 8th quorum seventies, Salt Lake City, and president of the mass quorum of Lehi. Was a member of the settlement exploring expedition to Salmon River, Oregon, 1857. Returning he was elected justice of peace at Lehi, and member of legislature again in 1859. Missionary to England 1860, and, returning, was immigration agent at Florence, fitting out 15 companies of Utah immigrants. In 1863 he was elected selectman of Utah county, and was mayor of Pleasant Grove for 10 years afterward. This county was represented again by him in the legislature in 1874-83. Bishop of Pleasant Grove for 29 years; presided over the southern states mission after the civil war for two years and returned again to Omaha as immigration agent. During this time he crossed the plains 15 times by team. Ordained patriarch 1893. Died Nov. 4, 1896, at Pleasant Grove.

BROWN, JAMES LEHI (son of John Brown and Elizabeth Crosby). Born Nov. 26, 1860, Lehi, Utah.
Married Selena Curtis Sept. 13, 1883, Salt Lake City (daughter of George Curtis and Emma Whaley), who was born Nov. 23, 1862. Their children: Sytha b. Dec. 10, 1884, m. Eugene Lusk Roberts; Gertrude b. Feb. 2, 1886, m. Andrew Theodore Rasmussen; James Curtis b. Feb. 9, 1888; Emma b. March 8, 1891, and Pauline b. Nov. 16, 1892, died; Hugh Crosby b. Aug. 15, 1895; Harold Whaley b. June 22, 1898; John Lyman b. Jan. 31, 1900; Ruth b. Nov. 4, 1903.
Married Ella Larson June 18, 1908, Salt Lake City (daughter of Niels Peter Larson and Karen K. Swenson of Pleasant Grove, Utah, pioneers 1859). She was born Feb. 22, 1871. Only child: Helen b. Dec. 30, 1909. Families resided Pleasant Grove and Provo.
High priest; superintendent Sunday schools Pleasant Grove; counsellor to President Leonard Harrington of stake Sunday schools. President normal department Brigham Young University (Provo) and teacher of chemistry. Also a teacher Pleasant Grove schools and superintendent Utah county schools.

BROWN, JOHN ZIMMERMAN (son of John Brown and Margaret Zimmerman). Born Sept. 2, 1873, at Pleasant Grove.
Married Alice Vivia Driggs Sept. 2, 1903, Salt Lake City (daughter of Benjamin Woodbury Driggs and Olivia Thankful Pratt of Pleasant Grove, pioneers 1852). She was born Sept. 28, 1877. Their children: John Zimmerman Jr. b. June 19, 1904; Hoke Woodbury Driggs b. May 7, 1908, d. June 29, 1910; Richard Lyman b. July 13, 1912. Family home Salt Lake City.
Fourth quorum seventies; missionary to southern states 1896-99; member Ensign stake Sunday school board. School teacher. Graduated from Utah State Normal School 1902; A. B. degree from University of Utah 1906, and head of its department of physiology 1907-10; received M. D. degree from Rush Medical College of Chicago 1911. Interne Groves L. D. S. Hospital 1911-12.

BROWN, JOHN (son of William Brown and Jane Mitchell). Born in 1808, Stirlingshire, Scotland.
Married Christiana Thompson in Scotland (daughter of John Thompson and Christiana Mitchell), who was born Feb. 6, 1806, Stonerig, Airdrie, Scotland, and died July 1892,

PIONEERS AND PROMINENT MEN OF UTAH

Salt Lake City. She came to Utah Sept. 15, 1868, John Gillespie company. Their children: Christiana, m. Edward Johnson; Jane, d. infant; William, m. Elizabeth Cook; Jane, m. Alexander Brown; John, m. Elizabeth Hillhouse; Elizabeth, d. aged 21; Isabelle, d. aged 23; Helen, m. Alexander Wade; Mary, d. aged 4; Agnes, m. William Campbell. Family home Salt Lake City, Utah.

BROWN, JOHN (son of William Brown and Elizabeth Illman of London, Eng.). Born Nov. 26, 1831, Limpsfield, Eng. Came to Utah Oct. 13, 1863, Rosel Hyde company.
Married Sarah Haynes Nov. 7, 1852, London. Eng. (daughter of John and Sarah Haynes of Leicestershire), who was born Nov. 20, 1830. Their children: Hyrum; Lorenzo John, m. Louise Folsom; Samuel Willard; Sarah Elizabeth, m. William W. Needham; Imri, m. Jane Jones; George, m. Tina Bates; Louisa Mary; Mamie Salina. Family home Salt Lake City.
Married Eleanor Caffal in April 1874, Salt Lake City (daughter of John and Mary Ann Caffal of Watton, Hertfordshire, Eng). She was born April 1844. Their children: William, died; Mabel and Irene, died; Samuel Vernon, m. Eliza Hugentuveller; Edna; Harold.
Married Mary Burkhardt July 19, 1887, Salt Lake City (daughter of Frederick Burkhardt and Elizabeth Stanfiger of Bern, Switzerland, who came to Utah 1891). She was born March 15, 1868. Their children: Orson, died; Frank; Earl; Ada; Meloin; Frederick; oliver.
Missionary to England 1887-88; member 10th quorum seventies; high priest; bishop's counselor of 9th ward for 23 years. Teacher. Helped build Gardo house and temple in Salt Lake City.

BROWN, JONATHAN (son of Jonathan Brown, born April 23, 1794, Bristol, Eng., and Frances Mary Primrose, born Oct. 8, 1796, Norfolk, Eng.). He was born July 31, 1818, in England. Came to Utah Sept. 20, 1853, Claudius V. Spencer company.
Married Sarah Couzins Oct. 31, 1838 (daughter of George Couzins and Ann Herridge), who was born March 7, 1819. Their children: Henry William b. Oct. 10, 1839, m. Sarah A. Killpack March 15, 1869; Edwin b. June 24, 1841, m. Desdemona Fox June 12, 1865; Elizabeth b. Jan. 28, 1843, m. Chancey C. Webb April 7, 1868; Charles b. Jan. 14, 1845, d. June 24, 1860; Emma b. Jan. 12, 1850, m. Job Reading Feb. 8, 1870; Sarah Ann b. Sept. 1, 1846, m. J. C. Peterson Dec. 31, 1864; Ellen b. Aug. 3, 1851, d. April 29, 1853; Maria Ellen b. March 23, 1853, d. Oct. 5, 1853; Mary Frances b. April 9, 1857, m. James B. Henry July 25, 1878; Albert G. C. b. Dec. 13, 1859, m. Hannah Thompson April 24, 1881. Family home Murray, Utah.
Married Ann Langfield Nov. 22, 1856, Salt Lake City (daughter of James Langfield). She was born at Newbury, England. Only child: Elizabeth Ann b. Sept. 1857, m. Alexander Bowman.
Member 23d quorum seventies; treasurer of Reading branch of London, Eng.

BROWN, HENRY W. (son of Jonathan Brown and Sarah Couzins). Born Oct. 10, 1839, Newbury, Eng.
Married Sarah Ann Killpack March 15, 1869, Salt Lake City (daughter of John and Frances Killpack, former a pioneer 1864). She was born Aug. 8, 1851. Their children: Henry J. b. March 12, 1870, d. Aug. 20, 1889; Frances Sarah b. Dec. 19, 1871, d. Sept. 22, 1877; Charles b. Sept. 28, 1873, m. Hilma Johnson Jan. 18, 1899; Elizabeth Rachel b. July 22, 1875, m. James Dunster Oct. 23, 1894; George E. b. Aug. 12, 1877, m. May Rawlings Oct. 31, 1903; Arthur W. b. June 24, 1879, m. Ivie May Turner Oct. 21, 1903; John Louis b. July 6, 1881, m. Lucy E. Fisher Sept. 2, 1903; Lavinia Louisa b. April 20, 1884, m. James W. Cahoon June 20, 1906; Esther Lillace b. June 15, 1886, m. Melvin R. Fisher Feb. 27, 1907; Zina Merl b. July 7, 1890, m. Andrew H. Bennion Oct. 15, 1907. Family home Murray, Utah.
Member 61st quorum seventies; missionary to England 1881-83; councilman for 72d quorum seventies. Road supervisor South Cottonwood 20 years; president East Jordan Irrigation company, also serving as secretary, treasurer and director. Chairman board of canals; school trustee 15 years.

BROWN, JOSEPH. Born in Manasquam, N. J. Came to Utah in early days.
Married Ann Curtis at Salt Lake City. Their children: Benjamin, m. Rebecca Webb; Elizabeth, m. Elbert Eastmond; Sidney, m. Eleanor ——; Samuel, m. Katherine ——; Prudence, m. Lafayette Granger. Family home Salt Lake City.
Ship builder; carpenter; merchant.

BROWN, JOSEPH SMITH (son of James Brown and Mary McCrea of Ogden, Utah, pioneers July 29, 1847, with Mormon Battalion). Born Jan. 4, 1856, Ogden, Utah.
Married Sarah Wealthea Patton March 8, 1876 (daughter of William Cornwall Patton and Welthea Eddy of Payson, Utah, pioneers). She was born Oct. 22, 1858. Their children: Joseph Smith Jr., m. Ada Myrtle Stanford; Welthea May, m. Job E. Hemsley; Henry Alonzo, m. Lola Smith; Mary Josephine, m. George Oakey; James William died; George David, m. Blanch Smith; Margaret Viola, m.

Adnia E. Bramwell; Leroy Patten, m. Hazel Smith; Sidney Earl; Wendell Eddy died. Family home Plano, Idaho.
Farmer. Died March 22, 1903, Idaho Falls, Idaho.

BROWN, HENRY ALONZO (son of Joseph Smith Brown and Sarah Welthea Patton). Born June 30, 1880, Oxford, Idaho.
Married Lola Smith June 7, 1912, Salt Lake City (daughter of William Smith and Annie Mathews of Egin, Idaho). She was born Dec. 22, 1885. Only child: Esther b. March 27, 1913.
Missionary to California 1908-10. Farmer.

BROWN, PHILANDER (son of William Brown and Diantha Soreland). Born April 10, 1826, Rush, Monroe county, N. Y. Came to Utah Sept. 4, 1860, Franklin Brown company.
Married Orilla Leavitt Oct. 13, 1848 (daughter of John Leavitt and Lucy Fish), who was born Feb. 10, 1829. Only child: Horace b. July 23, 1849, d. Aug. 7, 1849.
Married Elizabeth Dobney Short Feb. 6, 1864, Salt Lake City (daughter of William John Short, pioneer Sept. 4, 1863, Capt. Patterson company, and Elizabeth Curtis, married Oct. 27, 1834, Islington, Eng.). She was born Nov. 24, 1841, London, Eng. Their children: Zina Elizabeth b. Oct. 17, 1865, m. Harold Hardy Nov. 19, 1884; Emily Orilla b. Dec. 8, 1866, m. T. H. Maxfield July 14, 1892; Philander Franklin b. Dec. 21, 1868, died; Charles Hyrum b. March 13, 1870, m. Ella Harton Oct. 24, 1891; Mary Emiline b. June 26, 1871, m. H. B. Hales April 1, 1903; Harvey Alfred b. Sept. 24, 1872; William John b. Jan. 24, 1874, m. Etta Clinger Dec. 6, 1895; Ellen Adell b. May 19, 1875, m. Ellis Maxfield Aug. 11, 1897; B. Jarrel b. Feb. 6, 1877, died; Phebe Diantha b. Dec. 26, 1878, m. W. E. Hardy Sept. 7, 1898; George Albert b. Feb. 23, 1880, m. Julia Ramsy Nov. 14, 1900. Family home Provo, Utah.
President 74th and 34th quorum seventies; missionary. Road supervisor; railroad foreman between Salt Lake City and Frisco, Utah.

BROWN, GEORGE ALBERT (son of Philander Brown and Elizabeth Dobney Short). Born Feb. 23, 1880, Provo, Utah.
Married Julia Ramsey Nov. 14, 1900, Salt Lake City (daughter of George W. Ramsey and Amanda Ross), who was born Jan. 27, 1881. Their children: Emily H. b. Aug. 7, 1901; Ellis S. b. Feb. 17, 1904; Albert R. b. Dec. 6, 1905; Mervin M. b. June 13, 1908; Erma F. b. Jan. 22, 1911. Family home Provo, Utah.
Missionary to New Zealand three years. Merchant.

BROWN, RICHARD DANIELS (son of William Daniels Brown and Grace Fairhurst of Wigan, Lancashire, Eng.). Born March 1, 1811, at Wigan. Came to Utah Oct. 4, 1864, William S. Warren company.
Married Margaret Parkinson Sept. 11, 1830 (daughter of Thomas Parkinson and Sarah Southworth), who was born May 12, 1811, and came to Utah with husband. Their children: William D. b. Jan. 1836, m. Hannah Hardman 1865; Thomas b. Dec. 16, 1838, m. Esther Wardle March 19, 1861; Mary Ann b. Jan. 1840, m. John McCullough; Elizabeth b. Oct. 28, 1841, m. Peter Later May 25, 1863; Catherine b. June 8, 1844, m. James Fields Aug. 1868; Richard Daniels b. May 27, 1846, m. Lucy A. Enzlow Field Dec. 5, 1870; Margaret b. May 6, 1849, m. Edward Hemsley; Rebecca b. Nov. 30, 1850, m. Noah Wardle; Sarah Jane b. Oct. 1852, m. Abraham Hedford; Josiah Hyrum b. Jan. 6, 1856, m. Sariah Rawson.
Elder. Farmer. Died June 22, 1893, Harrisville, Utah.

BROWN, RICHARD DANIELS (son of Richard Daniels Brown and Margaret Parkinson). Born May 27, 1846, Manchester, Lancashire, Eng.
Married Lucy A. Enzlow Field Dec. 5, 1870 (daughter of Elza Enzlow and Maria Howland, married 1848). She was born Nov. 30, 1849, and came to Utah 1851. Their children: Herbert b. March 20, 1873, m. Margaret Robson Nov. 8, 1893; Richard Roy b. May 10, 1875, m. Geneva Miller Nov. 14, 1903; Mary Margaret b. April 5, 1877; Elza b. July 29, 1878, m. Lucy Effie b. Dec. 9, 1901; Lucy Effie b. Dec. 9, 1901; Arthur E. Wilson March 4, 1898.
Married Mary Elizabeth Olmstead July 15, 1885, Logan, Utah (daughter of Hyrum Olmstead and Sarah Elizabeth Hammond, pioneers 1847, Company C, Mormon Battalion). She was born Nov. 29, 1851, Riverdale, Utah.
Married Betsy Fish July 29, 1889, Salt Lake City (daughter of Jabez Fish and Henrietta Stott). Only child: Thomas Lawrence Brown.
Married Emily Schofield May 20, 1904, Layton, Utah (daughter of Joseph Schofield and Lavina Parkinson). Their children: Verna Elizabeth; William Ray; Victor Leland.
Filled two missions to Europe; president 60th quorum seventies 10 years; secretary to 60th quorum seventies 12 years; superintendent Sunday schools 10 years; assistant superintendent Sunday schools 20 years. Postmaster Harrisville six years; city sexton at Ogden 1906-10, 1912-13.

BROWN, ROBERT (son of Charles and Jane Brown). Born May 14, 1831, St. Paul's, Bristol, Gloucestershire, Eng. Came to Utah Oct. 1, 1862, Joseph Horne company.
Married Ann Evans Nov. 18, 1852 (daughter of William Evans and Frances Russell, latter a pioneer Oct. 1, 1862).

776 PIONEERS AND PRO M

She was born July 28, 1834. Their children: Henry William Evans b. July 14, 1854, m. Charlotte Elizabeth Taylor Dec. 9, 1880; Robert William b. June 20, 1856, m. Mary T. Todd Jan. 8, 1896; Edmund J. b. March 3, 1864, m. Olive T. Butterfield Oct. 25, 1886; William A. b. June 6, 1866, m. Emily Todd Jan. 15, 1890; Rachel Emily Jane b. Sept. 30; 1872, m. Albert S. Gibbs Jan. 13, 1892; George T. b. June 30, 1875, m. Emeretta Miller Sept. 16, 1898; Ellen Maria b. June 17, 1878, m. Charles W. Malustrom Feb. 28, 1898. Family home South Murray, Utah.
Farmer and rancher.

BROWN, HENRY WILLIAM EVANS (son of Robert Brown and Ann Evans). Born July 14, 1854, St. Nicholas parish, Bristol, Eng.
Married Charlotte Elizabeth Taylor Dec. 9, 1880, Salt Lake City (daughter of Peter Taylor and Sarah Brent), who was born Sept. 5, 1858, Middlesex, London. Their children: Maude Elizabeth b. June 26, 1882, m. Royal Bateman; Tresas b. March 2, 1884. Family home South Murray, Utah.
Miner and smelterman.

BROWN, SAMUEL A. M. (son of Samuel Brown and Julia Maland of Salt Lake City). Born September, 1888.
Married Ethel Lees Jan. 29, 1908, Salt Lake City, Bishop McMillan officiating (daughter of Josiah Lees and Mary Ann Boyden, pioneers Sept. 3, 1860, James W. Ross company). She was born Jan. 11, 1887, Salt Lake City. Only child: Jack M. b. July 15, 1912.

BROWN, THOMAS B. (son of Thomas Brown and Jemima Rodgers of Salt Lake City). Born Dec. 27, 1824, Bath, Somersetshire, Eng. Came to Utah Sept. 25, 1856, Richard Ballantyne company.
Married Jane White May 13, 1857, Salt Lake City (daughter of Isaac White of North Ogden, Utah), who was born 1830. Their children: Thomas F., m. Susan Dudman; Louise d. aged 2; Jane M. d. aged 16; Elizabeth A., m. Lorenzo Waldram; Mary E., m. John Shaw; Rose E., m. William Bailey; Kate E., m. John Ward; Celia E.
Married Eliza Brown March 14, 1863, Salt Lake City (daughter of John Brown of North Oregon). Their children: John H., m. Elizabeth A. Roylance; George, m. Maud Dudman; Ellen, m. Arthur G. Barrett; Emily, m. Joseph Folkman; William C. d. infant; Harriet, m. Thomas Barrett; Nephi J., m. Vilate Taylor. Family resided North Ogden, Utah.
Member 10th quorum seventies: high priest. Cabinetmaker and farmer. Died June 18, 1899.

BROWN, THOMAS JAMES (son of James and Mary Brown of New Jersey). Born Sept. 20, 1837, in New Jersey.
Married Althea Chamberlain 1860, Salt Lake City (daughter of John Chamberlain and Amy Airy of New Jersey). She was born May 1846. Their children: James A., m. Rose Frances Morris; Mary Emma, m. James Kelly; Alice A., m. Thomas Taylor, who died, m. Henry Heaton; Charles W., m. Adele Lee; Ernest W.; Edna L., m. Clyde L. Bailey. Family home Salt Lake City, Utah.
Seventy; teacher. Florist and nurseryman. Died Oct. 22, 1905.

BROWN, JAMES A. (son of Thomas James Brown and Althea Chamberlain). Born Oct. 27, 1867, Salt Lake City, Utah.
Married Rose Frances Morris Dec. 18, 1890, Salt Lake City (daughter of Elias Morris and Mary Parry of Newmarket, Wales, pioneers of 1869). She was born Sept. 20, 1864. Their children: Sydney Vaughn b. Feb. 2, 1892; Irvin W. b. Dec. 22, 1894; Morris S. b. June 27, 1897; Florence L. b. Sept. 15, 1898; Allen J. and Vernon b. March 29, 1900. Family home Salt Lake City, Utah.
Real estate and investment agent.

BROWN, WILLIAM (son of John and Eliza Brown of London, Eng.). Came to Utah 1852.
Married Hannah Richardson (Hatton) October, 1852, Salt Lake City (daughter of Aaron Richardson and Sarah Higgins of Salt Lake City, pioneers Sept. 1852). Their children: Hannah b. Aug. 15, 1853, m. Heber Odekirk; Catherine Elizabeth b. Oct. 31, 1855, m. Samuel J. Merrill.
Hannah Richardson was the widow of William Hatton, whom she married at Plumbley, near Knutsford, Cheshire, Eng. He was drafted in the army and went to Mexico, where he died. Their children: Sarah b. Sept. 2, 1842, m. Robert Mickel; Mary b. June 6, 1844, m. Austin Merrill; Fannie b. Dec. 25, 1846, d. infant.

BROWN, WILLIAM PARKER. Born May 6, 1816, Nottinghamshire, Eng. Came to Utah Sept. 4, 1863, Capt. Patterson oxteam company.
Married Charlotte Parker March 28, 1841. She was born July 16, 1818, and died July 4, 1854, St. Louis, Mo. Their children: Emma b. Dec. 24, 1841, d. June 28, 1855; Henry b. July 31, 1843, d. Sept. 20, 1843; Henry b. Aug. 16, 1844, d. April 18, 1845; Ann b. March 1846, d. Aug. 5, 1846; Joh b. Jan. 29, 1848, m. Esther Sargent; William b. May 25

BROWNELL, RUSSELL GIDEON. Came to Utah Sept. 22, 1849 with William Miller, Captain of ten in that company. Married Betsy Wheeler. Only child: Julia A. b. Feb. 12, 1826, m. James Myler Oct. 5, 1843.
Musician and corporal Co. C, of Mormon Battalion. Died April 6, 1895, Fresno, Cal.

BROWNING, DAVID ELIAS (son of Jonathan Browning and Elizabeth Stockup of Nashville, Davidson county, Tenn.). Born Jan. 19, 1829, at Nashville. Came to Utah, Sept., 1852, Capt. Miller company.
Married Charilla Abbott, Jan. 1853, at Ogden, Utah (daughter of Stephen Abbott and Abigail Smith; latter a pioneer Oct. 27, 1849, with her children, Smith company). She was born July 4, 1829. Their children: Charilla Emily b. Jan. 29, 1854, m. William McGregor May 1, 1876; David Elias b. Aug. 8, 1856, m. Mary Anderson; Stephen Abbott b. Dec. 3, 1858, m. Emily Chetlain, m. Annie Baird; Jonathan Abbott b. March 9, 1861, m. Lucy Bateman; James Smith b. April 19, 1864; Westley M. b. April 3, 1867; Arbarilla Fastday b. Oct. 1, 1868, m. John Lowe; Abigail b. May 14, 1871. Family home Ogden, Utah.
Sergeant-major first regiment territorial militia, 1866. Inventor and gunsmith of world renown, as Browning automatic firearms are imported, patented and made in every country. Died Dec. 14, 1901.

BROWNING, JAMES GREENE (son of Edmund Browning, born Nov. 14, 1761, Culpeper county, Va., and Sarah Allen, born in Pottawattamie county, Iowa; married in 1790). He was born May 2, 1808, in Sumner county, Tenn. Came to Utah in 1850.
Married Mary Ann Neal, in 1827. Their children: Clifton Smith b. Sept. 15, 1828, m. Rachel Middleton Oct. 2, 1854; Sarah Ann b. Oct. 10, 1830, m. Edward Bunker 1856; Edmund Thomas b. Nov. 30, 1833, m. Charlotte McArty; David Henry b. March 16, 1835, m. Elizabeth Jane Garner 1854; Jane Neel b. Aug. 4, 1838, m. William A. Stewart 1854; Isaac Austin b. Dec. 25, 1840, m. Martha Lloyd 1858; Eliza Elizabeth M. A. A., b. Aug. 4, 1848, m. George A. Richardson 1866; Delilah Charilla b. Aug. 4, 1848, m. William A. Hunt 1864; Mary Ann b. 1852; Emeline b. Sept. 17, 1854. Family home St. George, Utah.
Married Ann Wood Sept. 6, 1861, Salt Lake City (daughter of James Wood and Alice Hollins), who was born March 18, 1834, in North Chestershire, Eng. Their children: James Greene b. Nov. 3, 1862, m. Amanda Vilate Elmer 1883; George Andrew b. June 27, 1865, m. Emma C. Matson Nov. 4, 1891; Edmund b. Oct. 16, 1867, m. Amanda E. Wetzel April 13, 1892; Jonathan b. Feb. 18, 1870, m. Jane Barker 1897; Lewis Wood b. April 11, 1872.
Second bishop of Weber county; missionary to England 1860; member territorial legislature; Ogden city councilman. Died Nov. 20, 1878.

BROWNING, GEORGE A. (son of James Greene Browning and Ann Wood). He was born June 27, 1865, Ogden, Utah.
Married Emma C. Matson Nov. 4, 1891, Logan, Utah (daughter of John and Christina Sophia Matson), who was born Oct. 5, 1870, in Sweden. Their children: George A. b. Sept. 27, 1892, Esther Sophia b. Dec. 17, 1894; Ruth Matilda b. Nov. 18, 1895; Gleen Wood b. Feb. 9, 1898; Golden Matson b. Nov. 10, 1891; Lester Matson b. Nov. 5, 1902; Rulon Matson b. Oct. 22, 1906; Roland James G. b. Dec. 27, 1908; Vera Emma b. Feb. 21, 1912. Family home Annis, Idaho.
Bishop Annis ward. Merchant and farmer.

BRUNSON, LEWIS (son of Seymour Brunson, born Dec. 1, 1798, in Vermont, and Harriet Gould, born Aug. 22, 1802, in New York). He was born Jan. 27, 1831, Mantua, Portage Co., Ohio. Came to Utah in September, 1851, Rosewell Stevens company.
Married Amanda Louisa Park (daughter of John Park and Matilda Wallace, pioneers 1851). She was born March 30, 1834, and came to Utah with husband. Their children: Mary Louisa b. Sept. 3, 1853, m. George Bryan; Joseph Lewis b. Jan. 6, 1855; Harriet Matilda b. Sept. 10, 1857, m. Ephraim Allred; Adaline b. Jan. 3, 1861, m. Joseph D. Smith Oct. 7, 1880; George Cannon b. 1859; Peter Lorenzo b. July 20, 1866, m. Clarinda Alta McCullough March 11, 1887. Family home Fillmore, Utah.
Married Lamira Mace Jan. 13, 1857 (daughter of Hyrum Mace and Elizabeth Armstrong, former a pioneer 1852, Capt. Miller company). She was born Jan. 14, 1840, Sevesten, Mich. Their children: Seymour Lewis b. Aug. 6, 1858, m. Anna Laura Tompkinson Dec. 25, 1876; Reuben E. b. Aug. 20, 1863; Arthur Mace b. Nov. 30, 1864, m. Sarah E. Carling Sept. 1, 1886; Hyrum b. Oct. 1, 1867, m. Clairilla A. Howard; Daniel b. March 20, 1870; Clairilla b. Oct. 19, 1872, m. William Wade; Harvey b. Oct. 29, 1882.
Married Catherine Carling March 31, 1887 (daughter of John Carling and Emaline Katon), who was born June 1, 1835. Their children: Annie b. March 13, 1859, m. Hans C. Hansen June 6, 1877; Jeanette b. Feb. 24, 1861, m. M. M. Bishop; John L. b. July 27, 1865, m. Emma Jane Wildon Nov. 11, 1887; James William b. April 17, 1866, m. Lois Warner Jan. 25, 1888; Isaac F. b. April 1, 1870, m. Nellie Beaston; Lewis b. Nov. 20, 1872; Charles A. b. Oct. 2, 1875, m. Christie Enckeul Jan. 29, 1897.
Bishop of Fillmore six years; missionary; president high priests quorum of Millard stake; high councilor.

BRUNSON, PETER LORENZO (son of Lewis Brunson and Amanda Louisa Park). Born July 20, 1866, Fillmore, Utah.
Married Clarinda Alta McCullough March 11, 1887 (daughter of Henry J. McCullough and Helen MacCallister), who was born Nov. 20, 1867, Fillmore, Utah. The'r children: Peter Lorenzo, Jr. b. Dec. 26, 1887; Mary Altana b. Nov. 5, 1889; Amy Louisa b. Sept. 16, 1891; Helen b. Jan. 21, 1893; Harriet b. Aug. 27, 1895; Myrtle b. March 14, 1897; Henry b. June 14, 1900; Nora b. Dec. 29, 1902; Lewis Clark b. Aug. 5, 1906; Elbert LaStar b. Nov. 16, 1908; Max Eliot b. June 18, 1911. Family resided Fillmore, Marion and Panguitch, Utah.
Secretary Y. M. M. I. A. at Marion ward nine years and president one year. Bishop's counselor one year; bishop of Fillmore 1909-12; counselor to President Orvel K. Thompson of Millard stake. City councilman.

BRUNSON, SEYMOUR, Jr. (son of Seymour Brunson and Harriet Gould). Born Jan. 6, 1836, Tomkins county, Ill. Came to Utah in 1852, Capt. Miller company.
Married Elizabeth A. Mace in 1862 (daughter of Hyrum Mace and Elizabeth Armstrong), who was born in February, 1847. Their children: Seymour E.; Hyrum; William H.; Elizabeth Irena; Reuben; Walter; Freeman; Pearl; Emily; Deela.

BRUNSON, SEYMOUR E. (son of Seymour Brunson, Jr., and Elizabeth A. Mace). Born Sept. 15, 1863, Payson, Utah.
Married Annie Speakman Sept. 20, 1884, Fillmore, Utah (daughter of William Speakman and Sarah Young), who was born Aug. 17, 1867. Their children: Edna b. Sept. 10, 1885; William E. b. July 7, 1887; Lorinda b. July 17, 1888; Evelyn b. March 18, 1891; Velate b. Oct. 19, 1894; Freeman S. b. Oct. 19, 1897; Ava b. March 18, 1900; Osborn L. b. Aug. 25, 1902; Wanda b. Sept. 25, 1906.

BRYNER, HANS ULRICH. Born March 30, 1806, Bosserdorf, Switzerland. Came to Utah 1857, Edward Hunter company.
Married Verena Wintsch at Zurich, Switzerland (daughter of Friederich Wintsch and Susana Weise of Zurich). She was born Feb. 26, 1804, and came to Utah with husband. Their children: Hans Ulrich, Jr., m. Marie Mathis; Casper, m. Magdalena Gubler; Barbara, m. John Mathis; Verena, m. John C. Naglie. Family home St. George, Utah.
Went to Dixie in 1861. Died 1864, St. George, Utah.

BRYNER, HANS ULRICH, Jr. (son of Hans Ulrich Bryner and Verena Wintsch). Born April 29, 1827, at Zurich. Came to Utah Dec. 24, 1856, Martin and Tyler handcart company.
Married Marie Mathis at Zurich (daughter of Hans Heinrich Mathis and Dorthea Meyer, of Zurich, former a pioneer Dec. 24, 1856, the latter died at Price, Utah, 1893). She was born in 1823. Their children: Henry G., m. Isabella Burch; Pauline, m. John H. Pace; Elizabeth, m. George Wood; Albert, m. Mariah Jane Pace; Verena, m. A. Redd; Franklin Casper, m. Dora McIntyre; m. Ellen Redd.
Married Margret Kahun 1868, in Salt Lake City, who came to Utah 1862. Their children: Henry Kahun; Mary m. Heber Naglie; John U., m. Martha Smith; George William, died; Josephine, m. George A. Fawsett; Annie, m. Albert A. McMullen; James, m. Miss Babcock; Rosilla, m. Peter Anderson; Lilly, m. Rasmus Frandsen; Enoch, m. Miss Zabriskie; Edith, m. Thomas Sheppick; Alma, m. Ethel Porter. Family home Toquerville, Utah.
High priest; worked on St. George temple last five years of his life. Lived at New Harmony 1863, and Price in 1881. Died Feb. 8, 1905, St. George, Utah.

BRYNER, ALBERT (son of Hans Ulrich Bryner, Jr., and Marie Mathis). Born Feb. 5, 1862, St. George, Utah.
Married Mariah Jane Pace March 18, 1881, St. George (daughter of Harvey Alexander Pace and Elizabeth Redd of New Harmony, Utah). She was born Jan. 12, 1864. Their children: William Albert b. Dec. 30, 1881; Ulrich Alexander b. Aug. 15, 1883; Maggie M. b. Sept. 3, 1885; Annie Pearl b. April 7, 1887; Elmer Pace b. Jan. 16, 1889; Mary Evaline b. Sept. 27, 1890; first six died; Ruby b. July 21, 1890; Rulon Anton b. Nov. 14, 1896; Elmo b. Aug. 16, 1902; Harold Ernest b. Feb. 16, 1904, also are dead; Marie b. April 3, 1908. Family home Price, Utah since 1884.
President 81st and 101st quorum seventies; high priest; missionary to Germany 1893-95; counselor to Bishop Horsley 1896; bishop Price ward 1909; president Y. M. M. I. A.; assistant Sunday school superintendent of Price and New Harmony wards; president deacons' and elders' quorums. Vice president and assistant general manager Price Co-op.; vice president Eastern Utah Telephone company.

BUCHANAN, ARCHIBALD W. (son of John Buchanan of Scotland and Nancy Bache of Lexington, Ky.). Born Feb. 9, 1830, at Covington. Came to Utah Sept. 13, 1852, Captain Howell company.
Married Helen Amelia Whiting Aug. 2, 1855 (daughter of Edwin Whiting and Elizabeth Tillotson, pioneers Oct. 28, 1849, Ezra T. Benson company; married 1833 in Portage county, Ohio). She was born Aug. 21, 1836. Their children: Sarah Elizabeth b. Nov. 10, 1857, m. P. K. Lemoni; Archibald W. Jr. b. Jan. 21, 1859, m. Mary Peterson Dec. 7, 1881; Helen Amelia b. March 14, 1861, m. H. M. Payne; Lorenzo Dow b. May 12, 1866, m. Mary Larson Feb. 24, 1892; Theda Jane b. Dec. 29, 1867, m. A. Oldroyd; Effie Louisa b. May 29, 1871, m. G. F. Haskett Aug. 18, 1891. Family resided Manti and Glenwood, Utah.

PIONEERS AND PROMINENT MEN OF UTAH

Married Mary Ann Brown Jan. 1, 1860, at Manti (daughter of James Brown and Eunice Reesor, pioneers 1847; married 1826). She was born Oct. 2, 1842. Greenville, Ind. Their children: Eunice Rozina Snow b. March 11, 1858, m. C. W. Powell Nov. 1, 1875; James Alonzo b. Oct. 30, 1860; Mary Jane b. Dec. 28, 1862, m. I. R. Oldroyd Nov. 24, 1881; William Wallace b. March 26, 1865, m. Nancy Madora Poole Oct. 12, 1898; Eugene Deloss b. June 12, 1867, m. Hattie Ann Young Dec. 19, 1888; Henry Pomeroy b. March 13, 1871, m. Ida Brugger July 19, 1905; Amy Lorette b. Sept. 6, 1873, m. Alma J. Ence Nov. 22, 1893; Charles Vertener b. March 15, 1877. Family resided Manti and Glenwood, Utah.
Married Mariah Larson 1870 in Salt Lake City (daughter of H. P. Larson), who was born Oct. 1862, Slagelse, Sjaelland, Denmark. Their children: Osmond b. Sept. 1871, m. Mariah Killian; Arthur b. July 23, 1874; Mariah Costina b. Oct. 16, 1876, m. Knewell C. Young; James Carlos b. April 8, 1879; Ethel b. Feb. 10, 1882, m. M. H. Brainholt; Edna b. July 1884, m. Robert Beecroft.
Married Caroline S. Sorenson Sept. 27, 1876, Salt Lake City (daughter of H. Sorenson and Anna Nielson, who came to Utah 1870). She was born April 30, 1858, Slagelse, Denmark. Their children: John Soren b. Oct. 6, 1879; Anna Delia b. April 27, 1881, m. R. H. Poole June 5, 1900; Mae b. Sept. 7, 1883, m. J. A. Black Aug. 31, 1903; Aaron William b. April 5, 1885; Parley Ammon b. Jan. 10, 1888; Carrie Myrl b. March 25, 1892, m. George Brugger Nov. 15, 1911; Archie Earl b. March 25, 1892. Family resided at Manti and Glenwood, Utah.
Bishop Glenwood 1870-75. Indian war veteran. Indian missionary in the Elk mountains.

BUCHANAN, ARCHIBALD W., Jr. (son of Archibald W. Buchanan and Helen Amelia Whiting). Born Jan. 21, 1859, Manti, Utah.
Married Mary Peterson Dec. 7, 1881, St. George, Utah (daughter of Peter Christen Peterson, pioneer 1860, and Christina Sorenson, pioneer 1862). She was born Jan. 31, 1864. Their children: Archibald Lester b. Oct. 27, 1884, m. Odetta Cowley Nov. 15, 1911; Mary Lula b. July 16, 1886; Mabel b. Jan. 17, 1889, m. J. Hainsworth Dec. 27, 1910; Christen Leroy b. Jan. 3, 1891; Clancey Emeron b. Feb. 22, 1896; Clayona b. Aug. 2, 1904. Family home Glenwood, Utah.
Missionary to northern states 1882-1883.

BUCK, CHARLES (son of Charles Buck and Mary Dobb of England). Born Feb. 6, 1839, Woodlane, Hucknall Torkard, Nottinghamshire. Eng. Came to Utah Sept. 4, 1866, Thomas E. Ricks company.
Married Hannah Chantery Dec. 22, 1859, in England (daughter of John Chantery and Ann Bonnington of Nottinghamshire; former came to Utah 1869). She was born Feb. 25, 1841. Their children: William Henry b. Jan. 12, 1861, m. Rebecca Chadburn May 25, 1882; Joseph b. Jan. 10, 1864, m. Mather Bennington; Mary Ann b. Dec. 19, 1865; Hannah E. b. Jan. 5, 1868, m. Walter Farr; Sariah b. June 1, 1870, m. Lorin Farr; Charles J. b. May 27, 1872, m. Elizabeth Cox; Sarah b. Jan. 8, 1874, m. Thomas Mills; Selena b. Dec. 9, 1875, m. Alex Morrison; Eliza b. July 13, 1877; Nephi C. b. Jan. 15, 1881, m. Alice Woods. Family home West Weber, Utah.
Seventy; high priest; second counselor to President J. F. Hunter of elders' quorum. Died 1889.

BUCK, WILLIAM HENRY (son of Charles Buck and Hannah Chantery). Born Jan. 12, 1861, Woodlane, Nottinghamshire, Eng.
Married Rebecca Chadburn May 25, 1882, Salt Lake City (daughter of William Chadburn and Ellen Calivere of Seatway, N. J.). She was born April 2, 1865. Their children: Mary Ann b. April, 1883; Elizabeth Ellen b. Jan. 12, 1886; Hannah R. b. April 10, 1888; Charles H. b. Feb. 7, 1891; Sarah Ida b. April 17, 1893, m. John L. Wright June 7, 1911; Ruth Olive b. Sept. 14, 1895; Flora A. b. April 7, 1898. Family home West Weber, Utah.
Married Flora Buck Aug. 19, 1898, Salt Lake City, who was born March 5, 1872, Hucknall Torkard, Eng. Their children: Percy H. b. May 25, 1899; William Edwin b. Jan. 7, 1901; Elsie Agnes b. Jan. 9, 1903; Joseph Seeley b. Dec. 6, 1905; Flora Priscilla b. March 4, 1907; Pearl Irene b. 1909; James Harold b. June 11, 1911. Family home West Weber, Utah.
Elder.

BUCKLE, GEORGE (son of John Buckle and Anne Cooper of Salt Lake City). Born July 24, 1861, Manchester, Eng. Came to Utah 1870.
Married Esther E. Long at Salt Lake City (daughter of John and Elizabeth Long of England). She was born 1863. Their children: Adella, m. Theodore J. F. Mauss; George C., m. Minnie Gallacher; Lillian, m. Perry C. Rockwood; Leslie Long. Family home Salt Lake City.
City councilman three terms; president of city council one term. Foreman of bindery department at Desert News for thirty years.

BUCKLE, GEORGE C. (son of George Buckle and Esther E. Long). Born July 15, 1882, at Salt Lake City.
Married Minnie Gallacher at Salt Lake City (daughter of John Gallacher of Scotland). Family home Salt Lake City. Lawyer; assistant attorney general of Utah.

BUDD, CHARLES (son of Richard and Sarah Budd, of Beading, Sussex, Eng.). Born June 9, 1800, at Beading. Came to Utah Sept. 1859.
Married Louisa Capeland at Beading (daughter of Mr. Capeland and Miss French of Beading), who was born May 29, 1804, at same place. Their children: Charles Jr. b. April 29, 1821; Mary b. June 24, 1822; John b. May 23, 1824; Richard b. Oct. 17, 1826; Francis b. Aug. 24, 1828; Edward b. Aug. 13, 1831; Louisa. b. March 24, 1833; Elizabeth b. July 5, 1835; Henry b. Oct. 2, 1836; Martha b. May 31, 1838; James Frances Caroline b. Jan. 16, 1841; William b. Aug. 21, 1842; Daniel b. March 4, 1844; George b. Feb. 21, 1846.

BUDD, GEORGE (son of Charles Budd and Louisa Capeland). Born Feb. 21, 1846.
Married Sarah Jane Turpin April 7, 1872, Salt Lake City (daughter of Jesse Turpin and Jane Smith, pioneers Sept. 20, 1848, Brigham Young company). She was born June 2, 1850, Salt Lake City. Their children: Charles E. b. Jan. 25, 1873; Sarah Louise b. Nov. 7, 1874, m. Walter Duncombe; George Henry b. Aug. 15, 1877, m. Edith Farnese; William Alvin b. April 12, 1880, m. Hannah O. Jensen and Letha Jane Lay; James Hervey b. Nov. 12, 1883, m. Eva Isabel Dangerfield; Martha Hazel b. Jan. 9, 1887, m. Howard A. Davis; Frances Mary b. Dec. 30, 1889; Gerald Jesse b. March 24, 1893, m. Marie Hanson. Family home Salt Lake City.
Carpenter and millwright.

BUHLER, ULRICH (son of Christian Buhler and Anna Von Gunten of Achlisbuhl, Canton Bern, Switzerland). Born Dec. 7, 1823, at Heimondswand, Switzerland. Came to Utah July 4, 1872.
Married Anna Burgdorffer 1854, in Switzerland (daughter of Christian Burgdorffer and Susanna Egli, of Gunten, Switzerland, pioneers 1868). She was born in July 1824. Their children: Anna, m. John T. R. Hicks; Magdalena, m. Christen Berger; Elizabeth, m. Christian Kunz; Susanna, m. John T. R. Hicks; Gottfried F., m. Louisa Barben; Caroline, m. Christen Kunz; John Ulrich, m. Magdalena Haueter; Karl, m. Jane McGee; Gotlieb, m. Louisa Krebs. Family home Midway, Utah.
High priest. Farmer. Died Jan. 31, 1907.

BUHLER, GOTTFRIED F. (son of Ulrich Buhler and Anna Burgdorffer). Born Oct. 28, 1854, in Switzerland. Came to Utah in 1872.
Married Louisa Barbin Dec. 9, 1880, Salt Lake City (daughter of Jacob Barbin and Susan Bergener of Switzerland). She was born Jan. 1, 1865. Their children: Franklin Gottfried b. Jan. 10, 1883, died; William John b. Nov. 8, 1885, m. Rachel Wilson; Joseph b. July 11, 1887; Alma Herman b. July 16, 1891; Adeline Louisa b. Aug. 30, 1893; Francis Lyman b. Oct. 30, 1895; Ephraim Walter b. Aug. 12, 1897; Carl Rolhand b. Oct. 17, 1899; Orson Earl b. Jan. 26, 1902; Burnice Elmence b. Feb. 27, 1904; Vesta Amber; Thurman Jacob. Family home Midway, Utah.
Missionary to Switzerland and Germany 1888-90; high priest; ward teacher; president German branch. School trustee; member town board; justice of the peace. Established first creamery at Midway; stockraiser and merchant.

BULL, DANIEL D. (son of Joseph Bull and Sarah Bullock of Birmingham, Eng.). Born Sept. 16, 1814, at Birmingham. Came to Utah 1849.
Married Elizabeth Tantum, 1841, at Birmingham (daughter of William Tantum and Sarah Brown of that place, pioneers 1849, Enoch Reese company). She was born May 3, 1818. Their children: Charles b. Sept. 17, 1842, m. Jane Rounci; Sophronia Ann b. Sept. 22, 1844, m. Thos Harding; Elizabeth b. Jan. 15, 1853, m. W. B. Parkinson.
High priest. Was Brigham Young's gunsmith; built the first gunsmith shop in Utah on Main street, Salt Lake City. Moved to Morgan, Utah, in 1860, and engaged in cattle and sheep raising. Assisted in organization of Morgan Co-op store, of which he was director and treasurer until his death. Morgan City councilman; school trustee. Bandman in Salt Lake City and bandmaster at Morgan. Died Nov. 11, 1885.

BULLARD, EZRA NELSON (son of John Bullard and Prudence McNamara of Worcester, Mass.). Born March 15, 1833, at Worcester. Came to Utah in 1852.
Married Mary Harriet Burgess July 27, 1856, Salt Lake City (daughter of William Burgess and Marie Pulsipher of Pennsylvania, pioneers Sept. 20, 1848, Brigham Young company). She was born May 22, 1842. Their children: Prudence Marie b. Aug. 30, 1857 (d. 1884), m. John Wilson; William Austin b. Nov. 2, 1859, m. Mary Elizabeth Johnson; Mary Ellen b. Jan. 30, 1861, m. Benjamin Clark; Orpha Estella b. April 28, 1863, d. infant; Ezra Nelson Jr. b. Sept. 8, 1864, m. Mary Ann Brinkerhoff; Olive Celestia b. Nov. 19, 1871, m. Hyrum H. Huntsman; Charles McNamara b. Nov. 19, 1871, m. Jenny Vivian Mangum 1894; Viola b. April 23, 1873, m. Andrew Martinson; Edward Franklin b. Oct. 30, 1875, d. 1888; Margaret Burgess b. May 22, 1878, m. James Kelley; John Ellis b. Nov. 2, 1880; Lilly Maud b. Sept. 21, 1883, m. Arthur Combs; Frederick b. Sept. 2, 1889, d. infant; Francetta b. Sept. 2, 1889, m. Orr Wilson March, 1910. Family home Thurber, Utah.
Elder; member 9th quorum seventies. Veteran Echo canyon and Black Hawk Indian wars. Farmer. Died at Thurber, Utah.

BULLARD, JOHN ELLIS (son of Ezra Nelson Bullard and Mary Harriet Burgess). Born Nov. 2, 1880, at Thurber, Utah.

BULLEN, NEWELL (son of Jesse Bullen and Sally Lovell). Born Aug. 18, 1809, in Kennebec county, Maine. Came to Utah 1848. Oxteam company.
Married Clarissa Judkins Atkinson (daughter of William Atkinson and Mary Blunt), who was born May 20, 1806. Their children: Francis Andrew b. Aug. 24, 1837; Herschel b. Jan. 10, 1840, m. Lydia Malinda Knapp March 28, 1868; m. Emma Boston Gibbs Feb. 8, 1870; m. Mary Josephine Whittle Dec. 20, 1876; Cincinnatus b. Feb. 25, 1842; John Joseph b. Oct. 25, 1847, m. Elizabeth Van Ettan; Samuel b. April 27, 1850; Newell, Jr, b. Nov. 8, 1852, m. Marian Drusilla Pew Feb. 21, 1878. Family resided Salt Lake City and Richmond, Utah.

BULLEN, HERSCHEL (son of Newell Bullen and Clarissa Judkins Atkinson). Born Jan. 10, 1840, Mercer, Somerset county, Me. Came to Uta 1848.
Married Lydia Malinda Knapp March 28, 1868, at Salt Lake City (daughter of Albert Knapp and Rozina Shepard of Richmond, Utah). She was born April 4, 1851. Only child: Lorenzo H. b. May 9, 1869. Family home Richmond. They were divorced Dec. 27, 1869.
Married Emma Boston Gibbs. Feb. 8, 1870, Salt Lake City (daughter of George D. Gibbs and Eleanor Griffiths of Paradise, Utah, pioneers 1866). She was born Aug. 14, 1851, and died Oct. 1, 1873. Their children: Herschel, Jr. b. Nov. 13, 1870, m. Mary Hendricks; Nellie b. Feb. 22, 1872, m. Willard Langston.
Married Mary Josephine Whittle Dec. 20, 1876, at Salt Lake City (daughter of John Casper Whittle and Mary Ann Harris of Richmond, pioneers 1848). She was born July 19, 1857. Their children: Roy b. Dec. 12, 1877, m. Annie Nibley; Pearl b. Dec. 20, 1879, m. A. B. Harrison; Cyrus b. Feb. 19, 1882, m. Maud Pearl; Emma b. Nov. 28, 1884, d. Feb. 14, 1891; Asa b. Sept. 6, 1886; Bryant b. Feb. 24, 1890; Edith b. Dec. 9, 1892, m. D. Earle Robinson. Family home resided Richmond, Utah.
Seventy. Directed construction of R. G. W. railroad between Price and Salt Lake City; directed construction of O. S. L. railroad between Salt Lake City and Weston, Idaho. Member state board of land commissioners 1900-04. Farmer Died June 27, 1911.

BULLEN, LORENZO H. (son of Herschel Bullen and Lydia Malinda Knapp). Born May 9, 1869, Richmond, Utah.
Married Sarah Maud Johnson Nov. 19, 1903, Logan, Utah (daughter of William Leamon Johnson and Katie Wickham, pioneers October, 1860). She was born Oct. 27, 1882. Their children: Lorenzo Johnson b. Sept. 7, 1904; Dean Johnson b. April 12, 1908. Family home Richmond.

BULLEN, HERSCHEL, JR. (son of Herschel Bullen and Emma Boston Gibbs). Born Nov. 13, 1870, Richmond, Utah.
Married Mary Hendricks April 11, 1894, at Logan (daughter of William Doris Hendricks and Alvira Lavona Smith of Richmond). She was born Jan. 4, 1875. Their children: Herschel Keith b. July 17, 1898; Lavona b. April 1, 1902, d. Jan. 14, 1903; Helen b. Nov. 29, 1904; Reed b. Nov. 17, 1906; Thurlow b. Jan. 9, 1912. Family home Logan.
Seventy; missionary to England 1891-96. Member board of education Logan City 1900-04; member state senate 1907 and 1909.

BULLEN, NEWELL, JR. (son of Newell Bullen and Clarissa Judkins Atkinson). Born Nov. 8, 1852, at Salt Lake City.
Married Marian Drusilla Pew Feb. 21, 1878, Logan, Utah (daughter of Hyrum Pew and Henrietta Drusilla Weymouth, the former came to Utah Sept. 24, 1848, Heber C. Kimball company, the latter Sept. 25, 1850, Thomas Johnson company). She was born April 6, 1856, Farmington, Utah. Their children: Mabel b. Nov. 23, 1878, m. Wilford Van Cott Young June 3, 1903; Ethel b. Oct. 17, 1880, m. George Oliver Webb Dec. 9, 1903; Newell Francis b. Sept. 1, 1884, m. Anna Lenore Stoddard May 17, 1904; Russell Pew b. Aug. 29, 1887, m. Ethel Josephine Spackman Dec. 29, 1909; Milton Hyrum b. Feb. 25, 1892. Family home Richmond, Utah.

BULLOCH, DAVID (son of James Bulloch, born Jan. 8, 1808, and Isabella Dunn, born Dec. 13, 1813, both of Glasgow, Scotland). He was born Sept. 10, 1844 at Glasgow. Came to Utah September, 1851, Morris Snedaker independent company.
Married Alice Bladen April 5, 1869 (daughter of Thomas Bladen and Mary Cottle), who was born July 1849. Their children: David C. b. July 18, 1872, m. Clara Crane; Robert William b. July 29, 1875, m. Arminta McConnell; John Taylor b. May 28, 1878, m. Mary Jane Arthur; Mary Isabell b. Aug. 25, 1880, m. Henry Mackelprang; Thomas b. April 13, 1884, m. Rebecca Walker; Angus b. April 7, 1889.
Married Sarah Ann Higbee Jan. 5, 1390, Juarez, Mexico (daughter of John M. Higbee and Eunice Bladen, pioneers 1847 and 1851 respectively). She was born Nov. 27, 1861, Cedar City, Utah. Their children: Warren b. June 7, 1894; Norine b. Jan. 15, 1897. Families resided at Cedar City.
First white boy on site of Cedar City; early freighter to Nevada mining camps; in early days had charge of Co-op cattle and horse herds. Assisted in bringing immigrants to Utah. Member Cedar City council. Missionary to Scotland 1875-76.

BULLOCK, DAVID COTTLE (son of David Bulloch and Alice Bladen). Born July 10, 1872, Cedar City, Utah.
Married Clara Cram Jan. 3, 1893, St. George, Utah (daughter of Charles Cram and Maggie Smith), who was born Dec. 21, 1868, Salt Lake City. Their children: Della; Charles; Clara. Family home Cedar City, Utah.
Stock and sheepraiser.

BULLOCK, BENJAMIN KIMBALL (son of Benjamin Bullock and Dorothy Kimball of Grafton, Grafton county, N. H.). Born Jan. 27, 1821, at Grafton. Came to Utah Sept. 20, 1852, Isaac Bullock company.
Married Martha Elizabeth Hart Jan. 26, 1851, Bullock's Grove, Iowa (daughter of Thomas T. Hart and Mary Riggs of Oxford, Conn.—latter a pioneer Sept. 20, 1852). She was born Oct. 4, 1837, Oxford, Conn. Their children: Benjamin Kimball, Jr. b. June 11, 1852, d. Oct. 16, 1855; Thomas Henry b. Oct. 3, 1854, d. Feb. 11, 1889; Martha Melissa b. Jan. 1, 1857, m. A. E. Daniels Dec. 24, 1874; Joseph Isaac b. March 12, 1859, m. Maria Anderson March 12, 1892; John Kimball b. June 9, 1861, m. Addie Arnold Burton June 16, 1900; George Albert b. Sept. 25, 1863, m. Mary Jane Dugdale Nov. 27, 1886; David Charles b. April 19, 1866, d. Oct. 20, 1867; Seth Hart b. Sept. 5, 1868, d. Oct. 27, 1868; Gideon Riggs b. Nov. 10, 1869, d. Feb. 25, 1877; Frank Orin b. Jan. 12, 1873, d. Aug. 12, 1905; Burt Kilton b. Oct. 9, 1875, m. Annie L. Anderson March 20, 1900; Benjamin Hart b. Oct. 27, 1878, m. Nora Alice Broadbent April 20, 1904; Jared Asa b. Nov. 14, 1882, d. Feb. 2, 1884.
Married Ann Sykes Feb. 20, 1856, Provo, Utah (daughter of James Sykes and Sarah Hill), who was born Oct. 17, 1827, Brampton, Eng. Their children: James Alonzo b. March 30, 1858; Ernest Kimball b. Nov. 5, 1860; Amasa Sykes b. March 7, 1862; Ralph Arthur b. May 31, 1868. Families resided Provo, Utah.
Missionary to the Muddy 1868. Mayor of Provo three terms, 1855-61. Assisted in erection of public buildings at Provo.

BULLOCK, BENJAMIN HART (son of Benjamin Kimball Bullock and Martha Elizabeth Hart). Born Oct. 27, 1878, Provo, Utah.
Married Nora Alice Broadbent April 20, 1904, Salt Lake City (daughter of Thomas Broadbent and Chana Ellen Spainhower of Provo, pioneers Sept. 1862). She was born July 22, 1882. Their children: Grace Hart b. April 2, 1905; Benjamin Vern b. Feb. 25, 1908; Alice b. June 21, 1911. Family home Provo.
Missionary to England 1899-02; secretary 123d and member 34th quorums seventies; 2d counselor and later president 3d ward Y. M. I. A. of Provo; 2d assistant Sunday school superintendent, 1st ward; set apart bishop of Bonneville ward, Provo, Feb. 16, 1913. Miner; farmer.

BULLOCK, ISAAC (son of Benjamin Bullock and Dorothy Kimball, both of Grafton, Grafton county, N. H.). Born Oct. 23, 1825. Came to Utah Sept. 21, 1852.
Married Electa Wood Dec. 14, 1856. She was born July 15, 1834. Their children: Isaac, Jr., b. Sept. 19, 1857; Electa b. March 6, 1857; Hanna Christina b. Dec. 25, 1861; Frances Eva b. June 7, 1867; Ada Elizabeth b. May 12, 1869; Nettie May b. June 13, 1872; Gideon Owen b. Dec. 3, 1875; Abraham b. July 24, 1878. Family home Provo.
Married Emma Stoot April 6, 1857, Salt Lake City (daughter of William Stoot and Sarah Lees of England). She was born June 27, 1840. Their children: William b. Aug. 30, 1859; Edwin James b. Oct. 8, 1861, died; Allison b. 1864, died; Lyman b. 1867, died; Emma Jane b. July 24, 1870, died; Hezekiah b. 1873, died; Sarah b. Jan. 9, 1878; Celia Ann b. 1881, died; John b. 1884 and Jared b. 1887, died. Family home Provo, Utah.
Missionary to England 1863-66; president high priests' quorum. Mayor of Provo 1863; member Utah legislature; U. S. marshal 1867. Farmer. Died March 16, 1891, Provo, Utah.

BULLOCK, JAMES (son of Thomas Bullock and Jeanett Boyle, of Canada). Born 1805, in Scotland. Came to Utah Sept. 20, 1848, Brigham Young company.
Married Mary Hill in Canada (daughter of Alexander and Elizabeth Hill, pioneers 1850, independent company). Their children: Alexander b. 1838, m. Emily Harris; Elizabeth b. 1842, m. Donald D. McArthur 1857; Mary E. b. 1846, m. E. Farns; James O. b. 1849, m. Martha Brown. Family home Pleasant Grove, Utah.
Seventy; counselor to Bishops Brown and Thorne. City councilman, Pleasant Grove, four years. Farmer.

BULLOCK, ALEXANDER (son of James Bullock and Mary Hill). Born Sept. 22, 1838, in Canada. Came to Utah with father.
Married Emily Caroline Harris Nov. 9, 1861, at Salt Lake City (daughter of Moses McGee Harris and Mary Givens, pioneers Sept. 20, 1848, Brigham Young company). She was born Feb. 14, 1844. Their children: Emily Ellen b. Oct. 18, 1862, m. Thomas Admonson; William A. b. June 25, 1865, m. Clara E. Marrott; Newel H. b. Oct. 22, 1867, m. Mary Skillings; Effie D. b. April 15, 1871, m. William H. Marrott; Dessie b. June 6, 1874, died; McGee H. b. Nov. 6, 1876, m. Octavie Poulson; Florence H. b. Feb. 5, 1882, m. John P. Madsen.
Married Clarissa Melissa Herron Dec. 7, 1875, Pleasant Grove (daughter of Orlando F. Herron, pioneer 1847, and Hannah J. Driggs, pioneer April 1849, Aaron Farr company).

She was born April 1858. Their children: Jeanet C. b. 1877, m. Henry Johnson; Lamont b. April 19, 1879; Gertrude b. 1881, m. Lafayette G. Blackmont; Hannah b. 1884, m. O. Halladay. Family home Pleasant Grove, Utah.
Missionary to New Zealand 1887-89; high priest. City marshal Pleasant Grove 12 years. Farmer and stockraiser.

BULLOCK, THOMAS (son of Thomas Bullock and Mary Hall of Leek, Staffordshire, Eng.). Born Dec. 23, 1816 at Leek. Came to Utah July 24, 1847, Brigham Young company.
Married Henrietta Rushton at Leek, who was born Feb. 13, 1817. Their children: Thomas Honri, m. Mary Ann Wagstaff; Charles Richard, m. Susan Marinda Johnson; m. Wilhelmina Iverson; Pamela, m. James B. Mason; Willard Richard died; Mary Elizabeth, m. Walter Scott Halbrook; Brigham Maroni died; Henrietta Rushton, m. George Garretson Griffith; Francis Alonzo, m. Margaret Priscilla Smith; David Parley died. Family home 14th ward, Salt Lake City.
Seventy; missionary to England 1855-57; clerk for first pioneer company, and in office of church historian. Once a press corrector on Deseret News. First recorder Salt Lake City and county. Died Feb. 10, 1885, Coalville, Utah.

BULLOCK, FRANCIS ALONZO (son of Thomas Bullock and Henrietta Rushton). Born Aug. 5, 1855, Salt Lake City.
Married Margaret Priscilla Smith Nov. 7, 1882 (daughter of William Simmons Smith and Margaret Rebecca Bird of Salt Lake City, pioneers 1853). She was born Nov. 8, 1860. Their children: Alonzo Eugene b. May 27, 1883, m. Edna Elizabeth Rawlings; William Owen b. Aug. 4, 1886; Myrtle b. Sept. 19, 1888; Lester Rowland b. April 11, 1894; Margaret Arlene b. July 26, 1901. Family home Salt Lake City.
Elder. Yard-checker for Harriman railroads.

BULT, ROBERT (son of Robert S. Bult and Jane Coats, former of England, latter of Scotland, pioneers 1862). Born Dec. 7, 1865, Salt Lake City.
Married Mary Jane Haslam June 15, 1888, Salt Lake City (daughter of John R. Haslam and Margerite Howarth, pioneers Oct. 1853, Cyrus H. Wheelock company). She was born Aug. 6, 1868, Salt Lake City. Their children: Lester R. b. Dec. 18, 1889, m. Ethel Ball; Margerite J. b. Feb. 9, 1891, d. aged 20; Sarah A. b. Oct. 14, 1892, m. Thomas Seddon; Robert A. b. June 15, 1893; Lottie I. b. March 29, 1895; Carl H. b. Feb. 22, 1896; Ethel L. b. July 14, 1899; William E. b. April 2, 1903; Ralph b. June 1, 1908; Myrtle D. b. Jan. 16, 1911. Family home Salt Lake City.
Locomotive engineer and railroad switchman.

BUNCE, LEWIS DE MOTT. Born Sept. 29, 1827, Walcott, Wayne county, N. Y. Came to Utah 1852.
Married Elmira Vorhees Oct. 28, 1852, Salt Lake City (daughter of Elisha Vorhees and Nancy Ann Leak, of Manti, Utah, pioneers 1851, Ezra T. Benson company). She was born June 30, 1834. Their children. Esther Ann b. Sept. 20, 1853, m. Jasper Larson; Louis Avery b. Oct. 5, 1854, m. Betsey Jeffs; Mary Elizabeth b. Nov. 8, 1855, m. William Dixon; Warren Alonzo b. Jan. 14, 1857, died; Austin Moroni b. April 18, 1858, m. Ella Burns; Elmira Matilda b. April 6, 1860, m. Niels C. Christensen; Joseph Delaney b. Sept. 16, 1862, m. Retta Johnson; William Franklin b. Oct. 4, 1863, m. Mamie Pollock; Diantha Adaline b. Sept. 8, 1865; Jane b. Jan. 23, 1867; Rosabell b. March 30, 1868, and Arabell b. March 30, 1868, latter four died; Laura Luella b. Sept. 8, 1870, m. Peter Christensen; Urbin Ross b. June 14, 1875, m. Ethel Warnick; John Homer b. Aug. 25, 1890. Family home Parowan, Utah.
Seventy; missionary to England 1877-79. Lived at Manti, Springdale, and Parowan; moved to Sterling 1875. Veteran Black Hawk Indian and Mexican wars. Mason and farmer. Died Sept. 16, 1894, Price, Utah.

BUNNELL, DAVID EDWIN (son of Ithamar Bunnell). Born June 25, 1809, Newark, Essex county, N. J. Came to Utah Oct. 5, 1852, captain of ten in James C. Snow company.
Married Sallie Heller Conrad April 15, 1830, Elmira, N. Y., who was born Sept. 19, 1810. Their children: Daniel Kimball, m. Abigail Miller (Martin); m. Mary Muir (Hughes); Stephen Ithamar, m. Percia Cornelia Grover; Samuel Gardner, m. Ellen K. Zabriskie; George Henry, m. Margarette Sulzer; Phoebe Elizabeth, m. Joseph Cluff; Mary Armstrong, m. Sidney T. Horsley; Martha, died; Alfareda, m. Lorin S. Glazier; Rosetta, m. Vernie Lorenzo Halladay. Family home Provo, Utah.
Member 34th quorum seventies; high priest; missionary to eastern states 1849. Sent by Brigham Young to colonize the White Mountain section of Arizona. Provo city councilman and one of its first fruitgrowers. Carpenter and farmer. Died July 3, 1865.

BUNNELL, DANIEL KIMBALL (son of David Edwin Bunnell and Sallie Heller Conrad). Born Oct. 23, 1831, Brownstown, Wayne county, Mich. Came to Utah Oct. 5, 1852.
Married Abigail Miller (Martin) Nov. 28, 1856, Indiantown, Iowa (daughter of Branch Miller and Abigail Williams of Scotland county, Mo.). She was born June 15, 1840. Their children: Alphretta Jane b. Sept. 28, 1857, m. John Lee; Mary Ellen b. Sept. 28, 1859, m. Chill Brown; Daniel Edwin b.

John Henry b. Oct. 20, 1876, d. July 22, 1908. Family home Henefer, Utah.
Married Annie Hunt (Price) February, 1870, Salt Lake City (daughter of John and Ann Hunt (Price), pioneers 1869). She was born Sept. 1, 1852, Deptford, Eng. Their children: Edward b. 1870, d. 1872; Felix Leonard b. November, 1874, m. Mary Elizabeth Dearden, 1897; Charles and Charlotte (twins), both died; Myrah Adelaide Annie b. September, 1877; Lydia May b. May 17, 1880; Frederic Ludovic b. May 2, 1889; John Alma b. Nov. 18, 1886, married Nov. 7, 1906; Samuel Arthur b. May 17, 1899. Family home Henefer, Utah.
His grandfather was a captain-general, and his father receiver-principal, in the custom-houses of the French government. He fought in the French army, was in the campaign of Rome, 1848, and after leaving the army, located in Geneva, where he first married. Missionary from Utah to France, Switzerland and Italy 1882; president 27th quorum seventies; high priest; patriarch. Was arrested June 6, 1889, at Ogden, and again July 5, 1890, at Henefer, for following his religious beliefs. Watchmaker; civil engineer for Union Pacific Railroad company. Justice of the peace; elected surveyor of Summit county 1872. Retired farmer, stockraiser and sheepman.

BUNOT, WALTER (son of Joseph Almé August Bunot and Louise Richard). Born in April, 1869, Salt Lake City, Utah.
Married Sarah Ralphs Aug. 19, 1894, Salt Lake City (daughter of Fred Ralphs), who was born May 24, 1874, Plain City, Utah. They had five children, all girls.

BURBANK, DANIEL M. Born Dec. 3, 1814, in New York state. Came to Utah Oct. 6, 1852, captain independent company.
Married Abigail Blogit, who died en route to Utah. Among their children was: Mary L. b. Jan. 30, 1844, m. Henry L. Marble.
Married Sarah S. Burbank, who was born Feb. 10, 1835, Boston, Leeds Co., Canada, and came to Utah with husband. Among their children was: Sarah S. b. July 12, 1866, m. George Roland Williams Oct. 25, 1883.

DURBIDGE, JAMES RHOADES. Born Dec. 22, 1814, Bedford, Eng. Started for Utah in 1854, with ten-pound company and died en route.
Married Mary Brown (daughter of John Brown and Edith Atterton of Biggleswade, Bedfordshire, Eng.). She was born Dec. 16, 1816. Their children: James William b. Feb. 25, 1837, m. Sarah J. Humphery; Catharine Emma b. Nov. 17, 1839, m. Samuel P. Hoyt; Jesse Rhoades b. March 1, 1844, m. Catherine D. Pack; Mary Ann b. Jan. 17, 1851; Jane E. b. Oct. 31, 1848, m. John K. Lemon; Lucy, m. James McCormick.
Died May 15, 1854, Florence, Neb.

BURBIDGE, JESSE RHOADES (son of James Rhoades Burbidge and Mary Brown). Born March 1, 1844, Bedfordshire, Eng. Came to Utah Sept. 30, 1854, Darwin Richardson company.
Married Catherine Devalla Pack Aug. 14, 1871, Salt Lake City (daughter of John Pack and Ruth Mosher of Kingston, Canada, pioneers July 24, 1847, Brigham Young company). She was born June 8, 1853. Their children: Ruth Devalla b. Aug. 24, 1872, m. Robert Dee King April 28, 1896; Jesse Elias b. Jan. 28, 1874, m. Sarah Vivian Simpson Sept. 1898; Ward Parley b. May 4, 1876, m. Orinda Park Dec. 1901; Mary Ann b. Dec. 15, 1877; Emma Ursula b. Oct. 24, 1879, m. Samuel Turnbow June 28, 1899; Catherine Emily b. Oct. 4, 1881, m. Spencer Williams Jan. 15, 1902; James Rhoades b. Aug. 8, 1883, m. Florence J. Wilkinson Sept. 10, 1912; William Allen b. Nov. 28, 1885; Henry Eugene b. Sept. 8, 1887, m. Myrtle Woolstenhulme Oct. 4, 1910; John Ashahel b. Jan. 4, 1890, d. June 5, 1890; Lucy Celestia b. March 16, 1893, d. Oct. 20, 1906; Zoa Sarah b. June 6, 1893, m. George Williams Nov. 22, 1911; Anton Lemon b. Feb. 3, 1897; Laura b. July 30, 1898, died. Family resided Salt Lake City and Kamas, Utah.

BURCH, DANIEL (son of Daniel Burch and Rebecca Dumford). Born Nov. 5, 1803, Boone county, Ky. Came to Utah Sept. 20, 1848, Lorenzo Snow company.
Married Ann Wilson McClellen Nov. 11, 1829 (daughter of James McClellen and Ann Giffin), who was born Nov. 1, 1807, Hamilton county, Ohio. Their children: John Milton b. Oct. 1530; William b. July 4, 1832, m. Ida Hazleton; James b. Dec. 10, 1835, m. Nancy L. Stewart Dec. 18, 1861; Robert McClellen b. April 21, 1838, m. Catherine J. Jenkins, 1865; Belinda b. March 21, 1840, m. John Matthew Clark Jan. 24, 1858; Angeline b. 1842; Emma b. Dec. 21, 1844, m. John Westley Shoup 1870; Joseph b. Oct. 22, 1844; Elizabeth Nancy b. Jan. 31, 1849, m. George Richard Hill Dec. 18, 1872. Family resided Nauvoo, Ill.; Cincinnati, Ohio, and Ogden, Utah.
Built first sawmill and grist mill in Weber county, and first ferry boat on Weber river.

BURCH, JAMES (son of Daniel Burch and Ann Wilson McClellen). Born Dec. 10, 1835, Cincinnati, Ohio.
Married Nancy Lorena Stewart Dec. 18, 1861, Ogden, Utah (daughter of George Stewart and Ruth Baker, latter a pioneer Sept. 21, 1847, Abraham O. Smoot company). She was born Nov. 6, 1841, in Alabama. Their children: Ruth Ann b. May 12, 1863, m David Stowell April 17, 1884; Nancy Jane b. June 11, 1865; Emma Lorena b. May 30, 1868, m. Joseph B. Whitehead 1889; Eva Belinda b. April 10, 1871; Cynthia Ella b. Nov. 10, 1872, m. Lucius A. Humphrey June 30, 1898; Mary Elizabeth b. Oct. 11, 1875, m. James Brown July 6, 1904; Edith Matilda b. Dec. 29, 1877, m. Thomas H. Clifford Nov. 22, 1899; James Edward b. June 15, 1880, m. Martha Selman; Florence b. March 4, 1884, m. Joseph B. Clark May 9, 1904; George McClellen b. Oct. 3, 1886. Family home Ogden, Utah.
Bishop's first counselor and also second counselor at Ogden, Utah; high councilor twenty years. Policeman and school trustee at Ogden.

BURCH, ROBERT McCLELLEN (son of Daniel Burch and Ann Wilson McClellen). Born April 21, 1838, Hamilton county, Ohio. Came to Utah Sept. 24, 1847.
Married Catherine Jane Jenkins (daughter of Thomas Jenkins and Joanna Marshall, pioneers 1852). She was born Aug. 22, 1846. Their children: Robert M. b. Aug. 3, 1866, m. Edith A. Thompson Dec. 13, 1888; Daniel b. Dec. 8, 1868, m. Edith Stoker; Thomas G. b. Jan. 25, 1872; John William b. Dec. 28, 1873; James Karry b. Oct. 5, 1875; Samuel Furgeson b. June 7, 1878, m. Pearl Crandall; David Aaron b. April 6, 1880; Heber b. Dec. 29, 1881; Henry b. May 5, 1884, m. Susie Arnold; Wilford Woodruff b. March 4, 1886; Benjamin Jenkins b. Feb. 13, 1888; Lewis Marshall b. April 27, 1891. Family home Weber county, Utah.
High priest. Farmer and stockraiser.

BURGENER, JACOB (son of Jacob Burgener and Annie Touscher of Switzerland). Born April 13, 1824, in Switzerland. Came to Utah October, 1864, George W. Snow company.
Married Marie Müllenatter in Switzerland (daughter of John Müllenatter), who was born Sept. 22, 1819. Their children: Marie, m. Christy Shoney; Jacob and Annie, died; Christian, m. Emelie Sulzer; John, m. Mary Murri; Louisa, died. Family home Midway, Utah.
Married Elizabeth Christian at Salt Lake City, who was born in 1835. Family home in Switzerland.
Elder. Farmer and stockraiser. Died Aug. 7, 1895, at Midway, Utah.

BURGENER, CHRISTIAN (son of Jacob Burgener and Marie Müllenatter). Born Nov. 21, 1855, in Switzerland. Came to Utah 1864 with parents.
Married Emelie Sulzer Nov. 13, 1876, Heber Utah (daughter of Casper Sulzer and Kathryne Stiedler of Meiringen, Switzerland, pioneers Sept. 22, 1861, Joseph W. Young company. She was born Sept. 5, 1859. Their children: Emelie Irene b. Oct. 21, 1877, m. John Fausett; Anna Elizabeth b. June 11, 1879, m. John E. Berg; Christian Ernest b. June 12, 1881; Kathryne Bertha b. May 9, 1883, m. Fred Dummer; Margareth Agness b. March 16, 1885, m. Abram Shields; Jacob Casper b. March 30, 1887, m. Minnie May Bunnell; John Elmer b. Jan. 31, 1889, d. May 13, 1909; Frank Monroe b. Dec. 3, 1890; Charles Arthur b. Feb. 10, 1893; Mary Merle b. Oct. 6, 1895; Laverne b. Aug. 17, 1898; Maynard Lamont b. Nov. 7, 1899; Violet b. Jan. 22, 1904. Family home Midway, Utah.
High priest; ward teacher. Farmer and stockraiser.

BURGENER, JOHN (son of Jacob Burgener and Marie Müllenatter). Born March 31, 1858, in Switzerland. Came to Utah 1864 with parents.
Married Mary Murri Nov. 27, 1878, Midway, Utah (daughter of John Murri and Elizabeth Grosen of Affoltern, Switzerland). She was born April 16, 1861. Their children: John Jacob b. Jan. 3, 1879, m. Clara Durschi; George Albert b. April 13, 1880, m. Naomi Vail; Mary Elizabeth b. April 11, 1881, m. John Sulzer; Henry Alma b. April 15, 1883, m. Hazel McDonald; Edward Laverence b. Jan. 18, 1887; William Walter b. Sept. 15, 1889; Grace Eva b. Jan. o, 1893, m. Willard McDonald; Karl Andrew b. March 13, 1896, Joseph B. b. June 24, 1899; Hazel May b. Dec. 20, 1902. Family home Midway, Utah.
Elder; ward teacher. Stockraiser and horticulturist.

BURGESS, GEORGE MARTIN (son of Horace Burgess and Almira Pulsipher and grandson of William Burgess and Violate Stockwell). Born April 2, 1839, in Clay county, Mo. Came to Utah 1850, Capt. Johnson company. (Aaron Johnson came Sept. 8 and Thomas Johnson came Sept. 12.)
Married Rhoda Ann Dykes April 16, 1864, St. George, Utah (daughter of George Parker Dykes and Dorcas Keeling of Washington county, Ky., pioneers 1852, Ezra T. Benson company. She was born in 1846. Their children: George Edward, m. Emily Jeffery; Mary Alice, m. Samuel Alonzo Gardner; Lillian, d. child; Howard Lee, died; Ella May, m. Orrin Henry Snow; Willard; Horace Martin, died; Lucy, m. Daniel E. Hendrix; Ruth Fowler, m. David Cannon Gardner; Ernest Hungate b. Jan. 3, 1884, m. Donna Viola Miles; Clarence b. Jan. 29, 1886, m. Jessie Reid.
President 29th quorum of seventies. Crossed plains three times as blacksmith. Black Hawk Indian and Echo Canyon wars veteran. Missionary among the Indians. Tanner. Pioneer of Lehi and later St. George, Utah.

BURGESS, ERNEST HUNGATE (son of George Martin Burgess and Rhoda Ann Dykes). Born Jan. 3, 1884, in Pine Valley, Utah.
Married Donna Viola Miles June 3, 1908, Salt Lake City (daughter of William A. Miles and Lucretia A. Wightman

of Salt Lake City and Payson). She was born Jan. 18, 1884. Their children: William Miles b. March 11, 1910; Ernest Martin b. Oct. 28, 1911. Family home Roosevelt, Utah.
Missionary to Germany 1904-07; president Berlin conference 1906-07; clerk of Duchesne stake; Sunday school superintendent; stake instructor of elders' quorum. Deputy county attorney of Wasatch county. Principal of Roosevelt public schools 1911-12.

BURGESS, WILLIAM. Came to Utah Sept. 22, 1848, Brigham Young company.
Married Violate Stockwell, who came to Utah with husband. Their children: Horace, m. Almira Pulsipher; Harrison, m. Amanda Hammon; Hannah; Philope; William, Jr., m. Mariah Pulsipher; Rosina; John; Frederick; Violate, m. Richard Gibbons; Melancthon, m. Margaret McIntyre. Family home in Pine Valley, Utah.

BURGESS, WILLIAM, JR. (son of William Burgess and Violate Stockwell). Born March 1, 1822, Putnam county, N. Y. Came to Utah Sept. 22, 1848.
Married Mariah Pulsipher September, 1840, in Illinois (daughter of Zera Pulsipher and Mary Ann Brown, pioneers Sept. 22, 1848). She was born June 17, 1822. Their children: Mary Harriet b. May 22, 1842, m. Ezra Nelson Bullard; Cornelia b. Jan. 1843, m. James Hughes; Juliet, m. Joshua Chidester; William b. 1848, d. infant; Wilmer, m. Jane Heath; James, m. Mary Heath; Violate, m. Joseph Meeks; William Harrison, m. Mary Ann Davis; Anetta, m. Orson Robins. Family home Huntington, Utah.
Missionary among Indians; high priest; counselor to President Thomas S. Smith. Indian war veteran and took part in Echo canyon trouble; colonel 2d regiment territorial militia 1854; captain 3d company 5th regiment Nauvoo Legion. Farmer and sawmillman. Helped build Nauvoo temple. Died March 14, 1904

BURGON, WILLARD C. (son of James Burgon and Matilda Rook of Winchester, Hampshire, Eng.). Born Nov. 5, 1854, in Hampshire. Came to Utah July 4, 1872.
Married Emma Crouch July 26, 1875, Salt Lake City (daughter of William Crouch and Caroline Baker of London, Eng., who came to Utah Nov. 14, 1873). She was born March 3, 1857. Their children: Emma Matilda b. June 2, 1876, m. Thomas F. Greenwood; Minnie Josephine b. Sept. 13, 1878, m. William M. Cox; Willard Charles b. Sept. 28, 1880, m. Ann Walker; Heber James b. May 20, 1882, m. Lulu M. Hanson; Albert Edward b. July 15, 1884, m. Bertha E. Hansen; Horace William b. Sept. 7, 1888, m. Alice Graham; Franklin Ernest b. Sept. 25, 1890. Family home Union, Salt Lake county, Utah.
Bishop Union ward 1900-10; president high priests' quorum, Jordan stake; missionary to England 1895-97. Justice of peace. Mason and contractor.

BURKE, CHARLES PETER (son of Andrew Bjurke and Anna Nielsen, born June 29, 1799, in Sweden). He was born Aug. 11, 1837, Malmö, Sweden. Came to Utah Nov. 9, 1856, Abraham O. Smoot company.
Married Betsey Christina Jensen June, 1859 (daughter of Jens Jensen and Kristen Andersen). She was born Jan. 13, 1844, in Denmark. Their children: Betsey Ann b. Jan. 13, 1861, m. Richard Parker Jan. 28, 1880; Mary Jane b. April 11, 1864, m. Thomas R. Reeve; Amanda Jane b. Aug. 5, 1866, m. Amos J. Workman; Charles b. Dec. 2, 1868, m. Mary Sophia Peterson Jan. 20, 1891; Oscar b. July 16, 1871, m. Elizabeth Humphries; Andrew b. Sept. 23, 1873; Hyrum b. Dec. 19, 1876, m. Estella Pack.
Married Annie Batilda Johnson Sept. 1, 1880, St. George, Utah (daughter of Caroline Johnson), who was born Aug. 9, 1856, Helsingborg, Sweden. Their children: Wilhelmina b. Oct. 13, 1877 (adopted), m. Thomas Cook; Caroline b. July 6, 1882, m. Alma Wright; Walter G. b. Oct. 22, 1884, m. Amanda Johnson.
Married Annie Andersen July 27, 1887, St. George, Utah (daughter of Anders Mortensen and Maren Jacobsen Andersen), who was born Jan. 15, 1863 in Denmark. Their children: Lula b. Dec. 24, 1885, (adopted), m. Swan Burg; Alma b. June 14, 1888, m. Arintha Howard; Arthur b. Dec. 19, 1889; Emily b. July 2, 1892, m. Godfrey Johnson; Clarence b. Oct. 3, 1895; Norah b. April 1, 1900.
Settled at Spring City; moved to Dixie, then to Hinckley, Utah, and later to Woodville, Idaho.

BURKE, CHARLES (son of Charles Peter Burke and Betsey Christina Jensen). Born Dec. 2, 1868, Virgin, Utah.
Married Mary Sophia Peterson Jan. 20, 1891, Deseret, Utah (daughter of Nels Mathias Peterson and Mary Elizabeth Woodard), who was born Sept. 25, 1871, at Lehi, Utah. Their children: Charles Walter b. Jan. 29, 1892; Pacosa Dean b. March 1, 1894; Mary Juanita b. April 25, 1896; Denzil b. March 2, 1899; Newel Mathies b. Jan. 18, 1902; Elgin Alburn b. Nov. 7, 1905; Ferron P. b. May 23, 1910.

BURNETT, DAVID (son of Alexander Burnett, born 1783, at Carnoustie, and Margaret Robertson, born 1780, Abroath, Scotland). He was born Feb. 14, 1814, at Abreath. Came to Utah Sept. 12, 1861, John R. Murdock company.

nigna Day; Maud b. April 4, 1889; Bryant A. b. Feb. 12, 1894. Family home Bountiful.
Member 70th quorum seventies; missionary to England 1879-81; high priest; block teacher. School trustee at Bountiful. General merchant; gardener.

BURNINGHAM, THOMAS (son of Thomas Burningham and Sarah White). Came to Utah with father.
Married Ellen Hook 1861, Bountiful, Utah, Bishop Stoker officiating (daughter of Richard Hook and Alice Bryant of Walden, Sussex, Eng., latter a pioneer Aug. 27, 1860, Daniel Robinson handcart company). She was born Jan. 20, 1842. Their children: Mary E., m. Isaac Spencer March 4, 1879; Thomas A., m. Eliza Alford; William H., m. Sarah Burton; Emily R. d. infant; Madeline A., m. John Ashton; Heber J., m. Lavenia Porter; Frank A., m. Katie Tolman; m. Martha Lunsford; Louis L., m. Emma Lunsford; George E., m. Amelia Ixter; Charles Lester, m. Emma King; Annie L., m. Harvey Sessions. Family home Bountiful, Utah.
Married Lucina Sessions.
Member 70th quorum seventies; high priest; ward teacher; missionary to England 1893-94. Farmer and market gardener. Died 1893, Salt Lake City.

BURNS, CHARLES (son of Ellen Marsden of Nottingham, Eng.). Born Nov. 3, 1831, Nottingham, Eng. Came to Utah Aug. 19, 1868, John R. Murdock company.
Married Martha Fretwell Nov. 15, 1851, in England, who was born March 9, 1827. Their children: Mary Ellen, m. Edward Tomlinson; Joseph, m. Eliza J. Madden; Charles b. July 3, 1859, m. Susannah Stacey; Sarah m. James Stacey; Martha, m. Levi Hasker; Ellen, m. Benjamin Matkin; Hannah, m. John Blackburn. Family resided in England and Salt Lake City. Pioneer. Died Oct. 11, 1904.

BURNS, CHARLES, JR. (son of Charles Burns and Martha Fretwell). Born July 3, 1859, Brampton, Derbyshire, Eng.
Married Susannah Stacey Nov. 22, 1882, Salt Lake City (daughter of John Stacey and Susannah Worrall of England. She was born Feb. 22, 1860. Their children: Frank Charles b. Aug. 13, 1883, m. Esther Briggs; Martha b. June 9, 1885, m. George Briggs, Jr.; May b. April 30, 1887, m. James E. Haws; Joseph b. Jan. 14, 1890; Minnie b. March 24, 1892, m. Lawrence B. Squires; Edward Linus b. July 8, 1894; Henry Stacey b. Feb. 4, 1897; Susie Alice b. May 24, 1900; Lawrence Earl b. Jan. 2, 1907. Family resided at Salt Lake City, Utah, and at Archer, Idaho.
Bishop's counselor in 1902.

BURNS, ENOCH. Born Nov. 2, 1807, Ascot, Sherbrooke county, Lower Canada (Quebec). Came to Utah 1850.
Married Elizabeth Jane Pierce Jan. 11, 1842, Nauvoo, Ill. Their children: Bethsinah b. Nov. 5, 1842; Franklin b. Jan. 3, 1845; Enoch b. Aug. 6, 1847; Martha Jane b. Jan. 21, 1849; Elizabeth Ann b. Feb. 17, 1857; Mary Ellen b. Aug. 4, 1852; John Franklin b. Feb. 24, 1855; Ruth b. June 30, 1857; Amanda b. June 29, 1860; Jacob Armstead b. May 13, 1863; Sarah b. March 17, 1867.

DURRASTON, JOHN. Born April 21, 1837, Devonshire, Eng. Came to Utah 1852, James Cummings company.
Married Elizabeth Dall, who came to Utah 1854, Jacob Hofines company. Their children: Elizabeth, m. John R. Morgan July 23, 1890; William b. Oct. 5, 1865, m. Mary C. Morgan Jan. 1903; James b. Dec. 2, 1867, m. Esther Ercanbrack July, 1894; Albert b. March 24, 1870, m. Ella Brown Aug. 1894; John b. July 20, 1874, d. March 10, 1875; David b. May 6, 1876, m. Lucinda Nealson April, 1909; Maud b. Jan. 8, 1878, d. Oct. 30, 1880; Myrtle b. Feb. 27, 1880, m. Frank Sloan May, 1904; Eddie b. April 20, 1882, d. April 16, 1887; Rebecca b. Sept. 6, 1884, m. Irvin Jasperson April, 1909; Sarah b. Sept. 6, 1884; Anthony b. Aug. 10, 1887, d. Nov. 27, 1889; May b. July 4, 1896.
Came with first company taking the road from Council Bluffs, around the "Horn," and assisted in building this road. Took part in Walker Indian war 1853-67. He settled and has resided at Goshen. Member L. D. S. Church.

BURRIDGE, GEORGE WILCOX (son of Thomas Burridge, born April 17, 1782, and Annie Wilcox, born April 3, 1781, both in England). He was born Jan. 17, 1813, in Somersetshire, Eng. Came to Utah Oct. 24, 1855, Milo Andrus company.
Married Hannah Shaw Nov. 16, 1847 (daughter of John Shaw and Jane Norrie, latter a pioneer 1865). She was born Dec. 27, 1827, and came to Utah with husband. Their children: George Dennis b. Nov. 16, 1848, d. July 23, 1849; Charlotte Hannah b. March 23, 1851, m. Joseph W. Steele November, 1867; Thomas Lorenzo b. Dec. 2, 1853, m. Alice McIntosh Jan. 8, 1881; Annie Jane b. Jan. 24, 1856, d. Feb. 26, 1857; Pauline b. Feb. 26, 1858, m. Isaac James Neddo Jan. 8, 1880; Daniel Shaw b. Nov. 2, 1861, died. Family home St. John, Tooele county, Utah.
Missionary in Scotland and England; and to Italy 1853; high priest; bishop St. John ward 20 years. Manager St. John co-operative store 20 years. Farmer. Died September, 1894.

BURRIDGE, THOMAS LORENZO (son of George Wilcox Burridge and Hannah Shaw). Born Dec. 2, 1853, Valetta. Isle of Malta. Came to Utah with parents.
Married Alice Maria McIntosh Jan. 8, 1881, Salt Lake City (daughter of William McIntosh and Maria Caldwell of St. John, Utah, pioneers 1852). She was born Sept. 16, 1858. Their children: George Thomas b. Jan. 19, 1882; William McIntosh b. Oct. 6, 1883, d. Nov. 30, 1903; Franklin Dennis b. Dec. 7, 1885; Alice Marie b. Jan. 1, 1888, d. May 12, 1896; Jared b. Jan. 2, 1890, d. Sept. 15, 1890; Theol Lorenzo b. Nov. 18, 1891. Family home St. John.
Seventy; ward teacher; assistant Sunday school superintendent St. John ward. Justice of peace. Pioneer to Cottonwood Creek. Farmer and sheepraiser. Died April 12, 1891.

BURROWS, DAVID C. (son of William C. Burrows and Catherine Louder; former born Nov. 6, 1828, County Down, Ireland; latter Dec. 10, 1830, Grayson county, Virginia). He was born June 23, 1860, Salt Lake county.
Married Emeline Woodruff Aug. 18, 1887, Logan, Utah (daughter of President Wilford Woodruff and Sarah D. Stocking), who was born July 26, 1863. Their children: Wilford C. b. July 6, 1888, m. Treste Smith; David Elmer b. Sept. 13, 1890, m. Ethel Buick; Lewis L. b. May 8, 1892, m. Myrle Snyder; Lulu E. b. July 3, 1894, d. child; Ruby F. b. Feb. 25, 1896, d. infant.

BURROWS, JAMES BASCOM (son of William Henderson Burrows, born July 22, 1883, in East Tennessee, and Elizabeth Harmon Collins, born Oct. 27, 1845, Tyler, Texas; married May, 1860). He was born July 13, 1861, Denton county, Texas. Came to Utah September, 1890.
Married Lucy Emma Workman Sept. 11, 1891 (daughter of Abram Smith Workman and Millie Bethenia Devoo). She was born Nov. 21, 1874. Their children: James Henry b. Aug. 2, 1892; Effie Harmon b. Dec. 22, 1894, m. S. B. Riggs July 20, 1910; Lucy Myrtle b. Feb. 5, 1896.
Married Mary Ann Hatch June 14, 1905. Hatch, Utah (daughter of Meltiar Hatch and Mary Ann Ellis, former a member of the Mormon Battalion and pioneer October 1840, Enoch Reese company; married May 9, 1856, Bountiful, Utah). She was born March 10, 1880. Their children: Carl Bascom b. Feb. 24, 1906; Horace J. b. Sept. 15, 1907; Herbert C. b. July 30, 1909.
Missionary to eastern states 1899-91; bishop Hatch ward 1905. School teacher in Garfield 1890-99 and 1902-05; school trustee Georgetown 1894; postmaster there 1894, and of Hatch 1908; justice of peace Hillsdale 1898.

BURT, JAMES (son of Thomas Burt of Edinburgh, Scotland). Born Jan. 8, 1822, Ballantrae, Scotland. Came to Utah Oct. 19, 1862, Horton D. Haight company.
Married Mary McBride Dec. 4, 1841, Glasgow, Scotland (daughter of James McBridge of Ballantrae), who was born Aug. 28, 1821. Their children: Ellen, m. Robert Miller; James, m. Annie Hughes; John, m. Hulda ———; Elizabeth, m. Walter Lindsay; Mary Alice, d. aged 10; Mary, m. Thomas Atkinson; Christina, m. John Clark. Family resided Salt Lake City and Eden, Utah.
High priest and Sunday school superintendent at Eden. Blacksmith; farmer. Died July 15, 1904, Liberty, Utah.

BURT, JAMES, Jr. (son of James Burt and Mary McBride). Born Sept. 26, 1846, Merry Marder, Scotland. Came to Utah with father.
Married Annie Hughes July 12, 1867, Farmington, Utah (daughter of William and Katherine Hughes of Liberty, Utah, pioneers 1860). She was born Aug. 26, 1848. Their children: James T., d. aged 12; William, d. infant; Katherine, d. aged 2; John E., m. Salista Keyser; George S., m. Mary Flower; Robert m. Jennie ———; Samuel, m. Salista Short; Mary, m. Alfred Penrod; Albert, m. Florence Holmes; Bertha, m. Edward Clark; Ellen, m. Joseph Graham; Annie, m. William Sheetz; Jeanette, m. Amos Hall; LeRoy; Walter and Wilfred, d. infants.
Married Agnes Waldrum April, 1898, Salt Lake City (daughter of Lorenzo Waldrum and Maria Butler of North Ogden, Utah). She was born in 1860. Only child: Agnes b. April 1, 1901.
Member 60th quorum seventies; Sunday school teacher; 2d counselor to President E. W. Davis. Farmer. Died Feb. 19, 1907.

BURT, JOHN. Born 1817, Fifeshire, Scotland. Came to Utah Oct. 19, 1862, Horton D. Haight company.
Married Margerite Burt 1837, Fifeshire, Scotland, who was born 1823. Their children: Annie, m. George Irvine; Peter G., m. Ellen Condie; Marguerite, m. Andrew Scott; Jane, m. Robert Snedden; John, m. Mary Sedden; Mary, m. George Burt; Adam, m. Ann Reese. Family home 5th ward, Salt Lake City.
Seventy.

BURT, PETER G. (son of John and Margerite Burt). Born Dec. 24, 1840. Came to Utah 1862 with parents.
Married Ellen Condie Oct. 17, 1870, Salt Lake City (daughter of Gibson Condie and Cecelia Sharp of Salt Lake City,

PIONEERS AND PROMINENT MEN OF UTAH

pioneers 1850). She was born April 27, 1849, St. Louis, Mo. Their children: Margerite b. Oct. 20, 1871, d. infant; Elizabeth b. Jan. 30, 1873, m. William Shipley; Nellie b. Aug. 23, 1876, m. John D. Brown; Cecelia b. Aug. 9, 1880, m. William Brinton. Family home 6th ward, Salt Lake City.

BURTON, JOHN (son of William Burton of Lancashire, Eng.). Born 1832 in Lancashire. Came to Utah 1852. Married Hannah Thompson at Salt Lake City. Their children: John, m. Mary Wesley; William T., m. May Done; George O., m. Annie M. Calton; Walter E., m. Ophelia Bodden; Sarah J., m. Earnest Hamer. Family home Salt Lake City.
Elder; block teacher. Carpenter and builder. Died 1911, 6th ward, Salt Lake City.

BURTON, GEORGE O. (son of John Burton and Hannah Thompson). Born Sept. 23, 1869, 6th ward, Salt Lake City. Married Annie M. Calton Jan. 25, 1899, Salt Lake City (daughter of William Calton and Maria Gutteridge of Salt Lake City, pioneers Oct. 15, 1863, Samuel D. White company). She was born Nov. 26, 1871. Their children: LaVon b. March 2, 1900; George Alva b. Sept. 10, 1901, d. aged 1 year; Florence Lone b. March 27, 1905; Nellie b. April 4, 1908, d. aged 1 year; Lester LaMar b. Jan. 25, 1911. Family home Liberty ward, Salt Lake City.
Police officer; motorman; carpenter.

BURTON, JOSEPH F. (son of Joseph Burton and Eliza Cussworth). Born June 1, 1849. Came to Utah November, 1856. Married Nancy Brooks May 30, 1877, Salt Lake City (daughter of Alexander and Mary Brooks of Marion, Smythe county, Va.). Their children: Joseph, d. infant; John, m. Maybell Lundgreen; William, m. Marian Belle Allred; Mary, m. Frederick Larsen; James, m. Almira Allred; Eliza; Martha, m. Moroni Johansen; Susan; Clarence and Nancy, d. infants; Henry; Coleman; Ellis and Ella, d. infants. Family home Mt. Pleasant, Utah.
High priest; ward teacher. Served in Black Hawk war. One of the earliest settlers of Mt. Pleasant, Utah. Farmer.

BURTON, WILLIAM L. (son of Joseph F. Burton and Nancy Brooks). Born March 2, 1878, Mt. Pleasant, Utah. Married Marian Belle Allred Oct. 10, 1906, Salt Lake City (daughter of Milford A. Allred and Elizabeth Johnson of Salt Lake City). She was born May 8, 1883. Their children: Virginia Belle b. July 18, 1907; Milford L. b. Oct. 30, 1909; Joseph William b. Sept. 30, 1911. Family home Mt. Pleasant, Utah.
Missionary to southern states 1906-08; elder; ward teacher; home missionary; assistant Sunday school superintendent.

BURTON, ROBERT TAYLOR (son of Samuel Burton of Yorkshire and Hannah Shipley of Lincolnshire, Eng.). Born Oct. 25, 1821, Amherstburg, Ontario, Canada. Came to Utah Sept. 23, 1848, Capt. Allen's division of Brigham Young company.
Married Maria S. Haven Dec. 18, 1845, Nauvoo, Ill. (daughter of John Haven and Judith Temple of Holliston, Mass, pioneers 1848, Capt. Allen company). She was born April 10, 1826. Their children: Theresa, m. Louis S. Hills; William Shipley, m. Julia M. Horne, m. Eloise Crismon; Robt. Taylor, m. Roselia M. Salisbury; Charles Samuel, m. Julia Young, m. Josephine Beatty; John Haven, m. Catherine Ferguson; Lafayette Grant. m. Ella Mitchel; Albert Temple, died; Florence May, m. Edwin E. Wilcox; Mary Amelia, m. Ezra Stevenson; Heber Kimball, m. Clara Herman.
Married Sarah A. Garr Feb. 6, 1856, Salt Lake City (daughter of Fielding Garr and Pauline Turner of Indiana, pioneers 1847). She was born Sept. 24, 1833. Their children: Henry Fielding, m. Anna Gibbs; Franklin Garr, died; Alfred Jones, m. Elizabeth Peart; Alice Maria, died; Lyman Wells, m. Ella Cummings; Elbert Turner, m. Ida Larson; Edward Leon, m. Isabella Armstrong; Theodore Taylor, m. Florence Moyle; Ada May; Virginia Louisa, m. Ralph Cutler; Austin Garr, m. Leonora McMillen; Hardy Garr, m. Florence Self.
Married Susan E. McBride Feb. 6, 1856, Salt Lake City (daughter of William McBride and Ellen Borum of Pennsylvania, pioneers 1848). Their children: Willard Cushing, m. Mary Jane Gardener; Hosea McBride; George; Walter James, m. Lucy Brown; Sarah Elizabeth, m. Robert Fenton. Families resided Salt Lake City.
Bugler in 1st company of cavalry of Nauvoo Legion. Once a member of Nauvoo brass band. Constable of Salt Lake City 1852; U. S. deputy marshal 1853 and many years afterward: sheriff, assessor and collector Salt Lake county 1854-74. Went to meet belated handcart companies, 1856. Served in Echo canyon war. Territorial deputy marshal 1861. Commanded posse sent against seceding Morrisites June 12, 1862. U. S. internal revenue collector for Utah, by appointment of President Lincoln 1862-69. Missionary to Illinois, Michigan and Ohio; counselor to Bishop Andrew Cunningham of 15th ward, Salt Lake City, and in 1867 became bishop of that ward; missionary to eastern states 1869 and to Europe 1873; president London conference; second counselor to Edward Hunter, and after his death became first counselor to William B. Preston (presiding bishops). Took an active part in early Indian troubles; first a captain Company A, then commissioned major, and afterward major-general Utah militia by Governor Durkee in 1868; Assessor of Salt Lake county 1880; member city council 1856-73; and member legislative council (territorial senate) 1855-87. While serving in the legislature in 1876, he, Abraham O. Smoot, and Silas S. Smith, were appointed a committee to arrange, compile and publish all the laws of the Territory of Utah then in force. Member board of regents University of Deseret 1880-84. Died Nov. 11, 1907, Salt Lake City.

BURTON, WILLIAM SHIPLEY (son of Robert Taylor Burton and Maria Haven). Born Sept. 27, 1850, Salt Lake City. Married Julia Marion Horne March 6, 1872, Salt Lake City (daughter of Joseph Horne and Mary I. Hale of Nauvoo, pioneers 1847). She was born Aug. 12, 1851. Only child: Julia Horne b. Oct. 24, 1873, died. Family home Salt Lake City.
Married Eloise Crismon June 11, 1878, Salt Lake City (daughter of George Crismon and Mary L. Tanner of Nauvoo, pioneers 1847). She was born Sept. 26, 1857. Their children: Evaline b. Aug. 14, 1880, m. James W. Burt; Leone b. June 27, 1882; Theresa b. Sept. 28, 1883, m. Charles W. Brown; Eloise b. Sept. 30, 1885, m. John N. Scoville; Vernice b. Sept. 15, 1887, m. Edwin D. Hatch; Florence and Ralph Shipley b. Nov. 17, 1893; Helen Crismon b. Sept. 28, 1896; George Crismon b. Aug. 7, 1898, died. Family home Salt Lake City.
Member 2d quorum seventies; missionary to Great Britain 1877-79; counselor in bishopric of 14th ward 1909. County assessor; county sheriff. Mining man.

BURTON, ROBERT WALTON (son of James Burton and Isabella Walton). Born April 29, 1826, Arsgail, Yorkshire, Eng. Came to Utah September, 1851.
Married Mary Ann Mathews May 9, 1870, Salt Lake City (daughter of Jeremiah Mathews and Ann Martin), who was born Sept. 2, 1851, North Hill Parish, Eng. Their children: Mary Ann b. March 12, 1871, m. Michael Clark 1893; Charles H. b. Dec. 9, 1872, m. Sophia Loynd March 28, 1900; Christopher M. b. June 12, 1874, m. Emeline Hill April 14, 1897; Robert b. May 12, 1876, m. Mary A. Card September, 1901; Sarah E. b. Aug. 11, 1878, m. Joseph Mortenson June, 1904; Rachel b. April 24, 1881, m. George Hinkle Oct. 14, 1908; Thomas A. b. May 16, 1883; James A. b. April 10, 1885; Rosella b. March 9, 1887, m. Earl Tribe Dec. 23, 1909; Chancy W. b. April 30, 1891; Lillian M. b. May 6, 1897. Family home Kaysville, Davis Co., Utah.
A pioneer of Bear Lake valley, Utah. Veteran Black Hawk war. Sheriff 17 years.

BURTON, CHARLES H. (son of Robert Walton Burton and Mary Ann Mathews). Born Dec. 9, 1872, Kaysville, Utah. Married Sophia Loynd March 28, 1900, Salt Lake City (daughter of James Loynd, pioneer Nov. 30, 1856, Edward Martin handcart company, and Mary Earney, pioneer Sept. 15, 1866, William Henry Chipman company). She was born May 12, 1878, Farmington, Utah. Their children: Charles Kenneth b. Sept. 26, 1856, m. Fred Foulger Dec. 21, 1874; Sherman L. b. Nov. 28, 1906; Mildred b. July 10, 1908; Ralph Walton b. Oct. 11, 1910.

BURTON, WILLIAM WALTON (son of James Burton, born July 7, 1800, Arsgail, Yorkshire, Eng., and Isabelle Walton, born April, 1802). He was born March 23, 1833, Bradford, Yorkshire. Came to Utah Sept. 23, 1854, Job Smith company. Married Rachel Fielding March 28, 1856, Salt Lake City (daughter of Joseph Fielding and Hannah Greenwood, married June 11, 1838, Preston, Eng., pioneers 1848, Capt. Lott company). She was born June 27, 1839. Their children: Isabelle b. Dec. 26, 1856, m. Fred Foulger Dec. 21, 1874; Hannah b. Jan. 14, 1859, m. Moroni S. Poulter Sept. 5, 1878; Joseph Fielding b. March 3, 1861, m. Mary A. E. Driver March 31, 1886; William Fielding b. Nov. 10, 1862, m. Marian Treseder Aug. 1, 1888; Rachel b. Feb. 14, 1865, m. Zachariah Ballantyne 1884; Sarah Ellen b. Dec. 14, 1866, m. Fred Foulger 1886; James Fielding b. May 18, 1868; Mary Eliza b. July 4, 1870, died; Martha b. Oct. 11, 1872, m. Isaac M. Cooley Sept. 12, 1900; Christopher Fielding b. June 4, 1875, m. Miriam Van Orden April 10, 1906; Robert Ibbotson b. Feb. 9, 1879, m. Letitia Jane Richards Dec. 2, 1903; Vilate Pearl b. June 20, 1881; Julina May b. Oct. 21, 1884, d. child. Family resided Kaysville, Mill Crek and Ogden, Utah.
Married Ellen Fielding Nov. 2, 1861, Salt Lake City (daughter of Joseph Fielding and Hannah Greenwood), who was born Feb. 9, 1841, Preston, Eng. Their children: Mercy Rachel b. July 29, 1863, m. T. J. Stevens 1885; Margaret b. Sept. 11, 1865, m. Hyrum Barlow Jan. 2, 1889; Heber Fielding b. March 6, 1868, m. Delecta Ballantyne Dec. 14, 1889; Hyrum Fielding b. July 10, 1870, d. child; John Fielding b. June 26, 1873, m. Musetta Porter April, 1897; Lucy died; Mabel b. May 19, 1877, died; Reuben Fielding b. March 10, 1880, m. Caroline C. Call.
Married Sarah Ann Fielding May 23, 1870 (daughter of Joseph Fielding and Hannah Greenwood), who was born May 19, 1851, Salt Lake City. Their children: Thomas Fielding b. May 12, 1871, m. Alice Maud Call June 22, 1898; Arthur Fielding b. June 10, 1873, m. Kittie C. Dixon Oct. 10, 1894; Alice Ann b. Sept. 2, 1875, m. Clarence Gardener Oct. 8, 1897; Parley Parson b. July 10, 1878, died; Wilford Fielding b. May 17, 1882, m. Ivie Irene Rainey Dec. 22, 1910; Emma b. Aug. 10, 1884, died; Ephraim Fielding b. April 3, 1886; George Fielding b. April 27, 1888, m. Mary Frances Poulter June 14, 1911; Josephine b. Dec. 23, 1890.
Missionary to England 1851-53. Settled at Kaysville, 1854;

PIONEERS AND PROMINENT MEN OF UTAH 785

moved to Ogden 1860 and taught school 12 years: Weber county superintendent of schools. Member 17th quorum seventies; first counselor to Bishops Joseph Parry (Ogden) and George Osmond, president Star Valley stake; high councilor Weber stake. Ogden city councilman three terms; President William W. Burton & Sons company, Burton Mercantile association; Burton Creamery association, Afton, Wyo.

BURTON, JOSEPH FIELDING (son of William Walton Burton and Rachel Fielding). Born March 3, 1861, in Weber county, Utah.
Married Mary A. E. Driver March 31, 1886, Logan, Utah (daughter of William Driver and Charlotte E. Boulter of Ogden, Utah). She was born Aug. 28, 1865, Wandsworth, Surrey, Eng. Their children: Rachel Emblem b. July 4, 1889; Joseph Howard b. May 18, 1891; Lee Driver b. Feb. 19, 1893; Ida May b. Sept. 20, 1894; Vilate Pearl b. July 12, 1896; Charlotte b. Jan. 5, 1898; Mary Ellen b. July 8, 1899; Margaret b. Sept. 4, 1902. Family resided Ogden and Salt Lake City, Utah.
Member Ogden board of education 1894-96; vice president W. W. Burton & Sons company, Burton Mercantile company, and Burton Creamery association; manager, secretary-treasurer Utah Implement and Vehicle company.

BURTON, WILLIAM FIELDING (son of William Walton Burton and Rachel Fielding). Born Nov. 10, 1862, Kaysville, Utah.
Married Marian Treseder Aug. 1, 1888, Logan, Utah, who was born Oct. 18, 1862.

BURTON, JAMES F. (son of William Walton Burton and Rachel Fielding). Born May 18, 1868.
Assistant cashier First National Bank of Ogden.

BURTON, ROBERT IBBOTSON (son of William Walton Burton and Rachel Fielding). Born Feb. 9, 1879, Ogden, Utah.
Married Letitia Jane Richards Dec. 2, 1903, Salt Lake City (daughter of Charles C. Richards and Letitia L. Peery), who was born Feb. 2, 1879, at Ogden. Their children: Robert Richards b. April 24, 1906; Charles Richards b. Jan. 1, 1909. Family home Ogden, Utah.
Assistant stake superintendent Sunday schools Weber stake 2 years; 2d president 77th quorum seventies. Secretary Wm. W. Burton & Sons company, Burton Mercantile company, and Burton Creamery association.

BURTON, HEBER FIELDING (son of William Walton Burton and Ellen Fielding). Born March 6, 1868, Ogden, Utah.
Married Mary Delecta Ballantyne Dec. 14, 1898, Salt Lake City (daughter of Richard A. Ballantyne and Mary Ann Stewart), who was born April 7, 1877, at Ogden. Their children: Esther b. Aug. 7, 1900; Winfield Ballantyne b. May 26, 1902; Stewart Ballantyne b. Sept. 2, 1904; Richard Ballantyne b. Oct. 30, 1906; Margaret b. June 10, 1908; Katherine b. Jan. 5, 1910; Minerva b. Feb. 6, 1912. Family resided Ogden and Afton, Wyo.
Superintendent Sunday schools Star valley stake. Bookkeeper Z. C. M. I., Ogden, Utah, 1890-93, and for Shurtliff & Co., joint agent for R. G. W. and U. P. coal department, Ogden. Secretary Utah commission to Trans-Mississippi exposition 1898.

BURTON, REUBEN FIELDING (son of William Walton Burton and Ellen Fielding). Born March 10, 1880, Ogden, Utah.
Married Caroline Charlotte Call Feb. 22, 1908, Salt Lake City (daughter of Anson Vasco Call, Jr., and Alice Jeanette Farnham), who was born April 22, 1888, Afton, Wyo. Family resided Ogden, Utah, Afton and Freedom, Wyo.
Stake secretary Y. M. M. I. A. 1907-08; secretary California mission 1908-10; member Sunday school stake board. City treasurer, Afton, 1904-05.

BURTON, THOMAS FIELDING (son of William Walton Burton and Sarah Ann Fielding). Born May 12, 1871, Ogden, Utah.
Married Alice Maud Call June 22, 1898, Salt Lake temple (daughter of Anson Vasco Call, Jr., and Alice Jeanette Farnham), who was born July 12, 1881, Bountiful, Utah. Their children: Sarah Alice b. Oct. 13, 1899; Lila Maud b. July 3, 1901; Cumorah b. Aug. 12, 1903; Belva b. April 18, 1905; Ellen b. Oct. 28, 1906; Fielding b. July 18, 1908; Rachel b. May 29, 1910; Louise b. Jan. 18, 1912. Family home Afton, Wyo.
Ordained a high priest Aug. 14, 1892, by President Joseph F. Smith; served as counselor in bishopric of Afton ward up to Aug. 13, 1899; alternate high councilor 1899-1901; member high council Star valley stake from 1901 to present time; home missionary since 1899; member Sunday school and Y. M. M. I. A stake boards, also stake organist of same organizations, and of the latter since 1892; officer in Afton ward Sunday school since 1888. President Star Valley high school since its organization in 1910, and of Afton brass band. Manager William W. Burton ranch until October, 1908. Director and bookkeeper Burton Creamery association and Burton Mercantile company since 1908.

BURTON, WILFORD FIELDING (son of William Walton Burton and Sarah Ann Fielding). Born May 17, 1882, Ogden, Utah.
Married Ivie Irene Rainey Dec. 22, 1910, Salt Lake City (daughter of David William Rainey and Mary Marie Olsen), who was born Feb. 22, 1884, Richmond, Utah.

BURTON, EPHRAIM FIELDING (son of William Walton Burton and Sarah Ann Fielding). Born April 3, 1886.
In charge of Burton Creamery association; graduate of Agricultural college of Utah.

BURTON, GEORGE FIELDING (son of William Walton Burton and Sarah Ann Fielding). Born April 27, 1888, Afton, Wyo.
Married Mary Frances Poulter June 14, 1911, Salt Lake City (daughter of George Poulter and Mary Elizabeth Jackson), who was born Aug. 17, 1888, Ogden, Utah.

BUSBY, JOHN. Born March 10, 1833. Came to Utah with an oxteam company.
Married Harriet Emma Killian at Salt Lake City. Their children: John K., m. Eliza Knight; Andrew Edward, m. Julia Brooks; Ellen M., m. William Andrew Luke; Mary Emma, m. William Watkins; Lucy Alice, m. James Kelly; Latitia, died; Samuel George, m. Anna Dangerfield; Martha Jane, m. Ernest Harmon. Family home Salt Lake City.
Elder. Tanner. Conductor and driver of first mule streetcars in Salt Lake City.

BUSENBARK, ISAAC. Born in Niagara county, New York. Came to Utah 1849.
Married Abigail Manning, of New Jersey. She died on the plains en route to Utah. Among their children was Sarah Jane, who married Newton Daniel Hall in 1843. They came to Utah Sept. 28, 1847, with Vincent Shurtleff company.

BUSH, JAMES. Born Aug. 7, 1811. Came to Utah 1855. Cyrus H. Wheelock company.
Married Sophia Humphries of Newport, Monmouthshire, South Wales, Eng., who was born Nov. 16, 1814. Their children: William James, m. Angeline Luddington; Sophia, m. William Stradling; Henry Isaac b. April 17, 1846, m. Eveline Virginia Noe, Feb. 14, 1878; James Humphries b. November, 1848; Joseph b. 1854. Family home Pleasant Grove, Utah.
High priest and choir leader. Basket maker and farmer. Died March 10, 1879.

BUSH, HENRY ISAAC (son of James Bush and Sophia Humphries. Born April 17, 1846, Newport, Wales. Came to Utah 1855 with parents.
Married Eveline Virginia Noe Feb. 14, 1878, Salt Lake City (daughter of Abram Noe and Mary Jane Winslow of Cincinnati, Ohio). She was born Nov. 27, 1852. Their children: Mary Eveline b. Dec. 30, 1878; Henry Isaac b. Nov. 9, 1879; Joseph Edward b. Nov. 16, 1881, m. Rachel Harriet Easler; Emily Jane b. April 15, 1883; James Abraham b. June 14, 1885; Harmon Winslow b. Dec. 3, 1889; Benjamin Ray b. May 10, 1893. Family home Pleasant Grove.
High priest. Worked on Salt Lake temple. Farmer.

BUSH, JAMES HUMPHRIES (son of James Bush and Sophia Humphries). Born Nov. 28, 1848, Monmouthshire, Wales. Came to Utah September, 1855 with parents.
Elder. Veteran of Black Hawk war. Farmer.

BUSHMAN, MARTIN (son of Abraham Bushman, born April 12, 1767, Lancaster county, Pa., and Esther Franks, born Oct. 5, 1764—married Jan. 12, 1788). He was born April 1, 1802, Lascaster county, Pa., came to Utah October, 1851, Capt. Kelsey company.
Married Elizabeth Degen (daughter of John Casper Degen and Maria Graff). She was born Sept. 12, 1802. Their children: Henry b. Dec. 11, 1827, and Maria b. Jan. 31, 1829, died; Jacob b. July 27, 1830, m. Charlotte Turley March 2, 1858; Sarah A. b. Jan. 9, 1833, m. Alonzo D. Rhodes; Abraham b. July 19, 1835, and Elizabeth b. Nov. 9, 1837, died; Martin B. b. Feb. 5, 1841, m. Lucinda Goodwin; John b. June 7, 1843, m. Lois A. Smith Feb. 11, 1865; Hetty A. B. b. Nov. 28, 1845, died; Eliza A. b. Dec. 6, 1849, m. Margaret Zimmerman. Family home Lehi, Utah.
High priest. Died Oct. 8, 1886.

BUSHMAN, JACOB (son of Martin Bushman and Elizabeth Degen). Born July 27, 1830, in Lancaster county, Pa. Came to Utah October, 1851.
Married Charlotte Turley March 2, 1857, San Bernardino, Cal. (daughter of Theodore Turley and Frances Kimberley of San Bernardino—pioneers Oct. 19, 1848, Amasa M. Lyman company). She was born April 15, 1840. Their children: Priscilla Elizabeth, d. infant; Charlotte Amanda, m. John Sabey; Theodore Martin, m. Marilla Lambson; Frances Ann, d. child; Sarah Erminie, m. Henry Fowles; Mary E., d. infant; Grace Honor, m. Emanuel R. Lundquist; Jacob Isaac, m. Effie Bills; Ida Roxanna, m. A. R. Anderson; Ella Isadora, m. Rufus O. Backer.
Missionary to Pennsylvania, Ohio and Indiana 1872; bishop's counselor. Farmer and stockraiser. Pioneer to St. Johns, Ariz., four years. Resides Fairview, Utah.

BUSHMAN, MARTIN BENJAMIN (son of Martin Bushman and Elizabeth Degen). Born Feb. 5, 1841, Lancaster county, Pa. Came to Utah September, 1851, James Allred company.
Married Lucinda Ludelia Goodwin March 21, 1863, Salt Lake City (daughter of Isaac Goodwin and Laura Hotchkiss), who was born April 4, 1843. Their children: Mary Elizabeth

b. Sept. 29, 1864; Martin Isaac b. Oct. 9, 1865, m. Rule Holden June 4, 1890; Laura Ellen b. Oct. 9, 1865, m. William F. Butt Nov. 11, 1885; Nancy Lucinda b. Oct. 3, 1868; Sarah b. June 17, 1870; Lewis Jacob b. July 16, 1872, m. Martha Spencer Nov. 1, 1895; Edith b. March 3, 1875; Rhoda b. Sept. 5, 1877, m. William Oborn Aug. 14, 1902; Esther, twin of Rhoda; Emerett b. June 26, 1884. Family home Lehi, Utah.
Married Martha Worlton March 2, 1867, Salt Lake City (daughter of James Worlton and Elizabeth Borne, pioneers September, 1855—married Dec. 3, 1848, Somersetshire, Eng.). She was born Sept. 14, 1849, at Bath, Somersetshire. Their children: James Albert b. June 4, 1868, m. Emma Gurney Jan. 20, 1896; John Benjamin b. Nov. 16, 1870; Alva Alonzo b. Dec. 28, 1872; Flora Elizabeth b. Aug. 15, 1874, m. Suel Zimmerman Jan. 28, 1902; Eugene W. b. Dec. 14, 1876, m. Leah Christoferson March 27, 1901; Annie Lois b. April 27, 1880, m. Alma Miller Oct. 22, 1902; Martha Emma b. Sept. 3, 1882, m. William F. Gurney May 20, 1903; Cyrus William b. Sept. 23, 1884; Drucilla Jane b. Nov. 24, 1886; Vera b. June 22, 1891. President 68th quorum seventies; high priest; Sunday school teacher 30 years. Assisted in bringing in immigrants to Utah. Lehi city councilman. Territorial militiaman. Farmer.

BUSHMAN, JOHN (son of Martin Bushman and Elizabeth Degen). Born June 7, 1843, Nauvoo, Ill. Came to Utah 1851. Married Lois A. Smith Feb. 11, 1865, Salt Lake City (daughter of John Smith and Maria Foscue, pioneers Sept. 15, 1850, James Pace company). She was born Jan. 25, 1844, in Arkansas. Their children: John Albert b. May 28, 1866, died; Homer Frederick b. Aug. 6, 1868, m. Sariah A. Smith Nov. 19, 1890; Maria Elizabeth b. Dec. 17, 1869, m. Silas D. Smith Nov. 21, 1888; Martin Lester b. April 6, 1871, died; Lois Evelyn b. June 28, 1872, m. John W. Smith Nov. 5, 1892; Wickliff B. b. Feb. 10, 1874, died; Preston Ammaron b. Dec. 1, 1875, m. Anna Smith Oct. 1, 1902; June Augusta b. June 25, 1879, m. Hyrum Smith June 10, 1908; Jesse Smith b. June 10, 1881, m. Elva Porter; Florence C. b. Oct. 4, 1884, died; Alonzo Ewing b. Dec. 21, 1885; Jacob Virgil b. Jan. 4, 1889, m. Ruth Fuller Aug. 18, 1909. Family home Lehi, Utah.
Married Mary Ann Peterson March 2, 1877, St. George, Utah (daughter of Jens Peterson and Maren Frost, pioneers 1861). She was born May 24, 1857, Denmark. Their children: Elsie May b. Feb. 14, 1878, died; Lillian Ann b. Oct. 31, 1879, m. Wesley Palmer; Maren Adele b. Aug. 18, 1881, m. John L. Westover Oct. 1, 1902; John Lehi b. Sept. 14, 1883, m. Etna Cooper.
Bishop St. Joseph ward 1887; second counselor to President Lot Smith; high priest; called to settle in northern Arizona 1876. Veteran Black Hawk war. Member Snowflake stake board of education 23 years. Farmer and stockraiser.

BUSHMAN, HOMER FREDERICK (son of John Bushman and Lois A. Smith). Born Aug. 6, 1868, Lehi, Utah.
Married Sariah A. Smith Nov. 19, 1890, Manti, Utah (daughter of Jesse N. Smith and Janett M. Johnson—married Oct. 9, 1866, Salt Lake City; former a pioneer 1847, latter born in Utah). She was born Feb. 4, 1873, Parowan, Utah. Their children: Homer Frederick, Jr., b. Oct. 30, 1891; Silas Aiken b. May 15, 1893; Florence b. July 5, 1894; Martin Degen b. April 29, 1898; Curtis Johnson b. Dec. 9, 1899; Karl Mauser b. July 20, 1901; Mary b. Nov. 4, 1903; Lyman Smith b. Nov. 23, 1905; Marguerite b. July 1, 1908; Joel H. J. b. July 7, 1910.
Missionary to Germany and Switzerland 1894-97; superintendent religion classes Snowflake stake. Farmer.

BUTCHER, GEORGE (son of George Butcher and Barbara Hulme of Suffolk, Eng.). Born there 1799. Came to Utah Sept. 14, 1853, Claudius Spencer company.
Married Sophia Sayers 1826, Norwich, Eng. (daughter of John Sayers of London, Eng.). She was born in August, 1813. Their children: Harriet, m. Frederick Heath; Virtue, m. Daniel F. Clift; Charlotte, m. Jabez Taylor and afterward Watson S. Pierce; Elizabeth, m. Mr. Hyler. Family home London, Eng.
Landscape gardener. Died July 24, 1876, Salt Lake City.

BUTLER, CHARLES FRANKLIN. Born in Virginia. Came to Utah in 1860.
Married Louvisa Heron (Robinson) 1820, in Illinois. She was born in New York. Their children: Charles, died; Elizabeth, m. Daniel Dody; Major, died; Rebecca, m. Harrison Oliver; Thomas; Nancy, m. Matthew Caldwell; Sarah B., m. Hyrum W. Mikesell; George and Julia Ann, died; Louvisa Jane, m. George Chandler.

BUTLER, EDWIN (son of William Butler and Ann Dodd of Shropshire, Eng.). Born Feb. 11, 1846. Came to Utah in 1852.
Married Louisa S. Young, Aug. 12, 1867 (daughter of Josiah Young and Elizabeth Conava), who was born March 11, 1849, and came to Utah Oct. 29, 1855, Charles A. Harper company. Their children: Edwin William b. April 25, 1868, m. Jane Humble; Josiah Abraham b. Jan. 15, 1870, m. Eliza Robinson; Elizabeth Ann b. Sept. 7, 1872, d. Dec. 1, 1879; James Frederick b. Sept. 9, 1874, d. Sept. 20, 1879; Samuel Richard b. May 23, 1877, m. Leadya McIntyre; Franklin George b. Sept. 28, 1879, m. Leadya E. Martin; Louisa Sarah b. Oct. 3, 1881, d. March 20, 1896.

BUTLER, EDWIN WILLIAM (son of Edwin Butler and Louisa S. Young). Born April 25, 1868, Fairfield, Utah Co., Utah.
Married Jane Humble Sept. 22, 1898, at Victor, Idaho (daughter of George A. and Olive Humble). Their children: Louisa Sarah b. June 11, 1899; George Anthony b. Feb. 27, 1901; Edwin Humble b. Oct. 14, 1903; Warren Lee b. May 11, 1906; James Leroy b. Aug. 8, 1908; Olive Jane b. July 29, 1910; John Henry b. Nov. 17, 1912.

BUTLER, SAMUEL. Born Dec. 18, 1806. Came to Utah in September, 1857.
Married Hannah Barker, who was born Feb. 25, 1816. Their children: Mary b. Jan. 13, 1840, died; Philander b. March 18, 1841, m. Charlotta Berrell; Leander b. May 7, 1842, m. Eliza Chugg; Alma b. Aug. 20, 1843, m. Lucy Hale; Alva b. Jan. 13, 1845, m. Jane E. Labrum March 16, 1867; Samantha b. May 4, 1846, died; Veri b. Dec. 4, 1847, m. Emeline Hutchings; m. Mary McGhie; Erl b. Feb. 4, 1850, m. Elizabeth A. Gibson; Nephi b. May 4, 1851, died; Miranda b. March 7, 1854, m. Mr. Robertson; Lehi b. Feb. 22, 1854, died; Elbert b. March 17, 1856, died. Family home South Cottonwood, Utah. Moved to California settlement in 1858.

BUTLER, ALVA (son of Samuel Butler and Hannah Barker). Born Jan. 13, 1845, in Randolph county, Ind.
Married Jane E. Labrum March 16, 1867, Salt Lake City (daughter of Thomas Labrum and Elizabeth George), who was born July 4, 1846, Simpson Buck, Eng. Their children: Hannah E. A. b. April 24, 1868, m. Lewis E. Despain Feb. 20, 1889; Alva J. b. Aug. 26, 1869, m. Annie L. Despain Sept. 20, 1895; Prudence O. b. July 2, 1871, m. George F. Despain Feb. 20, 1899; Jane E. b. June 13, 1873, m. Edward C. Tucker Jan 13, 1897; George W. b. July 4, 1875, m. Ella M. Boyce Sept. 23, 1896; William W. b. Oct. 4, 1877, m. Mary Evalyn McGhie Nov. 18, 1908; Mary M. b. Dec. 10, 1881; Elva L. b. July 16, 1883, m. Asa L. Maxfield Oct. 24, 1907; Samuel T. b. June 17, 1885, died. Family resided Butlerville and South Cottonwood, Utah.
Bishop Granite ward 1886 and Butler ward 1909; counselor to Bishop Solomon J. Despain 1881-86. Assisted James Rawlings to bring immigrants to Utah. Died May 1, 1909.

BUTLER, ALVA J. (son of Alva Butler and Jane E. Labrum). Born Aug. 26, 1869, South Cottonwood, Utah.
Married Annie L. Despain Sept. 20, 1895, Salt Lake City (daughter of Solomon J. Despain and Susan Dean; pioneers Aug. 16, 1861, David H. Cannon company). She was born Sept. 1, 1871. Their children: Alva D. b. Dec. 22, 1895; Jennie D. b. July 6, 1897; Leo E. b. Nov. 8, 1898; Leon E. b. May 13, 1900; Laura S. b. Nov. 29, 1901; Norma b. July 6, 1903; Maude b. Jan. 10, 1905; Naoma E. b. July 23, 1908; Melva b. Feb. 1, 1911. Family resided Butlerville and Sandy, Utah.
Missionary to Samoa 1891; alternate high councilor, Jordan stake. Sandy city councilman 1908-10.

BUTLER, WILLIAM W. (son of Alva Butler and Jane E. Labrum). Born Oct. 4, 1877, Big Cottonwood, Utah.
Married Mary Evalyn McGhie Nov. 18, 1908, Salt Lake City (daughter of Alexander McGhie and Emma Rowan; former a pioneer Oct. 1, 1854, Daniel Garn company). She was born July 13, 1886, Butler, Utah. Their children: Virge M. b. Aug. 22, 1909; Florence M. b. Jan. 21, 1911; Rowan M. b. Oct. 19, 1912. Family home Butler, Utah.
Missionary to southern states 1899-1901; bishop Butler ward 1909; assistant Sunday school superintendent; home missionary Jordan stake seven years.

BUTTAR, DAVID (son of Daniel Buttar and Batheah Rattray, born 1788, both of Blairgowrie, Perthshire, Scotland. Born Dec. 2, 1822, at Blairgowrie. Came to Utah November, 1854, Capt. Taylor company.
Married Margaret Spalding Dec. 14, 1848, in Scotland (daughter of John Spalding and Marjory Meek Johnson), who was born January 1, 1822, and came to Utah with husband. Their children: Marjory Meek Johnson b. Sept. 16, 1849, m. Henry Mullet December, 1866; m. Joseph J. Harrison 1869; Batheah b. July 15, 1851, m. William Sparks Dec. 15, 1868; David b. November, 1853, d. February, 1854; John Spalding b. May 22, 1856, m. Sarah L. Tanner Jan. 1, 1880; Daniel b. Sept. 22, 1858, m. Emma Gover January, 1883; Robert Sutter b. April 6, 1861, m. Mary Godfrey 1891; Margaret b. Aug. 5, 1863, d. infant. Family home Lehi, Utah.
Married Sarah Keep Dec. 16, 1866, at Lehi (daughter of James Joseph Keep (high priest) and Ann Miller; married July 22, 1836; pioneers Oct. 22, 1866, Abner Lowry company). She was the widow of Thomas Francis, married May 15, 1865, and mother of Lucy Ann Francis, born March 26, 1866, who married Hans Jensen July, 1884). She was born June 28, 1840, Greenham, Berkshire, Eng. Their children: Sarah Isabell Buttar, b. April 16, 1868, d. June 15, 1868; Elizabeth Keep b. June 9, 1869, m. John Loosle Dec. 3, 1891; Charles William b. June 13, 1871, m. Angeline Stewart May 18, 1892; Thomas James b. Oct. 3, 1873, m. Annie Loosle; David Alexander b. Dec. 14, 1875, m. Rose Loosle; James Joseph Keep b. Feb. 26, 1878, m. Agnes Jordan; Mary Janet b. June 30, 1880, m. Louis Thompson; Emma Jane b. Oct. 8, 1882, m. David Thompson. Family home Clarkston, Utah.
Settled at Clarkston 1868. High priest. Shoemaker; farmer. Died Nov. 23. 1911.

BUTTAR, JOHN SPALDING (son of David Buttar and Margaret Spalding). Born May 22, 1856.
Married Sarah L. Tanner Jan. 1, 1880, who was born at Salt Lake City. Their children: Margaret Priscilla; John Tanner; David Wilham, m. Maud Summerhays; Rachel Batheah; Lucy Maud; Jessie Tanner; Harvey Louis; Dassey Marvilla; Golden; Lola; Lester. Family home Clarkston.

BUTTAR, THOMAS JAMES (son of David Buttar and Sarah Keep). Born Oct. 13, 1873, at Clarkston.
Married Annie Loosle (daughter of John K. Loosle and Annie Hinkern, of Switzerland, pioneers). Their children: Thomas James; Sarah Pearl; Annie; Royal; Jennie Lehon; Susie. Family home Clarkston.
Seventy. Farmer.

BUTTERFIELD, THOMAS (son of Zachariah Butterfield and Martha Hiscock, of Farmington, Kennebec county, Me.). Born June 17, 1811, Farmington, Me. Came to Utah Oct. 15, 1849, Allen Taylor company.
Married Mary Jane Parker in Maine (daughter of Samuel and Hannah Parker, of Parsonfield). She was born Jan. 18, 1816. Their children: Mary b. Jan. 18, 1836, m. Mr. Whittle; Eliza Ann b. Aug. 4, 1839, died; Almon b. July 14, 1844, m. Elizabeth A. Farmer; Martha b. Nov. 24, 1842, died; George b. Nov. 23, 1847, m. Emma Cook; Sarah b. March 13, 1849, m. William H. Freeman; Olive b. Feb. 5, 1851, m. George Miller; Thomas, Jr. b. April 23, 1853, m. Catherine F. Freeman; Samuel b. Feb. 27, 1855, m. Sarah Jane Farmer; Hannah b. Feb. 1, 1858, m. Franklin M. Carter. Family home Herriman, Utah.
Married Mary Jane Farmer 1857, Salt Lake City (daughter of Richard Farmer and Elizabeth Morris, of Herefordshire, Eng.). Their children: Richard b. April 19, 1858, and John b. July 11, 1859, died; Elizabeth M. b. July 20, 1861, m. Daniel Densley; Zachariah b. Jan. 4, 1864, m. Corille Warde; Emma Eliza b. June 4, 1866, died; Edwin James b. May 4, 1867, m. Vilate S. Newman; Lyman Thomas b. Dec. 28, 1872. Family home Herriman, Utah.
Member 3d quorum seventies; missionary to Salmon River, Idaho. Settled at Herriman 1850. Farmer.

BUTTERFIELD, ALMON (son of Thomas Butterfield and Mary Jane Parker). Born July 14, 1844, Nauvoo, Ill. Came to Utah with father.
Married Elizabeth A. Farmer Jan. 27, 1866, Salt Lake City (daughter of James M. Farmer and Sarah Trusler, pioneers 1856, settlers of Herriman, Utah). She was born Oct. 17, 1848. Their children: Elizabeth E. b. Nov. 5, 1866, d. Sept. 12, 1867; Agnes A. b. Sept. 29, 1867, d. Sept. 29, 1867; Almon T. b. July 5, 1868, m. Sarah Jane Crump; Joseph J. b. Nov. 14, 1870, m. Dora Peterson; Sarah Jane b. March 24, 1872, m. James G. Crane; Olive J. b. Nov. 14, 1873, m. Samuel H. Crump; George S. b. March 16, 1876, m. Hannah E. Stocking; Mary E. b. June 12, 1877, m. Hans B. Jensen; Fredrick R. b. April 14, 1879, m. Agnes Peckenbaugh; John E. b. Sept. 23, 1880, m. Gladys E. Hanson; Willard F. b. Dec. 29, 1882; Zachariah T. b. Dec. 14, 1885, d. Oct. 25, 1886; Mahonri b. Oct. 19, 1887, m. Hazel Bills; Parley P. b. Dec. 27, 1889; Hannah P. b. April 17, 1891; Lyman b. June 15, 1893, d. June 15, 1893. Family home Herriman, Utah.
Member 9th quorum seventies; missionary to eastern states 1900-02; assistant Sunday school superintendent; high priest. Justice of peace; constable. Assisted in bringing immigrants to Utah. Farmer and stockraiser.

BUTTERFIELD, ALMON T. (son of Almon Butterfield and Elizabeth A. Farmer). Born July 5, 1868, Herriman, Utah.
Married Sarah Jane Crump Oct. 14, 1896, Salt Lake City (daughter of William Charles Crump and Sarah Cornick, of Herriman, pioneers Sept. 3, 1852, Abraham O. Smoot company). She was born Sept. 2, 1873. Their children: Tira Arvilla b. Jan. 10, 1901; Amy Lucetta b. Feb. 27, 1903; Marva b. Nov. 3, 1905, died; Almon Floyd b. Nov. 6, 1906; Charles Ovid b. March 20, 1908; James Earl b. April 20, 1911. Family home Riverton, Utah.
President 94th quorum seventies; missionary to New Zealand 1896-1900; member stake board Sunday school; high councilor; missionary to central states 1908-10. President Jordan Valley bank; farmer and stockraiser.

BUTTERFIELD, THOMAS, JR. (son of Thomas Butterfield and Mary Jane Parker). Born April 23, 1853, Herriman, Utah.
Married Catherine E. Freeman Feb. 26, 1872, Salt Lake City (daughter of William H. and Angeline A. Freeman, of Herriman, Utah, pioneers 1851, Capt. Reese company). She was born Oct. 2, 1855. Their children: Mary Jane b. Dec. 13, 1872, died; Emmeline A. b. Oct. 20, 1874, died; Eliza Ann b. Oct. 28, 1876, m. Thomas Williams; Olive Jemima b. Aug. 2, 1878, m. Joseph Wright; Hannah R. b. March 30, 1880, m. Charles E. Crane; Sarah Rebecca b. July 22, 1882, m. Byron Hill; Harriet Serinda b. July 22, 1884, m. John C. Jensen; William W. b. July 28, 1887, died; Della Malinda b. Nov. 22, 1889; Samuel Heber b. March 10, 1892; Lucy Elizabeth b. June 17, 1894; Margaret Ellen b. April 28, 1897.
Married Lucy Wheadon Oct. 22, 1880, Salt Lake City (daughter of John and Jane Wheadon, of England). She was born Oct. 2, 1857. Their children: Martha Jane b. Nov. 15, 1880, m. Joseph H. Stocking; Thomas Solomon b. Oct. 17, 1882, m. Martha E. Bowlden; John Almon b. Sept. 10, 1884, m. Margaret E. Farmer; George Jefferson b. June 11, 1888; Emmeline Percilda b. July 21, 1891, m. Reuben B. Eastman; Edwin Parkber b. June 1, 1894; Lucy Marinda b. Dec. 9, 1896. Family home Herriman, Utah.

Bishop; superintendent Sunday school; ward teacher 1884-87; and first president Y. M. M. I. A. of Herriman ward; high councilor, Jordan stake; missionary to England, also to Arizona 1873, and to eastern states 1899; high priest.

BUTTERFIELD, THOMAS SOLOMON (son of Thomas Butterfield, Jr. and Lucy Wheadon). Born Oct. 17, 1882, Herriman, Salt Lake county.
Married Martha E. Bowlden at Salt Lake City (daughter of William and Sarah Bowlden of Riverton, Salt Lake county). She was born March 1, 1888. Their children: Thomas Ralph b. July 19, 1907; Martha Isabella b. March 1, 1909; Marjorie Elizabeth b. Dec. 5, 1910. Family home Herriman, Salt Lake county.

BUTTERFIELD, SAMUEL (son of Thomas Butterfield and Mary Jane Parker). Born Feb. 27, 1855, Herriman, Utah.
Married Sarah Jane Farmer Oct. 18, 1875, Salt Lake City (daughter of James Farmer and Mary Ann Biddell of Herriman). She was born Jan. 18, 1858. Their children: Samuel James b. Dec. 28, 1876, m. Edith E. Nichols; Mary Jane Delila b. Sept. 21, 1878, m. Orin R. Freeman; Lilly May b. Jan. 7, 1882, died; Clara E. b. June 13, 1883, died; Thomas Almon b. March 26, 1885, m. Ella Brown; Joseph W. b. Dec. 16, 1886, died; Sarah A. E. b. Jan. 1, 1888, died; Emma Lenora b. March 6, 1889, m. Walter E. Crane; Olive Percinda b. May 27, 1890, m. Alexander Fraser; Hannah Pearl b. Aug. 1, 1892; Agnes Annie b. May 12, 1894, died; George Nephi b. March 11, 1895; Edward Moroni b. Jan. 6, 1897, died; Gloria Beatrice b. March 10, 1901, died; Marvin Levern b. Feb. 23, 1904; Gladys Eurilda b. June 2, 1907, died; Ruth b. Nov. 23, 1908. Family home Herriman, Utah.
Married Sarah Ann Newman October, 1886, Salt Lake City (daughter of William Newman and Maria Hunt, of Riverton, Utah, who came to Utah September, 1886). She was born April 8, 1863. Only child; William P. b. Aug. 23, 1886.
Ward teacher; missionary to central states 1911-13.

BUTTERFIELD, ZACHARIAH (son of Thomas Butterfield and Mary Jane Farmer). Born Jan. 4, 1864, Herriman, Utah. Came to Utah 1849.
Married Crelia Wordell Oct. 31, 1884, Logan, Utah (daughter of Isaac J. and Martha Wordell), who was born Jan. 14, 1866. Their children: Anna May b. Aug. 3, 1885, m. Charles Myers March 7, 1906; Zachariah T. b. Nov. 9, 1888, m. Maud Page Sept. 30, 1909; Isaac John b. Feb. 25, 1891, died.
Married Isabelle J. Dansie 1897, Salt Lake City (daughter of Robert Dansie and Jane Wilcox). Their children: Bernice b. Sept. 26, 1900; Phyllis b. April 9, 1903; Maurice b. Sept. 26, 1904; Rheabell b. Aug. 27, 1906; Lavira b. Dec. 28, 1908; Lavell b. March 31, 1913.
Missionary to southern states 1893, to Society Islands 1909; high priest; seventy; second counselor to Bishop Bills 1900; attended B. Y. University. Farmer and sheepraiser.

BUTTERWORTH, EDMUND (son of Edmund Butterworth and Sarah Ann Platt). Born Jan. 15, 1826, Lancashire, Eng. Came to Utah Oct. 24, 1854, William A. Empey company.
Married Alice Fielding in 1856, Salt Lake City (daughter of James Fielding and Ann Enthorn of Lancashire, Eng., pioneers Oct. 24, 1854). She was born Nov. 1840. Their children: John, m. Elizabeth Amer; Robert, m. Maria Boyd; Sarah, m. Ranch Kimball; Margaret, m. Ernest Wright; Edwin F., m. Florence Boud. Family home, Salt Lake City.
High priest. Adobe maker. Died in Aug. 1903.

BUTTERWORTH, EDWIN F. (son of Edmund Butterworth and Alice Fielding). Born May 15, 1880, Salt Lake City.
Married Florence Boud May 18, 1904 (daughter of John W. Boud and Elizabeth Pollard of Salt Lake City). She was born Jan. 29, 1882. Their children: Wallace E. b. 1905; Florence b. 1906; Ruth b. 1907; Edwin b. Nov. 1912. Family home, Salt Lake City.
President second quorum seventies; ward clerk. President and manager Butterworth Real Estate and Investment Co.

BUYS, EDWARD (son of Hyrum D. Buys, born Oct. 22, 1802, in New York, and Elizabeth Huntington, born Feb. 10, 1813, Albany, N. Y.). He was born Oct. 22, 1841, La Harpe, Hancock county, Ill. Came to Utah Sept. 15, 1860, David Evans company.
Married Celestia C. Bromley March 23, 1867 (daughter of William Bromley and Sarah B. Bylemore, pioneers Sept. 6, 1866, Samuel D. White company). She was born June 26, 1849. Their children: Hyrum D. b. Jan. 25, 1868, died; William Edward b. March 3, 1869, m. Ada Jones Jan. 20, 1892; Sarah Elizabeth b. June 9, 1871, m. James W. Carlile Nov. 25, 1891; Amanda C. b. Sept. 14, 1873, m. Charles E. Shelton Sept. 14, 1893; Mary Ann b. Jan. 17, 1876, m. Joseph W. Cummings Dec. 1, 1897; Joseph H. b. April 5, 1878, m. Lillian Stagg April 5, 1904; Charlotte b. Oct. 15, 1880, m. William D. Johnston Dec. 25, 1899; Alma b. Jan. 30, 1883, d. Jan. 14, 1885; Martha R. b. April 15, 1885, m. Thomas M. Giles Oct. 17, 1904; Archie D. b. Jan. 6, 1888, m. Florence E. Bonner Aug. 28, 1907; Daniel H. b. March 7, 1889, died; Clara May b. May 11, 1890, m. Alma M. Cummings April 14, 1909; Celestia C. b. Aug. 7, 1894.
Married Margaret Hamilton June 14, 1876 (daughter of Henry and Margaret Hamilton, pioneers 1856). She was born Oct. 1, 1859, Spanish Fork, Utah. Their children:

Henry D. b. May 11, 1877, m. Lillie M. Newberg June 28, 1911; Alice J. b. Aug. 10, 1878, d. Aug. 29, 1883; Margaret J. b. May 31, 1880, d. Sept. 5, 1883; Melissa b. Feb. 17, 1884, m. Joseph Moss; Matta E. b. March 17, 1886, m. Jared Tanner April. 1902; Edna A. b. Sept. 5, 1888. Families resided Buysville and Heber City, Utah.
High priest; counselor to Bishop N. C. Murdock 15 years. County surveyor of Wasatch eight years; deputy sheriff for several years. Built first shingle roof house in Charleston. Opened first schoolhouse at Buysville, Utah.

BYBEE, BYRAM (son of John Bybee and Betsy Killey, of Virginia). Born Feb. 25, 1799. Barren county, Ky. Came to Utah Oct. 6, 1851, Alfred Cardon company.
Married Betsy Lane (daughter of David Lane), who was born June 24, 1801, and came to Utah with husband. Their children: Polly C. b. Oct. 28, 1820. m. Levi Hammon; Rhoda b. Nov. 19, 1823, m. David Bair; Elizabeth J. b. Jan. 23, 1825, m. Daniel Smith; Luann b. Jan. 3, 1827, m. S. Haufshitter; John M. b. Feb. 17, 1829, m. Polly Smith; Luseen Bird b. Feb. ¯, 1831, m. Henry Beckstead June 6, 1849; David B. b. Sept. 17, 1832, m Adelia Higley; Jonathan M. b. July 28, 1836, died; Robert Lee b. May 4, 1838, m. Jane Miller March 19, 1857; Byram L. b. May 4, 1841, m. Jane Robinson. Family home Uinta, Utah.
Married Maria Knutson. Only child: Betsy.
Bishop's counselor 1856-59. Justice of peace 1854-61.

BYBEE, ROBERT LEE (son of Byram Bybee and Betsy Lane). Born May 4, 1838, Clay county, Ind.
Married Jane Miller March 19, 1857, at Salt Lake City (daughter of Charles Miller), who was born Aug. 12, 1840, in Scotland. Their children: Betsy Jane b. March 20, 1859, d. child; Robert Lee b. Sept. 14, 1861, m. Lydia Forbush; Francis M. b. Oct. 2, 1862, m. Ann Ritchie; James A. b. July 2, 1865, m. Ozetta Eastman; Mary Alice b. Nov. 16, 1867, m. A. H. Boomer; Elizabeth b. June 17, 1870, m. C. W. Poole. Family home Uinta, Utah.
Married Harriett Raymond (daughter of Almon P. Raymond, member Co. D. Mormon battalion, and Clarinda Critler). She was born Oct. 3, 1852, West Jordan, Utah. Their children: Harriett R. b. Jan. 20, 1873, died; Clarinda b. Oct. 1, 1874, m. John W. Nowlin Dec. 14, 1892; Rhoda L. b. Sept. 22, 1876, m. Roy Stockman May 26, 1897; Walter R. b. Oct. 25, 1879, m. May Thompson; Minnie b. Sept. 28, 1881, m. A. C. Hancey Dec. 6, 1901; Jessie May b. April 17, 1883, Alonzo b. 1878, latter twin died; Ida b. Feb. 8, 1885, m. John Thomas Dec. 8, 1904; Stanley b. March 14, 1889, m. Lovina Lee Dec. 6, 1904; Venta b. Dec. 30, 1889, died; Leslie E. b. Jan. 5, 1892; Harold b. Dec. 23, 1895.
Mail carrier between Salt Lake City and Independence, Mo. Went with Y. X. company 1857. Missionary Salmon River 1858. Went south during general move. Bishop of Manti south ward four years; president of Menan (Idaho) stake four years; president of Bannock stake two years; moved to Bingham county, Idaho, where he was first counselor to President J. E. Steele 13 years and superintendent Iona ward Sunday school for four years. Senator in Idaho legislature 1901. Ordained patriarch 1908.

BYINGTON, HYRUM E. Born Oct. 4, 1830. Came to Utah in 1860.
Married Hannah Harr, who was born Aug. 3, 1836. Their children: Lorinda Hickman b. Jan. 25, 1858, m. Hyrum Stowe; Brigham Porthugh b. Jan. 6, 1860, m. Allie Hunt; Hyrum N. b. Dec. 30, 1862, died; Joseph H. b. Dec. 28, 1864, m. Rosetta Hunt; Stephen Elliott b. Jan. 12, 1866, m. Jane Larson; Sarah Jane b. Nov. 14, 1868, died; Hannah E. b. Oct. 12, 1870, m. Thomas Larson; Rebecca A. b. Aug. 25, 1872, and Alexander b. Feb. 3, 1874, died; Nora E. b. Feb. 3, 1876, m. Jason Pohmer. Family home Ogden, Utah.

BYINGTON, STEPHEN ELLIOT (son of Hyrum E. Byington and Hannah Parr). Born Jan. 12, 1866, Ogden, Utah.
Married Jane Larson Sept. 30, 1884, Oxford, Oneida county, Idaho (daughter of Thurston Larson and Elizabeth Fox, former a pioneer with Mormon battalion Co. C). She was born May 28, 1864, Salt Lake City. Their children: Stephen Millard b. Aug. 14, 1885, m. Lauretta West; Mary Ellen b. Jan. 5, 1887, died; Sarah Jane b. Jan. 5, 1889; Earnest Lorenzo b. Sept. 28, 1891; Hyrum Arthur b. Sept. 26, 1893; Raymond Thurston b. Nov. 9, 1895; Dyantha b. Feb. 16, 1898; Joseph Ephraim b. Feb. 8, 1900; Parley Grant b. Oct. 2, 1902; George Franklin b. Dec. 10, 1904; Elmer Norton b. Nov. 6, 1906; Isabell Maud b. Jan. 5, 1910.

BYINGTON, JOSEPH HENRY (son of Hyrum Norton Dyington and Sarah Hawkins). Born Jan. 25, 1829, in Ohio. Came to Utah Sept. 20, 1848, Heber C. Kimball company.
Married Nancy Avery 1850. Their children: Joseph Henry Jr., m. Ora Wakely; Mirandi. m. William Stowe; Sarah. m. Henry Hoffman; Hyrum Elliot. m. Cordelia Symons; Elizabeth. m. Julie Sorenson; John H., m. Lucinda Symons; Nettie, m. Christopher Sorenson; Ira, m. Sarah Walker; William, m. Emma Higgins.
Married Hannah Molland Feb. 26, 1864, Salt Lake City (daughter of James and Rebecca Molland, former a pioneer Oct. 4, 1852, Thomas E. Ricks company). She was born July 21, 1838, Liverpool, Eng. Their children: James Henry b. April 4, 1865, m. Sarah Mirah Carr Dec. 25, 1890; Hannah Mirah b. Aug. 8, 1866, m. William Burrup 1883; Charles Norton b. March 29, 1868, m. Ettie Smithies Feb. 11, 1903; Sarah Rebecca b. Nov. 24, 1869; Martha Jane b. May 25, 1872, m.

Frank Reed Nov. 27, 1894; Mary Ann b. Jan. 27, 1875; Susan Elizabeth b. Sept. 30, 1876, m. Ike Fisher Dec. 5, 1892; Joseph Henry, Jr. b. Nov. 18, 1878; John Parley b. March 23, 1880, m. Marguerite Smith Dec. 12, 1904; Clarence Spencer b. Dec. 19, 1881. Family home Ogden, Utah.
Seventy, and religious worker.

BYINGTON, JAMES HENRY (son of Joseph Henry Byington and Hannah Molland). Born April 4, 1865, Ogden, Utah.
Married Sarah Mirah Carr Dec. 25, 1890. Fremont county, Idaho (daughter of David Orlando Carr and Angeline Melvina Butler, pioneers Sept. 20, 1848, Brigham Young company). She was born Sept. 20, 1870. Their children: Roy Lovell b. Oct. 12, 1891; Emil Roldolph b. March 11, 1893; Florence Angeline b. June 12, 1895; Veda Evelyn b. Dec. 8, 1897; James Vernon b. July 2, 1900; Archie Delos b. Nov. 22, 1903; Clarence Arthur b. Dec, 3, 1905; Leonard Donald b. Oct. 29, 1909; Loren Richard b. Feb. 26, 1912.
Bishop's counselor and superintendent Sunday school of Lava ward.

C

CAFFEY, BENJAMIN F. (son of Benjamin F. Caffey and Mary E. Winn of Montgomery, Ala.). Born Jan. 12, 1862, at Montgomery. Came to Utah September, 1889.
Married Kate MacLean Aug. 17, 1892, at Salt Lake City (daughter of John MacLean and Agnes Flemming, Glasgow, Scotland, who came to Utah 1880). She was born Oct. 7, 1875. Their children: Benjamin F., Jr. b. July 20, 1893; John P. b. March 30, 1895; Andrew A. b. Dec. 5, 1897; Ian McConnie; Emma, m. Richard Winder; Louie, m. Lewis E. b. Feb. 11, 1908. Family home Salt Lake City, Utah.
Stock-broker.

CAHOON, REYNOLDS. Came to Utah 1848.
Married Thurza Stiles: Their children: Palaski; William F., m. Nancy M. Gibbs; Daniel; Andrew, m. Mary Carruth; m. Margaret Carruth; m. Jeannette Carruth; Mahonri. Family home Murray, Utah.

CAHOON, ANDREW (son of Reynolds Cahoon and Thurza Stiles). Came to Utah 1848.
Married Mary Carruth (daughter of William Carruth), who was born Oct. 1828. Their children: Joseph, m. Mary Ann McConnie; Emma, m. Richard Winder; Louie, m. Lewis A. Copeland. Family home Murray, Utah.
Married Margaret Carruth (daughter of William Carruth), who was born March 25, 1832. Their children: Alonzo A., m. Mary Ann Erickson; John P., m. Elizabeth Gordon; Albert m. Mary Clark; Reynolds, m. Margaret Davis; Maria A., m. David O. Mackay; Daniel Farrington, m. Naoma Tripp; Lucy, m. Harvey C. Carlisle; Margaret Melissa d. infant. Family home Murray.
Married Jeannette Carruth (daughter of William Carruth), who was born 1825. Their children: Rachel, m. Samuel Wooley; Jane W., m. Harry Haines; James W., m. Reuben, m. Melvina Morgan. Family home Murray.
Missionary to Scotland 1845-47; bishop of South Cottonwood ward fifteen years; served in Echo Canyon campaign. Surveyor; farmer. Died 1900 at Murray.

CAHOON, WILLIAM F. (son of Reynolds Cahoon and Thurza Stiles of Nauvoo, Ill.). Born Nov. 7, 1813 at Harperstield, Ohio. Came to Utah Sept. 1848.
Married Nancy M. Gibbs Jan. 17, 1836, Kirtland, Ohio (parents lived at Kirtland). She was born July 27, 1818. Their children: Nancy E.; Lerona E., m. Myron B. Durfee; John F., m. Margaret Sharp; Ermina Sarah Prudence. m. John Osborn Angell; Thurza Viola, m. Albert Angell; William M., m. Martitia Smith; Daniel C.; Joseph M. b. March 2, 1853, m. Mary E. Ensign Oct. 1, 1876; Henry R., m. Anna Durfee; Stephen T., m. Anna Irons; Andrew C. Family home Salt Lake City, Utah.
High priest; missionary. Carpenter. Said to have pulled first curtain on the famous Salt Lake theatre stage. Died April 1897, Salt Lake City.

CAHOON, JOSEPH M. (son of William F. Cahoon and Nancy M. Gibbs). Born March 2, 1853, Salt Lake City.
Married Mary E. Ensign Oct. 1, 1876, Salt Lake City (daughter of Lewman Ensign and Mary A. Garn of Massachusetts and Ohio. Came to Utah 1847). She was born Sept. 23, 1859. Their children: Joseph H. b. Jan. 22, 1877, m. Ceora D. Woody; Ashley E. b. Aug. 8, 1880; Eugene A. b. Oct. 14, 1882, m. Esther King; Ethel b. Jan. 23, 1885, m. Harlow Grove; Harold M. b. Jan. 21, 1889, m. Olive Shepard; Silvia D. b. Jan. 15, 1891; Margaret E. b. Jan. 13, 1894; Marian B. b. May 7, 1902. Railroad man.

CAIN, JOSEPH (son of James Cain born Sept. 18, 1797, Isle of Man, Eng., and Anne Moore born June 1793, Kirk Lanan, Eng). He was born Nov. 5, 1822, Douglas, Isle of Man. Came to Utah Sept. 18, 1847, John Taylor company.
Married Elizabeth Whitaker Feb., 1847 (daughter of Thomas Whitaker and Sophia Turner), who was born Aug. 4, 1828 and came to Utah with husband. Their children: Elizabeth Turner b. April 14, —, m. Charles Crismon June 1872; Joseph Moore b. May 14, —, d. Feb. 3, 1880.
Postmaster at Salt Lake City 1854-55; associated with Willard Richards and Elias Smith in publishing Deseret News.

CAINE, JOHN T. (son of Thomas Caine and Elinor Cubbon of the Isle of Man, Parish of Kirk Patrick). Born Jan. 8, 1829, on the Isle of Man. Came to Utah Sept. 20, 1852, captain of ten in the James McGaw company of fifty wagons.

Married Margaret Nightingale Oct. 22, 1850, St. Louis, Mo. (her grandmother, Mary Leach, was the second woman baptized into the L. D. S. church in Europe. She lived at Nauvoo, and later went to St. Louis).

The family record of Mr. and Mrs. Caine shows them to be the parents of thirteen children, eight of whom are living, namely, Agnes Ellen, who is Mrs. Arthur Pratt; John T., Jr., registrar in the Utah Agricultural College at Logan; Albion William, a rancher near Missoula, Mont.; Joseph Edgar, a former captain of the Utah Volunteer Cavalry in the Philippines, afterward cashier of the Utah Commercial and Savings Bank, secretary Salt Lake Commercial Club; and at this time secretary Oakland (Cal.) Commercial Club; Julia Dean, Mrs. George D. Alder; Charles Arthur, secretary of the Caine & Hooper Co.; Florence Nightingale, Mrs. Will G. Farrell; Margaret Nightingale, and Mrs. William G. Patrick.

He was a school teacher in Utah; missionary to Sandwich Islands; actor, stage manager and editor at Salt Lake City; territorial legislator; University regent and city recorder —such is a partial epitome of the pre-delegate record of this self-made man, rising step by step from the humblest walks of life to the high and honorable position of United States Congressman from Utah. As missionary to the Hawaiian mission, where he presided over the Oahu conference, the climate did not agree with him, and President Young recalled him. Reaching Utah October, 1856, he was made secretary of the legislature in session at Fillmore, which adjourned to Salt Lake City, and was with that body until its adjournment. He was secretary of a commission appointed by this legislature to codify the United States laws applicable to territories. He held the same positions in the legislatures for many years afterward. He was also military secretary (with the rank of lieutenant-colonel) on the staff of Gen. Daniel Wells, commanding the Nauvoo Legion, and once a private clerk to President Brigham Young.

Delegated to carry a protest from the people of Utah to Washington, D. C., against the Cullom bill, then pending in Congress, he created much favorable comment. Manager of Salt Lake Herald, established 1872, and third owner; member constitutional convention of 1882; elected to congress that year, taking his seat March, 1883; presided over the constitutional conventional of 1887, and strongly urged the adoption of a clause in the proposed constitution prohibiting polygamy, believing this to be the true solution of the "Mormon" problem, and the only course that would satisfy the government of the United States.

He presented the constitution and its accompanying documents to Congress, and on Feb. 18, 1888, before the Senate committee on territories, made a strong argument in support of the honesty and sincerity of the people of Utah in proposing this solution of the vexing question. During the same year, on the 2nd of August and the 4th of October, he delivered in the House his noted speeches, "Polygamy in Utah a Dead Issue," and "Mormon Facts Versus Anti-Mormon Fictions." In the beginning of 1889 he made an able and forcible argument before the House committee on territories in favor of Utah's admission as a State. All the while, in and out of Congress, he was stemming a perfect torrent of anti-Utah measures, one of which, by Senator Paddock of Nebraska, an ex-member of the Utah Commission, proposed the redistricting and reapportionment of Salt Lake City by the governor, secretary and members of that commission, in such a way as to give the "Liberals" control of the city government. Senator Cullom, of Illinois, and Delegate Dubois, of Idaho, presented legislative commission bills. Mr. Caine's plea to senators and members was that they should wait and see if the Edmunds-Tucker law would not accomplish all that was desired in the settlement of the "Mormon" question. He introduced a bill for an enabling act for Utah, and set on foot the movement that resulted in the appointment of a fourth federal judge for Utah. A pleasant episode in the midst of these stormy experiences was his attendance, as Utah's representative, in New York City, April 29, 30, and May 1, 1889, at the great celebration in honor of the centennial anniversary of the inauguration of George Washington as president of the United States.

The opening of the Fifty-first Congress found him at his post, fighting the infamous measures known as the Cullom and Struble bills, which proposed to disfranchise all members of the L. D. S church who were American citizens, and prevent the naturalization of Mormon aliens. On April 23, 1890, Mr. Caine, before the House committee on territories, delivered a masterful and convincing argument against the Struble bill, which though favorably reported, prevented it from coming before the House for action. Our delegate and his congressional friends also blocked the way of the new Edmunds bill, proposing to devote the funds escheated from the Mormon church to the public schools of Utah. Upon the passage of the bill for the admission of Idaho, he made a speech favoring statehood for that Territory; but opposing those provisions of the enabling act which disfranchised for their church membership, all Mormons citizens residing there.

But it was not alone in antagonizing measures inimical to his Mormon constituents, that our delegate's zeal and efficiency were shown. He fought repeatedly and successfully the proposed removal of the Southern Ute Indians from Colorado to Utah, and secured measures for the relief of the inhabitants of Ferron, Richfield, and Morgan, enabling them to increase the area of their townsite entries by filing upon school lands within their corporate limits. He obtained appropriations for the construction and completion of the Utah penitentiary, and for the benefit of the Shebit Indians in Washington county. He presented bills for the erection of government buildings at Salt Lake City and Ogden, for the creation of a land office at Ogden, and for the granting of a tract of sixty acres for a University site on the Fort Douglas military reservation. He also secured, during the anti-polygamy crusade, presidential clemency and full pardons for many old and feeble men who were undergoing imprisonment in the prisons of Utah and other places.

In these and all other matters requiring executive action Mr. Caine speaks in warm terms of the magnanimity and high sense of justice manifested by President Cleveland. With the president, the heads of departments, and the attaches of several government offices, he maintained the most cordial relations. Uniformly dignified and courteous, he enjoyed the confidence and respect of his associates in Congress, made no enemies, and had many warm friends. During the whole of his experience as delegate he served as a member of the National Democratic Campaign committee, representing Utah, and took an active part in all its deliberations for the advancement of Democratic interests in the several congressional districts. The influence thus gained was ever at the command of his constituents, and no citizen of Utah, nor even of Idaho or Arizona, Mormon or not, ever appealed to him in vain for assistance, when to give such assistance was proper and possible.

To recount the full story of his combats, victories and defeats in the Forty-eighth, Forty-ninth, Fiftieth and Fifty-second Congresses, to each of which he was elected by an overwhelming majority (his plurality at the last election being nearly ten thousand), would require much space. It might almost be said that a battle royal was waged from start to finish throughout his eleven years of service, the final victory coming to Mr. Caine and the people for whom he faithfully fought, in the practically unanimous consent of all parties to admit Utah into the Union. On Jan. 7, 1892, he introduced in the House the Utah Home Rule bill, duplicated by Mr. Faulkner in the Senate, and in February considered by the Senate and House committees on territories. Delegations from Utah, introduced by Mr. Caine, spoke for and against the measure: H. W. Smith, C. C. Richards, J. W. Judd, F. S. Richards, T. J. Anderson, J. L. Rawlins, F. H. Dyer, and ex-Governor West, in favor of it, and O. W. Powers, C. E. Allen, C. W. Bennett and John Henry Smith in opposition. The latter two argued in favor of statehood rather than against home rule. Before the Senate committee, Delegate Caine read the Mormon petition for amnesty, dated Dec. 19, 1891, and signed by the First Presidency and Twelve Apostles, thus securing its publication as a part of the proceedings. He worked zealously for the Home Rule bill, and on July 8, 1892, saw it pass the House, thus clearing the way for Statehood.

Upon the dissolution of the "People's" and "Liberal" parties, Mr. Caine, who had always been a Democrat in spirit, became identified with and one of the leaders of the Democratic party of Utah. In June, 1892, he attended as a delegate the National Democratic convention at Chicago which nominated Grover Cleveland for his second term as president. There was a contesting delegation, headed by Judge Powers, representing the "Tuscarora Society," mostly Democratic members of the fast dying "Liberal" party. Mr. Caine's acquaintance and influence with public men, members of the convention, was largely instrumental in seating the regular delegates—Judge Henry P. Henderson and himself. As a member of the committee on platform and resolutions, he secured a clause in the platform favoring statehood for all the Territories having the requisite qualifications. Back again in Congress, Jan. 14, 1893, he introduced in the House, a bill for an enabling act to admit Utah into the Union, and a similar bill at his request was introduced by Mr. Faulkner in the Senate. It failed of passage owing to the flood of business at the close of that session, and the change of administration, but practically identical with it was the bill that became a law in the next Congress.

With statehood in sight—the public boom for which he had toiled so long and faithfully—Delegate Caine was the logical candidate for re-election 1892, but it being suggested to him by personal friends among his fellow partisans, after the organization of the Democratic party of Utah, that in order to show the country that the dissolution of the "People's" party was an honest reality, it would be advisable to nominate a non-Mormon for delegate, he willingly sacrificed his own political interests, and heartily joined in the nomination and zealously worked for the election of Hon. Joseph L. Rawlins. The next year Utah went Republican, that party electing a majority of the members of the legislature. Fearing the effect upon Congress, which was strongly Democratic, and was then considering the Utah Statehood bill, which passed the House in December of that year, Mr. Caine was prevailed upon by prominent Utah Democrats, in January, 1894, to take a trip to Washington and consult with Democratic leaders in Congress over the Utah situation. The result was all that could be desired. While those leaders were disappointed at the outcome of the election, they declared that the Territory had all the qualifications for Statehood, and was entitled to admission into the Union. The enabling act passed the Senate in July, 1894, and on the 16th of that month was approved by President Cleveland.

As Chairman of the Democratic territorial committee, Mr. Caine, in the fall of the same year, waged an energetic campaign, many Democrats being elected to the constitutional convention, which, however, had a Republican majority; that party also elected the delegate to Congress, Hon. Frank J. Cannon. In August, 1895, Mr. Caine again went east in the interest of his party. At the Democratic convention for the nomination of State officers, held at Ogden, in anticipation of Statehood, on the 5th of September, he was almost unanimously nominated for Governor, but in the election, after a thorough canvass of the Territory with Hon. B. H. Roberts, he shared the fate of his party, receiving 18,519 votes as against 20,833 cast for the successful Republican candidate, Hon. Heber M. Wells. In 1896 he was nominated for the State Senate and elected, receiving a majority of 3,820 votes over any senatorial candidate on the opposition ticket. He served but one session in the Senate, having drawn the short, or one-year term.

In the interim of retiring from Congress in March, 1893, and the advent of statehood in 1896, Mr. Caine was Auditor of Public Accounts for the Territory. He was afterwards superintendent of waterworks for Salt Lake City. In business life he has also figured prominently. He was one of the original stockholders and directors of Zion's Savings Bank and Trust Company, and is a director, secretary and treasurer of the Josepa Agricultural and Stock Company, promoting the settlement of native Hawaiians on a large ranch in Skull Valley.

CALDER, GEORGE (son of George Calder and Anna Johnson of Dunnethead, Thurso, Scotland). Born Dec. 25, 1838, Edinburgh, Scotland. Came to Utah Sept. 1850, Captain Clawson company.
Married Mary Bennion April 6, 1861, at Taylorsville, Utah (daughter of John Bennion born at Hawarden, Wales, and Esther Wainwright born at Liverpool, Eng., pioneers Sept. 1847, John Taylor company). She was born May 4, 1844. Their children: Orson B. b. Jan. 8, 1862, m. Catherine Snedaker; George Washington b. June 1, 1863, d. infant; Louisa b. Dec. 21, 1864, m. William Orme Lee; Omni b. June 18, 1867, d. child; Lynus b. March 25, 1869, d. child; Ada b. May 23, 1871, m. Edwin J. Winder; Hyrum Bennion b. May 26, 1873, m. Agnes Ellen Hamilton June 27, 1900; Joseph b. May 26, 1873, d. infant; Georgiana b. Aug. 23, 1875, d. child; Rebeau b. Nov. 27, 1877, m. Stella Whitlock; Pontha b. Aug. 3, 1879, m. Rosella Soffe; Wallace b. March 1, 1882, m. May Hacking; Bruce b. June 23, 1885, m. Margaret Hamilton; Dora b. Nov. 14, 1887, m. William H. Cook. Family home Taylorsville, Mill Creek and Vernal, Utah.
Seventy; Sunday school superintendent; president Y. M. M. I. A. of Mill Creek ward. School trustee; school teacher. Founder of Calder's Park (Wandamere, Salt Lake county). Settled at Vernal 1905, where he engaged in stockraising. Died March 29, 1910, Vernal.

CALDER, ORSON BENNION (son of George Calder and Mary Bennion). Born Jan. 8, 1862, Taylorsville, Utah.
Married Catherine Snedaker July 28, 1886, Logan, Utah (daughter of John Frederick Snedaker and Elizabeth Rock of Mill Creek, Utah, pioneers Oct. 2, 1847, Jedediah M. Grant company). She was born Feb. 8, 1863. Their children: Orson Mentzer b. May 17, 1887; Mary Elizabeth b. May 25, 1889, m. John Robert Robinson; Leo b. Oct. 23, 1891; Alton b. Oct. 17, 1893; Zelph b. May 22, 1895; Sylvanus b. May 27, 1897, died; Greta Kathryn b. June 2, 1899. Family home Vernal.
High priest; missionary to England 1903-04; ward teacher 35 years; Sunday school superintendent; secretary of Y. M. M. I. A.; ward organist 28 years. Moved from Salt Lake county to Vernal 1886. Stockholder in Ashby Upper Irrigation Canal, Ashby Central Canal and Ouray Valley Irrigation Canal. Farmer and stockraiser.

CALDER, HYRUM BENNION (son of George Calder and Mary Bennion). Born May 26, 1873, Mill Creek, Utah.
Married Agnes Ellen Hamilton June 27, 1900, at Salt Lake City (daughter of James Campbell Hamilton and Isabell Hood Hill), who was born April 18, 1874. Their children: George Hamilton b. May 21, 1901, d. Feb. 6, 1913; James Hamilton b. Sept. 28, 1902; David Hamilton b. Aug. 9, 1904; Vera b. June 6, 1906; Grant Hamilton b. Aug. 1, 1909; Howard Bennion b. July 11, 1912.
Missionary to Scotland 1896-98; Sunday school teacher 19 years; set apart bishop of 1st ward of Vernal Sept. 18, 1910. Assisted his father in building Calder's Park (Wandamere) at Salt Lake City, and for many years assisted in its management. Moved to Vernal Oct. 1899, where he with his brother Pontha engaged in the ice business; later he became manager of Acorn Mercantile company and served three years; he then engaged in the creamery business with his brothers under the firm name of Calder Bros.

CALDWELL, ISAAC JAMES (son of David Caldwell and Mary Ann Vaughn of Canada). Born April 29, 1833. Came to Utah 1853, Captain Clawson company.
Married Eliza Ann Russell Feb. 16, 1858, Rush Valley, Utah (daughter of William Greenwood Russell and Louise Jones of Liverpool, Eng., pioneers Oct. 3, 1852, Isaac Bullock company). She was born Feb. 11, 1840. Their children: Isaac James Jr. b. Jan. 17, 1859, d. 1882; William H. b. Jan. 18, 1861, m. Margaret Park; John D. b. April 13, 1863, d. 1884; George b. May 11, 1865, m. Annie Morgan; Fanny C. b. July 12, 1867, d. 1873; Emily M. b. Dec. 23, 1869, m. Thomas Adams; Elizabeth J. b. April 1, 1872; Richard E. b. Sept. 27, 1875, m. Estella Neff; Margaret A. b. June 7, 1879; Herbert V. b. June 17, 1883, d. infant. Family resided St. John, Tooele and Salt Lake City, Utah.
Senior president seventies; assisted in bringing immigrants to Utah. Farmer and stockraiser. Died 1892 at Salt Lake City.

CALDWELL, RICHARD E. (son of Isaac James Caldwell and Eliza Ann Russell). Born Sept. 27, 1875, in Tooele county, Utah.
Married Estella Neff June 30, 1905, Salt Lake City (daughter of Benjamin Barr Neff and Mary Ellen Love of Dry Creek, Utah, pioneers, Lot Smith company). She was born Aug. 7, 1871. Their children: Richard Elmer b. Jan. 30, 1907; Mary b. Sept. 19, 1908; Eliza Bess b. March 12, 1910. Family home Salt Lake City.
Missionary to southern states 1896-98; seventy. Civil engineer.

CALDWELL, JOHN (son of Thomas Caldwell of Carlisle, Eng.). Born 1815 in Carlisle. Came to Utah Oct. 17, 1862, Henry W. Miller company.
Married Maria Hansum. Only child: Joseph Bridge b. May 7, 1848, m. Annie Petrena Fjeldsted July 24, 1874. Family home Gunnison, Utah.
Married Elizabeth Mien at Carlisle, who was born 1818. Their children: Siddens, died; Jane, m. Nephi Gledhill; William, m. Sylvia Metcalf. Family home Gunnison.
High priest. Killed in Echo Canyon Sept. 27, 1868, while working on Union Pacific railroad.

CALDWELL, JOSEPH BRIDGE (son of John Caldwell and Maria Hansum). Born May 7, 1848, Carlisle, Eng. Came to Utah with parents.
Married Annie Petrena Fjeldsted July 24, 1874, Gunnison, Utah (daughter of Lars Peter Fjeldsted, pioneer 1862). She was born Sept. 12, 1853. Their children: Joseph Edwin b. May 21, 1875, m. Virginia Eccles Sept. 3, 1902; John LeRoy b. Sept. 24, 1877, died; Peter William b. Feb. 25, 1880, died; Jessie, died; Edith b. Oct. 29, 1882, m. Edwin Beach; Junius b. June 3, 1888; Evelyn b. Aug. 3, 1893; Eudora b. Nov. 30, 1896. Family home Ferron, Utah.
Elder. First resided at Tooele; moved to Grantsville, later to Mt. Pleasant, to Gunnison, and in 1881 to Ferron. Superintendent Sunday schools Molen ward five years. Assisted in bringing immigrants to Utah 1868. School trustee three years. Black Hawk war veteran. Farmer.

CALDWELL, JOSEPH EDWIN (son of Joseph Bridge Caldwell and Annie Petrena Fjeldsted). Born May 21, 1875, Gunnison, Utah.
Married Virginia Eccles Sept. 3, 1902, Salt Lake City (daughter of John Hutchinson Eccles and Mary Richmond of Paisley, Scotland). She was born June 20, 1882, Ogden, Utah. Their children: Joseph Hutchinson b. June 1, 1903; Mary Evelyn b. July 14, 1905; David Junius b. Oct. 21, 1906; John Eccles b. March 8, 1909; Boyd L. Wood b. March 4, 1911. Family home Molen ward, Ferron, Utah.
Member 144th quorum seventies; missionary to North Carolina 1898-1900; bishop Molen ward 1910; president Y. M. M. I. A., Castle Gate and Clear Creek, Utah, and Baker City, Oregon; member Emery stake board Y. M. M. I. A. Member Business Men's Association, Baker City, Oregon.

CALDWELL, MATTHEW (son of Curtis Caldwell and Nancy Hood). Born June 11, 1822, Mt. Vernon, Jefferson county, Ill. Came to Utah Sept. 8, 1850, Aaron Johnson company.
Married Barzilla Guymon Oct. 17, 1843, in Illinois (daughter of Thomas Guymon and Sarah Gordon of Jackson county, Tenn., pioneers Sept. 8, 1850). She was born Dec. 31, 1823. Their children: Thomas Jefferson, m. Mary Ann Peterson; Rachel Almira, m. George Horace; Curtis Washington, m. Almira Chase; Melissa Jane b. April 7, 1851, m. William Henry Adams Jr.; Matthew, died; William Guymon, m. Emerett Gillespie; Sarah Elizabeth, m. Stephen Daniels; John Edgar, m. Mary King; Barzilla and James Martin, died. Family home Fountain Green, Utah.
Private in Co. "E" of Mormon battalion. Captain in Walker and Black Hawk Indian wars. Appointed one of the presidents of 50th quorum seventies May 19, 1857; ward teacher. First mayor of Spanish Fork. Justice of peace and school teacher. Delegate to legislature from Sanpete county. Died March 15, 1912, Dry Fork, Uinta county, Utah.

CALL, CYRIL (son of Joseph Call, born 1742, and Mary Sanderson, both of Woodstock, Vt.). He was born June 29, 1785, Woodstock, Vt. Came to Utah in 1849.
Married Sally Tiffany (daughter of Christopher Tiffany), who was born Nov. 27, 1790; died 1856. Their children: Harvey b. Sept. 6, 1808, m. Mary Ann Loga; Anson b. May 13, 1810, m. May Flint; Salmon b. 1812, d. young; Samantha b. Nov. 15, 1814, m. Jeremiah Nalloy; Fanney b. May 11, 1816, m. Chester Loveland; Lucina b. Sept. 29, 1819, m. Perrigrine Sessions; Josiah b. Aug. 12, 1822, m. Henrietta Williams; Mary b. Feb. 4, 1824, m. Perrigrine Sessions; Roseline S. b. Dec. 29, 1826, m. Fernuta Dustin; Sarah b. Dec. 13, 1828, m. Samuel Mecham; Melissa b. March 29, 1833, m. Russel Brownell; Omer b. Jan. 9, 1834, m. Sarah Ferrin; Homer b. Jan. 9, 1834, m. Nancy Merrill. Family home Bountiful, Utah.
Died May 23, 1873, Bountiful.

CALL, ANSON (son of Cyril Call, whose father, Joseph Call fought in the battle of Bunker Hill and served under Washington, and Sally Tiffany, daughter of Christopher Tiffany, a German immigrant to New England). He was born May 13, 1810, Fletcher, Franklin county, Vt. Came to Utah Sept. 19, 1848, in charge of 20 wagons of the Brigham Young company.
Married Mary Flint Oct. 3, 1833, Madison, Ohio (daughter of Rufus Flint and Hannah Hawes, who was born March 27, 1812, at Braintree, Vt. Their children: Anson Vasco b. July 9, 1834, m. Charlotte Holbrook, m. Eliza Dopp; Mary Vashti b. March 27, 1836, m. Ira Parke; Moroni b. Feb. 6, 1838, died; Chester b. May 13, 1841, m. Agnes Loveland, m Mary A. Packer, m. Sarah M. Dixon, m. Pamelia Barlow Thompson; Christopher b. May 13, 1841; Hyrum b. Dec. 3, 1845; latter two died. Family home Bountiful, Utah.
Married Ann Maria Bowen April 16, 1851 at Salt Lake City (daughter of Israel Bowen and Louisa Durham, latter a pioneer of 1851). She was born Jan. 3, 1834, Bethany, N. Y. Their children: Vilate b. July 27, 1852, d. June 10, 1862; Israel b. July 2, 1854, m. Medora White Dec. 21, 1874, m. Jane L. Judd Knight June 11, 1880; Vententia b. Feb. 14, 1856, d. April 19, 1862; Viola b. June 16, 1858, m. James George; Anson Bowen b. Oct. 20, 1863, m. Mary T. Thompson; m. Harriet Cazier, m. Dora Pratt; Harriet Louisa b. April 8, 1866, m. William C. Mann. Family home Bountiful, Utah.
Married Margaretta Clark Feb. 7, 1857, at Salt Lake City (daughter of John Clark and Mary Unwin), who was born May 26, 1828, Nottingham, Eng. Their children: Mary b. May 24, 1858, m. Thomas Waddoups; Cylista b. April 9, 1860, m. Mark Waddoups; Samantha C. b. Nov. 28, 1861, m. William C. Mann; Cyntha b. Feb. 20, 1864, m. Thomas Waddoups; Willard b. April 25, 1866, m. Adelaide White; Aaron b. July 3, 1868, m. Samantha A. Willey. Family home Bountiful.
Married Emma Summers Feb. 24, 1857, at Salt Lake City (daughter of Thomas Summers and Susannah Stockall), who was born Aug. 5, 1828, Broadheath, Worcestershire, Eng. Their children: Ann b. March 15, 1858, m. Kepler Sessions; Fanny b. Aug. 11, 1860, m. Truman H. Barlow; Lucins b. April 8, 1862, m. Jasper N. Perkins; David b. June 20 1868, m. Eliza Ditmore; Sarah b. Dec. 8, 1870, m. Truman H Barlow. Family home Bountiful.
Married also Henrietta (Williams) Call (widow of his brother Josiah) and Ann Clark.
In fulfillment of a prophecy of the prophet Joseph Smith in Montrose, Iowa, July 14, 1843, that, "He would come to the Rocky mountains, and that he would assist in building cities from one end of the country to the other," Anson Call built a home in Bountiful, then North Canyon ward, at which place he served as bishop 1849-50 and again 1873-77. In 1851 a special session of the legislature appointed him probate judge of Millard county with orders to organize that county, and in 1852 he represented that section in the legislature. In 1854 he founded Call's Fort, Box Elder county. In connection with his wife Maria he pioneered Parowan, Fillmore, Pauvan valley and Carson valley, built warehouse at Callville 1864, the head of navigation on the Big Colorado river. With his sons Anson V. and Chester, took part in the Echo Canyon campaign. At the organization of the Davis stake, June, 1877, he was made counselor to President William R. Smith. Promoter of the Davis and Weber Co. Canal company. A successful merchant and farmer. Died Sunday, Aug. 31, 1890.

CALL, ANSON VASCO (son of Anson Call and Mary Flint). Born July 9, 1834. Came to Utah with parents.
Married Charlotte Holbrook June 3, 1854 (daughter of Joseph Holbrook and Nancy Lampson; married Dec. 30, 1830). She was born Nov. 26, 1833. Their children: Charlotte Vienna b. Nov. 7, 1854, m. Chrestian Nelson Nov. 22, 1869; Anson Vasco b. May 23, 1855, m. Alice J. Farnham; Joseph H. b. Feb. 23, 1857, m. Sarah Isabel Barlow; Mary Vashti b. Jan. 24, 1859, m. Moses Muir; Ira b. March 23, 1861, m. Jane Barlow; Hannah b. Jan. 26, 1863, m. William Hatch; Lamoni b. Jan. 25, 1865, m. Annie Barlow. Family home Bountiful, Utah.
Married Eliza Dopp at Salt Lake City. Their children: Chester Vincent b. Oct. 6, 1860, m. Annis Barlow; Sidney B., m. Miss Loveland; Ida, m. Mr. Welton. Family home Bountiful.
Missionary to England 1864-67. Died Aug. 4, 1867.

CALL, ANSON VASCO, JR. (son of Anson Vasco Call and Charlotte Holbrook). Born May 23, 1855, Willard, Utah.
Married Alice J. Farnham May 17, 1876, Salt Lake City (daughter of Augustus Farnham and Caroline Pill), who was born Aug. 5, 1859, Bountiful, Utah. Their children: Anson Vasco b. May 18, 1877, m. Artemesia Dalrymple; Adolphus Alvin b. Feb. 28, 1879, m. Sarah Isabel Astle; Alice Maud b. July 12, 1881, m. Thomas H. Burton; Ella b. July 14, 1884, m. Carl Cook; Caroline Charlotte b. April 22, 1888, m. Reuben Fielding Burton; Farnham Lamoni b. Aug. 16, 1890, m. Lillie Welch; Chester Alfred b. Dec. 18, 1892; Lorna Louise b. Aug. 21, 1899. Family home Bountiful.
Married Lucy E. King Dec. 28, 1882 (daughter of Thomas F. King and Miss Ogden), who was born Sept. 21, 1865. Their children: Franklin b. Dec. 24, 1883; Ostella b. Jan. 21, 1888, m. Adelbert Kennington; Christian Joseph b. Nov. 21, 1889, m. Alice Walton; Mary Vashti b. Oct. 20, 1891; Frederick William b. Jan. 27, 1894; Walter Leroy b. May 9, 1896; Laura Ann b. March 7, 1898, d. April 13, 1898; Ira Edward b. March 22, 1899; George Albert b. June 7, 1901; Edgar Allen b. Feb. 1, 1904.
Married Rosa Emily Stayner Oct. 1, 1883, Salt Lake City (daughter of Thomas Stayner), who was born Dec. 11, 1856, Farmington, Utah. Their children: Thomas John b. Aug. 20, 1884, m. Ethel Grace Papworth; Charles Stayner b. Dec. 16, 1887; Charlotte Vienna b. Oct. 12, 1889; Horace Arthur b. July 28, 1892; Rosa May b. April 28, 1896; Mary Edith b. March 21, 1898, d. Nov. 3, 1899.
Superintendent M. I. A. Davis stake 1880-85; missionary to Europe 1885-87; superintendent Co.-op store Bountiful 1882-85; county school superintendent 1883-85; superintendent Sunday schools Afton, Wyoming 1889-92, counselor to Stake pres. 1892-04. Mayor Afton three terms.

CALL, ADOLPHUS ALVIN (son of Anson Vasco Call, Jr., and Alice Jeanette Farnham). Born Feb. 28, 1879, Bountiful, Utah.
Married Sarah Isabel Astle Aug. 9, 1899, Salt Lake City (daughter of John Astle and Isabel Jane Bradshaw), who was born Sept. 20, 1879, Montpelier, Idaho. Their children: Vera Isabella b. June 2, 1900; Adolphus Alwin b. May 5, 1902; Elworth Anson b. June 19, 1904; Alice Maud b. Sept. 13, 1906; Grace Carol b. July 18, 1908; Wilford Ray b. July 21, 1910. Family home Afton, Wyo.

CALL, ISRAEL (son of Anson Call and Ann Maria Bowen). Born July 2, 1854, Fillmore, Utah.
Married Medora White Dec. 21, 1874, Salt Lake City (daughter of John S. White and Ann Eliza Adelaide Everett), who was born April 9, 1855, Farmington, Utah. Their children: Israel Bowen b. Oct. 10, 1875, m. Martha Balfour; m. Charlotte V. Davids; John Anson b. Dec. 14, 1876, m. Annie B. Law; Medora Adelaide b. Dec. 21, 1878, m. Joseph Bergeson; Vasco b. July 24, 1880, m. Maud Dobie; Schuyler b. June 9, 1882, m. Edna M. Goff; Chester Monroe b. April 11, 1884, m. Maud Parkin; Hattie Jane b. June 3, 1886, m. Ezra L. Sainsbury; Ambrose b. Feb. 29, 1888; Chloe Irene b. Nov. 3, 1891, d. Dec. 12, 1891; Vinson Oro b. Jan. 22, 1893; Willard White b. Jan. 9, 1895; Eldred Odel b. March 12, 1897, d. May 5, 1901.
Married Jane L. Judd Knight June 11, 1880, St. George, Utah (daughter of Hyrum Judd and Lizania Fuller, pioneers 1849), who was born May 2, 1849, Pottawattamie, Iowa. Their children: Lydia b. Nov. 9, 1881, m. Joseph C. Hancock; Newel b. Sept. 26, 1883, m. Bathsheba Standiford; Leonard b. Aug. 16, 1885, d. Oct. 20, 1889.
Missionary with Lot Smith to Sunset, Arizona, from Feb., 1876, to 1885; member high council of Little Colorado stake; pioneer to Colonia Diaz, Mexico, 1885. Postmaster at Bountiful 1913.

CALL, OMER (son of Cyril Call and Sally Tiffany). Born Jan. 9, 1834, Madison, Ohio.
Married Sarah M. Ferrin at Salt Lake City. Their children: Omer S.; Sallie A. Cordon; Cyril J.; Albert J.; Nancy A.; Anson H.; Fanny M.; Lydia J.; George W.; Elihu; Eleanor S.
Married Eleanor Jones at Salt Lake City. Their children: Justin D. b. April 6, 1868, m. Lula Bryan; Mary L.; Cyrus J.; Sarah E.; Joseph; Benjamin C.; Esther; William V.; Margaret; Chancy H.; Waldemar A. Family home Willard, Utah.

CALL, JUSTIN D. (son of Omer Call and Eleanor Jones). Born April 6, 1868, Willard, Utah.
Married Lula Bryan at Salt Lake City (daughter of William A. C. Bryan and Elizabeth Parks, former pioneer of 1848). She was born Sept. 27, 1872, Salt La'e City. Their children: Justin Bryan; William Cornell; Verebal; Eleanor T.; Chancy C.; David H.; Elizabeth; Ruth A.
Principal Juab Stake Academy; graduate Cornell University; superintendent Sunday schools of Box Elder stake. Judge of the District court, First Judicial district. Member Utah society, Sons of American Revolution.

CALL, HOMER (son of Cyril Call and Sally Tiffany). Born Jan. 9, 1834, Madison, Ohio.
Married Nancy Merrill July 10, 1856 (daughter of Charles Merrill and Sarah Finley, pioneers 1852, who were married Oct. 12, 1834, Lewis county, Mo.). She was born Nov. 8, 1838. Their children: Nancy Henrietta b. Dec. 4, 1857, m. Frederick Pariah Dec. 27, 1875; Homer Charles b. Nov. 30, 1859, m. Mary Eveline Taylor March 6, 1885; Josiah b. April 18, 1862, m. Dove Facer Dec. 18, 1884; Sarah Elvira b. Aug. 17, 1864; Alonzo b. Nov. 17, 1866, m. Elvira Lessie Oct. 21, 1889; Orvis b. Jan. 8, 1868, m. Chloe Ryan April 19, 1892; Amber b. Aug. 12, 1870, m. Enoch Grover May 22, 1889; Oel Vasco b. Feb. 15, 1873; Cyril Sylvester b. July 31, 1877; Effie Salina b. June 11, 1875, m. Ira Pettengill Jan. 17, 1894; Fanny Arretta b. Nov. 30, 1880; Maney Arletta b. Nov. 30, 1880. Family home Willard, Utah.
Pioneer to Box Elder county. Imported first grist mill and threshing machine to Utah. Farmer and stock raiser. Died July 12, 1908.

CALL, HOMER CHARLES (son of Homer Call and Nancy Merrill). Born Nov. 30, 1859, Willard, Utah.
Married Mary Eveline Taylor March 6, 1885 (daughter of John Taylor, born May 6, 1838, and Lovisa Beecher, born Sept. 22, 1846, Iowa, pioneers to Utah). She was born Nov. 16, 1867, Willard. Their children: Charles Orvil b. Nov. 20, 1885; Nancy Irene b. Jan. 13, 1887; Alva Lovisa b. Sept. 29, 1889, m. Andrew Gray; Hazel Mary b. Jan. 14, 1892; Howard Leslie b. Sept. 7, 1895; Rose Amber b. Aug. 1, 1898; Martha Leone b. Nov. 5, 1907; Sarah Edrus b. Feb. 10, 1905; Homer Ray b. Sept. 15, 1907; Eva T. and Reva T. born July 3, 1907.
Rancher by vocation.

CALL, JOSIAH (son of Homer Call and Nancy Merrill). Born April 18, 1862, Willard, Utah.
Married Dove Facer Dec. 18, 1884, Logan, Utah (daughter of George Facer and Mary Pryor, pioneers 1859), who was born Jan. 10, 1867, Willard. Their children: Oel F. b. Nov. 24, 1885; Mary Nancy b. Nov. 28, 1887, m. William F. Chandier June 10, 1908; Ethel May b. April 21, 1890; Elmo Josiah b. Jan. 25, 1893; Dove Alida b. Oct. 3, 1895; Royal Glenn b. April 30, 1900; Vivian A. b. April 9, 1902; Allon Willard b. April 29, 1904; Leland b. May 9, 1906; Lola b. Aug. 8, 1908. Family home Rigby, Idaho.
Bishop's counselor 22 years; first counselor to president, Rigby stake. Justice of peace 1890-92; city councilman two terms.

CALLISTER, THOMAS (son of John Callister and Catherine Murphy of Isle of Man). Born July 8, 1821, Isle of Man. Came to Utah Sept. 25, 1847, Daniel Spencer company.
Married Caroline Smith Aug. 31, 1845, Nauvoo, Ill. (daughter of John Smith and Clarissa Lyman of Illinois, pioneers 1847, Daniel Spencer company). Their children: Thomas and Clarissa died; Clara C., m. Francis M. Lyman; Philomela d. 1879; Mary Miranda, m. Edward L. Lyman; Samuel J. d. 1856; Bathsheba B. d. 1860; Asahel S. d. 1865. Family home Salt Lake City.
Married Helen Marr Clark Dec. 16, 1845, Nauvoo, Ill. (daughter of Russell Kilburn Clark and Elizabeth Towne of Michigan, pioneers 1847, Daniel Spencer company). Their children: Helen Marr b. Sept. 26, 1846, m. Henry J. McCullough; Elizabeth Ann b. March 20, 1848, m. Cuthbert King; Katherine Eliza b. Feb. 10, 1850, m. William E. Hatton; Thomas Clark b. Aug. 2, 1852, m. Alice M. McBride Nov. 16, 1874; Sarah Melissa b. Oct. 29, 1854, m. Nephi Pratt; Isabella b. Oct. 5, 1856, m. Francis A. Webb; Margaret Jane b. Oct. 13, 1858, d. May 6, 1875; Daniel Porter b. Dec. 28, 1860, m. Malissa E. Davis; Susan Delilah b. May 25, 1863, m. Francis M. Lyman; Russel Kilburn b. Feb. 13, 1865, m. Melvie Smith; John Warren b. Oct. 15, 1867, m. Mercy Croft; m. Annie Ellison; Zina Prescinda b. May 25, 1871, d. June 17, 1871.
Married Mary Levina Phelps Dec. 1863 (daughter of Alva Phelps and Margaret Robison of Fillmore, Utah). Their children: Mary Levina b. Feb. 2, 1865, m. Jacob T. Robison; Alva Phelps b. Jan. 27, 1867, m. Ella Marcus; m. Jennie Jensen; George Albert b. Dec. 28, 1867; Ida and Ada b. Dec. 26, 1869; Joseph b. April 29, 1871; William Henry b. July 7, 1872, m. Inez Blood; Elida b. Aug. 5, 1874, m. William M. Elison; Juliet b. May 25, 1876, m. Clarence Carson; Orson Pratt b. Dec. 2, 1878, m. Francelia Jones; Walter Stanley b. July 19, 1880, m. Grace Carson.
Married Carlie E. Lyman Feb. 14, 1878, at Salt Lake City (daughter of Amasa M. Lyman and Caroline Eliza Partridge of Salt Lake City and Fillmore, Utah, pioneers 1847). Only child: Joseph Platte b. March 17, 1879, m. Sarah Elizabeth Christensen.
Served in Walker and Black Hawk Indian wars with rank of colonel. Missionary to Great Britain 1875-76; bishop of 17th ward, Salt Lake City 1855-61; bishop of Fillmore 1861-69; president Millard stake 1869-77; patriarch 1877-80. Member legislature 14 years. Farmer and stock raiser. Died Dec. 1, 1880, at Fillmore.

CALLISTER, THOMAS CLARK (son of Thomas Callister and Helen Marr Clark). Born Aug. 2, 1852, Salt Lake City.
Married Alice M. McBride Nov. 16, 1874, Salt Lake City (daughter of Reuben McBride and Mary Ann Anderson of Fillmore, pioneers 1851). She was born Dec. 4, 1853. Their children: Ruby Alice b. Nov. 29, 1875, m. Raymond Ray; Helen Angie b. June 9, 1878, m. Elmer E. Hinckley; Thomas Clark Jr. b. May 1, 1881, m. Millie Peterson; Wells Reuben b. Dec. 1, 1883, d. Jan. 26, 1886; Laura Adell b. March 27, 1886; Edna Louise b. July 15, 1888, m. John W. Starley; Mabel Venita b. June 26, 1891, d. Feb. 12, 1892; LaNola b. March 22, 1893. Family home Salt Lake City.
Bishop of Fillmore; high councilor; counselor in presidency of Millard stake; patriarch. Probate judge of Millard county, and assessor and collector; mayor of Fillmore; justice of peace; secretary State Board of Land Commissioners; county recorder; member legislature. Land attorney.

CALTON, WILLIAM (son of George Calton and Esther Hashurst, of Lancashire, Eng.). Born June 11, 1836, Manchester, Eng. Came to Utah Oct. 15, 1863. Samuel D. White company.
Married Maria Gutteridge Aug. 12, 1861, in England (daughter of Robert Gutteridge and Hannah Grover, of Berkshire, pioneers Aug. 20, 1868, Chester Loveland company). She was born Nov. 10, 1841, Reddington, Eng. Their children: William H. b. Nov. 6, 1864, m. Sarah I. Kingdom; Walter C. b. Dec. 10, 1866, m. Martha Chapman; Emily M. b. April 8, 1869, m. Charles H. Kammerman; Annie M. b. Nov. 26, 1871, m. George O. Burton; George A. b. Feb. 9, 1874, m. Helen Phillips; Isadore b. Jan. 28, 1877, m. Annie Christensen; Henry A. b. Jan. 15, 1880, m. Laura Cox; Pearl G. b. Nov. 25, 1884, m. Julian F. Smith.
Married Eliza Gutteridge Sept. 26, 1868, Salt Lake City (daughter of Robert Gutteridge and Hannah Grover), who was born April 17, 1846. Their children: Frederick b. Sept. 22, 1870, m. Anna L. Wilcox; Alfred b. Mar. 4, 1872, m. Catherine Ashler; Joseph b. June 25, 1874, m. Mary Inger Wilcox; Hyrum b. June 25, 1874, m. Mamie Hault; Rosanna b. March 31, 1878, d. aged 11; Mary Edith b. April 25, 1880, m. William Vaughan. m. James Hardy; James Herber b. July 12, 1883, m. Hazel Householder; David Carl b. Aug. 4, 1886. Families resided at Salt Lake City.
Chorister 1st ward Salt Lake City, and member Tabernacle choir 40 years. President Nauvoo Legion. Said to have dug first well in Utah. Died Feb. 4, 1912.

CALTON, FREDERICK (son of William Calton and Eliza Gutteridge). Born Sept. 22, 1870, Salt Lake City.
Married Anna L. Wilcox Jan. 4, 1893, Manti, Utah (daughter of Samuel A. Wilcox and Anna C. Peterson, of Cedar Valley, Utah), who was born Jan. 18, 1874. Their children: Anna V. born Nov. 5, 1893; Frederick L. b. Sept. 14, 1895; William Evan b. April 10, 1899; Reva May b. June 23, 1901; Clifton E. b. July 9, 1903; Leland Samuel b. May 2, 1906; Velma b. Oct. 22, 1907; Edith b. May 2, 1911. Family home Riverside, Utah.
Chorister Cedar Valley and Riverside wards, 15 years; Sunday school choir leader; supt. religion class. Carpenter; farmer.

CAMERON, JOHN (son of Alexander Cameron and Catherine McCullan of Scotland). Born Dec. 25, 1819. Came to Utah October, 1861.
Married Margaret Fairgrove. Their children: Catherine b. April, 1847, m. George Southam; James A. b. Sept. 22, 1851, m. Sarah E. Conley Dec. 6, 1875. Family home Randolph, Utah.
Married Mary McFall at St. Louis, Mo., who was born Sept., 1826. Their children: Margaret, d. young; Mary, d. April 6, 1857.
Married Alice Parkinson, who was born Feb. 4, 1829, Lancashire, Eng. Their children: John b. Sept. 9, 1859; Jannet b. June 9, 1861.
High priest.

CAMERON, JAMES A. (son of John Cameron and Margaret Fairgrove). Born Sept. 22, 1851.
Married Sarah E. Conley Feb. 6, 1875, Evanston, Wyo. (daughter of S. N. Conley and Eve Merckley). She was born April 14, ———, Centerville, Utah. Their children: James A., Jr. b. Jan. 16, 1876, m. Elizabeth Hamp; Sarah E. b. Oct. 18, 1877, m. Edwin Cornia; Mary P. b. Sept. 9, 1879, m. R. M. Horton; Hattie M. b. July 15, 1881, m. S. J. Clarke; Elizabeth A. b. Aug. 29, 1883, died; Ethel Pearl b. Aug. 13, 1885, m. James Jackson; Catherine Ruby b. Oct. 29, 1887, m. Melvin Cornia; Inez Estella b. Aug. 11, 1889; John G. b. Oct. 4, 1891; Albert G. b. Sept. 25, 1893; Hortense b. Jan. 26, 1896. Family home Blackfoot, Idaho.
High priest. Moved to Blackfoot, Idaho, 1895. Assisted in erecting many buildings at Blackfoot. Mason.

CAMPBELL, DAVID (son of John Campbell and Christina Cowan). Born 1809 in Stirlingshire, Scotland. Came to Utah Oct. 5, 1862, Ansel Harmon company.
Married Jane Izatt in Fifeshire, Scotland (daughter of Alexander Izatt and Margaret Mitchell, of Fifeshire), who was born in 1809. Their children: Margaret, m. William Kinghorn; John, m. Grace Izatt; William, m. Agnes Brown; Jane, m. Alexander Kinghorn; Christiana, d. infant; Alexander. Family home Airdrie, Lanarkshire, Scotland.
High priest. Block teacher. Laborer. Died in October, 1877, Salt Lake City.

CAMPBELL, WILLIAM (son of David Campbell and Jane Izatt). Born Aug. 12, 1841, Coatbridge, Lanarkshire, Scotland. Came to Utah with parents.
Married Agnes Brown March 29, 1869, Salt Lake City (daughter of John Brown and Christiana Thompson of Airdrie, Scotland—pioneers Sept. 15, 1868, John Gillespie company). She was born April 15, 1847. Their children: Christiana b. Jan. 5, 1870, m. John E. Sherlock; Jane b. Oct. 9, 1872, d. aged six; Mary E. b. June 24, 1875, m. John W. Gray; Margaret b. Aug. 21, 1878, d. infant; William D. b. Sept. 25, 1879, m. Lizzieetor Taylor; John A. b. Dec. 29, 1881, m. Jennie Kinder; Agnes M. b. Dec. 29, 1884; James B. May 17, 1887, d. infant; Albert A. b. Oct. 29, 1892. Family home Salt Lake City.
High priest; missionary to Scotland 1896-98; ward trustee; block teacher 40 years. Street car conductor; laborer; watchman.

CAMPBELL, JOHN Born Sept. 12, 1812, Nova Scotia, Canada. Came to Utah 1852.
Married Pernina Rose.
Settled at Cottonwood in 1852. Died Oct. 6, 1893.

CAMPBELL, JOSEPH H. (son of Benona Campbell, born Feb. 10, 1800, in Pennsylvania, and Mary Lenard, born Sept. 12, 1807, in New York state, married 1821). He was born Aug. 15, 1837, Kirtland, Ohio. Came to Utah 1850, Stephen Markham company.
Married Elizabeth Mathews Jan. 1, 1861 (daughter of Hopkin Mathews and Margaret Morris, pioneers Oct. 2, 1856, Edward Bunker Handcart company—married May 11, 1844, Merthyr Tydfil, Wales). She was born March 1, 1845, Combach, Wales. Their children: Joseph b. Oct. 26, 1861, m. Ella F. Hammond Sept. 29, 1887; Hyrum Alma b. April 30, 1863, m. Caroline Garr Sept. 8, 1886; Honkin B. b. Feb. 2, 1866, m. Jemima Low Dec. 27, 1890; David M. b. Feb. 27,

PIONEERS AND PROMINENT MEN OF UTAH 793

1869, m. Margaret Fife April 8, 1891, m. Libbie Rossiter May 9, 1894; Margaret E. b. April 19, 1872, m. C. M. Hammond Dec. 21, 1892; Mary Ann b. March 20, 1875, m. Henry H. Bullock June 28, 1893; Ezra T. b. Nov. 12, 1879, m. Lucy Pickett April 8, 1902; Nina Amanda b. Feb. 6, 1883, m. William Baer July 17, 1900; Kenneth R. b. Jan. 8, 1886, m. Aneona Smith Jan. 23, 1906. Family home Providence, Utah.
Pioneer to Cache Valley 1859. Assisted in bringing immigrants to Utah 1863. Took part in Echo canyon campaign. Ran a sawmill twenty-seven years at Providence; one of organizers of Providence co-operative store and a director of same 20 years. Farmer and miller.

CAMPBELL, JOSEPH (son of Joseph H. Campbell and Elizabeth Mathews). Born Oct. 26, 1861, Providence, Utah.
Married Ella Freelove Hammond Sept. 29, 1887 (daughter of Milton D. Hammond and Freelove Miller, married Jan. 29, 1861, Salt Lake City, the latter a pioneer 1858). She was born April 16, 1865. Their children: Ella Irene b. July 6, 1888, m. Godfrey Fuhriman March 24, 1909; Vesta Freelove b. March 26, 1891, m. Leon Alder March 6, 1912; Elizabeth b. Nov. 5, 1894; Genevieve b. July 7, 1896; Joseph M. b. Aug. 8, 1598; Alta and Alva b. June 18, 1901 (twins); Glen H. b. June 14, 1905. Family home Providence, Utah.
Missionary to England 1891-93, also to Northern States 1907-09; bishop 2nd ward Providence 1909; chairman church building committee for 2nd ward meeting house. Trustee Providence town two terms. School teacher in Cache county 1886-1907. Treasurer of Cache county school district 1911-1913.

CAMPBELL, SAMUEL (son of John and Deborah Campbell of Ohio). Came to Utah 1849, with members of Mormon Battalion.
Married Clarissa Rebecca Hall at Salt Lake City (daughter of William and Clarissa Hall of Missouri). Their children: Mary, d. infant; Lizzie, d. child; Joseph, m. Leona Reynolds, m. Matilda Frances Reynolds, m. Clarissy Reynolds; Benjamin, m. Annie Darling; Polly, m. Messrs. Whitney, Garr, Rhoades and Chatman; James Heber, m. Sarah Henry; Rozella, d. aged 14 years. Family home Vernal, Utah.
Seventy; high priest. Mexican war veteran; fought against Shoshone Indians. County commissioner. Farmer; carpenter. Died in 1908.

CAMPBELL, JAMES HEBER (son of Samuel Campbell and Clarissa Rebecca Hall). Born April 14, 1853, at Salt Lake City.
Married Sarah Henry in 1881, at Vernal (daughter of Calvin and Agnes Henry of Park City, Utah; pioneers oxteam company). Their children: Agnes Rozella b. Dec. 4, 1881, m. Harley Elmer Pope; May, d. aged 3 years; Clarissy, m. Alonzo Holmes, m. Jack Dunn; Marion, m. Frances Ellison; Raymond; Calvin Leroy; Hazel, d. infant; Fay.
Member of the church. Farmer and freighter. Died at Roosevelt, Utah.

CAMPBELL, CALVIN LEROY (son of James Heber Campbell and Sarah Henry). Born Jan. 20, 1894 at Vernal, Utah.

CAMPBELL, THOMAS (parents resided in Scotland). Born in Perthshire, Scotland. Came to Utah 1855.
Married Elizabeth Davis, who was born Sept. 17, 1826, and came to Utah with her husband. Their children: Alexander, m. Ann McNaughton; Janet, d. infant; Joseph, m. Margaret McNaughton; John b. Sept. 9, 1853, m. Marion Jane Todd March 19, 1890; Thomas, d. infant; Agnes, m. Richard Jones; William, m. Kate Johnson; Mary, m. James W. Clyde; James, m. Maud Whitt; Elizabeth, m. C. J. Wahlquist. Family home Heber City, Utah.
Coal miner; worked in first coal mine the Union Pacific opened at Bear River City, Utah; farmer in Wasatch county. Died April 25, 1894.

CAMPBELL, JOHN (son of Thomas Campbell and Elizabeth Davis). Born Sept. 9, 1853, Ayrshire, Scotland. Came to Utah 1855.
Married Marion Jane Todd March 19, 1890, at Heber City (daughter of Thomas Todd and Margaret Shankland of Dumfrieshire, Scotland, pioneers Oct. 1, 1854). She was born March 19, 1861. Their children: Mazie b. March 12, 1891; Jennie b. Dec. 31, 1893; Hugh J. b. Aug. 3, 1898. Family home Heber City.
Stood guard when nine years old in Sevier county during Black Hawk war. Farmer and stockraiser. Died Nov. 30, 1898, at Heber City.

CANFIELD, CYRUS CULVER. Born Dec. 20, 1817, near Columbus, Ohio. Came to Utah 1849 with members of Mormon Battalion.
Married Clarissa L. Jones, who came to Utah Sept. 24, 1848, Heber C. Kimball company. Their children: Eliza L., m. Thomas Stokes; Melissa, m. John W. Bolace; Maria T., m. Hyrum Goff; Hyrum, died.
Elder. Third lieutenant in Company D, Mormon Battalion. Went to California about 1851, where he died.

CANNON, ANGUS M. (son of George Cannon and Ann Quayle). Born May 17, 1834, Liverpool, Eng. Came to Utah October, 1849, Reddick N. Allred company.
Married Sarah Maria Mousley July 18, 1858, Salt Lake City (daughter of Titus Mousley and Ann McMenemy of Centerville near Wilmington, Del., pioneers 1857, Jacob Hollphine company). Their children: George M., m. Marian A. Morris; John M., m. Zina Bennion; Ann M.; Leonora M., m. Barnard J. Stewart; Henry M., d. infant. Family home, Salt Lake City.
Married Ann Amanda Mousley July 18, 1858, Salt Lake City (daughter of Titus Mousley and Ann McMenemy). Their children: Wilhelmina M., m. Abraham H. Cannon; Angus M., m. Katherine Lynch; David Henry, d. infant; Lewis M., m. Mary Alice Hoagland Cannon; Charles M., m. Ida M. Daynes; Eugene M., m. Edna C. Lambert; Mary M., m. J. Frank Chamberlin; Clarence M., m. Harriet Burns; Jesse F., m. Margaret McKeever; Quayle, m. Eugena Silver. Family home, Salt Lake City.
Married Clarissa Cordelia Moses June 16, 1875, Salt Lake City (daughter of Ambrose T. Moses and Lydia Ensign of Westfield, Mass.). She was born April 21, 1839. Their children: Samuel Ensign b. March 24, 1876, d. Jan. 10, 1880; Erastus Snow b. May 23, 1878, d. Dec. 8, 1878; Alice, m. Joseph Leroy Cheney Nov. 14, 1906.
Married Martha Hughes Oct. 5, 1884, Salt Lake City (daughter of Peter Hughes and Elizabeth Evans, pioneers Oct. 1, 1862, Joseph Horne company). She was born July 1, 1857. Their children: Elizabeth Rachel b. Sept. 13, 1885, m. Roy Hillman Porter; James Hughes b. May 10, 1891, m. Lavinna Hale April 5, 1911; Gwendolyn Hughes b. April 17, 1899.
Married Maria Bennion March 11, 1886, Salt Lake City (daughter of Johnson Bennion and Esther Wainwright of Nauvoo, Ill., pioneers 1847, John Taylor company). She was born Aug. 5, 1857. Their children: Hattie Bennion b. March 5, 1887; Ira Bennion b. Feb. 11, 1889; Eleanor b. Jan. 11, 1893, d. Dec. 29, 1901; Glenn b. July 6, 1897.
Missionary to eastern states 1854-58. Called to Parowan to assist in settling that country in 1850. Manager Deseret News 1868-74. Engaged in wagon and implement business in Salt Lake City. President Salt Lake stake 1876-1904. County recorder 1876-84. Patriarch. Has extensive mining interests.

CANNON, CHARLES MOUSLEY (son of Angus M. Cannon and Ann Amanda Mousley). Born Jan. 2, 1869, Salt Lake City.
Married Ida Maud Daynes Nov. 12, 1891, Logan, Utah (daughter of John Daynes and Rebecca Bushby of Salt Lake City, the former a pioneer 1862, the latter 1869). She was born March 6, 1871. Only child: Dorothy.

CANNON, QUAYLE (son of Angus M. Cannon and Ann Amanda Mousley). Born Dec. 30, 1879, Salt Lake City.
Married Eugena Silver Sept. 20, 1905, Salt Lake City (daughter of John Silver and Orthena Pratt of Salt Lake City). She was born April 15, 1884. Their children: Quayle b. July 5, 1906; Geneve b. Sept. 27, 1907; Orson Silver b. Nov. 21, 1910; Angus Welden b. July 6, 1910; Amanda Sylvia b. Sept. 1, 1912. Family home Bountiful, Utah.
Missionary to Germany and Switzerland 1902-05; bishop's counselor 1908-12. Member of firm of Cannon & Cannon.

CANNON, GEORGE Q. (son of George Cannon and Ann Quayle of Liverpool, Eng., and Isle of Man). Born Jan. 11, 1827, Liverpool, Eng. Came to Utah Oct. 3, 1847, John Taylor company.
Married Elizabeth Hoagland Dec. 10, 1854, Salt Lake City (daughter of Abraham Hoagland and Margaret Quick of New Jersey, Michigan, and Nauvoo, Ill., pioneers Oct. 3, 1847, John Taylor company). She was born Nov. 3, 1836. Among their children were: George H., d. infant; John Q., m. Annie Wells, m. Louie Wells; Abraham H. (deceased), m. Sarah A. Jenkins, m. Wilhelmina M. Cannon, m. Mary Croxall, m. Lillian Hamblin; Georgiana, George A., and Elizabeth—latter three died infants; Mary Alice (deceased), m. Lewis M. Cannon (cousin); Lillian Ann, d. infant; David H., died; Emily, m. Israel E. Willey; Sylvester Q., m. Winnifred Saville.
Married Sarah Jane Jenne April 11, 1857, Salt Lake City (daughter of Benjamin Jenne and Sarah Snider of Canada, pioneers 1848). She was born Sept. 1, 1833. Their children: Frank J., m. Martha Brown (died), m. Rose Brown; Angus J., m. Miriam Hawkins; Hugh J., m. May Wilcken; Rosannah, m. Alonzo R. Irvine; Joseph J., m. Florence Groesbeck; Preston J., m. Mabel Harker; Karl Q., m. Mary Silver.
Married Eliza L. Tenney 1864, Salt Lake City (daughter of William Tenney and Eliza Webb of Chicaque, N. Y., pioneers July, 1860). She was born Feb. 9, 1847. Their children: William T., m. Ada E. Croxall; Read T. (deceased), m. Ada White; Edwin Q., m. Luella Waring.
Married Martha Telle at Salt Lake City. Their children: Hester T., m. Daniel B. Richards; Amelia Telle b. Feb. 16, 1870, m. William H. Chamberlin, Jr.; Lewis Telle b. April 22, 1872, m. Martha Howell; Brigham Telle b. Aug. 3, 1874, m. Cecelia Farrell; Willard T., m. Caroline Croxall; Grace, m. Clarence Neslen; Radcliffe Q., m. Maud Riter; Espey T., m. Alice Farwarth; Collins T., unmarried.
Married Emily Hoagland (Little). No children.
Married (Mrs.) Caroline Young Croxall, who was born Feb. 1, 1851. Their children: Clawson Y.; Ann Y.; Georgius Y. Families resided Salt Lake City, Utah.
Missionary to Hawaii and England 1849-64; apostle and

member first presidency of L. D. S. church 20 years. Territorial delegate from Utah to U. S. Congress. Printer and editor of Deseret News. Died April 11, 1901, Ocean Park, Cal.
[See "History of George Q. Cannon" for additional and fuller data regarding this remarkable figure in Utah history.]

CANNON, DAVID H. (son of George Q. Cannon and Elizabeth Hoagland). Born April 14, 1872, Salt Lake City. Seventy; missionary to Soran, Silesia, Germany, 1891-92. Died there Oct. 7, 1892.

CANNON, HUGH J. (son of George Q. Cannon and Sarah Jenne). Born Jan. 19, 1870, at Salt Lake City.
Married May Wilcken Oct. 1, 1890 at Logan, Utah (daughter of Charles H. Wilcken and Eliza Reiche of Germany, former came to Utah 1857, with Johnston army, latter 1858). She was born Jan. 8, 1871. Their children: Hugh Harley b. Oct. 18, 1891, m. Florence Darch; May Maurine b. Jan. 29, 1897; Ruth M. b. Nov. 24, 1899; Charles W. b. Feb. 15, 1902; Constance Q. b. Dec. 30, 1905; Rosannah J. b. July 12, 1907. Family home, Salt Lake City.
President Swiss and German branch 1891-92 and 1901-05; member 110th and 138th quorums seventies; president Liberty stake. Executor and secretary of George Q. Cannon estate.

CANNON, JOSEPH JENNE (son of George Q. Cannon and Sarah Jenne). Born May 22, 1877, at Salt Lake City.
Married Florence Groesbeck Sept. 23, 1904, at Salt Lake City (daughter of John Groesbeck and Ann D. Bringhurst of Salt Lake City). She was born Aug. 7, 1880. Their children: Wayne Dilworth b. March 1, 1906; Jane b. Nov. 20, 1908; Grant Groesbeck b. May 6, 1911. Family home, Salt Lake City.
Missionary to England and Sweden 1899-1904; high priest. Member of legislature. Secretary of National Savings & Trust Co.

CANNON, WILLIAM T. (son of George Q. Cannon and Eliza Tenney). Born Sept. 5, 1870, Salt Lake City.
Married Ada E. Croxall April 27, 1892, Manti, Utah (daughter of Mark Croxall and Caroline Young of Salt Lake City, pioneers 1860). She was born Aug. 13, 1870, Salt Lake City. Their children: Helen b. May 14, 1894; Alma b. May 29, 1896; William b. July 23, 1898; Richard b. Nov. 5, 1902; Emily A. b. Aug. 9, 1904; George Q. b. May 23, 1908; Warren C. b. March 9, 1911. Family home, Salt Lake City.
Missionary to the Netherlands 1899-1901; member 8th quorum seventies. Physician and surgeon.

CANNON, LEWIS TELLE (son of George Q. Cannon and Martha Telle). Born April 22, 1872, at Salt Lake City.
Married Martha Howell June 12, 1901 (daughter of Joseph Howell and Mary Maughan), who was born Oct. 7, 1879. Their children: Martha Howell; Mary Aileen; Howell Quayle. Family home, Salt Lake City. Architect.

CANNON, BRIGHAM T. (son of George Q. Cannon and Martha Telle). Born Aug. 3, 1874, Salt Lake City.
Married Cecelia Farrell Oct. 11, 1905, Omaha, Neb. (daughter of Dan Farrell and Annie Howard of Omaha, Neb.). She was born March 9, 1885. Only child: Howard Raymond b. Feb. 5, 1908. Family home. Salt Lake City.
Missionary to Germany 1895-98; member 110th quorum seventies. Real estate dealer; colonizer.

CANNON, DAVID HENRY (son of George Cannon and Ann Quayle). Born April 23, 1838, Liverpool, Eng. Came to Utah October, 1849, Allen Taylor company.
Married Wilhelmina L. Mousley Jan. 15, 1859, Salt Lake City (daughter of Titus Mousley and Ann McMenemy, pioneers 1857, and sister of Sarah Maria, who married Angus M. Cannon). She was born Oct. 11, 1840, Centerville, Newcastle county, Del. Their children: David Henry, Jr., b. Oct. 15, 1860, m. Camilla E. Mason; Ann Mousley b. Aug. 8, 1864; George Quayle b. July 7, 1866; Elizabeth b. Jan. 12, 1869; Amanda Mousley b. June 10, 1870; Angus Munn b. May 12, 1873, m. Rachel Cunningham; Wilhelmina Mousley b. Nov. 29, 1875, m. Charles Sullivan; Lewis Ray b. May 28, 1878, m. Jenny Laub; Josephine b. Aug. 22, 1881, m. Shadrach H. Jones; Frank b. Sept. 17, 1873, m. Mary Bryner.
Married Josephine L. Crossgrove Oct. 19, 1867, Salt Lake City (daughter of Charles Crossgrove and Theressa Raymond), who was born Sept. 7, 1848, Centerville, Newcastle county, Del. Their children: Charles b. Dec. 25, 1869; John b. June 10, 1871; Mary A. b. April 7, 1873; Ethe b. May 14, 1875; Leonora b. Aug. 31, 1876; Erastus Snow b. Dec. 12, 1878; Bayard b. Feb. 4, 1881; Eugene b. March 17, 1883, m. Renna Laub; Theressa b. Oct. 20, 1885; Claud b. Dec. 22, 1887, m. Parthenia Hunt; Raymond b. Aug. 30, 1890.
Married Rhoda Ann Knell June 20, 1877, St. George, Utah (daughter of Robert Knell and Mary Crook, pioneers 1850 and 1849, respectively). She was born May 7, 1858, Salt Lake City. Their children: Evaline b. April 10, 1878, m. Joseph W. Webb; Robert Knell b. Nov. 9, 1879; Wilford Woodruff b. Nov. 20, 1880, m. Marie Anderson; Clarence b. March 20, 1883; Rhoda b. Sept. 10, 1885, m. Hyrum A. Bryner; Walter b. July 5, 1888, m. Leah Sullivan; Clara b. May 30, 1891, m. Milton Burgess; Vernon b. May 1, 1894; Douglas b. Aug. 15, 1897; Earl b. April 24, 1900; Harold b. March 14, 1903. Families resided St. George, Utah.

Missionary to California 1856. Assisted moving Deseret News plant to Fillmore, Utah, 1858. Member 30th quorum seventies 1858, and same year set apart one of council 23d quorum; missionary to England March 1861. A special messenger to Canada on account of blockade troubles between northern and southern states. Brought many immigrants to Utah; high councillor and high priest; second counselor to Erastus Snow, president Dixie mission; bishop 4th ward St. George; president St. George temple and counselor in stake presidency several years; member stake board of education. Printer; worked in office of Western Standard at San Francisco, Cal., 1856; later in Utah in office of Mountaineer.

CANTWELL, JAMES SHERLOCK (son of Simon Cantwell, born 1788, Castlecomer, Kilkenny, Ireland, and Wilhelmina Sherlock, born 1792, Carlow, Ireland). He was born Nov. 24, 1813, in Dublin. Came to Utah Dec. 14, 1856, Martin Tyler company.
Married Elizabeth Cotteral Hamer April 27, 1838, (daughter of William Hamer), who was born March 20, 1819. Their children: Robert Simon b. Dec. 22, 1838, and John b. Feb. 25, 1840, died; Francis Robert b. April 7, 1841, m. Dorcas E. Wall; James b. Feb. 28, 1843, m. Julia A. Collett Jan. 15, 1872; Alma b. April 26, 1845; William H. b. April 21, 1846, m. Lorena A. Downs 1871; Ellen b. Sept. 24, 1848, m. Joseph N. McCann; Wilhelmina b. Dec. 28, 1850, d. June 1, 1851; Stephen b. June 25, 1852, d. July 17, 1852; Mary Ann b. Sept. 9, 1853, m. Thomas Mather November, 1871; Elizabeth C. b. Dec. 16, 1855, m. Henry Burger; Lucius S. b. April 2, 1858, m. Percinda Tibbets.

CANTWELL, JAMES (son of James Sherlock Cantwell and Elizabeth Cotteral Hamer). Born Feb. 28, 1843, Liverpool, Eng.
Married Julia A. Collett Jan. 15, 1872, Salt Lake City (daughter of Daniel Collett and Esther Jones), who was born at Mill Creek, Salt Lake county, Utah. Their children: Daniel James b. Oct. 12, 1872, m. Mary C. Chambers March 15, 1894; William Hamer b. March 17, 1874, m. Eliza J. Mourirtsen Dec. 4, 1895; Elthura b. Jan. 1, 1876, d. March 13, 1897; Francis Rueben b. Dec. 6, 1878, d. Sept. 19, 1891; Stephen b. June 21, 1882, m. Mabel Pilkington; Julia b. Feb. 3, 1885, m. Wallace Raymond July 23, 1902; Leanora b. Aug. 24, 1886, m. James W. Kirkbride October, 1904; Esther b. Aug. 20, 1888, m. Daniel Littledyke Oct. 2, 1907; Milo b. July 15, 1890, m. Ella Reese June 1, 1910. Family home Smithfield, Utah.
Missionary in England 1843; clerk of the Liverpool conference; president branch at St. Louis 1852; high priest; appointed member high council 1854. Leaving St. Louis June 27, 1856, arrived at Florence, Neb., July 7 of the same year. Left Florence Aug. 17, 1856, with Capt. James G. Willie and arrived at Laramie Oct. 1, laid over until 17th from illness, when he joined the Hodgett wagon and Martin handcart company, arriving at Salt Lake City Dec. 14, 1856. Settled at Big Cottonwood; joined in the move south, 1858, and returned to Cottonwood in the fall. Moved to Smithfield May, 1862, and followed school teaching. Was president of high priest's quorum 20 years. School trustee and postmaster 1869 to 1887. Died Sept. 4, 1887, Smithfield, Utah.

CAPENER, WILLIAM (son of Daniel Capener, born March 12, 1780, and Elizabeth Capener). He was born July 30, 1806, at London, Eng. Came to Utah Oct. 2, 1852, Isaac Bullock company.
Married Sarah Verander Oct. 26, 1828, at Hanover Square, London, (daughter of William Verander), who was born Sept. 2, 1804, and came to Utah with husband. Their children: George b. July 23, 1829, m. Harriet Dunn; William b. Dec. 26, 1831, m. Harriet Hill; Louise Rebecca, m. Joseph Edward Taylor; Elizabeth Ann, m. Augustas P. Hardy; Jane Maria, m. William Hanks March 27, 1856, m. Joseph E. Taylor July 9, 1876, m. Thomas H. Giles Nov. 12, 1890; Charles Henry, d. child. Family resided Cleveland, Ohio and Salt Lake City, Utah.
Married Ellen Rigby March 23, 1861, Salt Lake City (daughter of Aaron Rigby and Elizabeth Ellison, pioneers Sept. 3, 1860, James D. Ross company). She was born Aug. 15, 1839, Lancaster Lane, Eng. Their children: Ellen Matilda Rigby b. Feb. 6, 1862, d. infant; Samuel Rigby b. Feb. 18, 1863, m. Fanny Celestia Garn; Mary Lucinda b. Aug. 11, 1864, m. Wilford H. Park; Margaret Alice b. May 27, 1866, d. infant; John b. Oct. 8, 1867, m. Angeline Cleveland; Arthur Rigby b. Jan. 20, 1869, m. Mary Larelda Garn; Sarah Ada b. Nov. 4, 1870, m. Wilford Woodruff Hill; Alfred Albert b. March 31, 1872, m. Myrtle Cleveland; Joseph Aaron b. Dec. 25, 1874, m. Ella Smith; Edward Theodore b. April 26, 1876, m. Fannie Turner; Daniel b. Nov. 13, 1878, d. child. Family resided Salt Lake City and Centerville.
Settled at Salt Lake City 1852; moved to Centerville 1874; carpenter and cabinetmaker. Died January, 1894, in Centerville.

CAPENER, ARTHUR RIGBY (son of William Capener and Ellen Rigby). Born Jan. 20, 1869, at Salt Lake City.
Married Mary Larelda Garn July 12, 1893 (daughter of Micah Garn and Fanny Wood, pioneers Sept. 27, 1855). She was born July 12, 1874, Centerville, Utah. Their children: Echo b. April 19, 1894; Arthur Dean b. May 24, 1896; Verna b. Nov. 21, 1898; Lavon b. Feb. 28, 1900; Ruth b. Jan. 29, 1903; Larelda b. March 14, 1906; Edna b. Sept. 1, 1908; Max Garn b. Aug. 29, 1911. Family home Salt Lake City, Centerville and Garland, Utah.

Located in Garland 1891. Sunday school superintendent at Garland 11 years; missionary to northern states 1905-07; bishop of Garland ward 1908-12. Road supervisor; treasurer Garland town board; director in first mutual fire insurance company in Utah. Farmer and stockraiser.

CARDON, ALFRED. For genealogy see page 821.

CARDON, PHILLIP. Born Oct. 7, 1801, Prarustin, Italy. Came to Utah Oct. 29, 1854, Robert Campbell company.
Married Marie Tourn 1823, Prarustin, Italy (daughter of Bartholemi Tourn of Roca, Italy). Their children: John, m. Anna Fourer; Louis Phillip, m. Sarah Hunt; Katherine, m. Moses Byrne; Mary M., m. Charles Guild; Paul, m. Susannah Goudin, m. Magdalene Beus; Thomas B., m. Lucy S. Smith. Family resided at Ogden and Logan, Utah.
Elder; high priest. Farmer. Died Aug. 1890, Hyrum, Utah.

CARDON, PAUL (son of Phillip Cardon and Marie Tourn). Born Dec. 28, 1839, Prarustin, Italy. Came to Utah Oct. 29, 1854, Robert Campbell company.
Married Susannah Goudin March 16, 1857, at Salt Lake City (daughter of Bartholomew Goudin and Martha Cardon of Prarustin, Italy). She was born July 30, 1833. Their children: Phillip, died; Mary C., m. M. W. Merrill Jr.; Susette C., m. Joel Ricks; Louisa, died; Sarah C., m. Fred Turner; John P., m. Euphemia King; Louis S., m. Rebecca Ballard; Lucy C., m. William Merrill; Joseph E., m. Sophia Wilson; Moses G., m. Myrtle Wood; Ezra B., died. Family home Logan, Utah.
Married Magdalene Beus Dec. 19, 1869, at Salt Lake City (daughter of Michael Beus and Marian Combe of Ogden, Utah, pioneers 1856, Edmund Ellsworth handcart company). She was born July 17, 1853. Their children: Marian M. and James, died; Hyrum M., m. Isabelle Roundy; George David, m. Elizabeth H. Ballantyne; Amanda, m. Silas Ricks; Ernest W., m. Annie Marshall; Violet P., m. E. L. Walker; Katie L. Family home Logan.
President 64th quorum seventies; missionary to Switzerland 1898-1900. First city treasurer and first policeman at Logan. Farmer.

CARDON, JOSEPH EMANUEL (son of Paul Cardon and Susannah Goudin). Born Oct. 28, 1872, Logan, Utah.
Married Sophia Wilson Sept. 16, 1894, Logan, Utah (daughter of Joseph Wilson and Mary Ann McCornick, both of Leeds, England. Came to Utah 1868, Simpson Molen company). She was born Oct. 5, 1870. Their children: Joseph LeGrand b. Apr. 28, 1900; Rula b. Sept. 14, 1901; Sybil b. March, 1903; Joseph E. b. Dec. 25, 1904; Bartell Wilson b. Oct. 28, 1906; Karma b. Nov. 1, 1908. Family home Logan, Utah.
High priest; president seventies; missionary to Northern States 1896-99; bishop; stake president; patriarch. Merchant and manufacturer. Representative Tenth Utah state legislature.

CARDON, GEORGE DAVID (son of Paul Cardon and Magdalene Beus). Born Dec. 1, 1877, Logan, Utah.
Married Elizabeth H. Ballantyne Nov. 10, 1902, Logan, Utah (daughter of Richard A. Ballantyne and Mary A. Stewart of Logan, Utah, pioneers 1847). She was born Oct. 28, 1879. Their children: Carvel Ballantyne b. July 19, 1903; George D. b. Aug. 30, 1905; Ardelle b. Feb. 13, 1908; Carlos Ballantyne b. Aug. 23, 1910; Winona b. March 29, 1913. Family home Logan, Utah.
President 4th quorum elders of Cache stake; senior class leader Y. M. M. I. A.; Sunday school teacher. Assistant manager and treasurer of Cardon company. Real estate and loans.

CARLILE, ROBERT (parents lived at Mission, Eng.). Came to Utah 1852, Capt. Jolley company.
Married Christiana Spouncer (parents lived at Mission, Eng.). She came to Utah with her husband. Their children: Mary b. Jan. 11, 1818, m. Joseph Cooper; Isaac b. Aug., 1820, m. Jane ——; John b. Sept. 16, 1822, died; John II. b. May 25, 1825, m. Elizabeth Williamson; James b. Jan. 31, 1829, m. Emily Ann Giles, m. Fannie Lee, m. Eliza Hallet Dowell Lowden, m. Annie Rachel Nageli Mosier; Robert b. Jan. 23, 1833; George b. April 11, 1836, m. Ann Giles, m. Susana Daybell Pollard. Family home Heber City, Utah. Farmer.

CARLILE, JAMES (son of Robert Carlile and Christiana Spouncer). Born Jan. 31, 1829, at Mission, Eng. Came to Utah, 1852, Capt. Jolley company.
Married Emily Ann Giles Oct. 31, 1857 (daughter of William Giles and Sarah Huskinson, both of Sturley, Nottinghamshire, Eng.). She was born June 6, 1837, died March 8, 1891. Their children: Sarah Ann b. Sept. 15, 1859, m. George Daybell; Evalina C. b. Oct. 16, 1862, m. Charles Henry Hurdsman; James William b. Oct. 14, 1855, m. Sarah Elizabeth Buys; Emily Jane b. Oct. 12, 1868, m. George Hyrum Barzee; Charles Robert b. July 21, 1872, m. Amelia Snow; Mary Elizabeth b. Jan. 1, 1877, died.
High priest. Located at Spanish Fork and then went to Heber City 1859. Indian war veteran.

CARLILE, JAMES WILLIAM (son of James Carlile and Emily Ann Giles). Born Oct. 14, 1865, at Heber, Utah.
Married Sarah Elizabeth Buys Nov. 25, 1891, at Logan, Utah (daughter of Edward Buys and Celestia Clarissa Bromley of Heber City, Utah). She was born June 9, 1871, Charleston, Utah. Their children: Lecil Emily b. Jan. 17, 1893, m. William Charles Murri; Sarah Viva b. Jan. 18, 1895; Clara b. March 13, 1897; James Edward b. Oct. 8, 1899; William Walter b. April 1, 1902; Orel May b. May 8, 1905; Glad Jane b. Aug. 29, 1909. Family home Heber Ctiy, Utahys
Member of the elders quorum; block teacher. Interested in Wasatch Irrigation Co., Sage Brush Irrigation Co., Timpanogos Irrigation Co., and Wasatch Extension Irrigation Co. Farmer and developer of Wasatch county's resources.

CARLILE, GEORGE (son of Robert Carlile and Christiana Spouncer). Born April 11, 1836. Came to Utah in 1851.
Married Laura Ann Giles Oct. 25, 1856, Provo, Utah (daughter of Thomas Giles and Elizabeth Susanna Moore, pioneers 1851). She was born April 19, 1837. Their children: Maria Ann, m. William Giles Rasband; Levina Elizabeth, m. F. O. Buel; Sarah Jane, m. Caleb Moore; George K., m. Marion Neal; Thomas Frank, m. Emma Christensen; Alfred Lorenzo, m. Jane Neal; William M., d. aged four. Family home Heber City, Utah.
Member of 20th quorum seventies; assisted to bring immigrants to Utah. Member Heber City council. Veteran of the Black Hawk, Tintic and Walker Indian wars; pensioned soldier. Died Jan. 29, 1909.

CARLING, JOHN (son of Abraham Carling, of Kingston, Ulster county, N. Y., and Sarah Green b. Jan. 10, 1779, Luzwardines, Herefordshire, Eng.). He was born Sept. 11, 1800, Kingston, Ulster county, N. Y. Came to Utah September, 1852, Henry Miller company.
Married Emeline Keaton Sept. 1, 1830 (daughter of Jacob and Catherine Keaton), who was born Nov. 1, 1806 and came to Utah with her husband. Their children: Isaac Van Wagoner b. Nov. 30, 1831, m. Asenath E. Browning 1854; Sarah Frances Wildey b. Sept. 6, 1833, d. Dec. 4, 1835; Catherine Keaton b. June 1, 1835, m. Lewis Brunson; Abraham Frier b. Aug. 19, 1837, m. Ann E. Ashman Sept. 28, 1862; John Warner b. Nov. 14, 1843, d. Sept. 5, 1844. Family home Fillmore, Utah.
Married Ann Dutson Feb. 10, 1844, Nauvoo, Ill., who was born Oct. 12, 1799, Herefordshire, England. Their children: Francis Caleb b. Aug. 9, 1845, m. Fannie Knixon; Joseph Mathew b. June 25, 1847, d. Jan. 5, 1866.
Bishop's counselor. Sheriff at Fillmore. Made wagons for use in crossing plains; assisted in wood carving of Nauvoo Temple. Moved to Fillmore 1875. Mason; tinner; cabinet maker; cooper and shoemaker.

CARLING, ISAAC VANWAGONER (son of John Carling and Emeline Keaton). Born Nov. 30, 1831, Klinesonup, Ulster county, N. Y.
Married Asenath E. Browning, 1854, Salt Lake City (daughter of Jonathan Browning and Elizabeth Stalcup, pioneers Sept. 1852, Henry Miller company). She was born Nov. 17, 1835, Adams county, Ill. Their children: Sarah Elizabeth b. Feb. 25, 1856, m. Edward M. Webb; Asenath Emeline b. Oct. 5, 1857, m. Howard O. Spencer; Ann b. April 7, 1859, m. Thomas Chamberlain Feb. 1876; Laura Malvina b. Dec. 30, 1860, m. Francis L. Porter Sept. 13, 1877; Olive Chrilla b. Nov. 14, 1862, d. Oct. 12, 1874; Catherine Areila b. March 11, 1865, m. Edson D. Porter; Martha Jane b. Jan. 26, 1867, m. Francis A. Webb; Phoebe Malinda b. Sept. 16, 1869, m. Edson D. Porter; Isaac VanWagoner b. Sept. 21, 1871, m. Elizabeth Johnson; Mary Alice b. Nov. 6, 1873, d. April 17, 1880; Walter Eliza b. Mar. 4, 1875, m. Edward K. Pugh; Barbara Amelia b. Aug. 17, 1878, m. James D. Duffin. Family reside Fillmore and Orderville, Utah.
Married Miriam E. Hobson (daughter of Jesse and Elizabeth Hobson), who was born Aug. 31, 1843, Camp Creek, near Nauvoo, Ill. Their children: John Henry b. Sept. 13, 1860, m. Elizabeth Lovell; Ellen Alvira b. Dec. 14, 1863, m. Thomas Chamberlain March 13, 1879; Lydia May b. March 1, 1866, m. John Corrugten 1883; Jesse Hobson b. June 3, 1869, m. Marie Jorgensen.

CARLISLE, RICHARD. Came to Utah with oxteam company.
Married. Their children: Joseph; Thomas; John; Richard; Alice, m. George Freestone; Mary. Family home in England.
Seventy. Farmer. Died at Alpine, Utah.

CARPENTER, JOHN STILLEY (son of John Steel Carpenter, born Aug. 6, 1822, and Margaret McCullough, born Oct. 15, 1822, both of Centerville, Newcastle county, Del.). He was born Feb. 11, 1849, at Centerville. Came to Utah 1857, Jacob Hoffines company.
Married Margaret E. Cutler Feb. 1, 1877 (daughter of Royal James Cutler, pioneer 1852, and Margaret Ross, pioneer 1853, Capt. Empey company, and who were married Dec. 8, 1857, Salt Lake City). She was born July 29, 1860. Their children: John Cutler b. Feb. 5, 1878, m. Annie M. Levanger Sept. 22, 1897; Rosanah b. Dec. 15, 1879, m. Hyrum Justet Aug. 18, 1900. Family home Glendale, Utah.
Married Ann Elizabeth Hopkins Jan. 10, 1890, Manti, Utah (daughter of Leprelet J. Hopkins, pioneer 1858, with Johnston's army, and Ann Spendlove, pioneer Oct. 4, 1864, Capt.

W. S. Warren company; they were married March 18, 1865, Virgin City, Utah). She was born Feb. 23, 1867, Toquerville, Utah. Their children: Ethel b. Oct. 27, 1890; Walter Stilley b. Oct. 29, 1894; Frank Gould b. Sept. 15, 1898; Ella b. Dec. 5, 1905.
Assisted to bring immigrants to Utah 1866; first and second counselor to Bishops James Leithead and M. D. Harris, Glendale ward, 1877-79; also to Bishop Royal J. Cutler 1879-94; presiding priest Glendale ward 1894-98; president Y. M. M. I. A. 1876; high councilor Sept. 2, 1900, to September 1908; missionary to southern states 1881-83. Director Glendale Irrigation Co. 25 years. Member district school board 22 years. Sunday school superintendent 1884-96; bishop Glendale ward 1908.

CARPENTER, WILLIAM H. (son of Hiram Carpenter and Elizabeth Schermerhorn). Born July 22, 1820, Glenville, Schenectady county, N. Y. Came to Utah July 29, 1847, James Brown company.
Married Cynthia Triphosa Wetherbee Nov. 28, 1849, Centerville, New York (daughter of William Wetherbee and Laura Doubleday of Gallands Grove, Pottawattamie county, Iowa, pioneers June. 1852). She was born Dec. 11, 1827, and died Nov. 30, 1854. Their children: Joseph Wetherbee b. March 17, 1852, m. Annie Burdett Randall Feb. 4, 1875; Cynthia, d. March 23, 1854. Family home Bloomington, Utah.
Married Marmora Sheffield Feb. 13, 1855, at Salt Lake City (daughter of Anson Sheffield and Maria Mott), who was born Aug. 8, 1838. Their children: William Sheffield b. May 13, 1856; Marmora C. Fawcett b. Aug. 22, 1866; Brigham Carpenter b. Feb. 8, 1876. Family home Bloomington, Utah.
Married Marie Aeschlimann. Their children: Alfred; Mary Agnes. d. aged 8 years. Family home Bloomington, Utah.
High priest. Broom maker and farmer. Died May 8, 1894, St. George, Utah.

CARPENTER, JOSEPH WETHERBEE (son of William H. Carpenter and Cynthia Triphosa Wetherbee). Born March 17, 1852, Gallands Grove, Iowa.
Married Annie Burdett Randall Feb. 4, 1875, at St. George, Utah (daughter of Joseph Henry Randall and Anne Burdett of St. George, pioneers 1853 and 1856, respectively). She was born Dec. 1, 1857. Their children: Annie May b. May 1, 1878, m. John A. Stringham; Leah Jemima b. Sept. 3, 1883, m. Joseph S. Hodges; Louisa b. Jan. 31, 1887, m. Edward Auguentine Guerrero; Ethel b. Jan. 30, 1891; Joseph Edgar b. May 26, 1894; Rudolph Adelbert b. June 29, 1898. Family home Central, Utah.
Member 29th quorum seventies; high priest. Justice of peace and postmaster, at Bloomington, Utah. Farmer and horticulturist; watch and clock repairer. Published "The Enterprise," then called "The Union," at St. George, Utah.

CARRUTH, WILLIAM (son of William Carruth and Mary Barr). Born March 11, 1825, in Renfrewshire, Scotland. Came to Utah Sept. 23, 1848, Brigham Young company.
Married Margaret Ellwood Feb. 12, 1848, in Renfrewshire (daughter of Gibson Ellwood and Margaret Duncan of Renfrewshire). She was born July 7, 1827. Their children: Margaret b. April 10, 1849, d. April 12, 1849; William b. April 29, 1850, m. Emma Wilde May 9, 1870; Mary Barr b. Aug. 2, 1852, m. Joseph A. Fisher; Ann Eliza b. Aug. 11, 1854, m. Samuel S. Cluff; John Gibson b. Feb. 1, 1857, m. Jane Black; Marion b. April 28, 1859, m. John L. Russell; Jane Agnes b. March 27, 1861, m. A. D. Chamberlain; George McKenzie b. June 29, 1863, m. Susan Elizabeth Daniels. Family home Coalville, Utah.
Counselor to Bishop Andrew Cahoon of South Cottonwood ward, 1858-61. Died Nov. 3, 1864.

CARRUTH, WILLIAM (son of William Carruth and Margaret Ellwood). He was born April 29, 1850, Murray, Utah. Married Emma Wilde May 9, 1870, Salt Lake City (daughter of Henry Brown Wilde and Sarah Hewlett of Southhampton, Eng., pioneers 1852). She was born Jan. 19, 1849. Their children: Margaret Emma b. May 21, 1871, m. Josiah Lewis Rhead; William Henry b. Aug. 27, 1872, m. Eliza Jane Barber; Joseph Theron b. Sept. 24, 1874, m. Sarah J. Hodson; Sarah Annie b. Sept. 26, 1876; Nellie Jane b. Oct. 6, 1878, m. Albert Becker; Mary Edith b. May 11, 1881, m. John J. Johnson; John Ellwood b. March 12, 1883, m. Eliza Jane Branch; Maud Marion b. Dec. 14, 1884; Ray Thomas b. Nov. 13, 1886; Effie Ellen b. Sept. 22, 1889; Frank Wilde b. April 26, 1893. Family home Coalville, Utah.
County commissioner, Summit county 1896-98. High councilor Summit stake, 1903-12.

CARSON, WILLIAM (son of George Carson and Anne Huff). Born Jan. 8, 1818, in Wayne county, Pa. Came to Utah 1851, Capt. Harrison company.
Married Crilla Egbert June 10, 1820. Their children: John A.; Mary Ann, m. J. R. Walker; George W., m. Agatha Morgan; Samuel, m. Marintha Burton 1868; William, m. Bennett Park 1880. Family home Fairfield, Utah.
Married Lula Goddard 1854, Salt Lake City. Their children: Stephen; Oscar; Isabell.
Married Ann McMind, who was born May 15, 1883. Their children: Washington; Julia, m. Thomas Walters; Mary, m. Mr. Daw 1886; M., m. James Park 1882; Lewis b. July 1867; Henry, m. Hattie McLane; Frank; Edith. Family home Fairfield, Utah. Died Dec. 25, 1901.

CARSON, GEORGE W. (son of William Carson and Crilla Egbert). He was born May 4, 1844, Hancock county, Ill.
Married Agatha Morgan Dec. 25, 1867, Fairfield, Utah (daughter of David Morgan and Hannah Turner of Fairfield, pioneers 1861, Ira Eldredge company). She was born March 30, 1850. Their children: Mary H. b. Oct. 5, 1867, m. Henry H. Hales; George W. b. Aug. 12, 1869, died; Charles H. b. Aug. 6, 1870, m. Ella Nixon; Crilla U. b. June 1, 1872, m. James Just; Agatha b. March 20, 1874, m. Abe Hodge; Maggie M. b. Nov. 29, 1876, d. 1880; George L. b. Sept. 29, 1878; Elsie M. b. Aug. 29, 1880, m. Myrlin Jones; Lenora b. May 29, 1882, died; Olive b. May 6, 1884, m. Arthur Dahlstrom; Edna b. Aug. 4, 1886, m. William Twitchell; Ernest b. June 19, 1888, d. 1903; Myrtle b. May 17, 1890; Jesse b. Jan. 11, 1892; James H. b. Jan. 14, 1894. Family home Fairfield, Utah.

CARTER, GEORGE (son of John Carter and Mary Pinner). Born April 2, 1841, Bridgenorth, Shropshire, Eng. Came to Utah 1868.
Married Fannie Brown (daughter of William Brown and Frances Sexton, latter pioneer 1868, McCarty company). She was born April 6, 1840. Their children: William H. b. March 7, 1866, m. Kate Willmore Sept. 1, 1886; Sarah Ada b. Oct. 9, 1869, m. William L. Taylor Feb. 4, 1886; Fannie b. May 9, 1872, m. Walter E. Moody Nov. 25, 1895; Thomas G. b. July 12, 1877, m. Luda E. Clayton March 27, 1901.
Assisted in bringing immigrants to Utah 1868. Settled at Nephi, Utah; later moved to Logan. Employe Utah Northern railroad until his death, July 24, 1905.

CARTER, WILLIAM H. (son of George Carter and Fannie Brown). Born March 7, 1866, Leamington, Eng.
Married Kate Willmore Sept. 1, 1886, Battle Creek, Idaho (daughter of Thomas Willmore and Louisa Baldwin), who was born Oct. 28, 1862, Birmingham, Eng. Their children: Clara May b. July 3, 1887, m. Jarvis Henderson Aug. 16, 1911; Frances Louisa b. Aug. 12, 1889, m. Isaac Elwell Oct. 16, 1911; Ernest W. b. Oct. 11, 1891; Jesse W. b. Oct. 16, 1893; George Washington b. Feb. 22, 1896; Kate Irene b. July 9, 1898; Emma Ada b. Oct. 21, 1900; Leah Maud b. Sept. 3, 1904. Family home Preston, Idaho.
Started to work for the old Utah Northern railroad at the age of fifteen, and is still engaged with Oregon Short line.

CARTER, JAMES PERRY (son of Josiah and Rebecca Carter). Born Feb. 23, 1827, Clutton, Somersetshire, Eng. Came to Utah September, 1861.
Married Harriet Wood Feb. 12, 1853, Tredegar, Wales (daughter of Thomas and Mary Wood), who was born June 6, 1830, Herefordshire, Eng. and died April 11, 1895. Their children: Josiah James b. July 20, 1854, d. May 6, 1859; Elizabeth Ann b. March 15, 1857, d. May 4, 1859; Catherine Esther b. May 12, 1859, m. Mosiah Evans Dec. 14, 1882; Mary Ann Rosalee b. Sept. 1, 1861, m. Charles Woodhouse; Harriet Jane b. Feb. 23, 1864, d. July 21, 1865; James b. Jan. 10, 1866, m. Ellen Gough; Clara Cleopatra m. April 1, 1868, m. Clancy S. Mowry; Nessey Maud b. Nov. 13, 1870, d. Oct. 18, 1878. Family home Lehi, Utah.
Married Amy Lewis Oct. 8, 1897, Salt Lake City (daughter of John Lewis and Elizabeth Griffith), who was born June 9, 1830, Cardiff, Wales.
Settled at Lehi. Leader of Lehi tabernacle choir twenty years; leader Lehi martial band. School trustee 13 years; member militia in early days. Died Oct. 11, 1898.

CARTER, JOHN (son of John Carter and Ellen Jackson). Born Jan. 26, 1846, Preston, Lancashire, England. Came to Utah Nov. 30, 1856. Edward Martin handcart company.
Married Almeda Janette McArthur March 10, 1868, Mount Pleasant, Utah (daughter of Washington Perry McArthur and Urania Gregg of Mount Pleasant, pioneers 1848, independent company). She was born Oct. 29, 1847, Fort Madison, Iowa, and died Dec. 19, 1900. Their children: John Perry b. Dec. 28, 1868, m. Rozette Howard; Ella Urania b. Sept. 19, 1870, m. Henry M. Todd; Charles Byron b. Aug. 9, 1872, m. Datilda O. Madsen; Abbie C. b. Oct. 10, 1874, m. Andrew C. Madsen; Carrie Louisa b. Nov. 1, 1876, m. Averett McCarty; Mary A. b. Aug. 7, 1879, m. Fred Stansfield; Samuel Anthnell b. Sept. 23, 1883, m. Susan Ashton July 30, 1913; Parlen b. July 23, 1886, m. Oceana Brandon; Almeda May b. April 14, 1890. Family home Mount Pleasant, Utah.
Married Annie Groves Nov. 27, 1901, Manti, Utah (daughter of Joseph Groves and Miriam Wood of Denholm, Yorkshire, Eng., both died in England). She was born April 25, 1869. Their children: Miriam May b. June 29, 1904; John Groves b. Aug. 6, 1906.
Member 66th quorum seventies. 1882; senior president 16 years; missionary to Georgia 1880-82; to England 1899-1900 and 1908-10; Sunday school superintendent five years; home missionary 20 years. County selectman two terms; sheriff two terms; constable ten years; councilman three terms; mayor one term; marshal three terms; justice of peace two terms. Minuteman in Black Hawk Indian war three years. First settled at Pleasant Grove, 1856, moved to Mount Pleasant April 1859. Farmer and stockraiser.

CARTER, SIMEON (son of Gideon Carter of Thillingworth, Middlesex county, Conn., and Joanna Simms of Connecticut). Born June 7, 1794. Came to Utah Aug. 15, 1850, Orson Hyde company.
His first wife bore him two daughters and one son. She presumably died at Nauvoo, where this family resided.

Married Louisa H. Gibbons Nov. 14, 1849 (daughter of Samuel Gibbons and Louisa Holland), who was born Jan. 25, 1828, Cheltenham, Gloucester, Eng., and came to Utah with her husband. Their children: Simeon b. Dec. 1, 1850, m. Ellen Sheffield March 13, 1877; Louisa Jane b. Aug. 23, 1852, m. Thomas H. Wilde 1877; Samuel b. April 1, 1853, m. Lena Christensen Nov. 7, 1877. Family home Brigham City, Utah.
Deacon; high priest; missionary to England and the states. Died Feb. 3, 1869.

CARTER, SIMEON (son of Simeon Carter and Louisa Gibbons). Born Dec. 1, 1850, Salt Lake City.
Married Ellen Sheffield March 13, 1877, at Brigham City (daughter of James Sheffield and Sarah A. Wilmer), who was born Feb. 5, 1860, Northampton, Eng. Their children: Louisa b. Jan. 15, 1878; Ellen F. b. Sept. 29, 1879, m. D. S. McQuee Nov. 4, 1901; Jane Aleda b. Jan. 21, 1882, m. Joseph H. Wallis Aug. 23, 1905; Vilate G. b. March 21, 1885, m. Joseph Primrose March 1, 1909; Eveline Lena b. June 21, 1887, m. Heber Stokes Oct. 26, 1910; Amelia A. b. Feb. 26, 1890, m. Vance H. Tingey Aug. 22, 1910; Wilmer Simeon b. Sept. 21, 1892; Vera Eliza b. March 14, 1895. Family home Brigham City.
Elder; high priest.

CARTER, WILLIAM (son of Thomas Carter and Sarah Parker). Born Feb. 12, 1821, Sudbury, Herefordshire, Eng. Came to Utah July 24, 1847, Brigham Young company.
Married Ellen Benbow Dec. 5, 1843, Nauvoo, Ill. (daughter of William Benbow and Mary Jones of Winslow parish, Eng.), who was born May 25, 1825. Their children: William John B. b. June 29, 1852, m. Lottie R. Smith Feb. 2, 1882; Marian B. b. Nov. 1, 1857, m. Frank Richard Bentley Nov. 8, 1877; Eunice B. b. Feb. 23, 1864, m. John Moody Feb. 26, 1883.
Married Harriet Temperance Utley Nov. 29, 1853, Salt Lake City (daughter of Samuel Utley and Maria Berry of Perry county, Alabama). She was born July 13, 1835. Their children: Samuel U. b. Sept. 22, 1854, m. Mary Ann Rankin; Isabella U. b. March 10, 1857, m. Willard Pixton; Willard U. b. July 19, 1859, m. Jane Thomas; Henry Lafayette U. b. Sept. 2, 1861, m. Alice Nelson; Jacob U. b. June 27, 1863, m. Mamie Blair; Sarah Elizabeth U. b. Feb. 8, 1866, m. Ephraim Harkes; Harriet Maria U. b. March 24, 1868, m. Preston Thomas; James U. b. Aug. 27, 1877. Family resided at Salt Lake City and St. George, Utah.
Married Sophrona Ellen Turnbow Feb. 8, 1857, Salt Lake City (daughter of Samuel Turnbow and Sylvia Caroline Hart, pioneers 1848). She was born Feb. 23, 1841. Their children: Adeline T. b. April 27, 1859, m. Walter Kemp; Wilford J. T. b. June 1, 1862; Franklin T. b. Aug. 4, 1864, m. Sarah Hemingway; Milton T. b. Feb. 7, 1867; Samuel Amos T. b. Sept. 13, 1869, m. Maggie Everett; Sylvira Caroline T. b. March 27, 1872, m. Milton Turnbow; Sophrona T. b. Oct. 13, 1874, m. Clifford Langdon; Mary Annie T. b. July 1, 1877, m. Charley Johnson; Austin C. b. Sept. 20, 1879. Family home St. George, Utah.
Seventy; high priest; counselor to Bishop Hoagland of Salt Lake City 1856-61; counselor to Bishop Robert Gardner of St. George; missionary to Florence, Neb. 1857-58. Plowed first half acre of land in Utah.

CARTER, WILLIAM JOHN BENBOW (son of William Carter and Ellen Benbow). Born June 29, 1852, Salt Lake City.
Married Lottie R. Smith Feb. 2, 1882, St. George, Utah (daughter of John L. Smith and Augusta Cleveland of Salt Lake City). Their children: John Cleveland b. Dec. 7, 1882, d. March 7, 1909; Ellen b. May 5, 1885; Augusta S. b. June 27, 1888; Metta B. March 12, 1890, m. R. A. Morris, Jr., Sept. 21, 1912; Don Smith b. May 31, 1892; Isabell b. Nov. 5, 1896, d. Nov. 19, 1896. Family home St. George, Utah.
Missionary to England 1877-79; member high council St. George stake. Pioneer to St. George. Indian war veteran. Farmer. Died March 9, 1908, St. George.

CARTWRIGHT, THOMAS (son of Thomas and Jane Cartwright). Born Dec. 23, 1814, Wigan, Lancashire, Eng. Came to Utah 1849, Milo Andrus company.
Married Jane Allen 1844 (daughter of Robert Allen and Jane Allen). She came to Utah with her husband. Their children: Joseph Henry b. March 6, 1845, m. Sarah Ann Grimshaw; Mary, m. John Matthews; Thomas Henry, m. Sarah Wardley; Caroline, m. William Anderson; Cedaresse C., m. Marcus L. Shepherd; Jane, m. Hyrum Baldwin. Family resided in Iron and Beaver counties, Utah.
Settled in Iron county, 1850, and followed the trade of blacksmith and made the first plows in Iron county, as well as the first woolen carding machine in southern Utah. He was a member of the high priest's quorum.

CARTWRIGHT, JOSEPH HENRY (son of Thomas Cartwright and Jane Allen). Born March 6, 1845, Liverpool, Eng.
Married Sarah Ann Grimshaw Feb. 8, 1866, Beaver, Utah (daughter of John Grimshaw and Alice Whitaker, pioneers 1863, Peter Neheker company). She was born Jan. 5, 1849, Tottington, Eng. Their children: Alice b. Nov. 6, 1866; Sarah Jane; Thomas b. April 20, 1869, m. Eliza Carlow; Elizabeth b. July 9, 1871, m. Charles Murdock; Joseph Hyrum; John; Vilate Sussannah; Wilford b. July 11, 1879; Duckworth; Frank b. Jan. 28, 1884; James; Charles b. Sept. 21, 1892; Ulysses. Family home Beaver, Utah.
High priest 14 years. Minuteman in Utah militia. Blacksmith.

CARTWRIGHT, JOHN (son of William Cartwright and Charlotte Hood of Church Gresley, Derbyshire, Eng.). Born July 2, 1837 at Derbyshire, England. Came to Utah Sept. 4, 1859, with George Rowley handcart company.
Married Ann Hardwick Jan. 30, 1859, at Burton-on-Trent, Derbyshire, Eng. (daughter of John Hardwick and Ann Sandiant of Woodville, Derbyshire, Eng.). They came to Utah Sept. 4, 1859 with George Rowley handcart company. She was born Aug. 6, 1837. Their children: John William died at 16 months; Thos. H., m. Elizabeth Smith; Edith H., m. J. G. McDonald; John A., m. Nellie Liddle; Annie E., m. Charles F. Solomon; Myrtle, m. William Murdock. Family home Salt Lake City.
Missionary to England 1883 to 1885; priest of 10th quorum of seventies; superintendent of Sunday school; bishop's counselor. Manufacturer of crockery; merchant.

CARTWRIGHT, THOMAS HYRUM (son of John Cartwright and Ann Hardwick). Born Oct. 5, 1863, at Salt Lake City.
Married Elizabeth Smith Sept. 1, 1892, at Logan (daughter of George Albert Smith and Susan E. West, who came to Utah July 24, 1847, with Brigham Young company). She was born Sept. 28, 1866. Their children: Priscilla b. Aug. 15, 1893; Hyrum b. Nov. 29, 1895; Marion b. May 10, 1899; Joseph F. b. Nov. 6, 1901; Richard b. Nov. 27, 1904, died. Family home Salt Lake City.
Missionary to England 1896 to 1898; secretary Sunday school and Y. M. M. I. A. of the eighth ward; counselor Y. M. M. I. A. seventeenth ward; secretary Salt Lake stake Y. M. M. I. A. Appraiser third judicial district. President and manager Home Agency Co.; insurance, real estate and loans.

CARVER, JOHN. Born Aug. 6, 1822, Clifford parish, Herefordshire, Eng. Came to Utah Sept. 3, 1852, independent company.
Married Mary Ann Eames (daughter of John Eames), who was born Aug. 8, 1828, in Orcop parish, Herefordshire. Their children: John W. b. July 28, 1852; George H. b. Nov. 11, 1854; Mary Ann b. Oct. 2, 1857; James S. b. Sept. 27, 1859; Josiah B. b. Sept. 3, 1861; Nancy C. b. Feb. 19, 1863; Willard C. b. Feb. 24, 1865; Parley P. b. Jan. 17, 1867, m. Elizabeth A. Pritchett Nov. 27, 1889; Orson b. Jan. 15, 1869. Family home Kaysville and Plain City, Utah.
Settled in Davis county 1852; moved to Weber county, and assisted in laying out Plain City. Active religion worker.

CARVER, GEORGE H. (son of John Carver and Mary Ann Eames). Born Nov. 11, 1854, Kaysville, Utah.
Married Elizabeth Geddes Nov. 24, 1881, Salt Lake City (daughter of William Geddes and Elizabeth Stewart of Scotland, pioneers to Plain City, Utah). She was born Aug. 8, 1862.
Member first Sunday school of Weber stake; ward clerk; missionary 1879-81; called by the church to assist in opening the Northwestern-States mission; bishop of third ward, of Oneida stake. Manager Oregon Lumber Company eight years; deputy county assessor and surveyor at Preston, Idaho 1900; member school board and held the office of chairman for many years. School teacher; farmer.

CARVER, PARLEY PRATT (son of John Carver and Mary Ann Eames). Born Jan. 17, 1867, at Plain City, Utah.
Married Elizabeth Ann Pritchett Nov. 27, 1889, at Harrisdale, Utah (daughter of Leonidas A. Pritchett, pioneer 1864, and Elizabeth Ann Heninger). She was born Feb. 19, 1869. Their children: Parley Leonidas b. Jan. 31, 1890; Walter Jerold b. Aug. 18, 1892; John Alfred b. Mar. 14, 1896; Parley Pratt b. April 18, 1899; Retta Elizabeth b. July 20, 1902; Durvard William b. Feb. 28, 1907.
Elder. Moved to Preston, Idaho, 1894.

CASE, ANDREW T. Born Jan. 31, 1819, in England. Came to Utah Aug. 19, 1868, John R. Murdock company.
Married Mary Ann Spruel in England (daughter of John Spruel of England), who was born Feb. 28, 1816. Their children: John; Mary Ann, m. Benjamin Wilson; Henry, killed at Promontory, Utah, Oct. 29, 1869; Alfred; Ellen G.; Eber, m. Mary Ann Mumford; Hyrum, m. Kate Davis; William, m. Ina Galsford. Family home Salt Lake City.
Seventy at Salt Lake City; high priest. Farmer. Died 1897, Salt Lake City.

CASE, EBER (son of Andrew T. Case and Mary Ann Spruel). Born Oct. 19, 1849, in England. Came to Utah Aug. 19, 1868, John R. Murdock company.
Married Mary Ann Mumford at Salt Lake City (daughter of Thomas Mumford and Mary Horsnel of England). Their children: Eber Sydney, m. Alice Saddler; Mary, m. Ernest H. Arnold; Leslie M.; Scott W., m. Clara Folsom; Lucille, m. Chester C. Pratt. Family home Salt Lake City.
Member 10th quorum seventies; high priest; clerk of 9th ward, Salt Lake City 37 years. Clerk.

CASPER, WILLIAM WALLACE (son of William and Everilla Casper). Born March 12, 1821, Richland, Ohio. Came to Utah Oct. 7, 1847, Ephraim Hanks company.
Married Sarah Ann Bean in 1844, Quincy, Ill. (daughter of James and Elizabeth Bean, pioneers Sept. 22, 1849, Jedediah M. Grant company). She was born Oct. 31, 1828, in Adams county, Ill., and died April 23, ——. Their children: Sarah Jane, m. Ebenezer Hanks; William Nephi, m. Agnes McFarland, m. Lucy Edwards; Elizabeth Ann, m. John Cook; James Moroni, m. Sarah Jean McFarland; Harriet Priscilla, m. Thomas Gunderson; Jedediah Grant, m. Annie Merrill; Emily Margaret, died; George Ether, m. Eliza Ray; Shermiah Ellen, m. George H. Luck; John, m. Rhoda Ann Williams; Ruben, m. Elizabeth Smith. Family home Mill Creek ward, Salt Lake county, Utah.
High priest; missionary to The Muddy in Nevada. Died July 17, 1908.

CASPER, WILLIAM NEPHI (son of William Wallace Casper and Sarah Ann Bean). Born Nov. 10, 1848, Mill Creek, Salt Lake county, Utah.
Married Agnes McFarland April 20, 1867, Salt Lake City (daughter of James McFarland and Sarah Mitchell of Granger, Utah, pioneers 1866, Joseph S. Rawlins company). She was born April 29, 1848. Their children: James William b. Feb. 20, 1868, d. infant; Mary Jane b. Aug. 6, 1869, m. Joseph Nelson; Margaret Priscilla b. June 4, 1872, m. John Hubbard Noakes; George Nephi b. Feb. 13, 1874, m. Maud Miles; Agnes Valeria b. March 17, 1876, m. Earnest Webb; John Reuben b. Sept. 7, 1878, m. Trisa Carlin; Elias Chemira b. Aug. 15, 1880, m. John Potter; Moroni Jedediah b. Nov. 13, 1882, m. Leah Thacker; Harriett Luella b. Oct. 13, 1884, m. Charles Carlin; Wallace Durbin b. Feb. 7, 1886, m. Lucy Wagstaff. Family home Charleston, Utah.
Married Lucy Edwards Nov. 29, 1877, Salt Lake City (daughter of Philip Edwards and Mary Simmons of Charleston, Utah). She was born Dec. 28, 1861. Their children: Philip Thomas b. Nov. 7, 1879, m. Mary Carlin; Emma Myrum b. March 10, 1881, m. Ernest Jacklin; Eliza Matilda b. Sept. 13, 1884, m. Owen Wright; Phoebe Lucy b. April 18, 1887, m. John Wright; Melissa Almyra b. Sept. 30, 1889, m. Daniel Street; Rachel Melvina b. Feb. 16, 1896; Mabel Jemimah b. Dec. 19, 1900; Joseph Warren b. Nov. 13, 1902; Wilford Raymond b. May 18, 1904. Family home Charleston.
President of 96th quorum seventies, eleven years; missionary to southern states 1895-97. Settled in Provo valley 1882 and has assisted in building up the country. Farmer.

CASPER, JAMES MORONI (son of William Wallace Casper and Sarah Ann Bean). Born Feb. 28, 1853, Mill Creek, Utah.
Married Sarah Jean McFarland Feb. 15, 1875, Salt Lake City (daughter of James McFarland and Sarah Mitchell of Paisley, Scotland, pioneers Oct. 1, 1866, Joseph S. Rawlins company). She was born Jan. 26, 1855. Their children: James Moroni, Jr., b. June 30, 1876, m. Margaret Price; William Jedediah b. Jan. 30, 1878, m. Mary Murdock; Cassius Roy b. Oct. 20, 1880, died; Arlington Nephi b. Nov. 30, 1882, died; Mary b. Dec. 26, 1884; Henry Mitchell b. Sept. 29, 1886; George Ether b. Oct. 5, 1888, died; Sarah Margaret b. Sept. 15, 1889; Minerva Jane b. Nov. 1, 1891; Evelyn E. Swin b. April 11, 1894; Nellie b. June 5, 1897; Nancy Ann b. Nov. 8, 1899. Family home Mill Creek, Salt Lake county, Utah.
Elder. Settled at Mill Creek; moved to Granger ward; lived there eleven years; moved to Charleston 1889. School trustee. Helped build canals, etc., around Charleston, Utah. Farmer, stockraiser and dairyman.

CASPER, DUNCAN SPEARS (son of William Casper, born July 30, 1784, in Culpepper county, Va., and Avarilla Durbin, born Nov. 26, 1790, Washington county, Pa.—married 1809). Born Dec. 8, 1824, Richland county, Ohio, pioneer Sept. 3, 1855, Captain Hindley company.
Married Matilda Allison May 24, 1845 (daughter of David Allison and Matilda Miner, married May 10, 1808). She was born Dec. 31, 1820 and came to Utah with husband. Their children: Rachel Louisa m. March 12, 1846; Amanda Elizabeth b. Feb. 18, 1848; Harriet Matilda b. Nov. 9, 1849, m. Albert George Henry Marchant Feb. 17, 1873; Rebecca Avarilla b. Nov. 21, 1851, m. Niles Pearson Dec. 11, 1871; Duncan Alonzo b. Nov. 2, 1853, m. Lucy Elizabeth Card March 25, 1884; Peter William b. Aug. 2, 1857, m. Margaret Maria Miles June, 1888; Mary Malinda b. Aug. 2, 1857, m. Edward Gunderson Sept. 1876; Cyrene Rosannah b. Aug. 18, 1859, m. James Hards 1877; Welthea Ann b. Aug. 6, 1862, m. Arthur Maxwell Jan. 5, 1881. Family home Big Cottonwood, Utah.
Married Elizabeth Clark Sept., 1872, Salt Lake City, Utah, who was born 1844 in England. Their children: David Allison b. Oct. 24, 1873; Emily b. Sep. 9, 1875, m. Samuel Oakley, 1895; Alice b. Jan. 5, 1878; George b. July 2, 1879; Arthur b. Sept. 13, 1881, m. in 1904; Beatrice Eliza b. Nov. 1885; Jesse C. b. Oct., 1888.
Ward teacher. School trustee. Participated in Echo Canyon war. Pioneer to The Muddy 1867. Charcoal burner, farmer and stockraiser.

CASTLETON, JAMES JOSEPH (son of Joseph Castleton, born in 1804, and Mary Smith, born in 1807). He was born Jan. 25, 1829, Lowestoft, Suffolk, Eng. Came to Utah Oct. 4, 1868, Thomas Ricks company.
Married Frances Sarah Brown Jan. 2, 1853, Yarmouth, Norfolk, Eng. (daughter of Robert Brown, born 1807, and Mary Ann Booty, born Aug. 11, 1811). She was born Dec. 13, 1834, Norfolk, Eng. Their children: Charles Lorenzo b. Oct. 2, 1854, m. Mary Ann Luff; William Joseph, m. Kate Roberts, m. Anna Pitchers; George Nephi, died; Frank Moroni, m. Elenore Hilton; James Samuel, m. Alice Gunn; Martha Ann, died; Arthur Robert, m. Ellen Wooley; Harry John, died; Wallace Claudius, m. Alice Bitner; Albert George, died. Family home Salt Lake City.
Gardener. Died Nov. 26, 1882.

CATROW, HENRY (son of Newton J. Catrow and Sarah Melissa Groby). Born June 22, 1878, at Miamisburg, Ohio. Came to Utah June, 1903.
Married Charlotte May Bettles April 7, 1904, Salt Lake City (daughter of Alfred J. Bettles and Grace Ann MacBain of Montana). She was born Feb. 23, 1884. Their children: Alfred Newton; Henry. Family home Salt Lake City.
Followed mining pursuits; was also connected with the theatrical business.

CAZIER, WILLIAM. Born Jan. 21, 1794 in Virginia. Came to Utah 1851, Captain Phelps company.
Married Pleasant Drake in Virginia (daughter of Thomas Drake of Virginia, pioneer 1851, Captain Phelps company), who was born March, 1796. Their children: James; Maranda; John; Benjamin; William; Elizabeth; Samuel; David; Charles Drake b. 1837, m. Harriet Gates June 12, 1858; Rosannah. Family home Nephi, Utah.
Married Margaret Ervin.
Married Sarah Winters.
High priest; patriarch. Cooper and farmer. Died February, 1872, at Nephi.

CAZIER, CHARLES DRAKE (son of William Cazier and Pleasant Drake). Born 1837, Brownsville, Oldham Co., Ky.
Married Harriet Gates June 12, 1858, Payson, Utah (daughter of Samuel Gates and Lydia Downer of Lynn, Utah, pioneers 1852). She was born March 19, 1839. Their children: Charles Gates, b. May 6, 1859; Pleasant Lydia b. March 7, 1861, died; Margaret b. Oct. 7, 1862, died; William Henry b. Feb. 6, 1864; Samuel b. Oct. 13, 1866; Sarah Ellen b. Dec. 14, 1868; Harriet b. April 13, 1870; Maranda b. Jan. 12, 1873; George b. June 8, 1874; Artello Byron b. July 8, 1876; Evelyn b. May 28, 1878 (latter four died); Willard Otis b. May 8, 1880. Family home Nephi.

CAZIER, CHARLES GATES (son of Charles Drake Cazier and Harriet Gates). Born May 6, 1859, Nephi, Utah.
Married Susan Bingham March 17, 1881, Salt Lake City (daughter of Willard Bingham and Amanda Snow of Wilson, Utah, pioneers 1847). She was born Dec. 1, 1864. Their children: Charles G. b. May 6, 1859; Pleasant Lydia, b. March 7, 1861, died; Margaret b. Sept. 7, 1862, died; William H. b. Feb. 6, 1864; Samuel G. b. Oct. 13, 1865; Sarah E. b. Dec. 14, 1867; Harriet b. April 13, 1870; Maranda b. Jan. 1873, died; George G. b. June 11, 1874; Artello Byron b. July 8, 1876, and Evelyn b. May 28, 1878, died. Family home Nephi, Utah.
Member 49th quorum seventies; president high priests quorum; first bishop of what is now known as the Star Valley stake; patriarch. State senator of Wyoming 1896-1900. Farmer.

CHADWICK, JOSEPH (son of William Chadwick). Born 1809, Yorkshire, Eng. Came to Utah 1857, John Smith company.
Married Mary Whitehead (daughter of James Whitehead and Hanna Heppeth). Their children: Benjamin; James; Adam, m. Eliza Fluit. Family home Franklin, Idaho.
Seventy. Farmer. Deceased.

CHADWICK, ADAM (son of Joseph Chadwick and Mary Whitehead). Married Eliza Fluit at Richmond, Utah (daughter of William Fluit and Mary A. Day of Franklin, Idaho, pioneers). She was born April 1, 1861. Their children: Mary Jane b. Sept. 23, 1884, died; Mary A. b. Sept. 21, 1885; James A. b. Dec. 4, 1887, m. Minnie M. Jensen Aug. 23, 1911; Bertha b. March 4, 1890; Earl b. June 2, 1892; Joseph b. Nov. 29, 1895. Family home Whitney, Idaho.
Farmer. Died April 1895, Logan, Utah.

CHADWICK, JAMES A. (son of Adam Chadwick and Eliza Fluit). Born Dec. 4, 1887, Whitney, Idaho.
Married Minnie M. Jensen Aug. 23, 1911, Logan, Utah (daughter of Christian J. Jensen and Christena M. Sorenson of Denmark; they came to Utah 1893). She was born Sept. 26, 1891. Their children: Cleo b. June 3, 1912. Family home Whitney, Idaho.
Seventy; missionary to central states 1907-09. Farmer.

CHAMBERLAIN, JOSEPH (son of Thomas Chamberlain, of Toms River, Ocean county, New Jersey). Born May 12, 1812, in Ocean county, N. J. Came to Utah Dec. 9, 1853, Preston Thomas company.
Married Amy Wilbert, Barnegat, Ocean county, N. J. (daughter of James Wilbert and Mary Gifford of Ocean

county, N. J.). Their children: Katherine, m. John Dickinson; John, m. Elizabeth Smart; Althea, m. James Brown; Rebecca, m. John Aldous; James Thomas b. March 18, 1847, m. Susanna A. Alston July 23, 1882; Josephine, m. Harold P. Johnson; Henry, m. Frances Brown; Hyrum, died. Family home Salt Lake City.
Owned first sawmill in Parley's canyon. Engaged in salt and lumber business. Died April, 1879.

CHAMBERLAIN, JAMES T. (son of Joseph Chamberlain and Amy Wilbert). Born March 18, 1847, Toms River, N. J. Came to Utah with parents.
Married Susanna A. Alston July 23, 1882, at Salt Lake City (daughter of Joseph Alston and Margaret Hall of Blackburn, Lancashire, Eng., pioneers 1848, Willard Richards company). She was born July 3, 1856. Their children: Lula b. Jan. 9, 1884; Gertrude b. Sept. 28, 1886; Thomas Roscoe b. March 30, 1889. Family home Salt Lake City.
Prominent sheep raiser; large real estate owner. Died June 7, 1889.

CHAMBERLAIN, THOMAS ROSCOE (son of James T. Chamberlain and Susanna A. Alston). Born March 30, 1889, Salt Lake City.
Graduate of Salt Lake high school; won the Dr. Mayo medal for the highest degree in the scientific course in 1907. Student University of Utah three years. Employed in government department of entomology, located at Sugar House, South Salt Lake City.

CHAMBERLIN, WILLIAM HENRY, JR. (son of William Henry Chamberlin and Frances Eliza Brown). Born Feb. 12, 1870, at Salt Lake City.
Married Amelia Telle Cannon Sept. 28, 1892, Logan, Utah (daughter of George Quayle Cannon and Martha Telle of Liverpool, Eng., former pioneer 1847, John Taylor company). She was born Feb. 16, 1870. Their children: Max Cannon b. Nov. 14, 1893; Hester b. Dec. 27, 1896; Martha b. Aug. 21, 1901; Paul b. June 17, 1904; Frances b. Sept. 24, 1906; Luke b. July 20, 1912.
Missionary to Society Islands 1896-99; high priest; church school professor.

CHAMBERS, JOHN GARRATT (son of Robert Chambers and Margaret Garratt of Alnwick, Northumberlandshire, Eng.). Born June 13, 1818, Alnwick, Eng. Came to Utah Oct. 7, 1853, Cyrus H. Wheelock company.
Married Maria Duffin Feb. 9, 1853, Manchester, Eng. (daughter of Abraham Duffin and Eliza Johnson of Manchester, former pioneer 1855). She was born Oct. 18, 1834. Their children: John Willard, m. Martha Mary Butterworth; Robert Heber, m. Gunda Anderson; Alma Duffin b. Feb. 16, 1858, m. Anne Pugh Holroyd June 2, 1881; Frances Maria, m. Henry William Gwilliam; Frederick William, m. Mary Leavitt; Annie Eliza, m. Nephi W. Anderson; Margaret Ellen; Clara Isabel, m. William Stowell Wallace; Letitia, m. Wilford Owen Ridges; Ida May, d. June 11, 1874; Josephine. Family home Ogden, Utah.
Seventy; high priest. Called in the Deseret News printing office, where he served about ten years; moved to Cache Valley and settled in Logan, where he farmed for five years; was identified with the publication of Ogden's first paper, the Telegraph, and later with the Ogden Junction for several years, subsequently establishing a book and stationery business in Ogden. Died Oct. 27, 1892, Ogden, Utah.

CHAMBERS, ALMA DUFFIN (son of John Garratt Chambers and Maria Duffin). Born Feb. 16, 1858, at Salt Lake City.
Married Anne Pugh Holroyd June 2, 1881, at Salt Lake City (daughter of Thomas Edward Holroyd and Dinah Williams of Ogden, Utah, pioneers September, 1861, Harvey Dilley company). She was born Dec. 2, 1856. Their children: Alma H. b. June 12, 1882, m. Lois Edna Daniels; Edward H. b. Oct. 8, 1885, m. Ellen Merintha Greenwell; Dinah R. b. June 5, 1887, d. Jan. 19, 1889; Ireta H. b. May 16, 1889; Lawrence H. b. Dec. 9, 1896, d. Aug. 23, 1898; Stanley H. b. July 14, 1898. Family home Ogden, Utah.
Member 77th quorum seventies; high priest. Clerk of 4th ward Ogden several years. Member of central board of Y. M. M. I. A. of Weber stake three years. Weber county treasurer 1897-1912. Foreman of "Ogden Junction" and later one of the proprietors; printer.

CHAMBERS, NATHANIEL GEORGE (son of George H. Chambers and Mary Hyde of Oakland county, Michigan). Born Dec. 31, 1836, Detroit, Mich. Came to Utah June 25, 1859, Capt. White company.
Married Mary Leone Spencer Feb. 17, 1861, Salt Lake City (daughter of Daniel Spencer and Sarah Lester of Great Barrington, Mass., pioneers Sept. 23, 1847, his own company). She was born Feb. 17, 1847. Their children: Sarah Leone, m. William Waples; Hattie Eliza, died; George Spencer b. Oct. 9, 1874, m. Anna Minor July 22, 1903. Family home Salt Lake City.
Elder; high priest. Went with Capt. White in 1866 to the Missouri river for immigrants. Rancher and stockman.

CHAMBERS, GEORGE SPENCER (son of Nathaniel George Chambers and Mary Leone Spencer). Born Oct. 9, 1874, Salt Lake City.

Married Anna Minor July 22, 1903, Salt Lake City (daughter of John W. Minor and Margaret Criswell of Danveldara, Ohio; came to Utah 1891). She was born Sept. 20, 1879. Their children: Baird Spencer b. June 25, 1905; Clara Margaret b. Sept. 1, 1908; Leone b. Oct. 2, 1911. Family home Salt Lake City.
In government postal service.

CHANDLER, STEPHEN G. (son of Stephen Chandler and Eliza D. Killick of Burgess Hill, Sussex, Eng.). Born Jan. 13, 1857, in Sussex. Came to Utah in November, 1870.
Married Sarah Ann Hemsley Oct. 30, 1879, Salt Lake City (daughter of Richard Hemsley and Christina M. Jenson of Salt Lake City, pioneers Sept. 11-12, 1857, Israel Evans company). She was born Nov. 27, 1862. Their children: Mary Jane b. Oct. 24, 1880; Eliza May b. June 8, 1882, m. Joseph F. White; Sarah Minnie b. Nov. 26, 1885, m. Joseph M. Peterson; Annie Christina b. Sept. 8, 1888; Ellen b. June 4, 1890; Rosa b. Aug. 14, 1893; Stephen George b. July, 19, 1895; Bertha Susan b. Oct. 25, 1898.
Bishop Plano ward, Fremont stake.

CHARD, DAVID (son of John Chard and Sarah Day). Born Sept. 24, 1810.
Married Mary Teagues June 24, 1840. She was born May 28, 1806 and died Aug. 21, 1886. Their children: Joseph b. Oct. 15, 1841; Alford b. Feb. 3, 1843; Sarah b. May 21, 1844; John b. Sept. 19, 1845; Hyrum b. Sept. 17, 1847; Mary Jane b. Feb. 13, 1852; Henry T. b. June 13, 1855, m. Mary Ann Berrett March 27, 1877. Family home Salt Lake City, Utah.
Held various positions in the ward. Died Sept. 25, 1881.

CHARD, HENRY T. (son of David Chard and Mary Teagues). Born June 13, 1855, North Somerset, Eng.
Married Mary Ann Berrett March 27, 1877, North Ogden, Utah (daughter of Alfred Berrett and Elizabeth Mathews), who was born Nov. 27, 1858, North Ogden. Their children: William Henry b. Jan. 9, 1878, m. Elizabeth A. Marshall, Nov. 19, 1902; Mary Elizabeth, b. Nov. 25, 1879, m. Charles A. Clark, Nov. 1, 1899; David E. b. Nov. 1, 1881, m. Sarah E. Jones, Jan. 7, 1903; Virtue Pearl b. Dec. 13, 1883, m. James E. Shaw, Oct. 20, 1903; Alford T. b. July 13, 1886; Ivan Edmund b. Dec. 5, 1888; Marcellus, b. Jan. 19, 1891; Sarah Ann, b. July 2, 1893; Stephen Hamlet b. Dec. 12, 1895. Family home North Ogden, Utah. Died Jan. 31, 1897.

CHARD, DAVID E. (son of Henry T. Chard and Mary Ann Berrett). Born Nov. 1, 1881, North Ogden, Utah.
Married Sarah Minerva Jones Jan. 7, 1903, at Salt Lake City (daughter of Richard Jones and Viola Cazier), who was born July 1, 1884, in Coltville (?), Utah. Their children: Henry David b. July 29, 1904; Viola Minerva b. Jan. 26, 1906; Lyslie J. b. Dec. 10, 1908; Ray Elery b. Aug. 14, 1910; Clarence Glen b. Sept. 28, 1911.
Lived at Liberty, Utah. At 15 years of age was called as secretary of ward Sunday school; when 21 years was chosen assistant superintendent; when 23 as superintendent; June 27, 1909, chosen as bishop's counselor, which position he now holds.

CHASE, EZRA (son of Timothy Chase of Rhode Island). Born Feb. 4, 1796, in Massachusetts. Came to Utah Sept. 20, 1848, Lorenzo Snow company.
Married Turzah Wells about 1825, in Massachusetts (daughter of Elisha Wells of Massachusetts), who was born 1797. Their children: Eliza, m. Clark Hubbard; Nancy, m. Lorine Farr; Charlotte, m. Constantine Hicks; Diana, m. William Shaw; Wells, m. Jane McGary; Henry, m. Mary Ann Baldwin; Dudley, m. Samantha Crismon; Newton, m. Elsie Tanner; Juliet, m. Hugh McClellan. Family home Ogden, Utah. Farmer. Died Oct. 24, 1873, Ogden, Utah.

CHASE, WELLS (son of Ezra Chase and Turzah Wells). Born April 21, 1830, in New York. Came to Utah Sept. 20, 1848, Lorenzo Snow company.
Married Jane McGary Nov. 23, 1853, Ogden, Utah (daughter of Charles McGary and Charlotte Earle of Ogden—pioneers Sept. 17, 1850, David Evans company). She was born June 8, 1835. Their children: Jane Diana b. Dec. 3, 1854, m. M. F. Cooper; Charles b. May 17, 1856, m. Amanda Taylor; William b. Jan. 14, 1858, m. Etta Mitchell; Ellen F. b. Nov. 18, 1859, m. Marshall Allan; Ernest b. Oct. 20, 1861, m. Minnie Crawford; Inez b. Dec. 31, 1862, m. William Cunningham; Turzah b. Aug. 23, 1864, m. Chauncy Leavitt; Charlotte b. Jan. 16, 1866, m. Allen T. Wood; Ezra b. May 12, 1867, m. Louise Lee; Clara b. Nov. 25, 1869, m. Robert Morton; James b. Sept. 12, 1871, m. Annie Clark; Ella b. May 15, 1873, d. infant; Ida b. May 1, 1875, m. M. A. Wood; Clarence b. Dec. 11, 1876, d. aged 3 years; David b. Dec. 26, 1879, d. infant; Genevieve b. July 6, 1883, m. J. W. Durkin. Family home Ogden, Utah.
Farmer.

CHASE, DUDLEY (son of Ezra Chase and Turzah Wells). Born May 27, 1835, Sportz, Livingston county, N. Y. Came to Utah Sept. 27, 1848.
Married Samantha Crismon July 19, 1857, San Bernardino, Cal. (daughter of Charles Crismon and Mary Hill of Illinois, pioneers, 1847). She was born March 27, 1840. Their children: Luella Crismon, m. Warren G. Child; Walter Dudley, m. Millie M. Richardson; Charles Ezra, m. Jane A. Dunn;

Mary Ellen and Cynthia, died; George Frank, m. Elsie J. Taylor; Henry Albert, m. Valla Van Winkle; Abigail Eliza, m. Myron A. Gudmundson; Juliette. m. Willard M. Spiers; John Weiler, m. Selina Greenwell. Family home Farr-West, Weber county, Utah.
Missionary to eastern states 1871-72. Settled Harrisville, Weber county, 1860, and engaged in farming and stockraising. Counselor to Bishop F. G. Taylor of Harrisville. Died Feb. 24, 1906, Idaho Falls, Idaho.

CHASE, JOHN DARWIN (son of Abner Chase and Amy Scott). Born Aug. 10, 1815, Bristol, Addison county, Vt. Came to Utah 1847, with a contingent of Mormon Battalion.
Married Priscilla McHenry. Their children: Amos, m. Ellen Coolidge; James.
Married Almira Higgins Feb. 17, 1846, on the plains (daughter of Nelson Higgins and Sarah Black, both of Vermont, pioneers 1847). Their children: Clarissa, m. Nathan Foux; John Darwin, d. child; Almira, m. Curtis Washington Caldwell; Amy, m. Ira Clark; George Albert, m. Julia Caldwell; Drusilla, d. child; Mary, m. Nathan Henry Stephens; Ruth, m. James Albert McKee; Samuel, m. Emma Ovard; Miriam, m. Edwin Mangum; Sarah, m. Clifton Gardner; Darwin John, died. Family home Moroni, Utah.
Married Elizabeth Tuttle. Their children: Sisson, m. Ruth Holly; Luther, m. Jane Brinton. Family home Nephi, Utah.
High priest; missionary to England 1863-1865; counselor in bishopric of Moroni ward; bishop at Manti; patriarch. Veteran Black Hawk war. Farmer. Died July 21, 1902, at Huntington, Utah.

CHASE, ISAAC (son of Timothy Chase and Sarah Simmons of Little Compton, Newport county, R. I.). Born Dec. 12, 1791, Little Compton, R. I. Came to Utah Sept. 20, 1847, Jedediah M. Grant company.
Married Phoebe Ogden Aug. 1818, Seneca county, N. Y. (daughter of Ezekiel Ogden and Abigail Brant of Seneca county, N. Y.). She was born Dec. 7, 1794. Their children: Silva b. Aug. 4, 1819, m. Mr. Van Fleet 1846; Desdemona b. April 3, 1821, m. John Gleason 1846; Maria b. 1823, died; Rhoda b. Sept. 29, 1830, m. Judson L. Stoddard 1845, m. Morgan Hinman; George Ogden b. March 11, 1832, m. Emily Hyde Dec. 25, 1854, m. Josephine Streeper March 25, 1856; Harriet Louisa b. April 28, 1834, m. John Whitney, m. Ephraim McLaughlin. Family home Salt Lake City.
Married Elizabeth Calvert July 7, 1850, Salt Lake City (daughter of William Calvert of Alabama, started to Utah with Brigham Young's company and died en route). She was born Feb. 2, 1825. Their children: Isaac b. July 21, 1851, m. Samantha Gardner Nov. 13, 1871, m. Priscilla Morgan Aug. 26, 1895; Nathan b. Dec. 6, 1852; Abraham b. Oct. 31, 1853, d. Oct. 31, 1853; Sarah b. Jan. 22, 1855, died; Elias b. Jan. 4, 1858, m. Carl Suisted 1876, m. Mr. Bird; Brigham b. May 14, 1861, d. 1884. Family home Centerville, Utah.
Married Charlotta Walters (Felshaw) April 15, 1855, Salt Lake City (daughter of William Walters of England, pioneer with first handcart company). Their children: Joseph b. Jan. 12, 1858; Charlotta b. Feb. 12, 1860, m. Woods Smith. Family home Centerville, Utah.
High priest; captain of 50 in Jedediah M. Grant's company. Built first mill and ground first flour in Utah. Miller. Died May 2, 1861, Salt Lake City.

CHASE, GEORGE OGDEN (son of Isaac Chase and Phoebe Ogden). Born March 11, 1832, Sparta, Livingston county, N. Y. Came to Utah Sept. 20, 1847.
Married Emily M. Hyde Dec. 25, 1854, Salt Lake City (daughter of Orson Hyde and Marinda Johnson, of Nauvoo, Ill., and Kirtland, Ohio, pioneers 1852). Their children: Emily Marinda b. Dec. 12, 1856, m. H. W. McKee Feb. 6, 1874, m. J. G. McAllister Oct. 15, 1889; Phoebe Ogden b. Oct. 2, 1857, m. W. H. McIntyre July 10, 1878; Maria b. Aug. 10, 1859, m. Owen Dix Oct. 30, 1877; George Ogden b. June 26, 1862, died; Rhoda, m. Albert Welker; Laura b. Nov. 4, ——, m. Walter Needham May 27, 1883, m. Richard McAllister Oct. 15, 1890, m. Alma Sadler. Family home Farmington, Utah.
Married Josephine Streeper March 25, 1856, Salt Lake City (daughter of Wilkinson Streeper and Matilda Wells of Philadelphia, Pa., pioneers October, 1851, Captain Kelsey company). She was born May 6, 1836. Their children: Kate Matilda S. b. April 22, 1857; Josephine S. b. Sept. 8, 1858, m. J. C. Woods Dec. 12, 1879; Fannie Dean S. b. March 22, 1860, m. J. R. Mathews June 1, 1881; Viola S. b. Sept. 30, 1861, m. C. O. Rollins Jan. 1, 1896; Alice S. b. Sept. 6, 1863, m. James S. Smedley Feb. 14, 1894; Frank Lesley S. b. Nov. 8, 1865, m. Emma Amelia Croft Feb. 3, 1891; Mary Ella S. b. June 6, 1867; George Angel S. b. Dec. 11, 1868, died; John Wilkinson S. b. June 19, 1871, m. Genevie Egbert; David Nelson S. b. April 10, 1872, m. Julia May Farr April 17, 1896; Ethel S. b. April 19, 1874; Leah S. b. April 12, 1875; Valentine S. b. Feb. 14, 1876; Clarissa Gretchen S. b. July 19, 1877, Luther four died; Emma Eckles S. b. Oct. 25, 1890. Family home Centerville, Utah.
High priest; organized the North Centerville Sunday school, of which he served as superintendent 23 years. Farmer. Died May 5, 1896, Centerville, Utah.

CHASE, FRANK LESLEY (son of George Ogden Chase and Josephine Streeper). Born Nov. 8, 1865, Centerville, Utah.
Married Emma Amelia Croft Feb. 3, 1891, Logan, Utah (daughter of John Croft and Amelia Mitchell of Manchester, Eng., pioneers Sept. 1860, J. D. Ross company). She was born April 7, 1868. Their children: Josephine Amelia Croft b. Nov. 14, 1892; Frank Ogden C. b. April 22, 1894; John Howland C. b. June 18, 1896; Annie Matilda C. b. April 22, 1898; Clara Dean C. b. March 3, 1900; David Harold C. b. Jan. 12, 1902; Beatrice Viola C. b. Dec. 30, 1904; Miranda C. b. Jan. 19, 1906; George O. C. b. May 17, 1909. Family home Centerville, Utah.
Elder. Postmaster. Farmer.

CHATELAIN, PETER LOUIS (son of Henry Louis Chatelain, born 1785, and Theresa Chatelain, born 1789, both in Switzerland). He was born Aug. 10, 1824, Piedmont, Italy. Came to Utah Nov. 30, 1856, Edward Martin handcart company.
Married Madeline Malan 1856 (daughter of Bartholomew and Mary Malan), who was born June 2, 1838. Their children: Henry Louis b. Dec. 8, 1857, d. 1878; Emily b. Oct. 6, 1859 (d. 1899), m. Stephen A. Browning Sept. 30, 1880; P. Edward b. Jan. 27, 1861, m. P. Isadora Allen Nov. 9, 1882; Alexander b. Feb. 1, 1866, m. Lola B. Allen Jan. 20, 1886; Bartholomew E. b. May 5, 1867, m. Albina Campbell Dec. 12, 1888. Family home Ogden, Utah.
Married Alice Johns, by whom he had one son.
Seventy. Farmer. Died July 18, 1900.

CHATELAIN, ALEXANDER (son of Peter Louis Chatelain and Madeline Malan). Born Feb. 1, 1866.
Married Lola B. Allen Jan. 20, 1886 (daughter of Elihu M. Allen and Mary Elizabeth Graham, former a pioneer Aug. 8, 1847, John Scott company). She was born July 1, 1868. Their children: Adelbert A. b. May 16, 1887, m. Gertie L. Shaw Sept. 1, 1908; Walter A. b. Aug. 3, 1889, m. Vesta Shaw Sept. 3, 1908; Edward M. b. Jan. 18, 1891, d. Aug. 1, 1892; Joseph L. b. Jan. 7, 1893; Mary E. b. May 21, 1896, d. 1895; Carl L. b. Oct. 18, 1899; Theodore B. b. May 15, 1903; Lola L. b. July 3, 1906; John M. b. March 16, 1912. Family home Ogden.
Member Weber stake Sunday school board; elder.

CHATTERTON, WILLIAM THOMAS (son of James Chatterton, born Oct. 23, 1813, Laughton, England, and Elizabeth Crofts, born Sept. 12, 1817, Everton, Eng.). He was born Nov. 16, 1842, Attercliffe, Yorkshire, Eng. Came to Utah Aug. 29, 1863, John R. Murdock company.
Married Mary Crossley Dec. 4, 1864 (daughter of John Crossley and Hannah Crabtree, former a pioneer 1863). She was born 1842 and came to Utah Sept. 25, 1863, Peter Nebeker company. Their children: Mary Elizabeth b. Aug. 14, 1865, m. James L. Daley Nov. 16, 1882; William James b. March 7, 1867; John b. Oct. 15, 1868; Hannah b. June 22, 1876; Maria b. Dec. 26, 1877; Ellen Rebecca b. Nov. 21, 1883. Family home Weston, Idaho.
Married Ellen Rebecca Howard June 15, 1882, Salt Lake City (daughter of John Howard), who was born Feb. 11, 1863, Rochdale, Eng.
Worked on the railroad 1868-69, and in woolen mills at Brigham City and Ogden, Utah, and Franklin, Idaho. Missionary to Oneida, Idaho, 1896-07. Appointed postmaster of Weston, Idaho, Dec. 10, 1908.

CHATWIN, WILLIAM (son of Joseph Chatwin). Born June 23, 1823, Bury, England. Came to Utah 1852.
Married Ann Sampson (daughter of Isaac Sampson). Only child: Joseph Isaac b. July 30, 1851, m. Arletta Carter July 23, 1872.
School teacher.

CHATWIN, JOSEPH ISAAC (son of William Chatwin and Ann Sampson). Born July 30, 1851, Kanesville, Iowa.
Married Arletta Carter July 23, 1872, Santaquin, Utah (daughter of William F. Carter and Roxena Mecham), who was born Sept. 6, 1855, Provo, Utah.

CHATTERLEY, JOHN (son of Joseph and Elizabeth Chatterley of Birmingham, Eng.). Born Dec. 1769, Birmingham, Eng. Came to Utah Sept. 25, 1851, John Brown company.
Married Ann Nuttall. Their children: Margaret b. Sept. 29, 1802; Joseph b. April 17, 1807, m. Nancy Morton; Mary b. Aug. 17, 1810; Helen b. June 16, 1812, m. Richard Sandiford; John b. Jan. 2, 1816; Sarah b. July 16, 1818, m. John Kay. Family home Radcliffe, Lancashire, Eng.

CHATTERLEY, JOSEPH (son of John Chatterley and Ann Nuttall). Born April 17, 1807, Bury, Lancashire.
Married Nancy Morton, at Pilkington, Eng. (daughter of Thomas Morton and Dorothy Seal), who was born Dec. 1806, Radcliffe, Eng. Their children: John b. July 4, 1835, m. Sarah Whittaker March 12, 1862; Ann b. March 3, 1837, m. J. M. Macfarlane Oct. 30, 1854; Morton b. March 3, 1840, m. Christina Mackelprang Feb. 1, 1862; Charlotte b. June 23, 1843, m. Thomas Walker Jan. 23, 1862. Family home Salford, Lancashire, Eng.
Married Catharine Clark, 1852, who was born Oct. 21, 1812, on the Isle of Man.
Lieutenant in territorial militia. Master wheelwright and blacksmith. Merchant.

CHATTERLEY, JOHN (son of Joseph Chatterley and Nancy Morton). Born July 4, 1835, Manchester, Eng.
Married Sarah Whittaker March 12, 1862, Cedar City, Utah (daughter of James Whittaker and Rachel Taylor, pioneers 1851, Morris Phelps company). She was born May 16, 1841, Heywood, Lancashire. Their children: Sarah Ellen b. Oct. 3, 1863, m. Caleb Haight June 24, 1891; Mary Joyce b. March 21, 1865, m. Richard H. Palmer April 27, 1891; Rachel Alice; Charlotte Ann b. Sept. 3, 1869, m. D. M. Perkins March 12, 1890; John Morton b. Jan. 23, 1871; Nancy May b. April 7, 1873, m. Edwin Walker Nov. 21, 1893; James Whittaker b. July 27, 1876; Martha Jane b. 1878; Catharine b. 1880. Family home Cedar City, Utah.
Mayor one term; postmaster 11 years; notary public 27 years; city recorder one term. Choir leader. Theatre manager.

CHEEVER, HENRY ALBERT (son of Amos Cheever and Abigail Chace Keech of Zanesville, R. I.). Born Nov. 7, 1826, Zanesville, R. I. Came to Utah Oct. 12, 1850, Edward Hunter company.
Married Mary Jane Nelson May 25, 1856, Salt Lake City (daughter of John Nelson and Agnes Ann Tennant of Ashton-Under-Lyne, Lancashire, Eng., latter a pioneer Oct. 8, 1853, Appleton Harmon company). She was born May 25, 1839. Their children: Agnes Abigail b. May 17, 1857, m. Christian Duseth; Mary Elizabeth b. April 19, 1859, m. John A. Brown; Sarah Jane b. March 20, 1861, m. Edward Rushton; Henry Albert b. Dec. 14, 1863, m. Margaret Ann Wright; Joseph Edwin b. Feb. 26, 1865, m. Grace Libby Smith; Caroline Augusta b. Dec. 8, 1866, m. John H. Dollen; John William b. Jan. 14, 1869, died; Lydia Maria b. July 16, 1871, m. A. H. Lavitra; Samuel Riter b. July 5, 1873, died; Ida Lenora b. Oct. 30, 1875, m. Samuel E. Hinckley. Family home Provo, Utah.
Member first quorum seventies; block teacher; high priest. Business man; gardener.

CHERRY, AARON BENJAMIN (son of John Cherry, born June 27, 1770, Huntington, Pa.). He was born Feb. 21, 1801, Hamilton county, Ohio. Came to Utah 1847.
Married Margaret Yelton June, 1827 (daughter of John Yelton), who was born Feb. 11, 1811. Their children: Rebecca Ann b. April 5, 1830, m. Nathan T. Porter Nov. 12, 1852; Jane b. Jan. 9, 1832, m. Jacob Winters; John James b. Jan. 13, 1834, m. Laura Bratton Oct. 25, 1856; Margaret b. March 11, 1836, m. Thomas Bratton May 6, 1856; Amelia Mariah b. May 9, 1838, m. William R. Smith May 6, 1856; Jesse Yelton b. June 10, 1842, d. May 21, 1865; Thomas b. Sept. 15, 1844; Caroline b. Aug. 4, 1846, m. Thomas Harris; Joseph b. 1847, m. Ellen Pender. Family home Centerville, Utah.

CHERRY, JOHN JAMES (son of Aaron Benjamin Cherry and Margaret Yelton). Born Jan. 13, 1834, Pendleton county, Ky.
Married Laura Bratton Oct. 25, 1856, Salt Lake City (daughter of George W. Bratton and Mary Graves, latter a pioneer Oct. 3, 1852, Harmon Cutler company). She was born Nov. 10, 1841. Their children: John James b. Oct. 16, 1867, m. Emeline Rich March 25, 1886; Mary Minetta b. Sept. 18, 1859, m. William H. Walton May 23, 1884; Jesse Yelton b. April 14, 1864, died; Aaron Benjamin b. Feb. 20, 1866; George Washington b. May 17, 1868, died; Thomas b. Sept. 27, 1870; Joseph Charles b. Dec. 19, 1874, died; Clarence Orvill b. May 31, 1878; Melvia Estella b. June 24, 1882. Family home Centerville, Utah.

CHERRY, JOHN JAMES, JR. (son of John James Cherry and Laura Bratton). Born Oct. 16, 1857, Centerville, Utah.
Married Emeline Rich March 25, 1886, Logan, Utah (daughter of Thomas Rich and Henriette Peck, former a pioneer 1850). She was born Jan. 11, 1868, Richville, Utah. Their children: Cora Emeline b. Feb. 8, 1887; Horace Rich b. May 28, 1889; Roland Lucian b. March 17, 1891, d. June 6, 1891; Henriette b. Sept. 23, 1893; Laura b. Feb. 28, 1897; Phoebe b. Nov. 30, 1898; Ann Amelia b. Jan. 31, 1901; John James, b. Oct. 20, 1904.

CHERRY, EBENEZER GRIFFIN. Born in Pennsylvania. Came to Utah 1847.
Married Mary Shumway at Logan, Utah (daughter of Charles Shumway and Wealthy Hicker, pioneers 1852). Their children: Charles; Thomas; Joseph b. 1865, m. Jennie Rideout; Wealthy; Clarissa; Margaret; Amanda; Porter; Levi; Samuel; Parley. Family home Lewiston, Utah.
Farmer. Died 1887.

CHERRY, JOSEPH (son of Ebenezer Griffin Cherry and Mary Shumway). Born 1865, in Utah.
Married Jennie Rideout 1896, Salt Lake City (daughter of John Rideout and Jane Terry, of Draper). She was born 1875. Their children: Wealthy b. 1898; Clarissa b. 1900; Griffin b. 1906; Joshua b. 1909; Cecil b. 1911. Family home Franklin, Idaho.

CHESHIRE, GEORGE (son of George Cheshire and Priscilla Evans of Kensworth, Herefordshire, Eng.). Born Dec. 16, 1822, Herefordshire. Came to Utah in September, 1863, independent oxteam company.
Married Elizabeth Keyse 1839 at Kensworth, Eng. (daughter of Thomas Keyse of Kensworth). She was born May 12, 1820. Their children: Mary Ann, m. Ralph Ramsey; Thomas, m. Mary Ann Elizabeth Abbott; Susan, m. Robert Golding; George, m. Sarah Maxeell; Eliza, m. John H. Brazier; William, m. Ella Rogers; Elizabeth, m. Samuel Baxter; Reuben, m. Mary ———. Family home Salt Lake City.
Married Elizabeth Turner at Logan, Utah (daughter of Catherine Turner). Their children: Charles, m. Emily ———; Maud, m. William Robinson; May, d. infant; Baby, d. infant; Baby, d. infant. Family home Salt Lake City.
High priest; teacher. Brickmaker and shoemaker. Died January, 1908, Huntington, Utah.

CHESHIRE, THOMAS (son of George Cheshire and Elizabeth Keyse). Born April 17, 1842, Kensworth, Eng. Came to Utah in December, 1864, oxteam company.
Married Mary Ann Elizabeth Abbott Jan. 7, 1866, Salt Lake City (daughter of William Abbott and Charlotte Ellerbons of Irchester, Northamptonshire, Eng., pioneers Sept. 15, 1865, Henry Chipman oxteam company). She was born Dec. 10, 1843. Their children: William G. b. April 13, 1867, m. Hattie Gustovesen; Thomas b. Nov. 12, 1869, d. aged 10 months; John R. b. Dec. 29, 1871, m. Caroline Batchelor; George b. Dec. 24, 1873, m. Sarah Bennett; Elizabeth b. Aug. 10, 1877, m. George Treseder; Charlotte b. Jan. 19, 1879, m. Horace Duncan; Sarah Jane b. Aug. 22, 1881, d. infant; Susan b. Aug. 2, 1883, m. John Westenskow; James Henry b. Aug. 21, 1887, m. Mabel Taylor; Hattie b. Nov. 4, 1891, d. aged 16. Family home Salt Lake City.
Elder. Worked on St. George temple. Marshal at Ferron, Utah, three terms; road supervisor; body guard of President Brigham Young and Daniel H. Wells 1875; policeman Salt Lake City. Experienced incessant Indian troubles while crossing the plains. Plasterer.

CHESLEY, ALEXANDER PHILIP (son of John Chesley and Elizabeth Brisker). Born Oct. 22, 1814, Fauquier county, Va. Came to Utah July 24, 1847, Brigham Young company.
Married Eliza Haws 1843 at Nauvoo, Ill. (daughter of Isabell Womack of Illinois, pioneer 1852). Their children: William Alexander, m. Matilda E. Robertson; John, m. Sarah Carter; Eliza Ellen, m. Nathan Barrett; James Edgar, m. Melissa A. Hamlin; Abner W., m. Jane Blair. Family home Provo, Utah.
Married Emily Haws (daughter of Isabell Womack). Their children: Emily, m. Joseph Nuttall; George B., m. Annie George; Martha, m. David Bowen; Frank, d. aged 14; Richard. Family home Provo.
Missionary to Australia 1856-57; elder. Constable at Provo 15 years. Member legislature from Fillmore. Farmer and stockraiser; lawyer. Died in Fauquier county, Va.

CHESLEY, WILLIAM ALEXANDER (son of Alexander Philip Chesley and Eliza Haws). Born Sept. 29, 1845, Sangamon county, Ill. Came to Utah 1852.
Married Matilda E. Robertson May 20, 1873 (daughter of James Robertson and Matilda Graham of Spanish Fork, Utah, pioneers Oct. 6, 1851, Alfred Cardon company). She was born May 6, 1856. Their children: Eliza b. March 26, 1874, m. Karl Olson; Matilda b. Jan. 14, 1876, m. Brigham Madsen; James A. b. Aug. 3, 1878; Grace D. b. Nov. 28, 1880, m. George E. Gordon; William Graham b. Feb. 14, 1883; Elmer b. July 7, 1885; Myrtle b. March 6, 1890, m. Albert J. Foulcer; Iva M. b. Aug. 14, 1892, d. aged 11; Paul R. b. Sept. 27, 1896. Family home Salt Lake City.
Seventy at Provo, Utah; ward teacher. Assistant city marshal of Provo City 20 years. Lumberman, farmer and stockraiser. Died March 27, 1910.

CHESLEY, JAMES A. (son of William A. Chesley and Matilda Robertson). Born Aug. 3, 1878, Provo, Utah. Resides at Salt Lake City.
Dairyman.

CHIDESTER, JOHN MADISON (son of John Madison Chidester). Born Jan. 22, 1809, Pompey, Onondaga county, N. Y. Came to Utah 1850.
Married Martha Parker in New York (daughter of Joshua Parker of New Haven, Conn.), who was born Aug. 2, 1809, Vernon, N. Y. Their children: John Peck, m. Susan Foy; David, m. Rebecca Ann Price; Eunice, m. Levi Harmon; Darwin, m. Caroline Goubler; Joshua Parker, m. Juliaette Burgess; Esther, m. William Pulsipher. Family home Spanish Fork, Utah.
Walker Indian war veteran. Carpenter and millwright. Died Aug. 30, 1893, Washington county, Utah.

CHIDESTER, JOHN PECK (son of John Madison Chidester and Mary Parker). Born Dec. 23, 1831, Somerfield, Monroe county, Mich. Came to Utah 1850.
Married Susan Foy Oct. 23, 1851, Salt Lake City (daughter of Thomas B. Foy and Catherine Fink, pioneers of 1851). She was born April 4, 1831, Wheatfield, Indiana county, Pa. Their children: John Foy b. Feb. 2, 1853, m. Almina Worthen; Susan Emma, m. George C. Dewey; Lodena Elizabeth, m. Amasa A. Ruby; Mary Catherine and Edgar, died; Emeline, m. Samuel Stewart; Evaline, m. Andrew Sprowl, Jr.; Myron, m. Sarah Ann Jackson. Family home Washington, Utah.
Bishop's counselor. Veteran Black Hawk Indian war. Carpenter and farmer. Died Jan. 10, 1897.

802 PIONEERS AND PROMINENT MEN OF UTAH

CHIDESTER, JOHN FOY (son of John Peck Chidester and Susan Foy). Born Feb. 2, 1853, Spanish Fork.
Married Mary Nicoll Oct. 22, 1874, St. George, Utah (daughter of Alexander and Sabina Nicoll), who was born March 22, 1856. Their children: Sabina b. Aug. 17, 1875, m. Steven Yates; Theodore b. May 17, 1877, m. Ida Sargent; John Nicoll b. Oct. 20, 1880, m. Elizabeth Workman; Mary Ceaveth b. Jan. 5, 1883, m. Elija Baker. Family home Washington, Utah.
Married Almina Worthen March 4, 1885, St. George (daughter of Samuel Worthen and Maria Louisa Grow), who was born Oct. 6, 1864. Their children: Worthen b. March 1, 1886, died; Almina b. July 7, 1887, m. Leonard Ogden; Samuel H. b. Oct. 11, 1889, m. Fern Dastrup; Aaron A. b. Nov. 6, 1891; Maria Louise b. Oct. 4, 1893; Fenton R. b. July 6, 1896; Susan Vera b. June 23, 1898; John Denzel b. Dec. 5, 1900; Thais E. b. Oct. 3, 1902; Alton Parker b. Jan. 25, 1905; Mae b. May 22, 1908, died. Family resided Panguitch and Richfield, Utah.
High priest; missionary to southern states 1889-90; Sunday school superintendent 1891-02. County clerk and recorder; county and district attorney ten years; city attorney and constable of Washington, each two years; member constitutional convention of Utah; member first state senate, and first state legislature, and land board.

CHIDESTER, JOSHUA PARKER (son of John Madison Chidester and Mary Parker). Born 1840, in Ohio. Came to Utah in 1853.
Married Juliaette Burgess 1861, Salt Lake City (daughter of William Burgess and Maria Pulsipher of Salt Lake City, pioneers Sept. 20, 1848, Brigham Young company). She was born in 1846. Their children: John William b. Nov. 25, 1864, m. Huldy Heath; Josephine b. Sept. 4, 1866, m. Jona than Hunt; Alfred G. b. Aug. 13, 1869, m. Sarah Susanna Hunt; Lafayette b. Sept. 25, 1871, m. Elsie Hicks; Parker Joshua b. Jan. 15, 1873, m. Althea Bunker; Juliaette b. 1875, d. infant; Esther Vilate b. Sept. 28, 1877, m. Raymond Burgess; Joseph Harrison b. April 3, 1879; Enoch b. May 3, 1881, m. Martha Heath; James b. Nov. 3, 1884, d. child; Charles b. June 27, 1887, m. Winnie Heath. Family home Pine Valley, Washington county, Utah.
Elder. Carpenter. Died April 17, 1894, Manti, Utah.

CHIDESTER, ALFRED G. (son of Joshua Parker Chidester and Juliaette Burgess). Born Aug. 13, 1869, Pine Valley, Utah.
Married Sarah Susanna Hunt Jan. 31, 1890, Richfield, Utah (daughter of Levi Hunt and Phebe Louisa of Nephi, pioneers of 1850). She was born Jan. 13, 1872. Their children: Phebe Louisa b. Dec. 1, 1891, m. Fayett Giles; Juliaette b. April 1, 1893; William Alfred b. Aug. 29, 1894; Amelia Emeline b. Feb. 23, 1896; Sarah May b. Oct. 30, 1897; Wanda D. b. April 8, 1900; Alta b. Oct. 13, 1901; Prealy b. April 8, 1904; Susanna b. June 25, 1905; Maria b. Feb. 21, 1907; Lovira b. May 13, 1909; Levi Parker b. Jan. 29, 1912. Family home Huntington, Utah.
Member 91st quorum seventies; elder. Farmer, carpenter and mason.

CHILD, JOHN (son of John Child and Deborah Steele of Middlesex, Eng.). Born Sept. 7, 1796, Middlesex, Eng. Came to Utah September, 1853, Moses Clawson company.
Married Eliza Newport in London, Eng. (daughter of Joseph Newport and Ann Wall, of London), who was born July 21, 1798. Their children: Jemima Elizabeth b. March 31, 1827, m. Enos Stookey; John, Jr., b. Oct. 9, 1831, d. infant; John Joseph b. Oct. 9, 1831, m. Elizabeth Ann De St. Geor; Mary Anne b. 1833 and James Newport b. 1836, d. infants; George Washington b. Jan. 2, 1839, died; Emma Eliza b. Aug. 13, 1841, m. David Henry Leonard. Family home Clover Creek, Tooele county, Utah.
Elder. Black Hawk Indian war veteran. Shoemaker, farmer and butcher. Died Feb. 1866.

CHILD, ALFRED BOSWORTH (son of Mark Anthony Child, born May 10, 1771, and Hannah Benedict, married Dec. 8, 1793). He was born Nov. 19, 1796, Greenfield, Saratoga county, N. Y. Came to Utah Oct. 1, 1852, Uriah Curtis oxteam company.
Married Polly Barber March 19, 1817 (daughter of Ichabod Barber and Anne Drake), who was born March 30, 1799, and came to Utah with husband; died Feb. 4, 1883. Their children: Polly Ann b. July 20, 1821, m. E. C. Richardson; Mark Alfred b. Oct. 19, 1823, died; Myron Barber b. Nov. 25, 1825, m. Emeline Elmer; Hannah Polina b. Jan. 24, 1828, m. William Elmer; John Lonson b. Oct. 28, 1830, m. Eliza J. Curtis; Phoebe Wooster b. Jan. 17, 1833, m. E. C. Richardson; Warren Gould b. Feb. 21, 1835, m. Hannah A. Wilder; Orville Rensselaer b. Oct. 11, 1837, m. Sarah Urinda Rawson. Family home Ogden, Utah.
Postmaster at Spring Prairie, Lee county, Iowa, 1841-47, until the persecutions of that time drove him westward. Settled in Weber county and started a sawmill. Died Dec. 22, 1852.

CHILD, MYRON BARBER (son of Alfred Bosworth Child and Polly Barber). Born Nov. 24, 1825, Hammond, St. Lawrence county, N. Y. Came to Utah Oct. 6, 1851.
Married Emeline Elmer Feb. 14, 1846 (daughter of Esquire and Lucy Elmer), who was born July 12, 1828. Their children: William W. b. Feb. 26, 1848, m. Jannette Fife Sept. 6, 1868; Asa L. b. Dec. 9, 1849, m. Sarah S. Grover; Alfred B. b. July 9, 1852, m. Sarah J. Stonebraker Oct. 8, 1872; Myron, Jr., b. July 3, 1854, d. Nov. 4, 1854; Mark A. b. Dec. 22, 1855, m. Eliza Wright; Emeline L. b. Nov. 21, 1858, m. Alexander Patterson 1875; Cynthia b. Dec. 14, 1860, m. Peter T. Nelson; John S. b. July 4, 1863, m. Susan Wadsworth; Chauncy b. Aug. 13, 1865, d. Aug. 6, 1878; Polly b. Nov. 13, 1868, m. William Allen; Henry J. b. Sept. 2, 1870, m. Maggie Stephens. Family resided Ogden and Riverdale, Utah.
Married Sarepta Jane Cole (daughter of William R. Cole and Nancy Sarepta Parrish), who was born Nov. 8, 1846, Iowaville, Iowa. Their children: Nathan b. Oct. 24, 1866, m. Julia (died) and Annie Wadsworth; Hannah b. July 12, 1868, m. William E. Stokes; Myron B. b. March 7, 1872, m. Caroline Carlsen; George C. b. Jan. 22, 1877, m. Etta M. Weaver Dec. 12, 1900; Emma T. b. July 26, 1879, d. Oct. 18, 1879; Drucilla b. Aug. 29, 1882, d. Sept. 15, 1882. Family resided Ogden and Riverdale, Utah.

CHILD, WILLIAM W. (son of Myron Barber Child and Emeline Elmer). Born Feb. 26, 1848, Lee county, Iowa.
Married Jannette Fife Sept. 6, 1868, Salt Lake City (daughter of Adam Fife and Ellen Sharp, pioneers Sept. 7, 1851). She was born March 1, 1851, St. Louis, Mo. Their children: William W. b. Aug. 30, 1869, d. Dec. 10, 1878; Myron B. b. Sept. 1, 1870, d. Dec. 7, 1890; Ellen b. April 1, 1873, m. John D. Hooper Dec. 21, 1899; John b. Nov. 21, 1875, d. Oct. 4, 1876; Mark A. b. Feb. 7, 1877, m. Emma Simpson April 28, 1897; Louisa E. b. June 5, 1879, m. Charles Towles Jan. 29, 1900; James O. b. Nov. 19, 1881, m. Blanche Manning Dec. 19, 1900; Vennetta b. April 1, 1884, m. John A. Martin Aug. 30, 1906; M. Evelean b. July 2, 1886, m. William Holmes Nov. 27, 1906; Jennie M. b. Nov. 18, 1888; Synthia b. Oct. 22, 1890, m. Heber Benz Oct. 26, 1910; Erbin L. b. April 18, 1884. Family resided Ogden and Riverdale, Utah.
Bishop of Hooper April 20, 1888, till present time. County commissioner Weber county 1889-90.

CHILD, JOHN L. (son of Alfred Bosworth Child and Polly Barber). Born Oct. 28, 1830, Greenfield, N. Y. Came to Utah Oct. 1, 1852, Capt. Uriah Curtis company.
Married Eliza J. Curtis Jan. 24, 1850, Pottawattamie county, Iowa (daughter of Uriah Curtis and Phebe Markin, of Ogden, Utah, pioneers Oct. 1, 1852). She was born April 30, 1830. Their children: Sarah A. b. Nov. 8, 1850; John L. b. March 3, 1852, m. Margaret Patterson; Mary R. b. Jan. 2, 1854, m. Cornelius T. Richmond; Charles Urich b. Nov. 21, 1855, m. Atelia A. Thompson; Lester A. b. Feb. 8, 1862, m. Emma Goodale. Family home Ogden, Utah.
Member 53rd quorum seventies. Farmer. Died Dec. 30, 1882, at Ogden.

CHILD, JOHN C. (son of John L. Child and Eliza J. Curtis). Born March 3, 1852, Council Bluffs, Iowa.
Married Margaret Patterson Oct. 4, 1875, Salt Lake City (daughter of Alexander Patterson and Mary Fife, of Riverdale, Weber county, Utah, pioneers 1851). She was born Oct. 13, 1858. Their children: Lettie b. Aug. 28, 1876; Mary E. b. May 12, 1878; Alice b. May 6, 1880; John b. Sept. 24, 1881; Ella M. b. July 9, 1883; E. A. b. July 17, 1885; Charles H. b. Feb. 6, 1887, drowned May 1, 1900; Andrew N. Jan. 5, 1890; Jennie R. b. May 2, 1892; Margaret A. b. Oct. 12, 1894; Florence b. Dec. 23, 1896; Lester A. b. Feb. 17, 1898; Adelbe b. Feb. 11, 1902. Family resided Riverdale and Roy, Utah.
Member 76th quorum seventies; first counselor to Bishop Sanford Bingham. County commissioner, 1895-1896; county road commissioner; director and superintendent of Davis and Weber county canal; member 1905 state legislature; superintendent county infirmary. Farmer; contractor of project construction.

CHILD, CHARLES URIAH (son of John L. Child and Eliza J. Curtis). Born Nov. 21, 1855, Ogden, Utah.
Married Atelia A. Thompson, at Riverdale, Utah (daughter of John C. Thompson of Riverdale). Their children: Charles C. b. June 5, 1878, m. Bessie Robinson; John L. b. June 12, 1882, m. Lenore Dwight; Vera, m. Francis F. Vanse; Colonel R. b. July 1, 1889, m. Stella Bingham; Mary Francelle b. April 5, 1890, d. aged 15; Georgia Atelia b. July 24, 1894. Family home Riverdale, Utah.
Farmer and contractor.

CHILD, WARREN GOULD (son of Alfred Bosworth Child and Polly Barber). Born Feb. 21, 1835, Greenfield, Saratoga county, N. Y. Came to Utah late father 1852.
Married Hannah A. Wilder Jan. 6, 1853 (daughter of Sally M. Wilder of Elba, Genesee county, N. Y.). She came to Utah 1852. Their children: Austin Wilder b. Feb. 11, 1854; m. Mary L. Thompson Oct. 28, 1872; Warren Gould, Jr., b. Aug. 15, 1856, m. Luella C. Chase Dec. 27, 1877; Hannah Maria; Rachel; Teresa; Henry Harrison; Heber Thomas, Julia Adelaide; Nella Dora; Jesse Alexander; Zilpha A.
In assisting to bring immigrants to Utah he crossed the plains in nine trips, five times with the most primitive means of locomotion, ox, cow and afoot.

CHILD, AUSTIN WILDER (son of Warren Gould Child and Hannah A. Wilder. Born Feb. 11, 1854, Ogden, Utah.
Married Mary L. Thompson Oct. 28, 1872 (daughter of John C. Thompson and Ann Clark, pioneers 1847). Their children: Ann Gertrude b. Feb. 18, 1875, d. Oct. 4, 1879; Austin b. Sept. 8, 1876, d. April 28, 1877; Hannah Elizabeth b. Nov. 25, 1877, d. Oct. 11, 1879; John Francis b. Feb. 8, 1879, m. Eva Noble of Oakland, Cal.; Raymond b. July 6, 1880, d. March 17, 1881; Earl Wilder b. April 22, 1882, m. Nettie Bra-

ley of Portland, Ore.; Florence Gladys b. Sept. 24, 1883, m. Frank W. Dice of Topeka, Kas., Jan. 15, 1902; Nell b. Jan. 2, 1886, m. Arthur Porter, Jr., of Rexburg, Idaho, June 24, 1908; Linzy Clark b. Aug. 14, 1887; Mary Alice b. Sept. 4, 1889; Matthew S. b. Jan. 9, 1892; Grace b. March 2, 1894; Cowley Warren b. Oct. 19, 1897. Family home Lima, Mont.

CHILD, WARREN GOULD, JR. (son of Warren Gould Child and Hannah A. Wilder). Born Aug. 15, 1856, in a wagon fifty miles east of Chimney Rock, Neb., while parents were crossing plains in one of their many return trips to the Missouri river.
Married Luella C. Chase Dec. 27, 1877, (daughter of Dudley Chase, pioneer 1848, and Samantha Crismon, pioneer 1847). Their children: Samantha Eloise, m. John Campbell; Warren Gerald, m. Julia Frank McGuire; Bessie Luella, m. Albert Purdy; Walter Dudley, m. Julia A. Taylor; Harold Lincoln; McLaren Chase.
Warren Gerald Child, the oldest son of Warren Gould Child, Jr., is now an ensign of the United States navy, commanding the U. S. S. Salmon, one of the new submarines.

CHILD, ORVILLE RENSSELAER (son of Alfred Bosworth Child and Polly Barber). Born Oct. 11, 1837, Ogdensburg, N. Y.
Married Sarah Urinda Rawson Feb. 3, 1859, Payson, Utah (daughter of Horace S. Rawson and Elizabeth Coffin, pioneers Oct. 1850, Wilford Woodruff company). She was born Feb. 8, 1844, Lima, Hancock county, Ill. Their children: Orville Rensselaer b. Jan. 8, 1860, m. Eunice Ellen Dewey Dec. 23, 1880; Sarah Annie b. Nov. 14, 1861, m. J. C. Dewey, Jr., Jan. 24, 1879; William Alfred b. April 3, 1864, m. Amanda Taylor Nov. 24, 1885; Polly Erminnie b. May 5, 1866, m. Levi Richardson April 17, 1883; Elizabeth b. Aug. 11, 1868, d. Feb. 11, 1871; Mary Eliza b. April 11, 1872, m. A. M. Harmon Sept. 25, 1892; Hannah Luella b. Oct. 15, 1874, m. John D. Wilkes Oct. 16, 1894; Ida Luetta b. May 19, 1877, m. Edgar Roberts Oct. 20, 1897; Edward Rawson b. Jan. 24, 1880, d. Aug. 27, 1903; Chloe Urinda b. Oct. 5, 1882, m. F. M. Hoopes Feb. 4, 1904; Horace Ezra b. Sept. 24, 1884, m. Jane Taggart Sept. 14, 1905; John Elmer b. April 10, 1888, died; Elva Pearl b. April 20, 1890, m. Robert M. Read Nov. 18, 1911. Family home Ogden, Utah.
Assisted in bringing immigrants to Utah, making two return trips east and fighting Indians who attacked along the way. Fought in Salmon River Indian trouble. Filled a five years' mission among the Indians of Malad valley; first counselor to John Cooke Dewey at Deweyville, Utah. In 1877, and to John Cyrus Dewey of Star Valley, Wyo., 1887. Took part in Echo Canyon trouble. Died March 27, 1897, Star Valley, Wyo.

CHILD, ORVILLE RENSSELAER, JR. (son of Orville Rensselaer Child and Sarah Urinda Rawson). Born Jan. 8, 1860, Ogden, Utah.
Married Eunice Ellen Dewey Dec. 23, 1880, Salt Lake City (daughter of John Cooke Dewey and Mary Allen, pioneers 1854 and 1852, respectively). She was born May 10, 1861, Call's Fort, Utah. Their children: Mary Ellen b. Nov. 6, 1881, m. Seymore B. Allred May 22, 1901; Effie Urinda b. March 4, 1884, m. Edward Sessions; Orville Rawson b. Dec. 22, 1885, m. Bertha Van Noy June 22, 1909; Annie Eugenia b. Dec. 23, 1887; John Rensselaer b. May 20, 1890; Eunice Emma b. March 5, 1894; Edna Verba b. March 31, 1897. Family home Fairview, Wyo.
Postmaster Deweyville, Utah, 1882-85, when he moved to Plain City, then to Ogden in 1888. Settled at Fairview, Star valley, Wyo., 1894. Superintendent Sunday school and president Y. M. M. I. A. at Deweyville, Utah, and Fairview, Wyo., for a number of years.

CHIPMAN, STEPHEN (son of Barnabus Chipman of England). Born Aug. 8, 1805, Leeds county, Canada. Came to Utah Sept. 23, 1847, Abraham Owen Smoot company.
Married Amanda Washburn in Canada (daughter of Stephen Washburn and Miss Sexton of Leeds county, Canada). She was born Sept. 8, 1805. Their children: Washburn, m. Mindwell Houston; m. Margaret Vance McNichol; m. Caroline Mayhew; Beulah, m. David Grant; Sinah, m. John Eldredge; William Henry, m. Martha Smith; James, m. Sarah Green; Martha, m. Theodore Herrington. Family home American Fork, Utah.
Farmer and stockraiser. Died in February, 1868.

CHIPMAN, WASHBURN (son of Stephen Chipman and Amanda Washburn). Born April 16, 1829, Leeds county, Canada. Came to Utah Oct. 20, 1847.
Married Mindwell Houston Nov. 1855, Alpine, Utah (daughter of Isaac Houston and Theodocia Keyes of Alpine, Utah, pioneers 1851, Captain Riggs company). Their children: Mindwell, m. Oscar F. Hunter; Louisa, m. John Hurbert; Amanda, m. George D. Chipman; Elizabeth, m. George Barney; James; Henry; Washburn and Isaac, died.
Married Margaret Vance McNichol Oct. 6, 1860, Salt Lake City (daughter of Alexander McNichol and Mary Ann Vance of Jackson, Tenn., both died on plains en route to Utah). She was born Dec. 10, 1840, and came to Utah Sept. 17, 1852, Thomas J. McCullough company. Their children: Sinah, m. Thaddeus King; Beulah, m. William Bromley; Celestia; Stephen, m. Ella Thornton; John W., m. Jane Clarke; Sidy, m. F. J. Noyes; Rhoda Adora, died; Martha; Thomas Jefferson; Melva; Romania, died.
Married Caroline Abigail Mayhew at Salt Lake City (daughter of Elijah Mayhew and Lydia Farnsworth of Pleasant Grove, pioneers Sept. 9, 1853, Daniel A. Miller company). Their children: Otto, m. Martha Hubbard; Lydia, m. Fred Houston; Walter; Luella, m. Mr. Montieth. Families resided American Fork, Utah.
President 67th quorum seventies; missionary to Iowa and Missouri 1870-71. Director and one of organizers of Z. C. M. I. and Provo Woolen Mills. Captain in Nauvoo Legion. Settled at American Fork 1850; called to help settle Iron county 1851; director in American Fork Co-op. Assisted in building the Parowan canal, first one in that country; it was nine miles long. One of the directors of County Co-op. Herd. Indian war veteran.

CHIPMAN, JAMES (son of Stephen Chipman and Amanda Washburn). Came to Utah Sept. 23, 1847.
Married Sarah Green at American Fork (daughter of Alphonso Green and Betsy Murdock of American Fork). Their children: James; Alphonso G., m. Fannie Dilworth; Stephen L., m. Sinah Nelson; Betsy, m. Richard Preston. Family home American Fork.
Mayor of American Fork. Merchant and banker.

CHIPMAN, WILLIAM HENRY (son of Stephen Washburn Chipman). Born 1834. Came to Utah 1847.
Married Eliza Filcher at American Fork, Utah (daughter of Thomas Filcher), who was born Feb. 18, 1840, in England. Their children: W. H., m. Elizabeth Parker; S. W., m. Sarah Southwick; Thomas J., m. ———; ———, m. Robert Booth; Jelphia, m. C. Beck; Leah; Squire, m. E. E. Adams; Eliza, m. A.———; Maude.

CHIPMAN, THOMAS J. (son of William Henry Chipman and Eliza Filcher). Born 1864, at American Fork, Utah.
Married Emily M. ——— at Logan, Utah (daughter of Eugene Alfonso ——— and Mary Thora Millett, former came to Utah with Captain Wheelock company, latter of Devonshire, Eng.). She was born 1871. Their children: Thomas Lester b. Feb. 17, 1890; Myron H. b. Sept. 17, 1891; Glen b. March 31, 1895; Arnold b. Dec. 27, 1901; Eugene b. Jan. 30, 1903; Frances L. b. April 5, 1909; Lucie.
Teacher; seventy. Assisted in building up American Fork. Farmer and stockraiser.

CHISLETT, JAMES (son of James Chislett and Lucy Ridley of Trowbridge, Wiltshire, Eng.). Born July 3, 1834, at Trowbridge. Came to Utah Oct. 19, 1862, Horton D. Haight company.
Married Mary Maria Harding Sept. 27, 1860, Wiltshire (daughter of Edward Harding and Mary Offer of Trowbridge, Eng.). She was born Aug. 9, 1836. Family home Provo, Utah.
Member 34th quorum seventies; high priest. Warper for Provo Woolen Mills. Died May 30, 1906, Provo, Utah.

CHISHOLM, WILLIAM WALLACE (son of Robert Chisholm of Elgin, Ill.). Born June 1841 in Wisconsin. Came to Utah in 1864.
Married Jennet Kendall in Illinois (daughter of John Kendall and Lillian Grant of Polo and Galena, Ill., who came to Utah 1884). She was born Sept. 18, 1843. Family home Salt Lake City.
Original opener of the Emma mine in Cottonwood canyon; principal owner in Centennial Eureka; mining man. Died March 18, 1909, Los Angeles, Cal.

CHITTOCK, SAMUEL (son of John Chittock and Ann Bloomfield of Hopton, Suffolk, Eng.). Born 1834, Livingston, Cambridgeshire, Eng. Came to Utah Aug. 8, 1869.
Married Margaret James Aug. 11, 1851, London, Eng. (daughter of David James and Margaret Gewey of London). She was born June 21, 1831. Family home 1st ward, Salt Lake City.
General blacksmith and gardener.

CHRISTENSEN, A. C. (son of Christen Christensen and Maren Andersen). Born Aug. 17, 1829, in Denmark. Came to Utah in 1862.
Married Ane Magrete Simonsen in Utah (daughter of Ole Simonsen of Bear River City, Utah, pioneer Oct. 28, 1866, Andrew H. Scott company). She was born Sept. 20, 1846. Only child: Rasmine, d. 1869. Family home Bear River City, Utah.
Ordained high priest 1895. Died April 7, 1902.

CHRISTENSEN, ANDREW (son of Christen Andersen and Katherine Jensen). Born Nov. 19, 1830, Copenhagen, Denmark. Came to Utah 1860, Oscar O. Stoddard company.
Married Nellie Widenberg, Sept., 1860, Mt. Pleasant, Utah, who was born 1839. Their children: Nicholine b. Oct. 24, 1861, m. Martin Rasmussen; Andrew b. Jan. 13, 1863, m. Caroline Larsen; David b. June 18, 1865, m. Christina Andersen Sweet; Christian b. 1868, d. child; Nephi b. Dec. 3, 1870,

m. Elsie Sorensen; Christine b. March 24, 1872, m. Frederick Moore; Hilda b. May 19, 1874, m. Jens Larsen; Jacob and Isaac, twins, d. infants. Family home Mt. Pleasant, Utah.
High priest; missionary to Denmark. Black Hawk Indian war veteran. Bricklayer and mason.

CHRISTENSEN, ANDREW, JR. (son of Andrew Christensen and Nellie Widenberg). Born June 13, 1863, Mt. Pleasant, Utah.
Married Caroline Larsen Dec. 21, 1888, Castle Dale, Utah (daughter of Hans Frederick Larsen and Julia Andersen of Castle Dale, who came to Utah 1874). She was born May 27, 1869. Their children: Nellie b. Jan. 27, 1890, m. Alvin Larsen; Eva b. July 12, 1892, m. Willis Ely; Andrew Emeal b. Oct. 19, 1894; Rollen b. April 19, 1897; Nephi b. July 3, 1899; Calvin b. Oct. 2, 1901; Huchie and Drewie (twins) b. Dec. 31, 1903; William G. B. b. Nov. 12, 1906; Hans Frederik b. March 23, 1909; Julia Ione b. April 17, 1912. Family home Sunnyside, Utah.
Elder. Road supervisor of Emery county 1897; settled at Castle Dale, where he assisted in building roads and irrigation ditches; preparer of miners' safety lamps for mines No. 1 and No. 4 of Utah Fuel Company.

CHRISTENSEN, CASPER (son of Christen Hansen and Boletta Marie Mathews). Born Sept. 5, 1837, Trondberg, Druning Lundsogn, Hjorring amt, Denmark. Came to Utah 1875.
Married Maren Christensen Lund 1866, Lyngbysogn, Aalborg amt, Denmark (daughter of Christian and Johanna Lund, of Terndsup, Lyngby). She was born Aug. 1, 1842, and came to Utah with husband. Their children: Johannas, died; Johanna b. Nov. 22, 1868, m. Isaac Allred; Hans C. b. Dec. 28, 1870, m. Elizabeth Christina Williams; Mary b. Jan. 16, 1873, m. Severene Albertsen; Sena b. April 4, 1875, m. John S. Lewis; Annie b. Nov. 14, 1877, m. John P. Nielsen; Bentena Cecila b. Jan. 29, 1881, m. C. T. Williams; Belletta Marie b. Aug. 26, 1883, m. Frank Pettey; Harriette Pauline b. Dec. 17, 1885. Family home Emery, Utah.
Married Johannah Maria Larson (Nielsen) Aug. 27, 1890, Manti, Utah (daughter of John Peter Larson and Annie Cecilia Bang, of Isteruttrup, Norsetranderssogn, Denmark). She was born June 16, 1854, and came to Utah 1877. Their children: Dertha Kistina b. June 11, 1891, m. Wilford Ervin Wilson; Minnie b. March 17, 1893, m. Henning Benjamin Olsen; Casper b. March 29, 1895; George b. Jan. 31, 1897, d. aged 11 years. Family home Emery.
President high priests' quorum Emery ward; bishop Emery ward ten years; ward teacher. Road supervisor ten years. Postmaster at Muddy. School trustee nine years. Farmer, stockraiser and apiarist.

CHRISTENSEN, CHRISTEN (son of Christen Christensen and Ane Katrine Lausen of Denmark). Born June 4, 1808, Ostrup, Aalborg, Denmark. Came to Utah Sept. 23, 1862, Christian A. Madsen company.
Married Buletta Sorensen (daughter of Soren Mortensen and Mette Nielsen), who was born Oct. 28, 1816. Their children: Christen b. March 11, 1843, m. Johaner Tomesen Feb. 17, 1867; Soren b. Nov. 1, 1844, m. Karlin Nielsen Feb. 21, 1870; Niels Christian b. Feb. 5, 1847, m. Johaner Tomesen 1887; Anthony b. Feb. 20, 1849, m. Castine Lovell April 14, 1873; Annie b. April 26, 1851, m. Christian Anderson April 17, 1871; Mette Christene b. 1853; Lauriz b. 1856.

CHRISTENSEN, ANTHONY (son of Christen Christensen and Buletta Sorensen. Born Feb. 20, 1849, Ostrup, Aalborg amt, Denmark. Came to Utah with father.
Married Castine Lovell April 14, 1873, Salt Lake City (daughter of John Lovell and Annie Gorgenson, former pioneer 1850, latter Oct. 5, 1854, Hans Peter Olsen company). She was born March 6, 1858. Their children: Christian b. March 6, 1874, m. Mary Jacobson Nov. 28, 1897; Annie Mette b. Dec. 17, 1875, m. Joseph Talbot Nov. 24, 1893; John A. b. Aug. 12, 1877, m. Frances E. Horward Nov. 21, 1896; Joseph M. b. June 7, 1880, m. Tillie Surilla Curtis June 24, 1903; Niels H. b. Jan. 23, 1882, m. Josephine Sorenson Feb. 8, 1906; Elizabeth S. b. Aug. 12, 1883, m. Joseph P. Colliater May 16, 1907; Edward P. b. March 29, 1885, m. Ida Bennett Sept. 11, 1912; Lorenzo H. b. Jan. 2, 1887; Willard R. b. March 10, 1889; Albert C. b. Sept. 2, 1891; Silva B. b. Nov. 4, 1894; Mary Pearl b. Feb. 26, 1896; Hilda C. b. Sept. 1, 1898; Anthony L. b. March 18, 1904. Family home Oak City, Utah.
Member council 3d quorum seventies and became its senior president Feb. 1, 1909; Sunday school superintendent 1888-91; missionary to Denmark 1891-93; home missionary at Scipio in 1906.

CHRISTENSEN, FREDERIK. Born in 1824, near Copenhagen, Denmark. Came to Utah Sept. 1862, Capt. Van Cott company.
Married Dorthea Sophia Thiessen about 1848 in Denmark. Their children: Anna Sophia b. Nov. 8, 1849, m. James Jensen; Soren S. b. 1861, m. Cammila Olsen.
First counselor to president of Bear River branch of Box Elder.

CHRISTENSEN, HANS (son of Christen Larsen, born Aug. 18, 1805, Gunderup, Hjorring, Denmark and Gjertrud Hansdatter, born Oct. 2, 1808, Rakkeby, Hjorring, Denmark, married in 1836). He was born Feb. 20, 1840, Rakkeby, Denmark. Came to Utah Sept. 27, 1862, John R. Murdock company.

Married Christiane S. Christensen Oct. 13, 1859. Their children: Anton b. Sept. 17, 1860, m. Maren Hansen; Mary L. b. Nov. 14, 1862, m. Chrest Peterson; Emma Margaret b. June 10, 1865, m. Alvin Stander; Lars C. b. April 21, 1868, m. Emilie Jorgensen; Erastus b. Feb. 24, 1871, m. Emma Larsen; Anna Marie b. Feb. 22, 1873, m. Isaac Burnhope; Orson Lorenzo b. Nov. 21, 1875, d. Sept. 3, 1892. Family home Bear River City, Utah.
Bishop's counselor many years. Died Jan. 19, 1903.

CHRISTENSEN, LARS NIELS (son of Niels Christiansen, born 1775, Meleby, Frederiksborg, Denmark, and Ellen Jorgensen, born Sept. 9, 1792, Evetofte, Frederiksborg, Denmark, married Oct. 4, 1811). He was born Aug. 11, 1812. Came to Utah Sept. 25, 1868, John G. Holman company.
Married Maren Kirstena Jorgensen (daughter of Jorgen Nielson and Karen Hansen, married 1817, Craguma, Frederiksborg amt). She was born Feb. 3, 1818. Their children: Karen Marie b. Jan. 8, 1853, m. Peter C. Jensen Aug. 16, 1876; Bertha Katrina b. Aug. 1, 1854; Dorthea b. Jan. 21, 1856; Anna C. Jan. 21, 1856; Jeppa J. b. Feb. 26, 1859. Family resided Brigham City and Newton, Utah.
Married Karen Margretta Larson April, 1869, Salt Lake City (daughter of Hans Larson and Karen Petersen, married 1838 at Meleby, Frederiksborg amt). She was born Jan. 9, 1839, at Meleby, Denmark. Their children: Lorenzo b. Dec. 1, 1872; Caroline Marie b. Nov. 30, 1875; Elizabeth M. b. Dec. 19, 1876.
Presided over Scandinavian organization of Newton ward several years. Died Sept. 10, 1890, Newton, Utah.

CHRISTENSEN, LARS PETER (son of Christen Larsen, born Aug. 18, 1805, Vreilev sogn, Hjorring amt, Denmark, and Gjertrud Hansdatter, born Oct. 2, 1808, Rakkeby, Hjorring amt). He was born Jan. 17, 1837, Vreilev, Denmark. Came to Utah Sept. 22, 1861, Samuel A. Woolley independent company.
Married Anne Marie N. Lee May 16, 1861 (daughter of Christian Nielsen Lee and Inger Magensen, former died 1865, Vreilev sogn, Denmark, latter a pioneer 1866). She was born Oct. 31, 1840, and came to Utah with husband. Their children: Peter b. Sept. 25, 1862, m. Isabeli D. Young; Christian b. Sept. 3, 1864, d. Oct. 2, 1876; Annie Christina b. Oct. 7, 1866, m. Joseph H. Thurber; Joseph L. b. June 24, 7, 1876, m. Julia Rasmussen; Emma Gjertrud b. Nov. 14, 1870, d. Nov. 20, 1876; Martha b. July 28, 1873, d. Jan. 9, 1877; Sarah b. March 17, 1876, m. H. J. Hansen; Alma b. June 27, 1878, m. Emily F. Moore. Family resided Farmington and North Kaysvreek, Utah.
Married Ane Marie (Mary) Petersen Sept. 8, 1866, Milton, Utah (daughter of Soren Petersen and Ane Magrethe Baltyersen, pioneers Sept. 5, 1863, John F. Sanders company). She was born Dec. 6, 1847, near Aarhuus, Denmark. Their children: George b. July 4, 1867, m. Hannah Eliza Greer; Hyrum S. b. Sept. 26, 1869, m. Elisabet Maria Hansen; Printha Levina b. Oct. 5, 1871, m. M. L. Brown; Ane Elisa b. April 30, 1874, m. John W. Ross; William Wester b. Oct. 7, 1876, m. Minerva Jensen; Mazgrie Mathilda b. Oct. 10, 1879, m. Hans P. Hansen April 26, 1899; Mary Rebecca b. July 7, 1884, m. John James Barton; Leo Carlos b. Feb. 21, 1887; Chester Hugh b. Oct. 24, 1889. Family resided Milton and Richfield, Utah.
Married Karen J. A. Jacobsen Dec. 13, 1883, Richfield (daughter of Andreas Jacobsen and Helena Larsen, former died 1888, in Denmark, latter came to Utah 1892, and died April 25, 1908). She was born Nov. 27, 1863, Astrup, Denmark. Their children: Helena b. June 13, 1885, m. B. Albern Allen; Lehi Peter b. Jan. 22, 1887; May Zather b. Dec. 25, 1888; Nephi Wilford b. Sept. 18, 1892; Heber Miller b. May 30, 1894, d. July 18, 1902; Mathew b. May 11, 1899, d. Oct. 26, 1899; Andrew b. May 11, 1899, d. Sept. 23, 1899; Ellen Vilate b. Nov. 23, 1903. Family home Richfield, Utah.
Presided over Milton branch of L. D. S. church ten years; counselor to Charles Peterson at that place; first counselor to Bishop Poul Poulsen of 1st ward 12 years; missionary to Denmark 1881-83, and president of Hjorring and Aalborg branches each one year. Captain in Utah militia. Settled at Milton 1863, and engaged in blacksmithing, farming and sawmilling; furnished ties and timber for U. P. R. R. Moved to Richfield 1875, and there joined the United Order and was elected a member of the board, and later its president.

CHRISTENSEN, NIELS (son of Chresten Andersen, born 1808, Rorbek, Jutland, Denmark, and Matte Marie Andersen, born Dec. 5, 1809, Jutland, Denmark). He was born July 11, 1842, Hvilsom, Jutland. Came to Utah 1864, Sharp and Spencer company.
Married Ane Marie Nielsen (daughter of Soren Nielsen and Ane Margrete Nielsen, pioneers Aug. 26, 1864). She was born Nov. 2, 1850. Their children: Niels Christian b. April 5, 1868, m. Tomine Marie Thompsen Feb. 26, 1890; Margaret Mariane b. May 6, 1870, m. Anton Nielsen Nov. 11, 1889; Ephraim Erastus b. Feb. 24, 1872, d. Nov. 22, 1894; Joseph Hyrum b. June 2, 1874, m. Hannah Thompsen 1898; Andrew Burten b. Oct. 27, 1876, m. Martine Mickelsen May 6, 1826; Delsine Eleonore b. Dec. 4, 1878, d. March 31, 1892; Dianthe Sophia b. Jan. 9, 1881, d. July 2, 1896; Peter Rudolph b. Nov. 25, 1883; James Marion b. March 24, 1886, m. Dorthelle Hansen June 29, 1910; John Precious b. Aug. 12, 1888, d. 1888. Family home Salina, Utah.
High priest. Farmer and blacksmith.

CHRISTENSEN, NIELS CHRISTIAN (son of Niels Christensen and Ane Maria Nielsen). Born April 5, 1868, Ephraim, Utah.
Married Tomine Marie Thompsen Feb. 26, 1890, Manti, Utah (daughter of Lars Peter and Kirsten Thompsen), who was born Dec. 23, 1869, Vendsyssel, Denmark. Their children: Niels Edward b. Jan. 4, 1891; James b. Feb. 1893; Tomine b. Sept. 1895; Walter b. Aug. 1898; Irene b. 1901; Ephraim b. 1907. Family home Salina, Utah.
Elder. Miner; train repairer.

CHRISTENSEN, NIELS (son of Christen Nielsen and Anne Marie Johansen of Stabrand, Randers amt, Denmark). Born Dec. 11, 1816, Stabrand, Denmark.. Came to Utah 1860.
Married Christine ———. Their children: Christian b. 1843, m. Karen ———; Christen b. 1845, m. Mina Petersen; Anna Marie b. 1847; Niels b. 1849, m. Anna Petersen. Family home Stabrand, Denmark.
Married Christine Johansen, who was born in Denmark. Their children: Joseph; Sophia b. Dec. 17, 1862, m. Lars Sorensen; Dorthe Christiane b. Aug. 8, 1864, m. Joseph Barstow; Samuel b. 1866; John b. 1868.
Married Christene Andersen Nov. 7, 1863, Salt Lake City (daughter of Anders Larsen and Kristen Petersen), who was born Oct. 28, 1843, in Denmark. Their children: Andrew b. May 23, 1865, m. Aldine C. Wilson 1889; Mary Anne Christene b. Sept. 2, 1867, m. Joseph J. Jensen 1889; Ezra b. July 18, 1869, m. May Killian 1900; Heber b. Aug. 25, 1871, m. Emma Nielson 1897; Joseph b. March 19, 1873; Hyrum b. Dec. 25, 1875, m. Lucy C. Wilson 1899; Nephi Levi b. Nov. 21, 1877; Wilford M. b. Oct. 24, 1879, m. Harriet Birdie Bates Oct. 11, 1904; Orsen b. May 14, 1891. Family resided Hyrum, Utah.
High priest.

CHRISTENSEN, WILFORD M. (son of Niels Christensen and Christene Andersen). Born Oct. 24, 1879, at Hyrum.
Married Harriet Birdie Bates Oct. 11, 1904, Salt Lake City (daughter of Ormes Eaton Bates and Augusta Eleason, pioneers 1862-63 respectively). She was born Dec. 8, 1886, Hyrum, Utah. Their children: Leatha b. Sept. 7, 1905; Harriet Lorrain b. May 11, 1907; Alice Augusta b. April 24, 1909; Genevieve Christene b. April 24, 1911. Family home Goshen, Bingham county, Idaho.
Missionary to Copenhagen 1900-03; member high council Blackfoot stake 1904; bishop Goshen ward 1906.

CHRISTENSEN, NEILS C. Born Feb. 6, 1832, Taars parish, Hjorring amt, Denmark. Came to Utah 1862.
Married Bertie Marie Sornson Nov. 11, 1853, in Denmark (daughter of Hans Sornson). Their children: Mary Ann, m. Carl C. Johnson; Hannah M., m. Joseph Newbold. Family home Smithfield, Utah.
Member 64th quorum seventies; missionary to Denmark; high priest; high counselor; Sunday school superintendent. Farmer. Died April, 1898, Lyman, Idaho.

CHRISTENSEN, PETER (son of Christian and Annie Cathaline Christensen). Born Aug. 26, 1833, Jutland, Denmark. Came to Utah in 1860.
Married Sophia M. Christensen 1852, North Bend, Utah (daughter of Christian Christensen and Ana Sophia Sorensen of Orep, Copenhagen, Denmark, pioneers 1860). She was born March 10, 1833. Their children: John Andrew; Parley Parker; Arthur Eugene, m. Christina Johnson; Elinora Blythe, m. John Russell Lamfiman; Florence Matilda; Lawrence Adolfus; Ester Sophia, m. Thur Cronholm. Family home Newton, Utah.
County commissioner and postmaster many years. Farmer.

CHRISTENSEN, PARLEY PARKER (son of Peter and Sophia M. Christensen). Born July 19, 1869, Weston, Idaho.
County superintendent schools two terms in Tooele county; first city attorney of Grantsville; secretary constitutional convention of Utah; Salt Lake county attorney. Attorney-at-law.

CHRISTENSEN, PETER CHRISTEN (son of Christen Nielsen and Maren Andersen). Born June 8, 1830, Asaa, Hjorring, Denmark. Came to Utah 1861.
Married Ane Kirstine Larsen 1849 in Denmark (daughter of Lars Sorensen and Bendine Rasmussen), who was born June 27, 1827. Their children: Ane Bendine, Cecelia Marie and Jens, died; Niels Christen, m. Elmyra Matilda Bunce, m. Hannah Bourdier; Larsine Bendine, m. Christen R. Nielsen; Joseph T. C., died; Hyrum, m. Ingra Gregerson, m. Elsena Sorensen; Peter, m. Laura Luella Bunce. Family home Mayfield, Utah.
Member 65th quorum seventies; high priest; ward teacher; missionary to Denmark 1872-74, and presided over Aalborg conference; again 1891-93, and 1895-97. First lieutenant to Warren S. Snow in Black Hawk Indian war. Mail carrier; farmer and sheepraiser. Died Nov. 24, 1908, Mayfield, Utah.

CHRISTENSEN, PETER (son of Peter Christen Christensen and Ane Kirstine Larsen). Born July 29, 1879, Manti, Utah.
Married Laura Luella Bunce Aug. 9, 1888, Manti (daughter of Lewis DeMott Bunce, born Sept. 29, 1827, Wolcott,

806 PIONEERS AND PROMINENT MEN OF UTAH

Wayne county, N. Y., and Elmyra Vorhees, born June 30, 1834, Hamilton county, Ohio, both of Wolcott, N. Y., pioneers 1852). She was born Sept. 8, 1870, Parowan, Utah.
President 149th quorum seventies; missionary to Denmark 1896-98; assistant Sunday school superintendent Emery stake. President Emery town board; school trustee 1904-08. Farmer.

CHRISTENSEN, RASMUS (son of Christen Christensen and Meta Rasmussen). Born Sept. 23, 1829, Aalborg, Denmark. Came to Utah Sept. 30, 1853, John Forsgren company.
Married Priscilla V. Mitchell (daughter of Hezekiah Mitchell and Sarah Malison), who was born Oct. 19, 1839, and came to Utah Sept. 29, 1854, James Brown company. Only child: Rasmus H. b. May 23, 1868, m. Nancy Melvina Bennett Sept. 19, 1889.

CHRISTENSEN, RASMUS H. (son of Rasmus Christensen and Priscilla V. Mitchell). Born May 23, 1868, Huntsville, Utah.
Married Nancy Melvina Bennett Sept. 19, 1889, Hooper, Utah (daughter of George Bennett and Nancy Melvina Taylor, former a pioneer 1852, Warren Snow company, latter 1848, Allen Taylor company). She was born in 1873, at Harmony, Utah. Their children: Nancy Elvira b. June 29, 1890, m. J. Edwin Thompson Oct. 5, 1910; Ethel Lovisa b. Dec. 28, 1891; Myrtle Chestina b. Nov. 25, 1893; Edsel Hezekiah b. Nov. 4, 1895; Irene Pearl b. Dec. 1, 1897; Wilford George b. June 30, 1900; Afton Priscilla b. July 18, 1902; Cora Naomi b. April 11, 1904; Clarence Earl b. May 27, 1906; Clover Bennett b. April 21, 1908; William Harvey b. July 10, 1911, d. same day. Family home Downey, Idaho.
Farmer and stockraiser.

CHRISTIANSEN, CHRISTIAN PETER (son of Christian Larsen and Ingeborah Kirstine Nielson). Born Aug. 18, 1838, Norre Sundby, Hjorring amt, Denmark. Came to Utah Sept. 12, 1861, John R. Murdock company.
Married Kirstine Marie Murman Sept. 28, 1856 (daughter of Abraham Godfred Murman and Karen Marie Skaksen), who was born May 30, 1838, and came to Utah with husband. Their children: Caroline b. April 7, 1857, m. Hyrum S. Washburn; Godfred Abraham Murman b. Sept. 14, 1861, m. Lydia Ziegelman Nov. 20, 1885; Peter b. Dec. 13, 1865, m. Edna Adams 1903. Family resided San Pete and Sevier counties, Utah.
Married Caroline Nazer July 8, 1865, Salt Lake City (daughter of Rudolph Nazer and Mary Ann Gonsour, pioneers Oct. 31, 1862, William H. Dame company). She was born Oct. 24, 1844, Zurich, Switzerland. Their children: Caroline Amelia b. Jan. 3, 1867, d. Oct. 7, 1867; Christina Maria b. Nov. 19, 1869, m. Lyman J. Collings; Martha Rosella b. Oct. 9, 1871, m. Erastus Johnson; Josephine Ingebar b. Oct. 13, 1873, m. D. Arthur Keeler; Hyrum Robert R. b. Dec. 16, 1875; Wilford Rudolph b. April 5, 1878, d. infant; Mary Lorena b. Sept. 20, 1879, m. Hyrum S. Johnson; Orson Christian, b. March, 1881, d. infant; Emma Geneva b. Dec. 25, 1883. Family home Monroe, Utah.
Married Inger Maria Christensen at Salt Lake City (daughter of Christen Neilason and Inger Maria Thompson), who was born Feb. 9, 1846, in Denmark. Only child: Carrie Torena (adopted) b. Oct. 19, 1859, m. Hillary Larsen Nov. 23, 1910.
Married Mary Magdalena Messerly May 29, 1878, St. George, Utah (daughter of Jacob Messerly and Magdalena Sigrist), who was born Sept. 14, 1862, Wattenwyl, Bern, Switzerland. Their children: Laura Magdalena b. July 24, 1884, d. infant; Bertha Eliza b. July 7, 1886; Harrold b. July 18, 1888; Mary Sarah b. Aug. 4, 1889, latter three died; Bert Marion, b. April 12, 1892; Nephi Jacob b. April 21, 1894, died; John Taylor b. Dec. 12, 1896; Wilford Owen b. Feb. 23, 1899; Heber Joseph b. May 5, 1901; Clara b. March 23, 1908. Family home Monroe, Utah.
President high priests' quorum at Monroe. Settled in San Pete county 1861; moved to Salina, then to Richfield and back to Monroe, Sevier county. Indian war veteran.

CHRISTIANSON, FREDERICK JULIUS (son of Christian Frederickson, born June 5, 1803, Hjorring, Denmark, and Marren Christensen, born July 14, 1803, Ruberg, Hjorring, married Nov. 4, 1825). He was born Dec. 25, 1826, Hjorring, Denmark. Came to Utah Sept. 20, 1856, Knud Peterson company.
Married Kirstena Marie Anderson Jan. 13, 1856, Taars, Hjorring, Denmark (daughter of Anders Anderson and Mary Anna Nielsen, pioneers Oct. 1859). She was born Oct. 15, 1838, and came to Utah with husband. Their children: Johannah Maria b. Sept. 29, 1857, m. Magnus Abilin March 15, 1875; Frederick Julius b. Aug. 7, 1859, m. Margrett M. Poulson June 17, 1880; Joseph b. May 10, 1861, m. Karren Mariah Jensen; Andrew Christian b. May 18, 1864, m. Anna Mariah Jensen Jan. 11, 1889; Mariah b. May 4, 1867, m. Mary b. June 28, 1869, m. Martin C. Jensen July 18, 1886; Hyrum Julius b. May 1, 1871, m. Hannah Mickelsen Nov. 11, 1892; Elizabeth b. May 3, 1873, m. Christian R. Christensen Oct. 6, 1892; Brigham Julius b. March 27, 1876, m. Loa Sanders; Erastus Julius b. Feb. 17, 1878, m. Katherine Christiansen Aug. 2, 1911; Orson J. b. Dec. 14, 1879, m. Nora Anderson Oct. 23, 1901; John J. b. Aug. 28, 1882, m. Mary Jorgensen Sept. 6, 1909. Family resided Ephraim and Mayfield, Utah.
Married Kirsten Maria Jensen July 16, 1864, Salt Lake City (daughter of Jens Jensen and Mette Johannah Madsen), who was born July 26, 1812, Tors Hjorring, Denmark, and came to Utah Oct. 5, 1854, Hans Peter Olsen company.
Married Elsa Margrette Larsen Jan. 15, 1868, Salt Lake City (daughter of Jens Larsen), who was born June 19, 1850, Stuberup, Falster, Denmark. Their children: Ephraim Julius b. Oct. 14, 1870; Juleanna b. Dec. 23, 1873, m. Alfred Lund; Kirstena b. March 8, 1875, m. Christian Sorensen; Albert J. b. May 31, 1878, m. Ellis Baxter; Mena b. Sept. 1, 1880; Ella b. Oct. 17, 1883, m. Nels Greagersen Dec. 17, 1901; Caroline b. Oct. 23, 1886, m. Leonard Sorensen Dec. 11, 1907. Family resided Ephraim and Mayfield, Utah.
President seventies at Ephraim, Utah. Farmer and cooper.

CHRISTIANSON, FREDERICK JULIUS, JR. (son of Frederick Julius Christianson and Kirstena Marie Anderson). Born Aug. 7, 1859, Ephraim, Utah.
Married Margrett M. Poulson June 17, 1880, Salt Lake City (daughter of Jens Poulson and Christena Christensen, who came to Utah Sept. 1877). She was born March 2, 1862, Voxlev, Denmark. Their children: Margrett Amelia b. Nov. 8, 1881, m. Louis D. Larsen Jan. 8, 1902; Myrtle Christena b. May 21, 1884; Frederick Arthur b. Dec. 12, 1885, m. Daisy G. Jensen Nov. 14, 1906; Alice Eveline b. Dec. 2, 1887; Ernest Milton b. Jan. 24, 1889; Russell Wilford b. Dec. 1, 1890; Cleveland Julius b. Nov. 9, 1892; Angus James b. Aug. 8, 1897; Orson Lorenzo b. May 28, 1899; Eva b. March 1, 1901; Reed Smoot b. Nov. 24, 1902; Stanley b. June 25, 1906. Family home Mayfield, Utah.
Bishop's counselor at Mayfield 1896-03; President elders' quorum five years 1888-93; missionary to northwestern states 1894-96; Sunday school superintendent at Mayfield. Constable; member Mayfield town board. Farmer.

CHRISTIANSEN, MADS. Born 1786, at Jutland, Denmark. Came to Utah 1862, oxteam company.
Married Annie Christena Halesen in Denmark, who was born 1810. Their children: Soren; Christian; Caroline, m. Soren Nielsen; Johanna Marie, m. Lars Jacobsen. Family home, Salt Lake City.
High priest. Farmer. Died 1878, Mt. Pleasant, Utah.

CHRISTIANSEN, SOREN (son of Christian Rudolph Phillip Jensen and Anne Johanna Rasmussen). Born Dec. 26, 1830, Aarhus amt, Denmark.
Married Caroline Theodora Loft 1854, in Denmark (daughter of Mikkel Christensen Loft and Anna Marie Nielson, who came to Utah 1873). She was born July 6, 1836, in Denmark. Their children: Christian John b. April 17, 1855, m. Ellen Jane Oldroyd 1876; Maria Mikkeline b. Sept. 29, 1856, m. Lars Nielson 1871. Family home Fountain Green, Utah.
President high priests quorum; ward teacher; Sunday school treasurer and librarian. Home guard in Nauvoo Legion. School trustee.

CHRISTIANSEN, CHRISTIAN J. (son of Soren Christiansen and Caroline Theodora Loft). Born April 17, 1855, in Denmark.
Married Ellen Jane Oldroyd May 29, 1876, Salt Lake City (daughter of Peter Oldroyd and Katherine Micklejohn; former came to Utah 1850, latter 1851). She was born Nov. 8, 1856, Ephraim, Utah. Their children: Christian T. b. Aug. 10, 1878, m. Estelle E. Cook 1898; Peter M. b. March 29, 1880; Agnes M. b. Nov. 8, 1881, m. James W. Chrestensen 1910; Ellen Jane b. April 1, 1885, m. Eugene Ivory Oct. 22, 1911; Soren A. b. Sept. 19, 1886; Archibald b. Oct. 8, 1888; Roy O. b. Jan. 29, 1892; Katherine J. b. Oct. 4, 1895; Leah B. b. Nov. 7, 1897; Joseph R. b. Sept. 26, 1898; John Eldon b. Feb. 27, 1901. Family home Fountain Green, Utah.
Sunday school superintendent; bishop; ward teacher. Band member. Town trustee.

CHRISTOPHERSON, MARTIN (son of Christopher Pedersen and Ellen Hansen). Born April 13, 1850, Lornnedalen Barum, Norway. Came to Utah July 1871.
Married Jennett Farquhar Ledingham Dec. 27, 1874, Salt Lake City (daughter of Alexander Morris Ledingham and Jennett Farquhar of Edinburgh, Scotland; former a pioneer Sept. 24, 1866, Capt. Watson company). She was born June 14, 1857. Their children: Martin E., m. Dagmar Mauger; Willard, m. Effie Askim; Victor, m. Bertha Bishop; Jessie, m. Traup Rigby; Ella, m. Carl Burton; Walter; Norma, m. Daniel Maskey; Alvin; Edna. Family home Salt Lake City.
President Scandinavian mission; missionary in Norway 1870-71; second to Norway 1883-85; high priest in Granite stake. County commissioner 1894-95. Nurseryman and landscape gardener.

CHUGG, MORONI (son of John Chugg, born March 19, 1819, West Down, Devonshire, Eng., and Hannah Lee, born Oct. 23, 1846, East Mersey, Essex, Eng.). He was born Jan. 23, 1879, Harrisville, Utah.
Married Ida Taylor Jan. 23, 1901, Salt Lake City (daughter of William A. Taylor and Philomela Lake, of Harrisville). She was born Jan. 3, 1881. Their children: Moron Orin b. Nov. 16, 1901, d. Dec. 14, 1901; Karl Willis b. June 11,

1903; Lelia Ida b. Dec. 17, 1904; Zola Philomela b. Feb. 26, 1907; John Andrew b. June 15, 1908; Melburne David b. Feb. 20, 1910; Oretta Hannah b. Oct. 13, 1912. Family home Farr-West. Utah.
Sunday school worker; member presidency Y. M. M. I. A., and president 1908-09; ward clerk 1902-09; ordained seventy March 3, 1904, and later president of 60th quorum; ordained high priest Aug. 2, 1908, and alternate member high council of North Weber stake; bishop of Farr-West ward.

CHUGG, WILLIAM (son of Philip Chugg, born at Caermarthen, Wales, and Johanna Stamberry, born at North Molton, Eng., married at West Down, Eng.). He was born Nov. 25, 1830, West Down. Came to Utah Oct. 16, 1862, Joseph W. Young company.
Married Mary Mitchell (daughter of John Mitchell and Mary Higgins), who was born in May, 1838, and came to Utah Oct. 4, 1863, Thomas E. Ricks company.
Their children: Sylvia Ann b. Dec. 15, 1864, m. Alfred B. Crabtree Dec. 18, 1884; William John b. Aug. 23, 1866, m. Bertha Zollinger Jan. 9, 1889; Mary Ann b. Oct. 31, 1868, d. Jan. 1881; Jane b. April 15, 1871, d. Sept. 15, 1871; Elizabeth b. Dec. 7, 1872, d. June 27, 1874; Parley Edward b. Oct. 7, 1876, m. Rosa Rindlishbacher June 12, 1902, died Aug. 8, 1902. Family home Providence, Utah.
Married Eliza Frederick June 4, 1880, Salt Lake City (daughter of Arnold Jacob Frederick and Elizabeth Enz, married June 22, 1866, Muelheim, Switzerland, and came to Utah 1870). She was born April 21, 1857, Muelheim, Switzerland. Their children: Willard Hyrum b. Feb. 20, 1881, m. Mary Josephine Rose March 4, 1908; Alvin Frederick b. April 2, 1882, d. Sept. 17, 1883; Ezra Albert b. Feb. 8, 1884, m. Lunetta Russon June 23, 1909; Nora Elizabeth b. Nov. 25, 1885, m. Auguste John Dissegger March 11, 1901, Nathaniel Benjamin b. Aug. 8, 1888; Mabel Eliza b. July 19, 1896.
High priest. Settled at Salt Lake City 1862, and acted as miller at Snider and Pugsley flour mills until 1866; moved to Cache valley and worked for Benson and Thatcher flour mills 1864-84; miller Box Elder mills 1884-86; miller Oneida mills 1888-91; miller South Cache milling company 1903-10. School trustee at Providence three years.

CHUGG, WILLIAM JOHN (son of William Chugg and Mary Mitchell). Born Aug. 23, 1865, Salt Lake City.
Married Bertha Zollinger Jan. 9, 1889, Logan, Utah (daughter of Ferdinand Zollinger and Louisa Meier, pioneers Oct. 1862. Capt. Davis company). She was born Aug. 3, 1867, Providence, Utah. Their children: William Duard b. Oct. 2, 1889; Retta Irene b. July 6, 1892, m. Newell Mathews Oct. 11, 1911; Gladys May b. April 6, 1895; Pearl Mitchell b. Sept. 13, 1897; Venna Bertha b. March 30, 1900; Leroy Edward b. July 8, 1902; Melvin Zollinger b. Aug. 1, 1904; Marion Byron b. May 11, 1907; Emma Louise b. Aug. 27, 1909. Family home Providence, Utah.

CHURCH, HADEN WELLS (son of Abraham Church of Hickman county, Tenn.). Born Aug. 29, 1817, Franklin, Williamson county, Tenn. Came to Utah July 24, 1847, Brigham Young company.
Married Sarah Ann Arterbery April, 1843 (daughter of Elias Arterbery and Matilda Wallace), who was born May 4, 1824, and came to Utah with husband. Their children: Hyrum Smith b. March 9, 1846, m. Clara Jane Randall Jan. 9, 1877; Abraham A. b. Feb. 26, 1854, m. Martha Ellen Alger; Paralee A. b. July 8, 1857, m. William Miles May 25, 1874; Robert R. b. Oct. 29, 1859, m. Charlotte Tolbert. Family resided Salt Lake City and St. George, Utah.
Married Catherine Gardner 1855, Salt Lake City (daughter of John Gardner), who was born in England.
Member Co. B, Mormon Battalion; missionary abroad and died in mission field.

CHURCH, HADEN WELLS (son of Haden Wells Church and Sarah Ann Arterbery). Born Sept. 8, 1848, Salt Lake City.
Married Clara Jane Randall Jan. 9, 1877, St. George, Utah (daughter of Joseph Randall), who was born Feb. 23, 1860, Spanish Fork, Utah. Their children: Sarah Ann b. April 11, 1878; Haden Wells b. Jan. 29, 1880, m. Clara Robison Jan. 29, 1902. Family home St. George, Utah.
Married Violet J. Pendleton June 28, 1883 (daughter of Benjamin F. Pendleton and Alice Jeffery). Their children: Mannettie b. Aug. 27, 1884; John Henry b. Jan. 5, 1887; Clara Jane b. June 10, 1889; Alice b. Jan. 11, 1892; Josephine b. Oct. 3, 1894; Vernon b. Nov. 9, 1896; Earl b. Jan. 19, 1899; Violet b. Dec. 17, 1901; Roma b. Sept. 29, 1906.

CHURCH, HADEN WELLS (son of Haden Wells Church and Clara Jane Randall). Born Jan. 29, 1880, St. George, Utah.
Married Clara Robison Jan. 29, 1902 (daughter of Joseph M. Robison, born March 29, 1852, Fillmore, Utah, and Sarah L. Staples, born Jan. 18, 1858, Lehi, Utah, pioneers 1852 and 1858 respectively). She was born Feb. 23, 1882, Kanosh, Utah. Their children: Wells Robison b. Aug. 2, 1903; Joseph Willard b. April 11, 1906; Della b. June 21, 1909; Willmer Haden b. Sept. 13, 1912.

CLARK, ANDREW A. (son of John Clark and Lillias Barber). Born Oct. 5, 1852, near Council Bluffs, Iowa. Came to Utah fall of 1853.
Married Mary Alice Lindsay, Logan, Utah (daughter of Walter Lindsay and Elizabeth Burt of Eden, Utah, pioneers 1862, William Brunson company). She was born Feb. 23, 1869. Their children: Walter A. b. Nov. 15, 1889, m. Zennia E. Hill; John W. b. June 15, 1891; Parley J. b. Aug. 19, 1893; Lillias b. Aug. 1, 1895. Family home Liberty, Utah. High priest. Farmer.

CLARK, BENJAMIN THOMAS (son of Thomas Benjamin Clark and Elizabeth Bell of Cambridge, Cambridgeshire, Eng.). Born Feb. 20, 1799 at Cambridge, Eng. Came to Utah Oct. 6, 1853, Cyrus H. Wheelock company.
Married Ann Shuker Sept. 24, 1819, Cambridge, Eng., who was born June 19, 1800. Their children: Thomas B., m. Sarah Nell; Joseph John, m. Maria Leach; Elizabeth, m. George Handley; Ann, m. Joseph Clark; Frances, m. James Stratton; Charles Jonas, m. Elizabeth Toladay; Martha, m. William Howard; William, m. Frances Davis; Benjamin T., m. Mary Hughes, m. Mary E. Ballard; Susanab, d. infant; Susanah, m. David King; Caroline, m. James Briggs.
Married Ann Southwell May 25, 1850, Cambridge, Eng. (daughter of Charles Southwell and Sarah Freestone of Cambridge, Eng.), who was born Sept. 18, 1815. Their children: Lorenzo S., m. Mary Rachel Wagstaff; Heber Abraham; Ellen, m. Robert Siddoway.
Married Ruth Butterworth Briggs June 28, 1857, Salt Lake City, who was born April 23, 1817. Only child: Alice, d. child.
Married Martha Larkins March 3, 1866, Salt Lake City (daughter of Henry Larkins and Ellen Spicer of Cambridge, Eng.), who was born April 15, 1822. Families resided at Salt Lake City.
Elder; high priest. Home builder; farmer; stockraiser. Died Sept. 4, 1867, at Salt Lake City.

CLARK, LORENZO SOUTHWELL (son of Benjamin Thomas Clark and Ann Southwell). Born May 14, 1852, Cambridge, Eng. Came to Utah Oct. 6, 1853, Cyrus H. Wheelock company.
Married Mary Rachel Wagstaff Aug. 17, 1874, Salt Lake City (daughter of William Wagstaff of Caldicote, Bedfordshire, Eng., and Maria Stuffs of Birmingham, Warwickshire, Eng.). She was born March 31, 1855. Their children: Lorenzo N. b. Aug. 4, 1875, m. Ada S. Sanford; Maria Ann b. Nov. 10, 1876, m. Don Carlos Kimball; Matilda Jane b. Oct. 30, 1878, m. Frederick C. Sanford; Mary Ellen, b. March 19, 1880, m. Walter Romney; William W. b. Aug. 13, 1881, died; Benjamin T. b. May 1, 1884, m. Nathala V. Jones; Cyrus Noble, d. infant. Family home Salt Lake City.
Member fourth quorum seventies; missionary to southern states. Constable; justice of peace. Music teacher; builder; contractor.

CLARK, EVAN O. (son of Osborn M. Clark, born July 27, 1855, Porter, Ohio, and Ida Catherine Cripps, born July 14, 1861, Bidwell, Ohio; married Nov. 1, 1876, Porter, Ohio). He was born Sept. 26, 1877, Addison, Gallia Co., Ohio. Came to Utah Feb. 13, 1899, independent company.
Married Mary L. Jones Oct. 30, 1897 (daughter of John L. Jones and Mary Susan Brightmell), who was born June 18, 1875. Their children: Ida Leona b. Aug. 30, 1898; Effie Susan b. Jan. 29, 1901; Evan Oscar b. March 14, 1903; Alice Melissa b. March 1, 1908; Virgie Opal b. March 30, 1910.
President Y. M. M. I. A. 1903-04; counselor in bishopric of Merran ward 1904-11; bishop Merran ward. City councilman at Merran 1907-08.

CLARK, EZRA T. (son of Timothy B. Clark and Polly Keeler). Born Nov. 23, 1823, in Illinois. Came to Utah in 1848.
Married Mary Stevenson May, 1845, who was born at Gibraltar, Spain, at the entrance to the Mediterranean, August 29, 1825. Their children: Ezra James, d. July 14, 1868; Timothy B., m. Lucy A. Rice; Mary Elizabeth, m. Joseph E. Robinson; William H., d. infant; Joseph S., m. Lucy Maria Robinson; Hyrum D. C., m. Eliza Porter; Edward B., m. Wealthea Richards; m. Alice Randall; Charles R., m. Mary Emma Woolley; m. Annie Waldron; Wilford W., m. Pamelia Dunn; Amasa L., m. Alice Steed (died); m. Susie Duncan; David P., d. infant.
Married Susan Leggett 1861 (daughter of William Leggett and Sarah Howe of Salt Lake City). She was born in England Aug. 25, 1838 and died Nov. 4, 1902. Their children: Seymour T.; Annie, m. Joseph Marion Tanner; Sarah, m. B. F. Knowlton, Jr.; Alice, m. Walter W. Steed; John A.; Eugene H., m. Sarah Ann Sessions; Nathan G., m. Esther Ford; Marion; Laura, m. Mark Cook; Horace W., m. Janette Denzon.
Married Nancy A. Porter Stevenson.
Spent winters of 1848-50 in North Canyon, southeast of Bountiful, and built a log cabin on his farm in Farmington, a few yards northwest of the present O. S. L. R. R. depot building. Moved into the cabin April 3, 1850. Missionary to Great Britain; to the States with Edward Stevenson and Nathan T. Porter; to Oregon with Alonzo Hyde; one of the presidents of 40th quorum seventies; high councilor; patriarch. Assisted in settling the Soda Springs country by locating at Georgetown; hauled the first load of timber with which to locate at Georgetown; built flour mill at Morgan; treasurer of Davis County; one of the organizers and president of the Davis County Bank. Died Oct. 17, 1901, at Farmington, Utah.

CLARK, TIMOTHY BALDWIN (son of Ezra Thompson Clark and Mary Stevenson). Born Nov. 23, ——.
Married Lucy A. Rice Nov. 23, 1867, Salt Lake City (daughter of William K. Rice and Lucy Witter Gees, pioneers Sept. 29, 1847, Edward Hunter company). She was born March 5, 1850, Farmington, Utah. Their children: Ezra Timothy b. May 1, 1869, d. Aug. 10, 1870; Lucy Evaline b. Jan. 14, 1871, m. Oliver S. Wilcox Nov. 23, 1892; Mary Elizabeth b. March 13, 1873, m. Orlando Barrus; William Joseph b. Jan. 12, 1875, d. Dec. 5, 1876; Zina Alice b. Feb. 22, 1877, d. May, 1879; Clara Maria b. Oct. 20, 1879, m. Edward Norr Feb. 24, 1908; Louisa Aurelia b. Sept. 28, 1881; Minerva Aurelia (twin of Louisa Aurelia); Ellen b. July 29, 1883, m. Martin Henderson June 14, 1905; George Amasa b. July 28, 1885, m. Eunice Thompson Sept. 15, 1910; Lera b. Feb. 7, 1887, m. Raymond Maughn Sept. 18, 1909.

CLARK, JOSEPH SMITH (son of Ezra T. Clark and Mary Stevenson). Born March 21, 1854, Farmington, Utah.
Married Lucy Maria Robinson Jan. 17, 1876, Salt Lake City (daughter of Oliver L. Robinson and Lucy Miller of Farmington), who was born Nov. 22, 1856. Their children: Lucy A. b. Oct. 1, 1876, m. William O. Robinson; Joseph S., Jr., b. Aug. 30, 1878, m. Mary L. Spencer May 10, 1906; Ezra T. b. Oct. 16, 1881, m. Margaret Jones; Ora Weltha b. Sept. 26, 1886, d. May 3, 1890; Mary b. Jan. 7, 1889, d. July 12, 1891; Oliver R. b. Sept. 16, 1891; LeRoy R. b. Nov. 15, 1894; Iris and Irvin B. b. May 13, 1898. Family home Farmington.
Missionary to southern states 1882-84; member 74th quorum seventies. First banker in Davies county; farmer.

CLARK, JOSEPH SMITH, JR. (son of Joseph Smith Clark and Lucy M. Robinson). Born Aug. 30, 1878, at Farmington.
Married Mary L. Spencer May 10, 1906, Salt Lake City (daughter of Isaac Spencer and Mary E. Burmingham of Bountiful, Utah), who was born Jan. 24, 1885. Their children: LaVerne b. July 11, 1907; Nedra b. Oct. 13, 1910.
Missionary to England 1901-04; member 55th quorum seventies; bishop of Fielding ward Oct. 14, 1906, to date. Farmer.

CLARK, WILFORD W. (son of Ezra T. Clark and Mary Stevenson). Born Feb. 2, 1863, Farmington, Utah.
Married Pamelia Dunn July 22, 1885, at Logan, Utah (daughter of John Dunn and Julia Ann McGuire of Plain City, Utah, and Bennington, Idaho, pioneers 1852). She was born April 4, 1863. Their children: W. Woodruff b. May 24, 1886, m. Ethel Cook; William O. b. July 17, 1887; Vera b. Sept. 13, 1888; Royal D. b. March 27, 1892, m. Mary E. Mumford; Ernest; Elmer R.; Homer b. April 4, 1898; Howard (twin of Homer); Russell b. Nov. 19, 1900; Legrand b. April 21, 1903; Leora b. April 27, 1907.
Bishop's counselor Georgetown 1891-93; bishop Montpelier Ward 1893-1912; high councilor and president of the high priests quorum of the Bear Lake Stakes. Member of Idaho house of representatives in the state legislature 1895-96, and of the senate 1903-04. Farmer and stockraiser.

CLARK, CHARLES RICH (son of Ezra T. Clark and Mary Stevenson). Born April 1, 1861, Farmington, Utah.
Married Mary Emma Woolley June 28, 1883, Salt Lake City (daughter of John W. Woolley and Julia Searle Ensign, former pioneer 1848, latter of Sept. 1847). She was born Jan. 31, 1862, Salt Lake City. Their children: Marion Charles b. April 4, 1884, m. Ella Shepherd June 14, 1907; Vernon John b. Aug. 27, 1888; Marvin Ezra b. Dec. 13, 1890; Carl Razel b. Jan. 31, 1895; Newell Siris b. April 25, 1896; Marie b. March 4, 1899; Julia b. July 22, 1902. Family resided at Farmington and Morgan, Utah, and Georgetown, Idaho.
Married Ann Elizabeth Waldron. Their children: Wallace R. b. Oct. 6, 1887; Lawrence W. b. Aug. 27, 1889; Gladys W.; Lela W.; Ella W.; Carlos; Myral G. Family home Morgan, Utah.
Traveling elder in Virginia 1891-1903; bishop's counselor; student Brigham Young university; normal graduate from University of Utah 1880. School teacher at Centerville, Morgan, Richville, and Minersville, Utah; Auburn, Wyo., and Georgetown, Idaho. Member Morgan city council; justice of the peace at Morgan. Sergeant under Capt. Wadsworth in Utah militia.

CLARK, MARION CHARLES (son of Charles Rich Clark and Mary Emma Woolley). Born April 4, 1884, Georgetown, Idaho.
Married Ella Shepherd June 14, 1907 (daughter of L. Tracy Shepherd and Sarah Clifton, former came to Utah 1877, latter 1863). She was born Sept. 5, 1886, Paris, Idaho. Their children: Ellsworth Marion b. Jan. 25, 1908; Hazel C. b. Aug. 10, 1909; Helen C. b. April 21, 1911; Clifton Shepherd b. March 7, 1913.
Missionary to northern states 1904-1907; president elders' quorum; stake and in Y. M. M. I. A. of Bear Lake stake; superintendent Sunday school Georgetown 1907. Member city council of Georgetown. Merchant.

CLARK, WALLACE RICH (son of Charles R. Clark and Ann Elizabeth Waldron). Born Oct. 6, 1887, Farmington, Utah.
Married Jean Boyce Sept. 6, 1911, Salt Lake City (daughter of John Boyce and Ella Despain of Granite, Utah). She was born April 4, 1890. Only child: Boyce Rich b. July 15, 1912.
Member 35th quorum seventies; class leader in Y. M. M. I. A.; member stake superintendency Sunday school. Farmer.

CLARK, GEORGE (son of James Clark and Martha England of Sommercote, Derbyshire, Eng.). Born July 8, 1826, Sommercote, Eng. Came to Utah Oct. 4, 1863, Horton D. Haight company.
Married Catherine Gascoigne 1850, Sommercote, Eng. (daughter of Jonathan Gascoigne and Charlotte Mountney of Normanton, Derbyshire), who was born Feb. 7, 1828, and died Dec. 9, 1901. Their children: Frederick Charles, m. Angela Vance; Sarah Ann, m. David McDaniel; Mary Ellen, m. Ewin Okey; Elizabeth, Willard Oliver, George Alfred and James Alvin, died.
High priest; president Nottingham branch, England; superintendent Sunday school; block teacher. Mayor of Alpine, Utah, three terms; justice of peace; road supervisor; sexton. Farmer. Died May 26, 1902, Alpine, Utah.

CLARK, GEORGE SHEFFER (son of Richard and Elizabeth Ann Clark, descendants of the William Penn settlement, Chester county, Pennsylvania). He was born Nov. 7, 1816, Jefferson county, Ohio. Came to Utah July 24, 1847, Brigham Young company. His name was inadvertently left off the pioneers' monument in Salt Lake City.
Married Susannah Dalley March 20, 1850 (daughter of William Dalley and Ann Davies), who was born Sept. 30, 1830, Leominster, Herefordshire, Eng., and died April 9, 1891, Pleasant Grove, Utah. Their children: Joseph Brigham, m. Louisa Pearson; George Heber, m. Lois Adeline Stewart; m. Luna B. Driggs; Susannah Matilda, m. James Evan Gamett; John Franklin, m. Leonia O. Alexander; William Edward, m. Cora Melinda Bromley; Hyrum Lorenzo, m. Mary Ellen Ward.
Member 13th quorum seventies; bishop north division Utah county 1851; first bishop of Pleasant Grove; missionary to Australia 1856-59, and later to eastern states. Elected probate judge of Utah county 1851. Walker Indian war veteran 1853; member Mormon Battalion, going as far as the Mexican line, sent back on sick list and joined the company at Green River, Wyo., arriving at Salt Lake City July 24, 1847. City councilman Pleasant Grove 1867-70. Settled Pleasant Grove Sept. 13, 1850; assisted in bringing immigrants to Utah. Farmer and merchant. Died Aug. 28, 1901, Pleasant Grove.

CLARK, WILLIAM EDWARD (son of George Sheffer Clark and Susannah Dalley). Born Feb. 9, 1864, Pleasant Grove.
Married Cora Melinda Bromley June 10, 1903, Salt Lake City (daughter of William Michael Bromley and Rosena Singleton of American Fork, Utah, pioneers 1853, Joseph Reynolds company). She was born Feb. 28, 1879. Their children: Melba Rosena b. March 17, 1904; Blanche Susannah b. Nov. 7, 1906; William Edward b. Jan. 24, 1908; Edna b. Nov. 14, 1910; George Bromley b. June 5, 1912. Family home Pleasant Grove.
Missionary to England 1896-98; president London conference 1898; president Y. M. M. I. A. Mayor Pleasant Grove 1901-02; justice of the peace 1891-92; city recorder 1893-94-95. Merchant.

CLARK, HARVEY. Came to Utah Oct. 2, 1847, Charles C. Rich company.
Married Lois Haws (daughter of Elijah Haws and Lois Patton of Illinois, pioneers 1849). Their children: Jason Edward, m. Ann M. Davies; William Wesley, m. May Davies; Esmerelda, m. H. E. Taylor. Family resided Salt Lake City and Payson, Utah.
Early settler in Utah county. Went to California by team twice (deceased).

CLARK, JASON EDWARD (son of Harvey Clark and Lois Haws). Born Sept. 21, 1862, Salem, Utah.
Married Ann M. Davies Dec. 25, 1881, Payson, Utah (daughter of Stanley P. Davies and Susan Fairbanks), who was born Dec. 27, 1863. Their children: Innes b. Oct. 1, 1882, m. Deronda C. Seegmiller; Edward Lee b. Aug. 24, 1884, m. Tillie Cuddeback; Mabel b. Oct. 22, 1886, m. W. A. Shepherd; Mazel b. Oct. 22, 1886, m. Percy Allred; Irma b. April 7, 1889, d. Aug. 18, 1909; Elon b. March 13, 1892, d. infant; Stanley b. Feb. 17, 1891, d. infant; Lelia b. Feb. 14, 1894; Ireta b. June 2, 1896; Ray b. July 24, 1899; La Mar b. Dec. 29, 1901; Harvey b. Oct. 10, 1903; Reed b. Feb. 18, 1905. Family resided Payson, Annabella and Richfield, Utah.
Director Central Utah Trout Co. at Richfield. Stockraiser.

CLARK, ISAAC (son of Robert Clark and Ruth Moore). Born May 7, 1806, Bowling Green, Ky. Came to Utah 1849.
Married Diana Herrick. Only child: Isaac L. b. Sept. 10, 1853, m. Romania Shaw.
Settled at Ogden, Utah, 1849, and was its first bishop, first postmaster and first probate judge. Died Jan. 24, 1854, at Ogden, Utah.

CLARK, ISAAC L. (son of Isaac Clark and Diana Herrick). Born Sept. 10, 1853.
Married Romania Shaw at Ogden (daughter of William Shaw and Diana Chase), who was born in that city. Their children: Isaac G., m. Marion Johnson; Ethel R., m. J. B Foulger; William C.; Jesse A., d. infant; Vera D.; Darrel G Family home Ogden, Utah.
Member high council of Ogden stake. Member city council 1893-95. President Weber Club one year. President I. Clark & Sons Co.; merchant 30 years.

CLARK, ISAAC G. (son of Isaac L. Clark and Romania Shaw). Born Nov. 13, 1878, at Ogden, Utah. Married Marion Johnson. Manager I. L. Clark & Sons company.

CLARK, ISRAEL JUSTICE (son of Eli Clark and Mary Smalage of Danville, Steuben county, N. Y.). Born Dec. 25, 1821, Danville, N. Y. Came to Utah 1848, John Smith company.
Married Emily Jane Pearson 1853, at Salt Lake City (daughter of Jesse Pearson, born June 13, 1813, in Georgia, and Mary Ann Brownell, born March 2, 1815, at Ascot, Lewis Co., Canada—they lived at Olive, St. Joseph Co. Ind., pioneers 1847). She was born March 16, 1837, Olive, Ind. Their children: Joseph b. Feb. 20, 1855; Mary Emily b. June 9, 1856, m. William Ricks; Harriet Louisa b. April 2, 1858, m. Ephraim Perks; Helen Cassandra b. Nov. 13, 1859, m. Peter Percy; William Henry b. Jan. 21, 1861, m. Printha Olive Downs; Henrietta Augustine b. Sept. 7, 1862, m. Jerry Hatch; Alice Melvina b. Jan. 8, 1864, m. W. D. Williams; Hannah Elizabeth and Ruth Matilda b. Dec. 13, 1866, died; Seth Benjamin b. Nov. 7, 1867, m. Mary Smith; George Albert b. Nov. 16, 1869, m. Ann McCurdy; Israel Jesse b. Dec. 13, 1871, d. Sept. 13, 1893; Richard James b. Nov. 7, 1873, d. infant; Sarah Jane b. Nov. 7, 1874, d. infant; Rachel Olive b. Feb. 24, 1876; Oliver Hazzard b. Jan. 4, 1877, m. Jane Mecham; Clarissa Antonett b. Nov. 4, 1880, m. George Bonner McCurdy; Martha Geribella b. July 31, 1882, d. infant. Family resided Logan, Farmington and Vernal, Utah.
Married Betsey Tuttle. Their children: Jesse Tuttle, m. Margarette Edwards; Cyrus, m. Sarah Jane; James, m. Annie Thompson.
Married Louisa Eynon. Their children: Edward, m. Mary Ann; Hyrum, m. Ceseltia; John, m. Theodosia Hatch; Eli, m. Clarinda Ricks; Ross Linda, m. Lafayette Harris.
Seventy; missionary among the Indians 1875-78. Indian war veteran. Died September, 1905. Vernal, Utah.

CLARK, JOHN E. (son of Israel Justice Clark and Louisa Eynon). Born May 22, 1854, Farmington, Utah.
Married Theadocia Hatch Oct. 14, 1877, Heber City, Utah (daughter of Jeremiah Hatch and Louisa Alexander of Vernal, Utah), who was born March 10, 1863. Their children: John Syemour; Theadocia, m. Charles C. Rich, Jr.; Jeremiah Hatch, m. Eliza Timothy; Alvah Justus, m. Nora Mecham; David Harvey. Family home Vernal, Utah.
Elder. Farmer.

CLARK, JAMES (son of Peter Clark and Catherine Telfer of Douglas, Scotland). Born May 17, 1845, Douglas, Scotland. Came to Utah Sept. 29, 1866, Daniel Thompson company.
Married Annie Osborn March 1, 1869, Salt Lake City (daughter of Allen Osborn and Annie Coventry of Glasgow, Scotland), who was born March 30, 1842, New London, Canada, and came to Utah Sept. 15, 1866, John Gillespie company. Their children: James b. Nov. 21, 1869, died; Peter O. b. Jan. 14, 1871, m. Julia Lynn; Annie b. July 27, 1872, d. Aug. 10, 1872; Cathrine b. Sept. 15, 1873, d. July 16, 1884; Nephi b. May 5, 1875, d. May 5, 1875; George H. b. April 6, 1876; Alice b. Aug. 12, 1878, d. July 2, 1879; Mary b. Oct. 8, 1881, d. Sept. 20, 1882; Nettie b. June 2, 1883, d. June 2, 1883. Family resided Salt Lake City, Utah, and Marion, Idaho.
Black Hawk war veteran. High priest; worked in Salt Lake Temple quarry several years. Called, with 200 others under Capt. Allen in 1876, to found St. Joseph, Arizona.

CLARK, JAMES. Born at Clathrope, Westmoreland, Eng. Came to Utah 1856, James P. Clark company.
Married Elizabeth England in England (daughter of John Purson and Mary Ann Dobson, pioneers Nov. 30, 1856, Edward Martin "frozen" handcart company. Their children: John P. m. Mary Ann Dobson; James; Thomas; Jane; Emma; Alice.

CLARK, JAMES P. (son of James Clark and Elizabeth Purson). Born 1833 at Clathrope.
Married Mary Ann Dobson at Salt Lake City (daughter of Alice Dobson, pioneers Nov. 30, 1856). Born 1832 at Preston, Lancashire, Eng. Their children: Alice Ann b. 1858; John Thomas b. 1859; Mary Elizabeth b. 1861; James Purson b. 1863; Culkrom b. 1865; William b. 1867; Emma b. 1869; Jane Eliza b. 1871; Clark Ward b. 1873.

CLARK, JOHN (son of Samuel Clark and Rebecca Garner of Clinton county, Ohio). Born April 20, 1832, in Clinton county. Came to Utah Sept. 24, 1848, Heber C. Kimball company.
Married Alvira Jane Pratt Nov. 25, 1859, Provo, Utah (daughter of Samuel Pratt and Louisa Tanner of La Porte county, Indiana, pioneers 1851, Harry Walton company). She was born March 27, 1843. Their children: Clarissa Alvira, m. James Henrie, Jr.; Ada, died; John Tanner, m. Alice Mathews; Osborne Samuel, m. Frances Elda Peay; Hyrum Milton, died; Florence Estella, m. Phillip Speckart; Tarza Pearl, m. Joseph E. Yates; Arvilla Jane, m. Willard Andelin. Family home Provo, Utah.
High priest; missionary to Elk Mountain mission 1855. Indian interpreter and veteran of many Indian ambuscades and skirmishes; served in all the Indian wars. Farmer.

CLARK, OSBORNE SAMUEL (son of John Clark and Alvira Jane Pratt). Born Sept. 2, 1867, Provo, Utah.
Married Frances Elda Peay Nov. 13, 1901, Salt Lake City (daughter of Edward Peay and Amanda Melvina Stubbs of Felpham, Sussex, Eng., pioneers Oct., 1852, Jerome Benson oxteam company). She was born July 29, 1873. Their children: Frances Estella b. March 25, 1903; Arvilla Amanda b. March 30, 1905; Eda Lucile b. Oct. 12, 1908; Osborne Peay b. Jan. 17, 1911. Family home Provo.
President of Y. M. M. I. A. Carpenter. Farmer.

CLARK, JOHN NORMAN (son of Nancy Norman of Virginia). Born Jan. 21, 1794, in Halifax county, Va. Came to Utah Sept. 28, 1851, Harry Walton, company.
Married Eliza Branch Sandifer (daughter of Matthew Sandifur), who was born Feb. 22, 1794. Their children: Elizabeth Caroline b. March 3, 1817, m. Jonathan Browning, m. Thomas Welr 1845; Mary Johnson b. June 1, 1819, m. John Ekless Truly; Ann Broye, b. Oct. 6, 1821, m. John Crow Thompson; America Morgan b. Feb. 23, 1824, m. Luke S. Johnson; Moses Sandifer b. July 10, 1828, m. Clarissa Abbie Allen; John Matthew b. Aug. 28, 1835, m. Belinda Burch. Family home Ogden, Utah.
Pioneer. Died June 7, 1864, Ogden, Utah.

CLARK, JOHN MATTHEW (son of John Norman Clark and Eliza Branch Sandifer). Born Aug. 28, 1835, in Patrick county, Va. Came to Utah with parents.
Married Belinda Burch Jan. 24, 1858, Ogden, Utah (daughter of Daniel Burch and Ann McLellan, pioneers Sept. 20, 1848, Lorenzo Snow company). She was born March 21, 1840, near Cincinnati, Ohio, and died Oct. 10, 1911, at Ogden. Their children: John Matthew b. Jan. 22, 1859, d. Sept. 7, 1891; Provo, m. Sarah Smith April 2, 1883; Daniel William b. May 5, 1861, m. Annie Borjenson May 3, 1896; Belinda Augusta b. April 23, 1863; James Norman b. July 20, 1865; Ann Eliza b. Jan. 13, 1868, d. Sept. 9, 1869; Emma Elizabeth b. Jan. 5, 1871; Joseph Boon b. Nov. 2, 1873, m. Florence Burch; Archie McLellan b. July 11, 1875. Family home Ogden, Utah.

CLARK, MICHAEL. Born June 12, 1832, at Chelmsford, Essex, Eng. Came to Utah 1857.
Married Harriet Smuin Sept. 24, 1859, Salt Lake City (daughter of Joseph Smuin of England), who was born July 22, 1836. Their children: Sarah Ann, b. Nov. 18, 1860, m. Harper Rudd; Jasper b. Sept. 19, 1863; Michael b. Nov. 26, 1867, m. Mary Ann Burton; Esther Hannah b Aug. 16, 1865, m. Joseph Ross; Elizabeth b. Dec. 5, 1869, m. John Trappit; Hannah b. June 26, 1872, m. James Kirkland; Edward b. April 12, 1875, m. Miss Despain. Family home Kaysville, Utah.
Married Eliza Smuin Oct. 27, 1861, Salt Lake City (daughter of Thomas Smuin, who came to Utah about 1869, and Sarah Hocok, pioneer 1861, of Kaysville, Utah). She was born Jan. 6, 1840. Their children: William Thomas b July 22, 1862, m. Annie M. Rasmussen; Sophia b. Nov. 5, 1863, m. Stephen E. Willis; David b. March 6, 1866, m. Elizabeth E. Barton; John b. Oct. 10, 1868; Edmuon b. Jan. 10, 1868; Eliza Jane b. Feb. 11, 1869, m. C. B. Lott; Irintha Maria b. Dec. 26, 1870, m. Harry Barber; Alice b. July 30, 1873; Charley b. April 19, 1875; Mary Ann b. March 23, 1877, m. William E. Barton; John b. Oct. 30, 1880; Sarah Lily b. Dec. 29, 1886; Goerge b. Nov. 4, 1884. Family home Kaysville.
Ward teacher. School trustee. Farmer; stockraiser. Died Jan. 21, 1891, Kaysville.

CLARK, DAVID (son of Michael Clark and Eliza Smuin). Born March 6, 1866, at Salt Lake City.
Married Elizabeth Butcher Nov. 3, 1890, at Farmington (daughter of William Butcher and Emma Wheatley, of Kaysville). She was born June 28, 1872, and came to Utah Oct., 1875. Their children: Millie b. Oct. 20, 1891, died; Asa David b. March 1, 1893; Andy William b. July 7, 1895; Joseph Oren b. Aug. 13, 1897; Effie Jane b. Sept. 8, 1899; Eugene b. March 24, 1902; Emma Eliza b. March 5, 1904; Glenn Smuin b. March 16, 1906; Leonard Butcher b. April 16, 1908; Elizabeth b. Oct. 20, 1910; Arthur Butcher b. Oct. 20, 1910. Family home Kaysville.
Member 56th quorum seventies; ward teacher Abram ward Deseret stake. Watermaster. Farmer and stockraiser.

CLARK, SAMUEL. Came to Utah Sept. 24, 1848, Heber C. Kimball company.
Married Rebecca Garner, who was born in Tennessee. Their children: Joseph b. April 26, 1828, m. Sarah Topham; m. Hannah Topham: m. Frances Carter; Riley Garner, m. Amanda Williams; Sarah, m. Miles Weaver; Mary, m. John M. Higby; Jane, m. John M. Baldwinkle; John, m. Elvira Pratt; Rebecca Ann, m. Solomon Hale: Samuel, died; Nellie, m. William Rawlins; James. Family home Provo, Utah.
Tanner.

CLARK, JOSEPH (son of Samuel Clark and Rebecca Garner). Born April 26, 1828, Clinton Co., Ohio. Came to Utah 1848, independent company.
Married Sarah Topham Oct. 17, 1849, Provo, Utah (daughter of John Topham and Jane Thornton of England, pioneers Sept. 15, 1850, David Evans company). She was born June 30, 1831, and came to Utah Oct. 2, 1847, Jedediah M. Grant company. Their children: Joseph b. Oct. 23, 1850, m.

PIONEERS AND PROMINENT MEN OF UTAH

Ann Elizabeth Whiteley Jan. 24, 1869; James Henry b. Jan. 15, 1852, died: Sarah Jane b. Dec. 31, 1852, m. Byron Colton; Rebecca Ann b. Nov. 6, 1854, m. Ezra Oakley; Samuel Moroni b. Jan. 14, 1857, m. Nellie Mitchell; Susannah b. April 12, 1859, m. David Cluff; Isaiah b. Feb. 9, 1863; William Riley b. Jan. 15, 1865, died; Mary Elizabeth b. Sept. 2, 1866, m. Albert Singleton; John Gideon b. Jan. 8, 1871, m. Emma Farrer; Byron Topham b. April 17, 1873, m. Jennie Provo, Utah.
Married Hannah Topham, who died March 31, 1913, childless.
Married Frances Carter.
High priest; second counselor to Bishop Myron Tanner. Member Co. A, Mormon Battalion. Farmer. Died March 9, 1895, Provo, Utah.

CLARK, JOSEPH (son of Joseph Clark and Sarah Jane Topham). Born Oct. 23, 1850, Provo, Utah.
Married Annie Elizabeth Whiteley Jan. 24, 1869, Salt Lake City (daughter of Thomas Whiteley and Harriett Saner, of Manchester, Eng., former a pioneer 1853). She was born Aug. 8, 1850. Their children: Harriett b. June 10, 1871, died; Joseph William b. May 13, 1874, m. Melvina Bennett; Jennie b. April 9, 1876, m. John S. Buckley; James Byron b. March 5, 1879, m. Mamie Stubbs; Marion Earl b. June 23, 1882, m. Annie Elizabeth James. Family home Provo, Utah.
Indian war veteran. Assisted in building the roads and canals in Utah county. Farmer and fruit grower.

CLARK, SAMUEL G. Born 1800. Came to Utah 1847. Ezra T. Benson company.
Married Roxine Frizzell, who was born 1800. Their children: Samuel G. b. 1833; William H. b. Jan. 10, 1838, m. Mary Ann Laing.
Member Co. E, Mormon Battalion. Died 1851 at Salt Lake City.

CLARK, WILLIAM H. (son of Samuel G. Clark and Roxine Frizzell). Born Jan. 10, 1838, Adams county, Ill.
Married Mary Ann Laing, at Toquerville, Utah (daughter of William T. Laing and Sarah Ann Browning, pioneers 1849, Orson Hyde company). She was born June 22, 1848, in Pottawattamie county, Iowa, and died March 30, 1906, Richfield, Utah. Their children: William H. b. Jan. 29, 1864, d. aged 2 years; Samuel G. b. Feb. 4, 1866, m. Melissa Bean Nov. 21, 1888; Mary E. b. April 6, 1868, m. Samuel Nebeker Nov. 21, 1888; Annabell b. May 22, 1870, m. Guy Lewis July 8, 1894; John Hyrum b. Oct. 14, 1873, died; Harriet b. Feb. 17, 1877, m. Alexander Elliott; Thomas E. b. Sept. 28, 1879; Sarah b. March 29, 1882, m. C. F. Hiki June 10, 1903; Wallace L. b. April 1, 1884, m. Hattie Williams Nov. 8, 1906; Jennie Neal b. May 23, 1888. Family home Richfield, Utah.
Deputy sheriff of Weber county; chief of police of Ogden; county sheriff and tax assessor and collector of Richfield 13 years; marshal at Richfield 8 years; city recorder at Richfield 3 years; recorder of Sevier county 2 years; county clerk 4 years. Chaplain in Utah legislature in 1893; missionary to Colorado two years; counselor in presidency of Sevier stake 16 years; member of high council Sevier stake.

CLARK, THOMAS H. (son of Thomas Clark). Born May 7, 1805, Acton, Herefordshire, Eng. Came to Utah Oct. 10, 1852.
Married Charlotte Gayley (daughter of William Gayley), who was born Jan. 27, 1803. Their children: John W. b. Jan. 12, 1826, m. Ann Micklewright Aug. 2, 1850; Ellen b. Jan. 21, 1828, m. George W. Bryan; Eliza b. May 17, 1829, m. Joseph Murdock; Hannah b. July 8, 1832, m. Charles G. Parkinson; Ann b. April 8, 1834; Thomas H. b. May 10, 1836, m. Margaret Quirk; Sarah b. Sept. 18, 1838; Mary Ann b. Nov. 28, 1843, m. John Anderson; Charlotte b. Aug. 25, 1845, m. John Rowberry. Family home Grantsville, Utah.

CLARK, JOHN WILLIAM (son of Thomas H. Clark and Charlotte Gayley). Born Jan. 12, 1826, Bishopsfrome, Eng.
Married Ann Micklewright Aug. 2, 1850 (daughter of William Micklewright and Sarah Hatch), who was born April 24, 1826, Cheltenham, Eng. Their children: Sarah Ann b. Dec. 21, 1852; Thomas H. b. Jan. 12, 1855, m. Rachel Hale Jan. 3, 1875; John William b. April 11, 1857, m. Selina Elizabeth Lee Dec. 26, 1878; George M. b. April 23, 1859, m. Mary Whittle; Lucy A. b. April 2, 1861, m. John A. Eliason Feb. 23, 1882; Emma Jane b. Sept. 18, 1863, m. William O. Jefferies; Ann Elizabeth b. Sept. 25, 1865, m. Eugene T. Wooley; Charles M. b. Jan. 8, 1869. Family home Grantsville, Utah.
High councilor; bishop's counselor. Farmer.

CLARK, JOHN WILLIAM (son of John W. Clark and Ann Micklewright). Born April 11, 1857, Grantsville, Utah.
Married Selina Elizabeth Jasper Dec. 26, 1878 (daughter of William Lee and Elizabeth Jasper, pioneers 1852), who was born Oct. 15, 1856, Grantsville. Their children: Rena b. Feb. 10, 1881, m. C. J. Anderson Dec. 10, 1902; George Sidney, m. Ethel M. Anderson Dec. 10, 1902; Vinnie Ann m. Gustav E. Anderson Dec. 5, 1906; Mamie, m. Parley P. Matthews Nov. 24, 1909; Alice Leon, m. Roy T. Brown Nov. 23, 1910.
First counselor to Bishop A. K. Anderson 7 years; second counselor to Bishop M. Wrathall 16 years. County commissioner 1908-12. Farmer and stockraiser.

CLARK, WILLIAM (son of Thomas Clark of Worcestershire, Eng.). Born July 26, 1825, in Worcestershire. Came to Utah 1852.
Married Jane Stephens 1852, at Council Bluffs, Iowa, who was born 1820, and came to Utah with husband. Their children: Emily Jane, m. Joseph Saby; William Wheeler, m. Polly Melissa Willies, m. Martha C. Ward; Martha Geneva, m. William Evans; Mary Ann, m. George Erastus Zimmerman; Hannah Mariah, m. George Albert Wall; Juliet, died; Rosilla, m. Hyrum Timothy. Family home Lehi, Utah.
Married Julia Ann Zimmerman (daughter of George Gottlob Zimmerman and Julia Ann Hoke of Franklin, Pa., pioneers 1851). Their children: Baby, died; Roseanna, m. Mr. Talbot.
Married Margaret Boardman. Their children: Thomas Henry, m. Margaret Ann Fox; Mary Jane; James B., m. Armetta Peterson.
Missionary to England; high priest; patriarch; bishop's counselor. Road supervisor; Lehi city councilman and alderman. Farmer, stockraiser and sheepman. Died May 7, 1910, at Lehi.

CLARK, WILLIAM WHEELER (son of William Clark and Jane Stephens). Born April 25, 1855, at Lehi, Utah.
Married Polly Melissa Willies (daughter of Ira Willies and Melissa Lott), who was born Nov. 7, 1856. Their children: Melissa Jane b. March 14, 1879, d. young; William Wheeler b. Aug. 29, 1880, d. aged 16; Asa Jones b. Sept. 24, 1882, m. Julia Bone; Mary Francell b. Dec. 4, 1884, m. Frank Fagan; Thomas Edgar b. Jan. 2, 1887, m. Edith Wales; Family home Lehi, Utah.
Married Martha Caroline Ward. Sept. 4, 1889, Manti, Utah (daughter of Burrell Ward and Catherine Livona Cooper, of Manchester, Tenn.), who was born May 27, 1860. Their children: Isaac Burrell, b. Sept. 28, 1890, d. infant; Sylvan Ward b. Sept. 2, 1892; Lexie Miri b. Sept. 21, 1897. Family home Lehi, Utah.
High priest; presiding elder; ward teacher. Member Lehi city council. Farmer and stockman.

CLARKE, AMOS (son of Edward Clarke, born 1795, and Ann Jarvis, born 1806, both of Denbighshire, Wales). He was born June 8, 1833, Rhosllanerchrugog, Denbighshire, Wales. Came to Utah Sept. 11, 1866, Samuel D. White company.
Married Ann Johnston (daughter of Richard Johnston and Ann Thomas), whc was born Jan. 7, 1832. Their children: Moses b. Sept. 6, 1864, d. Dec. 29, 1864; Anne b. March 18, 1856, m. John Jenkins; Elizabeth Jane b. Nov. 29, 1858, m. William H. Griffin; Sarah Angeline b. June 17, 1861, m. William F. Rigby; Mary Caroline b. May 27, 1863, m. George C. Rigby; Amos R. E. b. Dec. 12, 1868, m. Fidelia Haskell; Lemuel George b. Feb. 10, 1871, m. Sephorah Jones Oct. 2, 1907; Samuel Thomas b. Sept. 12, 1874, d. Sept. 21, 1899, while on mission in Cardiff, Wales, m. Olive Beck Dec. 23, 1897; David Robert b. Sept. 3, 1876, m. Martha Jane Cooley Jan. 24, 1901.
High priest; seventy; chorister of Newton ward 40 years. Justice of peace; school trustee three terms. Blacksmith.

CLARKE, FRANCIS (son of Thomas Clarke, born March 23, 1799, Lambourne, Essex, Eng., and Mary Ann Brown, born March 1, 1811, London, Eng., married 1840, Upminster, Essex, Eng.). He was born Jan. 1, 1840, Upminster, Essex, Eng. Came to Utah Sept. 12, 1861, Milo Andrus company.
Married Harriet Elvira Teeples March 28, 1867 (daughter of George B. Teeples and Huldah Colby; pioneers July 24, 1847, Brigham Young company). She was born Oct. 15, 1820. Their children: Francis b. June 4, 1869, m. Mary Ann Lindsay May 31, 1893; Thomas B. b. Nov. 3, 1872, m. Mary Atkinson 1897. Family home Eden, Utah.
Missionary to Great Britain 1893-95; teacher and clerk of Eden ward; high priest. Justice of peace at Eden 1893. Hauled freight across the plains with oxteams in 1863. Secretary and treasurer Eden Irrigation Company 1878-84.

CLARKE, JOHN H. Born April 9, 1831, Lambeth, Surrey, London, Eng. Came to Utah Sept. 25, 1855, Richard Ballantyne company.
Married Elizabeth Heaver Feb. 1854, in London (daughter of Benjamin Heaver of London). Their children: Catherine, m. Daniel Louis Hoopes; Elizabeth, m. A. A. Allen; Emily, m. Charles W. Knudsen; Emeline, m. Thomas Preston; Annie, m. William Preston; Herbert, died; Albert, d. aged nine years; Evelyn, m. Thomas Preston. Family home Weston, Idaho.
Member 88th quorum seventies; missionary to England 1889-91; bishop. Mgr. Weston co-op. Died May, 1904, at Weston, Idaho.

CLAWSON, HIRAM BRADLEY (son of Zepheniah Clawson and Catherine Reese of Utica, N. Y.). Born 1826, Utica. Came to Utah fall of 1848.
Married Ellen Curtis Spencer March 18, 1850, Salt Lake City (daughter of Orson Spencer and Catherine Curtis of Canaan Center, Conn.; former came to Utah 1849, captain of his own company, latter died en route). Their children: Hiram Bradley; Spencer; Diana; Ardelle; Georgia; Edith; Ivie; Winnie; Ruby. Family home Salt Lake City.
Member 17th quorum seventies. Diplomatic missionary in Salt Lake City and elsewhere 1855-77. First treasurer Salt Lake City. Adjutant-general Nauvoo Legion. First superintendent Zion's Co-operative Mercantile Institution. Died March 29, 1912, Salt Lake City.

PIONEERS AND PROMINENT MEN OF UTAH

CLAWSON, SPENCER (son of Hiram Bradley Clawson and Ellen Curtis Spencer). Born Aug. 15, 1852, Salt Lake City.
Married Nabbie Howe Young Feb. 15, 1876, Salt Lake City (daughter of Brigham Young and Clarissa Decker, pioneers July 24, 1847). She was born March 22, 1852, died 1894. Their children: Spencer; Claire, m. Chauncey Mott Benedict; Curtis; Grace; John; Neels.
Was buyer for the Zion's Co-operative Mercantile Institution in New York City for many years. Wholesale dry goods merchant. Prominent in political affairs of Salt Lake City. Secretary Utah exhibit at the Lewis and Clark Centennial Exposition at Portland, Ore., 1905. Associated with many industrial companies. Large real estate owner. Organizer and first secretary of the association for the preservation of relics of the pioneer days.

CLAWSON, MOSES. Married Sarah Inkley at Salt Lake City (daughter of Joseph Inkley, of Lincolnshire, Eng.). Their children: Georgiana, m. Henry Elliot; Joseph, m. Kate Gordon; Samuel, died; Charles M., m. Annie Fryer; Lola and Sarah, both died; Julia, m. Joseph Poulson; Henry; Lena, m. Clayton Brimhall; Lydia, m. James Lamb; Leslie; Rosa, died. Family home Toquerville, Utah.
High priest; in prison with the prophet. Died in June, 1877.

CLAYTON, ALBERT.
Married Frances Higginbottam. Among their children were: Mary Ann, m. Charles L. Rodebeck Oct. 16, 1872, and John b. Oct. 20, 1852, m. Elizabeth Tonks Aug. 13, 1874. Family home Pleasant Grove, Utah.

CLAYTON, JOHN (son of Albert Clayton and Frances Higginbottam). Born Oct. 20, 1852, Sheffield, Eng.
Married Elizabeth Tonks Aug. 13, 1874, Morgan, Utah (daughter of William and Martha Tonks of England). Their children: Elizabeth, m. John McAffee; John, m. Vinnie Toone; Amelia Louisa, m. Oswald Wilde; Joseph Alfred, m. Edith Davis; Frances Lillian, m. David Reese; Charles Raymond; Alveretta Gertrude; Albert Marlin; Luella Nadine. Family home Morgan, Utah.
Railroad engineer.

CLAYTON, WILLIAM (son of Thomas Clayton and Ann Critchlow of Manchester, Eng.). Born July 14, 1814, Preston, Lancashire, Eng. Came to Utah July 24, 1847, Brigham Young company.
Married Augusta Braddock Oct. 5, 1850, Salt Lake City (daughter of Thomas Braddock and Ann Reid of Bedford, Bedfordshire, Eng., pioneers Nov. 19, 1848, Willard Richards company). She was born Nov. 24, 1833. Their children: Walter Alfred, died; Nephi Willard, b. Oct. 8, 1855, m. Jane Thomas; m. Sybella White Young June 26, 1884; Carrie Gladys, m. Frank Amasa Lyman; Albert Cassus; Daniel John, d. child; Rose, m. O. S. Jackson. Family home Salt Lake City.
Married Sarah Walters. Only child: Archer Walters, b. April 10, 1858, m. Susan Ann Whipple.
Died Dec. 4, 1879, Salt Lake City.

CLAYTON, NEPHI WILLARD (son of William Clayton and Augusta Braddock). Born Oct. 8, 1855, at Salt Lake City.
Married Jane Thomas at Salt Lake City (daughter of Jacob and Ann Thomas, pioneers Levi Richards company). Divorced from Jane Thomas 1883. Their children: Nephi Willard b. March 25, 1880, m. Annie Margaret Jaenich June 26, 1906; Lafayette b. May 11, 1881, m. Hilda Stromburg Nov. 29, 1908. Family home Salt Lake City.
Married Sybella White Young June 26, 1884 at Salt Lake City (daughter of Lucus Lyman Johnson of Springfield, Mass., and Margarette McMinn of Philadelphia, Pa., pioneers Nov. 15, 1866, Mathew White company). She was born Jan. 27, 1854. Their children: Sybella White b. Oct. 3, 1886, m. W. S. Bassett; Charles Comstock b. April 27, 1889, m. Lydia Knudsen; Lawrence b. March 1, 1890; Irving Emerson b. Dec. 29, 1892; Robert McMinn b. May 4, 1894. Family home Salt Lake City.
Member 124th quorum seventies. Territorial librarian and recorder of marks and brands 1876; auditor of public accounts of the territory 1879-90; member of staffs of Governors Caleb W. West and Heber M. Wells; Mgr. Inland Crystal Salt Company 1898; organized and promoted the Salt Lake and Los Angeles Railway Company, and Saltair Beach Company, and served as its president and manager; president Clayton Inv. Company; president Consolidated Music Company 1904; president of the Delray Salt Co. at Detroit, Mich.; president Utah Sulphur Company; owner of Syndicate Insurance Company; president and owner Clayton Land and Cattle Company; director Utah State National Bank. President and owner N. W. Clayton Company.

CLAYTON, ARCHER WALTERS (son of William Clayton and Sarah Walters). Born April 10, 1858, Utah.
Married Susan Ann Whipple May 26, 1882, Salt Lake City (daughter of Nelson Wheeler Whipple, pioneer 1848, and Susan Ann Gay, pioneer 1851, Capt. Brown company). She was born Nov. 3, 1864, at Salt Lake City. Their children: Archer Lynne b. July 7, 1883, m. Marie Sorenson; Don Carlos b. Jan. 15, 1885, m. Bessie Widdesson; Phyllis b. June 28, 1887, m. Jessie R. Pettit; Susan A. b. Dec. 24, 1891; Alonzo H. b. April 25, 1893; Ruth b. Aug. 16, 1895, d. infant; William A. b. Aug. 30, 1897. Family home Salt Lake City, Utah.

CLEGG, BENJAMIN (son of Joseph Clegg and Mary Ogden). Born Sept. 1, 1827, Oldham, Lancashire, Eng. Came to Utah Oct. 28, 1849, Ezra T. Benson company.
Married Elizabeth Dodd April, 1850, Salt Lake City (daughter of Charles and Elizabeth Dodd, of Bilenga, Lincolnshire, Eng.). She was born Sept. 2, 1852, m. Moroni Pickett; Eliza b. April 9, 1856, m. Jonathan H. Hale.
Married Grace McIntyre Dec., 1853, Salt Lake City (daughter of Peter McIntyre and Agnes McCole). Their children: Elizabeth Mary; Benjamin; Peter McIntyre; Agnes; Grace Liliious. Family home Tooele, Utah.
Pioneers to Tooele and has lived there 56 years. High priest. Died Jan. 15, 1908.

CLEGG, PETER McINTYRE (son of Benjamin Clegg and Grace McIntyre). Born Oct. 15, 1859, at Tooele.
Married Edith M. Atkin Jan. 27, 1886, at Tooele, (daughter of Thomas Atkin and Mary Ann Maughan), who was born Oct. 30, 1864, at Tooele. Their children: Zella b. Sept. 13, 1887; Peter Vere b. Dec. 31, 1888, m. Annie May Bryan; Edith M. b. June 21, 1891.
Prominent business man at Tooele. President Tooele County State Bank.

CLEGG, HENRY (son of Henry Clegg and Ellen Cordwell). Born June 7, 1825, Preston, Lancashire, Eng. Came to Utah Sept. 25, 1855, Richard Ballantyne company.
Married Hannah Easton in 1848 at Preston. She was born 1825 and died en route to Utah. Their children: Israel, m. Verona Noakes; Thomas and James, died.
Married Ann Lewis Dec. 3, 1855, Salt Lake City (daughter of John Lewis and Ann John of Cardiff, Wales, former pioneer Sept. 30, 1854, Darwin Richardson company, later died). She was born June 25, 1836, and died April 11, 1913. Their children: John Henry, m. Martha Smith; William Jonathan, m. Jacobina Murdock; Fredrick L., m. Emma Caroline Luke; Lewis and Franklin, died; Amelia A., m. Livingstone Montgomery; Juventa, m. Frederick J. Tullidge; Cardwell, died; Brigham, m. Cloe Pearl Huffaker; Carlie, m. D. Alonzo Tidwell; Henrietta, died. Family resided at Heber and Springville, Utah.
Married Margaret A. Griffiths May, 1856, Salt Lake City (daughter of John Griffiths, born July 7, 1810, and Margaret Griffiths of London, Eng., former pioneer Nov. 30, 1856, Edward Martin company). She was born July 25, 1821. Their children: Thomas G., m. Rachel A. Sessions; Herbert L., m. Sarah C. Smith; Margaret, died; Henry J., m. Ella Chatwin; Hannah M., m. E. J. Cummings; George A., m. Sarah E. Giles; Charles D., m. Martha Niel: Heber, Josephus, Levi, latter three died; Jane E., m. Edward A. Jones. Family home Heber, Utah.
Member 20th quorum seventies; Sunday school superintendent; bishop; stake clerk; high councilor. Justice of peace; school teacher. Shoe manufacturer; merchant. Died Aug. 30, 1894.

CLEGG, WILLIAM JONATHAN (son of Henry Clegg and Ann Lewis). Born May 6, 1859, Springville, Utah.
Married Jacobina Wells Osborne Murdock Dec. 2, 1880, Salt Lake City (daughter of John Murray Murdock and Ann Steel of Heber City, Utah, pioneers Sept. 3, 1852, Abraham O. Smoot company). She was born Nov. 7, 1860. Their children: Tillie b. Sept. 24, 1881, died; Anna Isabella b. May 20, 1883, m. Albert Holdaway; Jacobina b. Nov. 13, 1884; Janetta Juventa b. Oct. 27, 1886, m. Joseph W. McDonald; William Francis b. Nov. 20, 1888, m. Geneva Aston; John Wallace b. Nov. 20, 1888; Mellicentt b. Sept. 18, 1890; Lewis b. Feb. 11, 1892; Jay Osborne b. Jan. 9, 1894; Elinora b. Jan. 6, 1896; Henry Murray b. Sept. 3, 1897; Brigham Otis b. July 7, 1899; Mary Merona b. July 7, 1899; Joseph Heber b. June 15, 1901; Thomas Edwin b. Sept. 27, 1903. Family home Vineyard, Utah.
Elder; ward teacher. Member band during Black Hawk war; assisted in building the first roads in Wasatch and Utah counties; ran shingle-mill in Daniel's canyon 1874. Farmer, stockraiser and miner.

CLEGG, FREDERICK L. (son of Henry Clegg and Ann Lewis). Born Aug. 6, 1861, Springville.
Married Emma Caroline Luke Nov. 30, 1882, Heber City (daughter of Henry Luke and Harriet Luce, former of Manchester, Eng., pioneer 1853, latter of Maine, U. S. A., a pioneer Oct., 1852, Capt. Walker company). She was born Aug. 29, 1861, Heber City. Their children: Henry b. Sept. 3, 1884; Florence b. March 10, 1886; Caddie and Carrie (twins) b. June 22, 1887, latter four died; Frederick M. b. Oct. 5, 1889; Henry b. Jan. 31, 1891; Lula b. Oct. 16, 1892; A. Luke b. April 25, 1894; Columbia b. Oct. 9, 1895; Guy b. April 23, 1897, died; Martelio b. Dec. 25, 1898; Rue L. b. Oct. 1, 1900; Juanita b. March 8, 1902; Russell b. Dec. 24, 1903, died; Reed Kenneth b. March 21, 1907; Genevieve b. Jan. 3, 1909. Family home Heber, Utah.
Probation officer; justice of peace in Wasatch county; city councilman; road supervisor. Contractor, farmer and stockraiser.

CLEGG, JONATHAN (son of Henry Clegg of Preston, Lancashire, Eng.). Born Feb. 26, 1817, near Preston, Lancashire, Eng. Came to Utah Nov. 30, 1856, Edward Martin handcart company.
Married Ellen Wombsley at Preston. She was born Jan. 8, 1817. Came to Utah with husband. Their children: James. m. Mary Ann; William, m. Louisa Gettings; Alice, m. Robert Broadbent; Henry, m. Christina Benson; Margaret Ellen, m. William Baynes. Family home Heber City, Utah.
High priest. Drum major and bandmaster. Pioneer of Heber City 1859. Died Jan. 11, 1901, at Heber City, Utah. Farmer.

CLEGG, ISAAC (son of Thomas Clegg and Ann Passey). Born Dec. 25, 1836, Manchester, Eng. Came to Utah 1860.
Married Dora Jackman Oct. 28, 1872, Salt Lake City (daughter of Permeno Adams Jackman and Phoebe Lodema Merrill, of New York state, pioneers 1847). She was born June 11, 1855. Their children: Luella, m. Charles Jackson; Dora Annie, m. Benjamin Leroy Rich; Chloe Elbina, m. Richard Osborn; Isaac, m. Susie Porter; Permeno Adams, d. infant; Thomas, d. infant; Duane, d. infant. Family home Rexburg, Idaho.
Seventy at Rexburg. Shoe merchant. Died Aug. 6, 1890.

CLEMENTS, ALBERT NEPHI (son of Albert Clements and Ada Winchell, born 1801, both of Warren county, N. Y.; married 1820). He was born in 1842, Hancock county, Ill. Came to Utah Nov., 1852, Warren Snow company.
Married Elizabeth Boice Aug. 20, 1865, Oxford, Idaho (daughter of John Boice and Mary Ann Barzee, pioneers 1852), who was born in 1850. Their children: Albert Nephi b. July 22, 1867; Mary Ann b. March 3, 1869, m. J. G. Sant June 28, 1883; Elizabeth Jane b. Dec. 3, 1870, m. G. F. Williams Nov. 11, 1886; Nephi David b. May 16, 1872; Isabelle b. Feb. 12, 1874, m. George Kingford Jan. 8, 1890; Ada Rebecca b. June 28, 1875, m. John Buckley Jan. 20, 1893; Louisa Torphna b. April 11, 1877, m. John McCoy June 13, 1898; Electa May b. Feb. 9, 1879, m. Edmund Buckley March, 1895; Racheal Sophia b. Dec. 24, 1880, m. Samuel Kennington 1899; John Benjamin b. Feb. 21, 1883; Esther Alveria b. Feb. 12, 1885; Dora Lucy b. Feb. 5, 1887, m. John Jensen April 17, 1905; Isaac Milo b. Jan. 28, 1895. Family home Oxford, Idaho.
Married Laura Georgeson Sept. 18, 1886, at Logan (daughter of Niels Georgeson and Johanna Kofoed, pioneers 1854). She was born May 21, 1868, Weston, Idaho. Their children: Niels William b. Jan. 30, 1888; Alice Alvira b. Sept. 3, 1891, m. George Barzee Jan. 5, 1910; John G. b. May 25, 1894; Ambrose G. b. March 1, 1896; Orris b. Nov. 20, 1897; Elias G. b. Jan. 23, 1904; Clifford G. b. Dec. 8, 1905; Norma G. b. Nov. 28, 1907; Owen G. b. May 24, 1901; Leora b. Nov. 9, 1902. Family home Oxford ward, Idaho.
Assisted to bring immigrants to Utah; president deacons' quorum three years; member high council Oneida stake 25 years; home missionary.

CLEMENTS, JOSEPH. Born Sept. 27, 1817, New Jersey. Came to Utah in 1855, Independent company.
Married Margaret Donaldson, who was born Jan. 4, 1837. They had several children, one of whom was: Mary Jane b. 1854, m. William B. Wood 1872. Family resided at Minersville and Frisco, Utah.
Shoemaker, farmer and stockraiser. Died July 15, 1880, Hay Springs, Beaver county, Utah.

CLIFT, GEORGE W. (son of George W. Clift, born 1793 in Ohio, and Lovia Farley, born at Greenbrier, Va.). He was born Feb. 24, 1817, Saunec, White county, Ill. Came to Utah Oct. 5, 1850.
Married Amanda C. Faucett July 9, 1844 (daughter of John Faucett), who was born Aug. 8, 1827. Their children: Eliza J. b. Jan. 25, 1846, m. Joseph Phelps; Ellen F. b. July 8, 1849, m. Ira N. Jacob; George A. b. April 12, 1851, m. Sarah H. Alexander May 3, 1875; Amanda Jane b. Jan. 19, 1854, m. Jess McCarl; Alzina b. Aug. 29, 1856, m. David Marchant; John E. b. April 14, 1859, m. Laura Wadkins; Mary M. b. May 7, 1861, m. John Wadkins, Jr.; Madora b. Aug. 27, 1862, m. W. J. Wilson; Vilete b. Nov. 29, 1868, m. Joseph Stevens; Francis E. b. April 1, 1871. Family resided Provo, Alpine and Midway, Utah.
High priest; member Joseph Smith's body-guard. Indian war veteran. Died Sept. 5, 1895.

CLIFT, GEORGE A. (son of George W. Clift and Amanda C. Faucett). Born April 12, 1851, Provo, Utah.
Married Sarah H. Alexander May 3, 1875, Salt Lake City (daughter of Henry S. Alexander and Sarah Miles), who was born Oct. 11, 1856, Genoa, Nev. Their children: Sarah Stella b. Aug. 11, 1876, m. Fred Hicken June 7, 1896; Lelia Luella b. July 6, 1879, m. Alfred T. Bond April 14, 1898; George A. b. June 2, 1881; Ida A. b. June 30, 1883, m. Isaac McDonald Oct., 1901; Henry M. b. May 6, 1886; Ruby M. b. April 5, 1888, m. Eugene A. Land May 12, 1908; Hazel D. b. March 20, 1890, m. Everett G. Ward, Jan. 9, 1911; William G. b. July 11, 1895; Frankie J. b. Aug. 7, 1898. Family home Heber City, Utah.
Bishop's counselor; missionary to southern states two years. Black Hawk war veteran.

CLIFTON, JOHN (son of George Clifton born 1800, Dunham, Nottinghamshire, Eng., and Martha Doe). Born March 31, 1829, Normanton, Eng. Came to Utah Sept. 13, 1861, Joseph Horne company.
Married Hannah Pettinger Nov. 26, 1851 (daughter of James Pettinger and Elizabeth Marshall), who was born August, 1827, and came to Utah with husband. Their children: Elizabeth b. July 31, 1852, m. John P. Passey; George b. Oct. 21, 1854, m. Alice Neat; Heber James b. March 5, 1857, m. Ann Parker; Mary Ann b. March 25, 1859, m. Samuel Humphreys; Hannah Martha b. May 12, 1864, m. Samuel Humphreys; John Henry b. Nov. 11, 1867, m. Elizabeth Hoge.
Married Ann Cook Oct. 30, 1861, at Salt Lake City (daughter of Barnabas Cook). She was born March 1, 1829, Crowle, Lincolnshire, Eng. Only child: Sarah Elizabeth b. April 17, 1863, m. L. T. Shepherd.
Married Catherine Randegger July 1, 1901 (daughter of Hans George Randegger and Catherine Gebendinger, who were married Feb. 19, 1850, Schaffhausen, Switzerland).

CLINGER, JAMES. Born Feb. 3, 1813, Bedford, Pa. Came to Utah Sept. 27, 1852, Capt. Whitehead company.
Married Harriet Chapin Dec. 7, 1845, in Illinois (daughter of Adolphus Chapin and Katherine Billings,' of Illinois, pioneers 1860, Independent company). She was born June 6, 1828. Their children: Martha Ann b. Nov. 19, 1846, m. Joseph S. Boren; James Henry b. Feb. 10, 1848, m. Paulina Mary Williamson; Elmira Zallota b. April 25, 1851, died; Mary Jane b. June 8, 1853, m. Peter Murie; William Carlos b. Nov. 4, 1855, m. Elizabeth Gillard; George Francis b. Jan. 25, 1858, m. Anna Johnson; Elinore b. Oct. 28, 1860, m. Miles Parker; Charles Edward b. Feb. 17, 1863, died; John Riggs b. Nov. 28, 1864, m. Lula Boyd; Laura Catherine b. Oct. 1, 1867, m. George Ball; Lucy E. b. May 6, 1871, m. Norman Davis; Elizabeth b. May 11, 1870, died.
Member 34th quorum seventies. Guard in Walker war. Farmer and stockraiser. Died Sept. 6, 1884, Pleasant Grove, Utah.

CLINGER, JAMES HENRY (son of James Clinger and Harriet Chapin). Born Feb. 10, 1848, in Iowa. Came to Utah Sept. 27, 1852.
Married Paulina Mary Williamson Feb. 10, 1868, Provo, Utah (daughter of Niels Williamson and Pernelia Blum of Brevig, Norway, pioneers Oct. 8, 1866, Andrew H. Scott company). She was born Sept. 15, 1848. Their children: Mary Jane b. March 9, 1869, died; James Henry b. Sept. 9, 1870, died; John William b. Dec. 3, 1871, m. Josephine Zoebell; Marion b. June 13, 1874, m. Rebecca Dorius; Henrietta b. Sept. 11, 1875, m. William J. Brown; Parley Browning b. April 5, 1878, m. Mary Williamson; Martin Albert b. Sept. 18, 1881, m. Tena Johnson; Harriet Ann b. Jan. 31, 1883, m. Angus Wride; Lillie May b. Sept. 14, 1888, m. Jesse Sumison. Family home Lake View, Utah.
Married Caroline Christensen Sept. 24, 1884, Salt Lake City (daughter of Peter C. and Marie Christensen, of Mayfield, Utah), who was born Dec. 4, 1866. Their children: Heber Christian b. May 31, 1889, m. Myrtle Alstrom; Myrtle Marie b. Nov. 14, 1893, m. Clifford Whitlock. Family home Mayfield, Utah.
High priest; missionary to Norway 1884-86; counselor to Bishop Johnson eight years. Constable at Provo eight years. Farmer and stockraiser.

CLOWARD, DANIEL (son of Jacob Cloward, born March 17, 1790, in Maryland, and Ann Pluck, born June 19, 1795, in Pennsylvania). He was born Aug. 30, 1820, in Chester county, Pa. Came to Utah Oct. 1852.
Married Ruth Bailey Logan, who was born Oct. 23, 1819, and came to Utah with husband. Their children: Catherine E. b. May 24, 1845, m. Lemuel Hegg; Daniel H. b. Feb. 11, 1848, m. Celestia A. Harwood Nov. 29, 1878; Heber C. b. Dec. 17, 1851; Mary J. b. 1853, m. Adelbert Searle. Family home Provo, Utah.

CLOWARD, DANIEL H. (son of Daniel Cloward and Ruth Bailey Logan). Born Feb. 11, 1848, Council Bluffs, Iowa.
Married Celestia A. Harwood Nov. 29, 1878, Salt Lake City (daughter of Thomas Harward and Sabrina Curtis), who was born March 13, 1858, Cedar City, Utah. Their children: D. Marion b. Aug. 2, 1885, m. Lillian Murphy May 2, 1907; Thomas H. b. July 20, 1888, m. Amanda Peterson March 11, 1908; Gertrude b. Jan. 7, 1891; Zellie b. Aug. 22, 1893; Mark b. Jan. 10, 1897. Family home Aurora, Utah.
Superintendent Y. M. M. I. A; bishop's counselor six years; ward teacher. Trustee Aurora school board.

CLUCAS, HENRY. Born May 15, 1805, Douglas, Isle of Man. Came to Utah Oct. 1855, C. A. Harper company.
Married Elizabeth Martin Feb. 3, 1835, at Trinity church, Whithaven, Eng. (daughter of William Martin and Lucy Walton), who was born July 31, 1805. Came to Utah with her husband. She died March 5, 1887. Their children: Henry Launcelot b. March 28, 1836, d. Nov. 30, 1857; Mary b. Jan. 2, 1841, m. Ephraim B. Sept. 2, 1843, m. Nephi Packard; Lucy b. Oct. 19, 1845, m. William Roylance.
Ward teacher. Settled at Springville, Utah, 1855. Pot printer. Died Oct. 17, 1882, Springville.

CLUFF, DAVID (son of William Cluff and Susannah Runnels of Durham, New Hampshire, and Provo, Utah). Born June 20, 1795, Durham, New Hampshire. Came to Utah Oct. 13, 1850, Edward Hunter company.
Married Betsy Hall Jan. 11, 1824, at Durham, N. H. Their children: Lavina, m. Hyrum Sweet; David, m. Sarah Ann Fleming, m. Anis H. Elmer; Moses, m. Rebecca Langman, m. Jane Johnson, m. Ann Bond, m. Eliza Langman; Benjamin, m. Mary Ellen Foster, m. Eliza A. Foster; William Wallace, m. Anne Whipple; Joseph, m. Phoebe Bunnell; Harvey Harris, m. Margaret Ann Foster; Samuel Sampson, m. Frances Worsley, m. Ann E. Carruth; Hyrum, m. Mary Worsley; Henry, m. Keziah Elizabeth Russell; Alfred, m. Jane Foster; Orson, m. Hattie Bean, m. Marinth L. Loveridge.
Married Anna Chapman at Provo, Utah. Only child: Jerry, m. Lydia Snow.
President seventies; missionary to Canada and New Hampshire 1867-69; patriarch. Provo city councilman. Carpenter and cabinet maker. Died Dec. 16, 1881, Smithville, Ariz.

CLUFF, BENJAMIN (son of David Cluff and Betsy Hall). Born March 20, 1830, Durham, New Hampshire. Came to Utah Oct. 13, 1850, Edward Hunter company.
Married Mary Ellen Foster (daughter of George Foster and Jane McCullough; former a pioneer 1852, latter died on the plains en route to Utah). She was born Dec. 24, 1837. Their children: Mary; Benjamin, Jr. b. Feb. 7, 1858, m. Mary Jane Johns, m. Harriet Cullimore; George, m. ——; D. Foster, m. Helena Cora Alexander; Walter, m. Gertrude Miller. Family home Provo, Utah.
Married Eliza Arnetta Foster February, 1856, Salt Lake City (daughter of George Foster and Jane McCullough), who was born Nov. 13, 1841. Their children: Eliza Ann, m. Alma U. Hobson; Josephine, m. Andrew Kimball; Margaret, m. Samuel Hobson; William K., m. Emma Moody; Bessie, m. Hyrum Willard Merrill; Karl V., m. Maud ——. Family home Logan, Utah.
Seventy; missionary to Sandwich Islands 1864-70; bishop of Center ward several years; patriarch. Mechanic and carpenter. Died 1910, Finca Lagunillas, Huimanguillo, Tabasco, Mexico.

CLUFF, WILLIAM WALLACE (son of David Cluff and Betsy Hall). Born March 8, 1832, at Willoughby, Ohio, pioneer 1850, Capt. Hunter company.
Married Anne Whipple Oct. 24, 1864, Pine Valley, Utah (daughter of Eli Whipple and Patience Foster of Pennsylvania, pioneers 1858). She was born March 15, 1844. Their children: William Wallace b. Aug. 31, 1865, m. Edith Atwood; Anne May b. May 10, 1866, m. Frank Olsen; Lilian b. Dec. 21, 1876, m. Jack Pawlos, who died; m. Given A. Light; Flora Marion b. June 9, 1879, m. Lawrence Eldredge; Erastus Eli b. June 11, 1869; Albion b. May 11, 1873; Edwin b. May 11, 1873; Joseph b. Jan. 5, 1884; the latter four died. Family home Coalville, Utah.
Member of 22d quorum seventies; missionary to Sandwich Islands 1854-58; to Denmark 1859-63 and 1870-73; bishop Summit, Morgan and Wasatch counties; president Summit stake twenty-eight years. First mayor of Coalville; member state legislature eight years. General manager coal mines, Coalville. Merchant.

CLUFF, HARVEY HARRIS (son of David Cluff and Betsy Hall). Born Jan. 9, 1836, at Kirtland, Ohio. Came to Utah 1850, Edward Hunter company.
Married Margaret Ann Foster Jan. 24, 1856, Provo, Utah (daughter of George Foster of Provo, Utah, pioneer 1852). She was born Jan. 23, 1840. Their children: Harvey Harris b. Oct. 28, 1857; Seth M. b. March 18, 1859; George H. b. May 30, 1862; Margaret Ann b. March 31, 1864; they all died. Family home Provo.
Married Emily Greening Till July 6, 1877, St. George, Utah (daughter of Robert A. Till and Mary A. Greening of Provo, pioneers 1854). She was born Feb. 26, 1858. Their children: Birdie J. b. 1879, m. H. R. Leedom; D. Lilly Ann b. 1884, m. Frank Alexander; Enbranim b. 1885, m. Emma Dixon; Gordon H. b. 1887, and Harold H. b. 1889, died; Ivy Isabell b. 1891, m. Albert T. Harding; Joy Robert b. 1893; Kenneth H. b. 1895; Lydia Laueritte b. 1898. Family home Provo, Utah.
Married Sarah Eggertson July 6, 1877, St. George, Utah (daughter of Simon P. and Johanna Eggertson, of Provo, Utah, pioneers 1852). She was born 1857. Their children: Alfred Peter b. 1879, died; Clara J. b. 1883, m. John Q. Ryan; Franklin L. b. 1885. Family home Provo, Utah.
President 45th quorum seventies; missionary to England 1865-68; bishop of 4th ward of Provo; president Utah stake; missionary to Sandwich Islands 1869-74. Assisted in colonizing Skull Valley 1889-01. City councilman at Provo. Cabinet-maker, farmer and rancher.

CLUFF, SAMUEL S. (son of David Cluff and Betsy Hall, of Vermont). Born Sept. 27, 1837, Kirtland, Ohio. Came to Utah Oct. 4, 1850, Edward Hunter company.
Married Frances Worsley March 16, 1861, Provo, Utah (daughter of John Worsley and Sarah Hamer, of England, pioneers Sept. 17, 1853, John W. Cooley company). She was born Nov. 8, 1841. Their children: Henry b. March 17, 1862, d. April 1863; Fannie b. March 21, 1865, m. Dave Bonnett; Sarah Jane b. April 6, 1867, d. Feb. 1868; Bessie b. July 10, 1870, d. Nov. 6, 1879; Harvey b. Oct. 24, 1872, m. Freda Barnum, Oct. 11, 1900; Samuel b. May 15, 1875, m.

Minnie Moyle; Elmo b. Sept. 20, 1880, m. Mamie Grain; Sidney b. May 1, 1882, m. Kadie Coivin. Family home Provo, Utah.
One of presidents 45th quorum seventies.

CLUFF, HARVEY (son of Samuel S. Cluff and Frances Worsley). Born Oct. 24, 1872, Provo, Utah.
Married Freda Barnum Oct. 11, 1900, at Salt Lake City (daughter of Guy C. and Amelia Barnum, of Provo. She was born March 14, 1876. Their children: Bernice b. Feb. 23, 1903; Frances b. March 30, 1907. Family home Provo.
Lawyer; attorney fourth judicial district, 1908-13; secretary state board of insanity.

CLYDE, GEORGE W. (son of George Washington Clyde, born 1798, and Cynthia Davis, born Jan. 28, 1806, both in New York state). He was born July 8, 1825, Ogdensburg, St. Lawrence county, N. Y. Came to Utah Sept. 15, 1850, David Evans company.
Married Jane McDonald Sept. 30, 1851, Springville, Utah (daughter of James McDonald and Sarah Ferguson of Crawfordsburn, County Down, Ireland; former died crossing plains; latter a pioneer Sept. 12, 1850). She was born July 17, 1827, at Crawfordsburn. Their children: George David W. b. Aug. 8, 1852; John b. Nov. 25, 1853, m. Fannie Jane Young Dec. 25, 1877; James William b. Aug. 30, 1855, m. Mary Campbell Dec. 12, 1884; Sarah Jane b. Aug. 16, 1858, m. Joseph Hatch Aug. 16, 1875; Robert b. Sept. 9, 1860, m. Margaret Cummings 1886; Mary Lorintha b. Sept. 24, 1862, m. William S. Willis Nov. 30, 1882; Edward D. b. Sept. 19, 1864, m. Clara Prudence Alexander Nov. 20, 1889; Georgiana b. Aug. 6, 1866, m. Nathan Alexander Neibaur April 1888; Sophia b. Nov. 25, 1868, m. John Henry Luke Nov. 25, 1890. Family home Heber, Utah.
Seventy. Commissioner Wasatch county 1884-85. Farmer and stockraiser.

CLYDE, EDWARD D. (son of George W. Clyde and Jane McDonald). Born Sept. 19, 1864, Heber, Utah.
Married Clara Prudence Alexander Nov. 20, 1889, Logan, Utah (daughter of Henry Samuel Alexander and Sarah Simons Miles, former of Ackworth, New Hampshire, latter of Freedom, N. Y., pioneers Oct. 28, 1849). She was born May 10, 1867. Their children: Edward Delbert b. Sept. 30, 1891; Lynden b. Aug. 10, 1893; Lionel Dean b. Dec. 19, 1894; Ednai Euilla b. Jan. 4, 1899; Elmo Miles b. May 10, 1904; Lily Clair b. May 16, 1906. Family home Heber, Utah.
Elder; missionary to Ireland 1864-67; to Boston 1901-03; and to Europe 1885-87; high priest; M. I. A. missionary in Millard and Juab stakes 1897-98; 1st counselor to bishop of Heber ward 1904-06; 2d counselor to stake president. Justice of peace; mayor. School teacher. Farmer and stockraiser.

CLYDE, WILLIAM MORGAN (son of George Washington Clyde and Cynthia Davis). Born April 8, 1829, Ogdensburg, N. Y. Came to Utah Sept. 17, 1850, David Evans company.
Married Eliza McDonald Jan. 24, 1851 (daughter of James McDonald and Sarah Ferguson, of Ireland, and came to Utah with her mother. Sept. 12, 1850. Their children: William b. Nov. 5, 1851, m. Ann Winget May 1, 1872; George W. b. March 26, 1854; James b. Aug. 26, 1856, m. Rhoda M. Potter Dec. 16, 1877; Almon b. Jan. 2, 1859, m. Electa Kendall Oct. 26, 1881; Hyrum S. b. Aug. 16, 1861, m. Elenora Johnson Jan. 9, 1887; Mary L. b. March 4, 1864, m. Abner Thorne Jan. 20, 1889; David b. Feb. 6, 1866, m. Ella W. Worden Jan. 18, 1900; Elva J. b. April 11, 1868, m. P. E. Houtz Aug. 28, 1889; John E. b. Jan. 19, 1870, m. Jesse Ervine April 13, 1904; Clara B. b. March 9, 1872; Lucy b. Dec. 21, 1874, m. W. O. Richard Jan. 1, 1896. Family home Springville, Utah.
Married Sarah Bateman Dec. 14, 1862, Salt Lake City (daughter of James Bateman and Bridget Medruth), who was born 1840, Coventry, Warwickshire, Eng. Their children: Edward b. Sept. 12, 1863; Lorinthy b. Sept. 12, 1864; Sarah A. b. Feb. 23, 1866, m. William Kemmar June 17, 1888; Joseph B. and Josephine b. Feb. 2, 1869; Julia b. Sept. 12, 1872, m. Andrew Johnson Jan. 27, 1898; Viola b. July 22, 1876, m. W. E. Beardell Oct. 17, 1895; Violetta b. July 22, 1876; Willis E. b. July 17, 1880; Elsa b. Oct. 5, 1882, m. John Forsyth Nov. 22, 1905.
Settled at Springville 1851. In 1862 went to Florence, Neb. for immigrants. He participated in Walker Indian war 1853, and in Black Hawk Indian war 1866-67. His was the first wedding at Alpine, Utah. Jan. 24, 1851, he was one of the two survivors to represent the first seven settlers of Alpine, Utah.

CLYDE, HYRUM S. (son of William Morgan Clyde and Eliza McDonald). Born Aug. 16, 1861, Springville, Utah.
Married Elenora J. Johnson Jan. 9, 1887 at Springville (daughter of Lorenzo Johnson and Mary A. Hall), who was born May 25, 1864, at Springville. Their children: Jesse James b. Sept. 17, 1887; Bessie b. Oct. 21, 1888; Wilford W. b. Oct. 27, 1889; Hazel b. Nov. 29, 1891; Grover b. Nov. 18, 1893; Edward b. Jan. 23, 1896; George Dewey b. July 21, 1898; Harry Schley b. Jan. 9, 1902; Clara b. April 10, 1906.
Member Springville city council one term; served two terms on Mapleton town board. Farmer.

COBBLEY, THOMAS. Born Jan. 22, 1820, Huntingdonshire, Eng. Came to Utah Sept. 27, 1862, John R. Murdock company.
Married Sarah Smith (daughter of John Smith and Hannah Sutton, pioneers Sept. 22, 1861, Samuel A. Woolley company). She was born April 16, 1823 and came to Utah with her husband. Their children: Robert b. 1844, m. Caroline Harris Dec. 20, 1869; James b. Sept. 21, 1846, m. Emmer Thorne Dec. 20, 1869; Emily, m. Amasa Lyman Mecham 1866; Jane, m. Edward Kahler; Charles A. b. 1860, m. Emma Davis; John b. 1862, m. Marie Halverson. Family home Pleasant Grove, Utah.

COBBLEY, JAMES (son of Thomas Cobbley and Sarah Smith). Born Sept. 21, 1846. Came to Utah Sept. 1862, Kimball and Lawrence freight company.
Married Emmer Thorne Dec. 20, 1869 (daughter of David Thorne and Elizabeth Reeves of Pleasant Grove, Utah, pioneers 1851, independent company). She was born March 16, 1848. Their children: Emma L. Norah b. Oct. 17, 1870, m. John S. Harper April 18, 1886; Sarah Elizabeth b. Sept. 2, 1872, m. William Parks March 1898; James David Orville b. July 14, 1874, m. Amanda I. Christianson Jan. 17, 1900; Emily Izella b. March 2, 1876, m. Willard Boulter June 1899; Clara Jenett b. March 18, 1879, m. William Ash Sept. 13, 1903; George Thomas b. March 5, 1881, m. Bertha Harper Sept. 12, 1907; Robert Henry b. Feb. 13, 1883, died; Effie Jane b. March 14, 1885, m. James Yancy Oct. 8, 1908; Etta May b. Oct. 30, 1887, m. Nels Sorenson Sept. 12, 1907; Joseph Eugene b. Dec. 6, 1889, m. Esther Wray June 7, 1912; Marian Reeves b. Feb. 4, 1891; Dorothy b. Oct. 6, 1900 (adopted).
Sunday school supt. 1885; president Y. M. M. I. A. 1891; bishop of Pleasant Grove 2d ward 1890-1904. Member city council of Pleasant Grove 1883; alderman 1886; member Pleasant Grove school board 1874-85. Went to Missouri River with Capt. Chipman in 1866, and with John Holman in 1868, for immigrants.

COFFIN, NATHAN HARRISON (son of William Barney Coffin, born Feb. 27, 1809, in North Carolina and Abigail Starbuck, born June 1, 1813, in Indiana; married Sept. 21, 1833). He was born Sept. 28, 1840, Richmond, Ind. Came to Utah, 1852, Captain Cutler company.
Married Chestina McMurtrey Dec. 7, 1863 (daughter of Samuel McMurtrey and Julia Ann Morris; pioneers 1849). She was born Jan. 27, 1847. Their children: Ester Vernetta b. Oct. 16, 1864, died; Amanda b. Sept. 26, 1866, m. John D. Kent Nov. 20, 1884; Eliza Ellen b. Nov. 21, 1868, m. Joseph A. Brim Jan. 12, 1886; Nathan Samuel b. Sept. 11, 1870, m. Margaretta Cooper Aug. 26, 1892; Jesse Thomas b. June 12, 1873, died; Effie May b. Oct. 11, 1875, m. Charles Johnson June 13, 1900; Henry Clay b. Nov. 25, 1878, m. Phoebe Richardson Oct. 10, 1900; William Barney b. June 4, 1880, m. Anna Johnson Nov. 14, 1901; Julia Abigail b. Nov. 16, 1882; Ella Lucile b. July 10, 1884, died; Mary b. June 13, 1881, m. Morgan Evans Oct. 8, 1906; Hattie b. March 20, 1890, died.
High councilor. Road supervisor; justice of peace.

COFFIN, NATHAN SAMUEL (son of Nathan Harrison Coffin and Chestina McMurtrey). Born Sept. 11, 1870, Huntsville, Utah.
Married Margaretta Cooper Aug. 26, 1892, McCammon, Idaho (daughter of Vincent Cooper and Mary Miller, pioneers 1852). She was born Dec. 14, 1870, Oxford, Idaho. Their children: Clarence James b. Aug. 1, 1893; Martha Irene b. Feb. 2, 1895; Mary Lucile b. Oct. 25, 1897; Nathan Sherman b. Nov. 16, 1899; Golden Agrippa b. June 24, 1903; Margaretta b. April 24, 1905; Fredric Samuel b. April 19, 1907; Hazel b. April 1, 1909; Jesse Cooper b. Oct. 18, 1912. Family home Marsh Center, Idaho.
School teacher. Secretary Sunday school and Y. M. M. I. A. several years; missionary to eastern states; president Y. M. M. I. A. Justice of peace. Is now bishop of Marsh Center ward, having been sustained Nov. 22, 1903.

COLBORN, THOMAS (son of Jonathan Colborn and Hannah Hamilton of Wayne county, N. Y.). Born Aug. 3, 1801, in Wayne county. Came to Utah Sept. 24, 1848, Heber C. Kimball company.
Married Sarah Bowers 1825, Lyons, Wayne county, N. Y. (daughter of Amos Bowers and Rosina Young of Lansing, Tompkins county, N. Y., pioneers Sept. 14, 1848, Heber C. Kimball company). She was born Nov. 4, 18—, and died Dec. 26, 1872, Peterson, Utah. Their children: Amanda b. Dec. 29, 1826, m. Winslow Farr; Thomas, died; Hannah b. Oct. 29, 1831, m. Samuel Miles; Sarah Matilda b. Nov. 4, 1834, m. Francis Martin Pomercy; Rosina b. April 16, 1837, m. William Godbe; Talma b. May 16, 1841, d. 1843. Family home Salt Lake City.
Missionary to Germany and England 1856; high priest; member Zion's Camp. Farmer. Died April, 1887 at Salt Lake City.

COLEBROOK, CHARLES. Born March 17, 1816, Midhurst, Sussex, Eng. Came to Utah 1851.
Married Meris Purser March 10, 1847. Only child: Nellie. Family home Salt Lake City.
Married Virtue Ann Bowthorne Jan. 1, 1854, at Salt Lake City (daughter of William Bowthorne and Mary Ann Tuttle, pioneers Oct. 14, 1853, Cyrus H. Wheelock company). She was born Feb. 28, 1836, Norwich, Eng. Only child: Charles b. Dec. 20, 1854, m. Sarah McGhie March 18, 1884. Family home Sandy, Utah.
Bookkeeper at tithing office; ordinance officer. Milliner.

COLEBROOK, CHARLES (son of Charles Colebrook and Virtue Ann Bowthorpe). Born Dec. 20, 1854, Salt Lake City.
Married Sarah McGhie March 18, 1884, Salt Lake City (daughter of William McGhie and Mary McBlain, pioneers Oct. 1, 1854, Daniel Garn company). She was born Nov. 5, 1865. Only child: Lewis b. Oct. 2, 1885. Family home Butlerville, Utah.
High priest; second counselor in bishopric ten years; Sunday school superintendent. Member Jordan school board three years; school trustee 57th school district nine years. Railroad builder.

COLEMAN, GEORGE (son of Prime Coleman, born 1802, Airsly, Herts. Eng., and Sarah Thornton, born 1806, Paxton Hants, Eng.—married 1826). He was born May 5, 1827, Warden parish, Bedfordshire, Eng. Came to Utah 1852.
Married Jane Smith Jan. 28, 1857 (daughter of Alexander Smith and May McEwan, the latter a pioneer Nov. 9, 1856, J. G. Willie handcart company). She was born Sept. 22, 1838; came to Utah with parents. Their children: Mary b. Dec. 6, 1858, m. Sylvester Williams Jan. 1, 1877; Sarah May b. Sept. 20, 1860, m. Charles Snow Jan. 28, 1885; Betsey A. b. Aug. 4, 1862, died; Emma Jane b. July 3, 1863, m. Heber J. Wilson Oct., 1885; George S. b. May 20, 1866, m. Angeline Hunt May 5, 1886; Alexander S. b. May 8, 1870, m. Anna Oetberg Jan. 12, 1892; Walter Prime b. Aug. 5, 1874, m. Leona Brinkerhof April, 1903; John A. b. Aug. 4, 1876, died; Maggie R. b. Oct. 2, 1878, died. Family resided Escalante, Lehi and Smithfield, Utah.
Married Olive Talseth June, 1865, Salt Lake City (daughter of Peter Olsen Talseth, pioneer Sept. 15, 1864, William B. Preston company). She was born April 3, 1834, in Norway. Their children: Samuel b. April 14, 1870, m. Sarah Burr Nov. 20, 1890; Joseph, died; Ann b. May 26, 1866, m. Robert Forsyth, Jr.
Missionary to Salmon river. "Indian war veteran; called to settle the country in Arizona in 1876 under George Lake. Bishop 1886-1900.

COLEMAN, GEORGE S. (son of George Coleman and Jane Smith). Born May 20, 1866, Smithfield, Utah.
Married Angeline Hunt May 5, 1886, St. George, Utah (daughter of Amos Hunt and Nancy G. Welborn, pioneers Sept. 24, 1852, Benjamin Gardner company). She was born Oct. 7, 1869, Hebron, Washington county, Utah. Their children: Nancy Angeline b. July 2, 1887, m. Lyman Taft April 6, 1906; Jane b. April 16, 1889, m. Neil Forsythe Nov. 24, 1909; Sarah Malinda b. Sept. 25, 1890; May b. Dec. 10, 1892; Bertha Ellen b. July 12, 1895; Sylvia b. June 12, 1902; George Burdett b. Feb. 20, 1906; Kenneth Hunt b. June 6, 1909.
Missionary to New Zealand; bishop Teasdale ward 1900-04.

COLEMAN, GEORGE. Born Nov. 30, 1815, Sherrington, Buckinghamshire, Eng. Came to Utah 1864.
Married Elizabeth Baily 1835 (daughter of John and Sarah Baily, of Sherrington, Eng.). She was born Oct. 17, —; died April 22, 1890, Big Cottonwood, Utah. Their children: Henry b. May 5, 1836, m. Mary Jane Threlkeld; Charles; William, m. Mary Clotworthy; George, m. Mary World; Lewis, m. Rachel O'Neil; Sarah, m. Preston Lewis; Elizabeth, m. Simon Lewis; Samuel; Annie, m. William McMillan. Family home Big Cottonwood, Utah.
High priest; choir leader at Big Cottonwood, Utah. Farmer; matting maker. Died June 15, 1888, Salt Lake City.

COLEMAN, HENRY (son of George Coleman and Elizabeth Baily). Born May 5, 1836, at Sherrington. Came to Utah 1850, Samuel McClaridge company.
Married Mary Jane Threlkeld Nov. 30, 1860, Big Cottonwood, Utah (daughter of John Threlkeld, born March 4, 1814, died 1875, and Elizabeth Barker, born Dec. 17, 1810, Glasgow, Scotland, died Dec. 19, 1870, both of Carlisle, Cumberland, Eng.). She was born May 15, 1842, at Carlisle, and came to Utah Aug. 28, 1860, Francis Brown company. Their children: Elizabeth b. Dec. 9, 1861, m. Charles Alonzo Epperson; Henry Threlkeld b. Nov. 20, 1863, m. Emily Matilda Springer Lucretia H. b. Dec. 23, 1865, m. Francis Ernest Wellman; Margaret E. b. Aug. 2, 1868, m. Alexander C. McKendry. Family home Midway, Utah.
Elder. Assisted in hauling the stone for Salt Lake temple. Indian war veteran; assisted in making canals and wagon roads. Lumberman. Died Dec. 25, 1867.

COLEMAN, HENRY THRELKELD (son of Henry Coleman and Mary Jane Threlkeld). Born Nov. 20, 1863, Salt Lake county, Utah.
Married Emily Matilda Springer Dec. 31, 1889, Midway, Utah (daughter of Nathan Chatmond Springer, born June 26, 1843, Providence, R. I., and Matilda Robey, both of Midway, Utah, pioneers 1862). She was born Sept. 6, 1868, at Midway. Their children: Henry Springer b. Jan. 13, 1891; Guy Ellsworth b. May 10, 1892; Lethe Belle b. Dec. 28, 1893; Nathan Chatmond b. April 23, 1895; Glen Robey b. March 17, 1897; Nathan Chatmond b. April 23, 1897; Keith Threlkeld b. April 10, 1901; Dale Franklin b. Jan. 16, 1904; Rhea Lillian b. May 19, 1907; Ruth May b. Nov. 3, 1909; Jessie Chloe b. March 17, 1911. Family home Midway, Utah.

PIONEERS AND PROMINENT MEN OF UTAH

High priest; bishop of 1st ward, Midway, Utah; 2nd counselor to presidency of elders' quorum; first counselor in Y. M. M. I. A.; County commissioner 1902-06; president Midway Water Works company six years; Midway city councilman six years. Blacksmith; farmer, sheepraiser; mining contractor.

COLLETT, DANIEL (son of Thomas Collett of Gloucestershire, Parish of Corse, Eng.). Born Dec. 9, 1809. Came to Utah 1849.
Married Esther Jones, who died 1858, Lehi, Utah. Their children: Sylvanus, m. Lydia Karren; Rhoda, m. John Eldredge; m. Philemon C. Merrill; Ruben, m. Elthurah Roseltha Merrill; Mary Ann, m. William Wamsley; Matilda, m. Ralph Teancum Merrill; Julia Ann, m. James Cantwell; Charles C., m. Anna Merrill; James Jones, m. —— Tidwell.
Married Mary Empey in 1860 (parents pioneers of 1847). Only child: Eliza, m. Robert Jones.
Married Elizabeth Gordon in 1859 (parents pioneers 1857, Edward Martin handcart company). She died 1859. Only child: William Gordon, m. Ada Rich.
Married Betsy Burke 1861. Their children: Thomas; Daniel. Families' home Smithfield, Utah.
High priest. Pioneer to Smithfield 1850. Wheelwright and farmer. Died in May, 1896.

COLLETT, REUBEN (son of Daniel Collett and Esther Jones). Born July 13, 1839, Gloucestershire, Parish of Corse, Eng. Came to Utah 1849.
Married Elthurah Roseltha Merrill Jan. 19, 1861, Smithfield, being first marriage performed in this place (daughter of Samuel B. Merrill and Elizabeth Runyon of Smithfield, pioneers of 1851). She was born Sept. 8, 1841. Their children: Reuben Samuel, m. Flora Elsie Colton; Sylvester Daniel, d. while on mission to Mexico; Sylvanus, m. Sarah Simpkins; m. Ethel Winnie Stringham; Julia Ann, m. William Postma; Adelbert T., m. Pernellie Goodrich; Charles M., m. Elnora Munk; Princetto, m. Albert Bills; Clarence J., m. Margarett Watkins; Roseltha, m. Albert W. Nielsen; George. Family home Smithfield.
High priest; missionary to Salmon River 1858-59; counselor to Bishop Thomas Jones of Lehi, Ariz.; member high council of Maricopa stake, Ariz., and also of Uinta stake; assisted in bringing immigrants to Utah. Pioneer to Lehi, Escalante, Vernal and Smithfield, Utah; Bennington, Idaho, and Cokeville, Wyo. Active in school and public enterprises. Indian war veteran.

COLLETT, REUBEN SAMUEL (son of Reuben Collett and Elthurah Roseltha Merrill). Born May 12, 1878, Provo, Utah.
Married Flora Elsie Colton Nov. 20, 1890, Logan, Utah (daughter of Sterling Driggs Colton and Nancy Adeline Williams of Vernal, Utah), who was born June 7, 1872, Provo, Utah. Their children: Gertrude b. July 9, 1892; Elsie b. Feb. 11, 1894; Reuben Sterling b. May 13, 1895; Mary b. Oct. 3, 1896; Karl Warren b. March 29, 1898; Merle b. June 21, 1900, died; Flora and Cora b. Feb. 19, 1902. Family resided at Roosevelt and Vernal, Utah.
Missionary to England 1884-86; high priest; 1st counselor to Samuel R. Bennion of Uinta stake presidency 1887-1906; high councilor Uinta stake 1909 to present time. Vernal city councilman eight years; postmaster; chairman of board of education of the Uinta Stake academy 1888-04. Organized Dry Gulch Irrigation company December 1905, served as president, director and secretary; farmer; merchant and real estate dealer.

COLLINGS, JAMES, SR. (son of John Collings and Elizabeth Robinson of Durham, Eng.). Born May 29, 1812, Sunderland, Durham. Came to Utah August 30, 1860, Jesse E. Murphy company.
Married Elizabeth Bewick (daughter of John Bewick and Catherine Stephanson), who was born Sept. 13, 1813, and came to Utah with her husband. Their children: John b. July 14, 1835, died; Elizabeth b. April 15, 1837, m. Simpson Moien; John b. Sept. 16, 1839, died; James b. Jan. 3, 1845, m. Frances P. Rich Oct. 5, 1874; Catherine b. Feb. 20, 1847, m. C. W. Maughan Sept, 1866; William John b. Sept. 15, 1849, died; Deseret b. Jan. 28, 1852, m. John T. Rich; Mahonri M. b. Jan. 17, 1856, m. Anne Horsley June 26, 1885.
High priest.

COLLINGS, JAMES [II] (son of James Collings and Elizabeth Bewick). Born Jan. 3, 1845, Depthford, Eng.
Married Frances Phoebe Rich Oct. 5, 1874, Salt Lake City (daughter of Charles Coulson Rich and Eliza Ann Graves), who was born June 30, 1850, Big Cottonwood, Utah. Their children: Elizabeth Ann b. June 13, 1876, m. Parley Pratt Parrish Sept. 14, 1905; James W. b. Aug. 6, 1898, m. Amelia Poulson; Eliza Ann b. Dec. 26, 1879; Charles R. b. Dec. 5, 1881; William B. b. May 5, 1883, died; Frances Phoebe b. Sept. 19, 1885, died; Catherine b. March 9, 1887; Joseph L. b. April 2, 1889; John b. Nov. 25, 1890; Mary F. b. Sept. 16, 1892; Leah b. July 23, 1895. Family home Paris, Idaho.

COLLINGS, RICHARD (son of Joseph and Sarah Collings). Born June 23, 1818, Tring, Buckinghamshire, Eng. Came to Utah Nov. 30, 1856, Edward Martin handcart company.
Married Emma Lawrence May 26, 1847 (daughter of Simon Lawrence and Ann Archer), who was born Nov. 26, 1826, and came to Utah with husband. Their children: Louise b. Nov. 1, 1849, m. J. W. Johnson March 6, 1866; Fred b. April 24, 1851, m. Fanny ——; David b. April 19, 1853, m. Frances Agusta Lisonbee Jan. 28, 1873; George b. Aug. 7, 1855, m. Mary Ann Lemons; Samuel b. Dec. 7, 1857, m. Lizzy Bertelsen; Will b. Aug. 3, 1859, m. Geneva Bean; Lyman b. Jan. 14, 1861, m. Marah Christianson; Sarah Ann b. Aug. 9, 1863, m. J. W. Taylor; Jane b. July 22, 1865, m. Samuel Dall. Family home Springville, Utah.

COLLINGS, DAVID (son of Richard Collings and Emma Lawrence). Born April 19, 1853, London, Eng. Came to Utah Nov. 30, 1856.
Married Frances Agusta Lisonbee Jan. 28, 1873, Monroe, Utah (daughter of Hugh Dobbins Lisonbee and Elma Hayman, the former of Alabama, the latter of Newart, Ill., pioneers 1850). She was born Jan. 28, 1858, Springville, Utah. Their children: David Owen b. Sept. 26, 1873, m. Minnie Nielsen; Ole Lavell b. Oct. 7, 1876, d. Aug. 29, 1877; Otto b. Aug. 11, 1878, m. Nora Bertelson; Luella Emma b. Oct. 6, 1880, d. Feb. 23, 1908; Elma ArDelcia b. Sept. 27, 1882, m. William W. Harmon; Roy b. Dec. 17, 1884, m. Florence Anderson; Mattie b. Jan. 7, 1887; Turner Wells b. July 15, 1889, d. Jan. 30, 1891; Guy Willis b. Oct. 16, 1892; Hazel Dotta b. Oct. 18, 1894; Frank Jay b. March 4, 1897; Fay Loring b. March 4, 1897, d. Sept. 16, 1897; Brett Adeline b. Aug. 9, 1899, d. Jan. 27, 1908; Welby Mae b. April 9, 1903. Family home Monroe, Utah.
Missionary to northwestern states 1887-89. State sheep inspector. Proprietor of "Monroe House." Farmer and stockraiser; contractor.

COLLINS, THOMAS (son of John Collins and Priscilla Sheffard, Collinbourn, Kingston, Wiltshire, Eng.). Born Jan. 12, 1832, at Collinbourn, Kingston, Eng. Came to Utah late in 1866 with ox and mule teams.
Married Mary Liddiard Feb. 23, 1877, Provo, Utah (daughter of Thomas Liddiard and Ann Tucker, Ogbourne, St. George, Wiltshire, Eng. Came to Utah June 1864 with ox-team). She was born March 4, 1860. Their children: John Thomas, m. Alfreda Jeppersen; Priscilla Ivy, m. Thomas Harding; Lemira Meta, m. George Halstead; Sarah Stella, m. Albert Jacobsen; Hazel May, m. Jesse Mitchell; Beatrice V., m. Parley D. Hindmarsh; Mary C., m. George Webb; Elva G.; Ann Sophia. Family home Provo, Utah. Farmer. Died Nov. 29, 1898.

COLLINS, JOHN THOMAS (son of Thomas Collins and Mary Liddiard). Born April 12, 1878, Provo, Utah.
Married Alfreda Jeppersen Oct. 13, 1903, Provo, Utah (daughter of Christian Jeppersen and Sena Nielson, Odense, Denmark. Their children: Leoia Alfreda b. July 24, 1904; John Wyman b. Jan. 3, 1908. Family home Provo, Utah.
Elder; Sunday school and ward teacher. Stonemason and farmer.

COLTON, PHILANDER (son of Charles and Polly Jones of Scipio, Cayuga county, N. Y.). Born Oct. 11, 1811, Clarence Hollow, N. Y. Came to Utah July 29, 1847 with members of Co. B, Mormon Battalion, under Capt. George P. Cook.
Married Matilda Merrill July, 1833, Utica, Mich. (daughter of Samuel and Phoebe Merrill), who was born Oct. 15, 1817, and came to Utah 1850. Their children: Charles Edwin b. Oct. 26, 1834, m. Mary Ann Kelton; Harriet Emily b. July 24, 1836, m. Daniel W. Jones; Eleanor Roseltha b. Aug. 26, 1838, m. Stephen Bliss Moore; Lamoni Andrew b. April 18, 1842, d. aged 22; George Philander b. Jan. 24, 1844, d. child; Sanford Lorenzo b. June 26, 1845, m. Nancy Workman (Reed); Byron Oliver b. Nov. 29, 1848, m. Sarah Jane Clark, m. Sarah M. Smith; Sterling Driggs b. March 22, 1851, m. Nancy Adeline Williams; Phoebe Albina b. Jan. 20, 1855, d. 1865; John Adelbert b. Jan. 30, 1858, m. Mary Susannah Wilson; Earnest Merrill b. Sept. 19, 1860, m. Eva Louisa Gill. Family home Provo, Utah.
Missionary to Las Vegas, Nev. Located at Provo and moved to Vernal in 1886. Mason; plasterer; brickmaker. Died Aug. 15, 1891, Vernal, Utah.

COLTON, BYRON OLIVER (son of Philander Colton and Matilda Merrill). Born Nov. 29, 1848, Council Bluffs, Iowa. Came to Utah 1850.
Married Sarah Jane Clark Jan. 24, 1870, at Salt Lake City (daughter of Joseph Clark and Sarah Topham of Provo, Utah, pioneers 1850). Their children: Minnie Jane b. April 23, 1871, m. George H. Wilson; May b. Feb. 25, 1874, d. March 14, 1874.
Married Sarah Maria Smith July 4, 1879, at Provo (daughter of George Albert Smith, Sr., and Hannah Libby of Provo and Salt Lake City, pioneers July 24, 1847, Brigham Young company). She was born Jan. 1, 1856. Their children: Stella Smith b. June 6, 1880, m. Charles A. Hardy; Byron Owen b. Feb. 15, 1882, m. Helen Merkley June 29, 1910; George Albert b. June 16, 1883, d. May 15, 1898.
Elder; ward teacher; secretary of Sunday schools several years. County clerk and recorder eight years; school trustee. Settled at Vernal 1884.

COLTON, BYRON OWEN (son of Byron Oliver Colton and Sarah Maria Smith). Born Feb. 15, 1882 at Provo.
Married Helen Merkley June 29, 1910 at Salt Lake City (daughter of Nelson Merkley and Keturah Peterson of Vernal, Utah). She was born April 9, 1890. Their child: Ruth b. May 17, 1911.
Ordained bishop of Maeser ward Sept. 18, 1910; ordained high priest and alternate high councilor Aug. 23, 1908; president Y. M. M. I. A.; Sunday school teacher. Member state board of education; school trustee. County surveyor 1904-08. Civil engineer.

COLTON, STERLING DRIGGS (son of Philander Colton and Matilda Merrill). Born March 22, 1851, Provo, Utah.
Married Nancy Adeline Wilkins March 21, 1870, at Salt Lake City (daughter of John G. Wilkins and Nancy Kennedy of Provo). She was born July 14, 1853, at Provo. Their children: Flora Elsie b. June 7, 1872, m. Reuben Collett; Sterling Leroy b. Jan. 16, 1874, m. Lula Camp; Don Byron b. Sept. 15, 1876, m. Mary Maria Hall; m. Grace Stringham; Frank Edwin b. Sept. 7, 1878, m. Elizabeth Jane Hacking; m. Jane Merkley; Warren Alfred b. March 29, 1883, m. Merle Crandall; Charles Henry b. Dec. 18, 1884, m. Nellie Hacking; Louis Lycurgus b. Nov. 30, 1886, m. Louise Fuller; Nancy Fern b. Feb. 25, 1890, d. April 28, 1892; Zora Maria b. Oct. 21, 1892; Hugh Wilkins b. Jan. 11, 1901.
Member seventies, Vernal, Utah; missionary of Illinois and Michigan 1895; high priest; bishop; superintendent Sunday school. Sheriff, Uinta county; county commissioner. Merchant; stockraiser; miner and smelterer. One of first discoverers of Gilsonite.

COLTON, DON BYRON (son of Sterling Driggs Colton and Nancy Adeline Wilkins). Born Sept. 15, 1876, Mona, Utah.
Married Mary Maria Hall Aug. 22, 1900, at Salt Lake City (daughter of Mark Hall and Mary Bingham of Vernal, Utah), who was born Aug. 17, 1878, and died July 9, 1905.
Married Grace Stringham June 17, 1908, at Salt Lake City (daughter of Philip Stringham and Caroline Crouch of Maeser ward, Vernal, Utah). She was born Aug. 26, 1878. Their children: Mera b. March 20, 1909; Alice b. Jan. 10, 1913.
Member 97th quorum seventies; missionary to England 1896-98; ordained president of Uinta stake Sept. 17, 1910; 1st counselor to president William H. Smart 1907-10; high councilor 1906-07; 1st counselor in bishopric of Maeser ward 1905-06; stake supt. of religion classes 1901-02; president Y. M. M. I. A. of Maeser ward 1898-1901; principal preparatory department of B. Y. A. at Provo; principal of Uinta Stake Academy 1902-03. Took course of law at Ann Arbor 1903-05. Served in Utah legislature 1903. Receiver U. S. Land Office at Vernal 1905-13. President Uinta Telephone company; president Vernal Express Publishing company. Rancher and stockraiser. Attorney-at-law.

COLVIN, LEVI ORSON ALAMANDER (son of William Colvin, born April 2, 1778, and Lydia Sherman, born Oct. 25, 1785, both of Dauby, Rutland county, Vt.). He was born Dec. 20, 1822, Ellsburg, Jefferson county, N. Y. Came to Utah Sept. 10, 1850.
Married Mary Ann Emeline Davis April 17, 1850, Mt. Pisgah, Iowa (daughter of Isaac and Sarah Davis, of Pennsylvania; the latter a pioneer Sept. 10, 1850). She was born Jan. 22, 1830, near Toronto, Can. Their children: Lydia Ann b. Jan. 13, 1851, m. Lester Taylor; Mary Melissa b. Oct. 28, 1853, m. John Henry Tanner; Levi Alexander b. June 12, 1857, m. Mary Alice Curtis; Orson Lamoni b. June 1862; Laconius Alamander b. in 1866, m. Julia Patten; William Albert b. Nov. 11, 1871, d. Nov. 27, 1907; Emma Potter (adopted), m. Ephraim Coombs. Family home, Payson, Utah.
High priest. Settled in Cottonwood and lived at Fillmore, Santaquin and Payson. Member Payson city council 1855-65. Farmer. Died Nov. 18, 1904.

COLVIN, LEVI ALEXANDER (son of Levi Orson Alamander Colvin and Mary Ann Emeline Davis). Born June 12, 1857, Payson, Utah.
Married Mary Alice Curtis Oct. 14, 1880, Salt Lake City (daughter of George Curtis, born Oct. 27, 1823, in Oakland county, Mich., and Mary Openshaw, born March 25, 1839, Brightmet, Lancashire, Eng., the former a pioneer Oct. 7, 1848, the latter of Nov. 30, 1856, Edward Martin "frozen" handcart company). She was born Aug. 30, 1858. Their children: Irene b. Aug. 6, 1881 (drowned April 15, 1912—victim of the "Titanic" catastrophe), m. Walter H. Corbett; Kady Emeline E. b. Nov. 1, 1882, m. Sidney H. Cluff; Levi Leslie b. May 24, 1884, d. Sept. 16, 1890; Curtis G. b. Nov. 16, 1885, d. Jan. 16, 1904; Tracy Sherman b. Nov. 14, 1887, m. Zella Ashton; Eleanor b. Nov. 16, 1889; Hattie Lucille b. Oct. 28, 1892. Family resided Payson, Pleasant View and Provo, Utah.
Member 34th quorum seventies; missionary to Iowa and Missouri 1895-97; bishop Pleasant View ward 1905-12; high priest; home missionary, Nebo stake. Payson city councilman eight years; first Utah county sheep inspector; chairman Payson school board six years. Farmer; stockraiser; fruitgrower.

COLTRIN, ZEBEDEE (son of John Coltrin and Sarah Graham). Born Sept. 7, 1804, Ovid, Seneca county, N. Y. Came to Utah July 24, 1847, Stephen Goddard company.
Married Mary Mott Feb. 5, 1841 (daughter of Samuel Mott and Elizabeth Dewitt, pioneers 1852), who was born Nov.

of Peter and Cecelia Sharp of Clackmannan, Scotian 1). She was born April 9, 1812. Their children: Mary, m. James C. Watson; Gibson S., m. Elizabeth Whitaker, m. Esther Palfreyman; Ellen, m. Peter G. Burt; Robert S.. m. Harriet Powell; Elizabeth, m. John Cowan; Peter S., m. Jeanette Watson; Thomas S., m. Marguerite Watson. Family home Salt Lake City.
S   . Contractor for building material. Died Nov. 17, 190&venty

CONDIE, THOMAS (son of Gibson Condie, born Dec. 25, 1774, and Jean Russel, both of Westfield, Scotland; they were married Aug. 15, 1794). He was born Sept. 27, 1806, Dunfernline, Fifeshire, Scotland. Came to Utah Sept. 2, 1852, Capt. Howell company.
Married Helen Sharp Aug. 21, 1830 (daughter of Luke Sharp and Janet White, married Nov. 9, 1900, Clackmannan, Scotland). She was born May 25, 1811, and came to Utah with husband. Their children: Janet b. Aug. 4, 1831, m. Joseph Sharp Aug. 28, 1849; Gibson b. March 10, 1835, m. Elizabeth Robinson Feb. 26, 1857; Helen b. July 24, 1837, m. George Thackeray July 1, 1854; Margaret b. Nov. 19, 1839; Thomas b. Feb. 9, 1842, m. Hannah Swan Sept. 17, 1864; Cecelia b. June 22, 1854, m. Arthur Kirk June 15, 1880; Joseph b. June 22, 1854, m. Elizabeth Walbie June 7, 1883.

CONDIE, GIBSON, son of Thomas Condie and Helen Sharp). Born March 10, 1835, Clackamannan, Scotland.
Married Elizabeth Robinson Feb. 26, 1857, Salt Lake City (daughter of George and Margaret Angus Robinson, pioneers of 1856. Edward Martin company). She was born June 28, 1838, Darlington, Eng. Their children: Margaret Helen b. June 28, 1858, m. William C. Palmer Oct. 31, 1881; Thomas R. b. July 7, 1861, m. Katie Jones Sept. 6, 1894; Gibson R. b. Sept. 17, 1863, m. Ettie Warrick June 16, 1907; Elizabeth Ann b. June 20, 1866, m. Willard C. Knight April 1, 1903; Joseph b. June 7, 1868, m. Minnie Johnson Feb. 8, 1899; Mary Jane b. Sept. 6, 1870, m. David H. Wickel Dec. 21, 1898; John W. b. Sept. 21, 1878, m. Reila May Pendleton Dec. 3, 1903; Agnes irene b. June 6, 1881, m. Frank Padkins March 30, 1904; George Moroni b. March 27, 1883, m. Caroline Johnson April 30, 1908. Family home Croydon, Morgan Co., Utah. Ward clerk. Active in Echo Canyon troubles. One of first settlers of Lost Creek on Weber river. Contractor in construction of Union Pacific R. R. in 1869.

CONDIE, JOHN W. (son of Gibson Condie and Elizabeth Robinson). Born Sept. 21, 1878, at Croydon, Utah.
Married Reila May Pendleton Dec. 31, 1903, at Wanship, Utah (daughter of Joshua Pendleton and Delphia Stewart, former born May 4, 1849, latter June 18, 1852, both of Salt Lake City; married in 1870). She was born May 4, 1881, Wanship, Utah. Their children: Melvina Lyman b. May 28, 1905; Mildred Evelyn b. June 18, 1907; Lucile b. Sept. 24, 1908; Vera b. Aug. 5, 1910. Family home Preston, Idaho.
Principal of Preston Central school 1906-08; teacher in Oneida Academy 1908-12. Mayor 1909-11. Bishop 4th ward since 1907.

CONLEY, SOLOMON N. Came to Utah July 24, 1847, Brigham Young company.
Married Eve Merckley (daughter of Christopher Merckley). Their children: Christopher Albert b. Feb. 4, 1844, m. Mary Whipple; Ransom N. b. Nov. 24, 1848; Hyrum J. b. May 19, 1850; Lyman b. April 13, 1855, m. Annie Harvey; Sarah E. b. April 14, 1857, m. James A. Cameron Feb. 6, 1872, Harriet M. b. April 21, 1859, m. Levi Hart Nov., 1874. Family home Centerville, Utah.
High priest.

CONNELL, WILLIAM F. (son of William Connell and Isabelle Leishman of De Kalb, Ill.). Born July 8, 1841, Darry, Lancastershire, Eng. Came to Utah May 6, 1864.
Married Henrietta Atkinson June 28, 1874, at Salt Lake City (daughter of Thomas Atkinson and Margerite Ann Field of Nauvoo, Ill., pioneers 1863), who was born Jan. 12, 1853. Their children: Margerite Isabelle, m. W. H. McKenna; James W., m. Sascha Stain; Anna L., m. Solomon K. Smith; Emma L., m. Claude M. Raybould; Maud H., m. Frank N. Huddleson; William A., m. Alice Taufer; Gladys R., d. aged 1 year; Hazel K. Family home 14th ward, Salt Lake City.
Justice of peace, Lincoln county, Nev.; general newspaper man.

CONNELL, WILLIAM SAMUEL (son of Samuel Connell and Martha Goodfellow of Birmingham, Eng.). Born June 3, 1851, in England. Came to Utah Sept. 25, 1863, Peter Nebeker company.
Married Emma Mariah Wright Sept. 25, 1870, at Salt Lake City (daughter of Thomas Wright and Sarah Ann Britt of Nephi, Utah, pioneers Nov. 20, 1856, Edward Martin handcart company). She was born Sept. 29, 1854. Their children: Sarah Ann, m. George W. Taylor; Amelia, died; Emma .ophronia, m. John Henry Weir; Birdie Lois, died; Gertrud . died; John Brit, died; Jessie, died; William, died; Samuel 'Vright; Barley Wright; John Robert; Walter; Geraldine. .'amily home Ogden, Utah.
Elder. Harness maker. Died Nov. 17, 1912, at Ogden.

CONOVER (COWNOVER), PETER WILSON (son of Peter Conover and Hannah Combs). Born Sept. 19, 1807, Woodford. Ky. Came to Utah Sept. 24, 1848, Heber C. Kimball company.
Married Eveline Golden Feb. 14, 1827, Morgan county. Ill. who died in 1847, at Winter Quarters. Neb. Their children: Houton; Charles; Abraham; Sarah; John; Jenett; Catherine; Zerelda; Alphis; Eveline.
Married Mary Jane McCorral Nov. 10, 1850, Provo, Utah (daughter of Jesse McCorral and Mary J. Lock of Louisiana, pioneers Sept. 24, 1848, Heber C. Kimball company). She was born March 11, 1829, in Louisiana. Their children: Mary E. b. Nov. 14, 1851, m. Charles Jenkins; Louisa H. b. Dec. 24, 1852, m. Robert Henderson; Peter Wilson, Jr., b. March 24, 1854, m. Myrtle Mason; Hanmer J. b. June 9, 1855, m. Viola Burdick; William C. b. April 22, 1858, m. Della Burdick; Martha J. b. Sept. 19, 1859, m. James Gillispie; Joseph b. Sept. 19, 1859, died; Alsetta b. May 4, 1862, m. W. E. Smith, m. James Hogan; Loretta b. May 5, 1862, m. Henry V. Smith; Ida b. Oct. 30, 1865, m. William H. Kenner; Ella b. Jan. 29, 1869, died; Ada b. July 29, 1872, m. Tight Snow; Robert Francis b. Dec. 23, 1873, m. Anna Richmond. Family home Provo, Utah.
One of Joseph Smith's body guards. Settled at Provo. It was reputed that his was the second wagon driven by a white man across the Provo river, and that he raised the first wheat produced in this part of the territory. In the 50's he commanded the militia in Utah county, one of the prominent military characters in territorial history. In 1854 he accompanied expedition of Colonel Steptoe to Carson Valley, Nev. Colonel in Black Hawk Indian war. Died Sept. 20, 1892, Richfield, ,Utah.

CONOVER, ROBERT FRANCIS (son of Peter William Conover and Mary Jane McCorral). Born Dec. 23, 1873, Eureka, Utah.
Married Annie Richmond Aug; 19, 1906, Provo, Utah (daughter of Benjamin B. Richmond and Martha James of Provo), who was born Nov. 4, 1885. Their children: Edna Afton b. Dec. 4, 1907; Bernice b. Nov. 7, 1909. Family home Pleasant View, Utah.
Member of Battery B, Utah Light Artillery Volunteers, and received special bronze medal (number 1807), which was issued in 1899 to members of the 8th army corps for service in the Philippines (Luzon), voluntary re-enlistment, patriotism, fortitude and loyalty, by an act of Congress, upon the recommendation of President McKinley. Farmer.

COOK, CHAUNCEY HARVEY (son of Milton Cook and Olive Amanda Smith). Born Nov. 26, 1844, Nauvoo, Ill. Came to Utah Sept. 24, 1848, Heber C. Kimball company.
Married Clarissa Curtis in February, 1869, at Salt Lake City (daughter of Enos Curtis and Tamma Durfee of Lennox, Madison county, N. Y., pioneers of September, 1850). She was born Oct. 13, 1851. Their children: Joseph Alma b. Aug. 23, 1871; Emma b. Aug. 16, 1872; Chauncey Harvey b. Dec. 5, 1874, m. Elsie Sonburg; Amelia b. May 11, 1877; Ray Curtis b. Aug. 27, 1878, m. Lydia Jane Babcock; Leroy Austin b. Aug. 24, 1881, m. Louisa Bennett; Marion b. March 14, 1884, m. Effie Elisonbee; Bertha b. March 9, 1886, m. Chas. B. Lewis; Dora b. March 26, 1888, m. William Clark Scott; Laura D. b. Dec. 11, 1889, m. Hyrum Hansen; Junius F. b. July 18, 1893. m. Vida Hardman.
High priest; 1st counselor to Bishop John T. Rowley, Emery stake; Sunday school superintendent, Sevier stake; ward teacher. Justice of peace, Spring Glen, Carbon county; postmaster, Caineville, Wayne county. Farmer and stockraiser.

COOK, GEORGE (son of George Cook and Mary Philpot of Brabourne, Kentshire, Eng.). Born Jan. 28, 1828, at Brabourne. Came to Utah Oct. 28, 1854, Robert L. Campbell company.
Married Hannah Burrows Jan. 31, 1854, Dover, Kentshire, Eng. (daughter of Henry Burrows and Mary Norton of Dover). She was born March 27, 1822. Their children: George Burrows, d. infant; Henry, d. infant; Samuel Norton, m. Margaret Lillian Wells and Stella Barker; Mary Burrows, m. Nephi Brunker; Elizabeth Jane, m. John A. Dalton; Hannah Louisa, d. infant; Rosetta Ellen, d. infant; Harbert Lorenzo, d. infant. Family home Willard, Utah.
Farmer. Died Jan. 1, 1906.

COOK, SAMUEL NORTON (son of George Cook and Hannah Burrows). Born April 26, 1857, Ogden, Utah.
Married Lillian Wells Dec. 27, 1883, Salt Lake City (daughter of Lyman B. Wells and Bithiah Fordham of Willard, Utah, pioneers of 1849). She was born April, 1865; died Dec. 5, 1890.
Married Stella Barker Oct. 12, 1892, at Logan, Utah (daughter of Byron Barker and Julia Hubbard of Willard, pioneers of 1852). She was born Oct. 17, 1870. Their children: George Byron b. Nov. 23, 1895; Merlin Norton b. Sept. 23, 1897; Francis Henry b. Nov. 13, 1899; Delbert Eugene b. Dec. 29, 1905. Family home Willard.
Member 59th quorum seventies; missionary to Great Britain 1892-94; counselor to bishops A. Zundel and George Facer; high councilor. County commissioner; member county board of education; mayor and justice of peace of Willard; member legislature 1896-98. Farmer and stockraiser.

818 PIONEERS AND PROMINENT MEN OF UTAH

COOK, HENRY FREEMAN (son of William Cook, born Sept. 6, 1780, and Lucy Chapman, born May 8, 1787, married Dec. 19, 1805). He was born Jan. 12, 1815. Came to Utah Oct., 1852, Warren Snow company.
Married Sophronia Strobridge April 9, 1837 (daughter of George Strobridge and Abigal Lull), who was born March 14, 1813, and came to Utah with husband. Their children: John b. May 22, 1838, m. Sarah Cook; James b. Jan. 11, 1840, m. Malinda Wilcox; Hannah b. Jan. 22, 1842, m. Rhone Dayton; Mary Jane b. Jan. 2, 1844, m. William Quail; Charles b. Feb. 21, 1846; William b. Oct. 19, 1847, m. Almina Weeks March 4, 1871; m. Rebecca Rhodeaback; George b. March 20, 1850, m. Ella Phippen, m. Alice Sparks; Harriet Ann b. May 20, 1853; Jenett b. March 17, 1855, m. Seth Ridgby; Maretta b. March 17, 1855, m. William H. Bassett. Family home Council Bluffs, Iowa.
Married Julia Ann Rocker in 1857, Salt Lake City. Their children: Franklin; George H.; Malinda; Ada.
Bishop Cedar Valley ward 1861-1881. Died in 1881.

COOK, WILLIAM (son of Henry Freeman Cook and Sophronia Strobridge). Born Oct. 19, 1847, Council Bluffs, Iowa. Came to Utah with father.
Married Almina Weeks March 4, 1871 (daughter of Allen Weeks and Sarah Jane Bennett), who was born Oct. 21, 1848. Only child: William Lucene b. March 4, 1873, m. Clara Clark Nov. 14, 1895. Family home Cedar Fort, Utah.
Married Rebecca Rhodeaback Oct. 25, 1875 (daughter of James Rhodeaback and Phebe Beagle), who was born May 2, 1846, Nauvoo, Ill. Their children: Edward b. Jan. 9, 1877, m. Nellie A. Chamberlain June 27, 1900; Helen b. April 6, 1879, m. Ralph Hardy Feb. 5, 1908; Clifford b. March 14, 1881, m. Arminta Wilcox Oct. 17, 1900; Mark H. b. April 26, 1884; Phebe R. b. July 12, 1885; Barnes Alma b. Oct. 11, 1887, m. Alice Southam April 29, 1908.

COOK, JAMES (son of John and Sarah Cook of England). Born Nov. 13, 1816, Shropshire, Eng. Came to Utah October, 1853, Joseph A. Young company.
Married Ann Lane at Wolverhampton, Staffordshire, Eng. Their children: Ann (d. Nov. 3, 1891), m. William K. Barton; Hyrum, m. Emily Alder; Maud, m. Christian Hicks; Mary, died; James N., died; Henry, d. aged 19 years; Brigham, died. Family home Manti, Utah.
Married Maria Davenport at Manti. They had one child who died in infancy. Family home Manti.
High priest. Black Hawk Indian War veteran. Wheelwright. Died Oct., 1906, at Manti.

COOK, JAMES M. (son of Thomas Cook and Mary Brundrett, of Choritoncum-Hardy, Lancashire, Eng.). Born June 3, 1850, Timperley, Cheshire, Eng. Came to Utah Nov., 1881.
Married Emily J. Radcliff (daughter of Samuel Radcliff and Ellen Hadkinson), who was born April 3, 1852.
High priest; missionary to England 1895-97; president 84th quorum seventies 1902; bishop Rexburg 2d ward 1907; high councilor Fremont stake, June 30, 1912.

COOK, JOHN. Came to Utah, Sept. 15, 1861, Ira Eldredge company.
Married Rachel Marson of Eastwood, Nottingham, Eng. Their children: Eliza, m. Robert Campbell Kirkwood, 1870; Elizabeth, m. Robert Campbell Kirkwood, July, 1860. They lived at Provo, Utah.

COOK, LUKE (son of George and Artulis Cook of Wales, Eng.). Born Jan. 25, 1824, Lath, Eng. Came to Utah, 1853, Vincent Shurtliff oxteam company.
Married Louisa Burton in England (daughter of George and Sarah Burton), who was born Oct. 6, 1831. Their children: Julia Emma, m. Hans Peterson; Liza B., m. Canby Scott; George H., m. Sarah Hooks; John E., m. Matilda Whipple; Louisa A., m. Andrew Eggertsen; Sarah, m. William Hoover. Family home Provo, Utah.
Member 34th quorum seventies; choir leader. Butcher. Deceased.

COOK, MELVIN D. (son of Edmund Cook and Amanda A. Bronson). Born Oct. 12, 1835, Akron, Ohio. Came to Utah 1863.
Married Sarah Duncombe Dec. 19, 1870, at Salt Lake City (daughter of Joseph Duncombe and Elizabeth Glover of Staffordshire, Eng., pioneers 1865, Thomas Taylor company). She was born Jan. 4, 1853. Their children: Aurelia E., d. infant; Alice May, d. aged nine; Annie Laurie, m. Charles Leonard; Melvin C. d. aged six; Lola M., m. Oscar Ahlbom; Rubin G., m. Amy Senior; Willard L., m. Gertrude Erickson; Arthur G.; Nellie, m. Samuel McNeil; Victor L.; Jennie Irene, m. Fred Hill; Ida Lillian.
Elder. Granger justice of peace two years. Mailcarrier; farmer and stockraiser.

COOK, PHINEAS W. (son of Welcott P. Cook and Irene Churchel). Born Aug. 28, 1819, Goshen, Conn. Came to Utah in 1848.
Married Johanna C. Polson Sept. 13, 1878 (daughter of James Polson and Johanna Ulrika Lundgren), who was born Aug. 8, 1815, Malmo, Sweden. Their children: Carl; Moses; Kib b. July 4, 1882; Emerson; Parley; Idaily.
His last short labon of Goshen, Utah.

COOK, KIB (son of Phineas W. Cook and Johana C. Polson) He was born July 4, 1882, Garden City Utah.
Married Rose Adline Dimick. June 17, 1903, Logan, Utah (daughter of James Heber Dimick and Rose M. Dalrymple) who was born Nov. 3, 1884, Wardboro, Idaho. Their children Maud Mae b. March 16, 1904; Fern b. Jan. 27, 1906; Phyllis b. Nov. 19, 1908.

COOK, THOMAS (son of Azarias and Mary Cook, of Wiltshire, Eng.). Born at Collingbourne, Eng. Came to Utah Sept. 15, 1868, John Gillespie oxteam company.
Married Joyce Collins, 1853, at Collingbourne (daughter of John Collins and Priscilla Shepperd of Collingbourne, pioneers Oct. 1, 1866, Joseph Rawlins oxteam company). She was born Feb. 8, 1830. Their children: Ellen, m. Joel A Johnsons; Charles, m. Hannah Allen; George E., m. Mary Ann Stradling; Emily Elizabeth, m. Geo. B. Peay; John; Sarah Ann; Mary Priscilla, latter three died. Family home Provo Utah.
Seventy; block teacher; member ward building committee Farmer; contractor; brickmaker. Died Sept. 10, 1890, Provo Utah.

COOK, GEORGE ELISHA (son of Thomas Cook and Joyce Collins). Born Sept. 13, 1857, Callingbourne, Eng. Came to Utah, Oct. 1, 1866, Joseph Rawlins company.
Married Mary Ann Stradling May 1, 1879, Salt Lake City (daughter of William Stradling and Sophia Bush, of Provo Utah, pioneers 1866, Captain Roylance company). She was born July 11, 1857. Their adopted child: Joseph P. b. April 28, 1900. Family home Provo, Utah.
Missionary to St. Johns, Ariz., 1880-90; Sunday-school teacher. Policeman at Provo. Farmer and fruitgrower.

COOK, WILLIAM (son of John Cook and Elizabeth Frith of Yorkshire, Eng.). Born July 24, 1845. Came to Utah in October, 1863.
Married Helen Wheatley in December, 1867, at Salt Lake City (daughter of John Wheatley of Sheffield, Yorkshire Eng.), who was born in 1843. Their children: Mathias, died Percilla, m. William Hartle; Lydia Ellen Elizabeth, m. Thomas O. Pichard; Helen, m. William Snellgrove. Family resided at Salt Lake City and Vernal, Utah.
Married Lydia Hartle, July 17, 1890, at Salt Lake City Utah (daughter of Samuel Hartle and Mary Ann McNickle of Leeds, Yorkshire, Eng.), who was born Jan. 10, 1855 Their children: Gertrude b. May 15, 1881, m. Gustave Frederickson; William Harry b. July 4, 1882, m. Dora Calder Moroni b. Nov. 11, 1883; Michael b. March 25, 1885, m. Lydia Ellen Hardy; Joseph Isaac b. Aug. 16, 1886; Minnie b. Jan 8, 1888, m. Heber Priest; Netta b. Jan. 9, 1890, died; Mark b Oct. 1, 1891; Alice b. March 1, 1896; Lydia May, b. April 16 1898. Family home Vernal, Utah.
Member 1st quorum seventies; ward teacher; high priest Active in Black Hawk war. Contractor and builder.

COOKE, HENRY (son of Abram Cooke). Born June 11, 1817 Chichester, Eng. Came to Utah Aug. 26, 1864, John R. Murdock company.
Married Martha Morris (daughter of James Morris), who was born Oct. 28, 1809, and came to Utah with her husband Their children: Benjamin Frederick b. Sept. 16, 1832, m Mary Joy April 1, 1861; Mary Ann b. 1834, died; Louisa Jan. 25, 1837, m. Aroet L. Hale Dec. 25, 1861; Charles March 14, 1839, m. Ann M. Fawson Dec. 25, 1865; Henry b. Aug. 24, 1841, m. Lily Butler; Elizabeth b. Sept. 27, 184 m. William H. Hobbs; Charlotte b. March 3, 1846, m. Aro L. Hale. Family home Grantsville, Utah.

COOKE, BENJAMIN FREDRICK (son of Henry Cooke and Martha Morris). Born Sept. 16, 1832, South Stoke, Susse Eng.
Married Mary Joy April 1, 1861, Chichester, Eng. (daughter of Walter Robert Joy and Sarah Masterson, pioneer Sept. 27, 1861, Sextus E. Johnson company). She was bo Jan. 25, 1837. Only child: Benjamin Henry b. April 23, 18 m. Annie Constance Hobbs.
Grantsville city recorder four years. Manager Hale Br mercantile business three years. Recorder at Lakes mining district three years; justice of peace, Grouse Cre Utah, fourteen years.

COOKE, BENJAMIN HENRY (son of Benjamin Fredri Cooke and Mary Joy). Born April 23, 1862.
Married Annie Constance Hobbs (daughter of William Hobbs, pioneer Sept. 27, 1861, Sextus E. Johnson compan She was born Nov. 19, 1861, Panguitch, Utah. Their childr Mary Elizabeth b. Oct. 16, 1881, m. Joseph Whittle Oct 1910; William R. b. May 9, 1890; Sarah Pearl b. Oct. 15, 18 Ethel b. Aug. 13, 1895. Family resided Grouse Creek, Ut and St. Anthony, Idaho.

COOLEY, ANDREW W. (son of Benjamin and Clari Cooley of Detroit, Michigan, pioneers 1864). Born May 1838. Came to Utah in 1864.
Married Rachel C. Coon Feb. 22, 1864, at Salt Lake C (daughter of Abraham Coon of Ohio and Elizabeth brough of Tennessee, pioneers, 1850). She was born Ma 22, 1848, Council Bluffs, Iowa, and came to Utah with ents. Their children: Samuel B. d. infant; Ida R. d. a two; Marrettie d. 14 years; Isabelle, m. Edwin Fish;

cretia; Oscar N., m. Margaret Bird; Andrew, m. Minnie Sorenson; Abraham C.; Frances, m. Samuel Rigby. Family home Salt Lake City, Utah.
High priest; bishop of Brighton ward. Farmer, stockraiser and butcher. Died Oct. 11, 1887.

COOMBS, ABRAHAM. Came to Utah in 1860.
Married Olive Olivia Curtis in 1849. Their children: Charles M., m. Elvira Ashbrook; Helen, m. George Clayton; Emily, m. J. J. Kenton and Al Davis; Arabelle, m. Joseph Smith; Ella b. March 27, 1857, m. William Henry Branch: Olive, m. John Fretwell. Family resided San Bernardino, Cal., and Cedar City, Utah.
Farmer. Died 1860 Beaver, Utah.

COOMBS, GEORGE (son of Richard Coombs). Born 1814, Staffordshire, Eng. Came to Utah Oct. 4, 1864, William S. Warren company.
Married Eliza Astubury (daughter of Joshua Astubary), who was born in 1812 and came to Utah with husband. Their children: William H., m. Eliza Morgan; Joshua, m. Fanny Bailey; George, m. Paulina Gulbranson; Harriet, m. James Dutton; Ephraim. m. Ruth Shawcroft; David, b. June 9, 1852, m. Theresa Billings Jan. 4, 1875. Family home Fountain Green, Utah.
Presiding elder Trent Vale (England) branch 1863. Black Hawk war veteran and Indian campaigner.

COOMBS, DAVID (son of George Coombs and Eliza Astubary). Born June 9, 1852, in Staffordshire, Eng. Came to Utah with parents.
Married Theresa Billings Jan. 4, 1875 (daughter of Titus Billings and Mary A. Tuttle), who was born Jan. 28, 1859. Their children: David J. b. Jan. 29, 1876, m. Ivy L. Thompson; Arthur W. b. Aug. 28, 1880, m. Lillian M. Bullard; Ray H. b. Sept. 29, 1882, m. Martha Bullard; Hephzibah E. b. Dec. 9, 1884, m. Floyd Ivie; George L. b. Jan. 7, 1887; Mary Eliza b. March 10, 1889, m. Frederick Baker; Ephraim H. b. April 25, 1891; Harriet T. b. Feb. 22, 1893; Emily b. Feb. 29, 1896; Vanever M. b. Nov. 22, 1897; Titus W. b. Aug. 12, 1899. Family resided Fountain Green, Joseph City, Thurber and Lyman, Utah.
Seventy and high priest; alternate high councilor, Wayne stake; presided over Allridge branch; Sunday school superintendent Trenton branch.

COON, ABRAHAM (son of John Coon, of Pennsylvania, and Rachel Smith, of Virginia). Born April 3, 1810, Herron Creek, Ohio. Came to Utah Sept. 17, 1850, William Wall company.
Married Elizabeth Yarbrough in 1830, St. Clair county, Ill. (daughter of William Yarbrough and Permelia Parker of Tennessee and St. Clair county, Ill.). She was born Dec. 23, 1808. Their children: Susanna, d. aged 12 years; John, m. Mary T. York; Permelia, d. aged 19 years; Sarah, d. aged 14 years; William, m. Sarah A. Moore, m. Emma Hiskey; Elizabeth W., m. James Hawkins; James D., m. Mary Horrocks; Frances Ann, m. Levi N. Hardman; Erastus, d. infant; Rachel C., m. Andrew Cooley. Family home Salt Lake City.
Married Frances Yarbrough at Nauvoo, Ill. (daughter of William Yarbrough and Permelia Parker). Only child: Abraham, d. aged 10 years.
Married Betsy Wilson at Council Bluffs, Iowa (daughter of Elijah and Elizabeth Wilson of Grantsville, Utah). Their children: Edna J., m. Albert Baker; Isaac, m. Catherine Mellen; Laura, d. infant; Jacob, m. Sarah Hirst; Mary E., m. Alfred Gardiner. Family home Salt Lake City, Utah.
Member 16th quorum seventies; missionary to Carson valley, Nev., 1856-57; high priest; bishop of Kirtland, Ohio, and Council Bluffs, Iowa. Salt Lake county road supervisor eight years. Farmer, stockraiser and cooper. Died March 27, 1886.

COON, JOHN (son of Abraham Coon and Elizabeth Yarbrough). Born Nov. 30, 1832. Came to Utah Sept. 17, 1850, William Wall company.
Married Mary T. York March 12, 1854, Salt Lake City (daughter of Benjamin F. York and Elizabeth York (3d cousins) of Salt Lake City, pioneers Sept. 22, 1847, Daniel Spencer company). She was born March 3, 1834, Nashville, Tenn. Their children: Mary T. b. Jan. 9, 1855, m. Olive Shafer; John A. b. Feb. 22, 1857, m. Charlotte Hirst; Amelia E. b. June 18, 1859, m. Joseph H. Smith; Frances Ann b. Sept. 22, 1861, m. George Susted; Sarah Jane b. April 30, 1864, m. William H. Smith; David F. b. April 30, 1866, m. Ellen Dearden; Isaac W. b. Aug. 11, 1869, m. Mary E. Bertoch; Rachel C. b. Aug. 29, 1872, m. William G. Staley; Emma M. b. Nov. 23, 1875, d. aged 8 years; George W. b. April 12, 1878, d. infant. Family home Pleasant Green, Utah.
Member 33d quorum seventies. Farmer and stockraiser. Died July 28, 1906.

COON, JOHN A. (son of John Coon and Mary T. York). Born Feb. 22, 1857, Salt Lake City.
Married Charlotte Hirst Jan. 6, 1881, Salt Lake City (daughter of John Hirst and Charlotte Brook of Yorkshire, Eng., pioneers Sept. 1868). She was born Dec. 9, 1859, Lancashire, Eng., and came to Utah with parents. Their children: John B. b. Nov. 15, 1881, m. Hannah E. K.; Bertha b. June 23, 1884, m. Frank L. Chambers; Charles L. b. March 18, 1887, d. aged two years; Myrtle b. May 19, 1889; Roswald H. b. Dec. 4, 1892; Rudger Y. b. March 30, 1896; Archie B. b. July 18, 1901; Clifford A. b. June 23, 1904. Family home Pleasant Green, Utah.
Member 14th quorum seventies; missionary to northern states 1896-98; ward teacher; president Y. M. M. I. A.; assistant Sunday school superintendent. Went to Arizona in 1876 with Lot Smith and his colony. Deputy assessor two years; school trustee in 83d district, Salt Lake county. Farmer and stockraiser.

COON, ISAAC W. (son of John Coon and Mary T. York). Born Aug. 11, 1869, Grantsville, Utah.
Married Mary Elva Bertoch Jan. 15, 1896, Salt Lake City (daughter of James Bertoch and Ann Cutcliff, of Italy and England, respectively, and later of Pleasant Green ward, near Salt Lake City). She was born June 23, 1877. Their children: Elva M. b. Oct. 24, 1896; I. Warren b. May 30, 1908; Vivian B. b. July 23, 1900; Stanley J. b. July 29, 1902; Lillian b. Sept. 4, 1905, d. infant. Family home Pleasant Green, Utah.
Member 14th quorum seventies; president elders' quorum 14 years; Sunday school superintendent. Road supervisor three years; trustee of 47th school district four years. Farmer and stockraiser.

COON, JAMES DAVID (son of Abraham Coon and Elizabeth Yarbrough). Born Dec. 7, 1842, Green county, Ill. Came to Utah July, 1850, Capt. Roundy company.
Married Mary Horrocks March 11, 1866, Huntsville, Utah (daughter of Edward Horrocks and Eliza Clark of Liverpool, Eng., pioneers Sept. 1857, Capt. Dunn company). She was born Feb. 7, 1850. Their children: James D. b. Feb. 18, 1867, m. Alida Elk; Abraham b. Sept. 18, 1869, d. aged one year; Joseph b. Feb. 17, 1871, m. Maud A. Dearden; Rose C. b. Feb. 4, 1873, m. George Kelson; Jacob b. Sept. 28, 1875, m. Martha Hancock; Effie M. b. Sept. 17, 1877, m. Waiter Sugden; Frank b. June 21, 1879, d. aged one year; Mary b. Jan. 7, 1880, m. John F. Thomas; Sarah b. Feb. 28, 1882, d. aged 16 years; Hyrum b. June 1, 1884, m. Nellie Brown; Maud b. Feb. 11, 1886, m. George Wilson; Walter b. Oct. 28, 1887, m. Ruby Hancock; Alonzo b. Aug. 2, 1889; Albert B. Aug. 4, 1891, m. Nellie Bellows; Flossie b. Sept. 2, 1893, m. Fred Rasmussen; Wilford b. Nov. 20, 1896. Family home Pleasant Green, Utah.
Elder; ward teacher. Farmer and stockraiser.

COON, JOSEPH (son of James David Coon and Mary Horrocks). Born Feb. 16, 1871, Huntsville, Utah.
Married Nancy M. Dearden June 5, 1893, Pleasant Green ward (daughter of Joseph Dearden and Nancy Hirst of Yorkshire, Eng., pioneers Sept. 1868). She was born July 11, 1874. Their children: Joseph E. b. Jan. 5, 1894; James L. b. July 30, 1897; Noble D. b. Jan. 2, 1899; Howard b. Dec. 9, 1901; Louis H. b. Feb. 5, 1905; Clyde b. April 18, 1907; Josephine b. Dec. 20, 1909; Maud Mae b. April 17, 1913. Family home Pleasant Green, Utah.
Member 14th quorum seventies; elder. Farmer and stockraiser.

COON, ISAAC (son of Abraham Coon and Betsy Wilson). Born June 18, 1850, on way to Utah.
Married Catherine Mellen Dec. 19, 1869, Salt Lake City (daughter of John Mellen and Jane Ramsden of Lancashire, Eng., pioneers 1854). She was born Nov. 29, 1851. Their children: Minnie M. b. Sept. 20, 1870, m. Charles Nealson; Isaac E. b. Jan. 1, 1873, m. Naoma Taylor; Fredrick b. Nov. 9, 1875, m. Louisa Perkins; John Abraham b. Dec. 10, 1877, m. Tillie Nealson; Susan b. Oct. 16, 1879, m. Lot Hancock; Laura b. Dec. 3, 1881, d. aged four years; Arthur b. Jan. 9, 1883, m. Ruth Breeze; Jane Edith b. Oct. 18, 1884, m. Claud Wilkins; George A. b. Jan. 19, 1886, m. Florence Smith; Herbert b. Jan. 29, 1887; Clara b. March 15, 1889; Frank b. Oct. 16, 1891, m. Georgie Rolph; Ralph b. Sept. 12, 1893; Katie M. b. May 31, 1895. Family home Pleasant Green, Utah.
Seventy; missionary to eastern states 1896-98; high priest; 1st counselor to Bishop Spencer. Farmer and stockraiser.

COOPER, ISAAC (son of Robert Cooper and Emmeline Marshall). Born Feb. 9, 1807, Mt. Earl, Lane county, Pa. Came to Utah 1848, David Spencer company.
Married Mary Murray Feb. 18, 1834, in Pennsylvania, who was born Feb. 16, 1815.
Married Nancy Lance May 1, 1852, in Utah, who was born Oct. 16, 1816. Their children: Isaac D. b. March 7, 1855, m. Rebecca R. Norton; John H. b. Sept. 14, 1857, m. Martha A. Olmstad; Cyrus W. b. Jan. 18, 1860.
Married Mary E. Stuart March 18, 1857, American Fork, Utah. Their children: Mary J. b. Jan. 12, 1860, m. Daniel Olmstead; Syntha b. June 20, 1862, m. Rufus W. Norton; Martha E. b. April 7, 1865, m. Leander D. Norton; Charles R. b. March 17, 1869; Joseph A. b. Feb. 3, 1873.
President high priests' quorum. With a wagon load of flour donated by himself, went to relieve a belated handcart company. Died Nov. 21, 1882.

COOPER, ISAAC D. (son of Isaac Cooper and Nancy Lance). Born March 7, 1855, American Fork, Utah.
Married Rebecca R. Norton Nov. 28, 1879, Lehi, Utah (daughter of James W. Norton and Nancy Hammer of Lehi, pioneers Sept. 24, 1848, Heber C. Kimball company). She was born Feb. 3, 1862. Their children: Isaac L. b. July

18, 1880, m. Mary Edmisten; Anna R. b. Dec. 28, 1881, m. Peter M. Fransden; James A. b. Oct. 10, 1883, m. Amanda Olson; Alfred A. b. March 9, 1886; Jesse E. b. Aug. 27, 1887; Nancy M. b. May 12, 1895; Ellis and Elsie (twins) b. Sept. 8, 1897; David A. b. Jan. 3, 1899; Basel b. March 10, 1901. Family home Idaho.
Missionary to St. Johns, Ariz., 1884-89.

COOPER, JOHN (son of James Cooper, born May 24, 1811, and Ann North, born Jan. 27, 1811, both in Loughborough, Leicestershire, Eng.). He was born May 27, 1834, at parents' birthplace. Came to Utah Nov. 30, 1856, Edward Martin handcart company.
Married Mary Ann Lewis June 8, 1857 (daughter of William Lewis and Ann Ward), who was born Nov. 11, 1833, and came to Utah with her husband. Their children: John Lewis b. June 20, 1858, m. Corrilla Carson Dec. 1879; Mary Ann b. July 13, 1860, m. Thomas Davis; Charles William b. Sept. 30, 1862, m. Hannah Anderson Jan. 5, 1884; James Henry b. Feb. 20, 1865, died; Isabella b. Feb. 26, 1867, m. William Speakman Nov. 20, 1884; Franklin b. March 26, 1869, m. Mary A. Kelly Oct. 17, 1894; Arthur b. March 27, 1871, m. Flora Day; Florence May b. April 17, 1873, m. Daniel Stevens Aug. 31, 1892. Family home Fillmore, Utah.
Married Sarah Ann Kate Newbold July 13, 1882, Salt Lake City (daughter of George Newbold and Emily Osgo Thorpe, the former came to Utah in 1881, the latter in 1883). She was born at Nottingham, Eng. Their children: George Albert b. Feb. 16, 1886, m. Irene Bartholomew; Katie May b. July 3, 1887, m. L. Alma Gee; Florence Emily b. March 19, 1889, m. Emory Johnson; Amy Ethel b. June 22, 1891; Robert Nelson b. March 23, 1893; Fred Wilford b. Nov. 27, 1898; Kimball Benjamin b. March 27, 1900.
Missionary to England 1854-56 and 1880-82. Assistant emigration agent to Daniel Spencer in Iowa City, May, 1856, to Sept., 1866; supt. Sunday schools, Fillmore, eight years and ward chorister two years. City councilman there one term and city watermaster four terms; justice of peace two terms; Millard county clerk and recorder two terms; Millard county treasurer five terms. Black Hawk war veteran. Endured perils of freezing and starvation assisting late comers through Devil's Gate winter 1856-57.

COOPER, WILLIAM (son of John Cooper, born 1785, and Elizabeth Row, born 1787, both at Houghton, Huntingdon, Eng.; married 1810). He was born Dec. 25, 1812, at parents' birthplace. Came to Utah 1861, Capt. Brown company.
Married Mary Ann Samworth (daughter of John and Mary Ann Samworth, married 1817), who was born 1818 and died at Leeds, Yorkshire, Eng. Their children: Frederick Alfred b. Dec. 19, 1837, m. Hannah Turpin Jan. 27, 1861; William b. Dec. 21, 1838, d. 1839; Henry b. Aug. 31, 1839, d. Sept. 18, 1839; William b. Aug. 18, 1840, m. Ann Jackson; Emma b. March 17, 1842 (d. 1888), m. William Mayne; Henry b. Jan. 13, 1844, d. March, 1844; Julia b. Feb. 22, 1845, m. Henry Wildman Leeds; Matilda b. Jan. 2, 1847, m. John Wood; Mary Maria b. Dec. 24, 1848, m. John Wood; Hyrum Smith b. April 6, 1850, m. Mary Green; Lorenzo b. March 25, 1852, d. April 8, 1853; Alma b. Feb. 20, 1854, d. May 24, 1856; Franklin b. Dec. 23, 1855, d. March 15, 1859; Eliza b. Nov. 15, 1857, m. Len Glenn; Charles Heber b. Jan. 19, 1860, d. 1861. Family resided Godmanchester and Leeds, Eng.
Married Sarah Peeling Mayne 1863, at West Jordan, Utah, who was born 1824, at Cosmin, Lancashire, Eng. Only child: Sarah Ann.
Married Sarah Bannfield 1883, at West Jordan, Utah (daughter of Thomas and Ann Bannfield), who was born Aug. 28, 1810, Gloucester, Eng.
Merchant and miller in England. High priest.

COOPER, FREDERICK ALFRED (son of William Cooper and Mary Ann Samworth, Eng. Born Dec. 19, 1837, Godmanchester, Eng. Came to Utah 1859, George Romney handcart company.
Married Hannah Turpin Jan. 27, 1861, West Jordan (daughter of William Turpin and Elizabeth Tidwell, pioneers 1848), who was born Nov. 25, 1842, Birkenshaw, Eng. Their children: Mary Ann b. Dec. 24, 1861, m. Leonard Huey; Elizabeth b. Nov. 28, 1863 (d. 1906), m. John B. Moreton Aug., 1884; Julia b. Oct. 13, 1865, m. Amos B. Moreton; Lavinia b. Feb. 1, 1868, d. Feb. 29, 1868; Alber Edward b. April 17, 1869, m. Mary Jane Lewis 1891; Arthur b. July 24, 1871, d. April 30, 1876; Hannah Maria b. Oct. 25, 1873, d. May 9, 1876; Clara Edith b. Nov. 16, 1876, m. William E. Park; Clarence LeRoy b. Sept. 7, 1879, m. Pearl C. Bradford; Frederick William b. Sept. 21, 1882, m. Ida Farmer Jan. 2, 1911; Effie Lenore b. Jan. 15, 1886. Family home West Jordan.
Married Mary Ellen Mayne April 3, 1863, Salt Lake City (daughter of George Mayne and Sarah Ann Peeling, latter a pioneer 1861). She was born Nov. 25, 1847, Bradford, Eng. Their children: Abraham Mills b. Dec. 1, 1863, d. Aug. 21, 1864; Mary Ellen b. July 11, 1865, m. W. J. Strickley March 6, 1886; Frederick Alfred b. Sept. 5, 1867, m. Margaret A. Jenkins Sept. 30, 1889; George Franklin b. Sept. 30, 1869; Rosetta b. Dec. 15, 1871, m. Josiah Wheeler Sept. 5, 1895; William Earnest b. April 3, 1874, d. May 9, 1876; Thomas Alma b. Apr. 24, 1876, d. May 12, 1883; John Herbert b. Dec. 15, 1879, d. Jan. 20, 1880; Horace Edgar b. Dec. 25, 1881, d. April 12, 1896; Inez Pearl b. Aug. 22, 1884, d. Nov. 9, 1889; Lucille b. Jan. 14, 1888, d. Nov. 14, 1889; Laura b. Feb. 1, 1890. Family home West Jordan.
Married Agnes McGregor Cutler Feb., 1871, Salt Lake City (daughter of William McGregor, pioneer 1851), who was born 1845, Glasgow, Scotland. Their children: Willard b. Dec., 1871, d. 1873; May b. 1873, d. 1877; Walter b. 1875, m. Thelma Lovendahl. Family home West Jordan.
Married Mary Ann Mills Oct. 13, 1898, Salt Lake City (daughter of Joseph Mills and Sarah Barton, pioneers 1858). She was born March 28, 1848, Gloucester, Eng.
Emigrated from England 1859 on ship "William Tubscot." Followed flour milling in early days; postmaster at West Jordan twenty-three years; merchant. Chorister and organist forty years; assistant Sunday school superintendent; in later years still an active ward teacher.

COPE, THOMAS (son of John Cope of Bradsfordshire, Eng.). Born Oct. 8, 1814. Came to Utah 1853, Ten-pound company.
Married Martha Newton. Leeds, Yorkshire, Eng. (daughter of Samuel Newton of Leeds). Only child: Thomas Henry b. Jan. 31, 1853, m. Amelia Jane Lloyd.
Died Sept., 1864.

COPE, THOMAS HENRY (son of Thomas Cope and Martha Newton). Born Jan. 31, 1853, Leeds, Eng.
Married Amelia Jane Lloyd Jan. 1, 1875, Pine Valley, Utah (daughter of Robert Lloyd and Eliza Goheen), who was born Jan. 22, 1856. Their children: Thomas Robert b. Feb. 21, 1876, m. Fanny Gale June 18, 1895; George Michael b. Dec. 13, 1877, m. Geneva Cox May 29, 1912; Martha Adaline b. Feb. 1, 1880, m. Michael H. Gale Nov. 15, 1898; Raphael b. Jan. 20, 1882; Maurice Nerton b. Feb. 24, 1888, m. DeZeta Stewart Nov. 19, 1906; Benjamin b. July 4, 1887, m. Elizabeth Gilger March 17, 1909; Jennie b. Dec. 27, 1890, m. Lenard Reynolds June 21, 1908; James Austin b. March 29, 1893; Elsie b. March 29, 1896; Hortense b. May 7, 1898; Orpha b. Sept. 6, 1900. Family resided Pine Valley, Panguitch and Tropic, Utah.
High counselor in Panguitch stake; bishop of Tropic ward. School trustee; county commissioner.

CORAY, HOWARD (son of Silas Coray and Mary Stephens of Luzerne county, Penn.; latter came to Utah with her children). Born May 6, 1817, Stevens county, N. Y. Came to Utah Oct. 1850, John Sharp company.
Married Martha Jane Knowlton Feb. 6, 1841, in Illinois. Member Nauvoo relief society; secretary first relief society organized in Salt Lake. Personal friend of the Prophet and Patriarch, Joseph and Hyrum Smith. Wrote a history of Joseph, including his mother's memory of him. She had a fair knowledge of law, philosophy, history, poetry, chemistry and geology. Was a member of the board of directors of the Brigham Young Academy, Provo. An earnest and efficient Sunday school worker. She was the daughter of Sidney A. Knowlton and Harriet Burnham of Illinois, pioneers 1849, and was born June 3, 1822. Their children: Howard Knowlton, m. Mary Elizabeth Lusk; Martha Jane, m. Theodore Belden Lewis; Harriet V., m. Wilson H. Dusenbury; Mary Knowlton, m. Orvil Clark Roberts; Eliza Elizabeth, m. Theodore Belden Lewis; Helena Knowlton, m. William D. Alexander; William Henry, m. Julia Ann Mundy; Sidney Agernon, m. Lydia Ann Lerwill; George Quincey, m. Catherine Ann Burt; Frank D., m. Elizabeth Sillers; Lewis Laville, m. Julia Ann Alred; Don Rathburn, m. Elizabeth Hyslop.
High priest; missionary to southern states; clerk in presiding bishop's office at Salt Lake City for five years; secretary to Prophet Joseph Smith, with whom he became acquainted at Nauvoo, Ill., April, 1840, and for whom he had unbounded trust and admiration during his entire life. Assessor in Utah county; school teacher at Salt Lake City and Provo; bookkeeper and accountant. Died Jan. 16, 1908, at Salt Lake City, Utah.

CORAY, HOWARD KNOWLTON (son of Howard Coray and Martha Jane Knowlton). Born April 10, 1842, at Augusta, Van Buren county, Iowa. Came to Utah 1850, John Sharp company.
Married Mary Elizabeth Lusk Sept. 15, 1872, at Salt Lake City (daughter of John Nicholson Lusk and Cythis Ann Beeler of Schuyler county, Mo.). She was born April 4, 1833. Their child: Edna Helena b. Aug. 27, 1875. Family home Salt Lake City, Utah.
Seventy; missionary to southern states 1867-69; bishop's counselor. Farmer and stockraiser.

CORBETT, DANIEL (son of Otis Corbett and Hannah Huscock). Born May 16, 1807, Farmington, Franklin county, Me. Came to Utah in 1849.
Married Elmira Wright, Farmington, Me., who was born July 18, 1811. Their children: Samuel b. Oct. 19, 1835, m. Cammilla D. Jacobsen; John b. June, 1837, m. Emily Woodard; Jonathan b. 1839; Betsy, m. John Casto; Elmira O. b. 1845; Mary b. Dec. 27, 1848, m. Martin Harris; Daniel, m. Alverett Packrell. Family resided in Nauvoo, Ill., Maine and Salt Lake City.
Married Ann Jones 1863, Salt Lake City, who was born Nov. 30, 1820.
Married Maria Roseland in Nov. 1865, Salt Lake City (daughter of John Roseland and Bole Jensen, of Sweden), who was born Nov. 1, 1826. Their children: George Q. b. Nov. 28, 1866; Otis b. Dec. 21, 1868; Oscar A. b. 1859; Ida C. b. May 4, 1863.
Missionary to Maine 1869; 2nd counselor to bishop of 2nd ward, Salt Lake City, 1864. Died June 25, 1892.

CORBETT, SAMUEL (son of Daniel Corbett and Elmira Wright). Born Oct. 19, 1835, Farmington, Me. Married Cammilla D. Jacobsen Oct. 2, 1860, Salt Lake City (daughter of Niels Jacobsen and Annie Dorothy Jorgensen, of Copenhagen, Denmark, pioneers 1849, handcart company). She was born Dec. 4, 1840. Their children: Samuel b. Oct. 31, 1861; Marion L. b. Jan. 20, 1864, m. Martha E. Woolstenhulme; Elmira V. b. Aug. 24, 1866; Annie C. b. Nov. 7, 1869, m. Terry B. Hallett; Walter N. b. March 19, 1872; Sophie b. March 15, 1874, m. Andrew Mathieson; Francis L. b. Oct. 23, 1876, m. Annie Taylor; Stella C. b. Jan. 13, 1879, m. John Jones; Mary E. b. June 14, 1881, m. Charles Percival; Florence R. b. Dec. 14, 1883, m. Harlen Gines; Thaddeus F. b. March 22, 1887, m. Mary F. Hoover. Family resided Salt Lake City and Kamas, Utah.
Seventy. Assisted to bring immigrants to Utah; Black Hawk war veteran; took part in Echo Canyon campaign. Farmer. Died Jan. 17, 1902.

CORBETT, MARION L. (son of Samuel Corbett and Cammilla D. Jacobsen). Born Jan. 20, 1864, Salt Lake City, Utah. Married Martha E. Woolstenhuime Jan. 15, 1890, Logan, Utah (daughter of James Woolstenhulme of England, and Julia M. Du Hamell of France, pioneers of 1852-54, respectively). She was born May 28, 1870. Their children: Ethel C. b. Nov. 5, 1890, m. Ovey A. Richardson; Marion L., Jr., b. Dec. 2, 1893; Martha E. b. Dec. 11, 1895; Otis R. b. Dec. 20, 1897; Freda E. b. May 10, 1900; Thora b. July 29, 1902; Linford b. Nov. 2, 1904; Robert S. b. Dec. 17, 1906; Reva J. and Rada M. b. Nov. 28, 1911. Family home Kamas, Utah.
Missionary to northern states 1901-02; seventy; high priest; 1st counselor to and later bishop of Francis, Utah. Farmer.

CORDINGLEY, THOMAS. Born in Yorkshire, Eng. Came to Utah 1853.
Married Mary Lee. Their children: William b. Aug 20, 1835, m. Permelia Haggins Dec. 25, 1856; Sarah Ann, m. Thomas Robertson.

CORDINGLEY, WILLIAM (son of Thomas Cordingley and Mary Lee). Came to Utah with parents. Born Aug. 20, 1835, Idle Bradsford, Yorkshire, Eng.
Married Permelia Haggins Dec. 25, 1856, Springville, Utah (daughter of William Haggins and Emeline Aker, pioneers Oct. 10, 1853, Anthony W. Ivins company). She was born May 23, 1841, Toms River, N. J. Their children: William Thomas b. Dec. 1, 1857; Sarah Alice b. Jan. 24, 1860; George Alonzo b. Dec. 22, 1861; Mary Emeline b. Jan. 14, 1864, m. Simon C. Drollinger April 20, 1884; Stephen Lorenzo b. April 4, 1866, m. Janett McKimbrick July 18, 1900; John Huggins b. Sept. 26, 1868, m. Jessie Jones Dec. 1, 1893; Howard Lee b. July 2, 1871, m. Lillie Deel May 17, 1906; Enoch Ernest b. April 23, 1874, m. Octora Keller April 3, 1907; Lula Permelia b. Aug. 9, 1877, m. Simeon Allen Jones Oct. 4, 1894; Hannah Flallio b. May 25, 1880, m. Heber B. Hardy March 10, 1897; Seymour David b. April 29, 1884, m. Martha May Jones March 7, 1905.
Indian War veteran; member martial drum and fife corps at Springville, Fountain Green and Huntington, Utah. His sons and daughters took part in the various pioneer activities as they grow to maturity, and are of the same stamp as those who have reclaimed the desert and made it blossom as the rose.

CORBRIDGE, WILLIAM. Born March 9, 1810, Thornley Lane, Eng. Came to Utah Aug. 29, 1852, John Parker independent company.
Married Ellen Parker Jan., 1840 (daughter of John Parker and Ellen Heskins, pioneers Aug 29, 1852, John Parker company). She was born July 7, 1817. Came to Utah with husband Their children: Helen b. Nov. 11, 1840, m. James Hutchins; John b. May 12, 1842, m. Hannah Lee Dec. 9, 1865; Margaret b. Jan. 9, 1844; Mary Ann b. Oct. 5, 1845; William Edward b. July 9, 1847, m. Elizabeth J. Lee; James N. b. Aug. 18, 1849; Samuel R. b. Oct. 29, 1851; Isabella P. b. Feb. 9, 1854; Alice A. b. Nov. 29, 1855, m. George F. Hampton; Amelia D. b. Feb. 8, 1858; Joseph H. b. Dec. 8, 1859, m. Esther Anderson; Lorenzo b. Feb. 10, 1862. Family resided Salt Lake City, Bountiful and Ogden, Utah, and Franklin, Idaho.
Lived at Bountiful, Utah, 1853; Slaterville, 1855, and Franklin, Idaho, 1860. High priest; ward teacher. Indian fighter.

CORBRIDGE, JOHN (son of William Corbridge and Ellen Parker). Born May 12, 1842, Thornley Lane, Eng.
Married Hannah Lee Dec. 9, 1865, Salt Lake City (daughter of George Lee and Sarah Peaker, the former a pioneer Aug. 29, 1852, John Parker company). She was born Dec. 30, 1847, Yorkshire, Eng. Their children: Sarah E. b. April 4, 1867, m. R. J. Hyde, Jr., Dec. 21, 1887; John William b. Dec. 14, 1868, m. Sarah L. Taylor Jan. 10, 1894; George A. b. Dec. 25, 1870, b. Salena Harris Jan. 10, 1894; James H. b. Dec. 16, 1872, m. Mary A. Thomson Jan. 10, 1900; Edward F. b. Dec. 26, 1874; Charles N. b. Oct. 28, 1877, m. Pearl Claypool March 13, 1903; Clarence F. b. May 29, 1880, m. Florence Golightly Dec. 5, 1906; Sylvester L. b. Sept. 5, 1882, m. Effie Stevens April 26, 1904; Leslie A. b. Nov. 4, 1884, m. Ruby Claypool Feb. 19, 1908; Olive H. b. Dec. 12, 1886, m. Francis Lewis April 17, 1907; Bertha M. b. Nov. 1, 1889, m. Albert Harding July 17, 1912. Family resided Franklin and Preston, Idaho.
Pioneer and Indian fighter Franklin. Idaho. Assisted building railroad in Cache Valley. Ward recorder; ward teacher; high priest.

CARDON, ALFRED (son of Sampson Cardon and Myra Hampson of Liverpool, Eng.). Born Feb. 28, 1817, in Liverpool. Came to Utah Oct. 5, 1851, with his own company.
Married Emma Parker 1836, Burslem, Staffordshire, Eng. (daughter of George Parker of Burslem, Staffordshire), who was born May 24, 1819. Their children: Elizabeth, died; George, died; Edwin Parker; Rachael Ann, died; Emma; Alfred, died; Adelaide Amelia; Myra Green; William Henry; Mary; Charles Edwin, latter four died; Eliza Almira; Sarah Jane; Ida Victoria. Family home Willard, Utah.
High priest; missionary to Vermont, Missouri and England 1844-51; bishop. Potter; brickmason; farmer. Died March 13, 1871, Willard, Utah.

CARDON, EDWIN PARKER (son of Alfred Cardon and Emma Parker). Born Oct. 7, 1841, Burslem, Staffordshire, Eng. Came to Utah Oct. 5, 1851, Alfred Cordon company.
Married Sarah Voss Dec. 14, 1867, Salt Lake City (daughter of Thomas Voss and Lucy Haddon, of Willard, Utah, pioneers Oct. 17, 1862, Henry W. Miller company.) She was born Sept. 11, 1847. Their children: Ida Pauline b. Sept. 10, 1868; Ada Amelia b. Sept. 29, 1870; Eliza Almira b. Oct. 23, 1872; Sarah Priscilla b. May 5, 1875; Alfred b. Jan. 9, 1878; Edwin Voss b. Feb. 3, 1882; Joseph Moroni b. Sept. 12, 1884; Rachael Alice b. Dec. 27, 1886. Family home Willard, Utah.
President 59th quorum seventies; high priest; patriarch; bishop's counselor; missionary to Missouri river, 1866. Farmer.

CORNWALL, ALEXANDER (son of Thomas Cornwall and Eliza Cloakson of Ireland). Born 1806, Drummond, Ireland. Came to Utah 1861, Capt. Asper company.
Married Eliza Nael 1827 (daughter of Joseph and Sarah Nael of Ireland). She died in Ireland. Their children: Deborn b. 1828; William b. 1830; Joseph b. 1832; Alexander b. 1835; Mary Jane b. 1837; Samuel b. 1842. Family home Mill Creek, Utah.
High priest. Farmer. Died in 1880, at Mill Creek.

CORNWALL, JOSEPH (son of Alexander Cornwall and Eliza Nael). Born Aug. 27, 1832, County Down, Ireland.
Married Charlotte Carter Nov. 29, 1862, at Salt Lake City (daughter of John Carter and Sarah Bowley), who was born June 21, 1840, in England. Their children: Joseph A. b. Oct. 4, 1863, m. Mary Ellen Spencer; Samuel A. b. Jan. 18, 1866, m. Mary Neff; John W. b. Sept. 13, 1869; Luetta b. Dec. 17, 1871, m. Joseph Hanson; Earnest b. Sept. 23, 1874, m. Maggie M. Miller; Mabel b. Nov. 26, 1878, d. 1880; Alma Mullen b. Feb. 18, 1883, m. Leonora Jane Hill.
Missionary to Ireland; high priest.

COTTAM, JOHN. Born 1798 in England. Came to Utah about 1856.
Married Catherine Livsey. Their children: Thomas; Jenny; John; Ellen. Lived at Salt Lake City, Utah.

COTTAM, THOMAS (son of John Cottam and Catherine Livsey). Born Oct. 21, 1820, in England. Came to Utah Sept., 1853.
Married Caroline Smith in 1849 at St. Louis (daughter of Samuel Smith and Mary West of England), who was born Oct. 9, 1820, and came to Utah in 1854. Their children: Mary Ann b. 1850; Emma b. June 27, 1851; George Thomas b. Oct. 29, 1853; Catherine Jane b. Jan. 7, 1855; Thomas Punter b. Sept. 23, 1857; Charles Smith b. Jan. 6, 1861; Sarah Ellen b. 1863.
Member of high priests quorum; ward teacher; superintendent of Sunday school of 4th ward, St. George, Utah. Janitor of St. George Tabernacle 18 years; turner and chairmaker. Died November, 1896, St. George, Utah.

COTTAM, GEORGE THOMAS (son of Thomas Cottam and Caroline Smith). Born Oct. 29, 1853, at Salt Lake City.
Married Rachel Holt Oct. 6, 1874, at Salt Lake City (daughter of James Holt and Parthenia Overton of North Ogden, Utah), who was born June 14, 1856. Their children: Mary Ann b. July 19, 1875; Rachel Parthenia b. March 2, 1877; Caroline b. Dec. 3, 1878; George Thomas b. Oct. 1, 1880; Ada b. Sept. 21, 1883; James Franklin b. Sept. 22, 1884; Maggie b. Sept. 21, 1886; John Henry b. Sept. 30, 1888; Effie b. Nov. 23, 1890; Bertha Jane b. Nov. 13, 1892; Vilate b. March 6, 1895; Joseph Milton b. Dec. 14, 1897. Family home St. George, Utah.
Member of high priests quorum; ward teacher; had charge of sacrament in Sunday school. County commissioner; city councilman. Farmer and stockraiser.

COTTAM, JOHN (son of John Cottam and Catherine Livsey of Clitheroe, Lancashire, Eng.). Born Dec. 10, 1832, at Clitheroe, Eng. Came to Utah October, 1852.
Married Anne Smith 1843, Chatburn, Lancashire, Eng. (daughter of John and Nancy Smith of Chatburn, Lancashire), who was born Feb. 18, 1824. Their children: William, m. Evelyn Allen; Alma, m. Elizabeth Foster; Katherine, d. infant; Smith; John; Thomas; Albert; Anne; Hyrum, d. aged 13 years; Daniel, d. infant; Heber. Family home Salt Lake City.
Teacher. Turner and chairmaker. Died July 21, 1904, at Salt Lake City.

COTTAM, HEBER (son of John Cottam and Anne Smith) Born June 27, 1858, at American Fork, Utah.
Married Alice M. Bailey May 11, 1888, at Salt Lake City (daughter of Charles Bailey and Martha Collier of England,

pioneers Sept. 15, 1868, John Gillespie company). She was born March 13, 1855. Their children: Alice M. b. Oct. 27, 1889; Leila A. b. Aug. 16, 1891; Minerva E. b. Jan. 14, 1896. Family home Salt Lake City. General workman.

COTTLE, HENRY (son of William Cottle). Born May 3, 1822, Horsley, Gloucestershire, Eng. Came to Utah 1866, independent company.
Married Elizabeth Brittle 1849 (daughter of Jesse Brittle and Mary Round). She was taken prisoner in fight with Indians July 24, 1866, near Laramie, and was never afterward seen. Her mother was killed, and father died three weeks later from tomahawk wounds. Their children: George, killed by Indians 1866; Thomas Edward; William Henry, m. Julia Miller; m. Elizabeth S. Dummer; Annie. Family home Ogden, Utah.
Elder. Died Dec. 19, 1872, Sacramento, Cal.

COTTLE, THOMAS E. (son of Henry Cottle and Elizabeth Brittle, of England). He was born Nov. 22, 1850, Dudley, Staffordshire, Eng. Came to Utah late in 1860, Capt. Duncan company.
Married Flora England Nov. 7, 1872 (daughter of John England and Jane Povard, pioneers 1860, Capt. Duncan company; married May 4, 1834). She was born Nov. 5, 1856. Their children: Floura Elizabeth b. Aug. 26, 1873, m. John Negus Nov. 6, 1895; Thomas Henry b. March 21, 1876, m. Ella Neal 1898; George Edward b. Jan. 26, 1878, died; Slener b. March 20, 1880, died; Annie Jane b. Dec. 30, 1881, m. Joseph P. Stock June 7, 1902; John b. Sept. 18, 1883, died; Charles W. b. Aug. 13, 1884, m. Rose Hutchins Feb. 2, 1906; Mary L. Beatrice b. Nov. 25, 1885, m. Claude Kimball Sept. 3, 1907; Myrtle b. Aug. 27, 1887, m. Morris Hodges April 3, 1908; Jesse L. b. Sept. 15, 1892; Violet Tressle b. Dec. 20, 1894, died; Reuben Francis b. April 27, 1896. Family home Plain City, Weber county, Utah.
Missionary to central states two years; Sunday school teacher. Settled at Ogden; moved to Plain City. Died March 28, 1908.

COTTLE, WILLIAM HENRY (son of Henry Cottle and Elizabeth Brittle). Born March 22, 1852, Dudley, Worcestershire, Eng. Came to Utah in September, 1866, independent company. On July 24, previous, he was badly wounded in fight with Indians. All of this party were either killed or wounded coming to Utah.
Married Julia A. Miller Feb. 5, 1872, Salt Lake City (daughter of Stephen Miller and Mary Ann Humpery of Plain City, Utah, pioneers Oct. 1860, Capt. Miller company). She was born June 18, 1854. Their children: Mary Ann b. June 20, 1873; William Stephen b. June 4, 1876; Julia Y. A. b. Nov. 2, 1878.
Married Elizabeth S. Dummer July 31, 1879, Salt Lake City (daughter of William Dummer and Sarah Hyde of Salt Lake City, pioneers Sept. 15, 1867, Capt. Seeley company). She was born Feb. 29, 1860, Southampton, Eng. Their children: Henry b. July 5, 1880; Sarah A. b. July 13, 1882; Walter b. Oct. 1, 1884; Emma J. b. Oct. 26, 1886; Lulla E. b. Oct. 27, 1888; Josephine b. April 20, 1891; Lorance N. b. April 27, 1894; Samuel A. b. May 28, 1896; George D. b. July 14, 1898; Eve D. b. Aug. 25, 1901; Gwendoline b. Feb. 3, 1904; Alphia b. March 31, 1907.
High priest; superintendent Sunday school, Poplar ward, ten years. Chairman Poplar school board three years.

COTTRELL, RAPHAEL HENRY KELTON (son of Edward Cottrell and Augusta Ann of London, Eng.). Born May 9, 1811, London, Eng. Came to Utah Nov. 1874.
Married Mary Edwards Sept. 1831, London, Eng. (daughter of John Edwards and Mary Dwen of London), who was born 1813. Their children: William and Mary, both died; James, m. Amy Alymead; Charles, m. Eleanor Whiteman; Martha Ann, m. Alfred Whiteman; Emma, m. Reuben Earl; Elizabeth; George, died.
Married Mary Ann Payne in London. Their children: Edward A., m. Vina Steed; William, died; Lucy, m. John Strange; August Ann; Lucy Mary; Raphael; George. Family home Kaysville, Utah.
Died Nov. 6, 1878.

COTTRELL, CHARLES (son of Raphael Henry Cottrell and Mary Edwards of London). Born April 3, 1835, in London. Came to Utah Nov. 12, 1880, John Nicholson company.
Married Eleanor Whiteman May 27, 1855, in London (daughter of Henry Whiteman and Hannah Pateman of London). She was born May 22, 1836. Their children: Charles R. H., d. infant; James A., m. Edith S. Layton; Raphael, m. Sarah Eamer; George, m. Eliza G. Slack; Eleanor S., m. William P. Burton; Charles, m. Erminia R. Layton; Emma E. M., d. child; Louisa, d. child; Henry, d. boy; Walter, m. Emilo Barton; Mary, d. infant; Emily; Alice, m. Louis J. Bowers; Annie F., d. infant. Family resided London, Eng., and Davis county, Utah.
President of high priest quorum of Davis county, Utah; president of Redding branch, England; block teacher. Plasterer and contractor.

COTTRELL, GEORGE (son of Charles Cottrell and Eleanor Whitman). Born May 27, 1861.
Married Eliza Cornelia Slack April 9, 1885, Kaysville, Utah (daughter of William Slack and Eliza Frost of Kaysville, pioneers 1859, Frederick Kesler company). She was born Aug. 1, 1860, at Kaysville. Their children: George H. and William C., d. child; James Alfred b. April 6, 1891, m. Martha Helen Whitman. Family home, Salt Lake City.

COTTRELL, JAMES ALFRED (son of George Cottrell and Eliza Cornelia Slack). He was born April 6, 1891, Kaysville, Utah.
Married Martha Helen Whitman Oct. 4, 1910, at Salt Lake City (daughter of Allen Heman Whitman and Christine Camilla Pederson of Salt Lake City; they came to Utah June, 1889). She was born June 23, 1892. Their child: Violet Ethelyn.
Blacksmith.

COTTRELL, SAMUEL (son of William Cottrell and Sarah Jefferson of Manchester, Eng.). Born May 7, 1816, Warrington, Lancashire, Eng. Came to Utah Sept. 9, 1852, Bryant Jolley company.
Married Ellenor Taylor April 4, 1838, Manchester Old Church, Eng. She was born March 5, 1819, Rimcon, Eng. Their children: William; Joseph T.; Mary Jane; Sarah; Alice; Laura Miranda; Samuel Henry; Ellenor Ann; Martha Ellen. Family home Farmington, Utah.
Member 27th quorum seventies; choir leader 20 years. Farmer. Died July 14, 1879, at Farmington.

COULAM, JOHN (son of John Coulam). Born Aug. 2, 1802, at Louth, Lincolnshire, Eng. Came to Utah Sept. 23, 1849, Orson Spencer company.
Married Sarah Cordon in Lincolnshire, Eng. (daughter of John Cordon of Lincolnshire). She died April 14, 1849. Their children: John, m. Sarah Jane Orton; Charles, died; Fannie, m. John Baker; Henry, m. Sarah Bean; Sarah Jane, m. John Heiner; George, m. Elizabeth Horrocks. Family home, Salt Lake City, Utah.
High priest. Carpenter. Died May 1877.

COULAM, HENRY (son of John Coulam and Sarah Cordon). Born March 13, 1842, Louth, Eng. Came to Utah with parents.
Married Sarah Bean Aug. 24, 1867, Salt Lake City, Utah (daughter of Joseph Bean and Sarah Beanland, of Bradford, Yorkshire, Eng.). She was born Feb. 11, 1847. Came to Utah late in 1859. Their children: John Bean b. Dec. 14, 1868, died April 5, 1871; Sarah Louisa b. March 21, 1874, died; Joseph Cordon b. July 25, 1876, died; William Ezra b. Nov. 30, 1878, m. Ellen May Geary; George Franklin b. March 31, 1881, m. Irene Romney; Alice b. Nov. 2, 1883, m. Willard B. Richards, Jr.; Eliza b. Feb. 7, 1887, died. Family home Salt Lake City.
Member 5th quorum seventies; missionary to England; high priest. Carpenter.

COULT, JAMES (son of William Coult and Elizabeth Hinton). Born April 26, 1837, in Essexshire, Eng. Came to Utah Sept. 23, 1859.
Married Sarah Ann Traveller March 23, 1859, Philadelphia, Pa. (daughter of Cornelius Traveller and Ann Eliza Atkins of London, Eng., pioneers April 1, 1860, John Smith company). She was born Oct. 19, 1841. Their children: William C. b. Feb. 10, 1860, d. child; Sarah Ann b. Dec. 18, 1861, m. Charles Collins; Joseph H. b. Dec. 21, 1863, drowned when twenty-one; Amy E. b. March 22, 1866, m. Joseph Gilbert; James F. b. March 20, 1868, d. child; James E. b. March 18, 1869, m. Amia L. Hicks; Minnie A. b. July 13, 1871, m. Everett Roberts; Jane A. b. Oct. 4, 1873, m. John H. McDonald; Annie L. b. Jan. 30, 1876, d. child; Charles A. b. Aug. 10, 1877, m. Iva Thomas; Della F. b. March 16, 1880, m. Carl I. Hallstrom. Family home Salt Lake City.
Plasterer and contractor. Died Feb. 9, 1893.

COULT, JAMES E. (son of James Coult and Sarah Ann Traveller). Born March 18, 1869, Salt Lake City.
Married Amia L. Hicks June 11, 1890, Logan, Utah (daughter of James H. Hicks of New York and Jane Ann Chase of Vermont, pioneers Sept. 1850, Capt. Johnson, and 1853, Joseph Thorne companies, respectively). She was born March 29, 1870. Their children: James Clyde b. Jan. 19, 1892; Delance Hicks b. Feb. 22, 1894, d. March 11, 1894; Althea Jane b. March 3, 1895; Viola Eloise b. March 12, 1899; Ernest Hicks b. Jan. 15, 1910. Family home Salt Lake City.
Elder. Plasterer and contractor.

COVEY, BENJAMIN (son of Walter and Sarah Covey). Born March 7, 1792, Dutchess county, N. Y. Came to Utah Sept. 20, 1848, Lorenzo Snow company.
Married Almira Mack Oct. 23, 1836, Kirtland, Ohio (daughter of Stephen and Temperance Mack, of Sharon county, Vt., pioneers Sept. 20, 1848). She was born April 28, 1805. Their children: Enoch b. Aug. 26, 1837, m. Janett Carruth Young; Joseph b. March 2, 1839, m. Elizabeth Parkinson; Alman b. June 20, 1841, died; Hyrum b. Aug. 6, 1843, m. Ellen Parkinson.
First bishop 12th ward, Salt Lake City. Farmer; shoemaker. Died March 13, 1868.

COVEY, ENOCH (son of Benjamin Covey and Almira Mack). Born Aug. 26, 1837, in Caldwell county, Mo.
Married Janett Carruth Young March 22, 1864, Salt Lake City (daughter of James Young and Janett Carruth, of

Houston Parish, Renfrewshire, Scotland, pioneers 1850). She was born Sept. 15, 1846. Their children: Grace C. b. May 10, 1865, m. O. T. Papworth; William B. b. June 12, 1867, m. Margaret A. Johnston; Stephen M. b. Nov. 7, 1869, m. Hannah Saunders; Janett A. b. July 2, 1870, m. James Klipple; Andrew A. b. June 3, 1876, m. Theodosia N. Kent; Hyrum T. b. Oct. 17, 1878, m. May Roberry; Mary E. b. June 19, 1881. Family home Salt Lake City. Sheepraiser. Died Nov. 11, 1902.

COVEY, WILLIAM BENJAMIN (son of Enoch Covey and Janett Carruth Young). He was born July 12, 1867, Salt Lake City.
Married Margaret A. Johnston Feb. 6, 1893, Coalville, Utah (daughter of James Johnston and Mary A. Fletcher, of Coalville, Utah, pioneers 1862). Their children: William W. b. Nov. 14, 1893; Grace M. b. May 20, 1895.
President Afton Harness company. Farmer and sheepraiser. Director Covey Investment Co., builder of Covey, La France and Kensington apartment houses at Salt Lake City.

COVEY, JOSEPH (son of Benjamin Covey and Elmyra Mack). Born March 2, 1839, in Caldwell county, Mo. Came to Utah Sept. 20, 1848, Lorenzo Snow company.
Married Elizabeth Parkinson, at Salt Lake City (daughter of Mr. Parkinson, who died while crossing the plains; parents lived in Missouri). She was born Sept. 1842. Their children: Joseph P., m. Alfreda Anderson; Elizabeth, m. Thomas Busby; Ellen; Jessie, m. Andrew Vissing; Rallar; William. Family home Salt Lake City.
Mining man.

COVEY, HYRUM (son of Benjamin Covey and Almira Mack). Born Aug. 6, 1843, in Illinois. Came to Utah Sept. 20, 1848, Lorenzo Snow company.
Married Ellen Parkinson July 19, 1867, Salt Lake City (daughter of John Parkinson and Ellen Smalley, of Preston, Lancashire, Eng.; both died en route to Utah). She was born 1850. Their children: Hyrum B. b. July 6, 1869, m. John T. E. Thompson; John P. b. Sept. 20, 1871, m. Phoebe Douglas; Kate C. b. Dec. 30, 1873, m. John Corbett; Almira R. b. July 25, 1876, m. Tom Cragehead; Frank J. b. Oct. 23, 1879, m. Birdie Mickle; Earl M. b. March 8, 1882, m. Lula Henderehot; Lorey b. Oct. 3, 1884; Mable b. Oct. 7, 1886, m. Joseph Pitcher; Nellie b. May 20, 1889, m. Leslie Scrowthers; Ivy b. Dec. 18, 1891, m. Arthur Simmons.

COWAN, JOHN (son of James Cowan). Born Aug. 1, 1784, Campsie, near Glasgow, Scotland. Came to Utah 1850, Levi Stewart company.
Married Agnes Barrey (daughter of Andrew and Nellie Barrey), who was born in 1785. Their children: James b. Dec. 12, 1808, m. Jessie Brown 1829; William b. April 1, 1811, died; Robert b. April 1, 1811, m. Dannon Faircloth; Margaret b. Sept. 17, 1813, m. John Henderson; John b. May 18, 1816, died; Mary b. Jan. 24, 1819, m. John Donelson; William Aug. 9, 1821, m. Mary Brown; Andrew b. Dec. 22, 1825, m. Ann Smiley; Alexander b. Nov. 9, 1827, died; Alexander b. 18, 1830. Jane Mitchell Jan. 22, 1860. Family home at Lake City.

COWAN, ALEXANDER (son of John Cowan and Agnes Barrey). Was born Dec. 18, 1830, Campsie, Scotland.
Married Jane Mitchell Jan. 22, 1860, Salt Lake City (daughter of William Mitchell and Helen Legg, latter a pioneer Sept. 25, 1866, John D. Holladay company). She was born July 24, 1835, Aberdeen, Scotland. Their children: Mary Jane b. Jan. 8, 1861, died; John M. b. Aug. 29, 1862, m. Loretta Lewis Dec. 19, 1889; Alexander, Jr., b. March 24, 1865, and James Brown b. Sept. 12, 1866, died; William M. b. Oct. 12, 1868, m. Mary I. Crook Nov. 27, 1890; Robert H. b. Feb. 21, 1872, m. Lillie P. Manwill April 22, 1896; Joseph B. b. April 4, 1874, m. Zella Pepper Dec. 22, 1903; Sarah b. Nov. 7, 1876, m. William E. Wilson Aug. 28, 1895; Emma M. b. Nov. 25, 1878, m. John D. Wimmer Oct. 24, 1900. Family home Payson, Utah.
Married Eliza Ratz Nov. 20, 1861, who was born April 20, 1834, in Switzerland. Their children: Agness b. Dec. 22, 1862, m. Frank A. Argyle Aug. 25, 1887; Frank W. b. Oct. 16, 1865, m. Mary E. Montague Feb. 28, 1893; Annie E. b. Dec. 20, 1867, m. John M. Manwill May 15, 1885; Hyrum b. Sept. 15, 1870, died; Mary L. b. Feb. 10, 1875, m. Christian Provstgard Sept. 1, 1890; George A. b. Dec. 30, 1877, m. Zina Montague Dec. 1898.
High priest. Farmer.

COWAN, JOHN M. (son of Alexander Cowan and Jane Mitchell). Born Aug. 29, 1862, Salt Lake City.
Married Loretta Lewis Dec. 19, 1889, Payson, Utah (daughter of J. W. Lewis and Mary A. Fuller; pioneers 1862). She was born Aug. 20, 1870, Provo, Utah. Their children: Hazel V. b. Nov. 19, 1890; John R. b. April 9, 1892; I. Glade b. June 5, 1894; Glenn F. b. Dec. 11, 1895; Martha A. b. April 20, 1898; Clarence E. b. April 22, 1901; Donna L. b. June 9, 1905; Deeth Lewis b. March 17, 1907, died; Max L. b. Jan. 31, 1909; Fawn b. Sept. 12, 1911. Family home Payson, Utah.
Elder. Farmer and stockraiser.

COWLEY, CHARLES CAESAR (son of Nicholas Cowley and Ellen Kelley, both of Isle of Man). Born Dec. 1, 1800, Isle of Man. Came to Utah 1850, Andrew Perkins company.
Married Ann Killip. Their children: Charles Caesar b. Nov. 17, 1834, m. Eleanor C. Curtis; William M. b. Sept. 29, 1835, m. Sarah Emily Wall; Eleanor, died; Ann Jane, m. William Partington; Nephi K., m. Unity H. Apperley; John Alma, m. Jeanette Davidson; Mariah E., m. A. A. Allen; Joseph Enos, m. Kate Worley; James Alma, m. Ann Lewis; Hyrum, died; Benjamin Franklin, deceased.
Settled at Salt Lake City, moved to Cache county.

COWLEY, CHARLES CAESAR, JR. (son of Charles Caesar Cowley and Ann Killip). Born Nov. 17, 1843, at Isle of Man. Came to Utah in 1850, Andrew Perkins company.
Married Eleanor Caroline Curtis Feb. 25, 1864, Logan, Utah (daughter of Joseph Curtis and Sarah Morrell, pioneers Oct. 1861, Capt. Harmon company). She was born Aug. 11, 1844, London, Eng. Their children: Eleanor Sarah b. Nov. 21, 1864, m. Joseph S. Wall; Ann Mariah b. April 23, 1866, and Charles Henry b. Sept. 5, 1867, died; Joseph Curtis b. Oct. 27, 1869, m. Minnie Wall; Edwin James b. March 19, 1872, m. Lydia Jackson; Ephraim Albert b. Aug. 4, 1874, m. Annie Dastrup; Fanny Louise b. Aug. 26, 1876, died; Angus A. b. June 29, 1878, died; Moses b. Aug. 2, 1880, and Luella b. Jan. 21, 1882, died; Benjamin Franklin b. April 4, 1883; David Curtis b. Oct. 13, 1895; Israel Abner b. June 18, 1889. Family home Logan, Utah.
Black Hawk Indian war veteran. Early settler of San Pete and Sevier counties. Made two trips across the plains for immigrants.

COWLEY, JOSEPH CURTIS (son of Charles Caesar Cowley, Jr., and Eleanor Caroline Curtis). Born Oct. 27, 1869, at Logan.
Married Minnie Ann Wall Sept. 6, 1891, Glenwood, Utah (daughter of Francis George Wall and Mary Bench, of England), who was born Oct. 20, 1875, Manti, Utah. Their children: Laura May b. Feb. 25, 1892; Elmo b. Dec. 21, 1894, deceased; Joseph Elmer b. Dec. 26, 1895; Fanny Louise b. Nov. 5, 1897; Francis Charles b. April 1, 1900; Naomi Clarissa b. Jan. 23, 1902; Anthony Oscar b. Oct. 30, 1903; Elva Clay b. Jan. 13, 1906; Angus Wayne b. July 29, 1910. Family home Venice, Utah.
Missionary to northwestern states 1907-09; secretary of Venice ward Sunday school; bishop of Venice ward 1900. School trustee at Venice. Merchant and farmer.

COWLEY, EPHRAIM ALBERT (son of Charles Caesar Cowley, Jr., and Eleanor Caroline Curtis). Born Aug. 4, 1874, at Logan.
Married Annie Maria Dastrup May 31, 1899, Manti, Utah (daughter of Hans Laurentz Dastrup and Annie Maria Anderson, Copenhagen, Denmark), who was born Dec. 26, 1875. Their children: Lamoin Ephraim b. Jan. 27, 1905; Waldo Valdez b. May 29, 1911. Family home Richfield, Utah.
Member 36th quorum seventies; missionary to Australia 1901-02; assistant stake Sunday school superintendent. Secretary Sevier Valley Canal company; manager People's Emporium.

COWLEY, RICHARD (son of John Lucas Cowley, born March 7, 1802, Simpson, Buckinghamshire, Eng., and Lucia Sear, born April 14, 1812, Bletchley, Buckinghamshire, Eng.). He was born May 10, 1834, at Simpson, Eng. Came to Utah Dec. 4, 1864, John M. Kay company.
Married Mary Labrum Nov. 10, 1865 (daughter of Thomas Labrum and Elizabeth George, latter a pioneer Oct. 1, 1862, Joseph Horne company—married 1837, Mursley, Buckinghamshire). She was born Feb. 20, 1838, and came to Utah Oct. 3, 1863, Daniel D. McArthur company. Their children: Fredrick Summerfield b. Oct. 22, 1866, m. Effie Elizina Despain Dec. 11, 1889; Richard Austin b. Sept. 22, 1868, m. Lucy Gull June 6, 1895; Lucy Elizabeth b. May 23, 1870, m. Peter Winward Dec. 4, 1895; Thomas Labrum b. Dec. 13, 1871, m. Janet H. Amelia Despain June 12, 1901; Maud Agnes b. Nov. 6, 1873, m. Charles Taysom March 6, 1895; Polley Jane b. Oct. 1, 1877, m. Charles Archibald June 16, 1898. Family home Sandy, Utah.
Settled at Mill Creek; moved to Meadow 1873-76, thence to Sandy 1878.

COX, DANIEL. Born May 5, 1800, in Maryland. Came to Utah Sept. 1850, William W. Wall company.
Married Mary Ann Frantom, of Maryland, who died in Illinois. Their children: Ann Maria, m. J. Lewis; m. Edward Walker; William, m. Elizabeth Smith; Jane, m. Jesse Doddie; Edward, m. Hannah Ashton; Jacob, m. Elizabeth Goodson; m. Julia Snow; Joseph, m. Julia Snow; Elsie, died.
Married Lucy Smith, in 1847 (daughter of Howard Smith of Green county, Ill.). Their children: Azuba Deseret, m. William Pratt; m. John Hardwick; Daniel, died; Charlotte, m. James Dawson; Lizzie, died; Daniel Howard, m. Sarah Jackson. Families resided at Lehi, Utah.
Assistant presiding elder at Lehi in 1850. Farmer.

COX, JACOB (son of Daniel Cox and Mary Ann Frantom). Born Aug. 5, 1837, in Green county, Ill. Came to Utah with parents.
Married Elizabeth Goodson March 9, 1860, at Lehi (daughter of John Goodson and Ann Sharon), who was born March 5, 1840, in Norfolkshire, Eng.
Married Julia Snow, in the fall of 1870, Salt Lake City (daughter of William and Sally Snow, of Lehi and Pine

Valley, Utah). She was the widow of Joseph Cox (son of Daniel Cox and Mary Ann Frantom). Their child: Joseph, Jr. She had one child by Jacob Cox: William Snow b. Jan. 14, 1872, m. Lizzie Cannon Gardner.
Elder. Indian war veteran. Early settler at Lehi. Road builder and irrigationist.

COX, EDWARD (son of Richard Cox and Sarah Beal of Herringford Abbotts, Huntingdonshire, Eng.). Born April 1, 1825, Haningford, Eng. Came to Utah Sept., 1860, Kimball-Lawrence freight train.
Married Lucinda Willis in 1846, at Lambeth, London (daughter of George Willis of London), who was born Jan. 24, 1825, Rochester, Eng. Their children: Edward George and Lucinda Mary, twins, Edward, William, and James George, first five died; Charles; Louisa, m. Hyrum Edwards; Lovina, Heber and Emeline Lavina Eugenia, latter three died. Family home 865 W. N. Temple, Salt Lake City.
Married Eliza Louisa Frost March 10, 1866, Salt Lake City (daughter of Henry Franklin of Bristol, Eng., who came to Utah Sept. 26, 1856, Edmond Ellsworth handcart company). She was born Nov. 2, 1830.
Married Eliza Helen Harvey Aug. 17, 1867, at Salt Lake City (daughter of Andrew Harvey and Eliza Helen Wheeler of Salt Lake City, pioneers Sept. 15, 1866, William Henry Chipman company). She was born June 2, 1849. Their children: Alfred Andrew; Ernest, m. Dora Christensen; Valentine Clifford; Lucius Edgar, m. Mary Newton; Nellie C., m. Fred Taylor; Royal Victor; May C., m. John A. Davis; Lucy Beal, m. Edward Wallace; Joseph Harvey, m. Ellen Mossberg; Richard; Frederick David.
High priest. Carpenter and joiner; foreman carpenter in finishing of Salt Lake temple.

COX, FREDERICK WALTER. Born Jan. 20, 1812, Oswego county, New York. Came to Utah 1852, Oxteam company.
Married Emeline Whiting 1835 (daughter of Edwin Whiting of Springville, Utah, pioneer with oxteam company). Their children: Frederick W., m. Lucy Allen, m. Elvira Coolidge; William Arthur, m. Christina Anderson; Razalia, m. Benjamin Driggs; Esther, m. Jane Reid; Emily, m. Luther Tuttle; Harriet, m. Henry M. Reid; Sylvester, m. Mary Ellen Parry; Lucia, m. Albert Tuttle; Baby, d. infant. Family home Manti, Utah.
Married Cordelia Morley Jan. 27, 1846 (daughter of Isaac and Hannah Morley of Moroni. Utah), who was born Nov. 28, 1823. Their children: Lavina, m. Andrew C. Van Buren; Emerett, m. Hayes Clark; Sarah Ann, m. Fred Anderson; Francis, m. Libby Johnson; Curlista, m. George Crawford; Arletta, m. Frank Tuttle; Evelyn, m. John Moffitt. Family home Manti, Utah.
Married Jemimah Losee Jan. 27, 1846. Their children: Adeline, m. William T. Reid; Ester, m. Gardiner Snow; Byron, m. Susan Henrie; Elvira, m. Al Alder; Jemimah, d. child; Elenor, m. Brig Peacock; Alice, m. Charles Tenent. Family home Manti, Utah.
Married Lydia Losee, who was born July 24, 1839. Their children: Samuel, d. child; Charles, m. Ella Stringham; Amanda, m. Horton Tuttle. Family home Manti, Utah.
Married Emma Smith (daughter of Albert Smith of Manti, Utah). Their children: Lacinda Bell; Walter; May. Family home Manti, Utah.
Seventy; president high priests quorum; missionary to England 1863. Farmer and lumberman. Died June 1865, Manti, Utah.

COX, FREDERICK WALTER, JR. (son of Frederick Walter Cox and Emeline Whiting). Born Nov. 6, 1837. Came to Utah 1852, Oxteam company.
Married Lucy Allen, Manti, Utah (daughter of Joseph Allen and Lucy Morley, pioneers with oxteam company). Their children: Frederick Walter, m. Maria Louisa Stevens, m. Lucy H. Woolman; Marion A., m. Elizabeth Demills; Lucy, d. child; Louisa, m. James Tatten; Arthur, m. Amanda Funk, m. Mary Thomas; Minnie, m. Charles Whitlock; Olive, m. Charles Christensen; Edwin and Elbert, d. infants; Roselyn; Louis, m. Louise Wintsch. Family home Manti, Utah.
Married Elvira Coolidge, Salt Lake City. Their children: Howard; Bruce, m. Miss Reed; Gene; Allie; Roy. Family home Manti, Utah.
Veteran Black Hawk Indian war. Seventy. Policeman; farmer and lumberman.

COX, FREDERICK WALTER. III (son of Frederick Walter Cox, Jr. and Lucy Allen). Born Sept. 1, 1858, Manti, Utah.
Married Maria Louisa Stevens Feb. 21, 1864, Ferron, Utah (daughter of Hyrum Stevens and Deby Lemmon of Paragonah, Utah, pioneers with oxteam company). She was born Oct. 10, 1865. Their children: Deby Louisa b. March 7, 1865, m. George Albert Huntsman; Frederick Leslie b. Feb. 22, 1887, m. Maria Huntsman; Clell Hyrum b. March 21, 1891; Ross W. b. Dec. 12, 1897; Lloyd Glen b. Sept. 28, 1903. Family home Ferron, Utah.
Married Lucy H. Woolman Nov. 16, 1907, Manti, Utah (daughter of Christopher Woolman and Agnes Robertson of Leicestershire, Eng.). She was born Oct. 16, 1878. Their children: Jennie b. July 30, 1908; Zella Agnes b. Sept. 16, 1910. Family home Ferron, Utah.
Ward teacher; counselor to Y. M. M. I. A. Farmer.

COX, CLELL HYRUM (son of Fredrick Walter Cox III and Maria Louisa Stevens). Born March 21, 1891, Ferron, Utah.
President priests, teachers and deacons quorums; usher in Sunday school eight years; ward teacher. Farmer.

COX, HENRY (son of Stephen Cox and Mary Ann May of New Swindon, Wiltshire, Eng.). Born Feb. 14, 1837, Aldbourn, Wiltshire. Came to Utah Sept. 25, 1866, John D. Holladay company.
Married Elizabeth Bellamy Feb. 1, 1877, at Salt Lake City (daughter of William Bellamy and Hellen Bedfern of Yorkshire, Eng.), who was born Feb. 1, 1841. Their children: Mary Jane, d. when eighteen months old; Laura, m. Henry Calton; Cora May, m. Harry Lieberthal. Family home Salt Lake City.
Assistant superintendent Deseret Telegraph company; general telegraph constructor.

COX, JEHU (son of Thomas Cox of Knox county, Ky., and Rachel Carr of Virginia). Born Sept. 5, 1803, Knox county, Ky. Came to Utah Sept. 24, 1848, Heber C. Kimball company.
Married Sarah Pyle Jan. 13, 1824 (daughter of Edward G. Pyle and Rosanah M. MacMahn; married Jan. 16, 1806). She was born July 22, 1807, and came to Utah with her husband. Their children: Rosanah b. Jan. 25, 1825, m. Benjamin Jones; Henderson b. Nov. 6, 1829; Sarah b. Feb. 28, 1832, m. David Jones; Mary Jane b. Sept. 19, 1833, m. Easton Kelsey; Elias b. Jan. 15, 1835, m. Martha Richards May 6, 1855; Rachel b. March 17, 1836, m. W. P. Brady May 6, 1855; Jehu b. June 15, 1837, m. Cordelia Merrill Dec. 24, 1854; Isaiah b. May 18, 1839, m. Henrietta Jones Jan. 1, 1856; Emma b. June 16, 1844, m. Jacob Jones; Martha E. b. Aug. 2, 1849, m. Frederick Fenn. Family resided Salt Lake City, Union and Fairview, Utah.
Road supervisor. First counselor to Bishop Silas Richards, also to James N. Jones, Amasa Tucker and A. Peterson, of Fairview, Utah; president high priests' quorum, Fairview, Utah.

COX, ELIAS (son of Jehu Cox and Sarah Pyle). Born Jan. 15, 1835, Putnam county, Ind.
Married Martha Richards May 6, 1855, Union, Salt Lake county, Utah (daughter of Silas Richards and Elizabeth McClanahan, pioneers Oct. 20, 1849, Silas Richards company). She was born May 23, 1839, Stark county, Ill. Their children: Elias Henderson b. Dec. 19, 1856, m. Ellen V. Sherman May 22, 1881.
Married Mary Elvia Sherman Nov. 10, 1880, Salt Lake City (daughter of Albey L. Sherman and Mary E. Swan; married June 10, 1854, pioneers 1854). She was born June 7, 1856, Santaquin, Utah. Their children: Albey Elias b. Aug. 10, 1881, m. Edith E. Hardee; Jehu b. Feb. 9, 1883; William E. b. Sept. 5, 1884, m. Margaret Black; Marion R. b. Oct. 12, 1886; Sarah E. b. March 12, 1888, m. Alvin Black; Orlo b. March 26, 1890; Margret B. b. Nov. 1892; George Francis b. Jan. 1895; Grace C. b. Aug. 25, 1897; Thomas Franklin b. June 9, 1900. Family home Union, Salt Lake county, Utah.
Bishop Huntington ward 1879; high councilor. Emery county selectman 1880; probate judge 1880; member state constitutional convention 1882. Assisted in bringing immigrants to Utah. Indian war veteran.

COX, JOHN. Born in England. Came to Utah July 29, 1847, with part of Mormon Battalion.
Married Eliza Roberts in England. She came to Utah 1847. Their children: Elizabeth, m. James Clemmons; Ann, died; Anna Mariah, died; Eliza, m. Richard Mills; Sarah, m. Edward Cheary; Margaret, m. Squire Hepworth; Martha, m. Thomas Smuin; Comfort Ann, m. Levi Cyrus Kendall; Jeanette; Mary Ann, m. Richard Mills.
High priest; teacher. Early settler at Oxford, Idaho. Died about 1880 at Oxford.

COX, LEVI ASHTON (son of Thomas Cox, born 1801, Wightoft, Eng., and Susannah Ashton, born Feb. 29, 1803, Swineshead, Lincolnshire, Eng.; married in 1820). He was born Oct. 13, 1863, Swineshead, Lincolnshire, Eng. Came to Utah Oct. 13, 1863, Rosel Hyde company.
Married Mary Sharp (daughter of Harrison Sharp and Mary James), who was born Nov. 26, 1826, and came to Utah with her husband. Their children: Robert H. b. June 25, 1854, m. Tirza D. Fisk Sept. 25, 1870; Levi A. b. Jan. 29, 1856, m. Edward Parker Oct. 31, 1870; Levi A. b. Jan. 29, 1865, m. Elnora Arave Sept. 22, 1886; Mary b. Jan. 29, 1865, m. Charles Fowers; Susan b. Sept. 7, 1867, m. Arthur Fowers Dec. 11, 1888. Family home Hooper, Utah.
President elders' quorum.

COX, ROBERT H. (son of Levi Ashton Cox and Mary Sharp). Born June 25, 1854, Finchley, Woodside, Eng.
Married Tirza D. Fisk at Salt Lake City (daughter of William R. Fisk and Tirza P. Warner, pioneers 1851), who was born June 12, 1859, in Utah. Their children: Robert H. b. April 4, 1877, d. Nov. 14, 1888; Mary P. b. Dec. 1, 1878, d. Oct. 11, 1887; Tirza D. b. Sept. 2, 1880, d. Nov. 18, 1880; Ann E. b. Dec. 3, 1881, m. David Hooper Jan. 29, 1898; Elnora D. b. Oct. 13, 1885, m. Robert Carr Nov. 14, 1901; Levi A. b. Dec. 4, 1886, m. Edith Douglas Feb. 28, 1905; Vernetta b. Oct. 27, 1888, d. March 6, 1905; Pearl b. Jan. 17, 1891, m. John Oster Dec. 16, 1908; Della b. Jan. 21, 1893, d. Jan. 23, 1893; Stella b. Jan. 21, 1893, d. March 17, 1893; Vera G. b. April 11, 1896; Kate I. b. March 8, 1898; Ziepha b. Aug. 19, 1904.
Leader Hooper ward choir 20 years.

COX, ORVILLE SOUTHERLAND (son of Jonathan Upham Cox, born 1770, Boston, Mass. and Lucinda Blood; married at Nelson, Portage county, Ohio). He was born Nov. 27, 1815, South Plymouth, Chenango county, New York. Came to Utah Oct. 23, 1847, Charles C. Rich company.
Married Elvira Pamelia Mills Oct. 3, 1839 (daughter of Robert Frederick Mills and Rhoda Hewlett), who was born March 2, 1820 and came to Utah with husband. Their children: Robert b. July 28, 1840; Adelia B. b. Dec. 1, 1841, m. George Sidwell April 13, 1864; Almer Bingley b. April 1, 1844, m. Martha Black Aug., 1865, m. Sarah Ellen Jones Nov., 1869; Orville M. b. Nov. 29, 1847, m. Rosanah Jones Aug. 6, 1874, m. Anna Brown Jan., 1894; Delaun Mills b. March 24, 1850, m. Charlotte Kelsey June 19, 1871, m. Susan Brown Aug. 8, 1877; Walter b. Sept. 4, 1852, m. Nancy Sanders Oct. 9, 1876; Philemon b. Jan. 21, 1857; Sylvanus b. Sept. 12, 1857; Tryphena b. Jan. 26, 1859, m. Conderceh Rowe Sept. 5, 1877, m. William Sidwell May 8, 1883; Amasa b. March 28, 1861, m. Caroline Hanson Nov. 12, 1890; Elvira Euphrasia b. May 11, 1864, m. Eli E. Day June 1883; m. Norman Mynor November, 1906. Family resided Manti and Fairview, Utah.
Married Mary Elizabeth Allen July 3, 1852, Salt Lake City (daughter of Joseph Stuart Allen and Lucy Diantha Morley; married Sept. 2, 1835, Clay county, Mo., pioneers Sept. 20, 1848, Brigham Young company). She was born Aug. 15, 1836, Clay county, Mo. Their children: Philena b. Dec. 30, 1854, m. H. W. Esplin Nov. 7, 1875; Amos b. Oct. 8, 1856, m. Sarah Arietta Palmer July 6, 1876, m. Grace Helen Chestnut 1894; Allen b. June 15, 1858, m. Harriet R. Caldwell July 29, 1885; Theressa Leanore b. Dec. 25, 1864, m. John M. Black 1877; Theodore b. Feb. 20, 1865, m. Almeda Eve Palmer Sept. 21, 1887; Lucy Elizabeth b. Jan. 29, 1866; Viola b. Nov. 2, 1868; Eleanor b. June 25, 1873, m. James M. Payne Nov. 1, 1899; Arthur b. Oct. 4, 1875, m. Sarah Esplin Oct. 25, 1902. Family resided Manti, Huntington and Orderville, Utah and Overton, Nev.
Married Eliza Jane Losee June 22, 1859, Salt Lake City (daughter of Isaac H. Losee and Sarah Gilbert, who were married 1840, pioneers Sept. 9, 1852, Bryant Jolley company). She was born Aug. 10, 1842, Lima, Hancock county, Ill. Their children: Lucinda Adeline b. May 13, 1863; Sarah Jane b. Nov. 15, 1866; Almira M. b. Oct. 20, 1867, m. John Henry Hatch Dec. 18, 1903; Phoebe Ann b. Sept. 30, 1870, m. Joseph Levi Stuart Feb. 20, 1895; Orlan L. b. Jan. 2, 1875, m. Ada Arsay Nov. 16, 1904; Lovisa b. Dec. 10, 1877, m. S. E. Johnson July 28, 1894. Family resided and pioneered Fairview, Manti, Mt. Carmel and Orderville, Utah and Overton, Nev.
Pioneer to The Muddy; bishop Bountiful ward two years; counselor to bishop Lowry of Manti 1849-60. Captain of minutemen during Walker Indian war. Member Nauvoo Legion brass band. Died Fairview July 4, 1888.

COX, DELAUN MILLS (son of Orville Southerland Cox and Elvira Pamelia Mills). Born March 24, 1850, Manti, Utah.
Married Charlotte Kelsey June 19, 1871, Salt Lake City (daughter of Easton Kelsey and Abigail Finch, pioneers 1851, captain of his own company). She was born Nov. 18, 1856, Little Cottonwood, Salt Lake county, Utah. Their children: Abigail b. June 22, 1872; Elvira Pamelia b. Feb. 3, 1875, m. Henry Blackburn Sept. 6, 1897; Leonard Delaun b. April 16, 1877, m. Jermmine Estella Esplin June 4, 1902; Charlotte b. July 22, 1879, m. Israel Hoyt Heaton Nov. 28, 1900; Margaret b. July 19, 1881, m. Charles Carrol Heaton Nov. 28, 1900; Louisa Euphrasia b. Nov. 17, 1884, m. Jesse W. Dobson Aug. 3, 1908; Easton b. Dec. 7, 1886; Delta b. June 9, 1888, m. Joseph Elijah Blake Aug. 15, 1908; Nancy b. April 24, 1890; Phoebe b. Oct. 5, 1891, m. Joseph Shelton Thurber Dec. 21, 1906; Zephyr b. May 3, 1894; Henry b. June 16, 1896; Orin Kelsey b. Oct. 15, 1899. Family resided Washington and Orderville, Utah.
Married Susan Brown Aug. 8, 1877, St. George, Utah (daughter of Robert H. Brown and Eunice Pectol, pioneers 1848 and 1847 respectively). She was born April 18, 1862, St. George, Utah. Their children: William Mills b. June 25, 1878, m. Eliza Olive Allen Oct. 11, 1905; Charles Robert b. April 9, 1880, m. Hannah Dora Blake Nov. 16, 1910; Eunice Ann b. Dec. 8, 1881; Edward b. July 13, 1884, m. Polly Estella Belnap Jan. 8, 1908; Susan b. Aug. 29, 1886; Amasa Brown b. May 31, 1889; Amy b. April 6, 1892; Clarissa b. Feb. 17, 1894; Orville Southerland b. May 12, 1901. Family resided Orderville, Utah and Moccasin, Ariz.
High priest; counselor in Y. M. M. I. A. 1880-81; Sunday school chorister 1892-97. Foreman blacksmith dept. Orderville 1875-77 and building dept. five years and of wagon dept. 1876-87. Violinist and musician. Farmer. Horticulturist.

CRABTREE, CHARLES (son of Joshua Crabtree and Lucy Webler). Born July 7, 1827 in Yorkshire, Eng. Came to Utah 1853, Lot Smith company.
Married Elizabeth Aston in 1846, Birkenhead, Chestershire, Eng. (daughter of William Aston and Mary Ellis of Hawarden, Flintshire, Wales). She was born Dec. 3, 1828. Their children: Eliza Ann. m. William A. Rossiter 1864; William Aston, m. Laura Wood 1867; Orson, d. Nov. 4, 1854; Mary Hannah, m. John Tout 1873; Charles Samuel, m. Elizabeth Blair; George Aston. m. Alice Poll Oct. 20, 1881; Frederick Aston. m. Margaret Blair Jan. 25, 1889; Alfred Brigham, m. Sylvia Chugg Dec. 18, 1884; Rose Aston, m. William D. Law Dec. 18, 1890; Lottie Aston, d. March 31, 1872. Family home Salt Lake City.
Farmer. Died Sept. 6, 1907, Rexburg, Idaho.

CRABTREE, CHARLES SAMUEL (son of Charles Crabtree and Elizabeth Aston). Born July 7, 1857, Salt Lake City.
Married Elizabeth Blair Oct. 10, 1881, Salt Lake City (daughter of Seth M. Blair and Elizabeth Fife of Salt Lake City, pioneers 1849). She was born Dec. 4, 1859. Their children: Margaret M. b. Aug. 6, 1882, m. W. J. Steele; Cliff b. Sept. 3, 1883, m. N. A. Packer; Charles S. b. Dec. 9, 1884, d. Jan. 1, 1885; Raymond b. Dec. 11, 1885, m. Barbara Donaldson; Elizabeth B. b. June 12, 1888, m. Charles Shirley; Loretta b. June 15, 1890; Ellen C. b. April 15, 1892, d. Dec. 12, 1894; William B. b. Jan. 18, 1894, d. Jan. 2, 1895; Glen B. b. March 5, 1896. Family home Providence, Utah.
Counselor in bishopric of Providence ward 1886-90; bishop of Idaho Falls ward Feb. 5, 1907. Contractor and builder.

CRAGHEAD, JOHN (son of Timothy Craghead and Mary Agey). Born 1808, Franklin county, Va. Came to Utah in July 1856.
Married Martha Furgeson (daughter of Martin and Martha Furgeson), who was born in 1807, and died Nov. 8, 1901, Brigham City, Utah. Their children: William Henry b. July 15, 1839, m. Mary Hedenson Aug. 30, 1870, d. June 22, 1911; Mary A. b. Dec. 16, 1840, m. George Reede Jan. 12, 1861; Thomas L. b. May 3, 1842, m. Harriet Wilson Nov. 1, 1865; George b. May 7, 1850; Nancy Arlin b. July 12, 1852, m. Jules Hancock Oct. 1, 1875; Sarah b. Aug. 13, 1854, d. Sept. 18, 1855; Elizabeth Catherine b. Oct. 18, 1856, m. Edward Cox Oct. 18, 1876, Joseph Hy. b. Aug. 3, 1850, m. Jane Sylvester Godfrey Nov. 28, 1884.
Settled at Brigham City, Utah, Aug. 1856, moved south in 1857 and returned to Brigham City 1858. Died June 16, 1864, Brigham City, Utah.

CRAGHEAD, THOMAS L. (son of John Craghead and Martha Furgeson). Born May 3, 1842, Franklin county, Va.
Married Harriet Wilson Nov. 1, 1865, Oxford, Idaho (daughter of Elijah Wilson and Martha Kelley), who was born Sept. 19, 1850, Pottawattamie, Iowa, and died Dec. 14, 1881, Smithfield, Utah. Their children: Martha Adeline b. Jan. 7, 1867, m. Isaac Britt May 2, 1887; Harriet Roset b. June 22, 1869, m. Benjamin Coleman Sept. 29, 1886; Mary Elizabeth b. Aug. 4, 1871, m. James Gittens Dec. 11, 1889; Rizila b. June 20, 1874, d. Jan. 13, 1889; Sarah Lenor b. April 28, 1877, m. John Gittens June 12, 1895; Thomas Henry b. March 18, 1879, m. Almira Covey Dec. 6, 1899; Katy May b. Dec. 9, 1881, d. Dec. 29, 1881.
Married Mary Jane Wilson Jan. 20, 1884, Logan, Utah (daughter of Elijah Wilson, born Feb. 14, 1801, and Martha Kelley, born Sept. 6, 1811, Fremont county, Ky.). She was born Oct. 17, 1846, Pottawattamie, Iowa, and died April 4, 1908, Smithfield, Utah.
Settled at Brigham City, Utah, Aug. 1856, moved south in 1857, and returned to Paradise, Utah, 1860; moved to Oxford, Idaho, 1866, and returned to Smithfield 1867. Assisted in bringing immigrants to Utah 1868. Indian war veteran.

CRAGUN, SIMEON (son of Elisha Cragun and Mary Osborne, former died at Council Bluffs, Iowa, latter at Pleasant View, Ind.). He was born Aug. 13, 1827, Richland, Rush county, Ind. Came to Utah Sept. 25, 1850, Jonathan Foote company.
Married Susannah Mower 1847, Kanesville, Iowa (daughter of Henry Mower and Mary Amik, former a pioneer 1848, died at Springville, Utah, latter died at Kanesville, Iowa; married Nov. 4, 1817). She was born July 11, 1829, Strongtown, Pa., and died June 16, 1899, Pleasant View, Utah. Their children: Mary Mahala, d. 1850; William Henry, d. aged three years; Wilford Elisha b. Dec. 4, 1853, m. Mary Ann Ellis; Willard U. b. Nov. 7, 1854, m. Luana Shaw; Wilson E. b. Oct. 14, 1856, m. Mary Hutchinson; Simeon W. b. Oct. 13, 1858, m. Mary Ann Clifford; m. Blanche Bingham; Wiley G. b. Oct. 6, 1860, m. Joanna D. Seaman.
Settled at Cold Springs, near Willard, Utah, 1851; moved to what is now Pleasant View, Weber county, the first settler at that place; served as first school trustee and gave his room for the first term of school at that place. Died Feb. 9, 1874, North Ogden, Utah.

CRAGUN, WILFORD ELISHA (son of Simeon Cragun and Susannah Mower). Born Dec. 4, 1853, North Ogden, Utah.
Married Mary Ann Ellis Jan. 2, 1870, Salt Lake City (daughter of Edmund Ellis and Sarah Barnaby of Melksham, Wiltshire, Eng., pioneers July 1868, Capt. Thatcher company). She was born Aug. 3, 1855. Their children: Mary Ann, m. Leroy Barker; Sarah Susan, died; Wilford S., m. Kate Burt; Julia A., m. George Douglass; Mahala, m. Joseph Hill; Mormon; m. Anna Budge; Edmund, m. Ella Mower; Wiley M., m. Delpha Hetzler; James Hyrum, m. Bertha Packham; Pearl Violet G.; Eva L. Family home Pleasant View, Utah.
High priest 38th quorum seventies; missionary to Indiana 1895-96; president Y. M. M. I. A.; ward teacher. School trustee. Farmer. Died Aug. 8, 1896.

CRAGUN, WILEY G. (son of Simeon Cragun and Susannah Mower). Born Oct. 6, 1860, Pleasant View, Utah.
Married Joanna D. Seaman Dec. 21, 1894, Salt Lake City (daughter of John Seaman, born Dec. 15, 1833, Ithaca, N. Y., and Susannah S. Brown, born April 15, 1838, Adams township, Sandusky county, Ohio). She was born March 2,

1867, Richville, Utah. Their children: John Wiley b. Dec. 8, 1906; Lucy Joanna b. Nov. 22, 1910.
Missionary to South Carolina 1883-86; high councilor. Director Utah State Fair association 14 years. Member Cragun Bros., fruit and produce firm.

CRAIG, WILLIAM J. (son of Josiah Craig and Adeline Manda Bunse). Born March 28, 1834, Rexville, Ohio. Came to Utah 1893.
Married Henrietta Zottman Nov. 1899, Salt Lake City. Family home, Salt Lake City.
Had charge of placing machinery in Mammoth Mill 1893; operated Sioux-Ajax tunnel. Owner Yampa mine, Bingham, Utah.

CRANDALL, MARTIN P. (son of David Crandall and Margaret Ann McBride). Born April 15, 1830, Villanova, N. Y. Came to Utah Sept. 8, 1850, Aaron Johnson company.
Married Mahala C. Fuller Dec. 3, 1852 (daughter of Edward M. Fuller and Hannah E. Eldridge), who was born Jan. 25, 1836, and came to Utah Sept. 20, 1848, Brigham Young company. Their children: Martin P., Jr., b. Sept. 25, 1853, d. July 20, 1861; Myron Lucius b. Oct. 30, 1856, m. Viola Cook May 16, 1886; Milan Lucian (twin of Myron Lucius), m. Deseret Bringehurst Nov. 30, 1879; Edward Mix b. Nov. 4, 1860, m. Mary Russel Dec. 3, 1889; Elenora b. Jan. 18, 1864, d. Sept. 26, 1864; Miranda L. b. Aug. 28, 1865, d. Jan. 19, 1868; Sarah A. b. Oct. 8, 1867 (d. March 13, 1913), m. N. L. Packard Jan. 10, 1886.
Married Harriet Taylor, who was born Oct. 11, 1848, and died Sept. 18, 1906. Only child: Mahala b. Dec. 12, 1866, m. J. F. Bringhurst Oct. 22, 1885.

CRANDALL, MYRON LUCIUS (son of Martin P. Crandall and Mahala C. Fuller). Born Oct. 30, 1856, Springville, Utah.
Married Viola Cook May 16, 1886, at Springville (daughter of Joseph Cook and Mary Lawson). Their children: Mary L. b. Dec. 5, 1888; Alta V. b. Aug. 24, 1890; Martin P. b. Jan. 13, 1893; Myron L. b. Dec. 14, 1894; Ora D. b. Aug. 25, 1896; Lawrence D. b. Oct. 15, 1898; Rulon S. b. Dec. 15, 1900; Louise b. Oct. 27, 1908.
Railroad-man and stockraiser.

CRANDALL, MYRON NATHAN (son of David Crandall and Margaret Ann McBride of Kirtland, Ohio). Born Aug. 17, 1818, Genesee county, N. Y. Came to Utah Sept. 8, 1850, Aaron Johnson company.
Married Tryphena Bisbee 1840, Nauvoo, Ill. (daughter of James Bisbee and Polly Packard of Chenango county, N. Y.). She was born April 4, 1819. Their children: Julia A., m. John S. Boyer; Hyrum Oscar, m. Margaret E. Guymon; m. Harriet Guymon; Myron Edgar, m. Mary Louise Metcalf; m. Eliza Adora Guymon; Lucian D., m. Elizabeth Cook; Daniel M., m. Ovanda Fuller; David Delos, m. Sarah West; m. Zina Crandall. Family home Springville.
Married Susan Wimmer at Springville, Utah.
Married Mary Hurst at Salt Lake City, Utah.
High priest: missionary to Fort Bridger 1868; bishop's counselor. Early pioneer to Springville. Justice of peace; alderman, and city councilman, Springville. Farmer and stockraiser. Died Aug. 4, 1880.

CRANDALL, MYRON EDGAR (son of Myron Nathan and Tryphena Bisbee). Born Feb. 17, 1848, Pottawattamie county, Iowa. Came to Utah Sept. 8, 1850.
Married Mary Louise Metcalf 1869, Salt Lake City (daughter of Levi Gregory Metcalf and Melissa Jane Guymon of Springville, pioneers 1850, Aaron Johnson company). She was born 1851. Their children: Clara Melissa b. Aug. 29, 1870, m. John E. Carlisle; Lucia Dean b. Nov. 3, 1872, d. May 10, 1873; Myron Edgar, Jr. b. May 17, 1874, m. Eva Maeser; Cora May b. Sept. 26, 1876, d. March 15, 1878; Erma Adelia b. Dec. 1, 1879, m. Moses Gudmundson; Bertha Tryphena b. Oct. 28, 1882, m. Cecil Woodward; Earl Metcalf b. Sept. 18, 1885; Sterling b. March 3, 1887, d. Jan. 3, 1889; Lavere Metcalf b. Dec. 1, 1889, m. Belle Curtis; Paul Gregory b. July 27, 1892, m. Amanda Lawrence. Family home Springville, Utah.
Married Eliza Adora Guymon March 18, 1887, Logan, Utah (daughter of James Guymon and Rhoda Leach Neice of Illinois), who was born Nov. 23, 1867. Their children: Dora Dee b. Jan. 15, 1888, m. J. George Barrett; Edgar Vernon b. Oct. 5, 1890, m. Sylva Hanson; Merrill Guymon b. May 7, 1896; Ray Erwin b. March 27, 1898; Rilla May b. Jan. 16, 1901; Robert Byron b. Feb. 1, 1903; Jessie Blair b. Aug. 10, 1905; Frank Leroy b. April 19, 1908; Louise b. April 27, 1910.
High priest. Farmer and stockraiser.

CRANDALL, MYRON EDGAR, JR. (son of Myron Edgar Crandall and Mary Louise Metcalf). Born May 17, 1874, at Springville.
Married Evelyn Maeser June 25, 1902, Salt Lake City (daughter of Karl G. Maeser and Anna Meith of Provo, Utah), who was born June 21, 1876. Their children: Myron Maeser b. April 10, 1903; Karl Kent b. Oct. 23, 1904; Gordon Edgar b. July 18, 1906; Keisch Carlisle b. March 7, 1909; Anna Emilie b. May 6, 1912. Family home Salt Lake City.
High priest; missionary to Chicago 1900-02. Deputy recorder 1904 and city councilman 1906 at Springville. Cashier for Springville Banking Company 1903-05; director Springville Canning company. Traveling auditor for Studebaker Bros. Co. of Utah 1906 to date.

CRANE, ELIAS (son of Joseph Crane, born in November 1796, Dunton Bassett, Leicestershire, Eng.). He was born Nov. 29, 1829, at Dunton Bassett. Came to Utah Sept. 9, 1857, Israel Evans handcart company.
Married Elizabeth Smith June 13, 1857 (daughter of William and Mary Smith), who was born June 25, 1829. Their children: Elias William b. Feb. 19, 1859, m. Mary Sophia Olsen; Elizabeth Ann b. Aug. 7, 1860, m. Joseph Bailey; Joseph Charles b. July 10, 1862, m. Roxanna Williams; John Thomas b. April 15, 1864, m. Martha Fenn; Mary Jane b. Aug. 1, 1866, m. W. H. Robinson; Hyrum Smith b. Aug. 8, 1868, m. Annie Christensen; George Francis b. Nov. 3, 1870, m. Rosa Jenson; James F. b. July 3, 1873, m. Nellie Allred; Alma S. b. June 25, 1875, m. Letisha Bench.
Pioneer to Salina, Utah, 1865; Black Hawk Indian war veteran. Bishop's counselor, Salina ward, 1876-84.

CRANE, ELIAS WILLIAM (son of Elias Crane and Elizabeth Smith). Born Feb. 19, 1859, Springville, Utah.
Married Mary Sophia Olsen Oct. 11, 1880, Salt Lake City (daughter of James C. Olsen and Fredricka Jenson, pioneers Sept. 15, 1864, William B. Preston company). She was born Feb. 9, 1865, Plain City, Utah. Their children: Elias William b. Aug. 16, 1881, m. Lizzie Stevens; Katie Fredricka b. Jan. 3, 1883, m. Arthur Brandt; James Clayton b. May 5, 1884; George Alford b. Oct. 12, 1885, m. Dora Colby; Maudie Juanita b. April 21, 1887; Rebecca C. b. Feb. 9, 1889, m. Frantz Matteson; Edwin Eugene b. March 14, 1891; Laura Elizabeth b. Oct. 17, 1892; Woodruff Harry b. Aug. 2, 1894; Walter b. Jan. 20, 1895; Lucile b. July 11, 1897; Leah Hortense b. July 16, 1899; Leo Hobsen b. July 16, 1899; John Daniel b. Sept. 22, 1900; Sophia b. Jan. 22, 1903. Family home Salina, Utah.
Married Elnor Melissa Murphy Jan. 18, 1905, Salt Lake City (daughter of William Columbus Murphy, a pioneer Aug. 30, 1860, Jesse E. Murphy company, and Mary E. Bean, pioneer Sept. 16, 1859, Edward Stevenson company). She was born March 24, 1884, Salina, Utah. Their children: Milton Ellwood b. June 27, 1906; Joseph Woodruff b. Feb. 15, 1913.
Settled at Salina; justice of the peace there 1890-93. Bishop's counselor 1887-91. President and secretary Vermillion Extension Irrigation Co. Sevier county commissioner 1909.

CRANNEY, HYRUM KING (son of William Cranney and Nancy M. Cranmer). Born Feb. 26, 1818, Northfield, Portage county, Ohio. Came to Utah August, 1862, Capt. Shirley company.
Married Elizabeth Boughey 1845, in Ohio (daughter of John Boughey of Frankfort, Ohio). She was born March 26, 1825, in Frankfort county, Ohio. Their children: Olivia Gennett; Willard Duane; Hattie Irene. Family home Logan, Utah.
Married Elizabeth Crook Aug. 25, 1864, Logan, Utah (daughter of William Crook and Margaret Lane of Gloucestershire, Eng.). She was born Oct. 7, 1828, came to Utah Nov. 9, 1856, James G. Willie handcart company and died March 15, 1891. Their children: Hyrum King; Frank Phylander, m. Eliza J. Kingston; Lorton Morton, m. Elisabeth Parsons; Adelbert Ezra, m. Mariah Garr; Wilford Woodruff, m. Laura Mickelson; Emaline, m. Frederick Lallathin; Clara.
Married Elizabeth White Jan. 18, 1868, at Salt Lake City (daughter of Thomas White and Hannah Williams of Monmouthshire, Eng., pioneers Oct., 1854). She was born Dec. 19, 1849. Their children: Loretta, m. Frank William King ston; Wilbur, m. Rose Monk; Kate, m. Thomas Barton; Ivy m. William Lohman; Hazel. Family home Logan.
High priest; high councilor. Probate judge; prosecutin attorney; city justice; alderman. Doctor. Died Feb. 2, 1896, at Logan.

CRANNEY, WILLARD DUANE (son of Hyrum King Cranney and Elizabeth Boughey). Born Aug. 24, 1848, at Sheboygan Wis. Came to Utah with father.
Married Hattie Wolfe 1882 at Salt Lake City (daughter of Absolom and Harriet Wolfe of Nephi, Utah, pioneers 1848 She was born July 8, 1862. Their children: Willard Duar b. July 16, 1883; Keith b. March 17, 1885; Kate Viva b. Ju 10, 1886; Vera b. Oct. 23, 1887; Martin Wyndon b. Dec. 2 1888; Cleo b. Oct. 13, 1891; Claire b. Jan. 26, 1892; Eldon March 20, 1893; Hattie Fay b. May 8, 1895; Leslie Lyons Oct. 21, 1896. Family home Logan, Utah.
Married Stensa Jensen April 3, 1901, at Logan, Ut (daughter of Hans C. Jensen and Celia Merie Larsen Hjorring Amt, Denmark; came to Utah June 27, 1873, Kanu Petersen company). She was born June 27, 1873. The children: Kimball J. b. Jan. 13, 1902; Monroe C. b. D 1905; Helen G. b. May 11, 1908.
High priest; high councilor; bishop. County commissioner. Farmer; miner.

CRAWFORD, JAMES (son of James Crawford and Eli beth Brown of Scotland). Born Feb. 8, 1827, Lanarkshi Scotland. Came to Utah Sept. 9, 1851, Abraham Day co pany.
Married Catherine Thompson Nov. 25, 1841 (daughter William Thompson and Catherine Cooper), who was b Dec. 21, 1821. Their children: James b. Aug. 28, 1853, Christenia Madson March 13, 1876; William G. b. Dec. 1854, m. Calista C. Cox Jan. 29, 1879; Jedediah G. b. Ma 2, 1857, m. Hannah Ellen Merriam Oct. 27, 1881; David M

March 8, 1859, m. Jemima A. Scott Jan. 17, 1894; Elizabeth b. June 11, 1863, m. Joseph C. Munk Nov. 14, 1884. Family home Manti, Utah since 1866.
Ward teacher at Kanesville in 1858; counselor to Bishop Bradley 1859-65; counselor to Bishop Jensen of South ward until 1892; Sunday school superintendent. City marshal of Monroe two years, and city councilman and school trustee until 1877. Indian war veteran. Died Jan. 30, 1911.

CRAWFORD, JEDEDIAH GRANT (son of James Crawford and Catherine Thompson). Born March 2, 1857, Kaysville, Utah.
Married Hannah Ellen Merriam Oct. 27, 1881, St. George, Utah (daughter of Amasa Edwin Merriam and Olive D. Lytle), who was born Nov. 14, 1861, San Bernardino, California. Their children: Ellen May b. July 25, 1882, m. Samuel W. Chapman Feb. 13, 1907; Edwin Merriam b. Sept. 12, 1884, m. Eliza May Larren Oct. 24, 1906; Jennie Leona b. Oct. 22, 1886, m. Earnest Eugene Munk Sept. 14, 1910; Jedediah Grant b. Jan. 6, 1890; Melvin b. Oct. 12, 1894, died; Lura b. Feb. 19, 1897. Family home Manti, Utah, since 1890.
Secretary Y. M. M. I. A., Manti 1877. One of the incorporators of Central Utah Wool company, Manti City Savings bank, Union Roller mills, Manti Publishing company and director in last named company.

CRAWFORD, JOHN. Born in Scotland. Came to Utah.
Married Celia Sharp at Salt Lake City. Their children: Elizabeth, m. John Thompson; John. d. aged 18; James, m. Nettie Moffitt; Celia, m. James Peterson; Nathaniel, m. Evalyn Lowry; William, m. Ella Callaway; Margaret, m. William Peacock; Delpha, d. child; Quince, m. Depha Jolly; Kate, m. William Fail. Family home Manti, Utah.
Married Elizabeth Snow (daughter of Gardiner Snow of Manti). Their children: Sarah, m. Joseph Tatton; Mary, d. infant; Martha, m. William Tatton; Gardiner, m. Sophia ———; George, m. Etta Anderson; Ida, m. Thomas Breathwaite; Charles; Nora, m. Thomas Breathwaite; Frank. Family home, Manti.
President of seventies at Manti; priest and teacher. Road supervisor. Burned lime for Manti temple. Assisted in protection against Indians at Manti. Called, together with John Lowry, to assist in colonizing Elk Mountain country, where they built a fort for protection against the Indians, who were very troublesome at that time. Mason; carpenter; farmer and rockraiser. Died at Manti.

CRAWFORD, NATHANIEL (son of John Crawford and Celia Sharp). Born Sept. 12, 1861, Manti, Utah.
Married Evalyn Lowry Oct. 22, 1885, St. George, Utah (daughter of John Lowry and Mary Allen of Manti). She was born Oct. 23, 1865. Their children: Serelda b. Nov. 17, 1886, m. Leon P. Ralphs: Venice b. July 20, 1890, d. infant; Elwood b. April 17, 1892, m. Matilda Olsen: Sadonia b. July 10, 1894, d. child; Theora b. Dec. 29, 1896; Carlyle b. March 19, 1900; Juanita b. March 16, 1905. Family resided at Manti and Ferron, Utah.
Member 48th quorum seventies; missionary to Indians 1907-09; home missionary; Sunday school superintendent. Farmer; stockraiser.

CREER, EDWARD (son of John and Mathias Creer, of Isle of Man, Eng.). Born Nov. 3, 1813, Bolton, Eng. Came to Utah Sept. 25, 1854, independent St. Louis company.
Married Ann Morris June 20, 1835, Preston, Eng. (daughter of William Morris, pioneer Sept. 25, 1854, Edward Creer company). She was born Dec. 27, 1813. Came to Utah with husband. Their children: William b. Dec. 18, 1836, m. Sarah Jane Bradley; Ellen b. March 1837; Mary b. Feb. 22, 1839; Willard Orson b. Feb. 2, 1841, m. Barbara Ferguson Nov. 13, 1862; Mathias b. May 2, 1842; Jane b. Feb. 3, 1845; Elenor A——— b. Apr. 18, 1847; Robert b. Jan. 27, 1849; Alice Ann b. ———, 1850, m. Llewelyn Jones Aug. 28, 1878; Edward, Jr. b. ———, 1858, m. Mary S. Davis Jan. 9, 1888; Ann b. March 21, 1857. Family resided Salt Lake City and Spanish Fork, Utah.
Married Mary Rambow.
Worked in rock quarry supplying stone for Salt Lake temple. Moved to Spanish Fork 1858. Indian war veteran. High priest. City councilman one term. Helped in constructing Provo Woolen mills; worked in mills 12 years; built canals and wagon roads in early days.

CREER, WILLARD ORSON (son of Edward Creer [I] and Ann Morris). Born Feb. 2, 1841, Preston, Lancashire, Eng. Came to Utah with parents.
Married Barbery O. Ferguson Nov. 13, 1862 (daughter of Andrew Ferguson and Catherine Douglas, pioneers 1861, Moses Thurston company). She was born Sept. 22, 1843. Came to Utah with parents. Their children: Barbara C. b. Dec. 31, 1863, m. D. A. Banks; Willard C. b. Nov. 28, 1866; William O. b. July 15, 1868, m. Ester Banks. Family home Spanish Fork, Utah.
Married Emma Elizabeth Robertson Jan. 15, 1872, Salt Lake City (daughter of William Robertson and Eliza Woodgate: married July 3, 1851, Council Bluffs, Iowa, the former a pioneer 1852, Isaac Stewart company). She was born April 9, 1854, Palmyra, Utah. Their children: Emma E. b. April 15, 1873, m. George Hitchings; John W. b. Aug. 4, 1874; Mary J. b. Jun. 22, 1876; Ralph b. Oct. 2, 1877, m. Elizabeth Banks; Eliza M. b. May 8, 1879, m. C. H. White; Morris b. Feb. 10, 1881, m. Mary A. Bowen; Grace b. Nov. 25, 1882; Elenor b. Aug. 13, 1884, m. L. W. Nelson; Roy R. b. July 31, 1886, m. Elenor Bowen; Ellareve b. Oct. 25, 1888; Christy D. b. Sept. 7, 1890; Alice b. Aug. 19, 1895.

Drove three yoke of oxen across the plains when thirteen years old; hauled rock for bee hive, lion and sugar houses, and for the penitentiary in 1854 and 1855; moved to Spanish Fork 1856 and served as policeman eight years; city marshal two years; city councilman two terms; school trustee two terms; served in second state legislature. Indian war veteran. Served on first committee of Strawberry Valley Irrigation Project.

CREER, EDWARD JR. (son of Edward Creer and Ann Morris). Born Oct. 7, 1853, St. Louis, Mo.
Married Mary S. Davis Jan. 9, 1878, Salt Lake City (daughter of John Tucker Davis, pioneer 1851, and Letitia Ann George). She was born Aug. 14, 1853, Salt Lake City. Their children: John Davis b. Feb. 17, 1879; Pearl b. Oct. 27, 1881, m. Lesley Gillett Nov. 15, 1906; Mary Hellen b. April 8, 1883, m. E. K. Ferguson Aug. 28, 1908; Letitia Ann b. May 29, 1885, m. Tracy Edmonds June 9, 1912; Edward Ray b. March 21, 1887; Reed b. May 24, 1889. Family home Spanish Fork, Utah.
Assisted in building canals and wagon roads in the early settlement of Spanish Fork. Elder in Mormon church.

CREAGH, SIMON P. (son of Richard Creagh and Margaret Cleary of Limerick, Ireland). Born Aug. 16, 1870, in Australia.
Married Eva Winberg June 13, 1912, at Salt Lake City.

CRIDDLE, CHARLES (son of Henry Criddle, born March 14, 1814, West Buckland, and Mary Bull, born July 23, 1813, Bradford, Eng.). He was born July 22, 1854, Taunton, Somersetshire, Eng. Came to Utah Oct. 1, 1866, Joseph S. Rawlins company.
Married Emma Jane Crofts July 6, 1874 (daughter of John Crofts and Ellen Rothwell who were married Jan. 1, 1854, in England, pioneers Oct. 17, 1862, Henry W. Miller company). She was born May 28, 1857 at St. Conama, Pa., and came to Utah with parents; died Aug. 15, 1905. Their children: Armena May b. Jan. 30, 1875, m. Daniel Taylor; Sylvia Luella b. July 1, 1876, m. Albert G. Winks; Mary Ellen b. Oct. 1, 1878, m. W. F. Russell; Charles Edward b. Jan. 4, 1881, m. Ethel Bybee April 20, 1904; Henry Preston b. May 30, 1883, m. Jane Skinner Oct. 20, 1902; Elsie Annetta b. March 25, 1885, m. James H. Lyon June 7, 1906; Daisy Dell b. Feb. 8, 1887, m. James Skinner June 2, 1904; Emma Elizabeth b. Dec. 4, 1889, m. George E. Lyon Oct. 10, 1907; John William b. March 4, 1892; George Arnold b. July 28, 1896; Lottie Marie b. March 10, 1900, d. Aug. 15, 1905. Family resided Morgan and Meadow, Utah, and Basalt, Idaho.
Married Dorothy Norwood July 15, 1880; Salt Lake City (daughter of Richard Norwood and Caroline Norton, former a pioneer 1847). She was born May 1, 1861, Morgan, Utah. Their children: Lillian Chloe b. March 21, 1883; Jennie Mabel b. April 22, 1884, m. Thomas Howell July 3, 1904; Richard Smith b. Sept. 10, 1885. Family home Morgan, Utah.
Married Harriet Habbeshaw Oct. 12, 1911, Salt Lake City (daughter of James Habbeshaw and Rachel Holt).
Settled at South Morgan, Utah. Secretary to Y. M. M. I. A. 1883; secretary of Sunday school 1883 to 1886; president of both seventies' theological class 1884, and Y. M. M. I. A. 1884-86; seventy. Moved to Basalt, Idaho, 1886. Postmaster there four years; justice of peace four years; secretary and director in Cedar Point and Basalt water company 26 years; member school board 15 years. Missionary to England 1904-06; called back by the drowning of his wife Emma Jane and daughter Lottie Marie on Aug. 15, 1905. Chairman of village board 1907-10. Secretary and treasurer Basalt meeting house committee; first counselor to Bishop A. O. Ingelstrom 16 years.

CRIDDLE, GEORGE (son of Henry Criddle and Mary Bull, married June 22, 1837). He was born April 15, 1838, Taunton, Eng. Came to Utah in Oct. 1862.
Married Mary Ann Locey (daughter of Barnard Locey and Priscilla Perry), who was born April 15, 1830. Their children: James Campion b. Sept. 14, 1854, m. Minnie Hanson July 5, 1877; Alice b. March 5, 1859, m. Edward Geary March 18, 1877; Sarah Jane b. Dec. 29, 1862, m. John W. Mantle March 28, 1882; Charles H. b. Oct. 9, 1864, m. Mary Gibson March 17, 1897; W. Edward b. Feb. 19, 1866, m. Cynthia O. Wilcox Feb. 13, 1895; Froderick b. Sept. 15, 1867; George b. Sept. 15, 1869, m. Blanch Rishton Nov. 28, 1894; Mary Ann b. June 28, 1874, m. Thomas F. Wilcox Nov. 28, 1894. Family home Littleton, Utah.
Member high council, Morgan stake. Morgan county commissioner. Died Aug. 1, 1891.

CRIDDLE, W. EDWARD (son of George Criddle and Mary Ann Locey). Born Feb. 19, 1866, Littleton, Utah.
Married Cynthia O. Wilcox Feb. 13, 1895, Salt Lake City (daughter of James D. Wilcox, a pioneer April 4, 1855, Isaac Allred company). She was born Feb. 13, 1875, Farmington, Utah. Their children: Frederick W. b. July 28, 1899; Ruth b. Feb. 18, 1901; Alline b. Aug. 31, 1902; Lewis I. b. Sept. 8, 1904; Lamar b. April 10, 1906; James E. b. Jan. 15, 1908; Claine L. b. April 25, 1909; George Henry b. April 25, 1911; Norma b. Oct. 4, 1912.
Senior president 35th quorum seventies. County commissioner Morgan county six years; chairman of charity commission. Farmer.

CRISMON, CHARLES (son of George Crismon, born 1765 in Virginia, and Elizabeth Hegley, born 1777, in Germany). He was born Dec. 25, 1807, Christian county, Kentucky. Came to Utah Oct. 2, 1847, Jedediah M. Grant company.
Married Mary Hill May 6, 1830 (daughter of John Hill and Patsy Carlton), who was born Oct. 1, 1814, and came to Utah with husband. Their children: Martha Jane b. Sept. 8, 1831, m. John Lewis 1848; George b. July 5, 1833, m. Mary L. Tanner 1856; James b. Sept. 8, 1835, d. January, 1837; Esther Ann b. Nov. 27, 1837, m. George Sirrine 1851; Samantha b. March 27, 1840, m. Dudley Chase 1858; Mary Ann b. Feb. 13, 1842, m. James Henry Horne 1860; Charles, Jr. b. June 14, 1844, m. Elizabeth. T. Cain June 1, 1872; Emily Percinda b. Jan. 18, 1846, m. Elijah M. Weller December, 1866; Ellen b. July 18, 1849, m. Hyrum C. Shurtliff Jan. 1867; John Franklin b. Feb. 14, 1852, m. Jane Taylor Feb., 1878; Cynthia Oxoline b. June 18, 1854, m. John C. Young March, 1879; Walter Scott b. Aug. 21, 1856, m. Fannie V. Little Feb., 1881.
Married Mary Gray (Winchester). Only child: William b. 1855 (she was a widow with two children: Katherine and Maria).
Built the first gristmill in Utah in City Creek canyon 1848.

CRISMON, CHARLES, JR. (son of Charles Crismon and Mary Hill). Born June 14, 1844, Macedonia, Ill.
Married Elizabeth T. Cain June 1, 1872, Salt Lake City (daughter of Joseph Cain and Elizabeth Whitaker, former a pioneer 1847, John Taylor company). Their children: Florence Elizabeth b. Jan. 1, 1875, m. John Rich 1895; Charles Cain b. Nov. 22, 1876, m. Gertrude Mayer 1905; Joseph Cain b. Feb. 10, 1878; George Whitaker b. Nov. 24, 1880; Aliene Sophia b. May 3, 1885.
Family home Salt Lake City.
Pioneer railroad builder and miner.

CRITCHFIELD, WILLIAM A. (son of Andrew Jackson Critchfield and Sarah Ann Polmentier, of Omaha, Neb.). Born Sept. 28, 1845, Coldwater, Mich. Came to Utah 1861.
Married Orissia M. Bates Sept. 11, 1864, Tooele, Utah (daughter of Ormus E. Bates and Phoebe M. Matison of Tooele, Utah, pioneers 1852). She was born Jan. 8, 1848. Their children: William A. b. April 8, 1865, m. Lizzy Wighall; Erin Eugene b. Nov. 29, 1867, m. Sletha Smith; Lewis Abraham b. Feb. 17, 1869, m. Jane W. Wilson; Ormus F. b. March 12, 1871; Clara E. b. Nov. 6, 1873, m. E. L. Wilson; Frederick H. b. Dec. 13, 1875, m. Matilda Dayley; Walter R. b. March 5, 1877; Arthur C. b. May 4, 1879, m. Lavina C. Cook; Orson P. b. June 30, 1881, m. May Dayley; Silva O. b. July 10, 1883, m. Fred Mahnkin; Delia M. b. Nov. 7, 1885, m. Reuben McEvers; Eva Pearl b. Aug. 4, 1887. Family resided Erda, Utah, and Oakley, Idaho.
Died Jan. 22, 1887.

CRITCHFIELD, LEWIS ABRAHAM (son of William A. Critchfield and Orissia M. Bates). Born Feb. 17, 1869, Tooele, Utah.
Married Jane W. Wilson Sept. 26, 1888, Logan, Utah (daughter of Robert Wilson and Anna Blood of Harrisville, Utah). She was born Feb. 16, 1868. Their children: Viola P. b. Dec. 17, 1889; Ethel Jane b. Nov. 5, 1891, m. Parley Martin; Lewis R. b. April 29, 1894; Roland A. b. May 12, 1896; Claud W. b. June 13, 1898; Orissa A. b. Sept. 27, 1900; Lloyd C. b. Aug. 30, 1902; Olive I. b. Oct. 19, 1904; Rhodetha W. b. Aug. 17, 1907; Odetta b. Aug. 17, 1907; Arnold M. b. Sept. 23, 1909. Family home Oakley, Idaho.

CRITCHLOW, WILLIAM (son of David Critchlow, born Nov. 3, 1787, and Margaret Coe, born April 12, 1758, both of Pennsylvania; married in 1806). He was born July 8, 1809, Tarantum, Pa. Came to Utah Sept. 24, 1851.
Married Harriett Hawkins 1832 (daughter of Caleb Hawkins and Sarah Griffith), who was born April 4, 1805, and came to Utah with her husband. Their children: Charles G. S. b. 1833; Lazurus b. 1834; Benjamin C. b. Dec. 20, 1835, m. Rhoda A. Garner, m. Elizabeth F. Fellow; Charlotte Rhoda b. 1837, m. Israel Canfield; William Fuller b. 1839. Family home Ogden, Utah, where he died June 7, 1834.

CRITCHLOW, BENJAMIN C. (son of William Critchlow and Harriett Hawkins). Born Dec. 20, 1835, Leechburg, Armstrong county, Pa.
Married Martha A. Garner Jan. 1, 1861, Ogden, Utah (daughter of Phillip Garner and Mary Hedrick, pioneers 1849, contingent Mormon Battalion). Their children: Benjamin P. b. Nov. 5, 1861, m. Georgiana Fellows March 3, 1886; Martha Luella b. Dec. 15, 1862, d. Aug. 25, 1865; William C. b. May 11, 1865, m. Berthenia Vest Oct. 20, 1886; Mary A. b. Nov. 30, 1866, m. George Wareing Sept. 7, 1887; Sarah H. b. April 16, 1868, m. James E. Ballantyne March 8, 1886.
Married Elizabeth F. Fellows April 5, 1887, Salt Lake City (daughter of George Fellows and Frances Goodwin). Their children: Georgiana B. b. Dec. 21, 1858, m. Alf E. Sorensen Oct. 23, 1907; George Q. b. Sept. 27, 1887, d. May 13, 1888; Charlotte R. b. July 31, 1890, m. Eric Ryberg Dec. 1, 1909; Charles C. b. April 28, 1894; Frances E. b. Nov. 3, 1895; Jessie C. b. Aug. 25, 1898.
Settled at Ogden in October 1851. Enlisted against Johnston's army. Went to Salmon river, Idaho, in 1858 to rescue a family from the Indians. Missionary in 1871-72; second counselor to Bishop Francis A. Brown, first ward of Weber stake; bishop of Ogden first ward 1888-89; high councilor of Weber stake; seventy; high priest. Farmer.

CRITCHLOW, BENJAMIN P. (son of Benjamin C. Critchlow and Martha Ann Garner). Born Nov. 5, 1861, Ogden, Utah.
Married Georgiana Fellows March 3, 1886, Logan, Utah (daughter of George Fellows and Frances Goodwin, of Bloxwich, Stafford, Eng., who came to Utah August, 1878). She was born Jan. 31, 1864. Their children: Frederick b. Jan. 11, 1887; Martha b. May 21, 1889; Ines b. Jan. 4, 1892; George P. b. Jan. 8, 1894; Helen b. Feb. 19, 1896; Viola J. b. Feb. 15, 1899; John B. b. May 11, 1901; Alvin C. b. Jan. 11, 1903; Carmen b. Jan. 12, 1909. Family home Ogden.
High priest; Sunday school superintendent first ward, Ogden 1899-1902. School teacher at Hooper, 1879, and Lewiston, 1880. Salesman and bookkeeper for Consolidated Wagon and Machine company 1887-93, and 1897-99. Principal of public schools at Lynn, 1883; principal Washington school of Ogden 1885-89, and 1893-97. Manager Co-operative wagon and machine company, Ogden 1899-1902; manager Ogden branch of Consolidated Wagon and Machine company, 1902-12.

CRITCHLOW, WILLIAM FULLER (son of William Critchlow and Harriet Hawkins). Pioneer school teacher of Weber county. Author.

CRITCHLOW, JOHN Q. (son of William F. Critchlow). Married Florence Augusta Snow (daughter of Lorenzo Snow and Phebe Augusta Woodruff), who was born Aug. 7, 1870, Brigham City, Utah. Their child: Lucile.
Organizer of Utah Implement Company, and Colonial Trust Company. Director Utah Pioneers Book Publishing Company. Member of the State Legislature. Member World's Panama-Pacific Exposition committee from Utah, 1913-15.

CROCKETT, ALVIN (son of David Crockett and Lydia Young). Born Oct. 19, 1831, Fox Island, Me. Came to Utah Oct. 19, 1849.
Married Sophia Reed June 26, 1851, (daughter of John Reed and Delia Curtis). Their children: Mary Sophia b. June 7, 1853, m. Robert H. Smith; Alvin David b. Oct. 24, 1854, m. Emma Hodge 1875; Ozro O. b. Nov. 29, 1856, m. Ruth Clarkson; Lydia L. b. Oct. 22, 1858, m. Alverda Lemeraux; Delia A. b. Oct. 22, 1860, m. Edwin Curtis; George Elmer b. 1865, m. Isabel Elizabeth Adams; Nora E. b. 1862, m. W. D. Ream; William J. b. 1866; Roxana b. 1868, m. John Hopkins; Hyrum E. b. 1870, m. Susa Facer; Henry W. b. 1876.
Married Anna Naomi Peel March 4, 1898, died. Their children: Anna Althera b. 1868; John A. m. Anna ———; Fred W. m. Bertha Wenderho; Della, m. Peter Lesenberg; Ella, m. Charles Smith. Family home Logan, Utah.
Settled at Cache Valley 1860. Member high council. First mayor of Logan city, served two terms; sheriff of Cache county 15 years.

CROCKETT, ALVIN DAVID (son of Alvin Crockett and Sophia Reed). Born Oct. 24, 1854, Payson, Utah.
Married Emma Hodges 1876, Salt Lake City (daughter of Abrahum Hodges and Rebecca Stedder), who was born Feb. 28, 1859, in England and died Oct. 24, 1900. Their children: Emma L. b. Jan. 25, 1877, (d. Dec. 29, 1912) m. Olef Christinsen; Alvin David b. Feb. 7, 1879, m. Emma Jensen; Irving Earnest b. Aug. 27, 1881, m. Alice Dees May 4, 1904; Ivy Maud b. March 4, 1884, m. John Kofoed; Royal Abraham b. June 30, 1886, m. Florence Simmonds; Amos Ozro b. Oct. 3, 1883, m. Alice McCarrel; Lydia Deliverance b. Jan. 13 1891; William George b. May 23, 1893; Edith Emerald b Aug. 3, 1896; Golden Loraine b. Oct. 19, 1900. Family hom Preston, Idaho.
Married Sarah Maughan Robbins Dec. 18, 1901.
High priest. Justice of the peace. Bishop's second counselor several years. Sunday school superintendent.

CROCKETT, GEORGE ELMER (son of Alvin Crockett and Mary Sophia Reed). Born Nov. 28, 1865, Logan, Utah.
Married Isabell Elizabeth Adams Feb. 27, 1889, Logan Utah (daughter of James Adams and Margerett Japp Moffatt, pioneers 1852, John M. Wood company). She was bor Sept. 23, 1869, at Logan. Their children: Margerett Eliza beth b. May 8, 1890, d. Oct. 18, 1891; Nora Sophia b. Oct. 1891, d. April 1908; George Alvin b. July 9, 1893; Guy Jame b. Aug. 25, 1895; Frank Lee b. Sept. 7, 1898; Elmo Ray b March 29, 1900; Irma b. April 10, 1902; Anna b. June 7, 190 Blanche b. July 11, 1906, d. April 4, 1908; Cora b. Aug. 2 1908, d. June 9, 1909; Kenneth b. May 12, 1911.
Sunday school superintendent 1890-94; seventy; wa teacher 15 years; secretary Y. M. M. I. A. Sheriff of Oneid county 1907-08; deputy sheriff and assessor and collect of Oneida county; city marshal of Preston; justice of t peace and road supervisor of Oneida county. Presider Whitney branch of Cache Valley Farmers' Association seven years. Director in Preston Riverdale & Mink Cre Canal Company six years; director Whitney-Nashville Wat Works Company and also Sand Hill Ditch Company.

CROFT, JOHN (son of John Croft and Ann Howland). Bo July 18, 1836, Wilsden, Yorkshire, Eng. Came to Utah Se 3, 1860, James D. Ross company.
Married Amelia Mitchell Jan. 8, 1860, Stockport, E (daughter of William Mitchell and Jane Ormsby), w was born May 3, 1840. Their children: William Howla b. Nov. 24, 1860, m. Rose J. Auger May 31, 1883; John Arth b. Aug. 24, 1862; George Albert b. Jan. 8, 1865, m. Mary D

Russell; Emma Amelia b. April 7, 1868, m. Frank L. Chase; Frank b. April 20, 1870, m. Geneva Fisher Dec. 12, 1895; Walter Leslie b. May 10, 1873, m. Sarah E. Smith April 22, 1913; James Herbert b. July 6, 1875; Alfred Mitchell b. July 29, 1877, m. Estia Heiner; Charles Milton b. Oct. 8, 1879, m. Fanny Heiner; Annie Miranda b. March 11, 1882, m. John Heiner; Jane b. June 16, 1886. Family home Peterson, Utah.
Married Emma Oliver Oct. 4, 1861, Salt Lake City (daughter of Edward Oliver, pioneer Sept. 27, 1860, Jane D. Ross company). She was born Feb. 16, 1821, Ralston, Eng. Bishop's counselor. County commissioner. Merchant.

CROFT, WILLIAM HOWLAND (son of John Croft and Amelia Mitchell). Born Nov. 24, 1860, Salt Lake City.
Married Rosa J. Auger May 31, 1883, Salt Lake City (daughter of Jabez Auger and Mary Ann Cosgrove, pioneers Sept. 10, 1866). She was born Sept. 13, 1866, Hoytsville, Utah. Their children: May Ann b. May 3, 1884, m. Wesley E. Tingey Feb. 22, 1905; William Parley b. June 10, 1886, m. Ida Harris; Ella Amelia b. Nov. 18, 1888, m. Horton Evans; John Henry b. Sept. 10, 1891; George Howland b. Sept. 15, 1895; Dora Leona b. Nov. 19, 1898.
Bishop's counselor. County commissioner 1880-93. Miner; merchant; stockraiser.

CROFT, ROBERT (son of John Croft and Alice Topping). Born Aug. 20, 1836, Preston, Lancashire, Eng. Came to Utah Sept. 2, 1861, Samuel A. Woolley company.
Married Louisa M. Leffen Oct. 29, 1856, London, Eng. (daughter of Frederick Leffen and Isabella Arnold), who was born Jan. 8, 1837, in London, Eng. Their children: Emily, m. Thomas H. Lewis; Elizabeth, m. William Buck; Meletia, m. Charles Wilkes; Louella, m. J. C. Jones; Robert, m. Ellen Thurkill; Isabella M., m. H. C. McDonald; Frederick, died; Charlotta. Family resided Logan and Salt Lake City, Utah.
High priest. Located at Logan in 1861. Established first foundry and machine shop in Cache Valley. One of the promotors of the United Order of Foundry & Machine Workers. Machinist and master mechanic on Utah and Northern Railroad eight years; settled at Salt Lake City 1880; held same position with Salt Lake and Fort Douglas Railway. Director and treasurer Utah Foundry and Machine Co.

CROMPTON, WILLIAM (son of John Crompton and Ann Stones). Born April 29, 1832, Kearnley, Eng. Came to Utah Sept. 29, 1866, Daniel Thompson company.
Married Hannah Hobson in 1852 (daughter of William Hobson and Phoebe Partington), who was born Oct. 2, 1835, and came to Utah with her husband. Their children: Jane b. July 19, 1853; David b. Feb. 9, 1856, m. Elizabeth Kennedy March 20, 1879; John b. Sept. 3, 1858, m. Matilda Johansen Feb. 15, 1878; Rachael b. Nov. 20, 1860, m. William H. Sims Feb. 7, 1879; Joseph G. b. Jan. 4, 1865, m. Mary E. Browning Jan. 4, 1899; William E. b. Aug. 1, 1867, m. Mary E. Parry Oct. 2, 1894; Mary H. b. Nov. 7, 1869, m. Orin Burleigh Aug. 19, 1899; Walter D. b. Oct. 1, 1872, m. Elizabeth Miller Sept. 20, 1900; Squire b. Feb. 17, 1874, m. Lillian Hutchinson Dec. 20, 1895; Sarah A. b. 1875; Carrie b. July 21, 1876, m. Frank Halverson Aug. 17, 1903; Lillie b. 1878. Family home Almy, Wyoming.
Married Mary Hobson, Salt Lake City (daughter of William Hobson and Phoebe Partington).

CROOK, JOHN (son of Dan Crook and Margaret Key). Born Oct. 11, 1831, Turtin Lancashire, Eng. Came to Utah Aug. 20, 1856, Philemon C. Merrill company.
Married Mary Giles in September, 1856, Provo, Utah (daughter of William and Sarah Giles of Provo, pioneers Sept. 20, 1856). She was born in April, 1833. Their children: John William b. April 9, 1858, m. Sarah E. Bourn; Sarah Elizabeth b. Nov. 28, 1859, m. John Carlisle; Heber Giles b. Sept. 18, 1861, m. Matilda Nicol; George Franklin b. Nov. 9, 1863, died; Mary Jane b. May 29, 1865, m. Jonathan O'Duke; Thomas Huskinson b. April 25, 1867, m. Julia Duke, (died), m. Gertrude Bond; Frederick b. Aug. 17, 1869, m. Minnie Mabel Lindsay; James b. Jan. 5, 1872, died; Margaret b. Jan. 18, 1876. Family home Heber City, Utah.
High priest; stake high councilor; counselor to Bishop William Forman. School trustee; road supervisor 1870-74.

CROOK, FREDERICK (son of John Crook and Mary Giles). Born Aug. 17, 1869, at Heber City.
Married Minnie Mabel Lindsay Feb. 22, 1893, Salt Lake City (daughter of James Lindsay and Agnes Watson, of Scotland, former a pioneer Sept. 24, 1862, Homer Duncan company; latter Sept. 8, 1861, Harvey Hulinger Independent company). She was born Oct. 30, 1874. Their children: Velma b. Dec. 14, 1893; Lindsay Watson b. Aug. 7, 1896; John Floyd b. July 4, 1898; Royal Don b. Jan. 3, 1902; James Ernest b. Jan. 4, 1906; Grace b. Aug. 28, 1907; Daniel b. Oct. 4, 1909; Ida b. Dec. 20, 1911. Family home Heber City.
Member 20th quorum seventies; missionary to Northern States 1900-02; bishop of third ward. Heber 1903; member stake Sunday school union board; school trustee six years. Farmer and sheepraiser.

CROOKSTON, JOHN. Born Dec. 5, 1849, in Scotland. Came to Utah in 1860.
Married Dinah Stoddard 1869 (daughter of Robert Stoddard and Margarette McCelvin of Carlisle, Cumberlandshire, Eng., latter a pioneer of 1856, 1st handcart company, former died en route with same company). She was born May 16, 1850. Their children: Margaret Elizabeth b. Dec. 25, 1869, m. Thomas Fugate; John b. June 17, 1871, d. Jan. 14, 1887.
Farmer. Died April 10, 1872, American Fork, Utah.

CROOKSTON, ROBERT (son of James Crookston and Mary Young). Born Sept. 21, 1821, Anstruther, Fifeshire, Scotland. Came to Utah September, 1851, Captain Betz independent company.
Married Ann Welch June 20, 1847, Winter Quarters, Neb. (daughter of Nicholas Welch, who died at Nauvoo, Ill., and Elizabeth Bugs, pioneer Captain Betz company). She was born Dec. 18, 1826. Their children: George b. July 27, 1848, d. March 6, 1862; William b. Oct. 18, 1849, m. Agnes McKeller; John b. June 1, 1851, m. Elizabeth Frances Fraton; James b. April 27, 1853, d. Sept. 15, 1854; Robert b. March 6, 1855, m. Elizabeth Welch b. Oct. 22, 1857, m. Alice M. Rice; Benjamin Franklin b. Oct. 20, 1860; David b. Oct. 24, 1862, m. Tena Josephus Hardvigner; Daniel b. Oct. 16, 1864, m. Nettie Rice; Marn b. April 7, 1870, m. Thomas P. Farmer; Ezra b. May 18, 1873.
First deacon 20th ward, Salt Lake City; member 64th quorum seventies; high priest; helped procure stone for Salt Lake temple; worked on Logan temple and tabernacle.

CROOKSTON, NICHOLAS WELCH (son of Robert Crookston and Ann Welch). Born Oct. 22, 1857, Salt Lake City.
Married Alice M. Rice Nov. 8, 1883, Salt Lake City (daughter of Oscar N. Rice and Jane C. Miller of Nauvoo, Ill.). She was born Feb. 13, 1860, Farmington, Utah. Their children: Nicholas Oscar b. May 1, 1885; Alice b. Oct. 9, 1886, m. Hyrum Egan b. Nov. 27, 1887; Lucile b. April 22, 1889, m. Dean C. Peterson; Newel James b. Aug. 8, 1890; Robert Burns b. Feb. 4, 1892; Spencer Cleveland b. April 22, 1893; Laurn Edgar b. Nov. 9, 1895; Hilda Edna b. June 3, 1899. Family resided Logan and Greenville, Utah.
Sheriff of Cache 1881-1909; marshal of Logan 1883-88; Cache county commissioner two years. Bishop Greenville ward 1891-1911.

CROPPER, GEORGE WISE (son of George Waters Cropper and Sebrina Land). Born May 4, 1846, in Harris county, Texas. Came to Utah Oct. 11, 1856, Jacob Croft independent company.
Married Mary M. Hurd May 4, 1871, Fillmore, Utah (daughter of Mr. Hurd and Sebrina Hurd), who was born Feb. 20, 1857. Their children: Dona, m. Peter Hansen; Vernetta; Earl, m. Ida Draper; Glen, m. Adair Taylor; Molinda, m. Wilford Warnick; Mattie, m. Alfred Bliss; Sebrina, m. Robert E. Robinson; Ward; Mammie; Molly. Family home Deseret, Utah.
Sheriff of Millard county. Drove a herd of cattle from Texas to Utah in 1872. Farmer.

CROPPER, THOMAS WATERS (son of George Waters Cropper and Sebrina Land of Harris county, Texas). Born Oct. 24, 1842, Harris county, Texas. Came to Utah Oct. 11, 1856, Jacob Croft independent company.
Married Mary Ann Dame Sept. 1, 1867 (daughter of Janvin H. Dame and Lovina Haze), who was born Dec. 14, 1851. Their children: Thomas Lloyd b. Sept. 3, 1868, m. Eliza Western Jan. 1893; Colmore b. Feb. 8, 1871, m. Cortima Black Oct. 24, 1894; Richard Marion b. Jan. 24, 1873, in. Lovina Wood.
Married Hannah Lucrecia Rogers Jan. 1, 1876, Fillmore, Utah (daughter of Theodore Rogers and Hannah Jones), who was born Oct. 30, 1858, at Fillmore. Their children: Georgiana b. Sept. 30, 1877, m. Willard Johnson; Hannah b. Dec. 13, 1879, m. Robert Ashby; Sebrina b. May 5, 1882, m. Mark Reynolds; Mary Amelia b. Sept. 19, 1884; Eda Elizabeth b. Sept. 15, 1887; Lyle b. Aug. 22, 1899.
Officer in Utah militia.

CROSBY, WILLIAM H. (son of David Crosby and Marial Thompson). Born March 29, 1836, Dunlap, N. Y. Came to Utah in 1848.
Married Caroline J. Ostrander Feb. 12, 1862, Salt Lake City (daughter of Walter Ostrander and Eliza E. Morrison of Waterford, Oakland county, Mich., latter a pioneer Sept. 1847). She was born July 13, 1842. Their children: William David, m. Emma S. Cromar; George H., died; Byron R., m. Lois B. Arnold; m. Alice Forbes; Robert M., m. Julia Colligher; Pearl E., m. Charles M. Evans. Family home Salt Lake City.
Seventy. Assisted to bring immigrants to Utah. Foreman of Troy granite barn. Died Nov. 9, 1912, Salt Lake City.

CROSBY, BYRON R. (son of William H. Crosby and Caroline J. Ostrander). Born Oct. 16, 1870, Salt Lake City.
Married Lois B. Arnold July 19, 1890, at Salt Lake City (daughter of Henry Arnold and Elizabeth Green of England, the latter a pioneer 1847). She was born Feb. 18, 1871, died. Their children: Byron R. b. May 28, 1892; Henry W. b. Nov. 8, 1895; Robert E. b. Dec. 9, 1898.
Married Alice Forbes June 1, 1909, at Salt Lake City. Assistant chief fire department; mounted policeman.

CROSSLEY, JAMES (son of James and Sarah Crossley of Yorkshire, Eng.). Born June 1, 1816, in Yorkshire. Came to Utah 1855.
Married Hannah Whiston Feb. 29, 1836 (daughter of Michael and Mary Whiston), who was born June 25, 1815, and died April 9, 1839. Their children: Ellen b. Jan. 8, 1837, d. May 28, 1839; Joseph b. April 8, 1839, d. April 9, 1839.
Married Mary Jarvis April 16, 1840, Eccles Church, near Manchester, Eng. (daughter of William and Betty Jarvis), who was born Nov. 25, 1811, in Yorkshire. Their children: Hannah b. Nov. 27, 1840, m. George Winn; Sarah b. Jan. 29, 1843, m. Perrigrine Sessions; William b. Nov. 15, 1845, d. child; Elizabeth b. March 20, 1848, d. child; Ephraim Jarvis b. June 4, 1850, m. Keziah Hall; Emma b. Oct. 6, 1852, died; Mary b. Jan. 30, 1855, died.
Married Mary Bentley Oct. 24, 1868, Salt Lake City (daughter of George and Sarah Bentley), who was born April 9, 1833, Craghall, Yorkshire, Eng. Their children: John Bentley b. Aug. 26, 1869; Priscilla Bentley b. Nov. 20, 1872; Jemima b. Sept. 18, 1876, m. Smith Furnace.
Settled at Three-mile Creek, Boxelder county; moved to Fillmore 1858; moved to Camp Floyd 1861; then to Bountiful, and in 1880 to Ogden. Brewer. Died June 15, 1894.

CROSSLEY, EPHRAIM JARVIS (son of James Crossley and Mary Jarvis). Born June 4, 1850, Lancashire, Eng.
Married Keziah Hall Oct. 8, 1870, Salt Lake City (daughter of Samuel Hall and Catharine Foden, pioneers Aug. 20, 1868, Chester Loveland company). She was born Nov. 22, 1847, Stafford, Eng. Their children: James Samuel b. Jan. 14, 1871, died; Joseph Ephraim b. Aug. 20, 1872, m. Rhoda Skinner; William Henry b. Nov. 10, 1874, m. Eva Arnold; Mary Ann b. April 8, 1877, died; Dennis George b. Dec. 15, 1879, m. Pearl Young; Hannah b. May 6, 1881, m. Albert E. Miller; Lucy b. Nov. 5, 1883, m. Thomas Smith; Samuel Hall b. May 15, 1886, died; Sarah Jane b. June 16, 1888, m. Walter L Hymas. Family resided Liberty and Sharon, Idaho.
Settled in Bear Lake county, Idaho, 1873. Farmer and lumberman.

CROW, CHARLES HENRY (son of Charles Henry Crow of Alve Church, Worcestershire, Eng.). Born Aug. 18, 1830, Alve Church, Worcestershire. Came to Utah 1859, Alexander Pyper company.
Married Mary Sharp Dec. 26, 1853, Atherston, Warwickshire, Eng. (daughter of Thomas Sharp and Moriah Spencer of Heather, Leicestershire, Eng.). She was born July 30, 1831. Their children: Charles; Mary; Heber C. and Sarah Jane, all d. infants; Annie Moriah, d. child; Alma H., m. Mary Brown; Orson H., d. infant; John E., m. Emily Wagstaff; Thomas W., m. Marie Rogers; Franklin, m. Maria Burrows; Charles S., m. Julina Markham; George H., m. Clara Kestler. Family home Salt Lake City.
President seventies. Constable of Salt Lake county; policeman; city alderman. Harnessmaker and saddler. Died Dec. 27, 1900, Salt Lake City.

CROW, FRANKLIN (son of Charles Henry Crow and Mary Sharp). Born Sept. 11, 1868, Salt Lake City.
Married Maria Burrows Sept. 12, 1894, Salt Lake City (daughter of William Burrows and Elizabeth Holmes of Nottingham, Eng., came to Utah 1872). She was born Nov. 5, 1870. Their children: Melvin B. b. Aug. 11, 1895, d. infant; Raymond F. b. Oct. 10, 1896; Lucile M. b. Nov. 28, 1899; Verna E. b. April 3, 1904; Lorene b. Nov. 7, 1906; Clyde B. b. May 28, 1910. Family home Salt Lake City.
President 154th quorum seventies; missionary to southern states 1900-02. Warehouse clerk.

CROWTHER, DAVID (son of Eli Crowther and Hannah Howe of Manchester, Eng.). Born 1843 Yorkshire, Eng. Came to Utah Sept. 20, 1864, Joseph S. Rawlins company.
Married Josephine Hultgren 1869 at Salt Lake City (daughter of Andrew Hultgren and Charlotte Erickson of Motalla, Ostergotland, Sweden, former pioneer 1863, Capt. Reese company). She was born 1847. Their children: Eli; Rose; Annie Josephine; Alice Charlotte; Clara Miranda, m. Samuel Smout; Walter Herbert; Adelia Emma; Albert Lawrence; May Evaline; Ethel Dolore; William Leslie. Family home Harrisville, Utah.
Elder. Road supervisor at Harrisville; worked on Utah Northern Railroad. Farmer.

CROXALL, MARK (son of Jonah Croxall and Eliza Orgyle of Church Gresley, Eng.). Born Oct. 7, 1844. Came to Utah 1860.
Married Mary Eliza Young at Salt Lake City (daughter of Brigham Young, pioneer July 24, 1847), who was born June 8, 1847. Their children: Mary Eliza, m. Abram Cannon; m. Albert Young Carrington; Mark, d. infant; Willard Y., m. Gertrude Pierce; Walter, d. infant. Family home 14th ward, Salt Lake City.
Married Caroline Young 1868, Salt Lake City (daughter of Brigham Young and Emily Dow Partridge of Salt Lake City, pioneers July 24, 1847). She was born Feb. 1, 1851. Their children: Emily Ada, m. William T. Cannon; Charles Y., d. infant; Maud Y., d. infant; Caroline Y., m. Willard Telle Cannon; Mark Y., m. Gertrude Winder; Tracy Y., m. Elsie Riter; m. Lettie Taylor; Vera Y., m. Henry Sharp; Verna Y., d. infant. Family home Salt Lake City.

Seventy at Salt Lake City; missionary to Australia 1876; block teacher. Musician. Telegrapher for Deseret Telegraph Company. Merchant and bookkeeper at Z. C. M. I. Died 1887, Butte, Mont.

CROXFORD, WILLIAM (son of John Croxford and Ann Croxford of Oxfordshire, Eng.). Came to Utah Sept. 26, 1862, James Wareham company.
Married Ellen Loader of Oxfordshire at Oxfordshire, she came to Utah with her husband. Their children: Ellen Elizabeth, m. William S. Ashton; Arbella, died; Stella, died; Ernest, m. Ella Miller; Barton, died. Family home Pleasant Grove, Utah.
Farmer. Died in 1905 at Pleasant Grove.

CRYSTAL, JAMES (son of James Crystal and Janet Kidd). Born Sept. 19, 1839, Boreland, parish of Dysart, Fifeshire, Scotland. Came to Utah Sept. 29, 1866, Daniel Thompson company.
Married Janet Smith Sept. 22, 1871, Salt Lake City (daughter of Alexander Smith and Elizabeth Young of Renfrewshire, Scotland, latter pioneer Sept. 12, 1861, Milo Andrus company). She was born June 2, 1846, Johnstone, Renfrewshire, Scotland; came to Utah with mother and family Sept. 12, 1861, Milo Andrus company. Their children: Janet b. Sept. 13, 1872, m. Ammon Shelley; James b. May 2, 1874, m. Laura Zufelt; Alexander F. b. Sept. 24, 1875, m. Easter Ingersoll. Family home American Fork, Utah.
High priest in 2d ward, American Fork; ward and Sunday school teacher many years. Regular literary contributor to the "Juvenile Instructor." Farmer; fruitgrower.

CULLEN, MATTHEW (son of Patrick Cullen and Catherine Rice of County Wicklow, Ireland). Born July 17, 1840, County Carlow, Ireland. Came to Utah January, 1858, with Johnston's army.
Married Anna J. Thompson Nov. 19, 1889 (daughter of Edward W. Thompson and Julia Fish). Their children: Ellen Marie, m. Fred L. Leonard; Julia Catherine, m. Garrett S. Wilkins.
Married Nellie I. Thompson (daughter of Edward W. Thompson and Julia Fish). Only child: Emma.
Left Camp Floyd May 15, 1860, with the army for Santa Fe, N. M.; joined General Rosecrans United States army in Maryland and took part in the Civil War at Louisville, Lebanon, Fort Donaldson, Nashville, Clifton Landing, Buel's Landing and East Point, Tenn. In charge of all trains to Florence, Ala. Returned to Louisville, hiring and buying teams for the government. Went to Tennessee as wagonmaster 20th army corps, then with Sherman's campaign to Atlanta, Ga., and on to the sea. Returned to Washington by way of the Carolinas and Fortress Monroe. Was at Harper's Ferry the night President Lincoln was assassinated. In 1865 went to Colorado. Helped build railroads and did general freighting into Salt Lake City. Conducted freighting outfits from Salt Lake to Ely, Nev., Silver Pack, Nev., and to the Star district in Beaver county, Utah, where in 1877 he became interested in the Horne silver mine, which yielded him a fortune, which he invested in the Cullen Hotel, Salt Lake Brewing Company, Walker Bros. Bank and many other large enterprises of Salt Lake City, at which place he now resides.

CULLIMORE, WILLIAM (son of John Cullimore and Grace Walker, both of Tockington, Gloucestershire, Eng.). Born Jan. 5, 1791. Came to Utah Sept. 16, 1859, Robert F. Neslen company.
Married Lettice Powell April 4, 1814, at Tockington, Gloucestershire, who was born Dec. 15, 1792. Their children: Mark b. Jan. 15, 1815; William b. Sept. 14, 1817, died; Luke b. Dec. 15, 1819, m. Caroline Rosser; George b. July 14, 1822, died; Robert b. Dec. 28, 1824; Elizabeth b. Aug. 22, 1829; William b. July 29, 1833, died; Sarah b. Jan. 11, 1835, m. William Owen; m. Mr. Montgomery; William b. March 3, 1837, died; James b. July 26, 1840, m. Clara Fowlke Feb. 10, 1864. Family home Lindon, Utah.

CULLIMORE, JAMES (son of William Cullimore and Lettice Powell). Born July 26, 1840, at Tockington, Gloucestershire, Eng. Came to Utah Sept. 16, 1859, Robert F. Neslen company.
Married Clara Fowlke Feb. 10, 1864, Pleasant Grove, Utah (daughter of John Fowlke and Harriet Raynor of Nottingham, Eng., pioneers Sept. 15, 1861, Ira Eldredge company). She was born Dec. 18, 1847. Their children: Elizabeth Lettice b. Jan. 31, 1865, m. George R. Ash; William James b. Oct. 26, 1866, m. Elizabeth Keetch; Harriet b. Oct. 2, 1868, m. Benjamin Cluff, Jr.; Maria Louisa b. Nov. 22, 1870, died; Albert Lorenzo b. Dec. 25, 1872, m. Luella Keetch Dec. 7, 1892; Clara Rosena b. April 18, 1875, m. James H. Kirk; Etta Caroline b. Dec. 20, 1877, m. William S. Greenwood; George Alfred b. April 15, 1880, m. Alice McBride; Vernie Angus b. July 25, 1883, died; Ernest b. May 1, 1882, died. Family home Lindon, Utah.
President high priests' quorum; assisted in building St. George Temple 1874; active Sunday school worker. School trustee several terms. Director in Pleasant Grove Co-op. several years. Representative of the Genealogical Society of Utah two years.

CULLIMORE, ALBERT LORENZO (son of James Cullimore and Clara Fowlke). Born Dec. 25, 1872, Pleasant Grove, Utah.
Married Luella Keetch Dec. 7, 1892, at Salt Lake City (daughter of Alfred G. Keetch and Emily Harris of Lindon, Utah, pioneers 1862). She was born Sept. 30, 1873. Their children: Luella Merle b. Feb. 6, 1894; Grace Lenile b. Nov. 24, 1895; Lloyd Lorenzo b. Dec. 10, 1896; Blanche b. July 17, 1899; Leland Keetch b. Sept. 21, 1901; Florence b. Nov. 30, 1903; James Alfred b. Jan. 17, 1906; Owen Stanley b. Nov. 26, 1908; Howard M. b. April 25, 1910; Albert Earl b. May 27, 1912. Family home Lindon.
Missionary to southern states 1895-98; high priest; bishop Lindon ward. Proprietor Cuilmore Mercantile Co., of Lindon. Merchant.

CUMBERLAND, HENRY. Born 1820 in Derbyshire, Eng. Came to Utah Sept. 3, 1852, Captain Layton company.
Married Elizabeth Kelly Oct. 12, 1852, Salt Lake City, Franklin C. Richards officiating (daughter of John Kelly and Catherine Clothier of Douglas, Isle of Man). She was born Aug. 16, 1830. Their children: Martha Ann, m. Joseph Mellen; Margerite, d. aged 17; Catherine E., m. Harry Walters; Eliza, m. Thomas Thomas. Family home, Salt Lake City.
Seventy; missionary to England two years. Blacksmith. Died 1893, Salt Lake City.

CUMMINGS, CHARLES M. (son of James W. Cummings and Aura Annetta Atwood).
Married Eva Winberg Aug. 1897, at Salt Lake City (daughter of Anders W. Winberg and Andrine W. Friese, pioneers 1854). She was born Jan. 20, 1872, at Salt Lake City. Their children: Leland M. b. May 15, 1898; W. Chester b. Jan. 20, 1901. Family home Salt Lake City.

CUMMINGS, JOHN (son of Harmon Cummings, born March 23, 1756, and Mary James, both of Maryland). He was born Dec. 2, 1802, in Anderson county, S. C. Came to Utah 1852, John Maxwell company.
Married Rachel Kennedy 1832 in Gibson county, Tenn. (daughter of Isaac Kennedy and Sarah Pritchet of Tennessee). She was born Jan. 20, 1813. Their children: Mary Jane b. Oct. 28, 1834, m. Richard Jones; William b. July 30, 1835, m. Mary Ann Meeks; Isaac b. May 31, 1837, m. Sarah Jones; Sarah Ann b. March 20, 1839, m. Elisha Jones; Malinda b. April 5, 1842, m. Jacob Baum; Nancy b. Sept. 7, 1843, m. Joseph McDonald; John J. b. March 25, 1846, m. Hannah Sophia Johnson and Lenora Duke; Harmon b. July 7, 1850, m. Isabel Florinda Dayton; Thomas b. 1852, and Joseph b. Jan. 6, 1857, died. Family home Provo, Utah.
Farmer. Died Sept. 8, 1895, Heber City, Utah.

CUMMINGS, WILLIAM (son of John Cummings and Rachel Kennedy). Born July 30, 1835, in Gibson county, Tenn.
Married Mary Annie Meeks Oct. 3, 1861, Provo, Utah (daughter of William Mecks and Mary Elizabeth Rhodes), who was born Nov. 22, 1844, Nauvoo, Ill. Their children: William C. b. Sept. 29, 1862, m. Jane Whatcott 1881; Mary Elizabeth b. Dec. 20, 1864, m. Thomas Gardner 1882; John b. Jan. 26, 1867, and Rachel b. June 9, 1869, died; Nancy Jane b. Sept. 2, 1871, m. William Winters 1896; Ada Evaline b. May 26, 1874, m. Charles Whitaker 1898; Sarah Ann b. Oct. 16, 1876, m. Charles George 1895; Mary Ann b. April 8, 1879, died; Harvey b. Nov. 12, 1881, m. Ida Bird 1902; Isaac b. May 26, 1884; Eva b. March 15, 1887, m. Stanley Johnson 1907. Family home Kanosh, Utah.
First settler in Provo valley, where he ploughed the first ground. Black Hawk and Walker Indian war veteran. Assisted to bring immigrants to Utah.

CUMMINGS, JOHN J. (son of John Cummings and Rachel Kennedy). Born March 25, 1846, Montrose, Iowa. Came to Utah 1852, John Maxwell company.
Married Hannah Sophia Johnson Feb. 27, 1865, Heber City, Utah (daughter of Gustave Johnson and Louise Erickson of Ulricehamn, Skaraborg, Sweden; pioneers Oct. 1, 1862, Joseph Horne company). She was born April 9, 1849. Their children: Louise b. Nov. 28, 1866, died; Hannah Malinda b. Jan. 9, 1868, m. Elisha Duke John Gustave b. April 15, 1870, m. Agnes Strong; Joseph W. b. June 6, 1874, m. Mary A. Buys; Harmon b. March 17, 1877, m. May Duke; Alma M. b. June 2, 1879, m. Clara Buys; Clara b. June 22, 1882, died; Lyman F. b. June 10, 1884; Myrtle b. Nov. 27, 1886, m. John N. Austin; May b. Sept. 27, 1888, m. John Floyd. Family home Heber City, Utah.
Married Lenora Duke May 7, 1890, Logan, Utah (daughter of Robert S. Duke and Anna R. Young of Heber City), who was born Dec. 18, 1862. Their children: Erda b. April 12, 1891, m. Clifford Austin; Wade A. b. Oct. 13, 1892; Lita b. March 19, 1895; Sadie b. Aug. 31, 1896; Birdie b. May 4, 1898; Golda b. Nov. 1, 1901, died; Ida b. July 3, 1903; Nellie b. Oct. 25, 1905; Grace b. April 2, 1907. Family home Heber City.
President 22d quorum seventies; high priest. Farmer; stockraiser.

CUNNINGHAM, ANDREW (son of Adam Cunningham, born Nov. 29, 1787, and Millia Lyons, born May 7, 1788, both of Harrison, W. Va.). He was born Oct. 21, 1816, Harrison, W. Va. Came to Utah Oct. 12, 1848, Amasa M. Lyman company.
Married Lucinda Rawlins, 1841 (daughter of James Rawlins and Jane Sharp, pioneers Oct. 12, 1848, Amasa M. Lyman company). She was born March 12, 1817, and came to Utah with husband. Their children: James A. b. June 14, 1842, m. Jannet Forsyth Jan. 1, 1870; Adam J. b. Aug. 15, 1843; Andrew H. b. July 9, 1845; Maranda J. b. March 29, 1848; Samantha A. b. Feb. 4, 1850; Lucinda A. b. March 29, 1852, m. Julian ———— June 6, 1868; Hyrum R. b. Jan. 12, 1855, m. Olive Wiser; Joseph R. b. June 11, 1858, m. Eda Rogers; Eustacia R. b. April 30, 1862, m. John Wiser. Family home Salt Lake City.
Married Mary Ann Ramsey March 1, 1862, Salt Lake City (daughter of William Ramsey and Mary Cameron, latter a pioneer 1861, Joseph S. Rawlins company). She was born Jan. 9, 1840, London, Eng. Their children: Georgena b. June 17, 1863; Mary Jane b. Sept. 5, 1864; Della b. Sept. 5, 1866, m. Hyrum Prady.
Missionary to eastern states 1855-57; 2d counselor to Bishop N. V. Jones of 15th ward, Salt Lake City; bishop same ward 1859-67. He, together with 100 men, went to Salmon River to protect the settlers against the Indians 1858.

CUNNINGHAM, HYRUM RAWLINS (son of Andrew Cunningham and Lucinda Rawlins). Born Jan. 12, 1855, Salt Lake City.
Married Mary Olive Wiser at Salt Lake City (daughter of John M. Wiser, pioneer 1850, and Martha M. Frost, pioneer Sept. 26, 1848, Heber C. Kimball company). She was born Feb. 11, 1856, Alpine, Utah. Their children: Andrew H. b. Feb. 10, 1876, m. Amy M. Wilson March 22, 1899; Mary M. b. March 29, 1878, m. Edgar L. Gee Nov. 23, 1898; John A. b. Dec. 19, 1880, m. Minnie Larson Jan. 9, 1901; Inis I. b. April 13, 1882, m. Frank McGavin Aug. 19, 1903; Minnie L. b. May 18, 1885, m. Joseph F. Loosli Nov. 7, 1906; Della A. b. May 20, 1888, m. James W. Stott April 18, 1905; Emery W. b. Sept. 18, 1891, m. Eliza M. Farnsworth July 5, 1911; Oral b. Feb. 10, 1894; Ora b. Feb. 10, 1894, m. George C. Farnsworth June 28, 1911; Leland C. b. Aug. 17, 1906. Family home Ashton, Idaho.
Married Christianna R. Farley Nov. 21, 1907, Salt Lake City (daughter of Winthron Farley and Mary E. Read, latter a pioneer with F. D. McAlister company). She was born Nov. 2, 1857, Ogden, Utah.
First counselor to Bishop M. J. Keer of Ashton ward 1907-09; bishop of Ashton ward 1909-12.

CUNNINGHAM, GEORGE WILLIAM (son of James Cunningham and Jessie Syme of Edinburgh, Scotland). Born Dec. 21, 1843, in Edinburgh. Came to Utah Oct. 4, 1863, Thomas E. Ricks company.
Married Mary McBride Dec. 10, 1864, Salt Lake City (daughter of James McBride and Elizabeth Main, both of Ayrshire, Scotland), who was born May 1, 1847. Their children: Elizabeth b. June 2, 1866, m. James Baker; Jessie b. Oct. 24, 1867, and James b. March 18, 1869, died; Susan b. Dec. 1870, m. William Edwards; Ellen b. June 18, 1872, m. George Brown; Janey b. April 25, 1874, m. George Brown; Sarah b. March 9, 1876, m. James Nair; Agnes b. Jan. 24, 1878, died; George b. Jan. 7, 1880, m. Mary Hammer; Maggie b. Oct. 18, 1882, m. Willard N. Meservy; John b. April 16, 1884, m. Larue Hammer. Family resided Salt Lake City and Idaho.
High priest. Black Hawk and Indian war veteran.

CUNNINGHAM, JAMES (son of Robert Cunningham and Katherine Currie of Scotland). Born 1805, Borland, Scotland. Came to Utah Nov. 9, 1856, James G. Willie handcart company.
Married Elizabeth Nicholson at Borland, Scotland (daughter of Alexander Nicholson and Agnes Allen of Fifeshire, Scotland), who was born 1878. Their children: Robert, m. Ann Wilson; Katherine, m. Azra Adams; George, m. Mary Rigley; Elizabeth, m. William Kelly; Margaret, m. John Binnoi. Family home American Fork, Utah.
High priest; ward teacher. Miner. Died May 29, 1873, at American Fork.

CURTIS, DORR P. (son of Beriah and Phoebe Curtis of Cayuga county, N. Y.). Born Jan. 21, 1819, Cayuga county, N. Y. Came to Utah 1847.
Married Sarah L. Van Orden 1854, at Salt Lake City (daughter of William Van Orden and Julia A. Haight of Davis county, Utah), who was born Sept. 25, 1836. Their children: William V. O. b. Dec. 29, 1855, m. Eliza A. Maxfield; Dorlesca B. b. 1858; Mary Louisa b. Oct. 9, 1860, m. George E. Lee; James Calvin b. Nov. 14, 1863; Lewellyn b. April 28, 1865; Arthur Eugene b. Jan. 27, 1868, m. Julia Samuelson; Marie Antonette b. Oct. 4, 1871, m. Joseph McMurray; Charlotte A. b. Nov. 22, 1873, m. Joseph Milward; Ella b. Jan. 21, 1876; Sarah E. b. Nov. 23, 1879, m. Raymond Fawson; Fay Alanson b. Nov. 9, 1881. Family home Springville, Utah.
Married Catherine A. Haight 1847 (daughter of Caleb and Keturah Haight), who was born Nov. 28, 1820. Their children: Phoebe b. Oct. 7, 1848; Dorr P. b. Nov. 16, 1850, m.

832 PIONEERS AND PROMINENT MEN OF UTAH

Jemima Frazier; Eva b. Sept. 4, 1855; Ida b. Oct. 25, 1857, m. E. S. Totten; May b. May 27, 1860, m. Patrick Rooney. Missionary to England 1852; counselor to bishop of Springville; patriarch 20 years. Member Mormon Battalion. Died Nov. 8, 1904.

CURTIS, WILLIAM VANORDEN (son of Dorr P. Curtis and Sarah L. VanOrden). Born Dec. 29, 1855, Kaysville, Utah. Married Eliza A. Maxfield May 22, 1884, Oakley, Idaho (daughter of John E. Maxfield and Rebecca Welch of South Cottonwood, Utah, pioneers 1849). She was born Feb. 11, 1866. Their children: Albert W. b. Feb. 23, 1885, m. Viola Hale; LeRoy b. Oct 6, 1887; Raymond b. Oct. 11, 1889; Elwin J. b. Sept. 28, 1891; Kenneth b. June 26, 1897. Family home Oakley, Idaho.

CURTIS, ENOS (son of Edmond Curtis of New York). Born in New York. Came to Utah 1848. Married Ruth Franklin. Their children: Lydia b. Feb. 5, 1808; Maria; Martha; Edmond b. Nov. 5, 1814; Jeremiah b. Nov. 12, 1815; Seth b. March 8, 1817; Simmons P. b. March 26, 1818; David Avery b. Aug. 10, 1820, m. Amanda Starr; John Whitte b. Aug. 10, 1820, m. Almira Starr; Ezra Houghton b. Feb. 19, 1823, m. Lucinda Carter, Dec. 18, 1846; Ruth b. June 4, 1825; Ursula b. Dec. 14, 1826, m. Samuel Gifford; Sabrina b. April 3, 1829, m. Thomas Harward; Celestia b. April 12, 1832, m. Jabez Durfee. Carpenter; wheelright.

CURTIS, DAVID AVERY (son of Enos and Ruth Franklin of Pennsylvania). Born Aug. 10, 1820, in Pennsylvania. Came to Utah July 24, 1847, Brigham Young company. Married Harriet Howard (Watson) (daughter of Edward Howard and Elizabeth Bramwell, latter pioneer 1857, ox-team company). She was born Aug. 15, 1831. Their children: Amanda H. b. Aug. 10, 1858, m. Robert Gillespie; m. Lorenzo Childs; Harriet Elizabeth b. March 11, 1860, d. child; Edward Enos b. March 24, 1862, m. Sarah Alexander; Ruth b. July 15, 1864, m. Franklin P. Hadlock; William Avery b. Oct. 2, 1866, m. Clarissa Morgan; David John b. Nov. 2, 1868, m. Sarah Alice Andrews; Eliel Elijah b. May 4, 1871, m. Hulda Ann Henry Jan. 4, 1892; Gideon Daniel b. April 23, 1873, m. Mary Bennett; Semar Granson b. June 25, 1875. Family resided Fountain Green and Aurora, Utah. Married Amanda Starr. Their children: Heber, m. Sarah Ann ——; Lucilla; Portland Adelbert, d. aged 4. Family home Springville, Utah.
. Seventy; missionary to England; patriarch. Black Hawk Indian war veteran; served in Echo Canyon trouble; assisted in bringing immigrants to Utah. Farmer and sheep-raiser. Died at Aurora, Utah.
Harriet Howard (Watson) was the wife of William Watson and the mother of Benjamin Howard Nephi Watson, who married Elizina Curtis; they lived at Aurora, Sevier county, Utah.

CURTIS, ELIEL ELIJAH (son of David Avery Curtis and Harriet Howard). Born May 4, 1871, at Fountain Green, Utah.
Married Hulda Ann Henry Jan. 4, 1892, Vernal, Utah (daughter of Calvin William Henry and Agnes Taylor of Heber City, Utah, pioneers oxteam company). She was born Oct. 14, 1873. Their children: Edna b. Nov. 6, 1892, m. Julius Guy Murray; Claude b. May 29, 1895; Agnes b. Jan. 21, 1898; Harriet b. Feb. 6, 1900; Amanda b. Feb. 21, 1904; Lila b. Nov. 13, 1905; Ralph b. Oct. 29, 1908; Mollie b. July 17, 1910; Babe b. ——. Family home Vernal, Utah.
Deacon; elder. Farmer; freighter. Died at Roosevelt, Utah.

CURTIS, JOHN W. (son of Enos Curtis and Ruth Franklin). Born Aug. 10, 1820, in Pennsylvania. Came to Utah 1850.
Married Almira Starr. Their children: Elial S., resides in Springville; the other d. infant.
Married Matilda Miner Oct. 21, 1855, Salt Lake City (daughter of Albert Miner and Tamma Durfee). Their children: Ellen b. Jan. 4, 1858, m. Smith Parker; John F. b. Sept. 11, 1859, m. Sadie E. Broadhead; Diantha b. July 27, 1861; Rozilla b. July 18, 1863, m. Norman McDonald; Courtland b. Jan. 5, 1865; Crepta b. Jan. 25, 1867; Frances Eva b. Feb. 17, 1869, m. Ozias Harward; Tamma Arminta b. June 19, 1871, m. James L. Deaton; Enos b. Nov. 30, 1873, m. Martha Murphy; Alfred b. July 13, 1876, m. Margret Anderson; Almira b. March 15, 1878; Asael b. Aug. 19, 1880, m. Grace Murphy; Wallace b. Jan. 29, 1882, m. Amanda Watson; Polly b. July 9, 1885. Family home Aurora, Utah. High priest. Farmer. Died Oct. 7, 1892, at Aurora.

CURTIS, JOHN FRANKLIN (son of John W. Curtis and Matilda Miner). Born Sept. 11, 1859, Springville, Utah.
Married Sarah Elizabeth Broadhead Jan. 29, 1885, St. George, Utah (daughter of Jabez Broadhead and Eunice Sevle Baxter of Aurora, pioneers 1849). Their children: Alva b. June 22, 1886; John Irvin b. Dec. 2, 1887; Lero b. Oct. 21, 1889, m. Hazel Kennedy; Jabez Earl b. Dec. 30, 1890; Sadie b. Nov. 10, 1892; Eunice Ellen b. March 18, 1895; Mabel b. Feb. 9, 1897; Kenneth b. June 11, 1901; Lora and Ruel (twins) b. Oct. 19, 1903; Verda b. April 24, 1908. Family home Aurora.
Elder. Farmer.

CURTIS, EZRA HOUGHTON (son of Enos Curtis and Ruth Franklin). Born Feb. 19, 1823, in Pennsylvania.
Married Lucinda Carter Dec. 18, 1846, Kanesville, Iowa (daughter of Dominicus Carter and Lydia Smith, of Maine, pioneers 1851, Joseph Horne company). She was born Jan. 14, 1831. Their children: Lida b. Sept., 1848; Malissa Jane b. July 25, 1850, m. James H. Kennedy; Delia b. May 24, 1852, m. William Jenkins; Ezra b. Aug. 13, 1854, m. Mary Ann Whipple; Sidney b. Jan. 15, 1858, m. Mary Ann Andrews; Lorenzo b. Nov. 5, 1861, m. Eliza Mott; Ruth b. March 4, 1870, m. Harry Payne; Hannah Eliza b. Feb. 2, 1863; Wilford b. May 27, 1874, m. Bertha Harward; Olive Lucinda b. Oct. 30, 1856, m. Samuel Harding; Laura b. Oct. 23, 1864; Isabell b. Dec. 31, 1866, m. Earnest A. Shepherd. Family home Provo, Utah.
Married Juliaette Everett, who was born April 15, 1839. Their children: Isaac b. Dec. 22, 1856; James b. Sept. 13, 1858; Elizina b. March 3, 1866, m. Benjamin Watson; Franklin b. June 3, 1872; Adelbert b. April 9, 1879; Elizabeth Elnora b. Jan. 25, 1863; Everett M. b. Aug. 31, 1870, m. Sarah E. Draper. Family home Provo, Utah. Farmer.

CURTIS, GEORGE (son of Nahum Curtis and Millicent Waite, of Oakland county, Mich.). Born Oct. 27, 1873, Silver Lake, Oakland county, Mich. Came to Utah Oct. 7, 1848.
Married Emma Whaley Oct. 30, 1850, at Salt Lake City. Their children: Emma, m. Quincy Simons; George William, m. Parmelia Haws; Horace, m. Martha J. Wightman; Harriet Elizabeth, m. Joseph H. Greer; Lillias Millicent, m. Jonathan B. Page; Selena, m. James L. Brown; Lexia, m. Hyrum S. Harris; Arzie, died. Family home, Payson, Utah.
Married Mary Openshaw Nov. 2, 1857, Salt Lake City (daughter of William Openshaw and Ann Greenalch, of Brightment, Lancashire, Eng., pioneers Nov. 30, 1856, Edward Martin and Daniel Tyler "frozen" handcart company). She was born March 25, 1839, at Brightment, Eng. Their children: Mary Alice b. Aug. 30, 1858, m. Levi Alexander Colvin; Clariss Irene b. March 2, 1860, m. William A. Hardy; Ann Millicent b. Jan. 12, 1862, died; Lodena Lucina b. May 22, 1863, m. Harry McClelland; George Phineas b. May 15, 1868, m. Elizabeth Crook; Martha Esthma b. March 18, 1871, m. Caleb Tanner; May b. May 16, 1875, died; Erwin Ray b. May 16, 1875, m. Lydia Crook. Family home Payson, Utah.
High priest; teacher. Surveyed first canal taken from Spanish Fork river on west side; laid out county road between Payson and Spanish Fork; located Payson City cemetery; member building committee Payson tabernacle. Farmer. Died Feb. 5, 1911, at Payson.

CURTIS, JOSEPH (son of Joseph Curtis of London, Eng.). Born Sept. 22, 1812, in London. Came to Utah Sept. 23, 1861, Ansel P. Harmon company.
Married Sarah Morrell 1837, in London (daughter of John Morrell of London, pioneer Sept. 23, 1861, Ansel P. Harmon company). She was born Nov. 23, 1814. Their children: Sarah C., m. William Husbands; Edwin, m. Fanny Harrison, m. Delia Crockett; Annie, m. Thomas Armstrong; Eleanor, m. Charles Cowley; Eliza M., m. Benjamin Pearson; Salina, m. Mr. Stout; Henry W., m. Lula Benson, m. Agnes Mackey. Family home Salt Lake City.
Missionary to England. General overseer in woolen and velvet works; weaver. Died April 1877, at Salt Lake City.

CURTIS, JOSEPH (son of Nahum Curtis and Millicent Waite). Born Dec. 24, 1818, Erie county, Pa. Came to Utah Oct. 12, 1848.
Married Sarah Ann Reed Jan. 1, 1844, Nauvoo, Ill. (daughter of Tillison Reed and Delia Byum of Illinois, the former died in Illinois; latter came to Utah). She was born March 6, 1826. Their children: Sarah Jane b. Sept. 27, 1847, m. Alvin Kempton; Delia Presendia b. Dec. 9, 1847, m. J. S. Whitehead; Zilpha Zobedia b. Nov. 13, 1851, m. Charles Hancock; Joseph Hyrum b. Dec. 14, 1853, m. Tabitha Richardson Tillison b. Sept. 25, 1855, m. Marion Hill; Frederick Rees b. May 17, 1866, m. Mary L. Stewart; Edward Alma b. April 20, 1870, died 1872. Family home Payson, Utah.
Missionary to Northern States; counselor to Bishops' Cross and Hancock of Payson ward; bishop o Payson 4th ward. One of the first settlers of Payson. Indian war veteran. Farmer. Died Aug. 1, 1883, at Payson.

CURTIS, LYMAN (son of Nahum Curtis and Millicent Wait of Salem, Mass.). Born Jan. 21, 1812, at Salem. Came t Utah July 22, 1847, Brigham Young company.
Married Charlotte Alvert, who came to Utah in 184 Their children: Julia, m. A. H. Rawleigh; Samuel B., n Lucinda Stewart; m. Susan Gardner; m. Ellen Gardne Adeline, m. Peter Elliott; Joseph Nem. m. Sarah D. Gard ner; m. Marilla Gardner; William F., m. Alice A. Higgin Charles G., m. Virginia Killian.
Married Sarah Wells Hartley Aug. 28, 1862, at Salt Lak City (daughter of Samuel Hartley and Eliza Gill of She field, Eng.). She was born Aug. 10, 1836, and came to Uta Nov. 30, 1856, Edward Martin and John Tyler handcart con pany. Their children: Sarah b. May 22, 1863, m. Robert

PIONEERS AND PROMINENT MEN OF UTAH

Snyder; Eliza J. b. Feb. 23, 1865, m. Jerome Durfee; Millesent b. June 16, 1867, m. James Edwin Smith; Emma K. b. July 31, 1869, m. Charles Hanks; Josephine Matilda b. Nov. 30, 1871, d. aged six; Asa Lyman b. Feb. 3, 1877, m. Annie Littlewood.
One of seven presidents seventies; missionary to the Indians. One of the founders of Salem, Utah, where helped build roads and canals. Surveyed the first canal at Price, Utah. Died Aug. 5, 1898, Salem, Utah.

CURTIS, MOSES (son of Nahum Curtis and Millicent Waite of Connaught, Erie county, Pa.). Born May, 1816, Connaught, Pa. Came to Utah Oct. 1, 1850, Stephen Markham company.
Married Aurelia Jackman May 29, 1839, Nauvoo, Ill. (daughter of Levi and Angeline Jackman, of Nauvoo, pioneers Oct. 1, 1850, Stephen Markham company). Their children: Moses Monroe b. Oct. 28, 1840, m. Martha Sims Feb. 10, 1862; m. Josephine Mecham; m. Miriam Malina Rudd; Levi Nahum and Angeline, died; Evaline Medora b. Aug. 22, 1850, m. John Plum; Delia, m. Libbeus Coons; Marie Melvina, died. Family resided Provo, Salem and Brigham City, Utah, and Eden, Ariz.
Married Elizabeth Hanks Jan. 11, 1870 (daughter of George Hanks and Jane Davis), who was born April 15, 1852, Gloucestershire, Eng. Their children were two sons and five daughters. Family home Eden, Ariz.
Rafted timber for Nauvoo temple. Drove two yoke of oxen and two yoke of cows across the plains. Settled at Provo in 1852. Assisted to set up first telegraph line between Provo and Salt Lake City. Directed by Brigham Young, together with other families, to settle along the Little Colorado River; moved to Eden, Ariz., on the Gila river. Patriarch; high councilor; presiding elder at Salem and Eden. Farmer. Died in 1907 at Eden.

CURTIS, MOSES MONROE (son of Moses Curtis and Aurelia Jackman). Born Oct. 28, 1840, Nauvoo, Ill. Came to Utah Oct. 1, 1850.
Married Martha Sims Feb. 10, 1862, Provo, Utah (daughter of George and Caroline Sims, former pioneer Oct. 1, 1850, the latter of Sept. 24, 1862, Homer Duncan company). She was born in 1844, Cheltenham, Eng. Their children: Martha Irene b. Nov. 21, 1863, m. S. C. Richardson; Mariah Miscliva b. Oct. 5, 1865, m. Andrew Anderson; Lorenzo Monroe b. Sept. 8, 1867, died; George O'Bostic b. Oct. 20, 1868, m. Lizzie Esler; Albert Permeno b. Feb. 17, 1871, died; Mary Septennish b. Oct. 3, 1873, died; Ami John b. Aug. 21, 1876, m. Rilla Oliver; Leah Caroline b. May 17, 1879, m. Cyrus Webb; Nahum b. April 24, 1881, died. Family resided Salem and Brigham City, Utah, and Eden, Ariz.
Married Josephine Mecham Oct. 10, 1876, Salt Lake City (daughter of Samuel Mecham and Sarah Call, of Salem, Utah), who was born in 1850, Sessions, Utah. Their children: Effie b. Aug. 13, 1877, m. Samuel Tanner; Myron Monroe b. Nov. 21, 1879; Violet Sarah b. Nov. 7, 1882, m. James Martin; William Ray b. Oct. 11, 1886, m. Effie Smithison; Iris Gertrude b. March 26, 1890, m. Adelbert Holladay; Wallace Leroy b. Oct. 30, 1892, m. Cynthia Gibson.
Married Miriam Malina Rudd July 24, 1879, St. George, Utah (daughter of Erastus H. Rudd and Carolina Bradford). Their children: Laura Amelia b. April 25, 1880, m. William J. Markham; Elijah E. b. March 22, 1882, m. Anna Rogers; Alta Jane b. Nov. 23, 1885, m. Henry Plum; Zella Pearl b. May 19, 1888, m. William Salene; Elda Eliza b. July 18, 1890, m. William Hawkins.
Settled at Salem, Utah. Assisted to bring immigrants to Utah. Was an orderly sergeant in Black Hawk war. High priest; high councilor; bishop of Eden ward. Constable at Salem. Farmer and carpenter.

CURTIS, URIAH (son of Charles Curtis). Born at New York in 1807.
Married Phoebe Martin. Their children: Ann, m. M. A. Benson; Erastus, m. Mary Caroline Barton; m. Joanna Price Fullmer; m. Margaret Stump; Lehi; Eliza, m. John Childs; ——, m. John Childs; Uriah Martin; Emeline, m. Morman Miroy.
Died in September, 1883, at Salem, Utah.

CURTIS, ERASTUS (son of Uriah Curtis and Phoebe Martin). Born May 15, 1828, Georgetown, Ohio.
Married Mary Caroline Barton. Their children: Phoebe A., m. Henry N. Larlin; Matilda C.; Joseph Boulden; William D., m. Prudence J. Miles; Erastus, m. Agnes Fullmer; Joanna E., m. George H. Bruno; Florilla, m. John C. Fullmer; Eliza J., m. James S. Fullmer; Rosetts P., m. William Miles; Joseph B.; Homer, died.
Married Joanna Price Fullmer Feb. 14, 1860, Spanish Fork, Utah (daughter of John S. Fullmer and Mary Ann Price). She was born Dec. 13, 1839, Murfreesboro, Tenn., and came to Utah Oct. 7, 1848, Willard Richards company. Their children: Uriah Erastus, m. Lucinda Catherine Black; John Solomon, m. Susan E. Young; m. Mary J. E. Allred; Charles Romine, m. Susan Cornelia Stillson; William Edwin, m. Mercy Miles; Don Alonzo, died; Joanna Price, m. Edward B. Jones; Mary Ann, died; Irwin Leroy, m. Evelyn Johnson.
Married Margaret Stump. Their children: Elvira, m. Gustavus Hash; Jacob Lehi; Morman Cornelius, m. Nina Marks; Erastus. m. Miss Blackham; Marion, m. Nancy Stoot. Family home Moroni, Utah.
Died Jan. 20, 1902, Barton, Idaho.

CURTIS, JOHN SOLOMON (son of Erastus Curtis and Joanna Price Fullmer). Born April 19, 1863, Moroni, Utah.
Married Susan E. Young July 19, 1900, Manti, Utah (daughter of Franklin W. Young and Nancy Green, pioneers September, 1847). She was born Oct. 8, 1865, and died Dec. 8, 1901. Family home Orangeville, Utah.
Married Mary Jane Elizabeth Allred Sept. 28, 1910, Manti, Utah (daughter of William Alma Allred and Nancy Susan Miles of Emery, Utah). She was born Jan. 8, 1890. Only child: John, died.
High priest; missionary to Virginia; ward teacher. Justice of the peace. Farmer; stockman.

CURTIS, SAMUEL THOMAS (son of Thomas Curtis and Purcy Baldwin of Chautauqua county, N. Y.). Born Dec. 20, 1834, Chautauqua county, N. Y. Came to Utah Sept. 15, 1852, Captain Walker company.
Married Mary Augusta Sheffield Jan. 29, 1866, Salem, Utah (daughter of Anson Sheffield and Mariah Noll of Payson, Utah). She was born July 27, 1848. Their children: Purcy Mariah, d. Sept. 26, 1869; Lura Augusta, m. William Hartell; Thomas, d. Sept. 28, 1870; Jasper Delano; Mary Alice, d. March 22, 1873.
Married Sarah Olive Butler Feb. 23, 1874, Salt Lake City (daughter of Kennion Taylor Butler and Olive Durfey of Spanish Fork, Utah, pioneers 1852, Captain Miller company). She was born Nov. 15, 1855. Their children: Sarah Olive b. Dec. 24, 1874, m. Edmond Loveless; Charity Lovisa b. Feb. 21, 1876, m. Henry Dickman; Francetta b. Jan. 2, 1878, m. George H. Pepper; Emma Jane b. Nov. 12, 1879, m. Gilbert Loveless; Samuel Thomas b. Nov. 27, 1881, m. Nina Johnson; George Washington b. Feb. 22, 1883, m. Minnie Christensen; William Henry b. Sept. 13, 1885, m. Tillia Stratford; Kennion Taylor b. Oct. 29, 1887, m. Emma Taylor. Family home Salem, Utah.
Councilor in elders' quorum; high priest in Mormon church; ward teacher. Justice of peace; jailer; poundkeeper; road supervisor. Indian war veteran 1853-67. Farmer.

CUSHING, JAMES (son of James Cushing, born Jan. 16, 1800, and Dina Foster, born in 1801). He was born Nov. 2, 1830, Wyndham, Norfolk, Eng. Came to Utah Oct. 10, 1852, John W. Young company.
Married Myrea Long Oct. 13, 1850 (daughter of John Long and Elizabeth Minns), who was born Aug. 2, 1829. Came to Utah with husband. Their children: Helen E.; Georgiana; Clara; James William b. Feb. 11, 1859, m. Mary Rebecca Humphrey March 18; Charles Henry b. Jan. 4, 1863, m. Nellie E. Ludlow Oct. 28, 1883; John Robert b. Feb. 18, 1865, m. Alena Amelia Swenson Feb. Jan. 6, 1884; George Edward b. Feb. 28, 1867, m. Georgiana Hawkins April, 1889; Rosette. Family home Salt Lake City.
Early Salt Lake City merchant.

CUTLER, HARMON (son of Samuel Cutler, born Feb. 26, 1773, and Cordelia Young). He was born July 15, 1779, Dover, N. Y. Came to Utah in September, 1852.
Married Susanna Barton Nov. 13, 1825, who died at Nauvoo, Ill., Nov. 21, 1840. Their children: Clarinda b. Jan. 9, 1827, m. Alonzo Raymond Dec. 1845; Royal James b. Feb. 1, 1828, m. Thida Ann Morton March 25, 1852; Almira b. Oct. 17, 1829, m. William W. Raymond Dec. 6, 1844; Anna b. April 25, 1834, m. Charles W. Galloway March 11, 1849; Samuel Bradford b. Feb. 23, 1835; Benjamin Louis b. Dec. 25, 1836; Orson Parley Pratt b. Oct. 21, 1839. Family resided Dover, N. Y., Council Bluffs, Iowa, and West Jordan, Utah.
Married Lucy Ann Pettigrew in 1842, at Nauvoo. Their children: Susanna; Harmon Jr.; Zachariah; Lucy Ann; Matilda b. June 2, 1853, m. Ephraim Burnett Feb. 28, 1870; Elizabeth Ann b. June 22, 1861; William b. March 20, 1868; Jane Susan b. Jan. 21, 1865; Young; Edwin.
Married Elizabeth Shields.
Married Agnes McGregor, who was born Aug. 13, 1843. Family home West Jordan, Utah.
Wagon maker; farmer. Died Jan. 29, 1869.

CUTLER ROYAL JAMES (son of Harmon Cutler and Susanna Barton. Born Feb. 1, 1828, Amboy, N. J.
Married Thida Ann Morton March 25, 1852, Liberty, N. Y. (daughter of John Morton and Lucy Gillett). She was born August, 1827, and came to Utah in 1852. Their children: Morton b. Brigham b. Sept. 18, 1853, m. Mary Irene Foot Dec. 2, 1878; m. Artemesia Foot; Thida Ann b. March 12, 1855, d. July 27, 1875; Rosanna Viola b. Dec. 11, 1856, m. George Brinkerhoff Nov. 1898; Sarah Lovinah b. March 3, 1858, m. Sylvester Williams March 3, 1878; Ida Estella b. Nov. 26, 1859, m. George Brinkerhoff; Royal James, Jr. b. Oct. 26, 1861, m. Frances Harris Jan. 10, 1855; Allen Riley b. Dec. 22, 1862, m. Lucy May Hardy May 23, 1890; Minnie b. Dec. 28, 1865, d. July 1, 1867; Edwin b. April 12, 1868, m. Minda Harris 1899; Frank H. b. Jan. 26, 1871, m. Margaret Sparks.
Missionary to New York 1851-52; bishop Glendale ward. Member legislature of Arizona; justice of peace at Glendale.

CUTLER, ALLEN RILEY (son of Royal James Cutler and Thida Ann Morton). Born Dec. 22, 1862, American Fork, Utah.
Married Lucy May Hardy May 23, 1890, Logan, Utah (daughter of Charles W. Hardy and Marinda Andrews), who

833

53

was born Dec. 29, 1873, Salt Lake City. Their children: Lucy May b. May 2, 1891, d. Sept. 24, 1893; Allen Riley, Jr. b. April 5, 1894; Karl Hardy b. April 19, 1896; Charles William b. 1898; Edwin James b. July 3, 1901; Orvid Ray b. July 21, 1903; Minnie Viola b. Nov. 12, 1904; Eurilla b. April 13, 1906; Ercil Marinda b. June 9, 1907; Morton b. June 26, 1909; Mary b. June 26, 1909; Milton b. March 10, 1912.
Missionary to southern states; bishop of Preston ward 1902-07; member high council Oneida stake 1907-11. Organized Panguitch Stake Academy; principal Sevier Stake Academy 1890-91 and 1893-94; principal Orderville, and superintendent schools, Kane county. Graduate Baltimore Medical school 1899.

D

DACK, PHILIP (son of William Dack, born 1795, Shipdham, Norfolkshire, Eng., and Sarah Billham of Swatham; Eng.). He was born June 28, 1837, Shipdham. Came to Utah Sept. 25, 1855. Williams and Jackman freight train.
Married Cyntha Sildona Maxham May 15, 1859 (daughter of Charles Maxham and Matilda Russell, pioneers Aug. 13, 1852). She was born Aug. 29, 1843. Their children: Sarah Matilda b. April 15, 1860, m. Levi Bown Feb. 1, 1877, d. Jan. 1, 1884; Eva Charlotte b. Jan. 17, 1862, m. John C. Mellor 1880; Ida Eliza b. March 9, 1864, m. Almeron A. Dalton 1880, d. Aug. 27, 1909; Philip Asa b. Dec. 14, 1865, m. Annie Shanks 1886; Agnes Annie b. July 13, 1868, m. Luther C. Palmer 1885; Clarissa Jane b. April 19, 1871, m. Lafayette Brown 1891; Cyntha Sildona b. Jan. 5, 1873, d. Dec. 13, 1880; Hope Wayne b. June 3, 1875, m. Henry Roper 1892; Daisy Dean b. June 10, 1878, m. Andrew Jensen 1899; William Charles b. May 2, 1881, m. Mattie Anderson 1905; Earl Maxham b. May 2, 1886, m. Auransla May Myrup 1907.
Assisted in bringing immigrants to Utah. Took an active part in Echo Canyon and Black Hawk wars.

DAILEY, MILTON (son of Luther Dailey, born April 27, 1786, and Minerva Townsend, born Dec. 9, 1797). He was born Oct. 14, 1827, Falls township, Luzerne county, Pa. Came to Utah 1850, Slaughter and Cavett company.
Married Sarah Jane Wilson 1850 (daughter of Whitford G. and Mary Wilson), who was born Dec. 21, 1830, and died Oct. 22, 1873. She came to Utah 1850 with husband. Their children were three daughters.
Married Mary Malinda Wilson June 14, 1874, Salt Lake City (daughter of Henry Hardy Wilson and Frances Kelley), who was born Feb. 6, 1851, Pottawattamie county, Iowa. Their children: Marion Dailey b. Aug. 11, 1877; Wilson, b. Nov. 12, 1881, m. Ellen L. Benson May 19, 1909; Milton Luther b. Nov. 25, 1884, m. Emily Reynolds Oct. 19, 1905; Ephraim b. Jan. 16, 1887.
Settled at Ogden. Assisted in bringing immigrants to Utah. Member 38th quorum seventies. Member territorial militia; called to Salmon river to protect settlers from Indians. Resided in Farmington two years; helped settle Dixie and lived there 13 years. Called to preside over Harrisburg ward; superintendent Harrisburg Sunday school. Harrisburg watermaster 12 years. Moved to Arizona, where he resided 13 years, returning to Utah, settled at Paragonah.

DALEY, PHINEAS (son of Moses Daley and Almira Barber of New York).
Married Adaline Grover at Salt Lake City (daughter of Thomas Grover, pioneer Oct. 3, 1847, and Caroline Whiting, who died 1841). She was born Feb. 10, 1834. Their children: Phineas M. m. Ellen Oliverson; Addie, m. George Passey; Serretta, m. Warren Sirrine; Ornetus, m. Millicent Babbitt; Emma, m. William Ellsmar. Family home San Bernardino, Cal.
Early day freighter. Died at Mesa, Ariz.

DALL, HENRY DAVID (son of James Dall and Ann Morris, of England). Born April 22, 1820, Wimpole, Cambridgeshire, Eng. Came to Utah October 1857, independent company.
Married Rebecca Carier, London, Eng. (daughter of Richard Carier and Mary Ann Parkinson), who was born in Cambridgeshire, Eng. Their children: Henry David Jr., m. Eliza Gold Weech, m. Jane Ogden; William, m. Phena Hansen; Elizabeth Ann, m. John Burrison; Sarah, m. Hyrum Weech; Mary Ann, m. Simon Miller; James, died; Rebecca, m. John Holliday. Family resided Pleasant Grove and Goshen, Utah.
Married Fanny Saunders at Salt Lake City (daughter of William Saunders). Their children: James, d. infant; Arthur, m. Nettie Paulson; David, m. Lydia Johnson; Clara and baby sister died. Family home Goshen, Utah.
President Bishopstafford branch at Hertfordshire, Eng. Farmer. Died May 5, 1876, Goshen, Utah.

DALL, HENRY DAVID, JR. (son of Henry David Dall and Rebecca Carier). Born Dec. 13, 1839, Cambridgeshire, Eng. Came to Utah October 1857, independent company.
Married Eliza Gold Weech Dec. 25, 1861, Payson, Utah (daughter of Samuel Weech and Elizabeth Gold, latter pioneer 1856). She was born March 3, 1841, and died Dec. 28, 1863. Their children: Samuel Henry b. 1862, m. Mary Jane Collins; Eliza Elizabeth b. Dec. 24, 1863, d. infant. Family home Goshen, Utah.
Married Jane Ogden Oct. 9, 1871, Salt Lake City (daughter of William Ogden and Mary Vickers, of Lancashire, Eng., pioneers September 1868). She was born Jan. 26, 1852. Their children: Mary Alice b. June 22, 1872, d. May 31, 1874; Eliza Jane b. Jan. 29, 1874, m. Joseph Nelson; Sarah Elizabeth b. Nov. 13, 1875, m. Claude Thurber; Rebecca Ann b. March 11, 1878, m. Lehi Ence; James William b. July 23, 1880, d. March 11, 1887; Henry David b. Oct. 28, 1882; Mary Ann b. April 15, 1885, d. March 7, 1887; John Thomas b. May 23, 1887; Ethel Geneva b. Oct. 2, 1889; Allie Fern b. Aug. 11, 1893; Pearl b. May 2, 1897. Family home Richfield, Utah.
High priest; bishop's counselor Pima, Ariz. Assisted in bringing immigrants to Utah.' Farmer.

DALLEY, JAMES. Came to Utah in the early days.
Married Emma Wright and among their children were: Richard Henry b. June 18, 1867, m. Mabel Jane Bryant; Charles R. b. Nov. 27, 1873, m. Ellen M. Allen.

DALLEY, RICHARD HENRY (son of James Dalley and Emma Wright). Born June 18, 1867, Summit. Iron county, Utah.
Married Mabel Jane Bryant at St. George, Utah (daughter of Richard Bryant and Clara Jones, who came to Utah 1880). She was born Sept. 11, 1871, St. Louis, Mo., and died July 20, 1897, Cedar City, Utah. Their children: Myrtle Bryant b. Aug. 16, 1891, m. Osburne Golightly Jan. 19, 1910; Clara Bryant b. Jan. 24, 1893, m. Abel Stevenson May 11, 1910; Thurza Bryant b. Feb. 22, 1895; Emma Mabel Bryant b. June 15, 1897. Family home Summit and Cedar City, Utah.
Married Clara Christensen April 19, 1899, Manti, Utah (daughter of Simon Christensen and Bertha Maria Jensen), who was born Nov. 23, 1878, Richfield, Utah. Their children: Armorel b. Jan. 25, 1900; Marguerite b. April 12, 1902; Veleta b. May 21, 1905. Family home Summit and Circleville, Utah, and Preston, Idaho.

DALLEY, CHARLES R. (son of James Dailey and Emma Wright). Born Nov. 27, 1873.
Married Ellen M. Allen Nov. 27, 1895, Manti. Utah. Their children: Charles Leland b. Nov. 13, 1896; Letha b. June 28, 1901; Marcella b. Aug. 18, 1906; Zelma Helen b. April 11, 1908. Family home Summit, Utah.
Bushop of Summit ward.

DALLIMORE, WILLIAM J. (son of George Dallimore and Harriet Harris). Born Dec. 11, 1844, Bath, Somersetshire, Eng. Came to Utah 1854.
Married Eliza Caroline Slater Dec. 7, 1866. Their children: Emily Davis; Ida C.; George W., m. Effie Browning; Julia; Pearl.

DALRYMPLE, EDGAR (son of Luther Dalrymple and Sally Hammond). Born May 25, 1837, Bolton, Warren county, N. Y. Came to Utah Oct. 3, 1863, Horton Haight company.
Married Eliza Theodocia Noble Nov. 10, 1865, Salt Lake City (daughter of Joseph Bates Noble and Mary Adeline Beman, of Bountiful, Utah, pioneers September 1847, Jedediah M. Grant company). She was born Aug. 12, 1847, on plains, 50 miles from Heber Springs. Their children: Mary Eliza; Joseph Edgar; Artemesia, m. Anson Vasco Call; Erastus Snow; Theodocia, m. William A. C. Keetch; Parley Noble; Newell Noble, m. Vera Collings. Family resided Bountiful, Utah, and Wardboro, Idaho.
Bishop's counselor; superintendent Sunday schools over 20 years. Died June 18, 1907, Paris, Idaho.

DALRYMPLE, JOSEPH EDGAR (son of Edgar Dalrymple and Eliza Theodocia Noble). Born Jan. 12, 1872, Bountiful, Utah.
Elder; missionary to northern states. Farmer. Died July 25, 1902, Wardboro, Idaho.

DALRYMPLE, OSCAR (son of Luther Dalrymple and Sally Hammond). Born Aug. 27, 1845, Bolton, N. Y. Came to Utah Oct. 3, 1863, Horton Haight company.
Married Mary M. Potter May 1862 (daughter of Ansel Potter and Kesiah Ward), who was born Nov. 20, 1841. Their children: John H. b. May 1863, died; Onila E. b. Feb. 12, 1866, m. Calvin Booth Nov. 2, 1888; Calista E. b. Jan. 31, 1868, m. Serenas Bagley Feb. 1890; Oscar A. b. April 19, 1871, died; Arthur B. b. May 29, 1874; Frank L. b. Feb. 4, 1880.
Early settler in Cache and Bear Lake valleys. In bishopric Wardboro, Idaho, six years; counselor; president Y. M. M. I. A.

DALTON, MATHEW WILLIAM (son of John Dalton and Mary McGovern of Arbroken, East Meath, Ireland). Born Jan. 11, 1829, Madrid, St. Lawrence county, N. Y. Came to Utah Sept. 5, 1850, independent company.
Married Rozilla Whitaker Dec. 5, 1850, Ogden, Utah (daughter of Ja... Whitaker and Malinda Fishel of Council Bluffs, Iowa, ...oneers Oct. 5, 1850). She was born Dec.

PIONEERS AND PROMINENT MEN OF UTAH 885

12, 1830, and died June 3, 1898. Their children: James Mathew b. Oct. 31, 1851, m. Isabella Perry April 5, 1875; William Albert b. June 21, 1853, m. Mary Jane Williams Feb. 8, 1875; Mary Malinda b. April 12, 1855, d. Sept. 14, 1855; Rozilla Marilla b. Dec. 10, 1856, d. Oct. 11, 1870; John Alma b. Oct. 26, 1858, m. Elizabeth Cook Jan. 22, 1880; Jane Emeline b. March 19, 1861, m. Alma Walter Compton Feb. 25, 1886; Martha Melissa b. May 10, 1862, d. July 25, 1880; Ellen Maria b. Feb. 8, 1864, m. Alexander Stowell June 1886, d. July 14, 1892; George Alfred b. Oct. 12, 1866, d. March 31, 1867. Family home Willard, Utah.
Married Alice Ophelia Miller Sept. 6, 1868, Salt Lake City, Utah (daughter of John and Mary Ann Miller), who was born July 19, 1846, Southampton, Eng. Only child: William Fredrick b. April 7, 1870, m. Annie Benson Dec. 16, 1902.
Married Sarah Ann Hymas June 7, 1899, Logan, Utah (daughter of George Hymas and Sarah Ann Carter), who was born Aug. 6, 1859, Hackley, Essex, Eng. Their children: Ada May b. May 5, 1900; Moroni Hymas b. Feb. 15, 1903.
President 59th quorum of seventies for 48 years; high priest; missionary to Europe, Mexico and four missions U. S. A. from 1869 to 1891; bishop's counselor. Justice of peace; delegate to territorial convention one term; captain of territorial militia. Built one of first two houses in Ogden 1850. Author of "Key to this Earth." Inventor and has secured many patents: carpenter and farmer. The first to illustrate by allegorical decoration the difference between pioneer days and later days in Utah. First to introduce putting in stone ditches or aqueducts to carry water for irrigation. Student of astronomy and inventor of a planetarium system. Made a suggestive map of travels of Nephite nations. Worked three years in Logan temple and did a work for 3,000 persons.

DALTON, JAMES M. (son of Mathew W. Dalton and Rozilla Whittaker). Born Oct. 31, 1851, Ogden, Utah.
Married Isabella Dock Perry April 5, 1875, at Salt Lake City, Utah (daughter of Alexander Perry and Marion Shanks of North Willard, Utah, pioneers of Oct. 1855, Charles A. Harper company). She was born March 27, 1857. Their children: Marion b. Jan. 5, 1876, m. John A. Ward Sept. 14, 1898; Rozilla b. Jan. 18, 1878, d. May 16, 1881; Isabella b. April 24, 1880; James M. b. Nov. 27, 1882, at Willard, Utah; Alexander Perry b. Aug. 5, 1885; Robert Dock b. Nov. 10, 1887; William Shanks b. July 22, 1890 (in Cassia county, Idaho); Edella b. May 23, 1893; Myrtle b. Aug. 17, 1896; Howard Linwood b. Dec. 24, 1898. Family resided Willard, Utah, and Cassia county, Idaho.
Elder. Member Willard school board three terms, and city councilman two terms; precinct constable; mayor two terms, and was instrumental in completing waterworks for Willard; also granted franchise to Ogden Rapid Transit company electric lines from Ogden to Brigham City. Farmer, stockraiser and lumberman.

DALY, JOHN J. (son of James Daly and Mary Moxin of Ireland). Born Oct. 18, 1853, Grundy county, Ill. Came to Utah 1873.
Married Eliza M. Benson March 1, 1880. They are the parents of three sons and five daughters, all but one of them living. Family home Salt Lake City.
Engaged in mining in Montana. In 1871 went to White Pine, Nevada, where he followed the occupation of miner and prospector. About two years later, visited Utah on a prospecting tour, but returned to Nevada. Took part in the Indian troubles in eastern Nevada 1875. Returned to Utah 1876, and became a prospector in the mountains near Park City, locating several claims. General manager Crescent mine; organized Daly Mining Company 1883 and served as its vice-president and general manager until 1888. Took a contract for driving a tunnel of 3,000 feet for the Anchor Mining Company. After completing his contract with the Anchor company, he began the work of developing what subsequently became the Daly West Mine. His struggle in overcoming the many obstacles encountered in the opening up of this great mine, forms one of the most interesting chapters in the history of the famous Park City district, and demonstrates what interest the indomitable pluck and perseverance of John J. Daly. Pres. Daly-Judge Mining Company; pres. Syndicate Inv. Company; interested in many banking institutions; vice-president of the Utah Savings and Trust Company. Elected one of the delegates of the National Republican Convention which nominated Benjamin Harrison for president. In 1889 was appointed member of the Territorial Loan Commission. Member Salt Lake City Council 1890; member Board of Regents University of Deseret; pres. Alta Club 1898-99; one of the presidential electors 1896. Capitalist.

DAME, JANVARIN HAYES (son of Simon Dame and Margarette Hayes, of Stratford county, N. H.). Born May 9, 1808. Came to Utah 1848.
Married Sophia Andrews 1833, in Hancock county, Ill. (daughter of Richard Andrews and Sarah Brockway), who was born 1818 in Ohio. Their children: Phidelin B. b. 1834, m. James Farrer; Laura A. b. 1836; Wesley W. b. 1838, m. Emma McBride; Tamson P. b. 1840, m. Hyrum Roy McBride; Margarette b. 1842; Simon R. b. 1844; Sarah Elsie b. 1846. Family home Fillmore, Utah.
Farmer and stockraiser. Died Dec. 26, 1885, Meadow, Millard county, Utah.

DAMRON, JOSEPH W. (son of John Damron, born 1791 in Missouri, and Sarah Shultz, born 1799, who resided in Missouri and Texas). He was born Jan. 6, 1841, in Missouri. Came to Utah Sept. 13, 1861, Homer Duncan company.
Married Margaret Phoebe Freeman (daughter of John Freeman and Nancy B. Smoot, pioneers 1853, David Lewis company). She was born Sept. 27, 1840, and came to Utah with parents. Their children: George A. b. April 18, 1863, m. Belle G. Erickson; Joseph W. Jr. b. June 9, 1866, m. Mary A. Kelly April 8, 1896; Milton W. b. April 1, 1868, m. Amy Lytle; Jemima C. b. Aug. 13, 1870, m. J. J. Barron; Charles S. and Sarah E. b. Sept. 10, 1872; William R. b. April 18, 1874, m. Orena Duggins; Arthur J. b. Aug. 29, 1876, m. Eudora Bishop; Luella B. b. Oct. 13, 1878, m. Oscar Warnick; Lizzie M. b. May 3, 1881, m. E. J. Whicker. Family resided Kanosh and Deseret, Utah.

DAMRON, JOSEPH W., JR. (son of Joseph W. Damron and Margaret P. Freeman). Born June 9, 1866, Lower Kanosh, now Hatton, Utah.
Married Mary Abiah Kelly April 8, 1896, Salt Lake City (daughter of Virgil Kelly and Amanda Barron), who was born Nov. 2, 1873, Panaca, Nev. Their children: Norma V. b. Feb. 14, 1897; Mary Lucile b. Dec. 1, 1898; Joseph Ladd b. Jan. 9, 1900; Marguerite b. Nov. 7, 1901; William Aileen b. Dec. 1, 1905; Virgilia b. March 28, 1911; Ruth Lauriel b. Nov. 28, 1912. Family resided Kanosh and Deseret, Utah.
Missionary to Society Islands Oct. 1891 to June 1895. Manager Kanosh Co-op. Oct. 1886 to Oct. 1891. Sunday school superintendent Dec. 1897 to June 1908; bishop of Deseret ward, Millard stake, 1908-12.

DANA, CHARLES ROOT. Born Nov. 8, 1802, in New York. Came to Utah 1849.
Married Jane Cully 1856 at Salt Lake City (daughter of Benjamin and Mary Ann Cully), who was born Jan. 2, 1834. Their children: Elizabeth b. Aug. 18, 1858, m. C. O. Rudd June 16, 1884; Joseph B. b. Nov. 24, 1860, m. Maggie L. Summers; Chauncey A. b. Dec. 2, 1862, m. Nellie Clark; Hattie b. May 15, 1865, m. A. A. Bright. Family home Ogden, Utah.
Missionary to England. Member first territorial legislature 1851. Died Aug. 7, 1868.

DANA, JOSEPH B. (son of Charles Root Dana and Jane Cully). Born Nov. 24, 1860, Ogden, Utah.
Married Maggie L. Summers Feb. 24, 1892 (daughter of Stephen J. and Sarah Twig Summers), who was born Aug. 19, 1870. Their child: Joseph Bertrand b. Aug. 1, 1903.
Member Ogden city council 1908-12. Gardener.

DANGERFIELD, JABEZ (son of Thomas Dangerfield and Caroline Buckwell, of London, Eng.). Born Nov. 12, 1840, at London. Came to Utah Sept. 1, 1859, Horton D. Haight company.
Married Mary Ann James Dec. 23, 1867, Salt Lake City (daughter of William James and Jane Haines, of Pinvin, Worcestershire, Eng., pioneers Nov. 9, 1856, James G. Willie handcart company). She was born Dec. 16, 1844. Their children: Annie Louvina, m. George Busby; Jabez William, m. Alice Dixon; Martha Mae; Mary Etola, m. Parley Dixon; George Earnest, m. Maud Ward. Family home Salt Lake City.
Married Elizabeth Morris at Salt Lake City (daughter of Charles Morris of England). Their children: Robert Wallace; Abraham Clarence; Ethel, m. Earl Duke; Moroni Alma. Family home Salt Lake City.
Member 67th quorum seventies; high priest. Plasterer; gardener.

DANIELS, DANIEL. Born Aug. 9, 1807, Caermarthenshire, South Wales. Came to Utah Oct. 27, 1849, George A. Smith company.
Married Mary Jeremy, who was born 1796 and came to Utah with husband. Their children: Thomas Daniels b. Jan. 18, 1831, m. Mary Davis; David Daniels, m. Hannah Thomas. Family resided Salt Lake City and Brigham, Utah, and Malad, Idaho.
President Malad Co-op. 1869-79; bishop of Malad ward 1866-77; missionary to South Wales four years. Assisted in building first bridges and wagon roads in Malad valley.

DANIELS, THOMAS (son of Daniel Daniels and Mary Jeremy). Born Jan. 18, 1831, Carmarthenshire, S. W.
Married Mary Davis May 20, 1852, Salt Lake City (daughter of Daniel and Mary Davis), who was born Dec. 22, 1832, Carmarthenshire, S. W. Their children: Mary Jane b. Aug. 15, 1853, m. William H. Jones; Thomas D. m. Aug. 28, 1855, m. Sarah Dives; Daniel B. b. Dec. 20, 1856, m. Mary Jones; m. Catherine Owens; David M. b. March 26, 1859, m. Gertrude Dives; Sarah Ann. b. April 29, 1861, m. Jedediah Jones; John M. b. April 21, 1863, m. Martha Richards; Joseph D. b. April 13, 1866, died. Family home Malad, Idaho.
Married Jennett Thomas 1867, Brigham, Utah (daughter of William H. Thomas and Ann Williams, pioneers with Joseph Young company). She was born May 26, 1837, Carmarthenshire, S. W. Their children: Jennett Maria b. Dec. 12, 1868, m. Thomas E. Price; Elvia b. Feb. 12, 1870, m. Lorenzo Griffiths; Catherine b. Feb. 22, 1872, died; Henry b. Aug. 17, 1873, m. Elizabeth Williams; George b. July 23, 1875, m. Mary Bolingbroke; Theodore b. Feb. 21, 1877, died; Dora b.

Feb. 21, 1877, died; Ann Eliza b. April 19, 1882, m. John S. Williams. Family home Brigham, Utah, and Melad, Idaho. Chairman board of county commissioners, Oneida county, Idaho; member Malad school board.

DANIELS, DANIEL M. (son of Thomas Daniels and Mary Davis). Born Dec. 20, 1856, Brigham, Utah.
Married M. Ellen Jones March 1883, who died 1884.
Married Catherine Owens (daughter of John E. Owens and Mary Thomas, pioneers 1853). She was born Dec. 27, 1868, Malad, Idaho. Their children: Mary D. b. Feb. 27, 1887, m. Thomas R. Williams; Daniel O. b. Jan. 1, 1889; Leroy O. b. Nov. 10, 1890; Catherine E. b. Sept. 10, 1892; Luther O. b. Nov. 1, 1894; Flora Bell b. Jan 20, 1896; Russell b. April 7, 1899; Lenna O. and Lona O., twins, b. Sept. 4, 1902; Pearl O. b. Aug. 13, 1908; Sarah Fern b. Nov. 26, 1911.
Settled in Malad 1865. High councilor Malad stake. Oneida county commissioner two years; member Malad city council.

DANIELS, DAVID MORONI (son of Thomas Daniels and Mary Davis). Born March 26, 1859, Brigham, Utah.
Married Gertrude Dives April 10, 1880 (daughter of Verulam Dives and Janette Thomas, pioneers 1853), who was born at Salt Lake City. Their children: Walter b. March 11, 1881, m. Alice Thews; David b. April 13, 1883, m. Amelia Davis; Mary Pearl b. Nov. 10, 1884, m. John Tuttle; Eli b. Jan. 20, 1886; Anna b. April 19, 1888, m. Bert Eliason; Jannette b. Aug. 27, 1893; Sarah Mabel b. Oct. 11, 1897; Oscar LaMar b. Oct. 15, 1905. Family home Malad, Idaho.
Settled at Malad in 1865. Cattle raiser in Southern Idaho.

DANIELS, JAMES E. (son of James Daniels and Elizabeth Salthouse of Manchester, Eng). Born Feb. 9, 1825, at Manchester. Came to Utah 1850.
Married Elizabeth Jane Jones, whose parents came to Utah 1850. Their children: La Prele, m. A. L. Towle; Eliza Luella, m. John R. Twelves; James Edward, m. Emma M. Spafford; Ida, dead; Joseph Ephraim, m. Lillian Spafford, m. Hannah Billings, m. Amelia Gallacher; Emma Isabella, died.
Married Marilla L. Miller (widow William Miller), June 13, 1878, Manti, Utah (daughter of Aaron Johnson and Polly Zerviah Kelsey of Nauvoo, Ill., pioneers Sept. 1850). She was born Oct. 2, 1830. Family resided Provo, Utah.
Patriarch; stake chorister. County recorder and clerk; assessor. Cabinet maker. Died June 16, 1902.

DANIELSON, HERMAN HANS (son of Daniel Rasmussen born Dec. 15, 1807, at Bogelund, and Anna Marta Hendrickson, born Dec. 17, 1822, at Wensiow, Denmark). He was born Aug. 3, 1862, at Bogelund. Came to Utah July 20, 1878.
Married Clara Jemima Kerr Nov. 21, 1889 (daughter of Robert Meriam Kerr, pioneer 1858, and Nance Jane Rawlins, pioneer Oct. 19, 1848, Amasa M. Lyman company, married Jan. 1, 1860, Draper, Utah). She was born June 6, 1868. Their children: Herman Kerr b. Aug. 30, 1890; Clara Maria b. Feb. 10, 1892; Esther b. Oct. 25, 1893, Myrtle b. Jan. 13, 1896; Vivian b. April 19, 1898; Lena b. April 9, 1902; Ina b. Sept. 16, 1908.
School trustee Lewiston, Utah, seven years. Y. M. M. I. A. counselor and also librarian six years; Sunday school teacher seven years; assistant Sunday school superintendent; missionary to Scandinavia 1903-05; second counselor to President Skidmore, high priests quorum Benson stake; president Y. M. M. I. A. 1905-07; bishop second ward Lewiston.

DANSIE, ROBERT (son of James Dansie, born 1790, and Sarah Cheney, both of Boxford, Eng.; married 1811). He was born Feb. 5, 1825, at Boxford. Came to Utah Oct. 5, 1862, Ansel T. Harmon company.
Married Charlotte Rudland April 8, 1849, Newton, Suffolk, Eng. (daughter of William Rudland and Mary Reason Hatch of Newton). Their children: Robert, Jr., b. 1850, m. Rosena Silcock, 1C75, m. Paulina Silcock 1880, m. Christinia Madsen 1882; Alfred John b. 1852, m. Martha Ann Wright; Charles N. b. 1855, m. Mary Crump, m. Nina Silcock; Sarah Ann b. 1857, m. James S. Crane; William Heber b. July 18, 1860, m. Eliza Jane Wright. Family home Herriman, Utah.
Married Jane Wilcox, Salt Lake City (daughter of John and Melissa Wilcox; latter came to Utah 1869). She was born Aug. 24, 1836, Bristol, Gloucestershire, Eng. Their children: James W. b. 1863, m. Alice Smith Dec. 28, 1885; George Henry b. Jan. 31, 1866, m. Sarah Anna E. England; Francis Hyrum b. 1867, m. Eliza Evans 1892; Benjamin W. b. 1868, m. Katie Taylor 1893; Isabella J. b. 1869, m. Zachariah Butterfield 1897; Charlotte L. b. 1871, m. John Wheeler 1897; Ada Amelia b. 1873, m. George Webster 1892; Alma Heisman b. 1876, m. Agnes Kuritz 1909.
Member 93d quorum seventies; missionary to England 1877; bishop of Herriman ward. Road supervisor. Farmer and stockraiser. Died Oct. 12, 1896, Salt Lake City.

DANSIE ROBERT, JR. (son of Robert Dansie and Charlotte Rudland). Born May 5, 1850, Boxford, Eng. Came to Utah with parents.
Married Rosena Silcock March, 1875, Salt Lake City (daughter of Nicolas T. Silcock and Jane Heath of South Jordan, Utah, pioneers Oct. 13, 1850, Edward Hunter company). She was born Jan. 27, 1856. Their children: Charlotte J. b. April 2, 1876, m. David Shelley; Robert M., died.

Married Paulina Silcock Sept., 1880, Salt Lake City (daughter of Nicholas T. Silcock and Jane Heath), who was born Oct. 4, 1862. Their children: Nicholas b. Sept. 6, 1881, and Rosena Harriet b. Oct. 7, 1883, died; Annie Louise b. Sep 29, 1885; Mahonri M. b. Sept. 1, 1887; Charles A. b. April 1889, and Edna Pearl b. Nov. 20, 1890, died; Electa H. b. De 21, 1891; Mary Isabell b. Aug. 2, 1894, died; Chauncy M. Nov. 7, 1896; Roberta b. Aug. 7, 1899; Percy J. b. Nov. 2 1901; Ida P. b. Sept. 26, 1906. Family home Salt Lake Cit
Married Christiania Madsen 1882, Salt Lake City, who wa born Sept., 1861. Their children: James H. b. March 1 1886; Joseph H. b. March 23, 1893; Ingra M. b. Nov. 2, 189 Elsie b. 1896. Family home Riverton, Utah.
Seventy. Constable Salt Lake City three years. Stock raiser.

DANSIE, WILLIAM HEBER (son of Robert Dansie an Charlotte Rudland). Born July 18, 1860, Boxford, En Came to Utah with parents.
Married Eliza Jane Wright Sept. 8, 1881, Salt Lake Cit (daughter of Thomas Wright and Ann Tanner of Lakepoin Utah), who was born April 29, 1863. Their children: Emm Jane b. Oct. 9, 1882, m. Christon Lovendahl; William Hebe Jr., b. June 27, 1885, m. Jennie Goates; Charlotte Mary June 30, 1887; Eva Isabell b. Oct. 7, 1889; Lenora Ada b. De 28, 1891, m. William Codell; Leroy Samuel b. July 8, 189 Robert Erva b. March 18, 1896; Olive May b. May 30, 189 Archie Robison b. March 21, 1902; Eliza Lillian b. Oct. 2 1904; Leslie Earl b. May 25, 1910. Family home Riverto Utah.
Elder. Laborer.

DANSIE, WILLIAM HEBER, JR. (son of William Heb Dansie and Eliza Jane Wright). Born June 27, 1885, Rive ton, Utah.
Married Jennie Goates Feb. 18, 1913, Salt Lake City (daugh ter of George Goates and Rose Munns of Lehi, Utah), wh was born May 15, 1885.
Seventy. Engineer.

DANSIE, GEORGE HENRY (son of Robert Dansie and Jan Wilcox). Born Jan. 31, 1866, Bingham Canyon, Utah.
Married Sarah Ann E. England Sept. 20, 1893, Salt Lal City (daughter of William England and Eliza Seamons, pineers Sept. 13, 1861, Homer Duncan company). She wa born Dec. 16, 1867, Hyde Park, Utah. Their children: Iv Jane b. Aug. 27, 1894; Roseanna Eliza b. Dec. 5, 1895; In Elizabeth b. Oct. 21, 1899; Hulon George b. March 18, 190 Marvin England b. Dec. 14, 1902; Lorin Jesse b. Nov. 24, 190 d. April 9, 1908; Connie Leora b. Oct. 31, 1907; Elvoy Henry Jan. 31, 1910. Family home Riverton, Utah.
President 94th quorum seventies; missionary to Englar 1896-98; first assistant Sunday school superintendent. Ju tice of peace. Farmer and stockraiser.

DAVENPORT, EDWARD HATHAWAY (son of Jeremi Davenport and Alice Hathaway of Rhode Island). Bo Sept. 20, 1822, in Rhode Island. Came to Utah 1851.
Married Clarissa Crapo Aug. 10, 1848 (daughter of Jose George Crapo and Mary Collins), who was born Aug. 1828, and came to Utah 1852. Their children: Joseph Cra b. Aug. 6, 1849, m. Charlotte E. Sperry Feb. 3, 1871; Jer miah Franklin b. June 17, 1853, m. Helen Badger Remingt Nov. 2, 1874; John Edward b. Oct. 13, 1855, m. Albatena Chr tensen Sept. 11, 1890; James Albert b. June 1, 1857, di William E. b. March 4, 1859, m. Alzina Hendrickson July 1900; Mary Alice b. April 4, 1861, m. Thomas J. Pearce N 10, 1881; Marcus M. b. Oct. 24, 1863, m. Maggie M. Christ son Feb. 5, 1900; Eudora A. b. April 9, 1866, m. Jesse Fra Short Jan. 1, 1884; Charles R. b. April 9, 1868, died; Will E. b. May 19, 1871, m. Marrentena Hendrickson March 5, 19 Family resided Draper and Paradise, Utah.

DAVENPORT, JEREMIAH FRANKLIN (son of Edwa Hathaway Davenport and Clarissa Crapo). Born June 1853, Salt Lake City.
Married Helen Badger Remington Nov. 2, 1874, Salt L City (daughter of Jerome Remington, pioneer 1850, Lydia Badger, pioneer 1851, Captain Duston company). was born Dec. 13, 1857, at Salt Lake City. Their childr Helen R. b. Dec. 16, 1875, m. Frederick Newby Sept. 1899; Franklin R. b. July 15, 1878, m. Kate Naomi Luf 1901; Emory R. b. May 25, 1880, m. Nellie Larsen J 4, 1901; Marion R. b. Oct. 24, 1881, m. Ella Boyes March Sept. 22, 1883, m. Lucile Barber May 25, 1903; Earl R March 4, 1886, m. Tillie Franzen; May R. b. Feb. 28, 18 Bery. R. b. Sept. 18, 1889, died; Winnie R. b. April 14, 1 Clarice R. b. Sept. 19, 1894; Marie R. b. June 22, 1896; I R. b. Dec. 21, 1898; Fay R. b. April 19, 1908. Family resi Paradise and Logan, Utah.
Elder. Pioneer to Oregon. Minuteman and Indian figh Built first irrigation canal on Egin bench, Idaho. Move Hood River, Ore., 1891; there he organized an irriga company and built canals. Lumberman.

DAVENPORT, FRANKLIN REMINGTON (son of Jere Franklin Davenport and Helen Badger Remington). I July 15, 1878, Paradise, Utah.
Married Kate Naomi Lufkin Oct. 3, 1901, Logan, l (daughter of George W. Lufkin and Martha Ann Town pioneers October, 1852). She was born Jan. 3, 1880, Lake City. Their children: Franklin Lufkin b. Oct. 31, Dorothy Lufkin b. Aug. 14, 1904; Hazel Lufkin b. Jul

1906; Violet Lufkin b. March 31, 1908; Kenneth Lufkin b. April 21, 1910. Family resided Logan and Salt Lake City, Utah.
Seventy; missionary to northwestern states. Bookkeeper and cashier.

DAVENPORT, JAMES N. (son of James Davenport and Almira Phelps). Born Aug. 14, 1814, Walnut Grove, Ill. Came to Utah 1848.
Married Margaret J. Petty Feb. 3, 1865, Salt Lake City (daughter of Robert C. Petty and Margaret J. Wells of Richmond, Utah, pioneers 1849). She was born Sept. 13, 1848. Their children: Martha J., m. Albert Heath; John W., m. Mamie Heath; Minnie A., m. A. L. Shaw; Lewis A.; Susie Valentine; Thomas P., m. Nettie Skiles; Alvin L., m. Grace Paul. Family home Richmond, Utah.
Farmer. Died July 10, 1902.

DAVID, MORGAN (son of Thomas and Mary David, of Llanelly, Caermarthenshire, South Wales). Born March 3, 1804, at Llanelly. Came to Utah Sept. 19, 1852, William Morgan company.
Married Elizabeth Bowen (daughter of William Bowen), who was born Oct. 23, 1803 and died of cholera at St. Louis. Their children: Mary, b. Jan. 24, 1825, m. David Bowen; Elizabeth, b. July 7, 1830, m. William Thomas; Ann b. April 15, 1833, m. William Warner; Hannah, b. March 3, 1837, m. Morgan Hughes; Emma, b. Aug. 9, 1839, m. Alfred Reece; Rachel, b. March 3, 1842, m. George Chambers. Family home Palmyra and Spanish Fork, Utah.

DAVIES, MORGAN (son of Thomas and Gwenllian Davies of Wales). Born May 10, 1847, in Wales. Came to Utah 1853.
Married Annie Keep March 1, 1865, Lehi, Utah (daughter of James Joseph Keep and Anne Miller of that place, pioneers 1852). She was born April 26, 1837. Their children: Thomas James, m. Alice Earl; Edward, m. Lillian Diamond; Lucy L. m. Joseph T. Harris; Daniel William, died; Morgan Alford, m. Louise Walsh; Gwenllian, m. Frank A. Sange. Family home Salt Lake City.
High priest. Contractor.

DAVIES, T. J. (son of Morgan Davies and Anne Keep). Born Sept. 5, 1866, Salt Lake City.
Married Alice Earl Dec. 18, 1889 (daughter of Jonathan Earl and Jane Wright of Salt Lake City, pioneers Aug. 7, 1852). She was born July 8, 1867. Their children: Rosella b. Nov. 7, 1890; Thomas Jesse b. April 7, 1892; Morgan Joseph b. Dec. 6, 1893; Viola May b. Oct. 6, 1895; Earl Jay b. Feb. 25, 1897; Alice Jane b. Feb. 19, 1900; Paul J. b. Aug. 15, 1902; Daniel Jones b. Nov. 25, 1904; Frank Joel b. March 15, 1908; Ruth b. Oct. 14, 1910. Family home Salt Lake City.
High priest; second counselor in bishopric 10th ward, Salt Lake City. Contractor.

DAVIS, ALEXANDER G. (son of Isaac Davis and Sara Saulsbury of New York state). Born Dec. 15, 1828, Holloman, Can. Came to Utah September, 1852, Captain Stewart ox-team company.
Married Emily Frances Oliver Dec. 8, 1861, Payson, Utah (daughter of Harrison Oliver and Hannah Martin of Louisville, Ky., pioneers September, 1850, Perrigrine Sessions company). She was born Jan. 10, 1843. Their children: Alexander b. Oct. 3, 1862, m. Mary Morrill; William Edward b. Sept. 30, 1864, m. Eveline Judd; Levi Alonzo b. May 17, 1866, m. Mary Brunette Niles; Sarah Melissa b. April 26, 1868, m. Walter E. Price; George Willard b. March 1, 1870, m. Eliza Luella Gentry; Clarissa Calista b. Dec. 28, 1874, d. aged two months; Amy T. b. Oct. 30, 1876, m. Levi Barton; Luther Llewellyn b. Feb. 8, 1878, m. Catherine Davis; Isaac Harrison b. Jan. 15, 1880, m. Elnora Wiseman; Lydia Elder b. May 1, 1882, m. Van Oscar Fullmer. Family resided Payson, Summit City Creek, Monroe and now at Spring Glen, Utah.
Elder. Veteran Echo Canyon and Black Hawk wars. Farmer.

DAVIS, ALEXANDER (son of Alexander G. Davis and Emily Francis Oliver). Born Oct. 3, 1862, Payson, Utah.
Married Mary Morrill June 6, 1883, Circleville, Piute Co., Utah (daughter of Laban Morrill and Lydia Davis of Junction, Utah), who was born May 31, 1863. Their children: Melissa b. March 3, 1884, m. John Jensen; Alonzo Alexander b. Nov. 16, 1886; Bert b. Jan. 11, 1888; Bertha b. Aug. 7, 1890, m. Nels Jensen; Vard b. Nov. 27, 1892; Lydia Cassie b. Sept. 21, 1894; Delma b. April 16, 1897; Emma Frances b. April 5, 1900; Arnold b. March 27, 1903; John Clarence b. Aug. 6, 1909. Family home Junction, Piute Co., and Dry Gulch, Uinta Co., Utah.
Farmer; carpenter.

DAVIS, CALEB HERSEY (son of Caleb Hersey Davis and Trifena Atherton). Born March 22, 1839, in New York state. Came to Utah Sept. 12, 1850, Thomas Johnson company.
Married Hannah Strong Dec. 6, 1862, Salt Lake City (daughter of John Strong), who came to Utah 1855. Their children: Hannah Trif.,* b. Sept. 6, 1863, m. J. H. Hales Sept.

22, 1886; Agnes E. b. Sept. 4, 1865, m. Morgan D. Evans Aug. 1, 1888; Hersey John b. April 12, 1868, m. Margret Bunnell June, 1893; Sophia Strong b. Nov. 5, 1871, m. James Evans March 5, 1900; Mary b. April 16, 1873, m. Stephen Hales March 2, 1898; Annie Marilla b. July 8, 1875, m. J. M. Brown June 26, 1901; Caleb Miles b. Aug. 16, 1877, m. Mina Penrod Aug. 16, 1902; Julia Strong b. Sept. 20, 1880, m. E. R. Kirkman Feb. 15, 1906; Zella Strong b. March 25, 1883, m. A. C. Miner Aug. 24, 1904.

DAVIS, CHARLES A. (son of James Davis born Oct. 5, 1786, and Myranda Jones born Nov. 16, 1784, both at Princeton, Mass.). He was born Oct. 13, 1810, at Princeton. Came to Utah 1849.
Married Ruth Kennan April 11, 1839 (daughter of Andrew Kennan, Jr., and Ruth Parminter), who was born Oct. 13, 1821. Their children: Emily b. June 9, 1840, m. William Munro Sept. 9, 1858; Charles E. b. Sept. 5, 1842; Andrew A. b. Sept. 10, 1845; [1] Warren Edgar b. June 13, 1848, m. Almira Stoker Dec. 18, 1871; Lydia Ann b. Jan. 7, 1851; Sarah H. b. March 5, 1852; Mary M. b. June 23, 1854, m. Isaac Losee Sept. 8, 1873; Ruth E. b. Dec. 23, 1856, m. John H. Hayes April 28, 1873; Lucretia R. C. b. Jan. 29, 1859, m. Moses Beckstead July 29, 1878; Elijah D. A. b. Dec. 16, 1861, m. Caroline M. Holm Jan. 16, 1882; Amelia T. b. May 4, 1863, m. William Adamson Nov. 15, 1878; John G. b. June 22, 1867, m. Alice McDaniels. Family resided Little Cottonwood, Palmyra and Spanish Fork, Utah.
High priest. Postmaster at Spanish Fork 25 years.

DAVIS, WARREN EDGAR (son of Charles A. Davis and Ruth Kennan). Born June 13, 1848, in Iowa. Came to Utah 1849 with parents.
Married Almira Stoker Dec. 18, 1871, at Salt Lake City (daughter of William Stoker and Almira Winegar, pioneers 1852, Isaac Stewart company). She was born Aug. 1, 1855, Palmyra, Utah. Their children: [a] Warren Edgar b. Oct. 26, 1872, m. Barbara E. Mooney Dec. 8, 1892; William C. b. Nov. 27, 1874; Sarah A. b. Jan. 29, 1877; John S. b. Feb. 24, 1879, m. Mary Beck Jan. 18, 1899; James A. b. Oct. 31, 1881, m. Vera Lund Dec. 12, 1906; Ida M. b. June 11, 1884, m. Clarence Hardman Feb. 22, 1907; Ruth E. b. Dec. 18, 1886, m. Mitchell Beck Dec. 5, 1905; Archie D. b. Aug. 29, 1889, m. Sarah J. Clyde Oct. 27, 1909. Family home Spanish Fork, Utah.
High priest. Deputy county road supervisor. Director in Spanish Fork Creamery company; also in Spanish Fork Co-op.

DAVIS, WARREN EDGAR, JR. (son of Warren Edgar Davis and Almira Stoker). Born Oct. 26, 1872, at Spanish Fork, Utah.
Married Barbara E. Mooney Dec. 8, 1892 (daughter of James Mooney and Mary McLean), who was born Oct. 28, 1872, Rome, Ga. Their children: [d] Warren Edgar and Barbara b. Feb. 20, 1895; James A. b. Jan. 23, 1897; Daniel J. b. Dec. 24, 1897; Erton R. b. June 21, 1900; Ora b. Oct. 16, 1902; Ruth b. Feb. 9, 1904; Mary D. b. March 30, 1906; Otto L. b. April 10, 1908. Family home Spanish Fork, Utah.

DAVIS, DAVID W. (son of William and Mary Davis). Born March 28, 1828, Hairwin, Brecknockshire, South Wales. Came to Utah 1855.
Married Charlotte Notte Jeremy July 18, 1853, at Aberdare, Wales (daughter of Evan Jeremy and Eleanor Davis—married Jan. 15, 1822, Llanuwchllyn, Wales). She was born Dec. 10, 1828. Their children: David Peter; Mary Ann; Ellen Jane; Hannah; William Gomer; George; Charlotte Notte. Family home Provo and Logan, Utah, and Malad, Idaho.
Farmer. Died Oct. 20, 1907.

DAVIS, WILLIAM G. (son of David W. Davis and Charlotte Notte Jeremy). Born June 14, 1865, at Logan.
Married Margaret A. Hawkins May 20, 1890, at Logan (daughter of William E. Hawkins, pioneer 1853, and Margaret Thomas, born 1854 in Farmington, Utah). She was born Nov. 25, 1873, Samaria, Idaho. Their children: William Ray; Eva; Pearl; Rulon H.; Lyman H., died; Margret Seldon H. Family resided Logan, Utah, Burley and Malad, Idaho.
Missionary to England 1906-08; 1st counselor to Bishop L. W. Robbins at Burley. Founder, president and manager of Burley opera house.

DAVIS, EDWARD WILLIAM (son of William Davis of Wales). Born Feb. 1, 1794, at London. Came to Utah Sept. 8, 1852, A. O. Smoot company.
Married Sarah Drabble Jan. 13, 1822, at London (daughter of Joshua Drabble and Hannah Goods of that place). Came to Utah with husband. She was born Jan. 16, 1802, at London and died Oct. 29, 1876. Their children: Samuel; Edward William b. Nov. 18, 1826, m. Sarah Elizabeth Hyder; m. Jemima Nightingale; Lydia, m. George B. Wallace; Martha, m. George B. Wallace; Hannah, m. George B. Wallace; Josiah. Family home Salt Lake City, Utah.
Silk and cloth weaver. Died Oct. 1, 1878.

DAVIS, EDWARD WILLIAM, JR. (son of Edward William Davis and Sarah Drabble), born Nov. 18, 1826, at London. Came to Utah Oct. 15, 1851, Orson Pratt company.
Married Sarah Elizabeth Hyder April 22, 1852, at Salt Lake City (daughter of Richard Hugh Hyder and Sarah Jarrold

838 PIONEERS AND PROMINENT MEN OF UTAH

of London, who came to Utah 1851, Orson Pratt company). She was born March 15, 1829, at London. Their children: Sarah Ann b. Jan. 18, 1853, m. William Heber Pitt; Heber Hyder b. Nov. 16, 1854, m. Martha Ann Webster Twitchell; m. Sarah Ann Tall; Willard Hyder b. March 6, 1857, d. Aug. 29, 1878; Edward Hyder b. March 23, 1860, m. Rene Brown; m. Amy Ball; Martha Hyder b. Jan. 18, 1862, d. Sept. 14, 1863; Charlotte Isabella b. March 17, 1865; Hannah Hyder b. Jan. 28, 1867, m. W. D. Bowering; Alma b. Dec. 20, 1869, m. Sophia Holmes; Thomas Stafford b. Feb. 18, 1872, m. Olive Van Cott.
Married Jemima Nightingale Feb. 26, 1857, at Salt Lake City (daughter of John Nightingale and Jane Archer of Stafford, near Manchester, Eng., pioneers Nov. 30, 1856, with Martin handcart company). She was born Nov. 19, 1834; died July 4, 1885. Their children: Jane Nightingale b. Jan. 3, 1858, m. George Careless; Joseph N. b. Aug. 18, 1860, d. July 23, 1910; Franklin N. b. Sept. 6, 1862, died; John N. b. Oct. 19, 1864, m. Minnie Jasperson; Allice N. b. Dec. 23, 1866, died; Kate N. b. Aug. 23, 1871, m. George Lloyd; William N. b. April 21, 1873, m. Nora Groo; Mary N. b. Dec. 16, 1874, d. Feb. 22, 1876. Families resided Salt Lake City.
Became president elders' quorum Oct. 9, 1874, and president 1st quorum; clerk of 17th ward Salt Lake City in 1855-96 at reorganization of Salt Lake City stakes; missionary to Arizona 1873; captain in the Nauvoo Legion. Major Utah militia; took part in Indian wars and Johnston's army trouble. Carpenter and builder. Died Sept. 10, 1896, at Salt Lake City, Utah.

DAVIS, HEBER HYDER (son of Edward William Davis and Sarah Elizabeth Hyder), born Nov. 16, 1854 at Salt Lake City. Married Martha Ann Webster Twitchell Feb. 28, 1877, at Salt Lake City (daughter of Luther Twitchell of Dublin, N. H., and Elizabeth W. Woodville Hovey, Cambridgeport, Mass). She was born Dec. 30, 1858, at Salt Lake City and died April 27, 1903. Their children: Mattie Orpha b. Sept. 19, 1886, died same day; Inez Twitchell b. Oct. 30, 1887, m. Gustave H. Schuster; Myrtle b. Feb. 3, 1889, d. April 26, 1897; Sarepta b. April 7, 1903, d. Dec. 5, 1903. Family home Salt Lake City.
Married Sarah Ann Tall June 15, 1904, at Salt Lake City (daughter of George Tall and Elizabeth Ormond, former a pioneer September, 1853, Jacob Gates company, latter Sept. 19, 1852, Captain Outhouse company). She was born Sept. 13, 1868. No children.
Seventy; missionary to Great Britain 1899-1901; Salt Lake City sexton 1904-05. Carpenter and builder.

DAVIS, JOHN N. (son of Edward William Davis, Jr., and Jemima Nightingale). Born Oct. 19, 1864, at Salt Lake City. Married Minnie Jasperson, Feb. 1, 1893, Manti, Utah (daughter of Lars C. and Augusta V. Jasperson of Parker, Utah), who was born July 12, 1868, and came to Utah 1874. Their children: Harold Edward b. Nov. 3, 1893; John Clive b. April 13, 1896; Paul Jasperson b. April 25, 1899; Jemima b. Feb. 14, 1900; Elfreda Augusta b. Sept. 12, 1901; Marie Nightingale b. May 15, 1903; Melbe b. Jan. 31, 1905, died; Carl Garrett b. March 8, 1906; George Careless b. June 28, 1907; William Lawrence b. Dec. 6, 1908. Family home Vernal, Utah.
High priest; missionary to northern states 1895-97; presided over Indiana conference; bishop Vernal ward July 24, 1898-1910. Member Utah house of representatives 1906-10. Interested in livestock, farming, mercantile and banking enterprises; secretary and director Bank of Vernal.

DAVIS, EDWIN ALBERT. Born in Iowa. Came to Utah 1859.
Married Mary E. Walker 1857, Nauvoo, Ill. (daughter of John Walker and Lydia Holms of Iowa, pioneers 1859), who was born Feb. 11, 1840. Their children: Benoni b. 1858, m. Mary Parson April, 1878; Charles H. b. June 23, 1860, m. Lizzie Rogers 1885. Family home Farmington, Utah.

DAVIS, CHARLES H. (son of Edwin Albert Davis and Mary E. Walker). Born June 23, 1860, Farmington, Utah.
Married Lizzie W. Rogers April 1, 1885, Logan, Utah (daughter of William Rogers and Cathrine Walker—pioneers 1847), who was born March 22, 1864, Ruby Valley, Nev. Their children: Charles Edwin b. Feb. 24, 1886; Mary Edna b. Sept. 29, 1888, m. Charles Robinett 1910; Cathrine b. June 17, 1890; Ruby L. b. June 2, 1893; Lizzie C. b. Jan. 30, 1896; Lydia May b. May 9, 1899; Lucy Myrtle b. Aug. 4, 1901; Lewis A. b. May 13, 1904; John W. b. April 20, 1905. Family home Brigham City.
Member 133d quorum seventies; missionary to eastern states 1906-08. Fruit grower.

DAVIS, ELIAKIM SPOONER (son of Nathan Davis and Abigail Spooner of Lowell, Mass.). Born Oct. 12, 1812, Lebanon, N. H. Came to Utah Sept. 12, 1861, Milo Andrus company.
Married Orpha Hopkins 1841 at Lowell, Mass. (daughter of Abram Hopkins and Miss Brown of Grantham, N. I). Their children: George Augustus, m. Harlett Elizabeth Weaver; Helen Maris, m. Thomas J. Thurston; m. Frank Reeder; Charles Hopkins, m. Elizabeth Walker; Elizabeth, m. Michael Gehrum; Ida; Emma, m. Frank Meyers. Family resided Salt Lake City and Milton, Morgan Co., Utah.
Elder; president of Branch at Lowell, Mass. Lived in Milton about one and a half years. came to Salt Lake. working on the buildings at Fort Douglas. Painter and builder. Died 1878, Atchison, Kas.

DAVIS, GEORGE AUGUSTUS (son of Eliakin Davis and Orpha Hopkins). Born Aug. 22, 1842, Lowell, Mass. Came to Utah with parents.
Married Harriet, Elizabeth Weaver Nov. 9, 1866, Littleton, Morgan Co., Utah (daughter of William Weaver and Hannah Carter of Lewes, Sussex, Eng., latter came to Utah 1868). She was born May 6, 1850, at Brighton, Sussex, Eng. and came to Utah 1866. Their children: Elizabeth Helen b. Oct. 10, 1867, d. child; Emily Ida b. Nov. 19, 1869, d. child; William George b. March 18, 1872, m. Margeret Luzina Bird; Charles Henry b. Sept. 14, 1874, m. Sarah Matilda Hall; Fannie Orpha b. Jan. 17, 1881, and Thomas Davey b. Nov. 14, 1878, d. infants; Mildred Lillian b. June 23, 1884, m. Joseph S. Murray; Harriet Weaver b. Nov. 5, 1886, m. Morris Thompson; Annie May b. May 19, 1889; Edith Carter b. Feb. 24, 1893. Family home, Vernal, Utah.
High priest; high counselor to S. R. Bennion 1884-88; pres. Merrell (Naples) Branch ward 1881-84; stake clerk, Uintah stake 1908-12 to Prest. William Smart and Don B. Colton; School superintendent for six years; ward teacher for several years. Justice of peace 1887-89; deputy county recorder; treasurer Uintah county 1901-07; came to Ashley Fork 1881 from Morgan, Utah; went to Morgan from Eagle Rock (Idaho Falls), Idaho. Locomotive engineer. Farmer.

DAVIS, FRANKLIN JUDSON (son of Powell Davis of New York). Born in New York state. Came to Utah 1852, Captain McCullough company.
Married Ann Richmond (daughter of Nathan Richmond). She died on the plains coming to Utah. Their children: Esther Mariah b. May 4, 1838, m. Nymphus C. Murdock: Stanley Powell b. April, m. Susan Fairbanks; Ann Eliza b. Aug. 8, 1842, m. Simeon C. Drollinger Dec. 4, 1859; Emily Amelia b. 1844, m. Cornelius Fairbanks April 6, 1865; Franklin Judson; Frederick. Family home New York state and Canada. Bishop at Council Bluffs. School teacher in Salt Lake City.

DAVIS, GEORGE (son of James Davis, born 1803, Bodenham, Herefordshire, and Elizabeth Goodwin, born March 10, 1805, Ombersly, Worcestershire, Eng.). He was born Dec. 8, 1824, Waterbury, Worcestershire, Eng. Came to Utah Oct. 24, 1854, William A. Empey company.
Married Mary Ann Sparks Dec. 27, 1853 (daughter of George Sparks and Hannah Lask; latter died in New York). She was born Dec. 10, 1833, and came to Utah with husband. Died July 2, 1905. Their children: Margaret Caroline b. July 1, 1854, on the plains; George James b. Nov. 25, 1855, m. Tryphena L. Terry Jan. 11, 1877; Hannah Elizabeth b. Nov. 15, 1857, m. James G. Thompson, b. Dec. 3, 1903; Alfred William b. Oct. 3, 1859, died Oct. 11, 1859; Nelson Franklin b. Oct. 15, 1860, m. Sarah E. Thorn Feb. 24, 1881; Orson Charles b. March 15, 1863, d. Feb. 10, 1865; Vinson Frederick b. Feb. 8, 1865; Vinson Frederick b. Sept. 13, 1883; Mary Laurn b. Feb. 1, 1867 (d. Jan. 12, 1885), m. Henry Matthews Dec. 7, 1882; Olivia Fullerton Rebecca b. May 6, 1869, m. John S. Holton Dec. 20, 1893; Benjamin Ephraim b. May 15, 1872, d. July 30, 1875; Arthur Nephi b. Sept. 10, 1876, d. Oct. 17, 1894. Family resided Clarkston, Perry, Lehi, Utah.
Married Alice E. Goodey Feb. 24, 1865, Salt Lake City. She was born Sept. 12, 1845. Their children: William Henry b. Feb. 2, 1866, m. Mary E. Young Dec. 16, 1885; Alice Mary b. Jan. 9, 1868, m. Isaac Thorn Sept. 13, 1883, died; Samuel Arthur b. Jan. 5, 1870, d. Nov. 15, 1889; Herbert John b. April 10, 1872, d. Nov. 14, 1889; Louisa Jane b. Dec. 14, 1874, m. Hyrum Thorn Dec. 18, 1895; Elizabeth Ann b. May 9, 1877, m. David Morgan Dec. 19, 1900; Emma Ellen b. Oct. 21, 1879, m. Willard Facer Oct. 25, 1899; Sarah Eliza b. Jan. 20, 1882, d. May 11, 1883; George Alma b. May 30, 1884, d. Sept. 10, 1891; Parley Ernst b. Jan. 16, 1887, m. Maria Jacobsen Jan. 16, 1907; Jonathan b. March 13, 1891, m. Mabel Miller Aug. 28, 1911. Families resided Clarkston, Lehi and Perry, Utah.
Worked for the church as wheelwright, repairing wagons for immigrants to cross the plains 1855-57; was in Echo Canyon winter 1857 resisting Johnson's army. Settled at Lehi 1858; moved to Clarkston 1868; moved to Perry 1875 and served there as Sunday school superintendent eighteen years; one of seven presidents 50th quorum seventies many years; missionary to Liverpool, Eng., 1900-02. Helped to build several towns in Utah; was an excellent shot with rifle; very diligent ecclesiastical worker; stood the hardships of pioneer life without complaint. Precise in all his labors. Died June 14, 1903, Perry, Utah.

DAVIS, VINSON FREDERICK (son of George Davis and Mary Ann Sparks). He was born Feb. 8, 1865, Lehi, Utah.
Married Melissa Emeline Perry Dec. 13, 1883, Salt Lake City (daughter of Lorenzo Perry and Mary Wray Walker). She was born Dec. 24, 1866, Perry, Utah. Their children: Melissa Emeline b. Sept. 7, 1887; Laura May b. Aug. 31, 1888, m. Isaac Allen Jan. 26, 1910; Ethel b. Jan. 25, 1891, m. William Wood Jan. 20, 1909; Annie b. March 27, 1893, m. Charles Ottley Oct. 16, 1912; Arthur b. March 12, 1895, d. Nov. 10, 1900; Benjamin Vinson b. March 13, 1897, d. April 13, 1898; Ruth b. Jan. 9, 1899; Vinson Frederick b. Sept. 13, 1900; Gwenith b. July 31, 1904; Eugene Russell b. Aug. 27, 1905; George Lorenzo b. Oct. 16, 1907; Dan Perry b. Nov. 1, 1909. Family home Perry, Utah.
Member bishopric Perry ward. President Perry Electric Light and Power company. President Perry town board. President Perry military band. Secretary and treasurer Three Mile Creek Land and Live Stock company; superintendent Bear River Club company. Reputed to be the greatest field and duck shot in the world.

PIONEERS AND PROMINENT MEN OF UTAH

DAVIS, GEORGE (son of William Davis born 1800, Witch Dorsetshire, and Lucy Davis born Nov. 14, 1806. Stoke Abbott, Dorsetshire, Eng.). He was born Nov. 4, 1833, at Stoke Abbott. Came to Utah Oct. 16, 1853, John Brown company.
Married Elizabeth M. Hammon Feb. 5, 1859 (daughter of Levi Hammon and Polly C. Bybee—pioneers September, 1851, Alfred Cardon company). She was born July 31, 1841, and came to Utah with parents. Their children: Elizabeth J. b. Jan. 17, 1860, m. William R. Howard; Rhoda A. b. Jan. 6, 1862, m. Hobert E. Thompson; Lucy E. b. Feb. 9, 1864, m. Frederick Stimpson; George A. b. Feb. 4, 1866, m. Emma S. Rice; Polly V. b. May 28, 1868, m. James M. Thompson; Sarah B. b. June 4, 1870; Joseph L. b. Feb. 29, 1872, m. Annie Sorensen; Nancy S. b. March 25, 1874, m. Charles W. Singleton; Samuel H. b. June 2, 1876, m. May L. Rice; Lydia M. b. May 12, 1878, m. Hyrum M. Thompson; William H. b. Jan. 19, 1881; John B. b. Jan. 25, 1884. Family resided South Hooper, Utah, Wilford, and Thomas, Idaho.
First counselor to Bishops Henry B. Gwilliam 1877, and Edwin Parker 1883, South Hooper; bishop Wilford ward, Bannock stake, 1887-93. Died May 5, 1912, at Thomas.

DAVIS, GEORGE PRESTON (son of Rachel J. Hunter of Mt. Pisgah, Iowa). Came to Utah, 1847.
Married Sarah Elizabeth Lewis at Ogden, Utah (daughter of Benjamin Lewis). Their children: Sarah Elizabeth, m. George Hanks; George Henry, d. aged 8; Rachel Johanna, m. Robert A. Powell; Benjamin Marian, m. Lilly Evans; William Preston; John Oliver, m. Sarah Lacretia McKindrick. Family home Springville, Utah.
High priest; ward teacher. Veteran Black Hawk Indian war. Farmer. Died December, 1909, Salem, Utah.

DAVIS, NATHAN C. (son of Ichabod Davis and Lydia Cutler of Warren county, N. Y.). Born in Warren county, N. Y. Came to Utah Aug. 10, 1860.
Married Isabel Wells in Warren county (daughter of George B. Wells and Rebecca Green of Bolton, Warren county, N. Y.). Their children: Allen, m. Matilda Robison; Cora, m. Lycurgus Johnson; Lydia Rebecca, m. Joseph Hardy; Huldah, d. infant; Julia Ellen, m. Simon Peter Dillmon. Family home, Salt Lake City.
High priest; first counselor to Jeremiah Hatch, president of Uinta stake; patriarch. Commissioner Uinta county, Utah, and Bear Lake county, Idaho. Lived in Nauvoo from its settlement until it was abandoned. Built the first gristmill at Wellsville; built sawmill in Kamas in 1861; built molasses mill in Salt Lake 1860. Master mechanic; farmer and stockraiser.

DAVIS, JAMES L. (son of George Davis and Mary A. Timson of London, Eng.). Born Aug. 9, 1840, at London. Came to Utah October, 1862, Kimball and Lawrence freight train.
Married Mary L. Fretwell April 23, 1864 (daughter of William K. Fretwell and Mary Ann Raby, married May, 1842, Yorkshire, Eng.). She was born April 14, 1843, and came to Utah Oct. 3, 1863, Daniel D. McArthur company. Their children: Mary F. b. Feb. 7, 1865; Edward F. b. April 4, 1866, m. Isabelle Budge Oct. 1, 1890; George William b. Oct. 24, 1868; James H. F. b. Oct. 28, 1870, m. M. E. Humphries Sept. 25, 1895; Emily E. b. June 2, 1873, m. R. W. Wallentine Oct. 11, 1893; Kate E. b. Jan. 21, 1875; John Orson b. Sept. 10, 1876, m. M. Hibbert Sept. 16, 1895; Norah Jane b. Feb. 21, 1878; Ethel Olive b. Aug. 2, 1879, m. J. Humphries Sept. 15, 1897; Cordelia A. July 15, 1881, m. D. Hyrnus Sept. 18, 1901; Stella b. July 22, 1883, m. D. L. Hays Sept. 18, 1901.
High priest; assisted in settlement of San Juan Valley, Utah, 1879-84; ward teacher over 28 years, and Sunday school worker 25 years.

DAVIS, JOHN CATLIN (son of John Davis and Elizabeth Catlin of London, Eng.). He was born 1821 at London. Came to Utah Sept. 16, 1859, Edward Stevenson company.
Married Phoebe Oxenbauld at Handsworth, Staffordshire, Eng. (daughter of William and Elizabeth Oxenbauld of England). Their children: Walter, m. Julia Harris; Frederick William, d. 1858; John Edward; Sylvia Jane, m. William Broomhead; Alfred, m. Margaret Bateman; Elizabeth, m. William Henry Stewart; Phoebe.
Married Caroline Young Jan. 16, 1860, at Salt Lake City (daughter of John Young of that place, pioneer 1858, Brigham Young company). Their children: Joseph b. 1862, d. 1862. Families resided Salt Lake City.
Gunsmith and locksmith. He died Feb. 18, 1878, Brigham City, Utah.

DAVIS, JOHN MEEKS (son of William Davis and Margarette Elsie Meeks, who came from Wales and later from Nauvoo, Ill., and Council Bluffs, Iowa). Born Sept. 9, 1823. Came to Utah 1854.
Married Elizabeth Abshire 1846, Nauvoo, Ill., who was born Dec. 28, ——, in Pennsylvania and came to Utah with her husband. Their children: Martha Jane b. June 27, 1847, m. David Toyn; Margarette Elsie b. 1849, d. child; Anniel b. Oct. 21, 1851, m. Winfield Scott Hullimer Nov. 22, 1869; John Spencer b. Feb. 22, 185-; Thomas b. 1856, m. Mary Lee; Sarah Ann b. 1858, m. James Wheeler; Angeline b. 1860, m. Lorenzo Dow; Olive b. 1862, m. James Graham; Abraham b. 1864; James b. 1866, m. Catherine Johnson; Frank d. child.
Married America Jane Overland 1857, Beaver Co., Utah (daughter of William Overland of Indiana, pioneer Autumn of 1856). She was born 1826. Their children: Elizabeth b. June 21, 1858, m. Richard Papworth Oct. 21, 1874; Atha, m. Mary Ford; Susanna, m. John Wall; Mary Ann, m. Dell Wall. Family home Beaver, Utah.
Elder; counselor in bishopric of Beaver ward. Settled at Vernal 1878 and helped build up the Uinta country. Blacksmith; farmer. Died Feb. 16, 1896, at Vernal, and was buried in Beaver county.

DAVIS, JOHN TUCKER. Born March 3, 1806, Genford, Pembrokeshire, South Wales. Came to Utah 1851.
Married Letitia Ann George 1842, Liverpool, Eng. (daughter of John George and Letitia Ann Harris of Liverpool, pioneers 1851, Daniel Jones company). She was born 1815. Their children: William George; John G.; Alma C.; Ephraim G.; Mary S.; Letitia A.; Sarah Jane; Martha H. Family home, Spanish Fork, Utah.
High priest; supervised block and tackle work on Salt Lake temple; pioneered making canals and wagon roads; settled at Spanish Fork 1855. Farmer. President of West Field farming district ten years. Died Dec. 20, 1888.

DAVIS, JOSEPH C. (son of John Davis and Elizabeth Cadwallader both of Pembrokeshire, South Wales). Born Dec. 6, 1836, in Parish St. Michael, Wales. Came to Utah Sept. 1, 1859, Horton D. Haight church train.
Married Maria Williams April 1, 1859, at Iowa City (daughter of Owen Williams and Ann Thomas of Abergele, Denbighshire, Wales, pioneers September, 1860). She was born Dec. 15, 1839, and came to Utah with husband. Their children: Annie M-, m. Joseph Houston; Elizabeth F., m. John Hatch; Alice Ann, m. Joseph S. Clark; Joseph W., m. Mary Schow; Hyrum, m. Lysade Craig; George H., m. Jenny McKeller; Margaret E., m. John C. Swenson.
Married Louisa Williams June 6, 1863, Salt Lake City (daughter of Owen Williams and Ann Thomas). Their children: John O.; Heber J., m. Christana Thompson; Wilford, m. Pearl Judd; Robert, m. Leona Reece; Rastus, m. Ethel McKeller; Susie, m. John C. Williams; Harriet, m. John Negley; Ettie; Pearl. Family home, Juarez, Old Mexico.
Bishop 1st ward of Panguitch eight years; missionary 1859-67. Died Sept. 20, 1905, at Juarez, Old Mexico.

DAVIS, JOSHUA (son of Dennis J. and Betsy Davis of Black Oak, Caldwell county, Ill.). Born Dec. 20, 1820, Alton, Ill. Came to Utah Sept. 3, 1850.
Married Susanna Cole Nov. 12, 1840, Alton, Ill. (daughter of Owen Cole of Illinois, pioneer Sept. 3, 1850). She was born June 13, 1827, Rochester, N. Y. Their children: William Dennis b. July 8, 1842, died; Henry L. b. Dec. 20, 1844, m. Rachel Baum; Joshua Martin b. Sept. 3, 1847, m. Sarah Cloward; Heber Carlos b. Oct. 23, 1849, died; Emily Anner b. Dec. 23, 1851, m. Jesse Buckner; Susanna b. 1852, m. John J. Baum; Orson b. May 20, 1854, died; Marion Albert b. Dec. 10, 1855, m. Anna Haws; Burdell Thomas b. Jan. 14, 1858, m. Martha Hall; Rachel Emma b. Jan. 21, 1860, m. William Graham; George Alvaro b. June 9, 1865, died.
Married Hanner Anderson Nov. 9, 1856, Provo, Utah (daughter of Ole Anderson and Anna Borkerson of Sweden, pioneers Sept. 4, 1855). She was born Sept. 5, 1839. Their children: Honner Andrew b. Oct. 20, 1858, m. Mary Ellen; Dennis J. b. April 7, 1861, m. Ada Draper; Norman Taylor b. July 14, 1863, m. Lucy Clinger; Anna Louisa b. July 7, 1867, m. Thomas Collins; Hanna Alwilda b. May 3, 1871, m. Gilbert York; Mary Caroline b. Oct. 11, 1873, m. George Powelson. Family home Provo, Utah.
Member 45th quorum seventies; missionary to eastern states. Sheriff Utah county. Farmer. Died Nov. 21, 1902, at Provo.

DAVIS, BURDELL THOMAS (son of Joshua Davis and Susanna Cole).
Married Martha Hall Sept. 28, 1876, at Provo (daughter of Henry Hall and Amanda Andrews, of St. Clair county, Ala., who came to Utah 1869). She was born June 24, 1858. Their children: Martha Ann b. Aug. 5, 1877; William Burdell b. Oct. 2, 1880; Dennis Raymond b. Aug. 19, 1882; Elnora L. b. March 31, 1885; Frona Myrtle b. April 12, 1888; Don R. b. September, 1889; Zora b. Dec. 5, 1893; Dean L. b. Feb. 11, 1898; Doss E. b. Nov. 21, 1899; Dell B. b. Nov. 21, 1902. Family home Pleasant View, Utah.
High priest; counselor to Bishop Levi A. Colvin, Pleasant View ward seven years; set apart bishop April 28, 1912; president elders' quorum seven years. Farmer and fruit grower.

DAY, M. L. (son of Melvin Davis and Permelia Lockwood of New York state). Born May 12, 1825, at Honeoye Falls, N. Y. Came to Utah 1859.
Married Mary Kenner 1854 in Missouri (son of Robert H. Kenner and Hannah Foster of Tennessee, pioneers 1857). She was born Feb. 2, 1832. Their children: Ella, died; Hay, m. Lucy Smith; Olive A., died; Martha, m. Newton Farr; Mary L., m. Ralph Savage; Robert Harrison, died. Family home, Salt Lake City, Utah.
Physician and surgeon. Died Aug. 3, 1882.

DAVIS, NATHAN. Born 1814 Rochester, Columbiana Co., Ohio. Came to Utah 1851.
Married Sarah Woolley 1836 (daughter of John Woolley of Chester county, Pa.). Their children: Edwin; Albert W. b. April 25, 1841, m. Melissa Jane Lambson 1865; David F. b. June 7, 1857, m. Martha M. Sheets; Sarah, m. John Thatcher. Family home 17th ward, Salt Lake City.
High priest; bishop of 17th ward. City sealer of weights and measures. Founder of Davis-Howe Foundry and Machine company. Machinist. Died Dec. 29, 1894.

DAVIS, ALBERT W. (son of Nathan Davis and Sarah W. Woolley). Born April 25, 1841, Rochester, Ohio. Came to Utah 1851.
Married Melissa Jane Lambson 1865, Salt Lake City (daughter of Alfred B. and Melissa J. Lambson of Nauvoo, pioneers Sept. 25, 1847, Elijah E. Fuller company). She was born Nov. 13, 1846. Their children: Albert J., m. Margerite D. Forsyth; Melissa E., m. Daniel F. Callister; Edna May; Nettie M., m. Robert H. Bradford; Wesley, d. aged 6 weeks; George A., m. Lucy S. Whittaker; Sarah W., m. Wilford Whittaker; Helen; Ethel. Family home Center ward, Salt Lake City.
Missionary to Sandwich Islands two years; high priest; patriarch; counselor in bishopric of 17th ward; bishop Center ward 14 years. Member city council. Foundryman and machine manufacturer.

DAVIS, GEORGE A. (son of Albert W. Davis and Melissa J. Lambson). Born July 7, 1877.
Married Lucy S. Whittaker Feb. 4, 1904, Salt Lake City (daughter of David M. Whittaker and Mary A. Smith of 16th ward, Salt Lake City). She was born Jan. 5, 1885. Their children: George W. b. Dec. 1, 1904; David M. b. Dec. 24, 1906; Willard W. b. April 14, 1908; Lucile b. Aug. 19, 1911. Family home Center ward, Salt Lake City.
Third president in council 109th quorum seventies; missionary to Sandwich Islands 1899-1903. Policeman under Hawaiian government.

DAVIS, DAVID F. (son of Nathan Davis and Sarah W. Woolley). Born June 7, 1857.
Married Martha M. Sheets March 26, 1885, Salt Lake City, Angus M. Cannon officiating (daughter of Elijah F. Sheets and Susannah Musser of Salt Lake City, pioneers Sept. 22, 1847, Perrigrine Sessions company). She was born May 3, 1861, 8th ward, Salt Lake City. Their children: Edna b. May 28, 1887; David F., Jr., b. March 9, 1890, m. Luella Howard; Olive b. April 11, 1893; Leah b. April 15, 1896. Family home Center ward, Salt Lake City.
High priest; high councilor; missionary to eastern states two years. Pattern maker.

DAVIS, JOHN R. (son of David Davis and Ann Thomas of Whitland, Wales. Born March 3, 1805. Came to Utah Sept. 15, 1861, Ira Eldredge company.
Married Mary Miles of South Wales (daughter of John Miles and Leah Phillips of South Wales). She was born March 19, 1813, and died April 25, 1889. Their children: William, David, Leah, and David, all died; Thomas, m. Mary Edwards, Jan. 2, 1860; John and William died; Leah, m. Hyrum Bennett North; Richard and Ann died. Family home Mill Creek, Utah.
High priest. Miner; contractor; farmer.

DAVIS, RILEY (son of James Ward Davis and Elizabeth J. Gordon of Fremont Co., Iowa). Born Nov. 26, 1851, Sidney, Fremont Co., Iowa. Came to Utah Sept. 4, 1866, Thomas E. Ricks company.
Married Jennette McMurrin Dec. 25, 1872, Salt Lake City (daughter of Joseph McMurrin and Margaret Lang of Glasgow, Scotland and Salt Lake City, pioneers 1856). She was born Dec. 23, 1854. Their children: James W. b. Dec. 23, 1882, m. Harriett E. Bybee June 5, 1907; Dora May b. April 22, 1885, m. William E. Larsen Sept. 2, 1903; Maud b. Feb. 18, 1884, m. Leander M. Boyce Dec. 13, 1905; Irvine b. Aug. 24, 1890. Family home, Clifton, Idaho.
Worked in Weber Canyon on first railroad in Utah 1867; pioneer to southern Idaho where he assisted in quelling early Indian disturbances. Missionary to southern states 1900-01; missionary to California.

DAVIS, WILLIAM (son of David Davis, born March 28, 1767, and Elinor Black). He was born Sept. 12, 1795, Union, Westmoreland county, Pa. Came to Utah 1848, Lorenzo Snow company.
Married Sarah McKee Oct. 3, 1822, who was born Sept. 22, 1799, and came to Utah with husband. Their children: David Varner b. Aug. 22, 1823, m. Caroline Angel March 26, 1847; Elinor Jane b. Nov. 21, 1824, m. William Summerville Feb. 4, 1844; Joseph McKee b. Dec. 12, 1826, m. Charlotte Condit Dec. 11, 1851; Sarah Bell b. April 15, 1829, m. John E. Fosgreen Feb. 15, 1849; James Spencer b. Feb. 24, 1831, m. Susannah Clapper March 2, 1856; John Fowler b. Nov. 26, 1832; Margaret Ann b. July 19, 1836, m. Elisha Grenard Dec. 25, 1855; Alma b. Dec. 14, 1838; Jared M. b. Nov. 30, 1839, m. Jane Osborne Nephi b. Dec. 28, 1842. Family home, Brigham City, Utah.

Married Christina Eureka Forsgren Feb. 20, 1854, Salt Lake City (daughter of John Olof Forsgren and Annie C. Holistran), who was born April 26, 1820, Geflea, Sweden. Their children: Abraham Peter b. Nov. 2, 1855, m. Lottie Van Noy Feb. 26, 1880; Oliver Frederic b. Jan. 2, 1859, m. Susannah Pulsipher Sept. 17, 1884; George William b. July 15, 1861, m. Eliza R. Watkins Nov. 11, 1885 and Vilate Cole Sept. 3, 1903. Family home Brigham City, Utah.
Settled at Brigham City 1850; ordained bishop of Brigham City 1851.

DAVIS, OLIVER F. (son of William Davis and Christina E. Forsgren). Born Jan. 2, 1859, Brigham City, Utah.
Married Susannah Pulsipher Sept. 17, 1884, Logan, Utah (daughter of Orson Hyde Pulsipher, pioneer 1852). She was born Jan. 27, 1865, Brigham City, Utah. Their children: Elfy A. b. Aug. 9, 1885, m. William C. Hubbard Aug. 15, 1904; May E. b. Dec. 8, 1887; Asa Oliver b. March 29, 1890; Jesse b. June 28, 1892; Zina Pulsipher b. Dec. 18, 1894; Zera Pulsipher b. March 15, 1899. Family home Brigham City, Utah.
Brigham City councilman; justice of peace at Avon, Utah. Ward clerk.

DAVIS, GEORGE WILLIAM (son of William Davis and Christina Eureka Forsgren). Born July 15, 1861, Brigham City.
Married Eliza Roxy Watkins Nov. 11, 1885 (daughter of William L. Watkins and Mary Hammond), who was born Oct. 5, 1863, Brigham City. Only child: Marguerite N. (adopted) b. March 6, 1892.
Married Vilate Cole Nuhn Sept. 3, 1903, Logan, Utah (daughter of Moroni Cole b. April 12, 1833, Jackson county, Mo., came to Utah 1850, Capt. Lake company, and Rhoda Ann Hubbard—who were married Sept. 28, 1854, Willard, Box Elder Co., Utah). She was born Sept. 16, 1859, at Willard, and was the mother of George C. Nuhn b. Jan. 10, 1890, and Leslie C. Nuhn b. Feb. 28, 1892.
Sunday school teacher; Sunday school superintendent Fourth ward Brigham city; missionary to New Zealand 1887-90; second counselor to Brigham Wright; president of Y. M. M. I. A.; moved to Avon, Utah, 1893; bishop of Avon ward 1895-04; alternate high counselor of Hyrum stake; missionary to eastern states 1905-07; ward clerk; high council June 6, 1908.

DAY, ABRAHAM (son of Abraham and Flavilla Day of Windhall, Vt.). Born Sept. 24, 1817, at Windhall. Came to Utah with other members of Mormon Battalion.
Married Elmira Buckley Feb. 16, 1838, in Pennsylvania (daughter of Noah Summers Buckley, pioneer, and Annie Newman of Council Bluffs, Iowa). She was born Jan. 30, 1820. Their children: Joseph Smith, m. Mary Anderson, m. Triny Bertelson; Melinda Ann, Harriet Jane. and Amelia, latter three d. infants; Jenette, m. Frank Whitmore; Ezra Jonas; Juliett, m. Henry Bonheu; Alice, m. Walter Christopherson; Abraham Nelson, m. Elizabeth Staker; Laura Annie, m. Ole Nielsen Tuft; Ira Alfred, m. Polly A. Noaks; Edward Summers, m. Maria Johnson; Ellie Jenora, d. infant; Albert Arlington, m. Emma Jean Loveless.
Married Charlotte Broomhead, Nov. 7, 1851, Salt Lake City. Their children: Dora Elmira, m. John Gustavus Johnson; Albert Demasaou, d. infant; Herbert Steven, m. Mary Wilcox; Eli Eseriah, m. Eliza Jane Staker and Euphrasia Cox; Benjamin Franklin d. infant; Hannah Flavilla, m. A. E. Smith; Ephraim Arthur; Harriet Ann, m. James Wilcox; George William, m. Ellis Staker; Harry Hazleton d. infant; Mary Ellen, m. Joseph Prows; m. Joseph Wilder; Joseph Abraham d. infant. Family resided Lawrence, Emery Co., Utah.
Counselor to Bishop Wm. J. Seeley of Mount Pleasant. Served in the Walker and Black Hawk wars. Built first grist mills in Springville, Mount Pleasant, and Nerhi. Farmer. Died April 30, 1890, at Lawrence.

DAY, HU_H (son of William Day and Betsy Johns). Born July 31, 1809, Leeds, Upper Canada. Came to Utah 1850, William Snow company.
Married Rhoda Ann Nicols 1830. Their children: Almeda; Mariah; William S.; John.
Married a widow, Boyce, with two children: John and Susan. Their children: Rhoda Jane; Arza; Rosana; Hugh; Florena; Laronzo.
Settled in 16th ward, Salt Lake City, where he lived until his death.

DAYBELL, FINITY (son of Samuel and Rebecca Ann Daybell of Lincolnshire, Eng.). Born March 14, 1815, in Lincolnshire. Came to Utah Sept. 20, 1864, Joseph S. Rawlins company.
Married Mary Draper March 10, 1841, Falkingham, Eng. (daughter of Richard Draper and Ann Green of Lincolnshire). She was born Jan. 6, 1820, Lincolnshire, Eng. and died Sept. 2, 1899. Their children: Robert b. July 3, 1842. m. Agnes Ann Bancroft; Annie b. April 14, 1846, m. William Webster; Susan b Aug. 14, 1849, m. John Pollard; m. George Carlile; Sarah b. March 11, 1851, m. George T. Giles; George T. b. Aug. 2, 1852, m. Sarah Ann Carlile; Elizabeth b. July 27, 1853, m. Franklin M. Giles; William b. Feb. 24, 1858, m. Annie Price. Family home Charleston, Utah.
High priest; ward teacher. Settled at Charleston Dec. 24, 1864, and died there Oct. 25, 1897.

PIONEERS AND PROMINENT MEN OF UTAH 841

DAYBELL, ROBERT (son of Finity Daybell and Mary Draper). Born July 3, 1842.
Married Agnes Ann Bancroft at Sheffield, Eng. (daughter of William Bancroft of Athlone, Ireland, and Mary Newham of Breaston, Derbyshire, Eng.). She was born April 26, 1847, and came to Utah Sept. 5, 1866, Samuel D. White company. Their children: Mary Hannah b. Jan. 9, 1866, m. George Price; Kate Elizabeth b. Jan. 11, 1867, m. Levi Carlos Snow. Family resided at Charleston and Provo, Utah.
While coming to Utah he left camp near the North Fork of the Platte river Aug. 16, 1866, hunting game for the immigrants, and has never been heard of since.

DAYBELL, WILLIAM (son of Finity Daybell and Mary Draper). Born Feb. 24, 1858, Derbyshire, Eng. Came to Utah Sept. 20, 1864, Joseph S. Rawlins company.
Married Annie Price Nov. 12, 1877, Heber City (daughter of James Price and Ann Powell of Staffordshire, Eng.; pioneers Sept. 21, 1864, Joseph S. Rawlins company). She was born June, 1858. Their children: John William b. Aug. 6, 1878, m. Jessie Fowers; Mary Ann b. May 5, 1880, m. Moroni Moulton; James Finity b. July 5, 1882, d. Sept. 25, 1882; Phoebe Elizabeth b. Dec. 8, 1883, m. John W. Simmons; Joseph Franklin b. Sept. 1, 1888, m. Hilda Dahlman; Myrtle b. Aug. 31, 1890, m. Archie Borhan; Violet B. b. Oct. 5, 1892; Lulla b. Oct. 21, 1894; Ernest b. March 15, 1899; Warren b. June 19, 1901. Family home Charleston, Utah.
Seventy; missionary to southern states 1885-87; bishop of Charleston ward; high counselor 1891-1901; Sunday school superintendent 14 years; president Y. M. M. I. A.; ward teacher; school trustee. County commissioner two years; town trustee.

DAYNES, JOHN (son of Thomas Daynes and Bridget Carter of Norwich, Norfolkshire, Eng.). Born April 15, 1831, at Norwich. Came to Utah Sept. 24, 1862, Homer Duncan company.
Married Eliza Miller 1850, in England (daughter of John Miller of Norwich, pioneer 1865). She was born May 20, 1831. Their children: Lyle; Joseph J., m. Mary J. Sharp.
Married Rebecca Bushby June 6, 1870, Salt Lake City (daughter of Thomas Bushby and Eater Rich of Hull, Eng., pioneers September, 1867). She was born Feb. 13, 1851. Their children: Ida Maud, m. L. W. Snow; John Frederick, m. Mary Anson; Della Rene, m. Lewis B. Hills; Royal Walter, m. Amy Rich; Arthur Vincent and Melvin Bushby, died; Dean Rich, m. Mina Rogers. Families resided Salt Lake City. Elder; choir leader. Jeweler and dealer in musical merchandise. Died March 30, 1905.

DAYNES, JOSEPH J. (son of John Daynes and Eliza Miller). Born April 2, 1851, Norwich, Eng. Came to Utah 1862.
Married Mary J. Sharp Nov. 18, 1872, Salt Lake City (daughter of Joseph Sharp and Jennette Condie of Salt Lake City). She was born Oct. 13, 1854. Their children: Joseph J. b. Nov. 7, 1873, m. W. Blanche Woodruff; Irene b. April 25, 1877, died; Harold Sharp b. July 15, 1881, m. Agnes Leona Taylor; Stella b. July 18, 1883, m. N. C. Christensen, Jr.; Raymond E. b. July 21, 1887; Marguerite b. June 21, 1891; Viletta b. May 22, 1896. Family home Salt Lake City.
High priest. Dealer in musical merchandise.

DAYNES, J. FRED (son of John Daynes and Rebecca Bushby). Born Dec. 7, 1872, Salt Lake City.
Married Mary Anson Sept. 28, 1904, Salt Lake City (daughter of Perry Anson and Jennie Lyon of Salt Lake City). She was born Sept. 10, 1880. Their children: Jean b. July 18, 1905; Marie b. Dec. 24, 1906; Arline b. Sept. 3, 1908; John b. Sept. 25, 1910. Family home, Salt Lake City, Utah.
Member 12th quorum seventies; missionary to England 1898-1900. Teacher; jeweler.

DAYTON, HYRUM (son of Abraham Dayton of Dayton, Ohio). Born at Dayton. Came to Utah 1849.
Married Permelia Bundy. Their children: Hyrum M., m. Ann Chamberlain; Lysander, m. Matilda Nay; William, m. Phenerata Whitaker; Moroni, m. Sarah Nichols; m. Elizabeth Nichols Berry; m. Hannah Cook; Permelia, m. Charles Bassett; Ann, m. Freeman Phippin; Myriah, m. William Higley; Lauvura, m. George Dockstater; Louisa Namy. Family home Council Bluffs, Iowa.
Married Syphia Thornton. Their children: Alma, m. Amanda Hudson; Charles, m. Sarah A. Berry; Joseph; William P., m. Josephine Dayton; Florenda, m. Hyrum Cummings; Louisa, m. Enoch Davis. Family home, Cedar Fort, Utah.
President 12th quorum elders at Nauvoo, Ill.

DAYTON, MORONI (son of Hyrum Dayton and Permelia Bundy). Born Sept. 3, 1834. Parkman Co., Ohio.
Married Sarah Nichols Aug. 12, 1855, Salt Lake City (daughter of Joseph Nichols and Sarah Newland), who was born March 28, 1834, Warwickshire, Eng. Their children: Francis Moroni b. Nov. 14, 1856, m. Isabella Follick Jan. 11, 1877; Charles Henry and William Henry b. April 5, 1859; Hyrum Alwin b. April 22, 1860, m. Louisa Neat; Sarah Jane b. Sept. 1, 1862; Theodore A. b. March 4, 1865, m. Lucy A. Neat; Etta Cereida b. July 20, 1867, m. Frederick E. Neat; Frederick b. Sept. 16, 1869; George Claudius b. April 26, 1872; Elizabeth Ann. m. Cook b. 5, 1874, m. William Quayle October, 1896; Permelia Mindwell b. Feb. 17, 1878, m. Henry L. George.
Married Hannah Cook 1860. Their children: Mary Saphronia b. Oct. 28, 1862, m. Boyd E. Wilcox; Helen Isolde b. Sept. 18, 1864, m. Joseph Johnson; Charlotte b. Aug. 8, 1866, m.

William Berry; Henrietta b. May 27, 1868, m. John H. Sparks; William Freeman b. March 20, 1870, m. Mary J. Follick; John Henry b. March 20, 1870, m. Caroline H. Sparks; Forest b. July 18, 1872; Oliver Lee b. Aug. 24, 1874, m. Laura J. Bird; Morette b. Oct. 13, 1876; Elmo b. March 6, 1879, m. Sarah J. Sparks; Marvin M. b. Aug. 1, 1881, m. Rebecca Bird.
Married Elizabeth Nichols Berry 1866. She was born April 7, 1847, Warwickshire, Eng. Their children: Selena b. Aug. 2, 1867, m. Hyrum Oakey; Alfred b. June 16, 1870. Families resided Cedar Fort, Utah.
Indian war veteran. Furnished a team for hauling stone for Salt Lake temple.

DAYTON, FRANCIS MORONI (son of Moroni Dayton and Sarah Nichols). Born Nov. 14, 1856, Cedar Fort, Utah.
Married Isabella Follick Jan. 11, 1877, Tooele, Utah (daughter of George A. Follick and Nancy Parker, the former pioneer September, 1868, the latter August, 1867). She was born Oct. 20, 1858, Mills Co, Iowa. Their children: George Francis b. Dec. 18, 1877, m. Lillian G. Lewis Nov. 5, 1902; Sarah Elizabeth b. June 23, 1880, m. William George Dec. 18, 1901; David Frederick b. March 28, 1882; Joseph Hyrum b. Nov. 5, 1884; Gertrude Isabella b. June 15, 1887, m. John Edmund Barkdull Oct. 9, 1907; William Nichols b. Oct. 16, 1891, m. Maud Allred Aug. 28, 1912; Nancy Josephine b. Dec. 16, 1893. Family home Dingle, Idaho.
Missionary to northern states; superintendent of Sunday school at Dingle five years. President Dingle Irrigation Co., 10 years.

DEAKIN, WILLIAM (son of William Deakin, born 1765, Big Sutton, Staffordshire, Eng., and Hannah Bates, born 1765, Little Sutton, Eng.). Born May 4, 1811, in Staffordshire. Came to Utah 1854.
Married Mary Jones (daughter of John Jones and Mary Roberts; former died in England, the latter in Wales). She was born Dec. 28, 1802, Wrexham, Eng., and came to Utah with husband. Their children: William Price b. July 11, 1832, m. Anna Maria Fordham Pepper May 9, 1868; John, m. Sarah Stone; Robert, m. Mary Celman; m. Margaret Thomas. Family resided England; Wellsville, Utah; Brooklyn, N. Y.; Connecticut.

DEAKIN, WILLIAM PRICE (son of William Deakin and Mary Jones). Born July 11, 1832, Brooklyn, N. Y.
Married Anna Maria Fordham Pepper May 9, 1868, Salt Lake City (daughter of Elijah Fordham and Anna Bibbins Chaffee, pioneers Oct. 13, 1850, Edward Hunter company). She was born May 21, 1844, Nauvoo, Ill. Their children: Mary Jane b. March 1, 1869, m. George Gardner March 12, 1887; John M. Feb. 19, 1871, m. Elizabeth Griffiths; Elijah James b. Oct. 4, 1873, died; Sarah Minerva b. Sept. 30, 1875, d. infant; Robert Price b. April 19, 1877, m. Maud House, holder; Lillian Delilah b. Nov. 14, 1879, m. Charles Schlicker; Serine May b. Sept. 26, 1881, m. William W. Jordan Dec. 17, 1900; Joseph Amos b. Oct. 18, 1883, m. Lulu George May 15, 1909; Charles Fremont b. Oct. 6, 1885; Lottie Adelia b. Dec. 7, 1888, m. Samuel Smith. Family home Wellsville, Utah.
Second lieutenant in home guards under Capt. John C. Reeder; Indian war veteran. Worked on Salt Lake theatre (1862) until completion; also worked on Logan temple.

DEAMER, JAMES (son of Charles Deamer born 1810, Whiteweil, Hertfordshire, Eng., and Elizabeth Foster born 1812, Kempton, Hertfordshire). He was born May 4, 1847, at Whitewell. Came to Utah October, 1866, Daniel Thompson company.
Married Annie Spackman Dec. 24, 1870 (daughter of William Spackman and Sarah Ward—married 1846, Pewsey, Wiltshire, Eng. Came to Utah in September, 1869, Capt. Ensign company). She was born May 25, 1851, and came to Utah with parents. Their children: James b. Oct. 7, 1871, d. Oct. 29, 1871; Mary Ellen b. Oct. 23, 1873, m. Isaac Lee Shupe May 24, 1893; William Charles b. March 20, 1877, m. Flora C. Waldram Oct. 22, 1902; Frederick John b. Aug. 13, 1880, d. Aug. 6, 1883; Sarah Elizabeth b. Dec. 16, 1885, d. same day; Nettie Luella b. March 30, 1887; Joseph Conwell b. June 18, 1890. Family home North Ogden, Utah.
Sunday school librarian several years; ward teacher; elder. Road supervisor two years, also constable two years at North Ogden.

DEANS, JAMES (son of David Deans and Helen Haswell of West Houses, Scotland). Born Feb. 14, 1844, West House, Scotland. Came to Utah 1852.
Married Susannah Hammond at Salt Lake City (daughter of Joseph Hammond and Elizabeth Egbert of St. George, Utah, pioneers 1848), who was born Jan. 10, 1850. Their children: James H., d. Oct. 26, 1897; Helen L., m. John Cook; head; Elizabeth D., m. Samuel Johnston; Joseph H., m. Elizabeth Fuller; David W., m. Lourainna Perry; Susannah D., m. H. George Wardle; Archibald H., d. child; Robert A., m. Jennie Wallace; Isabel I. Family home Woodruff, Ariz.
Elder. Justice of peace Woodruff, several forms. Minuteman in early Indian troubles. Farmer; railroad contractor. Died Dec. 23, 1897, Orangeville, Utah.

DEANS, DAVID WOODRUFF (son of James Deans and Susannah Hammond). Born Feb. 25, 1879, Woodruff, Ariz.
Married Louraina Perry March 13, 1912, at Salt Lake City (daughter of George W. Perry and Charlottie Fullmer of

Springville, Utah), who was born April 3, 1888, at Springville. Family home Vernal, Utah.
Assistant Sunday school superintendent; missionary to Kentucky, 1907; assistant superintendent Y. M. M. I. A.; counselor in deacons quorum; member 97th quorum seventies; ward clerk. Moved from Arizona to Uta 1893. Farmer.

DEANS, ROBERT ALEXANDER (son of James Deans and Susannah Hammond). Born Oct. 28, 1884, Woodruff, Ariz.
Married Jennie Wallace, May 12, 1908, at St. George, Utah (daughter of Hamilton Milton Wallace and Jane Staply of Toquerville, Utah, pioneers 1847). She was born Dec. 28, 1888. Their child: James Spencer b. Sept. 26, 1909.
Elder. School teacher. Miner.

DEAN, SAMUEL (son of James Dean and Emily Thatcher). Born June 4, 1830, Salt Fleet Township, Ontario, Canada. Came to Utah 1854.
Married Emma Norvill Sept. 25, 1856 (daughter of George Norvill and Catherine Force), who was born July 12, 1843, and came to Utah 1851. Their children: George Samuel b. Aug. 26, 1857, m. Alice S. Daniels Sept. 15, 1884; David Z. b. May 25, 1859, m. Alice A. Jenkins September, 1885; James R. b. April 1, 1861, m. Elizabeth Eveline; John A. b. Jan. 10, 1867; Mary T. b. Aug. 20, 1868, m. W. D. Olden; Rose E. b. Dec. 11, 1870; Martha M. b. June 22, 1872, m. George E. Worton. Family home North Ogden, Utah.
School trustee; manager first Co-op. store and captain of militia at North Ogden. Merchant. Died June 20, 1886.

DEAN, GEORGE SAMUEL (son of Samuel Dean and Emma Norvill). Born Aug. 26, 1857, North Ogden, Utah.
Married Alice S. Daniels Sept. 15, 1884, at North Ogden, who was born May 18, 1867, Tillyhead, Eng. Their children: George S. b. Sept. 14, 1885, m. Pearl Weatherman March 5, 1908; Ines E. b. March 23, 1888, m. J. P. Spackman Dec. 19, 1909; Irene E. b. March 23, 1888, m. William M. Alvord Jan. 22, 1908; John W. b. Nov. 1, 1889; Lester C. b. Sept. 30, 1891; Levi N. and B. Violet b. Aug. 20, 1897; Melba b. Feb. 9, 1906. Family home, North Ogden.
Member house of representatives Utah legislature 1905-07; notary public 1884-1913; lawyer, admitted to bar 1884; secretary N. O. I. and C. W. C. I. companies twenty years; printer and publisher; owner first printing plant in North Ogden; librarian North Ogden library.

DEARDEN, JOSEPH (son of James Dearden and Nancy Finney of Yorkshire, Eng.). Born Dec. 9, 1838, in Yorkshire. Came to Utah Sept. 20, 1868.
Married Nancy Hirst Nov. 15, 1867, in Yorkshire (daughter of John Hirst and Charlotte Brook of Yorkshire, pioneers Sept. 20, 1868). She was born Nov. 15, 1844. Their children: Emerald, m. William Hartley; Ellen, m. David F. Coon; Charlotte Hannah m. Jacob Hardman; Nancy Maud, m. Joseph Coon. Family home Pleasant Green, Utah.
High priest. Miner; farmer and stockraiser.

DEARDEN, WILLIAM (son of Thomas Dearden born in Lancashire, Eng., and Ann Forrest of Haydock, Lancashire). He was born July 7, 1826, at Haydock. Came to Utah Oct. 17, 1862, Henry W. Miller company.
Married Mary Greenall 1850 (daughter of James Greenall and Elizabeth Fairhurst), who was born 1826 and died 1852 in England. Their children: James b. May 12, 1851, m. Mary Bird Oct. 29, 1876; Thomas b. Dec. 20, 1852, m. Elizabeth Creechley Nov. 26, 1876.
Married Ann Agnes Arkwright November, 1855, Wigan, Lancashire (daughter of James Arkwright and Mary Buller, both of whom died in England). She was born March 7, 1824, at Wigan, Eng., and died July 8, 1889. Their children: Betsy E. b. April 27, 1861, m. John Creechley Dec. 23, 1880; Mary E. b. Sept. 7, 1864, m. George J. Kershaw Dec. 6, 1894; Sarah A. b. Feb. 7, 1868, d. 1886. Family home Porterville, Utah.
Presided over Wigan branch in England. Settled at Centerville 1862; moved to Porterville 1863, where he resided until his death Feb. 18, 1910.

DEARDEN, JAMES (son of William Dearden and Mary Greenall). Born May 12, 1851, in Lancashire, Eng.
Married Mary Bird Oct. 29, 1876, Henefer, Utah.

DEARDORFF, HARRY E. (son of John M. Deardorff and Elizabeth M. Pettigrew of Springfield, Ohio). He was born there June 26, 1860. Came to Utah Aug. 1, 1892.
Manufacturer of paper boxes in Salt Lake City.

DECKER, ISAAC (son of Peter and Hannah Decker of Holland). Born Nov. 29, 1800, in Holland. Came to Utah 1847.
Married Harriet Page Wheeler 1820 in New York state (daughter of Oliver and Hannah Wheeler), who was born Sept. 7, 1803, and came to Utah July 24, 1847, Brigham Young company. Their children: Lucy b. May 17, 1821, m. Brigham Young; Charles F. b. June 21, 1824, m. Vilate Young;

Harriet A b. March 13, 1826, m. Ephraim Hanks; Clarissa F. b. July 2, 1828, m. Brigham Young; Fanny M. b. April 24, 1830, m. Ferramorz Little; Isaac Perry b. Aug. 7, 1840, m. Elizabeth Ogden. Family home Provo Valley, Utah.
Farmer. Died 1873.

DECKER, HARLES FRANKLIN (son of Isaac Decker and Harriet Pre Wheeler). Born June 21, 1824, in New York state. Came to Utah Oct. 2, 1847, Jedediah M. Grant company.
Married Hate Young Feb. 24, 1847, Winter Quarters, Neb. (daughter f Pres. Brigham Young and Miriam Works), who was brn June 1, 1830. Their children: Miriam Vilate b. Jan. 15, 48, m. Louis L. Granger; Alice Luella b. July 21, 1851, m. Joseph Pitt; Charles Franklin b. May 24, 1854, m. Annie Thomas; Louie Isaac b. June 4, 1857; Brigham Lester b. Jan. 14, 859, m. Fannie Taylor; Patty Smoot, m. Emma Kammerms; Loretta Elmina b. Dec. 24, 1861, m. Heber C. Sorenson; is Elizabeth b. June 19, 1865; Fera Wallace b. Jan. 26, 18, m. Leila Rogers, m. Emma Decker. Family home Salt Lake City.
U. S. mail carrier 1851-55. Trail blazer and scout. Brought first pianin and door mill to Utah. Died March 22, 1901.

DECKER. ISAAC PERRY (son of Isaac Decker and Harriet Page Wheeler). Born Aug. 7, 1840, Winchester, Scott county, Ill. Came) Utah July 24, 1847, Brigham Young company.
Married lizabeth Ogden Jan. 3, 1860, Draper, Utah (daughter f Edward and Sarah Ogden of Salt Lake City, latter a pioneer October, 1853). She was born Sept. 24, 1842. Their child n: Charles F. b. Sept. 15, 1863, m. Elizabeth A. Dunn; Ferorz b. Nov. 8, 1868, m. Pearl Gay; Elizabeth b. July 30, 18, m. W. E. Brown; Joseph b. Aug. 22, 1874, m. Lily Parrie; Le Roy t. April 14, 1877, m. Milla Stevens; Roy b. Dec 27, 1879, m. Lottie Brown; Ira Otis b. Aug. 30, 1882, m. Soa King. Family home Salt Lake City.
Elder. Cried U. S. mail by pony express in early days.

DECKER. HARLES FRANKLIN (son of Isaac Perry Decker and Elizabeth Ogden). Born Sept. 15, 1863, Salt Lake City.
Married lizabeth A. Dunn Oct. 29, 1888, Provo, Utah daughter James Dunn and Hannah Fielding, pioneers 852). She as born Aug. 24, 1871. Their children: Charles Veri b. Aug 9, 1889, m. Essie Cook; Ethel b. June 12, 1891; Elmer J. b. sept. 1, 1893; Stanley D. b. Sept. 6, 1896; Harold Glenn b. Fe. 18, 1898; Edna b. Jan. 11, 1902; Alice b. July 12, 1905; Do b. Feb. 12, 1911. Family home Provo.
Member ovo city council two terms; mayor two terms—the first to elected under the commission form of government, sisted in locating springs and supervised collecting water and installing new water system for Provo city.

DEE. THOMAS HILL (son of John Dee). He was born 11, 1812, M thyr Tydfil, Glamorganshire, W. Utah Sept. 1860, James D. Ross company.
Married lizabeth Reese May 8, 1877, at ton, who was born Nov.
March 25, 1 2, Ogden.
13, 1839, m. ames Ta
25, 1912, m. liza W
b. Nov. 10, 14, m.
d. Nov. 10, 116. Fan
Pioneer d d Aug.

DEE, THOS. DUN
Elizabeth Iese). B
thenshire, 5 th Wales
Married Anie Tay
(daughter f John Tay
Eng., and d Dec. 4, 1
ders, born Spt. 18, 1828,
July 6, 1854—married May
17, 1860, ca.ain of his c
1852, at Loockgalen. 7
Feb. 27, 187, d. Dec. 18, 1
m. Richard Porter Aug
27, 1878, m mbrose A. S
9, 1880, m. Jank E. Hig
b. May 3, 83,
Emily b. F., 12
21, 1910; La rence
Rosabelle C a, b.
Settled a Ogden
schools 1871905;
1877-85; juste of
87; membercity c
city fire depament
member sta board
motors of at budi
a part of the S. P. L
intendent 2 years.
Ogden 12 yers.

DE LA MAE, PE
March 18, 1 4, an
St. Helier, rsey.
April 3, 18 in
November, 52, c
Married ary
Christopher ark
1823. Their hild
Francis b. F. 1

lus b. 1851, died; Esther Jane b. March 11, 1855, m. ples Walters May 5, 1872; Joseph Wilam b. Sept. 1859, m. e Atkin 1884; Hyrum b. April 6, 186 died.
arried Mary Chevalier 1851, St. Loui Mo. (daughter of lef Mathew Chevalier and Elizabet Le Corneu), who born Feb. 20, 1823, Trewly, Jerseysland. Their chili: Francis b. 1853, died; Elizabeth . Dec. 8, 1854, m. 1 W. Tate 1875; Sophia b. Aug. 10, 187, m. John McLaws 27, 1876; John b. April 8, 1859, m. Agnes McKendrick 12, 1879; Mary Eliza b. Jan. 6, 186 m. Alvin McCulp Dec. 23, 1880; Thomas b. July 23, 134, m. Loretta McDrick Dec. 23, 1884; Alice b. Feb. 7, 366, m. James Gow- Feb. 12, 1885.
arried Jeanetta Meiklejohn July, 185 at Salt Lake City ighter of Robert Meiklejohn and Mry McLackan, pio- 's Oct. 24, 1855, Milo Andrus compay). She was born d 13, 1840, in Dumbartonshire, Sc land. Their chili: Robert M. b. Oct. 6, 1859, d. 1860; Idia M. b. March 2, ; Mary Agnes b. Feb. 8, 1867, died; Josephine M. b. Jan. 1869, m. William W. H. Boyce Aug. , 1891; Colin M. b. 11, 1871. m. Caroline Green June 2: 1892; Franklin M. ov. 16, 1873, m. Ellen Holstein Jan.1, 1893; Ann Jean- a b. Dec. 30, 1875. m. Henry W. Drabay June 8, 1898; 'enee Philip b. July 12, 1884. Famlcs resided Tooele , Utah.
rought machinery for sugar mill to merica.

LA MARE, PHILIP FRANCIS (son c Philip de la Mare Mary Parkins). Born Feb. 16, 18!, Jersey, Channel nds.
arried Elvina Lucas Mallet June 16, 80, Salt Lake City ughter of George Philip Mallet and Jane Lucas, who e to Utah in 1869). She was born Fb. 11, 1856, also in ley. Their children: Mary Jane b. ov. 16, 1881, died; el M. b. March 14, 1885; Mabel Cla. b. June 23, 1887, : Theophilus George b. Sept. 10, 18!; Alma Joseph b. . 8, 1892. Family home Tooele, Utah

NISON, HANS (son of Rasmus Denisc. born March 1788, lgendrup, Fyen Island, Denmark, id Inger Mortens. n 1872 in Sweden). He was born July 0, 1824, Gjentofte, enhaexen Amt, Denmark. Came to lah Sept. 30, 1853, n Forsgren company.
arried Johanah Christofferson Nov. 2, 1845, who was n Dec. 4, 1825. Their children: Rasrus b. Dec. 6, 1846, an. 25, 1847; Jens b. Jan. 10, 1849. , Johanne Madsen , 21, 1875; Keratine b. Sept. 3, 1851 d. Sept. 10, 1851; traim b. March 19, 1853, m. Mary Ell Johnson Jan. 12, ; Hans b. July 29, 1856, m. Mary enes Braithwaite , 8, 1878; Joseph b. March 19, 1860, mMarie Larsen Dec. 880; Johanah b. Jan. 8, 1863, m. Chstian Henningson 1891; Hyrum b. Jan. 6, 1866, m. Barbara Stutzenegger , 7, 1891. Family home Manti, Utah.
arried Anne Margrette Hansen Oct. 3, 1873, Salt Lake y, who was born June 24, 1839, Sjellar, Denmark. Their ldren: Christian M. b. July 14, 1874, n Mary C. Apelgren r. 2, 1898.
arried Anna Nielsen Nov. 3, 1880, St. George, Utah, who s born Nov. 13, 1846, Sanded, Sjollan Denmark. Their ldren: Johannes b. June 14, 1882, d. ct. 20, 1887; Inger rie b. July 19, 1883; Emanuel b. June 1, 1889.
ettled at Manti 1853, where he serv: as ward teacher. listed in building the Salt Lake, Mati and St. George ples. Died Jan. 13, 1904.

NISON, EPHRAIM (son of Hans Deson and Johanah ristofferson). Born March 19, 1853, a New Orleans, La. ne to Utah with parents.
arried Mary Ellen Johnson Jan. 12,1873, Manti, Utah ; was born Aug. 16, 1851, Stockport, Cshire, Eng. Their ldren: Mary Elizabeth b. Dec. 16, 1873,n. Rasmus Nielson ril 20, 1898; Joseph Ephraim b. Nov. 1, 1875, m. Electia auregard March 28, 1956; Robert Tran b. July 22, 1877, Amanda Willardson Dec. 19, 1906; Aba Arthur b. June 1880, m. Hazel A. Voorhees June 5, 117; James Nephi b. c. 9, 1882, d. Sept. 22, 1883; Ellen Hanrh b. Aug. 18, 1884, Jefferson Bradley June 14, 1905; Willin Hans b. May 15, 16, m. Mary Jensen June 30, 1909; Gree b. May 24, 1888, Oct. 5, 1903; Margret b. Sept. 11, 192. Family home rling, Utah.
ishop's counselor, Sterling ward, 189:1910.

ENNING, JAMES (son of Henry Deaing and Martha chols of Colford, Eng.). Born Marc 2, 1830, Cofford, lmerston, Somersetshire, Eng. Cane to Utah Oct. 17, 53, Christopher Arthur company.
Married Sarah Merrifield July 8, 18(Tahowan, Mon- uthshire, Eng. (daughter of Uthur Derrifield and Jane nning of Kilmerston Parish). She as born Aug. 19, 32, and came to Utah with husban Their children: ne b. May 4, 1850, m. Joseph Astle De 5, 1866; James H. an. 25, 1853, m. Rosanna Williams D. 21, 1874; Joseph thur b. July 28, 1855, m. Lydia Dahlrom Dec. 9, 1887; hn A. b. Nov. 4, 1857, m. Dora M. Haison Nov. 4, 1890; ary M. b. Feb. 24, 1860, m. George G. Campbell Feb. 24, 78; Ephraim M. b. Dec. 3, 1862, m. Lyd Dahlstrom; Mar- a M. b. Jan. 3, 1864, m. Dan W. Kent D. 9, 1880; Elizabeth b. Feb. 11, 1866, m. Ayriah F. Willia March 4, 1885; Dan . b. April 11, 1869, m. Sarah A. Jones I, 16, 1898; Philip . b. June 9, 1870, m. Mary A. Ashdown Fb. 24, 1894; Elvira , b. Feb. 28, 1872, m. Ullock Gleed July 24, 1889; Uriah M.

b. June 22, 1874, m. Agnes Henderson; William M. b. 1876, d. Dec. 24, 1878. Family resided at Bountiful and Logan, Utah, and Montpelier (1863-77) and Malad, Idaho.
Assisted in bringing immigrants to Utah. Took part in Echo canyon war. Elder. Died May 2, 1898, Malad, Idaho.

DENNING, JAMES HENRY (son of James Denning and Sarah Merrifield). Born Jan. 25, 1853, on board ship in Irish Channel.
Married Rosanna Williams Dec. 21, 1874, at Salt Lake City (daughter of John Jones Williams and Mary Jones of Brigham City, Utah, and Malad, Idaho; former came to Utah Oct. 17, 1853, Christopher Arthur company, the latter October 1856, Edward Bunker company). She was born Dec. 13, 1859, at Brigham City. Their children: James Henry b. Nov. 3, 1875, m. Martha K. Wetzel Oct. 28, 1897; Mary W. b. Oct. 8, 1877, m. Cadwalander Owens Dec. 1, 1897; John W. b. Oct. 2, 1881, m. Almira Flitton June 1, 1904, m. Eva Ainsworth Dec. 10, 1908; Sarah Adell W. b. July 28, 1884, m. Peter H. Westergard Dec. 21, 1904; Rosanna W. b. Aug. 15, 1887, m. Edwin L. Jennings Oct. 8, 1902; Effie W. b. June 3, 1891, d. Nov. 14, 1898; Martha b. Dec. 19, 1902; George W. b. Dec. 18, 1894; Oliver W. b. Nov. 17, 1897. Family home Iona, Idaho.
Married Emma Jane Squires March 22, 1883, Salt Lake City (daughter of Henry A. Squires and Emma C. Slade, pioneers 1856 and 1857, respectively—married Oct. 21, 1858, Salt Lake City). She was born Oct. 22, 1868, Salt Lake City. Their children: Matilda Jane b. Oct. 17, 1884, m. John W. Duncan Nov. 24, 1904; Myrtle b. Oct. 8, 1887; Jeddie S. b. Aug. 18, 1890, m. Cornelia Moss Sept. 12, 1911; Ester b. April 15, 1893; Harriet b. Nov. 17, 1894; Lucy b. Nov. 8, 1896; Olive b. Oct. 31, 1898; Clara Bell b. July 6, 1900; Emeline b. Dec. 20, 1902; Pearl b. Jan. 21, 1905; Echo b. June 26, 1909.
High priest; high councilor in Bingham stake; counselor to Bishop James P. Harrison of St. John ward. Farmer.

DENNIS, WILLIAM TAYLOR. Born Jan. 18, 1810, in Lincoln county, Tenn. Came to Utah 1855, Gilbert I. Gavin company.
Married Tabitha Bankhead Dec. 8, 1836, in Tennessee. She was born Dec. 13, 1809. Their children: Dorothy Jane b. June 16, 1838, m. David P. Rainey Feb. 9, 1857; Sina; Mary E.; Grace; Delia C.; Tabitha.

DERRICK, ZACHARIAH WISE. Born March 1, 1814, Heysham, Somersetshire, Eng. Came to Utah in 1847.
Married Mary Shepherd, who was born Aug. 12, 1812, Longthorp, Yorkshire, Eng. Their children: Mary Ann Shepherd b. Jan. 8, 1837, d. Nov. 3, 1870; Zachariah Thomas b. Jan. 19, 1840; Elizabeth b. Nov. 29, 1842; John b. Aug. 19, 1847; Ursula Shepherd b. Sept. 21, 1851; William Henry b. April 23, 1854; Alfred Matthews b. April 9, 1856.

DERRICOTT, CHARLES (son of John Derricott and Tittle, of Shropshire, Eng.). Born 1806, Shropshire. Came to Utah Sept. 2, 1868, Daniel D. McArthur com Married Mary Ashley in England (daughter of Y Ashley and Martha Larrens of Shropshire, Eng.). Sh born Aug. 8, 1805. Their children: Sarah; Martha; Ch Ann; Susannah; Josiah; Mary Ann; Caroline; Rebecca. died March, 1885, Liberty, Idaho.

DERRICOTT, JOSEPH (son of Charles Derricott and Mn Ashley). Dorn Aug. 25, 1849, Wolverhampton, Staffordshir Eng. Came to Utah with parents.
Married Marintha Watkins Sept. 11, 1871 (daughter of Thomas Watkins and Lydia Meyers), who was born Sept. 1, 1852, and came to Utah in '71. Their children: Joseph T. b. Sept. 13, 1872, m. Lydi 'l ht 1903; Josiah b. 1874, m. Alice Butler 1906; Char 1 76, m. Leverna Hymas 1901; Alitha n b. May, 18 nk Wood 1900; Ors b. Nov. 1, 1880, m. Effie Kin ry L b. Jan. 2, 18: m. Joseph Hoge; Martha A 17, 1885; Paulina Aug. 1, 1887, m. Frank Ski In b. April 27, 1 William b. Sep. 19, 1892. . Liberty, Idaho. Married Annie E. Gami 1901, at Salt City (daughter of Elizab d Thomas Car of Southampton, Sept. 9, 1871, at Sou 6, 1869). ti, b. March 20, 1902; Ila 81, 1903; I. Oct. 13, 1904; Ascheal Ray 06; Mildre 1908; Elizabeth Wyona 11. Family erly, Idaho.
Drove herd of lame c across pl school superintendent I 81-1902

DESPAIN, SOLOMON dale county, Ala. (Cannon company.
Family home was i Married Susan D 17, 1843, in Arkansas. 1862, m. William Tho 1864, m. Hannah E. A 23, 1866, m. F. S. Cow 1869, m. Prudence G.

Springville, Utah), who was born April 3, 1888, at Springville. Family home Vernal, Utah.
Assistant Sunday school superintendent; missionary to Kentucky, 1907; assistant superintendent Y. M. M. I. A.; counselor in deacons' quorum; member 97th quorum seventies; ward clerk. Moved from Arizona to Utah 1893. Farmer.

DEANS, ROBERT ALEXANDER (son of James Deans and Susannah Hammond). Born Oct. 28, 1884, Woodruff, Ariz. Married Jennie Wallace, May 12, 1908, at St. George, Utah (daughter of Hamilton Milton Wallace and Jane Staply of Toquerville, Utah, pioneers 1847). She was born Dec. 28, 1888. Their child: James Spencer b. Sept. 26, 1909.
Elder. School teacher. Miner.

DEAN, SAMUEL (son of James Dean and Emily Thatcher). Born June 4, 1830, Salt Fleet Township, Ontario, Canada. Came to Utah 1854.
Married Emma Norvill Sept. 25, 1856 (daughter of George Norvill and Catherine Force), who was born July 12, 1843, and came to Utah 1851. Their children: George Samuel b. Aug. 26, 1857, m. Alice S. Daniels Sept. 15, 1884; David Z. b. May 25, 1859, m. Alice A. Jenkins September, 1885; James R. b. April 1, 1861, m. Elizabeth Eveline; John A. b. Jan. 10, 1867; Mary T. b. Aug. 20, 1868, m. W. D. Olden; Rose E. b. Dec. 11, 1870; Martha M. b. June 22, 1872, m. George E. Worton. Family home North Ogden, Utah.
School trustee; manager first Co-op. store and captain of militia at North Ogden. Merchant. Died June 20, 1886.

DEAN, GEORGE SAMUEL (son of Samuel Dean and Emma Norvill). Born Aug. 26, 1857, North Ogden, Utah.
Married Alice S. Daniels Sept. 15, 1884, at North Ogden, who was born May 18, 1867, Tillyhead, Eng. Their children: George S. b. Sept. 14, 1885, m. Pearl Weatherman March 5, 1908; Ines E. b. March 23, 1888, m. J. P. Spackman Dec. 19, 1909; Irene E. b. March 23, 1888, m. William M. Alvord Jan. 22, 1908; John W. b. Nov. 1, 1889; Lester C. b. Sept. 30, 1891; Levi N. and B. Violet b. Aug. 20, 1897; Melba b. Feb. 9, 1906. Family home, North Ogden.
Member house of representatives Utah legislature 1905-07; notary public 1884-1913; lawyer, admitted to bar 1884; secretary N. O. I. and C. W. C. I. companies twenty years; printer and publisher; owner first printing plant in North Ogden; librarian North Ogden library.

DEARDEN, JOSEPH (son of James Dearden and Nancy Finney of Yorkshire, Eng.). Born Dec. 9, 1838, in Yorkshire. Came to Utah Sept. 20, 1868.
Married Nancy Hirst Nov. 15, 1874, in Yorkshire (daughter of John Hirst and Charlotte Brook of Yorkshire, pioneers Sept. 20, 1868). She was born Nov. 15, 1844. Their children: Emerald, m. William Hartley; Ellen, m. David F. Coon; Charlotte Hannah m. Jacob Hardiman; Nancy Maud, m. Joseph Coon. Family home Pleasant Green, Utah.
High priest. Miner; farmer and stockraiser.

DEARDEN, WILLIAM (son of Thomas Dearden born in Lancashire, Eng., and Ann Forrest of Haydock, Lancashire). He was born July 7, 1826, at Haydock. Came to Utah Oct. 17, 1862, Henry W. Miller company.
Married Mary Greenall 1850 (daughter of James Greenall and Elizabeth Fairhurst), who was born 1826 and died 1852 in England. Their children: James b. May 12, 1851, m. Mary Bird Oct. 29, 1876; Thomas b. Dec. 20, 1852, m. Elizabeth Creechley Nov. 26, 1876.
Married Ann Agnes Arkwright November, 1855, Wigan, Lancashire (daughter of James Arkwright and Mary Buller, both of whom died in England). She was born February 7, 1824, at Wigan, Eng., and died July 8, 1889. Their children: Betsy E. b. April 27, 1861, m. John Creechley Dec. 23, 1880; Mary E. b. Sept. 7, 1864, m. George J. Kershaw Dec. 6, 1894; Sarah A. b. Feb. 7, 1868, d. 1886. Family home Porterville, Utah.
Presided over Wigan branch in England. Settled at Centerville 1862; moved to Porterville 1863, where he resided until his death Feb. 18, 1912.

DEARDEN, JAMES (son of William Dearden and Mary Greenall). Born May 12, 1851, in Lancashire, Eng.
Married Mary Bird Oct. 29, 1876, Henefer, Utah.

DEARDORFF, HARRY E. (son of John M. Deardorff and Elizabeth M. Pettigrew of Springfield, Ohio). He was born there June 26, 1860. Came to Utah Aug. 1, 1892.
Manufacturer of paper boxes in Salt Lake City.

DECKER, ISAAC (son of Peter and Hannah Decker of Holland). Born Nov. 29, 1800, in Holland. Came to Utah 1847.
Married Harriet Page Wheeler 1820 in New York state (daughter of Oliver and Hannah Wheeler), who was born Sept. 7, 1803, and came to Utah July 24, 1847, Brigham Young company. Their children: Lucy b. May 17, 1821, m. Brigham Young; Charles F. b. June 21, 1824, m. Vilate Young; Harriet A. b. March 13, 1826, m. Ephraim Hanks; Clarissa C. b. July 22, 1828, m. Brigham Young; Fanny M. b. April 24, 1830, m. Peramorz Little; Isaac Perry b. Aug. 7, 1840, m. Elizabeth Ogden. Family home Provo Valley, Utah.
Farmer. Died 1873.

DECKER, CHARLES FRANKLIN (son of Isaac Decker and Harriet Page Wheeler). Born June 21, 1824, in New York state. Came to Utah Oct. 2, 1847, Jedediah M. Grant company.
Married Vilate Young Feb. 24, 1847, Winter Quarters, Neb. (daughter of Pres. Brigham Young and Miriam Works), who was born June 1, 1830. Their children: Miriam Vilate b. Jan. 15, 1848, m. Louis E. Granger; Alice Luella b. July 23, 1851, m. Joseph Pitt; Charles Franklin b. May 24, 1854, m. Annie Thomas; Louie Isaac b. June 4, 1857; Brigham LeRoy b. Jan. 14, 1859, m. Fannie Taylor; Patty Smoot, m. Emma Kannermann; Loretta Elmina b. Dec. 24, 1861, m. Heber C. Sorenson; Lois Elizabeth b. June 19, 1865; Fera Wallace b. Jan. 26, 1872, m. Leila Rogers, m. Emma Decker. Family home Salt Lake City.
U. S. mail carrier 1851-55. Trail blazer and scout. Brought first planing and door mill to Utah. Died March 22, 1901.

DECKER, ISAAC PERRY (son of Isaac Decker and Harriet Page Wheeler). Born Aug. 7, 1840, Winchester, Scott county, Ill. Came to Utah July 24, 1847, Brigham Young company.
Married Elizabeth Ogden Jan. 3, 1860, Draper, Utah (daughter of Edward and Sarah Ogden of Salt Lake City, latter a pioneer October, 1853). She was born Sept. 26, 1842. Their children: Charles F. b. Sept. 15, 1863, m. Elizabeth A. Dunn; Feramorz b. Nov. 8, 1868, m. Pearl Gay; Elizabeth b. July 30, 1871, m. W. E. Brown; Joseph b. Aug. 23, 1874, m. Lily Parrish; Le Roy b. April 14, 1877, m. Milla Stevens; Roy b. Dec. 2, 1879, m. Lottie Brown; Ira Otis b. Aug. 30, 1882, m. Nora King. Family home Salt Lake City.
Elder. Carried U. S. mail by pony express in early days.

DECKER, CHARLES FRANKLIN (son of Isaac Perry Decker and Elizabeth Ogden). Born Sept. 15, 1863, Salt Lake City.
Married Elizabeth A. Dunn Oct. 29, 1888, Provo, Utah (daughter of James Dunn and Hannah Fielding, pioneers 1852). She was born Aug. 24, 1871. Their children: Charles Veri b. Aug. 9, 1889, m. Essie Cook; Ethel b. June 12, 1891; Elmer J. b. Sept. 1, 1893; Stanley D. b. Sept. 6, 1895; Harold Glenn b. Feb. 18, 1898; Edna b. Jan. 11, 1902; Alice b. July 12, 1905; Beth b. Feb. 18, 1911. Family home Provo.
Member Provo city council two terms; mayor two terms—the first to be elected under the commission form of government. Assisted in locating springs and supervised collecting water and installing new water system for Provo city.

DEE, THOMAS HILL (son of John Dee). He was born May 11, 1812, Merthyr Tydfil, Glamorganshire, Wales. Came to Utah Sept. 3, 1860, James D. Ross company.
Married Elizabeth Reese May 28, 1837, at Swansea, Glamorganshire (daughter of Thomas Reese and Margaret Dolton), who was born Nov. 25, 1812, at Swansea, and died March 25, 1892, Ogden, Utah. Their children: Annie b. Aug. 13, 1839, m. James Taylor March 23, 1861; James L. b. Feb. 25, 1842, m. Eliza Webb, m. Ellen Brown; Thomas Duncombe b. Nov. 10, 1844, m. Annie Taylor; Elizabeth b. Aug. 13, 1851, d. Nov. 10, 1866. Family home Ogden.
Pioneer died Aug. 21, 1877.

DEE, THOMAS DUNCOMBE (son of Thomas Hill Dee and Elizabeth Reese). Born Nov. 10, 1844, Llanelly, Caermarthenshire, South Wales.
Married Annie Taylor April 10, 1871, Salt Lake City (daughter of John Taylor, born Sept. 7, 1823, at Chester, Eng., and died Dec. 4, 1884, at Salt Lake City, and Ann Sanders, born Sept. 18, 1828, at Lostockgalen, where she died July 6, 1854—married May 25, 1848, former a pioneer Sept. 17, 1860, captain of his company). She was born Nov. 4, 1852, at Lostockgalen. Their children: Thomas Reese b. Feb. 27, 1873, d. Dec. 18, 1894; Annie Maude b. Nov. 20, 1875, m. Richard B. Porter Aug. 11, 1907; Mary Elizabeth b. Jan. 27, 1878, m. Ambrose A. Shaw Dec. 9, 1903; Margaret b. July 9, 1880, m. Frank E. Higginbotham Jan. 1, 1906; Edith May b. May 3, 1883, m. Glenn Mack July 10, 1901; Florence Emily b. Feb. 12, 1886, m. George S. Barker June 17, 1908; Rosabelle Cora b. July 11, 1888, m. Joseph F. Barker Dec. 21, 1910; Lawrence Taylor b. Aug. 3, 1891.
Settled at Ogden 1860. Closely identified with public schools 1870-1905; president school board; city assessor 1877-85; justice of peace, police judge and alderman 1883-87; member city council 1891-92, during which time the city fire department building and city jail were constructed; member state board of equalization 1896-1905. One of promoters of and builders of Utah & Pacific railroad 1891, now a part of the S. P. L. A. & S. L. R. R. Sunday school superintendent 30 years. Vice-president First National bank of Ogden 12 years.

DE LA MARE, PHILIP (son of Francis de la Mare, born March 18, 1794, and Jane Esther Ahier, born 1794, both at St. Helier, Jersey, Channel Islands, Eng.). He was born April 3, 1823, in Grouvil Parish, Jersey. Came to Utah November, 1852, captain of his own company.
Married Mary Parkins September, 1846 (daughter of Christopher Parkins and Isabel Plviss), who was born May 16, 1823. Their children: Mary Jane b. May 16, 1848, died; Philip Francis b. Feb. 16, 1849, m. Elvina Mallet June 16, 1880; The-

ophilus b. 1851, died; Esther Jane b. March 11, 1855, m. Charles Walters May 5, 1872; Joseph William b. Sept. 1859, m. Alice Atkin 1884; Hyrum b. April 6, 1867, died.
Married Mary Chevalier 1851, St. Louis, Mo. (daughter of Daniel Mathew Chevalier and Elizabeth Le Corneu), who was born Feb. 20, 1823, Trewly, Jersey Island. Their children: Francis b. 1853, died; Elizabeth b. Dec. 8, 1854, m. John W. Tate 1875; Sophia b. Aug. 10, 1857, m. John McLaws Dec. 27, 1876; John b. April 8, 1859, m. Agnes McKendrick Feb. 12, 1879; Mary Eliza b. Jan. 6, 1861, m. Alvin McCuistion Dec. 23, 1880; Thomas b. July 23, 1864, m. Loretta McKendrick Dec. 23, 1884; Alice b. Feb. 7, 1866, m. James Gowans Feb. 12, 1885.
Married Jeanetta Meiklejohn July, 1857, at Salt Lake City (daughter of Robert Meiklejhon and Mary McLackan, pioneers Oct. 24, 1855, Milo Andrus company). She was born April 13, 1840, in Dumbartonshire, Scotland. Their children: Robert M. b. Oct. 6, 1859, d. 1860; Lydia M. b. March 2, 1865; Mary Agnes b. Feb. 8, 1867, died; Josephine M. b. Jan. 30, 1869, m. William W. H. Boyce Aug. 1, 1891; Colin M. b. Jan. 11, 1871, m. Caroline Green June 22, 1892; Franklin M. b. Nov. 16, 1873, m. Ellen Holstein Jan. 8, 1893; Ann Jeannetta b. Dec. 30, 1875, m. Henry W. Droubay June 8, 1898; Clarence Philip b. July 12, 1884. Families resided Tooele City, Utah.
Brought machinery for sugar mill to America.

DE LA MARE, PHILIP FRANCIS (son of Philip de la Mare and Mary Parkins). Born Feb. 16, 1849, Jersey, Channel Islands.
Married Elvina Lucas Mallet June 16, 1880, Salt Lake City (daughter of George Philip Mallet and Jane Lucas, who came to Utah in 1869). She was born Feb. 11, 1856, also in Jersey. Their children: Mary Jane b. Nov. 16, 1881, died; Isabel M. b. March 14, 1885; Mabel Clara b. June 23, 1887, died; Theophilus George b. Sept. 10, 1890; Alma Joseph b. Feb. 8, 1892. Family home Tooele, Utah.

DENISON, HANS (son of Rasmus Denison, born March 1788, Skalgendrup, Pyen Island, Denmark, and Inger Mortens, Copenhagen Amt, Denmark. Came to Utah Sept. 30, 1853, John Forsgren company.
Married Johanah Christofferson Nov. 22, 1845, who was born Dec. 4, 1825. Their children: Rasmus b. Dec. 6, 1846, Jan. 25, 1847; Jens b. Jan. 10, 1849, m. Johanne Madson Nov. 21, 1875; Kerstine b. Sept. 3, 1851, d. Sept. 10, 1851; Ephraim b. March 19, 1853, m. Mary Ellen Johnson Jan. 12, 1873; Hans b. July 29, 1856, m. Mary Agnes Braithwaite Nov. 8, 1878; Joseph b. March 19, 1860, m. Marie Larsen Dec. 3, 1880; Johanah b. Jan. 8, 1863, m. Christian Henningson April 1891; Hyrum b. Jan. 6, 1866, m. Barbara Stutzenegger Jan. 7, 1891. Family home Manti, Utah.
Married Anne Margrette Hansen Oct. 13, 1873, Salt Lake City, who was born June 24, 1839, Sjelland, Denmark. Their children: Christian M. b. July 14, 1874, m. Mary C. Apelgren Nov. 2, 1898.
Married Anna Nielsen Nov. 3, 1880, St. George, Utah, who was born Nov. 13, 1846, Sanded, Sjelland, Denmark. Their children: Johannes b. June 14, 1882, d. Oct. 20, 1887; Inger Marie b. July 19, 1883; Emanuel b. June 19, 1885.
Settled at Manti 1853, where he served as ward teacher. Assisted in building the Salt Lake, Manti and St. George temples. Died Jan. 13, 1904.

DENISON, EPHRAIM (son of Hans Denison and Johanah Christofferson). Born March 19, 1853, at New Orleans, La. Came to Utah with parents.
Married Mary Ellen Johnson Jan. 12, 1873, Manti, Utah (daughter of Robert and Elizabeth Johnson, pioneers 1853). She was born Aug. 16, 1851, Stockport, Cheshire, Eng. Their children: Mary Elizabeth b. Dec. 16, 1873, m. Rasmus Nielson April 20, 1898; Joseph Ephraim b. Nov. 13, 1875, m. Electia Beauregard April 26, 1906; Robert Francis b. July 22, 1877, m. Amanda Williardson Dec. 19, 1906; Alma Arthur b. June 23, 1880, m. Hazel A. Voorhees June 5, 1907; James Nephi b. Dec. 3, 1882, d. Sept. 23, 1883; Ellen Amanda b. May 24, 1885, m. Jefferson Bradley June 14, 1905; William Hans b. May 16, 1886, m. Mary Jensen June 30, 1909; Grace b. May 24, 1888, d. Oct. 5, 1903; Margret b. Sept. 11, 1892. Family home Sterling, Utah.
Bishop's counselor, Sterling ward, 1893-1910.

DENNING, JAMES (son of Henry Denning and Martha Nichols of Colford, Eng.). Born March 2, 1830, Colford, Kelmerston, Somersetshire, Eng. Came to Utah Oct. 17, 1853, Christopher Arthur company.
Married Sarah Merrifield Aug. 8, 1849, Tahowan, Monmouthshire, Eng. (daughter of Uriah Merrifield and Jane Denning of Kilmerston Parish). She was born Aug. 19, 1832, and came to Utah with husband. Their children: Jane b. May 4, 1850, m. Joseph Astle Dec. 9, 1866; James H. b. Jan. 25, 1853, m. Rosanna Williams Dec. 21, 1874; Joseph Arthur b. July 28, 1855, m. Lydia Dahlstrom Dec. 9, 1887; John A. b. Nov. 4, 1857, m. Dora M. Rawson Nov. 4, 1890; Mary M. b. Feb. 24, 1860, m. George C. Campbell Feb. 24, 1878; Ephraim M. b. Dec. 9, 1862, m. Lydia Dahlstrom; Martha M. b. Jan. 3, 1864, m. Dan W. Kent Dec. 9, 1880; Elizabeth M. b. Feb. 14, 1866, m. Avriah F. Williams March 4, 1885; Dan M. b. April 14, 1869, m. Sarah A. Jones Feb. 6, 1885; Philip M. b. June 9, 1870, m. Mary A. Ashdown Feb. 24, 1896; Elvira M. b. Feb. 28, 1872, m. Lilock Gheed July 24, 1889; Uriah M.

b. June 22, 1874, m. Agnes Henderson; William M. b. 1876, d. Dec. 24, 1878. Family resided at Bountiful and Logan, Utah, and Montpelier (1863-77) and Malad, Idaho.
Assisted in bringing immigrants to Utah. Took part in Echo canyon war. Elder. Died May 2, 1898, Malad, Idaho.

DENNING, JAMES HENRY (son of James Denning and Sarah Merrifield). Born Jan. 25, 1853, on board ship in Irish Channel.
Married Rosanna William Dec. 21, 1874, at Salt Lake City (daughter of John Jones Williams and Mary Jones of Brigham City, Utah, and Malad, Idaho; former came to Utah Oct. 17, 1853, Christopher Arthur company). She was born Dec. 13, 1859, at Brigham City. Their children: James Henry b. Nov. 3, 1875, m. Martha K. Wetzel Oct. 28, 1897; Mary W. b. Oct. 8, 1877, m. Cadwalander Owens Dec. 1, 1897; John W. b. Oct. 17, 1881, m. Almira Flittom June 1, 1904, m. Eva Ainsworth Dec. 10, 1908; Sarah Adell W. b. July 28, 1884, m. Peter H. Westergard Dec. 21, 1904; Rosanna W. b. Aug. 15, 1887, m. Edwin L. Jennings Oct. 8, 1902; Effie W. b. June 3, 1891, d. Nov. 14, 1898; Martha b. Dec. 19, 1902; George W. b. Dec. 13, 1894; Oliver W. b. Nov. 17, 1897. Family home Iona, Idaho.
Married Emma Jane Squires March 22, 1883, Salt Lake City (daughter of Henry A. Squires and Emma C. Slade, pioneers 1856 and 1857, respectively—married Oct. 21, 1858, Salt Lake City). She was born Oct. 22, 1868, Salt Lake City. Their children: Matilda Jane b. Oct. 17, 1884, m. John W. Duncan Nov. 24, 1904; Myrtle b. Oct. 8, 1887; Jeddie S. b. Aug. 18, 1890, m. Cornelia Moss Sept. 12, 1911; Ester b. April 15, 1893; Harriet b. Nov. 17, 1894; Lucy b. Nov. 6, 1896; Olive b. Oct. 31, 1898; Clara Bell b. July 6, 1900; Emeline b. Dec. 20, 1902; Pearl b. Jan. 21, 1905; Echo b. June 26, 1909.
High priest; high councilor in Bingham stake; counselor to Bishop James P. Harrison of St. John ward. Farmer.

DENNIS, WILLIAM TAYLOR. Born Jan. 18, 1810, in Lincoln county, Tenn. Came to Utah 1855, Gilbert I. Gavin company.
Married Tabitha Bankhead Dec. 8, 1836, in Tennessee. She was born Dec. 13, 1809. Their children: Dorothy Jane b. June 16, 1838, m. David P. Rainey Feb. 9, 1857; Sina; Mary E.; Grace; Delia C.; Tabitha.

DERRICK, ZACHARIAH WISE. Born March 1, 1814, Heysham, Somersetshire, Eng. Came to Utah in 1847.
Married Mary Shepherd, who was born Aug. 12, 1812, Longthorp, Yorkshire, Eng. Their children: Mary Ann Shepherd b. March 3, 1837, d. Nov. 3, 1870; Zachariah Thomas b. Jan. 19, 1840; Elizabeth b. Nov. 29, 1842; John b. Aug. 19, 1847; Ursula Shepherd b. Sept. 21, 1851; William Henry b. April 23, 1854; Alfred Matthews b. April 9, 1856.

DERRICOTT, CHARLES (son of John Derricott and Mary Tittle, of Shropshire, Eng.). Born 1806, Shropshire, Eng. Came to Utah Sept. 2, 1868, Daniel D. McArthur company.
Married Mary Ashley in England (daughter of William Ashley and Martha Larrens of Shropshire, Eng.). She was born Aug. 8, 1805. Their children: Sarah; Martha; Charles; Ann; Susannah; Josiah; Mary Ann; Caroline; Rebecca. He died March, 1885, Liberty, Idaho.

DERRICOTT, JOSEPH (son of Charles Derricott and Mary Ashley). Born Aug. 25, 1849, Wolverhampton, Staffordshire, Eng. Came to Utah with parents.
Married Marintha Watkins Sept. 11, 1871 (daughter of Thomas Watkins and Lydia Mathews), who was born June 1, 1852, and came to Utah in 1871. Their children: Joseph T. b. Sept. 13, 1872, m. Lydia A. Slight 1903; Josiah b. 1874, m. Alice Buttler 1906; Charles b. 1876, m. Leverna Higman 1901; Althara b. Sept. 15, 1878, m. Frank Wood 1900; Orson b. Nov. 1, 1880, m. Effie King 1902; Mary L. b. Jan. 2, 1883, m. Joseph Hoge; Martha Ann b. May 17, 1885; Paulina b. Aug. 1, 1887, m. Frank Skinner 1908; Ida b. April 27, 1890; William b. Sept. 19, 1892. Family home Liberty, Idaho.
Married Annie E. Gambling April 4, 1901, at Salt Lake City (daughter of Elizabeth Powell and Thomas Gambling of Southampton, Eng.—married July 26, 1869). She was born Sept. 9, 1871, at Southampton. Their children: Marintha b. March 20, 1902; Harold b. May 31, 1903; Raymond b. Oct. 13, 1904; Ascheal Ray b. May 13, 1906; Mildred b. July 20, 1908; Elizabeth Wyona b. Oct. 26, 1911. Family home Liberty, Idaho.
Drove herd of lame cows and oxen across plains. Sunday school superintendent Liberty ward 1881-1902.

DESPAIN, SOLOMON JOSEPH. Born Dec. 3, 1823, Lauderdale county, Ala. Came to Utah Aug. 16, 1861, David H. Cannon company.
Married Ruth Amelia Newell (daughter of Asael Newell). Family home was in Tennessee.
Married Susan Dean May 17, 1862, Salt Lake City (daughter of William Dean and Nancy Mullen), who was born Nov. 17, 1843, in Arkansas. Their children: Martha E. b. Feb. 23, 1863, m. William Thompson Sept. 27, 1878; L. E. b. Sept. 2, 1864, m. Hannah E. A. Butler Feb. 20, 1889; Effie E. b. Nov. 23, 1866, m. F. S. Cowley Dec. 11, 1889; George F. b. Sept. 21, 1869, m. Prudence G. Butler Sept. 20, 1899; Anna L. b. Sept.

844   PIONEERS AND PROMINENT MEN OF UTAH

1, 1871, m. Alva J. Butler Feb. 20, 1895; Charles R. b. Nov. 5, 1873; De Bart b. Sept. 17, 1875, m. Bertha Kenner Sept. 21, 1899; Frank P. b. Sept. 2, 1878, m. Margaret Butler Nov. 5, 1897; A. R. b. Dec. 28, 1880; Ida E. b. Dec. 12, 1883, m. Amos E. Jensen March 1906. Family home Granite, Utah.
Bishop Granite ward 1877-86. Justice of peace and also postmaster at Granite. Died Feb. 17, 1895.

DEVEY, JOHN (son of William Devey and Ann Kershaw, of Wolverhampton, Staffordshire, Eng.). Born Jan. 28, 1849, at Wolverhampton. Came to Utah Sept. 24, 1868, Edward T. Mumford company.
Married Hannah A. A. Timms June 20, 1868, at Liverpool, Eng. (daughter of William Timms and Mary Ann Avery, of Birmingham; the former came to Utah Aug. 16, 1871, the latter Aug. 1, 1873). She was born April 24, 1851. Their children: Fannie Ann b. Aug. 19, 1869, m. Samuel O. Strong Dec. 15, 1886; Alfred John b. Sept. 29, 1871, m. Elizabeth Marsh 1892; Albert William b. Aug. 3, 1873, d. Oct. 11, 1873; Joseph Franklin b. Oct. 27, 1874, m. Mary Ruth Oakey Aug. 23, 1889; Amy Demarias b. Nov. 8, 1876, m. Hyrum Smith Jan. 16, 1907; John b. Aug. 28, 1878, m. Olive Marsh Feb. 23, 1900; Hannah Alice Avery b. Nov. 9, 1880, m. Samuel A. Hutchings Sept. 27, 1900; Walter Avery b. Sept. 14, 1882, m. Maacha Ellen Boley March 19, 1902. Family home Alpine, Utah.

DEWEY, JOHN H. (son of Ashbell Dewey and Harriet Adams of Little River, Mass.). Born Feb. 7, 1832 at Little River. Came to Utah Sept. 26, 1847, A. O. Smoot company.
Married Ann Lamoreaux 1855, at Salt Lake City (daughter of Andrew Lamoreaux and Isabella Wilson of Glasgow, Scotland—pioneers 1848). She was born April 8, 1834. Their children: Annette, m. Thomas K. Stephens; Luella; Emily; John H., m. Annie Smith; Caroline, m. Arthur Moulton; Abigail, m. Oscar Bourne; William G., d. aged 19; Charles H., d. aged 27; Isabella. Family home Salt Lake City.
Freighter; carpenter; sawyer; miner.

DIAMOND, JAMES (son of James and Nancy Diamond of Ireland). Born June 22, 1833, Crossland, County Kerry, Ireland. Came to Utah 1847, independent company.
Married Mary Ann Burton Aug. 14, 1859 (daughter of John Burton and Harriet Bradshaw, pioneers 1852, Mark Hall company). She was born June 14, 1843, and came to Utah with parents. Their children: James Burton b. Aug. 6, 1860; John Michael b. Jan. 18, 1862, d. March 14, 1866; Theodore Edwin b. Nov. 20, 1863; Harriet Izola b. Aug. 13, 1865, d. Jan. 22, 1868; William Henry b. March 27, 1867; Thomas Byron b. July 26, 1869, d. March 26, 1870; Alice Lillian b. May 9, 1871; Martin Vaughn b. June 18, 1873, d. Sept. 26, 1879; Leonard Lorus b. May 21, 1875, m. Harriet Pearl Lee; David Delbert b. Oct. 25, 1877; Nancy Mabel b. Oct. 28, 1879; Marvin Vell b. March 27, 1882; Mark Irvin b. Aug. 22, 1884.
Settled at Manti, where he did the first plowing. Moved to Springville, where he died April 12, 1908.

DIAMOND, LEONARD LORUS (son of James Diamond and Mary Ann Burton). He was born May 21, 1875, Springville, Utah.
Married Harriet Pearl Lee April 29, 1903, at Mapleton, Utah (daughter of John H. Lee and Emma Kelsie). Their children: Leonard Lee b. May 23, 1904; Louise b. Aug. 14, 1906, d. July 25, 1910; Russel b. Aug. 7, 1908.

DICKSON, BILLA (son of John Dickson, born Aug. 24, 1781, and Mary Henderson, born April 11, 1775, both in New York state). He was born March 8, 1816, Elizabeth, Upper Canada. Came to Utah October 1852, Captain Walker company.
Married Mary Ann Stoddard (daughter of Judson Stoddard and Samantha Hodge), who was born Oct. 18, 1817, and came to Utah with husband. Their children: Samantha Jane b. Feb. 25, 1838, m. Everett Van Norton; Albert Douglass b. Jan. 26, 1840, m. Nancy E. Shipley, m. Harriet R. Flint; Judson b. April 20, 1843; Alvira Aurelia b. Jan. 26, 1846, m. Eliza J. Henderson; William Henderson b. March 22, 1850, m. Martha Slade; John Henry b. Nov. 13, 1853, m. Avilda Hickman. Family home Rickville, Utah.
Settled at American Fork 1852, and opened a blacksmith shop; moved to Davis county 1853, and to Richville, 1863. Watermaster and justice of peace at Richville. Died Jan. 30, 1878, Salt Lake City.

DICKSON, ALBERT DOUGLAS (son of Billa Dickson and Mary Ann Stoddard). Born Jan. 26, 1840, in Porter county, Ind.
Married Nancy Elizabeth Shipley March 28, 1561, Kaysville, Utah (daughter of John Shipley and Sarah Perkins, who was born Dec. 12, 1840, in Illinois). Their children: Mary Alvira b. May 20, 1862; Albert b. April 12, 1865, m. Emma Francom; Lucy Louisa b. Oct. 4, 1867, m. Henry Lee; John Sheldon b. Sept. 18, 1870, m. Jennie Creager; William Jasper b. May 24, 1875, m. Annie Belle Creager; George Henry b. Sept. 10, 1878, d. June 6, 1898; James Douglass b. Aug. 17, 1880; Moroni Denzil b. Sept. 4, 1882. Family home Richville, Utah.

Married Harriet Rosella Flint (daughter of William Flint and Mary Jane Goodridge, married Dec. 24, 1850, pioneers 1848 and 1850, respectively). She was born Jan. 22, 1861, Bountiful, Utah. Their children: Abel Josiah b. Dec. 3, 1880, m. Annie Cottom Dec. 4, 1901; Asa Leonard b. Sept. 29, 1883; Nancy Elizabeth b. Oct. 1, 1885, m. George Hansen Jan. 10, 1912; Rufus b. Jan. 23, 1887; Sophia b. Sept. 12, 1888, m. David Weaver Feb. 23, 1910; Harriet b. Sept. 15, 1890; Bert Stoddard b. May 2, 1892; Jared b. Nov. 24, 1896; Eibern b. Aug. 4, 1899; Ford b. Oct. 6, 1902. Family home Richville, Utah.
Assisted in bringing immigrants and freight to Utah. Settled at Richville 1863 and assisted in building canals and wagon roads. Water master, road commissioner and trustee at Richville. Bishop Richville ward 36 years.

DIEHL, CHRISTOPHER (son of Aldoth Diehl and Barabah Meisinger of Germany). Born March 22, 1831, Butzbach, Grand Duchy of Hesse-Darmstadt, Germany. Came to Utah April 1, 1866.
Married Ann Bothardt May 13, 1860, San Francisco, Cal. (daughter of Christopher and Elizabeth Bothardt of Germany), who was born Aug. 6, 1835. Their children: Anna, m. Frank B. Willis; Christopher B. m. Lena Preston.
Member of city council two terms; assessor and collector of water rates. Grand Secretary Grand Lodge of Utah, F. & A. M., from 1882-1886. Treasurer and Secretary 1870-74 and 1882 until time of his death. Died Sept. 17, 1912, Salt Lake City, Utah.

DIEHL, CHRISTOPHER BOTHARDT (son of Christopher Diehl and Anna Bothardt). Born Jan. 10, 1874, Salt Lake City.
Married Lena Preston at Salt Lake City (daughter of Robert Preston and Mary Perry of England). Their children: Christopher Bothardt, Jr., b. July 11, 1903; Mary Mavia b. Feb. 28, 1906; Dorothy, b. Sept. 24, 1909. Family home, Salt Lake City.
City judge; prosecuting attorney; attorney at law.

DILLE, DAVID B. (son of David B. Dille and Harriet Lucretia Welch of Ohio). Born in Ohio. Came to Utah October, 1850, Captain Bennett company.
Married Harriet L. Welch in Ohio. Their children: Israel; Arvis C. b. Oct. 26, 1839, m. Mary Ann Bradley; Ruth L. Feb. 1848, m. Thomas E. Ricks 1865.

DILLE, ARVIS C. (son of David B. Dille and Harriet Lucretia Welsh). He was born Oct. 26, 1839, in Indiana. Came to Utah 1850, with father.
Married Mary Ann Bradley March 15, 1863, Logan, Utah (daughter of John Bradley and Mary Ann Williams, pioneers Sept. 24, 1862, Homer Duncan company). She was born June 10, 1845, Staffordshire, Eng. Their children: Mary Elizabeth b. Jan. 8, 1864, m. Daniel Cochrane Aug. 1887; Arvis Thomas b. Jan. 6, 1866; Anna L. b. April 8, 1868; Clara E. b. July 4, 1870; Minerva b. Sept. 10, 1872, m. Charles B. Valentine Sept. 12, 1893; Hiram b. Nov. 3, 1874, m. Rachel Walker June 1, 1898; Martha b. March 30, 1877, m. Wilford E. Anderson Oct. 9, 1896; John b. April 15, 1879, m. Adell Gibbs Dec. 16, 1903; Nancy Jane b. Sept. 19, 1881, m. James Cherry Feb. 28, 1901; George H. b. Nov. 7, 1885, m. Rosa Klinger; Harriet L. b. Jan. 12, 1888, m. George A. Watson Nov. 2, 1908; Ida Maud b. Feb. 12, 1890, m. Amos Gallup Nov. 2, 1908.

DILLE, HIRAM (son of Arvis C. Dille and Mary Ann Bradley). Born Nov. 3, 1874, Hyrum, Utah.
Married Rachel Walker June 1, 1898, Neeley, Idaho (daughter of Rufus Walker and Cyntha Ann Mikesell, pioneers Aug. 1, 1860, David H. Cannon company). She was born Nov. 14, 1877, Little Cottonwood, Utah. Their children: Vernice b. March 10, 1899; Vera b. May 11, 1902; Bernice W. b. Jan. 10, 1906; Norma b. April 9, 1907; Baby b. Nov. 25, 1910; Grace Dille b. July 19, 1912.

DITTMORE, HENRY (son of George Nicholas Dittmore and Mania Heiner). Born June 8, 1836, Saxony, Germany. Came to Utah 1861.
Married Rachel Smuin March 11, 1864, Salt Lake City (daughter of Thomas Smuin and Sarah Hook of England) who was born May 6, 1844, and died May 8, 1908. Their children: Henry Arthur, died; Caroline Mary, m. Thomas Stratton; George Nicholas, m. Minnie B. York; Eliza m. David Call; David Martin, m. Annie Rosengreen; Ann Eva m. Benjamin Heaps; Emily Ellesa, m. Andrew A. Johnson Lewis Henry, m. Lorintha Iverson; Esther Sarah, m. Samuel H. Kirk; Louisa, died; Alice. Family home Pleasant Grove, Utah.
Elder. Tailor. Early settler in Morgan county. Died January 6, 1893.

DITTMORE, LEWIS HENRY (son of Henry Dittmore and Rachel Smuin). Born Dec. 20, 1880, at Pleasant Grove, Utah
Married Eda Lorintha Iverson Feb. 12, 1908, at Salt Lake City (daughter of Alma Nicholas Iverson and Sarah Jan Tuckett of Pleasant Grove), who was born April 4, 1887 Their children: Marlin Lewis b. Feb. 17, 1909.
Missionary to Australia and New South Wales; war teacher. Farmer.

DIXON, HENRY ALDOUS (son of John Henry Dixon, born May 28, 1786, died April, 1874, London, Eng., and Judith Boardman, born Nov. 16, 1796, at London, and died Sept. 23, 1865, both of South Africa). He was born March 14, 1835, Grahamstown, Cape Colony, South Africa. Came to Utah Sept. 12, 1857, Jesse B. Martin company.
Married Sarah DeGrey January, 1865, Salt Lake City (daughter of John DeGrey—born 1804, died 1845—and Maria Brooks—born April 10, 1805, died April 2, 1876, both of Dudley, Worcestershire, Eng.—pioneers Sept., 1857, Jesse B. Martin company). She was born Jan. 27, 1845, at Dudley. Their children: Henry Alfred b. Nov. 14, 1865, d. July 1, 1867; John DeGrey b. July 16, 1867, m. Sarah Ann Lewis; Arthur De-Grey b. Oct. 5, 1869, m. Catherine M. Morgan; Maria Louisa b. Jan. 5, 1872, m. Arthur Nichols Taylor; Ernest b. Dec. 22, 1873, m. May Paintnc; Charles Owen b. Nov. 22, 1875, m. Virginia Beckstead; Walter b. Nov. 15, 1877, m. Louie Maiben; LeRoy b. Oct. 16, 1881, m. Electa Smoot; Arnold b. May 30, 1884, m. May Banks.
Married Mary Annie Smith April 13, 1869, at Salt Lake City (daughter of Robert Smith and Mary Ann Brown of Hull, Yorkshire, Eng., latter a pioneer Sept. 26, 1868). She was born Oct. 3, 1852, at Hull. Their children: Alice Smith b. April 29, 1870, m. Jabez W. Dangerfield; Sarah Anne b. Dec. 7, 1871, m. Alexander McConachie; William Aldous b. April 21, 1873, m. Harriett Hands; Robert Smith b. Nov. 10, 1874, d. Dec. 18, 1874; Albert Frederick b. March 31, 1876, m. Sena Rasmussen; Parley Smith b. June 9, 1878, m. Mary Etola Dangerfield; Harriet Amelia b. May 24, 1882, m. George W. West. Family home Provo, Utah.
Member 45th quorum seventies; missionary to England and Africa 1860-64, and again to England 1879-81. Provo city treasurer and councilman; Utah county treasurer 1872-78. Secretary Provo Woolen Mills; manager Provo branch Z. C. M. I.; bookkeeper. Died April 4, 1884.

DIXON, JOHN DeGREY (son of Henry Aldous Dixon and Sarah DeGrey). Born July 16, 1867, at Salt Lake City.
Married Sarah Ann Lewis Sept. 18, 1889, at Manti temple, Utah (daughter of William John Lewis and Jane Davis of Wales—pioneers with Dan Jones handcart company). She was born April 23, 1868. Their children: Henry Aldous b. June 29, 1890; John Williams b. Sept. 6, 1892, d. June 6, 1894; Stanley Lewis b. March 3, 1895; Rulon Sterlin b. Sept. 9, 1898; Maud b. Feb. 28, 1901; Lucian DeGrey b. June 17, 1903, d. March 22, 1904; Grant b. March 30, 1905, d. Dec. 18, 1905. Family resided Salt Lake City and Provo, Utah.
High priest; missionary to Viriginia 1896-97. City councilman and city recorder at Provo; secretary Provo school district, also of state land board; state treasurer 1901-05. Bookkeeper Provo Lumber Company; secretary and treasurer Taylor Bros. Co.; cashier Farmers' and Merchants' bank at Provo. Bishop's counselor, 30th ward, Salt Lake City; president 45th quorum seventies; Sunday school superintendent, president and secretary Y. M. M. I. A., 3d ward, Provo; member high council.

DIXON, WILLIAM WILKINSON (son of John Dixon of England). Born Nov. 14, 1818, Cumberlandshire, Eng. Came to Utah 1851.
Married Sabra Lake Aug. 16, 1842, Hancock county, Ill. (daughter of James Lake and Millie Smith of Canada, pioneers 1850, James Lake company). She was born July 17, 1824. Their children: Henry b. June 1, 1843, m. Amelia Garser; Harvey b. Sept. 12, 1844, m. Kittie W. Pritchett, m. Susie Harmon; Emma Jane b. Sept. 2, 1846, m. Dudley Chase; Lydia Ann b. Oct. 22, 1848; Mary Lucy b. April 12, 1850, m. Cyrus Rawson; Electa F. b. June 2, 1852, m. Lyman Skeen; Sarah E. b. Oct. 1, 1861, m. Charles D. Drown; Riley G. b. Nov. 9, 1866, m. Mary Ann Taylor; Alfred b. Jan. 3, 1869, m. Ida Ellen Harris; Dudley; James; Bailey; John; Esther; Sabra; latter six died. Family home Harrisville, Utah.
High priest. Farmer. Died June 10, 1891.

DIXON, ALFRED (son of William Wilkinson Dixon and Sabra Lake). Born Jan. 3, 1869, Harrisville, Utah.
Married Ida Ellen Harris May 15, 1901, Salt Lake City (daughter of Martin H. Harris and Louise Sargent of Harrisville, Utah), who was born Nov. 27, 1875, at Harrisville. Only child: Fern Louise b. Sept. 20, 1910. Family home Harrisville.
Missionary 1897-99; high councilor North Weber stake.

DIXON, HENRY (son of William W. Dixon and Sabra Lake). Born June 1, 1843, Scott county, Ill.
Married Amelia Jane Garner Nov. 13, 1871, Salt Lake City (daughter David Garner and Dolly Durfee of North Ogden, pioneers 1850). She was born Aug. 23, 1872, d. July 8, 1881; David W. b. April 20, 1874, d. April 21, 1874; Amelia E. b. Feb. 20, 1876, m. C. U. Meyers Jan. 8, 1902; Riley L. b. Jan. 27, 1878, m. Finnis Fife Oct. 30, 1901; Etta L. b. Sept. 22, 1880; Earnest E. b. April 30, 1882, m. Myrtle Adler Nov. 1, 1905; Chloa A. b. Oct. 19, 1884; Albert G. b. Sept. 30, 1887, d. March 7, 1889; Alma A. b. April 6, 1890, d. infant; Coral Carlson b. April 18, 1897. Family home Clifton, Idaho.
Assisted in bringing immigrants to Utah in 1868. High priest. Farmer. Died July 30, 1908, Preston, Idaho.

DIXON, EARNEST E. (son of Henry Dixon and Amelia Jane Garner). Born April 30, 1882, Clifton, Idaho.
Married Myrtle Alder Nov. 1, 1905, Logan, Utah (daughter of Alfred W. Adler and Sarah Jensen of Preston, Idaho,

pioneers Sept. 23, 1853). She was born Oct. 26, 1884, at Preston. Their children: Henry Adler b. Oct. 19, 1908; Alfred Adler b. May 1, 1910; Douglas Alder b. Sept. 27, 1911. Family home Banida, Idaho.
Missionary to northern states 1905-07; president Y. M. M. I. A. 1908-09; 2nd counselor Clifton ward bishopric 1910-12.

DOBBIE, JOHN (son of John and Jane Dobbie of Lanarkshire, Scotland). Born May 24, 1826. Came to Utah 1853.
Married Ellen Livingston (daughter of James and Christina Livingston), who was born May 30, 1831, and came to Utah Oct. 2, 1855, Richard Ballantyne company. Only child: William Dobbie Kuhre (adopted) b. Jan. 21, 1863, m. Alice A. Drown April 14, 1886.
Pioneer mining and sawmillman.

DOBSON, JOSEPH (son of Thomas Dobson and Ellen Ravenscroft, both of Outtonlew, Chestershire, Eng.). Born June, 1805, in Chestershire. Came to Utah 1848, with part of Mormon Battalion.
Married Elizabeth Frain 1836 in Chestershire (daughter of Thomas Frain). She was born 1801 and died 1843 at Nauvoo, Ill. Their children: Thomas F., m. Annie G. McIntyre 1854; William, m. Ann Hill 1860; Joseph, died. Family resided Salt Lake City, Lehi, and Richmond, Utah.
Seventy and high priest. Assisted in building temple at Nauvoo; member Mormon Battalion. Settled at Salt Lake City 1848; moved to Lehi, and from there to Richmond. Lived in Fredonia, Ariz., 30 years. Died 1864 Richmond, Utah.

DOBSON, THOMAS (son of Joseph Dobson and Elizabeth Frain). He was born Feb. 19, 1837, Macclesfield, Chestershire, Eng. Came to Utah 1850, Warren Foote company.
Married Annie G. McIntyre 1855, Farmington, Utah (daughter of Robert McIntyre and Isabell Watson, of Dannockburn, Scotland—pioneers 1848). She was born 1837 and died 1867. Their children: Thomas M. b. June 1856, m. Amanda Gee; Joseph b. 1857, m. Agnes Beeby; William M. b. 1860, m. Elee Egar; Henry b. 1863, d. aged 15; Adam b. 1867; Isabell, died.
Married Elizabeth Wiseman 1881, St. George, Utah. Their children: Jesse b. 1883, m. Eufrasia Cocks 1909; George b. 1885, m. Rhoda Ogden, 1909; John b. 1891; Annie m. Ray Botton 1908; Elizabeth b. 1887, m. John Pearson 1911; Ellen b. 1888, m. Orson Jensen; Susie.
Member 40th quorum seventies. School teacher. Worked on Salt Lake and St. George temples. Drove a herd of stock across the plains. Settled at Richmond; moved to Farmington, then to Kanab, Utah. Was first settler in Fredonia, Ariz., and resided there for past 30 years.

DOMVILLE, THOMAS (son of William Domville of Liverpool, Eng.). Born March 6, 1794. Came to Utah Oct. 4, 1851, Morris Phelps company.
Married Mary Peters Dec. 20, 1834, at Liverpool (daughter of Edward Peters and Elizabeth Pierce of Flencher, Eng.). She was born July 10, 1796. Their children: Peter; Jane; Elizabeth Emma, m. Frederick W. Rose. Family home 7th ward, Salt Lake City.
Asst. Sunday school superintendent; block teacher; high priest. Carpenter and builder. Died April 4, 1869.

DONALDSON, JOHN (son of William Donaldson, born at Haddington, and Rachael Notman of Slateford, near Edinburgh, Scotland). Born Sept. 30, 1842, London, Eng. Came to Utah 1863, Wm. B. Preston company.
Married Mary Ann Kent April 21, 1864 (daughter of James Kertin Kent and Alice Dickson, who were married in England). She was born Aug. 21, 1840, and came to Utah 1863, Thomas E. Ricks company. Their children: William Kent b. Dec. 21, 1865; Mary Alice K. b. Oct. 12, 1867, m. John E. Butt; Marion Elizabeth b. Aug. 8, 1869; Rachael Kent b. April 30, 1871, m. Jesse E. Bigler; James Kirtin b. May 1873; Rhoda Irene b. June 15, 1874, m. Isaac Clark; Marionetta Kent b. June 29, 1786, m. Harry M. Croft; Jane Ann Kent b. May 29, 1878, m. James Jensen; John Alexander Kent b. June 1, 1880, m. Rosy Maude Greene; Alma Kent b. Jan. 21, 1886, m. Sally Janette Allen Nov. 1, 1907. Family resided Mendon, Utah, and Teton, Idaho.
Second counselor to Bishop Hughes, Mendon ward 1877; Missionary to England 1880-82. Moved to Snake river valley 1883; bishop of Teton ward. Admitted to the bar as an attorney 1903; probate judge Fremont county 1903-11.

DONALDSON, ALMA KENT (son of John Donaldson and Mary Ann Kent). Born Jan. 21, 1886, Teton Idaho.
Married Sallie Jennett Allen Nov. 1, 1907, Salt Lake City (daughter of John R. Allen and Sarah Jannett Leavitt of Lewiston, Utah, pioneers Feb. 21, 1862). She was born March 27, 1885. Only child: Allen b. Aug. 15, 1911. Family home Teton, Idaho.
Member 149th quorum seventies; missionary to southern states 1907-09; teacher in Y. M. M. I. A. Farmer.

DONEY, JOHN (son of Elias Doney, born March 22, 1795, at Quethoich, and Maria Roberts of St. Stephens, both in Cornwall, Eng.). He was born May 3, 1821, at St. Stephens. Came to Utah in early days.

Married Ann George Jan. 22, 1853, at St. Stephens (daughter of William and Temperance George), who was born Nov. 28, 1831, and came to Utah Sept. 26, 1856, Edmund Ellsworth handcart company. Their children: Ann Temperance b. Nov. 1, 1854; Mary Jane b. July 29, 1856, m. Robert G. Lowe; Sarah b. Oct. 17, 1858, m. L. L. Hatch Dec. 28, 1883; Lucy Mariah b. March 28, 1861, m. George C. Parkinson; Anah Eliza b. Aug. 17, 1863, m. Joseph G. Lowe; John Franklin b. Dec. 16, 1866, m. Sarah Cutler Dec. 17, 1890; Elias William b. May 28, 1869, m. Susanna M. Mendenhall Dec. 16, 1891; Robert George b. Dec. 15, 1872; Bessie Ann b. Jan. 28, 1875, m. Fred S. Parkinson. Family resided Payson, Utah, and Franklin, Idaho.
Married Marinda Roberts. Their children: Henry Levi b. Aug. 1, 1874, m. Johanna Mecham; Joseph b. March 20, 1876, m. Isabelle Johnson.
Settled at Franklin, Idaho, 1860. High priest.

DONEY, ELIAS WILLIAM (son of John Doney and Ann George). Born May 28, 1869, Franklin, Idaho.
Married Susanna M. Mendenhall Dec. 16, 1891, Logan, Utah (daughter of Thomas Mendenhall and Louisa Smart), who was born Nov. 29, 1871, Bear River, Idaho. Their children: John Vernon M. b. Sept. 22, 1892; William M. b. Aug. 21, 1894; Verda M. b. Sept. 9, 1896; Levar M. b. Sept. 22, 1901; Horace M. b. Sept. 2, 1902; Grant M. b. May 27, 1904; Parley M. b. May 27, 1906; Alfonda M. b. Sept. 22, 1908.
Missionary to Great Britain 1898-1901; member council 18th quorum seventies 1901-09, also secretary and treasurer; high priest.

DORCHEUS, NIELS (son of Thue N. Dorcheus and Marianne Nielson of Lemvig, Jutland, Denmark). Born June 21, 1812, at Lemvig. Came to Utah Sept. 9, 1860, James D. Ross company.
Married Angelica C. Lund 1840, Copenhagen, Denmark, who was born June 24, 1808. Their children: John T. b. April 25, 1842, m. Ellen Jensen; Laura M. b. June 23, 1846, m. John England. Family resided Plain City, Gunnison, Scipio and Monroe, Utah.
High priest; member high council, Sevier stake. Carpenter on St. George temple. Died Oct. 22, 1892.

DORCHEUS, JOHN T. (son of Niels Dorcheus and Angelica C. Lund). Born April 25, 1842, Copenhagen, Denmark. Came to Utah with father.
Married Ellen Jensen Feb. 18, 1865, Gunnison, Utah (daughter of Knud Jensen and Bodil Olson of Gunnison, Utah, pioneers 1862). She was born Aug. 11, 1844; came to Utah Sept. 15, 1859, Robert F. Neslen company, and died March 10, 1913, at Monroe, Utah. Their children: John J. b. Dec. 19, 1866, m. Julia Maria Larsen Nov. 8, 1893; Niels O. b. Feb. 28, 1871, m. Lydia Webb; Constant b. March 12, 1874, m. Birdie A. Hesse Sept. 1, 1897; Angelica b. Dec. 3, 1877, died; Caroline b. July 24, 1885, m. Andrew Staples 1906. Family resided Gunnison, Scipio and Monroe, Utah.
Married Alice P. Wasden June 14, 1868, Salt Lake City (daughter of Thomas Wasden and Mary Brooks, the former pioneer 1859, Robert F. Neslen company). She was born Nov. 28, 1842, Ashton, Eng. Their children: Mary E. b. March 31, 1871, m. Orson Washburn; Ismilda b. Dec. 19, 1872, m. William England Jr.; Laura b. Nov. 11, 1874, m. Charles England; Eugenia D. b. 1877, m. Joseph Howes; Parley b. April 29, 1880, m. Irene Ward; Alma M. b. Jan. 8, 1881.
Married Mary McDonald Dec. 20, 1882, St. George, Utah (daughter of Edward McDonald and Elizabeth Kellun, pioneers 1866). She was born March 5, 1863, Bishopsbriggs, Lannarkshire, Scotland. Their children: Elizabeth A. b. Oct. 18, 1883, m. W. M. Humphreys; Edward W. b. July 4, 1885; Rhoda B.; Ellen L.; Gladys; John A. b. May 1, 1894; Jessie J.; Mary Irene; Robert A.; Charles H.; Alvin E.
Missionary to Kansas 1865-70; high priest. Black Hawk war veteran.

DORCHEUS, EDWARD W. (son of John T. Dorcheus and Mary McDonald). Born July 4, 1885, Monroe, Utah.

DORIUS, NICOLI. Born Sept. 21, 1804, Copenhagen, Denmark. Came to Utah Sept. 13, 1854.
Married Annie Sophia Christofferson, who died June 27, 1895. Their children: Carl C. N.; John F. P.; Augusta D., m. Stevens. Family resided in Denmark, and at Ephraim, Utah.
Missionary to Sjealland, Denmark. Shoemaker. Died July 10, 1872, at Ephraim.

DORIUS, CARL CHRISTIAN NICOLI (son of Nicoli Dorius and Annie Sophia Christofferson). Born April 5, 1830, Copenhagen, Denmark. Came to Utah Sept. 13, 1857, Chr. Christiansen handcart company.
Married Ellen G. Rolfson April 24, 1857, Liverpool, Eng. (daughter of Bent and Gertrude Maria Rolfson, latter pioneer Sept. 13, 1857, Christiansen handcart company). She came to Utah with husband. Their child: Charles Rolfson b. July 10, 1858, m. Margaret Neilson Dec. 11, 1879.
Married Tomena Frederickson 1864 at Salt Lake City (daughter of Canute Frederickson and Annie Larsen, former pioneer 1864, oxteam company). She was born Aug. 4, 1840, Risor, Norway. Their children: Canute Frederick b. Aug. 7, 1865; Anna Sophia b. Aug. 13, 1870, m. Soren J. Johnson Sept. 18, 1891; Ella Nicholena b. Oct. 7, 1872, m. Ephraim Hansen June 6, 1901.
Married Julia Peterson (daughter of John Peterson and Encer Anderson). Their children: Rebecca b. Jan. 6, 1874, m. Marion Clinger May 8, 1898; John N. b. April 6, 1876, m.

Ethel Rees Dec. 24, 1982; Julia b. April 24, 1878, m. Andrew Jensen July 16, 1902; Erastus b. Aug. 7, 1884; Maybell b. June, 1889.
Married Mary Williams.
Married Charlotta Otterstrom April, 1885, at Salt Lake City (daughter of Jonas Otterstrom and Hilda Amelia Algren, former pioneer 1855, Canute Peterson company, latter 1857, Chr. Christiansen handcart company). She was born Sept. 13, 1858, Ephraim, Utah. Their child: Mamie b. Oct. 5, 1887.
Bishop of Ephraim, South ward, 1877-94; missionary to Scandinavia 1862-64. City councilman Ephraim six years. Died March 4, 1894.

DORIUS, CHARLES ROLFSON (son of Carl Christian Nicoli Do i and Ellen G. Rolfson). Born July 10, 1858, Ephraim, Utahus
Married Margaret Neilson Dec. 11, 1879 (daughter of Christian Neillson and Karen Hansen, pioneers Sept. 13, 1854, P. O. Hansen company). She was born April 21, 1861. Their children: Caroline Maria b. Feb. 5, 1881, m. R. D. Rasmussen Oct. 2, 1907; Orpha Olevia b. Aug. 7, 1892; Sarah Magdalene b. Jan. 27, 1895; Elda Elizabeth b. Oct. 7, 1898; Inez b. April 27, 1902. Family home Ephraim, Utah.
Missionary to Norway 1886-88; set apart bishop south ward Ephraim, 1894. City treasurer; collector 1896-97; city councilman 1894-96; mayor; school trustee; representative state legislature from 14th district 1907-09.

DOUGALL, HUGH MacSWEIN (son of John Dougall of Muthill, Scotland, and Catherine MacSwein). He was born April 24, 1837, at Muthill. Came to Utah Sept. 7, 1855, Noah T. Guymon company.
Married Mary Catherine Streeper Dec. 6, 1862 (daughter of Wilkinson Streeper and Matilda Wells), who was born May 3, 1842. Their children: Hugh MacSwein born Dec. 9, 1863, m. Rhoda R. Groesbeck Nov. 25, 1891; Catherine Matilda b. Jan. 19, 1867; William Bernard b. July 23, 1872; John Wilkerson b. Nov. 19, 1874, m. Harriet Wheeler November, 1900; George Moses Patrick b. Nov. 23, 1879, m. Alice Paul Feb. 5, 1907; Mary Emma Josephine b. Nov. 13, 1883; Charles Stewart b. Feb. 22, 1869. Family home Springville, Utah.
Contractor on Union Pacific railroad. Postmaster 25 years at Springville, Utah. Died Feb. 28, 1906.

DOUGALL, HUGH MacSWEIN, JR. (son of Hugh MacSwein Dougall Sr. and Mary Catherine Streeper). Born Dec. 9, 1863, Springville, Utah.
Married Rhoda Rebecca Groesbeck Nov. 25, 1891, at Springville (daughter of Nicholas Harmon Groesbeck and Rhoda Sanderson), who was born Nov. 16, 1864, at Springville. Their child: Catherine Rhoda b. June 1, 1896.
City councilman 1909. Manager Dougall Live Stock company; merchant; rancher and stockraiser.

DOUGLASS, RICHARD (son of George Douglass and Ellen Briggs). Born Feb. 27, 1828, Downham, Lancashire, Eng. Came to Utah Aug. 28, 1852.
Married Elizabeth Wadsworth Jan. 29, 1849 (daughter of James and Agnes Wadsworth), who was born Aug. 10, 1833 Manchester, Eng., and came to Utah with husband. Their children: Ellen b. April 14, 1850, m. James Wilson; Elizabeth ab. March 31, 1852, m. John W. Hooper; Richard b. Jar 23, 1854, died; Agnes Vilate b. July 29, 1856, m. Charles c Wheat; James Henry b. Aug. 29, 1858, m. Irintha Pratt; Mar b. July 31, 1860, died; Jeannetta b. Aug. 10, 1861, m. George B. Smyth Jr., m. John Brown; Isabell b. Oct. 7, 1863, m. J McLaren Boyle; Benjamin Edmund b. Nov. 6, 1865, died Alice b. Nov. 29, 1867, m. Ashby Stringham; Mariah; Josep b. July 1, 1870, died; David George b. Oct. 25, 1871; Charle Walter b. Oct. 19, 1873, died; Wealthy b. Nov. 11, 1875; Ad Catherine b. Jan. 4, 1879, m. Charles F. Carlson. Famil home Ogden, Utah.
Married Eliza Joyce 1875, Salt Lake City (daughter o Thomas and Mary Ann Joyce, who were married in Bedford shire, Eng.). She was born in Bedfordshire. Their chil dren: George b. Nov. 22, 1857, died; Thomas Moroni b. Jul 12, 1859, m. Sophia Larson; John b. Feb. 4, 1861, m. Letti Shurtliff; William b. March 2, 1863, m. Chloe Leischma Ralph Heber b. April 2, 1865, m. Jennie Pickering; Sara Eliza b. July 30, 1867, m. William Reeve; Mary Ann b. Fe 22, 1870, died; Roseitha b. Jan. 8, 1873, m. David Georg Revore; Walter Joyce b. Sept. 2, 1880.
Member 25th quorum seventies; missionary to Englan Assisted in bringing in immigrants to Utah.

DOWDING, THOMAS (son of David Dowding born 1794 an Mary Smith, both of Wiltshire, Eng.). Born 1816 in Wil shire. Came to Utah Sept. 15, 1866, William Henry Chipm company.
Married Hannah Nash (daughter of James Nash), w was born May 1, 1830, and came to Utah with husbar Their children: David b. April 19, 1851, m. Henrietta V Tassell Dec. 8, 1872; Elizabeth, m. Allen Hall; William Oct. 10, 1854; Nephi b. Nov. 20, 1856, m. Jane Condor; Louim. Benj. Camp Oct. 5, 1879; Mary, m. Charles Engler; Jamt Martha, m. Benjamin Orlett; Sarah J. b. July 15, 1868; Em Nov. 2, 1869. Family home West Jordan, Utah.

DOWDING, DAVID (son of Thomas Dowding and Hann Nash). Born April 19, 1851, in Wiltshire.
Married Henrietta Van Tassell Dec. 8, 1872, Salt Lake Ci (daughter of Henry Van Tassell and Emily L. Street, pi

PIONEERS AND PROMINENT MEN OF UTAH

neers 1864, Ansel P. Harmon company), who was born Sept. 29, 1857, in New York city. Their children: David L. b. Oct. 30, 1873, m. Ann Goff June 19, 1907; Sarah J. b. June 25, 1875, m. Eric Nelson July 7, 1898; George W. b. July 2, 1878, m. Elizabeth Goff Nov. 16, 1898; Maud b. Jan. 1, 1881, m. S. H. Smith Sept. 20, 1899; Etta b. Oct. 10, 1888; James b. July 30, 1891; Arthur b. Jan. 18, 1892; Mae b. Sept. 16, 1894; Raymond b. March 12, 1896; Blanch L. b. Nov. 25, 1899. Family home Sandy, Utah.

DOWDELL, ABSALOM PORTER. Came to Utah 1847 with oxteam. Married Sarah Ann Halladay. Their children: William; Thomas; Louisa Jonathan; Martha Jane, m. Jeremiah Albert Robey. Family home Santaquin, Utah. Missionary to Australia. Farmer.

DOWDLE, ROBERT HUGHES (son of Robert Dowdle and Sarah Ann Robinson of Alabama). Born April 6, 1830, in Franklin county, Ala. Came to Utah 1849 with government freighters.
Married Henrietta Messervy March 27, 1858, Santaquin, Utah (daughter of Joshua Messervy and Jane Roberts of Jersey Island, Eng., pioneers Oct. 10, 1853, Joseph W. Young company). She was born March 20, 1837. Their children: Robert, Joseph and John E., all died; Elvira, d. aged 15; William Robert, died; Moroni Jerome, d. aged 5; Henriette Jane, m. Benjamin P. Porter Dec. 19, 1878; Sarah Ann, m. Jesse M. Baker Oct. 22, 1885; Annie Elizabeth, m. Joseph Bryant Hawks Dec. 5, 1885; Louisa, m. Joseph P. Daynes July 7, 1907; Hugh Joshua, m. Lettie Miles March 20, 1896. Family home Franklin, Idaho.
Seventy; ward teacher. Justice of peace; Indian interpreter. Farmer. Died Oct. 27, 1909.

DOWNARD, GEORGE. Born Dec. 27, 1822, in Kent. Eng. Came to Utah Nov. 1862.
Married Mary Emma Carlisle 1865 at Salt Lake City (daughter of William and Jane Carlisle of Kent), who was born Nov. 8, 1833, and came to Utah November, 1862, and died Dec. 5, 1897. Their children: William b. July 12, 1867, m. Annie Catherine Dahl; John Lewis b. Sept. 1869, m. Angeline King; Emma Jane. Family home Spring City, Utah.
High priest. Settled at Spring City 1862; moved to Richfield. from which place he was driven by Indians; went to Emery county, 1881. Carpenter; painter. Died July, 1902, Price, Utah.

DOWNARD, WILLIAM (son of George Downard and Emma Carlisle). Born July 12, 1867, Spring City, Utah.
Married Annie Catherine Dahl Aug. 3, 1887, Logan, Utah (daughter of Niels Peter Dahl and Bertha Mane Christensen, of Ulano, Denmark, who came to Utah 1878 by rail). She was born April 7, 1866. Their children: Emma Annetta b. April 19, 1888, m. John Sax; Bertha Matilda b. April 7, 1890, m. George McGahn; Arnold William b. March 21, 1892; Ernest Peter b. June 25, 1894; Arthur Lewis b. Aug. 4, 1897; Hazel b. Nov. 6, 1899; Ray Vermont b. June 15, 1902, died Rulon b. April 8, 1905; Ella b. Sept. 5, 1908; Alden b. June 19, 1911. Family home Price, Utah.
Settled at Price 1889 and has helped to build canals and wagon roads. President 101st quorum seventies; Sunday school superintendent at Price; counselor in presidency T. M. M. I. A.; superintendent Woodside branch, Emery county. Trustee of Woodside school district two years. Carpenter; farmer.

DOXEY, THOMAS (son of Thomas Doxey, born October, 1801, and Susannah Brearly, who was born June 5, 1802, at Derby, Eng., married July 6, 1821). He was born March 27, 1829, in Derby. Came to Utah 1853, Appleton Harmon company.
Married Ann Elizabeth Hunt July 10, 1853, Council Bluffs, Iowa (daughter of John Hunt and Mary Danby), who was born Dec. 20, 1830, and came to Utah with husband. Their children: Alma T. b. July 14, 1854, m. Leonora L. Eaton June 23, 1880; Mary Ann b. Aug. 28, 1856, m. Joseph H. Watkins April 30, 1879; David Hunt b. June 13, 1858, m. Ann E. Clark Oct. 31, 1889, d. Nov. 2, 1910; Moroni Hunt b. Aug. 13, 1860, m. Olive J. Riley June 11, 1887, d. Dec. 6, 1903; Jane b. Nov. 27, 1863, d. Aug. 10, 1865; Samuel b. Feb. 17, 1866, d. Feb. 8, 1907; m Margret N. Moyes Aug. 31, 1898; Thomas b. April 11, 1868, m. Bessie A. E. Watkins April 30, 1889. Family resided Salt Lake City and Ogden, Utah.
Married Mary Rhodes Feb. 26, 1872, at Salt Lake City (daughter of George Rhodes and Alice Mellor), who was born Sept. 11, 1850, St. Louis, Mo. Their children: James b. Aug. 15, 1873, d. March 24, 1894; Ellen Mellor b. Sept. 26, 1875, m. Nels Sorensen Oct. 9, 1895; Rosetta b. Jan. 7, 1878, m. Wallace Fife Nov. 22, 1899; John b. Oct. 14, 1879, m. Loretta Dingham May 10, 1899; Mary Alice b. Nov. 16, 1881, m. Henry A. Hill Jan. 7, 1902; George R. b. Dec. 22, 1883, m. Chloe Woods Nov. 23, 1910; Albert b. Dec. 2, 1885, m. Minnie Baird Jan. 1, 1905; William R. b. Aug. 14, 1888, d. Jan. 2, 1890; Clara b. Nov. 7, 1890; Susannah B. b. June 1, 1893, m. Frederick Paul Nisbitt Jan. 22, 1913. Family home, Ogden.
City watermaster 15 years; road supervisor 1888; member State Irrigation association 1895. Captain in Nauvoo Legion. Second counselor to Bishop Robert McQuarrie 1879; member Weber state high council; superintendent 2d ward Sunday school. Member city council. Farmer.

DOXEY, ALMA T. (son of Thomas Doxey and Ann Elizabeth Hunt). Born July 14, 1854, Salt Lake City.
Married Leonora L. Eaton June 23, 1880, St. George, Utah (daughter of John S. Eaton and Emily Ann Robins), who was born May 31, 1864, Scipio, Utah. Their children: Alma T. b. Feb. 5, 1882, m. Orpha Gould Oct. 28, 1901; Bella b. Sept. 2, 1884, d. Dec. 20, 1890; John Riley b. Nov. 22, 1886, d. Jan. 1, 1890; Ray Eaton b. June 18, 1890, d. May 31, 1907; Myrtle b. July 6, 1892; Leo Samuel b. May 9, 1895; Nora Eva b. March 31, 1897; Paul Dee b. Jan. 8, 1899.
Lived at Ogden until 1876; moved to Arizona, settling on Little Colorado river at Sunset, later at St. Johns; returned to Ogden 1890. Missionary to Australia 1894. Member high council in St. Johns (Ariz.) stake.

DRAKE, DANIEL (son of Seth and Chloey Drake of Vermont). Born Jan. 14, 1789, Vermont. Came to Utah Sept. 19, 1847, Daniel Spencer company.
Married Patience Perkins Dec. 3, 1813 (daughter of John Perkins and Hannah Gardner, married in Vermont), who was born Dec. 19, 1873, and came to Utah with husband. Their children: Joseph b. Dec. 17, 1814; Diantha b. Dec. 15, 1815, m. Elisha Barnes; Daniel N. b. June 27, 1819, m. Hannah Kempton; Sarah b. Sept. 10, 1821, m. William Paine; Orson F. b. Sept. 27, 1823, m. Betsy Parsons; Horace b. April 19, 1826, m. Diana E. Holbrook Oct. 3, 1850. Resided Salt Lake City and Ogden, Utah.

DRAKE, HORACE (son of Daniel Drake and Patience Perkins). Born April 19, 1826, Hartford, Trumbull Co., Ohio.
Married Diana E. Holbrook Oct. 3, 1850, Salt Lake City (daughter of Chandler Holbrook and Eunice Dunning), who was born Oct. 27, 1833, Genesee county, N. Y. Their children: Horace Louis b. March 23, 1852; Cyrus Henry b. Aug. 20, 1863; Eunice Diana b. Sept. 7, 1855, m. Willard R. Pickering; Samuel b. Aug. 2, 1857; Joseph b. Aug. 20, 1859; Hyrum b. March 19, 1861, m. Mary E. Derrick Jan. 18, 1883; Alice Emma b. Feb. 27, 1864, m. Sidney F. Worsley Jan. 18, 1885; Jedediah M. b. Aug. 1, 1866; Daniel C. b. Aug. 15, 1868; Rosetta b. 1870; James A. b. 1873; Edith L. b. June 29, 1878, m. Joseph F. Tingey March 28, 1907. Family resided Salt Lake City and Centerville, Utah.

DRAKE, DANIEL NEWELL (son of Daniel Drake and Mrs. Peachville Perkins). He was born June 22, 1819, in New York state. Came to Utah 1848, Daniel Miller company.
Married Hannah Kempton of Salt Lake City (daughter of John Kempton). Their children: Hannah M. b. Aug. 25, 1851, m. David W. Wilson; Daniel N., b. Feb. 20, 1853, m. Mary J. Cheney; John H. b. Jan. 23, 1855, m. Margaret P. Cheney; Ann E. b. April 17, 1857; Nathan L. D. b. Dec. 13, 1859, m. Sarah Westom; Alvin L. b. Sept. 19, 1866, m. Lora Lukis; Marim O. b. Dec. 22, 1869, m. N. Nickels; Richard M. b. May 25, 1872. Family home Weber Co., Utah.
Elder. Died in 1879.

DRAKE, DANIEL N. (son of Daniel Newell Drake and Hannah Kempton). Born at Ogden, Utah, in 1853.
Married May J. Cheney in Weber county in 1874 (daughter of E. W. Cheney and Lucy H. Cheney of Weber county; pioneers 1849, George A. Smith company). She was born April 9, 1857. Their children: Daniel N. Jr. b. May 4, 1876, died; Louis Daniel; Louis W. b. March 11, 1878, m. May Hill; Lawrence b. March, 28, 1880; Clarence E. Drake b. March 28, 1880, m. Anna Johnson; Elvira D. b. April 25, 1882; John H. b. Jan. 25, 1885, m. Alice Mow; Rosel b. Nov. 24, 1889, m. George Hadley; Charles W. b. Feb. 27, 1891, m. Clara Manning. Family home Weber county.
Elder.

DRAKE, ISAAC (son of David B. Drake and Caroline Nelson of New York). Born October 1831, in New York. Came to Utah 1869, independent company.
Married Marian Colt in May, 1865, Montreal, Canada (daughter of William and Mary Colt). She was born in 1831. Their children: Caroline b. 1864, d. 1874; David B. b. 1866, m. Sarah Metcalf.
Married Weltha Willer 1876 in Lawrence county, N. Y. (daughter of John Willer and Betsy Carpenter of that county). She was born there in April, 1855.
Settled at Malad City, Idaho. Doctor of medicine. Died 1895.

DRAKE, DAVID B. (son of Isaac Drake and Marian Colt). He was born 1866 in Lawrence county, N. Y.
Married Sarah Metcalf 1871, Malad City, Idaho (daughter of Anthony and Mary Metcalf). Their children: Molly b. 1893; Frank b. 1896; Miril b. 1898; Ann b. 1899.

DRAPER, CHARLES. Came to Utah with Capt. Seeley company.
Married Mary Ann Wann. Their children: William; Eliza, beth; Jane; Polly; Mary; Annie, m. George Morby. Family home, Hoytsville.
Elder.

DRAPER, WILLIAM (son of Charles Draper and Mary Ann Wann). Born Nov. 12, 1861, Croland, Lancastershire, Eng. Came to Utah with Capt. Seeley company.

DRAPER, THOMAS (son of Thomas Draper of Leicestershire, Eng.). Born in 1824 in England. Came to Utah about 1870.
Married Sarah Ward (daughter of William and Sarah Ward). Their children: Ebenezer, died; Rachel, m. James Richards; Sarah, m. Thomas Hardy; Thomas Ward, m. Truelove Miller; Martha, m. Robert Bates; Elizabeth, m. Hyrum S. Bellows; Phoebe, m. William Henry Tracy; Emma, m. James Andrews. Family home Spanish Fork.
Elder. Farmer. Died in 1906 at Plain City, Utah.

DRAPER, WILLIAM. Came to Utah 1849.
Married Muriel Thompson. Their child: Nephi b. March 23, 1847, m. Charlotte Elizabeth Johnson.

DRAPER, NEPHI (son of William Draper and Muriel Thompson), born March 23, 1847, at Little Pigeon River, Iowa). Came to Utah 1849.
Married Charlotte Elizabeth Johnson November, 1868, at Salt Lake City, Utah (daughter of Luke S. Johnson and America Clark. Came to Utah 1847). She was born 1850 at Little Pigeon River, Iowa. Their children: Muriel b. Aug. 7, 1870, died in infancy; Lovinia Ann b. Nov. 23, 1873, m. John Huggins; Walter Nephi b. Nov. 20, 1875, m. Clara Maud Critchlow; Emily Elizabeth b. June 17, 1878; Edith b. Aug. 4, 1880, deceased; Asa b. Jan. 6, 1882, m. Mamie Anderson; Ona b. June 24, 1885, m. Clyde Russell; Amoret b. Sept. 6, 1888, m. Leonard Scott; Eldra b. July 3, 1890; Lois b. Sept. 26, 1893. Family home St. John, Tooele county.
Farmer and stockman.

DRAPER, WALTER NEPHI (son of Nephi Draper and Charlotte Elizabeth Johnson). Born Nov. 20, 1875, St. John, Tooele Co., Utah.
Married Clara Maud Critchlow Sept. 27, 1900, Salt Lake City (daughter of John Carner Critchlow and Nancy Jane Cumberland of Butler county, Pa.). She was born Jan. 25, 1878; came to Utah June 29, 1900. Their children: Kenneth Floyd b. July 16, 1901; Asa Leroy b. March 13, 1903; Irene May b. Aug. 23, 1904; Clare b. Oct. 16, 1907, d. April 10, 1909; Walter Howard b. Sept. 21, 1909; Gladys Pearl b. Oct. 30, 1911. Family home Wellington.
Missionary to eastern states 1897-99; ward teacher; president Y. M. M. I. A.; Sunday school superintendent. Farmer and stockraiser.

DRAPER, WILLIAM (son of Thomas Draper, born 1748). Born Sept. 6, 1776, Little Nine, Padners, Dutchess county, Pa.
Married Lydia Lathrop. Their children: William Zemira b. Feb. 27, 1812, m. Amy Terry Jan. 30, 1842; Alfred; Carson; Polley; Phoebe, m. Ebenezer Brown; Lucretia, m. Mr. Gayland; Lydia, m. Fred Vanloovan; Fannie, m. Mr. Vanloovan; Charles. Family home Lavorran, Upper Canada, and Pennsylvania.

DRAPER, ZEMIRA (son of William Draper and Lydia Lathrop). He was born Feb. 27, 1812, Northumberland Co., Upper Canada. Came to Utah September, 1848, Daniel Hendricks company.
Married Ellen Agnes Bradshaw, Sept. 15, 1838. She died Aug. 15, 1839. Their child: Joseph Edward, d. 1839.
Married Amy Terry Jan. 30, 1842, Nauvoo, Ill. (daughter of Parshel and Hannah Terry). She was born June 5, 1821, York Home district, Upper Canada. Their children: Ellen Agnes b. Feb. 27, 1843, m. James Green Jan. 15, 1860; Rebecca Jane b. Sept. 1, 1846, d. Oct. 4, 1847; Lydia Hannah b. Oct. 4, 1848, m. Bateman H. Wilhelm March 1864; Susannah Catilda b. Aug. 3, 1851, m. James M. Ballard 1871; Fannie Lucretia b. Jan. 8, 1854, m. John P. Terry April 23, 1875; Phoebe Marrilla b. Oct. 9, 1857, m. James A. Terry Oct. 1880; Zemira Terry b. March 16, 1859, m. Olga J. Polson Oct. 26, 1887; Jilpha Amy b. Sept. 26, 1861, m. Hanner Duzett March 10, 1881; Carson Clark b. Jan. 29, 1866, m. Vilate Draper Jan. 2, 1888.
Settled in tenth ward, Salt Lake City; moved to Draper in the fall of 1850, from there he went to Alpine and to Rockville 1862. Served as bishop's counselor and justice of peace several years at Rockville, Utah. Died Jan. 9, 1876, Rockville, Utah.

DRAPER, CARSON C. (son of Zemira Draper and Amy Terry). He was born Jan. 29, 1865, Rockville, Utah.
Married Vilate Dalton Jan. 2, 1888, Rockville, Utah (daughter of John Dalton and Marrey A. Gardial—latter came to Utah 1856, Ellsworth handcart company). She was born April 27, 1872, Virgin City, Utah. Their children: Ellen Agnes b. Nov. 18, 1888, m. Walter R. Funk Oct. 9, 1908; Amy Vilate b. Dec. 25, 1890; Carson Melvan b. Nov. 22, 1892; Zemira Heuard b. May 25, 1895, d. Sept. 13, 1909; Vernon b. Jan. 28, 1898, d. Feb. 28, 1898; Marey Elva b. Jan. 20, 1900; Leona Josephine b. April 1, 1902; Ruby Florina b. July 1, 1906; Lawrance Luvell b. Jan. 11, 1910; Clark Lindon b. June 6, 1912.
First assistant Sunday school superintendent Kimball, Idaho, 1906; Sunday school teacher 1908-09 at Hinckley, Utah.

DREDGE, JESSE RICHARD (son of Richard Dredge, born Dec. 25, 1795, Proom, Somersetshire, Eng., and Sarah Sharp, born 1798, Gloucestershire, Eng. Came to Utah November, 1861, Godbe and Wright company.
Married Ellen Rhees April 29, 1854 (daughter of Horatio Nelson Rhees, born July 3, 1802, England, and Sarah Ann Green, born July 25, 1798, Bath, Eng.). She was born Feb. 12, 1836. Came to Utah October 1861, Capt. Horne company. Their children: Ellen H. b. March 24, 1855, d. Aug. 1, 1860; Sarah A. b. Oct. 27, 1856, d. Aug. 11, 1860; David C. b. Feb. 18, 1859, d. July 28, 1860; Elizabeth A. b. March 5, 1861, m. John L. Roberts May, 1881; Hannah A. b. March 28, 1863, m. George Thomas March 28, 1881; Lucy G. b. May 13, 1865, d. Dec. 23, 1865; Emma b. Sept. 27, 1866, m. James Harrison Nov. 27, 1884; Alice b. Dec. 7, 1868, m. David S. Thomas April 13, 1888; Nora b. Feb. 14, 1871, d. Sept. 16, 1890; Jesse H. b. March 29, 1873, m. Eliza Kunz Sept. 30, 1898; Hettie M. b. May 3, 1875, m. Alma Lusk Dec. 16, 1896; Richard H. b. Jan. 16, 1878, m. Esther Heward January, 1899; William R. b. May 28, 1880, m. Maud Mecham March 25, 1903. Resided at South Wales, Kaysville, Utah, and Malad, Idaho.
Married Rose Kunz (Bischoff) Oct. 21, 1885, Logan, Utah (daughter of John Kunz and Rosina Knutti, of Bern, Switzerland; married February, 1842). She was born Oct. 20, 1845, Bern, Switzerland.
Settled at Salt Lake City 1861, moved to Kaysville 1862, then to Malad, Idaho, 1866. Second president to 62d quorum seventies at Malad, Idaho, and high priest and high councilor for nineteen years; patriarch in Mormon church.

DROLLINGER, SIMEON COOK (son of Samuel Drollinger, born May 6, 1801, Hamilton Co., Ohio, and Rachel Cook, born June 14, 1798, Mason county, Ky.—they were married Dec. 21, 1819). He was born March 22, 1833, Fountain county, Ind. Came to Utah Sept. 10, 1853, John W. Cooley company.
Married Ann Eliza Davis Dec. 4, 1859 (daughter of Franklin Judson and Ann Davis, the former a pioneer 1852, McCullan company, the latter died on the plains). She was born Aug. 8, 1842. Came to Utah with her father in 1852. Their children: Simeon Cook b. Feb. 2, 1861, m. Mary Emeline Cordingley; Ann Eliza b. Aug. 20, 1862; Emily Estella b. Nov. 25, 1864; Rachel Mariah b. July 20, 1866; Franklin John b. Nov. 20, 1868, m. Lydia E. Williams; Clarissa Jane b. Oct. 16, 1870, m. John Haskell Pomroy July 13, 1889; Stanley Bert b. Jan. 6, 1873, m. Lydia E. Williams Drollinger. Resided at Payson and Spring Creek, Utah, St. Thomas, Nev., and Arizona.
Settled at Moapa Valley, Nev., 1865. Died July 1, 1911, Marysville, Fremont Co., Idaho.

DROLLINGER, SIMEON COOK, JR. (son of Simeon Cook Drollinger and Ann Eliza Davis). Born Feb. 2, 1861, Payson, Utah.
Married Mary E. Cordingley April 20, 1885, Huntington, Utah (daughter of William Cordingley and Permelia Huggins). She was born Jan. 14, 1864, Fountain Green, Utah. Their children: Cook Eugene b. May 24, 1886; Mary E. b. Oct. 21, 1887; Lottie P. b. Oct. 29, 1889, m. Chester Hansen May 23, 1911; William Lee b. Aug. 26, 1891; Stephen F. b. Nov. 25, 1893; Rachel Flavilla b. Dec. 24, 1895; Simeon Guy b. Feb. 7, 1898; Bert Cordingley b. April 25, 1899; Cecil John b. Jan. 20, 1902; Emeline Fern b. Sept. 13, 1904; Alfonzo b. Sept. 8, 1906. Resided at Huntington, Utah, Mesa City and Pima, Ariz., and Marysville, Idaho.

DROWN, CHARLES (son of Solomon Drown, born Oct. 10, 1789, of Illinois, and Fannie Drown born Feb. 2, 1803). Born Oct. 28, 1815. Came to Utah 1849.
Married Sarah Tarbell. She died in New York. Their children: James; David T. b. Dec. 9, 1837, m. Sarah O. Newall Dec. 18, 1860.
Married Mary Ann Sweazy. Their children: Carlos, m. Rose Drown; Brigham; Elizabeth.
Married Louise Jones Canfield.
Missionary to California in 1857.

DROWN, DAVID TARBELL (son of Charles Drown and Sarah Tarbell). Born Dec. 9, 1837, at Oswego, N. Y.
Married Sarah O. Newell Dec. 9, 1860, at Provo, Utah (daughter of Almon Newell and Alvow Comstock; the former came to Utah Oct. 5, 1852, the latter died in Nauvoo 1846). She was born Jan. 22, 1844, at Nauvoo, Ill. Their children: Ellen Elizabeth b. May 3, 1862, m. J. V. Blasdell Feb. 22, 1890; David Almon b. March 15, 1864, m. Elizabeth Warbarton Dec. 23, 1888; Alice Adelia b. Dec. 18, 1865, m. William D. Kuhre April 14, 1886; Charles Matison b. Oct. 10, 1867, m. Ella Perry Dec. 9, ——; Olive Maria b. May 7, 1870, m. William Erickson Oct. 22, 1891; Alfred Carlos b. June 15, 1872; Eva Geraldine b. July 4, 1874, m. O. J. Roberts Nov. 19, 1901; Clara Valeria b. Jan. 25, 1877, m. William Erickson March 8, ——; Melvin Ernest b. Jan. 17, 1882, m. Myrtle Hewlett July 2, 1908; Ivy Ruby b. Feb. 24, 1884, m. A. E. Custer March 12, 1901. Family home West Jordan, Utah.

DRUCE, JOHN (son of John Druce and Sophia Bragg of Mitcham Merton, Surrey, Eng.). Born June 18, 1818. Came to Utah Sept. 16, 1861, Ira Reed company.
Married Julia Ann Jinks June 19, 1842, Manchester, Eng., by Elder Charles Miller (daughter of John Jinks and Mary Woodfield of Manchester, Lancashire, Eng., the latter came to Utah Sept. 16, 1861, Ira Reed company). She was born April 17, 1824, Stone, Staffordshire, Eng. Their children: Julia Ann; Mary Sophia, m. Joseph Hyrum Phippen; Lilly Harriet Almira, m. Charles John Lambert; Eliza Jane. d. aged 60 years; John Alma, m. Elizabeth M. Kingsbury; Ada

Eugenia, m. Orville E. Hartwell; Amanda May, m. George Culver; Edgar Woodfield. m. Ann Elizabeth Bennett; Kate Agusta, d. aged 2. Family home Salt Lake City.
Missionary to and president of eastern states mission 1876-77; high priest; president 21st quorum seventies; counselor to bishop Pyper of 12th ward 1877-82, and to Bishop Clawson 1882-97; ordained patriarch Sept. 29, 1897. Engraver; carpenter; contractor and builder. Died Oct. 7, 1897, Salt Lake City.

DRYSDALE, JOHN (son of James Drysdale and Margrate Arnold). Born Oct. 10, 1839. Came to Utah 1853, Capt. Dailey company.
Married Emma Clark (daughter of James Clark and Elizabeth Pierson). She was born August, 1847. Their children: Margrate Pysdale b. 1862, m. Henry Goodale Dec. 18, 1882; Andrew C. b. 1871, m. Julia Gray Feb. 22, 1893; Mary Jane b. 1864; James b. 1867; John b. 1869; Henry R. b. 1876, m Sarah Jackson May 14, 1902; Nora R. b. 1878, m. Fremont Cook; Ann Adlin b. 1881; Edward F. b. 1887.
Indian fighter. Charcoal burner.

DUDLEY, JOSEPH (son of James Dudley of Nauvoo, Ill.). Born July 8, 1817, Kentucky. Came to Utah Oct. 3, 1852, oxteam company.
Married Sarah D. Stevens, who was born March 14, 1816. Their children: Martha, d. child; Sarah Ann, m. Alexander Williams; m. Charles Eldridge Smith; Andrew, m. Mary Ellen Packett and Mary Lucy Markham; Justus Manvill, m. Emily Packett; Helen, m. Alma Pace; William, d. child; Joseph, m. Sarah King.
Married Caroline Petty, Salt Lake City (daughter of Robert Petty of Fort Herriman, Utah, oxteam pioneer). She was born July 8, 1835. Their children: Percinda Jane, m. Mr. Pace; James; Celia, m. Isaac Robins; Warren, m. Sarah Jones; Marion, m. Louisa Jane McKee; Robert, m. Margaret Evans; Harriet, m. Mr. Stewart; Margaret, m. Ruben Hatch; Polly, m. John Evans. Family home Alpine, Spanish Fork and Provo, Utah.
Seventy. He was sent to Nevada and California to recall the people at the time of the invasion of the Johnston army; endured many hardships while crossing the desert. Echo Canyon war veteran. Died Aug. 24, 1893, Spanish Fork, Utah.

DUDLEY, ANDREW (son of Joseph Dudley and Sarah Stevens). Born June 6, 1844, in Illinois. Came to Utah Oct. 3, 1852, oxteam company.
Married Mary Ellen Packett Feb. 5, 1866, at Spanish Fork, Utah (daughter of Charles Packett of Spanish Fork, Utah, oxteam pioneer). She was born Feb. 10, ——. Their children: Mary Ellen b. Feb. 10, 1866, m. Charles Hollingshead; m. Albert Wilkins; Melissa and Lucy Emily, d. infants. Family home Spanish Fork, Utah.
Married Mary Lucy Markham July 19, 1869, Salt Lake City (daughter of Stephen Markham, pioneer July 24, 1847, and Mary Curtis of Spanish Fork, Utah). She was born April 2, 1853. Their children: Andrew b. Aug. 8, 1870, m. Sina Jensen; William b. Aug. 8, 1872, d. infant; Sarah Ann b. Nov. 3, 1873, m. Ephraim Rasmussen; Helen Aurelia b. April 20, 1876, m. L. H. Woodard; Stephen Markham b. July 28, 1878, m. Anna Bingham; Joseph Stratton b. Sept. 8, 1880, m. Mina Moon; Maryatta b. Jan. 3, 1883, m. Henry Chatwin; Guyletta Jane b. Feb. 10, 1885, m. Fitzgerald Stewart; Hosmer Marion b. May 28, 1887; Hyrum Sanford b. June 27, 1889; Arvilla Julina b. March 2, 1892, m. Jasper Otis Butcher; Bertha b. Dec. 8, 1894; Bernice b. Dec. 8, 1894, and Louis Marville, d. infants; Porney Trilby b. Dec. 21, 1897. Family resided Spanish Fork and Jensen, Utah.
Elder. Assisted in bringing immigrants to Utah 1863. Veteran Black Hawk war. Took active part in protecting settlers against Indians in the early days. Farmer.

DUDLEY, OLIVER HUNT (son of Steven Dudley and Harriet Haws of Vermont). Born Feb. 29, 1809, in Vermont. Came to Utah Oct. 13, 1850, Edward Hunter company.
Married Mary Ann Robinson 1831, Deerfield, Rockingham county, N. H. (daughter of Noah and Susannah Robinson, pioneers Oct. 13, 1850, Edward Hunter company). She was born March 3, 1811. Their children: Mary Ann b. Aug. 11, 1834, m. Edmund Ellsworth; Susan Jane Katherine b. June 8, 1836, m. Heber Hubbard; Oliver Noah b. Oct. 18, 1841; Brigham Simeon b. Aug. 28, 1845, m. Delilah Allen; Charles H. b. Aug. 18, 1848, m. Dora Wallace; Joseph Smith b. Sept. 30, 1851, m. Dora Snow; Hyrum Smith b. Sept. 30, 1851, m. Fidelia S. Tippets. Family home Willard, Utah.
Married Hannah Pullen.
Died 1897.

DUDLEY, HYRUM SMITH (son of Oliver H. Dudley and Mary Ann Robinson). Born Sept. 30, 1851, Salt Lake City. Married Fidelia S. Tippets March 30, 1874, Salt Lake City, (daughter of William P. Tippets and Sophia B. Mead, pioneers 1850, Capt. Hunt company). She was born March 28, 1854, Perry, Utah. Their children: Delin Elizabeth b. May 11, 1875, m. Benjamin Neibaur June 26, 1906; Mary Ann b. June 2, 1877, m. D. J. Bell April 5, 1905; Sophia Burnham b. Aug. 22, 1879, m. George C. Corey Nov. 13, 1904; Emma Druzilla b. April 15, 1881, m. George S. Davis March 26, 1901; Hyrum Smith b. April 30, 1883; Susan Rebecca b.

June 2, 1885, m. Perry B. Woodward Oct. 23, 1901; Olive Harriet b. Aug. 15, 1887; William P. b. Nov. 10, 1889; Joseph Clyde b. Oct. 14, 1891; Percy Lois b. May 25, 1894. Family home Rexburg, Idaho.
Pioneer Snake river valley. Superintendent Sunday school, Burton, Idaho, and bishop's counselor six years.

DUDLEY, JOSEPH SMITH (son of Oliver Hunt Dudley and Mary Ann Robinson). Born Sept. 30, 1851, Salt Lake City. Married Dora Snow Dec. 18, 1884, Logan, Utah (daughter of Larino Snow and Adilme Goddard), who was born Feb. 24, 1855. Their children: Joseph S. b. Sept. 26, 1885, m. Jennie Smith; Devere Snow b. 1888.
Married Agnes Allred.

DUERDEN, RICHARD (son of Richard Duerden and Martha Hudson of Marsden, Lancashire, Eng.). Born Feb. 19, 1830, at Marsden. Came to Utah Sept. 15, 1868, John Gillespie company.
Married Elizabeth Bradshaw 1851. Their children: Martha, m. Thomas Walton 1869; Nephi b. June 6, 1860, m. Augusta Boynton March 20, 1891.
Married Sarah Ann Starkie Feb. 1865, at Burnley, Eng. (daughter of James Starkie and Sally Spencer), who was born July 1, 1840, at Blacko, Lancashire, Eng.. Their children: Edmundson b. Dec. 14, 1866, m. Alice Hatch Dec. 11, 1890; Samuel b. Dec. 11, 1868; Richard b. Aug. 26, 1870, m. Susan Holt Dec. 28, 1893; Sarah Jane b. July 3, 1874, m. Jens Knud Neilson Oct. 28, 1897; Joseph Hudson b. Dec. 16, 1876; Spencer b. Jan. 10, 1877; Elizabeth b. Jan. 10, 1879, m. Elijah Pleggenas; William S. b. Jan. 2, 1881; Margret b. March 27, 1882, m. Vernon Felt. Family home Bountiful, Davis Co., Utah.
Member of high council Davis stake for thirty years. Merchant.

DUFFIN, ABRAHAM (son of James Duffin and Sarah Greaves). Came to Utah 1855.
Married Eliza Johnson, who died in Manchester, Eng. Their children: Maria, m. John Garratt Chambers; Sarah, m. Henry Foulkes.

DUKE, JONATHAN OLDHAM (son of James Duke and Mary Oldham of Derby, Derbyshire, Eng.). Born Aug. 31, 1807, in Derby. Came to Utah Sept. 15, 1850, James Pace company.
Married Mary Stone Dec. 30, 1828, at Derby, Eng. (daughter of Robert and Charlotte Stone of Derby). Their children: James b. Dec. 21, 1829, m. Almira Moore, m. Mary Murdock; Sarah Jane b. Nov. 11, 1832, m. James Smith; John b. Nov. 19, 1834, m. Martha D. Young, m. Mary Jones; Robert Stone b. April 14, 1837, m. Annar W. Ross Young; m. Rachel Horrocks; Mary Ann, died; Jonathan Moroni b. Oct. 23, 1844, m. Sarah Montgomery. Family home Provo, Utah.
Married Sarah Thompson Oct. 19, 1855, Salt Lake City (daughter of George and Jane Thompson of England). Their children: Charlotte b. Sept. 3, 1856, m. Dominicus Carter; George Jonathan b. May 25, 1858, m. Sarah T. Meacham; Sarah Ann b. Jan. 9, 1860, m. Jonathan Gledhill, m. Brigham Smith; Thomas William b. April 23, 1863, m. Pauline Smith; Elizabeth b. May 9, 1865, m. Jonathan Mecham. m. Halma Smith; Almira b. April 1, 1867, m. Richard Harrison; Mary b. April 1, 1867, died; Heber b. Aug. 19, 1869, m. Elizabeth Agnes Bouraine. Family home Provo, Utah.
Married Martha Thompson Dec. 3, 1855 (daughter of George and Jane Thompson). Their children: Mary Ann b. Dec. 21, 1857, m. Alma Brown; Charles Thompson b. April 24, 1860, m. Emily Williams; Jane b. Aug. 23, 1862, m. Thomas Alexander Meldrum; Joseph b. Nov. 23, 1864, m. Lucy Harrison; Hyrum b. Nov. 14, 1866, m. Elenor Ann Farrer; Alma b. Jan. 3, 1866, d. Nov. 16, 1866; Emma b. Aug. 9, 1868, d. Aug. 18, 1868. Family home Provo, Utah.
Member 11th quorum seventies. Settled in 12th ward, Salt Lake City, 1850, and worked as stone mason; moved to Provo 1851. Served there as city councilman. Bishop of 1st ward. Justice of peace and lieutenant of Silver Grays. Also followed farming. Died Dec. 31, 1868, Provo, Utah.

DUKE, JAMES (son of Jonathan Oldham Duke and Mary Stone). Born Dec. 21, 1829, Albany, N. Y. Came to Utah 1849, Amasa M. Lyman company.
Married Almira Moore 1854, Provo, Utah (daughter of Ethan Allen Moore and Sarah Weber of New York, pioneers 1849). She was born Feb. 21, 1836. Their children: James Moore, m. Mary L. Allred; Almira Jane, m. Moroni M. Meacham; Ethan Allen, m. Martha Jane Parcell; Robert Stone, m. Elizabeth B. Vanosdel; Joseph Moroni, m. Emily Jane Nysonger; John C., m. Loraney Ross; Helaman, died; Mahonri M., m. Willmuth Lamanda Wall; Bernice Gertrude, m. George A. Thomas; Roy Lamoni, m. Lotty Nye; Sarah Figena, m. James Albert Provost. Family home Wallsburg, Utah.
Married Mary Murdock.
High priest. Stone mason; farmer and stockraiser. Died May 21, 1892.

DUKE, ETHAN ALLEN (son of James Duke and Almira Moore). Born Sept. 23, 1857, Salt Lake City (daughter of John C. Parcell and Esther Lewis of Wallsburg, Utah, pioneers 1854, Capt. Bullock company). She was born Jan. 9, 1858. Their children: Martha Cloe b. Dec. 21, 1882; Hester Almira b. Nov. 11, 1883; Allen Parcell b. Feb.

1885, m. Florence Varley; Rose b. Sept. 28, 1886; Elizabeth b. Jan. 1, 1889; Emily Gertrude b. Oct. 6, 1890, m. Perry W. Harper; Ethan Moore b. Dec. 1, 1891; James Curtis b. May 11, 1894; Gerald B. Jan. 10, 1896; Violet b. Aug. 23, 1898; Lorin Wells b. March 1902.
Member 123d quorum seventies; high priest. Farmer and fruit raiser.

DUKE, JOHN (son of Jonathan Oldham Duke and Mary Stone). Born Nov. 19, 1834, Albany, N. Y. Came to Utah 1850.
Married Martha D. Young, 1857, Salt Lake City (daughter of Dolph and Rhoda Young). Their children: John H., Rhoda; Sarah Jane; Alfred; Annie; Louis; Joseph; Celistia; Ada M. Family home Provo, Utah.
Married Mary Jones 1857, Salt Lake City (daughter of Eliza Jones and Margrate Talbot, married in Morgan Co., Ohio, pioneers 1250). She was born 1840 in Ohio. Their children: Margrate; Elizabeth; Jonathan; Eliza A.; Laura Linona; Julia; Olive; May; Estella; Sylvia; Hannah.
Black Hawk war veteran. President 20th quorum seventies; counselor in high priests' quorum; patriarch.

DUKE, ROBERT STONE (son of Jonathan Oldham Duke and Mary Stone). Born April 14, 1837, Albany, N. Y. Came to Utah with father.
Married Anna W. Ross Young March 6, 1857, Provo, Utah (daughter of Adolphia Young, who died on the way to Utah, and Rhoda Jared, pioneer Sept. 25, 1852, John Tidwell company). She was born July 13, 1840. Their children: Robert b. Dec. 4, 1857, m. Anna J. Peterson; Adolphia Young b. Jan. 25, 1860, m. Emma Nilsson; Anna Lenora b. Dec. 18, 1862, m. John Cummings; Mary Maranda b. Sept. 23, 1864, d. April 22, 1881; Frances Marion b. Dec. 11, 1866, d. Sept. 2, 1879; Lawrence Brigham b. Jan. 10, 1869, m. Sarah K. Hicken; Rhoda Matilda b. Aug. 31, 1872, m. John A. Smith; Alma b. Jan. 15, 1874, d. June 18, 1879; William Wade b. July 20, 1876, d. July 14, 1879; Martha Jane b. Sept. 27, 1878, m. James William Rooker.
Married Rachel Horrocks Nov. 11, 1872, Salt Lake City (daughter of John and Ann Horrocks of Chesmore, Bolton, Lancashire, Eng., pioneers 1866). She was born Dec. 26, 1853. Their children: Mary Ann b. Dec. 10, 1876, m. Aldoras E. Dayton; Adelia B. Jan. 10, 1877, m. Albert Richens; Robert Roger b. Oct. 7, 1878; Emily Jane b. March 11, 1881, m. John J. Sellers; Lyman b. April 13, 1885; Betsy b. Oct. 12, 1888, m. Nels Anderson; Katy Lenhart b. Nov. 25, 1890. Family home Heber City, Utah.
Missionary to Pennsylvania 1882-84; high priest and patriarch; bishop of East ward, Heber City, 1884-1901; counselor to Pres. William Wall of Wasatch stake 1862. Assisted in bringing immigrants to Utah 1866. Settled at Heber City 1859 and helped to make first canals and wagon roads.

DUKE, ROBERT (son of Robert Stone Duke and Anna W. Ross Young). Born Dec. 4, 1857, Provo, Utah.
Married Anna Josephine Peterson Feb. 9, 1882, Salt Lake City (daughter of Swen August Peterson and Bety Dahlman of Trollhettan Falls, Sweden, who came to Utah 1872 by rail). She was born Feb. 21, 1860. Their children: Adolphia R. b. Nov. 16, 1882, m. Christina V. Lindsay; Joseph Pratt b. May 28, 1884; Mable Regina b. June 21, 1886; Seymour B. and Sterling S. b. July 1, 1888; Mina Laprele b. March 27, 1893; Dessie b. Dec. 20, 1894; Jerald Boyd b. Jan 13, 1897. Family home Heber City, Utah.
President Y. M. M. I. A. 1880; member 20th quorum seventies 1891-1901; missionary to Indiana and Ohio 1890-92; bishop of 1st ward Heber City 1901. Secretary and treasurer Heber Mercantile company 1905-12; director of Heber City bank 1908-12. Member city council 1908-12; president town board 1902-04, and 1908-12; treasurer Wasatch county. Farmer.

DUKE, GEORGE JONATHAN (son of Jonathan Oldham Duke and Sarah Thompson). Born May 25, 1858, Provo, Utah.
Married Sarah Temperance Meacham Oct. 26, 1881, at Provo (daughter of Lewis Meacham, born Sept. 4, 1814, Grafton county, N. H., and died March 22, 1895, Provo, Utah. and Lydia Wells, born Aug. 6, 1817, Onondaga county, N. Y., and died Oct. 20, 1890, at Provo; they later resided at Mercer, Pa.—pioneers Oct. 5, 1851). She was born May 3, 1863, Bountiful; Lydia b. Oct. 18, 1882, m. George M. Fuller; Sarah Emeline b. Nov. 18, 1883, m. Sidney T. Harding; George b. Feb. 25, 1885, m. Hilda Young; Albert b. Jan. 20, 1887, m. Fern Tanner; Lewis b. Dec. 18, 1888; Alice b. Sept. 27, 1890, m. Claud Carter; Orlando b. Dec. 22, 1891, died; Lenore b. Aug. 10, 1893; Matilda b. Sept. 29, 1895, died; Leila b. July 12, 1897; Florence b. Sept. 23, 1899; Thomas Alden b. March 16, 1901; Ralph b. Jan. 20, 1904, and Hilda b. Feb. 13, 1908, died. Family home Provo, Utah.
Farmer and ranchman.

DUNCAN, CHAPMAN (son of John Duncan and Betsy T. Putnam of Barnet, Caledonia county, Vt.). Born July 1, 1812, Bath N. H. Came to Utah Oct. 16, 1848, Barney Adams company.
Married Rebecca Rose. Only child: Ellen J., m. Charles Franklin Randall.
Married Locky Jones. One child: Emily D.
Married Rosanna Taylor Aug. 23, 1862. Their children: Taylor D.; Becky D.
Died Dec. 22, 1900, Loa, Utah.

DUNCAN, HOMER (son of John Duncan and Betsy Taylor Putnam of Barnet, Caledonia county, Vt.). Born Jan. 19, 1815, at Barnet. Came to Utah Oct. 16, 1848, Barney Adams company.
Married Asenath M. Banker 1841 in New York state (daughter of Platt N. M. Banker). Their children: Julia Emily b. April 25, 1845, d. April 26, 1873; John Chapman b. Sept. 9, 1846, m. Teresa Ann Urie; William Platt b. April 2, 1848, d. March 10, 1850; Permelia Asenath b. May 20, 1850, m. Frank C. Foster; Lydia Maria b. Nov. 24, 1852, d. Oct. 25, 1854; Homer Putnam b. Aug. 13, 1855, d. Aug. 2s, 1859, Mary Putnam b. Oct. 14, 1858, m. Louis Fisher; m. James Underwood; Lillies Isabel b. Aug. 30, 1862, d. Aug. 10, 1863; Emma Jane b. Oct. 20, 1864, m. William J. Strong; Don Delamore b. June 29, 1868, m. Anna H. Derrick.
Married Sarah Trippess July 11, 1863, at Salt Lake City (daughter of John Trippess and Susannah Barr of Foleshill, Eng.), who was born March 20, 1839, Coventry, Eng., and came to Utah 1862. Their children: Densmore Trippess b. Feb. 4, 1866, m. Nida Fuller; Sarah Ellen b. April 1, 1868, m. Robert Morris; May b. Sept. 17, 1871, d. March 9, 1901; Homer Horace b. May 26, 1873, m. Lottie Cheshire; Louis Chapman b. April 25, 1875, m. Zella Barton (deceased), m. Alice Foster; George b. July 8, 1877, d. same day; Israel Putnam b. May 20, 1880; Martha Putnam b. Jan. 25, 1885, m. Rodney W. Bartlett. Family resided Salt Lake City, Cedar City and St. George, Utah.
Missionary to Texas and England 1855-61; senior president 3d quorum seventies. Crossed the plains eleven times with oxteams. Called to help settle St. George 1863, later moved to Cedar City, returning to Salt Lake City 1885, where he died March 23, 1906.

DUNCAN, JOHN CHAPMAN (son of Homer Duncan and Asenath Malvina Banker). Born Sept. 9, 1846, Des Moines, Iowa. Came to Utah October, 1848, Barney Adams company.
Married Teresa Ann Heyborne May 27, 1872, at Cedar City, Utah (daughter of John Heyborne and Sarah Ann Melborn of Sydney, Australia, latter pioneer 1860, David H. Cannon company). She was born Jan. 27, 1854. Their children: Asenath Melvina b. May, 1873, m. Charles Perry; Julia Emily, m. William Hitchcock; Sarah Jane, Naomi Bell, Jessie Agnes, Emma Teresa, latter four died; George, m. Jennie Macdonald; John, d. infant; Bertha Roxana, m. Howard Pettie; Homer Chapman, d. infant. Family resided Cedar City and Ferron, Utah.
Missionary to eastern states 1875-76; member 91st quorum seventies; ward clerk and teacher. County commissioner; justice of peace. Farmer and stockraiser.

DUNCAN, DENSMORE TRIPPESS (son of Homer Duncan and Sarah Trippess). Born Feb. 4, 1866, Cedar City, Utah.
Married Nida Fuller June 22, 1893, Salt Lake City (daughter of William and Elizabeth Fuller of that place, pioneers 1862). Their children: Virginia b. Feb. 19, 1894; Marie b. July 14, 1900; Lora Bernice b. May 28, 1903. Family home Salt Lake City.
Missionary to eastern states.

DUNCAN, JAMES (son of John and Lydia Duncan). Born May 1, 1794, in Robertson County, Tenn. Came to Utah Sept. 24, 1848, Heber C. Kimball company.
Married Rebecca Herring Feb. 20, 1823, who was born March 25, 1807, and died June 11, 1830. Their children: James M. b. Sept. 12, 1826, died; Malinda b. June 14, 1827, d. July 17, 1844; Susan b. June 17, 1829, m. Joseph Henrie. Family home Bountiful, Utah.
Married Huldah Jones, March 7, 1833 (daughter of Chapwin and Ellen Jones), who was born May 4, 1813, in Wilson county, Tenn., came to Utah with husband and died Feb. 22, 1887. Their children: William Riley b. May 16, 1834, died; Matilda Ann b. April 25, 1836, m. Charles Henry Stoddard; Rebecca Jane b. June 14, 1842, m. John Poorman; John b. April 24, 1845, d. (Feb. 1, 1878), m. Martha Lewis. Family home Bountiful, Utah.
Presented the prophet Joseph Smith with a horse which the prophet named Joe Duncan, after himself and the donor. Farmer. Died May 4, 1874.

DUNCAN, JAMES (son of James Duncan and Mary McLaughlin of Lanarkshire, Scotland). Born Feb. 5, 1828, Greenend, Lanarkshire. Came to Utah September, 1852, John Higbey company.
Married Jennett Snedden 1850 (daughter of David Snedden and Christenia Lyle, pioneers 1852, John Higby company). She was born April 21, 1830, and came to Utah with husband. Their children: Mary J. b. April 15, 1854, m. James M. Stewart; David b. Feb. 4, 1855, m. Mary J. Stott; John b. Jan. 7, 1861, m. Annie Prisby; Christena b. March 24, 1863, m. Hugh Larson; Elizabeth E. b. Feb. 8, 1866, m. James M. Stewart; Adam b. Feb. 3, 1868, d. infant; Richard b. Feb. 8, 1869, m. Anna M. Martin; George, d. infant. Family home Meadow, Utah.
Early settler at Meadow. Bishop's counselor 18 years. Black Hawk Indian war veteran. Farmer. Died Jan. 4, 1912.

DUNCAN, WILLIAM (son of Henry and Jane Duncan of Scotland). Came to Utah Sept. 13, 1861, Joseph Horne company.
Married Mary Brown (daughter of Adam and Catherine Brown of Tranent, Haddington, Scotland). Their children:

PIONEERS AND PROMINENT MEN OF UTAH 851

Adam, m. Isabella Robbs; Peter, m. Annie McNeal; Henry, d. aged 4; Henry, d. aged 2; Catherine b. Dec. 28, 1846, m. John Thomas Moon; James, died. Family home Salt Lake City, Utah.
High priest. Died March 1874.

DUNCOMBE, JOSEPH (son of Henry Duncombe and Martha Etano of Dorliston, Staffordshire, Eng.). Born March 15, 1806, at Dorliston. Came to Utah November 1865, Thomas Taylor company.
Married Elizabeth Glover February 1833, Dorliston, Staffordshire (daughter of John Glover and Ann James, of that place). She was born Dec. 2, 1815. Their children: Caroline, m. Edward Kendrick; Martha d. aged 17; Henry m. Nancy Turner; Joseph, Thomas and Hannah, died; Ann, m. John Halmberg; Thomas Elijah, died; Nehemiah David, m. Fannie Haines; Eliza, m. Edwin F. Fletcher; Return, d. infant; Sarah, m. Melvin D. Cook; Franklin, m. Dora Hanson; Albert Joseph O., m. Mary Mackay. Family home Granger, Utah.
Seventy; president Willenhall branch in England. Farmer; miner. Died 1895.

DUNFORD, ISAAC (son of John Dunford of Trowbridge, Wiltshire, England). Born June 24, 1823, Trowbridge, England. Came to Utah Oct. 4, 1856, John Banks company.
Married Leah Bailey 1843 at Trowbridge, England (daughter of Jacob Bailey of Trowbridge, England). She was born September, 1825. Their children: Mary, died; William, m. Melvinia C. B. Whitney; Savinia, died; Alma B., m. Susa Young; Seaborne, died; Moroni, m. Sarah Bridwell; Albert, m. Mary Nelson; Eliza, died; Parley, m. Mary Jacobson; Oliver, m. Ida Osmond; James, m. Eliza Jacobson; Leah, m. David A. Brogue. Family home, Bloomington, Idaho.
Seventy; president of branch of church at St. Louis. Merchant. Died Oct. 4, 1877, Salt Lake City.

DUNFORD, ALMA B. (son of Isaac Dunford and Leah Bailey). Born Aug. 19, 1850, Trowbridge, England; came to Utah Oct. 4, 1856, John Banks company.
Married Susa Young Feb. 23, 1873, Salt Lake City (daughter of Brigham Young and Lucy Bigelow of Salt Lake City—pioneers July 24, 1847, Brigham Young company). She was born Feb., 1855. Their children: Leah E. b. Feb. 27, 1874. m. John A. Widtsoe; Alma B. b. Aug. 18, 1875. Family home Salt Lake City.
Married Lovenia T. Clayton Feb. 27, 1882, Salt Lake City (daughter of William Clayton and Margarette Moon of England—pioneers July 24, 1847, Brigham Young company). Their children: Isaac Clayton b. April 16, 1883; Carlos LeRoy b. May 19, 1884; Margarette, b. Aug. 10, 1886; Alice Amelia b. July 31, 1888; Rachel Grant b. Dec. 16, 1890; Ruth Olive b. Oct. 6, 1892; William Chauncey b. Sept. 10, 1895; Mary Lovenia b. Dec. 18, 1897.
Missionary to England 1877-78; member 52nd quorum seventies. Dentist.

DUNN, SIMEON ADAMS (son of Simeon Dunn and Sally Bath of Williamstown, Ontario county, now Groveland, Livingston county, N. Y.). Born Aug. 7, 1803, at Williamstown. Came to Utah Sept. 27, 1848, Brigham Young company.
Married Adeline Rawson July 3, 1828 (daughter of Amariah Rawson and Betsy Carpenter), who was born Nov. 27, 1811. Their children: Adeline b. June 11, 1830, m. Alpheus Haws 1845; Francis b. Dec. 5, 1831, d. 1834; Mary b. Nov. 2, 1833, m. Martin Luther Ensign; Maria b. March 3, 1836; Mosiah D. and Amariah b. Feb. 19, 1837; Betsy b. May 22, 1840, m. Alpheus P. Haws. Family home Nauvoo, Ill.
Married Margaret Snyder June 19, 1842, Nauvoo, Ill. (daughter of Jacob Snyder and Hannah Anderson), who was born March 12, 1812. Their children: Susanna b. May 6, 1843, m. Allen Hunsaker April 24, 1859; Simeon b. Feb. 9, 1846.
Married Jane Caldwell. Their child: Joseph Moroni b. Feb. 12, 1847, m. Susanna E. White Dec. 27, 1866.
Married Harriet Atwood Silver Jan. 3, 1847, Winter Quarters, Iowa (daughter of Arad Silver and Sophia Nichols), who was born July 22, 1818. Their children: Sarah Sophia b. July 8, 1849, m. John Dunn Jan. 12, 1867; Simeon Adams b. Jan. 13, 1851, m. Eunice E. Harmon Nov. 6, 1876; Eveline S. b. Sept. 12, 1853, m. Allen Hunsaker Oct. 5, 1868; Emeline S. b. Sept. 12, 1853, m. Frances R. Cantwell; Charles Oscar b. Oct. 13, 1855. m. Letitia Smith, m. Martha Jane Welch; Harriet S. and Henry S. b. Dec. 31, 1857. Family home Brigham City, Utah.
Married Elizabeth Wickham 1865, Salt Lake City, who was born Feb. 14, 1836, London, Eng. Their children: Ephriam W. b. April 15, 1866, m. Marian Whitney June 12, 1899; Lorenzo W. b. March 11, 1868.
President 15th quorum seventies 1845; missionary to Canada 1841; to New York 1844; Society Islands 1848-51; to Eastern states 1852. Settled at Brigham City, Utah, 1853.

DUNN, JOSEPH MORONI (son of Simeon Adams Dunn and Jane Caldwell). Born Feb. 12, 1847, Winter Quarters, Iowa.
Married Susanna Elizabeth White Dec. 27, 1866, Tooele, Utah (daughter of Jonathan White and Elizabeth Dodd, pioneers 1849, E. T. Benson company). She was born Feb. 4, 1848, Tealby, Eng. Their children: Joseph Owen b. Dec. 16, 1867, m. Mary Ann Craner Sept. 24, 1890; Elizabeth b. Dec. 13, 1869; Martha Jane b. Feb. 9, 1872, m. Frank Dramet May 10, 1894; Ann Eliza b. Jan. 7, 1875, m. Edgar Victor Ander-

son Dec. 8, 1897; Mary Adeline b. June 24, 1877, m. Herbert H. Vowles Jan. 5, 1898; Eveline b. Dec. 25, 1879; Effie Susanna b. Dec. 5, 1880, m. John Alfred Lindberg Oct. 9, 1901; Edith May b. Feb. 25, 1884, m. George F. Richards Jr. Dec. 18, 1902; Llewellyn Crandall b. Feb. 6, 1888, m. Terresa V. Jensen June 9, 1909. Family resided Bountiful, Brigham City and Tooele, Utah.
President elders' quorum 1884; member 43d quorum seventies; high priest. Served two terms in city council. Died Aug. 3, 1913.

DUNN, CHARLES OSCAR (son of Simeon Adams Dunn and Harriet Silver). Born Oct. 13, 1855, Brigham City, Utah.
Married Letitia Smith Oct. 18, 1876, at Brigham City (daughter of Samuel and Janet Maria Smith, who was born May 8, 1860, at Brigham City. Their children: Levi b. June 3, 1883, m. Mary Ann Miller Jan. 8, 1902; Oscar Smith b. Oct. 17, 1886, m. Media E. Nuttall Sept. 19, 1906; Harriet L. b. June 9, 1890, m. Victor J. Allen Dec. 18, 1913; Samuel A. b. March 12, 1898; Leslie S. b. April 15, 1900. Family resided Brigham City, Millville and College, Utah.
Married Martha Jane Welch Oct. 24, 1888, Salt Lake City (daughter of John Welch and Eliza Billington), who was born Feb. 24, 1859, Centerville, Utah. Their children: Charles Welch b. April 16, 1885, m. Lula M. Schenk Sept. 19, 1906; Eliza Jane b. Dec. 10, 1886, m. John A. Israelson Dec. 23, 1908; John William b. March 18, 1889; Eveline Silver b. Oct. 9, 1893; Simeon A. b. March 2, 1896; Lester W. b. Aug. 18, 1898.
Superintendent M. I. A. and assistant superintendent Sunday school Brigham City, Utah; labored in St. George temple 1882; bishop College ward 1831-1912. Moved to Cache county 1882, and labored in Logan temple 1884-85.

DUNN, WILLIAM G. (son of James Dunn and Jane Milner, of Staffordshire, Eng.). Born Feb. 16, 1812, in Staffordshire. Came to Utah June 6, 1851, freight company.
Married Elizabeth Howells Oct. 2, 1837, in Lancashire, Eng. (daughter of John and Elizabeth Howells of Manchester). She was born June 17, 1817. Their children: Elizabeth b. Jan. 1840, m. Peter Stubbs; James b. June 2, 1841, m. Hannah Fielding; Selina; Asenith; Hannah b. July, 1848, m. Alfred Dunkley; Elisha. Family resided Salt Lake City and American Fork, Utah.
Married Sarah Bradshaw. Their children: William B.; John S.; Joseph W.
Member 36th quorum seventies; member tabernacle choir 1851-55; member Nauvoo brass band 1851. Farmer. Died Dec. 25, 1894, Provo, Utah.

DUNN, JAMES (son of William G. Dunn and Elizabeth Howells). Born June 2, 1841, at Manchester, Eng. Came to Utah September 1853, A. O. Smoot company.
Married Hannah Fielding Jan. 10, 1861, Provo, Utah (daughter of James Fielding and Ann Henshaw, of Lancashire, Eng., pioneers 1855). She was born Aug. 9, 1843, and died March 12, 1888. Their children: James P. b. Oct. 1, 1861, m. Harriet Ann Snow; William F. b. July 2, 1863, m. Harriet Wilkins; Joshua F. b. July 30, 1866, m. Fanny Elliott; John Peter b. Dec. 14, 1867, 2. child; Henry F. b. March 3, 1869, m. Zina Cluff; Elizabeth Ann b. Aug. 24, 1871, m. Charles F. Decker; Hannah A. b. Nov. 11, 1873, d. child; Alice Eva b. Dec. 3, 1875, m. Robert Cunningham; Mary Ellen b. May 17, 1878, m. Arthur Craven; Emma May b. May 20, 1880, m. George A. Startup. Family home Provo, Utah.
Married Mattie Fitzgerald at Salt Lake City. Their children: Fern, m. Mr. Furner; Vera Earl; LeRoy. Family home Robinson, Utah.
High priest; member high council. Provo city councilman, alderman and commissioner. Lieutenant in Utah militia. Manager West Co-operative Association, also Provo woolen mills 10 years, and Mammoth Mining Company's mills 12 years.

DUNN, JAMES FIELDING (son of James Dunn and Hannah Fielding). Born Oct. 1, 1861, American Fork, Utah.
Married Harriett Ann Snow Feb. 1, 1882, Salt Lake City (daughter of John C. Snow, born in Lima, Ill., and Harriett Baker, born in Herefordshire, Eng., pioneers Oct. 9, 1852). She was born Nov. 6, 1861. Their children: Hannah H. b. Jan. 2, 1884, m. Nephi C. Hicks; Maud H. b. Feb. 9, 1886, m. Joseph A. Passey; Spencer S. b. Nov. 14, 1887, died; Erma A. b. Dec. 28, 1891, m. C. R. Stark; Marcus J. b. Oct. 20, 1893; Lora b. Aug. 23, 1896; Leon b. Oct. 15, 1898. Family home Provo, Utah.
Member 34th quorum seventies. Provo city councilman 1885-86. Commercial traveler; merchant.

DURFEE, JABEZ (son of Edmund Durfee and Lainey Pickle of Nauvoo, Ill.). Born May 10, 1828, New York. Came to Utah 1850, oxteam company.
Married Celestia Curtis Dec. 25, 1850, Salt Lake City (daughter of Enos Curtis and Ruth Franklin of Pennsylvania—pioneers 1850, oxteam company). She was born April 21, 1832. Their children: Mariah Elizabeth, m. Numan Van Luven; Jabez Erastus m. Sarah E. Kendall; Eliel, died; Celestia, died; Edmund Franklin, m. Nancy E. Martin; Celestia Chloe, m. Franklin D. Spencer; John Devalde, m. Zabrina E. Draper; LeGrande, m. Mary Jane Crowther; Vilate, m. C. M. Ivie. Family home Springville and Aurora, Utah.
First bishop of Aurora ward. Early settler to Aurora. Carpenter; farmer and fruitgrower. Died Dec. 27, 1884.

852   PIONEERS AND PROMINENT MEN OF UTAH

DURFEE, THOMAS. Came to Utah 1861, oxteam company. Married Charlotte Sanford. Their children: Henry, d. aged 18; Ellen, m. Abraham Penrod; Olive, m. George Pickup; Ida, m. Jep Dinsdale: Rolla, m. John Dinsdale; Fannie, m. John Faulkner. m. Elisha Wilbur. Family resided Ogden and Provo, Utah.
Elder. Carpenter and sawyer. Died February 1897, at Ogden.

DURRANT, JOHN (son of William Durrant and Mary Stewart of Bovington, Herefordshire, Eng.). Born April 8, 1837, Bovington, Eng. Came to Utah Oct. 13, 1861, E. R. Wright freight train.
Married Jemima Berry Henson (Turner) Dec. 24, 1862, Endowment House, Salt Lake City (daughter of James Henson and Hetty Lancaster of Deans Hanger, Eng., came to Utah about 1872). She was born Aug. 2, 1835.
Married Elizabeth Jane Ginger Aug. 9, 1870, Endowment House, Salt Lake City (daughter of William Ginger and Jane Childs of Herefordshire, Eng., latter came to Utah Aug. 20, 1868, Captain McMaster company, part of way on railroad). She was born Sept. 17, 1854. Their children: William A. b. Oct. 30, 1871, m. Eliza Conder; John Edward b. Dec. 23, 1873, m. Minnie Elizabeth Baxter; Lorenzo James b. Oct. 4, 1876, m. Agnes Priscilla Lewis; Mary Stewart b. Jan. 25, 1879 (d. Dec. 31, 1903), m. Albert Sagers Mott; Katie Jane Childs b. July 17, 1881, d. Aug. 11, 1890; Joseph Smith b. March 2, 1884, m. Lenora Holding; Lucy Hetty b. Sept. 23, 1885, m. John W. Wright; Jemima Berry Henson b. April 19, 1888, m. George E. May; Rosa Emmeline b. Nov. 13, 1893; Hyrum Sterling b. Feb. 11, 1895, d. infant. Family home American Fork, Utah.
Member 67th quorum seventies; high priest. Janitor many years; watermaster 1878 to 1908; gardener, vine dresser, farmer; conducted a molasses factory in American Fork from 1863 to 1900.
Jemima Berry Hensen was the widow of William Turner. Only child: a son, died infant.

DURRANT, THOMAS HOAR (son of William Durrant, born July 1814, and Phoebe Hoar, born May 23, 1816, both of Deanshanger, Northamptonshire, Eng.). He was born March 27, 1842, at Deanshanger. Came to Utah Aug. 20, 1868, Chester Loveland company.
Married Agnes Nish Dec. 28, 1874 (daughter of Robert Nish and Agnes Wilson—married Jan. 14, 1855, on Atlantic ocean, pioneers 1855, Richard Ballantyne company). She was born Feb. 10, 1857. Their children: Agnes Elvira b. Sept. 23, 1875, m. L. M. Mendenhall Dec. 15, 1897; Thomas William b. Dec. 20, 1876, m. Elizabeth M. Biggs Dec. 15, 1897; Phoebe Sarah b. Sept. 18, 1878, m. J. B. Robinson Sept. 15, 1898; James LeRoy b. Aug. 26, 1880, m. Lizzie Baker Dec. 17, 1902; Alonzo Robert b. Aug. 11, 1882, m. Elnora Morrison Dec. 21, 1906; Ida Maud b. July 14, 1885, m. Jerome B. Porter Dec. 24, 1903; Annie Eveline b. Nov. 11, 1886, m. Reuben Lowe Dec. 19, 1906; Ethel May b. Nov. 13, 1889, m. Hugh Sloan Nov. 9, 1910; Fredric Elmo b. May 5, 1892, m. Myrtle Whitehead Nov. 1, 1911; Jennie Ray b. Oct. 9, 1894; Isaac Alma b. May 22, 1889.
President Y. M. M. I. A; 2d counselor to bishop L. L. Hatch at Franklin; high priest; secretary of Sunday school Oneida stake 1884-97. Settled in Morgan City; assisted in building Union Pacific and Utah Northern Ry. Agent and telegraph operator in Corinne, Utah, and two years in Preston, Idaho. Member sixth session Idaho state legislature; member village board of trustees; village clerk; justice of peace; notary public and village magistrate in Franklin. Engrossing clerk for seventh session of Idaho state legislature.

DUSENBERRY, MAHLON. Born March 1, 1808, Frenchtown, N. J. Came to Utah July 18, 1860, Capt. Williams independent company.
Married Aurilla Coray May 21, 1831, at Easton, Pa. (daughter of Silas Coray, who died in Illinois, and Mary Stephens, both originally of Danville, N. Y., the latter a pioneer 1852). Their children: John b. Aug. 2, 1832, m. — Montague; Mary Ann b. Feb. 2, 1835, m. James F. Long, m. David Watson, m. Eliel Ogden; Warren N. b. Nov. 1, 1836, m. Adelaide Elizabeth Webb; Silas b. Dec. 11, 1838, d. child; Wilson Howard b. April 7, 1841, m. Harriet Virginia Coray, m. Margaret Thompson Smoot; Martha Jane b. April 15, 1843, b. Charles Dean Glazier; William b. June 12, 1845, d. infant; George b. July 7, 1848, and Albert B. Dec. 20, 1850, both died in childhood. Settled in California. Carpenter and cabinet-maker. Died Aug. 22, 1899, Sacramento, Cal.

DUSENBERRY, WILSON HOWARD (son of Mahlon Dusenberry and Aurilia Coray). Born April 7, 1841, Perry, Pike county, Ill. Came to Utah July 18, 1860, independent company.
Married Harriet Virginia Coray Dec. 4, 1864, Provo, Utah (daughter of Howard Coray and Martha Jane Knowlton, of Danville, N. Y., pioneers 1852). She was born Aug. 13, 1848, and died June 26, 1872. Their children: Charles Wilson b. June 2, 1866; May b. Nov. 25, 1867, d. Sept. 16, 1869; Blanche b. April 20, 1870, m. Edwin L Parker; Harriet Virginia, d. infant.
Married Margaret Thompson Smoot Nov. 25, 1874, Salt Lake City (daughter of Abraham Owen Smoot and Emily Hill, of Provo, Utah, pioneers September, 1847, Daniel Spencer company). She was born Aug. 27, 1854, Sugar House ward, Salt Lake county, Utah. Their children: Abraham Owen b. Dec. 5, 1875, m. Gertrude Louder; Lorena b. April 3, 1878; Ada b. April 6, 1881, m. Joseph F. Nibley; Cora b. Sept. 13, 1883; Eva b. Jan. 23, 1887, d. April 2, 1890; Edith b. May 16, 1891. Family home Provo, Utah.
High priest; member high council 1878. School teacher in Utah county 1863-75; county superintendent schools 1874-80; with his brother organized Timpanogos branch of University of Deseret 1870; secretary and treasurer of Brigham Young University since its organization in 1875. Member Provo city council 1872-88; mayor of Provo; county clerk 1875-82; member state legislature 1880, 1882 and 1884; chairman of house committee on education. Cashier First National Bank of Provo 1882-91; cashier Utah County Savings Bank 1891-1901; assistant postmaster of Provo 1901-13.

DYE, RICHARD (son of Thomas Dye and Sarah Gower, of Hertford, Hertfordshire, Eng.). Born Jan. 2, 1832, at Hertford. Came to Utah Sept. 20, 1858, Iver N. Iverson company.
Married Mary Peek Nov. 23, 1859, South Weber, Utah (daughter of Thomas Peek and Mary Malden, of Soham, Cambridgeshire, Eng.; latter pioneer Sept. 13, 1861, Joseph Horne company). She was born Aug. 21, 1841. Their children: Mary Adelaide b. Oct. 15, 1860, d. June 4, 1869; Richard Thomas b. Feb. 4, 1863, m. Elizabeth Jones; William Malden b. March 26, 1865, m. Julia A. Child; James Henry b. March 30, 1867, m. Nellie A. Child; Elizabeth b. Aug. 14, 1869, d. March 2, 1879; James b. Jan. 16, 1872, m. Mamie Pike; Walter Ernest b. July 16, 1874, m. Nellie Crofts; Samuel G. b. Oct. 10, 1876, m. Lydia Hobson; Sarah Gower b. Dec. 24, 1879, m. Walter Jarrell. Family home Riverdale, Utah.
Justice of peace 1872-1902; public school trustee 1876-1906; Sunday school superintendent 1876-1901; ward clerk 1880-1908; president 76th quorum seventies 1884-91.

DYE, SAMUEL G. (son of Richard Dye and Mary Peek). Born Oct. 10, 1876, Riverdale, Utah.
Married Lydia Hobson Oct. 22, 1902, Salt Lake City (daughter of Jesse D. Hobson and Joannah Lewis of Utah and Arizona). She was born Jan. 16, 1882. Their children: Eldon Hobson b. July 29, 1903; Melvin Lewis b. Feb. 18, 1906; Samuel Wayne b. June 22, 1910. Family home Ogden, Utah.
Clerk of board of education 1905-09; clerk Weber county 1909-14. First counselor to bishop of Riverdale ward; member high council Weber and Ogden stakes.

DYET, WILLIAM (son of Joean Campbell). Born 1836, Kelvin Grover, Scotland.
Married Martha Barnes Dec. 24, 1858, Polnan Parish, Sterlingshire, Scotland (daughter of Mark Barnes and Ann Armstrong of England, came to Utah July, 1881, with Ross Kelly). She was born Dec. 29, 1838. Their children: William B. b. March 7, 1860, m. Isabella Simpson; Joseph B. b. April 6, 1865, m. Katie Smith; Alexander b. April 4, 1865; Martha B., m. David Miller; James B. b. Aug. 29, 1867, m. Clara Lilya; John B. b. Dec. 29, 1869; Annie B. b. Jan. 22, 1871, m. Dougals McWilliams; Sarah B. b. July 3, 1874, m. Albert Butcher; Elizabeth b. Jan. 1, 1882. Family resided Salt Lake City, Utah, and Rock Springs, Wyoming. Ordained high priest June 2, 1907.

DYET, WILLIAM B. (son of William Dyet and Martha Barnes). Born March 7, 1860, Bo'ness, Scotland.
Married Isabella Simpson Jan. 11, 1892, Rock Springs, Wyo. (daughter of William Simpson and Frances Bell of England, came to Utah May, 1880). She was born Jan. 19, 1869. Only child: Mark W. b. March 31, 1900. Family resided Salt Lake City, Utah, and Rock Springs, Wyo.

DYKES, GEORGE P. Married Dorcas Keeling, who came to Utah 1852, Ezra T. Benson company. Their children: Lee, m. Lillie Cook; Rhoda Ann, m. George Martin Burgess.
Missionary ten years in England, Holland, France, Sweden and Denmark. Captain in Mormon Battalion. Died in Arizona.

DUZETT, EDWARD P. Came to Utah Sept. 24, 1848, Heber C. Kimball company.
Married Mary Adaline Ewing at Salt Lake City (daughter of Samuel Ewing and Elizabeth Schaffer of Little Britain, Lancastershire county, Pa., pioneers 1847). Their children: Alveretta, m. Joseph Pettey; Minerva; Marjorie, m. Nathan Terry; Urselia, m. Joseph A. Smith; Edward Hanmer, m. Rosa Hannah Slaughter; Rachel Vilate, died; Huldah, d. child. Family home Rockville, Utah.
The children of the second wife were: Clarissa, m. Johnson; Eliza, died; Jane, m. Frank Farnsworth; Emma.
Drummer in Nauvoo Legion. Teacher. Died November 1874, Rockville, Utah.

DUZETT, EDWARD HANMER (son of Edward P. Duzet and Mary Adaline Ewing). Born Jan. 1, 1861, at Salt Lake City.
Married Rosa Hannah Slaughter Feb. 1, 1882, at Rockville Utah, George Washington Terry officiating, daughter of Charles Merriwether Slaughter and Fanny Piety of Missouri—pioneers 1847, Mormon Battalion). She was born Sept 11, 1863, Grafton, Washington county, Utah. Their children: Edward Hanmer b. May 5, 1883, d. infant; Rosa Blanche

Nov. 10, 1884, m. Lewis W. Peterson; Virtue b. July 6, 1888, m. Arthur M. Anderson; Mable b. Oct. 23, 1891; Melvin b. June 10, 1894, d .infant; Melburn b. July 20, 1896; Robert b. March 17, 1899. Family home Emery, Utah.
Settled at Rockville when five years of age, where he assisted in making ditches, wagon roads, bridges, and in developing the country; moved to Hinckley 1890 and to Emery 1891. Farmer and stockraiser; merchant.

E

EAKLE, HENRY KENNEDY (son of John B. Eakle and Miss Kennedy, of Newhope, Va.). Born Nov. 28, 1828, in Virginia.
Married Mary Jane Johnson, in Virginia (daughter of Francis Johnson and Mary Jane Hall). Their children: Sarah Catherine, m. William B. Folsom; Betty Kerr, m. Eugene Peel; Millard F., m. Minnie Wilchen; Edgar F., m. Emma Cox; Mary Abi, m. Thomas Tidwell; Henry Francis, m. Ida Gochenhour; Julia Everiot; John Brigham, died; Anna Asenath. Family lived in Virginia.
Elder. Farmer and stockraiser.

EAMES, DAVID (son of Nathaniel and Cathrine Eames of Wales). Born Nov. 16, 1826, in North Wales. Came to Utah Sept. 17, 1850, Jonathan Foote company.
Married Esther Cullen in 1850, St. Louis, Mo. (daughter of James Cullen of England). She was born Oct. 15, 1830. Their children: David G., m. Elizabeth Greaves; Joseph C., m. Rebecca Williams; Cathrine, m. Joseph O. Greaves; Nathaniel; Arthur, m. Lydia Kidd; Rowland; Brigham; James; Ezra, m. Tressie Pink; Henry. Family resided Salt Lake City and Logan, Utah.
Seventy. Took part in Echo Canyon war. Carpenter and wheelwright. Died Nov. 17, 1885, at Logan.

EAMES, DAVID C. (son of David Eames and Esther Cullen). Born Sept. 1, 1851, at Salt Lake City.
Married Elizabeth C. Greaves Dec. 29, 1877, at Logan (daughter of Joseph Greaves and Sarah Priscilla Chesley of Logan). She was born Oct. 21, 1856, Provo, Utah. Their children: David G. b. Sept. 29, 1879; Sarah G. b. Nov. 1, 1881; Elizabeth G. b. June 6, 1884; Rebecca May b. Dec. 28, 1886; Aerial G. b. July 18, 1889; Nathaniel H. b. Aug. 3, 1892; Joseph Leland b. June 23, 1895; Rowland b. May 14, 1899, d. May 16, 1899; Ilah b. June 18, 1902. Family resided Logan, Utah, and Preston, Idaho.
High priest; home missionary Oneida stake 1900-01; counselor Preston ward bishopric nine years; member Oneida stake high council eight years. President and director of Cub River and Wormcreek Canal Co. 25 years. Farmer and stockraiser.

EAMES, DAVID G. (son of David C. Eames and Elizabeth C. Greaves). Born Sept. 29, 1879, Logan, Utah.
Married Pearl L. Geddes Jan. 25, 1905, Logan, Utah (daughter of Joseph S. Geddes and Dora Neeley of Plain City, Utah, and Preston, Idaho). She was born Feb. 22, 1882. Their children: David Ivo b. April 25, 1906; Melba Geddes b. May 14, 1909; Waldo Geddes b. April 11, 1911. Family home Preston, Idaho.
High priest; missionary to Northwestern states 1902-04; president of Mutuals at Preston; superintendent 3d ward Sunday school at Preston four years; first counselor to Bishop Carver of 3d ward, Preston, 18 months; stake Mutual superintendent. Vice-president and director of Riverdale Fruit and Farming Co. Farmer and stockraiser.

EARDLEY, JAMES (son of Edward Eardley and Elizabeth Grocket of Swadlincote, Derbyshire, Eng.). Born Feb. 25, 1830, at Swadlincote. Came to Utah Sept. 29, 1854, James Brown company.
Married Zurviah G. Fuller March 15, 1852, St. Louis, Mo. (daughter of Waiter Fuller, of Ludlow, Mass., and Eunice Gleason of Rowe, Mass., the former came to Utah 1855, the latter 1854, James Brown company). She was born Sept. 13, 1834. Their children: Edward A. d. infant; James W., m. Catherine A. Woolley; Eunice E., m. Barton Snarr; Adeline Z., d. infant; Bedson M., d. infant; Mary E., m. Thomas J. Curtis; Reuben H., m. Charlotte Solomon; Annie Z., m. William A. Sperry; Delia A., m. Mark W. Calder; Louisa E., m. Edward P. Midgley. Family home Salt Lake City.
Married Martha A. Preece 1871 (daughter of John Preece and Mary Ann Steel). Their children: John A., m. Elizabeth E. Brown; Albert W., d. infant; Martha M., m. Heber Donaldson; Ernest L.; George A.
Missionary to England 1884-86; superintendent Sunday school 3d ward, 33 years; high priest; patriarch. Captain of company in Echo Canyon war. Potter and merchant.

EARDLEY, JOHN (son of Edward Eardley and Elizabeth Grocket of Derbyshire, Eng.). Came to Utah in pioneer times.
Married Ann Crofts of Derbyshire. Their children: Elizabeth, died; Clara Elizabeth, m. James H. Mason; Agnes Ann, m. Joseph S. Smith; Hyrum Edward; Louisa Eliza, m. George

Faucett; Mary Ellen, m. Thomas Riding; John, m. Lottie Law; Emaline Phoebe; Florence, m. Joseph Hawk; Henrietta Drucilla. Family resided Salt Lake City and St. George, Utah.
High priest. Pioneer to St. George. Potter. Died March 1909.

EARL, BISHOP COLLIER (son of Charles Earl and Nancy Vinna Allen of Monroeville, Ohio). Born March 15, 1843, at Monroeville. Came to Utah July 4, 1861, by overland stage.
Married Sarah Ann Goates Dec. 28, 1868, Salt Lake City (daughter of William Goates and Susan Larkin of Lehi, Utah). She was born Oct. 29, 1846, and came to Utah late in 1852. Their children: Charles William b. Oct. 23, 1869, m. Jennie Fowler; Susan b. Jan. 8, 1872, died; Elida Vierna b. Nov. 15, 1874, died; Rebecca b. July 4, 1877, died; Olive b. May 15, 1879, m. Clarence Lott; John Hinckley b. May 12, 1881, died; Clara b. Nov. 5, 1883; Alma b. July 26, 1885, m. Elizabeth Candor; Jesse Allen b. Oct. 3, 1887, m. Lyle Boyle; Sarah A. b. Oct. 4, 1891, m. Junius McEwan. Family home Lehi, Utah.
Helped bring last immigrants that came overland from Ft. Benton, Wyo.

EARL, CHARLES WILLIAM (son of Bishop Collier Earl and Sarah Goates). Born Oct. 23, 1869, Lehi, Utah.
Married Jennie Fowler Dec. 7, 1898, Lehi, Utah (daughter of Henry Charles Fowler and Sarah Lee). She was born Sept. 29, 1877. Their children: Mildred Jennie b. Oct. 28, 1900; Lowell Allan b. Feb. 19, 1902; Harold Lee b. Dec. 8, 1903; Charles Franklin b. March 8, 1906.
Miner, contractor and electrician.

EARL, JONATHAN (son of George Earl and Sarah Earl of London, Eng.). Born July 29, 1816, Framlingham, Eng. Came to Utah Aug. 7, 1852.
Married Jane Wright March 22, 1847, in England (daughter of William Wright and Maria Downing of England). She was born Jan. 6, 1822. Their children: John, died; Joseph, m. Nettie Paul; George, m. Mary Harrison; Josephine, m. Benjamin Bright; Edwin, m. Lily Edmons; Alford, m. Agnus Harvy, Jesse died; Harry, m. Rachel Badley; Harriet, m. John W. Lunn; Frank, m. Sarah Olson. Family home Salt Lake City.
Farmer. Died Sept. 11, 1873.

EARL, MICHAEL (son of Launcelot Earl and Sarah Jackson). Born Jan. 3, 1835, Kendal, Westmoreland, Eng. Came to Utah Oct. 3, 1863, Daniel D. McArthur "Dixie" oxteam company.
Married Elizabeth Woolnough June 20, 1859, Islington, Middlesex, Eng. (daughter of Mark Woolnough and Rachel Skinner of London). She was born Sept. 7, 1832, in London, and came to Utah with husband. Their children: Elizabeth, m. John F. Lee; L. M.; M. W. Family home Salt Lake City.
Member 13th quorum seventies; performed many ordinances in the temple, and was ardent religious worker. Followed business of merchant tailor at 130 Main street (near what was called Teasdale alley) for many years. When he built his permanent residence, 436 G street, now a choice residence district, he was ridiculed, as it was far out of town, and inaccessible to water. Was an omniverous reader and accumulated a large library of choice literature. Was grandfather to nineteen and great-grandfather to five children, when he died Jan. 27, 1896, Salt Lake City.

EARL, SYLVESTER HENRY. Born Aug. 16, 1815, Scioto county, Ohio. Came to Utah July 24, 1847, Brigham Young company.
Was twice married, and the father of thirteen children, among whom was Joseph Ira born Sept. 6, 1852, who married Elethra Calista Bunker on March 15, 1880, and afterward Agnes Viola Bunker.
Performed several missions in the United States before coming to Utah; first counselor to Bishop A. H. Raleigh of 19th ward, Salt Lake City; missionary to England 1862-65. Died July 23, 1873, St. George, Utah.

EARL, JOSEPH IRA (son of Sylvester Henry Earl). Born Sept. 6, 1852, Salt Lake City.
Married Elethra Calista Bunker March 15, 1880 (daughter of Edward and Emily Bunker), who died in 1901.
Married Agnes Viola Bunker Dec. 11, 1885 (daughter of Edward and Mary Bunker).
Set apart as bishop of Bunkerville ward, St. George stake January 1908.

EARL, IRA JOSEPH (son of Joseph Ira Earl). Was born Dec. 16, 1884, and was an elder.

EASTMOND, ELBERT (son of John Eastmond and Margaret Lawrence). Came to Utah in 1858.
Married Elizabeth Brown (daughter of Joseph Brown and Ann Curtis, of Manasquam, New Jersey). Their children: Jefferson, m. Esther Hindley; Mary; Annie, m. John L. Snow; Joseph. Family resided Salt Lake City and American Fork, Utah.
Was sometimes kindly termed the father of free public schools in Utah. Carpenter and builder.

EASTMOND, JEFFERSON (son of Elbert Eastmond and Elizabeth Brown). Born at Great Kills, Staten Island, N. Y. Came to Utah in 1858.
Married Esther Jane Hindley Sept. 6, 1875, Salt Lake City (daughter of Jno. Hindley and Jane Charters Robinson, of American Fork, Utah). Their children: Elbert H. b. June 1, 1876; Jno. H. b. June 22, 1877, died; Jane May, m. Jas. Johnson; Elizabeth Ruby; Frank; Jefferson b. Sept. 16, 1880, died. Family home American Fork, Utah.
Elder. Carpenter, builder and architect. Died July 1, 1899.

EASTMOND, ELBERT HINDLEY (son of Jefferson Eastmond and Esther Jane Hindley). Born June 1, 1876.
Elder; member seventies; special missionary to New York city, 1900-1902. Instructor of manual training and art and design in Brigham Young University.

EATON, JOHN SEGERS (son of Joseph Eaton and Merniva Segers). Born April 2, 1842, Montrose, Lee Co., Iowa. Came to Utah 1849.
Married Emily Ann Robbins March 30, 1861 (daughter of Thomas F. Robbins and Ann Johnson), who was born Aug. 20, 1845. Their children: Lillian b. Dec. 25, 1862, d. Feb. 1, 1863; Leonora L. b. May 31, 1864, m. A. T. Doxey June 23, 1880; John Riley b. Sept. 5, 1866, m. Minnie Nicol; Annette M. b. Oct. 3, 1868, m. Lewis Ivie; Emily Ann b. Feb. 21, 1871, (d. Dec. 25, 1896), m. Frank Cherry; Bernice b. Feb. 18, 1873, m. Thomas Harris; Nora C. b. April 19, 1875, m. W. Slade; Daniel W. b. Dec. 5, 1877; Pheba A. b. Jan. 27, 1880, d. July 22, 1880; Chlorila Usler b. June 19, 1881; Wallas R. b. April 8, 1884, m. Evaline Biggs; Thomas L. b. June 22, 1887, m. Ida B. Maxwell. Family resided at Scipio, Utah, St. Johns, Ariz., and Breen, Colo.
Died March 25, 1912.

EATON, JOSEPH ORLANDO BECKWITH. Came to Utah by oxteam.
Married Victorine Elizabeth Walker at Pleasant Grove, Utah (daughter of Hanson McKowen of Pleasant Grove, Utah). Born at Pleasant Grove. Their children: Joseph, died; Manson, m. Percilla Richens; Elmer B., m. Rose Merrill; Elizabeth, m. William Winn; John B., m. Periettie Ross; Ernest, m. Susana McKowen; Benjamin; Irvin, m. Mary Fuller; Lewis, m. Sina Cook; Byron, m. Lucilla Hadlock; Zera, m. Alice Starkie; Vernee, m. Myrtle Wardle; Lthel, m. Reuben Hunting; Eva. Family resided Pleasant Grove and Vernal, Utah, where he died.

EATON, JOHN BURTON (son of Joseph Orlando Beckwith Eaton and Victorine Elizabeth Walker). Born Dec. 7, 1872.
Married Periettie Ross Sept. 26, 1902, Salt Lake City (daughter of Stephen Ross and Ginevra Molen of Lehi, Utah). She was born July 20, 1881, and came to Utah with Captain Tidwell company. Their children: Baby b. Sept. 1906, died; Baby b. July 12, 1908, died. Family home Vernal, Utah.
Missionary to Illinois and Indiana; Sunday school and ward teacher; bishop's counselor. Farmer. Died at Vernal, Utah.

EATON, ERNEST (son of Joseph Orlando Beckwith Eaton and Alice McKowen Eaton and Victorine Elizabeth Walker). Born Jan. 12, 1875, Pleasant Grove, Utah.
Married Susana McKowen March 10, 1897, Vernal, Utah (daughter of Phillip McKowen and Mary Hughes of Manchester, Eng., pioneers 1853 by wagon from Colorado). She was born March 6, 1877. Their children: Ernest Vernal b. Jan. 19, 1898; Mary E. b. Feb. 15, 1900; Joseph Lovell b. May 16, 1903; Clement b. May 3, 1905; Stanley b. April 18, 1910; Reba b. April 12, 1910.
Missionary to Manitoba, Canada, 1906-08; counselor to President Don B. Colton of Uinta stake; counselor to Bishop Glens Ward, Uinta stake; president Y. M. M. I. A., and superintendent of Sunday schools of Glens Ward. Teacher; trustee school district 14, Uinta county. Home-builder, farmer, stockman and merchant.

EATON, IRVIN (son of Joseph Orlando Beckwith Eaton and Victorine Elizabeth Walker). Born Nov. 21, 1879, Pleasant Grove, Utah.
Married Mary Adaline Fuller Feb. 25, 1903, Vernal, Utah (daughter of Ruben Calton Fuller and Anna Adaline Preece of that place, pioneers 1848). She was born Nov. 3, 1882. Their children: Mary Elva, b. June 18, 1904; Eunice Marsale b. Sept. 23, 1906; Baby, b. Aug. 26, 1912.
President Y. M. M. I. A. 1908-12; ward teacher. City councilman 1911-12. Butcher.

EBY, JOHN. Born Oct. 6, 1814, Lancaster, Pa. Came to Utah in 1848.
Married Elizabeth Pierce at Lancaster, Pa. (daughter of Edward Pierce and Posey Pierce), who was born April 1, 1820. Their children: Margaret, d. infant; Jacob; Eliza, m. John W. Phillips.
Married Mary Winchel of Salt Lake City. Their child: John.
Farmer and lived at Salt Lake City. Died May 18, 1900.

ECCLES, WILLIAM (son of William Eccles and Margaret Miller of Carlisle, Eng.; former died in England; latter came to America in 1843, and died at Nauvoo, Ill.). He was born April 6, 1826, Old Kilpatrick, Dumbartonshire, Scotland. Came to Utah Oct. 4, 1863, Thomas E. Ricks company).
Married Sarah Hutchinson (daughter of William Hutchinson and Mary Speers), who was born March 17, 1820, County Donegal, Ireland, and died June 11, 1907, Ogden, Utah. Their children: John H. b. May 12, 1846, m. Mary Richmond; David b. May 12, 1849, m. Bertha Marie Jensen; m. Ellen Stoddard; Stewart b. Jan. 15, 1852, m. Marintha E. Bingham March 4, 1878; Sarah b. Dec. 31, 1854, m. Robert Baird Oct. 17, 1870; Margaret b. July 1857, m. John Hiatt, m. Charles Swinger; William Hutchinson b. March 15, 1860, m. Marian Scow; Samuel b. Feb. 17, 1862, m. Jeanette Hiatt June 22, 1883. Family home Ogden, Utah.
Settled at Eden, Weber county, 1865. Patriarch. Wood turner. Died Dec. 4, 1903, Ogden, Utah.

ECCLES, JOHN HUTCHINSON (son of William Eccles and Sarah Hutchinson). Born May 12, 1846, Paisley, Renfrewshire, Scotland.
Married Mary Richmond Dec. 10, 1865 (daughter of John Richmond, and Jeanette Barr), who was born Dec. 6, 1845. Their children: Mary, William, Sarah, Maggie and David, all of whom died; John b. Sept. 29, 1878, m. Hannah Davis; Jeanette b. Dec. 29, 1880, m. Charles Conrad; Virginia b. June 20, 1882, m. Joseph Edwin Caldwell; David Richmond b. March 20, 1887, m. Myrtle House.
Cabinetmaker and turner. Contractor and builder. President Eccles Mercantile Co., Baker City, Idaho; merchant.

ECCLES, DAVID (son of William Eccles and Sarah Hutchinson). Born May 12, 1849, Paisley, Renfrewshire, Scotland. Came to Utah Oct. 4, 1863, with father.
Married Bertha Marie Jensen Dec. 27, 1875, Salt Lake City (daughter of Christen Jensen, born Sept. 25, 1818, Aabey, Denmark, died May 7, 1875, Huntsville, Utah, and Mary Anderson, born April 8, 1825, Panerup, Aarhus, Denmark, died 1858, at Aarhus. The father with his family came to Utah Oct. 5, 1867, Leonard G. Rice company). She was born Jan. 30, 1856, Panerup, Aarhus, Denmark. Came to Utah with her father in 1867. Their children: David Christen b. Nov. 29, 1877, m. Julia Wright Feb. 8, 1905; LeRoy b. Nov. 20, 1879, m. Myrtle Banks Feb. 9, 1905; Vida b. July 9, 1882, m. George H. Davis; Royal b. Dec. 9, 1885; Bertha Olivia b. Jan. 22, 1887, m. William Arthur Wright; Joseph Merrill b. Aug. 22, 1889; Lila b. Nov. 26, 1891; Laura b. May 9, 1894; Flora b. May 9, 1894; Marintha A. b. Aug. 8, 1895; Annie Vivian b. April 18, 1897; Homer Gordon b. April 18, 1901. Family home Ogden, Utah.
Married Ellen Stoddard Jan. 2, 1885, Logan, Utah (daughter of John K. Stoddard and Emma Stoddard, pioneers 1856). She was born Jan. 28, 1867. Their children: Marriner S. b. Sept. 9, 1890; Marie b. Nov. 2, 1892; Spencer b. July 20, 1894; Jesse b. May 12, 1896; Emma b. March 6, 1898; George b. April 9, 1900; Norah b. July 18, 1902; Ellen b. June 23, 1905; Willard b. Feb. 22, 1909. Family home Logan, Utah.
Member 160th quorum seventies. Member Ogden city council 1885-87; mayor of Ogden 1887-89. When the L. D. S. church authorized its $1,000,000 bond issue, David Eccles, with L. S. Hill was the trustee and negotiated this loan; he carried $100,000 of it. At the time of his death he was identified with some fifty-six industrial corporations and twenty banking institutions, extending and operating in Utah, Oregon, Washington, Idaho, Nevada, Wyoming, California, Colorado and Canada. He was president and director of sixteen industrial corporations and a director of twenty others; president and director of seven banking corporations, and director in four others. He conceived and organized the Utah & Pacific Railway company, which later became a part of the Oregon Short Line R. R. Co., and finally that part of the San Pedro, Los Angeles & Salt Lake railroad between Milford and Uvada; this construction was the nucleus of the great railroad system last above named. Among the major enterprises with which he was connected as the president and a member of the board of directors are: Amalgamated Sugar company; Lewiston Sugar company; Sumpter Valley Railway company (Oregon); Utah Construction company; Oregon Lumber company (Oregon); Vinyard Land and Livestock company (Nevada); Promontory-Curlew Land company; First National Bank of Ogden; Ogden Savings Bank; Lion Coal company (Wyoming); Wyoming Coal company (Wyoming); Ogden Rapid Transit company; Logan Rapid Transit company; and Eccles Lumber company. Some of the more important corporations with which he was identified as a director are: Utah-Idaho Sugar company; Deseret National Bank of Salt Lake City; Deseret Savings Bank of Salt Lake City; and Mount Hood Railroad Company of Oregon. Died Dec. 5, 1912, Salt Lake City, Utah, buried at Ogden.

ECCLES, STEWART (son of William Eccles and Sarah Hutchinson, of Glasgow, Scotland). Born Jan. 15, 1852, Glasgow, Scotland. Came to Utah with father.
Married Marintha E. Bingham Mar. 14, 1878, Salt Lake City (daughter of Erastus Bingham and Susan Green, of Huntsville, Utah, pioneers July, 1847, with Mormon Battalion. She was born May 26, 1862. Their children: Christabella b. May 9, 1879, m. David Johnson; Stewart b. March 12, 1881, m. Anna Rasmussen; Marintha A. b. Sept. 20, 1883.
Missionary to Great Britain 1894-96 and 1903-05; member high council Ogden stake.

ECKERSLEY, JOSEPH (son of Abraham Eckersley, born 1836, West Houghton, Lancashire, Eng., and Ellen Cleworth, born June 18, 1839, Davyhulme, Lancashire, Eng., married 1854). He was born July 19, 1866, Eccles, Lancashire, Eng. Came to Utah May 24, 1890.

Married Sarah Ellen Wilkinson Dec. 10, 1890, Manti, Utah (daughter of James Wilkinson of Hindley, Lancashire, Eng., and Alice Wright, married 1866 at Burnley, Lancashire, and came to Utah 1896). She was born Jan. 29, 1870, and came to Utah Aug. 1890. Their children: Joseph Smith b. Sept. 8, 1891; Alice Ellen b. June 19, 1893; George Teasdale b. May 6, 1895; James Wilkinson b. Feb. 21, 1897; Abraham Cleworth b. May 21, 1899; Daisy Hermine b. May 16, 1904; Lyman Wilkinson b. March 24, 1907; Hyrum Wilkinson b. March 15, 1909.
Settled first at Springville and later at Loa, Utah. County attorney; county superintendent of district schools; state senator. President 82d quorum seventies; stake superintendent of Sunday schools 1894-1901; missionary to Great Britain 1888-90, 1901-03; high priest; 2d counselor to Willis E. Robison, president of Wayne stake 1903; 1st counselor to Gearsen S. Bastian, president of Wayne stake 1906; president Wayne stake 1910.

EDGEL, GEORGE (son of William Edgel). Born July 19, 1829, Headly, Hampshire, Eng. Came to Utah Oct. 1, 1863, Daniel D. McArthur company.
Married Mariah Noble Apgood Oct. 8, 1864 (daughter of William Noble and Carolina Hansen, latter a pioneer 1859). She was born 1826; came to Utah with her mother in 1859. The only child was Sarah Ann b. Aug. 14, 1865, m. Shadrach Roundy 1887.
Married Elizabeth Bailey Dec. 20, 1865, Coalville, Utah (daughter of Francis Bailey and Eliza Smith; former came to Utah 1864, Warren Snow company). She was born Sept. 23, 1842, Hardway, Hampshire, Eng. Their children: Albert b. Dec. 13, 1866; Mary E. b. Dec. 9, 1868, m. Civilian Winters Dec. 25, 1890; Louisa b. March 19, 1871, m. Alma L. Sargent May 26, 1898; John F. b. Aug. 30, 1873, m. Maud E. Hillier; Alberta b. March 19, 1875; Franklin J. b. Aug. 24, 1878, m. Florence A. M. Warner Aug. 18, 1909; Hattie b. Oct. 25, 1880; William R. b. July 6, 1882, m. Olive V. Lemon Aug. 4, 1909; Clara A. b. July 18, 1884; Ruby b. July 30, 1886.

EDGEL, JOHN F. (son of George Edgel and Elizabeth Bailey). Born Aug. 30, 1873, Hoytsville, Utah.
Married Maud E. Hillier Jan. 5, 1910, Salt Lake City (daughter of John W. Hillier and Edith E. Banham), who was born Jan. 3, 1888, London, Eng. Their children: Herman H. b. May 27, 1911. Family home Hoytsville, Utah.

EDGEWORTH, JOSEPH (son of William and Martha Edgeworth). Born Sept. 16, 1844, at Candle Green, Gloucestershire, Eng. Came to Utah Sept. 5, 1866, Samuel White company.
Married Prudence Jones Nov. 10, 1867 (daughter of William Jones and Mary Shill). She was born July 4, 1847; came to Utah 1866, Capt. Chapman company. Their children: Elizabeth Prudence b. Aug. 20, 1868, m. Alfred R. Jones Nov. 11, 1880; William b. Feb. 23, 1871, m. Eva Norwell Aug. 7, 1908; Jane Sophia b. May 7, 1873, m. Henry E. Randell Nov. 10, 1893; Martha Jones b. March 25, 1875, m. Iden G. Bond Sept. 30, 1896; Mary Ann Shill b. Sept. 3, 1879, m. Thomas Ovard Aug. 9, 1899. Family home Henefer, Utah.
Farmer.

EDWARD, ALEXANDER D. (son of Alexander Edward and Mary Taylor of Scotland). Born Feb. 20, 1865.
Married Ann E. Parker Dec. 17, 1896, at Salt Lake City (daughter of Joshua Parker and Drucilla D. Hartley, pioneers 1852, Robert Wimmer company). She was born Jan. 21, 1863, at Salt Lake City. Family home Salt Lake City.

EDWARDS, JOHN (son of Owen Edwards and Ester Davis). Born Jan. 17, 1817, Langoedmore Parish, Cardiganshire, South Wales. Came to Utah in 1853.
Married Margaret Roberts Aug. 28, 1843, Vanor, South Wales. Their children: Ann, m. Mr. Nelson; Margarette, m. Mr. Clarke; J. R.; Hyrum; Thomas, died; William; Edward; Mary Jane, m. Mr. Davis.
Settled at Brigham City, Utah; moved to Logan 1859. Coal miner and farmer. Died Feb. 26, 1886, at Logan.

EDWARDS, WILLIAM (son of John Edwards and Margaret Roberts). Born Oct. 22, 1857, Brigham City, Utah.
Married Mary Ann Lewis Dec. 16, 1880, Salt Lake City (daughter of Enoch Lewis and Emma Farrell of Wales). Their children: Annie R., m. Geo. W. Flamm; W. Lewis; Mae; McLairon; Oliver Wendell; Don C.
Member Logan city board of education 1893-94; chairman Cache county commissioners 1901-02; mayor of Logan 1908-09.

EDWARDS, WILLIAM LEWIS (son of William Edwards and Mary A. Lewis). Born Aug. 13, 1886, at Logan, Utah. Elder; missionary to Great Britain 1909-10. Musician and merchant.

EDWARDS, PHILIP. Came to Utah 1860.
Married Mary Simmons February, 1860, in Sussex, Eng. Their children: Lucy, m. William N. Casper; Philip W., m. Bertha Webster; Eliza, m. George H. Bagley; George H., m. Mary A. Hartle; Emma, m. Eliska Webster; John O., m. Minerva Anne Bagley; J. Parley, m. Clara Bagley; Alice M., m. Robert S. Lindsay. Family home, Charleston, Utah. High priest. Butcher.

EDWARDS, JOHN O. (son of Philip Edwards and Mary Simmons). Born Aug. 20, 1873, at Millcreek, Utah.
Married Minerva Anne Bagley Jan. 18, 1897, at Charleston, Utah (daughter of Joseph Bagley and Ann Van Wagoner of Charleston, Utah). She was born April 8, 1878. Their children: Clarence O. b. May 26, 1898; Minerva b. Oct. 11, 1900; Maud b. Sept. 22, 1904; Viola b. Dec. 31, 1908; Dana b. Aug. 26, 1911. Family home Charleston, Utah.
Missionary to Missouri 1905-07; president elders' quorum; superintendent Sunday schools; bishop's counselor; home missionary. President of town and city council; school trustee. Manager co-op. at Charleston.

EGBERT, SAMUEL (son of John Egbert, born 1776, Staten Island, N. Y., and Susanna Kahn, born Aug. 10, 1770, Staten Island, N. Y., both of South Cottonwood, Utah). He was born March 24, 1814, Breckinridge county, Ky. Came to Utah Oct. 15, 1849, Allen Taylor company.
Married Margrett Mariah Beckstead 1839 in Illinois (daughter of Alexander Beckstead and Catherine Lince of West Jordan, Utah, pioneers 1848). She was born Dec. 9, 1823. Their children: William Henry b. 1840, died; John Alexander b. March 28, 1842 [marriages below]; Martha Ann b. March 1, 1844, m. Isaac Wardell; Andrew Jackson b. Feb. 4, 1846, died; Susannah b. Feb. 14, 1848, m. Mr. Vannetten, m. Daniel Jerman; Catherine Mann b. Sept. 21, 1850, m. Henry Byrum Beckstead; Samuel Wesley b. Aug. 26, 1852, m. Ann Gardner, m. Lucinda Beckstead; Harriet b. Sept. 13, 1854, m. Samuel Bateman; Amanda Jane b. Jan. 5, 1857, m. Henry Byrum Beckstead; Joseph Smith b. Jan. 10, 1859, m. Sarah Pierce; Hyrum Smith b. Dec. 30, 1860, m. Annie McGhie; Mary Ellen b. Feb. 21, 1863, m. Hyrum Steadman; George A. Smith b. Nov. 18, 1865, died; David Alonzo b. Aug. 4, 1868, m. Hannah Aylett. Family home West Jordan, Utah.
Married Louisa Minerva Pettie at Salt Lake City (daughter of Robert C. Pettie and Margret J. Wells, pioneers 1848). She was born Dec. 22, 1839, Benton county, Tenn. Their children: Margret b. Aug. 8, 1858; Polly Ann b. April 21, 1860, m. Samuel Boyd; Galletta b. May 18, 1862; Robert C. b. Sept. 4, 1864, m. Clara Bradford; Henry Lewis b. Dec. 12, 1866, m. Sarah Farmer; Emily b. Nov. 6, 1869, m. Isaac Wardell; Louisa b. Feb. 22, 1872, m. Joseph Allsop; William Lafayette b. Nov. 22, 1876, m. Clara Farmer. Family home West Jordan, Utah.
School teacher, West Jordan. Indian war veteran. Farmer and stockraiser. Died Dec. 11, 1888.

EGBERT, JOHN ALEXANDER (son of Samuel Egbert and Margrett Mariah Beckstead). Born March 28, 1842, Hancock county, Ill.
Married Emma Grimmett March 22, 1860, West Jordan, Utah (daughter of John Grimmett and Sarah Pettie, both of Bear Lake, Idaho, pioneers of 50's). She was born July 12, 1842, in England. Their children: Sarah Zerelda b. April 5, 1861, m. John Harris and Joseph Hammer; John Alma b. May 16, 1863, died; Samuel Alexander b. Jan. 20, 1865, m. Eunice S. Prim, m. Louisa Corilla White; Emma Mariah b. Sept. 27, 1866, m. R. W. Barnes; Martha Ann b. March 17, 1869, m. John Aylett; Annie Generra b. Sept. 2, 1871, m. Frank M. Young; Rosina b. Feb. 17, 1874, died; Adelbert Leroy b. Oct. 22, 1876, m. Verna Pack; Lorus Edgar b. April 30, 1879, died; Etna Lulu b. June 11, 1880, died. Family home West Jordan.
Married Arminta Elizabeth Bateman March 9, 1882, Salt Lake City (daughter of Samuel Bateman and Marinda Allen), who was born Dec. 4, 1862, West Jordan. Their children: Laura Marinda b. Jan. 5, 1883, died; John Alonzo b. Oct. 16, 1884, m. Nellie Beckstead; Cora b. Jan. 2, 1887, died; Ethel Laurelda b. Feb. 9, 1888, m. George Sivell Smith; Marinda Lisetta b. March 1, 1890, died; Elija Jenetta b. Dec. 23, 1891, died; Wilford Earl b. Nov. 8, 1893; Verd Irene b. Dec. 12, 1895; Margrett Arminta b. Jan. 5, 1897; Alma Mark L. Dec. 26, 1899; Arvill B. b. Jan. 15, 1902; Harold Allen b. April 17, 1904; Ross Duane b. Oct. 24, 1906, Ida Lathield b. Nov. 23, 1910. Family home West Jordan.
President seventies' quorum; president 12th quorum elders; ordained bishop June 1, 1890, which office he held 20 years; went on a mission to help settle the Dixie country. Farmer and stockraiser.

EGBERT, SAMUEL ALEXANDER (son of John Alexander Egbert and Emma Grimmett). Born Jan. 20, 1865, West Jordan, Utah.
Married Eunice S. Prim Dec. 24, 1885, Lander, Wyo. (daughter of Wyrum P. and Mariah Prim of Sugar House ward, Salt Lake county). She was born Sept. 22, 1867. Their children: Roland L. b. Jan. 10, 1886, died; Keith Eugene b. Oct. 20, 1887, m. Margrett Nannie; Grace Marguerite b. Dec. 12, 1893, m. Joseph Parley White; Emma Maria b. Nov. 3, 1897; Loyal Douglas b. Jan. 15, 1900. Family home Grace, Idaho.
Married Louisa Corilla White July 22, 1908 (daughter of Joseph Egbert and Louisa Taylor, pioneers July 24, 1847, Brigham Young company).
One of first school trustees of Grace, Idaho.

EGBERT, ROBERT C. (son of Samuel Egbert and Louisa Minerva Pettie). Born Sept. 4, 1864, Salt Lake City.
Married Clara F. Bradford March 13, 1889, West Jordan, Utah (daughter of Larkin H. Bradford and Annie Rex), who was born April 12, 1866, at Salt Lake City. Their children: Tessie F. b. Oct. 11, 1889, m. William B. Turner; R. Glenn b. Aug. 13, 1891, m. Maude Bateman; Ferrell C. b. Oct. 25, 1892; Moss L. b. June 11, 1900; Valgie M. b. Nov. 7, 1901; Larkin H. b. March 8, 1906. Family home Salt Lake City.
Died March 19, 1908, at Salt Lake City.

EGGERTSEN, SIMON PETER (son of Peter Eggertsen and Caroline Larsen of Fyen, Denmark). Born Feb. 7, 1826, Fyen, Denmark. Came to Utah Sept. 13, 1857, Christian Christiansen company.
Married Johanne Thompson Feb. 7, 1858, Salt Lake City (daughter of Thomas Andreason and Sarah Louisa Nyegreen of Jutland Hals, Denmark, pioneer Sept. 13, 1857, C. Christiansen company). She was born Jan. 2, 1825. Their children: Sarah Louisa, m. Harvey H. Cluff; Simon Peter, m. Henrietta Nielsen; Andrew, m. Artie Louise Cook; Lars Echert, m. Annie Nielsen. Family home Provo, Utah.
High priest; missionary to Denmark 1853-56. Farmer. Died Sept. 27, 1900.

EGGERTSEN, SIMON PETER (son of Simon Peter Eggertsen and Johanne Thompson). Born Sept. 15, 1860, Provo, Utah.
Married Henrietta Nielsen June 26, 1884, Salt Lake City (daughter of Soren Nielsen and Amelia Berg of Provo, pioneers Sept. 25, 1868, John G. Holman company). She was born Sept. 8, 1861. Their children: Achsa Henrietta b. June 28, 1886, m. W. Monroe Paxman; S. Bernard b. Jan. 6, 1888; Doressa b. April 12, 1890, m. John S. Smith; Lorie Louisa b. March 3, 1892, m. Robert P. Fairbanks; Eudora b. Feb. 26, 1894; Grant N. b. May 1, 1898; Paul b. July 11, 1901. Family home Provo, Utah.
Member high council; missionary to northern states 1886-87; bishop; Sunday school teacher and superintendent; home missionary. School trustee and school teacher. Merchant and farmer.

EGGLESTON, SAMUEL (son of Samuel Eggleston and Elisabeth Hill of Ogden, Utah). Born March 30, 1804, Marcellus, Onondaga county, N. Y. Came to Utah August 1862, James Wareham Independent company.
Married Lurania P. Burgess Aug. 23, 1827, Cayuga county, N. Y. (daughter of Harvey and Mary Burgess of Niles, Cayuga county, N. Y.). She was born Aug. 15, 1808, died July, 1870. Their children: Dwight b. Aug. 9, 1828, and Benjamin b. April 6, 1830, both died infants; Reuben Burgess b. July 24, 1831 (d. March 1890), m. Emeline Allen; Edwin b. Oct. 25, 1833, m. Eliza Spinning; Harvey Burgess b. Feb. 8, 1836, d. Feb. 12, 1864; Orson Hyde b. Oct. 3, 1841, m. Constant A. Stephens; Samuel E. b. Aug. 16, 1847, died in infancy; Mary Elizabeth b. Sept. 22, 1849, m. Enoch Farr. Family home Ogden.
Married Elizabeth Mumford.
Married Catherine Kat.
Second counselor to Bishop Robert McQuarrie of 2d ward, Ogden, several years; patriarch. Died May 26, 1884.

EGGLESTON, ORSON HYDE (son of Samuel Eggleston and Lurania Burgess). Born Oct. 3, 1841, Niles, Cayuga county, N. Y. Came to Utah Aug. 16, 1861, David H. Cannon company.
Married Constant A. Stephens (daughter of John Stephens and Elizabeth Briggs), who was born Feb. 17, 1849. Their children: Ida Evaline, d. infant; Mary Lurania, m. John Jewett; Elizabeth Jane, m. Benj. F. Welch; Orson Burgess, m. Anna Peterson; Samuel Lee d. in childhood; John Stephens; William Jessy, m. Jenaina Peterson; Walter Moroni, m. Emma Call; Laura, m. Elijah Cutler; Metta; Charles Alton d. infant.
Married Mariett O. Forley (daughter of Winthrop Forley and Angeline Calkin). Their children: Nellie, m. Wallace Gardner; Clara, m. Charles Berg; Constant A., m. Charles J. Dewey; Asa Winthrop; Rachel, m. Oliver Williams; Wilford; Vedia; Lottie; Ezra C. d. infant.
Married Anna Christine Johnson (daughter of Peter Johnson and Anna Mariah Madsen). Their children: David Orson d. infant; Joseph Smith; Mattie May, m. Harold J. Stock; Florence; Theron Johnson.
Settled in Ogden. Assisted the poor in immigrating to Utah several times. Missionary to Michigan 1876-77. Moved to Eden, Utah, where he served as Sunday school superintendent and 2d counselor to Bishop Josiah M. Ferrin; later 1st counselor. Postmaster at Eden three years. Moved to Afton, Wyo., where he served as Sunday school superintendent, clerk of high priests quorum and member of high council. Sergeant, lieutenant and captain in Utah militia.

EK, CARL AUGUST (son of Carl Larsen). Born July 10, 1845, in Sweden. Came to Utah July 1, 1878, with company of which he was captain.
Married Matilda Ekstrom Oct. 10, 1878, at Salt Lake City (daughter of Margarett Ekstrom of Upsala, Sweden), who was born Dec. 24, 1850. Their children: Carl Enoch b. July 17, 1879, m. Elizabeth Mitchell; Alma August, m. Mary Ellen Worthen; Sigma Elizabeth, m. William White; Logena, m. August J. Tadje; Royal Julius, m. Margarett Sneddon; Ebba Florence, m. Goddard Quist; Louise Christiana, m. Frank Quist; Violet Eugenia, m. Frank Mallory. Family home Salt Lake City.
Married Mary Anderson August 1885 at Logan, Utah, who came to Utah in fall of 1884 and died July, 1912.
Married Hildegard Quist Nov. 10, 1904, at Salt Lake City (daughter of John Quist of Gothenberg, Sweden). She was born July 7, 1875, and came to Utah in 1901, Peter Quist company; Their children: Frank Augustus; Ethel Leona; Hilda Constance.
Bishop of 25th ward for 11 years. Sheriff of Cache county. Worked on temple in Logan. Stonecutter. Died Nov. 8, 1912, at Salt Lake City.

ELDREDGE, ALANSON (son of Micah Eldredge, born March 17, 1758, and Annie Hanks, both of New England). He was born Nov. 16, 1780, in New England. Came to Utah Sept. 19, 1847, Daniel Spencer company.
Married Esther Sunderlin in New England, where she was born Jan. 4, 1787; died 1824, Brutus, N. Y. Their children: Ira b. March 30, 1810, m. Nancy Black July 4, 1833; Horace Sunderlin b. Feb. 6, 1816, m. Betsy Ann Chase, m. Sarah W. Gibbs; m. Hannah Adams; m. Chloe Antoinette Redfield; Lurana, m. John Hoagland; Ann Cady, m. Joseph Busby; John Sunderlin b. April 30, 1821, m. Sinah S. Chipman; m. Rhoda Silvia Collett. Family home Salt Lake City.
Farmer; tanner. Died December 1857.

ELDREDGE, IRA (son of Alanson Eldredge and Esther Sunderlin). Born March 30, 1810, Middleton, Vt. Came to Utah 1847, Daniel Spencer company.
Married Nancy Black July 4, 1833, Indianapolis, Ind. (daughter of Joshua Black and Elizabeth Burgess), who was born Nov. 22, 1812, in Maryland. Their children: Eliza. beth b. March 21, 1834, d. next day; Edmond b. May 1, 1835, m. Hannah Huffman Jan. 24, 1863; m. Emma Staley; Diana b. March 28, 1837, m. Abraham Owen Smoot May 6, 1856; Esther Ann b. March 24, 1839, m. Thomas Garn March 14, 1868; Alma b. Oct. 13, 1841, m. Marinda Merrill Jan. 24, 1863; Hyrum b. April 13, 1844, m. Julia Fippin July 28, 1861, d. Aug. 18, 1884; Alanson b. Dec. 5, 1846 (d. Oct. 22, 1893), m. Martha Neff; m. Bertha Pollisen; Ira Edgar b. May 4, 1850, m. Sarah Staker May 13, 1872; Hannah Matilda b. Feb. 9, 1853, d. June 17, 1854; Horace b. Sept. 7, 1855, m. Anna Cummings March 23, 1883; William Owen b. Jan. 24, 1859.
Married Hannah Mariah Savage Feb. 28, 1852, Salt Lake City (daughter of Levi Savage), who was born Jan. 10, 1832, in Ohio. Their children: Chancy Marion (d. Dec. 3, 1864) and Nancy Mariah, twins, b. Dec. 5, 1852, she m. Edward Garn; John Albert b. Jan. 23, 1854, m. Eliza Wilkinson; Laura Sunderlin b. Jan. 20, 1856; Mulford b. Nov. 20, 1857, d. Dec. 2, 1897; Sabrina b. July 13, 1859, m. Charles B. Wright; Jesse b. Feb. 8, 1861, d. Nov. 13, 1871; Levina b. July 30, 1863, d. Dec. 2, 1905; Content b. April 16, 1865.
Married Helvena Maria Jensen Nov. 22, 1861, Salt Lake City, who was born March 20, 1843, in Denmark. Only child: Mary Ann b. March 16, 1864, m. ——— Pitcher.
Member Utah legislature in early 50's. Captained three trips across the plains for immigrants. Member (first) high council of Salt Lake stake; bishop Sugar House ward 1858-66. Died Feb. 6, 1866, Coalville, Utah.

ELDREDGE, EDMOND (son of Ira Eldredge and Nancy Black). Born May 1, 1835, Warren, Ind.
Married Hannah Huffman Jan. 24, 1863, Salt Lake City (daughter of Jacob Huffman and Margaret Staley, pioneers Sept. 15, 1861). She was born Dec. 6, 1845, Nauvoo, Ill.
Married Emma Staley, who was born Feb. 10, 1839, in Canada, and died Dec. 30, 1854, in Iowa. They had one child born December, 1854, which died in infancy.
Came to Salt Lake 1847; moved to Coalville 1860. Crossed the plains with the last mail before Echo Canyon war 1857; took active part in early Indian troubles. Coalville city councilman several terms; director of Coalville Co-op, and vice president of same for 25 years. Missionary to England 1868-69; missionary to Hawaii; high councilor in Summit stake 1877-1901.

ELDREDGE, HORACE SUNDERLIN (son of Alanson Eldredge and Esther Sunderlin). Born Feb. 6, 1816, Brutus, Cayuga county, N. Y. Came to Utah Sept. 15, 1848, Brigham Young company.
Married Betsy Ann Chase July 20, 1837, Buffalo, N. Y. (daughter of Benjamin Chase and Mehitabel Russell of New England), who was born Sept. 23, 1818. Their children: Lurana b. Feb. 21, 1838, m. Joseph W. Young Feb. 9, 1856; Mary Aurelia b. Jan. 20, 1840, m. Amini D. Jackman Sept. 9, 1858; Selina Mehitabel b. Oct. 12, 1842, d. March 10, 1844; Betsy Ann b. April 11, 1845, d. Feb. 26, 1846; Helen Louisa b. Jan. 9, 1847, d. Aug. 30, 1847; Horace Alonso b. June 8, 1847, d. Sept. 12, 1847; Alice b. Oct. 26, 1848, m. David Treasley Jan. 11, 1871, d. Sept. 19, 1912; Zina Presinda b. Jan. 17, 1853, m. Moroni Reese Dec. 29, 1870.
Married Sarah W. Gibbs April 20, 1851, Salt Lake City (daughter of Aaron Gibbs and Prudence Carter of Benson-town, Rutland county, Vt.), who was born June 11 1827, and came to Utah Sept. 4, 1848, Daniel A. Miller company. Their children: Horace S. b. Feb. 7, 1853, d. Jan. 27, 1865; Eliza Evaletta b. May 29, 1855, m. Joseph H. Grant Oct. 17, 1874, d. Oct. 15, 1911; Jessie b. Nov. 17, 1857, m. Briant Stringham June 6, 1877; Byron Gibbs b. Feb. 7, 1867, d. April 9, 1879. Family resided Salt Lake City and Bountiful, Utah.
Married Hannah Adams Feb. 2, 1855, Salt Lake City (daughter of James Adams and Betsy Leavitt of Centerville, Utah, former a pioneer September, 1851, James Allred company, latter died 1848, Council Bluffs, Iowa). She was born Jan. 11, 1833. Their children: James A. b. Feb. 15, 1857, m. Jane Jennings June 23, 1879; Clara Ursula b. Nov. 8, 1861, d. Nov. 23, 1862; Adelbert U. b. Aug. 23, 1863, m. Edith Pack Dec. 2, 1885; Christie b. July 19, 1866, m. John L. Fackrell Nov. 1, 1887; Clarence b. June 1, 1869, m. Effie Peck Oct. 14, 1890; Horton A. b. Aug. 22, 1872, m. Lillie Hatch Oct. 26, 1892. Family home Bountiful, Utah.
Married Chloe Antoinette Redfield Feb. 14, 1857, Salt Lake City (daughter of Harlow Levi Redfield and Alpha L. Foster of North Madison, Conn., pioneers Sept. 8, 1850, Aaron Johnson company). She was born Aug. 10, 1812, Pittsfield, Pike county, Ill. Their children: Harlow Moroni b. Dec. 12, 1861, d. Dec. 23, 1862; Alpha May b. Aug. 6, 1863, m. Reed Smoot

PIONEERS AND PROMINENT MEN OF UTAH 857

Sept. 17, 1884; Ben R. b. May 4, 1866, m. Lizzie Sharp Aug. 18, 1887; Ernest R. b. Feb. 20, 1868, m. Kate Sharp Oct. 1, 1890 (she d. July 1893); m. Cora Hooper Oct. 28, 1897; Horace R. b. June 17, 1869, m. Eleanor Groesbeck Feb. 3, 1897; Chloe Addie b. Aug. 14, 1871, m. William J. Bateman Dec. 17, 1891; Esther b. Oct. 5, 1874, m. Edwin C. Coffin Nov. 1, 1893 (divorced 1903); m. Theodore L. Genter Feb. 15, 1906; David Harold b. Aug. 29, 1878, m. Barbara Mayr of Munich, Germany, April 24, 1906; Mary Jane b. July 23, 1880, m. Lee Green Richards Aug. 18, 1908; Guy S. b. March 12, 1882, m. Bess Shores of Ashland, Wis., April 9, 1903.
Marshal of wagon train Brigham Young company; territorial marshal state of Deseret; collector and assessor of territory; brigadier-general Utah militia. High priest; one of seven presidents 1st quorum seventies; immigration agent St. Louis 1852; president and superintendent Z. C. M. I. Merchant and banker in Salt Lake City. Died Sept. 6, 1888.

ELDREDGE, JAMES ALANSON (son of Horace S. Eldredge and Hannah Adams). Born Feb. 15, 1857, Salt Lake City, Utah.
Married Jane Jennings June 23, 1879, at Salt Lake City (daughter of William Jennings and Jane Walker, pioneers 1852). She was born March 19, 1856. Only child: Afton b. Jan. 9, 1892.

ELDREDGE, JOHN SUNDERLIN (son of Alanson Eldredge and Esther Sunderlin). Born April 30, 1821, Brutus, Cayuga county, N. Y. Came to Utah Sept. 24, 1847, A. O. Smoot company.
Married Sinah S. Chipman March 24, 1849, Salt Lake City (daughter of Stephen Chipman and Amanda Washburn, pioneers July 24, 1847). She was born Sept. 13, 1831. Their children: Mary A. b. Dec. 19, 1849, m. George Hoggard; John b. Sept. 20, 1851, died; Jedediah b. April 14, 1857; Ann b. Feb. 22, 1859, m. Heber Hoggard; Martha b. May 20, 1861, m. William Jackson, m. William Thomas Brown; Zinah b. July 18, 1863, died. Family home American Fork, Utah.
Married Rhoda Silvia Collett at Salt Lake City (daughter of Daniel Collett, born Dec. 12, 1808, and Esther Jones, born Oct. 10, 1814). She was born April 20, 1837. Their children: Ira b. Oct. 3, 1854; Esther Ann b. May 3, 1860, m. John S. Merrill; Daniel b. Nov. 1, 1863, m. Lola Kimball; Horace b. Feb. 5, 1865, m. Hannah A. Phillips. Family home American Fork, Utah.
One of first to plow in Salt Lake valley. Missionary to Australia 1852-56. Farmer. Died May 5, 1871, in Wasatch Co., Utah.

ELDREDGE, HORACE (son of John S. Eldredge and Rhoda S. Collett). Born Feb. 5, 1865, American Fork, Utah.
Married Hannah A. Phillips Nov. 23, 1892, Dayton, Idaho (daughter of Thomas Phillips and Sarah Boden of Clifton, Idaho), who was born Jan. 15, 1875. Their children: Zella b. Jan. 9, 1894; Ernest b. Feb. 15, 1896; Ivan H. b. Nov. 30, 1897; Jennie b. Jan. 13, 1898; Elva b. Jan. 3, 1901; Annora b. April 19, 1903; Horace S. b. Aug. 1, 1905; Ross P. b. Jan. 27, 1908; Dell B. b. Oct. 22, 1909; Demar b. Jan. 25, 1912. Family resided Dayton and Preston, Idaho.
Elder.

ELEASON, ERICK. Born May 11, 1815, Sweden. Came to Utah Sept. 12, 1863, John Royal Young company.
Married Anna Nielsen 1840 (daughter of Hans Nielsen), who was born Feb. 9, 1819. Their children: Andrew Eleason b. July 22, 1841, m. Johanne Nielsen; Johanne b. 1843, m. Steven Worthington; Betsy b. 1845, m. Dyerre Asmussen; Charles b. 1848, m. Mary Worthington; Alfred b. 1850, m. Sophia Andersen; Augusta b. 1854, m. Ormes Eaton Bates; Fredrick b. 1857, m. Eva Yeates. Family resided Grantsville and Millville, Utah.
Married Christine Anderson. Their children: Joseph b. 1870, m. Esther Yeates; Edith b. 1872, m. William Gray; Emma b. 1874. Family home Millville, Utah.
High priest.

ELEASON, JOHN ALFRED (son of Erick Eleason and Anna Nielsen). Born July 22, 1841, at Arlingsas, Skaraborg, Sweden.
Married Sophia Anderson April 1, 1877, Grantsville, Tooele Co., Utah (daughter of Andrew Anderson and Mary Swenson of Grefbeck, Sweden, pioneers Sept. 12, 1863, John R. Young company). She was born Nov. 19, 1854. Their children: Amanda b. Dec. 30, 1877, m. William C. Tolman; John Alfred Jr. b. June 14, 1880, m. Mary E. Adams; Augusta Geneva b. July 28, 1882, m. J. Fred Adams; Elia Alvaretta b. Nov. 28, 1884, m. Lewis A. Ward. Family home Oakley, Idaho.

ELEASON, JOHN ALFRED, JR. (son of John Alfred Eleason and Sophia Anderson). Born June 14, 1880, Grantsville, Utah.
Married Mary E. Adams Oct. 5, 1904, at Salt Lake City (daughter of John Adams and Anna Belle Warburton of Tooele, Utah. Their children: Thera Comorah b. Sept. 21, 1905; Lorada b. Feb. 17, 1908; Lano A. b. Sept. 28, 1910. Family home Oakley, Idaho.
President high priests quorum Cassia stake; bishop Oakley, 2d ward. City councilman two terms.

ELIASON, ANDERS. Born Jan. 15, 1806, Alingsas, Sweden. Came to Utah Sept. 12, 1863, John R. Young company.
Married Mrs. Anna Christina Eliason. Their children: Charles, m. Annie Anderson; Andreas b. 1838, m. Headvig Carlson; Andrew Gustave b. 1841, m. Matilda Johnson.

Married Christina Anderson in Sweden (daughter of Eric Anderson), who was born 1826 in Sweden. Their children: John Alfred b. 1854, m. Lucy Clark; August b. 1856, m. Emma Anderson; Annie Christina b. 1859, m. Jacob Dayley; Claus b. 1861 and Joseph b. 1863 died; Clara b. 1864, m. William Dahlquist; Manda Matilda b. 1866, died; Etta b. 1869, m. Mr. Whitehouse. Families resided Grantsville, Utah.
High priest. Assisted in bringing immigrants to Utah. Settled at Grantsville and was one of its active and progressive citizens.

ELIASON, ANDREW GUSTAVE (son of Anders and Anna C. Eliason). Born Feb. 12, 1841, in Sweden.
Married Matilda Johnson Aug. 8, 1868, Salt Lake City (daughter of Andreas Johnson and Anna Kaza Anderson, pioneers 1863). She was born Feb. 10, 1851, Alingsas, Sweden. Their children: Gustave Albin b. 1869, died; Edith Matilda b. 1870, m. Peter Sorenson; John Andrew b. 1872, m. Eliza Williams; Richard Alfred b. 1875, m. Lovina Jensen; Anna Josephine b. 1877, m. John C. Nielson; Ernest William b. 1879; Charles August b. 1882, died; Elmer Leroy b. 1885, m. Frances Jensen; Alma Lorenzo b. 1887; Effie Arletta b. 1890, died.
Settled at Grantsville, Utah, 1863; moved to Hyrum 1884. High priest.

ELIASON, JOHN ANDREW (son of Andrew Gustave Eliason and Matilda Johnson). Born Oct. 22, 1872.
Married Eliza Williams at Salt Lake City (daughter of Thomas Williams and Emily Allen, former of Wales, latter of Michigan). She was born Oct. 12, 1876, Hyrum, Utah. Their children: Lila b. Nov. 27, 1899; John Thomas b. Aug. 11, 1902; Charles Ross b. April 15, 1906; George Earl b. Nov. 4, 1906; Emily Matilda b. Sept. 14, 1909. Family home Hyrum, Utah.
Elder. Farmer.

ELKINS, PAUL A. (son of John Elkins and Charlotte Roberts of Wiltshire, Eng.). Born July 15, 1849, in England. Came to Utah 1868, working on railroad.
Married Mary Miller Dec. 26, 1870, at Salt Lake City (daughter of David Miller and Mary Hamilton of Ayrshire, Scotland), who was born April 28, 1852. Their children: Mary R., m. Radford Ostler; Amos b. Nov. 12, 1873, m. Sarah Bullock; Lottie, m. George L. Sneff; Annie d. aged 21; John; Alma, m. Laura Widdison; William d. aged 3; Lily; Roy. Family home Salt Lake City.
High priest. School trustee. Carder and spinner in woolen mills. Died Jan. 8, 1911, at Salt Lake City.

ELKINS, AMOS (son of Paul A. Elkins and Mary Miller). Born Nov. 12, 1873, at Salt Lake City.
Married Sarah Bullock Feb. 22, 1899, at Salt Lake City (daughter of Edwin Bullock and Mary Marguerite Parry, the former of England, came to Utah 1869, the latter of Wales, both later resided at Salt Lake City). She was born Nov. 9, 1873. Their children: Adelbert b. July 1, 1901; Ruth b. Nov. 12, 1903; Marguerite b. Sept. 18, 1905; Pearl b. Jan. 5, 1908; James b. May 3, 1910. Family home Salt Lake City, Utah.
Plasterer.

ELLERBECK, THOMAS WITTON (son of Thomas Ellerbeck and Mary Witton). Born May 14, 1829, Pendleton, near Manchester, Eng. Jan. 27, 1851, sailed from Liverpool on the "Geo. W. Bourne," and arrived at Salt Lake City Oct. 7 same year.
Married Emma Spence (daughter of John Spence and Marjorie Mary Leisk). Their children: George E., m. Winnie Clawson; Ettie V., m. Thomas D. Lewis; Mary, m. Elmer E. Darling; William Leon, m. Claire Clinton; Edith, m. Charles Read; Clarissa M.; Marjorie Mary; Aurania.
First engineer for Salt Lake City water-works; superintendent of gas and electric light works, Salt Lake City. Pioneer nurseryman; also engaged in banking. Died April 2, 1895, at Salt Lake City.

ELLERBECK, WILLIAM LEON (son of Thomas Witton Ellerbeck and Emma Spence). Born Sept. 7, 1874, at Salt Lake City, Utah.
Married Claire Clinton Jan. 26, 1898, at Salt Lake City (daughter of James E. Clinton and Rosella S. Peacock of Manti, Utah), who was born Sept. 22, 1877. Their children: Rosella Clinton b. Dec. 20, 1899; Katharine Claire b. July 22, 1905. Family home Salt Lake City.
Original promoter Clinton-Ellerbeck Fire Clay company, later changed to Utah Fire Clay company; managing director of Nephi Plaster & Manufacturing company; doctor of dental surgery.

ELLETT, JOHN JAMES (son of John Ellett and Frances Price of London, Eng.). Born Dec. 29, 1820, at London, Eng.). Came to Utah 1851, Orson Pratt company.
Married Eleanor Davison April 22, 1840, who was born May 13, 1824. Their children: Eleanor b. Jan. 4, 1841, m. George Sweetser; Sarah Ann b. Oct. 29, 1835, m. Willis Robison; John Davison b. June 1, 1857, m. Jeanette McArthur. Family home Fillmore, Utah.
Married Mary Turner Clarkson (widow of John Clarkson) Nov. 11, 1861, at Fillmore, Utah (daughter of David Turner and Rose Collier, pioneers 1861, John R. Murdock company). She was born Feb. 3, 1840, near Leeds, Eng. Their children: John Alonzo b. Nov. 21, 1862; David William b. Feb. 21, 1864,

858   PIONEERS AND PROMINENT MEN OF UTAH

m. Hannah A. Pierce Sept. 6, 1892; Mary Louise b. April 16, 1866, m. F. A. Young Dec. 21, 1881; Edwin Clarkson b. Nov. 10, 1867; Frances Rose Ann b. Jan. 27, 1870, m. Isaac W. Pierce Jr. Dec. 9, 1886; Joseph Henry b. June 20, 1872, m. Clara B. Shiner Jan. 23, 1891; Charles Arthur b. Jan. 4, 1874, m. Millie F. Maxfield March 19, 1901; Sarah Elizabeth b. Nov. 25, 1875, m. Albert W. Shiner Dec. 6, 1892; Martha Josephine b. Dec. 10, 1877, m. William C. Jensen Nov. 25, 1896; Susanna b. Jan. 25, 1880. Family home Fremont, Utah.
Member 42d quorum seventies; high priest. Held various prominent positions of trust and responsibility.

ELLIOTT, GEORGE (son of Benjamin D. Elliott and Ann Withers of New Radford, Nottinghamshire, Eng.). Born Oct. 15, 1815, in Nottinghamshire. Came to Utah August 1861, independent company.
Married Eliza Vinton 1840, in Nottinghamshire (daughter of George Vinton and Eliza Hamilton of Kilkenny, Ireland). She was born July 10, 1816. Their children: Edwin b. March 25, 1841, m. Fannie A. Peck; Sabina b. 1842, died 1847; Annie b. 1844, m. Frank Richardson; George b. Oct. 6, 1846, m. Mary Sweet, m. Annie E. Smart; Henry b. Feb. 28, 1848, m. Georgiana Clawson; Simon b. 1852, died 1855; William b. Oct. 30, 1850, m. Julia Ann Flemming; Eliza b. May 6, 1854, m. Harry R. M. Atkinson; Frederic b. 1856, died 1873; Hattie b. Oct. 1, 1858, m. John Westphal. Family home Provo, Utah.
Member 45th quorum seventies; high priest. Machinist; farmer. Died Dec. 18, 1904, Provo, Utah.

ELLIOTT, EDWIN (son of George Elliott and Eliza Vinton). Born March 25, 1841, in Nottinghamshire, Eng. Came to Utah Oct. 15, 1860.
Married Fannie A. Peck Dec. 1, 1864, Salt Lake City (daughter of Harrison G. O. Peck and Margaret R. Augier, both of Stoughton, Mass., pioneers October, 1852, Capt. Tidwell company). She was born Nov. 6, 1845. Their children: Fannie Eliza b. Nov. 6, 1865, m. Joshua Dunn; Margaret Vilate b. April 22, 1868; Mary Elenor b. Aug. 31, 1870, m. David J. Vincent; Leah Nora b. Feb. 26, 1875, and Emma Sabina b. June 7, 1876, died; Harriet Amelia b. June 20, 1879, m. Alphonso Adamson; Kathryn b. Nov. 7, 1882; Hazel R. b. Nov. 16, 1886, m. Clarence Ericksen; Genevieve b. Feb. 24, 1889, m. Thomas W. Shelley. Family home Provo, Utah.
Elder. Sawyer; engineer.

ELLIOTT, GEORGE (son of George Elliott and Eliza Vinton). Born Oct. 6, 1846. Came to Utah 1862.
Married Mary Sweet.
Married Annie Elizabeth Smart November 1885, Logan, Utah (daughter of H. B. Smart and Eliza Windsor of Somersetshire, Eng., pioneers 1868). She was born May 20, 1859, and died July 13, 1909, at Provo, Utah. Their children: Edwin H. b. Nov. 12, 1886, m. Ruby McKellar; Irene b. Aug. 5, 1888, m. Vern Searls; George died; Windsor; Florence; Clifford.
President Y. M. M. I. A., 4th ward. Provo, Utah, three years. Watermaster; superintendent Wild Dutchman mine at American Fork three years. Farmer; contractor; miner.

ELLIOTT, EDWIN H. (son of George Elliott and Annie E. Smart). Born Nov. 12, 1886, Provo, Utah.
Married Ruby McKellar June 3, 1909, at Salt Lake City (daughter of Hugh McKellar and Mary Henry of Scotland, who came to Utah by rail). She was born Oct. 16, 1889. Their children: George McKellar b. May 20, 1910; Gordon b. Nov. 2, 1911.
Operator Knight Power Co., Elkhorn, Utah. Electrician and engineer.

ELLIOTT, HENRY (son of George Elliott and Eliza Vinton). Born Feb. 28, 1848, Boulogne, France. Came to Utah July 1862.
Married Georgiana Clawson March 17, 1871, at Toquerville, Utah (daughter of Moses Clawson and Sarah Inkley of Nauvoo, Ill.), who was born Aug. 3, 1854. Their children: George Henry b. May 17, 1873, m. Bertha Irinda McEwan; Hattie b. Aug. 14, 1875, died; Effie Eliza b. April 6, 1877; Raymond b. Sept. 25, 1879; Moroni b. Oct. 15, 1881; Annie Lucile b. Jan. 29, 1884; Lizzie b. March 20, 1886; Sabina b. Nov. 2, 1889; Joseph E. b. Dec. 7, 1892; Lena Dotty b. Sept. 6, 1899. Family home Provo, Utah.
Member 45th quorum seventies. Farmer.

ELLIOTT, GEORGE HENRY (son of Henry Elliott and Georgiana Clawson). Born May 17, 1873, Provo, Utah.
Married Bertha Irinda McEwan Dec. 16, 1896, Salt Lake City (daughter of Joseph Thompson McEwan and Irinda Naoma Crandall of Springville, Utah). She was born Dec. 17, 1874. Their children: Erma Eliza b. April 21, 1898; Ethel b. March 21, 1900; Leah b. Aug. 17, 1901; Alma Raymond b. Jan. 28, 1903; Clawson Spicer b. Sept. 17, 1904; Walter Simon b. May 21, 1906; Bessie b. March 21, 1908.
Elder; counselor in presidency elders' quorum Timpanogos ward, Provo, 1908-10; ward and Sunday school teacher. Printer; farmer and fruitgrower.

ELLIS, ALEXANDER (son of William Ellis and Mary White of Crediton, Devonshire, Eng.). Born July 31, 1842. Witheridge, Devonshire, Eng. Came to Utah Oct. 15, 1863, Samuel D. White company.
Married Maria Elsimore May 14, 1863, London, Eng. (daughter of Thomas Elsimore and Martha Sandal of London, who came to Utah 1870 by rail). She was born Feb. 19, 1845. Their children: Rosina Marie b. June 19, 1864, d. 1868; James Alexander b. May 26, 1865, d. 1865; William Thomas b. June 17, 1866, m. Anna Christine Hansen; Mary Jane b. July 27, 1868, m. John A. Richins; Walter Alexander b. July 8, 1870, m. Nellie Catell; Alfred John b. July 31, 1872, d. 1903; Alonzo Edmond b. Oct. 16, 1874, m. Ellen Peterson; Burley Elizabeth Martha b. Aug. 14, 1876, m. Benjamin West; Horace Bertram b. April 20, 1878; Lewis George b. Jan. 15, 1880, m. Lenne Waddall; Florence Helen b. Feb. 8, 1882, m. Vance McHan; Belle Maude b. May 22, 1884, m. James Baxter; Pearl Bertha b. May 28, 1887. Family home Pleasant Grove, Utah.
Justice of peace; road supervisor. Owner and manager "Pioneer Nursery" at Pleasant Grove.

ELLIS, JOHN (son of George Ellis and Elizabeth Hague of Manchester, Eng.). Born Jan. 5, 1828, Derby, Derbyshire, Eng. Came to Utah Sept. 26, 1856, Daniel D. McArthur handcart company.
Married Mary Ann Emmett June 4, 1853, St. Louis, Mo. (daughter of John Emmett and Sarah Boothman of Clitheroe, Eng.), who was born Oct. 3, 1822. Their children: George b. March 31, 1854, d. infant; Mary Ann b. March 6, 1857, d. Jan. 16, 1882, m. J. H. Watkins; John G. b. Aug. 22, 1859, m. Rose A. Drake; Elizabeth b. Aug. 26, 1861, m. George Shorten. Family home Ogden, Utah.
Missionary to England 1881-83. Carpenter; building inspector of Ogden. Died Sept. 26, 1901.

ELLIS, JOHN GREGORY (son of John Ellis and Mary Ann Emmett). Born Aug. 22, 1859, Ogden, Utah.
Married Rose A. Drake May 24, 1883, Salt Lake City (daughter of George Drake and Emily White of Iowa, who came to Utah April, 1876). She was born Dec. 15, 1863. Their children: John F. b. Feb. 8, 1884, m. Telitha Browning; George b. Jan. 24, 1886, d. infant; Willard D. b. April 8, 1887, m. Elda I. Pingree; Paul b. Dec. 20, 1889; Oliver G. b. July 22, 1892; Wallace H. b. Jan. 5, 1896; Mary A. b. Oct. 30, 1898; Rose E. b. June 9, 1901; Grant b. Oct. 2, 1903. Family home Ogden, Utah.
Missionary to southern states 1892-95. Member board of education 1898-1901.

ELLIS, JOHN (son of John Ellis and Hannah Stoner). Born Jan. 4, 1814, Scarborough, near Toronto, Canada. Came to Utah 1851, Horton D. Haight company.
Married Harriet Hales Oct. 31, 1839 (daughter of Stephen and Mary Ann Hales), who was born June 10, 1824, and came to Utah with husband. Their children: Mary Ann b. Dec. 30, 1840, m. Melitre Hatch; Hannah Isabella b. Dec. 31, 1843, m. Samuel Henrie; Stephen Hales b. Oct. 18, 1846, m. Helen Marr Lee Feb. 13, 1871; John Henry b. March 18, 1849, m. Phebe Clark; Harriet Louisa b. Dec. 21, 1851, m. Daniel C. Lee; Joseph Ezra b. March 28, 1854, m. Elnora Burnham; Sarah Ann b. Jan. 8, 1856, m. Joseph Hogan; Elizabeth Jane b. Jan. 3, 1859, m. Stearne Hatch; Laura Victoria b. Oct. 12, 1861, m. John E. Hatch; Charles William b. April 13, 1864, m. Robenia Marshall; George Franklin b. Aug. 30, 1866; James b. Aug. 12, 1868. Family home Woods Cross, Utah.
Assisted in bringing immigrants to Utah. Helped haul stone for Salt Lake temple. Carpenter; cooper; miller; sawyer. Died April 3, 1871.

ELLIS, STEPHEN HALES (son of John Ellis and Harriet Hales). Born Oct. 18, 1846, Fort Madison, Iowa.
Married Helen Marr Lee Feb. 13, 1871, Salt Lake City (daughter of William Henry Lee and Harriet Carter), who was born May 4, 1853, at South Cottonwood, Utah. Their children: John Henry b. Jan. 27, 1872, m. Mary A. Howard; Helen Marr b. May 17, 1874, m. Charles H. Atkinson; Stephen Hales b. Sept. 10, 1876, m. Rachel Ann Briggs; Harriet Amelia b. Oct. 5, 1878, m. William Riley; Ruth Clarisa b. Oct. 28, 1880, m. William Hardy; LeRoy Lee b. Dec. 28, 1882, m. Emma McFarland; Ralph Ezekiel b. Jan. 21, 1885, m. Fannie Richards; Cordelia b. July 11, 1887. Family home Woods Cross, Utah.
Married Axeline P. Engebretsen March 30, 1902, Salt Lake City (daughter of Carl Peterson and Wilhelmina Scroll, pioneers Sept. 22, 1861, Samuel A. Woolley company), who was born March 12, 1873, at Salt Lake City. Their children: Owen William b. Dec. 21, 1903; George Edwin b. Feb. 24, 1905; Carl Reed b. Jan. 30, 1907; Orson Hales b. Oct. 16, 1908.
Black Hawk war veteran. Superintendent South Bountiful Sunday school 16 years.

ELLISON, JAMES (son of Adam Ellison and Ellen Glover). Born June 18, 1807, in Lancashire, Eng. Came to Utah Oct. 14, 1853, Cyrus H. Wheelock company.
Married Alice Haltwell 1842, in England. Their children: Ellen, m. John Bennett; George A., m. Hathern Morgan; John W., m. Amanda Miller; Jane A., m. Andrew D. Park; Mary E., m. James P. Bennett; Alice S., m. David F. Park. Family home Nephi, Utah.

ELLISON, JOHN (son of Matthew Ellison, born Sept. 15, 1793, and Jane Wilson, born June 5, 1797, both of Yorkshire, Eng.—married 1817). He was born May 23, 1818, in Yorkshire. Came to Utah Sept. 13, 1852, Capt. Howell company.

Married Alice Pilling Feb. 4, 1841 (daughter of John Pilling and Peggy Banks, pioneers 1853—married 1816). She was born Nov. 20, 1820, and came to Utah with husband. Their children: Margaret Jane b. Aug. 11, 1842, m. William Riley Taylor Sept. 1857; John Ammon b. April 22, 1845, d. Aug. 15, 1847; David Samuel b. March 4, 1848, d. July 24, 1849; Ephraim Peter b. June 10, 1850, m. Elizabeth Whitesides Jan. 1873; Matthew Thomas b. March 25, 1853, m. Jane Rowen July 1882; Susanah Ellen b. March 28, 1855, m. Joseph T. Robine March 1875; Elijah Edward b. Aug. 1, 1857, m. Harriet Morgan Jan. 1883; Mary Alice b. Oct. 29, 1859, m. William Wallace Feb. 1892; Sarah Ann Dinah b. Jan. 23, 1862, d. Jan. 29, 1863; Joseph Heber b. May 12, 1864, m. Lavena Wiggill Nov. 1884. Family resided in Nauvoo, Ill., St. Louis, Mo., and in Utah.
Married Catherine McClaine 1856, Salt Lake City.
Married Mary Ann Kidd June 20, 1869, Salt Lake City.
Married Grace Stewart June 1894, Salt Lake City.
Settled on Jordan river 1852; moved to Kaysville October 1853. Assistant stake Sunday school superintendent; high counselor; patriarch. Selectman Davis county. Died Sept. 9, 1903, Kaysville, Utah.

ELLISON, EPHRAIM PETER (son of John Ellison and Alice Pilling). Born June 10, 1850, St. Louis, Mo.
Married Elizabeth Whitesides January 1873, Salt Lake City (daughter of Lewis Whitesides and Susanah Perkins, pioneers 1852), who was born Nov. 13, 1851, Council Bluffs, Iowa. Their children: James Edward b. Sept. 9, 1873, m. Jane Watt Feb. 1897; Mary Annette b. Aug. 28, 1875, m. Warren S. Stevenson Feb. 9, 1898; Lawrence Ephraim b. April 27, 1879, m. Katherine M. Adams June 1907; Morris Heber b. Oct. 20, 1881, m. Margaret J. Cowley March 1905; John Parley b. Oct. 14, 1886; Alice Louise b. Jan. 27, 1889, m. Jabez S. Adams June 1911; Evan Lewis b. July 13, 1891; Marion Whitesides b. Nov. 27, 1893. Family home Layton, Utah.
Superintendent Sunday school at Layton; member high council, Davis stake. Farmer; stockraiser; miller; merchant.

ELMER, WILLIAM (son of John Elmer and Sally Peaque). Born Sept. 16, 1820, Norwich, Orange county, Vt. Came to Utah Oct. 3, 1852.
Married Hannah Plina Child March 26, 1846, in Lee county, Iowa (daughter of Alfred B. Child and Polly Barber), who was born Jan. 24, 1828, and came to Utah with husband. Their children: John Samuel b. Oct. 13, 1847, died; Mark Alfred b. Dec. 1, 1848, m. Minnie Jost; William Warren b. Nov. 23, 1850, m. Adelaide Hall; Cynthia Tryphenia b. Dec. 16, 1852, m. John Q. Leavitt Aug. 16, 1869; Hannah Plina b. Feb. 13, 1854, d. 1857; Polly Anna b. Dec. 6, 1856, m. M. D. Taylor Dec. 27, 1875; Phebe Arinda b. Sept. 19, 1858, m. Mark Hall Dec. 7, 1874; Sally Rosa Bell b. Nov. 16, 1861, d. 1878; Sanah Josephine b. April 15, 1863, m. W. W. Browning; Electa Ann b. Jan. 28, 1866, m. Lewis J. Brown; Charles Asa b. Aug. 17, 1869, d. July 3, 1870; Hiram Barney b. Feb. 11, 1871, d. May 21, 1872. Family home Ogden, Utah.
Married Mary Ann Gean April 1857, Salt Lake City (daughter of William A. Gean and Esther Ann Pierce, pioneers 1850). She was born Dec. 29, 1832. Their children: Levi James b. Oct. 1, 1858, m. Treen Louise Peterson Feb. 20, 1895; Esther Ann b. Dec. 27, 1861, m. Francis Keyes Oct. 27, 1878; Amanda Vilate b. July 5, 1863, m. James Green Browning April 26, 1883; William Heber b. Feb. 13, 1869, m. Inga Peterson Dec. 20, 1899.
Lieutenant-colonel Nauvoo Legion; captain cavalry Company A. Assisted in building first railroad in Ogden, and first road in Ogden Canyon. Assisted in bringing immigrants to Utah 1856. High priest.

ELMER, LEVI JAMES (son of William Elmer and Mary Ann Gean). Born Oct. 1, 1858, Payson, Utah.
Married Treen Louise Peterson Feb. 20, 1895, Salt Lake City (daughter of Jorgan Peterson and Ellen Anderson), who was born July 8, 1874, Copenhagen, Denmark. Their children: Joseph Levi b. May 10, 1896; William Jorgan b. Aug. 9, 1898; Ellen Louise b. Sept. 23, 1900; Polly Ann b. Nov. 27, 1902; Ezra James b. April 21, 1905; George Wilfred b. Nov. 2, 1907; Hannah Plina b. Oct. 18, 1910. Family home Marriott, Utah.
High priest. Farmer.

ELLSWORTH, EDMUND (son of Jonathan Ellsworth and Sarah Galley of New York state). Born July 1, 1819, Paris, Oneida county, N. Y. Came to Utah July 24, 1847, with Brigham Young.
Married Elizabeth Young (daughter of Brigham Young and Miriam Works). Their children: Charlotte b. 1843; Edmund b. 1845, m. Ellen Blair Nov. 6, 1864; Rowenah b. 1848, m. John Howard; Elizabeth M. b. 1850, m. Helen Gibson; Alice V. b. 1852, m. James O. Swift; Laura C. b. 1854, m. Richard F. Jardine; John W. b. 1858, m. Jennie Hanson; Minnie b. 1861, m. Emmett Horsley. Family home, Salt Lake City.
Married Mary Ann Dudley Dec. 24, 1853, Salt Lake City (daughter of Oliver H. Dudley and Mary Ann Robinson of Willard, Utah), who was born Aug. 11, 1834. Their children: Mary A. b. June 26, 1855, m. Spencer V. Raymond; Albert Lovel b. Sept. 27, 1857, m. Isabel Hoggs, m. Elizabeth Eames; James D. b. Oct. 31, 1859; Oliver Dudley b. Oct. 4, 1861, m. Dina Blumquist; Susan Lorena b. Jan. 19, 1864, m. W. W. Stephens; Asa Charles b. Sept. 17, 1866, m. Emily E. Theurer; Jerome D. b. Feb. 11, 1869, m. Anna Mary Clinger; Hannah D. b. Nov. 4, 1872, m. Lewis Henry Poole. Family resided at Salt Lake City and West Weber, Utah, and in Arizona.
Married Mary Ann Bates. Their children: William b. June 24, 1857, m. Emma Dailey; George F. b. Dec. 26, 1859, m. Sarah Fallet; Fanny b. April 28, 1862, m. C. H. Greenwell; Orson b. Dec. 31, 1864, m. Lucy Oakley; Nellie b. June 1, 1866, m. A. J. Merrill; Loritta b. April 12, 1867, m. Hans Hansen; Julia b. Dec. 16, 1869, m. S. E. West; Annie M. b. Dec. 1, 1871, m. Calvin Phelps.
Married Mary Ann Jones Oct. 10, 1856, at Salt Lake City (daughter of Thomas Jones and Hannah Paine). Their children: Abner b. Nov. 24, 1857, m. Betsy Merrill in 1884; Agnes b. April 28, 1858, m. James Hoage; Charles H. E. b. Dec. 23, 1860, m. Isabell Miriot; Frank b. Feb. 26, 1863, m. Edna Merrill; Louis b. Sept. 18, 1865, m. Josephine Crismon; William b. Oct. 13, 1867, m. Martha A. Passey; Ernest b. Dec. 13, 1869, m. Estella Johnson; Wilford b. Feb. 18, 1872, died; Sarah V. b. Sept. 9, 1873, m. Ernest Crismon; Laura b. Oct. 28, 1575, m. John Hall; Harry b. May 3, 1877, m. Annie Hall; Byron b. Feb. 9, 1879, m. Clara Hall.
Veteran Walker war. Counselor to bishop; missionary to England. Member Nauvoo Legion. Alderman Salt Lake City. Superintendent construction of Utah Northern Railroad; lumberman.

ELLSWORTH, EDMUND (son of Edmund Ellsworth and Elizabeth Young). Born 1845 at Hancock, Mo.
Married Ellen Blair Nov. 6, 1864, at Salt Lake City (daughter of Seth M. Blair and Jane Eapy), who was born Oct. 12, 1846, in Tennessee. Their children: Edmund b. Aug. 9, 1868; Seth M. b. Aug. 30, 1870; Frank B. b. Oct. 23, 1872; Clara Cornelia b. Oct. 21, 1874; John M. b. Oct. 21, 1878; Elizabeth b. July 6, 1880; Alonzo G. b. Sept. 16, 1883; Preston B. b. May 6, 1887.
Member Nauvoo Legion. President Parks and Lewisville Irrigation company; probate judge; superintendent of schools; president and director of Little Feeds Canal company.

ELLSWORTH, EDMUND (son of Edmund Ellsworth and Ellen Blair). Born Aug. 9, 1868, St. Joseph, Ariz.
Married Edwina Walker (daughter of William Walker and Louisa Bingham, pioneers 1847), who was born Jan. 24, 1870, Oak Creek, Utah. Their children: Lydia b. April 25, 1889, m. Orson Greenwood; Clara b. Dec. 4, 1890; Orba b. Nov. 1, 1892; Edmund F. b. Sept. 22, 1894; Genieve b. Sept. 14, 1896; Byron Y. b. Jan. 30, 1899; John Willard b. Nov. 20, 1901; Herald b. Nov. 9, 1904; Louisa b. Aug. 19, 1906; Ellen b. June 19, 1909. Family resided Lewisville and Rigbey, Idaho. State hay and grain inspector for Idaho.

ELLSWORTH, ASA CHARLES (son of Edmund Ellsworth and Mary Ann Dudley). Born Sept. 17, 1866, West Weber, Utah.
Married Emily E. Theurer July 3, 1889, Logan, Utah (daughter of John Theurer and Barbara Welfly, Providence, Utah—pioneers), who was born Aug. 30, 1865. Their children: a Bidney b. April 7, 1890, died; John Orval b. Nov. 15, 1892; Idetta T. b. Nov. 8, 1894; Von T. b. June 6, 1896; Barbara T. b. June 18, 1898; Reho William b. Feb. 1, 1900; Spencer T. b. March 9, 1904; Heber Michal b. March 29, 1907; Joseph T. b. Dec. 14, 1909, died. Family resided West Weber, Utah, and Rexburg, Idaho.
Elder; president deacons quorum; 1st counselor in presidency Y. M. M. I. A.; home missionary. Marshal; deputy game warden. Farmer; commission agent.

ELLSWORTH, GERMAN (son of Israel Ellsworth of Atica, LaPeer Co., Michigan). Born 1812, in New York. Came to Utah Sept. 4, 1848, Captain Allen company.
Married Experience (Speedy) Brown, in New York State. Their children: Eveline, m. James Ellsworth; Esther, m. William Doudle; Ephraim; Minerva; Elizabeth; German, m. Christena Parsons.
Elder; missionary in Michigan. Died October, 1848, Salt Lake City.
Experience Brown (Ellsworth), after her husband's death, married Philo Johnson, who was one of the original pioneers of 1847. Their children: Reuben; Emily; Hannah; Lettie; Philo; Speedy.

ELLSWORTH, GERMAN (son of German Ellsworth and Experience Brown). Born Sept. 27, 1848, Salt Lake City.
Married Christena Parsons Dec. 25, 1869, Payson, Utah (daughter of Peter and Chorsta Parsons), who was born July 13, 1848, and came to Utah 1859. Their children: Speedy Armina b. Sept. 13, 1870, Delos Tanner; German Edgar b. Oct. 12, 1871, m. Mary Rachel Smith; Reubin William b. May 2, 1873, m. Isabelle Barnes; George Arthur b. October, 1874, m. Charlotte Ellen Eyre; Albert Heber b. Sept. 28, 1876, m. Jane D. Thorne; Lewis Norman b. Feb. 28, 1880, m. Pearl Hale; Nellie b. 1882, died; Jesse Hyrum b. July, 1884; Sarah Eveline b. 1886, m. Elmer Madsen; Cyrus Wells b. Feb. 28, 1891; Wilford James b. 1893; Mary Cecila b. 1895.
Member 127th quorum seventies; counselor to bishop Jesse Taylor. City councilman. Bee and fruit inspector. Farmer, carpenter and builder.

ELLSWORTH, GERMAN EDGAR (son of German Ellsworth, Jr., and Christena Parsons). Born Oct. 12, 1871, Payson, Utah.
Married Mary Rachael Smith June 29, 1898, Salt Lake City (daughter of Jesse Smith and Mary Ann Price of

Lehi, Utah, pioneers September, 1865, Washburn Chipman company). She was born April 18, 1876. Their children: German Smith b. May 18, 1899; Blanche b. Aug. 10, 1901; Ruth b. March 11, 1907; Helen b. Dec. 3, 1909; Russell Smith b. May 29, 1913.
Member 127th quorum seventies; missionary to California 1896-98; Assistant Superintendent Jordan Stake Sunday school; president Northern States Mission 1903-13. Member Board of Education. Instrumental in publishing more than 250,000 of Book of Mormon. President Zions Printing and Publishing Co., of Independence, Mo. School teacher.

EMMETT, THOMAS (son of John Emmett and Sarah Boothman of Downan, Lancashire. Eng.). Born Sept. 19, 1827, at Downan. Came to Utah Sept. 13, 1854, Capt. Field company.
Married Nancy Hitchon Feb. 24, 1850, Sabdin, Lancashire. Eng. (daughter of Robert Hitchon and Margaret Irving of Downan), who was born Sept. 11, 1832. Their children: Henrietta A. b. Dec. 21, 1851, m. R. B. Wilson May 15, 1871; Thomas F. b. Jan. 27, 1856, m. Alice A. Hill Jan. 23, 1879; Robert W. b. Feb. 29, 1860, m. Mary Jensen Sept. 27, 1883; Nancy Ellen b. Nov. 6, 1861, m. George H. Greenwell May 24, 1883; Sarah E. b. Jan. 24, 1864, m. Edwin F. Tout Sept. 24, 1884; James H. b. Nov. 9, 1868, m. Elizabeth Pingree May 29, 1895; Mary A. b. Jan. 4, 1870, m. Edgar A. Ensign May 2, 1900; Walter R. b. Feb. 18, 1875, m. Joan Woodmansee Oct. 10, 1900; Irving C. b. March 15, 1878, m. Nellie Young Aug. 11, 1904. Family home Ogden, Utah.
Member high council Weber stake. School trustee two terms. Soda water manufacturer; farmer. Died Feb. 1, 1894.

EMMETT, THOMAS F. (son of Thomas Emmett and Nancy Hitchon). Born Jan. 27, 1856, Ogden, Utah.
Married Alice A. Hill Jan. 23, 1879, Salt Lake City (daughter of Thomas Hill and Alice Mellor of Ogden, Utah—pioneers 1853), who was born Oct. 9, 1855. Only child: Walter S. b. Sept. 3, 1881.
In early days, assisted his father in farming and in the soda water manufacture. Railroad conductor; contractor and builder.

EMERY, HENRY (son of George Emery of Doncaster, Eng.). Born at Doncaster. Came to Utah in the 50's.
Married Elizabeth Brewerton at Council Bluffs, Iowa, who was born March 13, 1825, Doncaster, Eng., and came to Utah with mother in the 50's. Their children: Harry B., m. Katie Putman; Elizabeth, m. Theodore McKean; George R., m. Rose Wilding; John, died; Isaac, m. Marian Ajax; David S., m. Mary Port; Mary, m. Edward Mitchell; Charles Frank, m. Elizabeth Simpson; Sarah, m. John Thomspon; Annie, m. James Roskelly; William, m. Lorina Nebeker; Ada, m. John Stowe; Frederick, m. Mamie Lamb; Martha, died; Edith, m. Edwin Rich; Fanny, died.
Seventy; bishop's counselor; choir leader. Manager shipping department Walker Bros. Co., Salt Lake City, Utah. Died July, 1881, at Salt Lake City.

EMERY, CHARLES FRANK (son of Henry Emery and Elizabeth Brewerton). Born Jan. 5, 1864, Salt Lake City.
Married Elizabeth Simpson March 5, 1890, Logan, Utah (daughter of Frank Simpson and Elizabeth Hutchinson of Durham. Eng., pioneers 1865), who was born March 16, 1866. Their children: Frank S. b. Dec. 22, 1893; Henry b. Oct. 1, 1895; Vidate b. Jan. 8, 1897; Vida b. Nov. 27, 1899; Elvie b. Aug. 18, 1901; Jessie b. May 13, 1903; Helen b. March 17, 1905; David b. Sept. 24, 1908; Elizabeth b. Sept. 4, 1910; Thaddeus b. Oct. 5, 1912. Family home, Salt Lake City.
Seventy; missionary to southern states 1890-92; superintendent Sunday school; sheriff Salt Lake county 6 years; state sanitary inspector.

EMPEY, CHARLES (son of Samuel Empey and Ann Peacock of Salt Lake City). Born 1847, Kanswarth, Eng. Came to Utah 1866.
Married Sarah Ann Shipley 1878, Ogden, Utah (daughter of Robert and Sarah Shipley of Ogden), who died December, 1898. Their children: Charles B. S., m. Katie M. Meyers; Sarah L., m. Peter Minoch; George, m. Amadille Calloway; Clarence. Family home, Ogden.
Engaged in dray business. Died Oct. 1, 1898.

EMPEY, CHARLES B. S. (son of Charles Empey and Sarah Ann Shipley). Born March 15, 1879, at Ogden.
Married Katie M. Meyers Feb. 28, 1904, Ogden (daughter of Ephraim Meyers and Cora M. Volker of Ogden, who came to Utah by rail). She was born Sept. 11, 1885. Their children: Charles Henry b. July 18, 1906; Philip Howard b. March 13, 1910. Family home, Ogden.
Manager and part owner of Ogden Wholesale Drug Company.

EMPEY, SHADRACH (son of Joseph Empey, born 1790, and Elizabeth Kempson of Bedfordshire, Eng.). Born June 21, 1822, Eatonbray, Bedfordshire. Came to Utah Oct. 11, 1852, George Kendall company.
Married Ann Athes Oct. 12, 1847 (daughter of William Athes and Elizabeth Prior), who was born Nov. 5, 1827, and came to Utah with husband. Their children: Elizabeth Ann b. Oct. 18, 1848; Caroline b. Nov. 16, 1849; Jane Ann b. March 20, 1851; Ephraim S. b. May 27, 1852, m. Sarah A. Rhodes April 19, 1875; George b. March 20, 1855; William b. Aug. 31, 1856; Joseph b. Nov. 26, 1858, m. Christie Lewis Dec. 28, 1878; David Hyrum b. Feb. 25, 1861; Alfred b. Jan. 20, 1863, m. Mariah Lewis May 12, 1886; John b. March 25, 1865, m. Almira Norton Dec. 15, 1896; Amos b. Feb. 26, 1868; Orrin b. March 25, 1870. Family home Lehi, Utah.
Married Ann Folks 1858 at Salt Lake City, who was born Nov. 5, 1829, Tottenhoe, Bedfordshire, Eng.
Member 44th quorum seventies; missionary to England 1875-76. Director in Lehi Co-op.

EMPEY, EPHRAIM S. (son of Shadrach Empey and Ann Athes). Born May 27, 1852, Eatonbray, Eng.
Married Sarah Ann Rhodes April 19, 1875, at Salt Lake City (daughter of Alonzo D. Rhodes and Sarah Bushman—pioneers 1850), who was born March 4, 1857, Lehi, Utah. Their children: Sarah Ann b. April 14, 1876, m. Perry Molen Feb. 21, 1895; Ephraim Elias b. Feb. 25, 1878, m. Jane Powell Oct. 22, 1897; Alonzo Ernest b. March 28, 1880, m. Olive Mitchell Dec. 7, 1904; Elsie Elizabeth b. May 6, 1882, m. Richard Tracy Sept. 18, 1901; Alfred Burton b. Aug. 5, 1884, m. Iola Simmions March 27, 1905; Martin Lester b. March 6, 1887, m. Hallie Simmions March 20, 1907; Alva M. b. April 29, 1889; Pearl Lorena b. Oct. 9, 1891, m. Antone L. Peterson Jan. 11, 1910; Ray Shadrach b. Dec. 20, 1893; Homer Rhodes b. May 28, 1896; Edna Mary b. March 25, 1901. Family home Ammon, Bingham Co., Idaho.
Missionary to eastern states 1897-99; 2d counselor in bishopric at Ammon 1903.

ENGEBRETSEN, BERNT (son of Engebret Engebretsen and Malene Johnsen). Born Oct. 22, 1841, Eidsvold, Akershus Amt, Norway. Came to Utah 1884.
Married Kirstine Anderson 1870. Their children: Ole Anaker, m. Seline DeGray; Einar Marcus, m. Exeline Pedersen; Bernhart Gunerius; Jennie Matilde, m. Perrigrine Sessions; Carl Johan, m. Ethel Abbott; Elize Marie, m. Henry Winter; Syverin Theodore, died; Moses Gustaph, m. Hazel Moyer; Martha Lovisa, m. Aderen Clinger; Adaubtet. Family home Lorenzo, Idaho.
High priest; ward teacher. Moved to Idaho in 1906.

ENGLAND, JOHN. Born March 20, 1815, at Stafford, Eng. Came to Utah May 4, 1862, Homer Duncan company.
Married Jane Pavard May 4, 1834, at Berwick Church, Eng. (daughter of Thomas Pavard of Stafford, Eng.), who was born Aug. 22, 1815. Their children: George b. March 10, 1835; Anny b. June 30, 1837; Mina b. June 25, 1838; Martha b. 1839; David b. March 5, 1840; John b. Sept. 4, 1843; William b. 1845; William b. July 29, 1846; Emma b. March 5, 1848; Lillian b. Nov. 30, 1849; James b. May 24, 1851; Elizabeth b. Feb. 8, 1852; Esther; Florio; Thomas b. July 3, 1861. Family home Plain City, Utah.
High priest. Died April 16, 1894, at Plain City, Utah.

ENGLAND, JOHN (son of John England and Jane Pavard). Born Sept. 4, 1843, at Bridport, Dorsetshire, Eng. Came to Utah Oct. 15, 1861, working on telegraph line.
Married Laura H. M. Thuesen Oct. 11, 1863, at Plain City, Utah (daughter of Niels Thuesen and Englika Christina Lund of Copenhagen, Denmark—pioneers Sept. 3, 1860, James D. Ross company). She was born June 2, 1846. Their children: Laura Christina b. March 28, 1865, d. February, 1866; John Vesilo b. March 20, 1867, m. Emma Stewart June 1, 1887; Julia b. July 11, 1869, d. Dec. 18, 1869; Ellen b. Feb. 1, 1871, m. Albert Miller Nov. 5, 1890; William T. b. Jan. 25, 1874, m. Eliza M. Geddes Sept. 5, 1894; Charles Milo b. May 24, 1876, m. Susie Geddes Aug. 15, 1900; Alice Louisa b. Sept. 28, 1878, m. John Griffith Oct. 21, 1889; Violate Lorena b. Aug. 24, 1880, d. March 16, 1892; Ida Adelinda b. Feb. 17, 1883, m. H. Andrew Benson April 6, 1905; Little May b. Nov. 27, 1881, m. Eugene Liljenquist Nov. 8, 1905; Alta Adelia b. Aug. 9, 1889. Family home Plain City, Utah.
Counselor to president of high priests quorum, Blackfoot stake, 1907-09. Black Hawk war veteran. Director Plain City Ditch Co., 1870-82, and president of same 1871-76; director of Peoples Canal Co. of Moreland, Idaho, 1895-99.

ENGLAND, WILLIAM T. (son of John England and Laura H. M. Thuesen). Born Jan. 25, 1874, Plain City, Utah.
Married Eliza M. Geddes Sept. 5, 1894, at Salt Lake City (daughter of William and Emma Geddes—pioneers October, 1864), who was born Sept. 25, 1873. Their children: William H. b. July 15, 1895; Lurlea E. b. Oct. 26, 1898; Violet M. b. Feb. 16, 1902; Martha Louisa b. Oct. 5, 1908; Prescilla b. July 20, 1912. Family home Moreland, Idaho.
Member stake Sunday school board five years; set apart and ordained bishop Moreland ward Jan. 11, 1908.

ENGLAND, JAMES (son of John England and Jane Pavard). Born May 24, 1851, at Bridport, Dorsetshire, Eng.
Married Rose Hannah Smith Jan. 24, 1870, at Salt Lake City (daughter of George Andrew Smith and Sarah Hues of Birmingham, Eng., who came to Utah 1865). She was born May 6, 1854, at Birmingham. Their children: Rose Hannah b. Oct. 9, 1871, m. Joseph Winn; James Henry b. June 13, 1875, m. Elizabeth Draper; m. Maggie Griffiths; George Albert b. Nov. 23, 1877, m. Hattie Hartvidgson; Sarah Jane b. Oct. 24, 1879, m. Jesse Davis; Willard Victor b. Jan. 13, 1882, m. Alice Ammondsen; Belle Harris b. Aug. 10, 1883,

m. E. H. Bench; Minnie b. Dec. 10, 1885, m. Earl Lamb; Emma b. Aug. 19, 1887, m. Robert Baxter; Carlos Smith b. Aug. 15, 1889; Nellie Smith b. Nov. 12, 1890; Charles William b. Sept. 26, 1892; Lizzie Smith b. April 13, 1894; Katy May b. June 4, 1896; Leona Smith b. April 17, 1898. Family resided Plain City and Collinston, Utah, Preston, Burley and Moreland, Idaho, LaGrande and Union, Oregon.
Moved from Plain City to Collinston, Utah, 1888; to Preston, Idaho, 1890; and to Moreland, Idaho, 1896, where he was ordained a high priest and set apart as 1st counselor to Bishop H. P. Christensen; moved to LaGrande, Ore., 1900; set apart bishop of LaGrande ward 1901, and of Union ward 1902; patriarch. One of the incorporators of Peoples Canal at Moreland, Idaho.

ENNISS, JOHN (son of John Enniss, born 1772, Forest of Dean, Gloucestershire, Eng., and Hannah Park, born April 14, 1778, parish of English Bidener; married Feb. 4, 1808). Born Dec. 10, 1821, Forest of Dean. Came to Utah 1852, Thomas Tidwell company.
Married Elizabeth Boulter Dec. 14, 1845 (daughter of Thomas Boulter and Comfort Davies, both of whom died at Council Bluffs, Iowa). She was born Aug. 11, 1824, and came to Utah with husband. Their children: Augusta Comfort b. Aug. 18, 1847, m. Ruel M. Rogers June, 1862; John Heber b. April, 1855, m. Annie M. Garfield 1874; Willard Boulter b. June 8, 1857, m. Mary Emily Wadley Dec. 14, 1882. Family home Draper, Utah.
Married Jane Okey (daughter of Thomas Okey). Only child: Rozella Jane b. Feb. 7, 1862, m. Joseph D. Wadley Dec. 30, 1884.
Settled at Draper 1853. Presided over Pontshill branch in England. Assisted in bringing immigrants to Utah.

ENNISS, WILLARD BOULTER (son of John Enniss and Elizabeth Boulter). Born June 8, 1857, Draper, Utah.
Married Mary Emily Wadley Dec. 14, 1882, Salt Lake City (daughter of Joseph Wadley and Hannah Dorney; former pioneer 1853, latter 1856), who was born Aug. 17, 1859, Pleasant Grove, Utah. Their children: John Wadley b. Sept. 27, 1883, m. Laura Peart Dec. 5, 1906; Hannah Mabel b. Dec. 30, 1884, m. Earl S. Allen Dec. 20, 1906; Annie Estella b. April 13, 1886, m. Alma Terry Jan. 7, 1904; Alva Benjamin b. Dec. 3, 1892; Vern Wilson b. Nov. 12, 1894; Maysel Augusta b. July 7, 1897; Emily Elizabeth b. March 31, 1899; Franklin Dorney b. Nov. 23, 1900; Elmer Marr March 31, 1906. Family home Draper, Utah.
Member 73d quorum seventies; high priest; bishop Draper ward 1898-10; missionary to England 1906-08. School teacher. Justice of peace two terms; instrumental in incorporating all water rights of settlers at Draper; director and active manager Draper Irrigation company 1890-95; then president till 1904. School trustee of 22d district Salt Lake county 16 years. One of organizers of Draper Mercantile company 1898.

ENSIGN, LUMAN DANIEL (son of Luman Ashley Ensign). Born March 25, 1854, Salt Lake City.
Married Rosa Belle Dee Oct. 11, 1885, Ogden, Utah (daughter of Thomas and Ann Dee of Ogden), who was born April 21, 1861.

ENSIGN, MARTIN L. (son of Horace and Mary Ensign). Born March 31, 1831, Westfield, Hampden county, Mass. Came to Utah Sept. 22, 1847, Ira Eldredge company.
Married Mary Dunn Jan. 8, 1852 (daughter of Simeon A. Dunn and Adaline Rawson, married July 3, 1828). She was born Nov. 2, 1833. Their children: Mary Adaline b. Nov. 10, 1852, m. John L. Roberts; Georgiana b. April 6, 1854, m. William J. Hill; Emma Lovinia b. Aug. 22, 1856, m. Siveren N. Lee; Harriet Camilla b. April 24, 1859, m. Isaac Smith; Martin Luther b. Jan. 15, 1862, m. Martha Wright Jan. 15, 1888; John Henry b. May 8, 1864; Horace b. March 29, 1866; Effie Celestia b. Sept. 7, 1871, m. Lewis A. Merrill June 6, 1895; Adams Wesley b. Jan. 1, 1875, m. Charlotte Winnifred Boden Dec. 20, 1901. Family home Brigham, Utah.
High councilor. Justice of peace; coroner. Built ferries at, and bridges over Bear river at Standings, Bear River City, and Corinne, Utah; helped build first house on Church Farm, Cache Valley; built sawmills in Box Elder and Logan Canyons, Blacksmith Fork, Three Mile, Willard and Honeyville.

ENSIGN, ADAMS WESLEY (son of Martin L. Ensign and Mary Dunn). Born Jan. 1, 1875, Brigham, Utah.
Married Charlotte Winnifred Boden Dec. 20, 1901, Logan, Utah (daughter of Heber Coleman Boden and Charlotte Welch), who was born Jan. 16, 1881, at Brigham. Their children: Hugo B. b. Oct. 30, 1902; Wesley B. b. July 19, 1904; Coleman B. b. Feb. 28, 1906; Olive b. April 19, 1908; Mary Winnifred b. Jan. 1, 1910; Eliza Boden b. May 9, 1913. Family home Brigham, Utah.
Missionary to southern states 1900. Dental surgeon, 1903; dairyman.

ENSIGN, SAMUEL (son of Isaac Ensign and Lydia Noble of Westfield, Mass). Born May 24, 1805, at Westfield. Came to Utah Sept. 22, 1847, Ira Eldredge company.
Married Mary Everett Gordon Nov. 29, 1832, Westfield, Mass. (daughter of Conrad Gordon and Julia A. Searles of that place), who was born May 15, 1811, and died Feb. 12, 1868. Their children: Julia Searles b. Sept. 16, 1833, m.

John W. Woolley March 20, 1851; Samuel Lozene b. Jan. 24, 1836, m. Mary Angell Dec. 29, 1858; Horace Sobieski b. April 6, 1848, m. Martha Triplett March 7, 1870; m. Thurza Case; Harriet Ann L. Dort (adopted) b. July 1, 1850, m. Henry B. Rugg Jan. 25, 1870; Lorin Gordon b. Feb. 12, 1855, d. Feb. 12, 1855.
Married Ruth Kelson Dec. 27, 1857, at Salt Lake City. Their child: Mary Jane b. March 17, 1859, m. Henry B. Rugg.
High priest. Worked as carpenter on Nauvoo temple 1844 until completion; aided in building many grist and sawmills in Utah, worked on Salt Lake temple and lost his life by falling from its wall June 24, 1885. Millwright.

ENSIGN, SAMUEL LOZENE (son of Samuel Ensign and Mary Everett Gordon). Born Jan. 24, 1836, Westfield, Mass. Came to Utah Sept. 20, 1847, Ira Eldredge company.
Married Mary Angell Dec. 29, 1858, Salt Lake City (daughter of Solomon Angell and Eunice Clark Young of Providence, R. I.), who was born Nov. 22, 1842. Their children: Orpha Adella b. Feb. 4, 1860; Julia Angeli b. Dec. 21, 1861, d. April 24, 1871; Samuel Lozene Jr. b. May 9, 1863 m. Mary Ann Gibson; George Albert b. July 22, 1865, m. Mary C. Woodruff, d. Feb. 29, 1912; Amy Eunice b. June 8, 1867, d. Sept. 29, 1882; Alfred Horace b. Sept. 19, 1869, m. Edith Lucile Hyde; Mary Elizabeth b. Aug. 8, 1871; Frank Victor b. May 5, 1873, m. Gracie F. Free; Louis Osborn b. March 16, 1875, m. Florence May Papworth; John Woolley b. April 15, 1877, m. Florence Louise Hughes; Herman Ross b. Jan. 21, 1881, d. Jan. 15, 1900; Stanley b. Nov. 14, 1882, m. Anna Mork; Ivie Jean b. Nov. 29, 1889. Family home, Salt Lake City.
High priest. Assisted in bringing immigrants to Utah; carried mail from Salt Lake City to Fort Kearney for the Y. X. Co. 1857; was member of Nauvoo Legion, member of territorial militia.

EPPERSON, SIDNEY HYRUM (son of Elias Epperson and Nancy Dalton of Indiana). Born 1832 in Indiana. Came to Utah 1852, David Wood company.
Married Mary Jane Robey 1853 at Provo, Utah (daughter of Jeremiah Robey and Ruth Tucker—pioneers 1852, David Wood company), who was born 1836, and came to Utah with parents. Their children: Sidney Theophelis b. Jan. 23, 1854, m. Eliza Van Wagoner; Charles Alonzo b. March 15, 1856, m. Libbie Coleman; Mary Louverna b. July 28, 1858, m. Dean Forrest; Albert b. Sept. 10, 1860; Elias Tipton b. Sept. 16, 1862, m. Janey Bonner; Viola Delphina b. Sept. 26, 1864, m. Adelbert Alexander; Robert Ross b. Jan. 20, 1867, m. Bertha Springer; William Henry b. Dec. 17, 1868; Simon S. b. Jan. 12, 1871, m. Lydia M. Smith April 4, 1889; Daniel D. b. Feb. 17, 1873; Ruth Lunica b. May 20, 1875, m. William J. Mathews; Frank S. b. June 26, 1877, m. Ada Mohlman; Elmer Drew b. Dec. 23, 1879, m. Maud Barker.
Settled at Provo 1852; moved to Snake Creek 1859. Bishop of Midway ten years. Member Utah militia; captain of Provo Valley cavalry three years; major. Indian war veteran. Farmer and stockraiser.

ERCANBRACK, W. T. (son of Smiton Ercanbrack and Lucinda Caroline Page of Niles, Mich). Born Dec. 16, 1840, at Niles. Came to Utah July, 1853.
Married Ruth Ann Seabury Nov. 11, 1864, Kamas Prairie, Utah (daughter of Wesley Hudson and Louisa Keith of Vermont—pioneer July, 1848). She was born Nov. 14, 1848. Their children: William Wesley b. Feb. 13, 1866, m. Mary Ella Morgan; George Grey b. April 8, 1868, m. Luella Girley; John b. July 3, 1870, died; Charles Frank b. Sept. 30, 1871, m. Lena Jensen; Ruth Ester b. Nov. 3, 1873, m. James Burston; Alice Velma b. Feb. 22, 1876, died; Caroline Lucinda b. March 23, 1878, died; Otis Lsrary b. July 13, 1880, m. Julia Bartholomew; Alta Malissa b. Aug. 29, 1883, m. Ezra B. Walker; Bertha Leonora July 4, 1885, died; Byron Abner b. July 16, 1887; Olive Mihely b. Feb. 6, 1891; Raymond Gilbert b. July 8, 1893; Arvilla Louisa b. May 14, 1896. Family home Goshen, Utah.
High priest. Merchant. Died June 17, 1911, Provo, Utah.

ERICKSON, GUNNER. Born at Christiania, Norway. Came to Utah 1852.
His only child: Jens Gunderson, m. Marie ——. Family home Mt. Pleasant, Utah.
Veteran Black Hawk Indian war. Carpenter and farmer. Died at Mt. Pleasant.

GUNDERSON, JENS (son of Gunner Erickson). Born Sept. 21, 1830, Christiania, Norway. Came to Utah 1852.
Married Marie ——, Salt Lake Endowment House, who was born Jan. 28, 1844. Their children: James P. b. March 4, 1865, m. Jennie Jensen Renburg; Gunner b. Jan. 19, 1867, m. Lucinda Madsen; Christine b. Jan. 28, 1869, m. Charles Jensen Renburg; Annie b. March 3, 1871, m. Joseph Coates; Mary b. Jan. 24, 1873, m. Charles Files; Caroline b. 1875, m. Marvel Fowles; Tina and Charles, d. infants; Henry b. Sept. 16, 1889. Family home Mt. Pleasant, Utah. Veteran Black Hawk Indian war; high priest; ward teacher. Early settler to Mt. Pleasant. Farmer and carpenter. Died Nov. 4, 1902, Mt. Pleasant.

GUNDERSON, JAMES P. (son of Jens and Marie Gunderson). Born March 4, 1865, Mt. Pleasant, Utah.
Married Jennie Jensen Renburg April 10, 1884, Salt Lake City (daughter of Charles Jensen Renburg and Maren Jen-

sen of Eling, Hjorring amt, Denmark; pioneers 1855). She was born Sept. 26, 1865. Their children: Charles J. b. Feb. 9, 1885; Dortha b. Aug. 7, 1887, m. Ira Cloud; Hazel b. March 24, 1891, m. Ivin Simmons; Levar b. Jan. 9, 1893; Foletta b. July 26, 1895, d. infant; Famia b. May 29, 1898; Virgil b. Oct. 27, 1901; Fredericka b. May 24, 1904. Family home Clear Creek, Utah.
High priest; ward teacher. Miner. Employed by Utah Fuel Company.

ERICKSON, OLSON LOUIS ERICK (son of Erick Erickson Olson, born April 26, 1835, Wingaker, Sweden, and Maria Christina Anderson, born Aug. 29, 1834, Lennes, Sweden, who came to Utah July 10, 1882). Born June 22, 1866, Wingaker, Sweden. Came to Utah July 10, 1882.
Married Christina Olson Nov. 6, 1890, Logan, Utah (daughter of Ola and Batilda Bartelson of Sweden), who was born Feb. 11 1867, Jeslof, Sweden. Their children: Alben L. b. Sept. 13, 1891; Chrestina Lovenia b. Feb. 25, 1894; Viola b. April 4, 1897, d. Nov. 22, 1903; Eugenia b. Jan. 31, 1901; Genette Josephine b. May 10, 1904; Verna Hortense b. March 16, 1906; Flora Vilate b. Nov. 4, 1911. Family home Glencoe ward, Idaho.
Missionary to Sweden 1898-99; bishop of Glencoe 1909.

ETHERINGTON, JOHN (son of John Etherington, born Jan. 10, 1757, and Alice Burdess, both of Bishop Auckland, Durhamshire, Eng.). He was born April 28, 1794, at Bishop Auckland, Eng. Came to Utah Sept. 7, 1855, with second company of Noah T. Guymon.
Married Elizabeth Hemsley (daughter of William Hemsley and Frances Dawson, married 1818). She was born Feb. 12, 1800, and came to Utah Sept. 7, 1855, with second company of Noah T. Guymon. Their children: John b. Aug. 23, 1818; Jane b. Nov. 29, 1820, m. Appleton Elcoat; James b. Dec. 5, 1822, m. Mary Hopper; Frances b. March 16, 1825, m. James Bulmer; Elizabeth b. July 31, 1827, m. William Pew; Ann b. Jan. 24, 1830, m. Thos. Heslop; m. John Newey June 2, 1856; William; Mary b. Aug. 12, 1834, m. George Stanger; Thomas b. Nov. 1, 1836, m. Sarah Wheeler March 9, 1853; George b. July 13, 1839. Family home Faceby, Yorkshire, Eng.
Ward teacher; high priest; helped many families in the emigration to Utah. Died Jan. 13, 1865.

ETHERINGTON, THOMAS (son of John Etherington and Elizabeth Hemsley). Born Nov. 1, 1836, at Bishop Auckland, Durham, Eng.
Married Sarah Wheeler March 9, 1858, at Salt Lake City (daughter of John Wheeler and Elizabeth Gillings, who came to Utah 1857, William Walker company). She was born Oct. 21, 1840, at Gravely, Cambridgeshire, Eng. Their children: Elizabeth Ann b. Dec. 29, 1858, m. Samuel Hadley April 16, 1877; Sarah Jane b. Jan. 30, 1860, m. Hyrum Goodale, June 30, 1881; Mary E. b. July 19, 1862, m. James R. McFarland April 13, 1882; Susan A. b. April 2, 1864, m. Charles B. McFarland, April 2, 1882; Frances A. b. March 9, 1886, m. Edward C. Charlton Nov. 26, 1884; Ellen Maria b. Jan. 4, 1868, d. Nov. 24, 1858; Thomas W. b. Sept. 29, 1869, d. Oct. 5, 1869; Emily E. b. Oct. 22, 1870, d. Aug. 24, 1873; Laura M. b. June 2, 1873, m Joseph Blanch Jan. 20, 1897; Esther C. b. Feb. 3, 1876, m. Peter F. McFarland Feb. 3, 1897; George W. b. Oct. 31, 1879, m. Hannah Clark March 7, 1900; James A. b. Oct. 31, 1882, m. Hannah M. Bingham Nov. 26, 1903; m. Rachel Hoskins Feb. 26, 1908.
Married Margaret Newby 1867 at Salt Lake City (daughter of John Newby and Elizabeth Smurthwaite), who was born Sept. 4, 1835, at Sunderland, Durhamshire, Eng. Their children: John b. Feb. 24, 1869, m. Ann Skeen Jan. 7, 1890; Margaret b. July 31, 1872, m. Henry B. Dance March 7, 1889; Isabella A. b. Nov. 13, 1875, m. Nathaniel Montgomery Jan. 1904. Family home West Weber, Utah.
Missionary to England 1886-1888; assistant superintendent of Sunday school in West Weber 1881 to 1883 and superintendent 1884 to 1889. Constable of West Weber from 1872 to 1878; trustee of West Weber public schools. President of Slaterville Consolidated Creameries from 1897 to 1905. Died Jan. 20, 1907.

ETHERINGTON, GEORGE W. (son of Thomas Etherington and Sarah Wheeler). Born Oct. 31, 1879, at West Weber, Utah.
Married Hannah Clark March 7, 1900, at Salt Lake City (daughter of John Clark and Ellen Wootton), who was born July 16, 1880, at Ogden, Utah. Their children: Sarah H. b. Aug. 3, 1901; Thomas W. b. Sept. 1, 1903; John A. b. June 3, 1905; Walter R. b. Feb. 18, 1908; George L. b. Oct. 26, 1909, d. June 14, 1911; Myrtle L. b. Aug. 9, 1911. Family home West Weber, Utah.
Missionary to southern states 1905 to 1907; 2d counselor to bishop in West Weber ward 1909-1910, and bishop since March 27, 1910.

EVANS, BENJAMIN (son of Evan Evans and Margaret Richards of New Court, Cardifanshire, South Wales). Born Sept. 16, 1826, New Court, Cardifanshire, South Wales. Came to Utah May, 1879.
Married Mary Eynon 1847 in Carmarthenshire, South Wales (daughter of Daniel Eynon and Mary Jones of Carmarthenshire, South Wales), who was born May 28, 1826. Came to Utah 1880. Their children: John, m. Ann Lewis; Evan, m. Hannah Prosser; Margaret, m. John Davis; Polly Brinton; Daniel; David, deceased; William, m. Margaret Gardner; Morgan, m. Agnes Elenor Davis; James, m. Sophia Davis; Thomas, m. Elizabeth Chambers; Benjamin, m. Rose Jones; Daniel (adopted). Family home Spanish Fork, Utah.
High priest. Farmer. Died June 13, 1912, Spanish Fork, Utah.

EVANS, MORGAN (son of Benjamin Evans and Mary Eynon). Born Jan. 2, 1863, at Yestalyfera, South Wales. Came to Utah June, 1880.
Married Agnes Elenor Davis August, 1888, at Provo, Utah (daughter of Caleb Hersey Davis and Hannah Strong of Provo, Utah—pioneers 1852, Milo Andrus company). She was born Sept. 4, 1865. Their children: Mary Eldera b. May 14, 1889, m. George Hayes; James Irvin b. Nov. 25, 1891; Hannah Sophia b. Aug. 30, 1893; Ruth b. July 25, 1897; Lois Emma b. June 3, 1899; Margaret Agnes b. Jan. 7, 1902; Zeia Fern b. March 24, 1904; Leiand b. June 8, 1905; Winona b. June 17, 1908, died Oct. 5, 1908. Family home Castle Gate, Utah.
Presiding elder of Castle Gate ward 1909-11; set apart bishop of Castle Gate ward Oct. 1, 1911; ward clerk; president and secretary of Y. M. M. I. A.; Sunday school superintendent. Justice of peace of Castle Gate. Miner.

EVANS, CHARLES M. (son of David J. Evans and Sarah Minshul of Liverpool, Eng.). Born Jan. 27, 1831, Liverpool. Came to Utah 1852.
Married Annie Reeves June 6, 1863, Salt Lake City (daughter of George Reeves and Charlotte Phillips of Sussex, Eng.), who was born Feb. 15, 1841. Came to Utah, Ansel Harmon company. Their children: John R., m. Mary Bowman; Charlotte A., m. Thomas Homer; Charles R.; George E. Sydney; Jessie E., m. August A. Hedberg; Edward G.; Ernest W., m. Chloe Bitner. Family home Salt Lake City.
Married Mary Stoner June 1, 1867, Salt Lake City (daughter of William Stoner and Harriet Davis of Brighton, Sussex, Eng., pioneers Sept. 23, 1866, Captain Halladay company). She was born Feb. 9, 1841. Their children: William S.; Mary J.; David; Sarah Jeannette; Arthur E.; Ethel A. Family home, Salt Lake City.
Seventy. Theater musician. Bugler in Lot Smith company. Bookkeeper and clerk. Died Sept. 20, 1902, Salt Lake City.

EVANS, DAVID (son of Thomas Evans of Cathrays, Cardiff, Monmouthshire, South Wales). Born Aug. 25, 1810, in Cardiff. Came to Utah Sept. 1, 1860, John Smith company.
Married Amy Hughes 1833 at Cardiff (daughter of William Hughes and Ann Wattes of Cardiff), who was born 1808. Their children: Job b. Jan. 9, 1833, m. Letta Thomas; Moses. b. Dec. 20, 1835, m. Louisa Pollard; Emma b. March 2, 1839, m. Robert G. Taylor; David b. Sept. 10, 1841, d. boy; Sarah b. June 11, 1844, m. John L. Rutherford; John b. April 12, 1847, m. Zina Bascom. Family resided Salt Lake City and Mona, Utah.
Elder; home missionary; ward teacher. Lived in Salt Lake, Ogden and Mona, Utah, where he assisted in developing the country. Farmer. Died in 1872 at Mona, Utah.

EVANS, JOHN (son of David Evans and Amy Hughes). Born April 12, 1847, in Cardiff. Came to Utah with father.
Married Zina Bascom June 25, 1877, at Mona, Utah (daughter of Joel Almon Bascom and Alice Jane Bell of Mona and Vernal, Utah, pioneers 1856 and 1857. She was born Dec. 1, 1858, Provo, Utah. Their children: John Almon b. May 9, 1878, m. Laura Gardner; David Watson b. Feb. 24, 1880; William Franklin b. Feb. 12, 1882, m. Rose Hodgkinson; Sarah Alice b. March 2, 1884, m. Stephen Adams; Zina Silitoa b. July 22, 1888, m. Albert Smith; Annie Louise b. Aug. 2, 1890, m. Clayborn Brimhall; Mary Amy b. Nov. 1, 1892; Flossie Rose b. Feb. 10, 1895; Joel Andrew b. Jan. 13, 1901; Pearl Bell b. May 24, 1903. Family home Naples ward, Utah.
Member Nephi quorum seventies; missionary to South Wales; high priest; president 1st Y. M. M. I. A., Mona, Utah; superintendent Sunday school, Naples ward; ward teacher 30 years. Road supervisor; school trustee at Mona, Utah. Moved to Naples ward in 1891. Located home, helped build canals and roads. Farmer.

EVANS, DAVID (son of Israel and Abigail Evans of Maryland). Born Oct. 27, 1804, Cecil county, Md. Came to Utah Sept. 18, 1850.
Married Mary Beck July 25, 1826 (daughter of Henry and Margaret Beck), who was born Oct. 18, 1804; died June 20, 1841, Adams county, Ill. Their children: Eliza Jane b. April 16, 1827, m. Ira Hinkley; Israel b. Oct. 2, 1828, m. Matilda Thomas; Henry b. Oct. 25, 1830, m. Anna Bruun; Mary Ann b. Sept. 2, 1832, m. John Glines; Margaret b. Jan. 3, 1835, d. Aug. 27, 1836; Araminta b. Aug. 21, 1838, d. Oct. 1, 1838; Emma b. Jan. 12, 1840, m. Prime Coleman.
Married Barbara Ann Ewell Nov. 23, 1841 (daughter of Pleasant and Barbara Ewell), who was born May 16, 1821, Albemarle county, Va. Their children: Martha b. Oct. 20, 1842, m. William Winn; Amanda b. April 21, 1844, m. Edward Marcus; Abigail b. Jan. 27, 1846, m. Oley Ellingson; Joseph b. April 7, 1847, m. Jane Scofield; Sarah b. April 27, 1849, m. Jacob Hodge; Susannah b. May 6, 1850, m. Isaac Aldridge; David b. Jan. 28, 1852, m. Leah Naegle; Hyrum b. July 8, 1853, d. July 29, 1862; Barbara Ann b. March 16, 1855, m. John P. Bush; Rozilla b. May 4, 1856, m. William E. Tacker; Ephraim b. July 11, 1858, d. May 15, 1863; Eleazar b. Feb. 24, 1861, d. March 24, 1884; Mosiah b. Sept. 22, 1862, m.

Esther Carter Dec. 14, 1882; Mary b. May 17, 1864, m. William P. Wanless; Jacob b. April 26, 1867, m. Ann Nelson.
Married Sarah Thornton at Salt Lake City (daughter of William and Elizabeth Thornton), who was born June 11, 1807, Little Paxton, Eng.
Married Edna Hinchliff (daughter of Elijah and Hannah Hinchliff), who was born March 24, 1846, Calico Bridge, Eng. Their children: Samuel b. Nov. 3, 1855, d. Nov. 3, 1855; Hannah b. Jan. 4, 1857, d. Feb. 15, 1857.
Married Clymenia Shaw March 16, 1854, Salt Lake City (daughter of Benjamin Shaw and Phoeba Whipple), who was born Feb. 2, 1834, Medina Co., Ohio. Their children: Phebe Jane b. Dec. 1, 1855, d. Dec. 18, 1855; James b. Aug. 17, 1857, m. Mary Wanless; Edwin b. Feb. 2, 1860, m. Catharine Lewis.
Married Rebecca Coleman Nov. 18, 1856, Salt Lake City (daughter of Prime and Sarah Coleman), who was born Oct. 4, 1838, Bedfordshire, Eng. Their children: George Coleman b. May 18, 1858, m. Agnes Taylor; Prime b. May 10, 1860, m. Sarah Taylor; Harriet b. June 11, 1862, m. John Wilson; Sarah b. Sept. 22, 1864, m. Samuel Taylor; Rebecca Susannah b. July 10, 1868, d. Jan. 4, 1869; Emma Jane b. Dec. 11, 1869, m. John Roberts; Martha Ann b. July 24, 1872; Ellen b. Dec. 23, 1875, m. Mr. Manning.
Married Margaret Christina Holm May 4, 1861, Salt Lake City (daughter of Jens Holm and Margaret Christina), who was born Sept. 5, 1843, Bornholm, Denmark. Their children: John Holm b. Nov. 29, 1863, d. Oct. 3, 1864; Margaret Christina b. Aug. 27, 1865, m. James Turner; Jane b. Dec. 18, 1867, m. Richard Bradshaw; Hannah b. Feb. 4, 1870, m. Andrew B. Anderson; Rachel b. April 25, 1874, m. William Wing; Clara b. Dec. 21, 1876, m. Joseph Goates.
Seventy; assisted in bringing immigrants to Utah; ordained bishop of 11th ward at Nauvoo 1842 by the prophet Joseph Smith; bishop at Lehi 30 years. Laid off the city of Lehi with a pocket compass and a square. Member first legislature of Utah and acted as a member of that body several terms; colonel in state militia; mayor of Lehi several terms. Died June 23, 1883.

EVANS, MOSIAH (son of David Evans and Barbara Ann Ewell). Born Sept. 22, 1862, Lehi, Utah.
Married Catherine Esther Carter Dec. 14, 1882, Salt Lake City (daughter of James P. Carter and Harriet Wood, pioneers 1861), who was born May 12, 1859, Tredegar, Wales. Their children: Mosiah David James b. Sept. 23, 1883, m. Bessie Preston Aug. 28, 1906; Esther Maud b. March 28, 1885, m. David B. Foulger May 1, 1907; Howard b. Feb. 20, 1887, m. Grace Harding Feb. 10, 1908; Hazel May b. Jan. 8, 1889, m. David C. Chapman Sept. 1, 1909; Eleazar Carter b. Jan. 16, 1892; John Roscoe b. July 14, 1893; Glenn Merrill b. Aug. 15, 1895; Earl William b. March 9, 1898; Jessie Virginia b. March 30, 1902; Lyra Alice b. Oct. 7, 1904, d. Oct. 7, 1904.
Lehi City recorder 1893-1904; mayor of Lehi four years; member house in fourth legislature from Utah county 1901; first president Garland town board 1905, and Garland Commercial Club 1907 and 1912; president Bank of Garland and the athletic association; resident manager Utah-Idaho Sugar company.

EVANS, DAVID MINSHALL (son of David Jones Evans and Sarah Minshall of Liverpool, Lancashire, Eng.). Born July 20, 1821, Liverpool. Came to Utah September, 1852.
Married Mary Holding 1842, at Liverpool (daughter of John Holding and Mary Fitten of Liverpool), who was born July 16, 1821. Their children: William H. b. Dec. 22, 1843, d. May 29, 1838; David H. b. April 24, 1845, d. Dec. 22, 1847; John H. b. May 17, 1847, d. Dec. 26, 1847; Edward Holding b. April 25, 1849, m. Catherine Van Dam; Charles H. b. March 27, 1852, m. Elizabeth M. Smith; Josephine H. b. Jan. 2, 1855; Herbert Van Dam; Sarah J. b. Oct. 29, 1859, m. George Brigham Kelly. Family home Salt Lake City.
Married Jane Owen Court July 20, 1867, Salt Lake City (daughter of Thomas Court and Amelia Owen of Salt Lake City, who came to Utah Oct. 23, 1849; James Needham company). She was born Sept. 12, 1837. Came to Utah Sept. 24, 1863.
One of presidents of 23d quorum seventies; high priest; member of band that played at breaking of ground for Salt Lake temple and laying of cornerstone of same, 1853; choir leader 7th ward. Contractor and builder. Died Aug. 20, 1911, Salt Lake City.

EVANS, EDWARD HOLDING (son of David Minshall Evans and Mary Holding). Born April 25, 1849, New Orleans, La.
Married Catherine Van Dam Nov. 8, 1875, Salt Lake City, who was born June 28, 1856, in Holland and came to Utah 1864. Their children: David Edward V. D. b. July 20, 1876, m. Lucile Margaret Hanson; Leonard V. D. b. Aug. 16, 1878, m. Ida Bates; Maud V. D. b. Nov. 3, 1881, m. Joseph Neve; Cornelius V. D. b. Aug. 8, 1883, m. Maude Tall; Margaret V. D. b. July 22, 1885, d. July 22, 1885; Harold V. D. b. Feb. 19, 1888, m. Pearl Harvey; Clarence V. D. b. Nov. 19, 1890; Clifford V. D. b. March 14, 1893; Moses T. V. D. b. Jan. 8, 1896; Vera V. D. b. Feb. 22, 1899. Family home Salt Lake City.
Elder. Carpenter.

EVANS, FREDERICK HENRY (son of William Evans and Elizabeth Bowring of Whitechurch, Wales). Born Aug. 2, 1842, Cardiff, Wales. Came to Utah 1852. Claudius V. Spencer company.
Married Emma Raymond November, 1870, Salt Lake City (daughter of Grandison Raymond and Celia Hall of Kaysville, Utah, pioneers 1852). She was born May 23, 1852. Their children: Celia Alice b. Aug. 7, 1871, m. Franklin A. Dimick; Frederick Charles b. Sept. 21, 1872, m. Caroline Eschler; Joseph Alvin b. Jan. 14, 1877, m. Nancy Pope; Asa Clarence b. Sept. 21, 1881; Andy Lawrence b. Sept. 21, 1881; Albert Max b. Dec. 18, 1887; Grandison b. Sept. 21, 1884, died in infancy. Family home Raymond, Idaho.
Made three trips to Missouri river after immigrants 1859-67. Settled at Thomas Fork Valley, Idaho, 1877. Died Feb. 11, 1910.

EVANS, FREDERICK CHARLES (son of Frederick Henry Evans and Emma Raymond). Born Sept. 21, 1872, Kaysville, Utah.
Married Caroline Eschler June 10, 1903, Logan, Utah (daughter of Gottfried Eschler and Rose Kunz, both of Raymond, Idaho. Came to Utah 1879). She was born Jan. 25, 1883. Their children: Roscoe Eschler b. April 18, 1904; Alice b. Sept. 24, 1905; LaGrande Eschler b. April 13, 1908. Family home Raymond, Idaho.
Missionary to England 1900-02; superintendent religion class, Raymond, Idaho; bishop's counselor 1902-12.

EVANS, JACOB (son of David Evans and Barbara Ann Ewell of Lehi, Utah). Born April 26, 1867, at Lehi, Utah.
Married Anna R. Nelson Nov. 17, 1886, at American Fork, Utah (daughter of Niels Nelson and Karren Pedersen of American Fork), who was born Feb. 22, 1867. Their children: Barbara Irene; Effie June; Jacob Sterling; Virginia Lucile. Family home Provo, Utah.
Utah county attorney 1899-1900 and 1908-12; city attorney Provo City 1904-6; Provo City councilman 1907; president Commercial Club at Provo 1908. Admitted to bar Feb. 23, 1895, to supreme court of United States Oct. 7, 1897; republican candidate for district judge 1912. Lawyer.

EVANS, JOHN (son of John Evans, born March 12, 1796, Kilcoom, South Wales, and Hannah Williams, born 1800, Llandovery, Wales). He was born Jan. 9, 1829, Llandovery, Carmarthenshire, Wales. Came to Utah Sept. 8, 1861, Harvey Hullanger company.
Married Elizabeth Davis Nov. 15, 1852 (daughter of Thomas Davis and Ann Price, who were married at Llandovary, Wales). She was born Feb. 22, 1825. Came to Utah with husband. Their children: Moroni b. Oct. 24, 1853 (St. Louis), died in childhood; Thomas M. b. Feb. 4, 1856 (St. Louis), m. Rachel Wright Dec. 21, 1882; Ann Jane b. Dec. 6, 1859 (Genoa), m. John H. Porsgren Aug. 12, 1880; John G. b. March 1, 1862 (Brigham City), m. Sarah Ann Jones March 13, 1888; Joshua Davis b. March 4, 1864 (Brigham City), died in childhood; Mary Elizabeth b. April 7, 1867 (Brigham City), m. John W. Irens Nov. 7, 1884; Martha Madora b. Nov. 20, 1871 (Brigham City), m. Laurit Berg Feb. 27, 1889. Family home Brigham City, Utah.
Seventy and high priest; missionary to Llandovary 1851 and to Nebraska 1857. Assisted in building first telegraph line across the plains. Settled at Brigham City 1861; labored at Bear River City 1866 to 1868. Served as watermaster; labored at Honeyville 1868. Assisted in building the tabernacle, and ward meeting houses. Worked on C. P. railroad. Member martial band 30 years; worked on Utah Northern railroad 1870. Missionary to Europe 1880-82. Member tabernacle choir 30 years.

EVANS, JOHN (son of John and Elizabeth Evans of Liverpool, Eng.). Born April 2, 1807 at Liverpool. Came to Utah 1855.
Married Ann Dinwoodey at Liverpool, Eng. She was born 1806. Came to Utah 1855. Their children: Elizabeth b. May, 1832, m. Jacob Hayball; John b. Oct. 7, 1834, m. Mary Ellison. Family home Salt Lake City.
Tailor. Deceased.

EVANS, JOHN (son of John Evans and Ann Dinwoodey). Born Oct. 7, 1834, Liverpool, Eng.
Married Mary Ellison Dec. 25, 1854, at St. Louis, Mo. (daughter of John Ellison and Mary Goulden, both of Bowdon, Cheshire, Eng.). She was born July 11, 1830. Their children: Mary Elizabeth b. Sept. 26, 1856, m. Ephraim Briggs; John Edward b. Oct. 11, 1858, m. Mary A. Andrew; Ephraim Sept. 7, 1860, m. Ephraim Briggs; William Ellison b. June 10, 1863, m. Lucy Onkey; James Dinwoodey b. Sept. 2, 1865; Elizabeth Mills b. May 24, 1867, m. D. H. Wood; Chancy Levi b. Sept. 13, 1869, m. Christene Jensen; Joseph b. Dec. 15, 1873; Jesse G. b. Sept. 23, 1877, m. Inez W. Wood. Family home Bountiful, Utah.
Married Emma Vine March 30, 1862, Salt Lake City (daughter of George Henry Vine and Rebecca Mary Langdon), who was born June 2, 1842, Portsmouth, Hampshire, Eng. Their children: George Henry b. May 1, 1863; Robert Alma b. March 25, 1864; Emma b. Nov. 23, 1866; Walter James b. Feb. 26, 1869; Wilford Thomas b. June 12, 1871; Rebecca Jane b. Nov. 27, 1873; David Charles b. Dec. 17, 1876; Willard Vine b. June 1, 1879.
Was 1st president of 29th quorum of seventy; ordained by H. S. Eldredge; ward clerk. Bookkeeper at Dinwoodey's Furniture company.

EVANS, JESSE G. (son of John Evans and Mary Ellison). Born Sept. 23, 1877, at Bountiful, Utah.
Married Inez W. Wood Nov. 27, 1901, at Salt Lake City (daughter of Joseph C. Wood and Josephine Chase, both of Woods Cross, Utah). She was born Nov. 16, 1879. Their

children: J. Goulden b. Sept. 20, 1902; Wells L. b. Aug. 31, 1904; John b. July 28, 1906; Mary Josephine b. Jan. 10, 1909; James b. Aug. 27, 1912. Family home Bountiful, Utah.
Missionary to England 1899-01; president 100th quorum seventies.

EVANS, THOMAS (son of Thomas and Hanna Evans of Kaysville, Utah). Born 1817, Cardiff, South Wales. Came to Utah 1856, Edward Martin company.
Married Ann Johns 1845, Cardiff, Wales (daughter of Williams Johns), who was born 1817. Their children: Thomas b. Feb. 17, 1846, m. Sarah Campkin; Emma b. 1848, m. William N. Naulder; Hyrum b. 1851, m. Annie King.
High priest. Died November, 1857.

EVANS, THOMAS (son of Thomas Evans and Ann Johns). Born Feb. 17, 1846, Cardiff, Wales. Came to Utah with parents.
Married Sarah Campkin Jan. 23, 1878 (daughter of George Campkin and Elizabeth Bell, pioneers 1850, Thomas Halmon company). She was born March 6, 1853. Their children: Elizabeth Bell b. Nov. 6, 1879, m. Isaac Adams; Ann E. b. June 29, 1882, m. John Wallen; Martha b. Dec. 5, 1885, m. David Green; Emma C. b. Dec. 5, 1887, m. Joseph Archie Allen; Ruth Campkin b. April 8, 1889, d. Aug. 1, 1890; Sarah L. b. March 15, 1890; George T. b. Jan. 31, 1892, died; Walter Elmer b. Aug. 18, 1895; John Campkin b. Jan. 17, 1897. Family home Layton, Utah.
Farmer and stockraiser. Black Hawk war veteran.

EVANS, WILLIAM M. (son of David J. Evans and Sarah Minshall). Born March 12, 1825, Liverpool, Eng. Came to Utah Oct. 2, 1851, Orson Pratt company.
Married Charlotte J. Hyder July 15, 1852, at Salt Lake City (daughter of Richard Hyder and Sarah Jarrold of Cambridge, Eng., pioneers Oct. 2, 1851, Orson Pratt company). She was born Sept. 24, 1834. Their children: Charlotte H. m. Henry Adams; John William, died; Alice H. m. Charles H. Bird; Lucy J. H., m. William McLachlan; Charles H., died; David M., died; Richard Hugh H. m. Retty Webb; Sarah Jane H., m. Charles W. Love; Martha E. H. m. George Paxman; Edward W. H., m. Louisa Burton; m. Nora Lewis; Grace H. m. Albert Sowby; Ernest I. H., m. Belle Tennent. Family home Nephi, Utah.
High priest; missionary to England 1875-76; high councilor; presided over Bristol conference, England. Indian war veteran. Farmer and carpenter; mechanical engineer. Died Jan. 5, 1877, at Nephi, Utah.

EVERETT, ADDISON (son of Ephraim Everett and Hetty Corwin). Born Oct. 10, 1815, Orange county, N. Y. Came to Utah July 24, 1847, Brigham Young company.
Only child: Mary D., m. Revilo Fuller.
Bishop at Nauvoo, also at Winter Quarters; bishop of 8th ward, Salt Lake City, 1848-60. Assisted in building Fort Supply. Called to help settle St. George 1860, and lived there until his demise, which occurred Feb. 12, 1885.

EVERILL, JOSEPH (son of John Everill of New Jersey). Born 1824, Herefordshire, Eng. Came to Utah Oct. 4, 1861, James Brown company.
Married Jane Bannister 1843 in Herefordshire, who was born 1814. Their children: Thomas, d. infant; John, m. Ruth Powell; m. Lois Chapman Williams; William R., m. Ellen Hilton; Mary Ann, m. William Hammond; m. John Spencer; Thomas J., m. Hannah Griffith; Joseph, d. infant. Family home Kaysville ward, Salt Lake City, Utah.
Seventy; high priest. Farmer and stockraiser. Died 1906, Salt Lake City.

EVERILL, JOHN (son of Joseph Everill and Jane Bannister). Born Oct. 6, 1845, Herefordshire, Eng. Came to Utah Oct. 4, 1861, James Brown company.
Married Ruth Powell May 2, 1870, Salt Lake Endowment house, by Daniel H. Wells (daughter of Jane Parks of Tunbridge Wells, Sussex, Eng., who came to Utah 1869). She was born Jan. 20, 1851. Their children: Jennie H. b. Feb. 25, 1872, m. Frank H. Stevens; Maud b. Jan. 29, 1873, d. infant; John Joseph b. Jan. 15, 1875, d. aged 21 years; Minnie b. April 6, 1877, m. Charles Donalson; Emily, d. aged three years; William, d. infant; Mamie b. Feb. 8, 1882, m. Richard A. Williams; Mattie b. Jan. 11, 1885, m. Garfield McDonald; Frank L. b. March 29, 1890, m. May Newman; Ruth E. b. May 14, 1894, m. James Sagres. Family home 15th ward, Salt Lake City.
Married Lois Chapman Williams (daughter of Ann Chapman) Nov. 2, 1908, Salt Lake City.
Elder. General contractor.

EWELL, FRANCIS MARION (son of William F. Ewell and Mary Bland, both of Ray county, Mo.). Born Nov. 3, 1835. Came to Utah 1849.
Married Francis Mary Weech July 27, 1858, in Provo, Utah (daughter of Samuel Weech and Elizabeth Gold of Somersetshire, Eng.). Came to Utah October, 1856, with John Banks company; born Oct. 9, 1838. Their children: Sarah Eliza b. June 8, 1860, m. Teancum Pratt; Franklin Marion b. Feb. 6, 1862, m. Kate Thompson; Torenzo Hyriam b. Feb. 25, 1865, m. Mary Jane Dennis; Mary Elizabeth b. Feb. 25, 1868, m. John Biglow; William Walter b. Jan. 12, 1870, m.

Tilliam Biglow; Tanra Ann b. Aug. 20, 1872, m. Daniel Dennis; Ether b. May 27, 1877, deceased; Permit Samuel b. Aug. 20, 1879, m. Ethel Savage. Resided Cassel Valley, Payson and Provo, Utah.
Senior president 101st quorum of seventy; presiding elder over Spring Glenn branch of Price ward 1883-89; teacher and superintendent of Sunday schools. Veteran of Blackhawk war. Manufacturer of shingles and farmer. Died Jan. 1, 1905, near Helper, Utah.

EWING, SAMUEL. Born 1803 in Pennsylvania. Came to Utah Oct. 2, 1847, Jedediah M. Grant company.
Married Esther Shaffer April 17, 1828 (daughter of Anderson Shaffer, pioneer Oct. 2, 1847, Jedediah M. Grant company). She was born 1866 in Little Britain, Lancaster county, Pa., died 1847, near Laramie, Wyo. Their children: Rachel b. May 4, 1829, m. Miles Miller 1848; William H. b. July 10, 1830, m. Sarah Zabriskie; Adeline M. b. May 31, 1833, m. Edward Duzette; John Jackson b. May 12, 1835, m. Rebecca F. Smith Nov. 30, 1861; Samuel Porter b. July 25, 1838, m. Emma Baldwin 1860; Anderson Shaffer b. Oct. 11, 1840, m. Liberty Parker 1865; Eliza Matilda b. Nov. 1, 1842, m. Robert Hills; James Clark b. March 2, 1845, d. 1847, crossing plains. Family home Provo, Utah.
Settled at Provo 1849. Farmer and blacksmith. Died 1882, Provo.

EWING, JOHN JACKSON (son of Samuel Ewing and Esther Shaffer). Born May 12, 1835, at Little Britain, Lancaster county, Pa.
Married Rebecca Florence Smith Nov. 30, 1861, at Salt Lake City (daughter of John Smith and Maria Foscue; the former died crossing plains, the latter came to Utah October, 1850, Byron Pace company). She was born February, 1842 Coosa county, Ala. Their children: John Smith b. Aug. 26, 1862; Esther Maria b. Oct. 6, 1863; Frederick Miles b. Aug. 15, 1865, all foregoing dead; Samuel Preston b. Nov. 4, 1866, m. Lana Hansen 1897; Jackson Elmer b. Sept. 20, 1868, m. Alice Hammond 1900; Wickliff Anderson b. March 25, 1870, m. Kate Meikle March, 1905; Florence May b. Dec. 15, 1872, m. George W. Lewis May, 1899; Cordelia Jane b. Aug. 19, 1873, m. Alma Raymond April, 1892; Porter b. May 8, 1875. m. Ione Thomas Oct. 30, 1902; Erle b. Feb. 18, 1877, m. Rose Pitcher; Lester b. Aug. 30, 1878; William b. May 23, 1880, m. Jane Merrill Dec. 1910; Russell b. Dec. 7, 1882; Lois Eliza b. Sept. 15, 1885. Family home Smithfield, Utah.
Moved to Smithfield 1866. Served as city marshal. Indian war veteran. Assisted in bringing immigrants to Utah 1864.

EYRE, EDWIN (son of James Eyre and Ann Naylor of Hecington, Lincolnshire, Eng., former died on plains, en route to Utah, latter died at sea). Born April 16, 1845, Dornsby, Lincolnshire, Eng. Came to Utah Oct. 12, 1865, independent freight train.
Married Melinva Myers Dec. 3, 1866, Minersville, Utah (daughter of William Myers and Martha Ogden; pioneers Sept. 5, 1866, Samuel D. White company). She was born April 1, 1848, and came to Utah with parents. Their children: Edwin b. Jan. 30, 1868, m. Arilla M. Guymon; Martha Ann b. Nov. 21, 1870, m. Solomon Walker; Melinva Elsie b. Sept. 18, 1872, m. John Hollingshead, died; James William b. Sept. 7, 1874, m. Rosilla Murdock; Joseph Hyrum b. Jan. 2, 1877, m. Lula Zealskie; Sarah Ellen b. Jan. 21, 1879, m. Fred W. Gillins; Paulina b. Aug. 24, 1880, m. Sidney Carter; 1888, died; Jedediah b. April 21, 1888, m. Linda Gates. Family home Minersville, Utah.
Presided over a branch of the church in England. Settled at Parowan upon arrival in Utah, and later moved to Minersville. Bishop's councilor, missionary to England 1881, returning home June, 1883; Sunday school superintendent of Minersville ward 11 or 12 years; ward teacher; choir member; performed a mission in St. George temple 1902-04; president elders quorum; instructor in high priests quorum. Has done much in the upbuilding of Minersville and surrounding country. Worked on St. George and Manti temples. Farmer.

EYRE, EDWIN, JR. (son of Edwin Eyre and Melinva Myers). Born Jan. 30, 1868, Minersville, Utah.
Married Arilla M. Guymon at Minersville (daughter of James Guymon and Rhoda Leach Neas). Their children: Guy Edwin b. March 30, 1888; Eugene A. b. April 11, 1891; Clifford b. March 9, 1893; Floyed b. Sept. 9, 1895; Robert Basil b. Jan. 2, 1898; Howard b. March 11, 1900; Gerilda b. Feb. 19, 1903; Trulan Orland b. Oct. 9, 1905; Vesta Arilla b. Nov. 24, 1907; Melvina Leach b. April 6, 1911.
Member high council Beaver stake. School trustee at Minersville several years; county commissioner; town marshal; watermaster.

F

FACER, GEORGE (son of Henry Facer born June 15, 1811, Colmworth, Bedfordshire, and Mary Jarvis born Aug. 31, 1810, Buckworth, Huntingdonshire, Eng.). He was born July 4, 1834, Eynesbury, Huntingdonshire. Came to Utah Aug. 27, 1860, Daniel Robinson company.

Married Mary Prior Sept. 6, 1857 (daughter of James Prior and Dove Brown), who was born Jan. 27, 1840, and came to Utah with husband. Their children: George H. b. Nov. 13, 1858, m. Caroline Erickson May 29, 1879; William J. b. July 13, 1861, m. Caroline P. Williams Jan. 3, 1884; Sarah Ann b. March 26, 1863, d. Jan. 18, 1864; Charles Heber b. Nov. 12, 1864, d. Jan. 27, 1867; Dove b. Jan. 10, 1867, m. Josiah Call Dec. 18, 1884; Prior b. July 14, 1869, m. Laura B. Williams Feb. 8, 1893; Joseph b. Nov. 7, 1871, m. Emma Richards Nov. 7, 1902; James Alma b. Feb. 11, 1874, m. Rose Dalton November, 1896; Willard b. Oct. 13, 1876, m. Emma E. Davis Oct. 25, 1899; Mary E. b. May 24, 1879, m. William Anderson Nov. 15, 1899; Mabel b. Sept. 3, 1883, d. Sept. 8, 1883; Royal G. b. Nov. 29, 1884, d. March 25, 1894. Family home Willard, Utah.
Married Sarah Thompson November, 1863, Salt Lake City (daughter of Thomas Thompson and Sarah Sewell—married in England), who was born June 2, 1832, in England. Their children: Emma L. b. Aug. 10, 1864, m. William Renshaw; James J. b. June 10, 1866, m. Myrtle Lechtenberg May 1, 1888; m. Emma L. Jackson Aug. 14, 1907; Annie Mariah b. Sept. 8, 1868.
Married Susanna Nebeker Sept. 6, 1875, Salt Lake City (daughter of Peter Nebeker and Elizabeth Davis), who was born April 9, 1848, Salt Lake City. Their children: Olive Nile b. Aug. 30, 1876; Susannah M. b. Sept. 26, 1878, m. Hyram E. Crocket 1898; Ethel Rose b. Aug. 20, 1880, m. Dr. P. W. Allison Jan. 12, 1891; Florence Zoe b. Sept. 20, 1882; Edna A. b. Jan. 24, 1884; Georgia Gretta b. June 7, 1886; Horace A. b. Sept. 20, 1887; Wanda L. b. May 18, 1889.
Married Hattie Shumway April 9, 1885, Logan, Utah (daughter of Andrew Shumway and Betsy Jenson), who was born April 9, 1867. Their children: George Andrew b. Jan. 4, 1887; Cleo b. Oct. 10, 1889; Charles b. April 22, 1892; Leo b. April 28, 1895.
Bishop of Willard two terms. Sub captain of ten handcarts under Daniel Robinson. Director of Brigham City Co-op. Director First ward bank of Brigham City; manager Box Elder Co-op. Sheep company. School trustee Salt Lake district several terms.

FACER, WILLIAM JOHN (son of George Facer and Mary Prior). Born July 13, 1861, Willard, Utah.
Married Caroline Williams Jan. 3, 1884, Salt Lake City (daughter of Mishach S. Williams and Elizabeth Lewis, pioneers 1854, Robert Campbell and A. Empey companies respectively). She was born July 13, 1861. Their children: William O. b. Dec. 3, 1884, m. Olive Harding 1911; Agnes C. b. March 8, 1886, m. Lorenzo Bailey 1903; Mary P. b. Oct. 31, 1887, m. George J. Marsh, Jr.; Martelio V. b. July 21, 1890, m. Hazel Wood 1912; Elizabeth L. b. June 22, 1893, m. Joseph Leroy Housley 1911; Carrie A. b. Oct. 13, 1824; Moyle E. b. Dec. 4, 1903; Parker b. May 10, 1907. Family home Willard, Utah.
Missionary to Bear Lake and Box Elder counties 1898; to Great Britain 1900-03; bishop Willard ward 1903-10. City councilman 1908-12.

FACER, WILLARD (son of George Facer and Mary Prior). Born Oct. 13, 1876, Willard, Utah.
Married Emma E. Davis Oct. 25, 1889, Logan, Utah (daughter of George Davis and Alice Eliza Goodey, former a pioneer October, 1854, Charles Empey company). She was born Oct. 21, 1879, Perry, Utah. Their children: Mattie b. Jan. 11, 1901; Emma Lavon b. Aug. 7, 1905; Reed W. b. March 30, 1910.
Settled at Willard. Farmer and stockraiser. President 59th quorum of seventy; first assistant superintendent of Sunday schools in Malad stake two years.

FACER, JAMES JARVIS (son of George Facer and Sarah Thompson). Born June 10, 1866, Willard, Utah.
Married Myrtle Lechtenberg May 1, 1888, Willard, Utah (daughter of Paul Lechtenberg and Susanna Nebeker), who was born Jan. 8, 1870, Salt Lake City. Their children: James Vere b. May 28, 1889, m. Bertha Rosenbaum October, 1912; George Lester b. June 10, 1891; Sarah Elizabeth b. March 16, 1897; Myrtle Rose b. June 15, 1903; Ethel Myer b. April 2, 1904. Family resided Willard, Paradise, Avon, Ogden and Logan, Utah.
Married Emma L. Jackson (daughter of A. O. Jackson and Emma Jane Obray), who was born Feb. 3, 1878, Paradise, Utah. Their child: Elden Jackson b. Nov. 15, 1908. Family home Hyrum, Utah.
Missionary to southern states 1898-1900; bishop of Avon ward 1904-06; Bishop Hyrum third ward. Elected county commissioner Cache county Nov. 5, 1912, term 4 years. Farmer.

FACER, WILLIAM O. (son of William John Facer and Caroline Williams). Born Dec. 3, 1884, Willard, Utah.
Married Olive Harding 1911 (daughter of George Harding and Mary Jones, former a pioneer 1851, John G. Smith company, latter October, 1863, Thomas Ricks company). She was born Nov. 8, 1883, Willard, Utah. Only child: Alice b. June 17, 1912.
Missionary to Samoa and Torigan Islands 1906-10; assistant Sunday school superintendent at Willard.

FAIRBANKS, AMOS (son of Caleb Fairbanks, who was born July 30, 1768, Berlin, Mass., and Mary Goddard, married Nov. 10, 1785). He was born Jan. 4, 1802, Madrid, N. Y. Came to Utah October, 1851.
Married Mary Bartholomew Nov. 11, 1832. Their children: Alva b. 1833; Karissa b. Oct. 29, 1838, m. Christopher Merkley; Jane b. Feb. 28, 1840.

FAIRBANKS, DAVID (son of Joseph Fairbanks and Polly White Brooks of Mount View, N. J., and Sandy Hill, N. Y.). Born March 14, 1810 at Peru, Bennington county, Vt. Came to Utah Oct. 6, 1847, with John Taylor company.
Married Susan Mandeville Nov. 26, 1838, Pompton Plains. N. J. (daughter of Cornelius W. Mandeville and Jane Jones of Pompton Plains), who was born Sept. 23, 1819. Their children: William Henry, m. Ann Ellsworth; m. Sarah Knight Jolly; m. Ann Elizabeth Hardy; Mary Jane, m. Warren Sidney Pace; Cornelius Mandeville, m. Emily A. Davis; Susan Jones, m. Stanley Davis; m. Philip L. Cauchet; Elizabeth Ann, m. George Montague; Barbara Matilda, m. Ezra Warren Simmons; Margaret, died; David Brooks, m. Hannah Johnson; Joseph Warren, m. Estelle V. Dixon; Ralph Jacobus, m. Celestia Johnson; Martha Alice, m. Joseph Brigham Keeler; Nicholas Jones and Nathaniel, died. Family resided Mountain View, N. J., and Payson, Utah.
President high priests quorum; missionary to The Muddy 1864-66; bishop 1st ward Salt Lake City 1849-51. Justice of peace at Salt Lake City; bishop 8th ward, winter quarters; pioneer to Payson, 1851; built dam that gave Salem, Utah, the name of Pond Town. City marshal; school trustee and c'ty councilman of Payson. Farmer; builder. Died Dec. 14, 1895.

FAIRBANKS, JOSEPH WARREN (son of David Fairbanks and Susan Mandeville). Born Jan. 2, 1856, Payson, Utah.
Married Estelle V. Dixon July 27, 1880, at Payson (daughter of Christopher Dixon and Jane E. Wightman; pioneers 1852). She was born Oct. 16, ———, Kirtland, Ohio. Their only child: Magdaline b. March 2, 1882, d. same day.
Settled at Annabella, Utah, 1881. Set apart bishop Annabella ward Feb. 20, 1893. President town board 1910. Active worker in the early development of Annabella.

FAIRBANKS, JOHN BOYLSTON (son of Joseph Fairbanks and Polly White Brooks of Mount View, N. J., and Sandy Hill, N. Y.). Born April 28, 1817, at Sandy Hill. Came to Utah September, 1847, captain 3d ten, Jedediah M. Grant company.
Married Sarah Van Wagoner Aug. 31, 1844, Mount View, N. J., Bishop John Leach officiating (daughter of Halmah Van Wagoner and Mary Tan Houten of New Jersey, latter pioneer September, 1847, Jedediah M. Grant company). She was born July 11, 1822. Their children: John J., d. infant; Harriett F., m. William J. Douglass; Henry, m. Elizabeth Oharra; Nathaniel, d. aged 8; Sarah Ann, d. aged 4; John B. b. Dec. 27, 1855, m. Lilly Annetta Huish; Mary F., m. Austin C. Brown; Allicia F., m. Patrick L. Simmons; Lillie Maria; Franklin, m. Louise Arminie Tanner; George A., m. Ann Worsencroft. Family home Payson, Utah.
Missionary to England 1871-73; bishop Payson 10 years; ward clerk. City councilman at Payson. Merchant; farmer. Died May 14, 1875.

FAIRBANKS, JOHN B. (son of John B. Fairbanks and Sarah Van Wagoner). Born Dec. 27, 1855, Payson, Utah.
Married Lilly Annetta Huish June 24, 1877, at Payson, Utah (daughter of Walter H. Huish and Ann Smith of Birmingham, Eng., pioneers 1861). She was born Feb. 24, 1857. Their children: John Leo b. April 30, 1878; Lillie A. b. July 27, 1879, m. Thomas J. Yates; Vernon W. b. Nov. 15, 1881, m. Esther H. Garnes; Erven H. b. Nov. 9, 1884, m. Harriet Jones; Leroy b. Feb. 26, 1886, m. Orissa Smith; Ortho Lane b. Sept. 29, 1887; Claude L. b. June 12, 1889; Larmar R. b. Jan. 13, 1894; Delmar R. b. Jan. 14, 1894, d. infant; Alma C. b. Sept. 9, 1895, d. infant. Family home Salt Lake City.
Member 47th and 152d quorums seventies; missionary to southern states 1881-83, and to South America 1900-02, a president in both missions; president mutual missionaries to Paris to study art 1890-92. Assessor and collector at Payson. Farmer; artist.

FARMER, EDWARD JOHN (son of Richard Farmer and Elizabeth Morris of Herefordshire, Eng.). Born Feb. 20, 1825. Came to Utah Sept. 12, 1861, John R. Murdock company.
Married Elizabeth Ellen Wright 1858, Philadelphia, Pa. (daughter of John Wright and Elizabeth Bailey of Scregington, Lincolnshire, Eng., pioneers Sept. 12, 1861). She was born Nov. 11, 1842. Their children: John Edward d. infant; Erastus Grenig, m. Mary Ellen Holt; Emma, d. youth; Mary Ann Theresa, m. Edwin Reese; Richard Wright, m. Margret McCann; Robert Fredrick, m. May Evalin Henderson; Sarah Jane Elizabeth, m. Henry Egbert. Family home Herriman, Utah.
Member 94th quorum seventies; ward teacher. School trustee. Farmer.

FARMER, ERASTUS GRENIG (son of Edward J. Farmer and Elizabeth E. Wright). Born June 29, 1861, Florence, Douglas county, Neb. Came to Utah with parents.
Married Mary Ellen Holt Jan. 10, 1887, Logan, Utah (daughter of Edward David Holt and Emma Billings, pioneers 1863). She was born June 5, 1867. Their children: Nellie Mabel b. April 23, 1888; Eva Grace b. Jan. 21, 1890, m. Marion H. Henderson; Erastus L. b. Nov. 8, 1891; Elsie May b. May 18, 1893; Ivie Pearl b. March 2, 1896; Golden Holt b. Oct. 28, 1897; Emma Ellen b. Feb. 15, 1900; Edward Truman b. Aug. 1, 1903; Cora H. b. Sept. 10, 1896. Family home Clifton, Idaho.
Member 95th quorum seventies; missionary to southern states 1883-85; counselor to Bishop William F. Garner July

26, 1893, to Jan. 12, 1896; bishop of Clifton ward Jan. 12, 1896, to May 14, 1911. Chairman Republican State Central committee four years. School trustee and justice of peace. State land examiner. Farmer.

FARNES, THOMAS SAMUEL (son of John Farnes and Harriett Cambell, of London, Eng.). Born Jan. 6, 1836, London, Eng. Came to Utah 1861.
Married Sarah Ann Harrison (daughter of James H. Harrison and Angelina Parry). She was born July 29, 1840. Their children: Thomas H. b. Dec. 13, 1861; Angelina H. b. Dec. 18, 1863, m. Edwin Batty June 13, 1882; Edwin James b. Dec. 16, 1865, d. Dec. 14, 1867; John Albert b. April 16, 1868, m. Ellen Lemor Jan. 4, 1897; Sarah Frances b. Nov. 25, 1870, m. Robert Slaughter June 17, 1888; Phebe Amelia b. Oct. 21, 1873, m. William R. Langston Nov. 17, 1890; Jane Elizabeth b. Nov. 27, 1876, d. April 16, 1876; Joseph Fritter b. Sept. 27, 1877; Cora Alvira b. Jan. 17, 1880, m. Levi DeMill Jan. 13, 1901; Fanny May b. May 24, 1882, m. Andrew Buchannah March 20, 1908; Retta b. Sept. 29, 1885.
Settled at "Dixie." Ward clerk there for years.

FARNES, JOSEPH FRITTER (son of Thomas Samuel Farnes and Sarah Ann Harrison). Born Sept. 27, 1877, Rockville, Utah.
Business man and merchant.

FARNSWORTH, STEPHEN MARTINDALE (son of Reuben Farnsworth and Lucinda Kent of Vermont). Born Oct. 9, 1809, Vermont. Came to Utah 1851, Capt. Higby company.
Married Julia Ann Clark Aug. 30, 1837 (daughter of Richard Clark and Miss Sheffer), who was born May 1, 1819, and came to Utah with husband. Their children: Austin Martindale b. Dec. 16, 1838, m. Dorcas Terry; Alonzo LaFayette b. Oct. 22, 1841, m. Mary Staker Sept. 8, 1866; Albert Stephen b. May 22, 1844, m. Martha Longmore; Stephen Martindale Jr. b. Feb. 17, 1847, m. Martha Loujean Jones; Caroline Elizabeth b. March 21, 1849, m. Henson Walker Oct. 24, 1868; Julia Ann b. Nov. 26, 1852, d. May 1, 1853; Cyrus Walter b. April 20, 1854, m. Mary Isabel Tidwell; Harriet Nancy b. Dec. 16, 1856, m. James Thorne; Reuben Richard b. Dec. 3, 1859, m. Lola Montez Bean. Family home Pleasant Grove, Utah.
Married Eliza Lewis (daughter of Nathan Lewis). Their children: Franklin Wallace, m. Anna Anderson; Clarinda; Alva Washington; Viola, m. William Shelton; Milford Bard; Curtis Edmund b. June 14, 1865; Olivia b. Sept. 15, 1867, m. Mr. Powell; Joseph; Eliza Jane; Benjamin. Family resided, Pleasant Grove and Richfield, Utah.
Married Ellen Louisa Showell. Only child: Cosmelia Ellen b. June 7, 1860, m. George Ogilvie.

FARNSWORTH, ALONZO LAFAYETTE (son of Stephen Martindale Farnsworth and Julia Ann Clark). He was born Oct. 22, 1841, South Bend, Ind.
Married Mary Ann Staker Sept. 8, 1866, Salt Lake City (daughter of Nathan Staker and Jane Richmond), who was born Jan. 21, 1848.
Married Christianna D. Bertelsen March 9, 1874, Salt Lake City (daughter of Niels Bertelsen and Mary Larsen, pioneers Sept. 10, 1863, William B. Preston company). She was born Jan. 8, 1852, Viberg amt, Denmark. Their children: Raymond Alonzo b. Nov. 15, 1876, m. Bertha Martineau May 7, —; Lester Burt b. Aug. 23, 1879, m. Rosina Nielsen Aug. 8, 1905; Mary A. b. Aug. 4, 1881, m. Joseph Fyans Dec. 26, 1906; Richard Kent b. Feb. 2, 1883, m. Hattie May Cluff Oct. 1, 1908; Elmer David b. April 8, 1885, m. Charity May O'Donnell Sept. 4, 1906; Franklin Lehi b. Oct. 24, 1889, m. Cora Walker; Anna Roine b. June 17, 1891, m. Thomas Dixon; Alonzo LaFayette b. Jan. 22, 1897, died. Family resided Tuba City, Ariz., and Colonia Garcia, Mexico.
Married Edith Henrietta Tietjen April 8, 1875, at Salt Lake City (daughter of August Tietjen and Edith Kreeger), who was born in Sweden. Their children: Ernest LaFayette b. July 20, 1878, m. Edith Nielsen Feb. 28, 1902; Ida Belle b. Sept. 25, 1880, m. George Turley Feb. 16, 1899; Stephen August b. Dec. 2, 1882, m. Ethel Bingham; Jesse Charles b. July 13, 1885, died; Orrin Fay b. Nov. 26, 1886; Byron Nephi b. Jan. 7, 1890, m. Maud Cluff March 6, 1911; Ellis b. July 8, 1892, m. Karl Nielsen Nov. 25, 1909; Earl Benjamin b. Jan. 24, 1894; Jennie Tietjen b. June 24, 1896.
Lieutenant Black Hawk war 1866. Member Richfield high council 1871; bishop of Joseph City 1873; went to Arizona on a mission 1877, and served as bishop Yuba City 1878. Moved to Mexico 1884.

FARR, WINSLOW (son of Ashael Farr, baptized March 23, 1776, at Chesterfield, Vt., and Lydia Snow, born March 18, 1772, Chesterfield, Vt.—married 1786). He was born Jan. 14, 1794, Chesterfield, Vt. Came to Utah Sept. 30, 1850, Joseph Young company.
Married Olive Hovey Freeman Dec. 5, 1816, Hanover, Vt. (daughter of Elijah Freeman, born Nov. 3, 1757, Mansfield, Conn., and Olive Hovey, born Oct. 30, 1761, died Oct. 21, 1820—married Dec. 27, 1781). She was born June 23, 1799, Lebanon, Vt. died March 10, 1893, Big Cottonwood, Utah. Their children: John b. Dec. 14, 1817, d. infant; Aaron Freeman b. Oct. 31, 1818, m. Persis Atherton Jan. 16, 1844; Lorin b. July 27, 1820, m. Nancy B. Chase; Olive Hovey b. March 18, 1825, m. William Walker Nov. 3, 1843; Diantha b. Oct. 12, 1828, m. William Clayton Jan. 1845; Winslow b. May 11, 1837, m. Emily Jane Covington Oct. 17, 1858. Family resided Waterford and Charleston, Vt., before coming to Utah. Appointed one of municipal high council of twelve 1846. Settled on Big Cottonwood river 1851. Died Aug. 25, 1867, Big Cottonwood, Utah.

FARR, LORIN (son of Winslow Farr and Olive Hovey Freeman). Born July 27, 1820, Waterford, Vt. Came to Utah Sept. 20, 1847, Daniel Spencer company.
Married Nancy B. Chase Jan. 1, 1845 (daughter of Ezra Chase, pioneer 1848, born Feb. 4, 1796, died Oct. 29, 1873, Ogden, Utah, and Tirzah Wells, who died April 4, 1867, at Ogden—married Aug. 22, 1818). She was born Jan. 27, 1823, Bristol, Vt.; died Sept. 10, 1892, Ogden, Utah. Their children: Enoch b. Dec. 28, 1845, m. Mary E. Eggleston Jan. 30, 1849, m. John Henry Smith Oct. 20, 1866; Tirzah b. May 3, 1852, m. John Gay Jan. 19, 1869; Lorin b. Feb. 21, 1854; Ezra b. Feb. 21, 1854, m. Elveretta Kay April 9, 1877; Newton b. May 31, 1856, m. Martha Davis; Diantha b. April 5, 1858, d. Oct. 30, 1858; Diana b. April 5, 1858, m. Ben E. Rich; Isabel b. March 3, 1861, m. Heber John Sears; Mary Belinda b. Oct. 16, 1863, d. July 21, 1864. Family home Ogden, Utah.
Married Sarah Giles July 26, 1851, Salt Lake City (daughter of Thomas Giles, born in Pembrokeshire, and Maria Davis, born Aug. 15, 1789, Norboth, Pembrokeshire, Wales, died June 1, 1866, Ogden, Utah—married Dec. 7, 1817, Bidwilly, Monmouthshire, Wales). She was born Jan. 1, 1831, Merthyr Tydfil, Glamorganshire, Wales, d. Feb. 26, 1892, in Ogden. Their children: Joseph b. Aug. 7, 1852, m. Sally M. Porter Dec. 7, 1874; Thomas b. March 16, 1854, m. Amanda Badger Sept. 1, 1879; March 2, 1856, m. Caroline Josephine Ballantyne Feb. 2, 1882; Sarah Maria b. March 30, 1858, m. Richard J. Taylor Aug. 7, 1876; Roxana b. Feb. 3, 1860, m. Jedediah Pidcock March 5, 1877; Winslow b. May 9, 1862, m. Mary Hannah Williams Nov. 8, 1883; Rachel b. Sept. 24, 1864, m. Fred Packard Oct. 11, 1883; Leonorah b. March 22, 1867, m. Thomas Pardee Dec. 9, 1883; Hiram b. Feb. 15, 1870, d. June 19, 1870. Family home Ogden.
Married Olive Ann Jones Feb. 28, 1852, Salt Lake City (daughter of Merlin Jones, pioneer 1852, born May 16, 1795, North Haven, Conn., died Dec. 4, 1879, in Ogden and Roxana Ives, born April 17, 1799, Wallingford, Conn., died Aug. 5, 1866, in Ogden—married Aug. 17, 1820, Wallingford, Conn.). She was born June 1, 1829, at Wallingford, and came to Utah Sept. 30, 1850, in Joseph Young's company. Their children: Laertes b. Jan. 23, 1853; Valasco b. Aug. 23, 1855, m. Diana Davis Fife Feb. 24, 1881; Olive Ann b. Aug. 3, 1857, d. May 1, 1866; Ellen b. Oct. 25, 1859, d. May 6, 1866; Merlin Jones b. Feb. 6, 1862, d. May 2, 1866; David b. April 5, 1864, m. Maggie Williams June 3, 1896; Ashael b. Oct. 17, 1866, m. Georgiana Julia Drake March 14, 1888. Family home Ogden.
Married Mary (Bingham) Snow Dec. 2, 1854, Salt Lake City (daughter of Erastus Bingham and Lucinda Gates, pioneers Sept. 19, 1847, Daniel Spencer company). She was born April 1, 1820, St. Johnsbury, Vt.; died Sept. 25, 1893, Ogden. Their children: Willard b. July 5, 1856, m. Mary Ballantyne; Erastus b. May 14, 1859, d. June 28, 1859; Isaac Farwell b. May 23, 1860, m. Isabel Poulter Feb. 23, 1882. Family home Ogden.
Married Nicholene Erickson Jan. 29, 1857, Salt Lake City (daughter of Neils Erickson, born 1803, Norway, died Sept. 14, 1873, in Ogden, and Maria Olsen, born 1801, and died 1873 in Frederikstadt, Aggerhuys, Norway, and came to Utah Sept. 7, 1855, Noah Guymon company. Their children: Lorenzo Erickson b. Oct. 25, 1858, m. Minnie Woodmansie March 23, 1882; Laura b. April 10, 1861, m. Winfred S. Harris Sept. 25, 1880; John b. Jan. 4, 1863, m. Rachel Ann Witten Dec. 20, 1884; Elnora b. April 2, 1865, m. James Wotherspoon Oct. 26, 1882; Elijah b. Dec. 28, 1867, d. May 27, 1906; Mary b. March 22, 1870, m. George W. Driver Sept. 11, 1889. Family home Ogden.
Settled at Ogden 1850. First president Weber stake; president high priests' quorum in 1850-51. Erected first grist mill and sawmill in Weber county. Member first territorial legislature from Weber county, in the earlier days represented Box Elder county from the time of the organization of the territory until 1887; first mayor of Ogden 1851-70, and re-elected in 1877. Missionary to Europe 1870. Prominent in building of railroads: superintendent of grading Central Pacific for two hundred miles west of Ogden, and also building of Utah Northern to Brigham City. Died Jan. 12, 1909, Ogden.

FARR, ENOCH (son of Lorin Farr and Nancy Bailey Chase). Born Dec. 28, 1845, Nauvoo, Ill. Came to Utah 1847.
Married Mary Elizabeth Eggleston Oct. 20, 1866, Salt Lake City (daughter of Samuel Eggleston Jr., born March 30, 1804, Marcellus, Onondaga county, N. Y., died May 27, 1884, at Ogden, and Lurania Burgess, born Aug. 15, 1808, Semproniua, Cayuga county, N. Y., died July 6, 1870, at Ogden—married Aug. 13, 1827, at Sempronius, pioneers Sept. 1863, Capt. Wareham company). She was born Sept. 22, 1849, Council Bluffs, Iowa. Their children: Enoch b. July 15, 1867, m. Mary Nelson Nov. 20, 1889; Mary Isabell b. Nov. 7, 1869, m. Christian Christensen Feb. 13, 1896; Julia Mary b. Feb. 29, 1872, d. Nov. 11, 1889; Reuben Ezra b. April 30, 1874, m. Nora Thornburg June 27, 1903; Frank b. Dec. 18, 1876, m. Mary Chapple Nov. 1902; Frederick b. Nov. 13, 1878, d. July 9, 1879; Walter Ray b. Dec. 7, 1879, m. Mary Carr May 18, 1901; Nancy Lurania b. Jan. 1, 1882, d. Sept. 1882; George b. Nov. 3, 1883, m. Mary Maria Roberts Sept. 28, 1910; Leslie b. June 4, 1886, m. Lydia Myers Dec. 14, 1910; Stanley Burgess b. Feb. 4, 1892. Family home Ogden.
Married Esther Myers Sept. 27, 1883, Salt Lake City (daughter of Thomas Myers, born Aug. 15, 1815, Skipton,

Yorkshire, Eng., died Sept. 11, 1886, at Ogden, and Isabell Bramley, born March 24, 1818, at Skipton, died Oct. 4, 1881, Ogden—married Dec. 14, 1837, Skipton, pioneers Sept. 27, 1855, Richard V. Morris company). She was born March 12, 1854, Burnley, Lancashire, Eng.

One of first seven presidents 76th quorum seventies; Oct. 1884 was ordained high priest; missionary to Sandwich Islands 1884-1887; was president of that mission and superintendent of the Lael plantation. Fruit grower; cement and general contractor.

FARR, EZRA (son of Lorin Farr and Nancy Bailey Chase). Born Feb. 21, 1854, Ogden, Utah.
Married Elveretta Kay April 9, 1877 (daughter of William and Mary T. Kay). Their children: Ezra Leon; Clare K.; Inez; Zelma; Cecil Earl; Mabel; Jennette Ruth. Family home, Ogden.

FARR, NEWTON (son of Lorin Farr and Nancy Bailey Chase). Born May 31, 1856, at Ogden, Utah.
Married Martha Davis Oct. 19, 1882, at Salt Lake City, Utah (daughter of M. L. Davis and Mary Kenner both of Salt Lake City. Came to Utah 1859). She was born May 15, 1863. Their children: Ethel LaBelle b. Sept. 17, 1883, m. W. J. Bennett; Morrill Newton b. June 17, 1885, m. Jean Spencer; Leah b. Oct. 12, 1887; Martha b. March 5, 1891, d. Jan. 4, 1892. Family home Salt Lake City, Utah.
Seventy; missionary to England 1880-82. Deputy sheriff of Weber county. Interested in and helped develop many mines.

FARR, JOSEPH (son of Lorin Farr and Sarah Giles). Born Aug. 7, 1852, in Ogden.
Married Sally M. Porter Dec. 7, 1874, Salt Lake City (daughter of Luther G. Porter and Aurora Ann Murry, of Antioun, N. Y., pioneers Oct. 2, 1862, Isaac A. Canfield company). She was born June 4, 1854. Their children: Joseph A. b. Jan. 1, 1876, m. Mabel M. Farr Aug. 16, 1897; Nellie R. b. Oct. 22, 1877, m. Andrea L. Farr Aug. 24, 1900; Marcia A. b. Aug. 29, 1880; Jennie L. b. May 14, 1882; Cora I. b. June 9, 1883; Hazel A. b. April 4, 1885; Hyrum A. b. Jan. 24, 1887; Leland N. b. March 15, 1889; Roxanna P. b. Nov. 27, 1892; Eugene b. Nov. 7, 1894.
Member 76th quorum seventies. Member city council two years; municipal judge two years. Miller and merchant.

FARR, MARCUS (son of Lorin Farr and Sarah Giles). Born April 2, 1856, Ogden.
Married Caroline Josephine Ballantyne Feb. 2, 1882, Salt Lake City (daughter of Richard Ballantyne, born Aug. 26, 1817, Whiteriggs, Scotland, and Caroline Albertine Sanderson, born Sept. 19, 1837, Rogen, Norway; married 1856). She was born Jan. 30, 1861, Salt Lake City. Their children: Josephine b. Feb. 17, 1883, m. William H. Olson July 15, 1903; Marcus Ballantyne b. April 11, 1885; Lionel B. b. Nov. 28, 1888; Beatrice Albertine b. April 24, 1892; Lorin B. b. July 1, 1896. Family home Ogden.
First counselor to 9th quorum elders July 13, 1891 to Dec. 13, 1897; missionary to Eastern states 1897; first assistant superintendent third ward Sunday school; senior member Ogden stake high council.

FARR, MARCUS BALLANTYNE (son of Marcus Farr and Caroline Josephine Ballantyne). Born April 11, 1885, Ogden.
Married Mary Elizabeth Watkins April 17, 1913 (daughter of Joseph Hyrum Watkins and Mary Ann Doxey).
Filled a mission to the southern states. Was one who assisted in building the first Mormon church in the city of Atlanta, Ga.

FARR, VALASCO (son of Lorin Farr and Olive Ann Jones). Born Aug. 29, 1855, in Ogden.
Married Diana Davis Fife Feb. 24, 1881, Salt Lake City (daughter of William Nicol Fife, pioneer 1853, born Oct. 16, 1831, Kincardine-on-Forth, Perthshire, Scotland, and Diana Davis, born April 12, 1837, Caermarthenshire, South Wales, died Sept. 11, 1884, Cochise county, Ariz.—married July 9, 1854, Salt Lake City). She was born Oct. 7, 1859, Ogden, died May 18, 1904. Their children: Diana Edith b. Nov. 28, 1881, m. Parley T. Moyes Feb. 22, 1906; Olive Ann b. Jan. 21, 1884, m. Harry Hales June 10, 1909; Raymond Valasco b. Nov. 20, 1886, m. Almira Shurtliff Oct. 29, 1909; Lamar Fife b. Feb. 1, 1889; Agnes Fife b. Nov. 6, 1891; Merlin Fife b. April 5, 1897; Ivan William b. Dec. 16, 1900. Family home, Ogden.
Farmer and fruit grower.

FARR, DAVID (son of Lorin Farr and Olive Ann Jones). Born April 5, 1864, Ogden.
Married Maggie Williams June 3, 1896, Salt Lake City (daughter of Thomas Lloyd William, born March 31, 1826, Santasaf, Flintshire, North Wales, died Feb. 24, 1889, Ogden and Elizabeth Rowlands born March 20, 1835, New Bridge, near Denbigh, Denbighshire, North Wales, died April 30, 1899, Ogden—married April, 1851, at Santasaf, pioneers Oct. 29, 1855, C. A. Harper company). She was born March 4, 1867, Ogden. Their children: David Rowland b. May 12, 1897; James Frederick b. Aug. 14, 1899; Dorothy b. Aug. 16, 1901. Family home Ogden.
Missionary to Alabama and Florida 1892-94. Merchant.

FARR, ASAHEL (son of Lorin Farr and Olive Ann Jones). Born Oct. 17, 1866, Ogden, Utah.
Married Georgiana Julia Drake March 14, 1888, Logan, Utah (daughter of George Drake, born Nov. 14, 1826, Cheltenham, Gloucestershire, Eng., died Feb. 5, 1913, at Ogden,

and Emily White, born Dec. 30, 1824, Newbury, Berkshire, died July 20, 1905, at Ogden—married Nov. 1, 1851, Newbury; former came to Utah 1878, latter 1877). She was born Sept. 11, 1866, Boomer, Pottawattamie county, Iowa. Their children: Georgiana Jennie b. Dec. 17, 1888, m. William Arthur Budge Oct. 11, 1911; Lawrence b. March 25, 1891; Mabel Ellen b. Sept. 8, 1893; Ashael b. Oct. 24, 1895; Dexter b. April 9, 1898; Verne b. June 9, 1901. Family home Ogden.
First counselor to Julius Farley; president Y. M. M. I. A. Mound Fort ward, Ogden; counselor to bishop James Taylor of same ward; first counselor to L. Jones. Member school board of Ogden City, 1905-13. Fruit grower; coal dealer.

FARR, ISAAC FARWELL (son of Lorin Farr and Mary Bingham Snow). Born May 23, 1860, Ogden.
Married Isabel Poulter Feb. 23, 1882, Salt Lake City (daughter of Thomas A. Poulter and Hannah Butler, of London, Eng., and Ogden, Utah, pioneers 1854, Capt. Shields company). She was born July 28, 1862. Their children: Chloe B., m. Alfred H. Summerville; Norman I.; Walter T., m. Nellie Brown; Orlando died; Archie; Orlaf; Rhea. Family home Ogden.
Manager Ogden flour mill 1876-83; bookkeeper; mining promoter.

FARR, JOHN (son of Lorin Farr and Nicholine Erickson). Born Jan. 4, 1863, Ogden, Utah.
Married Rachel Ann Witten Dec. 20, 1883, Salt Lake City (daughter of Samuel M. Witten, born Dec. 5, 1833, Jefferson City, Tazewell county, and Martha Jane Heninger, born May 14, 1840, Burks Garden, Tazewell county, Va.—married there Nov. 13, 1860, and came to Utah June 2, 1869). She was born Sept. 23, 1863, Jefferson City, Va. Their children: John Clement, m. Mary Alice Priest June 16, 1909; Mabel Grace; Fern, m. Adolphus Frank Moss June 6, 1911; Martha Pauline; Lyndall; Mildred; Rachel Afton; Roscoe Kenneth. Family home Ogden.
Missionary to England 1898-1900; second assistant superintendent third ward Sunday school, Ogden, 1901-03; first counselor to president of Y. M. M. I. A. third ward, Ogden, 1902-05; one of seven presidents 63d quorum, and later of 98th quorum seventies. Horticulturalist; coal dealer.

FARR, WINSLOW, JR. (son of Winslow Farr and Olive Hovey Freeman). Born May 11, 1837, East Charleston, Orleans county, Vt. Came to Utah October 1848.
Married Emily Jane Covington Oct. 17, 1858 (daughter of Robert B. Covington and Elizabeth Ann Thomas). Their children: Winslow Robert; Emily Olive; Lafayette Thomas; Lorin Freeman; David James; Moroni; Mohonri; Ida Almena; Silva May; William Henry; Mary Isabel; Barnard Elijah; Aaron Adelbert; Jonathan.
Walked and drove three yoke of oxen across the plains.

FARR, LAFAYETTE THOMAS (son of Winslow Farr, Jr., and Emily Jane Covington). Born Feb. 14, 1864, Paradise, Utah.
Married Nancy Hipwell Sept. 30, 1885 (daughter of William Hipwell and Elizabeth Barton). Their children: William Hipwell; Winslow; Emily Jane; Elizabeth; Aaron Lafayette; Lawrence; Harriet Olive; Flossie; Laura May; Glenn.

FARR, FRANKLIN (son of Elbrige Farr and Sarah Buss, Eastern Massachusetts). Born Oct. 12, 1837, Chatham, Medina Co., Ohio. Came to Utah 1852.
Married Anne Jones Dec. 22, 1866, Salt Lake City (daughter of John Prichard Jones and Mary Bevan of St. Brides, Glamorganshire, Wales, and Spanish Fork, Utah, pioneers Oct. 4, 1864, William S. Warren extra company). She was born Aug. 22, 1848, St. Brides, Wales. Their children: Anne E. b. Oct. 10, 1867, m. Z. P. Bomerill; Pamelia E. b. Aug. 13, 1869, m. John W. Lewis; Mary E. b. Jan. 27, 1872, m. Frank Abbott; Franklin J. b. March 12, 1874, m. Estell Jones; George Ansel b. July 10, 18—, died; Jeanette Bevan b. June 6, 1878, m. Peter Bomerill; Sarah Louisa b. Nov. 22, 1880, m. William Bomeril; T. Vaughan b. Sept. 5, 1884; Wilford Ivor b. Jan. 1888. Family home Spanish Fork, Utah.
Presided over elders quorum 1873-93; president deacons quorum four years; ordained high priest July 22, 1894; ward teacher; Sunday school teacher. Captain of ten in Utah militia; minuteman in Black Hawk Indian war. Farmer. Died April 24, 1901, Spanish Fork, Utah.

FARRELL, GEORGE LIONEL (son of William Farrell, born Jan. 1, 1785, Leek, Staffordshire, and Alice Saddler Bird, born Sept. 26, 1796, Minety, Wiltshire, Eng.). He was born Feb. 16, 1829, Hewelsfield, Gloucestershire, Eng. Came to Utah Aug. 12, 1859, James S. Brown company.
Married Amanda A. Steel April 29, 1860 (daughter of William Steel and Margaret Goodwin, pioneers Aug. 12, 1859, James S. Brown company). She was born Feb. 17, 1844. Their children: Margarett Alice b. Jan. 5, 1862, m. William Pilkington Oct. 4, 1883; Emma b. April 17, 1864, m. Herbert F. Barber Nov. 10, 1886; Annie Louisa b. Aug. 9, 1866, m. Solon Barber Nov. 14, 1887; Charlotte S. b. May 30, 1868, m. William Raymond March 8, 1889; May S. b. May 12, 1870, m. Peter Mack Dec. 4, 1896; Lionel S. b. Sept. 26, 1872, m. Florence Rainey May 8, 1901; Clara b. Aug. 1, 1875, died; Lewis S. b. Nov. 2, 1880, m. Namonia Naylor April 7, 1910; Francis D. b. March 13, 1883; Loraine b. Feb. 13, 1887, m. Ephraim Ralph July 5, 1911. Family resided Logan and Smithfield, Utah.

Married Mary Charlotte Lundburg April 11, 1862, Salt Lake City (daughter of Solomon Lundburg and Christina Anderson, pioneers 1861). She was born Dec. 15, 1842, Frothatta, Sweden. Their children: William G. b. May 24, 1864, m. Florence Caine Sept. 8, 1897; Laura L. b. Jan. 19, 1866, m. Don C. Musser 1899; Alfred L. b. March 4, 1868, m. Luna Thatcher July 15, 1897; George b. Aug. 24, 1870; Selma b. Aug. 1, 1875, m. David Robbins July 28, 1895; Vendla b. May 4, 1877; Lavene b. March 20, 1881. Family resided Salt Lake City and Logan, Utah.
Married Lydia A. Anderson June 25, 1878, Salt Lake City (daughter of Andrew Anderson and Sophia Sorenson, pioneers 1858, Rosel K. Homer company). She was born Oct. 4, 1858, Echo Canyon, Wyo. Their children: Andrew Otto b. Dec. 28, 1880, d. Dec. 28, 1880; Catherine Sophia b. Dec. 25, 1882, d. June 1893; Gladys Adline b. Oct. 1, 1885; Marion Lyman b. Dec. 1, 1890. Family home Smithfield, Utah.
Married Mary Elizabeth Groshaw May 12, 1887, Logan, Utah (daughter of Charles Crowshaw and Hannah Atkins; married Dec. 18, 1867, Barrow in Furness, Eng.). She was born Sept. 14, 1868, Williamsburg, N. Y. Their children: Mary b. Nov. 29, 1888, d. infant; Joseph b. July 9, 1890; Lola b. Dec. 17, 1893; Lillie Vale b. Jan. 14, 1897; Charles C. b. Dec. 16, 1898; Robert Atkins b. June 22, 1902; Florence b. Oct. 16, 1904; Leah b. Dec. 30, 1905; Amanda L. b. Feb. 19, 1901, died; Hyrum Russell b. Oct. 17, 1909. Family home Smithfield, Utah.
Tithing clerk Cache stake 1859-80; president elders' quorum 1859-76; president high priests quorum 1876-80. Cache county recorder 1860-84; postmaster at Logan 1862-74. Missionary to England 1874-76; bishop of Smithfield 1880-1900; patriarch 1900. Pioneer dry farmer.

FARRELL, WILLIAM G. (son of George Lionel Farrell and Marie Charlotte Lundburg). Born May 24, 1864, Logan, Utah.
Married Florence Caine Sept. 8, 1897, at Logan (daughter of John T. Caine and Margaret Nightingale, pioneers Sept. 20, 1853, James McGaw company). She was born Sept. 5, 1873, Salt Lake City. Their children: William Caine b. Sept. 28, 1898; Frederick Nightingale b. April 20, 1903.

FARREN, JOSEPH (son of Edward Farren and Elizabeth Young of New York, N. Y.). Born Dec. 21, 1837, in New York City. Came to Utah 1871.
Married Julia Sanders April 1868, at Austin, Nev. (daughter of Charles Sanders of Ohio), who was born 1840. Family home Salt Lake City, Utah.
Miningman. Had charge of Davenport-Matilda and City Rock Mining company; built two lead furnaces at Deep Creek, Utah; located Tacoma Lucine property and sold it to the Salt Lake copper plant.

FARRER. ROGER (son of Thomas Farrer and Jane Graveson of Helsington, Westmorland, Eng.). Born March 18, 1795, Westmorland, Eng. Came to Utah Sept. 17, 1850, David Evans company.
Married Catherine Adwin 1820, Westmorland, Eng., who died 1825. Their children: William b. Jan. 26, 1821, m. Elizabeth Kary; James b. March 12, 1823, m. Mary Jane McCune, m. Phidelia Dame. Family resided at Provo and Beaver, Utah.
Married Mary Stubbs Oct. 7, 1828, Westmorland, Eng. (daughter of John Stubbs of Westmorland, Eng., pioneer Sept. 17, 1850, David Evans company). She was born Dec. 23, 1800. Their children: Thomas b. Sept. 3, 1829, m. Mary Strong; Margaret b. Jan. 21, 1832, m. Hugh Syme; Jane b. Feb. 25, 1836, died; Roger b. April 17, 1838, m. Agnes Strong; Mary b. Sept. 22, 1844, died. Family home Provo, Utah.
Seventy; high priest in Mormon church. Farmer and miller. Died June 1, 1887.

FARRER. ROGER, JR. (son of Roger Farrer and Mary Stubbs). Born April 17, 1838, Westmorland, Eng. Came to Utah with father.
Married Agnes Strong Feb. 18, 1857, Provo, Utah (daughter of John Strong and Agnes Miller, of Provo, pioneers Oct. 3, 1855, Milo Andrus company). She was born Oct. 3, 1837. Their children: Agnes A. b. Dec. 18, 1857, m. Josiah W. Cluff; James H. b. March 25, 1860, m. Mary J. Roberts; John W. b. July 15, 1862, m. Alice Vilate Loveless; Joseph T. b. July 1, 1865, m. Sarah Chipman; Mary Ettie b. March 28, 1874, m. Walter P. Whitehead; Edward b. Dec. 6, 1878, m. Ruth Peay. Family home Provo, Utah.
Member 45th quorum seventies and high priest; high councilor Utah stake. Provo city councilman 13 years. Farmer.

FARRER, WILLIAM (son of Roger Farrer and Catherine Badwin, both of Brigstreer, Westmorland, Eng.). He was born Jan. 26, 1821, Brigstreer, Eng. Came to Utah 1847, Capt. Taylor company.
Married Elizabeth Ann Kerry Jan. 2, 1857, Salt Lake City (daughter of Thomas Kerry and Elizabeth Sharp, both of England). She was born Dec. 11, 1840. Their children: Mary Elizabeth, died; William K., m. Mary Ann Halliday; Roger C.; Catherine A., m. Hugh Ross; Frances J., died; Emma T., m. Hyrum F. Thomas; Sarah A.; Thomas, m. Rose Hardy. Family home. Provo. Utah.
Seventy; missionary to Sandwich Islands 1848-51. Farmer. Died Feb. 17, 1890, Provo, Utah.

FAUSETT, WILLIAM McGEE (son of Richard Fausett of Tennessee). Born Jan. 6, 1807, in Tennessee. Came to Utah September, 1851, Alexander Stephens company.
Married Matilda Caroline Butcher in Tennessee (daughter of Isaac Butcher and Narcissus Rebecca Rentfrow of Tennessee). She was born Aug. 18, 1809. Their children: Nancy Maria, m. William Follett; Martha Jane, died; Rebecca, m. Corneling Lott, m. Lewis Saunsosee; Mary Ann, m. John Lott; Harriet Catherine, m. James Addison Bean; Sarah Louisa, m. John Wesley Turner; Amanda Caroline, died; Joseph Smith m. Clarissa N. Wilcox; William, died; Isaac Romanzo, m. Samantha Louisa Mecham. Family home Provo, Utah.
Married Ruth Bailey Logan at Salt Lake City. Their child: Julia Ann, m. Thomas Holdaway. Family home Provo, Utah.
Married Elizabeth Bukie (Boshard) at Salt Lake City. Family home Provo, Utah.
Married Matilda Hardy. Family home Provo, Utah.
Bishop of Provo 21 years. Farmer. Died Sept. 6, 1896.

FAUSETT, ISAAC ROMANZO (son of William M. Fausett and Matilda Caroline Butcher). Born Dec. 19, 1853, Provo, Utah.
Married Samantha Louisa Mecham March 4, 1874, Provo, Utah (daughter of Lewis Mecham and Lydia Wells, pioneers 1852, James Snow company). She was born Dec. 12, 1856. Their children: William b. April 25, 1875, m. Bertha Herbert; Otis Eugene b. Sept. 8, 1876, d. infant; Raymond b. March 1, 1878, d. aged 11; Lydia Matilda. b. Oct. 3, 1879, m. Raymond Davis; Julia Ann b. Sept. 11, 1881, d. infant; Edna b. June 3, 1883; Sarah b. Jan. 5, 1885, m. Robert D. Young; Florence b. Sept. 27, 1896, m. Marian Adamson; Lewis b. Sept. 4, 1888, m. Lucy Bigelow; Elmer b. Sept. 4, 1890; Estella b. Dec. 5, 1892, m. Frank Simmons; Jennie b. Dec. 25, 1894, d. infant; Whitmor b. June 16, 1896; Arnold b. Sept. 11, 1898; Polly b. Feb. 3, 1901. Family home Wallsburg, Utah.
Elder. Farmer.

FAUSETT, LEWIS (son of Isaac Ramonzo Fausett and Samantha Louisa Mecham). Born Sept. 4, 1888, Provo, Utah.
Married Lucy Lavina Bigelow July 13, 1908, Heber, Utah (daughter of Daniel Bigelow and Clara Ostensen of Camp Creek, Mercer county, Ill., pioneers with Captain Snow company). She was born Jan. 21, 1890. Their children: Lucy Ella b. June 25, 1909; Lewis Earle b. Oct. 21, 1911. Family home Wallsburg, Utah.
Farmer.

FAWSETT, JOHN. Born Dec. 22, 1804, Illinois. Came to Utah by oxteam. His children: Amanda, m. Washington Clift; William, m. Julia Stevens.
Married Mary E. Shelton at Provo, Utah (daughter of Stephen Shelton and Nancy Brown of Jackson county, Mo.). She was born in 1825. Their children: Nancy, m. James Davis; Margaret Ann, m. John Van Wagner; Elizabeth, m. Phelix Murphy; Amanda, m. Heber Wardel; Sarah, m. John Hartnet; Julia, m. Charles Zufelt; Eliza, m. Thomas Hair; Jeanetta, died; Janie, m. William H. Graham; John W., m. Irene Burgner; Davin, died. Family home Midway, Utah.
Bishop of Midway, Utah. Veteran of Black Hawk war. Farmer and sheep raiser. Died 1873.

FAWSETT, JOHN W. (son of John Fawsett and Mary E. Shelton). Born Feb. 23, 1871, at Midway, Utah.
Married Irene Burgner Jan. 10, 1896, Heber, Utah (daughter of Christian Burgner and Amelia Sultzer of Switzerland). She was born Oct. 21, 1877. Their children: John William b. Nov. 6, 1896; Nancy Irene, b. Oct. 22, 1897; Sarah Jane b. Aug. 27, 1900; Charles Edmund b. Dec. 23, 1901; Amanda Elizabeth b. Oct. 29, 1903; Jessie Amelia b. Jan. 24, 1906; Walker Ray b. March 24, 1908; Violet May b. May 24, 1910. Family home Midway, Utah. Sheepraiser and miner.

FEATHERSTONE, THOMAS (son of John Featherstone and Eliza Berkinshaw of Kegworth, Leicestershire, Eng.). Born Sept. 15, 1834, at Kegworth. Came to Utah Sept. 11, 1857.
Married Emma Smith Jan. 11, 1853 (daughter of John Smith and Mary Ann Gauntly), who was born Aug. 9, 1832, Nottingham, Eng., and died April 12, 1913. Their children: John T. b. Nov. 16, 1853, d. Feb. 22, 1854; William Edwin b. July 12, 1856, d. Aug. 24, 1864; Mary Ann b. Nov. 10, 1859, (d. June 1, 1907), m. Hyrum Hoggard; Franklin Joseph b. Dec. 26, 1861, m. Martha Larson; Thomas b. Oct. 23, 1866, m. Mary Boley; Stephen b. July 9, 1867, d. May 17, 1912, m. Charlotte Rushton; Elizabeth b. Oct. 17, 1873, d. May 14, 1900, m. Frank Walker. Family home American Fork, Utah.
Married Martha Richards July 12, 1866, Salt Lake City (daughter of Isaac Richards and Ann Toulson), who was born Dec. 4, 1844, Attenborough, Derbyshire, Eng., and came to Utah 1864, John J. Rawlins company. Their children: Dolen b. July 10, 1869, d. July 11, 1869; Heber Chase b. May 25, 1874, m. Celestial Brown 1894; Joseph F. b. June 26, 1881, m. Marie Snow; James b. Nov. 5, 1878, d. Oct. 21, 1895. Settled at American Fork 1857. Seventy and high priest.

FELSHAW, WILLIAM (son of Elisha Felshaw and Sarah Hicks of New York state. Born Jan. 1, 1800, Granville, Washington county, N. Y. Came to Utah Sept. 9, 1851, Abraham Day company.

Married Mary Harriet Gilbert 1826 in Washington county, N. Y. daughter of Josiah Gilbert and Susannah Hyde of that state). She was born June 5, 1808, in Otsego county, N. Y. Their children: Betsy b. July 1831, d. young; Julia b. June 27, 1832, m. Clarence Merrille Dec. 7, 1867; William Alma b. July 3, 1834; Mary; Lemuel; Josiah, latter four d. young; John b. Nov. 23, 1836, m. Frances Croft; Anna Mary b. Dec. 28, 1839, d. young; Lucy b. March 1842, m. Frank Wilson; Carolina b. May 3, 1845, m. David R. Stephens; Olive b. Nov. 2, 1848, m. Amassa M. Lyman, Jr.; Sarah b. Feb. 3, 1851, d. young; Susannah b. Feb. 3, 1851, m. John Ashby.
Member 70th quorum seventies; went to Wyoming to assist in relief of handcarts company 1856; high priest. Member legislature 1854; mayor of Fillmore two terms; member town council. Worked on temples at Kirtland, Ohio. Nauvoo, Ill., and Salt Lake City, Utah. Contractor and builder. Died Sept. 24, 1867, at Fillmore, Utah.

FELT, NATHANIEL HENRY (son of Nathaniel Felt and Hannah Reeves of Salem, Essex county, Mass.). Born Feb. 6, 1816, at Salem. Came to Utah Oct. 6, 1850, Heywood and Woolley merchandise train.
Married Eliza Ann Preston Oct. 3, 1839, at Salem (daughter of Joseph Preston and Rebecca Peele of that place). She was born Nov. 10, 1820, and died June 19, 1875. Their children: Joseph Henry, m. Louise Bouton; Nathaniel Preston; Margaret Eliza, m. Thomas C. West; John G., m. Clara V. Hanks; Albert William, m. Ida Dalquist; George F. b. Dec. 15, 1854, m. Louise M. Ellerbeck Sept. 4, 1883; Charles B., m. Georgianna Spencer; Adaline Augusta; Mary Alice, m. Joseph G. Cutler; Annetta Rebecca. Family home Salt Lake City.
President Salem branch of L. D. S. church 1843; and president St. Louis conference 1847; member 29th quorum seventies; missionary to Great Britain 1865-67; and to New England states 1869-70; high councilor many years. Alderman of Salt Lake City 1851; elected to the house of representatives in first legislature August 1851; colonel and chaplain in Utah militia 1852. Assisted George A. Smith in locating and surveying town of Parowan. Established paper in New York City called "The Mormon." Grain merchant. Died Jan. 27, 1887, Salt Lake City.

FELT, GEORGE F. (son of Nathaniel Henry Felt and Eliza Ann Preston). Born Dec. 8, 1857, at Salt Lake City.
Married Louise M. Ellerbeck Sept. 4, 1883, at Salt Lake City (daughter of Thomas Witton Ellerbeck, born Sept. 14, 1829, and Henrietta Dyer, born April 28, 1842, former pioneer Oct. 15, 1851, Orson Pratt company). She was born May 10, 1864. Their children: Geneva E. b. July 7, 1884; Ethel b. March 3, 1886, m. J. P. Marshall; Alice b. Aug. 5, 1888; George Harold b. Aug. 13, 1891; Walter Lawrence b. Nov. 20, 1893; Richard Norman b. Oct. 10, 1890; Frank Allan b. Dec. 17, 1897; Marian b. June 20, 1907. Family home Salt Lake City.
Member 124th quorum seventies. Assistant county treasurer; secretary board of police and fire commissioners. Lumber merchant.

FENN, WILLIAM. Married Sarah Fenn. Their children: Martha, m. William Nuttall; George; Frederick; Sarah, m. William Thompson. Family home Provo, Utah. He was drowned in Provo river near Charleston, Utah.

FENTON, THOMAS (son of Robert Fenton and Mary Anderson of Sheffield, Eng.). Born April 7, 1821, at Sheffield. Came to Utah 1851.
Married Annie Maria Wilson 1862, at Salt Lake City (daughter of William Wilson and Elizabeth Jackson of Derbyshire, Eng.). She was born May 11, 1843. Their children: William and George A., both d. aged 2; Elizabeth C., d. aged 15; John Wilson, m. Eliza West; Joseph Jackson, m. Sarah J. Jensen; Beatrice, m. William Ebert. Family home Salt Lake City.
Married Emma Coombs. Their child: Robert Alfred b. Nov. 30, 1867, m. Sarah Elizabeth Burton Feb. 15, 1893.
High priest; block teacher. Nurseryman and florist. Died Jan. 21, 1890, at Salt Lake City.

FENTON, JOHN WILSON (son of Thomas Fenton and Annie Maria Wilson). Born March 3, 1873, at Salt Lake City.
Married Eliza West Aug. 15, 1895, at Salt Lake City (daughter of Jesse West and Isabella Windley of Derbyshire, Eng., pioneers 1850). She was born July 13, 1877. Their children: Thomas J. b. March 5, 1896; Irene I. b. April 22, 1898; John M. b. May 30, 1900; Edna A. b. May 11, 1903; Nellie T. b. Feb. 13, 1905; Russell W. b. Oct. 27, 1906; Leslie W. b. June 27, 1909. Family home Salt Lake City.
Elder; block teacher. Bricklayer.

FENTON, JOSEPH JACKSON (son of Thomas Fenton and Annie Maria Wilson). Born June 7, 1875, at Salt Lake City.
Married Sarah J. Jensen Nov. 4, 1896, at Salt Lake City (daughter of C. H. L. Jensen and Helbertine Nelsen of Copenhagen, Denmark, came to Utah June 23, 1878). She was born Jan. 7, 1876. Their children: Joseph J. b. April 23, 1898; Myrtle J. b. Nov. 28, 1899; Thomas J. b. Sept. 2, 1901, d. infant; Beatrice J. b. Sept. 2, 1901; Hyrum J. b. Dec. 1, 1903, d. infant; Gladys J. b. Nov. 18, 1903, died; David W. b. Sept. 9, 1905; Sarah E. b. May 17, 1908; John M. b. Jan. 23, 1910. Family home Salt Lake City.

High priest; president deacons quorum 6th ward; secretary 6th quorum elders; 2d counselor in bishopric 26th ward; Sunday school superintendent three years; ward clerk. Railway conductor; mail carrier; clerk in U. S. P. O. since 1902.

FENTON, ROBERT ALFRED (son of Thomas Fenton and Emma Coombs). Born Nov. 30, 1867, at Salt Lake City.
Married Sarah Elizabeth Burton Feb. 15, 1893, Logan, Utah (daughter of Robert T. Burton and Susan Ellen McBride, pioneers of Salt Lake City). She was born Feb. 29, 1868. Their children: Robert A. b. June 2, 1894; Harris Burton b. Sept. 6, 1898; Lee Coombs b. June 16, 1901; Ellen Clarissa b. Dec. 8, 1903; Burton Thomas b. July 30, 1908. Family home Salt Lake City.
Missionary to New Zealand 1895-98; home missionary; block teacher. Farmer. U. C. traveler.

FERGUSON, ANDREW (son of William Ferguson, born Nov. 5, 1792, Rutherglen, Lanarkshire, Scotland, and Barbara Orthur Lindsay, born Feb. 20, 1797, at Rutherglen). Born Sept. 6, 1818, at Rutherglen. Came to Utah Sept. 20, 1855, Moses Thurston company.
Married Catherine Douglas July 15, 1842 (daughter of Robert Douglas and Mary Bruce), who was born Oct. 6, 1819. Their children: Agnes Reid b. Sept. 21, 1843, m. Fredrick Lewis Jan. 28, 1865; Barbara Orthur b. Sept. 21, 1843, m. Willard O. Creer Dec. 16, 1862; Elizabeth Lock b. Nov. 19, 1846, m. John Houghton 1866; Eli B. K. b. Dec. 28, 1848, m. Christina Angus April, 1874.
Married Elizabeth Watson July 15, 1850, at Rutherglen, Scotland (daughter of William Watson and Ann White), who was born July 4, 1811, at Kilmorack, Scotland. Their children: William Watson b. May 22, 1851, m. Caroline Thomas Dec. 21, 1876; Andrew M. T. b. Aug. 23, 1855, m. Marie Simmons Feb. 18, 1878; John Robert b. April 23, 1856.
Missionary to Scotland 1879-80; president of Dundee conference, island of peace 1865-76; alderman 1883; city attorney of Spanish Fork. First president Spanish Fork Co-operative Mercantile Inst.

FERRE, ROSWELL C. (son of Daniel Ferre and Elizabeth Chapins of Kanesville, Pottawattamie Co., Iowa). Born Nov. 5, 1818, Bostard Township, Canada. Came to Utah October 1862.
Married Rachael Catherine Hollister Aug. 4, 1850, Kanesville (Miller's Hollow), Iowa. She was born Nov. 15, 1831, and came to Utah with husband. Their children: Alva Alonzo b. June 14, 1851, m. Polly Harding; Josephine b. Dec. 26, 1853, m. Erastus Snow; Roswell b. June 1, 1856, m. Eunice Martin; Ann Henry b. Sept. 9, 1858, m. Rosalia Potter; Rachel K. b. Dec. 26, 1860, m. Isaac McEwan; William b. June 16, 1863, m. Eva Davis; George A. b. Aug. 21, 1866, m. Susan Baum; Mary A. b. March 6, 1869, died; Warren S. b. Sept. 5, 1870, m. Emma Bowen. Family home Provo, Utah. Seventy. Farmer. Died Dec. 1885.

FERRIN, SAMUEL (son of Ebenezer Ferrin, born Sept. 4, 1777, and Lydia Phelps, born March 9, 1782, both at Hebron, Grafton county, N. H.—married Nov. 26, 1801). He was born Nov. 12, 1804, at Hebron. Came to Utah 1852.
Married Olive Fidelia Coon. Their children: Julia Fidelia, m. Hyrum Boynton; Jacob Samuel b. June 1, 1830, m. Janet A. McBride March 29, 1857.
Married Sally Powell (Marsh) Jan. 21, 1833, in Pennsylvania (daughter of James and Clotilda Powell), who was born March 21, 1811. Their children: Josiah Marsh b. Jan. 22, 1834, m. Martha A. Bronson Feb. 10, 1856; James Madison b. July 14, 1836, m. Eliza Jane Lincoln Dec. 25, 1861; Ebenezer; Moroni; Sarah Marie b. Dec. 1, 1840, m. Omner Call Oct. 26, 1855; Heber Chase Kimball b. Oct. 4, 1846, m. Martha J. Burns; Brigham b. January, 1849; Lydia b. March 8, 1852, m. George W. Williams Sept. 13, 1869. Family resided Salt Lake City and Ogden, Utah.
Married Ann Plant Aug. 24, 1861, Salt Lake City (daughter of Charles Plant and Ann Chapman), who was born Aug. 14, 1842, Calver, Derbyshire, Eng. Their children: Annie b. June 15, 1862; Samuel b. June 30, 1864; Anna b. May 4, 1866; Jesse b. Nov. 15, 1868; Francis b. May 13, 1871; Philip b. Jan. 24, 1874. Family resided Salt Lake City and Pleasant View, Utah.

FERRIN, JOSIAH MARSH (son of Samuel Ferrin and Sally Powell Marsh). Born Jan. 22, 1834, Cherry Creek, N. Y.
Married Martha Ann Bronson Feb. 10, 1856, Ogden, Utah (daughter of Leman Bronson and Lucy Brass), who was born June 13, 1834, Brownstown, Mich. Their children: Martha Jane b. Sept. 26, 1856, m. Zachariah Ballantyne Dec. 27, 1877; Josiah Leman b. Sept. 26, 1856, m. Ella D. Stallings Dec. 28, 1877; James Clinton b. Aug. 30, 1858, m. Elizabeth E. Edge Oct. 9, 1879; Thaddeus Marsh b. Sept. 9, 1860, m. Cornelia Nielson Jan. 24, 1884; Moroni Daniel b. July 6, 1862, m. Rosella Bachman Dec. 1884. m. Nancy V. Murphy June 19, 1895; George Elihu b. Aug. 30, 1864, m. Josephine Hortensen Oct. 25, 1893; Lucy Lorinda b. Aug. 26, 1866, m. William Stringham; Winslow Bronson b. May 27, 1871; Chariton Philip b. March 8, 1874, m. Ida Farley; Sally Lovella b. May 12, 1877, m. John F. Sharp. Family resided Ogden and Eden, Utah.
Bishop; high councilor. Member state legislature. Farmer and stock raiser.

870 PIONEERS AND PROMINENT MEN OF UTAH

FERRIN, JOSIAH LEMAN (son of Josiah Marsh Ferrin and Martha Ann Bronson). Born Sept. 26, 1856, Ogden, Utah.
Married Ella D. Stallings Dec. 27, 1877, Salt Lake City (daughter of Joseph Stallings, born Aug. 26, 1813, and Charlotte Jane Hussey, born July 8, 1838, Dover, N. H.). She was born June 3, 1859, Mill Creek. Utah. Their children: Joseph Leman b. Oct. 10, 1878, m. Minnie Slater March 30, 1899; Charles Leroy b. June 2, 1880, m. Delia R. Walker June 6, 1901; Arthur Moroni b. Dec. 10, 1881, m. Janet A. Lindsay Oct. 29, 1903; Lottie Jane b. Feb. 1, 1887, m. David C. Lindsay Sept. 15, 1909; Lorin Daniel b. Feb. 1, 1887; Florence May b. Feb. 8, 1889; Parley Ezra b. Sept. 14, 1891; Leonard William b. March 22, 1893. Family home Eden, Utah.
Bishop's counselor 15 years. Farmer.

FERRIN, ARTHUR M. (son of Josiah Leman Ferrin and Ella D. Stallings). Born Dec. 10, 1881, Eden, Utah.
Married Janet A. Lindsay Oct. 29, 1903, Salt Lake City (daughter of John Lindsay, pioneer 1862, and Marie Peterson, who came to Utah 1877). She was born Oct. 31, 1881, Eden. Their children: Leonard Arthur b. Aug. 6, 1904; Ada Maud b. Jan. 18, 1906; Clyde William b. Dec. 16, 1907; John Cyrus b. Dec. 17, 1909; George Albert b. Feb. 26, 1912. Family resided Eden and Liberty, Utah.
Bishop's counselor; bishop.

FERRY, EDWARD PAYSON (son of William M. Ferry and Amanda White of Grand Haven, Mich.). Born April 16, 1837, at Grand Haven. Came to Utah October, 1878.
Married Clara V. White June 1, 1870, at Grand Haven (daughter of Nathan White and Sarah Brittain of Grand Haven), who was born Dec. 4, 1844. Their children: William Montague, m. Ednah Truman; Edward S., m. Mabel Edie; Miriam, m. Charles C. Reynolds; Edith, m. Dane T. Merrill. Family home Grand Haven, Mich., until 1878.
Government director U. P. railroad; president Trans-Mississippi Congress at Denver, Colo., 1890; delegate to territorial legislature from Summit county 1888-92. Mining operator.

FERRY, WILLIAM MONTAGUE (son of Edward P. Ferry and Clara V. White). Born March 12, 1871, Grand Haven, Mich. Came to Utah July 1891.
Married Ednah Truman June 3, 1896, at Nashville, Mich. (daughter of George A. Truman and Juliet Frink of Nashville), who was born Aug. 18, 1872. Their children: William M. and Sanford T. b. Oct. 4, 1898. Family home Salt Lake City, Utah.
City councilman 1906-12; member state senate 1913. Mining operator; banker.

FIELD, JAMES (son of William Field, of Osberry Parish, and Mary Harding—latter born June 21, 1805, Bishop's Froom, Eng—both of Bosbury, Herefordshire, Eng.). He was born Feb. 17, 1830, Bosbury, Eng. Came to Utah Oct. 6, 1851, Alfred Cardon company.
Married Catherine D. Brown July 16, 1863, Lynn, Utah (daughter of Richard D. Brown and Margaret Parkinson, of Wigan, Lancashire, Eng., pioneers Sept. 20, 1864, Joseph S. Rawlins company). She was born June 8, 1844. Their children: Mary E. b. June 29, 1864, m. John H. Cole; James F. b. April 5, 1866; Ida A. b. Aug. 20, 1868, m. William R. Moore; Eva C. b. April 6, 1871, m. William Stevenson; William C. b. Feb. 23, 1873, m. Sarah Farnsworth (d.), m. Margaret Moran; Charles W. b. Jan. 17, 1875, m. Nellie Farnsworth; Margarett H. b. July 7, 1877, m. Joseph Baird; Riley O. b. Feb. 12, 1880, m. Lena Summers; Ruby M. b. May 14, 1882, m. Ernest E. Conlin; Zeffie Z. b. April 14, 1884. Family home Lynn, Utah.
Member 98th quorum seventies; bishop's counselor. School trustee. Farmer. Died Jan. 17, 1907, Lynn, Utah.

FIELD, JOHN (son of William and Mary Harding of England). Born Oct. 31, 1808, in Herefordshire, Eng. Came to Utah Sept. 17, 1860, David Evans company.
Married Susannah Cooper.
Married Alice Lavender April 5, 1862, Salt Lake City (daughter of Thomas Lavender and Charlotte Apthorpe—married Oct. 21, 1827, Bedford, Bedfordshire, Eng., pioneers 1861, Capt. Martineau company). She was born Aug. 23, 1828, at Bedford. Their children: John Joseph b. Feb. 16, 1864, m. Emma Moesser; Thomas Manasseh b. Jan. 5, 1865 m. Mary Riley Oct. 13, 1897; Judah George b. Nov. 6, 1866, m. Hannah Park May 5, 1889; Israel Charles b. Jan. 31, 1869; Joshua b. July 25, 1872.
High priest.

FIELD, JOHN J. (son of John Field and Alice Lavender). Born Feb. 16, 1863, Taylorsville, Utah.
Married Emma Moesser May 21, 1884, at Salt Lake City (daughter of Joseph Moesser and Elizabeth Rushton), who was born Jan. 16, 1866, Salt Lake City. Their children: Alice b. April 27, 1885, m. Canute Peterson March 1907; Maud M. b. May 14, 1887; Nellie Ray b. July 5, 1889, m. Parley War June 11, 1908; Emma b. June 13, 1892, m. Harry Empey Feb. 2, 1908; John Franklin b. Jan. 17, 1894; Bessie b. May 25, 1896, m. Hannah Park May 5, 1889; Israel Charles b. Jan. 31, 1869; President deacons' quorum, Taylorsville, Utah; counselor in presidency 20th quorum elders, Salt Lake City; also 1st counselor, 10th quorum elders, Granite stake; president 2d quorum elders; one of presidents of 146th quorum seventies.

FIELD, WILLIAM (son of William Field and Mary Harding). Born Jan. 16, 1836, in Herefordshire, Eng. Came to Utah Oct. 11, 1862, Warren Snow company.
Married Charlotte Bult Oct. 6, 1861 (daughter of Thomas Bult and Luesa Cuerfield, pioneers July 9, 1853, Horace S. Eldredge company). She was born Aug. 11, 1840, and came to Utah Sept. 14, 1861, Joseph Warren company. Their children: Charlotte Ann b. April 1, 1863, m. William Heber Perry; William Heber b. Jan. 1, 1865, m. Henrietta Leora Campbell; George Wesley b. Nov. 10, 1866, m. Ida Clifford; Elzy Howard b. Jan. 14, 1869, m. Olive Arvilla Perry; Lucy b. May 18, 1871, m. Haynes Robert Howell; Mary Olive b. June 7, 1873, m. James William Laughlin; Robert Warren b. Feb. 17, 1876, m. Ellen Randall; Levi Edward b. June 18, 1879, m. Mary Amelia Larson. Family home Slaterville, Utah.

FIELD, WILLIAM HEBER (son of William Field and Charlotte Bult). Born Jan. 1, 1865, Slaterville, Utah.
Married Henrietta Leora Campbell, Salt Lake City (daughter of Moroni Campbell). Their children: Eva Pearl b. Nov. 25, 1895; Heber Delbert b. Sept. 15, 1897.

FIELDING, JOSEPH (son of John Fielding and Rachel Ibbotson of Honiton, Eng.). Born 1817 at Honiton. Came to Utah September 1838, Captain Lott company.
Married Hannah Greenwood June 11, 1838, Preston, Eng. Their children: Rachel b. June 27, 1839, m. William W. Burton March 28, 1856; Mary Ann b. March 22, 1840, m. James MacKnight July 18, 1863; Ellen b. Feb. 9, 1841, m. William W. Burton Nov. 2, 1851; Heber d. 1868; Joseph; Josephine b. 1843, m. Orson Heath 1868; Sarah Ann b. May 19, 1851, m. William W. Burton May 23, 1870. Famfly home Salt Lake City.
Married Mary Ann Peak 1845, Nauvoo, Ill.
President first seven elders who went to England as missionaries. Farmer. Died December 1863, Mill Crek, Utah.

FIFE, ADAM (son of John and Margaret Fife of Sauchie, Scotland). Born July 4, 1806, at Sauchie. Came to Utah September 1851, David Wilkie company.
Married Helen Sharp at Sauchie, Scotland (daughter of John Sharp, later of Salt Lake City, pioneer 1850). She was born Nov. 10, 1808. Their children: Mary b. June 8, 1827, m. Alexander Patterson; Margaret b. July 25, 1829, m. David Fife, 1833, m. Jennette Triaddle; Andrew b. July 3, 1835, and Robert b. April 21, 1837, died; Adam S. b. July 24, 1838, m. Comfort Jelly; Cecelia b. Oct. 6, 1840, died; Joseph b. Sept. 9, 1842, m. Martha Ann Bingham; Ellen b. Sept. 25, 1844, died; Helen b. May 14, 1846, m. Sanford Bingham; Catherine b. Aug. 13, 1848, m. Francis Russell; Janet b. March 1, 1851, m. William Child; Jane b. May 7, 1853, m. Charles Densel; Sarah b. Dec. 26, 1855. Family home Riverdale, Utah.
Quarried stone in Red Butte canyon for wall around temple grounds at Salt Lake City. Died January 1864.

FIFE, ADAM S. (son of Adam Fife and Helen Sharp). Born July 24, 1838, Clackmannan, Scotland.
Married Comfort Jelly June 27, 1863, at Salt Lake City (daughter of William and Comfort Jelly of Herechester, Northamptonshire, Eng.—pioneers Sept. 30, 1854, Darwin Richardson company). She was born Jan. 6, 1846. Their children: Mary Ellen b. Jan. 24, 1865, m. William Jardine; Adam J. b. May 8, 1872, m. Agnes Shumway; William J. b. Oct. 22, 1876, m. May Jardine; Cecelia b. July 11, 1879, m. John Vaughn; John J. Fife b. Feb. 17, 1882, m. Elizabeth Terry; Joseph J. b. Nov. 28, 1884, m. Margaret Anderson; LeRoy b. June 2, 1887. Family home Brigham City, Utah.
Assisted in hauling stone for Salt Lake temple 1852-56; also assisted in hauling the cornerstone for that edifice.

FIFE, WILLIAM N. (son of John Fife and Mary Meek Nicol, of Kincardine-on-Forth, Perthshire, Scotland). Born Oct. 6, 1831, at Kincardine. Came to Utah Oct. 18, 1853, John Brown company.
Married Diana Davis July 9, 1854, Salt Lake City (daughter of Daniel Davis and Sarah Thomas of South Wales—pioneers Sept. 25, 1849, Daniel Jones company). She was born April 11, 1836. Their children: Sarah Jane, m. Barnard White; William Wilson, m. Elizabeth Stewart; Diana, m. Valasco Farr; John Daniel, m. Eliza Jane Stewart; Walter Thompson, m. Mary Jane Merrill; Agnes Ann; Emma; Robert; Bernard. Family home Ogden, Utah.
Member 37th quorum seventies; member Ogden high council. Coroner in Weber county 1869-80; Ogden city marshal 1861-76; deputy U. S. marshal 1866; colonel of 1st regiment Weber military district. Architect and builder.

FIFIELD, LEVI JOSEPH (son of David Fifield). Born Dec. 12, 1803, Grantham, N. H.; came to Utah June 5, 1848, with other discharged Mormon battalion soldiers.
Married Amy Tracy (daughter of Thomas Tracy and Amy Tibbits), who was born Sept. 10, 1803, and died Jan. 5, 1896, Nauvoo, Ill. Their children: Matthew P. b. June 18, 1830; Charles Byron.
Married Sarah Smith June 7, 1845, Nauvoo, Ill. (daughter of William Smith, pioneer 1848), who was born March 28,

1828, Solford, Eng. Their children: William John; Joseph Levi, d. child; girl, d. infant.
Member Mormon battalion. Died Aug. 16, 1850, Ogden, Utah.

FIFIELD, MATTHEW PHELPS (son of Levi Joseph Fifield and Amy Tracy). Born June 18, 1830, New Haven, Vt. Came to Utah Sept. 20, 1848, William G. Perkins company.
Married Almira Jane Gibson April 5, 1852, Bountiful, Utah (daughter of John and Elizabeth Gibson), who was born March 30, 1833. Came to Utah, Levi Murdock company. Their children: Almira Jane b. June 27, 1853, m. Andrew Quigley; Samuel b. July 5, 1855, and Elizabeth d. children; Orelia; Julia. Family home Ogden, Utah.
Married Rebecca Ann Hoopes March 30, 1862, Richmond, Utah (daughter of Warner Hoopes and Pricilla Gifford), who was born in Nauvoo, Ill. Their children: Charles Eugene b. Feb. 7, 1863, d. child; Naomi Adelaide b. Oct. 2, 1864, m. H. C. Heninger; Matthew Warner b. May 1, 1866, and Daniel Lewis b. May 27, 1868, d. children; William Phelps b. April 10, 1870, m. Amorett Allen; Joseph Levi b. Feb. 24, 1872, d. child; Edwin Willard b. March 27, 1874, m. Margarett Cowley; Wesley Andrew b. Dec. 21, 1875, m. Abbie Fife; Albert Moroni b. June 29, 1877, m. Sarah Price; Melissa b. March 31, 1879, m. Ambrose Maughn; Rebecca Ann b. April 16, 1881, m. Ethan Allen 1900; Thomas Alma b. July 10, 1883; Jesse Harold b. Sept. 29, 1885.
President high priests quorum; alternate high councilor, Oneida stake. Settled in Cache valley 1849; moved to Bear Lake valley. Went to the relief of Salmon river settlers.

FIFIELD, WILLIAM PHELPS (son of Matthew Phelps Fifield and Rebecca Ann Hoopes). He was born April 10, 1870, Weston, Idaho.
Married Amorett Allen Nov. 29, 1893, Logan, Utah (daughter of Alexander Allen and Maria Cowley), who was born April 21, 1876, at Logan. Their children: William Allen b. Nov. 7, 1894; Lois b. Feb. 29, 1896; Matthew Glen b. March 31, 1898; Reah Amorett b. Sept. 7, 1901; Rachel b. April 15, 1903; Melvin Joseph b. Aug. 19, 1905; Mae b. May 7, 1907; Inez b. March 21, 1909; Anna b. Feb. 28, 1911.
Missionary to southern states 1899-1900; clerk Rockland ward 1909-11.

FILLERUP, ANDREW PETER (son of Peter Fillerup and Karen Rasmussen of Pannerup, Denmark). Born May 30, 1831, in Denmark. Came to Utah Oct. 5, 1867, C. C. Rich company.
Married Caroline Rasmine Rassmussen 1867, Salt Lake City (daughter of Rasmus and Jensina Rassmussen of Denmark), who was born May 24, 1842. Their children: Caroline Rasmine b. Dec. 22, 1868, m. Solomon F. Kimball; Amelia Pedernell b. March 20, 1870, m. Silas Hutching; Andrew Peter b. Jan. 25, 1872, m. Emma Josephine Anderson; Carl Richard b. Nov. 11, 1873, m. Moneta Johnson; Erastus Kruse b. Feb. 16, 1875, m. Lula Johnson; Zenas Kimberly b. May 24, 1878, m. Clara Williamson; Albert Frederick b. May 24, 1878, m. Luella Lane; Sofus Alexander b. July 10, 1880; Rosena Eleonora Andrea b. Jan. 22, 1882, m. Hugh Parks. Family home Provo, Utah.
High priest missionary to Denmark 1893-95; ward teacher. Road supervisor. Assisted in building woolen mills and first jail at Provo. Farmer. Deceased.

FILLERUP, ANDREW PETER, JR. (son of Andrew Peter Fillerup and Caroline R. Rassmussen). Born Jan. 25, 1872, Provo, Utah.
Married Emma Josephine Anderson June 2, 1899, Salt Lake City (daughter of Andrew Anderson and Cecilia Hansen of Lake View, Utah. Came to Utah 1883). She was born May 10, 1874. Their children: Archie b. Feb. 27, 1900, and Andrew Pedro b. April 20, 1903, died; Vivian Gertrude b. Jan. 13, 1905; Delpha Valerie b. Feb. 23, 1911. Family home Vineyard, Utah.
Elder. Farmer; dairyman.

FILLMORE, NORMAN (son of Miland Fillmore and Jane Shadbolt). Born March 1, 1848, in Waukesha county, Wis. Came to Utah, John Smith company.
Married Eleanor Searle Dec. 31, 1867, Payson, Utah (daughter of Courtland Searle of New York state and Jerusha Hill of Petersburg, N. H.). She was born March 30, 1852. Came to Utah Oct. 21, 1850. Their children: Jerusha Jane, b. Dec. 1, 1868, m. Walter Gardner; Norman b. Oct. 19, 1870, and Millie Alameda b. Aug. 16, 1871, d. infants; Rosa Eleanor b. June 29, 1873, m. John Reese; m. David Curtis; Enes Estella b. March 3, 1875, m. Arden Elmer; Lillie May b. May 10, 1877, m. James Mitchell; Mary Effie b. Aug. 29, 1879, d. infant; Ada Agnes b. Dec. 2, 1881, m. James E. Blackburn; Clara Viola b. Jan. 24, 1884, m. Clarence Christensen; Chloe Amanda b. Aug. 23, 1886, m. Townsend Sampston; Orin Ezra b. Nov. 28, 1889, m. Clara Ivie; Dora Maud b. April 18, 1891, m. William Nebeker; Edith Pearl b. Aug. 26, 1894. Family resided Payson and Richfield, Utah.
High priest; bishop Burrville, Utah; ward teacher. School trustee, Salem, Utah. Farmer; merchant at Payson and Burrville, Utah.

FINCH, WILLIAM (son of Benjamin Finch of Tipton, Eng.). Born March 1803. Came to Utah Oct. 1, 1854, Daniel Garn company.
Married Rebecca Woodall (daughter of Joseph Woodall and Mary Harrison), who was born Oct. 2, 1796. Their children: Joseph b. Aug. 26, 1831, m. Jane Davis Feb. 8, 1855; Benjamin, m. Fanny Mathews; Jane, m. Joseph Argyle; William b. Aug. 19, 1837, m. Sarah Walker; Ann b. Aug. 6, 1839, m. Walter Weston; Maria died. Family home Birmingham, Eng.

FINCH, JOSEPH (son of William Finch and Rebecca Woodall). Born Aug. 26, 1831, Birmingham, Eng.
Married Jane Davis Feb. 8, 1855, at Salt Lake City (daughter of John T. Davis and Anna Burns, former pioner 1851, Harrison Pratt company). She was born Feb. 14, 1834. Their children: Maria b. Jan. 19, 1856, m. Theodora Barnchester; Jane b. March 25, 1858, m. Thomas Jarvis; Rebecca D. b. Feb. 11, 1860, m. Ezra Robertson; Mary E. Hanna b. May 8, 1862, m. Edward Heal; Joseph D. b. Aug. 2, 1864, m. Ruth Roach Dec. 30, 1885; Martha Helen b. June 1, 1867, m. Stephen Standford; John W. D. b. Dec. 29, 1869, m. Lizzie King; Benjamin H. D. b. Jan. 3, 1872, m. Margret Holm; Cicea b. March 16, 1874, m. Robert Snetten; Grace D. b. July 11, 1876, died; James Douglas b. Jan. 15, 1879, m. Augusta Anderson. Family home Spanish Fork, Utah.

FINCH, WILLIAM (son of Joseph Finch, born 1780, Witlame, Herefordshire, Eng., and Charlotte Freeman). Born May 19, 1819, at Witlame. Came to Utah 1853, Vincent Shurtliff company.
Married Margarette Edwards 1840, who was born 1820, Whitley, Eng. Their children: William b. 1845 and Rosetta b. 1847, died; John b. 1849, m. Ellen Jenkins; Hyrum b. 1851, m. Mary Ann Garbett; Sarah Ann b. 1854; Rossella, m. Henry Burnette; Jane, m. Ephraim Williams.
Married Eliza Fowler 1862 (daughter of George Fowler and Ellener Masefield, former pioneer with handcart company). Their children: William b. Feb. 2, 1866, m. Mary Ellen Jesperson; m. Caroline Ethel Cole; Ephraim, m. Emma Davis; Joseph, m. Alice Davis; Eliza Jane, m. John Draper; Minnie, m. George Gourley; Charlotte; Charles; Edwin, m. Geneva Page; Zella Noreen, m. Criss C. Johnson. Family home Goshen, Utah.
Settled at Pleasant Grove, Utah; moved to Goshen; presiding elder Bend ward Goshen, Utah; missionary in England eight years.

FINCH, WILLIAM, JR. (son of William Finch and Eliza Fowler). Born Feb. 2, 1866, Goshen, Utah.
Married Mary Ellen Jesperson Oct. 10, 1888, Manti, Utah (daughter of Hans Jesperson and Mandana Jepson, former pioneer Oct. 5, 1854, Hans Peter Olsen company, latter, 1853, John Forsgren company). She was born at Goshen, Utah. Their children: Dorcas Ellen b. July 15, 1890; Levern b. Jan. 4, 1892; Eugene b. May 11, 1893; Leroy William b. Aug. 29, 1895; Rulon b. Jan. 20, 1898; Sarah Eliza b. April 23, 1900; Edres Marinda b. Dec. 26, 1902; Gladys b. June 7, 1905. Family home Goshen, Utah.
Married Caroline Ethel Cole May 23, 1906, Salt Lake City (daughter of Gilbert G. Cole and Rosa Walsh), who was born Jan. 27, 1880, Overton, Texas. Their children: Homer b. May 11, 1907; John Mauris b. Nov. 16, 1908; Dora b. June 22, 1910. Willis Avery b. Nov. 20, 1912.
Member 15th quorum seventies; 2d assistant Sunday school superintendent Goshen ward; missionary to southwestern states 1902; 2d counselor to Bishop William Okelbery, later 1st counselor. President amusement committee. Justice of peace four terms; school trustee.

FINDLAY, HUGH (son of James Findlay and Mary Boyed of Scotland. Came to Utah 1855 and 1856, respectively). Born June 9, 1822. Came to Utah 1855.
Married Mary Ellen Smith April 22, 1857, Salt Lake City, President Young officiating (daughter of Arthur S. Smith and Elizabeth Logue of Salt Lake City; pioneers October, 1854, James Brown company). She was born March 8, 1841, Manchester, Eng. Came to Utah with parents. Their children: Arthur S. b. Nov. 8, 1858, m. Elizabeth Ann Kearl; Clara Jane b. July 23, 1860, d. aged 6; Brigham H. b. June 18, 1862, m. Anna Elizabeth Wilcox; James W. b. Feb. 29, 1864, m. Ida Wooley; Charles H. b. Dec. 9, 1865, m. Emma West; Nephi b Oct 6, 1865 d aged 1 year; Walter b. Aug. 15, 1869, m. Laura Smedley. Family home, Salt Lake City.
High priest; missionary to England 1878-80. Matchmaker. Died March 2, 1900, Paris, Idaho.

FINLINSON, GEORGE (son of Joshua Finlinson and Mary Thomlinson of Thursby, Eng.). Born Aug. 23, 1835, West Curthwait, Eng. Came to Utah 1864, John Ashmam company.
Married Susan Trimble 1866, Fillmore, Utah (daughter of Edward Trimble and Elizabeth Lennox), who was born Nov. 27, —. Their children: Elizabeth b. June 18, 1867, m. Walter C. Lyman Dec. 16, 1891; George E. b. Aug. 18, 1869, m. Mary C. Roper Oct. 9, 1895; William J. b. Sept. 29, 1871, m. Mary O. Walker Dec. 16, 1899; Margaret Ann b. Oct. 18, 1873, m. Lorenzo Lovell June 5, 1901; Joseph T. b. March 8, 1876, m. Edith E. Lyman Oct. 8, 1903; Joshua b. March 17, 1878, m. Ida Jacobson Oct. 3, 1907; Rachel b. Aug. 28, 1880, m. John L. Nielson Dec. 17, 1902; Leo b. Nov. 2, 1883, m. Lydia Lyman Oct. 3, 1907; Ray b. Sept. 4, 1887.
Counselor in bishopric Oak Creek ward 1878-1907; ward and tithing clerk. Millard county commissioner two terms; justice of peace at Oak City, Utah.

FINLINSON, JOSEPH TRIMBLE (son of George Finlinson and Susan Trimble). Born March 8, 1876, Oak City, Utah.
Married Edith E. Lyman Oct. 8, 1903, Salt Lake City (daughter of Frederic R. Lyman and Ann Lovell), who was born Aug. 4, 1879, at Oak City. Their children: Burns Lyman b. Nov. 24, 1904; Fred Lyman b. Sept. 30, 1906; Ann b. July 19, 1908; Joseph Lyman b. April 25, 1912. Family home, Oak City.
School teacher six years; Millard county school superintendent 1903-10; missionary to eastern states two years; bishop Oak Creek ward 1907-11; 1st counselor Deseret stake presidency.

FIRTH, JOHN (son of William Firth of Wakefield, Yorkshire, Eng.). Born Feb. 6, 1823, at Wakefield. Came to Utah Oct. 14, 1853, Cyrus H. Wheelock company.
Married Jane Kendell May 12, 1846 (daughter of William Kendell and Sarah Wilkerson), who was born March 6, 1821, and came to Utah with husband. Their children: William Henry b. April 2, 1847, m. Sarah C. Hickerson Dec. 7, 1870; m. Sarah A. Boulton Jan. 21, 1891; Arthur b. Jan. 18, 1849, m. Emily Firth Nov. 1869, d. Dec. 1, 1911; Heber John b. 1852, and John George b. August, 1855, died. Family resided Salt Lake City and South Weber, Davis Co., Utah.

FIRTH, WILLIAM HENRY (son of John Firth and Jane Kendell). Born April 2, 1847, Leeds, Yorkshire, Eng.
Married Sarah C. Hickerson Dec. 7, 1870 (daughter of George W. and Sarah Hickerson), who was born Aug. 3, 1852, and died Nov. 22, 1871. Only child: John George b. Nov. 16, 1871, died same day.
Married Sarah A. Boulton Jan. 21, 1891, Uinta, Weber Co., Utah (daughter of Thomas Boulton and Sarah Cook, pioneers 1860), who was born April 13, 1862, Ogden, Utah. Their children: John T. b. Feb. 6, 1892; Nellie b. Sept. 27, 1894; Jennie b. Aug. 11, 1898. Family home South Weber, Utah.

FISH, HORACE (son of Joseph Fish, born April 22, 1770, and Sarah Speare, born March 24, 1770, both in New Hampshire). He was born Jan. 6, 1799. Came to Utah 1850, Milo Andrus company.
Married Hannah Leavitt March 18, 1825 (daughter of Jonathan Leavitt and Sarah Shannon), who was born Dec. 26, 1805. Their children: Julia b. July 18, 1825, m. Edward W. Thompson 1849; Sarah b. October, 1828, m. John C. L. Smith 1848; Betsy Jane b. 1837, m. John A. West 1854; Joseph b. June 27, 1840, m. Mary C. Steele March 22, 1859; Anna Maria b. 1842, m. Sidney Burton March 22, 1859; Franklin b. April 12, 1848, m. Rebecca Wimmer 1866.

FISH, JOSEPH (son of Horace Fish and Hannah Leavitt). Born June 27, 1840, in Will county, Ill.
Married Mary C. Steele March 22, 1859, Parowan, Utah (daughter of John Steele and Catherine Campbell; pioneers July 29, 1847, James Brown company). She was born Dec. 23, 1840, Belfast, Ireland. Their children: Mary Josephine b. March 11, 1860, m. John Barraclough Oct. 9, 1879; Frances Amelia b. April 12, 1862, m. Samuel Carson Oct. 12, 1879; Delphina Catherine b. June 29, 1864, m. Joseph W. Smith 1887; Joseph Campbell b. Nov. 4, 1866, m. Kate Reedhead Oct. 19, 1887; John Lazell b. Oct. 28, 1868, m. Vina Cheney Sept. 5, 1888; Jessie May b. May 19, 1872, m. James Y. Lee Oct. 5, 1897. Family home, Parowan.
Sunday school superintendent Parowan 1869; member high council 1869. County clerk 1867; aide-de-camp with rank of major 1865; attorney at law; justice of peace.

FISHBURN, ROBERT LEEMING (son of Francis Fishburn, born Feb. 29, 1808, Darlington, Eng., and Eliza Jeffs, born Aug. 25, 1813, St. Ives, Eng.; married January, 1834). He was born Nov. 5, 1834, at St. Ives, Eng. Came to Utah Sept. 11, 1857, Israel Evans handcart company.
Married Eliza Priscilla Noble June 3, 1858 (daughter of William G. Noble and Mary Ann Harper; married Dec. 7, 1830, Irchester, Northampton, Eng.; pioneers Oct. 17, 1862, Henry W. Miller company). She was born April 3, 1836. Came to Utah with husband 1862, Henry W. Miller company. Their children: Eliza Priscilla b. Jan. 27, 1860, m. J. W. Sheffield Dec. 28, 1877; Laura Maria b. Feb. 26, 1862, m. Abraham Smith Dec. 23, 1880; Robert Leeming b. Dec. 31, 1863, m. Mary Ellen Mack Nov. 28, 1890; Francis William b. Nov. 24, 1865, m. Serepta L. Mack Dec. 23, 1887; Aquilla Noble b. Sept. 9, 1868, m. Elizabeth Dick Nov. 17, 1901; Zilphah b. June 27, 1870, d. April 2, 1873; Henriette b. Sept. 4, 1873, d. Oct. 22, 1874; Rachel b. Jan. 19, 1875, d. Dec. 13, 1875; Lavinia b. April 6, 1876, m. Thomas McMaster July 12, 1899; Leonora Louisa b. May 30, 1879, m. LeRoy Nelsen Dec. 17, 1902. Family home Brigham City, Utah.
Married Laura Matilda Noble March 9, 1869, at Salt Lake City (daughter of William C. Noble and Mary Ann Harper), who was born Feb. 17, 1850, Great Horton, Eng. Their children: Mary Ann b. Feb. 23, 1871, m. A. B. Chambers Jan. 31, 1895; Waterhouse Harper b. Oct. 24, 1872, d. Dec. 31, 1874; Arthur Goodwin b. April 5, 1875, d. Dec. 20, 1876; James Alfred b. April 14, 1877, m. Martha Callan June 22, 1904; Lilly Jane b. May 23, 1880, m. Everett Smith Sept. 10, 1901; Laurett b. March 11, 1885, m. Albert McCann June 10, 1903.
Organized first choir in Smithfield, Utah, 1860, and served as its leader until 1866; choir leader Brigham City 1866-80; missionary to Great Britain April to September, 1880; 1st counselor in presidency high priests quorum 1877-83; released account of ill health. Justice of peace Brigham City 1872-78; county collectors 1878-79.

FISHER, IRVIN F. (son of John Fisher and Josephine R. Lyon). Born Aug. 31, 1864, Bountiful, Utah.
Married Lydia E. Jones April 25, 1894, in Salt Lake temple (daughter of Evan Jones and Cynthia C. Porter of Porterville, Utah, who came to Utah 1869). She was born Sept. 14, 1873. Their children: John E. b. Feb. 13, 1895; Linnie May b. Feb. 14, 1897; Evan F. b. Feb. 4, 1899; Warren A. b. Feb. 12, 1901; Irvin A. b. Jan. 12, 1904; Byron P. b. Nov. 4, 1906; Marlow L. b. June 9, 1910; Audrey J. b. Dec. 17, 1911, d. infant; Hortense b. March 19, 1913. Family home, Bountiful.
Sixth president 100th quorum seventies; missionary to Sandwich Islands 1890-93; 2d assistant Sunday school superintendent Bountiful ward; ward teacher. Farmer and gardener.

FISHER, JAMES (son of Thomas Fisher and (——) Smith of St. Albans, Eng.). Born in England. Came to Utah 1853, oxteam company.
Married Emma Burrows (daughter of John Burrows of England). Their children: Frederick, died; Jane, m. W. R. Huscroft; James, m. Ann Nelson; George. Family home Provo, Utah.
Missionary in England. Died July, 1883, Provo, Utah.

FISHER, JAMES (son of James Fisher and Emma Burrows). Born Dec. 30, 1857, Provo, Utah.
Married Ann Nelson at Provo (daughter of Isaac Nelson and Margaret Wiston of Wales and England—pioneers 1854, Ten-Pound company). She was born Dec. 13, 1857. Their children: Effie b. Feb. 8, 1882, m. Louis Marriott; James Edward b. Oct. 16, 1883, m. Lillian Berkin; Henry Fisher b. Sept. 7, 1885, died; Dorothy Emma b. Aug. 29, 1886, m. William Frampton; Hazel Margaret b. Aug. 26, 1888, m. George Halladay; Emma B. b. March 14, 1891, m. Hans Christensen; Rosezella b. Sept. 21, 1893, died; Florence W. b. April 14, 1895; Janie Marie F. b. Aug. 18, 1898; Maud b. Jan. 24, 1901. Family home Provo, Utah.
Farmer and fruitgrower; stockraiser.

FISHER, JAMES (son of James Fisher of Scotland). Born March 6, 1802, in Scotland. Came to Utah Aug. 29, 1861, Lewis Brunson company.
Married Mary Douglas (daughter of Donald Douglas), who came to Utah with husband. Only child: Maggie.

FISHER, JOSEPH (son of Jessie Fisher and Betsy Martin). Born Oct. 20, 1800, in Pennsylvania. Came to Utah 1850, Gilbert and Garish company.
Married Evaline McLean 1826, at Freedom, Pa. (daughter of John Steel McLean and Elizabeth Kirk of that state), who was born Dec. 25, 1805. Their children: James Madison, m. Edith Pierce; m. Lydia Ann Rank; Curtis, d. infant; Helen Mariah, m. Patriarch John Smith; Elizabeth Jane, m. Isaac Seely; Joseph Armstrong, m. Sarah Lovina Harris; Henry Charles, m. Mary Freker; m. Mary Jane Kingsford; Rheuhannah, m. Joseph Brimm. Family home East Mill Creek, Utah.
High priest. Millwright; built several sawmills and gristmills in Utah. Died March 21, 1867.

FISHER, JOSEPH ARMSTRONG (son of Joseph Fisher and Evaline McLean). Born July 28, 1841, Nauvoo, Ill. Came to Utah with parents.
Married Sarah Lovina Harris Dec. 20, 1862, at Salt Lake City (daughter of Chancey Sumner Harris and Caroline Chonut of Salt Lake City), who was born July 20, 1846. Their children: Sarah Elizabeth b. July 6, 1864, m. John H. Salmon; Cora Avilliah b. Nov. 29, 1865, m. Willard Finley Smith; Geneva Jane b. April 20, 1868, m. Frank Croft; Edith Evaline b. April 25, 1871; Joseph Elmer b. July 17, 1873, m. Lenor Jensen; Ernest Sumner b. Aug. 20, 1875; Ella Florence b. Dec. 17, 1879, m. Spencer O. Squires; Belva Lovina b. Dec. 1, 1884, m. John Leslie Reynolds. Family home Coalville, Utah.
Married Mary Barr Carruth May 9, 1870, at Salt Lake City (daughter of William Carruth and Margaret Ellwood of Renfrewshire, Scotland—pioneers Sept. 23, 1848, Brigham Young company). She was born May 2, 1852. Only child: William George b. May 10, 1871, m. Magdalena Allison.
Married Margaret May Merrill Nov. 30, 1906, at Salt Lake City (daughter of Clarence Merrill and Bathsheba Smith of Nauvoo, Ill.; former pioneer 1851, Capt. Howell company, latter, 1849, George A. Smith company). She was born Feb. 5, 1872. Their children: Abba Josephine b. Feb. 23, 1908; David Merrill b. Dec. 25, 1909; Clarence Merrill b. Jan. 26, 1912.
High priest; member stake high council 25 years. Assisted in bringing immigrants to Utah 1863. Road supervisor; city councilman; chief of police. Indian war veteran; served under Capt. Lot Smith 1862. Carpenter and builder.

FISHER, THOMAS FREDERICK (son of Thomas Fisher and Elizabeth Powell of Woolwich, Kent, Eng.). Born Feb. 7, 1811, Llanfryllin, Wales. Came to Utah Oct. 28, 1854, Robert L. Campbell company.
Married Jane Christon 1832, Deptford, Eng. (daughter of William Christon and Mary Brown of Woolwich, Eng.). Their children: Thomas W. b. May 24, 1835, m. Elizabeth Prescott; William F. b. Nov. 16, 1839, m. Millennium Andrus;

John b. Feb. 7, 1842, m. Josephine R. Lyon Aug. 16, 1864, m. Harriet Knighton April 11, 1878; Minnie M. b. May, 1844, m. Richard E. Egan; Georgiana, d. aged 8. Family home Bountiful, Utah.
Shipbuilder for English government. High priest; home missionary. Justice of peace at Bountiful 12 years. Died Jan. 3, 1887.

FISHER, WILLIAM F. (son of Thomas F. Fisher and Jane Christon). He was born Nov. 16, 1839, Woolwich, Kent, Eng.; came to Utah with father.
Married Millennium Andrus Jan. 1, 1861, at Salt Lake City (daughter of Milo Andrus and Abigail Jane Daily—pioneers 1849 and 1848 respectively). She was born Aug. 31, 1845. Their children: William Edgar b. Nov. 21, 1861, m. Mary Rainey Oct. 8, 1880; Linnie May b. July 4, 1864, m. William Palmer June 18, 1884; Frederick James b. Nov. 5, 1870, d. Oct. 29, 1890; George Howard b. Dec. 5, 1872, m. A. Laura Lewis Sept. 20, 1893; Minnie Jane b. March 2, 1878, m. Frank Ellsworth Jan. 1, 1900; Stella Josephine b. Jan. 4, 1880, m. Louis Brossard Sept. 12, 1900; Ray Homer b. March 9, 1883, m. Blanche Dierden June 8, 1909; Victor Russell b. March 26, 1885, m. Cecil Tucker Dec. 23, 1908. Family home Oxford, Idaho.
Married Harriet Hougan Oct. 21, 1871, at Salt Lake City (daughter of Goudy Hougan and Christiana Christensen). She was born December, 1854, Richmond, Utah. Their children: Albert C. b. Feb. 8, 1873, m. Emma Harris; Hattie b. Aug. 6, 1875, m. Fred Christensen; Lorena b. Jan. 3, 1885, m. George Anderson. Family home Richmond, Utah.
Missionary to Oxford, Idaho, where he was made bishop 1878. County assessor three terms. Merchant.

FISHER, JOHN (son of Thomas F. Fisher and Jane Christon). Born Feb. 7, 1842, Woolwich, Eng. Came to Utah with father.
Married Josephine R. Lyon Aug. 16, 1864, Bountiful, Utah, James Stoker officiating (daughter of Winsor Lyon and Sylvia Sessions of Portland, Me., latter pioneers October, 1864, Perrigrine Sessions company). She was born Feb. 8, 1844. Their children: Ivan J. b. Aug. 31, 1865, d. aged 4; Irvin F. b. Aug. 31, 1865, m. Lydia Eliza Jones; Sylvia J. b. Oct. 6, 1867, d. aged 2; Minnie b. Oct. 4, 1869, d. infant; Perry C. b. Dec. 12, 1870, m. Della Harrison; Rosie L. b. Feb. 4, 1872, m. Edward Hanson; Erastus W. b. Feb. 18, 1874, m. S. Vina Major; Thomas L. b. Nov. 13, 1876, m. Josephine Eckman; Kirkwood b. Nov. 1878, d. aged 21; Horton b. April 25, 1880, m. Martha Stoker. Family home Bountiful, Utah.
Married Harriet Knighton April 11, 1878, Salt Lake Endowment House, Wilford Woodruff officiating (daughter of William Knighton and Elizabeth Marrott of Chesterfield, Derbyshire, Eng., who came to Utah November, 1869, James Needham company). She was born Jan. 1, 1860. Their children: George H. b. Jan. 27, 1879, m. Marie Hanson; John I. b. Feb. 2, 1881, m. Bertha Parker; Albert R. b. Sept. 1, 1882; Victor E. b. Sept. 12, 1885, d. infant; Frederick M. b. Jan. 31, 1887, m. Lucinda Tolman; Roy C. b. Sept. 15, 1890; William M. b. Aug. 11, 1892; Rulon Wells b. Sept. 10, 1898; Hattie E. b. Oct. 7, 1899; David M. b. Feb. 14, 1902; Minnie Jane b. June 5, 1904.
High priest; bishop's counselor. Probate judge; county commissioner; justice of peace; mayor; member legislature 1880-98. Pony expressman; expressman between Salt Lake City and Carson City, Nev. Merchant; farmer and stockraiser. Died Oct. 23, 1905, Bountiful, Utah.

FISHER, VARDIS. Born 1782 in New York. Came to Utah 1854, oxteam company.
Married Jane Fisher, who died on the plains on way to Utah. Their children: Elizabeth, m. William Avery, m. Jack Thomas; Lydia R., m. George Parsons, m. Leven Simmons; Joseph; Fanny, m. Ezekiel Lee; Sarah, m. Mr. DeVoll; Melissa, m. John Despain; Oliver. Family resided in Missouri.
Minuteman in Revolutionary war. Died February, 1866, Spanish Fork, Utah.

FISK, IRA (son of Hezekiah Fisk of Silver Creek and Mary Walker of Fredonia, N. Y.). Born Feb. 21, 1801, at Silver Creek, N. Y. Came to Utah 1861.
Married Lucretia Trask Feb. 16, 1832 (daughter of Lazarus Trask and Ruby Moulton), who was born Feb. 25, 1808, died in Pennsylvania.

FITT, GEORGE (son of Thomas Fitt and Ann Bennett of Yorkshire, Eng. Came to Utah 1873). Born June 7, 1855.
Married Caroline R. Wakefield, Nov. 14, 1877, Salt Lake City (daughter of John Wakefield and Caroline R. Wilson), who was born April 1, 1858, at London, Eng. Came to Utah September, 1866, Capt. Bullock company. Their children: Caroline E. b. Jan. 1, 1879, m. Adolph Hottizer; Louise b. Aug. 14, 1880, m. James Boyd; George W. b. July 21, 1882, m. Rosetta Neuson; Sarah E. b. Sept. 29, 1884, m. John Greenhalch; Cora I. b. Dec. 3, 1886, m. Henry Greenhalgh; Annie Laura b. Nov. 26, 1888; Hazel b. March 8, 1891; Leva B. b. March, 1893; Amy A. b. Nov. 15, 1894; Thomas W. b. Jan. 4, 1897; John W. b. Aug. 12, 1899; Charles P. b. Feb. 3, 1902. Family home, Salt Lake City.

FITZERALD, THOMAS H. (son of Jerome B. Fitzgerald and Isabel Sweet of Niles, Mich.). Born March 17, 1868, at Niles. Came to Utah 1906.
Married Edith Stevens Sept. 26, 1894, Niles, Mich. (daughter of Thomas L. Stevens and Hester B. Kimmel of Berrien Springs, Mich.), who was born Nov. 13, 1868. Their children: Mary; Isabel; Francis; Thomas. Family home Salt Lake City, Utah.
Real estate dealer.

FJELDSTED, CHRISTIAN DANIEL. Born Feb. 20, 1829, Sunibyvester, Denmark. Came to Utah Oct. 7, 1858, R. K. Homer company.
Married Karen Olsen 1849, Denmark (daughter of Ole Olsen of Amager, Denmark). She was born Jan. 1, 1821. Their children: Peter J. b. Aug. 10, 1853, m. Bertha Marie Jensen; Willard S. b. Aug. 10, 1853, m. Sarah C. Hansen; Veta Josephine b. Aug. 8, 1857, m. Ebenezer Farns; Sarah b. September 1861, m. John Ellis. Family home Sugar house ward, Utah.
One of seven presidents of seventies 1884; filled six missions; president Scandinavian mission 1861. Died Dec. 23, 1905.

FJELDSTED, PETER J. (son of Christian Daniel Fjeldsted and Karen Olsen). Born Aug. 10, 1853, Amager, Denmark.
Married Bertha Marie Jensen Oct. 12, 1875, Salt Lake City (daughter of Peter Jensen and Bodel Clawsen, of Finen, Denmark). She was born Oct. 30, 1857; pioneer Utah 1862. Their children: Peter C. b. Dec. 18, 1876, m. Martha Parsons; Amelia Mary b. May 7, 1879, m. John W. Rogers; Bertha Marie b. April 28, 1882, m. Oliver B. Kurtz; Martha Caroline b. Sept. 4, 1885, m. W. H. Thomas; Ada Bodella b. May 25, 1887; Edwin Leroy b. Jan. 7, 1890; Norman Samuel b. Nov. 11, 1893; Edith Irene b. March 19, 1896. Family home Blackfoot, Idaho.

FJELDSTED, LARS PETER. Came to Utah 1862, Ola Liljenquist and Christian Amadsen independent Scandinavian company. His children follow: James, m. Frederick Traolstrup; Andrew, m. Matilda Larson, m. Mary Merup; Peter, m. Ester Taylor; Morris, died; Annie Petrena, m. Joseph Bridge Caldwell.
High priest. Farmer.

FLETCHER, EDWIN FRANCIS (son of Francis Fletcher and Esther B. Fletcher of Westford, Mass.). Born in 1840, in Westford. Came to Utah Oct. 6, 1851. Married Eliza Duncombe at Salt Lake City (daughter of Joseph Duncombe of England). Their children: Francis Eugene, m. Edith K. Pearson; Melvina, m. William H. Jones; Rose, m. Dugal C. Wilson; Edwin, m. Emily G. Selley; Sarah Jane, m. Willis I. Chugg; Willard N., m. Emily Grether. Family home 10th ward, Salt Lake City.
Veteran fireman; veteran Black Hawk Indian war; carpenter. Died March 22, 1913, at Salt Lake City.

FLETCHER, EDWIN (son of Edwin Francis Fletcher and Eliza Duncombe). Born July 30, 1875, in Salt Lake City.
Married Emily Selley Aug. 1, 1900, at Salt Lake City (daughter of William Selley and Sarah Luke of Devonshire, Eng., who came to Utah Sept. 25, 1866, John Holliday company). She was born Nov. 23, 1877. Their children: Howard William b. March 17, 1902; Calvin Edwin b. Feb. 5, 1904, d. aged 4; Elva b. Feb. 13, 1907; Evelin Grace b. July 14, 1910. Family home Salt Lake City, Utah.
Priest. Carpenter.

FLINT, WILLIAM (son of Josiah Flint and Annie Woodard of New York). Born Jan. 28, 1814, Spafford, Onondaga county, N. Y. Came to Utah Sept. 26, 1848, Brigham Young and Heber Kimball company.
Married Mary Jane Goodridge Dec. 24, 1850 (daughter of Benjamin Goodridge and Penelope Gardner, pioneers 1850, Wilford Woodruff company). She was born June 11, 1825. Came to Utah with her parents. Their children: Sarah Jane b. Oct. 20, 1851, m. George Seaman Dec. 15, 1873; Valeria b. Jan. 14, 1853, m. Edward Laird Jan. 15, 1871; William Leonard b. March 24, 1854, m. Keturah Grover; Fidelia b. Oct. 21, 1856, m. Henry P. Jacobs Feb. 28, 1876; Abel Josiah b. Jan. 22, 1859, m. Persinda Winegar 1884; Harriet Rosella b. Jan. 22, 1861, m. A. D. Dickson June 26, 1879; George Martin b. Jan. 22, 1864, m. Catherine Smith Feb. 4, 1896; Sophia Lois b. Nov. 22, 1867, m. Robert Wills Dec. 21, 1887. Family home, Salt Lake City.
Indian war veteran. Presided over a branch of the Mormon church in New York state.

FOLEY, JAMES A. (son of Thomas Foley and Mary Jane Berner of Chicago, Ill.). Born Jan. 8, 1878, at Chicago, Ill. Came to Utah Aug. 28, 1902.
Married Rigmore M. Frisfeldt March 7, 1900, at Chicago, Ill. (daughter of Oscar Frisfeldt and Caroline Bouldau of Chicago, Ill.). She was born Sept. 22, 1880. Their children: Virginia; Patricia. Family home Salt Lake City, Utah.
Railroad commercial agent.

FOLKMAN, JEPPA G. (son of Jergen Christopher Folkman, born Sept. 10, 1792, Westmarie, Barnholm, Denmark, and Gertrude Kerstene Ipson, born March 19, 1790, Aokersogn, Denmark). Born Dec. 16, 1824, at Aokersogn, Denmark; came to Utah Oct. 5, 1854, H. P. Olsen company.

874 PIONEERS AND PROMINENT MEN OF UTAH

Married Anne Marie Petersen April 9, 1848 (daughter of Jens Petersen and Annie Catherine Knudsen). She was born Feb. 5, 1822. Came to Utah Oct. 5, 1854, H. P. Olsen company.
Married Catherine Kjerstne Lund Aug. 17, 1861, at Salt Lake City (daughter of Lars Peter and Wilhelmina Lund). She was born Oct. 6, 1826, at Copenhagen, Denmark. Their child: Lewis Peter b. Oct. 18, 1863.
Married Anne Serena Anderson at Salt Lake City (daughter of Gunder Anderson and Carry Anderson, pioneers Sept. 22, 1861, Wooley company). She was born Feb. 20, 1841. Their children: Jeppa George b. Feb. 29, 1864; Anne Maria b. Feb. 15, 1865; Ge Mary L b. May 13, 1867; Joseph Anton b. March 11, 1869. m. Marion Izatt 1896; Rachel Serena b. Aug. 20, 1871, m. N. D. Thatcher 1892; Gertrude Caressa b. Dec. 25, 1873, m. Willard Robbins 1892; George Benjamin b. May 1, 1876, m. Adeline Bevan 1902; William Tunder b. Jan. 1880; Matilda Caroline b. Sept. 16, 1881, m. John Gooch, Jr., 1902; Ezra Christopher b. March 11, 1884, m. Mable Call, 1908; Jessie Carloss b. March 22, 1887. Family home Thatcher, Idaho.
Married Olevia Nielson. Their child: Maggie Josephine b. Dec. 17, 1871, m. Chris O. Anderson 1891.
Missionary to Norway; first bishop of Soda Springs, where he aided in building up the country in 1873; moved to Gentile Valley 1876; member of high council of Oneida stake. Assisted in bringing immigrants to Utah.

FOLKMAN, JOSEPH ANTON (son of Jeppa G. Folkman and Anna Serena Anderson). Born March 16, 1869 at Plain City, Utah.
Married Marion Izatt Nov. 27, 1895, at Logan, Utah (daughter of David Izatt and Isabel McNeil). She was born July 15, 1870, at Logan. Their children: Joseph Tharen b. Oct. 15, 1896; Isobel Marion b. July 30, 1898; George Christopher b. Feb. 9, 1901; David Izatt b. Dec. 2, 1903; Basil b. July 14, 1906; Serena b. June, 1909.

FOLLETTE, WILLIAM TILLMON (son of Catharine Van Dyke of New York). Born March 26, 1819, New York. Came to Utah June 5, 1848, with contingent of Co. D, Mormon Battalion.
Married Esther Bayliss at Salt Lake City (daughter of Thomas Bayliss and Anne Savage of Horley, Oxfordshire, Eng.). She was born Feb. 4, 1828, Mollington, Oxfordshire, Eng., and came to Utah 1853, Claudius Spencer company. Their children: Esther Ann b. Oct. 4, 1856, m. Andrew Larsen; William T. Bayliss b. July 14, 1857, m. Annie Nielson; Mary Catharine b. June 2, 1862, m. William Clark; John Savage b. April 30, 1866; Emma Mathilda b. March 12, 1870, m. Charles Swindle. Family resided Mill Creek, Springville, Spanish Fork, Washington and Manti, Utah.
Early settler to Utah county; settled at Washington (in "Dixie"), 1861. Indian war veteran. Farmer and stockraiser. Died Jan. 21, 1887, Orangeville, Utah.

FOLLICK, GEORGE ALEXANDER (son of Mathias Follick and Rachel McLaughlin of Canboro, Canada). Born Oct. 12, 1831, Canboro, Canada. Came to Utah June, 1868, Capt. Taylor company.
Married Nancy Parker April 15, 1857, Canboro, Canada (daughter of Abel Parker and Isabel Marshall of Youngstown, N. Y.—pioneers June, 1863), who was born Sept. 8, 1838. Their children: Isabel, m. F. M. Dayton; David. m. Marian Bridges; Mattie, died in childhood; Claude, m. Mary Blaser; James and George, d. children: Mary Jane, m. William F. Dayton; Margaret Ann, m. Roy George; Abel Mathias, d. child; Martha, m. John R. George.
Blacksmith, carpenter and miner. Died Feb. 25, 1911, Montpelier, Idaho.

FOLLICK, DAVID (son of George Alexander Follick and Nancy Parker). Born Dec. 30, 1860, Egypt, Fremont Co., Iowa. Came to Utah August, 1867.
Married Marian Bridges Sept. 21, 1882, Salt Lake City (daughter of Charles Henry Bridges and Frances Elizabeth Pearson of Montpelier, Idaho—pioneers 1856 and 1860, Edward Ellsworth handcart company). She was born March 31, 1861, Salt Lake City. Their children: Sarah Elizabeth b. Oct. 12, 1883, m. John B. Hopkins; Marian Evaline, d. child; David Romaine b. Oct. 20, 1886, m. Mary Jane Randall; Charles Loraine b. Jan. 14, 1889; Minnie Ida b. May 11, 1892, m. Jesse Green; Mabel Ina b. May 11, 1892; Grace Irene; George Reuel; Sidney Bridges. Family resided Dingle and Montpelier, Idaho.
President 79th quorum seventies; missionary to southern states 1888-90; contractor, builder and lumberman.

FOLSOM, WILLIAM HARRISON (son of William Folsom. Born at Holliness, N. H., and Hannah Skinner, born at Lynn, Mass., of Grafton county, N. H., died at Buffalo, N. Y.). Born March 25, 1815, Portsmouth, N. H. Came to Utah Oct. 3, 1860, Joseph W. Young company.
Married Zerviah Eliza Clark Aug. 21, 1837, Pembroke, Mass. (daughter of Richard Clark and Susan Gillett. She was born Feb. 5, 1818, West Hartford, Conn. Came to Utah Oct. 3, 1860, died Aug. 16, 1863. Their children: Harriet Amelia b. Aug. 23, 1838, m. Brigham Young; Hyrum Pearse b. Sept. 1, 1841, m. Nancy Broadbent, m. Annie Eliza Lenzi; William B. b. Feb. 28, 1845, m. Sarah Eakle; Hinman D. b. Feb. 17, 1849, m. Barbara Romney, m. Gertrude Lingard; Frances Emily b. Sept. 20, 1853, m. George E. Wallace; Mary; Louisa F. b. Oct. 9, 1857, m. L. John Brown; Richard Clark b. July 22, 1862, died in infancy. Family home, Salt Lake City.
Married Elizabeth Gregory Dec. 25, 1863, Salt Lake City. She was born July 10, 1839. Their children: Henry G. m. Sarah Reid; Eliza; Ella; Elizabeth; William M.; Lucy d. child; Walter G.
Married Lavina Huff Oct. 13, 1865, Salt Lake City. She was born Nov. 22, 1845. Their children: Elsy, m. Jean Cox; Clara, d. child; Ruth. m. William Wantland; Olivia, m. Thomas Butler; Harrison, died; Martha, m. Albert Asper; Alice, m. Milton Miles; Eva; Edgar, m. Grace Miller; Amy, Rachel.
Died March 20 1901, Salt Lake.

FOLSOM, HYRUM PEARSE (son of William Harrison Folsom and Zerviah Eliza Clark). Born Sept. 1, 1841, Buffalo, N. Y. Came to Utah with father.
Married Nancy Broadbent Dec. 29, 1866, Salt Lake City (daughter of William and Mary Broadbent of Alton, Ill.). She was born May 18, Ashton-under-Lyne, Eng., 1842. Their children: Grace Amelia b. Oct. 25, 1867, d. child; Hyrum Burdett b. Oct. 13, 1869, d. 1870; Hugh B. b. April 6, 1871, m. Josephine Whitaker; Guy b. Oct. 20, 1873, d. child; Aaron b. Nov. 13, 1874, d. child; Paul b. March 2, 1877, d. in 1890; Mark b. May 23, 1879, m. Amy Thomas; Ida b. Aug. 29, 1881, m. Lafayette Lemmon; Mary Ella b. June 21, 1884, m. Clarence Lemmon.
Married Annie Eliza Lenzi Jan. 4, 1879, Salt Lake City (daughter of Martin Lenzi and Mary Ann Lutz of Philadelphia. Came to Utah 1857, Jacob Hoehne company). She was born Dec. 15, 1855, Philadelphia, Pa. Their children: Roy L. b. Dec. 19, 1880, m. Annie Draper, m. Martha Shaffer; Martin Ross L. b. Jan. 7, 1883, d. in childhood; Clara L. b. Jan. 24, 1885, m. James Alfred Neilson; Cornelia L. b. Jan. 7, 1888, d. in childhood; Cacia L. b. Jan. 29, 1890, m. John Margetts; Ralph L. b. April 4, 1892; Dee L. b. Sept. 8, 1894; Annie Laura L. b. April 13, 1897.

FOOTE, THOMAS (son of John and Martha Foote of Wales). Born Dec. 21, 1819, at Frome, England. Came to Utah Sept. 2, 1858, Horton D. Haight company.
Married Mary 2, 1857, at Williamsburg, N. Y. (daughter of William Barrett and Susan James of Monmouthshire, South Wales, pioneers, July 4, 1875, independent company). She was born March 16, 1837. Their children: William Charles, m. Emma Twelves; Thomas John, m. Sarah Louisa Haws; George Edwin, m. Dora White; John Samuel, died; Eliza, m. Thomas Shipley; Martha, m. Thomas Lawrence Walter. Lived at Provo and Spanish Fork, Utah. Watchman at the Provo woolen mills several years; coal miner; farmer. Died Nov. 7, 1875.

FOOTE, THOMAS JOHN (son of Thomas Foote and Eliza Barrett). Born Nov. 4, 1860, at Spanish Fork, Utah.
Married Sarah Louisa Haws Nov. 12, 1884, at Logan, Utah (daughter of Amos Whitcomb Haws and Mary Elizabeth Bean, of Provo City, Utah). She was born April 20, 1866. Their children: Thomas Earl b. Nov. 5, 1885; Ina Louisa b. Aug. 1, 1887, m. Thomas Joseph Lewis; Amos Eldred b. Dec. 19, 1892; Valeria b. May 10, 1891. Family home Pleasant View Ward, Provo, Utah.
High priest; Sunday school superintendent. Spinner Provo woolen mills; farmer and stockraiser.

FORBES, JOSEPH BARROW (son of Joseph Forbes and Sarah Ann Gillpatrick of Massachusetts). Born Jan. 29, 1847, Bangor, Maine. Came to Utah Aug. 1, 1865, Capt. Getchel company.
Married Nancy Cooper Jan. 1, 1866, American Fork, Utah (daughter of Isaac Cooper and Nancy Lance of American Fork). She was born Sept. 15, 1852. Their children: Amanda, m. Willard Done; Elizabeth, m. William Bust; Alice, m. Byron Crosby; Joseph Arthur m. Esther Hamlett; Emma; Catherine, m. Henry Foster; Isaac Roby, died; Olive E. m. Eli Bacley; Ellen Drew, m. C. L. Joy; Elbert Frederick, died; Charles Willard, m. Miss Green; Ruby.
Married Mary Jane Gardner April, 1886, at Salt Lake City (daughter of James Gardner and Jane Threlfall of American Fork—pioneers 1863). She was born June 15, 1854. Their children: Mabel, died; Zina Josephine, m. Thomas Purdy; Ida Anna, m. Heber J. Gledhill; James Gardner, died; Thomas Stanley, died; Ethel, died; William Gardner; Lenore Jennie, died; Kattie Marie, died.
High priest; Sunday school superintendent and teacher; president 1st Y. M. M. I. A. in American Fork; member choir of American Fork. Civil war veteran. School teacher and trustee; city councilman and recorder at American Fork; secretary school board.

FORD, ALFRED CHARLES (son of Charles and Hannah Ford of Tipton, Staffordshire, Eng.). Born Sept. 28, 1833, at Tipton. Came to Utah in 1847.
Married Matilda Rasmussen Dec. 26, 1864, at Salt Lake City (daughter of Rasmus Rasmussen and Johannah Holenberg of Trillaboro, Sweden: pioneers 1861). She was born Nov. 15, 1838. Their children: Hannah Matilda, m. Charles C. Ensign, Nov. 4, 1880; Isabel Caroline, m. Richard E. Ber-

rett, Dec. 22, 1887; Alfred R., m. Louise Toone; Alfreda, m. John M. Worthen May 18, 1894; Almeda, m. Thomas Carn; Charles Edwin, m. Susan Warren, Nov. 15, 1897. Family home Washington, Washington Co., Utah.
With exploring party to Green River; drove first mule team to California, during gold excitement. Rock and brick mason. Died Dec. 8, 1882 at Kanab, Utah.

FORD, ALFRED R. (son of Alfred Charles Ford and Matilda Rasmussen). Born Jan. 20, 1870, at Washington, Utah.
Married Louise Toone Dec. 16, 1896, at Salt Lake City (daughter of Edward Toone and Caroline Jackson of South Wales). Came to Utah Nov. 7, 1877, from Liverpool, Eng., with William Paxman company. She was born Sept. 25, 1872. No children.
Ordained an elder Dec. 13, 1896. Carpenter; builder; farmer and fruitgrower.

FORDHAM, ELIJAH (son of George and Mary Fordham of New York). Born March 8, 1798, New York City. Came to Utah November, 1850, Edward Hunter company.
Married Miss Fisher. Their children: Anne Eliza, died; George.
Married Miss Fisher. Their children: Bathiah, m. Lyman Wells; Mormon, died.
Married Anna Bibbins Chaffee (daughter of Amos Chaffee and Harmony Crary, who were married Oct. 1, 1797, at Ashford, Conn., the former d. Feb. 20, 1849, the latter Aug. 3, 1843, at Ashford, Conn.). She was born March 24, 1811 at Ashford Conn. Their children: Lidda Lovina d. infant; Amos Pierre, m. Elizabeth Hughes; Anna Maria, m. John Pepper March 7, 1863; Joseph, m. Mary Blake; Mary Louisa, d. infant; Emily Adelia, m. Jerrod Jericks. Family home, Salt Lake City.
Married Amelia Spencer at Salt Lake City.
Married Jane ———. Their only child was Elijah.
Married Elizabeth Hughes. Their child, Elizabeth, died in infancy.
Assisted in building the temples at Kirtland and Nauvoo. Member Nauvoo Legion.

FOREMAN, THOMAS CEPHAS. Born Feb. 20, 1824, Cartwright county, N. C. Came to Utah 1862.
Married Eliza Frances Biggs Aug. 17, 1843, North Carolina. She was born July 1827, Craven county, N. C. Their children: Thomas J., m. Roseane Day; Nephi, m. Mary Powell; Nancy, m. George Hicks; Charity, m. Richard A. Lowe; Joseph Hyrum, m. Rhoda Ann Baldwin. Family home Monroe, Utah.
High priest. Called to help settle the "Muddy." Early settler to Sevier county and also to St. George. Sailor and ship-calker; painter. Died Sept. 25, 1889.

FORRER, FRED. Came to Utah in September 1864.
Married Caroline ———. The only child was John Frederick, who married Rosetta Michel.

FORRER, JOHN FREDERICK (son of Fred Forrer). Born March 10, 1867, Camp Floyd, Utah.
Married Rosetta Michel Nov. 16, 1891, Heber, Utah (daughter of Samuel Michel and Elizabeth Thomas of Switzerland). She was born July 25, 1870. Their children: John Frederick b. July 22, 1892; Henry Hilman b. Dec. 14, 1894; Karl William b. June 19, 1899; Lida Hildtrude b. Feb. 17, 1901; Cuba Avilda b. Dec. 16, 1905. Family home Midway, Utah. Elder. Farmer and stockman.

FORSGREN, JOHN ERIK (son of John Oluff Forsgren, born Oct. 17, 1793, and Anna Christina Hollstrand, born Nov. 24, 1786). He was born Nov. 7, 1816, Gefle, Sweden. Came to Utah Oct. 16, 1847, with a part of Co. D, Mormon battalion.
Married Sarah Bell Davis (daughter of William Davis and Sarah McKee), who was born April 15, 1829. Their children: Charles William, m. Esther Smith; Sarah Alice, m. Hyrum Smith; John Heber b. Oct. 7, 1856, m. Ann Jane Evans Aug. 12, 1880, m. Cynthia Marie Thorn Dec. 16, 1885, m. Lydia Ann Walker July 1, 1903. Family resided Salt Lake City and Brigham City, Utah.
Member Mormon battalion. First L. D. S. missionary to Sweden 1849-53. Died Jan. 22, 1890.

FORSGREN, JOHN HEBER (son of John Erik Forsgren and Sarah Bell Davis). Born Oct. 7, 1856, Carson, Nev.
Married Ann Jane Evans Aug. 12, 1880, Salt Lake City (daughter of John Evans and Elizbaeth Davis), who was born Dec. 6, 1859, Geneva, Monroe county, Neb. Only child: Sarah Cleofa b. May 11, 1881, m. Victor E. Madson. Family home Brigham City, Utah.
Married Cynthia Marie Thorn Dec. 16, 1885, Logan, Utah (daughter of Richard Thorn and Rebecca Ann Osborn), who was born Sept. 4, 1864, Perry, Utah. Their children: John Claudius b. Nov. 19, 1886, d. May 3, 1888; Annie b. Aug. 15, 1888, d. Aug. 31, 1892; Ethleen b. Aug. 5, 1893; Eugene Richard b. Aug. 10, 1895; Virginia b. May 20, 1897; Charles Richard b. Aug. 23, 1899. Family home, Brigham City.
Married Lydia Ann Walker July 1, 1903, Salt Lake City (daughter of Dan Wray Walker and Barbara Ann Thorn), who was born Aug. 27, 1872, Perry, Utah. Their children: Afton b. April 8, 1904; Donald Walker b. June 28, 1906; Barbara b. March 26, 1908; Waldo Walker b. May 20, 1912. Family home Elwood, Utah.

Secretary and president Y. M. M. I. A. of Brigham 3d ward; member stake board M. I. A. Box Elder stake; assistant and superintendent Brigham 3d ward Sunday school; member 58th and 133d quorums seventies; superintendent religion classes of Bear River stake; missionary to Sweden 1890-92; now a high priest. Member Brigham city council one term.

FORSSELL, OLAF ALFRED T. Born Sept. 24, 1844, Sala, Westmanland, Sweden. Came to Utah 1856.
Married Eva Neilson Anderson in September 1869, Salt Lake City (daughter of Neils Anderson and Disa Orra of Vern Land, Sweden, who came to Utah August 1869, Olsie Olson company). She was born Nov. 27, 1835. Their children: Alfred T., m. Anna Hedberg; John W., m. May Felder. Family home 20th ward, Salt Lake City.
Missionary to Finland 1877-79. Block teacher. Teamster.

FORSSELL, ALFRED THEODORE (son of Olaf Alfred T. Forssell and Eva Neilson Anderson). Born July 18, 1870, Salt Lake City.
Married Anna Hedberg May 6, 1896, Salt Lake City (daughter of August L. Hedberg and Marie Catrina Swenson of Salt Lake City). Came to Utah July 23, 1875, John Anderson company. She was born Sept. 24, 1876. Their children: William R. b. Feb. 28, 1897; Stella C. b. June 21, 1899; Alfred L. b. Sept. 16, 1902. Family home 20th ward, Salt Lake City.
Block teacher. Mail clerk O. S. L. R. R. Co. 15 years.

FORSYTH, JOHN IRWIN (son of Andrew Forsyth and Sarah Irwin, of Carlisle, Eng.). Born July 27, 1816, at Carlisle, Eng. Came to Utah Sept. 12, 1861, Milo Andrus company.
Married Sarah F. Barker March 29, 1841, Carlisle (daughter of John Barker and Margaret Freeland, of Carlisle). She was born Oct. 14, 1815, Glasgow, Scotland. Their children: Jane B., m. James C. Snyder; Margaret B., died; Andrew Barker, m. Emily E. Moss; Sarah B., m. John B. Meldrum; Margaret R., m. Hyrum Yates; Mary E. B., m. William H. Harrison. Family resided Ogden, Salt Lake and E. T. City, Utah.
High priest. Put up machinery for woolen factory at Canyon Creek and managed same until he moved to Ogden 1867. Located at Provo 1888. Carder, spinner and farmer. Died Feb. 15, 1897, Provo, Utah.

FORSYTH, ANDREW BARKER (son of John Irwin Forsyth and Sarah Barker). Born Feb. 4, 1847, Port Richmond, Pa. Came to Utah with father.
Married Emily Elizabeth Moss June 24, 1872, at Salt Lake City (daughter of William Francis Moss and Eliza Crich, both of E. T. City, Utah, pioneers 1861, John H. Murdock company). She was born March 8, 1854. Their children: Mary E. b. April 11, 1873; Sarah E. b. Nov. 27, 1875, m. Chas. W. Penrod; Emily b. Aug. 19, 1878, m. Silas L. Allred; John A. b. March 2, 1881, m. Elsie Clyde; Jane M. b. Aug. 21, 1883, m. Colman Allred; Margaret Grace b. Feb. 9, 1886, m. John W. Madsen; Grover Cleveland b. Nov. 27, 1888, m. Emma Dahlquist; Claud D. b. Feb. 5, 1891, died: Barker M. b. Dec. 23, 1893, died; Stanley M. b. May 10, 1896. Family home Provo, Utah.
High priest; block teacher. Constable and road supervisor; school trustee; postmaster, Lake Point, Utah. Carder and farmer. Black Hawk war veteran.

FORSYTH, THOMAS R. (son of Thomas Forsyth, born 1782, Rexboro, Scotland, and Isabella Jackson of Kelso, Scotland). Born Sept. 10, 1813, Roxburghshire, Scotland. Came to Utah Oct. 1, 1850, Stephen Markham company.
Married Isabella Donald April 1839, who was born May 17, 1819, and came to Utah with husband. Their children: Thomas R. b. Sept. 10, 1840, m. Fredonia M. Goheen April 15, 1863; Jennett b. March 29, 1842, m. James A. Cunningham; George James b. May 23, 1844, m. Sarah Snow; Isabella Jane b. March 2, 1846, m. John Barnard; Marimma b. April 6, 1848, m. Charles Seegmiller; Neil Donald b. Aug. 4, 1849, m. Sophia Harrison; Saville Delina b. Sept. 28, 1851. Family resided Salt Lake City and Toquerville, Utah.
Married Mary Browett Aug. 20, 1853, Salt Lake City, who was born June 25, 1823, Leicester., Eng. Their children: George Joseph B. H. b. March 17, 1855, m. Mary Watts; Mary B. b. March 28, 1857, m. Brigham Jarvis Oct. 20, 1877; Christena b. Dec. 9, 1858, m. I. C. McFarlin; William H. b. Nov. 8, 1860; Agnes b. Oct. 10, 1863, m. J. F. Wolley; Eleanora b. Oct. 8, 1866, died; Benjamin H. b. Nov. 18, 1868, m. Barbara Lamb Dec. 30, 1890. Family home Toquerville, Utah.
Member Nauvoo Legion; crossed the plains with B. Y. express 1857; settled in Dixie 1861; moved to Pine Valley 1862, and to Ash Creek 1863; miller and lumberman; built a sawmill and a shingle mill at Ash Creek, then moved to Toquerville 1865.

FORSYTH, THOMAS R. (son of Thomas R. Forsyth and Isabella Donald). Born Sept. 10, 1840, Port Huron, Mich.
Married Fredonia M. Goheen April 15, 1863, Washington, Utah (daughter of Michel Roe Goheen and Dorinda M. Mondy —the latter came to Utah 1855, Preston Thomas company). She was born Sept. 10, 1845, Spring Creek, Harris Co., Texas. Their children: Thomas R. b. Feb. 7, 1864, m. Ann Coleman; George Michel b. Oct. 2, 1866, died; John W. b. March 25, 1869, m. Diantha Noyes Sept. 20, 1892; Charles D. b. Aug. 5, 1871, m. Sarah Symmons Dec. 29, 1892; William

R. b. Sept. 7, 1873, m. Isabelle Lund Sept. 10, 1895; Edward A. b. Dec. 1, 1875, died; James A. b. Dec. 1, 1877, m. Lorena Cook; Isabell D. b. Jan. 7, 1879, m. N. C. Hielerson; Mary A. b. April 5, 1881; Eliza O. b. April 22, 1883, m. Eric Torgerson June 13, 1906; Fredonia M. b. Feb. 5, 1885; Niel b. Nov. 11, 1887. Family resided Pine Valley and Thurber, Utah.
School trustee Pine Valley 1860-76. Assisted in bringing immigrants to Utah. Farmer.

FORSYTH, THOMAS R. JR. (son of Thomas R. Forsyth and Fredonia M. Goheen). Born Feb. 7, 1864.
Married Ann Coleman Oct. 6, 1886, Teasdale, Utah (daughter of George Coleman and Mary Talbet), who was born May 26, 1866, Smithfield, Utah. Their children: Thomas C. b. Aug. 24, 1887, died; George b. March 7, 1888; Robert J. b. Dec. 12, 1892; Alice T. b. Feb. 22, 1894; James, died; Annie E. b. Nov. 18, 1902; Chris b. March 17, 1904; Richard b. Feb. 10, 1907; Neil L. b. Oct. 24, 1908. Family resided Thurber and Grover, Utah, and Independence, Idaho.
Married Mira Christofferson 1890.
Married Ellen Norwood 1902 (daughter of Richard S. Norwood), who was born June 7, 1811, Green county, Tenn.
School trustee at Grover, Utah. First assistant Sunday school superintendent; bishop's counselor. Farmer.

FORSYTH, JOHN W. (son of Thomas R. Forsyth and Fredonia M. Goheen). Born Jan. 25, 1869, Pine Valley, Washington Co., Utah.
Married Diantha Noyes Sept. 20, 1892 (daughter of Fred F. Noyes, pioneer Sept. 25, 1865, Caldwell overland transportation company, and Meria Williams—who were married Jan. 22, 1869, Salt Lake City). She was born May 25, 1872, Glendale, Kane Co., Utah. Their children: Florence b. Dec. 30, 1893; John F. b. Oct. 8, 1895; Delores b. Oct. 2, 1897; Delta b. Feb. 24, 1900; Claude b. Aug. 18, 1901; Levurn b. Nov. 7, 1903; Floyd F. b. Dec. 25, 1905; Clell b. Sept. 27, 1908. Family home Teasdale, Utah.
Farmer.

FOSTER, GEORGE (son of George Foster and Mary Wallhene, both of Castlederg, Ireland). Born at Castlederg, Castledreg. Came to Utah 1852, Thomas Tidwell company.
Married Jane McCullough July 25, 1835 (daughter of Joseph McCullough and Mattie Hutchinson), who was born March 4, 1819. Their children: Sarah Jane b. July 31, 1836, m. Seth M. Blair; Mary Ellen b. Dec. 24, 1837, m. Benjamin Cluff; Margaret Ann b. Jan. 23, 1840, m. Harvey H. Cluff; Eliza Arnette b. 1842, m. Benjamin Cluff; Joseph b. Sept. 12, 1844, m. Clarise Emily Birdneau Oct. .867; Thomas James b. July 10, 1847, d. April 1858; Matilda Ruth b. Oct. 13, 1849, m. Lemuel Steel Oct. 1866; Jane b. March 4, 1853, m. Alfred Cluff.
Married Verena Fisher at Salt Lake City (daughter of Jacob Fisher and Annie Barbara Shufelbarger, the latter came to Utah 1855). She was born Aug. 15, 1829, Waningen, Switzerland. Their children: Berena b. March 31, 1861, m. Joseph S. Wright 1879; Barbara b. Oct. 11, 1859, d. infant; George Henry b. Feb. 17, 1863, d. infant; George F. b. April 17, 1864, m. Ruth Woodward May 5, 1892; Louisa b. March 19, 1866, m. William Neeley Dec. 24, 1887; Josephine b. May 20, 1868, m. Albert Beckstead Dec. 24, 1890.
Died June 1, 1888, Whitney, Idaho.

FOSTER, GEORGE (son of George Foster and Verena Fisher). Born April 17, 1864, Logan, Utah.
Married Ruth Woodward May 5, 1892, Logan, Utah (daughter of William Woodward and Rebecca Wright, the former came to Utah 1850, Robert Campbell company, the latter Sept. 15, 1868). She was born Sept. 25, 1874, Franklin, Idaho. Their children: Edna b. June 7, 1893; Winifred b. April 8, 1895; Georgia Ruth b. March 27, 1898; Gretchen b. May 25, 1901, d. March 12, 1905; George Woodward b. Aug. 18, 1904, d. Feb. 20, 1907; Lincoln Woodward b. Dec. 13, 1906; George Cecil b. Dec. 24, 1910. Family home Whitney, Idaho.
Missionary to England 1895-96. Member eighth session Idaho legislature 1905-06.

FOSTER, WILLIAM L. (son of William Foster). Born July 11, 1807, Lynn, Norfolk, Eng. Came to Utah in 1853.
Married Amelia Chaplin (daughter of William Chaplin), England. She came to Utah in 1853 with Joseph Young company. Their children: William H., m. Eunice Neslen; Sarah, m. Thomas Heath. The family home was Salt Lake City.
Weaver.

FOSTER, WILLIAM HENRY (son of William L. Foster and Amelia Chaplin of England). Born June 28, 1832, at Norwich, Eng. Came to Utah in 1852. Died Oct. 16, 1894, Salt Lake City.
Married Eunice Neslen Dec. 28, 1855, at Salt Lake City (daughter of Samuel Neslen and Eunice Francis, of Lowestoft. Suffolk. Eng.). She was born July 15, 1838. Their children: William Henry, died; Henry C., m. Lydia Ungar; Eunice Amelia, m. J. C. Lyon; Agnes Neslen, d. infant; William Neslen, m. Nellie West; Robert Francis, died; Alice N., m. Louis Duncan; Eleanor N., died; Franklin Pitt; Laura L.; Leo N., m. Ina Richie; Phoebe Neslen. Family home Salt Lake City.
Leading tenor singer tabernacle choir 45 years; leader of the old folks' choir from its beginning to the time of his death; choir leader of 7th ward. Wood turner and scroll sawyer.

FOULGER, JOHN (son of William Foulger and Sarah Larter of Harleston, Norfolk, Eng.). Born Aug. 14, 1820, Harleston. Came to Utah 1868, independent company.
Married Susannah Woolnough Jan. 1, 1846, St. Pancras church, London, Eng. (daughter of Mark and Elizabeth Woolnough of Harleston). She was born Nov. 23, 1819, and died Dec. 18, 1894. Their children: Wallace, m. Sarah E. Kay; Herbert J., m. Eliza Hagel; William T., m. Elizabeth Robinson; Frederick, m. Isabel F. Burton; Anna M., m. George H. Tribe; Arthur L., m. Nellie Lamph; Elizabeth H., m. George H. Tribe; Charles J., m. Libbie MacMaster. Family home 21st ward, Salt Lake City.
Tailor. Died June 23, 1889, Salt Lake City.

FOULGER, FREDERICK (son of John Foulger and Susannah Woolnough). Born Sept. 13, 1851, London, Eng. Came to Utah Sept. 26, 1866, John D. Holladay company.
Married Isabel Fielding Burton Dec. 21, 1874, Salt Lake City (daughter of William Walton Burton and Rachel Fielding of Ogden, pioneers Sept. 23, 1854, Capt. Jarvis company). She was born Dec. 26, 1856. Their children: Lottie B. b. Jan. 9, 1876, m. Burdette Smith; Frederick William b. Feb. 23, 1877, d. infant; Joseph B. b. May 16, 1878, m. Ethel Clark; Herbert B. b. May 29, 1879, m. Pearl Brown; Albert B. b. Sept. 26, 1883, m. Rae Thomas; David B. b. Dec. 6, 1881, m. Essie Evans; Heber C. b. Oct. 3, 1886; Franklin J. b. Oct. 8, 1888, m. Lucile Farr. Family home, Ogden.
Married Sarah Ellen Burton Feb. 26, 1886, Salt Lake City (daughter of William W. Burton and Rachel Fielding), who was born Dec. 14, 1866. Their children: Arthur B. b. Dec. 22, 1888; Ellen B. b. Nov. 21, 1890; Alvin B. b. Nov. 14, 1893; Delbert B. b. July 11, 1896; Thelma B. b. Feb. 10, 1902; Belva B. b. Feb. 13, 1904.
Senior president 77th quorum seventies 1883-1913; missionary to England 1899-1902. Contractor and builder; merchant.

FOULGER, HERBERT JOHN (son of John Foulger and Susannah Woolnough). Born Jan. 10, 1848, Islington, London. Came to Utah Oct. 3, 1863, Daniel D. McArthur company.
Married Eliza Mary Hazel April 24, 1871. Their children: Herbert J.; Ada E.; Isabelle L.; Nellie Pearl; Leslie H.; Vera K.
Carpenter and builder. Superintendent 20th ward Co-op. Bishop's counselor 21st ward. Wholesale grocer.

FOUTZ, JACOB (son of Conrad Foutz and Elizabeth Hinkle of Franklin, Pa.). Born Nov. 20, 1800, at Franklin. Came to Utah Oct. 1, 1847, Edward Hunter company.
Married Margaret Mann at Franklin. Pa. (daughter of David Mann of Franklin). She was born Dec. 11, 1801. Their children: Susan, m. James Brown; Polly; Nancy Ann, m. John Brown; Elizabeth, m. Hansen Walker; Sarah; Catherine, m. Samuel S. White; Alma; Joseph Lehi, m. Amanda Childs; Margaret, m. Hansen Walker; Hyrum; Jacob, m. Sarah Ann Thorne; Caroline Maranda, m. Thomas Bacon. Family home Pleasant Grove, Utah.
Bishop 8th ward Nauvoo, Ill.; bishop South fort, Salt Lake county. Brick-mason; farmer.

FOUTZ, JACOB, JR. (son of Jacob Foutz and Margaret Mann). Born Aug. 24, 1844, Nauvoo, Ill. Came to Utah with father.
Married Sarah Ann Thorne Jan. 7, 1866, Pleasant Grove Utah (daughter of David Thorne and Elizabeth Reeves of Nottig Hill, Eng., pioneers 1851). She was born Oct. 10, 1844. Their children: Jacob Fredrick b. Oct. 11, 1866, m. Olivia Warnick; Ida May b. May 17, 1868, m. John M. Smith; Joseph Earl b. June 22, 1871; Flora Elizabeth b. Dec. 11, 1873, m. James Waburton; David Hensen b. Oct. 7, 1876, m. Margaret Moffatt; Margaret Belle b. July 25, 1879, m. Charles Evans; George Thorne b. Sept. 18, 1881, m. Narcissus Edith Rogers; James Herbert b. Aug. 17, 1886, m. Rhoda Jacobson; Merle Reeves b. Feb. 17, 1889; Royal Lester b. Jan. 22, 1864, m. James C. Fitzgerald. Family home Pleasant Grove, Utah.
High priest; counselor to Alexander Bulloch, president of elders' quorum; ward teacher. City marshal of Pleasant Grove. Farmer and fruit grower.

FOUTZ, JOSEPH LEVI (son of Jacob Foutz and Margaret Mann). Born March 16, 1837, in Missouri. Came to Utah 1847.
Married Amanda Child Feb. 24, 1857, at Pleasant Grove, Utah (daughter of Ezbon Child, died in Ohio, and Mary Haskins of Athens Co., Ohio, came to Utah in October, 1851, John Brown company). She was born March 6, 1839. Their children: Joseph Lehi b. Dec. 29, 1857, m. Lorana Nelson; Jacob b. Feb. 14, 1860, d. infant; Caroline Amanda b. Jan. 10, 1861, m. James B. Morrison; Ezbon Alonzo b. May 6, 1863, m. Alice Packer; Jacob Haskin b. Dec. 29, 1865, d. infant; Mary Delilah b. Nov. 8, 1867, m. Andrew Anderson; Margaret b. July 31, 1869, m. Edmund Nelson; Catharine b. Nov. 1, 1872, m. John H. Van Pelt; John C. b. Aug. 22, 1877, d. infant. Family resided Pleasant Grove and Richfield, Utah, and Moweyaby, Ariz.
High priest. Indian war veteran. Pioneer. Farmer. Died March 22, 1909, at Fruitland, New Mexico.

FOWERS, JESSE (son of William Fowers and Ann Hardy of England). Born April 1819, Stenson, Derbyshire, Eng. Came to Utah Sept. 21, 1864, Joseph S. Hollins company.
Married Sarah Johnson November 1841 (daughter of John Johnson and Ann Ford), who was born Jan. 8, 1820; came to

Utah Sept. 21, 1864, Capt. Rollins company. Their children: John b. Sept. 27, 1842, m. Elizabeth Baird 1874; William b. March 1845, m. Hannah Dyson; Annie b. June 1848, m. James Byington Nov. 29, 1877; Joseph b. Sept. 28, 1850, m. Mary Ann Germes; George b. April 2, 1853, m. Laura Svenson July 28, 1874; Jesse b. June 20, 1855, m. Annie Byson; Franklin J. b. Nov. 5, 1857, m. Elizabeth Germes; Sarah b. 1860, m. James Simpson 1880; Charles A. b. Dec. 21, 1862, m. Mary Cox Nov. 10, 1885; Arthur D. b. April 27, 1867, m. Susie Cox Dec. 11, 1888.

FOWERS, JESSE, JR. (son of Jesse Fowers and Sarah Johnson). Born June 20, 1855, Derbyshire, Eng.
Married Annie Dyson July 28, 1874, Salt Lake City (daughter of John Dyson and Ann Crabtree, the latter came to Utah with A. Miner company). She was born June 6, 1856, Oldham, Eng. Their children: Jesse Dyson b. May 4, 1875, m. Emily M. Green Oct. 3, 1906; John Robert b. Dec. 3, 1877, m. Janie Douglass July 17, 1900; Sarah Ann b. May 7, 1880; David Arthur b. Oct. 23, 1882, m. Artie Douglass March 5, 1905; James Isaac b. Dec. 22, 1885, m. Martha Schult July 10, 1907; George Crabtree b. June 21, 1888, m. Annie Sumner July 29, 1908; Ida G. M. b. Nov. 19, 1890, m. Horace Clayton Sept. 29, 1910; Stanley; Cora May.

FOWERS, JESSE DYSON (son of Jesse Fowers Jr. and Annie Dyson). Born May 4, 1875, Hooper, Utah.
Married Emily M. Green April 22, 1871, at Salt Lake City (daughter of Ammon Green and Almira Mesick, the former came to Utah 1848). She was born Oct. 5, 1880, West Weber, Utah. Their children: Hazel Lenora b. Aug. 7, 1907; Cynthia Almira b. Dec. 6, 1908; Maurice Jesse b. July 29, 1910.

FOWLER, HENRY CHARLES (son of John Fowler of Yorkshire, Eng.). Born April 7, 1832, at Dover, Eng. Came to Utah in 1861.
Married Sarah Lee April 22, 1871, at Salt Lake City (daughter of George Lee and Sarah Peaker of Sheffield, Eng.). Came to Utah in 1859 with Edward Stephenson company. She was born Dec. 26, 1852. Their children: Lilly, b. Jan. 12, 1873, m. John J. McAfen; Jennie, b. Sept. 29, 1877, m. Charles William Earl: Henretta b. March 21, 1881, m. Harry Clay Allen; Sarah Elizabeth b. Dec. 31, 1879. d.; Pearl b. March 24, 1883, m. John Franklin Cuttler. The family home, Salt Lake City.
Missionary to England. Teacher. Bookkeeper. Died Feb. 29, 1884, at Salt Lake City.

FOWLKE, JOHN (son of John Fowlke and Anna May, both of Nottingham, Eng.). Born Dec. 26, 1803. Came to Utah Sept. 17, 1861, Horace S. Eldredge company.
Married Harriet Raynor about 1823 at Nottingham, Eng. (daughter of Mr. Raynor and Catherine Frost, of Nottingham, pioneers Sept. 17, 1861, Horace S. Eldredge company). Their children: Catherine Elizabeth b. Sept. 24, 1824, m. Thomas Windle; John b. April 20, 1826, m. Susannah Bonner; Harriet b. Sept. 20, 1828, died; Drucilla b. Dec. 22, 1830, William Aston; Eliza b. April 20, 1832, m. Elias Aston; Emma b. Aug. 4, 1836, died; William b. Nov. 11, 1837; Lueza b. May 26, 1840, m. William Marriott; Frederick b. July 21, 1842, m. Elizabeth Cook; Sarah Ann b. Feb. 15, 1845, m. John Truscott; Clara b. Dec. 28, 1847, m. James Cullimore. Family home Lindon, Utah.
High priest. Machinist and engineer; farmer. Died at Lindon.

FOXLEY, WILLIAM (son of James Foxley, born Dec. 25, 1807, and Elizabeth Mathews, born April 5, 1807, both of Bedfordshire, Eng.—who were married June 2, 1830). He was born April 6, 1831, Bedfordshire. Came to Utah 1855, Kaincaid company.
Married Ann Larkins 1852 (daughter of James Larkins, who died in Bedfordshire, and Martha Pack, who died 1851 at St. Louis, Mo.). She was born June 26, 1834; came to Utah with her husband. Family home Kaysville, Utah.
Married Alice Nicholls Sept. 25, 1889, Logan, Utah (daughter of Lemuel Nicholls and Emma Sarjent—who were married Dec. 31, 1861, Gravesend, County of Kent, Eng., they came to Utah 1885). She was born Nov. 30, 1870, Whitstable, County of Kent, Eng. Their children: William Lemuel b. June 29, 1890; Cora Ann b. Jan. 4, 1893; Emma Lydia b. Oct. 4, 1896; Mary Elizabeth b. Oct. 7, 1899; Leo Hebert b. Nov. 19, 1902. Family home Kaysville, Utah.
Black Hawk war veteran. One of the first men to make nails out of wagon tires in Utah. Died Jan. 17, 1906.

FOXLEY, WILLIAM LEMUEL (son of William Foxley and Alice Nicholls). Born June 29, 1890, Kaysville, Utah.

FOY, THOMAS B. (son of Frederick and Elizabeth Foy). Born Dec. 30, 1802, Lancaster county, Penn. Came to Utah 1850.
Married Catherine Fink, who was born 1807. Their children: Thomas; John M., m. Alice Jost; William, m. Lucinda Bingham; Elizabeth, m. John Durgman; Frederic L. b. Oct. 3, 1846, m. Rachel J. Slater; Susan, m. John Chidester; Sarah Jane, m. Thomas W. Jones; Emma, m. Newton Goodale; Catherine, m. Jaehue Blackburn; Mary, m. George Richard; Rhoda, m. Hyrum Jameson. Family home Washington, Utah.

High priest; missionary to Southern Utah 1863-74. He, with others, laid out the Harrisville Irrigation ditch. Farmer and stockraiser.
Died 1874 Washington, Utah.

FOY, FREDERIC L. (son of Thomas B. Foy and Catherine Fink). Born Oct. 3, 1846, Hancock county, Ill. Came to Utah with father.
Married Rachel J. Slater Dec. 25, 1863, at Slaterville, Utah (daughter of Richard Slater and Ann Corbridge of Slaterville, Utah, pioneers 1852, Thomas Howell company). She was born Jan. 8, 1847. Their children: Frederick R. b. Feb. 28, 1865; Delila b. Aug. 17, 1871; Ida b. May 17, 1877; Rachel b. July 15, 1880; Ora b. July 3, 1886. Family home Slaterville, Utah.
County selectman 1890; school trustee at Slaterville. Pioneer irrigator.

FRANDSEN, GEORGE (son of Frand Jorgensen and Maria Rasmussen of Longland, Denmark). Born May 31, 1834, Longland, Denmark. Came to Utah 1856, Canute Peterson company.
Married Karen Nielsen 1856, at Salt Lake City (daughter of Niels Christian Nielsen and Mary Larsen of Youland, Denmark, pioneers 1856, Canute Peterson company). She was born Sept. 19, 1838. Their children: Peter b. Oct. 15, 1858, m. Tena Otterson; Joseph b. May 19, 1860, m. Zina Madsen; George G. b. Nov. 25, 1861, m. Helga Sophia Rolfsen; Hyrum b. Feb. 28, 1863, m. Maria Jensen; Heber b. Feb. 11, 1865, m. Chasta Seely; Rasmus b. Jan. 10, 1867, m. Lillie Bryner; Lena b. Jan. 10, 1867, d.; Lars b. Aug. 16, 1870, m. Susan Cazar Stuart; Annie b. April 14, 1872, m. John Herbert Horr. Family resided Mt. Pleasant and Price, Utah.
Married Ingerbor Sinagaard. Their children: Ingerbor; Christian, died; Maria; Orson. Family home Mt. Pleasant, Utah.
Missionary to Denmark 1879-81; first bishop of Price, Utah, 1882-96. Together with the stake presidency located and surveyed the present town of Price. Gave the church land for meeting house, tabernacle, tithing office, public school and city hall at Price. Minuteman under C. C. Anderson at Mt. Pleasant in Black Hawk war. He moved from Mt. Pleasant to Price in 1859. Died May 21, 1898, Price, Utah.

FRANDSEN, GEORGE G. (son of George Frandsen and Karen Nielsen). Born Nov. 25, 1861, at Mt. Pleasant, Utah.
Married Helga Sophia Rolfsen March 30, 1886, at Mt. Pleasant, Utah (daughter of Jacob Rolfsen and Margaret Kjelson of Resor, Norway, pioneers 1861, Samuel A. Wooley company). She was born July 1, 1863. Their children: Hazel b. Jan. 31, 1887, m. John Reese Llewellyn; George Ray b. Nov. 21, 1888, died; Leo b. March 30, 1895; Lucile b. March 30, 1897; Rulen Rolfsen b. Aug. 19, 1899; Stella Margaret b. Dec. 2, 1902. Family home Price, Utah.
High priest; missionary to northern states 1906-08; member high council; ward teacher; assistant Sunday school superintendent. School trustee; county commissioner. Settled at Price 1896. Secretary, treasurer and director in Allred Canal company.

FRANDSEN, RASMUS (son of George Frandsen and Karen Nielsen). Born Jan. 10, 1868, Mt. Pleasant, Utah.
Married Lilly Agnes Bryner Jan. 2, 1900, at Price, Utah (daughter of Hans Ulrich Bryner and Margaret Kahun of Price, the former came to Utah Dec. 21, 1856, handcart company, the latter in 1863, with oxteam). She was born Oct. 13, 1879. Their children: Mona b. Dec. 24, 1900, d. April 12, 1902; Gertrude b. May 13, 1902; Waldo Rasmus b. March 21, 1904; Mildred b. Aug. 9, 1905; Lena b. Feb. 10, 1907; Ileen b. Nov. 28, 1910. Family home Price, Utah.
Elder. Settled at Price in 1887. Sheepraiser; farmer.

FRASER, ALEXANDER (son of Alexander Fraser of Inverness and Robena Strong of Rugland, Scotland). Born April 1, 1815, Glasgow, Scotland. Came to Utah Sept. 16, 1868, John Gillespie company.
Married Sarah Scott July 30, 1837 (daughter of George Scott and Jean Harvey), who was born in England and came to Utah with husband. Their children: Jane b. Dec. 6, 1838, m. James Dunn Sept. 9, 1877; Alexander b. Oct. 6, 1842, m. Robena Brown May 19, 1873; George b. Sept. 23, 1849, m. Ruth Hunt and Elizabeth Ramsay Feb. 15, 1875; Sarah b. July 13, 1852, m. James W. Elliott June 7, 1869; Emma b. Oct. 30, 1859, m. William Ogden Oct. 25, 1877.

FRAUGHTON, GEORGE (son of Augustus Fraughton and Margaret Corpron, of Nova Scotia, Canada). Born March 10, 1822, Champlain, Franklin county, N. Y. Came to Utah Aug. 3, 1854, James Ivie company.
Married Henrietta Case 1843 (daughter of Henry Case and Chloe Bancroft, of New York). She was born July 18, 1824, Enfield, Hartford county, Conn., died 1878. Their children: Edatha b. July 22, 1844, d. infant; Franklin Augustus b. Jan. 31, 1846, m. Juliett Mott; Flouretta Maranca b. Nov. 7, 1848, m. William Ryan; Henry Erastus b. Feb. 16, 1852, m. Christena Schage; George Homer b. Oct. 23, 1855, m. Eliza Peterson; Almyra Adelaide b. Feb. 3, 1859, m. Daniel Mitchell; Melissa O. b. Dec. 18, 1862, m. Oscar Eskelson. Family home Heber City, Utah.
Married Mary Jane Simpson December 1862, Salt Lake City (daughter of Thurston Simpson and Mary Sophia Bar-

leen), who was born June 22, 1840. Their children: Sarah Ellen, m. Frank Peters; Orson Alonzo; Julia Margaret, m. John Peterson; George Fredrick, d. May 26, 1879; William Alma; David Lorenzo; Joseph Hyrum; Martha Griselda, m. Rex Glynes. Family home Vernal, Utah.
Seventy and high priest. Assisted in bringing immigrants to Utah. Black Hawk war veteran. Died Aug. 9, 1905, Vernal, Utah.

FRAUGHTON, FRANKLIN AUGUSTUS (son of George Fraughton and Henrietta Case). Born Jan. 31, 1846, Westfield, Chautauqua county, N. Y. Came to Utah Aug. 3, 1854, with parents.
Married Juliett Mott Aug. 12, 1867, Salt Lake City (daughter of Daniel Richmond Mott and Elizabeth Graham, of Decatur, Green county, Wis., pioneers 1854, independent company). She was born Feb. 12, 1852, Decatur, Green county, Wis. Their foster children: Heber J. b. Dec. 3, 1876, m. Daisy Clark; Samuel; Francis b. March 1, 1879; Prudence Juliett b. Nov. 28, 1881, m. James McAffee; Daniel Alvie b. Oct. 23, 1883, m. Lucy Duncan; Purcies Elizabeth b. June 8, 1886, m. John Franklin Mecham; Mary Jane b. Sept. 3, 1888, d. infant; Jesse Monroe b. July 23, 1891; Thomas Arthur b. July 29, 1893, d. Nov. 6, 1906; Ruth Leone b. Jan. 3, 1896, m. William W. Merchant. Family resided Heber City and Wallsburg, Utah.
President 76th quorum seventies. Missionary to southern states 1885-87 and to northern states 1907-09; first counselor to Bishop Fullmer 1911; bishop of Wallsburg 1887-1903. Assisted in bringing immigrants to Utah 1866; scout in Black Hawk war. Wasatch county commissioner two terms. Lumberman, farmer and stockraiser.

FRECKLETON, JOHN ORR (son of William Freckleton, born 1799, Armagh, Ireland, and Jane Orr, born 1794, Tallanamalogue, Ireland, who were married 1818). Born March 3, 1835, Keady, Ireland. Came to Utah Oct. 5, 1862, A. P. Harmon company.
Married Jessie Gardner July 5, 1860 (daughter of Matthew A. Gardner and Elizabeth Leggett, married June 24, 1838, Airdrie, Scotland, the former came to Utah November, 1864, Joseph Sharp company, the latter October 1864, Homer Duncan company). She was born Feb. 22, 1840; came to Utah with husband. Their children: John b. May 12, 1861, d. infant; John Matthew b. Nov. 27, 1863, d. Sept. 3, 1882; Jessie Lina b. Sept. 22, 1865, m. William J. Harris Dec. 28, 1882; Samuel Hyrum b. March 23, 1867, m. Mamie Edwards Nov. 14, 1891; Wilford Woodruff, b. Feb. 2, 1869, m. Emma Kropf June 1, 1895; William Patterson b. Oct. 28, 1870, m. Louisa Frisby Aug. 14, 1893; Charles Lee b. June 7, 1872, m. Chloa Mickswell July 2, 1897; Elizabeth Jane b. Dec. 15, 1873, m. Hans J. Hassell June 11, 1895; Joseph Smith b. June 12, 1876, d. child; Josephine b. Sept. 27, 1877, m. Robert H. Towers May 25, 1901; Joanna G. b. Jan. 3, 1881, m. Albert Brass Jan. 15, 1903; Jennie Orr b. April 19, 1883, d. child. Family resided Salt Lake City, Goshen, Deseret, Homansville, Tintic and Eureka, Utah.
Missionary to Fifeshire, Scotland, 1887; Ireland 1900-02; superintendent Eureka Sunday school 1890-99; bishop's counselor 1893-1900. Quarried rock for Salt Lake temple 1862; worked on U. P. railroad 1868-69. Justice of the peace 1897-1900, 1909-11; member Eureka school board 1895-97. Indian war veteran.

FREDERICKSON, FERDINAND (son of Henry Frederick of Schleswig-Holstein, born in 1803, killed in 1837, and Stene Katrine Christensen of Tolne, Hjorring amt. Denmark). Born March 3, 1809, at Tolne, Hjorring amt. Came to Utah 1864 with Capt. Spencer company.
Married Nelsine Marie Larsen Miller Dec. 26, 1855 (daughter of L C Jensen Miller and Elsie Marie Petersen, both of whom died in Denmark). She was born Sept. 25, 1834, came to Utah with Monor G. Atwood company. Their children: Lars Frederickson b. Aug. 30, 1857, m. Stene Jensen March 1876; Marcus Frederickson b. Feb. 20, 1860, m. Elizabeth Hoopes. Family home western Idaho.

FREDRICKSON. LARS (son of Ferdinand Fredrickson and Nelsine Marie Larsen Miller). Born March 30, 1857, Hjorring, Denmark.
Married Stene Jensen, born Oct. 2, 1853, at Hjorring, Denmark. Their children: Fred. b. Dec. 3, 1876, m. Elizabeth Christensen Sept. 1903; Edwin b. May 21, 1879, m. Caroline Erikson; Almira b. Dec. 23, 1883, m. Carl Nelson April 17, 1899; Clara b. Sept. 5, 1884; Zelinda b. Dec. 20, 1886; Fernando b. Oct. 31, 1889; Chester b. Nov. 11, 1891; Eugene b. June 26, 1893.
Missionary to Denmark Nov. 20, 1908; labored in the Aalborg conference; returned July 4, 1910.

FREE, ABSALOM P. (son of Andrew Free and Mary Pennington of Burke Co., North Carolina). Born March 22, 1798, in Burke county. Came to Utah 1848, Captain Allen company.
Married Martha Belcher 1818, St. Clair county, Ill., who born 1802. Their children: Andrew Belcher; Minerva and Miranda b. May 22, ——, d. infants.
Married Betsy Strait 1823, St. Clair county, Ill. (daughter of Israel Strait and Mary Thompson of St. Clair county, Ill.). She was born Jan. 31, 1804. Their children: Louisa b. Aug. 6, 1824, m. John D. Lee, m. Daniel H. Wells; Emeline b. April 28, 1826, m. Brigham Young; Wesley b. Aug. 7, 1827, d. infant; Hannah b. June 9, 1829, m. Mr. Hodgkiss, m. Daniel H. Wells; Preston b. March 13, 1831, m. Mary Titcomb, m. Ruth Titcomb; Mary A. b. Sept. 25, 1833, d. aged 12; Telitha b. Oct. 5, 1835, m. Alma Smith; Findlay C. b. July 7, 1838, m. Julia Young; Sarah Alvira b. Aug. 30, 1840, m. Charles Kimball; William O. b. Nov. 18, 1842, m. Josephine Young. Family home, Salt Lake City.
Married Annie Hicks March 5, 1856, Salt Lake City (daughter of Daniel Hicks and Hannah Weniock of Barking, Essex, Eng.). She was born Jan. 8, 1837. Their children: Eleanor H. b. March 7, 1858, m. Brigham Jones; Lois b. July 9, 1860, m. Jacob N. Rock; Absalom P. b. May 10, 1862, m. Carrie Sorenson; Frances Wells b. Sept. 3, 1864, m. Henry Quayle; Joseph S. b. Oct. 17, 1868, m. Zina Peterson; Annie (Irene) b. Dec. 8, 1870, m. Robert Morris, m. Lorenzo D. Young; Wenlock A. b. Dec. 11, 1873, m. Rachel Wheeler. Family home Farmers Ward, Salt Lake City.
High priest and patriarch; home missionary. Farmer and stockraiser. Died July 23, 1882, Salt Lake City.

FREE, JOSEPH S. (son of Absalom P. Free and Annie Hicks). Born Oct. 17, 1868, Salt Lake City.
Married Zina Peterson Jan. 10, 1895, Salt Lake City (daughter of August (Jorgensen) Peterson and Margaret Peterson of Randers, Denmark, latter came to Utah 1884). She was born Dec. 17, 1875. Only child: Afton L. b. Aug. 20, 1896. Family home, Salt Lake City.
Deacon. Mining engineer.

FREEMAN, ELIJAH NORMAN (son of Elijah Norman Freeman, born April 17, 1822, in Vermont, died Nov. 28, 1846, in New Mexico en route to Utah; and Mary Bingham, born April 1, 1820, in Vermont). He was born May 20, 1845, La-Harpe, Hancock Co., Ill. Came to Utah Sept. 19, 1847, Daniel Spencer company.
Married Annie Maria Poulson March 11, 1872. She was born April 22, 1846. Their children: Annie Maria b. Dec. 11, 1872, m. W. I. Mallory Feb. 15, 1891. Family home Ogden, Utah.
Married Mary Ellen Farley April 24, 1876, Salt Lake City (daughter of Winthrup Farley and Mary Ellen Redd), who was born Jan. 5, 1855, Ogden, Utah. Their children: Mary Isidore b. May 1, 1877; Elijah Norman b. May 10, 1879, m. Mary Taylor Dec. 15, 1906; Zanie Ada b. Nov. 1, 1880, m. George Jesse Ruder Jan. 24, 1907; Olive Amelia b. March 14, 1882; Oscar Farley, b. Jan. 20, 1885, m. Lillian Nielson Jan. 18, 1909; Lorin Farr b. Jan. 1, 1887, m. Emma Crofts Jan. 25, 1909; Erastus Bingham b. Dec. 3, 1888; Deatric b. Feb. 18, 1891; Asa Farley b. May 28, 1893. Family resided Ogden, Utah, and St. Johns, Ariz.
Member 60th quorum seventies: high priest; high councilman in Winter stake: president Y. M. M. I. A.; missionary to England 1873-75; called to St. Johns, Ariz., 1881, where he served as counselor to Bishop D. K. Udall 1881-87; first counselor in St. Johns stake 1887-1905; moved to Basalt, Idaho, where he served as alternate high counselor in Blackfoot stake. Director in St. Johns Co-op. 17 years and in St. Johns drug store 18 years. School trustee; member Basalt village board two terms.

FREEMAN, JOHN (son of Arthur Freeman born 1772, and Nancy Ann Freeman born 1774). Came to Utah with John Freeman company. He was born Sept. 6, 1804, in Kentucky.
Married Nancy B. Smoot (daughter of Nancy Ann Smoot), who was born Feb. 24, 1807, in Kentucky. Their children: Adline C. b. Nov. 24, 1826, m. Charles Webb; Caroline b. Dec. 15, 1828, m. Charles Hall; Nancy A. b. Dec. 25, 1830, m. Edmund Wide; William H. b. Dec. 25, 1832, m. Angeline A. Stocking Nov. 10, 1854; Martisha b. Feb. 24, 1834, died; John W. b. April 15, 1836, m. Adline Collins; Columbus B. b. June 7, 1838, m. Lydia West; Margret H. b. Sept. 27, 1840, m. Joseph Damron; Levi b. Feb. 23, 1843, died; Jemima b. Feb. 23, 1843, m. Ruben Jolly; Rosaline B. b. July 15, 1845, died; Martha J. b. Feb. 27, 1848, m. Thomas Charles Worth. Deacon; teacher; elder.

FREEMAN, WILLIAM H. (son of John Freeman and Nancy B. Smoot). Born Dec. 25, 1832, at New Concord, Ky. Came to Utah October 1849, Enoch Reese company.
Married Angelina Stocking (daughter of John Stocking and Katherine Stocky), who was born 1833. Their children: Katherine E. b. Oct. 2, 1853, m. Thos. Butterfield; W. H. b. Feb. 4, 1858, m. Mary Ann Winters; John J. b. Feb. 2, 1860, m. Hetta Winters; Jurina b. Nov. 20, 1861, m. Emma J. Bodell; Levi b. March 28, 1864; Lida E. b. Feb. 1, 1866, m. Mabel Sorensen; Angeline B. b. Dec. 19, 1867, m. William B. Thomas; Margrate L. b. Feb. 23, 1872, m. Robert Swan; Orin R. b. April 9, 1874, m. Mary J. D. Butterfield; Melvina b. March 10, 1877; Albert Orin b. Jan. 2, 1879. Family home Fort Herrtman, Utah.
Married Sarah Butterfield 1867 at Salt Lake City (daughter of Thomas Butterfield and Mary Jane Parker), who was born 1849. Their children: Nancy Jane b. March 18, 1868, m. Thomas Nichols; Thos. b. Sept. 6, 1869, m. Ida Eastman; Ann Eliza b. Nov. 1, 1871, m. John Bodell; George W. b. Feb. 8, 1873; Adeline M. b. 1874; Orsen b. 1876, m. Sarah Seamore; Sarah E. b. April 5, 1878, m. Henry J. Tempest; Olive b. March 15, 1880, m. Alfred Holbrook; Arthur B. Sept. 24, 1882, m. Harriett Page; Joseph H. b. Aug. 1, 1885; Malinda M. b. March 21, 1889, m. James Henderson. Family home Fort Herrtman, Utah.

High priest; counselor to James Crane of Herriman branch; senior president of seventies; missionary to Southern Utah 1855. Participated in Echo Canyon trouble; member of Utah militia. Constable; deputy sheriff; justice of the peace.

FREEMAN, WILLIAM H. JR. (son of William H. Freeman and Angelina Stocking). Born Feb. 14, 1853, at Fort Herriman, Utah.
Married Mary Ann Winters at Salt Lake City, Utah (daughter of Oscar Winters and Mary Ann Sterns), who was born Jan. 3, 1862. Their children: William b. Aug. 22, 1881; Ivey L. b. Oct. 6, 1883, m. John W. Adams March 15, 1905; Junius O. b. Oct. 22, 1885, m. Myrtle Swensen Oct. 2, 1907; Albert O. b. Jan. 23, 1888; Ruby b. Nov. 7, 1890; Rintha b. Nov. 7, 1890; Laura b. Feb. 3, 1892; Archie L. b. Dec. 12, 1894; Marion G. b. Oct. 13, 1900; Mary B. b. June 26, 1902; Willie B. b. Sept. 18, 1903; Phoebe B. b. June 21, 1906; Clide B. b. July 12, 1907; Marinda b. Aug. 11, 1909. Family home, Salt Lake City.
President Y. M. M. I. A.; Sunday school teacher and superintendent; missionary two years. School teacher.

FREER, JOSEPH SLACK (son of William Freer, born March 19, 1838, Alfreton, Derbyshire, Eng., and Martha Slack, born March 21, 1832). Born Sept. 22, 1863, Leicestershire, Eng. Came to Utah Oct. 21, 1873.
Married Nancy P. Whitesides Dec. 16, 1885, Kaysville, Utah (daughter of Lewis Whitesides and Susan Perkins, pioneers 1852, John Walker company). She was born March 23, 1869, Kaysville. Their children: Lewis William b. July 30, 1886, m. Rhoda Alice Thompson June 27, 1906; Martha D. b. Dec. 25, 1887; J. Vooris b. Dec. 18, 1887; Jessie P. b. July 5, 1893; Mary S. b. Oct. 6, 1895; Parley W. b. Oct. 26, 1897; Elizabeth N. b. July 6, 1899; Eliza Josephine b. Nov. 2, 1902; E. Mark b. Dec. 10, 1904; Reed P. b. March 27, 1907; Boyd S. b. March 27, 1907; Lillie M. b. Sept. 21, 1909. Family home Twin Groves, Idaho.
President deacons' quorum; first counselor to President R. G. Wall of 4th quorum of elders, and later president of that quorum in Davis stake; second counselor Y. M. M. I. A. 8 years; second counselor to Bishop J. J. Willard of Twin Groves, Fremont stake Jan. 27, 1901; set apart as bishop Twin Groves ward Jan. 11, 1909; teacher in parents' class.

FREESTONE, THOMAS (son of George Freestone, born Dec. 10, 1760, and Anna Youngman, born Nov. 27, 1763, of Flixton, Suffolk, Eng.). He was born May 16, 1798, at Flixton. Came to Utah Sept. 9, 1853, Daniel Miller company.
Married Ann Fall on Prince Edward island (daughter of James Fall and Elizabeth Rouston of Prince Edward Island). She was born Aug. 6, 1812. Their children: George b. Aug. 13, 1838, m. Alice Carlisle and Jennie Lind; James, m. Poline Poulson; Elizabeth, m. Langston and Lars Jenson; Rhoda, m. John Vance; Phoebe, d. infant; Johanna, m. George Bennett; Emma, m. Thomas Whitby; Jane, m. Dan Johnson. Family home Hardin Co., Ohio.
Gardener and dyke builder. Killed July 1858 by Indians while crossing trail near Parowan, Utah.

FREESTONE, GEORGE (son of Thomas Freestone and Ann Fall). Born Aug. 13, 1838, on Prince Edward Island, N. S. Came to Utah with father.
Married Alice Carlisle at Alpine, Utah (daughter of Richard Carlisle of Alpine, Utah, came to Utah with ox-team company). Their children: Alice, m. John Bowden; Mary, m. Harrison Maughn; Rhoda, m. Robert Reynolds; Drucilla, d. child. Family home Alpine, Utah.
Married Jennie Lind Aug. 12, 1872, at Salt Lake City (daughter of Anton Lind and Mary Ann Nelsen, both of Aalborg, Denmark, came to Utah October, 1868, Jesaie Smith company). She was born March 26, 1855. Their children: George Oscar b. June 15, 1873, m. Ella Holliday; Georgine Marie b. May 10, 1875, d. May 11, 1879; Roselle Caroline b. Sept. 10, 1877, m. Stephen Beck; James Anton b. April 3, 1880, m. Vilate Batty; Emma Sine b. Jan. 22, 1883, m. Warren Beers; Louis Alonzo b. Oct. 17, 1885, m. Elmaide Labeau; Reuben Thomas b. April 11, 1888, m. Dora Batty; Henry Lind b. Aug. 30, 1890; Charles Royal b. April 19, 1893; May Atton b. May 26, 1895; Clarence Fall b. Feb. 26, 1898. Family home Vernal, Utah.
Missionary to England 1894-96; high priest; bishop of Vernal. Captain of company in Black Hawk Indian war. Sunday school superintendent. Farmer and beekeeper.

FREW, JOHN (son of James Frew and Jeanette Frew of Ayrshire, Scotland). Born June 17, 1826, Ayrshire. Came to Utah October, 1856, Daniel McArthur company.
Married Jane Clotworthy May 1, 1846 (daughter of Whugh Clotworthy), who was born June 10, 1821, and came to Utah with husband. Their children: James b. May 20, 1847, m. Ellen Woodward June 4, 1877; Jeanette b. Jan. 31, 1849, m. George O. Pitkin; Mary b. Sept. 1854, m. Ephraim Elsworth; William M. b. June 10, 1856, m. Elizabeth Smith Dec. 23, 1878; Emily Jane b. Sept. 3, 1858, m. John W. Riley; George b. June 10, 1860, m. Mary Ann Smith Feb. 11, 1885; Hyrum b. June 10, 1860, m. Hannah Everett Sept. 3, 1883.
Married Eliza Duce in Hooper, Utah (daughter of Thomas Duce, pioneer 1856). She was born in England. Their children: Robert B. b. June 13, 1880; Ronald M. b. Feb. 9, 1882; Walter Scott b. Sept. 11, 1884.

FREW, JAMES (son of John Frew and Jane Clotworthy). Born May 30, 1847, Delroy, Ayrshire, Scotland.
Married Ellen Woodward June 4, 1877, Logan, Utah (daughter of William Woodward and Sarah Davis), who was born June 7, 1858, Pleasant Grove, Utah. Their children: B. Myrtle b. Feb. 25, 1879, m. William Coburn June 14, 1897; James Leo b. Feb. 23, 1881, m. Louise Coburn Aug. 1900; Zina J. b. Nov. 22, 1882, m. J. W. Maxey Nov. 29, 1904; Mabel b. April 5, 1884, m. D. P. Whittle Sept. 23, 1908; Oscar b. March 14, 1886; Clarence b. Nov. 2, 1887, m. Abbie Murdock Sept. 28, 1911; Russell b. July 12, 1888, m. Laura Walker Dec. 14, 1910; Stanley b. April 7, 1890; Carl b. May 25, 1892; Jeanette b. April 14, 1895; Gertrude b. March 9, 1896; Afton b. May 17, 1899; Blenda N. b. Aug. 6, 1901.

FRISBY, EPHRAIM (son of William Frisby of Yorkshire, Eng.). Born Jan. 30, 1848, Yorkshire, Eng. Came to Utah 1866, oxteam company.
Married Sarah Ann Lowe Nov. 9, 1868, Coalville, Utah (daughter of Richard Lowe and Elizabeth Harper of Yorkshire, Eng.; latter came to Utah by railroad). She was born Nov. 4, 1849. Their children: Ephraim William b. Aug. 17, 1869, m. Ella Yates; Louisa E. b. Jan. 10, 1871, m. William Freckleton; Anna May b. Jan. 30, 1873, m. Eugene Pulver; Rachel Emily b. May, 1875, died; Edward James b. May, 1877, died; John Eddie b. Sept. 4, 1879, m. Hattie Gardner; Sarah Ann b. Aug. 26, 1881, m. John William Hill; Mary Lilly b. June 26, 1883, m. Francis Peterson; Katie Esther b. June 21, 1885, m. Guy Towers; Joseph Hyrum b. March 4, 1887, m. Alta Chase; Teatce Pear b. Jan. 23, 1890, died; Myrtle Levean b. Jan. 28, 1893. Family home Payson, Utah.
Teacher; elder. Mining man. Died Sept. 12, 1908, Eureka, Utah. Buried at Payson, Utah.

FRISBY, WILLIAM (son of David and Jane Frisby of Wolverhampton, Eng.). Born May 2, 1809, at Wolverhampton. Came to Utah 1866.
Married Elizabeth Ruff 1832 Birmingham, Eng. (daughter of James and Betty Ruff), who was born Oct. 7, 1813. Their children: William; Jane; Elizabeth; David; Emma; Ephraim; Joseph H.; Lorenzo; Esther; Rachel; Ann.

FRISBY, JOSEPH H. (son of William Frisby and Elizabeth Ruff). Born May 15, 1854, at Birmingham. Came to Utah 1864, Warren Snow company.
Married Dicy A. Staley (daughter of Merrit Staley and Rebecca Farley), who was born Feb. 22, 1860, Ogden. Their children: Priscilla b. Aug. 3, 1877, m. O. O. Shill 1908; Joseph Merrit b. Feb. 2, 1879; Dicy Ann b. April 13, 1880, m. W. G. Ritchie 1908; William b. May 6, 1883, m. Cora Ward 1911; Minnie E. b. Dec. 13, 1884; Cora L. b. Jan. 4, 1888, m. Arnold Zimmerer 1908; H. LeRoy b. April 27, 1892; Karl b. Sept. 10, 1895.
Missionary to England 1899-1901. Settled in Arizona 1877. Justice of peace 1880; Navajo, Ariz., county recorder 1896; moved to Provo 1903, where he served as mayor 1905. General manager Frisby Mercantile Co. of Provo 1905-11.

FROERER (GFROERER), FREDERICK G. (parents lived in Württemberg, Germany). Born May 21, 1825, in Germany. Came to Utah 1849.
Married Elizabeth Sabin (daughter of David and Elizabeth Sabin of Lancaster, Pa., pioneers 1848). She was born Nov. 10, 1832. Their children: Helen, m. David Wilson; Mary Elizabeth, m. Thomas Bingham; Margaret Louisa, m. Thomas Bingham; Frederick, m. Elizabeth Moffatt; David, d. youth; Anna Maria, d. child; Lester Herrick, m. Maria ——; Richard Henry; Hyrum, d. child; George, m. Lena ——. Family home Ogden.
Elder; missionary to Germany 1874. Carpenter. Died April 23, 1900, at Ogden.

FROST, BURR. Born March 4, 1815, Westfield, Conn. Came to Utah July 22, 1847, Brigham Young company.
Married Mary E. Potter at Westfield (daughter of James Potter of Westfield). She was born 1814. Their children: Elizabeth, d. infant; Emeline, m. Charles Hammer; m. Mr. Woods; m. Louis Marks; m. George Russell; infant, m. Eliza E. Palmer; Catherine, d. infant; Burr, Jr., d. aged 25; Mary, m. Aphonzo M. Palmer; Sarah, m. Kulus Ensign; William, d. aged two; Henry, m. Saline Simpson; George, twin of Henry. Family home Salt Lake City.
Married Eliza Nash. Resided at Salt Lake City.
Married Caroline Triplett 1863, who was born 1843. Their children: Albert, m. Catherine J. Forsyth; Isaac, m. Emma C. Nielson; Samuel, m. Alice Naylor; Rosa, d. infant; Martha, m. Edward S. Murphy; Laura, m. Eugene Dickenson. Family home Salt Lake City.
Member 16th quorum seventies; missionary to Australia 1852-54; one of presidents 70th quorum seventies. Blacksmith. Died March 16, 1878.

FROST, JOHN FRANKLIN (son of Edward and Eliza Frost of England). Born Aug. 16, 1851.
Married Elizabeth Grace Mackintosh Nov. 24, 1873, at Salt Lake City (daughter of Daniel Mackintosh and Elizabeth Ingles Hogg, pioneers 1852). She was born Jan. 29, 1853, at Salt Lake City. Their children: Grace Ingals b. Sept. 24, 1874; Frank Edward b. April 23, 1876, d. child.

FROST, SAMUEL BUCHANNAN (son of McCaslin Frost and Penima Smith of Carolinas, Tennessee and Illinois and Fremont Co., Iowa). Born Jan. 2, 1810, in Knox county, Tenn. Came to Utah 1861, William K. McKessack company. Married Rebecca Forman in Illinois (daughter of John Forman and Hetta Horre of Carolinas). She came to Utah 1861 with husband. Their children: Mary, m. Jerome Adams; Sarah, m. Valentine Acord; Nancy, m. Abram Acord; William Anderson, died; Hetta, m. Stephen Allred; Samuel Buchannan, Jr., m. Mary Patty; James McCasslin, died; George Washington, died; John Wesley, died; Clay, died. Family resided Fremont Co., Iowa, and Spring City, Utah, after 1861.
Married Ester Davis 1863 at Salt Lake City (daughter of William and Keziah Davis of Gloucestershire, Eng., pioneers 1861, Joseph Horne company). She was born April 24, 1839. Their children: Stephen, m. Sena Jensen; Chauncey, m. Lorevia Warner; Adolph; Rebecca, m. Peter Nielsen; Margaret, m. Organe Warner; Iven; Marion.
Missionary to southern states; ward teacher. Judge. Farmer and blacksmith. Died June 27, 1888, Cyote, Utah.

FRY, RICHARD (son of William Fry, born April 14, 1793, at East Down, Devonshire, Eng., and Mary Ridges, born 1800, at Devonshire). Born April 15, 1831, at East Down. Came to Utah Sept. 3, 1860, J. D. Ross company.
Married Ann Rawle (daughter of John Rawle and Ann Blackmore). She was born Sept. 3, 1830; came to Utah with husband in 1860. Their children: Mary Ann b. Feb. 2, 1851, m. William J. Eddington Oct. 13, 1882; Susan b. April 12, 1862, m. Henry Tonks May 1, 1884; Richard Rawle b. Jan. 20, 1864, m. Emeline Eliza Toomer March 31, 1887; Agnes b. Nov. 7, 1865; Emily b. June 23, 1867, m. Robert H. Welch Nov. 29, 1888; William John b. March 18, 1869; John Rawle b. Aug. 22, 1870; David James b. Feb. 22, 1873, m. Mare Campbell; Henry B. b. Dec. 13, 1876, m. Mable L. Nelson Aug. 29, 1904. Family home Morgan, Utah.
Married Susan Lerwill April 12, 1876, at Salt Lake City (daughter of William Lerwill and Mary Rawle). She was born May 14, 1850, at East Down, Devonshire, Eng. Their children: Thomas William b. Nov. 13, 1877, m. Lillian N. Gorder Dec. 20, 1899; Alfred George b. Aug. 27, 1879; Flora Mary b. Oct. 13, 1882, m. George F. Robison Dec. 18, 1902; Charles Lerwill b. Nov. 25, 1884, m. Laura Geary Oct. 17, 1904; Winnie May b. Dec. 13, 1886, m. Ebenezer T. Crouch.
Early settler in Morgan county. Presiding elder of Morgan stake and later 1st counselor to President W. G. Smith of same stake; president of Morgan stake. Morgan county treasurer four years; city treasurer four years; mayor of Morgan City; city councilman two terms.

FRY, RICHARD RAWLE (son of Richard Fry and Ann Rawle). Born Jan. 20, 1864, at Morgan, Utah.
Married Emeline Eliza Toomer March 31, 1887, at Logan, Utah (daughter of James Toomer and Mary Jane Cook), who was born Sept. 10, 1866. Their children Richard Toomer b. Feb. 25, 1888; Ada Emily b. March 27, 1889; Maud Eveline b. Feb. 5, 1891; Lee Ralph b. May 25, 1893; Dora Blancy b. Sept. 5, 1895; Paul Joseph b. Dec. 29, 1896; William Lester b. March 20, 1899; Lucille Jane b. March 2, 1901; Emeline Violet b. April 25, 1903; Alberta Ann b. Nov. 17, 1905. Family home Morgan, Utah.
Missionary to Canada and England 1884-86; member South Morgan bishopric 1887-1910. Sheriff of Morgan county two terms; mayor of Morgan two terms; city councilman twice. Member third state legislature 1900 and 1901.

FRYER, ROBERT C. (son of William Fryer, who died in 1849 at St. Louis, Mo., en route to Utah, and Ann Corts, who died Aug. 13, 1867, at Salt Lake City). He was born Sept. 28, 1845, Lincolnshire, Eng. Came to Utah Sept. 21, 1854, with James Buckland, afterward of Bountiful, Davis Co., Utah, in Capt. James Brown company.
Married Bashua Dorcas Kingsbury Oct. 4, 1867, at Salt Lake City (daughter of Joseph Cordon Kingsbury and Dorcas Adelia Kingsbury, pioneers Sept. 29, 1847, George B. Wallace company). She was born Ncv. 19, 1847, Salt Lake City. Their children: Robert William b. Oct. 10, 1870, d. Sept. 9, 1904; Joseph Thomas b. Dec. 20, 1872, d. May 13, 1887; Franklin George b. April 15, 1875, m. Rosa Steffensen; Rodney Hyrum b. July 16, 1877, m. Lucy Halladay; Nellie Dorcas b. Jan. 12, 1880, m. Peter C. Steffensen, Jr.
Went to Provo with Thomas Kerry late in 1855; assisted in building home at Provo; returned to Salt Lake City 1859; from 1865 to 1866 followed teaming in Big Cottonwood canyon for Joseph C. Kingsbury and James Jack of 11th ward, Salt Lake City; 1872 employed by Bishop Edward Hunter as night watchman on the property where now stands the Hotel Utah; 1872 built first home in 12th ward; same year built second home in Sugar House ward, Salt Lake county; 1877 to 1886 followed farming and fruit raising; 1886 moved to Deweyville, Box Elder county, followed farming and stockraising; 1902 built hotel and livery barn at Deweyville, and is following same business at this date.

FUGAL, CHRISTIAN. Born in Denmark. Came to Utah Sept. 25, 1868.
His wife came to Utah with him. Their children: Niels; Andreas, m. Hannah Carlson; Christian, m. Margarett Jensen; Mary, m. Peter Scow. Family home Pleasant Grove, Utah.
Missionary in Denmark. Shoemaker. Died at Mayfield, Utah.

FUGAL, CHRISTIAN (son of Christian Fugal). Born April 1, 1843, in Denmark. Came to Utah with father.
Married Margarett Jensen 1869 at Salt Lake City. She was born June 2, 1842. Their children: Stena Maria b. Oct. 10, 1870, m. Thomas W. Gillert; Annie Margarett b. Feb. 20, 1872, m. John Boren; Martha b. Jan. 10, 1874, d. Nov. 30, 1891; James P. b. Nov. 15, 1875, m. Annie R. Thorne; Louis b. Dec. 12, 1878; Lizzie b. June 28, 1885, m. James D. Thorne. Family home Pleasant Grove, Utah.
Missionary in Denmark. Tailor. Died Nov. 22, 1895, at Pleasant Grove, Utah.

FUGAL, JAMES P. (son of Christian Fugal and Margarett Jensen). Born Nov. 15, 1875, at Pleasant Grove, Utah.
Married Annie R. Thorne Feb. 27, 1906, at Salt Lake City (daughter of Frederick Thorne and Margarett A. Armitstead, both of Pleasant Grove, Utah). She was born Aug. 29, 1880. Their children: Levetta b. Jan. 31, 1907; Erma b. March 1, 1909; James Maynard b. Sept. 1, 1910. Family home Woodville, Idaho.
Bishop's counselor; missionary to Scandinavia 1900-02; ordained bishop of Woodville ward Nov. 13, 1910. Justice of peace. Sheepman and farmer.

FUGATE, HARRISON PERRY (son of Thomas Fugate, Clinton Co., Ohio). Born June 10, 1821, Clinton Co., Ohio. Came to Utah 1850, Lorenzo Snow company.
Married Sarah Shoemaker of Bennington county, Ky., and Nancy Golden of Quincy, Ill., pioneers 1847). She was born July 16, 1830, Bennington county, Ky. Their children: Harrison Moroni m. Jerusha Boswell; Theaphilus d. child; Jezreel b. Nov. 1, 1864, m. Mary Ellen Wrigley; Thomas, m. Margarete Elizabeth Crookston; Mary, d. child. Families resided Manti and Ferron, Utah.
Member seventies at Manti, Utah. Settled at Manti 1849, and at Richfield 1867; from the latter place he was driven away by Indians. Settled at Ferron, Utah, 1880. Died Jan. 4, 1902, Ferron.

FUGATE, JEZREEL (son of Harrison Perry Fugate and Sarah Shoemaker). Born Nov. 1, 1864, Manti, Utah.
Married Mary Ellen Wrigley Dec. 16, 1888, Ferron, Utah (daughter of Joseph Wrigley and Ann Singleton, both of Ferron). She was born Jan. 16, 1870. Their children: Ellen b. July 25, 1890, died; Alona b. March 2, 1892, d. child; Llewllss b. July 3, 1894, m. Jesse M. Killpack; Reul b. Aug. 13, 1896, d. child; Yukon b. June 13, 1898; Promice Wendal b. June 9, 1900, d. child; Oren b. May 4, 1904; Naomi b. Aug. 6, 1909. Family home Ferron, Utah.
Settled at Ferron 1880. Assisted in making the canals and wagon roads and building up the country. Farmer and stockraiser.

FUGATE, THOMAS (son of Harrison Perry Fugate and Sarah Shoemaker). Born Oct. 4, 1866, Richfield, Utah.
Married Margarete Elizabeth Crookston Dec. 25, 1889, Ferron, Utah (daughter of John Crookston and Dinah Stoddard, the former of Scotland and latter of Carlisle, England). She was born Dec. 25, 1869. Their children: Mary Lois b. Sept. 29, 1890; Delilah M. b. April 21, 1892, d. April 6, 1900; Ina, b. Aug. 30, 1894; Vera b. Nov. 25, 1898, d. Jan. 5, 1899; Leah b. May 24, 1901; Aldwin Lyle b. May 17, 1903; Fern b. Feb. 3, 1906; Jetta b. March 18, 1908; Margarete b. April 29, 1911. Family home Ferron, Utah.
Settled at Ferron 1880. Assisted in making canals, wagon roads and building up the country. Farmer.

FUHRIMAN, JACOB (son of Jacob Fuhriman, born Aug. 10, 1800, Oeschenback, Canton Bern, Switzerland, and Anna Maria Knuchel, born Dec. 12, 1802, Wadenswyl, Switzerland). He was born Jan. 15, 1831, at Oeschenback. Came to Utah Sept. 3, 1860, James T. Ross company.
Married Anna Barbara Loosli March, 1856 (daughter of Andreas Loosli and Barbara Kaser). She was born Sept. 14, 1833, at Durrenroth, Switzerland; died 1895. Their children: Gottfried b. June 15, 1859, m. Bertha May Frederick July 7, 1881; Jacob R. b. Dec. 23, 1861, m. Olga Aikle Jan. 7, 1898; Barbetta b. May 3, 1864, m. Emil Eliason March 9, 1887; Emelino b. Sept. 21, 1866, m. Ferdinand Zollinger Sept. 7, 1892; Joseph Henry b. May 28, 1869, m. Mary Ann Johnson Jan. 25, 1893; Elizabeth b. June 9, 1871, m. Isaac Smith; Hyrum b. Feb. 9, 1873, m. Emelle Aikle Jan. 30, 1901; John David b. Sept. 1, 1876, m. Margareth E. Rice Dec. 5, 1898.
Married Mory Loosli 1869 at Salt Lake City (daughter of Andreas Loosli and Barbara Kaser), who was born Sept. 7, 1846, at Durrenroth, Switzerland; died 1892. Their children: Andrew Ephraim b. Dec. 4, 1872, m. Effie Jones Dec. 15, 1897; Frank William b. June, 1874, m. Maud Brown Dec. 18, 1901; George Washington b. Jan. 14, 1879, m. Mary Scheonnais Dec. 12, 1906; Ezra b. July 4, 1887, m. Malinda Jones Dec. 15, 1909.
Married Carolina Bollschweiler May 12, 1897 (daughter of Jacob Frederick Bollschweiler and Emelie Otelie Maurer of Bavaria). She was born Nov. 24, 1854. Their children: Al- b. Jan. 27, 1902; Emelie b. April 20, 1903; Mary b. Sept. 6, 1904; Otto b. Dec. 26, 1906; Carl b. Jan. 27, 1912.
Presided over the Germans of Providence ward 33 years; acting teacher 40 years.

FUHRIMAN, GOTTFRIED (son of Jacob Fuhriman and Barbara Loosli). Born June 15, 1859, at Durrenroth, Canton Bern, Switzerland. Came to Utah Sept. 3, 1860, James T. Ross company.
Married Bertha Mary Frederick July 7, 1881 (daughter of Arnold Jacob Frederick and Elizabeth Enz. Came to Utah 1870). She was born Jan. 7, 1860; came to Utah with parents; died Feb. 11, 1898. Their children: Godfrey Jared b. Aug. 22, 1883, m. Irene Campbell Feb. 24, 1909; Arnold Jacob b. July 2, 1885, m. Rachel Partington June 3, 1908; Bertha Minerva b. Sept. 11, 1887, m. Leroy Jones Sept. 16, 1908; Rachel Elizabeth b. Feb. 25, 1890, m. William Kleopfer Dec. 20, 1911; Festus Marion b. Oct. 8, 1892; Oliver Wendell b. Feb. 9, 1895. Family home Providence, Utah.
Married Elizabeth Fluckiger July 10, 1895, at Logan, Utah (daughter of Ulrich Fluckiger and Anna Kaser). She was born May 25, 1860, at Durrenroth, Switzerland. Their children: Walter Ulrich b. July 8, 1896; Ruion Leroy b. Oct. 27, 1898; David Hyrum b. Nov. 30, 1900; Dora b. July 24, 1903. Missionary to Switzerland and Germany 1884; 2d counselor to Bishop Fredrick Theuer of Providence ward 20 years, bishop of Providence 1st ward May 1, 1909. Connected with many business affairs as president and director of Providence Co-operative Mercantile Institution; South Cache Milling Company; Providence Water Works Company; Providence Irrigation companies; Providence Canyon Land Company; director Cache Valley Banking Company.

FULLER, LUBURN LIVONIA (son of Asaheb Fuller and Esther Smith). Born Dec. 9, 1841, at Nashville, Iowa. Came to Utah in 1856.
Married Minerva Brown April 10, 1862, at Des Moines, Iowa (daughter of Aaron Brown and Margaret Corey of Elk Rapids, Iowa). She was born Feb. 10, 1843. Their children: Harvey; William; Minerva Esther; Maggie May; Jesse S.; Minnie D.; Perry B.; Amey Grace. Family home Provo, Utah.

FULLER, PERRY B. (son of Luburn Livonia Fuller and Minerva Brown). Born Nov. 23, 1876, Elk Rapids, Iowa. Came to Utah in 1879.
Married Zina Wilkins June 12, 1901, at Salt Lake City, Utah (daughter of Oscar Wilkins and Mary J. McEwen, of Provo, Utah). She was born Sept. 1, 1880. Their children: Livonia W.; Zina Naomi; Jenna Bert; L. Roy. Family home Knightsville, Utah.
Bishop of Knightsville ward since March 11, 1909. Superintendent of Beck Tunnel, Colorado & Iron Blossom Mining company.

FULLER, REVILO (son of Elijah K. Fuller and Harriet Loomis). Born Oct. 8, 1843, Windham, Greene county, N. Y. Came to Utah 1847.
Married Mary D. Everett (daughter of Addison Everett, pioneer July 24, 1847, Brigham Young company). Missionary at St. George, Utah, 1860, and to Tonto Basin in 1877.

FULLMER, ALMON. Came to Utah with the first pioneers.
Married Rachel Wyman, born May 26, ——. Their children: Thaddeus Edgar b. Jan. 13, 1853, m. Juliette Dallin; Franklin Pierce b. April 27, 1855, m. Roselle Dalton; John Hyrum b. Aug. 30, 1857, m. Ellen Lundblad.

FULLMER, JOHN H. (son of Almon and Rachel Wyman Fullmer). Born Aug. 30, 1847, Cottonwood, Salt Lake Co., Utah.
Married Ellen Lundblad, Beaver, Utah (daughter of James and Karoe Lundblad, pioneers with first oxteam). She was born Nov. 11, 1860. Their children: John Lorin b. Dec. 12, 1879, m. Lizzie Smith; Frank Wyman b. April 26, 1881. died; Edith Idel b. Nov. 12, 1887; Ida Dott b. April 22, 1885, m. Clement Tebbs; Dwight L. b. Aug. 29, 1887; Ellen Ina b. May 23, 1890, m. Ellis Chamberlain; Effie Maine b. Feb. 18, 1892; Arvil Elton b. Dec. 5, 1893; Nora Loreta b. May 17, 1897, died; Rolla Jay b. March 18, 1901, died; Ardis Nevoe b. Aug. 8, 1903.
Was deputy U. S. marshal from 1893 until statehood obtained and was representative to the state legislature in 1899.

FULLMER, JOHN LORIN (son of John H. Fullmer and Ellen Lundblad). Born Dec. 12, 1879.
Married Lizzie Smith, Circleville, Utah. Only child: Harry Smith b. Dec. 7, 1911.

FULLMER, DAVID (son of Peter Fullmer and Susannah Zerfoss, of Winter Quarters, Neb.). Born July 7, 1803, Chiliauquque, Northumberland county, Pa. Came to Utah Oct. 13, 1850, Edward Hunter company.
Married Rhoda Ann Marvin Sept. 18, 1831, Union township, Luzerne county, Pa. (daughter of Zera Marvin and Rhoda Williams of Union township). She was born Feb. 12, 1813, Union township, and died Aug. 18, 1892. Salt Lake City. She came to Utah Oct. 14, 1850, Edward Hunter company. Their children: Eugene Bertran, m. Sarah Jane Mitchell; Junius Sextus, m. Lucy Ellier; Hannibal Octavius, m. Rachel Brown; Elvira Martha, m. John Hickenlooper; Hortenla Jane d. aged 11 years; Susannah, m. Ephraim Stockwell Snyder; Rhoda Ann, m. Hyrum Chapman; David (twin of Rhoda Ann), m. Caroline Linnell; Don Peter Marvin, m. Ida Martin; Mary Vilate, m. Samuel Andrew; Esther, m. John S. Bowers. Family home 6th ward Salt Lake City.
High priest; high councilor of Hancock stake; missionary; president Garden Grove branch; home missionary, Salt Lake stake; first counselor to Daniel Spencer; president Salt Lake stake 1849; patriarch. Member of company appointed to explore southern Utah; captain of company sent to Independence Rock, to relieve a belated immigrant company. Member of territorial legislature from Salt Lake county; city councilman at Nauvoo, Ill. Treasurer of university of Deseret; treasurer, pro tem, Salt Lake county, and later of Salt Lake City. Delegate to territorial convention from 6th ward, at which convention he was appointed director of agricultural society. Farmer. Died Oct. 21, 1879, Salt Lake City.

FULLMER, EUGENE BERTRAND (son of David Fullmer and Rhoda Ann Marvin). Born May 3, 1833, Plymouth, Luzerne county, Pa.
Married Sarah Jane Mitchell (daughter of Benjamin Mitchell and Miss Treesbaugh of Jefferson Co., Ohio). She was born June 9, 1838. Their children: Rhoda Ann b. Jan. 20, 1856, m. George D. Deaton; David Eugene b. Jan. 21, 1858, m. Sarah A. Green; Sarah Lavina b. Jan. 7, 1860, m. Peter Frederick Goss; Emily b. Nov. 30, 1861, m. George S. Tall; Mary Adelaid b. April 19, 1864, m. Alma H. West;' Annie E. b. Oct. 7, 1866, died; Junius Bertran b. March 17, 1868, m. Adalaid Hart; George b. April 4, 1870, m. Catherine McLause; Benjamin b. May 4, 1872, m. Nellie Needham; Florence b. May 30, 1874, m. Robert McLause; Minnie b. Oct. 7, 1876. m. Harry Howe; Oscar b. 1878, m. Phoebe ——; LeRoy, died. One of presidents of 2nd quorum of seventies; high priest; ward teacher. Worked on Salt Lake temple 40 years. Died Oct. 21, 1879, Salt Lake City.

FULLMER, BENJAMIN (son of Eugene Bertrand Fullmer and Sarah Jane Mitchell). Born May 4, 1872, Salt Lake City.
Married Nellie Needham June 12, 1895, Salt Lake City (daughter of James Needham and Elizabeth Snalem of Salt Lake City). She was born April 23, 1873. Their children: Myrtle b. June 23, 1896; Earl b. June 20, 1900; Mildred b. Sept. 1, 1903; Arvilla b. May 25, 1905; Elizabeth b. Oct. 14, 1907; Sarah b. Dec. 13, 1909.
Bishop of Alpine ward 1907; missionary to eastern states 1897-99; president Y. M. M. I. A. Mayor of Alpine 1910-11. Superintendent water works of Alpine.

FULLMER JOHN SOLOMON (son of Peter Fullmer). Born July 21, 1807, Luzerne county, Pa. Came to Utah Oct. 10, 1848, Willard Richards company.
Married Mary Ann Price May 24, 1837 (daughter of John Price), who was born Sept. 16, 1815, and came to Utah with husband. Their children: Lavina Elizabeth b. March 5, 1838, m. Eli Ashcroft; Joanna Price b. Dec. 13, 1830, m. Erastus Curtis; Ann Adalaide b. Oct. 25, 1841, m. William T. Dennis; Mary Ann Frances b. May 19, 1844; John Solomon, Jr. b. Aug. 12, 1846, m. Juliet Fullmer Jan. 1, 1868, m. Miss Agatha Darow; William Price b. May 27, 1849, m. Maria Jane Curtis Jan. 2, 1871; Don Carlos b. Nov. 7, 1851, m. Eliza Ann Mason; Samuel David b. Nov. 4, 1856, m. Roxy Jane Kendall. Family resided Salt Lake City, Spanish Fork, Provo and Springville, Utah.
Married Olive Amanda Smith, who was born Sept. 26, 1826. Their children: Chauncy Harvey b. Nov. 26, 1843, m. Claricy Curtis; Mary Ann Smith b. Oct. 25, 1846, m. William Lisonbee; James Dickens Smith b. April 29, 1849, m. Mary Ann Babcock; Joseph L. Haywood Smith b. Nov. 25, 1850; Albert Heber Smith b. Sept. 17, 1852, m. Margaret Arzilla Oaks; Olive Amanda Smith b. Sept. 15, 1856, m. Gordon Taylor; Van Osden Smith b. May 26, 1858, m. Caroline Van Leuven; Edwin Smith b. March 13, 1860, m. Ada Mendenhall; Alonzo Smith b. March 17, 1862, m. Luella Perry; Alma Smith b. Sept. 14, 1864, m. Deseret Stilson; Charlotte Smith b. April 3, 1867, m. George Perry. Family resided Salt Lake City, Spanish Fork, Provo and Springville, Utah.
Married Sarah Ann Stevenson Oct. 12, 1856, Salt Lake City. She was born July 31, 1835. Loughborough, Leicestershire, Eng. Their children: M. Deseret b. Dec. 2, 1857, m. Jesse Baldwin Feb. 15, 1874; John Charles b. March 23, 1859, m. Floritta Ann Curtis July 14, 1881; Caroline Lucy b. March 20, 1860, m. Amos B. Warren July 23, 1876; Agnes b. Dec. 9, 1861; James Stevenson b. May 29, 1863; Thomas b. Jan. 11, 1865; George Wallace b. Dec. 29, 1867, m. Katie Estella Fall Aug. 18, 1891; Frank b. March 19, 1869, m. Altha Warren Jan. 11, 1890; Theodore b. Dec. 29, 1871, m. Sylvia Ada Sanford March 11, 1895; Sarah Ann b. Aug. 28, 1873, m. William Christofferson Oct. 25, 1892; Blanch Estell b. May 29, 1876; Leonard Ray b. May 14, 1878. Family resided Salt Lake City, Provo, Spanish Fork and Springville, Utah.
Missionary to England; member committee of three. John S. Fullmer, Joseph L. Haywood and Almon W. Babbitt, left at Nauvoo at time of exodus to complete business of those departing for Utah; high priest. Member legislature.

FULLMER, WILLIAM PRICE (son of John Solomon Fullmer and Mary Ann Price). Born May 27, 1849, at Salt Lake City.
Married Maria Jane Curtis Jan. 2, 1871, at Salt Lake City (daughter of David Avery Curtis and Lutitia Shearer, who were married Aug. 28, 1852, pioneers 1850). She was born Sept. 23, 1853, Springville, Utah. Their children: William Price, Jr. b. Nov. 10, 1871, m. Fannie Veroni Whiting;

Samuel Curtis b. June 8, 1874, m. Elizabeth Bromley; Lutitia May b. May 30, 1876, m. Silas W. Johnson; Mary Ann b. April 10, 1878, m. Harvey Edward Perry; Adelaide Maria b. Feb. 5, 1880, m. Erastus Jensen; Phebe Jane b. April 2, 1882, m. Marquis de Lafayette Perry; Gertrude b. March 1, 1884, m. James Shepherd; Beatrice b. March 4, 1886, d. April 17, 1887; Amy b. Feb. 18, 1888, m. Horace Either; Eva b. Aug. 1, 1890; Joseph Amon b. April 26, 1893; Elmer b. June 28, 1895; David John b. April 9, 1897. Family resided Springville and Mapleton, Utah.
Married Elizabeth Alice Salisbury June 19, 1884, at Salt Lake City (daughter of Martha Whiscombe and John Henry Salisbury), who was born July 9, 1866, Wyoming. Their children: Martha Ann b. Aug. 2, 1888; Hazel Bell b. July 6, 1890; Alice Geneva b. April 26, 1894; Myrtle Viola b. Dec. 24, 1896; Sarah Marie b. Oct. 5, 1900; Irma Leone b. Nov. 4, 1903.
Settled at Mapleton 1875. President 51st quorum seventies; superintendent Mapleton Sunday school; president Y. M. M. I. A.; counselor to Bishop Tew since 1896; missionary to Ohio and Pennsylvania 1887-89; assisted in bringing immigrants to Utah.

FULLMER, WILLIAM PRICE, JR. (son of William Price Fullmer and Maria Jane Curtis). Born Nov. 10, 1871, Springville, Utah.
Married Fannie Verona Whiting Jan. 15, 1896, Manti, Utah (daughter of Albert Milton Whiting and Harriet Perry of Mapleton, Utah). She was born 1877. Their children: William Ross b. March 6, 1890; Beatrice b. Oct. 12, 1896; Margarett Mary b. March 13, 1899; Richard Alvin b. May 29, 1901; Maud b. Nov. 20, 1902; Alice b. Sept. 3, 1905, d. April 3, 1912; Albert Whiting b. Feb. 5, 1907; John Howard b. July 29, 1908; Maria and Harriet b. Oct. 24, 1909, d. infants. Family home Wallsburg, Utah.
Moved to Wallsburg 1903. Member 76th quorum seventies; high priest; bishop Wallsburg ward 1911; counselor in Mutual; president elders' quorum. Superintendent Mapleton ditch and water distribution; superintendent road construction. Planted and raised first sugar beets. Farmer; rancher and stockraiser.

FULLMER, JAMES DICKENS (son of John S. Fullmer and Olive Amanda Smith). Born April 29, 1849, Salt Lake City, Utah.
Married Mary Ann Babcock Aug. 14, 1872, Monroe, Utah (daughter of Lorenzo Babcock and Amy Ann Marble, both of Nauvoo, Ill., came to Utah with oxteam company). She was born Aug. 20, 1856, Manti, Utah. Their children: Amy Amanda b. April 14, 1873, d. aged 16; James Dickens, Jr. b. Sept. 19, 1875, m. Frances Idona Mead and Margaret Ann Laura Miller; Mary Ann b. Oct. 1, 1877, m. Dora Davis; Veretta Jane b. Nov. 25, 1883, m. Samuel Eldridge; Olive Vera b. March 3, 1886, m. George Hanselman; Luella Chise b. Oct. 18, 1888, m. Albert Anderton; Lorenzo Babcock b. Oct. 27, 1890, m. Maggie Ferrish; Laura b. Dec. 18, 1892, d. aged 16; Joseph b. April 12, 1895, d. aged 14; Ada Pearl b. Sept. 30, 1896; Neva Glee b. Dec. 12, 1903. Family home Annabella, Sevier Co., Utah.
Elder; member of bishopric of Spring Glen; Sunday school teacher; ward teacher. Registration agent.

FULLMER, JAMES DICKENS, JR. (son of James Dickens Fullmer and Mary Ann Babcock). Born Sept. 19, 1875, Annabella, Sevier Co., Utah.
Married Frances Idona Mead July 6, 1900, Spring Glen, Utah (daughter of Orlanda Fish Mead, Lake Shore, near Spanish Fork, Utah). She was born March 17, 1872. Their children: Ruby b. Feb. 22, 1901, d. April 4, 1901; James Wallace b. May 12, 1902; Calvin Dickens b. Feb. 1, 1905. Family home Spring Glen, Utah.
Married Margaret Ann Laura Miller March 21, 1906, at Salt Lake City (daughter of William P. Miller and Martha Ellen Prows of Kanosh, Millard Co., Utah). She was born Oct. 6, 1884. Their children: Irma Cleo b. Jan. 12, 1907; William Evan b. July 23, 1908; Earl b. April 1, 1910; Lila Margaret b. Aug. 12, 1910. Family home Spring Glen, Utah.
Teacher; farmer; railroadman.

FUNK, DANIEL BUCKLEY (son of Susanna Stoner of Pennsylvania). Born in Ohio Came to Utah 1848.
Married Mariah DeMill (daughter of Freeborn DeMill and Ann Knight of Manti, Utah, pioneers 1848). She was born May 9, 1822. Their children: Sarah Ann, d. infant; William DeMill, m. Ingrie Sandbar; Ezra K., m. Mary Amanda Henrie; Daniel B., m. Mariah Terry; Irene, m. Dwight Atwood; Arseneth, m. Moroni Bradley; Emerett, m. Charles Musige. Family home Pennsylvania.
Married Mary Jane Pectol at Manti (daughter of William Pectol of Kentucky and Manti, Utah). Their children: Arlisha, m. Abner Lowry, Jr.; Jesse, m. Mina Nielson; Sylvia, m. Ira Allen Beal; George Alfred, m. Millie Hogan; Geneve; Andrew, m. Nora Mills; Frank, m. Myrtle Mills. Family home Manti.
Member 48th quorum seventies. Black Hawk Indian war veteran. Served in Echo Canyon trouble. One of the first settlers to Manti. Farmer; plasterer and builder. Died Nov. 30, 1888, at Funks Lake, Manti.

FUNK, EZRA K. (son of Daniel B. Funk and Mariah DeMill). Born June 1, 1846, at Quincy, Ill. Came to Utah 1848.
Married Mary Amanda Henrie Nov. 9, 1867, at Salt Lake City (daughter of Daniel Henrie and Amanda Bradley of Bountiful, Utah, pioneers 1848, contingent Mormon Battalion). She was born Sept. 4, 1850. Their children: Amanda b. Sept. 27, 1869, m. Arthur Cox; Myra L. b. Aug. 17, 1871, m. Joseph Hansen; Ezra K. b. Nov. 5, 1873, m. Etta Crawford; Emerett Lavern b. Oct. 1, 1875, m. Lewis Larsen; Olive Chelnishia b. Oct. 24, 1877, m. William Stringham; John Henrie b. April 16, 1879, m. Ann Conover; George B. b. May 18, 1882, m. Mary A. Olsen; William Arthur b. April 3, 1885, m. Zelma Westenskow; Alvira b. July 21, 1888, d. Oct. 23, 1911; Susie b. Oct. 22, 1890, d. infant; Ruby May b. March 20, 1892, m. Antone Hovgaard. Family home Manti, Utah.
Member 48th quorum seventies. Minuteman in Black Hawk Indian war. Farmer; carpenter; plasterer; builder and prospector.

G

GADD, ALFRED (son of Samuel Gadd, born July 25, 1815, and Eliza Chapman, born March 13, 1815, both in Cambridgeshire, Eng.—married April 12, 1836). He was born July 15, 1837, Orwell, Cambridgeshire. Came to Utah Nov. 9, 1856, James G. Willie handcart company.
Married Mary Ann Hobbs Jan. 10, 1864 (daughter of William D. Hobbs, pioneer, Captain Murdock company, and Mary Ann Pope—married Nov. 8, 1835, Brighton, Eng.). She was born June 16, 1841. Their children: William b. Jan. 18, 1865, m. John S. Linton Dec. 17, 1885; William Alfred b. Dec. 19, 1866, m. Laura B. Fly Sept. 29, 1890; Samuel George b. Dec. 5, 1868, m. Elizabeth Jackson; Arthur b. April 29, 1871, m. Jeanie Sinclair Oct. 6, 1897; Alice Jeanette b. Dec. 5, 1873; Walter Pentlow b. Oct. 26, 1875, m. Mary May Sutton Sept. 14, 1898; Ernest Alma b. Jan. 7, 1878; Alvin b. Dec. 11, 1879; Loris Albert b. Nov. 10, 1880; Albert Victor b. Dec. 17, 1882, m. Ethel Carter Dec. 23, 1908; Ethel Charlotte b. Aug. 23, 1884. Family home Nephi, Utah.
Indian war veteran. Horticulturist.

GADD, SAMUEL GEORGE (son of Alfred Gadd and Mary Ann Hobbs). Born Dec. 5, 1868, at Nephi.
Married Elizabeth Jackson May 10, 1895, at Nephi (daughter of John Jackson and Rachel Cope). Their children: Mary Fern b. Aug. 5, 1897; Ida Rachel b. Jan. 16, 1900; Bertha b. Sept. 2, 1904; George Aldew b. April 6, 1907; Melvin Roy b. May 1908. Family home Nephi.

GOGAN (GEOGHEGAN), WILLIAM HIGHLAND (son of James Geoghegan and Mary Highland, County Meath, Ireland). Born Aug. 22, 1860, North River, New York city. Came to Utah Oct. 12, 1875, independent company.
Married Lydia Ann Taylor Dec. 17, 1876, at Ogden, Utah (daughter of Joseph Taylor and Jane Lake of Harrisville, Utah, pioneers 1847, with a contingent of Mormon Battalion). She was born 1858. Their children: James William b. Nov. 3, 1877, d. infant; Joseph Albert b. Dec. 15, 1879, m. Emily G. Finch; Ira David b. March 17, 1882, m. Mary E. Smith; Marzela Jane, died; William Highland b. Jan. 28, 1887, m. Albie Glen.
Married Mary Augusta Goodrich Nov. 20, 1890, Logan, Utah (daughter of George Albert Goodrich and Eliza Ann Taggart of Vernal, Utah, pioneers 1853). She was born Jan. 4, 1868. Their children: Mamie Goodrich b. June 18, 1892, m. Marion H. Roberts; Fannie b. Jan. 10, 1894; Ella Rose b. Dec. 20, 1895; Leona May b. Dec. 3, 1897; George Raymond b. Jan. 17, 1901; Earl Golden b. Feb. 20, 1903; Carlie Maud b. May 21, 1905, died; Leslie Owen b. Sept. 17, 1907.
Clerk Duchesne stake 1910; member high councils Uinta and Duchesne stakes; president Y. M. M. I. A. of Naples ward; assistant Sunday school superintendent. Assessor and collector Uintah county 1892-98; Vernal city councilman two years. Settled in Ashley valley 1878; secretary and director Ashley Central Canal Company.

GALE, JAMES (son of James Gale, born May 10, 1801, and Sarah Tavinder, born 1798, both in Warminster, Wiltshire, Eng.). He was born May 14, 1829, in Warminster. Came to Utah Aug. 25, 1852, independent company.
Married Emma Blake (daughter of Isaac Blake and Sophia Wood), who was born March 4, 1829, Salisbury, Eng. Their children: Charles b. Aug. 30, 1849; Lorenzo b. March 17, 1851, and Henry Charles b. May 23, 1854, latter three d. infants; James Chancy b. Oct. 21, 1857, m. Lenoria Browning; Francis Albert b. July 25, 1860, m. Esther Malon; Edward Isaac b. April 4, 1868, d. infant; Heber Daniel b. Sept. 29, 1869, m. Harriet Robinson; Horace Ernest b. Dec. 7, 1871.
Married Mary Ann Derrick, Salt Lake City (daughter of Zacharias Derrick and Mary Shephard), who was born Jan. 8, 1837, London, Eng. Their children: Zacharias John b. Jan. 29, 1858; William Oreon b. Nov. 1, 1860; Joseph b. Jan. 17, 1863; latter three d. infants; Hyrum Edwin b. Feb. 13, 1564, m. Edna Stimpson.
Married Lilley Sutcliffe (daughter of Thomas Sutcliffe, born 1830, and Mary Sutcliffe, born 1836, both in Yorkshire, Eng.). She was born Feb. 2, 1861, in Yorkshire, Eng. Only child, Wilford b. Sept. 10, 1892, d. infant.

PIONEERS AND PROMINENT MEN OF UTAH 883

GALLOWAY, GEORGE CURTIS (son of Curtis Galloway and Harriet Annie Rowley). Born June 17, 1889, Meadow Creek, Utah.
Active teacher; priest. Farmer; inventor; poet. Family home Shelley, Idaho.

GAPPMAYER, BARTL (son of John Gappmayer and Anna Winken of Thompswig, Austria).
Married Mary Emily Nelson Jan. 1, 1895, Buysville, Utah (daughter of Henry Nelson and Sarah Ann Richmond), who was born Dec. 29, 1871, Heber City, Utah. Their children: Lewis Bartl b. July 8, 1896; Anna Lapriel b. Sept. 2, 1898; Roy Harry b. March 31, 1900; Reed Eigil b. Oct. 14, 1902; John Edwin b. June 23, 1904; Sarah Ella b. April 15, 1906; Hiram Nelson b. Sept. 20, 1911, died. Family home Provo, Utah.

GARDINER, JOHN WILLIAM (son of William Gardiner and Sarah Hughes of Chalford Hill, Gloucestershire, Eng.). Born May 17, 1840, at Chalford Hill. Came to Utah Sept. 12, 1864, John D. Chase company.
Married Harriet Dyer April 16, 1864, Brownshill, Eng. (daughter of Thomas Dyer and Sarah Weight of Avening, Eng.). She was born Aug. 30, 1840. No children.
Married Annie Nichols Aug. 30, 1883, Salt Lake City (daughter of William Nichols and Ann Webber of Viney Bridge, Crew Kerne, Eng., who came to Utah June 1, 1883). She was born March 9, 1863. Their children: Sarah Ann b. Aug. 8, 1884, m. Charles Weber; Matilda b. Oct. 8, 1885, m. Walter F. Healey; Hattie May b. Feb. 6, 1887, m. Edgar T. Healey; John William Jr. b. April 23, 1892; Heber b. July 22, 1893; Joseph N. b. Jan. 26, 1896; George Henry b. Nov. 2, 1897; Roy Hughes b. Feb. 10, 1900; Alma Edward b. April 2, 1901; Robert Lloyd b. Aug. 25, 1903. Family home Pleasant Grove, Utah.
Missionary to England 1880-81; high priest. Farmer.

GARDNER, BENJAMIN (son of Nathaniel B. Gardner, born Oct. 17, 1765, in New York state, and Hannah Briggs, born June 1, 1767—married Jan. 10, 1786). He was born Aug. 19, 1800, Johnstown, Montgomery county, N. Y. Came to Utah Sept. 28, 1852, captain of his company.
Married Electa Lamport May 29, 1822, in Erie county, Pa. (daughter of William Lamport, born July 17, 1778, and Martha Babbitt, born May 17, 1784, of Sharon, Schoharie county, N. Y.—married 1799, at Sharon). She was born March 5, 1800, and came to Utah with husband. Their children: Benjamin b. Nov. 24, 1823, d. same day; Hannah b. Dec. 19, 1824, m. George S. Mason b. March 22, 1855; William L. b. Feb. 3, 1827, m. Angeline Gould March 31, 1852; Belinda Sophia b. May 16, 1829, d. June 22, 1829; Nathaniel Bradley b. May 8, 1830, d. April 15, 1851; Mahala b. Feb. 5, 1833, m. Robert Hughs March 10, 1861; Milo Vandozen b. June 4, 1835, m. Margret Montgomery Sept. 29, 1859; Lucinda b. May 30, 1837, m. James Leithead March 7, 1856; Martha Belinda b. Oct. 12, 1839, m. Daniel W. Holdaway April 16, 1857; Electa E. b. March 8, 1842, m. John Montgomery Sept. 29, 1859; Joseph S. b. March 15, 1847, m. Mary Elizabeth Williams March 15, 1869. Family resided in Erie county, Pa., and at North Ogden and Deweyville, Utah.
President North Pigeon branch 1847-52; captain of tenth church train, which crossed the plains 1852; seventy. Settled at North Ogden 1857; later moved to Deweyville. Justice of peace at North Ogden 1865-69. Miller. Died July 3, 1875.

GARDNER, MILO VANDOZEN (son of Benjamin Gardner and Electa Lamport). Born June 4, 1835, in Erie county, Pa.
Married Margret Montgomery Sept. 29, 1859, at North Ogden (daughter of Robert Montgomery and Mary Willson of Scotland, pioneers Sept. 10, 1850, Jonathan Foote company). She was born July 31, 1839, Montreal, Canada. Their children: Mary I. b. March 27, 1861, m. Orson C. Loveland March 6, 1879; Milo Martin b. Oct. 25, 1862, m. Adalaide Anderson Jan. 12, 1886; Robert Nathaniel b. Jan. 23, 1865, m. Harriet A. Dewey Jan. 23, 1889; Benjamin Perry b. March 5, 1867, m. Johanah Foulsen Jan. 11, 1899; Margret Ann b. May 3, 1869, m. John T. Hansen Feb. 16, 1891; Hannah Lucinda b. April 18, 1871, m. William Loveland Nov. 18, 188—; Martha Lorett b. Jan. 30, 1873, d. Feb. 11, 1873; Hyrum Alma b. July 31, 1874, d. Dec. 5, 1885; James Alva b. Jan. 7, 1877, m. Harriet Eveline Dewey Dec. 27, 1904; Electa Buletie b. Sept. 29, 1880, m. Brigham Martelo Burbank Dec. 22, 1899; Estella b. Aug. 2, 1883, m. John A. Fryer Oct. 21, 1903. Family resided at North Ogden and Deweyville, Utah.
Drum major in Ogden band. Moved from North Ogden to Deweyville 1872. Farmer. Died March 26, 1908.

GARDNER, MILO MARTIN (son of Milo V. Gardner and Margret Montgomery). Born Oct. 25, 1862, North Ogden, Utah.
Married Adalaide Anderson Jan. 12, 1886, Deweyville (daughter of Oga Anderson and Carline Nelson), who was born July 14, 1856, in Sweden. Their children: Martin M. b. Nov. 10, 1886, m. Florence Loveland Feb. 10, 1909; Vivian A. b. Aug. 17, 1888, m. Cleone A. Hunsaker June 22, 1909; Margret b. Nov. 24, 1891; Lloyd M. and Floyd N. b. Dec. 7, 1898, latter d. Oct. 15, 1899. Family home Deweyville.
Moved from North Ogden to Brigham City; later to Deweyville. School trustee.

GARDNER, ROBERT NATHANIEL (son of Milo V. Gardner and Margret Montgomery). Born Jan. 23, 1865, North Ogden, Utah.
Married Harriet A. Dewey Jan. 23, 1889, Logan, Utah (daughter of John Cook Dewey and Harriet May of Deweyville, Utah, former pioneer Sept. 28, 1853, latter March 14, 1852). She was born Dec. 27, 1868, at Deweyville. Their children: Robert N. b. Feb. 21, 1890; George A. Dewey b. March 31, 1892; Leone D. b. April 14, 1895; Milo D. b. March 18, 1898; Alphonzo D. b. June 30, 1900; Rulon D. b. Nov. 2, 1903; Harriet E. b. Aug. 3, 1910, d. Sept. 13, 1910. Family home Deweyville, Utah.
Justice of peace 1909-12; juvenile court officer 1911. Superintendent Sunday school; counselor and president Y. M. M. I. A.

GARDNER, JOSEPH SMITH (son of Benjamin Gardner and Electa Lamport). Born March 15, 1847, Vernon, VanBuren Co., Iowa.
Married Mary Elizabeth Williams March 15, 1869, Salt Lake City (daughter of Ezra Granger Williams and Henrietta Elizabeth Crombie of that place, pioneers Oct. 25, 1849, Ezra T. Benson company). She was born Feb. 2, 1851, Salt Lake City. Their children: Joseph Nathaniel b. Jan. 30, 1870, d. Dec. 28, 1886; Lucinda Elizabeth b. Jan. 7, 1872, m. Richard Robinson Jan. 12, 1890; Hyrum Chauncey b. March 25, 1874, m. Mary Ellen Marshall Jan. 16, 1895; Emma Rebecca b. June 15, 1876, d. Dec. 4, 1886; Benjamin Ezra b. July 17, 1878, m. Effie Jane Walker Dec. 14, 1898; Electa Henrietta b. Oct. 4, 1880, m. Joseph Edward Southwick Feb. 27, 1900; William Frederick b. March 4, 1883; Isaac Moroni b. May 27, 1885, d. March 27, 1886; Francis Adna b. Sept. 5, 1887, m. Rose Percilla Randall Oct. 9, 1907; Andrew b. Nov. 11, 1889. Family resided at Deweyville, Pleasant View and Liberty, Utah, and Grant, Idaho.
Drummer boy in Utah militia. School trustee. Farmer.

GARDNER, CHARLES. Married Rhoda Kellogg. Their children: Charles Alma, m. Martha Timothy; Laura, m. John Nuttall. Family home Provo, Utah.
Farmer. Died 1886, Wallsburg, Utah.

GARDNER, CHARLES ALMA (son of Charles Gardner and Rhoda Kellogg). Born 1857.
Married Martha Timothy December 1879, Salt Lake City (daughter of John G. Timothy and Martha Davis of Wales). She was born July 3, 1863. Their children: John Alma b. Dec. 20, 1879, m. Ella Pike, m. Alice Long; Martha La Prele b. May 5, 1882, m. Fred Hoeft; Mary Alice b. Nov. 2, 1884, m. Charles Perry Bingham; Rhoda b. Aug. 12, 1886, d. aged 7; Mabel b. Sept. 12, 1887; Jeannette b. May 5, 1889, m. Ernest Hess; Cora Bell b. Nov. 30, 1890, m. Ira Belden. Family home Vernal, Utah.

GARDNER, ELIAS HARVEY (son of Walter A. and Martha A. Gardner of Salem, Utah). Born Dec. 5, 1855, Payson, Utah.
Married Caroline Ada Jackman 1878, at Salem (daughter of Albert Jackman of that place). She was born June 4, 1859. Their children: Ada Lucinda, m. Kenyon T. Davis; Daisy Martha, m. Charles W. Stone; Maud May, m. Howard B. Warnick; Harvey Elmer, m. Vera Rockhill; Frank Lynn. Carpenter; farmer.

GARDNER, HENRY (son of Henry B. Gardner, born Nov. 18, 1817, Bosham, Eng., and Harriett Ingram, born Jan. 29, 1816, Slindon, Sussex, Eng.—married Nov. 22, 1845). He was born Aug. 9, 1848, Oving, Sussex, Eng. Came to Utah Oct. 1, 1854, Daniel Garn company.
Married Madaleen Dalley Oct. 19, 1899 (daughter of Milton Dalley and Mary M. Wilson—married June 14, 1874, Salt Lake City, pioneers 1850, Slaughter and Cavett company). She was born Feb. 3, 1876. Their children: Bert B. Aug. 31, 1900; Merritt D. b. July 13, 1909; Grant H. Gardner, b. April 18, 1911.

GARDNER, JAMES (son of William Gardner and Ellen Beardworth of Langton, Lancashire, Eng). He was born June 4, 1829, Preston, Eng. Came to Utah Sept. 25, 1855, Richard Ballantyne company.
Married Jane Trelfull March 3, 1855, on the sea (daughter of Thomas Trelfull of American Fork, Utah; pioneer Sept. 25, 1855). She was born July 6, 1828. Their children: William, m. Frances B. Rondeau; Jane G., m. Joseph B. Forbes; Ellen, m. Robert Proctor; James T., m. Ruth Greenwood; Annie E., m. Washburn Chipman; Lydia, m. George F. Shelley.
High priest. City councilman and sexton. Farmer. Died Aug. 14, 1906.

GARDNER, JOHN (son of William Gardner and Ann Hudd, of Gloucestershire, Eng.). He was born May 31, 1805, Waterlane, Gloucestershire. Came to Utah Oct. 16, 1853, Appleton Harmon company.
Married Mary Ann Goodship (daughter of William Goodship and Mary Pettet), who was born Jan 2, 1805, and came to Utah with husband. Their children: William b. Oct. 18, 1825, m. Sarah Sisam; James b. Aug. 31, 1828, m. Hannah Gubbins; Sarah Ellen, d. child; Frederick b. Nov. 12, 1832,

m. Sarah S. Smith; Mary Ann b. Dec. 25, 1834, d. child; Joseph Hyrum b. Feb. 28, 1837, d. child; John Brigham b. Jan. 16, 1839, died; Henry b. May 14, 1840, m. Mary Walker; Alfred b. Sept. 25, 1842, m. Mary E. Coon May 29, 1871; Emma b. April 5, 1848, m. Martin L. Bird. Family resided Chalford Hill, Gloucestershire, Eng., and later in Utah.

GARDNER, JAMES (son of John Gardner and Mary Ann Goodship). Born Aug. 31, 1828, Chalford Hill, Gloucestershire, Eng. Came to Utah Nov. 9, 1856, James G. Willie company.
Married Hannah Gubbins (daughter of William Gubbins and Elizabeth Damsel). She came to Utah with husband. Their children: Mary Ann b. June 8, 1849, m. Alphonso Willie; Agnes E. b. Feb. 27, 1851, m. Henry Hughes; Frederick b. Dec. 28, 1852, m. Sedilia Bird; John W. b. June 28, 1855, m. Jennette Muir; Henry Stephen b. Nov. 2, 1857, and Elizabeth Jane b. Feb. 5, 1859, died; Hannah M. b. Nov. 29, 1860, m. Joseph Acock; Albert b. Aug. 27, 1863, m. Caroline Lawrence; Brigham b. Dec. 12, 1864, m. Nellie Robbins; Emma Z. b. Oct. 1868, m. Thomas Smith. Family resided Mendon Utah, and Teton, Idaho.

GARDNER, FREDERICK (son of James Gardner and Hannah Gubbins). Born Dec. 28, 1852, Chalford Hill, Eng.
Married Sedilia Bird Aug. 15, 1884, Logan, Utah (daughter of John P. K. Bird and Sarah Hoops), who was born Sept. 13, 1863, Mendon, Utah. Their children: Laura E. b. Aug. 26, 1885, m. Frederick Mace; Frederick b. Feb. 16, 1887, died; Elmer b. Nov. 7, 1888; Vera b. April 27, 1890, and Sylvia H. b. Aug. 12, 1892, died; Eras b. Sept. 16, 1893; Vernon b. May 19, 1897; Orval b. April 10, 1902, and Evan b. April 15, 1899, died. Family home Teton, Idaho.

GARDNER, ALFRED (son of John Gardner and Mary Ann Goodship). Born Sept. 25, 1842, Chalford Hill, Eng.
Married Mary Elizabeth Coon May 29, 1871, Salt Lake City (daughter of Abraham Coon and Elizabeth Wilson), who was born Jan. 12, 1856, Salt Lake City. Their children: Sarah Jane; Alfred Irvin b. May 11, 1875, m. Margaret E. Bird; Emma Maud; John Abraham; Henry Arthur; Alice Mabel; Esther Mae; Josephine; Amy Ione; Frederick Arnold; Hugh Raymond. Family home Mendon, Utah.
Ward clerk 30 years; counselor in bishopric 10 years; clerk high priests quorum 10 years; Sunday school teacher 38 years. City recorder 12 years; city treasurer nine years; notary public 1892-1912; postmaster Mendon five years; city councilman four years; justice of peace two years.

GARDNER, ROBERT (son of William Gardner and Christina Henderson of Huston, Scotland). Born March 12, 1781, Huston, Scotland. Came to Utah Oct. 1, 1847, Edward Hunter company.
Married Margaret Calinder (daughter of Archibald Calinder and Margaret Ewen, pioneers Oct. 1, 1847), who was born January 1777. Their children: William b. Jan. 31, 1803, m. Ann Lackey Jan. 1829; m. Janet Livingston 1841; Margaret b. Jan. 5, 1807, m. George Sweeten March 29, 1836; m. Roger Lackban Oct. 21, 1847; Archibald b. Sept. 2, 1814, m. Sarah Jane Hamilton June 17, 1857; m. Mary Larsen Dec. 22, 1869; Robert b. Oct. 12, 1819, m. Jane McEwen March 17, 1841.

GARDNER, ARCHIBALD (son of Robert Gardner and Margaret Calinder). Born Sept. 2, 1814, Killsyth, Scotland.
Married Sarah Jane Hamilton June 17, 1857, Salt Lake City (daughter of James Hamilton and Mary Ann Campbell of Mill Creek, Utah, pioneers 1852), who was born June 11, 1842. Only child: James Hamilton b. July 27, 1859, m. Rhoda Priscilla Huffaker. Family home West Jordan, Utah.
Married Mary Larson Dec. 22, 1869, Salt Lake City (daughter of Hans Larson and Karen Stene Olsen, pioneers Sept. 15, 1859, Robert F. Nelsen company). She was born June 15, 1850, Moen farm, Denmark. Their children: Andrew Bruce b. Feb. 5, 1874, m. Elizabeth Baxter May 23, 1894; Clarence b. Nov. 6, 1875, m. Alice Ann Burton Oct. 8, 1897; Ernest Adelbert b. Feb. 14, 1877, m. Kate Roberts Oct. 22, 1903; Royal b. Sept. 11, 1879, d. March 3, 1880; Edwin Leroy b. May 16, 1881, m. Dagmar Christensen 1905; Lillian Elnora b. March 2, 1883, m. James G. Widdison, Jr., Sept. 18, 1907; Wilford Woodruff b. May 17, 1885; Franklin Richards b. July 23, 1888. Family resided West Jordan, Utah, and Afton, Wyoming.
Bishop of West Jordan ward. Member territorial legislature two terms. Patriarch in Jordan stake. Constructed first sawmills at West Jordan, Spanish Fork, St. George, Utah, and Star Valley, Wyo. Died 1902.

GARDNER, JAMES HAMILTON (son of Archibald Gardner and Sarah Jane Hamilton). Born July 27, 1859, Mill Creek, Utah.
Married Rhoda Priscilla Huffaker Oct. 15, 1886, Logan, Utah (daughter of Simpson D. Huffaker and Rhoda P. Barnum of Cottonwood, Utah, pioneers Oct. 6, 1847). She was born Dec. 30, 1864. Their children: James Hamilton b. Jan. 4, 1888; Archibald Delos b. March 26, 1890; Viola b. April 24, 1892; Vera b. Jan. 10, 1894; Reid Huffaker b. May 20, 1897; LeRoi Barnum b. April 13, 1900; Marian b. Dec. 6, 1903; Ferne b. Dec. 23, 1905; Lois b. Feb. 20, 1908. Family resided Lehi, Utah, and Elba, Idaho.
Bishop of Lehi 2nd ward 1903. General consulting superintendent Utah-Idaho Sugar Company. City councilman Lehi; 1902-04; commissioner Utah county 1910-12.

GARDNER, ANDREW BRUCE (son of Archibald Gardner and Mary Larson). Born Feb. 5, 1874, West Jordan, Utah.
Married Elizabeth Baxter May 23, 1894, Afton, Wyo. (daughter of William Walton Burton and Sarah Ann Fielding), who was born Sept. 2, 1875, Ogden, Utah. Their children: Albert b. June 27, 1898, d. same day; Marian b. Nov. 17, 1901; Lawrence Alton b. Aug. 19, 1904; Rollin Elworth b. Oct. 9, 1906.
Second counselor to Bishop George Waite of Afton, Wyo., 1894-99; missionary to Eastern states 1898-1900; Star Valley stake Y. M. M. I. A. aid and stake high councilor 1900; Sunday school superintendent Afton ward 1900-01; first assistant Star Valley stake Sunday school superintendent 1901-02, 1909-12; stake superintendent Y. M. M. I. A. 1902-05; president Y. M. M. I. A. Afton ward 1907-10; alternate high councilor; secretary Sunday school. City councilman 1902-05; mayor 1905-08; member Wyoming state legislature 1909-10; school trustee; vice-president Afton commercial club.

GARFF, PETER N. (son of Nels Garff, born Jan. 20, 1811, and Marie Jackobson, born Dec. 9, 1820, both of Eskebjerg, Sjelland, Denmark; former died on plains, latter came to Utah). He was born Feb. 17, 1843, Sersiov, Holbek amt. Sjelland, Denmark. Came to Utah 1857, Christiansen's handcart company.
Married Antomina Sorensen July 26, 1869, Salt Lake City (daughter of Lars Sorensen and Maren Kerstine Petersen of Bjergby, Hjorring, Denmark, pioneers 1861, Samuel A. Wooley company). She was born May 6, 1852. Their children: George F. b. June 17, 1870, m. Phena Brimhall; Mary Ann b. Dec. 28, 1871, m. B. F. Fitzgerald; Huldah b. Jan. 23, 1873, m. F. C. Mickelson; Matilda b. April 1, 1874, m. B. M. Crossgrove; Heber N. b. Oct. 10, 1876, m. Louise Murphy; Royal B. b. Oct. 23, 1877, m. Rachel Day; Moses S. b. Nov. 10, 1879, m. Mary Rasmussen; Aaron Z. b. March 29, 1881; Mina C. b. May 7, 1883, m. S. J. Mickelson; Orson A. b. March 2, 1885, m. Bodel Lyngby; Connie M. b. Sept. 8, 1888, m. Enno Drown; Regnald W. b. May 6, 1890. Family home Draper, Utah.
Senior president 73d quorum seventies; high councilor; acting teacher since he was 18 years old; assisted in bringing immigrants to Utah in 1866; was one of a company of 500 who brought in about 4,000 people. As trustee he successfully established the first free public school at Draper (the Park school), and at Crescent taxing the railroads $1,800, which was used in supplying Draper with its first school house. School trustee. Teacher and superintendent of Sunday school at Draper 25 years; missionary to Linton, Brown county, Minn., where he organized a branch of the church; missionary to Norway, where he baptized 27 persons, 11 of them young ladies, who were organized into first Y. L. M. I. A. in Bergen, Norway; there he served as president of the conference in 1899, and until near the end of his mission, returning in 1902; home missionary; high councilor. Farmer and horticulturist.

GARN, PHILIP J. (son of John Garn, born 1771, and Susannah Pringle, born 1773, both at Bedford, Pa.—married 1794). He was born May 1, 1819, at Bedford. Came to Utah Sept. 28, 1855, Moses Thurston company.
Married Mary M. Vogt (daughter of Michael Vogt and Elizabeth Kline—married March 8, 1803, in Perry Co., Ohio). She was born Sept. 12, 1820, and came to Utah with husband. Their children: Mahala b. Feb. 4, 1840, m. Daniel Garn April 1856; Micah b. Oct. 14, 1841, m. Fanny Wood March 11, 1865; Philip J. b. Feb. 14, 1845, m. Sarah English Feb. 18, 1878; Samuel b. March 24, 1847, m. Lizzie Walker; Nathaniel b. May 1, 1849, m. Nettie Evans; Elizabeth b. April 19, 1851, m. John Ford Feb. 4, 1867; Daniel b. May 18, 1853, d. Jan. 1856; Mary M. b. March 31, 1855, m. W. H. J. Smith 1877; Emma b. Feb. 27, 1857, m. Joseph Ford Feb. 7, 1876.
Settled at Centerville 1855. High priest. Died Jan. 1, 1859.

GARN, MICAH (son of Philip J. Garn and Mary M. Vogt). Born Oct. 14, 1841, at Fremont, Ohio.
Married Fanny Wood March 11, 1865, Salt Lake City (daughter of John Wood and Fanny Coble, pioneers 1855, Moses Thurston company). She was born Oct. 11, 1841, Brighton, Eng. Their children: Fanny C. b. Oct. 22, 1866, m. Samuel Capener May 11, 1887; Micah A. b. Sept. 13, 1869, m. Mary M. Leonard Feb. 23, 1899; John H. b. Nov. 1, 1871, m. Nancy Udy Nov. 17, 1897; Mary Larelda b. July 12, 1874, m. Arthur Capener July 12, 1893; Daniel b. Aug. 15, 1877, m. Araminta Monahan Jan. 3, 1903; Nathaniel b. Aug. 15, 1877, m. Clara Monahan Aug. 20, 1908; Emma R. b. Jan. 29, 1879, m. William L. Aprood June 14, 1906; Mahala J. b. Sept. 7, 1882, m. Cooper Haffield April 14, 1909. Family home Fielding, Utah.

Seventy; missionary to the Muddy 1868-69; treasurer of Centerville Sunday school six years. Moved to Bear River valley 1887. Superintendent of first Sunday school in Fielding, and served for seven years. Postmaster eight years, and road supervisor seven years. Malad stake high councilor 17 years.

GARN, THOMAS (son of Martin Garn, born Feb. 17, 1814, and Catharine Croyl, born May 4, 1818, both in Bedford county, Pa.). He was born Aug. 11, 1839, in Fremont, Sandusky Co., Ohio. Came to Utah Sept. 17, 1861, Milo Andrus company.
Married Esther Ann Eldredge March 14, 1868 (daughter of Ira Eldredge and Nancy Black, pioneers Sept. 22, 1847, Daniel Spencer company). She was born March 24, 1839, and came to Utah with parents. Their children: Flavilla Catharine b. April 29, 1869, m. Henry Wright Aug. 27, 1890; Nancy E. b. April 24, 1871, m. David Birch March 9, 1892; Amanda Matilda b. March 30, 1873, m. Franklin R. Meadows Oct. 16, 1901; Thomas Martin b. Aug. 12, 1875; William Joshua b. Aug. 28, 1877, m. Ella Spriggs Dec. 12, 1900; Edmond b. March 22, 1880, m. Pearl Spriggs June 26, 1903. Family resided Salt Lake City and Coalville, Utah. Settled in Sugar House ward; moved to Coalville 1869, where he was ward teacher; high priest.

GARNER, DAVID (son of David Garner and Jane Stephens). Born Jan. 30, 1818, at Lexicon, N. C. Came to Utah July 28, 1847, with a section of Mormon Battalion.
Married Dolly Durfee Oct. 18, 1842 (daughter of Edmond Durfee, killed in raid by mob). She was born March 8, 1816. Their children: Louisa Ann b. July 12, 1844, m. Bailey Lake; Fannie Merilla b. July 2, 1845, m. William Tracey; David Edmond b. Jan. 10, 1847, m. Sarah Davis; William Franklin b. Dec. 12, 1848, m. Mary A. Barker; Mary Marinda b. Feb. 20, 1850, m. Abram Chadwick; Nancy Jane b. Sept. 7, 1851, d. child; Amelia Jane b. May 10, 1853, m. Henry Dixon; Charles Henry b. April 16, 1856; Lydia b. March 2, 1859, m. Elias Bybee. Family home North Ogden.
Married Bethzina Burns April 16, 1857, Salt Lake City (daughter of Enoch Burns and Elizabeth Moffet), who was born March 5, 1842, at Nauvoo, Ill. Their only child: Bethzina Elizabeth b. Oct. 3, 1858, and d. Nov. 5, 1859. Family home North Ogden, Utah.
Member Mormon Battalion; assisted bringing immigrants to Utah; one of the seven presidents of 78th quorum seventies. Farmer. Died April 27, 1889, North Ogden.

GARNER, WILLIAM FRANKLIN (son of David Garner and Dolly Durfee). Born Dec. 12, 1848, Council Bluffs, Iowa. Came to Utah 1851.
Married Mary Ann Barker Feb. 9, 1870, Salt Lake City (daughter of James Barker and Polly Emeline Blodgett of North Ogden, pioneers 1850, Benjamin Brown company). She was born Dec. 24, 1853. Their children: Olive Alberta b. Oct. 9, 1871, m. Oscar J. Maddox; William Henry b. Nov. 30, 1873, m. Mary D. Tolman; James Albert b. Oct. 2, 1875, m. Sarah K. Hill; Mary Emeline b. Feb. 20, 1878, m. Joseph E. Ward; Ida Louisa b. April 9, 1884, m. George H. Jones; Florence I. b. Dec. 7, 1886, m. James R. Rawlings; Hazel A. b. Oct. 1, 1889. Family home North Ogden, Utah, and Clifton, Idaho.
Seventy; bishop of Clifton ward 1886-97; president high priests' quorum; high councilman. Farmer.

GARNER, JAMES ALBERT (son of William Franklin Garner and Mary Ann Barker). Born Oct. 2, 1875, North Ogden, Utah.
Married Sarah K. Hill Dec. 19, 1900, Logan, Utah (daughter of John R. Hill and Margory Kerr, both of Wellsville, Utah, former coming to Utah 1852, latter 1861, Job Pingree company). She was born Oct. 1, 1882.

GARNER, PHILIP (son of David Garner and Jane Stephens of Council Bluffs, Iowa). Born Oct. 11, 1808, in Rowan county, N. C. Came to Utah Oct. 27, 1849, George A. Smith company.
Married Mary Hedrick April 4, 1830, Rowan county, N. C. (daughter of Francis Hedrick and Elizabeth Howard of Rowan county, pioneers Oct. 25, 1849, with George A. Smith company). She was born Sept. 25, 1811. Their children: Sarah b. Jan. 18, 1832, m. Lester J. Herrick; Henry b. Feb. 13, 1833, m. Mary M. Browning; David b. Aug. 13, 1834, m. Eliza Coffin; Jane b. Aug. 3, 1836, m. David II. Browning; Frederick b. Oct. 13, 1837, m. Ann Horrocks: Martha b. Jan. 18, 1840, m. Benjamin C. Critchlow; Asael b. June 6, 1843, m. Georgia Everett; Roemma b. April 7, 1845, m. Joel Terry; Joseph b. Nov. 22, 1847, m. Mary Phillips; Philip b. May 6, 1850, m. Mary Gaisford; William F. b. June 3, 1852, m. Sarah A. Furniss; John A. b. Sept. 11, 1856, m. Charlotte Pincock. Family home Ogden, Utah.
Member of the Mormon Battalion in Company B, under Capt. Jesse D. Hunter. He enlisted July 16, 1846. Was hurt on picket duty while en route to Santa Fe, N. M., by falling into a deep ravine and breaking three ribs. Was returned to Pueblo and was afterward honorably released and returned home to Council Bluffs, Iowa. In the spring of 1849 himself and family journeyed in a wagon drawn by oxteam over the plains to Utah. Farmer. Died Sept. 16, 1872.

PIONEERS AND PROMINENT MEN OF UTAH 885

GARNER, HENRY (son of Philip Garner and Mary Hedrick). Born Feb. 13, 1833, near Vincennes, Ind. Came to Utah Oct. 27, 1849, George A. Smith company.
Married Mary Melvina Browning June 22, 1854, Ogden, Utah (daughter of Jonathan Browning and Elizabeth Stolcup, who were married Nov. 9, 1826, Nashville, Tenn., pioneers Sept. 15, 1852, Henry Miller company). She was born Jan. 15, 1840. Came to Utah with her parents. Their children: Henry James b. June 9, 1855, m. Eliza A. Ballantyne Jan. 31, 1884; Jonathan Browning b. Aug. 31, 1857; Mary Ann B. b. March 4, 1860, m. Hyrum S. Wood Nov. 12, 1879; Emma Elizabeth b. May 4, 1862; Frederick Swen b. Feb. 5, 1864, m. Margaret Ann Gibbons Jan. 10, 1884; Enoch Charles b. Feb. 9, 1866; Barbara Alice b. Nov. 30, 1867; Rufus Alma b. Oct. 18, 1869, m. Rosa Belle Porter Dec. 2, 1891; Sarah Ida b. Oct. 8, 1871; Rosa Rebecca b. Dec. 8, 1872, m. Francis Horspool; Frank Philip b. Aug. 25, 1874, m. Katie Pratt Nov. 25, 1899; Hyrum Elihu b. Nov. 6, 1876, m. Mary V. Bigler Nov. 18, 1904; Reuben Page b. Jan. 9, 1878; Alta Charlotte b. May 22, 1880, m. Junius Cook Oct. 25, 1905.
High priest. Indian fighter; member of the Echo Canyon volunteers.

GARNER, HENRY JAMES (son of Henry Garner and Mary M. Browning). Born June 9, 1855, in Ogden, Utah.
Married Eliza A. Ballantyne Jan. 31, 1884 (daughter of Richard Ballantyne and Mary Pearce), who was born June 8, 1866, Eden, Utah. Their children: Richard H. b. Nov. 22, 1884; Ethel B. June 29, 1886, m. Ephraim W. Manning June 20, 1906; Mary Edna b. Aug. 8, 1888; Iona b. Aug. 2, 1893, m. James Bingham Dec. 20, 1911; Rulon B. b. March 31, 1900; Lyda b. July 24, 1902; Harold b. March 4, 1906; Milton Eugene b. Oct. 21, 1907. Family resided Ogden and Plain City, Utah.
Superintendent Plain City Sunday schools 1901-03; first counselor to Bishop George W. Bromwell 1903-06; bishop of Plain City ward 1906-10; high councilor in North Weber stake 1910. Merchant.

GARNER, RUFUS ALMA (son of Henry Garner and Mary M. Browning). Born Oct. 18, 1869, in Ogden, Utah.
Married Rosa Belle Porter Dec. 2, 1891, Logan, Utah (daughter of Charles A. Porter and Rachel L. Hall of Ogden). She was born Sept. 23, 1875. Their children: Vird Carlisle b. Sept. 22, 1897; Alma Edwin b. Aug. 29, 1901. Family home Ogden.
Member high council Weber stake. Assistant postmaster at Ogden. Bookkeeper and salesman.

GARNER, FREDERICK (son of Philip Garner and Mary Hedrick). Born Oct. 13, 1837, in Hancock county, Ill.
Married Ann Horrocks Jan. 1, 1862, Ogden, Utah (daughter of Edward Horrocks and Alice Houghton of England, the former coming to Utah in October 1857, Albert Carrington company, the latter dying in England). She was born May 4, 1844. Their children: Annie Elizabeth b. April 2, 1863, m. James Henry Pincock; William Frederick b. Feb. 16, 1865, m. Minnie Black; Aaron George b. Feb. 17, 1867, d. Oct. 17, 1879; Samuel Edward b. May 1, 1869, d. Sept. 8, 1879; James Nathan b. Aug. 7, 1871, m. Sylvia Layne; Alice Mozell b. Oct. 7, 1873, m. James William Banford; Horace Eugene b. June 29, 1876, m. Isabell Scott Ure; Burk LeRoy b. Sept. 3, 1878, m. Annie Elizabeth Clark; Benjamin Franklin b. March 28, 1881, m. Mary Salena Carr; Alpha b. June 4, 1887. Family home Ogden.
Second counselor to bishop of Ogden first ward 1878-89; home missionary 1889-95. School trustee; road supervisor; justice of peace. Brought first alfalfa seed into Utah in 1861.

GARNER, JOHN A. (son of Philip Garner and Mary Hedrick). Born Sept. 11, 1856, in Ogden, Utah.
Married Charlotte Pincock Nov. 24, 1881, Salt Lake City (daughter of John Pincock and Isabella Douglass of Ogden, pioneers 1852, John Parker company). She was born Oct. 7, 1861. Their children: John Earl b. Aug. 4, 1882, m. Edith Morgan; Violate Pincock b. May 22, 1884; George Albert b. Oct. 29, 1886; Walter Mack b. Sept. 21, 1890; Ray Douglass b. Nov. 27, 1892; Florence May b. Aug. 3, 1897; Lucile b. Oct. 6, 1901; Mary Ethel b. Nov. 14, 1902; Heber Ross b. Feb. 9, 1905. Family home Rexburg, Idaho.
Missionary to California 1898-01; high priest; member high council 1902; counselor to Bishop Oliver C. Dally of Rexburg 1st ward 1907-12.

GARNER, WILLIAM. Came to Utah Oct. 2, 1852, Harmon Cutler company.
Married Mary S. Holmes (Stowell) in 1852 (daughter of James Holmes and Millie Rossen of eastern New York, pioneers 1852). She was born Sept. 15, 1797, and came to Utah in 1852 with her family. There were no children.
Mary S. Holmes was the widow of Augustus Oliver Artemus Stowell. Their children: Sophia, m. William Parshall; William Rufus Rogers. m. Hannah Topham, m. Cynthia J. Maxwell; Mary L. m. Saphrona Kelly, m. Harriet Stowell; Minerva, m. Christopher Merkley; Laura. m. Nelson Baxter; Matilda, m. Orin Packard; Augustus, m. Emma Hill; Alice and Juliette, m. William Howard Perry; Mary Alvira, d. child. Family home New York.
High priest. Settled at Provo, and later moved to Cedar Valley, and farmed at Lynn. Died March 1872, Hooper, Utah.

GARRETT, JAMES (son of John Garrett of Quincy, Ill.). Born 1855. Married Mary E. Wallace May 2, 1880, at Salt Lake City (daughter of George B. Wallace and Martha Davis), who was born June 10, 1858, at Salt Lake City. Their children: James H. b: Sept. 9, 1881, m. Sucy D. Wardrupt; George E. b. Dec. 8, 1883, m. Martha J. Crookston; William A. b. Dec. 5, 1885, d. infant. Family home Salt Lake City.

GARRICK, HAMILTON MORRISON (son of John Garrick and Esther Wheatford of Gallowayshire, Scotland). Born Nov. 29, 1834, in Gallowayshire. Came to Utah Sept. 12, 1857, Jesse Martin company.
Married Elizabeth Tilley Dec. 8, 1857 (daughter of Richard Tilley and Phoebe Dukes), who was born at Newton, Lea Willis, Eng.; came to Utah in 1857 alone. Their children: Elizabeth Phoebe b. Feb. 1, 1860, m. Walter S. Carr 1881; Mary Jane b. Sept. 17, 1866, m. Herbert Tyzack 1885; John R. b. Nov. 19, 1870, m. Jane Mickleson 1897; Ellen b. June 27, 1873, m. Noah G. Kearns 1894; Esther b. April 16, 1876, m. J. H. Roylance 1893; Lillie May b. Oct. 16, 1879, m. William G. Barton 1900; Mabel b. Oct. 20, 1877, m. Edgar Fillmore 1901. Family home Gunnison, Utah.
President 48th quorum seventies; choir leader at Gunnison 20 years. Postmaster; treasurer of board of school trustees three years. Missionary to Ireland 1856. Black Hawk war veteran. Stockraiser.

GEARY, EDWARD (son of George Geary and Mary Heath, born 1788, both in Leicester, Leicestershire, Eng.). Born Nov. 25, 1830, in parents' birthplace. Came to Utah 1862, Joseph Horne company.
Married Elizabeth Ann Slater (daughter of Franklin Slater and Elizabeth Hewitt), who was born Oct. 6, 1833, in England. Their children: Elizabeth Ann b. Jan. 29, 1853, Claycross, Eng., m. Joseph Durrant July 12, 1874; Edward Long b. Aug. 18, 1854, at Claycross, m. Alice Criddle March 19, 1877; Mary Ellen b. Aug. 24, 1856, at Clay Cross, m. Larry Larson in Pennsylvania; George Samuel b. Aug. 26, 1858; Hyrum Phineas b. Oct. 19, 1860, in Pennsylvania, m. Isabell Gibby Oct. 13, 1887; William Joseph b. March 24, 1863, died; Thomas Hewitt b. May 10, 1866, Morgan, Utah, m. Laura Simmons; Eliza Catherine b. May 11, 1869, Morgan, Utah, m. James Jennings; Sarah Louisa b. April 11, 1870, Morgan, Utah, m. George London; Franklin Slater b. Sept. 8, 1872, Morgan, Utah; Agnes Hannah b. Oct. 14, 1874, Morgan, Utah, died; Daniel James b. June 20, 1876, Morgan, Utah, m. Josephine Littlefield. Family lived at Round Valley and Morgan, Utah.
Contractor and builder.

GEARY, EDWARD LONG (son of Edward Geary and Elizabeth Ann Slater). Born Aug. 18, 1854, Clay Cross, Eng. Came to Utah 1862, Joseph Horne company.
Married Alice Criddle March 19, 1877, Salt Lake City (daughter of George and Mary Ann Criddle of Morgan, Utah; pioneers October, 1862). She was born March 5, 1859. Their children: Edward George b. May 14, 1878, m. Grace Wakefield Feb. 3, 1905; William Frederick b. April 16, 1880, died; Mary Alice b. Feb. 25, 1882, m. H. D. Morgan; Ernest Leroy b. March 3, 1884, died; Maud Mary Ann b. May 27, 1886, m. James Mulliner. Family home Huntington, Utah.
Married Annie Guyman, Manti, Utah, March 13, 1889 (daughter of Noah T. Guyman and Louise Rowely of Fountain Green, Utah). She was born Oct. 12, 1870.
Married Isabella W. Walker, Manti, Utah, May 23, 1894 (daughter of John Walker and Ellen McSkelly of Manti, Utah).
Member 81st quorum seventies; ward teacher. Member Huntington canal and reservoir association board. three terms; member town board, three terms. Settled at Bountiful 1862; moved to Morgan county 1864; called to St. Johns, Ariz., spring of 1884, by Church of Jesus Christ of L. D. S., returning, settled at Huntington November, 1884; he has pioneered four new settlements and assisted in building communities. Farmer; stockman; freighter; capitalist.

GEARY, HYRUM P. (son of Edward Geary and Elizabeth Ann Slater). Born Oct. 19, 1861, Trevorton, Pa.
Married Isabell M. Gibby, Logan, Utah (daughter of John Gibby and Ellen Olphen) who was born Dec. 13, 1868, Round Valley, Utah. Their children: Hyrum George b. Sept. 22, 1888; Charles Calvin b. Sept. 7, 1891; Parley b. June 25, 1894; Austin Leo b. Sept. 20, 1896; Lillian May b. Feb. 17, 1900. Family home Morgan, Utah.
Seventy; superintendent Round Valley Sunday school.

GEDDES, WILLIAM (son of Hugh Geddes of Scotland). Born Dec. 8, 1832, Bilston, Lanarkshire, Scotland. Came to Utah Oct. 2, 1854.
Married Elizabeth Stewart June 3, 1855 (daughter of Archibald Stewart and Ester Lyle of Glasgow, Scotland). Their children: William S. b. April 5, 1856, m. Moran Carver; Joseph B. b. Dec. 18, 1857, m. Dora Neeley; Archibald b. Jan. 31, 1860, m. Nelley Reed; Hugh b. July 10, 1865, m. Martha Stodard; Elizabeth b. Aug. 8, 1863, m. George H. Carver. Family home Plain City, Utah.
Married Martha Stewart in Salt Lake City (daughter of Archibald Stewart and Ester Lyle of Scotland). She was born May 10, 1838, Glasgow, Scotland. Their children: Agness b. Aug. 17, 1857, m. Augustus Peterson; Hugh S. b. July 25, 1859, m. Martena Peterson July 12, 1883; Mary b. Sept. 18, 1861, m. James M. Thomas; Annie b. Sept. 20, 1865, m. Thomas Sutherland; John b. Feb. 18, 1867; Susan b. Feb. 9, 1868; Margret b. Jan. 9, 1871, m. Alfred N. Stevens; James S. b. May 18, 1873, m. Olive Nielsen; George b. Aug. 14, 1876.
Married Emma Hope (Stewart) (daughter of Archibald Stewart and Ester Lyle of Scotland). Their children: Robert; Eliza; Sarah; Susie; David; Hyrum S.; Joan C.; Gertrude.
Missionary for seven years in Europe; worked on Salt Lake temple from 1855 to 1860. Moved to Plain City 1859.

GEDDES, JOSEPH STEWART (son of William Geddes and Elizabeth Stewart). Born Dec. 18, 1857, Salt Lake City.
Married Isabell Dora Neeley Dec. 29, 1881, Salt Lake City (daughter of Aminus M. Neeley and Susan Morgan, the latter came to Utah with handcart company). She was born June 26, 1862, Brigham City, Utah. Their children: Pearl Lorena b. Feb. 22, 1883, m. David G. Eames Jan. 25, 1905; Joseph A. b. Nov. 27, 1884; Dora Blanch b. Sept. 30, 1887; Ruby L. b. April 22, 1889; Ivy M. b. May 8, 1891; Ira b. March 28, 1893; Hazel K. b. Oct. 30, 1894; Elizabeth Vera b. Feb. 7, 1898; Josie N. b. March 10, 1900; Paul Stewart b. Aug. 3, 1902; Elias Lyle b. Oct. 25, 1905.
Set apart to preside over Oneida stake Sept. 25, 1910.

GEDDES, HUGH S. (son of William Geddes and Martha Stewart). Born July 25, 1859, Plain City, Utah.
Married Martena Peterson July 12, 1883, Salt Lake City (daughter of Hans Peterson and Annie M. Hansen, pioneers 1853, first Danish immigration). She was born Oct. 14, 1864, Plain City, Utah. Their children: Estella b. March 18, 1885, m. Jacob A. Paten; Hugh Lester b. July 28, 1887, m. Lydia Lowe; Maud b. Feb. 28, 1892; Moses b. Sept. 18, 1895; Grant b. July 23, 1898; Elva b. March 31, 1900; Archibald b. Feb. 12, 1902, d. Jan. 5, 1907; Donald b. May 9, 1906, d. Jan. 12, 1907; William, d. infant; Ralph Thomas b. April 17, 1909. Family resided Plain City, Utah, and Preston, Idaho.
Moved to Preston, Idaho, 1884, where he worked two years on the canal. Missionary to New Zealand 1888-91; superintendent Preston Sunday school 10 years; second counselor to Bishop John Larsen, Preston ward; bishop of Preston 2d ward 1902-10; Oneida stake high council. Village trustee two terms; county commissioner two years. Secretary and director of Preston, Riverdale and Mink Creek Canal Company and of Cub River and Warm Creek Canal Company for several years.

GEE, GEORGE W. (son of George W. Gee and Mary Jane Smith). Born Oct. 9, 1841, Lee Co., Iowa. Came to Utah Sept. 28, 1851, Capt. John Brown company.
Married Sophina A. Fuller May 4, 1862, at Salt Lake City (daughter of Amos B. Fuller and Esther Smith), who was born May 6, 1843. Their children: George W. b. May 9, 1864, died; Elias A. b. June 29, 1868, m. Francis M. Bean; Georgiana b. Dec. 15, 1869, m. Joseph S. Smith; Mary Jane b. Oct. 8, 1871, m. Caleb A. Haws; Esther b. Oct. 29, 1873, m. George Hawn, m. Joseph B. Smith; Sophina A. b. Aug. 6, 1875, m. Joshua R. Hodson; Don Carlos b. April 20, 1878, m. Ida M. Loveless; Bertha V. b. May 31, 1880, m. Thomas Summer; Martha E. b. April 28, 1883, m. Hyrum G. Smith; Adelia M. b. May 14, 1885, m. Elvon L. Jackson.
Married Ursula Bandley March 2, 1877, St. George, Utah (daughter of Thomas Bandley and Ferena Lanieca of Provo, Utah; they came to Utah in 1872). She was born April 4, 1858. Their children: Asahel T. b. June 3, 1878, m. Eliza Jones; Dora b. Sept. 21, 1880, Theodora b. April 25, 1883, Amanda b. July 21, 1885, latter three died; Emma b. Nov. 1, 1887, m. Hugh E. Love; Pearl b. June 6, 1896. Family home Provo, Utah.
President 45th quorum seventies; missionary to England 1864-67. Deputy sheriff one year; school trustee; city watermaster. Farmer.

GEE, LYSANDER (son of Solmon Gee and Sarah Watson Crane of Ashtabula Co., Ohio). Born Sept. 1, 1818, at Austinburg, Ohio. Came to Utah 1849, George A. Smith company.
Married Amanda M. Sagers Sept. 5, 1838, at Far-West, Mo., who was born 1821 in New York state, and died Oct. 22, 1848, in St. Louis. Their only child was Orlando, m. Mary Bates.
Married Theresa Bowley Feb. 12, 1846, at Nauvoo, Ill. (daughter of John Bowley and Polly Reed of Maine). She was born Oct. 7, 1829, Carthage, Me. Their children: Rozella, m. Robert McGavin; Eudora, died; Andeca, m. Arish H. Brower; Electa, m. Erin Bates; Austin, m. Phoebe Bates; Newton, Elias, George, Louisa, latter four died; Sarah, m. Robert Skelton, Jr.; Almon, died. Family home Tooele, Utah.
Married Maryetta Rowe Feb. 10, 1850, in Salt Lake City, who was born Oct. 3, 1831, in Tompkins county, N. Y. Their children: Erasmus; Erastus, m. Geneva Telford; Augustus, m. Annie Dahlquist; Mary, m. Thorpe Luker; Stephen, m. Thalia Watson; Caroline, m. Robert McGavin; Emma, m. Brigham H. Telford; Robert, m. Alice Clark; John.
One of presidents of 31st quorum seventies; high priest Tooele stake; superintendent Sunday school. Prosecuting attorney; justice of the peace. Lawyer; carpenter. Died June 27, 1894, at Tooele.

GEORGE, JOHN (son of Thomas George and Ann Roberts of Glamorganshire. South Wales). Born April 19, 1818, Myrthyr Duggen, South Wales. Came to Utah 1850.
Married Elizabeth Morgan Jones 1854, Salt Lake City (daughter of Philip Jones and Elizabeth Morgan, both of Brecknockshire, South Wales). She was born Oct. 12, 1825. Their children: Harriet b. July 10, 1854, m. Peter Rossen; Thomas b. May 5, 1856, m. Margaret McMillan; Mary b. March 7, 1858; Joseph M. b. March 20, 1860, m. Medelliner Casto; Rachel b. May 8, 1862, m. F. W. Burrough; John b. Aug. 6, 1865, m. May Hawley. Family home 19th ward, Salt Lake City.
Elder. Died at Murray, Utah.

GEORGE, JOSEPH M. (son of John George and Elizabeth Morgan Jones). Born March 20, 1860, North Ogden, Utah.
Married Medelliner Casto Nov. 24, 1886, Independence, Utah (daughter of John Casto and Betsy Corbett, both of Salt Lake City). She was born April 7, 1861. Their children: Mary b. Oct. 10, 1887, m. C. E. Robertson; John L. b. July 25, 1889; Elizabeth b. April 2, 1891; m. R. J. Forsyth; Zenos F. b. Nov. 4, 1894; Paul b. April 2, 1898; Juanita b. April 16, 1900. Family resided Independence and Burton, Utah.
Member 34th quorum seventies; ward teacher. Laborer.

GEORGESON, NIELS (for his genealogy see Niels Jorgensen).

GEORGESEN, HANS HYRUM (son of Niels Georgesen and Johanna M. Kofoed). Born Dec. 25, 1871, Treasureton, Idaho. Idaho.
Married Minnie Berlips Oct. 23, 1907, Salt Lake City (daughter of Louis Derlips, born Oct. 27, 1841, died April 25, 1880 and Caroline Eugelhardt, born July 31, 1843). She was born Oct. 8, 1876, St. Peter, Minn. Their children: Wilbur Norval b. July 15, 1908; Donald LeMar b. Nov. 16, 1911.

GERBER, JOHN (son of Jacob Gerber of Bern, Switzerland). He was born Sept. 8, 1796, at Bern. Came to Utah October, 1854, Capt. Van Buren company.
Married Magdalena Hugh, who was born 1797. Their child: Susanna, d. child. Family home Sierra Leone, Africa.
Married Elizabeth Wagner, who was born 1799. Their child: Maria Susanna Wilhelmina. Family home, Sierra Leone.
Married Johanna Elenora Lessing, who was born Feb. 21, 1835. Their children: Frederick, d. child; John Theophilus, m. Mary ——; Louis Emanuel, m. Emily Jacob. Family home, Ohio.
Married Maria Ackeret 1843, in Indiana, who was born May 11, 1824. Their children: Julia Carolina, d. child; Julia Jemima, m. Ira Jacob; Helena Ellenora, m. Joseph Jacob; Anna Poulina, Benjamin Ulrich, d. child; Moroni, m. Emily Jane Jacob; Mary Matilda, m. Isaac Jacob; Sarah Elizabeth, d. child; Emily Adelia, m. Arthur Watkins. Family home, Utah.
High priest. Early settler to St. George; assisted in founding Washington, Utah, and later moved to Midway, Utah. Physician and surgeon. Farmer.
Died Nov. 22, 1870, at Midway, Utah.

GERBER, MORONI (son of John Gerber and Anna Maria Ackeret). Born Oct. 4, 1856, at Cedar City, Utah.
Married Emily Jane Jacob Nov. 11, 1880, at Salt Lake City (daughter of Lucian Jacob and Janet Clotworthy of Midway). She was born May 20, 1862. Their children: Janet Anderson b. Sept. 13, 1881, m. George S. Bingham; Mabel b. May 8, 1883, m. William Ralph Hacking; Jean Eleanor b. April 17, 1885, m. Ellis S. Merkley; Florence Rhoda b. March 27, 1887, m. Gilbert W. Richardson; Irvin Moroni b. May 6, 1891; Zetella Ackeret b. March 6, 1893; Ether Lyman b. April 17, 1896; Fern Elizabeth b. Sept. 17, 1898; Hugh Jacob b. March 18, 1901; John Wendell b. Aug. 6, 1904; Helen b. May 26, 1908. Family home Vernal, Utah.
High priest; missionary to Southern states 1887-91; ward teacher; president Y. M. M. I. A. at Midway and also of Maeser ward. Justice of peace at Midway 1895-97. Farmer.

GIBBONS, JOHN A. R. (son of William Gibbons and Dorothy Head of Berkshire, Eng.). He was born Feb. 10, 1794, Hillgreen, Berkshire. Came to Utah October, 1854.
Married Fanny Roby Aug. 18, 1818, Mapel Durham, Eng. (daughter of Aaron Roby and Mary Lowe of Berkshire, pioneers Oct. 1854). She was born Dec. 26, 1800. Their children: John b. May 2, 1823, m. Mary Schwving; James b. Jan. 27, 1825, m. Ann Shettelworth; William Belcher, b. Aug. 24, 1828, m. Mary Wilkes; Francis Lorenzo b. Nov. 5, 1831, m. Elizabeth Pearde; Thomas b. March 24, 1834, m. Ann Caroline Evans; Frederick b. Sept. 9, 1835, d. child; Henry b. Feb. 4, 1838, d. child; Dorothy Mary Caroline b. April 9, 1840, d. infant; John Aaron; Mary, d. infant. Family resided Berkshire, Eng. and South Wales.
High priest. Died March 1872.

GIBBONS, THOMAS (son of John A. R. Gibbons and Fanny Roby). Born March 24, 1834, Hillgreen, Berkshire, Eng. Came to Utah Oct. 1854, Thomas E. Ricks company.
Married Ann Caroline Evans May 6, 1860, Ogden, Utah (daughter of Thomas Evans and Margaret Powell of Merthyr, South Wales; pioneers 1858, Fredric Bussard company). She was born May 8, 1839. Their children: Thomas b. Dec. 13, 1861, d. Dec. 13, 1861; Thomas Francis b. Dec. 17, 1862, m. Mary Bashire Jan. 1899; Fanny Elizabeth b. Dec. 25, 1864, m. David B. Russell July, 1883; Margaret Ann b. Oct. 8, 1866, m. Frederick S. Garner Jan. 11, 1884; John Aaron Roby b. Aug. 10, 1868, m. Manerva D. Berry Oct. 7, 1886; Jennette Caroline b. Feb. 26, 1870, m. Matthew O. Callahan Oct. 25, 1885; Edward Evans b. Dec. 13, 1871, m. Anna Downs June 22, 1900; Evan Evans b. Nov. 1, 1872, d. June 23, 1886; Mary May b. Sept. 11, 1874, m. Oliver M. Davidson March 24, 1904; William Morgan b. June 10, 1876, d. Jan. 21, 1902; Elizabeth Latricia b. June 8, 1879, m. Francis L. Woods June 27, 1901, d. Aug. 7, 1905; David Howell b. Aug. 4, 1880, d. May 25, 1881; Wealtha Helena b. July 5, 1883, m. Parley E. Woods May 3, 1902.
Settled at Tooele 1854; moved to Ogden 1855 where he worked on Ogden tabernacle. on canyon road and on bench canal. Assisted in bringing immigrants to Utah 1863; moved to Huntsville 1865. Worked on U. P., Utah Central and Utah Northern railroads. Moved back to Ogden 1881. Road supervisor at Huntsville two years. Clerk 76th quorum seventies; high priest for 10 years at Ogden, Utah.
Farmer.

GIBBONS, THOMAS (son of George Gibbons of Carson, Eng., and Lucy Reed of Collorne, Somersetshire, Eng.). Born Dec. 25, 1820, at Collorne. Came to Utah Sept. 11, 1857, Israel Evans handcart company.
Married Sarah Elizabeth Lack (daughter of Frederick Lack and Mary Ann Blithe, married in 1839 at Norwich, Norfolk, Eng.; latter came to Utah with Milo Andrus company). She was born Jan. 16, 1845. Came to Utah Oct. 23, 1855, Milo Andrus company. Their children: Thomas b. Dec. 11, 1860, m. Elizabeth Agnes Stenbridge Dec. 28, 1882; Allbrey b. Dec. 20, 1861, m. Fannie Moore Sept. 19, 1887; Precinda Celestia b. July 23, 1863, m. William Cossey Dec. 28, 1881; Edward George b. Oct. 11, 1864, m. Annie Roundy April 14, 1886; Zina Diantha b. March 14, 1866, m. Hyrum Homer Sept. 22, 1892; Sarah Elizabeth b. Sept. 19, 1867, m. William D. Brown April 24, 1895; Joseph Alfred b. March 30, 1869, m. Ellen Beard; William Oliver b. Nov. 6, 1870, m. Mary Eliza Beecroft Nov. 27, 1895; Charles Frederick b. April 28, 1872; Emma b. April 19, 1874; Worthy b. Feb. 25, 1876, m. Elizabeth Ann Siddoway; Alma b. April 7, 1878, m. Cora M. Judd; Mary Eliza b. Aug. 21, 1880, m. Ezra Workman June 19, 1902; Luctia Adaline b. March 7, 1883, m. Claud Williams Dec. 16, 1904; Ward E. b. July 7, 1885; Orson b. July 24, 1887; Willard John b. Aug. 10, 1889, m. Mary Ellen Salsbury Feb. 16, 1910.
Settled at Salt Lake City 1857. Took active part in Echo Canyon war; one of guards left to care for the city at the time of the move south. Indian war veteran. Member 4th quorum seventies. Moved to Rockport 1862. Zealous in church work; high priest. Member city council. Sunday school superintendent 11 years. County commissioner 1869-70. Farmer. Died while visiting at Skaneateles, N. Y., June 12, 1893.

GIBBONS, THOMAS (son of Thomas Gibbons and Sarah Elizabeth Lack). Born Dec. 11, 1860, Rockport, Utah.
Married Elizabeth Agnes Stenbridge Dec. 28, 1882, Salt Lake City (daughter of William Stenbridge and Caroline Barter). Their children: Sadie b. Oct. 16, 1883, m. Frank Ford Dec. 1, 1909; Velate b. April 14, 1885, m. Lawrence Thompson Nov. 2, 1903; Belle b. Jan. 20, 1889, m. Joseph Wilson; Vera b. March 8, 1896.
Farmer.

GIBBS, JOHN DUGGAN (son of Francis Gibbs and Martha Duggan, both of Haverford, West Pembrokeshire, South Wales). Born Dec. 18, 1815, Haverford, West Pembrokeshire. Came to Utah Oct. 4, 1863, Thomas E. Ricks company.
Married Julia Ann Tompkins 1841, Bristol, Eng. (daughter of George Tompkins and Ann Stephens, both of Bristol, Eng.). She was born Feb. 20, 1820. Their children: George Francis, d. Sept. 2, 1842; Martha Ann, d. Aug. 14, 1844; William, d. Aug. 30, 1845; John Duggan, d. Oct. 14, 1846; Charles Tompkins, m. Sarah R. Thornton; William Henry, m. Letitia John; Samuel Willard, m. Saphrone McCray; Louisa Elizabeth, d. May 18, 1856; Joseph Edward, m. Elizabeth K. Parkinson; James Hyrum, m. Sarah M. Green; Matilda Jane, m. Joseph Salisbury. Family home Portage, Utah.
Married Mary Phillips (Rees) 1869, Salt Lake City (daughter of Richard Phillips and Elizabeth Pugh of Merthyr, Tydfil, Wales). She was born August 1815.
High councilor; started first Sunday school library in Box Elder county 1870; patriarch in Mormon church. Justice of peace; school trustee. Superintendent of first Sunday school in Willard county. Shoemaker; tanner. Died Feb. 28, 1892, Portage, Utah.

GIBBS, WILLIAM H. (son of John Duggan Gibbs and Julia Ann Tompkins). Born Feb. 7, 1851, Haverford, West Pembrokeshire, South Wales. Came to Utah Oct. 4, 1863, Thomas E. Ricks company.
Married Letitia John Feb. 5, 1872, Salt Lake City (daughter of Thomas John and Margaret Thomas of Merthyr Tydfil, Wales, pioneers Oct. 17, 1862, H. W. Miller company). She was born April 6, 1852. Their children: Thomas John b. Jan. 23, 1873, died April 16, 1873; William Henry b. Jan. 9, 1875, m. Elizabeth S. Zundel; Samuel Willard b. Dec. 26, 1875, d. Jan. 9, 1876; Joseph Edward b. March 1, 1877, m. Mary L.

888 PIONEERS AND PROMINENT MEN OF UTAH

Harkins; Julia Ann b. Dec. 22, 1878, m. Nathan D. Geaisley; Francis Dugan b. March 22, 1881, died April 2, 1881; Frances Letitia b. March 22, 1881, m. Isaac W. Allen; Charles Warren b. Jan. 26, 1884, d. Oct. 2, 1900; Amelia Naomia b. Dec. 6, 1887; Margaret Rosalie b. Feb. 6, 1889, m. Thomas L. Howell; Martha Louisa b. Sept. 17, 1890; James Hyrum b. Sept. 5, 1892; Matilda Priscilla b. Nov. 17, 1894; Lewis Hootchew b. Sept. 9, 1895 (adopted). Family home Portage, Utah.

High priest in Mormon church: missionary to southern states 1884-87; first counselor in presidency of Malad stake. Settled at Willard; moved to Portage. Second counselor to Bishop Oliver C. Hoskins of Portage ward; second counselor to President Oliver C. Hoskins of Malad stake; first counselor to President Milton H. Welling of Malad stake; first counselor to President William H. Richards of Malad stake. Member constitutional convention 1905; member first legislature; justice of peace, and school trustee; member Intermountain Good Road Convention at Pocatello 1911. Farmer and stockraiser.

GIBSON, GEORGE W. (son of Robert Gibson and Polly Evans of Monroe county, Miss.). Born June 17, 1800, Union county, S. C. Came to Utah, September 1847, John Brown company.

Married Mary Sparks March 15, 1822, South Carolina (daughter of Josiah Sparks and Lydia Tollison of South Carolina, who was born June 10, 1802. Their children: Robert M., m. Lucinda Henskaw; Mary D., m. William New; Lydia E., m. Gilbert Hunt; William, m. Centha Lockhart; Moses, m. Electa Badger; m. Lydia Badger; m. Lizzie Bube; Frances A., m. Alvin Green; Laura A., m. James Andrews; Neoma L., m. James Andrews; Joseph, m. Ruth Therebold. Family home South Cottonwood, Utah.

Seventy; bishop of South Cottonwood; high priest. Farmer and stockraiser. Died summer 1871, Duncan, Kane Co., Utah.

GIBSON, JACOB. Born Jan. 1, —, Philadelphia, Pa. Came to Utah, 1867.

Married Margaret Robinson (Lilya) January, 1868, at Salt Lake City (daughter of James Robinson and Ellen McWaters of Scotland—latter came to Utah 1868). She was born March 23, 1852. Their children: Stewart, died; John, m. Rose Warwood; Ellen, m. Andy Andersen; Margaret, m. Alford Aston; Andrew, m. Grace Newman; Roselen, m. Olf Larson. Family home Salt Lake City.

Seventy; missionary to Scotland; counselor to Bishops Smoot and Edward Wooley of Sugar House ward. Farmer; carpenter. Died May 1, 1882, at Salt Lake City.

GIBSON, JAMES B. (son of Robert Gibson and Eliza Campbell Brown; brother of William Gibson, pioneer). Came to Utah 1860, Capt. Warren Walling company.

Helped build the fort at Kamas for protection against Indians. Conducted a harness store at Beaver, Utah, and general trading stores at Ashley and on the Uintah agency, the latter by permission of the government. Died unmarried.

GIBSON, JOHN S. Came to Utah 1856, the wagon train.

Married Jeanette S. Barnard at Salt Lake City (daughter of James B. Barnard and Jeanette Snedden, married at Mt. Airdrie, Lanark, Scotland). She was born April 22, 1840. Their children: William B. (died aged 51 years), m. Augustin Nebit and Johan Barnard; James B., m. Sarah Jane Grant; Jeanette Barnard, m. James Elijah Malin; Eliza Jane b. David B. Smith; John S. (died), m. Annie Cunnington; Alexander, m. Elizabeth Brown; Thomas Nathaniel, m. Annie Cunnington.

GIBSON, JAMES B. (son of John S. Gibson and Jeanette S. Barnard). Born April 30, 1861, Salt Lake City.

Married Sarah Jane Grant Feb. 16, 1885, at Salt Lake City (daughter of David Grant and Elizabeth Williams of Mill Creek, Utah). She was born Feb. 17, 1862. Their children: James Grant b. Nov. 11, 1885, m. Sarah Ann Davis; Sarah Evelyn b. March 18, 1888, m. Edward Neilsen; Jeanette b. Jan. 30, 1891; Elizabeth E. b. March 11, 1894, m. William H. Dunn; Rena b. Feb. 3, 1897; George B. b. Feb. 24, 1902. Family home. Salt Lake City.

GIBSON, WILLIAM (son of Robert Gibson and Eliza Campbell Brown; of Ireland, latter a pioneer 1860). He was born April 25, 1845, Killmarnock, Scotland. Came to Utah Aug. 9, 1860, Captain Warren Walling company.

Married Mary Adelia Lambert May 6, 1872, Salt Lake City (daughter of John Lambert and Adelia Groesbeck, the former born in Lancashire, Eng., the latter in Trumbull Co., Ohio—pioneers 1850). She was born Sept. 11, 1851 Salt Lake City. Their children: James Lambert, m. Sarah Jane Pope; Mary Eliza, m. Nelson G. Sowards; Sarah Adelia, m. David C. Eccles. Family resided Salt Lake City, Kamas, Ashley and Vernal, Utah.

Settled in Salt Lake 1860; hauled rock for the Salt Lake temple of the L. D. S. church. Moved to Kamas 1864 and to Vernal 1877, but during many years 1860 to 1868 made seven trips across plains with many of the famous characters of that time, bringing back immigrants and supplies to Utah. Captain in Utah militia 1865-70, served in Black Hawk war, and in many campaigns and skirmishes with Indians when necessary. One of the builders of the forts at Peoa and Kamas: constable and school trustee at latter place and at Ashley, six years each; first sheriff of Uintah county, being a constable when county was organized, was made acting sheriff. Member first and second sessions of Utah legislature from 12th district. Stockman and rancher.

GIBSON, WILLIAM D. Born Sept. 26, 1838. Came to Utah Fall 1856, wagon train.

Married Johan S. Barnard July 12, 1863, Endowment House, Salt Lake City (daughter of James Barnard and Jeanette Snedden, pioneers October, 1853, David Wilkins company). She was born Nov. 12, 1845, Clackmannan, Scotland. Their children: William H. b. June 16, 1863, d. infant; Mary Ann b. Dec. 23, 1864, m. Loyene Ensign; Jeanette b. March 28, 1867, m. James Wright; James b. Dec. 15, 1869, m. Emma Huber; Alexander b. Nov. 30, 1871, m. Eliza Huber; John b. Dec. 1873, d. when nearly 16; Jane b. Dec. 13, 1875, m. Thomas Jones; William b. April 17, 1878; Arthur b. May 11, 1880, m. Annie Buck; Blanche b. Jan. 22, 1883, m. James Galligher; Ivie Bell b. Aug. 8, 1885, d. infant. Family home 20th ward, Salt Lake City.

GIFFORD, HENRY DILL (son of Alpheus Gifford, born Aug. 28, 1793, Barnstable, Mass., and Anna Nash, born Feb. 17, 1800, Butternuts, N. Y.). Born April 28, 1825, Recating, Wayne county, Pa. Came to Utah 1853, Captain Snow company.

Married Almira Ann Braffett, 1849 (daughter of George W. Braffett). Their children: Annie Amanda, m. Samuel Mackey; Henry Alpheus, m. Mary Ellen Hale; Almira Jane, m. Joseph Powell; George Washington, m. Louisa Hale; Alma, m. Alice Shelton; Levi, m. Sarah James. Family home Manti, Utah.

Seventy. Died May 5, 1901, Woodville, Idaho.

GIFFORD, GEORGE WASHINGTON (son of Henry Dill Gufford and Almira Ann Braffett). Born Jan. 10, 1857, Manti.

Married Louisa Hale Jan. 9, 1879, Hooper, Utah (daughter of James Hale and Lucy Clements), who was born Dec. 9, 1857. Their children: Lucy Ann b. Dec. 21, 1879; George Alvin b. Nov. 24, 1881, m. Florence Ellen Chaffin; Henry Elmer b. Jan. 6, 1884, m. Lilly M. Chaffin; Effie Louisa b. July 23, 1885; Helena b. Aug. 7, 1887, m. Arthur O. Moore; James Alma b. Sept. 10, 1889, m. Sarah Annie Mason; Lester b. Aug. 28, 1891, m. Elzada Hope; Martha Elnora b. Nov. 5, 1893, m. Wesley Huntsman; Moses b. Sept. 27, 1895; Milo b. Oct. 20, 1899. Family home Woodville, Idaho.

Settled at Woodville, Idaho, where he served as school trustee 1892-10; justice of peace 1898-04, and chairman of town board 1906-12. Farmer.

GIFFORD, LEVI. Came to Utah in 1850.

Married Deborah Wing. Their children: Ichabod; Daniel; William; Moroni; Priscilla; Levi. Family resided Farmington and Richmond, Utah.

GIFFORD, LEVI, JR. (son of Levi Gifford and Deborah Wing). Born March 14, 1827, Kirtland, Ohio. Came to Utah in 1859.

Married Caroline Jaques 1859 at Farmington (daughter of John Jaques). She was born Dec. 25, 1839. Their children: Melissa A. b. Jan. 5, 1860, m. Leander Clifford; Warren b. Feb. 18, 1861, m. Sophia Thompson; Theresa Ann b. April 21, 1863; Emma Caroline b. May 24, 1865; Homer b. July 9, 1868, m. Sarah Hoopes; Arthur b. Oct. 1, 1870, m. Jennie Bainbridge; William L. b. Oct. 18, 1876, m. Maggie Ann Hoopes. Family resided Farmington, Manti, Richmond and Bear Lake, Utah.

GIFFORD, ARTHUR (son of Levi Gifford and Caroline Jaques). Born Oct. 1, 1870, Weston, Idaho.

Married Jennie Bainbridge May 30, 1898, St. Anthony, Idaho (daughter of James Wesley Bainbridge and Sarah J. Lewis). She was born Sept. 23, 1877. Their children: Arthur Lamont b. April 4, 1899; Levi Wesley b. July 17, 1900; Rodney Joseph b. Jan. 15, 1905.

GIFFORD, SAMUEL KENDALL (son of Alpheus Gifford, born Aug. 28, 1793, Barnstable, Mass., and Anna Nash, born Feb. 17, 1800, Butternuts, N. Y.). Born Nov. 11, 1821, Milo, Yates county, N. Y. Came to Utah Sept. 11, 1850, Thomas Johnson company.

Married Lara Ann Demill Oct. 1, 1848 (daughter of Freeborn Demill and Anna Knight), who was born June 2, 1828, and came to Utah with husband 1850. Their children: Alpheus b. July 26, 1849, m. Sarah E. Hansen Sept. 11, 1873; Cornelia b. May 3, 1851, m. William R. Crawford; Cyrus b. March 18, 1853, died; Oliver Demill b. Dec. 10, 1854, m. Alice V. Allred Sept. 11, 1873; Samuel Kendall b. April 4, 1857; Freeborn Demill b. Jan. 4, 1860, m. Amelia J. Hepworth June 28, 1892; Lara Ann b. March 27, 1862, m. Christian Larson May 16, 1877; Adelia Mariah b. July 17, 1867, m. John T. Hall Feb. 15, 1888; Moses Elias b. June 18, 1869, m. Arannah Millet Feb. 13, 1889. Family home Springdale, Utah.

Married Ursula Curtis Jan. 2, 1871, Salt Lake City. Family resided Sanpete and Springdale, Utah.

Settled in Sanpete county 1850; moved to Springdale 1874. Sunday school superintendent at Springdale; president 9th quorum seventies; patriarch in Mormon church. School trustee and justice of peace at Springdale. Died there June 26, 1907.

GIFFORD, OLIVER DEMILL (son of Samuel Kendall Gifford and Lara Ann Demill). Born Dec. 10, 1854, Manti, Utah.
Married Alice V. Allred Sept. 11, 1873, Shonesburg, Utah (daughter of John Jones Allred and Mary Y. Bridgeman), who was born April 27, 1854. Their children: Olivia; William Henry b. Oct. 8, 1875, m. Eleanor Hepworth Dec. 10, 1894; Sarah Jane b. Oct. 27, 1876; John Jones b. Oct. 16, 1877, m. Fanny Crawford; Mary Emily b. May 6, 1879, m. Harold Russell Dec. 17, 1902; Lara Ann b. March 12, 1881, m. Samuel K. Larson Dec. 3, 1901; Emerett b. Nov. 30, 1882, m. Charles D. Johnson; Rosett b. Feb. 15, 1884, m. David W. Lemmon Nov. 8, 1906; Adelia b. Oct. 24, 1885, m. Daniel Q. Dennett May 5, 1902; Silva b. Feb. 9, 1888, m. Alexander Dailey. Family home Springdale, Utah.
Moved to southern Utah with parents 1863, where he helped to build up that country. High priest; second counselor to Bishop William R. Crawford, Springdale ward, 1887, and became bishop of that ward 1894.

GILES, JOSEPH SINKER. Born April 5, 1830. Came to Utah in 1853 with Johnson's army.
Married Sarah Huntsman (daughter of James Huntsman and Mary Huntsman, of Filmore, Utah). Their children: Joseph Riley, m. Polly Frances Harmon; Mary Maranda; Sarah Jane, m. Solomon Sprague; Emily Ann, m. David McKee; Jesse Huntsman, m. Emeline Carline; Melissa, m. Robert Miller; John Thomas, m. Mina Wilson; Salina, m. Mr. Sutherland. Family home Holden, Utah.
Physician; school teacher. County recorder; juvenile judge; county assessor and collector; surveyor; justice of peace of Millard county; county clerk; county attorney; United States surveyor.

GILES, JOSEPH RILEY (son of Joseph Sinker Giles and Sarah Huntsman). Born b. 8, 1860, at Filmore.
Married Polly Frances Harmon May 19, 1882, at Holden, Utah (daughter of Appleton Milo Harmon and Elemeda Stringham, both of Nauvoo, Ill. Came to Utah in 1847). She was born March 4, 1864. Their children: Elemeda b. Aug. 6, 1883, m. Mathew Carson; Dennis b. Aug. 17, 1886, m. Winifred Thomas; Mable b. Jan. 13, 1893; Robert Shirley b. Feb. 17, 1898; Donald b. March 14, 1905; Helen Jennet b. March 22, 1907. Family resided Holden and Lehi, Utah.
Blacksmith; farmer; wagonmaker.

GILLESPIE, WILLIAM (son of Peter Gillespie and Margerite McIntyre of Scotland, pioneers). Born April 13, 1855.
Married Sarah J. Lees Jan. 16, 1879, at Salt Lake City (daughter of John Lees Jr. and Martha Needham, pioneers October, 1855, Milo Andrus company). She was born Sept. 10, 1857, at Salt Lake City. Their children: William P. b. March 6, 1881, m. Melvina Ostler; Martha b. March 31, 1883, m. James H. Kirk; Sarah Edyth b. Aug. 25, 1886, m. Frank H. Manning; J. Earnest b. April 12, 1888; Elliott L. b. Sept. 23, 1893; Margerite Lovene b. Nov. 11, 1896.
Stonecutter.

GILLETT, GRANVILLE (son of Horace Gillett and Sarah C. Moore of Neversink, Sullivan Co., New York). Born April 5, 1847, at Neversink. Came to Utah Sept. 21, 1854, Capt. Fields company.
Married Fanny Ridout Feb. 11, 1875, at Salt Lake City (daughter of Samuel Ridout and Mary Ann Hart of Southampton, Eng., pioneers Oct. 27, 1854, William Hyde company). She was born April 17, 1856. Their children: Sarah Moore b. Dec. 2, 1875; Mary A. b Feb. 8, 1877; John Hugh Vincent; Granvill b. March 31, 1879, d. Jan. 18, 1884; Fanny J. b. June 21, 1886; Collins Horace b. Sept. 25, 1891, m. Florence Davis.
Lumberman and builder; landlord.

GILLETT, COLLINS MOORE (son of Horace Gillett and Sarah C. Moore of Neversink). Born Nov. 14, 1837, Neversink, New York.
Missionary to England. Pioneer lumberman. Died Aug. 20, 1866, near Lincoln City, Neb.

GILLIES, EBENEZER (son of John Gillies and Christina Gibb of Blair, Logie, Scotland). Born Nov. 18, 1819, at Blair, Logie, Scotland. Came to Utah 1854, William S. Empey company.
Married Esther Whittaker March 12, 1848. Their child: John Gillies, died in infancy.
Married Ann Gaitus 1853 at Sunderland, Eng. (daughter of John Gaitus of Newcastle on Tyne). She was born Oct. 22, 1833. Their children: Joseph S. Gillies, died; Mary Ann Gillies, m. Richard S. Horne; Ebenezer, m. Sarah Smith; Robert John, m. Isabel Black; Margaret C., m. Charles D. White; Duncan M., m. Minnie Gertrude Woolfenden; Isabella, m. Fred P. Kesler; Sarah J.; George B., m. Hannah Black and Ida Anderson; J. Ward. Family home Beaver City, Utah.
High priest. Carpenter and machinist.

GILLIES, DUNCAN M. (son of Ebenezer Gillies and Ann Gaitus). Born Oct. 12, 1865, at Beaver City, Utah.
Married Minnie Gertrude Woolfenden Nov. 1, 1899, at Salt Lake City (daughter of Abraham Woolfenden and Sarah Hewitt of Liverpool, Eng. Came to Utah Nov. 16, 1883). She was born Nov. 23, 1875. Their child: Gertrude Shirley b. Aug. 17, 1900. Family home Beaver City, Utah.
Missionary to Virginia 1892-94. High councilman; president Y. M. M. I. A. City councilman. Farmer and stockraiser.

GILMER, JOHN THORNTON (son of Charles Meriweather Gilmer and Mary Ann Ratliffe). Born Feb. 22, 1841, Quincy, Ill. Came to Utah 1864, Ben Halliday stage line.
Married Mary E. Vance Sept. 15, 1866, in Salt Lake City (daughter of John Vance and Elizabeth Campbell of McDonough, Ill., pioneers Oct. 4, 1847, John Taylor company). She was born Nov. 2, 1844. Their children: Charles Meriweather, m. Emma Merritt; Lucile b. 1870; Monroe Salisbury; Jay T., m. Elizabeth Watson; Thornton Meriweather, m. Elaine Hammell; Lloyd Jack, m. Eloise Sadler. Family home, Salt Lake City.
Manager Gilmer & Salisbury Overland Stage company. Government mail contractor; mining operator. Died May 8, 1892.

GILSON, WILLIAM (son of Edward and Lydia Gilson). Born 1811, Leicestershire, Eng. Came to Utah 1859, Edward Stevenson company.
Married Charlotte King (daughter of John King and Fanny Watkin of Nottinghamshire, Eng.), who was born 1810. Their children: Frances, m. Richard Gibbs, m. John Stock; Reuben, m. Caroline Liberty; Edward, m. Cynthia R. Drake; Elizabeth, m. Ebenezer Richardson; Anne, died; John King, died; Martha Ann, m. William H. Hall Nov. 22, 1869. Family home Melton, Leicestershire.
Seventy. Died 1877, Lynn ward, Ogden, Utah.

GIVINS, JAMES M. (son of John and Martha Givins, former of Ireland, latter of Scotland). Born Dec. 3, 1821. Came to Utah 1863.
Married Agness Murray (McCartney) 1855 (daughter of Robert Murray and Jane Robinson), who was born 1822, and came to Utah 1864, Ferramorz Little company. Only child: Elizabeth M. b. Feb. 4, 1867, m. Joseph H. Jordan Nov. 22, 1887.
Veteran Black Hawk Indian war. Helped bring immigrants to Utah.

GLAZIER, SHEPHERD (son of Calvin Glazier and Lydia Pierce of Massachusetts). Born Sept. 9, 1793, Holland, Worcester county, Mass. Came to Utah October, 1851, James Allred company.
Married Clarissa Withey Feb. 5, 1814, in Massachusetts, who was born Dec. 27, 1796. Their children: Caroline B. b. Aug. 29, 1815, m. Lavoirey Stebbins; Mary b. May 23, 1817, m. Deaucy Bacon; Edwin b. May 11, 1819; Merrick b. Jan. 10, 1821; Luther W. b. March 22, 1823, m. Martha Stevenson; Lewis G. b. March 8, 1829, m. Marinda Knapp; Joseph. Family home in New York state.
Married Rosetta Dean October, 1841, in Hancock Co., Ill. (daughter of Treadway Dean and Sarah Robinson of Vermont), who was born June 4, 1804. Their children: Charles Dean b. Sept. 26, 1842, m. Martha Jane Dusenberry; Mary R. b. Dec. 15, 1843, m. Joseph S. Faucett; Loren S. b. Dec. 26, 1845, m. Alpharetta Bunnell; Martha B. b. Oct. 8, 1848, m. John M. Haws. Family home Provo, Utah.
High priest; home missionary; bishop's counselor. Farmer and stockraiser. Died Feb. 23, 1881.

GLAZIER, CHARLES DEAN (son of Shepherd Glazier and Rosetta Dean). Born Sept. 26, 1842, in Hancock county, Ill. Came to Utah with parents.
Married Martha Jane Dusenberry Oct. 4, 1864 (daughter of Mahlon Dusenberry and Aurilia Coray of Provo, Utah, pioneers July, 1850, Capt. Williams company), who was born April 15, 1843, Perry, Ill. Their children: Charles Albert b. July 27, 1865, m. Agnes May Smoot; Belzora b. Nov. 28, 1866, d. Dec. 13, 1883; Wilson S. b. Oct. 11, 1868, d. Oct. 8, 1886; Jeannette b. June 8, 1871, d. Dec. 13, 1883; Lorin Dean b. Jan. 4, 1873; Warren R. b. Jan. 2, 1875, d. March 28, 1881; Helen R. b. Aug. 18, 1876, m. John B. Myers; Royal C. b. Sept. 16, 1881, d. April 2, 1882; Mary L. b. Feb. 15, 1884, d. March 24, 1880. Family home Provo, Utah.
High priest; missionary to southern states 1882-83; Sunday school superintendent; member high council Utah stake. Justice of peace; city councilman, Provo. Farmer; stockraiser; merchant.

GLAZIER, LOREN SCOVILL (son of Shepherd Glazier and Rosetta Dean). Born Dec. 26, 1845, Nauvoo, Ill. Came to Utah Oct. 8, 1851.
Married Alpharetta Jane Bunnell Jan. 17, 1870, Salt Lake City (daughter of David Edwin Bunnell and Sally Helen Conrad of Michigan, pioneers 1847), who was born Nov. 30, 1848, Pottawattamie, Iowa. Their children: Amy Jane b. Dec. 20, 1870, m. John P. Nicholson; Loren Adelbert b. March 11, 1873, m. Florence Brereton; David Shepherd b. Oct. 15, 1877, m. Maud Daley; Irvin Dean b. Nov. 4, 1887; Reed Conrad b. Aug. 31, 1891; Lilly Leane (adopted) b. July 6, 1890, m. Joseph Kendall. Family home Provo, Utah.

High priest; missionary to Tennessee 1893. Provo city councilman; chief of fire department at Provo, 1892-93. President Timpanogos and Rock Canyon Water company. Farmer and fruitgrower.

GLEASON, JOHN STREATOR (son of Ezekiel Gleason and Polly Howard of Worcester, Mass.). Born Jan. 13, 1819. Came to Utah July 22, 1847, Brigham Young company.
Married Desdemona Chase Nov. 8, 1839, Nauvoo, Ill. (daughter of Isaac Chase of Centerville, Utah, pioneer 1847, second company). She was born April 3, 1821. Their children: John b. 1844, died same year; Alviras Horne b. 1848, m. Maria Meady Lane; Ezekiel, died; Johannah Louisa, m. Leonidas Kennard; Joseph Hyrum b. June 19, 1855, died Feb. 26, 1890; Clara Maria, m. Andrew Locey Rogers. Family home Farmington, Utah.
Married Eliza Ann Malin 1852. Their children: Elijah M., m. Jane Garfield; Amasa L., m. Jane Walton.
Married Mary Ann Southerland 1864 at Salt Lake City (daughter of Thomas Sutherland born 1805, Ireland, and Mary Ann Timmings, born 1807, London, Eng.—pioneers 1859), who was born April 7, 1834, in London. Their children: John S. b. June 22, 1865, died June 22, 1865; Thomas Henry b. Feb. 8, 1867, m. Amanda Charlotte Jacobson; Eliza Ellen b. April 21, 1869, m. William Parley Broomhead; Lorenzo b. March 29, 1871, died Aug. 1872; Mary Ann b. Aug. 6, 1875. Family home Pleasant Grove, Utah.
One of presidents of 40th quorum seventies; high priest; president teachers' quorum at Farmington; missionary to England 1860-63, to Eastern states 1869-70 and to Eastern states 1842-44. Major Nauvoo Legion. Assisted in bringing immigrants to Utah. Settled at Little Cottonwood; moved into Salt Lake City 1849 where he operated a sawmill for two years; moved to Centerville 1851; to Tooele county where he served as county commissioner in 1852; returned to Farmington in 1853. Lieutenant Colonel Davis county militia. School teacher at Farmington; justice of peace 1864-65; Davis county clerk. Moved to Pleasant Grove 1873. Died Dec. 21, 1904, Pleasant Grove.

GLEASON, ALVIRUS HORNE (son of John Streator Gleason and Desdemona Chase). Born July 5, 1848, on the Elk Horn River, Neb.
Married Maria Meady Lane Jan. 18, 1869, Salt Lake City (daughter of Hyrum Mead Lane and Naomi Chase, the latter came to Utah 1853), who was born Aug. 15, 1847, in Wisconsin. Their children: Emma Louise b. Oct. 4, 1869, m. James A. Akers; Meady b. Sept. 19, 1871, m. C. E. Kason; Alvirus Horace b. Sept. 7, 1873, m. Liza Larsen; John Chase b. Aug. 1, 1875, m. Minnie Lewis; Delia; Phoebe b. Sept. 12, 1878, m. David Wood; Hyrum; Edward Carter b. March 31, 1882, m. Mildred Grover; Naomi b. Nov. 9, 1884, m. J. E. Grover; George b. Aug. 23, 1886, m. Anne Myrtle Jensen; Desdemona Florence b. Sept. 15, 1889; Lane b. March 15 1893, m. Pearl Jensen.
Resided in Salt Lake, Davis and Utah counties and on Elgin Bench, Idaho. Setled at Garland 1871. Black Hawk war veteran.

GLEASON, JOHN CHASE (son of Alvirus Horne Gleason and Maria Meady Lane). Born Aug. 1, 1875, Farmington, Utah.
Married Minnie Jane Lewis Dec. 15, 1904, Logan, Utah (daughter of William Davis Lewis born Sept. 7, 1858, at Provo, Utah, and Sarah Ann Harding born Feb. 25, 1862, Provo), who was born Nov. 11, 1883, Riverton, Utah. Their children: Beulah b. Jan. 5, 1906; Glenn Chase b. March 31, 1908; Elmo Lewis b. Aug. 16, 1909.
Missionary to Germany 1899-02; president of Y. M. M. I. A. at Garland ward; member stake board of Y. M. M. I. A.; home missionary.

GLEASON, ELIJAH M. (son of John S. Gleason and Eliza Ann Malin). Born Nov. 10, 1854, Salt Lake City.
Married Mary J. Garfield Aug. 23, 1879, Salt Lake City (daughter of Henry Garfield and Jane Ermissa, both of Kent, Eng., pioneers 1854), who was born June 21, 1858. Their children: Elijah M. b. June 19, 1880; James B. b. Dec. 25, 1882, m. Clara M. Sharer; Carrie M. b. Sept. 27, 1884, m. Werlie Sanders; Heber L. b. June 7, 1886; Elbert M. b. Sept. 12, 1888; Henry C., died; Athol G. b. Dec. 14, 1895; John S. b. Nov. 28, 1898; Lowell V. b. Aug. 23, 1902; Irma V. b. Oct. 1, 1904. Family home, Salt Lake City.
Elder. Teamster and lumberman.

GLEASON, THOMAS HENRY (son of John Streator Gleason and Mary Ann Sutherland). Born Feb. 8, 1867, Farmington, Utah.
Married Amanda Charlotte Jacobson Dec. 9, 1903, at Salt Lake City (daughter of Anton Jacobson and Amanda Larson of Skuna, Sweden, pioneers 1866, oxteam company), who was born July 7, 1875. Their children: Amanda Marie b. Jan. 20, 1905; Anton Jacobson b. Sept. 27, 1906; Jennie Eliza b. May 21, 1909; Thomas Henry b. Aug. 28, 1911, d. Sept. 7, 1911; Lilian b. Nov. 29, 1912. Family home Pleasant Grove, Utah.
One of the presidents of the 44th quorum of seventies; missionary to southern states 1896-97; superintendent 2d ward Sunday school at Pleasant Grove; stake aid Y. M. M. I. A. block teacher. Constable. Farmer.

GLEAVE, JOHN (son of John Gleave, born March 6, 1795, Altringham, Eng., and Lucy Potts, born June 4, 1798, Stockport, Eng.). Born March 2, 1822, at Stockport. Came to Utah Aug. 20, 1868, Chester Lovelard company.

Married Jane Brindley May 1, 1843 (daughter of Thomas Brindley and Jane Hanson, who were married Sept. 4, 1820, Stockport, Eng.). Their children: Lucy b. May 17, 1845; Hannah b. Oct. 23, 1846, m. Edward R. Roberts, April, 1869; Emma b. Aug. 26, 1848; Henry b. June 15, 1850; Walter b. May 31, 1852, m. Elizabeth Barronson, Aug. 1876; Herbert b. Nov. 31, 1854; Mary Jane b. Jan. 2, 1858, m. James Saffler, Feb., 1873; Samuel b. Feb. 11, 1860, m. Martha Mecham, Oct., 1893; Frances b. April 5, 1862; Bertha b. March 5, 1866, m. John Gardner.

GLEAVE, HERBERT (son of John Cleave and Jane Brindley). Born Nov. 24, 1854.

GLENN, WALTER (son of James Glenn). Born Oct. 6, 1821, Kirkliston, Linlithgowshire, Scotland. Came to Utah Oct. 24, 1854, William Empey company.
Married Elizabeth Stuart (daughter of James Stuart and Marion McKentire), who was born May 26, 1832. Came to Utah Oct. 24, 1854, William Empey company). Their children: James b. June 5, 1849, m. Ellen Reader; John b. Mar. 11, 1851, d. infant; Marion b. May 26, 1852, m. John Bankhead; Jonathan b. Sept. 6, 1854, d. infant; Walter S. b. March 12, 1856, m. Nancy Bankhead; Elizabeth b. March 13, 1858, m. Fred T. Bradshaw; Jenett b. June 6, 1860, m. Thomas Hendry; Thomas b. Oct. 20, 1862, d. infant; Adam b. June 20, 1864, m. Martha Bankhead; Margaret b. July 30, 1867, m. Samuel John Perkins Jan. 16, 1890; William b. Nov. 30, 1870, m. Christina Hendry; Anabell b. Oct. 6, 1873, m. Randolph Gee.
Veteran Echo canyon war. Early settler at Wellsville. Rock cutter; farmer. Died Sept. 27, 1909.

GLINES, JAMES HARVEY (son of James Pearsons Glines, born Aug. 31, 1796, and Ruth Brown, born April 17, 1802, both at Franklin, Merrimack county, N. H.). Born April 17, 1822, Franklin. Came to Utah July 28, 1847, with a section of the Mormon battalion.
Married Elizabeth Ann Mayer Oct. 20, 1845, Nauvoo, Ill. (daughter of George Mayer and Ann Yost, both of Bucyrus, Crawford Co., Ohio—pioneers 1848, Heber C. Kimball company), who was born Feb. 4, 1831, and died Nov. 3, 1876, in Salt Lake City. Their children: James Erastus b. Oct. 27, 1847, d. child; George Albert b. March 17, 1850, m. Mary Johannah Lundquist; Elizabeth Ann b. March 13, 1852, m. Frank Beers; Charles Harvey b. May 18, 1854, m. Melvie Amanda Bassett; Mary Jane b. May 6, 1856, m. Edison King; Annie Mariah b. May 11, 1858, m. James Hacking; John Franklin b. March 13, 1860, m. Mary McKowen; William Henry b. July 24, 1862, m. Adaline Workman; Emma Mayer b. April 8, 1865, died; Sarah Helen b. May 23, 1866, m. Peter Hansen; Andrew Lawrence b. Oct. 17, 1868, m. Mary Thornton; Alvin Clair b. May 6, 1870, d. Aug. 3, 1870; Alice Clara b. May 6, 1870, d. July 30, 1870; Moses b. Aug. 16, 1871, d. Aug. 16, 1871; Aaron b. Aug. 16, 1871, d. Aug. 16, 1871; Warren Carl b. Feb. 13, 1873, d. Aug. 16, 1890.
President 32d quorum seventies; high priest; missionary to eastern states from Aug. 12, 1899, to Oct. 28, 1899. Sergeant-major under Col. James D. Allen in Mormon battalion. Settled in Cedar Valley 1853, where he served as ward and tithing clerk and president teachers' quorum. Assisted in bringing immigrants to Utah. President Cedar Fort Irrigation company 1879; justice of peace 1880; moved to Ashley Valley 1883, where he reorganized the Ashley Central Irrigation Company 1884; president Upper Canal Company; probate judge two terms; bishop of Glines ward 1884; justice of peace 1891. Died Aug. 31, 1905, Vernal, Utah.

GLINES, CHARLES HARVEY (son of James Harvey Glines and Elizabeth Ann Mayer). Born May 18, 1854, Cedar Fort, Utah.
Married Melvie Amanda Bassett Dec. 19, 1875, Cedar Fort (daughter of Charles Henry Bassett and Mary Elizabeth Knight, of Salt Lake City—pioneers 1852), who was born July 29, 1856. Their children: Charles Herbert b. Sept. 14, 1876, m. Martha Gallaway; Roscoe Bassett b. June 12, 1878, m. Martha Jeanette Dingman; Reginald Harvey b. Sept. 18, 1880, m. Martha Yrisledla Fraughton; Leah Melvie b. Aug. 22, 1883, m. Miles Melvin Scofield; William Ernest b. July 22, 1885, m. Ada Lathoma McGuire; Junius Philip b. Sept. 30, 1887, died Jan. 2, 1891; Mary Elizabeth b. Dec. 1889, died Dec. 6, 1891; Diantha Merle b. Aug. 26, 1893; Henry Glines b. Nov. 19, 1895, died Nov. 19, 1895; Lois Knight b. Oct. 9, 1897; Byron Clawson b. Aug. 13, 1901.
High priest; president elders' quorum ten years; superintendent Mill ward Sunday school eight years; ward teacher 28 years. Settled at Cedar Fort; moved to Tooele City 1876, returned to Cedar Fort 1877; from there went to Vernal in 1910. Justice of peace 1909-10. Farmer and breeder of thoroughbred horses.

GLOVER, WILLIAM (son of William Glover and Catherine Amer of Kilmarnock, Ayrshire, Scotland). Born March 31, 1813, at Kilmarnock. Came to Utah 1849, Samuel Brannan company.
Married Jane Cowen 1832 at Pottsville, Pa. (daughter of John Cowen and Jane Mitchell of Pottsville, pioneers 1849, Samuel Brennan company, via California), who was born Dec. 9, 1816, in Lanorkshire, Scotland. Their children: William; Jacob; John; David; Ann; Jane, m. Barnett Rigby; Catherine, m. William Rigby; Joseph Smith, m. Ellen Mariah

Rice; William, m. Sarah J. Dapp; Mary Ann, m. Joseph Hancock; Abraham; Marian, m. Henry Dapp; Sarah, m. Elijah Fuller.
Married Zelnora Snow 1851, in Salt Lake City. She came to Utah 1849. Their children: Asinath b. 1852, m. Melvin Potter; Andrew; Brigham. m. Lucy (——); Prince Alma; Nora Eliza, m. George Smith.
Married Margaret Loteed 1856, in Salt Lake City. She was born in Scotland and came to Utah 1855. Their children: Ellen; Seth, m. Elizabeth Smith; James, m. Catherine Barber; Margrett Jane, m. William Jenkins; David, m. Sarah Barber; George, m. Margret (——).
Member of seventy; missionary to England 1852-55. Farmer. Died August, 1892, at Farmington, Utah.

GLOVER, JOSEPH SMITH (son of William Glover and Jane Cowen). Born Sept. 13, 1846, in Pennsylvania. Came to Utah 1849.
Married Ellen Mariah Rice Dec. 26, 1869, in Salt Lake City (daughter of William R. Rice and Lucy Witter Gees of Farmington, Utah, pioneers Sept. 13, 1847, Bishop Hunter company), who was born Sept. 13, 1846. Their children: Joseph Hyrum b. April 16, 1869, m. Edith Van Orden; Jane b. Nov. 25, (——), m. William E. Davis; Ellen b. July 28, 1874, m. William Wheeler Thompson; Catherine, m. William V. Hodges; Delila Adeline b. Jan. 20, 1879; Caroline b. May 2, 1881, m. Clarence O. Cherry; Sarah M. b. April 25, 1885, m. Shem G. Furnelle; Orvill W. b. May, 1890, m. Eve Hutchinson; Lewella Marian b. Oct. 10, 1892.

GLOVER, JOSEPH HYRUM (son of Joseph Smith Glover and Ellen Mariah Rice). Born April 15, 1869, at Farmington, Utah.
Married Edith Van Orden Feb. 19, 1891, in Idaho (daughter of Everett Clark Van Orden and Elizabeth Harris of Lewiston, Idaho), who was born Dec. 4, 1870. Their children: Edith Lourena b. Jan. 11, 1893, m. J. E. Martindale; Alta May b. Nov. 12, 1894; Joseph Everett b. Sept. 6, 1896; Esther Leroy b. Aug. 26, 1898; Leland Smith b. Aug. 22, 1900; Raymond b. June 7, 1902; Hyrum b. Dec. 21, 1903; Arvid F. b. Feb. 3, 1905; Clement b. Dec. 11, 1906; Audessa L. b. July 25, 1908; Eva E. b. Aug. 24, 1911. Family home Marysville, Fremont Co., Idaho.
Member 113th quorum seventies; missionary in Fremont stake; ward teacher. Constable and justice of peace, Marysville, Idaho. Farmer.

GLOVER, WILLIAM F. (son of William Glover). Born at San Francisco, Cal. Came to Utah in early days.
Married Sarah Jane Barnes (daughter of Sarah Barnes). Their children: William Henry b. April 14, 1870, m. Nettie May Rosenbaum; Alice Asenth, m. Harmon Wiser; Marion Armeda, m. James Hodges; Andrew; Ada, m. Julius Allen; Stella, m. Ephraim Blair; Carl, m. Luella Pope; Burt; Chester, m. Elva Wheeler.
Soldier; farmer; stockraiser.

GLOVER, WILLIAM HENRY (son of William F. Glover and Sarah Jane Barnes). Born April 14, 1870, Brigham City.
Married Nettie May Rosenbaum and Abigail Snow). Their children; William Lamont b. Feb. 14, 1897; Alice Maude b. Oct. 16, 1900; Wynn Eddy b. March 9, 1904; Morris Wayne b. Aug. 23, 1909; Afton b. April 24, 1911. Family home, Brigham City.
City councilman 1906-10. Liveryman; farmer and stockraiser.

GOASLIND, JOHN (son of John Goaslind, born 1788, Flemon, Ky., and Hannah Cornog, born 1789, Kentucky—married 1813). Born Jan. 26, 1818, Augusta, Bracken county, Ky. Came to Utah 1854, Texas company.
Married Matilda White Jan. 24, 1838, who was born 1813. Their children: Amanda b. 1838, d. infant; Levi b. 1840; John b. 1842, m. Mary J. Alder 1867; Edmond b. 1844; Willis b. 1846, died; Jacob b. 1848, died; Joseph b. 1850. Family home Houston, Texas.
Married Susan Allen July 4, 1858, Provo, Utah (daughter of Andrew Lee Allen and Clarinda Knapp, married 1825, Burton, N. Y., pioneers 1852, John Higby company). She was born Dec. 31, 1837, Kirtland, Ohio. Their children: Lydia Susannah b. April 22, 1859, m. Ernest A. Purnell Jan. 1, 1877; Charles David b. Nov. 18, 1860, m. Clara C. Parkinson March 25, 1885; Clarinda Hannah b. March 21, 1862, m. Elias S. Larsen Jan. 4, 1883; Mary Eugene b. Jan. 27, 1865, m. Thomas E. Tittansor April 10, 1882; George Knapp b. April 27, 1867, d. Dec. 1, 1883; Francis Zina b. Jan. 27, 1870, m. William Stockdale Feb. 22, 1888; James Orin b. Feb. 17, 1872, d. Dec. 26, 1883; Julia Sophronia b. Feb. 6, 1875, m. Heber Hanson Sept. 28, 1898, d. Feb. 10, 1910; Eliza R. b. Dec. 7, 1877, d. child. Family resided in Franklin, Idaho, and Coalville, Utah.
Assisted in building a gristmill at Provo, 1858, and at West Weber 1859. In 1860 he built a sawmill at Richmond and in 1862, the first sawmill at Franklin, Idaho. In 1864 he built the first gristmill at Logan and in 1865 the first gristmill at Franklin. Aided in bringing immigrants to Utah 1866-67. Operated the first threshing machine at Franklin, Idaho. School trustee at Franklin 1870-75; organized Coalville school and was its trustee 1875-77. Organized first Sunday school at Coalville 1877. High priest. Died June 6, 1878.

GOASLIND, CHARLES D. (son of John Goaslind and Susan Allen). Born Nov. 18, 1860, Richmond, Utah.
Married Clara Janat C. Parkinson March 25, 1885, Logan, Utah (daughter of Samuel R. Parkinson and Arabella Ann Chandler, pioneers 1854, Capt. Field company). She was born April 18, 1865, d. Jan. 20, 1897. Only child: Charles Earl b. April 28, 1889.
Married Caroline Matilda C. Parkinson Feb. 23, 1898, Logan, Utah (daughter of Samuel R. Parkinson and Arabella Ann Chandler). She was born Nov. 20, 1866. Their children: Clara P. b. June 25, 1899; Caroline F. b. Jan. 14, 1902; Ione P. b. Dec. 12, 1904; George David P. b. Sept. 9, 1908. Family resided in Franklin and Preston, Idaho.
School trustee at Franklin, Idaho, 1884; missionary to Great Britain 1885-87; Oneida stake clerk 1889-1907, and stake tithing clerk 1896-1907; Oneida stake high counselor 1900-07; second counselor to Pres. George C. Parkinson 1907-10. State insurance commissioner and ex-officio state examiner of Idaho, two terms.

GOATES, WILLIAM (son of James Goates and Ann Dockery of Wimpole, Cambridgeshire, Eng.). Born May 11, 1817, Wimpole, Eng. Came to Utah Sept. 3, 1852, A. O. Smoot company.
Married Susan Larkin at Cambridgeshire, Eng. (daughter of Thomas Larkin and Ann Raynor of Chesterton, Cambridgeshire, Eng., pioneers Sept. 3, 1852, A. O. Smoot company), who was born Aug. 1, 1821. Their children: Mary Ann, d. child; Sarah, m. Bishop C. Earl; Martha, m. John William Wing; Joseph W. m. Malissa Losee; James Thomas, m. Mary Losee; John, d. child; William, m. Elizabeth Annie Munns; George Hyrum, m. Louisa Munns. Family home Lehi, Utah.
Married Rebecca Pilgrim 1858, Lehi, Utah (daughter of Samuel Pilgrim and Elizabeth Cootes of Cambridgeshire, Eng., pioneers Sept. 1826, Cambridge, Eng. Came to Utah, 1856, Capt. Willie handcart company; d. April 18, 1909. Family resided at Lehi.
President elders quorum of Utah county; first counselor to Bishop David Evans of Lehi ward; president high priests quorum Utah stake. Gardener and farmer. Died Oct. 23, 1895, Lehi, Utah.

GOATES, WILLIAM (son of William Goates and Susan Larkin). Born Jan. 1, 1861, Lehi, Utah.
Married Elizabeth Annie Munns May 1, 1884, at Salt Lake City (daughter of James Munns and Elizabeth Collin of Orwell, Cambridgeshire, Eng.), who came to Utah Nov. 7, 1877). She was born July 7, 1865. Their children: Agnes Viola b. March 22, 1885, m. Horace Denton Woffinden; Adela b. April 17, 1887, m. Robert S. Fox; Leo Walman b. Aug. 20, 1889; William Rayner b. Nov. 1, 1891; Elsie b. June 3, 1894, d. infant; Essie Lerene b. Sept. 6, 1896. Family home Lehi, Utah.
Elder. Member Lehi Silver band 1887-96. Carpenter and farmer. Died April 16, 1896, Lehi, Utah.

GOATES, LEO WALMAN (son of William Goates and Elizabeth Annie Munns). Born Aug. 20, 1889, Lehi, Utah.
Elder; missionary to Germany 1908-10; president Austrian conference in 1910; member Sunday school superintendency of Lehi, 1910. Member Lehi Silver band. Sugar boiler at Lehi and Austin, Utah.

GODBE, WILLIAM SAMUEL (son of John Godbe and Sarah LaRevere of London, Eng.). Born June 26, 1833, London, Eng. Came to Utah 1851, independent company.
Married Mary Hampton (daughter of Benjamin Hampton and Patience Skuill of Philadelphia, Pa., pioneers 1856). She was born Aug. 12, 1838, at Philadelphia, Pa. Their children: Millicent, m. Charles Peter Brooks; Anthony Hampton, m. Ruby Clawson; Miriam, m. Charles Peter Brooks; Ernest Lacy, m. Sally Wertheimer; Murray Charles, m. Alta Young; Elva Bertoch, m. Patrick Sheahan. Family home Salt Lake City, Utah.

GODBE, ANTHONY HAMPTON (son of William Samuel Godbe and Mary Hampton). Born Nov. 22, 1862, Salt Lake City.
Married Ruby Clawson Sept. 15, 1898, at Salt Lake City (daughter of Hyrum B. Clawson and Ellen Curtis Spencer of Salt Lake City). She was born March 15, 1876. Their children: Virginia b. Dec. 13, 1899; Margaret b. June 18, 1901; Mary b. May 21, 1906.
One of organizers and developers of Ohio-Kentucky Mine and the Prince Consolidated M. & S. Co. Assayer; chemist; superintendent of mines; mine mill builder. Family home Salt Lake City.

GODBE, ERNEST LACY (son of William Samuel Godbe and Mary Hampton). Born Sept. 13, 1867, Salt Lake City.
Married Sallie Wertheimer Jan. 21, 1888, Salt Lake City (daughter of Leopold and Henrietta Wertheimer of San Francisco; latter came to California 1849). She was born Oct. 23, 1866. Their children: Viola, m. E. E. Work; Millie; Bertha; Marian; Benjamin, died; Billie; Lillian; Jack; Ernest.
One of the promoters of the Prince Consolidated Mining Co. and the Ohio-Kentucky Mining Co. Mining man; metallurgist. Family resides Salt Lake City.

892 PIONEERS AND PROMINENT MEN OF UTAH

GODBE, MURRAY CHARLES (son of William Samuel Godbe and Mary Hampton). Born Sept. 20, 1870, Salt Lake City, Utah.
Married Alta Young March 17, 1892 (daughter of Heber Young and Vilate Clayton of Salt Lake City). She was born Sept. 7, 1871. Their children: Ruth b. Jan. 14, 1893; Mary b. Sept. 28, 1895; Helen b. July 12, 1898; Murray b. June 23, 1901. Family home Salt Lake City.
Electrical engineer; mine operator.

GODDARD, GEORGE (son of Cornelius Goddard b. Dec. 28. 1783, at Leicester, Eng., and Mary Grace b. Jan. 27, 1780, at Leicester). Born Dec. 5, 1815, at Leicester. Came to Utah Sept. 15, 1852, Captain Tidwell company.
Married Elizabeth Harrison Sept. 10, 1839 (daughter of John Harrison and Elizabeth Pipes. Came to Utah with son-in-law), who was born March 17, 1817. Their children: George b. Sept. 23, 1840; Eliza b. Oct. 20, 1841; Joseph b. April 5, 1843; Mary b. Nov. 22, 1844; Annie b. April 2, 1846; Betsey b. March 14, 1847; Henry b. Jan. 10, 1849; Cornelius b. June 7, 1850; Edward b. Nov. 1851; John b. July 23, 1853; Almah b. April 22, 1855; Hyrum H. b. Jan. 3, 1857; Brigham H. b. Sept. 28, 1859.
Missionary to Canada; superintendent 13th ward S. S. 1867-1876; stake superintendent of Salt Lake stake Sunday school 1877-1882; assistant general superintendent of Sunday schools 1872-1898; clerk to presiding bishop 1856-1883; of general conference 1874-1884 and of school of prophets; ward teacher; member of Tabernacle choir, and Old Folks committee.

GODDARD, HYRUM HARRISON (son of George Goddard and Elizabeth Harrison). Born Jan. 3, 1857, Salt Lake City.
Married Martha Williams April 11, 1898, at Salt Lake City (daughter of David Williams and Sarah Lockwood), who was born in March, 1857, in Wales. Their children: Geo W. b. Sept. 22, 1879, m. Bertha Lessinger; Hyrum W. b. Feb. 15, 1882, d. Jan. 10, 1891; Frederick W. b. Oct. 14, 1884, d. Jan. 5, 1891; Albert W. b. Sept. 28, 1896, m. Melvina Omer Oct. 24, 1910; Clara W. b. Oct. 26, 1889, m. Alonzo A. Browning, Oct. 26, 1910; Irma W. b. Nov. 10, 1893; David W. b. April 11, 1896. Family resided Salt Lake City and Ogden, Utah.
Married Elizabeth M. Stanford March 11, 1886, at Logan, Utah (daughter of Jos Stanford and Elizabeth Young), who was born Oct. 31, 1863, at Logan. Their children: Ivy S. b. Jan. 29, 1888, m. Samuel F. Whittaker Sept. 25, 1907; Elizabeth S. b. July 1, 1893; Raymond S. b. May 26, 1895; Laura S. b. Feb. 24, 1897; Myrtle S. b. May 14, 1899; Joseph S. b. Feb. 14, 1901; Ruth S. b. Jan. 27, 1903; Ruth S. b. Dec. 18, 1905.
Secretary first Y. M. M. I. A.; member seventies. Sewing machine business 1880-1889; railroad contractor.

GODDARD, GEORGE W. (son of Hyrum H. Goddard and Martha Williams). Born Sept. 22, 1879. Married Bertha Lessinger (daughter of Mark Lessinger). Only child: George W.

GODDARD, BRIGHAM HARRISON (son of George Goddard and Elizabeth Harrison).
Married Helena Lucretia Kelly Sept. 28, 1880, at Salt Lake City (daughter of John B. Kelly and Helena Quirk, both of Salt Lake City, pioneers 1863). She was born July 4, 1861. Their children: Brigham Kelly b. July 4, 1881, d. April 15, 1891; Leo Kelly b. March 29, 1883, d. April 6, 1891; Edna Kelly b. Sept. 28, 1885; Francis Kelly b. June 12, 1888; Azalia Kelly b. May 2, 1890; Ella Kelly B. Aug. 24, 1893; Helen b. Jan. 24, 1896; John b. Oct. 30, 1897, d. Nov. 13, 1897; George b. Oct. 30, 1897; Lucretia b. April 5, 1901. Family home, Ogden and Salt Lake City.
Member Weber stake Sunday school board; superintendent 3d ward Sunday school, Ogden; high priest; 2d counselor to Bishop D. H. Ensign of Ogden 1st ward 1907-09; superintendent Weber stake Sunday schools. Deputy assessor of Cache county 1879; member board of education which started the first free school system at Ogden 1888. In 1882 formed copartnership with Heber J. Grant in the insurance business; one of the original incorporators of Heber J. Grant & Co.

GODDARD, HENRY (son of Enoch Goddard and Charlotte Mayfield of Nottingham, Eng.). Born Feb. 16, 1821, Nottingham. Came to Utah October, 1855, Captain Harper company.
Married Hannah Astill Dec. 11, 1847, Nottingham, Eng. (daughter of Joseph Astill and Harriet Wild of Nottingham). She was born June 20, 1823. Their children: Joseph b. Jan. 28, 1853, died; Hannah Charlotte b. Dec. 11, 1856, m. Thomas Leonard; Henry J. W. b. Nov. 20, 1858, m. Betsey A. Kay; Enoch Samuel b. June 27, 1861, m. Annie Cox. Family home Provo, Utah.
High priest. Farmer. Died April 9, 1901, Provo.

GODDARD, HENRY J. W. (son of Henry Goddard and Hannah Astill). Born Nov. 20, 1858, Provo, Utah.
Married Betsy Ann Kay Dec. 17, 1886, Payson. Utah (daughter of John Kay and Esther Howorth of Darwin, Lancashire, Eng., came to Utah July 16, 1890). She was born Feb. 14, 1863. Their children: Ernest Henry b. Sept. 18, 1887; Ester Janette b. July 15, 1889; John William b. Nov. 12, 1891; Elvin Kay b. March 9, 1898; Hugh Kay b. March 12, 1901; Estella Jane b. Oct. 14, 1904. Family home Provo, Utah.
High priest. Commissioner Provo City. Farmer.

GODFREY, JOSEPH (son of William Godfrey and Margaret Bauer). Born March 1, 1800, Bristol, Somersetshire, Eng. Came to Utah October, 1852, David Wood company.
Married Eliza Rheeves 1840, New Jersey. There were five children. Two, a son and a daughter, died at Winter quarters, and were the first to be laid away in the graveyard at that place. She died Jan. 7, 1857.
Married Mary Rheeves Coleman, who was the widow of George Coleman, who died while in California with the Mormon battalion, and mother of Moroni Coleman.
Married Sarah Ann Price.
Followed the sea for 19 years, and served English army in Canada. Worked for Joseph Smith, at Nauvoo. Settled at North Ogden, Utah, 1852. Member 28th quorum seventies; counselor to Bishop Thomas Dunn. Died Dec. 16, 1880.

GODFREY, RICHARD (son of Thomas Godfrey, born Jan. 30, 1798, and Elizabeth Ainge, born March 18, 1798, both of Worcestershire, Hanbury, Eng.). He was born March 11, 1835, Worcestershire, Eng. Came to Utah Nov. 9, 1856, James G. Willie company.
Married Jane Jelley 1868 (daughter of William Jelley and Comfort Allibone, married at Irchester, Eng.; the former died May 16, 1854, in Kansas, the latter came to Utah Sept. 30, 1854, Darwin Richardson company). She was born Oct. 8, 1841. Their children: William R. b. Sept. 21, 1864, m. Sophia Peterson 1883; Thomas H. b. May 23, 1866, m. Roselinda Loosie; John Edward b. June 21, 1868, m. Rosa Grover; Joseph A. b. April 5, 1873, m. Julia M. Myler Nov. 2, 1891; George A. b. Jan. 14, 1882, d. Feb. 22, 1882; Franklin M. b. March 16, 1883, d. March 11, 1884; Comfort E. b. Jan. 13, 1861, m. William S. Flinders; Maria J. b. Sept. 17, 1862, m. M. W. Nish; Mary E. b. March 30, 1871, d. March 16, 1875; Sarah E. b. Aug. 24, 1876; Agnes M. b. Dec. 22, 1878, m. Joseph M. Larson June 28, 1899. Family resided Salt Lake City, Riverdale and Clarkston, Utah.
Married Mary Ann George February, 1865, at Salt Lake City (daughter of Spencer George and Ann Allibone), who was born Sept. 17, 1837, Irchester, Eng. Their children: Spencer G. b. June 13, 1866, m. Christena Hansen 1901; Annie E. b. March 30, 1869, d. Oct. 23, 1873.
Worked on construction of Salt Lake temple and tabernacle. Served in Lott Smith company during Echo Canyon campaign. Pioneer of Clarkston, Cache county, and clerk of Clarkston ward.

GODFREY, WILLIAM R. (son of Richard Godfrey and Jane Jelley). Born Sept. 21, 1864, Salt Lake City.
Married Sophia Peterson January, 1883, at Salt Lake City (daughter of Hans and Margaret Peterson, who died in Denmark). She was born Jan. 2, 1865. Their only child: Martha L. b. Oct. 26, 1883, d. Feb. 24, 1884. Family home Clarkston, Utah.
Married Sarah Amelia Avery (daughter of John Avery and Josephine Roberts, who were married May 26, 1866, Kanosh, Utah, the former pioneer 1849, Capt. Allred company). She was born April 13, 1871, Kanosh. Their children: Eva Amelia . Jan. 1, 1890, d. Jan. 1, 1890; Elva Adella b. Feb. 1, 1891, m. Harford Baxter March 6, 1907; Clara Josephine b. March 27, 1893, m. Bert Potter Aug. 17, 1910; Clarence William b. June 10, 1895; John Viri b. July 3, 1897; Cora Jane b. Nov. 13, 1899; Enid Dorthelin b. April 10, 1902; Elma Ethlyn b. Oct. 29, 1906. Family home Dempsey, Idaho.
Married Drusilla Bell March 8, 1910, Dempsey, Idaho (daughter of William Bell and Esther Jane Booth, who were married Dec. 17, 1857, at Salt Lake City, the former pioneer 1850, Capt. Sharp company, the latter 1851, Capt. Davis company). She was born Nov. 7, 1873, Franklin, Idaho.

GOFF, ISAAC (son of Abraham Goff, born 1768, and Alice Lester, both of Longwhatton, Leicestershire, Eng.). Born July 1, 1813, in Longwhatton. Came to Utah 1863, Rosel Hyde company.
Married Mary Naylor 1833 (daughter of Samuel Naylor and Ann Smith—both died in England). Their children: William b. Oct. 16, 1833, m. Emma North; Thomas b. Aug. 12, 1836, m. Harriet Smith; Tamer b. July 25, 1838; Emma b. Sept. 6, 1840, m. Levi Naylor Oct. 5, 1862; Sarah b. April 17, 1842, m. John C. Stevenson October, 1862; Isaac Jr. b. May 21, 1844, m. Ann Sisam March 9, 1867; Henry; Alice; Hyrum b. July 29, 1849, m. Maria T. Arnold Jan. 2, 1871; Jedediah b. July 5, 1851, m. Sarena M. Grange March 2, 1880.

GOFF, ISAAC, JR. (son of Isaac Goff and Mary Naylor). Born May 21, 1844, Longwhatton, Leicestershire. Came to Utah 1862, William S. Godbey company.
Married Ann Sisam March 9, 1867, at Salt Lake City (daughter of Joseph Sisam and Catherine Payne, pioneers August, 1866, James Haight company). She was born Oct. 11, 1847, Worcestershire, Eng. Their children: Rebecca b. Dec. 4, 1867, m. Alberto Bateman 1888; I. Frank b. Dec. 30, 1869, m. Almina Bateman Feb. 22, 1893; Joseph H. W. b. Nov. 25, 1872, m. Naomi Lawrence April 9, 1897; Mary Ann b. Feb. 6, 1878, d. March 13, 1891. Family home East Jordan, Utah.
Assisted in bringing immigrants to Utah 1866. Died Jul 24, 1908.

GOFF, I. FRANK (son of Isaac Goff, Jr. and Ann Sisam) Born Dec. 30, 1869, at West Jordan, Utah.
Married Almina Bateman Feb. 22, 1893, Salt Lake Cit (daughter of William L. Bateman and Sophronia Watkins who were married Dec. 26, 1870, Salt Lake City; forme

came to Utah 1850, Farrymore and Little freight train, latter September, 1852, William Craighead company). She was born April 1, 1873, West Jordan, Utah. Their children: Frank Deverne b. Sept. 11, 1897; Merle b. Sept. 25, 1899; Glen Doral b. Feb. 27, 1902; Wesley Darwin b. Sept. 16, 1904; Zelda b. Aug. 26, 1906; Stanley Delmont b. April 23, 1909; Verlie b. Feb. 7, 1911. Family home Sandy, Utah.
President first quorum deacons at West Jordan; secretary of Y. M. M. I. A. 1887-90; missionary to Society Islands 1893-96. Justice of peace of seventh precinct, Salt Lake county, 1910. Farmer and stockraiser.

GOFF, HYRUM (son of Isaac Goff and Mary Naylor). Born July 29, 1849, Longwhatton, Leicestershire, Eng. Came to Utah Sept. 24, 1862, Homer Duncan company).
Married Maria T. Arnold Jan. 2, 1871 (daughter of Josiah Arnold and Clarissa L. Jones—married July, 1854, Salt Lake City, pioneers 1848, Brigham Young company). She was born May 1, 1855. Their children: Cora M. b. Nov. 27, 1871; Hyrum H. b. July 29, 1873; Hyrum L. b. July 23, 1875; Clifford I. b. July 27, 1877, m. Sabina J. Larson Sept. 2, 1903; George A. b. Nov. 28, 1879, m. Josephine Morris May 24, 1905; Ellen A. b. March 2, 1882, m. Nels H. Hallstrom Aug. 12, 1903; Harold b. June 13, 1884, m. Lulu Ormsby Aug. 16, 1911; Alma A. b. Aug. 4, 1886; Irene L. b. Dec. 25, 1888; Melissa L. b. Oct. 26, 1890; Clarissa L. b. Feb. 23, 1893; Alicia M. b. June 12, 1895. Family home West Jordan, Utah.
Married Marinda P. Bateman Oct. 24, 1878, Salt Lake City (daughter of Samuel Bateman and Marinda Allen—married Nov. 27, 1854; former came to Utah 1850, with merchandise train, latter 1853, Daniel Miller company). She was born Sept. 29, 1861, West Jordan, Utah. Their children: Clara M. b. April 12, 1880, m. Walter R. Wilson Aug. 28, 1891; Samuel H. b. Oct. 12, 1882, m. Irene Maginness June 17, 1903; Edna Ray b. Jan. 14, 1884, m. Schuyler Call Oct. 12, 1904; Edith May b. Jan. 14, 1884, m. David Bennion June 19, 1907; Dora A. b. Dec. 8, 1885, m. Joseph S. Bennion March 26, 1908; Edgar A. b. Feb. 6, 1888; Mary b. March 13, 1892, m. James Nielsen March 13, 1913; Wilford J. b. Feb. 8, 1896; Harvey L. b. Dec. 18, 1901. Family home West Jordan, Utah.
Member of presidency of 33d quorum seventies 1887-91; first counselor to bishop of West Jordan ward 1891-95; bishop of East Jordan ward 1895-1900; first counselor to Pres. O. P. Miller of Jordan stake 1900-01; president Jordan stake 1901. First mayor of Midvale, 1909. Merchant.

GOFF, THOMAS (son of Abraham Goff and Alice Lester of Long Whatton, Leicestershire, Eng.). Came to Utah 1863, Rosel Hyde company.
Married Harriett ——. Their children: Heber, m. Ellen Ellwood; Mary, m. Hyrum Lancaster; Ruth, m. John Lloyd; Naomi, m. William Hardcastle; Joseph, m. Phoebe Ann Hardcastle; Tamer, m. Barnard Anderson; Harriett, m. Benjamin Ainsworth; Jane, m. Walter Dumas; Isaac; two others who died infants.

GOFF, HEBER (son of Thomas and Harriett Goff). Born 1854. Came to Utah with father.
Married Ellen Ellwood 1874, Endowment House, Salt Lake City (daughter of Robert and Elizabeth Ellwood), who was born November 22, ——. Their children: Heber Robert b. Dec. 12, 1875, m. Mary Josephine Neilsen; Elizabeth Ellen b. 1877, m. George Downing; Joseph Hyrum, m. Bella Erickson; Dora Ann. m. George Hansen; William Henry; George Ellwood; Edith Ann, m. William Olesen; Alma, d. child.
Seventy; assistant superintendent Sunday school, Sandy ward, Sandy, Utah. Located in Sandy, where he engaged in farming.

GOFF, HEBER ROBERT (son of Heber Goff and Ellen Ellwood). Born Dec. 12, 1875, Sandy, Utah.
Married Mary Josephine Neilsen Jan. 14, 1903, Salt Lake tempie (daughter of Jens Christian Neilsen and Ann Maria Christensen of Duchesne (Theodore), Wasatch Co., Utah, came to Utah about 1883). She was born Aug. 30, 1885. Their children: Heber Lawrence b. June 12, 1904; Arvil Robert b. June 24, 1908; Laverne Marie b. Jan. 23, 1911.
Elder. Moved to Theodore, Wasatch Co., Utah, from Sandy, August, 1907, as a pioneer, and located a homestead there. Has assisted in building about 200 miles of water ditches and has built wagon roads, bridges, homes and many public improvements. Farmer.

GOLDER, EBER. Came to Utah 1857, Captain Babbit company.
Married Viola Shippee. Their children: Richard James, m. Mary Lee; Zaben Henry, m. Cora Grube; Lorena Arminda, m. Charles Pickle; Albert Ishmael, m. Rachel Hill; Lois May, m. George Bertsch.

GOLDER, ALBERT ISHMAEL (son of Eber Golder and Viola Shippee). Born June 15, 1870, in Iowa.
Married Rachel Hill Sept. 26, 1892, at Salem, Idaho (daughter of William Hill and Mary A. Williamson of England). She was born Sept. 22, 1872. Their children: Lauretta b. July 2, 1893, m. Parley Evans; Elva b. Feb. 17, 1897; Albert b. March 6, 1899; William b. Nov. 6, 1901; Ralph b. Sept. 3, 1903; Dora b. Dec. 11, 1905; Gladys b. March 7, 1910. Family home Rexburg Idaho.

GOLIGHTLY, RICHARD. Born in Northumberland. Eng.
Married Elizabeth Jessop (daughter of Edward Jessop and Frances Milward of Salt Lake City, Eighth ward). Their child: J. J., m. Millicent Williams. Family home, Salt Lake City.
Baker.

GOLIGHTLY, J. J. (son of Richard Golightly and Elizabeth Jessop).
Married Millicent Williams. Their children: Joseph W. b. 1879, m. Mabel Chatterton; Florence; Osburn.

GOLIGHTLY, JOSEPH W. (son of J. J. Golightly and Millicent Williams). Born 1879, Preston, Idaho.
Married Mabel Chatterton Feb. 18, 1903, Logan, Utah (daughter of Wilford Chatterton and Nellie E. Card, of Preston). She was born 1882. Their children: Joseph E. b. 1903; Virginia b. 1906; Card b. 1908; LaRue b. 1911. Family home Preston, Idaho.
Elder; missionary to southern states 1905-06; president Florida Conference one year; councilor in Sunday school stake board two years. Manager Studebaker Bros. Co.

GOODALE, I. N. Born Feb. 6, 1815, Berkshire, Tioga county, N. Y. Came to Utah September, 1847.
Married Maria L. Bingham January, 1849, Salt Lake City. Family home Ogden, Utah.
Was the oldest member of the high council of Weber stake; bishop's counselor. Settled in Iron county. Missionary to Canada 1841. Superintended construction of road through ogden canyon to Bear Lake; also Ogden Bench canal. City councilman of Ogden 15 years; school trustee 20 years.

GOODHUE, JUSTIN A. Born 1841 in Ohio. Came to Utah 1885. Resided in Salt Lake City, where he died July 23, 1908.

GOODRICH, BENJAMIN (son of Joseph Oliver Goodrich and Elizabeth Hastings of Lunenburg Mass.). Born Oct. 3, 1794, at Lunenburg. Came to Utah Oct. 14, 1850, Wilford Woodruff company).
Married Penelope Randall Gardner April 1, 1823, in Massachusetts (daughter of Abel Gardner, born Feb. 12, 1763, at Hingham, and Lousanna Bryant born August, 1767, Plymouth, Mass.). She was born Dec. 27, 1793, at Hopkinton, Mass. Their children: Mary Jane, m. William Flint; Sophia Lois, m. Leonard Hardy; Harriett Ann, m. Leonard Hardy; Lenard Burridge, died; Sarah Louisa, m. Joseph Hovey; Lousanna Emeline, m. Joseph Hovey; Estes Smyimda, m. Leonard Hardy; George Albert, m. Eliza Taggart, m. Harriett Taggart, m. Rhoda Slade. Family home, Salt Lake City. Farmer. Died Dec. 1, 1859.

GOODRICH, GEORGE ALBERT (son of Benjamin Franklin Goodrich and Penelope Randall Gardner). Born March 3, 1839, Lunenburg, Mass. Came to Utah 1850.
Married Eliza Ann Taggart in 1863, Salt Lake City (daughter of George W. Taggart and Harriet Atkins Bruce of Nauvoo, Ill.), who was born Jan. 28, 1844. Their children: George Leonard, m. Marion Remington; Eliza C., m. John B. Carlyle; Mary Augusta, m. William H. Goegan; Louis Henry, m. Josephine Merrill; Harriett Penelope, m. Adelbert Collett; Charles and Edith, died; Rhoda, m. Marion Roberts; Abbie Viola, m. Marion Flayer; Leslie Bruce, m. Elvina Hancock; Byron, m. Violet Starkey.
Married Harriet Taggart May 5, 1866, Salt Lake City (daughter of George Washington Taggart and Fannie Parks of Morgan county, Utah, pioneers (October 1852). She was born Sept. 2, 1848. Their children: Benjamin Franklin, and Fannie Sophia, died; Albert Gardner, m. Lydia Merrill; Rachael Maria, m. George A. Slaugh; William Burrage, Julia Louisa, Hyrum Parks, and Wallace, all died; Parley Herbert, m. Viva Hunting; Vilate, m. Julian Jensen; Leona, m. Elmer Manwaring; Lucy.
Married Rhoda Slade at Salt Lake City. Their children: Marion, died; Leroy, m. Sarah Bingham; Amelia Eliza, m. John Cook; Gardner L.; Alfred; John; Arthur; Edith; Ruth. Families resided Vernal, Utah.
Seventy; missionary to Tennessee 1894-96. Sheriff of Morgan county. Farmer and miller. Died Sept. 19, 1911.

GOODRICH, GEORGE LEONARD (son of George Albert Goodrich and Eliza Ann Taggart). Born Oct. 30, 1863, Salt Lake City.
Married Marion Vilate Remington Oct. 28, 1886, Logan, Utah (daughter of Jerome N. Remington and Lydia Ripley Badger of Salt Lake City and Paradise, Utah). She was born April 8, 1863. Their children: Laura Violet b. Aug. 28, 1887; George Remington b. Aug. 1, 1889; Charlie Remington b. Dec. 31, 1891; Jerome b. June 5, 1893; Birchell b. Oct. 21, 1894; Helen b. Feb. 6, 1897; Joseph Afton b. Aug. 23, 1901; Esther b. May 5, 1910. Family home Naples ward, Uintah, Utah.
High priest; counselor to superintendent of Sunday schools at Richville ward, and to Wm. H. Gagon, superintendent Y. M. M. I. A.; counselor in deacons' quorum, and to Bishop Thomas J. Caldwell of Naples ward; ward teacher. Road supervisor eight years; constable ten years. President Ashley Central Irrigation company; proprietor George L. Goodrich Mercantile business. As a settler in Ashley Valley since 1885, he has assisted in building up the country.

GOODRICH, ALBERT GARDNER (son of George Albert Goodrich and Harriet Maria Taggart). Born May 1, 1871, Mt. Carmel, Kane Co., Utah.

Married Lydia Merrell Oct. 14, 1892. Logan, Utah (daughter of Porter William Merrill and Harriet Amelia Badger Remington of Naples ward, Uintah, Utah, pioneers 1850), who was born Feb. 20, 1876. Their children: Fannie b. Sept. 7, 1893, died; Elma b. March 12, 1895, m. Jacob Norman Lybbert; Albert b. Oct. 1, 1897; Karl Iver b. May 11, 1901; Pearl b. Feb. 7, 1903, died; Ruth b. Aug. 5, 1905; Frank b. April 14, 1909; Merrell b. Aug. 24, 1911. Family home Uintah, Utah.
Bishop of Naples ward 1910; high counselor 1904; assistant Sunday school superintendent; ward teacher; ward chorister 1900-09; counselor to Bishop James M. Shaffer of Naples ward 1906-10; secretary Y. M. M. I. A.; member 97th quorum seventies; missionary to Michigan 1898-1900. School trustee twelve years; county register agent eight years. Secretary Central Irrigation Canal company. Carpenter; farmer; miller.

GOODRIDGE, JAMES WILLIS. Born May 1, 1843, Haverhill, Mass. Came to Utah 1852.
Married Eliza Frances Deuel 1871, Kanarraville, Utah (daughter of William Henry Deuel and Mary Avery Whiting, of Centerville, Utah), who was born June 23, 1854. Their children: William Willis b. Jan. 16, 1872, m. Josephine Johnson; George Milton b. 1875, m. Ada Bateman; Mary Avery b. May, 1877, m. Charles Wilkins; Eliza Mabel b. 1878, m. George Smith; Amelia Emeline b. 1880, m. William Anderson; Lewis Barnard b. Feb. 13, 1883; Byron Deuel b. April 14, 1885; Minerva, m. Nick Docas; Hazel, m. Parley Glover; Geneva, m. Theodore Johnson; Josephine; Jessie. Family home Midvale, Utah.
Member elders' quorum; assisted in bringing immigrants to Utah; drove oxteam across plains with machinery for first woolen mills in Utah. Smelterman.

GOODRIDGE, WILLIAM WILLIS (son of James Willis Goodridge and Eliza Frances Deuel). Born Jan. 16, 1872, Kanarraville, Utah.
Married Josephine Johnson Oct. 31, 1894, Salt Lake City (daughter of John Johnson and Inger Sward, of Provo, Utah, pioneers 1864, John Smith company). She was born May 22, 1874. Their children: Effie Josephine b. Aug. 4, 1895, died; Zettella b. Sept. 27, 1896; Mourine b. Nov. 2, 1899; Barbara b. July 13, 1901; Willma b. Feb. 29, 1904; Lynn Willis b. Nov. 13, 1906; Helen b. Aug. 15, 1911. Family home Lake View, Utah.
Member 70th quorum seventies; superintendent Lake View Sunday school ten years. Justice of peace of Lake View six years. Agricultural superintendent for Utah Sugar Beet company.

GOODWIN, ISAAC R. (son of Isaac M. Goodwin and Rhoda Richards). Born June 18, 1810, North Hartford, Conn. Came to Utah 1856.
Married Laura Hotchkiss (daughter of Benjamin Hotchkiss and Elizabeth Tyrell), who was born April 3, 1813, and died in 1846. Their children: Isaac H.; Lewis; Emerette E.; Edwin A.; Nancy Eleanor; Lucinda L.; Albert S.
Married Mary Cox, who was born Aug. 3, 1827, Sussex, Eng. Settled at Lehi and served as mayor. High priest. Said to be the first to introduce lucern into southern Utah. Farmer; carpenter; gardener. Also lived 12 years at San Bernardino, Cal.

GOODWIN, ISAAC H. (son of Isaac R. Goodwin and Laura Hotchkiss). Born Aug. 25, 1834, Hartford, Conn. Came to Utah with father.
Married Betsey Smith Dec. 1, 1859, Salt Lake City (daughter of Alexander Nichol Smith and May McEwan, the latter and her daughter pioneers Nov. 9, 1856, James G. Willie handcart company). She was born March 7, 1843, Dundee, Scotland. Their children: Isaac Smith; Laura May; Albert S.; Mary Jane; Alexander S.; Lewis Henry; Edwin A.; James E.; John McEwan. Family resided Lehi, Smithfield, Escalante, Thurber and Beaver, Utah.
Elder. Merchant and farmer.

GOODWIN, ISAAC SMITH (son of Isaac H. Goodwin and Betsey Smith). Born Feb. 8, 1861, Lehi, Utah.
Married Mary Jane Adams March 20, 1885, St. George, Utah (daughter of David Cook Adams and Mary Eleanor Armstrong), who was born July 14, 1868, Adamsville, Utah. Their children: Isaac A.; Lewis Adams; Laura E.; Betsey May; William J.; Lucinda; Martin Cook; Vernon McEwan; Vera Leona. Family resided Teasdale, Frisco, and Beaver, Utah.
Farmer; carpenter. Elder.

GORDON, JOHN (son of Foster and Sarah Gordon of Newcastle-on-Tyne, Eng.). Born at Newcastle, Eng. Came to Utah Sept. 10, 1861, oxteam company.
Married Hannah Hudson March 21, 1848, who was born Aug. 1, 1828, and came to Utah Sept. 10, 1861, with husband. Their children: Fannie, m. William Mills; Foster, m. Mary Parks; Robert, m. Agnes Davis; John, m. Mary Bolton; Samuel, m. Jane ——; George; Minnie, m. Plum Haslet. Family resided St. John and Salt Lake City, Utah.
Elder; ward teacher. Stone mason. Last heard from at Blackfoot, Idaho.

GORDON, ROBERT (son of John Gordon and Hannah Hudson). Born March 14, 1851, Newcastle-on-Tyne, Eng. Came to Utah 1863.

Married Agnes Davis June 3, 1870, Panaca, Nevada (daughter of James and Catherine Davis of Panaca, Nevada). She was born June 3, 1851. Their children: William b. May 3 1871, d. infant; Robert James b. June 5, 1872, m. Gertrude Estelle Sherman; Agnes Katherine b. Dec. 26, 1875, m. O. L. Sherman; Joseph Henry b. Feb. 28, 1878, m. Augusta Johnson; Samuel Raymond b. July 3, 1880, m. Katy Johnson Hannah Frances, m. G. A. Johnson; George Edward, m Elizabeth Burgess; Rose Ellen b. 1886, d. aged 22; Katy Hudson, m. A. V. Leonard; Emily Jane, m. Lawrence Leonard; Ruty; Clarence. Family home Huntington, Utah Elder; Sunday school superintendent. School trustee Town marshal 1906-08. Farmer and stockraiser.

GORDON, ROBERT JAMES (son of Robert Gordon and Agne Davis). Born June 5, 1872, Rush Valley, Utah.
Married Gertrude Estelle Sherman Oct. 18, 1894, Hunting ton, Utah (daughter of Alby L. Sherman and Mary E. Swa of Fountain Green, Utah). She was born Oct. 18, 1874 Their children: Corine Cornelia b. June 1, 1896; Robert Dor b. Jan. 22, 1898; Von b. Oct. 14, 1900; Luella b. Nov. 23 1904; Florence b. Dec. 10, 1905; Edna b. Sept. 13, 1908; Elli b. Oct. 17, 1910. Family home Huntington, Utah.
Farmer.

GORDON, JOHN HENRY (son of John Gordon and Hannal Hudson). Born Jan. 19, 1880, Salt Lake City.
Married Mary Bolton Nov. 19, 1876, Salt Lake City (daugh ter of Curtis E. Bolton and Mary Bunker of Long Island Queens county, N. Y., and Nauvoo, Ill., the former trans lated the Book of Mormon into the French language). She was born Nov. 15, 1857. Their children: Frances Maud b Dec. 12, 1877, m. Otto Olsen; Lewis Waterman b. Dec. 18 1879, m. Jennie Carter; John b. Jan. 19, 1882, m. Nellie Scott m. Eliza Boberg; Minnie b. April 16, 1884, m. Oliver Knowles Hannah b. April 4, 1886, m. Wallace Baum; Guy b. Feb. 26 1888; Robert b. Jan. 26, 1890, m. Lydia Whitely; Leon b July 7, 1892, m. Ethel Ashton; Curtis b. Dec. 29, 1894 Vera b. Feb. 29, 1896; Alphretta b. May 23, 1899. Family resided Pleasant View and Provo, Utah.
Elder. Moved from Salt Lake City to Provo Bench 1886 and was among the first to plant orchards at that place raised the first lucerne seed in Utah county. He assisted in making the canals and wagon roads and worked ten years on the Blue Cliff canal; he also assisted in planting the orchard on the farm known as the Carry farm. Took part in protecting the settlers against the Indians.

GORDON, JOHN (son of John Henry Gordon and Mary Rebecca Bolton). Born Jan. 19, 1880, Salt Lake City.
Married Eliza Boberg June 17, 1808, Salt Lake City (daughter of Niels Boberg of Gotland, Sweden, and Mary Anderson of Denmark, both of Provo, Utah, came to Utal 1874). She was born Nov. 24, 1882. Their children: Dorothy b. April 23, 1909; Donna Mary b. Sept. 13, 1910; Howard John b. March 12, 1912.
Elder; ward teacher. Farmer and fruitgrower.

GORDON, JOHN THOMAS (son of John A. Gordon an Emaline Wells). Born Oct. 11, 1871, York county, S. C Came to Utah 1888.
Married Margret Miller Dec. 24, 1895, American Fork Utah (daughter of Martin Miller and Christena Peterson o Lehi; pioneers Sept. 27, 1862, John R. Murdock company) She was born June 1, 1873. Their children: Myrtle Levhon b. Oct. 15, 1896; Erma Lee b. March 4, 1898; Rudger Mosiah b Nov. 9, 1899; Alta b. Nov. 12, 1901; Franklin John b. June 1909. Family home Lehi, Utah.
Seventy and ward teacher.

GORLEY, LEVI, of Alabama. Came to Utah 1857, by cow team.
Married Martha Isabel Scott in Illinois, who was bor in Alabama. Their children: Ann, m. Mr. Weeze; Esthe m. Ole Eddingberg; David, m. Sarah ——; Thomas, d. age 22; Mary, m. Joseph Truax; Keturah C., m. Francis Smit Jonathan E., m. Sarah Higgins; George W., m. Lizz Montague; James Henry Creswell, m. Mary Jane Grame Family home Provo, Utah.
Farmer. Died at Provo.

GORLEY, JAMES HENRY CRESWELL (son of Levi Gorle and Martha Isabel Scott). Born Oct. 27, 1855, in Illinoi Came to Utah with parents.
Married Mary Jane Grames Aug. 14, 1875, Spanish For Utah (daughter of Charles William Grames and Mar Lillywhite of Cote, Eng., pioneers with Captain Hor oxteam company). She was born July 13, 1857, Paktli Sussex, Eng., and came to Utah with parents. Their chi dren: Ella b. Feb. 4, 1878; Millie b. July 25, 1881, m. Le Tryon; James b. April 15; Charles Henry; Cora Isabel, Victor Hendrickson; Peter LeRoy; Mary Keturah; Franc Walter; Leonard. Family resided Garden Creek and Carbo ville, Utah.
Black Hawk Indian war veteran. Farmer. Died Aug. 1 1909, Salem, Utah.

GOUGH, JAMES (son of James Gough, born 1800, and Ele Jones, born 1810, both of Monmouthshire, Eng.). Born Ja 14, 1840, Murbridge Hill, Herefordshire, Eng. Came to Ut Oct. 5, 1862, Ansel P. Harmon company.

Married Charlotte Crockett Oct. 17, 1863 (daughter of William Crockett and Ann Williams), who was born April 25, 1840, and came to Utah 1863, Thomas E. Ricks company. Their children: Mary Ann b. Oct. 28, 1864, m. Soren Sorenson April 24, 1884; Lavina Jane b. Feb. 17, 1866, m. Moroni Thayne Nov. 24, 1881; James Charles b. Sept. 14, 1868, m. Elizabeth Trinnaman Feb. 14, 1894; Elenor b. June 19, 1870, m. James Carter Dec. 24, 1889; Harriet b. March 26, 1873, m. Thomas A. Taylor Nov. 2, 1891; William b. May 19, 1895, m. Lucy Shaw; Samuel b. July 22, 1877, m. Luella Anderson Nov. 26, 1902; Thomas E. b. April 21, 1879, m. Linda Day June, 1901; Richard b. May 20, 1881, m. Pearl Clift June 22, 1904; Charlotte b. Feb. 8, 1884, m. William Hadfield June 28, 1900; Robert b. March 5, 1886. Family home Lehi, Utah. President teachers quorum.

GOULD, ROBERT (son of Robert Gould and Mary Boyd of Stirling and Edinburgh, Scotland). Born Jan. 21, 1830, Edinburgh. Came to Utah 1861, Homer Duncan company.
Married Annie Simpson 1855, Philadelphia, Pa. (daughter of John Simpson and Elizabeth Carig of Edinburgh, Scotland). She was born Feb. 2, 1831. Their children: Elizabeth, m. Heber McBride; Robert, d. aged 20; Mary J., m. H. J. Fuller; John S., m. Mary Mortensen; William S., m. Maria Peterson Lindsay. Family home Eden, Utah.
Married Elizabeth Eube 1870, Eden, Utah, who was born 1845. Their children: Henry; Robert; Richard; Joseph, m. Miss Littlefield. Family home Ogden, Utah.
Ward teacher. Joiner and mechanic.

GOULD, JOHN S. (son of Robert Gould and Annie Simpson). Born July 10, 1855, Liberty, Utah.
Married Mary Mortensen Nov. 29, 1889, Huntsville, Utah (daughter of Neil C. Mortensen and Mary Christensen of Huntsville, Utah—pioneers 1864, John Smith independent company), who was born Aug. 14, 1871. Their children: Florence M. b. Oct. 2, 1892; Glenard A. b. July 7, 1894; Merrill J. b. Oct. 24, 1898; Arvena M. b. Oct. 20, 1903; Eileen G. b. Aug. 29, 1908; Clarissa E. b. Dec. 21, 1912; Claire C. b. Dec. 21, 1912.
Member 75th quorum seventies; ward teacher. Farmer.

GOWANS, ANDREW (son of Alexander Gowans and Mary Bowden of Canei, Scotland). Born December, 1800, at Canei. Came to Utah October, 1855, Milo Andrus company.
Married Anne McLeish (daughter of James McLeish and Betsy Gibb of Canel), who was born Feb. 26, 1788. Their children: James b. July 25, 1824; Mary b. March 30, 1826, m. George Cook; Barbara b. May 27, 1828, m. John Simpson; Betsy b. Feb. 22, 1832, m. Hugh S. Gowans. Family home Tooele, Utah.
Florist and landscape gardener. Died Nov. 20, 1891.

GOWANS, HUGH S. (son of Robert Gowans, born May 12, 1811, Arbroath, Forfarshire, and Grace McKay, of Perth, Perthshire, Scotland). He was born Feb. 23, 1831, in Perth. Came to Utah Oct. 24, 1855, Milo Andrus company.
Married Betsy Gowans in March, 1854, Arbroath (daughter of Andrew Gowans and Anne McLeish, married in Arbroath, 1823, pioneers Oct. 24, 1855, Milo Andrus company). She was born Feb. 22, 1832, and came to Utah with husband; died Sept. 25, 1912. Their children: Barbara b. Feb. 13, 1856, m. Benjamin L. Bowen July 24, 1876; Robert M. b. Oct. 9, 1856, d. July 31, 1863; Hugh G. b. June 10, 1858, d. May 21, 1863; James b. Nov. 21, 1860, m. Alice de la Mare Feb. 12, 1885; Andrew b. Sept. 8, 1862, m. Willena Henson, Feb. 12, 1894; Betsy b. Dec. 7, 1864, m. Francis M. Lyman, Jr., Oct. 16, 1889; Ephraim G. b. Feb. 1, 1868, m. Mary C. Lyman June 1, 1893; Alonzo G. b. Dec. 7, 1869, m. Deseret Leaver Nov. 15, 1899; Charles A. b. Jan. 21, 1872, m. Harriet Martineau June 12, 1904. Family home Tooele, Utah.
Married Elizabeth Broomhead April, 1883, Salt Lake City (daughter of Thomas Broomhead and Margaret Morton), who was born Feb. 24, 1847, Sheffield, Eng. Their children: Barbara E. b. Feb. 24, 1884, m. Edward Nelson; Thomas E. b. Feb. 26, 1886; George H. b. Aug. 4, 1887; Albert H. b. Aug. 10, 1889.
Assessor and collector Tooele county; mayor Tooele City; probate judge Tooele county. President Tooele stake. Died Sept. 10, 1912.

GOWANS, EPHRAIM G. (son of Hugh S. Gowans and Betsy Gowans). Born Feb. 1, 1868, Tooele, Utah.
Married Mary Crismon Lyman June 1, 1893, Salt Lake City (daughter of Francis M. Lyman and Rhoda Ann Taylor of Fillmore, Tooele and Salt Lake City, Utah). She was born July 29, 1571. Their children: Louis Lyman b. April 22, 1894; Lois b. Dec. 20, 1895; Marjorie b. June 7, 1899; Emerson Lyman b. Jan. 19, 1906; Marion Lyman b. May 17, 1908. Family home, Salt Lake City.
Member 47th quorum seventies; missionary to Great Britain 1888-90. Judge of juvenile court 3d judicial district 1907-09; superintendent State Industrial school since 1909. Physician; teacher.

GOWER, THOMAS (son of Thomas Gower and Catherine Cresswell of Stourbridge, Worcestshire, Eng.). Born May 23, 1816, at Stourbridge. Came to Utah Oct. 1854, Joseph Field company.
Married Jane Cresswell (daughter of Richard and Ann Cresswell of Mt. Pleasant, near Stourbridge), who was born July 17, 1817, and died at St. Louis, Mo. Their children: Thomas b. March 17, 1839; Elizabeth B. June 7, 1841; Ann b. Oct. 10, 1843, m. Henry Lunt; Richard Henry b. June 2, 1846.
Married Martha Ann Stockdale Nov. 4, 1850. Their children: John Thomas, m. Harriet Jane Corry; Joseph, died; Albert Francis, m. Mary Grace Condie; Betsy Ann b. May 26, 1857, d. June 2, 1857; Jane Elizabeth b. May 12, 1858, m. James McHamilton May 2, 1881, divorced 1886; m. William E. Yardley Nov. 12, 1889; Martha Ann b. April 30, 1860, d. Aug. 29, 1861; Mary Isabelle b. Jan. 16, 1862, d. March 6, 1879; Catherine Katura b. Nov. 27, 1863, m. Thomas Urie; Charlotte b. Nov. 3, 1865, m. Joseph A. Rosenburg; Horace Tidswell b. Dec. 13, 1867, d. Jan. 12, 1901; Louisa May b. May 31, 1870, m. William James Condie April 25, 1899.
Married Annie Williams April 4, 1863. Their children: David Stephen b. Dec. 17, 1863, d. Oct. 21, 1902; Jared, d. June 18, 1867; Benjamin b. Sept. 14, 1869, d. April 10, 1903. Family home Cedar City, Utah.
Called by Brigham Young to go to Iron county to smelt iron. Took part in early Indian troubles at Long Valley. Assisted in building canals, roads and sawmills in early days. Farmer. Died May 1, 1877.

GRACE, ISAAC (son of John Grace and Margaret Abbott, of Liverpool, Eng.). Born April 17, 1820, at Liverpool. Came to Utah 1851.
Married Elizabeth Williams, 1843, at Liverpool (daughter of John Williams and Ann Jones, of Liverpool). Their children: Elizabeth, m. Henry F. McCune; Amelia, d. infant; Margaret, m. James Jenkins Jr.; Annette, d. infant; Harriet Ann, m. Alexander Pyper; Celestia Jane, m. Lyman L. Hudson; Isaac Henry, m. Helen H. Hudson; John William, m. Tacy Whitmore; Emma Lorette, d. infant; Charles Howard, m. Elizabeth A. Laub. Family home Nephi, Utah.
Member 49th quorum seventies. Ship-builder and farmer. Died May 21, 1871, at Nephi.

GRACE, ISAAC HENRY (son of Isaac Grace and Elizabeth Williams). Born Aug. 9, 1857, at Nephi.
Married Helen H. Hudson Jan. 19, 1882, at Salt Lake City (daughter of Christopher Columbus Hudson and Annajenette Sisson of Oberlin, Ohio; the latter came to Utah 1880), who was born Dec. 18, 1850. Their only child: Helen Grace b. April 22, 1884. Family home, Nephi.
High priest; missionary to Hawaiian Islands 1891-94; high counselor; counselor to stake president; superintendent M. I. A.; counselor to stake mutual superintendent 1888. County school superintendent; county commissioner; city councilman; mayor of Nephi; school trustee. Contractor; carpenter; farmer.

GRAEHL, GEORGE LOUIS (son of Johan Ludvic Graehl and Marie Magdalena Renner of Böhl, Germany). Came to Utah Oct. 1864, Robert L. Campbell company.
Married Louise Charlotte Leuba Aug. 31, 1844, Geneva, Switzerland (daughter of Henry Francois Leuba of Neufchatel, Switzerland, and Audrienne Elizabeth Elger; pioneers October, 1854, Robert L. Campbell company). She was born Sept. 15, 1822, and died October, 1904. Their children: Eliza, Emile, Lena and Emma, died infants; Mary Adeline, m. Henry C. Jensen; Fanny; George Louis b. March 17, 1853, m. Ada Reese; Henry, d. child; Lorenzo, m. Elizabeth Bott; Joseph Serge, m. Mima Robie; Hyrum Henry; Amelia. Family home Geneva, Switzerland.
Married Katherine Isenman, at Salt Lake City. Their children: Mary Louise, d. child; August; Clara; Eli, m. Miss Goodliffe; Ellen, d. child; Edmund, m. Maud Hatch. Family home Brigham City, Utah.
High priest. Confectioner; farmer. Died Feb. 19, 1896.

GRAEHL, GEORGE LOUIS, JR. (son of George Louis Graehl and Charlotte Louise Leuba). Born March 17, 1853, Geneva, Switzerland. Came to Utah Oct. 1854, with parents.
Married Ada Reese Jan. 6, 1885 (daughter of John D. Reese and Zillah Mathias of Wales), who was born Dec. 8, 1866. Their children: Ada Louise b. Dec. 22, 1886; Hortense Zillah b. Sept. 10, 1888; Geneve b. March 28, 1890; George Leuba b. Feb. 24, 1892; Florence Laprille b. July 23, 1895; Adele Fanny b. July 22, 1895; Helen b. April 6, 1900, d. infant; Leland b. March 28, 1902; Harold b. Oct. 12, 1905. Family home, Salt Lake City.
Missionary to Switzerland twice; high priest. County clerk Box Elder county; city treasurer, Brigham. Merchant and mining man.

GRAHAM, ALEXANDER STEWART. Born Dec. 31, 1831, Glasgow, Scotland. Came to Utah in its early history.
Married Elizabeth Jane Nuttman at St. Louis, Mo. (daughter of George Nuttman of England), who was born Oct. 2, 1832. Their children: George, died; Jane, m. Joseph Checketts; Agnes McDonald, m. Charles Odd; Charles, died; Elenor Elizabeth, m. Willard Bishop; Margaret I., died; Jeannette Ennis, m. Daniel Lockhart, Jr.; Alexander Stewart, d. child; Henry James, m. Annie Weaver; John Thomas, m. Eliza ———. Family home Kaysville, Utah.
Married Maggie ———. She lived at Kaysville, Utah.
Married Ann Malan. Their only child was Sarah. Family home, Kaysville, Utah.
Railroader. Died Sept. 1882 at Leamington, Utah.

PIONEERS AND PROMINENT MEN OF UTAH

GRAHAM, ROBERT (son of William Graham and Jane Ross of Edinburgh, Scotland, latter born Feb. 12, 1820). Born Oct. 2, 1850, in Edinburgh. Came to Utah with Captain Scott company.
Married Gertrude Stallings Dec. 27, 1875 (daughter of Joseph Stallings and Caroline Hartford of Council Bluffs, Iowa, pioneers 1850, Stephen Wareham company), who was born Oct. 28, 1854. Their children: Joseph William b. Sept. 2, 1876, m. Ellen Elizabeth Burt Nov. 2, 1905; Robert Orson b. Aug. 31, 1878, m. Annie Hogge May 8, 1901; Caroline Gertrude, m. Ray B. Thompson Aug. 2, 1905; Jane Charlott b. May 11, 1886; Perry James b. July 10, 1892. Family home Eden, Utah.
Member bishopric of Eden ward. Road supervisor eight years; school trustee. Farmer. Died Sept. 2, 1901.

GRAHAM, ROBERT ORSON (son of Robert Graham and Gertrude Stallings). Born Aug. 31, 1878, Eden.
Married Annie Hogge May 8, 1901, Salt Lake City (daughter of George William Hogge and Margaret Ann Rirrie of West Weber, Utah), who was born Feb. 22, 1879. Their children: Orvil Robert; Nina Margret. Family home Eden. Missionary to Central states 1909-11; counselor in bishopric of Eden ward. Farmer.

GRAHAM, THOMAS B. Born Aug. 12, 1807, in Pickens county, Ala. Came to Utah 1849.
Married Sarah E. McCrary Jan. 27, 1828, in Pickens county. She was born May 1, 1810, and died in Iowa, on way to Utah. Their children: Jane; James M., m. Sarah J. Brandon; John; Martha; Caroline; Francis; David; Amanda; George A. Jane and Francis did not come to Utah.
Killed by a bear in 1864, at Mendon, Cache county, Utah.

GRAHAM, JAMES M. (son of Thomas B. Graham and Sarah E. McCrary). Born Sept. 17, 1829, in Alabama. Came to Utah with parents.
Married Sarah J. Brandon Feb. 12, 1854 (daughter of Thomas J. Brandon and Martha E. Bunch—married 1834, pioneers 1847, Jared Roundy company, latter died at Nauvoo, Ill.), who was born Dec. 25, 1833. Came to Utah with father. Their children: James F. b. Nov. 5, 1854, m. Alice Hardman; John M. b. Oct. 29, 1856; Sarah b. Jan. 28, 1858, m. J. S. Brady Nov. 17, 1870; George A. b. Aug. 14, 1861, m. L. Cole April 14, 1886; David b. April 4, 1864, d. 1864; Martha E. b. Oct. 17, 1863, m. F. Kemmer April 4, 1884; Joseph H. b. Feb. 12, 1866, m. Villey Green 1887; Alice A. b. March 17, 1874, m. A. MacMillian 1892; Merretta b. April 19, 1879, m. E. Bacchus April 12, 1902; Thomas B. b. April 2, 1883, d. 1883. Family home, Salt Lake City.

GRAHAM, JAMES F. (son of James M. Graham and Sarah J. Brandon). Born Nov. 5, 1854, Sugarhouse ward, Salt Lake City.
Married Alice Hardman Nov. 6, 1879, at Salt Lake City (daughter of Joseph Hardman and Nancy Booth, pioneers Sept. 25, 1855, Richard Ballantyne company), who was born Aug. 29, 1858, in England. Their children: Matilda F. b. Aug. 9, 1880, m. S. Schwendiman March 6, 1901; Roy b. April 25, 1882, m. Pearl Harris May 6, 1902; Ida L. b. Oct. 18, 1884, m. Mark Fullmer Nov. 27, 1905; Cady M. b. Aug. 26, 1887; Claude V. b. Dec. 24, 1890, m. Hannah Gardner April 14, 1910; Harry V. b. April 25, 1892; Olive b. Jan. 5, 1894; Luella b. Dec. 4, 1897.
He was an elder.

GRAMES, CHARLES WILLIAM (son of Charles and Mary Grames of England). Born at Finden, Sussex, Eng. Came to Utah 1861, Joseph Horne company.
Married Mary Bird in England. Their children: Walter, m. Julia ——; Ellen, m. William Lake. Family home Finden, Eng.
Married Maria Lillywhite, at Finden, Eng. (daughter of Joseph Lillywhite and Maria Stafford of Finden, Eng.). Their children: Alfred, m. Sarah Sparks; Emily, m. Peter Bell, m. William Campbell; Esther, d. aged 2; Frederick, m. Mary Seaberry, m. Martha Powell; Charles, m. Rhoda Chestina Hill; Mary Jane, m. James Henry Creswell Gorley; Albert, m. Casilia Donnard; m. Lilly Bass. Family home Ephraim, Utah.
High priest. Veteran Black Hawk Indian war. Tinker, watchmaker and tailor. Died March 17, 1901, Price, Utah.

GRAMES, CHARLES (son of Charles Henry Grames and Maria Lillywhite). Born May 16, 1855, Finden, Eng. Came to Utah 1861, Joseph Horne company.
Married Rhoda Chestina Hill Jan. 1, Price, Utah (daughter of James and Melissa Hill of Logan, Utah, pioneers with oxteam). Their children: Henry; George, m. Miss Davis; Rhoda; Sina, m. Hy Chittendon. Family home Wellington, Utah.
Rancher and stockraiser.

GRANGE, SAMUEL (son of John Grange and Nancy Atkinson of Yorkshire, Eng.). Born Feb. 11, 1826, Yorkshire, Eng. Came to Utah 1852.
Married Ann Bunting Jan. 2, 1850, on shipboard (daughter of Abraham Bunting of England). Their children: Ann Elizabeth, died; Lydia Ellen, m. R. H. Barnard; Samuel, died; Almyra Maria, m. Jedediah Goff; John William, died. Family home Springville, Utah.

Married Charlot Lee 1862, Springville, Utah, who was born Oct. 8, 1843. Only child: Charlot, died. Family home Springville, Utah.
Married Esther Stevenson Feb. 11, 1864, Springville, Utah (daughter of James Stevenson and Martha Charles of England—pioneers October, 1857, Capt. Hoffine company), who was born Jan. 17, 1848. Their children: Samuel Stevenson b. Dec. 25, 1864, m. Clara Belle Brasher; Joseph b. Oct. 14 1866, died; James b. Aug. 27, 1867, died; Ulysses Wallace b. Nov. 11, 1868, m. Margaret Elizabeth Jones; Ernest James b. Dec. 28, 1870, m. Rose Ramsey; Elizabeth Letitia b. Oct 10, 1872, m. S. M. Whitmore; Beryl Ann b. July 6, 1875, died Violet b. July 3, 1877; Ethel Tamer b. May 27, 1879, m. J. H Stevenson; John Atkinson b. April 13, 1881, died; Arthur b Nov. 3, 1883, m. Hilma Pterson; Ray Clifford b. May 29, 1885 m. Verda Jensen; Franklin Charles b. June 24, 1887, m. Mary Welby; Esther Maud b. March 31, 1889, m. Ferdinand Anderson. Family home Huntington, Utah.
High priest; ward teacher. Settled at Springville, 1852 moved to Huntington 1883, where he assisted in building up the country. Member board of education; school trustee File cutter; shoemaker; mining man. Died Dec. 1, 1893 Huntington, Utah.

GRANGE, SAMUEL STEVENSON (son of Samuel Grange and Esther Stevenson). Born Dec. 25, 1864, Springville, Utah.
Married Clara Belle Brasher Oct. 1, 1886, Logan, Utah (daughter of John Leisal Brasher and Eliza Cheshire of Kentucky), who was born Jan. 4, 1867. Their children Leisal Samuel b. Sept. 14, 1887, m. Coreila Taylor; Nida b Dec. 14, 1888; m. Byronel Howard; Nora b. June 1, 1891, m Ezra Harrison; Nellie S. b. Sept. 30, 1893; Florence b. Feb 12, 1896, died; Ida b. July 7, 1892; Ada b. July 7, 1892; Clifford b. June 3, 1905. Family home Huntington, Utah.
Member 81st quorum seventies; ward teacher fifteen years in Huntington ward. Member town council two terms district trustee three years. Fruitgrower and farmer.

GRANGE, ULYSSES WALLACE (son of Samuel Grange and Esther Stevenson). Born Nov. 11, 1868, Springville, Utah.
Married Margaret Elizabeth Jones Oct. 12, 1893, Huntington, Utah, by Daniel Tyler (daughter of Elisha Warren Jones and Georgana Jane Pierce of Nauvoo, Ill., and Kanesville Iowa), who was born Oct. 4, 1874. Their children: Wallace Guy b. Oct. 3, 1894; Elisha Myron b. July 14, 1896; Elli Lucile b. March 28, 1898; Ruby b. Jan. 17, 1901; Elizabeth Erma b. May 26, 1907; Hilma b. April 25, 1908; Samuel Lloyd b. July 24, 1911. Family home Huntington, Utah.
Missionary to northwestern states 1903-04; president high priests quorum of Emery stake; member high council; home missionary; president Y. M. M. I. A. 1909; Sunday school superintendent 1906-08; counselor to Bishop Peter Johnson of Huntington ward; counselor in Y. M. M. I. A. of Hunting ton ward; and counselor in elders quorum. President Hunt ington town board 1906-07; member Huntington town board 1910-11; road supervisor. Settled at Huntington 1883, where he has done much in the upbuilding of the country.

GRANGER, WALTER (son of Robert Granger and Catherin McDonald). Born Aug. 4, 1821, Edinburgh, Scotland. Cam to Utah Sept. 26, 1856, D. D. McArthur company.
Married Catherine Guthrie 1841 (daughter of John Guthri and Agnes Emought), who was born January, 1819. Thei children: Robert b. Jan. 18, 1842; Catherine b. December 1848, m. David Gibson 1868; Peter b. August, 1857; Nelli Emma; Walter, John, both died. Family home St. Georg Utah.
Settled at Spanish Fork 1856; moved to St. George 186 where he served as bishop of third ward and later of secon ward 1869-92; moved to Cedar City 1892; high priest. Die May 6, 1904.

GRANT, GEORGE DAVIS (son of Joshua Grant and Thali Howard of Neversink, N. Y.). Born Sept. 10, 1812, Windso N. Y. Came to Utah June, 1848.
Married Elizabeth Wilson Jan. 22, 1834, Naples, N. (daughter of Thomas Wilson of Tuley, Onondaga count N. Y.), who was born April 25, 1816, Tuley, N. Y. The children: Thalia Elizabeth, m. Joseph Angell Young; Georg Wilson, m. Lucy Curtis Spencer; William Smith, m. Ma Ann Mulr; Josephine, m. Benjamin Franklin Snyder; D Carlos, died; Julia Caroline, m. Edwin W. Gilman; Jose Smith, died. Family home. Salt Lake City.
Married Elizabeth Lamb. Their children: Pauline; Charl Albert; David, died; Georgiana, m. Mr. Pace; Andrew, died.
Married Margaret Baxter. Their children: Ella, m. M Cross, Utah; Jedediah and Nettie, died. Family home Woo Cross, Utah.
Married Susan Grant. Only child: Frank. Family hom Woods Cross.
Married Jennie Baxter. Their children: Caroline, Cla and Willard, died. Family home, Woods Cross.
He, with William H. Kimball, picked the "minute men bodyguard of Joseph Smith; general in Indian wars; capta of handcarts of Nauvoo Legion 1857; captain of "life guards Trader and farmer. Died Sept. 2, 1876. Woods Cross.

GRANT, JEDEDIAH MORGAN (son of Joshua Grant an Thalia Howard). Born Feb. 21, 1816, at Windsor, Broom county, N. Y. Came to Utah Sept. 1847, with own compan Married Susan Noble Fairchild (came to Utah Sep 1847, with George B. Wallace company), who was born Ju

25, 1832. Their children: Joseph Hyrum b. Oct. 17, 1853, at Salt Lake City, m. Eliza Evaeletta Eldredge Oct. 18, 1875, at Salt Lake City; Susan Vilate b. Sept. 19, 1855, m. William S. Muir, Jr., 1871. Family home Bountiful, Utah.
Married Rossetta Robinson. Their children: Jedediah Morgan b. Oct. 9, 1853, m. Lucy Fackrell; Henrietta b. 1855, m. D. S Marshall.
Married Maryette Kesler 1854, Salt Lake Endowment house (daughter of Frederick Kesler and Emeline Parker of Salt Lake City, pioneers 1852). She was born Feb. 23, 1839. Only child: Brigham Frederick, b. Oct. 15, 1856, m. Johanna Schluter.
Married Rachel Ridgeway Ivins November, 1855, Salt Lake Endowment house (daughter of Caleb Ivins and Edith Ridgeway of Toms River, N. J., and Philadelphia, Pa.). She was born March 7, 1821, Hornerstown, N. J., died Jan. 27, 1909. Only child: Heber Jeddy b. Nov. 22, 1856, m. Lucy Stringham, m. Huldah Augusta Winters, m. Emily Harris Wells. Family home, Salt Lake City.
One of the presidents of the first council of seventies 1845; chosen second counselor to Brigham Young April 7, 1854. First mayor of Salt Lake City and continued in that office until his death, Dec., 1856; was speaker of the house of the territorial legislature from 1852 to 1855; superintendent of public works of Salt Lake City. Plowed the first furrow in Morgan county, which county was named after him. Farmer and stockraiser.

GRANT, JOSEPH HYRUM (son of Jedediah Morgan Grant and Susan Noble Fairchild). Born Oct. 17, 1853, at Salt Lake City.
Married Eliza Evaeletta Eldredge at Salt Lake City, Oct. 18, 1875 (daughter of Horace S. Eldredge who came to Utah with his own company, and Sarah W. Gibbs). Their children: Joseph H. b. July 20, 1876, m. Algie Lydia Hatch, June 30, 1898; Sarah b. Dec. 20, 1877, m. Fred J. Pack, Nov. 25, 1896; Susan E. b. Aug. 7, 1879, m. D. David Mann Jan. 13, 1899; Jessie E. b. June 13, 1881, m. David E. Reed June, 1906; Walter E. b. March 29, 1883, m. Ellen Smith Sept. 2, 1908; Carter E. b. Dec. 31, 1885, m. Pamela E. Smith April 2, 1905; Eva E. b. Aug. 13, 1888, m. Daniel Roy Moss April 2, 1908; Howard E. b. Nov. 11, 1890; m. Hazel Howard June 14, 1912; Lyle b. Aug. 25, 1893; Horace James b. Oct. 7, 1895. Family home Bountiful, Utah.
Bishop of West Bountiful ward from 1888 to 1889; second counselor to Pres. Wm. R. Smith of the Davis stake 1890 to 1893; first counselor to Pres. John W. Hess of the Davis stake; called to the presidency of Davis stake Sept. 25, 1904. Farmer; stockraiser.

GRANT, JOSEPH HYRUM (son of Joseph Hyrum Grant and Eliza Evaeletta Eldredge). Born July 20, 1876, at Bountiful, Utah.
Married Algie Lydia Hatch June 30, 1898, at Salt Lake City (daughter of Orvin Hatch, one of the battalion, 1847, and Elizabeth Perry, who came to Utah 1847), who was born June 5, 1877, at Bountiful. Their children: Van Hatch b. April 15, 1900; Adelaide b. March 16, 1902; Myra b. March 26, 1905; Dale Eldredge b. Feb. 23, 1908. Family home Kaysville, Utah.
Missionary to Colorado 1897-98; high councilor in the Davis stake. Justice of the peace at Kaysville. Dentist.

GRANT, BRIGHAM FREDRICK (son of Jedediah M. Grant and Maryetta Kesler). Born Oct. 17, 1856, Salt Lake City.
Married Johanna Schluter, Nov. 22, ... (daughter of William Schluter and Phoebe Ann Wickel of Salt Lake City, pioneers 1867, independent company). She was born March 4, 1862. Their children: Fredrick W. b. May 11, 1890, m. Margret Smith; Jedediah b. March 16, 1882, m. Lavina Sainsbury; Hazel Maude b. March 9, 1884, m. J. V. Needham; Eugene S. b. July 17, 1887, m. Ella V. Owen; Luella Belle b. Nov. 9, 1889, died; Heber b. Nov. 16, 1899; Delora b. May 5, 1902. Family home, Salt Lake City.
Member high council Salt Lake stake; member Y. M. M. I. A. of Salt Lake City. Chief of police of Salt Lake. Engaged in mining, insurance, general merchandising, farming and stockraising.

GRANT, HEBER JEDDY (son of Jedediah Morgan Grant and Rachel Ridgeway Ivins). Born Nov. 22, 1856, Salt Lake City.
Married Lucy Stringham Nov. 1, 1877, St. George Temple, Utah (daughter of Bryant Stringham and Susan Ashby of Salt Lake City, pioneers July 24, 1847, Brigham Young company). She was born April 27, 1858, and died Jan. 3, 1893. Their children: Susan Rachel b. Aug. 30, 1878, m. John H. Taylor; Lucy Grant b. Oct. 22, 1880, m. George Jenkins Cannon; Florence b. Feb. 7, 1883, m. Willard Richards Smith; Edith b. April 2, 1885, m. Clifford Earl Young; Anna b. Dec. 28, 1886, m. John George Midgley, Jr.; Heber, b. Dec. 9, 1888, d. Feb. 27, 1896.
Married Huldah Augusta Winters May 26, 1884, Salt Lake City (daughter of Oscar F. Winters and Mary Ann Stearns of Pleasant Grove, Utah, pioneers). She was born July 7, 1856. Only child: Mary b. Feb. 6, 1889.
Married Emily Harris Wells May 27, 1884, Salt Lake City (daughter of Daniel H. Wells and Martha Harris of Salt Lake City, pioneers 1848). She was born April 22, 1857, and died May 25, 1908. Their children: Martha Deseret b. April 21, 1886, m. Ashby Douglas Boyle; Grace b. Dec. 21, 1888, m. Isaac Blair Evans; Daniel Wells b. Nov. 21, 1891, d. March 10, 1895; Emily b. June 5, 1896; Frances Marion b. Sept. 23, 1899. Families resided Salt Lake City.
Secretary Y. M. M. I. A. Salt Lake stake 1879-80; ordained high priest and set apart as president Tooele stake Oct. 30, 1880; ordained member Twelve Apostles, Church of Jesus Christ of Latter-day Saints Oct. 16, 1882; member 30th quorum seventies; missionary to Japan 1901-03; president European mission 1903-06; has been doing missionary work throughout the stakes of Zion for the past 30 years; one of the counselors of the first mutual organization (13th ward), under the personal direction of President Young, Salt Lake City. Member Salt Lake City council 1883-86; member legislative council (senate) of the territory of Utah 1883-84. President Home Fire Insurance Co., of Utah; president Heber J. Grant and Co.; president Utah Implement & Vehicle Co.; vice-president Utah State National bank, Salt Lake City; director Utah-Idaho Sugar Co., and Zion Coöperative Mercantile Institution; was president State Bank of Utah, which he organized, and president Salt Lake Theatre Co.; president Coöperative Wagon & Machine Co.; vice-president Salt Lake Herald Co., (morning newspaper, since Herald-Republican) and owned control of the stock.

GRANT, JOSHUA FREDERICK. Born July 24, 1818, in Stueben county, N. Y.
Married Louise Marie Goulay Aug. 27, 1843 of Vevey, Switzerland county, Ind. She was born May 28, 1826. Their children: Adelaide b. Oct. 4, 1845, Kanesville, Iowa; Florence Caroline b. May 11, 1851, Council Bluffs, Iowa; Joshua Frederick b. April 19, 1856, Woods Cross, Utah. Their early residence was at Vevey and later Salt Lake City.
He, with his brother, Jedediah Morgan Grant were the youngest missionaries to labor in the southern states (when boys in their teens). Migrated to Utah in 1847 with a private freighting outfit hauling material for the United States army part way.
Died Salt Lake City, Utah, Nov. 21, 1851. Buried in the city cemetery, lot 7, block 8, plat C, near corner of Main street and 8th avenue.

GRAVES, DANIEL (son of Daniel Graves born April 3, 1770, Carbook, Norfolk, Eng., and Mary Blanchflower born at Sahamtorry, Norfolk, Eng.). Born April 17, 1806, Yarmouth, Eng. Came to Utah 1854, Capt. Harker company.
Married Elizabeth Sarah Baker, who was born April 16, 1810. Their children: Elizabeth b. July 24, 1824; William Durrant b. Nov. 8, 1829; Isabella b. Sept. 27, 1833; Joseph b. June 11, 1834; Robert; Maria Ann b. Feb. 7, 1836; Jane b. June 20, 1837; Isabella b. May 18, 1838. Family home Yarmouth, Eng.
Married Mary Newman June 7, 1840, St. Olives, Southwork, London, Eng. (daughter of Henry G. Newman and Elizabeth Bull), who was born March 27, 1817, Hayres, Middlesex, Eng. Their children: Edward Henry b. Aug. 12, 1841; Elizabeth Sarah b. June 24, 1843; Daniel Robert b. April 17, 1845; Charlotte M. b. Nov. 1, 1847; Joseph Nephi b. Jan. 16, 1849; Lehi Moroni b. Nov. 4, 1850; Mary Ann b. Dec. 5, 1852; Ebenezer b. Sept. 28, 1855; Alma b. Nov. 4, 1857; Joshua b. Dec. 16, 1859. Family home Provo, Utah.
Elder. President agriculture association. Artist. Died 1892 at Provo.

GRAVES, JOSHUA (son of Daniel Graves and Mary Newman). Born Dec. 16, 1859, Provo, Utah.
Married Mary B. Vanwagoner June 11, 1881, Provo (daughter of John Vanwagoner and Elizabeth Young). She was born May 19, 1866, Provo. Their children: Daniel B. b. Nov. 26, 1881; Tessie May b. Nov. 12, 1882, m. Fred Herron May 20, 1907; Lizzie Maud b. Jan. 16, 1885, m. Joseph Chambers Oct. 25, 1905; Jessie b. May 19, 1887; Jennie b. March 12, 1898.
Married Martha Hansen Graves Sept. 3, 1890, Manti, Utah (daughter of Hans Frederick Hansen and Cathron Nielson, the former a pioneer 1854, Hans Peter Olsen company, the latter with Capt. Christenson company). She was born March 3, 1872, Spanish Fork, Utah. Their children: Frederick Joshua b. Sept. 1, 1891; James Henry b. April 18, 1894; Mary Cathron b. June 21, 1896; Lavera Charlotte b. Aug. 7, 1898; Zina Jane b. Nov. 26, 1900; Bertha Loretta b. March 28, 1903; Leona Martha b. Oct. 2, 1905; Walter Stoddard b. Dec. 31, 1908; Velma Lavern b. Dec. 17, 1910.

GRAY, JOSEPH REEVES (son of James Gray of Dorchester, Eng.). Born May 29, 1824, Dorchester, Eng. Came to Utah October, 1854, John Brown company.
Married Mary Franklin 1851, Dorchester, Eng., who was born 1832, and came to Utah with husband. Their children: Franklin Thomas b. Dec. 9, 1852, m. Mary Jane Titcomb; Joseph, died; James b. Dec. 31, 1856, m. Elizabeth Holdsworth; William b. 1858, m. Phoebe Yates; Charles b. 1860, m. Eunice Brown; Mary Rachael, died. Family home Lehi, Utah.
Married Elizabeth Marshall 1867, Salt Lake Endowment house (daughter of John and Elizabeth Marshall). Their children: Rhoda Ann, died; Rosa, m. William Makin; Lilly and George, died; John, m. Goldie Cummings; Edward, died; Elizabeth, m. George Webb. Family home Lehi, Utah.
Secretary high priests quorum; Sunday school teacher. Located at Lehi 1854. Indian war veteran; veteran Echo Canyon war. Assisted in building the first canals, wagon roads, and in the development of the country. Shoemaker and farmer. Died Feb. 2, 1877, Lehi, Utah.

GRAY, FRANKLIN THOMAS (son of John Reeves Gray and Mary Franklin). Born Dec. 9, 1852, Dorchester, Eng. Came to Utah October, 1854, John Brown company.
Married Mary Jane Titcomb Nov. 18, 1872, Salt Lake City (daughter of Luke Titcomb and Lydia Jane Tanner of Cot-

tonwood, Salt Lake county, pioneers September, 1850, William Wall company). She was born Dec. 31, 1855. Their children: Winfield Franklin b. Oct. 20, 1873, m. Eliza Bolin; James H. b. April 7, 1876, m. Winifred Price; Mary Susan b. May 30, 1877, m. Seth Littleford; Joseph William b. Dec. 28, 1879. —. Jane Saby; Lydia Rebecca b. June 7, 1881; Charles Delos b. Dec. 7, 1883, m. Leverne Anderson; Thomas M. b. March 12, 1886, m. Ethel Fox; Ina Gladis b. Oct. 31, 1888; Ezra Tollman b. Sept. 30, 1890. Family home Lehi, Utah.
Elder. Settled at Lehi when a boy and has spent his entire life in developing the country, building canals, wagon roads, irrigation ditches and bringing timber from the mountains for building purposes. Farmer.

GRAY, WILLIAM STYLUS (son of Joseph Reeves Gray and Mary Franklin). Born Nov. 28, 1858, Lehi, Utah.
Married Phoebe Yates Aug. 3, 1887, Logan, Utah (daughter of William Yates and Mary Ann Peck of Bath, Eng.). She was born Feb. 26, 1872. Their children: Mary Edith b. June 12, 1888, m. Murray O. Hayes; Phoebe Louisa b. Sept. 19, 1889, m. Claud Emmett Hayes; William Edward b. Aug. 9, 1891, m. Ethel Roberts; Archie Charles b. June 21, 1893; Hyrum Richard b. Aug. 18, 1895; Elisha Franklin b. July 15, 1897; Jesse Sylus b. Oct. 28, 1898; Myrton James b. June 13, 1901; Eldon Leroy Gates b. Jan. 11, 1903; Ruland Joseph b. Dec. 14, 1904; Alvin Stanford b. Nov. 13, 1906; Duaine Yates b. Feb. 27, 1909; Elaine b. Feb. 27, 1909; Ernest Elipton b. Jan. 8, 1912. Family home Lehi, Utah.
Elder. Has spent his life in developing the country in and around Lehi, building irrigation ditches, canals, wagon roads and bridges. Freighter and farmer.

GRAY, SAMUEL R. (son of Samuel W. Gray, born June 27, 1823, Kirkintilloch, Scotland, and Sarah Gray, born Oct. 31, 1830, who were married March 5, 1852). Born Jan. 19, 1853, Kirkintilloch. Came to Utah 1861, Joseph W. Young company.
Married Nancy Stewart Aug. 1880 (daughter of William A. Stewart and Jane Browning; the former came to Utah 1847). She was born Nov. 10, 1861. Their children: Eugene b. Nov. 10, 1881; John S. b. Feb. 21, 1885; Hazel b. Feb. 1, 1888; Wallace b. May 6, 1891; Archie b. Nov. 7, 1893; Lucille b. May 30, 1897; Mildred b. March 4, 1900; Leland b. May 5, 1905. Family home Central, Utah.

GREAVES, PETER (son of Thomas Greaves, born 1800, and Dorothy Gescal of Lancashire, Eng.—married 1825 in Lancashire). He was born Aug. 26, 1837, Paterson, N. J. Came to Utah 1852, Capt. Howell company.
Married Elizabeth Motley June 20, 1858 (daughter of William Motley and Elizabeth Hughes—married 1823, Hereford, Eng.; former died at Nauvoo, Ill., latter pioneer, William Wall company). She was born June 10, 1837, and came to Utah with mother. Their children: Peter b. Sept. 17, 1859, m. Catherine Mortenson; John b. Jan. 24, 1867, m. Hannah Frost; Albert M. b. March 10, 1872, m. Lorinda Peterson.
Member first city council of Ephraim eight years; member last territorial legislative council (senate); commissioner San Pete county, holding position as chairman two years.

GREEN, ALPHONZO. Born July 8, 1810, Brookfield, N. Y. Came to Utah 1847.
Married Betsey Murdock Dec. 29, 1838, Hamilton, N. Y., who was born May 6, 1810. Their children: Alva Alphonzo; m. Ellen Gibson; Sarah Annadellah, m. James Chipman; Joseph Daniels, and John Murdock, died. Family home American Fork, Utah.
Married Elizabeth Chadwick, at Salt Lake City, who came to Utah 1867. Their children: Rastus, m. Emily Adamson; Alice, m. Joseph Oler. Family home, American Fork.
Died Aug. 6, 1875, at American Fork.

GREEN, ALVA ALPHONZO (son of Alphonzo Green and Betsey Murdock). Born Nov. 14, 1859, at American Fork.
Married Elizabeth Buckwater (daughter of John and Sarah Buckwater). Their children: Alva Alphonzo b. Nov. 14, 1859, m. Mary H. Hindley; John Buckwater b. Jan. 31, 1861, m. Annie Proctor; Rastus, died; Sarah Mariam, m. David P. Pratt; Delia Betsey, m. John I. Chipman; Perry, died; Jesse, m. Elizabeth Boley; William Quincy, m. Emma ———; Margaret Vilate, m. Peter G. Clark; Fred Leroy, m. Jessie Clark. Family home, American Fork.
Married Ellen Gibson May 2, 1884, Salt Lake City (daughter of William Gibson and Liza Kennedy of Scotland, pioneers 1862, William Hicks company). She was born Nov. 26, 1847. Their children: Junia Elizabeth b. June 15, 1885, died; Alphonzo b. April 18, 1887, m. Hilda Boley; Ross Rodney b. Sept. 16, 1889. Family home, American Fork.
Seventy; ward teacher. City councilman. Farmer and stockraiser. Died March 2, 1901, at American Fork.

GREEN, ALVA ALPHONZO, JR. (son of Alva Alphonzo Green and Elizabeth Buckwater). Born Nov. 14, 1859, at American Fork.
Married Mary Hindley Green Jan. 13, 1880, Salt Lake City (daughter of John Hindley and Jane C. Robinson of England). She was born Oct. 22, 1860. Their children:

Mary L., died; Mark Hindley b. Dec. 12, 1880; Jane Ferne b. Feb. 28, 1891; Bessie Irene b. July 6, 1892; Minnie b. Oct. 1, 1898; Anna Maybelle b. July 12, 1901. Family home, American Fork.
Elder. Farmer and stockraiser.

GREEN, ALVIN (son of Robert Green and Fanny Greely). Born May 27, 1829. Came to Utah Sept. 19, 1847, Ira Eldredge company.
Married Frances A. Gibson Dec. 27, 1850, Brigham Young officiating (daughter of George W. Gibson and Mary Sparks of South Cottonwood, Utah, pioneers 1848, John Brown company). She was born May 15, 1823, in Mississippi and came to Utah with parents. Their children: Mary J., m. Isaac Ferguson; Frances A., m. Robert Oakden; Alvin W., m. Alice White; Robert A., m. Carrie Neilson; William A., m. Cena Jensen; Moses K., m. Sarah Wood; George A., m. Lucy Graham; Harriet A., m. Joseph Graham. Family home Brinton ward, Murray, Utah.
High priest. Water master at Big Cottonwood 20 years. Miner; farmer and stockraiser. Died Aug. 3, 1912.

GREEN, GRANDFATHER came to Utah in 1851.
Married Floretta ———. Their children: Riley, m. Addie Lambert; Ephraim, m. Sidney Florence Thayne; Sandford, m. Elnora Elckenson; Benjamin, m. Julia Lark.

GREEN, EPHRAIM. Came to Utah with oxteam.
Married Sidney Florence Thayne at Salt Lake City. Their children: Chas. Ephraim; John Edward, m. Esther Allen; Millie May; Amanda Elizabeth, m. Don Carlos Pope; Floretta. m. David Toliver; Elmera, m. Warren L. Allen; Alma. and Ada. d. infants; Matilda, m. Frank Searle; Sadie Florence. Family home Vernal, Utah.
Elder. Veteran Black Hawk war. Farmer.

GREEN, HERVEY (son of Ebenezer Green, born Sept. 22, 1777, and Ruth Weed). Born Dec. 4, 1806, in New York state. Came to Utah Sept. 24, 1848, Heber C. Kimball company.
Married Sally Ann Pickard April 14, 1828 (daughter of Henry Pickard and Jane Coleman). She was born April 14, 1811, and died in Jackson county, Mo. Their children: Henry Sheldon b. April 22, 1833, d. at birth; Ammon (twin of Henry Sheldon), m. Almira Mesick. Family home, Salt Lake City.
Married Jane Rich September, 1837 (daughter of Joseph Rich and Nancy O'Neal, who were married June 23, 1808, pioneers 1847, Charles C. Rich company). She was born Nov. 5, 1813, in Indiana. Their children: Mary Ann b. Aug. 11, 1836, m. William Hyde April 7, 1858; Nancy Jane b. Feb. 7, 1840, m. James H. Raser 1858; Celestia Artemesia b. Jan. 14, 1847, m. George Davis; Joseph Hervey b. July 30, 1850.

GREEN, AMMON (son of Hervey Green and Sally Ann Pickard). Born April 22, 1833, Kaw township, Jackson county, Mo.
Married Almira Mesick April 22, 1855. San Bernardine, California (daughter of Peter I. Mesick and Maria Spencer, former pioneer July 27, 1847, James Brown company; latter died in New York state). She was born Nov. 8, 1835, Leyden, Lewis county, N. Y. Their children: Ammon b. April 1, 1859, m. Annie Peterson Sept. 6, 1888; Cynthia Lois b. Nov. 25, 1860, m. George Heslop Nov. 1, 1880; Almira b. March 11, 1862, d. Feb. 22, 1863; Henry Peter b. June 3, 1863, m. Robina Noyes Nov. 5, 1890; George b. April 22, 1865, m. Charlotte I. Bartholomew Dec. 16, 1891; William Hervey b. Sept. 28, 1867, m. Mary Ann Bartholomew Dec. 16, 1891; Albert b. Aug. 5, 1869, m. Minerva Knight; Mary Ann b. March 13, 1871, m. Merlin J. Bartholomew; Edward S. b. Nov. 26, 1872, m. Martha E. Aldous June 13, 1900; Harriet Ann b. June 13, 1874, m. Elias Peterson; Charles Lawrence b. April 19, 1876, m. Margaret Peterson; Benjamin F. b. Dec. 28, 1878, m. Ellen Bartlett Sept. 18, 1901; Emily Maria b. Oct. 5, 1880, m. Jesse Fowers. Family home West Weber, Utah.
Presiding elder; president seventies; superintendent Sunday schools; missionary. Justice of peace; constable. Died April 23, 1911.

GREEN, AMMON (son of Ammon Green and Almira Mesick). Born April 1, 1859, Beaver, Utah.
Married Annie Peterson Sept. 6, 1888, Logan, Utah (daughter of Christian and Maren Peterson, who came to Utah 1875). She was born Nov. 28, 1865, Ringsted, Sorö amt, Tyvilsa, Denmark; and died Nov. 21, 1910, West Weber, Utah. Their children: Annie b. July 11, 1889; Leonie b. Dec. 5, 1891; Bertha Marguerite b. July 5, 1894; Ammon b. Sept. 26, 1896; Almira Flint b. Sept. 24, 1902.

GREEN, JOHN H. (son of William Green). Born in Worcestershire, Eng. Came to Utah 1849, Captain Clark company.
Married Susannah Phillips 1834, Acton, Eng. (daughter of William Phillips), who was born October 1815. Their children: Thomas; Ann; Charlotte; Robert, m. Sarah Ann Harris; James; Elizabeth; Emma; Amelia; John H.; Alice Maud. Family home Kaysville, Utah.
High priest; bishop's counselor. Farmer. Died April 16, 1886.

GREEN, ROBERT (son of John H. Green and Susannah Phillips). Born April 4, 1842, Nauvoo. Came to Utah with father.
Married Sarah Ann Harris Jan. 2, 1865, Layton, Utah (daughter of Robert Harris and Hannah Maria Egles of Apperley, Gloucestershire, Eng., pioneers 1850). She was born June 11, 1845. Their children: Sarah Maria b. Nov. 6, 1866, m. James H. Gibbs Feb. 4, 1886; Elizabeth Browett b. April 22, 1867, m. John W. Moss Jan. 27, 1897; Ada Ann b. March 4, 1869, m. George Moss Jan. 5, 1893; Lucy Emma b. Nov. 28, 1870, m. Edwin Williams Dec. 25, 1888; Susannah b. Sept. 4, 1872, m. David W. Morris Jan. 3, 1895; John Robert b. Oct. 9, 1874; Daniel Milton b. Nov. 19, 1876, m. Ella Clark Dec. 3, 1902; James William b. Sept. 22, 1878; Joseph Albert b. Sept. 3, 1880, m. Edna Evans Dec. 19, 1907; Alice Elvira b. April 27, 1882, m. Joseph S. Morris Dec. 24, 1902.
High councilor Malad stake; bishop's counselor at Woodruff, Idaho. Farmer.

GREEN, PETER C. (son of Christian Petersen Green, born May 2, 1789 and Elsie Jensen Bek, born Feb. 2, 1789, both in Denmark). He was born March 1, 1827, in Denmark. Came to Utah Sept. 26, 1862, oxteam company.
Married Elsie Marie Bertlesen Nov. 5, 1853, who died April 9, 1899. Their children: Peter B. b. Feb. 4, 1864; Elsie Marie b. April 25, 1866; Annie Josephine b. March 31, 1868; Eliza Godelia b. Dec. 22, 1871.
Seventy; presiding teacher Plain City ward; high priest; bishop's counselor 27 years.

GREEN, ROBERT (son of Kinyon Green of New Hampshire, and Nancy Austin of England). Born August, 1806, in New Hampshire; came to Utah Sept. 19, 1847, Ira Eldredge company.
Married Fanny Greely (daughter of Ezekiel and Annie Greely, former pioneer Sept. 19, 1847). She was born Aug. 12, 1806, and came to Utah with husband. Their children: Alvin b. May 27, 1828, m. Frances Gibson 1849; Austin G. b. March 26, 1834, m. Mary Ann Marchant 1858.

GREEN, AUSTIN G. (son of Robert Green and Fanny Greely). Born March 26, 1834, in New York state.
Married Mary Ann Marchant 1858. Their children: Austin A. b. Dec. 18, 1860, m. Sarah Hawkes; Oscar W. b. April 10, 1862, m. Christina Pool; Robert A. b. Feb. 8, 1864, m. Hattie Shippen; Albert b. Oct. 7, 1865; Alma L. b. Jan. 3, 1870, m. Meda Stephens; Amasa b. Jan. 2, 1872; Gilbert M. b. Feb. 4, 1874, m. Eva Ballantyne; Justin M. b. May 26, 1878, m. Julius Ballantyne.
Farmer.

GREEN, WILLIAM (son of James Green and Ann Mellows of Shelford, Nottinghamshire, Eng.). Born March, 1803, at Shelford. Came to Utah with Christiansen handcart company.
Married Harriet Hulet, who was born 1813. Only child: John (stepson) b. May 12, 1835, m. Mary Partington Dec. 25, 1857. Family home Fountain Green, Utah.
Veteran Black Hawk Indian war. Pioneer in irrigation.

GREEN, JOHN (stepson of William Green and son of Harriet Hulet). Born May 12, 1835, Lambly, Nottinghamshire, Eng. Came to Utah Aug. 18, 1856, Philemon C. Merrill company.
Married Mary Staford (Partington) Dec. 25, 1857 (daughter of James Staford and Hannah Williams), who was born Sept. 25, 1830, and came to Utah 1854. Their children: Elizabeth Herbert b. Sept. 5, 1859, m. James Green; William J. b. Nov. 3, 1861, m. Margret A. Johnson May 20, 1880; John b. Dec. 11, 1863; Allace b. Jan. 14, 1865, m. Isaac Huff Nov. 24, 1881; Allen b. Jan. 14, 1865, died.
Married Hephzibah Mathews Nov. 11, 1866, Salt Lake City (daughter of William Mathews and Hephzibah Jarvis, who were married Dec. 31, 1832, Radford, Eng.—former pioneer Oct. 4, 1863, Thomas E. Ricks company, latter Oct. 4, 1864, William S. Warren company). She was born Feb. 10, 1844, Belston, Nottinghamshire, Eng. Their children: John Henry b. Oct. 28, 1867; Mary Eliza b. March 14, 1869; Charles Mathews b. April 12, 1870, m. Eva May Bailey Dec. 25, 1899.
Married Elizabeth Ann Willson Jan. 16, 1879, Salt Lake City (daughter of John Willson and Allace Smith, married Feb. 9, 1859, St. Louis, Mo.). She was born Nov. 8, 1859, at St. Louis. Their children: George W. b. Jan. 20, 1880, m. Sarah Ann A. Taylor Jan. 24, 1909; Richard Edgar b. Nov. 20, 1881, m. Nellie May Anderson Sept. 2, 1908; Thomas Franklin b. Jan. 10, 1884; Wallace and Wilford b. March 22, 1886; James Arthur b. July 23, 1888; Frances Maud b. Dec. 9, 1890, m. Edward Bailey July 28, 1909; Orson b. March 8, 1893; Genevra Alice b. Sept. 24, 1898; Rea Harriet b. March 10, 1903. Families resided Fountain Green, Utah.
Served in Echo Canyon war; Black Hawk Indian war veteran. Pioneer in irrigation.

GREENE, EVAN MOLBOURNE (son of John Portineus Greene and Rhoda Young of New York, and Kirtland, Ohio). Born Dec. 22, 1814, Aurelius, Cayuga county, N. Y. Came to Utah Oct. 12, 1852, Allen Weeks company.
Married Susan Kent Aug. 29, 1835, in New York state (daughter of Daniel Kent and Nancy Young of Kirtland, Ohio, and New York state, latter pioneer Sept. 26, 1857, William G. Young company). She, Susan Kent, was born April 3, 1816, in Vermont. Their children: Emily Frances, d. infant; Evan Flavius, m. Mary E. Kennedy; Rhoda, m. J. J. Bullock; Nancy Leonora, m. Franklin W. Young; Susan Eveline, m. Edmond Homer; Ann Eliza, d. June 16, 1846; Melissa, m. Edmond Homer; Louisa Lula, m. Levi W. Richards; John Portineus, d. March 3, 1852; Admanzah, d. Jan. 30, 1863; Jasper W., d. infant; Daniel Kent, m. Adaline Allen; Edwin M.
Married Susie Platt April 12, 1869, at Salt Lake City (daughter of John Platt and Betty Dutterworth of Royton, Lancashire, Eng., latter pioneer 1863, Theron Spencer company). She was born Oct. 13, 1844. Their children: Joseph Platt b. Jan. 15, 1872, m. Mary Ann Read; Zerviah Susie b. Jan. 28, 1874, m. George Y. Smith: Molbourne Platt b. Oct. 26, 1876, m. Eva Bertha Bennett; Elizabeth Fanny b. April 28, 1879, d. Oct. 21, 1902; John Platt b. June 15, 1881, m. Effie Allsop.
Missionary to eastern states; patriarch; high councilor. Mayor of Provo two years; postmaster of Provo; member legislature four years; compiled book of laws for Utah territory; school teacher. Farmer; stockraiser; merchant. Died May 2, 1882, in Sevier Co., Utah.

GREENE, EVAN FLAVIUS (son of Evan M. Greene and Susan Kent). Born Feb. 22, 1838, Kirtland, Ohio.
Married Mary E. Kennedy March 17, 1873, at Salt Lake City (daughter of William Kennedy and Sarah Warren of Tazewell county, Va.—former died in Indiana, latter came to Utah 1869). She, Mary E., was born July 14, 1843. (Her children by Milburn Whitt, former husband: Sarah b. Aug. 12, 1865, m. Francis P. McNeil; Josephine b. Dec. 3, 1866, m. Robert Hamilton; Reece B. b. March 3, 1868, d. aged 18.) Their children: Mary E. b. Jan. 15, 1874, m. Frank P. Ellis; Susan Y. b. March 19, 1876, m. —— Fennessy; Rachel M. b. Jan. 19, 1878, d. Dec. 12, 1884; Hyrum S. b. May 25, 1880 and Rhoda M. twins) b. May 25, 1880, d. infants; Evan Flavius b. Nov. 2, 1882, d. aged 27. Family home Salt Lake City.
High priest; assistant Sunday school superintendent Springdale, Utah; ward teacher. Freighter; farmer and stockraiser.

GREENEWALD, AARON (son of Jacob and Tina Greenewald of Germany). Born March 28, 1831, in Germany. Came to Utah April 6, 1866.
Married Lena Lang Oct. 12, 1856, Philadelphia, Pa. (daughter of Isaac Lang of Baden, Germany), who was born Oct. 12, 1833. Their children: Bertha, m. Jacob E. Bamberger; Sarah, died; Lillie, m. Joseph Oberndorfer; Jacob A., m. Mildred Rheinstrom; Isadore and Clara, died. Family home Salt Lake City, Utah.
Hotel keeper and merchant.

GREENEWALD, JACOB A. (son of Aaron Greenewald and Lena Lang). Born Aug. 1, 1866, Salt Lake City, Utah.
Married Mildred Rheinstrom June 1, 1908 (daughter of Edward Rheinstrom and Ida Lang of Portland, Ore.), who was born June 2, 1881. Their children: Richard I. b. June 6, 1909. Family home, Salt Lake City.
President Greenewald Furniture Company. Colonel 1st regiment Utah national guard; member Governor John C. Cutler's staff 1904-08. Richard I. Greenewald, his first son, said to have been the first Jewish child born in Utah.

GREENHALGH, ABRAHAM II. Came from England to Utah 1853.
Married Sarah Hope in England. Their children: Jane, died; Sarah; Ellen, m. Hyram Bennett; Peter, m. Mary Ann Fisher; m. Jennette Stewart; Margaret, m. Robert Fergeson; William, Abraham and Lizzie, died; Joseph, m. Jane Adams; Jane, died. Family home Meadow, Utah.
Block teacher; choir leader. Road supervisor; postmaster 20 years at Meadow. Farmer.

GREENHALGH, PETER (son of Abraham H. Greenhalgh and Sarah Hope). Born May 3, 1853, on the banks of the Mississippi river in Iowa. Came to Utah with parents.
Married Mary Ann Fisher 1872 at Salt Lake City (daughter of James Fisher and Hannah Stott of Meadow, Utah), who was born February, 1853, and died 1880. Their children: Emma, m. George Lamburn; Peter, m. Anne Duncan; Mary, m. Charles Smith; Hannah, m. Wesley Barton. Family home Meadow.
Married Jennette Stewart May, 1882 (daughter of William Stewart and Jane Jenkins of Meadow). Their children: Jane, m. William Sutherland; Neil, m. Hilda Swenson; Jennette, m. Harry Hamburg; Rhoda, m. Roy Aubrey; Leona; Ruby; Luceil. Family home Salt Lake City.

GREENHALGH, PETER (son of William Greenhalgh, born 1790, and Margaret Hope, both of Leigh, Lancashire, Eng.). Born March 1, 1830, at Leigh. Came to Utah Oct. 21, 1854, William A. Empey company.
Married Sarah Heald May 3, 1852 (daughter of Henry Heald and Margaret Milligan). She was born Nov. 17, 1827. Their children: Margaret b. Dec. 12, 1852, Lorenzo b. Aug. 23, 1853, and William m Henry b. May 26, 1854, latter three died infants; Peter b. Nov. 9, 1855, m. Rebecca A. Weller Sept. 29, 1881; Thomas Alma b. Nov. 28, 1857, m. Josephine Kroener; Sarah Ann b. April 1, 1860, and Catherine b. May 1, 1862, d. children; Mary Ellen b. Jan. 13, 1864, m. David A. Nelson

Adelia b. June 27, 1867, m. Charles H. Hart; Franklin b. July 13, 1870, m. Frances Thomas. Family home Willard, Utah, and Bloomington, Idaho.
Settled first at Willard, Utah; served in Echo Canyon war 1857; moved to Bloomington, Idaho, 1863. Served two years as 1st counselor to president of elders' quorum at Willard; Feb. 8, 1858, ordained a seventy and set apart a president of 59th quorum, which position he held until Aug. 26, 1877, when he was ordained a high priest and set apart as a member of high council of Bear Lake stake, holding this position about 20 years; superintendent Bloomington Sunday school 1871-1909; choir leader 35 years. Director and secretary Bloomington Co-op. store 35 years. Farmer and stockraiser.

GREENHALGH, PETER, JR. (son of Peter Greenhalgh and Sarah Heald). Born Nov. 9, 1855, Willard, Utah.
Married Rebecca A. Welker Sept. 29, 1881, at Salt Lake City (daughter of James W. Welker and Annie Pugh, pioneers 1852). She was born Jan. 24, 1864, at Willard. Their children: Sarah Annie b. June 17, 1882, m. Christian Hansen Sept. 6, 1900; Peter Asa b. Jan. 27, 1884, died; Leonard b. Sept. 12, 1886, m. Annie M. Allen Nov. 25, 1908; Elliot Severe b. Nov. 7, 1888; Adeline b. June 5, 1891, m. Hugh Stewart Dec. 19, 1907; Alma W. b. Aug. 2, 1894; Gilda b. Aug. 5, 1898; Eielyn Pearl b. Nov. 20, 1902, Family home Wilford, Idaho.

GREENHALGH, THOMAS (son of William Greenhalgh, born Jan. 12, 1790, and Margret Greenhalgh, born Feb. 10, 1793, both at Swinton, near Manchester, Lancashire, Eng.). He was born Jan. 15, 1821, Worsley, Lancashire. Came to Utah Oct. 6, 1866, Joseph S. Rawlins company.
Married Mary Morecroft Sept. 26, 1847, Eccles, Eng. (daughter of James Morecroft and Hannah Downing of Macclesfield, near Manchester). She was born Feb. 24, 1827. Their children were: Mary Ann, m. George Mace; Sarah, m. James L. Newton; Martha, died; Abraham, m. Maria Nelsena Henrichsen; Thomas, m. Elizabeth Greenhalgh; Margaret Alice, m. William Wallace Billings; William, m. ——Jolley; Frances, d. child; Ruth Elizabeth, m. Charles S. Cram; George, m. Elizabeth Mackleprang. Family home Washington, Washington Co., Utah.
Married Harriet Wardle 1873 at Salt Lake City, who came to Utah 1872 from Lancashire, Eng. Their children were Thomas John; Henry; Esther.
Home missionary England 1840-65. High priest and ward teacher. Settled first in Sugar House ward, Salt Lake City, moving to Washington, Utah, in 1867, where he took charge of weaving department of Brigham Young cotton factory. Died May 2, 1882.

GREENHALGH, ABRAHAM (son of Thomas Greenhalgh and Mary Morecroft). He was born April 12, 1855, Manchester, Eng. Came to Utah with father.
Married Maria Neisena Henrichsen March 9, 1882, at Salt Lake City (daughter of Peter Henrichsen and Jacobine Ernst of Veile, Denmark, latter came to Utah July 12, 1872, Anthon H. Lund company). She was born Jan. 18, 1862, came to Utah with mother. Their children: Ernest Abraham b. Feb. 26, 1883, m. Hazel Adams; Thomas Charles b. Oct. 14, 1884; Leo Morecroft b. July 17, 1887; Earl Henrichsen b. April 11, 1891; Erma Mary b. Feb. 28, 1896; Jacobine b. Jan. 30, 1931, died.
Worked in cotton mill under father at Washington, Utah; moved to Kanab, Utah, 1873, and to Provo 1875, where he worked in Provo Woolen Mills until 1895. Settled at Schofield, Utah, 1899, where he engaged in the mercantile business, serving also as postmaster 1901-09; justice of the peace; town councilman. President of deacons' quorum; Sunday school and ward teacher; high priest; 2nd counselor in Schofield bishopric 1904-12, becoming first counselor Jan. 17, 1912.

GREENWOOD, WILLIAM (son of Robison Greenwood of Yorkshire, born 1782, and Elizabeth Cryer, born 1784, both at Burnley, Eng.). He was born Aug. 7, 1822, at Burnley. Came to Utah Oct. 25, 1847.
Married Alice Houghton May 30, 1843 (daughter of William Houghton), who was born May 1, 1823. Their children: Joseph R. b. March 16, 1844; Elizabeth b. March 8, 1845; Benjamin Y. b. Feb. 9, 1846, m. Jane Julian; Margaret A. b. Feb. 25, 1847, m. James Carter; Alice b. Feb. 26, 1849, m. Alfred Moyle; William b. April 13, 1850, m. Charlotte Wood; Samuel b. March 3, 1852, m. Ellen Julian; Jacob b. Feb. 25, 1853, m. Melissa Snow; Alma b. Oct. 18, 1854, m. F. M. Brown; Rachel b. Feb. 23, 1856, m. William H. Hunter; Jedediah M., m. Barbara Boley; Mary E. b. March 26, 1859, m. Frank Herbert; Joshua b. July 29, 1860, m. Josephine Payne; Ruth b. June 2, 1862, m. James Gardner.
Married Emma Julian Jan. 1864, Salt Lake City. Their child: William J. b. Jan. 30, 1865.
Married Bertha C. L. Eyring March 22, 1864 (daughter of Edward C. Eyring and C. L. Von Blomberg), who was born June 12, 1836, in Germany. Their children: Stephen b. Feb. 26, 1870; Bertha E. b. April 20, 1872, m. Perry Webster; Francis Charlotte b. Nov. 14, 1874; Abraham O. b. Feb. 5, 1877. Family resided American Fork.
One of first conference clerks in L. D. S. church in Utah. Active in manufacturing and building school houses. Member of first bishopric and first school teacher in American Fork. Pioneer surveyor of Utah county.

GREENWOOD, JOSHUA (son of William Greenwood and Alice Houghton). Born July 29, 1860, at American Fork, Utah.
Married Josephine Payne Jan. 18, 1883, Salt Lake City (daughter of Joseph Payne and Harriet McBride), who was born May 25, 1861, Fillmore, Utah. Their children: Marian J. b. Oct. 24, 1883, m. Louis Melville April 1905; Hattie E. b. Oct. 18, 1886, m. C. A. Kimball June 10, 1907; Lucile E. b. Nov. 1, 1891; Norma M. b. Oct. 31, 1894; Ruth Afton b. Aug. 30, 1897; Evangeline b. July 2, 1900. Family home Fillmore and Nephi, Utah.
One of first graduates of Brigham Young University. Territorial deputy school commissioner; justice of peace; mayor; city attorney; county attorney; county treasurer; county superintendent of schools; probate judge; district attorney and at present judge fifth judicial district of Utah.

GREENWOOD, WILLIAM (son of William Greenwood and Sarah Hartley of Burnley, Eng., and Warsaw, Hancock county, Ill.). Born March 4, 1819, at Hepinstall, Eng. Came to Utah 1852, Benjamin Gardner company.
Married Ann Hartley 1841 at Burnley (daughter of Barnard Hartley and Mary Beck of Burnley), who was born July 26, 1821. Their children: Martha, d. child; Sarah, m. Isaac Turley 1861; Foster, d. infant; Barnard Hartley, m. Eunice Howd; William, m. Matilda Stewart; Mary Ann, m. Charles D. White May 4, 1875; Adam, m. Henrietta Young; Nathan, m. Alice Parkinson; Titus, m. Edith Sidwell June 19, 1897; Rachel, d. infant; Ruth, m. William A. Twitchell. Family home, Beaver, Utah.
High priest; missionary to Iron Co., Utah, 1852-56; ward teacher. Road supervisor. Farmer. Died Oct. 11, 1899, at Riverside, Millard Co., Utah.

GREENWOOD, BARNARD HARTLEY (son of William Greenwood and Ann Hartley). Born Sept. 9, 1849, at Warsaw, Ill. Came to Utah July, 1852.
Married Eunice Morecraft Dec. 19, 1871, Beaver City, Utah (daughter of Simeon F. Howd and Lucinda Morgan—former pioneer July 24, 1847, and latter Sept. 1847). She was born Aug. 8, 1852, at Beaver City. Their children: Hartley b. March 13, 1873, m. Bertha Hawley; Rachel b. June 6, 1875, m. Wing Ence; Amelia b. Feb. 7, 1878, and Adelia b. Feb. 7, 1878, d. infants; Carlos B. b. Oct. 31, 1879, m. Esther Stevenson; William Simeon b. Feb. 18, 1882, m. Stena Christensen; Ernest Morgan b. March 4, 1884, m. Florence Reese; Ray Howd b. June 8, 1886, m. Hazel Gray; Lester Duane b. May 3, 1888; Raleigh Vern b. Dec. 6, 1890; Rhoda Lucinda b. March 5, 1895. Family home Inverury, Utah.
High priest; bishop Inverury ward 1892-1906. Sevier county selectman 1883-90; representative two terms in state legislature, 1896-99. Director in Elsinore Roller Mills Co., Sevier Valley Canal Co. and Richfield Canal Co. Died June 27, 1906.

GREENWOOD, HARTLEY (son of Barnard Hartley Greenwood and Eunice Howd). Born March 13, 1873, at Beaver, Utah.
Married Bertha Hawley Sept. 6, 1893, Inverury, Utah (daughter of Asa Smith Hawley and Mary Beers of that place, former pioneer 1852, James Shaw company, latter 1848, Zera Pulsipher company). She was born June 21, 1875. Their children: Mary Eunice b. June 7, 1894; Jennie b. Dec. 4, 1898; Irene b. April 24, 1899; Priscilla b. June 3, 1901; Sylvia b. March 4, 1905; Lavon b. April 21, 1908. Family home Inverury, Utah.
High priest; bishop Inverury ward. Farmer.

GREENWOOD, CARLOS B. (son of Barnard Hartley Greenwood and Eunice Howd). Born Oct. 31, 1879, Inverury, Utah.
Married Esther Stevenson June 10, 1901, Salt Lake City (daughter of Thomas Stevenson and Josephine Myers), who was born Dec. 15, 1880, at Kersor, Denmark. Their children: Melba b. Feb. 14, 1905; Fern Josephine b. Jan. 11, 1907; Reed Barnard b. Nov. 10, 1908; Eunice Ileen b. Jan. 7, 1911. Family home Inverury, Utah.
Missionary to southern states 1902-04; bishop Inverury ward 1906-11. Director Elsinore Canal Co.; president Centra Rural Telephone Co.; vice-president Central Water Works Co. Farmer.

GREER, DIXON HAMLIN (son of Nathaniel Hunt Greer died 1855, and Nancy Ann Roberts of Georgia and Texas). Born April 16, 1834. Came to Utah Sept. 10, 1855, Seth M Blair company.
Married Mary Sprouse in 1857, Salt Lake City (daughte of John Sprouse and Catherine Handley of that place pioneers 1854, Benjamin L. Clapp company). She was bor 1839. Their children: Nathaniel Dixon b. 1858, m. Sarai Howorth; Catherine b. 1861, d. infant. Family resided Walls burg and Provo, Utah.
Married Harriet Camp Murphy in February 1863, Salt Lak Lake City (daughter of William Camp and Dianah Greer of Sa Lake City, pioneers 1850). She was born Jan. 9, 183! Their children: John C. b. Feb. 15, 1864, m. Annie Gardner Dianah b. Feb. 1865, d. infant; William b. 1867, d. 1891; Nanc b. 1868, d. child; Stephen b. 1871, m. Susa Gardner; Susie t 1873, and Mark b. 1875, d. infants; Grace b. 1877, m. W. A Nuttall; Willmirth b. 1879, m. William Boshard; Alice b. 1881 m. Mors S. Duffield. Family home Wallsburg.

Left Mormon Grove on the Missouri river June 1855 with freight in company with his father; the father dying at Grasshopper Creek near Atchison, Kan., he and brothers brought goods to Salt Lake City and set up a store at corner of 1st South and Main streets. School teacher at Heber, Utah, 1862, and at Wallsburg 1864; at latter place was first school trustee, organized first school district and built first school house, 1865.

GREGORY, ROBERT (son of John Gregory, born 1786 at Pitminster, Somersetshire, Eng., and Elizabeth Sylvester, born 1791). He was born Nov. 30, 1826 at Pitminster. Came to Utah Oct. 18, 1862.
Married Mary Stevens Nov. 12, 1854, who died Sept. 15, 1862, near Fort Laramie, while en route to Utah.
Married Selena Marshall Jan. 2, 1863, Franklin, Idaho (daughter of Thomas Marshall and Sarah Good, pioneers Sept. 26, 1856, Edmond Ellsworth and Daniel McArthur company). She was born Feb. 22, 1844, Lintonhill, Eng. Their children: Mary Levenia b. Oct. 17, 1863, m. David Davis Jan. 4, 1883; Sarah Selena b. Jan. 6, 1866, m. Mark Porter Dec. 3, 1884; Charlotte Maria b. Feb. 1, 1868, m. M. H. Preece May 20, 1885; R. F. b. March 17, 1872, and R. A. b. Sept. 28, 1873, died; J. W. b. Nov. 17, 1874, m. L. M. Albiston Nov. 20, 1895; E. T. b. Dec. 25, 1877, m. J. R. Hansen April 19, 1900; E. L. b. Feb. 28, 1878, m. H. Hatch Sept. 20, 1888; George F. b. April 19, 1880, m Delila Bright June 11, 1903; T. J. b. July 16, 1882, m. Mary Hawkeswood Sept. 14, 1904; Amy L. b. Oct. 23, 1884, m. A. Morrison March 8, 1906; S. Cirling b. Jan. 5, 1887; Evea Vonie b. Feb. 13, 1888, m. J. Christofferson Nov. 8, 1905.
Missionary. Settled at Franklin, Idaho, 1862. Died Dec. 28, 1900.

GREGORY, GEORGE F. (son of Robert Gregory and Selena Marshall). Born April 19, 1880, Cove, Utah.
Married Delila Bright June 11, 1903, Logan, Utah (daughter of John Bright and Phoebe Smith). She was born March 16, 1884, at Lewiston, Utah. Their children: G. R. b. April 24, 1904; F. L. b. July 1, 1905; Edith b. Dec. 31, 1906; C. b. Dec. 14, 1908; A. B. b. April 28, 1910; J. M. b. Jan. 19, 1912.
Missionary to Missouri Jan 4, 1900, to March 26, 1902; member superintendency Cove and Mountain Home Sunday schools.

GRIFFETH, PATISON DELOSS (son of Judah Griffeth and Mariah Rockwell). Born Jan. 3, 1824, in Orleans county, N. Y. Came to Utah Oct. 1851, William H. Walton company.
Married Elizabeth Carson April 20, 1841 (daughter of George Carson, born July 17, 1794, and Ann Hough, born June 17, 1794). She was born July 7, 1822. Their children: Phebe Ann b. Feb. 9, 1847, m. William Hyde; George A. b. Jan. 5, 1849, m. Mary Thurman; Louisa E. b. Sept. 19, 1851, m. Samuel Seamons; Lovina S. b. Feb. 15, 1860; Lodicy Ann b. March 17, 1862, m. William Herbert Leroy Olsten Nov. 27, 1884; Julien Perkins b. Nov. 15, 1864, m. Emma Kathrine Rainey Oct. 12, 1887; Hortense Vilate b. Aug. 8, 1867, m. James Isaac Shepard Feb. 24, 1886; Anna Jemima b. Dec. 15, 1869; Orion Thomas b. Sept. 6, 1872; Ute Eion b. March 10, 1875, m. Millie Redford Feb. 17, 1904.
Member acting teachers' quorum under Bishop Tidwell at Richmond, Utah, 1863; president elders quorum; high priest; officer in Richmond Sunday school fifteen years. At annual exhibition of Deseret Agricultural and Manufacturing Society at Salt Lake City in Oct. 1856, was awarded silver medal for building first model steam engine in Utah territory; assisted in designing and making tools for manufacture of first firearms and nails in Utah. Left Salt Lake City and settled at Richmond in 1860, conducting a machine and blacksmith shop. Leader of Richmond Brass Band; Richmond city councilman 1884, 1890 and 1897; mayor of Richmond 1866, 1888, 1892, 1893, 1893 and 1903; commissioner of Cache county 1891; commissioned to locate university lands 1892; member federal grand jury at Salt Lake City 1911; school trustee. Director of Richmond Co-op, several years; administrator of estate of C. H. Monson.

GRIFFIN, WILLIAM HYRUM (son of William H. Griffin and Mary Pitts of Worcestershire, Eng.). Born Nov. 8, 1847, in Worcestershire. Came to Utah Aug. 20, 1863, James R. Miller company.
Married Elizabeth Trehern Oct. 3, 1870 (daughter of James Trehern and Ann Holder), who was born Nov. 9,

1840, and came to Utah in Oct. 1865. Their children: William Henry b. Jan. 11, 1872, m. Lydia Ballard, 1897; Franklin T. b. March 1, 1874, m. Jennie Ballard, 1899; Bessie b. March 17, 1877, m. W. R. Ballard June 10, 1896.
Married Elizabeth Clarke (daughter of Amos Clarke and Ann Thomas), who was born Nov. 29, 1858, in North Wales Their children: George Heber b. April 20, 1885; Nettie Ann b. Dec. 14, 1886, m. Pearl Jenkins 1909; Amos R. b. May 7, 1891; David H. b. July 20, 1894; Samuel H. b. Sept. 18, 1896; Lula Viola b. June 24, 1898; Spencer G. b. Sept. 7, 1901. Families reside Newton, Utah.
Bishop of Newton ward 1893-1904.

GRIMMETT, JOHN (son of George and Elizabeth Grimmett). Born Jan. 5, 1827, in England. Came to Utah 1855.
Married Sarah Passey (daughter of Thomas and Margret Passey), who was born June 24, 1818. Their children: George b. Jan. 11, 1848; Orson b. March 5, 1850, m. Ella Berneley 1876; Rosina b. Feb. 20, 1852, m. James W. O'Neill; Hyrum b. Jan. 6, 1854, m. Emma A. Pomeroy Oct. 14, 1875, m. Hannah A. Sleight June 17, 1894; Sarah Jane b. May 23, 1856, m. Alfred W. Sparks; John Henry b. May 23, 1856, m. Louisa Nate. Family resided Cedar Fort, West Jordan, Utah, and Bear Lake Co., Idaho.

GRIMMETT, HYRUM (son of John Grimmett and Sarah Passey). Born Jan. 6, 1854, Birmingham, Eng.
Married Emma Adelia Pomeroy Oct. 9, 1875, Salt Lake City (daughter of Francis Martin Pomeroy and Irene Ursula Haskell, former came to Utah July 24, 1847, Brigham Young company). She was born June 16, 1858, Provo, Utah. Their children: Hyrum Alberto b. Jan. 24, 1877, m. Annie McBride Feb. 24, 1897; Rosa Ella b. Dec. 23, 1878, m. Olen Ockerman; John Francis b. June 15, 1880, m. Bertha C. Benson; Chester Pomeroy b. May 1, 1883; Sarah Emma Francelle b. Aug. 29, 1888, m. W. W. Young. Family resided Paris, Dingle, Blackfoot, Idaho, and Lander, Wyo.
Married Hannah Ann Sleight June 17, 1894, Dingle, Idaho (daughter of Thomas Sleight and Mary M. Wixom of Salt Lake City). Their children: Fruel Arvina b. Nov. 14, 1895; Archibald Thomas b. May 2, 1898; Wayne Waldo b. Dec. 21, 1899; Medora Alice b. Nov. 30, 1901; Gordon Edmund b. April 14, 1904; June Estella b. Aug. 1, 1906; Juno Arvella b. Aug. 1, 1906; Norma Jane b. July 31, 1910; Carma Mary b. July 31, 1910.
Deputy sheriff of Bear Lake county 1891-92; deputy treasurer and assistant postmaster; postmaster at Bryan, Idaho 1896-1904. Justice of peace 1911-12.

GRIMMETT, HYRUM ALBERTO (son of Hyrum Grimmett and Emma Adelia Pomeroy). Born Jan. 24, 1877, Dingle, Idaho.
Married Annie C. McBride Feb. 24, 1897 (daughter of James Oliver McBride and Elizabeth Christanson), who was born June 13, 1892, Hyrum, Utah. Their children: Chester Alberto b. Nov. 1, 1898; Pearl Adelia b. Dec. 17, 1900; Annie Ulilla b. Jan. 3, 1903; Violet Ella b. March 23, 1906; Rosa May b. June 23, 1907; Emma Mildred b. July 30, 1910. Family home Moreland, Idaho.

GRIMSHAW, JOHN (son of Lawrence Grimshaw and Alice Whittaker). Born June 12, 1811, at Accrington. Came to Utah Sept. 25, 1863, Peter Nebeker company.
Married Alice Whittaker in 1836 at Accrington (daughter of Lawrence and Mary Whittaker of Accrington). She was born Dec. 28, 1809. Their children: James, d. infant; Mary, died; Elizabeth; Duckworth b. March 3, 1842, m. Mary Jane Moyes; Susannah, d. infant; Sarah Ann; Alice. Family home Tottington, Lancashire, Eng.
High priest. Laborer. Died May 25, 1894, Beaver, Utah.

GRIMSHAW, DUCKWORTH (son of John Grimshaw and Alice Whittaker). Born March 3, 1842, Tottington, Eng. Came to Utah Sept. 26, 1862, James Wareham company.
Married Mary Jane Moyes April 4, 1867 (daughter of William Moyes and Mary Eastcott, married Oct. 3, 1840, Ottraham, Cornwall, Eng., pioneers February 1858, San Bernardino company). She was born June 6, 1850. Their children: John G. b. March 15, 1868, m. Mary Elizabeth Bradfield Jan. 1, 1894; Elizabeth Alice b. May 7, 1870, m. Archie Fotheringham July 4, 1889; Mary Ann b. Aug. 19, 1872, m. Josiah Rogerson May 4, 1894; Martha Jane b. Jan. 6, 1875, m. William T. Rogerson Feb. 6, 1895; Franklin b. March 13, 1877; William Henry b. May 12, 1879, m. Mary May Hunter Sept. 16, 1902; Ray b. June 12, 1881; Ida b. Jan. 15, 1884; Lawrence b. Jan. 19, 1886, m. Della Parkinson March 18, 1908; May b. May 1, 1888; Arnold b. Sept. 2, 1890, m. Myrtle Hodges Jan. 1, 1910; Randolph b. Dec. 28, 1893; George Whittaker b. Feb. 22, 1896.
Married Ellen Muir April 12, 1887, St. George, Utah (daughter of John Walter and Grace Muir, married 1850, pioneers 1852, Capt. Miller independent company). She was born Feb. 12, 1855, Cedar City, Utah. Their child: Thomas Duckworth b. July 7, 1891. Families reside at Beaver, Utah.
Assisted in organizing Sunday school at Beaver in June. 1865, and acted in the superintendency for same for twenty-five years. Has been member of Beaver ward choir for forty-seven years and still acting; member Beaver stake high council twenty-six years; clerk of high priest's quorum

a number of years. Worked on St. George temple 1874, and on Manti temple 1878. Ward teacher; home missionary. Black Hawk war veteran. City councilman 1881-82, and 1887-88; Beaver city treasurer 1908-09; school trustee; precinct justice 1905-06 and 1909-12.

GROESBECK, JOHN A. (son of Nicholas Groesbeck and Elizabeth Thompson of Springfield, Ill.). Born July 14, 1849, at Springfield. Came to Utah 1856.
Married Ann D. Bringhurst 1871, Salt Lake City (daughter of William Bringhurst and Ann Dillworth of Germantown, Pa., pioneers 1847). She was born Aug. 14, 1854. Their children: John A., m. Tessie Clawson; Frank, m. Nell Young; Clara, died; Louise, m. E. V. McCune; Florence, m. J. J. Cannon; Scott; Emma, m. J. O. Nibley; Mark; Milton, died; Allen.
Seventy; missionary. Sheriff. Mining. Died 1905, Peru, South America.

GROESBECK, JOHN A., JR. (son of John A. Groesbeck and Ann D. Bringhurst). Born March 22, 1872, Salt Lake City.
Married Tessie Clawson Nov. 29, 1892, Salt Lake City (daughter of Hiram B. Clawson and Margaret Judd of Salt Lake City, pioneers 1849). She was born Jan. 26, 1872. Their children: Gay b. Sept. 26, 1895; J. D. b. May 30, 1903; Katherine b. April 3, 1906. Family home, Salt Lake City.
County treasurer four years. Merchant.

GROESBECK, NICHOLAS (son of Harmon Groesbeck and Mary Bovee of Springfield, Ill. and New York). Born Sept. 5, 1819, Buskirk Bridge, Rensselaer county, N. Y. Came to Utah Oct. 2, 1856, John Banks company.
Married Elizabeth Thompson March 25, 1841, Springfield, Ill. (daughter of John A. Thompson and Ruth Peterson), who was born Aug. 16, 1820. Their children: Nicholas H. b. April 27, 1842, m. Rhoda Sanderson Dec. 16, 1862; Stephen W. b. Sept. 18, 1844, d. Sept. 24, 1846; William b. Jan. 17, 1847, m. Elenor Pack Nov. 2, 1867; John A. b. July 14, 1849, m. Ann D. Bringhurst Feb. 27, 1871; Helen M. b. Feb. 7, 1852, m. John Morgan Oct. 24, 1868; Hyrum b. July 19, 1854, m. Ann E. Maycock Feb. 28, 1878; Josephine b. Oct. 13, 1857, m. John H. Smith April 4, 1877; Samuel S. b. July 14, 1860, m. Josephine Pettit Dec. 14, 1882; Joseph S. b. Dec. 18, 1864, m. Sarah A. Blood March 24, 1887; James T., died.
Married Elizabeth McGregor in 1857 at Salt Lake City. Families resided at Salt Lake City.
High priest; missionary to England 1875. Had charge of eastern division of Young Express company March to December, 1857. Salt Lake City councilman one term. Capitalist. Died June 29, 1884.

GROESBECK, NICHOLAS H. (son of Nicholas Groesbeck and Elizabeth Thompson). Born April 27, 1842, Springfield, Ill. Came to Utah Oct. 2, 1856.
Married Rhoda Sanderson Dec. 16, 1862, Springville, Utah (daughter of John and Rebecca Sanderson, pioneers 1861, David H. Cannon company). She was born Dec. 15, 1846, at Farsley, near Leeds, Eng. Their children: Nicholas H. b. Jan. 12, 1864, d. Dec. 24, 1865; John Sanderson b. March 11, 1866, m. Nettie Kerr Feb. 2, 1893; Rhoda R. b. Nov. 16, 1868, m. H. M. Dougall; Elizabeth M. b. July 10, 1871, d. March 8, 1872; Mary b. Aug. 7, 1873, m. M. W. Bird; Sarah b. March 10, 1876, m. A. O. Packard; George W. b. April 29, 1878, m. Emma Worsencroft; Louisa b. Aug. 31, 1880; d. June 6, 1881; Phillip E. b. June 5, 1883, m. Dora A. Novacovich Sept. 6, 1908; Ralph Amos b. March 6, 1886.
Married Cornelia Melissa Sanford June 28, 1869, Salt Lake City (daughter of Ira Sanford, pioneer of 1862, and Susan Clark). She was born Aug. 11, 1849, Augusta, Ill. Their children: Wm. Jesse b. Sept. 3, 1870, m. Hila McKenzie April 12, 1893; Cornelia E. b. July 18, 1873, m. Clarence Snow Sept. 5, 1900; Abby b. Oct. 21, 1875; Susan b. July 23, 1879, m. P. M. Kelly June 8, 1905; Marion b. July 22, 1881; Edgar b. Sept. 14, 1883, d. same date; Josephine b. Sept. 30, 1884; Helen Mar b. Dec. 13, 1886, m. Benj. Carlisle Dec. 2, 1906.
Married Katherine Houtz July 21, 1882, Salt Lake City (daughter of Jacob Houtz, pioneer 1847, John Taylor company, and Bridget Daley). She was born Oct. 6, 1862, Springville, Utah. Their children: Jacob M. b. Dec. 11, 1884, m. Berdena Rothwell Aug. 15, 1907; Katherine b. Nov. 8, 1886; Karl M. b. Aug. 1, 1888, m. Helen E. Ruff Feb. 1, 1910; Eunice b. March 2, 1892, d. March 17, 1892. Families reside Springville, Utah.
Engaged in mercantile business at Springville 1862-69; assisted in opening up Flagstaff mine in Little Cottonwood mining district 1870. Missionary to eastern states 1872, and to New Zealand 1881-82.

GROESBECK, HYRUM (son of Nicholas Groesbeck and Elizabeth Thompson). Born July 19, 1854, Springfield, Ill. Came to Utah Oct. 2, 1856.
Married Ann Elizabeth Maycock Feb. 28, 1878, Salt Lake City (daughter of John Maycock and Helen Leslie of Springville, Utah, pioneers 1852). She was born Aug. 23, 1855. Their children: Hyrum b. Dec. 21, 1879, m. Lena Badger, m. Lue Emma Stephenson; Leslie b. Dec. 24, 1881, m. Hazel A. Calder; Ethel E. b. Feb. 10, 1884; George M. b. Aug. 11, 1886, m. Lucille C. Clinton; Roy b. May 10, 1889; Nicholas Mack b. Feb. 7, 1893, d. Dec. 6, 1907. Family home, Salt Lake City.
High priest. Custodian of Salt Lake City street department property. Executor of his father's estate.

GROVER, THOMAS (son of Thomas Grover and Polly Spaulding of Whitehall, Washington county, N. Y.). Born July 22, 1807, Whitehall, N. Y. Came to Utah Oct. 3, 1847, Charles C. Rich company.
Married Caroline Whiting 1828 (daughter of Nathaniel Whiting and Caroline Young), who was born in 1809, and died at Nauvoo, Ill., 1841. Their children: Jane b. March 30, 1830, m. James Stewart 1848; Emeline b. July 30, 1831, m. Charles C. Rich 1846; Mary E. b. 1832, m. Wm. Simmons 1848, m. David Robinson; Adeline b. Feb. 1834, m. Phineas Daley 1854; Caroline b. 1836, m. John Heath 1855; Eliza Ann b. March 3, 1839, m. Wm. Simmons, m. Wyman M. Parker; Emma b. Jan. 1841, d. infant. Family home Nauvoo, Ill.
Married Caroline Eliza Nickerson (Hubbard) Feb. 20, 1841, Nauvoo, Ill. (daughter of Freeman Nickerson and Huldah Chapman, of Nauvoo, Ill., pioneers Sept. 24, 1850. Jackson Stewart company). She was born June 25, 1808. Their children: Pereia Cornelia b. 1842, m. Stephen I. Bunnell; Marshall Hubbard, m. Belle Orr; Leonard, d. infant; Data, d. child.
Married Hannah Tupper Dec. 17, 1844, Nauvoo, Ill. (daughter of Silas Tupper and Hannah Ladd of Nauvoo, Ill.) She was born March 23, 1823, at Parishville, N. Y. Their children: Thomas b. 1846, m. Elizabeth Heiner, m. Louise Picton, m. Annie B. Saunders; Hannah; Joel. m. Mary Asenath Richards; Pauline, m. Charles A. Brown; Jedediah Morgan Grant, m. Eliza Bigler, m. Emma Blackburn, m. Nettie Lazenby. Died in infancy or early childhood: James, Evelyn, Hyrum Smith, Silas, Josephine, Jerome, Maria Louisa, Ezra, John Ladd, Charles Coulson Rich. Family home Farmington, Utah.
Married Lodoiska Tupper 1846, Nauvoo temple (daughter of Silas Tupper and Hannah Ladd, latter pioneer 1853). She was born May 22, 1829; came to Utah Oct. 12, 1847, Charles C. Rich company, driving an oxteam across plains. Their children: Lucy, m. David A. Sanders; Moroni, d. infant; Jacob, m. Anna Smith; Napoleon, m. Armelia Bigler; Edward Partridge, m. Fannie Clawson; Inez, d. aged eight years; Don Carlos, d. infant. Family home Farmington, Utah.
Married Elizabeth Walker 1856, Salt Lake City (daughter of John William Walker and Elizabeth Coleman of England, latter a pioneer Oct. 1855, Edmund Ellsworth handcart company). She was born Oct. 17, 1839. Their children: Clara, d. child; Walter L., m. Celia Millard; Nettie, d. child; Zeruah, m. Thomas Poulton; Enoch, m. Amber Call; Pollie, m. Lorenzo Smith; Alma Fredrick and Samuel, d. in childhood; Lafayette, m. Ella Parkinson. Family home Farmington, Utah.
Married Emma Walker in 1857 at Salt Lake City (daughter of Henry Walker), who was born March 15, 1837, Bristol, Eng. Came to Utah with Edmund Ellsworth handcart company, Sept. 26, 1856. Their children: Keturah b. May 8, 1858, m. W. L. Flint June 1877; Rosella b. March 1860, m. Henry Simpson 1875; Henry A. b. April 12, 1862, m. Esther B. Smith Oct. 18, 1885; Amy Blanche b. 1864, m. Charles W. Vernisha b. Nov. 1866, m. Ira Poulton 1886; William Frank b. March 1868, m. Lettie Pierce; Abner and David, d. in childhood; Albert Isaiah b. June 7, 1874, m. Hortense Hess. Family home Farmington, Utah.
Member of first high council held at Nauvoo; lifeguard of Joseph Smith; assisted in burial obsequies of martyrs Joseph and Hyrum; missionary to eastern states, 1844, and 1870; member of Davis stake high council. Probate judge Davis county two terms; member Utah state legislature at Fillmore, Farmer. Died Feb. 19, 1886, Farmington.

GROVER, THOMAS (son of Thomas Grover and Hannah Tupper). Born Nov. 17, 1845, Nauvoo, Ill. Came to Utah Oct. 3, 1847, Charles C. Rich company.
Married Elizabeth Heiner Feb. 10, 1865, Salt Lake City (daughter of Martin Heiner and Adelgunda Deitzel of Morgan, Utah). She was born April 4, 1847. Their children: Thomas Martin b. Nov. 27, 1866, m. Isabel Hogg; Evelyn Maria b. Sept. 3, 1868, m. William Voriton; Hannah b. Nov. 26, 1870; Adelgunda b. June 7, 1873, m. Alfred J. Hemming; Daniel Wells b. April 8, 1876, m. Martha May Rich; Pauline Elizabeth b. Nov. 25, 1878; Freeman Tupper b. Aug. 6, 1882. Family resided Morgan and Nephi, Utah.
Married Louisa A. Picton December 1877, St. George, Utah (daughter of James Picton and Jane Phillips of England) who was born Aug. 20, 1854. Their children: Ethel b. Feb. 6, 1879, m. George Wheaton; Louisa Winnette b. March 26, 1880, m. Daniel A. Robinson; Rosetta b. Aug 24, 1882; James Picton b. June 14, 1884, m. Lottie Robison; Fanny Joyce b. May 5, 1887, m. Howard Thackray; Ellen Genevieve b. June 21, 1889; Lilian b. Feb. 11, 1991; Pearl b Nov. 11, 1894; Lula b. Dec. 3, 1896. Family home Morgan Utah.
Married Annie B. Saunders 1885, Logan, Utah. Their children: Annie May b. 1886; Charles b. 1889; Jerald b 1902. Family home Morgan, Utah.
President 35th quorum seventies; missionary to The Mudd; 1868-71; ordinance worker in Logan temple 1885; war teacher; Sunday school teacher; high priest. Assisted in bringing immigrants to Utah. Constable Nephi, Utah. Member Captain Burton company during Morrisite war. Stone mason; farmer; blacksmith.

GROVER, WALTER L. (son of Thomas Grover and Elizabeth Walker). Born Dec. 25, 1860, Farmington, Utah.
Married Celia Millard Jan. 18, 1883, at Salt Lake City (daughter of James Radford Millard and Kathryne Richard of Farmington, pioneers Oct. 1853, Joseph W. Young company). She was born June 16, 1862. Their children: George

PIONEERS AND PROMINENT MEN OF UTAH

Fredrick b. Jan. 8, 1884, m. Mary Vilate Clayton; Walter Leslie b. June 21, 1885, m. Thorburn Murie; Mary b. April 22, 1888, m. Thomas W. Innes Aug. 21, 1912; Alice b. Sept. 24, 1889, m. J. C. Jensen Sept. 25, 1912; James Millard b. Feb. 27, 1891; Thomas Odell b. June 30, 1895; Leland Raleigh b. May 10, 1893; Preston Legrand b. Nov. 21, 1900; Edna Kathryne b. Sept. 10, 1907. Family home Garland, Utah.
Pioneer of Bear river valley. Presiding elder and bishop, Garland ward 1894-1909; member Bear River stake high council. Elected mayor of Garland Nov. 8, 1911. Merchant.

GROVER, HENRY A. (son of Thomas Grover and Emma Walker). Born April 12, 1862, Farmington, Utah.
Married Esther Beart Smith Oct. 15, 1885, Farmington, Utah (daughter of Alkanah J. Smith, and Mary Eade Fulcher of England). She was born April 9, 1869, Farmington, Utah. Their children: Henry Abner b. June 6, 1886, d. infant; Royal Andrew b. Aug. 6, 1888, m. Minnie I. Larson 1907; Mary Emma b. March 31, 1890, d. Aug. 13, 1891; David Smith b. Nov. 19, 1891; Thomas b. Feb. 16, 1894; Ester B. b. June 10, 1898, d. same day; Ella Spaulding b. Oct. 8, 1900; Birdie Marie b. Nov. 19, 1904; George Albert b. March 31, 1908; Roscoe b. Sept. 24, 1909, d. in infancy. Family home Parker, Idaho.
Missionary to southern states and to England; president 113th quorum seventies; high councilor Yellowstone stake.

GROW, HENRY (son of Henry Grow and Mary Riter of Philadelphia, Pa. Born Oct. 1, 1817, at Norristown, near Philadelphia, and came to Utah Oct. 1, 1851, with James Cummings company.
Married Mary Moyer 1834 (daughter of Charles and Elizabeth Moyer). She was born in 1818. Their children: Maria L. b. Sept. 10, 1837, m. Samuel Worthen April 27, 1856; Charles M. b. Jan. 6, 1840, m. Elizabeth Langlois Jan. 26, 1863; William M. b. May 30, 1842, m. Esther Coffin July 2, 1865; George W. b. Sept. 10, 1845; John W. b. Dec. 21, 1848; m. Cathrine McKay Nov. 8, 1869; Ann Grow b. Dec. 15, 1851, m. Henry Smith June 21, 1869; Elizabeth b. Jan. 30, 1854, m. Iowa Hall Feb. 8, 1870. Family home Salt Lake City.
Married Julia M. Veach April 17, 1858, Salt Lake City (daughter of William Veach and Nancy Ann Elliott of Pittsburgh, Pa. pioneers Oct. 1, 1851). She was born March 10, 1842. Their children: Theodore M., m. Sadie Stuart; Sylvester Veach b. Aug. 29, 1861, m. Matilda Ann Smith and Hanna Michelson; Mary Ann, m. Walter Worthen; Julia Ellen, m. Andrew Leonard; George Elliot, m. Rose Griffiths; Amelia, m. John Dobbs; Walter V., m. Belle Bryson; Maud Rose, m. Will Lowrie; William Henry, m. Elizabeth Adams; Sarah Elizabeth. m. Ora Maddi; Oto Sylvanus, m. Phebe Argil; Eugene Parnell, m. Lillie Hablan; Frank V., died; Marco Bartlett, m. Selma Fernstrom. Family home Salt Lake City, Utah.
Served as bishop of 19th ward, Salt Lake City. Prominent architect and builder. Among the buildings he erected in Salt Lake City were Social Hall, Mormon Tabernacle 1865-1867; Salt Lake Theater, C. M. I. 1868, Assembly Hall 1877; also built first suspension bridge in Utah, 1853, across Ogden river; the first sugar factory in Utah, 1854, at Sugar House; built several saw mills for President Young in 1855; the first woolen mills, 1859; the first suspension bridges over the Jordan and Weber rivers, 1861; and completed the New Deseret Paper Mills, the first in Utah, in 1883. Missionary to Pennsylvania 1876. City councilman Salt Lake City 1870-76. Played in the first martial band in Salt Lake City. Died Nov. 4, 1891.

GROW, WILLIAM M. (son of Henry Grow and Mary Moyer). Born May 30, 1842, at Philadelphia, Pa.
Married Esther Coffin July 2, 1865, at Huntsville, Utah (daughter of William B. Coffin and Abigail Starbuck, latter a pioneer Oct. 3, 1852, Harmon Cutler company). She was born Aug. 15, 1844, Richmond, Ind. Their children: Mary Abigail b. March 27, 1866, m. Joseph H. Owen Aug. 15, 1883; William N. b. Sept. 3, 1867; James A. b. March 16, 1872, m. Maud Hays Dec. 1892; David H. b. Nov. 19, 1873, m. Mary Luette Rawson Oct. 1893; Jesse M. b. Oct. 22, 1875, m. Christa Edith Empey Oct. 1900; Horace I. b. Aug. 8, 1877, m. Rosella Rounds March 7, 1900; Cyrus L. b. March 10, 1879, m. Cecilia Yittings June 1899; Charles E. b. Nov. 30, 1882; Esther E. b. April 16, 1885, m. L. C. Poulter Sept. 6, 1911.
Assisted in locating Huntsville, Utah. In 1867 moved to western Oregon and on the way assisted in making the first brick manufactured at Boise City, Idaho; later engaged in freighting from Umatilla, Ore., to mines of northern Idaho. Returned to Huntsville, Utah 1871 and moved to Ammon, near Idaho Falls, Idaho, in 1880. Farmer.

GROW, JOHN W. (son of Henry Grow and Mary Moyer). Born Dec. 21, 1848, in Platte county, Mo.
Married Cathrine McKay Nov. 8, 1869, at Salt Lake City (daughter of William McKay and Ellen Oman, pioneers 1856, Captain James Brown company). She was born May 1, 1851, at Thurso, Scotland. Their children: Lena Faverett b. Sept. 2, 1871; John M. b. June 26, 1874, m. Amelia Wanggaard Oct. 18, 1895; Mary Janett b. Sept. 1, 1876, m. John Halls Feb. 14, 1895; David Henry b. Nov. 8, 1878, m. Mary Lofzneen Feb. 22, 1905; Charles Isaac b. Nov. 3, 1880, Adelia Abbot Sept. 5, 1899; William Angus b. June 17, 1883; Cathrine Rosel b. April 3, 1885; Arthur W. b. Sept. 15, 1887, m. Ella Thurston Nov. 25, 1909; Lorin M. b. Sept. 15, 1889; Clarence Oman b. Oct. 1, 1891; Isabell b. June 12, 1894. Family home Huntsville, Utah.
Member of bishopric of Huntsville ward.

GROW, SYLVESTER VEACH (son of Henry Grow and Julia M. Veach). Born Aug. 29, 1861, at Salt Lake City.
Married Matilda Ann Smith Dec. 21, 1880, at Salt Lake City (daughter of John and Mary Smith of Huntsville, Utah, formerly of England). She was born May 2, 1861. Their children: Julia Ellen b. Aug. 21, 1881, m. Christan Peterson; Mary Ann b. Sept. 2, 1882, m. George Gwilliams; Sadie M. b. May 25, 1884, m. Sam Slater; Henry b. Nov. 29, 1885, m. Ruth Halls; Sylvester b. Feb. 4, 1889; Ethel b. Aug. 15, 1887, died; Amelia b. Aug. 24, 1891, m. Levi Walker; Theodore b. Feb. 21, 1892, died. Family home Huntsville, Utah.
Married Hanna Michelson Jan. 29, 1896, at Salt Lake City (daughter of Joseph Michelson and Alberta Agnes Laason of Huntsville, Utah, who came to Utah from Denmark, arriving in June 1880). She was born Oct. 7, 1869. Their children: Veach C. b. Oct. 11, 1896; Theo Matilda b. April 30, 1898; Parnell b. Feb. 24, 1900; Wayne J. b. April 30, 1902; Nevii Leo b. April 24, 1904; Samuel Elmo b. Nov. 20, 1906; Sylva Johanna b. Oct. 10, 1908. Family home Huntsville, Utah.
Ward teacher. County game warden six years; deputy game commissioner two years; representative to state legislature. Farmer and sheepman.

GRUNDVIG, FRANTZ CHRISTIAN (son of Frederik H. Grundvig and Katherine Maria Frandsen of Jutland, Denmark). Born March 27, 1836. Came to Utah in 1865, Miner G. Atwood company.
Married Jensenia Hostmark in 1857, Copenhagen, Denmark. She was born March 26, 1837, and was captured by Indians while crossing the plains and has never since been heard from. Their only child, Severin Holger, was born March 27, 1858, and married Catherine Alfina Palmer.
High priest; missionary to Norway 1863-64. First settled in Salt Lake and afterward in Cottonwood, Richfield and Fayette, Utah; later he moved to Wellington, Utah.

GRUNDVIG, SEVERIN HOLGER (son of Frantz Christian Grundvig and Jensenia Hostmark). Born March 27, 1858, at Copenhagen, Denmark. Came to Utah 1865.
Married Catherine Alfina Palmer in 1883 (daughter of Abram Whitney Palmer and Huldah Catherine Hill of Ogden and Fayette, Utah). She was born Sept. 8, 1863. Their children: Severin Francis b. March 7, 1884, m. Beatrice Adelia Pinesar; Orville Abram b. Feb. 14, 1886; Abram b. Feb. 14, 1886; Reuben b. Nov. 20, 1887, died; William Earl b. Jan. 2, 1889; Don Carlos b. Nov. 29, 1890; Joseph Taylor b. March 29, 1893; Lenard Allen b. May 31, 1895; Lester Oron b. July 25, 1897; Daniel Richard b. Nov. 25, 1899; Alfina Charlotte b. Dec. 10, 1901; Inez Catherine b. Sept. 1, 1904; Laura Jensenia. b. June 26, 1907; Ruby Delilah b. March 5, 1911.
Moved from Fayette to Wellington, Utah, 1888. Ward teacher; counselor in presidency of Y. M. M. I. A.; choir leader; Sunday school teacher. Constable. Farmer.

GUDMUNDSON, SAMUEL (son of Gudmund Sommundson, born Dec. 27, 1804, and Mary Olsen, born July 29, 1805, both at Kurtsoe, Tellimarken, Norway). Born May 13, 1831, at Kurtsoe. Came to Utah in early days.
Married Ellen Marie Mork July 1861. Their children: Samuel T. b. July 29, 1862, m. Mary K. Birchinail April 17, 1907; Emma M. b. July 18, 1864, m. Bertrand A. Tanner; C. Amalia b. Feb. 18, 1866, m. J. M. Wilson; Nephi b. Jan. 25, 1868. Family resided at Fairview and Springville, Utah.
Married Inger Anntina Olsen May 16, 1869, at Salt Lake City (daughter of John Kelly and Gunhilda Olson), who was born Feb. 5, 1851, at Skein, Norway. Their children: Heber G. b. Oct. 6, 1870, m. Lucy Nielson; Mary J. b. Oct. 12, 1872, m. John D. Childs; Myron A. b. April 3, 1874, m. Abbie Chase; Octavius F. b. May 7, 1876, m. Anna Mae Clark Nov. 1906; Gunhilda E. b. March 7, 1878, m. Parley E. Burt; Moses S. b. Sept. 16, 1879, m. Erma Crandall; Inga M. R. b. July 20, 1881, m. Albert J. Knudsen Nov. 1905; Bessie E. b. May 13, 1883, m. Heber O. Hale Dec. 1905; Erma L. b. April 25, 1885, d. aged 5. Family home Springville, Utah.
Missionary to Norway 1867; conference president at Christiania. Indian war veteran. One of first settlers of Fairview 1863.

GUDMUNDSON, SAMUEL T. (son of Samuel Gudmundson and Ellen Marie Mork). Born July 29, 1862, at Salt Lake City.
Married Mary K. Birchinail April 17, 1907, at Salt Lake City (daughter of John Kelly and Honora Meagher, both of whom died in New York). She was born Nov. 29, 1868, at New York City. Family home Springville, Utah.
Served in all the degrees of priesthood to high priest.

GULL, JOHN (son of William Gull, born Aug. 11, 1811, and Sarah Bryant, born Aug. 9, 1809, both at Caples. St. Marys, Suffolk, Eng.—married Aug. 4, 1831). He was born Nov. 20, 1832, at Caples. Came to Utah Dec. 5, 1864, William Darling freight train.
Married Elizabeth J. Skeets April 6, 1857 (daughter of Samuel and Elizabeth Skeets, who were married 1827 at Bentley, Suffolk, Eng.). She was born Oct. 8, 1838, and died in England. Only child: John P. b. July 27, 1859, m. Elizabeth J. Bills April 9, 1884.

Married Harriet Pennell Nov. 8, 1861, Holbrook, Eng. (daughter of Shadrach Pennell and Hannah Farthern—married 1827 at Holbrook). She was born Oct. 8, 1843, at Holbrook.
Married Mary A. Nickerson April 1866 (daughter of Levi Nickerson and Mary A. Nyrman, pioneers 1851), who was born Aug. 5, 1852. Only child: Emma Jane b. 1867, m. Mr. Gates 1886.
Married Charlotte Criddle Jan. 12, 1867, at Salt Lake City (daughter of Henry Criddle and Mary Bull—married June 22, 1837, at West Buckland, Eng., pioneers Oct. 1, 1866, Joseph S. Rawlins company). She was born Nov. 21, 1847, in Somersetshire, Eng. Their children: Harriet E. b. April 17, 1868, m. F. H. Stewart; William H. b. July 2, 1869, m. Bessa A. Adams; George A. b. March 26, 1871; Mary J. b. Feb. 23, 1873, m. R. A. Cowley; Charles R. b. Dec. 21, 1874, m. Martha Martin; Albert E. b. May 17, 1877, m. Martha A. Adams; Harry A. b. Sept. 10, 1879, m. Emma Stewart; Sarah L. b. Dec. 28, 1881; Joseph B. and Hyrum B. b. Sept. 25, 1883, latter m. Lula Duncan; Jesse A. b. Oct. 4, 1886; A. Leonard b. March 7, 1889; A. Ezra b. May 13, 1891. Family home Meadow, Utah.
Missionary to England; church teamster bringing immigrants to Utah 1866.

GUNNELL, FRANCIS WILSON (son of Christopher and Ann Gunnell of England). Born March 3, 1831, Houghton, Nottinghamshire, Eng. Came to Utah Oct. 29, 1849, Ezra T. Benson company.
Married Polly Ann Edwards July 24, 1851 (daughter of Essias Edwards), who was born Oct. 25, 1836. Their children: Francis Chruther b. Aug. 4, 1853, m. Sarah Ann Owen Dec. 23, 1872; Sarah E. b. Oct. 16, 1856, m. Louis Howell; Ann E. b. March 12, 1858, m. Dan Walters; Mary b. March 14, 1860, d. July 8, 1860; Charlie b. Sept. 8, 1861, m. Sarah Ann Brown Feb. 23, 1882. Family home Wellsville, Utah.
Married Elizabeth Bickmore April 7, 1859, Salt Lake City (daughter of Isaac Bickmore and Martha Hawley), who was born May 31, 1842. Their children: John b. Feb. 18, 1861, d. April 5, 1861; Martha b. Dec. 14, 1862, m. Joseph Lloyd July 3, 1879; George b. March 9, 1865, m. Janet Hill Dec. 13, 1883; Polly Ann b. July 12, 1867, m. John Darley Dec. 23, 1885; Jemima b. Oct. 2, 1869, m. Thomas W. Hall Jan. 20, 1886; Printha b. Jan. 8, 1872, m. Daniel Leroy Hill Jan. 16, 1890.
Married Esther Lewis July 2, 1864, Salt Lake City (daughter of Thomas Lewis), who was born Nov. 18, 1848, in Wales. Their children: Thomas L. b. June 18, 1865, m. Sarah Poppleton Jan. 6, 1886; Mary Catherine b. July 16, 1867, m. Daniel G. Hill Dec. 13, 1883; Franklin L. b. Oct. 7, 1869, m. Mary E. Hill Nov. 30, 1892; Zina b. April 20, 1873, m. Robert H. Maughan June 7, 1893; Lionel b. April 20, 1873, d. July 17, 1893; Laura b. March 11, 1876, m. Thomas Williamson Jan. 12, 1898; Evan b. March 1, 1878, d. July 17, 1893; David b. April 7, 1882; Nora b. Sept. 27, 1884, m. Henry Brezze, Jan. 27, 1904; Maggie b. April 18, 1886, d. same day.
Married Emma Jeffs (daughter of William Jeffs and Mary Ann Ashard, married 1848, Birmingham, Eng., pioneers 1852). She was born Oct. 5, 1850. Their children: Emeline b. Jan. 24, 1873, m. Robert Brown Jan. 16, 1895; William J. b. July 7, 1875, m. Mary Bailey Dec. 5, 1901, m. Annie Poppleton April 27, 1910; Peter J. b. June 5, 1878, m. Olive Ward June 6, 1907; Llewellyn b. Dec. 18, 1880, m. Sarah Hawkins Dec. 14, 1910; Sarah Elizabeth b. July 1, 1883, m. Orson Bailey March 8, 1905. Family home Wellsville, Utah.
Married Jane Baxter April 7, 1869 (daughter of Robert Baxter and Eva Love, married Jan. 10, 1848, Greenock, Scotland, pioneers Sept. 26, 1855, Richard Ballantyne company). She was born Oct. 31, 1851. Their children: Robert B. b. Sept. 28, 1870, m. Agnes Kerr March 1893; Ezra B. b. March 10, 1872, m. Mary Mitton March 8, 1898; Essie May b. May 17, 1875, d. Feb. 28, 1877; Archibald B. b. Oct. 31, 1877, m. Maude Parke Feb. 8, 1905; Parley B. b. Oct. 12, 1880, m. Eva Haslem March 1905; Joseph B. b. Aug. 7, 1883, m. Alice Redford Dec. 19, 1906; Preston B. b. Feb. 28, 1886.
Settled in Cache Valley, Utah, Sept. 16, 1856; first school teacher and first choir leader there, and associated with William Maughan in first mail contract for that valley, carrying mail from Brigham City. First agent of Utah Northern railway at Mendon. Agent for care of church property in Cache Valley. Home in later life, Rexburg, Idaho, where he died Oct. 20, 1889.

GUNNELL, FRANKLIN L. (son of Francis Wilson Gunnell and Esther Lewis). Born Oct. 7, 1869, Wellsville, Utah.
Married Mary E. Hill Nov. 30, 1892, Logan, Utah (daughter of William J. Hill, pioneer September 1853, and Georgiana Ensign). She was born Nov. 21, 1874, at Wellsville. Their child: Maud b. Feb. 16, 1898. Family home, Wellsville.
Missionary to Colorado 1905-07; set apart bishop Wellsville ward July 25, 1909. One of organizers and vice-president of Wellsville City Bank. City councilman of Wellsville four years. Farmer and stockraiser in early life.

GUNNEL, ARCHIBALD B. (son of Francis Wilson Gunnell and Jane Baxter). Born Oct. 31, 1877, Wellsville, Utah.
Married Maude Parke Feb. 8, 1905, Logan, Utah (daughter of I. H. Parke and Hannah Dover), who was born July 6, 1878, Salt Lake City. Their children: Essie P. b. Jan. 9, 1906; Merrill P. b. Sept. 19, 1907; Gerald A. P. b. Oct. 1, 1909.

GURR, ENOCH ELDRIDGE (son of James and Sarah Gurr, of England). Born July 29, 1813, in Sussex, Eng. Came to Utah April 1857, Ezra Curtis company.
Married Ruth Buckman in Australia (daughter of Jas. Buckman and Susanna Price of that country), who was born Sept. 23, 1809. Their children: William; Mary; James; Susanna; Sarah; Peter; Reuben. Family home Benjamin, Utah.
High priest. Farmer.

GURR, REUBEN (son of Enoch Eldridge Gurr and Ruth Buckman). Born Dec. 29, 1849, in Australia. Came to Utah 1857 with father.
Married Elyadie Miles in 1868, Salt Lake City (daughter of John Miles and Lucy Polina Ford). Their children: William R.; Enoch Elijah; Elizabeth; John Miles; Lucy Polina; Delbert; Sarah.
Elder. Farmer.

GURR, WILLIAM R. (son of Reuben Gurr and Elyadie Miles). Born 1869, Provo, Utah.
Married Ida Harmon 1898, in Mexico (daughter of Levi Harmon of Joseph City, Utah). Their child: Reuben.

GUTTERRIDGE, ROBERT (son of William Gutteridge and Mary Houx of Berville, Berkshire, Eng.). Born in Berkshire. Came to Utah Aug. 20, 1868, Horton D. Haight company.
Married Hannah Grover December 1840, Berville, Eng. (daughter of William Grover and Hannah Chamberlain). Their children: Maria b. Nov. 10, 1841, m. William Calton Aug. 12, 1861; Mary Ann, m. Jonas H. Ingersoll; Eliza. m. William Calton; George, died; Fredrick, d. aged 11; William, d. infant. Family home Berville, Eng.
Presiding elder at Liverpool, Eng. Iron worker. Died April, 1879, Salt Lake City.

GUYMON, THOMAS (son of Isaiah Guymon). Born March 10, 1787. Came to Utah Sept. 8, 1850, Aaron Johnson company.
Married Sarah Gordon Feb. 23, 1809 (daughter of John Gordon), who was born Nov. 20, 1791. Their children: Isaiah b. Feb. 15, 1810; John b. Nov. 28, 1811; William b. Jan. 23, 1815; James b. Dec. 27, 1816; Noah T. b. June 30, 1819; Martin b. June 12, 1821; Barzilla b. Dec. 31, 1823, m. Mathew Caldwell; Elizabeth b. July 19, 1826; Polly Ann b. July 11, 1829, m. R. Johnson; Sarah Jane; Melissa Jane b. Feb. 14, 1833, m. Levi Gregory Metcalf.
Died Oct. 20, 1855, Springville, Utah.

GUYMON, NOAH THOMAS (son of Thomas Guymon and Sarah Gordon). Born June 30, 1819. Came to Utah Sept. 8, 1850.
Married Mary D. Dudley Dec. 24, 1837, at Caldwell, Mo. Their children: Mary Jane, m. Geo. B. Matson Jan. 25, 1854; Lucinda, m. Phillip Hurst; Emma M., m. H. H. Kearnes.
Married Margaret Johnson. Their children: Elizabeth, m. Oscar Crandall; Martin Lewis, died; Harriet, m. Oscar Crandall; Julia Luella, m. Geo. Maycock; Edward Wallace, m. Elizabeth Preator; Lillian M., m. Lou Pearson.
Married Elizabeth Ann Jones (daughter of James and Sarah Ann Jones), who was born Feb. 12, 1829. Their children: William Albert b. April 25, 1849, m. Marcillia Fowles; Clarissa E. b. Aug. 29, 1851, m. Amasa Scovial; Noah Thomas, Jr. b. April 18, 1853, m. Caroline M. Hanson; Sarah Ann b. Aug. 30, 1856, died; Amy Amelia b. Jan. 18, 1859, m. A. G. Jewkes; Elizabeth Ann b. Jan. 8, 1861, died. Family home Fountain Green, Utah.
Married Louisa Rowley March 2, 1857, who was born May 8, 1831. Their children: James W. b. Sept. 17, 1858, d. Nov. 17, 1858; John Wesley b. Aug. 7, 1860; Wm. Lee. m.——Black; David R. b. Feb. 21, 1862, died; Willard R. b. Sept. 20, 1864; Owen W. b. April 16, 1866; Thos. H. b. Oct. 23, 1868; Ann Louisa b. Oct. 12, 1870, m. Edward Gorry; Sarah Jane b. Oct. 21, 1872; Joseph H. b. Aug. 20, 1874; Melissa L. b. May 31, 1876; Laura E. b. April 7, 1879; Franklin b. May 12, 1883.
Missionary to Great Britain 1852-55; president 51st quorum seventies. Merchant; farmer; stockraiser. Died Jan. 7, 1911, Orangeville, Utah.

GUYMON, EDWARD WALLACE (son of Noah T. Guymon and Margaret Johnson). Born Dec. 15, 1859, at Springville, Utah.
Married Elizabeth Preator Jan. 27, 1883, at Salt Lake City (daughter of Richard Preator and Mary Harper, handcart pioneers from England). She was born May 31, 1860. Their children: Edward Ray b. Oct. 24, 1884, m. Ida J. Dayley; Beatrice Blanche b. March 15, 1886, died; Mary Margaret b. Dec. 26, 1887; Gregg Eugene b. Feb. 2, 1890; Martin Lewis b. Nov. 10, 1891; Beulah Grace b. Nov. 8, 1893; Leslie Lynn b. Oct. 20, 1895; Hazel b. March 12, 1897; Vernon Melvern b. Dec. 2, 1898; Richard Nathan b. Dec. 19, 1900; Leora Olga b. Jan. 24, 1902; Eva Wilda b. Dec. 13, 1903. Family resided Huntington and Vernal, Utah; Otto, Wyo., and Oakley, Idaho.
Ward teacher; president Y. M. M. I. A. Road supervisor; constable, Burley, Idaho. Railroad contractor; farmer.

PIONEERS AND PROMINENT MEN OF UTAH

GUYMON, NOAH THOMAS, JR. (son of Noah Thomas Guymon and Elizabeth Ann Jones). Born April 18, 1853, at Springville, Utah.
Married Caroline Maria Hanson Nov. 8, 1875 (daughter of Soren Hanson and Anna Maria Bendixen of Denmark, former pioneer Sept. 12, 1863, John R. Young company, latter killed on way to Utah in stampede of oxen). She was born Oct. 3, 1856. Their children: Ophelia Alzada b. Oct. 19, 1876, m. Jasper N. Robertson; Annie Laura b. July 29, 1878, and Lavina b. March 16, 1880, died; Noah Thomas b. Jan. 1, 1882, m. Isabella Sanderson; Louis Wealey b. Oct. 30, 1883, m. Pearl Mackleprang; Mary Caroline b. Jan. 2, 1886, m. Ralph Oliphant; William Lee b. May 25, 1888; Alvin Clarence b. Nov. 20, 1891. Family home Orangeville, Utah.
High priest. Farmer; apiarist.

GWILLIAMS, HENRY B. (son of Henry B. Gwilliams of Shrewsbury, Eng.). Born May 7, 1835, Shrewsbury, Eng. Came to Utah Oct. 24, 1855, Milo Andrus company.
Married Jane Fisher Oct. 1854 at Birmingham, Eng., who was born 1834 and died 1855 at Atchison, Kans.
Married Elizabeth Palmer March 21, 1856, Salt Lake City (daughter of Richard Palmer and Mary Chambers of Sheffield, Eng.), who was born Dec. 11, 1834, and came to Utah Oct. 28, 1853. Their children: Henry William b. Feb. 21, 1857, m. Frances Mariah Chambers; Charles John b. April 8, 1859, d. aged 6; George Washington b. July 22, 1861, m. Mary Grow; Benjamin Franklin b. July 22, 1861, m. Amelia Stanford; Josephine b. Oct. 22, 1863, m. Joseph Manning; Harry Chambers b. Aug. 6, 1865, m. Lea Moore; Orson Pratt b. March 29, 1867, m. Minnie Parker; Elizabeth Jane b. Feb. 16, 1869, d. aged 3; Carrie b. July 16, 1871, m. Orson Wadsworth. Family resided Salt Lake City, Draper, Paradise, Logan and Hooper, Utah.
Missionary to Salmon River, Idaho, 1868-69;; bishop of South Hooper 1874-78. Farmer; merchant. Died Sept. 22, 1907, at Hooper.

GWILLIAMS, HENRY WILLIAM (son of Henry B. Gwilliams and Elizabeth Palmer). Born Feb. 21, 1857, Salt Lake City.
Married Frances Mariah Chambers Jan. 13, 1881, at Salt Lake City (daughter of John Garratt Chambers and Mariah Duffin of Salt Lake City, Logan and Ogden, Utah, pioneers 1853). She was born Feb. 29, 1860. Their children: Florence M. b. May 9, 1882, m. Horace G. Nebeker; Henry Chambers b. Nov. 24, 1883, m. Arvilla West; Maria Elizabeth b. Jan. 13, 1886, m. Frank J. Chamberlain; Roscoe Chambers b. Sept. 13, 1891; Ralph Chambers b. June 1, 1897.
Member 53d and one of the presidents of 77th quorum seventies; high priest; first counselor to Bishop Stratford, also to Bishop E. T. Wooley, and later bishop 4th ward, Ogden, Utah; bishop 6th ward, Salt Lake City. Weber county assessor 1897 and 1898; street commissioner 1895-96; member board of education 1901-08. Engaged in lumber business.

H

HACKING, JOHN SAMPSON (son of James Hacking of Burton Eng. (died Sept. 12, 1840), and Jane Pearson of Whitehaven, Eng.). Born Sept. 16, 1835, at Preston, Lancashire, Eng. Came to Utah in 1851, Captain Cardon company.
Married Jane Clark May 5, 1856, at St. Louis, Mo. (daughter of James Clark and Elizabeth Pearson of Preston, pioneers 1856, John Banks company). She was born Feb. 21, 1839, at Preston. Their children: James b. Dec. 23, 1856, m. Annie M. Glines Aug. 11, 1876; Harriet Ambersine b. Nov. 14, 1858; Phoebe Ann b. Dec. 8, 1860, m. George D. Merkley Oct. 10, 1881; Jane Elizabeth b. March 29, 1863, m. George H. Southam Oct. 10, 1888, d. July 12, 1890; Eleanor b. March 5, 1865, m. Alfred Anderson April 17, 1885; John S. b. June 23, 1867, m. Mary E. Hall March 29, 1893; Henry Franklin b. Nov. 28, 1869, m. Martha Wilcox Oct. 28, 1895; Charles Lorenzo b. Jan. 18, 1872, d. June 30, 1896; Joseph Pearson b. Feb. 5, 1874, m. Carrie Claire Stringham June 22, 1898; George Alfred b. April 5, 1876, m. Frances Briggs June 20, 1900; Mary Emily b. April 15, 1878, d. April 30, 1878; Martha Caroline b. March 18, 1880, m. Earl Cook May 27, 1901; Orson Ezra b. Sept. 16, 1882, m. Ida Brown Feb. 22, 1901; Thomas William b. April 15, 1885, m. Keren Bingham Oct. 16, 1912. Family home Cedar Fort, Utah.
High priest. Settled first in American Fork, moved to Cedar Fort in 1853. Went with Gunnison party to California in 1854, thence via Isthmus of Panama and New York to St. Louis, where he married, returning to Utah with wife and latter's parents in 1856. Served as militiaman in Walker war, during which time drove the "Sow" cannon from Provo to Salt Creek (now Juab). Served on home guard in Black Hawk war. Director Cedar Fort Co-op. store 1868-76, for which he was purchasing agent 15 years; director of water board 25 years, and has been watermaster since 1860 continuously. School trustee nine years. Blacksmith; farmer.

HACKING, JAMES (son of John S. Hacking and Jane Clark). Born Dec. 23, 1856, at Cedar Fort, Utah.
Married Annie M. Glines Aug. 11, 1876, at Salt Lake City (daughter of James Harvey Glines and Elizabeth Ann Mayer, pioneers 1852, Robert Wimmer company). She was born May 11, 1858, at American Fork, Utah. Their children: James C. b. Jan. 1, 1878, m. Harriet Bodily Jan. 3, 1900; Elizabeth Jane b. April 23, 1879, m. Frank E. Colton; John Glines b. Jan. 18, 1881, m. Isabell M. Bodily; William Ralph b. Aug. 26, 1882, m. Mabel Gerber; Ambrosine b. Aug. 22, 1884, m. Stephen W. Ashby Aug. 30, 1906; Nellie b. Feb. 26, 1886, m. Charles H. Colton June 28, 1906; Anna Myrtle b. Jan. 4, 1888, d. Sept. 19, 1906; Ray b. Nov. 1, 1889, d. Aug. 28, 1890; May b. Aug. 24, 1891, m. Wallace Calder; Cora b. Sept. 19, 1893; Fern b. Aug. 28, 1895; Finnie b. May 28, 1898; Owen b. Dec. 15, 1900. Family home Vernal, Utah.
Ward Sunday school superintendent; stake superintendent Y. M. M. I. A.; stake superintendent Sunday schools; 2nd counselor in stake presidency; high councilor. Chairman People's party; county commissioner six years; county bee inspector; county tree inspector. Director in several corporations.

HACKING, JOSEPH PEARSON (son of John S. Hacking and Jane Clark). Born Feb. 5, 1874, at Cedar Fort, Utah.
Married Carrie Claire Stringham June 22, 1898, at Salt Lake City (daughter of Philip Stringham and Caroline Crouch of Vernal, Utah), who was born Nov. 3, 1874. Their children: Lucile b. May 3, 1899; Josephine Marie b. Dec. 3, 1900; Rulon Stringham b. Dec. 19, 1903; Sterling Don b. Sept. 21, 1905; Joseph Ferron b. Dec. 11, 1906; Grant Leland b. Feb. 23, 1908; Harold Lorenzo b. July 11, 1909; Junius Paul b. Aug. 28, 1910. Family home Vernal, Utah.
Member 97th quorum seventies 1904-10; missionary to Germany 1900-03; high priest; member bishopric 1910. Farmer; sheepman.

HADDOCK, JOHN (son of John Haddock and Betty Beech of Barnton, Cheshire, Eng.). Born July 17, 1827, Barnton. Came to Utah Sept. 12, 1861, Milo Andrus company.
Married Maria Collins Feb. 10, 1856 (daughter of John Collins and Jane Proverbs), Home South Cottonwood, Utah.
Married Margaret Penman Sept. 5, 1866 (daughter of George B. Penman and Mary Cowan), who was born Jan. 19, 1847, at Airdrie, Scotland. Their children: Mary b. Dec. 15, 1867, m. William A. Bee Nov. 20, 1883; Maria Elizabeth b. May 30, 1869, m. James C. Thomas; John George b. July 8, 1871, m. Alzina A. Kent Nov. 10, 1893; Jessie Christeena b. Jan. 29, 1873, d. childhood; William Penman b. Oct. 6, 1874, d. infant; Thomas b. Oct. 8, 1875, d. at 16 years; Margaret Ann b. Oct. 12, 1879, m. Joseph Nye May 1900; Arthur Edward b. Jan. 4, 1881, m. Marintha Briscoe Dec. 1899; James b. Nov. 17, 1882, d. at 20 years; Joseph b. Jan. 17, 1884. Family home Bloomington, Idaho.
Early settler in Bear Lake valley. Died May 8, 1911.

HADDOCK, JOHN GEORGE (son of John Haddock and Margaret Penman). Born July 8, 1871, Bloomington, Idaho.
Married Alzina Adelaide Kent Nov. 10, 1893, Logan, Utah (daughter of Sidney W. Kent, m. Anna Adelaide Ward). She was born March 25, 1873, Bountiful, Utah. Their children: George Elmer b. Aug. 13, 1894; John Alton b. April 6, 1896, d. June 18, 1896; Elna Adelaide b. Nov. 5, 1897; Jesse Warren b. Jan. 26, 1900; Blain Kent b. March 28, 1902; Ruth Ella b. Sept. 27, 1904; Myra Alzina b. Aug. 15, 1909. Family home Wardboro, Idaho.
Presiding elder, Diamondville, Wyoming branch, July 23, 1899 to Sept. 1, 1901; chosen 1st councilor in bishopric of Wardboro, Idaho, Dec. 8, 1901; set apart as bishop of Wardboro, Jan. 3, 1909.

HADDON, THOMAS C. (son of Thomas Haddon and Sarah Bayes of Norfolk, Eng.). Born Dec. 25, 1815, at Norfolk. Came to Utah 1852, A. O. Smoot company.
Married Elizabeth Cherry April 12, 1857, Salt Lake City (daughter of Mr. Cherry and Sarah Boyes of Norfolk), who was born Feb. 5, 1830. Their children: William Alvin, d. aged 48 years; Mary Elizabeth, m. Nicolas C. Hair; Ellen Maria, m. Edward Middlemess; Mahala, d. infant. Family home Ephraim, Utah.
Sunday school superintendent; high priest. Farmer. Died May 31, 1899.

HADFIELD, JOSEPH (son of George Hadfield and Alice Hazelrim, of Hazel Grove, Eng.). Born March 3, 1827, Hazel Grove. Came to Utah Oct. 1, 1854, Daniel Garn company.
Married Jane Walker Redfern Dec. 25, 1853, in England (daughter of Joseph Redfern and Janett Walker, pioneers Oct. 1, 1854, Daniel Garn company). She was born Jan. 12, 1821. Their children: Joseph, Jr. b. Oct. 24, 1854, m. Mary Jane Oliver; George Samuel b. June 26, 1856, m. Laura Smith; Janett Alice b. April 5, 1858, m. James Henry Steed; Mary Elizabeth b. Dec. 8, 1859, d. Oct. 14, 1860; Jane Ann b. Nov. 2, 1862, m. William A. Hess.
Member 56th quorum seventies; high priest; acting teacher. Pioneer silk weaver; brick-maker. Died Jan. 16, 1894, at Portage, Utah.

HADFIELD, JOSEPH, JR. (son of Joseph Hadfield and Jane Walker Redfern). Born Oct. 24, 1854, Salt Lake City.
Married Mary Jane Oliver Aug. 26, 1877, at Farmington, Utah (daughter of Francis Oliver and Elizabeth Bailey of Brown Candover, Eng., pioneers Sept. 25, 1866, John Holliday company). She was born Jan. 30, 1859. Their children: Joseph Francis b. May 20, 1878, d. Sept. 4, 1879;

George S. b. June 21, 1880, m. Mary I. Smith; Elizabeth J. b. Oct. 1, 1881, m. Delbert Bowers; Janett E. b. July 1, 1883, m. Ebenezer Lefler; Alice A. b. Feb. 14, 1885, m. Fredric W. Buxton; Mary L. b. June 26, 1887, d. Sept. 2, 1888; Job O. b. Nov. 18, 1888; William E. b. March 13, 1890, d. Aug. 10, 1891; John H. b. March 2, 1892, m. Louisa Hancock; Ida May b. Jan. 6, 1894; Hazel b. March 29, 1896; Myron Ralph b. Dec. 2, 1901. Family home Riverside, Utah.
Member 74th quorum seventies; Sunday school superintendent 25 years. Constable ten years; statistical recorder. Farmer.

HADFIELD, JOSEPH (son of Samuel Hadfield and Mary Ann Godby, of Manchester, Eng.). Born April 13, 1832, in Manchester. Came to Utah Oct. 11, 1856, Jacob Croft company.
Married Jeanette Goudie Dec. 25, 1857, Pine Valley, Utah (daughter of James Goudie and Isabelle Tenuck, of Scotland), who was born Sept. 18, 1841. Their children: Henry J. b. Oct. 13, 1858; Mary Jane b. Nov. 26, 1861; Sarah E. b. July 25, 1863; Annie b. Nov. 7, 1864, m. George Jensen; Emma A. b. Nov. 17, 1866, m. Edgar Burk; Joseph S. b. July 25, 1867; Jeanette b. July 25, 1868; Lillian b. Sept. 21, 1870, m. Charles Averette; William F. b. April 28, 1872; John L. b. Sept. 1, 1873; William A. b. Aug. 8, 1874; Albert T. b. Sept. 26, 1875, m. Sarah E. Housekeeper; Alford Charles b. Sept. 29, 1878, m. Julia Young; Laura M. b. June 20, 1881, m. Eli Kirkham.
Elder. Cabinet maker and carpenter.

HADLEY, GEORGE (son of Joseph Hadley of Derby, and Mary Ann Harper of Bilper, Eng., latter born 1795 at Shropshire, Eng.). He was born Nov. 14, 1816, in parish of St. Peters, Derbyshire, Eng. Came to Utah Oct. 4, 1863, Thomas E. Ricks company.
Married Hannah Brown 1840 (daughter of Thomas Brown, died in England), who was born Aug. 15, 1817. Their children: Alonzo b. 1840, d. childhood; Louisa b. 1842, d. infant; George b. Jan. 7, 1844, m. Mary Ann Kennel; Walter b. June 5, 1845, m. Elizabeth Hunter; William b. Sept. 11, 1847, m. Ann Welch; Mary Ann b. Aug. 21, 1849, m. James Lockland; Lorenzo b. Nov. 6, 1851, m. Elizabeth Jane Bitton; Samuel b. Nov. 15, 1854, m. Elizabeth Ann Etherington; Ezra Richard b. Nov. 14, 1859, m. Harriet Hipwell. Family home West Weber, Utah.
High priest. Blacksmith; worked several years in erection of Salt Lake temple making boilers and sharpening chisels; boiler maker by trade in England.

HADLEY, LORENZO (son of George Hadley and Hannah Brown). Born Nov. 6, 1851, at Werborghs, Derby, Eng.
Married Elizabeth Jane Bitton Nov. 6, 1876, at Ogden, Utah (daughter of John E. Bitton and Sarah Wintle, pioneers handcart company, 1857). She was born May 26, 1861, at West Weber, Utah. Their children: Hannah b. Sept. 3, 1877, m. Henry Williams; Sarah Jane b. April 27, 1879, m. Wheatley H. Gibson; Louisa b. Feb. 25, 1881, m. George Folkman; Mary Ann b. Jan. 2, 1883, m. George Goodell; Ida b. Oct. 23, 1885, m. Joseph Butler; Lorenzo B. b. March 30, 1887; Joseph E. b. Sept. 11, 1889, m. Florence Greenwell Feb. 12, 1908; Oscar E. b. April 4, 1892, m. Verna Greenwell July 2, 1910; Ada b. Sept. 25, 1895.

HADLEY, SAMUEL (son of George Hadley and Hannah Brown). Born Nov. 15, 1854, at Derby, Eng.
Married Elizabeth Ann Etherington April 16, 1877, at Ogden, Utah (daughter of Thomas Etherington and Sarah Wheeler), who was born Dec. 29, 1858, at Slaterville, Utah. Their children: Sarah Jane b. Feb. 21, 1878, deceased; Clara b. March 26, 1880, m. James J. Gibson June 17, 1901; John Etherington b. Aug. 24, 1882, m. Amy Alvord Dec. 1903; Edith Hannah b. Nov. 20, 1884, m. Thomas McLean Feb. 17, 1904; Elizabeth Ann b. Aug. 25, 1887, m. James B. Hunter, Jr. Dec. 1907; Samuel b. Nov. 22, 1889; Emily Alice b. Feb. 16, 1892; Thomas Albert b. Aug. 7, 1894; George Leland b. Sept. 30, 1896. Family home West Weber, Utah.
Seventy; missionary to England 1898-1900. Farmer and stockraiser.

HAFEN, JOHN GEORGE. Born in 1803 at Scherzligen, Canton Thurgau, Switzerland. Came to Utah Sept. 27, 1861, Sextus E. Johnson company.
Married Magdalena Hafen. Their children: Barbara b. 1835 (d. 1873), m. Ignaz Willi Oct. 18, 1861 (who died July 24, 1863); John George b. Oct. 17, 1838, m. Sussette Bosshard. Settled at Santa Clara, Utah, in 1861. Died in 1863.

HAFEN, JOHN GEORGE (son of John George and Magdalena Hafen). Born Oct. 17, 1838, at Scherzligen, Canton Thurgau, Switzerland. Came to Utah Sept. 27, 1861, Sextus E. Johnson company.
Married Susette Bosshard Oct. 18, 1861, Salt Lake City (daughter of John Bosshard and Katherine Egile). Their children: John; Emma; Edward, died; Herman; George, died; Adolph; Hermina, died; Sussette; Mina, died; Ernest.
Married Mary Ann Stucke in 1873 (daughter of Samuel Stucke and Magdalena Stadler). Their children: Albert; Mary; Bertha; Selina; Wilford, died; Lovina; Leroy.
Married Anna Elizabeth Huber in Nov. 1884 (daughter of Andreas Huber and Anna Elizabeth Gizar). Their children: August, died; Joseph; William and Heber, died; Franklin; Eliesi; Janette, died; Walter.

Married Rosena Stucke Blickenstorfer Feb. 28, 1885 (daughter of Samuel Stucke and Magdalena Stadler). Their children: Charles; Ellen; Viola.
Missionary to northern states in 1877 and to Switzerland 1882-84; bishop of Santa Clara ward, Nov. 1884 to Oct. 1912.

HAGUE, JAMES (son of James Hague of Sheffield, Eng.). Born in 1823. Came to Utah in 1852.
Married Sarah Ann Beaver in Sheffield in 1842. She was born Dec. 25, 1823. Their children: James, Jr., m. Sarah Carson; John Henry, m. Jane R. Peacock; Frank; Joseph, died; Sarah, m. D. G. Calder; George, died. Family home, Salt Lake City.
Gunsmith. Died in 1871; shipwrecked between U. S. A. and England on steamship Cambia.

HAGUE, JAMES, JR. (son of James Hague and Sarah Ann Beaver). Born Jan. 28, 1844, at Sheffield. Came to Utah in 1852.
Married Sarah Carson Jan. 1871 at Fairfield, Utah (daughter of John Carson and Elvira Egbert of Fairfield, pioneers 1851). She was born March 28, 1850. Their children: Margaret b. June 16, 1872; Charles b. Sept. 19, 1874, m. Ida Harmon; Dilla b. Nov. 10 1876; Effie b. Sept. 28, 1879, m. McCandless Moffet; Hazel b. March 2, 1885, died. Family home, Salt Lake City.
Business man. Died Aug. 13, 1911.

HAIGHT, CALEB (son of Samuel Haight of Dutchess county, N. Y.). Born Aug. 22, 1778. Came to Utah Sept. 22, 1847, Daniel Spencer company.
Married Keturah Horton Feb. 11, 1799. She was born May 28, 1777, and died Nov. 18, 1843, at Nauvoo, Ill. Their children: Oscar b. Nov. 14, 1800; Harriet Helen b. April 9, 1802, m. John Southard; Julia Ann b. Oct. 6, 1805, m. William Van Orden; David Bateman b. Oct. 18, 1808, m. Clarice Buckmyre; Hector Caleb b. Jan. 17, 1810, m. Julia Van Orden 1829; Isaac Chauncy b. May 17, 1813, m. Eliza Ann Snider; Eliza Caroline b. Feb. 2, 1816, m. Wesley Snider; Maria Antoinette b. July 25, 1818, m. Gob Canp Dibble; Catherine Adelia b. Nov. 28, 1820, m. Dorr P. Curtis. Family home Sempronius and Windham, N. Y.

HAIGHT, HECTOR CALEB (son of Caleb Haight and Keturah Horton). Born Jan. 17, 1810, in New York. Came to Utah in 1847 with second company.
Married Julia Van Orden (daughter of Peter Van Orden and Mary Crocker), who was born Jan. 19, 1811. Their children: Mary Adelia b. Jan. 1830, m. John L. Smith; Hector b. June 20, 1831, d. young; Horton David b. June 20, 1832, m. Louisa Leavitt 1854; Caleb b. July 22, 1834, d. young; William Van Orden b. Sept. 18, 1841, m. Louise Turner July 4, 1861. Family home Farmington, Utah.
Married Miss Weiler. Only child: Hector W., m. Nellie Clawson. Family home, Farmington.
Married Margaret Stewart 1876, Salt Lake City (daughter of David Stewart and Millie Wilson of Iowa), who was born March 27, 1850. Their children: Duane Miller (adopted); Isaac, died; Millie, m. John Duzan, m. Harry Thoburn; Meta, died; Cora, m. William H. Smith. Family home, Salt Lake City.
Missionary to Denmark 1855-58. Captain of infantry in Utah militia. Served as assessor and collector, sheriff and probate judge 1865-74, all in Davis Co., Utah. Hotel proprietor; farmer and stockraiser. Died June 29, 1882, at Farmington.

HAIGHT, WILLIAM VAN ORDEN (son of Hector Caleb Haight and Julia Van Orden). Born Sept. 18, 1841, in Stevenson county, Ill.
Married Louise Turner July 4, 1861, at Farmington, Utah (daughter of Henry Turner and Ann Steed, pioneers 1857, Captain Martin company). She was born Sept. 12, 1845, at Malvern, Worcestershire, Eng. Their children: William A. b. June 15, 1862, m. Mary E. France Dec. 7, 1882; Julia A. b. Dec. 8, 1864, m. William France Dec. 20, 1888; Henry C. b. July 24, 1868, m. Josephine Oviatt June 4, 1889; Alice L. b. March 9, 1871, m. Albert D. Ford Dec. 11, 1900; Lillian F. b. Jan. 20, 1879, m. James C. Brown Feb. 21, 1901; Grace E. b. Oct. 21, 1887, m. Alma Norman Jan. 26, 1910. Family home, Farmington.
Member of relief party sent to meet Martin handcart company in winter of 1856. Assisted in settlement of southern Utah in 1865. Served in Black Hawk War in 1866. Missionary to eastern states April 21, 1897-May 11, 1899. Farmer and stockraiser.

HAIR, JOHN (son of Jeremiah Hair and Bridget Murphy of Ireland). Born Aug. 15, 1821, at Newcastle, Northumberland, Eng. Came to Utah in Sept. 1864, Captain Chandler's train bringing freight.
Married Elizabeth Copeland in Oct. 1858 at Ryap, Durham, Eng. (daughter of Nicholas Copeland and Johanna Crazes of Sunderland, Eng.), who was born Feb. 3, 1838. Their children: Nicholas C., m. Mary E. Haddon; James, m. Martha Christianson; Elizabeth, d. infant; Joseph C., d. infant; Charles W., d. aged 4 years; George C., d. aged 2 years; John D., d. aged 2 years. Family home, Salt Lake City.
High priest; block teacher. Manager of lumber company. Died June 26, 1893, Salt Lake City.

HAIR, NICHOLAS C. (son of John Hair and Elizabeth Copeland). Born Oct. 21, 1859, at Southwick, Durham, Eng. Came to Utah Sept. 5, 1866, Captain White company.

Married Mary E. Haddon April 27, 1882, at Salt Lake City (daughter of Thomas C. Haddon and Elizabeth Cherry of Salt Lake City, pioneers 1852, A. O. Smoot company). She was born Feb. 15, 1860. Their children: John C. b. March 17, 1883, m. Lillie Waters; Thomas C. b. Nov. 19, 1885; William N. b. April 29, 1888, d. aged 23 years; Clifford b. July 7, 1890; Clarence b. Oct. 23, 1892, d. aged 4 years; Joseph b. Jan. 3, 1899. Family home, Salt Lake City. High priest; missionary to England 1904-06; Sunday school superintendent nine years; first counselor to Bishop William P. Waters of Bingham ward. Member school board of 43d district. Miner and engineer.

HALE, ALMA HELAMAN (son of Jonathan Harriman Hale and Olive Boyington, both of whom died at Council Bluffs, Iowa). Came to Utah 1848.
Married Elizabeth Walker. Their eldest child, Alma Helaman, m. Elizabeth Percinda Hendricks.
Married Sarah Ann Clark. Their eldest child, Ernest Frederick, m. Drucilla Harris.
Married Ellen V. Clark Aug. 19, 1865, Salt Lake City (daughter of Daniel Clark and Elizabeth Gower—the latter came to Utah Oct. 26, 1864, with William Hyde company, the former died crossing the plains to Utah). She was born Jan. 6, 1848, Colchester, Essex, Eng. Their children: Edgar Daniel b. Jan. 3, 1868, m. Emma Louisa Seamons Oct. 1, 1890; Aroet Clinton b. Aug. 17, 1869, m. Elizabeth A. Seamons Nov. 15, 1893; Arthur Willard b. July 3, 1871, m. Alice Jacobson Dec. 24, 1903; Franklin George b. July 10, 1874, m. Cora Hammond Nov. 17, 1897; Rosa Ellen b. Dec. 28, 1876, d. Aug. 13, 1897; Alvin Wilford b. Feb. 19, 1879, m. Julia Dean Oct. 9, 1907; Eugene Clark b. March 26, 1886, m. Sylvia L. Jensen June 2, 1909; Zina Emeline b. June 11, 1888, m. Melvin Barrus Dec. 22, 1909.
President of 31st quorum seventies, and later of 17th quorum; high priest; high councilor in Benson stake; missionary to eastern states; assisted in organizing first Sunday school in Grantsville, of which he served as teacher; stake superintendent of Sunday schools. Settled at Grantsville 1854. Participated in Echo Canyon war 1857, and also did considerable service as guard during the "Move" in 1858. In 1862 went to the Missouri river in Capt. Horne's company to assist the poor immigrants; on the return trip acted as wagonmaster and commissary. Moved to Cache Valley where he served as superintendent of Tooele County Co-op. Grist Mill. Constable and city marshal. Commissioned by Governor Durkee as captain's adjutant in territorial militia. Moved to Smithfield in 1888. Died March 30, 1908, Logan, Utah.

HALE, ALMA HELAMAN, JR. (son of Alma Helaman Hale and Elizabeth Walker).
Married Elizabeth Percinda Hendricks (daughter of Joseph S. Hendricks and Sariah Pew), who was born Dec. 16, 1867, Richmond, Utah. Their children: Elizabeth Percinda b. Sept. 5, 1886, m. Jasper M. Hammon Dec. 18, 1907; Mabel Fidelia b. March 20, 1889, m. Justin A. Knapp Aug. 17, 1909; Joseph A. b. May 16, 1893; Alta b. Aug. 25, 1895; Theolia b. Jan. 16, 1899; LeGrand Sheldon b. Oct. 1, 1901; Leila b. Aug. 10, 1905; Harold Hendricks b. Jan. 21, 1911. Family home Marysville, Idaho.
Oneida stake clerk; first counselor in presidency Y. M. M. I. A. Oneida stake; clerk Marysville ward; high councilor of Yellowstone stake.

HALE, ERNEST FREDERICK (son of Alma Helaman Hale and Sarah A. Clark). Born Sept. 4, 1863, Grantsville, Utah.
Married Drusilla Harris Feb. 23, 1887, Logan Temple, Utah (daughter of Eli McGee Harris and Elizabeth Gammell, who was born Sept. 25, 1868, Richmond, Utah. Their children: Drusilla b. Dec. 25, 1887, m. John Sorensen March 30, 1909; Grace b. June 8, 1890, m. Jesse Ford March 30, 1909; Pearl b. May 18, 1892; Ernest Grant b. April 3, 1894; Golden Harris b. April 12, 1897, d. May 20, 1907; Alminnie b. Jan. 31, 1901, d. May 28, 1907; Almannia b. Jan. 31, 1901; Douglas Ross b. July 22, 1903.
Married Mary Amanda Peterson June 19, 1907, Logan, Utah (daughter of John August Peterson and Maria Hansen, married 1854, Salt Lake Endowment House). She was born April 10, 1882, Logan. Their children: Leah b. June 12, 1908; Gladys b. March 26, 1910.
Ward teacher four years and Sunday school teacher several years; seventy. Settled in Gentile valley 1887, and served as superintendent of Sunday schools and home missionary. On Aug. 24, 1888, was called to preside over Mormon ward, Gentile valley; ordained high priest and bishop by Apostle Moses Thatcher; bishop of Cleveland ward; home missionary of Groveland ward, Blackfoot stake; missionary to Lost River country; member high council and superintendent religion classes Blackfoot stake. In his early years he was very skillful in handling wild horses, having broken to work about 200 head before he was 21 years old. Chief promoter of Gentile valley creamery, and served as its first manager; was overseer of the building of the plant and installing of the machinery. Founded the Cleveland Co-op. and became its first president. Assisted in the management and building of the bridges over Bear river in that section of the country. Member building committee and did a great deal of work on the Central building; worked as carpenter on Thatcher meeting house, and donated extensively toward the erection of the Preston academy. Moved to Groveland ward. Blackfoot, Idaho, 1905. Overseer of all the canals along the Sanke river through the southern part of Bingham county four years.

HALE, JONATHAN H. (son of Alma H. Hale and Sarah Ann Clark). Born Aug. 10, 1875, Grantsville, Utah.
Married Mary R. Moss April 28, 1897, Salt Lake City (daughter of Joseph Moss and Sarah P. Sessions, both born at Woods Cross, Utah). Their children: Blanch b. June 25, 1898; Horace b. March 26, 1900; Owen Moss b. Aug. 19, 1901; Mary b. Feb. 8, 1903; Joseph b. July 18, 1905; Sarah b. March 1, 1907; Nathan b. May 16, 1909; Ezra Foss b. May 29, 1911; Olive b. April 5, 1913. Family resided Smithfield, Utah, and Groveland, Idaho.
One of presidency 147th quorum seventies; missionary to Tennessee 1894-96; Sunday school superintendent; stake superintendent Mutual Improvement Association; president elders' quorum. School trustee. Farmer and dairyman.

HALE, EDGAR DANIEL (son of Alma Helaman Hale and Ellen V. Clark). Born Jan. 3, 1868, at Grantsville, Utah.
Married Emma Louisa Seamons Oct. 1, 1890, at Logan, Utah (daughter of Samuel Seamons and Louisa Emily Griffith, the former a pioneer with William B. Preston company). She was born April 18, 1871, at Hyde Park, Utah. Their children: Varian Edgar b. June 25, 1891; Raymond Seamons b. June 4, 1893, m. Faunt Killian Dec. 14, 1911; Arden Delos b. Oct. 3, 1895; Rhoda Louisa b. Sept. 24, 1898; Lyman Maesar b. March 17, 1901; Merlin Alma b. Nov. 16, 1903; Clayton Samuel b. Nov. 24, 1906; Calvin Leroy b. Aug. 1, 1909; Karl Griffith b. Dec. 2, 1911. Family resided Grantsville, Utah. Gentile Valley and Blackfoot, Idaho.
Engaged in Sunday school work as teacher and in superintendency almost continuously 1887-1909. Secretary elders' quorums 1891-1903 and 1905 to present. Justice of peace in Bingham county, Idaho, 1910. Farmer.

HALE, AROET CLINTON (son of Alma Helaman Hale and Ellen V. Clark). Born Aug. 17, 1869, at Grantsville, Utah.
Married Elizabeth Alferetta Scamons Nov. 15, 1893, at Logan, Utah (daughter of Samuel Seamons, pioneer, William B. P. company, and Louisa E. Seamons). She was born July 28, 1873, at Hyde Park, Utah. Their children: Elmer Clinton b. Nov. 1, 1894; Katie Louisa b. Oct. 12, 1897; Orvin Melrose b. April 27, 1900; Delos Griffith b. Sept. 19, 1902; Ferrin Alma b. May 1, 1905. Family resided Grantsville, Utah, Gentile Valley and Groveland, Idaho.
Member Mound Valley ward bishopric four years; member Blackfoot stake Sunday school board since June 1905, and of the religion class board since Aug. 1911. Farmer.

HALE, ARTHUR WILLARD (son of Alma Helaman Hale and Ellen Victoria Clark). Born July 3, 1871, at Grantsville, Utah.
Married Alice Evangeline Jacobson Dec. 24, 1902, at Logan, Utah (daughter of Julius W. D. Jacobson and Hannah Evangeline Hall, who came to Utah in July 1877). She was born Nov. 3, 1879, at Salt Lake City. Their children: Rosalind b. May 13, 1906; Whitney Bryan b. May 3, 1911, d. May 16, 1911; Bernice, b. April 20, 1912. Family resided Logan, Utah, and Blackfoot, Idaho.
Missionary to Logan Temple 18 months 1897-98; missionary to California 1898-1902. At time of marriage settled in Logan, Utah; moved to Blackfoot, Idaho 1905. Class leader and president Y. M. M. I. A.; ward and Sunday school teacher.

HALE, AROET LUCIUS (son of Jonathan Harriman Hale, born Feb. 1, 1800, and Olive Boyington, born July 19, 1805, at Bradford, Mass.—married Sept. 1, 1825). Born May 18, 1828, at Dover, N. H. Came to Utah Sept. 1848 with Heber C. Kimball company.
Married Olive Whittle Sept. 5, 1849 (daughter of Thomas Whittle and Amelia Fullmer, pioneers of Sept. 1848 with Heber C. Kimball company), who was born Dec. 9, 1833, in Canada; died Sept. 14, 1860, at Grantsville, Utah. Their children: Aroet Lucius b. June 6, 1850, m. Eliza Ann Lee Sept. 11, 1869; Olive Amelia b. July 11, 1852, m. Henry Sagers Oct. 11, 1869, died, and Robert E. Reed April 17, 1906; Jonathan Harriman b. Jan. 19, 1854, m. Eliza Clegg Jan. 3, 1876; Thomas Whittle b. Nov. 29, 1855, d. Nov. 13, 1880; Rachel Susan b. Dec. 1, 1857, m. Thomas Clark Jan. 4, 1875; Solomon Elliphet b. March 22, 1859, m. Louisa Hunter May 7, 1889. Family home, Grantsville, Utah.
Married Louisa Phippen; divorced three months after marriage. Their child: Esther b. Nov. 28, 1859, m. Joseph Acuff Aug. 17, 1878.
Married Louisa Cook Dec. 24, 1861, at Grantsville, Utah (daughter of Henry Cook and Martha Morris, pioneers of Sept. 1864), who was born Jan. 25, 1837 at Chichester, Essex, Eng. Came to Utah Sept. 15, 1851, with William B. Preston company. Died May 20, 1910, at Grantsville, Utah. Their children: Aroetta b. Nov. 24, 1862, m. Thomas A. Judd Jan. 6, 1886, d. April 4, 1889, and John H. Holgate Sept. 12, 1894; Clarissa Louisa b. Sept. 30, 1864, m. William S. Matthews May 7, 1889; Henry Little b. Oct. 28, 1866, d. Nov. 21, 1866; Leonard Wilford b. March 2, 1869, m. Rosa Judd April 11, 1887; Phoebe Elizabeth b. Aug. 7, 1877, m. Joseph P. Mecham May 29, 1890; Sarah A. b. Sept. 4, 1874, d. Dec. 5, 1888; Frank George b. March 27, 1877, m. Grace Robinson April 23, 1907; Janet b. March 6, 1880, m. John W. Anderson Oct. 21, 1903. Family home Grantsville, Utah.
Married Charlotte Cook March 18, 1866, at Salt Lake City (daughter of Henry Cook and Martha Morris, pioneers with John Murdock company). She was born March 7, 1844, in Sussex, Eng. Their children: George Edward b. April 4, 1867, d. Sept. 18, 1881; Alma Fredrick b. March 11, 1870, m. Eliza S. McCombs May 16, 1889; Lottie b. Dec. 5, 1872, m.

Davis Hunter May 19, 1890; Benjamin Walter b. Nov. 20, 1874, m. Susan Idella Cazier Feb. 5, 1903; Martha Harriet b. Feb. 25, 1876, d. July 21, 1892; Morris James b. May 19, 1878, m. Lois Call May 9, 1900; Mary Lulu b. Oct. 20, 1882, m. Ira A. Call April 3, 1903; Amy Lucile b. April 5, 1884, m. William A. Osmond March 13, 1907; Louie Ann b. Oct. 10, 1887, m. Willard Call Sept. 23, 1909. Family home Afton, Wyo.
Drummer boy in Nauvoo Legion at time of martyrdom of Joseph and Hyrum Smith. Scout and hunter on journey to Utah. First settled at Salt Lake City, but later moved to Tooele. Served in Walker Indian war; commissioned by Brigham Young, June 10, 1854, second lieutenant Company A battalion of life guards, cavalry, G. S. L. military district; commissioned by Governor Durkee, May 16, 1868, adjutant second battalion infantry, Nauvoo Legion at Tooele; paymaster of G. S. L. military district. In company with Dimick B. Huntington secured the body, papers, etc. of Lieutenant Gunnison after he was killed by the Indians in southern Utah. Assisted in settlement of "Muddy" and Las Vegas, Nev.; served as member of bishopric at former. Member first bishopric Grantsville, Utah; member Tooele stake high council 24 years; patriarch. Died Dec. 13, 1911.

HALE, AROET LUCIUS II. (son of Aroet Lucius Hale and Olive Whittle). Born June 6, 1850, at Salt Lake City.
Married Eliza Ann Lee Sept. 11, 1869, at Salt Lake City (daughter of Isaac Lee and Julia Ann Chapman, pioneers 1852). Their children: Aroet Lucius b. Dec. 20, 1870, m. Eliza E. Yeaman May 7, 1890; Isaac Lee b. Aug. 8, 1872, m. Mary Hyde Oct. 11, 1900; Jonathan Harriman b. Oct. 9, 1875, m. Alice Moffett April 3, 1900; William W. b. May 14, 1878, m. Ella Brown Oct. 5, 1905; Casper A. b. Dec. 11, 1880, m. Matilda Thurman July 1, 1903; George A. b. Feb. 22, 1890; Thomas E. b. Jan. 9, 1893. Family home Afton, Wyo.
Teamster in Captain Mumford's company, one of last to cross the plains with immigrants in 1868. Settled in Bear Lake Valley 1869, and in Star Valley, Wyo., 1885. Member of first high council Star Valley stake. City councilman. Business manager of the building of the Star Valley Stake Tabernacle.

HALE, AROET LUCIUS III. (son of Aroet Lucius Hale and Eliza Ann Lee). Born Dec. 20, 1870 at Liberty, Idaho.
Married Eliza E. Yeaman May 7, 1890 (daughter of Thomas Yeaman and Martha Moore), who was born Sept. 27, 1872, at Huntsville, Utah. Their children: Eliza Pearl b. Sept. 1, 1891, m. Joseph Michaelson Oct. 5, 1910; Aroet Leo b. June 18, 1893; Myrtle A. b. Nov. 8, 1895; Louis Holbert b. Dec. 17, 1897; Hazel Bell b. Oct. 17, 1900; Eugene b. Oct. 29, 1902; William Le Roy b. Nov. 13, 1904; Edward Everett b. Oct. 28, 1906; Walter Barber b. March 20, 1908. Family home Afton, Wyo.

HALE, BENJAMIN WALTER (son of Aroet Lucius Hale and Charlotte Cook). Born Nov. 20, 1874, at Grantsville, Utah.
Married Susan Idella Cazier Feb. 5, 1903, at Logan, Utah (daughter of Charles Gates Cazier and Susan Bingham), who was born June 20, 1884, at Bennington, Idbo. Their children: Izora b. May 10, 1904; Charles Benjamin b. Oct. 6, 1907; Edward Cazier b. Dec. 3, 1911.
Seventy; missionary to southwestern states.

HALE, MORRIS J. (son of Aroet Lucius Hale and Charlotte Cook). Born May 19, 1879, at Grantsville.
Married Lois Call May 9, 1900, at Logan, Utah (daughter of Joseph H. Call and Sarah Isabel Barlow of Bountiful, Utah), who was born May 28, 1880, at Bountiful. Their children: Lamar M. b. March 21, 1901; Hattie L. b. Dec. 28, 1902; Vasco Lester b. Feb. 10, 1905; Charlotte Isabel b. March 15, 1907, d. July 4, 1908; Clarence b. June 14, 1909; Wilford b. May 30, 1911. Family home Afton, Wyo.
Member 103d quorum seventies; president elders quorum 1899-1905; stake superintendent Y. M. M. I. A. since 1909. At Afton served as city marshal 1902-04; member city council 1906-11; mayor of Afton 1911-13. Farmer and stockraiser.

HALE, SOLOMON HENRY (son of Jonathan Harriman Hale and Olive Boyington of Quincy, Ill., both of whom died at Council Bluffs, Iowa, Sept. 1846, leaving four children, Aroet Lucius, Rachel, Alma Helaman and Solomon Henry, all of whom came to Utah in 1848). Born April 25, 1833, at Quincy, Ill. Came to Utah 1848 with Heber C. Kimball company.
Married Anna Clark April 17, 1863 (daughter of Samuel Clark and Rebecca Garner), who was born April 19, 1841. Their children: Solomon Henry b. May 30 1864, m. Ginerva Nowlin Dec. 8, 1886; Jonathan Joseph b. July 26, 1867, d. March 12, 1876; Samuel Clark b. April 24, 1870, d. Feb. 7, 1876; Hattie Vilate b. Sept. 18, 1872, m. Milton H. Thatcher June 11, 1890, d. Aug. 1908; Arta D'Christa b. April 19, 1877, d. June 29, 1878; Heber Quincy b. March 5, 1880, m. Bessie Gudmundson Jan. 17, 1906; Aroet Alma b. Oct. 29, 1881, m. Florence Belnap Nov. 5, 1906; Anna LaVinna b. Aug. 14, 1884, m. James H. Cannon April 5, 1911.
After coming to Utah resided at Salt Lake and Farmington until 1854. Went with herd of cattle with first settlers to Cache Valley 1856, but returned to Salt Lake at time of Johnston's army invasion in 1857. Expert horseman, broke wild horses for pony express company in 1862; commissioned by President Abraham Lincoln as wagonmaster for Utah volunteers company, which set in order stage stations and telegraph line between Salt Lake and Missouri river, which had been destroyed or damaged by Indians. Headed exploring party into Bear river valley 1856, and into Bear lake valley 1857. Settled at Liberty, Idaho, 1865, and at Soda Springs 1872, and in Gentile valley 1875. Engaged heavily in stockraising. Member Bear lake stake high council 1865-75; first counselor in Oneida stake presidency 1884-1907. Moved to Preston, Idaho, 1890, where he superintended erection of Oneida stake academy. Indian interpreter. Commissioner Oneida county, Idaho; elected mayor of Preston, 1907.

HALES, CHARLES H. (son of Stephen and Mary Ann Hales, of Rainham, Kent, Eng.). Born June 17, 1817, in Kent. Came to Canada in 1832, and to Utah in September, 1852.
Married Julia Ann Lockwood Oct. 31, 1839, at Quincy, Ill. (daughter of George Lockwood and Anas Gillet, of Buffalo, N. Y., pioneers Sept. 1852). She was born Aug. 10, 1824. Their children: Julia A.; Stephen F.; Eliza Ann; George G.; Mary L.; Charles H.; Joseph L.; John T.; William H.; Mariah J.; Jonathan H.; Harriet E. Family home Spanish Fork, Utah.
Seventy; home missionary; member Spanish Fork choir. School trustee; member city council. Farmer and brickmason. Died July 1, 1889, at Spanish Fork.

HALES, JOSEPH LOCKWOOD (son of Charles H. Hales and Julia Ann Lockwood). Born Jan. 16, 1851, at Garden Grove, Decatur county, Iowa. Came to Utah with parents.
Married Mary Jane Berry Feb. 21, 1875, at Salt Lake City (daughter of John W. Berry and Jane E. Thomas, of Spanish Fork, pioneers 1847, Jedediah M. Grant company). She was born Aug. 24, 1855. Their children: Jane I. b. June 6, 1876; Julia E. b. March 16, 1878; Lauretta b. April 9, 1880; Elenor b. Jan. 27, 1882, d. Feb. 21, 1882; Zina D. b. April 8, 1885; Lester J. b. April 26, 1894. Family home Spanish Fork.
High priest; missionary to Arizona 1881-89; bishop's aid; member presidency of elders' quorum. Farmer and stockraiser.

HALES, HENRY WILLIAM (son of Stephen and Mary Ann Hales, of Kent, Eng.). Born Aug. 7, 1829, at Rainham, Kent, Eng. Came to Utah in September, 1857.
Married Eliza Ann Ewing May 19, 1850, at Garden Grove, Iowa (daughter of Alexander Ewing and Sarah Ann Lehman, latter a pioneer, Sept. 17, 1850, David Evans company). She was born April 4, 1830, at Philadelphia, Pa. Their children: Stephen Alexander b. Feb. 22, 1851, m. Nancy Ann Peterson; Rebecca Jane b. Dec. 27, 1852, m. Wm. Spencer and J. R. Hall; Eliza Ann b. June 9, 1855; Henry William b. Dec. 23, 1857, m. Mary Hannah Carson; Thomas Bradford b. May 14, 1860; Mary Isabel b. Nov. 21, 1862, m. Nathan W. Bailey; George Lawrence b. Oct. 17, 1865; Harriet b. Feb. 5, 1867, m. Geo. F. Stanley; Richard b. Jan. 13, 1871, m. Elizabeth Wilson. Family resided Little Cottonwood, Cedar Fort, Enterprise and Deseret, Utah.
Married Sarah Jane McKinney Jan. 11, 1857, at Salt Lake City (daughter of Hugh McKinney and Sarah Ann Lehman, pioneers Sept. 17, 1850, David Evans company). She was born Oct. 30, 1838, at Philadelphia, Pa. Their children: Sarah Jane b. March 2, 1858, m. Taylor Crosby; Charles Henry b. Nov. 19, 1859, m. Eliza McKinney; Hugh b. March 27, 1861; Joseph William b. Nov. 22, 1862, m. Christena Hansen; Jacob Lehman b. March 11, 1864, m. Mary Crafts; Albert b. Nov. 27, 1865, m. Emma Sloan; Mary Ann b. Oct. 9, 1868; Matilda b. March 11, 1870; Martha Elizabeth b. Sept. 26, 1871, m. Percy Crafts; George Alven b. May 16, 1873, m. Anna Warnick; Lillie May b. May 20, 1875, m. Joshua R. Mickleson; John Smith b. Feb. 19, 1877, m. Rebecca Mickleson; Horace Franklin b. April 21, 1879, m. Erma Hansen; Roy b. June 9, 1881; Isa b. Oct. 1, 1883. Family home, Deseret.
Member bishopric Peterson ward, Morgan stake, 1861; presiding elder Lake town 1867-91; patriarch 1901, until his death. County road commissioner. Died June 25, 1909, at Woods Cross, Utah.

HALES, STEPHEN ALEXANDER (son of Henry William Hales and Eliza Ann Ewing). Born Feb. 22, 1851, at Appanoose, Ill.
Married Nancy Ann Peterson May 30, 1868, at Salt Lake City (daughter of Charles S. Peterson and Ann Patten of Alpine, Peterson and Plymouth, Utah, pioneers Feb. 1850). She was born March 30, 1852. Their children: Nancy Ann b. Oct. 24, 1869, m. Joseph Kelley; Stephen Alexander b. Sept. 12, 1871, m. Mary Ellen Fox; Charles Henry b. Sept. 29, 1873, m. Joanna L. Kennard; George Robert b. Feb. 9, 1876, m. Kate Kennard; Albert William b. May 19, 1878, m. Maud Chamberlain; Rosalie b. July 1, 1880, m. John McComie; Mable b. Oct. 20, 1882, m. David McComie; John Alma b. May 9, 1885, m. Edith May Covenington; Earl Bradford b. Feb. 11, 1888, m. Marion Nye; Manetta b. Jan. 21, 1891. Family resided Peterson, Enterprise, Cedar Fort and Riverside, Utah.

HALES, HENRY WILLIAM (son of Henry William Hales and Eliza Ann Ewing). Born Dec. 23, 1857, at Riverside, Utah.
Married Mary H. Carson June 12, 1889, at Iona, Idaho (daughter of George W. Carson and Agatha Morgan, of Iowa). She was born Oct. 5, 1867. Their children: Ethel b. Aug. 28, 1890; Lenorda b. Nov. 23, 1892; Hazel b. Oct. 21, 1894; Clara b. Aug. 21, 1897; Clarence b. Aug. 21, 1897; Florence Edna b. Oct. 26, 1901; Olive b. Oct. 5, 1903; Harold Wynne b. Aug. 28, 1908. Family home Park City, Utah.
City councilman 1899; county commissioner 1908-12. Teamster.

HALES, RICHARD FRANKLIN (son of Henry William Hales and Eliza Ann Ewing). Born Jan. 13, 1871, Enterprise, Utah. Married Lizzie Linzy Wilson June 23, 1897, Park City, Utah (daughter of William Walter Wilson and Emily Mansfield Gray, Midway, Utah, pioneers Aug. 7, 1856). Their children: Mont Richard b. July 31, 1898; William Mansfield b. July 9, 1902. Family home Park City, Utah. Superintendent of Daly Judge mill.

HALES, GEORGE (son of Stephen Hales of Province of Ontario, Canada). Born 1813, in England. Came to Utah with a contingent of the Mormon Battalion. Married Sarah Ann Gregory, Nauvoo, Ill. (daughter of William Gregory of Ione, Ill.). She was born Jan. 26, 1814. Their children: Mary, m. Hyrum Burgess; Charles, m. Eva May Burgess. Family home Beaver, Utah. Married Louisa Tripp, Salt Lake City (daughter of John Tripp and Jess Ess of Salt Lake City). She was born 1825. Their children: Libbie, m. William Bird; Willard, m. Jean Frasier; Rena, m. Sheff Tanner; Caroline, m. Frank Talton; Harriet, m. Julius Bearnson; Rhoda, m. Rollin Tanner; Bartlet. Family home Beaver, Utah. High priest; ward teacher. Justice of peace. Member Nauvoo Legion. One of the earliest workers in Deseret News printing office at Richfield, Utah. Printer and shoemaker. Died 1898, Beaver, Utah.

HALES, CHARLES (son of George Hales and Sarah Ann Gregory). Born March 26, 1865, Beaver, Utah. Married Eva May Burgess Oct. 24, 1887, Huntington, Utah (daughter of Wilmer Burgess and Jane Heath of Huntington). She was born May 1, 1872. Their children: Tressa b. Aug. 6, 1888, d. infant; May b. Feb. 27, 1890, d. child; Leona b. Feb. 6, 1892, m. Lewis Conrad; Edgar b. Oct. 2, 1893; Bertha b. April 16, 1896; John b. May 14, 1898; Vera b. Aug. 10, 1900; Afton b. Jan. 18, 1903; Frank b. March 22, 1905; Feron and Fern b. Oct. 21, 1908; Clarence b. Jan. 9, 1911, d. infant. Family home Winter Quarters, Utah. Elder; ward teacher. Carpenter and car repairer for Utah Fuel company 12 years.

HALGREN, TRULS A. (son of Asser Sven Halgren and Ingre Truelson of Klorup, Malmöhuslan, Sweden). Born Jan. 5, 1835, at Klorup. Came to Utah Oct. 5, 1864, Isaac Canfield company. Married Clara Bjurling May 22, 1864, on Atlantic ocean (daughter of John Eric Bjurling and Anna Greta Isaacson of Kulla, Sweden). She was born April 11, 1840. Their children: Asser Theodore, died; Ellen Wilhelmina, m. Daniel Hamer; Annie Magdalene, m. Parley T. Wright; Alma, died; Clara Sophie and Olivia Victoria, died; Joseph; Ottelia, m. Parley M. Perry. Family home Ogden, Utah. Member 53d quorum seventies; missionary to Sweden 1858-64 and 1889-91. Machinist. Died Sept. 4, 1892.

HALL, BENJAMIN K. Born Nov. 7, 1793, New York. Came to Utah in October, 1850, Captain Bennett company. Married Mehitabel Sawyer 1827, Maine (daughter of Amos Sawyer of Maine), who was born Oct. 1, 1806. Their children: Horace Loomis b. March 3, 1828; Eliza M. b. May 22, 1830; Dorothy Merrill b. Dec. 31, 1831; Mary K. b. Aug. 19, 1833; Katherine b. July 9, 1835; Helen S. b. April 18, 1837; Louisa Maria b. Dec. 30, 1839; William Henry b. Sept. 30, 1842; Benjamin Frank b. April 15, 1847. Family home Ogden, Utah. Seventy. Broom-maker and farmer. Died in 1882, Ogden, Utah.

HALL, DAVID (son of William Hall, born Feb. 13, 1778, and Anna Copeland, of Danville, Ill., born April 23, 1786). Came to Utah Aug. 29, 1862, Lewis Brunson company. Married Jane Hale July 23, 1850, in Vermilion county, Ill. (daughter of Elijah B. Hale and Mary Hoskins), who was born Nov. 20, 1832; pioneers, Lewis Brunson company. Their children: Mary Ann b. Oct. 25, 1852, m. Levi John; Leroy b. Nov. 13, 1865, m. Julia A. Harris; Racine b. Oct. 23, 1857, m. Anna Green; Philene b. Aug. 26, 1863, m. Isaac E. D. Zundel; Almira b. Dec. 5, 1865, m. William Orgill; David W. b. Oct. 10, 1867, m. Eliza Halford; Jane Orgill; Julia B. b. Oct. 16, 1869, m. Isaac David Zundel; Letha Jane b. Oct. 6, 1873, d. Oct. 23, 1874; Elijah Dotson b. Oct. 23, 1875. Family home West Portage, Utah. Served as superintendent of Portage Sunday school 1883-88; as superintendent of Malad stake Sunday school 1888-90. High councilor. Died April 10, 1902.

HALL, EBER W. (son of Selden S. and Larinda M. Hall of Burlingame, Kan., but formerly of Ohio). He was born March 21, 1868, at Brighton, Ohio. Came to Utah April 11, 1897. Married Artie L. Pratt April 8, 1897, Burlingame, Kan. (daughter of Hyrum B. Pratt and Mary Hoover of Burlingame), who was born Feb. 19, 1874. Their children: Bernice; Howard Pratt; Gwendolyn; Genevieve. Family home Salt Lake City, Utah. Funeral director.

HALL, EDWARD (son of Jacob Hall and Polly Pritchard of Waterbury, New Haven county, Conn.). Born Nov. 15, 1813, Waterbury. Came to Utah Sept. 2, 1850, David Evans company. Married Nancy Eleanor Ballinger Feb. 2, 1842, at Jamestown, Russell county, Ky. (daughter of Thomas Ballinger and Mary Ann Hartley of Jamestown, Ky., pioneers Sept. 2, 1850, David Evans company). She was born Oct. 23, 1826. Their children: Mary Ann, m. Lorenzo Johnson; William Isaac, m. Lydia Thorn; Sarah Jane, m. Philip Houtz; John Thomas, died young; James Edward, m. Katie Wiggins; Nephi Edwin, killed by accident; Joseph Smith, m. Sarah Sophrona Perry; Martha Elennor, m. Richard H. Thorn; Harriet Elizabeth, m. Robert A. Hutchinson; Julia Roseltha and Lydia Mariah, died young. Family home Springville, Utah. Elder. Farmer. Died Aug. 26, 1886, Provo, Utah.

HALL, HENRY, of St. Clair, Ala. Married Amanda Elizabeth Andrews 1855, in Floyd county, Ga. (daughter of Samuel Andrews and Elizabeth Potts, who lived seven miles north of Rome, Floyd county, Ga., came to Utah Oct. 1, 1869). She was born June 6, 1833. Their children: Mary Elizabeth, m. Peter Brown; Martha Frances, m. Burdell Davis. Family home Provo, Utah.

HALL, JOSHUA. Came to Utah with oxteam. Married Sally ——. Their children: Lee, m. Emma Richardson; Gord; Iowa, m. Mary Elizabeth Grow; Chellis, m. Lola Elmer; Orson, m. Eliza Tracy; Mary, m. George Ramey. Family home Beaver, Utah.

HALL, IOWA (son of Joshua and Sally Hall). Born in Iowa. Married Mary Elizabeth Grow, at Salt Lake City. Their children: Henry C. b. Oct. 2, 1871, m. Elizabeth Merkley; Mary Elizabeth, m. John Hacking; Sarah Melissa, m. Charles Davis; Iowa Jefferson, m. Mina Adams; Mark, m. Myrtle Arnold; Joseph, m. Ethel Dolman; Rutha May, m. Lee Caldwell; Orson E., m. Marinda Allen; Charles William, m. Effie Peters; Cloe Mariah, m. Quince Johnson; Alfred. Family home Huntsville, Utah. Farmer. Died April 9, 1905, Dry Forks, Utah.

HALL, HENRY C. (son of Iowa Hall and Mary Elizabeth Grow). Born Oct. 2, 1871, Huntsville, Utah. Married Elizabeth Merkley Dec. 24, 1893, Maeser ward, Vernal, Utah (daughter of Nelson Merkley and Sarah Jane Sanders of Cedar Fort, Utah). She was born Dec. 29, 1871. Their children: Henry Grant b. July 22, 1895; James Arthur b. Oct. 21, 1897; Wallace Edgar b. Sept. 30, 1900; Mary Elizabeth b. Dec. 30, 1902; Nelson Albion b. Aug. 18, 1904; Helen Laverne b. April 9, 1906; Sarah May b. June 18, 1911. Family resided Dry Fork and Hayden, Utah. Road supervisor. Farmer and lumberman.

HALL, NEWTON DANIEL (son of Daniel Hall and Sarah Loomis). Born March 12, 1819, at Byron, N. Y. Came to Utah Sept. 28, 1847, Vincent Shurtliff company. Married Sarah Jane Busenbark 1843 in New York state (daughter of Isaac Busenbark and Abigail Manning of Niagara county, N. Y.; the former came to Utah in 1849, the latter died on the plains), who was born March 2, 1825. Their children: Louisa Jane; Newton D.; Mary E.; Lemira; Lewna; Byron H.; Alice; Ephraim; Lydia; Calvin, m. Cenia Iverson. Seventy; ward teacher. Died March 11, 1889, at Washington, Utah.

HALL, CALVIN (son of Newton Daniel Hall and Sarah Jane Busenbark). Born Aug. 6, 1865, at Providence, Utah. Married Cenia Iverson June 26, 1885, at St. George, Utah (daughter of Hans Peter Iverson and Anne D. Niason of Denmark, pioneers 1859, Robert F. Neslen company), who was born Dec. 5, 1865. Their children (adopted): Caddie. Family home Washington, Utah. Bishop; superintendent Sunday school; missionary to central states 1898 to 1901. City recorder. Merchant; farmer.

HALL, THOMAS (son of Robert Hall of Scotland and Elizabeth Miller of England). Born Sept. 1, 1816, at Liverpool. Came to Utah 1851 with Alfred Cardon company. Married Ann Hughes 1840 (daughter of Samuel Hughes and Hannah Bevan), who was born Dec. 30, 1817. Their children: Samuel P. b. March 17, 1841, m. Margaret Williamson Feb. 2, 1864; Joseph S. b. Aug. 21, 1843, m. Margaret Hill; Thomas E. b. Jan. 18, 1846, m. Henrietta Pearce; James H. b. Sept. 8, 1850, m. Cyrenia Nebeker; Hannah M. b. July 27, 1854, m. Ellis W. Wiltbank; Brigham Y. b. Sept. 29, 1856, William H. b. June 24, 1859. Family resided Salt Lake City, Wellsville and St. George. Married Hannah Stephens. Their child: Sarah A. b. Oct. 26, 1856, m. Charles Brizzie. Resided in Salt Lake City from Oct. 1851 to 1860; later went to Las Vegas, Nev., then to Wellsville, Utah, and later was called to Dixie, settling at St. George. Missionary to Canada. Died at St. George at age of 78 years.

HALL, SAMUEL P. (son of Thomas Hall and Ann Hughes). Born March 17, 1841, at Liverpool, Eng. Married Margaret Williamson Feb. 2, 1864, at Wellsville, Utah (daughter of James Williamson and Mary Rae, the former a pioneer, 1851, Alfred Cardon company). She was born Jan. 25, 1844, at Slamannan, Scotland. Their children: Samuel W. b. Nov. 29, 1864, m. Catherine Stuart; Thomas W. b. Oct. 7, 1866, m. Jemima Gunnell; James W. b. Dec. 2, 1868, m. Martha Owen; William W. b. Jan. 4, 1871, m. Antoinette Larsen; Hyrum W. b. Aug. 27, 1873, m. Margaret Hill; Margaret W. b. Feb. 18, 1876; John Rae W. b. Nov. 26, 1878, m. Alice Nuttall; David W. b. July 1, 1881, d. April 1888; Leroy W. b. Oct. 6, 1883, m. Barbara Allan. Family home Wellsville, Utah.
Farmer.

HALL, JOSEPH SMITH (son of Thomas Hall and Ann Hughes). Born Aug. 21, 1843, at Hawarden, North Wales. Came to Utah 1851 with Alfred Cardon company.
Married Margaret Hill Jan. 20, 1865, at Salt Lake City (daughter of John Hill and Margaret Brice), who was born Nov. 28, 1844. Their children: Margaret A. b. Dec. 2, 1865, m. Daniel Price (died in 1895) and John Timothy (died in 1899); Mary E. b. Dec. 26, 1867, m. Absalom Bybee; Joseph H. b. Nov. 28, 1869, m. Henrietta Bronson; Rebecca b. Oct. 22, 1871, m. Parley Inglet; Hannah M. b. Jan. 30, 1874, m. Thomas Thompson; Thomas J. b. Oct. 29, 1876, m. Carrie M. Cafferty (died Aug. 4, 1904), m. Harriet Bodily Aug. 7, 1907; Julia b. Dec. 21, 1878, m. William E. Steers; Sarah A. b. Feb. 14, 1881, m. Thomas W. Jenkins; William Roy b. May 5, 1883, m. Caroline Smith; Zina b. March 15, 1886, m. Thomas Eugene Peck; Loretta b. Nov. 29, 1887, m. William D. Gilbert; Wilford b. Sept. 25, 1889, m. Ada Gilbert. Family home Fairview, Idaho.
Died April 9, 1908, at Fairview.

HALL, JOSEPH H. (son of Joseph Smith Hall and Margaret Hill). Born Nov. 28, 1867, at Wellsville, Utah.
Married Henrietta Bronson Feb. 8, 1893, at Logan, Utah (daughter of E. H. Bronson and Lydia Cole of Fairview, Idaho), who was born Dec. 24, 1873, at Willard, Utah. Their children: Joseph H. b. July 14, 1894; Henry I. b. March 28, 1896; Orva C. b. Dec. 19, 1897; Orlan E. b. Jan. 2, 1902; Margaret A. b. July 16, 1904; Willis Loyd b. May 14, 1911.

HALLS, JOHN (son of William Halls and Louisa C. Enderby). Born July 11, 1872, Huntsville, Utah.
Married Mary J. Grow Feb. 15, 1895, Logan, Utah (daughter of John W. Grow and Catherine McKay), who was born Sept. 1, 1874, Huntsville, Utah. Their children: Milton E. b. Feb. 4, 1901; Julian W. b. Dec. 10, 1903; Edna b. Sept. 9, 1909. Family home Huntsville, Utah.
Second counselor in bishopric of Huntsville ward; bishop same ward. City councilman at Huntsville; member county board of education of Weber county 1908. School teacher.

HALLADAY, ABRAHAM (son of William Halladay and Sarah Batchalor of Allesley, Warwickshire, Eng.). Born Aug. 24, 1824, at Fillongley, Warwickshire. Came to Utah Sept. 13, 1852, with Warren Snow company.
Married Mary Ann Beesley Jan. 27, 1845, at Chilverston, Eng. She was born May 25, 1825. Their children: William A. m. Mary Ann Price; George, died; Daniel Henry, m. Harriet Carter; Sarah Ann, m. Albert Jones; Abraham E., m. Mary Chadwick; George; Mary Elizabeth, died; Mary Ann, m. William K. Farrer; John Franklin, m. Elizabeth A. Jones. Family home Provo, Utah.
Married Ellen Reese at Salt Lake City (daughter of Thomas Reese and Hagar Pugh of Wales). Their children: Thomas, died; Joseph R.; Ellen Ann, m. William Mildenhall; Walter R., m. Rachel McDonald; David R., m. Annie Cooper; James A., m. Isabell Lamb; Mary E., m. Alvin Boardman; Arthur A., m. Agnes Florence Sorenson; Phyllis, m. William R. Horne.
High priest; missionary to England 1881; high councilor; assistant Sunday school superintendent; acting bishop. Deputy sheriff; city councilman. Farmer; merchant.
Died May 12, 1906, Provo, Utah.

HALLADAY, ABRAHAM E. (son of Abraham Halladay and Mary Ann Beesley). Born Feb. 17, 1856, at Provo, Utah.
Married Mary Chadwick May 13, 1885, at Logan (daughter of William R. Chadwick and Susannah Drew of London, Eng.; the latter came to Utah Sept. 1852). She was born May 24, 1864. Their children: William R. b. May 4, 1886, died; Lydia S. b. April 7, 1888; George A. b. June 21, 1890; Raymond b. Jan. 13, 1893; Clyde b. Aug. 16, 1900, died; Claude b. Aug. 16, 1900, died. Family home, Provo.
Elder. Farmer.

HALLS, WILLIAM (son of John Halls, Orsett, Essex, Eng., and Susanna Selstone, born Jan. 24, 1801, West Thurrock). Born May 25, 1834, Orsett, Essex. Came to Utah Sept. 15, 1861, Ira Eldredge company.
Married Louisa C. Enderby April 15, 1861 (daughter of William Enderby and Elizabeth Carritt). She was born Oct. 31, 1840. Their children: Mosiah b. March 12, 1862, m. Rosa Walton; William b. Sept. 6, 1863, m. Ella Barker; Thomas b. June 18, 1865, m. Luella Hammond; George Henry b. June 20, 1867, m. Celia Raymond; Louisa E. b. April 5, 1870, m. Christian Wangsgaard; John b. July 11, 1872, m. Mary J. Grow Feb. 15, 1895. Family home, Huntsville.

Married Johanna M. Frandsen June 26, 1871, Salt Lake City (daughter of Jens Frandsen and Kjersten Christensen, pioneers with Captain Hunt company; came from Denmark). She was born Aug. 21, 1855, Denmark. Their children: Johanna Susanna b. Jan. 29, 1873, m. John Smith; Mary b. Aug. 29, 1875, m. Charles S. Brown; David b. Oct. 12, 1877, m. Lillian E. Dean; Lucy and Emma (twins) b. Nov. 4, 1879, latter m. P. C. Lansing; Sarah b. Nov. 21, 1881; James Louis b. June 23, 1883, m. Elvira Burnham; Eliza M. b. Feb. 15, 1885; Franklin b. July 12, 1887; Herbert b. Oct. 5, 1891; Florence b. March 12, 1894. Family home Mancos, Colo.
Married Eleanor Howard Jan. 8, 1880, who died March 7, 1884. Their child: Lottie b. April 25, 1881.
Missionary to England 1854-61. Taught school at Kaysville 1861-62. Moved to Huntsville 1862. Assisted in bringing immigrants to Utah, 1864, William B. Preston company. Set apart as first counselor in Huntsville bishopric June 1877. March 1885 went on mission to assist in settlement of San Juan Co., Utah; and on organization of San Juan stake June 1885 was chosen first counselor in stake presidency. Moved from Bluff, Utah, to Mancos, Colo. 1886. Acting president San Juan stake, with exception of few weeks, from Nov. 1900 to May 1902, when he was again set apart as first counselor. Ordained patriarch May 17, 1908. Stake tithing clerk. Secretary Huntsville Co-op. store and postmaster of Huntsville, Utah, several years. In Colorado, director public schools in Mancos; served two terms as county superintendent of schools, Montezuma county; also justice of the peace. Farmer and stockraiser.

HALVERSON, SIMON FREDERICK (son of Halver Simonson and Moren Frederickson, both of Onse, Norway). Born Oct. 2, 1829, at Onse. Came to Utah, via Copenhagen, Denmark, and Hull and Liverpool, Eng. 1854-55, reaching Salt Lake City Sept. 7, 1855, Noah T. Guymon company.
Married Torbeg Kistene Gunderson March 25, 1855, while en route to Utah (daughter of Gunder and Annie Erickson), who was born May 18, 1838, Risor, Norway, and came to Utah, at Ogden, Utah. Their children: Mother b. March 2, 1856, d. May 4, 1856; Matilda b. July 4, 1857, m. Winslow Farr Dec. 12, 1878; Samuel Franklin b. July 15, 1859, m. Emily Farr; Annie b. Feb. 4, 1862, b. Feb. 4, 1879; Simon b. April 6, 1864, d. July 2, 1874; Hyrum b. June 25, 1866, m. Ann Ritchie; George b. Nov. 25, 1868, m. Evelyn Whittaker; James b. Nov. 25, 1868, m. Lillian M. Robbins; Mary Ellen b. July 8, 1871, m. John W. Owen; Bertha Elinda b. Nov. 15, 1874, m. William Swinyard; Owen Walter b. March 21, 1878, m. Geneva Driggs. Family home Marriott, Weber Co., Utah.
Married Ingvor Gurena Fredrickson Dec. 10, 1854, Salt Lake City (daughter of Knude Fredrickson and Ann Carson), who was born May 18, 1838, Risor, Norway, and came to Utah 1861, Captain Thompson company. Their children: Mary Ann b. Sept. 3, 1865, d. July 29, 1875; Fredrick b. April 18, 1867, m. Maude Worthington; Amelia b. June 6, 1869, m. Reuben M. Wright; Charles Albert b. Jan. 19, 1871, m. Diana Watson Sept. 6, 1899; Bearsh b. March 6, 1873, d. Feb. 13, 1876; Francis Theodore b. April 5, 1875, m. Frances Bitton; Ann Etta b. Jan. 13, 1878; Arthur b. April 27, 1880, m. Elizabeth J. Pierce June 12, 1907. Family home, Marriott.
First president Marriott district 1863-77; justice of the peace; school trustee. Died Jan. 5, 1901.

HALVERSON, GEORGE (son of Simon Frederick Halverson and Torbeg Kistene Gunderson). Born Nov. 25, 1868, at Marriott, Weber Co., Utah.
Married Evelyn Whittaker Nov. 17, 1897, Salt Lake City (daughter of Thomas S. Whittaker and Elizabeth Mills, former a pioneer). She was born Jan. 1, 1875, Centerville, Utah. Their children: George Byron b. Aug. 21, 1900; Spencer Lyndon b. March 20, 1905.
Graduated from normal school university of Utah 1888; taught school two years—principal South Washington school, Ogden, Utah, one year. Graduated university of Michigan, 1894, with degree LL. B. and began practice of law at Ogden same year. Weber county attorney two terms; district attorney about seven years; admitted to practice before supreme court of U. S. April 23, 1901.

HALVERSON, CHAS. A. (son of Simon Frederick Halverson and Ingebor Gurena Fredrickson). Born Jan. 19, 1871.
Married Diana Watson Sept. 6, 1899, at Salt Lake City (daughter of John Watson and Sarah Mortimer of Goole, Eng.; came to Utah June 1887). She was born June 17, 1877. Their children: Edna W. b. Nov. 2, 1902; C. Alton b. July 16, 1904; Marlowe b. Jan. 28, 1907; Phyllis b. Aug. 19, 1910. Family home Ogden, Utah.
Missionary to Norway 1899-1902; member Weber stake high council.

HAMBLIN, ISAIAH (son of Barnabas Hamblin, born 1739, and Mary Bassett). Born 1790, Falmouth, Mass. Came to Utah Oct. 27, 1850, Milo Andrus company.
Married Daphney Haynes of North Hero, Vt., Nov. 30, 1812 (daughter of William Haynes and Miss Stoddard), who was born 1797, and died en route to Utah. Their children: Melissa Daphney b. Feb. 1, 1814, m. Isaac Fuller Sept. 14, 1833; Emily Haynes b. Oct. 30, 1816, m. James Fuller June 3, 1832; Jacob Vernon b. April 2, 1819, m. Lucinda Taylor April 30, 1839; Olive H. b. May 1, 1821, m. Henry Johnson Aug. 27, 1838; Adaline Amarilla b. Sept. 18, 1823, m. Lyman D. Littlefield; Obed b. Feb. 25, 1826; Alsen Haynes b. April 28,

1828, m. Hester A. Stoddard 1849; William Haynes b. Oct. 28, 1828, m. Mary Leavitt 1850; Oscar b. April 4, 1833, m. Mary Ann Corbridge Feb. 14, 1854; Edwin b. May 20, 1835, m. Hannah Mariah Cook 1855; Francis Marion b. Nov. 27, 1839, m. Arminda Crow Oct. 31, 1859; Fredrick b. Feb. 12, 1841, m. Frances Jane Prudum May 29, 1859. Family home Bainbridge, Ohio.
High priest.

HAMBLIN, EDWIN (son of Isaiah Hamblin and Daphney Haynes). Born May 20, 1835, Bainbridge, Geauga Co., Ohio. Came to Utah with father.
Married Hannah Mariah Cook May 24, 1855 (daughter of Joseph P. Cook and Hannah M. Lashmelia), who was born 1834, and came to Utah Oct. 24, 1854, William A. Empey company. Their children: Obed Edwin b. Feb. 13, 1856, m. Margret Aycock July 19, 1883; Isaiah b. Nov. 8, 1857; Hannah Mariah b. Dec. 12, 1859, m. Thomas Logan May 27, 1883; Catherine Monsell b. Nov. 1, 1861; Sarah Ann b. Aug. 11, 1863, m. David R. Sinclair Sept. 19, 1889; Josephine b. Nov. 9, 1864, m. Joseph Rice July 1, 1891; Joseph Peter b. Nov. 28, 1866, m. Charlotte Adair 1895; Emma Elizabeth b. Dec. 18, 1869, m. Andrew Hamblin 1892; William Haynes b. July 18, 1872, m. Morey James; Mary Ellen b. Aug. 6, 1873, m. Alonzo Johnson. Family home Clover Valley, Lincoln county, Nev.
Missionary among the Indians of Southern Utah 1858-61; high priest. First lieutenant in militia Tooele county; minuteman. Justice of peace at Clover Valley, Nev.

HAMER, SAMUEL (son of Samuel and Jane Thornley of Bolton, Lancashire, Eng.). Born Aug. 31, 1831, Bolton, Eng. Came to Utah Oct. 1851, Orson Pratt company.
Married Ann Albion Nov. 5, 1857, Salt Lake City, Bishop Kesler officiating (daughter of James Albion and Ann Byers of Eng., formerly a pioneer 1851, handcart company). She was born May 2, 1835. Their children: Ann M., d. youth; Jane; Samuel, d. youth; John, m. Nellie Jones; Daniel, m. Ellen W. Halverson; Jessie, d. young; Clara, m. Robert A. Moss; Joseph, d. aged 3; David H., d. aged 1; Willard, m. Maria Stevenson.
Married Sarah Openshaw July 8, 1870, Salt Lake City, Brigham Young officiating (daughter of Job Openshaw and Nancy Beswick of Manchester, Eng., came to Utah June 1865). She was born Dec. 21, 1848. Their children: Nancy Ellen b. Aug. 20, 1871, m. Albert S. Teiser; Samuel Ernest b. May 1, 1873, m. Sarah Jane Burton; Martha Matt b. Jan. 19, 1875, m. Oscar W. Nyberg; Mary b. June 19, 1877, m. Hyrum E. Smith; Walter b. Sept. 10, 1879, m. Mary Stevenson; Emma b. March 9, 1882, m. Newton C. Schellenger; William Franklin b. Sept. 22, 1884, d. infant; Elsie b May 22, 1890, m. Frank Taysum. Families resided Salt Lake City.
Seventy; home missionary; counselor to James Henry, bishop of Panaca ward, Nev.; high priest. Patrolman at Salt Lake City. Machinist and blacksmith. Died Feb. 8, 1895.

HAMILTON, ANDREW M. (son of James Baker Hamilton of Ohio). Born in Ohio. Came to Utah 1852, Bryant Jolly company.
Married Ella Wilson, in Tennessee. Their children: Ivy, m. Sarah Orton; Zachariah; David, m. Ellen Bennett; Lovisa, m. John Butler, m. Moroni Oliver; Joseph, d. aged 9; James B., m. Martha Shelton; Brigham, d. aged 46; Catherine, m. Ephraim Van Wagonen; Malissa, m. Moses Reeves; William, d. infant. Family resided Springville and Richfield, Utah.
Seventy; bishop's counselor at Midway, Utah; presiding bishop of Juniper, Arizona; missionary. Veteran Walker, Black Hawk and Tintic Indian wars. He was sealed to Joseph Smith's family. Miller and carpenter. Died at Springville, Utah.

HAMILTON, DAVID F. (son of Andrew M. Hamilton and Ella Wilson). Born May 27, 1833. Came to Utah 1847, oxteam company.
Married Martha Ellen Bennett Nov. 18, 1858, at Springville, Utah (daughter of David Bennett and Jenna Lowell, both of Illinois). Came to Utah 1847, Rodolphus Bennett oxteam company). She was born March 1, 1840. Their children: David William b. April 22, 1860, m. Eliza Bird; James Alma b. Jan. 18, 1862, m. Susan Waggner; Robert b. Jan. 20, 1864, d. aged 13; Rodolphus b. Dec. 11, 1866, d. infant; Henry b. May 11, 1868, m. Ellin Gentry; Calvin b. July 20, 1871, m. Melia Hunt; Ellen b. Sept. 4, 1873, m. Frank D. Warren; Emma b. March 14, 1875, m. Frank Wiseman. Family home Richfield, Utah.
Member of the church. Indian War veteran. Farmer; stockraiser. Died Nov. 18, 1893, at Price, Utah.

HAMILTON, JAMES B. (son of Andrew M. Hamilton and Ella Wilson). Born Nov. 2, 1842, Hancock county, Ill. Came to Utah with father.
Married Martha Shelton Dec. 17, 1865, Mound City, Utah (daughter of Stephen Shelton and Abigail Harris, pioneers 1850, Melvin Ross company). She was born June 22, 1844. Their children: Ella A. b. Nov. 4, 1866, m. Levi Snyder; Nancy J. b. Nov. 13, 1868, m. Joseph Nielson; James A. b. March 6, 1870, m. Lizzie Kummer; Lovisa b. March 25, 1873, m. Kimball Snyder; Margaret b. May 7, 1876, m. William Campbell; William B. b. June 19, 1878; Mary b. Feb. 16,

1882, m. Theopholis Chambers; Hyrum T. b. Aug. 19, 1884; David b. Nov. 11, 1887, m. Delia VanWagonen; Emma A. b. Dec. 8, 1888, d. aged 4. Family home Midway, Utah.
Member 66th quorum seventies; ward teacher. Assisted in bringing immigrants to Utah 1862. Veteran Black Hawk Indian war. Farmer.

HAMILTON, JAMES McDONALD (son of John Hamilton, Jr. and Mary McDonald of Hamilton's Fort, Iron county, Utah). Born Oct. 15, 1859.
Married Jane Elizabeth Gower May 2, 1881, at Cedar City, Utah (daughter of Thomas Gower and Martha Ann Stockdale). Their children: James Donald; Martha Isabelle. Family home Hamilton's Fort, Utah.

HAMMER, HANS ANDERSON (son of Hans Hammer of Burgholm, Denmark). Born Oct. 11, 1829, at Burgholm, Denmark. Came to Utah 1854.
Married Anna C. Reese 1853. Their children: George b. 1858; Maggie b. 1860, m. Edward Cox 1886; Aldora b. 1862, m. Henry Ashton 1887; Julius; John; William. Family home Lehi, Utah.
Married Anna Christina Orego 1868 (daughter of Christian Larsen Orego, pioneer of 1866, and Maria Peterson), who was born 1839. Their children: Myria b. 1868; Elizabeth b. 1869; Joseph b. 1871, m. Zerelda Egbert 1897; Christian b. 1873; Alma b. 1875; Moses b. 1877; Samuel b. 1879, m. Linda Stewart 1899.
Settled at Salt Lake City 1854, moved to Lehi, Utah, 1858. Worked on temple. Trader; hotel and livery keeper. Died 1905.

HAMMOND, FRANCIS ASBURY (son of Samuel Smith Hammond and Charity Edwards of Patchogue, Long Island, N. Y.). Born Nov. 1, 1822, Patchogue, N. Y. Came to Utah Nov. 1848.
Married Mary Jane Dilworth Nov. 17, 1848, Salt Lake City (daughter of Caleb Dilworth and Eliza Wollerton of Lionville, Chester county, Pa., former came to Utah July 24, 1847, Edward Hunter company, latter 1848, Jedediah M. Grant company). She was born July 29, 1831. Their children: Francis Asbury, d. while on a mission; Samuel Smith, m. Eleonora Marie Sorensen; Fletcher B. m. Chalista Bronson; Mary Moiselle, m. George Halls; Eliza Dilworth, m. Mons Peterson; Luella Adelaid, m. Thomas Halls; Joseph Heber, m. Isa Wright; George Albert, died; William Edmond, died; Maybell Ophelia, m. Hyrum W. Fielding; Lizzie Fontella, d. child; Amelia May (died) m. J. U. Allred. Family home Huntsville, Utah.
Member 59th quorum seventies; missionary to Sandwich Islands 1850-55; 2d counselor to Bishop C. W. West of Ogden; president of a branch; bishop; president San Juan stake. County commissioner; justice of peace; member legislature. Farmer; stockraiser; dealer in boots, shoes and saddlery. Died Nov. 27, 1900, Largo, N. M.

HAMMOND, SAMUEL SMITH (son of Francis Asbury Hammond and Mary Jane Dilworth). Born April 15, 1853, Lahaina Maui, Sandwich Islands.
Married Eleonora Marie Sorensen July 14, 1881, Salt Lake City (daughter of Christian Sorensen and Nelsine Anderson of Huntsville, Utah, who came to Utah July 2, 1872, Anthon H. Lund company). She was born May 4, 1863, in Denmark. Their children: Samuel Smith, m. Vera Wilde; Zina Eleonora, m. Alfred Agren; Clara May, died; John Henry; Eda May, died; Genevieve. Family reside Huntsville, Utah, Mancos, Colo., and Moreland, Idaho.
One of presidents of 76th quorum seventies; missionary to Sandwich Islands 1889-92; to Navajo Indians 1887; president high priests' quorum; bishop's counselor. Farmer and stockraiser.

HAMMOND, JOHN. Born 1799 in England; came to Utah 1848, Brigham Young company.
Married Mary Luvica Parker 1821 in New York, who was born September 1797. Their children: Joseph; Mary; Sarah; Sufrona. Family home South Cottonwood, Utah.
Died 1859 at South Cottonwood, Utah.

HAMMOND, JOSEPH (son of John Hammond and Luvica Parker). Born June 14, 1822, in New York. Came to Utah 1848 with his father.
Married Elizabeth Egbert March 1844, Hancock Co., Ill. (daughter of John Egbert and Susanna Hann both of Little Cottonwood, Utah, pioneers 1848, Brigham Young company). She was born March 22, 1824. Their children: John E. b. Jan. 1, 1844, m. Saling Walker; Robert A. b. Oct. 1845, m. Sarah Wilson; Joseph, d. child; Susannah b. Jan. 10, 1850, m. James Deans; Elizabeth, m. Hosen Stout; Luvica Ann, d. infant; Helen Josephine, m. Peter Hanson. Family home St. George, Utah.
Married Delta Kelsy at St. George, Utah. Their children: Orson; Abigail. Family home St. George, Utah.

HAMMOND, JOHN EGBERT (son of Joseph Hammond and Elizabeth Egbert). He was born Jan. 1, 1844, Hancock county, Ill.
Married Selina W. Walker Nov. 21, 1862, at South Cottonwood, Utah (daughter of Henry Walker and Anne Preece of Herefordshire, Eng. Came to Utah Sept. 20, 1853, with Claudius V. Spencer company). She was born April 19,

1841, at Little Elm, Herefordshire. Their children: John H. b. Dec. 29, 1863; Joseph E. b. April 8, 1866, d. Sept. 17, 1867; Elizabeth J. b. June 5, 1868; Corilla S. b. Oct. 24, 1870; Wilford E. b. Oct. 24, 1872; Annie V. b. June 13, 1875; Nellie S. b. Dec. 20, 1877; Lillie b. April 18, 1880; Rose E. b. Sept. 14, 1882, d. Aug. 6, 1884; Alice H. b. Dec. 17, 1886, d. July 20, 1893. Family home Eagle Valley, Nev.
Moved to St. George, Utah, 1862; and from there to Eagle Valley, Lincoln county, Nev., 1865. Presiding elder Eagle Valley branch of Panaca ward in Nevada five years. Farmer and gardener.

HAMMOND, MILTON D. (son of Nathaniel R. Hammond and Alzina Spencer of Michigan). Born Oct. 7, 1831, in New York. Came to Utah 1850.
Married Lovisa Miller Dec. 11, 1853, Farmington, Utah (daughter of Daniel A. Miller and Clarisa Palm of Farmington, pioneers 1848). She was born Oct. 1, 1834. Their children: Melvin M., m. Sarah Thornton; James T., m. Leonora Blair; Clarisa Alzina, m. J. H. Brown, Jr.; Estus W., m. Ida Pitkin; Lionel, m. Ester Gamble; Datus R., m. Sarah Gamble; Lovisa, m. Andrew A. Allen, Jr.; Viola; Daniel A.; Minnie, m. Robert Allen. Family home Providence, Utah.
High priest; bishop Providence ward; counsellor to president of Cache stake. Probate judge of Cache county many years. Farmer; machine and implement dealer.

HAMMOND, JAMES T. (son of Milton D. Hammond and Lovisa Miller). Born Dec. 11, 1856, Farmington, Utah.
Married Leonora Blair Dec. 18, 1884, Logan, Utah (daughter of Seth M. Blair and Sarah Jane Foster of Logan, Utah, pioneers 1849). She was born Dec. 22, 1860. Their children: James T. b. Dec. 11, 1886; Wendell B. b. Oct. 31, 1888; Roscoe E. b. Feb. 19, 1891. Family home, Salt Lake City.
Member 124th quorum seventies; missionary to southern states 1881-83. Clerk, recorder and attorney Cache county; president board of education, Salt Lake City; member state legislature two terms, and state senate one term; secretary of state 1895-1904. Attorney-at-law.

HAMPTON, BENJAMIN (son of Benjamin Hampton and Patience Schull). Born Feb. 11, 1827, Philadelphia, Pa. Came to Utah October 1853, Moses Clawson company.
Married Adelaide Eugenia Grant Jan. 30, 1864, Salt Lake City (daughter of Joshua Grant and Louise Marie Goulay of Salt Lake City, pioneers Sept. 2, 1851, private company). She was born Oct. 4, 1845. Their children: Adelaide; Grant, m. Catherine Aurelia Lowe; William Goulet, m. Hattie Lyman; Horace Benjamin, m. Jean Pearson; Robert Roy, m. Margaret Howat; Joseph Eugene, d. Dec. 1, 1877. Family home, Salt Lake City.
Miner and smelting man.

HAMPTON, GRANT (son of Benjamin Hampton and Adelaide E. Grant). Born Sept. 8, 1867, Salt Lake City.
Married Catherine Aurelia Lowe Sept. 15, 1904, Salt Lake City (daughter of George A. Lowe and Anna M. Dewing). Their children: Anna b. July 21, 1905; Aurelia b. Aug. 28, 1910.

HANCEY, JAMES (son of George Hancey, born 1806, and Hannah Reynolds, born June 16, 1811, both of Suffolk, Eng.). He was born May 1, 1835, Chedeston, Suffolk. Came to Utah Sept. 4, 1860, Franklin Brown company.
Married Rachel Seamons Oct. 12, 1855 (daughter of Henry Seamons, who died Feb. 14, 1860, Omaha, Neb., and Mary King, pioneer Sept. 4, 1860, Franklin Brown company—married 1832). She was born May 31, 1834. Their children: James Sands b. March 24, 1856, m. Ellen Balls Oct. 9, 1879; George Henry b. June 21, 1858, d. Sept. 25, 1859, Omaha; Horace William b. Feb. 25, 1860, m. Jensine Christensen March 5, 1890; Mary Eliza b. Feb. 1, 1862, m. William Metcalf July 8, 1880; Henry Edwin b. Feb. 19, 1864, m. Nellie M. Hyde July 7, 1892; Amelia Rachel b. Jan. 19, 1866, m. John A. Woolf May 8, 1884; Alvin David b. Feb. 15, 1868, d. Feb. 25, 1868; Jesse Samuel b. June 8, 1869, m. Christine Erhartsen March 5, 1890; Alma John b. June 6, 1871, m. Ellen E. Thurston Dec. 16, 1897; Hannah Elizabeth b. Aug. 2, 1873, m. William Henry Price Nov. 16, 1891; Arthur Claudius b. April 14, 1876, m. Minnie Bybee Dec. 6, 1901. Family home Hyde Park, Utah.
Married Louise Purser April 9, 1865, Salt Lake City (daughter of Francis Purser, pioneer Thomas Ricks company, and Frances Eynon, died while crossing ocean to America—married in Pembrokeshire, Wales). She was born July 17, 1843, in Wales. Their children: Frederic P. b. Sept. 24, 1866, m. May Emily Hebdon April 24, 1897; Laura Louise b. Dec. 15, 1867, d. Feb. 21, 1868; Lottie Lorenne b. Dec. 19, 1869, m. Joseph Broadbent Dec. 8, 1886; Lillian b. Oct. 13, 1870, d. Jan. 7, 1877; Lettie Bell b. Aug. 27, 1872, m. George Q. Rich Dec. 9, 1891; Leonora b. May 15, 1874, d. June 22, 1874; Lula b. May 9, 1875, m. Otto B. Erlandson Oct. 28, 1895; Moses Moroni b. Oct. 28, 1877; Justus Edmund b. April 4, 1880, m. Elizabeth Monk July 27, 1910. Family home, Hyde Park.
Married Annie Marie Christopherson Oct. 10, 1879, Salt Lake City (daughter of Christian Christopherson and Christine Nielsen; married 1860, Aalborg, Denmark, and came to Utah 1875). She was born March 9, 1863, at Aalborg. Their children: Rachel May b. May 3, 1881, m. George Kirby Feb. 5, 1902; James Alfred b. July 2, 1883, m. Susan Arnold June 27, 1900; Mary Menetie b. Oct. 7, 1885, m. Martin C. Reeder May 19, 1905; George Ernest b. Jan. 17, 1888; Leander b. May 12, 1890; Leslie Peter b. Oct. 1, 1892; Evan Homer b. Dec. 25, 1894; Clarence b. March 8, 1897; Georgiana b. May 23, 1899; Kelvin b. June 26, 1902; Aleda b. May 2, 1904.
Elder. Assistant surgeon in Utah militia in 60's. Carpenter and builder; cabinet maker; wheelwright; machinist; dentist. Inventor of automatic spill-gate used in Logan Canyon. Registration and health officer of Hyde Park, Utah. Died April 5, 1913.

HANCEY, JAMES SANDS (son of James Hancey and Rachel Seamons). Born March 24, 1856, on the ship Caravan on Atlantic ocean.
Married Ellen Balls Oct. 9, 1879, Salt Lake City (daughter of John Balls and Sarah Baxter, pioneers Sept. 2, 1868, Simpson M. Molen company). She was born Nov. 3, 1859, Chedeston, Eng. Their children: Sarah Ellen b. Sept. 7, 1881, m. Willon Wildmun June 4, 1903; James Sands, Jr. b. Nov. 10, 1883, m. Florence I. Merrill June 28, 1905 (died 1908), m. Mabel Benson Jan. 15, 1912; John Willard b. Nov. 7, 1885, m. Vira C. Hansen Nov. 3, 1909; George Leonard b. May 15, 1888; Susie b. June 27, 1890; Norval Heber b. Dec. 8, 1892; Vilate b. April 6, 1896; Manila b. Feb. 12, 1899. Family home Hyde Park, Utah.
Elder. Snare drummer Utah militia in '60's. Organist for church choir and Sunday school 1875-1903; organist for all priesthood meetings; teacher and leader of first brass band 10 years, of second brass band eight years; member of present brass band, and of Home Dramatic Company nine years. Carpenter and builder; painter and paperhanger; keeps furniture and repair shop.

HANCOCK, C. B. (son of Solomon Hancock, born Aug. 14, 1793, Springfield, Mass., and Sarah Herrick Adams, born May 17, 1795, Pawlet. Vt.—married March 12, 1815). He was born in 1823 at Columbus, Ohio. Came to Utah 1847 with an independent company.
Married Samantha Rawson in 1850 at Salt Lake City (daughter of Horace Rawson and Elizabeth Coffin, pioneers 1849). She was born in 1830. Their children: C. B. b. Jan. 1, 1851, m. Louisa Shurtliff 1874; Cornelia Samantha b. Aug. 16, 1852, m. Noah Shurtliff; Alta Percillia b. Dec. 27, 1853, m. Francis Shurtliff. Family resided Harrisville, Weber Co., Utah.
High priest; second bishop of Payson, Utah. Farmer; stockraiser.

HANCOCK, C. B., JR (son of C. B. Hancock and Samantha Rawson). Born Jan. 1, 1851.
Married Louisa Shurtliff Sept. 28, 1874, Salt Lake City (daughter of Luman Shurtliff and Mary Adams), who was born in 1856 at Ogden, Utah. Their children: Charles William b. March 1, 1876, m. Martha Richardson; Mary Samantha b. Aug. 22, 1877, died; George b. Dec. 25, 1879, m. Pheney Bennett 1904; John Riley b. March 5, 1881; Ida Luella b. Dec. 6, 1883, m. Hyrum Bowman; Cyrus Alvin b. Dec. 8, 1885, m. Nettie Criddle; Chloe Larinda b. May 13, 1887, m. Hyrum Curtiss; Alma b. Aug. 16, 1889, m. Lucella Baker; Louisa Adeline b. June 27, 1893, m. John Hatfield Jan. 19, 1911; Louis Delbert b. July 2, 1895.

HANCOCK, JAMES (son of William Hancock and Susan Hooper of London, Eng.). Born Aug. 27, 1827, London. Came to Utah 1852, Abraham O. Smoot company.
Married Ann Melsom Hughes (daughter of John Hughes and Sarah Stephenson), who was born June, 1825, and came to Utah with husband. Their children: Joseph Hiram b. April 27, 1849, m. Mary Anna Glover; Susan b. Nov. 13, 1852, m. Jacob Sorensen; James Brigham b. July 10, 1856, m. Emma Sorensen; Anna Mary b. April 7, 1857, died. Family resided Salt Lake City and Mendon, Utah.
Veteran Echo Canyon war. Guard of Brigham Young's residence. Helped to build the walls of temple and tabernacle. Ward teacher; high priest. Was in first settlement at Mendon. Assisted in irrigation and making ditches.

HANCOCK, JOSEPH HIRAM (son of James Hancock and Ann Melsom Hughes). Born April 27, 1849, Bradford, Yorkshire, Eng.
Married Mary Anna Glover 1872, Salt Lake City, her birthplace. Their children: Joseph William b. April 10, 1876, m. Agnes Richards; Jane Melsom, m. Walter J. Sloan; Mary Luella b. July 10, 1878, m. Julius Hauerbach; James Antic b. Aug. 23, 1880; Orson; Oscar; Chloe May b. Nov. 8, 1889. Family home, Salt Lake City.
Drove team to Weeping Water, Mo., for immigrants. Member cavalry under Colonel Ricks. High priest. Farmer. Hotel keeper.

HANCOCK, LEVI W. Came to Utah in 1847, with contingent Mormon Battalion, Company E.
Married Clarissa Reed of Vermont. Among their children was John, born April 19, 1845, married Julia C. Huntington July 24, 1865.
Fourth of the seven presidents of first quorum seventies organized in the L. D. S. church. Musician in Company E of Mormon Battalion. Delegate from Utah county to first legislative assembly 1851.

HANCOCK, JOHN (son of Levi W. Hancock and Clarissa Reed of Vermont, pioneers 1847, Mormon Battalion). Born April 19, 1845. Came to Utah with parents in 1847.
Married Julia C. Huntington July 24, 1865, Salt Lake City, by Dimmick B. Huntington (daughter of Dimmick B. Hunt-

ington and Fannie M. Allen of Salt Lake City, pioneers July 28, 1847, Mormon Battalion). She was born June 21, 1846, Salt Lake City. Their children: Caroline b. April 19, 1866, d. infant; John E. b. June 3, 1867, m. Elizabeth Moss; Dimmick B. b. Feb. 10, 1870, m. Annie White; Julia b. April 3, 1872, d. aged 8; Fannie b. Oct. 9, 1874, d. aged 5; Lot b. Aug. 18, 1876, m. Susan Coon; Martha b. Dec. 19, 1879, m. Jacob Coon.

HANCOCK, THOMAS (son of William Hancock and Hannah Harvey of Derbyshire, Eng.). Born July 3, 1844, Derbyshire. Came to Utah Oct. 7, 1866, Captain Scott company.
Married Sarah A. Macduff May 29, 1864, Chesterfield, Eng. (daughter of John Robertson Macduff and Ellen Hancock of Chesterfield, pioneers Oct. 1864, Captain Warren company). She was born Oct. 16, 1844. Family home, Salt Lake City.
High priest; missionary to England 1896-98; block teacher. Lime burner.

HANDLEY, GEORGE (son of George Handley and Jane Smith of Boston, Lincolnshire, Eng.). Born June 2, 1826. Came to Utah Oct. 6, 1853, Cyrus H. Wheelock company.
Married Elizabeth Clark June 26, 1846, Chesterton, Cambridgeshire, Eng. (daughter of Benjamin Clark and Ann Shuker, pioneers 1853, Captain Wheelock company, settled in Salt City). She was born June 5, 1824, Cambridge, Eng., and came to Utah in 1853 with husband. Their children: Elizabeth Ann, d. aged 18 months; George B., d. aged 11 months; Ann Elizabeth, d. aged 10 years; Lewis, d. infant; John George, m. Ruth B. Stratton; William F., m. Sarah A. Stratton; Clara Jane, d. infant; Joseph H., d. infant; Charles Caleb, d. aged 2 years; David Thomas, d. infant; Charles Ira, m. Wilhelmina Garn; Emma N., m. Lorenzo Price, Jr.

HANDY, SAMUEL (son of Joseph Handy, born at Clifford-upon-Stour, Gloucestershire, and Rebecca Harris, born at Chesterton, Cambridgeshire, Eng.). He was born March 23, 1819, at Alveston, Derbyshire, Eng. Came to Utah in September 1859, James Brown company.
Married Hannah Watts Oct. 25, 1841, Atherston, Gloucestershire (daughter of William Watts and Mary Hayden), who was born March 14, 1820. Their children: Hannah Rebecca b. July 30, 1842, m. Mary Ann Day (Flueitt) Nov. 11, 1885; Joseph b. April 10, 1844, d. Sept. 18, 1855; Mary b. Dec. 5, 1847, m. Isaac H. Vail 1863; Eliza b. Dec. 20, 1849, m. David Boice Nov. 17, 1866; Samuel b. Nov. 5, 1853, d. May 27, 1854; James Henry b. April 18, 1855, m. Lucy Day Dec. 2, 1872. Family resided Clifford, Eng., Provo, Utah, and Franklin, Oneida Co., Idaho.
First watermaster of Franklin, holding position until 1880; minuteman during early Indian troubles. High priest. Farmer. Died Jan. 15, 1882, being thrown from horse and instantly killed.

HANDY, WILLIAM (son of Samuel Handy and Hannah Watts). Born July 30, 1842, Halestone, Warwickshire, Eng.
Married Mary Ann Day (Flueitt) Nov. 11, 1886, at Franklin, Idaho (daughter of Joseph Day and Ann Harvey, pioneers to Utah 1853, Jacob Gates ten-pound company). She was born Jan. 14, 1840, Essex, Eng. Their children: Hannah Rebecca b. Nov. 3, 1867, m. Edgar West Dec. 7, 1885; Lucy Elenora b. Oct. 22, 1869, m. Fredrick Harding Dec. 25, 1888; Elsie Catherine b. Oct. 29, 1871, m. George Sprunt Oct. 3, 1892; Phoebe Ellen b. Nov. 27, 1873, m. Al Dorsey May 11, 1895; William James Flueitt b. Dec. 6, 1875, d. May 20, 1877; Hulda Almeda b. Jan. 25, 1877, m. George John Newbold July 15, 1897; Alonzo Hazelton b. Nov. 6, 1879, m. Nettie Pearl Mendenhall Nov. 19, 1902; Samuel Preston b. Dec. 13, 1881, m. Lydia Adela Bybee Dec. 8, 1899, d. Aug. 11, 1909; David E. b. Sept. 19, 1887. Family resided Whitney, Idaho.
Married Jane Day Nov. 24, 1869, at Salt Lake City (daughter of Joseph Day and Ann Harvey), who was born Feb. 21, 1853, Lancashire, Eng. Their children: Emeline b. Aug. 24, 1870, m. William Lundergreen; William Thomas b. Dec. 17, 1872, m. Annie Stone Naef Dec. 23, 1909; Joseph Henry b. Oct. 15, 1875, d. June 10, 1877; Cloie Ann b. May 12, 1878, m. Joseph Titnesor Dec. 15, 1897. Family home Franklin, Idaho.
Minuteman during early Idaho history; settled at Whitney in 1873. High priest.

HANDY, JAMES HENRY (son of Samuel Handy and Hannah Watts). Born April 18, 1855, Stratford-on-Avon, Eng.
Married Lucy Day Dec. 2, 1872, Salt Lake City (daughter of Joseph Day and Ann Harvey), who was born Nov. 14, 1855, Bountiful, Utah. Their children: James Harvey b. Sept. 19, 1873, d. Feb. 26, 1874; Lucy Ann b. April 2, 1875, m. Uriah Wilkinson; George Henry b. April 15, 1877, m. Ruby Mendenhall; Samuel Joseph b. May 3, 1879, m. Mabel Hobba June 30, 1901; Leonard Thomas b. May 22, 1881, m. Jennie Tomason June 22, 1904; Emma b. Aug. 27, 1883, m. Lester Garrett June 18, 1903; Elmer Day b. March 28, 1886; m. Mae Biggs; Newell Day b. Jan. 18, 1888; Nora Day b. Dec. 18, 1889, m. W. M. Daines, Jr., Nov. 17, 1910; Elgin Day b. March 11, 1892; Ida Day b. Aug. 15, 1894, d. June 16, 1895; Martha May b. May 1, 1896, d. same day; Edna Day b. May 2, 1898. Family home Franklin, Idaho.

HANKS. EPHRAIM KNOWLTON (son of Benjamin Hanks and Martha Knowlton). Born March 21, 1826, Madison, Lake Co., Ohio. Came to Utah July 29, 1847, James Brown contingent Mormon Battalion, Company B.
Married Harriet Amelia Decker (Little) Sept. 22, 1848, who was born March 13, 1826, and came to Utah Oct. 5, 1847. Their children: Ephraim Marcelles b. June 21, 1849; Marcia Amelia b. July 3, 1851; O. Alvarus b. Sept. 15, 1853; Harriet Page b. Feb. 25, 1856; Clara Vilate b. July 10, 1858; Charles Decker b. Dec. 22, 1860; Perry Isaac b. Jan. 20, 1863. Family home, Salt Lake City.
Harriet Amelia Decker was the widow of Edwin S. Little, who died shortly after leaving Nauvoo. They had one child: George Edwin b. Aug. 6, 1844, who came to Utah with his mother.
Married Jane Maria Capener March 27, 1856, Salt Lake City (daughter of William Capener and Sarah Verander of London, Eng., pioneers Oct. 2, 1852, Isaac Bullock company). She was born Oct. 16, 1840, Dry Brook, Ulster county, N. Y. Their children: William Albert C. b. Feb. 17, 1859, m. Eunice L. Murdock; Alice Maria b. Jan. 15, 1861, m. Moroni S. McAffee; Sarah Elizabeth b. March 10, 1863, m. Ethan Leonard Brown; Ephraim Knowlton b. May 18, 1865, m. Lottie Bagley; George Augustus b. Jan. 3, 1868, m. Malissa Merrell, m. Bessie Johns; David C. b. March 6, 1870, m. Mary Baum; Louisa Rebecca b. June 27, 1872, m. George W. Lowe.
Jane Maria Capener (Hanks) married Joseph E. Taylor. Their children: Jane, m. George Alexander; Margret Wicks, m. Fred Cluff.
Married Thisbe Quilly Read April 6, 1862 (daughter of Samuel and Georgiana Read), who was born April 26, 1847, London, Eng., and came to Utah with Daniel Tyler handcart company. Their children: Ella M. b. Nov. 3, 1863, died; Walter Ernest b. June 19, 1865, m. Mary E. Stewart April 15, 1887; Martha Georgiana b. Aug. 20, 1867, m. Daniel Allen March 20, 1886; Amy Alicia b. Jan. 29, 1870, m. John Giles Dec. 21, 1887; Thisbe b. March 28, 1872, m. Samuel Allen Oct. 27, 1892; Knowlton b. Jan. 26, 1874, died; Sidney Alvarus b. April 4, 1875, m. Martha Hubber; Ray Elijah b. Aug. 24, 1877, d. Sept. 3, 1910; Lillie Maria b. Aug. 2, 1879, m. James Wodscow; Arthur Eugene b. May 14, 1882, m. Mattie Little; Nettie May b. Nov. 8, 1884, m. Henry Giles; Clara Ellen b. Aug. 9, 1888, m. Robert Kittley.
Assisted in bringing immigrants to Utah. First counselor to Bishop Henry Giles of Blue Valley ward; patriarch. Mail carrier in early days. Died in Grass Valley, Utah.

HANKS, WILLIAM ALBERT CAPENER (son of Ephraim Knowlton Hanks and Jane Maria Capener). Born Feb. 17, 1859, Salt Lake City.
Married Eunice Louisa Murdock in May, 1880, Salt Lake City (daughter of Nymphus Murdock and Esther Davis of Charleston, Utah). She was born May 27, 1862. Their children: William Murdock b. Dec. 1, 1882, m. Ida Folland; Nymphus Coridan b. Nov. 3, 1883; Hattie Josephine b. Nov. 29, 1885, m. Stanley Marchant; Fredrick E. b. Sept. 7, 1887; Esther M. b. Oct. 16, 1889, m. Ernest Foulks; Alvan M. b. Jan. 25, 1891; Joseph E. b. Dec. 13, 1894; Reed H. b. Jan. 23, 1896; Clyde C. b. Sept. 5, 1900; Eunice L. b. Feb. 10, 1904. Family home Charleston, Utah.
Missionary to Tennessee 1881; high priest. Justice of peace. Farmer and stockraiser. Died Aug. 19, 1912.

HANKS, WALTER ERNEST (son of Ephraim Knowlton Hanks and Thisbe Quilly Read). Born June 19, 1865, Provo, Utah.
Married Mary E. Stewart April 15, 1887, Logan, Utah (daughter of Urban Van Stewart and Ellen Adams, former a pioneer September 1847). She was born July 20, 1867, Beaver, Utah. Their children: Ellen Josephine b. Jan. 23, 1890, m. Sidney C. E. Rymer Aug. 17, 1910; Walter Benjamin b. April 4, 1892; Thisbe Alicia b. Aug. 23, 1894; Ephraim Knowlton b. Sept. 4, 1896; Edna Mary b. Oct. 9, 1898, d. Jan. 6, 1904; Urban Van b. Nov. 29, 1900; Verd Arthur b. June 12, 1904; Retta Arthella b. April 22, 1907. Family home Caineville, Utah.
Missionary to northwestern states 1887-89; bishop of Caineville ward 1893-1910; superintendent Y. M. M. I. A. of Wayne stake; president high priests' quorum Wayne stake; high councilor. Conductor on first electric car in Salt Lake City. Forest ranger on Powell reserve 1904.

HANKS, SIDNEY ALVARUS (son of Benjamin Hanks and Martha Knowlton of Madison, Lake Co., Ohio). Born Aug. 16, 1820, Madison. Came to Utah July 24, 1847, Brigham Young company.
Married Mary Ann Cook June 7, 1862, Salt Lake City (daughter of Benjamin Cook and Mary Jones of St. Johns, Worcestershire, Eng.). She was born June 23, 1830. Their children: Knowlton; Mary Ann, m. Thomas B. Brighton; Lydia H., m. Joseph H. Parry. Family home, Salt Lake City.
Missionary to Society Islands. Farmer. Died March 9, 1870.

HANKS, STANLEY ALONZO (son of Alfred Frederick Hanks of Gloucestershire, Eng., and Ellen Taylor Lyman, latter a daughter of Francis M. Lyman and Ann Taylor). Born Dec. 3, 1878, Tooele, Utah.
Married Maude Frame Feb. 15, 1905, at Salt Lake City (daughter of Archibald Frame, pioneer 1865, Capt. Sidney Miller company, and Hellen Duff Dick, pioneer 1868, John Gillespie company, settled at Taylorsville, Utah). She was born April 1, 1883. Their children: Lincoln Frame b. Nov. 10, 1905; Maurine Helen b. Aug. 26, 1907; Janetta b. March 1, 1910. Family home, Salt Lake City.
Counselor Y. M. M. I. A.; one of presidency 17th ward, Salt City; home missionary. Justice of the peace, Salt Lake City precinct, 1909-10. Lawyer.

914   PIONEERS AND PROMINENT MEN OF UTAH

HANKS, ALFRED LYMAN (son of Alfred Frederick Hanks and Ellen Taylor Lyman). Born Aug. 28, 1880, Tooele, Utah.
Married Mary Alice Tate June 14, 1905, Salt Lake City (daughter of John William Tate and Elizabeth de la Mare of Tooele, Utah). She was born Nov. 8, 1882. Their child: Ellen Romona b. March 16, 1906. Family home Tooele, Utah.
Member 43d quorum seventies; secretary Y. M. M. I. A. Tooele ward. Postmaster of Tooele.

HANSEN, ANDERS K. (son of Peter Hansen and Metta Hansen of Sjelland, Denmark). Born Jan. 27, 1818, Sjelland, Denmark. Came to Utah 1861, John R. Murdock company.
Married Aurelia Quistgaard Feb. 2, 1863, Salt Lake City (daughter of Julius Quistgaard and Louisa Puilike of Sjelland). She was born Sept. 22, 1842. Their children: Matha Louisa, died; Caroline, m. C. W. Walker; Henrietta, died; Anders K., Jr., m. Amelia L. Heppler; Julia (died), m. J. E. Heppler; Isaac, m. Sophia Sorenson; Abraham, m. Effie Sorenson; Jacob. Family resided Draper and Glenwood, Utah.
High priest; missionary in Denmark before coming to Utah. Farmer and stockraiser. Died Aug. 1, 1903, Glenwood, Utah.

HANSEN, ANDERS K., JR. (son of Anders K. Hansen and Aurelia Quistgaard). Born Dec. 12, 1870, Draper, Utah.
Married Amelia L. Heppler Oct. 13, 1897, Manti, Utah (daughter of Andrew Heppler and Louisiana Seegmiller of Canada—came to Utah 1872 by railroad). She was born Oct. 27, 1871. Their children: Arndale Kelch b. Feb. 12, 1899; Velva b. Oct. 27, 1900, d. infant; Leland Anders b. Oct. 12, 1901; Lina b. Jan. 23, 1903; Alta b. Dec. 17, 1905; Phil b. Oct. 26, 1907. Family resided Draper and Richfield, Utah.
Member 36th quorum seventies; missionary to northern states 1897-99; counselor Sevier stake Y. M. M. I. A.; counselor in bishopric of Richfield second ward; Sevier county assessor 1900-04; town president Glenwood; city councilman Richfield. Farmer and stockraiser.

HANSEN, ANDREW (son of Hans Andersen, born June 23, 1766, of Jerskow, Skilo, Odense Amt, Fyen, Denmark, and Maren Andersen, born May 6, 1792, Norup, Odense Amt). He was born July 10, 1809, at Egense, Norup, Odense Amt. Came to Utah 1853.
Married Karen Jacobsdaughter 1857, at Salt Lake City (daughter of Jacob Nielsen and Maren Petersdaughter), who was born May 3, 1825. Came to Utah Sept. 13, 1857, Christian Christensen company. Their children: James b. Nov. 20, 1860, m. Elizabeth Frandsen March 8, 1883; Andrew , Nov. 4, 1863, m. Carlina Anderson. Family home Ephraim, Utah.

HANSEN, JAMES (son of Andrew Hansen and Karen Jacobsdaughter). Born Nov. 20, 1860, Ephraim, Utah.
Married Elizabeth Frandsen March 8, 1880, at Salt Lake City (daughter of Niels Frandsen), who was born Feb. 12, 1861, in Denmark. Their children: Erma b. Dec. 14, 1884, m. Horace Hales; James Orvill b. May 25, 1886; Niels Andrew b. March 11, 1888, m. Olive Sorensen; Delbert b. March 25, 1890; Ruth Maria b. Aug. 8, 1895. Family home Redmond, Utah.
Member 1st city council Redmond, Utah. Vice-president Rocky Ford Irrigation company 1895-1905; vice-president Vermillion Extension Irrigation company. Deputy road supervisor, District 9, Redmond, Utah.

HANSEN, ANDREW N. (son of Hans Larsen, born Sept. 24, 1776, and Anna Nielsen, born Aug. 30, 1790, Ide, near Frederikshald, Norway—married 1815). He was born March 6, 1836, at Ide. Came to Utah Sept. 25, 1863, with Peter Nebeker company.
Married Jensine A. Petersen April, 1865 (daughter of Christian Petersen and Anna Elizabeth Jensen, pioneers Sept. 23, 1862, Madsen company). She was born May 3, 1844. Their children: Andrew b. Feb. 16, 1866, m. Zina Taylor April 22, 1887; Parley b. Nov. 25, 1868, m. Emma Johnson; Adolph b. Jan. 30, 1871, m. Julia Richie; Zina b. Feb. 26, 1873, d. March 6, 1874; Joseph b. July 30, 1874, m. Sarah Olsen; Thorwald b. April 3, 1877, m. Laura Jensen Jan. 20, 1903; Hans Christian b. Aug. 2, 1879, m. Hulda Andersen; Anna Elizabeth b. Aug. 25, 1884, m. Fred Hunt Jan. 7, 1903; Ida Augusta b. Aug. 1, 1884, d. Feb. 1885. Family home Ephraim, Utah.

HANSEN, CHRISTEN. Born Jan. 11, 1819, at Senglose, Kjobenhavn amt, Denmark. Came to Utah 1857.
Married Ingar Mortenson. Their children: Martin, m. Mary Elizabeth Steele; Caroline, m. Joseph Adams; Hannah, m. John Conder; Hans, m. La Vina Herbert; Joseph, died; Ingar, m. Richard Mitchell. Family home American Fork, Utah.
High priest. Farmer; shoemaker. Died July 8, 1906.

HANSEN, MARTIN (son of Christen Hansen and Ingar Mortenson).
Married Mary Elizabeth Steele Aug. 14, 1871, at Salt Lake City (daughter of Richard Steele and Mary Ann Reese of

Aug. 10, 1851, and came to Utah October 1851. Their children: Richard Henry b. Aug. 19, 1872, m. Margarette Thornton; Charles Edward b. Sept. 15, 1874, and Martin Ephraim b. Dec. 20, 1876 died; William Reese b. Nov. 25, 1877, m. Rosabelle Wilcox; Moses Albert b. Dec. 31, 1879, m. Mary Elizabeth Radmall; Isaac Walter b. Aug. 14, 1882, m. Hattie Waggstaff; Georg Heber b. Oct. 1, 1884, m. Maude Lowe; Mary Elizabeth b. Sept. 22, 1886, m. Gilbert Lesley Wootton; Thomas Crafton b. Feb. 22, 1892. Family home American Fork, Utah.
High priest; number American Fork 4th ward bishopric 10 years. Farmer and fruit grower.

HANSEN, HANS (For his genealogy see Hans Jorgensen, his father.)

HANSEN, HANS CHRISTIAN (son of Andrew Hansen and Regena Anderse of Denmark). Born May 6, 1824, in Denmark. Came to Utah 1853 John Forsgren company.
Married Annie E. Jensen 1849 (daughter of John Jensen). She was born 1826. Their children: Praben A. b. July 12, 1850, m. Emma Petersen 1875; Josephine b. 1852, m. C. J. Thomson 1870; Jephi b. 1856, m. Mae Monk 1896; Annie M. b. 1859, m. J. S. Lingham 1880; Hans C. b. 1863; m. Jane R. Bingham 1882; Cauncy E. b. 1865, m. Laura ——— 1888; Dorcose R. b. 1866, m John Eames.
Married Annie Catherine Neilsen March 21, 1863, at Salt Lake City (daugter of A. C. Neilsen), who was born June 5, 1842, at Fly, Denmark. Their children: Joseph E. b. Dec. 4, 1865, m. Sara Wayment 1897; Hyrum R. b. Feb. 2, 1868, and Moroni b. Jne 14, 1870, died; Joanna b. July 13, 1872, m. Sanford S. Bigham 1894; Louis A. b. Feb. 29, 1896, m. Martha Waymer 1898; Lorenzo E. b. June 13, 1879, died; Martin G. b. Jun 14, 1883, m. Alice King 1906; George P. b. July 19, 1886, m Zebonia Anderson 1911. Families resided Plain City, Utah
Member 7th corum seventies; missionary to Denmark 1860.

HANSEN, PRADEN A. (son of Hans Christian Hansen and Annie H. Jensen. Born July 12, 1850, Copenhagen, Denmark.
Married Emma Peterson 1875 (daughter of Hans Peterson and Martena Hisen, pioneers 1853 with John Forsgren company. She was born October 1857, Lehi, Utah. Their children: Annie L. b. March 15, 1877, m. Oscar Jensen 1895; Lorenzo E. b. July 9, 1879, m. Ethelmaid Bosworth 1900; Leonard E. b. Nov. 29, 1882, m. Laura Lebo 1901; Clarence b. March 13, 1885, m. Clarebell Berzon 1903; Delilah b. June 5, 1887, m. J. A. Tavlor 1906; Samuel N. b. Sept. 29, 1889, m. Annie Jenkins 1911; Sylvia H. b. Aug. 15, 1892. Family home Preston, Idaho.
Elder in Mormon church.

HANSEN, HANS '. (son of Hans Nielsen born May 12, 1791, at Eukrod, Denmark, and Anna Olsen). Born April 23, 1831, at Kaierod, Denmark. Came to Utah Oct. 26, 1852.
Married Anna Maria Sorensen (daughter of Rasmus Sorensen), who was bon June 16, 1832, and came to Utah Oct. 5, 1856. Hancock company. Their children: Anna Sophia b. Jan. 22, 1858, m. Michal Johnson Jan. 1, 1877; Peter O. b. March 3, 1860, m. Sarah A. Jensen March 11, 1885; Gertrude b. Feb. 5, 1862, m. W. Leishian Oct. 22, 1884; Maria b. June 27, 1864, m. John Wilckins D. 19, 1884; Emma b. Aug. 14, 1868; Sarah b. March 13, 1870, m J. A. Leishman.
Missionary to Denmark 1865-66. Stone cutter on temples at Salt Lake City and Logan, Utah. Indian war veteran.

HANSEN, PETE IORSON (son of Hans F. Hansen and Anna Marie Sorensen). Born March 3, 1860, Salt Lake City.
Married Sarah Ann Jensen March 11, 1885, Logan, Utah (daughter of Andrew C. Jensen and Anna Maria Carlson), who was born F. 25, 1867, and died April 12, 1899. Their children: Eulalia. May 25, 1886, d. Aug. 30, 1905; Sylvia b. Dec. 15, 1887, d. April 19, 1889; Orrin P.
Married Udeta ose Hansen. She died July 18, 1905. Their children: Valare . b. Sept. 10, 1891; Elva R. b. Dec. 17, 1893; Monta M. b. May, 1896. Family home Logan, Utah.
Monument dealer and cut stone contractor.

HANSEN, JACOB son of Hans Petersen, born May 17, 1808, Hvedstrup, Denmark, and Johanna Jacobsen, born 1803, Svogerslov, Denmark). He was born Nov. 21, 1842, at Klovtofte, Denmark. Came to Utah Oct. 5, 1867.
Married Karen Andersen Oct. 2, 1871 (daughter of Anders Andersen and In r Nielsen), who was born April 27, 1850. Their children: Hannah Roseline b. Dec. 18, 1872, m. Alma Nelsen; Hyrum Pb. Jan. 2, 1875, m. Hettie Howell; Joseph Waldemar b. Apr. 18, 1877, died; Nancy Ingebor b. July 17, 1879, m. Albe. Holmgren; Richard T. b. Nov. 9, 1882; Agnes b. April 1. 1885; Lorin E. b. April 19, 1890; Flora b. April 30, 1895. Family home Bear River City, Utah.
Married Isador Leutz Nov. 24, 1881, at Salt Lake City (daughter of Ole Leutz and Maren Olsen), who was born May 10, 1840, at Oskilde, Denmark.
Married Mary ansen Feb. 14, 1884, at Salt Lake City (daughter of Har Jorgensen), who was born Nov. 22, 1854, at Thorby, Denmark. Their children: Bernard b. Sept. 10, 1885, m. Lucinda anson.
Bishop's counsel 1884-1900, and 1904 to the present time.

PIONEERS AND PROMINENT MEN OF UTAH 915

HANSEN, JENS. Born in Denmark. Came to Utah 1862, oxteam company.
Married Bertha Christena Petersen, in enmark (daughter of Chris Petersen of Denmark). Their children: Martha, d. infant; Emma, d. infant; Caroline, . Mr. Anderson; Mary, m. Matt Peters; Joseph; Minnie, m. Chris Halverson; Josephine, m. Levi Anderton; Sophia, m. ET. Jones; Bertha, m. Charley Salt; Margaret, m. Harry Dniels; James, m. Sarah Wiseman; Hyrum, m. Laura Cook Family resided Monroe and Helper, Utah.
Seventy; home missionary. Echo Canyon war veteran. Farmer and railroad contractor. Died at Monroe, Utah.

HANSEN, HYRUM (son of Jens Hansen an Bertha Christena Petersen). Born Feb. 18, 1875, Monroe, Uth.
Married Laura Cook April 6, 1908, Spring Glen, Utah (daughter of Chauncy Cook and Clariss Curdith of Salt Lake City, pioneers with oxteam). Sh was born Dec. 11, 1889. Their children: Hyrum, Jr., March 9, 1909; James Peter b. Oct. 22, 1911. Family home Spring Glen, Utah.
Farmer.

HANSEN, JENS (son of Hans Sorensen and Karen Lucy Nielsen of Denmark). Born Feb. 15, 1822, Illgart, Denmark. Came to Utah Sept. 29, 1853, John Forsgrn company.
Married Charlotte Sophia Dorthea Pet'sen (Mickelsen) June 19, 1847 (daughter of Peter Michelse and Maria Rasmussen of Denmark). She was born Jan. 7, 1828, and came to Utah with husband. Their children: Karen Maria b. July 20, 1848, m. Peter H. Madsen; Hans hristian b. Sept. 14, 1850, m. Mary Leonora Morley; Geraldine b. Feb. 14, 1853, m. Louis Hougard; Dorthea b. M'ch 20, 1856, m. Niels Jorgensen; Ellen b. July 18, 185 m. William B. Lowry; Sophia b. Dec. 19, 1860, m. Jacob Finch; Jens J. b. June 12, 1863, m. Jeanette Ritchey; Emeli b. Nov. 13, 1865, m. Joseph H. Jenson; Joseph b. March 11868, m. Elmira Funk. Family home Manti, Utah.
Married Mary Anderson Sept. 2, 1864 Salt Lake City (daughter of Hans Anderson of Denmark Their children: Jens Peter b. Aug. 5, 1866, m. Karen Raburg; Albina b. Jan. 2, 1968, m. Joseph Bemus; Mary An b. July 5, 1875, m. James Breathwaite. Family home Manti, Utah.
High priest; ward teacher; superintendent teacher's quorum of North Manti ward. One of th first settlers of Manti; city councilman; school trustee. Bck Hawk Indian war veteran. Farmer and stockraiser. Led Nov. 29, 1884, Manti, Utah.

HANSEN, HANS CHRISTIAN (son of ns Hansen and Charlotte Sophia Dorthea Petersen (Mickeen). Born Sept. 14, 1850, Roskeld, Denmark. Came to Uta September, 1853, with father.
Married Mary Leonora Morley Jan. 3 1870, Salt Lake City (daughter of Isaac Morley and Hann Blaisley Finch of Montague, Mass., pioneers 1847). Shewas born March 26, 1852. Their children: Hannah Charlott b. March 4, 1871, m. John William McDonald; Effie Leonor b. June 20, 1872, m. Christian Christiansen; Jens Isaac b. Nov. 11, 1874, d. infant; Lafayette b. Dec. 31, 1875, m. Emi Pulsinher; Ellen b. Feb. 6, 1879, d. child; Hans Willis b. Sept. 3, 1881, d. child; Mary Rosalind b. Feb. 7, 1885, m. Leroy Livingston; Joseph Morley b. May 21, 1887, d. child; Lucy Cdelia b. June 1, 1889; Francis Leon b. Sept. 1, 1892. Faily home Molen (Ferron), Utah.
High priest; counselor to Bishops Lynn S. Beach and Hans Peter Rasmussen; presiding elder of Molen ward; Sunday school superintendent; ward christer; president Y. M. I. A. Has assisted in making canals. wagon roads, and in developing the country in and round Manti and Ferron. Black Hawk Indian war vetem. Farmer and apiarist.

HANSEN, JENS J. (son of Jens Hansen and Charlotte S. D. Petersen). Born June 19, 1863, Mant Utah.
Married Margaret Ann Ritchey March 4, 886, Manti, Utah (daughter of William B. Ritchey and Johana Mariah Hougaard of Manti, pioneers 1849, oxteam co pany). She was born Nov. 3, 1868. Family home, Manti.
Married Jeanette J. Ritchey May 30, 88, Manti. Utah (daughter of William D. Ritchey and Johana Mariah Hougaard), who was born July 25, 1871, Manti. Utah. Their children: Margaret Ann b. Sept. 7, 1889, m Elmer Sorensen; William J. b. Oct. 9, 1891; Jay B. b. Nov. 19, 1893; Lois b. Feb. 6, 1896; Joseph Wayne b. July 3, 1897; Howard F. b. May 7, 1900; Lamar R. b. Aug. 4, 1902; Audria E. b. June 30, 1904; Alton L. b. Sept. 1, 1906, d. Dec. 31, 1908; Mary Willina b. Dec. 17, 1911. Families sided Manti and Ferron, Utah.
Member 48th and 139th quorum seventis; Sunday school teacher. Horticultural inspector for Emer county; observation inspector and crop reporter. Farmer nd builder.

HANSEN, NIELS PETER (son of Hans Pelsen and Karen Rasmussen of Alindamogle, Sjelland, Denrk). Born April 1, 1841, at Alindamogle. Came to Utah ct. 5, 1864, John Sharp company.
Married Anna Marie Lofgren Nov. 15, 1 6, Brigham City, Utah (daughter of John August Lofgren and Karna Niels of Rostunen, Sweden). She was born June 4, 1838. Their children: Mary A.; Elizn; Rachel; Neeley L..; Dorothea Madsen June 14, 1899; Joseph J.; John A., aged 8 months. Family resided Brigham City and Smithfid, Utah.
Missionary to Scandinavia 1862-63; home missionary; elder. Shoemaker; watchmaker.

HANSEN, NEELEY LOFGREN (son of Niels Peter Hansen and Anna Marie Lofgren). Born July 25, 1873, Smithfield, Utah.
Married Dorothea Madsen June 14, 1899, Lake View, Utah (daughter of Peter Madsen and Caroline Knudson of that place). She was born March 9, 1875. Their children: Lola M. b. May 6, 1900; Ted b. June 3, 1904; Rama M. b. May 27, 1909. Family home Brigham City, Utah.
Missionary to Denmark 1911-13; Sunday school superintendent; bishop's counselor. Merchant.

HANSEN, OLE. Born Sept. 26, 1825, Lunde, Denmark. Came to Utah 1870.
Died Sept. 16, 1908.

HANSEN, PETER (son of Hans Christen and Johannah Marie Hansen). He was born March 27, 1837, Hyssten Torg Sovet amt, Syeland, Denmark. Came to Utah September, 1862, Capt. John Van Cott company.
Married Beata Gustava Burresen November, 1863, Manti, Utah (daughter of Mr. Burresen of Halmstam, Sweden). She was born November, 1837; came to Utah 1863. Their children: Eda b. Nov. 1864, m. John Ralphs; Peter b. Feb. 1866, m. Martha Stevens; Frederick b. Aug. 1867; Hannah, m. Parley Ralphs; Mary, m. Richard Keele; Beata, m. Lewis Olsen; Alfred William b. Jan. 23, 1875, m. Lydia Ann Jolly; Niels b. Feb. 15, 1877, m. Carrie Williams; William b. Sept. 7, 1879, died; Andrew b. March 28, 1881, m. Nora Abaline. Family home Emery, Utah.
Called by Brigham Young to help settle "The Muddy." Moved to Castle Dale 1880. Moved to Manti 1862, where he worked as a mason in constructing stone buildings and also on the Manti temple for two years; moved to Ferron; moved to Emery in 1893, where he assisted in making canals and wagon roads. Indian war veteran.

HANSEN, ALFRED WILLIAM (son of Peter Hansen and Beata Gustava Burresen). Born Jan. 23, 1877, Manti, Utah.
Married Lydia Ann Jolly Sept. 4, 1901, Manti, Utah (daughter of Williamson Wesley Jolly and Lydia A. Brimhall, both of Emery, Utah). She was born May 11, 1882. Their children: Screlda b. June 25, 1902; Wesley b. July 28, 1904; Farrel b. Oct. 21, 1906; Vera b. Feb. 22, 1909; Everett b. Feb. 25, 1912. Family home Emery, Utah.
Member 197th quorum seventies; counselor to superintendent of Sunday schools; aid in Y. M. M. I. A.; ward teacher at Emery. Farmer.

HANSEN, PETER (son of Hans Jorgenson and Anna Danielson of Haulykke (Maribo), Denmark). Born Sept. 29, 1827, Haulykke, Denmark. Came to Utah Oct. 22, 1866, Captain Lowry company.
Married Anne Danielson 1851, Haulykke, Denmark (daughter of Daniel Neilson and Anne Marie Jensen of Haulykke). She was born Feb. 5, 1827. Their children: Jorgen, m. Mary Nielson; Neils Antone, Hans Daniel and Marius (Anders), died. Family home Provo, Utah.
Married Mary Kathryne Hansen (Ludvigsen) December, 1875, Salt Lake City (daughter of Matta Hansen and Karren Steffensen of Vindeny, Denmark). She was born Aug. 24, 1840. Their children: Charles Peter, m. Nora Nebcker; Annie, m. Karl Gren; Sarah Rebecca, m. Lee Nauce; Karoline, m. Edward Vincent; Enoch Elbert, m. Fern Gatherum; Ephriam E., m. Maude Hawkins.
Member 34th quorum seventies; high priest. Farmer. Died June 21, 1903, Provo, Utah.

HANSEN, JORGEN (son of Peter Hansen and Anne Danielson). Born Aug. 1, 1852, Haulykke, Denmark. Came to Utah with father.
Married Mary Nielsen May 13, 1877, Provo, Utah (daughter of Seren Nielsen and Amelia Berg of Provo, Utah, pioneers Sept. 25, 1868, John G. Holman company). She was born Nov. 14, 1857. Their children: Amelia A. b. Feb. 15, 1878, m. Andrew Anderberg; Francis J. b. Feb. 24, 1881, died; Birdie B. b. June 26, 1883, m. Ernest Moore; Calvin C. b. May 2, 1886; Edna E. b. Sept. 28, 1888, m. Ivan Ben George G. b. Aug. 28, 1890; Henrietta B. Aug. 15, 1892 Tone I. b. Sept. 17, 1894; Julina J. b. August 31, 1896 May 10, 1899; Louis L. b. Feb. 7, 1904, died,
Married Alma Nielson Oct. 9, 1885, Logan, Ut of Hacon and Sophia Nielson of Salt Lake was born May 4, 1864. Only child: Donizett 27, 1886, m. Jane Chapman.
Member 34th quorum seventies; high priest; to Denmark 1883-85; bishop's counselor; Sunday sch intendent. County road supervisor. Farmer a grower.

HANSON, CHRISTIAN (son of Hans Andersen and Christensen of Fyen, Denmark). Born April 2, 1822, at mark, Fyen, Denmark. Came to Utah Oct. 6, 1862, Cap Murdock company.
Married Gertrude Kirstine Rasmussen (daughter of Rmus Neilsen and Abelone Marie Knudsen, both died in Der mark, Fyen, Denmark. She was born Nov. 8, 1826. Their children: Hans C. b. Sept. 16, 1849, m. Annie Brunson June 6, 1876; Abelone Marie and Maren, d. Denmark; Erasmus Martin b. March 26, 1859, m. Caroline Christianson April 6, 1881; Joseph Henry, m. Dinntha Black.
Member of Millard stake high council. Carpenter, did work on Manti and St. George temples. Died Aug. 1, 1889.

914   PIONEERS AND PROMINENT MEN OF UTAH

HANKS, ALFRED LYMAN (son of Alfred Frederick Hanks and Ellen Taylor Lyman). Born Aug. 28, 1880, Tooele, Utah. Married Mary Alice Tate June 14, 1905, Salt Lake City (daughter of John William Tate and Elizabeth de la Mare of Tooele, Utah). She was born Nov. 8, 1882. Their child: Ellen Romona b. March 16, 1906. Family home Tooele, Utah.
Member 43d quorum seventies; secretary Y. M. M. I. A. Tooele ward. Postmaster of Tooele.

HANSEN, ANDERS K. (son of Peter Hansen and Metta Hansen of Sjelland, Denmark). Born Jan. 27, 1818, Sjelland, Denmark. Came to Utah 1861, John R. Murdock company. Married Aurelia Quistgaard Feb. 2, 1863, Salt Lake City (daughter of Julius Quistgaard and Louisa Pulilke of Sjelland). She was born Sept. 22, 1842. Their children: Matha Louisa, died; Caroline, m. C. W. Walker; Henrietta, died; Anders K., Jr., m. Amelia L. Heppler; Julia (died), m. J. E. Heppler; Isaac, m. Sophia Sorenson; Abraham, m. Effie Sorenson; Jacob. Family resided Draper and Glenwood, Utah.
High priest; missionary in Denmark before coming to Utah. Farmer and stockraiser. Died Aug. 1, 1903, Glenwood, Utah.

HANSEN, ANDERS K., JR. (son of Anders K. Hansen and Aurelia Quistgaard). Born Dec. 12, 1870, Draper, Utah. Married Amelia L. Heppler Oct. 13, 1897, Manti. Utah (daughter of Andrew Heppier and Louisiana Seegmiller of Canada—came to Utah 1872 by railroad). She was born Oct. 27, 1871. Their children: Arndale Kelch b. Feb. 12, 1899; Velva b. Oct. 27, 1900, d. infant; Leland Anders b. Oct. 12, 1901; Lina b. Jan. 23, 1903; Alta b. Dec. 17, 1905; Phil b. Oct. 26, 1907. Family resided Glenwood and Richfield, Utah.
Member 36th quorum seventies; missionary to northern states 1897-99; counselor Sevier stake Y. M. M. I. A.; counselor in bishopric of Richfield second ward; Sevier county assessor 1900-04; town president Glenwood; city councilman Richfield. Farmer and stockraiser.

HANSEN, ANDREW (son of Hans Andersen, born June 23, 1766, of Jerskow, Skilo, Odense Amt, Fyen, Denmark, and Maren Andersen, born May 5, 1792, Norup, Odense Amt). He was born July 10, 1809, at Egense, Norup, Odense Amt. Came to Utah 1853.
Married Karen Jacobsdaughter 1857, at Salt Lake City (daughter of Jacob Nielsen and Maren Petersdaughter), who was born May 3, 1825. Came to Utah Sept. 13, 1857, Christian Christensen company. Their children: James b. Nov. 20, 1860, m. Elizabeth Frandsen March 8, 1883; Andrew b. Nov. 4, 1863, m. Carlina Anderson. Family home Ephraim, Utah.

HANSEN, JAMES (son of Andrew Hansen and Karen Jacobsdaughter). Born Nov. 20, 1860, Ephraim, Utah.
Married Elizabeth Frandsen March 8, 1880, at Salt Lake City (daughter of Niels Frandsen), who was born Feb. 12, 1861, in Denmark. Their children: Erma b. Dec. 14, 1884, m. Horace Hales; James Orvill b. May 25, 1886; Niels Andrew b. March 11, 1888, m. Olive Sorensen; Delbert b. March 25, 1890; Ruth Maria b. Aug. 8, 1895. Family home Redmond, Utah.
Member 1st city council Redmond, Utah. Vice-president Rocky Ford Irrigation company 1895-1905; vice-president Vermillion Extension Irrigation company. Deputy road supervisor, District 9, Redmond, Utah.

HANSEN, ANDREW N. (son of Hans Larsen, born Sept. 24, 1776, and Anna Nielsen, born Aug. 30, 1790, Ide, near Fredrikshald, Norway—married 1815). He was born March 6, 1836, at Ide. Came to Utah Sept. 25, 1863, with Peter Nebeker company.
Married Jensine A. Petersen April, 1865 (daughter of Christian Petersen and Anna Elizabeth Jensen, pioneers Sept. 23, 1862, Christian A. Madsen company). She was born May 3, 1844. Their children: Andrew b. Feb. 16, 1866, m. Zina Taylor April 22, 1887; Parley b. Nov. 25, 1868, m. Emma Johnson; Adolph b. Jan. 30, 1871, m. Julia Richie; Zina b. Feb. 25, 1873, d. March 6, 1874; Joseph b. July 30, 1874, m. Sarah Olsen; Thorwald b. April 3, 1877, m. Laura Jensen Jan. 20, 1903; Hans Christian b. Aug. 2, 1879, m. Hulda Andersen; Anna Elizabeth b. Aug. 26, 1884, m. Fred Hunt Jan. 7, 1903; Ida Augusta b. Aug. 1, 1884, d. Feb. 1885. Family home Ephraim, Utah.

HANSEN, CHRISTEN. Born Jan. 11, 1819, at Senglose, Kjobenhavn amt, Denmark. Came to Utah 1857.
Married Ingar Mortenson. Their children: Martin, m. Mary Elizabeth Steele; Caroline, m. Joseph Adams; Hannah, m. John Conder; Hans, m. La Vina Herbert; Joseph, died; Ingar, m. Richard Mitchell. Family home American Fork, Utah.
High priest. Farmer; shoemaker. Died July 8, 1906.

HANSEN, MARTIN (son of Christen Hansen and Ingar Mortenson).
Married Mary Elizabeth Steele Aug. 14, 1871, at Salt Lake City (daughter of Richard Steele and Mary Ann Reese of Aug. 10, 1851, and came to Utah October 1851. Their children: Richard Henry b. Aug. 19, 1872, m. Margarette Thornton; Charles Edward b. Sept. 15, 1874, and Martin Ephraim b. Dec. 20, 1875, died; William Reese b. Nov. 25, 1877, m. Rosabelle Wilcox; Moses Albert b. Dec. 31, 1879, m. Mary Elizabeth Radmall; Isaac Walter b. Aug. 14, 1882, m. Hattie Wagstaff; George Heber b. Oct. 1, 1884, m. Maude Lowe; Mary Elizabeth b. Sept. 22, 1886, m. Gilbert Lesley Wootton; Thomas Grafton b. Feb. 22, 1892. Family home American Fork, Utah.
High priest; member American Fork 4th ward bishopric 10 years. Farmer and fruit grower.

HANSEN, HANS. (For his genealogy see Hans Jorgensen, his father.)

HANSEN, HANS CHRISTIAN (son of Andrew Hansen and Regena Andersen of Denmark). Born May 6, 1824, in Denmark. Came to Utah 1853 John Forsgren company.
Married Annie H. Jensen 1849 (daughter of John Jensen). She was born 1826. Their children: Praben A. b. July 12, 1850, m. Emma Petersen 1875; Josephine b. 1852, m. C. J. Thomson 1870; Nephi b. 1856, m. Mae Monk 1896; Annie M. b. 1859, m. J. S. Bingham 1880; Hans C. b. 1863; m. Jane R. Bingham 1882; Chauncy E. b. 1865, m. Laura —— 1888; Dorcose R. b. 1866, m. John Eames.
Married Annie Catherine Neilsen March 21, 1863, at Salt Lake City (daughter of A. C. Neilsen), who was born June 6, 1842, at Fly, Denmark. Their children: Joseph E. b. Dec. 4, 1865, m. Sarah Wayment 1897; Hyrum E. b. Feb. 2, 1868, and Moroni b. June 14, 1870, died; Joanna b. July 13, 1873, m. Sanford S. Bingham 1894; Louis A. b. Feb. 29, 1876, m. Martha Wayment 1898; Lorenzo E. b. June 13, 1878, died; Martin G. b. June 14, 1883, m. Alice King 1906; George E. b. July 19, 1886, m. Zebonia Anderson 1911. Families resided Plain City, Utah.
Member 7th quorum seventies; missionary to Denmark 1860.

HANSEN, PRABEN A. (son of Hans Christian Hansen and Annie H. Jensen). Born July 12, 1850, Copenhagen, Denmark.
Married Emma Peterson 1875 (daughter of Hans Peterson and Martena Hansen, pioneers 1853 with John Forsgren company). She was born October 1857, Levis, Utah. Their children: Annie M. b. March 15, 1877, m. Oscar Jensen 1895; Lorenzo E. b. July 9, 1879, m. Ethelmaid Bosworth 1900; Leonard E. b. Nov. 29, 1882, m. Laura Lebo 1901; Clarence b. March 13, 1885, m. Clarebell Berzon 1903; Delilah b. June 5, 1887, m. J. A. Taylor 1906; Samuel N. b. Sept. 29, 1889, m. Annie Jenkins 1908; Sylvia H. b. Aug. 15, 1892. Family home Preston, Idaho.
Elder in Mormon church.

HANSEN, HANS F. (son of Hans Nielsen born May 12, 1791, at Bukrod, Denmark, and Anna Olsen). Born April 23, 1831, at Kalerod, Denmark. Came to Utah Oct. 26, 1852.
Married Anna Maria Sorensen (daughter of Rasmus Sorensen), who was born June 16, 1832, and came to Utah Oct. 5, 1856, Hancock company. Their children: Anna Sophia b. Jan. 22, 1858, m. Michael Johnson Jan. 1, 1877; Peter O. b. March 3, 1860, m. Sarah Ann Jensen March 11, 1885; Gertrude b. Feb. 5, 1862, m. W. Leishman Oct. 22, 1884; Maria b. June 27, 1864, m. John Wilckins Dec. 19, 1884; Emma b. Aug. 14, 1868; Sarah b. March 13, 1870, m. J. A. Leishman.
Missionary to Denmark 1865-66. Stone cutter on temples at Salt Lake City and Logan, Utah. Indian war veteran.

HANSEN, PETER ORSON (son of Hans F. Hansen and Anna Marie Sorensen). Born March 3, 1860, Salt Lake City.
Married Sarah Ann Jensen March 11, 1885, Logan, Utah (daughter of Andrew C. Jensen and Anna Maria Carlson), who was born Feb. 25, 1867, and died April 12, 1890. Their children: Eulalia b. May 25, 1886, d. Aug. 30, 1905; Sylvia b. Dec. 15, 1887, d. April 19, 1889; Orrin P.
Married Udeta Rose Hansen. She died July 18, 1905. Their children: Valare R. b. Sept. 10, 1891; Elva R. b. Dec. 17, 1893; Monta M. b. May 5, 1896. Family home Logan, Utah.
Monument dealer and cut stone contractor.

HANSEN, JACOB (son of Hans Petersen, born May 17, 1808, Hvedstrup, Denmark, and Johanna Jacobsen, born 1803, Svogerslov, Denmark). He was born Nov. 21, 1842, at Klovtofte, Denmark. Came to Utah Oct. 5, 1867.
Married Karen Andersen Oct. 2, 1871 (daughter of Anders Andersen and Inger Nielsen), who was born April 27, 1850. Their children: Hannah Roseline b. Dec. 28, 1872, m. Alma Nelsen; Hyrum J. b. Jan. 2, 1875, m. Hettie Howell; Joseph Waldemar b. April 30, 1877, died; Nancy Ingebor b. July 17, 1879, m. Albert Holmgren; Richard T. b. Nov. 9, 1882; Agnes b. April 16, 1885; Lorin E. b. April 19, 1890; Flora b. April 30, 1895. Family home Bear River City, Utah.
Married Isadore Leutz Nov. 24, 1881, at Salt Lake City (daughter of Ole Leutz and Maren Olsen), who was born May 10, 1840, at Roskilde, Denmark.
Married Mary Hansen Feb. 14, 1884, at Salt Lake City (daughter of Hans Jorgensen), who was born Nov. 22, 1854, at Thorby, Denmark. Their children: Bernard b. Sept. 10, 1885, m. Lucinda Hanson.
Bishop's counselor 1884-1900, and 1904 to the present time.

HANSEN, JENS. Born in Denmark. Came to Utah 1862, oxteam company.
Married Bertha Christena Petersen, in Denmark (daughter of Chris Petersen of Denmark). Their children: Martha, d. infant; Emma, d. infant; Caroline, m. Mr. Anderson; Mary, m. Matt Peters; Joseph; Minnie, m. Chris Halverson; Josephine, m. Levi Anderton; Sophia, m. E. T. Jones; Bertha, m. Charley Salt; Margaret, m. Harry Daniels; James, m. Sarah Wiseman; Hyrum, m. Laura Cook. Family resided Monroe and Helper, Utah.
Seventy; home missionary. Echo Canyon war veteran. Farmer and railroad contractor. Died at Monroe, Utah.

HANSEN, HYRUM (son of Jens Hansen and Bertha Christena Petersen). Born Feb. 18, 1875, Monroe, Utah.
Married Laura Cook April 6, 1908, Spring Glen, Utah (daughter of Chauncy Cook and Clarissa Curdith of Salt Lake City, pioneers with oxteam). She was born Dec. 11, 1889. Their children: Hyrum, Jr., b. March 9, 1909; James Peter b. Oct. 22, 1911. Family home Spring Glen, Utah.
Farmer.

HANSEN, JENS (son of Hans Sorensen and Karen Lucy Nielsen of Denmark). Born Feb. 15, 1822, Hulgart, Denmark. Came to Utah Sept. 29, 1853, John Forsgren company.
Married Charlotte Sophia Dorthea Petersen (Mickelsen) June 19, 1847 (daughter of Peter Michelson and Maria Rasmussen of Denmark). She was born Jan. 17, 1828, and came to Utah with husband. Their children: Karen Maria b. July 20, 1848, m. Peter H. Madsen; Hans Christian b. Sept. 14, 1850, m. Mary Leonora Morley; Geraldine b. Feb. 14, 1853, m. Louis Hougard; Dorthea b. March 20, 1856, m. Niels Jorgensen; Ellen b. July 18, 1858, m. William B. Lowry; Sophia b. Dec. 19, 1860, m. Jacob Winch; Jens J. b. June 19, 1863, m. Margaret Ann Ritchey; Emeline b. Nov. 13, 1865, m. Joseph H. Jenson; Joseph b. March 9, 1868, m. Elmira Funk. Family home Manti, Utah.
Married Mary Anderson Sept. 2, 1864, Salt Lake City (daughter of Hans Anderson of Denmark). Their children: Jens Peter b. Aug. 5, 1866, m. Karen Ranburg; Albina b. Jan. 2, 1868, m. Joseph Bemus; Mary Ann b. July 5, 1875, m. James Breathwaite. Family home Manti, Utah.
High priest; ward teacher; superintendent teacher's quorum of North Manti ward. One of the first settlers of Manti; city councilman; school trustee. Black Hawk Indian war veteran. Farmer and stockraiser. Died Nov. 29, 1884, Manti, Utah.

HANSEN, HANS CHRISTIAN (son of Jens Hansen and Charlotte Sophia Dorthea Petersen (Mickelsen). Born Sept. 14, 1850, Roskeld, Denmark. Came to Utah September, 1853, with father.
Married Mary Leonora Morley Jan. 3, 1870, Salt Lake City (daughter of Isaac Morley and Hannah Blaisley Finch of Montague, Mass., pioneers 1847). She was born March 26, 1852. Their children: Hannah Charlotte b. March 4, 1871, m. John William McDonald; Effie Leonora b. June 20, 1872, m. Christian Christianson; Jens Isaac b. Nov. 11, 1874, d. infant; Lafayette b. Dec. 31, 1875, m. Effie Pulsipher; Ellen b. Feb. 18, 1877, m. John Frederick Larsen; Edveinetta b. Feb. 6, 1879, d. child; Hans Willis b. Sept. 13, 1881, d. child; Mary Rosalind b. Feb. 7, 1885, m. Leroy Livingston; Joseph Morley b. May 21, 1887, d. child; Lucy Cordelia b. June 1, 1889; Francia Leon b. Sept. 1, 1892. Family home Molen (Ferron), Utah.
High priest; counselor to Bishops Lyman S. Beach and Hans Peter Rasmussen; presiding elder of Molen ward; Sunday school superintendent; ward chorister; president Y. M. M. I. A. Has assisted in making canals, wagon roads, and in developing the country in and around Manti and Ferron. Black Hawk Indian war veteran. Farmer and apiarist.

HANSEN, JENS J. (son of Jens Hansen and Charlotte S. B. Petersen). Born June 19, 1863, Manti, Utah.
Married Margaret Ann Ritchey March 4, 1886, Manti, Utah (daughter of William B. Ritchey and Johanna Mariah Hougaard of Manti, pioneers 1848, oxteam company). She was born Nov. 3, 1868. Family home Manti.
Married Jeanette J. Ritchey May 30, 1888, Manti, Utah (daughter of William B. Ritchey and Johanna Mariah Hougaard), who was born July 25, 1871, Manti, Utah. Their children: Margaret Ann b. Sept. 7, 1889, m. Elmer Sorensen; William J. b. Oct. 9, 1891; Jay B. b. Nov. 19, 1893; Lola Feb. 6, 1896; Joseph Wayne b. July 30, 1897; Howard F. b. May 7, 1900; Lamar R. b. Aug. 4, 1902; Audria E. b. June 30, 1904; Alton L. b. Sept. 1, 1908, d. Dec. 31, 1908; Mary Willina b. Dec. 17, 1911. Families resided Manti and Ferron, Utah.
Member 48th and 138th quorum seventies; Sunday school teacher. Horticultural inspector for Emery county; observation inspector and crop reporter. Farmer and builder.

HANSEN, NIELS PETER (son of Hans Nielsen and Karen Rasmussen of Alindamogle, Sjelland, Denmark). Born April 1, 1841, at Alindamogle. Came to Utah Oct. 5, 1864, John Sharp company.
Married Anna Marie Lofgren Nov. 15, 1866, Brigham City, Utah (daughter of John August Lofgren and Karna Niels of Rostunga, Sweden). She was born June 1, 1838. Their children: Mary A.; Eliza; Rachel; Neeley L., m. Dorothea Madsen June 14, 1899; Joseph F.; John A., d. aged 8 months. Family resided Brigham City and Smithfield, Utah.
Missionary to Scandinavia 1862-63; home missionary; elder. Shoemaker; watchmaker.

HANSEN, NEELEY LOFGREN (son of Niels Peter Hansen and Anna Marie Lofgren). Born July 25, 1873, Smithfield, Utah.
Married Dorothea Madsen June 14, 1899, Lake View, Utah (daughter of Peter Madsen and Caroline Knudson of that place). She was born March 9, 1875. Their children: Lola M. b. May 5, 1900; Ted b. June 3, 1904; Rama M. b. May 27, 1909. Family home Brigham City, Utah.
Missionary to Denmark 1911-13; Sunday school superintendent; bishop's counselor. Merchant.

HANSEN, OLE. Born Sept. 26, 1825, Lunde, Denmark. Came to Utah 1870.
Died Sept. 16, 1908.

HANSEN, PETER (son of Hans Christen and Johannah Marie Hansen). He was born March 27, 1837, Hyssten Torg Sovet amt, Scandinavia, Denmark. Came to Utah September, 1862, Capt. John Van Cott company.
Married Beata Gustava Burresen November, 1863, Manti, Utah (daughter of Mr. Burresen of Halmstam, Sweden). She was born November, 1837; came to Utah 1863. Their children: Eda b. Nov. 1864, m. John Ralphs; Peter b. Feb. 1866, m. Martha Stevens; Frederick b. Aug. 1867; Hannah, m. Parley Ralphs; Mary, m. Richard Keele; Beata, m. Lewis Olsen; Alfred William b. Jan. 23, 1875, m. Lydia Ann Jolly; Niels b. Feb. 15, 1877, m. Carrie Williams; William b. Sept. 7, 1879, died; Andrew b. March 28, 1881, m. Nora Abaline. Family home Emery, Utah.
Called by Brigham Young to help settle "The Muddy." Moved to Castle Dale 1880. Moved to Manti 1882, where he worked as a mason in constructing stone buildings and also on the Manti temple for two years; moved to Ferron; moved to Emery in 1893, where he assisted in making canals and wagon roads. Indian war veteran.

HANSEN, ALFRED WILLIAM (son of Peter Hansen and Beata Gustava Burresen). Born Jan. 23, 1877, Manti, Utah.
Married Lydia Ann Jolly Sept. 4, 1901, Manti, Utah (daughter of Williamson Wesley Jolly and Lydia A. Brimhall, both of Emery, Utah). She was born May 11, 1882. Their children: Screida b. June 25, 1902; Wesley b. July 28, 1904; Farrel b. Oct. 21, 1906; Vera b. Feb. 22, 1909; Everett b. Feb. 25, 1912. Family home Emery, Utah.
Member 197th quorum seventies; counselor to superintendent of Sunday schools; aid in Y. M. M. I. A.; ward teacher at Emery. Farmer.

HANSEN, PETER (son of Hans Jorgensen and Anna Danielson of Haulykke (Maribo), Denmark). Born Sept. 29, 1827, Haulykke, Denmark. Came to Utah Oct. 22, 1866, Captain Lowry company.
Married Anne Danielson 1851, Haulykke, Denmark (daughter of Daniel Neilson and Anne Marie Jensen of Haulykke). She was born Feb. 5, 1827. Their children: Jorgen, m. Mary Nielson; Nells Antone, Hans Daniel and Marius (Anders), died. Family home Provo, Utah.
Married Mary Kathryne Hansen (Ludvigsen) December, 1875, Salt Lake City (daughter of Matts Hansen and Karren Steffensen of Vindeny, Denmark). She was born Aug. 24, 1840. Their children: Charles Peter, m. Nora Nebeker; Annie, m. Karl Green; Sarah Rebecca, m. Lee Naucer; Karoline, m. Edward Vincent; Enoch Elbert, m. Fern Gatherum; Ephriam E., m. Maude Hawkins.
Member 34th quorum seventies; high priest. Farmer. Died June 21, 1903, Provo, Utah.

HANSEN, JORGEN (son of Peter Hansen and Anne Danielson). Born Aug. 1, 1852, Haulykke, Denmark. Came to Utah with father.
Married Mary Nielsen May 13, 1877, Provo, Utah (daughter of Seren Nielsen and Amelia Berg of Provo, Utah, pioneers Sept. 25, 1868, John G. Holman company). She was born Nov. 14, 1857. Their children: Amelia A. b. Feb. 15, 1878, m. Andrew Anderberg; Francis J. b. Fe. 24, 1881, died; Birdie B. b. May 26, 1883, m. Ernest Moore; Calvin C. b. May 2, 1886; Edna E. b. Sept. 23, 1888, m. Ivan Bean; George G. b. Aug. 28, 1890; Henrietta b. Aug. 15, 1892, died; Iona I. b. Sept. 17, 1894; Julina J. b. March 21, 1897; Cora K. b. May 10, 1899; Louis L. b. Feb. 7, 1904, died.
Married Alma Nielson Oct. 9, 1885, Logan, Utah (daughter of Hacon and Sophia Nielson of Salt Lake City). She was born May 4, 1864. Only child: Donizett D. b. Sept. 27, 1886, m. Gary Draper.
Member 34th quorum seventies; high priest; missionary to Denmark 1883-85; bishop's counselor; Sunday school superintendent. County road supervisor. Farmer and fruitgrower.

HANSON, CHRISTIAN (son of Hans Andersen and Maren Christensen of Fyen, Denmark). Born April 2, 1822, at Hasmark, Fyen, Denmark. Came to Utah Oct. 6, 1862, Captain Murdock company.
Married Gertrude Kirstine Rasmussen (daughter of Rasmus Neilsen and Abelone Marie Knudsen, both died in Denmark). She was born Nov. 8, 1826. Their children: Hans C. b. Sept. 16, 1848, m. Annie Brunson June 5, 1876; Abelone Marie and Maren, d. Denmark; Erasmus Martin b. March 26, 1859, m. Caroline Christianson April 6, 1881; Joseph Henry, m. Dintha Black.
Member of Millard stake high council. Carpenter, did work on Manti and St. George temples. Died Aug. 1, 1889.

HANSON, HANS C. (son of Christian Hanson and Gertrude Kirstine Rasmussen). Born Sept. 16, 1849, at Bederslev, Denmark.
Married Annie Brunson June 5, 1876, Salt Lake City (daughter of Lewis Brunson and Catherine Carling), who was born March 3, 1859, at Fillmore, Utah. Their children: Catherine b. June 9, 1877, d. July 9, 1879; Mary Abelene b. June 29, 1879, m. Frank Russell; Francis b. Jan. 29, 1882, d. Feb. 1, 1882; Joseph Lewis b. Sept. 13, 1883, m. Eva Paul July 13, 1910; Jenett b. Sept. 3, 1889; Harriet Annie b. Feb. 22, 1893; Hans Alma b. May 10, 1896; John b. June 16, 1901, died same day.
One of presidents of 42d quorum seventies; missionary to Denmark 1908. Carpenter; farmer.

HANSON, ERASMUS MARTIN (son of Christian Hanson and Gertrude Kirstine Rasmussen). Born March 26, 1859, Bederslev, Denmark.
Married Caroline Christiansen April 6, 1881, Salt Lake City (daughter of Hendrick Christiansen [died in Denmark] and Anne Marie Petersen). She was born July 6, 1862, in Denmark. Their children: Carrie K. b. Dec. 29, 1881, m. Edward Davis, Jr. March 16, 1904; Annie Laura b. July 19, 1885, m. Orin C. Black Oct. 11, 1907; Martin Henry b. June 18, 1887, m. Loa Black May 26, 1909; Lorenzo Christian b. Aug. 28, 1889; Peter Grantley B. Nov. 4, 1891; Lillian Olive b. May 1, 1894; David Arden b. Sept. 27, 1897; Gladys Marie b. Aug. 28, 1899; Nephi Burton b. Dec. 4, 1903; Celia Roselin b. Nov. 23, 1905; Millard August b. Aug. 13, 1905. Family home Fillmore, Utah.
Missionary to Sandwich Islands 1881-84. Carpenter.

HANSON, CHRISTOPHER O. (son of Ole Hanson and Kon Christenson of Denmark). Born Nov. 18, 1832, in Denmark. Came to Utah in October 1861, Captain Woolley company.
Married Johanna Gibson Nov. 29, 1862, Salt Lake City, who was born June 29, 1829. Their children: Josephine b. Jan. 1, 1864, m. Soerene Godwin; Martin b. April 5, 1867, died; John b. Feb. 12, 1871, m. Caroline Hanson; Martin b. April 1, 1873, m. Eliza Miles; Matilda b. April 2, 1875, m. Joseph Miles. Family home Spanish Fork, Utah.
High priest. Helped in settlement of Sevier valley and Kanab; veteran of Black Hawk war. Farmer.

HANSON, EMIL (son of Elias Hanson, born 1839, and Elizabeth Thor, born 1835, both at Gothenburg, Sweden—married 1857). He was born Oct. 30, 1861, at Gothenburg. Came to Utah 1868.
Married Martha Heep July 1889, Montpelier, Idaho (daughter of William Heep and Sarah Marsh, pioneers to Utah 1865). She was born Nov. 22, 1870. Their children: Ida May b. March 27, 1890, m. Otto Moser; Olive Hanson b. Aug. 20, 1892, m. Alvin Robinson; Lorin b. Sept. 20, 1894; Mammie b. Nov. 25, 1896, and Lyman b. Sept. 5, 1902, died; Selma b. Aug. 30, 1904; Laura b. April 11, 1907; Orel b. Sept. 14, 1909. Family home Freedom, Wyo.
Elder; member Sunday school superintendency 1892.

HANSON, HANS A. Born Jan. 10, 1814, in Denmark. Came to Utah 1855.
Married Anna Margaret Mickleson in Denmark, who was born Aug. 9, 1812. Their children: Rasmus, d. in Utah; Michael A. b. April 11, 1848, m. Lena Jenson. Family resided Ephraim and Elsinore, Utah.
Pioneer. Died at Elsinore.

HANSON, MICHAEL A. (son of Hans A. Hanson and Anna Margaret Mickleson). Born April 11, 1848, in Denmark. Came to Utah 1855.
Married Lena Jenson Nov. 2, 1867, at Salt Lake City (daughter of Thomas C. Jenson and Karen Maria Iverson of Denmark, pioneers 1865). She was born Nov. 15, 1848, and came to Utah 1864. Their children: Peter Michael b. Jan. 26, 1869, m. Emma M. Anderson; Hans Daniel b. Feb. 27, 1871, m. Clara Kirkman. Family resided Ephraim and Elsinore, Utah.
Missionary to Denmark; president of seventies. Black Hawk war veteran. Road supervisor. Watermaster Elsinore Canal company; farmer. Died Nov. 27, 1907.

HANSON, PETER M. (son of Michael A. Hanson and Lena Jenson). Born Jan. 15, 1869, Ephraim, Utah.
Married Emma Martha Anderson Jan. 2, 1895, Manti, Utah (daughter of J. August Anderson of Sweden and Marie Nielson of Denmark). She was born Oct. 25, 1872. Their children: Zereta b. Nov. 1, 1895, d. March 25, 1903; Leland Aurelian b. Feb. 19, 1897; Delora Marie b. Oct. 18, 1899; Maud Augusta b. Aug. 5, 1901; Boyd Peter b. Aug. 12, 1903; John LeRoy b. June 27, 1906; Morris August b. May 26, 1909. Family home Elsinore, Utah.
Elder. Farmer and stockraiser.

HANSON, HENRY (son of Henry Hanson). Born in Schleswig, Germany. Came to Utah in October 1868, Hans Jensen Hall company.
Married Annie C. Oleson in Denmark (daughter of Jorgen Oleson, came to Utah in October 1868, Hans J. Hall company). She was born March 4, 1847. Their children: Henry, died; George, m. Stena Williamson; Sarah C., m. Moroni P. Stark Feb. 10, 1897; Joseph, m. Elizabeth Williams; Augusta, m. James Finch; Jacob C., m. Lillie Brown; Hyrum, m. Eva Peterson; Annie E., m. Ferris Holley.

HANSON, JAMES J. (son of Hans Neilsen born 1791, Berkered, Denmark, and Anna Frederike Olsen born 1801, Denmark). Born Nov. 8, 1844, Kaierod, Frederiksborg, Denmark. Came to Utah in 1856, Knud Peterson company.
Married Caroline Christene Hanson (daughter of Hans and Karen Hanson), who was born in 1847 and came to Utah in 1863, Capt. Preston company.
Married Anna Katrena Jensen (daughter of Peter Jensen, pioneer 1856, Knud Peterson company), who was born March 14, 1860, Hyrum, Utah. Their children: Verda Christene b. Dec. 8, 1893; Ivy Carolina b. March 3, 1896; May Elizabeth b. Aug. 9, 1898; James J. b. April 20, 1901.
President 62d quorum seventies; first counselor to bishop of third ward at Hyrum. Justice of peace eight years. Second lieutenant in Black Hawk war in San Pete county 1866.

HANSON, MADS (son of Hans Peterson and Gertrude Hanson of Foslev, Denmark). Born Dec. 6, 1830, at Foslev. Came to Utah Sept. 23, 1862, with Ola N. Liljenquist company.
Married Mattie Petersen June 23, 1855, at Vemmelev, Denmark (daughter of Niels Petersen and Chesty Olsen of Foslev, pioneers 1862, Ola N. Liljenquist company). She was born May 17, 1837. Their children: Minnie Dorothy b. Feb. 22, 1856; Hans Peter b. March 2, 1858; Carrie Mariah b. March 27, 1860; Peter b. Aug. 30, 1862; Elias Peter b. Oct. 24, 1863, m. Margaret Bullock March 16, 1887; Hyrum William b. Jan. 20, 1866, m. Emma Jensen Feb. 10, 1897; Joseph b. March 1, 1868; Henry b. 1870; George David b. July 18, 1871, m. Hannah Lula Hammond Oct. 20, 1897; James Edward b. March 10, 1874, m. Elaine Smith Feb. 6, 1901; Emma Matenia b. May 2, 1877; Annie b. July 14, 1880. Family home Providence, Cache county, Utah.
Elder; ward teacher. School trustee. Farmer. Died Dec. 20, 1910.

HANSON, GEORGE DAVID (son of Mads Hanson and Mattie Petersen). Born July 18, 1871, Providence, Utah.
Married Hannah Lula Hammond Oct. 20, 1897, at Salt Lake City (daughter of Milton Datus Hammond born Oct. 7, 1832, Randolph, N. Y., and Chesty Transtrom, born July 7, 1851, at Onslonda, Sweden—former pioneer July 22, 1850; latter Sept. 23, 1862, Ola N. Liljenquist company). She was born Dec. 20, 1872. Their children: George Hammond b. Nov. 17, 1900; Lula Gwendol b. Aug. 2, 1904; Wynona Mae b. April 13, 1908; Clyde Winston b. Feb. 26, 1912. Family home, Providence.
Member 32d quorum seventies; missionary to Denmark 1897-99; ward teacher. School trustee. Farmer.

HANSON, SOREN (son of Hans Jacobsen and Anne Maria Lauridsen of Denmark). Born Feb. 16, 1817, Gjerslev, Denmark. Came to Utah 1863, Capt. Young company.
Married Anna Maria Bendixen (daughter of Benedix Petersen and Karen Jensen), who was born in 1835 and was killed by stampeding oxen while crossing plains in 1863. Their children: Hans, m. Ernestine Buchanan; Caroline Maria b. Oct. 3, 1856, m. Noah T. Guymon; Benedix, m. Nancy Curtis; Lars, b. Dec. 28, 1860, m. Laura Lund. Family home Fountain Green, Utah.
Married Myran Hansen. Their children: Soren, m. Clara Seeley; Maria, m. Victor Olsen; Paul.
Died Aug. 10, 1909, at Castledale, Utah.

HANSON, SOREN (son of Hans Larson and Myriah Jenson of Neoodager, Denmark). Born Dec. 4, 1823. Came to Utah 1862, Capt. Madison independent company.
Married Karen Salmonsen (daughter of Jacob Salmonsen and Annie Jacobensen), who came to Utah with Capt. Madison independent company. Their children: Maria b. Jan. 26, 1850, m. Peter Christiansen; Hans b. Nov. 17, 1856, d. 1874; Caroline b. Jan. 9, 1865; Soren b. May 2, 1863; Solomon b. March 25, 1875. Family home Hyrum, Utah.

HANSON, SOREN (son of Soren Hanson and Karen Salmonsen). Born May 2, 1863, Hyrum.
Married Martha Eva Unsworth (daughter of James Unsworth and Alice Cockshott), who was born Feb. 13, 1870, Hyrum. Their children: Leo b. Aug. 6, 1889, m. Marie Jensen; Ruby Alice b. March 6, 1891, m. Archy Stout; S. Russell b. Jan. 28, 1897; Ferry LeGrande b. Jan. 16, 1899; James Carroll b. Dec. 31, 1901; Eva Lila b. Nov. 23, 1903, in California; Zola Melba b. March 10, 1906; June Ella b. June 11, 1909.

HANSON, WILLIAM LAWRENCE (son of Paul Hanson and Maria Sophis Kannt of Copenhagen, Denmark). Born May 20, 1838, Copenhagen. Came to Utah in 1854.
Married Mary Jane Judson Aug. 21, 1859, Salt Lake City (daughter of Samuel Judson and Arilia Rice of Frisky, Iowa; started with Charles C. Rich's company and died on way).

She was born Oct. 26, 1843. Their children: William L., m. Nellie Cooper; Mary Jane and Sarah Jane, died; Fannie E., m. James M. Mack; Martha Ella, died; Emelius Godfred. m. Caroline Kimball Knowlton; Alice, m. Henry M. Mack; Victoria Eugenia, m. Alexander Judson; Florence May, died; Albert J., m. Louise Estella Clark; Leslie Raymond. Family home, Salt Lake City.
Seventy; ward teacher. Worked for church in public blacksmith shop; had charge of Singer machine department of Z. C. M. I. several years. Active member territorial militia. Died April 9, 1904.

HARDING, DWIGHT (son of Ralph Harding and Nancy Goodale, latter born 1780, Woodstock, Conn.). Born April 27, 1807, Sturbridge, Worcester county, Mass. Came to Utah Sept. 15, 1851. John G. Smith company.
Married Phebe Holbrook in February, 1833 (daughter of Moses Holbrook), who was born March 16, 1810. Their children: George b. Dec. 18, 1833, m. Mary Jones July 2, 1864; Alma b. June 29, 1835, m. Margaret Jones Nov. 1867; Charles b. April 2, 1838, m. Matilda Zundel Sept. 30, 1865; Elizabeth b. Oct. 23, 1840, m. Isaac Zundel Sept. 30, 1865; Nancy Ann b. Nov. 8, 1843; Phebe b. Aug. 23, 1845, m. Amos Warner Dec. 9, 1865.
Representative from Box Elder county to first state legislature. First counselor in first bishopric of Willard ward. Erected first school house in Willard, 1852.

HARDING, GEORGE (son of Dwight Harding and Phebe Holbrook). He was born Dec. 18, 1833, Wethersfield, Conn. Married Mary Jones July 2, 1864, Salt Lake City (daughter of Benjamin Jones and Esther Davis, former a pioneer 1863 Thos. E. Ricks company). She was born Feb. 17, 1839, Lampeter, Caermarthenshire, South Wales. Their children: Dwight b. Aug. 18, 1865; Eliza J. b. Aug. 24, 1867; Mary L. b. Aug. 6, 1869; Ralph J. b. June 6, 1871, m. Martha Williams Oct. 1895; Nancy A. Harding b. July 4, 1873, m. Leslie Nichols Aug. 15, 1900; George D. b. April 11, 1875, m. Margaret Thomas Sept. 1907; Phoebe E. b. Jan. 18, 1877; Sarah A. b. Oct. 20, 1878, m. Clarence E. Horsley Jan. 18, 1905; Alice C. b. May 6, 1881; Olive E. b. Nov. 8, 1883.
President Willard Z. C. M. I.; one of first directors of Willard City Co-op. Farmer and stockraiser.

HARDING, CHARLES (son of Dwight Harding and Phoebe Holbrook). Born April 2, 1838. Came to Utah 1859.
Married Matilda Zundel Sept. 30, 1865 (daughter of Jacob Zundel and Sarah Forstner), who was born Jan. 18, ——. Their children: Joseph; Charles Don Carlos, m. Jennie Lloyd; George Forstner b. Oct. 3, 1869, m. Flora Bell Birdie Snow; Matilda, m. Alma Carvine; Daniel, m. Edeth Blackburn; Jacob, m. Ada White; Sarah Phoebe, m. William T. Davis; Clarice, m. Charles Hardy; Elizabeth; Jennie Lavern, m. George Brim; Louis H., m. Hazel ——. Family home, Salt Lake City.
Member seventy; teacher and merchant Willard City, Utah. Made three trips across the plains for freight. Died June 1899, at Willard City.

HARDING, GEORGE FORSTNER (son of Charles Harding and Matilda Zundel). Born Oct. 3, 1869, Willard City, Utah. Married Flora Bell Birdie Snow June 26, 1899, Salt Lake City (daughter of Lorenzo Snow and Mary Houtz of Brigham City and Salt Lake City, Utah, pioneers 1853). She was born July 19, 1871. Their children: Vortia b. Sept. 10, 1901; George Rush b. March 21, 1904; Virginia b. Nov. 10, 1906; Mercedes b. April 10, 1910. Family home, Salt Lake City.
Member 33d ward seventies; missionary to California 1896-98; ward teacher. Member state and county medical society; secretary Utah state board of medical examiners 1909 to date. Member staff of L. D. S. hospital. Graduate University of Utah Normal School 1891; Rush Medical College 1903. Physician and surgeon.

HARDING, EDWARD C. (son of Edward G. Harding of Trowbridge, Wiltshire, Eng.). Born Nov. 2, 1832, at Trowbridge. Came to Utah 1874.
Married Sarah Ann Meeks June 28, 18——, Cambridge, Eng. (daughter of Robert Meeks and Elizabeth Sheldrick, of Cambridge). She was born Nov. 23, 1837. Their children: Edward Robert, m. Alice Talmage; Alfred William, m. Martha Lewis; Alice E., m. Austin Bennett; Sidney Thomas, m. Emma Duke; Heber Samuel, m. Elizabeth Bray; Minnie S., m. William B. Meldrum; Rosa Elizabeth, m. William A. Kerr; Anna Maria, died; Mary Maud, m. Lorenzo Taylor. Family home Provo, Utah.
High priest; missionary in England. Foreman of looms in woolen mills at Provo. Died Dec. 11, 1903.

HARDING, THOMAS (son of Charles Harding and Betsy Hinctable of Kentisbury, Devonshire, Eng.). Born Feb. 19, 1846, in England. Came to Utah 1873.
Married Sophronia Ann Bull Jan. 17, 1875, Logan, Utah (daughter of Daniel B. Bull and Elizabeth Tantam, pioneers 1849). She was born Sept. 22, 1849, at Sweetwater, Wyo., while her parents were en route to Utah. Their children: Evelyn B. b. Dec. 23, 1875, m. Peter J. Christensen; Thomas C. b. Dec. 5, 1877, m. Pearl Rollins; Daniel B. b. May 23, 1880. Family home Morgan, Utah.
Farmer and gardener.

HARDING, THOMAS C. (son of Thomas Harding and Sophronia Ann Bull). Born Dec. 5, 1877, at Morgan, Utah.
Married Pearl Rollins Sept. 17, 1902, Salt Lake City (daughter of William Rollins and Elizabeth A. Morris of Centerville, Utah). She was born in Utah. Their children: Erma b. Dec. 2, 1904; DeWelt b. Oct. 16, 1906; Twila b. Jan. 16, 1910. Family home Morgan, Utah.
Member of seventy; missionary to Great Britain. County recorder two years; city councilman two years.

HARDY, CHARLES MARCUS (son of Rudolph Hardy and Lizetta Mater of Lenzburg, Canton Aargau, Switzerland). Born March 13, 1828. Came to Utah Sept. 26, 1851.
Married Maria Sophia Doldi Aug. 2, 1852, Zurzach, Switzerland, who was born Feb. 24, 1831. Their children: Sophie, m. Henry Snyder; Charles Herman; Pauline Emelia, m. James William Bean; Paul Emil; Mary; Hermine, m. Herman E. Osterloh; Josephine. Family home Provo Utah.
Tailor by trade. Died Nov. 3, 1903.

HARDY, CHARLES W. (son of Josiah G. Hardy and Sarah C. Parker of Groveland, Mass.). Born July 28, 1843, Groveland, Mass. Came to Utah 1852.
Married Marinda Andrus March 31, 1872, Salt Lake City (daughter of Milo Andrus and Mary Ann Webster of Lancastershire, Eng., pioneers 1851). She was born May 18, 1856. Their children: Lucy May, m. Allen R. Cutler; Sarah Alice, m. Sther Esplin; Marinda Maud, m. Mathew Spiers; Mary Edna, died; Charles Jesse, m. Clarice Harding; Minnie Viola, m. Harry Gillett; Bertha A., m. Nephi Reynolds; Cynthia. Family home, Salt Lake City.
Member 8th quorum seventies; missionary to southern states 1881-83; bishop's counselor; high priest. County surveyor eight years. Civil engineer.

HARDY, ELISHA PHILBROOK (son of Zacariah Hardy and Eliza Philbrook of Nauvoo, Ill.). Born July 26, 1837, Camden, Me. Came to Utah 1852, Benjamin Gardner company.
Married Flora Worlton Jan. 13, 1867, Morgan, Utah (daughter of James T. Worlton and Elizabeth Bourne of Bath, Eng., pioneers Sept. 25, 1855, Richard Ballantyne company). She was born May 9, 1851. Their children: Eliza, beth b. Jan. 4, 1868, m. Brigham Robison; Martha A. b. Dec. 17, 1870, m. William Wadsworth; Lucinda S. Sept. 19, 1872, m. Lorenzo Olsen; James E. b. April 17, 1874, m. Elizabeth Toone; Nellie C. b. Dec. 29, 1875, m. George West; Margrette b. July 8, 1877, m. John Toone; Charles W. b. April 22, 1879, m. Eliza Ann West; Rosabelle b. May 22, 1881, m. Robert J. Durrant; Bertha E. b. Oct. 14, 1887, m. Wallace H. Dickson; Lillian b. Nov. 17, 1891, m. Alonzo D. West. Family home Hooper, Utah.
Early bridge and road builder. Railroad contractor.

HARDY, JOSEPH. Born 1810, Camden county, Maine. Came to Utah 1850.
Married Lucy Blandeon. Their children: Robert, m. Ann Kempton; Pamelia, m. Moroni Edmonds, m. Nathan Kington; Caroline, d. youth; Adelia, m. Stephen Oheen; Deborah, m. Alfred Johnson; Adeline, m. Charles Robinson; Joseph, m. Lydia Rebecca Davis; George A., m. Mary Jane Mayberry; Maryette, m. Lafayette Pierce; Sarah, m. Myron Higby, m. John Walsh. Family home Ogden, Utah.
Elder; ward teacher. Member Nauvoo Legion. Farmer. Died Feb. 24, 1888, Vernal, Utah.

HARDY, JOSEPH, JR. (son of Joseph Hardy and Lucy Blandeon). Born April 8, 1848, near Council Bluffs, Iowa. Came to Utah with father.
Married Lydia Rebecca Davis Oct. 3, 1868, Salt Lake Endowment house (daughter of Nathan C. Davis and Isabel Wills of Salt Lake City, pioneers Aug. 10, 1860). She was born Sept. 15, 1850, Bolton, Warren county, N. Y. Their children: Cora Adelia b. Oct. 17, 1869, m. William Temple, ton; Joseph Hyrum b. March 11, 1871, m. Rose Reynolds; Nathan Cutler b. Jan. 24, 1874, m. Jane Fisher; Charles Allen b. Nov. 20, 1876, m. Stella Colton; Albert Alvin b. April 17, 1878, m. Clara Griffin; Ernest LeGrand b. Aug. 15, 1881, d. infant; Ruby May b. May 30, 1882, m. Pardon Dodd, Jr.; Lydia Ellen b. March 9, 1886, m. Michael Moroni Cook; Hulda Viola b. April 2, 1890, m. Marion Westover; Flossie Marie b. April 2, 1895. Family home Vernal, Utah.
Elder. Constable of Uinta county six years. Farmer stockraiser and fruitgrower.

HARDY, JOSEPH HYRUM (son of Joseph Hardy, Jr., and Lydia Rebecca Davis). Born March 11, 1871, Laketown, Rich Co., Utah.
Married Roseltha Melissa Reynolds Jan. 6, 1897, Vernal, Utah (daughter of William George Bardwell Reynolds and Elizabeth Maria Peterson of Vernal, Utah, pioneers 1855). She was born Jan. 23, 1874. Their children: Iris Afton b. Oct. 19, 1897; Doris Merle b. Aug. 15, 1899; Lowell Reynolds b. Oct. 4, 1901; Gladys b. Oct. 20, 1905; Bernice b. July 5, 1907.
Missionary to southern states 1902-04; counselor to President Smart in presidency of Duchesne stake 1910; high councilor; Sunday school superintendent Vernal ward; presi-

dent Y. M. M. I. A. of Maeser ward; president Mississippi conference 1902-03; secretary southern states mission; counselor to Benjamin E. Rich, president of southern states mission. One of the founders, and assisted in issuing the first number of the "Elders" Journal, later it became the Liahona Elders Journal. City recorder at Vernal. Manager Roosevelt Mercantile Co.; president Roosevelt Realty Co.; secretary Sego Lilly Bee Co.; president Roosevelt Water Works Co.; manager Uinta Creamery Co.; credit manager and cashier Ashley Co-op. Merc. Co. of Vernal; secretary Vernal Drug Co. Postmaster at Vernal 1897-1900.

HARDY, LEONARD WILFORD (son of Simon and Rhoda Hardy of Bradford, Essex county, Mass.). Born Dec. 31, 1805, Bradford. Came to Utah Oct. 14, 1850, Wilford Woodruff company.
Married Elizabeth Nicols. Their children: Clarissa, m. Alonzo Russell; Charles, died; Rufus, died.
Married Sophia Lois Goodridge in 1850, Salt Lake City (daughter of Benjamin Goodridge and Penelope Gardner of Bradford, Mass., pioneers Oct. 14, 1850, Wilford Woodruff company). She was born July 2, 1826. Their children: Leonard G., m. Miriam Young; Oscar Harvey, m. Esther A. Margetts; William Bell, m. Tacy Woodford and Mary E. Laird; Sophia M. H., m. Samuel W. Jenkinson; Jesse W., m. Elizabeth Skidmore; George G., m. Sarah Ann Skidmore; Penelope Marian, m. Don Carlos Young; Susannah J., m. Henry T. McEwan; Martha Leis, m. Reginald McKaig. Family home, Salt Lake City.
Married Esther Smilinda Goodridge. Their children: Owen S., m. Lilly Hansen; Esther Isabell, m. Peter Hansen; Rhoda A., m. Martin Garn; Sarah, d. infant; Edward, d. infant.
Married Harriett Ann Goodridge. An only child: Frank, d. infant.
High priest; missionary to England 1844-45 and to the States 1869-70; presided over Manchester conference; bishop of 12th ward, Salt Lake City, 1851-76; first counselor to Bishop Edward Hunter 1856-80; counselor to Bishop Preston 1880-84. Member legislature. Captain of police. Captain of Company B, Nauvoo Legion. City councilman. Merchant and stockraiser. Died July 31, 1884, Salt Lake City.

HARDY, LEONARD GOODRIDGE (son of Leonard Wilford Hardy and Sophia Lois Goodridge). Born June 24, 1852, Salt Lake City.
Married Elizabeth Skidmore Nov. 25, 1880, Salt Lake City (daughter of Henry B. Skidmore and Sarah Ann Elliott of Philadelphia, Pa., pioneers Sept. 1855, John Hindley company). She was born May 3, 1860, East Mill Creek, Utah. Their children: Wallace E. S. b. Sept. 4, 1881, d. aged 31; Leonard W. S. b. Jan. 1, 1883, m. Ethel Allred; Elizabeth S. b. Oct. 18, 1884; Hazel S. b. Nov. 23, 1886, m. William D. Fawns; Jesse Victor S. b. July 16, 1888, d. aged 18 months; Alta S. b. Sept. 18, 1892, m. Bert E. Crockett; Frank S. b. Feb. 15, 1896; Aretta S. b. March 3, 1900; Virtue S. b. June 13, 1905, d. infant. Family home, Salt Lake City.
High priest; missionary to Canada 1899-1905; block teacher; high councilor Alberta stake. First overseer, Sterling, Canada. Chairman of school board. Merchant; farmer and stockraiser.

HARDY, JESSE WALLACE (son of Leonard W. Hardy and Sophia Lois Goodridge). Born Dec. 30, 1857, Salt Lake City.
Married Miriam Young Aug. 28, 1878 (daughter of Brigham Young and Emily Partridge of Salt Lake City, pioneers July 24, 1847, Brigham Young company). She was born Oct. 13, 1856. Their children: Miriam b. Aug. 7, 1879, m. Roy S. Hawkins; Eugenie b. Sept. 20, 1881, m. James H. Hampton; Emily b. Feb. 1, 1883, m. Thomas Blair; Leonard G. b. Feb. 25, 1885; Alice b. Dec. 8, 1887, died; Aaron b. May 14, 1890; Georgia b. Jan. 1, 1893; Lucile b. April 23, 1895, died; Brigham b. June 9, 1897; Vernon b. Jan. 7, 1900; Dorothy b. Sept. 23, 1902.
Missionary to Indiana 1879-80; bishop's counselor 12th ward; bishop of 2d ward 1889-99; member high councils of Liberty and Alberta stakes. County collector, Salt Lake county, 1886-93; city councilman. Director Zion Savings & Trust Company; Brigham Young Trust Company; president Silver Dipper Mining Company, American Fork, Utah; director Iron Canyon Gold Mining Company of Nevada; general manager Lucky Deposit Mining Company of Nevada; director Woolley, Young & Hardy Company and Burton Gardner Lumber Company; senior member Hardy, Young & Company, merchants. Mining expert.

HARDY, LEWIS O. Born Oct. 15, 1803, Camden, Me. Came to Utah with Lewis O. Hardy handcart company.
Children through first marriage: Henry; Phoebe, m. Lewis Donitis; Robert; Mary, m. —— Lawson; Lucy; Lewis.
Married Claridia Jane Doffelmyre (daughter of Louisa Doffelmyre, who came to Utah with handcart company). She was born April 3, 1840. Their children: William, m. Matilda King; Louisa, m. Thomas Wilson; Nathan; Lucetta, m. Samuel Nichols; Patience, m. Hyrum Smith Meeks; Adeline, m. George Haws; Nettie, m. Charles Wall; Esther, m. John T. Rassmussen; George, m. Clara Rudd; Albert, m. Celestia Poisey. Family home Marysvale, Utah.
Member of seventies. Served in Echo Canyon campaign; minuteman; Indian war veteran. Settler of southern Utah. Farmer. Died March 27, 1895, in Session's Settlement, near Salt Lake City.

HARDY, MILTON H. (son of Josiah G. Hardy and Sarah C. Parker). Born Sept. 26, 1844, Groveland, Mass. Came to Utah 1852.
Married Libby Smoot 1879 (daughter of Abraham O. Smoot and Diana Eldredge of Provo, Utah, pioneers Sept. 1847, A. O. Smoot company). They had five children, three sons and two daughters. Family home Provo, Utah.
Missionary to England, returning in 1878. First assistant to Dr. Karl G. Maeser of the Brigham Young Academy at Provo 1876-83; student in the University of Utah, and later took charge of a department. Pioneer organizer of Y. M. M. I. A. Took his degree from the medical department of the University of New York 1885. Utah county physician; Utah county superintendent district schools; president Teachers' Association of Utah county; principal Provo city schools; territorial superintendent district schools. Gained schools' reputation as superintendent of state insane asylum, or mental hospital. Died Aug. 23, 1905, Provo, Utah.

HARDY, WILLIAM (son of Robert Hardy and Jeanette Wilson of Falkirk, Scotland). Born Feb. 21, 1842, Glasgow. Came to Utah Oct. 29, 1855, C. A. Harper company.
Married Harriet Ann Wood Dec. 25, 1865, Farmington, Utah (daughter of John Wood and Fanny Goble of Brighton, Sussex, Eng., pioneers Sept. 28, 1855, Moses Thurston company). She was born June 11, 1847. Their children: William John b. April 19, 1867, m. Susie Wilcox; Harriet Ann b. Feb. 16, 1870, m. George Sanders; Edward Agustus b. Oct. 8, 1872, m. Millie Lindquist; Robert James b. Oct. 14, 1876, m. Alice E. Hess; Fanny Janet b. Aug. 7, 1880, m. Edward Haskell; Alice Estella b. Oct. 13, 1883; Bertha Adelia b. Feb. 23, 1887, and Clyde Cyril b. Jan. 16, 1890, died in infancy; Katie Ella b. Jan. 9, 1892, m. Arthur Sanders. Family resided Farmington and Fielding, Utah.
Indian war veteran; one of first to drive mail stage from Salt Lake to Montana, 1862. Died March 10, 1905.

HARDY, ROBERT JAMES (son of William Hardy and Harriet Ann Wood). Born Oct. 14, 1876, Farmington, Utah.
Married Alice E. Hess Dec. 19, 1906, Logan, Utah (daughter of James H. Hess and Elizabeth White of Fielding, Utah). She was born Aug. 14, 1885. Their only child: Harriet Bell b. Dec. 11, 1907.
Farmer and stockraiser.

HARMON, ALPHES AMULECK (son of Alphes Amuleck Harmon and Hulda Dimrus Vaughn, both of Kirtland, Ohio). Born April 14, 1839. Came to Utah 1854, oxteam company.
Married Eliza Bramwich (daughter of John Dramwich and Mary Brown, latter pioneer 1864, Milo Andrus company). She was born March 29, 1834. Their children: John Henry Moulton, d. aged 12; Henrietta Terrill, m. Edward Orr Covington; Harriet Elizabeth, m. Niels Larson Marsing; Almeda, m. Joseph A. Moore; Susan, d. infant; Eliza Riddle, d. aged seven. Family home Ogden and Salt Lake City, Utah. Assisted in bringing immigrants to Utah.

HARMON, CHARLES (son of Charles Harmon of Carmarthenshire, South Wales). Born in Carmarthenshire, South Wales. Came to Utah 1860.
Married Mary Mathias in Carmarthenshire. Their children: Benjamin, m. Ann Powell; William, m. Ann Michiel; David, m. Sarah Evans and Mary Williams; Charles, m. Martha Powell; Ann, m. William Crowther; Robert, m. Amanda Mitchell; George, m. Eliza Reese; Edwin, m. Catherine Williams; Isaac, m. Margaret Morgan.
Member of seventy; president of missions, Wales. Shoemaker to Brigham Young. Died at Salt Lake City.

HARMON, DAVID (son of Charles Harmon and Mary Mathias). Born June 8, 1838, Carmarthenshire. Came to Utah 1864, Thomas Jeremy company.
Married Sarah Evans 1858 in South Wales (daughter of Joseph and Sarah Evans). Their children: Benjamin, m. Rachel Williams and Sarah Jones; Mary Ann, m. Samuel H. Williams.
Married Mary Williams Oct. 1866, Salt Lake City (daughter of David Williams and Sarah Ludwig of South Wales, pioneers 1864, Thomas Jeremy company). She was born May 17, 1842. Their children David b. May 23, 1867, m. Mary Bullock; Sarah b. March 6, 1870, and Catherine b. Sept. 13, 1872, died; Margareth b. July 10, 1874, m. Heber C. Anderson; Martha b. July 8, 1876, m. Steven T. Durant; Charles b. July 6, 1878; Elizabeth Ann b. Dec. 22, 1885, died. Families resided Salt Lake City, Utah.
Member of seventies 34 years; high priest and teacher 29th ward. Foreman on railroad built from El Paso, Texas, to the colonies; built the railroad from Salt Lake to Ogden and to the mines at Scofield, Utah, also from Kelcham to Hailey, Idaho. Railroad and canal contractor.

HARMON, JESSE P. (son of Martin and Triphena Harmon of Vermont). Born Aug. 11, 1795, Rupert, Bennington county, Vt. Came to Utah Oct. 5, 1848, Heber C. Kimball company.
Married Anna Barnes April 29, 1819, Springfield, Pa. (daughter of Abijah and Abie Barnes of Springfield, Pa.) She died Jan. 1847, Winter Quarters, Iowa. Their children: Appleton M. b. May 29, 1820, m. Elmeda Stringham;

Saphronia Malinda, d. 1847; Amos Washington. m. Mary Jane Old; Ansel Perce, m. Rosaline Chandler. Family resided Springfield, Pa., Salt Lake City and Holden, Utah.
One of seven presidents 11th quorum seventies 1844. Alderman first municipal ward Salt Lake City at time of organization; colonel in Utah Nauvoo Legion. Moved to southern Utah 1861 and settled at Holden 1868. Died Dec. 24, 1877.

HARMON, APPLETON MILO (son of Jesse P. Harmon and Anna Barnes). Born May 29, 1820, Conneaut, Pa). Came to Utah July 24, 1847, Brigham Young company.
Married Elmeda Stringham Jan. 1, 1845, Nauvoo, Ill. daughter of George Stringham and Polly Hendrickson of Nauvoo, pioneers Sept. 24, 1848, Isaac Haight company, later residing at Salt Lake City and Holden, Utah). She was born Dec. 31, 1829. Their children: Milo and Mary, died; Willis M., m. Martha E. Spillesberry; Bryant, died; Appleton S., d. 1896; Hosea F., m. Julia Stringham; Anna. m. George W. Cherrington: Hyrum. m. Luella Tuttle; Polly, m. Joseph R. Giles; Julia, m. B. L. Kesler; Jesse M. b. July 19, 1868, m. Sarah E. Holman. Family resided Salt Lake City, Toquerville and Holden, Utah.
Member 11th quorum seventies; missionary to England 1850-53; bishop's counselor. Pioneer sawmill operator of Salt Lake, Millard and Washington counties, Utah. Built furniture factory at Toquerville and woolen mills at Washington, Utah. Indian war veteran. Blacksmith; contractor and builder. Died Feb. 27, 1877, Holden, Utah.

HARMON, JESSE M. (son of Appleton M. Harmon and Elmeda Stringham). Born July 19, 1868, Toquerville, Utah.
Married Sarah E. Holman Dec. 27, 1892, Holden, Utah (daughter of John G. Holman and Rachel Stevens, pioneers 1847, Brigham Young company). Their children: Clarence H. b. Oct. 24, 1893; Appleton J. b. July 3, 1895; Ardell b. Feb. 25, 1897; Warren T. b. Oct. 27, 1900, died; Dorothy b. April 24, 1904; Bryant b. Sept. 9, 1906; John b. Feb. 23, 1910; Robert Holman b. April 5, 1912. Family home Provo, Utah.
Sheriff of Utah county 1903-09; school trustee. Stockraiser; merchant; lumber and coal dealer; president of Utah Timber and Coal company.

HARMON, ANSEL PERCE (son of Jesse P. Harmon and Anna Barnes). Born April 5, 1832, Conneaut, Pa. Came to Utah Oct. 5, 1848, Heber C. Kimball company.
Married Rosaline Chandler Nov. 29, 1862, Salt Lake City (daughter of Abel Chandler and Mary Ann Jerome of New York), who was born March 15, 1841, and came to Utah 1862. Their children: Anna Rose b. Nov. 11, 1863, m. Jacob Stringham; Milo Ensel b. March 1, 1866, m. Elizabeth Jane Hunter; Mary Saphronia b. July 24, 1869, m. William Adam Seegmiller; Lucy Elmeda b. Sept. 23, 1871, m. James Jenson; Emma Theresa b. Oct. 17, 1874, m. John Reeve; Jane Marinda b. Jan. 10, 1877, m. Thomas Pratt; Zina Belle b. July 15, 1879, d. infant; Lillie Orilla b. March 31, 1881, d. Jan. 7, 1887. Family home Provo, Utah.
Assisted in bringing emigrants to Utah 1860-61. Teamed to Los Angeles for supplies 1862; captain of a company of immigrants 1862. Bishop's counselor; high priest; missionary to Pennsylvania 1874. Farmer and stockraiser. Died Sept. 12, 1908, Holden, Utah.

HARPER, RICHARD (son of Richard Harper of Swineshead, Eng., and Harriett Edwards of Sleaford, Eng.). Born April 5, 1827, Swineshead. Came to Utah Oct. 17, 1862, Henry W. Miller company.
Married Susann Faulkner Anwick, Eng. (daughter of William Faulkner and Ellen Fox), who was born June 17, 1827, and came to Utah with husband. Their children: Betsy Ann b. June 9, 1850, m. Joseph Hill Dec. 6, 1871; William F. b. July 3, 1852, m. Ellenor Morrell Nov. 28, 1878; Eliza L. b. Aug. 18, 1853, m. Joseph Richardson Nov. 1869; Richard N; Harriet, b. July 1867, died; Ellen b. July 1857, m. James Hill; Harriet Louvisa b. Oct. 25, 1859, m. Willis Kelsy Dec. 9, 1880; Emma b. July 31, 1861, m. William Hillyard Oct. 15, 1881; Alice b. Jan. 18, 1865, m. Lorenzo Toolson Oct. 22, ——; Lucy Jane; Ida b. Dec. 24, 1866, m. A. J. Merrill Nov. 14, 1890; Tacy, m. Joseph Burton.

HARPER, WILLIAM F. (son of Richard Harper and Susann Faulkner). Born July 3, 1852.
Married Ellenor Morrell Nov. 28, 1878, Salt Lake City (daughter of William Morrell and Matilda Kelsey), who was born Aug. 22, 1859, Smithfield, Utah. Their children: Ellen G. b. Dec. 31, 1879, m. William Homer Nov. 28, 1900; Richard S. b. May 12, 1881, died; William F. b. March 31, 1883, died; Archie John b. Feb. 15, 1885, m. Ellenor Homer Dec. 4, 1907; Joseph H. b. Nov. 12, 1885, died; Ruby M. b. April 18, 1889; Earl S. b. Dec. 12, 1891. Families resided at Smithfield, Utah.

HARRINGTON, LEONARD E. Born Jan. 7, 1816, New York state. Came to Utah Oct. 1, 1847, Edward Hunter company.
Married Lois Russell prior to coming west. Their children: Theodore S.; Sarah E., m. —— Robinson; Jane, m. —— Tanner.
Married Mary Jones in 1855. Their children: Daniel; Mary, m. —— Duncan.
Married Harriet Noon in 1858. Their children: Heber A.; Leonard S.; Chancey Delos.

Chairman judiciary committee Utah legislature 28 years; mayor of American Fork City. Promoter of first Utah free school 1866; trustee of B. Y. Academy 1870-83. Died June 1883.

HARRINGTON, DANIEL (son of Leonard E. Harrington and Mary Jones). Born March 15, 1860, American Fork, Utah.
Married Leonora Taylor March 17, 1886, Logan. Utah (daughter of John Taylor and Margaret Young; former came to Utah 1847, latter 1858). She was born March 25, 1864. Their children: Jennie; Daniel T.; Florence; John; Russell; Mary; Everett.
Superintendent Sevier county schools 1881-85; assistant Lake county district attorney 1895-96. Attorney at Salt

HARRIS, EMER (son of Nathan Harris, born March 23, 1758, Providence, R. I., and Rhoda Lapham, born April 27, 1759, Providence). He was born May 29, 1781, Cambridge, N. Y. Came to Utah 1850.
Married Roxana Peas July 22, 1802, who was born Dec. 5, 1781. Their children: Selina b. Oct. 10, 1803; Elathan b. Oct. 7, 1805; Alvira b. Aug. 7, 1807, m. Mr. Howles; Sephrona b. Aug. 17, 1809, m. Mr. Manchester; Nathan b. Sept. 26, 1811; Ruth b. Sept. 7, 1813. Family home New York.
Married Deborah Lott Jan. 16, 1819, in Pennsylvania (daughter of Zephaniah Lott and Rachel Brown), who was born Nov. 1799, in New York. Their children: Emer b. 1819; Martin H. b. Sept. 29, 1820, m. Georgeann Aldous; Harriet T. b. Dec. 26, 1822, m. Judson Daly; Dennison L. b. Jan. 17, 1825, m. Sarah Wilson; Deborah.
Married Parna Chapel March 29, 1826, who was born November 1792. Their children: Fannie M. b. Jan. 1827; Joseph M. b. July 19, 1830, m. Mary Pons; Alma b. June 6, 1832, m. Sarah Earl; Charles b. July 2, 1834, m. Louisa Hall; Rebecca b. Dec. 25, 1845.
Patriarch; elder. Brother of Martin Harris, one of three witnesses to Book of Mormon; obtained first bound copy of the Book of Mormon. Worked as carpenter on Kirtland temple; missionary in New York, Pennsylvania and Ohio. Settled at Provo 1850. Died Nov. 28, 1869, Logan, Utah.

HARRIS, MARTIN H. (son of Emer Harris and Deborah Lott). Born Sept. 29, 1820, Mahoney, Pa.
Married Georgeanna Aldous Jan. 18, 1855 (daughter of Robert Aldous), who was born Aug. 5, 1838. Only child: Emer M. b. Aug. 6, 1856, m. Hannah M. Poulter Jan. 5, 1883, and Louisa Kearns 1895.
Married Louisa Sargent April 3, 1859, Ogden, Utah (daughter of John and Ann Sargent, former pioneer 1852). She was born Dec. 18, 1841, Newbury, Berkshire, Eng. Their children: Leander S. b. April 20, 1860, m. Alice Jenson Sept. 19, 1888, m. Eliza Barlow Oct. 10, 1900; Lovisa G. b. March 4, 1862, m. David Davis Jan. 1883; Nathan J. b. March 20, 1864, m. Emma E. Oakaron July 1887; Martin D. b. May 4, 1866, m. Lillie R. Hayes Feb. 6, 1890; Louisa P. b. May 30, 1868, m. William H. Anderson March 4, 1897; Ida E. b. Nov. 27, 1875, m. Alfred Dixon May 15, 1901.
First presiding elder of Harrisville, Utah; first Sunday school superintendent of Harrisville 1865; missionary to Fort Limhi, on Salmon River, 1857; secretary of 38th quorum seventies; missionary to eastern states 1876-77. Member Nauvoo Legion. Settled at Harrisville 1851, where he planted the first crop. Road supervisor 1858-69. Fife major in martial band. First school teacher of Harrisville; school trustee. Farmer. Died Feb. 14, 1888.

HARRIS, CHARLES (son of Emer Harris and Parna Chapel of Harrisville, Utah). Born July 2, 1834, in Huron Co., Ohio. Came to Utah in October, 1852, Captain Cutler company.
Married Louisa Maria Hall April 20, 1855, Ogden, Utah, later in Endowment house, Salt Lake City (daughter of Benjamin K. Hall and Mehitable Sawyer of Maine, pioneers October, 1850, Captain Bennett company). She was born Dec. 30, 1839, Exeter, Scott county, Ill. Their children: Charles Elisha b. Jan. 23, 1857, m. Nellie Warner (Harris); Alva b. Feb. 28, 1859, m. Nellie Warner; Isabelle Maria b. April 15, 1861, m. Clarence Merrill, m. U. L. Nelson; Jesse Orson b. March 29, 1864, m. Louise Buckley; Mary Aderine b. June 3, 1866; m. Milo A. Hendrix; Eugene b. Jan. 10, 1869, m. Nellie Barton (Hopkins); Silas Albert b. June 11, 1871, m. Chasta Olsen; Ida May b. Oct. 5, 1873, died; Ole Van b. Dec. 5, 1875, m. May Perry; Clarence Earl b. May 24, 1878, m. May Bell Booth; Mertie Adell b. July 27, 1883. Family resided Washington and Junction, Utah.
Married Elizabeth Anderson. Their children: Juanita, died; Susan; Milo. Family home Junction, Utah.
First located at Ogden, and afterward moved to Willard, Toquerville, and Parowan, finally settling at Junction 1878; called to settle "Dixie" 1862, locating in Washington. He has been a pioneer to many places where it was necessary to build wagon roads, canals, ditches, homes, subdue the wilds and turn a desert into a habitable place. Participated in the Indian wars of northern Utah and southern Idaho, also the Black Hawk and Walker Indian wars and the troubles in southern Utah with the Utes and other tribes.

HARRIS, CLARENCE EARL (son of Charles Harris and Louisa Maria Hall). Born May 24, 1878, Parowan. Utah.
Married May Bell Booth June 25, 1902, Salt Lake temple (daughter of John Roston Booth and Elizabeth Hourth of Provo, Utah; former came to Utah 1875). She was born Oct. 4, 1881. Their children: Clarence Elroy b. Aug. 10, 1903; Wanda May b. March 17, 1907; Lurline b. Jan. 25, 1910.

Seventy; assistant superintendent Sunday school; president Y. M. M. I. A.; stake aid Sunday school. Moved from Junction to Provo, where he attended the Brigham Young university; then to Pocatello and Salt Lake City; finally settled at Schofield 1907, where he is engaged in the mercantile business under the firm name of the Schofield Mercantile Co.

HARRIS, NATHAN J. (son of Martin H. Harris and Louisa Sargent). Born March 29, 1864, Harrisville, Utah. Married Emma E. Oakason June 15, 1887, Logan, Utah (daughter of Hans Oakason and Mary Swenson; former came to Utah Sept. 24, 1861, Heber Kimball company; latter October 1861, Captain Horne company). She was born July 8, 1866. Their children: Lawrence E. b. April 30, 1888; Leo A. b. Jan. 13, 1890; Everett C. b. Dec. 25, 1891; Mabel b. March 20, 1894; Irene Louise b. Sept. 19, 1896; Wilford D. b. April 29, 1899; Ruth Evelyn b. Oct. 28, 1901; Luella May b. Jan. 19, 1905; Nathan J. b. Jan. 10, 1908. Family home, Harrisville. Missionary to southern states 1901-03; Sunday school superintendent and member bishopric of Harrisville ward; member high council of Weber and Ogden stakes. District judge of Ogden; school trustee; justice of peace; member of two state legislatures; county and district attorney. Graduate Ann Arbor Law School 1894.

HARRIS, MARTIN D. (son of Martin H. Harris and Louisa Sargent). Born May 4, 1866, Harrisville, Utah. Married Lillie R. Hayes Feb. 6, 1890 (daughter of Richard Hayes and Anna M. Turner; came to Utah 1869). She was born Jan. 28, 1869, in Wales. Their children: Louie Grace b. Dec. 23, 1891; Emma E. b. Feb. 24, 1893; Fern R. b. March 8, 1895; Priscilla E. b. Jan. 25, 1897; Martin H. b. March 8, 1898; Alma R. b. Aug. 1, 1901; Lillie S. b. Dec. 20, 1904; Albert D. b. March 19, 1911. Family home, Harrisville. Senior president 60th quorum seventies; Sunday school superintendent 1906-08; president Y. M. M. I. A. 1900-04 at Harrisville. Justice of peace 1890-96; deputy assessor 1904-10; road supervisor 1894-96, 1913.

HARRIS, GEORGE HENRY ABBOTT (son of James Harris, born April 26, 1793, Hayle, Copperhouse, Cornwall, and Eliza Rawlings Harris, born Feb. 1, 1791, Marazion, Cornwall, Eng.—married Oct. 22, 1822). Born Dec. 7, 1830, Ilfracombe, Devonshire, Eng. Came to Utah Oct. 2, 1852, Henry Miller company. Married Ann Burraston March 27, 1855 (daughter of William Burraston and Sarah Johnson—married 1830, Ashton, Eng.—latter pioneer 1855). She was born March 20, 1833. Came to Utah 1854. Their children: Eliza Jane Harris b. Jan. 16, 1856, m. Hyrum Tremayne Dec. 8, 1873; George Henry Burraston b. April 10, 1857, m. Victoria Sandgreen April 3, 1884; Cyrus Richard James b. Dec. 9, 1858, m. Mary Celestia Black Dec. 4, 1885; John William Shorland b. May 5, 1860, m. Rhoda Mason Aug. 1882; Marianne Desdenory b. July 25, 1861, d. Aug. 30, 1861; Annie B., d. Sept. 13, 1861. Family home Pleasant Grove, Utah. Married Sarah Loader May 30, 1862, Pleasant Grove, Utah (daughter of James Loader and Amy Britnel; former died on plains, latter pioneer 1857, handcart company). She was born May 1, 1844, Oxfordshire, Eng. Their children: James Loader b. Feb. 21, 1863, m. Mary Anne Morris June 10, 1887; Sarah Ellen b. April 29, 1865, m. William Ricks 1886; Amy C. b. April 29, 1865, d. Sept. 1879; Bernice Rawlings b. March 6, 1867, m. Annie Martha Fogg Dec. 19, 1894; Darwin R. b. Nov. 23, 1868, m. Euphensa Lutz April 3, 1894, m. Sarah Rebecca Bell June 9, 1897. Married Mariah (Loader) White. Her children by previous marriage: Emma Mariah b. March 3, 1858, m. Samuel Radmel May 15, 1876; James Henry b. 1859, d. April 28, 1865; Alexander Roswell b. Dec. 23, 1861, m. Minerva Thomas April 18, 1891. Their children: Abner Britnel b. March 1, 1867; Carlos Vivian b. Oct. 14, 1868, m. Emma Fox 1884; Frank L. b. May 19, 1871, m. Annie E. Cutler Aug. 25, 1891, and Julia Mitchell Sept. 8, 1902. Member 37th quorum seventies 1851; constable 1856; high priest. Moved to Salem 1888. Appointed commissioner of education at Salem 1889.

HARRIS, BERNICE R. (son of George Henry Abbott Harris and Sarah Loader). Born March 6, 1867, Pleasant Grove, Utah. Married Martha Ann Fogg Dec. 19, 1894, Logan, Utah (daughter of Mr. Fogg and Martha Ann Woodard; former d. March 13, 1891, latter aged 32). Their children: Bernice Leon b. Nov. 30, 1895; Martha L. b. Sept. 24, 1897; Luella b. Nov. 19, 1899; Leah b. Aug. 9, 1902; Ruth b. May 29, 1904; Agness b. Dec. 29, 1906; Vernon Fogg b. May 26, 1909. Family home Salem, Idaho. Moved to Rexburg, Idaho. 1884, where he quarried and did a general freighting business. In 1898 engaged in general merchandising business with his father at Salem. Appointed postmaster of Salem March 14, 1903. High priest and high councilor; superintendent of Sunday schools; president of mutual organizations; ex-executive member of the stake board of education; assistant stake superintendent Sunday schools; chosen bishop of Salem ward Jan. 29, 1905. Instrumental in erection of $18,000 meeting house at Salem.

HARRIS, JOHN (son of Jacob Harris and Susannah Hartman of Michigan). Born 1808, in Pennsylvania. Came to Utah 1848. Married Lovina Eiler Jan. 5, 1831, in Indiana (daughter of Daniel Eiler and Barbara Stutsman of Pennsylvania.

pioneers 1848). She was born Dec. 17, 1807. Their children: Daniel b. March 13, 1831, m. Lydia Harr; Lucinda b. Nov. 13, 1832, m. Abner Blackburn; Angeline b. Nov. 21, 1834, m. William Hyde; Jacob b. March 10, 1837, m. Eliza Carpenter; Susannah b. Feb. 14, 1840, m. Clark Fabin; Rebecca b. Aug. 21, 1842, m. William S. Warren; Joseph b. Nov. 28, 1844, d. child; Oliver b. June 13, 1847, m. Lodemia Sly; George b. May 18, 1850, m. Martha Thornton. Family home Farmington, Utah. Died May 4, 1899.

HARRIS, JOHN (son of Charles Harris and Mary Sutton of Worle, Somersetshire, Eng.). Born Nov. 5, 1837, at Worle. Came to Utah Sept. 18, 1860, John Taylor company. Married Annie Maddock Jan. 12, 1861, Salt Lake City, Counselor Carter officiating (daughter of Thomas Maddock, died in England, and Mary Taylor of Cheshire, Eng., pioneer Sept. 18, 1860). She was born Oct. 8, 1842. Their children: Emily; Harriet, m. Ephraim N. Morris; John O., died; Elizabeth, m. Willard Smith; Jessie, m. Robert Hunt; Edward J., m. Lillian James; William H., m. Catherine Miller; Walter T. Family home, Salt Lake City. Member 2d quorum elders. Cooked for the men in Cottonwood while quarrying rock for Salt Lake temple. Worked for Brigham Young in Globe Bakery. One of first candymakers in Utah.

HARRIS, JOSHUA (son of Isaac Harris, born 1810, Cardiff, South Wales, and Esther Bowerning, born 1807, Somersetshire, Eng.—married 1832). He was born June 23, 1848, Glamorganshire, South Wales. Came to Utah 1853, Vincent Shurtliff company. Married Ann D. Whitesides May 28, 1868 (daughter of Louis and Susan Whitesides—married May 5, 1850, Council Bluffs, Iowa—pioneers Oct. 1852, John Walker company). She was born Dec. 20, 1853, Kaysville, Utah. Their children: Susan b. June 22, 1869, m. Rosel Taylor Nov. 3, 1892; Ester E. b. Aug. 30, 1871, m. Hans Monson March 1, 1888; Lavisa b. Feb. 7, 1873, d. Feb. 6, 1880; Selena b. Dec. 16, 1875, m. Alonzo Corbridge Jan. 10, 1894, d. Sept. 26, 1900; William L. b. Dec. 1, 1877, m. Lottie Bronson Feb. 8, 1899; Joshua b. Dec. 22, 1879, d. April 24, 1895; Alvin b. March 28, 1881, m. Hayner Marler Nov. 21, 1901; Jabez M. b. June 29, 1884, m. Etta Van Luvin Dec. 17, 1902; Mary b. July 20, 1886, m. Winfred Jones Aug. 30, 1906; Ella b. April 17, 1888, m. William Settles March 26, 1910; Myrtle b. May 28, 1891, m. Bryant Tilford Feb. 7, 1908; Laura Bell b. June 15, 1892, m. Marl Beckstead Nov. 3, 1909; Edna b. Aug. 8, 1893. Family resided Kaysville, Utah, and Fairview and Preston, Idaho.

HARRIS, McGEE. Born in 1800. Came to Utah 1848. Married Mary Givens of Kentucky, who was born in 1802. Their children: Alexander, m. Mary Craner; William, m. Emeline Whittle Aug. 30, 1861; Ely, m. Elizabeth Gamble; Martha, m. Daniel H. Wells; Mary Ann, m. Casper Whittle; Emily, m. Alexander Bullock. Family home, Salt Lake City.

HARRIS, ROBERT (son of Robert Harris, born 1778, Oglecut, Gloucestershire, and Sarah Okey, born 1781, Saunter, Gloucestershire, Eng.). He was born Dec. 26, 1809, in Gloucestershire. Came to Utah 1850, Joseph Horne company. Married Hannah Maria Eagles in Gloucestershire, Eng. (daughter of Thomas Eagles and Ann Sparkes), who was born 1817 and came to Utah with husband. Their children: Joseph b. March 26, 1836, m. Charlotte Green March 18, 1855; Elizabeth b. April 1, 1838, m. Everett Van Orden March 12, 1857; William E. b. March 23, 1839, m. Lucinda Landon Sept. 23, 1865; Thomas E. b. Nov. 29, 1841, m. Mary Ann Payne Jan. 14, 1866; Enoch b. May 29, 1843, m. Jane Hoskins Dec. 31, 1866; Sarah Ann b. June 11, 1845, m. Robert Green Jan. 3, 1865; Robert b. Feb. 3, 1847, d. July 30, 1847; Daniel Browett b. Oct. 30, 1848, m. Elizabeth Ann Thornley April 1876; Marria b. June 20, 1851, d. June 20, 1851; Lucy Emma b. June 17, 1852, m. John Phillips Dec. 19, 1870; Jennett b. Aug. 11, 1854, m. James Parkinson Nov. 26, 1873; Henriette b. Aug. 11, 1854, m. John Milton Bernhisel Jan. 3, 1876; Robert Charles b. April 27, 1856, m. Sarah Green 1882; Julia Ann b. April 1, 1858, m. Leroy Hall Jan. 20, 1875; Mary Ellen b. Sept. 26, 1860, m. Don McCrary Feb. 8, 1879. Family resided Salt Lake City and Kaysville, Utah. Settled in Salt Lake City 1850; moved to Kaysville 1854 and to southern Idaho 1869; returned to Kaysville 1874. President of 56th quorum seventies. Farmer and stockraiser. Died in 1876.

HARRIS, ENOCH (son of Robert Harris and Hannah Maria Eagles). Born May 29, 1843, Nauvoo, Ill. Married Jane A. Hoskins Dec. 31, 1866, Kaysville, Utah (daughter of Oliver C. Hoskins and Lucinda Howell), who was born Feb. 30, 1847, Decator Co., Iowa. Their children: Laura Bell b. Sept. 30, 1867; Emma E. b. March 30, 1870, m. John F. Conley; Ranson E. b. June 30, 1872, m. Emma Elizabeth Morris Nov. 14, 1894; Robert C. b. Dec. 23, 1874, m. Sylvia Green March 30, 1897; William D. b. April 14, 1877, m. Zina E. Gibbs May 15, 1901; George F. b. Feb. 6, 1880; Wilford T. b. Feb. 24, 1882, m. Jennie McCrary; Annie J. b. Nov. 23, 1883, m. Jonas Heaton; Eliza A. b. July 15, 1885, m. David R. Anthony Oct. 19, 1904; Parley B. b. March 28, 1887; Mary L. b. May 15, 1888, died; Grace E. b. June 23, 1889 (died), m. Deeroy Hanks June 6, 1905; Lovina

H. b. July 25, 1892, died: Ellen R. b. Aug. 24, 1893. Family resided Kaysville and West Portage, Utah.
Missionary to northwestern states 1895; high priest; counselor to Bishop Hoskins of Portage ward; bishop Portage ward; president high priests quorum of three wards in Malad stake. Black Hawk Indian war veteran.

HARRIS, DANIEL BROWETT (son of Robert Harris and Hannah Maria Eagles). Born Oct. 30, 1848.
Married Elizabeth Ann Thornley April 10, 1876, Salt Lake City (daughter of John Thornley and Martha Seed), who was born 1851, Lancaster, Eng. Their children: Robert Thornley b. Jan. 10, 1877, m. Nora Robinson; Daniel Browett b. May 27, 1879, d. Aug. 15, 1879; Elizabeth Ann Thornley, d. June 24, 1879.
Married Mary Ann Parkinson Jan. 6, 1881, Salt Lake City (daughter of Thomas Parkinson and Elizabeth King, pioneers Captain Brown company). She was born Aug. 9, 1858, Ogden, Utah. Their children: Fred b. Sept. 3, 1881, m. Mary Ellen Thornley Aug. 17, 1904; Thomas J. b. Feb. 19, 1883, m. Chloe Louise Layton June 23, 1909; Daniel D. b. Oct. 7, 1884, m. Jennie Caroline Anderson Dec. 12, 1906; Mary Elizabeth Ann b. Aug. 19, 1886, m. James H. Walker Feb. 21, 1912; Chloe Marriah b. July 21, 1888, m. Franklin Hawks Dec. 12, 1909; David Oscar b. Dec. 12, 1890; Sarah Cecil b. June 28, 1893; Ezra Parkinson b. July 20, 1895. Family home Layton, Utah.
Bishop of Layton ward 1889-1909. Worked on first Utah railroad; hauled rock for Salt Lake temple. Farmer and stockraiser.

HARRIS, THOMAS (son of Thomas Harris, born 1780, and Mary Parre—married 1815). Born 1816, Caerleon, Monmouthshire, South Wales. Came to Utah Sept. 1863, independent oxteam company.
Married Ann Williams April 1, 1844 (daughter of John and "Grandmother" Williams). She was born Dec. 31, 1819, died in 1873—came to Utah with husband. Their children: Thomas Edwin b. Dec. 31, 1844, m. Catherine Davis 1870; Micah Francis b. Aug. 3, 1848, m. Mary Jane Bond Jan. 15, 1868; Daniel Richard b. May 5, 1853, m. Jennette Fife March 17, 1882.
Settled in Summit county. Miner.

HARRIS, MICAH FRANCIS (son of Thomas Harris and Ann Williams). Born Aug. 3, 1848, Nanty Glow, South Wales. Came to Utah 1863 with parents.
Married Mary Jane Bond Jan. 15, 1868, Henefer, Utah (daughter of William Bond, who died April 29, 1910, and Mary Ann Barker—pioneers Dec. 10-16, 1856, William B. Hodgett handcart company, rescued by relief trains sent to meet them). She was born Jan. 15, 1850, Fall River, Mass. Their children: Thomas William b. Sept. 26, 1868, d. Sept. 26, 1868; Micah b. Nov. 25, 1869, d. Nov. 25, 1869; George Richard b. Dec. 31, 1870, m. Elizabeth Deardon; Daniel Heber b. March 21, 1873, d. Oct. 12, 1874; Willard Bond b. Aug. 29, 1874; Eldora Ann b. Nov. 25, 1876, m. William George Richins 1897; Joseph Bond b. March 22, 1878, d. Aug. 1901; Lucy David Oscar b. Nov. 30, 1882, m. Rebecca Gustavson 1905; Mary Ida b. July 9, 1885, m. Parley Croft 1909; Hyrum Bond b. Dec. 3, 1882; Myrtle Jane b. Aug. 2, 1890, m. William O. Stephens Sept. 1911. Family home Henefer, Utah.
Married Mrs. Agnes C. Peterson (daughter of Carl Samuel Peterson and Annie Anderson), who was born July 3, 1870, Orebro, Sweden. Came to Utah Nov. 1, 1886.
Ordained seventy 1876, and high priest 1889; first counselor to Bishop John Paskett of Henefer ward 1889-1902, and made bishop of Henefer ward May 26, 1902; president Mutual Improvement Association; assisted in building stake tabernacle at Coalville; member stake high council two years. President Henefer Irrigation Company; stockraiser.

HARRIS, WILLIAM (son of McGee Harris of Illinois, born 1800, and Mary Givens of Kentucky, born 1802). He was born June 8, 1836, Williamson county, Tenn. Came to Utah 1848, Captain Kimball company.
Married Emeline Whittle Aug. 20, 1861 (daughter of Thomas L. Whittle and Mary Fullmer—married 1833, Montreal, Canada—pioneers 1848, Zera Pulsipher company). She was born March 7, 1845. Their children: William McGee b. May 23, 1862, m. Harriet Ann Carson Feb. 4, 1885; Charles Z. b. March 9, 1864, m. Sarah Alice Anderson April 14, 1886; Casper W. b. May 31, 1871, m. Tena Christensen 1892; Alexander L. b. Oct. 20, 1873, m. Olive Kerr Dec. 23, 1898; Emma b. March 20, 1878, m. Albert C. Fisher Dec. 19, 1900. Family home Richmond, Utah.
Member city council and school trustee at Richmond for many years. Farmer and stockraiser.

HARRIS, WILLIAM McGEE (son of William Harris and Emeline Whittle). Born May 23, 1862, Richmond, Utah.
Married Harriet Ann Carson Feb. 4, 1885, Logan, Utah (daughter of David Carson and Millie Jane Rawlins of Richmond, Utah, pioneers Brigham Young company). She was born June 18, 1861. Their children: Millie E. b. Nov. 27, 1885, m. Theo. Mickelson; David Earl b. June 14, 1890; Thomas Alan b. Oct. 7, 1892; Guy b. April 25, 1895; Viola b. April 12, 1898; Florence b. Oct. 1, 1901. Family home Lago, Idaho.
Bishop. Member legislature 1896. School trustee and road supervisor. Rancher and farmer.

HARRIS, CHARLES ZERA (son of William Harris and Emeline Whittle). Born March 9, 1864, Richmond, Utah.
Married Sarah Alice Anderson April 14, 1886 (daughter of George Anderson and Mary Ann Davis, pioneers 1852, Brigham Young company). She was born Jan. 10, 1870, Richmond, Utah. Their children: Melvin C. b. Sept. 21, 1887; William Z. b. July 5, 1890; George McGee b. Oct. 30, 1904. Family home Richmond, Utah.
Graduate University Deseret 1885. Assistant superintendent Richmond Sunday school 1887-89. Member state legislature 1889 and 1900; member Cache county school board 1908-09. Founder and owner of People's Mercantile Company, Richmond; one of founders Utah Condensed Milk Company and superintendent of same 1903-07. Farmer and dairyman.

HARRISON, GEORGE (son of William Harrison and Hannah Ellis of Springville, Utah). Born Aug. 24, 1841, Manchester, Eng. Came to Utah 1856, Martin and Tyler handcart company.
Married Rosella D. White 1865 at Springville (daughter of Noah White and Arvilla Lewis of Nauvoo, Ill., and New Hampshire). She was born 1838. Their children: George W., m. Ada Bissell; Rosella A., m. Joseph H. Storrs; Lewis E., m. Clara Stewart; Anna May, m. George Smith; William W., m. Myrtle Hall; Gertrude, m. William M. Packard; Winfred H., m. Martha Fereday. Family home, Springville, Utah.
Member of seventies; high priest; president elders' quorum; choir leader 20 years. Black Hawk Indian war veteran. Director Springville Banking Company; proprietor Hotel Harrison, Springville.

HARRISON, HENRY JAMES (son of James Harrison, born Jan. 13, 1804, and Ann Harrison). He was born Feb. 6, 1834, in Martines, Eng. Came to Utah Aug. 27, 1860, Daniel Robinson handcart company.
Married Sarah Elizabeth Burningham Oct. 6, 1860 (daughter of Thomas Burningham and Sarah White, latter pioneer 1861). She was born May 25, 1834, and came to Utah with handcart company. Their children: Arthur b. 1861; Thomas b. 1862; Harold Henry b. 1863, m. Clara Mold Sept. 21, 1882; Elizabeth Burningham b. 1865, m. Riley Burnham; James Alfred b. 1867; William John b. 1870, m. May Miller; Gertrude Anne b. 1873, m. David Fenwick.
Married Mary Acocks April 29, 1897 (daughter of George Acocks and Elizabeth Dodd, former came to Utah 1869, latter 1871). She was born Oct. 16, 1852, in England.
Deputy sheriff. Brick and rock mason.

HARRISON, HAROLD HENRY (son of Henry James Harrison and Sarah Elizabeth Burningham). Born 1863, Bountiful, Utah.
Married Clara Mold Sept. 21, 1882, Salt Lake City (daughter of Thomas Mold and Jane Spencer), who was born June 5, 1865. Their children: Lillian Clara b. Sept. 13, 1883, m. John Poorman; Harold Roy b. Dec. 26, 1885, m. Sarah Beatrice Steele Oct. 3, 1906; Ross Leo b. March 24, 1887; Ona Alvin b. June 24, 1893; Vivian Cecil b. Oct. 20, 1899; Rex Leland b. March 15, 1901; Lema LaRell b. July 10, 1903; Lola Leila b. Feb. 13, 1905; Thora Arenith b. June 22, 1906.

HARRISON, JAMES H. (son of Joseph Harrison and Sarah Hobday of London, Eng.). Born April 9, 1817, Birmingham, Eng. Came to Utah Oct. 5, 1862, Ansel P. Harmon company.
Married Angelina Parry Aug. 11, 1839, Birmingham (daughter of Thomas Parry and Mary Hidson of Birmingham). She was born Aug. 22, 1816. Their children: Sarah Ann, m. Thomas S. Farnes; Martha, died; Henrietta, died; Fannie, m. Edwin Curtis; James Parry, m. Elvira Williams; Joseph Hidson, m. Mary Ann Slight; Angelina, m. W. N. Shilling; William Hobday, m. Mary Ann Poll; Heber Chase, m. Capitola Birdno; Mary Elizabeth, m. George W. Earl; Edwin Daniel, m. Ellen Simmons.
High priest; teacher. Engraver. Deceased.

HARRISON, WILLIAM HOBDAY (son of James H. Harrison and Angelina Parry). Born June 18, 1852, London, Eng. Came to Utah with father.
Married Mary Ann Poll Aug. 1877, Salt Lake City (daughter of William Flint Poll and Charlotte Long of Lofoham, Eng., pioneers fall of 1857). She was born Dec. 28, 1858. Their children: Alta Maud b. April 13, 1880, m. Duke Lawrence; Verne David b. April 30, 1889; Angelina b. May 2, 1893, d. Jan. 29, —; Moroni Duval b. April 6, 1893; Clifford Charles b. March 11, 1896; Glen Poll b. Dec. 15, 1900. Family home, Salt Lake City.
Married Catherine Mary Louisa Jones May 7, 1907, Salt Lake City (daughter of Thomas Conforth Jones and Eliza Jesson of Birmingham, Eng., pioneers Sept. 1, 1868, Daniel D. McArthur company). She was born Aug. 30, 1869.
High priest; counselor in elders' quorum. City registrar 1904-06. Foreman cooperage department of Salt Lake Brewery Company. Merchant.

HARRISON, JOHN (son of Elizabeth Harrison of St. Ellen, Lancashire, Eng.). Born Dec. 13, 1839, at St. Ellen. Came to Utah 1862, oxteam company.

Married Nancy Platt (daughter of James Platt of St. Ellen, pioneer 1862, oxteam company). Their children: Isabel Josephine, m. Peter M. Hiskey; Jane, m. Edward Wilkins; James W. b. April 14, 1865, m. Victoria Sprouse; Peter b. Nov. 9, 1867, m. Margaret Murray; Elizabeth, m. Ephraim Roberts; Nancy, d. child. Family home Mona, Utah.

Married Margaret Vest 1880, Mona, Utah (daughter of John and Elizabeth Vest of England). Their children: John, m. Beatrice Neil; Alice, m. Ray G. Labrum; Joseph, m. Ollie Labrum. Family home Mona, Utah.

Member of seventy; Sunday school superintendent. District No. 11 school trustee Deepcreek, Utah, twelve years. Indian war veteran. Sheepraiser; railroader; farmer.

HARRISON, PETER (son of John Harrison and Nancy Platt). Born Nov. 9, 1867, Nephi, Utah.

Married Margaret Murray Nov. 2, 1892, Vernal, Utah (daughter of Jeremiah H. Murray and Mary Ashby of Spanish Fork, Utah). She was born Sept. 9, 1876. Their children: Nancy Noble b. May 23, 1893, m. Franklin Jenkins; Jeremiah Hatch b. Oct. 22, 1894; Lavina b. June 17, 1896, d. Aug. 13, 1896; Elzina b. June 17, 1896; Russell Peter b. Sept. 9, 1898; Hazel Pearl b. Aug. 15, 1900; Mary Ruth b. Nov. 14, 1902; Bertha b. Oct. 10, 1904, d. infant; Frances Ellen b. June 10, 1906; Carl Reed b. May 7, 1911. Family home Vernal, Utah.

Trustee District No. 11 for twelve years, Deep Creek, Utah. Farmer.

HART, JAMES (son of Richard Hart). Born April 17, 1806, Devonshire, Eng. Died Dec. 25, 1879. Came to Utah Oct. 17, 1862, Capt. Miller company.

Married Mary Cape, who was born 1810 and died 1858. Their children: Harriet b. June 4, 1836, m. Christopher Brown; Emma b. Oct. 14, 1838, m. James Notton; Ann b. Nov. 20, 1840; Sarah b. Sept. 18, 1842; William b. Jan. 2, 1845, m. Ann Horne; Mary Ann b. 1847; Charlotte Louise b. 1849; Levi Richard b. March 2, 1851, m. Harriet Maria Conley Nov. 24, 1874; Samuel Walter b. Oct. 31, 1853, m. Martha Raymond; Henry James b. Jan. 1857.

Worked on Salt Lake Temple. Mason.

HART, LEVI RICHARD (son of James Hart and Mary Cape). Born March 2, 1851, Bristol, Eng. Came to Utah with father.

Married Harriet Maria Conley Nov. 24, 1874, Evanston, Wyo. (daughter of Solomon Nelson Conley and Eve Merkley, pioneers 1848). She was born April 21, 1857, Centerville, Utah. Their children: James R. b. Aug. 28, 1875, d. April 14, 1903; William Augustus b. Sept. 7, 1877, m. Susan Birch June 7, 1907; Albert Leslie b. June 11, 1879, m. Amelia Escher April 4, 1907; Harriet Eve b. March 2, 1882, d. Aug. 18, 1882; Mary Caroline b. Oct. 17, 1884, d. July 22, 1899; Franklin b. July 5, 1887; Willard Edward b. Sept. 7, 1895.

Settled in Bear Lake county, Idaho, 1872.

HART, SAMUEL WALTER (son of James Hart and Mary Cape). Born Oct. 31, 1853, Devonshire, Eng. Came to Utah with father.

Married Martha Raymond Feb. 20, 1880, Woodruff, Utah (daughter of Grandison Raymond and Celia Hall, pioneers 1852). She was born Jan. 1, 1850, Council Bluffs, Iowa. Their children: Melvin Ray b. March 16, 1881, m. LeNore Dalrymple June 7, 1905; Celia Eva b. July 2, 1983, m. Wiley Call Dec. 15, 1904; Mary C. b. Aug. 28, 1887; Celdon Raymond b. May 17, 1890; Henrietta b. May 11, 1893. Family resided at Raymond, Idaho.

Settled in Salt Lake City; moved to Kaysville 1869; to Woodruff 1874; to Raymond, Idaho, 1878. First counselor to Bishop N. P. Larson; presiding high priest 1900, and bishop of Raymond ward.

HART, JAMES HENRY (son of Thomas Hart and Elizabeth Maryatt of Hemingford, Huntingdonshire, Eng.). Born June 21, 1825, at Hemingford. Came to Utah 1856.

Married Emily Ellingham 1850, England (daughter of Thomas and Elizabeth Ellingham), who was born July 15, 1820. Only child: James E. Hart b. Jan. 17, 1856, m. Elmira Birdneau. Family resided Salt Lake City and Provo, Utah, and Bloomington, Idaho.

Married Sabina Scheib May 4, 1861, Salt Lake City (daughter of John P. Scheib and Catharine Neinmann, pioneers Sept. 20, 1852, Capt. McGaw company). She was born March 2, 1839, London, Eng. Their children: Anna Maria b. July 22, 1862; Alice C. b. Sept. 14, 1864, m. Anson C. Osmond; Eugene S. b. Dec. 16, 1864, m. Nellie Osmond June 16, 1897; Charles H. b. July 5, 1866, m. Adelia Greenhalgh 1889; Arthur W. b. Oct. 16, 1869, m. Ada D. Lowe Aug. 22, 1900; Alfred A. b. Oct. 9, 1871, m. Sarah Patterson Oct. 11, 1905; John Thomas b. Jan. 22, 1874, d. infant; Sabina Hermoine b. July 18, 1875, m. David Roberts Feb. 2, 1911; Emily Rosina b. March 31, 1880, m. Ivan Woodward Nov. 13, 1901.

First probate judge Rich county; member Idaho legislature from Bear Lake county. Bishop of Bloomington, Idaho, for several years; first counselor to president of Bear Lake stake for thirty-five years; Mormon immigration agent at New York for several years. Had charge of President Young's nail factory in Sugar ward. Died Nov. 12, 1906, Bloomington, Idaho.

HARTWELL, ELLIOTT (son of Stephen Hartwell of Massachusetts). Born July 11, 1820, in Massachusetts. Came to Utah in 1853.
Married Hortense Rogers (daughter of Anne Slade of New York, pioneer 1853), who was born Aug. 18, 1823. Their children: Helena G., m. Joseph Hicks; Geneva A., m. Edwin Kimball; Orville, m. Ada Druce; Byron E., m. Margaret Mulholland; Inez H., m. John Livermore; May I., m. Oliver C. Lockhart; Ella M., died; Nina Rosabelle; Oscar L., m. Sarah Martin; Louis D., m. May Saunders. Family home, Salt Lake City.
Seventy. Nurseryman. Died Oct. 11, 1901.

HARVEY, DANIEL (son of John Harvey, born 1780, Prittywell, Essex, and Elizabeth Eastwood born 1800, Stanford, Eng.). Born May 29, 1830, Stanford. Came to Utah Oct. 13, 1863, Rosel Hyde company.
Married Hannah Smuin (daughter of Joseph Smuin), who was born Sept. 28, 1836. Came to Utah with husband in 1863. Their children: Annie b. June 21, 1856, m. Limon S. Conley; James Smuin b. Nov. 1, 1858, m. Mary Rosworth Feb. 2, 1898; Daniel Jr. b. Nov. 21, 1860, m. Olive Welker Nov. 2, 1896; Susannah b. June 9, 1865, m. J. H. Morgan Nov. 7, 1885; Mary b. Jan. 8, 1868, m. E. M. Whitesides 1892; Martha b. March 30, 1870, m. J. H. Hutchens 1893.
Married Ellen Wooten Dec. 17, 1868, Salt Lake City (daughter of William Wooten and Ruth Smuin, married at Eatonbray, Bedfordshire, Eng.). She was born Nov. 1, 1843, Eatonbray. Their children: George W. b. Jan. 8, 1870, m. Mary Baker May, 1896. Families resided at Kaysville, Utah.
Ordained seventy 1875. Died Sept. 15, 1899.

HARVEY, DANIEL JR. (son of Daniel Harvey and Hannah Smuin). Born Nov. 21, 1860, London, Eng.
Married Olive Welker Nov. 2, 1896, Bloomington, Idaho (daughter of Gilbert Welker and Charlotte Nelson), who was born Sept. 24, 1875, Bloomington. Their children: Daniel Orval b. July 26, 1897; James Evert b. Jan. 15, 1900; Demo Welker b. Jan. 14, 1902; Charlotte b. March 15, 1904; Olive Annie b. July 29, 1906.
Ordained seventy Oct. 30, 1910.

HARVEY, JOHN. Born Dec. 12, 1816, Balleston, Lanarkshire, Scotland. Came to Utah July 24, 1847, Brigham Young company.
Married Eliza Everett March 31, 1841, who was born July 12, 1814; died on way to Utah. Their children: John, d. April 27, 1900; Murray, d. March, 1903; Margeret A., m. Thomas Ross.
Married Ann Coope (Minchell) July 23, 1854, Salt Lake City, who was born April 13, 1826. Their children: Ester (Minchell) b. Oct. 1, 1846, m. Dr. L. Coons; Jenett b. June 1, 1855, m. Albert Walch; Alice Young b. June 1, 1857, m. Manassa Gallagher; Rhoda E. b. May, 1861, m. Joseph Foster; Frencea Ireeta b. May 21, 1863, m. William Hundley; Richard Coope b. Oct. 5, 1865, m. Mildred Cluff; Hugh William b. Feb. 15, 1868, m. Arbelia Howe. Family home Heber, Utah.
High priest. Farmer. Died July 4, 1887, Center Creek, Utah.

HARVEY, HUGH WILLIAM (son of John Harvey and Ann Coope). Born Feb. 15, 1868, Heber, Utah.
Married Arbelia Howe Feb. 14, 1894, Salt Lake City (daughter of Thomas Howe and Mary Jane McLider of Tonis Brook, Virginia), who was born July 2, 1870. Their children: Annie b. Nov. 25, 1894; Hugh b. May 7, 1896; James b. July 7, 1902; John b. Sept. 28, 1894; Myrth b. Aug. 16, 1909.
High councilor; missionary to northern states 1898-1901; bishop of Center ward 1903; president of Y. M. M. I. A.
Farmer and sheepraiser.

HARVEY, LOUIS (son of Jonathan Harvey and Sarah Harbert of Harrison county, W. Va.). Born Feb. 1, 1822, in Harrison county. Came to Utah in 1850.
Married Lucinda Clark April 6, 1849 (daughter of Richard Clark and Mary Ann Shaffer of Pennsylvania, pioneers 1850), who was born April 18, 1824. Their children: Maria Josephine, m. John A. Booth; Sarah Elizabeth, m. Wilford Baker; Jonathan Louis, m. Mary Helen Alexander; Lucinda Jane, m. Orlando Herron; Clarinda, died; Flora Samantha, m. Theo R. Sundberg; Rosetta and George Alfred, died. Family home Pleasant Grove, Utah.
President of seventies; high priest. City councilman two terms. Farmer. Died in 1900.

HARVEY, JONATHAN LOUIS (son of Louis Harvey and Lucinda Clark). Born March 5, 1854, Utah.
Married Mary Helen Alexander Dec. 30, 1880, Salt Lake City (daughter of Horace M. Alexander and Catherine Houston of Springville and Provo, Utah—pioneers 1847, Mormon battalion Company B). She was born Jan. 16, 1854. Their children: Effie Jane b. May 7, 1882, m. Stephen Roy Chipman; Catherine Fredonia b. May 7, 1884, m. Robert McCombie; Jonathan Louis Jr. b. May 23, 1886, m. Mae Langstaff; Helen Ora b. March 1, 1889, m. D. R. West; William C. b. March 1, 1891; Maria Lucile b. May 8, 1894; Leo P. b. May 1, 1896; Florence B. b. April 9, 1898; Dean Alexander b. March 19, 1900. Family home Pleasant Grove, Utah.
Home missionary; city councilman 1881-95; justice of peace 1898-99; precinct justice 1902-03; member school board 1889-1902. Farmer and stockraiser.

HASLAM, JAMES HOLT (son of John Haslam, born 1796, and Alice Young of Bolton, Lancashire, Eng., who were married 1823). Born Sept. 16, 1825, Bolton. Came to Utah Sept. 17, 1851, Philip Morgan company.
Married Mary Bough April, 1846 (daughter of John Bough and Rachel Bailey, the former died at St. Louis in 1849, the latter did not come to Utah). She was born March 20, 1825, and came to Utah 1851 with husband. Their children: Mary Alice b. June 4, 1848; Martha Ann b. Aug. 19, 1849; Sarah Jane b. Dec. 17, 1850; Rachel B. b. Nov. 19, 1852, m. Heber Bankhead; Lucy Elizabeth b. March 23, 1855, m. George Bankhead; Ellen Liza b. Oct. 20, 1857; Rosalie b. June 23, 1861; James Holt b. March 15, 1863, m. Amelia Riggs; Hannah b. Sept. 23, 1865; John b. June 15, 1868, m. Katherine Anderson.
Married Ann Redford May 21, 1869, Salt Lake City (daughter of Robert Redford and Letta Eckersely). She was born May 27, 1846, Pilkington, Halfacre, Lancashire, Eng. Their children: John Ephraim b. Jan. 11, 1870, m. Clara Tellefson; Mary b. Oct. 7, 1871; Robert b. Nov. 22, 1873; Letta Ann b. Dec. 21, 1877, m. Levi Broadbent; Samuel b. Dec. 27, 1875, m. Eliza Broadbent; Richard b. Feb. 2, 1880; Emily b. Nov. 27, 1881; Florence b. Nov. 26, 1884, m. Thomas W. Archibald Nov. 22, 1905; Maud b. June 26, 1886; Brian b. Aug. 3, 1888.
Settled in Salt Lake City 1851; moved to Iron county 1855, to Cache county 1860. Carried the dispatch of the Mountain Meadow massacre to Brigham Young.

HASLAM, RICHARD R. (son of James Holt Haslam and Ann Redford). Born Feb. 2, 1880, Wellsville, Utah.
Missionary to Great Britain, Oct. 17, 1910.

HASLAM, JOHN R. (son of Robert Haslam and Mary Nuttall of Manchester, Eng.). Born Jan. 10, 1828, Berry, Lancashire, Eng. Came to Utah October, 1853, Cyrus Wheelock company.
Married Marguerite Howarth May, 1851, Berry, Eng. (daughter of Robert Howarth and Mary Kay of Berry, Eng.), who was born Feb. 2, 1828. Their children: Robert H., m. Esther C. Williams; Margerite A., m. Thomas Francis; John W., m. Mary E. Kidd; James N., m. Mary E. Eardley; Joseph H., m. Sarah Bohling; Brigham, m. Jane and Elizabeth Breese; Mary Jane, m. Roert Bult.
Married Annie Catherine Brabandt May, 1865, Salt Lake City, by Brigham Young (daughter of Peter Brabandt and Sophia Willberg of Copenhagen, Denmark), who was born Jan. 30, 1836. Their children: Florence M., m. Joseph Brady; Ernest, m. Nellie Ash; Thomas, d. child; Heber C., m. Anena Anderson; Annie C., m. Harry McDonald; William, m. Minnie Schafer. Family home 28th ward, Salt Lake City.
Seventy; high priest; block teacher. Store-keeper and commissary 20 years. Gardener and gardener. Died Dec. 14, 1899, 28th ward, Salt Lake City.

HASLAM, ROBERT HOWARTH. Son of John R. Haslam and Marguerite Howarth. Born Aug. 15, 1854, at Salt Lake City. President 24th quorum seventies; Sunday school superintendent.

HASLAM, JOHN W. (son of John R. Haslam and Marguerite Howarth). Born April 7, 1860, at Salt Lake City.
Married Mary E. Kidd January, 1880, at Salt Lake City (daughter of William B. Kidd and Emma Lake of Devonshire, Eng.—came to Utah 1871), who was born Sept. 25, 1862. Their children: Emma L. b. Oct. 2, 1880, d. infant; Mary Ann b. Oct. 23, 1881, m. Robert E. Jones; John W. b. Aug., 1884, d. child; Nellie M. b. Sept. 5, 1886, m. Arthur B. Winter and John J. Bird; Bessie F. b. March 17, 1889, m. Richard M. Haddock; Cora M. b. May 5, 1892, m. E. D. Shelley; Harvard Y. b. May 13, 1894, m. Antonia Millicarn; Matthew R. b. Oct. 8, 1899; Josephine E. Holm b. Feb. 5, 1902. Family home, Salt Lake City, Utah.
Seventy; missionary to England 1900-03; secretary of elders quorum 34 years; Sunday school and block teacher. Carpenter and contractor.

HASLAM, ERNEST (son of John R. Haslam and Annie Catherine Brabandt). Born Sept. 6, 1870, 28th ward, Salt Lake City.
Married Nellie Ash Oct. 28, 1892, Salt Lake City, by Alexander Garrick (daughter of Thomas Ash and Sarah Ann Hick of Birmingham, Eng., came to Utah 1890), who was born March 6, 1870. Their children: Nellie A. b. July 17, 1893; Ernest W. b. July 29, 1895; Richard B. b. June 23, 1899; Annie M. b. Oct. 2, 1902. Family home Salt Lake City.
Gardener.

HASLAM, HEBER C. (son of John R. Haslam and Annie Catherine Brabandt). Born Jan. 18, 1874, Salt Lake City.
Married Arena Anderson April 4, 1898, Salt Lake City, by Bishop Kesler (daughter of Peter Anderson and Annie Oleson of Aarhus, Denmark, came to Utah 1888), who was born Oct. 12, 1875. Their children: Heber R. b. Oct. 8, 1898; Senter A. b. March 9, 1902; Annie E. b. July 4, 1907; Ruth H. b. March 19, 1900. Family home 28th ward, Salt Lake City.
Gardener.

HATCH, IRA STEARNS (son of Ira Hatch, born 1772, and Lucinda Rice of Rochester, N. Y.). Born Feb. 9, 1800, Winchester, Cheshire county, N. H. Came to Utah September, 1849, Enoch Reese company.
Married Welthea Bradford Jan. 26, 1824, at Farmerville, N. Y., who was born 1803, d. Nov. 3, 1841, Hancock county,

Ill. Their children: Meltiar b. July 15, 1825, m. Permelia Snyder Jan. 1, 1846; Ransom b. Nov. 13, 1826, m. Frances C. Atkinson Dec. 18, 1854; Orin b. May 9, 1830, m. Elizabeth M. Perry Oct. 10, 1855; Rhoana b. May 19, 1832, m. James Henry Dec. 28, 1850; Ira b. Aug. 5, 1835, m. Mandy Pace Sept. 17, 1859; Ephraim b. Nov. 20, 1837, m. Roseellen King June 13, 1864; Ancil b. June 18, 1840, m. Phebe Brown.
Married Abigal Whitley March 1842 (daughter of John and Margaret Whitley), who was born Dec. 19, 1797.
Married Jane Bee McKechine Nov. 27, 1852 (daughter of George Bee and Jennett Atchison), who was born Feb. 25, 1827. Their children: Stearns b. Dec. 6, 1853, m. Elizabeth Jane Ellis Oct. 9, 1876; Phllander b. June 2, 1856, m. Priscilla Muir Sept. 25, 1883; Abram b. June 22, 1857, m. Ida J. Levitt Dec. 9, 1880; Reuben b. July 23, 1859, m. Nora Ure April 24, 1884; Lucinda Jannett b. April 5, 1861; Lenord b. April 9, 1863; Alvin Willard b. April 17, 1865, m. Elizabeth Jackson; Ira Ette Eizina b. May 8, 1869, m. Stephen Ure Jan. 5, 1898. Family home Bountiful Utah.
Married Jane Ann Stuart March 20, 1857, Salt Lake City, who was born Dec. 27, 1824, Aberdeen, Scotland. Their children: Welthea Ann b. Jan. 23, 1858. m. Hyrum Hartley Dec. 6, 1875; Gilbert Stuart b. Jan. 15, 1860, m. Ellen Moss Oct. 4, 1884; Stephen Cornelius b. Aug. 20, 1861, m. Sarah Jane Atkinson Oct. 10, 1881.
Joined the church in 1832; ordained elder 1852; member Nauvoo Legion; member Mormon battalion. Settled at Bountiful, 1849. Ordained seventy 1869. Died Sept. 20, 1869.

HATCH, MELTIAR (son of Ira Stearns Hatch and Welthea Bradford). Born July 15, 1825, Cattaraugus county, N. Y. Came to Utah October, 1849, Enoch Reese company.
Married Permelia Snyder Jan. 1, 1846, Jobes Creek, Hancock county, Ill. (daughter of Samuel Snyder and Henrietta Maria Stockwell of Hatch, Utah, pioneers Oct., 1849, Enoch Reese company), who was born Oct. 7, 1827. Their children: Meltiar; Orson; Samuel; Ira Wilder; George S.; Welthea Maria; Permelia Eizina; Octavia; Jesse; Laura Ann.
Married Mary A. Ellis May 5, 1856, Salt Lake City (daughter of John Ellis and Harriet Hales of Hatch,Utah, pioneers 1850), who was born Dec. 30, 1840. Their children: John Henry; Elias; Julia; David; Harriet; Myra; Margret; Rhoana; Mary A.; Permelia.
Called in 1856 to go to Carson Valley to preside over a colony, and in 1871 to go South, and later went to Eagle Valley where he was set apart as bishop, from there went to Panguitch, where he served as high councilor.

HATCH, JOHN H. (son of Meltiar Hatch and Mary A. Ellis). Born July 22, 1857, Carson Valley, Nevada.
Married Elizabeth Frances Davis Nov. 26, 1879, St. George, Utah (daughter of Joseph C. Davis and Maria Williams of Tropic, Utah), who was born Feb. 25, 1862. Their children: Elizabeth Frances b. July 28, 1880; John Henry b. April 1, 1882; Rose Ettie b. March 17, 1883; Maria Vaughn b. Oct. 29, 1884; Mary Permelia b. Oct. 17, 1887; William Arthur b. Feb. 1, 1890; Ira Stearns b. Sept. 24, 1892; Joseph Aaron b. March 27, 1895; Orville C. b. April 22, 1897; Rachel b. May 13, 1899; Francis Ellis b. Feb. 8, 1902. Family home, Tropic.
Married Almira M. Cox Dec. 18, 1902, Manti, Utah (daughter of Orville S. Cox and Eliza J. Losse, Tropic, pioneers 1850), who was born Oct. 20, 1867. Their children: Ancell Alva b. Nov. 14, 1903; Orlan Earl b. Dec. 31, 1905; Merlin Vance b. June 6, 1908; Reid M. b. June 23, 1911.
Farmer and stockraiser.

HATCH, ORIN (son of Ira Stearns Hatch and Welthea Bradford). Born May 9, 1830, Farmersville, N. Y. Came to Utah 1848 with a section of Mormon battalion.
Married Elizabeth M. Perry Oct. 10, 1855 (daughter of John and Grace Ann Perry), who was born Sept. 13, 1836. Their children: Orin Perry b. July 28, 1856, m. Marinda Woodard; John Edward b. Jan. 26, 1859, m. Laura Ellis Oct. 16, 1879; Grace Ann b. Oct. 18, 1860, m. William Moss; Elizabeth Amelia b. Sept. 30, 1862, m. David Jackson; Joseph E. b. Oct. 30, 1864, m. Margaret Benson; James Ernest b. Nov. 11, 1866, m. Elizabeth Mann; Alice b. April 8, 1868, m. James Jackson; Chloe b. Jan. 11, 1870, m. Andrew Grant May 10, 1894; Ezra T. b. Dec. 29, 1871, m. Edith Folsom July 19, 1904; Wilder T. b. Nov. 14, 1873, m. Patty Sessions; Myra b. Oct. 12, 1875, m. Charles B. Mann; Algie Lydia b. June 5, 1877, m. Hyrum Grant, Jr., June 30, 1898; Jabez B. b. Aug. 5, 1879, m. Annie Putman. Family home, Bountiful, Utah.
Married Maria Thompson May 2, 1856, Salt Lake City (daughter of William G. Thompson and Elizabeth McCauley), who was born Aug. 16, 1838, Davis county, Mo. Their children: William Ira b. March 10, 1857, m. Maggie Muir Jan. 12, 1881; Orvil b. Jan. 1, 1860, m. Mary Albrand Nov. 17, 1886; Daniel b. March 4, 1863, m. Ida May Pace Nov. 16, 1885; David b. Jan. 22, 1867, died; Walter b. April 17, 1868, m. Charlotte Atkinson Nov. 9, 1892; Elizabeth b. Nov. 3, 1871; George b. April 28, 1874, m. Lillie L. Vance Dec. 18, 1901; Ella Maria b. July 10, 1876, died. Family home Bountiful, Utah.
Assisted in colonizing Green River country 1852, moved to Carson valley; ward teacher; president 74th quorum seventies; high priest; ordained patriarch 1898. Farmer and stockraiser.

HATCH, WILLIAM IRA (son of Orin Hatch and Maria Thompson). Born March 10, 1857, Eagle Valley, Carson county, Nev.
Married Maggie Muir Jan. 12, 1882, Salt Lake City (daughter of William S. Muir and Jane Robb, former came to Utah with the Mormon battalion). She was born June 17,

building canals, irrigation systems and wagon roads in and around Ashley Fork; county commissioner two terms; school trustee. Director in Central Canal company. Farmer; miller; tockraiser.

HATCH, LORENZO HILL (son of Hezekiah Hatch, born Dec. 2, 1798, Charlotte, Vt., and Aldurah Sumner, born May 4, 1803, Bristol, Vt., married 1819). Born Jan. 4, 1826, Lincoln, Vt. Came to Utah Sept. 15, 1850, David Evans company.
Married Hannah Elizabeth Fuller Feb. 3, 1846, who was born Feb. 24, 1827.
Married Sylvia Savonia Eastman Feb. 27, 1851, Salt Lake City (daughter of James Eastman and Clarissa Goss, married Jan. 1, 1812; former died on way to Utah, latter came Sept. 23, 1848, Heber C. Kimball company), who was born Nov. 4, 1826, New Fane, Vt. Their children: Lorenzo Lafayette b. Dec. 25, 1851, m. Annie Scarborough Dec. 1, 1873; Clarissa Aldurah b. Nov. 28, 1853, m. Sheldon Bela Cutler May 20, 1885; Hezekiah Eastman b. Dec. 16, 1855, m. Georgia Thatcher Oct. 6, 1884; Ruth Amorette b. Dec. 31, 1859; Elizabeth Ann b. Dec. 23, 1861, m. William M. Daines Jan. 18, 1883.
Married Catherine Karren Nov. 11, 1854, Lehi. Utah (daughter of Thomas Karren and Ann Ratcliff), who was born Aug. 12, 1836, Liverpool, Eng. Their children: Celia Ann b. March 19, 1856, m. John A. Woolf April 10, 1876; Catherine Alvenia b. Feb. 13, 1859, m. Thomas Smart Jan. 11, 1875; Lydia Lenora b. Sept. 1860, m. Levi M. Savage Dec. 24, 1879; Thomas b. Oct. 22, 1862, m. Viola Pearce Sept. 24, 1883; Hyrum b. Jan. 8, 1865, m. Esther L. Gregory Sept. 20, 1888; Hannah Adeline b. March 24, 1867, m. Levi M. Savage Sept. 28, 1883; Sarah Ella b. Sept. 6, 1870, m. Clarence E. Owens July 17, 1889; Chloe b. March 4, 1872, m. William M. Daines; Ephraim b. July 30, 1874; Achsah May b. Aug. 29, 1875, m. Louisa A. Decker; Lorenzo Wilford b. Dec. 31, 1878, m. Adelia Owen Oct. 9, 1901.
Married Alice Hanson Jan. 2, 1860, who was born Dec. 10, 1837, Bradford, Eng. Their children: John b. Oct. 26, 1860, m. Jane Stanford Oct. 21, 1885; Willard b. June 10, 1862, m. Priscilla Stanford Sept. 11, 1895; Ezra Taft b. Feb. 16, 1864, m. Maria Stanford Feb. 3, 1891; George Jeremiah b. Nov. 11, 1866, m. Elnora Brimhall March 16, 1887; Heber Albert b. Aug. 26, 1868, m. Abigail A. Webb Nov. 7, 1890; Maria Annett b. Oct. 30, 1870, m. James J. Shumway Dec. 9, 1887; Joseph Lorin b. Dec. 24, 1873, m. Louisa Lyrola June 6, 1901; Lulu Jane b. May 22, 1876, m. Samuel F. Smith April 5, 1900.
Member Utah legislature 1855. Bishop of Franklin, Idaho, 1863-76. Representative of Idaho legislature 1872-73. First counselor to Lot Smith in presidency of Little Colorado stake, and to Jesse N. Smith of Eastern Arizona stake.

HATCH, LORENZO LAFAYETTE (son of Lorenzo Hill Hatch and Sylvia Savonia Eastman). Born Dec. 25, 1851, Lehi, Utah.
Married Annie Scarborough Dec. 1, 1873, Salt Lake City (daughter of John Scarborough and Elizabeth Brook; the latter came to Utah Sept. 1861, Milo Andrus company), who was born June 1, 1853, Leeds, Eng. Their children: Lorenzo Fayette b. Jan. 16, 1875, m. Georgiana Smith Oct. 31, 1900; Della Savonia b. June 30, 1877, m. Ernest E. Gayman Oct. 30, 1901; Ina Elizabeth b. June 22, 1882; Ruth Blanche b. Aug. 3, 1883, m. Daniel P. Woodland June 24, 1909; Hezekiah James b. Oct. 5, 1887; Unita b. April 5, 1890; Leah Annie b. Nov. 14, 1892; Aura Charles b. Aug. 16, 1895; Catherine Clarissa b. Sept. 27, 1896. Family home Franklin, Idaho.
Married Sarah Doney Nov. 22, 1883, Payson, Utah (daughter of John Doney and Ann George, pioneers with Edmund Ellsworth handcart company), who was born Oct. 17, 1858, Payson. Their children: Elmer Doney (adopted) b. Sept. 4, 1890, m. Phoebe Preece Feb. 28, 1911; Cora Doney (adopted) b. Jan. 15, 1903. Family home Franklin, Idaho.
Bishop of Franklin, Idaho, 32 years. Chairman of board of county commissioners.

HAWES, WILLIAM. Came to Utah in early pioneer days.
Married Emily Meekham at Provo, Utah (daughter of Moses Meekham and Elvira Mekeham of Provo). Their children: William; Emily, m. John Timothy; Martha, m. David Timothy. Family home, Provo.
Married Celestia Mecham (daughter of Ephraim Mecham and Polly Durphy of Wallsburg, Utah). Their children: Ephriam, m. Effie Arminta Smith; Sarah, died.
Elder. Black Hawk Indian war veteran. Drove pony express between Salt Lake City and Provo. Died at Teton Basin, Idaho.

HAWKES, NATHAN (son of Peter Hawkes, born June 20, 1802, Stow Marus, Essex, Eng. and Ann Brookiman). Born Nov. 15, 1840, Hockley, Essex, Eng. Came to Utah Sept. 19, 1866, Benjamin Holliday company.
Married Elizabeth Bowman Dec. 1869, Salt Lake City (daughter of John Bowman and Margaret Piggott), who was born March 25, 1838. Their children: Margaret A. b. Sept. 1870, d. Jan. 16, 1897; Sarah E. b. Aug. 7, 1872, m. D. W. Adamson Nov. 5, 1904; Julia E. b. Oct. 6, 1874, m. James B. Birie Oct. 14, 1908; Nathan A. b. Dec. 15, 1876, m. Ethel Jackson Jan. 13, 1903; Peter B. b. Aug. 26, 1879, m. Emma Anderson May 13, 1905. Family home West Weber, Utah.
Settled at West Weber 1866.

HAWKINS, JAMES RICHARD. Born in England. Came to Utah, 1853.
Married Ann Suel in England. She came to Utah in 1853. Their children: William Edward b. Jan. 31, 1844; Charles b. June 26, 1845, m. Susan Sophia Jenkins Dec. 1, 1865; Eli B.; Joseph; Susanna, died.

HAWKINS, WILLIAM EDWARD (son of James R. Hawkins and Ann Suel, pioneers 1853). Born Jan. 31, 1844, London, Eng. Came to Utah, with parents.
Married Margaret Thomas May 3, 1870 (daughter of Thomas S. and Mary Thomas of Ogden, Utah). Their children: Mary, Margaret, William, Ida, James R., Alice, Thomas, Jedediah, Sarah, Oswald, Seth and Irvine. Family home Logan, Utah.
Pioneer of Tooele Co., Cache Co., Utah, and Malad Valley, Idaho. Died April 27, 1911.

HAWKINS, CHARLES (son of James R. Hawkins and Ann Suel). Born June 26, 1845 at Notting Hill, London, Eng. Came to Utah 1853.
Married Susan Sophia Jenkins Dec. 1, 1865, at Salt Lake City (daughter of William Ed. Jenkins and Mary Roeberry of Wellsville, Utah), who was born Oct. 13, 1847. Their children: Mary Eliza b. Dec. 1, 1866, d. 1880; James b. Sept. 9, 1868, d. 1880; William b. Sept. 9 1868, d. 1880; Ann b. Dec. 25, 1871; Charles E. b. Aug. 27, 1814; Elijah D. b. Oct. 21, 1880, m. Lillie Hone Sept. 25, 1901. Family home Benjamin, Utah.
President elders quorum; superintendent Sunday school; high priest. Member high council of Payson. Farmer. Died Aug. 21, 1912, Payson, Utah.

HAWKINS, CHARLES E. (son of Charles Hawkins and Susan Sophia Jenkins). Born Aug. 27, 1874.

HAWLEY, WILLIAM JOHN (son of Henry Hawley and Mary Wooden, former of Old Redding, Conn., later of Boyham, Middlesex Co., Canada). Born Nov. 25, 1803, Fishkill, N. Y. Came to Utah 1852, James Snow company.
Married Elsie Ellis Smith 1821, Boyham, Canada (daughter of Asa Smith and Hannah Kellum of Boyham, pioneers 1852). She was born June 4, 1804. Their children: William Henry, m. Mary Webb; Elizabeth, m. Henry Pinnell; George Washington, m. Lodenia Rogers; Anna, m. William Fletcher Reynolds; Cyrus Benjamin Edwin, m. Rachel Mary Ann Allred; Asa Smith, m. Mary Beers; Hannah, d. infant; James Ephraim, m. Susan McArthur. Family home, Pleasant Grove.
Married Sarah Jane Staker (daughter of Nathan Staker and Jane Richmond of Pleasant Grove, pioneers November 1852, Henry Miller company). She was born 1836, Pickering, Canada. Their children: Francis Marion b. Oct. 5, 1855, d. child; Sarah Ellis b. Sept. 10, 1860, m. Benjamin Pearson June 30, 1879; Anna Elnora b. Oct. 25, 1862, b. child. Family home Pleasant Grove.
Built first road in American Fork canyon. Alderman 1855. Appointed to open up the mining district. Judge of Piute county. Furnished nails, glass and putty for first school house in Pleasant Grove 1853. Trail blazer, miner, pioneer surgeon; farmer and miller. Died March, 1881, at Pleasant Grove.

HAWS, EPHRAIM (son of William Haws and Emily Mecham). Born March 15, 1869, Wallsburg, Utah.
Married Arminta Smith June 9, 1890, Midway, Utah (daughter of Phillip Smith and Eliza Ann Frampton of Mt. Pisgah, Iowa, pioneers 1852, oxteam). She was born June 8, 1869. Their children: William Elmer b. May 14, 1891; Laura Pearl b. July 26, 1893, m. William J. Lindeberg; Ineza b. Aug. 27, 1897. Family resided Midway and Heber, Utah.
Teacher. Farmer and cattleraiser.

HAWS, GILBERTH (son of Jacob Haws and Hannah Neil of North Carolina). Born March 10, 1801, in Kentucky. Came to Utah Sept. 23, 1848, Lorenzo Snow company.
Married Hannah Whitcomb June 2, 1822, in Illinois (daughter of Oliver Whitcomb and Olive Bidlock of New York), who was born April 17, 1806, in Madison county, N. Y., died Aug. 21, 1880, at Provo, Utah. Their children: Caroline b. Jan. 7, 1825, m. Walter Barney 1848; Matilda b. Oct. 31, 1826, d. June 4, 1849; Lucinda b. Oct. 20, 1828, m. Shadrach Holdaway Dec. 24, 1848; Eliza b. March 29, 1830, m. George Pickup 1848; Francis Marion b. Dec. 8, 1831, m. Sarah Ann Jones 1856; Amos Whitcomb b. July 10, 1833, m. Mary Bean; William Wallace b. Feb. 18, 1835, m. Barbara Mills; Albert W. b. Feb. 15, 1837, m. Nancy Haws; Caleb W. b. Oct. 1, 1838, m. Eliza Snow; George Washington b. March 12, 1841, m. Elizabeth Worsley; Emma Smith b. Aug. 6, 1843, m. Lyman Carter; Mary Olive b. June 28, 1845, m. James C. York; John Madison b. March 24, 1847, m. Martha B. Glazier; Gilbert Oliver b. Oct. 8, 1849, m. Luella Newell. Family home Provo, Utah.
High priest. Pioneer of Provo. Farmer. Died March 3, 1877, Provo.

HAWS, AMOS WHITCOMB (son of Gilberth Haws and Hannah Whitcomb). Born July 10, 1833 at Greentown, Wayne county, Ill.
Married Mary ... Bean Dec. 27, 1855, at Provo, Utah (daughter of James ... n and Elizabeth Lewis both of Provo), who was born April 17, 1839 in Adams county, Ill. Their children:

Elizabeth Caroline b. Oct. 6, 1856, m. Arthur Newell and William Hundley; William Amos b. May 23, 1858, d. Dec. 23, 1865; Mary Ellen b. June 10, 1860, m. William McEwan, d. June 3, 1909; James Gilberth b. March 4, 1862, m. Belle Williams; Cornelia Ann b. Jan. 27, 1864, d. March 12, 1864; Lewis Milo b. Jan. 13, 1865, d. Feb. 1, 1865; Sarah Louisa b. April 20, 1866, m. Thomas John Foote; George Whitcomb b. Nov. 20, 1868, died; Caleb Arthur b. Nov. 4, 1871, m. Mary Gee; Junius Orlando, m. Sarah Meznen. Family home Provo, Utah.
High priest. Carpenter and builder. Died May 28, 1888, at Provo.

HAWS, JAMES GILBERTH (son of Amos Whitcomb Haws and Mary Elizabeth Bean). Born March 4, 1862, Provo, Utah.
Married Nancy Isabella Williams Dec. 23, 1885, Logan, Utah (daughter of Nathaniel Williams and Eliza Helen Wall of Provo, Utah, pioneers 1847, second company). She was born Aug. 14, 1865. Their children: Gilbert Lynn b. Jan. 31, 1888, m. Evelyn Smith; Amos Waldo b. Oct. 24, 1889, died; Erma b. Jan. 20, 1891; Wilford Bruce b. Feb. 15, 1893; Guy Murice b. Dec. 7, 1894; James Noel b. May 20, 1897; Mary Vivian b. March 30, 1899, died; Alvah Merrill b. May 12, 1901; Helen Lucile b. Jan. 19, 1905. Family home Provo, Utah.
Ward teacher. Carpenter.

HAWS, WILLIAM WALLACE (son of Gilberth and Hannah Whitcomb). Born Feb. 18, 1835, in Wayne county, Ill. Married Barbara Mills. Was baptized into the church by Apostle Erastus Snow in Salt Lake City, November 1848. He located at Provo in the spring of 1849, helped to build the first old Fort on Provo river, and was put on military duty when a boy 14 years old. He served in the fight with the Indians when Joseph Higbee was killed; was made captain of a company of infantry which was sent into Echo Canyon to meet Johnston's army in 1857; helped to build the fortifications and was commissioned a major. He was a member of the Provo police force for 20 years. He was priest, teacher, elder, seventy and on his 59th birthday (Feb. 18, 1894) was ordained a high priest by Elder John Henry Smith; missionary to Illinois 1871. Pioneer settler to Mogollon mountain district, Arizona, 1879; to Gila Valley in 1882; and to Casas Grandes, Mex., 1885; moved to Colonia Dublan, Colonia, Juarez, and finally Colonia Pacheco, being among the early settlers in the Corrales basin. He has a large family of 20 children and 38 grandchildren—and a multitude of friends.

HAWS, ALBERT (son of Gilberth Haws and Hannah Whitcomb). Born Feb. 15, 1837, Wayne county, Ill. Came to Utah 1848, Lorenzo Snow company.
Married Nancy Haws Jan. 16, 1857, at Provo, Utah (daughter of John and Martha Haws of Provo), who was born Dec. 25, 1840. Their children: Albert Alonzo; Elnora, m. Almon Bascom Oct. 28, 1885; Joseph Marlow d. Jan. 22, 1863; Marion Oliver; Mary Olive; Emily Melisa, d. March 17, 1890; Owen Alpheus, d. Feb. 6, 1872; Lydia Alberta, d. Oct. 4, 1873; John Elmon, d. July 22, 1885. Family home Provo, Utah.
Married Harriet Mayberry September, 1879, at Salt Lake City (daughter of Thomas Mayberry and Mary Ann Chittenden of Australia. Came to Utah 1879). She was born May 6, 1860. Their children: Lillian Lestra; Jane Harriet; Nancy Elizabeth; Martha May, d. Sept. 18, 1905; Heber Bertel; Caleb Alfred, d. Jan. 4, 1910; Wilfred; Mary Ann; Gilbert LeRoy b. Sept. 17, 1898; Alice Amber b. Jan. 17, 1899.
Seventy. Sheriff and watermaster at Provo. Carpenter, wheelwright, blacksmith and farmer. Died May 20, 1912, at Naples, Utah.

HAWS, GEORGE WASHINGTON (son of Gilberth Haws and Hannah Whitcomb). Born March 12, 1841, Wayne county, Ill. Came to Utah Sept. 23, 1848, Lorenzo Snow company.
Married Elizabeth Ann Worsley Dec. 25, 1861, Provo, Utah (daughter of John Worsley and Sarah Hamer of Nauvoo, Ill., latter came to Utah), who was born Dec. 6, 1843. Their children: George Juan b. Nov. 23, 1862, m. Miss Moffatt; Elizabeth Ann b. Feb. 12, 1865, m. Albert E. Davis; Charles Henry b. Aug. 6, 1867, m. Elizabeth Richman; Mary Jane b. Dec. 21, 1869, m. John Anderson; Matilda b. Oct. 6, 1872; Electa P. b. Dec. 14, 1874, m. Wlear Baker; June Edwin b. June 17, 1877; John Ervin b. Sept. 12, 1879, m. Vera Loveland; Morilla Maude b. Dec. 23, 1887; Cortland b. Nov. 16, 1884; Effie May b. May 20, 1885, m. Henry M. Garn; Zina Vera b. June 13, 1890, m. Hugh Byrne.
Member Teton, Idaho, town board. Farmer.

HAWS, JOHN MADISON (son of Gilberth Haws and Hannah Whitcomb). Born March 24, 1847, Wayne county, Ill. Came to Utah Sept. 23, 1848, Lorenzo Snow company.
Married Martha Bitner Glazier March 6, 1866, Provo, Utah (daughter of Shepherd Glazier and Rozetta Dean of Pottawattamie Co., Iowa, pioneers 1851. Isaac Allred company). She was born Oct. 8, 1848, died Jan. 30, 1912. Their children: John Kimball b. May 18, 1868, m. Alice Fiorilla Wight Jan. 6, 1897; Lorin Dean b. Feb. 5, 1870, m. Mary Evans Jan. 1, 1896; Joseph Willman b. Jan. 19, 1872, m. Inez E. Rose March 3, 1897; Gilbert Shepherd b. Jan. 26, 1875, m. Meda J. Hansen Jan. 6, 1897; Oliver Caleb b. June 10, 1877, d. Sept. 13, 1877; Martha Lovica b. March 31, 1879; Francis Orlin b. April 2, 1882, m. Grace E. Munns June 21, 1905; Mary Olive b. April 26, 1885, m. Warren Elmer Hall Dec. 19, 1906. Family resided Mona and Elwood, Utah.

Married Laura Jane Partridge Nov. 22, 1869, at Salt Lake City (daughter of Charles Partridge and Mary Smith of Pottawattamie Co., Iowa; pioneers 1852). She was born Oct. 10, 1851. Their children: Laura Rozetta b. March 18, 1871, m. Thomas Kay; Mary Ann b. Aug. 1, 1872, m. James G. Higginson; Charles Madison b. Sept. 11, 1874, m. Harriet V. Hunsaker Jan. 6, 1897; Wallace Smith b. Aug. 18, 1876, m. Zoe May Thompson Jan. 1899; Rowena b. March 15, 1879, m. Joseph M. Jenson Jr. Sept. 15, 1896; Hannah Eliza b. Dec. 29, 1881, m. Alson H. Nihart; Matilda D. Feb. 2, 1887, d. Feb. 17, 1888. Family home Mona, Utah.
Settled at Provo, Utah, 1848; moved to Mona, 1868, where he served as presiding elder in 1876. High priest; bishop of Mona ward 1877-86; missionary to southern states 1899-1901. Assisted in bringing immigrants to Utah. County commissioner four years; president of Mona town board several years. Farmer.

HAWS, GILBERT OLIVER (son of Gilberth Haws and Hannah Whitcomb). Born Oct. 8, 1849, Provo, Utah.
Married Luella Isola Newell Oct. 3, 1870, at Salt Lake City (daughter of Elliott Alfred Newell and Maria Louisa Roberts; pioneers October, 1852), who was born April 2, 1852, Springville, Pottawattamie Co., Iowa. Their children: Myrta Isola, m. John W. Baum; Ruby Lorena, m. Orson Baum; Edna Murl, m. William E. Andrews; Zora Dee, m. Lester E. Holman. Family home Provo, Utah.
Member 45th quorum seventies. Road supervisor 12 years 1883-95. Second white child born in Provo. Assisted in making roads and canals in Provo and vicinity. Farmer and freighter.

HAY, ROBERT, of Glasgow, Scotland. Came to Utah in 1856. His children by first wife: William; James; Robena; Jean. Resided at Glasgow.
Married Mary Haley in Glasgow (daughter of John Haley and Mary Haley of Glasgow). Their children Isabel, m. John Lards; Alexander, m. Eliza Watson; George Smith; Annie, m. Abram Warburton; Elizabeth; Albert. Family home Pleasant Grove, Utah.
She was also the widow of Mr. Durfey, whom she married at Glasgow. Their child: Mary, m. James Smith; John Powell. Resided in Glasgow.
Elder; home missionary. Coal miner and farmer. Died February 1879 at Pleasant Grove, Utah.

HAYES, ALMA (son of Thomas Hayes and Polly Hess). Born Jan. 18, 1846, Nauvoo, Ill. Came to Utah in 1852.
Married Annselina Thomas Dec. 9, 1867 (daughter of Robert Thomas and Catherine Lewis), who was born Dec. 12, 1852, in Missouri. Their children: Elizabeth b. Nov. 13, 1868, m. Albert F. Rolph July 23, 1884, died March 13, 1908; John R. b. Oct. 3, 1870, m. Emma Dunn June 10, 1892; Alma H. b. Sept. 28, 1874, m. Lota Smart Oct. 19, 1897; Mary Jane b. Dec. 21, 1872, d. Dec. 7, 1872; Catherine b. April 23, 1877, m. George King Nov. 9, 1899; Alice L. b. Sept. 11, 1880, m. Robert Weber June, 1903; Margaret b. Jan. 19, 1882, m. Wilford King Sept. 11, 1901; Robert b. July 16, 1885, d. July 30, 1886; Edith b. July 29, 1887, d. Jan. 7, 1895; Harriet Ann b. March 13, 1889, m. Glee Lyb March 17, 1913; Esther b. May 23, 1891, m. Fred Smart Aug. 20, 1908; David W. b. Feb. 19, 1894, d. Dec. 28, 1895.
Married Louisa Jane Sheffield July 1, 1872, Salt Lake City (daughter of Thomas Sheffield and Jane Fowles). Their children: Joseph S. b. March 6, 1874, m. Elizabeth Smitt Oct. 19, 1894, and Roxena b. Jan. 26, 1892; Jane b. Sept. 10, 1877, m. William Hoff Oct. 21, 1896; Walter b. Dec. 8, 1875, d. March 20, 1889; Thomas b. Aug. 18, 1879, m. Margaret G. Bee March 27, 1905; Ann Selina b. July 1, 1881, d. Aug. 28, 1881; Zinn R. b. July 16, 1883, m. Mr. Armitage June 25, 1902; Horace b. April 13, 1886, m. Alice Roberts April 12, 1911; Wilford b. Sept. 10, 1890, m. Althea Rasmussen April 12, 1911; Hattie b. Nov. 11, 1892, m. Mr. Payne June 9, 1909; Lucy b. March 1, 1895. Family home Georgetown, Idaho.
Indian war veteran. Bishop of Georgetown ward, Bear Lake stake.

HAYWARD, HENRY J. (son of Gammon Hayward and Sarah A. Cripps of London, pioneers Sept. 30, 1863, Jacob Roach company). Born Sept. 2, 1852. Came to Utah with parents.
Married Elizabeth Ann Pugsley Dec. 23, 1875, at Salt Lake City (daughter of Philip Pugsley and Martha Roach), who was born Dec. 23, 1854. Their children: Henry G. b. Oct. 16; Emily J. b. July 11, 1878; Philip P. b. June 5, 1880; Sidney A. b. Sept. 4, 1883; Martha R. b. July 8, 1885; the first four died in childhood; Hazel G. b. March 20, 1887, m. Henry R. Wessman; Merle b. Dec. 8, 1889, d. child; Elizabeth C. b. Jan. 12, 1892; John E. b. June 19, 1895. Family home Salt Lake City.

HAZEN, SAMUEL B. (son of Robert Hazen and Mary Ann Bainbridge of New Castle, Eng., pioneers 1852). Born Jan. 1, 1867.
Married Clara E. Lane Sept. 9, 1891, Logan, Utah (daughter of James Lane and Sophia S. Brown of Brighton ward, Salt Lake City, pioneers 1861, James S. Brown company). She was born Dec. 22, 1866, Salt Lake City. Their children: Samuel C. b. July 29, 1892, d. child; Ruth M. b. Aug. 30, 1894; Laura S. b. Oct. 28, 1899; James L. b. June 29, 1902, and Clara L. b. April 8, 1903, d. infants: Leone M. b. July 18, 1904; Ida Lucretia b. Oct. 8, 1907. Family home Center ward, Salt Lake City.

HEALEY, JAMES (son of Joseph Healey and Mary Eggleyshaw of Commonside, Derbyshire. Eng.). Born March 31, 1824, Derbyshire. Came to Utah September 1854, Job Smith company.
Married Elizabeth Smith 1846, Wittake, Leicestershire, Eng. (daughter of William Smith and Mary Ethcott of Wittake, Leicestershire, former died on way to Utah, latter came September, 1854, Job Smith company). She was born 1825, died March 29, 1854. Their children: Ephraim b. Jan. 26, 1847, m. Mary Matilda Watkins, m. Mary Read; William b. 1849, m. Clara Hansen; Mary Ann b. 1852, died. Family home Leicestershire, Eng.
Married Mary Carlisle (James) 1855, Alpine, Utah (daughter of Richard Carlisle of Alpine, came to Utah 1847, John Taylor company). Their children: Alice, m. William T. Brown; Elizabeth, m. Jacob Beck; Jane, m. Hans Olsen; Martha, m. David J. Strong; James, m. Hannah Devey; Richard, m. Jane Winn. Family home Alpine, Utah.
Settled at Alpine 1855. High priest; teacher. Farmer. Died November 1907, Alpine.

HEALEY, EPHRAIM (son of James Healey and Elizabeth Smith). Born Jan. 26, 1847, Wittake, Leicestershire, Eng. Came to Utah September 1854, Job Smith company.
Married Mary Matilda Watkins Jan. 15, 1869, at Salt Lake City (daughter of Robert Watkins and Mary Smallman of England, Nauvoo and Alpine, pioneers 1852). She was born July 8, 1849, Garden Grove, Iowa. Their children: Rosella b. Nov. 10, 1869, m. William Jenkins; Ada b. May 29, 1871, d. Aug. 15, 1872; Ida Delilah b. Oct. 2, 1874, m. Otto Steinbock; Mary Edith b. Sept. 21, 1876, m. George Nielson; Olevia b. Feb. 13, 1879, m. Thomas McGregor; Margeret May b. March 9, 1881, m. Guy Shoemaker; Ephraim Franklin b. March 22, 1883, m. Lucy Elizabeth Okey; Fred Smith b. May 27, 1887, m. Gertrude Nash; Sarah Gertrude b. July 27, 1889, m. Mark Bennett. Family home Alpine, Utah.
Married Mary Read May 6, 1908, at Provo (daughter of Robert Read and Mary Fletcher Greensmith of Lenton, Nottingham, Eng.). She was born Jan. 23, 1859. Came to Utah 1888.
High priest. County justice of peace twenty years; alderman and city councilor. Settled at Alpine 1861; lived at Pleasant Grove seven years. Assisted in bringing immigrants to Utah in 1866. Indian war veteran. Farmer and stockraiser.

HEAP, WILLIAM (son of William Heap and Margaret Beasley of Cedar Grove, Ind.). Born Jan. 2, 1837, in Indiana. Came to Utah October, 1862, oxteam company.
Married Sarah Marsh Oct. 19, 1867, at Salt Lake City (daughter of James Henry Marsh and Martha Miller of Salt Lake City, pioneers October 1850). She was born April 18, 1852. Their children: Marion; Martha, m. Emil Hanson July 3, 1889; William; John; Joseph; Aaron; Eli, died; Maggie; Ella; Henry; Ira.
Elder. Farmer and rancher.

1900; delegate to state convention at Boise 1902; state senator of Fremont county 1902-03; Fremont county treasurer 1904-08. Chairman executive committee of Fremont stake tabernacle 1911. Deputy sheep inspector of Bannock county 1895. Director and secretary Independent Canal Co., Fremont; director of First National bank, Rexburg, 1911. Police judge at Rexburg 1913. School teacher 1885-1901. Farmer.

HEATH, FREDERICK (son of John and Barbara Heath of Henley, Staffordshire, Eng.). Born May 1, 1833. Came to Utah September, 1847, Captain Hunter company.
Married Harriett Butcher Dec. 2, 1855, Salt Lake City (daughter of George Butcher and Sophia Sayers of Norwich, Eng., pioneers 1855, Claudius Spencer company). She was born April 4, 1833. Their children: Frederick G. b. Aug. 23, 1856, m. Henrietta Haigh; John Franklin b. Aug. 8, 1858, m. Sarah M. Husbands; Henry O. b. Oct. 14, 1860, m. Nana Chapman; William E. b. Oct. 15, 1862, d. infant; Joseph A. b. Sept. 18, 1863, m. Mami Yeager; Horace A. b. April 29, 1866, m. Sarah Wheeler, m. Eva Ward; Harriett K. b. April 12, 1871, d. infant; Francis D. b. Aug. 15, 1876.
Drove a team to Salt Lake and settled at Old Fort Square on arrival. One of those participating in the farming of "The Family Farm," where was inaugurated the first system of irrigation in Utah; assisted in making the first dam and making the canal that carried the stream to the east side of the bench farm. Took part in the Indian fight at Battle Creek (now Pleasant Grove). Engaged in contracting supplies for the troops at Fort Douglas 1858 to 1893. Indian war veteran.

HEATH, FREDERICK GEORGE (son of Frederick Heath and Harriett Butcher). Born Aug. 23, 1856, at Salt Lake City.
Married Henrietta Haigh July 24, 1878, at Salt Lake City (daughter of John Haigh and Sarah Kershaw, Bradford, Yorkshire, Eng. They came to Utah 1870). She was born Dec. 19, 1858. Their children: Sarah H. b. Feb. 6, 1880; Rosenia b. Oct. 21, 1881, m. Hazel W. Kartchner; Frederick John b. Sept. 1, 1883, m. Emma C. Cahocn; Hazel E. b. Sept. 21, 1885; Arthur R. b. Dec. 10, 1888; Otto D. b. May 16, 1890; Warren H. b. March 18, 1892, d. infant; Dora b. Sept. 1, 1893, d. infant; Howard W. b. May 12, 1895; Florence b. Dec. 3, 1898; Mabelle A. b. May 1, 1901; Olive b. Jan. 5, 1903.
Engaged in real estate and loans. Farmer and contractor.

HEATH, JOHN FRANKLIN (son of Frederick Heath and Harriett Butcher). Born Aug. 6, 1858, at Salt Lake City.
Married Sarah M. Husbands Feb. 8, 1888, at Salt Lake City (daughter of William Husbands and Sarah Curtis of Salt Lake City, pioneers 1866). She was born March 29, 1867. Their children: Ivy Pearl b. Nov. 25, 1888; Alta P. b. Oct. 5, 1891; Frank b. Dec. 25, 1892, d. infant; John C. b. June 21, 1894; Clifford H. Family home, Salt Lake City.
Road supervisor five years. General contractor and real estate agent. Builder and owner of Salt Palace. Gardener.

Married Terissa ——. Their children: Jefferson Smith b. Feb. 28, 1837, died; George Fluker b. March 13, 1838. m. Annie Marker; Sarah Ann b. Dec. 3, 1839, and Mary Jane b. Oct. 7, 1841, died.
Married Abigail Unpstead. Their children: James Harvey, m. Susianna ——; William, m. Celia Mott.

Member 75th quorum and later senior president of 60th quorum seventies; high pest: missionary in Denmark seven years and presided over to Wensyssel and Copenhagen conferences. Settled in Salt Lake City 1865, and moved to Huntsville 1866, from her he went to Harrisville March 20, 1876, and later moved to Idaho.

HEATH, THOMAS. Came to Utah July 24, 1847, Brigham Young company.
Married Sarah Foster at Salt Lake City (daughter of William Foster of England. Came to Utah 1853). She was born March 26, 1835. Their children: Thomas, m. Sarah Brown; Amelia and Barbara, died; William, m. Margaret Shelton; Henry F., m. Sarah Shelton; Clara, m. Charles Skewes; Camilla and Drucilla, died; Lillian, m. O. T. Carlson; Chaplain, died. Family home Salt Lake City.
Farmer. Died March, 1879, Salt Lake City.

HEATH, HENRY F. (son of Thomas Heath and Sarah Foster). Born July 28, 1865, Salt Lake City.
Married Sarah Shelton Feb. 14, 1887, Salt Lake City (daughter of Robert Shelton and Margaret Slother of England, pioneers 1865). She was born Jan. 14, 1867. Their children: Delcie, m. Kenneth Britton; Walter; Bertha; George; Barbara. Family home, Salt Lake City.
Park keeper; superintendent parks. Carpenter. Died Dec. 4, 1911, Salt Lake City.

HEATON, JOHN (son of Jonas Heaton and Ann Richardson, Yorkshire, Eng., former died 1851, St. Louis, Mo.). Born 1828, Thorn Hill, Eng. Came to Utah 1863.
Married Janet Sinclair 1859 (daughter of William Sinclair and Christina Archibald, pioneers 1863). She was born June 11, 1843. Their children: Jonas b. Aug. 19, 1860, m. Laura Bell Hill Oct. 1881; Elizabeth Ann b. Dec. 19, 1862, m. Solomon M. Hale; Christina Archibald S. b. Marche 1, 1863, m. William A. McCrary July 26, 1880; Mary Jane b. March 18, 1864, m. Thomas J. Howell April 7, 1881; Martha b. Nov. 11, 1865, m. James W. Howell Feb. 15, 1884; John b. July 8, 1867, m. Annie L. Lewellyn Jan. 18, 1888; Sarah Agness, died April 1873; William Sinclair b. Jan. 17, 1871; James Henry b. 1872, died Jan. 1873.

HEDGES, GEORGE W. (son of James Hedges and Maria Andrews of Surrey, Eng.). Born June 20, 1842, Surrey. Came to Utah 1847.
Married Christina Olson April 25, 1867, Salt Lake City, by Bishop Speers (daughter of Hans Olson and Johanna Anderson of Svedala, Sweden, pioneers Sept. 20, 1862, John R. Murdock company). She was born June 12, 1847. Their children: Drucilla M. b. Feb. 23, 1868, m. J. G. Kelsom; Annie M. b. April 24, 1870, d. aged 3; Edith B. b. Feb. 15, 1873, m. William R. Turner; George A. b. Jan. 1, 1877; Chester J. b. April 1880, d. infant; Frank L. b. May 5, 1885, d. aged 23; Harrison S. b. 1900. Family home Salt Lake City.
Musician. Died March 12, 1906, Salt Lake City.

HEGGIE, ANDREW WALKER (son of Andrew Heggie, born March 19, 1796, Forgan parish, Fifeshire, Scotland, and Catherine Walker, born 1795, Hilland, Scotland). Born Jan. 3, 1825, Fraistown, Forgan parish. Came to Utah Aug. 27, 1860, Daniel Robinson company.
Married Annie T. Stewart Feb. 3, 1865 (daughter of William Stewart and Sarah Thompson, married Janh 18, 9, Belfast, Ireland, the former pioneer 1862, Captain Rollins oxteam company). She was born Dec. 11, 1839 and came to Utah with father. Their children: Annie S. b. Nov. 20, 1865, m. James B. Jardine Sept. 17, 1884; Cathrine W. b. March 4, 1867, m. William J. Griffiths Jan. 6, 1886; Andrew S. b. Nov. 15, 1868, m. Mary Loosie June 10, 1897; Sarah S. b. Jan. 7, 1871, m. John Helga Dohle Dec. 13, 1894; William S. b. Oct. 9, 1872, d. March 13, 1874. Family home Clarkston, Utah.
Settled at Salt Lake City 1860; moved to Clarkston 1865. Sunday school superintendent 25 years; president 7th quorum seventies; second counselor to Bishop John Jardine of Clarkston for 13 years beginning Nov. 25, 1888. School trustee; justice of peace.

HEGSTED, HANS CHRISTIAN SORENSON (son of Soren Christian Hansen, born 1797, and Johanna Christiansen, born 1802, Hjorring Amt, Denmark). Born Aug. 17, 1830, Wrejlev parish, Hjorring, Denmark. Came to Utan Nov. 8, 1865, Miner G. Atwood company.
Married Mary Borglum Dec. 10, 1861, Hjorring, Denmark (daughter of Augustine and Anna Borglum of Hjorring), who was born March 2, 1837, Hjorring, died March 29, 1909, Salem, Idaho. Their children: Victor Charles b. April 18, 1865, m. Ada Martin; Jacob b. May 5, 1871. Family resided Harrisville, Utah, and Salem, Idaho.
Married Christena Olson Jan. 20, 1866, at Salt Lake City (daughter of Iver John Olson and Anna Christensen, they came to Utah 1873). She was born Jan. 4, 1844. Their children: Hans C. S. b. April 6, 1871, m. Edna Porter Nov. 10, 1909, 1895; John b. Feb. 9, 1875, m. Edna Porter Nov. 10, 1909. Family home Salem, Fremont Co., Idaho.
Married Karen Nielsen April 14, 1866, at Salt Lake City, who was born April 8, 1840, died Sept. 25, 1879. Their children: Joseph b. Nov. 1, 1873, m. Mabel McKensie April 21, 1909; Isaac b. May 20, 1876.

HEINER, MARTIN (son of Johanas Heiner born Oct. 16, 1777, and Anne Eliza Hondorf, arn Aug. 9, 1790, Saxe-Muningen, Germany, who were marred 1814). Born March 17, 1818, Waldorf, Saxe-Muningen. Came to Utah Sept. 16, 1859, Edward Stevenson compan.
Married Adelgunda Dietzl Jan. 6, 1839 (daughter of Michal Dietzel and Sophia C. Krusa, who were married July 12, 1803, Germany). She was born June 11, 1815. Their children: Mary b. July 28, 1840m. Arza E. Ninckley 1862; Amelia b. Feb. 20, ——, m. George A. Black July 31, 1844; John b. July 2, 1842, m. Sarah Colan March 23, 1867; Anthony b. June 24, 1844, m. Lucinda I nderson Sept. 16, 1865; George b. March 26, 1846, m. Mary Hoderson Dec. 22, 1866; Elizabeth b. April 24, 1848, m. Thomas Grover Feb. 10, 1865; Daniel b. Nov. 27, 1850, m. Martha Strens March 31, 1873; Susannah C. b. Oct. 15, 1852, m. Joseph Ward June 28, 1875; Emma Ann b. Aug. 17, 1856, d. 1865; Rachel b. Sept. 16, 1858, d. 1862; Eliza b. Oct. 22, 1860, d. 265.
High councilman and petriarch. School trustee, and city councilman. Assisted in buding first canal on north side of Weber river; planted first ande and fruit trees in Morgan; cleared sage brush from p sent site of North Morgan City.

HEINER, ANTHONY (son f Martin Heiner and Adelgunda Dietzel). Born June 24, 144. Came to Utah Sept. 16, 1859, Edward Stevenson compan.
Married Lucinda Henderson 1865 (daughter of David E. Henderson and Mary MacFigeon, pioneers 1856). She was born May 30, 1842. Their children: Anthony b. July 6, 1866; Rachel b. Feb. 8, 1868; Lucida Ann b. June 20, 1870; David Martin b. Jan. 1, 1873; Joh Wesley b. Sept. 27, 1876; Mary Agnes b. Oct. 11, 1881, d. april 6, 189—; Henry Melvin b. April 29, 1884. Family hoe Morgan, Utah.
Married Sarah Elizabeth Morrison (Morris), who was born April 3, 1844. Childre: Eliza Morris b. May 22, 1866; Lucinda Morris b. Oct. 22, 867; Canway Morris b. May 17, 1869, by her former marrige. Their children: Evaline b. Nov. 5, 1875; Agatha H. b. Feb. 8, 1877; Joseph Anthony b. Jan. 17, 1879; Sparle b. Nov 27, 1881, d. June 7, 1882; Royal Oscar b. Sept. 1, 1882; Lafsette b. Aug. 21, 1885; Maryette b. Aug. 1885.

HEINER, DANIEL (son of Martin Heiner and Adelgunda Dietzel). Born Nov. 27, 180, Franklin county, Pa.
Married Martha A. Steven March 31, 1873, Salt Lake City (daughter of Roswell Stevus and Mary Peterson, former came to Utah with Mormon battalion). She was born Dec. 14, 1855, Peterson, Utah, fit white child born in Morgan county. Their children: Dael Nephi b. July 14, 1874; Roswell M. b. Dec. 22, 1875, m.day Littlefield March 20, 1809; Moroni b. Feb. 12, 1877, m. Ea Pernell Dec. 14, 1898; George A. b. Dec. 7, 1879, m. Sara Cobison June, 1902; Charles b. April 13, 1881, m. Perses Far June 1904; Geber J. b. Nov. 18, 1882, m. Theresa Tribe De. 14, 1904; Martha Sophia b. April 26, 1884, m. James A. Aderson 1906; Estella b. May 14, 1887, m. Alford Croft Aug. 2 1908; Mary Elizabeth b. Aug. 13, 1889, m. T. V. Thomas April 17, 1912; Brenton Wells b. June 24, 1891; Spencer b. No 22, 1894; Disc b. Dec. 1, 1896; Cash b. Feb. 7, 1899. Family home Morgan, Utah.
Married Sarah Coulam arch 31, 1873, Salt Lake City (daughter of John Coulam ad Sarah Cordon, former came to Utah 1848). Their children: Adelgunda b. Feb. 1874, m. James Taggart 1894; John b. Feb. 7, 1876, m. Anni Croft 1903; Daniel Hanmer b. Feb. 24, 1878, m. Hattie Robi n 1897; Frankie b. Aug. 6, 1880, m. C. M. Croft 1903; Henry bSept. 11, 1882, m. Lissie Robison 1911; George Sylvester b arch 2, 1886, m. Ellie Clawson 1911.
President of Morgan stak; Mayor of Morgan; member first state legislature; presid t Black Hawk Coal Co.; president Morgan County Commercial Club; president First National bank of Morgan.

HELM, ABRAHAM (son of Drid Helm and Elizabeth Bookmap). Born Feb. 22, 1813, umberland county, Pa. Came to Utah 1855, Moses Thursto company.
Married Mary Richards (aughter of Phillip Richards), who was born July 21, 1812, i Germany and came to Utah with husband. Their child n; Joseph b. July, 1837, m. Emma Smith; John b. Ap 1839, m. Emeline Verres; Bartrum b. 1840, m. Emily Ginn; Samuel b. 1845, m. Elizabeth Gardner; Marshall b. 18, m. Margaret Mitchell; Andrew b. 1849, m. Rachel Mitcell; David b. 1856, died 1862; Levi Phillip b. 1851, m. Viola. Ward Jan. 6, 1886.

HELM, LEVI PHILLIP (son of Abr ... m Helm and Mary Richards). Born Oct. 22, 185 Sandusky Co., Ohio.
Married Viola J. Ward at Lean. tah (daughter of James F. and Louisa Ward; former 1853; latter 1860). She was born July 21, 1856. Their c ldren: Seth Ward b. Feb 1, 1887; Orion b. Sept. 24, 1890; ola Joy b. July 20, 1894.
High priest; president 61st, nd member 91st quorum seventies; 1st counselor and pre dent. in the San Luis stake. Col. Member Utah legislatur 1887. Farmer and stockraiser.

HEMMING, WILLIAM (son of Jan Hemming, born 1805, at Burford, and Sarah Embra, born Dec. 21, 1807, Hooknorton, Oxfordshire, Eng.). He was bon June 8, 1827, at Hooknorton. Came to Utah Aug. 27, 1860, Daniel Robinson handcart company.
Married Emma Sanford Aug. 3 1851 (daughter of James Sanford and Elizabeth Powell) who was born Sept. 26, 1829, Warwickshire, Eng. Their hildren: Fanny b. June 9, 1852, m. John Foomee 1868; Hriet b. June 6, 1854, and William b. April 16, 1856, both c infants; Emma Elizabeth b. 1859, m. James T. Rich Dec. ", 1877; Mary Ann b. Feb. 1, 1862, d. infant; Frederick Wilam b. 1864, m. Olive Porter Doc. 4, 1895; Sarah Jane b Sept. 1866, m. Roswell B. Stevens March 24, 1891; Alfred Jrn b. Feb. 1, 1869, m. Adelgunda Grover March 24, 1891; Chriotte Matilda b. March 18, 1872, m. Aaron B. Cherry Nov. 21 1894. Family home, Morgan, Utah.
One of the first to push a handcart across the plains. Settled in Weber Valley 1860, and has devoted the greater portion of his life in actively developing the resources of his adopted commonwealth. Patriarch. City councilman two terms.

HEMMING, FREDERICK WILIAM (son of William Hemming and Emma Sanford). Born April 23, 1864, Morgan, Utah.
Married Olive Porter Dec. 4, 1/5, Salt Lake City (daughter of Lyman Wight Porter and Iecta Maria Kilborn), who was born March 20, 1870, Porter lie, Utah. Their children: Frederic C. b. 1896; Ella Maria). 1897; James Sanford b. 1901; Jessie Mardell b. 1905.

HEMSLEY, RICHARD (son of Mr. Hemsley and Dinah Fuller, Brighton, Sussex, Eng. Born Oct. 20, 1801, at Ditchling, Sussex. Came to Uta Sept. 16, 1866, Samuel H. Hill company.
Married Sarah Potter 1835 (daghter of Henry Potter who was married about 1798, Cookfiel, Sussex, Eng.). She was born Feb. 3, 1807. Their children: Richard b. May 25, 1836, m. Christina Maria Jensen 1861 Edward b. April 22, 1839, m. Meriam Simmonds 1861; Eliz b. Dec. 24, 1841; Ellen b. May 10, 1844, m. John Halford; Jb b. Jan. 6, 1847, m. Elizabeth Kensett. Family home Supr, Utah.

HEMSLEY, RICHARD (son of lchard Hemsley and Sarah Potter). Born May 25, 1836, Dihling, Sussex, Eng. Emigrated to Utah 1856, handcart company.
Married Christina Maria Jense 1861, at Mill Creek, Salt Lake county (daughter of O. oristen Jensen and Anna Hedilwick, pioneers 1861, oxtea company). She was born Aug. 18, 1842, Aryling, Denmark, ied June 27, 1867, San Pete Co., Utah. Their children: Sarahnn b. Nov. 27, 1862, m. Stephen G. Candler Oct. 30, 1879; Ichard b. Oct. 12, 1864, m. Mary Ann Davies Feb. 16, 1887 James b. Feb. 23, 1866, m. Anne Robinson June 1, 1896. Family home Mill creek, Utah.
Married Sarah Frances Heator who was born Feb. 2, 1846, and died July 5, 1878. Their cildren: Mary Jane; Joseph Hyrum; Christina Maria; Georg Edward; Francis Joseph.
Married Mary Roxbury. Their hildren: Ellen; Job; Maggie; Edward; Hamilton.
Settled at Mill Creek 1857. issionary to Dixie, 1865, from where he was driven by ndians, returning to Mill Creek. Moved to Egin Bench, rement Co., Idaho. Member bishopric of Hiatt ward; jesiding elder of Brighton Branch for many years.

HEMSLEY, RICHARD (son of lchard Hemsley and Christina Maria Jensen). Born Oct. 2, 1864, Mill Creek, Utah.
Married Mary Ann Davies 1 b. 16, 1887 (daughter of John Thomas Davies and Ann ilia, former came to Utah Nov. 18, 1886, latter June 6, 13—married March 7, 1864, Pontypool, Wales). She was bon Jan. 20, 1865, Pontypool, South Wales, came to Utah 1883 Their children: Sarah Ann b. Jan. 28, 1888, m. Herbert E Perrenond April 11, 1906; Richard John b. Feb. 23, 1889, m Avilda H. Jackson May 12, 1907; Mabol Christena b. Sept. 25,896, m. Weber C Weatherston Dec. 20, 1912; Emily May May 20, 1892, m. Albert R. Heath Sept. 13. 1911; Clyde Da es b. Sept. 8, 1893; Agnes Lepwretta b. March 15, 1895; Ja es Jensen b. June 25, 1896; Josephine Jane b. Nov. 8, 1897; one b. Jan. 27, 1899; Job b. Feb. 20, 1901; Lila Bertha b. Dec. 8, 1902; Mary Ellen b. Jan. 31, 1904; Myrtle Martha b. July 3 1905; Frances Charlotte b. Nov. 19, 1907. Family home Plao, Idaho.
Worked in brickyard at Salt ake City 1879. Moved to Plano, Idaho 1901, and was ordined 2d counselor to Bishop Hyrum J. Lucas May 26, 1902 ordained 1st counselor to Bishop Albert Heath May 26, 13; bishop Plano ward July 30, 1905; missionary to Great I tain Jan. 28, 1908, returning May 16, 1910. Bricklayer ax contractor; merchant and farmer.

HENDERSON, SAMUEL NEWTC (son of James Henderson, born Nov. 27, 1805, and Annie .rris, born 1812, both died at Nauvoo. Ill.). He was born pril 18, 1838, in Crawford county, Mo. Came to Utah Sep 12, 1847.
Married Esther Dewhurst Jn. 11, 1869 (daughter of James Dewhurst and Elizabet Fielding), who was born Feb. 17, 1847, Blackhaven, Lanc hire, Eng., and died March 15, 1872, Randolph, Utah. Thr child: Elizabeth Ann b. April 12, 1870, d. April 13, 188 Family home Randolph, Utah.
Married Sarah Jane Pugmire 1y 16, 1877, Randolph Utah (daughter of Joseph Ilyrum Igmire, pioneer 1847, John Taylor company, and Eleanor Craton, pioneer with a handcart company). She was born April 18, 1858. Their children: Samuel Henry b. Feb. 23, 1878, m. Isabel Sims June 15, 1904; Esther Eleanor b. April 23, 1880, m. John Thomson Barker Sept. 18, 1902; Florence Celeste b. Aug. 20, 1883, m. Riley Day, Jan. 20, 1905; Mary Maud b. Aug. 20, 1885, m. Joel Melvin Schenck June 22, 1904; James b. Oct. 10, 1887, d. Oct. 13, 1903; Jasper b. Jan. 14, 1889, m. Nancy Alice Barker Oct. 22, 1909; Annie Adelia b. Feb. 25, 1890, d. Sept. 12, 1901; Harriet Lilian b. April 2. 1892, m. Ole Mattson, Nov. 29, 1910; Martin b. March 10, 1895; Clifford Newton b. June 8, 1897; Nancy Josephine b. Nov. 25, 1899; George Allen b. June 30, 1902; Ira Pugmire b. Oct. 15, 1904. Family home Laketown, Utah.
Settled at Mill Creek 1848. Major in Utah militia 1855; veteran Black Hawk war. Moved to Randolph, Utah, 1870, and to Laketown 1880. Member 61st quorum seventies. Sheriff Rich county two terms; constable of Randolph one term. Assisted in bringing immigrants to Utah. Took an active part in Echo Canyon campaign.

HENDRICKS, JAMES (son of Abraham Hendricks and Charlotte Hinton). Born June 1808 Franklin, Ky. Came to Utah 1847, Jedediah M. Grant company.
Married Drusilla Dorris 1825 (daughter of William Dorris and Catherine Frost), who was born May 5, 1810. Their children: Elizabeth Mahala; William Dorris; Catherine Tabitha; Rebecca; Joseph Smith. Family home Salt Lake City.
Married Hannah Riggs.
Bishop of 19th ward Salt Lake City 1850-57. Justice of peace in Salt Lake City. Moved to Richmond 1860. Badly wounded in battle of Crooked River in Missouri, Oct. 25, 1838. Died July 8, 1870, Richmond, Utah.

HENDRICKS, WILLIAM DORRIS (son of James Hendricks and Drusilla Dorris). Born Nov. 6, 1829, Franklin, Ky. Came to Utah 1847, Mormon battalion.
Married Mary Jane Andrus March 12, 1851, at Salt Lake City, Brigham Young officiating (daughter of Milo Andrus and Abigail Jane Daley of New York, pioneers 1848, Heber C. Kimball company). She was born Nov. 16, 1833. Their children: Mary Jane, m. A. B. Harrison; Drusilla, m. I. K. Hillman; Brigham Andrus, m. Mary R. Stoddard; William Henry, m. Emma Traveler; Charlotte, m. William Underwood; Milo Andrus, m. Adeline Harris; Elizabeth, m. N. R. Lewis; Hildah Hannah, m. Andrew Morrison; Chloe, m. C. D. Merrill; George Gideon, m. Susa Eldridge. Family home Richmond, Utah.
President Oneida stake; bishop of Richmond ward; patriarch in Benson stake. Mayor of Richmond. Farmer; railroad contractor; banker. Died May 6, 1909, Lewiston, Utah.

HENDRICKS, JOSEPH SMITH (son of James Hendricks and Drusilla Dorris). Born March 23, 1838, Far West, Caldwell county, Mo.
Married Sariah Pew Tibbetts Jan. 4, 1857, Salt Lake City (daughter of John H. and Caroline Tibbetts, pioneers on July 24, 1847, and in 1848, respectively). She was born Aug. 11, 1833. Their children: Drusilla; Fidelia; Joseph; Elizabeth; Inez. Family resided Salt Lake City and Oxford, Utah.
Married Lucinda Bess 1866, Salt Lake City. She was born in New York state. Their children: Juel Joseph; Laura; William D.; John Henry; Lola; Lorinda; Asa; Hyrum. Family e e Oxford, and Marysville, Idaho, and Lewiston, Utah. aid d
Member Oneida stake high council. Moved to Oxford, Idaho 1876, from whence he went to Marysville, Idaho, where he served 15 years in the bishopric.

HENDRICKS, BRIGHAM ANDRUS (son of William Dorris Hendricks and Mary Jane Andrus). Born Nov. 27, 1857, at Salt Lake City.
Married Mary Rebecca Stoddard Jan. 13, 1881, at Salt Lake City (daughter of Charles Henry Stoddard and Anna Telford of Bountiful, Utah, pioneers 1851, Harry Walton company). She was born May 1, 1862. Their children: George B. b. Nov. 25, 1881, m. Caroline A. McAlister; Mary Lalene b. Aug. 24, 1885; Odessie Lepreal b. June 3, 1889; Nellie b. Oct. 22, 1890, m. Ralph Bernhisel; Brigham Victor b. June 30, 1895; Charles Durrell b. Nov. 17, 1899. Family home Lewiston, Utah.
Member 70th quorum Seventies; missionary to Southern states 1885-87, to Northwestern states 1897-98, and to South Africa 1909-11; counselor in presidency of Benson stake. County commissioner; school trustee at Lewiston; member Utah legislature. Farmer and stockraiser.

HENDRICKS, GEORGE B. (son of Brigham Andrus Hendricks and Mary Rebecca Stoddard). Born Nov. 25, 1881, at Lewiston, Utah.
Married Caroline Armeda McAlister June 5, 1912, at Salt Lake City (daughter of John A. McAlister and Clarissa Snow of Logan, Utah). She was born March 17, 1887. Family home Logan, Utah.
Member elders' quorum. Member faculty of Utah Agricultural College. Professor.

HENDRICKSON, JOHN A. (son of Andreas M. Hendrickson, born 1821, and Maren Andrea Olsen, born May 3, 1823, both of Fredrikstad, Norway). He was born Aug. 19, 1960, Fredrikstad, Norway. Came to Utah 1863, oxteam company.

Married Terissa ———. Their children: Jefferson Smith b. Feb. 28, 1837, died; George Fluker b. March 13, 1838, m. Annie Marker; Sarah Ann b. Dec. 3, 1839, and Mary Jane b. Oct. 7, 1841, died.
Married Abigail Unpstead. Their children: James Harvey, m. Susianna ———; William, m. Celia Mott.

HEATH, THOMAS. Came to Utah July 24, 1847, Brigham Young company.
Married Sarah Foster at Salt Lake City (daughter of William Foster of England. Came to Utah 1853). She was born March 26, 1835. Their children: Thomas, m. Sarah Brown; Amelia and Barbara, died; William, m. Margaret Shelton; Henry F., m. Sarah Shelton; Clara, m. Charles Skewes; Camilla and Drucilla, died; Lillian, m. O. T. Carlson; Chaplain, died. Family home Salt Lake City.
Farmer. Died March, 1879, Salt Lake City.

HEATH, HENRY F. (son of Thomas Heath and Sarah Foster). Born July 28, 1865, Salt Lake City.
Married Sarah Shelton Feb. 14, 1887, Salt Lake City (daughter of Robert Shelton and Margaret Slother of England, pioneers 1865). She was born Jan. 14, 1867. Their children: Delcie, m. Kenneth Britton; Walter; Bertha; George; Barbara. Family home, Salt Lake City.
Park keeper; superintendent parks. Carpenter. Died Dec. 4, 1911, Salt Lake City.

HEATON, JOHN (son of Jonas Heaton and Ann Richardson, Yorkshire, Eng., former died 1851, St. Louis, Mo.). Born 1828, Thorn Hill, Eng. Came to Utah 1863.
Married Janet Sinclair 1859 (daughter of William Sinclair and Christina Archibald, pioneers 1863). She was born June 11, 1843. Their children: Jonas b. Aug. 19, 1860, m. Laura Bell Hill Oct 1881; Elizabeth Ann b. Dec. 19, 1862, m. Solomon M. Hale; Christina Archibald S. b. March 1, 1863, m. William A. McCrary July 26, 1880; Mary Jane b. March 18, 1864, m. Thomas J. Howell April 7, 1881; Martha b. Nov. 11, 1865, m. James W. Howell Feb. 15, 1884; John b. July 8, 1867, m. Annie L. Lewellyn Jan. 18, 1888; Sarah Agness, died April 1873; William Sinclair b. Jan. 17, 1871; James Henry b. 1872, died Jan. 1873.

HEDGES, GEORGE W. (son of James Hedges and Maria Andrews of Surrey, Eng.). Born June 20, 1842, Surrey. Came to Utah 1847.
Married Christina Olson April 25, 1867, Salt Lake City, by Bishop Speers (daughter of Hans Olson and Johanna Anderson of Svedala, Sweden, pioneers Sept. 20, 1862, John R. Murdock company). She was born June 12, 1847. Their children: Drucilla M. b. Feb. 23, 1868, m. J. G. Kelsom; Annie M. b. April 24, 1870, d. aged 3; Edith B. b. Feb. 15, 1873, m. William R. Turner; George A. b. Jan. :, 1877; Chester J. b. April 1880, d. infant; Frank L. b. May :, 1885, d. aged 23; Harrison S. b. 1900. Family home Salt Lake City.
Musician. Died March 12, 1906, Salt Lake City.

HEGGIE, ANDREW WALKER (son of Andrew Heggie, born March 19, 1796, Forgan parish, Fifeshire, Scotland, and Catherine Walker, born 1795, Hilland, Scotland). Born Jan. 9, 1825, Hjorring, Forgan parish. Came to Utah Aug. 27, 1860, Daniel Robinson company.
Married Annie T. Stewart Feb. 3, 1865 (daughter of William Stewart and Sarah Thompson, married Jan. 1839, Belfast, Ireland, the former pioneer 1862, Captain Rollins oxteam company). She was born Dec. 11, 1839 and came to Utah with father. Their children: Annie S. b. Nov. 20, 1865, m. James B. Jardine Sept. 17, 1884; Cathrine W. b. March 4, 1867, m. William J. Griffiths Jun. 6, 1886; Andrew S. b. Nov. 15, 1868, m. Mary Loosie June 10, 1897; Sarah S. b. Jan. 7, 1871, m. John Helga Dohle Dec. 13, 1894; William S. b. Oct. 9, 1872, d. March 13, 1874. Family home Clarkston, Utah.
Settled at Salt Lake City 1860; moved to Clarkston 1865. Sunday school superintendent 25 years; president 7th quorum seventies; second counselor to Bishop John Jardine of Clarkston for 13 years beginning Nov. 25, 1888. School trustee; justice of peace.

HEGSTED, HANS CHRISTIAN SORENSON (son of Soren Christian Hansen, born 1797, and Johanna Christiansen, born 1802, Hjorring Amt, Denmark). Born July 17, 1830, Wreliev parish, Hjorring, Denmark. Came to Utah Nov. 8, 1865, Miner G. Atwood company.
Married Mary Borglum Dec. 10, 1861, Hjorring, Denmark (daughter of Augustine and Anna Borglum of Hjorring), who was born March 2, 1837, Hjorring, died March 29, 1902, Salem, Idaho. Their children: Victor Charles b. April 18, 1865, m. Ada Martin: Jacob b. May 5, 1874. Family resided Harrisville, Utah. and Salem, Idaho.
Married Christena Olson Jan. 20, 1866, at Salt Lake City (daughter of Iver John Olson and Anna Christensen, they came to Utah 1873). She was born Jan. 4, 1844. Their children: Hans C. S. b. April 6, 1871, m. Mary Walker Oct. 30, 1887; John S. b. Feb. 9, 1875, m. Edna Porter Nov. 10, 1909. Family home Salem, Fremont Co., Idaho.
Married Nelsina Nielsen April 14, 1866, at Salt Lake City, who was born April 8, 1840, died Sept. 25, 1879. Their children: Joseph b. Nov. 1, 1873, m. Mabel McKensie April 21, 1909; Isaac b. May 20, 1876.

Member 75th quorum and later senior president of 60th quorum seventies; high priest; missionary in Denmark seven years and presided over the Wensyssel and Copenhagen conferences. Settled in Salt Lake City 1865, and moved to Huntsville 1866, from here he went to Harrisville March 20, 1876, and later moved to Idaho.

HEINER, MARTIN (son of Johanas Heiner born Oct. 16, 1777, and Anne Eliza Hondorf, born Aug. 9, 1790, Saxe-Muningen, Germany, who were married 1814). Born March 17, 1818, Waldorf, Saxe-Muningen. Came to Utah Sept. 16, 1859, Edward Stevenson company.
Married Adelgunda Dietzel Jan. 6, 1839 (daughter of Michal Dietzel and Sophia C. Kniesa, who were married July 12, 1803, Germany). She was born June 11, 1815. Their children: Mary b. July 28, 1840, m. Arza E. Ninckley 1862; Amelia b. Feb. 20, ——, m. George A. Black July 31, 1864; John b. July 2, 1842, m. Sarah Coulan March 23, 1867; Anthony b. June 24, 1844, m. Lucinda Henderson Sept. 16, 1865; George b. March 26, 1846, m. Mary Henderson Dec. 22, 1866; Elizabeth b. April 24, 1848, m. Thomas Grover Feb. 10, 1865; Daniel b. Nov. 27, 1850, m. Martha Stevens March 31, 1873; Susannah C. b. Oct. 15, 1852, m. Joseph Ovard June 28, 1875; Emma Ann b. Aug. 17, 1856, d. 1865; Rachel b. Sept. 16, 1858, d. 1862; Eliza b. Oct. 22, 1860, d. 1865.
High councilman and patriarch. School trustee, and city councilman. Assisted in building first canal on north side of Weber river; planted first shade and fruit trees in Morgan; cleared sage brush from present site of North Morgan City.

HEINER, ANTHONY (son of Martin Heiner and Adelgunda Dietzel). Came June 24, 1844. Came to Utah Sept. 16, 1859, Edward Stevenson company.
Married Lucinda Henderson 1865 (daughter of David E. Henderson and Mary Macfadgeon, pioneers 1856). She was born May 30, 1842. Their children: Anthony b. July 6, 1866; Rachel b. Feb. 8, 1868; Lucinda Ann b. June 20, 1870; David Martin b. Jan. 1, 1873; John Wesley b. Sept. 27, 1876; Mary Agnes b. Oct. 11, 1881, d. April 6, 189—; Henry Melvin b. April 29, 1884. Family home Morgan, Utah.
Married Sarah Elizabeth Henderson (Morris), who was born April 3, 1844. Children: Eliza Morris b. May 22, 1866; Lucinda Morris b. Oct. 22, 1867; Canway Morris b. May 17, 1869, by her former marriage. Their children: Evaline b. Nov. 5, 1875; Agatha H. b. Feb. 8, 1877; Joseph Anthony b. Jan. 17, 1879; Sparle b. Nov. 27, 1881, d. June 7, 1882; Royal Oscar b. Sept. 1, 1882; Lafayette b. Aug. 21, 1885; Maryette b. Aug. 1885.

HEINER, DANIEL (son of Martin Heiner and Adelgunda Dietzel). Born Nov. 27, 1850, Franklin county, Pa.
Married Martha A. Stevens March 31, 1873, Salt Lake City (daughter of Roswell Stevens and Mary Peterson, former came to Utah with Mormon Battalion). She was born Dec. 14, 1855, Peterson, Utah, first white child born in Morgan county. Their children: Daniel Nephi b. July 14, 1874; Roswell B. b. Dec. 22, 1875, m. May Littlefield March 20, 1909; Moroni b. Feb. 12, 1877, m. Eva Pernell Dec. 14, 1898; George A. b. Dec. 7, 1879, m. Sara Robison June, 1902; Charles b. April 13, 1881, m. Perses Farr June 1904; Geber J. b. Nov. 18, 1882, m. Theresa Tribe Dec. 14, 1904; Martha Sophia b. April 26, 1884, m. James A. Anderson 1906; Estella b. May 12, 1887, m. Alford Croft Aug. 20, 1908; Mary Elizabeth b. Aug. 13, 1889, m. T. V. Thomas April 17, 1912; Brenton Wells b. Jan. 24, 1891; Spencer b. Nov. 21, 1894; Disc b. Dec. 1, 1899; Cash b. Feb. 7, 1899. Family home Morgan, Utah.
Married Sarah Coulam March 31, 1873, Salt Lake City (daughter of John Coulam and Sarah Cordon, former came to Utah 1843). She was born Jan. 19, 1846, England. Their children: Adelgunda b. Feb. 1, 1874, m. James Taggart 1894; John b. Feb. 7, 1876, m. Annie Croft 1893; Daniel Hanmer b. Feb. 24, 1878, m. Hattie Robison 1897; Fannie b. Aug. 6, 1880, m. C. M. Croft 1903; Henry b. Sept. 11, 1882, m. Lissie Robison 1905; George Sylvester b. January 2, 1886, m. Elfie Clawson 1911.
President of Morgan stake. Mayor of Morgan; member first state legislature; president Black Hawk Coal Co.; president Morgan County Commercial Club; president First National bank of Morgan.

HELM, ABRAHAM (son of David Helm and Elizabeth Bookman). Born Feb. 22, 1813, Cumberland county, Pa. Came to Utah 1855, Moses Thurston company.
Married Mary Richards (daughter of Phillip Richards), who was born July 21, 1812, in Germany and came to Utah with husband. Their children: Joseph b. July, 1837, m. Emma Smith; John b. April 1839, m. Emeline Verres; Bartrum b. 1840, m. Emily Griffin; Samuel b. 1845, m. Elizabeth Gardner; Marshall b. 1847, m. Margaret Mitchell; Andrew b. 1849, m. Rachel Mitchell; David b. 1856, died 1862; Levi Phillip b. 1851, m. Viola J. Ward Jan. 6, 1886.

HELM, LEVI PHILLIP (son of Abraham Helm and Mary Richards). Born Oct. 22, 1851, Sandusky Co., Ohio.
Married Viola J. Ward at London, Utah (daughter of James F. and Louisa Ward; former d. 1869; latter 1866). She was born July 21, 1856. Their children: Mrs Holly b. Feb. 10, 1887; Orion b. Sept. 24, 1890; Iola Jay b. July 20, 1894.
High priest; president 61st, and member 91st quorum seventies; 1st counselor and president, in the San Luis stake, Col. Member Utah legislature 1897. Farmer and stockraiser.

PIONEERS AND PROMINENT MEN OF UTAH

HEMMING, WILLIAM (son of John Hemming, born 1805, at Burford, and Sarah Embra, born Dec. 21, 1807, Hooknorton, Oxfordshire, Eng.). He was born June 8, 1827, at Hooknorton. Came to Utah Aug. 27, 1860, Daniel Robinson handcart company.
Married Emma Sanford Aug. 31, 1851 (daughter of James Sanford and Elizabeth Powell), who was born Sept. 26, 1820, Warwickshire, Eng. Their children: Fanny b. June 9, 1852, m. John Foomee 1868; Harriet b. June 6, 1854, and William b. April 16, 1856, both d. infants; Emma Elizabeth b. 1859, m. James T. Rich Dec. 27, 1877; Mary Ann b. Feb. 1, 1862, d. infant; Frederick William b. 1864, m. Olive Porter Dec. 4, 1895; Sarah Jane b. Sept. 1866, m. Roswell S. Stevens March 24, 1891; Alfred John b. Feb. 1, 1869, m. Adelgunda Grover March 24, 1891; Charlotte Matilda b. March 18, 1872, m. Aaron B. Cherry Nov. 28, 1894. Family home, Morgan, Utah.
One of the first to push a handcart across the plains. Settled in Weber Valley 1860, and has devoted the greater portion of his life in actively developing the resources of his adopted commonwealth. Patriarch. City councilman two terms.

HEMMING, FREDERICK WILLIAM (son of William Hemming and Emma Sanford). Born April 23, 1864, Morgan, Utah.
Married Olive Porter Dec. 4, 1895, Salt Lake City (daughter of Lyman Wight Porter and Electa Maria Kilborn), who was born March 20, 1870, Porterville, Utah. Their children: Frederic C. b. 1896; Ella Maria b. 1897; James Sanford b. 1901; Jessie Mardell b. 1905.

HEMSLEY, RICHARD (son of Mr. Hemsley and Dinah Fuller, Brighton, Sussex, Eng.). Born Oct. 20, 1801, at Ditchling, Sussex. Came to Utah Sept. 16, 1866, Samuel H. Hill company.
Married Sarah Potter 1835 (daughter of Henry Potter who was married about 1798, Cookfield, Sussex, Eng.). She was born Feb. 3, 1807. Their children: Richard b. May 25, 1836, m. Christina Maria Jensen 1861; Edward b. April 22, 1839, m. Meriam Simmonds 1861; Eliza b. Dec. 24, 1841; Ellen b. May 10, 1844, m. John Halford; Job b. Jan. 6, 1847, m. Elizabeth Kensett. Family home Sugar, Utah.

HEMSLEY, RICHARD (son of Richard Hemsley and Sarah Potter). Born May 25, 1836, Ditchling, Sussex, Eng. Emigrated to Utah 1856, handcart company.
Married Christina Maria Jensen 1861, at Mill Creek, Salt Lake county (daughter of O. Christen Jensen and Annie Headiwick, pioneers 1861, oxteam company). She was born Aug. 18, 1842, Aryling, Denmark, died June 27, 1867, San Pete Co., Utah. Their children: Sarah Ann b. Nov. 27, 1862, m. Stephen G. Candler Oct. 30, 1879; Richard b. Oct. 12, 1864, m. Mary Ann Davies Feb. 16, 1887; James b. Feb. 23, 1866, m. Anne Robinson June 1, 1896. Family home Mill creek, Utah.
Married Sarah Frances Heaton, who was born Feb. 2, 1846, and died July 5, 1878. Their children: Mary Jane; Joseph Hyrum; Christina Maria; George Edward; Francis Joseph.
Married Mary Roxbury. Their children: John; Ellen; Job; Maggie; Edward; Hamilton.
Settled at Mill Creek 1857. Missionary to Dixie, 1865, from where he was driven by Indians, returning to Mill Creek. Moved to Egin Bench, Fremont Co., Idaho. Member bishopric of Hiatt ward; presiding elder of Brighton Branch for many years.

HEMSLEY, RICHARD (son of Richard Hemsley and Christina Maria Jensen). Born Oct. 12, 1864, Mill Creek, Utah. Married Mary Ann Davies Feb. 16, 1887 (daughter of John Thomas Davies and Ann Ellis, former came to Utah Nov. 18, 1886, latter June 6, 1888—married March 7, 1864, Pontypool, Wales). She was born Jan. 20, 1865, Pontypool, South Wales, came to Utah 1883. Their children: Sarah Ann b. Jan. 28, 1888, m. Herbert E. Perrenond April 11, 1906; Richard John b. Feb. 23, 1889, m. Avilda H. Jackson May 12, 1907; Mabel Christena b. Sept. 25, 1890, m. Weber C. Weatherston Dec. 20, 1912; Emily May b. May 20, 1892, m. Albert R. Heath Sept. 13, 1911; Clyde Davies b. Sept. 8, 1893; Agnes Lepwretta b. March 15, 1895; James Jensen b. June 25, 1896; Josephine Jane b. Nov. 8, 1897; Irene b. Jan. 27, 1899; Job b. Feb. 20, 1901; Lila Bertha b. Dec. 8, 1902; Mary Ellen b. Jan. 31, 1904; Myrtle Martha b. July 30, 1905; Frances Charlotte b. Nov. 19, 1907. Family home Plano, Idaho.
Worked in brickyard at Salt Lake City 1879. Moved to Plano, Idaho 1901, and was ordained 2d counselor to Bishop Hyrum J. Lucas May 26, 1902; ordained 1st counselor to Bishop Albert Heath May 26, 1903; bishop Plano ward July 30, 1905; missionary to Great Britain Jan. 28, 1908, returning May 16, 1910. Bricklayer and contractor; merchant and farmer.

HENDERSON, SAMUEL NEWTON (son of James Henderson, born Nov. 27, 1805, and Annie Harris, born 1812, both died at Nauvoo, Ill.). He was born April 18, 1838, in Crawford county, Mo. Came to Utah Sept. 12, 1847.
Married Esther Dewhurst Jan. 11, 1869 (daughter of James Dewhurst and Elizabeth Fielding), who was born Feb. 17, 1847, Blackhaven, Lancashire, Eng. Their child: Elizabeth Ann b. April 12, 1870, d. April 13, 1883. Family home Randolph, Utah.
Married Sarah Jane Pugmire May 16, 1877, Randolph, Utah (daughter of Joseph Hyrum Pugmire, pioneer 1847, John Taylor company, and Eleanor Craten, pioneer with a handcart company). She was born April 18, 1858. Their children: Samuel Henry b. Feb. 23, 1878, m. Isabel Sims June 15, 1904; Esther Eleanor b. April 23, 1880, m. John Thomson Barker Sept. 18, 1902; Florence Celeste b. Aug. 20, 1883, m. Riley Day, Jan. 20, 1905; Mary Maud b. Aug. 20, 1885, m. Joel Melvin Schenck June 22, 1904; James b. Oct. 10, 1887, d. Oct. 13, 1903; Jasper b. Jan. 14, 1889, m. Nancy Alice Barker Oct. 22, 1909; Annie Adelia b. Feb. 25, 1890, d. Sept. 12, 1901; Harriet Lilian b. April 2, 1892, m. Ole Mattson, Nov. 29, 1910; Martin b. March 10, 1895; Clifford Newton b. June 8, 1897; Nancy Josephine b. Nov. 25, 1899; George Allen b. June 30, 1902; Ira Pugmire b. Oct. 15, 1904. Family home Laketown, Utah.
Settled at Mill Creek 1848. Major in Utah militia 1855; veteran Black Hawk war. Moved to Randolph, Utah, 1870, and to Laketown 1880. Member 61st quorum seventies. Sheriff Rich county two terms; constable of Randolph one term. Assisted in bringing immigrants to Utah. Took an active part in Echo Canyon campaign.

HENDRICKS, JAMES (son of Abraham Hendricks and Charlotte Hinton). Born June 1808 Franklin, Ky. Came to Utah 1847, Jedediah M. Grant company.
Married Drusilla Dorris 1825 (daughter of William Dorris and Catherine Frost), who was born Feb. 8, 1810. Their children: Elizabeth Mahala; William Dorris; Catherine Tabitha; Rebecca; Joseph Smith. Family home Salt Lake City.
Married Hannah Riggs.
Bishop of 19th ward Salt Lake City 1850-57. Justice of peace in Salt Lake City. Moved to Richmond 1860. Badly wounded in battle of Crooked River in Missouri, Oct. 25, 1838. Died July 8, 1870, Richmond, Utah.

HENDRICKS, WILLIAM DORRIS (son of James Hendricks and Drusilla Dorris). Born Nov. 6, 1829, Franklin, Ky. Came to Utah 1847, Mormon battalion.
Married Mary Jane Andrus March 12, 1851, at Salt Lake City, Brigham Young officiating (daughter of Milo Andrus and Abigail Jane Daley of New York, pioneers 1848, Heber C. Kimball company). She was born Nov. 15, 1833. Their children: Mary Jane, m. A. B. Harrison; Drusilla, m. I. K. Hillman; Brigham Andrus, m. Mary R. Stoddard; William Henry, m. Emma Traveler; Charlotte, m. William Underwood; Milo Andrus, m. Adeline Harris; Elizabeth, m. N. R. Lewis; Hildah Hannah, m. Andrew Morrison; Chloe, m. C. E. Merrill; George Gideon, m. Susa Eldridge. Family home Richmond, Utah.
President Oneida stake; bishop of Richmond ward; patriarch in Benson stake. Mayor of Richmond. Farmer; railroad contractor; banker. Died May 6, 1909, Lewiston, Utah.

HENDRICKS, JOSEPH SMITH (son of James Hendricks and Drusilla Dorris). Born March 23, 1838, Far West, Caldwell county, Mo.
Married Sariah Pew Tibbetts Jan. 4, 1857, Salt Lake City (daughter of John H. and Caroline Tibbetts, pioneers on July 24, 1847, and in 1848, respectively). She was born Aug. 11, 1833. Their children: Drusilla; Fidelia; Joseph; Elizabeth; Inez. Family resided Salt Lake City and Richmond, Utah.
Married Lucinda Bess 1866, Salt Lake City. She was born in New York state. Their children: Juel Josiah; Laura; William D.; John Henry; Lola; Lorinda; Asa; Hyrum. Family resided Oxford, and Marysville, Idaho, and Lewiston, Utah.
Member Oneida stake high council. Moved to Oxford, Idaho 1876, from whence he went to Marysville, Idaho, where he served 15 years in the bishopric.

HENDRICKS, BRIGHAM ANDRUS (son of William Dorris Hendricks and Mary Jane Andrus). Born Nov. 27, 1857, at Salt Lake City.
Married Mary Rebecca Stoddard Jan. 13, 1881, at Salt Lake City (daughter of Charles Henry Stoddard and Anna Telford of Bountiful, Utah, pioneers 1851, Harry Walton company). She was born May 1, 1862. Their children: George B. b. Nov. 25, 1881, m. Caroline A. McAlister; Mary Lalene b. Aug. 24, 1885; Odessie Lapreal b. June 3, 1889; Nellie b. Oct. 22, 1890, m. Ralph Bernhisel; Brigham Victor b. June 30, 1895; Charles Durrell b. Nov. 17, 1899. Family home Lewiston, Utah.
Member 70th quorum Seventies; missionary to Southern states 1885-87, to Northwestern states 1897-98, and to South Africa 1909-11; counselor in presidency of Benson stake. County commissioner; school trustee at Lewiston; member Utah legislature. Farmer and stockraiser.

HENDRICKS, GEORGE B. (son of Brigham Andrus Hendricks and Mary Rebecca Stoddard). Born Nov. 25, 1881, at Lewiston, Utah.
Married Caroline Armeda McAlister June 5, 1912, at Salt Lake City (daughter of John A. McAlister and Clarissa Snow of Logan, Utah). She was born March 17, 1887. Family home Logan, Utah.
Member elders' quorum. Member faculty of Utah Agricultural College. Professor.

HENDRICKSON, JOHN A. (son of Andreas M. Hendrickson, born 1821, and Maren Andrea Olsen, born May 3, 1823, both of Fredrikstad, Norway). He was born Aug. 19, 1860, Fredrikstad, Norway. Came to Utah 1863, oxteam company.

930 PIONEERS AND PROMINENT MEN OF UTAH

Married Mary D. Lloyd Jan. 1, 1885 (daughter of Thomas Lloyd and Susanna Stone, pioneers 1855 and 1856, respectively). She was born Oct. 16, 1866, Wellsville, Utah. Their children: Mary Irene b. March 25, 1891; Dorothy b. Nov. 6, 1907. Family home Logan, Utah.
Missionary to Norway and England 1887-89; and in 1904. Opened knitting industry in the state in 1890. Organized College Pure Food company, manufacturers of Koffee-et and other cereals, 1908; also Farmers' and Merchants' savings bank of Logan, which began business March 26, 1913.

HENEFER. JAMES. Born 1820, in Staffordshire, England. Came to Utah 1853.
Married Sarah Hulks Aug. 30, 1846, in England, who was born Nov. 25, 1823, and came to Utah with husband. Their children: Lehi; Charlotte; Phoebe; Sarah Ann; James E.; William T.; Mary; Jane; Elizabeth; Rachel; Rebecca Ann; Edward Richard.
High priest. Blacksmith. Died August 1898, at Henefer, Utah.

HENEFER, LEHI (son of James Henefer and Sarah Hulks). Born July 5, 1847, Staffordshire, Eng. Came to Utah 1853.
Married Margaret Bond Jan. 15, 1868, at Henefer (daughter of William Bond and Mary Ann Barker of Boston, Mass., pioneers 1857). She was born July 5, 1847. Their children: Margaret Ann b. Oct. 26, 1869; Sarah Jane b. May 25, 1870; May Emma b. Aug. 7, 1872; Lehi Alma b. May 30, 1874; Hannah B. b. Aug. 25, 1876; James William b. Feb. 3, 1879.
Married Mary Ann Randall Jan. 6, 1881 (daughter of Henry Randall and Susannah Jones), who was born July 23, 1862. Their children: Heber C. b. Sept. 23, 1882; Mary May b. March 24, 1885; Theodore b. June 15, 1888; Irvin b. Feb. 11, 1892; Marcus b. March 31, 1894.
Elder. School trustee; constable. Drove an oxteam across the plains in 1867. Helped to build roads and bridges in Henefer. Member Canal board. Farmer.

HENRIE, WILLIAM. Came to Utah July 24, 1847, Brigham Young company.
Married Myra Mayall. Their children: Daniel, m. Amanda Bradley and Susan Brown; James, m. Lorana Hatch, m. Christena Skow, m. Augusta Skow; Joseph, m. Susan Leslie, m. Susan Duncan; Margaret, m. Moses Dailey; Samuel, m. Isabell Ellis. Family home Bountiful, Utah.
Millwright. Died at Bountiful, Utah.

HENRIE, DANIEL (son of William Henrie and Myra Mayall). Born Nov. 15, 1824, in Hamilton county, Ohio. Came to Utah 1848, with part of Mormon Battalion.
Married Amanda Bradley Oct. 29, 1849, Salt Lake City (daughter of George W. Bradley and Elizabeth Betsy Kroll). She was born Jan. 15, 1829. Their children: Mary Amanda b. Sept. 4, 1850, m. Ezra K. Funk; Myra Elizabeth b. Jan. 28, 1852, m. John Olsen; Susan Lucretia b. April 29, 1853, m. Byron Cox; Daniel Jr. b. Dec. 24, 1854, m. Elzina Stringham; Diantha b. Nov. 4, 1856, m. William Stringham; James b. Jan. 25, 1858, m. Hannah Snow; Jerome B. b. Nov. 25, 1859, m. Mary C. Westenskow; William b. Oct. 12, 1861, m. Hannah Westenskow; Malinda b. Nov. 16, 1863, m. William Millpack; Margaret E. b. Oct. 1866, m. Alma Johnson; Luna A. b. Sept. 13, 1869; Jefferson b. Nov. 1872; Jedediah G. b. Nov. 1874, and Loran b. Nov. 1876, last three died infants. Family home Bountiful, Utah.
Married Susan Coleman at Salt Lake City. Their children: Margaret, d. infant; Joseph T., m. Mary Sorensen; Rachel, m. Charles Patten; Arthur, m. Mary Jorgensen; Maud, d. infant; Samuel, m. Hannah Boyington; Elizabeth, m. Ed Reid; Cora, m. Frank Maylet; Ellis; Ethel, died. Family home Manti. Utah.
President 48th quorum seventies 35 years. Captain minutemen in Black Hawk Indian war. Mayor and marshal of Manti; road supervisor at Manti. Butcher, farmer and stockraiser.

HENRIE, DANIEL, JR. (son of Daniel Henrie and Amanda Bradley). Born Dec. 29, 1854, Manti, Utah.
Married Zina Stringham Jan. 17, 1875, Manti, Utah (daughter of William Stringham and Eliza Lake of Salt Lake City, Provo and Manti, Utah; pioneers 1855). She was born Nov. 5, 1857. Their children: May Francelle b. Oct. 19, 1875, m. Smith Herring; Daniel Eugene b. Jan. 16, 1878, m. Hattie Thomas; Rosslynn b. May 25, 1880, d. infant; Lila b. Aug. 15, 1882, m. John Bohlens; Roscoe b. July 2, 1885, d. aged 5; William Herbert b. Dec. 20, 1887; Zina b. April 28, 1890, m. John LeRoy Bell; Maryetta b. Oct. 7, 1892; LeGrande b. April 26, 1895; Ada Ray b. Oct. 13, 1900. Family home Manti and Ferron, Utah.
Ward teacher. Farmer and stockraiser.

HENRIOD, EUGENE A. (son of Jean Louis Henry Henriod, born Nov. 5, 1802, Boussens, Canton de Vaud, Switzerland, and Domitille de Ligne, born March 18, 1798, Brest, France—married Nov. 25, 1826). He was born March 9, 1833, Havre de Grace, France. Came to Utah Oct. 6, 1853, Cyrus H. Wheelock company.
Married Mary T. Mallett Nov. 5, 1854 (daughter of Henry Mallett born at Starcross, Devonshire, and Mary Brimacombe born at Oldsworthy, Devonshire). She was born June 11, 1828; came to Utah in 1853. Their children: Eugene Henry b. Aug. 12, 1855, m. Rachel Conder Jan. 16, 1880; William b. July 4, 1857, m. Emma Conder Nov. 3, 1877; Mary Henrietta b. May 12, 1859, m. Don M. Bigler Jan. 16, 1880;

Helen b. Jan. 10, 1861, m David C. Adamson Jan. 12, 188 Edward b. July 1, 1864, d. infant; Frederic Augustus b. Sep 29, 1865, m. Lena Greenwood June 4, 1900; Thomas b. Se 8, 1867, d. infant; Emily Mallett b. Nov. 23, 1869, m. Thom J. Chipman Nov. 28, 1888. Family resided at Salt Lake Ci and American Fork, Utah.
Settled at Salt Lake City 1853; moved to American Fo 1855. Captain of Home Guards 1856-57. Missionary France 1860. Assisted in bringing immigrants to Utah 18 Assisted in organizing the first Free school in Utah 18 and was its first teacher. City recorder 1882-86. Memb Nauvoo Legion and captain of Company B in Colon Washburn Chipman's regiment. Notary public 1882- County surveyor one term and deputy county surveyor t terms.

HENRY, WILLIAM CALVIN (son of James Henry of Rho Island and Huldah Menerva Murray of Connecticut. Th lived at Cambria, Niagara county, N. Y.). He was born Ju 16, 1827 at Cambria, N. Y. Came to Utah in 1854.
Married Priscilla Barnum in 1850 at Pontiac, Oakla county, Mich. They came to Utah in the fall of 1853. S was born in 1834. Their children: James Barnum b. Ju 30, 1851, m. Mary Frances Brown; Lauretta Ann b. April 1854, m. Alma L. Johnstun.
Married Agnes Taylor in the fall of 1862, in the Salt La Endowment house. (She was the daughter of John Tayl and Agnes Robinson of Glasgow, Scot. and came to Utah Se 24, 1862, Horner Duncan company). She was born April 1837. Their children: Chas. Thos. b. July 4, 1863, died; Sar Lois, m. Heber J. Campbell; Calvin DeLos and William Ale ander, died; John Meari, m. Ada Beebe; Rhoda Melis Hulda Ann, Agnes Minerva and Mary Priscilla, died; Cel Jane b. Aug. 31, 1879, m. John W. Hicks. Families resid Heber City, Utah.
Located in Cottonwood in 1855, went to Heber City, 186 to Lyderville in 1874, and to Ashley Valley 1879. In these places he was a pioneer and helped in the first wor to open up the country.

HENRY, JAMES BARNHAM (son of William Calvin Hen and Priscilla Barnum). Born June 30, 1851, at Pontiac, Mic Came to Utah 1853.
Married Mary Frances Brown July 25, 1878, in Salt La City Endowment house. (She was the daughter of Jon than Brown and Sarah Couzins of England, and came Utah in 1853 with Jacob Gates company). She was bo April 9, 1857. Their children: James Calvin b. April 1879, d. 1901; Sarah Priscilla b. May 5, 1881, m. Joseph McKea; Albert Monroe b. Sept. 3, 1883, m. Abigal Goo rich; Emma May b. Oct. 11, 1885, m. James Hofeltz; Franc Mary b. Nov. 4, 1887; Lauretta b. Sept. 23, 1890, m. Mur Merkley; Merrell b. April 8, 1894; Bartlett b. Dec. 9, 1895 infant; Bertha b. April 16, 1899.
High priest; high councilor Unita stake 19 years; w teacher. Constable. Went to Heber City with early settl in 1860; went to Snyderville, Summit county, 1874, thenc Vernal Nov. 7, 1878, and built the first cabin on the site Vernal. In the spring of 1881 he, with David P. Woodr and Peter Peterson, went to Green River City for provisi for the settlement. On the morning before their ret the settlement had but little food and asked Jeremiah Ha what to do. He told them to eat all they had, because boys would be there next day, and sure enough there ca

HENSON. ALFRED (son of James Henson). Born June 1830, in England. Came to Utah 1868.
Married Mary Anna Robinson in England. Their childr Lucy R., m. Knute Hill; Agnes M., m. Joseph Marrison; Oliver
Married a second time, Dec. 11, 1857. The children we Alma S., d. infant; Orson S., d. on ocean; Livonia S., Chris Monson; Albert T., m. Elizabeth Vale; Livinia S., Levi Allen; Ameziah T., m. Minnie Bailey; Lizzie T., m. J Lewis; Laura S., m. Mibre Scott; Alonzo S., m. Ella Pre Missionary to England two years. One of guards w crossing plains. Died Nov. 2, 1902, Franklin, Idaho.

HENWOOD. JOHN (son of John Henwood, born June 1782, and Elizabeth Eath, born 1786, both of Cornw Eng.). He was born June 29, 1809, in Cornwall. Came to l 1856, Edmund Ellsworth handcart company.
Married Jane Treganna (daughter of Richard Tregan and Elizabeth Hancock). who was born May 16, 1813. T children: Richard b. Dec. 5, 1837, m. Ann Kirk; Eliza T.; John Edwin; Charles E.; Mary Jane.
Married Elizabeth Stockdale at Plymouth, Eng. She born in Cornwall, Eng.

HENWOOD, RICHARD (son of John Henwood and Treganna). Born Dec. 5, 1837, Cornwall, Eng. Cam Utah 1856, Edmund Ellsworth handcart company.
Married Ann Kirk Jan. 3, 1866, South Cottonwood, (daughter of Philip Kirk and Mary Ann Taylor, pio Joseph S. Rawlins company). She was born July 14, Their children: John R. b. Nov. 8, 1866, m. Emma Joseph H. b. Jan. 3, 1871; Ann E. b. Nov. 4, 1873, m. J H. Dayton; Charlotte M. b. Sept. 15, 1876, m. Caleb O Sarah S. b. July 14, 1880, m. Orin Skelton; Willard S. b. 23, 1884, m. Susie Bates; Mabel B. b. March 29, 1887.
Assisted in bringing immigrants to Utah under Nebeker in 1863, and again as teamster of Captain R company in 1866.

HEPWORTH, EDMUND (son of Joseph Hepworth, born Sept. 11, 1816, Yorkshire, and Mary Hurst born Nov. 8, 1820, Bristol, Eng.) He was born March 7, 1841, Yorkshire. Came to Utah Oct. 15, 1863. Samuel D. White company.
Married Hannah Cowling. Sept. 17, 1862, Bristol, Yorkshire, Eng. (daughter of David Cowling and Eliza Schofield), who was born April 2, 1834, and came to Utah with husband in 1863. Their children: Sarah Cathrine b. June 23, 1863; Joseph Edmund b. June 26, 1865, m. Mary E. Thurman 1889; William Henry b. Aug. 30, 1867, m. Artemicia Noble Oct. 10, 1888; Hannah Eliza b. July 25, 1869, m. James Jensen, Jr. Nov. 1, 1889; Mary Jane b. March 12, 1871; Emily Anice b. Sept. 23, 1872; Lauretta b. Sept. 26, 1874; m. John F. Astle Sept. 9, 1891; David Edgar b. Nov. 28, 1879, m. Mary E. Simons May 15, 1902. Family resided at Smithfield, Springdale, American Fork and Bountiful, Utah; Oxford, Idaho, and Grover, Wyo.
Married Eliza Sant March 9, 1869, Salt Lake City (daughter of John Sant and Mary Shaw), who was born Jan. 15, 1855, Runcorn, Cheshire, Eng. Their children: John Edmund b. Oct. 10, 1870, m. Mary Bee Sept. 3, 1896, m. Caroline Thompson Oct. 10, 1900; George William b. Sept. 20, 1872, m. Camera B. Thurman Nov. 1, 1895. m. Annie Matthewson Jan. 4, 1911. Family home Oxford, Idaho.
Married Lydia Wells Feb. 9, 1882, Salt Lake City (daughter of Joshua Wells and Margaret Farrer), who was born Oct. 11, 1857, Netherthong, Yorkshire, Eng. Their children: Clarence Joshua b. Feb. 24, 1883, m. Rose Ellen Dutson Sept. 16, 1904; Margaret Ann b. June 11, 1885, m. Anson V. Call; Emma b. Oct. 10, 1887, m. Joseph N. Anderson Oct. 12, 1910; Lovisa Matilda b. Aug. 29, 1889, m. Gustave Larsen June 16, 1911; Estella b. Oct. 20, 1892; Lydia Grace b. Oct. 19, 1894; Florence Rachel b. Feb. 6, 1899. Family home Grover, Wyo.
High priest; presiding elder of Oxford branch, Idaho, 1871. Moved to Smithfield 1864, to Oxford, Idaho, 1865, to "Dixie" 1871, to American Fork 1880, to Bountiful 1882, and to Star Valley, Wyo., 1887. Presiding elder in "Dixie" 1877-80. First counselor to Bishop James Jensen of Grover ward, Star Valley, for 16 years.

HEPWORTH, JOSEPH E. (son of Edmund Hepworth and Hannah Cowling). Born June 26, 1865, Smithfield, Utah.
Married Mary E. Thurman Oct. 20, 1889, Grover, Wyo. (daughter of Edward M. Thurman and Lavina S. Griffith, the former came to Utah 1862, Henry W. Miller company). She was born March 24, 1871, Hyde Park, Utah. Their children: Joseph Eugene b. Sept. 12, 1890, m. Myrtle Nielson June 19, 1912; George William b. Oct. 23, 1892; John Leonard b. Oct. 3, 1893; Edward Mondell b. Jan. 22, 1895; Mary Ethel b. April 10, 1898; Edith Lovina b. Oct. 14, 1901; Gerald Delynn b. Jan. 23, 1906; Hannah Leone b. June 25, 1909. Family home American Fork, Utah; Grover, Fort Briger and Star Valley, Wyo., and Kimball, Idaho.
Moved to Wyoming when 17 years of age where he spent five years, working on cattle ranches and carrying U. S. mail. Settled at Grover 1889; moved to Kimball, Idaho, 1909. First counselor to Bishop William B. Taylor of Kimball ward, Kimball, Idaho.

HERBERT, ROBERT (son of Thomas Herbert and Mary Jane Hone). Born Jan. 1, 1874, Benjamin, Utah.
Married Helen Lindstrom Dec. 6, 1900, Benjamin, Utah (daughter of John E. Lindstrom and Zelima Cederstrom of Benjamin, who came to Utah June 23, 1893). She was born Dec. 6, 1882. Their children: Violet b. Nov. 10, 1901; Elwood R. b. Jan. 10, 1904; Elsie C. b. March 13, 1908; John Lenden b. May 22, 1911. Family home Benjamin, Utah. Farmer.

HERBERTSON, CHRISTIAN PETERSON (son of Mr. and Mrs. Pongren of Randoth, Denmark). Born 1798, Denmark. Came to Utah 1861, Martin Lund oxteam company.
Married Anna Christiansen in Denmark. Their children: Ahketren; Christian Peterson, m. Mary Christiansen.
High priest; missionary to Denmark. Farmer. Died 1872, Pleasant Grove, Utah.

HERBERTSON, CHRISTIAN PETERSON (son of Christian Peterson Herbertson and Anna Christiansen). Born Dec. 14, 1830, Denmark. Came to Utah September 1866, Joseph S. Rawlins company.
Married Mary Christiansen 1854, Denmark (daughter of Christian and Mitkastine Saling). Their children: Annie m. Niels Hlesel and Dorias Kundel; Heber; Rasmus Christian, m. Lottie Peck.
Married Lena Doll 1865, Denmark (daughter of Jens Doll of Kisten, Denmark). Their children: Lewis; Charles, m. Cora Phillips. Family home Pleasant Grove, Utah.
High priest; Sunday school teacher at Pleasant Grove, Utah. Veteran Black Hawk war. Farmer.

HERRICK, LEMUEL (son of Amos Herrick and Eunice Scerl of Charleston, N. Y.). Born March 13, 1792, at Charleston. Came to Utah Sept. 12, 1850. Thomas Johnson company.
Married Sally Judd April 29, 1813, Hamilton, Madison county, N. Y., born March 17, 1792. Their children: Clinton Jeremiah; Eliza Ann, m. Harrison Keyes; Alonzo Tarquin, m. Mary Elizabeth (Reed) Ayers; Lucinda, m. Perry Keyes; Clinton, m. Lucinda Green; Mary Elizabeth, m. E. P. Coffin; Amanda, m. William O. Blanton; Lester James, m. Sarah Ann Garner; Lucy Jane, m. Barnabus Lake; Nelson, m. Harriet Hellen Sprague; Diana, m. Isaac Clark. Family resided Jackson county, Mo. and Ogden, Utah.
Tailor. Died Sept. 1, 1861, Ogden.

HERRICK, LESTER JAMES (son of Lemuel Herrick and Sally Judd). Born Dec. 14, 1827, Nelson, Portage Co., Ohio. Came to Utah Sept. 12, 1850, Thomas Johnson company.
Married Sarah Ann Garner July 13, 1851, Ogden (daughter of Phillip Garner and Mary Hedrick of Rowan, N. C., pioneers Oct. 27, 1849, Capt. George A. Smith company). She was born Jan. 18, 1832. Their children: Lester Alonzo b. April 23, 1852, m. Lydia Esther Ensign.
Married Mary Eliza Brooks Aug. 25, 1857, born Oct. 14, 1839, Flintshire, North Wales. Their children: James Albert b. Sept. 7, 1859, m. Susan Child; Sarah Eliza b. Sept. 18, 1861, m. O. G. Randall; Nelson Amos b. May 28, 1864, m. Lucinda Browning; Francis Brooks b. Sept. 14, 1867, m. Florence May Ryan; Samuel b. Nov. 21, 1869.
Married Agnes McQuarrie June 22, 1867, born Dec. 9, 1841, Kilmalcolm, Renfrewshire, Scotland. Their children: John Lester b. June 2, 1868, m. Jane Richards West; Lemuel b. Oct. 4, 1869; Aggie b. Nov. 18, 1870, m. Frank J. Stevens; Clyde b. April 16, 1872; Lucy Jane b. Oct. 19, 1873; Nettie May b. May 1, 1875; Diana Letitia b. July 8, 1877, m. William E. Purdy; Robert Peery b. Feb. 21, 1879; Walter b. Jan. 20, 1881. Family home, Ogden.
Settled in Ogden 1850. Appointed second counselor to Bishop Bunker of second ward of Ogden 1856. Sheriff of Weber county 1858. His commission from Governor Cummings being first official document issued by Mr. Cummings as governor of Utah territory; elected county selectman three terms; policeman; city councilor 1861. Bishop of 2nd ward 1861. Alderman 1864-67. Presiding bishop of Weber county 1872-75. Mayor of Ogden 1871-75 and 1879-83. Missionary to England 1873-74; appointed to take charge of European mission 1873. Formed partnership with D. H. Peery and W. W. Burton in milling and merchandise 1875. First counselor to David H. Peery in presidency of Weber stake 1877. Member implement company of Burton, Herrick & White. Member 38th quorum seventies; alternate high councilor. Farmer; miller and general merchant. Died April 18, 1892, Ogden.

HERRICK, JOHN LESTER (son of Lester J. Herrick and Agnes McQuarrie). Born June 2, 1868, Ogden.
Married Jane Richards West June 1, 1894, Salt Lake City (daughter of Joseph A. West and Josephine Richards of Ogden), who was born Dec. 29, 1873. Their children: Josephine b. May 25, 1896; John West b. Aug. 3, 1897; Lester James b. June 12, 1902. Family home Ogden, Utah.
Member stake board Y. M. M. I. A. of Weber and secretary from 1887 to 1899; stake superintendent Y. M. M. I. A. 1899-1908; high priest; member high council 1905; president Western States mission 1909. Clerk and bookkeeper Z. C. M. I. five years; bookkeeper First National bank five years. Assistant postmaster of Ogden six years; secretary and treasurer Boyle Furniture company two years. Partner with George J. Kelly 1903-08, real estate loans and insurance.

HERRON, ALEXANDER (son of Daniel Herron and Mary Anderson of Scotland). Born April 5, 1832, in Scotland. Came to Utah September, 1851, Captain Browning company.
Married Mary White Dec. 8, 1856 (daughter of Jonathan White and Elizabeth Dodd, latter came to Utah Oct. 28, 1849, Ezra T. Benson company). She was born Feb. 9, 1839, and came to Utah with mother. Their children: Alexander, Jr. b. Nov. 2, 1857, died; Mary b. Dec. 29, 1859, m. William Mc— April 28, 1890; Elizabeth, b. Jan. 25, 1862, m. Harvey Walters Dec. 29, 1887; Ella b. May 8, 1864, m. George McLaws Dec. 28, 1886; Maggie b. July 6, 1867; Annie b. March 25, 1870, m. R. H. Rowberry 1890; Joseph April and Ross May, died 1870; Howard b. May 24, 1876, died; Ruby b. Sept. 2, 1878, m. G. M. Nuttall Aug. 10, 1901; Elmer W. b. April 24, 1883; Mabel b. Oct. 3, 1886, m. Ernest H. Minns Dec. 8, 1908. Family home Tooele, Utah.

HERRON, ORLANDO FISHER (son of James Herron and Catherine Boulk of New York). Born Dec. 26, 1835, Washtenaw county, Mich. Came to Utah Oct. 2, 1847, Charles C. Rich company.
Married Hannah Jane Driggs May 5, 1856, Pleasant Grove, Utah (daughter of Shadrick H. Driggs and Elizabeth White of Pleasant Grove, pioneers 1852, independent company). She was born June 5, 1839. Their children: Emma Jane b. 1857, m. William Stewart; Clarice Melissa b. 1859, m. Alexander Bullock; James Orlando b. 1861, m. Lilly Nesbitt; Mary Louisa b. 1865, m. James Adamson; Fay Clifton; Myrtle, m. Frank Blair; Ruth, m. Thomas Crompton; Catherine. m. Mr. Ryan.
Married Lucinda Jane Harvey May 25, 1874, Salt Lake City (daughter of Louis Harvey and Lucinda Clark of Pleasant Grove, pioneers October, 1850, Captain Lake company). She was born June 19, 1857. Their children: Lucinda. m. Charles Furron; John L., m. Louisa Hendrickson; Gideon Ernest; Rosella, m. Benjamin Miller; Grace; Mirl; George Leroy. Family home Pleasant Grove, Utah.
Member 44th quorum seventies; high priest; first Mormon convert from Michigan who went to Utah. Served three terms in the state penitentiary for unlawful cohabitation. Farmer.

HESLOP, GEORGE (son of Thomas Heslop and Ann Etherington, born Jan. 24, 1830, in England). Born Feb. 19, 1855, Liverpool, Eng. Came to Utah September 1855, independent company.
Married Cynthia L. Green Nov. 1880 (daughter of Mr. Green and Almira Mesick—married April 2, 1855, San Bernardino, Cal.). She was born Dec. 25, 1860. Their children: George A. b. Aug. 19, 1881, m. Sarah E. Gibson Dec. 12, 1906; Almira b. July 7, 1883; Cynthia Lois b. Dec. 26, 1884, m. Hyrum Peterson March 16, 1910; John A. b. March 20, 1886; William b. May 3, 1888; Charles L. b. Jan. 12, 1890; Jesse b. Dec. 22, 1892; Edward T. b. Nov. 11, 1894; Franklin b. March 14, 1897; Austin b. Nov. 8, 1898; Herbert S. b. May 20, 1900; Elsie Ann b. May 28, 1902. Family home West Weber, Utah.
President of 5th quorum elders. Director in Hooper Irrigation company.

HESS, ALMA (son of Jacob Hess and Elizabeth Foutz of Farmington, Utah). Born June 3, 1839, Bay county, Mo. Came to Utah July 28, 1849.
Married Mary Elmira Miller at Salt Lake City (daughter of Henry William Miller and Elmira Pond of Farmington, and St. George, Utah). Their children: Alma Clarence b. Oct. 23, 1862, m. Eliza Flamm; Lucia b. April 2, 1864, m. William Cook. Family home Farmington, Utah.
Died Aug. 9, 1863.

HESS, ALMA CLARENCE (son of Alma Hess and Mary Elmira Miller). Born Oct. 23, 1862, Farmington, Utah.
Married Eliza Flamm Feb. 17, 1888, Logan, Utah (daughter of Henry Flamm and Helena Bock of Cottonwood and Logan, Utah, pioneers 1862). She was born Dec. 15, 1866. Their children: Alma Clarence b. March 13, 1889; Henry Leron b. Oct. 12, 1890; Charles Ellis b. July 15, 1892; George Irvin b. July 29, 1894; Iva b. Oct. 12, 1896; Ferrel Emerson b. Oct. 31, 1899; Leland b. May 13, 1902; Thelma Irena b. Nov. 9, 1904; Eliza Mae b. Dec. 1, 1907. Family reside Rexburg, Idaho and Union, Ore.
Member fifth session of Idaho legislature; chairman of board of trustees of Rexburg, 1899-1900.

HESS, JOHN W. (son of Jacob Hess, born May 21, 1792, and Elizabeth Foutz, born June 4, 1797, both of Franklin county, Pa.—married in 1816). Born Aug. 24, 1824, in Franklin county. Came to Utah July 28, 1847, with Capt. James Brown's contingent of Mormon battalion.
Married Emeline Bigler Nov. 2, 1845, Nauvoo, Ill. (daughter of Jacob Bigler and Elizabeth Harvey, pioneers 1851). She was born Aug. 20, 1824, and came to Utah with husband. Their children: Jacob b. Jan. 6, 1848; John Henry b. May 14, 1850, m. Susan Smith; Sarah Jane b. Jan. 11, 1852; Hyrum b. April 20, 1853, m. Adeline Earl; Eizada b. Aug. 11, 1854, m. David Sanders; Moroni b. Dec. 30, 1855, m. Emma Smith; Jedediah M. b. July 8, 1857, m. Mary Earl; Joseph Wells b. Oct. 11, 1859, m. Minnie Palmer 1881; Albert C. b. March 17, 1861, m. Lucetta Smith.
Married Emily Card March 30, 1852, Salt Lake City (daughter of Simeon Card, pioneer 1850, and Ruhanna Lancaster). She was born Sept. 27, 1831, in Maine. Their children: Ruhanna b. May 2, 1853, m. Joseph Ovard 1871; Emma Rebecca b. June 26, 1854, m. M. C. Udy 1875; Harriet Sophrona b. March 18, 1857, m. Milton Earl; Elizabeth Jane b. Jan. 26, 1859; Mary Lovina b. April 10, 1861, m. Hyrum Moon; Maud b. Aug. 4, 1862; Joseph Lancaster b. Aug. 16, 1864, m. Alice Udy; Joel Preble b. Feb. 4, 1866; Alma Riley b. Aug. 16, 1868; Dexter Waterman b. Feb. 9, 1870.
Married Julia Helena Person Nov. 6, 1856, Salt Lake City (daughter of Per Person and Ingeborg Halvorson), who was born Sept. 30, 1837, and came to Utah 1854, Jacob Secrist company. Their children: Heber Chase b. Nov. 12, 1859; Arthur b. May 22, 1861, m. Nellie Moon; John Frederick b. Jan. 14, 1864, m. Elenor Udy; Emeline R. b. July 22, 1868, m. John A. Bourne 1902.
Married Mary Ann Steed March 1857, Salt Lake City (daughter of James Steed and Caroline Holland; pioneers 1850, Milo Andrus company). She was born Nov. 27, 1837, in England. Their children: James Henry b. March 6, 1858, m. Elizabeth White 1881; Alma William b. Sept. 3, 1859, m. Jane Ann Hadfield 1881; George A. b. July 20, 1861, m. Lucy Sanders 1889; Madeline Eudora b. Aug. 20, 1863, m. William Miller 1881; Eliza b. June 29, 1865, m. Jonathan D. Wood 1882; Wilford b. March 5, 1868, m. Sarah Capener; Mary Elizabeth b. Jan. 18, 1870, m. George Smith; Caroline Rebecca b. March 25, 1872, m. Henry Moon; Orson Pratt b. Feb. 25, 1874, m. Francis Tubbs; Lorenzo Snow b. June 29, 1878.
Married Caroline Workman April 12, 1862, Salt Lake City (daughter of Abraham S. Workman, pioneer 1851, and Martha Witcher, who died on the way to Utah 1851. She was born March 28, 1844, and came to Utah 1851. Their children: Josephine b. Aug. 12, 1864; David C. b. Aug. 16, 1865, m. Lois Kimball; John W. b. Sept. 20, 1867, m. Ann King; Adaline b. Dec. 11, 1869, m. Charles Udy; Franklin b. March 10, 1872, m. Sarah A. Compton; Charles C. b. March 7, 1874, m. Jane Owen; Lot b. Jan. 27, 1876; Caroline b. March 29, 1878; Minerd Lyman b. Aug. 5, 1880, m. Nellie Holt; Mark b. June 19, 1884, m. Elsie Hughes.
Married Sarah Lovina Miller May 30, 1868, Salt Lake City (daughter of Daniel A. Miller and Hannah Bigler; pioneers 1848, Daniel A. Miller company). She was born June 24, 1850, Farmington, Utah. Their children: Sarah Jane b. March 30, 1869, m. Lewis E. Abbott 1888; James T. b. Jan. 25, 1871; Alice Malinda b. March 16, 1873, m.

Asa Pierson 1890; Josephine A. b. June 3, 1875, m. J. R. Mellus 1894; Hellen Lovina b. Aug. 23, 1879, m. Lewis Mellus 1896; Horace Arnold b. Sept. 17, 1880, m. Mildred Smith 1907; Milton Miller b. Dec. 23, 1882, m. Margaret Steed 1908; Hannah Lenore b. July 26, 1885, m. S. R. Butterfield 1910; Jesse Eugene b. Aug. 9, 1890.
Married Frances Marion Bigler July 28, 1875, Salt Lake City (daughter of Adam Bigler and Sarah Ann Compton; pioneers 1859, J. W. Cooley company). She was born Oct. 22, 1859. Their children: Claudius b. June 21, 1879; Clarissa b. Aug. 1880, m. Jessy J. Chipman 1896; Harriet b. May 21, 1882, m. Charles A. Secrist 1902; Edward b. May 8, 1884; Amy b. Jan. 22, 1885; Joseph J. b. May 6, 1886; Andrew b. May 19, 1889; Florence Ireta b. April 14, 1892; Lucy b. Jan. 19, 1895; Reuben b. Feb. 27, 1897; Carl Bigler b. March 27, 1899. Families resided at Farmington, Utah.
Settled at Mill Creek 1847; moved to Farmington 1849. Assisted in bringing immigrants to Utah. Bishop of Farmington ward 27 years; first counselor to President William R. Smith. Davis stake; president of Davis stake 1894; called by President Young in 1875 to take charge of a band of Indians and assist them in the arts of civilization. Representative to state legislature from Davis county three terms; delegate to Trans-Mississippi Congress at Omaha, Neb. Died Dec. 16, 1903.

HESS, JOSEPH WELLS (son of John W. Hess and Emeline Bigler). Born Oct. 11, 1859, Farmington, Utah.
Married Minnie Palmer Nov. 24, 1881, Salt Lake City (daughter of George Palmer and Eliza Howes, who came to Utah 1874). She was born July 4, 1864, Broome, Eng. Their only child was Minnie Laurite (adopted) b. Jan. 23, 1906. Family resided Elba, Idaho and Farmington, Utah.
President fifty-sixth quorum seventies 1904; counselor in stake presidency two years and stake president two years of Y. M. I. A. at South Davis stake; missionary to Oklahoma and Indian Texas 1896-98; president North Texas conference eleven months; Sunday school and ward teacher; home missionary three years.

HESS, JAMES H. (son of John W. Hess and Mary Ann Steed). Born March 6, 1858, at Farmington, Utah.
Married Elizabeth White Nov. 24, 1881, Salt Lake City (daughter of John S. White and Adilad Everette of Farmington; pioneers). She was born April 24, 1866. Their children: Mary Jane b. Aug. 31, 1882, m. Vinson Knight; Annie Eliza b. Nov. 5, 1884, m. Wilford B. Farnsworth; Alice E. b. Aug. 14, 1885, m. Robert Hardy; James H., Jr. b. Nov. 1887, m. Alice Tovey; Russell b. July 14, 1891, m. Louise Hansen; Wilda E. b. Oct. 12, 1889; Alvin b. March 13, 1893; Hazel b. Jan. 4, 1895; Elwood b. Feb. 20, 1897; Emery b. Oct. 31, 1898; Carter b. Nov. 26, 1900; Clara b. Dec. 20, 1903; Ella b. Aug. 19, 1906; Evelyn b. April 6, 1908. Family home, Fielding.
Settled at Bear River Valley 1877. Bishop's counselor and Sunday school superintendent of Plymouth ward 1884-94; bishop of Fielding ward 1904-1906.

HIBBERT, BENJAMIN (son of James Hibbert and Hannah Brown, Newton Heath, Eng.). Born March 16, 1841, at Newton Heath; came to Utah 1859 with one of the handcart companies.
Married Mary Mills Jan. 1, 1862, Peterson, Utah (daughter of Charles Edmund Mills, pioneer 1863, Rosel Hyde company, and Frances Far, both of Southampton, Eng.). She was born April 5, 1836. Their children: George W., m. Elizabeth Walton; Mary E., m. Andrew B. Kennedy; Annie J., m. William H. Bennett; Sarah E., m. Henry D. Auger; Melinda, m. Samuel J. Bennett; Eugene, m. Dolores Bartlett; Lillian M., m. John Bright; Maud, m. Claude O. Fulton: Angeline, died; Benjamin C., m. Evelyn Thompson. Family home Enterprise, Morgan Co., Utah.
Elder; Sunday school superintendent; home missionary. Constable. Farmer. Died Nov. 1894.

HIBBARD, GEORGE (son of John Hibbard and Mary Brown of Honslow, Middlesex, Eng.). Born Aug. 22, 1836, Honslow, Eng. Came to Utah 1854.
Married Hannah Williams 1855, Salt Lake City (daughter of Abraham Williams and Hannah Maddy of Bedford, South Wales; former started for Utah, but died on the way). She was born Aug. 25, 1840. Their children: George m. Julia C. Lemmon; Mary Ann, m. Thomas E. Ricks; James Edwin, m. Mary Jen Luttz; Charles Albert, m. Mary Wiliham; Flora, d. Jan. 1885; Rose, m. James E. Togg; Emaline, m. Evans. Family home Logan, Utah.
Elder. Shoemaker and tanner. Died Oct. 30, 1890, Hibbard, Idaho.

HIBBARD, GEORGE A. (son of George Hibbard and Hannah Williams). Born July 18, 1857, Farmington, Utah.
Married Julia C. Lemmon Oct. 29, 1884, Logan temple (daughter of Willis Lemmon and Anna E. Homer of Smithfield. Utah, pioneer company with Russell K. Homer company). She was born May 31, 1865. Their children: Mabel J. b. Sept. 3, 1885, m. Henry Arnold; Georgia b. Aug. 30, 1887, d. Jan. 26, 1888; Nellie May b. May 8, 1889, m. William Sheppard; Stella b. Aug. 27, 1890, d. Aug. 31, 1901; Willis L. b. March 24, 1892; Alice L. b. Aug. 12, 1894, d. March 26, 1910; Rhoda L. b. June 12, 1896; Julia L. b. Nov. 13, 1898; Silas L. b. March 4, 1903; Don T. b. June 20, 1906. Family home Hibbard, Idaho.
High priest; bishop Hibbard ward June 9, 1895; bishop Warm River ward Nov. 10, 1907. Farmer and stockraiser.

HICKEN, THOMAS (son of Thomas Hicken and Ann Ward of Leicestershire, Eng.). Born June 15, 1826. Came to Utah 1852, Eli B. Kelsey company.
Married Catharine Fewkes June 1845, Whitwick, Eng. (daughter of Benjamin and Culloden Fewkes of England). She was born 1825. Their children: Elizabeth, m. William Everet; Orzon, m. Emily Rasband; Addison, m. Elizabeth Molton; Thomas, m. Sarah McMullan; John, m. Isabel Todd; Benjamin, d. aged 2; David William, m. Kate Murdock. Family home Heber, Utah.
Married Margaret Powell Aug. 15, 1865, Salt Lake City (daughter of George Powell and Maria Mously of Tipton, Staffordshire, Eng., pioneers Oct. 15, 1864, Jos. S. Rawlins company). She was born March 8, 1848. Their children: Maria, m. William Baum; Sarah Ann, died; Rachael Emma, m. Adolphus Sessions; Charles Willard, m. Minnie Cummings; Ruth, m. Albert Douglas Dixon.
High priest; presided over Whitwick ward in England; seventy and patriarch. Veteran Black Hawk Indian war, 1853-54. Farmer and stockraiser.

HICKEN, JOHN HENRY (son of Thomas Hicken and Catharine Fewkes). Born June 14, 1859, Provo, Utah.
Married Isabel Ellen Todd Jan. 14, 1885, Heber, Utah (daughter of Thomas Todd and Margaret Shankland, of Heber). She was born March 17, 1863. Their children: Margaret Catharine b. Sept. 1, 1886, m. George Thomas Rasband; John Thomas b. Dec. 15, 1888, d. Dec. 15, 1888; Ethel Ione b. Dec. 22, 1892; Lizzie Belle b. Nov. 3, 1895; Irwin Todd b. Nov. 8, 1898; Geneve b. Sept. 8, 1901; Nellie Melva b. Feb. 23, 1907. Family home, Heber.
Elder. Member Heber city council. Butcher; farmer and stockraiser.

HICKENLOOPER, WILLIAM HAINEY (son of Andrew Hickenlooper and Rachel Long of Westmoreland county, Pa.). Born Sept. 22, 1804, in Westmoreland county. Came to Utah Sept. 19, 1847, Daniel Spencer company.
Married Sarah Hawkins Aug. 29, 1837, in western Pennsylvania (daughter of Caleb and Sarah Hawkins of Indiana county, Pa.). Their children: Jane, m. Stratton Thornton; Belinda, m. Edward Wade; John T., m. Elvira Fullmer. Family home, Salt Lake City.
Married Sarah Ward. Their children: William, m. Emily Gould; Rebecca, m. Thomas McEwan.
Married Ann Ham. Their children: Orson Hyde, m. Elizabeth C. Wallace; Rachel, m. Duncan McLain; Charles Andrew, m. Medora Blanchard; George.
Bishop 6th ward, Salt Lake City. City councilman. Manager Co-op. store; farmer. Died Jan. 14, 1888, Salt Lake City.

HICKENLOOPER, CHARLES ANDREW (son of William Hainey Hickenlooper and Ann Ham). Born Jan. 23, 1862, Salt Lake City.
Married Medora Blanchard Dec. 13, 1883, Salt Lake City (daughter of Alma Moroni Blanchard and Emma Bocock of Springville). She was born Feb. 23, 1866. Their children: William Alma b. Dec. 4, 1884; Luella b. March 19, 1886; Della Ann b. Sept. 24, 1888; Florence b. Aug. 4, 1890; Ray Charles b. Aug. 28, 1892; Meri Horace b. Feb. 14, 1896; Lottie Emma b. July 26, 1900; Glen Andrew b. July 7, 1903; Melva b. Feb. 18, 1907. Family home Pleasant View, Utah.
Missionary to southern states 1895-97; bishop's counselor; bishop of Pleasant View ward. County fruit tree and horticultural inspector; constable; secretary state board horticulture; director state fair association. Fruitgrower and shipper; general horticulturist.

HICKENLOOPER, WILLIAM ALMA (son of Charles Andrew Hickenlooper and Medora Blanchard). Born Dec. 4, 1884, Pleasant View, Utah.
Member stake board religion classes of Weber and Ogden stakes. Real estate dealer.

HICKS, JAMES M. (son of Sylvanus Hicks and Eveline A. Marvin, both of New York state). He was born June 29, 1833, in New York. Came to Utah 1850, Captain Johnson company.
Married Jane Ann Chase, at Salt Lake City (daughter of Sisson A. Chase and Miriam Gove of Vermont, pioneers 1852, Joseph Thorne company). She was born June 15, 1839. Their children: Emma J. b. Jan. 6, 1858, m. Smith Covert; Marvin J. b. Aug. 16, 1859, d. Aug. 23, 1884; Miriam E. b. April 27, 1862, m. Jabez Taylor; Sisson A. b. April 3, 1864, m. Hannah Scoby; John D. b. May 25, 1866, d. Feb. 2, 1874; Henry S. b. April 3, 1868, m. Viola Smith; Amia L. b. March 29, 1870, m. James E. Coult; Charles A. b. Sept. 19, 1872, m. May Robinson; George A. b. April 20, 1875, m. Elizabeth Edmonds; Levi D. b. May 15, 1877, d. Aug. 13, 1878; Annie L. b. July 20, 1879, m. Horace Fielding. Family home, Salt Lake City.
Elder. Died June 27, 1892.

HICKS, JOHN T. R. Born April 19, 1826.
Married Harriet Doe in England, who came to Utah and lived and died in Salt Lake City.
Married Anna Buhler, Salt Lake City (daughter of Ulrich Buhler of Zurich, Switzerland). She was born April 1, 1846. Their children: Harriet and Emeline, d. infants; John W. B. b. May 25, 1873, m. Amy Erickson; Anna J. b. Aug. 5, 1875, m. Frederick Pipegrass; Meily J. b. Feb. 9, 1878, m. Heber C. Nielsen; Heber C. b. Oct. 20, 1880; Nephi C. b. Feb. 1, 1883, m. Hannah Dunn; Olive M. b. July 28, 1885, died; Bertha P. b. April 27, 1888. Family home South Cottonwood, near Murray, Utah.
Seventy. Participated in Echo Canyon campaign. Shoemaker. Died Dec. 16, 1890.

HIGGINS, JESSE (son of William Higgins, born March 20, 1809, at Skitascotters, Eng., and Harriet Kennard, born 1810, Doddington, Eng.—married 1828). Born June 25, 1830, Lenham, Eng. Came to Utah Aug. 24, 1868, Horton D. Haight company.
Married Frances Hampshear in 1853 (daughter of William Hampshear and Ann Hales), who was born Oct. 6, 1834. Their children: William b. June 19, 1854, m. Cena Christopherson Nov. 24, 1882; Alfred John b. April 8, 1857, d. infant; George b. March 25, 1858, m. Martha Rice July 14, 1882; Frances b. April 28, 1862, m. John Nielsen Nov. 17, 1882. Family home West Jordan, Utah.
Married Louisa Ann Swinyard Jan. 16, 1866, Tunstall, Kent, Eng. (daughter of Edward Swinyard and Sarah Jennings), who was born April 5, 1829, at Tunstall. Their children: Louisa Ann b. Aug. 2, 1867, m. Hyrum Bateman Sept. 27, 1893; Lovina R. b. Feb. 3, 1870, m. Christopher Bateman Sept. 12, 1888. Family home West Jordan, Utah.

HIGGINS, NELSON. Born 1806, Otswego, Canada. Came to Utah with a contingent of the Mormon Battalion, captain of Company D.
Married Nancy Marybah Behunin (daughter of Elijah Behunin), who was born Feb. 8, 1840. Their children: Melvin, died; Nelson W., m. Christina M. Hanson; Joseph H., m. Margaret A. Luster; Isaac M., died; Lewis; Hyrum and Marybah Elmina, died; Nancy Loretta b. March 31, m. Samuel B. Harmon. Family resided Nephi, Richfield and Elsinore, Utah.
First bishop of Richfield before and after the Indian wars. Major-general of Sevier county troops in Black Hawk Indian war. Justice of peace, Elsinor. Farmer. Died 1890, Elsinore.

HIGGINS, LEWIS (son of Nelson Higgins and Nancy Marybah Behunin). Born Dec. 15, 1870, Nephi, Utah.

HIGHAM, THOMAS ROBERTS (son of Ambrose Higham and Cathrine Roberts of Eydon, Northamptonshire, Eng.). He was born July 27, 1821, Eydon, Northamptonshire. Came to Utah Oct. 7, 1851, Orson Pratt company.
Married Annie Stewart July 11, 1855, Salt Lake City (daughter of Archibald Stewart and Esther Lyle of Glasgow, Scotland, pioneers Oct. 1, 1854, Daniel Garn company). She was born Jan. 5, 1833. Their children: Thomas S., m. Ida Young Dec. 21, 1882, m. Hannah Gould July 7, 1885; Mary S., m. Charles W. Brewerton Nov. 20, 1884; Robert S., died; Archibald S., m. Hattie Dixon May 1883; George S., died; Annie S.; John S., m. Gwendolyn Vernetta April 16, 1906; William S., m. Ida Cope Sept. 19, 1894; Ambrose S., m. Clara Hoffman July 12, 1898; James S., died. Family home, Salt Lake Cty.
Member 4th quorum seventies; high priest. Veteran Indian war. Landscape gardener. Died Oct. 19, 1902.

HIGHAM, AMBROSE S. (son of Thomas Roberts Higham and Annie Stewart). Born March 3, 1873, Salt Lake City.
Married Clara Hoffman July 12, 1898, Salt Lake City (daughter of Herrman Hendrich Martin Hoffman and Christine Marie Frölander of Malmö, Sweden—latter came to Utah July 12, 1886). She was born Oct. 23, 1879. Their children: Lyle H. b. July 8, 1900; Mary H. b. Aug. 11, 1902; Ambrose H. b. Oct. 1, 1904; Harding H. b. Oct. 27, 1906; Clare H. b. June 15, 1909; Ruth H. b. July 12, 1911. Family home, Salt Lake City.
Member 4th quorum seventies. Master plumber; member of firm of Higham Brothers.

HIGLEY, GEORGE W. (son of Myron Spencer Higley and Priscilla Eberson). Born Nov. 20, 1831, Leeds county, Canada. Came to Utah in 1851.
Married Nancy Ellen Wadsworth July 24, 1855, who was born Aug. 23, 1839.
Settled at Salt Lake City; in 1852 moved to Green River, Wyoming, where he bought an interest in the Ferry. He went to meet his parents at Laramie, Wyo., and assisted them to Salt Lake City in 1852. Went to Marsh Valley, Idaho, and built a bridge across the Marsh Creek, and opened a trading post at that pace.

HIGLEY, MYRON SPENCER (son of Job Higley and Dorcas Eggleston). Born Dec. 29, 1801. Came to Utah 1852.
Married Priscilla Eberson in 1826, Leeds, Can. Their children; Viz Nelson b. April 1, 1827, d. 1828; Clarissa b. Oct. 21, 1829, d. 1873; George W. b. Nov. 20, 1831; Edwin b. Nov. 12, 1833, d. April 10, 1852; Adelia b. June 23, 1836; Abigail b. Oct. 6, 1838; James b. 1841, d. 1841; Dorcas b. Dec. 2, 1843,

d. Oct. 1864; Mary Jane b. Feb. 13, 1847; Elizabeth Ann b. April 1, 1850; Myron b. Feb. 6, 1853. Family home Mountain Green, Utah.
Settled in Salt Lake valley 1852; lived in Morgan and Davis counties till 1872; moved to Hooper, Weber county, 1872. Bowl-turner; farmer. Died in 1887 at Hooper, Utah.

HIGSON, JOHN (son of Jerrard Higson and Anne Hopkins of West Houghton, Lancashire, Eng.). Born Dec. 29, 1836, West Houghton, Eng. Came to Utah Sept. 15, 1859. Robert Neslen company.
Married Caroline Kidgell June 10, 1858, Wigan, Lancashire, Eng. (daughter of Charles Kidgell and Miss Loftus of Lancashire, pioneers Sept. 15, 1859, Robert Neslen company). She was born Sept. 15, 1836. Their children: Charles J., m. Georgia Smith; Henry, m. Mary O'Rork; Etta, m. Thomas H. Atkins; Frank E.; Alford, m. Miss Evans; Hugh H., m. Miss Peterson; John W., m. Blanch Becker. Family home Salt Lake City.
Seventy. In charge of Salt Lake City Sewerage department two and one half years. Mining man.

HIGSON, CHARLES J. (son of John Higson and Caroline Kidgell). Born April 8, 1859, in New York. Came to Utah with father.
Married Georgia Smith Nov. 8, 1882, Salt Lake City (daughter of George Smith and Catherine Wootton of Farmington, Utah, pioneers October, 1855, Milo Andrus company). She was born Jan. 23, 1859, Farmington, Utah. Their children: Roy C. b. Aug. 29, 1883, m. Effie Swanner; Earl K. b. Aug. 9, 1885, m. Maud West. Family home Salt Lake City.
Plumbing, heating and contracting.

HILL, ALEXANDER. Born October 1779 Skipness, Argyleshire, Scotland. Came to Utah Sept. 9, 1851, Abraham Day company.
Married Elizabeth Curry. Their children: Daniel; Agnes b. June 6, 1808, m. John Richards; John b. Jan. 14, 1814, m. Margret Brice, m. Agnes Steele; Archibald N. b. Aug. 20, 1816, m. Isabella Hood, m. Margaret Fotheringham; m. Mary Milam, m. Caroline Graham; Alexander; Mary, m. James Bullock; Elizabeth.

HILL, JOHN (son of Alexander Hill and Elizabeth Curry). Born Jan. 14, 1814, Renfrewshire, Scotland. Came to Utah 1850.
Married Margret Brice (daughter of Robert and Elizabeth Brice), who was born Dec. 15, 1816, and died in 1858. Their children: Elizabeth B. b. 1839, died; Mary B. b. Jan. 25, 1841, m. D. D. McArthur Feb. 13, 1857; Isabell B. b. 1843, died; John B. b. March 17, 1846, m. Margery Kerr Dec. 15, 1876; Margret B. b. Nov. 28, 1848, m. Joseph Hall; Sarah B. b. Oct. 9, 1850, m. Bradford Bird; Agnes Christy B. b. Jan. 20, 1853, died; Martha Ann B. b. May 19, 1856, m. A. B. Hill; Robert B. b. 1858, died.
Married Agnes Steele Nov. 26, 1859, Salt Lake City (daughter of Alexander Steele), who was born Dec. 25, 1823. Their children: Jane S. b. Sept. 23, 1860, m. J. J. Hill; Jennett S. b. Jan. 18, 1862, m. Charles Hill; Archibald S. b. Jan. 18, 1862; Frances S. b. June 30, 1863, m. Charles Hill.
Settled at Wellsville, Cache Valley, 1860, where he and his brother built and owned the first grist mill. Cooper; carpenter. Accidentally shot and killed while hunting 1863.

HILL, JOHN B. (son of John Hill and Margret Brice). Born March 17, 1846, Nauvoo.
Married Margery Kerr Dec. 15, 1876, Logan, Utah (daughter of David Kerr and Agnes Archibald; pioneers 1861, Job Pingree company). She was born July 27, 1859, in Pennsylvania. Their children: Laura K. b. Oct. 22, 1877; Mary K. b. April 24, 1880; Sarah K. b. Oct. 1, 1882, m. J. A. Garner Dec. 19, 1900; James K. b. Nov. 11, 1885, m. Nettie Leishman Sept. 11, 1907; Margery K. b. June 26, 1889, m. Fred Robinette Dec. 20, 1911; Lozena K. b. Jan. 3, 1892; Gladys K. b. Nov. 24, 1894; Margery K. b. Dec. 14, 1898; Beatrice K. b. July 11, 1905. Family home Wellsville, Utah.
President and secretary of elders' quorum; president Y. M. M. I. A.

HILL, ARCHIBALD N. (son of Alexander Hill and Elizabeth Curry). Born Aug. 20, 1816, at Johnstown, Scotland. Came to Utah Sept. 27, 1847, Abraham O. Smoot company.
Married Isabella Hood Feb. 21, 1840 (daughter of James Hood and Margaret Bisien of Toronto, Canada). She died at Winter Quarters on way to Utah. Their children: Samuel Hood, m. Audrey Payne; Hannah Hood, m. Miles Romney; Rebecca Hood, m. Edwin Pettit.
Married Margaret Fotheringham July 12 1851. Their children: Charlotte (adopted); Isabella; Lizetta; Newel; Frank.
Married Mary Milam Dec. 25, 1855. Their children: Emma; William.
Married Caroline Graham April 7, 1857. Their children: Loiza; Martha; Perley A.; Daniel; Audrey, m. Mary Houes Jan. 22, 1872.
Was in charge of tithing office at Salt Lake City 15 years. Missionary to England 1865-67, returning to Utah in charge of a company of emigrants; missionary to United States and Canada 1887-88; watchman at Z. C. M. I. and Constitution Building five years. Died Jan. 2, 1900.

HILL, GEORGE WASHINGTON (son of Richard Hill, born Nov. 29, 1793, near Fredericksburg, Md., and Sarah Strait, born March 26, 1799, Dutchess conty, N. Y.). Born March 5, 1822, Amesville, Athens Co., Ohio; came to Utah Sept. 18, 1847, Abraham O. Smoot company.
Married Cynthia Utley Stewart Sept. 18, 1845. In Missouri (daughter of George Stewart, died in Missouri, and Ruth Baker, pioneer Sept. 1847, Abraham O. Smoot company, Tuscaloosa, Ala.). She was born Jan. 15, 1823. Came to Utah Sept. 1847 with mother. Their children: George Richard b. Aug. 22, 1846, m. Elizabeth N. Burch Dec. 18, 1871; Clarinda Cynthia b. Oct. 19, 1848, m. James Beus Oct. 19, 1868; Heber James, d. child; Ruthinda Evelyn b. Nov. 3, 1853, m. Lewis F. Moench; Isaiah Lorenzo, d. child; Joseph John, m. Martha Stowell; Charles Washington, m. Janett Hill; Parley Pratt, m. Mary J. Roylance; Edna Rebecca, d. child. Family resided at Ogden and Salt Lake City, Utah.
High priest; patriarch; missionary among the Indians at Salmon River, Idaho, 1855; assisted in bringing immigrants to Utah 1849 and 1864; Indian interpreter; worked among the Indians on the Malad River Valley, establishing them on their farms. Farmer. Died Feb. 21, 1891, Salt Lake City.

HILL, GEORGE RICHARD (son of George W. Hill and Cynthia Utley Stewart). Born Aug. 22, 1846, Mt. Pisgah, Iowa; came to Utah Sept. 10, 1847.
Married Elizabeth N. Burch Dec. 18, 1871 (daughter of Daniel Burch and Ann W. McClellan), who was born Jan. 31, 1849, Ogden, Utah. Their children: George R. b. April 10, 1884; Daniel B. b. Dec. 4, 1885; Reuben L. b. March 4, 1888; Anna Elizabeth b. April 11, 1890, m. James R. Hindley June 1909.
Married Charity J. Shelton (daughter of William Shelton and Delphina Kirkman), who was born Jan. 22, 1858, Mt. Airy, N. C. Their children: John Shelton b. Aug. 30, 1884, m. Minerva Johnson; Mary D. b. Aug. 9, 1886; Cynthia J. b. May 18, 1895; William Richard b. Sept. 28, 1896.
Assisted in bringing immigrants to Utah 1866; hauled rock for Salt Lake temple; school teacher 1869 and 1870; missionary to southern states 1879-81; Sunday school superintendent at Ogden first ward 1884-89; moved to Springville 1889 and he was ordained bishop of third ward April 17, 1892; served as home missionary two years. County commissioner 1901.

HILL, CHARLES W. (son of George W. Hill and Cynthia Utley Stewart). Born May 30, 1861, Ogden, Utah.
Married Jannett Hill Aug. 26, 1880, Salt Lake City (daughter of John Hill and Agnes Steele both of Scotland, the former came to Utah). She was born Jan. 18, 1862. Their children: Charles W. b. June 30, 1881, m. Etta Marshall; Jennette b. Jan. 8, 1883, m. Edward P. Dahle; Cynthia A. b. Aug. 21, 1885, m. Moses Dahle; George W. b. Sept. 26, 1887, d. infant; Disa C. b. Sept. 26, 1887, d. infant; Archie G. b. Aug. 11, 1889; Noble b. Feb. 21, 1891, d. infant. Family home, Salt Lake City.
Married Frances Hill Sept. 26, 1882, Salt Lake City (daughter of John Hill and Agnes Steele), both of Scotland, the former came to Utah). She was born June 30, 1863. Their children: Edith F. b. June 8, 1883; Zina H. b. March 14, 1888; Mercy R. b. April 10, 1891, m. Henry K. Bytheway; Ruby M. b. May 13, 1893. Family home, Salt Lake City.
High priest; member high council of Pocatello stake; block teacher. Merchant. Died Oct. 14, 1908.

HILL, ISAAC (son of John Hill and Mary Ward of Pennsylvania). Born Sept. 29, 1808, in Ohio. Came to Utah 1849.
Married Mary Jane Miller, at Salt Lake City (daughter of James Miller and Sarah Surcey of Ohio, pioneers 1849, latter with Capt. Hooper company). She was born Jan. 9, 1834. Their children: Elizabeth b. Sept. 21, 1854, m. Phineas Cook; m. Chris Johnson; Isaac b. June 25, 1857, m. Rebecca Tremellin; Jacob. d. infant; Eliza b. Jan. 3, 1860, m. William Howard, Jr.; Samuel b. Jan. 11, 1862, m. Christy Reed; Margaret b. Jan. 21, 1864, m. Thomas Smith; Joseph b. March 17, 1866; Sylvia b. May 14, 1868, m. Beeman L. Oviatt; Emeline b. April 6, 1870, m. David A. Johnson; Hyrum S. b. Aug. 6, 1873, m. Miss Hendrickson. Family home Salt Lake City.
Missionary to Missouri 1857-58; bishop 2d ward. Salt Lake City. Blacksmith. Died June 25, 1879, Fish Haven, Idaho.

HILL, JAMES came to Utah by oxteam.
Married Malissia ——. Their children: Sally Malissia; James; George; Rhoda, m. Charles Grames, Jr.
Seventy; high priest. Farmer. Died 1910, Wellington, Utah.

HILL, JOSEPH (son of Joseph Hill of Gloucestershire, Eng.). Born March 17, 1806. Came to Utah 1851, Capt. Caldwell company.
Married Ann Marsden in England, who was born about 1808 and came to Utah with husband. Their children: John, m. Mary Bennett; Joseph, m. Ellen Sheen; Alice Ann, m. John Bloxom.
Farmer and stockraiser Died Aug. 21, 1889, Layton, Utah.

HILL, JOSEPH (son of Joseph Hill and Ann Marsden). Born about 1841, Santers Parish, Gloucestershire, Eng. Came to Utah with parents.

Married Ellen Sheen Dec. 25, 1858, Kaysville, Utah (daughter of James Sheen and Maria Loverage of Gloucestershire, pioneers Sept. 26, 1856, Edmund Ellsworth company). She was born Feb. 14, 1838. Their children: Joseph William b. April 18, 1860, m. Caroline Layton; Alice San Cordelia b. Jan. 1862, died; Jeanette Maria b. Dec. 1863, m. George W. Layton; Sarah Ann b. Dec. 14, 1865, m. Rufus Adams; Louisa b. Dec. 2, 1869, m. Marion F. Adams; Emeline b. Oct. 6, 1874, m. Christopher Burton; David Franklin b. Sept. 27, 1886, m. Amanda Jane Bennett. Family home Layton, Utah.
Elder. Took part in Echo Canyon trouble; went to Salmon River with Horton Haight company; went to San Pete and also to Skull Valley to protect the settlers against Indians. Horse herder for the pony express; stockman and farmer.

HILL, RICHARD (son of Richard Hill and Sarah Strait of Athens county, N. Y.). Came to Utah 1850, Independent company.
Married Rhoda Wheeler. Their children: Catherine, m. Mr. Palmer; Sarah, m. George Lake; Newton, m. Lucy Ann Henson (Packer); Frank, m. Sarah Edwards; James, m. Clara ———.

HILL, NEWTON (son of Richard Hill and Rhoda Wheeler). Born March 19, 1846, Athens county, N. Y. Came to Utah with father.
Married Lucy Ann Henson (Packer) (daughter of Alfred Henson, who came to Utah 1868). She was born Aug. 15, 1853. Their children: George Newton; James; Laura; Annie; Rhoda; Franklin Oliver b. Sept. 20, 1884, m. Vera Glenn; Obert; Mary; Elva; Orlin; Lee; Ruford Wade.
Elder. Located at Ogden.
Lucy Ann Henson was the widow of James Packer. Their children: Alfred Packer and Nathan Packer.

HILL, FRANKLIN OLIVER (son of Newton Hill and Lucy Ann Henson). Born Sept. 20, 1884, Doven, near Gunnison, Utah.
Married Vera Glenn Sept. 20, 1910, Vernal, Utah, by James M. Shafer (daughter of John Glenn, born at Vernal, Utah, and Olive Haws, born at Provo, both of Wallsburg, Utah). She was born Sept. 13, 1892. Only child: Lena May b. July 22, 1911.
Deacon. Merchant at Wellington.

HILL, SAMUEL HOOD (son of Archibald Hill and Isabel Hood of Toronto, Canada). Born Dec. 23, 1840, Toronto, Canada. Came to Utah 1851.
Married Jane G. Seaman Nov. 7, 1879, Salt Lake City (daughter of Joseph Seaman and Rachel Rand of Littlesbury, Eng., pioneers 1867). She was born Aug. 6, 1843. Their children: Ernest S. b. May 26, 1881, m. Annie Andrews; Ethel Jane b. Dec. 14, 1882; Jane S. b. Sept. 5, 1884; Joseph S. b. Sept. 4, 1889. Family home, Salt Lake City.
Bishop's counselor several years. Member constitutional convention of 1895. Indian war veteran. Died Feb. 10, 1903.

HILL, THOMAS (son of Thomas Hill and Betty Riggs of Yorkshire, Eng.). Born Dec. 25, 1820, Lancashire, Eng. Came to Utah 1853.
Married Alice Mellor 1851 at St. Louis, Mo. (daughter of John Mellor and Mary Hardman of Lancashire, Eng., pioneers 1853, Captain Clawson company). She was born April 27, 1815. Their children: Sarah, m. Allen Hondry; Alice A., m. Thomas F. Emmett; Betsy A., m. Dan Zundel. Family home Ogden, Utah.
High priest. Plasterer. Died March 1, 1887.

HILL, WILLIAM JAMES (son of Richard Hill and Sarah Strait and brother of George Westernton Hill). Born March 3, 1834, Athens Greene Co., N. Y. Came to Utah 1850, with an independent company.
Married Cellicia Hadlock Feb. 25, 1855, Ogden, Utah (daughter of Stephen Hadlock and Sally Alton of Vermont, pioneers Sept. 20, 1850, Edward Bunker company). She was born Sept. 23, 1836, in Cuyahoga Co., Ohio, and died June 30, 1895, Spanish Fork, Utah. Their children: Stephen William b. Nov. 27, 1855, died; Mary Elizabeth b. March 2, 1857, died; Solly Luvina b. Feb. 25, 1858, m. ——— Parker; James Henry b. Feb. 20, 1860, m. Nancy Matilda Beckstrom; Sarah Melvina b. April 1, 1862, m. John C. McKendrick; Henrietta Augusta b. Nov. 28, 1864, m. Rentew Smith; George Richard b. March 18, 1866, m. Rose Davis; Rozina Emeline b. July 23, 1868, m. Hyrum Chittenden; Nancy Naoma b. Feb. 13, 1873, m. Robert Bruce Martin; Rhoda Christina b. April 16, 1875, m. Henry Olsen; Adaline Precinda b. June 3, 1878, m. David Davis; Zoula Cilicia b. Aug. 15, 1880, died. Family home Ogden and Wellington, Utah.
Married Henrietta Hadlock Sept. 20, 1867, Salt Lake City (daughter of Stephen Hadlock and Sally Alton), who was born July 10, 1843, in Brown county, Ill. Their children: April 10, 1870, d. Jan. 17, 1911; Emily Celicia b. Aug. 4, 1871, M. John Calstrom; Cyntha Calista b. July 19, 1873, m. George Dimmick; Charles Sylvester b. Oct. 11, 1874, m. Florence Rollinson; Esther Marinda b. Aug. 20, 1876, m. William Mildrege; Zina Balinda b. Oct. 11, 1877, m. Brigham Von

Victor Gould; Henrietta Perisina b. July 16, 1879, m. William Park; Hulda Clarinda b. Oct. 19, 1881, m. William Norton; Betty Petty b. Sept. 4, 1884, m. Seamon Golden; William Strait b. Feb. 23, 1886.
Member 60th quorum seventies; high priest; Sunday school superintendent at Ogden and Wellington, Utah; ward teacher. Settled in Ogden where he remained until 1884, when he moved to Wellington, Utah, and assisted in building canals and wagon roads. Minute-man in Indian war. Assisted in the survey of Ogden city. Farmer. Died Dec. 26, 1910, Wellington, Utah.

HILL, WILLIAM JOHN (son of William Hill and Lucy Gibbons of England). Born Jan. 9, 1856, in England. Came to Utah 1866.
Married Charlotte Emily Holbrook June, 1878, Endowment House, Salt Lake City (daughter of Jonathan Holbrook and Melissa Smith of Canada). She was born 1879. Their children: John William, m. Sarah Ann Frisby; Jonathan; Charlotte (died), m. David Groves; Lucy; Millie; William; Alfred; Lyman; Bryan. Family home Bountiful, Utah.
Teacher; high priest. Road Supervisor and Watermaster at Bountiful. Farmer and market gardener.

HILL, JOHN WILLIAM (son of William John Hill and Charlotte Emily Holbrook). Born Nov. 1, 1879, Bountiful.
Married Sarah Ann Frisby November, 1900, Salt Lake temple (daughter of Ephraim Frisby and Sarah Ann Lowe, pioneers 1866). She was born Aug. 26, 1881. Their children: John Ephraim b. July 22, 1901; Percy b. Nov. 25, 1902; Guy b. Nov. 12, 1904; Elsie b. Oct. 22, 1906; Lloyd b. May 12, 1909; Ralph b. April 22, 1911.
Member high council Carbon stake; bishop Wellington ward Sept. 6, 1910; Sunday school teacher and stake chorister; teacher and class leader Y. M. M. I. A. Principal Wellington schools Feb. 3, 1905-12. General merchant.

HILTON, HUGH (son of John Hilton). Born 1819, Bolton, Eng. Came to Utah 1852.
Married Jane Hewet 1846. Only child: Charles b. 1847, m. Annie Johnson 1868. Family home Salt Lake City, Lehi, and Virgin, Utah.
Married Isabella Pilkington 1852, St. Louis, Mo. She was born 1826, Bolton, Eng. Their children: Hugh b. 1853; Sarah A. b. 1855, m. George Hunt 1874; John Hugh b. Nov. 17, 1857, m. Maria Parker June 1, 1881; Joseph b. 1860, m. Ellen M. Richards; Hyrum b. 1864, m. Sarah J. LaFevre. Family home Virgin, Utah.
High priest.

HILTON, JOHN HUGH (son of Hugh Hilton and Isabella Pilkington). Born Nov. 17, 1857, Salt Lake City.
Married Maria Parker June 1, 1881, St. George, Utah (daughter of John Parker and Maria Jackson, former a pioneer 1852—latter with first handcart company, Edmund Ellsworth, 1856). She was born May 19, 1862, Taylorsville, Utah. Their children: Isabel b. March 13, 1882, m. Bernard Hinton April 24, 1906; Annie M. b. Dec. 10, 1884, m. Riay Bishop Feb. 8, 1910; Hugh b. June 10, 1887, m. Chloe S. Black Aug. 17, 1910; Eugene b. Nov. 12, 1890; Wilford b. March 21, 1892; Ray P. b. Oct. 22, 1895; Ivin b. Jan. 21, 1897; Virgil b. Sept. 14, 1899; Clement b. April 19, 1902; Hazel b. May 13, 1905; Lyda b. Nov. 5, 1907. Family home Virgin, Abraham, and Hinckley, Utah.
Assistant Sunday school superintendent; presiding elder Abraham branch, Hinckley ward.

HINCHCLIFF, CHARLES W. Born Jan. 2, 1850, in Lancashire, Eng. Came to Utah Sept. 10, 1861, Milo Andrus company.
Married Mary Allen Aug. 21, 1871, Salt Lake City (daughter of Albern and Marcia Allen of Ogden, pioneers 1847). She was born Jan. 14, 1850. Their children: Ella; Marcia, m. Gomer A. Nicholas; Charles A., m. Carrie Wanseraard; Francis W., m. Lizzie Evans; Edmond A., m. Amelia James; John R., m. Effie Bullock; Estella, d. aged 25; Lorin A., m. Mamie Hipp; Lester G.; Lulu V. Family home Ogden, Utah.
High priest; choir leader. Shipping clerk.

HINCKLEY, ARZA ERASTUS (son of Nathaniel Hinckley, who lived at Leeds, Can.—born Dec. 5, 1794, in the United States—and Lois Judd of Upper Canada, born Sept. 15, 1805, at Leeds—married 1821). He was born Aug. 15, 1826, in Leeds. Came to Utah July 27, 1847, with company B, Mormon battalion.
Married Amelia Woodhouse March 1853 (daughter of Charles Woodhouse, who died in Illinois, and Ann Long, who came to Utah with Capt. Jepson company 1852—married Oct. 6, 1829, in the United States). She was born April 17, 1834; came to Utah with her parents. Their children: Amelia Ellen b. Dec. 22, 1853; Arza Erastus b. June 15, 1855; Ira Nathaniel b. March 15, 1857, m. Elizabeth Rock 1878; Lois Amelia b. Feb. 28, 1859, m. Wm. Vance 1881; Daniel Hanmer b. Jan. 3, 1861. Family home, Salt Lake City.
Married Temperance Ricks Dec. 18, 1857, at Salt Lake City (daughter of Joel Ricks and Elinor Martin, who came to Utah with H. C. Kimball company, Sept. 24, 1848; mar-

936 PIONEERS AND PROMINENT MEN OF UTAH

ried May 1, 1827, in Kentucky). She was born Jan. 4, 1837, at Edwardsville. Madison county, Ill. Their children: Lois Elinor b. Sept. 17, 1858; Joel b. Nov. 5, 1860, m. Lucy Woodard 1880; Ann Elizabeth b. Jan. 1863; Edwin Lewis b. March 28, 1865; Elia Clarinda b. Sept. 17, 1867, m. T. B. Cardon June 11, 1884; Rhoda Adelaide b. Nov. 6, 1869, m. J. T. B. Mason Dec. 28, 1887; Silas Ricks b. Jan. 28, 1872, m. Lilly Bell Nov. 1894; Arthur Seymour b. April 30, 1874, m. Clara Mason Dec. 20, 1900; Minnie Mary b. March 8, 1877, m. F. C. Bowen Sept. 2, 1903; Nathan Roy b. Dec. 20, 1880. Family resided Salt Lake City, Coalville, Richville, Cove Creek, Utah, and Rexburg, Idaho.
Married Mary Christina Heiner April 1861, Salt Lake City (daughter of Martin Heiner and Adlegunda Dietzel, married Jan. 6, 1837, in Germany, and came to Utah with Edward Stevenson company 1857). She was born July 20, 1839, in Germany. Their children: Heber b. July 10, 1862; Mary Loiza b. Aug. 28, 1864, m. C. A. Welch April 5, 1883; Martha Adiegunda b. May 13, 1866, m. F. S. Branwell June 11, 1890; Luna Ardell b. March 18, 1868, m. J. R. Paul May 20, 1886; John Heiner b. March 15, 1870, m. Jessie Taggart June 13, 1906; Frances Amelia b. Feb. 18, 1873, m. Joseph Roakelly June 13, 1900; Franklin Arza b. Feb. 18, 1873, m. Ellen Rowberry Aug. 6, 1902; Harvey b. July 10, 1875. Family resided at Salt Lake City, Morgan, Coalville, Richville and Cove Creek, Utah, and Rexburg, Idaho.
As a boy of nine years of age was teamster in Zion's camp. Helped bring immigrants to Utah. Policeman, Salt Lake City. Black Hawk war veteran. Probate judge. Summit county high priest; high councilor; missionary to Arizona Indians; bishop Papago ward; patriarch.

HINCKLEY, IRA NATHANIEL (son of Nathaniel Hinckley, born Dec. 5, 1794, and Lois Judd, born Sept. 15, 1805, Leeds, Canada, both of Rochester, N. Y., later. He was born Oct. 30, 1828, Johnstown Dist., Canada. Came to Utah 1850, David Evans company.
Married Eliza Evans (daughter of David Evans), who died 1850 crossing plains. Their child: Eliza, m. Edward L. Robertson.
Married Adelaide C. Noble Dec. 11, 1853 (daughter of Lucian Noble and Emily Wilcox of Livona, Mich., pioneers 1850, William Snow company). She was born Aug. 15, 1834. Their children: Minerva, m. William A. Ray; Lois, m. James Frampton; Delia, m. James H. Mace; Lucian N., m. Ada Robison; Frank, m. Helen Moody; Edwin Smith, m. Addie Henry; Nellie, m. Joseph H. Robison; Samuel Ernest, m. Ida Cheever; Sarah, m. Mosher F. Pack. Family home Salt Lake City, Coalville, Cave Fort and Fillmore, Utah.
Married Angeline Wilcox Noble (daughter of Lucian Noble and Emily Wilcox of Livona, Mich., pioneers 1850). She was born 1832. Their children: Angeline, m. Lafayette Holbrook; Laverne, m. James M. George; Ira N., m. Lillian King; Bryant S., m. Tenie Johnson and Ada Bitner; Alonzo A., m. Rosa M. Robison; Elmer E., m. Angie Callister; two children died in infancy.
Married Maggie Harley. Their child: Mary, m. Mr. Carter.
President of Millard stake 26 years. Captain of a company to guard U. S. mail from depredations of Indians. Pioneer to Arizona and New Mexico. Called by President Young to build Cove Fort 1867. Policeman at Salt Lake City; mayor of Fillmore. Blacksmith; farmer and stockman. Died April 10, 1904, Provo, Utah.

HINCKLEY, EDWIN SMITH (son of Ira Nathaniel Hinckley and Adelaide Cameron Noble). Born July 21, 1868, Cove Fort, Utah.
Married Addie Henry Sept. 3, 1890, Manti, Utah (daughter of Robert Henry of Ireland and Elizabeth Bacon of England, pioneers 1850, settled at Fillmore, Utah). She was born Jan. 12, 1868. Their children: Robert Henry b. June 8, 1891; Leonore Adelaide b. April 17, 1894; Edwin Carlyle b. July 25, 1896; Norma Elizabeth b. Oct. 12, 1897; Claudius Warren b. May 30, 1899; Paul Bryant b. Oct. 8, 1900; Frederick Russell b. May 28, 1902; John Noble b. aug. 6, 1903; Evaline Marguerite b. March 5, 1905; Gordon Holbrook b. June 12, 1906; Muriel Aileen b. Sept. 4, 1907; Marion b. March 1, 1909; Angela Ruth b. May 30, 1910. Family home Provo, Utah.
Missionary to Colorado 1897; high priest; first counselor to Bishop Moroni Snow of 5th ward, Provo, Utah. Member Provo city council. Second counselor to George H. Brimhall, president of Brigham Young University of Provo; professor of geology and physiography at Brigham Young University of Provo, Utah.

HINDLEY, JOHN (son of Thomas Hindley and Mary Seden Lumis of Lancashire, Eng.).
Married Jane Charters Robinson Feb. 1856 at Salt Lake City (daughter of John Robinson of England). Their children: Esther Jane, m. Jefferson Eastmond; Elenor Edith, m. Richard Preston; Mary Helena, m. Alva Greene; John Robinson, m. Ann Chipman; James Ernest, m. Emily Huggard; Anna Elizabeth, m. Oscar F. Hunter; William Hyrum, m. Maud Karen. Family home, American Fork. Bishop's counselor. Mayor of American Fork; justice of the peace. American Fork. Painter; farmer; merchant.

HIPWELL, WILLIAM (son of John Hipwell and Harriet Grucock of Hansby, Eng.). Born Jan. 11, 1836, Dunton, Bassette, Eng. Came to Utah Sept. 15, 1861, Sextus Johnson company.

Married Elizabeth Barton March 1, 1863 (daughter of William Barton and Nancy Kay of West Weber, Utah, pioneers Oct. 1862, Thomas Rich company). She was born Feb. 15, 1842. Their children: Harriet Handley; Ephraim; Nancy Farr; John; Mary Ann; Martha Knight; Elizabeth Hadley; Margeth Ann Walker; Sarah May Stone; Lizzie McLane. Family home West Weber, Utah.
Farmer.

HIPWELL, EPHRAIM (son of William Hipwell and Elizabeth Barton). Born April 22, 1866, West Weber, Utah.
Married Mary Jane Walker Dec. 2, 1885, Logan (daughter of Samuel F. Walder and Sarah Dixon of West Weber, pioneers 1861, Captain Hooper and Captain Thomas Rex companies). She was born May 1, 1865. Their children: Sarah Elizabeth b. May 5, 1887; Mary Jane b. Sept. 20, 1888; William Barton b. Dec. 23, 1890; Margaret Eliza b. Jan. 7, 1893; John Ephraim b. Nov. 7, 1895; Samuel Fredrick b. March 26, 1902; Willis Thomas b. Jan. 11, 1907. Family home West Weber, Utah.
Farmer.

HIRSCHI, ARNOLD DANIEL (son of Jacob Hirschi, born June 21, 1830, Reutigen, Bern. Switzerland, died June 18, 1909, Montpelier, Idaho, and Susanna Katerinna, born Oct. 28, 1834, Zwischenflüh, Bern, Switzerland, died July 2, 1902, Montpelier, Idaho). Born Dec. 20, 1868, in Zwischenflüh. Came to Utah Sept. 23, 1883, Captain Goss company.
Married Sophie Haehlen Sept. 12, 1894 (daughter of Jacob Haehlen and Rosena Katerine Dubach, who were married Sept., 1859, Borchlen, Diemtigen, Bern, Switzerland). She was born Nov. 14, 1870; came to Utah July 17, 1894. Their children: Arther b. June 20, 1895; Arnold Fredrick b. April 6, 1897; Sophie Katerina b. April 12, 1898; Clara Virginia b. Jan. 7, 1901; Rose Eliza b. Dec. 12, 1904; Gladis Lena b. June 11, 1910. Family home Geneva, Idaho.
Bishop of Geneva ward 18 years; missionary to Switzerland 1892-94; teacher in Montpelier ward. Business man.

HIRSCHI, GOTTLIEB (son of Ulrich Hirschi, born Aug. 7, 1812, Schaugnaw, Switzerland, and Anna Amacher, born 1800, Wilderswiel, Switzerland. He was born Jan. 16, 1837, Danbreson, Switzerland. Came to Utah Aug. 1860.
Married Mary Ann Rupp Sept. 14, 1861, Salt Lake City (daughter of Christian Rupp, who died at Sbotfo, and Susanna Winkler, who came to Utah from Shoffo Ct., Neufchatel, Bern, Switzerland). She was born Jan. 12, 1838. Their children: Albert b. July 18, 1862, d. Feb. 23, 1881; Mary Anna b. June 10, 1864, d. Oct. 11, 1865; Joseph b. Dec. 16, 1866; Henry b. June 28, 1867, m. Mary C. Stout; John b. July 25, 1869, d. June 16, 1871; David b. Dec. 13, 1870, m. Mary M. Petty Oct. 3, 1890; Samuel b. Aug. 29, 1872, d. Oct. 10, 1872; Daniel b. May 17, 1874, m. Amelia V. Petty June 27, — ; Susanna b. April 25, 1876, m. James N. Stanworth; Eliza b. Dec. 28, 1882, m. Oliver DeMill III. Family home Rockville, Utah.
Bishop of Rockville ward 1891-1900; missionary to Switzerland 1883-85. Settled in Santa Clara 1861, moved to Rockville 1863. Died Jan. 24, 1900, at St. George, Utah.

HIRSCHI, DAVID (son of Gottlieb Hirschi and Mary Ann Rupp). Born Dec. 13, 1870, Rockville, Utah.
Married Mary Matilda Petty Oct. 3, 1890, Rockville (daughter of Joseph H. Petty and Alfaretta M. Duzett, former a pioneer 1848, Captain Chase company, latter was native born). She was born Aug. 20, 1872, at Rockville. Their children: Claudius b. Sept. 13, 1892; Margery b. March 8, 1894, d. Aug. 24, 1905; Heber b. Nov. 19, 1895; Kenneth b. June 22, 1897; Susie b. May 5, 1899; David Milo b. Feb. 26, 1900; Wraph b. June 16, 1903, d. June 16, 1903; Hugh b. June 15, 1905; Annona b. May 6, 1907; Junius b. July 14, 1909; Jennie b. July 24, 1910; Karl Albert b. Aug. 26, 1912. Family home. Rockville.
Missionary to Switzerland 1902-04; bishop Rockville ward; school teacher 1892-1902. Director of Bank of St. George; member stake board of education.

HIRSCHI, DANIEL (son of Gottlieb Hirschi and Mary Ann Rupp). Born May 17, 1874, Rockville.
Married Amelia V. Petty Jan. 27, 1895 (daughter of Joseph H. Petty and Alfaretta M. Duzett, pioneers 1848, Captain Chase company). She was born May 5, 1875. Their children: Mary A. b. Oct. 9, 1895; Gottlieb A. b. May 18, 1897, d. April 1, 1897; Daniel A. b. Dec. 3, 1898; Walden b. Dec. 9, 1900, d. Dec. 16, 1900; Dewey b. Jan. 29, 1902; David L. b. Jan. 5, 1904.

HIRST, JOHN (son of Abraham Hirst and Nancy Dykes of Yorkshire, Eng.). Born March 7, 1816, Yorkshire, Eng. Came to Utah September 1868.
Married Charlotte Brook about 1839, Yorkshire, Eng. (daughter of William and Hannah Brook). She was born 1818. Their children: Abraham, d. infant; James, d. infant; Harriet, m. Thomas Marshall; Hannah, d. aged 17; Nancy, m. Joseph Dearden; Eliza, m. Jonathan Gledhill; Mary, m. George Wood; Martha, m. James Taylor; Fannie, m. William Jenkins; John, m. Elvira Spencer; Sarah, m. Jacob Coon; Charlotte, m. John A. Coon; Ellen, m. Daniel Whipple.

HISKEY, BENJAMIN. Born 1822 at Schuylkill Haven, Pa. Came to Utah Oct. 17, 1862, Henry W. Miller company.
Married Mary Ann Dankel, Lehi county, Pa. (daughter of Mr. Dankel of Schuylkill Haven, pioneers Oct. 1862, Capt.

Miller company). She was born 1818 and came to Utah with husband. Their children: W. F. and Emma Linda, both died; Peter M.; Clara; Augusta S.; John S.; Thomas A.; Cassa; Alfred D.; Allen. Latter three died.
Teacher. Car repairer. Died 1884, Erda, Utah.

HISKEY, JOHN S. (son of Benjamin Hiskey and Mary Ann Dankel). Born May 22, 1864, Salt Lake City.
Married Mary Lyman May 12, 1902, Boulder, Utah (daughter of Amasa Mason Lyman, Jr., and Rosanna Reynolds). She was born July 20, 1885. Only child: Max Lyman b. Aug. 2, 1909. Family home Teasdale, Utah.

HITCHCOCK, JOHN CHESTER (son of Seth Hitchcock and Sally Ann Rhodes, both died in Missouri). He was born March 3, 1832, Warsaw, Genesee county, N. Y. Came to Utah 1848, Heber C. Kimball company.
Married Petrea Jensen March 5, 1857, Ephraim, Utah (daughter of Soren Jensen and Kistina Maria Jensen, Torse, Hjorring amt, Denmark, pioneer 1854, Capt. Olson company). She was born March 1840. Their children: John Seth b. Dec. 28, 1857, d. infant; Franklin b. March 8, 1859, m. Anna Rosetta Cook; Louisa Jane b. May 11, 1861; Mary Ann b. Nov. 20, 1863, d. infant; Petrea Melissa b. Jan. 30, 1865, m. Moses Burdick; Maria Lavina b. Jan. 26, 1868, d. infant; Violet b. Feb. 18, 1869, d. infant; William Henry b. May 26, 1870, m. Julia Emily Duncan; Willard b. Feb. 16, 1873, m. Mary Thomas; James Edward b. Oct. 16, 1875, d. aged 11; Leonora b. Aug. 4, 1878, d. Oct. 23, 1878; Sarah Elizabeth b. June 23, 1880, d. Sept. 6, 1880. Family home Ferron, Utah.
High priest; ward teacher 40 years. Finally settled at Ferron 1883. Lieutenant in Blackhawk war 1865-68. Assisted bringing immigrants to Utah.

HITCHCOCK, WILLIAM HENRY (son of John Chester Hitchcock and Petrea Jensen). Born May 26, 1870, Spring City, Utah.
Married Julia Emily Duncan Nov. 2, 1892, Manti (daughter of John Chapman and Teressa Duncan, of Scotland and Ferron). She was born April 13, 1875. Their children: Dora Evelyn b. March 31, 1894, m. LaMar Kilpack; Blanche b. Oct. 25, 1896; Louis William b. May 18, 1899; Rulon John b. March 15, 1905; Helen b. March 24, 1913. Family home, Clawson.
Bishop Clawson ward, Oct. 25, 1904. Settled at Ferron 1884. County road commissioner 1912. Farmer and stockraiser.

HITCHCOCK, FRANKLIN (son of John C. Hitchcock and Petrea Jensen). Born March 8, 1859.
Married Anna Rosetta Cook. Their children: Delos, m. Rachel Thomas; Seth, m. Sarah Felstead, died; Olive, m. Livy Olsen; Monte; Ruth, m. Peter Alfred Knudson; Val; Reeva; Cleo.
Elder. Farmer.

HJORTH, PETER H.—See page 944.

HOBBS, WILLIAM DOWN (son of Henry Hobbs and Ann Down of Framfield, Sussex, Eng.) Born Jan. 6, 1814, Framfield, Sussex, Eng. Came to Utah Nov. 2, 1864, Warren Snow company.
Married Mary Ann Pope Nov. 9, 1835, Brighton, Eng. (daughter of Thomas Pope and Ann Grenier), who was born April 11, 1815. Their children: Annie b. April 30, 1837; William Down, Jr. b. Nov. 1839, m. Elizabeth Cook 1864; Mary Ann b. June 16, 1841, m. Alfred Gadd Jan. 1864; Emma Lucy b. Feb. 21, 1843, m. Alexander Meads Oct. 1864; Tryphena Jane b. April 29, 1847, m. William West 1867; Sarah Elizabeth b. Feb. 3, 1852, m. Henry H. Harriman; Ellen Agnes b. June 1853, m. Hyrum Fielding; George Brigham b. Feb. 22, 1856, m. Julia Broadhead Oct. 1883; Alice Lavina b. 1858, m. William Banks. Family home, Parowan.
Helped settle Iron county, 1885. Carpenter; builder and farmer.

HOBBS, WILLIAM DOWN (son of William Down Hobbs). Born in November 1839. Came to Utah Sept. 27, 1861, Sextus E. Johnson company.
Married Elizabeth Cooke (daughter of Henry Cooke), who was born Sept. 27, 1843, and came to Utah 1865, John R. Murdock company. Came to Utah Aug. 30, 1860, Jesse E. Murphy company.
Nov. 27, 1866, m. Benjamin H. Cooke March 10, 1886; William Henry b. Sept. 5, 1871, m. Mary E. Hathaway; Benjamin George, m. May G. Southworth; Amy, d. aged 3; Jesse T., m. Ethel Molyneux 1904; Franklin M., m. Mary Bault 1901; Edith Pearl, m. Rasmus Mickleson; Alvin M. b. Feb. 17, 1891. Family reside Parowan, Utah, and Wilford, Idaho.

HOCHSTRASSER, RUDOLPH (son of Rudolph Hochstrasser, born 1803, Fahrwangen, Canton Aargau, Switzerland, and Margaret Miller, born July 15, 1814, Reitnau, Canton Aargau, Switzerland). He was born Sept. 1, 1839, Wikermos, Canton Luzerne, Switzerland. Came to Utah Aug. 30, 1860, Jesse E. Murphy company.
Married Maria Sutter March 10, 1859, mid-Atlantic, on ship Emerald Isle (daughter of Daniel Sutter and Margaret Witmer of Bozberg, Aargau, Switzerland). She was born Aug. 13, 1824. Their children: Jacob b. Nov. 25, 1860, d. infant; Mary b. Jan. 15, 1863, m. Frederick Theurer Aug. 5, 1880; Joseph b. Jan. 9, 1866, m. Alice Fullmer. Family home Providence, Utah.

Married Mary Ann Lanz Nov. 1, 1861, Salt Lake City (daughter of Ulrich and Maria Lanz), who was born Sept. 5, 1841, Lotzuil, Bern, Switzerland. Their children: Rudolph Hyrum b. Aug. 20, 1865, m. Alice Fullmer; Nephi W. b. Feb. 26, 1867, m. Jane Fullmer; Eva Liottea b. May 8, 1869, m. Neils Hansen 1887; Sarah Ann b. July 11, 1871, m. Frank Hinman; Rachel Eliza b. Aug. 24, 1873, m. Thomas Low; Mary Ann b. Oct. 6, 1875, m. Julius Jacobsen; Alma b. Oct. 16, 1878.
Married Ursula Kerner May, 1865, Salt Lake City (daughter of Thomas Kerner and Ursula Trichler), who was born Sept. 9, 1837, Hamereisenbach, Baden, Germany. Only child: Thomas O. b. March 1866, d. infant.
Married Anna Maria Torbjornson Oct. 20, 1881, Salt Lake City (daughter of Neils Torbjornson and Mary Mason), who was born May 5, 1864. Their children: Martha b. Nov. 7, 1882, m. Charles Bradley; Elizabeth b. Jan. 26, 1886, m. Samuel Ahlman Dec. 24, 1910; Samuel b. Feb. 1888, d. April 1890; Daniel b. Jan. 15, 1890, d. same year.
Married Rhoda Jane Kietten Feb. 10, 1892, Salt Lake City (daughter of Eugene and Sarah Jane Fullmer of Salt Lake City). She was born 1856, Salt Lake City. Their children: Leah Lavon H. b. Aug. 1893, m. Mr. Webb 1911; Ruby Drucilla H. b. July 1895; Chloe Margaret H. b. Aug. 18, 1897.
Married Matilda A. Jahnke Dec. 10, 1907, Salt Lake City (daughter of Louis Jahnke and Ernstena Nixdorf of Germany). She was born Sept. 9, 1876, Milwaukee, Wis. Member 32d quorum seventies; missionary to Switzerland 1883-85; bishop's counselor 1885-89; high priest. Shoemaker and farmer.

HODGES, NATHANIEL MORRIS (son of William Hodges and Ann Sweet of Bristol, Eng.). Born Jan. 4, 1847, Sparksford, Eng. Came to Utah Sept. 2, 1868, Captain S. M. Molen company.
Married Louisa Weston Oct. 11, 1869, Salt Lake City (daughter of Nehemiah Weston and Rosanna Gifford of East Harptree, Somersetshire, Eng., came to Utah Aug. 11, 1870). She was born Feb. 11, 1847. Their children: William Nehemiah b. July 15, 1870, m. Edith Pearl; Nathaniel John b. Aug. 15, 1872, m. Rose Early; Hyrum b. Sept. 20, 1874, d. Feb. 11, 1888; Edward b. Oct. 20, 1876, m. Eva Olene Kimball; Mary Louisa b. July 15, 1879, m. Reuben Hyden; Samuel b. May 31, 1881; Orson Henry b. July 10, 1887; Leonora b. May 28, 1889, m. Frank Linford; Hortense b. June 26, 1892, d. Oct. 14, 1894. Family home, Laketown.
Missionary to England 1883-84. Built first roller flourmill and steam sawmill in Laketown 1876. Stock raiser.

HODSON, WILLIAM (son of William Embleton Hodson and Anna Pigford of Durham county, Eng.). Born Aug. 30, 1841, Gayrington Hill, Durham county. Came to Utah Sept. 9, 1863, John R. Young independent company.
Married Isabella Williamson Dec. 25, 1861, Pomeron, Meigs Co., Ohio (daughter of Thomas Williamson and Ann Robinson of Durham county, Eng.). She was born July 6, 1845. Their children: Ann Williamson b. Feb. 7, 1864, m. William G. Rhead; Isabella b. Oct. 11, 1866, died May 31, 1867; William Williamson b. June 18, 1868, m. Agnes Walker; John Thomas b. July 28, 1870, m. Coralie Elvira Smith; Benjamin Franklin b. May 3, 1872, m. Evar Martell; Margaret Elizabeth b. March 27, 1876, m. John Ambrose Pack; Sarah Juliet b. Nov. 22, 1878, m. Joseph Theron Carruth Sept. 29, 1909; Mary Isabell b. Dec. 25, 1880, m. Leo L. Robertson, later Vincent Shepherd; Edward Elmore b. Aug. 15, 1883; Ethel Irene b. Sept. 11, 1885, m. Joseph E. White; Alvin Claude b. Nov. 9, 1888, d. aged 7. Family home, Coalville.
Settled at Coalville Sept. 9, 1863. Counselor to Bishop Robert Salmon of Coalville ward from its organization to 1877. When divided into three wards he was made bishop of North ward 1889-95; stake tithing clerk; superintendent of Sunday school; ward teacher; ward clerk; high councilor of Summit stake since 1901. School trustee; city surveyor 1877-78; city councilman 1877-93; member school board of examiners 1879 and 1880. Assisted in organizing Coalville co-operative work; salesman; bookkeeper; half owner of Robinson and Fletcher-Hodson coal mines; also of Hodson-Olson coal mine of Coalville; had big interest in Summit County Railroad; helped organize a cattle company and grist mill company in Coalville. Secretary and treasurer of Summit stake tabernacle 1878-98.

HODGSON, HENRY WILLIAM SUTLIFF (son of Jonathan Hodgson and Grace Sutliff of Yorkshire, Eng.). Born July 26, 1824, in Yorkshire. Came to Utah Sept. 28, 1856, Daniel Thompson company.
Married Mary Shaw 1846, Yorkshire, Eng. (daughter of John Shaw and Ann Greenwood of Yorkshire), who was born May 4, 1826. Their children: Hannah, m. Jeffrey Hodgson; Miriam, m. Jeffrey Hodgson; Oliver, m. Ann Pickard Hollingworth; m. Mary E. Simmons, Nephi; Grace Ann, m. Richard Sidoway; Moroni, m. Clara Skidmore; Mercey, m. Henry Williams. Family home, Salt Lake City. Elder. Weaver and machinist. Died 1892, Salt Lake City.

HODGSON, OLIVER (son of Henry William Sutliff Hodgson and Mary Shaw). Born March 8, 1851, Yorkshire, Eng.). Came to Utah Sept. 28, 1866.
Married Ann Pickard Hollingworth Nov. 27, 1871, Salt Lake Endowment House, Daniel H. Wells officiating

938 PIONEERS AND PROMINENT MEN OF UTAH

(daughter of Thomas and Mary Hollingworth). Came to Utah July, 1871, R. Read company). She was born July 24, 1851.
Married Mary Ettie Simmons April 12, 1875, Salt Lake Endowment House, Wilford Woodruff officiating (daughter of Joseph M. Simmons and Rachel E. Woolley of Salt Lake City, former came to Utah 1850, latter 1848). She was born Nov. 15, 1856. Their children: Oliver Leroy b. March 11, 1876, d. aged five; Leslie Simmons b. Dec. 18, 1879, m. Louie Taylor; Rachel b. Jan. 3, 1882, m. Isaac B. Ball; Mary b. Dec. 18, 1883, d. infant; Frederick William b. March 12, 1886, m. Elinor Bingham; Philip b. June 15, 1888, d. infant; Maud '. May 13, 1889, m. Frank Fullmer; Clifford Shaw b. Jan. 15, 1893; Edgar Dilworth b. April 5, 1896; Russel Beales b. Dec. 6, 1897; Jasper Henry b. March 13, 1898, d. infant; Paul Sutliff b. July 21, 1900. Family home Salt Lake City.
Seventy; high priest; bishop 3d ward five years. City councilman four years. Building contractor.

HODSON, JOHN (son of William Hodson and Ann Wignough of Pendleton, Eng.). Born Jan. 10, 1808, Pendleton, Eng. Came to Utah Sept. 10, 1853, Jesse Crosby company.
Married Maria Gillard January, 1834, Pendleton, Eng. (daughter of George and Maria Gillard of Pendleton, Eng.). She was born Jan. 10, 1811. Their children: William b. Sept. 18, 1834, m. Ruth Ware; Elizabeth b. Jan. 20, 1836, m. Joseph Allen; Ann b. 1837, d. infant; John H. b. Oct. 10, 1844, m. Rebecca Marriott; Thomas H. b. Nov. 10, 1846, m. Millie Flint; Alma b. 1848, d. aged 23; Jane b. March 1850, m. James Bowler; Rebecca b. Feb. 12, 1854, m. William Flint; Ann b. Sept. 1839, m. Thomas Finley. Family home Kaysville.
Seventy; one of first Mormon converts in England. Built first flour mill at Kaysville 1854; helped plan and work out first irrigation system from Kays creek 1854. Farmer. Died Oct. 7, 1881, Kaysville.

HODSON, WILLIAM (son of John Hodson and Maria Gillard). Born Sept. 18, 1834. Came to Utah Sept. 10, 1853, Jesse Crosby company.
Married Ruth Ware Feb. 9, 1859, Kaysville (daughter of George Ware and Naomi Bigg of Kaysville, pioneers Sept. 1855, Richard Ballantyne company). She was born Feb. 14, 1840. Their children: William J. b. Dec. 7, 1859, m. Adaline Terry; George A. b. Feb. 11, 1861, m. Susanna Green; Sarah M. b. Sept. 1, 1862, d. aged 3; Naomi E. b. July 9, 1864, d. aged 2; James R. b. April 14, 1866, d. aged 3; Joseph S. b. March 31, 1868, d. aged 5; Mary A. b. March 21, 1870, m. Rodolph Parry; Thomas H. b. March 13, 1872, d. aged 5; Leonard B. b. June 3, 1874; Drusilla R. b. Aug. 7, 1878, m. Joseph T. Covington; Delbert F. b. Sept. 28, 1880, m. Elizabeth O. Butler. Family home Marriott.
Member 55th quorum seventies. Justice of peace. Farmer.

HODSON, WILLIAM JOHN (son of William Hodson and Ruth Ware). Born Dec. 7, 1859, Marriott.
Married Henretta A. Terry Oct. 6, 1880, Marriott (daughter of Partial P. Terry and Esther Adlock of Marriott—pioneers 1847, Brigham Young company). She was born Feb. 24, 1863. Their children: William A. b. April 4, 1881, m. Sarah Richardson; Sarah L. b. March 4, 1883, m. Leonard Wayment; Parley P. b. Dec. 19, 1887, m. Mary Anderson; Muraid b. March 8, 1889; Ruth b. Sept. 4, 1892, m. Frederick Wheeler; Bertha b. Aug. 1, 1893; Esther M. b. Nov. 11, 1900. Family home, Plain City.
Teacher. Farmer.

HOFF, HENRY HERMAN (son of John Gottlieb Hoff and Catherine Phitzenmaier, both born at Wetzheim, Germany). Born March 16, 1849, at Philadelphia, Pa. Came to Utah Oct. 19, 1872.
Married Harriet Bacon March 8, 1875, Pleasant Grove, Utah (daughter of Chauncey Bacon and Celestia F. Sisson—pioneers 1851). She was born 1856, Salt Lake City. Their children: Beatrice H.; Henry Herman; Edmund C.; Ernest P.; Celestia G.; Myrtle D.; Frank E. Family home Georgetown, Idaho.
Settled in Georgetown, Idaho, 1875; appointed regent of University of Idaho by Governor McConnell 1893; in 1895 appointed director Albion state normal school by Governor Steunenberg; commissioner Bear Lake county three terms. Counselor to Bishop Alma Hayes 1896; bishop Montpelier 2d ward 1909. Mayor Montpelier, Idaho, 1911 and 1912.

HOGENSEN, CHRISTIAN (son of Hoken Nielson, born April 17, 1789, and Ingborge Olsen, born 1791, natives Lear, Norway). He was born Feb. 9, 1830, Lear, Norway. Came to Utah Sept. 4, 1859, George Rowley company.
Married Peteria Larsen May 6, 1859 (daughter of Lars Neilsen and Anna Petersen), who was born Dec. 20, 1830. Came to Utah Sept. 4, 1859, George Rowley company. Their children: Caroline b. July 26, 1861, d. Dec. 1867; Agnes b. Nov. 9, 1863, m. Charles Rodwell Pearce Sept. 22, 1882; Mary Jane b. Dec. 9, 1867, m. Ole Swensen Nov. 1889; Charles Henry b. Aug. 12, 1871, m. Emily Andersen Dec. 1897; Lorenzo b. Dec. 26, 1873, d. July 23, 1881. Family home Montpelier, Idaho.
Married Mary Jensen Aug. 2, 1884, Logan, Utah. / Their children: James b. May 9, 1885; Clara b. Dec. 9, 1887, m. Walter Hancock Oct. 2, 1912.
Seventy; missionary 1880-82. Home guard during Indian wars. Early settler to Cache valley, moved to Bear Lake county, Idaho, 1863 and to Montpelier, 1864.

HOLBROOK, JOSEPH (son of Moses Holbrook, born May 15, 1779, Massachusetts, and Hannah Morton, born March 15, 1788, Rhode Island—married 1805). He was born Jan. 15, 1806, in New York City. Came to Utah Sept. 20, 1848, Brigham Young company.
Married Nancy Lampson Dec. 30, 1830, Western Massachusetts (daughter of David and Sarah Lampson), who was born Aug. 14, 1804, and died at Nauvoo, Ill. Their children: Sarah Lucretia b. Jan. 21, 1832, m. Judson A. Tolman 1846; Charlotte b. Nov. 26, 1833, m. Vasco Call Jan. 28, 1853; Joseph Lamoni b. Jan. 31, 1837, m. Catharina Waterson July 24, 1855; Mary Jane b. Jan. 27, 1839; David b. Feb. 11, 1840.
Married Hannah Flint Jan. 1, 1843, Nauvoo, Ill. (daughter of William Angel and Phebe Marton). Their children: Caroline Tunis b. Oct. 21, 1851, m. John Corbridge Nov. 13, 1871; Joseph Hyrum b. Feb. 8, 1854, m. Catharine Cooper Jan. 13, 1878; Brigham Angel b. Feb. 10, 1856, m. Hannah Cook Dec. 17, 1876; Moses Angel b. Jan. 16, 1858, m. Jane Ann Throughton Nov. 23, 1882; James Angel b. April 3, 1860; John Angel b. Dec. 9, 1861; Ephraim Angel b. April 18, 1863; Enoch Angel b. July 12, 1865, m. Mary Smedley Nov. 14, 1894; Heber Angel b. Jan. 5, 1867, m. Martha Sweeten Jan. 4, 1893. Family home, Bountiful.
Married Lucy Jones Nov. 10, 1855, Salt Lake City (daughter of William and Lucy Jones). Their children: Lucy Ann b. Oct. 7, 1856; Joseph b. Jan. 23, 1858, m. Alice Ceah Dec. 19, 1878; William b. Jan. 4, 1860, m. Polly Burmingham Dec. 28, 1880.
Married Louisa Haitt Jan. 2, 1864, Salt Lake City, who was born June 4, 1822.
Seventy. Worked on Kirtland, Ohio, and Nauvoo, Ill., temples. Special policeman at Nauvoo; took part in Crooked river battle. Member territorial legislature two terms; probate judge of Davis county three terms. Counselor in bishopric of Bountiful ward. Helped bring immigrants to Utah.

HOLDAWAY, DANIEL W. (son of Timothy Holdaway, born Dec. 3, 1801, Jefferson county, Tenn., and Mary Trent, born Feb. 8, 1803, Hawkins county, Tenn.). He was born July 14, 1834, Putnam county, Ind. Came to Utah Nov. 17, 1850, immigration company.
Married Martha Belinda Gardner April 16, 1857 (daughter of Benjamin Gardner and Electa Lamport, who were married May 29, 1822—pioneers Sept. 28, 1852, Train No. 10). She was born Oct. 12, 1839; came to Utah with parents in 1852. Their children: Mary Ann b. Feb. 23, 1858; Daniel Timothy b. May 27, 1859, m. Minnie Petersen April 27, 1890; Electa Emaline b. May 3, 1861, m. Andrew Patterson May 27, 1883; William Benjamin b. Sept. 27, 1864, m. Minnie Hossfeld March 6, 1898; James Nathaniel b. Jan. 2, 1868, m. Louisa Bragger March 6, 1900; Martha Vilate b. Oct. 20, 1871, m. Charles A. Kroksh April 23, 1891; Hannah Lestie b. June 28, 1876, m. Guy N. Rose April 10, 1901. Family home Deweyville, Utah.

HOLDAWAY, JAMES N. (son of Daniel W. Holdaway and Martha B. Gardner). Born Jan. 2, 1868, North Ogden, Utah.
Married Louisa Bragger March 6, 1900, Brigham City, Utah (daughter of Abraham Bragger and Solema Grunder, and came to Utah in 1887). She was born May 2, 1901; in Germany. Their children: Etta b. May 2, 1901; Vesta b. Dec. 27, 1902; Solema b. April 11, 1905; Alice b. May 29, 1906; James Daniel b. July 24, 1909. Family home Deweyville, Utah.
Box Elder county surveyor 12 years. Irrigation engineer.

HOLDAWAY, DAVID (son of Timothy Holdaway and Mary Trent, of Hawkins county, Tenn.). Born March 9, 1832, in Hawkins county. Came to Utah 1850.
Married Elizabeth Haws June 1852, Salt Lake City (daughter of John Haws and Martha Sessions of Wayne county, Ill.; the latter came to Utah 1850). She was born June 23, 1830. Their children: David William b. Nov. 23, 1850, m. Bertha Potter; Martha Angeline b. Jan. 2, 1852, m. Monte Edwards; George Timothy b. Nov. 4, 1854, m. Deseret Durfy. Family home Provo, Utah.
Married E. Prater Dec. 1855, Provo, Utah (daughter of Thomas Prater and Sarah Kinsworthy of Brownstown, Jackson county, Ind.—widow of John Huntsman, whom she married June 7, 1846, Bonaparte, Iowa. Their children: Sarah Katherine b. Sept. 12, 1847, m. William A. Woolsey; Julia, m. Hyrum Smith and Mr. Liberty. They lived at Kanesville, Iowa). She was born Jan. 12, 1828. Their children: Thomas Teancum b. Aug. 24, 1857, m. Julia Fossett and Mary White; Mary Milvina b. June 24, 1859, m. Robert Blackburn and David Lucas; Joseph Alma, m. Sarah Robinson; Elizabeth Rachel, m. Edward W. Robinson. Family resided at Vernal and Provo, Utah.
High councilor; member 44th quorum seventies. Probate judge. Machinist. Died March 13, 1907, Provo, Utah.

HOLDAWAY, SHADRACH (son of Timothy Holdaway and Mary E. Trent of Hawkins county, Tenn.). Born Oct. 15, 1822, in Tennessee. Came to Utah Oct. 24, 1848, with division of Mormon Battalion company.
Married Lucinda Haws Dec. 24, 1848, Salt Lake City (daughter of Gilbert Haws and Hannah Whitecomb of Salt Lake City, pioneers Sept. 21, 1848, Lorenzo Snow company). She was born Oct. 20, 1828. Their children: George Bradford and Timothy died; William Shadrach, m. Pebe

Pratt; Amos David, m. Lydia Thrower; John Madison, m. Jane Gillispie; Mary Elizabeth, m. Charles C. Conrad; Levi Stewart, m. Caroline Anderson and Rebecca Clark; Logan Gilbert, m. Mary Blair; Syntha Mahala and Nancy Emeline, died; Andrew Nathan, m. Lydia Ann Riddle; Louisa Diantha, died; Warren Hacos, m. Lilly Riddle; Amanda Lucinda, m. Almono Loeto Young and James King Pierpont; Marion, m. Prudence Peay. Family home Provo, Utah.

Member 31st quorum seventies; high priest. Brought first carding and wool spinning machine to Utah Dec. 31, 1850; made first threshing machines in Utah from wagons left by Johnston's army; made first canal out of Provo river to lake bottoms. Lumberman; engineer; miner; rancher and farmer. Died Dec. 24, 1902, Provo, Utah.

HOLDAWAY, MARION (son of Shadrach Holdaway and Lucinda Haws). Born Feb. 25, 1855, Provo, Utah.

Married Prudence Eliza Peay Nov. 25, 1876, Provo, Utah (daughter of Francis Peay and Eliza Baker of Provo, pioneers 1853). She was born March 7, 1854. Their children: Clara Eva b. Nov. 3, 1877, m. Dudley Chase; Francis Marion b. July 6, 1879, m. Nellie Handley; Albert Arthur b. June 5, 1881, m. Annabel Clegg; Prudence Eliza b. April 21, 1883, m. William C. Chase; Florence Rosetta b. Jan. 30, 1887, m. Frank Carter; Zelda Maud b. Jan. 17, 1889, m. Joel Bunnell; Jennie Arville b. Nov. 30, 1891. Family home Vineyard, Utah.

Helped to construct roads in canyons. Farmer and stockraiser.

HOLDAWAY, ANDREW NATHAN (son of Shadrach Holdaway and Lucinda Haws). Born Dec. 27, 1864, Provo, Utah.

Married Lydia Ann Riddle June 10, 1884, Coyote, Utah (daughter of Isaac Riddle and Mary Ann Eagles of Coyote and Provo). She was born Sept. 15, 1866, Beaver, Utah. Their children: Wallace, died; Wilford; Murl M.; Rhoda A.; Cyrus N.; Orrin C.; Illa L., died; Cleo L. Family home Provo, Utah.

Missionary to West Virginia 1893-94. Miner and stockraiser.

HOLDAWAY, WILLIAM SHADRACH (son of Shadrach Holdaway and Lucinda Haws, Provo, Utah). Born Dec. 12, 1851, Provo.

Married Pebe Soper Pratt Sept. 11, 1872, Spanish Fork, Utah (daughter of Parley P. Pratt and Pebe E. Soper of Salt Lake City; came to Utah in Sept. 1847, Daniel Spencer company). She was born May 19, 1852. Their children: William Shadrach b. June 5, 1873, m. Vina C. Holt; Parley P. b. Feb. 1, 1876; Lucinda May b. April 23, 1879, d. infant; Gilbert Orson b. Aug. 27, 1881; Hall H. b. March 27, 1888, m. Mrs. Owens; Hazel Pebe b. Nov. 7, 1890; Lorus Trent b. June 27, 1894; Eva (adopted) b. June 19, 1903. Family home Provo, Utah.

Member of 123d quorum seventies. Member Provo city council 1894-98. Patentee of Holdaway button sewing attachment and Holdaway sugar beet harvester. Mechanical engineer.

HOLDAWAY, WILLIAM SHADRACH (son of William Shadrach Holdaway and Pebe Soper Pratt). Born June 5, 1873, Provo, Utah.

Married Vina C. Holt Dec. 9, 1896, Springville, Utah (daughter of Jessie Patten Holt and Sarah Naoma Carr of Spanish Fork, Utah). She was born Dec. 31, 1875. Their children: Vaughn LaMar b. Sept. 27, 1897; Reva Lucile b. June 16, 1890. Family home Provo, Utah.

Doctor of dental surgery; professor of music.

HOLDAWAY, AMOS DAVID (son of Shadrach Holdaway and Lucinda Haws). Born Jan. 23, 1853, Provo, Utah.

Married Lydia Thrower Oct. 10, 1872, Beaver, Utah (daughter of Thomas Thrower, who died on the plains en route to Utah, and Lydia Pilch, pioneer Sept. 24, 1862, Homer Duncan company; they were married 1841, Norwich, Eng., she was the daughter of James and Lydia Pilch of Norwich). She was born Oct. 19, 1826, Norwich. Their children: Amos Claud b. Aug. 2, 1873, and Don Alvin b. Jan. 23, 1877, died; Elmer Thomas b. Oct. 13, 1879, m. Ellen Ekins; Elsie Alberta b. Sept. 27, 1881, died; Milton Leroy b. April 20, 1884; Leland Eugene b. Jan. 20, 1887; Walter Roland b. Nov. 25, 1889, m. Edna Knudsen; Edna Lydia b. Aug. 6, 1892. Family home Provo, Utah.

High priest. County commissioner Utah county 1882-93; Provo city councilman 1880-89; member state fair board; member state mental hospital at Provo 1886-90; director of Deseret Agriculture Manufacturing Society 1890-96. Railroad builder and financier. Died April 30, 1900, Provo, Utah.

HOLDAWAY, ELMER THOMAS (son of Amos David Holdaway and Lydia Thrower). Born Oct. 13, 1879, Provo, Utah.

Married Ellen Ekins March 11, 1903, Provo, Utah (daughter of George Ekins and Mary Mezener of Pleasant View ward, Provo). She was born Jan. 6, 1880. Their children: Lucile b. Feb. 14, 1904; Elmer Harold b. July 6, 1909. Family home Vineyard, Utah.

Elder. Farmer and dairyman.

HOLDAWAY, JOHN MADISON (son of Shadrach Holdaway and Lucinda Haws). Born April 30, 1854, Provo, Utah.

Married Jane Peterson Gillispie Dec. 5, 1870, Salt Lake City (daughter of Robert Gillispie, born Feb. 8, 1829, and Mary Sharp of Fifeshire, Scotland, pioneers Aug. 1869, independent company). She was born March 11, 1852, Fifeshire. Their children: Mary Jane b. March 27, 1872, d. child; John Shadrach b. March 23, 1874, m. Margerett

Adamson; Edith Lucinda b. Feb. 8, 1876, m. Edward H. Holt; Ruby May b. Sept. 29, 1877, m. Webster Hoover. Family home Provo, Utah.

Missionary to northern states 1904-06; president Y. M. M. I. A. Provo city councilman; superintendent Provo city water works four years. Contractor and constructor of D. R. G. railway 12 years; carpenter; miner and civil engineer.

HOLDAWAY, LOGAN GILBERT (son of Shadrach Holdaway and Lucinda Haws of Provo, Utah). Born Aug. 1, 1859, Provo, Utah.

Married Mary Blair March 18, 1880, Salt Lake City (daughter of Seth Millington Blair and Sarah Texanna East of Salt Lake City, pioneers 1850). She was born Oct. 1, 1859. Their children: Dora b. Aug. 8, 1881, died; Ethel b. March 21, 1883; Etna Neal b. March 6, 1884, m. Ernest Foulger; LeRoy Logan b. Aug. 17, 1886; Emma Sarah b. Jan. 26, 1889; Helen b. Nov. 1, 1890, m. Ernest Pierce; Willmarth b. Dec. 25, 1893; Seth Millington, died; Mary B. b. Sept. 6, 1897. Family home Provo, Utah.

Deputy county assessor of Utah county several terms. Real estate, insurance and loans; carpenter and builder.

HOLDSWORTH, JONAS (son of Thomas Holdsworth, born June 13, 1788, and Nancy Bibby, born June 26, 1794, in England). Born May 22, 1821, Leeds, Yorkshire, Eng. Came to Utah 1862.

Married Dorothy Harriet Brook 1852 (daughter of Richard Brook and Ann Doe). She was born Dec. 9, 1825. Their children: Thomas b. April 20, 1853; John b. March 20, 1855; Elizabeth b. April 8, 1859, m. James G. Gray Dec. 29, 1877; Harriet b. Sept. 22, 1864; Jonas b. Sept. 22, 1864, m. Harriet Bahr Aug. 3, 1896; Martha Ann b. July 23, 1866, m. Joseph E. Dorton Dec. 3, 1884; Sarah Jane b. Nov. 10, 1869. Family home Lehi, Utah.

High priest. Tanner.

HOLDSWORTH, JONAS (son of Jonas Holdsworth and Dorothy Harriet Brook). Born Sept. 22, 1864, Lehi, Utah.

Married Harriet Bahr Aug. 3, 1896, Lehi (daughter of William Bahr and Harriet Jackson). She was born Feb. 12, 1875, Salem, Utah. Their children: William J. b. July 3, 1897; Alice b. June 23, 1899; Hazel b. Jan. 3, 1903; Louis B. b. Feb. 9, 1907. Family home Lehi, Utah.

HOLLAND, JOHN (son of William Holland, born 1802, died 1844, Nauvoo, Ill., and Sarah Tomlinson of Barton-under-Needwood, Staffordshire, Eng.). Born March 23, 1836, in England. Came to Utah October, 1850.

Married Mary Burton (daughter of James and Isabelle Burton). She was born Feb. 26, 1844, pioneer 1855, died Jan. 15, 1874. Their children: John William b. Oct. 25, 1861, m. Anna Stucker March 7, 1901; Sarah Isabella b. Sept. 8, 1863, died Jan.; Hyrum Thomas b. July 15, 1865; Joseph b. Oct. 29, 1867; James Heber b. Oct. 3, 1869; Christopher b. Nov. 7, 1871. Family resided Weber Co., Utah, fifty years, and Lorenzo, Idaho.

HOLLAND, JOHN WILLIAM (son of John Holland and Mary Burton). Born Oct. 25, 1861, Ogden, Utah.

Married Anna Stucker March 7, 1901, Salt Lake City (daughter of John and Elizabeth Stucker of Switzerland; former came to Utah 1900). She was born June 10, 1882. Their children: Dora b. Jan. 19, 1902; Pearl Irene b. June 19, 1908; Lila Isabelle b. March 30, 1913.

HOLLEY, HENRY. Born April 3, 1828, Hereford, Eng. Came to Utah 1854, Thomas Thomas company.

Married Ann Hutchins 1859, Slaterville, Utah (daughter of William Hutchins and Anne Putman, former died at St. Louis, Mo., latter came to Utah 1853, locating at Slaterville, Utah). She was born September, 1829. Their children: Henry, m. Amanda Knight; John, m. Margret Ellen Kelly; Edwin, m. Samantha Parry; William C., m. Annie Jensen; Annie Edith, m. William A. Taylor; Lucy, m. Chris Lee. Family home Slaterville, Utah.

Grocery and dry goods merchant. Farmer.

HOLLEY, JOHN (son of Henry Holley and Ann Hutchins). Born May 29, 1862, Slaterville, Utah.

Married Margret Ellen Kelly Dec. 19, 1881, Ogden, Utah (daughter of George Kelly and Mary Ann Slater of Slaterville, Utah, pioneers 1850, contingent of Mormon Battalion). She was born Sept. 18, 1862. Their children: Edith Ann b. Nov. 29, 1883, m. Joseph C. Westwood; Nellie b. Nov. 13, 1886, m. Joseph P. Bailey; John C. b. Oct. 5, 1891; Lincoln James b. Jan. 5, 1894; Margerite b. March 19, 1897; Henry George b. Feb. 25, 1901; Louis Edwin b. June 25, 1904. Family home Salt Lake City.

Elder. City councilman 1907-12. Engaged in wholesale produce.

HOLLIDAY, GEORGE T. (son of Thomas M. Holliday and Ann H. Mathews of Santaquin, Utah). Born Jan. 10, 1857, at San Bernardino, Cal.

Married Alveretta C. Jones Sept. 18, 1879, at Salt Lake City (daughter of Thomas E. Jones and Mary Ann Males). She was born Jan. 4, 1857, at Kaysville, Davis Co., Utah. Their children: Mary A. b. Sept. 17, 1880, m. Osbourn

Richins; George T. b. Aug. 10, 1882, m. Annie Thomson; James E. b. Feb. 9, 1885, died; Effie A. b. Oct. 1, 1887, d. child: Catherine M. b. Dec. 15, 1889. Family home Salt Lake City, 17th ward.

HOLLIDAY, JOHN (parents South Carolinians). Born in South Carolina. Came to Utah July 29, 1847, William Crosby company.
Married Catherine B. Higgins 1822 in South Carolina (parents Carolinians). Their children: Susannah F., d. infant; Luticia H., m. Alicia Smithson; Katherine B., m. Braxton Acres; John D., m. Mahala Matthews; Sarah Ann, m. Porter Dowdle; Keren Happuich, m. Thomas Bingham; David, m. Henriet Taylor; Keziah, m. Henry Boyle; Thomas, m. Ann Matthews; Lenernorah, d. child. Family home Santaquin, Utah.
Elder; missionary to San Bernardino, Cal., 1851-59. Farmer. Resides Santaquin, Utah.

HOLLIST, HENRY (son of William Hollist and Elizabeth Draby of Amberly, Sussex, Eng.). Born March 2, 1816, Amberly. Came to Utah Sept. 13, 1861, Joseph Horne company.
Married Elizabeth Chandler Dec. 25, 1837, Dorking, Surrey, Eng. (daughter of William Chandler and Hannah Taylor of Buckland, Eng.). She was born March 31, 1806. Their children: Elizabeth b. Feb. 14, 1842, m. John R. Stinger Oct. 1, 1859; William C., d. Nov. 11, 1846; Deborah b. July 25, 1846, m. Eli Manning March 24, 1865. Family home, Farmington.
Married Frances Berry Nov. 1865, Salt Lake City (daughter of Richard Berry and Sarah Randals), who was born Nov. 17, 1835, Cookfield, Sussex, Eng. Their children: Henry William b. Aug. 18, 1867, m. Rachel D. Lovesy Jan. 1, 1896; John T. b. Nov. 12, 1870, m. Nancy Oviatt March 8, 1890. Family home. Farmington.
Sunday school teacher 1865-70; president branch of church at Omaha, Neb., and also in England. Died 1870.

HOLMAN, JAMES S. (son of Jonathan Holman). Born Sept. 17, 1805, Templeton, Mass. Came to Utah 1847, Franklin D. Richards company.
Married Naomi R. Le Baron, who was born Oct. 7, 1816. Their children: James A.; Harriet N.; Sarah M.; Zilpha; Susan A.; Sanford; Silas William; Emma Jane; David E.; Charles S.; Lydia B.; Isaac Lester.
Bishop at Santaquin, Utah Co., Utah. Died June 21, 1873, Holden, Millard Co., Utah.

HOLMAN, ISAAC LESTER (son of James S. Holman and Naomi R. Le Baron). Born Dec. 21, 1859, Fountain Green, Utah.
Married Phoebe Kenney Feb. 21, 1883, Salt Lake City (daughter of John Kenney and Elizabeth Bennett), who was born Jan. 11, 1867. Their children: Lester E. b. Oct. 7, 1885; James W. b. Dec. 30, 1887; Benjamin Earl W. b. Dec. 18, 1889; Clarence b. Dec. 4, 1892; Elizabeth b. Sept. 28, 1894; Leona b. March 15, 1897; Rulon b. March 31, 1900; Naomi Grace b. Nov. 21, 1902; Vivian b. Jan. 22, 1905; Raymon K. b. June 27, 1907; Rea Mabel b. July 11, 1909; Emma Kathleen b. July 31, 1911.
Seventy; ward teacher. Farmer and stockraiser.

HOLMAN, JAMES A. (son of James S. Holman, pioneer 1847, and Naomi Le Baron of Illinois). Born 1836 in Pennsylvania. Came to Utah in 1848 with Lorenzo Snow.
Married Sarah Mathis Nov. 30, 1857, Payson, Utah (daughter of Isaac Mathis and Elizabeth Mathis of Payson). She came to Utah in 1852 with Chas. C. Rich, who was born Dec. 7, 1837. Their children: James L., m. Lucy Johnson; Jane, m. Appollos Benjamin Walker; John A., m. Fannie Coombs; David W., m. Mary Hanson; Nancy, m. John Low; Parley, m. Mary Llewellyn; Warren, m. Mary E. Jackson; Robert, m. Mary Brown; Naomi, m. Joseph Huggins; Ray, m. Catherine Brown.
High priest. Railroad contractor. Was present at the time of the driving of the golden spike which connected the Southern Pacific and the Union Pacific. Indian war veteran. Farmer.

HOLMAN, JOHN GREENLEAF (son of Joshua Sawyer Holman and Rebecca Greenleaf, of Kirtland, Ohio). He was born Oct. 18, 1828, Genessee county, N. Y. Came to Utah Sept. 19, 1847, Daniel Spencer company.
Married Nancy Clark Aug. 23, 1849, Kanesville, Iowa (daughter of Richard Clark and Annie Lizzie Shafer of Indiana, pioneers Sept. 13, 1850, Bailey Lake company). She was born Feb. 26, 1829. Their children: John Dennis b. Sept. 2, 1851; Artemus b. Sept. 25, 1852, m. Annie M. Rawlings; Nancy Elizabeth b. Nov. 25, 1854, m. Joseph E. Thorne; John Clark b. Nov. 8, 1857, m. Mary Ann Openshaw; Rebecca b. Jan. 17, 1861, m. George T. Tomlinson; Margaret Josephine b. Jan. 14, 1864, m. Samuel Green; Clarinda b. Oct. 10, 1867; Benjamin Franklin b. Dec. 26, 1869, m. Margaret Harvey; Lewis Clark b. July 30, 1873, m. Myrtle Groo. Family home Pleasant Grove, Utah.
Married Rachel Stevens Feb. 3, 1856, Salt Lake City (daughter of William Stevens), who was born Dec. 1, 1835. Their children: Rachel Marinda b. March 6, 1858, m. George Hollday, Jr.; Chastina b. Nov. 30, 1859, m. John Walker; Joshua Stevens b. Feb. 5, 1862, m. Kate Nielsen; Ordell b.

Sept. 27, 1866, m. Peter Johnson, Jr.; William Rielly b. Oct. 8, 1868, m. Lizzy Foster Oct. 8, 1892, Fillmore, Millard county; Sarah Ellen b. Sept. 12, 1871, m. Jesse M. Harmon; Elinora b. Sept. 19, 1873, m. German Buchanan. Family home. Pleasant Grove.
Married Sarah Harris (Loder). Their children: Zilpha Ann; Jane; Albert; Ezekiel. Family home, Pleasant Grove.
Member city council. Bishop's counselor for a number of years; missionary to England 1862-65. Called to Fort Bridger in 1855 to build Fort Supply. Assisted in bringing immigrants to Utah. Indian war veteran. Moved from Pleasant Grove to Santaquin in 1878, and from there moved to Rexburg, Idaho, in 1883. Member city council, Pleasant Grove. Died Nov. 5, 1888, Rexburg, Idaho.

HOLMAN, ARTEMUS (son of John Greenleaf Holman and Nancy Clark). Born Sept. 25, 1852, Pleasant Grove, Utah.
Married Annie Marie Rawlings Dec. 2, 1877, Provo, Utah (daughter of Eber B. Rawlings and Ann Skinner of England, pioneers 1860). She was born Feb. 27, 1860. Their children: Artemus Ezekial b. June 19, 1879, m. Luella Patten; George Eber b. July 16, 1882, m. Alice Thorton; Annie Edith b. June 7, 1884, m. Marten Monson; John Henry b. March 29, 1886, d. Jan. 1, 1888; Willard Rawlings b. May 26, 1888, m. Nellie Dorothy McQuivey; Leroy Benjamin b. Aug. 22, 1890, d. Nov. 20, 1891; Clarinda b. July 11, 1892; Tursey Nancy b. Aug. 5, 1894, died; Ora Velma b. March 3, 1896; Charles Milton b. March 13, 1899; Ida Mame b. Aug. 9, 1901. Family home Pleasant Grove, Utah.
Road supervisor at Pleasant Grove. Early freighter; worked on railroad in Echo and Weber canyons; farmer and stockraiser.

HOLMES, JONATHAN H. (son of Nathaniel Holmes and Sarah Harriman of Georgetown, Essex county, Mass.). Born March 11, 1806, Georgetown. Came to Utah 1848 with a division of the Mormon Battalion.
Married Marrietta Carter. Their children: Sarah E., m. Mr. Weaver; Mary Emma. d. infant.
Married Elvira Anna Cowles at Nauvoo, Ill., who was born June 13, 1813. Their children: Marrietta b. July 17, 1849, m. Job Welling May 12, 1866; Phoebe Louisa b. Feb. 5, 1851, m. Job Welling Dec. 21, 1868; Emma Lucinda b. Feb. 1, 1856, m. Job Welling April 28, 1875.
Member Mormon Battalion. Died 1881, Farmington, Utah.

HOLMES, HENRY (son of John Holmes and Mary Ann White). Born May 8, 1837, Hochliffe, Bedfordshire, Eng. Came to Utah 1853.
Married Ellen Anderson March 21, 1857, Salt Lake City (daughter of William and Elizabeth Anderson). Their children: Henry J.; William R.; Elizabeth A.; Heber C.; Mary E.; Milton C.; Margaret; Lamonia.

HOLROYD, THOMAS EDWARD (son of Richard Holroyd and Hannah Hebden of Halifax, Yorkshire, Eng.). Born Jan. 7, 1820, at Halifax. Came to Utah Sept. 16, 1861, Joseph Horne company.
Married Dinah Williams Jan. 2, 1845, Everton, Lancastershire, Eng. (daughter of Robert Williams and Anne Pugh of Mynarsh, Denbighshire, North Wales). She was born Nov. 14, 1814. Their children: Richard, d. infant; Mary Hebden, m. James Moroni Thomas; Robert Williams, m. Mary Emeline Eggleston; Ellen Taylor, m. Joseph Argyle; Thomas, d. infant; Dinah, d. child; Hannah Sutcliffe, m. Jesse Franklin Brown; Anne Pugh, m. Alma Duffin Chambers; Elizabeth Smith, d. infant. Family home Ogden, Utah.
High priest. Merchant and tailor. Died May 27, 1888, Ogden, Utah.

HOLT, ROBERT (son of John Holt and Eleanor Newman). Born Dec. 27, 1802, Droadwindsor, Dorsetshire, Eng. Came to Utah Oct. 3, 1863, Daniel D. McArthur company.
Married Mary Ann Toms (daughter of Matthew and Gatherwood Toms), who was born July 15, 1799. Their children: Ellen G., m. Jesse Vincent; Matthew, m. Ann Harrison; Edward David, m. Emma Billings; Francis, m. Elizabeth Baker; William, m. Jane Mabey; Albert, m. Maria Mabey. Family home, Salt Lake City.
Weaver and gardener. Died March 20, 1881, South Jordan, Utah.

HOLT, MATTHEW (son of Robert Holt, born Dec. 27, 1802, and Mary A. Tornes, born 1803, Britport, Eng.). Born Dec. 23, 1828, at Britport. Came to Utah Oct. 3, 1863, Daniel D. McArthur company.
Married Ann Harrison May 9, 1851, Dorchester, Eng. (daughter of Thomas Harrison and Harriet Hann). She was born Aug. 3, 1827, and came to Utah with husband. Their children: Ellen G. b. March 10, 1859, m. Gordon S. Bills Sept. 27, 1875; William M. b. May 7, 1861, m. Anna Hemmingsen Oct. 21, 1904; Rosa Ann b. Aug. 31, 1863, m. Samuel H. Howard Dec. 2, 1891; Arthur J. b. Dec. 10, 1865, m. Catherine Beckstead July 15, 1885; Samuel E. b. Aug. 30, 1868, m. Geneva Beckstead Aug. 16, 1893; Edward H. b. June 1, 1872, m. Edith Holdaway June 26, 1895. Family home South Jordan, Utah.
High priest. Settled on west side of Jordan River. Assisted in building the canals in Salt Lake county. Sunday school superintendent; ward teacher. Farmer.

HOLT, WILLIAM M. (son of Matthew Holt and Ann Harrison). Born May 7, 1861, Britport, Eng.
Married Emma Thatcher at Salt Lake City. She died Sept. 1890.
Married Anna J. Hemmingsen Dec. 21, 1904, Logan, Utah (daughter of Peter and Christina Hemmingsen). She was born Nov. 8, 1879. Their children: Ann b. Dec. 3, 1905; Essie b. May 13, 1907; Arnold W. b. May 2, 1908; Hyrum P. b. June 20, 1909; Ida b. Oct. 30, 1911.
Missionary to southern states 1893-96. High priest. Farmer and stockraiser.

HOLT, SAMUEL E. (son of Matthew Holt and Ann Harrison). Born Aug. 30, 1868, South Jordan, Utah.
Married Margaret G. Beckstead Aug. 16, 1893, at Salt Lake City (daughter of Henry B. Beckstead and Catherine M. Egbert). She was born April 2, 1874, South Jordan, Utah. Their children: Samuel Adelbert b. Feb. 22, 1895; Ivy G. b. Nov. 23, 1896; Oral Ann b. Feb. 9, 1899; Verda C. b. Dec. 21, 1901; Rosamond B. Dec. 15, 1903; Mabel b. Sept. 21, 1905; Byrum Matthew b. Dec. 11, 1907; Reola b. Oct. 6, 1909; Allen Leslie b. Oct. 12, 1912.
Missionary to Missouri 1899 and 1900; first counselor to Bishop Blake eight years. Bishop of South Jordan ward 1911. Farmer and stockraiser.

HOLT, EDWARD DAVID (son of Robert Holt and Mary Ann Toms). Born May 23, 1839, at Broadwindsor, Eng. Came to Utah with his parents.
Married Emma Billings March 10, 1895, Salt Lake City (daughter of William Billings and Emily Chesson, of Norfolk, Eng.), who was born May 8, 1849. Their children: Emma Mary Ann b. May 13, 1866, m. James A. Oliver; Mary Ellen b. June 6, 1867, m. Erastus B. Farmer; Edward David, Jr. b. Aug. 15, 1868, m. Sarah E. Jackson; Annie Jane b. Aug. 26, 1870, m. Byron H. Beckstead; Robert Newman b. Dec. 8, 1871, m. Hannah Wendle; Elizabeth Abigail b. Feb. 27, 1873, m. Milton H. Henderson; William Billings b. Feb. 20, 1874, m. Effie Sellus; Alma Matthew b. Nov. 11, 1875, d. March 6, 1878; Albert John b. Feb. 3, 1878, d. March, 1878; Jesse Henry b. July 10, 1879, m. Eva Porter; Olive Blanche b. Jan. 16, 1884, d. July 16, 1889; Rosa Alberta b. Aug. 14, 1885, d. March 26, 1886; Joseph Hyrum b. Jan. 29, 1887, m. Nancy Knoffell; Victor Chesson b. April 14, 1894.
Family home South Jordan, Utah.
Senior president 93d quorum seventies; ward clerk. Farmer. Died Oct. 24, 1900, Salt Lake City.

HOLT, ALBERT (son of Robert Holt and Mary Ann Toms of Broadwindsor, Dorsetshire, Eng.). Born July 23, 1841, at Broadwindsor. Came to Utah September, 1861, independent company.
Married Maria Mabey October, 1862, Salt Lake City (daughter of Thomas Mabey and Esther Chalker of Loscombe, Dorsetshire, Eng., pioneers Dec. 1, 1862; Ansel P. Harmon company). She was born Dec. 23, 1838. Their children: John, m. Mary Ann Soffe; Albert Francis; Mary Ann; Thomas Mabey, m. Bertha Chipman; Robert Mabey, m. Edna Palmer; Joseph Mabey, m. Delia M. Stocking Nov. 28, 1894; Celestine; Lawrence Ackerman; Samuel; Maria Annie; Mathew Eugene, m. Louie Gardner; Royal Ernest, m. Edith Beckstead; Florence Maria, m. Delos Gardner. Family home South Jordan, Utah.
High priest; missionary to England 1885-86; Sunday school superintendent. School trustee. Contractor; farmer. Died Sept. 29, 1907, at South Jordan, Utah.

HOLT, JOSEPH MABEY (son of Albert Holt and Maria Mabey). Born Jan. 20, 1872, at Salt Lake City.
Married Emma Margaret Stocking Nov. 28, 1894, at Salt Lake City (daughter of Ensign Israel Stocking and Elizabeth Ellen Arnold of South Jordan, Utah, pioneers Sept. 1849). She was born Feb. 5, 1876. Family home South Jordan, Utah.
Member 95th quorum seventies; high priest; member stake high council; missionary to southern states 1899-1901; assistant stake Sunday school superintendent. Member Utah legislature 1909 and 1910; justice of peace; school trustee. Merchant; farmer.

HOLT, JOHN (son of Albert Holt and Marie Mabey).
Married Mary Soffe January, 1878, Salt Lake City (daughter of George L. and Mary N. Soffe of Salt of Salt Lake City and Provo, Utah, pioneers 1851). She was born Jan. 4, 1860. Their children: Virginia, m. D. R. Coombs; Louise; Daisy, m. C. L. King; Claudia; John A.; Mable; Glenn; Leland. Family home, Salt Lake City.
Contractor.

HOLYOAK, GUY (son of Isaac Holyoak and Ann Bird of Worcestershire, Eng.). Born Jan. 17, 1799, in Worcestershire. Came to Utah October, 1854, Dr. Rich company.
Married Sarah Green of Mosely Ware, Green Common, near Birmingham, Eng. (daughter of Daniel Green and Edith Hopkins of that place), who was born July, 1798, and died in 1854, while crossing the plains of Nebraska. Their children: William; Mary, m. John Knowles; George; Ann. d. on plains; Daniel, died; Sarah. m. Joseph James; Henry b. March 5, 1839, m. Sarah A. Robinson; Hannah, m. William LeFevre Dec. 25, 1855. Family home Parowan, Utah. Died 1882, Parowan.

HOLYOAK, HENRY (son of George Holyoak and Sarah Green). Born March 5, 1839, Worcestershire, Eng.
Married Sarah A. Robinson Jan. 29, 1869 (daughter of John R. Robinson, born March 6, 1815, Yorkshire, Eng., and Alice Cupp, died at Council Bluffs; former a pioneer 1852), who was born Dec. 22, 1842, Nauvoo, Ill. Their children: Sarah Ann b. Oct. 27, 1865, died; Alice Jane b. Jan. 25, 1869, m. J. C. Thompson; Henry John b. Oct. 29, 1871, m. Hattie Luetz; Mary Luellen b. Jan. 17, 1873, m. A. J. Young; Eliza Ellen b. April 1, 1875, m. John McConkie; Albert Daniel b. Sept. 1, 1879; Richard James b. March 15, 1882, died. Family resided Parowan and Moab, Utah.

HONE, GEORGE (son of George Hone of Warmington, Eng.). Born March 10, 1810, at Warmington. Came to Utah May 30, 1866, Daniel Thomson company.
Married Mary Boss (daughter of William Hoseman and Mary Boss), who was born Aug. 7, 1813—pioneer 1866, Daniel Thomson company. Their children: Sarah A., m. William Chitham; David b. July 3, 1837; Sarah Adams; George b. Jan. 24, 1840, m. Jane Mills; Emma, m. George Evans; Caleb, m. Alice Taylor; Mary Jane b. Sept. 18, 1847, m. Thomas Herbert; Joshua b. May 30, 1851, m. Susan Losser; Henry b. April 16, 1856, m. Rebecca Mills. Family resided Provo and Benjamin, Utah.

HONE, HENRY (son of George Hone and Mary Boss). Born April 30, 1856, Fonsil, near Coventry, Eng.
Married Rebecca Mills (daughter of Thomas Mills and Ann Clegg; former came to Utah in 1874, Capt. Birch company, the latter died in England). She was born July 3, 1866, Bedford, Lancaster, Eng. Their children: Henrietta b. Sept. 3, 1876, m. George William June 29, 1898; Charley H. b. June 28, 1878, m. Alena Ludlow; Mabel Florence b. June 21, 1880, m. Jessie Ludlow; Edward b. Dec. 23, 1882; Edith b. May 16, 1885; Lucy b. June 2, 1887; Arthur b. June 9, 1889, m. Ida Tietjen Jan. 1, 1909; Pearl b. Jan. 15, 1892; Norman F. b. Dec. 11, 1894; Wilford W. b. March 1, 1897; Arlyin b. May 10, 1903. Family home Benjamin, Utah.
Judge of election in Benjamin.

HOOTON, JOSEPH RAYNER (son of Peter Hooton and Catherine Beswick, born 1827, Bolton, Eng. Came to Utah 1858, Smith and Amies company). Born May 21, 1851, Philadelphia, Pa. Came to Utah with parents.
Married Mary Jane Parkingson Oct. 11, 1875 (daughter of Thomas Parkinson and Mary A. M. Bryant; former came to Utah with Captain Limans company). She was born Oct. 15, 1856, San Bernardino, Cal. Family home Beaver, Utah.
Married Lucy A. Jensen May 17, 1882, St. George, Utah (daughter of Jens L. Jensen and Ingra Pearson, who were married in Salt Lake City). She was born in 1865, at Mt. Pleasant, Utah. Their children: Joseph R. b. April 4, 1883, m. Elmora Nielson Dec. 13, 1909; Ephraim Levan b. May 24, 1888, m. Ednia Bates June 19, 1911; James Earl b. Oct. 29, 1895; Walter Ambrose b. Aug. 16, 1898.
Sunday school superintendent 1893-1907. Postmaster 12 years; precinct justice of the peace 10 years; road supervisor in Sevier county for 25 years. Lumberman.

HOOVER, JOHN WHITMER (son of Abraham Hoover and Mary E. Adair of Bridgeport, Pa.). Born Nov. 13, 1834. Came to Utah 1851, Captain Horner company.
Married Mary Elizabeth Coursa Dec. 23, 1855, at Salt Lake City (daughter of John Coursa and Mary Moore; former died near Nauvoo, Ill.). She was born Sept. 30, 1839, came to Utah Sept., 1849, Howard Egan company. Their children: John Whitmer, m. Margret Naomi Park; Mary, m. James Snyder; Agnes. m. Louis Meacham; William, m. Sarah Cook; Upton James, m. Barbara Loveless; Joseph, Diantha, both died; Florence, m. George Swan; Webster, m. Ruby Holdaway; Elsie; Frank, m. Eugene Noyae; Mertice, m. John Russell. Family home Provo, Utah.
Miller. Died May 29, 1902, at Provo, Utah.

HOOVER, JOHN WHITMER (son of John Whitmer Hoover and Mary Elizabeth Coursa). Born Dec. 2, 1857, at Springville, Utah.
Married Margret Naomi Park Jan. 8, 1880, at Salt Lake City (daughter of John Park and Louisa Smith of Provo, Utah, pioneers Oct. 1847, Edward Hunter company). She was born May 13, 1858. Their children: John Whitmer III b. Oct. 25, 1880, m. Emma Brown; Albert Andrew b. Nov. 22, 1883, m. Hazel Emily Carter; Margaret Floss b. Nov. 17, 1886, m. Don R. Davis; William Ralph b. July 5, 1890; Joseph Roy b. July 6, 1890, died; Ferris Webster b. June 26, 1892; Glen Park b. Aug. 23, 1894, m. Jean Arvill b. May 8, 1898; Reed Park b. Dec. 22, 1900; Mary Louisa b. Aug. 12, 1905. Family home Provo, Utah.
Elder. City councilman of Provo. Miller.

HORMAN, CHARLES (son of Charles Horman, born 1800, and Mary Gallichan, born about 1802, on Isle of Jersey). He was born March 3, 1825, Isle of Jersey. Came to Utah Sept. 15, 1868, John Gillespie company.
Married Margaret De La Haye, widow of William Powell (daughter of Francis De La Haye and Nancy Le Marchant, the latter a pioneer of Sept. 15, 1868, John Gillespie company). She was born Feb. 16, 1828, and came to Utah with husband. Their children: Charles D. b. June 18, 1854;

942 PIONEERS AND PROMINENT MEN OF UTAH

Francis D. b. Oct. 6, 1855, m. Thecla Lindholm Nov. 17, 1886; Mary D. b. July 18, 1859, m. Arnald Cooner; Edmund D. b. Dec. 25, 1860, m. Martha Smith; George D. b. July 31, 1863, m. Floranda Vowles; Ann D. b. Oct. 3, 1866, m. Ed. Green; William D. b. May 26, 1870, died; Thomas D. b. Nov. 7, 1871, m. Sarah Ann Vowles May 11, 1891.
Dentist; shoemaker; farmer.

HORMAN, FRANCIS D. (son of Charles Horman and Margaret De La Haye). Born Oct. 6, 1855, Iona, Idaho.
Married Thecla Lindholm Nov. 17, 1886, Logan, Utah (daughter of Carl Eric and Johanna Lindholm), who was born Jan. 29, 1868, Tooele City, Utah. Their children: Francis L. b. Nov. 19, 1887; Clara L. b. March 31, 1889, m. Joseph C. Moss Dec. 18, 1907; Albert L. b. Aug. 26, 1891; Lulu L. b. Feb. 25, 1893; Maud L. b. Nov. 1, 1895; Ross L. b. April 18, 1898; Charles L. b. April 13, 1900; Johanna L. b. May 6, 1901; Martha L. b. Nov. 19, 1903; Phyllis L. b. May 8, 1906; Merrill L. b. June 10, 1908; Leroy L. b. March 12, 1912.
Manager of Iona Coal & Lumber Yard, Iona, Idaho. Justice of the peace of Iona precinct.

HORNE, JOSEPH (son of Joseph Horne and Maria Maidens of London, Eng. Settled near Toronto, Canada, 1818). He was born Jan. 17, 1812, London. Came to Utah Oct. 5, 1847, captain of fifty in Edward Hunter company.
Married Mary Isabella Hales May 9, 1836 (daughter of Stephen Hales of England), who was born Nov. 20, 1818, Rainham, Eng., and came to Utah with husband. Their children: Mary Ann b. Jan. 22, 1837, and Robert (twin of Mary Ann) both died infants; Henry James b. July 24, 1838, m. Mary Ann Crismon July 24, 1860; William Joseph b. 1840, d. infant; Joseph Smith b. May 14, 1842, m. Lydia Ann Weiler Nov. 7, 1868; Richard Stephen b. July 9, 1844, m. Lizzie Price 1868; Elizabeth Ann b. June 3, 1846, m. Edward M. Webb; Leonora Taylor b. Jan. 16, 1849, m. George B. Spencer; Julia Maria b. Aug. 12, 1851, m. William S. Burton; Mary Isabella b. Nov. 9, 1853, died; John Parley (twin of Mary Isabella), m. Sonhronia Spencer; Permelia Eliza b. Dec. 9, 1855, m. David W. James; Cornelia Harriet (twin of Permelia Eliza), m. James L. Clayton; Martha Jane b. Oct. 15, 1857, m. Joseph S. Tingey; Clara Ella b. April 5, 1861, m. Henry C. James. Family resided Farr West, Mo., Nauvoo, Ill. and Salt Lake City.
Married Mary Shepard Nov. 30, 1855, Salt Lake City. Their children: Annie Elizabeth b. Jan. 1, 1857, d. infant; William Joseph b. Jan. 1, 1859, m. Lorilla Little; Edward b. July 25, 1862, d. infant; George Henry b. Nov. 5, 1864, m. Alice Merrill; Emma Eliza b. Nov. 9, 1866, d. infant; Thomas Richard b. July 5, 1868, m. Etta Murphy; Fred Andrew b. Dec. 29, 1870, d. infant; Albert Shepard b. Nov. 25, 1872, m. Alice Saunders; Margaret Nettle b. June 12, 1875, m. Alexander Pyper; Lillian Mary b. May 12, 1880, m. Mr. Woolley.
Was in the troubles in Missouri and Nauvoo, Ill. Left Nauvoo February, 1846, captain of 50 crossing the plains. Aided in exploring San Pete, Sevier, Piute and Iron counties; built the first log cabin in Parowan. School trustee. bishop's counselor; Sunday school superintendent; high priest; high counselor patriarch. Justice of peace; city councilman and city watermaster. Captain of immigrant trains in 1862 and 1863. Superintended labor on temple block 1854-58. Spring of 1858, went in charge of a company of men to make cotton farms on Rio Virgen River. Died April 27, 1897.

HORNE, JOSEPH SMITH (son of Joseph Horne and Mary Isabella Hales). Born May 14, 1842, Nauvoo, Ill.
Married Lydia Ann Weiler Nov. 7, 1868, Salt Lake City (daughter of Jacob Weiler and Annie Maria Malin), who was born Sept. 20, 1844, Nauvoo, Ill. Their children: Annie Maria b. Oct. 13, 1869, m. Marquis L. Bean Nov. 12, 1890; Joseph Leo b. Sept. 10, 1871, m. Flora D. Bean; Lydia Isabella b. Aug. 22, 1875, m. Thomas Yates; Jacob Weiler b. Aug. 15, 1878, d. Feb. 13, 1895. Family resided Gunnison and Richfield, Utah.
Settled at Salt Lake City 1847; moved to Gunnison 1868, to Richfield 1873. Ordained a teacher 1858; elder 1860; seventy 1864; high priest and bishop August, 1878; missionary to Switzerland 1865-68 and again in 1876, where he presided over the Swiss and German mission; was called to take charge of Gunnison ward 1868, and presided there eight years; bishop Richfield second ward 1878, 15 years; Sunday school superintendent; stake tithing clerk; counselor to William H. Seegmiller, president of Sevier stake, 1894, for 16 years; patriarch. County superintendent of schools; city councilman; mayor. First to establish undertaking business in Sevier county.

HORROCKS, EDWARD (son of John Horrocks and Alice Hulme of Bolton, Lancashire, Eng.). Born 1806 at Bolton. Came to Utah Sept. 12, 1857, Jesse B. Martin company.
Married Alice Houghton (daughter of Samuel Houghton, born Jan. 13, 1779, Ashton, Eng., and Betty Eaton, born Aug. 2, 1780, died July 5, 1860, in England). She was born 1803 at Ashton, and died 1856 at Macclesfield, Eng. Their children: Elizabeth b. Aug. 5, 1826, m. Aaron Jackson and Mr. Kingsford; Martha b. Nov. 9, 1828, m. Joseph Harrop; John b. Feb. 1831, and Sarah, died; Samuel b. July 7, 1834, m. Catherine Sarah Buckingham; Mary b. Sept. 11, 1836, m. Nathaniel Leavitt April 4, 1857; Alice b. March 3, 1841, m. Charles Wood; Edward b. May 4, 1843, died; Annie b. May 4, 1845; Aaron b. Dec. 3, 1872, m. Theresa Carter

March 27, 1890; Mabel b. May 25, 1876, m. E. S. Rolapp Oct. 19, 1894; Richard James b. Aug. 11, 1880, m. Gertrude Tackett April 22, 1908. Family home Ogden, Utah.
Located at Ogden, where he engaged in the mercantile business, establishing the firm now known as Horrocks Bros.

HORROCKS, EDWARD G. (son of John Horrocks and Mary Gregory of Macclesfield, Chestershire county, Eng.). Born 1842 in England. Came to Utah 1856.
Married Ida M. Johnson June 1873 at Salt Lake City (daughter of Charles Johnson and Mary Peterson of Sweden. Came to Utah 1870). She was born Aug. 15, 1856. Their children: Ida, and Augusta, died; Mary, m. William A. Lewis; Minnie, m. Harvey P. Randall; Effie, m. Charles R. McGregor. Family home, Ogden, Utah.
Elder. Died May 14, 1886.

HORROCKS, SAMUEL (son of Edward Horrocks and Alice Houghton). Born July 7, 1834, Macclesfield, Cheshire, Eng. Came to Utah Oct. 24, 1854, William A. Empey company.
Married Catherine Sarah Buckingham Jan. 23, 1853, Presbury, Eng. (daughter of William Henry Buckingham and Jane Ann Abbott), who was born Nov. 19, 1834, London, Eng., and came to Utah with husband. Their children: Samuel b. Oct. 10, 1854, d. March 18, 1855; Elizabeth Ann b. Jan. 9, 1856, m. Joseph Baxter Feb. 9, 1874; Jane b. March 25, 1858, m. James E. Davis Aug. 16, 1876; Catherine b. March 22, 1860, d. April 10, 1860; William Henry b. Aug. 22, 1861, d. Oct. 4, 1861; Mary b. July 2, 1862, d. same day; Martha b. June 13, 1863, m. H. H. Rolapp Dec. 9, 1885; Alice b. Feb. 25, 1866, d. same day; Edward J. b. Feb. 14, 1867, m. Adaline Dana Aug. 15, 1888; Maria b. April 24, 1870, d. Sept. 7, 1870; Joseph Aaron b. Dec. 3, 1872, m. Theressa Carter March 27, 1890; Mabel b. May 25, 1876, m. E. S. Rolapp Oct. 19, 1894; Richard James b. Aug. 11, 1880, m. Gertrude Tackett April 22, 1908.
Located at Ogden where he engaged in the mercantile business, establishing the firm now known as Horrocks Bros.

HORSLEY, HARRY (son of John Horsley and Susan Clements of Soham, Cambridgeshire, Eng.). Born Oct. 24, 1857, in London. Came to Utah Sept. 13, 1861.
Married Lois M. Hook Sept. 2, 1865 (daughter of Richard Hook and Alice Saunders, pioneers 1860, handcart company). She was born Sept. 6, 1848, and came to Utah with parents. Their children: Lois M. b. July 7, 1866; Henry D. b. Jan. 9, 1868; Harriet E. b. Aug. 29, 1869, m. Eugene Lambourne 1893; Louis W. b. Nov. 11, 1871; Alice R. b. April 27, 1873, m. Edward Rushten 1900; Lilles P. b. Oct. 24, 1874, m. Stephen Reed; Clements H. b. Aug. 10, 1876, m. Florence Anderson 1904; Joseph H. b. April 11, 1878; Susan M. b. Aug. 22, 1879, m. Joseph Van Steeter; Permelia M. b. June 6, 1881; Annie M. b. May 24, 1883, m. Richard Fletcher 1903; Gertrude b. Sept. 10, 1885; Eugene Ray b. Jan. 6, 1890; Ralph b. Dec. 28, 1892. Family home, Salt Lake City.
Married Margaret L. Foreman July 16, 1907, Salt Lake City (daughter of Joseph Foreman and Margaret Jane Mousley, married 1845 at Centerville, Newcastle county, Del., pioneers of Sept. 1857, Captain Hoffines oxteam company). She was born July 14, 1857, at Prairie Creek, Neb., and came to Utah with parents.
Went to St. George 1867 to help settle country. Missionary to England 1900. Worked at Salt Lake theatre 16 years; motorman and conductor for Utah Light Company since Oct. 11, 1889.

HORSLEY, HERBERT (son of Thomas Horsley, born May 5, 1816, at Alcester, Eng., and Ann Maiden, born June 6, 1818, at Birmingham, Eng.). He was born Sept. 6, 1845, Alcester. Came to Utah Nov. 1862, Henry W. Miller company.
Married Sarah Edghill Jan. 1864 (daughter of Thomas and Harriott Edghill, the latter a pioneer in 1863, John W. Wooley company). She was born July 23, 1845. Their children: Thomas H. b. Feb. 22, 1865, m. Louisa Lay; James M. b. Feb. 6, 1866, m. Matilda Jensen; Harriett b. Sept. 22, 1867, m. John Montrose; Elizabeth b. Feb. 19, 1869, m. Hugh Dorrien; Sarah Ann b. June 12, 1870, m. D. H. Rowley; Sodine b. March 13, 1872, m. Jessie Moore; Laura b. Sept. 17, 1873, m. W. G. Carr; George b. Jan. 18, 1875; Willard b. Oct. 9, 1876; Harry b. June 30, 1878, m. Ella Jensen; Sophia b. Jan. 4, 1880, m. J. J. Hayes; Alice b. July 9, 1882, m. Brig. Skinner.
Married Lucy Smith Skinner Jan. 1, 1899, at Soda Springs, Idaho (daughter of William Smith and Mary Mole, the former a pioneer with Captain Seeley company). She was born Aug. 18, 1857, at Bristol, Eng. Their child: Mabel Lucy b. March 20, 1901.
Seventy; missionary to Great Britain 1896-97, and also in 1905. Justice of the peace and notary public.

HORSLEY, JOHN P. (son of Robert Horsley and Mary Ann Pickett of Rochester, Eng.). Born Feb. 15, 1844, coming to Utah with the first oxteam company.
Married Frances Jane Mills March 3, 1864, at St. George and later Endowment House, Salt Lake City, Utah (daughter of Thomas Mills, who lived at Bogner, Sussex county, Eng., until they came to Utah about 1850). She was born July 1, 1845. Their children: Eliza Ann b. Feb. 24, 1865, m.

PIONEERS AND PROMINENT MEN OF UTAH

Henry G. Mills; Mary Ann b. July 1, 1867, m. John Joseph Rhodes; Lottie, d. child; John P. b. July 26, m. Hannah Jenson; Rosetta b. Oct. 21, m. Thomas H. Jones; Caroline, died; Agnes L. b. Sept. 12, m. James Bearnsen; Robert Thomas, died; Frances Jane b. Feb. 5, 1883, m. Walker Shellenberger; Samuel Ensign, died; Jemima, m. David Harris. Family home Ferron, Utah.
Elder; home missionary. Called by Brigham Young three times to haul supplies for the people. Mason; farmer and stockraiser. Now living at Preston, White Pine county, Nev.

HORTON, EDMUND. Came to Utah 1860, oxteam company.
Married Maria ———. Their children: John; Harriet; Ann, m. Charles Machaw; Esther, m. John Morehouse; Jane, m. George Edward Bench, Sr.; Eliza, m. William Henry Stevens; Elijah, m. Christie Frazier. Family home Wanship, Utah.
Farmer and stockraiser. Died at Wanship, Utah.

HOUGAARD, RASMUS H. Came to Utah, 1848. Oxteam company.
Married Mary Magdaline, in Denmark. Their children: Peter, m. Mary Steffisen; Kirstine; Johanna Maria, m. William B. Richey; John H., m. Petrea Petersen; Mary, m. Jens Madsen; Louis H., m. Jeredine Hougaard; Annie, m. Robert Johnson. Family home Manti, Utah.
Member 48th quorum seventies. Farmer. Died at Manti, Utah.

HOUSLEY, GEORGE F. (son of Charles Housley and Harriet Cook of Sutton Ashfield, Nottinghamshire, Eng.). Born 1836 at Sutton Ashfield. Came to Utah 1856, Martin and Tyler handcart company.
Married Myra Jacobinson at Salt Lake City, who was born 1844, and came to Utah with independent company. Their children: Harriet b. Nov. 28, 1860, m. Robert Wilson; Charlotte b. April 1, 1863, m. John C. Jackson; George J. b. March 29, 1865, m. Ida Obrey; Lewis b. Nov. 28, 1866, m. Mona Singleton; Benjamin b. March 28, 1871, m. Paulina Allen; Julia b. March 1, 1873, m. James Farley; Elizabeth b. Sept. 16, 1875, m. George Crapo; Nellie b. Feb. 16, 1876, m. Andrew Hanson; Emma b. Aug. 15, 1878, m. Dennis McNulty; Carrie b. Sept. 24, 1883, m. James Squires.
Married Mary Ann Buckley 1896, Logan, Utah (daughter of Edmund Buckley and Alice Grun, married 1859, Manchester, Eng.; former a pioneer, Joseph W. Young company). She was born 1860 in Manchester, Eng. Their children: George Jezu; Florence; Vilate.
Brought to Utah the paper that the first Deseret News was printed on. Made two return trips to bring immigrants to Utah. Indian scout and war veteran. Miller.

HOUSTON, ISAAC (son of Samuel Houston and Phoebe Mayo). Born Oct. 15, 1799, in New Hampshire. Came to Utah 1850.
Married Theodocia Keys July 19, 1827, who was born Sept. 27, 1804. Their children: Jane Mariah, m. Mr. Alexander; Louisa and Silson C., died; Emiline, m. James W. Preston; Minderell, m. Washburn Chipman; Alma, died; Isaac. Family home Alpine, Utah.
Died Aug. 23, 1856, at Alpine.

HOUSTON, JAMES (son of John Houston and Mary Demster of Paisley, Scotland). Born June 1, 1817. Came to Utah 1848.
Married Margaret Crawford August 1845 (daughter of James Crawford and Elizabeth Brown, former a pioneer Lorenzo Snow company). She was born March 1, 1825, and came to Utah with husband. Their children: Elizabeth b. June 1, 1846, m. Albert Delong; John b. April 13, 1848; James b. Feb. 6, 1850, m. Rebecca Lucy Cooper Nov. 18, 1875; m. Sarah Ann LeFevre April 22, 1881; Joseph b. Dec. 21, 1851, m. Elizabeth Clark Dec. 28, 1874; Thomas b. Sept. 6, 1853, m. Christena R. Schow May 2, 1880; Margaret b. Dec. 1, 1855, m. R. G. Clark Dec. 28, 1874; Mary Demster b. June, 1858; m. Ira W. Thatch; Hyrum b. Sept. 9, 1860; Brigham b. Aug. 7, 1863. Family home, Salt Lake City until Oct. 1861; then St. George until April 1873, and Panguitch since.
Counselor to bishop first ward Salt Lake City. Died Jan. 3, 1863, St. George, Utah.

HOUSTON, JAMES (son of James Houston and Margaret Crawford). Born Feb. 6, 1850, Salt Lake City.
Married Rebecca Lucy Cooper Nov. 18, 1875, Washington, Utah (daughter of Wm. D. Cooper and Lydia Rochester), who was born Jan. 10, 1855, in Georgia. Their children: John Cooper b. Aug. 24, 1876, m. Addie Asay; James William b. July 22, 1878.
Married Sarah Ann LeFevre April 22, 1881 (daughter of William LeFevre and Hannah Holyoak; former pioneer Sept. 17, 1852, Captain Wood's 6th company; latter Oct. 2, 1854; Dr. Rich company). She was born Sept. 20, 1860. Their children: Alonzo b. May 25, 1882; Lorin b. Nov. 14, 1887; William Wallace b. Nov. 17, 1889; Lucy Edna b. March 18, 1892; James Marion b. Dec. 18, 1893; Ozro b. July 4, 1896; Hannay Aza b. Aug. 27, 1898; David Crawford b. April 5, 1901. Family home Panguitch, Utah.

High councilor in Panguitch stake 1878; missionary to Arizona, New Mexico, and Colorado 1880; missionary to Central States 1884-1885; counselor to Bishop Allen Miller, and to president David Cameron of Panguitch stake 1900-08; became president Panguitch stake Aug. 1, 1908. County selectman Iron and Garfield counties; commissioner Garfield county.

HOUTZ, CHRISTIAN (son of Christian Houtz). Born July 16, 1805, near Philadelphia, Pa. Came to Utah Sept. 22, 1848, Lorenzo Snow company.
Married Susan Pawling at Philadelphia, Pa., who was born June 19, 1811. Their children: John S., m. Eleanor Palmer; Elleanor, m. Lorenzo Snow; Henry, m. ——— Ensign; Philip, m. Sarah J. Hall; Watson, m. Sophia Bohny; Levina, died; Heber, killed by Indians; Lorenzo, died. Family home Salt Lake City.
High priest. Farmer. Died 1852, Salt Lake City.

HOUTZ, J. S. (son of Christian Houtz and Susan Pawling). Born 1833, in Pennsylvania. Came to Utah with father.

HOUTZ, PHILIP (son of Christian Houtz and Susan Pawling). Born Sept. 13, 1838, Harrison county, Pa. Came to Utah with parents.
Married Sarah Jane Hall May 1, 1856, Springville, Utah (daughter of Edward Hall and Nancy Elleanor Ballinger of Jamestown, Ky., pioneers Sept. 2, 1850, David Evans company). She was born Oct. 12, 1846. Their children: Philip E. b. Sept. 23, 1865, m. Elva J. Clyde; Christian W. b. April 1, 1867, m. Esther Waters; Sarah Rozina b. June 11, 1869, m. Alfred Whitehead; John T. b. March 16, 1871, died; Nancy E. b. March 16, 1871, died; Lettie May b. Dec. 23, 1872, m. John T. Beardall; Susan Inzie b. March 18, 1875, m. George Russon; Mary Catherine b. July 18, 1877, m. Zuince King; Heber Hall b. Oct. 28, 1879; Esther b. March 12, 1881, died; Pearl b. April 16, 1884, m. James Coombs; James Elvan b. Oct. 13, 1887, m. May Metcalf. Family home Springville, Utah.
Member 51st quorum seventies; high priest. Farmer.

HOUTZ, PHILIP EDWARD (son of Philip Houtz and Sarah Jane Hall). Born Sept. 23, 1865, Springville, Utah.
Married Elva Jane Clyde Aug. 28, 1889, at Manti, Utah (daughter of William M. Clyde and Eliza McDonald of Springville). She was born April 11, 1868. Their children: Vida b. July 10, 1891, m. G. Dell Wood; Clyde Ervine b. Feb. 16, 1893, died; Verian b. Jan. 11, 1896, died; Glenden E. b. Sept. 5, 1897; Karl G. b. Feb. 25, 1902; Ray C. b. Jan. 21, 1907. Family home, Springville.
Member 51st quorum seventies. County recorder; city recorder. Accountant.

HOUTZ, DANIEL D. (son of Jacob Houtz and Bridget Daly). Born March 11, 1859, at Salt Lake City.
Married Edna Lyman June 23, 1886, Logan, Utah (daughter of Francis M. Lyman and Rhoda Ann Taylor of San Bernardino, Cal.). She was born Sept. 8, 1866. Their children: Martell b. March 25, 1887; Zula b. June 28, 1888, m. Joseph W. Bishop; Ithoda b. July 29, 1890; Elwood b. May 24, 1892; Edith b. April 12, 1894; Virginia b. July 23, 1901; Maxime b. March 6, 1903. Family home, Salt Lake City. Seventy. Prosecuting attorney Tooele county; district attorney of 3d district two terms. Lawyer.

HOVEY, JOSEPH GRAFTON (son of Thomas Hovey, born Aug. 8, 1766, at Roxbury, Mass., and E'izabeth Sever born Jan. 31, 1770, at Brighton, Mass.). Born Nov. 17, 1812, at Middlesex county, Mass. Came to Utah Sept. 26, 1848, Brigham Young and Heber C. Kimball companies.
Married Martha Ann Webster (daughter of Josiah and Hannah Webster), who was born in 1816. Their children: Elizabeth W. b. May 11, 1835; Martha J. b. May 11, 1837; Grafton W. b. Jan. 11, 1838; Joseph G. b. June 8, 1839, m. Mary Ann Hulse, 1865; Thomas J. b. Dec. 17, 1842; George W. b. June 14, 1844; Hannah A. b. July 17, 1845.
Married Sarah Baley Dec. 23, 1847, at Winter Quarters, Iowa, who was born at Lowell, Mass. Their child: Sarah E. b. Oct. 18, 1850, m. Luge Oviatt.
Married Sarah L. Goodridge Nov. 28, 1850 (daughter of Benjamin Goodridge and Penelope Gardner, pioneers of 1850, Wilford Woodruff company). She was born in 1832. Came to Utah with her parents in 1850. Their child: Orson G. b. Sept. 28, 1851.
Married Lusannah E. Goodridge Jan. 14, 1852, Salt Lake City (daughter of Benjamin Goodridge and Penelope Gardner, pioneers 1850, Wilford Woodruff company). She was born March 24, 1834, at Luxenberg, Mass. Their children: Penelope L. b. April 29, 1853, m. Samuel Clark; James A. b. June 13, 1855, m. Esther M. Pitkin 1879; Olive A. b. Aug. 24, 1857; Willard Reve; Mary L. b. July 18, 1859, m. Charles J. Lambert; Martha C. b. Sept. 10, 1861, m. Richard Lambert; Esther A. b. Feb. 22, 1863; George B. b. May 16, 1866; Grafton F. b. Sept. 7, 1869.
Missionary to southern Utah in the early fifties; counselor to Bishop Raleigh of the 19th ward, Salt Lake City, several years; arrived in Cache valley April 25, 1860, where he served as bishop of Millville, Cache county, Utah. Stone cutter on Salt Lake temple.

HOVEY, JAMES A. (son of Joseph Grafton Hovey and Lusannah E. Goodridge). Born June 13, 1855, Salt Lake City.
Married Esther M. Pitkin April 10, 1879, at Salt Lake City (daughter of George O. Pitkin and Mariah L. Wood,

pioneers 1848, Heber C. Kimball company). She was born Aug. 28, 1861, Millville, Utah. Their children: Maria L. b. Sept 24, 1880, m. Guy H. Hill Jr. Nov. 16, 1904; James Archie b. July 25, 1882, m. Josephine Cox June, 1907; George Orin b. Oct. 25, 1883; Rex b. Oct. 22, 1888; Angus Ray b. April 5, 1885, m. Hazel Garr Dec. 20, 1907; Merlin R. b. Sept. 21, 1886, m. Lauretta Johnson, 1907; Sidney G. b. March 29, 1891; Izene b. Oct. 10, 1892; Leslie Wilford b. Nov. 6, 1859.
Served as ward clerk from 1902 to 1912. School trustee 15 years; on town board two years; justice of the peace from 1906 to present time.

HJORTH, PETER H. (son of Niels Peter Hjorth and Dorthea Larson). Born Jan. 23, 1843, Copenhagen, Denmark. Came to Utah Sept. 22, 1861.
Married Anna Jensen Dec. 7, 1868 (daughter of Jens Jensen and Elsa Neilson, pioneers Sept. 29, 1866, Peter Nebeker company). She was born Aug. 15, 1853. Their children: Joan Vilate b. Dec. 12, 1869, m. ²Israel Barlow Sept. 21, 1892; Hannah Augusta b. April 2, 1872, d. Feb. 9, 1879. Family home Millville, Cache Co., Utah.
Ward teacher; assisted bringing immigrants from Missouri. Died March 17, 1872.

HOWARD, JOHN RICHARDS (son of Richard Howard, born at Gosport, Hampshire, Eng., and Martha Richards, born at Landport, Portsea, Hampshire; former drowned Feb. 26, 1852, in wreck of H. M. S. S. "Birkenhead," which sank off Cape of Good Hope). He was born Sept. 13, 1841, Fareham, Hampshire. Came to Utah Sept. 1864, Arthur Brown company.
Married Harriet Spinks Brooks 1866, Salt Lake City (daughter of Robert Brooks and Maria Stanly of Morley, Norfolk, Eng.). She was born Dec. 4, 1843, Morley; died Sept. 10, 1883. Their children: Richard Fitz Alan, d. July 6, 1884; John Fitz Alan, m. Drucilla Sears; Mary Fitz Alan and Martha Fitz Alan, infants; Alice Fitz Alan, m. Dan McIntosh; Josephine Mowbray, m. Albert C. Mathleson; Marguerite Mowbray, m. Hyrum Jensen. Family home, Salt Lake City.
Married Sarah Herwin (Manning) 1873, Salt Lake City, who was born Feb. 1829, died Dec. 25, 1912, Salt Lake City. Only child: Franklin Fitz Alan, d. infant.
Married Mary Browne Aug. 24, 1884, Salt Lake City (daughter of William Wesley Browne and Eliza Wolley of Derby, Eng.). She was born June 25, 1863, Derby, died June 26, 1913. Their children: Vere d'Albini b. Dec. 25, 1885, m. Ray Wagstaff; William d'Albini b. Nov. 26, 1887, m. Elizabeth Jones; Ernest Maltravers b. Feb. 12, 1890; Llewellyn D'Bresse b. Nov. 30, 1893, died; Elizabeth Marie Stuart b. Oct. 13, 1897; Amy Vengham b. Jan. 8, 1901; Ann Olding b. July 2, 1903. Family home Sandy, Utah.
Member 93d quorum seventies; missionary from Cape of Good Hope to England 1863-64; and from Utah to England 1880-82; block teacher; tithing clerk. Was the first to start public bathing; this was at Lake Side, on Judge Haight's property at Farmington, in 1870. Brought the first mowing machines to Utah 1864. Shipping clerk for Z. C. M. I. 10 years. Survivor of H. M. S. S. "Birkenhead," which sank off Cape of Good Hope Feb. 26, 1852, 462 lives lost. Manufacturer.

HOWARD, JOSEPH (son of William Howard of Kings Norton, Eng., born 1789, in Worcestershire, Eng., and Tamar Mills of Dickensheath, born 1789, in Worcestershire). He was born Nov. 12, 1819, Warwickshire, Eng. Came to Utah Oct. 28, 1864, William Hyde company.
Married Ann Shelton 1842, Birmingham, Eng. (daughter of Joseph Shelton of Birmingham, who was born 1816, and died on way to Utah. Their children: Thomas b. Sept. 14, 1843, m. Mary Lowe Dec. 25, 1864; William b. Nov. 2, 1844, m. Betsey J. Fackrell; James b. Jan. 29, 1846, m. Juliet Fackrell April 19, 1869; Joseph b. May 11, 1849, m. Jane Kenney, m. Mary Ann Perkins; Mary Ann b. March 21, 1851, m. Adam Tolman; Emma b. July 31, 1852, m. William Corbridge; John b. March 12, 1854, m. Josephine Johnson. m. Sarah Downs; Samuel S. b. June 3, 1856, m. Sarah Ann Taylor; Elizabeth b. July 20, 1859, m. John Dean; Matilda b. July 20, 1859, d. aged 5; Tamar b. June 13, 1861, d. child. Family home Bountiful, Utah.
President Hokley branch at Birmingham, Eng., six years, and of Ashted branch five years; high priest; Sunday school superintendent at West Bountiful; ward teacher. Farmer and gardener. Died Oct. 17, 1896, Bountiful, Utah.

HOWARD, THOMAS (son of Joseph Howard and Ann Shelton). Born Sept. 14, 1843, Birmingham, Eng. Came to Utah Oct. 7, 1861.
Married Mary Lowe Dec. 25, 1864, Bountiful, Utah. Wilford Woodruff officiating (daughter of Richard Lowe and Sarah Dudley of Staffordshire, Eng.; they came to Utah 1874). She was born Nov. 30, 1837. Their children: Thomas J. b. Dec. 15, 1866, m. Hattie Pack; William J. b. March 23, 1867, m. Rose Oliver; Charles J. b. March 5, 1869, m. Eva C. Larson; Sarah b. Feb. 3, 1871, m. Wilford Tuttle Jan. 23, 1889; Mary L b. April 6, 1875, m. John Ellis; Richard E. b. Aug. 26, 1877, m. Catherine Lukar. Family home Bountiful, Utah.
Member 70th quorum seventies; high priest, and president of same at Bountiful; Sunday school superintendent; ward teacher; presiding teacher. Farmer and gardener.

HOWARD JAMES (son of Joseph Howard and Ann Shelton). Born Jan. 29, 1846, Birmingham, Eng.
Married Juliet Fackrell April 19, 1869, at Salt Lake City (daughter of Joseph Fackrell and Clarrisa Dempsey), who was born Jan. 19, 1849. Their children: Juliet b. Feb. 18, 1870, m. George C. Wood Jan. 6, 1886; William b. Dec. 15, 1871, d. Feb. 19, 1874; Joseph b. Oct. 28, 1873, d. Sept. 9, 1893; Matilda Ann b. Nov. 29, 1874, m. John Johnson March 9, 1893; Lucy Jane b. Sept. 23, 1876, m. Richard Purcell June 29, 1898; James Henry b. Feb. 25, 1880, m. Effie Rose Sept. 22, 1898; Clara Shelton b. March 18, 1882, m. G. Q. Hatch Dec. 18, 1901; Maud Tamar b. Jan. 12, 1884, m. Eugene Ludwig June 17, 1903; Rachel Mary b. Aug. 9, 1885, m. Joseph E. Davis April 17, 1907; Owen Isom b. June 8, 1888, d. Sept. 3, 1889; Luella b. March 25, 1891, m. D. F. Davis, Jr., June 22, 1911; Leona b. Jan. 21, 1894, m. Emer S. Arbuckle Jan. 29, 1913. Family home Bountiful, Utah.

HOWARD, SAMUEL L. (son of Samuel Lane Howard and Betsey Park of St. Louis, Mo.). Born Oct. 16, 1840, Bedfordshire, Eng. Came to Utah Sept. 20, 1856, Helm family handcart company.
Married Sarah Jane Hamilton April 1, 1864, at Salt Lake City (daughter of James Lang Hamilton and Mary Ann Campbell of Goodridge, Canada, pioneers Oct. 6, 1852, John Wimmer company). She was born June 11, 1842. Their children: Mary Ann, m. S. H. Beckstar; Samuel H., m. Rosa A. Holt; Sarah L., m. J. S. H. Bodell; Elizabeth V. and John W., died; Robert L., m. Sytha Terry; Lenora E., m. Elamse Olsen; Joseph R., m. Millia Robesarn. Family home Riverton, Utah.
High priest; Sunday school superintendent 20 years. Died Sept. 10, 1906, Riverton, Utah.

HOWARD, SAMUEL HAMILTON (son of Samuel L. Howard and Sarah Jane Hamilton). Born Oct. 21, 1867, Mill Creek, Salt Lake county.
Married Rosa A. Holt Dec. 2, 1891, at Manti, Utah (daughter of Mathew Holt and Ann Harrison of England, pioneers Oct. 31, 1863, Daniel D. McArthur company). She was born Aug. 31, 1863. Their children: Samuel E. b. Sept. 27, 1893; Eva P. b. March 18, 1894; Lorenzo M. b. Dec. 20, 1896; Virginia A. b. Jan. 9, 1898; Sarah b. Nov. 29, 1900; Leroy H. b. July 9, 1902; Orin P. b. July 25, 1904; James W. b. April 1906, d. Aug. 11, 1910. Family home Riverton, Utah.
Elder; teacher. Road commissioner. Farmer.

HOWARD, WILLIAM (son of Stott Howard and Catherine Babbington of Belfast, Ireland). Born Jan. 17, 1815, Belfast. Came to Utah September, 1853.
Married Elizabeth Anderson June 9, 1841, at Belfast (daughter of Robert Anderson and Lucretia Ward of Northern Ireland, pioneers September, 1853). She was born Oct. 12, 1823. Their children: Catherine Alice b. April 25, 1843, m. Isaac Brockbank; Lucretia b. May 27, 1845, m. John Arrowsmith; William Howard b. Jan. 5, 1847, m. Mary Pead. m. Lenora J. Perkins, m. Eliza Hill; Robert Anderson b. June 21, 1848, d. April 13, 1849; Elizabeth Bennett b. Feb. 20, 1550, d. March 20, 1870; Lucas Babbington b. May 7, 1851, m. Sena Anderson; Mary Webster b. Jan. 9, 1853, m. Joseph H. Brinton; Thomas Anderson b. Oct. 30, 1854; Lockhard Anderson b. March 25, 1856, m. Mary Crystal; Erin Anderson b. Feb. 23, 1858, m. Clara E. Luce, m. Catherine Kirby, m. Edna J. Thompson. Family resided Salt Lake City and Holliday, Utah.
Seventy; missionary to England and Ireland 1868-69; Real estate and iron foundry. Died Dec. 19, 1890, Holliday, Utah.

HOWARD, WILLIAM, Jr. (son of William Howard and Elizabeth Anderson). Born Jan. 13, 1847, Belfast, Ireland. Came to Utah with father.
Married Mary Pead Dec. 21, 1868, Salt Lake City (daughter of James Pead and Elizabeth Wilkerson of Bedfordshire, Eng.; latter came to Utah 1868, Captain Rawlins company). She was born Jan. 13, 1847. Their children: Elizabeth Wilkerson b. Sept. 9, 1869, m. Joseph D. Johnson; William James b. Sept. 10, 1870, d. July 2, 1878; Catherine Alice b. March 24, 1872, d. 1883; Robert Anderson b. April 28, 1874, m. Vilate Meeks; Levi Howard b. May 10, 1876, m. Elizabeth Johnson; Mary May b. May 12, 1878, m. Lewis P. Oveson; Maud b. April 4, 1880, m. Thomas F. McElprang; Erin T. b. April 19, 1882, m. Marion Mangram. Family resided at Randolph and Huntington, Utah.
Married Lenora J. Perkins June, 1873, Salt Lake Endowment house (daughter of John and Elizabeth Perkins of Bountiful, Utah), who was born November, 1856. Their children: Charles Leroy b. June 17, 1874, d. April 6, 1893; Lenora Webster b. Jan. 28, 1876, m. William Howard Lockhard b. May 16, 1877, d. June 3, 1893; John b. Nov. 6, 1879, m. Gertrude Musser; Wilson Allen b. Sept. 1881. Family home Salt Lake City.
Married Eliza Hill Oct. 11, 1878, Salt Lake Endowment house (daughter of Isaac Hill and Mary Jane Miller, latter came to Utah 1849). She was born Jan. 3, 1860. Their children: Sarah Ella b. July 9, 1879, m. Charles Stewart; Jane b. Jan. 31, 1881, m. George W. Rowley; Joseph E. b. Oct. 29, 1883, m. Sarah E. Gardner; Lucas b. April 12, 1884 d. aged 5; Eliza Amy b. Feb. 11, 1886, m. Lawrence R. Staker; Frank Arthur b. Dec. 16, 1888; William Roy b. Dec. 6, 1890, d. aged 1; Louisa b. March 1, 1894; Lucretia Zina b. Oct. 19, 1897. Family home Huntington.
Member 72d quorum seventies; member high council of Emery stake; bishop's counselor; counselor to C. G. Larsen.

PIONEERS AND PROMINENT MEN OF UTAH 945

president of Emery stake; ward teacher. Director and secretary Huntington Co-op; director, secretary and treasurer Huntington Canal Agricultural Association; member Huntington school district two terms. Superintended the building of the Huntington school house. President Huntington town board. Lieutenant in Nauvoo Legion. Took an active part in Black Hawk Indian war. Chairman of Peoples party eight years. Mailing clerk of the Utah Senate. Justice of peace three terms. Delegate to National Irrigation Convention held at Salt Lake City; member National Irrigation Congress at Ogden 1903. Member Constitutional convention of Salt Lake City 1895. Notary public. Member first legislature of Utah. Emery county attorney 1896. Postmaster of Randolph 10 years. U. S. Commissioner for Utah 1872. County and probate clerk; county recorder; county assessor and collector; county attorney 1875. Called to assist in settling the Bear Lake country 1870. Superintended the building of the first meeting house in Emery county 1880. Chairman of board of federation of Emery county. Appointed and received commission as member world's congress, auxiliary of the World's Columbian Exposition held in Chicago Oct. 16, 1893. Blacksmith.

HOWD, SIMEON FULLER (son of Samuel Howd and Eunice Fuller of Camden, N. Y.). Born May 13, 1813, Camden. Came to Utah July 24, 1847, Brigham Young company.
Married Lucinda Morgan March 16, 1847, Winter Quarters, Iowa, who was born Nov. 1, 1820, and came to Utah Sept 1847. Their children: Elmira b. Sept. 23, 1848, m. James Blincsley; Lucinda b. June 30, 1850, m. Gideon A. Murdock; Eunice b. Aug. 8, 1852, m. B. H. Greenwood; Flora b. Feb. 7, 1855, m. Allen Russell; Sarah b. June 30, 1857, m. James Yeater; Simeon Fuller b. March 5, 1859, m. Julia Levi June 3, 1881; Abigail b. March 13, 1861, m. Thomas Parkinson; Frances b. May 11, 1863, m. Asa Hawley. Family home Beaver, Utah.
Died May 20, 1878, at Beaver City, Utah.

HOWD, SIMEON FULLER (son of Simeon Fuller Howd and Lucinda Morgan). Born March 5, 1859, Beaver City, Utah.
Married Julia Levi June 3, 1881, St. George, Utah (daughter of David Levi and Ann Gillispie; the latter came to Utah 1852, Captain Smoot company). She was born June 29, 1859. Their children: Jennie b. March 5, 1882; Levi b. Dec. 9, 1884, m. Clara Henderson; James b. Jan. 31, 1890, m. Eva Oakden; Zora b. Aug. 17, 1895. Family home Beaver, Utah.
City marshal and member city council of Beaver City, Utah.

HOWE, AMOS (son of Eli Howe, New York city). Born Feb. 19, 1830, New York. Came to Utah Oct. 25, 1864.
Married Julia Cruse June 9, 1850, St. Louis, Mo. (daughter of James Cruse and Mary Jane Joyce, Boxford, Berkshire, Eng.), who was born June 17, 1823. Their children: Edgar, m. Annie Talmage; George E., m. Sarah A. Barney; Charles R., m. Nettie Taylor; Amos, Horace and Eli James, died. Family home, Salt Lake City.
Member 3d quorum seventies; member church board of education. Farmer; mechanical engineer. Died June 16, 1908, Salt Lake City.

HOWE, CHARLES R. (son of Amos Howe and Julia Cruse). Born Aug. 28, 1860, St. Louis, Mo. Came to Utah Oct. 25, 1864.
Married Nettie Taylor Sept. 11, 1884, Logan, Utah (foster daughter of John Taylor and Sophia Whittaker of Salt Lake City), who was born June 12, 1864. Their children: Charles Ralph b. June 30, 1885; Sophia T. b. Aug. 9, 1887, died; Harold T. b. Jan. 18, 1889; Cruse T. b. Feb. 6, 1891; Lucile b. Dec. 10, 1893; Jennetta b. Aug. 5, 1896; Bessie b. Nov. 2, 1900; Amos Ross b. Oct. 18, 1903. Family home, Salt Lake City.
Member 3d quorum seventies; missionary to Virginia 1885-87; Sunday school and block teacher. City councilman 1900-91. Partner in Davis Howe Company.

HOWE, GEORGE E. (son of Amos Howe and Julia Cruse). Born July 14, 1858, St. Louis, Mo. Came to Utah with father.
Married Sarah A. Barney Sept. 27, 1883, Salt Lake Endowment House, Joseph F. Smith officiating (daughter of Royal A. and Esther Barney), who was born Aug. 8, 1858. Their children: Effie B. b. Sept. 3, 1884, m. John O. Mellor; Amos B. b. June 12, 1886, m. Zinna Hoover; Esther Hazel b. March 4, 1889, m. Fred A. Caine; Charles F. b. Feb. 10, 1891; Edna b. Jan. 11, 1893; Royal G. b. Jan. 28, 1895; Julia b. June 6, 1901. Family home, Salt Lake City.
Member 4th quorum seventies; missionary to southern states 1881-82.

HOWELL, ELIAS WILLIS (son of Edmond W. Howell and Sarah Vail, Long Island, N. Y.). Born April 29, 1836, Long Island. Came to Utah in 1852 with Captain Wood.
Married Martha Jane Rigby February 1858 at Salt Lake City (daughter of James Rigby). Their children: Sarah Lovenia, m. Otis Lysander Perry; Martha A., m. Christian Peter Jensen; Rosalie F., m. Peter Hansen; Bruella, m. Thomas Hackford. Family resided Union and Fairview, Utah.
High priest. Associated with all the principal movements for growth of Fairview. Farmer; miller; stockman. Died about 1909 at Fairview.

HOWELL, JAMES (son of James Howell and Jane Copeland). Born Oct. 15, 1828, Vermilion county, Ill. Came to Utah Aug. 29, 1863, William Patterson company.
Married Rosannah Monk Jan. 29, 1857 (daughter of John Monk and Sarah Hatfield), who was born Feb. 1, 1842, and came to Utah with husband. Their children: Sarah Jane b. March 16, 1858, m. Levi Thornton Nov. 14, 1875; Thomas Jefferson b. March 7, 1860, m. Mary Jane Heaton April 7, 1881; Nancy Melvina b. Feb. 26, 1862, m. William H. Thornton Jan. 28, 1878; James William b. July 29, 1865, m. Martha Heaton Feb. 15, 1884; Mohonri Moriancumer b. Aug. 13, 1870, d. Sept. 30, 1898; John Cromwell b. March 7, 1874, m. Margaret Rebecca John Nov. 1899; Leroy b. Oct. 6, 1875, m. Hannah Sariah John Dec. 29, 1898, d. May 31, 1913, Blackfoot, Idaho; Rosie Annie b. April 23, 1879, m. Adam Bigler Nov. 18, 1900. Family resided Kaysville and Portage, Utah, and Woodruff, Idaho.
Teacher at both places 1875-1902. Pioneer to Portage and was active in making canals and roads in early days. Died June 1, 1906.

HOWELL, THOMAS JEFFERSON (son of James Howell and Rosannah Monk). Born March 7, 1860, Franklin, Decatur Co., Iowa. Came to Utah Aug. 29, 1863, William Patterson company.
Married Mary Jane Heaton April 7, 1881 (daughter of John Heaton and Janet Sinclair, married 1859, St. Louis, Mo., pioneers 1863). She was born March 18, 1864, Wellsville, Utah. Their children: Rosa Janet b. Aug. 2, 1882, m. James Heber Yearsley Nov. 10, 1899; Thomas Leslie b. April 30, 1884, m. Margaret Rozella Gibbs April 8, 1909; Mary Melvina b. Oct. 4, 1885, m. George Samuel Young April 27, 1904; Ruby b. Sept. 4, 1887, m. Benjamin Lundberg Sept. 4, 1907; Laura Leona b. April 26, 1889, m. Ernest Hyrum Sorenson Dec. 6, 1911; Oliver Cromwell b. March 7, 1891; Sarah Elizabeth b. May 27, 1893; James Herald b. Sept. 3, 1896; Mildred b. Dec. 30, 1900; Lillian Heaton b. Jan. 21, 1903; Ida Luvena b. Nov. 16, 1905; Grace Avelda b. Dec. 23, 1907. Family home Woodruff, Idaho.
First assistant Sunday school superintendent of Portage ward 1877-84; secretary 52d quorum seventies 1884-91; counselor in Y. M. M. I. A. of Muddy Creek branch; ward teacher Cherry Creek ward 1885-90; first counselor to Bishop Thomas A. Davis of Cherry Creek ward 1891-1902; missionary to northern states 1897-99; president of branch in Omaha; clerk of Nebraska conference; president of Nebraska conference; president high priests quorum of Malad stake 1902-08; member high council since 1907. School teacher. Religious class superintendent.

HOWELL, THOMAS C. D. (son of Caleb Howell and Celia Boyett of Waynesborough, Wayne county, N. C.). Born Feb. 22, 1814, North Carolina. Came to Utah 1852, his own company.
Married Sarah Stuart July 5, 1835 (daughter of Samuel Stuart and Ann Wallace, latter died in Iowa). She was born Jan. 15, 1815, and came to Utah with husband. Their children: Jason E. b. Sept. 2, 1837, m. Jane M. Thomas; Henry Nelson b. May 23, 1840, m. Elizabeth W. Bird Dec. 16, 1861; William J. b. April 8, 1842, m. Lydia A. Beebe; Charles D.; Thomas A. b. Sept. 17, 1855, m. Harriet A. Henderson Feb. 19, 1875. Family resided Payson, Utah, and Franklin and Clifton, Idaho.
Member Mormon Battalion. Enlisted in war with Mexico 1847. Appointed captain of third company of 1852 to come to Utah. Settled at Payson 1853; moved to Franklin, Idaho, 1860, where he served as justice of peace five years. Took active part in early Indian wars. Moved to Clifton, Idaho, 1865, where he resided until his death.

HOWELL, HENRY N. (son of Thomas C. D. Howell and Sarah Stuart). Born May 23, 1840, Yorkville, Gibson county, Tenn.
Married Elizabeth W. Bird Dec. 16, 1861, Salt Lake City (daughter of Edmund F. Bird and Mary Montgomery, former pioneer 1850, latter died Jan. 3, 1846, Boston, Mass.). She was born Jan. 1, 1846, Cambridge, Mass. Their children: Henry J. b. Sept. 2, 1862, m. Lucy L. Bingham Oct. 13, 1883; Sarah A. b. Feb. 22, 1864, d. infant; Mary M. b. April 7, 1866; Lydia L. b. July 10, 1868, m. William A. Lewis; Amelia E. b. Sept. 3, 1870; Edmund F. b. Nov. 11, 1872, m. Annie Henderson; Ida A. b. Dec. 4, 1874, m. George E. Porter; Clara E. b. Nov. 8, 1877, m. C. M. Alston; John E. b. Dec. 18, 1879, m. Maud Henderson; Wallace B. m. March 1, 1882, m. Elizabeth Sant Nov. 28, 1907; Angus b. Oct. 2, 1886. Family home Clifton, Idaho.
School teacher Oxford and Clifton, Idaho, three years each. Sunday school superintendent, Clifton; ward clerk 20 years. Built first house in Clifton, 1869; postmaster there 17 years.

HOWELL, WILLIAM (son of Stephen Howell and Margarette Williams, latter of Lambstoneparish, South Wales). Born Aug. 15, 1819, Lambstoneparish, Pembrokeshire. Came to Utah Sept. 12, 1861, Homer Duncan company.
Married Louisa Thomas 1842 (daughter of James Thomas and Ann Harris), who was born June 12, 1823, and came to Utah with husband. Their children: Martha Leah b. Nov. 21, 1843, m. William Wheeler Nov. 15, 1861; Richard b. March 23, 1846, m. Ann Nov. 19, 1869; Mary Moore 1870; Maria; William; Ann b. Nov. 19, m. Pauley Smout; Arthur; Margarette, m. John Slater June 1875; Stephen; James Parley b. Nov. 25, 1861, m. Lois Perry May 1890; Frances Jane; Louisa b. July 25, 1863, m. McGraw Vandyke. Family home Slaterville, Utah.
Elder.

HOWELL, JAMES P. (son of William Howell and Louisa Thomas). Born Nov. 25, 1860, Fristrap, Wales. Came to Utah 1861.
Married Lois L. Perry May 1890 (daughter of Stephen W. Perry and Mary Bishop), who was born 1871.

HOYT, SAMUEL PIERCE (son of James Hoyt and Pamelia Brown). Born Nov. 21, 1807, Devonshire, N. H. Pioneer 1850, independent company.
Married Emily Smith April 17, 1832 (daughter of Asael Smith), who was born Sept. 1, 1806. Family resided Fillmore and Hoytsville, Utah.
Married Catherine Emma Burbidge June 3, 1856, Salt Lake City (daughter of James Rhoades Burbidge and Mary Brown, the latter a pioneer 1854, Captain Richardson company). She was born Nov. 17, 1839, in England. Their children: James William b. Sept. 28, 1858, d. Nov. 17, 1859; Mary b. Aug. 9, 1863, m. J. W. Lee; Pamelia b. May 22, 1865, m. Alonzo A. Mills Aug. 10, 1891; Elizabeth b. May 31, 1867, m. J. P. Stonebraker Feb. 22, 1898; John B. b. Jan. 16, 1869, m. Inez Park Dec. 4, 1907; Elias B. b. March 6, 1871, d. April 6, 1871; Martha b. May 18, 1872, m. William Myrick; Joseph B. b. Dec. 6, 1873, m. Sarah J. Johnson; Aphia b. May 13, 1875, d. April 17, 1879; Emma b. Aug. 27, 1878, m. H. H. Stevens June 3, 1902; Samuel b. Aug. 2, 1880, d. March 17, 1892.
Pioneer to Fillmore. Located at Hoytsville. Seventy. Brought the first iron turning lathe to Utah and owned the first flour mill in Summit county. Member of the first constitutional convention and helped to make the first territorial laws. County commissioner. Farmer; tanner; rancher; merchant. Died Aug. 12, 1889, Rhoade's Valley.

HUBBARD, CHARLES WESLEY (son of Noah Hubbard, born Oct. 20, 1778, Sheffield, Mass., and Cynthia Clark of Michigan,). He was born Feb. 7, 1810, Sheffield. Came to Utah 1848, Heber C. Kimball company.
Married Mary Ann Bosworth 1832, Monroe county, Mich. (daughter of Jared Bosworth and Lucy Hubbard), who was born Aug. 12, 1816. Their children: Noah Eli b. Feb. 9, 1834; Emma b. Feb. 13, 1836; Rhoda Ann b. June 22, 1839, m. Moroni Cole; Lucy b. Aug. 16, 1841; John b. Oct. 22, 1843, m. Rosabell Shaw; Heber William b. Jan. 31, 1845, m. Susan Dudley; Julia C. b. April 3, 1848, m. Byron Barker; Albert b. Feb. 27, 1850; Mary Malinda B. b. Dec. 31, 1851, m. Charles William Merrill; Charles N. b. Dec. 5, 1853, m. Rebecca J. Davis; Permelia S. b. June 25, 1856; David Clark b. Feb. 7, 1860, m. Charlotte Morgan. Family home Willard, Utah.
Married Mary Edwards in February 1856, Salt Lake City (daughter of John Edwards and Ann Jones, married in Cardiganshire, South Wales, former pioneer 1855). She was born May 30, 1835, Cardiganshire. Their children: Mary Elizabeth b. Nov. 5, 1856, m. Thomas Taylor Jan. 18, 1875; Joseph b. Oct. 20, 1859, m. Salley Marsh March 4, 1880; David b. Nov. 30, 1861, m. Ida Cordon Nov. 10, 1881; Ann Rebecca b. March 14, 1864; John Hyrum b. April 18, 1867; Lucynthia b. May 22, 1869, m. Lorenzo Robbins; Jane b. Feb. 8, 1872, m. Ezra Lloyd Dec. 23, 1897; Alma E. b. April 12, 1874; Sarah Gevennie b. Oct. 4, 1877, m. T. L. Redford Dec. 22, 1904. Family home Willard, Utah.
Married Sophia Pollard June 4, 1856, Salt Lake City (daughter of James Pollard and Sarah Robertshaw), who was born Feb. 26, 1831, and came to Utah in 1853, Cyrus Wheelock company. Their children: James Willard b. Feb. 12, 1861, m. Emma M. Pettingill; Sarah Ann b. Feb. 7, 1863.
First bishop of Willard ward 1851-56; missionary to England and Scotland 1856-58. Moved to the Muddy, where he lived six years, 1864-70. Mail carrier to the Muddy four years. Returned to Willard 1871. Died Dec. 19, 1903.

HUBBARD, CHARLES N. (son of Charles W. Hubbard and Mary Ann Bosworth). Born Dec. 5, 1853, Willard, Utah.
Married Rebecca J. Davis 1877, Brigham, Utah (daughter of Richard and Rebecca Davis of Willard), who was born July 31, 1856, died 1891. Their children: Mary Ann b. Nov. 19, 1878, m. John M. White; William b. Nov. 21, 1880, m. Mary E. Powlsen; Lucy Jane b. May 8, 1882, m. Lawrence Abeggien; Morgan P. b. Oct. 31, 1884, m. Merrit J. Wood. Family home, Willard.
Missionary to southern states 1888-90.

HUBBARD, JAMES WILLARD (son of Charles Wesley Hubbard and Sophia Pollard). Born Feb. 12, 1861, Willard, Utah.
Married Emma M. Pettingill Jan. 8, 1880, Salt Lake City (daughter of Elihu Pettingill and Jane C. Marsh), who was born April 20, 1862, Willard. Their children: Sarah Paulina b. July 31, 1880; Clotilda b. Dec. 6, 1881, m. Henry Mickelsen July 31, 1903; Edith Mariah b. Dec. 26, 1883, m. John Whitehead Oct. 13, 1904; Rhoda Ann b. Nov. 6, 1885; Charles W. b. May 25, 1888; Ida b. May 31, 1890, m. Nephi Petersen Oct. 5, 1909; Jane b. Feb. 5, 1893; Vara b. May 5, 1898; Cora b. July 22, 1900. Family home Raft River and Trout Creek, Idaho.
Missionary to southern states 1895-96; bishop of Bench ward three years; high councilor of Bannock stake.

HUBER, JOHN (son of Johannes Huber, born 1810, Weinfelden, and Anna Elizabeth Huber, born 1815, Dodtnacht, Switzerland—married in 1840). Born in 1840, at Dodtnacht. Came to Utah 1863, Peter Nebeker company.
Married Mary Magdalena Munz Oct. 18, 1863 (daughter of Henry and Margaret Munz), who was born Jan. 21, 1843, and came to Utah with husband. Their children: John Martin b. Oct. 22, 1865, m. Elizabeth Gertsch; Henry Albert b. Oct. 7, 1867, m. Margaret Abegglen; Mary Magdalena b. Oct. 15, 1869, m. Jacob Brobst 1891; Emma Elizabeth b. Dec. 19, 1871, m. James Gibson; Otillia Eliza b. March 29, 1875, m. Alexander Gibson; Matilda b. May 8, 1877, died; Nephi b. Oct. 10, 1879, m. Anna Bronson; Joseph Emanuel b. Aug. 18, 1881; Ida b. May 7, 1883, m. William W. Abplanalp. Family home, Midway, Utah.
Missionary to Switzerland 1860-63, 1871-74; ward clerk at Midway 1878-1908; ward chorister 1880-1910. Black Hawk war veteran. Agent for Wasatch & Jordan valley railroad, shipping granite for Salt Lake temple 1875-78; took U. S. census 1880 and 1900; member school board 24 years; secretary of Midway Irrigation Company 10 years; compiled history of Midway ward from 1859 to 1905; justice of peace two years; agent of crop reporting for agricultural department of U. S. A. Composer of numerous songs and poetical compositions in German and English.

HUBER, HENRY ALBERT (son of John Huber and Mary Magdalena Munz). Born Oct. 7, 1867, Midway, Utah.
Married Margaret Abegglen Dec. 9, 1891, Logan, Utah (daughter of Gottlieb Abegglen and Anna Gertsch of Gundlischwand, Bern, Switzerland, came to Utah September, 1873). She was born March 16, 1871. Their children: Elmer b. Sept. 19, 1892; Henry Lyman b. March 1, 1894, d. March 17, 1894; Frank Ervin b. June 1, 1895; Leroy b. April 1, 1897; Albert Dean b. Jan. 11, 1899. Family home Midway, Utah.
High priest. Road supervisor. Member town board. Farmer.

HUCKVALE, JONATHAN (brother of Mrs. George Osmond, the mother of Alfred Osmond).
Married Sarah Huckvale. Their children: Frederick, m. Ella —; Ethel, m. Charles Stone; Perkins, died. Family home, Bloomington, Idaho.
Farmer and painter. Deceased.

HUDMAN, JOHN (son of Thomas Hudman and Ann Dancose of Ripple, Worcestershire, Eng.). Born Oct. 23, 1821, at Ripple. Came to Utah 1856 with Knud Peterson company.
Married Sophia Langley Nov. 12, 1848 (daughter of Mathias Langley and Diana Connell), who was born Jan. 7, 1822, and came to Utah with husband. Their children: Emma b. June 25, 1851, m. William H. Manning June 9, 1873; Alvin J. b. April 4, 1864, m. Jane A. Webb; Henry Heber b. Aug. 14, 1859, m. Annie Cowan; Ellen Maria b. Dec. 6, 1861, m. James Cowan Jr. Family home Slaterville, Utah.
Ordained high priest, April 14, 1855.

HUFF, JOSEPH (son of John Edwards Huff and Hilda Hicks of Canada). Born April 24, 1818, Upper Canada. Came to Utah Sept. 20, 1861, Joseph Young company.
Married Mary Jane Losee Nov. 10, 1836, Lower Canada (daughter of David Losee and Lydia Huff), who was born Oct. 4, 1820, Canada; came to Utah with husband. Their children: James b. July 24, 1837, m. Sena Nibley, m. Sophia Atkins; Jemima b. Dec. 24, 1839, d. child; John Edwards b. Dec. 3, 1843, m. Sarah Ann Robinson; David Losee b. April 10, 1845, m. Amelia Robinson Jan. 21, 1866; Joseph b. July 10, 1847, m. Jane Hodgetts; Mariah b. Aug. 26, 1849, m. Nephi Williams; Mary b. March 6, 1852, m. Robert Pope; George W. b. May 7, 1854; Elvira b. June 2, 1856, m. Samuel Robinson; Isaac b. Nov. 22, 1859, m. Alice Green; Abraham b. Oct. 6, 1862, m. Annie Clark. Family home Coalville, Utah.
Bishop of Upton ward 1864-76. Forced from Upton by Indians and moved to Coalville. Built several sawmills in Summit county. Farmer. Died in February, 1895, Spanish Fork, Utah.

HUFF, DAVID LOSEE (son of Joseph Huff and Mary Jane Losee). Born April 10, 1845, Nauvoo, Ill. Came to Utah Sept. 20, 1861, Joseph Young company.
Married Amelia Robinson Jan. 21, 1866 (daughter of William Robinson and Mary Dexter—married 1845, in England; pioneers 1868, Captain Murdock company). She was born Nov. 29, 1847. Came to Utah in September, 1864, Captain Rawlins company. Their children: William Edward b. Jan. 24, 1867, m. Sarah Tippetts; David B. b. June 22, 1869, m. Lettacie Hayes; Joseph Hyrum b. Dec. 10, 1871, m. Lulu Myers April 10, 1895; Mary Amelia b. Feb. 24, 1874, m. John Ballard; Rosalia b. Nov. 22, 1876, m. Thomas Hone; John Rufus b. March 27, 1879, m. Martha Larson; George Elmer b. Aug. 5, 1881, m. Annie Westernie; Earnest James b. Oct. 31, 1883, m. May Hall; Jane b. Aug. 15, 1886, m. David Evans; Ralph b. Nov. 15, 1888. Family home Lake Shore, Utah.
Moved from Upton, Summit county, to Randolph in 1870; assisted in erection of first sawmill in Randolph; in 1877 moved to Lake Shore. Freighter.

HUFF, THOMAS. Born June 22, 1788, Roanoke, Va. Came to Utah in September 1853, Captain Dailey company.
Married Betsy Adams March 7, 1815, Hancock county, Ga. (daughter of Jonathan Adams and Charlotte Lawrence of Pontotoc, Miss., pioneers 1853, Captain Dailey company). She was born Sept. 19, 1798. Their children: Alivia, m. Asa A. Felts; Willaim T.; Pheriba; Sarah Jane, m. William

PIONEERS AND PROMINENT MEN OF UTAH 947

Hall; Maragaret, m. John C. Bowman; Rebecca, m. Tillery Mitchell; Bethena. m. John Ellege; Jonathan G.; Joel, m. Annie Winters; Thaddeus, m. Frances Russell; Betsy V., m. David N. Shanahan; Lucy Ann; Mary F., m. John C. Lemmon; Jefferson Adams, m. Mary Emeline Moore. Family home Pontotoc, Miss.
Farmer. Died Oct. 15, 1855.

HUFF, JEFFERSON ADAMS (son of Thomas Huff and Betsy Adams). Born May 12, 1842, Chambers county, Ala. Came to Utah September 1853, with parents.
Married Emeline Moore Oct. 15, 1884, Logan, Utah (daughter of Joseph Webber Moore and Hannah Seely Young of Moab, Grand county, Utah, pioneers 1847, John Taylor company). She was born July 24, 1864. Their children: Jefferson A. b. Dec. 7, 1885; Joseph Thomas b. Dec. 22, 1886; Jonathan Rile b. June 22, 1888; Enos Marion b. Sept. 1, 1889; William Lee b. Feb. 22, 1891; Sarah Blanche b. June 6, 1892, m. Francis Jean Rogerson; Archie Ross b. March 14, 1894; Cyrus b. May 6, 1895; Ivy Emeline b. April 22, 1897; Francis Seth b. Dec. 14, 1898; Joel Roaf b. Dec. 14, 1900; Ruth Elizabeth b. June 6, 1903; Clarence b. March 29, 1905; Acil Wayne b. April 23, 1907. Family home, Moab.
Member 84th quorum seventies; high priest; bishop's counselor. Probate judge; county commissioner Grand county, Utah. Farmer and stockraiser.

HUFFAKER, SIMPSON D. (son of Jacob Huffaker and Margaret Bodkins of Kentucky). Born July 23, 1812, in Wayne county, Ky. Came to Utah Oct. 6, 1847, Jedediah M. Grant company.
Married Susan Green Robinson Feb. 25, 1836, Morgan county, Ill. (daughter of Joel Robinson), who was born Oct. 16, 1817. Their children: Rozella, m. John Pulsipher; Sarah M., died; Lewis Albert, m. Martha Sarah Murray; Sidney, Sarah and Augusta, d. young.
Married Elizabeth Richardson in January 1846, Nauvoo, Ill. (daughter of Stephen Richardson and Erepta Wilder of New Hampshire, pioneers 1847, Jedediah Grant company). She was born May 28, 1829, died April 26, 1911, Salt Lake City. Their children: David S., m. Eva Neff; Elizabeth M., m. W. H. Perry; Susan L., m. D. B. Brinton; Della, m. H. G. Williams; Welby R., m. Martha Winn; Wilford D., m. Jane McMillian; Ray E., m. Etta Davis; Earl P., m. Matilda Scott; Etta B., m. Livingston Gardner.
Married Elizabeth Brady in September, 1852, Salt Lake City (daughter of Lundson and Elizabeth Brady of Union, Utah), who was born 1839. Their children: Frances M., m. W. K. Wallon; George M., m. Abigail Bradford; Arardna T., m. Joseph Gardner; Simpson L.; Beatrice; Mary; Franklin.
Married Priscilla Barnum March 24, 1856, Salt Lake City (daughter of James and Loretta Barnum), who was born Oct. 3, 1834. Their children: Shelby V., m. Sophia Neville; Eugenia, m. George D. Gardner; Herman, died; Rhoda P.. m. James H. Gardner. Families lived at South Cottonwood, Salt Lake county.
One of presidents 7th quorum seventies. Selectman. Farmer. Died Oct. 25, 1891.

HUFFAKER, LEWIS ALBERT (son of Simpson D. Huffaker and Susan Green Robinson). Born March 19, 1841, Bureau county, Ill. Came to Utah in 1847, Jedediah M. Grant company.
Married Martha Sarah Murray July, 1863, South Cottonwood, Utah (daughter of Asahel Plumb Murray and Lauretta Barnum, of Knox county, Ill., pioneers with Perrigrine Sessions company). She was born March 28, 1848. Their children: Susan A., m. John Cutler, m. Charles O. Harmon; Simpson D., d. infant; Sarah Maria, m. Parley Cutler; Lewis Albert, d. aged 7 years; Francis D., d. young; Mary Lois. m. Albert Larson; Asahel C.; Lauretta L., m. William C. Melogue; Esther R., m. Geeorge Mast; Dermont and Martha Melvina, d. infants.
Married Sarah Ann Ilse Oct. 3, 1897, Salt Lake temple (daughter of Jeremiah Ilse and Mary Ann Taylor, who came to Utah in July, 1891). She was born Aug. 19, 1866. Their children: Sarah Maud and Lewis John, d. infant. Families lived at Salt Lake City.
Member 105th quorum seventies; missionary to England 1900-1902; high priest; home missionary 21 years; acting president high priests of Bingham stake, Idaho, three years; president block teachers. Constable of Summit county four years. Took part in Echo Canyon war; Indian war veteran. Farmer and stockraiser.

HUFFMAN, JACOB (son of George Huffman and Hannah Johnson, born July 31, 1806, Albany, later of Buffalo, N. Y.). He was born Aug. 28, 1823, West Waterloo, Canada. Came to Utah September 1861, Milo Andrus company.
Married Margaret Staley in 1843 (daughter of Conrad Staley and Hannah Tripp), who was born June 4, 1826, and came to Utah with husband, died 1862, at Coalville. Their children: Hannah b. Dec. 6, 1845, m. Edmond Eldredge Jan. 4, 1863; George b. Feb. 1, 1848, m. Ellen Mariah Wild; Harriet b. Oct. 6, 1851, m. Joshua Misemor; Susan Alvira b. Sept. 13, 1854, m. Edward Henry Rhead Jan. 27, 1873.
Married Elizabeth Frisby Dec. 13, 1864, Coalville, Utah (daughter of William and Elizabeth Rebeca Frisby), who was born July 17, 1838. Their children: Margaret b. Oct. 19, 1865, m. Samuel Haslam; Sarah Ann b. Nov. 20, 1867; May b. Dec. 12, 1868, m. Alfred Blonzuist; Jacob William b. April 6, 1871, m. Elizabeth Swainston; Joseph Henry b. May 27, 1873. m. Annie Underwood; Eliza J. b. July 12, 1875.

m. Aaron Densley; Emma P. b. Jan. 4, 1878, m. Moses Densley; Gertrude b. Jan. 2, 1880, m. William Bagnell; Frank b. Sept. 24, 1882, m. Mary Wilson. Family home Coalville, Utah.
Settled at Coalville 1861. Member high council Summit stake. Brought first threshing machine to Summit county; built first meeting house in Coalville. Justice of peace. Died Aug. 22, 1899.

HUFFMAN, JACOB WILLIAM (son of Jacob Huffman and Elizabeth Frisby). Born April 6, 1871, Coalville, Utah.
Married Elizabeth Swainston June 15, 1897, Coalville (daughter of Elijah Swainston and Mary Ann Williamson; former came to Utah 1868, latter 1873). She was born July 19, 1877, Coalville. Their children: Vera E. b. May 11, 1898; Mildred M. A. b. July 12, 1900; Wyona H. b. Jan. 8, 1908; Orville b. Aug. 21, 1912. Family home, Coalville.

HUGGINS, WILLIAM (son of John Huggins). Born June 2, 1811, in New Jersey. Came to Utah Oct. 10, 1853, Anthony Ivans company.
Married Emeline Aker (daughter of Stephen Aker and Elizabeth Lemon), who was born March 14, 1816, and came to Utah Aug. 10, 1853. Their children: Elizabeth; George Aker b. April 5, 1839, m. Eliza Adams April 3, 1866; Permelia b. May 23, 1841, m. William Cordingley Dec. 25, 1865; Hannah P. b. June 8, 1844, m. Alonzo Nay June 8, 1861; Mary Ann b. Aug. 24, 1847, m. Hyrum Johnson April 9, 1867; Sarah b. July 2, 1850, m. Joshua Combs.
High priest. Assisted in bringing immigrants to Utah. Deceased.

HUGHES, JOHN (son of John Hughes and Ann Jones, both of Llanedan, Denbighshire, North Wales). Born December 1815, in Wales. Came to Utah Sept. 1, 1860, John Smith company.
Married Sarah Jones in August 1840, in Wales (daughter of William Jones and Grace Owens, both of Wales, pioneers August 1860, John Smith company). She was born in 1811, and died June 26, 1887. Only child: Ann Hughes, m. William Treharne. Family home, Salt Lake City.
He died April 16, 1901.

HUGHES, MORGAN. Born Oct. 30, 1824, in Wales. Came to Utah in 1852.
Married Hannah David Dec. 3, 1853 (daughter of Morgan David of Spanish Fork, came to Utah 1852). She was born March 3, 1837. Their children: Morgan J.; Hannah E., m. Ephraim G. Davis: William B., m. Louise S. McKell, m. Margaret Black, m. Alice E. Payzant; David F., m. Ellen McKell; Thomas D., died; John B., m. Katherine Banks; Henry, m. Mary E. Myler, m. LaRene King; Benjamin, m. Belva Werner; Alfred. m. Carrie Nielson; George, m. Alice Moore; Joseph, m. Delila Gardner; Ephraim G., m. Katherine Jones; Mary, died. Family home Spanish Fork, Utah.
Elder. Farmer and stockraiser. Died Jan. 11, 1890.

HUGHES, WILLIAM B. (son of Morgan Hughes and Hannah David). Born Feb. 27, 1859, Spanish Fork, Utah.
Married Louisa B. McKell Dec. 18, 1879, Salt Lake City (daughter of Robert McKell and Elizabeth Boyack of Spanish Fork, pioneers 1852, Captain Tidwell company). She was born Jan. 1, 1860. Their children: William M. b. Dec. 5, 1880, m. Retta Kahn; Hannah E. b. Feb. 25, 1883, d. Feb. 28, 1883; Delbert B. b. May 27, 1884, m. E. Lois Wright; Jennie M. b. Dec. 12, 1886, m. Albert G. Brockbank; Robert Edward b. Aug. 21, 1889, d. July 3, 1892; Louise S., d. Aug. 30, 1889.
Married Margaret Moore (Black) July 20, 1892, at Manti, San Pete county, Utah (daughter of John Moore and Jennette Henderson of Scotland), who was born May 12, 1862, and died May 3, 1896. Their children: Janet L b. July 5, 1894; Morgan J. b. Aug. 8, 1895, d. Sept. 28, 1911.
Married Alice E. Payzant 1897, Salt Lake City (daughter of John Payzant and May Emma Bucher of Spanish Fork, Utah). She was born in 1876. Their children: George D. b. April 22, 1898; Mary E. b. Nov. 18, 1899; David b. Sept. 20, 1902, died; Gladys b. April 2, 1904; Myrtle b. Nov. 27, 1905; Ronald b. Sept. 19, 1909.
Elder; teacher. Utah county commissioner; Spanish Fork city councilman. Merchant.

HULLINGER, HARVEY COE (son of John Hullinger and Olive Coe of Mad River, Champaign Co., Ohio). Born Dec. 2, 1824, Mad River. Came to Utah Sept. 16, 1859, Edward Stephenson company.
Married Julia Bloce 1847 in Champaign Co., Ohio (daughter of John Bloce and Omelia Pence), who was born March 21, 1821. Their children: Winfield Scott b. Jan. 5, 1848, m. Anniel Davis, Nov. 22, 1869; Omelia, d. Nov. 30, 1852.
Married Marrett Woolworth Dec. 24, 1854, Comanche, Clinton Co., Iowa (daughter of Joshua Woolworth and Philecta Morley), who was born Dec. 4, 1828. Their child: Adelbert (adopted), m. Abby Shelton.
Married Christena Peterson Nov. 22, 1869, Salt Lake City (daughter of Soren Peterson and Marn Jensen of Denmark), who was born Jan. 3, 1842. Their children: Mary Olive b. July 6, 1872, d. infant; Marrett b. Aug. 24, 1873, d. Aug. 21, 1876; John Frank b. May 7, 1876, d. June 2, 1878; Rhoda Ann

b. June 15, 1879, m. Eli Lee; Sarah C. b. June 5, 1884, m. Seth B. Perry.
Member 15th quorum seventies of Salt Lake City; missionary to Council Bluffs 1860-61; counselor in 77th quorum seventies of South Cottonwood; missionary to Ohio 1902. Called to St. George as a physician 1862-64; first physician of Uintah county. County surveyor four years; county commissioners four years; school treasurer. Volunteer surgeon in U. S. army 1862; assisted in bringing immigrants to Utah; member Utah State Medical Association. Recorder at Big Cottonwood mining district three years. Worked on Nauvoo temple and all temples in Utah.

HULLINGER, WINFIELD SCOTT (son of Harvey Coe Hullinger and Julia Bloce). Born Jan. 5, 1848, Tremont, Ohio. Came to Utah in 1859 with parents.
Married Anniel Davis Nov. 22, 1869, Salt Lake City (daughter of John Meeks Davis and Elizabeth Abshire of Nauvoo, Ill., pioneers 1854). Their children: Winfield Scott b. Sept. 23, 1870, m. Emma Theresa Lybbert Jan. 1, 1895; John Harvey b. Feb. 22, 1872, m. Elnora Bergeson; Julia Elizabeth b. Oct. 4, 1873, m. Arthur Gardner; Mary B. b. June 24, 1875, d. young; Susan b. April 22, 1878, m. Henry Merkley; Jesse b. Nov. 5, 1880, died; Dora b. Jan. 3, 1883, m. Alfred Hunting; Spencer b. June 24, 1886, died; Anniel b. June 16, 1888, m. George McCarrel; Sarah C. b. Nov. 20, 1892, m. Monroe Hatch. Family home Vernal, Utah.
High priest; ward and Sunday school teacher. Settled in Uintah county 1883, assisting in building up the country. Farmer.

HULLINGER, WINFIELD SCOTT, JR. (son of Winfield Scott Hullinger and Anniel Davis). Born Sept. 23, 1870, Salt Lake City.
Married Emma Theresa Lybbert Jan. 1, 1895, Vernal, Utah (daughter of Christian Frederick Bernard Lybbert of Germany and Antonetta Meria Olsen of Norway, pioneers 1847). She was born April 11, 1873. Their children: Harvey L. b. Nov. 18, 1895; Mary Theresa b. Oct. 25, 1897; Herold Everett b. Dec. 11, 1899; Jesse Enoch b. Nov. 30, 1901; Norma Anniel b. Oct. 17, 1903; Jacob Neldon b. March 24, 1906; Emma Elvera b. June 2, 1908; Adelbert Owen b. July 30, 1910.
Ward and Sunday school teacher; counselor to president of Y. M. M. I. A. of Naples ward; elder. Road supervisor 1906-07; deputy road commissioner 1908-12. Assisted in building up country around Vernal.

HULLINGER, ADELBERT (adopted son of Harvey Coe Hullinger and Marrett Woolworth). Came to Utah Sept. 16, 1859, with adopted father.
Married Abby Shelton. Their children: Harvey b. Dec. 22, 1874, m. Minerva Cook; Adelbert b. Dec. 31, 1876, d. Dec. 31, 1879; Philecta b. April 2, 1878, m. John Mott; Phidelia b. Dec. 2, 1880, m. Walter Anderson; Hyrum b. Feb. 4, 1884; William b. March 25, 1887; Stephen b. March 28, 1891; James E. b. Dec. 7, 1894.

HUMPHERYS, GEORGE (son of Thomas Humpherys, born April 20, 1812, Nottinghamshire, and Mary Sudberry, born April 19, 1811, Mansfield. Eng.). He was born April 19, 1842, in Nottinghamshire. Came to Utah Oct. 2, 1856, John Banks company.
Married Sarah Ann Eaton Oct. 9, 1864 (daughter of William Eaton and Zillah Wayne, the latter pioneer Oct. 15, 1864, Joseph Rawlina company). She was born June 5, 1845, and came to Utah with her mother 1864. Their children: George William b. Feb. 23, 1866, m. Kate Weible; Thomas Heber b. Nov. 19, 1867, m. Amelia Bolton Sept. 14, —; Zillah Ann b. July 1, 1870, m. Frank Bolton, d. Dec. 31, 1899; Mary Elizabeth b. May 7, 1872, m. James Henry Davis; Joseph b. Sept. 28, 1874, m. Ethel Davis; Sarah Ann b. June 20, 1877, d. April 16, 1878; Emeline b. July 13, 1879, m. John Skiner; Harriet b. Aug. 4, 1882, m. James S. Poulsen July 19, 1905; John Henry b. April 18, 1885, m. Lillian Lulu Lindsay June 28, 1912; David Ray b. Feb. 19, 1888.
Missionary to Great Britain 1896-98. Assisted in bringing immigrants to Utah in 1864.

HUMPHERYS, HYRUM THOMAS (son of Thomas Humpherys, born April 20, 1812, Nottinghamshire, and Mary Sudberry, born April 19, 1811, Mansfield, Eng.). Born May 13, 1850, in Nottinghamshire. Came to Utah in October 1856, with older brothers.
Married Caroline Whiting Rich Oct. 7, 1878 (daughter of C. C. Rich and Emeline Grover, former pioneers 1847). She was born Jan. 2, 1852, San Bernardino, Cal. Their children: Thomas Hyrum, m. Carrie Stewart; Charles Rich, m. Constant Price; Ray Rich, m. Jennette Gardner; LeGrande Rich, m. Nettie Wright; Emeline; Caroline; Asia. Family resided at Salt Lake City, Ogden and Springville, Utah, and Paris, Idaho.
Bishop of Paris 1st ward sixteen years. City councilman two years.

HUMPHERYS, SAMUEL (son of Thomas Humpherys, born April 20, 1812, Nottinghamshire, and Mary Sudberry, born April 19, 1811, Mansfield Eng.). Born Jan. 31, 1846, Nottinghamshire. Came to Utah October 1856 with older brothers.
Married Mary Ann Clifton Oct. 2, 1876 (daughter of John Clifton and Hannah Pettinger—married at Crawl, Yorkshire, pioneers 1861, Joseph Horne company). She was born March 25, 1859, and came to Utah with parents. Their children: Samuel G. b. March 5, 1878, m. Christina Sorensen July 3, 1903; Mary E. b. Oct. 29, 1880, m. John A. Berry Nov. 1898; Emma S. b. Jan. 27, 1882, m. Joseph Hansen June 8, 1899; Vinnie b. April 7, 1890, m. Jacob C. Jensen, in June 1907; Phoebe M. b. Sept. 23, 1896; Ivy M. b. Oct. 17, 1898.
Married Hannah M. Clifton Sept. 3, 1884, Logan, Utah (daughter of John Clifton and Hannah Pettinger, pioneers 1861, Joseph Horne company). She was born May 12, 1864, Paris, Idaho. Their children: Louisa b. Aug. 17, 1885, m. Earnest Sparks Dec. 16, 1910; Oliver b. Jan. 12, 1888; Alfred b. Dec. 20, 1899; Alta b. Feb. 11, 1892; Ella b. July 14, 1894; Nora L. b. Sept. 4, 1896; Irene b. May 19, 1899; David B. Aug. 16, 1902; Vera b. Feb. 28, 1905; Edna b. July 27, 1910. Families resided at Dingle, Idaho.
Bishop of Dingle ward since 1887.

HUMPHRYS, GEORGE, of Gloucester, Eng. Came to Utah Nov. 9, 1856, with James G. Willie company.
Married Harriet Harding in Gloucester. Their children: Richard, m. Elizabeth Brown; George, d. aged 10 years; Edwin, m. Mary Jewet; Ann, m. Henry Webber; Mary, m. Bishop Amos Maycock; Elizabeth, m. William Hill; Hannah, m. George Wheeler; Salena, m. Stacy Fairbanks; James.

HUMPHRYS, EDWIN (son of George Humphrys and Harriet Harding). Born Dec. 14, 1838, at Gloucester, Eng. Came to Utah Nov. 9, 1856.
Married Mary Jewet March 23, 1876, at Pleasant View, Utah (daughter of William Jewet and Margaret McCartney), who was born June 2, 1857. Their children: Margaret A. b. Oct. 23, 1877; Mary E. b. May 30, 1879; Edwin b. July 11, 1881; Ellen b. Sept. 23, 1883, and Riller, b. Oct. 23, 1885, all died; George E. b. May 26, 1892; Bertha b. May 17, 1894. Family home, Pleasant View.
Farmer.

HUNSAKER, ABRAHAM (son of Jacob Hunsaker, born Nov. 4, 1781, in Pennsylvania, and Polly Luce, born Mullenberg, Ky.—married in 1808). Born Nov. 29, 1812, Jonesboro, Union county, Ill. Came to Utah Oct. 3, 1848, Andrew Cunningham company.
Married Eliza Collins Jan. 3, 1833 (daughter of Allen Collins and Mary Broady), who was born March 5, 1817, and came to Utah with husband in 1848. Their children: Jacob b. Oct. 22, 1833; Mary J. b. Dec. 3, 1835, m. David Grant; Elizabeth b. Nov. 17, 1837; Lewis J. b. April 6, 1839; Allen C. b. July 9, 1840, m. Susannah Dunn April 24, 1858, m. Eveline Dunn Oct. 5, 1868; Nephi b. Aug. 31, 1842; Nephi b. Dec. 11, 1844; Abraham b. Sept. 16, 1848, m. Hannah Andersen, m. Annie Wright; Isaac b. Oct. 11, 1850, m. Eliza M. Hansen 1863; Israel b. Sept. 28, 1852, m. Ester L. Neeley; Franklin b. July 2, 1855, m. Laura E. Neeley; Eliza b. Oct. 29, 1857, m. Heber Rampton. Family home Honeyville, Utah.
Married Harriet V. Beckstead at Salt Lake City (daughter of Alexander Beckstead and Catherine Lince, pioneers 1849, Allen Taylor company). She was born June 17, 1831, West Canada. Their children: Alexander b. May 9, 1852, m. Malissa C. Johnson; Katherine b. Aug. 8, 1853, m. John W. Winward; Hyrum b. March 12, 1855, m. Julia V. Hansen; Joseph b. May 1, 1856, m. Emily Graham; Polly b. Dec. 24, 1857; Elnora b. June 31, 1859; Enoch b. Sept. 8, 1860, m. Martha E. May; Cyrus b. July 20, 1862, m. Mary Anderson; John L. b. July 11, 1864, m. Celestia C. Allen; Gordon b. March 27, 1866, m. Annie Peterson; Elzarus b. June 15, 1867, m. Eveline May; Ruplie1 b. Dec. 29, 1869; Harriet b. March 9, 1871, m. Hyrum S. Lewis; Daniel W. b. Sept. 13, 1872, m. Alfrurette M. Neeley; Walter H. b. Sept. 28, 1874. Family home, Honeyville.
Married Margaret Sweeten at Salt Lake City (daughter of Robert Sweeten and Mary Gardner), who was born Dec. 23, 1837, Brook City, West Canada. Their children: Mary Ann b. Sept. 16, 1856, m. William P. Willie; George b. July 27, 1857; Lorenzo b. March 21, 1859, m. Florida I. Castele; Idumea b. Dec. 8, 1860, m. Isaac D. E. Zundel; Robert S. b. Oct. 12, 1862, m. Minnie M. Whealy.
Married Katherine Jensen at Salt Lake City (daughter of Hans P. Jensen and Anna M. Clauson), who was born Feb. 12, 1843, in Denmark. Their children: Annie M. b. Feb. 10, 1862, m. Lewis Grant; Margaret b. Dec. 5, 1863, m. Joshua Hawks; Julia b. Nov. 28, 1865, m. David Loviand; Esther b. Feb. 29, 1868, m. Allen Wagstaff; Hans Peter b. July 9, 1871, m. Matilda Allen; Benham b. July 5, 1873, m. Emily Summeral; Ila b. Jan. 16, 1875; Frederic b. June 28, 1878; Leo b. Feb. 15, 1879, m. Thuresa Neumeyer May 4, 1903; Newman b. July 7, 1881, m. Myrtle Smith July 22, 1903.
Married Mary Leukham (daughter of Roger Leukham and Mary Gardner), who was born Aug. 15, 1845, in Canada. Their children: Susannah b. Feb. 25, 1867, m. Frederic G. Graham Oct. 25, 1901; Martha b. April 8, 1869, m. George Harper; Roger b. June 8, 1871; Thomas L. b. Oct. 13, 1873; Weldon N. Nov. 20, 1875, m. Rose V. Allen; Mintn b. Feb. 16, 1878; Oakhan b. Dec. 14, 1880; Amos.
First Sergeant Co. D., Mormon Battalion; bishop of Honeyville ward 25 years.

HUNSAKER, ALLEN C. (son of Abraham Hunsaker and Eliza Collins). Born July 9, 1840, Payson, Adams county, Ill.
Married Susannah Dunn April 24, 1858, Brigham City, Utah (daughter of Simeon A. Dunn and Margaret Snyder, former pioneers 1848). She was born May 6, 1842, in Hancock county, Ill. Their children: Eliza b. March 17, 1862, m. John S. Willie Nov. 12, 1885; Allen D. b. Sept. 2, 1865, m. Ivy M. Green Dec. 17, 1885; Abraham b. April 22, 1870; Jacob A. b. July 8, 1873; Martin L. b. Oct. 26, 1876, m. Anna A.

Christensen June 20, 1909, m. Calla L. Frisby Sept. 6, 1906.
Married Eveline Dunn Oct. 5, 1868, Salt Lake City (daughter of Simeon A. Dunn and Harriet A. Silver, pioneers 1848, Brigham Young company). She was born Sept. 12, 1853, Brigham City, Utah. Their children: Simeon A. b. July 20, 1869, m. Mary A. Green Dec. 27, 1893, m. Matilda Teuber July 19, 1896; Lewis b. Jan. 17, 1871, m. Sarah E. Warner Feb. 6, 1898; Louisa b. Oct. 4, 1872, m. Hyrum Christensen Nov. 12, 1891; Lily M. b. April 28, 1874, m. Seymour L. Miller Nov. 12, 1891; Emeline M. b. Jan. 15, 1876, m. Henry Seeger Sept. 9, 1896; Harriet V. b. Oct. 27, 1877, m. Charles Haws Jan. 6, 1897; Ethel b. April 2, 1879, m. J. William Smith Oct. 3, 1901; Adaline b. Dec. 3, 1880; Letitie b. Jan. 19, 1882, m. Lester L. Hansen Dec. 14, 1904; Margaret b. Nov. 24, 1883, m. Parley W. Christensen Nov. 25, 1903; Susie b. Nov. 20, 1885, m. Wilford W. Christinsen Oct. 11, 1904; Aleen b. March 13, 1887, m. John N. Thomas June 22, 1910; Nephi b. July 10, 1889; Oscar b. June 1, 1891; Lorenzo S. b. May 29, 1892; Amy b. Oct. 18, 1894; Harold b. Nov. 6, 1897. Family home Honeyville, Utah.
Presiding elder of Bear River City ward ten years. Assisted in bringing immigrants to Utah. Served in Echo Canyon war.

HUNT, AMOS. Born Feb. 18, 1819, at Muklingburg, Ky. Came to Utah in October, 1852, Benjamin Gardner company.
Married Rebecca Wiggins Salt Lake City, who was born March 14, 1843. Their children: Elias b. Oct. 14, 1858, m. Luna Terry; Eliza Ellen b. Dec. 10, 1860, m. John A. Peterson; Cena Ann b. Oct. 3, 1863, m. Mathew W. Mansfield. Family home Hebron, Utah.
Married Nancy G. Welborn. Their child: Angeline b. Oct. 7, 1869, m. George S. Coleman May 5, 1886.

HUNT, LEVI (son of William Hunt of Worcestershire, Eng.). Born Aug. 21, 1833, in Worcestershire. Came to Utah in 1850.
Married Jane Gadd June 26, 1858, at Nephi. Their children: Joseph William, m. Marie ——; Levi Alderman, m. Elvira Hyatt; Samuel Sylvester, d. infant. Family home Nephi, Utah;
Married Phebe Louisa Fellows April 1, 1863, at Nephi (daughter of William Fellows of Nephi), who was born Aug. 4, 1846. Their children: Samuel Isaac, m. La'——. L. Lott; Eliza Jane, m. Thomas Ould; Mary Ellen, m. Thomas Shepherd; Sarah Susanna, m. Alfred G. Chicester; Amelia Emeline, m. Charles Grundy; Alice M., m. William Nay; Rosetta, m. Orson Talbot, m. James Harman; Wilfred. Family home Richfield, Utah.
Married Elizabeth McDonald March 15, 1886, at Joseph City, Utah. Family home Monroe, Sevier Co., Utah.
Seventy. Farmer. Lived at Joseph City, Utah.

HUNT, THOMAS (son of John Hunt, born July 1802, Derby, Eng., and Sarah Hunt, born March 29, 1804). He was born June 15, 1826, at Derby. Came to Utah in 1862.
Married Hannah Moon 1848 in England (daughter of James Moon of Derby), who was born Dec. 27, 1827. Their children: Sarah b. March 16, 1850, m. Charles Hale; Moroni b. May 5, 1852, m. Emma Casto; Frederick Nephi b. Sept. 2, 1854, m. Tomina Larsen; Ruth b. April 3, 1857, m. George Frazer; Fanny Moon b. Feb. 28, 1860, m. Hans Hansen; Thomas Alvin b. March 14, 1862, m. Alice Mary Jenson; Ammon b. March 26, 1865, m. Albertina Okerlund; Eliza Ann b. April 2, 1867, m. George Okerlund; Teancum b. Oct. 16, 1870, m. Ella Robinson; Hannah Isabella b. Jan. 6, 1872, m. John Andersen. Family resided Moroni, Gunnison and Monroe, Utah.
Member high council of Sevier stake. Director in United Order at Monroe 1873-77. Farmer; sheepraiser; miner. Died March 16, 1899, Monroe.

HUNT, FREDERICK NEPHI (son of Thomas Hunt and Hannah Moon). Born Sept. 2, 1854, in England. Came to Utah in 1864.
Married Tomina Larsen at Monroe, Utah. Their children: Harriet Isabella b. Oct. 11, 1876, m. Robert Orland Pope; Mary, m. Chris Andersen; Frederick Nephi, Jr., m. Lizzie Hansen; Franklin; Birdie; John Nathan; Maud, d. infant; Leah; Teancum. Family home, Monroe.
Elder. Farmer.

HUNT, THOMAS ALVIN (son of Thomas Hunt and Hannah Moon). Born March 14, 1862, Alton, Ill.
Married Alice Mary Jenson March 27, 1889, Manti, Utah (daughter of Jens Jenson and Celia Anderson of Monroe, Utah), She was born May 4, 1865. Their children: Delma b. Dec. 26, 1889, m. Irvin Olsen; Edna b. Sept. 9, 1891; Horace b. March 22, 1893, d. child; Theron b. Jan. 15, 1895; Irwin Jay b. Sept. 5, 1896; Byron b. Sept. 3, 1898; Ruth b. Sept. 28, 1901, d. March 26, 1910; Dona b. Jan. 22, 1904, d. March 5, 1905; Alice Helen b. Nov. 16, 1905; Maggie Alva b. Dec. 5, 1909. Family home, Monroe.
Missionary to England 1898-99.

HUNTER, ADAM PATTERSON (son of David Cook Hunter and Margaret Patterson of Fifeshire, Scotland). Born April 16, 1818, at Fifeshire. Came to Utah Aug. 13, 1852.
Married Elizabeth Patterson April 25, 1847 (daughter of William Patterson and Elizabeth Blair), who was born Oct.
6, 1822. Their children: Elizabeth b. July 2, 1843, m. David Cook Feb. 4, 1859; David P. b. Oct. 15, 1845, m. Mary Hughes Aug. 9, 1867; Margaret b. Sept. 28, 1847, m. Abraham Van Orman March 6, 1867; Mary b. Nov. 18, 1849, m. Archie Moffat June 14, 1875; Janette b. Oct. 27, 1852, m. John Kingdon Aug. 22, 1870; Isabella b. Oct. 27, 1852, m. George Perkins July 18, 1870; Christina b. May 10, 1855, m. James Brown July 27, 1882; George P. b. Sept. 13, 1857, d. infant; Gean b. Aug. 21, 1858, m. Dave Mullholland 1880; Adam P. b. Nov. 25, 1860, m. Estella Sephson Nov. 11, 1886; Eller, b. Oct. 22, 1863, m. William McCammeron June 15, 1887; William P. b. Aug. 20, 1865, m. Jane McDuff Oct. 24, 1895; Lorena G. b. Nov. 19, 1870, m. Alma Burdett 1893.
Quarried stone for Salt Lake temple 1852-79. Elder. Died Jan. 25, 1879.

HUNTER, DAVID P. (son of Adam Patterson Hunter and Elizabeth Patterson). Born Oct. 15, 1845, Fifeshire, Scotland.
Married Mary Hughes Aug. 9, 1867, Farmington, Utah (daughter of William and Cathrine Hughes), who was born July 28, 1847, Liverpool, Eng.

HUNTER, ALEXANDER (son of Alexander Hunter and Sarah Maine of Scotland). Born April 3, 1849, in Ayrshire, Scotland. Came to Utah Sept. 2, 1868, Simpson M. Molen company.
Married Elizabeth McBride Dec. 22, 1877 (daughter of James McBride and Elizabeth Glenn, pioneers Sept. 2, 1868, Simpson M. Molen company). She was born Feb. 16, 1857. Came to Utah with parents. Their children: Elizabeth M. b. Dec. 20, 1878; Alexander b. Feb. 8, 1881, m. Nora Smout Oct. 18, 1905; Sarah b. May 16, 1884, m. Orson P. Linford June 3, 1909; James S. b. Jan. 24, 1887, m. Stella Rogerson Nov. 22, 1911; John Angus b. Oct. 14, 1889, m. Ruby Ipsen Oct. 7, 1910; William Clyde b. Aug. 5, 1893; Hazel May b. Feb. 23, 1896; Lawrence Glenn b. Feb. 17, 1898; Clarence E. b. May 27, 1904. Family home Slaterville, Utah.
Seventy. Ward teacher.

HUNTER. ALEXANDER Jr. (son of Alexander Hunter and Elizabeth McBride). Born Feb. 8, 1881, Slaterville, Utah.
Married Nora Smout Oct. 18, 1905, Ogden, Utah (daughter of William Smout and Sarah Moore), who was born March 10, 1892, Slaterville, Utah. Their children: Elton Glenn b. March 20, 1907; Hazel L. b. Oct. 20, 1908; Darrell W. b. Oct. 15, 1910.

HUNTER, EDWARD (son of William Hunter and Mary Ann Davis). Born March 29, 1821, Newtown Square, Delaware county, Pa.
Married Mary Ann Whitside November 1843 (daughter of James Whitside and Penina Evans). Their children: Sarah Ann; Margaret; Elizabeth; Emily J.; William E.; Mary Ann; Penina; Hyrum L.; Ada Rosetta.
Married Martha Ann Hyde March 30, 1856 (daughter of Rosel Hyde and Mary Ann Cowles). Their children: Rosel; Louisa; Herman; Ida; Davis; Mary Ann; George A.; Edward; Edna; Martha M.; J. Austin.
Member Mormon Battalion; bishop Grantsville ward.

HUNTER, ISAAC (son of Isaac Hunter and Elizabeth Taylor). Born Aug. 14, 1816, Haversham Parish, Westmoreland-shire, Eng. Came to Utah 1849.
Married Ann Lund Nov. 8, 1840, Brigstaee, Eng. (daughter of Robert Lund and Mary Wilson of Brigateer), who was born May 9, 1815. Their children: Jacob, m. Mary Shaffer; Mary Ann; Margaret, m. Isaac Groo, m. Joseph M. Phelps; Martha, m. Levi Wolstenholme; Abraham, m. Harriet Astle; Ann Elizabeth, m. John R. Clawson; Isaac, m. Mary Hansen; Ellen, m. Francis L. Ball. Family home, Salt Lake City.
Member 42d quorum seventies; ward teacher. One of President Young's guards. Captain of home militia; policeman. Worked on Salt Lake theatre and temple. Stonecutter and contractor. Died May 28, 1898, Salt Lake City.

HUNTER, WILLIAM (son of James Hunter and Marian Patterson, the former of Newtonshaw, Clackmanan, Scotland). Born August 1794, Newtonshaw. Came to Utah 1851.
Married Mary Sandon May 13, 1813 (daughter of Joseph Sandon and Mary Hunter), who was born March 1789 and came to Utah Jan. 14, 1849. Their children: James H. b. March 17, 1816, m. Janet Reid; Joseph b. Aug. 20, 1818, m. Elizabeth Davidson Jan. 5, 1840; John b. July 23, 1820, m. Ann Davidson 1849; Mary b. April 5, 1823, m. George Condie; William b. Nov. 1825; George b. March 30, 1828, m. Mary Muir Dec. 23, 1858; Janet b. July 28, 1810, m. Robert Strang 1849; David b. Nov. 4, 1833. Family home Cedar City, Utah.

HUNTER, JOSEPH (son of William Hunter and Mary Sandon). Born Aug. 20, 1818, Rekyrow, Clackmannan, Scotland.
Married Elizabeth Davidson Jan. 5, 1840, at Clackmannan, Scotland (daughter of John Davidson, pioneer 1852, Jasen Howell company). Their children: Alexander (adopted) b. Dec. 31, 1837; William D. b. March 30, 1841, m. Emma Freeman; John D. b. May 19, 1842, m. Elizabeth Bennett Oct. 27, 1863; Joseph Sandon b. Nov. 20, 1844, m. Eliza C. Pincock Jan. 1, 1866; Euphenia b. March 24, 1848, died. Family home Cedar City, Utah.
Early settler to Cedar City 1852. Farmer and stockraiser.

HUNTER, JOHN D. (son of Joseph Hunter and Elizabeth Davidson). Born May 19, 1842, Clackmannan, Scotland. Married Elizabeth Bennett Oct. 27, 1863, Fillmore, Utah (daughter of John Bennett and Jane Roberts, pioneers Oct. 15, 1863, Samuel D. White company). She was born Aug. 25, 1844, in Connahs Quay, North Wales. Their children: John Edward b. Oct. 8, 1864, m. Margret Hulda Teepler April 21, 1886; Elizabeth Jane b. Oct. 14, 1866, m. Milo Harmon April 1887; Catherine b. July 18, 1869, m. Thomas Memmott May 1900; Joseph B. b. Dec. 23, 1871, m. Lillias J. Morris Feb., 1896; Mary Ann b. April 11, 1874, m. George Milburn Mills Jan. 6, 1897; Benjamin b. Nov. 28, 1876, m. Ellen Lewis Dec. 1901; George William b. March 26, 1879, died; Emma b. June 3, 1881, m. Charles Edmond Lewis Dec. 1905; Lavinia b. April 30, 1883, m. Joseph Alvin Lyman Feb. 1, 1905; James Samuel b. May 9, 1885, m. Della C. Allred Dec. 1907. Family home Holden, Utah.
Worked on St. George temple. Assisted in bringing immigrants to Utah 1863. Farmer and stockraiser.

HUNTING, JAMES (son of Nathan Hunting of Earls Commons, Worcestershire, Eng.). Born 1791, Earls Common, Eng. Came to Utah 1853, Appleton Harmon company. Married Elizabeth King, Grafton, Worcestershire, Eng. (daughter of Abel King), who was born April 24, 1803, and died May, 1891. Their children: James, d. infant; Elizabeth, m. George Ballard, m. Thomas Smith; Hannah b. Dec. 1832, m. William Smith and Mr. Reynolds; George, died; Benjamin, died; William James. m. Martha Ann Hale, m. Laura Wiscomb (Sainsbury). Family home Springville, Utah.
Farmer. Died 1871, Cottonwood, Utah.

HUNTING, WILLIAM JAMES (son of James Hunting and Elizabeth King). Born June 24, 1839, Earls Commons, Eng. Married Martha Ann Hale June, 1866, Springville, Utah, later in Endowment House, Salt Lake City (daughter of James and Lucy Hale of Weber county, came to Utah by oxteam). She was born Jan. 20, 1845. Their children: Annie b. July 4, 1867, m. John Schofield; William b. 1869, m. Susie Cherry; Lucy b. 1871, m. John Ritchens. Family home Springville, Utah.
Married Laura Wiscomb (Sainsbury) Feb. 16, 1882, Endowment House, Salt Lake City (daughter of James Wiscomb and Mary Ann Fleet of Portfield [Chidester], Eng., came to Utah 1871). She was born June 14, 1850. Their children: Benjamin Franklin b. Dec. 1882, d. infant; Elizabeth A. b. Oct. 22, 1883, d. child; Laura b. April 22, 1886, d. infant; George Q. b. June 11, 1887; Minnie Mary b. Nov. 26, 1890, m. James Joseph Tromley. Family home Roosevelt, Utah.
Member 72d quorum seventies; high priest. Participated in the Echo Canyon war; veteran Walker and Black Hawk wars. First located in Cottonwood ward, and after moved to Springville 1858, Malad, Idaho, Ashley valley, locating in Jensen ward 1889, finally settled at Roosevelt, Utah, 1906, when the Uintah Indian Reservation was opened. Pioneer irrigation canal and wagon road builder. Farmer.
Laura Wiscomb married John Sainsbury October, 1871, Endowment House, Salt Lake City. His parents lived at Portsmouth, Eng., and came to Utah about 1867. He was born Dec. 6, 1826, and died 1876, Springville, Utah. Their children: James b. Aug. 26, 1872, d. infant; Ellen Marie b. June 22, 1874, m. Alma N. Timothy; Charles b. June 14, d. infant. Family resided Minersville and Springville, Utah.

HUNTINGTON, DIMMICK B. (son of William Huntington and Zina Baker of Watertown, N. Y.). Born May 26, 1808, at Watertown. Came to Utah July 28, 1847 with Captain James Brown, Contingent, Mormon battalion.
Married Fannie Maria Allen April 28, 1830, Watertown, N. Y. (daughter of Clark Allen and Martha Thompson of Watertown), who was born Oct. 26, 1810. Their children: Clark A., m. Rosanna Galloway; Lot E., m. Naomi Gibson; Margett, d. infant; Fannie M., d. infant; Martha Zina, m. Edmon Paul; Betsy P., d. infant; Julia C., m. John Hancock, m. John R. Mellen; Sarah A., d. infant.
High priest; Indian missionary, forty years; Indian interpreter; patriarch. Farmer. Drum major in martial band. Early settler at Provo. Died Feb. 1, 1879.

HUNTINGTON, OLIVER B. (son of William Huntington). Born 1825 in New York state. Came to Utah July 24, 1847, Brigham Young company.
Married Mary Melissa Neal 1843, Cambria, Niagara county, N. Y. (daughter of George A. Neal and Aseneth Cooley of Cambria, pioneers 1852, Captain Brown company). Their children: Mary A., m. Andrew Cooley; Baby, d. infant; George W., m. Elizabeth Sprouse and Rosetta A. Squires. Family home Salt Lake City.
High priest; missionary to England two years; patriarch; superintendent Sunday school at Springville, Utah. Bee inspector. School trustee. Farmer and stockraiser. Died January 1909, at Springville, Utah.

HUNTINGTON, GEORGE W. (son of Oliver B. Huntington and Mary Melisa Neal). Born Sept. 13, 1848, Cambria, N. Y. Came to Utah with father.
Married Sarah Elizabeth Sprouse Sept. 1870, at Salt Lake City (daughter of John Sprouse and Catherine Woldridge of Texas); she was born Oct. 27, 1844. Their children: Mary Zina b. Aug. 14, 1871, d. young; George Augustus b. Nov. 1, 1872, m. Elizabeth Ross; Mabel Elizabeth b. June 1, 1874, m. Louis O. Knight; John William b. Jan. 17, 1876, d. infant. Family home Salt Lake City, Utah.
Married Rosetta Agnes Squires, Feb. 14, 1878, at Salt Lake City (daughter of Henry Augustus Squires and Sarah M. Cottlin of Salt Lake City, pioneers Nov. 30, 1856, Edward Martin handcart company). She was born March 14, 1855. Their children: Zina Ida b. Jan. 4, 1879, d. infant; Minnie Precinda b. Oct. 15, 1880, d. young; Rosetta Agnes b. June 16, 1883, m. William J. Bronson; William C. b. Dec. 10, 1885, d. infant; David Oliver b. May 10, 1887, d. 1890; Henrietta b. April 18, 1890, d. infant; Bessie Clestia b. Nov. 3, 1892, d. infant, Chauncy Boardman b. Sept. 26, 1897. Family home, Salt Lake City, Utah.
Elder; block teacher. Farmer and stockraiser.

HUNTINGTON, GEORGE AUGUSTUS (son of George W. Huntington and Sarah Elizabeth Sprouse). Born Nov. 1, 1872, at Salt Lake City.
Married Elizabeth Ross March 30, 1904, at Salt Lake City (daughter of Robert E. Ross and Ella Gertrude Alexander, of Midway, Utah). She was born Feb. 12, 1882. Their children: George Ross and William Rex b. March 12, 1905; Don Clifford b. Oct. 26, 1906; Ella Mourine b. June 17, 1909. Family home Midway, Utah.
Member 109th quorum seventies; home missionary 1905-07; high priest; Sunday school superintendent. Justice of peace. Farmer and stockraiser.

HUNTSMAN, JAMES. Came to Utah July 24, 1847, Brigham Young company.
Married Mary Johnson, who came to Utah Aug. 17, 1861, with her children. Their children: Lavinia; Katy Ann, m. Gilbert Bickmore; Isaiah, m. Rebecca Ames, m. Emma M. King, m. Sophia Egbert; Isaac, died; William, m. Mary Bickmore; Jacob, m. Jane Bickmore; Gabriel, m. Eunice Holbrook; Jesse Peter, m. Emma Crompton; Sarah, m. Joseph Gills; Kesiah, m. Levi Huntsman. Family home Fillmore, Utah.
Farmer. Died at Fillmore.

HUNTSMAN, ISAIAH (son of James Huntsman and Mary Johnson). Born Sept. 14, 1826, in Richland county, Ohio. Came to Utah in 1849.
Married Rebecca Ames Jan. 16, 1849, at Kanesville, Pottawattamie county, Iowa (daughter of Ira Ames and Charity Carter of Vermont, pioneers 1851). She was born 1830, Mooers at Fork, Clinton county, N. Y. Their children: Ezra b. Nov. 12, 1849, m. Mary Ann Walton and Mary (Williams) Chandler; Harriet b. Sept. 25, 1852, m. John H. Bankhead, m. Daniel Dalton; Ira b. Oct. 6, 1854, m. Anna (Palmer) Hutchinson; Clarissa b. Dec. 11, 1858, m. Benjamin Stewart, m. Orson Dalton; Isaiah b. Sept. 24, 1856, m. Mary Ann Meller Palmer, m. Susan Dalton, m. Thursa Lewis; Isabella b. Nov. 21, 1862, m. John William Dalton; Estella b. Jan. 24, 1863, m. Lewis Monroe Nebeker, m. William Nelson Spafford, Jr.; James b. April 13, 1865, m. Eunice Pritchett; Nila Ann Norton; Ida Rebecca b. Nov. 13, 1873, m. Thomas Mitchel Pritchett. Family home Annabella, Utah.
Married Emma Melissa King 1856, Salt Lake City (daughter of John Morris King and Sarah Ann Jewell, of American Fork, pioneers Sept. 17, 1852, John Tidwell company). She was born Sept. 18, 1840; died Jan. 10, 1905 in Cassia county, Idaho. Their children: Sarah, d. infant; Mary, m. Philander H. Bell; Edson, m. Elizabeth Johnson; Jane. m. John Tolman; John, m. Lucy Hardy; Amanda, m. Ebenezer Dalton; Ada, m. Isaac Dalton. Family home Annabella, Utah.
Married Sophia Egbert 1868, Salt Lake City. Widow of Robert Egbert with six children. Their only child: Louisa, died. Family home Wellsville, Utah.
Member company B Mormon battalion.
Settled at Fillmore and took an active part in the Indian warfare of that period. Moved to Wellsville 1864, then back to Fillmore 1870; in fall of 1874 moved to Annabella and died there June 3, 1878. Justice of peace; blacksmith and general mechanic.

HUNTSMAN, EDSON (son of Isaiah Huntsman and Emma King). Born March 16, 1863, Fillmore, Utah.
Married Elizabeth Johnson Sept. 7, 1884, Spring City, Utah (daughter of Andrew and Hannah Johnson), who was born Feb. 14, 1865. Their children: Grace b. June 10, 1885, m. John Cook; Ada b. Oct. 3, 1886; Ethel b. July 13, 1888, m. Clifford Jones; Mamie b. March 24, 1890; Ray b. Dec. 22, 1892, d. 1898; Vaurice b. Dec. 25, 1894; Furl b. Nov. 24, 1896; Thelma b. Dec. 2, 1898; Owen and Ona b. June 28, 1900; Austin b. April 12, 1902; Blenda and Blanche b. Jan. 26, 1904, both d. infants. Family resided Spring City and Ferron, Utah. Elder. Farmer.

HURD, WILLIAM BAKER (son of John Hurd and Fanny Baker of Devonshire, Eng.). Born Sept. 20, 1835, Devonshire. Came to Utah Sept. 15, 1861, Milo Andrus company.
Married Frances Taylor Jan. 1, 1858, at St. Louis, Mo. (daughter of Edward Ebenezer Taylor and Mary Ann Tarrant of London, Eng., pioneers October 1868). She was born June 2, 1833. Their children: John William b. Oct. 20, 1860, m. Eliza Williams; Francis b. Oct. 6, 1862, died; Joseph Hyrum b. Dec. 20, 1864, m. Blanche Duke; William Henry b.

Dec. 20, 1864, m. Margaret Leukel; Ruben Arthur b. March 17, 1867, m. Anna Gillott; David Elmer b. Aug. 29, 1869, m. Edith Frome; Albert Edwin b. Jan. 20, 1872, m. Emily J. Clark; Sarah A. b. Jan. 10, 1876, m. Thomas W. Bell; Walter Clarence b. Feb. 3, 1880, m. Kate M. Erskine. Family home Salt Lake City.
Elder. Bailiff of third district circuit six years. Contractor, plasterer and painter.

HURREN, JAMES (son of William Hurren, born Feb. 24, 1795, Chediston, and Mary Fisher Martin, born Nov. 27, 1786, Suffolk, Eng.; married in 1813). Born Feb. 24, 1827, Suffolk. Came to Utah Nov. 9, 1856, James G. Willie hand cart company.
Married Eliza Reeder, 1847 (daughter of David Reeder and Lydia Balls, former died at Omaha, Neb.; latter in 1839, in England). She was born Jan. 31, 1830, came to Utah with husband. Their children: Mary b. July 29, 1848, m. Joseph M. Wight Oct. 1864; George b. March 30, 1851, d. infant; Emma b. Feb. 21, 1852, m. James Woolf Dec. 1869; Sarah b. March 23, 1854, m. Samuel K. Seamons April, 1875; Selena b. July 14, 1856, d. infant; Rosannah b. Nov. 5, 1857, m. William Hyde Jan. 1879; James William David b. Dec. 8, 1859, m. Margaret A. Ashcroft June 10, 1886; Martin Francis b. Sept. 8, 1862, d. Nov. 2, 1863; Eliza Marietta b. Jan. 7, 1865, m. Stephen Thurston April 7, 1884; Phebe Jane b. April 15, 1867, m. Rosel Homer Hyde Oct. 15, 1886; Frank Edmund b. Sept. 1, 1873, d. infant. Family resided at Brigham City and Hyde Park, Utah.
Presided over Chediston branch in England; counselor to Bishop Robert Daines of Hyde Park ward; teacher and priest. Served in Echo Canyon trouble.

HURREN, JAMES WILLIAM DAVID (son of James Hurren and Eliza Reeder). Born Dec. 8, 1859, Brigham City, Utah.
Married Margaret A. Ashcroft June 10, 1886, at Logan, Utah (daughter of Henry Ashcroft and Mary Glover, pioneers with Isaac Allred company). She was born Feb. 10, 1865, Hyde Park, Utah. Their children: James William b. Dec. 2, 1889; Mary Ione b. Feb. 19, 1892; Clarence Ashcroft b. May 14, 1894; Carrie b. Jan. 26, 1897; Henry Reeder b. Aug. 27, 1899; David Glover b. Feb. 27, 1902; Eulalia b. April 4, 1906. Family home Hyde Park, Utah.
Officer in Y. M. M. I. A. 13 years. Member school board. Worked on Logan temple 1887-89. Missionary to Holland 1901-04; bishop's counselor 1903. School teacher eleven years.

HUSBANDS, CHARLES THOMAS (son of Thomas Husbands and Maria Weight of London, Eng.). Born March 15, 1844, London. Came to Utah Sept. 1, 1860, John Smith company.
Married Elizabeth Slater Oct. 3, 1868, at Salt Lake City (daughter of John Slater and Jane Booth of Lancashire, Eng., and Beaver, Utah; pioneers Sept. 15, 1868, John Gillesple company). She was born Aug. 17, 1851, Lancashire, Eng. Came to Utah 1868 with her parents. Their children: Charles Henry, d. infant; Rosetta, m. Alma Chalker; Charles Millard, m. May Wilson; John Eugene, m. Martha M. Axton; Herbert Henry, m. Ada Thomas; Albion C., m. Emily McMillian; Hazel, d. young. Family home Salt Lake City, Utah.
Elder. Made two trips to Omaha, Neb., for immigrants 1862, and to Rawlings, Wyo., 1868. Locomotive engineer.

HUSBANDS, WILLIAM (son of Thomas Husbands and Maria Margarett Weight of London, Eng.). Born Feb. 27, 1838, in London. Came to Utah September, 1861, Capt. Harmon company.
Married Sarah Curtis March 19, 1869, at London, Eng. (daughter of Joseph Curtis and Sarah Morrell that place; pioneers Sept. 23, 1861, Ansell P. Harmon company). She was born April 12, 1836. Their children: William C. b. May 13, 1861, m. Lucy Goodfellow; Charles T. b. Nov. 17, 1863, m. Julia Mikesell; Sarah M. b. March 29, 1865, m. John F. Heath; Hewson H. b. Sept. 29, 1866, m. Lamie Amy; Edwin M. b. Jan. 9, 1869, m. Esther Sandberg; Francis J. b. March 21, 1871; Lillian L. b. Dec. 17, 1872, m. Arthur Kent; Arthur D. b. Sept. 6, 1875, d. infant; Thomas Carlos b. Nov. 16, 1876, m. Alvira Edler; Amy A. b. Nov. 6, 1879, m. George L. McKeaver. Family home, Salt Lake City.
Employed on construction of Salt Lake theatre about two months; worked on Salt Lake temple about three years. On Feb. 6, 1885, received an appointment to a position in U. S. treasury department, during administration of President Chester Arthur and has continued an officer in that department to date; U. S. storekeeper in the service of U. S. Internal Revenue, collection district of Montana.

HUSSEY, DANIEL AGUSTUS (son of Elijah Hussey and Caroline Hartford of Dover, N. H.). Born Nov. 29, 1833, Dover. Came to Utah November, 1851, Stephen Markham company.
Married Sarah Louisa Bridges 1861, Salt Lake City (daughter of Henry Mallion Bridges and Sarah Louisa Lowe of Birmingham, Eng., the former came to Utah in September, 1864, the latter died on the plains). She was born March 29, 1841. Their children: William Agustus, d. infant; Florence Marian, m. James M. Brown; Charles Henry, m. Mary Alice Lambert; Caroline Rosella, m. Joseph T. Grover; Sarah Louisa, m. William Delbert Grover; Charlotte Agusta, m. Heber Burch; Daniel Warren, m. Rose Riley; Elijah, d. infant; Julia Isabell, d. aged seven; Joseph Seymour, d. infant. Family home East Mill Creek, Salt Lake county.
Went to the Missouri river in 1864 for immigrants with Joseph Rawlins' company. Lumberman.

HUSSEY, CHARLES HENRY (son of Daniel Agustus Hussey and Sarah Louisa Bridges). Born July 10, 1866, East Mill Creek, Salt Lake county, Utah.
Married Mary Alice Lambert 1896, Salt Lake City (daughter of Charles John Lambert and Lilly Harriet Druce, the former of Nauvoo, Ill., the latter of Haverstraw, N. Y.; pioneers September, 1848, Allen Taylor company and Sept. 16, 1861, Ira Reid company). She was born Jan. 26, 1871. Their children: Warren Lambert b. 1896; Alice Lambert b. 1899; Norma Lambert b. 1901; Elton Charles 1903; John Daniel 1906; Marian Iown 1910. Family home Ogden, Utah.
President fourth quorum elders of Veber stake; first counselor of Y. M. M. I. A. of first ward, Ogden; first assistant Sunday school superintendent of first ward, Ogden: member Weber stake board of religion class; superintendent Weber stake religion classes seventies. Real estate brokerage and Tungston industry. President Idaho Tungston Co. Lumberman, working in both mills and forests.

HUTCHINGS, WILLIAM WILLARD (son of Elias Hutchings, born April 20, 1784, in New York, and Sally Smith, born Feb. 26, 1794; married in 1816). Born April 3, 1823, in Ohio. Came to Utah Dec. 29, 1849, in a company of which he was captain.
Married Ruth C. Chase March 12, 1845. Their children: Sarah Ann; Emeline J.; Ruth C.; Mariam. Family home, Salt Lake City.
Married Sarah Ann Baldwin March 4, 1851, at Salt Lake City (daughter of Junius and Sarah Baldwin; pioneers 1849), who was born Nov. 25, 1837, Ledsvery, Hartfordshire, Eng. Their child: William Willard b. Nov. 23, 1851, m. Sarah Agnes LeBoron April 7, 1874.
Major in Black Hawk war and Utah militia.

HUTCHINGS, WILLIAM WILLARD (son of William Willard Hutchings and Sarah Ann Baldwin). Born Nov. 23, 1851, Salt Lake City.
Married Sarah Agnes LeBoron April 7, 1874, Salt Lake City (daughter of Alonzo E. LeBoron and Sarah Jeffs). She was born Jan. 9, 1875, m. A. B. Cline; Ellace Matilda b. Dec. 4, 1876; Lydia Monah b. Feb. 10, 1878, m. Edward Bohn; Mary Emeline b. March 2, 1881, m. James Rollins; Julia T. b. Aug. 25, 1883, m. W. T. Boyle; Emma Jane b. July 28, 1885, m. Ray Cuttler; Edna b. July 21, 1887; Effie Luciel b. Feb. 12, 1891; Suson Baldwin b. Nov. 3, 1894; William LeBoron b. April 24, 1896. Family home Beaver, Utah.
President of elders quorum; ward teacher; president Y. M. M. I. A. Sheriff of Beaver county, two terms, and city marshal of Beaver City two years. City councilman two years. Deputy U. S. marshal two years.

HUTCHINS, JAMES. Born in England. Came to Utah 1855.
Married Ellen Corbridge in April, 1859, Salt Lake City (daughter of William Corbridge and Ellen Parker of Franklin, Utah; pioneers 1852, John Parker company). She was born Nov. 17, 1840. Their children: John James, m. Mary M. Knight; Ellen E., m. John W. Stanger.
Elder. School trustee; justice of peace. Farmer, stockraiser and merchant. Died April 16, 1891, Slaterville, Utah.

HUTCHINS, JOHN JAMES (son of James Hutchins and Ellen Corbridge). Born March 27, 1860, Slaterville, Utah.
Married Mary M. Knight Dec. 23, 1881, Salt Lake City (daughter of John Knight and Sarah Taylor of Slaterville, Utah; pioneers 1854, independent company). Their children: Mary M. b. Oct. 4, 1882, m. Eli Lund; Ellen b. Sept. 9, 1884; James b. July, 1885; Rosina b. Sept. 15, 1886, m. Charles W. Cottel; Edeth b. April 24, 1889; Luella b. Sept. 23, 1891, m. Frank A. Bingham; Delwin b. Jan. 25, 1894, m. Elizabeth Farr; Iva b. March 20, 1896, d. Dec. 3, 1898; Marie b. Aug. 15, 1899.
Married Mattie L. Bragg May 24, 1905, Salt Lake City (daughter of James M. Bragg and Martha E. Tucker of Mississippi). She was born Oct. 5, 1873, Lexington, Miss. Their children: James Spencer b. July 8, 1906; Anna Ellen b. May 8, 1908; Louis B. b. May 6, 1910.
Elder; ward teacher. Constable six years; justice of peace two years. Judge of election. Member state convention.

HUTCHINSON, JACOB FLYNN (son of Solomon Hutchinson and Catherine P. Flynn of Nashua, N. H.). Born Aug. 14, 1816, East Wilton, N. H. Came to Utah Oct. 13, 1850, Edward Hunter company.
Married Constantia E. C. Langdon 1837 (daughter of Nathaniel Langdon and Pernelopy Sampson of Bowdoinham, Maine). She was born Nov. 11, 1818. Their children: Pernelope and Henrietta, d. infants; Nathaniel b. Nov. 5, 1841; Catherine b. Feb. 14, 1843, m. Newton Zyrick 1862; Margret b. 1844, died; Jacob Flynn b. June 15, 1846, m. Rhoda Jane Smith Aug. 8, 1870; George Henry b. May 3, 1849, m. Edwina Walker; Sarah Ellen b. Aug. 9, 1850, m. Henry Ketcham 1868; David Langdon b. April 30, 1852, m. Sarah Dudge Nov. 8, 1885; Mary, d. infant; Ruth b. Jan. 21, 1858, m. Peter Liddell Feb. 3, 1875.

Married Alice Peniston Wasden June 9, 1861, at Gunnison, Utah (daughter of Thomas Wasden and Mary Upson of Gunnison, Utah, pioneers Sept. 16, 1859. Edward Stevenson company). She was born Aug. 29, 1842. Their children: Joseph b. May 28, 1862, m. Rosanna Stratton; Orson b. Dec. 9, 1863, m. Martha M. Sorenson; Alice A. b. Jan. 17, 1866, m. Harmon Esklund.
First bishop of Gunnison ward. Tithing bookkeeper. Notary at Springville; assessor and collector of Salt Lake county 1850. Member legislative assembly from Salt Lake City at Fillmore in the early fifties. Painter; barber; bookkeeper and salesman.
Died May 7, 1867, Springville.

HUTCHINSON, JACOB FLYNN (son of Jacob Flynn Hutchinson and Constantia E. C. Langdon). Born June 15, 1846, Council Bluffs, Iowa. Came to Utah with parents.
Married Jane Smith Aug. 8, 1870, at Salt Lake City (daughter of Lott Smith and Jane Walker of Farmington, Utah), who was born Sept. 26, 1853. Their children: Jacob Lot b. Oct. 29, 1871; Rhoda Jane b. June 16, 1873; Joseph Flynn b. Aug. 10, 1874, m. Margaret E. Butchart Dec. 25, 1910; Clementina b. July 30, 1876, m. John Drew Dec. 30, 1894; William b. Feb. 7, 1878, m. Nellie McCurdy Dec. 1, 1902; Harriet S. b. Dec. 30, 1880; Jean b. Feb. 4, 1883, m. Rebecca Edwards Oct. 4, 1904; Ida Effie b. Feb. 2, 1885; Quincy David b. Dec. 13, 1886, d. April 16, 1889; Estella b. March 4, 1889; Leila b. Jan. 20, 1892; Earl b. July 3, 1894, d. infant;•Dewey b. Oct. 12, 1897. Family home Kimball„Idaho.
Settled at Salt Lake City. Elder. Moved to Farmington in 1870, to Randolph, Utah, 1874, from there to Rockland, Idaho, 1883, and in 1887 went to Kimballward, Idaho. Worked on Salt Lake tabernacle. Assisted in the erection of the meeting house at Randolph. Assisted in the organization of the first, school district at Rockland, Idaho, and served as trustee for three years; built the circular water power sawmill at Rockland, also• mills at Randolph and Kimball. Carpenter and lumberman.

HUTCHINSON, JAMES (son of William Hutchinson. born Jan. 28, 1814, Woodhouse,• and Mary Wilson, born Oct. 25, 1818, Bradford, Yorkshire, Eng.). Born July 25, 1838, Woodhouse, Eng. Came to Utah October, 1862, Kimball and Lawrence Merchandise company.
Married Ellen Redman March 29, 1862, at St. Louis, Mo., (daughter of Thomas Redman and•Alice Rothwell; pioneers 1862). She was born. May 17, 1833. Came to Utah 1862. Their children: John W. b. July 11,, 1864, m. Catherine Erickson Nov. 23, 1886; Alice b. April 26, 1866, m. Samuel Western, Sr.; James b. Aug. 3, 1868, d. infant; Sarah Ellen b. Oct. 12, 1869, d. Sept. 3, 1885; George H. b. Jan. 3, 1872, d. infant; Annie E. b. July 3, 1873, m. James Garrett; Luvenia b. Aug. 15, 1875, m. Edward Davis.
Ward teacher; Sunday school superintendent; choir leader; high priest. Black Hawk war veteran. Died in 1905.

HUTCHINSON, JOHN W. (son of James Hutchinson and Ellen Redman). Born July 11, 1864, Salt Lake City.
Married Catherine Erickson Nov. 23, 1886, Deseret, Utah (daughter of Nells Erickson and Christina Peterson, who came to Utah 1870). She was born June 1, 1869, in Denmark. Their child: Claris (adopted). Family home Hinckley, Utah. Seventy; missionary to southern states.

HYDE, HEMAN (son of James Hyde and Betty Pennock of Stratford, Orange county, Vt.). Born June 30, 1788, Stratford. Came to Utah September, 1849.
Married Polly W. Tilton, Stratford, Vt. (daughter of Mr. Tilton and Tabitha Bullock), who was born Jan. 20, 1786. Their children: Heman Tilton b. June 18, 1812, m. Eunice Sawyer; Charles W. b. July 16, 1814; Rosel b. May 20, 1816, m Mary Ann Cowles and Hannah Maria Simmons; William b. Sept. 11, 1818; Mary Ann b. Sept. 18, 1820, m. Mr. Grant. Family home Stratford, Vt.; Livingston, New York; Nauvoo, Ill.; Salt Lake City.
Veteran war 1812. Died June 11, 1869.

HYDE, ROSEL (son of Heman Hyde and Polly W. Tilton). Born May 20, 1816, York, Livingston county, N. Y. Came to Utah with father.
Married Mary Ann Cowles Dec. 12, 1839 (daughter of Austin Cowles and Phebe Wilbur), who was born Dec. 31, 1820. Their children: Martha Ann b. Nov. 20, 1841, m. Edward Hunter March 30, 1856; Rosel Maria b. April 20, 1843, m. James C. Taylor Jan. 8, 1860; Rosel James b. May 25, 1845, m. Jane Driggs; Mary Louisa b. March 9, 1851, m. James Bodily; Helen Elvira b. Dec. 6, 1852, m. Arthur Staynor Sept. 17, 1879; Heman b. Feb. 3, 1855, m. Urmina T. Griffeth May 9, 1878; Austin Cowles b. April 12, 1858, m. Mary W. Griffeth Feb. 12, 1880; Charles Croydon b. May 9, 1860, m. Mary Galbreth; William Alonzo b. June 6, 1863, m. Maria Reddich June 16, 1886. Family home, Kaysville.
Married Hannah Maria Simmons Feb. 22, 1862, Salt Lake City (daughter of Samuel Simmons and Hannah Maria Shekles), who was born Sept. 2, 1843, Bristol, Eng. Their children: Samuel b. Aug. 22, 1863, d. Oct. 1, 1863; Henry b. Aug. 4, 1864, d. Sept. 20, 1866; George Tilton b. Nov. 25, 1866, m. Emma Nibley Nov. 18, 1897; Clara Maria b. Dec. 25, 1868, m. Christopher E. Layton Nov. 27, 1895; John Simmons b. Dec. 18, 1870, m. Josephine Kennett 1901; Mabel b. Oct. 20, 16, 1872, m. Francis Stortevant Oct. 11, 1900; Mabel b. Oct. 20, 1875. m. Frank B. Flint March 9, 1904; Rosel T. b. Aug. 24, 1877, m. Lula Wray Sept. 7, 1903; Frank b. Jan. 25, 1881, m. Winnifred Barnes May 25, 1904; Ida b. Jan. 10, 1883, m. Mark L. Johnson Sept. 9, 1908. Family home, Kaysville.

HYDE, HEMAN (son of Rosel Hyde and Mary Ann Cowles). Born Feb. 3, 1855, Kaysville, Utah.
Married Urmina F. Griffeth May 9, 1878, Salt Lake City (daughter of Pattison Deloss Griffeth and Elizabeth Carson, pioneers 1851), who was born Jan. 12, 1860, Lehi. Utah. Their children: Heman b. April 14, 1879, m. Elizabeth Alhdown; William A. b. May 4, 1881, m. Lucy Wheelock; Dora E. b. Aug. 8, 1885. Family lived in Kaysville; home, Lewiston.
Bishop Fairview ward, Oneida stake, 1884. Moved to Star Valley, Wyo., 1888. Served there as counselor to Bishop William E. Crobridge, Auburn ward; bishop Auburn ward. 1894.

HYDE, WILLIAM ALONZO (son of Rosel Hyde and Mary Ann Cowles). Born June 6, 1863, Kaysville.
Married Maria Reddish June 16, 1886, Logan, Utah (daughter of Henry Reddish and Eliza Hurst), who was born Sept. 3, 1864, Brimmington, Eng. Their children: Myrtle Presindia b. Oct. 21, 1888; Elaine Maria b. Aug. 5, 1892; Charles Wilkis b. Sept. 18, 1894. Family lived Layton, Utah; Downey, Idaho; home Pocatello, Idaho.
Bishop Cambridge ward 1895; counselor to Pres. William C. Parkinson 1898; president Pocatello stake 1901. Member Idaho legislature 1898-99.

HYDE, GEORGE TILTON (son of Rosel Hyde and Hannah Maria Simmons). Born Nov. 25, 1866, Kaysville.
Married Emma Nibley Nov. 18, 1897, Salt Lake City (daughter of James Nibley and Fannie Gibbs), who was born Nov. 6, 1873, Paradise, Utah. Their children: George Osmond b. Dec. 17, 1898; Rosel Hirschel b. April 12, 1900; Emma and Enna (twins) b. May 15, 1902; Charles Corydon b. Aug. 7, 1904; Donald b. Aug. 20, 1909; Reed Tilton b. Nov. 9, 1911. Family lived Kaysville, Utah; home Downey, Idaho.
Missionary to Kentucky 1893-95; bishop Cambridge ward. Pocatello stake 1899-1907, Downey ward 1907. Settled at Downey, Idaho, 1895. Chairman board county commissioners Bannock county 1903-08. President and manager W. A. Hyde company, Downey, Idaho; director Gate City Furniture company, Pocatello, Idaho; president Downey state bank; president Downey townsite and deve'opment company; treasurer Portneuf-Marsh Valley Irrigation company.

HYDE, WILLIAM (son of Heman Hyde and Polly W. Tilton). Born Sept. 11, 1818, York, Livingston county, N. Y. Came to Utah Sept. 22, 1849, Captain Gulley company.
Married Elizabeth How Bullard Feb. 23, 1842, Nauvoo, Ill. (daughter of Joel and Lucretia Bullard), who was born Oct. 2, 1813, Holliston. Mass. Their children: J'ne Elizabeth b. Feb. 12, 1843, m. Simpson M. Molen; Angeline F. b. July 12, 1845, d. March 30, 1849; William b. Jan. 7, 1847, m. Matilda Card; Mary L. b. Dec. 23, 1848, m. John A. Woolf; Ellen M. b. Oct. 16, 1850, m. Isaac Woolf.
Married Sally Allred Sept. 1, 1850, Salt Lake City (daughter of Martin Allred and Polly Hesket), who was born Dec. 31, 1834, Salt Creek, Mo. Their children: Sariah b. July 25, 1851, d. July 25, 1851; Eliza Elvira b. July 6, 1852, m. Fred Turner; Don Carlos b. April 1, 1857, m. Zina Roakelly; Roselitha b. Feb. 8, 1859, m. Martin Woolf; Clara b. Feb. 28, 1861, m. Luther C. Burnham; Heman Tilton b. Jan. 3, 1863; Emma b. July 24, 1865, d. May 5, 1866; George b. July 24, 1865, d. May 11, 1866; Arthur Frank b. March 26, 1867, m. Lettie Woolf; Annie Laura b. Jan. 10, 1869, m. Robert W. Reeder; Ezra b. Jan. 25, 1871; James Martin b. Feb. 8, 1874.
Married Sarah Hamlin Pratt Jan. 1, 1860, Salt Lake City (daughter of Otis Pratt and Clarissa Hamlin, pioneers Oct. 11, 1859, Abraham R. Wright company), who was born July 4, 1861, m. Henry E. Hancey.
Married Abigail Gloyd Jan. 1, 1860, Salt Lake City (daughter of Charles Gloyd and Abigail Pratt, pioneers Oct. 11, 1859, Abraham R. Wright company), who was born Nov. 16, 1820, Cummington, Hampshire county, Mass. Their children: Charles Gloyd b. Nov. 13, 1861, m. May Daines Feb. 5, 1891; Abbie b. Jan. 19, 1863, m. B. F. Cowley; Rosel Homer b. Oct. 24, 1864, m. Phebe Hurren.
Married Phebe Ann Griffeth Aug. 31, 1867, Salt Lake City (daughter of Pattison D. Griffeth and Elizabeth Carson), who was born Feb. 9, 1847, Garden Grove, Iowa. Their children: Martha Elizabeth b. May 11, 1868, d. June 1, 1868; Wilford A. b. July 20, 1869; Delos William b. Oct. 10, 1871; John Alma b. Feb. 12, 1874.
Elder, Oct. 7, 1839; member seventy April 17, 1840; filled missions in Illinois, Indiana, Michigan, Maine, Vermont, New York and Australia; first bishop Hyde Park 1860 to death. Member Mormon Battalion. Probate judge of Cache county 1865 to death.

HYDE, CHARLES GLOYD (son of William Hyde and Abigail Gloyd). Born Nov. 13, 1861, Hyde Park, Utah.
Married May Daines Feb. 5, 1891, Logan, Utah (daughter of Robert Daines and Mary Glover; former pioneer 1859, Feramorz Little company, latter :853, Isaac Allred company). She was born May 26, 1872, Hyde Park. Their child: May b. Oct. 28, 1891, d. Oct. 28, 1891.
Married Sarah C. H. Parry (daughter of John Parry and Harriet Roberts). Born Feb. 27, 1866. Their children: Lavinia b. June 16, 1896; Willard Parry b. Aug. 30, 1899; Onofre b. Aug. 26, 1899; Hattie b. Dec. 9, 1902, d. Jan. 6, 1903; Nettie b. Sept. 4, 1904; Irma b. June 18, 1908. Family home, Hyde Park.
President deacons quorum 1877; president elders quorum 1885; missionary to Illinois and Indiana two years; member seventy Feb. 9, 1891; bishop March 19, 1893. Justice of peace; county recorder; president Hyde Park board of trustees ten years.

HYER, CHRISTIAN (son of Lars Hyer and Ann Olsen of Norway). Born Sept. 17, 1817, Christensen, Norway. Came to Utah Oct. 25, 1849, Ezra T. Benson company.

Married Carlina Hogan Nov. 23, 1850 (daughter of Eric Gaudyson Mibben Hogan and Halga Hanutedater Nestabe, married Dec. 1828 in Norway, pioneers Sept. 22, 1848, Zera Pulsipher company). She was born July 24, 1831. Came to Utah with parents. Their children: Carline b. Aug. 28, 1851, m. Robert Lewis; Ann b. Jan. 25, 1853, m. William Budge April 4, 1868; Harriet b. Sept. 14, 1854, d. Nov. 1, 1861; Christian b. April 30, 1859, d. Dec. 16, 1881; Andrew L. b. Dec. 1, 1860, m. Ellen Gilbret Feb. 14, 1880; Lizzie Helen Telfort b. May 20, 1885; Orson b. Sept. 3, 1862, d. Feb. 24, 1878; Elizabeh R. b. June 23, 1865, d. Aug. 23, 1880; Joseph b. July 11, 1867, m. Sarah Ann Tittensor June 1, 1892; Ellen b. Sept. 23, 1869, m. Fred Tittensor Dec. 11, 1889; Heber P. b. Sept. 3, 1872, d. Nov. 17, 1873; Brigham b. Dec. 6, 1874, m. Emma May Bright Nov. 24, 1897.

Married Lovina Hogan March 4, 1854, Salt Lake City (daughter of Eric Gaudyson Mibben Hogan and Halga Hanutedutter Nestabe), who was born July 14, 1836, Christensen, Norway. Their children: Lovina b. March 4, 1855, m. Hyrum A. Watson May 11, 1874; Ira b. July 27, 1859, d. July 9, 1881; Oliver b. Jan. 14, 1862, d. Sept. 16, 1862.

Married Rozina Shepard. Salt Lake City (daughter of Issa Shepard and Sarah Sackore, latter died May 7, 1847 in Missourri), who was born Jan. 31, 1829, in Denmark. Their children: Ezra Taft b. Dec. 11, 1869, d. Sept. 1870; Esther Jane b. Sept. 27, 1871, m. Samuel W. Hendricks Dec. 28, 1892, Family home Richmond.

High priest; member seventy, 1846; missionary to Scandinavia 1855-58; president teachers' quorum 1861-77; first counselor Richmond bishopric. Moved from Richmond to Bountiful 1860. Indian war veteran. Member territorial legislature. Helped bring immigrants to Utah. Died Sept. 20, 1901.

HYER, ANDREW L. (son of Christian Hyer and Carolina Hogan). Born Dec. 1, 1860, Richmond.

Married Ellen Gilbret Feb. 14, 1880, Richmond (daughter of James Gilbret and Sarah Choles), who was born May 24, 1862, Crafton, Eng. Their children: Annie Eliza b. Dec. 1, 1880, m. John Henry Kemp June 4, 1902; Andrew William b. Aug. 9, 1882, m. Emma Elaine Hillyard June 29, 1910; Orson Urban b. March 4, 1884; Elizabeth Ellen b. Jan. 31, 1886, m. Walter F. Hogan June 24, 1908; Ira and Ora (twins) b. Feb. 5, 1889, latter m. Blanche Benson Nov. 1, 1911; Sarah b. Nov. 15, 1890; Saul Edward b. Aug. 4, 1892; Ralph James b. June 25, 1894; Mere Gilbret b. June 17, 1896; Seneth b. May 16, 1898; Lovell b. June 12, 1900; Zethel b. April 7, 1902; Estell b. May 29, 1904.

Married Lizzie Helen Telford May 20, 1885, Logan, Utah (daughter of John Dodds Telford and Sarah Mitalda Coltrin; former pioneer 1850, latter Sept. 1850, Ben Hawkins company). She was born Oct. 21, 1862, Richmond, Utah. Their children: Lois Hellen b. March 7, 1886, d. Sept. 13, 1901; Norma b. Feb. 2, 1889; John Christian b. Sept. 10, 1890; Orvil b. Sept. 3, 1892, d. Oct. 5, 1892; Beatrice b. Feb. 18, 1895; Mardean b. Oct. 22, 1896; Eunice b. Feb. 8, 1898; Ross Telford b. July 28, 1900; Violeet b. June 4, 1902; Clester Wallace b. Dec. 13, 1903; Dorris Dale b. May 2, 1905. Family home, Lewiston.

President 39th and 117th quorum seventies; bishop Lewiston ward 1905; missionary to Europe 1885-88. One of organizers of Lewiston; member first town board 1904. Interested in Cache Valley creamery; director Union Creamery company and Utah Condensed Milk company. Farmer.

HYMAS, WILLIAM. Born July 26, 1806, at Rayleigh, Essex, Eng. Came to Utah Oct. 1862, James Wareham company.

Married Mary Ann Atkins Jan. 6, 1834. Their children: George b. 1835, d. in England; William Alfred b. March 22, 1837, m. Mary Edwards May 7, 1861; John A. b. Sept. 1, 1839, m. Mary Ann Pitman Nov. 10, 1861; Sarah M. b. 1841, m. Ormus Bates; Susan b. 1844, m. Noah Wardle; Benjamin b. May 6, 1846, m. Hannah Thurston 1868; James b. March 14, 1849, m. Sarah C. Evans; Mary Ann b. 1851, m. Thomas Duce. Family home Liberty, Idaho.

HYMAS, JOHN A. (son of William Hymas and Mary Ann Atkins). Born Sept. 1, 1839, at Rayleigh, Essex, Eng. Came to Utah Oct. 1861, Creighton telegraph train.

Married Mary Ann Pitman Nov. 10, 1861 (daughter of James Pitman and Ann King, latter pioneer 1862, James Wareham company), who was born Oct. 4, 1846. Came to Utah with husband 1861. Their children: John W. b. Feb. 22, 1865, m. Rossa Lee Orr; Mary Ann A. b. April 20, 1866, m. Thomas H. Watkins; Joseph M. b. Oct. 21, 1867, m. Emma Lyons; Benjamin P. b. Aug. 7, 1869, m. Elizabeth Price; Hyrum H. b. Oct. 10, 1870, m. Julia Poulsen; Mary R. b. May 8, 1872, m. John S. McMurray; Caddie C. b. Nov. 27, 1873, m. David R. Morgan; Arthur J. b. March 18, 1875, m. Della Davis; Alice L. b. June 12, 1876, m. Heber Johnson; David M. b. Jan. 9, 1878, m. Mary Agerter.

Married Mary Jane Watkins Oct. 24, 1878, Salt Lake City (daughter of Thomas Watkins and Ann Derricott), who was born Aug. 18, 1859, St. Louis, Mo. Their children: Thomas N. b. July 24, 1879, m. Mary J. Boyle; Martha J. b. April 7, 1881, m. Isaac Johnson; Bertha A. b. Nov. 30, 1882, died; Rebecca R. b. Nov. 11, 1884, m. Christian Jensen; Charles E. b. Jan. 7, 1887, m. Lora M. Pratt; Emily E. b. Feb. 4, 1889, died; Wilford W. b. March 6, 1890; Lottie b. June 26, 1892; Melvin M. b. June 9, 1894; Mabel b. May 12, 1896.

HYMAS, BENJAMIN (son of William Hymas and Mary Ann Atkins). Born May 6, 1846, Essex, Eng. Came to Utah 1862.

Married Hannah Thurston 1868, Salt Lake City (daughter of James Thurston and Mary Siamons, pioneers 1860, independent company), who was born June 1854. Their children: Mary Monitta b. Nov. 2, 1869, m. Wilfred Hyde; Binnie b. May 5, 1872, d. aged 8 months; Almidia b. Nov. 8, 1874, m. Phillip Quail; Emma b. Nov. 1875, died; Caroline b. Dec. 1876, m. Charles M. Shumway; Alma b. Nov. 1878, Willard b. Nov. 1879, Ida b. Dec. 1880, and Ada b. March 1882, died; Burt b. Sept. 16, 1887; Sarah Edith b. 1890; Jennie Clarissa b. 1893, m. Laura Neeley; Dell Grover b. 1895.

Bishop Treasuretown ward 19 years. Postmaster. Helped bring immigrants to Utah.

HYMAS, WILLIAM ALFRED (son of William Hymas and Mary Ann Atkins). Born March 22, 1837, Rayleigh, Essex, Eng. Came to Utah Sept. 26, 1862, James Wareham independent company.

Married Mary Edwards May 7, 1861, Omaha, Neb. (daughter of Thomas Edwards and Elizabeth Lewis of Merthyr Tydfil, Wales, pioneers Sept., 1861, Job Pingree company). She was born Oct. 12, 1839. Their children: Mary Ann; Elizabeth Ann; William T.; Samuel E.; Margret V.; Charles V.; May Janett; Alfred C.; Susan; Mary E. Family home Liberty, Ida.

High priest; stake president Y. M. M. I. A. 1888-96; first counselor to bishop Liberty ward 30 years. Farmer.

HYMAS, SAMUEL EDWARD (son of William Alfred Hymas and Mary Edwards). Born Dec. 10, 1867, Liberty, Idaho.

Married Fanny L. McMurray Oct. 17, 1900, Salt Lake City (daughter of James McMurray and Elizabeth Stevenson of Grantsville, Utah, pioneers 1852, Warren Snow company). She was born Nov. 2, 1873. Their children: Denail S. b. Oct. 22, 1902; Jesse R. b. May 28, 1904; Douglas b. July 28, 1905; Winnie b. Dec. 29, 1907; Willard A. b. Sept. 8, 1909; Gladys b. Aug. 12, 1911. Family home Sharon, Idaho.

Bishop Sharon ward 11 years; missionary to Northwestern states 1898-1900. County commissioner 1906-10; justice of peace four years. Farmer.

I

INGRAM, JAMES (son of Samuel Ingram and Kezia Coggins of Bicester, Oxfordshire, Eng.). Born June 17, 1833, at Bicester. Came to Utah Sept. 28, 1853, Vincent Shurtliff company.

Married Charlotte Holland March 26, 1862, Salt Lake City (daughter of John Holland and Ann King Renall of Molden, Essex, Eng.—pioneers Sept. 2, 1860, James D. Ross company). She was born Nov. 16, 1839. Their children: George W., m. Aurelia Amererte Mecham; Mary Ellenor, m. Abraham Zundel; Drusilla Louise; Fanny Ann, m. Thomas J. Morgan; James Oliver, m. Lula Gertrude Frodsham. Family home Brigham City, Utah.

Carpenter; farmer; wood turner.

INGRAM, JAMES OLIVER (son of James Ingram and Charlotte Holland). Born June 17, 1873, at Brigham City, Utah.

Married Lula Gertrude Frodsham 1904, Salt Lake City (daughter of Joseph Seymour Frodsham and Adelia Avasta Rudd), who was born March 31, 1882. Their children: Olive Ingram b. July 5, 1905; Douglas F. b. April 26, 1907; Burnace Gertrude b. April 11, 1909; Grace b. May 12, 1911. Family home Brigham City, Utah.

Member 58th quorum seventies; missionary to California 1889-1900. Farmer.

IRVINE, WILLIAM (son of Thomas Irvine and Agnes Shaw of Scotland). Came to Utah 1855, Milo Andrus company.

Married Agnes Kerr in Scotland. She came to Utah with husband. Their children: Margaret, m. James E. Leatham; George, m. Annie A. Burt; William, m. Jane Fife; John, m. Ellen Egan; Lizzie, m. Henry Nesbit; Lorenzo, died; James, m. Janie Richardson; Robert, m. Josephine Peterson. Family home, Salt Lake City.

Elder. Miner. Died 1855.

IRVINE, GEORGE (son of William Irvine and Agnes Kerr of Scotland). Born April 6, 1839, Lanarkshire, Scotland. Came to Utah 1855, Milo Andrus company.

Married Annie A. Burt Sept. 20, 1864, Salt Lake City (daughter of John and Margaret Burt of Scotland; pioneers Oct. 19, 1862, Horton D. Haight company). She was born Nov. 13, 1838. Their children: George b. Oct. 30, 1866, m. Clara Lyon; Thomas b. May 13, 1868, died; Margaret b. Jan. 3, 1870, m. Orson Harper; John William b. July 9, 1872, m. Edna May; Agnes Kerr b. Sept. 20, 1875, George Burt (adopted) b. Aug. 8, 1879, m. Sadie Kilpatrick; Edna Morrisey (adopted), b. Oct. 2, 1877, m. Emil Mossburg. Family home, Salt Lake City.

Drove three yoke of oxen across the plains. Lumber contractor and miner.

PIONEERS AND PROMINENT MEN OF UTAH

IRVINE, GEORGE, JR. (son of George Irvine and Annie A. Burt). Born Oct. 30, 1866, Salt Lake City, Utah.
Married Clara Lyon Sept. 15, 1897, Salt Lake City (daughter of Matthew Lyon, Salt Lake City, pioneer 1853). She was born Sept. 14, 1870. Their child: Annie b. June 20, 1898, died. Family home, Salt Lake City.
Missionary to southern states 1892-95; seventy. Merchant.

IRVING, WILLIAM (son of John Irving and Elizabeth Heron of Gatehouse of Fleet, Scotland). Born June 22, 1845, at Gatehouse of Fleet, Scotland). Came to Utah Oct. 15, 1863, William Hyde company.
Married Rebecca Williams Nov. 17, 1878, in Montpelier, Idaho (daughter of Thomas Williams and Janet Rogers), who was born 1862 and came to Utah 1875. Their children: William Thomas b. July 29, 1880, m. Mary Lindsay April 3, 1901; Samuel James b. Dec. 3, 1881, m. Minnie Hunter Sept. 27, 1910. Family home Montpelier, Idaho.
Married Christina Larsen Jan. 25, 1887, Paris, Idaho (daughter of Christian Larsen and Anna Sophia Peterson, married in 1862—pioneers 1862, Capt. Lindquist company). She was born Feb. 22, 1865, at Hyrum, Utah. Their children: John Leo b. Dec. 15, 1887; Washington b. Jan. 18, 1890; Alonzo Chester b. Feb. 22, 1892; Beatrice Sophia b. May 8, 1894, m. Albert Bowcutt July 19, 1911; Vivian Zora b. March 11, 1899. Family home Montpelier, Idaho.
Farmer.

ISAAC, JOHN PHILLIP (son of Reese Isaac and Margarette Phillip of Trevaughan, Carmarthen, South Wales). Born Feb. 2, 1833, Trevaughan, South Wales. Came to Utah Sept. 3, 1860, John Smith company.
Married Rachel Williams April 27, 1855, St. Clear, Carmarthen, South Wales (daughter of Theophilus Williams and Mary Wilkin of St. Clear), who was born Aug. 27, 1835, and came to Utah with husband. Their child: Mary Ann b. Feb. 10, 1856, d. March 16, 1856. Family home, Salt Lake City.
High priest. Worked on Salt Lake temple. Stone mason. Died Nov. 25, 1875.

ISAACSON, NEILS (son of Isaac Neilson and Massa Evans, both of Christiania, Norway). Born Jan. 6, 1817, at Christiania, Norway. Came to Utah Sept. 13, 1861.
Married Bertha Catherine Ogis Sept. 8, 1850 (daughter of Ogis Johnson and Hila Anders), who was born April 6, 1826, in Norway and came to Utah Sept. 13, 1861. Their children: Mary Ellen b. Nov. 21, 1851, m. William Thompson; Ingeborg Maria b. March 5, 1857; m. Jens Christian Johnson; Petra Annette b. Oct. 21, 1854; Lorenza b. Oct. 18, 1859; Isaac b. Feb. 9, 1864; Caroline b. May 14, 1865, m. Justin V. Shepard; Martha Ann b. July 27, 1867; Neils Henry b. April 4, 1870.

ISGREEN, ANDREW JENS (son of Jens Isgreen and Kerstena Tuffras of Sodermanland, Skone, Sweden). Born May 24, 1830, Skonsbeck, Skaninge, Sweden. Came to Utah Aug. 29, 1859, James S. Brown company.
First wife died, leaving one son, John M., who married Jane Dick.
Married Anna B. Stromberg at Salt Lake City (daughter of John Frederick Stromberg and Ulrika Juliana Johnson of Benggstorp, Kyrefalla, Sweden—pioneers Sept. 13, 1861, Joseph Horne company). She was born Feb. 1, 1833. Their children: Anna Wilhelmina, m. Charles Pocock; Emil Benjamin, m. Minnie Peterson; William Charles, m. Ida Jane Lindsay; Solomon, m. Alice Thomas; Martha Matilda, m. Charles C. Bush; Emily Jane, m. Lafayette Orme. Family home Tooele, Utah.
High priest; missionary in Sweden 1856-58. City sexton. Blacksmith; tinsmith; farmer and stockraiser. Died Oct. 6, 1909.

ISRAELSEN, TELLIF JOHN (son of Israelsen Tellif and Anna Christena Zacharisen, born Aug. 3, 1803, both of Kasfjorden, Norway). Born Feb. 18, 1826, at Kasfjorden. Came to Utah Oct. 1864, Captain Christoffersen independent company.
Married Mary Dorthea Markusen (daughter of Markus Andreas Nielsen and Mary Anna Rasmussen, married at Kasfjorden, Norway). She was born Aug. 9, 1836. Came to Utah with husband. Their children: Andrew Martin b. Jan. 9, 1857, m. Doletta Wilson; Mary Ann b. July 11, 1858, m. Christen Jensen; Annie Christine b. Sept. 17, 1860, m. John Jensen; Israel, died; Zacharias Ward b. Feb. 24, 1865, m. Edith F. Janes April 24, 1907; Maria Dorthea b. April 27, 1867, m. Ezra Wilson; Ellen Sophia b. Nov. 4, 1869, m. Joseph S. Allen; Clara Matilda b. Aug. 22, 1871, and Tellif John b. Nov. 14, 1873, both d. children; Emily Caroline J. b. May 17, 1876, m. Jeremiah Christiansen; Ida Malinda b. Nov. 11, 1878, d. child; Willard F. b. Aug. 26, 1879, m. Sadie Ames. Family home Hyrum, Utah.
Settled at Hyrum 1864; high priest; missionary to Norway two years 1881-83. Teacher. Died Dec. 5, 1897.

ISRAELSEN, ZACHARIAS WARD (son of Tellif John Israelsen and Mary Dorthea Markusen). Born Feb. 24, 1865, Hyrum, Utah.
Married Edith F. Janes April 24, 1907, Salt Lake City (daughter of Jacob Janes and Mary Ann Harrison, pioneers Sept. 15, 1862, William Henry Chipman company). She was born Nov. 9, 1877.

Missionary to Norway 1897-1900; president 62d quorum seventies 1906; first counselor to Bishop James J. Facer (3rd ward) Hyrum. Treasurer Hyrum 1892; deputy assessor west side Cache county 1897; registration officer for Hyrum precinct 1895. Manager Allen Bros. Mercantile company.

IVIE, WILLIAM FRANKLIN (son of James R. Ivie and Eliza M. Foset of Bedford county, Tenn.). Born Dec. 18, 1826, Bedford county, Tenn. Came to Utah 1848.
Married Malinda Jane Young, Provo, Utah (daughter of A. D. and Rhoda Young). Their children: John Franklin, died; William Alfred, m. Marlette Johnson; Jacob Alma, m. Lydia Okerlawd; Eliza Ann, m. J. J. Ivie; James Riley, m. Jensina Nielsen; Wilford, m. Matilda Okerlawd; Louis F., m. Nettie Eden; Della, m. William A. Taylor; Calvert Milton, m. Vilate Durfee. Family home Scipio, Utah.
Married Emily Young, Provo, Utah (daughter of A. D. and Rhoda Young). Their children: Addie, m. Warren Peck; Edwin, m. Lette Porter; Rosie, m. Thomas Memmott; Arthur; James; Estella; Burt. Family home Scipio, Utah.
Seventy. Indian war veteran. Assisted in bringing immigrants to Utah. Farmer and stockraiser. Died May 4, 1880.

IVIE, CALVERT MILTON (son of William Franklin Ivie and Malinda Jane Young). Born April 7, 1869, Scipio, Utah.
Married Vilate Durfee Nov. 25, 1892, Richfield, Utah (daughter of Jabez Durfee of New York, and Celestia Curtis of Pennsylvania, pioneers oxteam company). She was born June 29, 1873. Their children: Milton b. Sept. 9, 1893; Wilford Byron b. Oct. 6, 1895; Raymond b. Dec. 16, 1897; Elvada Jane b. Aug. 4, 1901; Otto Verlin b. March 7, 1904; Theresa Lucile b. April 9, 1907; Golden La Voy b. Aug. 10, 1909; Vergil June b. June 6, 1912. Family home Aurora, Utah.
Missionary to Eastern states 1898-1900; ward clerk 11 years; ward teacher; Sunday school superintendent of Aurora ward 5 years; bishop of Aurora ward since 1906. School trustee Aurora district 12 years. Farmer and stockraiser.

IVERSEN, JEPPE (son of Iver and Elsie Sorensen of Aarhuus Amt, Denmark). Born Aug. 16, 1814, Orslev Kloster, Denmark. Came to Utah Sept. 24, 1856, Knud Peterson company.
Married Annie Christina Mortensen, at Esterborg, Aarhuus Amt, Denmark (daughter of Andrew Mortensen and Christina Anderson of Roivi, Aarhuus Amt, Denmark). She was born Sept. 13, 1802. Their children: Hans Peter, m. Annie Nilson; Elsie Maria, m. Stephanus Moss; Martin, d. 1862; Ceroline Christina, m. William Morrison; Elizabeth Catherine, m. Ole Salisbury. Family home Mt. Pleasant, Utah.
High priest. Farmer. Died 1899, Washington, Utah.

IVERSEN, MAGNUS (son of Iver Klemensen and Gunhild Olsen of Engen, Buskerud, Norway). Born Dec. 22, 1816, at Engen.
Married Ingeborg Kirstine Nielsen (daughter of Ole Nielsen and Ann Margrette Nielsen of Haugsund, Norway), who was born Dec. 9, 1845. Came to Utah 1875. Their children: Iver; Gustave Arnt, m. Mary Olsen. Family home Christiania, Norway.
Died Aug. 24, 1874, Christiania, Norway.

IVERSEN, GUSTAVE ARNT (son of Magnus Iversen and Ingeborg Kirstine Iversen). Born Nov. 17, 1871, at Drőbak, Norway. Came to Utah July 24, 1875, L. S. Anderson company.
Married Mary Olsen Oct. 23, 1895, Manti, Utah (daughter of Fredrick Olsen and Matilda Jensen of Ferron, Emery county, Utah), who was born Aug. 6, 1873. Their children: Maude May b. March 31, 1897; Glendon Gustave b. Dec. 11, 1898; Clarence Magnus b. Jan. 4, 1899; Richard Donald b. March 15, 1902; Ray Clifford b. Nov. 24, 1903; Ethel Jean b. Sept. 23, 1905; Kenneth Ross b. May 25, 1909; Evelyn Augusta b. June 1, 1911. Family resided Manti and Price, Utah.
Missionary to Norway 1892-4; second counselor in presidency South San Pete stake; president Carbon stake, Price. County recorder of San Pete county 1896; Utah state senator 12th district 1911-14; assistant attorney general of Utah 1913. Attorney.

IVERSEN, PETER (son of Christian Iversen, born Aug. 24, 1805, and Anna Elizabeth Jensen, born April 27, 1807, both at Viele, Denmark—married 1829). Born Jan. 21, 1840, Viele, Denmark. Came to Utah Oct. 1, 1862, Joseph Horne company.
Married Kiersten Rasmussen Feb. 16, 1863 (daughter of Rasmus Clausen and Karen Eabensen), who was born March 1840. Came to Utah with husband. Their children: Peter Martin b. Jan. 31, 1865, m. Augusta Nelsen Sept. 15, 1893; Niels Carl b. Oct. 8, 1866, m. Hilda Lundquist March 16, 1898; Richard b. Aug. 22, 1868, m. Annie K. Larsen 1891. Family home Mill Creek, Utah.
Married Karen Rasmussen Sept. 17, 1871, Salt Lake City (daughter of Rasmus and Knudsine Petersen, who were married in 1836, Aarhuus, Denmark). She was born April

23, 1844, Aarhuus, Denmark. Their children: Lelian Sine b. March 21, 1880, m. John Calvin Cobb Oct. 19, 1904; Emma Carrie b. Sept. 16, 1882, m. Reeves D. Heigh Dec. 16, 1903; Amanda b. May 10, 1884, m. Joseph Israel Pierson Oct. 3, 1906. Family home Bear River City, Utah.
High priest and ward teacher. Assisted in erection of St. George, Manti, Logan and Salt Lake temples. Settled in Mill Creek ward 1862 and moved to Box Elder county 1867. Helped build canal from Cottonwood to Salt Lake City to convey water to Temple. Worked on Canadian Pacific from Ogden to Promontory, also on Utah Northern narrow gauge from Brigham to Logan. Pound-keeper 7 years; watermaster 25 years; mailcarrier from Bear River City and Corrine 8 years; registrar agent 4 years.

IVERSON, IVER NICHOLAS (son of Nicholas and Mary Catherine Iverson of Schleswig-Holstein, Denmark). Born March 19, 1821, in Schleswig. Came to Utah Sept. 27, 1853, Moses Dailey company.
Married Catherine Williams Jan. 19, 1854, Salt Lake City (daughter of Christopher Williams and Millicent Van Nostran of Upper Canada, former a pioneer, 1848, Brigham Young company). She was born June 6, 1826. Their children: Mary Catherine b. Feb. 15, 1855; Alma N. b. Aug. 7, 1857, m. Sarah Jane Tuckett; Christopher W. b. Dec. 30, 1859. Family home Pleasant Grove, Utah.
Missionary to Denmark 1857-58. Had charge of a company of emigrants from Denmark. Died Aug. 19, 1860, Pleasant Gorve.

IVERSON, ALMA NICHOLAS (son of Iver Nicholas Iverson and Catherine Williams). Born Aug. 7, 1857, Pleasant Grove, Utah.
Married Sarah Jane Tuckett Oct. 16, 1884, Salt Lake City (daughter of John Tuckett and Sarah Ann Gee of Salt Lake City and Springville, Utah). She was born Jan. 2, 1863. Their children: Thalia b. Aug. 10, 1885, m. Arthur Laycock; Eda Laryotha b. April 14, 1887, m. Louis Ditmore; Eltha May b. Oct. 10, 1889, m. Niels L. Monson; Alma Nicholas b. Dec. 5, 1891; Nellie b. Jan. 21, 1894; Olive b. Aug. 8, 1896; Reva Caroline b. March 13, 1899; Jessie Catherine b. Oct. 21, 1901; Laid Dewayne b. Nov. 25, 1904; John G. b. May 18, 1907. Family home Pleasant Grove, Utah.
Worked for 43 years in canyons building roads, trails, hauling logs, running a sawmill and cutting lumber for houses, beginning when he was 13 years of age, and taking a man's place; built the trail over which the first sacks of ore were brought from American Fork canyon. Also conducted a farm.

IZATT, ALEXANDER (son of William Izatt and Grace Adamson of Fife, Scotland; latter came to Utah Oct. 4, 1864, William S. Warren company). Born May 14, 1843, Fifeshire. Came to Utah Oct. 4, 1864, William S. Warren company.
Married Elizabeth Boyle 1865, Salt Lake City (daughter of George Boyle and Mary McDugall). Their children: Mary and Grace, died; William B., m. Rhoda Ann Turner; Elizabeth, m. John S. Andrews; Janett. m. Albert Hugo; Margaret, m. Alfred Osborn Shelton; Jane. m. Robert Briggs; Anne, m. Joseph E. Wilson, Jr.; Alexander G., m. Rebecca Turner; Georgena, m. Edward J. Clark. Family home Logan. Utah.
High priest; temple wokrer. Stone mason. Died Jan. 1913.

J

JACK, JAMES (son of John Jack and Margret Cooper of Scotland). Born 1829, in Scotland. Came to Utah 1853, independent company.
Married Jemima Innis Feb. 11, 1853, in Scotland (daughter of James Innis), who was born 1829. Their children: James C. died; Jemima M., m. H. M. Weight; John M., died; William H., m. Ann Meek; Jane A., m. T. L. Halliday; Jessie E., died; Rolla I., m. Mable Longfellow; Joseph C., m. Louise Young. Family home, Salt Lake City.
Member eighth quorum seventies; chief clerk and treasurer to first presidency. Director Saltair Beach Co. Director Inland Crystal Salt Co.; director Grass Creek Coal Co.; vice president Salt Lake & Los Angeles R. R. Co.; Utah territorial treasurer many years. Died March 2, 1911, Salt Lake City.

JACK, WILLIAM H. (son of James Jack and Jemima Innis). Born Jan. 2, 1859, Salt Lake City.
Married Ann Meek July 9, 1883, Salt Lake City (daughter of Benjamin Meek and Louisa Rogers of Salt Lake county; pioneers 1866, independent company). She was born June 12, 1861. Their children: Myrtle; James E.; William L., died; Joseph E.; Jemima E.; Ruth A., died; Rolla L.; Jessie; Anita J.; John M. Family home, Salt Lake City.
Member eighth quorum seventies. Superintendent Inland Crystal Salt Co.; president Holliday Drug Co.

JACKSON, HENRY CLARK (son of Robert Jackson, born Jan. 12, 1788, and Hannah Clark, born June 13, 1790, Crowle, Lincolnshire, Eng.). He was born June 3, 1819, Gainsborough, Lincolnshire. Came to Utah Oct. 7, 1852, James C. Snow company.

Married Ann Oades Feb. 22, 1843 (daughter of William Oades and Elizabeth Sowersby), who was born May 7, 1823. Their children: Henry William b. July 24, 1851, m. Mary Adeline Montierth; Elizabeth Sarah b. May 21, 1854, m. Jerome E. Remington; Alma Oades b. March 25, 1856, m. Emma Jane Obray; Hannah Ann b. Dec. 13, 1857, d. Sept. 23, 1861; John Clark b. Aug. 31, 1859, m. Charlotte Housley; Frederick Walter b. Dec. 4, 1863, m. Hannah Evans.
Married Mary Gilmore White May 4, 1861, Salt Lake City (daughter of William White and Martha Griffith), who was born Dec. 27, 1837, at Fishguard, Pembroke, Wales. Their children: Mary Jane White b. May 3, 1862, d. Aug. 24, 1863; Bessie White b. Feb. 18, 1865, m. Joseph Cowley; Amanda White b. Jan. 25, 1867, d. July 8, 1869; Robert William White b. Jan. 8, 1870, m. Eliza Welch Sept. 17, 1891; Thomas Franklin White b. Jan. 11, 1873, m. Hannah Welch.
President 36th quorum seventies; first counselor in bishopric of Paradise ward 1877-84; bishop of Paradise ward 1873-76; president high priests quorum 1894; ordained patriarch May 8, 1898. Participated in Echo Canyon campaign 1857-58. Built sawmill at Paradise in 1860, and in 1865 built gristmill at same place. Moved to Hyrum in 1869. Died Jan. 9, 1905, Paradise.

JACKSON, HENRY WILLIAM (son of Henry Clark Jackson and Ann Oades). Born July 24, 1851, Kanesville (Council Bluffs), Iowa.
Married Mary Adeline Montierth Feb. 5, 1871, Paradise, Utah (daughter of Alvin M. Montierth and Harriet Crapo), who was born Nov. 27, 1853, Salt Lake City. Their children: Henry Somes b. Nov. 4, 1871, m. Mary Jane Flint; Charles William b. Aug. 28, 1873, m. Luella Clegg; Alvin Somes b. Aug. 8, 1875, m. Effie M. Mangum; Laura May b. June 27, 1877, m. Edward D. Jones; Eugene Somes b June 6, 1879, m. Edith Dayley; Ann Somes b. Sept. 17, 1881, m. Orin M. Hess; Frederick Clark b. Aug. 11, 1883, m. Ann Karlson; Harriet Somes b. Sept. 9, 1885, m. Edward Teeples; Mary Elizabeth b. Sept. 15, 1887, m. Sidney Nielson; Esther Somes b. Aug. 22, 1890, m. George F. Rudd; Hazel b. Jan. 29, 1894. Family home St. Anthony, Idaho.
Settled at Salt Lake City 1852, moved to Paradise with his parents in 1865. Presiding elder at Old Paradise branch of Paradise ward: bishop of Avon 1891-94; counselor to Bishop E. Z. Carline 1896-97; high councilor of Fremont stake; ordained patriarch March 15, 1908. Moved to Parker, Idaho, 1894.

JACKMAN, LEVI (son of Moses French Jackman, born June 16, 1767, and Elizabeth Carr, born Sept. 19, 1763, both of Salisbury, Essex county, Mass.). Born July 28, 1797, Corinth, Vt.; pioneer July 24, 1847, Brigham Young company.
Married Angeline Myers (daughter of Henry Myers and Ruth Rodgers), who died at Kirtland, Ohio. Their children: Albert Brady, m. Lucinda Stone; William Ruel b. Oct. 6, 1818; Aurilla Peckham b. Sept. 20, 1820, m. Moses Curtis; Parmenia Adams b. Aug. 6, 1822, m. Phebe Loderna Merrill; Ammi Rumsey b. Feb. 6, 1825, m. Aurilla Eldredge; Levi b. May 2, 1828. Family resided at Kirtland, Ohio, and Salt Lake City, Utah.
Married Lucinda Harmon Nov. 18, 1849, Salt Lake City (daughter of Oliver and Sarah Harmon), who was born March 15, 1822, Conneaut, Pa. Their children: Sarah Lucinda b. March 20, 1851, d. young; Levi Harmon b. Sept. 6, 1853, m. Sarah E. Hatch; Almira Sophronia b. June 30, 1856, m. Joseph Hanks Oct. 29, 1876; Daniel Wells b. April 18, 1860, m. Sarah M. Marble Nov. 1, 1878. Family home Salt Lake City, Utah.
Member of high council. Worked on Kirtland and Nauvoo temples. First counselor to Bishop Roundy of the sixteenth ward and acted as bishop during the bishop's mission to England; patriarch. Died July 23, 1876, Salem, Utah.

JACKMAN, LEVI HARMON (son of Levi Jackman and Lucinda Harmon). Born Sept. 6, 1853, Palmyra. Utah.
Married Sarah Elizabeth Hatch April 12, 1875, Salt Lake City, Utah (daughter of Lewis Hatch, pioneer Sept. 17, 1850, Jonathan Foote company, and Sarah Ann Lloyd of Salem, Utah). She was born July 25, 1856, Payson, Utah. Their children: Levi Lewis b. Jan. 12, 1876, m. Annie M. Petersen July 28, 1897; Reuben Oliver b. Nov. 6, 1877, m. Mary Pearl son July 10, 1897; Clarence Manning b. May 31, 1880, d. young; Francis Albert b. April 11, 1882, m. Nancy Pearl Baldwin Dec. 23, 1903; Sarah Lucinda b. June 15, 1885, d. young; Wallace Arthur b. Oct. 20, 1888, m. Velma A. Foreman May 21, 1913; Wilford Hamner b. May 26, 1891, m. Ella Pearl Hanks, Dec. 18, 1912; Ezbon Laton b. March 26, 1895; Necha Estella b. April 9, 1898. Family home Joseph, Utah.
Seventy; clerk of quorum of elders; clerk of Salem ward 1885. Settled at Salem, 1864, moved to Joseph February, 1870. Assistant Sunday school superintendent. Joseph ward for 20 years; high priest; ward clerk of Joseph ward Dec. 5, 1909. Acted as member of town board 1904-6; town clerk.

JACKSON, AARON (son of Samuel Jackson of England). Born Sept. 30, 1823, Eyrne, Derbyshire. Came to Utah Nov. 30, 1856, Edward Martin handcart company.
Married Elizabeth Horrocks May 28, 1848, Macclesfield, Eng. (daughter of Edward Horrocks and Alice Houghton of England, pioneers 1857). She was born 1823. Their children: Martha b. Feb. 6, 1849, m. T. R. Thomas; Mary E. b. July 23, 1851, m. George Boulter; Aaron b. Jan. 18, 1854, m. Eliza J. Rawson. Family home Ogden, Utah.
Died while crossing plains Oct. 25, 1856.

956　　　PIONEERS AND PROMINENT MEN OF UTAH

JACKSON, AARON (son of Aaron Jackson and Elizabeth Horrocks—stepson of William Richard Kingsford, pioneers Nov. 28, 1854, Robert L. Campbell company). Born Jan. 18, 1854, Macclesfield, Eng.
Married Eliza J. Rawson Jan. 26, 1878, Salt Lake City (daughter of William C. Rawson and Eliza J. Cheney of Indiana and Ohio, pioneers 1850). She was born Aug. 31, 1857. Their children: Grace Eliza b. Dec. 24, 1878, m. Martin R. Barrows Dec. 6, 1899; Ethel Elizabeth b. March 6, 1880, m. Nathan A. Hawkes Jan. 13, 1904; Mary Vanetta b. Oct. 28, 1882, m. Leland K. Nelson Aug. 31, 1904; Aaron William b. Nov. 29, 1884, d. Aug. 3, 1906; Samuel Francis b. Sept. 22, 1886; Zina Geneva b. Feb. 8, 1889, m. Gerard G. Klomp June 23, 1909; Emma Isabell b. Sept. 12, 1893, d. Sept. 30, 1909; Myrtle Florence b. Oct. 19, 1896; Joseph Rawson b. Oct. 29, 1898. Family home Ogden, Utah.
Member 77th quorum seventies; high priest; missionary to Great Britain 1891-1902. Merchant. Worked on state roads and temples.

JACKSON, JOHN (son of John Jackson of Oscroft, Cheshire, Eng.). Born March 7, 1819, at Barrow, Cheshire. Came to Utah Aug. 19, 1868, John R. Murdock company.
Married Mary Joynson 1837 (daughter of Thomas Joynson and Mary Clay), who was born Aug. 30, 1819. Came to Utah with husband. Their children: Henry; John, m. Ann Jones; Thomas, d.; Enos b. Feb. 27, 1845, m. Ellen Ferington Feb. 24, 1863; Hyrum; Joseph; Daniel; Ephraim, m. Christena Jorgensen; Moses, m. Mary Dalimore. Family home Lehi, Utah.
Elder. Painter.

JACKSON, ENOS (son of John Jackson and Mary Joynson). Born Feb. 27, 1845.
Married Ellen Ferington Feb. 24, 1863. Their children: Eugene b. Feb. 8, 1882, m. Lucy Hitesman March 8, 1904; Charles b. June 8, 1884, m. May Wheeler; John b. Sept. 14, 1886, m. Victoria Coledge Jan. 7, 1906; James b. March 24, 1888; Ernest b. Sept. 4, 1891; Alvin b. May 16, 1896. Family home Lehi, Utah.
Painter.

JACKSON, THOMAS (son of John Jackson, born Feb. 7, 1802, and Susannah Grundy born Feb. 5, 1795, Blockley, Eng.; married 1822). Born Sept. 13, 1823, at Blockley, Eng. Came to Utah September, 1856, Nicholas Groesbeck company.
Married Alice Crompton Aug. 14, 1842 (daughter of William Crompton and Alice Hall), who was born Aug. 14, 1820. Came to Utah September, 1856, Nicholas Groesbeck company. Their children: Maria b. June 2, 1845, m. Henry Jackman Aug. 21, 1870; John William b. June 4, 1849, m. Sarah E. Bingham Aug. 7, 1878; Elizabeth b. Jan. 18, 1851, m. John K. Reid; Joseph Brigham b. Oct. 18, 1852, m. Mary Beckstead; David Franklin b. July, 1854, died; Thomas Edward b. Oct. 7, 1856, m. Eliza Shaw; Alice Ann b. May 15, 1858, m. Franklin Jones; Amileent b. Feb. 23, 1861, m. A. T. Oldroyd; James b. 1862, died. Family resided at Nephi, Payson and Glenwood, Utah.
Married Dinah Burres. Their children: Fanny; Lydia; George; Frederic; Horace; Alice; Bertha; Hermion.
Missionary to eastern states 1869-70 and to England 1880-81. Indian war veteran. Cabinet-maker.

JACKSON, JOHN WILLIAM (son of Thomas Jackson and Alice Crompton). Born June 4, 1849, at Manchester, Eng.
Married Sarah E. Bingham Aug. 7, 1870, at Payson, Utah (daughter of Jeremiah Bingham and Sarah Keel), who was born April 15, 1850, in Pottawattamie Co., Iowa. Their children: John Henry b. June 13, 1873, m. Mariah Vandyke July 24, 1891; Jeremiah b. Aug. 9, 1874, m. Cloe Merrell Jan. 18, 1895; William Thomas b. Sept. 5, 1876, m. Mary J. Allen Jan. 4, 1911; James Perry b. Aug. 10, 1878, died; Sarah Ellener b. Oct. 5, 1880; Alpheus b. Sept. 9, 1882, m. Hattie Vandyke March 8, 1905; Joseph Bert b. Aug. 30, 1884; Ernest b. Aug. 16, 1886, m. Ida May Larsen April 18, 1910; Susa b. June 17, 1888; Minnie b. Oct. 3, 1891. Family resided Payson, Glenwood and Lyman, Utah, and in Arizona.
Married Margaret Josephine Nordford Nov. 4, 1883, at St. George, Utah (daughter of Andrew M. Nordford and Cathrine Olsen; married at Krongeade, Sweden). She was born Oct. 13, 1864, at Kongeade, Sweden. Their children: Alice Cathrine b. Oct. 21, 1887, m. Junius F. Ogden June 4, 1909; William Andrew b. April 8, 1889, died; Junius Wilford b. Sept. 27, 1891, m. May Baker Jan. 4, 1912; Margaret Emily b. Sept. 21, 1893; Victor Leroy b. July 26, 1896; Orvill Q. b. Aug. 2, 1899; Cora Luella b. Feb. 18, 1902; Thelma Matilda b. Nov. 16, 1904.
High priest; missionary to Arizona 1876; missionary to Michigan and Wisconsin 1880-81. Veteran Indian wars 1865-67.

JACOB, LUCIAN (son of Norton Jacob and Emily Heaton). Born Feb. 28, 1836.
Married Janet Anderson Clottworthy, Midway, Utah (daughter of Hugh Clottworthy and Jean Maitland of Scotland—pioneers 1854), who was born Sept. 4, 1846. Their children: Emily Jane b. May 20, 1862, m. Moroni Gerber; Hugh Alexander b. Sept. 4, 1864, m. Isabel West; Lucian Heaton, d. child; Mary Elizabeth, m. John Gibson. Family home Midway, Utah.
Elder. Farmer. Died 1875, Midway, Utah.

JACOB, NORTON (son of Udney H. Jacob, born April 24, 1781, Sheffield, Mass., and Elizabeth Hubbard born Aug. 24, 1881, Middletown, Conn.). He was born Aug. 11, 1804, at Sheffield, Berkshire county, Mass. Came to Utah July 24, 1847, Brigham Young company, himself captain of ten.
Married Emily Heaton Nov. 20, 1830, who came to Utah 1848, Heber C. Kimball company. Their children: Lucian Heaton b. Feb. 22, 1836, m. Janet Clottworthy; Ira Norton b. Oct. 16, 1840, m. Julia A. Gerber and Ellen Clift; Joseph b. May 29, 1845, m. Ellen H. Gerber. Family resided Salt Lake City, Payson and Midway, Utah.
Married Elizabeth Harris, Salt Lake City. Their children: Norton Kellog; Frank; Sidney; Lonzo.
Presiding elder Snake Creek branch 1863-64. Mechanic.

JACOB, JOSEPH (son of Norton Jacob and Emily Heaton). Born May 29, 1845, Nauvoo, Ill.
Married Ellen H. Gerber May 8, 1864, Midway, Utah (daughter of John Gerber and Anna Maria Ackeret, pioneers 1854, Captain Van Buren company). She was born Sept. 26, 1847, Huntsville, Ala. Their children: Mary Jane b. April 24, 1865; Joseph b. Aug. 1, 1867, m. Lucy Baker April, 1898; Emma b. Sept. 14, 1869, m. John M. Parry May 7, 1895; Ann Eliza b. Dec. 1, 1871, m. John A. Phillips March 1899; Milton b. May 20, 1874, m. Mary Carlson Nov. 1904; Isaac b. May 11, 1876, m. Thea Anderson June, 1905; Nellie b. July 10, 1878, m. George A. Anderson Sept. 1906; Tillie b. May 17, 1881; Elmer Acred b. Nov. 25, 1883, m. Maude M. Beeley Aug. 30, 1910; Clarence Cecil b. June 9, 1886, m. Florence Johnson June 13, 1910; Irvin Heaton b. Aug. 24, 1889. Family resided Midway, Vermillion, Daniels, Pleasant Grove and Provo, Utah.
Priest. Black Hawk Indian war veteran. Farmer and tailor.

JACOBSON, OLE JOHN. Born March 17, 1824, Christiania, Norway.
Married Ossa ———, in Norway. Their children: Matilda, m. Frank Hanson; Rachel, m. William Dennison; Benjamin; Jacob, m. Clara Larson; Calaman, d. aged 14-17. Family home Ephraim.
Married Caroline Frederickson (Christensen), Ephraim, Utah (daughter of Carl and Annie Frederickson of Sjelland, Denmark), who was born Dec. 5, 1835, and came to Utah with handcart company. Their children: Daniel John b. March 13, 1874, m. Sophia Schwalbe; David Olius b. Nov. 27, 1876, m. Juliette Stevens, m. Agnes Ellen O'Neil. Family home Ephraim, Utah.
Caroline Frederickson first married Antone Christensen in midocean. Their children: Neils, m. Annetta Larson; Charles, drowned, aged 21; Sarah, m. H. P. Larsen; Mary, m. Oliver M. Larsen; Antone, m. Stena Peterson; Rosetta, m. Charles Christensen; Frank, m. Augusta Dorius. Family home Ephraim, Utah.

JACOBSON, DAVID OLIUS (son of Ole John Jacobson and Caroline Frederickson). Born Nov. 27, 1876, Ephraim, Utah.
Married Juliette Stevens June 15, 1898, Ephraim, Utah (daughter of Henry Stevens and Augusta Dorius of Canada and Denmark, respectively), who was born Jan. 5, 1875. Their children: David Wells b. March 12, 1901; Vernon b. April 3, 1903; Marcella May b. May 14, 1905. Family resided Ephraim, Salt Lake City and Vernal, Utah.
Married Agnes Ellen O'Neil Aug. 14, 1907, Salt Lake City (daughter of James O'Neil and Mary Elizabeth Alexander of Midway and Vernal, Utah; former a pioneer 1864, oxteam company). She was born Jan. 24, 1887. Their children: Florence Louise b. June 3, 1908; Anthony Olius b. Nov. 6, 1909; Daniel John b. Jan. 2, 1911; Audrey Ione b. July 27, 1912. Family home Vernal, Utah.
Member 97th quorum seventies; ward teacher; 1st counselor in Y. M. M. I. A. Farmer and stockraiser.

JACOBSON, OLE WILLIAM (son of Ole H. Jacobson and Rebecca D. Dutson). Born Oct. 5, 1880, Oak City, Utah.
Married Silvia Alice Anderson Oct. 4, 1905, Salt Lake City (daughter of Peter Anderson and Martha Ann Lovell former pioneer 1854, latter 1852). She was born Feb. 25, 1881, Oak City. Their children: Milan William b. July 24, 1906; Wilmer Thurlow b. Sept. 17, 1908. Family home Oak City, Utah.
Missionary to central states Nov. 2, 1908, to April 4, 1911 Chorister, organist, religion class teacher and ward clerk Oak City ward.

JACOBS, JOHN (son of Sven Jacobsen and Johanna John sen of Norway). Born Dec. 7, 1825, at Byglandsfjord Berjnisley, Norway, pioneer 1849, Ezra T. Benson company.
Married Elizabeth Coleman (daughter of Prine Coleman and Sarah Thornton—former died in Norway; latter pionee 1850, David Evans company). She was born 1831. Cam to Utah with mother. Their children: John S. b. Aug. 7 1856, m. Sarah Jane Savage 1875; George P. b. Feb. 9, 1858 m. Cynthia Duell Sept. 15, 1896; Hyrum b. March 9, 1859 died; Prine b. May 11, 1860, m. Ellen Ashton Aug. 25, 1881 Aaron b. July 9, 1862, died; Sarah Elizabeth b. Jan. 9, 1867 m. Heber Allred Aug. 1885; Swen A. b. Jan. 16, 1865, died Hanna Myren b. July 24, 1867, m. William Ralph March 27, 1888 Isaac N. b. Nov. 11, 1869, died; Andrew B. Nov. 5, 1872, n Jane Clough Dec. 30, 1903. Family home Lehi, Utah.
Married Harriet Austin March 23, 1867, Salt Lake Cit (daughter of James O'Neil and Emma Grace, married Marc

20, 1847, Studham, Eng., pioneers 1866, Captain Chipman company). She was born Aug. 5, 1847, at Kenwith Hot, Eng. Their children: Joseph Rawlins b. Aug. 20, 1868; Emma Ann b. Dec. 23, 1869; Franklin b. Dec. 3, 1871, m. Sarah E. Wing June 19, 1895; Harriet Elizabeth b. March 13, 1874, m. George H. Wing June 19, 1895; Julia b. Aug. 22, 1877; Lud b. Feb. 29, 1880, m. Florence Gilchrest Feb. 25, 1903; Dell Ray b. Oct. 17, 1883; Della b. Oct. 17, 1883, m. B. D. Lott Nov. 18, 1903; Josephine b. May 13, 1886; Clara M. b. Sept. 21, 1887; Isre Thomas b. Feb. 7, 1889. Settled Lehi 1851, moved to Cedar City 1853 and back to Lehi in 1858. Indian war veteran. Counselor in deacons quorum 32 years.

JACOBSEN, LARS (son of Jacob Larsen and Marie Larsen of Jutland, Denmark). Born Oct. 26, 1833, Denmark. Came to Utah Sept. 13, 1857, Chr. Christiansen handcart company. Married Inger Andrea Thompsen Feb. 7, 1858, Salt Lake City Utah (daughter of Thomas Andreasen and Sarah Louisa Johansen of Denmark), who was born 1829. Their children: Lars b. March 1859, m. Sarah May Scott; Sarah b. Sept. 3, 1861, m. Harry Williams; Marie b. March 17, 1863, m. Jasper Davis; Josephine b. April 11, 1867, m. Geo. C. Scott Jr.; Brighamina b. April 11, 1866, m. Mads Johnsen; Caroline b. Jan. 3, 1869, died; Johhanna b. June 24, 1871, died. Family home Lake View, Utah.
Married Marie Christensen May 3, 1870, Salt Lake City (daughter of Mads Christensen and Annie Christina Halesen of Mt. Pleasant, Utah, pioneers 1862, ox team company). She was born Feb. 6, 1855. Their children: Christian b. Feb. 9, 1871, died; Annie Christina Marie b. June 9, 1873, m. William Christian Williamson; Emily b. Dec. 14, 1876, m. Hyrum Clark Scott; Hyrum b. Jan. 30, 1878, died; Wilford b. July 22, 1880, died; Albert b. Jan. 14, 1882, m. Stella Collins; Parley Louies b. Sept. 12, 1884, m. Myrtle Grua; John b. Feb. 14, 1890, died; Dora Elmina b. Oct. 31, 1894. Family home Lake View, Utah.
Member 70th quorum seventies; missionary to Minnesota 1883; high priest; ward teacher. Participated in Echo Canyon trouble. Farmer; stockraiser; fisherman. Died March 12, 1912, Lake View, Utah.

JACOBSEN, LARS (son of Lars Jacobsen and Inger Thompson). Born March, 1859, Lake View, Utah.
Married Sarah May Scott Sept. 7, 1892, Manti, Utah (daughter George Comb Scott and Cornelia Kennedy of Lake View), who was born May 6, 1873. Their children: Inger May b. May 10, 1894; Cornelia b. Oct. 24, 1896; Frances Grace b. Aug. 11, 1899; Heneretta b. Nov. 19, 1902; Reva b. March 30, 1907; Lola b. Oct. 23, 1909. Family home Lake View, Utah.
High priest; counselor in elders quorum; ward teacher. Farmer and stockraiser.

JACOBSEN, LAURITZ (son of Severine Jacobsen and Anna Marie Abrahamsen of Albeck, Denmark). Born Feb. 2, 1844, in Denmark. Came to Utah Sept. 23, 1862, C. A. Madson company.
Married Matilda Nielsen April 4, 1867, Salt Lake City, Utah (daughter of Andrew Nielsen and Anna Mary of Slagnlshe, Denmark). She was born May 18, 1850. Their children: Anna Matilda. m. John Watkin; Minna Marie; Lauritz, m. Elizabeth Wright; Rosetta Elinore, m. C. W. Glasier; Joseph William Hyrum, m. Elizabeth Sim; George Albert, m. Anna Lorena Jensen; Oscar Peter; Nephi Moroni, m. America Wall; Wilford Alexander Benjamin; Rebecca Berdina Josephine, m. Orson W. Badger; Rhoda Elizabeth, m. Herbert Foutz; Olive Goldie b. Sept. 9, 1890; Hazel May b. Aug. 5, 1895. Family home Pleasant Grove, Utah.
High priest. Helped bring immigrants to Utah 1863 and 1868. Veteran Black Hawk war. Farmer.

JACOBSEN, OLE H. (son of Hans Jacobsen of Kloutofte, Denmark, and Maren Hansdatter). Born Jan. 1, 1853, at Kloutofte. Came to Utah, 1867.
Married Rebecca D. Dutsen (daughter of John Wm. Dutsen and Elizabeth Jane Cowley; former pioneer Sept. 20, 1857—married Aug. 10, 1850, St. Louis, Mo.). She was born Jan. 28, 1855. Their children: Mary Ellen b. May 8, 1879, m. Christian C. Christensen; Ole William b. Oct. 8, 1880, m. Silvia Alice Anderson Oct. 4, 1905; Ida Jane b. Feb. 14, 1882, m. Joshua Finlinson Oct. 3, 1907; Maggie Ann b. Aug. 14, 1883; Eddie Matthias b. Nov. 28, 1884, m. Sarah Delilah Anderson Aug. 19, 1907; Elizabeth b. Oct. 9, 1886, m. Lem Roper Dec. 4, 1907; Nellie b. Feb. 14, 1888; Irvin Elmer b. Aug. 12, 1889; Joseph Alfred b. Oct. 13, 1891; Alma Evan b. Aug. 20, 1893; Ruby Rebecca b. April 5, 1895. Family home Oak City, Millard Co., Utah.

JACOBSEN, THOMAS E. (son of Thomas Jacobsen and Anna M. Larson of Ebeltoft, Denmark, who came to Utah 1883). Born May 30, 1853.
Married Elizabeth A. Mumford Nov. 18, 1886, at Logan, Utah (daughter of Thomas Mumford and Elizabeth Moore of Salt Lake City, pioneers Sept. 24, 1862, Homer Duncan company). She was born Dec. 7, 1866, at Mill Creek, Utah. Their children: Elmon T. b. Jan. 27, 1888, d. infant; Anna

E. b. July 12, 1889, m. Daniel C. Kesler; Marius J. b. Feb. 8, 1892; Joseph M. b. June 24, 1896; Lillian M. b. Jan. 10, 1900; Wilford M. b. Jan. 29, 1909. Family home Salt Lake City, Utah.

JACQUES, THOMAS (son of Alexander Jacques and Mary Durling of Aylesford, Nova Scotia). Born Aug. 8, 1805, Nova Scotia. Came to Utah Oct. 4, 1854, Orson Pratt and Horace S. Eldredge company.
Married Sarah Farnsworth 1828, Aylesford, Nova Scotia (daughter of Daniel Farnsworth), who was born May 21, 1804. Their children: Mary Jane, died; Jerusha Ann. m. John Patterson; Susan, m. George Mathew Dow Phillips; Daniel, died; George W., m. Louisa Phillips; Caroline, m. Zamira Palmer. Family home Provo, Utah.
Shoemaker. Died at Provo, Utah.

JAKEMAN, JAMES THOMAS (son of James Jakeman and Ann Field of Leeds, Yorkshire, Eng.). Born Aug. 28, 1853, at Leeds. Came to Utah September 1863, Daniel D. McArthur company.
Married Ellen Lee 1888, Beaver, Utah (daughter of John P. Lee and Eliza Foscue of Beaver, pioneers 1858), who was born 1859. Their children: Howard Lee, died; Cora Ellen, m. Percy Block; James Franklin; Gladys Annetta, m. Mr. Saunders; Spencer Wells. Family home Beaver, Utah.
Married Hulda Pauline Swanson 1900, Salt Lake City (daughter of August Swanson of Sweden), who was born July 5, 1880. Their children: James Glen b. 1901; Theodore G. b. 1905. Family home, Salt Lake City.
Counselor in deacons quorum; recorder elders quorum; Sunday school teacher. Publisher.

JAMES, ABRAHAM (son of Abraham James of Kentucky). Born 1824. Came to Utah 1867, independent company.
Married Elizabeth Jane Ragsdale who came to Utah with husband. Their children: Louise M. R. b. May 22, 1847, m. William Powers; William Irvin, m. Emily Hale; Augustus, m. Sarah ——; Mary Jane, m. Nathan Huckleby; James Marion; Margarett Elizabeth, m. Mr. Thompson; Martha Ann, died; David, m. Julia ——.
Elder. Died 1882, Flagstaff, Arizona.

JAMES, DAVID, JR. (son of David James). Born Nov. 5, 1833, in England. Came to Utah 1852.
Married Jane Humphreys 1851, in England, who was born Nov. 29, 1835. Their children: David W., m. Permelia Horne; Henry C., m. Clara Horne; Mary A., m. Samuel O'Bray; Jennette, m. Mark Spencer. Family home Salt Lake City.
Seventy; bishop in Cache county. Plumber and gas fitter. Died April 27, 1909, at Salt Lake City.

JAMES, DAVID W (son of David James, Jr., and Jane Humphreys). Born April 2, 1857, Draper, Utah.
Married Permelia Horne Jan. 21, 1880, Salt Lake City (daughter of Joseph Horne and M. Isabella Hales of Salt Lake City, pioneers October, 1847, John Taylor company). She was born Dec. 9, 1855. Their children: Minnie H. b. Oct. 12, 1880, m. L. T. Whitney; David W., Jr., b. May 27, 1883, m. Mabel Wills; Cornelia b. Nov. 29, 1888, m. H. L. Mulliner; Frank b. Sept. 29, 1890; Marie b. June 1, 1894; Louise b. Dec. 19, 1907.
Seventy. Plumber and gas fitter.

JAMES, JOSEPH (son of Thomas and Ann James of Pembrokeshire, South Wales). Born in 1798 in Pembrokeshire. Came to Utah Sept. 24, 1854, Job Smith company.
Married Alice Mohn 1834, in Pembrokeshire (daughter of James John and Alice Sayse of Pembrokeshire, married in 1789—pioneers Sept. 24, 1854, Job Smith company). She was born Aug. 10, 1801. Their children: Thomas John, m. Emma Jones; Joseph, died. Family home 10th ward, Salt Lake City.
Farmer and stockraiser. Died Dec. 19, 1877.

JAMES, THOMAS JOHN (son of Joseph James and Sarah John). Born Oct. 31, 1835, in Pembrokeshire. Came to Utah Sept. 24, 1854, Job Smith company.
Married Emma Jones Feb. 28, 1858, Salt Lake endowment house, Brigham Young officiating (daughter of Edward Jones of Manchester, Eng., pioneer 1852). She was born Aug. 29, 1841. Only child: Thomas Edward b. Dec. 7, 1858. Family home, Salt Lake City.
Married Elizabeth Newton Nov. 18, 1864, Salt Lake City (daughter of James Newton and Elizabeth Blackburn of Manchester, Eng.), who was born Dec. 12, 1844. Their children: Thomas Alma b. Aug. 12, 1865, m. Maggie Syme; James Ammon b. Dec. 6, 1867, m. Olive Judd; Joseph Irwin b. Jan. 28, 1870, m. Martha Swaner; Elizabeth Amelia b. April 19, 1872, m. Amos Cardwell; Lilly Maria b. July 11, 1875, m. Edward Harris; Sarah Alice b. Dec. 22, 1877, m. Hyrum Vincent; Hyrum Ernest b. Aug. 31, 1880, Ada b. July 28, 1882, and Adam Samuel b. Dec. 28, 1883, all died. Family home, Salt Lake.
Married Mary E. Taylor Aug. 31, 1887, Logan, Utah (daughter of Edward Taylor and Sarah Turner; first couple married in 10th ward, Salt Lake City—pioneers 1852). She was born in 1854. Only child: Eva May b. Sept. 5, 1894.

Elder and high priest, 10th ward, Salt Lake City. Worked on Salt Lake temple 16 months and public works for the church about three years; head carpenter and wagon maker for Brigham Young.

JAMES, JOSEPH. Born Feb. 26, 1830, at Halse, Denmark. Came to Utah Sept. 30, 1854, David Jones company.
Married Sarah Holyoak Oct. 3, 1854 (daughter of George Holyoak and Sarah Green; former pioneer Sept. 30, 1854, Darwin Richardson company, latter died on plains en route). She was born Aug. 4, 1835, and came to Utah with father. Their children: Joseph H. b. Oct. 22, 1855, m. Elizabeth Bloomfield; William F. b. April 30, 1857, m. Julia E. Whitehead; George R. b. May 4, 1859; Edward B. b. Dec. 11, 1860; Charles W. b. Sept. 9, 1862, m. Eveline Backer March 18, 1887; Sarah H. b. Sept. 20, 1864, m. Francis Rushton Dec. 6, 1883; Mary E. b. June 17, 1866, m. Eleazer Jones Oct. 7, 1887; Abinidi b. March 28, 1869, m. Edith Bowers April 29, 1891; Frederick b. Feb. 22, 1873; Heber b. .Dec. 24, 1874; Hyrum R. b. Feb. 23, 1878; Harriot b. Jan. 14, 1881.

JAMES, WILLIAM F. (son of Joseph James and Sarah Holyoak). Born April 30, 1857, at Ogden, Utah.
Married Julia E. Whitehead Sept. 5, 1877, St. George, Utah (daughter of George Whitehead and Julia Morris), who was born Feb. 19, 1860, Somersetshire, Eng. Their children: William H. b. June 14, 1878; Julia R. b. Oct. 6, 1879; George M. b. March 4, 1882; Clara b. Nov. 8, 1888; Lillian b. June 30, 1890; Evaline b. Feb. 14, 1892; Florence b. Nov. 8, 1894; Pearl b. Nov. 8, 1896; Myrtle b. Nov. 8, 1898; Alfred b. Jan. 22, 1902; Laura b. Oct. 22, 1903. Family home, Ogden.
President and manager of James Coal & Ice company and the Pioneer Plate Ice plant.

JAMES, REES D. (son of Howell James, born April 3, 1816, at Brecknockshire, and Mary Jones, born April 13, 1817, at Carmarthenshire, South Wales). Born Dec. 31, 1842, at Merthyr Tydfil, South Wales. Came to Utah Sept. 5, 1866, Captain White company.
Married Jane Hopla Feb. 3, 1873 (daughter of John Hopla and Cathrine Edwards, pioneers Captain Stephenson company; married in 1845 at Pembrokeshire). She was born Nov. 12, 1848. Their children: Harriet E. b. Dec. 14, 1873, m. Robert Starling; Mary Ellen b. Nov. 20, 1875, m. Niels Peter Larsen; David H. b. Jan. 22, 1877, m. Mary Ann Sorenson; Howell b. July 19, 1883; Rees William b. Oct. 3, 1886; Jane b. Dec. 6, 1888, m. William Roundy.
Choir and band leader. Constable. President East Bench Water, Creamery and Canning company; director Spanish Fork Co-op.

JAMES, SYLVESTER (son of Sherman James and Jane E. Manning of Salt Lake City, pioneers in September, 1847, Captain Eldredge company). Born March 1, 1835. Came to Utah with parents.
Married Mary Perkins Jan. 31, 1865, Salt Lake City (daughter of Franklin and Esther Perkins, pioneers 1848, A. Perkins company). She was born April 6, 1940, in Grundy county, Mo. Their children: William H. b. Oct. 28, 1866; Esther J. b. Feb. 14, 1869, m. Henry Leggroan; Nellie b. April 28, 1870, d. aged 16; Sylvester b. Feb. 12, 1874, and Albert S. b. Jan. 31, 1876, (infants: Nettie b. July 29, 1877, m. Louis Leggroan; Manissa b. May 8, 1881, and Mary b. June 14, 1885, d. infants. Family home, Salt Lake City.
Farmer.

JAMES, WILLIAM (son of Lee James of Eckington, Worcestershire, Eng.). Born in 1809 in Worcestershire. Frozen to death in 1854 at last crossing of Sweetwater river, Wyo., on way to Utah.
Married Jane Haines 1836, Pinvin, Eng., who was born Jan. 1, 1815, Bristol Hampton, Worcestershire, and came to Utah Nov. 10, 1856. James G. Willie handcart company. Their children: Sarah b. Aug. 13, 1837, m. Aaron Johnson; Emma b. June 3, 1840, m. Lorenzo Johnson; Reuben b. June 15, 1842, m. Sarah B. Allen; Mary Ann b. Dec. 16, 1844, m. Jabez Dangerfield; Martha b. June 8, 1846, m. Benjamin Richmond; George b. June 16, 1849, m. Matilda Saussasee, m. Mary Elizabeth Wordsworth; John b. July 12, 1852, m. Elizabeth Warner, m. Jenett McKinley; Jane b. Aug. 16, 1855, d. on ocean; William Maud b. May, 1862 (latter a son of Mathew Maud and Jane Haines by a later marriage). Family home Provo, Utah.

JAMES, REUBEN (son of William James and Jane Haines). Born June 15, 1842, Pinvin, Eng. Came to Utah in 1856 with mother.
Married Sarah B. Allen Feb. 20, 1878, St. George, Utah (daughter of William Allen, who died on plains). She was born Feb. 24, 1835, and came to Utah in 1852.
High priest; pioneer to St. George. Badly frozen on the plains. Farmer.

JAMES, GEORGE (son of William James and Jane Haines). Born June 16, 1849, Pinvin, Eng. Came to Utah Nov. 10, 1856, with mother.
Married Matilda Saussasee in April, 1869, Salt Lake City (daughter of Louis Saussasee and Rebecca Fawcett of Provo, Utah; pioneers 1850). She was born in 1852. Their children: Estella b. March 26, ——, m. Warren Fenn: Albert, m. Elizabeth Snyder; Louis, m. Annie Davis; Susie and Emma, died.

Married Mary Elizabeth Wordsworth Sept. 23, 1883, Springville, Utah (daughter of William Wordsworth and Nancy Ann Vance of Lehi, Utah; pioneers July 24, 1847, Brigham Young company). She was born Feb. 9, 1854. Their children: Glenn Lee b. Jan. 2, 1887; Annie Elizabeth b. Sept. 20, 1889, m. Earl Clark; Willis b. Feb. 14, 1892, m. Lorena Carlson; Leo b. Aug. 8, 1894; Clarence b. Nov. 26, 1897; Minnie b. Feb. 7, 1899. Family home Pleasant View, Utah.
Elder. Pioneer of Pleasant View in 1872. Teamster; farmer and horticulturist.

JAMESON, CHARLES. Born in Scotland; came to Utah 1847, contingent Mormon Battalion company.
Married Mary Shadrick, who died while crossing plains. Their children: Julia Ann, m. Jehu Blackburn; Mary Ann, m. James Hirors; Alexander; Lucinda, m. Hyrum Woolsey; Susann, m. Jehu Blackburn; Margarett, David and Agesee, died; Hyrum, m. Rhoda Foy; Charlotte, m. Mr. Hubbs.
Wounded at Hauns Mill massacre in Missouri and died at Minersville, Utah.

JANES, JACOB (son of Joseph Janes and Elizabeth Cavil of Abertillery, Monmouthshire, Eng.). Born Feb. 18, 1844, Carston, Somersetshire, Eng. Came to Utah 1866, William Henry Chipman company.
Married Mary Ann Harrison Jan. 11, 1869, Salt Lake Endowment House (daughter of Ralph Harrison and Mary Jane Edmonds—pioneers 1866, Joseph S. Rawlins company), who was born July 2, 1847. Came to Utah with her parents. Their children: Allice Elizabeth, m. Frank W. Owen; Mary Eliza, m. Alma L. Sargent; Jacob Ralph, m. Margaret Lavrina Jacobsen; Emily Louisa, m. William O. Dearley; Edith Frances, m. Zachariah W. Israelsen; Susan Annie; Ruth Ellen; Caroline Sarah, m. George F. Ellsworth; Joseph Cavil, d. child; Clare Ann, m. Sargent A. Rice; Royal Benjamin; Viola, d. child. Family home Hyrum, Utah.
Member 27th quorum seventies; president branch of Coalville ward, Grass Creek, Summit stake. Worked on Salt Lake tabernacle 1866. Engineer of mines at Grass Creek. Worked on telegraph line from The Muddy to Green River, 1866, and on railroad in Echo Canyon.

JANNEY, THOMAS A. (son of James Janney and Maggie Gillespie of Virginia). Born July 26, 1816, in Virginia. Came to Utah in 1857.
Married Mary Anna Whittaker Aug. 14, 1858, Salt Lake City (daughter of Isaac Whittaker and Sarah Hemison of Salt Lake City, pioneers Oct. 14, 1850, Wilford Woodruff company). She was born July 2, 1840. Their children: E. M., m. Maggie Player; William H., m. Lou K. Gibson; Frank G., m. Flower B. Player; George W. Family home, Salt Lake City.
Bookkeeper and accountant. Died Dec. 15, 1881.

JANNEY, E. M. (son of Thomas A. Janney and Mary Anna Whittaker). Born June 21, 1860, Salt Lake City.
Married Maggie Player June 21, 1887, Salt Lake City (daughter of William Player and Nancy Hamer of Salt Lake City). She was born in November, 1861. Their children: Maggie b. June 11, 1888, m. William H. McDonald; E. b. Aug. 2, 1893; Vivian b. July 23, 1897. Family home, Salt Lake City.
City marshal; turnkey at state penitentiary; detective police force Salt Lake City.

JANSEN, JOHN A. (son of Johnsen Jansen of Norway). Born Sept. 19, 1792, in Norway. Came to Utah in September, 1863, with the Dorius company.
Married Andrea Petersen in Norway (daughter of Amon Petersen and Andrea Munsen, of Norway), who was born March 3, 1829. Their children: Matilda, m. C. D. Jorgensen; Josephine, m. N. L. Christensen; Joseph Y., m. Margaret Andersen; Maria, died; Amanda, m. Andrew C. Nelsen; Julia, died; Amelia, m. Fred Christensen; Hannah, m. Hiram Brimhall; Anna, died. Family home Ephraim, Utah.
Member seventies; missionary to Norway. Sea captain; farmer. Died June 6, 1872.

JARDINE, JAMES (son of Richard Jardine and Sarah Wilson of East Killbride, Lanark, Scotland). Born May 6, 1819, East Killbride. Came to Utah Sept. 16, 1859, Edward Stevenson company.
Married Isabella White July 17, 1840, East Killbride, Scotland (daughter of John White and Isabella Scott of East Killbride), who was born June 14, 1822. Their children: Isabel b. July 1, 1841, m. William Simpson; Sarah b. June 1, 1843, d. July 29, 1851; Janie b. March 9, 1845, d. July 19, 1846; Elizabeth b. Jan. 25, 1847, m. Charles Shumway; Richard F. b. Dec. 30, 1848, m. Luna Ellsworth; Sarah b. July 21, 1851, d. Nov. 29, 1853; James b. Sept. 10, 1854, d. Aug. 18, 1855; Mary b. June 22, 1856, m. Jacob Gibson; Isadora b. April 21, 1858, m. Hyrum Thompson; Margaret b. March 21, 1860, m. Thomas Moore; John b. March 19, 1863, d. Sept. 5, 1864; William H. b. Feb. 11, 1865, m. Georgina L. Morrison. Family home Taylor ward, Utah.
Farmer. Died Aug. 7, 1891, West Weber, Utah.

JARDINE, WILLIAM H. (son of James Jardine and Isabella White). Born Feb. 11, 1865, Wellsville, Utah.
Married Georgina L. Morrisen Feb. 11, 1885, Logan, Utah (daughter of Jens Morrisen and Dorothy Larsen of Denmark), who was born Aug. 26, 1864. Their children: Minnie I. b. Aug. 23, 1886; James E. b. Dec. 16, 1888, m. Ida R. Dar-

ton; Dorothy E. b. March 14, 1891; Margaret A. b. Sept. 21, 1894; Mary H. b. Dec. 20, 1896; Florence b. July 21, 1900; William H. b. Aug. 11, 1906. Family home West Weber, Utah.
Member 54th quorum seventies; missionary to Central states 1897-99; high priest; bishop's counselor; bishop Taylor ward. Farmer.

JARDINE, JOHN (son of Richard Jardine of Minnagaff, Scotland, born 1792, and Sarah Wilson of Townhill, Scotland, born Aug. 2, 1786). Born Oct. 31, 1830, at Middlequarter, Scotland. Came to Utah Sept. 17, 1859, Edward Stevenson company.
Married Agnes Beveridge Aug. 15, 1851, Parkhead, Scotland (daughter of John Beveridge and Mary Burns of Parkhead), who was born May 29, 1829. Came to Utah with husband. Their children: Sarah b. Dec. 7, 1854, m. Charles Shumway Sept. 1874; John B. b. Nov. 24, 1856, m. Marinda Homer Jan. 1, 1880; Richard H. b. Sept. 10, 1858, m. Emily Homer Sept. 17, 1879; James B. b. Dec. 6, 1860, m. Annie S. Heggie Sept. 17, 1884; Agnes B. b. March 23, 1863, m. Charles Shumway Sept. 17, 1879; Mary B. b. April 1, 1865, m. Alma Jenson; William B. b. Dec. 17, 1867, m. Mary E. Fife. Family home Wellsville, Utah.
Married Elizabeth Griffiths July 1884, Logan, Utah (daughter of John and Theo Griffiths), who was born July 23, 1866, Clarkston, Utah.
Acting bishop of Wellsville ward 1875-76; bishop of Clarkston ward 1876-1902; patriarch. Farmer. Died Aug. 8, 1903, Clarkston, Utah.

JARDINE, JOHN B. (son of John Jardine and Agnes Beveridge). Born Nov. 24, 1856, at St. Johns, Ill. Came to Utah Sept. 17, 1859, Edward Stevenson company.
Married Marinda Homer Jan. 1, 1880, Salt Lake City (daughter of Russell K. Homer and Elija Thornton, Salt Lake City, pioneers 1858, Russell K. Homer company). She was born Jan. 18, 1861. Their children: John P. b. Jan. 9, 1881, m. Ellen Clark; Russell K. b. April 16, 1886, m. Effie Clark; Lilly b. Nov. 19, 1889; Irene b. Sept. 24, 1892; Leo b. June 8, 1895; William H. b. March 30, 1898; James E. b. Feb. 9, 1900. Family home Clarkston, Utah.
School trustee. Farmer.

JARDINE, JAMES B. (son of John Jardine and Agnes Beveridge). Born Dec. 6, 1860, at Wellsville, Utah.
Married Annie S. Heggie Sept. 17, 1884 (daughter of Andrew W. Heggie and Annie T. Stewart; former came to Utah 1860, handcart company). She was born Nov. 20, 1865. Their children: James b. June 2, 1885, m. Margaret Buttars April 17, 1907; Annie b. Feb. 17, 1888, m. Herman Thompson Dec. 11, 1907; Andrew b. Dec. 18, 1889; Agnes b. March 5, 1892; Lottie b. Dec. 5, 1894; Electa H. b. Sept. 25, 1896; Peru H. b. Oct. 26, 1898; John S. b. March 5, 1901; La Reu b. Oct. 5, 1903. Family home Clarkston, Utah.
President deacons quorum 1877; home missionary 1877-81; president of Y. M. M. I. A. 1881-85; bishop of Trenton ward 1885-88. Moved to Clarkston 1889; missionary to Great Britain 1889-91; 1st assistant Sunday school superintendent; secretary of Sunday school; first counselor to Samuel Roskelly high priests quorum of Clarkston ward; superintendent Sunday school at Clarkston ward two years. Member Clarkston town board six years; justice of peace four years; school trustee six years.

JASPERSEN, JENS. Born March 14, 1809, Jylew, Denmark. Died 1854, on Missouri river while en route to Utah.
Married Maria Hansen, who was born Sept. 12, 1809, Gaverslund, Denmark. Their children: Catherine; Hans; Yearn. Family first resided Fort Ephraim, San Pete county; moved to Provo, later to Goshen, Utah.

JASPERSEN, HANS (son of Jens Jaspersen and Maria Hansen). Born Aug. 5, 1843, Uhlan, Denmark. Came to Utah Oct. 5, 1854, Hans Peter Olsen company.
Married Marinda Christena Ipsen Nov. 6, 1864, Goshen, Utah (daughter of Andrew and Christena Maria Ipsen; former died on ocean 1852; latter came to Utah Sept. 15, 1853, John Forsgren company). Their children: Julia Maria b. Dec. 5, 1865, m. Peter Okelberry Jan. 28, 1886; Marinda Christena b. Feb. 22, 1868, m. Peter Peterson Dec. 20, 1892; Mary Ellen b. Aug. 20, 1870 (d. Sept. 15, 1905), m. William Finch Oct. 10, 1888; Lydia Catherine b. Feb. 6, 1873, m. Alva Moore Feb. 3, 1897; Annie Matilda b. June 11, 1875, m. Walter Manlove May 18, 1898; Minnie Margaret b. Jan. 28, 1878, m. Albert Manlove; Alma Hans b. April 16, 1881, m. Rhoda Manlove May 11, 1904; James Andrew b. Jan. 1, 1884, d. March 18, 1884; Stephen Johnson b. June 28, 1886, m. Emma Stark Nov. 2, 1910; Joseph Brigham b. March 24, 1889, d. infant. Family home Goshen, Utah.
Married Laura Alice Dean April 8, 1885 (daughter of James and Esther Dean of Virginia), widow of Jefferson Horton whom she had married in Virginia Dec. 26, 1878. To this union were born: Gastan S. b. Oct. 1, 1879, d. Nov. 18, 1884; James A. b. April 18, 1881, d. Nov. 13, 1884; Oscar F. b. Oct. 8, 1882, m. Annie Thomas; Belva Ann b. Oct. 14, 1884, m. Edd Rudd. She was born March 29, 1857, in Virginia. Their children: Esther Jasperson b. Jan. 16, 1890, d. March 8, 1910; Calvin Joseph b. Nov. 1, 1893; Dean b. Sept. 18, 1896. Family resided at Virginia and Goshen, Utah.
High priest; seventy; assisted in bringing immigrants to Utah 1864; assisted in the "move" South 1858. Pioneer to Ephraim, Utah.

JEFFS, RICHARD. Born in England. Came to Utah 1862, Captain Murdock company.
His child: William Walker, m. Emma Summers.

JEFFS, WILLIAM WALKER (son of Richard Jeffs). Born in England. Came to Utah October, 1862, Captain Murdock company. Married Emma Summers 1853, in England (daughter of Richard and Ann Summers of England, pioneers), who was born 1832. Their children: Arthur James b. May 17, 1855, m. Lucinda Seely; Ephraim Rastus. m. Miss Zabriskie; Elizabeth, m. Louis Buntz; Lorenzo, m. Harriet Fauscott. Family home Manti, Utah.
Married David V. Bennett 1864, Manti, Utah. Their children: Annie Jane, m. Fred Nicholas; Emma Rosetta, m. Riley Pace. Family home Manti, Utah.
Seventy; president Staffordshire branch in England. Died September, 1862, Laramie, Wyo.

JEFFS, ARTHUR JAMES (son of William Walker Jeffs and Emma Summers). Born May 17, 1855, in England.
Married Lucinda Seely Dec. 12, 1876, Mt. Pleasant, Utah (daughter of William Stewart Seely and Elizabeth Delfart of Mt. Pleasant, pioneers Sept. 29, 1847, John Taylor company). She was born Nov. 1, 1859. Their children: William Arthur b. March 12, 1878, m. Sarah A. Stott; Moroni Raymond b. March 6, 1881, m. Merlie Bouldin; Emma Elizabeth b. Oct. 24, 1883, m. Alford D. Dixon; Alice Seely b. Aug. 12, 1886; George Nephi b. April 5, 1889; Jimmie Clifford b. Jan. 26, 1891; Elmer b. Aug. 26, 1895; Ada Fay b. April 19, 1897; Jella Lucinda b. Dec. 1, 1899; Dustin Valjane b. April 21, 1902. Family home Castle Dale, Utah.
Elder. Fruitgrower and stockraiser.

JEFFERIES, WILLIAM (son of William Jefferies, born Oct. 20, 1808, and Lita Flower, born Feb. 19, 1804, of Somersetshire, Eng.—married 1827). He was born March 8, 1831, at Goodeaves, Somersetshire, Eng. Came to Utah Sept. 23, 1861, with Ansel P. Harmon company.
Married Mary Frances Ould April 3, 1861 (daughter of William Ould and Mary Fox, who was born May 29, 1840; Mary Fox was a pioneer Sept. 23, 1861, with Joseph W. Young company—married 1820, at Lelant, Cornwall, Eng.). Their children: William Ould b. Feb. 12, 1862, m. Emma Jane Clark Feb. 19, 1885; Mary Frances b. Oct. 31, 1863, m. Joseph R. Olsen, June 19, 1889; James Frederic b. Nov. 1, 1865; Richard b. Nov. 29, 1867, m. Jane E. Rydalch. Nov. 26, 1890; Franklin b. Oct. 3, 1869; Lita b. Sept. 11, 1871; Matilda b. April 28, 1873, m. Mahonri M. Stookey Sept. 24, 1896; Frederic b. March 25, 1875; Albert b. Sept. 6, 1876, m. Maud M. Boshard Sept. 11, 1901; Henry b. March 11, 1879, m. Edith E. Cooley Sept. 10, 1902; Murray b. June 23, 1881, m. Martha M. Hunter Jan. 21, 1903; Sarah b. Nov. 10, 1884. Family home Grantsville, Utah.
Married Mary Fox March 17, 1865, at Salt Lake City (daughter of Richard Fox). She was born March 14, 1809, at Lelant, Cornwall, Eng.
Settled at Grantsville, Tooele county. Tithing clerk 1861-78; president elders' quorum 1864; member of bishopric 1869-73; second counselor to Pres. Francis M. Lyman Tooele stake 1877; superintendent Sunday schools of Tooele stake 1882-88; member presidency high priests of Tooele stake 1882-88. First postmaster 1866-78; city councilman; mayor two terms, 1879 and 1881. Assisted in establishing Grantsville Co-op. store March 1869, of which he was secretary and treasurer, and in 1882 became manager.

JENKINS, EVAN. Born June 22, 1817, Cowbridge, Glamorganshire, South Wales. Came to Utah 1861, Homer Duncan company.
Married Ann Davis, who was born Feb. 8, 1823. Came to Utah 1861, Homer Duncan independent company. Their children: John, m. Mary Oviatt; Ann, m. John Steed; Moroni, m. Martha Benson; William, m. Margaret Jane Glover; Sarah Ellen, died; Juliette, m. Lemuel Rice; Henry, m. Catharina Rice; Mary, m. Will Smith; Margaret, m. Allie Lamb, David, m. Mary Porter. Family home Farmington, Utah.

JENKINS, JOHN (son of Evan Jenkins and Ann Davis). Born May 8, 1845, at Cowbridge, Glamorganshire, Wales.
Married Mary Oviatt Dec. 18, 1867, at Salt Lake City (daughter of Ira Oviatt and Ruth Bennett, pioneers 1851, independent company). She was born Feb. 1, 1850, at Council Bluffs, Iowa. Their children: John F. b. Sept. 13, 1868, m. Mary Haskell March 17, 1890; William E. b. Sept. 14, 1870, m. Lena Weber October, 1891; Alice b. Sept. 28, 1872; Chris. Christensen March 7, 1894; Eva b. Oct. 9, 1874, d. Oct. 6, 1887; Lewis I. b. Jan. 4, 1877, m. Mary Ann Griffin Dec. 15, 1898; Ruth b. Sept. 27, 1878; Edmund D. b. Sept. 2, 1880, m. Elvena Erickson March 27, 1902, Rosabel b. June 11, 1884, m. Leroy Sparks March 27, 1902; Rhoda b. Dec. 28, 1886, d. May 11, 1889; Philip b. Dec. 15, 1889, m. Ida Haderlie Sept. 1912.
Married Ann Clarke at Salt Lake City (daughter of Amos Clarke and Ann Johnston). She was born March 18, 1856. Their children: John Henry b. Oct. 3, 1874, d. Jan. 20, 1875; David Robert b. Jan. 18, 1876, and Sarah Ann (twins), b. Jan. 18, 1876, d. infant; Mary Elizabeth b. July 30, 1877, d. infant; Sophora b. Nov. 25, 1879, m. Eli Hansen Dec. 19, 1902; Junius F. b. Sept. 28, 1881, m. Mary Ann Peterson March 24, 1909; Ida b. July 21, 1884, m. Arthur Crookston June 6, 1906; Stella b. Jan. 16, 1887, m. Carl Jorgensen Feb. 20, 1907; George Edgar, d. infant; and Edna Almira b. Nov. 5, 1890, d. infant; Lorin Amos b. Jan. 7, 1892; Archie A. b. May 1, 1894; Veneta b. Sept. 23, 1896; Donald Thomas b. June 19, 1899; Spencer Samuel b. Feb. 7, 1902.

PIONEERS AND PROMINENT MEN OF UTAH

Married Maria Jensen Oct. 12, 1882, Salt Lake City (daughter of Hans and Maren Jensen), who was born Aug. 9, 1863, while parents were crossing the plains. Their children: James Oliver b. Aug. 10, 1884, m. Maria Stevens July 20, 1904; Marian Lorena b. Nov. 16, 1886, d. child; Peter Moroni b. March 19, 1889; John Raymond b. May 15, 1891; Ann Olivia b. Oct. 2, 1893; Wilford Lorenza b. Nov. 12, 1895; David Seymore b. May 13, 1898; Media Lucile b. May 28, 1900; Lavon b. Sept. 17, 1903; Burton b. Feb. 8, 1909. Family home Newton, Utah.
Missionary to Wales 1882-83; high priest; counselor to Bishop William H. Griffin. Took part in early Indian troubles. Assisted in bringing immigrants to Utah; drove oxteam across the plains seven times. One of first settlers in Cache Valley 1869.

JENKINS, EVAN (son of David Jenkins, born 1814, Llandwr, South Wales, and Anna Evans, born June 9, 1820, Merthyr Tydfil, South Wales, married 1841). He was born May 18, 1849, Cwm Batch, Galmorganshire, South Wales. Came to Utah Sept. 20, 1868, Captain Loveland company.
Married Ann Williams (daughter of David Williams and Sarah Ludwig of Llanelly, Caermarthenshire, South Wales; latter came to Utah 1869, Elias Morris company). She was born Feb. 8, 1854, and came to Utah with mother. Their children: Evan b. June 14, 1878, m. Alice Hawkins; Sarah b. March 27, 1880, m. William J. Powell; Anna b. Feb. 26, 1882, m. David Crowther; David b. May 11, 1884; Mary Ann b. July 23, 1886, m. Henry J. Thomas; Rachael b. April 24, 1889; Vida b. March 2, 1891; Esther b. Jan. 7, 1893; Samuel b. Oct. 3, 1894. Family home Samaria, Oneida Co., Idaho.
Married Sarah Jenkins March 18, 1903, Logan, Utah (daughter of John Jenkins and Ann Deer), who was born Jan. 28, 1860, Swansey, Glamorganshire, South Wales.
Peace officer four years. First counselor to Bishop Daniel E. Price of Samaria ward.

JENKINS, JAMES (son of Thomas Jenkins and Mary Thomas of South Wales). Born October, 1817, South Wales. Came to Utah October 1854, Dorr P. Curtis company.
Married Elizabeth Davis 1843, Llanelly, Wales (daughter of John Davis of Wales), who was born 1807. Their children: Jane, m. Andrew W. Cooley; John, m. Rosella Morris; William, m. Fannie Hirst. Family home West Jordan, Salt Lake Co., Utah.
Elder; block teacher. Farmer and stockraiser. Died March 6, 1904.

JENKINS, JOHN (son of James Jenkins and Elizabeth Davis). Born May 27, 1846, Llanelly, South Wales. Came to Utah Sept. 4, 1854, Captain Richards company.
Married Rozella Morris Nov. 25, 1870, Salt Lake City, by Bishop Hoagland (daughter of George Morris and Hannah Newberry of Ohio, pioneers 1848). She was born March 29, 1848. Their children: John M. b. April 21, 1873, m. Florence Brown; Zina E. b. March 2, 1875, m. Valton M. Pratt; George E. b. April 11, 1877, m. Elma Stogell, m. Rosella Brown; Ada R. b. Sept. 20, 1878, m. Frank L. Clark; Arthur V. b. July 23, 1880, m. Grace Moss; Mary M. b. March 16, 1885, m. Everett Watrous; Viola P. b. Dec. 18, 1892. Family home Pleasant Green, Salt Lake Co., Utah.
Elder. Farmer and stockraiser.

JENKINS, WILLIAM (son of James Jenkins and Elizabeth Davis). Born Oct. 7, 1848, South Wales. Came to Utah October 1854, Dorr P. Curtis company.
Married Fanny Hirst Dec. 20, 1869, Salt Lake City (daughter of John Hirst and Charlotte Brook of Yorkshire, Eng., pioneers Aug. 25, 1868, Hans Jensen Hals company). She was born May 10, 1852. Their children: John W. b. Dec. 13, 1870, m. Harriet Davis; Hannah E. b. Jan. 1, 1873, d. aged 6; Sarah J. b. April 1, 1875, m. Leroy Morris; Fanny C. b. Aug. 26, 1877, d. infant; James H. b. June 30, 1880, m. Helma Ek; Annetta Eve b. Dec. 5, 1882, m. A. W. Exstrand; Mary C. b. July 9, 1885, m. W. H. Smith; Henry A. b. Aug. 23, 1887, m. Pearl Smith; Amos B b. Nov. 16, 1889, m. Edith Wagner; Thaddeus b. Dec. 25, 1892, d. infant; Annis b. July 18, 1894. Family resided in Salt Lake Co., Utah.
Member 8th quorum seventies; high priest; missionary to Indiana 1896-97; block teacher; president Y. M. I. A. Farmer and stockraiser.

JENKINS, JAMES HARDY (son of John Jenkins and Ellen Hardy of Stirlingshire, Scotland). Born July, 1822. Came to Utah October 1863.
Married Jeanett Laird 1842 (daughter of Charles Laird). She was born 1822. Their children: John Laird b. Jan. 17, 1844, m. Emma Louisa Taylor, m. Annie Maria Sorenson; Charles B. Oct.. 1845. m. Mary Conover; Jane, m. William Stewart; Ellen, m. John Finch; Henry, m. Emma Stanfield; Elizabeth, m. Heber Stanfield; Jeanette, Agnes, James, Margeret, James. Isabel, latter six d. young.
Married Miriam Saunders 1880, Salt Lake City. Their children: William b. January, 1882, m. Lucile Cook; Francis M.; Robert Lusie. Family home Goshen, Utah.
High priest. Died February, 1891, Salt Lake City; buried at Goshen.

JENKINS, JOHN LAIRD (son of James Hardy Jenkins and Jeanett Laird). Born Jan. 17, 1844, in Scotland. Came to Utah October, 1863.
Married Emma Louisa Taylor (daughter of George Taylor and Louisa Gwyther, Candle Green, Gloucestershire. Eng.).
She was born Aug. 13, 1854, Parish Besley, Eng., and came to Utah Oct. 3, 1862, Capt. Duncan company. Their children: Emma Louisa b. June 23, 1872, died; Jeanett Laird b. Sept. 6, 1874, m. Charles H. Wentz; James Hardy b. Nov. 20, 1876, m. Mary Elizabeth Bucklar; Son b. July 28, 1878, died; Alice Taylor b. Aug. 28, 1879, m. Lars L. Olsen; Lucy Jane b Dec. 2, 1881. m. Peter N. Anderson; Louisa Gwyther b. July 2, 1883, died; John Laird b. March, 1885, died; George Taylor b. July 10, 1888; Joseph b. March 13, 1892; Hyrum b. March 13, 1892; Junis Paxman b. June 13, 1894; Hattie Eva b. April 10, 1896; May Afton b. May 30, 1899.
Married Annie Maria Sorenson November, 1878, Salt Lake City (daughter of Jeppa Sorenson and Catherine Ceila Johnson, Koosharem, Utah). She was born April 26, 1859. Their children: Annie Maria b. July 9, 1880, died; Catherine Ceila b. July 15, 1882, m. Albert Earl Davis; Henry J. b. April 24, 1885, died; David William b. May, 1887, died; Isabell b. June 28, 1888; Wilford W. b. April 28, 1892; Gilbert b. July 14, 1895; Jennie Marretta b. May 5, 1900. Family home Goshen, Utah.
Member of presidency of 15th quorum of seventies; missionary to Scotland 1889-1890; counselor to Bishop Peter Okelberry, Goshen ward; superintendent of Sunday school; counselor to president Y. M. M. I. A. School trustee. Assisted in bringing immigrants to Utah 1866. Worked on St. George temple. Carpenter; miner; farmer. Died May 22, 1905.

JENKINS, JAMES HARDY (son of John Laird Jenkins and Emma Louisa Taylor). Born Nov. 20, 1876, Goshen, Utah.
Married Mary Elizabeth Bucklar June 24, 1908, Salt Lake City (daughter of George Bucklar of Burton Overy, and Jane Fant of Swineshead, Lincolnshire, Eng.). She was born Nov. 9, 1876. Their children: Ruth Mary b. Feb. 18, 1910; John Laird b. Dec. 5, 1911; Pearl Fant b. June 8, 1912.
Missionary to Missouri 1902-04; bishop Grand View ward; secretary elders quorum, Goshen, Utah. Fruit raising; mining.

JENKINS, LEWIS (son of Thomas Jenkins and Margaret Griffeth, Glamorganshire, South Wales). Born March 28, 1834, in Glamorganshire. Came to Utah 1859.
Married Eliza Ann Harrison May 22, 1870, Salt Lake City (daughter of Isaac Harrison and Hanna Dore of Belper, Derbyshire, Eng., came to Utah 1879). She was born Nov. 24, 1840. Their children: Lewis R. b. April 2, 1871, m. Laura Cynthia Moench Dec. 22, 1899; Rosa, m. Thomas, m. Florence Turner; Clara Jane; Margaret; George Albert, m. Lillian Malquist. Family home Plain City, Utah.
Member 54th quorum seventies; president Y. M. M. I. A.; first assistant Sunday school superintendent. Justice of peace. Farmer. Died July 30, 1903.

JENKINS, LEWIS ROBERT (son of Lewis Jenkins and Eliza Ann Harrison). Born April 2, 1871, Plain City.
Married Laura Cynthia Moench Dec. 22, 1899, Salt Lake City (daughter of Louis F. Moench and Ruthinda Eveline Hill of Ogden, Utah). She was born Sept. 13, 1875. Their children: Genevieve Eliza b. Nov. 22, 1900; Lewis Rulon b. Sept. 12, 1902; Laurence William b. Nov. 5, 1904; Gwendolyn b. June 28, 1907; Ruthinda La Rue b. March 26, 1909; Donald Moench b. Aug. 7, 1910, d. young; Donna Mae b. Nov. 4, 1912. Family home Plain City, Utah.
One of presidents 87th quorum seventies; missionary to Hawaiian Islands 1895-99; assistant Sunday school superintendent; first counselor and secretary Y. M. M. I. A.; secretary elders' and seventies' quorums. Farmer.

JENKINS, THOMAS (son of David Jenkins and Jane Fergeson of Lancaster county, Pa.). Born 1808 in Lancaster county. Came to Utah 1852.
Married Joanna Marshall April 19, 1838, in Lancaster county (daughter of Joseph Marshall and Joanna Halze of Philadelphia, Pa.). She was born April 21, 1816. Family home Ogden, Utah.
High priest. Blacksmith and farmer. Died Dec. 3, 1893.

JENKINS, THOMAS (son of John Jenkins and Hanna Cartwright of Herefordshire, Eng.). Born Feb. 18, 1829 in Herefordshire. Came to Utah Sept. 22, 1848, Lorenz Snow company.
Married Anna Smith Jan. 16, 1851 (daughter of Thomas Smith, pioneer John Young company). She was born Dec. 2, 1833. Their children: Mary Ann, m. Richard G. Lambert Alice, m. David L. Dean; Sarah J., m. Abraham H. Cannon Annie, m. Frank Wilcox; John A., Eva, George B. Thomas W., last four died.
Married Mary R. Avery Oct. 27, 1855, Salt Lake City (daughter of Ernestus and Jerusa Avery), who was bor Oct. 19, 1834. Their children: William B., m. Maria Kimball; Sophia, m. W. A. Aubrey; Rachel (deceased), m. Charle Slade; Thomas H., m. Minnie Moffat; Cyrus F., m. Matild Burrows; Maud, m. J. U. Eldredge, Jr.; Joseph J., Jerusa A James A., latter three died.
Married Mary A. Fuller Dec. 22, 1866, at Salt Lake City No children.
Married Mahala Elmer Dec. 19, 1870, Salt Lake Cit (daughter of Edward Elmer and Elizabeth Ann Blunde of Suffolk, Eng.). She was born Dec. 12, 1847. Came Utah 1870. Their children: Edward Elmer, m. Elizabe Cutler; Harrison E., m. Julia Wieser; Rose, m. Carl Badger; Emily, m. David A. Smith.

Married Mary Buckley at Salt Lake City. Only child: May (deceased), m. Albert B. Needham. Family home, Salt Lake City.
High priest; bishop of 4th ward. City councilman. Contractor; stockraiser. Died at Salt Lake City Oct. 21, 1905.

JENKINS, EDWARD ELMER (son of Thomas Jenkins and Mahala Elmer). Born Nov. 25, 1873, at Salt Lake City.
Married Elizabeth Cutler Oct. 14, 1897, at Salt Lake City (daughter of John C. Cutler and Elizabeth Taylor of England). She was born Oct. 5, 1874. Their children: Elmer C. b. Oct. 6, 1898; Irving E. b. March 12, 1902; Harold C. b. Dec. 28, 1905; John C. b. May 3, 1908.
Missionary to England 1898-1901; high priest. Member firm Ashton & Jenkins, real estate dealers.

JENKINSON, SAMUEL WILFORD (son of Noah Jenkinson and Hannah Smith of Oldham, Lancashire, Eng.; came to Utah May, 1878). Born Dec. 18, 1851. Came to Utah Oct. 14, 1850.
Married Sophia M. Hardy May 21, 1878, Salt Lake City (daughter of Leonard Wilford Hardy and Sophia Lois Goodridge of Salt Lake City, pioneers Oct. 14, 1850, Wilford Woodruff company). She was born April 21, 1856, Salt Lake City. Their children: Wilford b. Sept. 17, 1879, d. infant; Frank N. b. April 21, 1881, m. Edna M. Hemphill; Florence S. b. Jan. 21, 1883, m. Fred Jacobson; Samuel W. b. May 30, 1886, m. Susie Johnson; Lena V. b. Sept. 16, 1888, d. infant; Isabel b. Oct. 22, 1890, d. infant; Joseph A. b. Oct. 22, 1890; Alma H. b. Dec. 13, 1892; Leonard H. b. Feb. 19, 1895; Harold H. b. Oct. 18, 1896, d. child; Wallace H. b. April 8, 1899. Family resided Smithfield and Salt Lake City, Utah.
Chaplain state legislature; superintendent home for the blind; justice of the peace, Smithfield, and member city council. Superintendent 20th ward Sunday school, Salt Lake City.

JENNE, BENJAMIN (son of Prince Elisha Jenne and Olive Lincoln). Born May 16, 1806. Came to Utah 1848, George Snyder company.
Married Sarah Snyder Jan. 20, 1830 (daughter of Isaac Snyder and Louisa Comestock of New York). She was born April 11, 1813. Their children: Hyrum; Isaac; Louisa b. June 15, 1832, m. Jared Curtis Roundy; Olive b. Oct. 1, 1835, m. William Peck; Chester; Sarah Jane b. Sept. 11, 1839, m. George Q. Cannon; Roseanna, m. Peter Hanson; Maria; Brigham; William H. b. April 22, 1848, m. Minnetta Johnson; Robert; Lucy.
Died in Idaho in 1897.

JENSEN, ANDREW. Born February, 1810, Klotofte, Denmark. Came to Utah 1860.
Married Methei Catherine Nilsen, Copenhagen, Denmark, who was born May 22, 1810, in Denmark, came to Utah with husband, and died Aug. 14, 1878.
Died Nov. 29, 1883.

JENSEN, ANDREW NIELSON (son of Neils Jensen and Gunilla Eriandsen of Sweden). Born May 7, 1829, Herestad, Sweden. Came to Utah Oct. 5, 1864, Isaac Canfield company.
Married Caroline Nielson in Oct. 1860, at Malmö, Sweden (daughter of Ola Nielson and Petronilla Larsdatter of Malmö). She was born Aug. 25, 1839. Their children: Gunilla b. Dec. 18, 1861, d. while crossing the Atlantic; Niels b. Dec. 23, 1862, d. Oct. 16, 1864; Andrew b. Dec. 20, 1865, d. Sept. 16, 1866; John b. Aug. 11, 1867, m. Elma Sanberg; Mary Caroline b. July 30, 1869, m. Charles L. Bean; James b. Oct. 14, 1871, m. Lucy Harmon; Martha Sophia b. Feb. 24, 1874; Lewis b. Aug. 17, 1876, m. Adele Gottfridson; Alexander b. Nov. 20, 1878, m. May Harmon. Family resided in Sweden and at Fountain Green and Richfield, Utah.
High priest; counsellor in bishopric of Richfield ward. Farmer and stockraiser. Died May 14, 1893, at Richfield.

JENSON, JAMES (son of Andrew Nielson and Caroline Nielson). Born Oct. 14, 1871, Richfield, Utah.
Married Lucy Harmon April 30, 1902, Manti, Utah (daughter of Ansel P. Harmon and Rosaline Chandler, pioneers 1848 and 1862 respectively). She was born Sept. 23, 1871. Their children: Ruth b. Sept. 8, 1903; Carrie b. Oct. 19, 1905; James Harmon b. Nov. 13, 1907; Rose b. Feb. 3, 1910; Milo Andrew b. Feb. 23, 1912. Family home Richfield, Utah.
Elder and ward teacher at Richfield. Farmer and stockraiser.

JENSEN, CHRISTIAN (son of Jens Jensen and Metta Maria Jensen of Laasby, Skanderborg amt, Denmark). Born June 6, 1841. Came to Utah Oct. 8, 1854, Hans Peter Olsen company.
Married Albertina Carlsten Nov. 10, 1863, at Manti, Utah (daughter of Charles Anton and Amanda Carlsten of Sölvesborg, Blekinge, Sweden). She was born Jan. 23, 1841, and came to Utah Sept. 5, 1863, John P. Sanders company. Their children: Amanda b. Aug. 17, 1864, m. Joseph Ralphs; Jens Christian b. July 30, 1866, m. Agnes Christie Brown; Albert b. Sept. 6, 1868, m. Olive Stephens; James b. Aug. 13, 1870, died; Carl Anton b. March 23, 1873, died; Albertina Annetta b. April 16, 1875, m. Andrew Samuelson; Cora Josephina b. Aug. 16, 1877, m. Hans Nelson.
Settled at Manti, Utah, 1854. Veteran Black Hawk war. Quarried stone for St. George temple. Brought immigrants from Missouri river to Salt Lake City in 1863, with Capt. Sanders company. Moved to Ferron, Utah, 1896.

JENSEN, JENS CHRISTIAN (son of Christian Jensen and Albertina Carlsten). Born July 30, 1866, Manti, Utah.
Married Agnes Christie Brown Jan. 22, 1886, Manti, Utah (daughter of James Cant Brown and Margarette Christie of Lochee, three miles west of Dundee, Scotland). She was born June 10, 1869, and came to Utah in 1882. Their children: Christian b. Dec. 13, 1886, m. Blanche Caldwell; Agnes Bertha b. Sept. 2, 1888, m. William Ralphs; James Stanley b. June 7, 1890; Eva b. Nov. 26, 1899; Maggie Vera b. April 7, 1901; Gerald Quintin b. April 13, 1905. Family home Ferron, Utah.
Moved from Manti to Ferron, Utah, 1890. Farmer; brickmaker.

JENSEN, CHRISTIAN (son of Jens Christensen and Anna Jensen of Aaby, Denmark). Born Sept. 25, 1818, Aaby, Denmark. Came to Utah Oct. 5, 1867, Independent company.
Married Karen Petersen Aug. 12, 1860 (daughter of Peter Andersen and Kjarstin Jensen), who was born May 16, 1825. Their children: Bertha M. b. Jan. 30, 1858, m. David Eccles; Mary b. Sept. 2, 1863, m. R. W. Emmett; Peter M. b. Jan. 22, 1868, m. Elizabeth Bronson.
Farmer.

JENSEN, PETER M. (son of Christian Jensen and Karen Petersen). Born Jan. 22, 1868, Huntsville, Utah.
Married Elizabeth Bronson June 20, 1889, Logan, Utah (daughter of Wilmer W. Bronson and Elizabeth Fisher), who was born March 10, 1870, Huntsville, Utah. Their children: Wilmer C. b. Dec. 23, 1890; Floyd C. b. Nov. 17, 1892; Ronald V. b. March 18, 1895; Clarice b. June 7, 1897; Royal Q. b. Nov. 9, 1899; Lillian b. Sept. 10, 1901; Myrtle b. Sept. 19, 1905; Oren L. b. Jan. 28, 1902; Dillworth D. b. Oct. 1, 1910. Family home, Huntsville.
Farmer.

JENSEN, CHRISTIAN RUDOLPH PHILLIP (son of Jens Kristiansen, born 1751, and Maren Jensdatter). Born March 8, 1796, Horhaven, Aarhuus Amt, Denmark. Came to Utah in 1864.
Married Anne Johanna Rasmusen (daughter of Bendix Sorensen), who was born March 15, 1790. Their children: Jens b. April 16, 1814; Niels b. June 15, 1824, m. Karen Jensen 1851; Soren b. Dec. 26, 1830, m. Caroline Theodora Loft 1854. Family resided Ephraim and Fountain Green, Utah.

CHRISTIANSEN, SOREN (son of Christian Rudolph Phillip Jensen and Anne Johanna Rasmusen). Born Dec. 26, 1830, Aarhuus Amt, Denmark.
Married Caroline Theodora Loft in 1854, in Denmark (daughter of Mikkel Christensen Loft and Anna Marie Nielson, who came to Utah in 1873). She was born July 5, 1836, in Denmark. Their children: Christian John b. April 17, 1855, m. Ellen Jane Oldroyd 1876; Maria Mikkeline b. Sept. 29, 1856, m. Lars Nielson 1871. Family home Fountain Green, Utah.
School trustee; Sunday school treasurer and librarian; ward teacher; president high priests quorum.

CHRISTIANSEN, CHRISTIAN JOHN (son of Soren Christiansen and Caroline Theodora Loft). Born April 17, 1855, in Denmark.
Married Ellen Jane Oldroyd, at Salt Lake City (daughter of Peter Oldroyd and Katharine Micklejohn; former came to Utah 1850, latter 1851). She was born Nov. 8, 1856, Ephraim, Utah. Their children: Christian T. b. Aug. 10, 1876, m. Estelle E. Cook 1892; Peter M. b. March 29, 1880; Agnes M. b. Nov. 8, 1881, m. James W. Christensen 1910; Ellen Jane b. April 1, 1885, m. Eugene Ivory Oct. 22, 1911; Soren A. b. Sept. 19, 1886; Archibald L. b. Oct. 8, 1888; Roy O. b. Jan. 29, 1892; Catharine J. b. Oct. 4, 1895; Leah B. b. Nov. 7, 1897; Joseph R. b. Sept. 26, 1898; John Eldon b. Feb. 27, 1901. Family home Fountain Green, Utah.
Town trustee. Ward teacher; Sunday school superintendent; bishop 20 years. Member brass band.

JENSEN, DAVID J. Born April 15, 1835, Tolton, Norway. Came to Utah in 1863.
Married Birta Serena Peterson, who was born Aug. 20, 1844, Norway. Their children: Segvart Julius, d. Norway; Josephine, d. on plains; David Henry, d. Lehi, Utah; Sarah Christina, m. Alfred Alder Jan. 1884; Hyrum Daniel, m. Augusta Alder Nov. 23, 1891; David Oscar, m. Martina Hansen; Nora Elvina, m. James Smart; Anton Henry, m. Nellie Bowen; Carl Fredrick, m. Dagmar Lund; Joseph William, m. Sarah Chadwick; Naham, m. May Monson.
Married Margaret Ann Alder Sept. 1, 1898, Logan, Utah (daughter of Alfred Alder and Susan Field), who was born Aug. 10, 1864, Kaysville, Utah. Their children: Olean Alder b. Nov. 24, 1899; Winifred b. May 1, 1904; Lenard Alder b. Sept. 2, 1907.
Bishop's counsellor of Preston; first Sunday school superintendent of Preston stake; high councilor of Oneida stake. Farmer and stockraiser. Died Jan. 1909, at Preston, Idaho.

PIONEERS AND PROMINENT MEN OF UTAH

JENSEN, HYRUM DANIEL (son of David J. Jensen and Birta Serena Peterson). Born Feb. 22, 1868, Franklin, Idaho.
Married Augusta Alder Nov. 23, 1891, Preston, Idaho (daughter of Alfred Alder and Silsan Field of St. Louis, Mo., pioneers Sept. 23, 1853, Cladius V. Spencer company). She was born Aug. 27, 1866. Their children: Alta b. Sept. 2, 1892, m. William H. Anger; Serena Jensen b. Dec. 29, 1893. Family home Ogden, Utah.
Missionary to Norway 1896-98; member presidency Scandinavian organization, Oneida stake. First marshal of village of Preston. Farmer.

JENSEN, HANS (son of Jens Andersen and Anna Katrina Jespersen). Born April 10, 1842, Frybjerg, Orte Sogn, Denmark. Came to Utah 1865.
Married Cecelia Jensen in April 1864 (daughter of Peter and Martha Jensen), who was born Feb. 28, 1848. Their children: Waldemar b. June 1, 1867, m. Selma Johnson Sept. 1, 1894; Hans b. April 3, 1869; Jacob b. Sept. 1, 1871; Martha b. Jan. 20, 1874, m. John C. Johnson; Jens Mikkle b. July 8, 1876; Anne Katrine b. Oct. 4, 1878, m. John Lerwell Jan. 1, 1898; Maria Christina b. March 19, 1881, m. Delos F. Tanner April 9, 1902; Alma b. Dec. 23, 1884; Moses b. 1888, m. Eva Francom Nov. 28, 1906; Cecelia and Emilia, twins, b. 1896. Family home Goshen, Utah.
Married Maren Hansen Oct. 11, 1870, Salt Lake City (daughter of Lars Hansen and Karen Peteradatter), who was born Jan. 13, 1848, Meby, Denmark. Their children: Lars b. June 21, 1872; Johanas b. Jan. 20, 1874; Hans b. March 14, 1875; Peter Christian b. Nov. 11, 1877; Andrew Jorgen b. June 7, 1878; Joseph b. Nov. 19, 1879; Hyrum b. Oct. 3, 1881; Carl Moroni b. March 22, 1884; Adam b. Feb. 22, 1888; Dan Frederick b. June 9, 1890; John b. July 31, 1892; Albert b. Jan. 7, 1896.
Missionary to Sjælland, Denmark, 1862-65. High priest and seventy. First settler at Salt Lake City, afterwards moved to Goshen and lived there until his death. Tailor by occupation.

JENSEN, WALDEMAR (son of Hans Jensen and Cecelia Jensen). Born June 1, 1867, at Salt Lake City.
Married Selma Johnson Sept. 1, 1894, Santaquin, Utah (daughter of Ludvick and Christine Johnson; came to Utah Aug. 1893). She was born Feb. 15, 1875, in Sweden. Their children: Edmund Walter b. July 23, 1896; Emma Christen b. Sept. 3, 1898; Elmer Ludvick b. Oct. 21, 1901; Agnet Cecelia b. Feb. 8, 1903; Hans Delos b. Aug. 20, 1905; Robert Franklin b. Aug. 30, 1907; Sylvia Selma b. Oct. 14, 1909; Ruth Carrie b. March 8, 1912.
Missionary to Aalborg and Aarhuus, Denmark, two years; 2d counselor to Bishops Peter Okelberry (dead), and later to Wm. P. Okelberry.

JENSEN, HANS RICHARD. Married Mary S. Christensen, Denmark (daughter of Carrie Marie Madsen, Denmark). She was born Feb. 23, 1852. Their children: Hans Richard, Jr., m. May Pitt; Carrie Marie, m. Joseph Ellison Murray; Julius, m. Vilate Goodrich. Family home Vernal, Utah.

JENSEN, JAMES (son of Niels Jensen, born in 1817 at Starup, and Inger Marie Madsen, born March 17, 1819, at Fleisborg, Denmark). Born July 14, 1847, at Starup. Came to Utah Sept. 12, 1861, John Murdock company.
Married Anna Sophia Christensen Sept. 26, 1868 (daughter of Frederick Christensen and Dorthea Sophia Tiesen, married in 1848; former pioneer 1862, Capt. Van Cott company, latter died in Denmark). She was born Nov. 8, 1849; came to Utah with father in 1862. Their children: James B. b. Sept. 9, 1869, m. May Cushing; Niel C. b. Jan. 23, 1872, m. Rose Graham; Joseph F. b. April 12, 1874, m. Isabell Sidoway Sept. 24, 1902; Mary A. S. b. Sept. 27, 1876, m. A. G. Cushing Dec. 16, 1896; Amos E. b. July 2, 1879, m. Ida Despain March 28, 1906; Mabel E. b. Nov. 22, 1881, m. August M. Nelson April 25, 1906; Sarah Florence b. Aug. 16, 1884, m. Louis E. Van Dam April 20, 1905; Evan Orlando b. April 16, 1887, m. Edith Brown Sept. 20, 1911. Family home Draper, now Sandy, Utah.
Bishop of Sandy ward, Salt Lake county, May 15, 1892; counselor in presidency, Jordan stake of Zion, 1900. Veteran Black Hawk war. Precinct constable, Draper, 1876-1880; justice of peace 1882; postmaster 1879-1892.

JENSON, JAMES B. (son of James Jenson and Annie Sophia Christensen). Born Sept. 9, 1869, Bear River City, Utah.
Married Ellen May Cushing Feb. 25, 1896, Salt Lake City (daughter of A. J. and Ellen M. Cushing of Sandy, Utah; former came to Utah 1869, latter 1850). Their children: James Arthur b. Jan. 16, 1896; Irma May b. Jan. 21, 1898. Family home Salt Lake City.
Member 57th quorum seventies. Mining engineer.

JENSEN, JAMES (son of James Jensen, born 1797, Kendertofte, Denmark, and Mary Nielsen, born at Kirkehealsange, Denmark). He was born Oct. 3, 1832, Lyra Rye, Gorlovsogn, Denmark. Came to Utah Sept. 27, 1862, Captain Murdock company.
Married Bodel Larsen April 20, 1862, on board ship (daughter of Lars Pederson and Anne Olsen of Wortingborg, Denmark). She was born Dec. 23, 1832, and came to Utah with husband. Their children: Mary Josephine b. April 17, 1863, d. infant; James, Jr., b. April 16, 1864, m. Hannah Eliza Hepworth Nov. 8, 1889; Lars Peter b. Sept. 12, 1866, m. Elizabeth Colton Oct. 26, 1886. Family resided Brigham City and Mantua, Utah.
Married Henrietta Christensen July 6, 1869, Salt Lake Endowment house (daughter of Jacob and Maren Christensen), who was born Jan. 22, 1843, came to Utah 1866, independent company. Their children: Joseph b. April 16, 1870 d. March, 1892; Hyrum b. May 8, 1871, m. Sarah Ellen Allen Oct. 21, 1903; Martin b. Sept. 30, 1874, m. Elnora Nielsen Oct. 24, 1895; Henrietta b. March, 1874, m. Richard T. Astle Oct. 24, 1895. Family home Mantua.
Married Albine Jensen Sept. 25, 1879, Brigham City, Utah (daughter of Jens Karstiane Jensen and Annie Maria Petersen), who was born March 1, 1859. Their children: Alfred b. July 15, 1881, m. Ina Griffith Nov. 20, 1902; Lorenzo b. Sept. 8, 1883, m. Kattie A. Carpenter Oct. 19, 1907; Nephi b. July 21, 1886, m. Luella Esther Allender July 29, 1909; Annie Elizabeth b. Oct. 26, 1888, m. William Kirby Feb. 13, 1907; Nellie Bodel b. Oct. 1, 1891, m. Louis J. Jensen April 12, 1911; Heber Charles b. March 9, 1894; Wilford Lavon b. June 18, 1896; Leland Levere b. Oct. 23, 1899; Leo James b. June 20, 1904.
Settled at Brigham City 1862; moved to Mantua, and in 1883 went to Curlew Valley, where he resided until 1886 and then went to Star Valley, Wyo. Presiding elder of the Grover ward from 1888 to 1889, when he was set apart as bishop of that ward and served till 1905.

JENSEN, JAMES, JR. (son of James Jensen and Bodel Larsen). Born April 16, 1864, Brigham City, Utah.
Married Hannah Eliza Hepworth Nov. 8, 1889, Logan, Utah (daughter of Edmond Hepworth and Hanna Cowling, pioneers 1863, Captain White company). She was born July 5, 1869, Oxford, Idaho. Their children: James Edmond b. Sept. 13, 1890, d. Oct. 11, 1906; Jesse Lyman b. Oct. 26, 1892; Ruben Adelbert b. Aug. 8, 1894; Willis Clifford b. Nov. 16, 1896; Maud Bodel b. April 9, 1901; Hannah Rowena b. March 27, 1903; Mabel Anice b. June 24, 1906; Ira Wilford b. Oct. 2, 1908; Lyle Hepworth b. Jan. 30, 1911. Family home Grover.
President Y. M. M. I. A.; missionary to Norway 1897-1900; high councilor in Star Valley stake; bishop Grover ward 1905; Sunday school teacher. School trustee 15 years. Deputy district assessor six years.

JENSEN, JAMES CHRISTIAN (son of Soren Peter Jensen, born Oct. 30, 1836, Glimsholt, Ugilt, Denmark, and Kirsten Marie Christensen, born Nov. 24, 1834; married Ugilt church Oct. 24, 1862; came to Utah July 14, 1877). Born Sept. 9, 1863, at Glimsholt. Came to Utah July 14, 1877.
Married Joannah Eliza Jennings Oct. 16, 1884, Salt Lake City (daughter of Mansfield Jennings and Fanny Jane Perri of Springville and Levan, Utah). She was born Sept. 2, 1866. Their children: James Christian, d. infant; Jay Clai b. Sept. 1, 1888; Erma Inez b. March 9, 1892; Glen Marti b. Jan. 18, 1895; Ralph Owen b. Aug. 3, 1897; Perrie Sore b. Feb. 5, 1902; Leo Ray b. July 26, 1906; Eva Frances b. April 10, 1908. Family resided Salt Lake City and Hebe City, Utah.
President Y. M. M. I. A. of 13th ward, Salt Lake Cit 1888; secretary Granite stake Sunday schools 1897-190; County recorder, Salt Lake county 1897-1901. First coun selor in presidency of Wasatch stake. Abstractor; in surance; real estate and loans.

JENSEN, JAMES IVER (son of Thomas C. Jensen an Karne Marie Iverson, both of Denmark). Born Aug. 1846, in Denmark. Came to Utah Oct. 5, 1867, Independen company.
Married Inger Sejnedegaard Nielson May 22, 1868, in Denmark (daughter of Christian Nielson of Denmark). She wa born Feb. 17, 1845. Their children: James Iver, died; Charles, m. Sarah Peterson; Daniel, m. Matilda Lee; Carolin died; Walter, m. Elizabeth Sylvester; Emma, m. Herbert Lund; Wilhelmina, m. F. Horace Guymon; Clementine, John Hagen. Family home, Salt Lake City.
Seventy; missionary to Denmark 1865-67 and 1880-8 high priest; bishop; patriarch. Merchant.

JENSEN, DR. CHARLES (son of James Iver Jensen an Inger Sejnedegaard Nielsen). Born Dec. 21, 1872, Ephrai Utah.
Married Sarah Peterson September, 1895, Salt Lake Ci (daughter of Peter C. Peterson and Hannah Thompson Norway), who was born Feb. 27, 1872. Their childre Charles Easton b. Dec. 19, 1896; Ethel b. July 23, 190 Dorothy b. Feb. 1906. Family home Ephraim, Utah.
Seventy. School trustee, Ephraim. County physicia Physician and surgeon.

JENSEN, JAMES PETER (son of Andrew Jensen and Bertl Maria Jensen). Born Aug. 2, 1835, Kastberg, Randers, Denmark. Came to Utah 1867.
Married Mary Christina Jensen Nov. 12, 1865, Ginerv Randers amt, Denmark (daughter of Christian Jensen), w was born Feb. 1, 1844, and came to Utah 1867. Their children: Andrew, d. on North Platte River; Niels, d. infar Mary Christina, m. N. E. Mortensen; Eliza Martha, m. Jose Mortensen: James Peter, m. Laura Baker; Joseph Willi m. Viola Thompson; Sarah Merretta, m. John McMaste

Bertha Lenora, m. Joseph H. Smith; Hyrum Edward, m. Mary Anderson. Family home Newton, Cache Co., Utah. Postmaster six years. Farmer. Died April 6, 1901.

JENSEN, JAMES PETER, JR. (son of James Peter Jensen and Mary Christina Jensen). Born Oct. 12, 1875, Newton, Utah.
Married Laura Baker June 5, 1901, Logan temple (daughter of Albert Mourey Baker and Edna Jane Coon of Mendon, Utah, pioneers Oct. 2, 1847). She was born June 11, 1881. Their children: Mabel b. March 4, 1902; Peter Raymond b. July 15, 1903; Laura Le Rue b. Aug. 5, 1904; Royal Baker b. Oct. 1, 1905; Edna b. Jan. 26, 1908; Albert Rex b. Sept. 6, 1910. Family resided Brigham, Utah, and Malad, Idaho.
Member Sunday school board of Box Elder stake three years; second assistant to superintendent of Malad stake Sunday schools; bishop Malad ward from 1908. Member school board. Corporal in Battery A, Utah Artillery, during Spanish-American war, serving in the Philippines. Merchant.

JENSEN, JENS (son of Jens Larsen and Metta Hansen of Sundstrup, Sjælland, Denmark). Born March 22, 1829, Sundstrup. Came to Utah in September 1857, Mathias Cowley company.
Married Hannah Hansen in 1851 at Hosterkjob, Denmark (daughter of Hans Jensen and Christine Rasmussen of Hosterkjob). She was born April 22, 1830. Their children: James, m. Hannah Larson; John, m. Annie Israelson; Christine, m. Andrew Larson; Sophia, died; Emma, m. Hyrum McBride; Joseph, m. Mary A. Christensen; Benjamin, m. Hlena Christiansen; Martha, died.
Elder. Farmer. Died April 10, 1902, Hyrum, Utah.

JENSEN, JAMES (son of Jens Jensen and Hannah Hansen). Born Dec. 17, 1853, Sundstrup, Denmark. Came to Utah in September 1857 with parents.
Married Hannah Larson Jan. 1, 1875, Hyrum, Utah (daughter of Peter Larson and Cecelia Peterson of Trode, Sweden, pioneers 1863, W. W. Cluff company). She was born Sept. 2, 1857. Their children: Joseph b. Oct. 7, 1876, died; Amanda b. June 16, 1878, m. Joseph J. Hall; Edith b. Jan. 6, 1881, m. Clarence Nielsen; Hilda b. May 8, 1883, m. Estelle Smith; Clara b. Aug. 1, 1885, m. Emery Mitton; Victor b. Nov. 10, 1887; Alice b. Nov. 22, 1889, m. Henry Danielsen; Harvey b. Oct. 14, 1893; Phyllis b. Nov. 19, 1901, died. Family home Hyrum, Utah.
Elder. City councilman; watermaster; member water board; member first irrigation congress in Utah. Director South Cache Mill Co. Farmer.

JENSEN, JENS LARSON (son of Jens Larson and Kirsty Monsen of Sweden). Born July 14, 1827, Dalby, Scona, Sweden. Came to Utah in October 1860.
Married Ellen Jepson in 1858 at Copenhagen, Denmark. She was born Oct. 6, 1838. Their children: Anna Sophia b. Aug. 12, 1860, m. Bennett Monk; John L. b. Nov. 1, 1862, d. infant; Emma Kirsty b. Dec. 18, 1864, m. William Jarvis; Ellen b. May 9, 1867, m. Charles Barnhart. Family resided at Lehi, Mill Creek and Mt. Pleasant, Utah.
Married Engre Parson in 1862, Salt Lake City (daughter of Andrew and Lucy Parson of Sweden; former came to Utah in 1874, latter in 1861). She was born Oct. 13, 1832. Their children: Joseph L. b. March 20, 1864, m. Hannah Peterson; Lucy Amelia b. Aug. 3, 1865, m. Joseph R. Hooton; Andrew L. b. July 2, 1868, d. June, 1869; Ephraim b. Oct. 16, 1869, d. March 9, 1883; Edith Josephine b. March 1, 1872, d. Feb. 24, 1883; Mary Ann b. Jan. 28, 1876, m. P. C. Hansen.
Married Emma C. Roseberry Jan. 2, 1874, Salt Lake City (daughter of Charles Roseberry and Helena Erickson, Malmö, Sweden, pioneers Sept. 4, 1859, Captain Rowley handcart company). She was born Sept. 10, 1858, at Malmö. Their children: John Roseberry b. Oct. 11, 1874, m. Emma Jane Barlow; James L. b. Aug. 30, 1876, d. Jan. 17, 1905; Anna H. b. Oct. 24, 1878, m. J. W. Lund, m. Joseph E. Dennis; Julia b. July 12, 1881, m. Clarence Isabelle; Charles J. b. May 6, 1884; Cora Elizabeth b. Aug. 31, 1886, d. infant; Lillian E. b. Oct. 25, 1887, m. Clarence Isabelle; Almo O. b. May 12, 1891, d. child; Rachel L. b. March 3, 1894; George W. b. Feb. 22, 1898.
Missionary in Sweden; high priest; second counselor to Bishop Greenwood, central ward, in 1891. Veteran Black Hawk war; early settler in Sevier and Sanpete counties. Farmer and lime burner. Died at Richfield, Utah, Jan. 3, 1907.

JENSEN, JOHN ROSEBERRY (son of Jens Larson Jensen and Emma C. Roseberry). Born Oct. 11, 1874, Santaquin, Utah.
Married Emma Jane Barlow Jan. 12, 1899, Manti, Utah (daughter of John and Lunes Barlow of England, former came to Utah in 1852). She was born June 17, 1881. Their children: Viola Hortense b. Dec. 14, 1900; Kindon Roseberry b. Aug. 10, 1902; Noel b. Jan. 4, 1905; Montel B. b. April 27, 1907; Madeline b. Dec. 31, 1911. Family home Richfield, Utah.
Farmer and stockraiser.

JENSEN, JENS PETER (son of Hans Jensen and Anna Kjerstine Hansen of Honsinge, Holbek amt, Denmark). Born Dec. 12, 1845, Honsinge. Came to Utah Oct. 22, 1866, Abner Lowry company.

Married Dorthea Gregersen Oct. 23, 1866, at Salt Lake City, by Edwin D. Wooley (daughter of Gregers Jensen and Kjersten Christensen of Reersnes, Laaland, Denmark, latter came to Utah 1868). She was born June 16, 1841, died Feb. 23, 1913. Their children: Jens Joseph August b. Aug. 10, 1867, d. June 15, 1868; Peter Daniel, m. Sarah Jane Rees; Adolph Willard, m. Elizabeth James; Sophia Kjerstine; Anna Cathrine b. May 6, 1875, d. Oct. 12, 1875; Hans Ephraim, m. Kirstene Marie Andersen; Josephine Eline b. Nov. 7, 1878, d. Sept. 13, 1879; Christian Nephi, m. Mary Ann Blackham, who died Aug. 28, 1907, m. Marian Lee Choate Dec. 21, 1909. Family home Ephraim, Utah.
Missionary to Denmark 1882-84; high councilor 17 years; Sunday school superintendent; stake president high priests' quorum South Sanpete stake. City councilman; school trustee 13 years. Farmer and stockraiser.

JENSEN, PETER DANIEL (son of Jens Peter Jensen and Dorthea Gregersen). Born May 17, 1869, Ephraim, Utah.
Married Sarah Jane Rees Sept. 26, 1894, Manti, Utah (daughter of Nephi Rees and Mary Ann Jones of Wales, Sanpete Co., Utah, pioneers 1855, Captain Murphy company). She was born Dec. 13, 1873. Their children: Eva Dorthea b. July 3, 1895; Dellisle Rees b. June 30, 1897; Ruby Uarda b. Jan. 9, 1900; Daniel Talmage b. May 30, 1903, d. April 5, 1905; Sarah Utahna b. Oct. 13, 1905; Joel Peter b. Nov. 2, 1907; Mary Zoe b. Nov. 9, 1912. Family home Ephraim, Utah.
Member 41st and 47th quorums seventies; Sunday school superintendent; assistant superintendent religion classes of Sanpete stake. County superintendent of schools Sevier county five years; mayor of Ephraim; principal of Ephraim public schools.

JENSEN, JENS PETER (son of Jens Christian Jensen of Holme, Aarhuus amt, Denmark, and Anne Marie Jensen). Born Aug. 10, 1838, Holme, Denmark. Came to Utah Oct. 8, 1866, Andrew H. Scott company.
Married Christiane Andersen May 5, 1866 (daughter of Anders Jensen). She was born Sept. 10, 1832, and came to Utah with husband. Their children: Mary Christiane b. Sept. 24, 1867, m. J. P. Holmgren, 1889; Andrea Christiane b. Nov. 5, 1869, m. Ben E. Rich 1888; James Peter b. June 28, 1872, m. Annie Anderson Nov. 24, 1897; Eleonora b. Nov. 5, 1874; Alfred Christian b. Jan. 5, 1878, m. Elvina Anderson 1902. Family home Bear River City, Utah.
High priest. Active pioneer. School trustee three terms.

JENSEN, JENS PETER (son of Jens Anderson and Johanna Maria Jensen of Vensysel, Denmark). Born Sept. 4, 1831, Vensysel. Came to Utah autumn 1857.
Married Inger Nielsen Jensen Oct. 22, 1861, first couple wedded at Hyrum, Utah (daughter of Hans I. Nielsen and Johanna Christina Andersen of Clausbölle, Tullebölle Sogn, Denmark, pioneers Sept. 22, 1861, Captain Wooley company). She was born Oct. 27, 1843. Their children: Peter B. b. Oct. 17, 1863, m. Christina Mortensen; James P. b. Dec. 19, 1865, m. Caroline Larsen; Johanna M. b. Feb. 9, 1868, m. Jens Peter Mortensen; Hyrum B. b. Feb. 12, 1870, m. Charles R. Jensen; Hyrum b. April 14, 1872; Martha Ann b. July 24, 1875, m. William C. Nielsen. Family home, Hyrum.
Seventy. Member city council. Farmer and stockraiser. Died Jan. 20, 1889.

JENSEN, KNUT (son of Jens Knutsen and Margaret Rassmussen of Torbey, Laaland, Denmark). Born 1810 in Denmark. Came to Utah Sept. 23, 1862, Ola N. Liljenquist company.
Married Boddell Olsen in Denmark. She was born 1807. Their children: James; Anna b. Nov. 2, 1834, m. Mats Jorgenson; Boddell b. Sept. 1836, m. Mr. Tuesen; Caroline b. April 3, 1838, m. Peter Madsen; Dorothy b. April 26, 1840, m. Morten Peterson; Elizabeth b. April 11, 1842, died; Ellen b. April 11, 1844, m. John Tuesen; Elsa Margaret b. April 21, 1846, and Ola b. April, 1847, died. Family home Round Valley, Utah.
Farmer and stockraiser. Died at Round Valley, Utah, in 1875.

JENSEN, OLOF. Born in Sweden. Came to Utah 1866, ox-team company.
Married Alice ———, in Sweden. Their children: Niels, m. Bertha Davis; Hannah, m. James Brown; Van, d. aged 27; John, m. Melissa Davis; Christena, d. infant.
Carpenter. Died 1864, in Sweden.

JENSEN, JOHN (son of Olof and Alice Jensen). Born March 8, 1863, in Sweden. Came to Utah in 1866, with father.
Married Melissa Davis Feb. 24, 1903, Price, Utah (daughter of Alexander Davis and Mary Morrill of Junction, Utah), who was born March 3, 1884. Their children: John William b. Feb. 18, 1905; Lloyd Alexander b. Jan. 20, 1907; James Howard b. Jan. 26, 1910. Family home Spring Glen, Utah.
Director Spring Glen Canal Co. School trustee. Justice of peace. Watermaster. Farmer and sheepraiser.

JENSEN, OLE ANDREW (son of Andres Jensen and Ane Christena of Sjælland, Denmark). Born Sept. 21, 1839, at Allisege, Sjælland, Denmark. Came to Utah Sept. 15, 1863, Captain Young company.
Married Annie Maria Larsen July 4, 1863, at Florence, Neb. (daughter of Lars Magnes and Annie Christens Peter-

sen), who was born Dec. 16, 1829, Norvenge, Denmark. Their children: Alma L. b. July 4, 1864, m. Mary B. Jardine, d. July 8, 1909; Annie Christena b. April 6, 1866, d. Dec. 22, 1866. Family home Clarkston, Cache Co., Utah.
Married Margaret Ann Jolley Feb. 29, 1868, at Clarkston (daughter of John Jolley and Susan Carter of Logan, Utah). Their children: John J. b. Jan. 16, 1869, d. Jan. 19, 1869; Susanab J. b. Dec. 2, 1869, m. Ammi Alonzo Shumway Oct. 22, 1888; William J. b. July 31, 1871, m. Clarissa Ames Sept. 30, 1892; Mariah b. May 4, 1873, m. Phillip Ames; Ole Andrew b. Feb. 17, 1874, d. Jan. 5, 1894; Mary b. Nov. 19, 1876, m. Seth B. Neild Dec. 25. —; Sarah Ann b. Sept. 26, 1878, m. Oliver Ames Nov. 21, 1896; Thomas J. b. Oct. 13, 1880, d. Dec. 31, 1905; Margret J. b. May 3, 1883, m. Orson Harmon Sept. 28, 1904; Joseph b. April 12, 1885, m. Isabella McJavin Sept. 21, 1905; Hannah Agnes b. Dec. 18, 1887, m. Willard G. Brown Sept. 14, 1910; Ralph LeRoy b. Sept. 19, 1888; Rubin R. b. Sept. 23, 1894; Murland Wall b. Aug. 3, 1896.
Married Caroline Margaret Nelsen Feb. 22, 1883, Salt Lake City (daughter of Niels and Ane Hansen, Nablerod, Sjælland, Denmark; came to Utah in 1881). She was born Oct. 26, 1858. Their children: Lena b. Dec. 27, 1883; Jorgen b. Sept. 9, 1885, m. J. G. Jensen Dec. 13, 1909; Annie b. July 28, 1887; Nephi b. June 1, 1891, d. June 6, 1891; Hyrum b. March 10, 1893; Ella Nora b. Aug. 24, 1895.
Married Caren Marie Nelsen Dec. 21, 1883 (daughter of Nails and Ane Hansen of Nablerod, Sjælland, Denmark). She was born March 11, 1855. Their children: Peter b. June 28, 1885, d. Jan. 5, 1911; Henry b. Oct. 12, 1889; Mary Annie b. July 28, 1890; Ezra Parley b. Nov. 12, 1895.
Missionary to Denmark 1859-63; counsellor to Bishop John Jardine of Clarkston; high councillor Star valley stake. Road overseer six years Uinta county, Wyo.

JENSEN, ALMA L. (son of Ole Andrew Jensen and Annie Maria Larsen). Born July 4, 1864, Mendon, Cache Co., Utah.
Married Mary Beveridge Jardine Oct. 27, 1886, Logan, Utah (daughter of John Jardine and Agnes Beveridge, pioneers of Utah Sept. 15, 1859, Edward Stevenson company). She was born April 1, 1865, and died July 8, 1909. Their children: Annie Marie b. May 23, 1888, m. Ezra Wickham Nov. 24, 1909; Agnes Jardine b. Sept. 1, 1891, m. Jorgen G. Jensen Dec. 13, 1909; Mary J. b. Jan. 28, 1894, m. George L. Jones June 22, 1911; Sarah Elizabeth b. Sept. 8, 1895, d. Nov. 6, 1895; Alma J. b. Oct. 8, 1897.
Married Eldena Wilhelmina Ericksen March 23, 1910, Logan, Utah (daughter of Bendt J. Ericksen and Anna Sophia Danielsen of Preston, Idaho, pioneers of 1864). Their children: Lavor E. b. Jan. 16, 1911; Reta Jensen b. Aug. 9, 1912.
Missionary to Bingham Co., Idaho, 1886-87; assistant superintendent Bannock stake Sunday schools 1887-1909; bishop of Dayton ward, Oneida stake, Idaho.

JENSEN, PETER (son of Jens Jensen of Denmark). Born 1812, Skanderberg, Denmark. Came to Utah 1862.
Married Kjesten Anderson who died 1880, Moroni, Utah (daughter of Andres Anderson), who was born 1808, came to Utah 1862, Christian Madsen company. Their children: Jens W. b. 1837; Ellen M. b. 1839; Andres b. 1841; Soren P. b. Aug. 17, 1843, m. Maren Christensen, m. Dorthea Fulkersen, m. Martina Ring; Andres B. Dec. 4, 1844; Christian b. 1846; Karen K. b. 1848. Family home Moroni, Utah.
Died 1872, Moroni, Utah.

JENSEN, SOREN P. (son of Peter Jensen and Kjesten Anderson). Born Aug. 17, 1843, Farre, Denmark.
Married Maren Christensen Nov. 8, 1866, Ephraim, Utah (daughter of Christian Christensen and Kjesten Nielsen, latter came to Utah 1863). She was born April 12, 1845, Jerslev, Denmark. Their children: Mary K. b. Jan. 18, 1868, m. Jens Sandrup 1888; Peter R. b. Aug. 29, 1869, m. Anna C. Christensen 1892; Maria b. Jan. 25, 1872, m. James E. Larsen 1893; Christian R. b. Sept. 24, 1874; Hyrum b. March 10, 1876, d. Sept. 25, 1882; Soren P. b. Feb. 17, 1878, m. Laura Abbott 1903; Elvena N. b. Sept. 18, 1882, m. Ras C. Larsen 1900; Carrie Mabel b. May 8, 1888, d. Sept. 1888. Family home Ephraim, Utah.
Married Dorthea Fulkersen (daughter of Christian Fulkersen and Ersger Hansen), who was born Aug. 11, 1853. Their children: Sedonia b. July 18, 1889; Elmer b. June 25, 1891; Wilford b. March 15, 1893. Family home Ephraim.
Married Martina Ring Sept. 8, 1897, Manti, Utah (daughter of Peter Martin Ring and Gonelda Christensen), who was born May 11, 1864, Aarhus, Denmark. Their children: Harold M. b. Sept. 23, 1903; Gonelda M. b. Jan. 21, 1908.
Black Hawk Indian war veteran. Assisted in bringing immigrants to Utah. Missionary to Europe 1889-90; high priest; ward teacher,

JENSEN, PETER (son of Jens Madsen, born April 17, 1793, Sneilerup, Holbeck, Denmark). He was born Nov. 27, 1836, Sneilerup, Denmark. Came to Utah September, 1860.
Married Annie M. Hansen (daughter of Soren Hansen and Annie Jensen, pioneers Sept. 30, 1862, Joseph Horne company). She was born June 27, 1835, in Denmark, and came to Utah with husband. Their children: Annie Christena b. Aug. 17, 1859; Lena C. b. Aug. 20, 1861, m. Martin M. Jensen; Peter b. Nov. 11, 1863, m. Christena Larsen Dec. 29, 1886; Hyrum b. May 2, 1866; Joseph b. Nov. 29, 1868, m. Mantina Keller April 16, 1890; Lewis b. April 6, 1871; James B. April 5, 1874, m. Sarah Jeppsen April 8, 1897; Annie M. b. Dec. 17, 1879, m. Alvin Keller. Family home Mantua, Box Elder Co., Utah.
Assistant superintendent of first Sunday school organized at Mantua ward; second and later first counsellor to the first bishop of Mantua ward; missionary to Scandinavia. School teacher; justice of peace; school trustee; superintendent and manager of the Co-op store 12 years; county assessor. Died Nov. 24, 1897.

JENSEN, JOSEPH (son of Peter Jensen and Annie M. Hansen). Born Nov. 29, 1868, Mantua, Utah.
Married Mantina Keller April 16, 1890, Logan, Utah (daughter of James Keller and Margaret Larsen, who resided at Mantua, Brigham and Garland, Utah). She was born March 3, 1870.
Second assistant superintendent Mantua Sunday school Jan. 14, 1894, first assistant March 19, 1899, superintendent April 21, 1901; ward chorister 1895 to 1902; second counsellor in bishopric of Garland ward, until the organizing of Bear river stake, when he was chosen second counsellor to the president of that stake. Succeeded his father as superintendent and manager of the Mantua Co-op store, which business he successfully managed for a number of years. School trustee. Clerk Box Elder county Nov. 6, 1900, and again Nov. 4, 1902. Moved to Brigham City, December, 1902. Moved to Garland, Utah, 1906, where with his three brothers, organized the company of Jensen Brothers, dealers in lumber, furniture and hardware, also operating a large dry farm in the Blue Creek Valley. Member board of trustees Garland.

JENSEN, PETER. Came to Utah with oxteam company.
Married Mary ——, in Denmark. Their children: Margaret, m. Hans Thunnisen; Rasmus, m. Ingre ——; Jens, m. Dorothy Petersen, m. Elvena Bj Hans; m. Margaret ——. Family home in Denmark.
Farmer. Died at Gunnison, Utah.

JENSEN, JENS (son of Peter and Mary Jensen).
Married Dorothy Petersen at Salt Lake City. Their children: Mary Dorothy, m. D. W. Woolsey; Lena, d. aged 4 years; Anne Josephine, m. Harrison Edwards, Jr.; Eliza Andrea, m. Andrew Hamilton Kearns; James Peter, d. aged 21 years; Matilda Eleanor b. Jan. 14, 1878, m. Orson Hyrum Lowry July 20, 1897; Isabel b. 1880, d. aged 1 year; Francis Marion; Lydia, m. Mark Brewer. Family home Gunnison, Utah.
Married Elvena Bj at Manti, Utah. Their children: Ruby; Herold, d. aged 5 years; Heber; Edna. Family home Centerfield, Utah.
President elders quorum 25 years; choir leader at Gunnison. School trustee. Farmer. Died in 1906.

JENSEN, PETER (son of James A. Christensen and Johannah Larsen of Bybyarg, Denmark). Born July 16, 1831, at Bybyarg. Came to Utah Sept. 12, 1863, John R. Young independent company.
Married Bodelia Marie Jacobson Feb. 12, 1859, in Denmark (daughter of Ole Jacobson and Ana Poulsen of Gjorlewby Frederiksborg, Denmark, pioneers Sept. 12, 1863, John R. Young independent company). She was born July 8, 1839. Their children: Johannah Maria b. June 1860, d. July 1863 on plains; Ole Peter b. June 27, 1863, m. Eliza Whitehead; Lars P. b. Nov. 24, 1864, m. Margarett V. Hymas; Anna Hannah b. April 6, 1866, d. May 1866; Annie Christena b. Aug. 10, 1867, m. Abel Smart; Johannah Christena b. Oct. 9, 1868, m. Alonzo Cook; James A. b. May 16, 1870, m. Johannah Overgaard.
Married Marie Sorenson in 1870, Ovid, Idaho (daughter of Lars P. Sorenson and Gertrude M. Gregersen, of Vesstershassing, Aalborg, Denmark, pioneers 1869). She was born March 18, 1852. Their children: Georgiana Sicilia b. Jan. 17, 1882, m. John Osborne; Christian Peter b. Sept. 24, 1883, m. Rebecca Hymas; Lorenzo Wilford b. April 5, 1886, m. Minnie Hymas; Mary Bodelia b. Dec. 13, 1888; Alvin Hans b. Dec. 27, 1891. Family resided at Ovid, Idaho.
Bishop of Ovid ward nearly 16 years. Postmaster many years.

JENSEN, LARS P. (son of Peter Jensen and Bodelia Marie Jacobson). Born Nov. 24, 1864, Ovid, Idaho.
Married Margarett V. Hymas Oct. 19, 1887 (daughter of William Hymas and Mary Edwards, pioneers Sept. 26, 1862, James Wareham company). She was born March 4, 1870. Their children: Maggie Ann b. Sept. 9, 1888, m. Arthur Porter; Lars William b. April 20, 1890, m. Ethel Findley; Asa Ray b. April 15, 1892, m. Venice Johnson; Ethel b. Dec. 10, 1893; Archie b. March 8, 1896; Charles Telbert b. Feb. 19, 1898; Idell b. Feb. 6, 1900; Leda b. April 10, 1903; Alfred Ona b. Feb. 10, 1907; La Vaun b. Dec. 8, 1910; Dean Wesley b. Sept. 9, 1912. Family home Ovid, Idaho.
Missionary to Denmark two years; high councillor, Bear Lake stake and superintendent Ovid Sunday school for many years.

JENSEN, PETER CHRISTIAN (son of Christian and Boletta Jensen of Svenstrup, Denmark). Born Feb. 18, 1833, Svenstrup. Came to Utah Oct. 6, 1854, Hans Peter Olsen company.
Married Mary Anderson in Oct. 1853, Thornbergh, Denmark (daughter of Christian Anderson and Caroline Anderson of Svenstrup, pioneers 1854). She was born Aug. 16, 1825. Their children: Ingerbor; Mary Christena; Heber

C.; Peter C.; Alma; Caroline Cecelia. Family home Mt. Pleasant, Utah.
Married Kisten Jensen Jan. 15, 1865, Salt Lake City (daughter of Soren Jensen and Mary Christensen of Barimer, Denmark). She was born March 27, 1844. Their children: Anna Kistena; Judith Cecelia; Hans Peter; James Christian; Mary Boletta; Nilsine Sorine; Joseph; John Frank; Hyrum C.; Ella S.; Wilford M.; Stella L. Families resided at Fairview and Milburn, Utah.
Member bishopric; seventy; teacher. Marshal at Fairview. Farmer.

JENSEN, SOREN (son of Jense Peter Sorenson, born Sept. 23, 1809, Hvirring, Denmark, and Anna Kjerstine Jenson, born 1807, Honum—married 1834). Born June 14, 1838, Hvirring, Denmark. Came to Utah 1860, last handcart company.
Married Elma Peterson, who was born 1824 in Sweden. Their children: Soren b. Sept. 22, 1861, died; Elna Annie b. March 9, 1863, m. Severen Nelson; Kjerastine b. May 25, 1869, d. July 30, 1878.
Married Kjerstine Rasmuscn March 9, 1867, Salt Lake City (daughter of Rasmus Hansen). She was born March 22, 1837, in Denmark. Their children: Joseph Erastus b. April 21, 1868, m. Grace Horton; Kaermtha Mora b. Aug. 6, 1870, died; Jense Peter b. March 9, 1872, died; Jense Jule b. Dec. 25, 1873, m. Seela Wilden; Nephi U. C. S. b. Feb. 16, 1876, m. Margaret Smith; Alma Christian b. April 6, 1879.
Married Karen Juliusen April 18, 1868, Salt Lake City (daughter of Julius Peterson), who was born Nov. 28, 1836, in Denmark; died Dec. 1906. Their children: Hyrum Julius b. March 13, 1869, m. Bodil Jensen; Nelse Peter b. Oct. 11, 1870, d. 1885; Brigham Miles b. Nov. 20, 1872, m. Kate Samars; Caroline Elizabeth b. Dec. 9, 1874, m. Alma Squires; Julie R. b. Nov. 15, 1876; Daniel Christian b. Sept. 2, 1879, m. Adelia Decker.
Married Ann Johanna Jensen Sept. 12, 1878, Salt Lake City (daughter of Henry Jensen, came to Utah 1878). She was born April 29, 1855, in Denmark, died Sept. 11, 1883. Their children: Katerina Kristena b. July 10, 1879, m. Andrew Jackson Stephens; Sarah Myriah b. Sept. 24, 1880; Anne Christina b. Jan. 23, 1883, d. 1883.
Married Petrea Cathrina Hansen Feb. 21, 1884, Salt Lake City (daughter of Hans Peter Hansen, born 1817, and Margreta Christena Kirstine Kofoed, born March 16, 1825—married in 1848; former came to Utah with William Christensen company). She was born April 3, 1859, Bornholm, Denmark. Their children: Petrea b. Oct. 13, 1886, d. infant; Ann Margaret b. May 6, 1888; Soren M. b. May 8, 1890; Morgan Moroni b. Aug. 23, 1894; Mary Grace b. May 23, 1896.
Missionary to Denmark 1876-78; high priest; settled in Salt Lake City 1860; worked on tabernacle three years, joining together the circular arch supporting the roof at both ends of the building; built tithing house and relief room at St. Johns, Ariz. Moved to Mancos, Colo., and remained there 25 years. Farmer and carpenter.

JENSEN, SOREN. Born May 6, 1810, Torse, Hjorring amt, Denmark. Came to Utah 1854, Captain Olsen company.
Married Kistina Maria Jensen 1834 (daughter of Jens Jensen and Mette Johana Madsen of Torse, Denmark). She was born July 26, 1812, d. Nov. 1891. Their children: Jens Christian and Andrew Peter, died; Petrea b. March 5, 1840, m. John Chester Hitchcock; Nettie Maria, m. Ole Olsen; Henry Godfredt, m. Stina Nielson Skow; Peter. Family home, Ephraim, Utah.
Elder. Farmer. Died 1906 at St. Joseph, Mo.

JENSEN, SOREN PETER (son of Jens Pedersen and Maren Sorensdatter of Glimsholt, Ugilt Sogn, Denmark). Born Oct. 30, 1836, at Glimsholt, Denmark. Came to Utah July 14, 1877.
Married Kirsten Marie Christensen Oct. 24, 1862, Ugilt Church, Ugilt Sogn, Denmark (daughter of Christen Christensen and Inger Jensdatter of Horsevad, Ugilt Sogn—came to Utah July 14, 1877). She was born Nov. 24, 1834. Their children: James Christian, m. Joannah E. Jennings; Charles, m. Lettie Christensen; Martin, died; Anders Christian, d. child; Inger Marie, and Soren Peter, d. infants; Andrew Christian, m. Emma Lefgren. Family home Levan, Utah.
High priest. County selectman in Denmark several terms. Farmer. Died Jan. 15, 1905, Levan, Utah.

JENSEN, THOMAS CHRISTIAN (son of Christen Kyer and Maren Mickelsen). Born Jan. 16, 1818, Jersley, Hjorring amt, Denmark. Came to Utah in November 1866, Captain Lowry oxteam company.
Married Karen Marie Iversen in 1842, Vreislev, Denmark (daughter of Iver and Maren Hansen), who was born Jan. 12, 1817. Their children: Marie b. June 12, 1842; Mary Ann b. April 1844; Jens Iver b. Aug. 8, 1846; Micaline b. in Nov. 1848; Stena b. Aug. 4, 1853; Christian Julius b. July 1, 1855; Niels Peter b. in Dec. 1856; Mathilda b. in Feb. 1858. Family home Elsinore, Utah.
Elder. Brass molder and mechanic. Died July 6, 1903.

JENSEN, JENS IVER (son of Thomas Christian Jensen and Karen Marie Iversen). Born Aug. 8, 1846, Jersiev, Hjorring amt, Denmark. Came to Utah Oct. 5, 1867, Captain Rice oxteam company.
Married Ingar Nielsen Sondergaard May 24, 1867, Aalborg, Denmark (daughter of Jens Nielsen Sondergaard and Karen Madsen of Vorsaa, Hjorring amt, Denmark). She was born Feb. 17, 1845, and came to Utah with husband in 1867. Their children: James Iver b. Nov. 25, 1868, d. April 30, 1879; Dr. Charles b. Dec. 21, 1870, m. Sarah Peterson; Daniel P. b. Sept. 1, 1872, m. Mathilda Lee; Carolina, died; Walter b. July 14, 1877, m. Elizabeth Sylvester; Emma b. in June, 1879, m. Dr. H. Z. Lund; Wilhelmina b. April 16, 1883, m. F. H. Gunn; Clementina b. April 14, 1885, m. Dr. J. W. Hagen. Family home Elsinore, Utah.
Married Inger Anna Christiansen Oct. 24, 1883, Salt Lake City (daughter of C. Christiansen and Anna Kirstina Jensen), who was born April 23, 1857, Hormestad, Denmark. Their children: Hannah, died; Sarah b. June 21, 1888; Oscar b. Jan. 4, 1893.
Missionary to Denmark twice; bishop of Elsinore ward 1887-1911; patriarch. Superintendent of Elsinore Co-op. about 25 years.

JENSEN, CHRISTIAN JULIUS (son of Thomas Christian Jensen and Karen Marie Iversen). Born July 1, 1855, Söby, Denmark. Came to Utah with parents.
Married Celina Anderson in 1875, Salt Lake City (daughter of Ralph Smith and Sophia Hansen of Kolding, Denmark, pioneers 1862, San Pete ox team company). She was born Feb. 16, 1856, died Dec. 10, 1900. Their children: Eva b. March 17, 1876; Elnora b. April 10, 1878; Zionlena b. Dec. 6, 1881; Blanche b. Aug. 19, 1884; Afton b. June 15, 1892; Hope b. Sept. 4, 1896.
Married Anna Johanna Katter. Their children: Margaret b. Dec. 9, 1907; Grace Louisa b. Sept. 19, 1912. Families resided at Elsinore.
Elder. Farmer.

JENSON, JENS (son of Jens Knutson of Sweden). Born Feb. 12, 1829, Felestad, Sweden. Came to Utah in 1857 with handcart company.
Married Celia Anderson in 1862, Salt Lake City, who was born Dec. 28, 1832, Helsingborg, Sweden, and came to Utah in 1860 with oxteam company. Their children: Emma C. b. Sept. 23, 1863, m. Samuel W. Collings; Alice M. b. May 4, 1865, m. Thomas A. Hunt; Joseph Henry b. Aug. 23, 1867, m. Emmaline Hansen, m. Ellen Louise Anderson. Family home Monroe, Utah.
Missionary to Sweden 1879-81; high priest; ward teacher. Early settler in Morgan and Sevier counties. Farmer. Died July 2, 1900.

JENSON, JOSEPH HENRY (son of Jens Jenson and Celia Anderson). Born Aug. 23, 1867, Round Valley, Utah.
Married Emmaline Hansen Nov. 5, 1890, Manti, Utah (daughter of Jens Hansen and Charlotte S. D. Peterson of Denmark, pioneers Sept. 29, 1853, John Forsgren company). She was born Nov. 13, 1865, at Manti and died April 12, 1904. Their children: Josephine b. Oct. 1, 1891; Evan Henry b. Feb. 15, 1893; Charlotte b. Nov. 10, 1894; Celia b. Feb. 22, 1896; Emmaline b. Dec. 29, 1897; Wilford Wells b. July 21, 1900.
Married Ellen Louise Anderson Aug. 12, 1908, Salt Lake City (daughter of Claus Anderson and Sophia Anderson of Sweden). She was born Dec. 31, 1879, in Sweden. Their children: Sophia b. Oct. 20, 1909, d. May 27, 1910; Claus b. June 10, 1911, d. infant. Families resided at Monroe, Utah.
Missionary to Sweden 1901-03; high priest; president and clerk of 41st quorum seventies; bishop of Monroe North ward 1904; president of deacons quorum; president of teachers quorum. President of Monroe town board two terms. President of Monroe Creamery Corporation. School trustee six years. Farmer and stockraiser.

JENSON, LARS (son of Jöns Jönson of Anderslöf, Sweden). Born Sept. 30, 1823, at Anderslöf. Came to Utah 1866, Peter Nebeker company.
Married Engar Andersen March, 1852, Ostra Torp, Sweden. She was born Aug. 11, 1822, and came to Utah with husband. Their children: James L., m. Bertha Maria Carlson; Olof, m. Mary Frances Ralph; Nels, m. Minna Holmgren.
High priest. Stone mason and farmer. Died at family home, Bear River City, Utah, Sept. 24, 1896.

JENSON, OLOF (son of Lars Jenson and Engar Andersen). Born Jan. 18, 1856, Ostra Torp, Sweden. Came to Utah 1866, Peter Nebeker company.
Married Mary Frances Ralph May 22, 1876, Salt Lake City (daughter of Thomas Ralph and Sarah Johnson of Brigham City, Utah). She was born Feb. 15, 1857. Their children: Sarah Irena b. Feb. 25, 1877, m. Hyrum Hogensen; Olof Lionel b. Oct. 5, 1880, m. Henrietta Hudson; Viola Sophia b. March 3, 1882, m. Nels Enoch Iversen; Ernest Ralph b. Oct. 6, 1884, m. Leona Taylor; Orestes b. June 5, 1886, m. Amanda Johnson; Conrad Heber b. Oct. 16, 1890; Myrtle Geneva b. Jan. 28, 1894. Family home, Bear River City.
Member 58th quorum seventies; missionary to Sweden 1877-89; Sunday school superintendent 12 years. Farmer.

JEPPESEN, CHRISTIAN (son of Jeppe Jeppesen of Odense, Denmark). Born Oct. 6, 1817. Came to Utah fall of 1857, Captain Nelsen company.
Married Christina Orsted Christensen 1852, Nakskov, Sjelland, Denmark (daughter of Niels Christensen and Mary Hansen of Kublen, Sjelland). She was born April 16, 1807. Their children: Minnie b. Jan. 3, 1853, m. Thomas H. Jones; Matina b. March 4, 1855, died.
Married Abelle Steffena 1863, Salt Lake City. She was born in Nakskov, Sjelland, Denmark.
Married Hansena Nielson Jan. 22, 1867, at Salt Lake City (daughter of Hans and Mary Nielsen of Odense, Denmark). She was born Feb. 11, 1850. Their children: Christian b. Jan. 22, 1868, m. Adlie Christina Anderson; Nephi b. Nov. 8, 1869, m. Minnie Jorgensen; Christina b. Oct. 24, 1871, died; Mary b. Dec. 7, 1873, died; Zina Johanna b. Nov. 12, 1875, m. John B. Seamounto; Daniel b. Sept. 3, 1877, m. Pearl Loverridge; Ephraim b. Aug. 1, 1880, m. Martha Selmon; Sarah Elizabeth b. March 2, 1882, m. Benjamin Wride; Alfreda Jacobina b. Dec. 29, 1883, m. John Collins. Families resided Lake View, Utah.
Ward teacher. Sailor; farmer; stockraiser. Died May 13, 1884, Lake View, Utah.

JEPPESEN, CHRISTIAN (son of Christian Jeppesen and Hansena Nielsen). Born Jan. 22, 1868, Provo, Utah.
Married Adlie Christina Anderson July 1, 1903, Manti, Utah (daughter of Andrew Anderson and Cecilia Gertrude Pherson, Gothland, Sweden). She was born Dec. 4, 1870. She came to Utah Nov. 17, 1883. Their children: Christian Rhodes b. April 7, 1904; Geraldine Christina b. Aug. 25, 1905; Oden Cecil b. Aug. 12, 1907; Chrissie Lucile b. May 22, 1909; George Nephi b. June 15, 1910. Family home Lake View, Utah.
Ward teacher; assistant Sunday school superintendent Lake View. Farmer.

JEPPESEN, PETER NIELSEN (son of Niels Jeppesen, born Sept. 3, 1788, Vegersted, Denmark, and Marie Rasmussen, born 1786, same place—married Nov. 25, 1814). He was born Sept. 19, 1816, Sigersted, Denmark. Came to Utah 1868, oxteam company .
Married Caroline Sophie Sorensen April 12, 1845 (daughter of Soren Sigvardsen and Karen Sorensen, married June 11, 1819, in Denmark). She was born Sept. 28, 1822, Kirke Hvalso, Denmark. Their children: Annie b. March 3, 1846, m. A. P. Schow; Karen Marie b. Aug. 20, 1848, m. H. N. Jeppesen; Sigvard b. Oct. 23, 1851; Niels Peter b. Aug. 2, 1854, m. Anne M. Jeppesen; Sophia b. May 2, 1857, m. Joseph Ricks; Christian Peter Edward, d. on plains. Family home Mantua, Utah.

JEPPESEN, NIELS PETER (son of Peter Nielsen Jeppesen and Caroline Sophie Sorensen). Born Aug. 2, 1854, Hvalso, Denmark. Came to Utah with parents.
Married Anna M. Jeppesen Jan. 25, 1876, Brigham City, Utah (daughter of Rasmus N. Peppesen and Ellen Catherine Ottosen, pioneers 1854). She was born June 9, 1860, Brigham City, Utah. Their children: Niels P. b. June 17, 1877, m. May Call (died), m. Luella Nelsen; Caroline Sophia b. Nov. 21, 1879, m. Anton Jensen; Albert Edward b. March 25, 1882, m. Emelia Ipson; Agnes Millicent b. July 27, 1884; Oscar Arnold b. Nov. 10, 1886; Meda Christena Elizabeth b. Feb. 11, 1889; William Wallace b. April 15, 1891; Evelyn Catherine b. March 29, 1893; Ronald Olsen b. June 30, 1895; Hazel Geneva b. Jan. 5, 1898. Family home Mantua, Utah.
Member 59th quorum seventies; high priest; missionary to Scandinavia 1907-09. Justice of peace two terms; school trustee three terms. First postmaster of Mantua. Director and secretary Mantua Co-op, now owner of same. Director in Mantua Land and Live Stock Company.

JEPSON, JAMES. Came to Utah 1849, oxteam company.
Married Eleanor Nightingale, who was born July 4, 1816, and came to Utah 1849, with husband. Only child: Eleanor b. Sept. 1, 1858, m. John Alfred Spendlove. Family home Virgin City, Utah.
High priest; first counselor in bishopric of Virgin City ward. Farmer. Died at Virgin City.

JEPSON, JAMES (son of Mikel Jepson and Alice Headock of Lancashire, Eng.). Born June 24, 1816, Artly Bridge, Lancashire. Came to Utah 1852, ox team company.
Married Eleanor Nightingale June 27, 1838 (daughter of Miles Nightingale and Lucy Thornly). She was born July 4, 1816, and came to Utah with husband. Their children: James, Jr., b. Oct. 13, 1854, m. Lucinda Stratton Dec. 28, 1876; Mary Ellen b. Nov. 1851, m. M. M. Steele April 1874; Eleanor b. Sept. 1, 1857, m. Estelvin Owens Dec. 28, 1876, m. John Alfred Spendlove 1886. Family home Virgin City, Utah.
Missionary to England 1841-42; first counselor to Bishop John Parker, Virgin City 1865-81. Farmer. Died Sept. 1881 at Virgin City.

JEPSON, JAMES (son of James Jepson and Eleanor Nightingale). Born Oct. 13, 1854, Centerville, Utah.
Married Lucinda Stratton Dec. 28, 1876, Virgin City (daughter of Anthony J. Stratton and Martha Jane Lane). She was born Jan. 15, 1857, Cedar City, Utah. Their children: James Anthony b. March 2, 1878, m. Louisa Cox Oct. 16, 1905; Martha b. May 12, 1880, m. John H. Hastings Sept. 12, 1900; Mary Eleanor b. Oct. 18, 1881, m. Richard Isom Sept. 12, 1905; Rozilpha b. July 27, 1883, m. George Q. Knowlton Sept. 11, 1907; Lucy b. Sept. 21, 1886, m. Calvin D. Barnum Sept. 16, 1909; Jesse N. b. April 21, 1888, m. Brenda Angell Dec. 27, 1910; Artemissia b. Feb. 19, 1893. Family home Virgin City, Utah.
President Y. M. M. I. A., Virgin City; first counselor to Bishop John Parker 1881-83; second counselor to Bishop Beebe 1899-1903; first counselor to Bishop Samuel Isom 1903-07; bishop of Virgin ward 1907-09. President Hurricane Canal Company 1902-09.

JEREMY, THOMAS E. (son of Thomas Jeremy and Sarah Evans of Carmarthenshire, South Wales). Born July 11, 1815, in South Wales. Came to Utah Oct. 28, 1849, George A. Smith company.
Married Sarah Evans March 16, 1838, in South Wales. She was born April 27, 1815. Their children: John, m. Sarah Riley; Thomas E., Jr., m. Elizabeth W. Pettit; Hannah; Margaret; Esther, m. David L. Davis; Sarah, died; Mary, died; Ann, m. Sarge Stenhouse; Eliza, m. Harvey Hardy; Martha, m. Samuel Wallace; Francis, died. Family home, Salt Lake City.
High priest; missionary to Wales. Farmer; gardener. Died April 17, 1891, at Salt Lake City.

JEREMY, THOMAS E. (son of Thomas E. Jeremy and Sarah Evans). Born Dec. 1, 1839, Carmarthenshire, South Wales, Came to Utah with father.
Married Elizabeth W. Pettit Feb. 10, 1866, Salt Lake City (daughter of Ethan Pettit and Margaret Ellsworth of Long Island, N. Y.). She was born Sept. 27, 1846. Came to Utah Sept. 1848 with Heber C. Kimball company. Their children: Ethan J. b. April 17, 1869, m. Minnie Hodges; Margaret A. b. July 27, 1872, m. Thomas I. Irvine; Chloe b. May 28, 1875, m. Calvin Kempf; Mary O. b. Aug. 2, 1877, m. Grant Andrus; Stella W. b. July 23, 1879, m. William B. Taylor; Emily b. April 27, 1881, m. Walter Wright; Ernest L. b. Aug. 18, 1884, m. Vera Jamison. Family home, Salt Lake City.
High priest. City councilman. Farmer.

JESSOP, RICHARD (son of Edward Jessop, born Aug. 9, 1805, Lincolnshire, Eng., and Frances Millward, born Sept. 30, 1800, Kirptown, Derbyshire, Eng.). Born May 3, 1838, Stoke Rogford, Lincolnshire, Eng. Came to Utah Sept. 10, 1862.
Married Mary Ellen Shaffer Nov. 26, 1863 (daughter of Joseph Russel Shaffer and Gilead Taylor, pioneers Oct. 1853, Heber C. Kimball company). She was born Nov. 27, 1848. Came to Utah with her parents. Their children: Richard Edward b. March 3, 1865, died; Mary Alice b. April 18, 1867, m. James Greene Taylor March 31, 1886; Joseph Smith b. Jan. 25, 1869, m. Martha Moore Yeates Oct. 16, 1889; Louise Frances b. April 29, 1871, m. Martin Olson Jan. 22, 1890; Nephi b. July 16, 1873, died; Moroni b. Nov. 3, 1874, m. Bertha Jackson June 24, 1903; Tessie Geneva b. Dec. 5, 1881; Lilleth Ethel b. Sept. 13, 1884, m. George Timothy Cummings, Jr., Oct. 4, 1902; Ellen b. Nov. 29, 1887, m. Edmund J. Bailey Sept. 5, 1911; Gilead b. July 29, 1889, m. William Daniel Saurey March 4, 1911. Family home Millville, Utah.
Married Jenett Levronia Shaffer Nov. 26, 1873, Salt Lake City (daughter of Joseph Russel Shaffer and Gilead Taylor, pioneers Oct. 1853, Heber C. Kimball company). She was born May 11, 1858, Cottonwood, Salt Lake county. Their children: Sarah Cathrine b. Feb. 3, 1876, m. Joseph Grafton Hovey, Jr., March 6, 1895; William Oscar b. Sept. 21, 1879, d. Dec. 13, 1897; George Henry b. Dec. 5, 1881, m. Frances Stephens; Lester Russel b. June 1, 1887, m. Leone Telford; Alma b. Feb. 10, 1889; Parley b. April 18, 1893; Agnes Merle b. Jan. 7, 1895, m. Edward Hanson Feb. 13, 1913; Jenett b. Feb. 15, 1897.
Assisted in bringing company of immigrants to Utah 1868. Stood guard during early Indian troubles. President and watermaster Providence and Millville Irrigation Company; assisted in organizing in 1887 and served as first president of Millville Stock and Agriculture Association; an organizer of Millville Broom Company, and United Order; president of the former 1878-81. Died March 13, 1899, at Millville, Utah.

JESSOP, JOSEPH SMITH (son of Richard Jessop and Mary Ellen Shaffer). Born Jan. 25, 1869, Millville, Utah.
Married Martha Moore Yeates Oct. 16, 1889, Logan, Utah (daughter of Frederick Yeates and Sarah Webb, former came to Utah Sept. 21, 1857, Capt. Hoffines company, latter Oct. 1861, Milo Andrus company). She was born July 8, 1871, at Millville. Their children: Sarah Genevieve b. Oct. 3, 1890; Joseph Lyman b. Feb. 10, 1892; Richard Seth b. Jan. 22, 1894; Dowayne Neor b. Sept. 9, 1895; Violet b. Jan. 10, 1897; Ruby b. Dec. 9, 1898; Martha b. Sept. 14, 1900; Vergel Yeates b. Oct. 31, 1902; Sylmar Green b. Nov. 25, 1904; Fawnetta b. Dec. 31, 1906; Millicent b. Nov. 20, 1908, died; Fredrick M. b. April 20, 1910; John Millward b. March 19, 1912. Family home Millville, Utah.

JEX, WILLIAM (son of William Jex and Ann Ward of Norfolk, Eng.). Born Sept. 5, 1831, Crostwick, Norfolk. Eng. Came to Utah Sept. 30, 1854, Darwin Richardson company.
Married Eliza Goodson Feb. 22, 1854 (daughter of John Goodson and Sarah Trexon), who was born Jan. 1, 1826, and

PIONEERS AND PROMINENT MEN OF UTAH

came to Utah with husband. Their children: Sarah Ann Trexon (adopted) b. April 1, 1851, m. Joshua Brockbank March 7, 1868; Emma Eliza b. Oct. 11, 1855, m. Robert W. McKell Feb. 28, 1876; Alice Velat b. Aug. 28, 1857, m. Henry J. McKell Jan. 9, 1879; Rosetta Coreline b. March 30, 1859, m. Heber Robertson Dec. 18, 1880; Artemesia Jane b. Oct. 6, 1860, m. Lars O. Lawrence May 13, 1880; Richard Henry b. April 7, 1862, m. Ruth Jex Feb. 24, 1886; George Hyrum b. Dec. 28, 1863, m. Burl Christena Larsen Jan. 31, 1889; Ann Melinda b. Sept. 25, 1865, m. Albert T. Money Jan. 9, 1889; Hanna Eliza b. Oct. 6, 1867, m. Roswell Bradford March 22, 1893; John William b. Oct. 5, 1867, m. Emily Hedquist March 22, 1893; Heber Charles b. Aug. 12, 1871, m. Emeline Bird Dec. 23, 1898.
Married Jemima Cox Jan. 1865, Salt Lake City (daughter of George Cox and Ann Elizabeth Newby), who was born Jan. 15, 1836, in Leicestershire, Eng. Their children: George William b. Dec. 3, 1865, d. Oct. 25, 1866; James Henry b. Oct. 4, 1867, d. Jan. 3, 1879; Jemima Sophia b. Dec. 22, 1869, d. Feb. 24, 1879; David Walter b. April 23, 1872, d. Jan. 3, 1885. Families resided at Spanish Fork, Utah.
Senior president 50th quorum seventies 20 years; high priest; presided over Norwich conference 1885; missionary to England 1883; presiding teacher Spanish Fork ward several years. Worked on Salt Lake temple in 1854. Took active part in early Indian troubles and in Echo Canyon campaign 1857. Chosen to supervise the work of opening up roads into canyons near Spanish Fork; had charge of co-op. saw mill for a time; general watermaster 1861-62; city councilman and school trustee, Spanish Fork. Assisted financially in bringing immigrants to Utah in 1910. Descendants number 110 grandchildren and 59 great-grandchildren. Made patriarch 1912.

JOHANSON, CARL. Came to Utah in 1862.
Married. His children: August, m. Christina Jorgensen; Sophia, m. Mads Larsen. Family home Ephraim, Utah.
Had charge of co-operative sheep herd. Sheepman and farmer. Died about 1872 at Ephraim, Utah.

JOHANSEN, LARS (son of Johan Christiansen and Kjersten Mortensen of Orum, Veile amt, Denmark). Born Feb. 8, 1792. Came to Utah Oct. 5, 1854.
Married Anna Margreta Sorensen (daughter of Soren Christensen and Cecelia Larsen), who was born Aug. 17, 1797; came to Utah Oct. 5, 1854. H. P. Olsen company. Their children: Soren b. March 23, 1821, m. Maria Frederickson Dec. 1854; Johannes b. Dec. 18, 1824, m. Anna Jorgensen Oct. 19, 1850; Sesel Kjestine b. May 11, 1826, m. Jens Blak 1855; Chresten G. b. Dec. 17, 1828, m. Marie K. Sorensen April 1, 1857; Christian J. b. March 21, 1831, m. Barbara J. D. Olsen Oct. 30, 1853; Lauritz b. Jan. 25, 1834, m. Maria Thompsen April 1, 1857; Mary b. Aug. 2, 1836, m. Chr. Willarsen July 18, 1868. Family resided Spring City, Ephraim, Castledale and Logan, Utah.
High priest. Settled at South Weber City, moved to Ephraim 1858, and to Spring City 1862. Died in 1884, Spring City, Utah.

JOHN, THOMAS (son of William John and Letitia Phillips of Wood Roach parish, Pembrokeshire, Wales). Born Jan. 29, 1820. Came to Utah Oct. 17, 1862, Henry W. Miller company.
Married Margaret Thomas July 14, 1840 (daughter of William Thomas and Ann James), who was born Aug. 14, 1815; came to Utah with husband in 1862. Their children: Henry J. b. Jan. 9, 1841, m. Sarah Ann Ashton; Charles b. April 21, 1843, m. Elizabeth Williams; Ann b. Feb. 1, 1844, m. Edward W. Smith; James b. Nov. 10, 1846, m. Hannah Abbott; Levi b. Feb. 4, 1849, m. Mary Ann Hall; Henry b. Feb. 15, 1851, m. Margaret Rees; Letitia b. April 6, 1853, m. William H. Gibbs; Mary Jane b. Nov. 18, 1855, m. Joseph B. Hawkley. Family resided Wellsville and Malad Valley, Utah.
Married Jane Green Oct. 28, 1872, Salt Lake City (daughter of Thomas and Ann Green), who was born Nov. 8, 1819, Preston, Eng.
Ward teacher; high councilor. Settled at Wellsville 1862, moved to Malad Valley 1867. Planted first wheat on west side of Malad river; helped found town of Portage.

JOHN, JAMES (son of Thomas John and Margaret Thomas). Born Nov. 10, 1846, Mathry parish, Pembrokeshire, Wales. Married Hannah S. Abbott May 9, 1869, Wellsville, Utah (daughter of Jacob Abbott), who was born at Council Bluffs, Iowa. Their children: Thomas Jacob b. Aug. 27, 1866; Mary Jane b. Oct. 19, 1867, m. Henry Parkinson Jan. 18, 1888; Martha Jane b. Oct. 17, 1869; Elizabeth b. Jan. 24, 1870, m. Frank Hall Jan. 18, 1888; Emily Ann b. Jan. 18, 1872, m. Edwin Vaughn July 4, 1889; Harriet b. Nov. 15, 1874, m. C. W. Hall: James b. Sept. 25, 1876; Angline b. Oct. 4, 1877, m. Joseph Olsen April 19, 1892; Sarah b. Feb. 21, 1879; Margaret S. b. May 13, 1880; David A. b. Jan. 18, 1883; Letha b. Nov. 16, 1884, m. Samuel Smith Nov. 21, 1901; Rosella b. July 26, 1886. Family resided Wellsville and Portage, Utah.
Married Mary James May 16, 1877, St. George, Utah (daughter of Thomas James and Sarah Vaughn, who were married Aug. 1, 1843, Castle Braith, Wales, the former came to Utah July 1876). She was born Aug. 22, 1844, Castle Braith. Their children: Emma b. March 20, 1867, m. Hyrum

Ashton Aug. 18, 1884; Annie b. June 20, 1870, m. John Heaton; Thomas b. March 14, 1878, m. Rose E. Ward Feb. 27, 1903; Hannah S. b. May 9, 1880, m. Leroy Howell; Minnie I. b. May 3, 1883; m. Lorenzo Hoskins April 19, 1899; Mirinda I. b. Jan. 20, 1884, m. Richard Ward April 26, 1904; Henry Edgar b. Nov. 21, 1886.
High priest. Farmer.

JOHN, HENRY (son of Thomas John and Margaret Thomas). Born Feb. 15, 1851, Mathry Parish, Pembrokeshire, Wales.
Married Margaret Rees Dec. 8, 1876, Portage, Utah (daughter of Thomas Rees and Rebecca Williams, they came to Utah 1872). She was born Nov. 15, 1858, Broadway, Pembrokeshire, Wales. Their children: Thomas Parley b. May 17, 1878, m. Annie M. Wells Feb. 15, 1899; Margaret Rebecca b. May 25, 1880, m. John C. Howell Nov. 15, 1899; Elizabeth b. July 15, 1881, d. July 15, 1881; Brigham Henry b. Feb. 20, 1883, m. Letha J. Landon Jan. 19, 1910; Ethel Mary b. Sept. 13, 1884, m. John Roderick Nov. 12, 1902; Ruth b. Sept. 5, 1886, d. Sept. 8, 1906; Samuel Franklin b. Feb. 23, 1888, d. Aug. 28, 1888; Bertha Naomi, b. Sept. 21, 1889; William Arthur b. May 24, 1891; Noah James b. Dec. 2, 1894; Edwin b. Dec. 23, 1898, d. Dec. 25, 1898. Family home Portage, Utah.
President 52nd quorum seventies; Sunday school superintendent; missionary to Great Britain and to California. Justice of the peace and school trustee.

JOHNS, JOHN (son of Morgan Johns of Glamorganshire, South Wales). Born May 26, 1805, Wells, St. Donats, South Wales. Came to Utah Sept. 27, 1861, Sextus E. Johnson company.
Married Margaret Thomas in 1835, Prisk parish, South Wales (daughter of Morgan and Blanch Thomas), who was born Feb. 19, 1810. Their children: Jonathan b. April 2, 1840, m. Mary Jenkins; Jonathan b. April 27, 1843, m. Elizabeth A. Bishop; William b. Nov. 27, 1845, and Meriam b. Aug. 13, 1848, d. infants; David b. March 19, 1853, m. Sarah A. Thomas. Family resided North Ogden, Pleasant View, Utah.
President Pendylon branch in Wales; high priest. Died March 20, 1884.

JOHNS, DAVID (son of John Johns and Margaret Thomas). Born March 19, 1853, Wells, St. Donats, South Wales.
Married Sarah A. Thomas March 1, 1878, Salt Lake City (daughter of Jacob Thomas and Elizabeth Philips of Brigham City, Utah, pioneers Sept. 12, 1861, Milo Andrus and John R. Murdock company). She was born July 15, 1858. Their children: David J. b. July 13, 1880, m. Susan V. Maycock; Diana B. b. May 4, 1882; William M. b. Oct. 25, 1883, m. Anna E. Chamberlain Nov. 20, 1912; Robert J. b. April 6, 1885, d. child; Margaret b. Aug. 2, 1887; Elizabeth b. May 4, 1890, m. William H. Shaw; Sarah b. Nov. 11, 1891. Family home Pleasant View, Weber Co., Utah.
Missionary among the Indians 1876; missionary to Great Britain 1892-93; presiding teacher, Pleasant View ward.

JOHNSON, AARON (son of Didymus Johnson and Rheuama Stephens of Haddam, Conn.). Born June 22, 1806, Haddam. Came to Utah Sept. 18, 1850, captain of his own company.
Married Polly Zerviah Kelsey Sept. 13 1827, New Haven, Conn. (daughter of Willis Kelsey and Polly Parmalee, Killingworth, Conn.). She was born Sept. 1, 1808, and died June 27, 1850. Their children: Willis Kelsey b. Sept. 13, 1828, m. Laura Crandall; Marilla b. Oct. 12, 1830, m. William Miller, m. James E. Daniels; Mary Ann, died; Emma Marie b. Sept. 13, 1836, m. William N. Spafford. Family home Killingworth, Conn.
Married Jane Scott July 12, 1845, Nauvoo, Ill. (daughter of George and Abigail Scott of Nauvoo, pioneers 1850, Aaron Johnson company). She was born May 10, 1822. Their children: Don Carlos b. July 1, 1847, m. Lydia M. Boyer; Aaron b. May 22, 1850, m. Louisa M. Whiting; Sophia b. Nov. 20, 1853, d. Aug. 24, 1854; Stephen D. b. Oct. 5, 1856, m. Luella Curtis; Mose b. April 14, 1860, m. Annie Kearns; Heber C. b. June 4, 1864, d. Feb. 1, 1866. Family home Springville, Utah.
First bishop of Springville 1850-72; president high council Utah stake; high councilor Nauvoo, Ill. for 14 years; missionary to eastern states 1843-44. Chief justice Utah county for eight years; major general Utah militia; speaker of first legislature at Fillmore; member Utah legislature 20 years; postmaster of Springville for 26 years. Founder of Springville. Died May 10, 1877, Springville.

JOHNSON, AARON (son of Aaron Johnson and Jane Scott). Born May 22, 1850, Garden Grove, Utah.
Married Louisa M. Whiting Oct. 8, 1871, Salt Lake City (daughter of Edwin Whiting and Elizabeth Tilotson, Springville, Utah, pioneers 1849, Capt. Morley company). She was born May 17, 1850, at Manti, San Pete Co. Their children: Aaron Wayne b. July 14, 1873, m. Anna Whitney; Winifred b. Nov. 17, 1874, d. child; Claudia b. June 12, 1877, m. Harvey A. Whitney; Willis K. b. Sept. 16, 1879, m. Annie E. Clark and Hattie Lee; Frank b. Oct. 25, 1881, m. Rosa Francis; Elmer b. Nov. 14, 1874, m. Luella Snow; Hugh Dougral b. July 27, 1887, m. Maggie Van Orman; Louisa A. b. Dec. 8, 1889, m. Alice Jackson; Leland b. Aug. 15, 1893; Bryan b. June 20, 1897. Family home Springville, Utah.
Elder; Sunday school teacher; president T. M. M. I. A.; colonizer in Arizona in 1878; at Kanab was chosen captain of the company. Member educational board; justice

of the peace; assessor and collector; sergeant-at-arms of Utah legislature in 1895; postmaster at Taber, Alta., Canada, for four years. At age of 16 crossed plains in Capt. Scott's train of 78 wagons in 1866, acting as night guard; was in Alberta, Canada, 1901-07. Dramatist and elocutionist.

JOHNSON, ANDREAS (son of Jonas Larson, born Feb. 21, 1798, and Katrina Olson, born May 4, 1794, at Alingsaa. Sweden). Born Nov. 29, 1827. Came to Utah 1863, Capt. Edwards company.
Married Annie Kaza Anderson. Their children: Matilda Christina b. Feb. 10, 1851, m. Andrew Gustave Eliason; Anna Sophia b. 1854, m. Fred Pederson; Edith Charlotte b. 1859, died; John Andrew b. 1866, m. Mattie Parkinson; Nettie Tillula b. 1871, died.
High priest. Settled at Moroni, Utah, 1863; moved to Sevier county 1865; to Ephraim 1866; to Spring City 1866; to Grantsville 1868, and to Hyrum, Cache county, 1886. Indian war veteran. Farmer and carpenter. Died 1889, Hyrum, Utah.

JOHNSON, ANDREW. Came to Utah in 1866.
Married Hannah Johnson. Their children: Lena, m. Jacob Kofford; Elizabeth, m. Edson Huntsman; Andrea, m. Alfred Smith. Family home, Spring City, Utah.
He was killed Aug. 13, 1867, in a Black Hawk Indian ambush while hauling hay into Spring City.

JOHNSON, ANDREW J. (son of Johanas Hokanson, born July 30, 1768, and Elra Pehrson, born May 1782, of Asige, Halland, Sweden). Born June 14, 1827, Asige. Came to Utah in 1859, Capt. Rawlins company.
Married Elna Petronela Pehrson in 1854 (daughter of Nels Pehrson and Engeborg Mouson). She was born April 28, 1822. Their children: Nels J. b. June 12, 1856, m. Agness Murray; John E. b. April 4, 1858, m. Josephine Sedelius; Hannah b. Sept. 6, 1861, m. John Bowen; Emma b. March 12, 1863, m. George Atkin; Andrew b. April 14, 1866; Samuel b. March 30, 1869, m. Clara S. Johnson. Family home Tooele Utah.
Farmer.

JOHNSON, SAMUEL (son of Andrew J. Johnson and Elna Petronela Pehrson). Born March 30, 1869, Tooele, Utah.
Married Clara S. Johnson March 19, 1890, at Logan, Utah (daughter of Andrew G. Johnson and Anna Sophia Bjork). She was born Nov. 23, 1871, Grantsville, Utah. Their children: Samuel H. b. Oct. 15, 1892; Clara Fesmetta b. June 18, 1894; Lucile M. b. June 29, 1896; Delbert b. Feb. 8, 1899; Vera b. Oct. 27, 1901; Bernice b. July 1, 1909. Family home Tooele, Utah.
Deputy county assessor; county treasurer Tooele county. Farmer.

JOHNSON, BENGT (son of John and Hanna Bengston of Sodervidinge, Sweden). Born Jan. 31, 1822, Sodervidinge. Came to Utah October 1862, Joseph Horne company.
Married Guinala Benson in May 1850 at Sodervidinge, Sweden (daughter of Mr. Benson, pioneer 1862, Joseph Horne company). She was born Oct. 28, 1821. Their children: Bengt, m. Betsie Christoferson; Nels B., m. Laura Larsen; Peter B., m. Hester Robbins; Abraham B., m. Eliza Ross; Guinala, m. Frank Tucker. Family home Provo, Utah.
Farmer. Died March 13, 1912.

JOHNSON, BENGT (son of Bengt Johnson and Guinala Benson). Born June 13, 1850, Sodervidinge, Sweden. Came to Utah with father.
Married Betsie Christoferson March 7, 1871, at Salt Lake City (daughter of Nels Christoferson and Hanna Polson Gulf of Sweden, the latter came to Utah by rail). She was born Dec. 23, 1848. Their children: Emma B. b. April 29, 1872; Hanna S. b. Jan. 7, 1875, m. John B. Cardall; Benjamin A. b. Aug. 18, 1877, m. Ellen Johnson; Aleda N. b. June 29, 1880; Alvin C. b. March 9, 1883, died; Reed T. b. Nov. 4, 1885, m. Alfrida Blomquist; Vernie C. b. May 25, 1888; Bessie R. b. June 20, 1891. Family home Provo, Utah.
High councilor; missionary to Sweden 1888-89 and in 1910. Farmer.

JOHNSON, BENJAMIN (son of William and Fanny Johnson Northampton, Northamptonshire, Eng.). Born 1813 Buckinghamshire. Came to Utah Aug. 20, 1868, Joseph S. Rawlins company.
Married Charlotte Budd in 1838, Aston, Clinton Newmill Chapel, Herefordshire, Eng. (daughter of George Budd and Rebecca Ford of Whipsnade, Bedfordshire, Eng.). She was born Aug. 20, 1812. Their child en: Sarah F., m. Joseph Bishop; William, m. Annie Hammond; Fanny, m. William Bishop; Rebecca F., m. William Hammond; Benjamin, m. Harriet Cross; Charlotte, m. Thomas Plyer; Joseph T., m. Elizabeth Rawlins; Susannah E., m. William Pead; Mary Ann, m. Edward Brain. Family home, Salt Lake City, 14th ward.
Died Dec. 23, 1869.

JOHNSON, [1]BENJAMIN FRANKLIN, of Palmyra, N. Y. Born July 28, 1818. Came to Utah July 24, 1847, Brigham Young company.
Married Melissa LeBaron. Their children: [2]Benjamin F., m. Mary Eliza Williams and Caroline Butterfield; David Albion, m. Christine Jensen; Julia Diadma, m. David Wilson; Esther, m. Samuel Openshaw; Melissa, m. Don Carlos Babbit; Delcina, m. Almon W. Babbit. Family home Spring Lake Villa. Juab Co., Utah.
Missionary to Sandwich Islands; seventy; patriarch; private secretary to Joseph Smith. Farmer, orchardist and freighter. Died in 1904, Mesa, Ariz.

JOHNSON, [2]BENJAMIN FRANKLIN (son of Benjamin F. Johnson and Melissa LeBaron). Born Dec. 29, 1842, Palmyra, N. Y. Came to Utah July 24; 1847, Brigham Young company.
Married Mary Eliza Williams Sept. 18, 1877, at Santaquin, Utah (daughter of Elias Willard Williams and Lucy Hendricks of Whitinsville, Mass., pioneers 1852). She was born June 8, 1856. Their children: Mary Eliza b. Jan. 10, 1878, m. Herman A. Miller; Benjamin Willard b. Sept. 19, 1880, m. Dora E. Slaugh; Charles A. b. July 22, 1882; Lucy Dadma b. May 24, 1884, m. Thomas Kendall. Family home Mona. Utah.
Married Caroline Butterfield. Their children: Evaline (d. Aug. 1912), m. John Dodge; [3]Benjamin F., m. Maim Cloward; Elmer, died; Melissa (died), m. John Dussard; Marcus, died; Julian H.; Inez (died), m. Ernest Ellworth; Carrie, m. Heber K. Maxham.
Elder. Orchardist and farmer. Died Jan. 21, 1884, Tempe, Ariz.

JOHNSON, BENJAMIN WILLIAM (son of [2]Benjamin Franklin Johnson and Mary Eliza Williams). Born Sept. 19, 1880, Spring Lake. Utah.
Married Dora Elizabeth Slaugh Oct. 21, 1899, at Naples. Utah (daughter of John Jacob Slaugh, Sr., and Matilda Smuin), who was born Aug. 22, 1879. Their children: Mary Matilda b. July 11, 1900; Charles Willard b. Feb. 26, 1902; George Elias b. June 23, 1903; Florence Melissa b. Jan. 4, 1905; Dora Nell b. March 5, 1906; Carl Hentherly b. Sept. 21, 1907; Lucy Ellen b. Oct. 28, 1909; Benjamin Franklin b. Jan. 30, 1911; Ruth b. Aug. 9, 1912. Family home Naples. Utah.
Elder; ward and Sunday school teacher; Sunday school superintendent Naples ward. Farmer.

JOHNSON, CHAS. A. (son of [2]Benj. F. Johnson and Mary Eliza Williams). Born July 22, 1882, Mona, Juab Co., Utah. Family home Vernal, Utah.
Elder: second assistant superintendent Davis Sunday school and Sunday school teacher. Farmer. Ward teacher. Ex-mailcarrier.

JOHNSON, C. P. W. (son of Lars Johnson, born March 1, 1785, and Maria Holm, born May 3, 1793, both of Copenhagen, Denmark). Born Dec. 29, 1823, Copenhagen. Came to Utah in 1862.
Married Albiena Henrietta Weiss July 24, 1852, at Copenhaaren (daughter of Christian Frederick Weiss, born Dec. 11, 1786, and Johanna Christina Mork, born Jan. 15, 1794). She was born April 22, 1833. Their children: William b. 1853; Sophus W. W. b. Dec. 24, 1854, m. Maria Sorenson March 31, 1877; Edmund H. C. b. Nov. 7, 1856, m. Josephine V. Nielsen Jan. 20, 1882; Arnold E. C. b. Oct. 5, 1858; James J. A. b. Oct. 12, 1860.

JOHNSON, EDMUND H. C. (son of C. P. W. Johnson and Albiena Henrietta Weiss). Born Nov. 7, 1856, Copenhagen. Denmark.
Married Josephine Nielsen Jan. 20, 1882 at Mt. Pleasant, Utah (daughter of Fredrick P. and Christina Nielsen), who was born Feb. 14, 1862, Mt. Pleasant. Utah. Their children: Edmund A. b. Dec. 6, 1882, m. Clida Dodge Feb. 12, 1907; Pearly L. b. Aug. 3, 1884; Ferrington W. b. Aug. 10 1886; Eugene W. b. June 23, 1899; Virtue L. b. Dec. 12, 1892; Mary A. b. Sept. 7, 1896; Josie b. Sept. 11, 1902; Viola J. b. April 14, 1905.

JOHNSON, DANIEL (son of Jonas Danielson and Marie Jensen, both of Elvingstorp, Calmarian, Sweden). Born July 24, 1820, Elvingstorp. Came to Utah Oct. 1854, Hans P. Olson company.
Married Catherine Jensen at Bornholm, Denmark (daughter of Rasmus Jensen and Johanna Christena Nielsen, both of Bornholm, Denmark, pioneers 1854, Hans P. Jensen company). She was born March 6, 1827. Their children: Wilhelmine b. July 10, 1850, m. Erastus Petersen; Joseph b. May 11, 1855, m. Mary Annette Sorensen; Jacob b. April 22, 1857, m. Marian Perry; Daniel b. Aug. 22, 1859; Erastus b. July 31, 1862, m. Ruth Pulsipher; Catherine b. April 22, 1864; Emma b. Nov. 25, 1865; George A. b. Aug. 3, 1870, m. Alice Lucy Kilgore; Clara Rosetta b. Dec. 4, 1871, m. Charles Spierman, m. James Ainsworth; Alice Florence b. May 31, 1874, m. Nephi Smith. Family resided Logan, Utah, and LaGrande, Ore.
Married Sena Hansen at Salt Lake City. Their children: Fredrick b. Nov. 28, 1870, m. Clara Larence Jensen; Anna Maria b. 1872, m. Nephi Andrews: Hyrum m. Berta Guimanal; Aaron: Moses, m. Ella Pulsipher.
Mason by trade and assisted in building three Mormon temples. Died Dec. 4, 1890.

JOHNSON, GEORGE WASHINGTON (son of Ezekiel Johnson and Julia Hills of Uxbridge, Mass. Born Feb. 19, 1823, Pomfort, Chautauqua Co., N. Y. Came to Utah Sept. 21, 1851, Alfred Cardon company.
Married Maria Jane Johnston April 14, 1844, Macedonia, Ill. (daughter of Oliver Campbell Johnston and Hanna Hall Buckley, of Wilson county, Tenn.). She was born Oct. 28, 1824, at Wartrace Creek, Tenn. Their children: George Washington b. March 20, 1845, d. child; Amos Partridge b. Sept. 25, 1846, m. Elizabeth F. Stone; Ezekiel Albert b. July 7, 1848, d. child; William Oliver b. Dec. 9, 1849, d. child; Milas Edgar b. July 31, 1851, m. Alice Malena Wilkins; Maria Jane b. Dec. 11, 1852, m. Thomas G. Wakefield; Julia Ann b. Feb. 28, 1855, m. John F. Wakefield; Joseph Ellis b. Jan. 31, 1858, m. Catherine Annie Johnson; m. Elizabeth Howard; Nancy Loretta b. Sept. 23, 1860, m. Andrew Jackson Woodward. Family home Mona, Juab Co., Utah.
Married Eveline Burdick Oct. 1, 1851, in Salt Lake City (daughter of Alden Burdick and Jerusha Parks of Nauvoo, Ill., the latter pioneer 1852). She was born Sept. 18, 1832. Their children: Joseph Horace, m. Julia Hills Eagar; Margaret Ellen, d. child; Mary Eveline, m. Orris C. Newell; Charlotte, d. child; George Washington, m. Sarah Partridge; Laura Marinda, m. Stanley Keat; m. John E. Jones; David Almon, m. Emeline Hill; Jerusha Annetta, m. Stephen Jones; Herbert Ernest, d. child; Esther Minnie, m. David B. Farnsworth; Charles Edwin, m. Maud Carter; m. Florence Crapo. Family home Mona, Utah.
Helped to build the Nauvoo temple, and in 1848, in connection with David T. LeBaron had charge of it, and was present and saw it while it was burning. Physician; Indian interpreter; compiled the first dictionary of the languages of the Utah Indians. High priest; bishop of Fountain Green ward 1860-65. Postmaster for 35 years. Poet. Seedsman and florist. Died Jan. 22, 1900, Moab, Grand Co., Utah.

JOHNSON, MILAS EDGAR (son of George Washington Johnson and Maria Jane Johnston). Born July 31, 1851, 15 miles north of Platte river. Came to Utah Sept. 21, 1851, Alfred Cardon company.
Married Alice Malena Wilkins March 15, 1874, at Mona, Utah (daughter of Alexander Wilkins and Alice Malena Barney of Provo, Utah; they came to Utah in 1851). She was born Feb. 28, 1857. Their children: Milas Partridge b. March 28, 1875, m. Eliza Viola Loveless; George Alexander b. March 9, 1877, m. Hannah Frances Gordon; Joseph Buriah b. Aug. 13, 1879, m. Alice Allen; Edgar Vernon b. May 27, 1881, m. Ethlind Bradley; Inez Geraldine b. April 7, 1884, m. John Edward Johnson; Hattie Minerva b. Nov. 18, 1885, d. infant. Family home Huntington, Utah.
Married Hannah Eliza Rowley Aug. 25, 1887, at Logan, Utah (daughter of Samuel Rowley and Ann Taylor of Parowan, Utah). She was born Jan. 20, 1872. Their children: Alice Malena b. Oct. 18, 1888, d. infant; Rolla Virgil b. Dec. 17, 1889; Irene Ann b. Oct. 6, 1891, m. George Gardner; Margaret Ellen b. April 25, 1893; Jerold Rowley b. April 1, 1895, d. child; Senate Jane b. Feb. 17, 1897; Norma Delsa b. Feb. 24, 1899; Byron Francis b. Sept. 23, 1901, d. infant; Mildred Erma b. Jan. 3, 1904; Milton Erman b. Jan. 3, 1904; Sarah b. Dec. 12, 1906, d. infant; Lowell b. Sept. 29, 1909. Family home Huntington, Utah.
High priest: stake secretary Y. M. M. I. A. Emory stake 1890-96. Water commissioner; jury commissioner; registration officer; town clerk; trustee; notary public; state senator for twelfth senatorial district; postmaster 20 years. Merchant; traveling salesman. Commander Indian war veterans for department of Emory and Carbon counties and secretary Huntington commercial club.

JOHNSON, GUSTAVE (son of John and Ann Maria Snygg of Sweden). Born July 23, 1821, Gathered, Sweden. Came to Utah Oct. 1, 1862, Joseph Horne company.
Married Louise Erickson March 25, 1845, in Sweden (daughter of Jacob and Johana Erickson of Sweden). She was born March 25, 1815. Their children: Hannah Sophia b. April 9, 1849, m. J. J. Cummings; Eda b. Sept. 7, 1861, m. Andrew Johnson.

JOHNSON, HANS PETER (son of Johanas Paurigg and Magretha Paurigg). Born Oct. 7, 1816, in Sjælland, Denmark. Came to Utah in 1866.
Married Annie Dorthea Jensen in 1843. She was born in 1814. Their children: Dorthea Christina b. March 4, 1843, m. James Hansen April 1869; Grete Bergitha b. Feb. 2, 1849, m. August Swenson Nov. 14, 1868.
Married Helen Anton in the spring of 1881.
Settled at Provo 1866; moved to Spanish Fork 1868; to Fountain Green 1870; to Spring City 1873; to Spanish Fork 1886. Musician; farmer.

JOHNSON, JAMES (son of John Johnson and Ellen Jensen of Brigham City, Utah). Born March 14, 1830, in Denmark. Came to Utah July, 1857, Captain Nesbitt company.
Married Mary Nielsen, in Denmark (daughter of Lars Nielsen and Maron Hanson of Denmark), who was born June 11, 1830. Their children: Ellen; Lars; Christina; Mary, m. John Halling; James, m. Harriet E. Lamb Dec. 23, 1880; Laura, m. Peter Hansen Dec. 28, 1877; Joseph, m. Olive R. Lamb Oct. 28, 1884; Sarah; Lorenzo, m. Mary E. Hansen Nov. 25, 1891; Jane. Family resided Brigham City and Hyde Park, Utah.
High priest. Died May 16, 1891, Hyde Park, Utah.

JOHNSON, JAMES Jr. (son of James Johnson and Mary Nielsen). Born Nov. 20, 1859, Brigham City, Utah.
Married Harriet E. Lamb Dec. 23, 1880, Salt Lake Endowment house (daughter of Suel Lamb and Elizabeth Zimmerman of Hyde Park, Utah), who was born Feb. 23, 1862. Their children: James E. b. Sept. 25, 1881, m. Annie A. Lewis Nov. 16, 1894; Laurence b. Nov. 5, 1883, m. Mary A. Stephens October, 1907; Edna b. May 19, 1886, m. Harrison R. Merrill Jan. 27, 1909; Louis b. Sept. 2, 1888; Floyd b. Sept. 8, 1892; Howard b. Feb. 21, 1895; Harriet b. Aug. 14, 1897; Hazel b. Nov. 5, 1899; Orene L. b. Oct. 12, 1904. Family home Preston, Idaho.
Missionary to Denmark 1900-03, and presided over the Aalborg conference at that place; counselor to Bishop Larson of Preston ward; and also to G. H. Carver of 3d ward, Preston; counselor to Joseph S. Geddes, president Oneida stake.

JOHNSON, JOSEPH (son of James Johnson, Sr., and Mary Nielsen). Born July 19, 1865, Brigham City, Utah.
Married Olive Lamb October, 1884, Logan, Utah (daughter of Suel Lamb and Elizabeth Zimmerman), who was born May 30, 1864, Lehi, Utah. Their children: George b. July 25, 1885, m. Linna Heldsted Dec. 12, 1909; Willard b. Oct. 1, 1887, m. Margie Oliverson 1909; Leonard b. April 21, 1890; Wallace b. Oct. 28, 1892; Leslie b. Feb. 20, 1895; Jessie b. June 9, 1899; Ina b. July 5, 1901; Frank b. April 19, 1904; Bertha b. March 16, 1906. Family resided Brigham City, Utah and Preston, Idaho.
Married Nellie Elizabeth Thomas June 30, 1909, Logan, Utah (daughter of Harrison Ayers Thomas and Ann Morehead, former a pioneer with John Brown company, latter with Aaron Johnson company—married Feb. 12, 1858, Salt Lake Endowment house). She was born Sept. 25, 1870, Smithfield, Utah. Only child: Harrison Thomas b. June 10, 1910.
Missionary to southern states 1906. Railroad contractor in Montana and Idaho. Member board of education of Preston. Engaged in farming and stockraising. Sawmill owner.

JOHNSON, JAMES NICHOLAI (son of Niels Sorensen and Christena Mickelsen of Denmark). Born Nov. 11, 1838, Risegaard, Denmark. Came to Utah November 1856, Knud Peterson company.
Married Nellie Truelson 1859 at Salt Lake City, who died June 1888. Their children: Niels; Soren, d. infant. Family home Brigham City, Utah.
Married Elna Bodelson May 1865, Salt Lake City (daughter of Bodel Olson and Christena Parson, former came to Utah with Captain Baker, latter came Sept. 1864). She was born May 20, 1835, Broby, Sweden. Their children: James Lorenzo b. Jan. 23, 1869, d. Dec. 1888; Niels Oscar b. Dec. 4, 1871, d. Dec. 1888.
Called to assist in settling the Muddy at St. Thomas, Nev., where he resided three years and moved to Panguitch; moved as a pioneer to Richfield, Sevier Co., Utah, 1871. Pioneer farmer and canal builder. Died Oct. 26, 1900, near Galiana, Mexico.

JOHNSON, JARVIS (son of Peter Johnson and Lurina Roberts of Vermont). Born July 6, 1829, at Lincoln, Addison county, Vt. Came to Utah 1847 with division of Mormon Battalion.
Married Heater Ann Jackson Aug. 5, 1849. Their children: Mary Charlotte b. Dec. 14, 1850, m. Rais B. Cahoon; Malissa Caroline b. Feb. 19, 1853, m. Alexander Hunsaker; Lusina b. April 6, 1855, m. Denmark Jensen; William Leaman b. Jan. 27, 1857, m. Katie Wickham; John H. b. Jan. 29, 1859, m. Sophena Hansen. Family home Brigham City, Utah.
Married Sarah Jane Angel 1861 at Salt Lake City (daughter of T. O. Angel and Polly Johnson). She was born May 28, 1834, in New York state. Their children: Martha Ann b. Aug. 19, 1862, m. Orsen Burrell; Jarvis Truman b. Dec. 1, 1863, d. child; Race Alphalus b. Oct. 4, 1865, m. Charlotte Whitworth March 28, 1888; Alice A. b. Dec. 17, 1866, m. George Simmons; Alonzo A. b. Dec. 17, 1866, m. Eva Boothe; Sarah Jane b. March 21, 1869, d. child; Peter b. March 21, 1869.
Married Mary Jane Ainsworth Jan. 17, 1870, at Salt Lake City, Utah (daughter of Joseph Ainsworth and Mary Hupp). She was born in Staffordshire, Eng. Their children: Mary Emerets b. Feb. 6, 1871, m. L. W. Standing; Sarah Adelaide b. Jan. 18, 1873, m. Wilford Stevenson; Jarvis b. Sept. 27, 1876, m. Effie Busenback; Joseph Seaman b. Nov. 28, 1880, m. Katie Yates; Cyntha Delilah b. Feb. 20, 1884, m. Harry Goodsell; Hazel Emmer b. Jan. 30, 1886, m. Alma Knapp; Myrtle Inez b. Aug. 6, 1888, m. Chester Webb; Owen Ainsworth b. Feb. 2, 1891, m. Sarah Elizabeth Coombs; Wallace b. Oct. 11, 1892; Ruby b. March 8, 1896. Family home Beaver Dam, Box Elder Co., Utah.
Machinist.

JOHNSON, WILLIAM LEAMAN (son of Jarvis Johnson and Hester Ann Jackson). Born Jan. 27, 1857, Otoe county, Neb.
Married Katie Wickham Nov. 11, 1877, Brigham City, Utah (daughter of John Wickham, who came to Utah Aug. 20, 1868, Chester Loveland company, and Sarah Andrews, who came to Utah Aug. 14, 1868). She was born May 11, 1859. Their children: William Leroy b. Aug. 25, 1878, m. Lillie Scott: Warren Edward b. Sept. 5, 1880, died; Sarah Maud b. Oct. 27, 1882, m. L. H. Bullen; Sylvanus b. Dec. 31, 1884, died; Hester Ann b. March 24, 1886, died; Lola

May b. June 18, 1888, m. George E. Pulsipher; Leona Minnie b. June 18, 1888; Walter Leslie b. Dec. 15, 1890; John Wickham b. April 10, 1892, and Ethel b. Jan. 22, 1894, died; Lester R. b. May 23, 1895.
High priest. Settled at Brigham City; moved to Avon. Farmer.

JOHNSON, RACE ALPHALUS (son of Jarvis Johnson and Sarah Jane Angel). Born Oct. 4, 1865, Brigham City, Utah.
Married Charlotte Whitworth March 28, 1888, Logan, Utah (daughter of George Whitworth and Mary Wheatley). She was born Oct. 22, 1868, at Calls Fort, Utah. Their children: Pearl b. Dec. 16, 1888, died Jan. 9, 1889; Mary Lavona b. March 23, 1890; Vedia b. March 30, 1892, d. Oct. 5, 1904; Alphalus b. May 2, 1894; Florence b. June 3, 1896; Martha Fern b. July 22, 1898, d. Jan. 18, 1905; Catherine b. Aug. 11, 1900; George Elmer b. Sept. 2, 1902; Charlotte b. April 6, 1905; Alice Virginia b. Feb. 28, 1907; Benjamin Francis b March 25, 1909. Family home Beaver Dam, Box Elder Co., Utah.
Engaged in Sunday school work 17 years; missionary to eastern states; high piest; bishop of Beaver Dam, Utah.

JOHNSON, ALONZO ALVARO (son of Jarvis Johnson and Sarah Jane Angel). Born Dec. 17, 1866, Brigham City, Utah.
Married Eva Boothe Oct. 9, 1895, Logan, Utah (daughter of Lewis Nathaniel Boothe and Mary Jane Reese, the former pioneer 1851, Captain Smith company). She was born April 2, 1875, Brigham City. Their children: Alvero b. Aug. 19, 1896, Jarvis Glen b. Dec. 28, 1897; Alice Alviretto b. Aug. 5, 1899; Mary Jane b. Jan. 16, 1902; Martha E. b. Dec. 8, 1903; Louis Alonzo b. Oct. 15, 1905; Mauda June b. June 19, 1907; Leah b. Sept. 21, 1909; Mertle Ladine b. Oct. 11, 1911.

JOHNSON, JARVIS (son of Jarvis Johnson and Mary Jane Ainsworth). Born Sept. 27, 1876, Brigham City, Utah.
Married Effie Busenbark March 22, 1899, Logan, Utah (daughter of Elias Monroe Busenbark and Sarah Ann Smith, the former was born in Farmington, Utah, latter came to Utah with Captain Murdock company). She was born Sept. 22, 1879, Beaver Dam, Utah. Their children: Jarvis Erwin b. July 10, 1900; Marcellisa B. b. Feb. 3, 1906, Lawrence M. b. Feb. 18, 1904; Farren B. b. Feb. 3, 1906, d. Sept. 15, 1907; Wilford B. b. April 16, 1908; Elmer Carlisle b. April 30, 1909; Ray Lavor b. May 5, 1911.
Moved from Brigham City to Beaver Dam in 1880. Ward clerk, Fielding, Utah. 1909-10; high priest; member bishopric of Fielding, Utah.

JOHNSON, JOEL H. (son of Ezekiel Johnson and Julia Hill). Born March 23, 1802, Grafton, Mass. Came to Utah Oct. 19, 1848, Willard Richards company.
Married Annie P. Johnson Nov. 2, 1826, at Pomfort, N. Y. (daughter of Timothy Johnson and Dimmis Welch, of Pomfret, N. Y., pioneers 1848, Willard Richards company). She was born Aug. 7, 1800. Their children: Sixtus E.; Sariah; Nephi b. Dec. 13, 1833, m. Mandana R. Merrill; Susan T.; Seth b. March 6, 1839, m. Lydia Ann Smith.
Missionary to Iowa and Nebraska 1857-60; bishop; high councilor; patriarch. Member city council; chaplain of territorial legislature at Fillmore. Farmer and stockraiser. Was present at the dedication of the Kirtland temple. Died Sept. 24, 1882, Johnson, Utah.

JOHNSON, NEPHI (son of Joel H. and Annie P. Johnson). Born Dec. 12, 1833, Kirtland, Ohio. Came to Utah Oct. 19, 1848, Franklin D. Richards company.
Married Mandana R. Merrill Jan. 4, 1856, at Cedar City, Utah (daughter of Justin Merrill and Lovinna Manchester of Nauvoo, Ill.; came to Utah in 1848). She was born Oct. 4, 1838, Shelby, Mich. Their children: Lovinna A., m. Frank L. Farnesworth; Nephi, m. Julia Shumway; Joel H., m. Harriett Broadbent; Justin M., m. Emma Fuller; Editha M., m. John C. Stewart; Susan E., m. William Hamlin; Sixtus E., m. Ann Hamlin; William W., d. infant; Lillian C. m. William Jolley; Seth J. Family resided Virgin City and Kanab, Utah.
Indian missionary 1853-65; bishop's counselor; patriarch. County commissioner four terms; road commissioner 10 years; town president; justice of the peace. Mail contractor and farmer.

JOHNSON, SETH (son of Joel H. and Annie P. Johnson). Born March 6, 1839, Carthage, Ill. Came to Utah 1848, Willard Richards company.
Married Lydia Ann Smith Nov. 11, 1861, Parowan, Utah (daughter of Thomas P. Smith and Mary Dugard, of Fort Johnson, Utah). She was born Feb. 17, 1847. Their children: Mary Julia b. Nov. 13, 1862; Seth Alvin b. Nov. 9, 1864; George W. b. June 27, 1866; Lydia Annie b. Sept. 13, 1868; Joel Hills b. July 6, 1870; Sixtus Ellis b. July 29, 1872; Nephi b. Dec. 15, 1874; Seth b. Dec. 17, 1876; Janet Matilda b. Jan. 13, 1878; Susan Sariah b. Nov. 29, 1880.
In 1863 called to the Missouri river with a company of teams to assist immigrants to Utah. Bishop of Hillsdale ward and Cannonville ward; high councilor 24 years; patriarch. County superintendent of district schools; mail carrier. Farmer and stockraiser.

JOHNSON, JOHN (son of John Erickson, born Aug. 26, 1835, Westmanland, Sweden, and Christina Person, born Feb. 3, 1835. Westmanland). He was born April 20, 1864, Westmanland. Came to Utah June 24, 1889.

Married Edla Lundell Oct. 22, 1869, Uta'h (daughter of Andrew Gustave Lundell and Carolina G. Erickson, who were married 1844 in Westmanland). She was born Dec. 5, 1865. Their children: J. Edward b. Oct. 2, 1890; Edna b. Jan. 31, 1892; George Q. b. March 21, 1894; Nora b. March 20, 1896; Elsie b. Dec. 28, 1896; Lorenzo Carl b. Jan. 17, 1899; Vera b. April 1, 1902; Halver T. b. Jan. 13, 1904; Wilma b. Nov. 9, 1906; Darwin W. b. Nov. 20, 1910.
Joined L. D. S. church Sept. 12, 1886; missionary in Sweden 1887-89, and to Sweden 1899-1902; bishop Benjamin ward, Nebo stake 1904. Moved from the northern part of the state to Benjamin in 1891. First president Benjamin Electric Light & Telephone Company 1904.

JOHNSON, JOHN (son of Jorgen Esberson and Gertrude Larsen of West Maria, Bornholm, Denmark). Born Sept. 20, 1812, at West Maria, Bornholm, Denmark. Came to Utah Oct. 6, 1854, Hans Peter Olsen company.
Married Karen Kirstine Jensen Aug. 8, 1835, at Aaker Sogn, Bornholm, Denmark (daughter of Christen Jensen), who was born Sept. 1, 1809, in Klemersker Sogn, Bornholm, Denmark. Their children: Sine Cathrine b. May 14, 1837, m. Niels Mikelsen 1855; Mary Ann b. July 23, 1841, m. Alvin Nichols April 8, 1857; Lewis Peter b. March 12, 1844, m. Susan Elizabeth Watkins Jan. 25, 1869; Teah Jensina b. Dec. 14, 1847, m. William Lampard Watkins July 13, 1867; John Peter b. Nov. 16, 1850, m. Mary Klenn June 9, 1873. Family home Brigham City, Utah.
Married Annie C. Petersen in 1860, at Salt Lake City (daughter of Hans N. Petersen and Caroline Sophia Andriasen, pioneers 1856, with Knud Peterson company). She was born April 4, 1844, Sjøelland, Denmark. Their children: Sophia b. April 19, 1861, m. Frank W. Earl March 21, 1909; Eliza b. June 30, 1864, m. Nels Madson Feb. 12, 1885; Aurelius E. b. June 26, 1879, m. Hattie Forrest June 7, 1904; Harmon J. b. May 23, 1882, m. Sarah Nelson April 27, 1907; George L. b. Dec. 7, 1884, m. Loa Tingey June 26, 1907. Family home, Brigham City.
Married Annie Maria Nielsen Nov. 1865 (daughter of Christian Nielsen and Karen Larsen Olsen, the latter pioneer 1862). She was born July 18, 1834; came to Utah 1863, Captain Clapp company). Their children: Meda A. b. Aug. 11, 1866, m. Nels C. Jensen Dec. 21, 1892; Sarah b. March 13, 1868, m. David L. Reese Jan. 2, 1896; Oluf b. Oct. 24, 1859, m. Annie White June 25, 1902; Louisa b. Oct. 8, 1872, m. Lorenzo Peterson April 11, 1894.
High priest; member 1st bishopric of Bear River City, Utah. Helped found Brigham City in 1854, and Bear River City in 1866. Assisted in bringing immigrants to Utah. Died Feb. 21, 1896.

JOHNSON, LEWIS PETER (son of John Johnson and Karen Kirstine Jensen). Born March 12, 1844, West Maria, Bornholm, Denmark.
Married Susan E. Watkins Jan. 25, 1869, at Salt Lake City (daughter of William Lampard Watkins and Mary Almina Hammond, pioneers of Sept. 11, 1852). She was born Aug. 30, 1848, Little Pigeon, Pottawattamie Co., Iowa. Their children: Lewis Orlando b. April 29, 1870, m. Celine Anderson Nov. 9, 1898; Susan Almina b. April 23, 1874; Thomas W. Whittaker Jan. 1, 1896; John Watkins b. Aug. 20, 1876, m. Oralee Cheney June 18, 1908; Lucius Octavius b. Dec. 13, 1884, m. Florence R. Wilde June 13, 1906; George Wallace b. Nov. 1, 1889. Family home Brigham City, Utah.
High priest; member of presidency Y. M. M. I. A. of the first ward of Brigham City four years; usher in Box Elder tabernacle from 1877 to 1905. Assisted in founding Brigham City in 1854, and Bear River City in 1866. Assisted in bringing immigrants to Utah in 1864. City treasurer two terms; school trustee 1894-96; road supervisor 1888-93; city councilman in Brigham City 1896-1902. Had charge of Brigham Co-operative farm in Malad valley during seasons 1875-76-77. Fruit grower.

JOHNSON, OLUF (son of John Johnson and Annie M. Nielsen). Born Oct. 24, 1869, at Brigham City, Utah.
Married Annie White June 25, 1902, at Salt Lake City (daughter of Barnard White and Mary Williams), who was born July 12, 1876, at Ogden, Utah. Their children: Ruth Annie b. Jan. 18, 1906; Russel, died; Mildred b. Aug. 31, ——, died.
Missionary to Denmark; 3rd president 153d quorum seventies Bear River City.

JOHNSON, JOHN.
Married Bergite Larson Loken at Elverum, Hedemarken, Norway (daughter of Lars Loken of Elverum), who was born Dec. 23, 1834, and came to Utah Oct. 1, 1864, John Smith independent company. Their children: Ingere b. March 14, 1844, m. J. P. R. Johnson; Lena b. Dec. 9, 1846, m. Peter Madsen; John, Jr., b. June 7, 1849, m. Ingere Sward. Family home Provo, Utah.
Bergite Larson Loken later married Hans Knutson, (son of Knud Kokenson and Eli Neilsen) pioneer 1864. Their children: Christena, m Christian Nelson; Andrew, m. Chasty Sward; Herman, m. Amanda Evert; Bertha, m. Peter Madsen; Ellen died.

JOHNSON, JOHN (son of John Johnson and Bergite Larson Loken). Born June 7, 1849, Ostroveen, Lorten, Hedemarken, Norway. Came to Utah with father.
Married Ingere Sward June 13, 1870, Salt Lake City (daughter of Aake Aakeson Sward and Lena Olson of

Ostravram, Skaane, Sweden—came to Utah August, 1874). She was born May 2, 1848. Their children: Ellen Bergite b. April 3, 1871, m. Leslie L. Bunnell; Josephine b. May 22, 1873, m. William W. Goodridge; Ingere Julia b. Nov. 20, 1875, m. Ted Hatton; Emma b. Dec. 30, 1877, m. Conrad Marg, Jr.; John b. July 20, 1880, d. Sept. 21, 1881; Tenie b. June 26, 1882, m. Martin Clinger; Alfred Henry b. Sept. 3, 1884; m. Murel Holdaway; Nora b. Nov. 19, 1886, m. William W. Taylor; August Jeremiah b. Feb. 4, 1888; Anna Goldie Halverson (adopted) b. April 27, 1884, m. John McCune.

Member 45th quorum seventies; missionary to Norway 1889-91; high priest; bishop Lake View ward since Feb. 14, 1892; presiding teacher since 1877; president Y. M. M. I. A. and Sunday school superintendent. Peace officer. Farmer and stockraiser.

JOHNSON, JOHN A. (son of James and Josephine Johnson of Denmark). Born April 14, 1883.
Married Sarah Jane Thomas (Matthews) July 7, 1908, at Salt Lake City (daughter of Samuel Thomas and Mary Darknell, of Salt Lake City). She was born Oct. 15, 1874, at Salt Lake City. Their children: John W. b. Jan. 3, 1909; Stanley T. b. Sept. 23, 1910.
Motorman; stationary engineer.

JOHNSON, JOHN PETER RASMUS. Born April 10, 1824, near Copenhagen, Denmark. Came to Utah Oct. 5, 1854.
Married Caroline Maria Nelson Tuft in 1845, in Denmark (daughter of Lars Nielson, who resided near Copenhagen). She was born Feb. 2, 1822. Their children: John T., m. Dortha Merk; Niels b. Sept. 1848, m. Josephine Johnson; Hans Christian, Dortha and Rebecca, died; Andrew Christian, m. Anna Rosser; Annie Maria, m. Samuel Stephen Jones; Minnie; Johanna Patrina Rasmina, m. Samuel Jepperson; Peter, died; Hyrum, m. Julia Shepherd.
Married Mary Poulsen at Salt Lake City (daughter of Mads Poulsen of Copenhagen, Denmark, who came to Utah about 1854). Their children: Elias, m. Mary Greenough; Brigham, m. Nora Peay; Maria, died; Pauline, m. Joseph Kirkwood. Family home Provo, Utah.
Married Inger Johnson at Salt Lake City (daughter of John Johnson and Bergeta Knutson; they came to Utah in 1864). Their children: John Joseph, m. Emma Brown; Ellen; Marietta; Abraham Owen, m. Alice Henrickson; Hans, m. Juliet Stewart; David, m. Grace Gay; Hannah, m. John Smith; Inger. Family home Provo, Utah.
High priest; missionary to Denmark 1860-64; president Christiania conference in Norway; bishop 1st Provo ward 1864-83. Took active part in the early Indian troubles. Helped build tabernacle. Railroad contractor in Echo Canyon; cabinet maker and carriage builder; farmer and stockraiser.

JOHNSON, NIELS (son of John Peter Rasmus Johnson and Caroline Maria Nelson Tuft). Born Sept. 1848, near Copenhagen, Denmark. Came to Utah with parents.
Married Josephine Johnson May 3, 1869, Salt Lake City (daughter of John J. Johnson of Fredricksted, Christiania, Norway, and Inger Jensen; she came to Utah Oct. 7, 1866, Andrew Hunter Scott company). She was born Dec. 17, 1846. Their children: Christina, b. June 4, 1870, m. B. S. Hinckley; Caroline b. March 30, 1872, m. Walter M. Wolfe; Emma b. July 25, 1874, and George b. Sept. 9, 1875, died; William b. Jan. 22, 1878, m. Eliza Safford; James Edwin b. May 20, 1881, m. Marion Jones; Alfred b. Feb. 22, 1883, m. Josephine Brown; Stephen b. March 26, 1885, m. Winefred Overlaid; Josephine b. July 5, 1889, m. Curtis Cohn. Family home Provo, Utah.
High priest; counselor to his father, Bishop Johnson, 1st ward, Provo, Utah. Member Provo city council eight years; 1894-95, supervisor Provo city streets; superintendent of construction Provo city water works four years; president and director Upper Union Irrigation Company. Farmer and railroad contractor.

JOHNSON, JAMES EDWIN (son of Niels Johnson and Josephine Johnson). Born May 20, 1881, Provo, Utah.
Married Marion Jones Aug. 20, 1906, Salt Lake City (daughter of Thomas Jones and Florence Taylor), who was born Oct. 25, 1883. Their children: Norman Edwin b. Oct. 1, 1907; Alton Bryant b. Nov. 1, 1908; William Dazil b. April 21, 1910; Niels Shelly and Thomas Scott, twins, b. Aug. 25, 1912. Family home Provo, Utah.
Missionary to southern states 2 years; elder. Assisted in freighting material for Strawberry tunnel. Contractor.

JOHNSON, JOSEPH (WEAVER) (son of William Weaver and Catherine H. Beck Johnson). Born Feb. 28, 1866, Ogden, Utah.
Married Addie L. Morrill Sept. 25, 1891, Circleville, Utah (daughter of Horatio Morrill and Sarah Ann Ludweeks of Cedar City, Utah, pioneers 1852). She was born March 28, 1872. Their children: Elva Josephine b. Nov. 4, 1892, m. Erin Beal Nov. 8, 1911; Alta Merilla b. Dec. 11, 1894; Addie Ora b. Sept. 7, 1895; Marguerite b. May 13, 1897; Joseph Ottis, b. Nov. 15, 1899; Catherine Mertilia b. July 13, 1903; Aileen b. Feb. 8, 1905; Eldon b. March 13, 1908. Family resided Circleville and Richfield, Utah.
Missionary to southern states 1900-02. President Circleville Irrigation Co.; manager Richfield branch Consolidated Wagon & Machine Co.

JOHNSON, WILLIS (WEAVER) (son of William Weaver and Catherine H. Beck Johnson). Born Nov. 4, 1868, Ogden, Utah.
Married Emma Phedora Morrill April 1, 1891, Manti, Utah (daughter of Laban D. Morrill, pioneer 1852, and Emma W. Dailey of Circleville, Utah). She was born April 6, 1875. Their children: Dora Pearl b. March 2, 1892, m. Marion Seegmiller; Willis Franklin b. Sept. 21, 1895; Reginald Morrill b. May 10, 1898; Merlin Roland b. Aug. 2, 1900; Laban Owen b. Dec. 1, 1902, d. Jan. 2, 1906; Jacquita b. Dec. 13, 1907; Howard D. b. Sept. 4, 1910. Family home Richfield, Utah.
High priest; missionary to North Carolina 1892-94; 1st counselor to Sunday school superintendent; Sunday school superintendent; president Y. M. M. I. A. of Circleville, Utah. Member school board of Circleville. State senator from tenth district 1901-08. Member St. Louis World's Fair commission from Utah. Merchant; hotel proprietor; farmer.

JOHNSON, LARS FERDINAND (son of Hans Jorgensen and Marie D. Brinck). He was born Nov. 21, 1858, North Sjaelland, Denmark. Came to Utah in 1868.
Married Johanna Thomsen Sept. 4, 1893, Salt Lake City (daughter of Nels Peter Thomsen and Johanna A. Andersen of Hjorring, Denmark). She was born Aug. 10, 1874. Their children: Edward L. b. Oct. 25, 1894; Norman M. b. June 27, 1896; Lerve H. b. March 19, 1898; Lorenza J. b. Sept. 27, 1899; Edna Viola b. July 21, 1901; Vernald F. b. Aug. 3, 1902; Alvin Oleen b. May 16, 1904; Erma Marie b. May 12, 1906; Raymond b. June 4, 1909, d. Oct 29, 1909. Family home, Bear River City.
Member 5th quorum seventies; missionary to Denmark 1891-93; alternate high councilor 1899; bishop Bear River ward. County commissioner two terms, school trustee; trustee town board. Farmer and stockraiser.

JOHNSON, LOUIS (son of D. C. Johnson and Matilda Madison). Born Nov. 9, 1858, at Richmond, Utah.
Married Clarinda H. Allen June 19, 1907 (daughter of Levi Allen and Livinia Henson). She was born Nov. 3, 1889, at Cove, Utah. Their children: Louis Allen b. June 4, 1908; Lyman Leon b. Aug. 30, 1909; Ora Wendell b. Nov. 24, 1911.

JOHNSON, JOHN LYCURGUS (son of Willis Johnson and Nancy Greer of Brennen, Tex.). Born Aug. 25, 1844, Brennen. Came to Utah in 1854.
Married Cora Isabella Davis March 1, 1867, at St. Charles, Idaho (daughter of Nathan Cutler Davis and Isabella Wells, Bolton, Warren county, N. Y., pioneers to Utah Oct. 1857 with John Smith company). She was born Oct. 25, 1847, Bolton, N. Y. Came to Utah Oct. 1857. Their children: Edward L. b. Oct. 25, 1870, m. Minerva Wilkins; Nathan b. April 2, 1872, d. infant; Alfred N. b. April 2, 1872, m. Mary De Freeze; Snellen b. Sept. 3, 1874, m. Genevieve Sprouse; Eugene b. Feb. 28, 1876, d. child; Le Roy b. Sept. 18, 1877, d. child; Clarence Irwin b. March 23, 1879, m. Ada May Rich; Nancy Pearl b. April 16, 1881, m. Brigham Christensen; Cora Myrtle b. April 21, 1884, m. Edward Harvey Belcher; Hazel b. Sept. 23, 1886.
High priest; high councilor; ward teacher. Settled at St. Charles, Idaho, in 1864; moved to Vernal, Utah, 1879. Delegate to state constitutional convention; member of state legislature in 1898; United States marshal several years; county sheriff; county commissioner; mayor of the city; school trustee. Farmer.

JOHNSON, CLARENCE IRWIN (son of Lycurgus Johnson and Cora Isabella Davis). Born March 23, 1879, Vernal, Utah.
Married Ada May Rich April 11, 1900, at Salt Lake City, Utah (daughter of Charles Coulson Rich, Jr., and Jane Susannah Stocks of Vernal, Utah). She was born March 23, 1880. Their children: Clarence Etheridge b. Nov. 10, 1901; Narvol Rich b. Sept. 28, 1903; Therma May b. May 13, 1906; Nila Hazel b. May 19, 1909, d. May 19, 1911. Family home Roosevelt, Utah.
High priest; alternate high councilor; first superintendent Sunday school at Roosevelt; ward teacher, Vernal and Roosevelt; first superintendent Y. M. M. I. A. at Roosevelt; first president Duchesne stake M. I. A. and president Y. M. M. I. A. at Vernal four years; president of deacons' and elders' quorum at Vernal; junior president of seventies, Roosevelt. Registration officer in Uintah county. Vice-president Dry Gulch Irrigation Co., Roosevelt. Merchant.

JOHNSON, NELS PETER (son of Jens Johansen and Johanne Christine Simonsen).Born March 21, 1871, Skanderborg, Denmark. Came to Utah July 13, 1886.
Married Olga Caroline Winkler March 23, 1892, Logan, Utah (daughter of Jens Winkler and Chatrina Felt, both of Sweden, the latter came to Utah from Denmark Aug. 1890). She was born April 12, 1873, at Copenhagen, Denmark. Their children: Eldora Cathrina b. Dec. 13, 1892; James John b. Feb. 9, 1908; Oscar b. Feb. 10, 1912.
Missionary to Denmark 1899-1901; first bishop of eighth ward, Logan, Utah. Street supervisor of Logan. Merchant; farmer.

PIONEERS AND PROMINENT MEN OF UTAH

JOHNSON, PETER (son of Jens Benson and Hannah Anderson of Skona, Sweden). Born Jan. 1, 1825, Skona, Sweden. Came to Utah 1854, Captain Olsen company.
Married Dorthea Madsen 1854, Manti, Utah (daughter of Mads Monk of Brestroup, Denmark), who was born 1823. Their children: Peter, Jr., b. Dec. 30, 1855, m. Mina Zoebell; Mads, m. Brignamina Jacobson; Annie, m. George Klinger; Abraham, m. Merby Davis.
High priest; ward teacher. Farmer and stockraiser.

JOHNSON, MADS (son of Peter Johnson and Dorthea Madsen). Born March 6, 1860, Lake View, Utah.
Married Brighamina Jacobson March 21, 1888, Logan, Utah (daughter of Lars Jacobson and Inger Thompson of Denmark, pioneers 1857, Christian Christiansen handcart company). She was born April 11, 1867. Their children: Florence Minnie b. Feb. 23, 1889; Lafayette Mads b. March 4, 1891; Clarence Peter b. Sept. 30, 1894; Jennings Bryan b. Oct. 20, 1897; Vera Dorthea and Vesta Inger (twins) b. July 19, 1899; Vernile Independent b. July 4, 1902; Clifford Oline b. May 4, 1906, died; Elden Lamar b. Aug. 7, 1909. Family home Lake View, Utah.
Elder; home missionary; secretary of Sunday school; secretary and treasurer Y. M. M. I. A. Constable and justice of peace at Lake View; sheriff at Provo. Built first meeting house at Lake View, also first store at that place. Farmer, fruitgrower and carpenter. Manager Lake View Dramatic Organization.

JOHNSON, PETER (son of Jens Johanson and Margaret Marquet of North Jutland, Viborg, Denmark). Born May 1, 1839, Orum, Denmark. Came to Utah October 1854, Captain Olsen company.
Married Annie Catherine Anderson May 29, 1861, Ephraim, Utah (daughter of Lars and Maron Anderson of Sistrop, Viborg, Denmark, pioneers 1856). She was born Feb. 16, 1843. Their children: Catherine Ann b. June 28, 1862, m. Joseph E. Johnson; James Peter b. Nov. 11, 1863, m. Jane Leonard; Margaret Ann b. Oct. 15, 1865, m. William J. Green; Mary Ann b. Oct. 19, 1867, d. young womanhood; Peter Ellis b. Oct. 31, 1869, m. Orelia Overson; Lewis William b. April 3, 1872; Hannah Matilda b. March 19, 1874, m. Heber Leonard; Elizabeth May b. May 1, 1876; Charles Robert b. May 7, 1878; Heber Andrew b. Feb. 8, 1880, d. infant; Petreren Estell b. July 21, 1881, m. Amos Petersen; Fanny U. b. Jan. 12, 1885, d. child. Family resided Cleveland and Huntington, Utah.
Married Annie Margaret Hansen Nov. 19, 1865, Salt Lake City (daughter of Abraham and Mary Hansen of Denmark, pioneers Oct. 1854). She was born May 1, 1841. Their children: Andrew F. b. Sept. 1865; John P. b. July 1867, m. Oscena Olson; Daniel A. b. April 1871, m. Carrie Mortensen; Helen b. Nov. 1873, m. Bowther Erickson; Eliza b. March 1876, m. George H. Oviatt; Ellen B. b. Oct. 1878. Family home Huntington, Utah.
Superintendent of Sunday school in Fountain Green 1874 in Huntington 1882 and general superintendent of Sunday schools Emery stake 1883; member of high council of Emery stake 1883; bishop of Huntington 1891-1902; patriarch. Indian war veteran. Helped to bring in last oxteam company of immigrants. Member Huntington town board; registration officer 1910. Sheep herder; farmer; carpenter.

JOHNSON, REED TAYLOR (son of Bengt Johnson, Jr. and Betsy Christopherson). Born Nov. 4, 1885, Provo, Utah.
Married Bertha Alfrida Bloomquist Jan. 28, 1909, Salt Lake temple (daughter of John Alfred Bloomquist and Carlina Sophia Johanason of Malmo, Sweden, came to Utah July 8, 1909). She was born Feb. 1, 1881. Their children: Alvin Eben b. Oct. 17, 1909; Wellis Regdon b. April 22, 1911. Family home Provo, Utah.
Elder; missionary to Sweden May 1, 1906-Oct. 3, 1908; block and Sunday school teacher; president religion class second ward; first counselor in elders quorum; acting chorister in priesthood meetings; member stake choir.

JOHNSON, ROBERT (son of William Johnson, born Sept. 14, 1785, Sutton, Cheshire, Eng., and Ann Edwards, born 1786—married Jan. 12, 1845, in England). He was born Sept. 4, 1823, Guilden Sutton, Cheshire. Came to Utah 1853, Captain Brown company.
Married Elizabeth Johnston Jan. 12, 1845 (daughter of Joseph Johnston and Elizabeth Clark). She was born Oct. 20, 1825. Their children: William b. Sept. 4, 1845, died; John b. Feb. 19, 1848; Robert b. March 3, 1849, m. Anna Hougaard Jan. 26, 1873; Mary Ellen b. Aug. 16, 1851, m. Ephraim Denison Jan. 12, 1873; Elizabeth Ann b. Jan. 19, 1855, m. Francis M. Cox Jan. 12, 1873; Joseph b. Oct. 17, 1853, died; Samuel b. Sept. 6, 1857, died; Alma b. Dec. 2, 1858, m. Margret E. Henry Nov. 25, 1886; Martha b. May 1, 1861, m. Robert Counliffe March 7, 1880; Nephi b. Oct. 12, 1868, m. Marien Hogen Dec. 5, 1894; Cicley b. Sept. 6, 1866, died; Sarah Jane b. June 14, 1864. Family home Manti, Utah.
Settled at Manti 1854. Guard in Black Hawk war. Missionary to England 1883-85. Farmer.

JOHNSON, ROBERT (son of Robert Johnson and Elizabeth Johnston). Born March 3, 1849, Stockport, Eng.
Married Anna Hougaard Jan. 26, 1873, Manti, Utah (daughter of Rasmus and Magdalena Hougaard, former came to Utah 1862). She was born April 13, 1855, Falster, Denmark. Their children: Robert W. b. Feb. 21, 1874, m. Tresie Willson Oct. 14, 1898; Rasmus R. b. Jan. 24, 1876, died; Annethy E. b. Jan. 16, 1877, m. Oliver Wakefield Sept. 2, 1897; Alma Eugene b. Nov. 12, 1879, m. Stella Collard July 10, 1902; John Edward b. Dec. 26, 1881, m. Ing Johnson Feb. 26, 1904; Louis Nephi b. Jan. 7, 1883, m. Nettie Nielson Dec. 29, 1903; Mary Magdelien b. April 2, 1885, m. Hyrum Peterson Oct. 21, 1903; Hannah Evlin b. Dec. 27, 1887, m. Leo Moffit March 14, 1905; Samuel Richard b. March 10, 1889; Verona Gertrude b. Jan. 22, 1891, died; Clarane P. b. Feb. 10, 1893. Family home Orangeville, Utah.
Settled at Manti 1854; moved to Orangeville 1881. Black Hawk war veteran. Farmer; musician.

JOHNSON, THOMAS SMITH (son of Isaac Johnson and Grace Smith of New York). Born Jan. 1, 1818, Schenectady, N. Y. Came to Utah with his own company.
Married Mary Harrison. Their children: Parhant b. May 4, 1852, m. John Hill; Thomas Smith b. Dec. 18, 1854, m. Eliza Anne Higley; Louisa b. 1857; Deece b. 1860, m. Charles Higley; Adeline b. 1864, m. George E. Higley; Eliza b. 1866, m. George Haynes; Charles b. 1869, m. Martha Priest; Annice b. July 31, 1876, m. Charles Cunningham.

JOHNSON, THOMAS SMITH, Jr. (son of Thomas Smith Johnson and Mary Harrison). Born Dec. 18, 1854, Salt Lake City.
Married Eliza Anne Higley July 6, 1880, Hooper, Utah (daughter of George Higley and Nancy Wadsworth), who was born May 4, 1862, Riverdale, Utah. Their children: Thomas Smith b. July 31, 1881, m. Leveta Olive Lewis 1908; Charles Warren b. Aug. 22, 1883, m. Nellie Childs 1908; George Edwin b. Aug. 23, 1885; Maud Eden b. Feb. 8, 1888, m. Clarence Bates 1906; Ola b. Oct. 16, 1891, d. Aug. 3, 1908; Leroy b. Jan. 29, 1893; Delia May b. Feb. 23, 1895; Mary Lillian b. Sept. 20, 1898; William Lloyd b. Dec. 30, 1900.

JOHNSON, WILLIS KELSEY (son of Aaron Johnson and Polly Zeviah Kelsey). Born Sept. 13, 1828, Haddam, Middlesex county, Conn.
Married Laura Crandall Jan. 1, 1850, Kanesville, Iowa (daughter of David Crandall and Margaret McBride). Their child: Willis Kelsey b. Oct. 2, 1850, m. Sarah Mendenhall.

JOHNSON, WILLIS KELSEY (son of Willis Kelsey Johnson and Laura Crandall). Born Oct. 2, 1850, Salt Lake City.
Married Sarah Mendenhall (daughter of William Mendenhall and Sarah Lovell, the former came to Utah Sept. 18, 1862). She was born May 12, 1853, Springville, Utah. Their children: Willis Kelsey b. June 30, 1875, m. Eva Clark; James Bayard b. Oct. 20, 1877, m. Alice Whitney; Franklin M. b. Sept. 9, 1879, died; Minerva b. Dec. 6, 1881, m. John S. Hill; Harrison b. Dec. 17, 1883, died; Chester b. Jan. 12, 1886; Richard M. b. Feb. 20, 1888; Thursa b. Sept. 17, 1890; Mary Edna b. Oct. 10, 1892; George Leo b. Sept. 10, 1895. Family home Springville, Utah.
Member of quorum of seventies for 25 years; president of quorum of seventies for 10 years. Early settler in southern Utah. District school trustee of Springville, Utah, for two terms; member of city council for two terms.

JOHNSTUN, JESSIE WALKER (son of James Johnstun and Amity Welsh of New Jersey). Born Jan. 21, 1820, in Ohio. Came to Utah July 28, 1847, with section of Mormon Battalion.
Married Betsy Ann Snyder March 2, 1848, Jamestown, Mo. (daughter of Samuel Cainstock Snyder and Henrietta Mona Stockwell of Canada, came to Utah in 1847). She was born July 17, 1836. Their children: Alma James, m. Loretta Henry; Maria Amity, m. Jacob Reader Workman; Laura Menetta, m. William Jennie; Elizabeth Rebecca, m. John Blankenship; Anny Lovess, m. John Toone.
Presiding elder at Snyderville, Utah. Lumberman. Died May 8, 1860, Parley Park, Summit county.

JOHNSTUN, ALMA JAMES (son of Jesse Walker Johnstun and Elizabeth Ann Snyder). Born July 23, 1853, Big Cottonwood, Salt Lake Co., Utah.
Married Loretta Muriel Henry May 30, 1875, Endowment House, Salt Lake City (daughter of Calvin William Henry and Priscilla Barnham, pioneers 1854). She was born April 25, 1855. Their children: Minnetta b. March 20, 1876, m. Charles B. Atwood, Jr.; Emily b. Sept. 2, 1878, d. child; James b. Oct. 27, 1880, m. Mary Timothy; William b. March 10, 1883, m. Fedelia Labrum; Eugenie b. Aug. 23, 1885, m. Harvey Mashall; Elizabeth b. Jan. 2, 1888, m. Elvin Hodson; Jeremiah b. Jan. 13, 1890, d. infant; Joseph b. March 15, 1892; Derrell and Delpha b. May 30, 1894; George b. Oct. 28, 1896; Owen b. July 16, 1899. Family home Vernal, Utah.
High priest; second counselor to Bishop Joseph Black of Snyderville ward 1877. Called as home missionary to settle Ashley Valley (now Vernal) April 6, 1878, by President John Taylor, and his homestead was where the tabernacle, academy, stake office and town of Vernal now stands. With him were Joseph H. Black and David Johnston. During the same fall, there were families by the names of Clark, Bird, Hatch, Morrison and Bodly located at Vernal. He built the first house, made the first canal for water, opened the first coal mine, brought the first threshing ma-

PIONEERS AND PROMINENT MEN OF UTAH

chine, the first steam sawmill, the second grist mill and many of the other public improvements in Vernal. Went to Snyderville as a child with parents, where his father conducted a sawmill, and he remained there until he moved to Vernal. County commissioner 1891-92. Operates saw, lumber, flour and planing mills; is engaged in farming; is interested in the Uinta State Bank, Acorn Mercantile Company and the Vernal Drug Company.

JOLLEY, HENRY BRYANT MANNING (son of Henry Jolley and Frances Manning of North Carolina). Born Sept. 18, 1813, Bedford county, N. C. Came to Utah Sept. 16, 1852, captain his company.
Married Brittania Mayo in Weakley county, Tenn. (daughter of John Mayo and Gatsey Franklin of Bedford county, N. C.). She was born 1814. Came to Utah Sept. 1852 with husband. Their children: Mary b. Dec. 25, 1834, m. Thomas Keele; Elizabeth, m. George Hicks; Wesley, m. Annie Chambers, m. Lydia Ann Brimhall; Henry, died; Frances, m. Robert Moncur; Nephi, m. Mary Ann Harris, m. Mary Daily; Bryant Heber, m. Orissa Taylor; Ruben, m. Emily Pace; Joseph, m. Martha Ann Brown.
Married Cintha Ann Shurtcliff Sept. 16, 1852, Salt Lake City (daughter of Haskel of Massachusetts). Came to Utah Sept. 15, 1852, Henry Bryant Jolley company. Their children: Haskel Shurtcliff, m. Effie Leathhead, m. Nellie Harrison; Lorenzo, m. Maletta Spencer, m. Mary Mayo at St. George, Utah.
Seventy; missionary to North Carolina 1890-92. Indian war veteran. Settled at Palmyra; moved to Springville; later to Long Valley. Farmer; stockman; storekeeper. Died March 4, 1895, at Mt. Carmel, Utah.

JOLLEY, BRYANT HEBER (son of Henry Bryant Manning Jolley and Brittania Mayo). Born Feb. 26, 1851, Council Bluffs, Iowa. Came to Utah Sept. 15, 1852, with his father's company.
Married Orissa Taylor Dec. 25, 1869, New Harmony, Utah (daughter of Allen Taylor and Reddicka Allred of New Harmony, came to Utah 1848, Brigham Young company). She was born Oct. 13, 1851. Their children: Bryant Heber b. Oct. 4, 1870, m. Annie Pernella Nisson and Annie Sproul; Joseph Allen b. Oct. 14, 1872, m. Ingre Emerett Nisson; Alma Franklin b. May 9, 1876, m. Annie Schlappey and Dora Hutchings; Riley Taylor b. March 28, 1879, m. Sadie Neilsen, m. Nora Winn; Gatsey Lorisa b. Nov. 5, 1881, m. Silas E. Hutchings. Family resided at Elseeora, Theodore and Duchesne, Utah.
Elder. Settled at Spanish Fork 1855; later moved to Duchesne, Idaho. Veteran Indian war. Farmer and stockraiser.

JOLLY, WILLIAMSON WESLEY (son of George Jolly). Born July 16, 1835, in Tennessee. Came to Utah by team.
Married Lydia Ann Brimhall (daughter of John Brimhall and Ann Reddy, pioneers 1847). Their children: John Manning, m. Drewey Hartley; Malinda, m. Steven Wilson; Donald, m. Emma Allred; Heber, m. Letta Whetstone; Aurilia, m. Erastus Bastian; Lydia Ann b. May 11, 1852, m. Alfred William Hansen; Louise, m. Ola Olsen; Magneus; Wesley. Family resided Mt. Carmel, and Emery, Utah, and Heyburn, Idaho.
High priest. Settled at Mt. Carmel in early '60s and one of the leaders in the Order of Enoch at that place. Farmer and freighter. Died Jan. 10, 1911, Heyburn, Idaho.

JONES, BENJAMIN. Born Feb. 24, 1796, in Cattaraugus county, N. Y. Came to Utah 1848.
Married Rosannah Cox in January ——— (daughter of Jehu Cox and Sarah Pyle of Knox county, Ky., pioneers Sept. 24, 1848, Heber C. Kimball company). She was born Jan. 25, 1825. Their children: Heber C., m. Rosannah Brady; Benjamin, m. Sarah Jane Cheney; Sarah, m. Almir B. Cox; Rosannah, m. Orville Cox. Family home Union Fort, Utah.
Elder; ward teacher. Shoemaker and farmer. Died April 4, 1875, Fairview, Utah.

JONES, BENJAMIN (son of Benjamin Jones and Rosannah Cox). Born July 10, 1850, Union Fort, Utah.
Married Sarah Jane Cheney June 28, 1875, Fairview, Utah (daughter of Elam Cheney and Martha Taylor, pioneers), who was born Sept. 7, 1857. Their children: Martha Ellen b. April 4, 1876, m. Lyman Sherman; Elam L. b. May 1, 1877, m. Ada C. Sherman; Celestia Castel b. Dec. 15, 1878, m. Marion J. Brady; Benjamin b. Sept. 7, 1880, m. Mary Frances Foote; Sarah Jane b. Sept. 10, 1882, m. Andrew Johansen; David H. b. Aug. 29, 1884; Rosannah b. May 1, 1886, d. child; Orin Samuel b. April 12, 1888; Jehu b. Jan. 2, 1890; Hettie b. Dec. 7, 1891, d. infant; Zelma b. Jan. 7, 1896, d. infant. Family home Huntington, Utah.
Married Mary Maria Burrison Oct. 1, 1907, Castledale, Utah (adopted daughter of Philip and Rachel Burrison of Denmark).
Member 31st quorum seventies; elder; ward teacher 1890-'90⁰. Farmer and stockraiser.

JONES, CHARLES H. (son of John Jones and Maria Mather New York). Born Aug. 30, 1836, in New York. Came Utah 1857, Johnston's army.
Married Viola Maria Russell Dec. 20, 1862, Grafton, ne Co., Utah (daughter of Alonzo H. Russell and Nancy

B. Foster of Grafton, pioneers, Wilford Woodruff company). She was born Oct. 27, 1848. Their children: Charles Alvin, m. Harriet Spendlove; Annie Viola; George A., m. Clara Wilson; William Alfred; Edwald D., m. Rhoda A. Ballard; Philetus, m. Annie Laura Stout; Lavenia; John Frank, m. Hilda Coleman. Family home, Grafton.
Elder. Printer. Died April 30, 1903.

JONES, PHILETUS (son of Charles H. Jones and Viola Maria Russell). Born Jan. 13, 1875, Grafton, Utah.
Married Annie Laura Stout Dec. 23, 1898, St. George, Utah (daughter of Alfred Fisk Stout and Mary Emma Langston, Rockville, Utah). She was born April 14, 1881. Their children: Alvin Vernon b. Oct. 10, 1899; Madge b. Aug. 22, 1901; Vernessa Fern b. Feb. 2, 1904; Mary Viola b. March 6, 1906; Iona b. Feb. 9, 1908; Ada b. Feb. 26, 1909; Winnie b. March 5, 1911. Family home Rockville, Utah.
Member 21st quorum seventies. Farmer.

JONES, DAN (son of Thomas Jones and Ruth Jones of Swansea, South Wales). Born Aug. 4, 1811, in Flintshire, Wales. Came to Utah September 1849, Captain Jones company.
Married Elizabeth Jones Dec. 1849, Salt Lake City (daughter of Thomas Jones and Elizabeth Jones of Cleddy, South Wales). She was born April 5, 1813. Their children: Thomas, died; John, m. Augusta Smith; Eliza, m. Isaac Vorhees; Cannan. m. Sarah Reese; Louis; Ruth, m. George B. Squires; Brigham, m. Ella Free. Family home, Salt Lake City.
Missionary to Wales; president of Wales mission 1852-55. Seaman; built first boat on Great Salt Lake. Died Jan. 3, 1862, Provo, Utah.

JONES, DAVID PROSSER (son of David Jones and Elizabeth Prosser of Rosa, near Beaufort and Abywaie, Monmouthshire, Wales). Born 1836, near Brecknocktown, Brecknockshire, Wales. Came to Utah Sept. 25, 1866, John D. Holladay company.
Married Ellnor Smart (Corns) about 1858, Rhymney, Wales (daughter of Joseph Corns of Pontypool, Monmouthshire). She was born in 1814. Family resided Willard City and Cherry Creek, Utah, and Malad, Idaho.
Bishop; chorister. Poet. Mason, freighter and farmer.

JONES, EDWARD (son of Edward Jones and Margrett Roberts of Ruthin, Denbigh, Wales). Born March 10, 1832, at Ruthin. Came to Utah 1856.
Married Hannah Pendlebury Oct. 11, 1852, Manchester, Eng. (daughter of James Pendlebury and Sarah Walker), who was born June 10, 1832. Came to Utah Sept. 12, 1857, Israel Evans handcart company. Their children: Emily Jane b. Dec. 11, 1860, m. John L. Sperry Aug. 21, 1877; Margrett b. 1862 and James Edward b. 1864, died; Martha Ann b. April 1, 1865, m. Robert G. Pyper Jan. 7, 1884; George b. 1866, died; Selena Bell b. May 29, 1869, m. Thomas M. McCune Feb. 11, 1891; Mary Jane b. May 29, 1871, m. John William McPherson Sept. 11, 1895.
Married Martha Jackson, Salt Lake City (daughter of Benjamin Jackson and Ann Grimshaw of Manchester, Eng., pioneers Sept. 12, 1857, Jesse B. Martin company). She was born April 22, 1830, Manchester, Eng. Their children: Edward b. Nov. 23, 1857, m. Sarah Jane Tolley; William b. May 11, 1859, m. Elizabeth Ann Tolley April 11, 1883; Ellen b. Feb. 11, 1861, m. Nephi Jackson 1879; Elizabeth b. Feb. 7, 1863, m. John H. Cazier March 1, 1882; Louisa b. April 1865, m. William Broadhead March 10, 1886; Benjamin b. 1867, died; Samuel b. 1869; Joseph b. 1875, m. Maud Salisbury; John Henry, died; Martha Maud, m. Bertrand Kendall July 6, 1897. Families resided Nephi, Utah.
Elder. Blacksmith and farmer.

JONES, EDWARD (son of Edward Jones and Martha Jackson). Born Nov. 23, 1857, Nephi, Utah.
Married Sarah Jane Tolley Feb. 10, 1881, Salt Lake City (daughter of William Fisher Tolley and Sarah Warren, pioneers, Captain Stenhouse company). She was born Feb. 7, 1863, Fountain Green, Utah. Their children: Edward Leonard b. Dec. 26, 1881; William Louis b. Dec. 5, 1883; Jenerva b. Jan. 27, 1886, m. William M. Jenkins June 13, 1906; Franklin Roger b. Dec. 30, 1889; Charles Warren b. April 17, 1891; Harry Tolley b. June 11, 1893; Ruth Colen b. June 24, 1895; Donald Q. b. Aug. 11, 1897; Raymond Leon b. Dec. 30, 1900; Elma Louise b. Feb. 10, 1903; Waldo Leroy b. Aug. 13, 1905. Family home Nephi, Utah.
High priest. Farmer and stockraiser.

JONES, ELISHA (son of Thomas Jones and Mary Naylor). Born June 11, 1813, in Jefferson county, Ohio. Came to Utah 1850, Matthew Caldwell company.
Married Margeret Talbott, Jefferson Co., Ohio (daughter of Absalom Talbott and Sarah Mullholland of Maryland). Their children: Martha, m. Erastus D. Meacham; Thomas, died; Richard, m. Mary Cummings; William and James, died; John, m. Elizabeth Young; Mary, m. John Duke; Sarah, m. Isaac Cummings; Elizabeth, m. James Knight; Margaret Ellen, died; Elisha Warren b. June 7, 1849, m. Jane A. Pierce; Jacob Absalom, died; Joseph, m. Metta Maria Nielson, m. Sybil Seeley; Hyrum, m. Alice Ryan.
Married Sarah Ann Cummings (daughter of John Cum-

mings and Rachel Ann Canada, Heber City, Utah). She was born March 20, 1839. Their children: Samuel b. July 12, 1858, m. Margaret Fisher; Rachel Ann b. Jan. 8, 1861, m. Orson Henry Lee; Mary Malinda b. March 23, 1864, m. Joseph McDonald; Nancy Jane b. March 26, ——, m. Elmer Mahoney; John, m. Minnie Davis; Harmon, died; Susan, m. Albert Mitchell; Louisa, m. Harry Morris.
Married Anna Poulson at Provo, Utah.
Married Caroline Delight Allen (daughter of Joseph S. Allen and Lucy Morley, both of Nauvoo, Ill.). Their children: Simeon, m. Lulu Cordingley; Heber, died; Eliza, m. Thomas Houlton; Edward, m. Jane Clegg; Leonora, died; Caroline, m. Marion Lewis.
High priest; bishop of east ward, Heber City. Indian war veteran. Justice of the peace. Farmer; blacksmith and shoemaker. Died Aug. 1880, at Heber City.

JONES, ELISHA WARREN (son of Elisha Jones and Margeret Talbott). Born June 7, 1849, Kainesville, Iowa. Came to Utah with father.
Married Jane A. Pierce March 6, 1871, Heber City, Utah (daughter of George W. Pierce and Margeret Watson, Lockgalley, Scotland, pioneers, Thomas Watson company). She was born Nov. 7, 1853. Their children: William Thomas b. March 16, 1872, m. Margeret McKelprang; Margeret Elizabeth b. Oct. 4, 1874, m. Ulysses W. Grange; Jessie Squire b. Nov. 27, 1875, m. John Huggins Cordingley; Edward Franklin b. Aug. 30, 1877, died; Joseph Myron b. July 26, 1879, m. Alice Horrocks; Hyrum b. June 21, 1880, died; Sarah Jane b. Oct. 23, 1882, m. Quartus Sparks Catlin; Agnes Malinda b. June 3, 1885, m. Charles William Kimber; Martha May b. Sept. 9, 1887, m. Seymour D. Cordingley; Richard Warren b. Dec. 23, 1889, m. Jennie Provost; John Samuel b. Oct. 25, 1891; Hazel G. b. May 17, 1894; Francis Lamont b. March 2, 1897. Family home Heber City, Utah.
High priest; teacher; home missionary; secretary and counselor elders quorum. Assessor and collector Emery Co., Utah.

JONES, JOSEPH (son of Elisha Jones and Margeret Talbott). Born May 18, 1854, Provo, Utah.
Married Metta Maria Nielsen June 1880, Heber City, Utah (daughter of Jens Nielsen and Annie Christina, Heber City, Utah). She was born Sept. 6, 1864, died Oct. 24, 1894. Their children: Margaret Ellen b. April 3, 1881, m. Carl R. Marcusen; James b. July 30, 1883, m. Laura Gallaway; Elisha Ernest b. May 25, 1885, m. Maud Ward; Joseph Alvin b. Nov. 20, 1887, d. Feb. 12, 1892; Noah b. March 14, 1890, d. child; Christine Myrtle b. April 16, 1891, d. April 20, 1891; Metta Mable b. June 4, 1892; Annie Christina b. Oct. 15, 1894. Family home Price, Utah.
Married Lottie Sybil Seeley June 20, 1901, at Salt Lake City (daughter of Don Carlos Seeley and Hannah E. Seeley Reynolds). Their children: Clarissa Elizabeth b. June 25, 1903; Reta Hannah b. July 5, 1905; Wilton Carlos b. July 28, 1908; Ivan b. Dec. 17, 1910, d. Dec. 29, 1910; Rolland Seeley b. Dec. 16, 1912.
Member of presidency of seventies; missionary to southern states 1889, to California 1903-04; Sunday school superintendent; high priest. Farmer and merchant.

JONES, EVAN (son of John Jones of Llanegwad and Susannah Titus of Brechfa, Caermarthenshire, South Wales). Born July 13, 1829, at Felingwon, Caermarthenshire. Came to Utah Sept. 2, 1868, Simpson M. Molen company.
Married Jane Thomas January, 1858, Swansea, Glamorganshire (daughter of David Thomas and Elizabeth Nash of Neyland, Pembrokeshire, pioneers Sept. 4, 1866, Thomas E. Ricks company). She was born April 10, 1838. Their children: Elizabeth Susannah b. Jan. 20, 1859, m. Parley W. Price; Sarah Jane b. Dec. 12, 1860, m. John H. Lloyds; John Claudius b. Feb. 3, 1863, m. Luella Croft; Joseph Hyrum b. Oct. 24, 1864, died; Parley Parker b. July 4, 1867, m. Margaret Jyort; Evan James b. Feb. 10, 1870, m. Eliza E. Tanner; David William b. March 8, 1872, m. Clara Parks; Leander Thomas b. March 26, 1879, m. Ida Carlson; Mary Ann b. aug. 1, 1877, m. David Andrew; Charles Henry b. March 6, 1880, died. Family home Logan, Utah.
High priest; missionary to South Wales 1893-95. Ran first steam plow on President Young's farm, Jordan River; first train to Logan, Utah, to Idaho and Montana on the Utah Northern; also steamer "Garfield" on Salt Lake for three years.

JONES, HOPKINS (son of Thomas and Mary Jones, both of Neath, Wales). Born Jan. 25, 1824, Neath, Wales. Came to Utah 1865, Captain Willis oxteam company.
Married Winnifred Morris July 4, 1846, at Neath (daughter of William Morris and Lucy Hughes), who was born Oct. 12, 1828. Their children: Mary b. March 7, 1848, m. Currie H. Banks; Martha b. Nov. 19, 1851, m. Bernard McAdams; Lucy b. Dec. 4, 1854, m. Abraham Liddell, Family home Neath, Wales.
Member seventies; missionary to St. George, Utah; teacher; president of branch in Neath, Wales. Guard in Salt Lake City against Indians. Mason and stonecutter. Died April 28, 1897, Salt Lake City.

JONES, JAMES NAYLOR (son of Thomas Jones and Mary Naylor). Born April 3, 1810. Came to Utah in 1850.
Married Caroline Delight Allen. Their children: Mary b. Dec. 4, 1856, m. Henry Boren; Lucy b. September, 1859,

burned to death Oct. 25, 1860; Isaac Morley b. Aug. 3, 1862, m. Anne Elizabeth Starkie; Lovina b. Feb. 8, 1864, m. William Coleman Boren; James Naylor b. Nov. 18, 1865, m. Mary Ann Bodily. Family resided Heber and Fairview, Utah.
High priest; bishop's counselor. Called to The Muddy. First white man that ever wintered at Marysville. Farmer and stockraiser. Died Aug. 14, 1865, North Bend, Utah.
Caroline Delight Allen married Elisha Jones after the death of her husband—James Naylor Jones. Their children: Leonora b. Jan. 30, 1868, d. infant; Eliza b. June 7, 1869, m. Thomas E. Moulton; Simeon b. Dec. 30, 1872, m. Lula Cordingly; Heber b. June 3, 1874, d. Aug. 11, 1891; Edward A. b. Nov. 8, 1877, m. Jane Clegg; Caroline A. b. Dec. 22, 1879, m. Marian Lewis. Family home Heber, Utah.

JONES, ISAAC MORLEY (son of James Naylor Jones and Caroline Delight Allen). Born Aug. 3, 1862, Fairview, Utah.
Married Anne Elizabeth Starkie Dec. 4, 1890, Merrills ward, Uinta Co., Utah (daughter of Edward John Starkie and Ann Spray of Yorkshire, Eng., came to Utah July 3, 1878). She was born Oct. 11, 1869. Their children: Morley b. Oct. 30, 1891; Mary Elizabeth b. March 15, 1893; Sarah Rosalin b. March 5, 1895; Isaac Allen b. Dec. 16, 1897; Caroline Mabel b. Oct. 22, 1899; Lucy Viola b. Dec. 23, 1901; Warren Starkie b. Feb. 21, 1904; Rachel Ann b. March 28, 1906; Olive Florette b. April 14, 1909; Albert Edward b. July 19, 1911. Family home Maeser, Uinta Co., Utah.
High priest; president Y. M. M. I. A.; assistant Sunday school superintendent nine years; president deacons' quorum; counselor in elders' quorum; ward teacher 25 years. Boss-farmer, teaching the Indians how to farm, on Uinta Reservation, and later transferred to White Rock, Indian Agency 1886. Farmer and miller.

JONES, JENKIN (son of Thomas Jones, born Feb. 13, 1814, Penfra Farm, and Elizabeth Jenkins, born June 10, 1813, Ton Farm, both of Ystradyfodog, South Wales). He was born July 17, 1840, Park Isha Farm, Ystradyfodog. Came to Utah fall of 1867, handcart company.
Married Mary E. Jones Aug. 31, 1870 (daughter of Griffith Jenkins), who was born June 20, 1846. Their children: Catherine Palmer b. March 29, 1872, m. W. H. Palmer Nov. 3, 1907; Annie b. Oct. 17, 1873, m. James T. Jones Jan. 23, 1905; Mary E. b. Sept. 5, 1875; Margaret b. June 10, 1876, M. E. R. Jones June 8, 1908; Jenkin b. Nov. 25, 1880; Evan b. Oct. 21, 1882; Thomas b. June 12, 1884. Family home Malad City, Idaho.
Bishop of Malad ward five years; missionary to Wales. Treasurer of Oneida county; mayor of Malad City.

JONES, JENKIN, JR. (son of Jenkin Jones and Mary E. Jones). Born Nov. 25, 1880, Malad City, Idaho.
Connected with city government, Malad, last eight years; clerk district court, Fifth judicial district, Oneida county; also deputy auditor and recorder, Oneida county.

JONES, JOHN D. (son of Moses Jones of Mt. Pisgah, Iowa). Born at Mt. Pisgah. Came to Utah by ox team.
Married Susan Boren. Their children: John E., m. Laura Johnson; Billie, died; Minerva, m. Grayham Daley; Sharles E., m. Martha J. Jones; Rosy B., m. Jed Robinson; Annie; Irvine, m. Millie Barrett. Family home Provo, Utah.
Married Lena B. Sims Dec. 18, 1907, Provo, Utah (daughter of Frederick Sims and Margaret Nelson of Lee County, Ill., came to Utah 1885). She was born June 18, 1869. Only child: Ralph Waldo b. Sept. 28, 1908.
Assisted in bringing immigrants to Utah. Farmer.

JONES, CHARLES E. (son of John D. Jones and Susan Boren). Born April 19, 1868, San Bernardino, Calif.
Married Martha J. Jones May 15, 1888, Provo, Utah, at Manti temple (daughter of John G. Jones and Mary John of Lancashire, Eng., pioneers 1852). She was born April 6, 1867. Their children: Charles Alma b. Sept. 3, 1890, m. Julia Sackett; La Real b. Dec. 7, 1892; John Gilbert b. Dec. 21, 1901; Martha Adelaid b. Oct. 27, 1903, died; Etta Jane b. June 7, 1905; Florence Irene b. Aug. 8, 1908. Family home Provo, Utah.
Member 134th quorum seventies; missionary to southern states 1898 to 1901; Sunday school and block teacher. Farmer. School teacher.

JONES, JOHN G. Born Nov. 27, 1830, in Wales. Came to Utah 1852.
Married Mary John. Their children: Adelaid, m. John Meldrum; David H., m. Dianthia Petty; Mary Ann, m. Richard Nuttall; Daniel, died; Eleazor, m. Mary James; Martha m. Charles E. Jones; Shadrach, m. Josephine Cannon; Lizzie Thomas, m. Susa Barton; Bennie, died. Family home Provo Utah.
Seventy; missionary to Wales; patriarch. Farmer. Stone mason.

JONES, JOHN PIDDING (son of Isaac Jones and Mary Pidding of Wiltshire, Eng., latter born May 1774). He was bor June 10, 1819, Greenber Field, Yorkshire. Came to Uta Oct. 6, 1852, James K. Maxwell company.
Married Margaret Lee about 1840 (daughter of Joseph Le and Margaret Crosby of England). She was born April 1

1821, Liverpool, Eng. Their children: John Lee b. May 18, 1841, m. Rachel Simkins Jan. 14, 1862; Joseph William b. Oct. 26, 1843; Daniel L. b. May 6, 1847; Sylvester F. b. Dec. 5, 1848, m. Susannah Melling 1871; Frederick Isaac b. Feb. 6, 1851, m. Mary McKelprang Dec. 23, 1874; Elizabeth b. Dec. 13, 1853, m. Joseph Perry; Isaac Charles, d. infant; Hyrum b. May 3, 1859, m. Lucy Jones; Margretta Jane b. Sept. 16, 1861, m. William W. Dailey; Mary Crosby b. July 3, 1864, m. Nelson B. Dailey. Family home Cedar City, Utah.
Adjutant Company D, Iron Military district, 1857-59. Iron molder and machinist with Deseret Iron Company five years.

JONES, JOHN LEE (son of John Pidding Jones and Margaret Lee). Born May 18, 1841. Came to Utah with father.
Married Rachel Simkins Jan. 14, 1862, Cedar City, Utah (daughter of James Simkins and Jane Kirkbride), who was born Nov. 3, ——. Their children: John James b. Oct. 14, 1862, m. Louisa Dover June 4, 1884; Isaac b. Sept. 22, 1864, m. Elizabeth Melling 1884; Jane Kirkbride b. June 1, 1866, m. James A. Bryant; Samuel Bell b. Jan. 8, 1869; Ward b. Aug. 16, 1870, m. Ada Smith 1893; Rachel Margret b. March 6, 1872, m. Jesse Sterling; Rachel Margret b. Dec. 31, 1874, m. Alma Mathews Sept. 7, 1898; James Simkins b. March 17, 1877, m. Esther Alice LeFevre Sept. 15, 1904; Violet Ann b. March 4, 1879, m. Elroy Wood Oct. 2, 1907; Orson Pratt b. Feb. 10, 1882; Myron Simkins b. March 4, 1884; Jessie Lee b. Dec. 17, 1886; Lilly Maud Simkins and Pearl Simkins (twins) b. Nov. 16, 1888; Leonard Willemont b. Dec. 6, 1893. Family resided Enoch and Cedar City, Utah.
Married Betty Marsden Walker Feb. 6, 1879, St. George, Utah (daughter of Joseph Walker and Emma Smith), who was born March 15, 1858, Cedar City, Utah. Their children: Rosetta b. Dec. 19, 1878; Emily Rachel b. Dec. 23, 1882; Mattie Walker b. Jan. 27, 1885; Ida Walker b. Feb. 24, 1887; Ruben Walker b. June 9, 1889; George Wilford b. March 6, 1892; Willard Walker b. Jan. 7, 1895; Blanche Walker b. April 20, 1887; Grace Ashton b. Oct. 16, 1899.
Missionary to Great Britain 1879-81. Settled at Cedar City 1853. Participated in Echo Canyon campaign. Assisted in bringing immigrants to Utah. Indian war veteran. Assisted in establishing fort in Long Valley, Utah.

JONES, JAMES SIMKINS (son of John Lee Jones and Rachel Simkins). Born March 17, 1877, Enoch, Iron Co., Utah.
Married Esther Alice LeFevre Sept. 15, 1904, St. George (daughter of William LeFevre and Hannah Hollyoak of Orton [now Spry], Utah). She was born Sept. 3, 1883. Their children: James Chester b. Sept. 20, 1905; La Fevre b. May 26, 1907; Lavawn b. Oct. 12, 1909; Devor b. April 16, 1910; Eddie Lee b. Aug. 7, 1912. Family home Tabby, Wasatch Co., Utah.
Member 97th quorum seventies; missionary to Society Islands 1900-03; bishop Tabiona ward, Tabby, Utah; 2d assistant superintendent Sunday school, Enoch, Iron Co., Utah; president Y. M. M. I. A. at Enoch. Farmer.

JONES, JOHN R. (son of Roger and Amelia Jones of Hereford, Herefordshire, Eng.). Born July 24, 1829. Came to Utah 1860.
Married Agnes Martin July 15, 1864, Salt Lake City (daughter of George L. Martin and Janet Osborne of Kilmarnock, Ayrshire, Scotland, came to Utah 1872). She was born Oct. 17, 1829. Their children: George M. (adopted), m. Hortense M. Lang; Henry, d. infant; John, d. infant; Janet, m. Frank McDonald; Allen, d. aged 2. Family home, Salt Lake City.
Seventy; high priest; 2d counselor to Bishop Schoenfeld. Farmer; sheepraiser; freighter. Died 1909 in Mexico.

JONES, GEORGE MARTIN (adopted son of John R. Jones and Agnes Martin). Born June 19, 1858, Kilmarnock, Ayrshire, Scotland. Came to Utah Sept. 20, 1864, Joseph S. Rawlins company.
Married Hortense Marie Lang Oct. 26, 1882, Salt Lake City (daughter of John Daniel Lang and Josephine Laporte of Geneva, Switzerland, came to Utah 1869). She was born July 2, 1859. Their children: Josephine Lang b. Aug. 5, 1883, m. Orson F. Christensen Oct. 12, 1904; Hortense Lang b. Feb. 8, 1885; Agnes Lang b. Sept. 5, 1886, m. Jonathan Lloyd; Jeanette Lang b. June 5, 1888, m. Nathan O. Fullmer; George Lang b. March 25, 1890, d. Aug. 1, 1902; Daniel Lang b. Jan. 10, 1892, d. July 27, 1902; Louise Lang b. Aug. 29, 1894, d. Sept. 12, 1902; Allan b. June 26, 1898, d. June 26, 1898; Evan Stevens b. Nov. 4, 1899, d. Aug. 4, 1902. Family resided Salt Lake City and Richfield, Utah.
High priest; president first elders' quorum Sevier stake; Sevier stake chorister 1897-1910; Sevier stake tithing clerk; stake clerk; clerk of high council; clerk of high priests' quorum. Railroader in Salt Lake City on Utah Central, Union Pacific, O. S. L., and Saltair lines. Merchant.

JONES, MERLIN (son of Samuel Jones, born 1761 at North Haven, died May 21, 1810, and Sally Macks, born 1763, Wallingford, Conn., died Feb. 3, 1815). He was born May 16, 1795, North Haven, Conn. Came to Utah Sept. 15, 1852, Captain Tidwell company.
Married Roxana Ives Aug. 17, 1820, Wallingford, Conn. (daughter of Joel Ives, born April 16, 1760, died June 2, 1808, and Olive Ives, born April 20, 1758, died March 14, 1822, of Wallingford—married Oct. 22, 1778). Their children: Horace b. May 24, 1821, d. July 17, 1821; Minerva Leantine b. June 4, 1822, m. Amos Pease Stone; Ruth Ives b. Nov. 19, 1824, m. Davis Bartholomew, d. March 10, 1911; Olive Ann b. June 1, 1829, m. Lorin Farr; Miles Hudson b. Jan. 27, 1835. Family resided Wallingford and North Haven.
Married Mary Ann Pinfield (Heath) Feb. 9, 1867, Salt Lake City (daughter of John Pinfield and Mary Gray), who was bo n Aug. 25, 1819, in England; died Dec. 20, 1896, Ogden, Utah.

JONES, MILES HUDSON (son of Merlin Jones and Roxana Ives). Born Jan. 27, 1835, at North Haven. Came to Utah with father.
Married Ann Elizabeth Rollins Jan. 27, 1864, Ogden, Utah (daughter of David Rollins, born April 1811, Eaton Bray, died Sept. 12, 1870, Ogden, Utah, pioneer 1852, and Mary Ann Sharrett, born Jan. 6, 1814, London, Eng., died March 13, 1880, Ogden, Utah). She was born Sept. 12, 1846, Eaton Bray, Bedfordshire, Eng., died Nov. 27, 1877, Ogden, Utah. Came to Utah Sept. 3, 1852, Abraham O. Smoot company. Only child: Miles L. b. Oct. 31, 1866, m. Isabell Chase. Family home, Ogden.
Married Rachel Morton Dec. 29, 1881, Salt Lake City (daughter of John Morton, born Nov. 15, 1806, Cheshire, Eng., died Dec. 26, 1884, Salt Lake City, and Ann Jones, born June 7, 1812, Stockport, Cheshire, died June 1, 1888, Ogden, Utah). She was born April 6, 1851, Macclesfield, Eng.
First counselor to President Amos P. Stone, Mound Fort district. Served in Echo Canyon campaign. Assisted in bringing immigrants to Utah.

JONES, MILES L. (son of Miles Hudson Jones and Ann Elizabeth Rollins). Born Oct. 31, 1888, Logan, Utah (daughter of Elisha Wells Chase, born April 21, 1830, Sparta, Livingston county, N. Y., pioneer 1848, and Harriet Barker, born Aug. 29, 1836, LeRay, Jefferson county, N. Y.—married April 30, 1860, Salt Lake City). She was born May 12, 1868, at Ogden. Their children: Harriet Ann b. July 30, 1889; Raymond Miles b. Oct. 8, 1891; Ezra Byron b. Aug. 20, 1893; Olive May b. Oct. 14, 1895; Marion b. April 28, 1897; Wilbur b. Aug. 11, 1899; Elizabeth b. Dec. 10, 1902; Lois b. Aug. 9, 1905.
Bishop of seventh ward; missionary to England 1905-07; superintendent Y. M. M. I. A.; assistant superintendent Mound Fort Sunday school. City councilman.

JONES, NATHANIEL VARY (son of Samuel Jones and Lucinda Wheelock of Brighton, now Rochester, N. Y.). Born Oct. 13, 1822, Brighton, N. Y. Came to Utah July 20, 1849, with contingent of Mormon Battalion.
Married Rebecca Maria Burton March 14, 1845, Nauvoo, Ill. (daughter of Samuel Burton and Ann Shipley of Leamington, West Canada, former a pioneer), who was born Feb. 16, 1826. Their children: Clara L., m. John W. Young; Harriet C., m. Richard V. Morris, m. J. W. Pickett; Nathaniel V., m. Janet I. Swan, m. Elizabeth D. Barlow, m. Barbara E Morris; Mary A, m. Stanley H. Clawson; Fredrick B., d. 1881; William B. Family home, Salt Lake City.
Married Caroline M. Garr Oct. 9, 1856, Salt Lake City (daughter of Fielding Garr). The only child was Mark V. b. Jan. 3, 1863, m. Elizabeth Taylor, m. Lovinia A. Talbot.
Married Eliza Reed March 21, 1857, Salt Lake City. The only child was Mary L. b. Dec. 21, 1859, m. Adeline M. Monteith; Seth V. b. May 16, 1862, m. Annie B. Layton.
Bishop 15th ward, Salt Lake City; missionary to eastern states, Hindoostan, India and England; elder. Took part in Echo Canyon campaign; 1st lieutenant cavalry, Nauvoo legion life guard battalion. First alderman of 2d ward; city councilman Salt Lake City. Carried mail from Salt Lake City to Deer Creek, Wyo. Died Feb. 15, 1863.

JONES, NATHANIEL VARY (son of Nathaniel Vary and Rebecca M. Burton). Born Nov. 9, 1850, Salt Lake City.
Married Janet I. Swan Dec. 24, 1872, Salt Lake City (daughter of George Swan and Agnes McDonald of Edinburgh, Scotland), who was born Aug. 1, 1850. Their children: Agnes S. b. Oct. 20, 1873, m. John W. Twigges; Julia B. b. May 23, 1875, m. Henry E. Sharaven; Janet I. b. March 21, 1877, m. P. P. Targetta; Isabel b. March 14, 1879; Nathala V. b. Nov. 4, 1881, m. Benjamin T. Clark.
Married Elizabeth D. Barlow (daughter of James M. Barlow and Susan Mott). Their children: Lillian V. b. Nov. 17, 1886, m. C. Grant Bird; Clara L. b. Jan. 12, 1890; Calvin B. b. May 31, 1892; Aaron B. b. Oct. 17, 1895. Family resided at Salt Lake City.
Member 32d quorum seventies; high priest; missionary to northern states 1876-77; counselor in bishopric of 15th ward; counselor in presidency high priests quorum Salt Lake stake; president high priests quorum Granite stake. Collector and deputy sheriff of Salt Lake county 1875-86. Lawyer.

JONES, RICHARD (son of Richard Jones, born 1790, and Elizabeth Greenland, born 1791, London Eng.). Born Oct. 4, 1824, London. Came to Utah Oct. 4, 1863, Thomas E. Ricks company.
Married Naomi Parsons in 1850, who was born May 22, 1830, and came to Utah with husband. Their children: Richard Jr. b. Sept. 21, 1850, m. Viola Cazier November 1870; Elizabeth b. March 9, 1852, m. David J. Evans; John b. Oct. 7, 1853, m. Rhoda Berrett Feb. 16, 1874; Sarah

b. Feb. 12, 1855; m. David Francis; Charles A. b. Dec. 30, 1857, m. Catherine Beckstead Oct. 16, 1879; William b. March 2, 1860; Mary Ann b. Oct. 30, 1862, m. Joseph Rhodes Dec. 1881. Family home North Ogden, Utah.
Married Elizabeth Mickham 1870, Salt Lake City, who was born Feb. 14, 1836, London, Eng. Their children: Emma G. b. Oct. 24, 1870, m. George E. Chadwick March 8, 1893; Rosabel b. April 3, 1872, m. Frederick Berrett 1893; Abraham b. March 17, 1873, m. Mary Brunker Sept. 4, 1896; Mary E. b. Dec. 13, 1874, m. A. G. Graham June 19, 1893; Joseph E. b. Jan. 18, 1877, m. Vilda A. Perks; Eva b. May 25, 1878, m. Melvin Godfrey March 4, 1897. Family home, Ogden and Greenville, Cache Co., Utah.
President of branch in London two years; president of elders' quorum in North Ogden 33 years. Sailor and stevedore 25 years in Europe, Asia, Africa and America.

JONES, RICHARD Jr. (son of Richard Jones and Naomi Parsons). Born Sept. 21, 1850, London, Eng. Came to Utah with parents.
Married Viola Cazier in November 1870, Salt Lake City (daughter of Benjamin Cazier and Olive Shaw, former pioneer Oct. 10, 1863, Thomas E. Ricks company). She was born at North Ogden, Utah. Their children: Olive Naomi b. Oct. 21, 1871; Permelia b. Nov. 7, 1874, m. Frank Carpenter; Richard B. b. Oct. 27, 1876, m. Dianna Weisinger; John Clarence b. Oct. 3, 1878, m. Myrtle Lucile Nov. 14, 1907; Viola Ann b. Sept. 9, 1884, m. Phillip Ferrin Sept. 15, 1897; Sarah Manerva b. July 1, 1884, m. David Chard.
Clerk of elders quorum.

JONES, JOHN (son of Richard Jones and Naomi Parsons). Born Oct. 1, 1853, at London, Eng. Came to Utah with parents.
Married Rhoda Berrett Feb. 16, 1874, at Salt Lake City (daughter of Robert Griffin Berrett and Sarah Ann Woodhead, of North Ogden, Utah), who was born Jan. 19, 1856, at North Ogden. Their children: John Arthur b. Jan. 3, 1875, m. Rachel Heninger; Charles William b. Oct. 14, 1876; Sarah Naomi b. Nov. 27, 1878, d. Aug. 14, 1879; Rhoda Pearl b. Aug. 2, 1880; Mary Elizabeth b. Dec. 23, 1882, m. Samuel Randall; Jennie May b. Sept. 25, 1884, m. William E. Shaw; Charlotte Emily b. Aug. 29, 1886, m. Nathaniel Bailey; Robert Berrett b. Sept. 4, 1888, d. Dec. 23, 1888; James Edmund b. April 16, 1891, m. Hazel Bell Berrett; Elsie Ireta b. Oct. 30, 1893; Carl Henry b. June 28, 1897. Family home, North Ogden.
Ordained elder Feb. 16, 1874. Farmer and miner. Died May 15, 1910.

JONES, RICHARD (son of William and Mary Thomas Jones of Llangranog, Cardigan, South Wales; former born March 18, 1771, and latter Jan. 1, 1783). He was born March 5, 1819, at Llangranog. Came to Utah Sept. 27, 1851.
Married Mary Evans Jones Aug. 20, 1848 (daughter of William and Ellinor Hughs Evans), who was born Nov. 8, 1825, and came to Utah with husband. Their children: Ellen b. Aug. 29, 1850, m. Oliver Haskins May 7, 1873; Mary Jane b. Jan. 17, 1853, m. Benjamin D. Evans Oct. 10, 1872; Rachel Ann b. May 30, 1855, m. Benjamin L. Thomas; Richard E. b. Nov. 10, 1857, m. Louisa Lusk Dec. 20, 1883; William E. b. March 18, 1860, m. Cynthia M. Lusk Dec. 2, 1885; Hannah M. b. Oct. 24, 1864, m. Enoch Sawyer 1898; David E. b. April 7, 1867, m. Catherine Evans May 23, 1890.
Active church worker. Settled at Salt Lake City, moved to Brigham City in 1853, and in 1865 moved to Malad City, Idaho.

JONES, RICHARD E. (son of Richard Jones and Mary Evans). Born Nov. 10, 1857, Brigham City, Utah.
Married Louisa Lusk Dec. 20, 1883, Salt Lake City (daughter of John W. and Martha Tidwell Lusk), who was born July 9, 1862, Wellsville, Utah. Their children: Darias L. b. Dec. 28, 1884; Daniel L. b. Jan. 24, 1886; John L. b. Jan. 21, 1887; Richard L. b. Nov. 11, 1888; Harvey L. b. Aug. 3, 1891, m. Catherine Price Sept. 4, 1911; Lavern b. Aug. 9, 1897; Mary A. b. May 21, 1904.
Missionary to Great Britain 1899-1901; seventy.

JONES, SAMUEL STEPHEN (son of Samuel Jones and Sarah Bradshaw of Rose Cottage, Ealing Lane, Brentford, Middlesex, Eng.). Born Feb. 9, 1837, seven miles from London, Eng. Came to Utah Sunday, Nov. 30, 1856, Edward Martin and Daniel Tyler "frozen" handcart company. This was the handcart company that endured so much suffering on the plains, loosing fully one-third of their number. About 586 persons started on this memorable journey. He was the secretary and clerk of the company.
Married Lydia E. Hooker Feb. 9, 1857, Provo, Utah (daughter of William Hooker of Kent, Eng.), who was born Aug. 18, 1837, and died Dec. 21, 1874. Their children: Mary Ann Sarah b. July 7, 1858, m. W. C. A. Smoot, Jr.; Samuel William b. Feb. 11, 1861, d. Oct. 18, 1861; Ady Rosena b. Aug. 18, 1862, d. Nov. 13, 1863; Annie L. b. Sept. 24, 1864, m. George Atkin, Jr.; Charles Albert b. Oct. 7, 1866, d. Sept. 17, 1867; Grace Darling b. Nov. 24, 1868, d. October, 1869; Arthur Wellington b. Jan. 28, 1870, d. Feb. 12, 1870; Vermelia b. July 21, 1871, d. August, 1871; Lydia Maud b. Sept. 30, 1874, d. April 15, 1875. Family home Provo, Utah.
Married Julia Ipson, Aug. 27, 1867, Endowment House, Salt Lake City. Her parents lived at Bornholm, Denmark. She was born Jan. 11, 1847, Bornholm, and came to Utah 1854. Their children: Christina Maria b. Aug. 28, 1868, m. Frank Thomas; Albert Stephen b. Jan. 15, 1871, m. Sadie E.

Fletcher; Rasmus Eugene b. June 16, 1874, m. Alice Teasdale; Alma Andrew b. Jan. 5, 1877, d. June 28, 1880. Family home Provo, Utah.
Married Annie Maria Johnson Dec. 27, 1875, Endowment House, Salt Lake City (daughter of John Peter Rasmus Johnson and Caroline Maria Tuft of Denmark, pioneers 1854). She was born Sept. 15, 1858. Their children: Samuel Johnson b. Oct. 16, 1876, m. Effie May Fenn; John Milton b. Oct. 3, 1878, m. Lulu Lameraux; Horatio b. Oct. 23, 1880, m. Elizabeth Silver; Lydia Geneve b. Feb. 19, 1883; Pearl b. Feb. 7, 1886; Ralph Harry b. May 23, 1888; Eva Caroline b. Oct. 14, 1891; Lucille Emma b. Aug. 17, 1893, d. March 29, 1894. Family home Provo, Utah.
Married Emma Jane Allman July 26, 1878, Endowment House, Salt Lake City (daughter of Thomas and Jane Allman), who was born Nov. 18, 1853, Salt Lake City, and died July 9, 1879. Only child: Ernest Allman b. June 18, 1879, d. Aug. 29, 1879.
One of the presidents of the 52d quorum seventies; high priest; missionary to Great Britain 1872-73; traveling elder London Conference; president Sheffield Conference; assistant editor "Millennial Star." Was instrumental in starting co-operative movement in Provo with A. O. Smoot and E. F. Sheets; the Provo Co-op antedated the Z. C. M. I, about one year. Owner of the S. S. Jones Mercantile Co., Provo and Price, Utah. Tie contractor, furnishing the Utah Southern Railway with ties at its beginning, and the Rio Grande Western with 147,000 in one year, between Provo and Price. He with T. R. Cutler organized the Sioux and Utah mines at Tintic, and has been largely interested in mining 1900-12. Made the big cut at the Jordan River narrows for power and irrigation. Interested with John T. Pope in asphalt, iron and oil properties in Uinta Co., Utah. Charcoal manufacturer; saw mill operator; railroad contractor. Author of "Adown Provo River," and many poems on Utah, especially "Utah's Natal Days" which was rendered on the state's 21st birthday, under the Bowery in President Brigham Young's presence, part of which he (Young) had repeated. "Home of the Old Years" and "The Life of the Master" are some of the masterpieces from his pen.

JONES, THOMAS (son of John and Ann Jones of South Wales). Born July 20, 1827. Came to Utah 1851.
Married Sage Treharne October, 1852 (daughter of William and Ann Treharne). Born Nov. 27, ——, came to Utah 1852, Dan Jones company. Their children: Alma Treharne b. Aug. 21, 1853, d. aged 4; Lehi Willard b. Nov. 15, 1854, m. Henrietta Lunt Feb. 12, 1878; Kumen b. May 5, 1856, m. Mary Neilson Dec. 19, 1878; Thomas Jedediah b. June 5, 1858, m. Ellen Eva Lunt Nov. 17, 1878; William Treharne b. Sept. 12, 1860, m. Keturah Arthur b. Dec. 27, 1881; Uriah Treharne b. Feb. 11, 1861, m. Mary Alice Cluff Feb. 7, 1883; Sarah Ann b. Feb. 11, 1861, m. Samuel A. Higbee Dec. 27, 1881. Family home Cedar City, Utah.

JONES, LEHI WILLARD (son of Thomas Jones and Sage Treharne). Born Nov. 15, 1854, Cedar City, Utah.
Married Henrietta Lunt Feb. 13, 1878, St. George, Utah (daughter of Henry Lunt and Mary Ann Wilson, latter pioneer 1857, Jessie B. Martin company). She was born Nov. 12, 1858, Cedar City. Their children: Thomas Willard b. Dec. 5, 1878, m. Sophia Forsyth June 25, 1902; Kumen Lunt b. Feb. 21, 1881, m. Ann Elizabeth Leigh June 26, 1907; Henry L. b. July 20, 1883; Henrietta Lunt b. Feb. 2, 1886, m. Ferdinand F. Hintze Sept. 3, 1908; Ann b. June 15, 1888, m. Robert S. Gardner Dec. 21, 1910; Lehi Milton b. Oct. 4, 1890; Martha b. Feb. 15, 1893, d. same day; Erastus L. b. Dec. 2, 1895; William b. Sept. 14, 1897. Family home Cedar City.
Mail contractor and carrier between Cedar City, Utah, and Bullionville, Nev. Justice of peace, city treasurer, city councilman, mayor and county commissioner. Member ward bishopric. Has done much for the development of southern Utah.

JONES, THOMAS (son of John R. Jones and Ann Evans of Dawlais, South Wales). Born July 24, 1858, at Dawlais. Came to Utah in August 1866, William Henry Chipman company.
Married Florence Taylor Jan. 1, 1883, at Lehi, Utah (daughter of James W. Taylor and Ann Rogers of Oldham, Eng., pioneers 1853). She was born Aug. 7, 1862, at Lehi. Their children: Marion, m. J. Edwin Smith; Gordon AD. 1906, Salt Lake City; Florence, m. David Firmage; J. Leonard; Maurice; Earl F.; Clarence; Verna Margrette; Norma; Alice; Leyland. Family home, Lehi.
Elder. Farmer.

JONES, THOMAS B. (son of Richard Jones of Denbighshire, North Wales). Born Oct. 16, 1820, at Denbighshire. Came to Utah in 1860, Captain Corbett company.
Married Diana Roberts 1840, Denbighshire, who was born in 1820. Their children: Amelia, m. John Griffiths; James R., m. Mary Ann ——; Robert R., m. Agnes Squires; Jane. aged 1; George D., m. Ann Thomas; Jane, m. Theodore (Augusta) Reamer; Samuel, d. infant. Family home 15th ward. Salt Lake City.
President of a branch in Wales. Coal miner; stone cutter for Salt Lake Temple. Died March 20, 1904.

JONES, GEORGE D. (son of Thomas B. Jones and Diana Roberts). Born Aug. 23, 1849, Denbighshire, North Wales. Came to Utah in 1860 with parents.
Married Ann Thomas 1868, Salt Lake City (daughter of Samuel Thomas and Sarah Jeremy of Caermarthenshire,

South Wales, pioneers 1849, Daniel Jones company). She was born June 22, 1848. Their children: Mary Ann b. Jan. 27, 1869, m. Sheridan Smith; George D., m. Hilda Lundgren; Eva, m. Robert E. Currie, d. aged 1; Benjamin, m. Mr. Parsons; Ada, d. aged 6; Samuel, m. Angie Anderson; Bertha D., m. Frederick Anderson; Claud, m. Celia Sanders. Family home 15th ward, Salt Lake City.
Miner; blacksmith; machinist. Died Dec. 10, 1902.

JONES, SAMUEL (son of George D. Jones and Ann Thomas). Born Jan. 1, 1879, Salt Lake City.
Married Angie Anderson Feb. 21, 1890, Salt Lake City. Bishop Ashton officiating (daughter of John Anderson and Awrey Little of Augusta, Ga., who came to Utah in 1889). She was born Nov. 25, 1882. Their children: Samuel Oddus b. Dec. 21, 1900, d. infant; George S. b. July 5, 1901; John Melvin b. May 12, 1904; Mildred E. b. June 9, 1907; Lena G. b. Jan. 23, 1909; Fred Norman b. Sept. 9, 1911. Family home 15th ward, Salt Lake City.
Brass and iron molder.

JONES, THOMAS C. (son of William Jones and Sarah Cornforth of Birmingham, Eng.). Born Feb. 11, 1825, Birmingham. Came to Utah Sept. 2, 1868, Daniel D. McArthur company.
Married Elizabeth Clarissa Blincke July 22, 1849, Birmingham (daughter of Edward Blincke of Birmingham), who was born April 27, 1826. Their children: Merentha Althera, m. Peter Miller, m. George Austin; Jeter Edward, m. Emma Thayne; Clarissa Elizabeth; Franklin Thomas; Brigham William. Family home, Salt Lake City.
Married Eliza Jesson Feb. 12, 1865, Birmingham (daughter of John Jesson and Elizabeth Beesley, former came to Utah Sept. 2, 1868, Daniel D. McArthur company). She was born Oct. 19, 1832. Their children: Sarah Elizabeth; John Heubert; Eliza Celestial; Cathrine Mary Louisa, m. William H. Harrison; Joseph Hyrum; Emma Susannah; Martha Amelia.
Married Mary Orgill June 27, 1870, Salt Lake City (daughter of Thomas and Mary Ann Orgill, pioneers Sept. 2, 1868, Daniel D. McArthur company). She was born May 31, 1848. Their children: Heber Lorenzo, m. Jemima Derrick; Charlotte Anne; Rhoda Ellen; Willard Charles; Joshua Wilford, m. Harriet Bagshaw; Julia Kate.
Member 13th quorum seventies; president New Hill district, England, 1851; recorder of 10th ward, Salt Lake City, 1880-87; member Tabernacle choir. Brushmaker. Died Sept. 11, 1887, Salt Lake City.

JONES, JETER EDWARD (son of Thomas C. Jones and Elizabeth Blincke). Born Feb. 9, 1852, Birmingham, Eng.
Married Emma Thayne Feb. 10, 1873, Salt Lake City (daughter of John Johnson Thayne and Sidney Boyer of Mill Creek, Utah, pioneers Sept. 3, 1861). She was born Sept. 10, 1855. Their children: Emma Clarissa b. Jan. 8, 1874, m. William J. Tidwell; William Edward b. Dec. 30, 1875, m. Mary Ann Rowley; John Johnson b. April 23, 1883, m. Rebecca Lusk. Family home, Salt Lake City.
Died July 16, 1883, in Idaho, killed by a train.
Emma Thayne afterward married George Millner, and they had the following children: Esther, m. George Brigham Grundvig, m. William Tidwell; George Bush; Arnold Seaton; Ernest Yardly.

JONES, WILLIAM EDWARD (son of Jeter Edward Jones and Emma Thayne). Born Dec. 30, 1875, Salt Lake City.
Married Mary Ann Rowley July 2, 1908, Logan, Utah (daughter of John Thompson Rowley and Mary Jane Smith of Spring Glen, Utah). She was born Dec. 5, 1887. Their children: Lewella b. Nov. 5, 1909; Irene b. Dec. 7, 1911. Family resided at Wellington and Spring Glen, Utah.
High priest; missionary to southern states 1904-06; first counselor to president of South Carolina mission; president deacons quorum of Sunnyside 1902-03; president Y. M. M. I. A. of Wellington 1906-08; member Emery stake Sunday school union board 1907-09; president third quorum elders 1908-09; second counselor to Bishop Edgar H. Thayne of Wellington ward 1908-11; superintendent Sunday school at Spring Glen. Justice of peace at Wellington 1906-07.

JONES, HEBER LORENZO (son of Thomas C. Jones and Mary Orgill). Born March 18, 1871, Salt Lake City.
Married Jemima Derrick Feb. 22, 1898, Salt Lake City (daughter of Zacariah Derrick and Mary Emma Horspooll of London, Eng., pioneers 1859, James S. Brown company). She was born May 17, 1872. Their children: Jemima b. Oct. 26, 1896, died; Heber Derrick b. Jan. 23, 1898; Hyrum Clifford b. Sept. 30, 1900; Mary Leon b. Oct. 15, 1902; Thelma b. March 10, 1905; Emma Marie b. June 1, 1907; Zacariah Thomas b. Oct. 14, 1910; Mamie Irene b. Sept. 28, 1912. Family home, Salt Lake City.
Elder; teacher. Engineer on D. & R. G. R. R. eight years. Member B. of L. E.

JONES, THOMAS E. (son of William Jones, born about 1779, and Catherine Jones, born about 1780, of Brosbury, Eng.). He was born April 5, 1811, Bishop's Frome, Herefordshire, Eng. Came to Utah Sept. 26, 1848, Heber C. Kimball company.
Married Mary Parson in 1836, who was born about 1805, died in England. Their child: William Parson b. Aug. 20, 1837, m. Elizabeth Shaw Feb. 25, 1858.
Married James Ann Males Jan. 16, 1842, at Nauvoo, Ill. She was born Oct. 25, 1816, Easnor, Herefordshire, Eng. Their children: Hannah; Isabell; John; Mary Ann, d. infant;

Robert Easnor, m. Sarah E. Nelson March 15, 1874; Thomas Males, m. Phebe Watts; Catherine Elizabeth, m. Archibald McFarland; Alverita C., m. George T. Halladay; James H., m. Sopha Deucheux March 22, 1884; Henry and Easnor, d. infants.
Married Jane Nelson in 1857 at Salt Lake City (daughter of William Nelson), who was born Sept. 26, 1823, Cumberland, Eng. Their children: Eliza b. July 4, 1858, m. Martin Mahnkin; Richard Nelson b. Feb. 2, 1860, m. Sarah Homme; Mary Ellen b. Dec. 21, 1861, m. T. Alma Sayer; Joseph Wilford, m. Harriet A. Robinson Dec. 9, 1896.
High priest.

JONES, JOSEPH WILFORD (son of Thomas E. Jones and Jane Nelson). Born Aug. 27, 1864, West Weber, Utah.
Married Harriet A. Robinson Dec. 9, 1886, at Lewisville, Idaho (daughter of Joseph Lee Robinson and Mary Taylor), who was born Oct. 1, 1871. Their children: Joseph Thomas b. Nov. 18, 1887, m. Coara M. Tall Oct. 11, 1905; Emma J. b. June 4, 1889, d. July 11, 1889; Mary Eliza b. June 24, 1890, m. William P. Sharp Oct. 4, 1911; Mabel b. Nov. 16, 1892, d. March 15, 1894; Ada A. b. Sept. 24, 1894, d. Jan. 22, 1895; Lee Albert b. Feb. 11, 1896; Sadie b. Oct. 27, 1899, d. Oct. 30, 1899; Clarence Wilford b. March 22, 1901; Francis Gilbert b. Sept. 11, 1903; Lulu Margarett b. Sept. 8, 1905; Louis Harold b. Jan. 22, 1909; Julius Melvin b. May 21, 1911; Ruth b. Jan. 31, 1913. Family home Lewisville (now Bybee), Utah.
Superintendent Sunday schools Center ward: bishop of Bybee ward; missionary to Nebraska 1897-98 and to Great Britain 1907-08; high councilor; home missionary. Early settler in Snake River valley. Farmer; stockraiser.

JONES, THOMAS J. Born 1804, South Wales. Came to Utah Sept. 23, 1854, Job Smith company.
Married Elizabeth Rees, Cefn Coyd Cymar, Brecknockshire, Wales. Only child: John R., m. Mary A. S. Ridd.
High priest. Killed by railroad accident 1886, Salt Lake City.

JONES, JOHN REES (son of Thomas J. Jones and Elizabeth Ree). Born 1847 in Brecknockshire. Came to Utah with father.
Married A. S. Ridd April 3, 1874, Salt Lake City (daughter of William Ridd and Sarah Squires of Devonshire, Eng., pioneers 1854, Job Smith company). She was born 1855, Salt Lake City. Their children: John R. b. April 7, 1875, m. Louise Meyer June 29, 1898; Thomas H. b. Oct. 28, 1876, m. Jane Gibson Sept. 25, 1901; William A. b. Dec. 14, 1878, m. Salina Evans Sept. 23, 1903; Albert J. b. July 26, 1882, m. Lilly Conday June 14, 1906; Ernest B. b. Aug. 17, 1884, m. Clara Folger June 5, 1909; Clarence E. b. July 18, 1888; Agnes M. b. March 31, 1890, m. Leroy Colton Sept. 5, 1911.
Elder; high priest; ward teacher. Worked on Salt Lake temple 10 years, and on assembly hall. Black Hawk Indian war veteran 1866.

JONES, JOHN REES, JR. (son of John Rees Jones and Mary A. S. Ridd). Born April 7, 1875, Salt Lake City.
Married Louise Meyer June 29, 1898, Salt Lake City (daughter of Christian Meyer and Louise Amstead of Berlin, Germany), who was born May 18, 1879. Their children: Vera Lose b. April 3, 1899; John Meyer b. Sept. 7, 1900; Alfred Clyde b. March 14, 1906; Edna b. Sept. 30, 1909, died; Alice Meyer b. March 12, 1912.
Elder; teacher. Foreman of Gallagher Trunk Company 20 years.

JONES, WILLIAM. Born 1798, Cayo, Caermarthenshire, South Wales. Came to Utah 1866.
Married Eleanor Evans in 1838, Llansawel, South Wales (daughter of John Evans of Bryndafydd), who was born in 1820. Came to Utah 1866. Their children: James, d. infant; James E.; David E.; William E.; Mary; John E.; Daniel; Elenor; Annie. Family home Malad City, Idaho.
Elder and president over branch in Wales. English soldier 21 years. Died in 1873, Malad City.

JONES, JAMES E. (son of William Jones and Eleanor Evans of South Wales). Born 1842, Lwynkelyn, Wales. Came to Utah Oct. 4, 1864, W. S. Warren company.
Married Anne Williams July 20, 1866, Malad Valley, Idaho (daughter of Thomas Williams and Anne Jones of Morganshire, South Wales, pioneers 1864, W. S. Warren company). She was born 1849. Their children: Olive Ann, m. Jan. 28, —; Eleanor J., died; Margaret; James T.; John W.; Daisy M.; Gwenfred. Family home Malad, Idaho. Commissioner. Railroader; farmer.

JONES, WILLIAM (son of William and Elizabeth Jones of Brimpsfield, Gloucestershire, Eng.). Born June 7, 1805, Brimpsfield. Came to Utah Aug. 18, 1868, Captain Murdock company.
Married Mary Shill June, 1828, at Brimpsfield (daughter of Robert Shill and Prudence Golding of Caudle Green, Gloucestershire, Eng.). Their children: Robert b. July 9, 1829, m. Harriet Tipper; Ann, d. child; Susan b. March 24, 1833, m. Henry Randall; Lucy, d. child; Rhoda b. Nov. 5, 1840, m. Samuel Bennion; Mary J. b. June 16, 1842, m. Thomas H. Stephens; Elizabeth b. Jan. 6, 1844, m. James Ure; Prudence b. July 4, 1847, m. Joseph Edgeworth. Family resided Brimpsfield, Eng., and Henefer, Utah.
Farm laborer. Assisted in building roads and ditches. Died July 7, 1889.

PIONEERS AND PROMINENT MEN OF UTAH

JONES, ROBERT (son of William Jones and Mary Shill). Born July 9, 1829, Washbrook, Gloucestershire, Eng. Came to Utah September 1866, Henry Chipman company.
Married Harriet Tipper Nov. 18, 1852, Cowley, Gloucestershire (daughter of William and Jane Tipper of Birdlip, Gloucestershire, Eng.). She was born May 2, 1824. Their children: Robert A. b. Feb. 19, 1854, m. Elizabeth J. Parker; William b. March 8, 1856, m. Caroline Toone; Mary Jane b. June 5, 1858, m. Albert F. Richens; George W. b. May 7, 1863, d. Jan. 29, 1865. Family home Nettleton, Gloucestershire, Eng., and Henefer, Utah.
Married Miriam Ann Richens Dec. 2, 1866, Croyden, Utah (daughter of William and Charlotte Richens, who were married at Sheepscombe, Eng., and came to Utah with Captain White company). Their children: Alfred R. b. Sept. 18, 1867, m. Elizabeth Edgeworth; Emma b. Nov. 9, 1869, m. James Salmon; John S. b. Feb. 18, 1871, m. Clara Toone; Amelia b. Nov. 26, 1872, m. Frank Rippon; Clara R. b. May 28, 1875, m. Charles S. Toone; Charles R. b. Feb. 12, 1877, m. Annie Faddies.
Married Agnes Caroline Peterson (daughter of Charles S. and Caroline Peterson), who was born in Denmark. The only child was Clarens Ray b. Sept. 18, 1893.
Sunday school superintendent 1870-92; first counselor to Bishop Richens 1869-92. Assisted in building Union Pacific railroad; worked on canyon and county roads, and on irrigating canals. Died April 27, 1906.

JONES, ROBERT ALLEN (son of Robert Jones and Harriet Tipper). Born Feb. 19, 1854, Birdlip, Gloucestershire, Eng.
Married Elizabeth Jane Parker June 16, 1873, Salt Lake City (daughter of Abraham Parker and Barbara Scott, who came to Utah March 31, 1871). She was born Sept. 16, 1855, Greencroft, Eng. Their children: T. A. b. June 4, 1874, m. Charlotte Judd; George F. b. Feb. 26, 1876, m. Isabel May Wright; John W. b. March 23, 1878, m. Lydia M. Marchant; Ellen M. b. June 28, 1880, m. Joseph W. Tanner; David W. b. Sept. 16, 1882; Barbara H. b. Nov. 5, 1885, m. Albert Peterson; Virginia b. May 23, 1888, m. Thomas Stevens; Irvin T. b. Aug. 28, 1890; Cheltina E. b. Aug. 11, 1893; Alice Isabel b. Jan. 9, 1896.
Missionary to England 1890-92; ward clerk 1885-1907. Justice of the peace 1884-90; school trustee 1893-97; surveyor of Summit county.

JONES, WILLIAM E. (son of Jenkin Jones of Vaynor, Breckcnockshire, South Wales). Born Feb. 18, 1824, Pantyskill, Vaynor, Brecknockshire. Came to Utah Sept. 24, 1851, James Brown company.
Married Mary Jones July 1, 1841, South Wales, who was born July 1, 1819. Their children: Ann b. Jan. 27, 1842; Jenkin b. April 21, 1843; Mary Ann b. Feb. 8, 1845; Elizabeth; Kesiah Jane b. July 16, 1855; Margret b. Oct. 10, 1857; Caroline b. Sept. 8, 1861; Martha b. Nov. 12, 1863. Family home Paragonah, Utah.
Bishop's counselor; bishop. Farmer. Died Feb. 24, 1897, Paragonah, Utah.

JONES, WILLIAM PARSONS (son of Thomas E. Jones, born April 5, 1811, Dosbery, Herefordshire, Eng., and Mary Parsons, who died in England in 1839). He was born Aug. 20, 1837, at Bosbery. Came to Utah in 1848, Heber C. Kimball company.
Married Elizabeth Shaw Feb. 25, 1858 (daughter of Paul Shaw and Ellen Fletcher), who was born May 23, 1837. Came to Utah 1857, Israel Evans company. Their children: William Clinton b. April 5, 1859; Thomas Lorenzo b. June 25, 1860, m. Mary Ann Hill Jan. 6, 1881; Elizabeth Ellen b. May 9, 1862; Annie Emily b. Oct. 9, 1863, m. Charles A. Peterson March 6, 1895; Mary Adaline b. Oct. 23, 1865, m. Joseph M. Thompson April 26, 1883; Agnes Elenor b. Oct. 13, 1867; James Franklin b. Jan. 18, 1869, m. Pamela Barlow Jan. 3, 1895; John Parsons b. April 15, 1871, m. Julett Wheeler June 15, 1899; Rebecca and Ruth b. March 13, 1874, Rebecca m. Arthur Whittar June 10, 1908, Ruth died; Cynthia Catherine b. June 9, 1877, m. Irvin Carrigan Dec. 15, 1903; Robert Joseph b. Nov. 25, 1879; Martha Alveretta b. Feb. 19, 1882, m. Dyan Taggart Oct. 5, 1905.
Missionary among the Indians; bishop; Sunday school superintendent. School trustee. Took part in Echo Canyon campaign; member of Utah militia; figured prominently in Morrisite trouble. Assisted in bringing immigrants to Utah. Settled at Salt Lake City; moved to Kaysville in 1851, and to South Weber in 1864.

JONES, JAMES F. (son of William Parsons Jones and Elizabeth Shaw). Born Jan. 18, 1869, South Weber, Utah.
Married Pamela E. Barlow Jan. 3, 1895, Salt Lake City (daughter of Israel Barlow and Annie Yates), who was born June 9, 1872, Bountiful, Utah. Their children: Leland Venice b. Jan. 1, 1896, Logan, Utah; Winford Franklin b. April 30, 1901, at Bountiful; Leora and La Vora b. Dec. 29, 1904, at Ogden; Erma b. Aug. 20, 1908. Family home South Weber, Utah.
Sunday school superintendent; ward clerk; counselor and secretary in Y. M. M. I. A.

JONES, WILLIAM R. (son of William Jones and Betsy Roberts of Manchester, Eng.). Born Feb. 4, 1821, in England. Came to Utah 1850.
Married Sarah Ann Wright 1853, Salt Lake City, John Taylor officiating. She was born July 13, 1829, and came to Utah with a handcart company. Their children: William R., m. Jessie Penrose; James S., m. Annie M. Sims; John T., d. infant; Patience Mary, m. Thomas W. Sims; Frank D., m. Carrie Mace. Family home 15th ward, Salt Lake City.
Seventy; high priest; block teacher. Tailor. Died May 24, 1906, Salt Lake City.

JONES, JAMES S. (son of William R. Jones and Sarah Ann Wright). Born Jan. 21, 1860, Salt Lake City.
Married Annie M. Silins March 17, 1886, Salt Lake City, by Bishop Pollord (daughter of Thomas Sims and Emma Amy Sharman of Morehanger, Bedfordshire, Eng., came to Utah May, 1895). She was born Sept. 7, 1865. Their children: Amy Florence b. Aug. 18, 1887, m. William H. Gourley; James H. b. May 28, 1889; Annie S. b. Jan. 31, 1891; Mary Clarice b. Dec. 25, 1901. Family home Salt Lake City. Elder; block teacher. Engaged in real estate. Capitalist.

JORDAN, JOHN (son of John Jordan, born June 21, 1775, Berkshire, Eng., and Charlot Townsend, born about 1777, Berkshire). He was born Jan. 4, 1812, Courtney, Berkshire. Came to Utah 1852, independent company.
Married Cynthia Elizabeth Phillips Feb. 18, 1842, who was born Dec. 7, 1813, died at Genessee, Kane county, Ill., March 25, 1847. Their children: Jacob Henry b. Dec. 6, 1842, in Michigan, d. San Pete county, Utah; John Phillips b. Aug. 31, 1845, m. Julia Smith, m. Dell McPeak.
Married Charlott Malinda Colvin Aug. 16, 1847, who was born Nov. 20, 1807, died b. 1851, in Iowa.
Married Eliza Humphreys Robins March 4, 1851 (daughter of Richard and Esther Humphreys), who was born March 2, 1814, Shropshire, Eng. Their children: Charlott Malinda b. Dec. 4, 1851, d. Oct. 22, 1856; Elizabeth Cynthia b. April 1, 1854, m. William Crawford; Joseph Hyrum b. June 4, 1856, m. Elizabeth M. Givens.
Married Mary Spiers 1864, at Salt Lake City. Their children: Eliza Dunlap b. March 5, 1865, d. Sept. 26, 1887; John James b. May 16, 1869; George B. b. Feb. 14, 1871; Mary Jane b. April 26, 1867, d. July 26, 1888; Allen S. b. July 1, 1874. Families resided at Heber City, Utah.
High priest; first counselor to John M. Murdock, president of high priests' quorum. Settled at Heber City 1859. Veteran Walker and Black Hawk Indian wars; took part in Echo Canyon trouble.

JORDAN, JOHN PHILIPS (son of John Jordan and Cynthia Elizabeth Phillips). Born Aug. 31, 1845, Michigan. Came to Utah in 1852.
Married Julia Smith Nov. 30, 1874, Scipio, Utah (daughter of Jackson Smith of Scipio), who was born May 1856. Their children: Mary Elizabeth b. Aug. 25, 1875, m. Charles Thompson; Eliza Ann b. April 24, 1877, m. William Barnes; Alice Maud and John Henry, died; Charlotte b. Sept. 7, 1882; Minnie Lenora b. April 24, 1884, m. John Wheeler; Edith Amy b. April 23, 1886, died.
Married Dell McPeak May 22, 1898, Daniel ward, Wasatch stake, who came to Utah 1887. Their children: Joseph b. June 1899, d. Oct. 19, 1910; Hyrum b. Dec. 28, 1900; Vera b. May 6, 1902; Charles William b. Nov. 22, 1904; Earl b. Jan. 30, 1906; Roy b. March 8, 1908.
Elder. Settled at Heber City in 1859. Black Hawk Indian war veteran. Farmer.

JORDAN, JOSEPH HYRUM (son of John Jordan and Eliza Humphreys Robins). Born June 4, 1856, Springville, Utah.
Married Elizabeth M. Givens Nov. 22, 1887, Wallsburg, Utah (daughter of James and Agness Givens, Heber City, Utah). She was born Feb. 4, 1867. Their children: William Elmer b. Feb. 26, 1889; James Alva b. March 5, 1891; Lenora b. March 30, 1894; Lillie b. April 11, 1898; Clarence b. July 30, 1900, d. Aug. 4, 1900. Family home Riverside, Idaho. Settled at Heber City 1860; moved to Snake River valley, Idaho, 1888; now lives at Blackfoot.

JORDON, GEORGE BORLAN (son of John Jordan and Mary Spears). Born Feb. 14, 1872, Heber City, Utah.
Married Emma Davis Oct. 12, 1897, Heber City, Utah, Robert Duke of Elkhorn ward officiating (daughter of William Davis and Mary Goddard of Elkhorn ward). She was born May 7, 1876. Their children: George Erving b. June 12, 1899; John William b. Feb. 26, 1901; Mary b. May 30, 1903; Minnie b. Aug. 28, 1908. Family resided Elkhorn ward and Heber City.
Elder. Farmer and ranchman.

JORGENSEN, HANS (son of Jorgen and Petra Nelsen of Fyen, Denmark). Born Oct. 13, 1827, Fyen. Came to Utah 1868.
Married Marie D. Brinck April 5, 1855, at Copenhagen, Denmark (daughter of Christopher Brinck and Maren Jacobsen of Stege, Moen, Denmark). She was born June 30, 1834. Their children: Lars Ferdinand Johnson, b. Nov. 21, 1858, m. Sine Smith and Johanne Thomsen; Sophie, m. Andrew Andersen; Caroline, m. David P. Rich; Anina, m. John E. Nielsen; Mary, m. Rasmus Andersen. Family home Bear River City, Utah.
High priest. Farmer. Died Nov. 5, 1889.

PIONEERS AND PROMINENT MEN OF UTAH

JORGENSEN, HANS. Born Nov. 29, 1795, Willinge Fyen, Denmark. Came to Utah 1853, John Forsgren company. Married Maren Christena Peterson, who was born Jan. 27, 1794. Their children: Jens, m. Mary Christensen; Lars; Jorgen Peter; Peter, m. Karen Peterson; Nels, m. Karen Jenson; Hans, m. Anna Helena Maryger.

HANSEN, HANS (son of Hans Jorgensen and Maren Christena Peterson). Born July 15, 1835, Trustrup Dorup, Fune, Denmark. Came to Utah 1859, Robert F. Neslen company. Married Anna Helena Maryger Jan. 8, 1860, Salt Lake City (daughter of Jorgen Maryger and Ellen Peterson of Venebar, Sjaelland, Denmark). She was born Aug. 23, 1840. Their children: Hans John b. Oct. 2, 1860, m. Alvida Marie Peterson; James b. March 15, 1862, m. Amelia Berg; Joseph Albert b. Jan. 3, 1864, d. Jan. 23, 1864; Niels b. Oct. 18, 1864, d. Oct. 18, 1864; Erastus Snow b. Nov. 30, 1865, m. Hanna Nette Mortensen, who died Dec. 22, 1866, and Mary S. Jensen; Lorenzo b. Sept. 30, 1867, m. Margaret Jane Williams; Mary Christena b. Oct. 8, 1869, m. James Orcen Welch; Alice Helena b. Oct. 8, 1869, m. James Olsen; Ephraim b. Nov. 4, 1871, d. Oct. 6, 1873; Emma Albertine b. July 12, 1873, m. Judson Welch; Abraham b. June 23, 1875, m. Mary Ellen Olsen; Willard b. April 4, 1877, m. Johanna Marie Steffensen; Sarah b. Nov. 25, 1878, m. Tim Parkensen; Caroline b. Nov. 7, 1880, m. Samuel D. Wilcox.
High priest. Justice of peace; policeman. Farmer; lumberman.

JORGENSEN, MADS (son of Jeppa Jorgensen of Cophenhagen, Denmark). Born March 7, 1832, at Copenhagen. Came to Utah 1859.
Married Eva Coderstrom of Göteborg, Sweden, who was born Feb. 23, 1842. Only child: Edward Johannas b. March 25, 1856, m. Eva Catherine Hansen Zobell.
Seventy; high priest; counselor to Bishops Madsen and John J. Johnson of Lake View ward; missionary to northern states 1878-81; to Scandinavia 1887-89; Sunday school superintendent; president of Y. M. M. I. A. of Lake View ward. Farmer. Died April, 1905, Lake View, Utah.

JORGENSEN, EDWARD JOHANNAS (son of Mads Jorgensen and Eva Coderstrom). Born March 25, 1856, Copenhagen, Denmark. Came to Utah July 24, 1870.
Married Eva Catherine Hansen Zobell Nov. 25, 1880, Salt Lake City (daughter of Ole Hansen and Annie Zobell of Sjeland, Denmark—came to Utah 1877). She was born Feb. 21, 1860. Their children: Edward Johannas b. Sept. 18, 1881, m. Chloe Blackburn June 10, 1903; Eva Catherine b. April 24, 1883, m. Oscar Blackburn Aug. 20, 1900; Joseph William b. Dec. 19, 1885, m. Mary Kelsey Oct. 24, 1905; m. Julia Akelund; Anna Maria b. Feb. 19, 1888, m. Albert Blackburn Nov. 21, 1906; Edna Marinda b. Nov. 30, 1890, d. June 11, 1891; Clara Minerva b. Dec. 8, 1891, m. Perry Miller Oct. 27, 1909; James Henry b. Sept. 10, 1895, died; Jesse Clarence b. March 23, 1901. Family home Clawson, Utah.
Member 95th quorum seventies; president Y. M. M. I. A. 1911; assistant Sunday school superintendent and ward teacher at Clawson. Settled at Provo 1870; moved to Clawson 1894, and was the first settler of that place; assisted in making canals, wagon roads and in developing the country.

JORGENSEN, MASS. Came to Utah 1859, oxteam company. Married Annie Jensen in Denmark. Their children: Margaret, d. aged 40; Hannah, m. John Madsen; Eva: Annie, m. Andrew Madsen; Rebecca. m. George Nixon; Ellen, m. Carl Christensen. Family home, Lake View.
Married Elvena Hansen, Salt Lake City. Their children: Mass; Alma; Heber; Abe, died young; Elvira; Sarah, d. aged 22. Family home, Lake View.
Missionary to Denmark; bishop of Lake View ward; Sunday school superintendent; Veteran Blackhawk war. Farmer. Died in 1907.

JORGENSEN (GEORGESEN), NIELS (son of Jorgen Knudson, born 1765, and Anna Sophia Nielsen, born Sept. 20, 1801, Karlebo, Denmark). Born Jan. 17, 1834, Hosterkjob, Birkerod, Fredericksberg, Denmark. Came to Utah October, 1884.
Married Johanna M. Kofoed July 24, 1863 (daughter of Hans Anker Kofoed and Cecelia Monk). Their children: Niels Oliver b. Dec. 12, 1864; William b. Oct. 21, 1866, m. Annie B. Hansen Sept. 6, 1893; Laura b. May 21, 1868, m. Albert N. Clements Sept. 8, 1886; Annie Cecelia b. May 10, 1870, m. Fred Berntsen Jan. 17, 1894; Hans Hyrum b. Dec. 25, 1871, m. Minnie Berlips Oct. 23, 1907; Alice Lenora b. May 5, 1874, m. James Kingsford March 12, 1890; Josephine b. June 3, 1876.
Married Mette Catharine Jensen June 16, 1877, Logan, Utah (daughter of Jens Jensen and Ane Kerstena Nielsen), who was born May 6, 1859, Silkaborg, Denmark. Their children: Niels Wilford b. April 30, 1878, m. Martha E. Rose April 12, 1899; Joseph b. Sept. 21, 1881, m. Mira Amelia Nielsen March 19, 1902; Mette Catharine b. Dec. 18, 1883; George Peter b. Oct. 10, 1885, m. Lis Churn Dec. 15, 1910; Anna Sophia b. March 25, 1888, m. Roland Williams Dec. 18, 1908; Lucy K. b. April 18, 1890; Heber Moroni b. Oct. 27, 1891; Ruby Margareta b. Dec. 21, 1893; Lorenza Knud b. Sept. 14, 1897. Families resided Weston, Idaho.
Patriarch of Oneida stake counselor of bishopric Weston ward; member high council Oneida stake; missionary to Scandinavia 1895-97. Resided at Pleasant Grove 1854,

Salt Lake City 1857; worked at Brigham Young's sawmill at City creek canyon. Resided at Oxford, Idaho, 1863 to 1866. Family home, Weston.

JORGENSEN, RASMUS G. (son of Jorgen Just Jorgensen and Anna Metta Rasmussen of Aärhus, Denmark). Born April 8, 1863, Aärhus, Denmark. Came to Utah June 4, 1884.
Married Thora D. Jensen April 28, 1886, Logan. Utah (daughter of Hans H. Jensen and Lise Lechbant of Sjaelland, Denmark, came to Utah June 4, 1884). She was born Dec. 21, 1866. Their children: Albert Erastus b. March 2, 1887, d. Jan. 5, 1888; Jennie Laura b. July 15, 1888; Anna Teresa b. April 6, 1890, m. Nahum Hancock; Pearl Elize b. Sept. 10, 1891, m. C. M. Christensen; Hans Helbert b. May 22, 1893; Dora Emelie b. Nov. 4, 1894, m. Otto Hegstrom; Klara Adela b. March, 1896, d. Oct. 6, 1896; Arthur Lorenza b. June 25, 1897; Rosette Arilla b. Dec. 19, 1899; Herman Rasmus b. Sept. 19, 1902; Lyla Amanda b. April 7, 1904; Jessie Just b. Nov. 26, 1905; Leo Lyman b. Jan. 18, 1908; Howard Chester b. Aug. 3, 1910. Family home Central. Idaho.
High priest; presiding elder East Lund branch; 1st counselor to Bishop Daniel Lloyd of Central ward; bishop of Central ward Jan. 18, 1904.

JOSEPHSON, ANDREW M. (son of Nels Josephson and Stena Greta Swenson of Pilfer, Sweden). Born April 14, 1824, Liungesocken, Jönköping, Sweden. Came to Utah 1863, John F. Sanders company.
Married Anna Anderson July, 1862, Florence, Neb. (daughter of Oka Anderson and Karna Nelson, pioneers Sept. 5, 1863, John F. Sanders company), who was born March 29, 1841. Their children: Olive Josephine, d. May 24, 1864; Joseph A., m. Sarah E. Zundel; Ephraim, m. Nellie Arbon; Christena Josephine, died; Emma Shorlett, m. Robert Lee Joyce; Nephi d. April 18, 1903; Alma, m. Ella Hudson; Anna Mary, d. June 1, ———; Josephine C., m. Joseph R. Olsen; Clara, m. William Wight. Family home Brigham City, Utah.

JOST, JOHN A. Born Dec. 17, 1811, in Nova Scotia. Came to Utah Dec. 16, 1856, Wooley & Atwood company.
Married Mary A. Zwicker, who was born July, 1811. Came to Utah with her husband. Their children: George H.; Eliza A.; Alice E.; Kate; John D.; Samuel E.; Thomas; Minnie; Alexander; Andrew. Family home Ogden, Utah.

JOST, SAMUEL EDWARD (son of John A. Jost and Mary Ann Zwicker). Born Dec. 1, 1844, Lunenburg, N. S.; pioneers Dec. 16, 1856, Wooley & Atwood company.
Married Elizabeth A. Baker (West) April 2, 1872, Ogden, Utah (daughter of Henry Baker and Jean Rio), who was born April 2, 1842. Their children: Mary A. Frances b. Feb. 23, 1873, m. Alexander Huss Nov. 1, 1893; Katie B. b. Aug. 27, 1874, m. George Huss Oct. 6, 1894; Lila E. b. Dec. 20, 1876; Samuel E. b. April 2, 1879, m. Ann Christiansen June 19, 1908; Walter H. b. Feb. 4, 1887. Family home, Ogden.
Married Flora B. Durling (Dilley) Oct. 5, 1909, at Ogden (daughter of John Durling and Elizabeth Reddig, married about 1848, in Pennsylvania). She was born May 14, 1860, Harrisburg, Penn.
As teamster brought first telegraph wire.

JUDD, ZADOK KNAPP (son of Arza Judd, born Jan. 10, 1798, and Lucinda Adams, born Dec. 13, 1799, natives Canada). He was born Oct. 15, 1827, Johnstown, Canada. Came to Utah September 1848 with Mormon Battalion contingent.
Married Mary Minerva Dart Nov. 14, 1852, Parowan, Utah (daughter of John Dart and Lucy Ann Robert, former pioneer at Parowan 1851, James Foote company, latter died en route), who was born March 31, 1838. Their children: Lucinda Abigail, m. Charles H. Olephant; Zadok K., m. Ada M. Howell; Harriet Polina, d. infant; Lois Sabina, d. infant; Henry Eli, m. Mary E. Johnson; Ezra Abner, d. infant; Esther Irene, m. John Mantripp Ford; Asa Walter, m. Alice M. Young, m. Liby Brown; Samuel Ami, m. Polly A. Johnson; James Arthur, d. infant; William Leonard, d. infant; Mary Gertrude, m. Charles S. Cottam; Arza Orange, d. infant; John Lael, d. infant. Family home, Kanab.
Member of seventy; missionary to Santa Clara 1855; bishop Santa Clara ward 1856. School trustee at Kanab. Member Company E, Mormon Battalion. Pioneer at Parowan; resided Santa Clara 1856; Kanab 1871. Farmer. Died Jan. 28, 1909.

JUDD, ZADOK KNAPP (son of Zadok K. Judd and Mary Minerva Dart). Born Nov. 25, 1855, Parowan, Utah.
Married Ada M. Howell Jan. 21, 1884, St. George, Utah (daughter of Robert Howell). Only child: Daniel K. b. Nov. 2, 1884, m. Elizabeth Church.

JUDD, ASA W. (son of Zadok K. Judd and Mary Minerva Dart). Born Aug. 28, 1868.
Married Alice May Young May 31, 1893 (daughter of Brigham L. Young and Ida F. Lewis), who died Jan. 6, 1898. Their children: Asa Walter; Amy Elizabeth, d. aged 14.
Married Thilly Leonore Brown Dec. 22, 1903 (daughter of A. W. Brown and Emma S. Sibley). Their children: Thora Mae; Rex Aberdeen, d. infant; Abia Waldemar; Verda Leonore; Whitney Carlyle; Elise Ione.
Bishop Fredonia ward; second counselor to Bishop Joel

980 PIONEERS AND PROMINENT MEN OF UTAH

Johnson of Kanab 1890-1903; missionary to Holland; president Netherlands mission 1895-96; second counselor to Bishop Fredonia one year; bishop Fredonia ward since December, 1901.

JUDGE, JOHN (son of John and Annie Judge), born 1845, County Sligo, Ireland. Came to Utah April, 1876.
Married Mary Harney Nov. 25, 1867, Port Henry, who became the mother of his five children. Family home Salt Lake City.
Enlisted in Union Army as private in Company K, second regiment, New York Volunteer Cavalry, and served a little over two years. Miner at Wood River, Idaho. Returning to Utah, he went to Park City where he did considerable prospecting and worked upon some of the most valuable properties in that section, notably the Daily mine. One of the original lessees of the "Mayflower." One of the organizers of the Silver King Mining Company. In his will, he provided for the building of the Judge Mercy Hospital, which was to be a home for destitute or sick men who had given their lives to mining and prospecting. The Judge building at the southeast corner of Main and Third South streets was built by his widow. Mining. Capitalist. Died Sept. 14, 1892, Salt Lake City.

JUDY, WILLIAM CLARK (son of Samuel Judy of Illinois). Born June 1, 1826, in Ohio. Came to Utah 1850.
Married Kesiah Benson March 22, 1846 (daughter of Alva Benson and Cynthia Vail, pioneers 1852, Uriah Curtis company), who was born March 10, 1825. Only child: William Alva b. Dec. 2, 1847, m. Alseoun Smith Nov. 15, 1869. Family home, Big Cottonwood.
Died July 5, 1851.

JUDY, WILLIAM ALVA (son of William Clark Judy and Kesiah Benson). Born Dec. 2, 1847, Council Bluffs, Iowa.
Married Alseoun Smith Nov. 15, 1869, Salt Lake City (daughter of Adam and Melissa Henry Smith, pioneers 1857). Their children: Melissa Kesiah b. Aug. 29, 1870, d. Aug. 1883; William Aaron b. Nov. 28, 1871, m. Mary Ann Ward Oct. 22, 1897; Elvira b. May 14, 1873, d. Aug. 17, 1890; Merilla b. Feb. 27, 1875, m. Charles H. Fogg April 15, 1896; Elmina b. March 31, 1877, m. Delonza Cherry Sept. 13, 1899; Angelia b. Nov. 18, 1878, d. Aug. 26, 1883; Charlotte b. Sept. 21, 1888, m. Joseph E. Anderson June 12, 1905; Ivie Josephine b. May 9, 1890, m. Wilfred J. Price April 8, 1909; Junius Victor b. April 6, 1895. Resided Hyrum, Cache Co., Utah, and Salem, Fremont Co., Idaho.
High priest; missionary.

JULANDER, JACOB A. Born April 8, 1805, Denmark. Came to Utah 1856, handcart company.
Married Johanna Christina Yacht, who died 1853. Came to Utah 1856 with husband. Their children: William, m. Ida Ingerberg Darling; Caroline, m. Ira Sutton; Brigham, m. Annie Johnson; Julia A., m. Henry John Rich; Jacob m. Mary Johnson; Lucretia, m. Martin Larsen.
High priest. Pioneer Sevier county. Indian war veteran. Farmer. Died June 1898, Monroe, Utah.

K

KAIGHN, MAURICE M. (son of William S. Kaighn and Nancy S. McElroy). Born March 30, 1843, Camden, N. J. Came to Utah October 1876.
Married Effie M. Coates July 31, 1901. His children by a former wife: Jean F., m. A. H. Gawler; Maurice E.; Walter H.; Herbert E.; Merill M.
First appointed receiver of United States land office, Salt Lake City, in February 1907; reappointed in March 1911. Department commander of Utah G. A. R. 1899. Admitted to the bar by Supreme court of Columbia 1870. Clerk in the interior department of law, Washington, D. C., 1869-76. Mining and corporation lawyer Salt Lake City. Served with the 44th and 197th regiments, Pennsylvania volunteer infantry, in the Civil war.

KARLSON, CLAUS HERMAN (son of Lars Karlson, born July 26, 1813, and Breta Anderson, born Sept. 23, 1822, both of Bergvik, Sweden). He was born Sept. 26, 1849. Came to Utah in 1857, Christiansen handcart company.
Married Henrietta Severe Jan. 10, 1875 (daughter of Harrison Severe and Elizabeth Orr), who was born June 3, 1853. Their children: Herman W. b. Sept. 23, 1876, died; Noel b. Oct. 15, 1879, m. Maud Cook; Raymond Karlson b. Nov. 15, 1883, m. Nellie Martindale Nov. 29, 1910; Lawrence b. Aug. 15, 1885, m. Eva Jenkins Feb. 1, 1904; Lewis b. March 28, 1890; Leo b. Jan. 14, 1899.
Missionary to Sweden 1887-90; member of high council in Cassia stake 1892-1900. Member of Grantsville city council 1875-80; justice of the peace of Oakley precinct 1883-87; chairman of Parker village board 1904-10.

KARREN, THOMAS (son of Thomas Karren, born in 1784, and Catherine Clark of Isle of Man). He was born in 1810 on Isle of Man. Came to Utah July 28, 1847, with part of Company E, Mormon Battalion.
Married Ann Ratcliff (daughter of John Ratcliff and Lydia Farecliff—married at Farnely, Eng.). She was born Nov. 1, 1815, Liverpool, Eng., and came to Utah 1850, Captain Dilley company. Their children: John b. 1834, m. Mariah Lawrence; Catherine K. b. 1836, m. Lorenzo Hatch; Lydia K. b. 1838, m. Silbvens Collett; Thomas, Jr., b. 1840, m. Sarah Reed; Joseph b. 1842, d. child; Hyrum b. July 9, 1844, m. Martha Langley Dec. 30, 1865; Charles H. b. 1846, m. Sarah Agnes Davis; Ann b. 1848, d. child; Mary K. b. Feb. 1852, m. Hyrum Bennion; Isabel K. b. Jan. 1, 1856, m. S. R. Thurman; David b. 1858, died. Family home Lehi, Utah.
Married Elizabeth Gilcrist at Salt Lake City. Their children: George b. 1865; Robert b. 1867; James b. 1869; Eliza b. 1871, m. Mr. Carns.
Married Hannah ——. Their children: Jane; Anna; one boy died young.
Missionary to Sandwich Islands in 1853; bishop's counselor. First man to plow a furrow and start the settlement of Lehi. Built first house in Lehi. Indian war veteran.

KARREN, THOMAS (son of Thomas Karren and Ann Ratcliff). Born Dec. 22, 1839, Liverpool, Eng. Came to Utah in 1852.
Married Sarah Garrett. Their children: Thomas b. March 4, 1864, m. Sarah Caldwell and Nettie Van Norton; David H. b. June 22, 1866, m. Elizabeth Haworth; Charles.
Married Ellen Wilkshire (Rolf) in 1876 at Lehi, Utah, who was born April 2, 1845. Their children: Virginia b. Aug. 8, 1877, m. Roy B. Anderson; Pearl b. Nov. 21, 1879, m. Hatch Murray; Merton b. April 22, 1883, m. Minerva Melvina Wilkins Johnson; Maud b. May 25, 1885, m. Frederick W. Richards; Margaret b. May 25, 1885, and Clarence, d. child. Family home Vernal, Utah.
Ellen Wilkshire was the widow of Jasper Rolf, a pioneer of 1847, to whom were born: William, m. Hannah Jacobs; Annie, m. Garabaldi Gamble; Lydia, m. J. M. Shaffer; Samuel, m. Hetta Crandall.
Missionary to England 1891-93; high priest; ward and Sunday school teacher. Early settler to Utah; moved to Vernal in 1879. Sheepman. Died November 1903 at Vernal, Utah.

KARREN, MERTON (son of Thomas Karren and Ellen Wilkshire). Born April 22, 1883, at Vernal, Utah.
Married Minerva Melvina Wilkins (Johnson) Nov. 22, 1900, Vernal, Utah (daughter of Oscar Wilkins and Mary Jane McEwan of Provo, Utah, pioneers. She was born Dec. 17, 1872.
Farmer and stockraiser.
Minerva Melvina Wilkins was the widow of J. Warren Johnson, whom she married May 29, 1895, Salt Lake City, and by whom were born: Warren L., April 8, 1896; Venice, Dec. 29, 1899; Isis, Oct. 10, 1902; Arvan, Aug. 16, 1903; Jessie, Aug. 25, 1905.

KARREN, HYRUM (son of Thomas Karren and Ann Ratcliff). Born July 9, 1844, Nauvoo, Ill.
Married Martha Langley Dec. 30, 1865, Salt Lake City (daughter of George Langley and Martha M. Frost, former came to Utah with Heber C. Kimball company). She was born Jan. 17, 1847, Winter Quarters, Iowa. Their children: George Hyrum b. Dec. 2, 1866, m. Ella Kent; Mary Isabel b. Sept. 29, 1868, m. E. M. Harris; Thomas Sylvester b. Aug. 12, 1870, m. Annie Pingray; Fredrich William b. May 12, 1873, m. Annie Pingray; Lydia Elnora b. Nov. 11, 1875, m. Edward Leavitt March 9, 1899; Dennina Ann b. Jan. 11, 1876, m. John Blair May 20, 1895; Vila May b. Dec. 2, 1882, m. George Elfonzo Pope Dec. 10, 1902. Family home Lewiston, Utah.
Hauled rock for Salt Lake temple, 1861. High priest. Drove cattle across the plains several times. Minuteman in early Indian troubles.

KARREN, THOMAS S. (son of Hyrum Karren and Martha Langley). Born Aug. 12, 1870, at Richmond, Utah.
Married Georgiana Leavitt (daughter of George Leavitt and Jeanette Brinkerhoff—married Aug. 29, 1852, Centerville, Utah—former came to Utah in 1847, Jedediah M. Grant company; later Sept. 25, 1847, Ira Eldredge company). She was born Oct. 29, 1873, at Lewiston, Utah. Their children: Liva b. July 6, 1892; Verta b. March 16, 1894; Leahfay b. Oct. 25, 1895; Lowell Sylvester b. Sept. 23, 1897; Myrtle b. Aug. 10, 1899; George Leavitt b. April 17, 1902; Zenda b. June 4, 1904; Langley Clawson b. May 14, 1906; Fred Velford b. June 16, 1909. Family home Lewiston, Utah.
Missionary to eastern states in 1898, and to southern states in 1901; member high council of Benson stake 1901-09; bishop of 3d ward at Lewiston in 1909.

KARTCHNER, WILLIAM DECATUR (son of John Christopher Kartchner and Prudence Wilcox, of Utah, Montgomery county, Pa.). Born May 4, 1820, Hartville. Came to Utah in 1847, Captain Emmett company, escorted by members of the Mormon Battalion.
Married Margaret Jane Casteel (daughter of Jacob I. Casteel and Sarah Nowlin, of Cooper county, Mo.), who was born Sept. 1, 1825, and came to Utah with husband. Their children: Sarah Amma, m. Ninian Miller; William Ammon, died; Prudence Jane, m. William J. Flake; John, m. Lydia A. Palmer; Mark Elisha, m. Phoebe Palmer; Alzada S.,

m. Alma Z. Palmer; James, died; Mary Marinda, m. Don C. Clayton; Nowlin D., m. Margaret Savage; Orrin, m. Annie Hunt; Euphemia A., died. Family home Beaver City, Utah.
Married Elizabeth Gale at Salt Lake City (daughter of Henry Gale of Australia, who came to Utah with oxteam company). Their children: Aaron, m. Margaret Blythe; Culver, m. Rebecca Stewart; Minnie, m. William E. Stratton; Byrtleson, m. Emma McCleve; Darien, m. Maggie McCleve; Elsie, m. George Gale; Etta, m. John McCleve; Melva, died. Family home Snowflake, Ariz.
Seventy; superintendent of Sunday school; ward and block teacher. Postmaster Panguitch, Utah. and Snowflake, Ariz. Blacksmith; farmer. Died May 14, 1892, Snowflake.

KARTCHNER, MARK ELISHA (son of William Decatur Kartchner and Margaret Jane Casteel). Born Dec. 10, 1853, San Bernardino, Cal. Came to Utah, spring of 1858.
Married Phoebe Palmer May 11, 1874, Salt Lake City (daughter of Zemira Palmer and Sally Knight of Provo, Utah, pioneers 1847, division of Mormon Battalion). She was born Feb. 18, 1858. Their children: Mark Elisha b. June 6, 1876, m. Nellia Loveless; Zemira b. April 12, 1879, died; Asael W. b. June 21, 1882, m. Rosina Heath; Ellora b. Oct. 24, 1889, m. Benjamin H. Knudsen; Lydia b. Oct. 30, 1891, died; Rachel b. March 1, 1895; Lyman Alma b. March 17, 1897; Jesse C. b. July 11, 1899. Family resided Snowflake, Ariz., and Provo, Utah.
Seventy; high priest; block teacher; superintendent of Sunday school; president Y. M. M. I. A. Farmer.

KATZ, MICHAEL S. (son of Michael Katz and Catherine Jolley of Philadelphia, Pa.). Born April 20, 1853.
Married Mary J. Thomas Dec. 25, 1880, Salt Lake City, Elias Smith performing ceremony (daughter of Samuel Thomas and Ann Jones of Salt Lake City, pioneers Sept. 25, 1849, Dan Jones company). She was born June 8, 1858, Salt Lake City; Their children: Edith b. Nov. 1, 1881; Vera b. Sept. 7, 1887; Harold T. b. Dec. 6, 1894. Family home, Salt Lake City.

KAY, THOMAS (son of John Kay and Margaret Batisby of St. Helens, Lancashire, Eng.). Born June 21, 1836. Came to Utah Oct. 1, 1854.
Married Margret Ann Vest April 15, 1864 (daughter of Elizabeth Barnaby), who was born March 31, 1849. Their children: John Thomas Kay, m. Laura Rosetta Haus Nov. 12, 1890; Amanda Melvina Kay, m. Andrew B. Roberts Nov. 13, 1890; Abraham Kay, m. Ellen Burgin; Lorenzo Kay, m. Martha Kay.
Married Eliza Day Dec. 13, 1869, in Salt Lake City (daughter of William Day and Mary Ann Leonard, came to Salt Lake City with Wheeler Duncan—married Nov. 20, 1840, St Augustine, Lancashire, Eng.). She was born Dec. 4, 1846, in Stock Port, Lancashire, Eng. Their children: Sarah Ann Kay, b. Aug. 3, 1871, m. Charles Henry Stark; Mary Elizabeth Kay, b. Nov. 8, 1874, m. James William Kay June 20, 1895.
Farmer. Died 1875, Mona, Juab Co., Utah.

KAY, JOHN THOMAS (son of Thomas Kay and Margret Ann Vest). Born Feb. 8, 1865, in Mona, Juab Co., Utah.
Married Laura Rosetta Haus Nov. 12, 1890, Provo, Utah (daughter of John M. Haus and Laura Jane Partridge, of Mona, Juab Co., Utah), who was born March 28, 1871. Their children: Calvin Kay b. April 25, 1894; Lucinda Kay, b. Nov. 16, 1895; Loren Kay b. May 4, 1897; Millie Rosetta Kay b. July 21, 1898; Laura Ann Kay b. Nov. 17, 1899; Lapreal Kay b. March 21, 1901; Leona Kay b. Nov. 1, 1902; Carma Alta Kay b. Aug. 29, 1904; Arvella Kay b. Dec. 5, 1906; Dorothy Kay b. Aug. 11, 1908; Enice Veril Kay b. Feb. 18, 1911; Lillian Marie Kay b. April 24, 1913.
Farmer and stockraiser.

KAY, WILLIAM (son of William and E'izabeth Mercer of Chailey, Lancashire, Eng.). Born April 11, 1811, Chailey. Came to Utah Oct. 10, 1848, Willard Richards company.
Married Mary Twinberrow Wattis 1844, Nauvoo, Ill. (daughter of Edmund Wattis and Sarah Twinberrow), who was born Aug. 26, 1819. Their children: Jeanetta, m. David George Nelson; Sarah Elizabeth, m. Willace Foulger; Maria Deborah, m. George Walker; Martha A., m. James Allen; Isabella, m. William David Littlefield; Elveretta, m. Ezra Farr. Family home Ogden, Utah.
Missionary in Great Britain 1840-44, and to Carson. Nev. 1856; bishop of Kaysville; president of West Weber district. Farmer. Died March 25, 1875, Ogden.

KEARNS, AUSTIN (son of Hamilton H. Kearns and Charlott White). Born Sept. 2, 1845, in Iowa.
Married Mary Jergensen Jan. 29, 1865, Gunnison, Utah (daughter of Andrew Jergensen and Elizabeth Snelson of Denmark, pioneers January, 1856, Martin and Willis handcart company). She was born July 15, 1846. Their children: William b. Jan. 12, 1866, m. Lillie May Whitlock; Charlott b. Dec. 15, 1868, m. William S. Roper; Mahala b. Sept. 18, 1869, m. William C. Martell; Andrew H. b. Nov. 29, 1871, m. Eliza Jenson; John M. b. Sept. 8, 1873, m. Fleata Long; Frances O. b. Dec. 3, 1875, m. Fred N. Swalberg; Nels Frank b. Oct. 2, 1877, m. Carrie B. Mayfield; Lydia b. April 26, 1881, m. Charles E. Ferre; Elmer E. b. Jan. 15, 1884; Blanche b. Aug. 3, 1886, m. Herbert Beck March 7, 1906. Family home Gunnison, Utah.
High councilor. Farmer.

KEARNS, HAMILTON H. (son of Matthew Kearns of Ohio and Mahala Frazier of Ireland). Born Sept. 17, 1817, Ohio. Came to Utah Sept. 8, 1850, Aaron Johnson company.
Married Charlott White in 1840, in Ohio (daughter of William and Elizabeth White of Ohio), who was born in 1825. Their children: Mahala; William b. Oct. 3, 1841, m. Martha Snellson; John; Austin b. Sept. 2, 1845, m. Mary Jergensen; Elizabeth b. May, 1848, m. Hans Jergensen. Family home Springville, Utah.
Married Emma M. Guymon Feb. 4, 1857, Salt Lake City (daughter of Noah T. Guymon and Mary D. Dudley of Nauvoo, Ill.; they came to Utah in 1850, Matthew Caldwell company). She was born July 8, 1842. Their children: Edwin J. b. Dec. 29, 1858, m. Ovanda Whitbeck; Emma Jane b. March 15, 1861, m. George H. Knighton; Marion D. b. Feb. 23, 1863; Helena M. b. March 15, 1865, m. William Parker; Harriet L. b. Oct. 12, 1867, m. Heber S. Goddard; Anna A. b. May 3, 1870, m. Moses Johnson; Noah G. and Margaret B. b. Dec. 24, 1873; Noah, m. Ella Garrick; Margarett, m. Samuel Dowse; Joseph A. b. June 17, 1875, m. Cordelia Peterson; Zina b. April 22, 1878; Zada b. March 2, 1880, m. Hubert T. Andrews; Leah b. Sept. 1884. Families resided at Springville and Gunnison, Utah.
Bishop of Gunnison. Indian war veteran. Wheelwright; millwright; blacksmith. Died Feb. 28, 1893.

KEARNS, EDWIN J. (son of Hamilton H. Kearns and Emma M. Guymon) Born Dec. 29, 1858, Springville, Utah.
Married Ovanda Witbeck Feb. 1, 1899, Gunnison, Utah (daughter of John C. Witbeck and Susan Roper of Gunnison, Utah, pioneers 1857). She was born March 3, 1876. Their children: Helen b. Nov. 25, 1899; Edwin J. b. April 28, 1901; Richard Dudley b. Dec. 18, 1906; Henry Witbeck b. May 27, 1910. Family home Salt Lake City.
Member board of sheep commissioners 1902-04.

KEARNS, THOMAS (son of Thomas Kearns and Margaret Maher of Ireland). Born April 11, 1862, Oxford county, Upper Canada. Came to Utah 1883.
Married Jennie Judge Sept. 14, 1890 (daughter of Patrick Judge of Ireland, and Jane Pattison of America). She was born Nov. 30, 1869, Fort Henry, Essex county, N. Y. Their children: Margaret, d. 1893; Edmund J.; Thomas F.; Helen Marie. Family home, Salt Lake City.
Worked on Denver & Rio Grande railroad until the completion of the line to Salt Lake City. In June, 1883, he went to Park City and entered the employ of the Ontario Mining Company; in 1889 went to work for the Woodside mine, which was then owned by Edward Ferry. That same year he bought into a lease on the Mayflower mine, the other lessees being David Keith, John Judge, A. E. Emery and W. V. Rice. In 1891 he, with David Keith and their partners, bonded the Silver King mine site, and purchased the same in 1892. He became its manager and through his enterprise and ability effected its rapid and successful development.
Member city council of Park City, and in 1894 was elected to the Constitutional Convention which, in 1895, framed the basic law of the present state of Utah. Delegate to the National Republican Convention held at St. Louis, Mo. Elected United States senator in 1901. Donated $50,000 for the erection and endowment of St. Ann's orphanage in Salt Lake City. Sole owner of the Pixton property on Main street; owner of the Kearns terraces at corner of Sixth South and State, and corner of First and G street. Part owner in the Grand Central, Raymond, Crown Point and other mines. Builder and owner of the Kearns building. With David Keith, principal owner of the Daily Salt Lake "Tribune." Capitalist.

KEELE, RICHARD. Came to Utah 1853, oxteam company.
Married Elenor ——. Their children: Aleck; Dabney; Thomas; Elizabeth; J. Polly. Family home Payson, Utah.
Indian war veteran. Farmer. Died 1877, at Mt. Carmel, Utah.

KEELE, THOMAS (son of Richard and Elenor Keele). Born Aug. 15, 1828. Came to Utah 1853, oxteam company.
Married Mary Jolly (daughter of Henry Bryant Jolly and Britannia Mayo, of Spanish Fork, Harmony and Mt. Carmel, Utah, came to Utah 1853, oxteam company). She was born 1834. Their children: Nancy E. b. Jan. 15, 1853, m. William H. Worthen; Susan Elizabeth b. Oct. 1854, m. Harvey Pace; Henry b. 1856, m. Maggie Enelestead; Mary b. 1858, m. Henry Jolly; William b. 1860, m. Annabell Bullock; Richard Bryant b. 1862, m. Mary Hanson; John b. 1864, m. Alice b. 1866, m. John Jolly; Nephi b. 1868, m. Martha Bolck; Cynthia Ann b. 1870, m. Chris. Larsen; Maggie b. 1873, m. Heber Petty. Family home Harmony, Mt. Carmel and Emery, Utah.
Elder. Veteran Black Hawk Indian war. Farmer. Died in Uinta reservation.

KEELER, DANIEL HUTCHINSON (son of John Budd Keeler and Amy Hutchinson of Pemberton, N. J.). Born July 25, 1811, at Pemberton, N. J. Came to Utah in September 1852 with Horace S. Eldredge company.
Married Ann Brown (Taylor) in 1853 (daughter of James Brown and Elizabeth Atkin of Tildsley, Eng.). Their children: Amy b. July 28, 1854, died; Joseph Brigham b. Sept. 8, 1855, m. Martha Alice Fairbanks May 17, 1883; Theodosia b. Aug. 31, 1858, m. Jacob Collier; Lucy b. Oct. 27, 1860, died. She was the widow of Benjamin Taylor, by whom she had the following children: James; Sarah; Ann; Mary Jane; Martha, died.
Married Philinda Eldredge (Merrick) in July 1843 at Nauvoo, Ill. Their children: Abner Eldredge, m. Jane Shaw; Daniel, died.
High priest; ward teacher. Mason; contractor; builder.

KEELER, JOSEPH BRIGHAM (son of Daniel Hutchinson Keeler and Ann Brown). Born Sept. 8, 1855, Salt Lake City.
Married Martha Alice Fairbanks May 17, 1883, Salt Lake City (daughter of David Fairbanks and Susan Mandville of Mountain View, N. J., came to Utah in October 1847, with John Taylor company). She was born June 29, 1860. Their children: Major Joseph b. Feb. 19, 1884, m. Esther Reese; Beulah May b. Oct. 25, 1885, m. Daniel H. McAllister; Karl Fairbanks b. Jan. 1, 1887, m. Kitty Leetham; Irvin Talmage b. Nov. 29, 1889; Hattie Brown b. April 3, 1891; Eva Josephine b. Oct. 25, 1894; David Hutchinson b. April 1, 1896; Ralph Budd b. Dec. 27, 1897; Daniel Mandeville b. Oct. 28, 1900; Paul Fortesque b. Feb. 12, 1904.
High priest; missionary to southern states 1880-82; superintendent of Y. M. M. I. A. of Utah stake 1893-95; bishop of 4th ward, Provo, 1895-1901; president of Utah stake of Zion 1908-13. County recorder 1882-84; city councilman 1876-79; member of board of trustees of Agricultural College at Logan 1894-96. Author and publisher; one of the presidency of the Brigham Young University, Provo, 1913.

KEELER, JAMES (son of George Keeler and Laura Thompson of Vermont). Born Jan. 4, 1817, Ferrisburg, Vt. Came to Utah in 1849.
Married Jane Herritt June 8, 1842, Jacksonville, Ill. She died in 1845. Their child: Sophia b. July 29, 1843.
Married Eliza Shelton March 3, 1856, Salt Lake City (daughter of David Booth Shelton and Bethiah Slawson of New Brunswick, N. S.). She was born Aug. 7, 1840, in New Brunswick, and came to Utah in 1854. Their children: Eliza Bethiah b. Sept. 10, 1856, died; Laila Ann b. July 7, 1859, m. Joseph Thurber; James Shelton b. Sept. 1, 1861, d. March 6, 1887; Margaret b. Dec. 28, 1863, m. Theodore Brandley; Alice Adell b. Oct. 29, 1865, m. George A. Hatch, m. Peter Gottfredson; Joel Gideon b. Jan. 31, 1867, d. Feb. 24, 1867; Martha E. b. Aug. 7, 1869, m. Christian Sorenson; Orson Olmsted b. Oct. 1, 1871, m. Emma Jeppeson, m. Ireta Davis; Susan b. March 10, 1873, died; Ernest William b. May 10, 1875, d. 1888; Audrey Cannon b. Sept. 29, 1879, m. C. R. Snowdon.
Married Emily Shelton April 22, 1857, Salt Lake City (daughter of David Booth Shelton and Bethiah Slawson of New Brunswick, N. S.), who was born July 21, 1842, in New Brunswick. Their children: Lucretia b. Nov. 3, 1858, m. Joseph Roseberry; George Albert b. Nov. 17, 1862, d. April 5, 1863; Charles Obid b. Jan. 3, 1864, m. Nora Johnson; Grace Arlettie b. Oct. 25, 1866, m. G. A. Norton; David Arthur b. Feb. 18, 1869, m. Josephine Christiansen; Hyrum Alfred b. March 15, 1870, m. Josephine Bulow; Joseph b. April 24, 1875, died; Ruth Ada b. Jan. 5, 1877, died. Families resided Santaquin, Goshen and Richfield, Utah.
Missionary to Sandwich Islands 1850-55. Built first grist mill at Goshen. Carpenter; farmer. Died April 18, 1909, Monroe, Utah.

KEELER, DAVID ARTHUR (son of James Keeler and Emily Shelton). Born Feb. 18, 1869, Santaquin, Utah.
Married Josephine Christiansen May 22, 1894, Monroe, Utah (daughter of C. F. Christiansen and Caroline Nazer of Monroe), who was born Oct. 13, 1873, in Monroe. Their children: Ivan Arthur b. Sept. 29, 1895; Charles Ernest b. Sept. 24, 1897, d. Oct. 24, 1897; Delbert B. b. March 18, 1900; Wilford Orson b. Aug. 2, 1903, d. April 6, 1904; Fern b. Nov. 2, 1905; Donna Rose b. July 30, 1908; Kenneth Wells b. Sept. 25, 1910. Families resided Monroe and Kimberley, Utah.
Farmer; fruitgrower; stockraiser.

KEEP, JAMES JOSEPH. Came to Utah in 1852.
Married Anne Miller of England. Their children: Annie, m. Morgan Davies; Mary Elizabeth, m. Alford Turner; Sarah, m. David Buttars; James Joseph, Jr., died; Lucy, m. Fred Dounward; Jane, William Richard, Harriet and Emma Martha, all four dead; Ruth, m. John Griffin.
Mason. Died in March 1899 at Lehi, Utah.

KEETCH, ALFRED GREENWORD (son of William K. Keetch and Ann Greenwood of Kempston, Bedfordshire, Eng.). Born Jan. 3, 1840, Kempston. Came to Utah Nov. 4, 1863, Willie and Atwood company.
Married Emily Harris Nov. 10, 1866, at Pleasant Grove, Utah (daughter of John Harris and Ann Stanley of Redditch, Worcestershire, Eng., pioneers Sept. 15, 1866, William Henry Chipman company). She was born April 3, 1840. Their children: Emily Ann, m. Edwin Aston; Lizzie, m. William James Cullimore; Martha J., m. Amasa Meacham; Luella, m. Albert Lorenzo Cullimore; Mary Eva, m. David B. Thorne; Alfred G., m. Martha Thorne; Ruthie M., m. Benjamin Walker; Effie, m. Enderson Wilson; William John, m. Lora Fage; Hazel Berthena, m. Parson Richards; Stanley Birdsell; Samuel Charles. Family home, Lindon ward.
High priest; bishop's counselor. Assisted in bringing immigrants to Utah in 1866; went to Bear Lake, Idaho, to assist in settling that country 1864-65; missionary to the Muddy, Ariz., 1867-71. Mayor of Pleasant Grove two terms; member city council three terms. Farmer and fruitgrower.

KEETCH, CHARLES GREENWOOD (son of William K. Keetch, born Sept. 3, 1811, and Ann Greenwood, born Dec. 18, 1811, both of Kempston, Eng.). He was born July 2, 1837, Kempston. Came to Utah Sept. 20, 1861, Joseph Young company.
Married Mercy Truth Barker Dec. 14, 1860 (daughter of Thomas Barker and Elizabeth Thomson), who was born Feb. 21, 1835, and came to Utah Sept. 20, 1861, with Joseph Young company. Their children: Charles Greenwood, Jr., b. Sept. 12, 1861, m. Ellen N. Pugmire July 22, 1885; Heber C. b. Dec. 22, 1862, m. Lizzie Bennet April 6, 1890; Eliza C. b. May 31, 1865, m. Annie S. Pugmire Nov. 19, 1889; Mercy T. b. Feb. 10, 1867; Elizabeth T. b. Jan. 27, 1869, m. Swan O. Arnell; William A. C. b. Oct. 13, 1871, m. Theodosha Dalrymple Nov. 10, 1904; Elisha C. b. July 16, 1873; Ann G. b. June 8, 1875, m. Rasmus Nelson April 5, 1905. Family resided Grantsville, Utah, and St. Charles, Bear Lake Co., Idaho.
Seventy; teacher. Worked on Logan temple; helped build road from Bear Lake valley to Cache valley. Died Sept. 3, 1908.

KEETCH, CHARLES GREENWOOD (son of Charles Greenwood Keetch and Mercy Truth Barker). Born Sept. 12, 1861, Gunnison, Utah.
Married Ellen N. Pugmire July 22, 1885, at Logan, Utah (daughter of Jonathan Pugmire and Caroline Nelson of St. Charles, Idaho). Their children: Charles P. b. July 18, 1886, m. Frances Bridges; Jonathan P. b. July 10, 1888; Elisha P. b. Aug. 7, 1895; Genevieve P. b. July 19, 1898.

KEITH, DAVID (son of John Keith and Margaret Ness of Scotland). Born May 27, 1847, Mabou, Cape Breton, Nova Scotia. Came to Utah in March, 1883.
The children of his first marriage were: Charles F.; Margaret; Etta; Lillian, m. Albert C. Allen.
Married Mary Patrick Ferguson June 12, 1894, Park City, Utah (daughter of James Ferguson and Jane Robinson), who was born Oct. 22, 1854, Salt Lake City. Only child: David F. Families resided, Salt Lake City.
Came to Utah from Nevada, and settled at Park City, where he became connected with several of the most prosperous mines—notably the Ontario and the Silver King. In 1884 he was elected representative to the constitutional convention from Summit county, which was held at Salt Lake City the year following. In 1888 he connected himself with the Woodside mine, taking charge of the underground work. The next year he bought into a lease on the Mayflower mine, the other lessees being Thomas Kearns, John Judge, A. B. Emery and W. V. Rice; in 1891 the same parties bonded the Silver King mine. Manager Anchor Mining company. Part owner, with James Ivers, of the Summit block, and sole proprietor of the Pioneer Roller mills, and the ten acre block known as the Tenth Ward square, containing the old exposition building; owner of the David Keith block. Principal owner, with Thomas Kearns, of the Daily Salt Lake "Tribune," and Silver King Mining company, being president of the latter. Capitalist.

KELLER, JACOB (son of Daniel Keller and Elizabeth Frischknecht, both of Schwellbrunn, Switzerland). Born June 22, 1837, at Schwellbrunn. Came to Utah in 1863.
Married Anna R. Hemman July 11, 1863, at sea (daughter of Jacob Hemman and Anna Catharina Dierauer, both of Berneck, Switzerland). She was born April 8, 1837, at Berneck. Their children: Anna b. Dec. 8, 1864, m. Peter H. Westenskow; Mary b. Dec. 9, 1865, m. Christian Munk; Jacob Hirum b. April 19, 1868, m. Annie Dorothy Westenskow; Emma b. June 1, 1870, d. Sept. 28, 1870; Louise b. Sept. 2, 1871, m. James W. Cherry; Eliza R. b. March 13, 1874, m. Luther A. Stringham; Emily Rebecca b. Nov. 29, 1875, m. Halbert S. Kerr; Daniel b. March 22, 1878, d. April 17, 1878.
High priest; seventy; elder; teacher. Farmer. Died Oct. 5, 1892.

KELLER, JAMES MORGAN (son of James Morgan Keller and Anne Pearson of Bjornsholm, Denmark). Born April 6, 1826, at Bjornsholm. Came to Utah Oct. 5, 1854, Hans Peter Olsen company.
Married Karen Margaret Valentine (daughter of Peter Velentine and Margaret Hansen), who was born July 9, 1821. Came to Utah with husband. Their children: Peter J., died; Lena E., died; Theodore b. Nov. 16, 1848, m. Christena Larsen Nov. 1873, m. Lydia Rasmussen Sept. 29, 1877; Julius P., died; Margaret, died; Lena b. Jan. 22, 1855, m. John Olsen; William b. Feb. 9, 1857; James E. b. April 24, 1859, m. Cathrine Larsen April 3, 1877; Jamina, died;

James M. b. June 9, 1865, m. Mary Ellen Baird Dec. 9, 1883. Family home Brigham City, Utah.
Married Annie Margaret Larsen 1856, Salt Lake City (daughter of Anders Larsen and Margaret Nelsen, former pioneer 1855, Peter O. Hansen company). She was born Feb. 27, 1836, Weiby, Fredericksborg, Denmark. Their children: Julius b. Sept. 28, 1857, m. Christena Jeppsen Dec. 8, 1881; Anton Keller b. Aug. 6, 1859; Emelia b. Jan. 19, 1862, m. Peter C. Jensen. Dec. 8, 1881; Annie M. b. Feb. 26, 1864, m. Moroni Jensen March 1888; Hans b. April 29, 1866, m. Mattie Sornsen Dec. 22, 1893; Mantina b. March 3, 1870, m. Joseph Jensen April 16, 1890; Lenora b. Feb. 11, 1872, m. Niels Nielsen Oct. 1, 1890; Alvin b. July 1, 1874, m. Annie Jensen Sept. 21, 1898. Family home Mantua, Utah.
Married Christena Larsen Jan. 5, 1888, Salt Lake City (daughter of Jens Larsen and Bartha Sophia Anderson, pioneers 1858, Captain Brown company). She was born August 1843, Helsingör, Denmark. Their children: Sophia b. Jan. 19, 1859, m. William Pratt Nov. 1884; Adelia b. Feb. 28, 1861; Maria b. Feb. 27, 1863, m. Peter Priest: Charlotte b. Aug. 6, 1865, m. William D. Baird July 23, 1884; Tora b. Oct. 28, 1868, m. Albert A. Wilde July 23, 1884; Towal b. Oct. 28, 1868, m. Delila Dudley Oct. 23, 1895; Romanta b. Dec. 1870, m. Oscar Dockstader 1889; Sylvanus b. Aug. 22, 1872; Adam b. Feb. 14, 1874, m. Adrian Clanton Jan. 3, 1900; Newgena b. Jan. 1, 1876, m. Lorenzo Baird Aug. 28, 1896; Urias b. April 6, 1878, m. Ada Smith Sept. 27, 1905; Sylvestres b. Dec. 7, 1879, m. Clara Egley Oct. 19, 1904; Ernest b. Aug. 13, 1883; Louella b. Oct. 3, 1885, m. Arthur Schwilder Oct. 3, 1907.
Married Sophie Marie Christensen Dec. 26, 1864, Salt Lake City (daughter of Frederick and Johanna M. Christensen, pioneers Sept. 15, 1864, William B. Preston company). She was born June 3, 1847, Helsingör, Fredericksborg, Denmark, Their children: Amos b. March 27, 1866, m. Hannah Roberts Oct. 21, 1884; Nephi b. Aug. 1867, d. infant.
Married Annie Petria Larsen 1879, at Salt Lake City, who was born 1859, Laaland, Denmark. Their children: Sylvester b. Dec. 6, 1880, m. Esther Jensen Oct. 19, 1904; Royal b. Dec. 8, 1882, m. Annie Oliverson Jan. 5, 1910; Allie b. Feb. 14, 1885, m. Hans C. Hanson Sept. 27, 1904; Octavia b. March 31, 1887, m. Ernest Cardingly March 4, 1907; Eli T., Elsadia b. Feb. 6, 1894. Family home Mink Creek, Oneida Co., Idaho.
Elder; missionary to Scandinavia 1876. Took part in Echo Canyon campaign.

KELLER, JAMES MORGAN (son of James Morgan Keller and Karen Margaret Valentine). Born June 9, 1865, Mantua, Utah.
Married Mary Ellen Baird 1883, Logan, Utah (daughter of Alexander Baird and Sarah Delacy), who was born Oct. 28, 1867, Brigham City, Utah. Their children: Thresse b. Oct. 21, 1884, m. Alvin Peterson Dec. 12, 1909; Mabel Carrie b. June 16, 1886, m. Hyrum James Bell Dec. 21, 1905; Ellen Lovene b. Feb. 14, 1888, d. Aug. 29, 1907; Kloa b. April 5, 1892, m. Elmer Larsen Dec. 22, 1909; James Leo b. March 25, 1894; Susie Lena b. March 29, 1897; Melvin M. b. Jan. 30, 1899; Rulon M. b. Jan. 21, 1901; Elmo M. b. Sept. 18, 1903; Tennie June b. June 28, 1906; Mary Ellen b. March 15, 1912. Family home Mink Creek, Oneida Co., Idaho.
Missionary to Denmark 1889-1891, and in 1907; bishop of Mink Creek ward; bishop's counselor 14 years; presided at Berger conference.

KELLY, JOHN (son of James Andrew Kelly, of Kilmarnock, Scotland). Born Aug. 5, 1824, at Kilmarnock. Came to Utah July 1854.
Married Mary Carmichael in Scotland. Only child: John, m. Mary Jane Melville.
Married Margaret Melville February 1867, Fillmore, Utah (daughter of Alexander Melville of Fillmore, pioneer 1856), who was born Dec. 22, 1843. Their children: Mary, died; Quentin Blair, m. Laura Dahlrymple; Alexander, m. Annie Jackson; Eugene, m. Anna Laura Dillon; Viola; Eva, m. Orson H. Holbrook; Ada, died; Irene, m. Don Townsend; Lincoln Grant, m. Jennie Reid.
Families resided at Fillmore, Utah.
Member of seventy. County assessor, treasurer and collector; clerk town board; school trustee; member council. School teacher; merchant. Died Aug. 2, 1905, at Fillmore.

KELSEY, ELI B. (son of Eli and Mary Oldfield). Born Oct. 27, 1819. Came to Utah September, 1852.
Married Letitia Sheets March, 1837 (daughter of Lewis Sheets and Naomi Agin), who was born October, 1818. Their children: George W. b. May 7, 1838; Mary Jane b. March 14, 1840, m. James Gillespie Brigham, d. 1844; Minerva; Emma Celestin, m. Alexander Munhack; Eli b. May 6, 1852; Lorenzo b. Jan. 21, 1855, m. Susanah Tanner; Lewis b. Nov. 22, 1857, m. Jennie Young; John b. May, 1860, m. Susanah Hickman.
Married Jane Waite in Pennsylvania; no children.
Married Mary McIntyre Nov. 20, 1853, Salt Lake City (daughter of Peter McIntyre and Agnes McCole). Their children: Margaret Anna b. Sept. 9, 1853, m. Roman Kouhn; Letitia b. Nov. 14, 1855, m. John A. Bevan 1876; Agnes b. May 10, 1858, m. Richard Adams 1877; Rachel b. Oct. 22, 1859, d. 1860; Grace b. April 14, 1861, d. 1872.
Missionary to Europe; president Scotch mission; president elders quorum at Tooele, Utah; president 43d quorum seventies. Prosecuting attorney Tooele county 1868. Owner and developer of mines in Bingham Canyon; first real estate dealer in Salt Lake City; farmer; merchant.

KELSEY, STEPHEN (son of Stephen Kelsey, born Aug. 17, 1782, and Rachel Allen, born Dec. 15, 1784, of Montville, Geauga Co., Ohio, married May 17, 1828). He was born Dec. 29, 1830, at Montville. Came to Utah July 24, 1847, Brigham Young company.
Married Lydia Snyder March 13, 1851 (daughter of John Snyder and Jane Noble; former died June 5, 1849, St. Louis, latter pioneer Oct. 6, 1850, independent company). She was born Feb. 25, 1833, and came to Utah with mother. Their children: Electa Abigail b. Dec. 8, 1851, m. Frederick Sleight July 20, 1874; Stephen Robert b. Oct. 9, 1853, m. Margaret Ann Wallantine July 20, 1885; Lydia Melissa b. Nov. 1, 1856, m. Samuel Payne Nov. 15, 1877; Sylvia b. Jan. 27, 1859, m. John A. Skinner Oct. 19, 1876; Alice Didame b. Feb. 15, 1861, m. Samuel Nate Feb. 5, 1878; Rachel b. July 5, 1863; Mary Eliza b. March 30, 1865, m. Edward Johnston July 14, 1886; Vienna b. Oct. 19, 1868, m. Martin Stork Dec. 24, 1903; Betsy Ann b. Oct. 19, 1870, m. Horace Chatman March 25, 1896; Minerva Jane b. Jan. 19, 1872, m. Matthew McMurtrie Sept. 18, 1903; Rosina Myranda b. Jan. 24, 1874, m. William Johnston Dec. 23, 1902; Easton John b. Nov. 18, 1876, m. Eliza Pritchell Nov. 26, 1903. Family home Paris, Bear Lake Co., Idaho.

KELSEY, STEPHEN ROBERT (son of Stephen Kelsey and Lydia Snyder). Born Oct. 9, 1853, Brigham City, Utah.
Married Margaret Ann Wallantine July 20, 1885, Logan, Utah (daughter of Christian Wallantine and Elizabeth Caldwell; former a pioneer Oct. 5, 1854, Hans Peter Olsen company, latter Nov. 9, 1856, James G. Willey handcart company). Their children: Robert Monroe b. April 15, 1886; Stephen Lee b. Aug. 10, 1887; Seth C. b. Dec. 19, 1888; Lucius R. b. Aug. 4; 1890; Newell b. Oct. 9, 1392; Zylpha Margaret b. Nov. 1, 1894; Myrtle Elizabeth b. Oct. 7, 1896; Lydia Jane b. Nov. 23, 1898; Mabel b. Oct. 21, 1899; Easton b. Nov. 17, 1901; Daniel b. June 2, 1904; George Delmar and Sarah Velma b. Sept. 28, 1906; Reed b. Dec. 2, 1907; Benjamin b. May 11, 1911.

KEMP, CHARLES (son of John Kemp and Ann Ferneough of Manchester, Eng.). Born Oct. 30, 1833, at Manchester. Came to Utah fall of 1855.
Married Sarah Blackham Dec. 27, 1857, Nephi, Utah (daughter of Samuel Blackham and Martha Robinson of Lancaster, Eng., pioneers 1856, Martin and Wheelock company). She was born June 24, 1840, died 1899. Their children: Charles, d. aged 24; Martha A., d. aged 17; Jessie; Seth; Mary, m. William B. Armstrong, Jr.; Sarah J., m. Daniel H. Morley; Olive, m. George F. Draper; Lizzie, m. Heber Morley; Hannah, m. Stephen M. Peterson; Maud, m. Robert C. Anthony; Charles L., d. aged 2. Family home Moroni, Utah.
High priest; Sunday school and block teacher. Commissioner in San Pete county. Millwright. Died October 1906 at Moroni.

KENDALL, LEVI NEWELL. Came to Utah July 24, 1847, Brigham Young company.
Married Eliza Clemmons 1848, Salt Lake City, who was born March 4, 1835. Came to Utah Oct. 2, 1847, Jedediah M. Grant company. Their children: Levi Cyrus b. Oct. 14, 1849, m. Comfort Ann Cox; Lerina, d. child; Joseph, m. Eliza Clemmons; Justus, died; Ada Mariah, m. Ruben Barsee; Charlotte, m. Richard Code; Nancy, m. Benjamin Boyce; Baby, d. infant; David, m. Mary Burningham. Family home Springville, Utah.
Married Elizabeth Clemmons 1851, Salt Lake City. Their children: Lucy; Sarah; Ruben; Electa; Samuel; and others.
High priest; member seventies. Veteran Echo Canyon and Indian wars. Located in Springville 1856. Farmer. Died 1902 at Springville, Utah.

KENDALL, LEVI CYRUS (son of Levi Newell Kendall and Eliza Clemmons). Born Oct. 14, 1849, Salt Lake City.
Married Comfort Ann Cox Oct. 14, 1872, at Oxford, Utah (daughter of John Cox and Eliza Roberts, both of Oxford, pioneer contingent Mormon Battalion). She was born July 16, 1857. Their children: Levi Cyrus b. Sept. 21, 1874, m. Effie Matilda Smuin; John b. July 25, 1876, m. Miss Bradford; Eliza Ann b. March 9, 1879, m. William Smuin; William Henry b. April 10, 1881, m. Metta May Atwood; Samuel A. b. July 26, 1883, d. child; Charles Thomas b. Sept. 14, 1886, m. Lucy Didama Johnson; Sarah Elizabeth b. Jan. 17, 1890, m. Henry Allen; Franklin Bradford b. Sept. 4, 1907. Family home Oxford, Idaho, and Vernal, Utah.
Deacon; assistant Sunday school superintendent. Moved to Idaho 1860; to Naples 1889. Worked on Logan temple.

KENDALL, LEVI CYRUS, JR. (son of Levi Cyrus Kendall and Comfort Ann Cox). Born Sept. 21, 1874, Oxford, Idaho.
Married Effie Matilda Smuin Dec. 23, 1900, Vernal, Utah (daughter of David and Emma Robison of Vernal), who was born Aug. 9, 1883. Their children: Charles Henry b. May 1, 1902; Bertha Ann b. July 2, 1903; Hazel Emma b. Nov. 27, 1905; Mirtle Adelia b. Oct. 3, 1907; Levi David b. Dec. 6, 1908; Jennie May b. Dec. 12, 1911.

KENDELL, WILLIAM (son of William Kendell and Sarah Wilkinson, Yorkshire, Eng.). Born June 20, 1828, Wickersly, Eng. Came to Utah October 1854.
Married Joanna Peck March 1854, Soham, Cambridgeshire, Eng. (daughter of John Peck and Sarah White of Soham),

who was born April 26, 1827. Their children: William Peek; George W.; John James; Elizabeth J.; Timothy; Sarah J.; Frederick W.; Ira N.; Emma. Family home Uinta, Utah. Missionary to England 1852-54; bishop's counselor 1867-77. District school trustee several terms. Farmer. Died April 12, 1883.

KENDELL, GEORGE W. (son of William Kendell and Joanna Peek). Born April 21, 1856, South Weber, Utah. Married Margery Adella Pingree April 3, 1876, Ogden, Utah (daughter of Job Pingree and Mary Morgan of Ogden, pioneers Sept. 19, 1853). She was born Dec. 5, 1858, died Nov. 2, 1910. Their children: George William b. Aug. 5, 1878; Mary Adella b. Feb. 14, 1880; Job P. b. July 22, 1882; Joanna b. Jan. 14, 1885; Myrtle b. Feb. 8, 1889; Henry Timothy b. Jan. 25, 1891; John W. b. March 7, 1894; Lillie N. b. Dec. 16, 1897. Family home South Weber, Davis Co., Utah. Bishop South Weber Jan. 25, 1891. Constable South Weber precinct six years. Prominent in irrigation matters, serving as director and watermaster. Merchant. Farmer and stockraiser.

KENNARD, LEONIDAS HAMLIN (son of James R. Kennard, born June 21, 1808, in Pennsylvania, and Elizabeth Martin, born March 12, 1812, in Ohio). He was born Jan. 29, 1842, Vinton Co., Ohio. Came to Utah Sept. 30, 1867, William Streeper merchandise train. Married Joanna Louisa Gleason Jan. 29, 1869, Farmington, Utah (daughter of John Streeter Gleason and Deasdemona Chase, former a pioneer July 24, 1847, Brigham Young company, latter a pioneer with Isaac Chase). She was born May 11, 1852, Tooele, Utah, died Jan. 17, 1901. Their children: Leonidas Hamlin b. Oct. 26, 1869, m. Frances C. Frankland May 15, 1901; Deasdemona b. June 12, 1871, d. 1872; Mary Elizabeth b. Jan. 6, 1873, m. Charles H. Tingey May 4, 1892; Geneva b. Dec. 8, 1875, d. 1879; Joanna Louise b. Aug. 10, 1877, m. Charles H. Hales Sept. 15, 1904; Clara Maria b. Dec. 28, 1879, m. Martin Matsen Oct. 25, 1905; James R. b. Sept. 6, 1881, m. Elizabeth Gertrude Jardine March 29, 1906; Kate b. July 9, 1884, m. George R. Hales May 28, 1903; Angie b. Feb. 15, 1886, m. George O. Nye June 15, 1905; Helen b. Dec. 12, 1887, m. Alfred Granger May 17, 1910; Viola b. Oct. 27, 1891; Teresa b. Jan. 22, 1893; Cecil b. Oct. 13, 1894. Family resided Farmington and Riverside, Box Elder Co., Utah. Missionary to Eastern states. School teacher. Clerk Bear River stake; state editor "Deseret News." President high priests quorum. Civil war veteran Co. B, 18th Ohio Vol. Infantry, and commander Maxwell-McKean G. A. R. Post No. 1. School teacher; superintendent schools in Davis county. Postmaster and merchant at Farmington and Riverside.

KENNARD, LEONIDAS HAMLIN, JR. (son of Leonidas Hamlin Kennard and Joanna Louisa Gleason). Born Oct. 26, 1869, Farmington, Utah. Married Frances C. Frankland May 15, 1901, Salt Lake City (daughter William R. Frankland and Elizabeth Anderson, pioneers Sept. 14, 1853, Claudius V. Spencer company). She was born at Salt Lake City. Their children: John Gleason b. March 27, 1902; Frankland James b. Oct. 6, 1903; Gordan Keith b. April 2, 1905; Marguerite b. Dec. 3, 1906; Joanna b. Jan. 22, 1909; Varna b. May 13, 1911. Family home Riverside, Utah. First counselor president; high priest quorum: Malad stake; seventy; first counselor in bishopric of Riverside ward; missionary to Society Islands; home missionary, Malad stake. Farmer.

KENNEDY, CHARLES (son of Alexander Kennedy and Jane McEwen of Edinburgh, Scotland). Born July 1, 1807, New York. Came to Utah Sept. 20, 1848, Brigham Young company. Married Cornelia Gates in Ohio. Their children: Charles Dota. Ellenor R., m. Mr. Mock. Married Frances Gates of Ohio. Married Hulda Elvira Clark Feb. 17, 1841, Illinois (daughter of Silas Clark and Elmina Beach of Illinois), who was born April 14, 1817. Their children: James Horace b. Feb. 3, 1842, m. Melissa Curtice; Cornelia Elmina b. Nov. 4, 1844, m. George Comb Scott; Silas Lorenzo b. Sept. 3, 1850, died; Hulda Elvira b. May 3, 1853; Henry Edward b. May 3, 1853, m. Lydia Palmer, and Charles and Chauncey b. Aug. 3, 1857, died. Families resided at Sugar House, Salt Lake Co., Utah. Member 17th quorum seventies; high priest; ward teacher. Adopted son of Brigham Young and lifeguard of Joseph Smith and Brigham Young while latter crossed plains. Died Jan. 1890, in Arkansas.

KENNER, SCIPIO AFRICANUS (son of Foster Ray Kenner and Sarah Catherine Kirkwood of Kentucky). Born in St. Francisville, Mo. Married Isabelle Gray Park (daughter of Hamilton Gray Park and Agnes Steele, pioneers 1852), who was born Feb. 23, 1863, Salt Lake City. Their children: Hamilton R., m. Dorlinskey Philipps; Jenette B., m. Daniel Lamborne; Edwin T., m. Maud Cook; Agnes S., m. Jesse L. Knight; Park, m. Laverne Farnes; Robert B.; Maud C.; Hazel M., m. George W. Potter; Dortha I., m. William J. Quinn. Family home, Salt Lake City.

KENNEY, JOHN (son of Daniel Kenney and Bridget Riley). Born March 31, 1836, in Ireland. Came to Utah 1858, oxteam company. Married Elizabeth Bennett 1860, Salt Lake City (daughter of Benjamin Bennett and Catherine Jones, both of Connorskay, Eng. Came to Utah 1858, oxteam company). She was born Sept. 26, 1838. Their children: John, m. Esther Fenn; Kate, m. David E. Stevens; Phoebe, m. I. L. Holiman; Benjamin, m. Ellen Nixon; Edward, m. Ellen Johnson; Bert, m. Bertha Textorius. Married Phoebe Alden 1860, Salt Lake City (daughter of William Alden of England), who was born 1837. Their children: Elizabeth, m. Joshua Stevens; William; Eleanor, m. William R. Probert; Daniel; Emma, m. William Johnson; Eliza, died. Families resided at Holden, Utah. Early settler Deseret and Holden, Utah. Veteran Black Hawk Indian war. Farmer.

KENNEY, LOREN E. (son of Parley Kenney and Ruth Hutchens of Maine). Born July 7, 1815, Sutton, Worcester county, Mass. Came to Utah 1847, Isaac Allred company. Married Hanner Nichols (daughter of Robert Nichols and Mary Appleton), who was born March 27, 1812. Their children: Ellen b. Sept. 10, 1843, m. George Sears 1856; Albert b. March 29, 1846, died; Dennis b. Nov. 22, 1852, died. Family home Millard county, Utah. Married Mary Tucker, Salt Lake City. Their children: James Baley b. Aug. 2, 1850; Mary D. b. Nov. 20, 1852, m. Fred Wagner; Selena b. November, 1854; Amasa b. April 9, 1857, m. Canny Fullgreen. Family home Fillmore, Utah. Elder. Member Mormon Battalion. Assisted in making the first adobes in Salt Lake.

KENNEY, AMASA (son of Loren E. Kenney and Mary Tucker). Born April 9, 1857. Married Canny Fullgreen 1875, Spring City, Utah (daughter of Axel and Ellen Fullgreen, pioneers 1855). She was born Aug. 16, 1858, Spanish Fork, Utah. Their children: Amasa b. March 9, 1877, m. Annie Hanson; Christena b. Jan. 12, 1879, m. January 8, 1897.

KENNINGTON, RICHARD. Born Oct. 18, 1804. Came to Utah Sept. 26, 1856, Edward Ellsworth and Daniel D. McArthur company. Married Mary Davison, who was born April 1, 1810, died Aug. 20, 1900. Their children: Sarah Jane b. 1839, m. David Adamson 1862; William Henry b. Aug. 7, 1842, m. Annie Rebecca Seward April 1, 1865; Eliza b. Aug. 23, 1844, m. John England 1863; Richard b. Aug. 7, 1846; Mary Ann b. May, 1854. Died Oct. 13, 1879.

KENNINGTON, WILLIAM HENRY (son of Richard Kennington and Mary Davison). Born Aug. 7, 1842, South Lincolnshire, Eng. Married Annie Rebecca Seward April 1, 1865, Salt Lake City (daughter of George Seward and Esther Sarah Frewin, pioneers Oct. 13, 1863, Rosel Hyde company), who was born Aug. 22, 1841, Newbury, Berkshire, Eng. Their children: Annie Esther b. Feb. 3, 1866, m. Samuel Mathews; Mary Caroline b. Jan. 22, 1868; William Henry b. July 30, 1869, m. Isabell B. Blanchard Oct. 22, 1891; Mary Ann b. April 29, 1872, m. Osborne Low Nov. 8, 1893; Alonzo Richard b. Sept. 2, 1874, m. Susan I. Dixon Sept. 29, 1899; Ida Eliza b. Jan. 6, 1876, m. Adolph S. Jensen June 15, 1898; George Seward b. Sept. 29, 1879, m. Ada Kimball June 24, 1908; Albert Edwin b. June 30, 1883, m. Stella Call Oct. 10, 1906. Married Elizabeth Lee (Bracken) (daughter of Isaac Lee and Julia Chapman; widow of Aaron Bracken; mother of Aaron Franklin and Isaac Lee Bracken). Their children: John b. May 6, 1876, m. Nellie Baxter Jan. 2, 1897; Joseph Hyrum b. Jan. 22, 1878, m. Sarah Jane Walton Oct. 10, 1902; Samuel b. Jan. 10, 1880, m. Rachel Clements Jan. 5, 1899; Alfred b. Dec. 23, 1882; Elizabeth Ann b. Jan. 29, 1884, m. James W. Buckley June 19, 1900; Lucius b. March 2, 1886; Julia Ann b. Oct. 17, 1887, m. Larone H. Stoffer Oct. 20, 1903; Ira Lee b. Dec. 25, 1889.

KENT, SIDNEY B. (son of Samuel Kent and Sarah Jane Standley of Portage Co., Ohio). Born Aug. 21, 1828, in Portage county. Came to Utah Sept. 4, 1848, Daniel A. Miller company. Married Mary Matilda Daley May 5, 1848, Council Bluffs, Iowa (daughter of Moses Daley and Almira Barber of Council Bluffs, Iowa, pioneers Oct. 1, 1849), who was born April 18, 1831. Their children: Mary Ann, m. Joseph Reed; Sarah Almira, m. Cyril Call; Sidney Warren, m. Adelande Ward; William Riley, m. Elsie Deseret Ward; George Albert, died; Charles Edward, m. Susan Valate Noble; Eliza Matilda, m. Edward France; Samantha Adaline, m. Frank Hoops; Alice Eveline, m. Charles Barber; Philo Alvaro, m. Margaret Thomas. Family home Bountiful, Utah. Member 28th quorum seventies; high priest. Captain of militia in Davis county. Farmer. Resides at Lewiston, Utah.

KENT, WILLIAM RILEY (son of Sidney B. Kent and Mary Matilda Daley). Born March 23, 1855, Bountiful, Utah. Married Elise Deseret Ward Jan. 30, 1877, Centerville. (daughter of Martin Ward and Caroline Dalrymple of New York state, m. came to Utah October, 1869). She was born Feb. 11, 1853, Hague, N. Y. Their children: Lillie Maud b. Nov. 1, 1877, m. Leo Nielsen Feb. 9, 1910; Carrie Mary b. March 9, 1881, m. Edwin Brough June 17, 1903; Cleo M. b. 1892. Family home Logan, Utah.

KERBY, FRANCIS, JR. (son of Francis Kerby and Jane Guilleaum of Isle of Jersey, Channel Islands, Eng.). Born Aug. 17, 1820, Isle of Jersey. Came to Utah Sept. 24, 1860, Oscar O. Stoddard handcart company.
Married Mary LeCornu Oct. 8, 1845, Island of Jersey (daughter of John LeCornu and Mary Renouf of same place). She was born Sept. 19, 1823. Their children: John b. April 20, 1846, d. March 13, 1852; Francis b. Aug. 9, 1847, m. Rachel Isabel Riggs, m. Leah P. Smith; Mary b. Oct. 25, 1850, m. Edward Stock; Alma b. Nov. 15, 1853, m. Bathsheba Wall, m. Elda Rogers; Harriet b. Jan. 13, 1855, m. Brigham Mecham; Joseph b. March 16, 1857, m. Nellie Murphy; Eliza b. April 26, 1859, d. Aug. 1, 1861; Alice b. Jan. 11, 1862, m. Robert Cook; Louisa Jane b. April 13, 1864, m. William Nuttall, m. Hyrum Mecham; Isabella b. Jan. 12, 1870, m. David A. Penrod. Family resided Salt Lake City and Wallsburg, Utah.
President of Sheffield conference, England; high priest. Painter. Died at Wallsburg, Utah.

KERSHAW, JOSEPH HYRUM WATKINS (son of George Frederick Watkins Kershaw, born May 6, 1824, and Eliza Byard, born Nov. 25, 1822, London, Eng., who were married Dec. 17, 1849, the latter a pioneer Nov. 1865, Thomas Taylor company). He was born Aug. 27, 1855, Uitenhage, South Africa. Came to Utah November, 1865, with mother.
Married Julia Annie Clift Dec. 17, 1877. Their children: Lydia Maria b. Oct. 24, 1878, d. July 25, 1888; Harriet Eliza b. Sept. 24, 1880, d. 1891; George Alfred b. Sept. 24, 1882, d. March 5, 1897; J. H. W. b. Nov. 25, 1884, d. Feb. 27, 1897; William Priestly b. April 11, 1887, d. Feb. 27, 1897; Edmund Byard b. Sept. 14, 1889, d. Feb. 22, 1897; Lillie Mabel b. April 10, 1892, d. March 6, 1897; Francis Daniel Clift b. Nov. 6, 1894, d. March 6, 1897; Frederick Guy b. April 5, 1896, d. March 9, 1897; Ferdinand Phineas b. Feb. 6, 1898; Julia Isabella b. May 11, 1899; John Wilber, d. Sept. 10, 1902; Charles Elmer b. March 22, 1902; Annie Melissa. Family home St. Anthony, Idaho.

KESLER, FREDERICK (son of Frederick Kesler and Mary Sarah Lindsey of Meadville, Pa.). Born Jan. 20, 1816, at Meadville. Came to Utah Oct. 1, 1851, Orson Pratt company.
Married Emeline Parker May 20, 1836, Augusta, Iowa, who was born March 26, 1818, and came to Utah with husband. Their children: Maryette b. Feb. 23, 1839, m. Jedediah M. Grant Aug. 16, 1855; Antoinette b. Nov. 9, 1840; Caroline Elizabeth b. Jan. 15, 1843, d. April 12, 1845; Joseph b. Jan. 11, 1845, m. Annie Pitts Feb. 4, 1864, d. Jan. 28, 1898; Frederick b. July 27, 1847, m. Sophia Howland, d. Jan. 25, 1896; Laura b. April 22, 1850, m. John Gressman Oct. 10, 1865, d. June 9, 1853; Elvira b. March 21, 1852; Emeline b. July 13, 1854, d. May 4, 1855; Leonard b. Feb. 16, 1856, d. Nov. 19, 1859; Julia b. Nov. 26, 1861, died same day.
Married Jane Elizabeth Pratt March 20, 1854, Salt Lake City (daughter of Anson Pratt), who was born Oct. 22, 1835, Long Island, N. Y., and died Nov. 23, 1912. Their children: Parthenia b. June 3, 1855, m. Joseph Hyrum Parry Sept. 4, 1876; George W. b. Jan. 8, 1857, d. July 27, 1879; Ellen b. Dec. 10, 1858, m. Jenkyn Thomas Oct. 14, 1885; Jacob b. Sept. 20, 1860, m. Ellen Whipple May 3, 1883; Anson b. April 17, 1862, m. Sarah Ann Wixcey April 17, 1884; Edgar b. March 31, 1864, m. Mary Emma Perkins Oct. 16, 1889; Arthur b. Feb. 3, 1866, m. Harriet Taylor Dec. 27, 1888; Alonzo P. b. Jan. 29, 1868, m. Donnette Smith Dec. 26, 1900; John Bert b. April 8, 1870, m. Alice Latham Sept. 22, 1892; Percy G. b. July 4, 1872, d. April 2, 1891; Florence M. b. March 19, 1874, d. April 22, 1874; Clara b. April 4, 1876, m. George H. Crow June 29, 1905; Archie B. b. Sept. 28, 1878, m. Frances Hackard Jan. 3, 1910. Families resided at Salt Lake City.
Married Abigail Snow April 21, 1857, Salt Lake City, who was born Oct. 5, 1837, Caldwell county, Mo. Their children: Alfred W. b. Nov. 28, 1860, m. Laura Olson Dec. 26, 1887; Lena b. Dec. 31, 1862, d. April 9, 1875; Vilate b. Jan. 27, 1865, d. April 18, 1867; Byron L. b. March 25, 1867; Ida b. April 24, 1869, m. B. B. Barnes Jan. 8, 1896; Murray b. Aug. 18, 1871, m. Mildred D. Kearns Sept. 29, 1898.
Bishop Salt Lake City 16th ward 43 years. Built first flour mills Iowa, Kansas, Nebraska and Utah. Constructed ferry boat at Council Bluffs, Iowa. Died June, 1900.

KESLER, JOSEPH (son of Frederick Kesler and Emeline Parker). Born Jan. 11, 1845, in Iowa. Came to Utah 1851.
Married Annie Pitts Feb. 4, 1864, who died Jan. 28, 1898.
A pioneer to southern Utah, one of the first settlers on The Muddy, spending his entire life in the "Dixie" country. Died March, 1898, at Caliente, Nev. He leaves a large posterity in the southern part of the state.

KESLER, ALONZO PRATT (son of Frederick Kesler and Jane Elizabeth Pratt). Born Jan. 29, 1868, Salt Lake City.
Married Donnette Smith December, 1900, Salt Lake City (daughter of Joseph F. Smith and Julina Lambson), who was born 1872, Salt Lake City. Their children: Donnette b. March 13, 1902; Marion b. March 3, 1903; Alonzo b. April 26, 1905; Henry b. April 1907; Imogene b. April 11, 1909; Mack b. August 1911.
Assistant postmaster at Salt Lake 1904 to date. Missionary to London 1894-96; president Eastern States mission, New York City 1897-99. Owner of the Kesler Ranch, where the Garfield Smelter and town now stands. Organized the Mount Pickle Company. Architect and constructor. Built Kesler apartment house. Instrumental in organizing several successful business enterprises.

KETTLE, JOHN (son of John Kettle and Elizabeth Greatrick of Newton, Lincolnshire, Eng.). Born Feb. 1, 1806, Newton. Came to Utah Oct. 5, 1856, Edmund Ellsworth handcart company.
Married Judith Ward 1831, Gosberton Bank, Lincolnshire, Eng. She was born July 28, 1812; died March 12, 1902, Uncompahgre, Montrose county, Colo. Their children: Charlotte b. Feb. 3, 1832, m. Thomas Eldredge; Elizabeth b. Feb. 1, 1834, m. John Rasbal; John b. Dec. 12, 1835, m. Mary Ann Kelley; Mary Ann b. April 19, 1838, m. John Middleton; Robert b. July 29, 1841, m. Mary Ann Kettle; Eliza b. Nov. 26, 1843, m. William Wood; James b. Sept. 22, 1846, m. Anna Belle Brower; Samuel b. Oct. 27, 1850, m. Nettie Hearld; Hannah b. Sept. 16, 1854, m. Oscar Smith. Family home American Fork, Utah.
Elder. Farmer. Died October, 1856.

KETTLE, ROBERT (son of John Kettle and Judith Ward). Born July 29, 1841, Grosberton Bank, Lincolnshire, Eng. Came to Utah Oct. 5, 1856, Edmund Ellsworth handcart company.
Married Mary Ann Kettle Dec. 31, 1866 (daughter of James Kettle and Mary Mackinder, Gosberton Bank. Came to Utah in 1878 by rail). She was born Sept. 1, 1837. Came to Utah Oct. 8, 1866, Andrew H. Scott (Provo, Utah) company. Their children: Mary Ann b. May 5, 1868, m. Samuel S. Boucher; George Robert b. Sept. 30, 1869, d. Oct. 20, 1869; Judith Elizabeth b. Aug. 30, 1871, m. Charles McClellan; Harriet Hester b. Jan. 1, 1874, m. George John Mulvey; John James b. Dec. 21, 1875, d. infant; Arthur Richard b. Nov. 28, 1877, d. infant; Samuel Bruce b. Aug. 19, 1878, m. Julia Smith. Family home Vernal, Utah.
High priest; ward teacher several years. Settled at American Fork 1856; moved to Wet Mountain, Colo., 1871, Kansas 1874, Ouray, Colo., 1875, and Vernal, Utah, 1903. Purchased meeting house and conducted ward branch at Ridgeway, Colo. Farmer and stockraiser.

KEYES, ELISHA BARRUS (son of Hyrum Keyes and Martha Barrus). Born March 28, 1806, in Chenango county, N. Y. Came to Utah Oct. 27, 1852, Eli B. Kelsey company.
Married Joanna Case Worden March 26, 1838, Grafton, Loraine Co., Ohio (daughter of Amos Worden and Mary Case of Antwerp, Jefferson county, N. Y.), who was born Feb. 17, 1822. Came to Utah with husband. Their children: Celia Anzinette b. May 10, 1841, m. Alma Taylor; Mary, m. Thomas M. (d. 1875), m. Alma Taylor; Sarah Ann, d. infant; Elisha B. (d. 1911), m. Lillis Barney; Hyrum H., d. infant; Joanna Isabell (died), m. Thomas Yardley. Family home Provo, Utah.
High priest. Worked on Salt Lake temple. Carpenter. Died Sept. 27, 1855.

KEYES, WILLIAM HENRY HARRISON. Born Nov. 20, 1812, Huron Co., Ohio. Came to Utah Sept. 12, 1850, Captain Johnson company.
Married Eliza Ann Herrick April 12, 1834, Clay county, Mo. (daughter of Lemuel Herrick and Salley Judd of Herkimer, N. Y., pioneers Sept. 12, 1850, Captain Johnson company). She was born Nov. 17, 1815, died November, 1895. Their children: Howard; William; Alma b. Aug. 10, 1839, m. Maria Eveline Tracy April 27, 1862; Sarah, m. D. M. Stewart; Edward; Lyman; Alfaretta, m. Buck Miller; Joseph R.; Francis.
Seventy. Farmer. Died May 9, 1895, Ogden, Utah.

KEYES, ALMO (son of William H. H. Keyes and Eliza Ann Herrick). Born Aug. 10, 1839, Adams county, Ill. Came to Utah Sept. 12, 1850, Captain Johnson company.
Married Maria Eveline Tracy, April 27, 1861, Clackamas county, Ore. (daughter of Joseph and Hannah Tracy of Clackamas county, Ore., pioneers Sept. 12, 1850, Captain Johnson company). She was born Sept. 10, 1847, died March 8, 1894. Their children: William Lemuel b. April 13, 1863; Willard Alonzo b. June 25, 1864; Lyman Henry b. Jan. 29, 1866; Joel Francis b. Jan. 29, 1868; Joseph Loren b. Oct. 2, 1869; Rosetta Mariah b. Sept. 2, 1871; George Alma b. Aug. 14, 1873; Elsie May b. Sept. 19, 1875, m. Samuel Yoeman; Alfred Lee b. Oct. 26, 1877; Eliza Jane b. Dec. 5, 1879; Charles Ray b. March 10, 1881; Alta Virginia and Ethel Esther b. Nov. 22, 1883, twins.
Married Jennie James. Their children: Harry b. Aug. 12, 1896; Evaline Jennie b. Oct. 3, 1898; Theodore McKinley b. Nov. 6, 1900.
Member 75th quorum seventies; high priest; president Y. M. M. I. A.; bishop of Uinta ward. President and later vice president, director and assistant manager Uinta Canning Co. Chief of first volunteer fire department of Ogden. Constable; school trustee; city marshal at Ogden. Chief of police. Farmer; fruit grower; carpenter; stockman.

KEYSOR, GUY MESSIAH (son of Henry Keysor and Elizabeth Scovill of Black Rock, N. Y.). Born Oct. 6, 1816, Black Rock. Came to Utah Oct. 1, 1850, contingent Mormon Battalion.
Married Mary Ann Elven, Salt Lake City, who was born June 8, 1822, died Sept. 5, 1860, Salt Lake City. Their children: Guy Henry b. June 5, 1852; Elizabeth M. b. Nov. 26, 1857, m. Martin Richard.

986   PIONEERS AND PROMINENT MEN OF UTAH

Married Ruth Wyllie Sept. 17, 1855, Salt Lake City (daughter of Oliver Wyllie and Mary Ann George of England; latter pioneer 1855, Captain Brown company). She was born May 1, 1830. Came to Utah 1855 with mother; died 1891. Their children: Mary Merselvia b. Aug. 10, 1856, d. May 3, 1875; James Barnard b. Jan. 14, 1858, m. Louie Felt; Rebecca H. b. Nov. 26, 1860, m. Joseph Orton; William George b. Nov. 21, 1862, m. Sarah A. Hawkins; Peter Moroni b. April 26, 1864, m. Martha Hellen Warren; Ephraim Manassa b. Sept. 11, 1867; Susan Independence b. July 4, 1870, m. William M. McCullough. Families resided at Salt Lake City.
Elder; block teacher; missionary. Stone mason. Died Oct. 3, 1885, Richfield, Utah.

KETSOR, WILLIAM GEORGE (son of Guy Messiah Kesyor and Ruth Wyllie). Born Nov. 21, 1862, Salt Lake City.
Married Sarah Ann Hawkins March 20, 1889, Logan, Utah (daughter of John Bennett Hawkins and Sarah Moulton of Salt Lake City, pioneers 1853 and 1856 respectively, she with handcart company). She was born Oct. 29, 1859. Their children: Sarah Ruth b. May 1, 1892; William Harold b. Sept. 16, 1893; Viola May b. June 7, 1902, d. Oct. 3, 1902. Family home, Salt Lake City.
Member eighth quorum seventies; missionary to Northern States 1901-03; block teacher; ward missionary. Carpenter.

KIESEL, FREDERICK JOHN (son of Friedrich Johann Christoff Kiesel and Louise Buhrer of Ludwigsburg, Württemberg, Germany). Born May 19, 1841, at Ludwigsburg. Came to Utah July, 1863, John Clayton division, Kimball & Lawrence company.
Married Julie Christiane Schanzenbach Arpil, 1872, in Germany (daughter of Christoff Schanzenbach and Wilhelmina Sommers of Ludwigsburg), who was born Nov. 10, 1850. Their children: Frederich William b. Feb. 11, 1874, m. Jane Birdsall Dec. 18, 1901; Wilhelmina P.
Mayor of Ogden; state senator; member constitutional convention. Wholesale merchant.

KIESEL, FREDERICH WILLIAM (son of Frederich J. Kiesel and Julie Christiane Schanzenbach). Born Feb. 11, 1874, Corinne, Utah.
Married Jane Birdsall Dec. 18, 1901, Sacramento, Cal. (daughter of Frederick Birdsall and Esther Stratton of Sacramento), who was born Oct. 9, 1879. Their children: Frederich Birdsall b. Sept. 29, 1905, d. May 26, 1906; Corinne b. Sept. 11, 1907; Phyllis b. March 31, 1910; Robert Allen b. Aug. 30, 1911.

KILLPACK, JOHN (son of Richard Killpack of Northamptonshire, Eng.). Born Jan. 1, 1813, Coventry, Warwickshire. Came to Utah Sept. 20, 1864, Joseph S. Rawlins company.
Married Frances Sheriff, who was born May, 1813, in England. Their children: John b. April 13, 1835, died; Charles, m. Fanny Coates; Louisa b. 1841, m. Abraham Fawson 1862; George, m. Emily Bailey; Joshua, died; Sarah Ann b. Aug. 8, 1851, m. Henry W. Brown March 15, 1869; John b. Aug. 17, 1853, m. Penelope Lambert Dec. 26, 1878.
High priest. Weaver.

KILLPACK, WILLIAM JOSEPH (son of John Killpack and Elizabeth Day of Dunton Bassett, Leicestershire, Eng.). Born Feb. 6, 1832, at Dunton Bassett. Came to Utah September, 1853, Jacob Gates company.
Married Eliza Sarah Sauza Aug. 6, 1854, Salt Lake City (daughter of William and Amy M. Sauza, of London, Eng.; pioneers September, 1853, Jacob Gates company). She was born July 6, (—). Their children: Baby, died; John David b. May 8, 1857, m. Helen Eugenie Peacock; Samuel, m. Maria Funk; William J., m. Malinda Henrie; Mary E., m. Amasa Marian; Frederick Arthur, m. Janie Richards, m. Emma Richards; Edward A., m. Gertrude Perry; Jonathan, m. Mary A. Bradley; Frank H., m. Addie Snow; Charles Rudolph, m. Henrietta Farbush; Grace, m. Lewis Madsen; Jesse M., m. Lewellis Fugate; Clara, m. Lawrence Tuttle.
Member seventies quorum Manti, Utah. Moved to Manti 1858; settled in Glenwood 1863. Black Hawk and Echo Canyon war veteran. Helped build both temple and tabernacle at Manti. Carpenter and millwright. Died Feb. 23, 1910, Manti.

KILLPACK, JOHN DAVID (son of William Joseph Killpack and Eliza Sarah Sauza). Born May 8, 1857, Salt Lake City.
Married Helen Eugenie Peacock Oct. 20, 1877, St. George, Utah (daughter of George Daniel Peacock and Sarah Bell of Manti, Utah; pioneers 1848), who was born June 14, 1860. Their children: John David b. July 29, 1878, m. Eva Bornetta Shipp; Blanche b. Sept. 15, 1880, died; Helen Eugenie b. Oct. 12, 1881, m. Arthur M. Truman; Sarah Elizabeth b. April 12, 1884, m. Alma Williams; William Leslie b. March 26, 1886; Gertrude b. Feb. 11, 1888, m. Theodore B. Bertelson; Calvin Lamar b. July 10, 1890, m. Dora Evaline Hitchcock; Montrose b. March 25, 1893, m. Lulla Bunnell; Uyudella b. Oct. 3, 1894; Ellis b. March 9, 1899; Cleo b. Sept. 13, 1901; Leah b. April 6, 190?.
High priest; first counselor to Bishop J. E. Caldwell; superintendent Sunday schools Molen ward; counselor to Bishop Frederick Olsen, and also bishop of Ferron ward 190?-??; president of Y. M. M. I. A., Manti. Assessor and collector four years. Farm r and stockraiser

KILLPACK, WILLIAM JAMES (son of William Joseph Killpack and Eliza Sauza). Born Oct. 6, 1861, Manti, Utah.
Married Malinda Henrie May 13, 1886, Logan, Utah (daughter of Daniel Henrie and Amanda Bradley, pioneers). She was born Nov. 17, 1864. Their children: Hettie b. Jan. 4, 1889, d. Dec. 30, 1903; Henry b. Nov. 15, 1890, d. Dec. 16, 1903; Amanda b. Dec. 23, 1892, d. same day; Llewellyn b. March 19, 1894; McLloyd b. May 30, 1896; Maralda b. March 18, 1898; Zona b. April 13, 1900; Marion b. Sept. 11, 1902; Alton Bradley b. May 29, 1905. Family home Ferron, Utah.
Elder; Sunday school and ward teacher. Moved to Ferron from Manti 1890; at these places he has used his life in the upbuilding of the country—making canals, wagon roads, bridges, breaking out the land and building the homes. Farmer and dairyman.

KIMBALL, EDWIN (son of Prescott Kimball and Mary Spaulding, New Hampshire and Massachusetts). Born Jan. 3, 1832, in Massachusetts. Came to Utah 1865.
Married Geneva A. Hartwell Nov. 29, 1876, Salt Lake City, Utah (daughter of Elliot Hartwell and Hortense Rogers of Massachusetts and New York; pioneers 1853), who was born July 20, 1853. Their children: Mary Hortense; Edwin Elliot; Douglas Brooks; Scott Prescott. Family home, Salt Lake City.
Mayor of Park City, Utah. Mine supplies business. Died Oct. 11, 1893, in Massachusetts.

KIMBALL, EDWIN ELLIOT (son of Edwin Kimball and Geneva A. Hartwell). Born March 10, 1882, Salt Lake City, Utah. Family home Schenectady, N. Y.
Electrical engineer.

KIMBALL, HEBER CHASE (son of Solomon Farnham Kimball, born 1770, in Massachusetts, and Anna Spaulding of Plainfield, N. H.). Born June 14, 1801, at Sheldon, Vt. Came to Utah July 24, 1847, Brigham Young company.
Married Vilate Murray Nov. 22, 1822, Victor, Ontario county, N. Y. (daughter of Roswell Murray and Susanah Gould of that place), who was born June 1, 1806, and came to Utah 1848. Their children: Judith Marvin; William Henry, m. Mary M. Davenport; m. Melissa Cora Burton; m. Naomi Eliza; Helen Mar, m. Horace K. Whitney; Roswell Heber; Heber Parley, m. Phoebe Judd; David Patten, m. Caroline Williams; Charles Spaulding, m. Elvira Free; Brigham Willard; Solomon Farnham, m. Zula Pomeroy; m. Caroline Fillerup; Murray Gould.
Married Sarah Peak of England at Nauvoo, Ill., who came to Utah in 1848, with husband. Their children: Adelbert Henry, Sarah Helen and Heber, all died.
Married Sarah Ann Whitney (daughter of Newel K. and Elizabeth Ann Whitney; pioneers Sept. 24, 1848, Heber C. Kimball company). She was born March 22, 1825, Victor, N. Y. Their children: David b. 1847, and Orson b. 1848, d. infants; David Heber b. Feb. 26, 1849, m. Lizzie Hammon; Newel b. May 19, 1852, m. Martha W. Winder; Horace H., m. Precilla Tufts; Maria, m. William Jenkins; Joshua H., m. Kate McClain.
Married Lucy Walker, in Nauvoo temple, who came to Utah with husband. Their children: Rachel Sylvia, died; John H., m. Adalaid Hopkins; Willard H., died; Lydia H., m. Mr. Lowry; Annie Spaulding, m. Mr. Knox; Eliza, m. Franklin Woolley; Washington; Franklin H., died.
Married Prescindia Lathrope Huntington, Nauvoo temple, who came to Utah with husband. Their children: Prescindia Celestia, died; Joseph, m. Lathilla Pratt.
Married Clarissa Cutler, Nauvoo temple (daughter of Alpheus Cutler), who died at Cutlerville, Iowa. Only child: Abraham Alonzo, m. Mary Eliza Hatton.
Married Emily Cutler, Nauvoo temple (daughter of Alpheus Cutler), who died at Cutlerville, Iowa. Only child: Isaac Alphonzo.
Married Mary Ellen Abel, Nauvoo temple, who came to Utah in 1847, John Taylor company. Only child: Peter, died.
Married Ruth Reese, Nauvoo temple, who came to Utah with husband. Their children: Susannah R., Jacob R., and Sarah M., all died.
Married Christeen Golden, Nauvoo temple, who came to Utah with husband. Their children: Cornelia C., died; Jonathan Golden, m. Jeanette Knowlton; Elias Smith, m. Miss Whitney; May Margaret, m. Mr. Motfit.
Married Annie Gheen, Nauvoo temple, who came to Utah with husband. Their children: Samuel H., m. Oradine Pratt; Daniel H. b. Feb. 8, 1856, m. Joan Okleberry; Alice, m. Joseph F. Smith; Andrew, m. Louis Seccles; Sarah.
Married Amanda Gheen, Nauvoo temple, who was born Jan. 15, 1830, in Pennsylvania, and came to Utah with husband. Their children: William G. b. March 3, 1851, m. Calista Thornton; Albert E., m. Hattie Partridge; Jeremiah, died; Moroni, m. Agatha Kelley.
Married Harriet Sanders, Nauvoo temple, who came to Utah with husband. Their children: Harriet, died; Hytum H.; Eugene.
Married Ellen Sanders, Nauvoo temple, who came to Utah with husband. Their children: Joseph Smith, Samuel and Augusta, all died; Jedediah; Rosalia, m. William Edward.
Married Frances Swan, Nauvoo temple, who came to Utah with husband. Only child: Frances, died.
Married Martha Knight, Nauvoo temple, who came to Utah with husband. Only child: Baby, d. infant.
Married Mary Smithies. Their children: Melvina; m. Mr. Driggs; James, died; Wilford A., m. Miss Free; Lorenzo, m.

In connection with the above genealogy the following is from the Life of Heber C. Kimball, by Orson F. Whitney.

"In the foregoing lists we have classed together the wives who were the mothers of his children. Besides these there were many others, most of them aged ladies and widows whom he merely supported, without living with them. Following is a list of their names: Mary Fielding Smith (widow of Hyrum Smith, sealed to Heber for time), Margaret McMinn, Hannah Moon, Dorothy Moon, Adelia Wilcox, Huldah Barnes, Eliza Cravath, Mary Ann Shefflin, Charlotte Chase, Theresa Morley, Ruth L. Pierce, Maria Winchester, Laura Pitkin, Abigail Pitkin, Ruth Wellington, Abigail Buchanan, Sophronia Harmon, Sarah Stiles, Elizabeth Hereford, Rebecca Williams, Sarah Buckwater, Mary Dull.

Thus it will be seen that Heber C. Kimball was the husband of forty-five wives (at the funeral of his wife Vilate, Heber, pointing to the coffin, said: "There lies a woman who has given me forty-four wives.") and the father of sixty-five children. Truly a patriarchal household.

It may well be surmised that the government and support of a family of such dimensions were no small tax upon the wisdom, patience and provident care of even the wisest and most opulent. Forever banished be the thought—aspersion upon reason and consistency as it is—that self-seeking, ease-desiring human nature would take upon itself such burdens and responsibilities from any motive less honorable and pure than that which Mormonism maintains is the true one. Luxury and lust so frequently hand in hand; licentiousness and honest toil but rarely.

Heber C. Kimball was a man of industry, a man of virtue, of self-denial, who would sooner have thought of severing his right hand from his body, than to have cherished an unchaste sentiment, or sacrificed a principle to sin or selfish ease. He was often heard to declare that the plural order of marriage, with its manifold cares and perplexities, had cost him "bushels of tears."

Yet his was an exemplary family—as much so as any in all Israel, polygamous or otherwise. His wives loved each other as sisters, and dwelt together in peace and unity; while his children, especially the males, sons of various mothers, clung together with an affection all but clannish in its intensity. Woe betide the luckless wight, who, even in childhood's days, imposed upon a "Kimball boy." The whole family of urchins would resent the insult, and that, too, with pluckiness surpassing even their numbers.

Family prayer was an institution in the Kimball household. Morning and evening the members were called in to surround the family altar and offer up praise and petitions to the Throne of Grace. It is a common remark to this day that such prayers are seldom heard as were wont to issue from the heart and lips of Heber C. Kimball. Reverence for Deity was one of the noticeable features that the God to whom he prayed was a being "near at hand and not afar off." He worshiped not as "a worm of the dust," hypocritically meek and lowly, or as one conscious of naught but the meanness of his nature, and the absence of merit in his cause. But in a spirit truly humble, confessing his sins, yet knowing something of the nobility of his soul, he talked with God "as one man talketh with another"; and often with the ease and familiarity of an old-time friend.

On one occasion, while offering up an earnest appeal in behalf of certain of his fellow-creatures, he startled the kneeling circle by bursting into a loud laugh in the very midst of his prayer. Quickly regaining his composure and solemn address, he remarked, apologetically: "Lord, it makes me laugh to pray about some people."

Heber loved his children, and was justly proud of his numerous noble posterity. If at times he appeared stern, and was severe in his correction, it was not that he loved them less, but their welfare and salvation more. He made no compromise with sin, but nipped it in the bud, though the soil wherein it grew were the hearts of his dearest friends and relations. His greatest desire for his family was that they should be humble, virtuous and God-fearing. The riches, fashions, and even culture of the world were as nothing in his eyes, compared with honesty, morality and the treasures of eternal truth.

Nor was he morose and sullen, because thus soberminded and religious. Mingling with his deeply earnest, profoundly solemn nature was a keen sense of humor, a continuous play of mirth, like "sunlight gilding the edges of a cloud."

First counselor to President Brigham Young in the presidency of the Church of Jesus Christ of Latter Day Saints until his death, 1868. Visited Kirtland, Ohio, late in 1832, and met the Prophet Joseph Smith on Nov. 8. In 1834 went to Jackson county, Mo., with Joseph Smith, Brigham Young and about 200 others. Feb. 14, 1835, was made a member of first body of the twelve apostles, and accompanied them in their first preaching to the eastern states and Canada. In 1837 was placed at the head of the first mission to England; returned in 1838. going to Far-West, Caldwell county, Mo. Returned to England 1840, founding the London conference with Wilford Woodruff and George A. Smith.

Returning to Nauvoo in 1841 and accepting the principles of plural marriage taught to him by the Prophet Joseph, Smith, who also practiced it, his eldest daughter, Helen Mar Kimball, was sealed to the Prophet in full ritualistic form. (See Whitney's history of Utah. Vol. IV, page 191).

Performed various missions to eastern states and constantly sustained President Young as the rightful successor to Joseph Smith after his death.

Left Nauvoo and joined the migrating church members at Sugar Creek, Iowa, Jan. 14, 1846. That summer he recruited the Mormon Battalion on the Missouri river; came to Utah with Brigham Young July 24, 1847; and returned with him to Winter Quarters. Dec. 27, 1847, when the first presidency of the church (unorganized since the death of the Prophet) was organized, he became first counselor to President Brigham Young, and Willard Richards second counselor. May, 1848, started on return trip to Utah, arriving there Sept. 20. First chief justice of the provisional government of Deseret, and lieutenant governor. He introduced at the general conference the subject of the Perpetual Immigration Fund Company, which was forthwith organized. President of the council branch (senate) of the State of Deseret legislature March, 1851, and again of the Territory of Utah September, 1851. Assisted President Brigham Young in laying the southeast cornerstone of the Salt Lake temple April 6, 1853, and offered thereon the prayer of consecration.

During the famine of 1856 he fed hundreds from his provisions, having to put his own families on short rations to feed those who were destitute. Sent his sons William H. and David P. with wagons of food and bedding in connection with the relief corps to assist the belated handcart companies caught in the early snows along the Platte and Sweetwater rivers, thus saving hundreds of lives from perishing, as their companions had.

Whitney, in his history, says of him:

"Preaching, colonizing, traveling through the settlements, encouraging the saints in their toils and sacrifices, sitting in council with church leaders, ministering in sacred places, and in various other ways playing the part of a public benefactor—so wore away the remaining earthly years of President Kimball. His name is a household word wherever his people dwelt, and 'Brother Heber' was everywhere honored and beloved—even the Gentiles esteemed him, admiring his high courage and outspoken candor."

He died at Provo June 22, 1868, principally as the result of an accident, by the overturning of a vehicle in which he was riding at night.

KIMBALL, WILLIAM HENRY (son of Heber Chase Kimball and Vilate Murray). Born April 10, 1826, Mendon, Monroe county, N. Y. Came to Utah Sept. 24, 1848, Heber C. Kimball company.

Married Mary M. Davenport (daughter of James and Marion Davenport, former a pioneer 1847, latter 1848). Their children: Helen Vilate, m. Charles E. Hilton; Marion M., m. Lindsay S. Sprague; Isabell M., m. William Pitts; John H., m. Margaret N. Clayton; William D., m. Emily Serine; Parolee, m. John Haley; Heber R.; Victoria, m. Frank Jackman. Family home, Salt Lake City.

Married Melissa Burton (Cora) (daughter of John Burton). Their children: Burton Shipley; Ida Maria; Charles; Robert Taylor b. Sept. 15, 1857, m. Amanda Hannah Evans Jan. 1, 1878; Rauch Stanley; Lawrence Prosper; Ernest Lynn.

Married Naomi Eliza Redden March 27, 1891 (daughter of Return Jackson Redden and Eliza Naomi Murray; pioneers July 24, 1847, Brigham Young company). She was born Oct. 6, 1858.

Missionary to England 1854-57. Deputy U. S. marshal three years; sergeant-at-arms in legislature two terms; brigadier-general of Utah militia. Assisted in bringing immigrants to Utah, and went to meet the Edward Martin "frozen" handcart company. Received reward for discovering the first coal mine within 40 miles of Salt Lake City, known as "Sprague" mine. Postmaster at Parley's Park. Captain of minutemen in early Indian troubles. Proprietor of Kimball hotel; drove mail and stage line between Salt Lake and Park City 1870-85. Second settler in Parley's Park. Died at Coalville, Utah, Dec. 30, 1907.

KIMBALL, JOHN HENRY (son of William Henry Kimball and Mary M. Davenport). Born Nov. 22, 1851, Salt Lake City.

Married Margaret C. Clayton (daughter of William Clayton and Ruth Moon, former a pioneer July 24, 1847, Brigham Young company, latter 1848). Their children: Henry F. b. 1873, m. Gertie Felt 1902; Elliot T. b. 1875, m. Edith Lowther 1904; Roy De Alton b. 1877; Claire b. 1879, m. William W. Roger 1902; Afton b. 1881, m. A. B. Pembroke 1903. Family home, Salt Lake City.

Hauled freight across plains in 1868; worked at Ontario Mills 11 years. Engaged in livery and transfer business in Salt Lake City 23 years.

KIMBALL, ROBERT TAYLOR (son of William Henry Kimball and Melissa Burton). Born Sept. 15, 1857, Salt Lake City.

Married Amanda Hannah Evans Jan. 1, 1878, Centerville, Utah (daughter of Parley Pratt Evans). Their children: Ada; Clara; Phyllis; Florence; Gilbert Gregor; Robert Walter.

KIMBALL, DAVID PATTEN (son of Heber Chase Kimball and Vilate Murray). Born Aug. 23, 1839, Nauvoo, Ill. Came to Utah in 1848.

Married Caroline Marian Williams (daughter of Thomas S. Williams and Allenry M. Merrill, coming with a contingent of the Mormon Battalion, pioneers 1847). She was born April 24, 1843. Only child: Thatcher b. Aug. 30, 1883, m. Mamie Lee Melton March 1, 1911.

Missionary to Europe; minuteman of early days; president of Bear Lake stake five years; deacon and elder; first counselor to President Saxton. Moved to Arizona and has assisted in developing that country.

KIMBALL, THATCHER (son of David Patten Kimball and Caroline Marian Williams). Born Aug. 30, 1883, St. David, Ariz.
Married Mamie Lee Melton March 1, 1911 (daughter of Robert Smith Melton and Mary Jane Bryant), who was born April 30, 1885, Madisonville, Ky. Only child: Doris Melton b. March 3, 1912.
Missionary to southern states 1908. Ranchman. Engaged in harness and hardware business.

KIMBALL, NEWELL W. (son of Heber Chase Kimball and Sarah Ann Whitney). Born May 19, 1852, Salt Lake City.
Married Martha W. Winder Nov. 28, 1870, Salt Lake City (daughter of John R. Winder and Ellen Walters, pioneers Oct. 10, 1853, John W. Young company). She was born July 7, 1852, Liverpool, Eng. Their children: Sarah Ellen b. July 26, 1872, m. Lorten Cranney; Newel W, Jr. b. Feb. 26, 1875, m. Lottie B. Goodwin Feb. 28, 1899; Mary E. b. Dec. 8, 1877, m. Leonidas Thatcher June 15, 1898; Winnifred b. June 20, 1880, m. Charles D. Priday Sept. 2, 1903; John R. b. Sept. 26, 1882, m. Irma Roza Feb. 6, 1906; Leroy W. b. June 13, 1886, m. Ethel Pilkin Feb. 6, 1904; Leo M. b. June 20, 1889, m. Marie Smith June 23, 1910; Laurence W. b. Sept. 1, 1891; Grant W. b. July 28, 1894, died. Family home, Logan City.
Missionary to southern states 1880; member bishopric in Logan second ward 18 years; member Cache stake presidency five years. Member city council of Logan City three terms; county commissioner two terms; mayor of Logan City in 1888. Branch manager of Cooper Wagon and Machine Co., of Logan for 16 years.

KIMBALL, JOSEPH (son of Heber Chase Kimball and Prescindia Lathrope Huntington). Born Dec. 22, 1851, Salt Lake City.
Married Lathilla Pratt Oct. 30, 1870, at Salt Lake City (daughter of Orson Pratt and Mary Merrill, pioneers July 24, 1847, Brigham Young company). She was born July 19, 1855. Their children: Joseph Raymon b. Nov. 4, 1871, m. Abbie H. Rice; Louie Prescindia b. Oct. 3, 1873, m. Lysander C. Pond; Florence b. June 15, 1875, m. John William Hyde; Ernest b. Sept. 12, 1876, m. Vienna Hortense Booth; Orson Heber b. May 8, 1878, m. Zule Chambers; Alma b. Jan. 3, 1880, m. Katie Wasden; Clark b. Dec. 1, 1881, m. Lydia Maud Partridge; Ethel Beatrice b. Jan. 20, 1884, m. Herbert Williams; Oliver b. Dec. 20, 1885, m. Etta Garrett; Naomi Pearl b. Jan. 15, 1888, m. Alfred Wooley Davis; Reba Geneva b. Sept. 23, 1889, m. Stanley Eugene Hooper; Willard Lathrope b. Dec. 16, 1892, m. Mae Hardy; Pratt b. Aug. 31, 1897. Family home, Salt Lake City.
Reared in Salt Lake City and attended the leading schools; finished with Morgan's Business College and Deseret University. Always took active part in church work. Moved from Salt Lake to Meadowville, Rich Co., Utah, 1871; bishop of that ward 1871-90, when he moved to Cache county; member bishopric 1st ward, Logan; selectman 1878-84, from 1887-89, and probate judge of Rich county 1884-85; chosen member of territorial legislature from districts of Cache and Rich counties; delegate to constitutional convention from Rich county 1882; member second legislature from Cache county; delegate to Trans-Mississippi Congress in Ogden and Salt Lake. Has been largely interested and materially aided in the development of the agricultural resources, stockraising and mining in this intermountain country. Was president and director of many irrigation and canal companies; made the first successful withdrawal of land under Carey Act in Utah; president and director of many mining companies; president of the Logan Chamber of Commerce; actively engaged in irrigation and land development in Southern Utah; extensively interested in the state of Oaxaca, Mexico.

KIMBALL, DANIEL H. (son of Heber Chase Kimball and Annie Gheen). Born Feb. 8, 1856, Salt Lake City.
Married Joan Okleberry Sept. 25, 1875, Salt Lake City (daughter of Paul and Cherstia Okleberry of Malmö, Sweden). She was born Nov. 11, 1854. Their children: D. Carlos b. July 16, 1877, m. Annie Clark; Ernest R. b. Sept. 1, 1878, m. Fannie Coulam; Joan Pearl b. Sept. 4, 1881; Louis C. b. Aug. 16, 1884, m. Lucretia Mangum Aug. 2, 1911; Lester E. b. Aug. 22, 1888, m. Emma Peterson; Charles V. b. Oct. 25, 1892; Sarah Katie b. March 24, 1894.
He became a seventy. Retired business man.

KIMBALL, LOUIS C. (son of Daniel H. Kimball and Joan Okleberry). Born Aug. 16, 1884, at Salt Lake City.
Married Lucretia Mangum Aug. 2, 1911, at Salt Lake City (daughter of Mary Trantery of Nephi, Utah), who was born Jan. 17, 1880. He was an elder.

KIMBALL, WILLIAM GHEEN (son of Heber Chase Kimball and Amanda Gheen, latter died Jan. 15, 1830). Born March 3, 1851, Salt Lake City.
Married Calista F. Thornton March 13, 1875, Salt Lake City (daughter of Samuel Thornton and H. J. Hickenlooper), who was born August 26, 1854. Their children: Florence b. May 11, 1876, m. Lars Francen; May b. Nov. 15, 1878, m. W. H. Mace: Temperance b. Nov. 24, 1880, m. Alma Hill; Pearl b. Dec. 4, 1882, m. John Layman; Birda b. Jan. 15, 1885; Calista b. May 6, 1887, m. William Crowther; Idaho b. Se , 10, 1889; Chase b. Aug. 24, 1891; Charles b. July 23, 1894.

KINDRED, EDMOND HENRY (son of Edmond Henry Kindred and Lucy Wright of Farthingham, Suffolk, Eng.). Born June 8, 1817, Farthingham. Came to Utah Oct. 24, 1855, Milo Andrus P. E. fund company.
Married Harriet Lord October, 1856, Salt Lake City (daughter of Reuben Lord and Charlotte Wright of Ipswich, Suffolk, Eng.), who was born June 3, 1817. Their children: Edmond Henry, died; Harriet, m. Edwin Lee; Lydia Mary, m. George Storrs; Martha, m. James Dowdle, m. John McTague; Charles Alfred; Fannie, m. Joseph William Allen; John Reuben, m. Luella Bird; Nephi (died), m. Annie Pennington.
Seventy; block teacher; ward clerk. Wheelwright and carriage-maker. Died Jan. 28, 1874, Springville, Utah.

KING, DAVID MORRIS (son of Thomas King and Mary Morris of Winfreth, Dorsetshire, Eng., married 1812). Born March 23, 1825, at Winfreth. Came to Utah 1855.
Married Susanna Clark Jan. 1, 1858, Salt Lake City (daughter of Benjamin Clark and Ann Shuker of Cambridge, Eng., pioneers Oct. 15, 1853, Cyrus H. Wheelock company). She was born Dec. 17, 1840, and came to Utah with parents. Their children: Maria Minnette b. Dec. 3, 1858, m. James F. Bunn 1876; Franklin Morris b. Oct. 16, 1860, m. Gertrude Sorensen 1887; Elizabeth Ann b. March 13, 1863, m. William G. Smith 1882; Emily Jane b. June 21, 1866, m. Thomas C. Orr 1885; David Charles b. Oct. 17, 1868, m. Rose Thornick 1894; Isabel Caroline b. Oct. 10, 1871, m. Frederick H. Wood 1897; Thomas Clark b. Oct. 10, 1874, m. Ruella Pearl Rogers 1897; Mary Olive b. April 10, 1878; Nellie May b. Feb. 15, 1880, m. Oliver Orr 1900; Effie Frances b. Sept. 22, 1882, m. Orson Derricott 1902. Family resided Salt Lake City, Utah, and Liberty, Idaho.
Elder. Worked on temple. Echo Canyon war veteran and guard at Salt Lake City. Farmer and stockraiser. Died Jan. 29, 1910.

KING, THOMAS CLARK (son of David Morris King and Susanna Clark). Born Oct. 10, 1874, Liberty, Idaho.
Married Ruella Pearl Rogers Nov. 3, 1897, Logan, Utah (daughter of Ruel Mills Rogers and Hannah C. Nelson of Pleasant Grove; latter pioneer 1867, handcart company), who was born Oct. 30, 1878. Their children: Rowean b. Feb. 28, 1900; Florence b. Feb. 22, 1905; Nellie May b. Oct. 2, 1906; Vilate b. Aug. 12, 1910. Family resided Liberty and Twin Falls, Idaho.
Elder; ward clerk.

KING, ELEAZAR.
Married Nancy Fowler. Their children: Nancy Diana; Abigail Moreney; John; Eleazar, Jr., m. Mary Caroline Fowler; Phoebe; Lorenzo Don; Alonzo; Enoch; Huldah; Mary; Robert.
Elder. Veteran Black Hawk Indian war. Farmer. Died at Spring City, Utah.

KING, ELEAZAR (son of Eleazar King and Nancy Fowler).
Married Mary Caroline Fowler. Their children: Caroline Matilda b. Dec. 11, 1836, m. Charles Whitlock; Eveline Jeanet b. April 15, 1838, d. child; Emily Jane b. March 24, 1840, m. Isaac M. Behunin; Susan Nancy b. Dec. 23, 1842, d. child; Mary Elizabeth b. Oct. 16, 1847, d. child; Abigail M. b. Sept. 16, 1849, m. Joseph S. Stevens; Samuel Eleazar Jan. 26, 1852, m. Cena Nielsen; Elsie Lovina b. March 17, 1854, m. Ole Olsen; George William b. Nov. 9, 1856; Francis Enoch b. Sept. 21, 1858, m. Julia Dodge; James Alonzo b. Dec. 12, 1861, d. child; John Lorenzo b. Jan. 19, 1864, d. aged 10. Family home Ephraim, Utah.
Seventy; elder. Mason and farmer. Settled at Spring City, but was driven from there by the Walker Indians. Was called to settle Circle Valley, and was driven from there by the Black Hawk Indians, losing his home and everything he owned, with the exception of what few things he could gather together, and a few head of cattle. Veteran Walker and Black Hawk Indian wars, and the Echo Canyon campaign in which he served as drummer boy. Died March 20, 1897, Spring City, Utah.

KING, JOHN (son of John King and Hannah Halls of Hockley, Essex, Eng.). Born Sept. 27, 1835, at Hockley. Came to Utah M. Sermon Nov. 15, 1861, who was born October, 1836, and came to Utah Sept. 15, 1861, Ira Eldredge company. Only child: Edith b. Aug. 1, 1871. Family home, Millville, Cache Co., Utah.
Married Elizabeth Griffin Nov. 1, 1868, at Salt Lake City, Utah (daughter of Henry Griffin and Maria Allen, pioneers Sept. 2, 1868, Simpson M. Molen company), who was born Feb. 7, 1851, Walsall, Eng. Their children: Lydia Eliza b. Sept. 5, 1869, m. George S. Obray Nov. 1888; Elizabeth Sarah b. May 19, 1871, m. William C. T. Peterson Jan. 1889; Rosebelle b. Sept. 12, 1873, m. P. L. Nielson Jan. 1896; Harriet Louise b. Sept. 16, 1875, m. William R. Andrew Dec. 1899; Maryette b. Oct. 4, 1877; John Hyrum b. Oct. 28, 1880; Camilla Victoria b. Sept. 25, 1881; Alice May b. April 2, 1883; Jennie Ilene b. July 21, 1887, m. Morgan P. Yeates June, 1907; Grace Evelyn b. Sept. 7, 1889, m. Alma L. Riggs Dec. 1910; Clara Beatrice b. May 4, 1891, m. Golden M. Fergus Oct. 1910; Pearl b. Sept. 14, 1894.
Bishop's counselor 1865-1897. School trustee 1870-85; justice of the peace 1875-79; notary public 1897-1909.

PIONEERS AND PROMINENT MEN OF UTAH 989

KING, JOHN MORRIS (son of Eleazer King and Nancy Fowler of Massachusetts, pioneers). Born Sept. 23, 1809, Sunderland, Bennington county, Vt. Came to Utah Sept. 17, 1852, John Tidwell company.
Married Sarah Ann Jewell February, 1833, Green, Allegheny county, Pa. (Parents lived at Three Rivers, Mich.). Their children: Robert Edson, m. Margaretta Lemon, Jane Purdy and Angeline Thrift Boley; Vemer, m. Isaiah Huntsman; Joseph H., m. Emma Julian; John, m. Effie Cable. Family home, Salt Lake City.
High priest; member Mormon Battalion. Died Nov. 13, 1855, at Salt Lake City.

KING, ROBERT EDSON (son of John Morris King and Sarah Ann Jewell). Born Nov. 1, 1834, Chagrin Falls, Ohio. Came to Utah with father.
Married Margaretta Lemon March 13, 1855, Salt Lake City (daughter of William McClure Lemon and Catherine Mayer of Cass county, Ind., pioneers Sept. 24, 1847, Perrigrine Sessions company). She was born Oct. 4, 1839. Their children: John E. b. Feb. 25, 1856, m. Mary Jane Glines; William b. April 12, 1858, m. Jane Proctor and Annie Johnson; Thaddeus C. b. Aug. 2, 1860, m. Sina Chipman; Mortimer b. Jan. 6, 1863, died; Eva M. b. May 24, 1865, m. Caleb Cotton; Sarah Ann b. July 27, 1867, m. Frank Allen; Catherine b. May 2, 1870, died; Lillian b. June 4, 1873, m. Joseph Brown; Laura b. March 5, 1876, m. Joseph L. Duntley; Martha b. Sept. 25, 1880, m. John F. Kirk. Family home American Fork, Utah.
Married Jane Purdy March 15, 1862, Salt Lake City, who was born April 5, 1838, Ayrshire, Scotland, pioneer, 1862. Their children: Mary Adretta b. Jan. 20, 1863, died; Robert E. b. April 15, 1864; James P. b. Oct. 2, 1866, m. Dot Smith; Melissa Jane b. Nov. 18, 1869, m. Leo T. Shelley; Joseph H. b. May 2, 1871, and David b. Dec. 11, 1873, died; Arthur B. Nov. 2, 1875; William b. Aug. 27, 1878, died.
Married Angeline (Thrift) Boley Feb. 18, 1865, Salt Lake City (daughter of Henry Boley [stepfather] and Elizabeth Davis of American Fork, Utah), who was born Nov. 23, 1843, in Missouri. Their children: Angeline b. Sept. 28, 1866, died; Frances Louisa b. Dec. 28, 1867, m. Joseph Payne; Sena b. Dec. 6, 1869, m. W. W. Rose; Guy T. b. Oct. 15, 1871; Arabella b. Jan. 5, 1876, died; Morris b. Oct. 21, 1877; Edson b. July 13, 1879. Family home American Fork, Utah.
Member 67th quorum seventies; Sunday school teacher. Black Hawk Indian war veteran. Located at American Fork 1856, and assisted in building up the country. City councilman. Farmer.

KING, THOMAS (son of Thomas King), born April 6, 1800, at Dernford Dale, near Stapleford, Cambridgeshire, Eng. Came to Utah Sept. 21, 1853, Claudius V. Spencer company.
Married Hannah Tapfield in 1824 (daughter of Peter Tapfield and Mary Lawson), who was born 1809. Came to Utah with husband. Their children: Georgina b. Oct. 4, 1830, m. Claudius V. Spencer, 1852; Louisa b. Aug. 12, 1833, m. Claudius V. Spencer Nov., 1853; Bertha Mary, b. Oct. 4, 1834, m. Brigham Y. Hampton 1855; Thomas Owen b. April 27, 1840, m. Dorcas Debenham May 23, 1868. Family home, Salt Lake City.

KING, THOMAS JEFFERSON (son of Enoch King and Rhoda Phillips of Ashford, Mass.). Born May 27, 1806, at Ashford. Came to Utah Aug. 9, 1854, Benjamin Thurman company.
Married Rebecca E. Olin July 8, 1827, Shaftsbury, Bennington county, Vt. (daughter of Jonathan Olin and Amy Johnson of Shaftsbury), who was born April 30, 1805. Their children: George E. b. Oct. 23, 1828, m. Sabrina Curtis; m. Mary Susan Kinsley; William J. b. July 13, 1833, m. Elizabeth Baer; Jonathan A. b. Feb. 2, 1835, d. Dec., 1849, Amy Jane b. Oct. 2, 1836, m. Elias Smith; Enoch E. and Rhode E. b. Oct. 3, 1839, d. young; Thomas Franklin b May 1, 1842, m. Lucy A. Ogden; m. Hannah T. Moon; Rebecca A. b. June 29, 1845, m. John O'Brien. Family home Kays Creek (now East Layton), Davis Co., Utah.
Hauled supplies from Camp Floyd, Utah, to Atchison, Kas, for General A. S. Johnston 1861; July, 1862, secured contract for carrying mail from Salt Lake to Brigham City; the Boise express is said to have been the oldest member of the L. D. S. church. Died Sept. 23, 1876.

KING, THOMAS FRANKLIN (son of Thomas Jefferson King and Rebecca E. Olin). Born May 1, 1842, Mantua, Portage Co., Ohio.
Married Lucy Ann Ogden Jan. 1, 1863, Salt Lake City (daughter of Edward Ogden and Sarah Garrett of Stalybridge, Lancashire, Eng., pioneers Oct. 18, 1853, John Brown company). She was born Sept. 23, 1865, m. Anson V. Call; Thomas Edward b. Jan. 17, 1867, m. Elizabeth Manning; Sarah Amy b. May 16, 1869, m. John W. Hess; Elias Silas b. Jan. 24, 1871, m. Elizabeth Shipley; George William b. June 20, 1873, d. young; Esther Ada b. June 20, 1784, m. Isaiah Howe Loveland; Alma b. 1875, d. young; Rebecca Jane b. July 7, 1877, m. Howard Perkins; Jonathan Olin b. Sept. 30, 1879, m. Helen May Gibson; Hyrum Otis b. Sept. 9, 1882, d. 1883. Family resided South Weber and Farmington, Utah.
Married Hannah Temperance Moon April 12, 1883, Salt Lake City (daughter of Henry Moon and Temperance Westwood of England, former pioneer Oct. 5, 1850, latter pioneer, Sept. 11, 1853, Jesse W. Crosby company). She was born Oct. 7, 1861. Their children: Hannah Elnora b. Nov. 22, 1884, m. Ira Decker; Olive Temperance b. Aug. 15, 1886, d. Jan. 13,

1901; Henry LeGrande b. March 19, 1888; Roland Roy b. Sept. 5, 1890; Herbert Moon and Lillian May (twins) b. Aug. 6, 1895; Reuel Franklin b. Jan. 19, 1898; Merle Moon b. Feb. 26, 1900. Family home Farmington, Davis Co., Utah.
Member first bishopric South Weber, 1877-81. Is said to have carried first passenger from Salt Lake City to Brigham City, 1862; assisted in building Union Pacific railway 1869. Assisted in quelling Morrisite disturbance at South Weber. Fruitgrower.

KING, THOMAS EDWARD (son of Thomas Franklin King and Lucy Ann Ogden; he died Jan. 8, 1913). Born Jan. 17, 1867, Mountain Dell, Salt Lake Co., Utah.
Married Elizabeth Manning June 6, 1888, Logan, Utah (daughter of Eli Manning and Deborah Hollist of Farmington, Utah, former pioneer Oct. 18, 1853, John Brown company, latter Sept. 13, 1861, Joseph Horne company). She was born Sept. 5, 1868. Their children: Lucy Elizabeth b. Aug. 3, 1890; George Edward b. Jan. 8, 1892; Deborah May b. Feb. 16, 1894; Rhoda Evaline b. March 25, 1896; Ralph Manning b. Sept. 29, 1898; Edna b. June 13, 1902; Rebecca b. Nov. 15, 1904; Lorus Olin b. Aug. 16, 1911. Family resided South Bountiful, Farmington, Salt Lake and Garland, Utah.
Ordained elder 1882; ward teacher; president of 153d quorum seventies; pioneer of Garland.

KING, THOMAS RICE (son of Thomas King and Ruth Hyde). Born March 9, 1813, Marcellus, Onondaga county, N. Y. Came to Utah 1851, Vincent Shurtliff company.
Married Matilda Robison Dec. 25, 1831 (daughter of John Robison and Cornelia Gumal), who was born March 11, 1811, at Charleston, N. Y., and came to Utah with husband. Their children: William b. April 8, 1834, m. Josephine Henry; Culbert b. Jan. 31, 1836; John R.; Thomas Edwin b. April 19, 1839, m. Rebecca Jane Murray; Delilah; Matilda; Volney LeRoy. Family home Fillmore, Utah.
Missionary to Michigan 1842; assisted in establishing United Order; member Millard stake presidency. Probate judge for years. Resident of Fillmore 25 years; moved to Kingston 1877.

KING, CULBERT (son of Thomas Rice King and Matilda Robison). Born Jan. 31, 1836, in Onondaga county, N. Y. Came to Utah 1851, Vincent Shurtliff company.
Married Eliza Esther McCullough Feb. 5, 1855 (daughter of Levi Hamilton McCullough and Clarinda Altainia Bartholomew), who died June 11, 1898. Their children: Culbert Levi b. June 11, 1856, m. Polly Ann Ross July 31, 1875; Esther Clarinda b. Sept. 24, 1858, m. George Black; Ida Roseltha b. Sept. 7, 1860, d. April 23, 1869; Matilda E. b. April 10, 1863, m. William Black; Deliah b. Feb. 4, 1865, m. Charles E. Rowan; Volney Henry b. Jan. 22, 1867, m. Maria Ross; Julia Frances b. Feb. 4, 1869, m. David Nichols; William b. April 3, 1871, m. Olive Dora Wallace; Elda H. b. Aug. 3, 1873, died; Parley b. Aug. 17, 1875; Alonzo b. May 24, 1877, m. Mary Ann Wallace. Family resided Fillmore, Kanosh and Coyote, Utah.
Married Elizabeth Ann Callister (daughter of Thomas Callister and Helen M. Clark), who was born March 20, 1848, and died December, 1901. Their children: Thomas C. b. May 6, 1868, m. Elizabeth Dunsire; Caroline b. May 6, 1869, m. Edward Savage; Elizabeth Ann b. March 22, 1871, m. Daniel T. Ross; Collins R. b. June 1, 1873; John b. March 16, 1876, d. April 17, 1892; Helen Lulu b. Sept. 2, 1878, d. March 31, 1884; Marion, m. Maria Antoinette Snow; Julina b. July 17, 1887, d. 1890.
Married Sarah E. Pratt (daughter of Parley P. Pratt and Sarah Houston). Their children: Orson Pratt b. Dec. 4, 1879, m. Irene McNally; Heber b. June 24, 1881; Larena b. Feb. 14, 1883, m. Henry Hughes; Junius; Catherine b. April 3, 1890.
Bishop of Petersburg 4 years, of Kanosh 16 years and of Marion ward 22 years; counselor to bishop in Kingston 6 years. Militiaman; Indian interpreter and scout. Express carrier.

KING, CULBERT LEVI (son of Culbert King and Eliza Esther McCullough). Born June 11, 1856, Fillmore, Utah.
Married Polly Ann Ross, Salt Lake City July 31, 1875 (daughter of Thomas Ross and Margret Mecham), who was born Oct. 18, 1858, Provo, Utah. Their children: Eva Clair b. Aug. 14, 1877, m. Robert O. Warner; Culbert Levi b. Nov. 28, 1879, m. Louisa May Gardner Jan. 9, 1902; Margret Ruby b. March 11, 1882, m. John E. Riddle; Thomas Ervin b. March 31, 1884; Lewis b. Feb. 5, 1886, d. Feb. 9, 1902; Elbert b. April 9, 1888, d. May 1, 1887; Florence b. July 18, 1889; Lyman b. April 27, 1892; Maud b. Jan. 13, 1898; Wells Rulon b. Feb. 5, 1900; Mabel Q. b. Aug. 11, 1902. Family resided Kanosh and Coyote, Utah.
Missionary to Southern States 1887; bishop of Marion ward eight years. Settled in Garfield county.

KING, THOMAS CALLISTER (son of Culbert King and Elizabeth Ann Callister). Born May 6, 1866, Petersburg, Utah.
Married Elizabeth Dunsire (daughter of Archibald Dunsire and Marian Brown), who was born July 9, 1887. Their children: Marian Ethel b. Sept. 30, 1887, m. Robert Burns Sherratt Sept. 28, 1910; Thomas Arthur b. Jan. 8, 1889. Family home Coyote, Utah.

KING, THOMAS EDWIN (son of Thomas Rice King and Matilda Robison). Born April 19, 1839, Schroupie, Oswego Co., N. Y. Came to Utah 1851, with father.
Married Rebecca Jane Murray April 29, 1862, Fillmore,

Utah (daughter of Robert Murray and Rebecca Henry), who was born Aug. 17, 1842, Woodstock, N. Y. Their children: Eva Matilda b. March 10, 1863; Ella Vilate b. Feb. 18, 1864, m. Wister B. Harmon June 1, 1881; Naomi b. June 27, 1866, m. Lewis Willis Dec. 16, 1889; Viola b. March 9, 1869; Josephine May b. June 28, 1872; Clifford Carroll b. Aug. 12, 1873; Murray Edwin b. Aug. 7, 1874.
Married Isabella Elicia Savage Jan. 16, 1878, St. George, Utah (daughter of David Savage and Mary Ward), who was born Oct. 28, 1859, Holden, Utah. Only child: Mary Laberna, m. John H. Stoney Dec. 10, 1902; Emily Louisa Heap (adopted) b. March 19, 1895.
Elder; first counselor to Bishop Allen, 2d counselor to Bishop John Morrill; assisted in building St. George temple; missionary to Michigan, Indiana and Illinois. County surveyor. School teacher; merchant; farmer.

KING, WILLIAM (son of Thomas Rice King and Matilda Robison of New York state).
Married Josephine Henry (daughter of Andrew Henry and Margaret Creighton of Ireland at Nauvoo, Ill., and Fillmore, Utah, pioneers 1850), who died 1868. Their children; William H., m. Louisa Ann Lyman; Lillian, m. Ira N. Hinckley; Josephine, m. John W. Thornley; Samuel A., m. Nettie Bagley. Family home Fillmore City, Utah.
Married Mary Ann Henry 1870, Salt Lake City (daughter of Robert Henry of Fillmore, Utah). Their children: Harry W. b. Feb. 28, 1871, m. Katie McBride; Margaret b. 1873, m. Frank Holbrook; Robert b. 1875, m. Hermie Robison; Claudius b. May 15, 1878, m. Daisy Holt; Arthur R. b. Aug. 18, 1880; Lester; Elmer.
Member of high council; bishop; in charge of mission at Hauvern, Ireland, five years. Merchant; manufacturer; stockraiser. Died 1892, Salt Lake City.

KING, WILLIAM HENRY (son of William King and Josephine Henry). Born June 3, 1863, Fillmore, Utah.
Married Louisa Ann Lyman March 17, 1889, Manti City, Utah (daughter of Francis M. Lyman and Rhoda Taylor, pioneers Oct. 19, 1848, Amasa M. Lyman company), who was born Dec. 28, 1868. Their children: Romola; Paul Browning; Josephine; Adrieinne. Family resided Provo and Salt Lake City, Utah.
Member 72d quorum seventies; missionary to Great Britain; member of high council. County attorney; clerk; assessor and collector. Member of city council; attorney recorder; member of legislature three times; president of council; judge Supreme Court; member of congress. Attorney at law.

KINGDOM, WILLIAM HUNTER (son of John Kingdom and Jennet Hunter of Salt Lake City). Born Feb. 21, 1873.
Married Annie May Peck June 21, 1898, Salt Lake City (daughter of Joseph Augustine Peck and Ann Miller of Salt Lake City, pioneers 1848, Brigham Young company), who was born Dec. 28, 1876. Their children: Gladys Mae b. June 15, 1899; William Douglas b. March 10, 1901; Phyllis Jeanette b. March 21, 1903; Joseph Herman b. Oct. 15, 1905; Bernice b. June 15, 1910; Annie b. Dec. 30, 1911. Family home Salt Lake City, Utah.

KINGFORD, WILLIAM RICHARD (son of John Kingford and Elizabeth Files, East Langden, Kent, Eng.). Born Jan. 9, 1820, at East Langden. Came to Utah Oct. 28, 1854, Robert Campbell company.
Married Louisa Burrows July 26, 1851, St. James Church, Dover, Kent, Eng., who was born Oct. 4, 1816. No children. Family home Ogden, Utah.
Member 76th quorum seventies; missionary to England 1886-87; high priest. Worked on Ogden tabernacle; assisted in making Ogden Bench canal, and did much for the upbuilding of Ogden and vicinity.

KINGSBURY, JOSEPH C. (son of Solomon Kingsbury and Bashua Amanda Pease of Enfield, Hartford county, Conn., and Painesville, Ohio). Born May 2, 1812, at Enfield. Came to Utah 1847.
Married Dorcas Adelia Moor March 4, 1845 (daughter of Thomas and Mahalia Moor), who was born Jan. 22, 1829, Bennington, N. Y. She died Dec. 27, 1869, Salt Lake City. Their children: Bashua Dorcas, m. Robert C. Fryer; Josephine Adelia, m. Joseph Fryer; Mary Ophelia, m. Joseph Miservy; Joseph T., m. Jany Mair; Elizabeth M., m. John Druce; Annis L.; Solomon S.; David P., m. Mary Morris; Melvina, died.
Married Loenza A. Pond, born Feb. 15, 1830, died June 15, 1853. Their children: Martha Ann; Vilate Elizabeth; Maria. Family home 12th ward, Salt Lake City.
A descendant of the "Pilgrim Fathers." A close associate of the prophet Joseph Smith. Bishop of 2d ward, Salt Lake, 1851; ordained patriarch 1883 by Wilford Woodruff and Franklin D. Richards. Keeper of the tabernacle gate for many years. His genial, kind disposition caused him to be loved throughout the community. Painesville, Ohio, is located on his father's old homestead. Superintendent of the tithing store many years, and filled many other useful positions during his active career. One of his forefathers came with the pilgrims who landed at Plymouth Rock in 1620, another to Boston Bay in June, 1630. He followed their example of pioneering and came to Utah 1847.

KIRK, JAMES (son of Philip Kirk and Mary Ann Taylor). Born April 11, 1845, Arnold, Nottinghamshire, Eng. Came to Utah Sept. 30, 1862, Joseph Horne company.
Married Mary Peasnall Dec. 20, 1869, Salt Lake City (daughter of William Peasnall and Eliza Sanders, Aldbury, Worcestershire, Eng., pioneers Sept. 15, 1868, Joseph S. Rawlins company). She was born April 18, 1851. Their children: Mary Eliza b. Sept. 17, 1870, m. Alvin James McCuistan Oct. 1, 1891; James b. Aug. 20, 1872, m. Irene Dalton Jan. 25, 1899; Sarah Ann b. Nov. 7, 1874, m. Charles Frederick McDonald Dec. 19, 1907; William Philip b. Nov. 11, 1876; Clair May b. May 1, 1879, died; Elizabeth b. Dec. 7, 1880, m. Edgar June Rich; Rosetta Olive b. April 5, 1885, m. Percy Marshall Oct. 4, 1899; Ada Viola, m. George Hickman Nov. 22, 1906; Spencer Benjamin b. Oct. 27, 1889, m. Vine Blair Jan. 28, 1911; Frank Actor Wakefield b. Aug. 11, 1893, m. Myrtle Helen Williams April 7, 1913.
Married Alice Tarrant Spray (daughter of John Robert Tarrant and Ellen Jarmane of Portsmouth, Hampshire, Eng.), who was born May 24, 1858.
Elder. Assisted in bringing last immigrants to Utah by oxteam 1868; also assisted in carrying provisions that year from Fort Benton to Bitter Creek with Crismon and Wylie militiamen. Worked on construction of Union Pacific and Western Pacific railroads.

KIRKWOOD, ROBERT CAMPBELL (son of Thomas Kirkwood and Margaret Campbell of Bridge-of-Weir, Scotland). Born Aug. 14, 1834, at Bridge-of-Weir. Came to Utah Nov. 9, 1856, James G. Willie handcart company.
Married Elizabeth Cook (Daft) July, 1860, Salt Lake City (daughter of John Cook and Rachel Marson of Eastwood, Nottingham, Eng., pioneers October, 1861, Ira Eldredge company). Their children: Della Maud b. Dec. 19, 1866, died; Katherine b. Aug. 22, 1868, m. Alfred Moyle; Rachel b. Aug. 13, 1870, m. Antone Sorenson; John Alfred b. Jan. 7, 1873, m. Mae Knight; Joseph b. June 13, 1875, m. Pauline Johnson; Milton; Zella. Family home Provo, Utah.
Married Mary Mathews Oct. 21, 1860, Salt Lake City (daughter of William Mathews and Hepzibah Jarvis of Nottingham, Eng., pioneers 1861). She was born Oct. 24, 1837, and came to Utah Sept. 24, 1860, Oscar O. Stoddard handcart company. Their children: Margaret b. Sept. 22, 1861, m. John E. L. Nelson; Thomas Mathews b. March 30, 1863, m. Sarah Jane Whitehead; Robert Campbell b. Dec. 3, 1868, m. Hilda Johnson; Ruth b. Aug. 15, 1870; William b. May 14, 1872; Annie M. b. Jan. 8, 1874, m. Alfred Masterman; Albert Centennial b. Jan. 1, 1876, died; Emma Blanche b. Sept. 9, 1877; Richard Colquhoun b. June 15, 1879, m. Martha Ellen Freshwater; Heber Charles b. April 17, 1882, m. Edith Eliza King. Family resided Salt Lake City and Provo, Utah.
Married Eliza Cook in 1870 Salt Lake City (daughter of John Cook and Rachel Marson). Their children: Tennie b. May 31, 1874; Eugene b. Jan. 7, 1876, died; Ella Mae b. March 26, 1879, m. Charles M. Beckstead; Alice Martha b. Jan. 22, 1881, m. Thomas Albert Bailey; Daniel b. Dec. 9, 1882, m. Bertha Berles; Tessie b. June 10, 1886. Family home Provo, Utah.
High priest; member 45th quorum seventies. Sealer of weights and measures and city councilman in Provo. Superintendent Co-op. stores 1874-85; merchant.

KIRKWOOD, JOSEPH SMITH CAMPBELL (son of Thomas Kirkwood and Margaret Campbell of Bridge-of-Weir, Scotland). Born June 21, 1851, in Scotland. Came to Utah Nov. 9, 1856, with older brother, James G. Willie handcart company.
Married Alice Elizabeth Pulley July 1, 1880, Salt Lake City (daughter of William Pulley and Sarah Morse of England), who was born Feb. 5, 1859. Their children: Olive Margaret b. July 7, 1881, m. George Linn; Joseph Robert b. Feb. 20, 1884; Charles Albert b. Feb. 15, 1886; James b. Aug. 20, 1891, and Leonard b. May 13, 1893, latter three died; Mary Alice b. June 1, 1901. Family home American Fork, Utah.
Elder. Fruit grower and farmer.

KJAR, LOUIS CHRISTIAN (son of Lars Christian Kjar, born in 1816 in Denmark). He came to Utah in 1852, Captain Martin company.
Married Annie Edith Jensen at Logan temple. Their children: Louis Melroy b. Oct. 25, 1885, m. Ephai L. Bird; Clinton b. March, 1887; Aldred Claudius b. July 18, 1890; Edith Pearl b. Jan. 1892; Curtis Anthon, died; Ruth Gelean b. Feb. 26, ——; Florence Cathrine; Lenard Jensen. Family home Manti, Utah.
Bishop of Manti south ward.

KJAR, LOUIS MELROY (son of Louis Christian Kjar and Annie Edith Jensen). Born Oct. 25, 1885, at Manti, Utah.
Married Ephai L. Bird June 18, 1909, Salt Lake City (daughter of Charles Heber Bird and Alice Ann Evans, of Nephi, Utah), who was born Oct. 31, 1886. Their child: Ronald Melroy b. Nov. 6, 1910. Family home Provo Bench, Utah.
Elder. Member M. I. A. of Sharon ward. Farmer and stockraiser.

KLEINMAN, CONRAD. Born about 1820 in Germany. Came to Utah in 1847.
First wife had no children. His second wife was Mary Ann Germer and of the children, a son is given below. The family home was St. George and Toquerville, Utah. He was a patriarch. Farmer and stock grower.

KLEINMAN, JOHN M. (son of Conrad Kleinman and Mary Ann Germer). Born March 10, 1868, Toquerville, Utah.
Did not marry. Lived at Marsh Center, Idaho. Was bishop's first counselor and a missionary to the Northwestern states 1900-1902. Farmer.

KNAPP, ALBERT. Born July 10, 1825, Antwerp, Jefferson county, N. Y. Came to Utah 1847, contingent Mormon Battalion.
Married Rozina Shepard at Salt Lake City (daughter of Isaac Shepard), who was born Jan. 21, 1827. Their children: Azlica Patena; Lydia M.; Sarah Armina, m. William Lobark Skidmore; Silas A.; Justin A.; Morgan A. Family home Farmington, Utah.

KNIGHT, ALONZO (son of Stephen Knight, born May 22, 1784, New Ipswich, N. H., and Polly Knight, born April 29, 1788, Hancock, N. H.; married June 5, 1806). He was born Oct. 14, 1830, Marlow, N. H. Came to Utah Sept. 30, 1850, Joseph Young company.
Married Catharine Meguire April 24, 1853 (daughter of William Wells Meguire and Charlotte Meguire; pioneers 1852, Captain Curtis company; married Dec. 10, 1828, in Pennsylvania). She was born Oct. 15, 1833. Their children: William b. May 31, 1854, m. Florence Dunne March 28, 1872; Charlotte b. May 2, 1857, m. Stephen Green Jan. 3, 1875; Catharine b. Oct. 16, 1858, d. Aug. 21, 1861; Alonzo b. Aug. 22, 1860, d. Sept. 16, 1878; Lucy b. Jan. 16, 1863, m. Robert J. Eames March 29, 1880; Julia Ann b. Dec. 25, 1864, m. Henry Eames Dec. 8, 1881; Stephen b. March 18, 1867, m. Ellen Carver Dec., 1888; Crandal b. March 13, 1869, d. May 10, 1870; Curtis b. Jan. 8, 1871, d. Sept. 4, 1872; Noah b. March 15, 1873, d. Sept. 8, 1878; Marion b. Feb. 6, 1876.
Married Martha Sanders Feb. 10, 1857, Salt Lake City (daughter of Amasa Sanders and Amanda Sanders, pioneers 1849-50), who was born May 25, 1836, in Montgomery county, Ill., and died Dec. 31, 1897. Their children: Amanda b. April 3, 1858, m. Charles Richardson Oct. 27, 1873; Dexter b. Jan. 28, 1860, m. Mary Jane Trappit Jan. 7, 1884; Martha b. Oct. 12, 1861, m. Frederick Wheeler March 7, 1883; Joseph b. Jan. 4, 1863, m. Julia Waymin Dec. 8, 1887; John F. b. Feb. 8, 1865; Samuel b. Oct. 9, 1866, m. Maggie Campkin Feb. 10, 1904; Catharine b. April 29, 1869, m. David Jeremy Dec. 17, 1890; Emma b. May 23, 1871, m. Robert Warring Feb. 18, 1890; Mark M. b. June 21, 1877, m. Sarah Rosetta Young June 12, 1907. Families resided at Plain City, Utah.
High priest; seventy. Teacher.

KNIGHT, JOHN ALLEN (son of James Knight and Charlotte Allen of Cape Colony, South Africa). Born Jan. 10, 1846, Eutenaug, South Africa. Came to Utah Sept. 4, 1864, Captain Patterson company.
Married Isadore M. Atwood July 25, 1868, Salt Lake City (daughter of Miner Atwood and Mary Julie of Connecticut; pioneers 1850). She was born Oct. 27, 1848. Their children: Lillie I.; John M., m. Florence R. Cornell; Adelaide, m. Frederick J. Hatt; William A., m. Effie Phippen; Mary, m. Warren Hilton; Jessie; Charles L., m. Elsie Glen; Milford D.; George H.; Ivey L., m. Harry White; Millan G. Family home, Salt Lake City.
Patriarch. Carriage manufacturer.

KNIGHT, JOHN M. (son of John Allen Knight and Isadore M. Atwood). Born Sept. 14, 1871, Salt Lake City.
Married Florence R. Cornell Dec. 21, 1893, Salt Lake City (daughter of Thomas Cornell and Helen C. Graves of Salt Lake City), who was born Jan. 22, 1870, London, Eng. Their children: Montague b. Oct. 13, 1901; Arthur C. b. May 7, 1896; Melvin J. b. April 7, 1899; Florence L. b. Dec. 24, 1900; Phillis L. b. Oct. 13, 1901; Arthur C. b. May 7, 1903; Richard K. b. April 4, 1905; Newell C. b. Feb. 11, 1909; Ralph D. b. Nov. 27, 1911 Family home, Salt Lake City.
Member eighth quorum seventies; missionary to central states 1895-98; second counselor in presidency of Ensign stake. Carriage manufacturer.

KNIGHT, JOSEPH (son of Joseph Knight and Polly Peck of Marlborough, Windham county, Vt.). Born June 22, 1808, Marlborough, Vt. Came to Utah Sept. 12, 1850, Thomas Johnson company.
Married Betsy Covert March 22, 1832, at Kirtland, Ohio (daughter of James Covert of Cuyahoga county, Ohio), who was born Apr. 27, 1813. Their children: Martha Ann, m. —— Windsor; Mary E., m. C. H. Bassett; Rhoda C., m. Thomas Moore; Joseph J., Orpha F., Ellen R., all d. infants. Family home, Salt Lake City.
Acting bishop of Winter Quarters and Council Bluffs, Iowa. Cooper. Died Nov. 3, 1866, at Salt Lake City.

KNIGHT, NEWEL (son of Joseph Knight, one of six men who laid the corner stone of Nauvoo temple and Polly Peck, of Nauvoo, Ill.). Born Jan. 11, 1800; died on plains on way to Utah.

Married Sally Colburn. Only child: Samuel b. Oct. 14, 1832. Family home Conesville, Broome Co., N. Y.

Married Lydia Goldthwaite Nov. 23, 1835, Prophet Joseph Smith officiating at Kirtland, Ohio (daughter of Jesse Goldthwaite and Lydia Goldthwaite Knight, pioneers Oct. 2, 1850, Edward Hunter company, Jesse Havens, Captain 10). She was born 1812. Their children: Sally, m. Zemyra Palmer; James; Joseph, m. Elizabeth Jones; Lydia, m. John R. Young; Newel, m. Caroline Loveless; Jesse, m. Amanda Melvina McEwan; Hyrum, died. Family home Salt Lake City, Utah.

Died Jan. 11, 1847, at Fort Niobrara, Neb. Jesse Knight has erected a monument at his burial place and that of his companions. This monument is seven miles northwest of Fort Niobrara.

KNIGHT, JESSE (son of Newel Knight and Lydia Goldthwaite. Born Sept. 6, 1845, at Nauvoo, Ill. Came to Utah Oct. 13, 1850, Edward Hunter company.

Married Amanda Melvina McEwan Jan. 18, 1869, at Salt Lake City (daughter of John McEwan and Amanda Higbee, born May 26, 1826, in Chestnut county, Ohio, pioneers 1848). She was born Nov. 13, 1851. Their children: Lydia Minerva b. May 20, 1870, d. 1888; Oscar Raymond b. April 8, 1872, m. Isabel Smith, m. Lottie Heneger; Jesse William b. Aug. 20, 1874, m. Lucy Jane Brimhall; Amanda Inez b. Sept. 8, 1876, m. R. Eugene Allen; Jennie Pearl b. Nov. 7, 1885, m. W. Lester Mangum Sept. 6, 1905; Addie Iona b. Dec. 18, 1891, m. Knight Starr Jordan Sept. 1, 1913. Family home Provo, Utah.

High priest. Founder of the town of Raymond, Canada; built first sugar factory in Northwest territory, being second sugar factory in Canada. President of all the Knight Investment Company's industries; sugar company, power company, woolen mills, smelter company, Iron Blossom mining company, Colorado mining company, Beck Tunnel, Black Jack and Dragon Consolidated Mining Companies; railroad, reservoir, light and irrigation companies. Served the party in many capacities and was unanimously nominated as democratic candidate for governor of Utah, but refused to accept. Large contributor to church and charity. Prime mover and principal contributor in the founding of Maeser Hall of the Brigham Young University at Provo. Director Utah Pioneer Book Publishing Co.

KNIGHT, JESSE WILLIAM (son of Jesse Knight and Amanda Melvina McEwan). Born Aug. 20, 1874, at Payson, Utah Co., Utah.

Married Lucy Jane Brimhall Jan. 18, 1899, Salt Lake City (daughter of George Henry Brimhall and Alsina Elizabeth Wilkins of Salt Lake City, Spanish Fork and Provo, Utah, pioneers of 1849). She was born Dec. 13, 1875.

Missionary to England 1896-98; first bishop of Raymond ward, Taylor stake, Alberta, Canada; second counselor to President Allen of the Taylor stake; first counselor in Utah stake presidency. Nominee for governor on democratic ticket 1908. Associated in the management of the Knight Investment Companies' interests.

KNIGHT, WILLIAM (son of Thomas Sargent Knight and Charlotte Maires, of Devonport, Devonshire, Eng.). Born Dec. 2, 1846, Devonport. Came to Utah Nov. 2, 1864, Warren S. Snow company.

Married Jane Eliza Holden March 21, 1868, Salt Lake City (daughter of Michael Holden and Eliza Orme of England, pioneer 1854). She was born July 25, 1848. Their children: William T., d. aged 14; Eliza, m. Charles Johnson; Amy C., m. William J. Burnett; Walter S., m. Emma Drysdale; Louis M.. m. Florence Smith, m. Lillian Gates; Caroline E., m. Ray E. Montrose; Ivy E., m. Clyde E. Miller; Hazel; Ruby, m. Eugenia M. Clark; Rebecca Gordon, d. infant. Family home Salt Lake City, Utah.

Member of 24th quorum seventies; high priest; block teacher. Boot and shoe salesman.

KNIGHTON, GEORGE (son of George Knighton and Katherine Rigley of Derbyshire, Eng.). Born April 23, 1845, Derbyshire, Eng. Came to Utah 1873, on railroad.

Married Eliza Johnson May 15, 1876, Salt Lake City (daughter of Thomas Johnson and Martha Collough of Bountiful, Utah, who came to Utah 1874, on railroad). She was born Nov. 22, 1858. Their children: George T., m. Mamie Gilbert; Samuel H., m. Hazel Levitt; Katherine, m. Herman A. Gardner; Mary E., m. Oliver A. Penrod; Martha H., m. William C. Penrod; Elizabeth M., m. William H. Oram; Daniel W.; Myrtle A., d. infant.

Elder and ward teacher. Farmer. Served in Civil war 18 months. Died Jan. 4, 1899, Benjamin, Utah.

KNOWLES, EDWARD AUSTIN (son of Samuel Knowles, born July, 1811, Kingsnorth, Eng., and Ann Austin born March, 1812, Parish of Wye, Kent, Eng.). Born March 4, 1848, at Parish of Wye. Came to Utah 1869, last company. Married Elizabeth Jane Smith Nov. 9, 1892, in temple at Logan, Utah (daughter of William Smith and Hannah Dufosee, married April 23, 1862, Salisbury, Wiltshire, Eng.,

Christensen of Holbek, Denmark). She was born Feb. 14, 1834. Came to Utah 1853, John Forsgren company). Their children: Charles William, m. Emily Clarke; Joseph, m. Josephine Carlson; Peter, m. Diniah Hanson; William O., m. Alice Larsen; James, m. Amelia Kaiser; Lauria Amelia, d. Nov. 8, 1864; Juliane Fatime, m. August Valentine; Jonathan C., m. Jennie Prichard; Lorenzo, d. July 16, 1869; Franklin, d. April 29, 1871; Rozella, m. Oluf Petersen; Williamine Dosine, d. Feb. 11, 1875; Hanna Lorinda, d. Dec. 29, 1877. Family home Brigham City, Utah.
One of the first nine converts of the L. D. S. church to sail from Copenhagen to America, Jan. 31, 1852. Settled at Brigham City 1854. Took part in Echo Canyon trouble. Guard during Indian troubles. Farmer and fruitgrower. Died April 20, 1900.

KNUDSON, CHARLES WILLIAM (son of William Knudson and Lauria Amelia Christensen). Born Jan. 18, 1855, at Brigham City, Utah.
Married Emily Clarke Oct. 23, 1879, at Salt Lake City (daughter of John H. Clarke and Elizabeth Heaver of Weston, Idaho, pioneers October, 1855, Richard Ballantyne company). She was born March 12, 1860. Their children: Charles Albert b. July 8, 1880, d. infant; Orville b. June 13, 1881, d. Nov. 18, 1882; Lylia Emily b. Sept. 19, 1883, m. C. C. Clayton; Vinna b. June 16, 1886, d. Jan. 29, 1890; Louella Emeline b. Sept. 16, 1888; Ethel Elizabeth b. Dec. 1, 1890; Earl John b. Sept. 16, 1893; Ray Evelin b. Nov. 17, 1896; Opal b. Oct. 9, 1898; Baby girl b. June 4, 1905, d. same day. Family home Brigham City, Utah.
One of council 58th quorum seventies; missionary to Scandinavia 1883-85; ward clerk seven years; city councilman. Fruit and produce dealer.

KNUTSON, HANS (son of Knud Kokenson and Eli Neilsen). Born Oct. 24, 1819, Finstadsveen, Lorten, Hedemarken, Norway. Came to Utah Oct. 1, 1864, John Smith independent company.
Married Bergite Larson Loken (Johnson) 1850, in Norway (daughter of Lars Loken of Elverum, Hedemarken, Norway). She was born Dec. 23, 1816. Their children: Christena, m. Christian Nelson; Andrew, m. Chasty Sward; Herman, m. Amanda Evert; Bertha, m. Peter Madsen; Ellen, died. Family home Provo, Utah.
Bergite Larson Loken first married John Johnson, pioneer, Oct. 1, 1864. Their children: Ingere b. March 14, 1844, m. J. P. R. Johnson; Lena b. Dec. 9, 1846, m. Peter Madsen; John b. June 7, 1849, m. Ingere Sward.

KOEEN, SVANTE JOHAN (son of Svante Anderson, born 1798 at Kil, Sweden, and Brita Anderson of Rada, Sweden). He was born Dec. 30, 1836, at Rada, Sweden. Came to Utah Oct. 8, 1866.
Married Anna Arvidson 1868 at Salt Lake City, who came to Utah with Captain Scott company. Only child: Oscar b. Sept. 22, 1872.
Married Johannah Louisa Karlson 1888, Logan, Utah (daughter of Anders Karlson). Their children: Frances b. July 17, 1789, d. 1906; Isaac b. Nov. 11, 1891; Ruth b. Sept. 14, 1893; Esther b. April 29, 1895; Mary b. Feb. 24, 1897; Enes b. April 1, 1399; Svean J. b. May 15, 1901.
Missionary to Sweden twice; high priest. Tailor; farmer; stockraiser.

KOFFORD, WILLARD.
Married Christena Neilson Nov. 14, 1881, at Mount Pleasant, Utah (daughter of Hokan Neilson and Johannah Larson). Their children: Anna Christena, died; Willard Hogan, m. Veda Mieling; Clarence Louis, m. Elnora Millett. Family home, Provo, Utah.

KOFFORD, WILLARD HOGAN (son of Willard Kofford). Born May 24, 1858, at Bornholm, Denmark.
Married Veda Mieling July 20, 1909, at Provo, Utah (daughter of James Christena Mieling and Hanna Peterson both of Mount Pleasant, Utah). She was born Aug. 31, 1888. Their children: Evelyn Viola b. April 3, 1910.

KOFFORD, CLARENCE LOUIS (son of Willard Kofford and Christena Nielson). Born July 31, 1887, Mt. Pleasant, Utah.
Married Nancy Lanora Millett Sept. 26, 1906, Provo Bench, Utah (daughter of Artemus Millett and Nancy Beal of Provo), who was born Feb. 8, 1890. Their children: Beria b. April 5, 1907; C. Clarence b. Dec. 17, 1908; Ned Millett b. Oct. 5, 1910.

KOTTER, HENRY HERMAN LUDVICK (son of Frederick Kotter born Nov. 22, 1806, of Housten Beck, Lippdetmoltd, Germany, and Johana Heid born March 13, 1807, at Lage, Germany, who were married Jan. 25, 1835). Born Nov. 20, 1837. Came to Utah Oct. 8, 1866, Andrew H. Scott company.
Married Patrenna Henrietta Boasroup August, 1866, Wyoming, Neb. (daughter of Riedelick Christian Boasroup and Anna Christen Mons). She was born Nov. 8, 1840, d. Aug. 3, 1920. Their children: William Fredrick b. Jan. 14, 1868, m. Ellen Jensen; Johanna b. March 8, 1870, m. J. Z. Stewart; Henry Ludvic b. Feb. 19, 1872, m. Alfreda Larsen

(died), m. Jean Bott; Patrenna b. Jan. 18, 1874, m. J. H. Selley; Ludvick Boasroup b. Oct. 29, 1877, died; Christena Sophia b. Feb. 21, 1876, died; Frederick Oscar b. Jan. 16, 1880; Elnora Henrietta b. Aug. 21, 1882.
Married Wilhelmina Erickson Feb. 22, 1893, at Logan, Utah (daughter of Carl Victor Erickson and Bertha Elizabeth Erickson; former came to Utah 1894). She was born April 6, 1868, in Sweden. Their children: Henrietta Wilhelmina b. May 4, 1894; Ruby Viola b. Aug. 4, 1895; Victor McKinley b. Nov. 3, 1896; Herman Bernard b. July 20, 1897; Homer Clifford b. Nov. 26, 1900; Gertrude Almina b. April 22, 1903; Norma Elizabeth b. Jan. 2, 1905; Elmer Henry b. Aug. 24, 1907; Vendell Carl b. March 31, 1909. Families resided at Brigham City, Utah.
Member city council of Brigham six years; superintendent of water works two years. Brickmaker; farmer, gardener and fruit grower.

KUHRE, MARTIN PEDERSEN (son of Peder Hansen Kuhre, born 1803, and Gundel Kristine Pederson, born May 26, 1802, both of Ronne, Bornholm, Denmark). Born Sept. 15, 1838, at Ronne. Came to Utah Sept. 26, 1862.
Married Hansine Katrine Jensen Feb. 1, 1862 (daughter of Hans Jensen and Ane Kjerstine Hansen), who was born July 27, 1838, and came to Utah with husband. Their children: William Dobbie b. Jan. 21, 1863, m. Alice A. Drown April 14, 1886; Kristine Maria b. Jan. 15, 1864. Family home Ephraim, San Pete Co., Utah.

KUHRE, WILLIAM DOBBIE (son of Martin Pedersen Kuhre and Hansine Katrine Jensen). Born Jan. 21, 1863, at Ephraim, Utah.
Married Alice Adelia Drown April 14, 1886, at Logan, Utah (daughter of David T. Drown and Sarah O. Newell), who was born Dec. 18, 1866, West Jordan, Utah. Their children: Leon William b. May 10, 1887; Helen b. May 12, 1889; Kenneth Drown b. Feb. 21, 1891; Martin Grover b. March 4, 1893; Alice b. June 12, 1895; Ella b. July 16, 1898; Newell John b. July 7, 1900; Thelma b. Sept. 9, 1903; Udell Jensen b. Aug. 21, 1908. Family resided Manti, Salt Lake City and Sandy, Utah.
Member bishopric 1892-1900; bishop of Sandy, Utah; missionary to Denmark. Member of school board; mayor of Sandy.

KUNZ, JOHN (son of John Kunz and Rosina Catharine Klossner). Born Jan. 20, 1823, Diemtigen, Canton, Bern, Switzerland. Came to Utah Aug. 5, 1870, Karl G. Maeser company.
Married Rosina Knutti Oct. 20, 1842 (daughter of David Knutti and Catharine Mani), who was born June 21, 1819, and came to Utah with husband. Their children: John b. Feb. 7, 1844, m. Magdaline Straubhaar Nov. 11, 1863, m. Sophia Straubhaar Oct. 26, 1874; m. Magdalena Linder Nov. 2, 1874; m. Louisa Weibel; m. Margerette Lauener; m. Elizabeth Boss; Rosina b. Oct. 21, 1845, m. Jesse Dredge Oct. 22, 1866; Christian b. Dec. 26, 1846, m. Eliza Buhler Oct., 1870; Catharine b. Sept. 20, 1848, m. James Chivers July 1903; Samuel b. May 18, 1851, m. Eliza Hanni 1872; Gottfried b. June 30, 1853; David b. Oct. 30, 1855, m. Louisa Jacobs Oct. 10, 1878; Jacob b. Aug. 5, 1859, m. Rosa Hirschi April 1883; William b. Dec. 5, 1860, m. Eliza Eschler May 4, 1882; Robert b. Dec. 16, 1862, m. Caroline Eschler May 4, 1882.
Married Catharine Zemp Oct. 29, 1884, Logan, Utah (daughter of Peter Zemp and Barbara Stadelmann), who was born Oct. 5, 1837, in Canton, Luzerne, Switzerland. Families resided at Bern, Idaho.

KUNZ, JOHN, JR. (son of John Kunz and Rosina Knutti). Born Feb. 7, 1844, Diemtigen, Switzerland. Came to Utah July 2, 1873.
Married Magdeline Straubhaar Nov. 11, 1863 (daughter of Peter Straubhaar and Johanna Eggen). Their children: William John b. March 14, 1865, m. Anna Schmid May 5, 1887; Jacob b. April 17, 1866; Rose b. May 16, 1867, m. Gottfried Eschler May 4, 1887; John b. July 14, 1869, m. Mary Schmid April 11, 1894; Magdelina M. b. Oct. 11, 1871.
Married Sophia Straubhaar Oct. 26, 1874, at Salt Lake City (daughter of Peter Straubhaar and Johanna Eggen). No children.
Married Magdalena Linder Nov. 2, 1874, Salt Lake City (daughter of Peter Linder). Their children: Mary M. b. Oct. 15, 1875; Catharine b. Jan. 20, 1878; Eliza R. b. June 19, 1880, m. Jesse H. Dredge Sept. 20, 1898; Wilford J. b. Sept. 24, 1883.
Married Louisa Weibel (daughter of Jacob Weibel and Louisa Kaufman). No children.
Married Margerette Lauener (daughter of Christian Lauener and Margerette Gertsch). Their children: Charles C. b. May 21, 1892; Lovina H. b. July 28, 1893; Abel C. b. Aug. 23, 1896; Heber C. b. Dec. 7, 1898; Melvin b. June 21, 1900; Milton L. b. Jan. 6, 1902; Jesse A. b. Oct. 5, 1903; George S. b. Sept. 20, 1905; Ursula G. b. March 8, 1908; Louisa b. Feb. 16, 1910.
Married Elizabeth Boss (daughter of John Boss and Mary Ann Gertsch). Their children: Agnes R. b. April 25, 1890, m. A. H. Dansie; Julia E. b. Jan. 20, 1893, m. A. Gertsch; Parley F. b. Oct. 28, 1894; Hedwig H. b. Sept. 29, 1896; Lucy M. b. Nov. 13, 1898; Lydia b. May 13, 1900. Families resided Bern, Idaho.
Bishop of Bern ward 1890-1913.

PIONEERS AND PROMINENT MEN OF UTAH

L

LAIRD, JAMES (son of Edward Laird and Sarah Barr of Bonebefore, County Antrim, Ireland). Born Dec. 25, 1825. Came to Utah Nov. 9, 1856, Captain Willie handcart company.
Married Mary Rainey Aug. 20, 1847, in Scotland (daughter of Hughey Mickle Rainey and Elizabeth Creelman of Scotland). She was born July 3, 1826. Their children: Joseph Smith, m. Persis McKee; Edward; Elizabeth, m. Richard Windmill; Almina, m. William Wright; Mary; James; Harriett Ann, Sophia, and Sarah, died; Alexander (died), m. Clarisa Riley. Family home, Salt Lake City.
One of the first settlers at Spanish Fork 1857, Heber City 1859 and Parley's Canyon 1862. Farmer.

LAIRD, EDWARD (son of James Laird and Mary Rainey). Born Feb. 12, 1852, at Anet Lodge, Irvin Parish, Scotland. Came to Utah Nov. 9, 1856, Captain Willie handcart company.
Married Valeria Ann Flint Jan. 15, 1872, Salt Lake City (daughter of William Flint 1848 and Mary Jane Goodrich 1850, pioneers 1848, Heber C. Kimball company). She was born Jan. 14, 1853, Farmington, Utah. Their children: Edward William b. Oct. 27, 1872, m. Annie McKean; Valeria Ann b. May 31, 1874, m. James Taggart; Mary b. Oct. 8, 1875, m. Henry Taggart; James b. May 14, 1877, m. Mayme Harris; Joseph Albert b. Sept. 12, 1878, m. Louie Davidson; Harriett Jane b. May 27, 1880, m. Howell H. Harries; Elizabeth Elmira b. Dec. 30, 1882, died; Rhoda Lois b. Dec. 5, 1883, m. Frank Naylor; Fidella Flint b. March 6, 1886, m. Charles F. Snelgrove; Royal Martin b. March 6, 1888, died 1892. Family home 820 East Twelfth South, Salt Lake City.
Farmer; freighter; general contractor; sheepman. Early settler to Idaho.

LAKE, WILLIAM (son of John and Nancy Lake of Brampton, Eng.). Born March 11, 1812, Brampton. Came to Utah in 1862, Milo Andrus company.
Married Maria Wight. Their child: Ann Maria b. July 9, 1844.
Married Ellen Grimes, Council Bluffs, Iowa. She was born April 16, 1840. Their children: John William b. April 13, 1862, m. Annie Elizabeth Everett; Robert b. Oct. 2, 1863, m. Lilly Coats; Emma Jane b. March 22, 1865, m. Mr. Thornstensen; James Henry b. March 2, 1867, m. Maggie Coats; Annie b. Aug. 2, 1868, deceased; Mary Ellen b. Sept. 23, 1870, m. John William Truscutt; Sarah Elizabeth b. Dec. 25, 1872, m. George Farnsworth; Edward b. Sept. 28, 1874; Rosaie b. Dec. 16, 1875, m. Herbert Farnsworth; Ella b. Aug. 11, 1878, died. Family home Mt. Pleasant, Utah.
Settled at Ephraim; moved to Circleville where he took an active part in the early Indian troubles. Physician. Died Nov. 5, 1891, Mt. Pleasant, Utah.

LAKE, JOHN WILLIAM (son of William Lake and Ellen Grimes). Born April 13, 1862, Ephraim, Utah.
Married Annie Elizabeth Everett March 13, 1883, Mt. Pleasant, Utah (daughter of Charles Washington Everett and Elizabeth Coats). She was born April 13, 1866. Their adopted child: Basil Guy b. Feb. 2, 1895. Family home Castle Dale, Utah.
President 91st quorum seventies; missionary to Oregon; ward teacher 18 years; Sunday school superintendent. Treasurer Castle Dale two years. Stockraiser and farmer.

LAMB, SUEL (son of Erastus Lamb, born 1805, and Abigail M. Jackson, born 1808, both of Connecticut, former died while crossing plains to Utah). He was born March 1, 1833, Huron, Wayne county, N. Y. Left Nauvoo 1846, arrived in Utah October, 1852, James Snow company.
Married Elizabeth Zimmerman Nov. 30, 1854, Lehi, Utah (daughter of George G. Zimmerman and Julia Ann Hoke), who came to Utah in William Critchlow's company. Their children: Elizabeth Victorine b. Oct. 19, 1855, m. William Hyde Jan. 20, 1873; Julia Ann b. Dec. 25, 1857, m. Joseph B. Roper Dec. 28, 1877; Susie b. Jan. 12, 1860, m. William Hawkes Oct. 11, 1878; Harriet Emeline b. Feb. 23, 1862, m. James Johnson Dec. 23, 1880; Olive Rosan b. May 30, 1864, m. Joseph Johnson Oct. 29, 1884; Suel Erastus b. Nov. 20, 1866, m. Phoebe A. Thurston Dec. 12, 1888; Margaret Elsie b. April 1, 1869, m. Joseph T. Sharp April 1, 1888; Myra Christenia b. April 19, 1871, m. Joseph B. Daines Oct. 24, 1889; George Zimmerman b. Aug. 2, 1878, m. Jane E. Grant June 6, 1894; John James b. Oct. 4, 1876, m. Tracy Thurston March 5, 1896.
Married Anna Wys in 1864 at Salt Lake City (daughter of Jacob Wys and Elizabeth Wayman, former a pioneer, handcart company). She was born Sept. 1, 1839, Zurich, Switzerland.
Married Susan Kirby in 1864 at Logan, Utah (daughter of John Kirby and Charlotte Wright), who was born May 5, 1835, Shipmeadow, Suffolk, Eng.
Missionary among the Indians 1853; bishop's counselor to Robert Daines of Hyde Park 15 years. School trustee of Hyde Park. Died Feb. 10, 1913.

LAMBERT, CHARLES (son of Charles Lambert and Sarah Greaves of Kirk Deighton, Yorkshire, Eng.). Born Aug. 30, 1816. Came to Utah October, 1849, was captain in Allen Married Mary Alice Cannon Nov., 1844, at Nauvoo, Ill. (daughter of George Cannon and Ann Quayle of Liverpool, Eng.). She was born Dec. 9, 1828. Their children: Charles J., m. Lillie Druce and Mary Hovey; George C., m. Mary Alice Needham and Rosina Cannon; Richard G., m. Mary Ann Jenkins and Martha Hovey; Mary A., m. Thomas H. Woodbury; Ann T. and Leonora E., m. Isaac M. Waddell; David H., m. Minnie Eldredge; Sarah M., m. Louis C. Shaw; Elizabeth, died; Angus M., m. Edna Snow; Joseph, d. infant; James C., m. Mary Waddell; Elias, died infant; Alma C., m. Mary Woods. Family home, Salt Lake City.
Married Euphemia Gillespy 1872 at Salt Lake City (daughter of Ralph Gillespy and Margaret Thompson, who came to Utah July 12, 1871). Their children: Elizabeth, m. Joseph Porter; William G., m. Olive Patten; Isaac G., m. Florence Cottrell; Thomas G., m. Pearl E. Tomlinson; Maggie G., m. John Carlson. Family home, Salt Lake City.
Senior president 23d quorum seventies; missionary to England, 1882-83 and 1870-71; block teacher. Stone cutter and mason. Died May 2, 1892, at Salt Lake City.

LAMBERT, GEORGE C. (son of Charles Lambert and Mary Alice Cannon). Born April 11, 1848, at Winter Quarters, Neb. Came to Utah October, 1849, Allen Taylor company.
Married Mary Alice Needham May 1, 1871, at Salt Lake City (daughter of James Needham and Alice Warburton, both of St. Louis, Mo., pioneers 1854). She was born March 25, 1853. Their children: May N. b. May 4, 1872, died infant; George C. b. Dec. 10, 1873, m. Kate Y. Clawson; James N. b. June 18, 1876, m. Maria G. James; Mary A. N. b. Aug. 10, 1878, m. John G. Pearr; William N. b. Nov., 1881, died when 10 years old; Lester N. b. Sept. 20, 1885, m. Afton Eldredge; Zina N. b. Nov. 17, 1887, m. W. Haven Willey; Grace N. b. May 19, 1890, m. George P. Frayner; Felicia N. b. April 27, 1893.
Married Rosina M. Cannon Nov. 4, 1872, at Salt Lake City (adopted daughter of George Q. Cannon, but daughter of James Mathews and Mary Oakey). She was born Oct., 1852. Their children: Edna C. b. April 27, 1874, m. Eugene M. Cannon; Leroy C. b. Dec. 23, 1877, d. infant; Ettie C. b. May 23, 1880, m. Emil Egli; Mamie C. b. Dec. 17, 1885, m. James Smith; Sidney C. b. Jan. 22, 1891, d. aged 15. Family home, Salt Lake City.
Missionary to England 1882-84; senior president 23d quorum seventies; worker in Salt Lake temple. Manager Deseret News 1887-92; President and manager Lambert Paper Company 1893; president Lambert Manufacturing Co., Lambert Roofing Co. and Lambert Calendar and Novelty Company.

LAMBERT, JOHN (son of Richard Lambert, born July 10, 1771, West Martin, Yorkshire, Eng., and Patience Vey of Yorkshire—married Oct. 6, 1811, in Yorkshire). Born Jan. 31, 1820, at Gargrave, Yorkshire. Came to Utah Sept. 11, 1850, Lorenzo Young company.
Married Adelia G. Groesbeck Feb. 6, 1846, at Sugar Creek, Iowa (daughter of Garret L. Groesbeck and Mercy Bosworth), who was born April 14, 1822; came to Utah Sept. 12, 1850, Thos. Johnson company. Their children: Martha Adelaide b. Feb. 24, 1847, m. William R. Green Feb. 24, 1866; John Carlos b. Sept. 20, 1849, m. M. A. Woodard 1882, and Olevia F. Anderson 1886; Mary Adelia B. Sept. 11, 1851, m. William Gibson 1873; Sarah Amelia b. March 9, 1853, m. Silas M. Pack Jan. 5, 1874; Richard Franklin b. Feb. 11, 1855, m. Elva E. Woolstenhulme 1886; Jedediah Grant b. July 10, 1857, m. Alice M. Myrick 1887; Ann Maria b. May 24, 1861, m. Thomas A. White 1883; Emma Cordelia b. Jan. 5, 1864, m. Don C. Pack 1896; Mercy Harriet b. March 21, 1866, m. Daniel B. Lewis Jan. 25, 1887. Family resided Salt Lake City and Kamas.
Married Elena Hansena Larsen in 1885, at Salt Lake City (daughter of Hans Larsen and Elena Dorothea Benson of Denmark, pioneers Sept. 30, 1853, Capt. John Forsgren company—married Aug., 1836, at Copenhagen, Denmark). She was born Sept. 13, 1838, in Denmark. Their children: Joseph Heber b. Oct. 27, 1856, m. Alice Matilda Mitchie Jan. 7, 1886; Ephraim b. Nov. 4, 1858, m. Agnes Catherine Harriette Mitchie April 1880; Dan b. March 2, 1861, m. May Young Mitchie April 1880; Dan b. March 2, 1861, m. May Young Moroni Mitchie Jan. 7, 1886; Mary Elizabeth b. June 14, 1865, m. Robert Booth Montgomery Oct. 18, 1885; Sarah Christine b. Aug. 20, 1867, d. Sept. 18, 1867; Rebecca Cornelia b. Aug. 30, 1868, m. Ephraim Merritt Jan. 26, 1885; John Benjamin b. March 10, 1871, m. Edith Lemon Oct., 1892; Laura Amanda b. July 1, 1873, d. July 3, 1875; Parley William b. July 28, 1876, d. Dec. 4, 1892; Emeline Agnes b. May 19, 1879, m. Frank Carpenter 1901; Alice Adelia b. Feb. 7, 1882, d. infant. Family resided, Salt Lake City and Kamas.
Member 9th quorum seventies. Settled at Salt Lake City 1850, moved to Kamas in 1861; at both places took an active part in upbuild of country. Member Nauvoo legion. Echo Canyon war veteran. Worked on Salt Lake temple. Brickmason. Died Nov. 25, 1893, at Kamas.

LAMBERT, JOHN CARLOS (son of John Lambert, born 1820, Yorkshire, Eng., and Adelia G. Groesbeck, born 1822, Trumbull Co., Ohio, married 1846). Born Sept. 20, 1849, at Kansas City, Mo. Came to Utah Sept. 11, 1850, L. Young company.
Married Margarete Ann Woodard Feb. 23, 1882, at Salt Lake City (daughter of Charles N. Woodard and Margarete Ann Malin, pioneers 1847). She was born Feb. 19, 1859, at Salt Lake City, died Jan. 6, 1883, at Kamas, Utah. The only child was Margarete Ann, who died young.
Married Olevia Frances Anderson April 14, 1886, Logan, Utah (daughter of William Oye Anderson and Dorothy

Erickson, pioneers 1847). She was born Nov. 11, 1860, at Salt Lake City. Their children: John Carlos b. Feb. 12, 1887, m. Laura Seymour Sept. 23, 1908; Roy Grant b. April 18, 1888; Olive Alberta b. Feb. 2, 1890, m. Clarence E. Jones June 1, 1910; Alfred William b. March 22, 1892; Harold Alma b. June 18, 1894; Parley Henry b. March 27, 1896; Lorraine b. April 27, 1900. Family resided, Salt Lake City and Kamas.
Ward clerk at Kamas eight years. County commissioner; county road commissioner; justice of peace; school trustee; constable; mayor of Kamas. School teacher. Indian war veteran. Farmer and stockraiser. Died June 29, 1912, at Kamas.

LAMBERT, JOHN CARLOS, JR. (son of John C. Lambert and Olevia Frances Anderson). Born Feb. 12, 1887, Kamas, Utah.
Married Laura Seymour Sept. 23, 1908 (daughter of Charles W. Seymour and Elizabeth Brown; former came to Utah 1853, latter in 1864). She was born June 8, 1885. Only child: Beth b. Aug. 3, 1911. Family home, Salt Lake City.
Elder; superintendent Sunday school at Kamas 1907-08; 2d counselor in Y. M. M. I. A. of Kanab ward 1909. School teacher 1907-09. Deputy state dairy and food commissioner 1911-13. Graduate B. Y. U. 1907. Bachelor of Science Utah Agricultural college 1911.

LAMBERT, JOSEPH HEBER (son of John Lambert and Elena H. Larsen). Born Oct. 27, 1856, at Salt Lake City, Utah.
Married Alice Matilda Mitchie Jan. 7, 1886, at Logan, Utah (daughter of Robert Mitchie of Scotland and Frances Potts of England, pioneers Aug. 1861). She was born Jan. 6, 1866. Their children: Joseph Robert b. Nov. 11, 1886; Ralph b. Nov. 14, 1888, d. infant; Della b. Feb. 13, 1893; Donald b. April 20, 1896, d. infant; Harold b. Aug. 1, 1898; Gladys b. Dec. 6, 1900; Minola b. July 28, 1903; Alta b. Oct. 5, 1905; Reed b. June 12, 1908. Family home Roosevelt, Utah.
President high priests quorum, Roosevelt; missionary to Holland 1889-92; high councilor; stake Sunday school superintendent; one of presidents of seventies; counselor to Bishop Hansen of Roosevelt ward; secretary Y. M. M. I. A. of Kamas ward. Member Heber City council. Settled in Kamas 1861; moved to Heber City 1885, and to Roosevelt 1908; at all these places has assisted in building up the country.

LAMBORN, JOSEPH THOMAS (son of John Lamborn and Ellen Bagley of Bath, Somersetshire, Eng.). Born Feb. 20, 1855, at Bath. Came to Utah 1864.
Married Emily Hulda Sprague, born Jan. 16, 1858 (daughter of Festus Sprague and Lydia Barrus). Their children: Joseph Edwin b. July 18, 1879; Mary Ellen b. Oct. 4, 1881; Emily Eliza b. March 23, 1883; Lydia Malinda b. Jan. 18, 1885; Cora b. May 6, 1889.
President of fourth elders quorum 1903-07; assistant superintendent of Sunday school; ward teacher. Village treasurer. Director in Marysville State bank and Farmers' elevator; stockholder in Marysville Mercantile Co. and Marysville creamery.

LAMBSON, ALFRED B. (son of Boaz Lampson and Polly Walworth of Niagara Co., N. Y.). Born Aug. 27, 1820, Niagara Co., N. Y. Came to Utah Sept. 25, 1847, Elijah E. Fuller company.
Married Melissa G. Bigler Nov. 25, 1845, Nauvoo, Ill. (daughter of Mark Bigler and Susanna Ogden of West Virginia). She was born April 21, 1825. Their children: Melissa J., m. Albert W. Davis; Julina L., m. Joseph F. Smith; Edna L., m. Joseph F. Smith; Alfred B., m. Eveline DeWitt. Family home 17th ward, Salt Lake City.
Seventy; missionary to West Indian islands 1852-54. Machinist and blacksmith. Died Feb. 26, 1905, 17th ward, Salt Lake City.

LANE, JAMES. Born March 1, 1834, Berkshire, Eng. Came to Utah 1861, James S. Brown company.
Married Sophia S. Brown in 1859, Redding, Berkshire, Eng. (daughter of Daniel Brown and Sarah Stopes of Oxfordshire, Eng.). She was born April 17, 1834. Their children: William J., d. aged 18 months; Louisa, m. James Herridge; Sophia J., m. Theodore McKean; Clara E., m. Samuel B. Hazen; Charlotte A., m. Nathan Gedye; Ida M., m. Peter Clegg; Camilla N., m. Horace Hollingworth. Family home Brighton ward, Salt Lake City.
Seventy; choir leader. Boiler maker and farmer. Died Feb. 10, 1879, Brighton ward, Salt Lake City.

LANEY, ISAAC (son of Culbert Means Laney and Margaret Cook of Simpson county, Ky.). Born Dec. 19, 1815, in Simpson county, Ky. Came to Utah in 1847, Captain Hunter company.
Married Sarah Ann Howard March 25, 1841, in Girard, Macoupin county, Ill. (daughter of Samuel Howard and Margaret Disher), who was born Nov. 16, 1822. Their children: Margaret Elizabeth b. Jan. 13, 1843, m. James Elijah Malin; George Culbert. Family home, Salt Lake City.
One of the presidents in seventies quorum. Died Oct. 31, 1873, at Salt Lake City, Utah.

LANGFORD, JEREMIAH EUCHLET (son of Jeremiah E. Langford and Mary Ann Jackson of Rome, Ga.). Born Sept. 18, 1848, at Rome. Came to Utah Sept. 11, 1856, Seth M. Blair company.

Married Sarah E. Olson March 18, 1880, Salt Lake City (daughter of Shure Olson and Ellen Jacobs of Salt Lake City, pioneers Oct. 25, 1849, Charles Hopkins company). She was born Dec. 30, 1854. Their children: Sarah Ellen and Mary Ann b. Oct. 29, 1881; Jeremiah E. b. March 1, 1884, m. Florence Tuddenham; Estella b. Jan. 16, 1887, m. Albert Leroy Taylor; Lester O. b. Nov. 14, 1890; Florence b. Dec. 22, 1892; Ralph Jackson b. Dec. 23, 1896.

LANGFORD, WILLIAM E. (son of Jeremiah Langford and Mary E. Jackson). Born Jan. 16, 1850.
Married Caroline A. Reed (daughter of Levi W. Reed and Matilda Pettit). She was born April 1, 1859, at Salt Lake City—married Oct. 10, 1876, at Salt Lake City. Their children: William L. b. April 25, 1878; Levi A. b. Oct. 31, 1879, d. aged 27; Pearl A. b. June 28, 1881; Jeremiah b. May 27, 1883, d. aged 8; Francis b. May 27, 1883, d. infant; Ira A. b. June 12, 1886, m. Lillian Baker; Ruby O. b. Sept. 16, 1890; Mary E. b. Dec. 28, 1892; John O. b. Nov. 5, 1894; Lewis W. b. Nov. 15, 1898; Archie C. b. Dec. 25, 1900. Family home, Salt Lake City.

LANGLEY, GEORGE. Born Sept. 20, 1818, in Tennessee. Came to Utah in September, 1848.
Married Mary Turner. Their children: Elsie; Mary; George.
Married Martha Frost Aches in 1845, Nauvoo, Ill. (daughter of McCleana Frost and Pirrina Smith of North Carolina pioneers Sept., 1856). She was born 1826, Knox county, Tenn. Their children: Martha McInna, m. Hyrum Karren; Perrina McCleane, m. James Allen.
Missionary to Memphis, Tenn; Brigham Young's bodyguard. Captain of police at Nauvoo. Captain of first company that came across the ice at Nauvoo. Standing guard at Nauvoo temple. Built first adobe house at Salt Lake City. Died Feb. 24, 1850, and was first man buried in Salt Lake cemetery.

LANGSTON, JOHN (son of Francis Langston and Elizabeth Heathecut). Born March 8, 1822, in London, Eng. Came to Utah in 1854.
Married Clarinda Phillips Sept. 5, 1844 (daughter of Israel Phillips and Dorothy Rose, the former came to Utah 1854). She was born Jan. 19, 1829. Their children: John F. b. Sept. 15, 1852, m. Ann Morris; Clarinda Jane b. Feb. 2, 1857, m. H. F. Stout; Mary Emma b. Feb. 15, 1859, m. Alfred F. Stout; Isaac Heber b. Nov. 28, 1860, m. Rosiipha Dalton; Jacob Heathecut b. Jan. 20, 1863, m. Alice M. Hall; Alice Ann b. Feb. 1865, m. Orley Dalton; Laura Matilda b. April 15, 1869, m. Brigham Dalton; William Robert b. Feb. 15, 1872, m. Phoebe Farnes. Family resided Alpine and Rockville, Utah.
Married Elizabeth Ann Freestone March 7, 1857, at Salt Lake City. She was born Jan. 26, 1841, in Harden Co., Ohio. Their children: Elizabeth Ellen b. April 4, 1858; George Heber b. Sept. 22, 1860.
Seventy. Indian war veteran. Settled in Dixie in 1862. Died Dec. 21, 1882, at Rockville.

LANGSTON, JACOB HEATHECUT (son of John Langston and Clarinda Phillips). Born Jan. 20, 1863, at Rockville, Utah.
Married Alice Maud Hall Oct. 1, 1884, at St. George (daughter of John C. Hall, pioneer 1851, and Kezia DeGrey). She was born April 5, 1864, at Rockville. Their children: Maud, m. D. Earl Bishop Dec. 20, 1906; Jacob Alma b. May 3, 1887, m. Jennie P. Camp Dec. 21, 1910; Ella b. Jan. 12, 1889; Sarah b. Sept. 26, 1890; Myrtle Kezia b. Dec. 15, 1892; Charles John b. March 24, 1895; Carrie b. Oct. 22, 1898; Tressie b. April 2, 1901; Enola b. Sept. 24, 1903. Family resided Rockville and Hinckley, Utah.
Bishop's counselor at Rockville and also at Hinckley. Member state legislature, 1910 session.

LAPISH, JOSEPH (son of Joseph Lapish and Ann Mitchel of Woodhouse, Yorkshire, Eng.). Born April 3, 1830, Woodhouse. Came to Utah Aug. 27, 1860, with Daniel Robinson handcart company.
Married Hannah Settle July 3, 1853, Bradford, Yorkshire, Eng. (daughter of William Settle and Hannah Strickland of Beeston, near Leeds, Yorkshire). She was born Nov. 2, 1834. Mrs. Lapish founded the society of the Daughters of the Handcart Pioneers April 14, 1910. Their children: Marhitha A. d. child; Laura J., m. William H. Bird; Emily V., m. Silas D. Beebe; Joseph S.; James W., m. May Kirby, m. Addie Brice; Sarah Ann, m. Phillip Stelzer; Rose Hannah, d. infant; Kate Amalia and Fanny Sherwood (twins), d. infants.
Missionary to eastern states and England, 1883 to 1886; president high priest's quorum; Sunday school superintendent at Salina. Upon arrival in Utah he settled at Lehi, where he taught school and engaged in farming. In 1866 and 1867, in company with Edward Webb, he made an overland trip for freight to Los Angeles, Cal.; in 1867 and 1868, in company with Gilbert Webb, he built a telegraph line between Cheyenne, Wyo., and Denver, Colo. In

1868 he moved to Salt Lake county, where he engaged in mining and smelting work; in 1876 he moved to Salina, where he served as school trustee, town clerk and justice of peace. Died March 2, 1909, Salina, Utah.

LAPISH, JOSEPH SETTLE (son of Joseph Lapish and Hannah Settle). Born Nov. 4, 1861, Lehi, Utah. Member 4th state legislature of Utah. Inventor.

LARAMIE, ONEZIME (son of Louis Laramie and Mary Vinet of Canada). Born Sept. 25, 1837, St. Rock, Canada. Came to Utah 1859.
Married Harriet Ground Dec. 16, 1861, Salt Lake City (daughter of Amond Ground), who was born 1840. Their children: Harriet Esther b. Jan. 25, 1863, m. Richard Wilson; Mary Elizabeth b. Sept. 21, 1865, m. David Allen; Onezime Louis, died. Family home Orangeville, Utah.
Married Alice Heaps Dec. 25, 1870, Panaca, Nev. (daughter of Henry Heaps and Susannah Turner of Garston, Eng., pioneers 1863). She was born March 18, 1855. Their children: Susannah b. April 18, 1872, m. Henry Davis; Alice Annis b. April 11, 1874, m. John W. Woolsey; John Henry b. Oct. 18, 1879, m. May Moffett; Armeline b. June 30, 1886, m. William Taylor; Josette b. Feb. 21, 1886, died; Henrietta b. June 8, 1890, m. Orsen Miles. Family home Orangeville, Utah.
Member 86th quorum seventies. Farmer; shoemaker; apiarist.

LARK, WILLIAM (son of Samuel and Miss Coe of Norfolk, Eng.). Born March 15, 1819, at Norfolk. Came to Utah Aug. 30, 1860, Jesse E. Murphy company.
Married Mary Clarkson in 1843 at Beverly, Eng. (daughter of Mathew and Elizabeth Clarkson of Beverly). She was born Oct. 28, 1824. Their children: Maria Elizabeth b. Jan. 11, 1844; Mary Francis b. May 3, 1846; Clarissa b. March 26, 1848, m. James Knight; Minus b. March 1, 1851; Erastus Robert b. Feb. 15, 1853, m. Mary Peterson; Isabella b. Aug. 23, 1855, m. James Knight; William Henry b. May 23, 1858; Angus Edward b. Aug. 9, 1859; Louisa b. Aug. 13, 1861; John Albert b. May 16, 1863; Julia Ann b. Nov. 1, 1866, m. Benoni Green. Family resided Beverly, Eng., and Salt Lake City, Utah.
Clerk for George Q. Cannon in immigration work; ward clerk. Died May 23, 1889.

LARK, ERASTUS ROBERT (son of William Lark and Mary Clarkson). Born Feb. 15, 1853, at Beverly, Yorkshire, Eng.).
Married Mary Petersen Feb. 13, 1879, at Salt Lake City (daughter of Christian Petersen and Elizabeth Jensen of Denmark, pioneers of Oct., 1860, John W. Young company). She was born March 3, 1860. Their children: Erastus Edward b. Jan. 26, 1880, m. La Verna Nelson; Mary Elizabeth b. Nov. 30, 1882, m. Eri W. Butler; Frank Theodore b. July 4, 1885; Clarissa Ellen b. June 7, 1888, m. Joseph D. Wilkins; William Charles b. March 16, 1891; Alice Lenora b. May 21, 1894; Robert Ozro b. Nov. 30, 1898; Milton Leland b. June 26, 1901; Hazel Geneva b. June 29, 1905. Family home Brinton, Utah.

LARKIN, ELIJAH (son of Thomas Larkin and Sarah Southwell of Cambridge, Eng.). Born April 20, 1829, at Chesterton, Cambridge. Came to Utah Oct. 3, 1863, Daniel D. McArthur company.
Married Sarah Parfey 1846 at Chesterton, Cambridge, Eng. (daughter of James Parfey and Mary Phillips of Chesterton). She was born Aug. 16, 1812. Their children: George William Larkin b. April 1, 1847, m. Ann Lane; Joseph S. Larkin b. Dec. 5, 1851, m. Harriett Chatterly.
Married Ruth Coe Nov. 17, 1863, at Salt Lake City (daughter of James Coe and Rose Gostling Barrett of East Dereham, Norfolk, Eng.). She was born April 27, 1833. Their children: Ruth b. Jan. 6, 1865, m. Orrin W. Bates; Susan b. Feb. 19, 1867, Elijah b. Jan. 16, 1869; John b. Dec. 31, 1871; James and Alma b. Oct. 29, 1874.
Died Jan. 4, 1905, at St. Johns, Tooele Co., Utah.

LARKIN, GEORGE WILLIAM (son of Elijah Larkin and Sarah Parfey). Born April 1, 1847, at Chesterton, Cambridge, Eng.
Married Ann Lane Aug. 2, 1869, at Salt Lake City (daughter of Henry Lane and Bridget Lyles of Leicester, Eng., pioneers of Sept. 6, 1864, Captain Rawlins company). She was born Dec. 16, 1850. Their children: George William b. July 30, 1870, m. Annie Trott; Elijah A. b. March 30, 1876, m. Aurelia Mary Kremer; Emily A. b. Aug. 19, 1873; Sarah J. Larkin b. July 29, 1879, m. William W. Shaw; Alma J. b. Dec. 12, 1881, m. Nellie Stark; Zina R. b. Aug. 23, 1884; Ellen E. b. Jan. 8, 1889, m. Lester H. Patterson; Josephine P. b Oct. 23, 1891. Family home, Ogden.
Counselor in first quorum of elders, Weber stake; later made president; first counselor to Bishop T. J. Stevens of fifth ward, Ogden; ordained patriarch July 21, 1901. Holds Royal Humane medal of Great Britain for saving lives of three persons.

LARSEN, ANDERS. Born Dec. 23, 1814, at Sunderstranders, Denmark. Came to Utah Sept. 12, 1861, John R. Murdock company.
Married Mary Jensen. She was born June 25, 1812; came to Utah with her husband. Their children: Lars C. b. Jan. 28, 1842, m. Clara C. Jensen Nov. 6, 1864; Ness b. May 4, 1843, m. Sarah Nelson; John b. May 1, 1845, m. Anna Jensen; Maria, m. Paul Hansen; Anna C., m. Jens C. Jensen. Family home Logan, Utah.
Farmer and stockraiser. Died Nov. 1864.

LARSEN, LARS C. (son of Anders Larsen, born Dec. 23, 1814, and Mary Jensen, born June 25, 1812, of Sunderstranders, Denmark). Born Jan. 28, 1842, at Guedumluned, Denmark. Came to Utah Oct. 10, 1861, Goodby and Wright company.
Married Clara C. Jensen Nov. 6, 1864 (daughter of Jens C. Jensen and Christina Peterson, the former pioneer 1862, Mattson company, the latter died at Florence, Neb., en route to Utah). She was born May 1, 1848. Their children: Clara C. b. June 9, 1866; Lars C., Jr. b. June 27, 1867, m. E. A. Hebdon March 29, 1890; Mary b. Dec. 21, 1869, m. Joseph Nelson Feb. 12, 1890; Andrew b. March 19, 1872; James b. Dec. 26, 1874, m. Olga F. L. Peterson Feb. 27, 1902; George b. June 16, 1877; Alma F. b. Dec. 19, 1879; Alice M. b. Aug. 1, 1882; Nephi Hyrum b. April 26, 1885, m. Cathrine McKinney Dec. 12, 1906; Annie L. b. July 23, 1888, m. Herbert Owen June 3, 1908. Family home Logan, Cache Co., Utah. Presided in absence of bishop 3rd ward, Logan, Utah; ward teacher 40 years; home missionary Cache stake 1890; worked on various church buildings. Assisted in building Utah Northern R. R. Farmer.

LARSEN, LARS, C., JR. (son of Lars C. Larsen and Clara C. Jensen). Born June 27, 1867, at Logan, Utah.
Married Elizabeth A. Hebdon (daughter of James R. Hebdon and Mary A. K. White, pioneers July 1869, Captain Loveland company). She was born April 6, 1875, at Paris, Idaho. Their children: Christina James b. Jan. 17, 1894; Clara Elizabeth b. March 14, 1895; Lars Harvey b. Feb. 11, 1897; Melinda Alice b. Nov. 22, 1898; Merlin Joseph b. March 21, 1902; Percy William b. Aug. 24, 1905; Arland Alvin b. Nov. 29, 1909; Vesta b. Sept. 1, 1911. Family home Glendale, Idaho.
First counselor in deacons quorum; president deacons quorum two years; assistant secretary of Sunday school, 3rd ward; director-secretary, 3rd ecclesiastical organization; ward clerk; first counselor to E. E. Hopkin of Worm creek branch of Preston ward; first counselor to Austin T. Merrill; bishop. Justice of the peace of Riverdale precinct two terms; school trustee.

LARSEN, JOHN (son of Anders Larsen and Mary Jensen). Born May 1, 1845, at Guedumluned, Denmark. Came to Utah in 1861.
Married Anna Nelson Nov. 25, 1866, at Logan, Utah (daughter of Ole Jensen and Enger Pearson, pioneers 1862, Captain Horne company). She was born Dec. 4, 1846, at Herby, Sweden. Their children: Mary Ann b. Sept. 3, 1867; John A. b. Sept. 14, 1869, m. Myra Allen Dec. 3, 1895; Nephi b. Aug. 1, 1872, m. Bertha S. Parkinson Dec. 7, 1898; Willard b. Jan. 8, 1875, m. Anna B. Cowley March 4, 1902; Alma b. Oct. 3, 1877, m. Martha Swainston Jan. 7, 1906; Charley b. March 10, 1880; Louisa b. March 10, 1880; Marinda b. April 15, 1886; George Lee b. Jan. 11, 1889; Blanch b. June 27, 1890, m. J. Eugene Cluff Oct. 12, 1910. Family home Logan, Utah, and Preston, Idaho.
Bishop's counselor 15 years; bishop of Preston three years; high councilor. Merchant and Banker.

LARSEN, ANDREW (son of Larse Andrews and Hannah Eskelson of Sweden). Born Jan. 26, 1819. Came to Utah Sept. 13, 1857, Christian Christensen handcart company.
Married Caroline Andrews in 1846, born Dec. 23, 1812, at Naima, Sweden. Their children: Lewis b. March 12, 1847; Anna Hannah b. Nov. 30, 1849, m. Dunham Van Leuven, Nov. 30, 1864; Mary Christine b. May 6, 1852, m. Henry F. Collin Feb. 7, 1872. Family home Springville, Utah.
Ward teacher; merchant. Died June 4, 1899, at Mapleton, Utah.

LARSEN, ANDREW (son of Ole Larsen and Ingeborg Maria Rholfsen of Reesoer, Norway). Born March 26, 1844, Reesoer, Norway. Came to Utah Sept. 25, 1863, Peter Nebeker company.
Married Esther Anne Follette Dec. 18, 1879, St. George, Utah (daughter of William Tillmon Follette and Esther Bayliss of San Pete Co., Utah, the former came to Utah with a division of the Mormon battalion). She was born Oct. 4, 1856.
Missionary to Norway 1892-94; first counselor to Bishop D. L. Harris of Monroe, Utah. President of Monroe town board; town trustee. Early settler in Sevier county. Veteran Indian war. Farmer and stockraiser.

LARSEN, CHRISTEN A. (son of Christen and Maria C. Larsen, of Denmark). Born March 6, 1836, in Denmark. Came to Utah Oct. 5, 1854, Captain Olsen company.
Married Mary Ann Jensen May 18, 1858, Ephraim, Utah (daughter of Andrew and Annie Jensen of. Loland, Denmark). She was born March 6, 1842. Their children: William A., m. Matilda Anderson; Mary C., m. H. P. Larsen; Anna b. July 12, 1866, m. James R. Larsen Dec. 2, 1885; m. Emil W. Larsen May 10, 1902; Christian, m. Sarah Sodo-

burg; Olivia, m. Heber Nielson; Alma C., m. Mamie Tucker; m. Vina Rockhill; Zenobia, m. Alma Jenson. Family home Ephraim, Utah.
Seventy. Leader in city affairs of Ephraim; councilman two year; postmaster seven years. Black Hawk Indian war veteran, and had a horse shot from under him in this war. Assisted in bringing immigrants to Utah. Director of co-op. at Ephraim. Strong believer in free speech and religious freedom. He erected a large hall and fitted it up, giving any and all denominations, without cost, the privilege of using it for many years. In 1891 took a trip to Europe, and visited his old home in Denmark; while on this trip he did a great deal of good for the people of Utah. Farmer; stockraiser and capitalist.

LARSEN, ALMA CLARENCE (son of Christen A. Larsen and Mary Ann Jensen). Born July 10, 1877, Ephraim, Utah. Married Mary E. Tucker April 19, 1899, at Ephraim, Utah (daughter of Amasa Tucker of Fairview, Utah). She was born May, 1879, died. Only child: Cecil Alma b. 1899.
Married Vina Garland Rockhill Aug. 2, 1903, at Nephi, Utah (daughter of John Rockhill and Cynthia Amelia Thurber of Spanish Fork, Utah, pioneers 1854). She was born June 20, 1877.
Hotel-keeper.

LARSEN, CHRISTIAN GRICE (son of Lars Johansen and Anna Margaret Sorensen). Born Dec. 17, 1828, Veile amt, Denmark. Came to Utah September, 1857.
Married Maria Caroline Sorensen April 1, 1857, at Copenhagen, Denmark (daughter of Peter and Margaret Sorensen of Bornholm, Denmark, pioneers Sept. 1857). She was born Oct. 27, 1838. Their children: Annie M., m. Rasmus Jensteen; Christian Grice, m. Emma Jane Seely; Hannah Margaret; Samuel Henry, m. Sarah Seely; Joseph Smith, m. Jeanetta Peacock and Carrie Olsen; Orson Albert, m. Ella Christensen; Franklin Peter, m. Ella Burresen; George Washington, died; Erastus Snow, m. Emma E. Petersen; Luella Minerva, m. William Petersen; Edna Elnora, m. Ray Olson. Family home Castle Dale, Utah.
Presided over Scandinavian mission 1873-75; president Emery stake; bishop of Spring City. Mayor of Spring City. Moved to Castle Dale 1880.

LARSEN, SAMUEL HENRY (son of Christian Grice Larsen and Maria Caroline Sorensen). Born Dec. 8, 1865, Spring City, Utah.
Married Sarah Seely Oct. 24, 1890, Manti, Utah (daughter of Orange Seely and Annie Olsen of Castle Dale, Utah, pioneers 1847). She was born Feb. 7, 1872. Their children: Horace Henry b. April 9, 1891; Glen Seely b. Feb. 25, 1894; Lyman Grice b. May 5, 1896; Thelma b. July 1, 1911.
Member 91st quorum seventies; missionary to northern states 1907-09; counselor Peter J. Akelund 1910-12; president T. M. M. I. A.; ordained high priest and bishop of Castle Dale ward Aug. 10, 1912; teacher in ward and Sunday school. School trustee seven years. Farmer.

LARSEN, CHRISTIAN J. (son of Lars Johansen and Anna Margreta Sorensen). Born May 21, 1831, at Griesvlei, Denmark. Came to Utah Oct. 5, 1854, himself as captain in Hans Peter Olsen company.
Married Barbara J. Dortha Olsen Oct. 30, 1853, Copenhagen, Denmark (daughter of Jens Olsen and Maria Berg), who was born April 4, 1833, Aalborg, Denmark. Their children: John Christian b. Jan. 13, 1855, m. Susannah Titensor Feb. 7, 1877; Maria b. April 11, 1857, m. Willard S. Hansen 1876; Brigham Louis b. Jan. 2, 1859, m. Anna Olsen June 8, 1892; Jacob Peter b. Oct. 26, 1860, m. Sophia Titensor Dec. 14, 1887; Julia Christina b. Oct. 16, 1862, d. April 27, 1864; Joseph Abraham b. Dec. 15, 1864, d. Dec. 8, 1873; Erastus Snow b. Jan. 14, 1867, m. Ruth Comish June 28, 1892; Anna Margreta b. July 30, 1870, d. July 30, 1870; Hyrum Christopher b. May 28, 1872, m. Carlin Comish June 28, 1893; Barbara Dorthea b. Oct. 17, 1875, m. Milton D. Hammond March 12, 1902. Family resided at Spring City, Logan and Cove, Utah, and Preston, Fairview and Rexburg, Idaho.
Married Ingeborg Ellefsen (daughter of Elef Ellefsen and Bertha Danielsen, former pioneer 1856, Knud Petersen company). She was born Oct. 30, 1821, Risor, Norway. Their children: Elias Saverin b. June 2, 1859, m. Clarinda Hannah Goaslind June 4, 1884; Mary b. Feb. 9, 1861, m. Daniel Clark Feb. 20, 1885; Anna Margreta b. Dec. 9, 1863, d. Dec. 9, 1863; Anna Louisa b. Dec. 9, 1863, m. Martin Hansen.
Married Inger Margreta Petersen Dec. 9, 1863, Salt Lake City (daughter of Alf Petersen and Osster Christensen, former pioneer 1863, Captain Needham company). She was born July 7, 1838, at Risor, Norway. Their children: Ellef Ellefsen b. Jan. 14, 1859, died (adopted); Almartin Ellefsen b. Aug. 1, 1861, died (adopted); Magdalene b. Sept. 9, 1864, d. Aug. 4, 1865; David Ellef b. July 1, 1866, m. Mary Alice Smith Sept. 9, 1886; Almartin b. Dec. 25, 1868, m. Ellen Comish Oct. 15, 1893; Joseph Franklin b. Oct. 4, 1874, d. Nov. 15, 1900; Alexander Willard b. Jan. 28, 1877, m. Anna Jameson Dec. 8, 1897.
Missionary in Denmark 1850-53; second counselor to Bishop Thomas Kinkton; first counselor to Bishop Ballard of Logan; bishop of Logan; high councilor 1872-77; patriarch. Veteran of Echo Canyon and Black Hawk Indian wars. Farmer.

LARSEN, JOHN C. (son of Christian J. Larsen and Barbara J. Dortha Olsen). Born Jan. 13, 1855, West Weber, Utah.
Married Susannah Titensor Feb. 7, 1877, Logan, Utah (daughter of Thomas Titensor and Sarah Robbins of Richmond, Utah, pioneers 1861). She was born Jan. 7, 1855. Their children: John C. b. Nov. 22, 1877, m. Hattie Comish; Oliver T. b. June 4, 1880, d. Sept. 27, 1881; Ida Larsen b. June 5, 1882, m. David Nash; Louis W. b. Oct. 27, 1884, m. Ada Hendricks; Joseph R. b. May 22, 1887, m. Charlotte Andersen; Hazen b. April 25, 1891, d. July 4, 1900; Hazel b. April 25, 1891, m. Louis Ricks. Family resided Logan and Coveville, Utah.
Married Mary Ellen Titensor Nov. 24, 1881, Salt Lake City (daughter of Thomas Titensor and Sarah Robbins of Richmond, Utah, pioneers 1861). She was born Jan. 13, 1859. Their children: Alice b. July 22, 1882, d. July 22, 1882; David b. June 23, 1883; Almeda b. Nov. 20, 1885, m. Alma Hendricks; Irene E. b. July 27, 1888, m. Thomas Rose; Inez S. b. July 27, 1888; Barbara Lavern b. Jan. 29, 1895; Edna Maria b. Nov. 16, 1897; Mary Teresa b. Dec. 8, 1900. Family home Coveville, Utah.
Married Emma Jane Howland April 27, 1887, Logan, Utah (daughter of Henry Howland and Martha Diana Case of Flaggtown, Ogle county, Ill., former died on the plains, latter pioneer 1852, Thomas Tidwell company). She was born Jan. 14, 1849. Only child: Newel H. b. Jan. 30, 1888, m. Louise Larsen. Family home Coveville, Utah.
Bishop of Coveville 1882 to date. Road supervisor. President Cove Water Works Corporation. Farmer.

LARSEN, EMIL W. (son of Even Larsen Laerum and Fredrike Wilhelmine Ohlsen). Born Feb. 28, 1859, Moss, Norway.
Married Anna Larsen May 10, 1902, Salt Lake City (daughter of C. A. Larsen and Mary Ann Jensen of Ephraim, pioneers Oct. 6, 1854, Captain Olsen company). She was born July 12, 1866.
Cashier of Stockville Bank in Nebraska. Bookkeeper for T. C. Martin Furniture Company, Pocatello, Idaho.

LARSEN, ERICK (son of Lars Ericksen and Dorothy Jorgensen of Sjelland, Denmark). Born June 20, 1845, at Seirslev, Denmark. Came to Utah Sept. 10, 1866, Captain Rawlings company.
Married Annie Elizabeth Ericksen April 4, 1868, at Salt Lake City (daughter of Jorgen Ericksen and Sidse Petersen of Tjornmard, Sjelland, Denmark, pioneers Sept. 29, 1866, Peter Nebeker company). She was born July 22, 1846. Their children: Emma Elizabeth b. May 21, 1869, m. Jeremiah Roby; Nancy Dorothy b. March 15, 1872; Alma E. b. Oct. 19, 1874, m. Harrietta Eden; Lars Peter b. May 11, 1877, m. Nora Oveson; Joseph Jorgen b. Aug. 3, 1879, m. Geneva Oveson; Elsina Sophia b. Dec. 20, 1884, m. James T. Johnson; Junius Benjamin b. May 3, 1889. Family home Cleveland, Utah.
High priest; bishop's counselor at St. Johns, Ariz., 1887-92, and at Cleveland, Utah, 1897-1910; patriarch; member high council of eastern Arizona stake. Assisted in settling St. Johns, Ariz. Farmer.

LARSEN, JOSEPH JORGEN (son of Eric Larsen and Annie Elizabeth Ericksen). Born Aug. 3, 1879, Spanish Fork, Utah.
Married Geneva Oveson Oct. 28, 1908, at Salt Lake City (daughter of Lars P. Oveson and Louisa Otterstrom of Larslev, Hjorring, Denmark, pioneers Oct. 12, 1863). She was born Sept. 5, 1885. Their children: Joseph Lavon b. March 28, 1910; Alma Verdell b. May 24, 1912. Family home Cleveland, Utah.
Missionary to eastern states 1905-07; president New England conference; ordained bishop of Cleveland ward Aug. 7, 1910. Farmer.

LARSEN, HANS PETER (son of Lars Rasmussen, born 1803, at Falster, Denmark, and Christina Petersen, born 1800, in Denmark). Born Sept. 24, 1835. Came to Utah Sept. 7, 1855, Noah T. Guyman company.
Married Eleanor Andersen Shelton Dec. 6, 1875 (daughter of Richard John Shelton and Mary Wann, pioneers Sept. 12, 1861, who were married May 15, 1854, at Philadphia, Pa.). She was born Jan. 4, 1859. Their children: Christiane b. Jan. 9, 1877, d. Jan. 26, 1877; Peter b. March 5, 1878, m. Hannah Acomb June 29, 1904; Mary b. Dec. 22, 1880, m. William Patrick Feb. 4, 1907; Joseph b. Sept. 10, 1882, d. June 18, 1883; Ellenor B. June 27, 1884, m. John Worley June 29, 1904; Annie Marie b. Feb. 9, 1886, m. Alfred Curtis March 28, 1909; Isabell b. Dec. 1, 1887, d. Aug. 30, 1888; Elizabeth b. Oct. 28, 1889; Lucy b. Oct. 20, 1891; Helen b. Dec. 6, 1893; Maggie b. Feb. 11, 1896; Wilford b. Dec. 6, 1897.
Presiding high priest 16 years. Settled in Big Cottonwood 1855; moved to Mendon, Cache county, 1859. Assisted in bringing immigrants to Utah in 1862. Served two terms in Mendon city council.

LARSEN, HANS S. (son of Lars Larsen and Sidre Christina Nielsen of Odden, Sjelland, Denmark). Born April 13, 1858, at Eyderly, Odden, Denmark. Came to Utah Sept. 24, 1868, Edward T. Mumford mule team.
Married Lucy Sephrona Janson Dec. 29, 1881, at Salt Lake City, Utah (daughter of Anthony A. Janson and Anna Christena Maria Pallisen of Brigham City, Utah, pioneers July 9, 1858). She was born Sept. 27, 1862, died March 16, 1885. Their children: Hans Ethelbert Larsen b. Oct. 17, 1882, m. Sophrona Johnson; Ruby Sophrona b. Sept. 25, 1884. Family home Brigham City, Utah.
Married Sophia Pertreia Sorensen Oct. 28, 1886, at Logan City, Utah (daughter of Lars Sorensen and Christena Petersen of Brigham City, Utah, who came to Utah 1871 by rail. She was born Jan. 14, 1869. Their children: Lucy C. b. Aug. 5, 1890; Milton N. b. April 17, 1892; Leland L. b. Nov. 10, 1893; Leora M. b. Jan 20, 1896; Tracy H. b. April 4, 1898; Alta b. July 10, 1900; Frank S. b. Dec. 9, 1903; Sopreal b. April 24, 1908. Family home Brigham City, Utah.
County commissioner 1911-12; city councilman, 1896-1900 and 1910-11; state senator 1900-05. Fruit grower and farmer.

LARSEN, HENRICK (son of Lars Jensen of Smeserop, Denmark, and Annie Hansen of Rumlesse, Denmark). Born June 20, 1833, at Rumlesse, Fordenkbough, Denmark. Came to Utah Sept. 15, 1864, W. B. Preston company.
Married Mary Hansen (daughter of Lars Hansen; came with W. E. Preston company). She was born May 29, 1831. Their children: Henry b. May 17, 1872, at Logan City, Utah, m. Mary E. Jensen Nov. 3, 1893; Hannah b. Nov. 12, 1859, m. Peter L. Larsen; Mary b. Oct. 27, 1865, m. Peter Nielsen Dec. 25, 1880; Emma b. July 16, 1869, m. Ole Hansen Oct. 15, 1893.

LARSEN, HENRY (son of Henrick Larsen and Mary Hansen). Born May 17, 1872.
Married Mary Elizabeth Jensen Oct. 3, 1892, at Logan, Utah (daughter of Niels Jensen and Annie Elizabeth Nielsen, the former a pioneer). She was born Feb. 16, 1867, at Mendon, Utah.
Bishop of Cleveland ward.

LARSEN, JACOB. Born Feb. 6, 1841, Deiret, Mols, Denmark. Came to Utah Sept. 30, 1862, Captain Massen independent company.
Married Anna Catherine Nelsen 1869, at Sale Lake City (daughter of Simon Nelsen of Lumby Mark, Odense, Denmark—came to Utah 1868). She was born Dec. 8, 1841, died May 4, 1899, Paradise, Utah. Their children: Jacob N.; Caroline S.; Martha J. N.; Eliza S. N.; Joseph S. N. Family home, Paradise.
Married Eva Larsen.
Missionary to Denmark 1893-95; member bishopric of Paradise ward. Member school board 15 years. Director of Paradise Co-op.

LARSEN, JACOB N. (son of Jacob Larsen and Anna C. Nelsen). Born March 11, 1871, at Paradise, Utah.
Married Ella Bickmore May 20, 1895, Logan, Utah (daughter of Isaac D. Bickmore and Ellen Oldham). Their children: Vincent b. April 20, 1896; Nelsen b. March 1902; Thelma b. Feb. 26, 1906; Paul b. March 22, 1909; Ellen b. Nov. 22, 1911. Family home Preston, Idaho.
Missionary to northern states 1898-01; 1st counselor in bishopric of 4th ward, Preston, Idaho. County clerk, Cache county 1902-06; justice of peace, at Paradise 1893-95; member city council of Preston, Idaho 1909-11; mayor of Preston 1911-15. Cashier of Idaho State & Savings bank, Preston 1906-09; director Lundetrom Furniture & Carpet Co., Logan, Utah; vice-president First National bank of Preston, Idaho.

LARSEN, JAMES R. (son of J. P. and Kisty Larsen). Born Dec. 29, 1863, Ephraim, Utah.
Married Anna Larsen Dec. 2, 1885, Ephraim, Utah (daughter of Christen A. Larsen and Mary Ann Jensen of Ephraim, pioneers Oct. 5, 1854, Captain Olsen company). She was born July 12, 1856. Only child: Urania M. Sept. 3, 1886, m. Harry G. Shafer. Family home Ephraim.
Seventy; high priest. Farmer and stockraiser. Died April 5, 1888, Ephraim.

LARSEN, LAURITZ (son of Lars Johansen and Anna Margreta Sorensen). Born Jan. 25, 1834, at Veile, Denmark. Came to Utah 1857.
Married Marie Thompson 1857, who died Dec. 28, 1887. Their children: Marie Catherine. m. Louis Olsen Feb. 19, 1880; Eliza M., m. James Crawforth.
Married Louise R. Jaspersen Jan. 15, 1864, Salt Lake City (daughter of Rasmus Jaspersen and Kiratina Olsen), who was born Sept. 25, 1838, at Nyborg, Denmark; died Oct. 28, 1892. Their children: Laura M. b. 1865, d. 1866; Lauritz Orsen b. Feb. 7, 1867, m. Deseret M. Anderson June 13, 1894; Emeline M. b. Aug. 18, 1871, m. John S. Blain 1900; Mary L. b. April 16, 1873, m. Charles Zabriskie Dec., 1893; Albert E. b. Sept. 2, 1875, m. Lizzie Behunin. Family home Spring City, Utah.
Married Minnie Jensen. Their children: Leona b. 1894, d. 1898; Lauretta b. 1896.

Missionary to Denmark 1867-70; 2nd counselor to Bishop James A. Allred of Spring City ward 14 years. Settled in Ogden 1867, moved to Spring City 1860. Member of constitutional convention 1895; mayor of Spring City two terms; justice of the peace four terms. Farmer. Died, Spring City, Utah 1896.

LARSEN, LAURITZ ORSEN (son of Lauritz Larsen and Louise R. Jaspersen). Born Feb. 7, 1867, Spring City Utah.
Married Deseret M. Anderson June 13, 1894, Manti, Utah (daughter of James Anderson and Matilda Cheney), who was born May 13, 1871, Fairview, Utah. Their children: Ruby Gladys b. Nov. 27, 1895, d. April 14, 1896; Sylvia Firl b. June 1, 1898; Liona Louise b. Dec. 25, 1900; Dora Fay and Flora May b. Sept. 15, 1909.
Missionary southwestern states 1897-1900; choir leader ten years; president of 80th quorum of seventies; ward superintendent Y. M. M. I. A.; bishop of Spring City; member of board of Snow academy; bishop 1905-11. City councilman four years; mayor two years. Merchant.

LARSEN, LAURITZ EDWARD (son of Lars Emanuelsen and Berthar Maria Olsen of Fredrikshald, Smaaleneno, Norway). Born Dec. 6, 1832, at Fredrikshald. Came to Utah with William B. Preston company.
Married Carolina Larsen Sept. 15, 1864 (daughter of Lars Larsen and Annie Christensen of Haegeland, Norway). She was born Feb. 21, 1835; came to Utah April 5, 1864, William B. Preston company. Their children: Carolina Maria b. May 20, 1865, m. George Petersen April 3, 1890; Edward Lauritz b. Dec. 6, 1865, m. Christina Andersen Feb. 13, 1907; Ludvig Joseph b. Jan. 22, 1870, m. Sarah S. Valentine Dec. 31, 1889; Orson Alfred b. Oct. 30, 1871, m. Nancy Rock Dec. 6, 1894; Alma Benjamin b. Oct. 18, 1875, m. Lydia Hales Dec. 1, 1904; Matilde Eliza b. Oct. 16, 1877, m. Henry Frank Hulze April 1907; Charles Wilford b. Dec. 15, 1879, m. Maria Jacobsen April 12, 1906; Anna Bolette b. Oct. 29, 1872, d. infant. Family resided Hyrum, Cache Co., Utah, and Salem, Fremont Co., Idaho.
Missionary to Scandinavia 1856-64 and 1897-99; high priest; teacher.

LARSEN, ALMA B. (son of Laritz Edward Larsen and Carolina Larsen). Born Oct. 18, 1875, at Hyrum, Cache Co., Utah.
Married Lydia Hales Dec. 1, 1894, at Logan, Utah (daughter of Stephen and Alice Jane Hales of Bountiful, Utah; the former came to Utah, but the latter did not). She was born Sept. 30, 1882. Their children: Gerald Leeland b. Feb. 3, 1906; Alice Melva b. March 15, 1910; Alma Melvin b. March 15, 1910; Gladys Lydia b. Aug. 14, 1911. Family home, Salem, Freemont Co., Idaho.
High councilman of the Fremont stake; missionary to Scandinavia 1907-09. Farmer. Presided over Christiania conference 13 months

LARSEN, PETER (son of Lars Larsen and Elizabeth Hartwick of Lobeher, Sjelland, Denmark). Born Oct. 14, 1843. Came to Utah October, 1868, Joseph S. Rawlings company.
Married Ellen Johnson May 9, 1870, at Salt Lake City (daughter of Jons and Annie Nelsen of Marthasholm, Sweden). She was born Jan. 30, 1844, came to Utah 1868, Captain Lowland company. Their children: Annie Elizabeth. m. Olander Pearson and Peter W. Nelson; Peter, died; Ellen Charlotte, m. James Peterson; Margarett Magdalene. m. John Peterson; Chestey, died. Family home Lehi, Utah.
Married Mathea Fredericksen Dec. 9, 1880, at Salt Lake City (daughter of Christian Fredericksen and Maria Olsen of Lueten, Hademarken, Denmark, who came to Utah by railroad). She was born Feb. 28, 1858. Their children: Frederick Peter b. Jan. 2, 1882, died; Marie Christina b. March 27, 1883, m. John H. Parker; Henry Christian b. April 12, 1885, died; Edward Orson b. Jan. 19, 1887, m. Clara Woodhouse; David b. Aug. 30, 1889, died; Leslie Franklin b. Feb. 19, 1892; Ernest Wilburn b. Jan. 15, 1893; Elvira Hellena b. Jan. 2, 1894; Oscar b. March 7, 1896, died; Ole Moroni b. June 11, 1897. Family home Lehi, Utah.
Teacher in 14th ward, Salt Lake City, and 4th ward, Lehi. Helped build railway to Promontory, Utah; had charge of material for construction Utah Southern R. R. United States grand juryman. Farmer and butcher.

LARSEN, SOREN (son of Lars Johansen and Anna Margreta Sorensen). Born March 28, 1821, at Copenhagven, Denmark. Came to Utah Oct. 5, 1854.
Married Maria Hansen of Denmark, who was born May 3, 1831. Came to Utah Oct. 5, 1854, died April 22, 1907. Their children: Hans Ephraim, m. Bell Davidson; Soren, m. Meta; Marenius, m. Anna Mena Mickelson; Daniel, m. Sarah Jane Farmer; Josephine, m. Christian Christiansen; Mary Ann, died; Otto, m. Hannah Ellis; David, died; Peter Christian b. March 23, 1874, m. Nellie Acord. Family home Spring City, Utah.
Married Christena Nielsen of Denmark. Their children: Maria, m. Fred C. Sorensen; Niels; Hyrum, m. Ann Ellis; Joseph, died; Fredrick, m. Maud Alfred; Ida Marinda, m. Vincent Bellington.
Elder. Settled at Ephraim, moved to Spring City. Minuteman. Carpenter and farmer. Died August, 1892.

LARSEN, PETER CHRISTIAN (son of Soren Larsen and Maria Hansen). Born March 23, 1874, Spring City, Utah. Married Nellie Acord April 19, 1899, at Manti, Utah, who was born July 7, 1879, at Spring City. Their children: Leslie Acord b. May 9, 1900; Henry Clarence b. Feb. 18, 1902; Hue Ernest b. July 7, 1907; David Arthur b. March 19, 1909, d. April 11, 1909.
High priest; ward teacher; assistant superintendent Sunday school; counselor to Bishop David McMillan of Clear Creek ward. Settled at Clear Creek 1904.

LARSON, CARL HENNING (son of Lars Olson and Anna B. Swenson of Snotorp, Sweden). Born Dec. 25, 1839, Halmstad, Halland, Sweden. Came to Utah Sept. 5, 1863, John F. Sanders company.
Married Elizabeth Swenson Sept. 7, 1863, Salt Lake City (daughter of Peter Swenson and Johannah Gilbert of Halmstad, Sweden). She was born Feb. 8, 1840. Their child: Amelia C., m. C. J. A. Lindquist. Family home Ogden, Utah.
Elder. Contractor and builder. Died March 11, 1877.

LARSON, CHRISTEAN S. Born May 9, 1802, in Denmark. Came to Utah Aug. 29, 1859, James S. Brown company.
Married Johanna Marie Christianson Feb. 19, 1836, Alborg, Denmark (daughter of Christian Christianson), who was born Jan. 21, 1813. Their children: Christian Peter, m. Mary Larson; Inger Marie, m. Peter Ahlstrom; James P., m. Kisty Larson; Lars C., m. Hansena Peterson; Maren Margretta, m. Louis Larson. Family home Ephraim, Utah.
Blacksmith and farmer. Died October, 1884, Ephraim, Utah.

LARSON, LARS C. (son of Christean S. Larson and Johanna Marie Christianson). Born Dec. 4, 1844, Alborg, Denmark. Came to Utah with parents.
Married Hansena Peterson Dec. 22, 1865, Circleville, Utah (daughter of Jens Peterson and Metta Christena Olsen of Hals, Denmark, former died en route to Utah, latter came in 1854). She was born Nov. 19, 1846. Their children: Christian A. b. Sept. 27, 1866, m. Cynthia Keel; Louis D. b. Aug. 18, 1868, m. Amelia Christianson; James E. b. Sept. 2, 1870, m. Nora Sorenson; Johanna Christena b. Feb. 22, 1873, m. Andrew Sorenson; Orvil L. b. May 25, 1875, m. Hazel Kimball; Zina R. b. Oct. 8, 1877, m. Peter C. Lund; Alma LeRoy b. Feb. 25, 1880; Malinda Ann b. Nov. 19, 1882, m. Albert Rosenlund; John M. b. Oct. 1, 1885, m. Vivian Whitlock; Helen C. b. Feb. 12, 1889, died. Family resided Ephraim and Mayfield, Utah.
Married Metta Polena Peterson June 5, 1871, Salt Lake City (daughter of Jens Peterson and Metta Christena Olsen, pioneers 1854). She was born March 12, 1849, Hals, Denmark. Their children: Peter Franklin born July 4, 1872, d. July 26, 1872; Joseph H. b. Nov. 19, 1873, m. Lottie Layton; Mary H. b. March 17, 1877, m. Hyrum Olsen; George O. b. Dec. 16, 1879, d. Oct. 25, 1905; Raymond D. b. June 15, 1882, m. Lilly Christianson; Wilford E. b. Feb. 25, 1885, m. Agnes Holland; Mabel Lena b. Dec. 26, 1887, m. Claud D. Michaelson.
Ordained teacher in 1862; elder May 2, 1868; seventy March 5, 1885; one of the council of 75th quorum seventies for many years; Sunday school teacher 25 years. In 1864 drove an oxteam from Ephraim to the Missouri river for immigrants in August Canfield company. Black Hawk Indian war veteran; took active part in early Indian troubles. Farmer and breeder of horses.

LARSON, CHRISTIAN HANSEN (son of Hans Larson, born 1809, at Torop, Frederiksborg amt, Denmark, and Karen Petersen, born April 27, 1817, at Craguma, Frederiksborg). Born Jan. 30, 1844, at Meleby, Frederiksborg. Came to Utah Sept. 25, 1868, J. G. Holman company.
Married Mary Ann Larson Dec. 21, 1868 (daughter of Lars Jorgensen and Maren Kirstena Jorgensen, who were married April 1840, pioneers of Sept. 25, 1868, J. G. Holman company—stepdaughter of Lars Niels Christensen, pioneer of Sept. 25, 1868, J. G. Holman company). She was born Nov. 11, 1841. Their children: Lorenzo C. b. Nov. 20, 1869, m. Altena Eriksen Aug. 24, 1892; Hyrum M. b. Feb. 3, 1872, m. Anna Petersen June 29, 1898; Joseph J. b. Sept. 27, 1873, m. Letta Christensen Oct. 18, 1900; Mary Ann b. Nov. 16, 1875, m. R. Amos Dowdle Nov. 11, 1903; Caroline B. b. June 25, 1878; William L. b. Feb. 24, 1883, m. Sarah Ada Porter Dec. 4, 1907. Family resided Brigham City, Kanab and Newton, Utah.
Missionary in Denmark three years; assistant superintendent of Sunday school; second counselor in bishopric at Newton; high priest.

LARSON, HANS (son of Lars Petersen, born 1766, died Nov. 26, 1833, and Maren Hansen, born 1770, died March 20, 1839, of Lunde, Lydersluw, Preasto amt, Denmark). He was born July 8, 1806, at Lunde. Came to Utah Sept. 30, 1853, John Forsgren company.
Married Elena Dorathea Bensen Aug. 5, 1836, at Copenhagen, Denmark (daughter of Christian Bensen and Pauline Kirstine Margrette Falkenberg), who was born Dec. 27,

1810, died March 4, 1877. Their children: Ellen Matine Paulen b. 1837, d. 1837; Elena Hansine b. Sept. 13, 1838, m. John Lambert; Carl Olof b. 1840, d. 1846; Peter b. 1843, d. 1843; Petrine Christine b. Aug. 13, 1844, m. Samuel Miller; Mary Magdalene b. March 11, 1847, m. John F. Oblade; Margrete Kjerstine b. 1849, d. 1853; John George Erastus b. Sept. 3, 1852, m. Mary Cecilien Smith. Family home Salt Lake City.
High priest. Worked on Salt Lake temple many years. Sailor. Died Feb. 27, 1876, at Salt Lake City.

LARSON, LARS (son of Lars and Martha Larson of eastern Iowa). Born Jan. 11, 1825, Hadngar, Norway. Came to Utah 1850.
Married Mary Adelphia Bellows 1848, en route to Utah (daughter of James Bellows and Judith Hopper of Nauvoo, Ill., the latter came to Utah 1850). She was born Aug. 17, 1832. Their children: Martha Ann, m. Thomas Baker, d. 1895; Mary Jane, d. 1852; Lars James, m. Isidore Andrus, m. Olena M. Peterson; John Thomas, m. Henrietta Riding; Thurston, m. Maria Perkins; Judith Marillia, m. James Alfred Larson; Charles William, m. Jane Riding; Elizabeth Detsy, (d. 1893) m. William B. Baker; Sarah Maria, m. Francis Y. Morse; Joseph Merlan. Family resided Mill Creek and St. George, Utah.
Member 29th quorum seventies; missionary to Ponca Indians in northern Nebraska and Dakota with W. C. Stames 1846 and to "Dixie" 1862; ward teacher. Brick and stone-mason; farmer. Died Feb. 7, 1903, at St. George, Utah.

LARSON, LARS JAMES (son of Lars Larson and Mary Adelphia Bellows). Born June 7, 1853, Mill Creek, Utah.
Married Isidore Andrus May 20, 1879, at St. George, Utah (daughter of Milo Andrus and Margaret Boyce of Price and St. George, Utah). She was born May 20, 1859. Their children: Martha Marillia b. March 6, 1880, m. Granville H. Fullerton; Milo b. May 20, 1882, d. June 26, 1894; Isidore b. May 4, 1884, m. Wallace Blake; Aaron b. Feb. 13, 1886, m. Clara Fawcett.
Married Olena M. Peterson Dec. 17, 1885, St. George, Utah (daughter of F. P. Peterson and Martha Neilson of Richfield, Utah). She was born April 25, 1868. Their children: Willard b. June 28, 1881, m. Emma L. Booth; Elsie Victoria b. Sept. 22, 1889, m. Alfred A. Carpenter; Reuben b. Nov. 26, 1892; Pearl b. Nov. 18, 1894; Charles b. Dec. 18, 1896; Martha Adelphia b. July 17, 1899; LeRoy b. Dec. 19, 1901; Ellis b. June 5, 1904; Elizabeth b. April 22, 1907. Family home Bloomington, Utah.
High priest; bishop's counselor; Sunday school superintendent and teacher; home missionary. Justice of peace. School trustee. Pioneer to Bloomington. Farmer and horticulturist.

LARSON, LARS C. (son of Christian Larson and Kjerstine Nielsen of Denmark). Born Jan. 1, 1808, in Denmark. Came to Utah Nov. 10, 1863, W. B. Preston company.
Married Maren Bertelsen in 1838, in Denmark (daughter of Christen Bertelsen and Johanna Christensen), who was born Nov. 22, 1815. Their children: Johanna Christena, m. Marcor Petersen; Christian Peter, m. Charlotte C. Johnson; Christina Marie, m. Charles Peter Warnick.
Farmer.

LARSON, MADS. Born April 21, 1837. Came to Utah in 1865.
Married Sophia Johanson in 1867, at Ephraim, Utah (daughter of Carl Johanson, of Sweden, later of Denmark; came to Utah 1862). She was born Dec. 21, 1843. Their children: John Frederick b. Sept. 19, 1868, m. Ellen Hansen; Alexander b. July 28, 1871. Family home Ephraim, Utah.
Married Cecilia —— about 1870. Their children: Annie, died; Louise, m. Walter Hickey.
High priest; bishop's counselor; high councilor; president of ward teachers.

LARSON, JOHN FREDERICK (son of Mads Larson and Sophia Johanson). Born Sept. 19, 1868, at Ephraim.
Married Ellen Hansen Oct. 27, 1897, at Molen, Utah (daughter of Hans Hansen and Mary Lenora Morley of Denmark). She was born Feb. 18, 1878. Their children: Pearl b. Dec. 21, 1898; Lavera b. May 9, 1900; John Frederick b. Oct. 23, 1901; Elmer Ray b. April 8, 1903; Aprilia b. April 1, 1905; Ella b. March 15, 1907; Leonard b. Dec. 3, 1911.
Bishop's counselor; president Y. M. M. I. A.; Sunday school superintendent. School trustee. Farmer.

LARSON, MONS (son of Lars Olson and Birtha Jonson of Sweden). Born June 6, 1823, Skaglinge, Sweden. Came to Utah Sept. 4, 1859, George Rowley handcart company.
Married Ellan J. Malstrum, in Sweden (daughter of Olof Jensen Malmstrum and Carna Parsen of Sweden). She was born Feb. 13, 1826. Their children: Betsy, m. Edwin L. Carter; Caroline, m. Wesley B. Robbins; Lehi, m. Letitia Carter; Olof, m. May Hunt; James M., m. Stella Wilkins; Emma E., m. Jesse N. Smith; Ellis J., m. Silas D. Smith. Family home in Sweden.
Seventy. Farmer. Died March 1890, Fairview, Utah.

LARSON, NIELS PETER (son of Lars Nielson and Metta Christian of Jutland, Denmark). Born April 20, 1826, Weiby, Denmark. Came to Utah Sept. 15, 1869, Robert F. Neslen company.
Married Karem K. Swensen in 1854 (daughter of Swen Larsen and Anne Pedersen of Weiby). She was born May 17, 1830. Their children: Anna, m. Alexander Gillespie; Lauritz, Emma, Peter and Clara, died; Maria Clarinda, m. James Bell Heywood; Joseph, m. Ostella Baker; Ella, m. James Lehi Brown; Alma, died. Family home Pleasant Grove, Utah.
Missionary to Omaha, Neb., 1880; missionary to Denmark in 1892; high priest. Farmer. Died Nov. 20, 1911.

LARSON, NILS (son of Lars Larson, born Oct. 6, 1800, and Elna Jacobson, born July 22, 1793, of Willie Parish, Malmö, Sweden). He was born July 17, 1833, Malmö. Came to Utah Oct. 1, 1862, Joseph Horne company.
Married Bengta Flaygare May 13, 1864 (daughter of Nils Flaygare and Anna Neilson, pioneers Aug. 29, 1863, John R. Murdock company). She was born May 11, 1835. Their children: Mary Ann b. April 1, 1865, m. George M. Smoot Dec. 19, 1888; Bettie Elenor b. Jan. 25, 1867, m. Joseph L. Wiggand July 17, 1902; Nils Olaf b. April 11, 1869, d. Sept. 29, 1870; Ester Johanna b. Sept. 19, 1871, d. June 26, 1877; John Lawrence b. Aug. 28, 1873, d. Sept. 25, 1877; Emma Christina b. July 21, 1875, m. Joseph Oliver Stone Jan. 19, 1898; Isaac Jacob b. Sept. 27, 1877, m. Jane Delila Stone Dec. 9, 1903. Family home Salem, Utah.

LASHBROOK, EDWARD LAKER (son of Henry Lashbrook, born 1801, Horson Sussex, and Elizabeth Finch, born at Readhill, Eng.). Born 1839 at Croydon, Surrey, Eng., died in Montpelier, Idaho. Came to Utah Oct. 6, 1862, Ansel Harmon oxteam company.
Married Mary Lenor Johnson, who was born Nov. 1854, in Denmark. Their children: Johann Elizabeth b. Oct. 18, 1875, m. John S. Green; Mary Ellen b. May 25, 1877, m. Carl Leisering; George Finch b. March 19, 1879; Charles Brigham b. Nov. 9, 1880; Laker John b. Sept. 22, 1882, d. April 4, 1902; Annie Alina b. April 21, 1884, m. Carl Stronborg; Minnie b. Nov. 27, 1885, m. David Bischoff; Lillie Jayne b. Jan. 25, 1889, m. Albert Preston; Edward Ancel b. Nov. 26, 1890; Lawrence b. June 13, 1892. Family home Geneva, Bear Lake Co., Idaho.
High priest; Sunday school superintendent Morgan, Weber stake, Utah; also in Ovid ward, Bear Lake stake. Worked on Salt Lake temple. Carpenter.

LATER, PETER (son of Peter Later, born 1796, Lancashire, and Margrate Barrington, born 1799, Mostyn, Eng.). Born May 30, 1835, Newton Heath, Eng. Came to Utah Sept. 4, 1859, George Rowley company.
Married Elizabeth D. Brown (daughter of Richard D. Brown and Margrate Parkinson, former pioneer 1864). She was born Oct. 28, 1841, Wigan, Eng. Their children: Samuel S. b. March 14, 1864, m. Helena M. Hayes Dec. 22, 1886; Elizabeth Ann b. Oct. 24, 1865, m. James L. Robson Feb. 7; Peter b. Dec. 3, 1867, m. Laura Ann Taylor Jan. 21, 1891; Richard b. Nov. 20, 1869, m. Mary A. Prophet Dec. 8, 1897; William b. Oct. 16, 1871, died; Mary b. Nov. 20, 1873, died; Rebecca b. March 28, 1875, died; Joseph b. April 16, 1877, m. Lucetta Taylor; Abner b. March 26, 1881, m. Alvira Myler. Family resided Sugar House and Lynn, Utah.

LATER, SAMUEL S. (son of Peter Later and Elizabeth D. Brown). Born March 14, 1864, Sugar House, Utah.
Married Helena Mary Hayes Dec. 22, 1886, Logan, Utah (daughter of Richard Hayes and Anna M. Turner, who came to Utah 1869). She was born Oct. 4, 1866, Yorkshire, Eng. Their children: Lewis S. b. Nov. 6, 1887, m. Chloe Call April 21, 1907; Lawrence R. b. Oct. 28, 1889, m. Mable Cordon Oct. 4, 1911; Hazel b. Jan. 5, 1891, died; Athel E. b. June 28, 1894; Curtis C. b. Aug. 25, 1896; Reta L. b. Jan. 21, 1898; Thelma G. b. May 31, 1901; Gladys M. b. Nov. 13, 1905; Jeston J. b. Oct. 31, 1907; Dillon W. b. July 7, 1909; Floyd H. b. May 10, 1911. Family resided Harrisville, Utah, and Rigby, Idaho.

LATIMER, THOMAS (son of Sarah Ann Jones of Staffordshire, Eng.). Came to Utah 1853.
Married Ann Hardy Feb. 10, 1856, Salt Lake City (daughter of Robert Hardy of Falkirk, Scotland). She was born June 3, 1838. Their children: Sarah Ann, m. John W. A. Timms; Thomas H., m. Annie M. Gant; William G., m. Amelia Hunter; John J., m. Ella Gant; Elizabeth H., m. Almond Rust; Leanette W. H., m. William D. Pyper; Richard H., m. infant; Euphelia H., m. William D. Pyper; Richard H., m. Emma McIntyre; Henry James, m. Nellie Halliday, m. Myrtle Brown; Lucy H., m. Benjamin Hunt; Warren N., m. Emily Grinsdell. Family home, Salt Lake City.
Lumber merchant and planing miller. Died Nov. 1881, at Salt Lake City.

LAUB, GEORGE (son of Jacob Laub and Barbara Resler of Lancaster county, Pa.). Born Oct. 5, 1814, Lancaster county. Came to Utah 1852.
Married Mary Jane Meginness Jan. 6, 1846, Nauvoo, Ill. (daughter of Benjamin Meginness and Sarah Johnston of Lancaster Co., pioneers 1860). She was born Jan. 11, 1831. Their children: Luemma E., m. John W. Snell; Sarah, m. Ute W. Perkins: George W., m. Willamma Terry; John F., m. Mary Pulsipher; Mary J., m. Arnold D. Miller; Alice, d. child; Rachel, m. William Perkins; William B., m. Mary Robison; Caroline, m. Frederick W. Richards; Corinda E., died. Family resided Salt Lake City and St. George, Utah.
Member 25th quorum seventies. Called to St. George in 1862 to help settle that country. Worked on Salt Lake theater. Built several saw and grist mills. Carpenter. Died Nov. 14, 1880, at St. George.

LAWRENSON, WILLIAM. Born 1799 at Liverpool, Eng. Came to Utah September, 1856, handcart company.
Married Ann Quick, born Feb. 1, 1801, who came to Utah with husband. Their children: Mary b. Aug. 24, 1824; Ann b. Oct. 2, 1826; William b. Dec. 18, 1830; James b. Oct. 5, 1832; Richard b. June 5, 1835; Eliza b. April 9, 1837; Jane b. Oct. 9, 1838, m. Abraham Shaw Dec. 2, 1856; Margret b. April 7, 1842, d. 1843; Margret b. May 9, 1845, m. William Sampson. Family home, Liverpool.

LAWSON, JOSEPH. Born Dec. 9, 1824, Isle of Man, Eng. Came to Utah 1854, Bishop Hogland company.
Married Ruth M. Greenway (daughter of John Greenway and Elizabeth Price), who came Dec. 6, 1826, and came to Utah with husband. Their children: Joseph b. Jan. 16, 1856, d. June 8, 1866; Brigham b. Jan. 18, 1858, m. Susa Poole; Sarah b. Dec. 6, 1860, m. Lamoni Grix; Benjamin b. Jan. 17, 1862, d. June 15, 1864; Ephraim b. Aug. 16, 1864, m. Mary Scott; David Cottier b. July 6, 1866, m. Orrilia Ann Stephens Feb. 5, 1889; John b. May 18, 1871, m. Martha Trott March 7, 1895.
Secretary of seventies 20 years and high priests 15 years. Black Hawk war veteran. Colonizer. Secretary and treasurer of Ogden Bench canal 1858-66; secretary and treasurer David Heber canal 1873-94. Assisted in bringing immigrants to Utah 1866-69 from Liverpool, Eng. Farmer.

LAWSON, DAVID COTTIER (son of Joseph Lawson and Ruth M. Greenway). Born July 6, 1866, Ogden, Utah.
Married Orrilla Ann Stephens Feb. 5, 1889, at Ogden (daughter of Cornelius J. Stephens and Harriet Corilla Shaw), who was born Nov. 5, 1870, at Ogden. Their children: David S. b. Oct. 15, 1889, m. Jane Greenwell; Lillian S. b. Nov. 13, 1890; William H. b. Aug. 6, 1892; Benjamin T. b. Dec. 29, 1893; Maxwell B. b. April 18, 1896; Sarah May b. May 3, 1898; Eyvonne Orrilla b. July 18, 1904; Harriet Jane b. April 11, 1906; Edward Nephi b. Feb. 11, 1908; Edith Marie b. Nov. 4, 1909; John Francis b. Jan. 21, 1911, died. Family home, Ogden.

LAYMAN, JOHN (Johannes Lehmann) (son of Felix Lehmann, born May 15, 1782, and Elizabeth Gassmann, born Oct. 9, 1784, both of Rümlang, Switzerland—married March 10, 1807). Born Sept. 23, 1815, at Rümlang, Zurich, Switzerland. Came to Utah October, 1861.
Married Anna Geering May 27, 1850, Rümlang, Switzerland (daughter of Kasper Geering and Elizabeth Roshlin, latter pioneer Oct. 1861—married Aug. 28, 1826). She was born April 16, 1833. Their children: Adolph b. Oct. 4, 1851, m. Annie E. Stanger Jan. 13, 1873; Gottlieb b. Dec. 11, 1853; Conrad b. July 1, 1855, m. Hannah Baird April 3, 1881; Mary b. March 23, 1860, m. Samuel L. Brown June 13, 1883; Betty Annie b. Oct. 20, 1861, m. Thomas Reed White Dec. 5, 1882; Herman b. Aug. 15, 1863, m. Mary Herzig Oct. 8, 1892; Anna Rosa b. Jan. 27, 1866, m. Samuel Harrop March 3, 1886; John b. April 26, 1867, m. Melissa M. Fogg May 3, 1899; Hyrum b. Oct. 8, 1868, d. March 5, 1871; William b. May 9, 1871, m. Caroline Baird April 7, 1894; Nettie b. Aug. 24, 1873, m. Francis W. Dudman May 31, 1899. Family home Lynn, Utah.
Active church worker. Assisted in bringing immigrants to Utah. Freighted carding mill across the country to Bingham Fort and erected it in 1863. Farmer and fruit grower.

LAYMAN, ADOLPH (son of John Layman and Anna Geering). Born Oct. 4, 1851, at Rümlang.
Married Annie E. Stanger Jan. 13, 1873, Salt Lake City (daughter of Thomas Stanger and Jane Wilson, pioneers Sept. 25, 1855, Richard Ballantyne company). She was born April 28, 1854, Faceby, Yorkshire, Eng. Their children: Edward Adolph b. Aug. 22, 1874, d. May 30, 1878; Thomas Wilson b. Aug. 14, 1877; Laura Jane b. May 15, 1885, m. Henry C. Meyerhoffer June 2, 1909. Family home Slaterville, Utah.
High priest. Farmer and dairyman.

LAYTON, CHARLES (son of Mr. Martin, who died about 1831, and Bathsheba Layton; son assumed mother's name, according to custom of that day). Born April 6, 1832, Sandford, Lincolnshire, Eng. Came to Utah 1852.
Married Elizabeth Bowler at Salt Lake City. Their children: S. J., m. Sarah Trappet; Charles A., m. Victoria Walker; William I., m. Rosa Warren; Eliza, m. Charles Wall; Orson, m. Ruthe Bodily; Phoebe, m. Mr. Warren;

Timothy, m. Harriet Jarmen; George, m. Annie Deshazo. Family home Kaysville, Utah.
Married Sarah A. Crockett at Salt Lake City, who was born April 12, 1833, Petersborough, Northamptonshire, Eng. Their children: Edith, m. James A. Cottrell; Christopher E., m. Clara M. Hyde Nov. 27, 1895; Nettie L. died; Erminie, m. Charles Cottrell; Frank L., m. Elizabeth Hall. Family home, Kaysville.
Seventy. Died April, 1901, at Kaysville.

LAYTON, CHRISTOPHER E. (son of Charles Layton and Sarah A. Crockett). Born September, 1867, at Kaysville.
Married Clara M. Hyde Nov. 27, 1895, Salt Lake City (daughter of Rosel Hyde and Hannah Simons of Kaysville), who was born Dec. 25, 1868. Their children: Gladys b. March 10, 1897; Corydon H. b. Jan. 1, 1899; Mabel b. Jan. 26, 1901; Lena b. Aug. 24, 1903; Willis H. b. Jan. 19, 1906; Charles H. b. Oct. 30, 1908; Alice b. April 6, 1911.
Missionary to southern states 1893-95; bishop of Hunter ward 1899-1901; high councilor in Pocatello stake. Furniture dealer.

LEATHAM, JAMES (son of Robert Leatham and Janet Urquhart, Lanarkshire, Scotland). Born Dec. 15, 1830, Lanarkshire. Came to Utah Oct. 5, 1853, Appleton M. Harmon company.
Married Margaret Irvine Dec. 31, 1852, Lanarkshire (daughter of William Irvine and Agnes Kerr of Lanarkshire, pioneers Oct. 25, 1855, Milo Andrus company). She was born Jan. 3, 1837. Their children: John, m. Annie Critchlow; Agnes, m. John Acomb; Janet; Margaret, m. R. C. Pitt; Jane; Selina, m. D. J. Mackintosh; James, m. Agnes Reid; Alice, m. J. B. Kesler; William A., m. Florence Beck; Robert; Sarah A., m. R. B. Wooley. Family home, Salt Lake City.
First counselor in presidency of high priests' quorum of Pioneer stake. Stone cutter.

LEATHAM, WILLIAM A. (son of James Leatham and Margaret Irvine). Born Feb. 12, 1872, at Salt Lake City.
Married Florence Beck at Salt Lake City (daughter of Peter Beck and Isidora Jameson of Provo, Utah). She was born Oct. 1, 1877.
Salt Lake county assessor. Bookkeeper.

LEAVER, SAMUEL H. (son of Samuel Leaver and Mary Ann Hartlett, England). He was born Nov. 5, 1847, Winter Quarters, Neb. Came to Utah 1850.
Married Mary Spriggs Sept. 5, 1868, Salt Lake City (daughter of John Spriggs of Wales, came to Utah 1853). She was born Jan. 9, 1851. Their children: Mary L., m. Frederick Stauffer; Edmund Spriggs, m. Netah Yearsley; Moroni, m. Cora Wilson; Hartlett S., m. Theresa Hopfenbach; Genevieve, m. George Hopfenbach; Barnes; Earl S., m. Florence Pratt; Sidnay A., m. Lenora Lewis; Thomas O.; Leona. Family home. Salt Lake City.
Seventy. Bookkeeper. Died Jan. 31, 1910.

LEAVITT, GEORGE (son of Wire Leavitt, born 1785, and Phoebe Cole of New Hampshire). Born Aug. 29, 1828, in Sherbrooke Co., Quebec, Canada. Came to Utah October, 1847, Bates Noble company.
Married Janet Brinkerhoff Aug. 29, 1852, Centerville, Utah (daughter of James Brinkerhoff and Sally Ann Snyder, pioneers Oct. 1847, Bates Noble company). She was born Oct. 30, 1836. Their children: Phoebe Ann b. June 13, 1853, m. A. B. Cherry Aug. 15, 1868; Sarah Janett b. April 17, 1855, m. John R. Allen Nov. 2, 1875; George b. Oct. 23, 1857, d. Sept. 23, 1861; James Brinkerhoff b. Aug. 31, 1858, m. Pennina J. Rawlins May 5, 1881; Leona b. Sept. 25, 1861, m. F. A. Rawlins Dec. 18, 1879; Hyrum b. Dec. 9, 1863, m. Jane F. Stoddard Feb. 23, 1888; Mary Edith b. Dec. 27, 1864, d. Feb. 22, 1878; Levie b. April 25, 1866, d. Feb. 3, 1888; John C. b. Feb. 16, 1868, d. July 16, 1869; Lucy E. b. April 14, 1870, d. March 14, 1871; Horton Brinkerhoff b. May 12, 1871, m. Lurinda A. Hendricks Nov. 15, 1895; Georgia Anna b. Oct. 29, 1873, m. Thomas S. Karren Dec. 2, 1891; Edward b. Nov. 18, 1876, m. Lydia C. Karren March 8, 1899; Wire b. Jan. 18, 1878, d. March 18, 1878. Family home Lewiston, Utah.

Married Sarah A. Porter April, 1857 (daughter of Chauncy Warriner Porter and Amy Sumner, former pioneer of 1847, latter died at Winter Quarters, Iowa). She was born 1841 at Green Plains, Hancock county, Ill. Their children: Nina Malinda b. Nov. 25, 1861, m. Sanford Marius Porter Sept. 4, 1879; Elva Armina b. Jan. 15, 1864, m. William Henry Bond 1881; Ada Permelia b. July 29, 1865, m. William H. Bond Jan. 6, 1886; Amy Teresa b. Feb. 1, 1868, m. Sullivan C. Richardson 1886. Family resided at Porterville, Utah, and Sunset and St. Joseph, Ariz.
Married Nancy Minerva Earl July 11, 1857, Salt Lake City (daughter of Asa Earl and Minerva Rich), who was born Oct. 13, 1840, Hancock county, Ill. Came to Utah Oct. 1847, Charles C. Rich company. Their children: Joseph Wire b. Nov. 14, 1859, m. Mary E. Rawlins May 4, 1882; Charles Coulson b. Oct. 7, 1861, m. Sarah E. Cazier; Louisa b. May 16, 1863, d. May 26, 1865; William b. July 17, 1864, m. Carline F. Corlage Aug. 12, 1889; Charlotte Ann b. Oct. 3, 1867, d. May 15, 1868; Landon b. April 15, 1869, d.

Dec. 20, 1869; Orson b. Feb. 23, 1871, m. Alice Spackman 1898; Henry b. Oct. 17, 1874, m. Hepsebeth Webster Aug. 26, 1893; Albert b. May 25, 1878, d. May 10, 1898; Julia b. March 9, 1882, m. Marriner W. Jackson Nov. 12, 1902. Family home Lewiston, Utah.
First settled at Salt Lake City, moved to Centerville. Assisted in settlement of Parowan, Cedar City and Lewiston, Utah, Muddy, Ariz., and Star Valley, Wyo. Member of bishopric; high priest. President Cub River Canal Company. Died Jan. 23, 1889, Lewiston, Utah.

LEAVITT, JOSEPH WIRE (son of George Leavitt and Nancy Minerva Earl). Born Nov. 14, 1859, Centerville, Utah.
Married Mary E. Rawlins May 4, 1882, Salt Lake City (daughter of Harvey M. Rawlins and Margaret E. Frost). Their children: Joseph McCaslin b. Jan. 2, 1883; William Francis b. Nov. 22, 1883; Eulalie Ardella b. June 7, 1885, m. Fredrick Taggart Dec. 17, 1902; Arden Odell b. Oct. 3, 1887; Charles Newel b. Feb. 1, 1891; Elden Harvey b. July 1, 1893; George Lamont b. June 11, 1895; Hettie Mildred b. Sept. 1, 1898; Edith Alvira b. March 29, 1901; Hyrum Andrew b. July 3, 1903. Family home Lewiston, Utah.
Officer in Y. M. M. I. A.; Sunday school teacher. Farmer; carpenter; dairyman.

LEAVITT, JOHN QUINCY (son of John and Lucy Leavitt, Compton, Quebec, Can.). Born Oct. 1, 1834, at Compton. Came to Utah September, 1860, Captain Brown independent company.
Married Malinda Minion Sept. 21, 1858, Pulaski, Jackson county, Mich. (daughter of Isaac Minion and Claricy Curn of Pulaski). She was born April 22, 1838. Their children: Elmer Brigham b. 1859, m. Mary Ellen Spitzer; John Julian b. Oct. 4, 1861, m. Annie World; Ida Josephine b. Feb. 3, 1863, m. Abram Hatch. Family home Farmington, Utah.
President 14th quorum seventies; ward teacher. Assisted in bringing immigrants to Utah. Assessor and collector of Davis county; county recorder; county clerk; justice of peace at Farmington. Lieutenant in Utah militia. Director Utah Central railroad. Vice-president Utah Live Stock Company.

LEAVITT, LEMUEL STURDIFONT (son of Jeremiah Leavitt and Sarah Sturdifont). Born Nov. 3, 1826, Compton, Canada. Came to Utah October, 1849.
Married Melvina Thompson Oct. 15, 1850, by whom he had seven children, among whom was Lovisa b. Oct. 22, 1861, m. Myron Abbott Jan. 11, 1878. She died 1862.
Married Betsy Mortinson Feb. 1864. She died 1867. Only child: Mary Matilda b. Nov. 6, 1864, m. Myron Alma Abbott April 14, 1881 (son of Myron Abbott above).
Married Mrs. Craig, an English widow, who died a year or two after marriage.
Married Mary Ann Adams, an English widow, by whom he had one son.
Married Mrs. Waite, an English widow, who died a few years later, bearing him one son and one daughter.
About 1850 settled near Pine Canyon, Tooele county; in 1856 assisted in planting the first grain in Cache valley; located at Santa Clara, Utah, 1857. In 1863 drove an ox team to Omaha, Neb., and returned with immigrants same year.

LEE, ALFRED (son of Samuel Lee, born April 14, 1778, Orange county, N. C., and Elizabeth Gilham). Born Sept. 12, 1805, in North Carolina. Came to Utah 1849.
Married Elizabeth La Flesh (daughter of Peter La Flesh and Polly Dudley), who was born Aug. 24, 1805. Their children: Isaac b. Sept. 12, 1826, m. Julia Ann Chatman; Thomas b. Jan. 12, 1828, m. Harriet Wolkitt; Eliza Ann b. July 30, 1830; Mary b. May 18, 1832, m. Andrew Blodget; Samuel Francis b. July 25, 1835, m. Ann White; Alfred L. b. April 21, 1837; Joseph Smith b. April 23, 1839; George Henry b. July 11, 1841; Eli b. Aug. 13, 1843; John b. Nov. 29, 1848. Family home Tooele, Utah.
Married Rebecca Orme, who was born Jan. 17, 1838, Leicester, Eng. Their children: Alfred O. b. April 6, 1858; Carolina b. April 6, 1860; William O. b. Nov. 28, 1861; James Alma b. Feb. 5, 1867.

LEE, THOMAS (son of Alfred Lee and Elizabeth La Flesh). Born Jan. 12, 1828, Winchester, Ind.
Married Harriet Wolkitt July 20, 1849, while crossing the plains (daughter of Samuel Wolkitt and Emmeline Neilson). Their children: Sarah Jane b. Feb. 19, 1851, m. Joseph Rowberry; Thomas W. b. March 23, 1853, m. Martha Bowen; Emmeline b. Sept. 6, 1854; Alfred b. July 13, 1855, m. Elizabeth Dorman; Elizabeth b. Sept. 14, 1857, m. Mr. Mythena; Samuel b. Aug. 18, 1859, m. Minnie Mythena; Mary b. Oct. 5, 1861, m. Charles Bassett; Emma b. July 1, 1863; Eli b. June 27, 1865; Henry b. March 3, 1867; Caroline b. March 24, 1869; Alice b. May 28, 1872; Franklin W. b. Aug. 15, 1876; Charles W. b. Jan. 1, 1879.
Married Primrose Shields March 10, 1857, at Salt Lake City (daughter of John Shields and Primrose Cunningham). She was born July 7, 1842, in Renfrewshire, Scotland. Their children: Harriet b. Nov. 6, 1859, m. James Whitby; Primrose b. Nov. 9, 1861, m. Brigham Davies; John Shields

b. Feb. 22, 1862, m. Harriet E. Sabine; Joseph b. Jan. 11, 1865, m. Polly Skelton; Hyrum b. Dec. 18, 1866; Eli S. b. Jan. 31, 1868, m. Grace Moss; Annie Elizabeth b. Sept. 6, 1871, m. Benjamin Henson; William b. May 10, 1874; Ida b. June 7, 1877, m. Walter E. Beers; Alma S. b. Feb. 12, 1881, m. Bertha Craner; Clara May b. April 16, 1884, m. Bert Drury.
Superintendent of Sunday school; president of Y. M. M. I. A.; seventy. Hunter for company crossing plains; captain of Indian militia.

LEE, JOHN SHIELDS (son of Thomas Lee and Primrose Shields). Born Feb. 22, 1862, Tooele, Utah.
Married Harriet E. Sabine Dec. 23, 1886, at Milton, Utah (daughter of Ara W. Sabine and Nancy Ann Hanes, pioneers Sept. 1850). She was born Aug. 27, 1867, at Grantsville. Their children: John Leroy b. Oct. 3, 1887, m. Emma Hufaker; Marion b. Oct. 11, 1889; Ida b. Oct. 21, 1893; Ralph b. Jan. 29, 1896; Amy b. Nov. 12, 1897; Ruth b. July 22, 1899; Eurilda b. March 9, 1902; Thomas b. April 9, 1906; Maurice b. Feb. 11, 1908. Family home Tooele, Utah.
Missionary two years; superintendent of religion classes; president of Y. M. M. I. A.; assistant superintendent of Sunday school; senior president of 43d quorum of seventies.

LEE, ELI S. (son of Thomas Lee and Primrose Shields). Born Jan. 31, 1868, Tooele City, Utah.
Married Grace Alice Moss Dec. 22, 1887, at Milton, Utah (daughter of William Francis Moss, who came to Utah 1856, and Eliza Crich of Lake Point). She was born Jan. 10, 1866. Their children: Alice May b. July 23, 1888, m. John Hansen; Florence b. June 15, 1890, m. Ernest Presbridge; Primrose b. Dec. 29, 1892; Lurilla b. Sept. 23, 1893; Eli Thomas b. Feb. 2, 1896; Eva b. Jan. 14, 1898; Della b. July 23, 1900; Ida Grace b. July 10, 1902; Helen b. May 13, 1904; William Moss b. July 18, 1906. Family home Lake Point, Utah.
Elder; teacher; assistant Sunday school superintendent. Constable of Tooele county 1891-92. Farmer; lumberman.

LEE, CHRISTEN C. (son of Christen C. Lee, Sr., and Dorothy Marie Jensen, of Narre-lie, Aabentorp, Denmark). Born Oct. 20, 1833, at Aabentorp. Came to Utah Sept. 13, 1857, Mathias Cowley company.
Married Kjersten Marie Jensen, 1853, in Denmark. She was born Sept. 24, 1824, and died Jan. 7, 1863, Brigham City, Utah.
Married Sophia Karen Madsen Nov. 19, 1862, Salt Lake City (daughter of Niels Madsen and Martha Marie Hansen, who came to Utah Aug. 8, 1860, Captain Wallings company). She was born May 3, 1846, in Denmark. Their children: Mary Lerinda b. Nov. 11, 1863, m. Joseph Waite, Nov. 11, 1887; Francis Christen b. Nov. 11, 1865, m. Julia P. Cash, Nov. 29, 1893; Peter Madsen b. May 1, 1859, d. Oct. 2, 1876; Martha Louisa b. Dec. 20, 1870, d. Nov. 1, 1876; Wilford Neils b. Jan. 10, 1874, d. Oct. 10, 1878; Alta Sophia b. Feb. 22, 1879, m. Wilford Daines Feb. 22, 1905; Edna Trudie b. Sept. 23, 1882; Orville Leonard b. Dec. 3, 1885, m. Martha W. Smith, Sept. 7, 1910; Royal Elmer b. March 3, 1888. Family home Hyde Park, Utah.
Married Tomine Petersen July 8, 1865, Salt Lake City (daughter of John C. Petersen and Christene Jensen, married Dec. 1843 in Denmark, came to Utah Sept. 20, 1856, Knud Peterson company). She was born June 9, 1847, Farso sogn, Denmark. Their children: Clara b. March 8, 1866, m. Walter Hawks Jan. 17, 1885; John Earnest b. Oct. 2, 1867, m. Jennie Reeder Oct. 12, 1898 (died), m. Hattie Vilate Reeder Oct. 1, 1903; Tomine C. b. July 16, 1869, d. Oct. 10, 1876.
Missionary to Denmark; temple worker; secretary during "United Order" move. Watermaster; farmer; merchant; sheepman; dairyman. Died Jan. 1, 1905, Logan, Utah.

LEE, FRANCIS CHRISTEN (son of Christen C. Lee and Sophia Karen Madsen). Born Nov. 11, 1865, Brigham City, Utah.
Married Julia Perier Cash Nov. 29, 1893, Logan, Utah (daughter of Lewis Lunceford Cash, and Juliet Perier Williams; former came to Utah Sept. 27, 1890; latter died Feb. 11, 1871, Howes Valley, Ky.). She was born March 14, 1868. Their children: Eva b. Oct. 18, 1894; Avon b. Sept. 8, 1896; Geneva b. Oct. 18, 1898; Eulalia b. April 18, 1902; Afton b. July 1, 1904; Inez b. Jan. 22, 1908; Francis Cash b. July 10, 1910, d. April 2, 1911. Family home Hyde Park, Utah.
Missionary to England; Sunday school teacher for 15 years. Treasurer of school board of trustees three years. Merchant.

LEE, EDDY ORLAND (son of Josiah Lee and Rockselana Davis of Quebec, Canada). Born Sept. 16, 1855. Came to Utah January, 1891.
Married Jennie Cummings Aug. 20, 1884, Sheffield. Ill. (daughter of Pitchyon Cummings and Ester Garrett of Sheffield). She was born Aug. 1, 1858.
Graduate Illinois State University. Prosecuting attorney Cheyenne county, Neb., 1888-90. Lawyer.

LEE, EZEKIEL (son of Charles Lee, born Oct. 15, 1763, Worcester county, Mass., and Rhoda Keith, born Dec. 2, 1768, Chesterfield, Mass., married, 1789). Born Nov. 8, 1795, Chesterfield, pioneer October, 1848.

Married Elizabeth Strong Jan. 31, 1822 (daughter of William Strong and Lydia Ferrin), who was born Nov. 17, 1795, and came to Utah Oct. 1, 1850, Aaron Johnson company. Their children: Marquis Fayette b. Dec. 1822, m. Ann Lee; Jane b. Aug. 17, 1824, m. Pardon Webb; William Henry b. May 12, 1827, m. Harriett Carter; Orrin Strong b. Dec. 7, 1835, m. Sally A. Miles. Family home, Salt Lake City.
Married Fanny Britton Fisher May 1857, Salt Lake City (daughter of Mr. Fisher), who was born Aug. 4, 1841. Their children: Elizabeth b. April 1858, m. Frank Peirce; Rhoda b. June 14, 1860, m. Parley P. Parker; John F. b. June 18, 1862, m. Elizabeth Earl; Lucy b. April 14, 1864, m. George Evans; Catherine b. April 15, 1866, m. Frank Raleigh; Adelia b. May 8, 1868, m. Chas. Brown; Irene b. July 17, 1870, m. George Nichols; Joseph Warren b. April 31, 1873.
Served in war of 1812. In October 1848 carried first mail to Utah. Settled at Cottonwood. Presiding elder of first branch of church in Comstock, Mich., 1843; bishop of Holliday ward 1851-58. One of the first physicians to practice in Utah. Died 1878, Salt Lake City.

LEE, ORRIN STRONG (son of Ezekiel Lee and Elizabeth Strong). Born Dec. 7, 1835. Came to Utah with parents.
Married Sally Ann Miles Oct. 30, 1859 (daughter of Albert Miles and Mariah Veich; came to Utah Oct. 1, 1850, Aaron Johnson company). She was born 1842, in Illinois. Their children: Luella M. b. Nov. 13, 1860, m. Jasper Horn, Dec. 7, 1882; Orrin S. Jr. b. April 13, 1862, m. Jane White Dec. 25, 1882; Joseph W. b. Dec. 17, 1863, m. Mary H. Hoyt Dec. 23, 1884; Clarissa J. b. Jan. 13, 1868, m. Sam'l Woolley Aug. 4, 1887; Sally A. b. Nov. 14, 1870, d. infant; Zella May b. Feb. 7, 1872, d. 1881; Frank A. b. Aug. 28, 1874; Edith A. b. July 27, 1877, m. Albert Roos July 19, 1899; Lucy I. b. July 26, 1880, m. John J. Angel April 23, 1901. Family home Peoa, Utah.
Counselor in the bishopric of Peoa ward 1861-66; superintendent of Sunday school five years; missionary to Michigan 1878. Assessor and collector Summit county three years; county commissioner four terms; member of the Utah legislature 1871-72. Walker and Black Hawk war veteran. Participated in Echo Canyon trouble.

LEE, ORRIN S. (son of Orrin Strong Lee and Sally Ann Miles). Born April 13, 1862, Peoa, Utah.
Married Jane White Dec. 25, 1882, Peoa, Utah (daughter of Wm. White and Martha Gray, the former came to Utah, California company). She was born at Bountiful, Utah. Their children: Zella M. b. Oct. 6, 1883, m. Dwight Henry 1903; Lavenia b. Nov. 25, 1885, m. Stanley Bybee 1906; Orrin Ward b. May 22, 1888, m. Lydia Tracey 1908; Mary Myrtle b. Feb. 24, 1890, died; Henry Stanley b. May 12, 1892; Mark White b. Jan. 25, 1897, and Bessie Fern b. July 10, 1899, died; Perry Arnold b. Aug. 11, 1903; Minnie b. Jan. 21, 1905; Marrion Albert b. March 25, 1905, died. Family home Leorin, Idaho.
County commissioner of Bingham Co., Idaho, for two years.

LEE, JOSEPH WARREN (son of Orrin Strong Lee and Sally Ann Miles). Born Dec. 17, 1863, Peoa, Utah.
Married Mary Hoyt Dec. 23, 1884, Hoytsville, Utah (daughter of Samuel Pierce Hoyt and Catherine Emma Burbidge, Marion, Utah). Their children: Ethel b. Nov. 14, 1885; Elmer H. b. June 7, 1888, d. May 10, 1901; Winifred b. March 17, 1890; Mary Lucile b. March 17, 1892; Fay Warren b. Dec. 7, 1893; Bertie H. b. Jan. 13, 1897; Ernest O. and Elbert O. b. Jan. 16, 1899, the latter d. Feb. 6, 1899; Merlin R. b. June 3, 1903; Kermit P. b. Feb. 15, 1908. Family home Hoytsville, Utah.
Justice of the peace 1904-06. Farmer; stockraiser; dairy and laundryman.

LEE, JOHN F. (son of Dr. Ezekiel Lee and Fanny Britton Fisher). Born June 18, 1862.
Married Elizabeth Earl Jan. 3, 1884, Logan, Utah (daughter of Michael Earl and Elizabeth Woolnough, pioneers Oct. 3, 1862, Captain McArthur "Dixie" oxtrain). Their children: Earl L.; Bessie; Myrtle; Mabel; Mark W.; Lucy; Oliver. Family home Rexburg, Idaho.

LEE, GEORGE. Born Sept. 27, 1824, Nottinghamshire, Eng. Came to Utah Sept. 16, 1859, Edward Stevenson company.
Married Sarah Peaker (daughter of George Peaker and Hannah Smith), who was born Nov. 14, 1825, and came to Utah with husband. Their children: Mary Ann b. Jan. 24, 1846, m. John Albiston Dec. 3, 1863; Hannah b. Dec. 20, 1847, m. John Corbidge Dec. 9, 1865; John b. Jan. 5, 1850; Sarah b. Dec. 24, 1851, m. Henry Fowler; Elizabeth J. b. Jan. 1, 1854, m. William Corbidge; Ellen b. Jan. 8, 1855; George b. Dec. 30, 1855; Willamina b. Jan. 4, 1858; Moroni b. July 11, 1859; William J. b. Sept. 2, 1860; Fannie E. b. Dec. 4, 1862, m. Elliott Butterworth; Joseph b. March 7, 1867.
Pioneer and member choir, Franklin, Idaho. Indian fighter. Died Oct. 29, 1868.

LEE, ISAAC (son of Alfred and Elizabeth Lee). Born Sept. 12, 1826, Randolph county, Ind., pioneer 1852.
Married Julia Ann Chapman. Their child: Eliza Ann, m. Aroet Lucius Hale, Jr., Sept. 11, 1869.
Assisted in building of Nauvoo temple; member Nauvoo martial band. On coming to Utah, settled in Tooele; ran saw and shingle mill. Tooele Canyon. Moved to Grouse

Creek, Utah 1879; and nine years later to Salt River Valley, Wyo.; and six years later to Marion, Idaho. President of seventies quorum in Wyoming. Died Jan. 30, 1899, at Marion, Idaho.

LEE, JOHN PERCIVAL (son of John Lee and Margaret Dudney of Lincoln county, Tenn.). Born April 26, 1824, in Lincoln county, Tenn. Came to Utah October or November, 1850, started with Thomas Johnson company, lost their way and later were picked up by Shadrach Roundy company.
Married Eliza Foscue Feb. 18, 1844, in Coosa county, Ala. (daughter of Benjamin Foscue and Eliza Skurlock of Clark county, Ala.). She was born Sept. 23, 1829, in Jackson county, Fla. Their children: John Rupard, m. Sarah Banks; Sarah Lucinda, m. Charles Wakeman Dalton; Ann Eliza, m. E. W. Thompson, m. Patrick Henry McGuire, m. Willard Amos Nixon; Mary Caroline b. 1850, m. Martin Luther Black Aug. 22, 1868; Emma R., m. Charles Dalton, m. Jabez Gilbert Sutherland; Charles Andrew, m. Julia Speck; Ellen, m. Elias Sims, m. James Thomas Jakeman, m. Martin Sanders; Rosamond, m. George Sutherland. Family home Beaver, Utah.
Married second wife 1879, her name and family unknown. Member 24th quorum seventies; missionary to southern states 1866-68. Superintendent of schools; school teacher. Farmer and stockraiser. Died April 30, 1907, at Thatcher, Ariz.

LEE, THOMAS OCTAVIOUS (son of Richard Lee and Lydia Lee, Nottingham, Eng.). Born Dec. 4, 1828, in Nottingham, Eng. Came to Utah Oct. 27, 1863.
Married Ellen Tadwell March 1844 in Rotherham, Yorkshire, Eng. Came to Utah in 1860 with handcart company. She was born July 15, 1819. Their children: Emma b. 1845, died; Mary b. Aug. 26, 1846, m. William D. Doulton; John b. Nov. 21, 1848, frozen to death near Park City Jan. 8, 1868; Orson Henry b. Oct. 28, 1850, m. Rachel Ann Jones.
Home missionary in England; Sunday school teacher; ward worker. Worked in quarries; carpenter. Aided in building up the community. Engineer and foundry man in England. Was killed March 1865 at Heber City in Crook's rock quarry.

LEE, ORSON HENRY (son of Thomas Octavious Lee and Ellen Tadwell). Born Oct. 28, 1850, in Sheffield, Eng. Came to Utah Oct. 27, 1861.
Married Rachel Ann Jones Feb. 12, 1880, in Salt Lake City Endowment House (daughter of Elisha Jones and Sarah Ann Cummings, family resided Heber City, Utah). She was born Jan. 8, 1861. Their children: Thomas b. Sept. 2, 1881, d. Oct. 3, 1881; Sarah Ann b. Aug. 5, 1884, m. Nymphus H. Murdock; Margeret Lydia b. April 15, 1889; Orson Monroe b. Aug. 22, 1891; Fay b. Dec. 21, 1894; Dell b. April 6, 1898.
Moved into the ward in 1883 among the first and has devoted his life to the good of the ward and building up the country. Bishop of Elkhorn ward, Wasatch stake; superintendent Sunday school since the ward was organized May 12, 1895; teacher and secretary 1891; elder May 19, 1878. Justice of the peace; school trustee. Farmer; ranchman; dairyman.

LEE, WILLIAM (son of Richard Lee, born April 16, 1799, at Upper Mitten, Eng., and Jane Baynum, born May 3, 1800, at Stourport, Eng.). He was born Sept. 6, 1820, at Upper Mitten, pioneer Oct. 8, 1850.
Married Elizabeth Jasper Jan. 8, 1844 (daughter of Thomas Jasper and Elenor Baker), who was born May 3, 1820, in England. Their children: William R.; Mary Jane; Sarah Ann; Alice Ann; John Jasper; George Henry; William Richard; Selina Elizabeth; Thomas Jasper. Family home Grantsville, Utah.
Married Jane Lyon April 10, 1855, Salt Lake City (daughter of William and Mary Lyon of England). She was born in England. Their children: Mary; Joseph; Emma; Rachel; Damsel; Isaac; Rosema; Charlotte.

LEE, WILLIAM RICHARD (son of William Lee and Elizabeth Jasper). Born Oct. 15, 1856, Grantsville, Utah.
Married Dorcas J. Whittle Oct. 10, 1876, Salt Lake City (daughter of George Whittle and Ann Janette Severe, the former pioneer 1849, the latter Oct. 1850). She was born Aug. 28, 1861, Grantsville, Utah. Only child: Gladys b. Oct. 15, 1895.
Missionary to southern states 1887-88, to Idaho 1896 and to Missouri and Texas 1904-06; first counselor to Bishop Hector C. Haight of Oakley, first ward, 1906; ordained first counselor in high priests quorum June 20, 1906.

LEES, JOHN (son of Joseph Lees of Manchester, Lancashire, Eng.). Born 1801 Lancashire. Came to Utah October, 1853, Cyrus H. Wheelock company.
Married Elizabeth Buckley about 1828, Lancashire, Eng. Their children: James, m. Elizabeth Walker; Joseph, died; Susanna, m. John Blackham; John, Jr., m. Mary Ann Needham; George, d. aged 72 years; Josiah, m. Mary Ann Boyden. Family home, Salt Lake City.
Elder; block teacher. Laborer. Died Jan. 28, 1886, at Salt Lake City.

LEES, JOHN (son of John Lees and Elizabeth Buckley). Born March 9, 1833, Lancashire, Eng. Came to Utah with parents.
Married Martha Needham in June 1853, Lancashire, Eng. (daughter of Joseph and Jane Needham of Lancashire). Their children: John N., m. Luella J. Balser; Amazon, m. Charles Player; Sarah Jane, m. William Gillespie; Elizabeth, m. Jonathan Openshaw; Josiah N., m. Ellen M. Perkins; Martha and Samuel, died.
Married Emma Chetham Oct. 27, 1881, at Salt Lake City (daughter of Thomas Chetham and Sarah Taylor of Birmingham, Eng.). She was born March 6, 1838.
Seventy; block teacher. Butcher.

LEES, JOHN N. (son of John Lees and Martha Needham). Born May 23, 1860, at Salt Lake City, Utah.
Married Luella J. Balser Feb. 15, 1883, at Salt Lake City (daughter of John Balser and Emma Evans of St. Louis, Mo., and England, pioneers 1852 Abraham O. Smoot company). She was born Jan. 8, 1862, Salt Lake City. Their children: Martha E. b. Dec. 28, 1885, d. aged seven; Luella G. b. Sept. 8, 1886; John Lewis b. Aug. 20, 1888, d. infant; Mary May b. Dec. 15, 1889; Frank D. b. Dec. 1, 1892; Earl B. b. Sept. 8, 1894; Nettie b. Dec. 30, 1897, and Nellie b. Dec. 30, 1897, d. infants; Evan B. b. April 18, 1899; Eugene A. b. Nov. 1, 1908; Willie b. May 15, 1902, d. infant. Family home, Salt Lake City.
Elder; block teacher. Employed by Utah Hide and Live Stock Company.

LEES, JOSIAH N. (son of John Lees and Martha Needham). Born Sept. 23, 1865.
Married Ellen M. Perkins Sept. 22, 1892, at Manti, Utah (daughter of John Perkins and Martha Filer, pioneers 1865). She was born March 22, 1873, at Salt Lake City. Their children: Lester J. b. March 5, 1899; Emma R. b. April 24, 1901; Murtice E. b. Oct. 27, 1904. Family home, Salt Lake City.
Elder; Sunday school and block teacher. Butcher.

LEES, JOSIAH (son of John Lees and Elizabeth Buckley). Born Dec. 27, 1840, Lancashire, Eng. Came to Utah 1862.
Married Mary Ann Boyden Nov. 13, 1865, at Salt Lake City (daughter of Charles Boyden and Sarah Korns, pioneers 1860, James D. Ross company). She was born Jan. 27, 1847, Newcastle-on-Tyne, England. Came to Utah with parents in 1860. Their children: Josiah Jr., b. Oct. 6, 1866, m. May E. Ridges; Sarah b. Dec. 3, 1868, m. Joseph Wood; Charles M. b. Feb. 13, 1870, m. Elizabeth Bishop; Susannah b. Aug. 26, 1873, m. Matery Duncombe; William b. Dec. 17, 1875, d. infant; John E. b. Sept. 28, 1877, d. aged 4; Clarence b. Dec. 16, 1879, m. Etta Hodson; Eva b. June 4, 1882, m. Emmett W. Bywater; Le Roy b. Oct. 25, 1885, m. Ivy Farr; Ethel b. Jan. 11, 1887, m. Samuel A. Brown; Frank E. b. Jan. 1, 1890.
Elder; home missionary. Deputy sheriff under Joseph Sharp, Salt Lake county, four years. Freighter and merchant. Died Feb. 21, 1908, at Salt Lake City.

LEES, JOSIAH (son of Josiah Lees and Mary Ann Boyden). Born Oct. 6, 1867, at Salt Lake City.
Married May E. Ridges Nov. 1889 at Logan, Utah (daughter of Joseph Ridges and Adelaide Whiteley of Salt Lake City). She was born March 1866. Their children: Leone b. Aug. 1891; Myrtle b. Feb. 1893, m. George Eastwood; Earl E. b. June 1895; Adelaide b. Feb. 9, 1899; Mary E. b. Jan. 15, 1902. Family home, Salt Lake City.
Member 109th quorum seventies. Car inspector. Freighter.

LE FEVRE, WILLIAM (son of John Le Fevre and Ann Dalton of Crowland, Lincolnshire, Eng.). Born Aug. 31, 1833, at Crowland. Came to Utah Sept. 17, 1852, David Woods company.
Married Hannah Holyoak Dec. 25, 1855, Parowan, Utah, and later in the Endowment house, Salt Lake City (daughter of George Holyoak and Sarah Green of Mosely Ware Green Common near Birmingham, Eng., pioneers Oct. 1 or 2, 1854, Dr. Rich company). She was born March 25, 1841. Their children: William Dame, b. Sept. 10, 1857, m. Cornelia Robinson; Sarah Ann b. Sept. 20, 1860, m. James Houston; John Henry b. May 2, 1861, m. Hattie Gale; Hannah Eliza b. March 6, 1864, m. Albert F. McEwen; Daniel James b. Oct. 29, 1867, m. Jane A. Robinson; Ann Elizabeth b. Aug. 28, 1870, m. William D. Haycock; Martha Jane b. Sept. 12, 1872; Jesse Holyoak b. Nov. 11, 1874, m. Nora McClelland; Mary Ellen b. March 7, 1877, m. Byron M. Orton; Clara Parthenia b. June 23, 1879, m. William E. Chatwin; Esther Alice b. Sept. 3, 1883, m. James Simkins Jones.
Married Frances Banks Oct. 3, 1863, Salt Lake City (daughter of William E. Banks and Ellen Eyre of Sidney, Australia, pioneers 1858). She was born Nov. 4, 1844, died July 30, 1911. Their children: Susannah Delfiney b. Aug. 15, 1864, m. Michael G. Lloyd; George Edwin b. March 13, 1866, m. Margaret A. DeLong; Luke Dalton b. Nov. 12, 1867, m. Julia A. Orton; Ellen Lovina b. Sept. 5, 1869, m. Edward R. McEwen; Joseph Ellis b. April 10, 1871, died; Charlotte Moore b. March 24, 1873, m. Mahonri M. Steele, Jr.; Frank Banks b. April 24, 1875, died; Sarah Alice b. Feb. 14, 1877, died; William b. Oct. 19, 1879, m. Jessie M. Robinson; Claudin Pernetta b. Jan. 10, 1882, d. July 24, 1893; Fannie May b. Oct. 9, 1883, m. James Burtown Davenport; Leon b. Feb.

15, 1886, m. Pearl Houston. Family resided Cleveland, Garfield Co., Utah.
Member 6th quorum seventies; missionary to St. George temple 1900-02; ordained high priest Aug. 29, 1897 and elder Oct. 31, 1852. Stockraiser and farmer.

LEFFLER, JAMES A. (son of Joseph Leffler, born Sept. 11, 1806, and Mary Rummons, born May 12, 1811, in Missouri). Born July 28, 1840, Boon county, Mo. Pioneer July 10, 1862, private company.
Married Mary Jane Gleave July 24, 1872 (daughter of John Gleave), who was born Jan. 2, 1858. Only child: Joseph Levingston b. 1873, d. child.
Married Anna Maria McGregor Jan. 4, 1875, Salt Lake City (daughter of William McGregor and Ann Hossack, married Dec. 28, 1841, in Scotland, pioneers Sept. 1852, Captain Wood company). She was born Aug. 21, 1853, Salt Lake City.

LEMMON, WILLIS (son of Washington Lemmon and Tamer Stevens of Big Cottonwood, Utah). Born Aug. 12, 1837, Quincy, Ill. Came to Utah 1852.
Married Anna E. Homer Nov. 1, 1859, Salt Lake City (daughter of Russell King Homer and Eliza Williamson, pioneers 1858). She was born March 19, 1844, and died July 5, 1911, Smithfield. Their children: Anna Eliza, m. Justin Knapp; Willis, died; Julia C. m. George A. Hibbard; Nancy M. m. Fred Saurey; Eva A., m. James Skeen; Alice, m. Axel Anderson; Lee, m. Nellie Richardson; Rozette, m. William Anderson; Nellie, m. Henry Barnes; Homer, m. Emma Anderson. Family home Smithfield, Utah.
High priest; missionary to Florence, Neb., 1863; assisted in bringing immigrants to Utah. Farmer. Died Feb. 4, 1909, Smithfield, Utah.

LEMON, WILLIAM McCLURE (son of Alexander Lemon and Margaret McClure of Pennsylvania). Born April 25, 1808, in Cumberland county, Pa. Came to Utah 1847, Perrigrine Sessions company.
Married Catherine Mayer in Pennsylvania (daughter of Abraham and Elizabeth Mayer). Their children: Alexander A. b. March 1, 1831; Elizabeth b. July 26, 1833, m. Barrol Covington; Samuel b. Oct. 4, 1836, died; Margaretta b. Oct. 4, 1839, m. Robert E. King; Mary Ann b. Sept. 1, 1843, m. Henry Pickering; John Knox b. Aug. 19, 1846, m. Jane Burgess; William b. April 15, 1849. Family home Salt Lake City, Utah.
High priest. Surveyor.

LENZI, MARTIN (son of John and Eliza Lenzi of Walbach, Switzerland). Born Oct. 19, 1815, at Walbach, Rhinefelden, Canton Aarogan, Switzerland. Came to Utah in September 1857, Jacob Hoffines company.
Married Jane Height in Philadelphia, Pa. She died 1877. Their children: Cornelia, m. John D. T. McAllister; Martin and William Tell, died. Family home, Salt Lake City.
Married Eliza Lutz in Philadelphia, Pa. (daughter of Charles Lutz and Mary Skidmore of Philadelphia; came to Utah with parents). She was born Feb. 1, 1835. Their children: John Alexander, m. Erenstine Holling; Annie Eliza, m. Hyrum Pearse Folsom; Charles Henry, m. Ada Ferguson; Samuel Frank, died; Sophia Elizabeth, Joseph Albert, George Washington, Wendell Leon, and Clara, d. in childhood. Family home, Salt Lake City.
Married Caroline Johnson. Their child: Gertrude.
High priest; counselor to Bishop Hoagland, 14th ward, Salt Lake City, Utah; president Zurich mission. Merchant. Died Oct. 18, 1898, Salt Lake City, Utah.

LEONARD, DAVID HENRY (son of James Leonard and Jane Caldwell of upper Canada). Born March 7, 1841, in upper Canada. Came to Utah Sept. 17, 1853, Moses Clawson company.
Married Emma Newport Child Jan. 7, 1861 (daughter of John Child and Eliza Newport of London, Eng., pioneers Sept. 17, 1853, Moses Clauson company). She was born Aug. 13, 1841. Their children: Emma Leu Alice b. July 25, 1866, m. William Willis Wimmer; David Heber b. July 13, 1869, m. Hannah Matilda Johnson; Myra Annie b. Jan. 6, 1872, m. Henry Charles; Mary Eliza b. Jan. 5, 1874 and George Alma b. June 25, 1875, d. infants; Alonzo Newport b. Feb. 22, 1878, m. Georgiana Spilsbury; Marian Lyman b. Jan. 9, 1885, m. Rosa Ward.
Married Elizabeth Charles Sept. 16, 1865, in Salt Lake City (daughter of David Charles and Elizabeth Thomas, of South Wales, pioneers 1852). She was born Dec. 7, 1846. Their children: William Henry b. Aug. 9, 1866, m. Annie Luce; Elizabeth Jane b. March 1868, m. James Johnson; James Vaughan b. April 4, 1870, m. Janet Collard; John Hyrum b. Dec. 18, 1871, m. Alice Rowley; Alice Ann b. April 2, 1874, m. George Westover; Margaret B. Dec. 1, 1876, d. infant; Agnes b. Dec. 9, 1877, d. child; Elsie Adeline b. Feb. 20, 1880, m. Robert Litster; Caroline Althera b. March 3, 1882, m. George A. Albright; Davis Charles b. April 26, 1884, m. Bessie Collard; Emma Eulila b. Sept. 23, 1886, m. Amasa Porter Clark; Alvin Eugene b. Aug. 7, 1888, m. Katy Gordon;

Myron Herald b. Sept. 1, 1890, m. Elsie Bartlett. Family home Huntington, Utah.
Missionary to frontier; elder. School trustee for several years in St. Johns, Tooele county. Bee and tree inspector. Black Hawk war veteran. Farmer; blacksmith and stockraiser. Missionary to settle Rush Valley, Tooele county, St. Joseph, The Muddy, Nevada and Emery county 1870, returned to Missouri river 1863 for immigrants for the church—crossing the plains with oxteams three times in all.

LEWIS, DAVID (son of David Lewis). Born April 10, 1814, in Simpson county, Ky. Came to Utah October, 1850.
Married Duritha Trail 1836, in Kentucky (daughter of Solomon Trail and Nancy Durant of Kentucky, pioneers Oct. 1850). She was born Jan. 5, 1813. Their children: Armita, m. George Baker; Preston, m. Virtue Ann Bowthorpe; m. Sarah Coleman; David, d. Oct. 30, 1866; Siney, m. Elizabeth Coleman; m. Elizabeth Blair; Olive, m. David Brenton; m. Hill Wylie; William Trail, d. aged 14. Family home Salt Lake City, Utah. Their children: Annie Elizabeth; Liza.
Married Elizabeth Huntsman at Salt Lake City. Their children: Annie Elizabeth; Liza.
Married Jane Huntsman at Salt Lake City.
Married Clarissy ——.
High priest. Photographer; cooper and farmer. Died in 1854 at Parowan, Utah.

LEWIS, PRESTON (son of David Lewis and Duritha Trail). Born Nov. 15, 1838, Simpson county, Ky. Came to Utah 1851.
Married Virtue Ann Bowthorpe Jan. 4, 1856, Salt Lake City, by Elija Sheets (daughter of William Bowthorpe and Mary Ann Tuttle of city of Norwich, Norfolkshire, Eng., pioneers Oct. 13, 1853, Cyrus H. Wheelock company). She was born Feb. 28, 1836. Their children: David W. b. Feb. 4, 1858, d. aged 2; Preston K. b. Dec. 21, 1859, m. Margeret R. Herbert; George S. b. Feb. 17, 1862, d. aged 10; Virtue Ann b. Feb. 4, 1864, m. Fredrick Kent; Marion T. b. March 10, 1867, d. aged 2; Mahaley A. b. Jan. 9, 1870, m. William H. La Pearl; Franklin T. b. Feb. 22, 1872, m. Lorett Butler; Emerelta b. July 23, 1875, d. aged 2; Ira A. b. March 22, 1877, m. Annie Quist. Family home, Big Cottonwood ward.
Married Sarah Coleman (daughter of George Coleman and Elizabeth Bailey, of Big Cottonwood, Utah).
Seventy at Big Cottonwood; missionary to "Dixie" one year and to The Muddy six months; priest; block teacher. Road supervisor at Big Cottonwood three years; school trustee. Farmer and stockraiser. Died Jan. 13, 1913, Heber, Utah.

LEWIS, PRESTON KING (son of Preston Lewis and Virtue Ann Bowthorpe). Born Dec. 21, 1859, Big Cottonwood, Utah.
Married Margeret R. Herbert Jan. 4, 1900, Vernal, Utah, by George A. Davis (daughter of Thomas Herbert and Ann Wardle of Vernal, Utah). She was born May 27, 1882. Their children: Margeret A. b. Feb. 24, 1901; Mary b. Jan. 16, 1903; Charles b. Dec. 22, 1904; Frank b. Oct. 24, 1906. Family home, Big Cottonwood.
Carpenter.

LEWIS, SINEY (son of David Lewis and Duritha Trail). Born Aug. 1, 1848, Council Bluffs, Iowa. Came to Utah 1850, oxteam company.
Married Elizabeth Coleman Jan. 5, 1874, at Salt Lake City (daughter of George Coleman and Elizabeth Bailey of England, pioneers with oxteam company). She was born Dec. 6, 1856. Their children: David b. Nov. 24, 1874, d. child; Lenorah b. Aug. 16, 1876, m. Alfred Watkins; m. E. W. Evans; Annie Elizabeth b. May 9, 1878, m. Joseph H. Carroll; Minnie b. Sept. 21, 1880, m. William Pierce; Siney Jr. b. June 6, 1883, m. Lena Hoft; Frank C. b. July 26, 1885; Mary Coleman b. Nov. 25, 1887, m. Charles Hatch; Georgeana b. July 12, 1890, m. Linn McClelland; Charles b. March 3, 1892; Aaron b. Jan. 17, 1892, d. child; Birdie b. June 9, 1898; Jennie b. Dec. 6, 1900. Family home, Salt Lake City.
Married Elizabeth Blair Oct. 10, 1876, at Salt Lake City (daughter of Harrison Blair and Mary McNutt). She was born May 9, 1856, died Nov. 19, 1887, at Big Cottonwood, Utah. Their children: Lottie b. Dec. 28, 1877, m. Allen Hodson; William Harrison b. Dec. 9, 1879, d. aged 16; Royal b. Dec. 6, 1881, died; Mary Elizabeth b. March 2, 1883, and Olive b. Aug. 13, 1884, d. child; Baby b. Nov. 15, 1887, d. infant. Family home Big Cottonwood, Utah.
High priest; Sunday school superintendent; superintendent Y. M. M. I. A: ward teacher. Assisted in bringing immigrants to Utah. School trustee at Vernal. Director in Wasatch water company at Midway. Indian war veteran. Farmer.

LEWIS, ENOCH (son of Thomas and Rachel Lewis). Born Nov. 25, 1824, in Wales. Came to Utah 1859, James Brown company.
Married Emma Farrell in 1849, at Newport, Wales. Their children: Alice, m. Mr. Kewley; Thomas H.; George, died; Mary, m. William Edwards; Enoch H.; Martha, m. Mr. Carlisle; Lewis, died.
Settled at Farmington, Utah; moved to Logan 1860. Died Feb. 7, 1890, Logan, Utah.

LEWIS, JESSE WILLIAM (son of John Lewis, born 1799, in Virginia, and Mary Douglas, born 1800, in Kentucky). Born Oct. 27, 1836. Came to Utah in 1861.
Married Mary A. Fuller Dec. 27, 1855, Des Moines, Iowa (daughter of Amos Botsford Fuller and Esther Smith, both born in St. Lawrence county, N. Y.). She was born Aug. 31, 1833. Their children: Oran Amos b. Nov. 2, 1857, m. Ellen Gillispie Aug. 2, 1883; m. Laura Larson June 30, 1887; Seth b. Jan. 30, 1860; Mary Esther b. March 2, 1863; Ella Sophina b. June 20, 1865; Alcesta Adelia b. May 21, 1867; Loretta Alice b. Aug. 20, 1870, m. John Mitchell Cowan Dec. 19, 1889; Jesse William, Jr. b. Oct. 15, 1872, m. Melissa Manwell June 30, 1897; Elmer Ray b. Dec. 23, 1874; Cora Cordelia b. Feb. 24, 1877; Ora Jane Gertrude b. Oct. 8, 1879, m. John August Allen Feb. 29, 1903. Family home Provo, Utah.

LEWIS, JOHN A. (son of Edmund Lewis, born 1771, and Amelia Preece, born 1780, of Cardiff, South Wales, who were married in 1800). He was born Jan. 15, 1814, at Llandaff, South Wales. Came to Utah Sept. 30, 1854, Darwin Richardson company.
Married Ann John (daughter of John and Elizabeth John, who were married about 1808). She was born May 3, 1818. Their children: Ann b. June 25, 1836, m. Henry Clegg 1855; Mary b. Nov. 22, 1839, m. Joshua Hawks Dec. 21, 1859; Fredrick b. May 29, 1844, m. Agnes Ferguson Jan. 28, 1865; William b. Jan. 6, 1847, m. Sarah Ann Malcom April 3, 1875. Family resided Salt Lake City, Brigham City and Spanish Fork, Utah.
Married Priscilla Merrimen in 1851 (daughter of Joseph and Mary Merrimen), who was born Feb. 22, 1811, at Pembrokeshire, Wales. Their children: Amelia Priscilla b. June 3, 1852, m. Moses B. Gay Feb. 22, 1874; John Samuel b. July 13, 1884, m. Mary Jane Warner Dec. 28, 1874.
Missionary to Wales 1872-74. Planted first orchard at Brigham City in 1856. Assisted in bringing immigrants to Utah in 1854. Contractor and builder

LEWIS, FREDRICK (son of John A. Lewis and Ann John). Born May 29, 1844, at Cardiff, Wales
Married Agnes Ferguson Jan. 28, 1865, at Spanish Fork, Utah (daughter of Andrew Ferguson and Cathrine Douglas, former came to Utah 1855, with Moses Thurston company). She was born Sept. 21, 1843, at Airdrie, Scotland. Their children: Priscilla b. Oct. 26, 1867, m. John O. Swenson Jan. 2, 1890; Agnes b. April 5, 1872, m. Myron Newton Crandall Feb. 13, 1895; Mary Cathrine b. March 21, 1874, m. Joseph Markham Jan. 28, 1899; Adlinda b. Jan. 8, 1877, m. Paul Ludlow June 28, 1899; Fredrick b. Aug. 17, 1880, m. Sarah Jane Amos Sept. 6, 1906. Family resided Salt Lake City, Brigham City and Spanish Fork, Utah.
Leader of military band 1862-76. Missionary to Wales 1883-85. Policeman and city marshal of Spanish Fork 1870-77.

LEWIS, JOHN MOSS (son of Benjamin Lewis and Joannah Ryan of Simpson county, Ky.). Born Feb. 16, 1829, in Simpson county. Came to Utah July 24, 1847, Brigham Young company.
Married Martha Jane Crismon in 1848, at Salt Lake City (daughter of Charles Crismon and Mary Hill of Simpson county, Ky., pioneers July 24, 1847, Brigham Young company). She was born Sept. 8, 1831, Jacksonville, Ill. Their children: Martha Joannah b. Oct. 15, 1851, m. Jesse Hobson; Charles Benjamin b. Aug. 15, 1853, m. Libbey Carpin; Clara Jane b. Nov. 24, 1855, m. Charles Peterson; Ida Francis b. June 24, 1857, m. Harve Blair; John Franklin b. May 19, 1861, m. Eliza Morris; Emily Ann b. Jan. 12, 1863, d. March 20, 1873; George William b. Oct. 29, 1865, m. Oleni Kemp; Walter Beers b. Nov. 21, 1866, m. Fannie Holly; Henry Mahalen b. Feb. 8, 1869, m. Rose Ingram; Leonard Ryan b. Nov. 6, 1870, m. Alice Ingram. Family home Mesa City, Ariz.
High priest in Maricopa stake, Arizona. Farmer. Died May 5, 1894, Mesa City.

LEWIS, NERIAH (son of Neriah Lewis of Kentucky). Born April 29, 1816, Simpson county, Ky. Came to Utah October, 1851, James Cummings company.
Married Rebecca Hendricks in Kentucky (daughter of Samuel Hendricks of Kentucky, who came to Utah with Orson Pratt company). Their children: William H., m. Martha Pitt; Benjamin Marion b. March 20, 1841, m. Barbara Crockett; Neriah R. b. March 10, 1843, m. Amanda Jane Allred Jan. 20, 1864; Rebecca Louisa b. Sept. 7, 1848, m. M. W. Merrell. Family resided at Salt Lake City and Richmond, Utah.
High priest. School trustee. Farmer.

LEWIS, BENJAMIN MARION (son of Neriah Lewis and Rebecca Hendricks). Born March 20, 1841, in Kentucky. Came to Utah with his father.
Married Barbara Crockett at Logan, Utah (daughter of David Crockett and Lydia Young of Maine). She was born April 5, 1845. Their children: Marion Alonzo, m. Lena Feist; Harriett, m. William Brown; Lettie.

LEWIS, NERIAH R. (son of Neriah Lewis and Rebecca Hendricks). Born March 10, 1843.
Married Amanda Jane Allred at Richmond, Utah, Jan. 20, 1864 (daughter of Isaac Allred and Julia Ann Taylor), who was born Nov. 16, 1843. Their children: Robert Charles b. Dec. 10, 1864, m. Mary Ann Anderson; William Alma b. June 1, 1867, m. Laura Howell; Rebecca Augusta b. March 6, 1869; Augusta Louisa b. March 6, 1869; Amanda Laura b. Aug. 7, 1870, m. Henry Johnson; Isaac Neriah b. Jan. 27, 1872, m. Jane Hillman; George Wara b. Sept. 28, 1874, m. Florence E. Ewing; Julia E. b. Dec. 31, 1876, m. Albert M. Merrill; Clarence Leroy b. April 29, 1879, m. Margaret Black; Nellie P. b. Feb. 16, 1882, m. C. A. Meeker; Lillie V. b. Oct. 17, 1884, m. Herbert W. Mauring; Edna V. b. Sept. 6, 1887, m. Moses Gustaveson. Family home Oxford, Idaho.
Settled at Richmond, Cache county, 1860. Assisted in bringing immigrants to Utah in 1861, making round trip to Florence, Neb., by oxteam. Moved to Oxford in 1883, where he served as bishop for 23 years; high priest. Farmer and stockraiser.

LEWIS, WILLIAM CRAWFORD (son of Benjamin Lewis, born April 20, 1803, at Pendleton, S. C., and Joanna Ryons, born April 6, 1808, in Clark county, Ky., who were married 1826). He was born Nov. 24, 1830, in Simpson county, Ky. Came to Utah Sept. 19, 1847, David Spencer company.
Married Sarah Jane Veach Feb. 27, 1853 (daughter of William Veach and Ann Elliot, the former died at Nauvoo and the latter came to Utah in September, 1851, Orson Pratt company). She was born Oct. 26, 1834; came to Utah with her mother. Their children: Mary E. b. Dec. 30, 1853, m. J. P. Collins 1889; Joanna S. b. April 9, 1855, m. J. W. Bainbridge 1874; Ellen b. Sept. 16, 1856; Adelaide H. b. Feb. 20, 1859, m. J. N. Van Noy Oct. 8, 1878; William W. b. Sept. 14, 1860, m. Julia A. Tidwell Nov. 28, 1882; Eliza J. b. Jan. 20, 1862, m. Frank V. Lamb March 24, 1882; Benjamin E. b. Nov. 13, 1864, m. Fanny Williams Oct. 16, 1890; Julia A. b. Jan. 4, 1866; Martha A. b. Sept. 14, 1867, m. Chas. Oakley Jan. 28, 1886; James Leonard b. Aug. 26, 1869; Lorette V. b. Nov. 11, 1871, m. H. A. Adamson Dec. 21, 1896.
Married Martha Ann Kingsbury Nov. 15, 1869, at Salt Lake City (daughter of Joseph C. Kingsbury and Loenza A. Pond, who were married Jan. 27, 1846, pioneers Sept. 29, 1847, A. O. Smoot company). She was born Oct. 17, 1850, at Salt Lake City. Their children: Abbie Loenza b. Nov. 30, 1871, m. H. S. Stephenson Oct. 4, 1905; Maria Lucinda b. Dec. 14, 1873; Vilate Elizabeth b. Dec. 4, 1875, m. Albert J. Elggren June 5, 1901; Bancroft Bingham b. July 8, 1878; Amy Frances b. May 19, 1882; Ray Crawford b. Feb. 27, 1891; Hazel Cosby b. Nov. 22, 1895.
Moved to Richmond 1896. Indian war veteran.

LIDDELL, WILLIAM. Born Jan. 13, 1822, in Lanarkshire, Scotland, died Jan. 16, 1862. Came to Utah Oct. 12, 1863, Rosel Hyde company.
Married Agnes Cassell Park Dec. 20, 1841, Rutherglen, Scotland (daughter of John Park), who was born Oct. 24, 1822, and died in May, 1912, Salt Lake City. Their children: Mary, William James and Margaret, died; Peter Gillespie, m. Ruth Voce Hutchinson; Agnes, died; Mary, m. Soren Peter Neve; Abraham, m. Lucy Jones; Elizabeth, m. Joseph Hyrum Felt. Family home, Salt Lake City.

LIDDELL, PETER GILLESPIE (son of William Liddell and Agnes C. Park). Born Sept. 12, 1851, Ervin, Ayrshire, Scotland. Came to Utah Oct. 13, 1863, Rosel Hyde company.
Married Ruth Voce Hutchinson Feb. 3, 1875, Randolph, Utah (daughter of Jacob Flynn Hutchinson and Constantia Elizabeth Clementis Langdon of Nashua, N. H.). She was born Jan. 24, 1858. Their children: William Barker b. May 1, 1876, m. Kate Blackburn; Jacob Flynn b. Aug. 25, 1877, died; Peter James b. Jan. 21, 1879, m. Elizabeth Jane Phelps; Mildred b. April 11, 1887, m. Frank Holmes; David Nathaniel b. Dec. 30, 1882; Wallace George b. June 10, 1883, died; Ruth Voce b. Sept. 8, 1887, m. Roscoe Philip Whitmore; Agnes Elizabeth b. Feb. 14, 1899, m. Abraham Ouellete; Abraham b. May 6, 1894, died; Frank b. May 16, 1893; Helen Mar b. Dec. 20, 1897.
Elder. Rancher; miner; farmer.

LIDDELL, ¹ABRAHAM (son of William Liddell and Agnes Cassell Park of Glasgow, Scotland). Born Oct. 5, 1855, Ervin, Ayrshire, Scotland. Came to Utah Oct. 15, 1868, with John Gillespie's mother's company.
Married Lucy Jones Sept. 21, 1875, Salt Lake City (daughter of Hopkins Jones and Winifred Morris of South Wales, pioneers Nov. 29, 1865, with William S. Willis oxteam company). She was born Dec. 4, 1854. Their children: Bernard Winifred b. Aug. 9, 1876, m. Stella Flower and Lillian Brown Clayton; Agnes Winifred b. May 6, 1878, m. Eugene Branch, Jr.; ²Abraham b. March 4, 1880, m. Mary Crawford; Hopkins Jones b. Jan. 26, 1882, m. Ethel Moss; Lucy May b. Jan. 26, 1832, m. Arthur Day; Mary Lillian b. Jan. 30, 1884, m. Ernest Miller; Martha Elizabeth b. July 31, 1887, m. Bliss Roberts; Iris Ruth b. Jan. 15, 1890, d. Jan. 28, 1891; Willis James b. Dec. 20, 1891; Carl Lynwood b. April 10, 1894; Beatrice Maud b. Sept. 16, 1897. Family home, Salt Lake City.
Elder; block teacher. Commissioner Carbon county four years; also assessor Carbon county. Carpenter; builder; farmer; stockraiser. Died at Salt Lake City.

LIDDELL, ²ABRAHAM (son of Abraham Liddell and Lucy Jones). Born March 4, 1880, Smithfork, Wyo.
Married Mary Crawford 1904, Sunnyside, Utah (daughter of John and Agnes Crawford of Scotland). She was born April 11, 1886. Their children: Willis Lynwood b. Jan.

12, 1905; Clarence Dyer b. Feb. 7, 1906; John b. April 1908; Agnes b. 1910. Family home Sunnyside and Myton, Utah. Deacon; Sunday school superintendent. Salesman; farmer; liveryman.

LIDDIARD, SAMUEL (son of James Liddiard and Mary Nippress). Born June 27, 1841, Aldbourne, Wiltshire, Eng. Came to Utah Oct. 3, 1863, Daniel McArthur company. Married Sarah Collins May 5, 1863, Collingbourne, Kingston, Wiltshire, Eng. (daughter of John Collins and Priscilla Sheffred of Collingbourne, came to Utah in October, 1863, in Daniel D. McArthur company). She was born March 31, 1844. Family home Provo, Utah.
Member 34th quorum seventies; high priest; Sunday school superintendent 1876-91; high councilor 1886-98. City councilman of Provo 1890-91; school trustee 1868-74 and 1878-90. Contractor and builder; manufacturer.

LIECHTY, JOHN (son of John Liechty and Christina Guggisburg of Langnau, Canton Bern, Switzerland). Born Nov. 27, 1827. Came to Utah October, 1863, Peter Nebeker company.
Married Louisa Wintsh, Provo, Utah (daughter of Casper Wintsh and Annie Willieman of Zurich, Switzerland, pioneers to Utah Oct. 1862, Captain Decker company). She was born Feb. 13, 1849. Their children: Louisa, died; John Nicholas, m. Mary Keppler; Abraham Brigham, m. Ida Stooki, m. Louisa Reinwald; Frederick Bernhart, died; Christian Hyrum, m. Elizabeth Andrews, died; Enoch, died; Josephine, m. John Nicholas Muhlestein; Josiah Nephi; Rosinna Ester, m. Stoyl Cheney; Ephraim Amon, Elizabeth Edna. Family home Provo, Utah.
Missionary in Switzerland; high priest; ward teacher. Guard against Indian invasion; pioneer canal and road builder. Farmer. Died Sept. 17, 1910.

LIECHTY, ABRAHAM BRIGHAM (son of John Liechty and Louisa Wintsh). Born March 10, 1870, Provo City, Utah.
Married Ida Stooki Jan. 20, 1897, Salt Lake City (daughter of Jacob Frederick Stooki and Elizabeth Morgenegg, of Bern, Switzerland). She was born April 3, 1873, died Dec. 15, 1900. Their children: Brigham Jacob b. Nov. 27, 1897; Eda Elizabeth b. Jan. 18, 1899; Heber J. b. Sept. 3, 1900.
Married Louisa Reinwald April 20, 1904, Salt Lake City (daughter of William Reinwald, born at Brackenheim, and Louisa Brauenberger, born Steinfeld, Germany, resided Heilbronn, Wurttemberg). She was born June 15, 1875, in Germany. Came to Utah in 1903. Their children: Ida Louisa b. July 14, 1905, Clear Creek, Utah; Gertrude b. Nov. 17, 1907; Helen Rose b. May 27, 1910. Families reside at Pleasant View, Utah.
Missionary to Germany 1901-03; high priest; second counselor to Bishop Gillespie of Pleasant View; president deacons' quorum; secretary Pleasant View ward; secretary of the Y. M. M. I. A. at Pleasant View and Scofield, Utah; ward teacher. Blacksmith; engineer; mechanic; farmer.

LILJENQUIST, OLE N. (son of Nils Tykerson and Bengta Larson, Ignaberga, Skaane, Sweden). Born Sept. 23, 1825, Ignaberga. Came to Utah Sept. 13, 1857, Mathias Cowley company.
Married Christine Hansen Jacobson 1848, Copenhagen, Denmark, who was born Jan. 1, 1822. Their children: Theodore, N., m. Henrietta Benson; Otto, died; Clara Josephine, m. Julius Johnson; O. Oscar, m. Emma Anderson; Harold F., m. Laurine Rasmussen; Nina, died. Family home Hyrum, Utah.
Children by second marriage: Joseph, died; Charles, m. Katurah Williams; Olivia, died; Waldamer O., m. Nora Antousen; Zina.
Children by third marriage: Conrad, died; Ezra, m. May Wilcox; Victor; Truel, died.
Missionary to Scandinavia 1859-62 and 1876-73; bishop of Hyrum ward 1862-72; president Scandinavian mission 1876; ordained patriarch June 22, 1873; president Copenhagen conference 1870. First mayor of Hyrum 1870; delegate from Cache county to constitutional convention 1871.

LILJENQUIST, HAROLD F. (son of Ole N. Liljenquist and Christine H. Jacobson). Born Jan. 19, 1857, Copenhagen, Denmark. Came to Utah Sept. 13, 1857, with parents.
Married Laurine Rasmussen Jan. 1, 1876, Hyrum, Utah (daughter of Jens Rasmussen and Bendta Nielsen of Aggebo, Denmark, pioneers Sept. 1863, John Young company). She was born May 28, 1858. Their children: James Harold b. Nov. 4, 1876, d. April 5, 1877; Olaf Leth b. June 30, 1878, m. Ida Allen; Otto E. b. Nov. 24, 1880, m. Ivy Y. Allen; Walace B. b. Aug. 8, 1883, m. Melinda Petersen; George E. b. Feb. 22, 1886; Warren M. b. Aug. 18, 1888; Willie S. b. Oct. 28, 1893. Family home Hyrum, Utah.
Member 62d quorum seventies; missionary to Denmark 1890-92; president Y. M. M. I. A.; Sunday school superintendent; ordained bishop of first ward, Hyrum, Aug. 25, 1901; president Copenhagen conference 1892. County commissioner of Cache county; city councilman three terms;

LIND, ANTON. Born Oct. 18, 1822, Aalborg, Denmark. Came to Utah 1868, Jesse Smith oxteam company.
Married Mary Ann Nelson, who was born April 8, 1824. Their children: Baby; Larsine; Niels Peter, first three died infants; Marie, m. James Freestone; Sine, m. Peter Mortesen; Jennie, m. George Freestone; Caroline, m. Edward Adams; James Christian, died at age of one year; George Christian b. April 4, 1863; Louis Peter b. June 17, 1865, m. Eliza Grey; Marion, m. Emery Williams, m. Henry Winslow, m. Edward Adams.
Elder. Iron molder. Died April 6, 1877, Weston, Idaho.

LINDHOLM, CARL ERIC (son of John Skantz and Brita Catherine Olsson, Fombo, Locksta county, Sweden). Born Nov. 16, 1835, at Fombo. Came to Utah 1861.
Married Johanna Nilsson May 15, 1861, on the Atlantic ocean (daughter of Nels Johnson and Christina Anderson, Greyby, Gothland county, Sweden). She was born July 29, 1836, at Greyby. Their children: Charles, d. Nov. 29, 1900; Franklin, m. Agnes Stewart; Parley, d. Oct. 5, 1867; Thecla, m. Francis D. Horman; Clara, d. Jan. 8, 1870; Martha, d. Feb. 26, 1888; Albert, m. Agnes Adams; Alma Eric, m. Agnes Smith. Family home Tooele City, Utah.
Tailor. Died April 19, 1876.

LINDQUIST, NILS AARON. Born Dec. 24, 1830, Norrala, Sweden. Came to Utah Sept. 5, 1863, John F. Sanders company.
Married Josephine Hagerlund Sept. 6, 1863, who was born Aug. 19, 1844 and came to Utah with husband. Their children: Charles John Aaron b. July 24, 1864, m. Amelia C. Ness Larson Aug. 15, 1888; Elizabeth Carolina; Selma b. July 2, 1869, m. Christian Olsen Jan. 13, 1892; George William b. Sept. 29, 1871, m. Mettine Olsen Dec. 3, 1890; Albert Reinhalt b. Oct. 6, 1873; Millie Christina b. Oct. 7, 1875, m. E. A. Hardy Dec. 1, 1891; Alfred Henning b. March 11, 1880, m. Ethel N. Ashcroft Dec. 1902; Jennie Harriett b. Nov. 27, 1882, m. James R. Dinsdale Dec. 14, 1904; Edward Elmer b. Dec. 17, 1884, m. Della Dinsdale Dec. 15, 1904; Niels Ernest b. April 7, 1888, m. Bergulat Simonson June 22, 1911.
High priest. Furniture dealer. Undertaker.

LINDQUIST, CHARLES JOHN AARON (son of Nils Aaron Lindquist and Josephine Hagerlund). Born July 24, 1864, Salt Lake City.
Married Amelia C. Ness Larson Aug. 15, 1888, Logan, Utah (adopted daughter of Carl Larson and Elizabeth Larson, pioneers Sept. 5, 1863, John F. Sanders company). She was born Jan. 12, 1867, Huntsville, Utah. Their children: Amelia b. Feb. 16, 1890; Carl Archibald b. Jan. 29, 1892; Myrtle Josephine b. March 4, 1894; Ruby Estella b. May 16, 1896; Milton Wilford b. June 4, 1898; Clyde Arthur b. Sept. 7, 1900; Norene May b. Oct. 6, 1908. Family home Ogden, Utah.
Missionary to Sweden 1883-85 and 1903-05; home missionary; second counselor to Bishop Robert McQuarrie. Undertaker.

LINDSAY, JAMES (son of William Lindsay and Christna Howie of Scotland). Born 1849, Hudson Bridge, Scotland. Came to Utah Sept. 24, 1862, Homer Duncan company.
Married Agnes Watson Jan. 9, 1871, Salt Lake City (daughter of James Watson and Jennett Cambell), who was born 1842. Their children: Jennett L. b. Nov. 4, 1871; Christna T. b. March 5, 1873, m. Jonathan M. Duke July 24, 1891; Minnie Mattie b. Oct. 30, 1875, m. Frederick Crook 1893; James W. b. July 30, 1877, m. Christina Bowers Nov. 17, 1908; Lizzie b. June 14, 1879, m. Edward Jones Oct. 5, 1899; Maggie B. b. Feb. 22, 1881, m. Eugene Brown July 18, 1906; Bennett b. Oct. 23, 1882, m. Sarah Sweat Nov. 23, 1905; Jean b. March 16, 1886, m. Alonzo Hicken Dec. 13, 1906; Hazel L. b. Nov. 8, 1890, m. Albert Giles Feb. 24, 1910; Gladys b. Oct. 13, 1892. Family home Heber and Center, Utah.
Farmer; miner.

LINDSAY, WALTER (son of Walter Lindsay and Janeta McLain of Lanarkshire, Scotland). Born April 1, 1837, Lanarkshire. Came to Utah fall of 1862, William Brunson company.
Married Elizabeth Burt about 1859 at Salt Lake City (daughter of James Burt and Mary McBride of Salt Lake City and Eden, Utah, latter came to Utah Oct. 19, 1862, Horton D. Haight company). She was born Sept. 2, 1851. Their children: Mary Alice, m. Andrew A. Clark; Jeanette May, m. Robert N. Ames; Christina, m. Charles McLaughlin; Walter A., m. Margaret Wade; James B., m. Christina Geissler; Ellen, m. Peter R. Geisler; Mirnen, m. Cornelius Vandenakker; Hulda, m. Niels Petersen; Hattie; William C.; John P., d. infant. Family home Liberty, Utah.
Member 67th quorum seventies; Sunday school superintendent at Liberty, Utah. Mail carrier at Liberty and Eden for 20 years. Farmer.

LINDSAY, WILLIAM BUCKMINSTER (son of Ephraim Lindsay and Mercy Willey). Born March 30, 1797, in Vermont. Came to Utah 1852, Captain Day company.
Married Sarah Myers, who was born July 9, 1800. Their children: Ephraim b. May 4, 1820, m. Jane Parish; William

B., Jr., b. Dec. 25, 1821, m. Julia Parks; Mary M.; Thomas M. b. Sept. 16, 1826; Edwin R. b. Sept. 25, 1828, m. Tabitha Cragun; Mercy M.; Sarah M. b. March 10, 1833; George R. b. Jan. 15, 1837, m. Sarah Shipley.

LINDSAY, WILLIAM BUCKMINSTER, JR. (son of William Buckminster Lindsay and Sarah Myers). Born Dec. 25, 1821, at Leeds, Upper Canada. Came to Utah 1852, Captain Walker company.
Married Julia Parks Feb. 19, 1845, Nauvoo, Ill. (daughter of William Parks and Fannie Hyde of Livonia, N. Y.) She was born Feb. 2, 1824, and came to Utah with husband. Their children: Mary Amanda b. May 4, 1847; Julia Ann b. Sept. 9, 1849, m. Hyrum Henderson Oct. 3, 1865; Fannie Louisa b. March 5, 1852; William Thomas b. Oct. 22, 1854, m. Hanna Sparks Sept. 22, 1881; Edgar Monroe b. Jan. 17, 1857, m. Sarah A. Beach Sept. 30, 1880; Norman A. b. Aug. 8, 1859, d. aged 10; Warren Parks b. July 22, 1862, m. Eveline Welker Oct. 23, 1885; m. Selma C. Hartigan; m. Annett S. Anderson; Marion David b. July 19, 1868, m. Luella Stewart Oct. 5, 1898. Family home Paris, Idaho.
Married Permelia Blackman Aug. 12, 1849, Kanesville, Iowa (daughter of Stephen Blackman of Nauvoo, Ill., pioneer 1852, Captain Walker company). Their children: Harriet B. Feb. 1, 1851, m. Morman Williams; Charles M. b. Sept. 1853, d. aged 16; Priscilla b. June 21, 1855, m. Morris Holmes; Philemon b. Aug. 23, 1857, m. Marintha Athay; William H. b. April 19, 1860, m. Mary Beck; Mary b. June 23, 1862, m. James Athay; Mercy b. March 1864, d. infant; Albert E. b. July 24, 1868, m. Mercy A. Clark; Joseph b. May, 1870, d. infant; Delila b. Oct. 23, 1873, m. George A. Humphreys. Family home Kaysville, Utah.
Married Sarah Henderson 1854, at Salt Lake City (daughter of James Henderson and Sarah Harris, pioneers 1852, Captain Walker company). Their children: George H. b. Dec. 12, 1855; Martha J. b. Jan. 13, 1858, m. Reuben Bingham; Annie M. b. March 1, 1860, m. Miles Weaver; Sarah E. b. March 8, 1862, m. Frank Weaver; Mary D. b. March 5, 1864, m. Isaac Biglow; Alvira D. b. March 16, 1867, m. F. W. Hurst; Jasper b. Aug. 6, 1869, m. Ellie Minson; Fredrick William b. March 11, 1873. Family home Kaysville, Utah.
Member Nauvoo Legion. Moved to Paris, Idaho, 1864. Counselor in bishopric of Paris ward several years. Died Jan. 3, 1889, at Paris.

LINDSAY, EDGAR MONROE (son of William Buckminster Lindsay and Julia Parks). Born Jan. 17, 1857, Kaysville, Utah.
Married Sarah A. Beach Sept. 30, 1880, Salt Lake City (daughter of Orson Gillett Beach and Sarah Palmer, former pioneer 1851, latter October 1852, Captain Wheelock company). She was born March 23, 1861, Logan, Utah. Their children: Edgar Charles b. Oct. 11, 1881; Warren Leroy b. March 3, 1884, m. Mary C. Anderson Sept. 7, 1911; George William b. July 19, 1886; Franklin David b. Nov. 28, 1890; Sarah Erma b. Dec. 7, 1893, d. infant; Denina b. Nov. 25, 1896; Julia b. Feb. 13, 1900; Rulon Beach b. June 5, 1903. Family home Nounan, Idaho.
Missionary to Great Brittain 1894-96; ordained bishop of Nounan ward Aug. 7, 1897.

LINDSAY, WARREN P. (son of William B. Lindsay and Julia Parks). Born July 22, 1862.
Married Susan Eveline Welker Oct. 23, 1885, Logan, Utah (daughter of Wilburn Welker and Susan Caroline Stephenson of Bloomington, Idaho). She was born March 19, 1866, died Oct. 23, 1898. Their children: Warren Jean b. Jan. 2, 1887; Lola Eva b. Aug. 25, 1889, m. Abram Hatch March 6, 1912; Maud Julia b. Dec. 7, 1890; James Russel b. Feb. 10, 1893; Ora Edgar b. Aug. 2, 1895; Jennie Caroline b. Jan. 10, 1898. Family home Moreland, Idaho.
Married Selma C. Hartigan, Logan, Utah, Sept. 8, 1899. She died Sept. 17, 1900.
Married Annett S. Anderson at Salt Lake City, Oct. 4, 1906.
Bishop. Farmer; merchant.

LINDSAY, WARREN J. (son of Warren P. Lindsay and Susan Eveline Welker). Born Jan. 2, 1887, Paris, Idaho.
Missionary to England 1912.

LINDSAY, PHILEMON (son of William Buckminster Lindsay and Permelia Blackman). Born Aug. 23, 1857, at Kaysville.
Married Marintha Athay Sept. 29, 1881, at Salt Lake City (daughter of James Athay and Ellen Morris of London, Eng., pioneers 1864). She was born July 25, 1861. Their children: Minnie b. Feb. 22, 1883, m. John C. Sorenson, Lago, Idaho; Philemon LeRoy b. June 25, 1884, m. Josephine Peterson; Ellen L. b. Jan. 6, 1889, d. March 7, 1889; Hazel b. May 22, 1890, m. Oliver Peterson; James C. b. May 7, 1892; Willard b. Jan. 27, 1895; Lyman b. Dec. 11, 1897; Beatrice b. Aug. 11, 1898, d. Sept. 12, 1898; Blanche b. Nov. 6, 1899; Wallace b. July 7, 1903. Family home Ovid, Bear Lake Co., Idaho.
Worked on Temple sawmill in Logan Canyon 1878. Missionary to southern states 1886-88; bishop of Ovid ward 1888. County coroner 1895; county commissioner three terms.

LINDSAY, EDWIN REUBEN (son of William Buckminster Lindsay and Sarah Myers). Born Sept. 25, 1828, Johnstown, Ont., Can.). Came to Utah 1852, Captain Day company.
Married Tabitha Cragun Dec. 25, 1850, who was born March 5, 1830, Boone county, Ind. Came to Utah with husband. Their children: Sarah Adeline b. Nov. 6, 1851, m. D. M. Burbank; Mary Jane b. Aug. 7, 1853, m. D. M. Burbank; George Edwin b. April 4, 1855, m. Mary A. Hawkins; William Nelson b. Feb. 11, 1857, d. March 7, 1911; James Samuel b. Nov. 9, 1858, m. Emma Dewey (died); Thomas Hyrum b. Aug. 25, 1860, d. Sept. 7, 1912; Ephraim b. Aug. 28, 1862, m. Mary E. Barton; Trisha E. b. Nov. 19, 1864, David E. b. Oct. 4, 1866, John C. b. Dec. 1, 1868, Tabitha A. b. Dec. 1, 1868, latter four died.
Married Emma Bowden in 1871 at Salt Lake City. She was born at Swansea, Wales. Their children: Trisha E., m. L. J. Dewey; Edwin R., m. Christena Van Orman (died); Warren T., m. Edith Tippetts; Alpheus (died), m. Annie Higgens; Eliza V., died; Lydia A., m. Clarence Flancher; Elizabeth, m. Mr. Marchant; Mary Irene, m. Mr. Marchant; Joseph Arley; Abigail.
Died Dec. 6, 1893.

LINDSAY, GEORGE EDWIN (son of Edwin Reuben Lindsay and Tabitha Cragun). Born April 4, 1855, Kaysville, Utah.
Married Mary A. Hawkins Aug. 7, 1876, Salt Lake City (daughter of George W. Hawkins and Amanda S. Boothe of California). She was born May 22, 1859, Santa Rosa, Cal. Their children: George E. b. Sept. 1, 1877; Mary T. b. July 30, 1880, m. Thomas William Irving April 1, 1901; Hyrum Lester b. Nov. 5, 1882, m. Vera Morteson Sept. 27, 1911; Amanda J. b. April 13, 1885, m. Albert G. Richards Aug. 3, 1904; Celestia, d. Dec. 3, 1900; Adaline b. Oct. 3, 1887, m. William Short Aug. 3, 1909; Edna Imogene b. Oct. 19, 1890, m. William Wildman; Reuben R. b. Dec. 14, 1893. Family home Bennington, Idaho.
Farmer and stockraiser.

LINFORD, JOHN (son of James Linford and Miss Ashcroft of Swavesey, Cambridgeshire, Eng.). Born 1808, Eltisley, Eng. Came to Utah Nov. 9, 1856, Captain Willie handcart company.
Married Marie Christian about 1832, Graveney, Cambridgeshire (daughter of William Christian and Mary Bently), who was born April 10, 1813. Their children: James H. m. Zillah Crocket; George John, m. Eliza Wheeler; Joseph W., m. Mary B. Rich; Amasa C., m. Miranda Savage. Family home Centerville, Utah.
Farmer. Died November, 1856, on the plains.

LINFORD, JOSEPH W. (son of John Linford and Marie Christian). He was born March 30, 1842, Graveney, Eng. Came to Utah Nov. 9, 1856, Captain Willie handcart company.
Married Mary B. Rich Dec. 6, 1866, Paris, Idaho (daughter of Charles F. Rich and Eliza Ann Graves of Nauvoo, Ill., pioneers Oct. 2, 1847). She was born Jan. 6, 1845, Swavesey, Eng. Their children: Joseph W. b. Sept. 2, 1867, m. Lois Esther Ricks; Eliza M. b. April 12, 1870, m. Joseph H. Denio; John C. b. Oct. 18, 1872, m. Hannah Morgan; James W. b. Feb. 26, 1875, m. Edna Hulme; George C. b. Sept. 7, 1877, m. Alice Peterson; Phebe A. b. April 8, 1880, d. Aug. 4, 1892; Mary E. b. Aug. 29, 1882, m. George E. Gibby; Amasa R. b. Jan. 31, 1885, m. Carrie Merrill; Frances L. b. Nov. 20, 1888, m. Hervin Bunderson. Family home St. Charles, Idaho.
Member of high priests quorum. Assisted in bringing immigrants to Utah 1863. County commissioner. Farmer.

LINFORD, AMASA (son of John Linford and Maria Christian). Came to Utah November, 1856, Captain W. Willie company.
Married Miranda Savage June 29, 1867 (daughter of David Savage and Mary A. White—married Oct. 17, 1841, Knox county, Ill., pioneers September, 1847, Perrigrine Sessions company). She was born April 24, 1851. Their children: Mary Maria b. Dec. 8, 1868, m. George H. Hall Feb. 2, 1887; Agnes Belzora b. Oct. 23, 1870, m. John S. Bryson May 30, 1889; George Clark b. April 1, 1874; John Amasa b. Oct. 1, 1876, m. Elizabeth Rowlan; Albert Henry b. May 25, 1879, m. Elizabeth Hess; Joseph Ernest b. Sept. 13, 1882, m. Addie Hess; James Franklin b. June 15, 1885, m. Leonora Hodges May 23, 1907.
High priest. Settled at Centerville, Utah, and moved to Bear Lake Valley, Idaho.

LINFORD, ALBERT HENRY (son of Amasa Linford and Miranda Savage). Born May 25, 1879, Garden City, Utah.
Married Elizabeth Hess Sept. 17, 1902, Logan, Utah (daughter of Jacob Hess and Hannah Thornock), who was born Dec. 1, 1882, Bloomington, Idaho. Their children: Fenton Hess b. March 5, 1904; Albert Hess b. May 25, 1908.
Elder and ward teacher; president Y. M. M. I. A.; ward historian.

LINTON, SAMUEL (son of William Linton, Philadelphia, Pa., and Elizabeth Selfridge, New Brunswick, Nova Scotia, Can.). Born June 27, 1827, in Ireland. Came to Utah in 1853.
Married Ellen Sutton April 26, 1858, Salt Lake City (daughter of John Sutton and Mary Ellison, Parestokes, Lancashire, Eng., who came to Utah October 1853, Joseph A. Young company). She was born Jan. 20, 1832. Their children: John Sutton b. April 6, 1859, m. Eliza Ann Gadd Dec. 17, 1885; Mary Ann b. Feb. 11, 1865, m. John Morgan; Samuel b. Jan. 7, 1867, m. Elizabeth Jenkins; Alice b. Dec. 30, 1869, m. Joseph Obard; Julia b. Feb. 4, 1873, m. Thomas

W. Crawley; William b. Sept. 29, 1877, m. Elmina Cox. Family resided at Nephi and Salt Lake City, Utah. Member 49th quorum seventies; high priest. Veteran Echo Canyon war. Farmer.

LINTON, JOHN SUTTON (son of Samuel Linton and Ellen Sutton). Born April 6, 1859, Salt Lake City.
Married Eliza Ann Gadd Dec. 7, 1886, Logan, Utah (daughter of Alfred Gadd and Mary Ann Hobba, of England, former pioneer of November, 1856). She was born Jan. 18, 1865. Their children: Mary Ellen b. Sept. 29, 1887, m. Frank William Crow; Leora b. Dec. 28, 1889; Zua Alice b. May 17, 1891; Genevieve b. May 7, 1894; Jeanette b. Aug. 14, 1895; Grace Idella b. Dec. 15, 1897; Wilma Belle b. Jan. 28, 1901; Heber John b. Aug. 27, 1904. Family resided at Nephi, Juab, and Provo, Utah.
Member 49th quorum seventies; missionary to southern states 1882-84; 1st counselor to Bishop Robert Stevenson of Juab; high priest. School trustee. Farmer.

LISH, JOSEPH LIONS. Born April 8, 1803, Orange, N. Y. Came to Utah 1850.
Married Harriet Ann Tripp Oct. 14, 1823, New York (daughter of Blakeley Tripp of New York), who was born May 24, 1807. Their children: William S., m. Fairzina C. Cornwell; Everet; Enos L. B. m. Marie Alexander; Peter; Timothy C., m. Huldah Wells; Ingraham, m. Matilda Langford; Henry D., m. Emily Allen; Harriet Angeline, m. Jacob Welker; George; Rhoda Jane, m. Henry Bell; Alma, d. infant; Charles. m. Sarah Teeters; Joseph, d. infant; Alva A., d. infant. Family resided at Ogden and Willard, Utah.
Seventy. Wheelwright. Died September, 1886, Albion, Cassia Co., Idaho.

LISH, WILLIAM SEELY (son of Joseph Lions Lish and Harriet Ann Tripp). He was born Nov. 9, 1824, Minisink, Orange county, N. Y. Came to Utah 1850.
Married Fairzina C. Cornwell Jan. 11, 1846, Nauvoo, Ill. (daughter of Lemuel Cornwell and Susan Darling of Michigan and New York, pioneers). She was born Jan. 9, 1822. Their children: George T. b. Jan. 3, 1847, m. Lydia R. Bingham; John B. b. March 10, 1849, m. Luella A. Norton; Albert J. b. Jan. 17, 1857, m. Delinda A. Norton; Harriet A. b. Oct. 3, 1853, m. S. H. Cotterel; William S. b. Oct. 22, 1855, m. Sarah J. Moss; Hyrum P. b March 8, 1857, m Erminie V. Norton; Charlotte L. b. Oct. 1859, m. Josiah Haskins; Annie M. b. April 12, 1861, m. Comadorl Moss; Charles E. b. May 12, 1863, m. Ethelda Palmer; Alta W. b. Oct. 12, 1865, m. Albert Cunningham; Annettle A. b. Sept. 12, 1868, m. William A. Norton. Family home Ogden, Utah.
Seventy; counselor to President F. A. Hammond at Huntsville, Utah. Wheelwright; merchant. Died July 16, 1896, McCammon, Idaho.

LISONBEE, HUGH DOBBINS. Born May 30, 1830. Came to Utah 1850.
Married Elma J. Haymond (daughter of Edward Owen Haymond and Margaret Ann Sissell, who were married March 15, 1825). She was born Feb. 17, 1837. Their children: Hugh E. b. Jan. 5, 1856, m. Susan Newby March 5, 1880; Frances A. b. Jan. 28, 1858, m. David Collings Jan. 28, 1873; Margaret A. W. b. Aug. 30, 1860, m. A. J. Sargent Dec. 29, 1877; Elma L b. June 6, 1863, m. Bally Kiner June 13, 1880; Martha J. b. Dec. 3, 1865; John A. b. June 23, 1868, m. Carrie D. Oldham; Lula D. b. Nov. 24, 1870, m. W. T. King June 22, 1893; Ola b. Jan. 25, 1874; Nellie b. April 12, 1875, m. R. E. Lawler June 4, 1895; Mae b. Oct 29, 1877, m Frank Chase Oct. 28, 1908.

LITTLE, EDWIN S. (see Ephraim Knowlton Hanks).
Married Harriet Amelia Decker (Hanks). Their child: George E. b. Aug. 6, 1844.
Died shortly after leaving Nauvoo.

LITTLE, FERAMORZ (son of James M Little and Susan Young, of Seneca county, N. Y.). Born June 14, 1820, Auriesville, Cayuga county, N. Y. Came to Utah 1851.
Married Fannie M. Decker Feb. 12, 1846, Nauvoo, Ill., Brigham Young performing ceremony (daughter of Isaac Decker and Harriet Page of New York, pioneers July 24, 1847, Brigham Young company). She was born April 24, 1830. Their children: James Tyler, m. Alice B. Souja; Juliett, m. Adelbert Roundy; Clair Susan, m. Bradley Carsson; Roselle L. m. Fredrick W. Gardiner; Janett Viola, m. John Relysimar; Frank C., m. Minerva Anderson. Family home, Salt Lake City.
Seventy; first counselor to Bishop Wooley of 13th ward. Vice president Deseret National bank; mayor; banker and capitalist. Died Aug. 14, 1886, Salt Lake City.

LITTLE, JAMES TYLER (son of Feramorz Little and Fannie M. Decker). Born Sept. 13, 1848, St. Louis, Mo. Came to Utah with father 1851.
Married Alice S. Souja June 5, 1883, Salt Lake City, his father performing ceremony (daughter of Theofial Souja and Mary Bowdidge, Paris, France, latter pioneers 1864, Captain DeLamar company). She was born Aug. 3, 1862. Their children: James J. b. May 15, 1884, d. aged 5; Fannie M. b. Aug. 6, 1885, m. Joseph W. Stringfellow; Clair B. b. Jan. 20, 1887; Alice S. b. March 11, 1890, d. infant; Romaine B. b. Jan. 30, 1892; Feramorz T. b. April 5, 1894; Decker J. b. March 27, 1897. Family home, Salt Lake City.
President Deseret Savings Bank; director Deseret National Bank; banker and capitalist. Died Feb. 27, 1898.

LITTLE, JAMES AMASA (son of George Edwin Little and Susan Young, of Auriesville, N. Y.). Born Sept. 14, 1822, at Auriesville. Came to Utah 1848.
Married Mary Jane Lytle Dec. 16, 1849, Salt Lake City (daughter of John and Christina Lytle, of Middletown, Butler Co., Ohio). She was born Aug. 6, 1834. Their children: Feramorz b. June 10, 1851, died; James b. Feb. 19, 1852, m. Emma Evans; Edwin b. Dec. 2, 1853, died; Phineas Howe b. June 2, 1858; Ada b. May 24, 1860, m. Alfred D. Young; Fannie Marie b. May 4, 1862, m. William T. Stewart; Leo Charles b. Feb. 14, 1865, m. Myra Johnson; Claudie Augusta b. July 22, 1867, m. John Robinson; Rose b. Jan. 6, 1872, died.
Married Anna Matilda Baldwin Dec. 21, 1857, Salt Lake City (daughter of David Baldwin and Elizabeth Cole, of Birmingham, Eng., pioneers 1861). She was born March 28, 1839. Their children: Mary Jane b. Dec. 31, 1858, m. Elmer W. Johnson; Christina b. Jan. 12, 1863, m. Leonard John Nuttall Jr.; Lorin Amasa b. April 29, 1864, m. Eliza Peugh; Willis Copland b. Sept. 8, 1869, m. Addie Jackson; Susan Elizabeth b. Jan. 6, 1871, m. Heber G. Robinson; Laura b. March 21, 1873, m. Fuller Broadbent; Harriet b. Nov. 14, 1874, m. James Jacobsen; Malcolm b. Nov. 14, 1876, m. Elizabeth Galbraith; David Baldwin b. Oct. 13, 1878, m. Hettie Acord, m. Harriet Fredricksen.
Married Elizabeth Tulledge Nov. 19, 1864, Salt Lake City (daughter of Edward Tulledge, of Salt Lake City). Their children: John Tulledge b. Jan. 20, 1869; Edward William b. Oct. 11, 1872; Frank b. March 29, 1875, m. Bessie Finley. Families resided at Kanab, Utah.
Missionary to England and also to eastern states; high priest; patriarch; counselor to Bishop Levy Stewart of Kanab. Veteran of Mexican war. Settled at St. George 1863; helped to survey and lay out the town of Kanab. Farmer. Historian.

LITTLE, JESSE C. Born 1808 in Maine. Came to Utah July 24, 1847, Brigham Young company.
Married Emily Hoagland at Salt Lake City (daughter of Abraham Hoagland and Margaret Quick of Michigan, came to Utah September 1847). She was born Sept. 20, 1840. Their children: Thomas N., m. Eliza Stewart; Mary, m. B. F. Jones; Ella, m. Dr. William H. Bucher; Abraham H., m. Dille Reese; Georgia, m. Paul J. Daly; Walter W., m. Jessie Martin. Family home, Salt Lake City.
High councilor. Fire chief and town marshal. Farmer and sexton. Died Dec. 26, 1894, Salt Lake City.

LITTLE, WALTER W. (son of Jesse C. Little and Emily Hoagland). Born Dec. 28, 1876, Salt Lake City.
Married Jessie Martin June 10, 1908, Salt Lake City (daughter of Lewis and Elizabeth Martin of Pennsylvania). Their children: Martin W. b. April 8, 1910. Family home, Salt Lake City.
Prosecuting attorney. Lawyer.

LITTLEFIELD, JOSEPH (son of William Littlefield, born 1803, Portsmouth, Eng. and Ann Toomer, born Nov. 18, 1818, Hummington, Eng.). He was born Nov. 24, 1854, in England. Came to Utah Nov. 2, 1864, Warren S. Snow company.
Married Agness A. Simmons Dec. 6, 1875, at Salt Lake City (daughter of George and Mary Ann Simmons, who came to Utah Sept. 25, 1855, Richard Ballantyne company). She was born Nov. 15, 1856. Their children: Joseph George b. Aug. 29, 1876, m. Kate Wadsworth Dec. 2, 1902; Mary Agness b. March 21, 1879, m. Rosewell M. Heiner March 1899; Maud Amelia Simmons b. Jan. 2, 1882, m. Robert Ellis June 1903; Sarah Isabelle b. Nov. 5, 1884, m. Fritz Eckhardt Oct. 1906. Family home Morgan, Utah.
First counselor to president of Y. M. M. I. A. Association of Morgan stake when Y. M. M. I. A. was first organized. Captain of Morgan city brass band for 30 years. Served two terms as city councilman.

LITTLEFIELD, JOSEPH GEORGE (son of Joseph Littlefield and Agness Simmons). Born Aug. 29, 1876, at Morgan, Utah.
Married Kate Wadsworth December 1902 at Ogden, Utah (daughter of Thomas Shore Wadsworth, who came to Utah September 1853, with David Wilkins company, and Catherine Moore, who came to Utah October 1864, with Captain Ricks company). She was born April 9, 1881, at Payson, Utah. Their children: Catherine b. Aug. 1903; Garnett b. June 1905; Bernice b. Oct. 1907; Joseph b. Aug. 1909; Isabelle b. Nov. 1911. Family home Morgan, Utah.

LLOYD, THOMAS (son of Benjamin Lloyd, born April 5, 1805, Wolverhampton, Eng., and Mary Elidge of Wolverhampton). Born June 15, 1833, Wolverhampton. Came to Utah 1855.

Married Susanna Stone Nov. 6, 1856, Salt Lake City (daughter of William Stone and Diana Grant), who was born Dec. 24, 1830. Came to Utah 1856, James G. Willie handcart company. Their children: Thomas William b. Sept. 21, 1857, m. Elizabeth Lea Feb. 26, 1877; Joseph Benjamin b. Nov. 28, 1858, m. Martha Gunnell July 1879; Jesse Willard b. June 3, 1860, m. Sarah Ellen Jones Nov. 25, 1885; Sarah Susanna b. Dec. 5, 1861, m. Robert Redford; Daniel David b. Feb. 8, 1863, m. Alice Haslem; Charles Edward b. Jan. 19, 1865, m. Janey Haslem. m. Lucy Parkinson; Mary Diana b. Oct. 16, 1866, m. John A. Hendrickson; Brigham Samuel b. Feb. 28, 1868, d. aged 7 months; Heber Lorenzo b. Sept. 8, 1869, d. infant; Annie Eliza b. Sept. 8, 1869, m. Alfred Osmond; Ezra Timothy b. Feb. 10, 1871, m. Jennie Hubbard; John Ephraim b. Sept. 17, 1872, d. aged 23; Olive Margret b. Aug. 2, 1874, m. Oscar Bjorkman; George Francis b. June 27, 1876, m. Beatrice Hoff. Family home Farmington, Utah.
President 28th quorum seventies; missionary to southern states 1877-79. Took part in Echo Canyon trouble. Settled at Farmington 1855; moved to Wellsville 1858. Saddle and harness maker. Died April 1894, Wellsville, Utah.

LLOYD, THOMAS WILLIAM (son of Thomas Lloyd and Susanna Stone). Born Sept. 21, 1857, Farmington, Utah.
Married Elizabeth Lea Feb. 26, 1877, Logan, Utah (daughter of John Lea and Elizabeth Lamb, who came to Utah 1873, John Needham company). She was born March 15, 1857, Salford, Lancashire, Eng. Their children: William Thomas Lea b. Dec. 9, 1877, m. Sarah Wyatt Myers Dec. 7, 1898; John b. March 21, 1879, m. Hortense Park March 13, 1901; Charles Alfred b. Nov. 20, 1880, m. Zena Conner March 9, 1904; Norman b. Aug. 28, 1883, m. Beatrice Jones Dec. 15, 1908; Parley b. March 23, 1885, m. Nettie Spence March 14, 1906; Archey b. Nov. 4, 1887, m. Agnes Neddo June 16, 1907; Ellis b. July 10, 1889, m. Mary Sorensen June 7, 1911; Lyman b. Jan. 1, 1892, d. aged 3. Family home Wellsville, Utah.
Seventy; missionary to Europe 1899; high priest at Logan. Farmer and cattleman.

LLOYD, WILLIAM THOMAS LEA (son of Thomas William Lloyd and Elizabeth Lea). Born Dec. 9, 1877, Wellsville, Utah.
Married Sarah Wyatt Myers Dec. 7, 1898, Logan, Utah (daughter of Alma Myers and Sarah Helen Wyatt, former came to Utah, latter born in 1856, Salt Lake City). She was born April 4, 1877, Wellsville, Utah. Their children: Beatrice Myers b. Dec. 1, 1899; Sarah Helen M. b. Nov. 1, 1901; Elizabeth M. b. Dec. 11, 1903; William Herman M. b. Feb. 11, 1906; Russell Carl M. b. Dec. 6, 1907; Oliver Freelen M. b. March 21, 1910; Gladys M. b. March 26, 1913. Family home Wellsville, Utah.
One of the seven presidents of 108th quorum seventies of Bannock stake, Idaho. Farmer.

LLOYD, EZRA T. (son of Thomas Lloyd and Susanna Stone). Born Feb. 10, 1871, at Wellsville, Utah.
Married Jennie Hubbard in 1897, Logan, Utah (daughter of Charles Hubbard of Willard, Utah). She was born in 1872. Their children: Gwendolyn b. March 25, 1899; Ezra T.; Donnette; Viola; Hubbard; Jennie. Family home, Salt Lake City.
Member 119th quorum seventies; missionary to England 1899-1902. Proprietor Lloyd Knitting Mills.

LLOYD, WILLIAM JOHN (son of John Lloyd and Mary Thomas of Carmarthen, Wales). Born Aug. 9, 1823, at Carmarthen. Came to Utah Sept. 30, 1853, Jacob Gates company.
Married Ann Thomas March 28, 1853, on board "Falcon" on Atlantic ocean (daughter of John Thomas and Ann Reese of Monmouth, Wales). She was born May 24, 1834. Their children: Mary Jane and Elizabeth Ann, died; William Thomas, m. Martha Lloyd; John Heber, m. Sarah Jane Jones; Thomas Hyrum, died; Benjamin Ira, m. Laura Morgan; Ann Isabel, died; George Willard, m. Kate Davis; Charles Henry, died. Family home, Salt Lake City.
Married Elizabeth Evans Dec. 7, 1867, at Salt Lake City (daughter of John Evans and Mary Thomas of Brechfa, Carmarthen, Wales). She was born March 25, 1829. Only child: David, died.
Member 62d quorum seventies; missionary to Wales 1874-75; ward teacher. Veteran Black Hawk Indian war. Shoemaker 1853-1903. Died May 29, 1903, Salt Lake City.

LLOYD, JOHN HEBER (son of William John Lloyd and Ann Thomas). Born July 23, 1857, Salt Lake City.
Married Sarah Jane Jones Aug. 5, 1880, at Salt Lake City (daughter of Evan Jones and Jane Thomas of Carmarthen, Wales, pioneers Sept. 2, 1868, Simpson M. Molen company). She was born Dec. 12, 1860. Their children: John Willard b. June 17, 1881, died; Florence May b. Aug. 22, 1883, m. George S. Soderborg; Elizabeth Jane b. Jan. 3, 1886, died; Luella b. Nov. 6, 1888; Charles Heber b. Feb. 15, 1891; Parley William b. June 20, 1894. Family home, Salt Lake City.
Member 2d quorum seventies; home missionary; president deacons quorum; ward teacher. Painting contractor.

LOCKHART, DANIEL. Born in Lanarkshire, Scotland. Came to Utah in 1868.
Married Margaret Glenn in 1854 at Lanarkshire, Scotland (daughter of David Glenn of Lanarkshire). Their children:

Brigham, died; Daniel, m. Murran M. Young and Jeannette Ennis Graham; Margaret, m. Speirs Wilson; Mary, m. Charles Lund; Elizabeth, died; Jeannette, m. Angus Buchanan. Family home Richfield, Utah.
High priest. Miner. Died 1879 at Richfield.

LOCKHART, DANIEL (son of Daniel Lockhart and Margaret Glenn). Born Feb. 24, 1855, Motherwell, Lanarkshire, Scotland. Came to Utah in 1873.
Married Murran Mitchell Young Sept. 27, 1881, at Richfield (daughter of Archibald Young and Mary Graham of Kirkintilloch, Scotland). Their children: Mary Graham b. Jan. 7, 1883, m. James William Boyden; Daniel b. April 15, 1884, d. infant; Archibald Bert b. May 29, 1885, m. Nessie S. Killacorn. Family home Neils Station, Utah.
Married Jeannette Ennis Graham Jan. 2, 1890, at Logan, Utah (daughter of Alexander Stewart Graham and Elizabeth Jane Nuttman of St. Louis, Mo.). She was born Oct. 2, 1872. Their children: Daniel Alexander b. Sept. 15, 1890; George William b. May 6, 1892; James Lee b. Nov. 14, 1894; Glenn Dewey b. March 6, 1898; Jeannette Oreen b. Aug. 15, 1900; Murran Elizabeth b. Dec. 23, 1902; Verl Dellis b. April 23, 1906; Eugene Lester b. May 24, 1909. Family home Wallsburg, Utah.
Elder. Railroader; farmer.

LOFTHOUSE, JAMES (son of Anthony and Ann Lofthouse, Downham, Lancastershire, Eng.). Born November 1833, Downham. Pioneer Oct. 6, 1853, H. C. Wheelock company.
Married Charlotte E. Woodhead Feb. 19, 1856, North Ogden, Utah (daughter of William Woodhead and Charlotte Spenceley, Goole, Yorkshire, Eng., pioneer Oct. 22, 1855, Milo Andrus company). She was born Oct. 19, 1837. Their children: Charlotte Ann b. Oct. 5, 1857; James Richard b. Feb. 22, 1860, d. at Paradise Sept. 9, 1869, m. Dorcas Crager; Anthony William b. Sept. 6, 1862, m. Sarah Housley; John Henry b. April 27, 1865, m. Josephene James; Joseph Thomas b. Sept. 18, 1867, m. Emma Bishop; George Frederick b. Feb. 16, 1870, m. Ellen M. Danielson; Margaret Elizabeth b. Jan. 12, 1873, d. Sept. 10, 1873; Sarah Helen b. Dec. 24, 1875, m. Elias T. Tarns; Charles Edwin b. Feb. 1, 1879, m. Rachel Weld; Parley W. b. Aug. 9, 1883, m. Jennie A. Miller.
Died June 6, 1908, Paradise, Utah.

LONDON, JOHN (son of George London of England, born 1806, and Sarah Garfield of Allcester, Eng., born March 25, 1805). He was born Nov. 7, 1840, at Allcester. Came to Utah Sept. 15, 1862, Homer Duncan company.
Married Hannah E. Smith Nov. 8, 1863 (daughter of Samuel Smith and Elizabeth Baldwin). She was born June 22, 1838; came to Utah Oct. 4, 1863, Horton D. Haight company. Their children: Annie Elizabeth b. Sept. 19, 1864, m. George R. Thackeray May 4, 1883; George Thomas b. June 25, 1866, m. Sarah L. Geary Aug. 15, 1888; Mary Louisa b. March 22, 1868, d. March 27, 1878; Alfred John b. March 28, 1870, m. Annie M. Kirkland; Alice Rebecca b. March 28, 1872, m. Thomas A. Condie Dec. 8, 1897; Emily Maud b. May 15, 1874, m. James Edwin Lingenfelter Oct. 9, 1907; William Henry b. Oct. 27, 1876, m. Lucy B. Robinson Feb. 1, 1905; Oliver Charles, m. Katie B. Blackwell Feb. 12, 1902. Family home Croydon, Utah.
High priest; superintendent of Croydon Sunday school 30 years. Postmaster of Croydon for 24 years.

LONDON, GEORGE THOMAS (son of John London and Hannah E. Smith). Born June 25, 1866, at Echo, Summit Co., Utah.
Married Sarah L. Geary at Logan, Utah, Aug. 15, 1888, who was born April 11, 1870, at Morgan. Their children: Walter George; Clarence Oliver; Cordelia; Mary Alice; Leone Seymour; Flora May; Ella Maud. Family resided Morgan and Ogden, Utah.

LONGHURST, WILLIAM HENRY. Born Jan. 22, 1818. Came to Utah in 1864.
Married Ann Preston, who was born in 1827 and died February, 1873, at Woodruff, Utah. Their children: Thomas, m. Emma Bruff; Amelia, m. William Rounds; Clara, m. Warren Tinner; William, m. Betsy Dean; Charles, m. Volare Davis; Marintha, m. George Whittington; George Heber, m. Mary E. Moore; Joseph, m. Lydia Bennett; Edwin John, m. Adalina Orno Orlendo Pope; Warren, m. Myra I. Alfred. Family home Woodruff, Utah.
Missionary in England; high priest. Resided at Bountiful, Utah, until 1872; moved to Woodruff, Utah. Was one of the original members of the United Order and remained in the order until its dissolution. Coffinmaker; wheelwright. Died April 1888, at Iona, Utah.

LONGHURST, EDWIN JOHN (son of William Henry Longhurst and Ann Preston). Born Jan. 22, 1865, at Salt Lake City.
Married Adalina Orno Orlendo Pope Oct. 2, 1884, at Logan, Utah (daughter of Robert Pope and Sarah La Duke of Vernal, Utah, pioneers 1855). She was born Sept. 24, 1869. Their children (all adopted): Elizabeth Pope; Charles Hinton; Syntha Margerin; Jerald V. Hunting. Family home Vernal, Utah.
Member of seventies at Garden City, Utah; missionary to England 1899-1900; president seventies at Vernal, Utah.

missionary to Colorado 1904-06; president of Colorado (Pueblo) conference; one of the first superintendents of Uintah stake Sunday schools; superintendent Riverdale Sunday school for nine years; president Y. M. M. I. A. several times. School trustee for nine years; deputy sheriff of Uintah county. Mine and smelterman at Dyer, 28 miles north of Vernal, Utah. Promoter of farms.

LONGSTRATH, STEPHEN. Came to Utah 1848, Brigham Young company.
Married Ann Gill in England (daughter of George Gill of Lancashire, Eng.). She was born 1793. Their children: Alice, m. Moses Whitaker; Sarah, m. Willard Richards; Nannie, m. Willard Richards; George, died; Mary, died; William, m. Lottie Baker; Ann, m. John K. Whitney. Family home Iron Cliff, Lancastershire, Eng.
Cabinetmaker. Died about 1859, Salt Lake City.

LONGY, FRANCIS (son of Peter Longy and Mary Ann Bywater, former of New York, latter of Canada). Born June 19, 1835, Toronto, Canada. Came to Utah in 1849.
Married Mary A. Warburton June 19, 1855 (daughter of Edward Warburton and Sophia Bywater, pioneers Oct. 28, 1849, Ezra T. Benson company). She was born May 29, 1839, and came to Utah with parents. Their children: Francis X. b. June 19, 1856, died; Edward W. b. Sept. 4, 1859, m. Mary A. Atkin Sept. 9, 1880; Mary Ann b. Dec. 25, 1861, m. Thomas Nix in 1879; Edgerton b. Nov. 28, 1863, m. May Smith; John b. June 19, 1867, died; Richard b. Oct. 29, 1869, m. Mary A. Martin; Sophia b. June 19, 1871, m. Hyrum Dronby; Isabell b. Dec. 12, 1873, m. James A. Smith; Clara b. May 11, 1876; Luetta b. June 21, 1879, m. William Nix. Family home Tooele City, Utah.
High priest. Took part in Echo Canyon trouble. Indian fighter of Tooele county.

LOOFBOUROW, CHARLES F. (son of Franklin S. Loofbourow of Ohio). Born 1841 in Ohio. Came to Utah February, 1889.
Married Fanny H. Hodgkins at Marshalltown, Iowa. Their children: Wade; Jesse H.; Leon L.; Frederick C., m. Maud H. Read. Family home, Salt Lake City.
Judge of 11th district of Iowa. President of city council at Salt Lake City.

LOOFBOUROW, FREDERICK C. (son of Charles F. Loofbourow and Fanny H. Hodgkins). Born Feb. 8, 1875, Atlantic, Iowa. Came to Utah February, 1889.
Married Maud H. Read Oct. 31, 1901, at Helena, Mont. (daughter of Francis S. Read and Laura Thoroughman of Helena). She was born July 7, 1880. Their children: Frederick Read b. Feb. 13, 1904; Leonidas T. b. March 31, 1906; Francis H. b. Nov. 17, 1907. Family home, Salt Lake City.
Graduate law department of University of California. Assistant county attorney at Salt Lake City two years; district attorney 1904; judge 3d judicial district of Utah 1911-12.

LOOSLE, JOHN KASPER (son of Andrew Loosle, born Dec. 11, 1803, in Canton Bern, and Barbra Kähser, born Oct. 15, 1807, Dürrenroth, Switzerland). He was born Oct. 21, 1831, at Bern, Switzerland. Came to Utah Sept. 1, 1860, John Smith company.
Married Anna Elizabeth Huncebager (daughter of Christen Huncebager and Elizabeth Mautidize, pioneers Sept. 1, 1860, John Smith company). She was born Aug. 18, 1835. Their children: George b. July 11, 1858, m. Anna Dahle March 29, 1906; Adolph b. Oct. 26, 1860; Elizabeth b. March 13, 1863; Emma b. June 24, 1865; John W. b. Aug. 11, 1867; Roslindy b. June 21, 1869; Sarah b. Aug. 19, 1872; Mary b. Nov. 17, 1874; Anna Elizabeth b. March 1, 1877; Rosette b. May 15, 1881. Family resided Providence, Clarkston and Ogden, Utah.
Married Anna Foster. She was born May 16, 1824, at Alkon, Zurich, Switzerland.

LOOSLE, GEORGE (son of John Kasper Loosle and Anna Elizabeth Huncebager). Born July 11, 1858, at Bern, Switzerland.
Married Anna Jeannette Dahle March 29, 1906, at Logan, Utah (daughter of John Dahle, born Nov. 16, 1837, at Bergen, Norway, and Jeannette B. Dahle, born February, 1846, at Trendagern, Norway). She was born in 1874 at Logan, Utah. Their children: George D. b. Dec. 11, 1906; John C. b. May 16, 1909; Normen D. b. Nov. 5, 1910. Family home Clarkston, Utah.

LOOSLI, ULRICH (son of Andrew Loosli, born 1803, and Barbra Kähser, born 1807, both of Switzerland). He was born April 22, 1830, Dürrenroth. Came to Utah Sept. 3, 1860, James D. Ross company.
Married Magdalin Aeschemann in 1852 (daughter of Christian Aescheman and Barbra Brand), who was born 1818 at Trachselwald, Switzerland; came to Utah with husband. Their children: Rosetta b. 1853, m. Jacob Zollinger; John b. 1854, d. 1862; Jabez b. August, 1859, d. 1898. Family home Newton, Utah.

Married Elizabeth Eggimann September 1869, at Salt Lake City, who was born 1842, Gumiswell, Switzerland. Their children: Anfaniel, died; Boundy Endore b. June 28, 1872; Dimond M. b. Oct. 20, 1876, m. Hattie Salisbury Nov. 11, 1898; Edward S. b. April 24, 1879, m. Nellie Price Oct. 5, 1904; Andrew b. 1881; Joseph b. May 14, 1884, m. Minnie Cunningham Nov. 7, 1906; Henry, d. infant. Family home Marysville, Idaho.
High priest; missionary to Switzerland 1868. Pioneer to Newton, Clarkston and Trenton, Utah, and Marysville, Idaho.

LOOSLI, DIMOND M. (son of Ulrich Loosli and Elizabeth Egemann). Born Oct. 20, 1876, Clarkson, Utah.
Married Hattie Salisbury Nov. 11, 1898, Logan, Utah (daughter of Joseph M. Salisbury and Miranda Ramsden, former a pioneer 1856, latter of 1863). She was born May 13, 1876, Brigham City, Utah. Their children: Dimond Herschel b. Sept. 26, 1899; Stanley b. Aug. 13, 1901; Anna Lisle b. June 5, 1903; Clayton Girr b. March 18, 1905; Adrienne b. March 12, 1907; Leo Arden b. March 18, 1909; Berlin Ramsden b. June 10, 1911.
Bishop's counselor; choir leader. Farmer and engineer.

LORDS, WILLIAM S. Born Oct. 13, 1820, in Massachusetts.
Married Mary Ann Nirden July 23, 1854, Pleasant Grove, Utah (daughter of Thomas Nirden and Elizabeth Dunn, pioneers Sept. 19, 1852, Captain Clawson company). She was born July 27, 1835, in England. Their children: Thomas B. April 25, 1857, m. Charlotte Long May 1, 1878; Henry B. b. Nov. 16, 1859, m. Anna Lance July 23, 1879; John S. b. Oct. 12, 1861, m. Isabell May; Joseph C. b. May 26, 1866, m. Agnes Cook July 23, 1887; David N. b. March 25, 1868, m. Morilla Locks May 14, 1893; Susan A. b. Nov. 14, 1871, m. Erastus Bingham Jan. 1, 1888; Daniel J. b. Nov. 10, 1873, m. Ella Cook Jan. 2, 1895; Amy L. b. Nov. 9, 1880, m. Joshua Cook Dec. 25, 1898.
Drummer boy and soldier in the United States army 10 years. Settled in Pleasant Grove. Captain in Black Hawk Indian war. Cattle herder.

LORENTZEN, CHRISTEN (son of Lorentzen and Margaret Christensen of Geisling, Denmark). Born March 26, 1821, Geisling, Denmark. Came to Utah July 3, 1878.
Married Dorthea Larsen, Follesslov, Denmark (daughter of Lars and Ane Larsen, Slagelse, Denmark). She was born March 26, 1824. Their children: Soren Peter b. April 13, 1847, d. 1888; Anna b. Feb. 15, 1863, m. Andrew Nelson; Ane Margaret b. Sept. 23, 1864, m. Christen Peterson; Marie b. July 19, 1870, m. Nephi Pierce. Family home Follesslov, Denmark.
Seventy. Farmer. Died Nov. 25, 1895, Ferron, Utah.

LORENTZEN, GODTFRED (son of Soren Lorentzen and Anna Helene Roager of Sclesvig, Denmark). Born Dec. 23, 1862, Sclesvig, Denmark. Came to Utah June 1884.
Married Chrestine B. Smith Dec. 15, 1887, Logan, Utah (daughter of Jens Smith and Fredricka Jepsen of Hjorup, Denmark, came to Utah June, 1881). She was born 1868. Their children; died May, 1900. Their children: Annie R.; Eden C.; Brnald G.; Verna C. Family resided Moroni and Salina, Utah.
Married Elmer Olivia Johnson Sept. 29, 1903, Manti, Utah (daughter of Gustaf Johnson and Marie Jansen of Stockholm, Sweden, came to Utah 1879). Their children: Ora M.; Emma L.; Vera. Family home Salina, Utah.
Member of 107th quorum seventies; bishop of Salina ward. Miller; farmer.

LOTT, CORNELIUS P. Came to Utah July 24, 1847, Brigham Young company.
Married Rebecca Fawcett (Saunsosee) (daughter of William Fawcett and Matilda Butcher of Kentucky and Tennessee. Came to Utah Oct. 5, 1851, Roswell Stephens company). Only child: Isiah Barkdell b. Nov. 12, 1846, m. Lavonia Andrews.
Rebecca Fawcett was the widow of Louis Saunsosee, pioneer 1852. Their children: Susan, m. Joseph Nuttall: Matilda, m. George James; Rosilla, m. William C. Hathenbrook. Family home Provo, Utah.

LOTT, ISIAH BARKDELL (son of Cornelius P. Lott and Rebecca Fawcett). Born Nov. 12, 1846, at Winter Quarters, Neb. Came to Utah Oct. 5, 1851, Roswell Stephens company.
Married Lavonia Andrews May 10, 1870, at Salt Lake City, Utah (daughter of Samuel Andrews and Elizabeth Potts, both of Rome, Ga. Came to Utah October, 1869). She was born Jan. 19, 1849. Their children: Walter J. b. Feb. 7, 1872, m. Margaret Norton; Daisy b. April 2, 1873, m. William Thorton; Alnora b. Dec. 10, 1874, m. Joseph Mills; Nellie b. Jan. 20, 1876, m. Millage Jaques; Willie b. Nov. 14, 1878; Charles W. b. Aug. 4, 1880, m. Minnie Gillespie and Myrtle Mowers; Frederick b. March 2, 1883, m. Tohitha Norton; Wallace b. Dec. 14, 1884, m. Elsie Cook; Lavona b. May 7, 1887, m. Nelson Seamount; Ella b. Dec. 13, 1889, m. Lafayette Baum; Ora b. Nov. 28, 1890, m. Myrtle Doudle.
Farmer. Located in Pleasant View ward in 1851, where he was active in building up the country.

LOTT, CORNELIUS P. (son of Peter Lott and Mary Jane Smyle of Holland). Born Sept. 27, 1798. Came to Utah September, 1847.
Married Permelia Darrow (daughter of Joseph Darrow and Mary Ward). Their children: Mellisa, m. Ira Willes; John S.; Mary E., m. Abraham Lossee; Almira H., m. J. R. Murdock; Jane, m. Abram Hatch; Alzina L., m. Sidney Willes; Amanda; Joseph; Peter, m. Sarah Snow; Cornelius; Benjamin S., m. Mary A. Evans. Superintendent of the Church farm for a number of years.

LOTT, BENJAMIN S. (son of Cornelius P. Lott and Permelia Darrow). Born Nov. 16, 1849, Salt Lake City.
Married Mary A. Evans Oct. 25, 1868, Salt Lake City (daughter of Israel Evans and Malita Ann Thomas, former came to Utah with the Mormon Battalion, latter 1847, Parley P. Pratt company). She was born Feb. 15, 1850, Salt Lake City. Their children: Lillian b. July 30, 1870, died; M. M. b. Oct. 16, 1872; B. C. b. Sept. 5, 1874, m. G. R. Broadbent; L. E. b. Aug. 6, 1877, m. Agnes Adamson; E. A. b. Oct. 17, 1880, m. Ellis A. Peterson; B. D. b. July 18, 1883, m. Della Jacobs; I. L. b. July 30, 1885, m. Emma Brown; M. S. b. July 30, 1885, m. R. B. Peterson.

LOTT, JOHN S. (son of Cornelius Lott of Pennsylvania). Came to Utah 1848, Heber C. Kimball company.
Married Mary Ann Faucett at Provo, Utah (daughter of William and Matilda Faucett of Provo, Utah, pioneers 1849). Their children: Cornelius, d. infant; Pemella, m. Richard E. Skinner; John W., m. Sarah J. Robison; Joseph A., m. Murai A. Twickell; Asa, d. child; Amosy, d. youth; Angelia H., m. Rodolp Lucre; Elmyra, m. Henry Berlin; Francis; Benjamin S.; Isaac R., d. youth. Family home Joseph City, Sevier Co., Utah.
High priest. Sheriff of Utah county 15 years; Black Hawk Indian war veteran. Took part in Tintic and Echo Canyon wars. Farmer. Died at Joseph City.

LOTT, JOHN W. (son of John S. Lott and Mary Ann Faucett). Born Oct. 24, 1850, Mill Creek, Utah.
Married Sarah J. Robison Feb. 23, 1873, at Petersburg, Utah (daughter of Peter Robison and Salina Chaffe of Pennsylvania). Their children: John S. b. Oct. 10, 1874, m. Otilda Johnson; James P. b. April 21, 1876, m. Annie Rowbury; Sarah M. b. Oct. 10, 1878, m. Anton Nielson. Family home Petersburg, Utah.
Married Hannah C. Johnson Jan. 27, 1882, Joseph City, Utah (daughter of Bengt Johnson and Annie Hogan of Sevier county, Utah). She was born in November, 1865. Their children: William b. Nov. 1, 1882, d. child; Emma C. b. Feb. 25, 1884, m. John S. Knight; Pary F. b. Dec. 14, 1884, d. infant; Adelbert J. b. Feb. 20, 1887, m. Vina J. Gardiner; Hyrum F. b. Jan. 14, 1889; Myrtie A. b. March 25, 1891; Pearl H. b. April 15, 1893; Ira F. b. May 22, 1895; Mary A. b. May 17, 1911. Family home Huntington, Utah.
Deacon. Trustee of town board of Huntington, Utah. Guard in Black Hawk Indian war. Farmer and stockraiser.

LOVE, DAVID. Born Jan. 1, 1822, at Blackbraes, Scotland. Came to Utah Aug. 12, 1852.
Married Margaret Hunter 1852 in St. Louis (daughter of James Hunter of Clackmannan, Scotland). Their children: David; Henry; Margaret; John; Stephen H.; James W.; Joseph H.; Neil; Winnifred. Fmaily home 6th ward, Salt Lake City.
Died at Salt Lake City 1888.

LOVE, STEPHEN H. (son of David Love and Margaret Hunter). Born Jan. 15, 1865, Salt Lake City.
Married Eleanor Wilding Feb. 8, 1883, Salt Lake City (daughter of George Wilding and Mary E. Layne of Salt Lake City, 19th ward, pioneers 1852). Their children: Eleanor Hazel; Geneva; Lucy; Stephen Russell; Milton H.; Viola; Steve Layne; Afton; Douglas; Doris; Eugene; Eloise. State senator eight years; Traffic manager of the Z. C. M. I. President Commercial Club traffic bureau.

LOVELESS, JOHN. Came to Utah in 1851.
Married Rachel Mahaley. Their children: Ellen, m. Charles White; James, m. Matilda McClelland; Nephi, m. Louisa Williams; Joseph J., m. Sarah Jane Scriggins; Parley Pratt, m. Ann Parry; Hyrum, m. Eliza Wimmer; William, m. Rebecca Gaines; Mary Elizabeth, m. Lucius Elmer; Priscilla, m. David Wilson. Family resided West Jordan and Payson, Utah.
High priest; elder. Farmer.

LOVELESS, JOSEPH J. (son of John Loveless and Rachel Mahaley). Born in Jackson county, Mo. Came to Utah in 1851, oxteam company.
Married Sarah Jane Scriggins at Provo, Utah (daughter of Samuel Scriggins and Ellen Printiss of Salem, Mass., pioneers 1852, Archibald Gardner oxteam company). She was born Aug. 13, 1839. Their children: Matilda Jane b. Aug. 7, 1863, m. William H. Wignal; Martha Ann, m. Charles Hawkins; Jedediah ; Joseph Henry, m. Hattie Savage; Rachel Mahaley, m. Morris Davis, m. A. Crump; Raphael Grant, d. aged 21; John Franklin, d. aged 12; Stella Emeline,

d. aged 3; Sarah Elizabeth, d. aged 9. Family home Payson, Utah.
Elder. Black Hawk Indian war veteran; veteran Echo Canyon war. Farmer. Died Jan. 6, 1882, at Payson, Utah.

LOW, SYLVESTER (son of David Low and Jane Oliver of parish of Tealing, Scotland). Born March 12, 1836, at Tealing. Came to Utah Nov. 13, 1855, Isaac Allred company.
Married Annie Allen Paton Feb. 28, 1858 (daughter of Jacobina Osborne, pioneer Nov. 13, 1855). Their children: James Paton, m. Sarah Ida Barber; Sylvester, m. Lillian Jones; Osborne b. April 1, 1865, m. Sylvia Merrill Dec. 21, 1887, m. Mary A. Kennington Nov. 8, 1893; William, m. Carrie Dahl; Annie, m. Robert Reid; Janetta, m. Charles Erickson; Lydia, m. George Nelson; Lawrena May, m. Joseph Richardson; Sylva Euphemia, m. June Jensen; Charles David, m. Grace Nelson; Millicent, m. Oliver Nilson. Family home Smithfield, Utah.
Married Mary Smith Nov. 13, 1884, Logan, Utah (daughter of Nathan Smith and Jane Sant). Their children: Jane; Sylvester; Joseph Smith; Brigham Young; Sterling; Oliver; Mabel.
Missionary to Scotland 1887-88. Early settler in Cache valley. Resided at Bear Lake, Idaho, and Smithfield, Utah, and Afton, Wyo.; finally settled at Cardston, Canada, 1892. Flourmiller.

LOW, OSBORNE (son of Sylvester Low and Annie Allen). Born April 1, 1865, Ovid, Idaho.
Married Sylvia Merrill Dec. 21, 1887, Logan, Utah (daughter of George Merrill and Alice Smith), who was born Oct. 10, 1867, Smithfield, Utah. Only child: Alice Ann b. Jan. 1, 1889, d. in July, 1889. Family home Afton, Wyo.
Married Mary A. Kennington Nov. 8, 1893, Logan (daughter of William H. and Annice Rebecca Kennington, former pioneer Sept. 26, 1856, Daniel B. McArthur company, latter pioneer Oct. 13, 1863, Rosel Hyde company). She was born April 1, 1865, Salt Lake City). Their children: Osborne b. Sept. 9, 1894; Jennie b. Nov. 3, 1896; Bessie b. Aug. 26, 1899; Wanda b. Sept. 2, 1903; Nora b. Oct. 15, 1905; Rolla b. July 1, 1908.
Ordained as bishop of Freedom ward, Wyoming, in 1894; moved to Afton and ordained bishop or that ward Aug. 12, 1899, to date. Mayor one term; city marshal; member board of education Star Valley stake. Manager telephone exchange.

LOWE, JOHN (son of Peter and Ellen Lowe of Ashton, near St. Helens, Lancaster, Eng.). Born April 24, 1818, Wigan, Lancaster, Eng. Came to Utah Oct. 14, 1853, Cyrus H. Wheelock company.
Married Mary Wilgoose 1839, Wigan, who was born Aug. 13, 1817. Their children: Richard, m. Mary Rebecca Warner 1872; William, m. Emma Cordon Oct. 14, 1864; Jarvis, d. 1845; Peter, m. Esther Ford (died), m. Martha Summers; Elizabeth, d. 1848; Elizabeth, d. 1862; John, m. Ann Elizabeth Ward; Mary Ellen, m. Alfred Ward; Alice, died; Sarah Jane, m. John Darington.
Married Elizabeth Dueherst in 1859, died; no children.
Married Mary Rebecca Warner 1872. Families resided Willard, Utah.
Blacksmith. Died Oct. 15, 1891.

LOWE, RICHARD (son of Richard Lowe). Born Dec. 25, 1826, Nottingham, Eng. Came to Utah in 1851.
Married Ada Clements at Grantsville, Utah (daughter of Alvin and Ada Clements; former came to Utah in 1849, latter in 1847, both of Missouri). She was born in 1841. Their children: Richard Alvin, m. Charity Foreman; Ada, m. William S. Lemmon; Joseph Hyrum, m. Rose Jensen; John, m. Annas Barlow; Harriet Louisa, m. Jack Lemmon; Juliaette, m. George Dallin; Adelia, m. Lee Daniels; Betsy Ann, m. C. B. Scoville; William Nephi, m. Mary Powell.
Married Jane Hale at Salt Lake City (daughter of James Hale and Lucy Clements of Hooper, Utah). Their child: James E., m. Almira Powell. Families resided Springville, Utah.
Settled at Springville in 1857. President of elders quorum of Springville. Early settler in Tooele and Box Elder counties. Veteran Indian war. Farmer; stockraiser and apiarist. Died Dec. 26, 1899.

LOWE, RICHARD ALVIN (son of Richard Lowe and Ada Clements). Born Sept. 13, 1856, Brigham City, Utah.
Married Charity Foreman Nov. 22, 1880, Monroe, Utah (daughter of Thomas Cephas Foreman and Eliza Biggs of North and South Carolina, pioneers 1863). She was born Aug. 6, 1864, Pine Valley, Utah. Their children: Richard Franklin b. Oct. 20, 1881, m. Lydia Yergensen; Thomas Cephas b. Dec. 15, 1882, m. Clara Anderson; Clara b. June 8, 1885, m. Joseph Ross; Eliza b. Oct. 9, 1887, m. Peter Washburn; William b. Dec. 16, 1889; Birdy b. June 30, 1893, m. Hyrum Peterson; Silvia b. March 26, 1896; Ada b. Nov. 13, 1898; Alvin b. June 26, 1901. Family home Monroe, Utah.
Farmer and apiarist.

LOWRY, JOHN (son of William Lowry of Nashville, Tenn., and Polly Norris). Born Aug. 10, 1799, at Nashville. Came to Utah Sept. 30, 1847, John Taylor company.
Married Susan Groom, who died in Missouri. Their children: William; Sarah, m. George Peacock April 4, 1840.

1012 PIONEERS AND PROMINENT MEN OF UTAH

Married Mary Wilcox (daughter of Hazard Wilcox and Sarah Seeley, latter came to Utah Sept. 30, 1847, John Taylor company). Their children: James Hazard b. June 3, 1825, m. Mary Ann Bryerly; Hyrum b. March 15, 1827, d. March 16, 1847; John b. Jan. 31, 1829, m. Sarah Jane Brown, m. Mary A. Allen; Abner b. Oct. 12, 1831, m. Louisa Bradley; Susan Lucretia b. March 13, 1834 (d. Oct. 21, 1859), m. William George Pettey Dec. 13, 1854; Mary Artemesia b. March 13, 1834, m. George Peacock Aug. 5, 1854; George Moroni b. Aug. 9, 1836, d. May 26, 1856; Sarah Jane b. Jan. 26, 1838, m. Nelson D. Higgins; Elizabeth b. March 16, 1841, d. Aug. 18, 1846; William Mahonri b. April 28, 1844, d. Sept. 14, 1846. Family home Manti, Utah.
First counselor to Bishop Hunter, the first bishop of Salt Lake City; also bishop of second ward, Salt Lake City, 1849; first bishop of Manti 1850. Justice of peace at Manti. Farmer and stockraiser. Sent with John Crawford, by Brigham Young, to colonize Elk Mountain country, Nevada. Died Jan. 7, 1867, at Manti.

LOWRY, JOHN, JR. (son of John Lowry and Mary Wilcox). Born Jan. 31, 1829, in Lewis county, Mo. Came to Utah Sept. 30, 1847, Edward Hunter oxteam company.
Married Sarah Jane Brown Nov. 27, 1851, at Manti (daughter of James Polly Brown and Eunice Reesor, pioneers July 29, 1847, Captain Higgins company of James Brown contingent Mormon Battalion). She was born Oct. 27, 1834, Greenville, Ind. Their children: John b. Oct. 3, 1852, m. Lorency Anderson March 14, 1876; James Hazard b. Dec. 8, 1853, m. Maria B. Larson March 8, 1877; Sarah Jane b. Sept. 22, 1855, m. James C. Reynolds May 9, 1878; William Brown b. Dec. 21, 1857, m. Ellen Hansen Nov. 11, 1879; Eunice b. April 16, 1860, m. Michael W. Molen; Olive b. Sept. 1, 1862, m. George Edward Anderson May 30, 1888; Ida May b. July 30, 1865, m. Samuel H. Allen June 8, 1892; Dora b. Nov. 9, 1869, m. Edwin Olsen June 8, 1892; Ethel b. July 6, 1873, m. Clare William Reid Oct. 9, 1895. Family resided Manti and Springville, Utah.
Married Mary Ann Allen in March 1857, Salt Lake City (daughter of Daniel Allen and Mary Ann Maurice, pioneers oxteam company). She was born March 10, 1837, Kirtland, Ohio. Their children: Daniel Allen b. Jan. 7, 1858, m. Emily Ludvigsen Oct. 22, 1885; Mary Artemesia b. March 30, 1860, m. Hyrum A. Nelson; Clara Bell b. March 7, 1863, m. Samuel Singleton; Evelyn b. Oct. 23, 1865, m. Nathaniel Crawford Oct. 22, 1885; Diantha b. March 31, 1868, m. William F. Reid; Orson Hyrum b. Aug. 23, 1873 (d. March 26, 1913), m. Matilda Eleanor Jensen July 20, 1897. Family home, Manti.
High priest; patriarch. Settled at Manti in 1849. Veteran Indian war. Commissioned, by Brigham Young, as paymaster in infantry of San Pete county 1855. Missionary to Elk mountains, under President Alfred Billings, 1855. Interpreter for Ute and Shoshone Indians. Member of legislature from Manti 1896; also city councilman four terms, 1851-59, and assessor and clerk four years. Farmer and stockraiser.

LOWRY, DANIEL ALLEN (son of John Lowry and Mary Ann Allen). Born Jan. 7, 1858, at Manti, Utah.
Married Emily Ludvigsen Oct. 22, 1885, at St. George, Utah (daughter of Eric Ludvigsen and Anna Steck of Manti, pioneers with oxteam company). She was born May 5, 1868. Their children: Mervin Daniel b. July 13, 1886; Mary Evelyn b. May 11, 1888; Ivy C. b. Oct. 26, 1890; Zora b. Oct. 30, 1893, d. Oct. 29, 1894; Lyle Revere b. Sept. 20, 1898; June Lamont b. June 14, 1903; Floyd b. June 29, 1905, d. infant. Family home Ferron, Utah.
Member 49th quorum seventies; missionary to central states 1897-99; Sunday school superintendent. School trustee 15 years. Mechanic.

LOWRY, ORSON HYRUM (son of John Lowry and Mary Ann Allen). Born Aug. 23, 1873, at Manti, Utah.
Married Matilda Eleanor Jensen July 20, 1897, at Manti (daughter of Jens Jensen and Dorothy Petersen of Denmark), who was born Jan. 14, 1878. Their children: LaFonta b. April 11, 1899; Aleda b. Feb. 8, 1901, d. Nov. 8, 1903; Allen b. Feb. 13, 1904. Family resided Manti and Ferron, Utah.
Manti city marshal. Farmer.

LOYND, JAMES (son of James Loynd of Bolton, Eng.). Born in May, 1815, Chatham, Eng. Came to Utah Nov. 30, 1856, Edward Martin handcart company.
Married Elizabeth Thompson in England (daughter of Joseph Thompson and Sarah Thompson of Lancaster, Eng.), who was born Sept. 22, 1810, Worksop, Eng. Their children: John b. Aug. 21, 1837, died; James B.; b. March 1, 1838, m. Sophis Dew; Thomas b. Sept. 19, 1840; Joseph b. Dec. 19, 1843, m. Mary Ann Hollingdrake; Richard b. Jan. 11, 1846, m. Larsine Sorenson. Family resided Cheshire, Eng., and Springville, Utah.
High priest. Pioneer of Davis and Utah counties. Gardener. Died in 1891

LOYND, JOSEPH (son of James Loynd and Elizabeth Thompson). Born Dec. 19, 1843, Dukinfield, Chestershire, Eng. Came to Utah Nov. 30, 1856, with parents.
Married Mary A. Hollingdrake, Dec. 18, 1864 (daughter of John Hollingdrake and Ann Swain, former pioneer Joseph S. Rawlins company Sept. 20, 1864—married at Bradford, Eng.). She was born Aug. 20, 1842, and came to Utah with father. Their children: Elizabeth A. b. March 6, 1866, d. same day; John b. Feb. 28, 1867, d. same day; Joseph S. b. July 25, 1868, m. Amelia Allsworth; Thomas b. June 11, 1871, m. Mary E. Gabitias; Mary A. b. Aug. 17, 1874, d. same day; James A. b. Nov. 16, 1877, m. Louise L. Daniels; Albert b. Sept. 26, 1883, m. Carry M. Ekker. Family home Springville, Utah.
Married Sarah Ann Briggs April 19, 1899, Manti, Utah (daughter of John Briggs and Amelia Hilton; former came to Utah in 1876, latter having died in England). She was born Jan. 16, 1875, Atherton, Eng. Their children: Amelia Gladys b. Jan. 15, 1901; Josephine b. Jan. 10, 1903; Sarah b. Jan. 21, 1905; Alice b. July 4, 1907; Elizabeth b. Nov. 1, 1909.
Bishop of 4th ward, Springville; ward teacher. City councilman; school trustee.

LOYND, JOSEPH S. (son of Joseph Loynd and Mary Ann Hollingdrake). Born July 25, 1868, Springville, Utah.
Married Amelia Allsworth February, 1898, Salt Lake City (daughter of James E. Allsworth and Emily Whitehead), who was born July, 1874, in England. Their children: Harry Joseph b. Feb. 1889; Elvery b. May 1900; Frank b. Aug. 1902; William b. 1903; Walter b. Nov. 1904.
Road supervisor and deputy marshal at Springville. President Y. M. M. I. A. and Sunday school teacher. Agricultural superintendent for the American Beet Sugar Co., in Colorado.

LOYND, RICHARD (son of James Loynd and Elizabeth Thompson). Born Jan. 11, 1846, at Hyde, Cheshire, Eng. Came to Utah Nov. 30, 1856, with parents.
Married Larsine Sorenson Sept. 1, 1872, Monroe. Utah (daughter of Soren Rasmussen and Annie Hogensen of Denmark, who came to Utah in October, 1862). She was born Feb. 21, 1851. Their children: Richard James b. Aug. 6, 1873, m. Ida Larson; Sine Annie b. Nov. 12, 1875, m. Steven Prince; John b. Feb. 8, 1878, m. Birdie McMurtury; Mary b. Aug. 11, 1880, died; Sarah Elizabeth b. July 13, 1882, m. Lars Christian Larsen; Martha Ann b. Aug. 1, 1885, and Josephine b. Dec. 17, 1886, died; Emma Jane b. Nov. 13, 1888, m. Edgar R. Lloyd; Thomas b. Jan. 5, 1891, died; Harriet b. June 21, 1892. Family home, Monroe.
Elder. Veteran Indian wars. Farmer; freighter.

LUDVIGSEN, ERIC.
Married Mary _____ in Denmark. Only child: Peter, who was killed by Black Hawk Indians. Family home Manti, Utah.
Married Stena _____. Only child: Baby, who died at birth. Family home, Manti.
Married Anna Steck (daughter of Jens Steck and Mariah Vosse, pioneers with oxteam company). Their children: Christina, m. Edward Clark, m. P. J. Goble; Mary, m. Chris K. Jensen; Emily, m. Daniel Allen Lowry Oct. 22, 1885; Anna, m. Arthur Nelson; Eric; Sophronia, m. John Wilson, m. Will Nelson; Lillian, m. George Bradley; Elmer, m. Pearl Snow; Leona, m. Alva Barrackman; Merelda, d. aged 18 months. Family home, Manti.
Weaver and farmer.

LUFF, GEORGE T. (son of George Luff and Mary Simpkins of Surrey, Eng.). Born Oct. 23, 1835, in Surrey. Came to Utah Sept. 13, 1861, Homer Duncan company.
Married Mary H. Dixon Dec. 11, 1859, London, Eng. (daughter of James W. Dixon and Hannah Taylor), who was born Aug. 29, 1835, and came to Utah Sept. 13, 1861, with husband. Their children: Mary A., m. Charles Castleton; George D. (d. April 12, 1893), m. Sarah Owen; Elbertha Louise, m. Lorenzo J. Aubrey; Elizabeth Jane, d. infant; Emily H., m. Albert Bargimer; Frank T., m. Kate Dunbar; Harry A., m. Callie Carter; Fred S., m. Myrtle Persell; Linvill J. (d. Oct. 9, 1910), m. Flora Longley. Family home, Salt Lake City.
Deacon; missionary in England 1856-58; high priest; block teacher. Carpenter and builder. Died Feb. 22, 1904, at Salt Lake City.

LUFKIN, SAMUEL (son of Samuel Lufkin, born March 29, 1762, and Sarah Livingston, born Feb. 14, 1766, both at Chelmsford, Mass.). He was born June 22, 1788, Chelmsford, Mass. Came to Utah October, 1852, Blind Lennard company.
Married Eleanor Johnson 1815 (daughter of James Johnson and Eleanor O'Brien), who was born 1795, and came to Utah with Captain Hawley company. Their children: Cyrus, m. Sarah Goodele; Sarah E., m. Eastman Reedham; Acenach E. b. Oct. 18, 1827, m. H. Taylor; George Washington b. June 30, 1831, m. Martha A. Townsend; Jane Ann b. Nov. 8, 1835, m. John Wesley Jennison; Charles H. b. July 18, 1839, m. Catherine Jones.
Married Olena Nelson 1856, who was born in Norway. Their children: Sarah Jane b. Dec. 1856, m. Henry Rudy; Eleanor Olena, m. Jedediah Kimball; Samuel, m. Martha Yates.
High priest; superintendent of Sunday school, Lehi, Utah.

LUFKIN, GEORGE WASHINGTON (son of Samuel Lufkin and Eleanor Johnson). Born June 30, 1831, Lincoln, Vt.
Married Martha A. Townsend 1853, Salt Lake City (daughter of James Foss Townsend and Susan Davis. Came to Utah with John M. Higby company). She was born March 2, 1832, Buxton, Me. Their children: John T. (adopted) b. Jan. 21, 1853, m. Hanna Barron; Florence May b. March 26,

1855, m. William A. Barron; George Eastman b. May 26, 1857, m. Hanna Hanson; Emma M. b. March 26, 1859, died; Susan Asenith b. Nov. 11, 1860, m. Adelbert Phippen; Jessie b. July 20, 1863, m. Ashmer Meloney; Jane Maria b. Feb. 14, 1866, m. Stephen Hailstone; Marion Davis b. Aug. 7, 1868, m. Douglas M. Todd; Vernie Isabell b. April 18, 1871, m. Samuel Thatcher; Kate Naomi b. Jan. 3, 1880, m. Franklin R. Davenport.

High priest. Went with Lot Smith to Fort Bridger to resist Johnston's army and, with 24 others, burned 79 wagons—destroyed provisions, captured over 1,000 head of oxen and some beef cattle, used by the army in hauling their outfit. Veteran Walker war. Owner Salt Lake Transfer Company five years. Furniture merchant. Cabinetmaker. President and manager North Point Canal Company of Salt Lake county. Watermaster and justice of peace two years at Logan, Utah. Farmer.

LUKE, WILLIAM (son of Charles and Hannah Luke of Manchester, Eng.). Born May 8, 1801, at Manchester. Came to Utah 1850, oxteam company.
Married Emma Perkins Dec. 31, 1824, at Manchester, Eng. She was born in 1803. Their children: Emma b. Sept. 29, 1825; John Henry b. Sept. 1827; Charles Oliver b. Jan. 25, 1829, m. Ann Beaver b. Feb. 27, 1853; Thomas William b. Nov. 3, 1830; William b. Sept. 2, 1834, m. Mary Haydock Jan. 10, 1857; Henry b. 1836; Uriah b. Oct. 10, 1838; Elizabeth b. 1840; Angelina b. 1841; Charlotte b. Sept. 25, 1843; Mary b. 1846. Family home Manchester, Eng.
Seventy; ward teacher. Settled at Manti 1850. Indian war veteran. Killed by Indians October, 1853, near Fountain Green.

LUKE, CHARLES OLIVER (son of William Luke and Emma Perkins). Born Jan. 25, 1829, at Manchester, Eng.
Married Ann Beaver Feb. 27, 1853, at Manchester (daughter of John Beaver and Ann Bradshaw, latter pioneer Oct. 9, 1853, Appleton Harmon company). She was born Dec. 25, 1826, at Shevlent, Eng. Their children: Emma Ann b. Aug. 15, 1854; Elizabeth Charlotte b. April 6, 1856, m. James C. Tooth Feb. 18, 1896; Charles William b. Dec. 25, 1857, m. Amanda Anderson Feb. 20, 1896; Sarah Jane b. Oct. 16, 1859, m. Henry Wintch; Mary Malinda b. July 27, 1861, m. Aaron D. Squire; Margret Beaver b. Sept. 22, 1863, m. Christian Poulsen; Thomas James b. July 24, 1865; Joseph Oliver b. Aug. 18, 1867, m. Levi Davis; Benjamin Franklin b. Aug. 6, 1871, m. Emily Jane Davis. Family home Manti, Utah.
High priest.

LUKE, CHARLES WILLIAM (son of Charles Oliver Luke and Ann Beaver). Born Dec. 25, 1857, at Manti, Utah.
Married Amanda Anderson Feb. 20, 1896, at Manti, Utah (daughter of Anders Anderson and Johannah Erickson), who was born May 11, 1866, at Aleverta, Kullsveden, Sweden. Their children: Delis Ann b. Aug. 16, 1902; Mabel Margret b. June 6, 1905; Melroy C. b. Nov. 9, 1908. Family home Manti, Utah.
Elder. Farmer.

LUKE, WILLIAM, JR. (son of William Luke and Emma Perkins). Born Sept. 2, 1834, at Manchester, Eng., pioneer Oct. 16, 1853, Captain Harmon company.
Married Mary Haydock Jan. 10, 1857, at Salt Lake City (daughter of William Haydock and Elizabeth Crompton, former died in England, latter pioneer 1857 with Robinson handcart company). She was born Jan. 2, 1835, at Little Eton Lance, Eng. Their children: William Haydock, Jr., b. Jan. 25, 1858, m. Anne Martina Ottoson March 14, 1878; George Henry b. Feb. 4, 1859, d. Dec. 6, 1880; John Thomas b. May 26, 1861, m. Henrietta C. Barlow Oct. 19, 1881; Joseph b. Aug. 4, 1863, d. Oct. 6, 1863; Mary Emily b. Nov. 6, 1864, m. N. W. Anderson Aug. 17, 1882; Elizabeth Ann b. Nov. 27, 1866, m. Willard Barlow May 5, 1887; Charlotte Jane b. March 3, 1869, m. Oliver C. Peacock; Alonzo b. Dec. 12, 1871, d. Jan. 4, 1873; Franklin b. April 21, 1874, d. same day; Albert Edward b. Aug. 2, 1875, m. Inger M. Ahlstrom Dec. 18, 1895. Family home Manti, Utah.
Settled at Manti in 1853. Veteran Indian war. One of the founders of the Co-op, at Manti and acted as its director for many years. School trustee; road supervisor 13 years; county commissioner three years; Manti city councilman six years; alderman four years; mayor of Manti two terms. Died Sept. 28, 1904, at Manti, Utah.

LUKE, WILLIAM HAYDOCK, JR. (son of William Luke, Jr., Mary Haydock). Born Jan. 25, 1858, at Manti, Utahand
Married Anne Martina Ottoson March 14, 1878, Salt Lake City (daughter of Jens Ottoson and Johannah Sorenson, former came to Utah in 1858, latter with last handcart company). She was born Nov. 15, 1854, at Goshen, Utah. Their children: William James b. Dec. 22, 1878, m. Levina Allen; Joseph Loinal b. March 12, 1880, d. Aug. 9, 1882; George Leroy b. Nov. 3, 1881, m. Della Connell June 30, 1902; Melvin b. Oct. 13, 1883, m. Clarissa Esplin June 13, 1907; Hannah Cleo b. Sept. 30, 1885; Mary Hazel b. April 12, 1887, m. John Pendleton June 16, 1909; Oden b. March 11, 1889; Jessie b. April 5, 1891; Clinton Lamar b. Feb. 20, 1893, m. Fern I. Morrill Sept. 20, 1910; Ottoson b. April 21, 1895; Isabell Martina b. Aug. 14, 1897; Lorenzo Franklin b. Oct. 14, 1899; Orral Stanford b. July 21, 1902; Alton Arnold b. April 8, 1905. Family home Junction, Utah.
Worked on St. George temple. Counselor to first president of Y. M. M. I. A. at Manti; ward teacher. Moved from Manti to Junction in 1888. School trustee. Sunday school superintendent at Junction; missionary to central states 1905-07; high priest; counselor to Bishop Morrill of Junction ward. Clerk Piute county two terms.

LUKE, HENRY (son of William Luke and Emma Perkins). Born March 17, 1836, Manchester, Eng. Came to Utah October, 1853, oxteam company.
Married Harriet E. Luce at Spanish Fork, Utah. Their children: Maria b. Jan. 30, 1858, m. Abram C. Hatch; William Andrew b. Jan. 29, 1860, m. Ellen M. Busby; Emma Caroline b. Aug. 29, 1861, m. Frederic L. Clegg; John Henry b. June 18, 1864, m. Sophia Clyde; Mary Ann b. March 28, 1866, m. Fred Davis. Family home Heber, Utah.
Assisted in settling the "Dixie" country. Indian interpreter. Farmer. Died June 26, 1876, at Heber City, Utah.

LUKE, WILLIAM ANDREW (son of Henry Luke and Harriet Luce). Born Jan. 29, 1860, Spanish Fork, Utah.
Married Ellen M. Busby Jan. 27, 1881, at Salt Lake City (daughter of John K. Busby of Glasgow, Scotland, and Harriet Emma Killian of Missouri, pioneers with oxteam company). She was born July 23, 1860. Their children: John Henry b. Dec. 28, 1881; William Andrew b. Dec. 30, 1883, m. Leona Jenson; Nellie May b. Oct. 1, 1885, m. William Gibson; George Edward b. May 20, 1887, m. Jennie Gibson; Charles Franklin b. Nov. 26, 1888, m: Cordelia Shelton; James Alfred b. Dec. 17, 1890, d. Sept. 4, 1891; Douglas b. Oct. 13, 1892, d. Aug. 22, 1899; Wallace b. Jan. 10, 1895; Otto b. July 26, 1896; Violet b. June 10, 1898, d. Jan. 21, 1899; Pansy b. May 18, 1900, died same day; Lawrence b. May 22, 1901; Avon b. April 18, 1903. Family home Midway, Utah.
Elder. Road supervisor. Farmer and freighter. Manager Lukes Hot Pots at Midway, Utah.

LUNCEFORD, WILLIAM (son of George and Nancy Lunceford, both of St. Clair county, Ill.). Born April 15, 1796. Came to Utah 1850, oxteam company.
Married Rawsey Robertson (daughter of Robert and Elizabeth Robertson of Illinois. Their children George b. Nov. 14, 1821, died; Mary Ann b. Aug. 1, 1823, m. Thomas Berry; Elizabeth b. March 6, 1825, m. William Padfield; John Dew b. Jan. 23, 1826, died; Joseph b. Dec. 12, 1828, m. Angeline Skinner; Martha Jane b. Nov. 8, 1830, m. William Ashmead; Samuel b. Dec. 22, 1832; Caroline b. Nov. 15, 1834, died; Rawsey b. Nov. 22, 1836, died. Family home, Illinois.
Married Mary Trent Holdaway in Illinois (daughter of Timothy Trent of Tennessee), who was born 1805. Their children; William Trent b. Aug. 7, 1838, m. Mary Jane Jamies; Mary Emaline b. Dec. 4, 1840, m. Sirus Snell, m. Silas Call; Sarah Melvina b. Feb. 18, 1884, m. William Keller; Synthia Mary Mahaly b. Sept. 6, 1847. Family home, Illinois.
Veteran Walker Indian war. Died 1886, San Luis Obispo, Cal.

LUNCEFORD, JOSEPH (son of William Lunceford and Rawsey Robertson). Born Dec. 12, 1828, in Illinois. Came to Utah 1850, Shadrach Holdaway company.
Married Angeline Skinner Oct. 18, 1860, Provo, Utah (daughter of Horace Billins Skinner and Elinore Clace of Nauvoo, Ill., pioneers October, 1852, Captain Walker oxteam company), who was born Oct. 4, 1843. Their children: Rawsey Angeline b. Aug. 20, 1862, died; Joseph William b. Aug. 7, 1864, m. Mary Cardner; John Hyrum b. Nov. 26, 1866, m. Melvina Hansen; Martha Elinore b. Oct. 21, 1869, m. Frank Birmingham; Emma Almeda b. Jan. 19, 1873, m. Lewis Birmingham; Hannah Elizabeth b. July 20, 1876, m. Lewis Olsen; Sarah Caroline b. April 3, 1879, m. Julius Johnson; Annie b. Aug. 27, 1883, m. George S. Wheeler; Alonzo b. Oct. 3, 1886, died. Family home Lake View, Utah.
Married Esther Jane Skinner, 1868, Provo, Utah (daughter of Horace Billine Skinner and Elinore Clace of Nauvoo, Ill., pioneers October, 1852, Captain Walker company). Their children: Elizabeth Esther, m. John Hick; Mary Ann, died; Cynthia Melvina; David Hyrum; Wilford; Ellen Orminda, m. Andrew Lovegrande; Alma, m. Sadie Randall; George, m. Lutty Hale.
Elder; ward teacher. Black Hawk and Walker Indian war veteran. Farmer. Died June, 1895, Lake View, Utah.

LUND, ANTHON H. (son of Henry Lund and Anna Christina Anderson of Denmark). Born May 15, 1844, Denmark. Came to Utah Sept. 23, 1862, C. A. Madsen independent company.
Married Sarah Ann Peterson May 2, 1870, Salt Lake City (daughter of Canute Peterson and Sarah Ann Nelson of Illinois, pioneers September, 1849). She was born Jan. 1, 1853. Their children: Anthony C., m. Cornelia Sorenson; Henry C., m. Julia A. Farnsworth; Sarah H.; Herbert Z., m. Emma Jensen; Canute L.; Othniel R., m. Mabel Hall; August William, m. Josephine Brown; George C.; Eva A. Family home, Salt Lake City.
Missionary to Denmark 1871-72; to Scandinavia 1883-85, to England 1893-95, to Palestine 1897-98 and to Europe 1909; first counselor to Joseph F. Smith in presidency; church historian. Member legislature 1896 and 1898; author of bills creating the industrial school at Ogden and the agricultural college at Logan. Vice president of Zion's Savings & Trust company; director of Z. C. M. I. and of Utah State

National bank; regent of the university of Utah; member of the capitol commissions and president of the genealogical society of Utah: president of the board of trustees of the L. D. S. university.

LUND, ANTHONY CANUTE (son of Anthon Henrik Lund and Sarah Ann Peterson). Born Feb. 25, 1871, Ephraim, Utah.
Married Laura Greaves Aug. 14, 1895, Ephraim, Utah. Their children: Weber Anthony b. July 16, 1896; Grant b. Oct. 2, 1898.
Married Cornelia Sorenson Dec. 24, 1902, Manti, Utah (daughter of Neils Christian Sorenson of Gunnison, Utah. and Sareh Christina Capsson, born July 31, Spanish Fork, Utah), who was born March 8, 1882. Their children: Anthon Henrik b. Dec. 11, 1903; Herschel Sorenson b. Feb. 11, 1905; Sarah Cornelia b. Sept. 20, 1907; Max Welton b. July 31, 1910. Families reside Provo, Utah.

LUND, HENRY C. (son of Anthon H. Lund and Sarah Ann Peterson). Born April 13, 1873, Ephraim, Utah.
Married Julia A. Farnsworth Sept. 20, 1899, Salt Lake City (daughter of P. T. Farnsworth and Julia P. Murdock), who was born Nov. 2, 1874, Beaver, Utah. Their children: Henry C. F. b. Sept. 8, 1900; Philo F. b. Jan. 9, 1902; Anthon F. b. Oct. 10, 1905, died; John C. F. b. March 3, 1907; Alton F. b. Jan. 29, 1909; Julia F. b. Oct. 26, 1911. Family home, Salt Lake City.
Member 124th quorum seventies; member general board of Y. M. M. I. A. Lawyer.

LUND, HERBERT Z. (son of Anthon H. Lund and Sarah Ann Peterson). Born Jan. 17, 1877, Ephraim, Utah.
Married Emma Iver Jensen May 15, 1902, Manti, Utah (daughter of James Iver Jensen and Inger Nielson Syndegard of Denmark. Came to Utah September, 1868, independent company). She was born June 29, 1879. Their children: Sarah Inger b. June 26, 1904; Herbert Z. b. July 19, 1907; Richard b. March 7, 1911.
Member seventy; missionary to southern states 1899-1901. Physician and surgeon state prison; member of state board of medical examiners. Physician and surgeon.

LUND, OTHNIEL R. (son of Anthon H. Lund and Sarah Ann Peterson). Born Feb. 28, 1882, Ephraim, Utah.
Married Mabel Hall Jan. 27, 1906, Salt Lake City (daughter of Edwin Hall and Clara Bringhurst), who was born 1885. Their children: Robert b. July 29, 1907; Elmo b. Feb. 15, 1912. Family home Ephraim, Utah.
Deputy treasurer of Salt Lake county four years. School teacher. Farmer.

LUND, ROBERT C. (son of Wilson and Eliza B. Lund). He was born May 29, 1847, New Diggins, Wis. Came to Utah 1850.
Married Mary A. Romney 1870.
Settled at Salt Lake City; moved to St. George 1860. Telegraph operater Deseret telegraph company, at St. George, Utah, and Pioche, Nev.; Wells Fargo express agent at St. George and Silver Reef, Utah: chairman board of county commissioners, Washington county; served in territorial legislature; member and president state board of equalization. Died Jan. 30, 1906.

LUNDBLAD, HANS. Born Sept. 29, 1821, in Sweden. Came to Utah 1855 with oxteam.
Married Karste Mortenson in Sweden (daughter of Andres Mortenson and Anna Pahrson of Sweden), who was born Sept. 10, 1821. Their children: Johanna, m. John T. Covington; Mary Christena, m. Joseph Ash; Charlotte Elena, m. Joseph Simkins; John Williard. Joseph and Emma Helena, died; Ellen, m. John H. Fullmer. Family home Beaver, Utah.
President Scandinavian mission before emigrating to America. Settled first in San Pete county, later in 1861 moved to Washington county. Tailor by trade. Died June 29, 1868, Beaver, Utah.

LUNDHOLM, ANDREW G. (son of Anders E. Lundholm and Maria Louisa Lindberg of Sweden). Born May 17, 1833, Tillinge Socken, Upsallalan, Sweden. Came to Utah August.
Married Gustava Charlotta Grindstrom, in Sweden, who died Jan. 12, 1903, Santaquin, Utah. They had two daughters, both of whom died in Sweden.
Married Louisa Gustafson May 27, 1903, Salt Lake temple. Settled at Santaquin in 1869. Teacher; president elders quorum; high priest; high councilor in Nebo stake. Engaged in farming at Santaquin, at which he was very successful. Died Feb. 19, 1911, Santaquin.

LUNDQUIST, AXEL THEODORE (son of Carl Gustav Lundquist born Dec. 7, 1804, and Katrine Abrika Hornstrand, both of Stockholm, Sweden). He was born Feb. 6, 1838, at Stockholm. Came to Utah October, 1863, Captain Fabus company.
Married Sarah Erson Nov. 27, 1865 (daughter of Anders Erson of Dalene, Sweden, and Sarah Miles), who was born Aug. 22, 1843 (deceased). Their children: Axel Jalmer b. Jan. 20, 1867, d. same year; Alexander Theodore b. Sept.

3, 1868, m. Alvilda Fonnesbeck; Sarah Josephine b. March 5, 1870, m. Willard Carlson March 23, 1892; Charles William b. Jan. 22, 1872, m. Catherine E. Kofoed Dec. 5, 1894, and Martha E. Olsen Jan. 22, 1902; Selma Catherine b. March 23, 1873, died; Andrew Enoch b. April 21, 1874; John Parley b. Sept. 5, 1876, m. Antonine Christina Nielsen March 6, 1901; Alvin Theodore b. March 3, 1878, died; Hulda Johanna b. Jan. 19, 1879, m. James J. Nelson Nov. 16, 1899; Albert Peter b. Dec. 28, 1880, died; Anna Sophia b. July 23, 1882, died. Family home Weston, Idaho.
Worked on Logan temple.

LUNT, EDWARD (son of John Lunt, born 1785, Walsall, Staffordshire, Eng., and Ann Elton). Born July 10, 1815, at Walsall. Came to Utah Sept. 12, 1857, Israel Evans handcart company.
Married Harriett Wood Sept. 17, 1844 (daughter of James Wood and Ann Amos), who was born Oct. 5, 1822, and came to Utah with husband. Their children: Alfred b. Sept. 27, 1845, m. Priscilla Pitt Dec. 8, 1865; Elizabeth b. Dec. 16, 1848, m. Eli Batchelor Jan. 1, 1866; Shedrach b. Oct. 2, 1850, m. Ann Pitt May 27, 1872; Henry Lunt Jan. 16, 1878; James Edward b. Aug. 11, 1858, m. Henry Lunt Jan. 16, 1878; James Edward b. Oct. 15, 1860, m. Mary Ann Shaw Sept. 1, 1881.

LUNT, ALFRED (son of Edward Lunt and Harriet Wood). Born Sept. 27, 1845, Willenhall, Staffordshire. Came to Utah with parents.
Married Priscilla Pitt Dec. 8, 1865 (daughter of John Pitt and Caroline Wright, pioneers 1866, Daniel Thompson's oxteam company), who was born Oct. 10, 1846, Willenhall, Eng., and came to Utah 1864, W. S. Warren company. Their children: Elizabeth Ann b. Nov. 17, 1866, m. Charles H. Grace; Shedrach James b. Oct. 26, 1869, m. Sarah Florence McCune; George William b. July 23, 1872, m. Rose Etta Morhan; Alfred Oscar b. Dec. 4, 1874, m. Jeanette Sperry; John Edgar b. May 3, 1880, m. Lydia Jane Kendall. Family home Nephi, Utah.
Member 71st quorum seventy; high priest. City councilman of Nephi six years. Helped bring immigrants to Utah 1864; Black Hawk war veteran. Rancher; sheepman; farmer.

LUNT, HENRY (son of Randle Lunt and Ann Morgan both of Midley Hall Farm, Eng.). Born July 20, 1824, Midley, Hall Cheshire, Eng.). Came to Utah October, 1850.
Married Ellen Whittaker March 25, 1852, Parowan, Utah (daughter of James Whittaker and Rachel Taylor both of Heywood, Lancashire, Eng., pioneers 1851, W. W. Phelps company), who was born June 6, 1830.
Married Mary Ann Wilson Oct. 7, 1857, Salt Lake City, who was born Jan. 19, 1832, Carlisle, Cumberland, Eng. Came to Utah 1857, Jesse B. Martin company. Their children: Henrietta Wilson; Ellen Eva W.; Henry Whittaker; Randle W.; William W.; Florence W.; Violet W.; Maude. Family home Cedar City, Utah.
Member 1854-57; bishop of Cedar City. County selectman; mayor and city councilman, Cedar City; member of legislature and state militia. Farmer. Died Jan. 22, 1902, Pacheco, Old Mexico.

LUNT, HENRY W, (son of Henry Lunt and Mary Ann Wilson). Born Jan. 25, 1863, Cedar City, Utah.
Married Rosella Hunter Dec. 10, 1884, St. George, Utah (daughter of George Hunter and Mary Muir, both of Scotland, pioneers 1850). She was born Feb. 25, 1866. Their children: Henry Hunter b. Nov. 24, 1885; George b. June 8, 1887; Raymond b. Nov. 19, 1889; Wallace b. July 14, 1891; Mary Ellen H. b. May 16, 1895; Corris H. b. June 18, 1897; June H. b. May 27, 1900; Harold B. b. Oct. 14, 1902; Willard H. b. Oct. 20, 1904; Rose Olive H. b. March 22, 1909. Family home, Cedar City.
Missionary to England 1892-94; bishop of Cedar City. County commissioner; mayor; city councilman; state senator. Farmer and stockraiser.

LUTZ, FREDRICK. Born Feb. 25, 1838. Came to Utah 1865.
Married Fannie Barton April 10, 1871, Salt Lake City (daughter of William Barton and Mary Ann Taylor of Salt Lake City, pioneers 1856, Edward Martin company). She was born Aug. 7, 1852, Southport, Eng.; came to Utah with parents. Only child: Fredrick P. b. March 6, 1872, d. aged 3.
Wells Fargo mailcarrier across the plains. Died Sept. 20, 1911, Salt Lake City.

LYBBERT, CHRISTIAN FREDERICK BERNHARD (son of Joachim Frederick Lybbert of Mecklenburg, Schwerin, Germany, and Margrethe Elsebethe Wilkelmine Evart of Denmark). Born Nov. 6, 1834, Flade, Hjorring, Denmark. Came to Utah Nov. 5, 1865, Miner G. Atwood company.
Married Mary M. Andersen June 15, 1862, Copenhagen, Denmark (daughter of Christian Andersen and Anna Christine Petersen), who was born May 27, 1833, and came to Utah with husband. There were no children.
Married Antonete M. Olsen March 10, 1866, Salt Lake City (daughter of Christian Olsen and Christine Halvarsen, pioneers 1868). She was born Jan. 6, 1845, Christiania, Norway, and came to Utah with husband. Their children: Enoch C. b. Nov. 26, 1867, m. Augusta O. Rinnon June 11, 1902; Waldemar C. b. Oct. 21, 1869, m. Ella Dora

Darnell Nov. 10, 1892; Emma T. b. Aug. 8, 1871, d. infant; Emma Theresa b. April 11, 1873, m. Winfield S. Hullinger, Jr. Jan. 1, 1895; Rachel C. b. July 27, 1875, m. John W. Bascom Jan. 1, 1895; Mary Sophia b. Sept. 25, 1877, m. William P. Merrill Oct. 5, 1896; Daniel Evert b. Oct. 26, 1879, m. Fannie M. De Friez Aug. 19, 1903; Charles Joachim b. Oct. 19, 1881, m. La Pearl Cook June 19, 1909; John Isaac b. March 6, 1884, m. Verda Elmira Timmons Sept. 23, 1903; Jacob Norman b. April 24, 1886, m. Elma Goodrich; Esther b. Feb. 2, 1890, m. Daniel F. Olsen. Family home Naples, Utah.

Priest; missionary to Randers June 1854; clerk of Aalborg conference and later of the pastorate, district and branch. While doing missionary work was called into the service of his native land as a soldier, and while serving in the army remained clerk of the Copenhagen conference. Member of the choir. Returned to Salt Lake City Nov. 9, 1865.

LYMAN, AMASA MASON (third son of Roswell Lyman, who was born in 1784, Lebanon, and Martha Mason, born June 7, 1787, at Grafton, both in New Hampshire—married March 14, 1810). He was born March 30, 1813, at Lyman, Grafton county, N. H. Came to Utah July 24, 1847, Brigham Young company.

Married Louisa Maria Tanner June 10, 1835 (daughter of John Tanner and Lydia Stewart—married 1801, Greenwich, N. Y.; former a pioneer Oct. 17, 1848, Amasa M. Lyman company; latter died May 31, 1825, Bolton, Warren county, N. Y.). She was born Nov. 28, 1818, and came to Utah with husband. Their children: Matilda b. Nov. 14, 1836, m. Isaac P. Carter Oct. 6, 1856; Francis Marion b. Jan. 12, 1840, m. Rhoda Ann Taylor Nov. 18, 1857 (see genealogy); Ruth Adelia b. Aug. 1, 1843, d. Feb. 27, 1848; Amasa Mason, jr. b. Feb. 22, 1846, m. Hannah Olive Felshaw Jan. 6, 1867; Maria Louisa b. May 8, 1849, m. William Clayton Oct. 3, 1866; Lelia Deseret b. Jan. 21, 1852, m. Edwin Bartholomew Dec. 25, 1871; Love Josephine b. April 25, 1854, m. Hyrum S. Coombs June 23, 1872; Agnes Hilda b. Dec. 5, 1857, m. George C. Veile Dec. 16, 1877. Family home Fillmore, Utah.

Married Caroline Ely Partridge Sept. 6, 1844, Nauvoo, Ill. (daughter of Edward Partridge and Lydia Clisbee— former died May 27, 1840, Nauvoo, Ill.; latter a pioneer Oct. 17, 1848). She was born Jan. 8, 1827, Painesville, Ohio, and came to Utah with mother and husband. Their children: Martha Lydia b. April 1, 1853, m. Alvin Roper Oct. 26, 1874; Frederick Rich b. Oct. 12, 1856, m. Ann Elizabeth Lovell Dec. 6, 1875; Annie b. July 2, 1860, m. Peter Anderson Oct. 9, 1882; Walter Clisbee b. Oct. 1, 1863, m. Sylvia Ann Lovell Oct. 4, 1883; Harriet Jane b. Aug. 17, 1866, m. John Edmond Lovell Oct. 4, 1883. Family home, Fillmore.

Married Eliza Maria Partridge Sept. 28, 1844, Nauvoo, Ill. (daughter of Edward Partridge and Lydia Clisbee), who was born April 20, 1820, Painesville, Ohio; came to Utah with husband's company. Their children: Don Carlos b. July 14, 1846, d. Dec. 12, 1846, Florence, Neb.; Platte DeAlton b. Aug. 20, 1848, m. Adelia Robinson May 18, 1867; Carlie Eliza b. Aug. 1, 1851, m. Thomas Callister Feb. 14, 1878; Joseph Alvin b. Dec. 13, 1856, m. Nellie Grayson Roper April 25, 1878; Lucy Zina b. Aug. 26, 1860, m. Lemuel Hardison Redd Oct. 31, 1883. Family resided Fillmore, Salt Lake City and Oak City, Utah.

Married Cornelia Eliza Leavitt Nov. 14, 1844, Nauvoo, Ill. (daughter of Enoch Virgil Leavitt and Abigail Leonora Snow, former pioneer Oct. 17, 1848, Amasa M. Lyman company). She was born Jan. 5, 1825, Warren, Ohio. Their children: Lorenzo Snow b. Nov. 6, 1851, m. Zuriah Rowley Nov. 21, 1874; Henry Elias b. July 4, 1854, m. Ina Caldwell Dec. 21, 1883. Family resided Salt Lake City and Parowan, Utah.

Married Diontha Walker in July, 1845, Nauvoo, Ill. (daughter of Oliver Walker and Nancy Crispy, pioneers Oct. 17, 1848, Amasa M. Lyman company). She was born March 10, 1816, Dayton, Ohio, and died childless. Family resided Salt Lake City and Minersville, Utah.

Married Paulina Eliza Phelps Jan. 16, 1846, Nauvoo, Ill. (daughter of Morris Phelps and Laura Clark), who was born March 20, 1827, Lawrenceville, Ill. Their children: Oscar Morris b. Dec. 16, 1847, m. Phebe Medora Benson April 5, 1869; Mason Roswell b. July 5, 1851, d. May 31, 1866, Parowan, Utah; Clark b. Oct. 5, 1853, d. April 7, 1854, Salt Lake City; Charles Rich b. Feb. 18, 1857, m. Barbara Alice Ward July 8, 1876; William Horn b. Feb. 19, 1859, m. Julia Hannah McGregor Oct. 26, 1888; Solon Ezra b. Aug. 9, 1863, m. Luella Ward Feb. 8, 1884; Laura Paulina b. Aug. 19, 1865, m. Porter van der Clark Dec. 21, 1883. Family resided Salt Lake City and Parowan, Utah.

Married Priscilla Turley Jan. 17, 1846, Nauvoo, Ill. (daughter of Theodore Turley and Frances Kimberley, former pioneer Oct. 17, 1849, ᴀ M. Lyman company). She was born June 1, 1829, Toronto, Canada. Their children: Theodore Kimberley b. April 13, 1853, m. Elizabeth Duggins Dec. 29, 1875; Ira Depo b. April 30, 1855, m. Elizabeth Ann Rowley Jan. 1, 1878; Isaac Newton b. Oct. 18, 1857, d. Sept. 27, 1858, Parowan; Albert Augustus b. Oct. 5, 1859, d. Oct. 25, 1860, Minersville, Utah; Stephen Alonzo b. Aug. 16, 1863, m. Ellen King Dec. 24, 1887; Frances Priscilla b. July 21, 1868, m. Robert Edward Barry April 20, 1884. Family resided Salt Lake City and Fillmore, Utah, and San Bernardino, Cal.

Married Lydia Partridge Feb. 7, 1853, Salt Lake City (daughter of Edward Partridge and Lydia Clisbee), who was born May 8, 1830, Painesville, Ohio. Their children: Edward Leo b. Jan. 4, 1857, m. Mary Maranda Callister Nov. 14, 1878; Ida Evelyn b. March 28, 1859, m. Hans

Joseph Nielson Nov. 30, 1881; Frank Arthur b. Sept. 9, 1863, d. April 26, 1864, Salt Lake City; Lydia May b. May 1, 1865, m. Kumin Treharne Jones Nov. 2, 1882. Family resided Salt Lake City and Fillmore, Utah.

He was early placed upon his own resources, for when he was about two years old his father left home for the western country, never to return, and is supposed to have died in New Orleans.

At the age of eighteen, just a year after the organization of the church, he became somewhat thoughtful on religious subjects. In the spring of 1832, Lyman E. Johnson and Orson Pratt visited the neighborhood where he lived and Amasa believed in their doctrine and was baptised by the former on April 27, 1832, being confirmed the following day by Orson Pratt.

On account of his joining the Latter-day Saints ill feeling arose against him, in his uncle's family where he resided, and for that reason he set off for a journey with only scanty provisions and clothing. He arrived at Lyons, Wayne Co., New York, and hired out to Thomas Lackey, who, by-the-bye, was the man who purchased Martin Harris' farm when he sold it to raise money for printing the Book of Mormon. He only stopped here a couple of weeks, and then made his way to Buffalo, and thence to Cleveland, Ohio, and later to Hyrum, Portage Co., Ohio, where he was received by Father Johnson and family. He soon met the Prophet Joseph Smith and was given a living testimony by the spirit that he was a man of God. He was called on a mission on the 23d of August, 1832, by the Prophet Joseph, who ordained him an elder, and labored during the following winter with Zerubabel Snow in southern Ohio and Cable Co., Virginia. They returned to Kirtland early the following spring having added forty souls to the church.

He filled a second mission with William F. Cahoon, leaving March 21, 1833, and journeying as far as Chautauqua and Cattaraugus counties, New York. During this mission he held 150 meetings and there were about a hundred souls added to the church. While on this mission the call reached him to go to Kirtland. Arriving in Kirtland on May 1st, 1834, a few days later he joined Zion's Camp at New Portage, and traveled with this organization to Missouri, suffering all the privations and difficulties of that famous trip. Having attended the dedication of the Kirtland temple, in the spring of 1836, in company with Elder Nathan Tanner he filled another mission that year to the state of New York.

In 1837, he went to Missouri and there experienced all the persecutions to which those of his belief were subjected. His family in the meantime were enabled to move to Illinois and he joined them in March, 1839. During that year he made two dangerous trips to Missouri for the purpose of assisting Elder Parley P. Pratt and his fellow-prisoners and to attend to unsettled business.

He settled in Iowa in the spring of 1840, building a cabin for his family on the half-breed Indian tract in Lee county. In 1841, with his family, he moved to Nauvoo and later was called on a mission to northern Illinois and Wisconsin. He was subsequently directed in company with Peter Hawa to go on a mission to secure means to build the Nauvoo temple and Nauvoo House, going as far east as Indiana.

In the spring of 1842 he was sent on a mission to the state of Tennessee with Horace K. Whitney and others. On the 20th of August, 1842, Elder Lyman was ordained to the apostleship, and the following month sent on a mission to southern Illinois in company with Elder George A. Smith, being a part of the time in company with Brigham Young and Heber C. Kimball.

He went through many of the privations and trials at Nauvoo and filled many other missions in the states around about. In the spring of 1844 he went to Nauvoo to attend the April Conference, and it was here determined that he should go to Boston. He had proceeded only as far as Cincinnati (remaining until July), when he received the news of the massacre of the prophet and patriarch, Joseph and Hyrum Smith. He was recalled to Nauvoo, arriving there July 21, 1844, and was present at the meeting at Nauvoo on August 8th following when the twelve apostles were acknowledged as the presiding quorum of the church. He rendered efficient aid during the exodus of his people from Illinois in 1846, and was one of the pioneers of Utah in 1847.

In 1848 he led a large company of immigrants to the great Salt Lake valley. In 1850 he went on a mission to California, returning September 30th, of that year, and in 1851 he and Apostle Charles C. Rich were appointed to lead a company of settlers to California. This company left Payson, March 24, 1851, and arrived at San Bernardino the following June. It was a few months later, in September, that the ranch of San Bernardino was purchased, and a settlement was located. This was continued until 1857, when the Johnston army-Echo Canyon hostilities caused it to disintegrate when most of the inhabitants had gone to Utah.

In 1860 he filled a mission to Great Britain, arriving July 27th, and in connection with Apostle Charles C. Rich presided over the European mission until March 14, 1862, when he returned home. It was while on this mission that he delivered the remarkable sermon at Dundee, Scotland, March 16, 1862, in which he denied the atonement of the Savior. Some time later he was summoned to answer the charge of having preached false doctrine, and he acknowledged his error, and signed a document January 23, 1867, in which he asked forgiveness of the authorities. Soon after, however, he again preached in the same strain, and was finally excommunicated May 12, 1870. He died at Fillmore, Millard county, Utah, February 4, 1877.

National bank; regent of the university of Utah; member of the capitol commissions and president of the genealogical society of Utah; president of the board of trustees of the L. D. S. university.

LUND, ANTHONY CANUTE (son of Anthon Henrik Lund and Sarah Ann Peterson). Born Feb. 26, 1871, Ephraim, Utah.
Married Laura Greaves Aug. 14, 1895, Ephraim, Utah. Their children: Weber Anthony b. July 16, 1896; Grant b. Oct. 2, 1898.
Married Cornelia Sorenson Dec. 24, 1902, Manti, Utah (daughter of Neils Christian Sorenson of Gunnison, Utah, and Sarah Christina Carlson, born July 31, Spanish Fork, Utah), who was born March 8, 1882. Their children: Anthon Henrik b. Dec. 11, 1903; Herschel Sorenson b. Feb. 10, 1907; Sarah Cornelia b. Sept. 23, 1909; Max Welton b. July 21, 1910. Families reside Provo, Utah.

LUND, HENRY C. (son of Anthon H. Lund and Sarah Ann Peterson). Born April 15, 1870, Ephraim, Utah.
Married Julia A. Farnsworth Sept. 13, 1893, Salt Lake City (daughter of P. T. Farnsworth and Julia P. Murdock), who was born Nov. 6, 1874, Beaver, Utah. Their children: Henry C. F. b. Sept. 5, 1899; Philo F. b. Jan. 9, 1901; Anthon F. b. Oct. 10, 1903, died; John C. F. b. March 3, 1907; Alton F. b. Jan. 29, 1909; Julia F. b. Oct. 16, 1911. Family home, Salt Lake City.
Member 104th quorum seventies; member general board of Y. M. M. I. A. Lawyer.

LUND, HERBERT J. (son of Anthon H. Lund and Sarah Ann Peterson). Born Jan. 17, 1877, Ephraim, Utah.
Married Emma Jensen May 15, 1912, Manti, Utah (daughter of James Iver Jensen and Inger Nielsen Syndegard of Denmark. Came to Utah September, 1898, independent company). She was born June 29, 1878. Their children: Sarah Inger b. June 26, 1914; Herbert J. b. July 16, 1915; Richard b. March 3, 1917.
Member seventy; missionary to southern states 1898-1901; Physician and surgeon state prison; member of state board of medical examiners. Physician and surgeon.

LUND, OTHNIEL F. (son of Anthon H. Lund and Sarah Ann Peterson). Born Feb. 18, 1880, Ephraim, Utah.
Married Mabel Hall Jan. 20, 1905, Salt Lake City (daughter of Edwin Hall and Clara Kingsbury), who was born 1885. Their children: Robert b. July 28, 1907; Elmo b. Feb. 15, 1912. Family home Ephraim, Utah.
Deputy treasurer of Salt Lake county four years. School teacher. Farmer.

LUND, ROBERT C. (son of Wilson and Eliza B. Lund). He was born May 15, 1847, New Diggins, Wis. Came to Utah 1857.
Married Mary A. Romney 1870.
Settled at Salt Lake City; moved to St. George 1861. Telegraph operator Deseret telegraph company, at St. George, Utah, and Pioche, Nev.; Wells Fargo express agent at St. George and Silver Reef, Utah; chairman board of county commissioners, Washington county; served in territorial legislature; member and president state board of equalization. Died Jan. 31, 1918.

LUNDBLAD, HANS. Born Sept. 21, 1810, in Sweden. Came to Utah 1859 with oxteam.
Married Margie Mortensen in Sweden, daughter of Andrew Mortensen and Anna Pahlson of Sweden, who was born Sept. 10, 1829. Their children: Johanna b. 1851; Christina b. Mary Christina b. ; Joseph; Ann; Charlotte b. m. Joseph Simkins; John Wm. and Joseph and Emma Helena (died) Ellen, m. John E. Palmer. Family home Beaver, Utah.
President Scandinavian mission before emigrating to America. Settled first in San Pete county, later to 1861, moved to Washington county. Farmer by trade. Died June 28, 1898, Beaver, Utah.

LUNDHOLM, ANDREW G. son of Anders E. Lundholm and ... Louisa Lindberg of Sweden. Born May ..., 1850, ... Sweden. Came to Utah August 1888, working in ... Pacific railroad.
Married Julieva Christina Lundstrom, in Sweden, who led Jan. 15, 1914, Santaquin, Utah. They had two daughters, both of whom died in Sweden.
Married Louisa Alfreds May 27, 1913, Salt Lake temple. Settled at Santaquin in 1888. Teacher; president L.D.S. Sunday School; high councilor in Juab stake. Engaged in farming at Santaquin, at which he was very successful. Died Feb. 15, 1915, Santaquin.

LUNDQUIST, AXEL THEODORE. son of Carl Sigfus Lundquist ... and Johanna Mathilda Efverstrom, born of Stockholm, Sweden. He was born Feb. 1, 1868, Stockholm. Came to Utah October, 1891, Alpine, Utah. ...
Married Signe Tegen Nov. 17, 1893, daughter of Anders Tegen of Oscar, Sweden, and Sarah Carlson, who was born ... and ... deceased. Their ...
Jan. 17, 1897, ... same year. Alexander Theodore b. Sept. ...

on of Caleb Lyons and Sarah
25, 1835. Came to Utah 1849.
869, Salt Lake City (daugh-
l Lydia Johnson, pioneers
851. Their children: Oscar
s; Abraham M., m. Jenetta
Ferbert A., m. Maude M.
y C., m. George Criddle;
dith. m. Frank Barnum;
Lake City.
  school superintendent;
ce of peace; postmaster.
nty; actor; farmer and
Summit Co., Utah.

Lythgoe, born July 12,
ury, Lancaster, Eng.,
5, died July 23, 1885,
iter, Eng.). He was
  Came to Utah Sept.
npany.
4, Manchester, Eng.
eth Singleton), who
ncaster, Eng., and
r children, born at
Sept. 22, 1865, m.
m. Mary Harston;
  Born at Henefer.
m. James Burton;
Elizabeth S. Jan.
Santaquin, Utah

Salt Lake City
and Ann Miller,
t, 1827, in Lan-
enefer.
852, Salt Lake
Vealding, born
  died Nov. 3,
, Eng. Their
2, 1883; Her-

Logan, Utah
etta Borsen,
he was born
ormer mar-
on Feb. 17,
c. 24, 1882;
884; Joseph
t Henefer;
y 2, 1895;
a Wilcox
14; Esther

ty; high
d bless-
ly name
ation in

cker-
1812,
rmon

' Jo-
was
l, m.
bert
June
, m.
Dan-

ther
in

Alb
4.

ria
13,
outh

assist-
School
n war,
ailroads
in Canal
28, 1912.

LYMAN, FRANCIS MARION (son of Amasa M. Lyman and Louisa Maria Tanner). Born Jan. 12, 1840, Goodhope, Ill.
Married Rhoda Ann Taylor Nov. 18, 1857, San Bernardino, Cal. (daughter of James Taylor and Ann Stanley Kingston, former died in Australia, latter a pioneer in February 1858, Capt. Bell Company). She was born Aug. 29, 1840, New South Wales, Australia. Their children: Rhoda Alice b. April 26, 1859, m. Charles R. McBride Nov. 20, 1875; Ellen Taylor b. Jan. 7, 1861, m. Alfred F. Hanks Jan. 24, 1878; Francis Marion Jr. b. Sept. 25, 1863, m. Betsy Ann Gowans Oct. 16, 1889; Edna Jane b. Sept. 8, 1866, m. Daniel D. Houtz June 23, 1886; Louisa Ann b. Dec. 28, 1868, m. William Henry King April 17, 1889; Mary Crismon b. July 29, 1871, m. Ephraim G. Gowans June 1, 1893; Lois Victoria b. Sept. 27, 1876, m. Phares Wells Dunyon Aug. 9, 1899; Ada Alta b. July 4, 1878, d. Nov. 6, 1881, Tooele, Utah; Hilda Olive b. Jan. 25, 1881, d. Jan. 21, 1882, Tooele. Family resided Beaver, Fillmore, Tooele and Salt Lake City, Utah.
Married Clara Caroline Callister Oct. 4, 1869, Salt Lake City (daughter of Thomas Callister and Caroline Smith, pioneers 1847), who was born April 18, 1850, Salt Lake City. Their children: Richard Roswell b. Nov. 23, 1870, m. Amy Cassandra Brown Sept. 9, 1896; George Albert b. Nov. 14, 1873, m. Susan Mae King Sept. 25, 1901, Salt Lake City; Lucy Smith b. Aug. 5, 1876, m. George Arthur Partridge Nov. 14, 1895; Ida b. Aug. 2, 1878, m. Eric Herman Anderson Nov. 18, 1908; John Callister b. Sept. 24, 1880, m. Zella Jane Brown Oct. 15, 1909; Amy b. Dec. 10, 1882; Don Callister b. June 21, 1886, d. Sept. 24, 1892, Manassa, Colo. Family resided Fillmore and Tooele, Utah, and Manassa, Colo.
Married Susan Delilah Callister Oct. 9, 1884, Salt Lake City (daughter of Thomas Callister and Helen Marr Clark, pioneers 1847), who was born May 25, 1862, Salt Lake City. Their children: Clark Callister b. July 4, 1891, d. same day; Waldo Wilcken b. March 2, 1893, Salt Lake City, Grant Herbert b. May 10, 1896, Fillmore; Floe b. July 6, 1898, Fillmore; Rudger Clawson b. Nov. 2, 1900, d. May 17, 1909; Helen Marr b. Oct. 30, 1904, Fillmore.
When Joseph Smith and his brother Hyrum were assassinated at Carthage jail, in his native state of Illinois, President Francis M. Lyman was four and one-half years old. Only as a child would know and remember such great personages was it possible for him to know them, but in his mature manhood he has had a thorough knowledge of all their successors and through them a better understanding of those who have gone before. At home and abroad for fifty years, President Lyman has been in the missionary service, beginning the work at the age of twenty. He has officiated in the offices of elder, seventy, high priest and an apostle during the past thirty years of his life. Three missions in Europe, occupying all together seven and one-half years, have been filled by him.
Elder Lyman's childhood was spent in Illinois, Indiana, Nebraska, Utah and California. For six years he lived at San Bernardino, Cal., and he was married there in 1857. During that year he returned to Utah, it being the time of the Echo Canyon imbroglio, and resided later in Cedar City, Beaver, and Farmington. After his first mission in 1860-2, he located with his father and family, under the direction of President Brigham Young, at Fillmore, and it was his home for fourteen years. During this time he engaged enthusiastically in all the activities of the people of Millard county, being much of the time their public and official servant.
On March 23, 1866, he was appointed assistant assessor of internal revenue for District No. 6 of Utah, by Hugh McCulloch, then secretary of the U. S. treasury. He served in this capacity under the following assessors: Col. J. C. Little, A. L. Chetiain, John E. Smith, Richard V. Morris, and Dr. John P. Taggart.
It was in 1866 that Elder Lyman with his father built the O. K. Flour Mills of Fillmore, and he was largely engaged in the flour and grain trade as well as in many more business enterprises.
In September, 1867, he was commissioned by Governor Durkee as lieutenant colonel of the first regiment of militia in the Pauvan military district. Two years later, 1869, he was elected a member of the house of representatives of the general assembly of the state of Deseret for Millard county and subsequently represented that county in the territorial legislature of Utah in the 17th, 18th, 22d and 23d sessions, and Tooele county in the 24th and 25th sessions. In the 25th session (1882), he acted as speaker of the house, while President Joseph F. Smith was president of the council (now senate).
He served as high councilor in Millard stake about six years, and in political activities occupied the positions of district attorney, superintendent of common schools, county and probate clerk and recorder. He was also secretary and treasurer of the county cooperative companies, and did the land business of the county, such as homesteading, preempting and the en..ing of townsites with Probate Judge Edward Partridge and Mayor Joseph V. Robison. It was during the organization of the stakes of Zion by President Brigham Young in 1877 [died Aug. 29 of that year], that Elder Lyman was called to preside over the Tooele stake of Zion when it was organized by [Apostle] President John Taylor and the other apostles on June 24, 1877. Later he was chosen by election of the people as a representative of Tooele county, and county clerk and recorder, serving in those positions about four years. He had a most thrilling experience in the fight with the liberals, and it was during his term of office that the people succeeded in redeeming Tooele county from their unrighteous rule.
With Elders Erastus Snow, Brigham Young, Jr., and eight others, he went on a mission, in 1880, to San Juan county,

Utah, and into Colorado, New Mexico and Arizona. During this trip they traveled 1,800 miles with teams. It was during this year and while at Orderville, Kane county, on the 10th of October, that he was chosen at the general semiannual conference of the church, one of the council of the twelve apostles, John Henry Smith being chosen at the same time. Both were ordained by President John Taylor and Wilford Woodruff on the 27th of October, 1880, in the Endowment House.
He filled a second mission to Europe in 1873-4-5, just before moving to Tooele. Since he was chosen an apostle he has been engaged exclusively in the spiritual and temporal welfare of the people of the church. He has visited the stakes of Zion over and over again and given counsel and advice to the people serving towards their spiritual growth and strength. In a temporal way he has served as a director in such institutions as Z. C. M. I., Zion's Savings Bank and Trust Company, Consolidated Wagon and Machine Company, Home Fire Insurance Company, Heber J. Grant & Company, Deseret National Bank, Beneficial Life Insurance Company, Zion's Coöperative Home Building and Real Estate Company, president and director Utah Pioneers Book Publishing Company, etc.
After the death of President Brigham Young, Jr., in 1903, he was sustained president of the council of the twelve and was blessed and set apart for that presidency in the temple by President Joseph F. Smith and his counselors and on the 7th of July, 1904, since which time he has filled another mission to Europe, presiding over the European mission, May, 1901, to January, 1904, besides laboring diligently in his office and calling at home. While on this last mission, he not only visited many of the European countries, including Russia, but also the Holy Land, and Egypt, and wherever he went he turned the keys for the establishment of liberty and the preaching of the Gospel. His traveling companions were Elders Sylvester Q. and Joseph J. Cannon.

LYMAN, FRANCIS MARION, JR. (son of Francis Marion Lyman and Rhoda Ann Taylor). Born Sept. 25, 1863, at Fillmore.
Married Betsy Ann Gowans Oct. 16, 1889, Logan, Utah (daughter of Hugh S. and Betsy Gowans, pioneers 1856, Milo Andrus company). She was born Dec. 7, 1864, Tooele, Utah. Their children: Manon b. Nov. 30, 1890, m. Charles Colson Smith April 16, 1909; Merl b. June 5, 1892, m. Irene Gray Nov. 6, 1909; Hugh Marion b. March 7, 1894; Taylor b. Dec. 14, 1895; Coral b. Feb. 6, 1898; Frank Gowans b. June 23, 1901; Donald Gowans b. Jan. 2, 1905. Family resided Tooele and Salt Lake City, Utah.
Civil and mining engineer and surveyor. At 20 years of age went on a 3 years' mission to Germany and traveled extensively in Russia, Palestine and Egypt, as well as in Turkey and Italy. Seventy.

LYMAN, RICHARD ROSWELL (son of Francis M. Lyman and Clara C. Callister). Born Nov. 23, 1870, Fillmore.
Married Amy Brown Sept. 9, 1896, Salt Lake City (daughter of John Brown and Margaret Zimmerman of Pleasant Grove, Utah, pioneers July 24, 1847, Brigham Young company). She was born Feb. 7, 1872. Their children: Wendell Brown b. Dec. 18, 1897; Margaret b. Sept. 15, 1903. Family home, Salt Lake City.
High priest; superintendent of M. I. A. of Salt Lake stake 1894-1902; supervisor of parents' classes of Ensign stake 1907. Vice chairman of State road commission 1909. Professor of civil engineering at University of Utah; civil and consulting engineer. Director in Inter-Mountain Life Insurance Co., and also in Delta State bank.

LYMAN, WALDO WILLKEN (son of Francis M. Lyman and Susan Delilah Callister). He was born March 2, 1893, Salt Lake City.

LYMAN, AMASA MASON, JR. (son of Amasa Mason Lyman and Louisa Maria Tanner). Born Feb. 22, 1846, Nauvoo, Ill. Came to Utah 1848.
Married Hannah Olive Felshaw Jan. 6, 1867, Fillmore, Utah (daughter of William Felshaw and Mary Harriet Gilbert), who was born Nov. 2, 1848, Callands Grove, Iowa. Their children: Olive Ethel b. Oct. 30, 1867, m. Seth Taft Sept. 23, 1885; Amasa Mason b. June 5, 1870, m. Elizabeth Jane Moosman Nov. 7, 1896; William Milton b. May 12, 1872, d. July 9, 1872.
Married Cynthia Wright Oct. 9, 1872, Fillmore, Utah (daughter of Jonathan C. Wright and Cynthia Martin), who was born Aug. 12, 1851, Big Cottonwood, Utah. Their children: Sarah b. May 1, 1873, d. May 1, 1873; Rachel b. May 1, 1873, d. May 1, 1873; Willard Henry b. April 9, 1874, m. Hildegard Sophia Schoenfeld Nov. 15, 1893.
Married Rosannah Reynolds May 16, 1877, Panguitch, Utah (daughter of John Reynolds and Mary Haskin), who children: Vern b. Jan. 5, 1878, m. Mary Wilcock Oct. 7, 1909; Haskin b. Feb. 20, 1880, m. Ruth Elizabeth Peters Dec. 12, 1901; Reynolds b. June 4, 1882; Mary b. July 20, 1884, m. John S. Hiskey May 12, 1902; Maria b. Aug. 9, 1886, m. Volney Emery King Aug. 9, 1904; Francis b. Nov. 28, 1888; Maurice b. Nov. 27, 1892, m. Inez Merl Shaw Oct. 9, 1911; Amasa b. Oct. 22, 1894, m. Fanny May Stewart Jan. 29, 1913.
Settled at Little Cottonwood 1848; moved to San Bernandino, Cal. 1851; returned to Utah 1855; and to California again in 1856. In 1859 went again to Utah and settled at Cedar; moved to Beaver 1860. In 1862 drove a ten mule team to Sacramento, Cal., for his uncle Freeman Tanner;

in 1864 went with Captain John R. Murdock to the Missouri river with a six mule team to assist a company of immigrants to Utah. Served in the Black Hawk Indian war under James C. Owens. Assisted in the erection of the O. K. flouring mill at Fillmore 1866; in 1879 and 1880 went with a company of Saints into San Juan county and assisted in the construction of the road known as the "Hole in the Rock," where the wagons were let down with ropes. Moved to Rabbit Valley in 1883, where he resided 7 years, assisting in developing the country; from here he went to Boulder, and resided there 20 years and did much in reclaiming the country and making it habitable; later he went to Teasdale, where he now resides.

LYON, ALBERT C. (son of John B. Lyon and Arvilla Olcott of Lunenburg, Vt.). Born Sept. 15, 1832, at Lunenburg. Came to Utah Aug. 17, 1859, Harlow Redfield company.
Married Susan R. Redfield Sept. 27, 1860, Salt Lake City (daughter of Harlow Redfield and Alpha P. Foster of Salt Lake City, pioneers Sept. 3, 1850, Aaron Johnson company). She was born Aug. 7, 1839, in Illinois. Their children: Clarissa A. b. Sept. 2, 1862, d. infant; Alpha b. Oct. 19, 1866, d. infant; Rachel E. b. July 31, 1869, d. aged eight; Albert M. b. June 24, 1873, d. aged four. Family home, Salt Lake City.
Elder. Farmer.

LYON, JOHN (son of John Lyon and Jennette McCarter of Kilmarnock, Scotland). Born March 3, 1803, Kilmarnock. Came to Utah Sept. 26, 1853, Jacob Gates company.
Married Janet Thompson Dec. 4, 1825, Kilmarnock (daughter of Robert Thompson and Janet Lamont), who was born March 15, 1809. Their children: Thomas, m. Mary Ann Huggins; Janet, m. George Spiers; Annie, m. Allen Hilton; Robert Thompson, d. aged 17; John, Jr., m. Mary E. Toone; Lillian, m. William C. Staines; David Carruthers, d. aged 11; Matthew Thompson, m. Sarah Shilltoe; Mary, m. Ami Shumway; Margaret, d. aged six; Agnes, d. infant; Franklin Richards, d. aged three. Family home, Salt Lake City.
Superintendent House until the dedication of the temple. Died Nov. 28, 1889, Salt Lake City.

LYON, JOHN, JR. (son of John Lyon and Janet Thompson). Born Jan. 18, 1835, Kilmarnock, Scotland. Came to Utah with father.
Married Mary Elizabeth Prosser Toone April 4, 1857, Salt Lake City (daughter of John Toone and Emma Elizabeth Prosser of Leamington, Warwickshire, Eng., pioneers 1852). She was born April 18, 1840. Their children: John James T. b. March 24, 1858; David Lyon b. Jan. 22, 1860, d. same day; William Henry b. July 5, 1861, m. Alice Brown; Matthew Thompson b. Jan. 25, 1864, m. Delia Mangum; Thomas b. Oct. 14, 1866, d. same day; Charles Ernest b. April 28, 1868; Emma Elizabeth b. Oct. 9, 1870, m. James B. Eddington; George A. b. April 6, 1873, d. April 7, 1873; Mary G. b. March 21, 1875, d. Aug. 19, 1875; Albert Edgar b. Feb. 25, 1877, m. Cora Mears; Janet M. b. Sept. 7, 1880, d. Oct. 4, 1880; Martha b. April 5, 1883, d. same day. Family home, Salt Lake City.
Member 36th quorum seventies.

LYON, WILLIAM HENRY (son of John Lyon, Jr., and Mary Elizabeth Toone). Born July 5, 1861, at Salt Lake City.
Married Alice Brown March 20, 1884, at Salt Lake City (daughter of William Brown and Sarah Apperley of Hereford, Eng., the latter came to Utah 1881). She was born March 29, 1861. Their children: William H. b. Dec. 16, 1884, d. Aug. 23, 1885; Alice D. b. Oct. 12, 1886, m. George W. Phillips March 4, 1908; John William b. Dec. 12, 1888, d. Dec. 16, 1888; Albert E. b. Dec. 20, 1889, d. Jan. 4, 1892; Archibald E. b. Jan. 14, 1892; George B. b. Dec. 26, 1893; Emma E. b. Nov. 25, 1895; Charles Leonard b. Aug. 21, 1897; Paul I. b. June 30, 1899; Mary M. b. May 24, 1902; Wilhelmina b. April 12, 1904. Family resided Salt Lake and Morgan, Utah.
Elder. Farmer.

LYON, JOSEPH DE (son of William and Hannah Tilley of Rainhill, Lancaster, Eng.). Born Feb. 19, 1836, at Rainhill. Came to Utah Sept. 7, 1855, Noah T. Guymon company.
Married Eliza Goddard April 5, 1854, Salt Lake City (daughter of George Goddard and Elizabeth Harrison of Leicester, Eng., pioneers 1852). She was born Oct. 20, 1841. Their children: Joseph Cornelius, m. Millie Foster; Mary Elizabeth, m. A. F. Angell; Katie Goddard, m. J. E. Wright; Gertrude Eliza, m. T. C. Patten; Lorretta Edna, m. Daniel Taylor; George Archibald m. Ella Grace Robertson; Ida Louise; Ruby Goddard, m. Ernest Rumell; Elsie Goddard, m. Harry Anderson. Family home, Salt Lake City.
Married Eliza Ann Rumell (daughter of John Rumell and Elizabeth Gray). No children.
High priest; bishop's counselor. Contractor; plasterer and builder.

LYON, JOSEPH CORNELIUS (son of Joseph De Lyon and Eliza Goddard). Born Jan. 31, 1865, Salt Lake City.
Married Millie Foster June 4, 1891, Salt Lake City (daughter of William and Neslen Foster of Salt Lake City). She was born 1853. Their children: Vera Foster b. April 13, 1891; Afton Foster b. Feb. 25, 1893; Marion Foster b. April 25, 1903. Family home, Salt Lake City.
Elder.

LYONS, OSCAR FITZALLEN (son of Caleb Lyons and Sarah Biglowe of Ireland). Born Dec. 25, 1838. Came to Utah 1849. Married Maria L. Marchant 1869, Salt Lake City (daughter of Abraham Marchant and Lydia Johnson, pioneers 1849). She was born Oct. 12, 1851. Their children: Oscar F.; Maria Louise, m. Albert Miles; Abraham M., m. Jenetta Wilkins; Gilbert, d. aged 9; Herbert A., m. Maude M. Herridge; Elbert, d. infant; Amy C., m. George Cridlle; Emory L., d. aged 18 months; Edith, m. Frank Barnum; Hazel; Gladys. Family home, Salt Lake City.
Missionary to England; Sunday school superintendent; ward clerk. County attorney; justice of peace; postmaster. Telephone operator in Summit county; actor; farmer and stockraiser. Died Jan. 1908, Peoa, Summit Co., Utah.

LYTHGOE, JAMES (son of Thomas Lythgoe, born July 12, 1905, died Sept. 30, 1887, at Pendlebury, Lancaster, Eng., and Esther Willcock, born April, 1806, died July 23, 1885, Henefer, Utah, both of Leigh, Lancaster, Eng.). He was born March 15, 1842, at Pendlebury. Came to Utah Sept. 22, 1864, Joseph S. Rawlins oxteam company.
Married Martha Heells April 17, 1864, Manchester, Eng. (daughter of Thomas Heells and Elizabeth Singleton), who was born Dec. 12, 1840, Breathmet, Lancaster, Eng., and died Aug. 14, 1881, Henefer, Utah. Their children, born at Porterville, Morgan Co., Utah: Joseph Sept. 22, 1865, m. Emily Harris; Thomas b. Oct. 5, 1867, m. Mary Harston; James Heells Jan. 24, 1870, m. May King. Born at Henefer, Summit county; Mary Jane April 5, 1872, m. James Burton; Edward Dec. 18, 1874, m. Mary Johnston; Elizabeth S. Jan. 14, 1880, m. Dée Roy Keithley. Born Santaquin, Utah county; John July 13, 1877, m. Clara Hines.
Married Esther Howarth Feb. 23, 1882, Salt Lake City (daughter of John Howarth, born in 1788, and Ann Miller, born Aug. 12, 1879). She was born March 1, 1827, in Lancashire, Eng., and died Aug. 11, 1889, in Henefer.
Married Elizabeth Ann Birks Feb. 23, 1882, Salt Lake City (daughter of James Birks and Mary Wealding, born March 12, 1837, Stockport, Lancaster, Eng., died Nov. 3, 1875). She was born Jan. 22, 1859, Stockport, Eng. Their children, born at Henefer; William B. Jan. 22, 1883; Herbert Howarth Nov. 7, 1886.
Married Hannah S. Peterson Aug. 16, 1892, Logan, Utah (daughter of Neils Peterson and Annie Bolletta Bornen, latter came to Utah with oxteam company). She was born March 21, 1861, in Norway. Her children by former marriage, born at Mill Creek, Utah: Mary Johnson Feb. 17, 1880, m. Edward Lythgoe; Hyrum Johnson Dec. 24, 1882, m. Gertrude Stevens; Ephraim Johnson Feb. 18, 1884; Joseph Sept. 21, 1886. Children of James Lythgoe, born at Henefer: Martha Heells Aug. 16, 1893; Neils Peterson July 2, 1895; Brigham Aug. 3, 1897, d. March 8, 1899; Bolletta Wilcox Dec. 8, 1899; Otto Jan. 8, 1902; Sophia Dec. 5, 1904; Esther March 1, 1907.
Ordained first a church teacher; elder; seventy; high priest. Justice of peace two terms. Has received blessings from three different patriarchs; all said, "Thy name shall be handed down from generation to generation in honorable remembrance."

M

MABEY, THOMAS (son of William Mabey and Sarah Ackerman of Mapperton, Dorsetshire, Eng.). Born Oct. 15, 1812, at Mapperton. Came to Utah Oct. 5, 1862, Ansel Harmon company.
Married Esther Chalker in Dorsetshire (daughter of Joseph Chalker and Mary Hoskins of Dorsetshire). She was born May 1, 1813. Their children: Maria b. Dec. 3, 1838, m. Albert Holt; Jane b. May 13, 1841, m. William Holt; Albert b. Sept. 4, 1843, m. Celestie J. Wood; Joseph T. b. June 30, 1845, m. Sarah L. Tolman; Esther b. July 4, 1850, m. Perrigrine Sessions; John James b. Nov. 22, 1857, m. Danielette Wood. Family home Bountiful, Utah.
Farmer. Died March 8, 1863.

MABEY, ALBERT (son of Thomas Mabey and Esther Chalker). Born Sept. 4, 1843, Wraxall, Dorsetshire, Eng. Came to Utah September, 1862, Kimball and Lawrence freight train, arriving about two weeks in advance of his family.
Married Celestie J. Wood May 12, 1873, Salt Lake City (daughter of Daniel Wood and Emma M. Ellis of Bountiful, Utah, former a pioneer July 24, 1847, Brigham Young company, the latter with Appleton Harmon company). She was born March 7, 1855. Their children: Thomas b. Aug. 24, 1874, and Ellen b. Dec. 17, 1875, died; Albert b. Feb. 4, 1878, m. Aileen Irvine; James E. b. July 4, 1879, m. Mary Lewis; Esther Verena b. March 30, 1881, m. William Newbold; Samuel, died; Daniel W. b. Aug. 16, 1895; Ella Maria b. Jan. 31, 1886, m. Samuel Newbold; Myrtle b. April 13, 1890, died; Walter A. b. Aug. 10, 1893. Family home South Jordan, Utah.
Bishop's counselor South Jordan ward 1892-1900; assistant Sunday school superintendent South Jordan ward. School trustee 35th district. Veteran Black Hawk Indian war. Worked on Union, Central and Southern Pacific railroads during their construction; director in South Jordan Canal Co. since 1896. Farmer and sheepman. Died March 28, 1912.

MABEY, JOSEPH THOMAS (son of Thomas Mabey and Esther Chalker). Born June 30, 1845, Wraxall, Eng. Came to Utah Oct. 5, 1862, Ansel Harmon company.
Married Sarah L. Tolman March 13, 1871, Salt Lake City (daughter of Judson Tolman and Sarah L. Holbrook of Bountiful, Utah, pioneers Sept. 28, 1848, Brigham Young company). She was born April 7, 1855. Their children: Joseph T. b. March 24, 1872, d. Oct. 17, 1873; Judson A. b. Nov. 26, 1873, m. Ruby P. Pickett Oct. 11, 1900; William A. b. Oct. 7, 1875, m. Nancy ———— Oct. 8, 1912; Charles R. b. Oct. 4, 1877, m. Afton Rempton Dec. 20, 1905; Joseph L. b. Aug. 30, 1879, m. Margaret Payne May 18, 1906; George E. b. July 30, 1881, m. Jennie Roberts June 15, 1906; Clarence b. Dec. 23, 1883, m. Sarah Wagstaff Oct. 1905; David b. May 2, 1886, m. Nellie Pack March 20, 1913; Sarah L. b. Feb. 14, 1888, m. Jasper Hepworth June 5, 1913; Orson H. b. Aug. 9, 1890; Alice E. b. Jan. 11, 1893; Esther b. Aug. 5, 1897. Family home Bountiful, Utah.
Member 100th quorum seventies; high priest; president Y. M. M. I. A.; Sunday school superintendent. County commissioner 1904-05; constable and city marshal. Sheepraiser and gardener.

MACDUFF, JOHN ROBERTSON (son of Malcolm Macduff and Mary Morrison, of Dumfrieshire, Scotland). Born Oct. 12, 1801, at Lochgilphead, Scotland. Came to Utah Oct. 4, 1864, William S. Warren company.
Married Ellen Hancock in 1859, Nottingham, Eng. (daughter of Joseph Hancock of Chesterfield, Eng.). She was born June 19, 1813. Their children: Mary E., m. William Varley; Malcolm b. May 17, 1842, m. Jane Lord; Sarah Anna, m. Thomas Hancock; John M., d. infant; Ada A., m. Henry Rampton; Jane R. M., m. William Butler. Family home, Salt Lake City.
Seventy; missionary to England 1854-64; block teacher. Laborer. Died Oct. 17, 1871.

MACDUFF, MALCOLM (son of John Robertson Macduff and Ellen Hancock). Born May 17, 1842, Nottingham, Eng. Came to Utah in 1861.
Married Jane Lord Aug. 11, 1866, Salt Lake City (daughter of William Lord and Mary Allen of Radcliffe, Eng.; latter died en route to Utah). She was born May 25, 1846. Their children: Sarah Hannah, d. infant; John Williams; Malcolm, m. Harriet Horsley; Ellen M., m. George E. Asper; Jane, m. William Hunter; Minnie E.; Thomas W., d. infant. Family home, Salt Lake City.
Elder. Lime-burner. Died Sept. 27, 1881.

MACFARLANE, JOHN MENZIES (son of John and Annabella Sinclair Macfarlane). Born Oct. 11, 1833, Stirling, Stirlingshire, Scotland. Came to Utah in 1852, A. O. Smoot company.
Married Ann Chatterley Dec. 30, 1854, Cedar City, Utah (daughter of Joseph and Nancy Morton Chatterley). Their children: Isaac Chancey; Charlotte Ann; Annabella; John Morton; Joseph Chatterley; Ellen; Elizabeth; Kate; Daniel Sinclair; William Chatterley.
Married Agnes Eliza Heyborn Oct. 9, 1866, Salt Lake City (daughter of John and Sarah Ann Heyborn). Their children: Sarah Ann; Agnes Eliza; Robert Urie; Catherine; Archibald; Jennie Bell; Ann; Menzies John; Ernatus.
Married Elizabeth Jane Adams Jan. 30, 1879, St. George, Utah (daughter of Samuel Lorenzo Adams and Emma Jackson). Their children: Emma; Donald; Samuel Alexander; Elizabeth; Jane; John; Hubert.
Pioneers of Cedar City, Utah. Died June 4, 1892, St. George, Utah.

MARFARLANE, ISAAC CHANCEY (son of John Menzies Macfarlane and Ann Chatterley). Born Nov. 5, 1855, Cedar City, Utah.
Married Hephzibah Smith Jan. 9, 1878, St. George (daughter of Charles Smith and Eliza Mathews). Their children: Ellen; Charlotte Ann; Della Maude; Isaac; Chancey, Jr.; Hephzibah.
Married Christina Forsyth March 16, 1892, St. George, Utah (daughter of Thomas Forsyth and Mary Browit). Their children: Christina; Lauree; Donald.

MACK, JAMES (McCracken) (son of Henry McCracken and Sarah Shaw). Born Nov. 15, 1836, at Duntocker, Scotland. Came to Utah Sept. 1855, Richard Ballantyne company.
Married Elizabeth F. Miller Jan. 15, 1858, Salt Lake City (daughter of Charles Miller and Mary McGowan of Glasgow, Scotland). She was born Sept. 3, 1842. Their children: Sarah E. b. Nov. 3, 1858, died; James M. b. Dec. 14, 1864, m. Pannie Hansen; Mary E. b. Oct. 4, 1852, m. Robert L. Fishburn; Sarepta L. b. Jan. 26, 1865, m. Frank Fishburn; Henry M. b. Jan. 30, 1867, m. Alice Hanson; Charles W. b. April 3, 1869, m. Alice M. Miles; Ada J. b. Sept. 25, 1871; Moses M. b. Nov. 12, 1876, m. Charlotte Douglas; Glen H. b. March 16, 1882, m. Edith Dee; Wanda b. Jan. 9, 1886; Pearl m. Foster Wardleigh; Lettie, Margaret and David, died. Family home Smithfield, Utah.
Counselor to Bishop Geo. Farrel 12 years; county commissioner of Cache county; city councilman two terms; mayor Smithfield one term; school trustee; president and manager Ogden Milling and Elevator company; vice-president Pingree National bank, Ogden; director Thatcher Bros. bank, Logan.

MACK, HENRY M. (son of James Mack (McCracken) and Elizabeth F. Miller). Born Jan. 30, 1867, Smithfield, Utah.
Married Alice Hanson Nov. 29, 1893, Salt Lake City (daughter of William L. Hanson and Mary Jane Judson, latter a pioneer Oct. 3, 1847, Charles Coulson Rich company). She was born March 8, 1867, Salt Lake City. Only child was Helen Mar. born Nov. 14, 1894. Family home Ogden, Utah.
Deputy recorder of Salt Lake county 1890-97; secretary and treasurer, and acting manager Ogden Milling & Elevator company of Ogden, Utah.

MACKAY, THOMAS (son of Mackay and Nancy Sloan of Ireland). Born July 23, 1810, Belfast, Ireland. Came to Utah Sept. 1847, John Taylor and Edward Hunter company.
Married Ann Rodgers on the Isle of Man (daughter of Peter Rodgers and Eleanor Cowley), who was born Sept. 1799. Their children: Margaret Ellen; John b. March 18, 1834, m. Isabella Calder Oct. 6, 1855; Thomas Rogers b. 1836; Annie R. b. Sept. 23, 1837, m. David O. Calder; Charles R. b. 1839. Family home Taylorsville, Utah.
Married Charlotte James in 1853, at Salt Lake City (daughter of Mary James of Taylorsville, pioneers 1852). She was born 1830. Their children: Hyrum b. June 1, 1854, m. Sarah and Newbold; Margaret b. Jan. 31, 1855, m. Charles Wright; Joseph b. Sept. 1, 1858, m. Susan Taylor; Mary A. b. June 7, 1860, m. Albert Duncombe; David b. June 10, 1862, m. Agnes Park; Edward b. July 6, 1865, m. Mary Park; Heber b. Sept. 13, 1868, m. Hattie Todd; Charlotte b. April 1871, m. William Clark; Jane b. May 10, 1872, d. Dec. 1896. Family home, Taylorsville.
Married Sarah Franks January 1857 (daughter of Joshua Franks and Sarah Stanley of American Fork. Utah, formerly of England, latter a pioneer Sept. 12, 1861, Milo Andrus company). She was born May 9, 1832. Their children: Elizabeth Ann b. Jan. 16, 1859, m. John Richardson; William b. Oct. 11, 1860, m. Miss Park; George b. March 10, 1862, d. Jan. 12, 1870; Emma b. Sept. 28, 1863, d. Feb. 1, 1865; Samuel b. Feb. 19, 1865, m. Miss Hill; Sarah Ellen b. Oct. 2, 1866, m. Mr. Park; Daniel b. Sept. 15, 1868, m. Elizabeth Smith; Joshua A. b. May 10, 1870, m. Laura Smith; Clara b. May 16, 1874, m. Charles Davis. Family home, Taylorsville.
School trustee 1868-71. Farmer and stockraiser. Died Feb. 19, 1880, at Taylorsville.

MACKAY, JOHN (son of Thomas Mackay and Ann Rodgers). Born March 18, 1834, on the Isle of Man.
Married Isabella Calder Oct. 6, 1855, Salt Lake City (daughter of George S. Calder and Ann S. Johnston of Scotland, latter a pioneer 1851, Captain Clawson company). She was born Sept. 20, 1833. Their children: Annie Johnston b. Oct. 2, 1856, m. Mark Murphy; John Calder b. Nov. 30, 1857, m. Catherine J. Moses Nov. 8, 1883; Isabella C. b. Feb. 1, 1860; David Orson b. May 8, 1862, m. Maria A. Cahoon Dec. 17, 1885; William Wallace b. Dec. 30, 1864, m. Mamie Jensen; Jane C. b. Feb. 12, 1868, m. Enos Bennion; George C. b. Oct. 4, 1869, Albert Thomas b. Sept. 30, 1871 and Arthur C. b. Sept. 18, 1872, latter three died; Walter Scott b. Nov. 8, 1873, m. Laura B.; Ellen Winder; Julian Benedict b. March 26, 1877, m. Lillie Tripp. Family resided Salt Lake City and Taylorsville, Utah.
High priest. Freighter. Farmer and stockraiser.

MACKAY, JOHN CALDER (son of John Mackay and Isabella Calder). Born Nov. 30, 1857, Salt Lake City.
Married Catherine J. Moses Nov. 8, 1883, Salt Lake City (daughter of George Moses and Alice Christie), who was born March 23, 1863, Salt Lake City. Their children: John Elmer b. Nov. 1, 1884, m. Abijail Tanner April 10, 1907; Eugene b. Feb. 1, 1886, m. Geneva Player June 12, 1907; Alice b. July 24, 1887, m. L. I. Acomb June 17, 1909; Alonzo b. April 17, 1889; Albert Calder b. Feb. 11, 1891; George Washington b. Jan. 11, 1893; Roland Carlisle b. Nov. 25, 1895; Harold Moses b. Aug. 1, 1897; Dewey Calder b. March 28, 1899; Wendell b. Dec. 20, 1901; Thomas Wayne b. March 30, 1903; Catherine Isabella b. May 3, 1905. Family home, Salt Lake City.
Chairman board of county commissioners, Salt Lake county. Member legislature of 1891. President Western Wyoming Land and Live Stock company; vice-president North Irrigation company. Graduate from university of Utah 1875; president of the Alumni 1907.

MACKAY, DAVID ORSON (son of John Mackay and Isabella Calder). Born May 8, 1862, Salt Lake City.
Married Maria A. Cahoon Dec. 17, 1885, Logan, Utah (daughter of Andrew Cahoon and Margaret Carruth of Murray, Utah, pioneers 1848). She was born April 11, 1865, Salt Lake City. Their children: Isabella b. Dec. 21, 1886, m. Edward L. Hoagland; David Orson, Jr. b. Nov. 9, 1888, m. Mary H. Collins; Winnie b. Oct. 3, 1891; Gertrude b. Dec. 14, 1893; Lincoln Clyde b. April 14, 1896; Genevieve b. Sept. 16, 1898; John W. b. Aug. 5, 1901; Thurza b. Sept. 29, 1903; Annie J. b. Oct. 20, 1906. Family resided Taylorsville, Jensen and Roosevelt, Utah, also Emmett, Idaho.
Ordained high priest Sept. 22, 1912; ward teacher; president deacons quorum 200 weeks T. M. M. I. A. at Taylorsville ward; superintendent Sunday school of Brammell (Idaho) ward; superintendent religion class Duchesne stake; missionary to Arizona 1884-85; senior president 162d quorum of seventy; home missionary. Postmaster of Roosevelt. Farmer.

PIONEERS AND PROMINENT MEN OF UTAH

MACKAY, DANIEL (son of Thomas Mackay and Sarah Franks). Born Sept. 15, 1868, at Taylorsville.
Married Elizabeth Smith, Logan, Utah (daughter of Daniel Smith and Caroline Burr of Murray, Utah; came to Utah 1876). She was born Jan. 13, 1870, Birmingham, Eng. Their children: Laura C. b. Feb. 13, 1890, d. Dec. 5, 1891; Daniel T. b. Nov. 11, 1891, m. Norma Christopherson; Hazel L. b. July 13, 1893; Elsie A. b. March 31, 1895; Velma M. b. Feb. 5, 1897; Frederick M. T. b. Dec. 26, 1899; Raynor J. b. Sept. 9, 1902; Clarice E. b. July 26, 1905, d. Dec. 12, 1907; Sterling b. July 10, 1907; Luella May b. May 22, 1909; Chadwick C. b. Dec. 8, 1910; Karma Aurania b. Sept. 14, 1911. Family home, Salt Lake City.
Stockraiser.

MACKEY, SAMUEL (son of Joseph Mackey of Scotland and Ann Kimmens, born 1755 in Pennsylvania). He was born Sept. 3, 1806, Lancaster, Pa. Came to Utah Oct. 28, 1852, Isaac Stewart company.
Married Phoebe Wilkinson Sept. 3, 1834 (daughter of Anthony Wilkinson of Ireland and Catherine Miller of Germany, both immigrants to Pennsylvania). She was born Feb. 17, 1804, and came to Utah Oct. 29, 1852, Isaac Stewart company. Their children: Joseph b. Nov. 22, 1836, died; Harriet b. Nov. 22, 1836, m. Alan Wilkinson Jan. 16, 1853; John b. Nov. 25, 1838, m. Marie Davenport; Ann b. Oct. 8, 1839, m. Welcome Chapman; Fanny b. Nov. 15, 1840, d. Sept. 6, 1846; Hannah b. Aug. 11, 1842, d. Aug. 16, 1846; Samuel, Jr., b. June 7, 1844, m. Annie Amanda Gifford Oct. 11, 1869; Phoebe b. July 14, 1846, d. Sept. 19, 1846; Elizabeth Catherine b. July 5, 1848, d. March 30, 1849; Sarah b. March 17, 1850, m. Samuel Davenport.

MACKEY, SAMUEL, JR. (son of Samuel Mackey and Phoebe Wilkinson). Born June 7, 1844, Nauvoo, Ill.
Married Ann Amanda Gifford Oct. 11, 1869, Salt Lake City (daughter of Henry Dill Gifford and Elmira Ann Braffet, latter pioneer 1852). She was born March 11, 1850, at Plum Hollow. Their children: Almira Ann b. Aug. 17, 1870, m. Don Carlos Ross Oct. 3, 1889; Samuel b. Oct. 1, 1872, m. Charlotte Jane Levy May 15, 1894; Mary Lucretia b. July 26, 1876, d. Sept. 20, 1876; Sarah Minerva b. Jan. 17, 1878, d. Sept. 18, 1879; Henry John b. June 19, 1880, m. Sarah Lottie Moore June 25, 1907; Anthony b. April 18, 1884; Phoebe b. Sept. 25, 1888, m. John Burgess Utley Oct. 16, 1906.

MACKINTOSH, DANIEL (son of James Mackintosh and Grace Stewart of Perthshire, Scotland). Born Aug. 12, 1821, Caline, Scotland. Came to Utah in 1852.
Married Elizabeth Ingles Hogg in 1846, Edinburgh, Scotland (daughter of Mr. Hogg and Miss Ray of Edinburgh). She was born June 1825. Their children: Daniel James, m. Emeline Young, m. Barbara S. Leatham, m. Elizabeth Ockey, m. Josephine Reiser; Thomas John, m. Rhoda Young; Charles S., d. infant; Elizabeth G., m. John F. Frost; Catherine Gow, m. Edwin S. Snelgrove; Laura Ray, m. George H. Snelgrove; William W., m. Elizabeth W. C. Young. Family home Edinburgh, Scotland.
Married Ellen Nightingale in 1855, Salt Lake City (daughter of Henry Nightingale and Agnes Leach of Preston, Eng.). She was born Dec. 2, 1835. Their only child was Agnes, who married Mahonni M. Young.
Member 39th quorum seventies; missionary to eastern states; private secretary to President Young. Merchant; bookkeeper.

MacKNIGHT, JAMES (son of John W. MacKnight of Cleveland, Ohio). Born, Irish Channel Islands. Came to Utah in 1852.
Married Mary Ann Fielding (daughter of Joseph Fielding).

MacKNIGHT, JOSEPH FIELDING (son of James MacKnight and Mary Ann Fielding). Born July 20, 1872, Salt Lake City.
Married Katherine Heystek June 6, 1900, Salt Lake City (daughter of Peter Heystek and Nellie Fountain of Zendam, Holland; they resided at Rotterdam, Holland, pioneers of 1854). She was born Dec. 5, 1880. Their children: Joseph b. Oct. 15, 1901; Helen Mirona b. April 15, 1903; Hallet Glen b. Dec. 27, 1905; Mary Virginia b. March 17, 1907; Baby b. Aug. 26, 1912. Family home Vernal, Uinta Co., Utah.
Member first quorum seventies of Vernal, Uinta Co., Utah. Superintendent Mutual Improvement Association of Uinta. Counselor elders' quorum; teacher; class leader. City land and water commissioner of Salt Lake City 1904-06; claim agent Utah Light and Railway Co. 1906-08; cashier Consolidated Wagon and Machine Co. 1907-1912. Republican nominee for city treasurer of Salt Lake City in 1906.

MADSEN, HANS PETER (son of Mads Petersen and Caroline Petersen of Denmark). Born Aug. 18, 1824, Aalborg, Denmark. Came to Utah 1860.
Married Christina Petersen in Denmark, who came to Utah with husband 1860. She was born Sept. 17, 1823, and died Aug. 8, 1902, at Willard.
Married Anne Mette Ericksen Dec. 19, 1863, Salt Lake City (daughter of Soren Ericksen, pioneer with Captain Young company, and Boletta Christina, Kyen). She was born Dec. 15, 1839, Morkholt, Gjersiev Parish, Veile amt. Denmark. Their children: Hans Peter, Jr., b. Oct. 25, 1864,

m. Edith Ella Robbins Dec. 31, 1888; Annie b. April 25, 1867, m. Omer S. Call Dec. 31, 1884; Christina b. March 1, 1869; Matthew b. Aug. 12, 1871, m. Olive Gray May 15, 1903; Serena b. Oct. 29, 1873, m. James S. Mason March 4, 1897; Charles b. Oct. 25, 1875; Zina b. Oct. 30, 1878. Family resided Big Cottonwood, Salt Lake county, and Willard, Utah.
Married Evangeline Brig Ida Nielsen Nov. 25, 1872, Salt Lake City (daughter of Soren Nielsen and Inger Andersen), who came to Utah 1871 with mother. Their children: Anthony Frederick b. Feb. 9, 1876; Marie b. March 29, 1878, m. George W. Jacobs April 3, 1900; Mary Ann b. March 29, 1878, m. D. B. Woodland, Jr., June 1, 1898; Caroline b. April 21, 1880; Ida b. Jan. 12, 1882, m. John H. Singleton May 3, 1899; Margaret b. June 13, 1884, m. Hobert A. Thompson June 17, 1908; Patrea Hancena b. Aug. 5, 1887; Cyril Peter b. Nov. 28, 1889.
Seventy; high priest. Settled at Salt Lake City; moved to Big Cottonwood 1861, and to Willard late in 1868. Carpenter; farmer; stockraiser.

MADSEN, HANS PETER, JR. (son of Hans Peter Madsen and Anne Mette Ericksen). Born Oct. 25, 1864, Big Cottonwood, Salt Lake Co., Utah.
Married Edith Ella Robbins Dec. 31, 1888, at Rigby, Idaho. Their children: LaVern P. b. Dec. 23, 1889; Dan; Howard; Loyal; Arnold; Edith Annie; Melvin; Theodore; Eva; Zenda.
Ordained member of high council of Rigby (Idaho) stake June 11, 1911.

MADSEN, MADS PETERSEN (son of Peter Madsen of Odense, Denmark). Born June 30, 1852, at Odense. Came to Utah July 17, 1876, Andrew Andersen company.
Married Minnie C. Christiansen July 24, 1876, Salt Lake City (daughter of Casper Christiansen of Aashus, Denmark; they came to Utah July 17, 1876, Andrew Andersen company). She was born June 27, 1858. Their children: Charles P., m. Ora Dooly; William F., d. infant; Roslla M., d. aged 17; Oscar H., d. infant; Lillian M., d. aged 3; Ida A. Family home, 4th ward, Salt Lake City.
High priest; missionary to Denmark 1872-76; counselor to Bishop H. Sperry of 4th ward, Salt Lake City. Salesman for F. W. Madsen, furniture merchant, 25 years. Died Oct. 29, 1906.

MADSEN, NELS (son of Mads Nelsen and Karen Nelsen of Denmark). Born March 27, 1813, Toreby Ryde, Denmark. Came to Utah Aug. 10, 1860.
Married Martha M. Hansen of Denmark (daughter of Nels Hansen and Catherine S. Jacobsen of Denmark, pioneers Aug. 10, 1860). She was born Sept. 16, 1816. Their children: Adolph b. June 12, 1841, m. Mary Wogensen; Peter F. b. Aug. 10, 1843, m. Emelia Dahlgren; Karen Sophia b. May 3, 1846, m. C. C. Lee; Caroline b. Jan. 9, 1849, m. G. B. Reeder; Trenia b. Jan. 6, 1851; Nels b. Aug. 14, 1853, m. Eliza Johnson; Josephine; Nephena b. Oct. 4, 1858, m. Joseph Frodsham.
Died May 18, 1891.

MADSEN, PETER F. (son of Nels Madsen and Martha M. Hansen). Born Aug. 10, 1843, at Sjaeland, Denmark. Came to Utah August, 1860, independent company.
Married Emelia M. C. Dahlgren Nov. 10, 1873, at Salt Lake City (daughter of Jacob Jorgen Ulrik Dahlgren and Anne Sophia Basse), who was born June 16, 1848, in Skjillskoi, Denmark. Their children: Waldemar T. F. b. Aug. 19, 1874, m. Adah Nichols Nov. 1901; unnamed b. Jan. 9, 1876, died; Emelia Maria b. Aug. 23, 1877, m. Frank Welling June 1911; Victor Emmanuel b. March 17, 1879; Roland Adolph b. Oct. 2, 1880, m. Abbie Reese Jan. 24, 1906; Lillie May b. March 19, 1882; Leo Dahlgren b. Feb. 1, 1884, m. Albertie West June 19, 1912; unnamed b. July 22, 1887, died; Sterling Dahlgren b. April 4, 1890; Constance b. June 12, 1892.
Missionary to Europe three years; bishop's counselor; high councilor. Bookkeeper tithing office. First man to subscribe to Edmunds-Tucker oath in Utah and voted in 1887. Justice of the peace; county clerk and recorder; commissioner and probate judge. First telegraph operator in Brigham 8 years.

MADSEN, VICTOR E. (son of Peter F. Madsen and Emelia M. C. Dahlgren). Born March 17, 1879, at Brigham City, Utah.
Married Beatrice Winnifrid Midgley April 23, 1902 Salt Lake City (daughter of Benjamin Midgley and Sarah J. Midgley, former pioneer May 1855, Milo Andrus company, latter of Nov. 2, 1864, Warren Snow company). She was born Aug. 28, 1877, at Nephi, Utah, died Oct. 6, 1902. Family home Brigham City, Utah.
Married Sarah Fleofa Forsgren June 24, 1908, at Salt Lake City (daughter of John H. Forsgren and Annie Jane Evans of Brigham City, Utah). She was born May 11, 1881. Their children: Victor Earl Madsen b. April 14, 1909; Irwin Denton b. Dec. 16, 1910, died Dec. 18, 1910. Family home Brigham City, Utah.
Missionary to Scandinavia 1905-07; high priest; chorister in 3d ward since 1900; leader of tabernacle choir. Manager of Box Elder creamery 1900-05. Editor Box Elder News. Member 32d ward bishopric.

MADSEN, NELS (son of Nels Madsen and Martha M. Hansen). Born Aug. 14, 1853, in Sjaeland, Denmark.
Married Eliza Johnson Feb. 12, 1885 (daughter of John

and Annie C. Johnson of Brigham City, Utah, pioneers Aug. 10, 1860). She was born June 30, 1864. Their children: Marcus N. b. Dec. 13, 1885; Francis M. b. Aug. 13, 1887; Stanley J. b. Aug. 13, 1889; Violet M. b. Oct. 24, 1891; Marco b. Dec. 30, 1893; Irving L. b. Aug. 21, 1896; Augusta b. Sept. 19, 1899. Family home Brigham City, Utah.
Missionary to central states 1877; assistant superintendent Y. M. M. I. A. Box Elder stake 20 years; stake superintendent of religion classes Box Elder stake 2 years; president of the 58th quorum seventies; second counselor in high priests' quorum; assistant superintendent Sunday school third ward; home missionary 20 years. Pound keeper Box Elder county; school trustee and city councilman Brigham City. Superintendent of construction of Brigham City water works.

MADSEN, PETER (son of Mads Madsen and Grandmother Madsen of Bredstrup, Denmark). Born April 6, 1824, in Denmark. Came to Utah Oct. 5, 1854, Hans Peter Olsen oxteam company.
Married Mary Ann Madsen 1847 in Denmark (daughter of Mads Monk of Bredstrup, Denmark). She was born 1832. Their children: Mads Peter b. Aug. 5, 1848, m. Johanna Gronnaman; m. Frances C. Scott; Anna Marie b. 1850, died; Hans Olof b. 1852, died; John b. 1855, m. Hannah Christine Jorgensen; Peter b. 1858, m. Bertha Knutsen. Family home Lake View, Utah.
Married Johannah Christine Anderson at Salt Lake City (daughter of Andrew Peter Anderson and Marie Kristine Ammutzobhl of Germany). She was born Feb. 19, 1827. Only child: Andrew B. Feb. 2, 1859, m. Ellison Archibould; m. Annie Jorgensen. Family home, Lake View.
Married Caroline Jensen April 1860 at Salt Lake City (daughter of Knud Jensen and Boddel Olsen of Toreby, Laaland, Denmark, pioneers Sept. 23, 1862, Ola N. Liljenquist company). She was born April 3, 1838. Their children: James b. Jan. 7, 1861, m. Priscilla Stephenson; Mary Ann b. Oct. 3, 1862, m. Christian Sorensen; Caroline b. Oct. 25, 1864, m. John Park; Ephraim b. May 28, 1867, died; Boddel Margaret b. March 6, 1869, died; Sarah Elizabeth b. July 15, 1872, m. Jacob Fullgreen; Dorothy b. March 9, 1875, m. Nels Hanson; Charles b. Oct. 23, 1877, m. Roxie Garner; Eliza b. March 22, 1880, m. Fred Starton. Family home, Lake View.
Married Wilhelmina Jorgensen May 14, 1864, Salt Lake City (daughter of Nels Jorgensen and Johanna Petersen of Pyren, Denmark, pioneers 1865, oxteam company). She was born Nov. 5, 1847. Their children: Nels Christian b. Oct. 7, 1865, died; Rasmina b. March 16, 1868, m. David Bowen; Johanna b. Jan. 11, 1871, m. Levy Carpenter; Brigham b. June 15, 1873, m. Mattie Chesley; George Abraham b. Nov. 25, 1876, m. Nettie Wilson; David Heber b. Feb. 12, 1878, m. Annie Hardy; Emma b. Aug. 11, 1880, died; Mary Josephine b. April 20, 1882, m. William Bean; Albert Ephraim b. Aug. 5, 1884, died; Annie Gulina b. Sept. 24, 1886, m. Alma Clare Ferguson; Clarence Elmer b. May 8, 1893. Family home, Lake View.
Married Lena Johnson at Salt Lake City (daughter of John Johnson and Bergite Larson of Hedemarken, amt. Norway, pioneers Oct. 1, 1864, John Smith independent company). She was born Dec. 9, 1846. Their children: Julia b. Nov. 27, 1866, m. Samuel E. Bunnell; John Joseph b. Feb. 23, 1869, m. Susan Elmina Scott; Ellen Bergite b. Nov. 29, 1870, d. Jan. 21, 1890; Hyrum b. Nov. 2, 1872, m. Clara Lovina Edwards; Marie b. Dec. 23, 1874, m. Rufus Daniel Babcock; Alma Theodore b. April 18, 1877, m. Sarah E. Carter; Parley William b. Oct. 22, 1879, m. Christina Nuttall b. Nov. 21, 1888; Inger B. b. March 20, 1883, m. Arthur James Harding; Edwin Anton b. July 18, 1885. Family home, Lake View.
Missionary to Denmark and also to Sandwich Islands; bishop of Lake View. Veteran Danish-German war 1848-50. Provo City councilman. Farmer; stockraiser and fisherman. Died in 1911 at Provo, Utah.

MADSEN, MADS PETER (son of Peter Madsen and Mary Ann Madsen). Born Aug. 5, 1848, Bredstrup, Denmark. Came to Utah Oct. 5, 1854, Hans Peter Olsen company.
Married Johanna F. W. Gronnaman 1871 at Salt Lake City (daughter of George L. Gronnaman and Andrea Rose of Provo, Utah, pioneers, 1864, John Smith independent company). She was born Dec. 25, 1851. Their children: Mary Ann Andrea b. Dec. 13, 1872, m. Heber W. Harrison; Johanna Dorothea b. Sept. 7, 1874, m. Henry Wing. Family home, Lake View.
Married Frances Cornelia Scott Dec. 18, 1885, at Logan, (daughter of George Comb Scott and Cornelia Elmina Kennedy of Provo, Utah). She was born Dec. 4, 1863. Family home, Lake View.
Member 45th and 123d quorums seventies; high priest; Sunday school superintendent; home missionary; president Y. M. M. I. A. two years. Justice of peace at Lake View; Provo city councilman; school trustee. Dairyman and fisherman.

MADSEN, JOHN (son of Peter Madsen and Mary Ann Madsen). Born May 15, 1855, Fort Ephraim, Utah.
Married Hannah Christine Jorgensen Jan. 26, 1882, at Salt Lake City (daughter of Mads Jorgensen and Annie Jensen), who was born Nov. 19, 1862. Their children: John Peter b. Feb. 16, 1884, m. Florence Bullock; Curtis Adolphus b. April 14, 1885, m. Ruby Bean; Ernest b. Oct. 25, 1887, m. Stella Roberts; Edith Hannah b. April 17, 1890; Leonard Jorgensen b. April 13, 1892; Margaret Ann b. Nov. 15, 1894,

died; Harold b. Aug. 31, 1897, died; Onetah Mabel b. Sept. 7, 1901; Alta Eva b. April 4, 1904; Sylvia b. April 8, 1907. Family home Vineyard, Utah.
High priest; Sunday school superintendent at Vineyard nine years; ward teacher. Farmer and stockraiser. Fisherman.

MADSEN, JOHN PETER (son of John Madsen and Hannah Christine Jorgensen). Born Feb. 16, 1884, Vineyard, Utah.
Married Florence Bullock, 1909, at Salt Lake City (daughter of Alexander Bullock and Emily Harris of Pleasant Grove, Utah). She was born Feb. 7, 1884. Their child: Emily b. July 10, 1911. Family home Duchesne, Utah.
Missionary to southern states 1902-05; Sunday school superintendent; president second quorum elders of Duchesne stake; ward teacher. Farmer.

MADSEN, PETER (son of Peter Madsen and Mary Ann Madsen). Born June 2, 1858, Lake View.
Married Bertha Knutsen June 2, 1881, at Salt Lake View, (daughter of Hans and Beget Knutsen of Lake View, pioneers, 1864, John Smith independent company). She was born Feb. 26, 1860. Their children: Peter Hans b. May 5, 1882, died; John William b. April 22, 1884, m. Margaret Grace Forsythe; Ann Pearl b. April 3, 1887, m. Don T. Allred; Clara b. Nov. 8, 1890; Evelyn b. June 12, 1893; Spencer b. Nov. 4, 1896; Raymond Lamar b. April 22, 1901. Elder; high priest; ward teacher; president Y. M. M. I. A. School trustee; religious teacher. Farmer and stockraiser.

MADSEN, ANDREW (son of Peter Madsen and Johannah Christine Anderson). Born Feb. 2, 1859, at Lake View.
Married Ellison Archibould April 1884 at Salt Lake City (daughter of ——— Archibould of Salt Lake City). Only child: Jessie b. 1885, d. same year.
Married Annie Jorgensen Feb. 20, 1892, at Logan (daughter of Mats Jorgensen and Annie Jensen of Lake View, pioneers 1859, oxteam company). She was born June 28, 1865. Their children: Ethel b. 1890; Josephine b. 1892; Andrew b. 1894; Luella b. 1900; Eugene b. 1900; Jessie b. 1902. Family home Provo, Utah.
Member 45th quorum seventies; high priest; counselor to Bishop Roundy of Knightsville ward; home missionary. School trustee of Vineyard precinct. Mine foreman. Farmer.

MADSEN, JAMES (son of Peter Madsen and Caroline Jensen). Born Jan. 7, 1861, at Lake View.
Married Priscilla Stephenson Jan. 25, 1888, Logan, Utah (daughter of Thomas Paul Stephenson and Jane Cobb of England, pioneers Sept. 25, 1856, Richard Ballantyne company). She was born Aug. 10, 1865.
Elder; home missionary. Justice of peace. Farmer.

MADSEN, CHARLES (son of Peter Madsen and Caroline Jensen). Born Oct. 23, 1877, at Lake View.
Married Roxie A. Garner Dec. 26, 1900, Lake View (daughter of Robert Nute Garner and Marie Ann Staley of Hunting Creek, N. C.). She was born Nov. 25, 1880. Their children: Gladys Mary Ann b. Sept. 20, 1903; Alfred James b. Dec. 24, 1905; Robert Peter b. Sept. 30, 1907; Herbert Charles b. Dec. 31, 1909; Helen b. Jan. 16, 1912. Family home, Lake View.
Elder; treasurer of Y. M. M. I. A.; Sunday school teacher at Lake View. Farmer and stockraiser.

MADSEN, BRIGHAM (son of Peter Madsen and Wilhelmina Jorgensen). Born June 15, 1873, Lake View, Utah.
Married Mattie Chesley March 23, 1896, at Provo (daughter of William Alexander Chesley and Matilda Robertson of Provo, pioneers oxteam company). She was born Jan. 14, 1876. Their children: Erma Esther b. Dec. 3, 1897; Leah b. June 23, 1899; Shirley Brigham b. Jan. 30, 1900; Gordon David b. July 1, 1903, d. May 9, 1911; Grace b. March 20, 1904; Stanley Alexander b. Aug. 17, 1906; Grant Chesley b. Jan. 2, 1909. Family home Lake View.
Elder; County game warden 1907-09; chief deputy state fish and game warden until his death. Died July 11, 1910, Springville, Utah.

MADSEN, JOHN JOSEPH (son of Peter Madsen and Lena Johnson). Born Feb. 23, 1869, at Lake View.
Married Susan Elmina Scott Jan. 11, 1893, Manti, Utah (daughter of George Comb Scott, Sr. and Cornelia Kennedy of Lake View). She was born Oct. 13, 1870. Their children: John Joseph b. Oct. 27, 1894; Leland Scott b. Dec. 14, 1896; Susan Elmina b. Nov. 25, 1899; Druzella b. Feb. 7, 1904; George Willis b. May 17, 1907. Family home Vineyard, Utah.
President elders quorum; Sunday school teacher four years; home missionary. School trustee of Lake View precinct; deputy state fish and game warden. Farmer.

MADSEN, PARLEY WILLIAM (son of Peter Madsen and Lena Johnson). Born Oct. 22, 1879, at Lake View.
Missionary to north-western states 1906-08; elder; assistant Sunday school superintendent of Lake View ward three years; member Utah stake Sunday school board; secretary of deacons quorum 10 years. Salesman for Consolidated Wagon & Machine Co.

MADSEN, EDWIN ANTON (son of Peter Madsen and Lena Johnson). Born July 18, 1885, at Lake View.
Elder; Sunday school teacher. Farmer.

MADSEN, HANS (son of Jacob and Dorothy Madsen of Denmark). Born Jan. 4, 1840, Randers, Denmark. Married Annie Broom (daughter of John and Elizabeth Heywood). Their children: John Franklin; Oscar B.; Delbert; Walter; Parley; Dorothy; Wilford; LeRoy; Carl; Lewis.

MADSEN, OSCAR B. (son of Hans Madsen and Annie Broom). Born March 28, 1870, at Ogden, Utah. Married Adella Bausoher Feb. 17, 1904 (daughter of Joseph and Eliza Bausoher). Their children: Kathryn; Dorothy; Josephine.
Weber county commissioner and prominent in Republican politics. Wholesale milk dealer and farmer.

MAIR, ALLEN (son of John Mair and Mary Fowles of Grasswater, Ayrshire, Scotland). Born April 28, 1815. Married Mary Murdock June 24—(daughter of James Murdock and Mary Murray of Common Dyke, Ayrshire, Scotland). She was born Nov. 19, 1819, and brought her family to Utah 1866 with Captain Scott company. Their children: John; James; Fowles; Mary m. William Lindsay; Andrew m. Mary Ann Thompson; Alexander Eliza Thompson. Family home Heber City, Utah.

MAIR, ANDREW (son of Allen Mair and Mary Murdock). Born Feb. 18, 1856, Grasswater, Scotland. Came to Utah 1868.
Married Mary Ann Thompson July 24, 1879, at Heber City, Utah (daughter of William Thompson and Sarah Fenn of Heber City, Utah). She was born Oct. 6, 1863. Their children: Wm. Allen b. Oct. 13, 1880, m. Isabell Burt; Mary b. Aug. 15, 1882, m. George D. Giles; Sarah b. Oct. 14, 1884, m. Thomas Horrocks; Esther b. Dec. 18, 1886, m. Thomas Davis; Andrew b. April 14, 1889, m. Myrtle Young; John b. Aug. 28, 1891, m. Alma Florence Harcourt; Franklin b. Sept. 1, 1893; Martha b. Jan. 17, 1895; Nellie b. Sept. 15, 1899; Mabel b. Sept. 24, 1902; Emma b. Nov. 6, 1905. Family home Heber City, Utah, since 1868.
Elder. Blacksmith.

MALIN, ELIJAH (son of Thomas and Hannah Malin). Born Feb. 1, 1774, in Chester county, Pa. Came to Utah 1848, Amasa M. Lyman company.
Married Catherine Essex March 19, 1799, in Chester county, Pa. (daughter of Rudolph and Mary Essex, both of Vincent township, Chester county, Pa.). She was born Jan. 3, 1779. Their children: Sidney Ann b. Oct. 20, 1800, d. Dec. 22, 1817; Ann Maria b. March 28, 1802, m. Jacob Weiler Aug. 12, 1830; Sarah b. Jan. 10, 1804, m. Brigham Young April 18, 1848; Nancy b. Nov. 9, 1806, m. Joshua Hookes Dec. 25, 1827; Elijah, Jr. b. March 11, 1808, m. Sarah McQuicken Feb. 4, 1830; Levi b. April 13, 1811, m. Eliza Lewis Nov. 6, 1835; Samuel b. June 29, 1813, m. Mary Ann Bosley Nov. 14, 1846; Rudolph b. Aug. 15, 1815, d. 1820; Thomas b. Aug. 14, 1818, d. 1818; Eliza Ann b. March 24, 1820, m. John Gleason April 20, 1851. Family home, Salt Lake City.

MALIN, ELIJAH, JR. (son of Elijah Malin and Catherine Essex). Born March 11, 1808, in Chester county, Pa. Died 1848, en route to Utah.
Married Sarah McQuicken Feb. 4, 1830, in Chester county, Pa. She was born Aug. 29, 1803. Their children: John McQuicken b. Aug. 16, 1833, m. Alice Smith Jan. 2, 1864; Margaret Ann b. Feb. 14, 1835, m. Charles Woodard April 27, 1856; Catherine b. April 6, 1837, d. July 19, 1837; James Elijah b. Sept. 10, 1839, m. Margaret Laney Nov. 29, 1861. Died May 5, 1848, at St. Louis, Mo.

MALIN, JAMES ELIJAH (son of Elijah Malin and Sarah McQuicken). Born Sept. 10, 1839, in Chester county, Pa. Came to Utah 1851, Ansel Harmon company.
Married Margaret Laney Nov. 29, 1861, Salt Lake City (daughter of Isaac Laney and Sarah Ann Howard of Girard, Macoupin county, Ill. pioneers Sept. 29, 1847, Edward Hunter company). She was born Jan. 13, 1843. Their children: James Elijah, Jr. b. Jan. 28, 1863, m. Jeannetta Barnard Gibson Feb. 2, 1888; Isaac Howard b. Dec. 29, 1865, d. Feb. 4, 1899, m. Jessie Brown; Sarah Ann b. June 28, 1871, m. George F. Baldwin Feb. 19, 1904; George Edwin b. Oct. 13, 1873, m. Sena Craig June 16, 1897; John Charles b. June 18, 1874, m. May Gray Sept. 9, 1907; Joseph Abiah b. June 30, 1880, m. Alice Phelps Sept. 2, 1908; Margaret Pearl b. Jan. 28, 1884, d. July 13, 1885; Ivy Hazel b. Aug. 28, 1885, m. Elva V. Black June 19, 1907. Family home. Salt Lake City.
Seventy; missionary to Wisconsin 1868-70; president elders quorum. Peace officer. Died Oct. 6, 1909.

MALIN, JAMES ELIJAH, JR. (son of James Elijah Malin and Margaret E. Laney). Born Jan. 28, 1863, Salt Lake City. Married Jeannette Barnard Gibson Feb. 2, 1888, Salt Lake City (daughter of John S. Gibson and Jeannetta Barnard). She was born March 13, 1863. Their children: Jeannetta G. b. June 15, 1889, and Margaret G. b. Oct. 29, 1890, d. infants; Sarah Ann b. May 6, 1891; James Elijah b. Oct. 20, 1892, d. infant; Raymond G. b. Oct. 18, 1893; Bar b. Aug. 5, 1895, d. infant.
First president street car drivers union. Drove mule street cars in Salt Lake City. Motorman on first electric car in Salt Lake City.

MALIN, SAMUEL (son of Elijah Malin and Catherine Essex). Born June 29, 1813, in Chester county, Pa.
Married Mary Ann Bosley (daughter of Edmund Bosley, came to Utah 1848, Ezra T. Benson company). Their children: Council B. June 19, 1849, m. Elizabeth Shortren Dec. 4, 1878; Millard F. b. Oct. 24, 1851, m. Annie Pinnock Jan. 22, 1885; Sarah A. b. Dec. 28, 1850, m. W. G. Seamands Sept. 26, 1886; Almira I. b. April 13, 1856, m. William Everett June 4, 1884; Samuel B. b. July 5, 1860. Family home, Salt Lake City.
Married Mary Ann Rodeback (daughter of Charles Rodeback and Jane Morgan), who was born June 30, 1839, Chester county, Pa. Their children: Freeman b. Nov. 25, 1857, m. Louise Anderson; Edmund b. Dec. 15, 1862; Millburn b. Sept. 6, 1862; Ida b. March 10, 1877, m. Gilbert Judd.
Salt Lake City councilman.

MALIN, FREEMAN (son of Samuel Malin and Mary Ann Rodeback). Born Nov. 25, 1857, Salt Lake City.
Married Annie Louisa Anderson Aug. 1, 1880, Hoytsville, Utah (daughter of Anders Anderson and Annie Marie Jacobson, who came to Utah Sept. 5, 1863). Their children: Frank A. b. Jan. 18, 1887; Annie Louisa b. Oct. 23, 1882, m. June 17, 1907; Chester F. b. April 5, 1884, m. Aug. 18, 1909; Edmund L. b. Nov. 14, 1885, m. Dec. 5, 1904.
County commissioner of Summit county. Superintendent Sunday school of Hoytsville ward.

MALLORY, LEMUEL. Born April 1801, Charleston, Canada. Came to Utah, 1850, Captain Bennett company.
Married. ——— Only child: Elisha b. 1830.
Married Elizabeth Canada. Their children: Eliza Jane, m. James Akins; Charles Henry b. Aug. 15, 1840, m. Caroline M. T. Lesueur March 10, 1866; Frances, m. James Furgeson. Family home Cache Valley, Utah.
Pioneer of Cache Valley, Utah. Helped build many mills. Millwright. Died at Logan, Utah.

MALLORY, CHARLES HENRY (son of Lemuel Mallory and Elizabeth Canada). Born Aug. 15, 1840, Macon, Mich. Married Caroline M. T. Lesueur, who was born Jan. 27, 1847, died July 2, 1878. Their children: Charles Lemuel b. Jan. 17, 1867, m. Emily S. Stoffers March 5, 1895; Warren James b. Oct. 23, 1868, m. Anna M. Freeman Feb. 15, 1893; Emma Jane b. Oct. 17, 1870, m. Chester S. Staley Dec. 25, 1891; Lorenzo b. March 3, 1873, m. Mamie Herrick; John Wilford b. Sept. 23, 1874, d. Nov. 14, 1874; Rosetta b. Nov. 27, 1875, m. John Boyer; Caroline M. b. June 23, 1878, d. July 22, 1878.
Made two trips across the plains to bring immigrants to Utah, also made one trip to California, pioneer of Cache valley and Bear Lake valley. Moved with family to Mesa, Ariz. in 1878 and helped to construct the Mesa canal; built the first house on the Mesa.

MALLORY, WARREN JAMES (son of Charles Henry Mallory and Caroline M. T. Lesueur). Born Oct. 23, 1868, Montpelier, Idaho.
Married Anna Marie Freeman (daughter of Elzah N. Freeman and Anna M. Poulsen, married 1872). She was born Dec. 31, 1872, Ogden, Utah. Their children: Warren Freeman b. Dec. 11, 1893; Anna Florence b. May 24, 1896; Charles Guy b. March 5, 1899; Elijah F. b. Jan. 29, 1902, d. Feb. 15, 1902; Wilford Gold b. Sept. 23, 1903, d. Jan. 3, 1904; Alta Leona b. June 28, 1905; Theola b. Nov. 3, 1907; Beatrice b. Dec. 18, 1909.
Bishop 2d ward Shelley, Idaho; president elders quorum and Sunday school superintendent of St. Johns ward; president elders quorum; stake secretary Y. M. M. I. A. and high counselor in St. Johns stake. Engaged in the drug and mercantile business at St. Johns, Ariz. Member of village board for two years, Shelley. Manager of the Shelly Merc. Co. After several months located at Shelley, Idaho, in the spring of 1907, where he engaged in the mercantile business.

MANGUM, JAMES MITCHELL. Born January, 1820, Mobile county, Ala. Came to Utah Sept. 29, 1847, Edward Hunter company.
Married Eliza Jane Clark (daughter of Samuel Clark and Miss Adair). Their children: Joseph Daniel; James Harvey b. Nov. 29, 1848, m. Amy Lorette Bigler Feb. 21, 1870; John William b. Nov. 14, 1850, m. Eliza Hamblin; Heber C. b. Oct. 7, 1852, m. Louisa Leavitt 1870; Martha Jane b. May 5, 1855, m. George W. Kendall; Lydia Ann b. Aug. 31, 1857, m. William H. Apperly. Family resided Salt Lake, Provo, Payson and St. George, Utah.
Married Mary Smith 1866, Salt Lake City (daughter of Thomas Smith). Their children: Frances; Robert; Albert; Carel.
Seventy. Expert millwright, conducting saw and grist mills on Mill Creek and at Provo and Payson, Utah.

MANGUM, JAMES HARVEY (son of James Mitchell Mangum and Eliza Jane Clark). Born Nov. 29, 1847, Salt Lake City. Married Amy Lorette Bigler Feb. 21, 1870, Salt Lake City (daughter of Jacob G. Bigler and Amy Lorette Chase, pioneers 1852). She was born July 17, 1852, at the crossing of the pioneer trail on the Platte river. Their children: James Harvey b. Nov. 18, 1870; W. Leland b. Nov. 27, 1873, m. Jennie Pearl Knight Sept. 6, 1905; Lewis Irvin b. Oct. 30, 1875; Ernest b. March 12, 1878; Mark LeRoy b. April 23, 1879; Effie Maud b. May 19, 1881, m. Alvin S. Jackson;

1022 PIONEERS AND PROMINENT MEN OF UTAH

Minnie Lorette b. June 23, 1884, m. C. H. Miles; Clark Chase b. Nov. 16, 1886, m. Mayme Kerr; Amy Ann b. Dec. 10, 1889, m. C. R. Jones Sept. 7, 1910.
Elder. Worked on St. George temple. Drove teams across the plains for church immigrants and supplies.

MANGUM, W. LESTER (son of James Harvey Mangum and Amy Lorette Bigler). Born Nov. 27, 1873, Nephi, Utah.
Married Jennie Pearl Knight Sept. 6, 1905 (daughter of Jesse Knight and Amanda Melvina McEwan—married Jan. 18, 1869, Salt Lake City, the former a pioneer of 1859, Edward Hunter company). She was born Nov. 7, 1885, at Provo. Their children: Gloria K. b. July 31, 1906; Max K. b. July 6, 1908; Beth K. b. Aug. 19, 1910; Dixie K. b. March 25, 1913.
Missionary to Asiatic Turkey. Tutor in Brigham Young university. Director, manager, secretary and treasurer in various mining, milling, smelting, railroad, banking and industrial companies. Director of Utah Pioneers Book Publishing Co.

MANGUM, JOHN. Born 1814. Came to Utah October, 1852, Jacob Bigler company.
Married Mary Ann Adair in Mississippi (daughter of Samuel Adair), who was born 1817. Their children: William, Laney and Martha, died; Francis, m. James Mangum; Joseph Esiem, m. Maria Lucinda Heath; John Wesley, m. Martha Ann Smith; Lucinda, m. James W. Wilkin; Cyrus, m. Unity Alexander; Harvey, twin of Cyrus, died; Abigail, m. William Hamlin, Jr.; Caroline, m. James Wilkins; David Newton, m. Elizabeth Thornton; Mary Ellen, m. Ebenezer Cherry; Julia, died.
Married Ellen Bargeley 1852, Payson, Utah (daughter of George and Ellen Bargeley). Their children: George, m. Jane Hamlin; Ellen, died. Family home St. George, Utah.
Married Mary Hamlin (daughter of Jacob and Priscilla Hamlin, pioneers 1852).
Seventy. Marshal at Nephi. Farmer and stockraiser. Died May 1881 in Arizona.

MANGUM, JOSEPH ESLEM (son of John Mangum and Mary Ann Adair). Born Dec. 12, 1850, in Iowa. Came to Utah October, 1852, Jacob Bigler company.
Married Maria Lucinda Heath July 21, 1872, Pahreah, Utah (daughter of James Harvey Heath and Mariah Holden of Louisiana, pioneers 1851). She was born Jan. 21, 1858. Their children: Samantha Lucinda b. Nov. 24, 1873, m. Benjamin J. Baker; Joseph Harvey b. Oct. 17, 1875, m. Malinda Johnson; Celestia b. Feb. 13, 1878 (died May 2, 1913), m. John W. Warf; Jennie Vivy b. March 16, 1880, m. Charles Bullard; Benjamin F. b. July 30, 1882, m. Minnie P. Smith; Tamar b. Nov. 13, 1883, m. Levi Christenson; John Ammon b. March 29, 1887, m. Eliza Jane Brinkerhoff; Wilford Woodruff b. April 16, 1889, died; William Arthur b. June 4, 1891, died; George Edwin b. July 27, 1893; Cora Ovilla b. Sept. 17, 1895; Burl Atellia b. Jan. 24, 1898; Ether b. Dec. 25, 1905. Family home Price, Utah.
High priest; missionary to Arizona and New Mexico 1880-87.

MANNING, JOHN RUSSELL (son of John Russell Manning and Eliza White of Bedminster, Bristol, Somerset, Eng., born 1795 and 1796 respectively, at St. Mary, Redcliff, Bristol—married Jan. 12, 1813). He was born May 9, 1823, at Bedminster. Came to Utah Sept. 13, 1861, Joseph Horne company.
Married Sarah Tucker Sept. 5, 1847 (daughter of James Tucker and Elizabeth Hill), who was born June 18, 1821, and came to Utah with husband. Their children: William Henry b. Nov. 6, 1848, m. Emma Hudman June 9, 1873; Emanuel b. Jan. 12, 1855, m. Sarah A. Singleton Jan. 31, 1878; Sarah E. b. Aug. 29, 1859, m. Hyrum Raylane Feb. 24, 1898. Family home Slaterville, Utah.
High priest.

MANNING, WILLIAM HENRY (son of John Russell Manning and Sarah Tucker). Born Nov. 6, 1848, Bedminster, Eng.
Married Emma Hudman June 9, 1873, Salt Lake City (daughter of John Hudman and Sophia Langley, pioneers Feb. 7, 1856, Knud Peterson company). She was born June 25, 1851, Alton, Ill. Their children: Emma S. b. June 10, 1874, m. John Wheeler June 13, 1894; Edith A. b. March 11, 1876, m. Arthur Barnett June 21, 1899; Clarence A. b. April 15, 1879, m. Mattie Hofer June 21, 1906; Amelia E. b. Feb. 25, 1882; Ephraim W. b. Dec. 16, 1884, m. Ethel Garner June 20, 1906; Nephi H. b. July 23, 1887, m. Florence E. Barker Nov. 4, 1908. Family home Slaterville, Utah.
Elder; high priest; ward teacher; president 60th quorum of seventies; ward clerk.

MANNING, WILLIAM C. (son of David Manning and Susan Callard of Devon, Eng.). Born Jan. 23, 1819, at Buckfastleigh, Devon. Came to Utah Oct. 16, 1853, with ox and cow for team. C. E. Bolton independent company.
Married Elizabeth Elliott June 12, 1843 (daughter of John Elliott and Ann (Webber), who was born Nov. 22, 1818, and came to Utah with husband. Only child: Eli b. April 15, 1844, m. Deborah Hollist March 24, 1865. Family home Farmington, Davis Co., Utah.
Elder. Settled at Farmington Oct. 19, 1853, and spent the first winter sawing lumber with hand saw. Assisted in building sawmill in Bears Canyon 1854; assisted in build-

ing first flour mill in Ogden 1854; assisted in building first carding mill in Farmington and the first in Utah. During the winter of 1857 and 1858 was in Echo Canyon with Capt. Philemon Merrill company resisting Johnston's army. Went south with the "move"; returned to Farmington fall of 1878, where he resided until his death, Sept. 9, 1887.

MANNING, ELI (son of William C. Manning and Elizabeth Elliott). Born April 15, 1844, Totnes, Devon, Eng.
Married Deborah Hollist March 24, 1865, Salt Lake City (daughter of Henry Hollist and Elizabeth Chandler, pioneers Sept. 13, 1861, Joseph Horne company). She was born July 25, 1864, Brighton, Sussex, Eng. Their children: David E. b. Sept. 9, 1866, m. Margaret R. Wilcox April 11, 1888; Elizabeth b. Sept. 5, 1868, m. Thomas E. King June 6, 1888; William H. b. March 29, 1871, m. Alice Taylor March 24, 1891; John C. b. Aug. 1, 1873, m. Mary A. Edmonds Dec. 18, 1895; George C. b. Nov. 5, 1875, m. Eliza J. Reddish April 29, 1896; Charles E. b. May 7, 1878, m. Nellie Butcher May 18, 1910; Alice D. b. Dec. 16, 1880, m. Francis H. Edmonds April 26, 1905; Annie S. b. July 6, 1883, m. Henry W. Talbot April 17, 1912; James E. b. Oct. 20, 1885, m. Zilla J. Walker Nov. 1, 1911; Joseph W. b. Nov. 25, 1890. Family home Farmington, Utah.
Assistant Sunday school superintendent; secretary North Farmington ward Jan. 25, 1885-1909. Delegate to several irrigation congresses 1902-10. Farmer and dairyman.

MANNING, DAVID E. (son of Eli Manning and Deborah Hollist). Born Sept. 9, 1866, Farmington, Utah.
Married Margaret Wilcox April 11, 1888, Logan, Utah (daughter of James D. Wilcox and Anna Maria Robinson, latter pioneer 1848). She was born Sept. 30, 1869, at Farmington. Their children: David Henry b. April 1, 1889; Alissa Maria b. Feb. 22, 1891; LeRoy Wilcox b. Sept. 1, 1893; Ruth b. Sept. 13, 1896; Rulon Hollist b. Dec. 9, 1898; Victor Eugene b. Jan. 19, 1901; Julia b. Oct. 4, 1903; Oleen Marion b. June 29, 1906; Margaret b. July 29, 1909; La Vera Alice b. June 22, 1912. Family home Garland, Utah.
Chosen and set apart as president of Y. M. M. I. A. of Sunset branch, at which he served 1896-98; first counselor in bishopric of Garland ward 1910; alternate high councilman of Bear River stake.

MANSFIELD, MATTHEW (son of John Mansfield and Sarah Pinket of Brambly parish, Surrey, Eng.). Born Oct. 25, 1810, Brambly parish. Came to Utah 1848.
Married Johannah Christine Winberg Petersen 1855, Salt Lake City (daughter of Swen Winberg and Elna Nielsen of Sweden, latter a pioneer 1865). She was born May 24, 1824. Their children: Isabel Maria, m. Brigham Reese; Mary Ann, m. W. O. Bentley; Matthew W., m. Cena Ann Hunt; Sarah. Family resided at Salt Lake City, Mill Creek and St. George, Utah.
Married Isabella Mansfield, who was born in Scotland, and died 1891, Mill Creek, Utah.
Married Margaret Haslam (daughter of John Haslam), who died 1870 at St. George. Only child: John M. b. Sept. 6, 1863, d. Feb. 10, 1884. Family home, St. George.
Pioneer. Died March 6, 1891, Mill Creek, Utah.

MANSFIELD, MATTHEW WINBERG (son of Matthew Mansfield and Johannah Christine Winberg). Born Jan. 15, 1862, St. George, Utah.
Married Cena Ann Hnut Feb. 23, 1882, St. George, Utah (daughter of Ames Hunt and Rebecca Wiggins of Hebron, Utah, former a pioneer Oct. 1, 1852). She was born Oct. 3, 1863. Their children: Matthew Lorenzo b. Jan. 20, 1883, m. Jennie Bastian; Mary Eliza b. Feb. 17, 1885; John Amos b. March 9, 1887, m. Maud Robbins; Eliza Edward b. June 14, 1889, m. Effie L. Pace; Ephraim b. May 10, 1892; Pearl b. Jan. 8, 1895, m. Charles Chappel; Cena Josephine b. April 26, 1897. Family home Thurber, Utah.
Married Annie M. T. Bastian Dec. 14, 1898, Salt Lake City (daughter of J. S. and Harriet Bastian). No children.
Member 112th quorum seventies; high priest; bishop Thurber ward; high councilor Wayne stake; stake superintendent and president Y. M. M. I. A. Wayne county attorney; assessor; collector; school trustee; justice of peace; representative state legislature. Attorney at law, Family home, Salt Lake City.

MANWILL, JOHN WORKLEY. Born May 8, 1791, in Maine. Came to Utah Sept. 9, 1852, Bryant Jolley company.
Married Patty Tracey (daughter of Samuel Tracey and Elizabeth Getchill), who was born May 20, 1807, and died in Iowa in 1847. Their children: Daniel Booker, m. Mary Shumway; John Ferrington b. Dec. 2, 1832, m. Emily Sophia Brown June 22, 1856; James B. b. Oct. 5, 1835, m. Sarah A. McClellan Feb. 25, 1863; Orson M. b. March 6, 1840, m. Alice Crandall Nov. 16, 1863; Mary Elizabeth b. May 6, 1843, m. Horatio Calkins May 28, 1859. Family resided Salt Lake City and Payson, Utah.
Married Losana September 16, 1852, Salt Lake City.

MANWILL, JOHN FERRINGTON (son of John Workley Manwill and Patty Tracey). Born Dec. 2, 1832, Oxford Co., Maine.
Married Emily Sophia Brown June 22, 1856, Salt Lake City (daughter of Samuel Brown, pioneer 1852, and Lydia Maria Lathrop, died en route to Utah). She was born April 16, 1837, in Davis county, Mo. Their children: Emily

Elizabeth b. April 19, 1857, m. Lorenzo Arayle; Lydia Maria b. Feb. 1, 1859, died; John Monroe b. Aug. 20, 1860, m. Ann Cowan May 14, 1884; Riley b. April 9, 1863, died; Mary Ann b. Oct. 16, 1864, m. Alpheus Bingham; Virginia b. May 16, 1866, m. Charles Bingham; George A. b. Aug. 14, 1868, m. Elmira Jensen; Melissa b. Aug. 5, 1874, m. William Lewis; Princessetta b. Jan. 9, 1876, m. Robert Cowan; Cynthia May b. May 1, 1870, died; David b. Dec. 11, 1872, m. Viola McBeth; Sarah b. July 1, 1877, m. James N. Hansen. Married Rosina Trevort Dec. 15, 1881. Their children: William Riley b. Nov. 17, 1882; Daisy b. Dec. 5, 1883, m. Frank Daley. Francom; Myrtle b. June 8, 1885, m. Frank Priest; elder; seventy; high priest. Farmer.

MARBLE, HENRY L. (son of Nathaniel Marble of Ohio, born Jan. 25, 1800, and Mary King, born Feb. 29, 1802, both of England). He was born June 2, 1836, in Geauga Co., Ohio. Came to Utah in October, 1851, Reddick N. Allred company. Married Mary L. Burbank (daughter of Daniel Burbank, came to Utah in 1852, John Walker company, and Abigail Blogit, died on plains). She was born Jan. 30, 1844. Their children: Henry L., Jr., b. April 1862, m. Sarah Abigail Burbank in 1887; Mary B. b. Jan. 10, 1864, m. Edwin Gittent in 1883; Abigail B. b. Feb. 22, 1866, m. Henry J. Rogers in 1889; Daniel B. b. July 20, 1868, m. Mary Hansen March 31, 1892; Nathaniel B. b. June 25, 1870, m. Jena Germer in 1901; Almeda B. b. Feb. 1, 1890, m. John Rumrell in 1903. Merchant; farmer; stockraiser.

MARBLE, DANIEL B. (son of Henry L. Marble and Mary L. Burbank). Born July 20, 1868, Brigham City, Utah. Married Mary Hansen March 31, 1892, Collinston, Utah (daughter of Christian Hansen and Anna Mortensen), who was born Dec. 23, 1872, Logan, Utah. Their children: D. Milton b. Feb. 23, 1895; H. Irving b. Feb. 20, 1897; Earl C. b. July 4, 1899, died; Harold H. b. June 29, 1900; John Leroy b. Feb. 27, 1903; Anna Alfreda b. July 2, 1905; Lettia G. b. Sept. 14, 1907; Eddie H. b. Jan. 3, 1910. Family home Deweyville, Utah. Bishop Deweyville since Sept. 20, 1911; high priest. School trustee; constable.

MARCHANT, ABRAHAM (son of Abraham Marchant of Bath, Somersetshire, Eng.). Born March 17, 1816, Bath, pioneer Oct. 28, 1854, Robert L. Campbell company. Married Lydia Johnson, who was born March 8, 1814. Came to Utah with husband. Their children: Mary Ann b. March 19, 1839, m. Austin Green; Sarah Matilda b. Sept. 1, 1841, m. John Newman; Abraham Robert b. April 5, 1843, m. Mary Ann Barter; Albert George Henry b. Jan. 3, 1845, m. Harriet Casper; Lydia Elizabeth b. Oct. 27, 1846, m. Stephen Walker; John Alma b. May 7, 1848, m. Hannah Russel; Franklin William b. Sept. 20, 1858, m. Annie Pearson; Gilbert Johnson b. Sept. 20, 1858, m. Elizabeth Wright; Maria Louisa b. Oct. 12, 1861, m. Oscar Lyons. Bishop of Peoa, Utah. Justice of the peace. Merchant; farmer. Died Oct. 6, 1881.

MARCHANT, ABRAHAM ROBERT (son of Abraham Marchant and Lydia Johnson). Born April 5, 1843, Bath, Eng. Married Mary Barter Nov. 30, 1869, Salt Lake City (daughter of William Barter and Emma Walden), who was born at Tedegar, South Wales. Their children: Mary Ann b. Nov. 15, 1867, m. Arthur W. Adams; Abraham Robert b. Dec. 25, 1870, and Marion Joshua b. Jan. 1, 1873, died. Married Annie Margaret Larson Jan. 8, 1880, Salt Lake City (daughter of Trols Larson and Ingra Larson), who was born July 20, 1861, Henras, Sweden. Their children: Robert Henry b. Feb. 23, 1881, m. Ivy Winigar; Franklin William b. Nov. 30, 1882, m. Annie Jensen; Lydia Ann b. Aug. 25, 1884, died; George b. Aug. 7, 1885; Reuben b. Aug. 28, 1887; Hannah Mabel b. June 13, 1889; Esther b. March 6, 1891; Alice Blanche b. June 1, 1892; Mariah Louisa b. Feb. 21, 1894; Alvin and Almina b. March 18, 1895; Edgar Walden b. Aug. 31, 1897; Howard Larson b. Jan. 17, 1900. Married Hannah Dora Larson Dec. 15, 1880, Salt Lake City (daughter of Trols Larson and Ingra Larson), who was born March 3, 1856, in Sweden. High priest; member of bishopric of Peoa 1871. Justice of the peace; school trustee. Farmer.

MARCHANT, ALBERT GEORGE HENRY (son of Abraham Marchant and Lydia Johnson). Born Jan. 3, 1845, Bath, Eng. Married Marriet M. Casper Feb. 17, 1873, Salt Lake City (daughter of Duncan Spears and Matilda Allison Casper, pioneers Sept. 3, 1855, Captain Hindley company). She was born Nov. 9, 1849, Platt county, Mo. Their children: Albert George b. March 22, 1874, m. Mary Harper Sept. 1, 1898; Duncan William b. Oct. 9, 1875, m. Malinda Anna Gunderson June 24, 1903; Lydia Maria b. Aug. 14, 1877, m. John William Jones June 18, 1902; Robert Henry b. Dec. 21, 1880, m. Agnes Taylor June 10, 1910; Matilda Casper b. April 6, 1879; Alonzo Justice b. Sept. 23, 1882; Abraham Franklin b. Sept. 9, 1884; Mary Ann Casper b. July 19, 1886; Edward Casper b. July 31, 1888; Stephen Casper b. Jan. 10, 1890; Harvey Allison b. Oct. 8, 1891; Harriet Casper b. July 5, 1894; Leroy Casper b. April 22, 1896. Family resided South Cottonwood and Peoa, Utah. Ward and Sunday school teacher. Justice of the peace; school trustee. Helped to bring immigrants to Utah with John D. Holliday company 1866. Veteran of Black Hawk

MARKHAM, STEPHEN (son of David Markham and Dina Hosmer of New York). Born Feb. 9, 1800, New York. Came to Utah July 24, 1847, with Brigham Young company. Married Mary Curtis Oct. 6, 1848, Salt Lake City (daughter of Jeremiah Curtis and Ruth Straton of Michigan and widow of Orren Houghten, by whom she had one child, Edgar Straton, who married Martha Ann Parnett). She was born Nov. 15, 1832. Their children: Orvill Sanford, William Don Carlos, m. Sarah Ann Warner; Sarah Elizabeth, m. William Ashby; Atta Ruth, m. Henry Angus Hosmer Merry, m. Jessie Geneva Cleveland; Emily Aurilia, m. William McKee; Margaret Eliza, m. Owen Morgan; Joseph, m. Mary Lewis; Julina Charlotta, m. Charles S. Crow; Ira Mitchen, m. Rose Patterson; Clarissa Maretta, m. Elias Bona; Carolina Louisa, d. child. Family home Spanish Fork, Utah. Bishop of Spanish Fork for several years; assisted in bringing immigrants to Utah in 1848; captain of Nauvoo Legion and bodyguard of Joseph Smith. Colonel, Walker Indian war. Farmer and stockraiser. Died March 10, 1878, Spanish Fork, Utah.

MARKS, LOUIS A. (son of Louis Marks and Emeline Frost). Born Nov. 10, 1865, Salt Lake City. Married Emma Pope Nov. 16, 1900, Fishhaven, Idaho (daughter of Charles Pope and Maria McCann of Garden City, Utah, pioneers 1857). She was born May 5, 1870. Their children: Louie Thelma b. Sept. 13, 1901; Lewis Lathair b. Oct. 25, 1904. Family home, Salt Lake City. Capitalist.

MARRIOTT, HENRY (son of Edward Marriott, born Nov. 22, 1788, and Mary Hallingsworth, born Oct. 30, 1788, both of Nottingham, Eng.—married September, 1812). He was born Aug. 18, 1813, at Nottingham. Came to Utah Oct. 5, 1862, Ansel P. Harmon company. Married Esther Spencer Jan. 18, 1836, who was born March 22, 1817, and came to Utah with husband. Their children: Joseph Marriott b. April 4, 1838, m. Elizabeth Williams; Thomas E. b. Nov. 30, 1842, m. Ann Paramore Feb. 27, 1865; Sarah Ann b. May 16, 1847, m. R. York 1865. Family home West Jordan, Utah. Elder; missionary to England 1877-78. Merchant in West Jordan for several years.

MARRIOTT, THOMAS E. (son of Henry Marriott and Esther Spencer). Born Nov. 30, 1842, Nottingham, Eng. Married Ann Paramore at Salt Lake City Feb. 27, 1865 (daughter of George Paramore, a pioneer with William S. Seeley company, and Rose Hannah Clark). She was born Oct. 16, 1849, Nottingham, Eng. Their children: Rose Hannah b. Jan. 15, 1866, m. Archibald Stuart; Henry G. b. April 26, 1868, m. Mary J. Gough July 30, 1890; Thomas E. b. Feb. 6, 1871; Samuel b. Sept. 14, 1873; Albert b. July 18, 1878, m. Zina Williams; Florence b. Aug. 20, 1882, m. L. L. Raddon; Laura b. Sept. 4, 1885, m. William Hughes Jan. 30, 1906; Roscoe b. April 21, 1888, m. Lillie Loveridge Sept. 1909; Zella b. March 16, 1890, m. Peter Clyde Swenson Sept. 1908. Family resided West Jordan and Sandy, Utah. Blacksmith originally, but was engaged for a time in mercantile business. City councilman; justice of the peace; was practicing optician at time of his death.

MARRIOTT, HENRY G. (son of Thomas E. Marriott and Ann Paramore). Born April 26, 1868, West Jordan, Utah. Married Mary J. Gough July 30, 1890 (daughter of Joseph H. Gough and Mary J. Stone, married Nov. 23, 1864). She was born Aug. 5, 1870, Ogden, Utah. Their children: Maud I. b. Feb. 8, 1891, m. Roy Mounteer Nov. 17, 1909; Leon Fay b. Jan. 9, 1898; Leavon b. Oct. 5, 1901; Leola b. July 18, 1905. Family home Sandy, Utah. Blacksmith; wagon maker. City councilman 1905.

MARRIOTT, JOHN (son of John Marriott and Frances Warren of Bedfordshire, Eng.). Born March 6, 1817, Rhode, Northamptonshire, Eng. Came to Utah May 1851, Livingston-Kinkade company. Married Susannah Folk 1840 (daughter of Samuel F. Folk and Susannah Holton), who was born July 2, 1825; came to Utah with husband. Their children: Caroline Swanton b. 1841, died; Lorenzo b. 1844, m. Melissa Baker; John b. 1850, m. Alberta Spiers; Susannah b. 1852, m. Andrew Lepper; Rebecca b. 1854, m. John Hodson; Martha b. 1856, m. Moroni Skeen; Benjamin b. 1858, m. Louisa Gampton. Married Elizabeth Stewart Feb. 26, 1854, at Salt Lake City (daughter of Charles Stewart and Sophia Tengey), who was born April 12, 1829, at Colmworth, Bedfordshire, Eng. Their children: Elizabeth b. April 12, 1855, m. David S. Tracy Nov. 13, 1872; Moroni Stewart b. Oct. 31, 1857, m. Rose W. Parry Jan. 29, 1879; Annie Treazer b. Aug. 7, 1859, m. Bernard Parry 1873; Louisa b. Oct. 28, 1864; died; Esther Amelia b. Dec. 6, 1863, m. Fredrick Brown 1881; Hyrum Willard b. Dec. 6, 1863, m. Ellen Morris Dec. 1, 1897; Caroline Emma b. April 8, 1866, m. James Hewitt Oct. 12, 1889; Ellen Maria b. March 6, 1868, m. James E. Morris Feb. 21, 1900; Franklin b. May 13, 1872, m. Maude Kimball Oct., 1894. Married Trezer Southwick Nov. 5, 1855, at Salt Lake City (daughter of Joseph Southwick and Ann Golden, former died 1849 at St. Louis, latter died in England). Their children: Mary Ann b. Sept. 10, 1860, m. James Shoupe; Edward b. Nov. 13, 1862, m. Lily Merrill; Lisle b. Dec. 4, 1867, m. William

Louder Feb. 21, 1893; David b. Aug. 18, 1868, died; Charles Arthur b. May 6, 1870, m. Mary Agnes Farley March 28, 1894; Brigham b. Dec. 30, 1873, m. Linda Fidella Leavitt June 1897; Ida May b. Aug. 8, 1875, m. Daniel A. Creamer Jan. 24, 1894; Israel b. June 25, 1878, died.
Married Margaret Burton Dec. 17, 1857 (daughter of James Burton and Isabell Walton, latter pioneer 1855, Milo Andrus company). She was born April 1839, at Bradford, Yorkshire, Eng. Their children: Annie b. Feb. 27, 1861, m. Hyrum Hogge; Isabell b. April 29, 1864, m. Charles Henry Ellsworth; Maggie b. Sept. 2, 1873, m. John R. Morris; Mary b. Feb. 22, 1876; Lucy b. Oct., 1880, m. John Lamoreaux.
First settler at Marriott, Utah, moving to that place from Kaysville 1855. Presided over Marriott ward eight years. Died June 10, 1899.

MARRIOTT, HYRUM WILLARD (son of John Marriott and Elizabeth Stewart). Born Dec. 6, 1863, Marriott, Utah.
Married Ellen Morris Dec. 1, 1897, Ogden, Utah (daughter of William Morris and Elizabeth Russell), who was born Dec. 14, 1869. Their children: Doris Elizabeth b. Aug. 6, 1898; John Willard b. Sept. 17, 1900; Ellen b. Dec. 29, 1902; Eva Fontella b. April 1, 1905; Paul Morris b. April 6, 1907; Kathryn Esther b. Sept. 30, 1909. Family home Ogden, Utah.

MARSDEN, WILLIAM (son of Abraham Marsden and Hannah Thornton of Oldham, Lancashire, Eng.). Born March 15, 1814, Oldham, Lancashire. Came to Utah April 15, 1855.
Married Jane Appleby (deceased) 1835, St. John's Church (Manchester, Eng. (daughter of David and Betty Appleby of Manchester). Their children: Samuel b. March 2, 1852; Mary Ann b. Oct. 22, 1853; Cornelia Phelps; Elizabeth; Abraham; William; Sarah.
Married Maria Dailey.
Married Sariah Scovil June 16, 1856, Salt Lake City (daughter of Lucius Nelson Scovil, who died 1889 at Springville, Utah, and Lura Snow of Provo, Utah). She was born May 27, 1837. Their children: Lura Alice b. April 3, 1857, m. Thomas Benson. Joseph William b. Jan. 14, 1859; Sarah Ellen b. Dec. 16, 1860, m. Joseph Smith; Lucius Nelson b. Oct. 11, 1862, m. Mary Matheson; Roxa Lenora b. June 10, 1865, m. John K. Paramore. Family resided Provo and Parowan, Utah.
Priest; missionary in New Jersey and New York. Settled at Provo in 1855. Deputy sealer of weights and measures 1882; justice of peace for city and county. Erected first factory at St. George, Utah. Cotton-spinner. Died June 4, 1890.

MARSDEN, LUCIUS NELSON (son of William Marsden and Sariah Scovil). Born Oct. 11, 1862, Parowan, Utah.
Married Mary Matheson Jan. 16, 1886, St. George, Utah (daughter of David Matheson and Mary Craig of Dundee, Scotland, pioneers Sept. 12, 1868, Daniel D. McArthur company). She was born Oct. 13, 1865. Their children: William b. Nov. 13, 1886; Mary Ellen b. Oct. 11, 1888, m. George H. Durham; Florence b. May 14, 1891, m. Arthur L. Joseph; Maggie Dean b. 1893; Lucius Nelson b. 1896; Albert Matheson b. 1900; Glena b. 1903; Milo Scovil b. 1906. Family home Parowan, Utah.
Missionary to southern states 1900; president Parowan stake. Superintendent Equitable Co-op. store of Parowan 1898. Parowan city councilman and mayor; Iron county commissioner; cashier. Farmer and sheepraiser. Early freighter between Silver Reef (near St. George) mining camp and Delamar, Nev.

MARSHALL, GEORGE THOMAS (son of George T. Marshall of Herefordshire, Eng., and Sarah Good, born March 22, 1822, Mitchelldean, Gloucestershire, Eng.). He was born Nov. 9, 1852, in Herefordshire. Came to Utah Sept. 26, 1856, Edmund Ellsworth company.
Married Alvira Van Curen Dec. 20, 1870 (daughter of Paul Van Curen and Alvira Teeples), who was born Jan. 8, 1855, Salt Lake City. Their children: George Thomas, Jr. b. June 23, 1872, m. Sarah Ann Parkinson March 23, 1892; Ellen Elvine b. Jan. 6, 1875, m. Charles Walker 1893; Sarah Rosella b. April 26, 1878, m. H. J. N. Adams 1896; Lovina b. June 28, 1880, m. Thomas M. Perkins 1900. Family home Franklin, Idaho.
Married Mary Jane Alder (Goaslind) Nov. 9, 1882, Salt Lake City (daughter of George Alder and Mary Ann Hamilton, pioneers with Daniel A. Miller company). She was born Aug. 7, 1853, at Sweetwater, Wyo. Their children: Francis b. Aug. 9, 1883; Mary Jane b. Nov. 23, 1884, m. Chase Chatterton; Charles Frederick b. Dec. 27, 1886; Percilla b. July 14, 1888; Bert b. Dec. 31, 1891; Carl b. Jan. 14, 1894; Lavon b. Jan. 5, 1896; Lola b. Aug. 2, 1898. Family home Franklin, Idaho.
Elder. Policeman of Franklin six years. Was in vanguard always in defending the settlers against Indians 1865-70.

MARSHALL, GEORGE THOMAS (son of George Thomas Marshall and Elvira Van Curen). Born June 23, 1872, Franklin, Idaho.
Married Sarah A. Parkinson March 23, 1892, at Logan, Utah (daughter of Samuel R. Parkinson and Maria Smart). She was born April 22, 1875, Franklin, Idaho. Their children: Ania S. b. Feb. 28, 1895; Sarah Phyllis b. March 16, 1896; Lavern S. b. Oct. 28, 1897; George P. b. March 18, 1899; Clifford P. b. April 21, 1901; Ellen Elvira b. Feb. 5, 1903;

Owen P. b. Nov. 22, 1905; Serge P. b. July 28, 1908; Paul Eugene b. May 24, 1911; Veda Maria b. Feb. 17, 1913. Family resided Franklin, Preston and Blackfoot, Idaho.
Missionary to north central states 1892-94. Sheriff of Oneida county 1905-07. Superintendent 1st ward Sunday school at Blackfoot 1909; alternate high councilor Blackfoot stake 1912. Salesman.

MARSHALL, JOHN (son of John Marshall and Jennet Wright of Yorkshire, Eng.). Born Dec. 10, 1821, Glasgow, Scotland. Came to Utah Aug. 20, 1868, Captain Roylance company.
Married Margarette Alexander Wood Rutledge Nov. 13, 1846, Southside, Glasgow, Scotland (daughter of Rev. Rutledge and Alexandria Wood of New Town, Glasgow, Scotland). She was born March 3, 1822. Their children: John; Margarette. Family home Mossend, Lanarkshire, Scotland.
Married Elizabeth Joyce Robson May 28, 1855, at Escomb Church, Witten Park, Durham, Eng. (daughter of Thomas Robson and Jane Joyce of Barley Mow, Chester Parish, Eng.). She was born June 20, 1835. Their children: Thomas; Eliza Jane; Jessie; William; Edmond James; Mary Ann; Robert; Elizabeth Katherine; Mercy Alice; Joseph Hyrum, m. Lettie Hickenlooper. Family home Bountiful, Utah.
High priest. Farmer. Refiner of iron and smelterman. Died Jan. 3, 1904, View, Weber Co., Utah.

MARSHALL, JOSEPH HYRUM (son of John Marshall and Elizabeth Joyce Robson). Born Oct. 24, 1876, Liberty, Utah.
Married Lettie Hickenlooper (daughter of Orson Hyde Hickenlooper and Elizabeth Charlton Wallace of View, Utah). She was born Nov. 27, 1886. Their children: Elizabeth Ann b. April 15, 1906; Jessie Letitia b. Nov. 8, 1909; Joseph Hyde b. April 1, 1913. Family home Logan, Utah.
Member second quorum elders; chorister 1st ward Sunday school. Manager of New Eagle hotel, Logan, Utah.

MARSHALL, WILLIAM (son of William Marshall of England). Born March 9, 1822. Came to Utah 1863.
Married Frances Bridger Kadewell of England, who was born July 2, 1817. Their children: John; George b. Oct. 5, 1846; Edward b. March 11, 1850; Jane b. April 25, 1852, m. George Fowler; Frances b. Jan. 5, 1855; William, Jr. b. Dec. 7, 1867, m. Martha P. Allen. Family home Parowan, Utah.
Married Martha Allen 1862, San Bernardino, Cal. (daughter of Rial Allen of Andrew county, Mo.). She was born March 2, 1819. Family home Parowan, Utah.
Ward teacher. Parowan city councilman. Farmer and stockraiser. Died Feb., 1894, Parowan, Utah.

MARSHALL, WILLIAM (son of William Marshall and Frances Bridger Kadewell). Born Dec. 7, 1857, San Bernardino, Cal. Came to Utah 1863.
Married Martha P. Allen April 17, 1878, St. George, Utah (daughter of Lewis Allen and Elizabeth Alexander, of Andrew county, Mo., pioneers 1862). She was born May 23, 1859. Their children: William Lewis b. Sept. 15, 1879, m. Sarah E. Otteson; John W. b. June 9, 1881, m. Martha E. Cox; James Ira b. May 14, 1883, m. Janet Otteson; Adelbert b. Feb. 6, 1885, m. Barbara Otteson; Elizabeth b. May 22, 1887, d. infant; Arley b. May 28, 1888; Loren b. July 18, 1891, d. April 6, 1903; Andrew Marion b. Jan. 20, 1896; Allison b. April 30, 1897; Jessie b. Nov. 25, 1903. Family home Huntington, Utah.
Member 81st quorum seventies; high priest; ward teacher; missionary to Texas 1900-02. School teacher. Member town board 1904-05. Farmer; stockraiser; apiarist.

MARSING, NIELS LARSON (son of Lars Marsing and Ingre Martenson of Malmohus Lan, Sweden). Born Dec. 23, 1828, in Malmohus. Came to Utah Oct. 5, 1860, Captain Anderson oxteam company.
Married Karn Nielson 1854 at Malmö Lün, who was born Aug. 14, 1814, and died Oct. 4, 1856. Only child was Niels, who died in childhood.
Married Katrine Christina Smith April, 1860, Florence, Neb. (daughter of Hans Peter Smith of Aalborg, Jutland, Denmark, died Dec. 7, 1865. Their children: Lars Julius b. July 13, 1861, m. Elvira Powell; Hans Peter b. Jan. 22, 1863, m. Sarah E. Powell; Martin L b. July 16, 1865, m. Lucy Powell. Family resided Salt Lake City, Corn Creek and Mt. Pleasant, Utah.
Married Klarsti Nielson Sept. 1866, Salt Lake City (daughter of Olf Nielson of Malmö Lün, Sweden, pioneer 1866, oxteam company). She was born 1841 and died Oct. 1869. Their children: Niels Olf b. Sept. 25, 1867; Joseph b. Oct. 1869, d. infant. Family resided Corn Creek and Bountiful, Utah.
Married Sarah Bedford (daughter of John Bedford and Charlotte Love of Bradford, Eng.). She was born April 29, 1834, and came to Utah with a handcart company. Their children: Sarah Betsy, m. Mason L. Snow; Hyrum, m. Alice Thyne; Alma, m. Annabel Thyne; Jane, m. d. aged 5. Family resided Koncom and Joseph City, Utah.
Married Harriet Elizabeth Harmon June 12, 1876, Salt Lake City (daughter of Alphes Amuleck Harmon and Eliza Brumwick of Leicestershire, Eng.). She was born Dec.

20, 1860, in Iowa. Their children: Alphes Amuleck b. Feb. 18, 1878, d. Feb. 10, 1891; John Henry b. May 24, 1880, d. Feb. 2, 1891; Carljohn b. Dec. 11, 1881, d. June 11, 1882; Huldah Eliza b. May 2, 1883, d. Feb. 8, 1891; Rachel Elena b. Dec. 22, 1884, d. Feb. 10, 1891; Edward Orrd b. Sept. 7, 1886, d. Feb. 8, 1891; Ether LeRoy b. May 25, 1887, d. Feb. 17, 1891; Chester Arthur b. June 2, 1889, d. Jan. 30, 1891; Henrietta b. Dec. 4, 1891; Lily Almeda b. June 2, 1893; Francis Marion b. March 1895; Dessie Julia b. Feb. 17, 1898; Ernest Lionel b. April 28, 1901. Family home Price, Utah.
Teacher in Millard county 12 years. Member 17th quorum seventies; high priest; first counselor to Bishop Gideon Murdock; called by President Young to The Muddy Mission; missionary in Sweden five years; superintendent Sunday schools Millard stake. Farmer.

MARTIN, JESSE BIGELOW. Born 1815. Came to Utah in 1848.
Married Ann Clark of Cheltenham, Eng. Only child: Esdras, b. 1860, m. Ella Beck Feb. 12, 1896. Family resided Cheltenham, Eng., and in Utah.

MARTIN, ESDRAS (son of Bigelow Jesse Martin and Ann Clark). Born at Lehi, Utah.
Married Ella Beck Feb. 12, 1896 (daughter of Frederick Beck and Henrietta Henson, pioneers Oct. 1, 1866, Joseph S. Rawlins company). She was born April 7, 1871. Their children: Huron E. b. Dec. 1, 1896; Emma b. March 22, 1898; Linn Beck b. Feb. 19, 1900; Inez b. Nov. 17, 1903; Cleone b. Dec. 13, 1906; Angus J. b. June 23, 1909, died.
President second quorum elders Millard stake; with Zion's Coöperative Mercantile Institution for five years. Merchant.

MARTIN, JOSIAH FLEMMING (son of Josiah Martin and Sarah Flemming). Born Dec. 15, 1815, in Huntingdon county, Pa. Came to Utah 1853.
Married Celinda Hannah Russell June 28, 1846 (daughter of Amasa Russell and Hannah Knight, pioneers 1850). She was born Feb. 29, 1832, and came to Utah with husband. Their children: Elizabeth b. Feb. 13, 1848, m. Charles A. West Feb. 13, 1863; Celinda Adeline b. Feb. 20, 1855; Josiah Flemming b. Aug. 12, 1857, m. Emma Fenn May 26, 1882; Catharine b. Nov. 11, 1859, m. Mans J. Gottfredson Oct. 21, 1885; Margaret A. b. Jan. 6, 1862, d. Feb. 2, 1865; Sarah Isabell b. Oct. 1, 1865, m. Carlos Rasmussen Jan. 22, 1885; Angeline b. Feb. 17, 1869, m. Jacob Gottfredson Nov. 25, 1887.
Married Catharine Fahy Nov 3, 1858, at Salt Lake City, who was born 1828 in Scotland. Their children: Hannah Jane b. July 30, 1860, m. Franklin Spencer Feb., 1875; Nancy Ellen, m. Edmond Durfee.
Moved to Payson from Salt Lake City 1858; to Moroni 1861; and in 1863 was called to help settle Salina, where he assisted in building up the country. He took an active part in protecting the settlers against the Indians 1850-72. Sevier county selectman several years. Died April 13, 1881.

MARTIN, JOSIAH FLEMMING (son of Flemming Martin and Celinda Hannah Russell). Born Aug. 12, 1857, at Salt Lake City.
Married Emma Fenn May 26, 1882, at St. George, Utah (daughter of George Fenn and Sarah Ann Jarvis, former pioneers 1851 and 1860 respectively). She was born March 17, 1864, Gunnison, Utah. Their children: Josiah Flemming b. Dec. 23, 1882, d. same day; Elizabeth b. Sept. 13, 1883, d. same day; Alfred b. Dec. 2, 1884, m. Minnie Shepherd Dec. 23, 1904; Rebecca b. Aug. 20, 1886, d. Oct. 23, 1887; Lucian b. May 17, 1888, m. Anna Larson April 3, 1906; William and Sarah b. June 7, 1891, d. same day; Edmond b. April 9, 1892; Jarvis b. May 4, 1894; Emmett b. Feb. 8, 1896; Emma Jettie b. March 16, 1902, d. Sept. 15, 1902; Arthur b. July 25, 1904, d. June 1, 1909. Family home Salina, Utah.

MARTIN, LEWIS D. (son of Henry H. Martin and Corine Denio of Nebraska). Born Dec. 23, 1861, Galena, Ill. Came to Utah April, 1889.
Married Grace Gallacher Dec. 23, 1890, Logan, Utah (daughter of James Gallacher and Jennet Izett of Scotland, who came to Utah 1870). She was born March 22, 1865, Glasgow, Scotland. Their children: Russel V.; Norma C.; Lewis D. Jr., died. Family home, Salt Lake City.
Member Salt Lake City council 1903 to 1910. Architect.

MARTIN, MARION M. (son of William Augustine Martin and Charlotte Roblon of Virginia). Born Nov. 16, 1825, near Richmond, Va. Came to Utah in early days.
Married Lucinda Busenbark Nov. 18, 1855 (daughter of Isaac Busenbark and Abigail Manning). Their children: Lucinda, m. Buckley M. Fullmer; Lerona Abigail b. Feb. 23, 1862, m. Joseph E. Wilson; Theodore M., m. Sarah Maria Bingham; William Henry, m. Irene ——; David Alvaro; Marcellus, d. infant. Family resided Ogden, Huntsville and Providence, Utah, and Clifton, Idaho.
Married Josephine Jensen 1885 at Clifton, Idaho (daughter of Ole Jensen and Bengta Olson), who was born April 13, 1861. Their children: Walter b. June 29, 1886; Victor b. Dec. 26, 1887; Joseph b. May 28, 1889 d. infant; Arthur

PIONEERS AND PROMINENT MEN OF UTAH 1025

b. Dec. 28, 1890; Louis b. March 26, 1892; Anna b. July 26, 1894; John b. April 11, 1896; Pearl b. April 27, 1901.
Served in war with Mexico 1846-48; in Echo Canyon war 1847-58. One of leaders of relief to Salmon river 1858. Worked on Logan temple 1882-83. Millwright; carpenter.

MARTIN, THEODORE MONROE (son of Marion M. Martin and Lucinda Busenbark). Born Oct. 1, 1864, Providence, Utah.
Married Sarah Maria Bingham Feb. 5, 1884, Clifton, Idaho (daughter of Perry Levi Bingham and Sarah Elizabeth Lusk), who was born Sept. 8, 1867, Three Mile Creek, Utah. Their children: Alta Ardella b. Nov. 12, 1884, m. Willard Deuain Bell Nov. 12, 1902; Ada Lucinda b. April 18, 1886; Sarah Viola b. Jan. 31, 1889, m. Earl Moss Nov. 19, 1908; Lucy Lerona b. April 17, 1892; Clara Elizabeth b. June 24, 1893, m. Fred Bond Dec. 16, 1910; Florence b. July 14, 1895; Hazel b. May 5, 1897; Theodore William b. Nov. 13, 1898; Leora b. July 31, 1900; Rhoda Alberta b. Nov. 14, 1902; Dora Lavon b. Oct. 22, 1904; Eva May b. Aug. 23, 1906; Irven Perry b. April 6, 1908; Lula Maria b. Dec. 1, 1910.

MARTINEAU, JAMES HENRY (son of Martineau of Staten Island, N. Y., and Eliza Mears of Eldridge, N. Y.). Born March 13, 1828, Amsterdam, N. Y. Came to Utah July 20, 1850, California Gold Seekers' Company.
Married Susan Ellen Johnson Jan. 8, 1852, Fort Johnson, Utah (daughter of Joel Hills Johnson and Anna Pixley of Kirtland, Ohio, and Nauvoo, Ill., pioneers Sept. 1, 1848). She was born July 11, 1836, in Kirtland. Their children: Henry Augustus, m. Editha Melissa Johnson; Moroni Helaman, m. Sarah Sophia Johnson; Susan Elvira, m. Benjamin Samuel Johnson; John William, d. aged 3½ years; Nephi, m. Emeline Pamelia Knowles; George Albert, m. Emma Pauline Allred; Joel Hills, m. Mary Ann Thurston; Gertrude, m. Everett Guy Taylor; Theodore, m. Josephine Thurston; Anna Sarah, m. Henry Samuel Walzer; James Edward, d. aged 3 years; Dora, d. aged 19 years.
Married Susan Julia Sherman Jan. 18, 1857, Salt Lake City (daughter of Lyman Royal Sherman and Delcena Diademia Johnson of Kirtland, Ohio and Missouri, pioneers 1853, Almon W. Babbit company). She was born Oct. 21, 1838, Far West, Mo. Their children: Delcena Diademia b. Nov. 27, 1857, died; Lyman Royal b. April 21, 1859, m. Alley Preston; Charles Freeman b. July 24, 1861, m. Eva Rosetta Rice; Jesse Nathaniel b. April 6, 1863, m. Eliza Bell Johnson; Julia Henrietta b. Feb. 4, 1865, d. Jan. 9, 1885; Elizabeth b. Aug. 13, 1867, m. Frank Knowlton Nebeker; Virginia b. July 16, 1870, m. Edward E. Sudbury; Joseph b. April 23, 1873, d. May 10, 1873. Family resided Logan and Salt Lake City.
Married Jessie Helen Anderson Russell Grieve April 18, 1887, Salt Lake City (daughter of Simon Grieve and Mary Anderson of Salt Lake City), who was born Nov. 23, 1867, died 1902 in Salt Lake City.
High priest; bishop's counselor. Regimental adjutant of Iron and Cache military districts, Nauvoo Legion; Indian war veteran. County surveyor; county clerk; sheriff; U. S. deputy internal revenue collector; U. S. deputy land and mineral surveyor. Located what is now called Oregon Short Line from Ogden City to Idaho; was topographical and construction engineer in construction of the Union Pacific Railroad; also located railway in Mexico.

MARTINEAU, LYMAN ROYAL (son of James Henry Martineau and Susan Julia Sherman). Born April 21, 1859. Parowan, Utah.
Married Alley Preston Dec. 29, 1881, Salt Lake City, Utah (daughter of William Bowker Preston and Harriett Ann Thatcher of California, former pioneer Jan., 1858). She was born March 2, 1863. Their children: Alley b. Dec. 20, 1882, m. Kenneth A. Crismon; Harriett Ann b. July 25, 1884, m. Charles A. Gowans; Lyman E. b. Sept. 17, 1886, m. Zayda Bothwell; Henrietta Julia b. Dec. 3, 1888, died; Preston b. Aug. 23, 1890, m. Eleanor Herringer; Martha Claytor b. Nov. 24, 1892; Allen Sherman b. Jan. 23, 1897; May b. Dec. 8, 1898, d. April 21, 1899. Family home, Salt Lake City.
Missionary to England 1879-81; high councilor, Cache stake 1884-1904; stake superintendent Y. M. M. I. A.; member general board Y. M. M. I. A.; a trustee of the Brigham Young college board of trustees. County assessor and treasurer 1882-87; member of Logan City council; member of reform school board 1893-95. Farmer and stockraiser.

MATHER, JAMES (son of John Mather, born Feb. 14, 1780, and Catherine Higginson, born 1780, both of Lancashire, Eng.). He was born Nov. 14, 1811, in Lancashire. Came to Utah Sept. 7, 1855, Noah T. Cuyman company.
Married Mary Ditchfield (daughter of William Ditchfield and Hannah Higginson), who was born Oct. 28, 1811, came to Utah with husband. Their children: John b. 1838; Thomas b. April 28, 1846, m. Mary Ann Cantwell Dec. 6, 1870; Hannah b. Nov. 1847; James b. 1848. Family home Cedar Valley, Utah.
Assisted financially in bringing immigrants to Utah.

MATHER, THOMAS (son of James Mather and Mary Ditchfield). Born April 28, 1846, Lancashire, Eng. Came to Utah 1855.
Married Mary Ann Cantwell Dec. 6, 1870, at Salt Lake City (daughter of James Shirlock Cantwell and Elizabeth

Hammer, former pioneer Nov. 30, 1856, Edward Martin handcart company). She was born Sept. 9, 1853, St. Louis, Mo. Their children: Mary Elizabeth b. Oct. 3, 1871, m. Ira E. Noble; James b. April 5, 1873; William b. Jan. 12, 1875, m. Bertha Done; Alice b. April 8, 1877, m. Harper W. Noble; Ellen b. Nov. 13, 1879; Rachel b. Sept. 20, 1880; Thomas Edgar b. Feb. 18, 1883; Zina May b. March 12, 1885, m. Hyrum Sorenson; John b. Sept. 23, 1887, m. Leon Robinson; Elias b. Dec. 31, 1889; Ethel b. April 9, 1892. Family home Smithfield, Cache Co., Utah.
Assisted in bringing immigrants to Utah 1866; director of ecclesiastical organization of Smithfield; seventy; missionary to England 1893; high councilman of Benson stake. City councilman of Smithfield.

MATHEWS, JAMES NICHOLS (son of Knowel and Martha Ann Mathews of the southern states). Born July 4, 1823. Came to Utah in 1849 by mule team.
Married Clara Slade at Washington, Utah (daughter of William Slade and Julian Higginbottam), who came to Utah 1848 from Texas (with Blair or Jolley). Born Dec. 25, 1842, and died Aug. 1891, Vernal, Utah. Their children: James b. March 6, 1858; Martha Ann b. March 9, 1860, m. Orlando Henry Bracken; Joseph, m. Mary Ann Marshall; Alice, m. John T. Clark; Jefferson, m. Edith Jones. Family home Pine Valley, Utah.
Missionary to southern Utah to make peace with the Indians and assisted in development of "Dixie." Elder and teacher. Farmer. Died June 27, 1871.

MATHEWS, JOSEPH D. (son of Thomas Mathews and Ann Davis of Triboth, Glamorgan, Wales). Born Sept. 20, 1819, Triboth, Wales. Came to Utah Sept. 3, 1852, Abraham O. Smoot company.
Married Ann Roberts 1840, Triboth, Wales (daughter of John Roberts of Llandilo, Wales). She was born 1818. Their children: Thomas, m. Abigail L. Baker; Joseph R., m. Fannie D. Chase; Mary Ann, m. Griffith Roberts. Family home, Salt Lake City.
High priest and block teacher. Stone and brick mason; contractor. Died at Pleasant View, North Ogden, Utah.

MATHEWS, THOMAS (son of Joseph D. Mathews and Ann Roberts). Born May 29, 1841, Triboth, Wales. Came to Utah Sept. 3, 1852, A. O. Smoot company.
Married Abigail L. Baker June 17, 1865, Salt Lake City, Edward Hunter performing ceremony (daughter of Simon Baker and Charlotte Leavitt of Nauvoo, Ill., pioneers Oct. 2, 1847, Jedediah M. Grant company). She was born Jan. 7, 1846. Their children: Thomas W. b. April 8, 1866, m. Annie Gray; Lottie Ann b. Jan. 5, 1868, m. Miles R. Taylor; Francis M. b. Dec. 10, 1869, m. Sarah Williams; Joseph S. b. Dec. 11, 1873, m. Bessie Ence; Mary M. b. Dec. 21, 1875, d. aged 9 years; Roy R. b. Nov. 25, 1878, m. Elizabeth Lawrence. Family home, Salt Lake City.
Deputy sheriff under Adam Naylor for two years. Freighter.

MATHEWS, WILLIAM (son of Richard Matthews and Elizabeth Byron of Radford, Nottingham, Eng.). Born Oct. 14, 1839, at Radford. Came to Utah Oct. 4, 1864, William S. Warren company.
Married Hephzibah Jarvis Dec. 31, 1832 (daughter of Joseph Jarvis and Mary Bedsley), who was born March 3, 1810. Came to Utah with husband. Their children: Eliza b. March 28, 1834, m. Charles Smith Nov. 5, 1855; Richard b. Dec. 29, 1835, m. Mary Ann Sanders; Mary b. Aug. 17, 1837, m. Robert C. Kirkwood Oct. 21, 1860; Elizabeth, d. infant; Annie b. Aug. 12, 1840, m. George Morris Dec. 24, 1863; Emma, d. infant; Hephzibah b. Feb. 10, 1844, m. John Green Nov. 11, 1866; William b. Nov. 14, 1845, m. Mary Hannah Partington Oct. 16, 1870; Thomas b. July 10, 1847. Family home Nottingham, Eng.

MATHIAS, THOMAS (son of John Mathias and Mary Michael of Wales). Born June 6, 1808, Carmarthen, Wales. Came to Utah 1852, William Morgan company.
Married Margaret Williams July 1, 1831 (daughter of William Williams and Elizabeth Jeremy), who was born Dec. 22, 1811. Came to Utah with husband. Their children: Jared b. Jan. 3, 1832; Ada b. Aug. 12, 1836, m. Leander H. Clifford 1855; Zillah b. Dec. 14, 1839, m. J. D. Rees Dec. 13, 1857; Jonah b. July 30, 1843, m. Abigail Burbank April 4, 1868; Ephraim S. b. March 9, 1850, m. Abi Gardner April 10, 1872. Family home Brigham City, Utah.

MATHIAS, JONAH (son of Thomas Mathias and Margaret Williams). Born July 30, 1843, Carmarthen, Wales.
Married Abigail Burbank April 4, 1868, Salt Lake City (daughter of Daniel E. Burbank and Abigail Blodget, former pioneer 1852, latter died on the plains). She was born Aug. 14, 1848, Council Bluffs, Iowa. Their children: Jonah B. b. May 10, 1869, m. Mary Ardelia Bingham Nov. 18, 1896; Margaret Abigail b. Oct. 11, 1870, m. J. S. B. Bingham Sept. 18, 1895; Thomas B. b. July 12, 1872, m. Harriet Reeves Nov. 18, 1896; Daniel B. b. April 4, 1874, m. Rebecca Tingey Oct. 7, 1909; John B. b. Oct. 29, 1875, m. Esther Marble June 21, 1905; Mary Elvira b. July 9, 1877, m. Ernest P. Horsley Oct. 27, 1897; Ephraim B. b. Aug. 11, 1879, m. Tilla Knudsen Oct. 3, 1908; Laura Liona b. Oct. 13, 1881; Sarah Luella b. July

8, 1884; Ada Vivian b. June 30, 1886, m. A. M. Reeder Oct. 2, 1906; Zillah Elevene b. Jan. 24, 1890; Ivy Hortense b. Dec. 24, 1892, d. Sept. 12, 1895. Family home, Brigham City.
Second counselor in bishopric of Brigham City, first ward. 1877-92. Assessor and collector of Brigham 1885-87; clerk of Box Elder county 1886-90; justice of peace 1889; collector 1890 of Box Elder county; justice of peace at Brigham City 1891, and city councilman 1893-95; county commissioner of Box Elder county 1894-96; mayor of Brigham City 1895-97, and school trustee four years. Assisted in bringing immigrants to Utah 1862-64. Minuteman in home guard eight years.

MATHIS, HANS HENRICH. Born Feb. 22, 1803, in Switzerland. Came to Utah 1864.
Married Anna Dorothea Myers 1827. Their children: Jacob; Anna Marie Dorothea, m. Hans Ulrick Bryner, Jr.; John. m. Barbara Bryner; Henry, m. Elizabeth Hubsmith. Family home Lehi, Utah.
Elder. Farmer. Financially assisted immigration of several families to Utah.

MATHIS, HENRY (son of Hans Henrich Mathis and Dorothea Myers). Born at Zurich, Switzerland, 1834. Came to Utah Oct. 29, 1862, William H. Dame company.
Married Elizabeth Hubsmith 1862 in Wyoming while coming to Utah (daughter of George Hubsmith of Hedigen, Canton Zurich, Switzerland, pioneers Oct. 29, 1862, William H. Dame company). She was born Sept. 30, 1839. Their children: George Henry b. Dec. 5, 1863, m. Louise Pace; Mary Elizabeth b. March 28, 1866, m. James F. Pace; Louise, died; James Samuel b. March 10, 1870, m. Mary Ann Robb; John Arnold b. May 3, 1875, m. Rachel Parthenia Cottam. m. Lilly Pearl Morrison; Albert Ferdinand b. April 27, 1877. Family home New Harmony, Utah.
Elder. Freighted across plains 1863-64; assisted in building wagon roads, canals, and getting out material for Deseret telegraph line. Settled at St. George 1862, and in this year he and his brother John built first log houses in St. George; moved to Harmony, then moved to Toquerville for two years, then moved back to New Harmony, where he has since made his home. Popularly known by inhabitants of southern Utah as "Uncle Henry," and as being very generous and liberal with his fellow citizens.

MATHIS, JAMES SAMUEL (son of Henry Mathis and Elizabeth Hubsmith). Born March 10, 1870, New Harmony, Utah.
Married Mary Ann Robb April 3, 1901, Salt Lake City (daughter of George Robb and Caroline Jones, pioneers 1857). She was born Sept. 1, 1878. Their children: Elwood James b. Jan. 3, 1904; Clair Robb b. Sept. 24, 1905; Rex Henry b. Aug. 13, 1908. Family home Price, Utah.
Elder; ward teacher; treasurer of Price Sunday school; first counselor and president Y. M. M. I. A. of New Harmony ward. Settled at Price 1897, where he assisted in building up the country.

MATHIS, JOHN ARNOLD (son of Henry Mathis and Elizabeth Hubsmith). Born May 3, 1875.
Married Rachel Parthenia Cottam May 5, 1899, St. George, Utah (daughter of George Thomas Cottam and Rachel Parthenia Holt of St. George, Utah). She was born March 2, 1877. Only child: Milton Arnold b. Oct. 5, 1900.
Married Lilly Pearl Morrison April 12, 1911, Salt Lake City (daughter of John Morrison and Mary Jane Warren of Price, Utah). She was born Feb. 20, 1891. Child of Bernard Henry b. April 5, 1912.
Member presidency 101st quorum seventy; missionary to Switzerland, Germany and Austria-Hungary 1903-06; president Y. M. M. I. A. Price ward 1899-1900; Sunday school teacher; secretary and treasurer Y. M. M. I. A. Carbon stake. Secretary and treasurer Tanners' Exchange and Implement Co. Settled at Price 1899 and served as school trustee and town councilman. Farmer and stockraiser.

MATHIS, JOHN (son of Hans Henrich Mathis and Anna Dorothea Myers). Came to Utah Nov. 30, 1856, Martin and Tyler handcart company.
Married Barbara Bryner at Salt Lake City (daughter of Hans Ulrick Bryner of Zurich, Switzerland). She was born Jan. 29, 1831, and came to Utah 1856. Martin and Tyler handcart company. Their children: Henry George b. May 2, 1861; John H., m. Emma Nixon; Barbara Anna, m. Brigham O. McIntyre; Louisa; Lena, m. Joshua Crosby; Albert; Pauline; Alma; Frank; latter four died; Julius, m. Minnie Miles. Family home St. George, Utah.
Elder; ward teacher. Settled at St. George, Utah, 1861. Worked on temple and tabernacle. Built first house in St. George. Died Aug., 1899.

MATHIS, HENRY GEORGE (son of John Mathis and Barbara Bryner). Born May 2, 1861, Ogden, Utah.
Married Mary DeFreize Jan. 30, 1890, St. George, Utah (daughter of William DeFreize and Mary Aurelia Venton of London, Eng. who came to Utah 1877). She was born Aug. 24, 1868. Only child: Mary Florence b. July 12, 1891. Family home Price, Utah.
Married Sarah Ann McFarlane Nov. 22, 1893, St. George, Utah (daughter of John Menzies MacFarlane of Sterling, Scotland, and Agnes Eliza Heybor of Australia, pioneers 1852, A. O. Smoot company). She was born July 21, 1867. Their children: George MacFarlane b. June 22, 1895; Iven b. Dec. 18, 1898; Zelma b. Aug. 31, 1903; Myrtle and Murray b. July 9, 1905, twins; LeGrande b. June 22, 1908. Family home Price, Utah.

High priest; second counselor to Ruben G. Miller of Emery stake 1898-1910; counselor to Bishop Horsley of Price ward 1896-98; president Y. M. M. I. A. several years. Farmer and implement dealer.

MATSON, GEORGE B. (son of George B. Matson and Ann Pierson, the latter born April 13, 1797, Chester county, Pa.—married Oct. 12, 1819). He was born Oct. 26, 1827, Centerville, Del. Came to Utah October, 1847, A. O. Smoot company.
Married Mary Jane Guymon Jan. 25, 1854, Salt Lake City (daughter of Noah T. Guymon and Mary H. Dudley—married Dec. 24, 1837, Caldwell, Mo., pioneers 1850, Aaron Johnson company). She was born Oct. 25, 1838. Their children. George Brinton; Evaline; Aaron Wesley; Mary Louella; Aymor Frederic; Noah Thomas; Ida Bernicia; Clarence Rafael; Raymond Marcellus; Dudley Guymon; Erma.
Assisted in building state house at Fillmore; assisted in bringing handcart company to Utah 1856. Veteran Indian war. Built Camp Floyd in 1857. Missionary to Philadelphia 1898. Springville city councilman. In 1864 he went to the Missouri river for freight. Moved to Fountain Green in 1865; to Moroni in 1856, and in 1867 he went to Springville. Contractor and builder; mason and freighter.

MATSON, GEORGE BRINTON, JR. (son of George B. Matson and Mary Jane Guymon). Born Feb. 1, 1855, Springville, Utah.
Married Jane Elizabeth Waters Feb. 14, 1877, at Springville, Utah (daughter of John Waters and Sarah Burch, pioneers Oct. 6, 1853). She was born Dec. 12, 1854, Big Cottonwood, Utah. Their children: George Ernest b. Feb. 14, 1878; William b. Aug. 11, 1880, m. Myrtle Robinson; Sarah Jane b. Sept. 11, 1882; Ella May b. March 30, 1886, m. Eugene Petrie; John Wesley b. Aug. 11, 1890; Afton Monroe b. June 23, 1896. Family home Springville, Utah.
In 1871 hauled ore from West to East Tintic with ox teams; assisted in making the wagon road into Pleasant Valley 1876; assisted in surveying the township; mined first load of coal out of Pleasant Valley. Moved to Mapleton ward 1890. Missionary to northern states 1893-95. Merchant; farmer and stockraiser.

MATSON, WILLIAM (son of George B. Matson and Jane Elizabeth Waters). Born Aug. 11, 1880, Springville, Utah.
Married Myrtle Robinson (daughter of Hugh Robinson and Margaret Stringfellow, who were married Sept. 11, 1864, at Cappel Church, Eng.). She was born July 9, 1881, at Farnsworth, Lancashire, Eng. Only child: Genevieve b. July 20, 1906. Family home Green River City, Utah. Machinist, fireman and engineer on D. & R. G. R. R.

MATTHEWS, WILLIAM (son of William Matthews and Elizabeth Rowney of North Hill, Bedfordshire, Eng.). Born Feb. 21, 1817, North Hill, Bedfordshire. Came to Utah Oct. 16, 1855, John Wardle company.
Married Elizabeth Flinders 1842 (daughter of Samuel Flinders and Sara Garner, who were married at Bedfordshire, Eng.). She was born at North Hill, Bedfordshire. Died at sea Oct. 1850. Their children: Samuel b. May 4, 1843, m. Elizabeth Keetch Oct. 12, 1864; George E. Dec. 1845, m. Elizabeth Hunter; Timothy b. April 1848, m. Mary Poulton. Family home Grantaville, Utah.
Married Sara —— at St. Louis, Mo., who died 1852. Only child, a son, died 1851.
Married Charlotte Swift at St. Louis, Mo., 1853 (daughter of William Swift, who came to Utah with John Wardle company, and Harrah Reynolds). She was born Aug. 12, 1821, at Pollokshill, Renfrewshire, Eng. Their children: Walter William b. Feb. 22, 1854, m. Martha E. McMurray; Joseph b. July 17, 1856; Hyrum b. July 17, 1856; Elizabeth Hannah b. April 23, 1858; Harrison H. b. March 24, 1860, m. Sara Ann Williams; William Swift b. Feb. 3, 1862, m. Clara Hale; Charlotte Ann b. March 26, 1867, m. James Barrus.

MATTHEWS, SAMUEL (son of William Matthews and Elizabeth Flinders). Born May 4, 1843, North Hill, Bedfordshire, Eng. Came to Utah Oct. 17, 1855, with William S. Godbe freight train.
Married Elizabeth Keetch Oct. 12, 1864 (daughter of William K. Keetch and Ann Greenwood), who was born April 7, 1842. Came to Utah Oct. 1862, David P. Kimball freight train. Their children: Samuel William b. Aug. 25, 1865, m. Caroline E. Orr; Elizabeth A. b. Feb. 5, 1877, m. Henry N. Pugmire; Emily M. b. July 9, 1869, m. William L. Rich; Charlotte A. b. July 2, 1872; Eliza A. b. March 7, 1874, m. Richard Toomer; Martha E. b. Dec. 12, 1877; Ella b. June 21, 1880, m. James A. Hymas.
Married Annie E. Kennington Feb. 28, 1884, at Salt Lake City (daughter of William H. Kennington, came to Utah 1856 with handcart company, and Annie R. Mason, who came to Utah Oct. 13, 1863, with Rosel Hyde company—married April 1, 1864, at Salt Lake City). She was born Feb. 3, 1866, in Tooele, Utah. Their children: George T. b. Jan. 29, 1886; Alonzo H. b. April 20, 1888; Ada b. July 5, 1890; Edna A. b. Dec. 13, 1892; Harvey K. b. Feb. 1895; Esther S. b. Aug. 14, 1897. Families resided at Liberty, Bear Lake Co., Idaho.
Assisted in bringing immigrants to Utah, 1863 and 1866. High priest; bishop of the Montpelier ward. Commissioner Bear Lake county 1883-85.

MATTHEWS, WILLIAM A. (son of William Matthews of Dunstable, Eng., and Rebecca Hill of Glasgow, Scotland, pioneers to Lehi 1852). Born July 2, 1871.
Married Sarah Jane Thomas April 27, 1899, Salt Lake City (daughter of Samuel Thomas and Mary Darknell of Salt Lake City). She was born Oct. 15, 1874, 15th ward, Salt Lake City. Their children: Mary R. b. Feb. 9, 1900; Samuel W. b. Sept. 3, 1901; Sarah Jane b. Oct. 28, 1903, d. infant; Abbey E. b. March 6, 1905, d. aged 2. Family home, 15th ward, Salt Lake City.
Farmer. Died Sept. 15, 1904.

MATTINSON, ROBERT (son of Peter Mattinson, born Dec. 2, 1803, and Ann Shaw, born Feb. 6, 1812, of Sunderland, Eng.). He was born July 16, 1835, Lancashire, Eng. Came to Utah Nov. 30, 1856, Edward Martin handcart company.
Married Betsy C. Burnhope (daughter of Isaac Burnhope and Elizabeth Charlton, latter a pioneer Aug. 19, 1868, John R. Murdock company). She was born in England. Their children: E. A., m. James Nolan; Laura S., m. Peter Borup; Marie, m. Richard Barrett; Anna, m. J. F. Rushter; R. Frank; H. B. b. Nov. 24, 1880; Effie M., m. E. O. Simons; Joseph B., m. Ella Balch; Roy B. b. Sept. 11, 1891; Veatus b. Oct. 16, 1893. Family home Payson, Utah.

MAUGHAN, PETER (son of William Maughan and Martha Walton of Alston, Cumberland, Eng.). Born May 7, 1811, Milton, Eng. Came to Utah Sept. 17, 1850, William Wall company.
Married Ruth Harrison 1830 at Alston, Eng. (daughter of Thomas Harrison and Agness Walton of Milton). She was born Feb. 26, 1812. Their children: John b. Oct. 8, 1830, m. Sarah M. Davenport July 24, 1853, m. Mary Nibley Aug. 1863, m. Hannah Toombs 1869; Agnes, m. Jonathan Teasdale; William Harrison b. May 7, 1834, m. Barbara Morgan Dec. 25, 1853; Thomas V. b. May, 1851, died; Mary Ann, m. Thomas Atkin; Ruth, died at sea. Family home E. T. City, Utah.
Married Mary Ann Weston December, 1841, at Nauvoo, Ill. Their children: Charles W.; Peter; Joseph; Hyrum; Willard, m. Lavina Parry; Elizabeth R. Cole; Martha R. Davis; Peter W., m. Mary Neff.
Presiding bishop. Probate judge. Quartermaster of 1st brigade of military district, Cache county, and representative to territorial legislature from Cache and Rich counties. Farmer. Died April 24, 1871, at Logan, Utah.

MAUGHAN, JOHN (son of Peter Maughan and Ruth Harrison). Born Oct. 8, 1830, at Alston, Cumberland, Eng.
Married Sarah M. Davenport July 24, 1853, at Tooele City, Utah (daughter of James Davenport and Almyra Phelps of Grantaville, Utah, pioneers 1851, Philo Merrill company). She was born Nov. 22, 1836. Their children: Sarah A. b. July 1854, m. W. C. Robbins; Mary A. b. Aug. 1856, m. C. A. Norton; John b. Jan. 1859, m. Agnes Olsen; Harrison D. b. Sept., 1861, m. Mary E. Freestone; Ruth E., m. Thomas Griffin; Peter D., m. Eliza Neilsen; Martha A., m. George A. Hansen; George, m. Matilda Jensen; Ambrose, m. Melissa Fifield; Elise, m. S. T. Merrell; Margaret, m. I. W. McKay; Hyrum; William; latter two died.
Married Mary Nibley August, 1863. Their children: Jane, m. Thomas Murphy; Charles, d. Oct. 9, 1869.
Married Hannah Toombs 1869. Only child: James.
Settled in Cache valley 1850; helped settle Bear Lake valley in 1863. Bishop of Preston, Idaho.

MAUGHAN, WILLIAM HARRISON (son of Peter Maughan and Ruth Harrison). Born May 7, 1834, at Alston, Cumberland, Eng. Came to Utah Sept. 27, 1850, William Wall company.
Married Barbara Morgan Dec. 25, 1853, at Salt Lake City (daughter of Morgan Morgan and Cecelia Lewis of E. T. City, Utah, pioneers 1852, William Morgan company). She was born Dec. 23, 1834. Their children: Ruth b. Oct. 7, 1854, m. Thomas Williamson; Mary E. b. July 8, 1856, m. Joseph Howell; Peter Morgan b. Oct. 18, 1858, m. Jerusha G. Baxter Feb. 23, 1882; William H. b. Oct. 17, 1860, m. Margret Baxter; Sarah A. b. Dec. 12, 1862, m. Walter W. Jones; Agnes b. March 19, 1865, m. Horman C. Allan; Thomas b. June 14, 1869, m. Emily Perkins; Joseph b. Sept. 26, 1872, m. Fannie Salsbury; Brigham b. Sept. 26, 1878, m. Jessie Hendry. Family home Wellsville, Utah.
Bishop of Wellsville ward; ward teacher; patriarch. County selectman; mayor of Wellsville several terms; member constitutional convention from Cache county. Farmer and contractor. Died Aug. 28, 1905, at Wellsville.

MAUGHAN, PETER MORGAN (son of William Harrison Maughan and Barbara Morgan). Born Oct. 18, 1858, at E. T. City, Utah.
Married Jerusha G. Baxter Feb. 23, 1882, Salt Lake City (daughter of Robert Wright Baxter and Jane Love of Wellsville, Utah, pioneers 1853, 1856, Richard Ballantyne company). She was born Jan. 6, 1859. Their children: Jane E. b. June 21, 1885, m. Thomas P. Walters; Peter Melvin B. b. July 27, 1887; William Harrison B. b. Jan. 25, 1889, m. Mary Ann Jackson; Robert Milton B. b. March 16, 1891; Adelbert B. b. Aug. 12, 1898; Parley B. b. July 1, 1902; Rulon B. b. Nov. 11, 1906. Family home, Wellsville.
Member 28th quorum seventies; president deacons', teachers' and elders' quorum; Sunday school superintendent; assistant stake Sunday school superintendent; first counselor

to bishop of Wellsville ward. County assessor two years; mayor two terms; city councilman two terms; justice of peace; city assessor and collector, Wellsville; member first and fourth state legislatures from Cache county. Merchant and farmer.

MAUSS, MICHAEL (son of Jacob Mauss, born Oct. 20, 1832, at Lothringen, Germany, and Lena Kelsch, born Aug. 28, 1841—married June 1867). He was born Nov. 2, 1871, at Papillion, Neb.

Married Charlotte Wright June 28, 1893, Salt Lake City (daughter of Benjamin Wright and Eliza Darton, pioneers Oct. 17, 1862, Henry W. Miller company). She was born Oct. 18, 1873, Murray, Utah. Their children: Myrtle E. b. Nov. 9, 1894; Mylo M. b. Jan. 26, 1897; Vinal G., Velma M., and Vilda C. (triplets) b. Oct. 16, 1900; Adella D. b. Nov. 26, 1903; Ruby L. b. April 25, 1906; Lowell b. Jan. 12, 1911. Family home Murray, Utah.

Deputy sheriff of Salt Lake county 1901-02; city marshal since 1903. Missionary to Ohio and Nebraska 1897-99; first counselor to Bishop Orson Sanders of South Cottonwood ward 1900-03; first counselor to Bishop William B. Erekson of South Cottonwood ward 1903-06; ordained bishop of Murray, first ward, Jan. 16, 1909.

MAW, EDWARD. Came to Utah Oct. 19, 1862, Horton D. Haight company.

Married Dina Gledall, who died in England in 1841. Their children: Robert, m. Ann Davis, m. Lois Reeves, m. Hertha Schoenfeld; Abraham, m. Eliza Tripp; Isaac, Jacob, d. infants; Sarah, m. William Coy; Ephraim; Aaron; Ellen, m. Hans Poulsen; Alice, m. Moroni Poulter; Susannah, d. on plains in 1862 (21 years old). Family home Ogden, Utah.

High priest. Shoemaker and farmer. Died Aug. 9, 1893.

MAW, ROBERT (son of Edward Maw and Dina Gledall). Born Sept. 12, 1834, Root, Eng. Came to Utah Sept. 30, 1854, Darwin Richardson company.

Married Ann Davis July 15, 1858, Lehi, Utah (daughter of Thomas and Mary Davis of Wales, pioneers 1855, A. O. Smoot company). Their children: Robert Edward b. Oct. 15, 1859, m. Victorine Sharp; Abraham Thomas b. Nov. 3, 1861; Mary Eliza b. Oct. 4, 1863, m. William Rawson; Katherine b. Oct. 17, 1865, m. J. A. Lampert; Rose Ann, d. child. Family home Plain City, Utah.

Married Lois Reeves Nov. 16, 1873, Salt Lake City (daughter of Abraham Reeves and Miss Straw of Kaysville, Utah, pioneers with oxteam company). She was born Feb. 6, 1844. Their children: Robert b. May 11, 1879, m. Mary Victoria Johnson; James Abraham b. April 29, 1880; Marintha b. May 23, 1881, d. infant.

Married Hertha Schoenfeld May 13, 1897, Salt Lake City (daughter of F. W. Schoenfeld and Henrietta Loman of Brighton, Utah, pioneers with John Smith company). She was born Oct. 11, 1873. Their children: Richard Fredrick b. June 19, 1898; Ralph Edwin b. Dec. 28, 1899; Howard Wilford b. July 19, 1901; Rudger Floyd b. Nov. 3, 1902; Orin b. May 24, 1906; Edna May b. Jan. 22, 1910. Family home Plain City, Utah.

Member 87th quorum seventies; high priest; missionary to England 1883-85. Farmer.

MAW, ROBERT (son of Robert Maw and Lois Reeves). Born May 11, 1879, Plain City, Utah.

Married Mary Victoria Johnson Dec. 22, 1909 (daughter of Victor Johnson and Hilda Kay of Woods Cross, Utah). She was born Feb. 2, 1887. Their children: Clarence Victor b. Sept. 17, 1910; Earl Lloyd b. Feb. 19, 1912. Family home, Salt Lake City.

Priest. Street car conductor.

MAW, ABRAHAM (son of Edward Maw and Dina Gledall). Born April 10, 1837, Root, Lincolnshire, Eng. Came to Utah with his father.

Married Eliza Tripp Aug. 1, 1859, in England (daughter of Thomas Tripp and Jane Snell). Their children: Robert William; Mary Jane; Dinah; Abram; John; Henry; Joseph; Charles; Florence Snell. Family home Plain City, Utah.

Married Olive Williams June 27, 1884, Salt Lake City. Only child: Albert William, m. Hattie P. Grant Dec. 7, 1910. Family home, Salt Lake City.

MAXFIELD, JOHN ELLIS (son of John Ellis Maxfield, born 1762, and Hannah Appleton, born 1760, both of Hull, Yorkshire, Eng.—married about 1782). He was born March 21, 1801, at Hull. Came to Utah Sept. 9, 1851, Abraham Day company.

Married Sarah Elizabeth Baker about 1827 (daughter of Jesse Baker and Sarah E. Schuerman—married about 1784 at Prince Edward Island, Canada). She was born May 10, 1810, and came to Utah with husband. Their children: Robert b. April 29, 1830, m. Emma Smith Jan., 1855; Richard b. May 5, 1831, m. Artie M. Harris Oct., 1854; Elijah H. b. Nov. 5, 1832, m. Helen A. Tanner Aug. 24, 1856; Jesse b. April 29, 1835, d. aged 15; James b. Jan. 14, 1837, m. Sophia Johnson 1861; John E. b. Nov. 15, 1838, m. Minnie Johnson 1859; William b. Dec. 10, 1839, m. Elizabeth Caldwell 1863; Sarah b. Jan. 18, 1844, m. George N. Stager 1859; Joseph S. b. June 13, 1847, m. Matilda Van Valkenburg Jan. 16, 1872; Quincy b. July 3, 1862, d. 1873; Henry b. Sept. 1, 1851, m. Helen Morrell 1873. Family home West Jordan, Utah.

Worked on Salt Lake temple. Settled at South Jordan 1851. High priest; ward teacher. Died Feb. 1, 1875.

1861, m. Samuel S. Ferrin: James A. b. April 21, 1864, m. Mary Ann Marshall; George H. b. April 4, 1866, m. Ruth Evans, m. Elizabeth Parrott; John L. b. April 16, 1868, m. Alice Marshall. Family home Pleasant View, Utah.
Married Mary Jane Hurst September, 1875, at Salt Lake City (daughter of William Hurst and Susannah Webley of Southampton, Eng., pioneers 1852, Captain Jepson company). She was born Nov. 7, 1838. Their children: Mary Helen b. March 3, 1877; Emma Elizabeth b. Nov. 14, 1878, m. William M. Wade; Susannah Vermell b. Dec. 11, 1882, m. David J. Johns.
Missionary to central states 1876-77; bishop of North Ogden ward; member of Pleasant View bishopric. Member of Young Express Co. Veteran Black Hawk and Walker Indian wars. Was one of the rescuers of the "Frozen" handcart company.

MAYCOCK, JAMES AMOS (son of Amos Maycock and Mary Humphreys). Born April, 1864, at North Ogden, Utah.
Married Mary Ann Marshall April 25, 1888, at Logan (daughter of John Marshall and Elizabeth Joyce), who was born Jan. 24, 1867. Their children: Ethel Maycock b. Feb. 25, 1889; Rhoda b. May 21, 1890; Cyril A. b. March 27, 1892; Herman J. b. May 21, 1893; George B. b. Aug. 24, 1894; Nona b. Sept. 7, 1895; William M. b. Nov. 23, 1896; Esther J. b. Nov. 22, 1897; Joseph W. b. Jan. 19, 1900; Laura b. March 1, 1902; Merril C. and Mariam b. Jan. 22, 1904.
Ward teacher; Sunday school teacher; assistant superintendent Sunday school. School trustee. Fruit grower and farmer. Died March 10, 1913.

MAYCOCK, JOHN EDWIN (son of Amos Maycock and Mary Humphreys). Born April 16, 1868, Pleasant View, Utah.
Married Alice Marshall Aug. 25, 1897, Salt Lake City (daughter of John Marshall and Elizabeth Joyce of Pleasant View, pioneers Aug. 20, 1868, Captain Roylance company). She was born July 19, 1874, died Aug. 1, 1910. Their children: Amos Joyce b. Sept. 11, 1900; Marshall Wright b. July 22, 1904. Family home Pleasant View, Utah.
Member 38th quorum seventies; missionary to eastern states 1897-99. Teacher; farmer.

MAYCOCK, JOHN (son of James Maycock and Esther Berry of Warwickshire, Eng.). Born in Warwickshire, Eng. Came to Utah 1852.
Married Helen Leslie 1853 at Springville, Utah. She was born May 2, 1826. Their children: George Henry, m. Julia Guyman; Ann Elizabeth, m. Hyrum Groesbeck; Helen Marilla, m. Romanzo A. Deal; John Berry, m. Tryphena Crandall. Family home Springville, Utah.
Missionary to England. Farmer. Died Feb. 14, 1888.

MAYER, GEORGE. Born 1805. Came to Utah Sept. 24, 1848, Heber C. Kimball company.
Married Ann Yost. Their children: Rachel Ann, m. George Washington Brimhall; Catherine, m. Jack Bivens; Elizabeth, m. James H. Glines; Maria Y., m. Leonard Smith; Sarah Jane, m. James Manly; Diantha, m. John Lollin; Benjamin, died at Ponca, Neb.; George Y., m. May Ann Whitney. Family home, Salt Lake City.
She died and he married Mary L. Wilson.
Married Maria Cable. Their children: Samuel, m. Jula Davis; Martha, m. Mosiah Handcock; Flora Ann, m. Everett Peck; Esther, m. Hosiah Handcock; John; Elizabeth, m. George A. Wilkins. Family home Spanish Fork, Utah.
Married Freda Johnson. Only child: Abraham, died.
President 22d quorum seventies; missionary to Switzerland; patriarch. Farmer

MAYHEW, ELIJAH (son of Elisha Mayhew and Abigail Tibbets). Born April 15, 1807, at Levant, Penobscot, Me. Came to Utah Sept. 9, 1853, Daniel Miller company.
Married Lydia Farnsworth Oct. 2, 1832, Shelbyville, Ind. She was born 1808 and came to Utah Sept. 9, 1853. Their children: Lucinda; Laurana; Otto Lyman; Austin Ship, m. Martha Walker; Elijah; Elisha; Caroline Abigail, m. Washburn Chipman; Elijah Warren; Walter Franklin, m. Eliza Dreinholt.
Married Elizabeth Seeley February, 1857, at Salt Lake City.
Married Sarah Young Peck July 10, 1859, Salt Lake City. She was born Oct. 8, 1834. Their children: Mary, m. Ferdinand Nelson; Elijah; Sarah, m. Fred Meachum; Elizabeth, m. James Astle; Charlotte; Grace.
Married Ann Rogers April 18, 1868, Salt Lake City. She was born Aug. 3, 1883. Their children: Lydia Ann, m. Samuel Kirk; Elisha Thomas, m. Miss Harper. Families resided Pleasant Grove, Utah.
High priest; tithing clerk; ward clerk at Pleasant Grove, Utah. County commissioner of Utah county; alderman Pleasant Grove. Railroad man. Died Jan. 17, 1896.

MAYHEW, OTTO LYMAN (son of Elijah Mayhew and Lydia Farnsworth). Born Oct. 2, 1836, Edinburg, Ind. Came to Utah Sept. 9, 1853.
Missionary to Alabama 1881-82; high priest. City recorder. Mail messenger. Farmer

MAYHEW, AUSTIN SHIP (son of Elijah Mayhew and Lydia Farnsworth). Born at Indianapolis, Ind. Came to Utah with oxteam company.
Married Martha Jane Walker at Salt Lake City (daughter of Hensen Walker and Sophrona Clark of Pleasant Grove, Utah, pioneers 1847). She was born May 18, 1853. Their children: Austin, Jr.; Elijah Walker b. July 11, 1871, m. Rosetta White; Martha Medora, m. Benjamin Gibbons; Berthenia, m. Rufus Stoddard; Cordelia, m. Hyrum Knight; Ernest, d. infant; Caroline, m. Myron Lance; Walter Franklin, m. Nellie May Abbott; Robert Ray; Luella, m. Joseph Pedersen; Otto Benjamin; Shelby. Family home Giles, Utah.
Elder; ward teacher; Sunday school teacher. Assisted in bringing immigrants to Utah. Veteran Indian wars. Farmer; stockraiser; mechanic. Died May 22, 1910, at Giles, Utah.

MAYHEW, ELIJAH W. (son of Austin Ship Mayhew and Martha Jane Walker). Born July 11, 1871, Pleasant Grove, Utah.
Married Rosetta White May 22, 1896, at Giles, Utah (daughter of John C. White and Mary Ann Ingram, of Nephi and Orderville, Utah, pioneers Sept. 20, 1853, Hyrum Clawson company). She was born Aug. 7, 1872. Their children: Wayne Elijah b. March 13, 1897; Melvin Ray b. Nov. 28, 1899; Burdett b. Dec. 3, 1901; Berney b. Aug. 22, 1903; Edna b. March 30, 1905; Fay White b. Jan. 7, 1907; Dora Helen b. Feb. 19, 1909; Rosey May b. April 17, 1910; Lillie White b. Nov. 6, 1911.
High priest; ward teacher; Sunday school superintendent; president Y. M. M. I. A.; counselor to Bishop White. Postmaster at Giles, Utah. Now lives at Duchesne, Uinta county. Farmer and stockraiser.

MAYNES, JOHN A. (son of John A. Maynes and Jane Watson of London, Eng., who came to Utah 1878). Born Oct. 28, 1859, Hull, Eng.
Married Selina J. Sabine March 16, 1882, Salt Lake City (daughter of James Sabine and Jane Holder), who was born July 29, 1861, at Wiltshire, Eng., and came to Utah Sept. 2, 1868, with parents. Their children: John A. b. March 21, 1883; Albert J. b. July 27, 1884; Edith L. b. March 15, 1886, m. Milton G. Wilson Nov. 27, 1907; Ernest E. b. Dec. 23, 1887, d. infant; Joseph S. b. July 23, 1889, d. infant; Frederick W. b. Dec. 4, 1890; Dorothy J. b. Oct. 21, 1903. Family home, Salt Lake City.
Manager and jewelry salesman.

MEAD, ORLANDO FISH. Came to Utah 1847, contingent of Mormon Battalion.
Married Lydia Aby Presley (daughter of Joseph Presley of Carthage, Mo., who died on the plains en route to Utah). Their children: Anna E., m. T. Pratt; Zina, m. Don Corbit, m. Mike Conners; Kiszer, m. E. Dimick; Emily Jane, m. Nephi N. Perkins; Amanda, m. Samuel Montgomery, m. John Thompson, m. Henry Checkett; Zolena, m. Heber Thompson, m. James Dickens Fullmer; Orlando, m. Pheney Davis; George, m. Sadie Thompson; Eleanor, d. infant. Family resided Spanish Fork and Price, Utah.
Guard in Indian troubles in Salt Lake Valley. Died Feb. 26, 1897, Price, Utah.

MECHAM, EDWARD (son of Joshua Mecham and Permelia Chapman of New Hampshire). Born Feb. 22, 1802, in New Hampshire. Came to Utah 1851, Morris Phelps company.
Married Irena Currier in Pennsylvania (daughter of John Currier and Sallie Silver of New Hampshire). Their children: Roxena, m. William F. Carter; Sallie Ann, m. William F. Carter; Amasa Lyman, m. Emily Cobbley and Lorena Boren.
Married Sophia Burris (Osman) May 1864, Provo, Utah.
Married Hannah Phillips at Provo, Utah (daughter of Mathew Phillips of same place). Only child: Mathew, m. Miss Phillips. Families resided Provo, Utah.
Seventy. Furniture dealer. Died July 31, 1895.

MECHAM, AMASA LYMAN (son of Edward Mecham and Irena Currier). Born March 30, 1848, Nauvoo, Ill. Came to Utah October, 1851, Morris Phelps company.
Married Emily Cobbley Dec. 1866, Provo, Utah (daughter of Thomas Cobbley and Sarah Smith of Pleasant Grove), who was born Feb. 21, 1851. Their children: Edward C. b. Dec. 15, 1867; Amasa Lyman, Jr. b. Feb. 21, 1870, m. Nettie Ketah; Irene b. Aug. 15, 1872, m. Frank W. Cromson; Eugene b. Aug. 1, 1875, died.
Married Lorena Boren (daughter of Colman Boren and Malinda Keller of Provo, pioneers Oct. 1851). She was born June 29, 1847, Mt. Pisgah, Iowa. Their children: Wells Osmond, m. Rachel Hood; Emily, m. Dean McEwen; Alma, m. Ava Rilla Hiatt, m. Mary Cook; Earl, m. Vera Burr; Pearl; Amy. Families resided Provo, Utah.
High priest; member bishopric 17 years 1886-1901; Sunday school superintendent. School trustee. Fruit grower.

MECHAM, EPHRAIM (son of Joshua Mecham and Permelia Chapman). Born March 6, 1808, Cannan, Grafton county, N. H. Came to Utah 1852, oxteam company.
Married Polly Derby Nov. 22, 1829, in Mercer county, Pa. (daughter of John Derby and Sarah Currier), who was born Aug. 13, 1813. Their children: Amos Mecham, d. infant; Permelia, m. Daniel Bigelow; Lewis, m. Esther Herbert;

Elvira, d. child; Emma, m. William Hill; Hyrum Moroni, m. Sarah A. Stephens; Sarah Ann, d. child; Ephraim Don Carlos, d. infant; Mary Henrietta, m. Miles Batty; Polly Celeatia, m. William Haws; John Albert, m. Rosella Ann Bigelow; Adelia Vilate, m. Robert Glenn. Family home Wallsburg, Utah.
Farmer and horticulturist. Died July 6, 1891.

MECHAM, LEWIS (son of Ephraim Mecham and Polly Derby). Came to Utah 1862, oxteam company.
Married Vasta Johnson (daughter of Luke Johnson). Their child: Lafayette (deceased), m. Sarah Ann Richens.
Married Ester Herbert. Their children: Luke R.; Polly Esther; Orson; George Fayette, m. Ida Viola Boren; Emma Naomi; Ephraim Liberty; Marquis Herbert; Mary; Gib Ami; Burnet; Alice. Family home Wallsburg, Ut
Seventy; second counselor to Bishop Frag— at Wallsburg, Utah. Veteran of the Black Hawk and the Walker Indian wars, and also took part in the Johnston army trouble. Farmer. Died Oct. 14, 1907.

MECHAM, GEORGE FAYETTE (son of Lewis Mecham and Ester Herbert). Born April 5, 1875, Wallsburg, Utah.
Married Ida Viola Boren April 29, 1896, at Salt Lake City (daughter of William Jasper Boren and Lucina Mecham, 1817. Their children: Arthur Fayette b. June 6, 1897; Amorie b. Sept. 5, 1898; Dean b. Aug. 9, 1901; Erma V. b. June 26, 1903; Viola b. April 26, 1907. Family home Wallsburg, Utah.
Elder. Farmer.

MECHAM, LEWIS (son of Joshua Mecham and Permella Chapman, Canaan, N. H.). Born Sept. 4, 1814, Canaan, N. H. Came to Utah Oct. 5, 1851, James Snow company.
Married Lydia Wells April 9, 1836, Mercer, Pa. (daughter of Judah Wells and Temperance Mecham of Mercer, Pa., the latter came to Utah Oct. 5, 1851). She was born Aug. 6, 1817. Their children: Emeline, m. Hyrum Sweet; Mosiah, died; Margaret, m. Thomas Ross; Joshua Josiah, m. Donna M. Mecham; Elmira Ann, m. Henry Meeks; Melissa, died; Brigham, m. Harriet Kirby; Lydia, m. James Herbert; Martha Jane, m. William Wall; Lewis, m. Agnes Hoover; Samantha, m. Isaac Romanzo Faucett; Johnathan, m. Elizabeth Duke; Judah, died; Sarah, m. George J. Duke. Family home Provo, Utah.
Member of bodyguard of Joseph Smith. Wheelwright; farmer; fruitgrower; nurseryman. Died March 22, 1895.

MECHAM, BRIGHAM (son of Lewis Mecham and Lydia Wells). Born Nov. 24, 1847, Garden Grove, Decatur Co., Iowa. Came to Utah 1851.
Married Harriet Kirby Oct. 20, 1873, at Salt Lake City (daughter of Francis Kirby and Mary Le Carnier of Channel Islands, Isle of Jersey. Came to Utah 1860). She was born Jan. 13, 1855. Their children: Mary Viola b. Dec. 2, 1874, m. Joseph Young; Harriet E. b. Oct. 22, 1876, m. Ephraim Mecham; Ray b. Aug. 29, 1880, died; Roy b. Aug. 29, 1880, died; Lewis Walter b. Sept. 3, 1881, m. Pearl Ivie; Francis b. Feb. 2, 1883, m. Alice Myler; Alice b. Nov. 4, 1886, m. Robert Sweet; Brigham Warren b. May 25, 1889; Margaret b. April 27, 1892, died; Albert Wells b. March 20, 1895; Herschell R. (adopted) b. May 7, 1898. Family home Wallsburg, Utah.
High priest; bishop for two years at Rosehill church of Wallsburg; teacher and home missionary; 1865 stood guard on Provo river and at Heber City. Veteran of Black Hawk war. Farmer.

MECHAM, LEWIS (son of Lewis Mecham and Lydia Wells). Born March 28, 1854, Provo, Utah.
Married Agnes Jane Hoover Nov. 28, 1878, Salt Lake Endowment house (daughter of John W. Hoover, Sr., and Mary Elizabeth Corsey of Provo, pioneers with oxteams). She was born Dec. 8, 1860. Their children: Daisy b. June 28, 1879, m. Gibson Condie; Mary Elizabeth b. Oct. 1, 1881, d. infant; William Whitmer b. Dec. 4, 1883; Elsie May b. Feb. 27, 1887, m. Joseph Smith Jr. Aug. 12, 1891; Ferris Earl b. Nov. 20, 1893; Agnes b. April 13, 1896; Joshua b. Feb. 13, 1899; Lynn b. July 11, 1901. Family resided Provo and Wallsburg, Utah.
Elder; ward and Sunday school teacher. Farmer. Died March 29, 1910, Wallsburg, Utah.

MECHAM, WILLIAM WHITMER (son of Lewis Mecham and Agnes Jane Hoover). Born Dec. 4, 1883, Provo, Utah.
Deacon. Farmer.

MEEKS, PRIDDY (son of Athe Meeks and Margaret Snead of Greeneville, S. C.). Born Aug. 29, 1795, Greeneville. Came to Utah Oct. 2, 1847, Jedediah M. Grant company.
Married Mary Bartlett March, 1815. She died in Spencer county, Ind., 1824. Their children: Lovin b. March 7, 1816, d. 1851; Eliza b. Dec. 10, 1817, d. 1825; Athe b. Oct. 4, 1819; Elizabeth b. July 2, 1823.
Married Sarah Mahurin (Smith) Dec. 24, 1826 (daughter of Steven Mahurin and Sarah Meeks), who was born Dec. 12, 1802, and came to Utah with husband. Their children: Susan Smith (adopted) b. May 30, 1819, m. O. B. Adams; Mary Jane b. Sept. 29, 1827; Steven Mahurin b. March 30, 1830; Eluldah b. Aug. 17, 1833; Margaret Jane b. May 8, 1838, m. Samuel Hamilton; Sarah Angeline b. Nov. 9, 1845.
Married Mary Jane McCleve Nov. 13, 1856, Salt Lake City (daughter of John McCleve and Nancy Jane McGovern, who came to Utah, Daniel D. McArthur company— married at Belfast, Ireland). She was born Aug. 21, 1842, Belfast, Ireland. Their children: Joseph b. Dec. 13, 1857, m. Mary Ellen Dorrity April 20, 1879; Nancy b. Aug. 12, 1859, m. Jerome Asay; Hyrum b. Oct. 4, 1861, m. Patience Maria Hardy; John Priddy b. Sept. 29, 1863, died; Sarah Deseret b. Dec. 9, 1864, m. J. B. Morris; Mary Ellen b. Jan. 31, 1867, m. Josiah M. Hoyt; Heber Jesse b. May 9, 1869, m. Clara Bowers; Charles Mason b. March 31, 1872, died; Elizabeth Dalton b. March 31, 1874, m. Norman P. Fackrell; Alfred Randall b. May 13, 1877, m. Linda Covington.

MEEKS, JOSEPH (son of Priddy Meeks and Mary Jane McCleve). Born Dec. 13, 1857, Parowan, Utah.
Married Mary Ellen Dorrity at Leeds, Washington Co., Utah, April 20, 1879 (daughter of James Bruse Dorrity and Amanda Jane Lee, who came to Utah in 1857 with William Moody company). She was born Sept. 21, 1861, Gunnison, Utah. Their children: Elsie b. March 16, 1880, m. Wilford Albert Halladay April 6, 1897; Ellen Amanda b. Dec. 11, 1881, m. Edgar Pierce Fullmer March 29, 1897; Sarah Susan b. Nov. 25, 1883, m. Wilford Rynearson Feb. 19, 1904; Ida b. Feb. 15, 1887, m. John Bolker May 1, 1908; Joseph Priddy b. Aug. 18, 1889; James Orson b. Dec. 15, 1891. Family home Leeds, Washington Co., Utah.
Second counselor in bishoporic, Circleville ward, Panguitch stake, 1894; stake superintendent of Sabbath school, Kanab stake, 1888-93. Commissioner Kane county 1891; justice of the peace seven years; school trustee for nine years. President of Y. M. M. I. A. Chief probation officer for Piute Co., Utah.

MEEKS, HYRUM SMITH (son of Priddy Meeks and Mary Jane McCleve). He was born Oct. 4, 1861, St. George, Utah.
Married Patience Hardy Feb. 21, 1882, Salt Lake City, Utah (daughter of Lewis O. and Clarinda Jane Doffelmyre, Ogden, Utah), who was born May 12, 1864. Their children: Hyrum b. July 2, 1883, d. child; Alfred James b. Aug. 31, 1885, m. Zilpha Caroline Wall; Belle B. b. May 9, 1888; Ora b. April 25, 1892, d. 1898; Virde b. May 29, 1894; Ida May b. May 8, 1903; Zara Thelda b. Dec. 12, 1905. Family home Jensen, Utah.
Elder; ward teacher. Marshal; deputy sheriff; supervisor of roads and watermaster two years, Vernal, Utah. Vice-president of Farmer Burns bench irrigation company and Jensen Irrigation company.

MEEKS, WILLIAM. Born 1815, Spencer county, Ind. Came to Utah 1852, Captain Nisonger company.
Married Mary Elizabeth Rhodes (daughter of George), who was born 1818. Their children: Harvey b. April 9, 1838, m. Catherine Dowie; Henry b. Jan. 1840, m. Ann Mecham; Elizabeth b. June 1841, m. Jared Bullock; May Annie b. Nov. 23, 1844, m. William Cummings; William b. 1846, m. Sarah Gardner; Joseph b. 1848, m. Vilate Burgess; Mary Jane b. 1850, m. James Pierce; Mary Melissa b. 1856, m. Willard Snow; Mary Louisa b. Aug. 23, 1859, m. James Gardner. Family home Provo, Utah.

MEGUIRE, WILLIAM WELLS (son of Thomas and Catherine Meguire, of Chester county, Pa.). Born June 25, 1819, Chester county. Came to Utah 1852, Captain Curtis company.
Married Charlotte — Dec. 10, 1828, Chester county, Pa. She was born Nov. 22, 1803. Their children: Catherine b. Oct. 15, 1833, m. Alonzo Knight April 24, 1853; Julia Ann, m. Mr. Dunn Feb. 11, 1855. Family home Plain City, Utah.
Seventy. Justice of peace; postmaster. School teacher. Died Dec. 8, 1887.

MEIKLE, JAMES (son of William Meikle, Hamilton, Scotland, and Margaret Jackson, born July 19, 1798, Cumbuslang, Scotland—married June 22, 1834). Born July 5, 1839, Hamilton, Scotland. Came to Utah Sept. 28, 1856, Daniel D. McArthur company.
Married Harriette Louisa Peacock Jan. 3, 1864 (daughter of William and Phillis Hyam Peacock, pioneers 1865—married Nov. 9, 1835, London, Eng.). She was born Nov. 10, 1837. Their children: James Jackson b. Sept. 24, 1864, m. Malinda Tidwell Feb. 23, 1888; Thomas William b. July 8, 1866, d. Oct. 27, 1867; Robert Gilbert b. June 5, 1868, m. Sophia Mack 1894; Alfred William b. Jan. 30, 1870, m. Amelia Allen Feb. 23, 1893, d. June 21, 1911; Isabell Merrion b. Jan. 22, 1872, m. Foster J. Gordon Dec. 29, 1898; Samuel b. March 20, 1874, d. Dec. 29, 1874; Joseph Arthur b. Jan. 10, 1877, m. Temperance Allen May 10, 1899; Harriette Louisa b. June 23, 1879, m. Samuel A. Gordon Feb. 27, 1901. Family home Smithfield, Utah.
Married Lovina Noble Oct. 17, 1872, Salt Lake City (daughter of William Noble and Mary Ann Waterhouse, pioneers 1863), who was born March 23, 1839, Hartford, Eng. Their children: Lavina Priscilla b. Sept. 25, 1873, m. James Kirby 1898; Katy Violett b. Aug. 16, 1875, m. Wickliff Ewing June, 1904; Margaret Jessey b. Jan. 17, 1877, d. May 4, 1877; Zilpha b. June 3, 1879, m. Lindsey Lightfoot Jan. 12, 1899; Mamie Rebecca b. April 7, 1882, m. Carl Nielson June 5, 1902; Birdie b. Sept. 11, 1884, m. Frank Covey 1902.
Missionary to England and Scotland 1892-84; president Birmingham conference, England; chairman old folks committee of Benson stake; president of the high priests of

PIONEERS AND PROMINENT MEN OF UTAH

Smithfield, Utah. Member of the university land board two years; county commissioner of Cache county two years; water commissioner seven years. Member of Lieut. Gen. James Furgeson's detachment Mormon Battalion; minute man in Cache Valley under Major Thos. E. Ricks.

MEIKLE, JAMES JACKSON (son of James Meikle and Harriette Louisa Peacock). Born Sept. 24, 1864, Smithfield, Cache Co., Utah.
Married Malinda Tidwell Feb. 23, 1888, Logan, Utah (daughter of Peter and Sophronia Hatch Tidwell, the former pioneer 1849), who was born Sept. 29, 1866, Smithfield, Utah. Their children: Clarence b. March 15, 1889; Rada b. July 14, 1891; Vivian b. May 11, 1898, d. Dec. 17, 1898; Jennie b. Dec. 31, 1905.
Smithfield city councilman two years and mayor of Smithfield four years; chairman of Cache county commissioners.

MEIKLEJOHN, ROBERT (son of Peter Meiklejohn and Jeannetta Wilson). Born March 10, 1812, Glasgow, Scotland. Came to Utah Oct. 24, 1855, Milo Andrus company.
Married Mary McLackan (daughter of Colin McLackan and Agnes McCroon), who was born April 14, 1812. Their children: Peter b. April 10, 1836, and Agnes b. March 15, 1838, died; Jeannetta b. April 13, 1840, m. Philip De La Mare July 16, 1857; Mary b. July 29, 1842, m. John A. Smith 1864; Jean b. Feb. 13, 1845, m. John C. Shields Dec. 22, 1865; Catherine b. Aug. 16, 1851, died; Robert (adopted) b. April 17, 1872, m. Elvenia H. Hanks 1896. Family home Tooele City, Utah.
Married Elizabeth Sanders Jan. 11, 1879, Salt Lake City (daughter of Thomas Sanders and Elizabeth Gordon), who was born Jan. 11, 1857, Salt Lake City. Their children: Mary E. b. Nov. 17, 1879, died; Robert William b. Jan. 27, 1882; Arthur b. Nov. 8, 1884; Sarah b. Feb. 16, 1890, m. George W. Eddins Jan. 3, 1912. Family home Tooele, Utah.

MELDRUM, GEORGE (son of John Meldrum and Agnes Hean of Carlston, Forfarshire, Scotland). Born Aug. 24, 1830, Carlston, Scotland. Came to Utah Sept. 24, 1860, Edward Martin and Daniel Tyler handcart company.
Married Jane Barclay Jan. 17, 1848, Leslie, Scotland (daughter of David and Jane Graham Barclay of Leslie). She was born Nov. 22, 1825, and came to Utah Sept. 24, 1860, with the last handcart company. Their children: John B. b. March 21, 1849, m. Sarah Forsythe (died), m. Adeline Jones; David b. July 31, 1851, m. Etta Hooks; James Low b. Aug. 5, 1853, m. Hannah Jane Haws; George b. April 21, 1856, m. Olive Penrod, m. Jane Richmond; William Barclay b. Nov. 14, 1859, m. Minnie Harding; Thomas Alexander b. Feb. 14, 1862, m. Jane Duke; Mary Jane, died; Margaret E. b. Sept. 5, 1866 (died), m. Thomas Dryber; Joseph b. April 17, 1869, m. Sonoma Richmond. Family home Provo, Utah.
Member of quorum seventies; missionary to Edinburgh, Scotland, 1877-79, and to Shetland Islands 1880; second counselor to Bishop John Edge Booth for 20 years, fourth ward. Interested in Provo Woolen Mills, East and West Company operative stores and other mercantile companies; shoemaker; farmer; fruitgrower.

MELDRUM, JAMES LOWE (son of George Meldrum and Jane Barcley). Born Aug. 5, 1853, in Leslie, Scotland. Came to Utah Sept. 24, 1860, Edward Martin and Daniel Tyler company.
Married Jane Hannah Haws Aug. 5, 1873, Salt Lake City (daughter of William Wallace Haws, pioneer 1848, and Barbara B. Mills of Provo). She was born in 1852. Their children: James, died; Lillie May, m. Frank Sackett; Elmer Cornelius; Nellie, m. Owen Hull; George; Donald Wesley (died), m. Sarah Moore; G. Gilbert; Effie; Calvin; Fleta; Vernal. Family home Provo, Utah.
Elder. County fruit tree inspector 1903-05; supervisor Provo-Olmstead county boulevard; planted first orchard in Pleasant View ward; director of Timpanogos canal company; owner in Fawcett Field canal company. Railroad tie and lumber business for 17 years; had charge of Holdaway's sawmill and loggers in Spanish Fork canyon 1880-82. Pioneer Gila. Ariz., 1882. Successful farmer and horticulturist Utah county.

MELDRUM, WILLIAM BARCLAY (son of George Meldrum and Jane Barclay). Born Nov. 14, 1859. Came to Utah 1860 with parents.
Married Minnie S. Harding Aug. 29, 1894, Salt Lake City (daughter of Edward G. Harding and Sarah Ann Meeks of Trowbridge, Wiltshire, Eng. Came to Utah Sept. 6, 1874). She was born Aug. 22, 1872. Only child: Nellie Irene Contaser (adopted) b. May 12, 1902. Family home Provo, Utah.
High priest. Carpenter and builder.

MELDRUM, THOMAS ALEXANDER (son of George Meldrum and Jane Barclay). Born Feb. 14, 1862, Provo, Utah.
Married Jane Duke Feb. 16, 1887, Logan, Utah (daughter of Jonathan Oldham Duke, pioneer 1850, and Martha Tompson, he of Derby and she of Oldham Parish, Eng.—married Dec. 3, 1855, at Provo). She was born Aug. 23, 1862. Their children: Emma b. Aug. 25, 1888; Thomas Albert b. Sept. 3, 1890; Reed Duke b. Sept. 28, 1892; Walter b. Oct. 11, 1894, d. July 17, 1895; Martha Jane b. Sept. 16, 1897; Ralph b. June 13, 1900. Family home Pleasant View, Utah.
Elder. Farmer and stockraiser; plasterer. Died May 9, 1912.

MELLEN, JOHN (son of John Mellen and Ann Horrick of Lancastershire, Eng.). Born Aug. 18, 1813, in Lancastershire. Came to Utah Sept. 20, 1848, Brigham Young company.
Married Jane Ramsden 1836, Lancastershire, Eng. (daughter of James Ramsden and Catherine Lever of Lancastershire). She was born Sept. 26, 1816. Their children: John R., m. Julia Huntington; Jane, m. John Winegar; William, d. young; Alice, m. George W. Perkins; Joseph, m. Martha Cumberland; Catherine Ann, m. Isaac Coon; Elizabeth, m. Richard Margetts; Mary, m. John F. Bouck; Sarah, m. Fredrick Mitchell; Martha, m. Judith Howell. Family home 16th ward, Salt Lake City.
Seventy; high priest. Stonemason. Died Feb. 16, 1896.

MELLEN, JOHN R. (son of John Mellen and Jane Ramsden). Born May 27, 1838, Bolton, Eng.). Came to Utah 1848, Erastus Snow company.
Married Julia Huntington June 7, 1885, Salt Lake City (daughter of Dimmick B. Huntington and Fannie M. Allen of Watertown, N. Y., pioneers July 29, 1847, Capt. James Brown's detachment of the Mormon Battalion). She was born June 21, 1848. Only child: Theresia b. Nov. 23, 1887, m. Martin Larson. Family home Pleasant Green, Utah.
Pony express rider. Veteran Black Hawk Indian war. Miner; farmer and stockraiser.

MELLEN, JOSEPH H. (son of John Mellen and Jane Ramsden). Born April 11, 1848, Winter Quarters, Neb. Came to Utah with his parents.
Married Martha A. Cumberland in September, 1870, Salt Lake City (daughter of Henry Cumberland and Elizabeth Kelly of Salt Lake City). She was born Sept. 4, 1851. Their children: John R. b. March 4, 1872, d. infant; Joseph W. b. March 8, 1873, m. Estella Jacobson; Frank b. May 24, 1875, m. Bessie Peterson; Edith J. b. Jan. 3, 1877, m. Edward A. Morehouse; Elizabeth C. b. March 31, 1879, d. aged 17; Clara b. Sept. 30, 1881, d. aged 25; Martha A. b. Jan. 27, 1884, d. aged 2; Flora b. Jan. 22, 1886, m. Lewis F. Harris; Inez L. b. June 1, 1893. Family home Salt Lake City, Utah.
Seventy. Contractor.

MELLEN, JOSEPH W. (son of Joseph H. Mellen and Martha A Cumberland). Born March 8, 1873, Salt Lake City.
Married Estella M. Jacobson Sept. 14, 1898, Salt Lake City, by Judge Bartch (daughter of Aaron Jacobson and Ann M. Simons of Bountiful). She was born Nov. 29, 1876. Their children: Ivy M. b. June 22, 1899; Harvey J. b. Dec. 13, 1900; Clyde L. b. March 8, 1909; Glen S. b. April 7, 1911. Family home 16th ward, Salt Lake City.
General contractor.

MELLOR, JOHN (son of William Mellor and Ann Dilks of Leicestershire, Eng.). Born 1811, in Leicestershire. Came to Utah 1868.
Married Mary Fletcher in England (daughter of William Fletcher and Mary Bellamy). Their children: John; Mary Ann; William; Edwin Dilks; Sarah B. Family home, Leicestershire.
Married Amy Bellamy (daughter of Charles Bellamy and Ann Dilks), who was born in Leicestershire, Eng. Their children: Sarah b. Aug. 9, 1848, m. Wilber Foss 1877; William b. Dec. 30, 1849; Amy b. Dec. 4, 1852, m. Amos Howe; James b. April 27, 1856, died; Annie b. July 15, 1858, m. Levi Brown; James Charles b. Nov. 8, 1860, died; Alice b. July 15, 1861, died; Edwin James b. May 20, 1862, m. Mary McBeemus; Elizabeth b. Aug. 19, 1864, died; Elizabeth Ann b. Jan. 1, 1867, m. J. W. Duffin; Rachel Dilks b. Aug. 25, 1869; Albert Charles b. Feb. 4, 1873.

MELLOR, EDWIN JAMES (son of John Mellor and Amy Bellamy). Born May 20, 1863, Leicestershire, Eng. Came to Utah with parents.
Married Mary Martha McBeemus 1884, Salt Lake City (daughter of George M. and Margerite McBeemus, pioneers 1858, among first settlers of Gunnison). She was born Sept. 6, 1866. Their children: Diana Elizabeth; William James; Amise Leone; Flossie Margerite. Family home Fayette, Utah.

MEMMOTT, WILLIAM (son of Thomas Memmott, born 1789, and Sarah Willden, born 1788, Aston, Yorkshire, Eng.). Born July 11, 1813, Aston, Yorkshire. Came to Utah Sept. 12, 1861, Milo Andrus company.
Married Ann Wilson (daughter of James Wilson and Martha Wilkinson), who was born Aug. 12, 1813. Their children: Thomas b. Feb. 27, 1838, m. Emma Whitham April 12, 1857; Martha b. Oct. 21, 1839; James Wilson b. Feb. 25, 1841, m. Elizabeth Hopkins 1861; John Wilson b. March 1, 1845; William b. Oct. 4, 1847, m. Elizabeth Monroe Jan. 17, 1875; Samuel b. July 18, 1850, m. Mary Ann Monroe Jan. 26, 1873; Sarah Ann b. Nov. 6, 1855, m. Jacob Miller June 22, 1870. Family home Scipio, Millard Co., Utah.
High priest; president of elders' quorum, Scipio, Utah; president of Deepcar and Rotherham branches, Sheffield conference, England, three years. Justice of the peace, Scipio precinct, two terms; postmaster of Scipio over 30 years.

MEMMOTT, SAMUEL (son of William Memmott and Ann Wilson). Born July 18, 1850.
Married Mary Ann Monroe Jan. 26, 1873, Scipio. Utah (daughter of George Monroe and Margaret Sanders), who was born April 16, 1853, Pentrabach, Merthyr Tidfil, Glamor-

PIONEERS AND PROMINENT MEN OF UTAH

ganshire, Wales. Their children: Niletta b. Dec. 4, 1873, m. Henry W. Schutter Oct. 1, 1894; Gilbert b. July 22, 1876; Mary Edna b. Aug. 9, 1877, m. Silas H. Carman Sept. 12, 1900; Florence b. Aug. 28, 1881, m. Joseph Brenchley April 12, 1905; Robert Lyman b. March 1, 1884, m. Emma K. Peterson Oct. 18, 1905; Angus b. March 30, 1887; Lizzy b. June 27, 1889. Family home Scipio, Utah.
Married Alice Arilla Hutchinson (daughter of Jacob Flynn Hutchinson, pioneer 1850, Edward Hunter company, and Alice P. Wasden, pioneer 1859, Edward Stevenson company). She was born Jan. 17, 1866, Springville, Utah. Their children: Ray Lincoln b. Sept. 20, 1902; Dorothy b. Oct. 9, 1903; Seymour Carl b. July 6, 1907; Samuel Paul b. July 29, 1909. Family home, Scipio.
High priest; high councilor in Millard stake; assistant Sunday school superintendent; president of Y. M. M. I. A. many times; ward teacher. School trustee; justice of the peace. Veteran Indian war.

MENDENHALL, THOMAS (son of Abraham Mendenhall, born March 28, 1766, Mill Creek, Newcastle county, Del., and Elizabeth Wells, born Dec. 15, 1778—married Jan. 4, 1798). He was born March 10, 1806, Wilmington, Mercer county. Came to Utah Sept. 15, 1852, David Wood company.
Married Mary Ann Synix, who was born Sept. 16, 1812, and came to Utah with husband. Their children: Susannah b. Sept. 26, 1834, m. Jacob Cloward; George Madison b. Sept. 29, 1836, m. Celestia Ann Mecham; Lewis Henry b. Sept. 26, 1838, m. Maria Gay; Edmund b. Sept. 29, 1841; Thomas Jr. b. Feb. 18, 1844, m. Louisa Fleet; Elizabeth b. Feb. 1847. Family resided Spanish Fork, Utah, and Franklin, Idaho.
Settler of Spanish Fork, Utah, and a pioneer of Franklin, Idaho. Farmer and trader. Died 1888, Dayton, Idaho.

MENDENHALL, GEORGE MADISON (son of Thomas Mendenhall and Mary Ann Synix. Born Sept. 29, 1836, Wilmington, Del.
Married Celestia Ann Mecham Sept. 28, 1867, Salt Lake City (daughter of Moses Warthen Mecham and Elvira Derby), who was born Sept. 12, 1848. Their children: Mary Elvira b. Sept. 3, 1868, m. Nephi M. Perkins; George Madison b. Jan. 1, 1870; Valeria Jane b. Dec. 24, 1872; Thomas Leslie b. Sept. 24, 1874; Moses Leroy b. June 24, 1876; Arthur John b. June 3, 1878, m. Olive Ann McCarrey; Estus Clinton b. Jan. 8, 1850; Effie Maria b. Oct. 7, 1881; James Mecham b. Aug. 16, 1883, m. Effie C. Perkins; Lucina b. May 9, 1885; Elsie Mecham b. June 9, 1887; Elmer Mecham b. Aug. 3, 1889; Zella Mecham b. Sept. 21, 1891; Willis b. Aug. 31, 1893. Family home Dayton, Oneida county, Idaho.
Early settler at Spanish Fork, Utah, and at Dayton, Idaho, in 1868. Minute man. Assisted in bringing immigrants to Utah.

MENDENHALL, ARTHUR JOHN (son of George Madison Mendenhall and Celestia Ann Mecham). Born June 3, 1878, Dayton, Idaho.
Married Olive Ann McCarrey Sept. 7, 1904, Logan, Utah (daughter of William McCarrey, pioneer 1852 and Hannah Melissa Hooper, pioneer 1859, Harlow Levi Redfield company). She was born Oct. 20, 1879, Richmond, Utah. Their children: Fern McCarrey b. Sept. 18, 1905; Donna Mae b. Oct. 25, 1906; Olive Mc. b. July 6, 1908; Wilma Mc. b. Oct. 25, 1910; Arthur John b. Nov. 22, 1912. Family home Richmond, Utah.
Assistant Sunday school superintendent, Dayton, Idaho; ward clerk; missionary Oct. 28, 1899 to March 15, 1902. Settled at Richmond May 15, 1906. Farmer.

MENDENHALL, THOMAS (son of Thomas Mendenhall and Mary Ann Synix). Born Feb. 18, 1844, Nauvoo, Ill. Came to Utah with parents.
Married Louisa Smart March 31, 1863, Franklin, Idaho (daughter of Thomas Smart and Ann Hayter of Franklin, pioneers Sept. 4, 1852). She was born Oct. 11, 1846. Their children: Catherine Ann b. Dec. 29, 1863; Thomas George June 7, 1865; Mary Ann b. May 3, 1867, m. Samuel Webster; Rhoda Kiziah b. July 25, 1869, m. John Wilkinson; Susanna b. Nov. 29, 1871, m. Elias W. Doney; William Henry b. Nov. 21, 1873, m. Naomi Herd Sept. 20, 1893; Lorin Matthew b. March 18, 1876, m. Elvira Durrant; Ada Louisa b. Jan. 12, 1878, m. Samuel Webster; Ruby May b. Nov. 16, 1880, m. George Handy; Nettie Pearl b. March 7, 1883, m. Alonzo Handy; Leo b. April 7, 1886, m. Agnes Turner; Bert b. July 4, 1888. Family home Franklin, Idaho.
Indian war veteran. Died March 21, 1909.

MENDENHALL, WILLIAM HENRY (son of Thomas Mendenhall and Louisa Smart). Born Nov. 21, 1873, Preston, Idaho.
Married Naomi Herd Sept. 20, 1893, Logan, Utah (daughter of James Herd and Grace Knowles, of Darwin, Eng., and Franklin, Idaho; came to Utah Oct. 5, 1875). She was born Aug. 25, 1873. Their children: Vernon Herd b. April 5, 1898; Lovell James b. Aug. 21, 1899; William Thomas b. Feb. 26, 1901; Murat Herd b. July 18, 1902; Millen Herd b. Feb. 26, 1904; Naomi Herd b. Nov. 28, 1905; Ruth Herd b. Feb. 17, 1910; Elease Herd b. March 24, 1912. Family home Thatcher, Idaho.
Member of seventy; missionary to Sandwich Islands; bishop of Mound Valley ward, Oneida stake; second counselor to Lewis S. Pond, Bannock stake; first counselor in the stake presidency; counselor in the superintendency of Y.

M. M. I. A. Oneida stake; ordained to Aaronic priesthood; first counselor to President Lewis S. Pond of Bannock stake, Zion. Merchant. Member 12th Idaho legislature; notary public. School teacher. Farmer.

MENDENHALL, WILLIAM (son of Abraham Mendenhall of Brandywine Springs, Del, and Elizabeth Wells). He was born April 8, 1815, Mill Creek Hundred, Newcastle county, Del. Came to Utah Sept. 18, 1852.
Married Sarah Lovell Feb. 21, 1838 (daughter of Richard Lovell and Frances Sawdon), who was born March 12, 1818. Their children: Mary Frances; Thomas Lovell; Abraham; Richard Lovell b. Aug. 19, 1845, m. Catherine Boyer Dec. 5, 1870; John Elizabeth Wells; Sarah Mariah Lovell; William Amasa; Hannah Matilda.
Pioneer to Springville, Utah, Sept. 26, 1852. Ordained elder and seventy at the October conference 1842, at Nauvoo, Ill.; high priest Sept. 28, 1884, and patriarch April 14, 1901; missionary to eastern states; presiding teacher and superintendent of Sunday school several years. Master mason; contractor and builder; helped build first meeting house and worked on the Mud Wall which was built around the fort, one half mile square as a protection from Indians, at Springville. Died June 5, 1906.

MENDENHALL RICHARD LOVELL (son of William and Sarah Lovell Mendenhall). Born Aug. 19, 1845, Nauvoo, Ill.
Married Maria Catherine Boyer Dec. 5, 1870, Salt Lake City, Utah (daughter of Augustus Sell Boyer, who died in Pennsylvania, and Catherine Houtz Boyer, latter a pioneer). She was born Oct. 13, 1850, near Freeburg, Union county, Pa. Their children: Irena Boyer b. Dec. 13, 1871, m. Joseph Jensen Dec. 23, 1896; Richard Lovell Jr. b. Nov. 15, 1873, m. Hannah Bird May 14, 1902.
Missionary to Colorado 1902-04. Pioneer to Springville, Utah. City marshal for several years. Moved to Mapleton, Utah, 1878. Indian war Veteran. Farmer and stockraiser.

MENDENHALL, RICHARD LOVELL Jr. (son of Richard Lovell and Maria Catherine Boyer). He was born Nov. 15, 1873, Springville, Utah.
Married Hannah Bird May 14, 1902 (daughter of Charles Monroe and Abigail Ann Whiting), who was born July 23, 1883, Mapleton, Utah. Their children: Helen b. Feb. 28, 1903; Wendell Bird b. Sept. 26, 1907; Louise b. Oct. 13, 1909; Arthur Lovell b. Feb. 13, 1913.
Elder. Missionary to southern states May 20, 1897; superintendent of Sunday schools and president of East Kentucky conference.

MERKLEY, CHRISTOPHER (son of Jacob Merkley and Elizabeth Stata of Williamsburg, Dundas county, Ontario, Can.). Born Dec. 18, 1808, at Williamsburg. Came to Utah Oct. 8, 1849, Enoch Reese company.
Married Sarah Davis, in February 1823 (daughter of Nathaniel Davis and Sarah Jacobs), who was born May 19, 1811, and came to Utah 1848. Their child: Nelson, m. Jane Sanders.
Married Minerva Stowell 1845, at Nauvoo, Ill.
Married Karissa Fairbanks 1858, at Salt Lake City (daughter of Amos Fairbanks, pioneer 1861, and Mary Bartholomew—married Nov. 11, 1822). She was born Oct. 29, 1838, Michigan City, Ind. Their children: Sarah Frances b. May 13, 1858, m. Amos Virgin 1875; Christopher Amos b. Feb. 28, 1859, m. Lydia Lavette Allred; Sarah Nathaniel b. March 18, 1866, m. George Y. Pugmire Oct. 1888; Mary Jane b. March 18, 1866; Susa b. July 11, 1875, m. Elmer Cleveland March 1892; Lucy b. July 11, 1875, m. Heber S. Pugmire 1893.
Missionary eight times. Assisted in building Nauvoo, Sal Lake, and Logan Temples. Indian war veteran.

MERKLEY, NELSON (son of Christopher Merkley and Sara Davis). Born Nov. 11, 1828. Came to Utah 1848, Amas Lyman company.
Married Sarah Jane Sanders (daughter of Ellis M. Sander and Rachel Roberts, of Delaware). She was born Dec. 1 1841, Wilmington, Del. Their children: Nelson Jr. b. Marc 25, 1857, m. Keturah Peterson; George Davis b. July 14, 1859 m. Phoebe A. Hacking; Sarah Jane b. Aug. 24, 1861, m William P. Colthorpe; Susan Maria b. Oct. 28, 1863, m. Georg Finly Britt; Christopher Ellis b. Aug. 26, 1865, m. Aldur Hatch; Mary b. 1867, d. infant; Charles Albert b. Jan. 11 1868, m. Mary L. Murray; Elizabeth b. Dec. 29, 1871, Henry Hall; John b. Aug. 29, 1874, m. Nellie Lanore Bartlett; Henry b. Dec. 3, 1877, m. Susan Hullinger; Willia b. July 1, 1880, m. Rose Walker; Rachel Ellen b. Sept. 2, 188 m. Jeremiah Hatch Murray; Jacob b. Feb. 5, 1886, m. Ann Hullinger. Family home Salt Lake City, Morgan Valle Cedar Valley, Cedar Fort, and Vernal, Utah.
Member of seventy. Veteran Echo Canyon war. Ca penter, farmer and stockraiser.

MERKLEY, NELSON, JR. (son of Nelson Merkley and Sara Jane Sanders). Born March 24, 1857, Genoa, Nev.
Married Keturah Peterson June 9, 1884, Vernal, Ute (daughter of Peter Peterson, born in Denmark, and Ma Elizabeth Thurman, born in Kentucky; came to Utah fa of 1869). She was born Oct. 8, 1867, in Hart county, K Their children: Ellis b. May 2, 1885, m. Jean Eleanor Gerbe Ezra b. Sept. 23, 1887; Helen b. April 9, 1590, m. Byron

Colton: Milton b. April 30, 1893, d. infant; Sarah b. April 30, 1894, d. infant; Mary Elizabeth Aug. 25, 1896; Asher b. July 19, 1899; Margaret Jane b. April 14, 1902; Kate b. Nov. 27, 1906, d. infant. Family home Vernal, Utah.
Bishop's counselor; patriarch; president of high priests' quorum; high councilor. Farmer.

MERKLEY, JOHN (son of Nelson Merkley and Sarah Jane Sanders). Born Aug. 29, 1874, Cedar Fort, Utah.
Married Nellie Lenorah Bartlett July 25, 1894, Salt Lake City (daughter of Charles Claymore Bartlett and Anna Jensen of Vernal, Utah), who was born Nov. 3, 1875. Their children: Christopher b. Oct. 22, 1893; John Golden b. Sept. 11, 1897; Sarah Madeena b. Jan. 4, 1900; Charles Nelson b. March 6, 1902; Rachel b. March 3, 1905; Clyde Emil b. Feb. 9, 1907; Loyal Ross b. Jan. 15, 1909; Nelda b. June 3, 1912.
High priest; bishop's counselor; assistant Sunday school superintendent; president elders' quorum; ward teacher; assistant to president Y. M. M. I. A. Farmer and honey producer.

MERKLEY, CHRISTOPHER AMOS (son of Christopher Merkley and Karissa Fairbanks—married 1858, Salt Lake City, Utah). Born Feb. 28, 1859, Salt Lake City.
Married Lydia Lavette Allred May 24, 1877, St. Charles, Bear Lake Co., Idaho (daughter of William More Allred, pioneer October, 1851, and Orissa A. Bates). She was born Sept. 23, 1859, Grantsville, Utah. Their children: Lettie Lavette b. April 3, 1878, m. John Bennett Oct. 28, 1897; Alva Christopher b. May 5, 1880, m. Ellen L. Allen June 27, 1906; Inez Orissa b. July 25, 1882, m. George L. Winslow Jan. 1, 1903; Lorin William b. June 22, 1885; Lavern Mathias b. May 3, 1887; Ray Edgar b. Dec. 8, 1889, m. Francis E. Peterson Jan. 20, 1910; Vera Allred b. July 31, 1892; Cecil Allred b. April 15, 1897; Ruby Allred b. Oct. 11, 1901.
High councilor; bishop of Wapello ward, Blackfoot stake, Idaho; missionary to southern states; ward teacher; Sunday school superintendent.

MERKLEY, ALVA CHRISTOPHER (son of Christopher Amos Merkley and Lydia Lavette Allred—married May 24, 1877, St. Charles, Idaho). Born May 5, 1880, St. Charles.
Married Ellen Leonora Allen June 27, 1906, Orderville, Utah (daughter of Albert Allen and Harriet Fowler), who was born April 27, 1881, Salt Lake City. Their children: Arlin Alva b. July 15, 1907; Della Leonora b. Nov. 24, 1908; Zeldon Allen b. Oct. 30, 1910.
Missionary to Samoan Islands four years; ward teacher; Sunday school teacher; ward chorister.

MERRELL, HOSEA (son of Simeon Merrell of Michigan). Came to Utah 1850.
Married Mary Saxton in Michigan, who came to Utah with husband. Their children: Alonzo, m. Eliza Bird; Jerusha, m. John Davis; Edna, m. Warren Reynolds; Joseph, died; John, m. Eliza VanLeuven; Silas Jerome, m. Lydia Eugenia Remmington; Porter William, m. Harriett Amelia Badger Remmington. Family resided Big Cottonwood, Salem, Mendon and Paradise, Utah.
Died February, 1863, Paradise, Utah.

MERRELL, SILAS JEROME (son of Hosea Merrell and Mary Saxton). Born Oct. 28, 1843, Oakland county, Mich. Came to Utah 1851, Harry Walton company.
Married Lydia Eugenia Remmington Jan. 28, 1866, Paradise, Utah (daughter of Jerome Napoleon Remmington and Lydia Ripley Chamberlain Badger of New York, pioneers 1849). She was born June 1, 1851. Their children: Lydia b. March 10, 1867; Millie b. Oct. 15, 1868; Rodney b. Oct. 24, 1870; Elwin b. Nov. 6, 1872; Elma b. Feb. 6, 1874; Joseph b. July 8, 1875; Vilate b. March 12, 1879. Family home Paradise, Utah.
Bishop Mountain Dell ward; ward teacher; Sunday school superintendent; president Y. M. M. I. A. Farmer.

MERRELL, PORTER WILLIAM (son of Hosea Merrell and Mary Saxton). Born Sept. 10, 1846, Garden City, Iowa. Came to Utah 1850.
Married Harriett Amelia Badger Remmington June 11, 1869, Salt Lake City (daughter of Jerome Napoleon Remmington and Lydia Ripley Chamberlain Badger of New York, pioneers 1849). She was born Feb. 7, 1854. Their children: William Porter b. 1870, m. Mary Sophia Elizabeth Olson Lybbert; Rosa Amelia b. Jan. 26, 1871, m. Elmer B. Eaton; Josephine b. Oct. 6, 1872, m. Louis F. Goodrich; Mary b. April 18, 1874, m. Avia Leonidas Lisonbee; Lydia b. Feb. 20, 1876, m. Albert Gardner Goodrich; Fuller b. Dec. 23, 1877, m. Christina Angus; Helen b. Aug. 6, 1880, m. David Richardson; Roxana b. Aug. 6, 1880, m. Albert Mott; Charles Elwin b. Feb. 13, 1882, m. Rhoda Knight; Franklin b. June 3, 1884, m. Mary Angus. Family home (Merrell), Naples ward, Uinta Co., Utah.
Seventy; presiding elder and Sunday school superintendent of Merrell ward, Wasatch stake 1883; called to work on Salt Lake temple. Went to Fort Benton for immigrants 1868. Settled at Vernal 1879. President Central Irrigation Canal Co. Farmer, freighter. Died Aug. 29, 1884, Merrell, (Naples ward), Utah.

MERRELL, WILLIAM PORTER (son of Porter William Merrell and Harriett Amelia Badger Remmington). Born Aug. 30, 1869, Paradise, Utah.
Married Mary Sophia Elizabeth Olson Lybbert Oct. 9, 1897, Salt Lake City (daughter of Christian Frederick Bernard Lybbert and Antonetta Olsen of Naples (Merrell), Utah, pioneers Nov. 9, 1865). She was born Sept. 25, 1878. Their children: Irene b. April 23, 1899; Porter b. Jan. 15, 1901; Lucile b. Nov. 20, 1902; Bernard b. Jan. 28, 1904; William Alton b. Jan. 28, 1906; Elva b. March 17, 1908; Victor b. March 25, 1910; Baby b. Sept. 14, 1912.
High priest; first bishop of Bluebell ward, Duchesne stake 1911; ward teacher; Sunday school superintendent; presiding elder of Bluebell; counselor in elders quorum; counselor in deacons quorum; counselor in Y. M. M. I. A. of Jensen and Naples wards. Member Dry Gulch Irrigation Co. Farmer.

MERRELL, JOSEPH (son of Charles Merrell and Sarah Finley). Born 1847, Council Bluffs, Iowa. Came to Utah 1852, Captain Weeks company.
Married Martha Ann Campkin May 6, 1872, Salt Lake Endowment house (daughter of Isaac Campkin, died at St. Louis, Mo., en route to Utah, and Martha Webb, both of England, latter a pioneer Nov. 9, 1856, James G. Willie handcart company). She was born Jan. 15, 1854. Their children: Charles M. b. May 22, 1873; Isaac George b. Sept. 24, 1874; Joseph L. b. Jan. 28, 1876; Jonathan b. Sept. 20, 1877; Martha Henrietta b. March 17, 1879; Archibald b. Aug. 5, 1881; James Ruben b. July 25, 1883; Sarah S. b. Dec. 26, 1884; Nancy M. b. Oct. 13, 1886; Benjamin B. b. Aug. 4, 1888; Emma Luella b. July 8, 1890; Elija Vilate b. April 8, 1892; Albert Ervin b. March 28, 1894.
Moved from Plymouth to West Portage 1872, and served as counselor in the Y. M. M. I. A. at that place; moved to Brigham City 1882, and served as Sunday school teacher, assistant Sunday school superintendent and counselor in the Y. M. M. I. A.; moved to Rich, Bingham Co., Idaho 1898, where he took an active part in the ward organizations, serving as high priest and high counselor; president Rich branch; moved to Blackfoot 1908. Assisted in bringing immigrants to Utah 1868. Took an active part in the early Indian troubles, and did much in the upbuilding of the state.

MERRICK, GEORGE (son of James and Elizabeth Merrick). Born June 13, 1838, Leamington, Warwickshire, Eng. Came to Utah 1854.
Married Hannah Green, at Pleasant Grove, Utah (daughter of William and Mary Green, former of Pleasant Grove, both of Bridgenorth, Shropshire, England, pioneers 1853). She was born March 15, 1844. Their children: George W., m. Almeda Davis, m. Elizabeth Edmondson; Mary E., b. Jan. 22, 1870, m. Franklin Anderson Miller; Hannah M., m. Thomas Simpers; Sarah J., m. John Dalton; Ann Eliza m. John Dalton; James D., m. Esther Miller; John F. Died Oct. 21, 1885, Mt. Pleasant, Utah.

MERRILL, ALBERT (son of Valentine Merrill, born Jan. 30, 1783, and Lydia Sisson, born Oct. 18, 1786, former of South Norwalk, Fairfield county, Conn., latter of Green Port, Long Island, N. Y.). He was born July 17, 1815, on Long Island, N. Y. Came to Utah Sept. 13, 1852, Captain Howell company.
Married Margaret Ann Richardson March 21, 1836 (daughter of William Richardson and Ann Jones), who was born Nov. 15, 1816, and came to Utah with husband. Their children: Amanda b. Sept. 10, 1837, d. 1846; Antoine b. July 23, 1839, d. 1846; Clarence b. May 18, 1841, m. Bathsheba Smith Jan. 3, 1861, m. Julia Felshaw Dec. 7, 1867, and Isabelle M. Harris Oct. 8, 1879; Franklin b. March 17, 1843, m. Elizabeth Peck; Austin b. Oct. 8, 1844; Alfred b. Aug. 6, 1846, d. infant; Albert b. Oct. 10, 1848, d. 1870; Margaret Elinor b. Dec. 19, 1850, d. 1904; Marion b. March 29, 1853, m. Lydia A. Young Oct. 27, 1873; Melville b. 1855, d. infant; Irene b. Jan. 14, 1855, d. 1864; Alice b. Sept. 28, 1859, d. 1865; Austin, d. infant. Family home, Salt Lake City.
Married Frances Machin Oct. 21, 1860, Salt Lake City (daughter of George Machin and Sarah Mcrmick), who was born Sept. 15, 1843, Sheffield, Yorkshire, Eng. Their children: Annetta b. Aug. 5, 1863, m. William Lunnen June 16, 1881; Valentine b. April 22, 1865, d. infant; Ada b. April 6, 1866, m. John Barrows; Annie b. May 19, 1868, m. Jake Mahone; Mark Earnest b. Jan. 10, 1870, m. Jane Norris; Clara b. Aug. 13, 1871, m. William Thompson Feb. 1901; Leo Sisson b. Feb. 4, 1873, d. infant.
President fifth quorum seventies, Salt Lake City; missionary to eastern states 1841-44 and 1869-70; ordained patriarch May 7, 1873. Captain of Hardie pendencement Rifle Company 1856, and major of battalion 1857 in Nauvoo Legion; captain of 17 families of Captain Howell company, which arrived in Utah September, 1852. Farmer. Pioneer hat manufacturer of Utah. Died Nov. 1, 1873, Salt Lake City.

MERRILL, CLARENCE (son of Albert Merrill and Margaret Ann Richardson). Born May 18, 1841, South Norwalk, Fairfield county, Conn. Came to Utah September, 1852, Captain Howell company.
Married Bathsheba Smith Jan. 3, 1861, Salt Lake City (daughter of George Albert Smith and Bathsheba W. Diglow of Nauvoo, Ill., former pioneer July 24, 1847, Brigham Young company, the latter 1849, Captain Jones company). She was born Aug. 14, 1844. Their children: Annella b. Dec. 19, 1861, d. infant; Lella b. 1863, m. David R. Allen; George Albert b. Feb. 2, 1866, d. aged 33; Alice b. Jan. 2, 1868, m. George H. Horne; Maud b. Feb. 7,

1870, m. B. T. Lloyd; Margaratt M. b. Feb. 5, 1872, m. Joseph A. Fisher; Clarence Jr. b. Jan. 7, 1874, m. Louisa Amott; Irene b. June 4, 1876, m. Stephen L. Richards; Alton b. July 15, 1878, d. aged 14 months; John H. b. Feb. 28, 1880, m. Marie Rounds; Joseph S. b. May 8, 1882 (killed April 23, 1913, in railroad accident), m. Jennie Nordvall; Thomas S. b. March 6, 1884, m. Mary Ridges; Lewis Bigler b. July 30, 1887; Charles S. b. April 27, 1890. Family home Salt Lake City and Fillmore, Utah.
Married Julia Felshaw Dec. 7, 1867, at Salt Lake City (daughter of William Felshaw and Mary Harriett Gilbert of New York, pioneers fall of 1851). She was born June 27, 1832. Their children: Frank F. b. Sept. 30, 1868, m. Fredereka Poulson, m. Elizabeth A. Petersen; Luta F., b. Aug. 3, 1870, d. aged 15.
Married Isabelle M. Harris Oct. 8, 1879, at St. George, Utah (daughter of Charles Harris and Louisa Hall), who was born April 15, 1861. Their children: Albert b. Feb. 16, 1881, m. Rosella Gertrude Seely; Horace G. b. July 19, 1882, m. Murl Miller.
Member 16th quorum seventies; high priest. First lieutenant to Major John L. Smith of Nauvoo Legion. Member city council of Fillmore two terms; superintendent schools of Piute county. Telegraph operator; hatmaker; farmer; stockraiser; merchant.

MERRILL, MARION (son of Albert Merrill and Margaret Ann Richardson). Born March 29, 1853, Provo, Utah.
Married Lydia Young Jan. 27, 1873, Salt Lake City (daughter of John Young and Sarah McCleave, former pioneer Oct. 22, 1847, latter 1853). She was born Nov. 7, 1854. Their children: Lydia Mable b. Dec. 17, 1873, died; Madelon b. May 18, 1875, m. Frank W. Merrill Sept. 9, 1893; Nellie Marie b. Feb. 14, 1877, died; John b. April 27, 1881, m. Jessie Busby April 2, 1906; Sarah b. March 22, 1884, m. Joseph E. McGinty Nov. 21, 1901; Albert b. Feb. 22, 1892. Family home, Salt Lake City.
Miner; owner of "Bill Nye" mine at Deep Creek, Utah.

MERRILL, AUSTIN S. (son of Epaphreas Merrill and Sarah Taylor of New York). Born 1805, in Massachusetts. Came to Utah 1848, Lorenzo Snow company.
Married Laura W. Harris (daughter of Joseph Harris, pioneer). Their children: Laura C., m. Jehu Cox; Ira E., m. Lucinda Olmsted; Horatio H., m. Jane Webb; Solomon S., m. Lucinda Jane Olmstead; Sarah C., m. Aquilla Noble; Austin T. m. Mary Hatton; Freborn S., m. Mary Davis. Family home Smithfield, Utah.

MERRILL, SOLOMON S. (son of Austin S. Merrill and Laura W. Harris). Born 1840, Will county, Ill.
Married Lucinda Jane Olmsted Sept. 26, 1862, Smithfield, Utah (daughter of Hyrum Olmsted and Eliza Winters), who was born 1841, Hancock county, Ill. Their children: Elias S. b. 1864, m. Melvina Scott 1889; Mary T. b. 1866, m. John F. Hillyard 1886; American C. b. 1867, m. J. A. Rainey 1886; Abarbara E. b. 1873, m. William Hawk 1894; Grace A. b. 1879, m. George Cunningham 1897; Elsie I. b. 1881, m. Pearls Raymond 1897; Warren L. b. 1885, m. Mary Hall 1906.
Minuteman in early Indian troubles, in the course of which he was wounded.

MERRILL, EDWIN DE LAFAYETTE (son of Oren Merrill, born 1805, and Emily F. Merrill, born Feb. 2, 1804, of New York—married 1825). He was born Jan. 8, 1836, Genesee county, N. Y. Came to Utah in 1851, Captain Williams merchandise train.
Married Eliza Ann Perkins (daughter of Lewis Perkins), who was born 1840, married 1863, died 1872. Their children: Edwin D. b. June 1871; Emily C. b. 1869, m. Samuel Hagraves.
Ordained elder 1862; president Y. M. M. I. A. four years. Minuteman several years; took part in several raids against the Indians; enlisted in U. S. service, Lot Smith company; guard for Brigham Young. Has six grandchildren and five great-grandchildren.

MERRILL, HORATIO HARRIS (son of Austin Taylor Merrill, born 1805, in Massachusetts, and Laura Wilder Harris). He was born Jan. 3, 1834, Alden, Erie county, N. Y. Came to Utah in 1850.
Married Jannette Webb July 28, 1861 (daughter of Charles Young Webb and Margaret Allen), who was born Oct. 24, 1876. Their children: Laura Margaret b. Oct. 13, 1863, m. Samuel C. Weeks Nov. 8, 1880; Horatio Epaphras b. Dec. 13, 1865, d. Sept. 12, 1884. Family home Smithfield, Utah.
Married Martha Mouritsen Dec. 24, 1866, at Salt Lake City (daughter of Lars Mouritsen and Maren Sorensen, pioneers September, 1859, Captain Nibley company). She was born Nov. 11, 1851, in Denmark. Their children: Joseph Harris b. March 10, 1868, m. Grace Emma Hale June 21, 1894; m. Katie Eliza Hale Sept. 6, 1889; Martin Herman b. Jan. 20, 1870, d. Aug. 16, 1870.
Married Sarah Ann Smith (daughter of John Glover Smith and Margaret Allen Webb), who was born Sept. 4, 1858, Mill Creek, Utah. Their children: Robert Wilson b. June 4, 1879; Ann Eliza b. July 27, 1881, d. Dec. 4, 1894; Ira Lafayette b. Jan. 27, 1885, m. Jessie Saphronia Smith Oct. 9, 1907; Ivin Allen b. Aug. 20, 1886, m. Carey Gray Jan. 30, 1909; Margaret b. Oct. 4, 1888, m. Dalus Hendricks May 25, 1902; Austin Smith b. Sept. 4, 1891, m. Clara Larsen Aug. 30, 1910.
Member 17th quorum seventies. Located at Big Cottonwood; moved to Smithfield in early '60s- Pioneer wheelwright and carpenter of Smithfield. Fifer in first martial band. Moved to Pima, Ariz., where he was shot from ambush and killed by Indians, Dec. 4, 1894.

MERRILL, JOSEPH HARRIS (son of Horatio Harris Merrill and Martha Mouritsen). Born March 10, 1868, at Smithfield, Utah.
Married Katie Eliza Hale Sept. 6, 1889 (daughter of Alma Helaman Hale and Sarah Annie Clark), who died June 29, 1890.
Married Grace Emma Hale June 21, 1894 (daughter of Alma Helaman Hale and Sarah Annie Clark), who was born March 16, 1873, Grantsville, Utah. Their children: Leland Hale b. May 19, 1895; Leonard Mouritsen b. Nov. 27, 1896; Melvin Horatio b. Jan. 14, 1899; Joseph Ernest b. Dec. 27, 1901; Alma Harold b. Jan. 6, 1904; DeMar b. July 14, 1905; Kenneth b. April 25, 1907; Katie Anona b. July 26, 1910; Donald Gower b. Sept. 20, 1912.
Missionary to Samoan Islands 1890, where he was instrumental in opening up several branches of the church and presided over Savii conference; released April 25, 1894; secretary and later one of the presidents of 17th quorum seventies; president of 147th quorum seventies; second mission to Samoa 1901-02; presided over the mission there. Moved from Smithfield, Utah, to Groveland, Idaho, 1894. Member Blackfoot stake Sunday school board three years; and of Y. M. M. I. A. three years. Farmer.

MERRILL, JUSTIN J. (son of Samuel J. and Phebe Odell Merrill of Salt Lake City, Utah). Born Feb. 18, 1806, Byron, Genesee county, N. Y. Came to Utah September, 1848, Willard Richards company.
Married Camilla Wirack in 1840, Pawpaw, Pawpaw Grove, De Kalb county, Ill. (daughter of Jacob and Camilla Wirack of Nauvoo, Ill., pioneers July 24, 1847). She was born Oct. 3, 1817. Their children: George G.; Justin J.; Maryette; Lucy; Julia; Jacob; Samuel J.; Jedediah; Morgan; Parmelia, d. child. Family home Smithfield, Cache Co., Utah.
Farmer. Died Jan. 14, 1887, Smithfield, Utah.

MERRILL, GEORGE G. (son of Justin J. and Carmilla Wirack, Salt Lake City). Born March 17, 1841, Nauvoo, Ill. Came to Utah in 1848, Willard Richards company.
Married Alice Smith May 30, 1864, Smithfield, Utah (daughter of Barnett and Delilah Hilock Smith of Logan, Cache Co., Utah. Came to Utah August, 1863, William B. Preston company). She was born Jan. 14, 1845. Their children: George Wallace b. July 31, 1865; Sylvia b. Oct. 14, 1867; Alice Adelia b. Feb. 10, 1870; Josephine b. July 5, 1872, and Frank b. Nov. 8, 1874, d. child: Maud Milly b. Sept. 13, 1877; Catie b. March 5, 1879; William Leroy b. Sept. 3, 1882; Delilah May b. May 6, 1885; Florence Ione b. Oct. 7, 1887; Rada Rane b. Feb. 11, 1895. Family home Smithfield, Utah.
Missionary to Omaha 1863-65. Marshal of Smithfield for 10 years. Farmer.

MERRILL, MARRINER WOOD (son of Nathan Merrill and Sarah Ann Reynolds of Sackville, N. B., Canada). Born Sept. 25, 1832, Sackville. Came to Utah September, 1853, William Atkinson company.
Married Sarah Ann Atkinson Nov. 11, 1853, Salt Lake City (daughter of William Atkinson and Phoebe Campbell of Sackville, pioneers September, 1853, William Atkinson company). She was born Sept. 28, 1834. Their children: Phoebe Ann, m. James R. McNeil; Marriner Wood, Jr., m. Mary M. Cardon, m. Lucina Shepard; Thomas Hazen, m. Emma B. Olsen, m. Margaret W. Thompson; Alma, m. Almira E. and Rebecca Hendricks; Rhoda Louisa, m. William S. Hendricks; Clarissa; William, m. Lucy Cardon; Louis Edgar, m. Clara Hendricks, m. Carrie Jane; Amos Newlove, m. Eliza Drysdale.
Married Cyrene Standley June 5, 1856, Salt Lake City (daughter of Alexander Standley and Philinda Upton of Nauvoo, Ill., pioneers 1852). She was born May 1, 1840. Their children: Nathan Alexander; Healon, m. William H. Jackson; Parley, m. Mary Jackson, m. Emma Griffeth; Ella Rebecca, m. Joseph R. Kerr; Alonzo David, m. Luisina Whittle; Ida, m. Peter E. VanOrden; Ezra J., m. Mary McCann; Alice.
Married Almira Jane Bainbridge April 1, 1865, Salt Lake City (daughter of Fredrick Bainbridge and Elizabeth Pond), who was born Aug. 27, 1849. Their children: Charles Edward, m. Ortencia and Chloe Hendricks; Elizabeth Almira, m. James W. Hendricks; Heber Kimball, m. Ora Dudley; Albert Marion, m. Julia Lewis; Lewis Alfred, m. Effie Ensign; Lorin Asa, m. Laura Reese; Fredrick Whitmore, m. Ida Homer; Emma Irene, m. Joseph Sharp; Preston Reynolds, m. Millie Lowe; Alvaretta, m. George A. Lewis.
Married Maria Loenza Kingsbury Oct. 4, 1867, Salt Lake City (daughter of Joseph C. Kingsbury and Loenza Pond), who was born Sept. 19, 1852. Their children: Joseph Francis, m. Annie Laura Hyde; Hyrum Willard, m. Bessie Cluff; Hattie Loenza, m. Andrew Morrison; Laura Vilate, m. Clarence Funk; Loenza, m. James W. Funk; Newel Alvin; Ambrose Pond, m. Lydia Stevens; Melvin Clarence; Nellie Maria, m. Erastus Johnson; Lenora Evaline.
Married Elna Jonson Feb. 11, 1885, Logan, Utah (daughter of Peter Jonson and Elsa Sajer Carlson of Sweden, who came to Utah 1882). She was born Oct. 20, 1863. Their

children: Elna b. Jan. 29, 1886, m. Victor Johnson April 1905; Hilda b. Feb. 7, 1889, m. Thomas W. Richards Aug. 28, 1907; Loretta b. Nov. 13, 1891; Luella b. June 17, 1896; Wilford b. Aug. 22, 1898. Family home Richmond, Utah.
One of the most prominent and personally well-known men of his day, a counselor to thousands, a peripatetic traveler and intermittent visitor. Past Utah histories are strangely brief concerning this wonderfully unique character, as only a glimpse here and there is given of his activities. Bishop of Richmond July 1861-79; first counselor to William B. Preston in stake presidency 1879-84; first counselor to Charles O. Card in stake presidency 1884-89; president Logan temple 1884-1906. Oct. 4, 1889, on reorganization of first presidency, with Anton H. Lund and Abraham H. Cannon, he was called to apostleship of the council of the twelve, succeeding the revered veteran Erastus Snow. In 1899, though a member of the council of the twelve to solve a difficult problem, he was appointed president of Cache stake, which office he held until the division of the stake in 1901. Member of the B. Y. College board for a number of years, 1896-1906; member of Agricultural College board nearly four years. Member Utah legislature 1876 and 1878, the first term in the lower house and the second in the council (senate); member county court Cache county for 10 years. One of the subcontractors on C. P., and succeeded Moses Thatcher as superintendent of Utah Northern in the '70's; then as contractor built this railroad from Franklin, Idaho, to Butte, Mont., 1877-81. Died Feb. 6, 1906, Richmond, Utah.

MERRILL, THOMAS HAZEN (son of Marriner Wood Merrill and Sarah Ann Atkinson). Born June 11, 1859, Bountiful, Utah.
Married Emma Boletta Olsen April 7, 1881, Salt Lake City (daughter of Christopher Marenus Olsen of Denmark and Caroline Christina Johnson of Norway), who was born Feb. 2, 1862. Their children: Thomas Hazen b. Nov. 25, 1885, d. May 26, 1897; Roscoe Cyril b. May 24, 1888; Edna Boletta b. Sept. 21, 1891; Veda Adella b. May 3, 1894; Emma Gwendoline b. Feb. 3, 1897; Reno Olsen b. June 6, 1899; Irma Berneice b. Jan. 15, 1903; Osmond Marriner b. Sept. 2, 1908.
Married Margaret Winifred Thomson April 22, 1884, Logan, Utah (daughter of George Thomson of Scotland and Alice Tomlinson of England, pioneers September, 1851). She was born March 16, 1860. Their children: George William b. Nov. 4, 1885, d. Nov. 6, 1885; James Newlove b. April 12, 1887, d. April 12, 1887; Ira Edgar b. March 7, 1889, d. June 18, 1899; Athel Wood b. Nov. 11, 1891, d. Feb. 3, 1892; Mazel Melburn b. Sept. 25, 1893; Alice Winifred b. Nov. 30, 1895; Rhoda Lucile b. March 15, 1898; Eva Thomson b. Jan. 26, 1901; Phyllis Janet b. May 18, 1904.
Bishop of Richmond ward since April 23, 1900. Member Richmond city council in 1881; state representative two terms, 1903-05; member state land board. Farmer; dairyman; stockraiser.

MERRILL, LEWIS A. (son of Marriner Wood Merrill and Almira J. Bainbridge). Born June 23, 1874, Richmond, Utah.
Married Effie Ensign June 6, 1895, Logan, Utah (daughter of Fuller Ensign and Mary Dunn of Brigham City, pioneers 1847). Their children: Lola b. Aug. 13, 1896; Myla b. June 11, 1898; Edna b. Aug. 4, 1899. Family home, Salt Lake City.
Bishop of 31st ward, Liberty stake, 1909-12. Director extension work of Utah Agricultural College; member state conservation commission. Agricultural expert.

MERRILL, JOSEPH FRANCIS (son of Marriner Wood Merrill and Maria L. Kingsbury). Born Aug. 24, 1868, Richmond, Utah.
Married Annie Laura Hyde June 9, 1898, Salt Lake City (daughter of Alonzo Eugene Hyde, born Feb. 28, 1848, Council Bluffs, Iowa, and Annie Taylor, born Oct. 21, 1849, Salt Lake City, both of Salt Lake City). She was born Dec. 25, 1871. Their children: Joseph Hyde b. March 18, 1899; Annie H. b. Nov. 2, 1900; Edith H. b. Jan. 5, 1902; Rowland H. b. Jan. 11, 1904; Taylor H. b. June 2, 1906; Eugene H. b. June 25, 1908. Family home, Salt Lake City.
Member 3d and 105th quorum seventies; first assistant superintendent Y. M. M. I. A. of Salt Lake stake 1897-03; second assistant Sunday school superintendent, Granite stake, 1904-07; stake superintendent Sunday schools 1907-11; second counselor in Granite stake presidency 1911. Trustee of Forest Dale 1911-12; member and secretary state conservation commission 1907-12; professor and director State School of Mines. Member of several technical and scientific societies, as American Institute Electrical Engineers, American Physiological Society, American Electrochemical Society, American Association Advanced Science, etc.

MERRILL, ALMA (son of Marriner Wood Merrill and Sarah Ann Atkinson). Born Nov. 9, 1861, Richmond, Utah.
Married Almira Esmerilda Hendricks March 19, 1885, Logan temple (daughter of William Dorris Hendricks and Almira Davenport, former came to Utah with the Mormon Battalion from California). She was born Oct. 29, 1866, Richmond, Utah. Their children: Alma Lowell b. Jan. 24, 1886; Wesley Hendricks b. April 5, 1887; Rhoda Mildred b. Oct. 18, 1888; Nathan Dorris b. Sept. 26, 1891; Annie Esmerilda b. Nov. 26, 1893; Ruby Leora b. Feb. 12, 1896; Eliza Zelka b. Nov. 9, 1899; Tenna b. April 8, 1901; Atha b. May 29, 1903; Denzal Reed b. Aug. 16, 1905; Juanita b. March 28, 1907.

Married Rebecca Hendricks, Logan temple (daughter of William Dorris Hendricks and Almira Davenport). She was born Jan. 30, 1868. Their children: Carrie Rebecca b. June 20, 1887, m. Amasa Linford Oct. 16, 1907; Alfred Adrian b. Dec. 12, 1890; Erma Almira b. May 31, 1889; Ruel Derby b. Jan. 24, 1893; La Rue Hendricks b. Aug. 3, 1895; Phebe Ann b. Dec. 12, 1897; Ethelia Fern b. Dec. 29, 1899; Marriner Hendricks b. Feb. 8, 1902; Ruth b. Jan. 5, 1904; Matthias Wood b. July 14, 1905; Rilda b. July 11, 1907; Vermont b. Nov. 15, 1909; Neomi b. Jan. 1, 1912.

MERRILL, HIRAM WILLARD (son of Marriner Wood Merrill and Maria L. Kingsbury). Born Jan. 19, 1870, Richmond, Utah.
Married Bessie Cluff March 26, 1891, Logan, Utah (daughter of Benjamin Cluff and Eliza Arnetta Foster of Logan, Utah, pioneers 1850). She was born May 25, 1873. Their children: Willard Alvin b. Feb. 19, 1892; Reynold Cluff b. Oct. 2, 1893; Aaron Utillus b. July 15, 1895; Maria b. Jan. 29, 1897; Rosley Cluff b. Oct. 17, 1899; Glaucus Godfrey b. May 27, 1905; Foster Cluff b. Sept. 26, 1908. Family home Richmond, Utah.
Missionary to western states 1901-03; ward teacher 15 years; member Benson stake Sunday school board 3 years; Sunday school officer at Richmond 12 years. An up-to-date, progressive farmer.

MERRILL, SAMUEL (son of Jared Merrill and Abigail Phelps of Sansbury, N. Y.). Born Sept. 28, 1780, Sansbury, N. Y. Came to Utah July 29, 1847, Capt. James Brown and his detachment of Mormon Battalion.
Married Phoebe Odell (daughter of Jones and Lucy Weaver Odell), who was born April 29, 1788.

MERRILL, SAMUEL B. (son of Samuel Merrill and Phoebe Odell). Born Jan. 4, 1812, Smithfield, N. Y. Came to Utah 1849, Captain Gardner company.
Married Elizabeth Runyan, in 1836, Utica, Mich. (daughter of Ralph Runyan and Rachel Gardner), who was born Aug. 16, 1818. Their children: Adelbert Owen b. Aug. 16, 1837; Cynthanah R. b. Nov. 10, 1840, m. William Douglass Nov. 9, 1862; Elthurah Roseltha b. Sept. 8, 1842, m. Ruben S. Collett Jan. 19, 1861; Samuel Adams, b. April 2, 1846, m. Elnora Noble Feb. 3, 1865; Ralph Teancum, b. June 13, 1849, m. Matilda Collett May 23, 1869; Sarah E. b. Oct. 22, 1852, m. Joseph Gold; Orrin Jackson b. June 22, 1855, m. Elizabeth White Feb. 15, 1875; Caroline b. June 12, 1858, died; Princetta R. b. May 2, 1861, m. James Christenson. Family home Mill Creek and Smithfield, Utah.
Counselor to Bishop John B. Smith, Smithfield, Utah, for a number of years; high priest. Farmer.

MERRILL, PHELEMON C. (son of Samuel Merrill and Phoebe Odell). Born Nov. 12, 1820, Byron, N. Y. Came to Utah July 29, 1847.
Married Cyrena Dustin, who was born Jan. 6, 1817. Their children: Sabina Ladena b. Aug. 21, 1841, died; Phelemon Alisandra b. Nov. 18, 1843, m. Lucinda Rowe; Lucy Cyrena b. April 7, 1846, died; Melissa Jane b. Sept. 10, 1848, died; Morgan Henry b. Feb. 17, 1850, m. Emma Fenemaker; Albina Altamira b. Oct. 31, 1851, died; Thomas Stephen b. Jan. 3, 1853, m. Eater Collett; Seth Adelbert b. Aug. 10, 1859, m. Lucy Ann Merrill. Family resided in Utah, Idaho and Arizona.
Married Mary Jane Smith. Their children: John Smith b. March 5, 1853, m. Rebecca Weaver; Jedediah Grant b. Dec. 14, 1857, m. Harriett A. Dunn; Hannah Ann b. Jan. 24, 1860, m. Charles C. Collett; Cyrena Imorjean b. Nov. 5, 1861, died; David Elmore b. May 4, 1863; Joseph Lott b. June 4, 1865; Henry Morgan b. March 4, 1867, m. Amy Welker; Peter Herbert b. June 6, 1869, died. Family resided in Utah, Idaho and Arizona.
Patriarch. Worked on the construction of first railroad in Utah. Died August, 1903.

MERRILL, JEDEDIAH GRANT (son of Phelemon C. Merrill and Mary Jane Smith). Born Dec. 14, 1857, Farmington, Utah.
Married Harriett Amelia Dunn Dec. 18, 1876, Paris, Idaho (daughter of John Dunn and Julian Ann McGuire of Utah and Idaho), who was born March 2, 1860. Their children: Catharine b. July 27, 1877, died; Mary Jane b. Aug. 22, 1878, m. C. A. Jensen; Ambrose Dunn b. Aug. 29, 1880, m. Ada Welker, m. Estella Hansen; Jedediah Grant b. Feb. 3, 1883, m. Marian McNiel; Mable b. Oct. 20, 1884, m. Mahonri Crane Aug. 19, 1912; Lorn Smith b. Sept. 12, 1885, m. Jennie Barrett Dec. 25, 1912; Harriet Amelia b. May 15, 1893, d. July 5, 1902; Julius LaRoue b. Dec. 9, 1905. Family home Bennington, Idaho.

MERRILL, ORRIN JACKSON (son of Samuel B. Merrill and Elizabeth Runyan). Born June 22, 1855, Little Cottonwood, Utah.
Married Elizabeth White Feb. 14, 1875, Salt Lake City (daughter of Samuel D. White and Elizabeth Thomas), who was born Feb. 11, 1855, Lehi, Utah. Their children: Orrin Preston b. Aug. 6, 1876, m. Alice N. Stephensen; Elmer S. b. March 12, 1878, m. Annie Neaf; Frank T. b. Feb. 1, 1880, m. Emma Bennett; Jessie b. Sept. 13, 1881; Harrison b. Nov. 11, 1884, m. Edna Johnson; Ralph b. April 23, 1888; Martil b. Nov. 4, 1890; Maddie b. Jan. 21, 1896; Maggie b. Jan. 22, 1898. Family home Preston, Idaho, where he settled in 1860.

1036　　PIONEERS AND PROMINENT MEN OF UTAH

MERRILL, ORRIN PRESTON (son of Orrin Merrill and Elizabeth White). Born Aug. 5, 1876.
Married Alice May Stephenson (daughter of Archibald B. Stephenson, born Sept. 13, 1843, pioneer 1861, and Mariah Simpkins, born in 1853, St. Louis; came to Utah 1863—married March 17, 1871, Adamsville, Utah). She was born June 9, 1886, Lewiston, Utah. Their children: Virginia b. Aug. 7, 1906; Donald b. Aug. 17, 1908; Levohn b. April 8, 1909. Family home Smithfield, Utah.
Formerly bishop's counselor, now a bishop; Sunday school superintendent. President of M. I. A. Farmer.

MERRITT, SAMUEL (son of George Merritt and Elizabeth Scott). Born Nov. 18, 1838, near Indianapolis, Ind. Came to Utah about 1864.
Married Emma Naylor July, 1865 (daughter of William Naylor and Diana Ireland), who was born Dec. 18, 1846, Bedford, Nottinghamshire, Eng. Came to Utah 1863. Rosel Hyde company. Their children numbered six sons and seven daughters. Family home Bedford, Wyo.

MEYER, CARL FREDERICK CHRISTIAN (son of Carl Frederick Meyer, born Jan. 8, 1797, and Marie Elizabeth Morgensen, born Nov. 2, 1795, both of Copenhagen, Denmark). He was born June 29, 1819, Rodie, Copenhagen.
Married Anne Jensine Jacobson Dec. 6, 1839 (daughter of Mr. Jacobsen and Sophia Amelia Krog), who was born Feb. 15, 1817, and came to Utah in 1862. Their children: Carl b. April 1841; Jacob b. Sept. 23, 1842; Carl b. March 30, 1845; Jacob b. May 21, 1847; Sophia. b. Sept. 11, 1849, m. Isaac Wardle; Enger b. Nov. 2, 1851; Bien Marie b. March 11, 1855, m. Christian Lovendahl; Carl Peter b. June 5, 1857, m. Wilhelmine Larson; Josephine Caroline b. April 9, 1860. Family home Murray, Utah.
Married Anne Mary Meyer in February, 1867, Salt Lake City, (daughter of Hans Jensen Meyer and Karen Rasmussen, latter a pioneer—married in Denmark). She was born June 1, 1842, Valsollille, Glngsted, Denmark. Their children: Hans Wilhelm b. Feb. 23, 1869, m. Rebecca Jenkins; Josephine b. Aug. 9, 1872; John Christian b. Oct. 5, 1875; Hannah Teoro b. Aug. 5, 1880, m. Edwin Charles Tame Dec. 20, 1905; Mary Ann b. Jan. 19, 1882, m. William Wood Sept. 23, 1904; Emma Christine b. June 6, 1884, m. Charles Rudger Larsen May 19, 1908.

MEYER, CHARLES PETER (son of Carl Frederick Meyer and Anne Jensine Jacobsen and brother of Jacob Myers on page 1052). Born June 5, 1851, at Ledole.
Married Wilhelmine Larsen Jan. 12, 1882, Salt Lake City (daughter of Hans and Karen Nielsen Larsen, who came to Utah 1877). She was born Jan. 9, 1862, Copenhagen, Denmark. Their children: Charles Henry b. Feb. 2, 1883, m. Mary Ann Hamilton June 23, 1905; Clara Jenette b. March 16, 1884, m. James Lundberg June 7, 1905; Minnie Elizabeth b. Aug. 30, 1886, died; Annie Helane b. Aug. 13, 1888, m. Lorenzo Jensen Dec. 9, 1908; Joseph Lawrence b. Aug. 16, 1890; Agnes Florentine b. May 24, 1892; Louis Edward b. April 27, 1897; John Raymond b. Sept. 21, 1899; Geo. Clinton b. May 29, 1904. Family home Grant Ward, Murray, Utah.
High priest. School trustee. Farmer.

MEYER, JACOB E. (son of Peter Meyer and Barbara Schmidt, of Calmar, Iowa). Born Dec. 26, 1864, Calmar, Iowa. Came to Utah 1899.
Married Ella Pierpont Jan. 6, 1904, Salt Lake City (daughter of Thomas Pierpont and Naomi King, of Toronto, Can., pioneers October, 1866, Abner Lowry company). She was born Dec. 29, 1878. Their children: Naomi; Edmond; Virginia. Family home, Salt Lake City.
Mining man.

MICHIE, ROBERT (son of John Michie and Agness Melculm, of Aberdeen, Scotland). Born Feb. 29, 1822, near Aberdeen. Came to Utah in 1861, having first located in Boston.
Married Frances Potts March 16, 1857, in Kent, Eng. (daughter of Thomas Potts and Harriett Pulling, of Centerbury, Eng.), who was born Dec. 22, 1836, and died July 20, 1904. Their children: Agnes Catherine Harriett, m. Ephraim Lambert; Eliza Ann Elena, d. infant; Robert Moroni, m. Elena Dorothea Lambert; Frances Harriett, d. infant; Alice Matilda b. Jan. 6, 1866, m. Joseph Heber Lambert; John and Mary Ellen, both died; Della, m. John James Horrocks; William George, m. Eliza Annie Murphy; Christiana, m. Louis H. Bisel. Family home Woodland, Utah.
Senior president 20th quorum seventy, Heber City; high priest. Settled at Nephi 1864; moved to Sugar House ward to run a flour mill and salt refinery; moved to Malad, to Salt Lake City, to Woodland, thence to Heber City, where he resided fifteen years and then returned to Woodland; postmaster there 1893-1901. Farmer. Died April 20, 1909.

MICKELSEN, JENS (son of Mickel Jenson). Born March 2, 1816, Denmark. Came to Utah Sept. 12, 1861, John Murdock company.
Married Margret Christenson, born Aug. 29, 1816. She came to Utah Sept. 12, 1861, John Murdock company. Their only child: James Peter was born April 18, 1847, m. Annie B. Hanson and Hannah Jensen. Family home Weston, Idaho.
High priest; ward teacher, Weston, Idaho.

MICKELSON, JAMES PETER (son of Jens Mickelson and Margret Christenson, pioneers Sept. 12, 1861, John Murdock company). Born April 18, 1847, in Denmark.
Married Annie B. Hanson Nov. 4, 1866, Bear Lake, Idaho (daughter of Bengta Hanson), who was born Dec. 3, 1843, in Sweden.
Married Hannah Jenson March 4, 1871, Logan, Utah (daughter of Jens Jenson and Elsie Nilson, pioneers Sept. 29, 1866, Peter Nebeker company).
In bishopric 1877-1902, Weston, Idaho. Assisted in bringing early immigrants to Utah.

MICKELSON, JENS (son of Mickel Sorensen and Petrine Hansen of Eig, Aarhus Amt., Denmark). Born May 2, 1853, Eig. Came to Utah September, 1861, Captain Wilhelmsen oxteam company.
Married Anne Christine Anderson, June 24, 1880, Salt Lake City (daughter of Niels Anderson and Ellen Cathrine Olsen, of Trellose, Presto Amt, Denmark, latter came to Utah Sept. 19, 1884). She was born Oct. 6, 1853. Their children: James M., m. Christine Anderson June 24, 1903; Ellen Cathrine, d. Oct. 31, 1884; Anna Christine, m. Fred E. Willardson March 9, 1910; Elmer A., m. Leora Billings Dec. 27, 1912; Minerva; Alice; Lydia M. Family home Manti, Utah.
High priest; high councilor; bishop's counselor. Woolgrower; farmer; stockraiser.

MICKLEJOHN, DAVID FORBES (son of George Micklejohn and Cathrine Forbes, of Glasgow, Scotland). Born in 1816, Kinross, Scotland. Came to Utah 1865.
Married Esther Cowan Martin (daughter of John Martin and Esther Cowan, of Kinross), who was born in 1821. Their children Elizabeth, m. George D. Watt; Mary C., m. Henry Enon Phelps; David F., m. Anna Clark.
Married Anna McGowan, who was born Dec. 25, 1815, and came to Utah in 1855. Their children: Jane b. 1847; Anna b. 1855; George b. 1857; Margaret b. 1859; Isabelle; Elmyra, m. John Noyes; Alice; m. Jeremiah Roach; Ellen; William b. 1864.

MIDDLETON, JOHN (son of William Middleton and Amy Parsons of England). Born Oct. 25, 1841, in England. Came to Utah November, 1856, Edward Martin handcart company.
Married Jane Withers (daughter of George Withers of Scotland), who was born in 1840. Their children: John, died; Amy, m. Frank Brown; George W., m. Margaret E. Palmer; Annie, m. Isaiah Cox; Mary A., m. Jethro Palmer; Francis, m. Sarah Holland; Katherine, m. William Pace. Family home Hamilton's Fort, Iron Co., Utah.
Missionary to England 1891-92. Farmer and stockraiser. Died September, 1896.

MIDDLETON, DR. GEORGE W. (son of John Middleton and Jane Withers). Born Dec. 10, 1866, Hamilton Fort, Utah.
Married Margaret E. Palmer Sept. 27, 1894, St. George, Utah (daughter of Richard Palmer and Johanna Reese of Cedar City, Utah, pioneers 1850). She was born Jan. 1, 1869. Their children: Roka b. July 3, 1895; Richard b. Aug. 10, 1901; Eugene b. Feb. 23, 1905; Anthony W. b. April 25, 1907; John b. May 12, 1910. Family home, Salt Lake City.
High priest; alternate high councilor. Mayor of Cedar City, Utah; regent of University of Utah. Physician and surgeon.

MIKESELL, HYRUM W. (son of John A. and Catherine Mikesell (cousins), of Hagerton, Md.). Born June 13, 1812, in Montgomery, Ohio. Came to Utah Oct. 15, 1852.
Married Ann Augusta Scott Feb. 21, 1844, Nauvoo, Ill. (daughter of Mathew and Nancy Scott). Their children on the plains en route to Utah. Their children: Ammoziah and Mathew Scott, died; Sarah Jane b. June 11, 1849, m. Osborn Angel; Sariah Ann b. Oct. 8, 1851, m. George Cheshire.
Married Sarah D. Butler Feb. 3, 1853, Salt Lake City (daughter of Charles Franklin Butler, born in Virginia Aug. 15, 1771, and Louisa Heron, born in New York). She was born Dec. 26, 1832, and came to Utah in 1852. Their children: Louisa, d. infant; Azariah H., m. Annie Hanson; Hyrum W.; Sarah Ann, d. infant; Elizabeth D.; Julia E., m. C. T. Husband; William W.; Alice; Eldora J., m. Reginald Anderson. Family home, Salt Lake City.
President 15th quorum seventies; block teacher; doorkeeper Tabernacle; helped to build Nauvoo temple; served three years' mission in Endowment House, Salt Lake City. Stonemason. Died May 8, 1883, at Salt Lake City.

MILES, ALBERT (son of Thomas Miles of New York, born 1790, and Sally Sexer, born at Newton, Mass., 1793). He was born Jan. 22, 1812. Came to Utah Sept. 3, 1848, Heber C. Kimball company.
Married Mariah Veits 1833 (daughter of Benjamin Veits and Sallie Donalson of Ohio—married at Southinaton, Ohio). She was born Jan. 31, 1810. Their children: Henry Albert b. Dec. 1833, d. Jan. 1834; Benjamin Adrian b. Dec. 3, 1835, m. Rachel M. Lockhart 1856; Edwin Ruthven b. May 25, 1838, m. Jane Ruth Warefield March 11, 1857; Franklin b.

Dec. 10, 1841, d. Dec. 26, 1850; Sally Ann b. Oct. 6, 1843, m. Orrin S. Lee 1859; Mariah Louisa b. Sept. 1849, d. 1861. Family resided Ohio, Illinois, Nebraska and Utah.
Married Hannah Daniels in 1856, Salt Lake City (daughter of David Daniels, pioneer 1856, handcart company), who was born at Caermarthenshire, Wales. Their children: Mariah b. Jan. 1857, m. Charles Powell 1866; Thomas b. Aug. 14, 1857, m. Elizabeth Merrill 1880; John, m. Alice Summers 1884; Hannah, m. Charles Montrose 1879; Daniel, m. Jane Walker; David, m. Lillie Rasmussen. Family resided Idaho and Utah.
Seventy. Member of Nauvoo Legion. Indian war veteran. Member of Utah militia.

MILES, EDWIN RUTHVEN (son of Albert Miles and Mariah Veits—married in 1833). Born May 25, 1838, Parkman, Geauga Co., Ohio.
Married Jane Ruth Wakefield March 11, 1857, Big Cottonwood, Salt Lake Co., Utah (daughter of Thomas Wakefield, who died in Nauvoo, Ill., 1843, and Mary Clark). She was born Feb. 3, 1840, Springfield, Ill. Their children: Edwin Ruthven b. Oct. 3, 1858, m. Annie Smith Jan. 9, 1879; Thomas b. Sept. 7, 1860, d. Sept. 7, 1860; Mary Jane b. Sept. 20, 1861, m. Parmenus Jones June, 1879; William Albert b. April 7, 1864, m. Eleanor Douglas Jan. 22, 1887; Lucinda Louetta b. March 29, 1866, m. Samuel P. Neilson Oct. 9, 1885; Harriet Ann b. July 16, 1868, m. Joseph Watts Dec. 19, 1889; Alice Mariah b. Dec. 20, 1869, m. Charles William Mack March, 1889; Sylvia May b. May 12, 1872, d. Oct. 31, 1873; Eleanor b. Jan. 25, 1874, m. John T. Hind May 8, 1901; Franklin Wakefield b. March 14, 1876, m. Amanda Neilson March 1897. Family resided Ohio, Illinois, Nebraska and Utah.
Married Jane Christianson Mouritzen May 5, 1870, Salt Lake City (daughter of Lars Mouritzen and Mary Mouritzen, latter born Oct. 17, 1825). She was born Jan. 29, 1853, Hjorring, Denmark. Their children: Lettie Luella b. Jan. 19, 1877, m. Hugh Dowdle March 20, 1895; Ruth b. March 13, 1879, d. Oct. 25, 1885; Jeddie Leroy b. Jan. 1, 1881, m. Myra Smith April 29, 1902; Mina b. Nov. 30, 1884, m. John W. Roundy Oct. 14, 1903; Leone b. Aug. 25, 1887, m. Hugh S. Rash Dec. 12, 1094; Ruby b. July 23, 1895. Family home Smithfield, Utah.
Married Jeanette Hendrickson Oct. 5, 1881, Salt Lake City (daughter of Nicholas Hendricks and Diana E. Kelsey), who was born Jan. 11, 1854, Springfield, Ill. Their children: Fred b. March 11, 1886, d. March 14, 1887; Harvey b. Nov. 9, 1887, m. Effie Elvina Tibbets Oct. 2, 1907; George b. Aug. 11, 1889, m. Ira Marie Corbet Sept. 8, 1909; Diana b. Dec. 25, 1890; Glen b. April 6, 1892; Olive b. Nov. 9, 1894; Zina b. Feb. 4, 1897; John b. April 12, 1899. Family home, Smithfield.
High priest; president of 17th quorum seventies 50 years; missionary to England and to southern states; helped in construction of all temples in Utah. Commissioner of Cache Co., Utah. City surveyor, Smithfield; president of Smithfield Z. C. M. I. Indian war veteran. Member of Cavalry Company A, First Brigade, Nauvoo Legion.

MILES, EDWIN RUTHVEN, JR. (son of Edwin Ruthven Miles and Jane Ruth Wakefield—married March 11, 1857). Born Oct. 3, 1858, Big Cottonwood, Salt Lake county.
Married Annie G. Smith Jan. 9, 1879 (daughter of George Young Smith and Johanna Suckle, latter pioneer 1852). She was born Nov. 9, 1859, Dundee, Scotland. Their children: George E. b. Dec. 25, 1879, m. Rae Nelson Jan. 4, 1905; Jane Ruth b. March 3, 1882, d. April 28, 1892; Edwin Ruthven b. July 9, 1884; Leonard Smith b. July 17, 1887; Johanna Pearl b. May 30, 1890; Hazel Vern b. Nov. 12, 1892; Mainice Kent b. Jan. 26, 1899. Family home, Smithfield.
Bishop of first ward, Smithfield, Utah. Merchant. President of the Bank of Smithfield; president of Smithfield Brick & Tile Company; first vice president of Trenton Irrigation Company of Utah; president Smithfield Lumber Company, and also of Smithfield Implement Company.

MILES, BENJAMIN FRANKLIN (son of Benjamin Albert Miles and Mahuldah Lockhart). Born in 1857, Wanship, Utah.
Married Rachel Emily Shippen in Wanship, Utah (daughter of Charles Shippen and Mary Alice Casper), who was born in 1859, Big Cottonwood, Utah. Their children: Zina Estella b. Sept. 2, 1878, m. George Edgar Wilkins; Jennie, m. William Wardell; Mary, m. Joseph Beecroft; Benjamin; Blanche; Pearl; Margaret. Family home Peoa, Utah.
Elder. Farmer.

MILES, SAMUEL, (son of Samuel Miles, born Sept. 3, 1779, Bransford, New Haven county, Conn., and Prudence Marks, born May 1, 1795, Rutland county, Vt.—married May 19, 1825). He was born April 8, 1826, Attica, Genesee county, N. Y. Came to Utah in 1848, with a portion of Company B, Mormon Battalion.
Married Hannah M. Colborn Sept. 6, 1849 (daughter of Thomas Colborn and Sarah Bower—married Aug. 11, 1825, Genoa, Cayuga county, N. Y.—pioneers Sept. 24, 1848, Heber C. Kimball company). She was born Dec. 29, 1831, and came to Utah Sept. 20, 1848, Brigham Young company. Their children: William Gustavus b. Sept. 13, 1851, m. Paralee A. Church May 25, 1874; Samuel b. Dec. 23, 1853, m. E. Louisa Worthen Dec. 6, 1875; Thomas Colborn b. March 12, 1856, m. Annie Pulsipher March 27, 1878; Ira b. Dec. 17, 1859, m. Alice Bell; John Salmar b. May 7, 1862, m. Merza Whitehead; Franklin Godbe b. April 7, 1865, m. Nellie Moss April

7, 1887; James Edwin b. Oct. 26, 1867; Charles Henry b. July 2, 1870, m. Minnie Mangum Aug. 2, 1905; Hannah Marinda 13, 1874, m. W. E. Mathis March 22, 1897. Family resides Salt Lake City, St. George and Price, Washington Co., Utah.
High councilor; Sunday school superintendent; patriarch. Justice of peace. School teacher. Adjutant in Nauvoo Legion. Secretary Price Irrigation Company.

MILLARD, JAMES RADFORD (son of John Millard and Martha Radford of England). Born March 22, 1827, Bidisham, Somersetshire. Came to Utah October, 1853, Joseph A. Young company.
Married Kathryne Richards (daughter of William Richards and Alice Howells, the former a pioneer Oct. 2, 1854, Daniel Garn company). Their children: John James b. Oct. 23, 1855, m. Katurah Haight; Alice Elizabeth b. March 16, 1857, m. William Watson; Mary Kathryne b. June 27, 1860; Celia b. June 16, 1862, m. Walter L. Grover Jan. 18, 1883; William Joseph b. Sept. 3, 1865, m. Maud Walker.

MILLBURN, HERBERT WEST (son of John B. Millburn and Jennie Tingley of Battle Creek, Iowa; they came to Utah 1887). Born Nov. 8, 1863, Battle Creek, Iowa. Came to Utah in 1887.
Married Olive Branch April 22, 1897, Salt Lake City (daughter of William Henry Branch and Ella Coombs, pioneers Oct. 14, 1850, Wilford Woodruff company). She was born Dec. 19, 1878, St. George, Utah. Their children: Amelia b. Dec. 7, 1897; Jennie Ruth b. June 12, 1900; John Herbert b. Feb. 15, 1908; Frank Branch b. Nov. 8, 1909. Family home Price, Utah.

MILLER, CHARLES J. (son of William Miller and Ann Ellis of Maresfield, Sussex, Eng.). Born Oct. 8, 1818, Fletching, Sussex, Eng. Came to Utah June 24, 1868, Harvey H. Cluff company.
Married Harriet Hill in England (daughter of John Hill and Elizabeth Budgen of England), who was born Feb. 16, 1785. Their children: James, m. Elizabeth ———; Harriet, m. John Duke; Charles, m. Amelia Hawkins, d. March 23, 1883; Jane, died; Eliza, m. George Barnett; Andrew, m. Caroline Saunders; Job, m. Alice Perkins, d. Feb. 28, 1873; Oliver, d. March 5, 1875; Emma, m. John Coes. Family home Cleveland, Ohio.
Railroader. Died Aug. 18, 1900, Cleveland.

MILLER, ANDREW (son of Charles Miller and Harriet Hill). Born March 8, 1852, at Clayton, England. Came to Utah with parents.
Married Caroline E. Saunders Dec. 16, 1872, Salt Lake City (daughter of William Gilbert Saunders and Phoebe Merrill of Soham, Cambridgeshire, Eng.). She was born March 5, 1853, and came to Utah in 1854. Their children: Andrew b. Aug. 22, 1873, m. Mary Buse; William Charles b. Aug. 2, 1876, died; Caroline Eliza b. Feb. 20, 1878, m. George G. Rose; Oliver Steven b. June 14, 1880, m. Rose Kershaw; Elizabeth Moyes; Rhoda Harriet b. Oct. 29, 1882, m. John Williams; James G. b. March 13, 1885, m. Elizabeth Browning; John H. b. Aug. 17, 1887, m. Gwenna Rhees; Parley b. Jan. 16, 1890, d. July 24, 1890; Albert Joseph b. April 14, 1891, m. Cordelia London; Wiley b. March 1, 1893; Carl b. June 27, 1895. Resided North Ogden, Utah.
Ordained elder Dec. 16, 1872; clerk of quorum; ordained high priest March 28, 1908. Brickmaker and poultry raiser.

MILLER, OLIVER STEVEN (son of Andrew Miller and Caroline E. Saunders). Born June 14, 1880, North Ogden, Utah.
Married Rose Kershaw April 30, 1902, Salt Lake City (daughter of Andrew J. Kershaw and Rose Whitten of England). Their only child died in infancy.
Married Elizabeth I. Moyes Oct. 22, 1905, Salt Lake City (daughter of John H. Moyes and Elizabeth Ingles of Ogden, pioneers with John Nicholson and P. C. Christenson companies. Family home Ogden. Utah.
Elder. Fruit, bee and poultry raiser.

MILLER, CHRISTIAN JENSEN (son of Jense Christian Miller, born 1808, Rorbek, Dastrup, Denmark, and Christina Myriah Christensen, born 1813, Dastrup, Denmark). He was born Aug. 6, 1840, Thrue, Denmark. Came to Utah 1863.
Married Mary Poulsen 1866, Hyrum, Utah (daughter of Jense Poulsen and Dorthea Andersen, former died on plains, latter came to Utah 1866, Peter Nebeker company). She was born 1847, Dastrup, Denmark, and came to Utah with mother. Their children: James C. b. March 3, 1869, m. Martha L. Bradshaw; Myriah b. Dec. 10, 1871, m. Theodore Peterson; Caroline b. Aug. 2, 1875, m. J. Wilford Munk; Emma Margrete b. April 1878, m. Hyrum N. Hanson; Lauritz W. b. May 18, 1882, m. Eliza Robins; Hyrum Jensen b. March 1885, m. Maud Anderson; Amanda Jensen b. June 8, 1887, m. Robert P. Lotham. Family home Hyrum, Utah.
Married Anna Poulsen 1869, Hyrum, Utah (daughter of Jense Poulsen and Dortha Andersen of Denmark). She was born Nov. 27, 1853, Eastrup, Denmark. Their children: Anna b. Nov. 11, 1873, m. Herman Johnson; Niels C. b. Aug. 24, 1876, m. Carrie ———; Milla Jensen b. April 7, 1878, m.

J. A. Lowry; Charles C. b. Nov. 7, 1881, m. Herman Fosley; Laura June b. Jan. 13, 1884, m. John Bankrod; Rosetta b. April 13, 1880, m. George B. Cannon; Agnes A. b. Sept. 30, 1885, m. George Banket; Pearl b. Jan. 8, 1887; Momel b. 1888, m. Will Nielson; Janin b. Jan. 25, 1890; Ruben Jensen b. Sept. 3, 1892.
Missionary to Denmark 1905-06; high priest. Has done much for the upbuilding of Hyrum and surrounding country. Farmer and stockraiser.

MILLER, DANIEL ARNOLD (son of James Gardner Miller and Ruth Arnold, born 1767, of Lexington, Green county, N. Y.—married Oct. 29, 1798). He was born Aug. 11, 1809. Came to Utah Sept. 4, 1848, captain of one of the large immigrant trains preceding the large number who came that year.
Married Clarissa Pond Dec. 29, 1833 (daughter of Thodeas Pond, born in 1770, died Aug. 20, 1847, and Lovisa Minos, born in 1777, died Oct. 30, 1844—married 1797). She was born Jan. 8, 1806, and died Sept. 1, 1844, near Carthage, Hancock county, Ill. Their children: Lovisa b. Oct. 1, 1834, m. Milton D. Hammon; Jacob b. Dec. 9, 1835, m. Hellen Mar Cheney; James Thodeas b. Dec. 19, 1837, d. Feb. 25, 1858; Susan Hulda b. Sept. 11, 1839, m. William Carbine; Clarissa Jane b. Aug. 11, 1841, m. Oscar Rice; Daniel Arnold b. Oct. 8, 1843, d. Oct. 8, 1843. Family home Adams, Hancock county, Ill.
Married Hannah Bigler Dec. 29, 1844, near Carthage, Ill. (daughter of Jacob Bigler, pioneer Sept. 4, 1848, Daniel A. Miller company). She was born Jan. 20, 1820. Their children: Isabella Clarinda b. Jan. 21, 1846, m. Adam Bigler; Joseph Smith b. Aug. 12, 1847, m. Lydia Steed; Emeline Elizabeth b. May 1, 1849, m. Calvin Wilson; Sarah Lavina b. June 24, 1850, m. John Hess; Ruth Abagail b. July 29, 1852, m. Charles Turner; Hannah Malinda b. June 23, 1854, m. Elija Jones; David Edgar b. Oct. 28, 1855, m. Julia E. Rogers; Bathsheba b. Jan. 12, 1857, m. Ira R. Steede; Daniel G. b. May 29, 1859, m. Nellie M. Smith; Henry William b. Oct. 5, 1860, m. Anniel Leonard. Family home Farmington, Utah.
Married Elenor Williamson Feb. 15, 1857 (daughter of Thomas Williamson and Hannah Robinson), who was born Sept. 28, 1827, and died Feb. 26, 1864. Their children: Clarissa Ruth b. May 28, 1859, m. Arthur Stayner; Charles Arnold b. May 22, 1861, m. Gertrude Stayner; Frederick Septimus b. Feb. 10, 1864, died. Family home Farmington, Utah.
High priest; missionary to Indiana in 1842; bishop of Kanesville, Iowa, 1846-47. Assisted in bringing immigrants to Utah in 1848, and again in 1853. Treasurer of Davis Co., Utah. Consecrated all his property ($3,871) to the Mormon Church. Moved to southern Utah May 2, 1858. Director of Z. C. M. I. Farmer and stockraiser.

MILLER, JACOB (son of Daniel Arnold Miller and Clarissa Pond). Born Dec. 9, 1835, Quincy, Adams county, Ill.
Married Helen Mar Cheney March 15, 1856, Farmington, Davis Co., Utah (daughter of Nathan Cheney and Eliza Ann Beebe, pioneers Oct. 6, 1850, with William Snow company). She was born July 25, 1835, Freedom. Cattaraugus county, N. Y. Their children: Jacob Franklin b. Dec. 10, 1856, m. Hulda Larson; Eliza Ann b. Jan. 15, 1859, d. Jan. 31, 1859; James Bertram b. April 22, 1860, d. May 14, 1860; Helen Vestina b. Nov. 10, 1861, d. Oct. 24, 1865; Nathan Wallace b. May 23, 1864, d. Sept. 25, 1864; Bertina Nathalia b. Aug. 21, 1865, m. James J. Steed; Daniel Thomas b. May 15, 1870, m. Hattie Knowlton.
Married Annie Sophia Christensen May 13, 1885, Logan, Utah (daughter of Mads Christensen and Mary Johannah Jenson, pioneers Sept. 13, 1857, with a handcart company). She was born March 4, 1864, Farmington, Utah. Their children: Joseph Royal b. May 18, 1890; Harold C. b. April 25, 1894, d. March 26, 1895; Annie Elna b. Aug. 3, 1896; Hyrum Julian b. Sept. 27, 1898; Horton C. b. Nov. 18, 1900.
Seventy; high priest; patriarch; called on a mission to Australia on June 12 and left on June 16, 1875-76; counselor to Bishop John W. Hess and first counselor to Bishop J. M. Secrist; stake tithing clerk; missionary to Indian mission at Limhi. Idaho. Moved to southern Utah May 2, 1858. School teacher 25 terms, 1858-69. Superintendent of Sunday school 1859-73. School trustee for three terms; president of the board of examination of teachers. Director, secretary and treasurer of Z. C. M. I. Justice of peace for two terms. Helped in the attempt to colonize the Little Colorado valley in Arizona, but the undertaking was a failure. Director, treasurer and assistant superintendent of a Farmington Co-op. for tanning, manufacturing and stockraising. Director and secretary and assistant superintendent of a Davis county company, successor to the Farmington Co-op. Agent for Hammond, Hendrecks & Co., Co. R. G. R. R. contractors for grading and track-laying. Served one term as county clerk of Davis county, 1883. Died Oct. 15, 1911.

MILLER, JACOB FRANKLIN (son of Jacob Miller and Helen Mar Cheney). Born Dec. 10, 1856, Farmington, Utah.
Married Hulda Larson Sept. 18, 1901, Logan, Utah (daughter of Ole Larson, who came to Utah Aug. 21, 1865, and Johanna Nelson). She was born June 26, 1872, Skane, Sweden. Their children: Joseph Larson b. Sept. 1, 1902; Helen Mar b. Nov. 13, 1903.
President 40th quorum seventies; missionary to Tennessee 1883-85; stake tithing clerk; member of board of Y. M.

M. I. A.; student of Deseret University. Professor of history and political science in the B. Y. C. 1892-96. In 1896 the degree of Bachelor of Didactics, and in 1902 the degree Bachelor of Arts were conferred upon him. Died March 25, 1906.

MILLER, DANIEL G. (son of Daniel Arnold Miller and Hannah Bigler—married Dec. 29, 1844, near Carthage, Ill.). Born May 29, 1859, Farmington, Utah.
Married Nellie M. Smith Dec. 23, 1880, Salt Lake City (daughter of Jesse W. and Catheren A. Vanvelver Smith), who was born Dec. 14, 1861, Farmington, Utah. Their children: Daniel Gardner b. Feb. 18, 1882, m. Sarah Luella Brower; Jesse Arnold b. April 8, 1885, m. Myrtle Eva Brower; Charles Henry b. Feb. 18, 1887, m. Olive May Orgill; Horace S. b. Feb. 2, 1889; Andrew b. Nov. 13, 1890; Wallace Arland b. Dec. 12, 1892; Ralph b. Jan. 8, 1895; Hellen b. March 30, 1900; Sarah b. Oct. 25, 1902; Stella b. Oct. 27, 1904. Family resided Farmington, Utah, and Parker, Idaho.
Second assistant superintendent Sundy school, north district, Farmington ward; president Y. M. M. I. A.; president Y. M. M. I. A. Egin (Parker), Idaho; assistant Sunday school superintendent Parker, Idaho; counselor to Bishop Carbine in 1893; bishop of Parker ward 1902-10; president of Yellowstone stake; missionary to southern states 1895-98.

MILLER, ELEAZAR. Came to Utah 1847.
Married Rebecca Rathbone. Their children: Gilbert; Van Rensler, died; Perry, d. aged 70; Harrison; Elliott; Subrina, m. John Hackshaw; Baby, d. infant; William, m. Margaret Neibaur, m. Christene ———.
Farmer. Ran church farm in early days. Died at Salt Lake City.

MILLER, WILLIAM (son of Eleazar Miller and Rebecca Rathbone). Born June 10, 1832. Came to Utah 1847.
Married Margaret Neibaur 1856, Salt Lake City (daughter of Alexander Neibaur of Salt Lake City, pioneer 1848, with oxteam). She was born Feb. 20, 1836. Their children: Ellen b. March 14, 1857, m. Fred Brind; Rebecca Jane b. Nov. 24, 1858, m. Herbert Savage; William Perry b. Jan. 7, 1860, m. Martha Ellen Prows, m. Mary Jane Birch; Van Rensler b. Jan. 3, 1861, m. Salina Gay; Alice, m. Robert Morgan, m. Richard B. Keffer; Gilbert, d. aged 21; Subrina, d. infant; Harrison, m. Elnora Wiseman; Elliott, m. Serepta Vicker; James Nathan, m. Lilly Stallings; Isaac Alexander, d. May 1, 1900; Heber John, d. infant; George Washington, m. Abigail Fullmer; Margaret. Family resided Salt Lake City and Kamas, Utah.
Married Christene ———. Salt Lake Endowment house. Their children: Joseph; Hyrum. Family home, Salt Lake City.
High priest. Farmer and freighter. Died July 5, 1910, Spring Glen, Utah.

MILLER, WILLIAM PERRY (son of William Miller and Margaret Neibaur). Born Jan. 7, 1860, Salt Lake City.
Married Martha Ellen Prows April 27, 1881, Kanosh, Utah (daughter of William Cook Prows and Lodesky Ann Roberts, pioneers 1850). She was born March 27, 1862, and died Feb. 4, 1889, Kanosh, Utah. Their children: Clara Ellen b. Aug. 17, 1882, d. infant; Margaret A. L. b. Oct. 6, 1884, m. James Dickens Fullmer; William Albert b. Sept. 19, 1886; Parley b. Jan. 23, 1889; Perry b. Jan. 23, 1889, m. Clara Jorgensen. Family home Kanosh, Utah.
Married Mary Jane Birch Dec. 1, 1892, Manti, Utah (daughter of Richard Birch and Mary Ann Hale of Hoytsville, Utah, latter a pioneer 1849—married Aug. 15, 1865, Salt Lake Endowment house). She was born Nov. 10, 1864. Their children: Gilbert b. Nov. 29, 1893; Helen Mar b. July 28, 1896; Woodruff b. Oct. 19, 1898; Isaac b. Dec. 20, 1900; James Earl b. July 26, 1902; George Ellis b. Nov. 27, 1904; Eleazar b. March 14, 1907. Family resided at Joseph City, Cleveland and Spring Glen, Utah.
Seventy; high priest; counselor to Bishop James Nathan Miller; counselor to Bishop J. T. Rowley; Sunday school superintendent; president Y. M. M. I. A.; ward teacher. Farmer and freighter.

MILLER, FREDERICK ANDRUS (son of Frederick Andrus Miller of Germany, born 1811, and Mary Wilson of Scotland, born Feb. 16, 1811—married in New York city). He was born March 24, 1838. Came to Utah Sept. 27, 1851, Morris Phelps company.
Married Geneva Shaw Oct. 31, 1870 (daughter of William Shaw and Diana Chase), who was born Feb. 5, 1854, Ogden, Utah. Their children: Frederick S. b. July 28, 1871, m. Polly Ann Taylor; William b. Aug. 11, 1873, died; James b. Dec. 27, 1874; Frank b. March 14, 1876, m. Anna Connan; Mary b. Nov. 14, 1877, m. Walter Taylor; Jerome b. Aug. 21, 1879; Geneva b. March 22, 1881, m. R. R. D. Brown; Diana b. April 10, 1883, m. Frank Blair; Margret b. Nov. 6, 1884, m. Isaac D. Fife; Reuben b. Sept. 13, 1886; Agnes b. March 2, 1888; Rosabell b. Nov. 26, 1889; Robert L. b. Dec. 4, 1891; Archie D. b. Feb. 15, 1893; Jesse E. b. Sept. 29, 1894; Juliet F. b. July 6, 1899.
Counselor to bishop, Harrisville, Utah, for four years; missionary to Lemhi, Idaho, 1857-58. Alderman for Ogden city two terms; justice of the peace for six years, Lynne precinct, Ogden, Utah; school trustee 20 years for Lynne and Harrisville districts.

MILLER, FREDERICK S. (son of Frederick Andrus Miller and Geneva Shaw). Born July 28, 1871, Lynne, Utah.
Married Polly Ann Taylor Dec. 2, 1897, Salt Lake City (daughter of Harvey G. Taylor and Emeline Rawson). She was born Aug. 22, 1873, Harrisville, Utah.

MILLER, HENRY WILLIAM (son of James Gardner Miller, born March 15, 1771, in Connecticut, and Ruth Arnold, born 1769—married Oct. 27, 1798). He was born May 1, 1807, Lexington, Greene county, N. Y. Came to Utah 1852.
Married Elmira Pond June 19, 1831 (daughter of Silas and Clarissa Pond), who was born Feb. 14, 1811, and came to Utah 1852, Captain Miller company. Their children; Elizabeth b. Sept. 25, 1832, m. Andrew Quigley; Ruth Ann b. March 30, 1834, m. George McBride; m. James McBride; Lucy b. Jan. 10, 1837, m. Oliver L. Robinson; Wm. Henry b. Dec. 22, 1838, m. Helen M. Hinmon; Alma b. Jan. 20, 1841, m. Louisa Jane Hall; Mary Elmira b. Sept. 10, 1843, m. Alma Hess; Freelove b. July 24, 1845, m. Milton D. Hammond; Hyrum Smith b. May 4, 1847, m. Caroline Smithson; Sarah Jane b. March 22, 1849, m. Wm. V. Carbine; David b. Feb. 14, 1851; Arnold Daniel b. March 2, 1852, m. Mary Jane Laub. Family resided Council Bluffs, Iowa, Farmington, and St. George Utah.
High priest. High councilor. Representative Iowa legislature. Missionary to Indian territory in 1852. Assisted in bringing immigrants to Utah; member of Mormon Battalion; pioneer to southern Utah 1865. Located at Farmington in 1882. Lawyer; farmer and stockraiser. Died October, 1885.

MILLER, WILLIAM H. (son of Henry W. Miller and Elmira Pond). Born Dec. 22, 1838, at Quincy, Ill. Came to Utah with father.
Married Helen M. Hinman, March 20, 1857, Salt Lake City (daughter of Lyman Hinman of Massachusetts—pioneer of Sept. 8, 1848), who was born Sept. 20, 1840. Their children: Edna, d. aged 13; William M., m. Udora Hess; Aurelia, d. infant; Lyman H., m. Mary J. Smith; Seymour L., m. Lillie Hunsaker; Eva, m. Franklin L. Walker; Maud, m. David Cook; Hattie, m. Harvey Moore; Rhoda, m. —— Raddon. Family home Farmington, Utah.
Fruitgrower and stockraiser.

MILLER, WILLIAM M. (son of William H. Miller and Helen M. Hinman). Born Feb. 12, 1861, Farmington, Utah.
Married Udora Hess, Nov. 24, 1881, Salt Lake City (daughter of John W. Hess and Mary Ann Steed, of Farmington, Utah—pioneers 1849). She was born Sept. 28, 1863. Their children; Helen M. b. March 26, 1883, d. aged 2; William M. b. March 11, 1885; George Lewis b. May 14, 1887, m. Alice Rohwer; Mary Ann b. Nov. 5, 1889, m. William T. Rogers; Clarence (Eugene) b. Aug. 15, 1892; John (Wilford) b. Nov. 17, 1894. Family home Penrose, Box Elder Co., Utah.
Married Olive Pierson, Sept. 8, 1895, Plymouth, Box Elder Co., Utah, (daughter of Harmon D. Pierson and Mary ——, of Plymouth, Utah—pioneers fall, 1847). She was born about 1870. Their children: James H. b. Sept. 3, 1897; Meud b. May 12, 1899; Olive U. b. Nov. 1901; Aurelia E. b. Dec. 12, 1902; Jessie b. Sept. 30, 1906; Irene (twin of Jessie); Helen b. March 19, 1909; Althea b. in 1911.
Elder. Farmer; fruitgrower; stockraiser.

MILLER, ARNOLD DANIEL (son of Henry Wm. Miller and Elmira Pond). Born March 2, 1852, Council Bluffs, Iowa.
Married Mary Jane Laub Dec. 14, 1873, Salt Lake City, Utah, (daughter of George and Mary Jane McGinnes Laub, pioneers 1852, Captain Higby company). She was born Nov. 29, 1856, Salt Lake City. Their children: Arnold Daniel b. Oct. 23, 1874, m. Effie A. Secrist; Bert Henry b. Dec. 15, 1876, m. Rose Davis; Franklin Alma b. Sept. 3, 1879, m. Bertha Flint; Erwin Stanley b. Aug. 11, 1882; George Wm. b. Dec. 26, 1885, m. Jennie Southworth; Mary Elmira b. Nov. 7, 1887, m. Lee Stanford; John Frederick b. Nov. 10, 1891; Edgar Ray b. Jan. 3, 1894; Leah Lurene b. July 13, 1896. Family resided St. George, Utah; Parker, Idaho, and St. Anthony, Idaho.
High councilor Zion stake, Oregon, 1902-3; bishop of St. Anthony, Idaho. Was a leading member of the building committee of the Yellowstone stake tabernacle. Pioneer in farming and stock raising in the Egin Bench (now Parker), Idaho. Assessor and collector of Fremont county, Idaho, 1896-98. Served in constructing and developing the irrigation system of the Upper Snake River valley. Freighter and railroader of the Rocky Mountain region 1870-84. Bishop's counselor at Parker, Idaho, 1884.

MILLER, ARNOLD DANIEL JR. (son of Arnold Daniel Miller and Mary Jane Laub). Born Oct. 23, 1874, St. George, Utah.
Married Effie A. Secrist Dec. 1, 1897, Salt Lake City (daughter of Heber Nephi Secrist and Florence Adelia Smith). She was born Feb. 1, 1878, Farmington, Utah. Their children: Vernessa Irene b. Dec. 26, 1899; Eunice Gertrude b. Jan. 8, 1902; Florence Mary b. Jan. 14, 1907; Effie Myrle b. May 20, 1909. Family home Parker, Idaho.
Bishop of Parker, Idaho; assistant superintendent of Sunday school; stake Sunday school board member; missionary to northwestern states 1897-99. Attended school at the B. Y. U., Provo, Utah. Pioneer of Idaho 1884. Assisted in the development of the upper Snake River valley. Member building committee Yellowstone stake tabernacle. Ward presiden' Y. M. M. I. A. eight years.

MILLER, JAMES. Born Nov. 20, 1829, Birtherglen, Lanarkshire, Scotland. Came to Utah with oxteam.
Married Margaret Anderson, at Salt Lake City. Their children: Mary Elizabeth, m. George Boyen; Margaret Ann. m. Alma Charles Davis; Charles William, m. Minnie Creamer; James David, m. Margaret Snell; Agnes Ann, m. Jo e Creer; John Archibald. Family home Spanish Fork, Utalph
Married Lavenia Andrus Dec. 6, 1869, Salt Lake Endowment house (daughter of Milo Andrus and Lucy Loomis of Big Cottonwood, Utah, pioneers with handcarts). She was born Feb. 28, 1854, Big Cottonwood. Their children: Brigham b. Nov. 24, 1870; Lucy b. Aug. 2, 1872; Lavenia b. July 29, 1873; Alma R. b. Jan. 12, 1876; June b. June 1, 1878; Francina b. Sept. 14, 1880; Amos b. Oct. 19, 1882, d. Aug. 22, 1909. Family home Spanish Fork, Utah.
Died October, 1904, Spanish Fork, Utah.
Lavenia Andrus later married James McComb, at Salt Lake City. Their children: Eleanor b. March 17, 1889, m. Jesse Miles, m. James Raymond; Mary Alma b. May 29, 1890, m. Clifford Robinson; Viola b. Dec. 2, 1891, m. Edward House; Ida b. July 14, 1893, d. aged 2; William James b. July 2, 1895. Family home Helper, Utah.

MILLER, JOHN. Born Jan. 11, 1811, Wymondham, Norfolk, Eng.
Married Mary Jolley, at Norfolk, Eng.
Married Jane Childs (Ginger) Nov. 1, 1868, Salt Lake Endowment house (daughter of George Childs and Rachel Proyer of Herefordshire, Eng., pioneers Aug. 20, 1868, Captain McMaster company). She was born Dec. 10, 1818.
Died Aug. 11, 1892, Salt Lake City.
Jane Childs was the widow of William Ginger.

MILLER, MARTIN (son of George Miller, born 1807, Denmark, and Margret Healey, born in Denmark). Born June 23, 1843, in Denmark. Came to Utah in 1853.
Married Christena Peterson Dec. 15, 1867, Salt Lake City (daughter of Andrew Peterson and Norma Anderson of Sweden, pioneers Sept. 27, 1862, John R. Murdock company). She was born May 21, 1845. Their children: Martin George b. Dec. 17, 1868, m. Lovina Williams July 4, 1892; Mary Ann b. Jan. 9, 1869, died; Margret b. June 1, 1873, m. John Thomas Gordon Jan. 24, 1895; Emma Christena b. Aug. 27, 1876, m. Boise A. Wells July 3, 1900; Alma, m. Anna Bushman Oct. 3, 1902; Franklin John; Hannah Lottie, m. Myron Harker Feb. 15, 1907; Anna, died; Elma, m. Earl Harker. Family first resided Lehi, then Mount Pleasant (1859), Utah, and Magrath (1892), Canada.
Seventy. Teacher. Black Hawk war veteran. Member water board Lehi for years. Made trip across plains with oxteam for immigrants 1862. Farmer. Died Dec. 5, 1912, Magrath.

MILLER, MILO (son of Josiah and Amanda Miller of Ohio). Born July 26, 1818, in Ohio. Came to Utah 1849. Ephraim Hanks company, by way of California with Mormon Battalion.
Married Rachel Ewing 1851, Salt Lake City, Brigham Young officiating (daughter of Samuel Ewing and Elizabeth Schaffer of Little Britain, Lancaster county, Pa., pioneers 1848, Heber C. Kimball company). She was born Aug. 12, 1829, and died August, 1898. Their children: Samuel, m. Maggie Sheppee; Daniel, m. Loanda Tidwell; James, died; Charles Andrew; John Edward, m. Mariah Jensen; Franklin Anderson, m. Ann Eliza Merrick (Toot); William Ashmer, m. Hannah Jensen; Sarah Frances, died; Joseph Henry; Ora Ann, died; Hyrum Emer, died. Family resided Nephi and Emery, Utah.
President seventies quorum; block teacher. Was called to settle Nephi, and his child, James, was the first child buried there; helped to build canals, irrigation ditches and wagon roads; moved to Rabbit Valley from Nephi 1875, then to Loa, and then to Emery county 1877, where there was but one family at the time he arrived, Casper Christensen. He was the upbuilder of this part of the country, and his work paved the way for the others that came. Veteran Black Hawk and Tintic Indian wars. Farmer. Died March 3, 1900, Nephi.

MILLER, FRANKLIN ANDERSON (son of Milo Miller and Rachel Ewing). Born Jan. 9, 1861, Nephi, Utah.
Married Ann Eliza Merrick (Toot) Dec. 25, 1886, on his ranch, seven miles south of Emery, David Jones officiating (daughter of George Merrick and Hannah Green of Mt. Pleasant and Emery, Utah). She was born Jan. 22, 1870. Their children: Franklin Edwin, died; Rachel b. Jan. 14, 1891, m. Alfred Jensen; Delphia b. Jan. 19, 1893; Ruth b. Dec. 5, 1894; May b. Feb. 27, 1897; Esther b. Dec. 1, 1899; William b. Nov. 5, 1901; Sherman b. June 16, 1904; George b. May 24, 1908. Family home, Emery.
Deacon. Came to Emery as a boy, where he passed his life in building up the county and town of Emery; all that has been accomplished in building the south side of the county to its present high state of cultivation and development has been done since he came here; the irrigation canals and wagon roads that have been the hardest to build has

been a part of his labor; he has devoted his time to farming, and owns the first farm taken up in this part of the country; it is where his father located in 1877; he was the first man to successfully raise corn in this part of Utah.

MILLER, REUBEN (son of Isaac Miller, born Jan. 19, 1782, Reading, Pa., and Esther Glime, born Feb. 27, 1789, in Lancaster county, Pa.). He was born Sept. 4, 1811, Lancaster, Pa. Came to Utah 1849.
Married Rhoda Ann Letts April 17, 1836 (daughter of David Letts and Martha Strawn), who was born Nov. 25, 1814. Their children: Edwin C. b. Feb. 9, 1837, d. July 26, 1838; James R. b. Oct. 2, 1838, m. Mary Jane Gardner; Martha b. March 17, 1843, d. May 12, 1843; Reuben P. b. Dec. 22, 1844, m. Margaret Gardner Oct. 1, 1868; Melvin M. b. Oct. 17, 1846, m. Martha Maria Shurtliff; Chillian L. b. Nov. 29, 1848, m. Harriett Jane Webb June 24, 1870; Edgar G. b. June 22, 1850, d. Jan. 2, 1853; Rhoda Ann b. June 28, 1852, d. April 20, 1854; Uriah G. b. Sept. 24, 1854, d. Dec. 9, 1857; David L. b. Oct. 8, 1856, m. Emerett Boyce Dec. 27, 1877. Family home Mill Creek ward, Salt Lake county, Utah.
Married Orace Burnham (daughter of Dyer Burnham and Orace Cone). She was born Nov. 20, 1815, Mexico, Oswego county, N. Y. Their children: Ellen Elizabeth b. Feb. 14, 1850, d. May 28, 1865; Julia Ann b. Oct. 8, 1854, d. June 3, 1865; Charles Eugene b. Aug. 25, 1852, m. Christeena McAllister.
Married Ann Cramer Dec. 9, 1856, Salt Lake City (daughter of George B. Cramer and Elizabeth West). She was born July 15, 1838, Warwickshire, Eng. Their children: Orrin Porter b. Sept. 11, 1858, m. Minnie Morgan; Mary Elizabeth b. Nov. 1, 1860, m. Thomas Boam; Louisa b. Nov. 23, 1862, d. Oct. 11, 1883; George Benjamin b. Feb. 19, 1865, m. Jane Merrill; Harriet Ann b. March 11, 1867, m. John W. Morgan; Lenora b. March 20, 1869, m. George Green; Milton Henry b. Aug. 8, 1871, d. Oct. 31, 1875; Walter Frederick b. Sept. 6, 1873; Marion John b. Sept. 20, 1877, m. Lydia Bolton; Nellie Cramer b. Sept. 30, 1880, m. Otto Headman Dec. 19, 1900; Deuane b. Jan. 15, 1883, m. Mary Elizabeth Burgon Sept. 7, 1904. Family home Mill Creek, Utah.
Married Jane Hughes Jan. 11, 1869, Salt Lake City (daughter of James Hughes and Elizabeth Swallon). She was born Jan. 21, 1849, Leominster, Herefordshire, Eng. Their children: Ella Jane b. Dec. 30, 1869, m. Ernest Croxford; Frank Hughes b. Sept. 7, 1872, m. Blanche Williams; Letts Glime b. March 5, 1874, d. March 5, 1875; Esther Elizabeth b. April 11, 1876, d. Sept. 6, 1878; Emma Maria b. Oct. 6, 1877, m. William Park; Elias Smith b. Aug. 5, 1882. Family home Mill Creek, Utah.
First located at Mill Creek. When the Mill Creek ward was organized in 1850, he was set apart as bishop of that ward, which position he held to his death. County commissioner 1850. He was known to be a hard worker and a keen business man, and succeeded in accumulating considerable worldly goods. Nearly, if not all of the many water ditches lying north of Big Cottonwood Creek were laid out by him, with an old water level and a teakettle that he used for an instrument. During his life as a commissioner he opened all of the roads both ways across the valley, and the present system of roads is due to his foresight and judgment.

MILLER, REUBEN PARLEY (son of Reuben Miller and Rhoda Ann Letts). Born Dec. 22, 1844. Beech Creek, LaSalle county, Ill. Came to Utah 1848.
Married Margaret Gardner Oct. 10, 1868 (daughter of Robert Gardner and Jane McCune, pioneers October, 1847, Edward Hunter company). She was born Sept. 1, 1844, and came to Utah with parents. Their children: Reuben Edgar b. Oct. 30, 1869, m. Janetta McMillan; Mary Elizabeth Dixon; Robert Gardner b. April 20, 1872, d. Nov. 29, 1878; David b. June 19, 1873, d. July 31, 1873; Uriah George b. Nov. 28, 1874, m. Rosamond Carlisle; Margaret May b. May 7, 1878, d. June 12, 1878; Edith Lyle b. Aug. 7, 1879; Melvin Parley b. April 30, 1882, m. Cora Brugger; Ernest Tay b. April 30, 1884, d. Dec. 20, 1892. Family home Mill Creek, Utah.
Member Nauvoo Legion from early 1860 until its disorganization 1870; 1862 was called by President Lincoln to guard mail route; crossed plains in all 13 times, making six trips for immigrants; 1867-68, freighted to Los Angeles; 1871, with his brother, Melvin, entered Cheny Creek in the cattle business; 1876 there they entered Castle Valley where they established a flourishing sheep and cattle industry; also engaged in farming, manufacturing and mercantile business. Just previous to his death, he secured controlling interest in what was known as the Inter-Mountain Milling Company. Died March 27, 1891.

MILLER, URIAH GEORGE (son of Reuben Parley Miller and Margaret Gardner). Born Nov. 28, 1874, Mill Creek, Utah.
Married Rosamond Pearl Carlisle (daughter of Joseph Carlisle and Isabell Sharp, married 1853, St. Louis, Mo., and came to Utah same year). She was born July 29, 1875. Their children: Uriah Lynn b. Dec. 12, 1902; Marvin George b. Sept. 2, 1905.
Missionary to northern states June 2, 1896 to Dec. 21, 1898; missionary to West Mountain mining district Nov. 15, 1899, and remained there until the Granite stake was organized, when he was chosen second counselor in the Y. M. M. I. A. When Murray first ward was organized Oct. 8, 1900, he was chosen as bishop; released January, 1909, on account of ill health. Engaged in fruitgrowing and general farming on Provo bench. President and manager Utah Products Company at Murray. Member school board. School teacher in Salt Lake City 1895-96. Graduate of University of Utah, 1895.

MILLER, WILLIAM (son of Seth Miller and Martha Tilden of Avon, N. Y.). Born Jan. 8, 1914, Avon, N. Y. Came to Utah Sept. 15, 1849, with his own company.
Married Marilla Lucretia Johnson Dec. 27, 1845, Nauvoo, Ill. (daughter of Aaron Johnson and Polly Zerviah Kelsey, of Nauvoo, Ill.; came to Utah September, 1850, the former's own company). She was born Oct. 12, 1830. Their child: Wm. Alonzo, died. Family home, Salt Lake City.
Married Phoebe Scott May 4, 1834, Avon, N. Y. She was born Aug. 19, 1816. Their children: George; Rebecca Scott.
Married Emeline Potter Feb. 7, 1846. She was born May 18, 1828.
Married Annie Lewis Sept. 3, 1859. She was born July 23, 1837.
Married Jane Lewis Oct. 22, 1864. She was born Nov. 20, 1840.
Member second quorum seventies; missionary to England 1860-63; president of Utah stake. Probate judge Utah county. Merchant; farmer; stockraiser. Died Aug. 7, 1875, Provo, Utah.

MILLETT, ARTEMUS (son of Artemus Millett and Susannah Peters of Kirtland, Ohio). Born June 15, 1836, Kirtland, Ohio. Came to Utah in 1856, independent company.
Married Nancy Jane Beal Oct. 11, 1865, at Glenwood, Utah (daughter of William Beal and Clarissa Allen of Glenwood, Utah; came to Utah in 1850, independent company). She was born Oct. 22, 1846. Their children: Artemus b. Dec. 4, 1866; Franklyn W. b. Sept. 23, 1868, m. Caroline Jarmin; Charley William b. April 18, 1871, m. Ethel Larson; Emma Maria b. Nov. 4, 1873, m. Edwin Lytle; Susan Harriett b. Aug. 15, 1876, m. Melvin A. Court; Eliza Lemira b. Nov. 4, 1878, m. William E. Barney; Paul Alma b. Dec. 12, 1880, m. Effie May Burr; Clarice Effie b. June 21, 1883, m. Joseph Hill, m. Elwood Davis; Sarah Jane b. April 19, 1885; Ella Augusta b. Aug. 15, 1887, m. Arthur Newell; Lenora Nancy b. Feb. 18, 1887, m. Clarence Kofford.
Farmer and fruitgrower. Died Oct. 31, 1902, Provo.

MILLETT, PAUL ALMA (son of Artemus Millett and Nancy Jane Beal). Born Dec. 12, 1880, Spring Valley, Nev. Came to Utah May, 1900.
Married Effie May Burr Dec. 9, 1903, at Manti, Utah (daughter of Henry Uriah Burr and Julia Caroline Beal of Grass Valley, Utah). She was born April 1, 1883. Their children: Maggie Edna b. Sept. 14, 1904; Lorin Elmer b. July 7, 1906; Archie Levon b. Oct. 18, 1908; Orson Paul b. Nov. 1, 1910; Hazel Ruby b. Nov. 13, 1912. Family home Provo, Utah.
High priest; assistant superintendent Sharon Sunday school 1903-11; superintendent 1911; bishop's counselor. Fruitgrower and farmer.

MILLS, CHARLES EDMOND THOMAS (son of Charles Mills and Frances Farr of Southampton, Eng.). Born Jan. 14, 1838, Southampton. Came to Utah Oct. 11, 1861, Willia Wright independent freight company.
Married Eliza Harriet Bailey at Southampton (daughte of Francis and Eliza Bailey of Southampton; they came t Utah in 1869). She was born Sept. 22, 1838. Their children Charles Frank b. Dec. 14, 1861, m. Caroline Daniels; Alonz Alvin b. Aug. 31, 1863, m. Pamelia Hoyt; Eliza Jane b. Aug 23, 1865, m. William Crittenden; Mary Ellen b. June 4 1867, d. June 5, 1878; Samuel James b. Oct. 2, 1869, m. Oliv Irene Crittenden; Ella Louisa b. Oct. 5, 1871, d. May 2: 1878; Maud Elizabeth b. April 6, 1873, m. Andrew Peterson Albert Edmond b. Nov. 8, 1874, m. Martha Ann Wilkinson Walter Louis b. July 18, 1876, d. Dec. 21, 1876; Ezra Thoma b. Jan. 15, 1878, d. Dec. 2, 1878; Amy Clara b. Nov. 9, 187 d. Feb. 24, 1893. Family home Hoytsville, Utah.
County superintendent of Sunday schools. County super intendent of schools.

MILLS, ALBERT EDMOND (son of C. E. T. Mills and Eliz Harriet Bailey). Born Nov. 8, 1874, Hoytsville, Utah.
Married Martha Ann Wilkinson June 27, 1906, Salt Lak City (daughter of Joseph and Martha Ann Wilkinson o Hoytsville, pioneers of 1852 and 1869, respectively). Sh was born April 7, 1883. Their children: Grace Bernice April 27, 1907; Alice Afton b. Sept. 15, 1908; Emma b. Sep 18, 1910. Family home Hoytsville, Utah.
Stake aid in Y. M. M. I. A.; second counselor in stak Y. M. M. I. A.

MILLS, RICHARD ISAAC (son of Thomas Mills and An Stevens of Walsall, Staffordshire, Eng.). Born Nov. 2 1836, Birmingham, Warwickshire, Eng. Came to Utah 1859.
Married Charlotte Giles Oct. 27, 1861, Salt Lake Ci (daughter of James Giles and Charlotte Napper of Utah the former died at Green River; latter came to Utah 1863). She was born Oct. 4, 1839. Their children: Jam

Thomas; Charlotte Ann; Sarah Jane; Richard Isaac. Family home West Weber, Utah.
High priest; ward teacher; Sunday school superintendent. Died Jan. 28, 1910, West Weber.

MILLS, JAMES T. (son of Richard Isaac Mills and Charlotte Giles). Born Jan. 29, 1863, West Weber.
Married Sarah Buck March 29, 1895, Salt Lake City (daughter of Charles Buck and Hannah Chantrey, pioneers 1866, Thomas E. Ricks company). She was born Jan. 8, 1874. Family home, West Weber.
Member 108th quorum seventies; missionary to Society Islands 1899-01; president elders quorum of Bannock stake 1899; assistant Sunday school superintendent; ward teacher. Farmer.

MILLS, THOMAS. Born April 4, 1814, Radcliff, Lancastershire, Eng.
Married Alice Allen in 1838, at Radcliff. She was born April 14, 1819, and died July 14, 1891, at Mt. Pleasant, Utah. Came to Utah Oct. 2, 1862, James B. Brown company. Their children: Mary and James, d. infants; Mary Ann, m. James Allen; Elizabeth, m. Joseph Page; Alice, m. Joseph Page; William, died; Samuel, m. Mary Jane Winegar; Sarah Jane, d. infant.
Died Sept. 5, 1858, Alton, Ill.

MILNER, STANLEY B. (son of John Milner and Sarah S. Bark of Lancaster, Wis.). Born Jan. 11, 1850, Little Grant, Wis. Came to Utah in June, 1891.
Married Truth Campbell, Sept. 26, 1875, Atlantic, Cass Co., Iowa (daughter of Stanton A. Campbell and Theresa Lamson of Mt. Washington, Mass), who was born Sept. 23, 1852. Their children: Archibald C. b. June 8, 1877; Clarence E.; Joy S., m. Hazel Robinson. Family home, Salt Lake City.
Promoter of the irrigation on the Snake river, in Idaho. President Twin Falls Irrigation Company. Mining and reclamation. Died May 2, 1901, Salt Lake City.

MILNER, ARCHIBALD C. (son of Stanley B. Milner and Truth Campbell). Born June 8, 1877, Atlantic, Iowa. Came to Utah in 1891. Resides at Salt Lake City.
Mining and reclamation operator.

MITCHELL, HEZEKIAH (son of Thomas Mitchell and Martha Haigh, of Bolton, Lancastershire, Eng.). Born May 31, 1810, Simondly, near Stockport, Eng. Came to Utah Sept. 29, 1854, James Brown company.
Married Sarah Mallinson, Oct. 7, 1832, Manchester, Lancastershire, Eng. (daughter of John Mallinson and Mary Shaw Mallinson, of Pitsmoor [near Sheffield], Yorkshire, Eng.). She was born Nov. 16, 1810. Their children: Martin Luther, d. infant; Frederick Augustus Herman Frank, m. Margaret Thompson; Lavinia, m. James Brown; m. John Horrocks; Manti Ann, d. infant; Maria, m. ———— and Ed. G. Horrocks; Elizabeth, m. Ed. G. Horrocks; Ebenezia, d. infant; Sarah Ann, m. Joseph Graham; m. Winslow Farr; Priscilla Victoria, m. Rasmus Christianson. Family resided Tooele, Ogden and Salt Lake City.
High priest; counselor in the bishopric of 1st ward, Salt Lake City, Utah. at the time of demise. Machinist; farmer. Died Sept. 25, 1872, Salt Lake City, Utah.

MITCHELL, FREDERICK AUGUSTUS HERMAN FRANK (son of Hezekiah Mitchell and Sarah Mallinson Mitchell). Born July 14, 1835, Sheffield. Yorkshire, Eng. Came to Utah September, 1854, James Brown company.
Married Margaret Thompson Nov. 15, 1856, Salt Lake City (daughter of Ralph Thompson and Ann Bently of Nauvoo, Ill., and later of St. Louis. Mo., pioneers September, 1852). She was born Jan. 31, 1840, Alston, Cumberland, Eng. Their children: Margaret Ann b. Aug. 28, 1859, m. Alfred H. Caine; Emily Lavinia b. July 13, 1861, d. infant; Ella b. Jan. 18, 1864, m. Lafayette Grant Burton; Francis Laura b. March 20, 1866, m. Alexander McMaster; Fredrick Augustus b. Dec. 30, 1867, d. infant; Eleanor Mary b. June 20, 1870, m. Hyrum Mickle Blackhurst; Ida Rachel b. Sept. 24, 1872; Herman Frank b. Oct. 18, 1874, m. Mary Maude Thompson; Ralph Thompson b. Feb. 4, 1877, m. Sarah Oliver Yeates; Alfred Hezekiah b. March 26, 1879, m. Beatrice Carlisle; M^cton Reuben b. Jan. 21, 1883, m. Helena Belinken; Edgar Ben^tley b. Sept. 13, 1885, m. La Prile Barber. Family resided Salt Lake City and Logan, Utah.
Member of 27th and 57th quorum seventies; missionary to Hawaiian Islands 1856-8 and 1873-5, to Great Britain 1899-1902; presided over Hawaiian mission from 1873-8; member of council 57th quorum seventy from 1860-1902; counselor in the high priest quorum of Cache stake of Zion; second counselor in bishopric of 15th ward. Salt Lake City; superintendent of Sunday school, twentieth ward, Salt Lake City. County surveyor Summit Co., Utah; commissioner to locate University lands, territory of Utah; deputy U. S. mineral surveyor 1887-1900. Merchant; civil engineer; farmer. Family home Logan, Utah.

MITCHELL, ALFRED HEZEKIAH (son of Frederick Augustus Herman Frank Mitchell and Margaret Thompson). Born March 26, 1879, Salt Lake City.
Married Beatrice Carlisle Nov. 19, 1902, Logan, Cache Co., Utah (daughter of John G. Carlisle, pioneer 1855, Wm. S.

Godbe company, and Margaret Kewley, who came to Utah Nov. 30, 1856, Edward Martin company, of Logan. Utah). She was born April 13, 1882. Their children: Beatrice b. Sept. 5, 1903; Lavinia b. Sept. 13, 1905; Margaret b. Nov. 3, 1908; Alfred Hezekiah b. June 19, 1911. Family home Logan. Utah.
Member of 8th quorum elders of Cache stake of Zion; second of 8th quorum of elders. Barber.

MITTON, SAMUEL CROWTHER (son of William Mitton and Hannah Crowther). Born May 27, 1835, Halifax, Yorkshire, Eng. Came to Utah 1857.
Married Mary Ann Bailey Dec. 25. 1861. Their children: Ann Maria; Samuel B.; John; William Edwin; Mary Ann. Family home Wellsville, Cache Co., Utah. Died Dec. 27, 1902, Logan, Utah.

MITTON, SAMUEL BAILEY (son of Samuel C. Mitton and Mary Ann Bailey). Born March 21, 1863, at Wellsville.
Married Mary Hawkins March 28, 1888 (daughter of William E. Hawkins and Margaret Hawkins). Their children: William Edwin; Ada; Annie; Leroy; Mary; Ruby. Family resided Wellsville and Logan, Utah.

MOFFAT, DAVID KAY (son of Alexander Moffat and Catherine Kay of Scotland). Born Dec. 30, 1811, Parish of Inveresis (Junction), Scotland. Came to Utah Aug. 27, 1860, Daniel Robison handcart company.
Married Janet Leishman July 1, 1842, Penston, Scotland (daughter of William Leishman and Janet Donaldson of Penston), who was born Sept. 10, 1816. Their children: Janet b. May 17, 1843, m. John McLain; Catherine b. Nov. 4, 1844; Joseph S. b. June 16, 1846, m. Mary Jane Brown; William b. Feb. 11, 1848, m. Eliza Barnes; Christine b. March 26, 1850, m. Henry Grow; Alexander D., m. Mattie Dewey; Marrian, m. Manass Williams; Millen A. b. Oct. 9, 1856, m. May Kimball; Mary J., m. Lorin Eldredge. Family home, Salt Lake City.
Laborer and coal miner. Died 1885.

MOFFAT, JOSEPH S. (son of David Kay Moffat and Janet Leishman). Born June 16, 1846, Crofthead, Scotland.
Married Mary Jane Brown Dec. 7, 1868, Salt Lake City (daughter of Robert Brown and Mary Dearden of Salt Lake City, pioneers 1847), who was born Dec. 12, 1849, and died February, 1881. Their children: David W. b. March 26, 1870, m. Sarah E. Howe; Mary M. b. Sept. 26, 1872, m. Thomas H. Jenkins; Percy D. b. May 4, 1875, m. Kate Johnson; Joseph S. b. March 31, 1878, m. Mary E. Karl; Mary Jane, d. Feb. 1881. Family home Meadowville, Utah.
Married Lois B. Gunn Jan. 5, 1886, Salt Lake City (daughter of John C. and Caroline B. Gunn of Salt Lake City, pioneers August. 1860), who was born March 7, 1858. Their children: Caroline B. b. Sept., 1886, m. Martin Kearl; John Kay b. May, 1888, m. Hannah Robinson; Lois L. b. June, 1889, m. Lawrence Johnson; Clarence G. b. Aug., 1890; Lucile J. b. Dec., 1891; Janet L. b. March, 1894, m. Simon Thornick; Roy A. b. July, 1896; Ralph S. b. Sept., 1898. Family home Meadowville, Utah.
Justice of peace; school trustee. Rancher; stockraiser.

MOLEN JESSE. Came to Utah Oct. 2, 1847, Jedediah M. Grant company.
Married Lurania Huffaker. Their children: Margaret Ann, m. Orris Murdock; Alexander C., d. aged 4; Simpson M., m. Jane Hyde; James Wesley, m. Jane Stoddard; Francis Marion, m. Emma Lawrence; Docey E., m. John Lott; Sophrona R., m. John Reese; Hannah E., m. Benson Roper; Nancy Jane, d. aged 3; Michael W., m. Eunice Lowry; Ginevra E., m. Stephen Weeks Ross, Jr.; Martha M., m. David Grant; Mary E., m. George Murdock. Family home Salt Lake City, Utah.
Elder. Farmer. Died at Salt Lake City.

MOLEN, MICHAEL W. (son of Jesse Molen and Lurania Huffaker). Born Jan. 15, 1842, Camp Creek, Bureau county, Ill. Came to Utah with father.
Married Eunice L. Lowry Aug. 14, 1879 (daughter of John Lowry and Sarah Jane Brown, who were married Nov. 27, 1850, at Manti, Utah; former pioneer September, 1847, the latter July 29, 1847, with contingent Mormon Battalion company). She was born April 15, 1861, Manti, Utah. Their children: Michael Kenneth b. April 15, 1882, m. Minerva Richards Feb. 14, 1907; Adrienne b. Aug. 6, 1880, m. Walter J. Park Sept. 30, 1903; Jesse Lowry b. Feb. 14, 1884; Simpson Hazelton b. Aug. 12, 1888, died; Vera b. Dec. 8, 1890; Verda b. Jan. 24, 1893; Ronald Lowry b. Feb. 26, 1896; Mildred b. Sept. 5, 1898, died; Reid Lowry b. Feb. 8, 1901; Sterling Lowry b. Aug. 16, 1903. Family home Ferron, Springville and Mapleton. Utah.
High priest; 1st counselor to Bishop William Taylor of Ferron ward; director of Manti temple. Justice of peace at Ferron; county commissioner of Emery county 1888-89.

MOLEN, MICHAEL KENNETH L. (son of Michael W. Molen and Eunice L. Lowry). Born April 15, 1882, at Ferron. Utah.
Married Minerva Richards Feb. 14, 1907 (daughter of Thomas and Adelaid Richards, both of St. Anthony, Idaho). Their child: Mildred b. 1910.
Elder; missionary to southern states 1902-04. Railroad contractor; engaged in implement business.

1042   PIONEERS AND PROMINENT MEN OF UTAH

MONSON, CHRISTIAN HANS (son of Hans Monson, born September, 1798, and Berte Nilsdater, born Aug. 10, 1795, both at Rakkestad, Norway). He was born June 16, 1837, Fredrikstad, Norway. Came to Utah 1857, handcart company.
Married Nilsine Hansen June 29, 1858, who was born Jan. 23, 1823, Copenhagen, Denmark. Their children: Christian b. May 22, 1860, m. Lavina Henson; Hyrum b. March 22, 1862, d. March 22, 1863. Family resided Lehi, Logan and Richmond, Utah.
Married Annie Catherine Peterson April 26, 1861, who was born Sept. 25, 1831, in Denmark. Their children: Joseph b. Feb. 2, 1862, m. Laura Larsen; Annie C. b. Dec. 10, 1863, m. Frank Whitehead; Hans b. June 4, 1866, m. Esther Harris; Elizabeth b. June 10, 1868, d. Oct. 25, 1868.
Married Ellen Monson March 16, 1867, Salt Lake City (daughter of Per Monson and Hanna Person; latter pioneer 1862, John R. Murdock company), who was born Sept. 5, 1850, Hufverod, Sogn, Sweden. Their children: Parley Herman b. Oct. 26, 1868, m. Matilda Ljungman June 13, 1890, m. Augusta Axelson Oct. 27, 1900; Charles Andrew b. March 2, 1870, m. Eliza Thomas Nov. 20, 1895; Ellen Marinda b. Dec. 1871, m. William A. Skidmore Dec. 13, 1893; Hyrum Moroni b. Nov. 1873, m. Cecil Funk Jan. 2, 1895; Walter Peter b. June 30, 1875, m. Leona Parksinson Oct. 30, 1896; Brigham b. Aug. 30, 1877, m. Matilda Anderson Nov. 7, 1900; Aaron A. b. April 11, 1879, m. Sarah Kirkup Sept. 26, 1900; Otto J. b. June 20, 1881, m. Mary Burnham June 21, 1905; Bertha Maria b. Aug. 9, 1883, d. Feb. 11, 1901; Lafayette b. Nov. 4, 1886, d. Feb. 12, 1901; Emma Chersta b. Aug. 19, 1888, m. Ernest Gilgen Oct. 19, 1910. Family home Richmond, Utah.
Married Karen Maria Olsen May 2, 1870 (daughter of Ola Nelson and Metha Larsen), who was born Aug. 9, 1843, in Denmark and came to Utah Sept. 10, 1863, William B. Preston company. Family home Richmond, Utah.
Married Ella Jenson Jan. 5, 1874, Salt Lake City (daughter of Peter Jenson and Boel Shunerson), who was born Oct. 23, 1850, near Malmö, Sweden. Came to Utah July 24, 1873, Erastus Snow company. Their children: Ezra Peter b. Sept. 30, 1874, m. Olive S. Parkinson Oct. 16, 1898; Emaline b. Oct. 25, 1876, d. Oct. 25, 1876; Ella Evaline b. Oct. 11, 1877, m. Albert H. Parkinson Oct. 2, 1901; Frederick Lorenzo b. May 2, 1881, m. Maggie Perkins Oct. 4, 1906; Julia Amanda b. June 7, 1883, m. Joseph S. Wright Nov. 30, 1904; Rachel b. July 31, 1885, m. S. W. Allen Dec. 20, 1905; Sarah b. Aug. 5, 1888, m. William Whitehead, Jr. Oct. 25, 1905; Franklin Leroy b. Jan. 10, 1891; Willard b. April 11, 1893, d. Nov. 15, 1893; William Aquilla b. Jan. 12, 1895. Family resided at Richmond, Utah, and Franklin, Idaho.
Married Vendla Jacobson April, 1883, Salt Lake City (daughter of Peter Jacobson and Christiana Peterson of Sweden), who was born Nov. 20, 1858, Sweden. Their children: Josephine b. Oct. 2, 1884, d. June 20, 1902; Ernest E. b. July 22, 1886; Eliza b. Dec. 2, 1887. Family home Richmond, Utah.
Senior president 39th quorum seventies; missionary to Scandinavia. First settled at Lehi, moved to Logan, and finally settled at Richmond. Guard in Echo canyon 1857-58; worked on St. George temple; second man to own and operate a planing machine in Utah; owned a saw and planing machine at Franklin, Idaho; pioneer builder and lumberman. Died Sept. 23, 1896, Richmond, Utah.

MONSON, EZRA PETER (son of Christian Hans Monson and Ella Jenson). Born Sept. 30, 1874, Richmond, Utah.
Married Olive Smart Parkinson Oct. 16, 1895, Logan, Utah (daughter of Samuel R. Parkinson and Maria Smart), who was born May 25, 1877, Richmond, Utah. Their children: Ezra Parkinson b. Nov. 7, 1896; Matthias Parkinson b. Jan. 10, 1900; Carol Parkinson b. Aug. 5, 1901; Roland Parkinson b. Aug. 20, 1904; Franklin D. b. Aug. 23, 1906; Irma b. Dec. 31, 1909. Family home Franklin, Idaho.
Missionary to southern states 1897-99; secretary of 18th quorum seventies; ward clerk at Franklin. Bookkeeper for Oregon Lumber Company 1900-08; entered in general merchandise business at Franklin, Idaho, 1908.

MONTAGUE, LEVI WEST (son of Nathaniel and Lucy Montague of Cambridge, Vt.), who was born Oct. 12, 1806, at Cambridge. Came to Utah 1852.
Married Elizabeth Durrant Ursula Graves 1859, Salt Lake City (daughter of Daniel Graves and Elizabeth Sarah Baker of Yarmouth, Norfolk, Eng., pioneers 1852), who was born July 24, 1825. Their children: Elizabeth, m. George Corley, m. Thomas Tait; Levi Zenith, m. Louisa Atwood; Sarah, m. Don Carlos Snow, m. George Ball; Charlott Louisa, m. John Willard Hawkins; Mary Emily, m. Frederick L. Hanson; Edward Ephraim, m. Esther Marriott; Madora, m. George Allsop. Family resided at Salt Lake City and Provo, Utah.
Seventy. Shoemaker and farmer. Died 1874, Provo, Utah.

MONTAGUE, EDWARD EPHRAIM (son of Levi W. Montague and Elizabeth Durrant U. Graves). Born April 1, 1864, Payson, Utah.
Married Esther Marriott Jan. 5, 1887, Provo, Utah (daughter of Joseph Marriott and Elizabeth Williams of Salt Lake City, pioneers 1861, Ira Eldredge company), who was born April 2, 1863. Their children: William Edward b. Nov. 29, 1887; Louis Claud b. April 2, 1889; Vivian Elizabeth b. May 14, 1891, m. Lawrence O. Stewart; Floy La Verna b. Aug. 11, 1893, m. John Darwin Walton; Easling Harold b. Oct. 11, 1895; Ralph Waldo b. Oct. 23, 1897; Grace Leona b. April 29, 1900; Marriott West b. Jan. 11, 1903; Warren DeVerle b.

Nov. 14, 1905; Calvin Orlando b. Jan. 20, 1907; Esther Mae, b. Sept. 2, 1908; Elwyn Murrel b. Jan. 31, 1912. Family home Grace, Idaho.
Elder; ward teacher; assistant president deacons quorum; member Y. M. M. I. A. School trustee seven years. Farmer.

MONTGOMERY, ROBERT (son of Robert Montgomery and Agnes Shepard of Churchtown, Ireland); born Jan. 7, 1825, at Churchtown. Came to Utah in 1861.
Married Mary Lourie 1846, in Ayrshire, Scotland (daughter of John Lourie and Agnes Gould of Whitletts Toll, Ayrshire. She was born April 25, 1830. Their children: Agnes, m. John Turner; Sarah, m. Moroni Duke; Mary, m. William Foreman; Robert, m. Sarah Young, m. Elizabeth Lambert; Alexander, died; Livingston, m. Amelia Ann Clegg; Christine, m. Joseph H. Simthers; Elizabeth, m. W. C. Britt. Family home Heber, Utah.
Machinist. Died Jan. 10, 1863 at Heber, Utah.
Mary Lourie's second husband was Joseph Booth, whom she married in 1863, Salt Lake City. Only child was Josephine, who married James Rasband.
Mary Lourie's third husband was John Horrocks, whom she married late in 1866 at Salt Lake City. Only child was John L. Montgomery, who married Nellie Moulton.

MONTGOMERY, LIVINGSTON (son of Robert Montgomery and Mary Lourie), born March 28, 1858, Waterside, Ayrshire, Scotland. Came to Utah Sept. 22, 1862, Homer Duncan company.
Married Amelia Ann Clegg Dec. 28, 1887, Logan, Utah (daughter of Henry Clegg and Ann Lewis of Heber, Utah, former pioneer 1854, latter 1855). She was born Jan. 19, 1863. Their children: Livingston Clegg, b. Oct. 3, 1888; Mary Ann, b. Dec. 28, 1899, d. March 3, 1891; Francis Clayton, b. Aug. 7, 1893; Juventa, b. Sept. 7, 1895; Walter, b. Oct. 3, 1904. Family home Heber, Utah.
Missionary to Indiana 1898-1900; teacher; elder; high councilor. Constable; justice of the peace. Farmer.

MOON, HENRY (son of Robert Moon and Ann Walton of Eccleston, near Shirley, Lancaster, Eng.). Born March 29, 1819, Walton Hall, Eng. Came to Utah Oct. 5, 1850, John Moon company.
Married Lydia Moon Jan. 30, 1841 in Pennsylvania (daughter of Hugh Moon and Alice Plumb of Eccleston, Eng.), who was born 1811. Their children: John T., m. Catherine Duncan; Joseph H., m. Alice Pully; Alice Ann, died. Family home, Salt Lake City.
Married Temperance Westwood March 18, 1856, Salt Lake City (daughter of Joseph Westwood and Ann Webly of Groms Grove, Worcestershire, Eng.), who was born Aug. 19, 1839. Their children: Robert H., m. Marriett Smith; Joseph H., m. Mary L. Hess; Hannah T., m. Thomas F. King; Helenora, m. Arthur Hess; Rowenah, m. Thomas J. Udy; Henry M., m. Caroline R. Hess; Edmund, m. Helen L. Barkdull; Philip W., m. Polly Smith; Lelia O., m. William E. Potter; Mercy E., m. George Q. Udy; Louisa W.; Albert; Franklin E. Family home Farmington, Utah.
Married Mary Ann Thayne Jan. 4, 1868, Salt Lake City (daughter of John J. Thayne and Sidney Boyer of Canada, pioneers 1861, Perrigrine Sessions company), who was born Aug. 27, 1849. Their children: Orson, d. May 16, 1896; Amanda Jane, m. Peter Duncan; William, m. Sarah Luella Swift; Charles Henry, d. March 11, 1884; Eliza Ann, m. Roger Horricks; Florence Sidney, m. Henry Vantassell; Heber, m. Emily H. Vantassel; Nephi, m. Malinda White; Parley, d. Sept. 1, 1886. Family home Woodland, Utah.
High priest; missionary to central states 1871-72; bishop of first ward Salt Lake City 1856-70; bishop of Woodland ward 1881-85. Member first company of L. D. S. immigrants that left England 1840. School trustee. Farmer and stockraiser. Died Nov. 14, 1894, Farmington, Utah.

MOON, JOHN THOMAS (son of Henry Moon and Lydia Moon). Born Sept. 13, 1844, Des Moines, Iowa.
Married Catherine Duncan Feb. 16, 1867, Salt Lake Endowment house (daughter of William Duncan and Mary Brown of Salt Lake City, pioneers 1861, Richard Horne company). She was born Dec. 28, 1846. Their children: John Thomas, Jr. b. Dec. 5, 1867, m. Hettie Bicell; William D. b. Nov. 10, 1869, m. Elmira Mecham; Lydia Ann b. Nov. 23, 1871, m. David Richardson; Catherine b. July 10, 1874, m. Lorenzo Pitt; Mary b. Sept. 19, 1876, d. aged 2; Jemima b. Jan. 29, 1880, m. Joseph S. Dudley; Henry Moroni b. Aug. 4, 1883, m. Maggie Bell Richardson. Family resided Salt Lake City and Farmington.
High priest; bishop Woodland ward. Called to assist in settling Arizona. Farmer, lumberman and stockraiser. Died September, 1910, Colonia Diaz, Chihuahua, Mexico.

MOON, HENRY MORONI (son of Henry Moon and Temperance Westwood). Born March 22, 1868, Salt Lake City.
Married Caroline R. Hess September, 1895, at Salt Lake City (daughter of John W. Hess and Mary Ann Steed, pioneers July 28, 1847, contingent Mormon Battalion). She was born March 25, 1872. Their children: Henry Hess b. April 26, 1897; Mary Laverne b. April 28, 1899; John Rutland b. Nov. 6, 1901; Joseph b. Oct. 9, 1904; Druscilla b. March 11, 1907; Herald b. Aug. 29, 1911. Family home Farmington, Utah.
Member fifty-sixth quorum seventies. School trustee four years. Sergeant Utah militia three years. Farmer and stockraiser.

PIONEERS AND PROMINENT MEN OF UTAH

MOON, HENRY MORONI (son of John Thomas Moon and Catherine Duncan). Born Aug. 4, 1883, Woodland, Utah.
Married Maggie Bell Richardson Dec. 4, 1907, Jensen, Utah (daughter of John Thornton Richardson and Isabella Muir of Heber, Utah, pioneers Oct. 1, 1863, Isaac C. Haight company). She was born Nov. 3, 1886. Their child: Vera Bell b. July 8, 1908. Family home Jensen, Utah.
Seventy; president Y. M. M. I. A.; ward and Sunday school teacher; counselor in deacons quorum. Constable. Watermaster for Burns Bench Irrigation Co. Farmer and freighter.

MOORE, DAVID (son of Dudley Moore—born Aug. 8, 1773, in Saratoga county, N. Y., died March 17, 1852, Eardley, Canada and Mary Moulton—born Aug. 8, 1774, in Windsor county, N. Y., died Oct. 10, 1845, Eardley—married at Rutland, Vt.). He was born Jan. 20, 1819, Eardley, Province of Quebec, Canada. Came to Utah Oct. 20, 1849, Allen Taylor company.
Married Susan Maria Vorce August, 1841, Eardley, Canada (daughter of Warren and Amanda Vorce), who was born Feb. 5, 1810, Windsor county, Vt., and died March 2, 1882, Ogden, Utah.
Married Sarah Barker Sept. 6, 1850, Salt Lake City (daughter of Frederick Barker—born at Diss, Eng., died Nov. 4, 1866, North Ogden, Utah and Ann Blygh—born Feb. 8, 1802, Tibbenham, Eng., died Sept. 18, 1876, Ogden, Utah; pioneers 1849). She was born Aug. 7, 1829 at Diss, Norfolk, Eng., and died July 12, 1908, Ogden, Utah. Their children: David Moulton b. July 1, 1851, m. Elizabeth Stone; Mary Ann b. March 17, 1853, d. April 2, 1882; Joseph Byron b. Feb. 9, 1855, m. Louisa M. Bybee, m. Alice Twitchell; Ellen Louisa b. April 26, 1858, m. John L. Wilson; Franklin b. Nov. 22, 1861, m. Julia G. Taylor; Leonard b. June 2, 1863, d. Sept. 22, 1863. Family home Ogden, Utah.
Early settler to Ogden, Utah. First recorder of Ogden 1851; county clerk and both city and county treasurer 1851-55; member city council. Colonel Utah militia. Member high council of Weber stake. Missionary to the Salmon River. Bishop of Mount Fort ward.

MOORE, DAVID MOULTON (son of David Moore and Sarah Barker). Born July 1, 1851, Ogden, Utah.
Married Elizabeth Stone Dec. 3, 1871, Ogden, Utah (daughter of Amos P. Stone and Dinah Rawlins, pioneers 1850). She was born Sept. 27, 1853 at Salt Lake City. Their children: Ida b. Oct. 9, 1872, m. Samuel Thomas; Clyde b. Oct. 5, 1874, d. April 24, 1878; Florence b. April 25, 1879, d. March 7, 1904, m. F. W. Bishop; Jesse B. Aug. 19, 1882, m. Winifred Goddard; Elberta b. Jan. 4, 1888, m. Joseph O. Read; Edna May b. March 3, 1893. Family home Ogden, Utah.
Horticulturist and nurseryman.

MOORE, DAVID (son of Thomas Moore and Hannah Horigan of Whitwick, Edmonton, Eng.). Born Aug. 1, 1847, Whitwick, Eng. Came to Utah Oct. 8, 1866, Andrew H. Scott company.
Married Mary Rees Dec. 26, 1870, Coalville, Utah (daughter of Edmund and Suriah Margret Rees of Pontaberbengum, Monmouthshire, Wales, and Coalville, Utah, pioneers September, 1859, Independent company). She was born Jan. 28, 1853. Their children: Morgan b. Nov. 11, 1871, m. Jennie Armstrong; William b. Nov. 15, 1873, m. Rose Leamaster; Thomas Ellis b. April 25, 1876, m. Emily Wilde; John Edmond b. Sept. 11, 1878, m. Jennie Izatt; Suriah Margret b. Sept. 3, 1880, m. W. S. Twornbly; David Edward b. Aug. 23, 1882, m. Pearl Powell; Elizabeth Mary b. March 22, 1885, m. J. Q. Lawson; Samuel b. Sept. 2, 1887; Carrie E. b. March 25, 1890, m. Ben J. Pye; Charles Henry b. Dec. 27, 1892.
First justice of peace and postmaster of Castle Rock, Utah. Black Hawk Indian War veteran 1866-67.

MOORE, THOMAS ELLIS (son of David Moore and Mary Rees). Born April 25, 1876, Castle Rock, Utah.
Married Emily Wilde Sept. 20, 1911, Salt Lake City (daughter of Thomas Wilde and Fanny Gunn of Coalville, Utah, pioneers Nov. 6, 1859, George Rowley handcart company), who was born Dec. 30, 1884.

MOORE, GEORGE S. (son of Joseph Moore and Maria Sharrat of Walsall, Staffordshire, Eng.). Born April 2, 1830, Birmingham, Eng. Came to Utah Sept. 24, 1861, Ansel Harmon and Joseph Young companies.
Married Agness Ann Bancroft (Daybell) May 15, 1871, Salt Lake City Endowment House (daughter of William Bancroft and Mary Newham of Dreaston, Derbyshire, Eng., who came to Fort Benton by rail and to Utah, Samuel D. White company). She was born April 28, 1847. Came to Utah Sept. 22, 1866. Their children: Robert, m. Jane Burton; William, m. Selma Anderson; Godfray Finity, died; Susie, m. Harmon David Baum; John Newham, m. Annie Lamb; Mabell, m. Edwin J. Sumners; Sarah Ann, m. Don Meldrum, m. Ruben Ernest Woolf; Ernest, m. Lirdie Hansen; James Edan, m. Ethel Hawks; Constance, m. John E. Bott; Florence.
Home missionary in England; teacher for many years; elder; member of school of prophets. Wood-turner and glazier.

MOORE, LEWIS D. (son of Isaac Moore and Sarah Dogart of New York City). Born June 13, 1864, Neponset, Bureau county, Ill. Came to Utah April 1900.
Married Mary A. Curtis September, 1898, Livingston, Mont. (daughter of Zenis and Margaret Curtis of Livingston). Their children: Eva; Birdena; Bessie. Family home, Salt Lake City.
Engaged in railroad work and mining.

MORE, CALVIN WHITE (son of Ethan Allen More and Soval Webber of Massachusetts). Born July 21, 1827, Taunton, Mass. Came to Utah in 1848, with 37 other members Mormon Battalion (Co. C).
Married Catherine Allred Jan. 13, 1853, Salt Lake City (daughter of Levi Allred and Abigail McMurtrie), who was born March 6, 1833. Their children: Calvin C.; Joseph Orlando; Louis Alexander, m. Rose Boren; Calvin White; William J.; Maryetta, m. Samuel David Bunnel; Eugene; Earl, m. Annie Abbey; LeRoy; Nellie, m. Fritz Earl Reynolds.
High priest of quorum at Lawrence, Utah. Took active part in Black Hawk war and Echo Canyon trouble. Died May 9, 1908, at Castledale, Utah.

MORGAN, DAVID (son of John Morgan and Letitia Anson). Born Oct. 10, 1812, Staffordshire, Eng. Came to Utah Sept. 15, 1861, Ira Eldredge company.
Married Hannah Turner. Their children: Mary b. Aug. 19, 1833, m. Job Pingree 1854; Olive b. June 3, 1835; Olive b. June 29, 1840, m. Thomas Howell 1862; Jesse b. Jan. 23, 1843, m. Lizzie Hadden 1874; David b. Feb. 25, 1845, m. Mary Walker 1877; Agatha b. March 30, 1850, m. George W. Carson 1867; Amanda b. April 27, ——, m. Joseph Darlow; Clara Eudora b. May 4, ——; Benjamin L. b. Dec. 20, ——, m. Lizzie Ewing 1876. Family home Fairfield, Utah.

MORGAN, EDWARD (son of Joseph Morgan and Elizabeth Hardman of Preston, Lancaster, Eng.). Born Oct. 20, 1838, at Preston. Came to Utah 1850, Stephen Markman company.
Married Louisa Scott Aug. 3, 1856, Salt Lake City, Brigham Young officiating (daughter of John Scott and Elizabeth Menery of Mill Creek, Utah, pioneers 1848). She was born March 20, 1840, d. Nov. 1, 1900. Their children: Louisa Matilda b. Nov. 7, 1857, m. George Smith Grant; Elizabeth M. b. Nov. 10, 1859, m. O. P. Miller; Edward M. b. March 3, 1862, m. Agnes Park; John William b. Sept. 29, 1864, m. Harriet Miller; Joseph M. b. Jan. 3, 1867, m. Louisa M. Miller; Isaac M. b. Sept. 29, 1869, m. Anna Louise Bell; Ephraim Royal b. Aug. 16, 1873, m. Adalade Spencer; Earnest Leroy b. Dec. 27, 1877, m. Josephine E. Bawden; Alvina E. b. June 20, 1878, m. Forrest N. Stillman; Louisa E. b. March 31, 1883, m. Leslie P. Bawden. Family home Mill Creek, Utah.
Married Sophia Scott Oct. 24, 1870, Salt Lake City (daughter of John Scott and Elizabeth Menerey of Mill Creek, pioneers with Captain Broomfield company), who was born Apr. 20, 1854, Mill Creek, Utah. d. May 28, 1874. Their children: Joseph Albert b. May 18, 1872, d. 1873; Sophia C. b. May 26, 1874, d. 1874.
High priest; seventy; missionary to England 1864. Took part in Echo Canyon war. Pioneer to Dixie country 1862. Indian war scout; minute-man. Took part in move South.

MORGAN, EVAN S. (son of William Morgan, born February, 1800, Langwick, Lnysymond, Glamorganshire, Wales, and Sarah Davies, born 1800). Born Nov. 29, 1833, at Lnysymond. Came to Utah Sept. 11, 1857, Israel Evans handcart company.
Married Mary Parry October, 1862, who was born 1840, and came to Utah 1861; died Feb. 7, 1862. Only child: John Parry b. Jan. 30, 1862, d. infant. Family home Shambip. Tooele Co., Utah.
Married Margaret Roberts May 1, 1863, at Shambip (daughter of Hugh Roberts and Mary Roberts Humphreys, pioneers 1864), who was born May 17, 1841, Eglwys Bach, Wales. Their children: Hugh Evan b. Sept. 12, 1864, died; David Roberts b. Sept. 12, 1867, m. Caddie C. Hynas Dec. 8, 1892, d. May 10, 1912; William Roberts b. July 27, 1870, m. Martha Christiansen June 15, 1898; Sarah Jane b. Dec. 12, 1873, m. Arta Austin June 14, 1901; Hannah b. March 11, 1878, m. John C. Linford Sept. 14, 1904; John Samuel b. Sept. 29, 1882, m. Ethel M. Rich Oct. 10, 1906. Family home Liberty, Idaho.
Missionary to Caermarthenshire, Wales, 1854; also to North Wales; high priest; member high council of Bear Lake stake; missionary to Great Britain 1889-92. Settled at Shambip, Tooele county, 1857, moved to Bear Lake valley 1864. Assisted in bringing immigrants to Utah 1861.

MORGAN, WILLIAM R. (son of Evan S. Morgan and Margaret Roberts). Born July 27, 1870, Liberty, Idaho.
Married Martha Christenson June 15, 1898, Logan, Utah (daughter of Jacob Christenson and Mary T. Myres, pioneers 1862, Joseph Horne company). She was born Oct. 18, 1869, Bloomington, Idaho. Their children: Iris Thersea b. Dec. 22, 1901; Evan William b. Jan. 7, 1903; Cassie Lucile b. Feb. 11, 1904; Clifford Christenson b. Dec. 11, 1906; Larue

1044   PIONEERS AND PROMINENT MEN OF UTAH

b. May 10, 1909; Eunice b. Oct. 23, 1911. Family home Liberty, Idaho.
Missionary to eastern states 1898-1900; Sunday school superintendent Liberty ward 1909-10; member bishopric of Liberty ward 1900; bishop of Liberty ward.

MORGAN, JOHN (son of Morgan Morgan, born 1800, and Catherine Jones, born 1808, both at Brecon, Wales, later of Caseyville, Ill.). Born Feb. 28, 1833, Merthyr Tydfil, Wales. Came to Utah Oct. 5, 1854, Hans Peter Olsen company.
Married Emma Richards May 1, 1854 (daughter of William Richards and Rachel Williams), who was born July 13, 1835. Their children: Cathrine, m. Peter Okelberry; Rachel, died; Emma, m. A. H. Pettis; John R., m. Lizzie Burraston; William, died; Mary Ellen, m. W. W. Ercanbrack; David, m. Ida White; Maggie, m. Thomas P. Stubbs; Pearl, m. Albert E. Cox; Lilliare; Maud. Family home Goshen, Utah.
Seventy; ward and Sunday school teacher 20 years; missionary to Wales. Settled at Cedar City 1854; moved to Goshen valley. Hotelkeeper at Goshen 40 years. Died Sept. 4, 1896.

MORGAN, JOHN R. (son of John Morgan and Emma Richards). Born Aug. 11, 1863, Goshen, Utah.
Married Elizabeth Burraston July 23, 1890, at Goshen (daughter of John Burraston, pioneer 1853, James Cummings company, and Elizabeth Dall, pioneer 1854, Jacob Hoffines company). She was born at Honeyville, Utah. Their children: John B. b. Jan. 21, 1891; William Leo b. April 10, 1894; Ireta b. Aug. 22, 1896; Lillian b. Feb. 23, 1899; Rachel b. Sept. 10, 1901; Bert b. April 25, 1903; David b. March 1, 1905; Albert b. Nov. 12, 1906; Sadie b. March 1, 1910; Willis M. b. March 8, 1903. Family home, Goshen.

MORGAN, JOHN (son of Gerard Morgan and Eliza Ann Hamilton of Greensburg, Ind.). Born Aug. 8, 1842.
Married Helen M. Groesbeck Oct. 24, 1868, Salt Lake City (daughter of Nicholas Groesbeck and Elizabeth Thompson, pioneers Oct. 2, 1856, John Banks company), who was born Feb. 7, 1852, Springfield, Ill. Their children: Helen M. b. Jan. 19, 1870, m. Andrew Burt; Elizabeth b. Oct. 7, 1872, d. infant; Eliza M. b. Feb. 8, 1875, m. James F. Smith; Ruth b. Oct. 4, 1877, m. Burke Kinkle; John b. Feb. 12, 1881, d. infant; Flora b. Sept. 19, 1882, d. infant; Nicholas G. b. Nov. 9, 1884, m. Ethel S. Tate; Gail b. April 3, 1888, m. John Clayton; Bessie b. Jan. 11, 1891, m. Percy H. Rex; Gerard E. b. Oct. 8, 1892; John H. b. Feb. 7, 1894. Family home, Salt Lake City.

MORGAN, SAMUEL (son of William Morgan of Forest of Dean, Gloucester, Eng.). Came to Utah 1866, oxteam company.
Married Elizabeth Beddis April, 1831, Little Deans Hill, Gloucestershire, Eng. (daughter of Thomas and Susanah Beddis of Little Deans Hill, pioneers 1868). Their children: Margaret, m. Frederick Firley; Joseph Rehoboam, m. Mary Margarett Jane Turner; Thomas, m. Elizabeth Tingle; Martha, m. William Burris; Emma, deceased; Absolom, deceased. Family home Salt Lake City, Utah.
Elder. Iron ore miner. Died at Salt Lake City.

MORGAN, JOSEPH REHOBOAM (son of Samuel Morgan and Elizabeth Beddis). Born April 26, 1835, Little Deans Hill, Eng. Came to Utah 1862, William H. Dame company.
Married Mary Margarett Jane Turner May 6, 1862, Cheltenham, Gloucestershire, Eng. (daughter of James M. Turner and Maria Simeons of Bishop's Cleave, Gloucester, pioneers 1862, William H. Dame company), who was born Oct. 15, 1841. Their children: Frederick Willard b. Aug. 12, 1863, m. Elizabeth J. Roberts and Isabel Penfold; Harry Thomas b. Nov. 30, 1864, died; Laura Elizabeth b. Aug. 15, 1866, m. Ben Lloyd; James Samuel b. Dec. 21, 1868, m. Pearl Pratt; Emma Zilpha b. Jan. 28, 1871, m. Thomas Gill; Maggie May b. Feb. 12, 1873, died; Joseph Charles b. July 23, 1874, m. Ada Marsh and Leah Wilson; Albert George b. Oct. 30, 1876, d. Feb. 15, 1880; Effie Mabel b. Oct. 15, 1878, m. James Rigby; Stanley Roy b. Aug. 6, 1882. Family home, Salt Lake City.
Home missionary five years; president seventies; bishop of 15th ward, Salt Lake City, four years. Worked on Salt Lake temple two years. Member tabernacle choir 25 years; leader of 15th ward choir two years. Connected with Z. C. M. I. 35 years as packer and salesman.

MORGAN, WILLIAM (son of Edward and Janett Morgan of Merthyr Tydfil, Glamorganshire, Wales). He was born 1813. Came to Utah October, 1852, with William Morgan company.
Married Mary Treharn 1835, Wales (daughter of Edward Treharn of Wales; came to Utah October, 1852). Only child: Edward Morgan, m. Rachel Cole. Family home Brigham City, Utah.
High priest. Died March, 1889, at Willard City, Utah.

MORGAN, EDWARD (son of William Morgan and Mary Treharn). Born Jan. 1, 1842, at Merthyr Tydfil, Wales. Came to Utah October, 1852, with William Morgan company.
Married Rachel Cole Jan. 27, 1865, Salt Lake City (daughter of John Cole and Charlotte Jenkins of Willard, Utah;

came to Utah 1850). She was born July 17, 1844. Their children: Charlotte E. b. Dec. 23, 1865, m. Mr. Hubbard Dec. 27, 1883; Mary Ann b. Feb. 18, 1868; Eliza J. b. Oct. 3, 1869, m. Mr. Mason; William E. b. Sept. 29, 1871; John R. b. Dec. 3, 1873; Robert H. b. Aug. 25, 1876; Joseph L. b. Nov 5, 1878; Pauline M. b. Feb. 13, 1881, m. Mr. Ramsey; Frank b. Nov. 12, 1887.
Member 59th quorum seventies.

MORGAN, WILLIAM (son of William Morgan and Johannah Williams of Blaernargarth Glamorganshire, South Wales). Born Sept. 14, 1834.
Married Malinda Rhoades (Williams) April 30, 1895 (daughter of Caleb Baldwin Rhoades, Sr., and Malinda Powell), who was born Dec. 23, 1862. Their children: Johannah b. June 3, 1895, d. infant; Mary Margaret b. May 5, 1900, d. infant.

MORLEY, ISAAC (son of Thomas Morley, born March 26, 1758, Ansonia, Conn., and Edetha Morley, born Oct. 2, 1762, Montague, Mass.—they lived at Kirkland, Ohio). He was born March 11, 1786, Montague, Mass. Came to Utah 1847.
Married Lucy Gunn June 20, 1812, Montague, who was born Jan. 24, 1786, and died Jan. 3, 1848, buried in grave No. 4, 13th row, camp of Israel, Omaha, Neb. Their children: Philena b. Oct. 2, 1813, m. Amos Cox; Lucy Diantha b. Oct. 4, 1815, m. Joseph Allen; Edetha Ann b. Jan. 25, 1818, m. Chauncy Whiting; Calista b. May 11, 1820; Cordelia b. Nov. 28, 1823, m. Walter Cox; Arathusa; Therissa B. b. July 18, 1826, m. Heber C. Kimball; Isaac b. May 2, 1829, m. Abiah Bradley.
Married Hannah Blaixley Finch 1844, Nauvoo temple (daughter of Daniel and Mary Finch of Waterbury and Woodbridge, Conn.). She was born March 19, 1811. Their children: Joseph Lamoni b. July 15, 1845, died; Simeon Thomas b. June 12, 1849, died; Mary Leonora b. March 26, 1852, m. Hans Christian Hansen. Family home Manti, Utah.
Married Leonora Snow (Leavitt) 1844, Nauvoo temple (sister of Lorenzo and Eliza R. Snow).
Ordained a patriarch by the Prophet Joseph Smith; first counselor to the first bishop of the Church of Jesus Christ of Latter-day Saints. Was the first man to settle in Manti; plowed the first furrow; built the first house; made the first table in that new settlement. Died June 21, 1864, Fairview, Utah, buried in Manti.

MORRILL, LABAN (son of Abner Morrill and Mary Carpenter of Wheelock, Vt.). Born Dec. 8, 1814, Wheelock, Vt. Came to Utah 1852, Daniel D. McArthur company.
Married Permelia H. Drury Feb. 22, 1844, in Illinois (daughter of Joel Drury and Tirzah Winters of Illinois, pioneers 1852), who was born Aug. 20, 1824, came to Utah with husband. Their children: Horatio; John; Laban D.; Joseph; Charles; Hyrum; George D.; Sarah P.; Horace. Family homes Iron and Piute counties, Utah.
High priest. Member of city council Cedar City, Utah. Blacksmith; farmer and stockraiser. Died Dec. 8, 1900, Junction, Utah.

MORRILL, JOHN (son of Laban Morrill and Permelia H. Drury). Born Feb. 21, 1848, Garden Grove, Iowa. Came to Utah about November, 1852, Daniel McArthur company.
Married Esther E. LeBaron May 18, 1874, Salt Lake City Utah (daughter of David T. LeBaron and Esther M. Johnson of Salt Lake City, pioneers of May, 1854), who was born Nov. 27, 1853. Their children: Ella Belle b. Feb. 27, 1875, d. 1904; John D. b. Oct. 3, 1877; Milo J. b. March 30, 1880, d. 1904; George Albert b. July 27, 1882, d. Sept. 21, 1882; Hattie P. b. Sept. 4, 1883; Myrtle C. b. Jan. 25, 1886, d. Dec. 10, 1890; Fern L. b. Sept. 30, 1892. Family home Junction, Piute Co., Utah.
Bishop of Junction ward 18 years, still acting. Recorder 1884-90; clerk 1884-94: elected county clerk 1912. Postmaster since 1881. Farmer.

MORRILL, LABAN D. (son of Laban Morrill and Permelia H. Drury). Born Oct. 4, 1850, Keg Creek, Iowa. Came to Utah 1852.
Married Emma W. Dalley Jan. 6, 1874, Summit, Utah (daughter of James Dalley and Emma Wright of Ohio, pioneers 1852), who was born Dec. 15, 1854. Their children: Emma Phedora b. April 6, 1875, m. Willis Johnson (Weaver); Mary Permelia b. April 2, 1877, m. M. D. Morgan; Annie D. b. Aug. 26, 1879, m. G. H. Johnson; Della b. April 19, 1882, m. Walter Farnsworth; Ida b. Dec. 23, 1885, m. H. D. Scott; Laban Rupert b Sept. 14, 1888; Rural D. b. July 5, 1892, d. Nov. 27, 1905. Family home Circleville, Utah.
High priest; member bishopric of Circleville, Utah. School trustee Circleville. Farmer Twin Falls, Idaho.

MORRIS, HYRUM BOWLES (son of Thomas Morris and Sophia Talbot of Bourbon county, Ky.). Born Dec. 23, 1821, in Bourbon county. Came to Utah Aug. 9, 1860, Warren Walling company.
Married Eleanor Crawford Roberts Aug. 8, 1852, Quincy, Ill. (daughter of Adonijah Roberts and Elizabeth Crawford

of Illinois. Utah and Arizona, pioneers Aug. 9, 1860). She was born Nov. 9, 1830, died Aug. 2, 1909, at Mesa. Their children: Laura Elizabeth b. April 20, 1854, m. David Franklin M. Rappleye; William Edwin b. Aug. 18, 1857, d. 1860; Hyrum Bowles b. Feb. 14, 1863, m. Eliza Smith; Eleanor Rebecca b. May 14, 1866, m. George A. Smith; Eliza Roberts b. April 10, 1870, m. Frank Lewis; Sophia Isadora b. April 10, 1873, m. Franklin Thomas Pomeroy. Family home Mesa City, Ariz.
High priest; patriarch in Maricopa stake. Justice of peace. Farmer; cooper. Died Jan. 23, 1908.

MORRIS, GEORGE (son of Joseph Morris and Elizabeth Vernon of Manchester, Eng.). Born Aug. 23, 1816, Manchester, Eng. Came to Utah Sept. 22, 1848.
Married Hannah Maria Newburry Aug. 23, 1842, Clay Co., Iowa (daughter of James Newburry and Mary Smith of Clay Co., Iowa), who was born March 13, 1823, d. Nov. 6, 1898. Their children: Lavina, m. Nathan Davis; Julia Ann, m. Thomas Golightly; Rozilla, m. John Jenkins; George V., m. Catherine Davis and Agnes LeCheminant; Maria R. J., m. Edward Sarace; Joseph N., m. Sarah A. Grow; Mary Ann, m. Alfred J. Ridges; James N., m. Harriet Elliott; Ellen M., d. young; Franklin N., m. Elizabeth Mitchell; Harriet N., m. Calvin Pendleton; Ephraim N., m. Harriet Harris.
Died Jan. 29, 1897, at Salt Lake City.

MORRIS, GEORGE V. (son of George Morris and Hannah Maria Newburry).
Married Agnes LeCheminant Nov. 29, 1884, Salt Lake City (daughter of Peter LeCheminant, d. in England, and Sarah Farr of Isle of Guernsey, Eng., latter pioneer 1854, William Taylor company). She was born Aug. 6, 1848. Their children: Edmund H. b. Sept. 28, 1885, d. aged 29, m. Lois Skelton; Agnes E. b. Dec. 28, 1886, m. Jasper Hobbs; Albert O. b. June 9, 1888; Sarah L. b. June 20, 1890; Lavenia b. April 18, 1892, d. aged 9. Family home, Salt Lake City.
Married Catherine Davis Nov. 9, 1869, Salt Lake City (daughter of James Davis and Ann Owen of South Wales and Salt Lake City; former came with Mormon Battalion, latter 1851). She was born June 22, 1852. Their children: Maria L. b. Dec. 8, 1870, d. aged 16 years; Delila b. Dec. 9, 1872, d. infant; George V. b. Feb. 27, 1874, m. Flora Foster; James D. b. Jan. 7, 1876, d. aged 28. m. Alice Jeff; Frank Eugene b. Nov. 23, 1877, m. Fredrica Rouche; Orin H. b. Jan. 3, 1881, m. Lillian Jeff. Family home, Salt Lake City.

MORRIS, ISAAC C. (son of William Morris—born Feb. 2, 1793, Llanfair, Montgomeryshire, North Wales. died Jan. 30, 1857, same place, and Sarah Morris—born March 21, 1799, Llansanan, Denbighshire, died April 24, 1875, at Llanfair). He was born April 26, 1828, at Llanfair. Came to Utah 1853.
Married Elizabeth Williams in Wales (daughter of Thomas L. and Caroline Williams of Eglwys Bach, Denbighshire, Wales, pioneers 1853). She was born April. 1828, at Eglwys Bach, died Oct. 25, 1865, Salt Lake City. Their children: Sarah E. b. Sept. 13, 1853, d. May 13, 1881, m. Charles Stevens; Mary b. Oct. 25, 1855, d. Feb. 14, 1895, m. Daniel Alexander Robison Aug. 31, 1873; William b. September, 1857, m. Amanda Rock; Isaac C. b. Aug. 23, 1859, m. Sarah E. Stewart Jan. 9, 1890; Lizzie Ann b. May 18, 1861, m. William Rollins; Priscilla b. Nov. 30, 1863, m. John Maranda; Eliza b. May 21, 1866; Lucinda b. Oct. 21, 1867; Conway b. May 17, 1869.
Died Nov. 27, 1868, Richville, Utah.

MORRIS, JOHN (son of John Morris and Catherine Vaughan of Llanfair, Talharine, Denbighshire, North Wales). Came to Utah Oct. 2, 1853, Joseph A. Young company.
Married Barbara Thomas (daughter of Elias Thomas). Their children: Price; William; Lucy; Elias b. June 30, 1825, m. Mary E. Parry and Mary L. Walker; John; Richard V. b. Sept. 3, 1830, m. Hannah Phillips, m. Hattie C. Jones, m. Levenia Robbins; Barbara; Hugh.
Died Sept. 18, 1871.

MORRIS, ELIAS (son of John Morris and Barbara Thomas). Born June 30, 1825, at Llanfair, Wales. Came to Utah Nov. 1, 1852, Philip De La Mar company.
Married Mary Parry May 23, 1852, Council Bluffs, Iowa (daughter of John Parry and Elizabeth Parry of New Market, Flintshire, North Wales, pioneers Oct. 2, 1856, Edward Bunker company). She was born Dec. 21, 1834. Their children Barbara b. May 30, 1853, m. Nathaniel Jones; Winifred b. Oct. 28, 1855, m. Peter T. Tibbs; Harriet b. Sept. 3, 1857, died; Elias Jr. b. Sept. 23, 1859; Mary E. b. March 11, 1862; Edward b. Sept. 20, 1864, died; Rosa Frances b. Sept. 20, 1864, m. James A. Brown; John Parry b. March 23, 1870; Ernest Edwin b. June 21, 1872; Albert Conway b. June 8, 1847, died; Jessie Pearl b. Aug. 22, 1876; Josephine Edna b. Oct. 23, 1879, m. George A. Goff.
Married Mary L. Walker May, 1856, Salt Lake City (daughter of William Gibson Walker and Mary Godwin of Manchester, Eng.; former pioneer October, 1853, Joseph W. Young company, latter died at St. Louis, Mo.). She was born May 14, 1835, Leek, Staffordshire, Eng. Their children: Effie Walker, m. Edward T. Ashton; Marion Adelaide, m. George H. Cannon; Nephi Lowell, m. Harriet Young; George Dunyle, m. Emma Ramsay; Katherine Vaughan; four children d. infants. Family home, Salt Lake City.

Missionary to Wales, 1865-69; president high priests quorum; bishop fifteenth ward. Member of Utah legislature; city councilman; member of constitutional convention. Builder; contractor; president sugar company. Died March 17, 1898, in Salt Lake City.

MORRIS, NEPHI LOWELL (son of Elias Morris and Mary L. Walker). Born Oct. 2, 1870, Salt Lake City.
Married Harriet Young June 5, 1907, Salt Lake City (daughter of Willard Young and Harriet Hooper of Salt Lake City, both born in Utah), who was born Feb. 25, 1885. Their children: Lowell Young b. March 12, 1908; Willard Young b. March 29, 1910; Mary Young b. Aug. 22, 1911. Family home, Salt Lake City.
Member second quorum seventies; missionary to Great Britain, 1892-95; president Salt Lake stake. Member state legislature; Progressive party nominee for governor of Utah, 1912. President Elias Morris & Sons Co., Deseret Building Society, and Utah Concrete Pipe company.

MORRIS, RICHARD V. (son of John Morris and Barbara Thomas). Born Sept. 3, 1830. Came to Utah 1855.
Married Hannah Phillips. Their children: Richard P., m. Sarah Isaacs, m. Florence Dinwoodey; A. V., m. Maggie Brian; Melvin C., m. Lydia Osborne. Family home, Salt Lake City.
Married Hattie C. Jones. Their children: Clara, m. Selden I. Clawson; Victor V.; Sidney H.; Hannah, m. John E. Hanson. Family home, Salt Lake City.
Married Levenia Robbins. Only child: Orvin, m. Nellie Patrick, m. Stella Barton. Family home, Salt Lake City.
Bishop of nineteenth ward, Salt Lake. Revenue collector. Stonecutter and bookkeeper.

MORRIS, RICHARD P. (son of Richard V. Morris and Hannah Phillips). Born Dec. 23, 1855, Salt Lake City.
Married Sarah Isaacs January, 1881 (daughter of Benjamin Isaacs and Phoebe Davis of Spanish Fork, Utah, pioneers 1860), who was born November, 1854. Their children: Emma b. Jan. 23, 1888; Benjamin P. b. Oct. 13, 1890, m. Hazel Tomlinson.
Married Florence Dinwoodey. Their children: Russell P. b. Dec. 31, 1900; Thornton D. b. Aug. 25, 1903; Marion b. Aug. 17, 1905. Family home, Salt Lake City.
Elder. Member Salt Lake city council 1893-1906; city treasurer 1897-1903; mayor 1904-05. Elected one of the five commissioners of Salt Lake City, 1911, for four years. In charge of streets, public improvements and engineering. Telegraph operator twenty-five years, and in railroad work; local freight agent for Union Pacific railroad 1888-90. Engaged in coal business under the firm name Woolstenholme & Morris 1890; organized Citizens Coal company. Director in Farmers & Stockgrowers Bank, Merchants Bank, and Dinwoodey Furniture company.

MORRIS, JOHN STEPHEN (son of Benjamin Morris, born Feb. 23, 1809, Letterston, Wales, and Charlotte Morse, born May 18, 1815, Fishguard, Wales—married 1832). Born Nov. 7, 1838, near Fishguard. Came to Utah Oct. 3, 1863, Thomas Ricks company.
Married Esther Williams (daughter of Isaac Williams and Esther Francis, latter a pioneer Oct. 6, 1863, Thomas Ricks company). She was born Nov. 6, 1842. Their children: John George b. Dec. 31, 1866, m. Emma Teresa Landon; David William b. March 27, 1869, m. Susanah Cover; Charlotte b. Feb. 14, 1871, m. Leonard Porter Hall; Benjamin Thomas b. Jan. 13, 1874, m. Helen May Neely; Mary Ann b. Dec. 24, 1875, m. George Moroni Ward; Joseph Stephen b. Sept. 16, 1877, m. Elvira Green; Martha Elizabeth b. July 21, 1879, m. Ransom Enoch Harris; Samuel Francis b. Aug. 13, 1881, m. Anna Pearl Hansen; George Williams b. June 3, 1883, m. Margaret Call; Parley Morse b. June 20, 1885. m. Anna Sarah Eliasen; Thomas Roskelly b. March 13, 1888. Family home West Portage, Utah.
Ordained patriarch by Rudger Clawson Dec. 21, 1902.

MORRIS, ROBERT (son of John Morris and Maria Billings of Barrowden, Rutland, Eng.). Born Sept. 13, 1843, at Barrowden. Came to Utah Aug. 16, 1861, David H. Cannon company.
Married Janet Watson Dec. 21, 1867, at Salt Lake City (daughter of William and Mary Ann Watson of Glasgow, Scotland), who was born Oct. 28, 1842, and came to Utah 1863. Their children: Robert b. Oct. 10, 1868, died, m. Irene Free; Mary b. Oct. 5, 1870, m. John L. Groo; William C. b. Aug. 21, 1872, died; Marie b. Oct. 10, 1874; Jeanette b. Aug. 3, 1876, m. Hugh T. Rippeto; Louise b. Aug. 27, 1880, m. George L. Weiler.
Married Josephine H. Meyer Oct. 14, 1878, Salt Lake City (daughter of Fredrick Henry John Meyer and Anna Dorothy Elizabeth Jensen of Schleswig-Holstein, Germany; latter with daughter came to Utah September, 1862, James Wareham company). She was born March 22, 1856. Their children: Fred Joseph b. Dec. 27, 1879, m. Susie Bitner; Charles Meyer b. June 18, 1882, m. Elizabeth Bowring; Leroy Meyer b. Jan. 9, 1884; Frank Meyer b. July 19, 1887; Logan b. Oct. 25, 1889.
Married Mary Monson July 16, 1884, Salt Lake City (daughter of Mons Monson and Cecelia Peterson of Porham, Blekinge, Sweden, who came to Utah 1882). She was born Dec. 26, 1854. Their children: Henry Monson b. July 2,

1885, died; Josephine Monson b. May 7, 1888, m. Joseph A. F. Everett.
Married Sarah E. Duncan July 18, 1900, Manti, Utah (daughter of Homer Duncan, pioneer Oct. 16, 1848, Barney Adams company, and Sarah Trippess, pioneer October, 1862, Homer Duncan company, both of Salt Lake City). She was born April 1, 1868. Their children: Isabelle b. July 4, 1902; Ella Viola b. Sept. 26, 1904; Rose Lucile b. Feb. 1, 1907, died; Myron Duncan b. March 16, 1909, died. Families resided Salt Lake City.
Member eighteenth quorum seventies; assistant Sunday school superintendent eleventh ward, Salt Lake City; president Y. M. M. I. A. eleventh ward prior to 1877; bishop of eleventh ward Nov. 1, 1891-Oct. 13, 1912. Member city council of Salt Lake City 1897-98. Participated in Indian expedition in San Pete county 1867. Tanner and wool merchant. Died April 25, 1913.

MORRIS, CHARLES M. (son of Robert Morris and Josephine H. Meyer). Attorney-at-law, Salt Lake City.

MORRIS, WILLIAM (son of William Morris, born 1794, Clee, Shropshire, Eng.). Born Feb. 27, 1821, Clee. Came to Utah 1854.
Married Harriett Evans, who was born Jan. 17, 1822. Their children: Elizabeth b. June 19, 1851; Sarah Ann b. Dec. 25, 1852; Mary Jane b. Dec. 3, 1854, m. D. M. Sheldon; William Edward b. Nov. 10, 1856; Elizabeth Ellen b. June 30, 1858; Martha b. March 25, 1860; John Thomas b. June 18, 1861; Lucy Emma b. June 15, 1863. Family home Weber Co., Utah.
Married Elizabeth Russel March 11, 1865, Marriott, Utah (daughter of John Russel and Ellen Blackwood), who was born July 2, 1836, Clackmannanshire, Scotland. Their children: William R. b. Jan. 17, 1866, died; Elizabeth b. Feb. 24, 1867, died; Ellen b. Dec. 14, 1869, m. Hyrum W. Marriott Dec. 1, 1897; John R. b. Feb. 3, 1871, m. Maggie Marriott March 2, 1894; James B. b. Jan. 27, 1873, m. Ellen M. Marriott Feb. 21, 1900; Peter Thomas b. Oct. 28, 1874, died; Catharine b. June 15, 1876, m. Thomas E. Powell March 16, 1910; George b. Nov. 12, 1878, died.
One of first settlers of Bingham Fort and Marriott, Utah. Died Dec. 23, 1892, Marriott, Utah.

MORRIS, JAMES B. (son of William Morris and Elizabeth Russel). Born Jan. 27, 1873, Marriott, Utah.
Married Ellen M. Marriott Feb. 21, 1900, Salt Lake City (daughter of John Marriott, pioneer Livingston Kincaid company, and Elizabeth Stewart, pioneer Hyrum Clawson company). She was born March 6, 1868, at Marriott. Their children: Verna b. Dec. 1, 1900; Wallace Floyd b. Jan. 11, 1902; James Russel b. March 10, 1905; Afton Marriott b. Feb. 27, 1907. Family home Marriott, Utah.

MORRISON, JOHN (son of Andrew Morrison). Born in 1805 in Ireland. Came to Utah Oct. 16, 1852, Eli B. Kelsey company.
Married Sarah Mark of Ireland, 1835, who was born in 1820. Their children: Jane, m. Samuel Pine, 1853; Andrew, m. Mary Anne Fleet, 1862; John, m. Mary Jane Warren; Joseph, m. Luey Annie Henson, Nov. 3, 1878; Ellen, m. Edward Clayton; Thomas, m. Marguerite Perkins. Family resided at Palmyra, Utah, and Franklin, Idaho.
High priest; assisted in building Nauvoo temple. Pioneer of Franklin, Idaho. Farmer.
Died April 1, 1881, Franklin, Idaho.

MORRISON, JOSEPH (son of John Morrison and Sarah Mark). Born Nov. 25, 1846, at Plymouth, Iowa. Came to Utah with father.
Married Luey Annie Henson Nov. 3, 1878, Franklin, Idaho (daughter of Alfred Henson and Mary Ann Frost of England, pioneers 1868). She was born March 3, 1861. Their children: John Alfred b. March 28, 1880, m. Annie Miller Sept. 11, 1907; Martha Ellen b. May 8, 1882, m. Peter G. Whitehead, Dec. 18, 1907; George Leo b. May 9, 1884; Alvin Oliver b. May 18, 1886, d. June 27, 1905; Sarah Violet b. Dec. 6, 1888, m. Fredrick Henry Campbell Nov. 18, 1908; Joseph Andy b. June 7, 1891; James Philemon b. Feb. 14, 1893, m. Ray Perkins April 10, 1912. Family home Franklin, Idaho.
High priest. Assisted in bringing immigrants to Utah 1868 with Chester Loveland company. Pioneer of Franklin, Idaho. Freighter; farmer.

MORRISON, GEORGE LEO (son of Joseph Morrison and Luey Annie Henson of Franklin, Idaho). Born May 9, 1884, Franklin, Idaho.
Missionary to southern states 1904 to 1906. Graduate of U. A. C. with degree of B. S. A. 1911. Agriculturist.

MORRISON, JOHN, JR. (son of John Morrison and Sarah Mark). Born Aug. 15, 1844, Nauvoo, Ill. Came to Utah Oct. 16, 1852, Eli B. Kelsey company.
Married Mary Jane Warren May 15, 1876, Salt Lake City (daughter of William James Warren and Sarah Jane Simmons of Spanish Fork and Price, Utah, pioneers 1853). She was born March 26, 1857. Their children: Sarah J.; Mary Ellen; John William; Colemus Maclaurin; Clarence Zenos; Luella Pauline; Lewis Franklin; Lilly Pearl, m. J. A. Mathis; Joseph Meliburn; Paul Desmon. Family home Spanish Fork and Price, Utah.
Elder. Mechanic. Died April 30, 1905, Hyrum, Utah.

MORRISON, WILLIAM (son of George Charles Morrison and Mary Ann Bruce of Aberdeen, Scotland). Born Sept. 7, 1820, at Inverury, Aberdeen, Scotland. Came to Utah 1856, Knud Peterson company.
Married Margaret Forquhar Cruikshank Dec. 22, 1843, Aberdeen, Scotland (daughter of William Cruikshank and Mary Forquhar of Aberdeen, Scotland), who was born June 5, 1823. Their children: Anthony Bruce b. Oct. 30, 1844, d. 1848; Andrew, Mary Margaret, Mary Isabella and Sarah, all died in childhood; William b. Dec. 9, 1856, m. Emma Sorenson; Mina b. March 13, 1859, m. Henry Erickson; Tina b. Feb. 15, 1863, m. Ferdinand Erickson. Family resided Aberdeen, Scotland, and Utah.
Married Caroline Christina Iverson. Ephraim, Utah (daughter of Jeppe Iverson and Anna Christina Jensen of Jutland, Denmark, pioneers 1856, Knud Peterson company). She was born Dec. 15, 1842. Their children: James Bruce, m. Caroline Amanda Foutz; Amanda Puella, m. John A. Hellstrom; Alexander, m. Cecelia Seare; Annie Christina, m. John W. Orrock; George Charles. m. Mary Avery; Walter William, m. Christina Sellers; William, died; Lorenzo Barr. Family resided Mt. Pleasant and Richfield, Utah.
Married Martha Maria Hansen Sept. 21, 1861, at Mt. Pleasant, Utah (daughter of Niels Hansen, died in Denmark, and Mette Maria Hansen of Denmark, pioneer 1860, handcart company). She was born Nov. 21, 1846, and came to Utah with mother. Their children: Martha b. April 20, 1863, m. Joseph S. Horne; Hannah, d. child; Charles Henry, m. Isabella Dunn; Robert Bruce, m. Lillie Seare; Mary Ann Bruce, m. Christopher D. Swan, m. Jeff Drake; Mary Margaret, d. infant; Cosmelia Jamima, d. infant; Henrietta Angelina, m. Chester A. Altsire; William Arthur, m. Esther Elgreen; Isabella, m. O. A. Cushing. Family resided Mt. Pleasant and Richfield, Utah.
President Woolwich conference of England. Settled at Richfield 1864. Sevier stake clerk; president high priests quorum; patriarch. Probate judge of Sevier county; representative Utah territorial legislature; clerk of Sevier county. Veteran Indian war; member Utah militia. Shipbuilder; farmer. Died Aug. 7, 1889, Clear Creek, Utah.

MORRISON, JAMES BRUCE (son of William Morrison and Caroline Christina Iverson). Born Nov. 7, 1860, Mt. Pleasant, Utah.
Married Caroline Amanda Foutz Jan. 30, 1882, St. George, Utah (daughter of Joseph Lehi Foutz, pioneer 1847, and Amanda Child, pioneer 1851, John Brown company). She was born Jan. 10, 1861. Their children: James Bruce b. Jan. 15, 1883, m. Anna McCthvie; Leith Lumsden b. Sept. 29, 1884, m. Flossie Preston; Estelle b. Oct. 16, 1886, m. Guy H. Goodlander; Reuel b. July 9, 1890; William b. Sept. 1, 1892; Bandera DeVara b. July 6, 1895; Gladys b. Jan. 14, 1898; Eliold and Ellolse (twins) b. April 20, 1900; Verona b. April 12, 1902; Sybil Foutz b. April 19, 1904. Family home Richfield, Utah.
Missionary to northwestern states 1888-89; high priest; superintendent Sevier stake Sunday school; high councilor. City recorder; justice of peace at Richfield; chaplain of territorial legislature and docket clerk of first Utah state legislature. President Otter Creek reservoir board. Farmer.

MORRISON, ROBERT BRUCE (son of William Morrison and Martha Maria Hansen). Born Nov. 28, 1868, Mt. Pleasant, Utah.
Married Lilly Jane Seare Sept. 5, 1894, Salt Lake City (daughter of William Seare and Jane Simmonds both of Abingdon, Berkshire, Eng.), who came to Utah Sept. 15, 1884). She was born April 17, 1864, at Abingdon. Their children: Walter Bruce b. Aug. 30, 1895; Von Seare b. Aug. 26, 1897; William b. March 12, 1899; Albert b. March 10, 1901; Lucile Elta b. May 20, 1903; Lillian Jane b. Sept. 14, 1907, d. April 14, 1908. Family resided Richfield, Helper and Mill Creek, Utah.
Presiding elder at Spring Glenn; bishop's counselor; president Y. M. M. I. A.; ward teacher; Sunday school teacher. Justice of peace at Helper; notary public of Carbon county; postmaster at Helper. School teacher; farmer; contractor; stockraiser.

MORSE, FRANCIS YOUNG (son of Ebenezer Morse and Lydia Young of Boston, Mass.). Born Jan. 25, 1834, at Boston. Came to Utah in 1859, Peter Nebeker company.
Married Elizabeth Thomas in 1859, Boston, Mass. (daughter of John Thomas and Phoebe Body of Wattford, near London, Eng.), who was born Jan. 19, 1830. Their children: Lydia Young, m. Joseph S. Rowley; Francis Young, m. Sarah Larson; John Thomas. m. Louisa Fay; William B., d. child; Jedediah, m. Hannah Cunningham. Family home St. George, Utah.
Elder; ward teacher; pioneer of St. George. Carpenter.

MORSE, RICHARD (son of William Morse of South Wales). Born July 10, 1837, at Llanelly, Caermarthenshire, South Wales. Came to Utah in October, 1863.
Married Maria Jones Oct. 11, 1856, at Merthyr Tydfil, South Wales (daughter of William and Martha Jones of South Wales), who was born Feb. 18, 1837, and died March 21, 1909. Their children: Mary Ann, m. Samuel Reese; Margret, m. Daniel J. Williams; Marthur and William, d. infants; Jane, m. Jonah Evans; Rebecca, m. John H. Williams; Sarah E.,

m. George H. Williams; Maria, m. David H. Anderson. Family home Samaria, Idaho.
Member 52d quorum seventies; missionary to South Wales 1887-89; first Sunday school superintendent of Samaria ward; high councilor of Malad stake. County commissioner; chairman of school board; chairman of town board. Merchant; farmer. Died Nov. 11, 1901.

MORSE, WILLIAM (son of William Morse and Mary Thomas of Mountain Ash, South Wales). Born June 6, 1830, Llanelly, Caermarthenshire, South Wales. Came to Utah Oct. 4, 1863, Captain Wight company.
Married Margaret Evans October, 1859, at Merthyr Tydfil, Glamorganshire, South Wales (daughter of Ebenezer Evans and Amy Jones of Cynwyl Elfed, Caermarthenshire), who was born Oct. 10, 1836. Their children: Mary Jane, m. Jeremiah Jones: Ann, m. William P. Camp; Emma, m. John E. Price; William E., m. Sarah A. Evans; Margaret, m. Hyrum W. Jones; Rachael, m. Joseph Williams; Sarah, m. Lewis Williams; Sophia, m. James R. Hawkins. Family home Samaria, Idaho.
Farmer. Died April 16, 1904.

MORSE, WILLIAM E. (son of William Morse and Margaret Evans). Born Oct. 31, 1867, Logan, Utah.
Married Sarah A. Evans Jan. 25, 1905, at Logan (daughter of Thomas Evans and Elizabeth Reese of Pembrokeshire, South Wales; came to Utah in June, 1882). She was born Sept. 29, 1883. Their children: William E. Jr. b. Nov. 19, 1905; Sarah Verla b. July 21, 1909.
Missionary to Great Britain 1897-99; secretary 52d quorum seventies; Sunday school superintendent. Mayor. Farmer.

MORTENSEN, ANDERS (son of Morten Christiansen and Metta Mortensdatter of Lille Rorbek, Fredericksborg, Denmark). Born Nov. 9, 1828, in Denmark. Came to Utah in July, 1873.
Married Anna Cathrina Hansen in 1865, Copenhagen (daughter of Hans Hansen and Mary Christina Christensdatter, Juderup, Holbek, Denmark), who was born May 18, 1839. Their children: Mary Julia; Metta Christena and Hans Christian, died; Andrew Daniel; Marten Christian; Paul, died. Family resided at Spring City, Utah, and Preston, Idaho.
High priest; ward teacher; president Worm Creek branch. Farmer. Died Dec. 7, 1892, at Preston.

MORTENSEN, ANDREW D. (son of Anders Mortensen and Anna Cathrina Hansen). Born July 15, 1874, at Spring City, Utah.
Married Christena Gregersen Dec. 14, 1904, at Logan, Utah (daughter of Laurids Gregersen and Metta Fredericksen of Brande, Denmark), who was born May 12, 1871. Their children: George A. b. Feb. 24, 1906; Ada M. b. July 12, 1907; Carl A. b. Oct. 14, 1908; Orson A. b. Feb. 14, 1911. Family home Glendale, Idaho.
Member 114th quorum seventies; missionary to Scandinavia 1900-1903; ward teacher; bishop. Farmer; stockraiser.

MORTENSEN, ANDREAS P. (son of Morten Swenson and Dorthea Sophia Rost). Born July 14, 1822, Dronningaard, Denmark. Came to Utah in 1864, William B. Preston company.
Married Ingeborg Petersen June 25, 1848, Sollerod, Denmark (daughter of Peter and Kjirsten Christiansen), who was born April 27, 1821, Overod, Denmark. Their children: Anna Sophia; Sine Maria; Niels William; Jens Christian; Adam Sophus. Family home Huntsville, Weber Co., Utah.

MORTENSEN, NIELS WILLIAM (son of Andreas P. Mortensen and Ingeborg Petersen). Born May 23, 1853, Dronningaard, Denmark. Came to Utah with parents.
Married Cecelia Schow Oct. 25, 1875 (daughter of Hans and Maren Schow). Their children: Niels William, Jr., b. Dec. 16, 1876; Anna Maria b. Feb. 17, 1879; Hans Andrew b. Feb. 25, 1882; Joseph Alma b. Nov. 3, 1884; Aaron b. June 26, 1888.
Married Johanna C. Christensen June 19, 1890, Logan, Utah (daughter of Hans and Wilhelmina Christensen). Their children: Adam b. June 9, 1891; Rhoda Cecelia b. Dec. 16, 1894; Nora Rosabell b. Nov. 6, 1897. Families resided at Huntsville, Utah.

MORTENSON, JOHN PETER.
Married Eva Rasmusson Feb. 20, 1862, Salt Lake City (daughter of Rasmus Rasmusson and Johanna Holmberg), who was born Jan. 2, 1836, Trelleborg, Sweden. Came to Utah 1861 with her sister in covered company, and died Sept. 4, 1911. Their children: Eva Hilma; Jennie Caroline. Family resided Salt Lake City and Logan, Utah, and in Idaho.
Married Caroline Rasmusson Oct. 4, 1868, Salt Lake Endowment house (daughter of Rasmus Rasmusson and Johanna Holmberg), who was born Feb. 10, 1831, Frau Alsted, Sweden; came to Utah Sept. 26, 1868, and died Dec. 13, 1912, Salt Lake City. Their children: Matilda; Rose Amelia. Family home, Salt Lake City.
Died Sept. 23, 1911.

MORTENSEN, KNUD (son of Christen Mortensen of Lille Rorbek, Denmark, born July 2, 1758, and Mette Knudsdatter of Olstykke, born Sept. 19, 1756). He was born Dec. 13, 1819, Lille Rorbek. Came to Utah Sept. 5, 1863, John F. Sanders company.
Married Karen Ericksen in March, 1845 (daughter of Erick Andersen and Karen Belersdatter—married Sept. 20, 1815). She was born May 8, 1822. Came to Utah with her husband. Their children: Morton C. b. June 3, 1846, m. Christene Knudsen Nov. 8, 1869; Marie b. Sept. 30, 1848, m. Hans P. Andersen Nov. 8, 1869; Elizabeth b. March 13, 1854, m. Lars Olsen in June 1880; Peter b. June 6, 1857, m. Mary Iversen Sept. 24, 1884; Moroni b. Oct. 3, 1864, m. Elizabeth Trenchard June 9, 1898.
Counselor to Bishop William Neely 1870-80 and to Bishop Carl Jensen 1880-99; ward teacher several years. Pioneer of Bear River City, Utah. Died Jan. 13, 1909.

MORTENSEN, PETER (son of Knud Mortensen and Karen Ericksen). Born June 6, 1857, Copenhagen, Denmark.
Married Mary Iversen Sept. 24, 1884, Logan, Utah (daughter of Nels Iversen and Maren Olsen), who was born July 21, 1867, in Denmark. Their children: Elvira b. Sept. 9, 1885, m. Henry Jensen June 4, 1905; Samuel b. Aug. 22, 1887; Jedediah M. b. Feb. 11, 1894; Benjamin P. b. June 30, 1896; Edna I. b. Dec. 28, 1898; Enos N. b. March 30, 1901; Heber R. b. June 24, 1903; Pearl b. Aug. 30, 1909; Ethel b. Oct. 4, 1911. Family home Tremonton, Utah.

MORTENSEN, NIELS CHRISTIAN (son of Martin and Inger Nielsen of Nykjobing, Sjelland, Denmark). Born July 4, 1833, in Denmark. Came to Utah in 1864, John Smith independent company.
Married Mariana Christensen in 1864 at Huntsville, Utah (daughter of Christian Mortensen and Anna Kathrina Petersen of Astrup, Denmark), who was born March 27, 1835. Their children: Emma Elizabeth, m. Charles S. Wood; Josephine Anderina, m. George E. Ferrin; Mariana, m. John S. Gould; Niels Christian, m. Nell Russell; Elvina Caroline, m. J. J. Allen; Ingar Sophia Amelia, m. Theron L. Rogers.
Married Thora Emalina Christensen. Their children: Nielzina Christena, m. Jens Jensen; Peter Andrew; Thora Etmalina, m. A. C. Schade; Ernest Joseph; Anna Cecelia; Irene Georgene. Families resided at Huntsville, Utah.
High priest; missionary to Denmark 1883-85; bishop's counselor. One of the first to go to the penitentiary for religious convictions. Farmer and merchant. Died Sept. 22, 1898.

MORTON, THOMAS FINCHER HARRY (son of William Harry Morton and Hannah Tanner of Aldridge's Run, Morgan Co., Ohio). Born Sept. 27, 1832, Pennsville, Ohio. Came to Utah Nov. 29, 1865, William S. S. Willis company.
Married Mary Ann Croy in 1853 at Pennsville (daughter of John Croy and Prudence Edgar of Virginia, who came to Utah, Sidney Willis company). She was born July 7, 1827. Their children: Jemima J. b. March 6, 1856; Hannah Ann b. July 27, 1857; Melissa E. b. March 16, 1861, m. Edward McLelland; Laura Geneva b. Nov. 29, 1865, m. Don C. Tufts; Flora Geneva b. Nov. 29, 1865, m. Robert Cowan; Prudence Luvera b. June 1, 1868; John William b. Nov. 27, 1870.
Married Julia Ann Conley June 15, 1874, Salt Lake City (daughter of Solomon N. Conley and Martha Smith, Morgan Co., Utah, pioneers 1849). She was born Feb. 6, 1855. Their children: Thomas Fincher Harry b. April 15, 1875, m. Nellie Pettit; Franklyn Willard b. July 12, 1877; Edgar Townsend b. Oct. 4, 1879; Amos Nelson b. Sept. 19, 1881; Julia Myrtis b. Feb. 10, 1884, m. Samuel H. Worthen. Families resided at Salt Lake City.
18President of fourth quorum of seventies. Died April 8, 1907.

MORTON, THOMAS FINCHER HARRY, JR. (son of Thomas Fincher Harry Morton and Julia Ann Conley). Born April 15, 1875, Salt Lake City.
Married Nellie Pettit Sept. 6, 1905, Salt Lake City (daughter of Edwin Pettit and Rebecca Hill of Salt Lake City, pioneers 1847). She was born Feb. 10, 1878. Their child: Paul Harry b. May 26, 1910. Family home, Salt Lake City.
Practicing physician; graduated in medicine and surgery in 1908 at Medico-Chirurgical College, Philadelphia, Pa.

MOSES, JAMES (son of Jesse Moses, born in June, 1774, South Manchester, Conn., and Ester Brown of Norfolk, Conn., born 1776—married in Norfolk in 1794). Born Feb. 28, 1806, Norfolk. Came to Utah Sept. 26, 1861, Ira Reed company.
Married Roxy M. Terry April 9, 1833 (daughter of Timothy Terry and Roxy Latimer, married at Simsbury, Conn.). Their children: James b. April 20, 1835, m. Ezra Pettit Nov. 28, 1860; John b. 1837, d. child. Family resided North Canaan, Conn., and Kirtland, Ohio.
Married Eliza Spencer Oct. 17, 1839, Nauvoo, Ill. (daughter of Solomon Spencer and Martha Jones), who was born June 15, 1813, Johnson, Ohio. Their children: Martha b. in October 1845; Jesse Tilton b. May 9, 1848, m. Phebe A. Woodruff June 14, 1875; Eliza b. in August 1850, m. Joseph Neuman; James b. Feb. 14, 1853, died; Fred F. b. June 5, 1856. Family resided at Nauvoo, Ill., Council Bluffs, Iowa, North Canaan, Conn., and Salt Lake City.

MOSES, JESSE TILTON (son of James Moses and Eliza Spencer). Born May 9, 1848, Council Bluffs, Iowa.
Married Phebe A. Woodruff June 14, 1875, Salt Lake City (daughter of Wilford Woodruff and Sarah Brown), who was born May 30, 1859, Salt Lake City. Their children: Sarah Eliza b. April 18, 1876, d. Feb. 16, 1877; Jesse Tilton b. Jan. 28, 1878, m. Lavine Harper Sept. 23, 1903; Sylva Arabell b. Aug. 24, 1880, m. B. F. Handley June 27, 1906; Wilford Newton b. Nov. 18, 1882; James Julian b. July 29, 1885, d. Aug. 5, 1885; David Courtney b. July 6, 1886; Clarence Frederick b. April 15, 1891; Elmer Woodruff b. June 5, 1894; Ethel Woodruff b. June 5, 1894, d. March 20, 1895; Phoebe Ester b. Jan. 20, 1896; Henry Brown b. Nov. 1, 1898; Mary Woodruff b. June 14, 1901; Brigham b. Nov. 22, 1903, d. Nov. 23, 1903. Family resided at Randolph, Big Cottonwood and Smithfield, Utah, and Mesa, Ariz.

MOSS, JOHN (son of Hugh Moss and Elizabeth Rushton of Newton, Yorkshire, Eng.). Born March 6, 1820, Newton. Came to Utah in 1848, Brigham Young company.
Married Rebecca Wood in 1845 in Pike county, Ill. (daughter of Daniel Wood and Mary Snyder, pioneers 1848, Brigham Young company). She was born May 11, 1826. Their children: Mary, m. Henry Moyle; Daniel, m. Melvina Rushton; Elizabeth, died; Joseph, m. Sarah Phoebe Sessions; John Hugh, m. Missouri V. Lincoln; William, m. Grace Ann Hatch; Moroni, m. Mary Ann Hale; Rebecca Jane, died; Ellen, m. Hilbert S. Hatch; Nephi, m. Rhoda Pace; Alice, m. Rastus Eagan; Henry, m. Minnie M. Atkinson. Family home Bountiful, Utah.
Married Emma A. Alexander March 25, 1865, Salt Lake City (daughter of Abel Alexander and Sarah Alexander [cousins] of Colne, Wiltshire, Eng., pioneers Nov. 3, 1864). She was born April 14, 1846. Their children: David A., m. Ellen B. Deppie; Alma, m. Amelia E. Cleaverly; Sarah, d. infant; Adaline, d. in September 1908; Alexander, m. Annie Jones; Robert A., m. Linnie Eagan; Stephen, m. Martha A. Jones; Margret, m. Ernest R. Grant.
President seventy-seventh quorum seventies. Farmer and stockraiser. Died Aug. 4, 1884.

MOSS, JOSEPH (son of John Moss and Rebecca Wood). Born Aug. 10, 1850, Bountiful, Utah.
Married Sarah Phoebe Sessions Dec. 18, 1871, Salt Lake City (daughter of David Sessions and Phoebe C. Foss of Bountiful), who was born Nov. 26, 1853. Their children: Sarah Phoebe b. March 28, 1873, m. Edwin P. Porter Feb. 1, 1899; Mary Rebecca b. Aug. 9, 1875, m. Jonathan H. Hale April 28, 1897; Joseph William b. Dec. 15, 1877, m. Lillian A. Porter Aug. 13, 1902; Olive Cerdenia b. Aug. 25, 1881, m. Ansel Hatch June 7, 1899; Carrie b. Sept. 18, 1884; Cora b. Sept. 8, 1884, m. Sylvenia Nelson May 27, 1908; Calvin b. Dec. 31, 1886, m. Olive P. Bolton Oct. 9, 1912; David S. b. May 4, 1889; Ellen b. Jan. 11, 1892.
High priest. Farmer.

MOSS, WILLIAM (son of John Moss and Rebecca Wood).
Married Grace Ann Hatch. Their children: Grace b. Nov. 19, 1879, d. Dec. 25, 1879; Leonard W. b. April 1, 1881, d. June 3, 1889; Ethel b. Dec. 22, 1883, m. Ezra Waddoups Jan. 6, 1904; Gertie M. b. Jan. 14, 1886, m. Joseph W. McMurrin, Jr.; Florence b. Oct. 7, 1887, m. M. E. Waddoups; Chloe E. b. July 27, 1890, m. William Roberts March 6, 1907; Ralph J. b. April 3, 1893; Delilah b. Jan. 12, 1896; Ezra O. b. Aug. 19, 1898; Amelia b. Aug. 13, 1900. Family home West Bountiful, Utah.
Missionary to England 1902-04; bishop of West Bountiful ward since March 27, 1909. Superintendent Deseret Live Stock Company.

MOSS, WILLIAM F. (son of William F. Moss, Sr., and Sarah Stokes of Derbyshire, Eng. Born Nov. 15, 1825, Nottinghamshire, Eng. Came to Utah in 1861, John R. Murdock company.
Married Eliza Crich in England (daughter of William Crich and Eliza Summers of England), who was born Oct. 27, 1829, Mansfield, Eng. Their children: Sarah Ann, m. Caleb Luker; Emily Elizabeth, m. Andrew Barker Forsyth; Rosenia, m. Heber Lorenzo Crockett; William Edward, m. Salina Paget; Eliza Charlotte, m. William Owens; Frances Ellen, m. Alfred F. Denney; Grace Alice, m. Eli Lee; Catherine Jane, died; George F., m. Ada Hammond; Joseph F. and Henry Crich; last two died. Family home E. T. City, Utah.
Bishop of E. T. City 30 years; patriarch. Justice of peace; postmaster; school trustee. Merchant. Died Sept. 20, 1909, East Garland, Utah.

MOTT, SAMUEL (son of John Mott and Eunice Thompson of Vermont). Born in 1782 in Vermont. Came to Utah in 1854, independent company.
Married Elizabeth Dewight in Vermont (daughter of Mr. Dewight and Electa Garret of Vermont), who was born in 1790 and died July 6, 1865. Their children: Maria Howe, m. Anson Sheffield; Wesley, d. infant; William Harrison, m. Almina Plato, m. Sallie Plato; Jeremiah and Harmon, m. Ann, m. Daniel Dye; Mary, m. Zebdee Coltren; Samuel, d. aged 3 years; John W., m. Caroline ———, who died; m. Catherine Holden; Daniel Richmond, m. Elizabeth Graham; m. Isabelle Wilkin McCleave; Electa, m. James Barlow; Susana, m. James Barlow; Thomas, died; Simon, d. aged 11 years. Family home Batavia, N. Y.
Farmer. Died Feb. 5, 1867, Payson, Utah.

MOTT, DANIEL RICHMOND (son of Samuel Mott and Elizabeth Dewight). Born April 23, 1826, Batavia, N. Y. Came to Utah with parents.
Married Elizabeth Graham in 1850, Decatur, Wis. (daughter of Sylvenus Graham and Electa Garret of Batavia), who was born July 8, 1828. Their children: Helen b. 1851, d. infant; Juliett b. Feb. 12, 1852, m. Franklin Augustus Fraughton; Dewight Graham, d. infant; Elizabeth Jane b. Dec. 25, 1856, m. Heber Taylor.
Married Isabelle Wilkin McCleave May 19, 1861, at Payson (daughter of John and Nancy Jane McCleave, the former died on way to Utah, the latter came in Sept. 1856, Daniel D. McArthur handcart company). She was born Jan. 29, 1843. Their children: Cecilia Arthemia, m. William R. Heath; Isabelle Eliza, m. Lorenzo Curtis; Daniel Richmond, d. 1869; Joseph Harrison, d. 1869; Jeremiah, m. Eliza C. Smith; Electa Rhoda Ann, m. Elias Arthur Johnson. Families resided at Payson, Utah.
Assisted in bringing immigrants to Utah. Black Hawk war veteran. Farmer; freighter. Died Jan. 18, 1904, Wallsburg, Utah.

MOURITSEN, LARS. Born Oct. 17, 1825, Fastropsogn, Denmark. Came to Utah in 1859, Captain Nibley company.
Married Maren Sorensen, who was born April 22, 1824, and came to Utah with husband. Their children: Johanna Marie b. June 17, 1846, m. Lars C. Petersen Nov. 25, 1860; Mourits b. Jan. 28, 1849, m. Lizzie Hillyard; Maren b. April 10, 1850, m. Anton Jensen 1865; Martine Martha b. Nov. 11, 1851, m. Horatio Harris Merrill Dec. 24, 1866; Johanna Kirstine b. Jan. 29, 1853, m. Edwin R. Miles.
Elder. Settled at Kaysville, but soon moved to Plain City and thence to Smithfield in 1864. Pioneer brickmaker. Died at Smithfield Feb. 1, 1913, being 87 years, 7 months, 14 days of age.

MOWER, HENRY (son of Michael Mower and Cathrine Geisinger of Frederick, Md.). Born in 1798 in Frederick. Came to Utah in 1851.
Married Mary Amick in 1816 (daughter of John Amick, Sr., of Bedford, Pa.), who was born in 1796. Their children: Catherine; Mahala, m. George Shaw; Leah; Henry, Jr., m. Susan Strong; John, m. Sarah Ann Bidwell; Susan, m. Simeon Cragun; Mary; Ezra; George, m. Emma Bidwell; Hannahette, m. Joseph Bidwell. Family home Bedford, Pa.
Married Lucretia Hupper Feb. 15, 1847 (daughter of William Hupper and Margaret Craig), who was born Sept. 15, 1818, Port Clyde, Maine. Their children: Matilda, died; Orson Hyde, m. Margaret Van Valkenberg; Oscar Middleton, m. Elizabeth Beardall; Eliza, m. Rubert Singleton; Lucretia, died; Deliah Jane, m. Seth Hansen.
Married Elmyra Wheeler 1855 (daughter of Levi Wheeler). Their children: Brigham and Heber, died; Henry Levi, m. Sarah Elizabeth Smith; Elmyra, m. William Brower; Joseph, m. Cynthia Mower; Hyrum, died; Michael F., m. Louisa Lewis; Andrew; William, died.
Missionary to eastern states; president high priests quorum. Member city council of Springville. Farmer. Died April 4, 1878, at Springville.

MOWREY, HARLEY (son of Barton Mowrey, Providence, R. I.). Born Aug. 9, 1822, Burrillville, near Providence, R. I. Came to Utah July 27, 1847, with Capt. James Brown contingent Mormon Battalion.
Married Martha Jane Sargent (Sharp), widow of Norman Sharp, who was accidentally shot during Battalion's march to Pueblo.
Member first high council of Bear Lake stake and later of Uinta stake; missionary in New Hampshire 1844. Worked on Nauvoo temple. Member first artillery company that left Nauvoo, Feb. 9, 1846; mustered into Co. C Mormon battalion July 6, 1846. Accompanied C. C. Rich and Amasa M. Lyman to California, residing there seven years. Took part in the move south, after which he lived at Centerville until 1864. Called to assist in settling Bear Lake valley, Idaho. He brought the first reaper, or mower, to Utah and Idaho. Moved to Vernal, Utah, in 1885. Stone and brick mason. Died in December 1905.

MOYES, ROBERT (son of James Moyes, born 1780, Paisley, and Margaret Mann, born 1780, Kilmarnock, Scotland). Born in 1812 at Belfast, Ireland. Did not come to Utah.
Married Elizabeth Hutchison in June, 1835, at Paisley (daughter of William Hutchison and Mary Spears), who was born in October, 1814, in County Donegal, Ireland, and died Aug. 16, 1907, at Ogden, Utah. Came to Utah with her family Sept. 29, 1866, Daniel Thompson oxteam company. Their children: James Hutchison b. April 13, 1838, m. Margaret Ann Barton; William b. May 17, 1841, m. Robina Gowans June 22, 1860; Robert Hutchison b. Jan. 1, 1844, m. Lucy Wilson, m. Esther Pingree. m. Agnes Stewart; John Hutchison b. March 22, 1846, m. Agnes Douglass. m. Elizabeth Ingals; Stewart Hutchison b. Aug. 11, 1848, m. Anna Rogers; Alexander Hill b. March 22, 1851, m. Nancy Marinda Tracy; Margaret b. April 28, 1853, m. Charles Larson, m. Bennett Anderson.
Died July 11, 1861, at Paisley. Mrs. Moyes five years later came to Utah with part of her family and settled at Ogden.

MOYES, WILLIAM (son of Robert Moyes and Elizabeth Hutchison). Born May 17, 1841, Paisley, Scotland. Came to Utah Oct. 8, 1868, Edward T. Mumford mule train.
Married Robina Gowans June 22, 1860, at Paisley (daughter of James Gowans, born 1799, at Paisley and died there March 7, 1849, and Robina Bryson, born in June. 1806, at Paisley, died there Aug. 12, 1876). She was born Nov. 15, 1843, at Paisley. Their children: Robert b. Jan. 29. 1861, d. Feb. 16, 1861; William Gowans b. Jan. 10, 1862, m. Sarah Ann Allen; James G. b. Jan. 14, 1864, m. Elizabeth Fields; Robina b. Feb. 14, 1866, m. Henry Green; Elizabeth Ivers b. Aug. 8, 1868, on board ship in American waters, d. Oct. 20, 1869; Elizabeth Ann b. Sept. 30, 1870, d. March 19, 1873; Robert Alexander b. Sept. 14, 1872, m. Clara Hamer; Jane b. Feb. 6, 1875, m. William Charles Schmalz; John b. Feb. 23, 1877, d. Feb. 25, 1877; May b. May 31, 1878, d. June 23, 1878; George Gowans b. May 26, 1879; Arthur Gowans b. Sept. 10, 1881, d. May 18, 1882; David Gowans b. June 28, 1883, d. Oct. 8, 1901; Eva b. Aug. 23, 1885. Family home, Ogden. Member 75th quorum seventies; high councilor 1903-08. Health inspector 1896-1901. Worked on Union Pacific R. R. 1868-87.

MOYES, JOHN HUTCHISON (son of Robert Moyes and Elizabeth Hutchison), born March 22, 1846, at Paisley, Scotland. Came to Utah July 14, 1866, John Nicholson company.
Married Elizabeth Ingles Sept. 4, 1876, at Salt Lake City (daughter of Robert Ingles and Elizabeth Eccles of Paisley). She was born Aug. 17, 1856, and came to Utah July 15, 1874, P. C. Christensen company. Their children: John I. Moyes b. Nov. 25, 1877, m. Maggie Cottam; Elizabeth I. b. April 27, 1880, m. Oliver Miller; Robert I. b. Aug. 29, 1883, m. Agnes Purdie; Jane I. b. March 12, 1886, m. William Curteman; Maggie I. b. July 5, 1888, m. Orville Rupe; Robena G. b. Oct. 19, 1891, m. Thomas Harris; Ella b. March 30, 1894; Alice M. b. April 14, 1897; Bertha M. b. Jan. 29, 1900. Family home Ogden, Utah.
High priest. Farmer and janitor.

MOYES, ALEXANDER HILL (son of Robert Moyes and Elizabeth Hutchison). Born March 22, 1851, at Paisley. Came to Utah Sept. 29, 1866, with mother.
Married Nancy Marinda Tracy in Oct. 1879, Salt Lake City (daughter of Walter and Nancy Tracy of Ogden). She was born in 1862. Their children: Margaret, m. Samuel Doxey; m. Arthur Long; Alexander Walter; Elizabeth; Robert, m. Ethel Hill; Dora, m. D. J. Pidcock; Norine; Julia; Helen; three died. Family home Ogden, Utah.
State deputy game warden.

MOYLE, JOHN ROWE (son of James Moyle and Elizabeth Rowe, of Wendron, Cornwall, Eng.). Born Feb. 22, 1808, in Wendron. Came to Utah Sept. 26, 1856, Edmund Ellsworth handcart company.
Married Phillippa Beer in 1834, Island of Guernsey, Eng. (daughter of William Beer and Elizabeth Cook of Devonport, Devonshire). She was born Dec. 13, 1815. Their children: James b. Oct. 31, 1835, m. Elizabeth Wood; Elizabeth b. Jan. 12, 1837, m. Chauncy G. Webb; Henry b. Jan. 23, 1839, d. child; Stephen b. Nov. 27, 1840, m. Mary Ann Kelley; Phillippa b. Dec. 12, 1842, d. child: Henry b. Jan. 3, 1844, m. Mary Moss; Alfred b. Oct. 11, 1846, m. Alice Greenwood; William b. Nov. 13, 1848, d. 1853; John b. May 25, 1851, m. Fanny Carlisle; Joseph Edward b. Nov. 19, 1857, m. Matilda C. Hansen. Family home Alpine, Utah.
Seventy; senior president of 68th quorum of seventies. Worked for several years on Salt Lake temple. Died Feb. 15, 1889.

MOYLE, JAMES (son of John Rowe Moyle and Phillippa Beer). Born Oct. 31, 1835, Rosmellen, Cornwall, Eng.
Married Elizabeth Wood July 22, 1856, Salt Lake City (daughter of Daniel Wood and Mary Snyder of Kingston county, Canada). She was born Dec. 20, 1839. Their children: James Henry b. Sept. 17, 1858, m. Alice Evelyn Dinwoodey; Mary Elizabeth b. Jan. 25. 1860; John Alma b. May 2, 1862, and Phillippa Ann b. Dec. 4, 1863, latter three died; Bertha May b. May 15, 1865, m. Andrew John Gray; Daniel Wood b. Jan. 28, 1866, died; Oscar Wood b. Jan. 20, 1868, m. May Preston; Steppen Lawrence b. Dec. 22, 1869, m. Charlotta H. Atkinson; Deseret Blanch b. Feb. 19, 1872, died; Idda b. Sept. 25, 1873, m. Ray VanCott; Walter b. May 28, 1875, Mahonria b. Aug. 8, 1878, and Ellen b. May 28, 1880, latter three died; Louise Rebecca b. May 28, 1881, m. James Watson Silver. Family home, Salt Lake City.

MOYLE, JAMES HENRY (son of James Moyle and Elizabeth Wood). Born Sept. 17, 1858, Salt Lake City.
Married Alice Evelyn Dinwoodey Nov. 17, 1887, Logan. Utah (daughter of Henry Dinwoodey and Sarah Kinnersley of England). Their children: Henry Dinwoodey b. April 22, 1889; James Hubert b. Feb. 5, 1891, d. Oct. 2, 1892; Alice Evelyn b. March 21, 1893; Walter Gladstone b. March 13, 1895; Gilbert Dinwoodey b. Jan. 5, 1898; James Douglas b. Oct. 26, 1901; Richard Granville b. Dec. 20, 1903, d. April 1904; Sarah Virginia b. Aug. 13, 1906. Family home, Salt Lake City.
Lawyer; city and county attorney.

MOYLE, HENRY (son of John Rowe Moyle and Phillippa Beer). Born Jan. 3, 1844, Plymouth, Eng. Came to Utah with parents.
Married Mary Moss Jan. 11, 1867, Salt Lake City (daughter of John Moss and Rebecca Wood of Bountiful, Utah, pioneers 1848). She was born Nov. 16, 1844. Their children: Henry Alonzo b. March 31, 1868; Mary Rebecca b. June 26, 1869, m. J. W. Booth; Elizabeth b. June 25, 1871, m. Martin Hanson; Phillippa b. Feb. 15, 1873, m. Joseph A. Stubbs; Phebba Malvina b. Jan. 12, 1875, m. Samuel S. Cluff; John Franklin b. March 30, 1877, m. Vernett Thomas; Ellen Ameilia b. June 1, 1879, m. Oscar Wilkins; Parley b. June 12, 1881, m. Maud Austin; Clara Vilate b. June 7, 1884, m. William Vincent; Sylvia Etta b. Nov. 6, 1886, m. Alma Bourne; Alletta b. April 25, 1889, m. Samuel S. Grant. Family home Alpine, Utah.
Missionary to Great Britain June 4, 1890, to July. 1892; set apart as president of 67th quorum seventies Oct. 28, 1883, and senior president 128th quorum seventies in fall of 1900; ordained high priest and patriarch Jan. 20, 1901; deacon; teacher; elder. Member first company of cavalry from Utah county in Indian war of 1866. Marshal; city councilman; justice of peace; postmaster of Alpine.

MUHLESTEIN, NICHOLAS (son of John Muhlestein and Elizabeth Luthy of Bern, Switzerland. Born Oct. 7, 1831, Toffen, Canton Bern, Switzerland. Came to Utah October, 1863, Peter Nebeker company.
Married Mary Hauenstein in April. 1858, Koelliken, Switzerland (daughter of Frederick Hauenstein and Verena Ashbough of Koelliken, Switzerland). She was born Nov. 26, 1835, Koelliken, Canton Argau, Switzerland. Their children: Mary, Rosalie and Emma, all three died; John Nicholas b. Sept. 23, 1864, m. Martha Josephine Liechty; Emil, m. Barba Richenbach; Joseph Aaron, m. Margarett Hitz; Christian Hyrum, m. Lizzy Conrad; Martha Josephine, m. Karl Hassler; Frederick B. June 7, 1884, m. William Wintsh; Mary Anna Caroline Wintsh April 9, 1867, Salt Lake City (daughter of Casper Wintsh and Annie Willieman of Zurich, Switzerland). She was born Jan. 11, 1851. Their children: Mary Ann, m. Joseph E. Smith; Louisa Bertha, m. Reece Hooks; Esther, m. Albert Brown; Enoch, m. Jennie Wintsh; A. Brigham, m. Pearl Brown; Israel, m. Dorthy Elva; Ida, m. Arthur Conrad; Ephraim A.; Edna, died. Family home Pleasant View, Utah.
High priest; one of the presidents of 34th quorum seventies. Veteran Indian wars. Musician; watchmaker; jeweler; farmer and fruitgrower.

MUHLESTEIN, JOHN NICHOLAS (son of Nicholas Muhlestein and Mary Hauenstein). Born Sept. 23, 1864, Provo, Utah.
Married Martha Josephine Liechty Jan. 20, 1897, Salt Lake City (daughter of John Liechty and Luisa Wintsh of Zurich, Switzerland, pioneers Oct. 1862). She was born Feb. 20, 1879. Their children: Louisa Mary b. Jan. 19, 1898; d. Jan. 19, 1898; John Wilford b. June 1, 1900; Zina Ann b. Dec. 6, 1901; Albert Nicholas b. Sept. 24, 1903; George b. March 15, 1905; Martha b. March 13, 1907, d. March 1, 1908; Roy Casper b. Sept. 5, 1909; Leah b. Aug. 5, 1911. Family home Pleasant View, Utah.
President 15th quorum elders; president deacons quorum; teacher. Assessor 1906. Farmer; fruitgrower; gardener.

MUIR, JAMES. Born in Scotland. Came to Utah 1853 by oxteam.
Married Mary Reid in Scotland. (She had one child by a former husband: James Reid, m. Elizabeth ——). Their children: John, m. Margaret Fotheringham; George b. Oct. 16, 1831, m. Margaret Hannah; Mary, m. William McCoslin; Isabella, m. James Shanks. Family home Heber City, Utah.
Seventy; high priest. Shoemaker. Died at Salt Lake City.

MUIR, GEORGE (son of James and Mary Reid). Born Oct. 16, 1831, in Scotland. Came to Utah 1856, handcart company.
Married Margaret Hannah (daughter of William Hannah and Jane Howie, pioneers 1856). She was born Jan. 1, 1829. Their children: Mary Jane, m. William Richardson; James; Margaret Ann; Isabella b. June 1860, m. John Thornton Richardson; Elizabeth; George; Christina Maria; Agnes. Family home Heber City, Utah.
Married Christina Howie (Lindsay) 1862, Salt Lake City. Their children: John, m. Sarah Rooker; George, m. Agnes Arinda Thomas.
Christina Howie was the widow of William Lindsay of Scotland and mother of the following children: Robert, m. Sarah Murdock; William, m. Mary Mair; James, m. Agnes Watson; Baby, died; Samuel, m. Mary Reid; Andrew, m. Sarah Jane Thompson; Jane, m. William Shepard; Isabel, m. Joseph Smith; Elizabeth, d. aged 14 months. Family home Heber City, Utah.
Seventy. Opened coal mines at San Pete. Veteran Indian wars; participated in Echo Canyon trouble. Farmer. Died May 16, 1908, Heber City, Utah.

MUIR, WILLIAM SMITH (son of Stephen Muir and Elizabeth Blackwood of Scotland). Born July 17, 1822, Bannockburn, Scotland. Came to Utah 1848 with a contingent of the Mormon battalion (first sergeant, Co. A).
Married Jane Robb at Bannockburn, Scotland, who was born Jan. 10, 1817. Their children: W. S. m. Vilate Grant; Moses, m. Mary Call; Aaron, m. Emeline Day; James; Dan, m. Lillian F. Fisher. Family home Bountiful, Utah.
Missionary to Scotland 1850-53. Farmer.

MUIR, MOSES (son of William S. Muir and Jane Robb). Born May 11, 1852, Bountiful, Utah.
Married Mary V. Call March 15, 1876, Salt Lake City (daughter of Anson Vasco Call and Charlotte Holbrook of Bountiful, Utah, pioneers Sept. 20, 1848, Brigham Young company). She was born Jan. 29, 1859. Their children: Charlotte b. Feb. 16, 1877, m. C. A. Higginson; Vasco b. Nov. 16, 1879, m. Elizabeth Grant; Jane b. Dec. 25, 1881, d. March 23, 1892; Stephen b. June 28, 1883, m. Ada C. Paull; Cathrine b. July 25, 1885, m. J. T. Whitworth; Cassie b. Sept. 18, 1887, m. William Lasley; William b. Sept. 15, 1890; Anson b. Nov. 4, 1892, d. July 5, 1899; Mary A. b. April 22, 1895; Lillie b. Jan. 4, 1900; Lillius b. Jan. 4, 1900, d. Jan. 4, 1900.
High priest; bishop's counselor. Justice of the peace 4 years. Farmer.

MULLETT, JOSEPH E. (son of James Mullett and Amelia Meade). Born Nov. 29, 1838, Charleton, Somerset, Eng. Came to Utah 1868.
Married Rhoda Pocock July 2, 1867, St. Louis, Mo. (daughter of John Pocock and Mary Hapgood), who was born Dec. 13, 1834, Newbury, Berkshire, Eng., and came to Utah Aug. 20, 1868, Chester Loveland company, from Laramie terminus of Union Pacific Railroad. Their children: Joseph E. b. Sept. 30, 1868, m. Charlotte Alquist; Rhoda A. b. Jan. 5, 1871, m. Richard Conely; Lydia M. b. May 3, 1873, d. infant; William H. b. Feb. 11, 1875, d. aged 5; Mattie S. b. May 15, 1878, m. Chester Hope. Family home, Salt Lake City.
Missionary to New Jersey April 7, 1881.

MULLINER, SAMUEL. Born Jan. 15, 1809, Haddington, Scotland. Came to Utah 1850.
Married Catherine Nisbet Dec. 4, 1830. Their children: Jeanette, m. Easton Kelsey; Elizabeth, m. John M. Jones. Married Harriet Berry. Their children: Heber J.; Martha J., m. William Ford; Katherine, m. Samuel Pollock; Samuel; Brigham; Amelia, m. Mr. Higgins; William; Albert, m. Sarah Willis; Robert; Cyntha, m. Mr. Varney. Family home, Salt Lake City.
Married Mary Richardson. She was born May 15, 1829, England. Their children: Ursula b. Nov. 26, 1834, m. Isaac H. Allred June 4, 1871; Joseph S. b. Dec. 10, 1856, m. Amelia Woodward; Sarah b. 1858, d. infant; Fannie b. Nov. 14, 1860, m. Isaac Gudmundson; Hyrum S. b. Feb. 18, 1863, m. Maggie Adams; Mary Ann b. Feb. 22, 1865, d. aged 6.
First missionary to Scotland 1839; one of presidents of 12th quorum seventies. Pioneer leather manufacturer in Utah.

MUMFORD, THOMAS (son of Thomas Mumford and Mary Horsnel of Essex, Eng.). Born Dec. 24, 1829, in Essex. Came to Utah Sept. 24, 1862, Homer Duncan company.
Married Elizabeth Moore Nov. 8, 1860, in Dorsetshire, Eng. (daughter of John Moore of Dorsetshire). She was born Feb. 11, 1826. Their children: Thomas M., m. Emily M. Wright; John W., m. Maud Saxton; Elizabeth A., m. Thomas J. Jacobsen. Family home, Salt Lake City.
High priest: missionary to England 1858-60; block teacher. Farmer and stockraiser.

MUMFORD, JOHN W. (son of Thomas Mumford and Elizabet Moore of England, pioneers 1862). Born April 27, 1864.
Married Maud Saxton Nov. 9, 1885, Coalville, Summit Co., Utah (daughter of Solomon Saxton and Matilda Dexter), who was born April 30, 1868, Coalville, Summit Co., Utah. Their children: Matilda E. b. Aug. 4, 1886; Daisy M. b. Jan. 7, 1888, m. Vern Metcalf; William J. b. July 8, 1892; Gladys S. b. April 20, 1894. Family home, Salt Lake City.

MUNK, HANS JORGEN (son of Jens Sigfred Munk and Annie Jorgensen of Bornholm, Denmark, married June 19, 1845). Born Aug. 17, 1831. Came to Utah Sept. 20, 1856, Knud Peterson company.
Married Petri Nellie Larson (daughter of Anders and Margritte Larson, former a pioneer 1855, Captain Hoggen company). She was born June 13, 1828. Their children: Andrew b. Feb. 15, 1858, m. Mary C. Jorgensen; Malvena b. March 8, 1860, m. Jacob Jorgensen. Family home Logan, Utah.
Married Sene Larson May 30, 1863, Salt Lake City (daughter of Magnus Larson and Mary Hanson, pioneers Oct. 1, 1862, Joseph Horne company). She was born Nov. 20, 1847, Sjaeland, Denmark. Their children: Emma b. March 25, 1868, m. Charles Wilkes; Rose b. Nov. 3, 1871, m. Wilber F. Cranney; Lottie M. b. Oct. 14, 1874, m. Joseph Carlson; Joseph Segfred b. Feb. 6, 1878; Albert Jacob b. Sept. 17, 1880; Elizabeth C. b. March 29, 1883, m. Edward Justus; Oliver Magnus b. Aug. 11, 1885. Family home Logan, Utah.
Married Kirsten Sorensen June 13, 1865, Salt Lake City (daughter of Jens Sorensen who came to Utah Sept. 15, 1864, William Preston company, and Nellie Sorensen). She was born June 21, 1844, Denmark. Their children: Eliza b. Jan. 11, 1866, m. Noah Williams; Alma b. Oct. 2, 1870, m. Ester Williams; Amanda b. May 19, 1877, m. Fred Smith; Aaron b. May 19, 1873, m. Sadie Bird; Sophia b. Feb. 9, 1880, m. T. A. Tarhenson. Family home Logan, Utah.
High priest; member Nauvoo legion. Took part in Echo Canyon campaign. One of the first school trustees of Logan, Utah. Pioneer of Logan 1860.

MUNSON, HANS (son of Peter Munson and Kirsten Mixkelsen of Sjaelland, Denmark). Born March 6, 1803, at Laaland, Denmark. Came to Utah in 1854.
Married Martha Jensen in Laaland (daughter of Hans Jensen and Anne Hansen Jensen of Laaland). Born Dec. 12, 1804. Their children: John Munson b. Jan. 7, 1836, m. Mary Christina Christensen; Yens Munson b. 1839, m. Anne Sophia Hansen.

MUNSON, JOHN (son of Hans Munson and Martha Jensen). Born Jan. 7, 1836, Laaland, Denmark.
Married Mary Christina Christensen Feb. 22, 1864, Salt Lake City (daughter of James Christensen and Maria Andersen), who was born Oct. 28, 1844. Their children: John Henry b. April 9, 1865, m. Mary Emma Crystal; Charles b. Aug. 23, 1867; Lorenzo b. June 5, 1874, m. Margarett Jane Yates.

MUNSON, JOHN HENRY (son of John Munson and Mary Christina Christensen). Born April 9, 1864, Hyrum, Utah.
Married Mary Emma Crystal Dec. 28, 1910, Salt Lake City (daughter of James Crystal and Lera Jane Barret), who was born April 19, 1883; came to Utah in 1853.

MURDOCK, DANIEL HALL (son of Levi Murdock and Elizabeth Campbell). Born Nov. 10, 1839, Warren county, Ind. Came to Utah 1850, Captain Bennett company.
Married Mary Murdock Feb. 16, 1864, and five sons and five daughters were born.
Settled at Mound Fort, near Ogden, where he assisted in developing the country. Took part in Echo Canyon campaign, served under Gen. C. W. West, and rose to first lieutenant under Charles C. Middleton. Moved to Fountain Green in 1894, to Provo in 1897, and to Lovell, Big Horn county, Wyo. In 1902, at which places he has done much for the upbuilding of the community. Hauled rock for Salt Lake temple and worked on the Ogden tabernacle. Hauled and planted the shade trees in Ogden. Farmer and chair-maker. Died Feb. 16, 1864.

MURDOCK, JOHN (son of John Murdock of Delaware county, N. Y., and Eleanor Riggs of New York, N. Y.). Born July 15, 1792, Kortright, Delaware county, N. Y. Pioneers Sept. 24, 1847, Captain Wallace company.
Married Julia Clapp. Their children: Orrice C., m. Margret Molen 1850; John R., m. Almira H. Lott 1849. Family home Lehi, Utah.
Married Electa Allen (daughter of Gideon Allen and Rachell Hand, pioneers 1848). She was born Dec. 5, 1806, Litchfield, Conn. Only child: Gideon A. Murdock, m. Lucinda B. Howd March 1, 1866.
Married Sarah Zufelt. Their children: George (adopted); Brigham.
First bishop of 14th ward, Salt Lake City. First missionary to Australia in 1851; patriarch. Member of the first legislature in Utah 1849. Died Dec. 23, 1871, Beaver, Utah.

MURDOCK, GIDEON A. (son of John Murdock and Electa Allen). Born Aug. 1, 1840, Lima, Ill.
Married Lucinda E. Howd March 1, 1866, Beaver City (daughter of Simeon F. Howd, pioneer Brigham Young company and Lucinda Morgan pioneer 1847). She was born June 30, 1850, Salt Lake City. Their children: Electa b. May 12, 1870, m. Francis M. Dirrity; Lucinda E. b. Oct. 13, 1872, m. Myron O. Cooley; Rosella M. b. July 19, 1876, m. James W. Eyre; Almira H. b. March 2, 1879, m. John McKnight; Simeon b. May 8, 1883, m. Ella Dotson; Orrin b. Aug. 12, 1885, m. Cassie Myers; Lucy b. July 12, 1889, m. Cyrus Osborn; Edmond H. b. Aug. 24, 1891. Family home Minersville, Utah.
Bishop of Joseph, Sevier Co., Utah 1877-93. Deputy sheriff of Beaver county 1868-75. Adjutant of cavalry; lieutenant of cavalry during the Black Hawk war.

MURDOCK, JOSEPH STACY (son of Joseph Murdock and Sally Bonny Stacy of Hamilton, Madison county, N. Y.). Born June 26, 1822, Hamilton, N. Y. Came to Utah Sept. 1847.
Married Eunice Sweet June 26, 1842, at Albany, N. Y. (daughter of William and Hanna Sweet of Augusta, N. Y.) She was born Oct. 27, 1818. Family home, Salt Lake City.
Married Eliza Clark June 2, 1852, Salt Lake City (daughter of Thomas and Carlotte Clark of Grantsville, pioneers 1850, Orson Pratt company). She was born May 17, 1830. Their children: Sarah Ann, m. Robert Lindsay; John Heber, m. Mary Gallagher; m. Emily A. Bond; Joseph Thomas, m. Margaret Duke; Rocksina, m. Isaac Nathaniel Brown; Charlotte, m. William Wright; George Calvin, m. Louisa Bagley; Ester Melissa, m. George Lindsay.
Married Jane Sharp June 18, 1854, Salt Lake City (daughter of Nathaniel and Cecilia Sharp of Clackmannan, Scotland, pioneers 1850). She was born April 13, 1836. Their children: David N. Murdock, m. Christine Watson; William Henry, m. Melissa Baum; Cecilia, d. child: Stanley Gibson, m. Annetta Solon; Margaret Ellen, m. George F. Murray; Sarah Jane, m. Owen Hilton; Royal Stacy, m. Margaret Molton; m. Nellie Duncan. Family home Heber, Utah.
Married Elizabeth Hunter June 11, 1854, Salt Lake City (daughter of Robert and Agnes Hunter of Clackmannan,

PIONEERS AND PROMINENT MEN OF UTAH 1051

Scotland). She was born April 17, 1839. Their children: Johnathan R., m. Hulda Mary Elm; Alvy M., m. Josephine Nichol; Parley A., m. Lucy R. Hunley; James S., m. Dora Nichol; Alphonso B., m. Phoebe Lee; Annie E., m. Leonard Coleman; Nelson, m. Levina Averette; Clara, m. Alfred Richeus; Joseph G. and Erastus, both died young; Andrew, m. Jane Horner. Family home Heber City, Utah.
Married Pernette (Piede Indian) June 28, 1859, Salt Lake City. She was born 1842. Their children: Benjamin, d. infant; Betsy, m. Thomas Blackley; Almy, d. June 1911; Edward T., m. Jenta Murdock; Franklin Judson, m. Stella McNaughton.
Missionary to Carson valley and to the Muddy in Nevada; bishop in Wasatch stake 1861. Member of legislature. Veteran Indian war. Died Feb. 4, 1899, Heber City.

MURDOCK, JOHN HEBER (son of Joseph Stacy Murdock and Eliza Clark). Born April 28, 1854, Old Church Pasture, four miles north of Salt Lake City.
Married Mary Elvira Gallagher Dec. 15, 1873, Salt Lake City (daughter of John Gallagher and Amelia Brittingham of St. Louis, Mo., pioneers 1863). She was born Feb. 22, 1852. Their children: John Gallagher b. Aug. 14, 1874, d. Feb. 22, 1880; Amelia Brittingham b. Dec. 26, 1875, m. William Witt; Eunice Sweet b. Dec. 11, 1877, m. Orson Thomas Hicken; Eliza b. Nov. 13, 1879, m. Archibald Sellers; Mary Elvira b. Jan. 8, 1882, d. Oct. 10, 1882; Pearl b. May 23, 1884, m. George Buckley; Joseph Stacy b. April 24, 1886, m. Zina Hill; Sarah Esther b. Jan. 31, 1888; Heber b. Dec. 13, 1889, m. Effie Morton. Family resided at St. Johns, Ariz., 1884-90, and since at Heber City, Utah.
Married Emily Ann Bond Dec. 4, 1895, Salt Lake City (daughter of Stephen Bond and Sarah Clark of Road, Somersetshire, Eng., pioneers 1857). She was born Oct. 30, 1873. Their children: Marella Irene b. Sept. 30, 1896; Leah b. June 26, 1898; Paul Bond b. Feb. 28, 1900; Thomas Calvin b. Jan. 7, 1902; Ellen b. March 7, 1907; Edith May b. May 28, 1909.
High priest; missionary to Arizona 1884-90, and to Virginia 1907; high counselor of Wasatch stake. President of St. Johns Irrigation Co. and Wasatch Irrigation Co., 1912. Farmer.

MURDOCK, JOSEPH THOMAS (son of Joseph Stacy Murdock and Eliza Clark). Born Dec. 15, 1855, near Bingham, Utah.
Married Margaret Sedenia Duke Feb. 14, 1875, Salt Lake City (daughter of John Duke and Mary Jones of Heber City, Utah; came to Utah Sept. 15, 1850, James Pace company). She was born Oct. 18, 1858. Their children: Joseph Thomas b. Jan. 8, 1876, died; Margaret Sedenia b. March 20, 1877, died; John Heber b. Oct. 1, 1880, m. Tessie Maria Thacker; Mary Alvina b. Nov. 20, 1882, m. William Jedediah Casper; Eliza Rocksina b. Dec. 12, 1884, m. William Lloyd; Claude b. Feb. 12, 1887; Carrie b. May 30, 1889, m. Frank Webster; Lawrence Lee b. March 20, 1892; Sylva b. June 1, 1895. Family home Charleston, Utah.
Member elders quorum; missionary to St. Johns, Ariz., 1884. Member Charleston town board 1908-12. Vice-president and director of Pioneer Irrigation company and was associated with Charleston Irrigation & Canal company. Settled at Heber City, Utah 1859. Indian war veteran. Has resided in Provo valley since 1862. Farmer and ranchman.

MURDOCK, NYMPHUS CORIDON (son of Joseph Murdock, died at Nauvoo, Ill., 1844, and Sally Stacy, died at Salt Lake City, both from Hamilton, Madison county, N. Y.). Born May 12, 1833, Hamilton, Madison county, N. Y. Came to Utah Sept. 22, 1847, Ira Eldridge company.
Married Sarah Malissa Barney Oct. 21, 1856, Salt Lake City (daughter of Royal Barney and Sarah Bowen Estabrook of Amherst, Ohio, came to Utah 1852, Samuel Wooley company). She was born March 31, 1834, died May 21, 1911. Their children: Nymphus Coridon, Sarah Malissa, both died; Joseph Royal; Betsey Emeline, died. Family home, Salt Lake City.
Married Esther Mariah Davis Nov. 12, 1857, Salt Lake City (daughter of Franklin Judson Davis and Anna Richmond of Salt Lake City, pioneers 1851). She was born 1838, died Nov. 12, 1909. Their children: Franklin Judson, died; Stanley b. May 27, 1865; Eunice Louisa b. May 27, 1865, m. William C. Hanks; Alphonso, died; Alva Nymphas, m. Margarett Watson; Ella b. Feb. 22, 1871, m. Harry Watson; Frederick, died; Anna; Melissa, died. Family resided Salt Lake City, Charleston and Heber City, Utah.
Married Elizabeth Chadwick Green, a former wife of Alphonso Green, Oct. 2, 1912 (daughter of John Chadwick and Elizabeth Tomlinson), who was born July 27, 1842, Liverpool, Eng.
Member 10th quorum seventy; missionary to eastern states 1867-68; deacon; elder; first bishop Charleston ward, Wasatch Co., Utah, 1877-1900; patriarch. Representative to constitutional convention to form state of Deseret; postmaster; second sheriff of Wasatch county; school trustee many years. Farmer; merchant; stockraiser and dairyman. Brought the first sheep to Utah; brought the first flaxseed and made the first linen thread made in Utah.

MURDOCK, JOSEPH ROYAL (son of Nymphus Coridon Murdock and Sarah Malissa Barney). Born Aug. 11, 1858, Salt Lake City.
Married Margaret Wright Nov. 28, 1878, Salt Lake City (daughter of William Wright and Jamima Dands of Liverpool, Eng., pioneers 1858). She was born Aug. 11, 1860

Their children: Mima Malissa b. Nov. 26, 1879, m. David A. Broadbent; Maggie Josephine b. Oct. 6, 1883, m. Sylvester Broadbent; Royal Joseph b. April 19, 1885, m. Zina Armandella Chipman; Nymphus Warren b. Aug. 17, 1887, m. Emma Hicken; Sarah Emeline b. April 14, 1889, m. Leonard C. Henroid May 7, 1913; Emer Wright b. Sept. 22, 1891, m. Tarza Henry; Chloe b. April 24, 1893; Cora b. Jan. 13, 1895; Ira Barney b. July 8, 1859, died June 6, 1904; Nellie b. Dec. 13, 1902; Erma b. July 5, 1904. Family home Heber City, Utah.
President Wasatch stake; counselor to Bishop Murdock, Charleston ward; president of Charleston Y. M. M. I. A. and superintendent Sunday school. Member of the constitutional convention 1895; representative to legislature 1896; member of state senate; commissioner Wasatch county six years; justice of the peace Charleston ward. Banker; merchant; farmer and rancher.

MURPHY, EMMANUEL MASTERS (son of Mark Murphy, born March 8, 1763, and Holly Duke, born Feb. 27, 1789,— married March 19, 1786). He was born Sept. 15, 1809, Union county, S. C. Came to Utah Aug. 30, 1860, Jesse E. Murphy oxteam company.
Married Nancy Judd Easters April 5, 1831 (daughter of Robert Easters and Celia Hyatt), who was born July 30, 1813, and came to Utah with husband. Their children: Jesse Easters b. Jan. 27, 1832, m. Grace Broadbent April 28, 1857; Holly Ann b. March 30, 1834, m. Martin Baxter May 1, 1855; Mark b. July 6, 1837, m. Harriet Kemp Dec. 24, 1860; Louisa Jane b. June 3, 1840, m. William Allman Nov. 1858; William Columbus b. April 1, 1842, m. Elizabeth Bean June 27, 1863; Martha Frances b. Dec. 11, 1843; Hyrum b. March 3, 1846, m. Martha Sarah Ann Murphy Nov. 1, 1869; Thomas Gaden b. June 22, 1848, m. Matilda Slater Oct. 6, 1868; Charles b. May 15, 1851; Emmanuel Bird b. Oct. 14, 1854, m. Eliza Lambert Oct. 16, 1878.
Married Sarah Elizabeth Alexander May 12, 1861, Salt Lake City. She was born June 14, 1845, Hancock county, Ill. Their children: Nancy Merzy b. May 17, 1862; Randolph b. Nov. 12, 1864; Joseph b. Oct. 25, 1866; Masters Alexander b. Sept. 22, 1868; Burilda b. Aug. 1, 1870; Clara b. Aug. 30, 1871.
Married Margret Denning April 1864. No children.
Married Elizabeth Irving August, 1864. Their children: Brigham Young b. Jan. 28, 1867; Robert E. Irving b. Oct. 5, 1870.
High councilor. Farmer.

MURPHY, WILLIAM COLUMBUS (son of Emmanuel M. Murphy and Nancy Judd Easters). Born April 1, 1842, Fayette county, Ga. Came to Utah 1860, Jesse Murphy company.
Married Mary Elizabeth Bean June 27, 1863, Salt Lake City (daughter of Joseph Bean and Sarah Beanland of Bradford, Yorkshire, Eng., pioneers 1859). She was born Feb. 16, 1845. Their children: Sarah Nancy b. May 27, 1864, m. Richard Humphrey; William C. b. April 1, 1866, m. Malone Casto; George W. b. June 12, 1868, m. Amanda Clawson; Annie E. b. July 19, 1870, m. Absalom Williams; Joseph B. b. Sept. 16, 1872, d. Oct. 7, 1873; Martha A. b. May 28, 1874, m. George Fenn; Emma B. b. Aug. 12, 1876, m. John Gribble; Eliza Lorna b. May 30, 1878, d. Aug. 3, 1881; Emmanuel Mark b. Oct. 23, 1881, d. Aug. 29, 1883; Malissa b. March 24, 1884, m. E. W. Crane; Amy Florence b. June 18, 1886, m. Peter Oldemalder; Richard Heber b. Feb. 17, 1890, m. Lavenia Johnson. Family home Salina, Utah.
Member 23d quorum seventies; missionary to Arizona 1876-77; first counselor to Jens Jensen 1883-87; acting bishop. School trustee. Minuteman in Black Hawk Indian war. Carpenter. Died Feb. 17, 1895, Salina, Utah.

MURPHY, HYRUM (son of Emmanuel Masters Murphy and Nancy Judd Easters). Born March 3, 1846, Fayette county, Ga. Came to Utah with parents.
Married Martha Sarah Ann Murphy (daughter of James D. Murphy and Anna Elizabeth Hudson), who was born July 9, 1853. Their children: Ida B. Aug. 17, 1870; Hyrum Daniel b. Feb. 20, 1872, m. Alta Baxter Nov. 11, 1896; Alma b. March 9, 1874, m. Mary A. Curtis Nov. 24, 1897; Ernest b. May 19, 1876, m. Carrie Nielsen Oct. 11, 1899; Martha A. b. Aug. 28, 1878, m. Enos Curtis Feb. 3, 1897; Alice b. Nov. 17, 1890, m. Orrin Williams Oct. 1, 1897; Grace R. b. June 12, 1883, m. Asel Curtis Dec. 27, 1902; Nancy Lillian b. Nov. 5, 1885, m. Marion Cloward May 1, 1907; Eva b. March 20, 1888, m. Eugene Christensen Aug. 16, 1909; Samuel Bert b. Sept. 20, 1890; Archie b. March 9, 1893; Euphema b. Sept. 2, 1895. Family home Salina, Sevier Co., Utah.
Married Arminta Curtis (Deaton) Sept. 12, 1906, Manti, Utah (daughter of John W. Curtis and Matilda Miner, married Oct. 21, 1855, Salt Lake City). She was born June 19, 1871, Springville, Utah. Their children: Ruby Rozilla b. Dec. 20, 1907; Matilda Mae b. May 13, 1910. Family home, Salina.

MURPHY, JESSE JEANES (son of John Murphy and Miss Jeanes, both of Union District, S. C.). Born June 22, 1834, at Union, S. C. Came to Utah February, 1854, Jesse Murphy company.
Married Jerusha Elizabeth Pledger Dec. 8, 1842, at Jonesboro, N. C. (daughter of Joseph P. Pledger and Elizabeth Chambers, both of Georgia). She was born July 10, 1823. Their children: Francis; John Joseph; Elizabeth Ann; C. M.; Sarah D.; William B.; George W.; Emma. Family home Ogden, Utah.
Medical doctor. Died March 17, 1894, at Salt Lake City.

1052 PIONEERS AND PROMINENT MEN OF UTAH

MURPHY, WILLIAM B. (son of Jesse J. Murphy and Jerusha L. Pledger, both of Georgia). Born Jan. 14, 1849, at Jonesboro, N. C. Came to Utah September, 1868, William S. Seeley company.
Married Mary A. Cousins Sept. 30, 1877, at Ogden, Utah (daughter of Moses Cousins of Harnerford, Wales). She was born June 12, 1852. Their children: Elwood Ray b. Nov. 5, 1878; William E. b. April 17, 1881; George Ernest b. March 30, 1882; Josephine Alta b. April 23, 1885; Moses A. b. Oct. 14, 1890. Family home Ogden, Utah.
Justice of the peace at Promontory, Box Elder Co., Utah. Locomotive engineer.

MURRAY, JOHN (son of Andrew and Christena Murray of Edinburgh, Scotland). Came to Utah 1852, with ox-team.
Married Sarah Bates, in Michigan (daughter of John Bates and Sophia Anderson of Ireland). Their children: John, m. Mary Ann Marlow, m. Rachel Allred; Richard, m. Margaret Beck. m. Martha Hicks: Elizabeth, m. John Moyes: Jeremiah, m. Maria Nelson, m. Mary Ashby; Edwin, Joseph and Albert, d. infants; Robert, d. aged 8. Family home Spanish Fork, Utah.
Patriarch; missionary to The Muddy where he endured many hardships, and took an active part in developing that country. Veteran Black Hawk and Walker Indian wars. Farmer and wheelwright. Died at Spanish Fork, Utah.

MURRAY, JEREMIAH HATCH (son of John Murray and Sarah Bates). Born July 11, 1844, Lucerne township, Monroe county, Mich. Came to Utah with father.
Married Maria Nelson Feb. 6, 1863, Salt Lake Endowment house, who was born Jan. 3, 1846, in Denmark. Their children: Jeremiah, m. Christine Nelsen; Sarah Ellen, m. Peter Petersen; Andrew, m. Stella Stewart, m. Delia Yegersen; William Riley, m. Emma Hunting; Elizabeth, m. Hugh Snow; Rebecca, m. Albert Snow; Stephen Robert; Hyrum Smith, m. Ethel Dudley; Jonathan Moyes, m. Anna Hollingshead, m. Miss Stewart. Family home Spanish Fork, Utah.
Married Mary Ashby March 4, 1867, Salt Lake City (daughter of Samuel Ashby and Hannah Ward of Leicestershire, Eng.). She was born April 1, 1852. Their children: John Richard, m. Anna Hodson: Elizabeth Ellen, d. infant; Thomas Ward, m. Maryette Caldwell, m. Zinnie Nichols; Mary Lavina, m. Charles Merkley; Samuel Ashby, m. Jane Hansen; Margaret, m. Peter Harrison: Jeremiah Hatch, m. Pearl Karren, m. Rachel Merkley; Joseph Smith, m. Lilly Davis; William Ashby, m. Beatrice Howarth, m. Stella Woodruff. Family home Spanish Fork, Utah.
Road supervisor and school trustee at Roosevelt. Farmer. Died Sept. 5, 1909, Maeser ward, Vernal, Utah.

MURRAY, RICHARD (son of John Murray). Born Dec. 16, 1852, in Michigan.
Married Margaret Fannie Beck, Salt Lake City Endowment House (daughter of Joseph Ellison Beck), came to Spanish Fork, Utah, 1849). She was born Jan. 11, 1840. Their children: Joseph Ellison b. Nov. 17, 1862, m. Carrie Marie Jensen; John Richard b. June 1863; Alfred. died; George, m. Charlotte Searles; Margaret, m. Edward Wilkins: Annie, died age 2 years; Hannah, m. Ormal Wilkins; James, m. Att Ashby; Thomas; Edward, Bert, both died. Family home Vernal, Utah.
Married Martha Hicks Salt Lake City (daughter of George Hicks, Spanish Fork, Utah, came to Utah in early days). Their children: Caroline, m. William Bradshaw; Moroni, m. Hall; Martha Ann, m. Henry Glines; Jeremiah Bates, m. Caldwell; Alice Nora, m. Robert Carroll; Wilson; Richard; Scott, m. Bessie Sprouse; William; Nathalia, m. Barnhill. Lived at Spanish Fork, Utah.

MURRAY, JOSEPH ELLISON (son of Richard Murray and Margaret Beck). Born Nov. 17, 1862, at Spanish Fork, Utah.
Married Carrie Marie Jensen Feb. 1, 1891, Vernal, Utah, and temple, Salt Lake City (daughter of Hans Richard Jensen and Mary S. Christensen of Salt Lake City). She was born Nov. 6, 1871, Salt Lake City. Their children: Richard Ellison b. Nov. 13, 1892; Carrie b. Sept. 21, 1894; Vera Mary b. Sept. 24, 1896; Grant b. July 5, 1898; Florence b. Nov. 28, 1902; Grant b. July 8, 1908; Carl Jay b. March 29, 1911, d. May 4, 1911; Thomas Jefferson b. Oct. 31, 1912. Lived at Vernal and Duchesne, Utah.
Member of the quorum of elders. Road supervisor; deputy sheriff; constable Duchesne, Utah. Farmer and stockraiser.

MURRAY, ROBERT. Born 1816, Scotland. Came to Utah Sept. 5, 1861, Job Pingree company.
Married Jessie Archibald, who was born 1824 and came to Utah Sept. 5, 1861, Job Pingree company. Their children: James b. Feb. 25, 1844, m. Emma L. Steward; David b. Feb. 23, 1849, m. Christina Archibald; William b. March 23, 1853, m. Sarah Parker; John b. Aug. 25, 1857, m. Mary Garrett; Thomas b. July 11, 1861, m. Agnes Hendry; Christin b. June 21, 1865, m. William Jones; George H. b. Jan. 9, 1867, m. Swian Baity. Family home Wellsville, Utah.

MURRAY, DAVID (son of Robert Murray and Jessie Archibald). Born Feb. 22, 1849, in Scotland.
Married Christina Archibald Dec. 11, 1871, Salt Lake City (daughter of Thomas Archibald and Elizabeth Russell, former died in Scotland, latter a pioneer 1862, Horton D. Haight company). Family home Wellsville, Utah.
Married Martha Ann Baugh Jan. 31, 1876, Salt Lake City (daughter of John Baugh and Martha Suttiff—married Jan. 22, 1853, Salt Lake City, died Jan. 24, 1877). She was born Jan. 22, 1853, Salt Lake City, died Jan. 24, 1877.
Married Martha J. Woodward Dec. 26, 1878, Salt Lake City (daughter of Joseph Woodward and Margaret Barnes, came to Utah 1853). Their children: D. Jessie b. Aug. 28, 1880, and Margaret b. Aug. 1, 1882, d. infants; David W. b. Sept. 5, 1884, m. Jennie Bayter; Joseph W. b. Sept. 10, 1854, m. Dulia Bradshaw; Martha Ann b. May 1, 1892, d. infant; Milton W. b. March 5, 1895.
Bishop of Mt. Sterling ward, Utah; member of high council of Hyrum stake; missionary in Scotland 1889-91. City councilman of Sterling two terms; mayor 1900-02.

MUSSER, A. MILTON (son of Samuel Musser and Ann Barr of Donegal township, Lancaster county, Pa.). Born May 20, 1830, Lancaster county, Pa. Came to Utah 1851.
Married Annie Seegmiller Jan. 30, 1874, at Salt Lake City (daughter of Adam Seegmiller and Anna Eva Knectle of Stratford, Perth county, Ont., Canada, the latter came to Utah 1865). She was born Jan. 31, 1841. Their children: Anna Eva S., m. Elias M. James; Frederick S., m. Mattie Petersen; Maroni S.; William S., m. Mae Arnold; Roscoe S., m. Louisa Judd; Orson P. Seegmiller, d. aged 17. Family home, Salt Lake City.
President 57th quorum seventies; missionary to Hindustan, India, Asia, 1852-56; missionary to Pennsylvania 1877; high priest; historian. Fish commissioner. Capitalist. Died Sept. 24, 1909, Salt Lake City.

MUSTARD, DAVID (son of William Mustard and Ann Jemeson of Blairgowrie, Perthshire, Scotland). Born July 6, 1819, Blairgowrie, Perthshire, Scotland. Came to Utah Sept. 3, 1852, A. O. Smoot company.
Married Margaret Kay April 1841, Edinburgh, Scotland (daughter of William Kay and Margaret Moyes of Burntisland, Fifeshire, Scotland). She was born March 9, 1822. Only child: Margaret b. March 9, 1842, m. George Sant Oct. 3, 1858. Family resided at St. Gorge, Utah, and Treasureton, Idaho.
Missionary to Scotland, 1859-61 and 1872-75; high priest; sent to St. George in 1861, where he resided seven and a half years and worked on the temple. Took part in Echo Canyon trouble. Carpenter and furniture maker. Died March 15, 1895, Treasureton, Idaho.

MYERS, ALMA THORNTON. Came to Utah Sept. 20, 1864, Joseph Rawlins company.
Married Sarah Hellen Wyatt. Their child: Sarah Wyatt, m. William T. Lloyd.

MYERS, JACOB (son of Carl F. C. Myers and Anna Jensine Jacobsen of Denmark). Born May 21, 1847, Ledo, Copenhagen amt, Denmark. Came to Utah Oct. 1, 1862, Joseph Horne company.
Married Anna M. Johnsen Aug. 23, 1876, Sugar House ward, Salt Lake City (daughter of John Peter Johnsen and Anna Carlsen of Denmark, pioneers 1866). She was born May 15, 1852. Their children: Anna Laura; Hyrum P., m. Cenia Andersen; Louis J., m. Ida M. Garrett; Lionel L., m. Stella Holley; Annie J. C., m. Aaron Garside; Clara S. E., m. Claude Hibbard; Lillie M. H., m. Raymond Boyakin; Charles F., m. Annie May Butterfield; Florence E., m. Mark Stokes; Wilford J.; Nellie C.; Mannie M.; Urban G. Family home Riverton, Utah.
High priest. Railroader; canal constructor; merchant; freighter. Farmer.

MEYER, CHARLES P. Brother of Jacob Myers.

MYERS, WILLIAM (son of Benjamin Myers of Idle, near Bradford, Yorkshire, Eng.). Born Aug. 22, 1812, Idle, Eng. Came to Utah 1866.
Married Martha Ogden 1834, at Idle, Eng. (daughter of William Ogden and Sarah Heaton of Idle, Eng). She was born March 12, 1813. Their children: Joseph, m. Eliza Bentley; m. Sarah Eyre: Sarah; Betty; Ezra; Sophia; Melvina; Paulina; Moroni; Emily.
High priest teacher and elder. Worked as stone cutter on Salt Lake and St. George temples. Died Jan. 9, 1891, Minersville, Utah.

MYERS, JOSEPH (son of William Myers and Martha Ogden). Born May 31, 1835, Idle, Yorkshire, Eng. Came to Utah Oct. 7, 1859. A. R. Wright company.
Married Eliza Bentley July 1855 (daughter of Nathan and Grace Bentley), who was born Aug. 26, 1835, and came to Utah with husband.
Married Sarah Eyre January, 1859 (daughter of James Eyre and Ann Naylor, former died on plains, en route to Utah, latter died at sea). She was born at Dowsby, Lincolnshire, Eng. Their children: John W. b. Jan. 25, 1860, m. Mary McKnight Nov. 11, 1884; Sarah Eliza b. Feb. 3, 1862, m. R. W. Dotson; Joseph E. b. Sept. 30, 1864, m. Lillie Corbridge; Moroni b. Dec. 4, 1866, m. Hattie Brandshaw; Martha b. Jan.

23, 1869, m. John Fotheringham; George L. b. July 25, 1871; James Heber b. Sept. 19, 1873, m. Edith Roberts, Francette b. May 29, 1875; Erastus Edwin (step son) b. May 9, 1857. Family resided at Salt Lake City and Minersville, Utah. Seventy and high priest. Judge of election.

MYLER, JAMES (son of James Myler, born Nov. 19, 1794, West Moreland, N. Y., and Olive Maine, born May 16, 1796, New York). Born Feb. 3, 1822, Butler Co., Ohio. Came to Utah Sept. 22, 1849, William Miller's contingent of Mormon battalion (Co. C).
Married Julia A. Brownell Oct. 5, 1843, Buchanan, Mich. (daughter of Gideon Brownell and Betsy Wheeler, pioneers Sept. 22, 1849—married at Dayton, Ohio). She was born Feb. 12, 1826 came to Utah with husband. Their children: Oscar b. Dec. 27, 1844, m. Christine Jensen April 1866; Joseph E. b. Jan. 31, 1846, m. Emma Godfry 1872; Calvin b. 1848, d. 1856; James b. 1850, d. 1860; Julia A. b. July 25, 1852, m. Arthur Goody Nov. 29, 1869; John b. June 14, 1854, d. June 1868; Orin Maine b. Sept. 14, 1856, m. Elizabeth Stokes Nov. 8, 1874; Margaret L. b. May 2, 1858, m. Martin H. Hannon 1877; Charles C. b. June 1860, m. Isabell Morton Oct. 1879; Rosetta E. b. April 1862, m. James Archibald Nov. 1880; Frank b. Aug. 1864, d. Nov. 1875. Family home Logan, Utah.
Member 5th quorum, and later one of the seven presidents of 6th quorum seventies at Farmington, Utah; president teachers' quorum. Resided at Farmington ten years, and moved to Logan in 1859. Took part in Echo Canyon campaign. Pioneer to Sanke River, Idaho. Died May 21, 1894, Lewisville, Idaho.

MYLER, ORRIN MAINE (son of James Myler and Julia A. Brownell). Born Sept. 14, 1856, Farmington, Utah.
Married Elizabeth J. Stokes Nov. 8, 1874, Clarkston, Utah (daughter of Henry Stokes and Elizabeth Hale, pioneers 1862, Henry Miller company). She was born Feb. 5, 1857. Their children: Sarah E. b. Sept. 2, 1875, m. William W. Selek Nov. 23, 1892; Mary J. b. Nov. 22, 1877, m. Harry S. Robinson Dec. 15, 1904; Eliza O. b. April 22, 1880, m. William Iaby Nov. 18, 1898; Alice A. b. March 4, 1883, m. Harry Howard May 1899; Orrin M. b. Nov. 20, 1886, m. Mary Walker Nov. 17, 1908; Joseph C. b. Nov. 17, 1887; Lorenzo b. Aug. 2, 1890; Lester b. March 21, 1892, d. Jan. 3, 1894; John H. b. Nov. 23, 1895, d. Feb. 28, 1904; William b. Nov. 23, 1895, d. Nov. 23, 1895; James M. b. April 26, 1898, d. April 8, 1904; Eullalia b. Aug. 20, 1899. Family home Lewisville, Idaho.
High counselor in Rigby stake, Idaho; bishop of Lewisville, Idaho; first counselor to B. P. Jardine 21 years; superintendent Sunday school; president of deacons' quorum. Teacher.

MYRUP, LARS CHRISTEN N. (son of Niels Larsen Christen Myrup, of Glade, Thisted, Denmark, born March 25, 1812, Farerster, Thisted, Denmark, and Mette Maree Pedersen, born 1811, Glade—married 1835). Born March 26, 1845, Glade. Came to Utah April 6, 1866, Abner Lowry company.
Married Maren Christen April 22, 1866 (daughter of Christen Christensen and Karen Larestysen of Denmark, pioneers April 6, 1856, Abner Lowry company—married March 25, 1845 Denmark). She was born Feb. 14, 1849; came to Utah April 6, 1856, with Abner Lowry company. Their children: Mary b. March 22, 1868; Lars Christen b. March 1, 1870; Niels Christen b. March 29, 1872; Adolph M. b. Aug. 24, 1874; Karen Laurene b. June 4, 1877; Joseph Henry b. May 10, 1879; Sarahann b. Nov. 10, 1881; Manda May b. May 24, 1883.
Married Josephine Marie Jensen Jan. 17, 1876 (daughter of Swen Jensen and Marian Larsen of Denmark—married Nov. 1, 1862, Denmark; came to Utah July 21, 1871, with Peter Madson company). She was born at Hjorring, Denmark. Their children: Mattie Marie b. Oct. 8, 1877, m. A. E. Sorensen; Josephine b. Dec. 28, 1879, m. Chas. B. Carr; Minnie Gustave b. Aug. 7, 1882, m. Alma Dorius.
Married Mary Ann Jensen Sept. 5, 1877, Wisconsin (daughter of Hans Jensen and Anna Jenson). Their children: Mary Ann Ella Onora b. Nov. 18, 1878, m. W. C. Metcalf Nov. 18, 1897; Anna Maria b. Oct. 25, 1881, m. A. E. Dalton May 1, 1907; Lars L. b. April 30, 1884, m. Luella Anderson July 22, 1908; Rany May b. May 29, 1886, m. Earl M. Dack Feb. 20, 1907; Stella P. b. March 1, 1888, m. Newman Beck Jan. 18, 1913; Bertie U. b. June 25, 1890; Joseph Christen b. July 15, 1894; Leah T., Levi Z. (twins) b. May 12, 1897; Almena b. Sept. 21, 1900.
Counselor elders quorum; member of the seventies; member of the high council of the South Sanpete stake of Zion. President Grim Irrigation Co. Missionary to Denmark. Pioneer of Gunnison, Utah 1870.

McAFEE, JOHN SHARP. Came to Utah by oxteam.
Married Ann Lyons of Scotland, who came to Utah with husband. Their children: Samuel; Sarah; Ephraim; Moroni; Lizzie. Family home Charleston, Utah.
Seventies. Died at Lehi, Utah.

McAFEE, SAMUEL (son of John S. McAfee and Ann Lyons). Born Aug. 4, 1842, in Scotland. Came to Utah by oxteam.
Married Ann Campbell Baird Nov. 21, 1870, Salt Lake City (daughter of John and Elizabeth Baird of Scotland). Their children: John, m. Elizabeth Ann Clayton; Samuel, m. Henrietta Graves; James, m. Juliet Taylor; Elizabeth, m. Elmer Broadhead; Barbara Ann, m. Thomas Broadhead; Martha, m. William Price; Melissa, m. John Bell; William, m. Mary Sims; Sarah Agnes, m. John Anderson; Leona Florence. Family home Charleston, Utah.
Seventies. Farmer.

McAFEE, JOHN (son of Samuel McAfee and Ann Campbell Baird). Born Nov. 21, 1871, Charleston, Utah.
Married Elizabeth Ann Clayton Oct. 15, 1895, Morgan, Utah (daughter of John Clayton and Elizabeth Tonks, of Morgan). She was born July 31, 1875. Their children: Leslie Nadine b. June 30, 1896; Samuel Maurice b. April 5, 1898; Albert Clayton b. Jan. 10, 1900; John Willis b. Nov. 4, 1901; Louis Raymond b. Dec. 17, 1903; Earl Leroy b. July 28, 1905; Charles Lester b. Feb. 11, 1907, d. infant; Bessie May b. Nov. 4, 1908; Vera Elizabeth b. Sept. 17, 1910; Harold b. May 1, 1912. Family home Wallsburg, Utah.
Priest. Farmer and stockraiser.

McALLISTER, DUNCAN McNEIL (son of George McAllister). Born June 24, 1807, at Kirkintulloch, Scotland, and Christina McNeil, born May 9, 1815, at Glasgow, Scotland). Born April 18, 1842, at Glasgow. Came to Utah Oct. 22, 1862, via Denver with private contracting company.
Married Catherine Perkes Oct. 20, 1866 (daughter of Henry Perkes and Charlotte Lowe, pioneers 1861). She was born at Liverpool, Eng. Feb. 16, 1846, and died Jan. 24, 1907. Their children: Duncan William b. Nov. 25, 1867, m. Anna Hatch Dec. 3, 1902; George Stanley b. May 26, 1869, m. Jeanette Masser June 17, 1896; Catherine b. June 4, 1871, d. July 25, 1871; Katie b. Nov. 27, 1872; Henry Perkes b. Dec. 31, 1874, d. Aug. 12, 1875; Malcolm b. Feb. 23, 1877, m. Johanna Zitzman Dec. 18, 1907; Christina V. b. April 22, 1880, m. N. Lamont Wilson June 16, 1909. Family home, Salt Lake City.
Clerk of general conference of C. of J. C. of L. D. S., since Oct. 1906; business manager L. D. S. church office. Liverpool, 1887-89; employed in Salt Lake temple recorders' office from the beginning, 1893; ordained a seventy in 1870; president of third quorum 1898; secretary of manufacturing departments of Z. C. M. I. 1869-87; clerk of 17th ward 1896-1913. Mail clerk Salt Lake City postoffice 1865-69. Appointed battalion adjutant of Box Elder cavalry, of Nauvoo legion 1864. Charter member of Genealogical Society of Utah and a director. Wrote numerous articles for Deseret News, on health, hygiene, etc., 1885-87. Associated, until recent years, with musical and dramatic organizations.

McALLISTER, JOHN DANIEL THOMPSON (son of William James Frazier McAllister and Elizabeth Thompson of Lewes, Sussex county, Del., and later of Philadelphia, Pa.). Born Feb. 19, 1827, at Lewes. Came to Utah Oct. 6, 1851, Alfred Cardon company, secretary of a fifty.
Married Ellen Handley July 5, 1847, in Philadelphia, who came to Utah with husband. Their children: Moroni H., m. Marinda Brown; John D. H., m. Alfreda Fitzgeralds; Ellen Handley, m. Nephi Sheets; Daniel H., m. Rhoda Young, m. Susie Barnett; Mary H., m. Schuyler Gates. Family home, Salt Lake City.
Married Angeline Sophronia Goforth Jan. 11, 1857, Salt Lake City, Brigham Young officiating (daughter of Dr. William Goforth and Martha Nelson, former of St. Louis, Mo., where he died, latter of Bellview, Ill., came to Utah in 1848, bringing her daughter and son, William Goforth). She was born July 10, 1840. Their children: Angeline b. Oct. 9, 1858, m. Amos Gabbott; James Goforth b. Dec. 22, 1860, m. Emily Marinda Chase; Allister b. 1864, d. infant; Richard G. b. March 25, —; Eliza Thompson b. Oct. 26, 1869, m. William Henefer; William Wallace b. July 1872; Effie Dean b. Oct. 2, 1878, m. Edward Sprout; Josephine, d. aged 5. Family home, Salt Lake City.
He also married Cornelia Agatha Lenzi, Alvina MacLean and Julia Nielson.
He was president of 16th quorum of seventies; missionary to England 1853-56; president of Belfast conference; missionary in Scotland and Wales; in 1860 missionary to the States, presiding over all branches of the church east of the Rocky mountains; missionary to England and presided over Birmingham conference; for many years in charge of Salt Lake Endowment House; moved to St. George in 1876; set apart as president of the temple; set apart 1877 as president of St. George stake and did missionary work among the Indians in southern Utah; moved to Manti 1893 and was set apart as president of Manti temple; counselor to Bishop Elijah F. Sheets and acting bishop of the 8th ward, Salt Lake City. Raised a company of life guards 1857; served major of cavalry for Great Salt Lake military district during the Echo Canyon war. In 1862 brought a company of immigrants to Utah. January, 1863 the legislative assembly elected him territorial marshal, which office he held until late in the '70s; 1866-76 Salt Lake City marshal and chief of the fire department; January, 1869 and January 1870 sergeant-at-arms of the territorial legislature. Jan. 10, 1870, marshal of the day at the celebration of the driving of the last spike of the Utah Central railway when it reached Salt Lake City. Sept 3, 1872, as chief of the fire department, assisted in breaking and dedicating the ground for the first Salt Lake City water works in City Creek canyon. Brigadier general of the Utah militia. School teacher; built many dwellings in Salt Lake City and mills in the canyons; was associated with the eighth ward industrial society, 8th ward co-op. store, the parent Z. C. M. I. organization; in charge of the Brigham Young Woolen Factory; ex-

president of the Rio Virgin Manufacturing Co., operating woolen and cotton factories in southern Utah; owned the real estate where the O. S. L. depot and Salt Lake fire department No. 1 now stand, and much land below Tenth South and West Temple streets; prominent in dramatics and one of the actors in the opening of the Salt Lake theatre 1862; was noted for his patriotism, and as the leading soloist of the Mormon tabernacle choir, for many years at conference time sang the "Star Spangled Banner" and other patriotic songs. Died in St. George Jan. 18, 1910.

McALLISTER, MORONI H. (son of John Daniel Thompson McAllister and Ellen Handley). Born July 28, 1848, Philadelphia, Pa. Came to Utah with father.
Married Marinda Brown Oct. 12, 1873, Salt Lake City (daughter of Robert Brown and Mary Deardon of Salt Lake City). She was born April 13, 1852. Their children: Edith B., died; Constance B. m. Arthur E. Handley; Harold, m. Nettie Chamberlain (Nichols); Robert; Sadie, m. Harmon Weight; Mary, died.
High priest; member tabernacle choir 45 years. Agent Utah Central, U. P. and O. S. L. railroad companies for 29 years.

McALLISTER, JOHN DANIEL HANDLEY (son of John D. T. McAllister and Ellen Handley). Born Jan. 9, 1851, Kanesville, Iowa. Came to Utah with father.
Married Alfreda Fitzgerald Oct. 23, 1875 (daughter of Perry Fitzgerald and Ann Wilson of Draper, Utah, pioneers 1847). Their children: Perry; Ethel; John D.; Laura; Archibald; Ellen; Joseph F.; Gale F.; Leon F.
High priest; missionary 1875-79. Surveyor.

McALLISTER, JAMES GOFORTH (son of John Daniel Thompson McAllister and Angeline Sophronia Goforth). Born Dec. 22, 1860, Salt Lake City.
Married Emily Marinda Chase (McKee) Oct. 15, 1889, Salt Lake City (daughter of George Ogden Chase and Emily Marinda Hyde of Centerville, Utah, pioneers Sept. 20, 1847, Jedediah M. Grant company). She was born Dec. 12, 1856. Their children: Emily Chase b. July 12, 1890; James Goforth b. June 1, 1892.
Emily Marinda Chase married H. W. McKee Feb. 5, 1874, he died 1879. Two sons: Hugh Chase b. Aug. 15, 1875; Earl Young b. June 15, 1878, m. Nellie Douglas—their child: Clela b. Aug. 13, 1900.
Mr. McAllister was born between Third and Fourth South on the west side of State street, Salt Lake City, and has spent his entire life in Utah. He served a carpenter's apprenticeship and worked on the tabernacle; helped to build the pipes for that famous pipe-organ. In the early days of his boyhood, the principal necessaries of life were food and clothes for his mother's family, and he turned his time to any occupation that would produce these necessaries. He followed farming, teaming and carpenter contracting. As he grew older and the mines opened at Park City, he became actively engaged in teaming and freighting, having a contract to haul the machinery for the Marasac mill, which was one of the first mills built at Park City. He served an apprenticeship as a wagonmaker and blacksmith, which occupation he followed for several years. In 1886 engaged in the real estate business; during 1887-88 engaged in mining in Marysvale, Utah, going from there to Ophir and then to Bingham. Provision inspector under Mayor Bascom two years. Head salesman and assistant manager of the Studebaker Bros. Co., 1897-1906. In 1902 organized the McAllister Bros. Sheep Co. (John D. H. and James G. McAllister), which in 1911 was incorporated as the McAllister Land and Ice Stock Company, of which he is now the president. In 1907 associated with Frank Esshom in the beginning of the history of the "Pioneers and Prominent Men of Utah," being the first president and director of the company, and a director until the completion of the work. He and C. B. Stewart were the originators, promoters and the organizers of the Farmers and Stockgrowers Bank, which was incorporated Jan. 20, 1913, when he was elected director and member of the executive board, and as one of the members of the board, purchased the ground and arranged for the construction of their banking house at 123-125 South Main street. Director and chairman of the executive board of the Bird's Eye Marble Company and director and adviser in other manufacturing, mercantile and industrial companies. Member of the state board of equalization 1911-13. One of the committee to organize the first republican party in the state, and has remained constantly with the party ever since. Stockgrower; banker and ranchman.

McALLISTER, RICHARD WESLEY (son of William James Frizen and Eliza Elizabeth Bell of Philadelphia, Pa.). Born Oct. 15, 1825, Pottsville, Del. Came to Utah Sept. 13, 1861, Joseph Horne company.
Married Elizabeth Elenor Bell in Philadelphia (daughter of James Bell of Delaware). Their children: William James Frizen; Joseph W.; Susanna Bell; Mary; Lillie; John; James; Rich.
Married Emma Wallen.
High priest. Deputy marshal in territorial days for a number of years. Died in 1905.

McALLISTER, WILLIAM JAMES FRIZEN (son of Richard Wesley McAllister and Elizabeth Elenor Bell). Born Aug. 15, 1845, Pottsville, Del. Came to Utah Sept. 25, 1861, Milo Andrus company.
Married Elenor Jackson Adams Oct. 3, 1868 (daughter of Samuel Lorenzo Adams and Emma Jackson, married in England). She was born Aug. 3, 1853, Sugar House, Salt Lake Co., Utah. Their children: William J. F., Jr. b. Nov. 17, 1870, m. Minnett Adams Jan. 6, 1890; Emma Elizabeth b. Jan. 13, 1872, m. John Q. Adams Jan. 4, 1888; Richard Samuel b. Oct. 27, 1874, m. Harriet L. Brown Nov. 19, 1895, m. Ida Young Jan. 10, 1903; Alma Leo b. June 3, 1877, m. Mary Elizabeth Lewis March 1, 1898, m. Luella Maud Dec. 31, 1908; Walter Adams b. May 23, 1880, m. Rachel Albe; John b. Aug. 1889, died; Arthur Dee b. Oct. 29, 1884, m. D. Hatch Oct. 1909; Melita Bell b. Oct. 7, 1887; Dellor Ray b. May 6, 1889.
Married Angeline Brown at St. George, Utah (daughter of Joseph Guinzey Brown and Harriet Musa Young, married at Salt Lake City). She was born Jan. 6, 1861, Draper, Utah. Their children: Granam Brown b. March 4, 1880, m. Aseneth Chamberlin 1904; Nellie b. Dec. 13, 1881, m. Edgar L. Clark 1906; Clara b. April 5, 1883; Symour Young b. May 17, 1887; Pursus b. Sept. 17, 1894; Wesley Theo b. Jan. 3, 1904. Families resided at Kanab, Utah.
Deputy marshal (territorial) for seven years. Served in court in Beaver and St. George. Indian war veteran. Moved to Kanab from St. George in 1876. Served as chorister Kanab ward for 30 years.

McARTHUR, WASHINGTON PERRY (son of Duncan McArthur and Susan McKein of Mt. Pleasant, Utah). Born Dec. 24, 1824, in Pennsylvania. Came to Utah in 1850.
Married Urana Gregg Oct. 25, 1846 (daughter of John Gregg and Elizabeth Roberts), who was born Feb. 13, 1826. Their children: Almeda Jennet, m. John Carter; Emma Lucretia; Duncan, m. Lucina Whalin; Perry Melvin, m. Carrie Jorgensen; Herbert Eldrege; Urana Loreta; William Henry, m. Zetta Hutchison; Charles; Silas Gregg, m. Christena Jensen; Annie, m. Erastus Frandsen; Agnes. Family home Mt. Pleasant, Utah.
High priest; bishop; counselor to W. S. Seely. City councilman. Farmer and doctor. Died at Mt. Pleasant.

McBRIDE, HARLUM (son of James McBride and Betsy Mead of Chautauqua county, N. Y.). Born Dec. 8, 1824, in New York. Came to Utah in 1849.
Married Jensine Gyldenlove Dec. 25, 1864, Hyrum, Utah (daughter of Andrew Gyldenlove and Johannah Jocbemsen of Randers, Denmark). She was born March 21, 1832. Their children: Betsy Sophia, m. Hans G. Johnsen; Harlum James, d. Jan. 20, 1894; Helen Maria, m. Andrew B. Nielsen. Family home, Hyrum.
High priest. Member Mormon battalion. City marshal several years. Farmer. Died Nov. 21, 1901.

McBRIDE, HEDER R. (son of Robert McBride of Rothesay, Scotland, born Nov. 16, 1803, and Margret Howard, born Dec. 21, 1814, at Churchtown, Lancashire, Eng.—married Nov. 25, 1833). He was born ——— 13, 1843, at Churchtown. Came to Utah Nov. 30, 1856, Martin and Taylor handcart company.
Married Elizabeth Ann Burns July 28, 1868 (daughter of Enoch Burns and Elizabeth Jane McGoth Pierce, married Jan. 11, 1842, Hancock county, Ill.). She was born Feb. 17, 1851. Their children: Elizabeth Jane b. April 30, 1869, m. Alexander Rirle Jan. 5, 1887; Margarett R. b. March 31, 1871, m. Joseph Bachmand Dec. 8, 1390; Anna Bethaina b. Nov. 24, 1873, m. Frank Biard Dec. 30, 1894; Heber R. b. Aug. 28, 1875; Enoch F. b. July 30, 1877; Orlando b. Jan. 24, 1880, m. Mary Wangsgaard Oct. 8, 1902; Thirza b. April 25, 1882, m. Leroy Fackrell April 24, 1901; Clarence Burns b. July 6, 1884, m. Helen Bennett Dec. 23, 1908; Parley b. June 26, 1886, m. Jeneva Day Nov. 21, 1909; Amber b. Dec. 26, 1888, m. Nels C. Petersen Dec. 9, 1908; Edna b. Jan. 15, 1891, m. George Rasmussen Jan. 13, 1909.
Married Elizabeth B. Gould Nov. 24, 1884, Logan, Utah (daughter of Robert Gould and Anna Simpson), who was born May 27, 1857, in New York. Their children: Elizabeth Elnora (adopted) b. March 20, 1879, m. Christen D. Peterson; Mary Evelee b. July 6, 1887, m. J. Norman Fackrell; Delecta b. June 12, 1895; Ira Robert b. Sept. 10, 1896; Detta Olive b. Nov. 7, 1898; Omer b. Feb. 7, 1901. Family home Eden, Utah.
Assisted in bringing immigrants to Utah in 1865. Veteran Indian war. President 75th quorum seventies; high priest; bishop's counselor.

McBRIDE, JAMES (son of Thomas McBride and Catherine John of Iowa). Born May 15, 1818, in Ohio. Came to Utah in October, 1850.
Married Olive M. Cheney (daughter of Aaron Cheney and Mahetable Wells, pioneers 1850). She was born May 16, 1817. Only child: Amos O., m. Mary E. Jenson.
High priest. Farmer. Died Jan. 6, 1881, Grantsville, Utah.

McBRIDE, AMOS O. (son of James McBride and Olive M. Cheney). Born Jan. 3, 1850, Appanoose Co., Iowa. Came to Utah with parents.
Married Mary E. Jenson May 22, 1871, Salt Lake City (daughter of Truits and Ingaber Jenson of Tooele, Utah).

She was born Feb. 14, 1854. Their children: Olive M.; James T.; Amos O., Jr.; Alvin H.; Andrew C.; Mary L.; Ellen E.; Edith L.; Leland L. Family home Grantsville, Utah.
High priest. Farmer and fruit raiser.

McCARREL, JESSE HUGHES (son of Jesse McCarrel and Mary Hughes). Born March 26, 1825, in Louisiana. Came to Utah 1852, oxteam company.
Married Amanda Wood in 1848 (daughter of David and Catherine Wood of Canada, pioneers 1852). She was born Sept. 2, 1829. Their children: Jesse David b. Feb. 7, 1849, m. Jane Cliff; Sidney Osborn b. Sept. 22, 1851, m. Susan Sulzer; Mary Catherine b. Sept. 25, 1853, m. Daniel Evans; Joseph Peter b. May 5, 1855, m. Elizabeth Sulzer; Amanda, m. Harmon Knoble; Charles Oscar, m. Margaret Gill; Agnes, m. John D. Mecham; William Mark, died; Eliza, m. Lafayette Woods; George Hughes.

McCARREL, SIDNEY OSBORN (son of Jesse Hughes McCarrel and Amanda Wood). Born Sept. 22, 1851, at Council Bluffs, Iowa. Came to Utah 1852, the oxteam company.
Married Susan Sulzer Jan. 24, 1878, Midway, Wasatch Co., Utah (daughter of Casper Sulzer and Catherine Stuedler of Pike Pond, Sullivan county, N. Y., the former of Midway, Utah, the latter of Esenbogan, Switzerland, pioneers 1861, Joseph Young company). She was born Nov. 24, 1853. Their children: Auriela b. April 24, 1879, m. Alfred Simpson; Amanda Catherine b. Jan. 12, 1881, died; Mary Elizabeth b. Dec. 31, 1881, m. Virden Thompson; Frank b. April 14, 1884, m. Carrie Holmes; Sidney Osborn b. June 30, 1886, m. Luetta Cook; Harriet b. March 26, 1890, m. David McHenry Keays; Vernon Monroe b. May 11, 1893.
Elder; president of deacon quorum. Located at American Fork, Utah, 1852; moved to Provo; then to Midway, Wasatch Co., Utah, and later to Ashley Fork (Vernal), Uinta Co., Utah, 1881.

McCARREY, WILLIAM (son of James McCarrey, born Sept. 21, 1799, and Catherine Crane, born July 5, 1793, Kirk Melew, Isle of Man—married in 1824, Kirk Melew). He was born Feb. 12, 1832, Peel, Isle of Man. Came to Utah Sept. 3, 1853.
Married Hannah Melissa Hoopes July 24, 1864 (daughter of Warner Hoopes and Priscilla Gifford, pioneers Aug. 2, 1859, Harlo Redfield company—married 1840, Kirtland, Ohio). She was born April 30, 1845. Their children: William, Jr., b. June 26, 1865; Catherine Priscilla b. March 6, 1867, m. Thomas Smith Oct. 22, 1890; Rebecca Jane b. June 27, 1869; James Lewis b. May 3, 1872, m. Alice Maiben Squires Sept. 6, 1899; Hannah Elizabeth Adelaid b. Aug. 21, 1874, m. George Ellis Daly June 26, 1901; John b. April 29, 1877, m. Gustina Roggencamp Dec. 21, 1904; Olive Ann b. Oct. 20, 1879, m. Arthur J. Mendenhall Sept. 7, 1904; Melissa May b. May 13, 1882. Family home Richmond, Utah.
Ordained seventy 1861. Pioneer of Richmond March 1860. Built first home at Lewiston, Utah, in August, 1871. Director of Richmond Co-op. 1875-1900. Minuteman 1861-62; militiaman Johnson army trouble.

McCARREY, JAMES LEWIS (son of William McCarrey and Hannah Melissa Hoopes). Born May 3, 1872, Richmond, Utah.
Married Alice Maiben Squires (daughter of John Fell Squires and Alice Penn Maiben, pioneers Sept. 30, 1853, Jacob Gates company). She was born Oct. 13, 1876, Logan, Utah. Their children: Alice Squires b. July 20, 1900; Florence Squires b. Feb. 1, 1902; James Lewis b. Jan. 30, 1906; Lucile Squires b. Feb. 7, 1908; Elva Squires b. May 24, 1910. Family home Richmond, Utah.
Missionary to northern states, returning 1899. Graduate Brigham Young College in June 1896. School teacher Richmond, Utah, Sept. 1899-June 1902; principal 1903-04; superintendent of schools Cache Co., Utah, Jan. 1, 1895-July 1909. Ordained high priest Jan. 5, 1908; superintendent Benson stake Sunday schools Jan. 5, 1908; superintendent of Richmond Sunday school May 1900 to Feb. 10, 1907. Director of Richmond Co-op.

McCARTY, NELSON. Born in 1812 in Canada. Came to Utah in September 1849, contingent Mormon battalion, Co. B, Jesse B. Martin captain.
Married Louisa Payne in 1833 in Canada and she died at Nauvoo, Ill., in 1842. Their children: Charlotte b. Feb. 22, 1834, m. Thomas Browning June 1, 1854; Susan Catherine b. 1836; Susan Maria b. 1837, d. 1844; Lemington b. Oct. 10, 1842, m. Hannah Williams, d. Feb. 21, 1903.
Married Mary Jane Morris in 1843, Nauvoo, Ill. (daughter of Jacob Morris, pioneer, died in 1856 at Ogden). She was born April 11, 1818, Kirtland, Ohio, died Dec. 4, 1893, Ogden. Their children: Sarah b. Oct. 11, 1844, m. Daniel Snell Oct. 30, 1870; Delilah b. April 4, 1846, m. Thomas Browning, m. Edward Keys 1864; Nelson b. Oct. 28, 1849, m. Mary Ann Outhouse.
October 18, 1847, he, with Co. D, Mormon battalion, went to winter quarters, arriving Dec. 18, 1847. In May 1849 he left with his family in Captain Horne's company for Utah. Family arrived at Salt Lake City in September 1849.

McCARTY, NELSON, JR. (son of Nelson McCarty and Mary Jane Morris). Born Oct. 28, 1849, Salt Lake City, died April 5, 1912, Ogden, Utah.
Married Mary Ann Danford Nov. 29, 1869, Salt Lake City (daughter of Samuel Danford, died 1856, Worcestershire,

PIONEERS AND PROMINENT MEN OF UTAH 1055

Eng., and Charlotte Farron, born Feb. 7, 1814, Worcestershire, died Nov. 12, 1905, Ogden Utah). She was born May 11, 1851, in Worcestershire. Left Liverpool March 28, 1857, ship George Washington. Came to Utah with mother Sept. 12, 1857, Jesse B. Martin company. Their children: Charlotte Jane b. Sept. 23, 1870, m. Robert Fields June 21, 1890; William N. b. Feb. 12, 1872, m. Fannie Foulke; Delilah b. Oct. 21, 1874, m. George Wahlen; m. Charles L. Mitchell June 11, 1909; John b. May 22, 1878, m. Belle Leavitt; Samuel b. Jan. 28, 1880, m. Anna Wilson.

McCHRYSTAL, JOHN (son of Philip McChrystal of Montreal, Canada). Born July 14, 1834, Belfast, Ireland. Came to Utah in 1857.
Married Sarah Hancock April 15, 1869, in Houghton county, Mich. (daughter of John Hancock and Margaret Gorham of Michigan). She was born Feb. 10, 1843. Their children: John H. H., m. Belle Robins; Jackson C., m. Miss Earls; Noah, m. Stella Lafeet; Alexander; Sadie, m. Edward Parsons; Mark A., m. Grace Schuster; Jason. Family home, Salt Lake City.
Miningman. Died July 14, 1897, Eureka, Utah.

McCLELLAN, JAMES (son of Hugh McClellan, born Feb. 8, 1773, and Polly McCall). He was born Aug. 8, 1804, York district, S. C. Came to Utah Oct. 6, 1850, William Snow company.
Married Cynthia Stewart Jan. 19, 1826, who was pioneer Oct. 6, 1850, William Snow company. Their children: William Carroll b. May 12, 1828, m. Almeda Day July 19, 1849; Matilda Elizabeth b. Dec. 15, 1829, m. James W. Loveless; Mary Jane b. Aug. 22, 1831, m. William Head; Samuel Wilburn b. Aug. 23, 1833, m. Arthusa Head; Hugh Miles b. Aug. 4, 1835; Hugh Jefferson b. Nov. 13, 1836, m. Juliet Chase; John Jasper b. Aug. 6, 1838, m. Eliza Walser; Louisa Ann b. April 11, 1841, m. Eli Bell; Sarah Amanda b. Nov. 5, 1844, m. James Mamoill; James b. Aug. 19, 1848; Cynthia Selena b. Aug. 22, 1850, m. David Brown; Araminta b. Aug. 11, 1852, m. Edward Bunker.
Married Elsie Jane Richardson April 14, 1873, Salt Lake City (daughter of John Richardson and Minerva Ann Williams Richardson—married 1836, came to Utah April 30, 1872, Henry G. Boyle company). She was born May 2, 1848, in Franklin county, Va. Their children: Laura Catherine b. June 9, 1874, m. Hyrum Whipple March 1, 1891; Lorenzo Carroll b. Nov. 17, 1876, m. Assenath Porter Sept. 30, 1908; Wilford b. Aug. 7, 1879, m. Clara Kingsford May 13, 1908; Orson Wells b. Nov. 17, 1882, m. Geneva Porter June 11, 1908; Joseph Earl b. March 28, 1884, m. Lois Hurst Oct. 5, 1907; Minerva Jane b. March 1, 1887, m. David Mayer June 8, 1910; Lois Elizabeth b. Oct. 23, 1889; Alta Willmerth b. Feb. 4, 1893.
Ordained high priest in Nauvoo, Ill. Moved to Payson 1851, where he resided for many years. Lumberman; gunsmith; blacksmith.

McCLELLAN, WILLIAM CARROLL (son of James McClellan and Cynthia Stewart). Born May 12, 1828, Bedford county, Tenn.
Married Almeda Day July 19, 1849, Pottawattamie, Iowa (daughter of Hugh Day, pioneer Oct. 6, 1850, William Snow company, and Rhoda Ann Nickles). She was born Nov. 28, 1831, Leeds, Lower Canada. Their children: Mary Almeda b. May 11, 1850, m. Alma E. Bagley Sept. 17, 1867; William Hugh b. March 24, 1852, m. Elizabeth A. Mitchell; Maria Matilda b. May 2, 1854, m. John Hutch March 14, 1873; Cynthia Lovesta b. May 2, 1856, m. George W. Bailey; James Jasper b. Dec. 23, 1858, m. Hannah Sorenson; Sarah Evaline b. Feb. 10, 1860, m. Elisha E. Bailey Sept. 13, 1878; John Henry b. April 12, 1863; David Alvin b. June 16, 1865, m. Esther Tusley; Samuel Edwin b. July 23, 1867, m. Bertha M. Lewis Sept. 27, 1891; Rhoda Ann b. Oct. 27, 1871, m. Joseph S. Cardon; George Alma b. June 13, 1872, m. Mary A. Wright Sept. 18, 1893; Charles Eli b. Feb. 8, 1875, m. Josephine Haws April 11, 1900.
Bishop of Pleasanton, N. M.; president 46th quorum seventies; member high council Juarez stake 17 years. Assisted in ferrying pioneers across Missouri river. Member Company E Mormon battalion. Came to Utah July 27, 1847, and in August 1847 started for Missouri to assist family, reaching Council Bluffs in November 1847; moved to Payson in March 1851. Called to Sunset, Ariz., Sept. 24, 1877; moved to Forest Dale, Ariz., and resided there one year, when called to preside over church at Pleasanton, N. M., where he remained three years. Veteran Indian war.

McCLELLAN, WILLIAM HUGH (son of William Carroll McClellan and Almeda Day). Born March 24, 1852, Payson, Utah.
Married Elizabeth A. Mitchell May 13, 1875, at Payson (daughter of David Mitchell and Christiana Frost, pioneers Sept. 1862, A. H. Patterson company). She was born May 3, 1859, in South Africa. Their children: Ethel Gertrude b. April 28, 1877; Almeda Ludell b. April 5, 1879, m. Lee Vannosdol Feb. 12, 1900; William Hugh b. July 15, 1882, m. Jennie Taylor April 13, 1902; Elizabeth Jane b. Jan. 11, 1884, m. John Gamwells Feb. 17, 1902; Christiana Mariah b. Dec. 27, 1886, m. Willard Ellertson Oct. 5, 1905; David Mitchell b. Feb. 4, 1888; James Samuel b. Feb. 12, 1890; Alfred A. b. May 18, 1892; Sarah Arminta b. March 3, 1894; Learah Deseret b. Jan. 5, 1896; Norah Marian b. Nov. 1, 1898. Family home, Payson.

1056   PIONEERS AND PROMINENT MEN OF UTAH

McCLELLAN, HUGH JEFFERSON (son of James McClellan and Cynthia Stewart). Born Nov. 13, 1836, Shelby county, Ill. Came to Utah in 1847, James McClellan company.
Married Juliet Chase Aug. 11, 1858, Ogden, Utah (daughter of Ezra and Tirzah Wells Chase of Harrisville, Utah). She was born Sept. 13, 1841. Their children: Hugh Manuel b. Sept. 11, 1859; Elsie b. Sept. 18, 1861; James Ezra b. Sept. 15, 1863; Tirzah Juliet b. Nov. 11, 1865; Cynthia Letticia b. Nov. 7, 1867; George B. b. July 12, 1870; Henry Vernon b. May 30, 1872; Ernest b. Aug. 25, 1874; Winfield Scott b. Feb. 7, 1877; Nellie b. Oct. 8, 1879; Ethel b. July 21, 1882; Albert L. b. Sept. 13, 1884.
Rancher; farmer; merchant; miller. Died Jan. 13, 1912, Loa, Utah.

McCLEMOND, SAMUEL. Born in Ireland. Came to Utah in 1853.
Married Mary Ann Hartle at Salt Lake City (daughter of Samuel Hartle and Mary Nichols of England, pioneers 1849). Their children: Lydia Jane b. May 8, 1888, m. Samuel R. Page; Sarah Ellen b. April 21, 1889, m. Francis Melvin Caldwell. Family resided Salt Lake City and Vernal, Utah.

McCLEVE, JOHN (son of John McCleve). Came to Utah with handcart company.
Married Nancy Jane McFarren (daughter of Margaret McHarra of Ireland). Only child: Mary Jane, m. Priddy Meeks.

McCRACKEN, HENRY (son of James and Sarah McCracken, of Letterkenny, near Londonderry, Ireland). Born in 1810, at Letterkenny. Came to Utah Sept. 27, 1862, John R. Murdock company.
Married Sarah Shaw 1834 at Duntocker, Scotland (daughter of Hugh Shaw and Sarah Summerville, of Duntocker). She was born in 1818 at Dumbarton. Their children: James, m. Elizabeth F. Miller; Henry; Robert; Sarah; John, m. Jane Downes; Joseph. m. Annie Scrowthers; Thomas, m. Emma Downes; Elizabeth. m. Charles Rash. Family home Smithfield, Cache Co., Utah.
Elder. President of Bradford district near Manchester, Eng. Chemist. Died May 4, 1879, Smithfield.
[Note—The son of Henry McCracken adopted the name of Mack.]

McCULLOCH, JOHN BLACK (son of George McCulloch, Puston, Scotland, born in 1801, and Marion Black, born Stubhill, Scotland). He was born in August, 1829. Came to Utah Aug. 27, 1860, Daniel Robinson company.
Married Margeret McNeill in June 1852 (daughter of Charles McNeil and Marion Dobie, pioneers Aug. 27, 1860, Daniel Robinson company—married in 1830, Penston, Scotland). She was born Jan. 1, 1834. Their children: George b. May 25, 1855, m. Katherine Smith 1876; Charles b. Aug. 14, 1857, m. Jane H. Smith 1879; Marian b. May 23, 1860, m. William Nelson 1878; John Henry b. Nov. 12, 1862; Isabell b. March 3, 1865, m. Frank Hubbard 1890; Alexander b. April 29, 1868, m. Ethel Mary Oct. 14, 1909; Margeret b. Dec. 9, 1870, m. Charles Davey, Jr. 1900; Agnes b. June 8, 1873, m. Richard Smith 1890; Anna b. June 24, 1881, m. Otto Bearson 1902; George b. Jan. 1885. Family resided Salt Lake City and Logan, Utah, and Rexburg, Idaho.
Pioneer of Logan, Utah, in 1861. Died in 1893 at Rexburg.

McCULLOCH, ALEXANDER (son of John Black McCulloch and Margeret McNeil). Born April 29, 1868, Logan, Utah.
Married Ethel Mayo at Towcester, Eng. (daughter of Valentine Joseph Mayo and Harriet Wheeler), who was born March 26, 1882. Their child: Hazel Marion b. July 19, 1910.

McCULLOUGH, LEVI HAMILTON (son of Levi McCullough and Isabel Hamilton). Born April 18, 1810, Norwich, Chenango county, N. Y. Came to Utah in 1848, Captain Howell company.
Married Clarinda Bartholomew Jan. 9, 1834 (daughter of Isaac Bartholomew and Jerusha Molby), who was born June 4, 1815, and died at Winter Quarters, Neb. Their children: Julia Frances b. July 26, 1836, m. Amos Bemis 1853; Eliza Esther b. Dec. 31, 1837, m. Culbert King 1854; Henry Judson b. April 13, 1842, m. Helen Mar Callister May 22, 1864; Emily Jerusha b. Aug. 11, 1845, d. Aug. 2, 1847.
Sheriff of Millard county 1854-55; mayor in Nauvoo legion 1853; member presidency 42d quorum seventies; member Co. C Mormon battalion. School teacher at Fillmore 1855-56. Member Fillmore city council.

McCULLOUGH, HENRY JUDSON (son of Levi Hamilton McCullough and Clarinda Bartholomew). Born April 13, 1842, Jackson, Mich.
Married Helen Mar Callister May 22, 1864, Fillmore, Utah (daughter of Thomas Callister and Helen Mar Clark, pioneers Sept. 25, 1847, Daniel Spencer company). She was born Sept. 26, 1846, Winter Quarters, Neb. Their children: Helen Mar b. March 12, 1865, m. John Elbert Wilcox; Caroline Eliza b. Nov. 13, 1866, d. Nov. 16, 1866; Clarinda Altana b. Nov. 20, 1867, m. Peter Lorenzo Brunson; Frances Melissa b. Nov. 1, 1870, m. David Oswell Wilcox; Henry Judson, Jr. b. June 12, 1874, d. June 7, 1876; Claribell b. Jan. 19, 1877, m. Parley Franklin Savage; Esther b. Dec. 7, 1879, d. July 6,

1894; Levi Hamilton b. March 27, 1833, m. Sarah Alvey March 26, 1903; Thomas Clark b. Dec. 15, 1885, m. Rose Day June 28, 1911; Eleanor b. March 26, 1888, m. Charles R. Sampson Dec. 21, 1910. Family resided at Fillmore, Marion ward, and Burtner, Utah.
Ward teacher; president Y. M. M. I. A.; superintendent Sunday school; second counselor to Bishop Alexander Melville; member high council of Millard stake; missionary to Great Britain 1867-68. Councilman at Fillmore; constable.

McCUNE, MATTHEW (son of Robert McCune, of Newtown Ards, Ireland, and Lucy Jane Fleming, of Scotland). Born July 23, 1811, Douglas, Isle of Man. Came to Utah Sept. 21, 1857, Delaware company.
Married Sarah E. C. Scott April 11, 1835, who came to Utah with husband and who was born Jan. 28, 1812. Their children: Henry F. b. May 31, 1840, m. Elizabeth Grace Dec. 24, 1861; George b. Dec. 27, 1846, m. Sarah E. Wright Jan. 11, 1868; Alfred W. b. July 11, 1849, m. Elizabeth A. Clarridge July 1, 1876; Edward J. b. Sept. 27, 1851, m. Margaret A. Hague Sept. 30, 1872.
Missionary to Great Britain twice. Military officer. Physician and surgeon. Pioneer of Nephi, Utah 1858. Died Oct. 27, 1889.

McCUNE, HENRY F. (son of Matthew McCune and Sarah E. Scott). Born May 31, 1840, Calcutta. India.
Married Elizabeth Grace Dec. 24, 1861, Nephi, Utah (daughter of Isaac Grace, pioneer Oct. 15, 1851, James W. Cummings company, and Elizabeth Williams Grace). She was born July 23, 1843, Liverpool, Eng. Their children: Henry M. b. Sept. 27, 1862, m. Esther E. Paxman April 9, 1885; Elizabeth Grace b. May 21, 1844, m. Adelbert Cazier Jan. 1890; Henrietta b. Sept. 2, 1867, m. Mark A. Coombs March 5, 1890; Alfred A. b. March 2, 1870, m. Sarah Broadhead June 22, 1892; George W. b. May 24, 1872, m. Sarah A. Scowcroft Nov. 21, 1900; Sarah Florence b. Sept. 16, 1874, m. S. J. Lunt Oct. 17, 1898; Royal Albert b. Jan. 29, 1877, m. Elizabeth May Rice Dec. 19, 1905; Mabel b. March 12, 1881, m. J. W. Ure, Jr. Sept. 12, 1906; Margaret Leah b. June 21, 1883, m. B. W. Musser Jan. 3, 1906; Rosa Hamilton b. Oct. 9, 1887; Clarence Scott b. June 8, 1890. Family resided Nephi and Ogden, Utah.
Veteran Black Hawk war. Missionary to East Indies and to New Zealand. Pioneer to Nephi 1858; moved to Ogden in 1906.

McCURDY, ALBERT GALLINTON (son of John Robert McCurdy and Mary Epperson, of Glenwood, Iowa). Born Nov. 5, 1844. Came to Utah in 1867.
Married Christena Bonner Sept. 7, 1869, at Midway, Utah (daughter of George Bonner and Margerette Edmiston, pioneers 1857). She was born Sept. 7, 1852, in Scotland. Their children: Ulmeda Loretta b. May 19, 1870, m. George Bird; Albert b. Feb. 8, 1872, m. Delia Workman; George Bonner b. April 4, 1874, m. Clarissa Antonette Clark; Margerett Edmiston b. May 1, 1876, m. Myron Roberts; Ann b. April 6, 1878, m. George Clark; Daisy b. Feb. 24, 1880, m. Lars Sorensen; Jane b. May 5, 1882, m. Louis Galley; Tina Lucretia b. Aug. 19, 1884, m. Archer Jenkins; Robert b. May 18, 1886, m. Allie Decker; Elizabeth b. April 29, 1888, and Ethel May b. May 2, 1890, latter two died.
Elder. Farmer. Died Jan. 24, 1892, at Vernal, Utah.

McCURDY, GEORGE BONNER (son of Albert Gallinton McCurdy and Christena Bonner). Born April 4, 1874, Heber City, Utah.
Married Clarissa Antonette Clark Jan. 1, 1897, Vernal, Utah (daughter of Israel Justice Clark and Emily Jane Pearson, pioneers 1848, John Smith company). She was born Nov. 4, 1880, at Vernal. Their children: Alice Melvina b. Aug. 7, 1898; Lavista Pearl b. Dec. 24, 1907.
Farmer.

McCURDY, JACOB WENTLING (son of John McCurdy, born in Ireland, and Elizabeth Wentling, born in Germany). He was born March 11, 1818, in Ocean county, N. J. Came to Utah Aug. 10, 1853, Abraham and Israel Ivans company.
Married Emerline Applegate in June 1845 (daughter of John Applegate), who was born Sept. 7, 1825, and came to Utah with husband. Their children: Martha Ann b. 1847, d. 1852; Charles Ivans b. 1849, d. 1852; Mary Emma b. 1852, d. 1852; France Anna b. 1854, m. J. S. Wing 1876; Jacob Ellwood b. Oct. 9, 1856, m. Olive L. Packard, Provo, Utah, Oct. 15, 1894; Anthony b. 1864, d. 1875.
Ironmolder. Veteran of Walker Indian war. Pioneer to Gunnison, Utah; moved to Springville in 1863. Pioneer miner.

McCURDY, JACOB ELLWOOD (son of Jacob Wentling McCurdy and Emerline Applegate). Born Oct. 9, 1856, Salt Lake City.
Married Olive L. Packard Oct. 15, 1894, Provo, Utah (daughter of Romanzo Packard and Mary Ross), who was born Nov. 10, 1870, in Iowa. Their children: J. R. b. Nov. 6, 1897; Howard E. b. July 10, 1899; Elsie L. b. April 7, 1910.

McDANIEL, JOHN (son of James McDaniel of Ohio and Zbinh McCarley). Born 1812 in Ohio. Came to Utah Oct. 29, 1852, Isaac Stewart company.
Married Christine Stocker in Ohio (daughter of David

PIONEERS AND PROMINENT MEN OF UTAH 1057

Stocker, pioneer Oct. 29, 1852, Isaac Stewart company). She was born in Hancock county, Ill. Their children: Electa Jane b. 1835, m. Eli Ashcraft; Tabitha b. 1837, m. Dale Norton; John R. b. 1839, m. Sarah Ann Watkins; Cathrine b. 1842, m. Alma Winn; George Washington b. 1844, m. Mary Jane Taylor; Matilda b. 1841, m. T. J. McCullough; James William b. 1847, m. Vina Mantle; David b. 1851, m. Sarah Ann Clark; Michael Sylvester b. 1857, m. Emma Beck. Family home Alpine, Utah. Settled at Alpine 1852. High priest. Farmer.

McDANIEL, GEORGE WASHINGTON (son of John McDaniel and Christine Stocker). Born 1844 in Hancock county, Ill. Came to Utah with parents. Married Mary Jane Taylor Dec. 29, 1867, Alpine, Utah (daughter of Mary Ann Taylor of England, pioneer Sept. 4, 1866, Thomas E. Ricks company). She was born in Birmingham, Eng. Their children: Mary Matilda b. Oct. 23, 1868, m. Francis Lyman Carlisle; George Willard b. Dec. 21, 1870, died; George Willard b. Dec. 1871, m. Cathrine Oakley; Charlotte Alice b. Dec. 19, 1874, m. John Gould Davis; Alvin Sylvester b. 1877, m. Alice Hunter; William John b. 1879, died; Delbert Carroll b. 1880, m. Hazel Rishens; Esther Eliza b. 1882, m. John S. Curzon. High priest; ward teacher. Builder. Indian war veteran.

McDONALD, EDWARD. Born Feb. 1, 1821, Ruskey, Tyrone, Ireland. Came to Utah in 1866. Married Elizabeth Kellun, who was born May 6, 1827, and died in April 1912. Their children: Isabella, m. John Batchelor; William; John Taylor; Mary b. March 5, 1863, m. J. T. Dorcheus Dec. 20, 1882; Jessie, m. Walter Bingham. Family home Riverdale, Utah. Died in 1891 at Ogden, Utah.

McDONALD, JOHN KILPATRICK. Came to Utah 1849. Married Rachel Burck Taaffe. Their children: Elizabeth Taaffe b. Dec. 27, 1823; William Taaffe b. Dec. 13, 1825; John Taaffe b. April 11, 1830; Alexander Taaffe b. April 8, 1833; Washington Taaffe b. Aug. 9, 1835; James K. Taaffe b. Aug. 4, 1837; Jane Taaffe b. in March 1840; Joseph Taaffe b. Jan. 1, 1842. All came to America except Elizabeth, who died in Ireland. William died in California; all the other children died in Salt Lake City.

McDONALD, JOHN TAAFFEE (son of John Kilpatrick and Rachel Burck Taaffe of Armagh, Ireland). Born April 11, 1830, in Armagh. Came to Utah with father. Married Eleanor Amelia Crossland May 17, 1858, Salt Lake City (daughter of Junius Crossland and Frances Otton of London, Eng., pioneers Sept. 11, 1853, Jacob Gates company). She was born April 5, 1841. Their children: Fannie Rachel, m. George B. Margetts; John Crossland. m. Laura Elvira Minor; Joseph Smith, died; Rachel, m. F. E. Margetts; James G., m. Edith Cartwright, m. Lillie Neal; Junius C., m. Alice Byetheway; William C., m. Annie Strongberry; Ronald C., died; Eleanor Amelia, m. Richard Chamberlain; George Washington C., m. Kate South; Ronald C. and Alexander, died. Family home, Salt Lake City. Seventy; high priest. Merchant. Died Aug. 15, 1910.

McDONALD, JAMES G. (son of John Taaffe McDonald and Eleanor Amelia Crossland). Born April 30, 1865, Salt Lake City. Married Edith Cartwright at Salt Lake City (daughter of John Cartwright and Ann Hartwick, pioneers 1862). She died. Their children: Florence; Irene; James G.; Lucile. Married Lillie Neal (daughter of Casper W. Neal and Elizabeth Hanna, came to Utah in 1869). Their children: Neal; Lillie Earl. Families resided at Salt Lake City. High priest. President and director of Utah State Fair Association. Manufacturer of candy, cocoa and chocolate. Director Utah State National Bank.

McDONALD, WILLIAM (son of James McDonald and Sarah Ferguson of Crawford's Burn, County Down, Ireland). Born in Ireland in 1805. Came to Utah Oct. 15, 1850, oxteam company. Married Seriah Shirts Dec. 10, 1853, Cedar City, Utah (daughter of Peter Shirts and Margaret Cameron of Cedar City, Utah, pioneers Oct. 1, 1850, oxteam company). Their children: Jane b. Oct. 19, 1854, m. Thompson McNaughton; Sarah Ann b. March 3, 1856, m. Brigham Young; William b. Dec. 16, 1857, m. Hannah Handberg; Margaret Seriab b. Jan. 15, 1860, m. Jonas Anderson, m. John Erickson; James b. Dec. 21, 1861, m. Sarah Broadhead; Mary b. Feb. 1, 1864, m. David Young; Eliza Ann b. July 4, 1865, m. John Blackley; George B. Dec. 12, 1866, m. Sarah A. Hamilton; Olive b. Aug. 20, 1868, died; Nancy b. April 11, 1870; Roda Frances b. Dec. 6, 1871, m. David Jones; Joseph b. Nov. 11, 1872, died; Lucy and Robert (twins) b. May 18, 1874, died; Fannie Levina b. Sept. 7, 1875, m. Henry R. Cluff; Ermina b. Sept. 2, 1876; Alma b. Jan. 11, 1878; John b. April 11, 1879; Lenora b. March 12, 1882; Allilea b. Sept. 18, 1885. These last five all died. Family home Heber City, Utah.
Married Elizabeth Ann Shirts Nov. 3, 1565, Salt Lake Endowment House (daughter of Peter Shirts and Margaret Cameron of Cedar City, Utah, pioneers Oct. 1, 1850, oxteam

company). She was born Feb. 15, 1849. Their children: Hyrum b. Feb. 7, 1867, died; Seriah Jane b. April 14, 1870, m. Andrew Johnston; Margaret Ann b. July 15, 1872, m. Daniel L. Griffith; Henry Carlos b. Nov. 21, 1874, m. Florence M. Enzi; Susan Sophia b. Aug. 4, 1877, m. Richard R. Giles; Elizabeth b. April 24, 1880, m. Jesse Munroe Witt; Joseph b. Aug. 24, 1882, m. Nettie Clegg; Elva Loretta b. Feb. 7, 1884, died; Clara b. Jan. 3, 1885, m. John McAfee; Edward b. May 4, 1888, m. Myrtle Clayborn; Daniel Lewis b. Nov. 25, 1890, m. Nina Sulcer; Maudie May b. July 27, 1893, died. Family home, Heber City, Utah.
High priest; ward teacher at Springville, Utah; appointed by Brigham Young to locate agricultural sections for settlement; worked on Nauvoo temple. First county treasurer Wasatch county; selectman same county. Scout in Echo Canyon campaign; veteran Walker and Black Hawk Indian wars. Farmer and stockraiser.

McEWEN, HENRY (son of John McEwen and Jane McAnley of Ireland). Born Feb. 14, 1802, Parish of Garvaby, County Down, Ireland. Came to Utah Sept. 3, 1860, James D. Ross company. Married Jane Thompson in Ireland (daughter of Joseph Thompson and Eliza Boyce of VanBridge, Down, Ireland). She was born Dec. 25, 1801. Their children: John, m. Amanda M. Higbee; Jane, died; Joseph, died; Robert T., m. Jeanette Hogg; Margaret, m. Agnes Hogg; Jane, m. William F. Reid; William, died; Joseph, died; Eliza, m. Joseph M. Brown; Joseph Thompson, m. Irinda Naomi Crandall. Family home Provo, Utah. High priest; president Edinburgh conference several years. Farmer. Died Sept. 24, 1882, Provo, Utah.

McEWEN, JOHN (son of Henry McEwen, born February 1802, County Down, Ireland, and Jane Thompson, born Dec. 25, 1801, Bonbricly, Ireland). Born February 1824 at Bonbride, County Down, Ireland. Came to Utah 1848. Married Amanda M. Higbee Dec. 23, 1845 (daughter of Isaac Higbee and Keziah String, married Feb. 11, 1819, former pioneer 1848, latter died at Nauvoo, Ill.). She was born May 20, 1826. Their children: Mary J. b. Nov. 17, 1846, m. Oscar Wilkins Nov. 27, 1866; William b. June 17, 1848, m. Ellen Haws; Joseph b. May 17, 1850; Amanda M. b. Nov. 13, 1851, m. Jesse Knight Jan. 18, 1869; John H. b. Sept. 22, 1854, m. Nellie Flemings; Isaac H. b. Dec. 3, 1856, m. Rachel Ferre; Julia R. b. Feb. 20, 1860, m. William Haws; David O. b. Aug. 6, 1863; Jesse b. July 7, 1867; Eleanor b. Oct. 10, 1869, m. John Roundy. Family home Provo, Utah.
President 22nd quorum seventies; secretary to Joseph Smith in Nauvoo, Ill. Clerk 3rd judicial district court; postmaster Provo.

McEWEN, JOSEPH THOMPSON (son of Henry McEwen and Jane Thompson). Born Sept. 1, 1840, Edinburgh, Scotland. Came to Utah with father. Married Irinda Naomi Crandall Aug. 25, 1867, Provo, Utah (daughter of Spicer Wells Crandall and Sophia Kellogg of Michigan and later Springville, Utah, pioneers Aug. 1850, Captain Johnson company). She was born Aug. 18, 1851, Springville, Utah. Their children: Joseph C. b. July 1, 1870, died; Laura Sophia b. Sept. 24, 1871, m. Louis William Nuttall; Robert Wells b. May 16, 1873, died; Bertha Irinda b. Dec. 17, 1874, m. George Henry Elliott; William Spicer b. Feb. 6, 1877, died; Daniel Dean b. Aug. 14, 1878, m. Emily Mecham; Mabel Ottillie b. Dec. 9, 1881, m. Reed A. Boren; Rhoda b. Aug. 16, 1883, m. Raymond Boren; Jennie Theresa b. Oct. 31, 1885, m. Frank C. Thorne; Ellatheria b. June 6, 1887, m. George V. Selman; Owen Crandall b. Jan. 10, 1889; Erma b. Sept. 20, 1892, m. J. Oliver Hood. Family home Provo, Utah.
High priest; president 45th and 123rd quorums seventies; ward clerk 4th ward, Provo. County commissioner; city councilman. One of those who started the Salt Lake Herald and started the first newspaper at Provo. Printer.

McEWAN, DANIEL DEAN (son of Joseph Thompson McEwan and Irinda Naomi Crandall). Born Aug. 14, 1878, Provo, Utah. Married Emily Mecham Nov. 16, 1898, Manti, Utah (daughter of Amasa Lyman Mecham and Lorana Boren of Provo, pioneers 1851, Morris Phelps company). She was born Nov. 23, 1879. Their children: Kenneth Eugene and Gilbert Dean (twins) b. Aug. 27, 1899; Murry Wells b. July 26, 1902; Vivian Lorana b. March 27, 1904; Inez b. Nov. 16, 1908; Marvin D. b. Jan. 13, 1912. Family home Provo Bench, Utah.
Member 123rd quorum seventies; missionary to eastern states 1908-10; bishop; president Y. M. M. I. A. Miller and farmer.

McFARLAND, JAMES (son of John McFarland and Mary Irvin of Paisley, Scotland). Born May 18, 1818, in Ireland. Came to Utah Oct. 1, 1866, Joseph S. Rawlins oxtrain. Married Sarah Mitchell in Ireland (daughter of Henry Mitchell and Mary McCalvay of Belfast). She was born Nov. 14, 1814. Their children: Mary, m. William Morrow: Margaret, m. William Morrow; Agnes, m. William Nephi Casper; William Henry, m. Tracie Brown; Sarah Jean, m. James Moroni Casper. Family home Mill Creek, Salt Lake Co., Utah.
High priest. Settled at Mill Creek and after seven years moved to Granger; lived there 15 years, then to Star Valley, Wyo. Farmer. Died April 10, 1891, at latter place.

1058 PIONEERS AND PROMINENT MEN OF UTAH

McFARLAND, WILLIAM (son of Archibald McFarland and Mary Blair of Dromora, Ireland). Born June 8, 1795, Trillick, Tyrone Co., Ireland. Came to Utah Sept. 25, 1855, Richard Ballantyne company.
Married Margret McCormick January, 1832, Dysart, Fifeshire, Scotland (daughter of James McCormick and Jennet Mitchel of Fifeshire). She was born April 11, 1804. Their children: Archibald b. Dec. 17, 1832, m. Isabell Mitchel; James b. Oct. 25, 1835, m. Hannah Boyck; William b. May 14, 1838, m. Rose Cole; Mary Ann b. Oct. 22, 1842, m. Hans D. Petterson; Robert b. Sept. 11, 1844, m. Mahale Wilson; Jennet b. Sept. 8, 1846, died. Family home West Weber, Utah.
Patriarch; high priest. Justice of the peace, West Weber precinct. Died Jan. 27, 1890, West Weber.

McFARLAND, ARCHIBALD (son of William McFarland and Margret McCormick). Born Dec. 17, 1832, Hawklymuir, Fifeshire, Scotland. Came to Utah Sept. 25, 1855, Richard Ballantyne company.
Married Isabel Mitchel Aug. 3, 1856, Boness, Linlithgow, Scotland (daughter of William Mitchel and Isabella Nimmo of Linlithgow). She was born March 5, 1837. Their children: James R. b. Dec. 20, 1859, m. Mary E. Etherington; Charles B. b. April 8, 1862, m. Susan A. Etherington; Isabella b. Sept. 25, 1864, m. Joseph Hogge; Archibald b. Jan. 15, 1867, m. Emiline Nelson; John b. Dec. 31, 1868, m. Grace McKay; Albert R. b. May 1, 1871, m. Elizabeth Greenwell; Margret E. b. Oct. 13, 1873, m. Joseph Nelson; Janet b. June 29, 1879, m. Thomas R. Faddis; Daniel b. May 17, 1882, m. Esther Greenwell. Family home West Weber, Weber, Co., Utah.
Presided over West Weber ward nearly ten years; filled three foreign missions. Two terms in legislature; justice of the peace ten years.

McFARLAND, CHARLES B. (son of Archibald McFarland and Isabell Mitchel). Born April 8, 1862, West Weber.
Married Susan A. Etherington April 2, 1882, Salt Lake City (daughter of Thomas Etherington and Sarah Wheeler of West Weber, Utah, pioneers 1855). Jacob Secrist company). She was born April 2, 1864. Their children: Ida b. March 2, 1883, m. Jacob W. Gibson; Charles H. b. Nov. 6, 1884, m. Esther E. Drake; Archibald J. b. Sept. 29, 1887; Thomas L. b. Sept. 24, 1891; William M. b. June 8, 1894; Roy b. May 14, 1896; Susan A. b. Aug. 9, 1898; Donald B. b. Oct. 18, 1900; Sarah Isabell b. July 26, 1903.
Second counselor elders' quorum. Died Oct. 16, 1909.

McFARLANE, PETER (son of George McFarlane and Agnes Bryson of Scotland). Born Aug. 28, 1819, Glasgow, Scotland. Came to Utah September, 1862, Israel Canfield company.
Married Mary Clark 1846 at Glasgow (daughter of John Clark of Johnston, Scotland). She was born June, 1820. Their children: James, m. Martha Smuin; Peter K., d. infant; John; Peter B.; Mary C., d. infant; Arthur, d. aged 33. Family home, Glasgow.
Home missionary 1864-68; president of branch, Grenock, Scotland; block teacher. First lieutenant territorial militia. Shoemaker. Died July, 1883, Ogden, Utah.

McFARLANE, JAMES (son of Peter McFarlane and Mary Clark). Came to Utah with father.
Married Martha Smuin Oct. 5, 1868, Salt Lake City (daughter of John Smuin and Jane Honey of London, Eng., pioneers 1869). She was born Aug. 8, 1848. Their children: James, m. Thursia Shaw; Mary Jane; Martha A.; Joseph C., m. Pearl Richards; John S., m. Alice Liddell; Louisa, m. Gilbert Mears; Arthur, m. Gertrude Rock; Harriet, m. Julias Millican; Florence; Lawrence C.; William C., d. aged 4. Family home Ogden, Utah.
Member 131st quorum seventies; missionary to England 1904-07; block teacher. Station baggage agent U. P. R. R. at Ogden.

McFERSON, DIMON (son of William McFerson and Miriam Runnels of New York state). Born June 15, 1809, Newport, N. H. Came to Utah in 1855, Isaac Allred company.
Married Mary Ann Neas Nov. 29, 1845, at Nauvoo (daughter of Peter Neas and Ellen Martin of Pennsylvania). She was born Jan. 29, 1824. Their children: Sarah b. Oct. 20, 1846, m. Peter Van Orden; Abner b. Sept. 14, 1849; Delila b. Jan. 6, 1852; m. William Bodily; Lydia b. Aug. 26, 1854; m. Levi Phillips; Jedediah b. Dec. 7, 1856; Miriam b. Oct. 12, 1858, m. J. G. M. Barnes; Mary Ann b. Nov. 4, 1860, m. Jacob Layton; Rhoda Matilda b. May 6, 1863, m. Irvin Keetely; Dolly b. March 7, 1865, m. Frank Brown; David b. March 31, 1867, m. Mary Ann Watte. Family home Kaysville, Davis Co., Utah.
Justice of the peace; orderly sergeant and color bearer; member of city council. Died Feb. 14, 1875.

McGARY, CHARLES. Born about 1810. Came to Utah 1850, Captain Evans company.
Married Charlotte Earle in Canada (daughter of William Earle of Logan, Utah, pioneers 1850, Captain Evans company). She was born 1816. Their children: William, m. Ellen Pratt; Jane, m. Wells Chase; Ellen, m. Potter Bowen; Sarah, m. James Browning; James; Malissa, m. Benjamin Garr. Family home Ogden, Utah.
Road supervisor several years. Blacksmith and farmer. Died April 1875.

McGAVIN, ROBERT (son of Robert McGavin and Janet Johnston of Glasgow, Scotland). Born July 5, 1843, at Glasgow. Came to Utah 1855, Hooper & Eldredge merchant train.
Married Rozelia Gee Oct. 7, 1865, Tooele City, Utah (daughter of Lysander Gee and Theresa Bowley of St. Louis, Mo., pioneers 1852). She was born June 1, 1848. Their children: Laura Theresa; Sarah Inez, m. 1898; Robert Lysander; Rozelia Irene, m. 1895; Almond E., m. 1900; Jeannette, m. 1900; George G. Family home Glen, Idaho.
Elder.

McGHIE, JAMES (son of Richard McGhie and Helen Anderson of Kilmarnock, Ayrshire, Scotland). Born Dec. 1, 1834, in Scotland. Came to Utah Sept. 15, 1861, Ira Eldredge company.
Married Isabella Lindsay Dec. 28, 1858, Liverpool, Eng. (daughter of Alexander Lindsay and Annie Mathie of Glasgow, who came to Utah Dec. 28, 1861). She was born Oct. 17, 1833. Their children: Isabella b. Dec. 15, 1859, m. A. F. Cummings; Annie b. Aug. 1, 1861, m. S. H. Igbert; James b. March 24, 1864, m. Susanna Wagstaff; Nellie b. March 1867, died; R. L. b. April 14, 1874, m. Angie Cabbot; Catherine b. Aug. 1877, m. A. A. Alkier. Family home, Salt Lake City.
Missionary to Scotland; patriarch. Manager Burton & Sharp woolen mills.

McGHIE, JAMES, JR. (son of James McGhie and Isabella Lindsay). Born March 24, 1864, Salt Lake City.
Married Susanna Wagstaff Sept. 10, 1886, Logan, Utah (daughter of William Wagstaff, pioneer from England September, 1854). She was born Jan. 18, 1867. Their children: James L. b. June 21, 1887, died; Arthur W. b. June 3, 1889, m. Emma Sylvester; Jesse Earl b. Oct. 8, 1891, m. Maude Fisher; Susie D. b. Aug. 15, 1893, m. Ralph Quayle; Joseph E. b. July 13, 1895, died; Richard D. b. April 19, 1896; Frank W. b. May 10, 1898; Rulon S. b. Jan. 2, 1900; Emily L. b. June 17, 1905; Isabelle b. June 17, 1905. Family home, Salt Lake City.
Member first quorum seventies of Granite stake; division president. Fire insurance agent.

McGHIE, WILLIAM (son of Mr. McGhie and Henrietta Gibson). Born 1811 Dumfrieshire, Scotland. Came to Utah Oct. 1, 1854, Daniel Garn company.
Married Elizabeth Collins in Scotland, who was born 1809 in Ireland. Their children: William b. Jan. 6, 1830, m. Mary McBlain Dec. 31, 1850; Elizabeth b. Jan. 6, 1832, m. Thomas Boam 1854; John; Sarah 1st; Henrietta 1st; Sarah 2d; Henrietta 2d; Agnes b. 1843, m. Mr. Robinson. Family home Cottonwood, Utah.
Member of seventy.

McGHIE, WILLIAM, JR. (son of William McGhie and Elizabeth Collins). Born March 6, 1830, in Scotland.
Married Mary McBlain Dec. 31, 1850, in Scotland (daughter of Alexander McBlain and Mary McMaster, former pioneer Oct. 1, 1854, Daniel Garn company). She was born July 27, 1832, in Scotland. Their children: William b. Dec. 20, 1851, m. Sarah J. Spillett; Alexander b. Nov. 8, 1853, m. Emma Rowan; Mary b. Oct. 25, 1855, m. Neri Butler; Agnes b. Sept. 2, 1857, m. Hyrum Covert; John b. Aug. 15, 1859, m. Rozetta Daw; Joseph b. Aug. 9, 1861, m. Christina Porter; Thomas b. July 22, 1863, m. Viola Draw; Elizabeth b. July 22, 1863, m. William O. Blair; Sarah b. Nov. 8, 1865, m. Charles Colebrook; Henrietta b. March 19, 1868, m. Parley Hansen; Jean b. Oct. 7, 1870, m. Charles Buhler; Annie b. March 27, 1873, m. Joseph I. Staker. Family resided Midway, Provo Valley and Butler, Utah.
Postmaster at Butler.

McGHIE, ALEXANDER (son of William McGhie and Mary McBlain). Born Nov. 8, 1853, Scotland.
Married Emma Rowan (daughter of Matthew Rowan and Jane V. Martin, pioneers Oct. 28, 1855, C. R. Harner company). She was born March 15, 1856, South Cottonwood, Utah. Their children: Raymond A. b. March 29, 1882, m. Hazel Staker Nov. 13, 1904; William Matthew b. Jan. 31, 1884, m. Jane Brady Nov. 18, 1904; Mary Evalyn b. July 13, 1886, m. William W. Belter Nov. 18, 1908; James Bertrand b. March 20, 1888, m. Marvel Huish Sept. 22, 1909; Oliver Calvin b. Aug. 16, 1890; Florence Jane b. June 16, 1892; Annie Caryl b. April 22, 1896. Family resided Park City and Butler, Utah.

McGREGOR, WILLIAM (son of William McGregor and Agnes Murray of Glasgow, Lanarkshire, Scotland). Born Oct. 4, 1842. Came to Utah 1850.
Married Charilla Emily Browning May 1, 1876, Salt Lake City (daughter of David Elias Browning, pioneer 1852, and Charilla Abbott, pioneer 1849, of Ogden, Utah). She was born Jan. 22, 1877, m. Hannah Victoria Larson; John Jonathan b. June 25, 1878, m. Evelyn Leona Woods; James Stephen b. Oct. 14, 1880, m. Agatha Georgiena Woods; Charles Roy b. July 1, 1882, m. Effie Horrocks; Charilla Abigail October b. Dec. 25, 1883, m. Ernest M. W. Jones; Frank Duncan b. Nov. 29, 1885, m. Annie Empey; Mary Agnes b. April 6, 1887, m. Lawrence Anderson; Joseph b. June 10, 1889, m. Hortense Young; Arthur b. Sept. 10, 1891; Arba May b. May 5, 1895. Family home Ogden, Utah. Died Oct. 15, 1906.

McGREGOR, JAMES STEPHEN (son of William McGregor and Charilla Emily Browning). Born Oct. 14, 1880, Ogden, Utah.
Married Agatha Georgiena Woods Nov. 25, 1903, Salt Lake City (daughter of Francis Charles Woods, who came to Utah Sept. 14, 1869, and Evelyn Pratt, born in Salt Lake City). She was born Dec. 18, 1883. Their children: Agatha Woods b. Sept. 14, 1904; James Edmond Woods b. July 12, 1906; Parley Wallace b. Jan. 18, 1908; Athleen Woods b. Oct. 12, 1909; Francis Walker b. June 11, 1911. Family home Ogden, Utah.
Seventy.

McGUIRE, PATRICK HENRY (son of Bernard McGuire and Susan McHugh of Derry Lahan, County Cavan, Ireland). Born June 14, 1844, at Derry Lahan. Came to Utah July 9, 1872.
Married Sarah Elizabeth Parcell May 31, 1875, Salt Lake City (daughter of John C. Parcell and Esther Lewis of Wallsborg, Utah, both formerly of Cambridge, Eng.). She was born May 19, 1855. Their children: John Parcell b. March 6, 1876, m. Amanda Elizabeth Anderson; Patrick Henry b. Oct. 15, 1877, died; Anna Elizabeth b. Aug. 19, 1879, m. William D. Bethers; Edna b. Jan. 12, 1881, m. Ephraim Bethers; Esther b. Oct. 16, 1883; Francis Preston b. Oct. 10, 1885; Bernard b. Dec. 7, 1887; Lewis Curtis b. Oct. 24, 1889; Ada b. Dec. 5, 1893, died; Orson b. June 16, 1897; James Ernest b. Nov. 2, 1899.
Married Annie Eliza Lee Jan. 1, 1881, St. George, Utah (daughter of John P. Lee and Eliza Foscue of Beaver, Utah). She was born Jan. 11, 1849. Their children: Rupert Lee b. March 12, 1882; Alice Hulda b. May 17, 1885, died.
Bishop Daniels ward Nov. 12, 1899; president elders' quorum; ward clerk; superintendent Sunday school, Washington ward, St. George stake; president of Daniels branch of center ward. County assessor of Wasatch county 1899-1910. Missionary to Ireland Oct. 5, 1910; returned Nov. 21, 1911.

McGURRIN, FREDERICK T. (son of Manis McGurrin and Ellen Malone of Grand Rapids, Mich.). Born 1869 Grand Rapids. Came to Utah 1889.
Married Estelle La Fitte McChrystal, Colorado Springs, Colo., 1903.
Attorney.

McINTIRE, WILLIAM PATTERSON (son of George McIntire and Sarah Davis of Wheatfield, Pa.). Born May 29, 1813. Came to Utah 1849, Orson Spencer company.
Married Anna Patterson in Pennsylvania (daughter of William Patterson and Margaret Weir), who was born in Pennsylvania Dec. 19, 1811, died June 28, 1880. Their children: Wallace M., m. Adelaide Hovey; Margaret Jane. m. Melancthon Burgess; Erastus W., m. Anna Birch; Alexander, m. Viola Paxton; Mary and Sarah, twins, d. infants; Caroline A., d. aged 16; John O., m. Alice Empey; Brigham Oscar, m. Barbara Mathis: Joseph H., m. Rose Clark. Family home St. George, Utah.
Missionary to eastern states in 1840; seventy. Called to St. George by President Young to build up that country. Tailor. Died Jan. 7, 1881.

McINTIRE, BRIGHAM OSCAR (son of William Patterson McIntire and Anna Patterson). Born Aug. 21, 1852, Salt Lake City.
Married Barbara Mathis Dec. 7, 1877, St. George, Utah (daughter of John Mathis and Barbara Brayner of St. George, pioneers 1855, Richard Ballantyne company). She was born Oct. 24, 1858. Their children: Zina b. Sept. 29, 1878, d. infant; Brigham Franklin b. March 4, 1880, m. Effie Cottam; Anna B. b. Feb. 26, 1882, m. Oliver Harmon; William Mathis b. June 28, 1884, m. Zelma Harmon; Oscar b. Sept. 7, 1888; Lena b. Dec. 28, 1890, m. J. W. Nelson; Leon b. Nov. 23, 1896, died aged 4; Evelyn b. March 2, 1901, d. infant. Family home Price, Carbon Co., Utah.
Elder; teacher; worked on St. George temple. Road supervisor. Minuteman in Indian war. Farmer and cattleraiser. Died Feb. 15, 1907.

McINTIRE, BRIGHAM FRANKLIN (son of Brigham Oscar McIntire and Barbara Anna Mathis). Born March 4, 1880, at St. George, Utah.
Married Effie Cottam June 23, 1910, at St. George (daughter of George Thomas Cottam and Rachel Holt of St. George). She was born Nov. 23, 1890. Their child: Wayne Franklin b. Sept. 7, 1911.
Missionary to Germany and Austria-Hungary 1893-96; high priest; member of high council; member of stake mutual 1897-99; president Y. M. M. I. A.; ward teacher; Sunday school teacher. Farmer and stockraiser.

McINTOSH, WILLIAM (son of John McIntosh and Isabell Rankin of highlands of Scotland). Born Sept. 16, 1819. Came to Utah in 1852.
Married Maria Caldwell Sept. 16, 1841, in Lanark county, Canada (daughter of David Caldwell and Mary Ann Vaughn of Lanark, the latter a pioneer 1852). She was born Feb. 17, 1827. Their children: John Ephraim, died; Mary Ann and David, died; William Henry (died), m. Mary Keelle; James Franklin (died), m. Annie Jordon; Malissa Jane, m. Jacob Keelle; Alice Maria b. Sept. 16, 1858, m. Thomas

Lorenzo Burridge; Abraham Edward b. March 4, 1860, m. Mary Ghould; Lillian Elizabeth, m. Heber McBride; Caroline Jennett b. Nov. 2, —, m. Joseph Jordon; Joseph Albert, m. Annie Russell. Family home Mt. Pleasant. Utah.
High priest; presided over St. John mission; missionary to Panaca, Nev., and Panguitch and Rush Valley, Utah.

McINTYRE, SAMUEL (son of William McIntyre and Margret Anglin of Texas). Born Dec. 16, 1844, in Texas. Came to Utah 1853, Captain Daily company.
Married Mary Alexander July 4, 1872, St. Louis, Mo. (daughter of Robert Alexander and Mary Melvin of St. Louis, who came to Utah 1872). Their children: Samuel G.; Frank; Lapere, m. Stella Switz; Mintha, m. Capt. R. H. Allen; Earl; Roy. Family home, Salt Lake City.
Stockraiser. With brother William he is owner of the Horn Silver mine.

McINTYRE, WILLIAM HOWELL (son of William McIntyre and Margret Anglin of Grimes county, near Anderson City, Texas). Born March 19, 1848, in Grimes Co., Texas. Came to Utah 1853 with his mother.
Married Phoebe Ogden Chase July 10, 1878, Salt Lake City (daughter of George O. Chase and Emily Marinda Hyde). Their children: June M. b. June 23, 1881, m. Frederick Carl Dern; Elizabeth G. b. Dec. 28, 1883, m. Arthur G. Hertzler; William Howell b. Jan. 2, 1887; Robert Bradford b. March 2, 1891; Margaret Anglin b. Aug. 11, 1894; Marion b. Nov. 19, 1898.
Director Z. C. M. I. and Deseret National bank. Owner and builder of the McIntyre building; owner McIntyre ranch of sixty-four thousand acres, Alberta, Canada. Engaged in cattle business. Freighter between Blackfoot, Idaho, and California; furnished the U. S. government at Ft. Douglas, Utah, with supplies. Went to Texas 1869, returning to South Tintic, Utah, the next year with 1,000 cattle. In 1872 brought 2,000 cattle to Utah from Fort Hayes, Kan., and has followed the cattle and land business ever since. In 1875 he and his brother Samuel bought an interest in the Mammoth mine. Tintic, Utah, and gained control of the mine 1879, own g it until 1901. This mine produced about two million dollars.

McKAY, ANGUS (son of William McKay and Grace Gunn of Kirtomy, Parish of Farr. Sutherlandshire, Scotland). Born June 3, 1839, Kirtomy, Scotland. Came to Utah Oct. 4, 1863, Thomas Ricks company.
Married Williamena McKay Dec. 14, 1866 (daughter of William McKay and Ellen Oman of Thurso Parish, Caithness, Scotland, pioneers Oct. 1859, James Brown company). She was born Dec. 23, 1846. Their children: Barbara E., m. A. E. Barnes Oct. 21, 1891; Cathrine G., m. John McFarland Oct. 17, 1889; Angus W., m. Christina Wanggsard Oct. 23, 1902; Isabella; Harriet C., d. 1878; Donald D., m. Ethel E. McLean Dec. 8, 1905; James G.; Mary, m. John Christy Dec. 24, 1902; Hugh Leroy, d. 1894; Ernest R. Family home Huntsville, Utah.
Senior president 75th quorum seventies; missionary to Arizona February, 1873, and March, 1876; to southern states November, 1882, and to Scotland October, 1883; president Y. M. M. I. A. 6 years; Sunday school teacher 40 years. Justice of peace; road supervisor; school trustee 19 years; state representative. First lieutenant Utah territorial militia. Farmer and stockraiser.

McKAY, WILLIAM (son of John McKay, born 1779, and Barbara Monroe, both of Sutherland, Scotland). He was born March 18, 1804, Scotland. Came to Utah September, 1859, James S. Brown company.
Married Ellen Oman (daughter of David Oman and Isabella Sutherland), who was born 1810, and came to Utah with husband. Their children: Isaac b. Nov. 3, 1839, m. Ellen Jesperson; Isabella b. Aug. 26, 1842, m. William Wadley 1858; David b. May 3, 1844, m. Jennette Evans April 9, 1867; Wilhelmina b. Dec. 23, 1846, m. Angus McKay Dec. 14, 1866; Barbara b. Dec. 23, 1846; John George b. 1848; Catherine b. May 1, 1849, m. John Grow Nov. 8, 1869. Family home Ogden, Utah.
President elders quorum, Weber stake. Founded first co-operative mercantile and drug company in Ogden, and was its president.

McKAY, DAVID (son of William McKay and Ellen Oman). Born May 3, 1844, Thurso, Caithness, Scotland. Came to Utah with father.
Married Jennette Evans April 9, 1867, Salt Lake City (daughter of Thomas Evans and Margaret Powell of Cefn-Coed, near Merthyr Tydfil, Wales, pioneers 1859, Captain Buzzard company). She was born Aug. 28, 1850, at Cefn-Coed. Their children: Margaret Elizabeth b. Jan. 22, 1869, d. March 25, 1880; Elena Odetta b. March 16, 1871, d. April 1, 1880; David Oman b. Sept. 8, 1873, m. Emma Ray Riggs Jan. 2, 1901; Thomas Evans b. Oct. 29, 1875, m. Faun Brimhall Sept. 11, 1912; Jennette Isabelle b. Nov. 12, 1879, m. Joseph R. Morrell June 19, 1907; Annie Powell b. April 17, 1881, m. Thomas B. Farr Sept. 20, 1905; Elizabeth Odetta b. Oct. 30, 1884; William Monroe b. Sept. 3, 1887; Katherine Fayorite b. Feb. 16, 1891; Morgan Powell b. June 25, 1893. Family home Huntsville, Utah.
One of presidents of 75th quorum seventies; missionary to Scotland 1891-93; president 75th quorum high priests; presi-

dent Scotch conference 1882-83; bishop Eden ward 1884; bishop Huntsville ward 1888. Member lower house of first state legislature, and later elected to the senate. Justice of peace. Farmer and stockraiser.

McKAY, DAVID O. (son of David McKay and Jennette Evans). Born Sept. 8, 1873, Huntsville, Utah.
Married Emma Ray Riggs Jan. 2, 1901, Salt Lake City (daughter of Obadiah H. Riggs and Emma L. Robbins of Salt Lake City). She was born June 23, 1877. Their children: David Lawrence b. Sept. 30, 1901; Llewelyn Riggs b. June 5, 1904; Louisa Jennette b. Oct. 13, 1906; Royle Riggs b. Oct. 21, 1909. Family home Ogden, Utah.
Secretary Sunday school; ward officer in Y. M. M. I. A.; president Scotch mission 1898-99; called as a member council of twelve apostles 1906; member superintendency Weber stake Sunday school. Principal Weber academy 1902-08. Teacher. Stockraiser.

McKEAN, THEODORE (son of Washington McKean and Margaret Ivins of Tom's River, Ocean county, N. J.). Born Oct. 26, 1829, Allentown, N. J. Came to Utah Aug. 11, 1853. Orson Pratt and Horace S. Eldredge company.
Married Mary Page Gulick 1847 at Tom's River (daughter of Stephen Gulick and Deborah Homes Page of Tom's River). She was born Aug. 6, 1825. Their children: George b. April 12, 1848; Sarah Ivins b. April 11, 1849, m. William Perry Nebeker; Mary Gulick b. Oct. 10, 1851, m. William J. Newman; Theodore b. Oct. 10, 1855, m. Sophia J. Lane; Stephen G. b. July 11, 1858; Margaret I. b. Sept. 3, 1861; Ruth Gulick b. May 28, 1864; Maud b. Sept. 30, 1868. Family home Salt Lake City, Utah.
Married Elizabeth Ann Emery 1875, Salt Lake City (daughter of Henry Emery and Elizabeth Brewerton of Salt Lake City). She was born March 1, 1854. Their children: John Emery; Elizabeth E., m. Idwill Ajax; Mabel; Dorothea E.; Samuel E.; Vida E., m. Jesse Argile; Edith E.; Bertha E., m. Claron Swan; Joseph E.; David; Salome E.; Theodoris E.; Naomi E.; Jean E.
Seventy 1859 and high priest 1877; high councilor Salt Lake stake; counselor to Bishop Kesler June, 1872 to December, 1884; missionary to eastern states 1869, to Europe July, 1891; Sunday school superintendent. Surveyor of Salt Lake county August, 1860; county treasurer September, 1860-76; collector internal revenue 1862-69; sheriff August, 1876 to October, 1883; road commissioner January, 1860; superintendent of water works; city councilman Sept. 30, 1860. Director Z. C. M. I. 1872. Colonel of Nauvoo Legion Feb. 1, 1868. Veteran Indian war.

McKEAN, THEODORE, JR. (son of Theodore McKean and Mary Page Gulick of Tom's River, N. J., pioneers Aug. 11, 1853). Born Oct. 10, 1855.
Married Sophia Jane Lane Feb. 7, 1884, Salt Lake City, Daniel H. Wells officiating (daughter of James Lane and Sophia S. Brown of Salt Lake City, pioneers 1861, James S. Brown company). She was born Jan. 24, 1864, 16th ward, Salt Lake City. Their children: Theodore L. b. Nov. 17, 1884, m. Nina Burnham; Howard J. b. Sept. 16, 1886, m. Mable Fredrickson; Franklin L. b. Nov. 18, 1888, m. Cora Millecam; Margaret b. April 7, 1891, m. Robert C. Newson; Alvin b. May 31, 1893; Royal L. b. March 10, 1896; Rachel I. b. March 10, 1896; Mary b. Jan. 18, 1900; Edna b. Nov. 11, 1901. Family home 29th ward, Salt Lake City.
High priest; bishop of 29th ward 1901-10. Sheep inspector and stockman.

McKEE, JAMES (son of David McKee and Mary Tweed McMillian, both of Butler county, Pa.). Born May 8, 1820, in Butler county, Pa. Came to Utah in 1850.
Married Matilda Sweat. Their children: James Albert, m. Ruth Chase; Sarah Jane, m. Andrew Stephensen; David D., m. Emily Giles. Family home Spanish Fork, Utah.
Elder. Veteran Walker Indian war. Farmer. Died July 14, 1861.

McKEE, JAMES ALBERT (son of James McKee and Matilda Sweat). Born Dec. 27, 1854, Palmyra, Utah.
Married Ruth Chase Jan. 17, 1878, Nephi, Utah (daughter of John Darwin Chase and Almira Higgins of Vermont, pioneers 1847). She was born Oct. 12, 1859. Their children: Ruth Almire b. April 15, 1880; James Albert b. Aug. 3, 1883, m. May Sherman; Laura Matilda b. Feb. 2, 1885; Goldie Euzell b. March 25, 1887, m. Robert C. Woodward; Archie Montell b. Feb. 17, 1889, died; Alma Dorus b. Dec. 14, 1892; Miriam Chloe b. May 27, 1895; Sarah Lazette b. March 27, 1897, both d. infants; David Vardine b. June 26, 1899. Family home Huntington, Utah.
Member 81st quorum seventies; high priest; president of priests, teachers and deacons 1883-87. Farmer; restaurateur.

McKEE, THOMAS. Came to Utah with oxteam company.
Married Percy Sweat. Their children: David, m. Rachel Dimmick; Polly, m. George Ainge; Harriet, m. John Babcock; Sarah, m. David Hutchinson; Elizabeth, m. George Gates; Susan, m. Charles Mechem. Family home Spanish Fork, Utah.
High priest. Farmer. Died at Salina, Utah.

McKEE, WILLIAM (son of David McKee of Pennsylvania). Born 1825 in Pennsylvania. Came to Utah 1852, captain of oxteam company.
Married Sarah Ann Hodgson at Salt Lake City, who was born in Bradford, Eng. Their children: David, d. infant; Mary Tweed, m. Thomas Butler; William, m. Emily Aurilla Markham; Joseph A. b. April 3, 1859, m. Laura Orser, m. Sarah Priscilla Henry; Sarah Ann, d. child; Louisa Ann, m. Marion Dudley. Family home Spanish Fork, Utah.
Member of seventy. Brought immigrants to Utah. Veteran Echo Canyon campaign and Indian wars. Captain police Spanish Fork 15 years. Farmer. Died 1900 Vernal, Utah.

McKEE, WILLIAM, JR. (son of William McKee and Sarah Ann Hodgson). Born Feb. 24, 1857, Spanish Fork, Utah.
Married Emily Aurilia Markham March 10, 1886, Spanish Fork, Utah (daughter of Stephen Markham and Mary Curtis of Spanish Fork, Utah, pioneers July 24, 1847, Brigham Young company). She was born Jan. 4, 1864. Their children: Mary b. Jan. 27, 1887; Joseph Ray b. Oct. 21, 1889; Emily Aurilla b. Feb. 28, 1892; Sarah Ann b. Jan. 15, 1895; Margaret Elsie b. Aug. 11, 1900; William Harvey and Stephen Harold b. Nov. 25, 1903; Lynn Curtis b. Jan. 12, 1912. Family home Maeser, Utah.
Elder; ward teacher. Farmer and stockraiser.

McKEE, JOSEPH A. (son of William McKee and Sarah Ann Hodgson). Born April 3, 1859, Spanish Fork, Utah.
Married Laura Orser Dec. 28, 1887, Vernal, Utah (daughter of Everet Orser and Mary America Mecham of Provo, Utah), who was born Nov. 13, 1868. Their children: Laura America b. Dec. 10, 1888, m. John Alma Workman; William F. b. Sept. 23, 1890; Eugene b. Feb. 12, 1892, d. infant; Mary Alice b. Jan. 15, 1896; Joseph Clair b. Feb. 20, 1899, d. aged 13; Ella Leon b. Aug. 31, 1902. Family home Vernal, Utah.
Married Sarah Priscilla Henry Sept. 7, 1904, Salt Lake City (daughter of James B. Henry, born in Michigan, and Mary Brown, born in South Cottonwood, who resided in Heber and Vernal, Utah). She was born May 5, 1881. Their children: Rena Permelia b. June 23, 1905, d. May 7, 1906; Josephine b. April 22, 1910; Vella b. Sept. 6, 1912. Family home Vernal, Utah.
President Y. M. M. I. A.; bishop's counselor; bishop Uinta. County commissioner. President Ashley Upper Irrigation Co.; president Ouray Valley Irrigation Co. Farmer.

McKELL, ROBERT (son of John McKell and Robena Wilson of Glasgow, Scotland. Came to Utah 1852, Captain Tidwell company). Born Feb. 23, 1823, Glasgow, Scotland. Came to Utah 1852 with parents.
Married Elizabeth Boyack January, 1856 (daughter of James Boyack and Elizabeth Mealmaker of Dundee, Scotland, who were married at Dundee; came to Utah Oct. 24, 1855, Milo Andrus company). She was born April 15, 1838, came to Utah with parents. Their children: Robert W. b. Nov. 16, 1856, m. Emma E. Jex; Henry J. b. May 25, 1858, m. Alice V. Jex; Louisa S. b. Jan. 1, 1860, m. William B. Hughes; Ellen R. b. Feb. 26, 1862, m. David A. Hughes; William B. b. Feb. 19, 1864, m. Marelda Andrus; Emma J. b. March 4, 1866, m. Joseph Brockbank; Margaret Ann b. April 19, 1868, m. Jacob A. Hansen; David A. b. March 8, 1870, m. Sarah Ann Wood; John E. b. Feb. 25, 1873, d. Dec. 5, 1896; Joseph G. b. April 27, 1875, m. Rebecca J. Sterling; Lucy M. b. Aug. 8, 1877, m. James Clayton Beck. Family home Spanish Fork, Utah.
President East Bench Irrigation and Manufactory Co. and director in board of Spanish Fork co-op. for several years. Pioneer blacksmith of Spanish Fork, Utah. Veteran Indian war. Helped forge first cannon used in Spanish Fork.

McKELL, ROBERT W. (son of Robert McKell and Elizabeth Boyack). Born Nov. 16, 1856, Spanish Fork, Utah.
Married Emma E. Jex Feb. 28, 1876, Salt Lake City (daughter of William Jex and Eliza Goodson, who came to Utah Sept. 30, 1854, with the Darwin Richardson company). She was born Oct. 11, 1858, Salt Lake City. Their children: Elizabeth R. b. Feb. 14, 1877, m. Peter Regtreep; Alice E. b. Oct. 28, 1878, d. March 10, 1891; Robert R. b. Dec. 18, 1880, d. Oct. 14, 1887; Effa B. Dec. 5, 1882, m. John T. Williams; Eva b. Dec. 5, 1885, m. E. Arthur Nielsen; Wilson S. b. March 24, 1885, d. March 5, 1891; Harriet C. b. Aug. 3, 1887, m. J. Delbert Banks; Ellen J. b. Aug. 14, 1889, m. Arnold Lee; Rodney W. b. April 4, 1892; Henry B. b. Oct. 21, 1894; Lenard E. b. Jan. 21, 1897; Ruby L. b. Dec. 1, 1899.
Bishop Spanish Fork; missionary to Illinois May 1, 1888. Director Spanish Fork Co-op.; director in Jex Lumber Co. City councilman of Spanish Fork three terms.

McKENZIE, RODERICK (son of Roderick McKenzie, died 1869, Howick, Canada, and Euphemia McKimron, died 1875, Keene, N. H., both of Winchendon Springs, Mass.). Born Aug. 25, 1865, at Howick, Canada. Came to Utah 1891.
Married Mable Scott Aug. 24, 1904, Salt Lake City (daughter of Rev. D. B. Scott of Windsor, Nova Scotia, and Sarah Ann Tibbits of New Brunswick, Conn; came to Utah 1905). She was born Oct. 29, 1884.
Member board of public works 1911; chief of police Salt Lake City, 1907.

PIONEERS AND PROMINENT MEN OF UTAH 1061

McKINLEY, GEORGE (son of James McKinley and Jane Hogg of Fernent, Midlothian, Scotland). Born Jan. 6, 1805, at Fernent. Came to Utah 1864.
Married Mary Hamilton (daughter of Richard Hamilton and Mary Forsythe of Fernent, Scotland), who was born in 1807. Their children: Mary, m. Alexander Gillespie; James, m. Augusta Mengies; Robert, m. Isabella Watson; George Hamilton, m. Jane Johnston, m. Agnes Johnston; Archibold, m. Hannah Adamson; Peter, m. Margaret Adamson. Lived in Scotland.
High priest. Died in 1876 at Provo, Utah.

McKINLEY, GEORGE HAMILTON (son of George McKinley and Mary Hamilton). Born Jan. 6, 1835, Preston Paus, Scotland. Came to Utah July, 1880.
Married Jane Johnston Dec. 21, 1855 (daughter of George Johnston and Ann Clark of Cowdensbeath, Scotland), who was born Dec. 22, 1830. Their children: Ann, m. John Birch March 22, 1856; Mary b. Jan. 10, 1858, m. John Henderson; George b. March 9, 1859, died; James b. Dec. 22, 1860, m. Sarah Willey; George b. Jan. 22, 1863; Jane b. April 9, 1865; Janet b. Aug. 9, 1867—three died; Elizabeth, m. Lee Warner; Agnes b. Oct. 6, 1872, m. Walter G. Taylor; Hannah b. July 22, 1870, m. Aimy Baker; Robina b. Oct. 8, 1875, m. Edward G. Tieke.
Married Agnes Johnston June 6, 1900, Salt Lake City (daughter of George Johnston and Ann Clark of Cowdensbeath, Scotland), who was born in 1844.
Missionary to Scotland 1876-80; high priest. Engineer and miner.

McLACHLAN, WILLIAM (son of Gilbert McLachlan and Hannah W. Glencorse of Scotland). Born May 3, 1840, Gatelawbridge, Dumfrieshire, Scotland. Came to Utah October, 1863, John W. Wooley company.
Married Caroline Filer 1860, Coggishal, Eng. (daughter of William Filer and Maria Stow of Essex, Eng.), who was born July 6, 1837. Their children: William, George, and Gilbert, died; Ellen, m. I. R. Wilson; Alice, m. Benjamin E. Rich; Lily, m. A. C. Sperry; Ida, died; Joseph, died; Hannah, m. Warren Lyon; Isabel, m. Adam Sharp. Family home, Salt Lake City.
Married Margret Naismith 1874, Salt Lake City (daughter of William and Margaret Naismith of Salt Lake City, who came to Utah 1873). She was born 1850. Their children: George, died; May, m. Alvin Cundick; Mary, m. David Lindblom; John, m. Nettie West; Robert, died; James, died. Family home Taylorsville, Utah.
Married Lucy J. H. Evans 1886, Salt Lake City (daughter of William Evans and Charlotte Hyder of Nephi, Utah, pioneers Oct. 2, 1851). She was born 1858. Their children: Nephi; Grace; Lucile, died. Family home, Salt Lake City.
Member 23d quorum seventies; missionary to New Zealand 1875-77; bishop's counselor; superintendent 7th ward Sunday school 40 years; president Pioneer stake. Carpenter and contractor.

McLAWS, JOHN (son of John McLaws, born June, 1793, Campsie, Scotland, and Sarah Whitworth, born July 23, 1802, Dalmottor, Scotland—married July 28, 1817). Born Nov. 27, 1827, Renfrew, Scotland. Came to Utah August, 1851.
Married Joanna Ross Dec. 5, 1850 (daughter of Daniel Ross and Agnes McKeller—married April 28, 1814). She was born Dec. 23, 1831. Their children: John b. Sept. 14, 1852, m. Sophia De La Mare 1875; Daniel Ross b. March 6, 1854, m. Julia Lee June 7, 1876; William b. Feb. 16, 1856, m. Mary Herron April 19, 1880; George b. March 9, 1858, m. Ella Herron; Robert Fleming b. April 7, 1860, m. Florence Fulmer; Agnes McKeller b. Dec. 31, 1861, m. Peter M. Clegg; Alexander b. Aug. 28, 1864; Sarah Whitworth b. June 30, 1866; Jane b. May 30, 1867; Catherine b. March 29, 1869, m. George Fulmer; Joanna b. Aug. 27, 1871; Mary Ann b. Aug. 14, 1874, m. A. M. Shields; James b. Aug. 14, 1874. Family home Tooele, Utah

McLAWS, JOHN, JR. (son of John McLaws and Joanna Ross). Born Sept. 14, 1852, Salt Lake City, Utah.
Married Sophia De La Mare Dec. 27, 1875, Salt Lake City (daughter of Philip De La Mare and Mary Chivlier, pioneers 1851), who was born Aug. 10, 1857, Tooele, Utah. Their children: John William b. Aug. 3, 1876, m. Ellen Elsie Bradshaw March 7, 1900; Joanna b. Nov. 22, 1877; Francis b. Feb. 24, 1880, m. Lydia Pearl Finke Sept. 27, 1901; Mary Alice b. Jan. 20, 1882, m. E. A. Wilkinson April 20, 1910; Walter b. Nov. 11, 1883; Agnes Estella b. Aug. 29, 1885, m. F. L. Cummins March 17, 1909; Robert b. Nov. 12, 1887; Philip Delmar b. July 4, 1889; Jennie b. March 1, 1891; Ruby Elizabeth b. Jan. 30, 1894; Millie May b. Dec. 6, 1895; Daniel Ross b. Dec. 31, 1897; Archie Leo b. Oct. 29, 1899. Family home St. Joseph, Ariz.
High priest; stake superintendent Sunday schools Little Colorado stake. First postmaster at Allen, now St. Joseph, Ariz. High counselor Snowflake stake.

McMASTER, WILLIAM ATHOL (son of Peter McMaster and Grace Henderson of Scotland). Born Sept. 20, 1816, Greenock, Renfrewshire, Scotland. Came to Utah Oct. 1, 1854, Daniel Garn company.
Married Margaret Drummond Ferguson 1841, Paisley, Scotland (daughter of James Ferguson and Margaret Drummond of Scotland). Their children: John Brigham b. Aug. 15, 1843, m. Elizabeth Forrest, m. Vera Forrest; Margaret Drummond b. Jan. 15, 1845, m. John Priestley; Grace, d. infant; Israelus, d. infant; William Athol, m. Rachel Smith; Virginia Faithful, m. William Major; Donald Henderson b. Aug. 16, 1855; Alexander b. Aug. 12, 1857, m. Frances Laura Mitchell; James Bruce, d. infant; Hannah E. b. March 16, 1860, m. Charles J. Foulger; Mary A. b. April 28, 1862, m. Charles M. Latyon; Joseph H. b. July 31, 1865. Family home, Salt Lake City.
Missionary to Great Britain 1865-69; member 11th ward bishopric; first superintendent of 11th ward Sunday school. First rope-maker in Utah. Merchant. Died Jan. 20, 1887, Salt Lake City.

McMASTER, JOHN BRIGHAM (son of William Athol McMaster and Margaret D. Ferguson of Scotland, married Sept. 2, 1842). Born Aug. 17, 1843, Dumfermline, Scotland. Came to Utah Oct. 1, 1854, Daniel Garn company.
Married Elizabeth Ferguson December, 1869, Salt Lake City (daughter of Thomas M. and Elizabeth Ferguson Forrest, Vale of Levon, Scotland; came to Utah June 25, 1869, Elias Morris company). She was born March 6, 1844. Their children: William O. b. March 25, 1871; Thomas M. b. July 21, 1872; Margaret D. b. Sept. 12, 1874; John b. April 14, 1877. Family home Brigham City, Utah.
High priest; missionary to Scotland 1895-96; bishop. Treasurer; commissioner; justice of the peace; school trustee; member of city council. Merchant.

McMASTER, ALEXANDER (son of William Athol McMaster and Margaret D. Ferguson). Born Aug. 12, 1857, Salt Lake City.
Married Frances Laura Mitchell Dec. 27, 1883, Salt Lake City (daughter of Frederick A. H. F. Mitchell and Margaret Thompson of Salt Lake City, pioneers 1853), who was born March 20, 1866. Their children: Lucile b. June 10, 1885, m. Daniel Coulam; Alexander b. March 11, 1888, m. Hazel Pepper; Frank Athol b. Sept. 24, 1890; Frances Laura b. April 12, 1897. Family home, Salt Lake City.
Member 57th quorum seventies; missionary to southern states 1887-89; member high council of Ensign stake; superintendent 11th ward Sunday school. Justice of peace, fifth precinct, two terms; judge of juvenile court, third district, Salt Lake, Summit and Tooele counties. Printer and editor; lawyer.

McMICHAEL, ROBERT (son of Thomas McMichael of Thornebank, Scotland). Born Aug. 9, 1811, in Ireland. Came to Utah Sept. 3, 1852, Abraham O. Smoot company.
Married Elizabeth McMullen, Scotland (daughter of John McMullen and Elizabeth Pickett of Scotland, pioneers Sept. 3, 1852, Abraham O. Smoot company). She was born March 20, 1816. Their children: Jane b. Jan. 3, 1836, died; Elizabeth b. Dec. 18, 1836, m. E. H. Rodeback; Mary Ann b. Dec. 27, 1838, m. Franklin Hodge; John b. Jan. 27, 1841, died; William b. Feb. 9, 1842, m. Arsula Brim 1863; Robert b. March 25, 1844, m. Celestia Griffiths; Sarah b. Oct. 7, 1845, m. George B. Lymes; Martha b. May 8, 1848, m. Adelbert Hillhouse; Joseph Clements b. Oct. 1, 1850, died; Maria b. July 14, 1853, m. Robert McQueen; Isabell Esther b. Feb. 13, 1855, m. Hugh H. McQueen; Emma b. Sept. 11, 1857, m. Jonah Birch. Family home Sugar House, Utah. Died in 1896.

McMICHAEL, WILLIAM (son of Robert McMichael and Elizabeth McMullen, pioneers Sept. 3, 1852, with Abraham O. Smoot company). Born Feb. 9, 1842, Scotland.
Married Arsula Brim 1863, Coalville, Utah (daughter of Verness and Margaret Brim of Nauvoo, Ill., pioneers 1852), who was born April 1844. Their children: Elizabeth b. 1864, m. John Leonard Frazier; Sarah Margaret b. 1865, m. Robert Birch; Martha Jane b. 1867, m. Alma Stonebreaker; William Frederick, died; Robert Vernoss b. 1871, m. Alice Alferetta Johnson, d. 1910; Deseret Amelia b. 1873, m. William Sargent. Family home Summit Co., Utah.
Married Elizabeth Robinson 1878, Coalville, Utah (daughter of Samuel and Ann Soar Robinson of Eastwood, Nottingham, Eng.; former came to Utah 1873 by rail, Samuel Robinson company). She was born Jan. 1, 1860. Their children: William Henry b. May 12, 1879, d. Sept. 4, 1879; Le Roy b. July 5, 1880, m. Margaret Fadlicat; Mary Anice b. June 9, 1886, m. John H. Yount; Theone Theressa b. Sept. 30, 1892. Family home Summit Co., Utah.

McMILLAN, DAVID (son of Hugh McMillan and Catherine Fowler of Ballyrick, County of Down, Ireland). Born March 10, 1860, at Ballyrick. Came to Utah October, 1890, independent company.
Married Agnes Bell March 2, 1888, Laramie, Wyo. (daughter of Thomas Bell and Agnes Cuningham of Springside, Ayrshire, Scotland; came to Utah October, 1890). She was born Dec. 17, 1869. Their children: Agnes Cuningham b. Dec. 16, 1889, m. Charles Henry Hill; Hugh b. Jan. 3, 1891; Catherine Fowler b. April 7, 1892; Thomas b. April 1, 1894; Margerite b. Nov. 18, 1901; Mary Burns b. Jan. 25, 1903; David b. Dec. 14, 1905, died; John M. Baxter b. March 1, 1908. Family home Clear Creek, Carbon Co., Utah.
High priest; bishop of Clear Creek ward, Carbon stake, Oct. 29, 1911, M. Kemmerer ward, Woodruff stake, Wyoming, Feb. 2, 1902; counselor to Presiding Elder Daniel Clark, Kemmerer branch; Sunday school superintendent. School trustee Clear Creek; coal mine inspector Clear Creek, 1907. Moved from Wyoming to Castle Gate, Utah, 1890; to Clear Creek, 1907. Engaged in coal mining.

1062 PIONEERS AND PROMINENT MEN OF UTAH

McMULLIN, HENRY (son of Archible and Sarah Lufkin McMullin of Vinal Haven, Me.). Born 1816 at Vinal Haven. Came to Utah Sept. 3, 1855, with John Hindley company.
Married Mary Pierce (daughter of Josiah and Elizabeth Hudson Pierce of Vinal Haven, pioneers Sept. 3, 1855, John Hindley company). She was born 1824. Their children: Albert Eats b. July 15, 1847, m. Nancy Jane Ross; Alphonzo Payson, m. Lucy Witt; Calvin Pendleton, died; Henry Lufkin, m. Nettie Murdock; Sarah Jane, m. Thomas Hicken; Susan, died; Edwin Pierce. Family home Heber City, Utah.
High priest; member of high council. Selectman; postmaster. Carpenter. Died May 2, 1886, Heber City, Utah.

McMULLIN, ALBERT E. (son of Henry McMullin and Mary Pierce, Vinal Haven, Me.). Born July 15, 1847, Vinal Haven. Came to Utah with father.
Married Nancy Jane Ross Dec. 15, 1868, Salt Lake City (daughter of Thomas and Rachel Smith Ross, Heber Utah, pioneers 1850), who was born Dec. 11, 1848. Their children: Estella Jane b. Oct. 26, 1869, m. Ernest Ekins Jan. 3, 1891; Albert Orlando b. Oct. 11, 1871, m. Annie Bryner Jan. 1, 1894; Bryant Ross b. Jan. 24, 1874, m. Manerva Ellis; Rachel Arletta b. Dec. 24, 1876, died; Mary Elizabeth b. Jan. 20, 1878, m. Lee Caunaday; Florence Lucinda b. Jan. 22, 1880, died; Elmer Henry b. Jan. 20, 1882, m. Ethel Jenson; Clara b. March 14, 1884, died; Chloe Clair b. March 14, 1884, m. Ianthus Barlow; Leanor b. Aug. 28, 1886, died; Thomas Nelson b. June 4, 1889; LeRoy b. Jan. 15, 1892.
Married Elizabeth F. Bell July 25, 1877, St. George, Utah (daughter of William Bell and Jane Laidlaw of Heber City, Utah, pioneers 1853), who was born Sept. 15, 1858. Their children: Jane Ann b. May 26, 1878, m. George N. Hill; Nellie Bell b. Dec. 31, 1880, m. Maroni Turner; Mary Lucile b. April 30, 1882, m. Van Tromp; William Bell b. Sept. 5, 1884, m. Bertha Ellis; Elizabeth Bell b. Oct. 5, 1886, died; Susan Bell b. Aug. 11, 1888, m. Lewis Ray; Althora Bell Feb. 14, 1898; Ruby Bell b. Oct. 15, 1900. Families resided at Wellington, Carbon Co., Utah.
High priest; member of high council Heber, Utah; bishop at Wellington, Emery Co., Utah. Constable of Heber; road supervisor. Contractor and farmer.

McMURRAY, JOHN (son of William McMurray). Born March 1798. Came to Utah October, 1852, Warren Snow company.
Married Mary Hutton Aug. 18, 1821 (daughter of Simeon Hutton and Mary Underwood, latter a pioneer October, 1852, Warren Snow company). She was born Nov. 6, 1801. Their children: James b. Dec. 24, 1829, m. Elizabeth Stevenson; Joseph b. April 13, 1832, m. Elizabeth Fairchild; Charles K. b. June 24, 1854, m. Melvina Wilson; Arrabella, m. Oliver Weatherby 1846; Matilda J. b. 1836, m. Willam C. Martindale 1851; Harriet Lucinda b. 1840, m. Moroni Fairchild 1853.
High priest. Died October, 1853, Salt Lake City.

McMURRAY, JAMES (son of John McMurray and Mary Hutton). Born at Hodgetown, Pa., Dec. 24, 1829.
Married Elizabeth Stevenson, Salt Lake City (daughter of John Stevenson, and Mary Vickers, pioneers 1862, Joseph Horne company). She was born Dec. 21, 1828, Breaston, Eng. Their children: James S. b. July 13, 1863, m. Sarah Orr Aug. 5, 1886; John S. b. March 6, 1865, m. Clarn D. Hymas April 9, 1891; Charles b. Nov. 30, 1866, d. infant; Jesse b. Oct. 3, 1867; Mary b. April 3, 1870, died June 1870; Hannah M. b. May 13, 1871; Fanny Lee b. Nov. 2, 1873, m. Samuel Hyrmas Oct. 17, 1900; Bertha b. Nov. 5, 1876, m. Julius Fairchild 1904; George V. b. Jan. 1, 1880, m. Nellie Austin Oct. 11, 1905. Family home Liberty, Bear Lake county, Idaho.
High priest; second counselor in Liberty ward a number of years.

McNEIL, THOMAS (son of Thomas McNeil, born March 20, 1769, and Emily Selkirk, of Scotland). Born Feb. 15, 1823, Tranent, Scotland. Came to Utah October, 1859.
Married Jannette Reid June 19, 1845 (daughter of Peter and Margaret Martin Reid), who was born Aug. 2, 1823. Their children: Margaret b. April 11, 1846, m. Henry Ballard May 5, 1861; Thomas b. Dec. 6, 1847, m. Mary J. Montgomery March 11, 1872; Emily b. June 19, 1849, m. Henry Ballard Oct. 4, 1867; James Reid b. Oct. 24, 1854, m. Phebe Ann Merrill March 15, 1875; Charles T. b. May 1, 1856, m. Emma Hibbard Dec. 1880; Joseph b. Jan. 14, 1859, d. 1875; Jannet Jane b. March 14, 1861, m. Robert Davidson; William R. b. May 3, 1863; Hyrum b. Oct. 30, 1864; George b. Oct. 1, 1866, m. Ellen Becket. Family home Logan, Utah.
Presiding elder Tranent, Scotland, 1849-56; first counselor to Bishop Robert Davidson May 31, 1877.

McNEIL, JAMES REID (son of Thomas McNeil and Jannette Reid). Born Oct. 24, 1854, Tranent, Scotland.
Married Phebe Ann Merrill March 15, 1875, at Salt Lake City (daughter of Marriner Wood Merrill and Sarah Ann Atkinson, pioneers 1853, William Atkinson company). She was born Oct. 24, 1854, Bountiful, Utah. Their children: Sarah Jannette b. Sept. 16, 1876, d. Sept. 16, 1878; Mary Margaret b. Sept. 16, 1876, d. Sept. 16, 1876; Phebe Deseret b. Oct. 29, 1878, d. Jan. 19, 1901; Chloe Leona b. Nov. 3, 1880, m. Thomas O. Howell July 17, 1901; Ida Ione b. Aug. 23, 1882; m. James A. Hadley July 6, 1905; James Reid b. Dec. 7, 1884, d. June 20, 1895; Marriner Wood b. Dec. 7, 1884, m. Lucy Elvira Cafferty; J. Taylor b. Nov. 12, 1886, d. Nov. 12, 1886; Rhoda Winnefred b. Feb. 20, 1888, d. Aug. 23, 1892; Preston Merril b. May 3, 1890, d. Oct. 7, 1891; Velma Ethel b. June 21,

1892, m. George H. Gardner Jan. 6, 1911; Elva Mahala b. March 27, 1895. Family home Preston, Idaho.
Married Jane Montgomery (McNeil) July 30, 1889, Salt Lake City, Utah (daughter of John and Ann Montgomery), who was born Aug. 2, 1853, England. Children by former marriage: Joseph Reid b. June 17, 1881, d. Sept. 14, 1898; Margaret Roxie b. May 13, 1884, m. Orson F. Lewis; Henry Ballard b. Feb. 1, 1887, m. Ruby Hakes.
Married Elizabeth Nielson April 5, 1882 (daughter of Peter Nielson and Huldah Fransiski Larson), who was born July 19, 1865, Peterson, Morgan Co., Utah. Their children: William Reid b. March 1, 1884, m. Edith Chedgzey Feb. 16, 1913; Thomas Peter b. Nov. 10, 1886, d. Sept. 18, 1887; Huldah Emily b. Oct. 22, 1889, m. Henry E. Larson Sept 14, 1910; Mary Elizabeth b. April 19, 1892; Esther Erastus b. May 24, 1895; James Russell b. July 19, 1898, d. March 8, 1900; Edgar Verne b. Dec. 7, 1901; John Nielson b. May 7, 1904; Vaughn b. Sept. 11, 1907, d. Sept. 11, 1907; Mar b. May 2, 1912, d. Jan. 29, 1913.
Missionary to Ramah, McKinley county, N. M. Moved to Fairview, Idaho, 1896, to Preston, Idaho 1907. Member Oneida stake high council; bishop of Ramah ward, New Mexico.

McPHERSON, JAMES RAMSAY (son of David McPherson, born 1804, Dundee, Forfarshire, and Mary Ramsay, born July 26, 1803, Arley, Scotland—married 1823). He was born March 31, 1831, Glenproson, Forfarshire. Came to Utah Dec. 9, 1853, Preston Thomas company.
Married Jane Ann Ollorton July 15, 1860, Eccleston, Lancaster, Eng. (daughter of John Ollorton and Alice Dancy, pioneers Nov. 20, 1856, Edward Martin company). She was born Jan. 2, 1841. Their children: Mary Lovina b. Nov. 27, 1861, m. William Andrews Wright Feb. 10, 1881; James b. April 5, 1863; Alice Ann b. Oct. 28, 1864, m. James Banford Riches Oct. 9, 1884; John William b. Jan. 28, 1867, m. Mary Jane Jones Sept. 11, 1895; Seth Ollorton b. July 13, 1869, m. Margaret Shaw July 18, 1894; Jane Ann b. Feb. 25, 1871; Elizabeth Helen b. Nov. 1, 1872, m. Marcus Lorenzo Swoby June 5, 1901; Rose b. June 3, 1874, m. Osmond Card July 19, 1907; Thomas Whitson b. Jan. 29, 1876; Janet b. Feb. 27, 1877; Esabell Estelle b. June 15, 1878; Heber Ernest b. June 28, 1880, m. Emeline Huggins Dec. 5, 1906; Amelia b. Aug. 15, 1882; Bertha b. Jan. 2, 1884; Ruby b. Nov. 23, 1886, m. Abner Bigler, Jr., Oct. 9, 1909.
Missionary to England 1884-85. Director of Nephi Irrigation Company. Councilman of Nephi 1889-92; member board of education 1890 and 1892. Vice-president of Nephi Co-op. 1896. Member of Captain Picton's company of infantry; transferred to Col. Warren S. Snow's regiment of cavalry. Member of Gen. Horace S. Eldredge's company in September, 1858. Captain of Home Guard, Monroe, Sevier county, 1865-67.

McQUARRIE, ALLAN (son of Hector McQuarrie, born 1759, Kildalton, Argyleshire, Scotland, and Annie McQuaig, born 1759). He was born Oct. 22, 1800, Kildalton. Came to Utah Sept. 12, 1857, Jesse B. Martin company.
Married Agnes Mathieson 1831 (daughter of Neil Mathieson and Agnes Graham—married at North Knapdale, Argyleshire). She was born Jan. 1, 1807. Their children: Robert b. Aug. 17, 1832, m. Mena Funk April 29, 1860; Hector b. Oct. 2, 1834, m. Agnes Gray Nov. 29, 1857; Mary G. b. Jan. 20, 1837, d. infant; Neil b. May 12, 1839, m. Margaret Thomson Aug. 12, 1869; Agnes b. Dec. 8, 1841, m. Lester J. Herrick June 22, 1867; John b. March 9, 1844, m. Mary E. Dixsen Nov. 13, 1871; Mary M. b. Aug. 23, 1846, m. Edward Bunker April 20, 1861.
Ordained high priest Feb. 1, 1859, by Charles R. Dana.

McQUARRIE, ROBERT (son of Allan McQuarrie and Agnes Mathieson). Born Aug. 17, 1832, North Knapdale, Scotland.
Married Mena Funk April 29, 1860, Ogden, Utah (daughter of Dedrick Funk and Christina Madsdaughter, pioneers 1859, James S Brown company). She was born Dec. 20, 1834, Brunholm, Denmark.
Married Hester Summerhays Ballam (widow of Mr. Ballam and mother of Alice M. b. July 25, 1874, d. infant; Isaac A. b. Feb. 6, 1876, d. infant; Frederick T. b. April 22, 1877, m. Lurany E. Grant Nov. 28, 1900; Florence b. Feb. 18, 1879, m. Frederick Elwood May 9, 1900; Willard b. March 18, 1881, m. Eliza E. Peterson June 8, 1905). Only child: Robert S. b. July 15, 1884, m. Lilly E. Mikkleson Nov. 21, 1906. Family resided Ogden and Hyde Park, Cache Co., Utah.
High priest; presided over second ward, Ogden; missionary to Great Britain two years; bishop of Ogden, second ward, 1877; stake tithing clerk for 12 years; Sunday school superintendent at Ogden, second ward, two years. County treasurer four years, Weber county; alderman second municipal ward of Ogden 1882-85; Ogden city councilman six years; Weber county treasurer eight years; school trustee six years; Ogden city treasurer two years; county commissioner three years.

N

NAEF, JACOB I. (son of Johannes Naef and Elizabeth Schweitzer of Ebnat, St. Gallen, Switzerland). Born Nov. 1, 1836, at Ebnat. Came to Utah Sept. 3, 1860, James D. Ross company.

Married Mary Frey May 29, 1860, Florence, Neb. (daughter of Jacob Frey and Barbara Erni of Babikon, St. Gallen, Switzerland, latter died at sea April, 1860). She was born April 9, 1840. Their children: Mary L. b. May 14, 1861, m. Peter W. Maughan; Jacob D. b. Jan. 11, 1864, m. Jennie L. Parker; Robert H. b. March 7, 1866, m. Rosali Haderli; Lydia E. b. Dec. 20, 1868, m. Halsey D. Fullmer; Annie E. b. April 8, 1870, m. Albert J. Hewlett; John A. b. April 7, 1872, m. Mary Parker; Joseph W. b. March 5, 1874, m. Minnie Parker; Rudolph G. b. May 9, 1876, m. Ellen Archibald; Elsie B. b. April 5, 1881, m. Ernest Kendrick. Family home Providence, Utah.

Married Anna Kathrina Tobler Oct. 29, 1873, Salt Lake City (daughter of Martin Tobler and Anna Kathrina Klarer of Herian, Switzerland), who was born May 21, 1855. Their children: Hyrum J. b. Sept. 6, 1874, m. Elizabeth Backer; Annie K. b. Feb. 6, 1876, m. Elmer S. Merrill; Ernest A. b. March 19, 1878, m. Violet Ivie; Franklin U. b. March 30, 1880, m. Annie M. Stone; Rhoda B. b. Feb. 26, 1882, m. Niels C. Olsen; Daniel C. b. April 27, 1884, m. Katie Scheibel; Elma E. b. April 26, 1886, m. Samuel Buckley; Lily J. b. Dec. 28, 1888, m. Jacob A. Wheeler; Elmer M. b. April 26, 1891; Arnold E. b. March 8, 1894. Family home Mapleton, Idaho.

Missionary to Switzerland and Germany 1885-87. Secretary of Irrigation Company; farmer; lumberman; weaver; rancher.

NATE, SAMSON (son of Richard Nate and Sarah New of Upton-on-Severn, Eng.). Born May 8, 1834, Worcestershire, Eng. Came to Utah Oct. 9, 1853, George Kendall company.
Married Mary Ann Cottrell December, 1852 (daughter of Benjamin Cottrell), who was born Dec. 23, 1831, and came to Utah with husband. Their children: Samson W. b. Oct. 24, 1854, m. Alice Kellsey; Mary Ann b. March 4, 1857, m. Joseph Lewis; Sarah Jane b. March 1, 1859, m. Reuben Oakey; Willard Benjamin b. April 18, 1861, m. Ann Bird Oct. 3, 1888; Elizabeth H. b. May 6, 1863, m. George H. Cook; George b. June 1866; Lucy Ann b. May 17, 1868, m. Theodore Dayton; Rosina M. b. June 19, 1870, m. James Sparks Oct. 3, 1888; Effie Minerva b. Dec. 27, 1872, m. Alfonso Quayle. Family home Fort Herriman, Utah.
Married Elizabeth Cornell Feb. 17, 1864, Salt Lake City (daughter of Frederick E. Cornell and Mary A. Munton, former a pioneer 1863, Captain McCarthy company). She was born Sept. 23, 1839, Enfield, Middlesex, Eng. Their children: Emma Elizabeth b. Jan. 6, 1865; Frederick Ebenezer b. April 24, 1866, m. Ettie C. Dayton Nov. 4, 1885; Louisa Adelaide b. Oct. 14, 1868, m. Hyrum A. Dayton Nov. 4, 1885; Henry William b. Nov. 18, 1870, m. Mary G. Sawyer Oct. 1891; Mary Ellen b. July 18, 1872, m. Charles H. Bridges Oct. 4, 1888; Charles Cornell b. June 13, 1874, m. Emma May Bird Feb. 14, 1899; Ettie Rebecca b. May 13, 1880, m. John H. Bird Sept. 29, 1899. Family home Paris, Bear Lake Co., Idaho.
First counselor to bishop 1879-1911.

NATE, SAMSON WILLIAM (son of Samson Nate and Mary Ann Cottrell). Born Oct. 24, 1854, Fort Herriman, Utah.
Married Alice Kellsey, at Dingle, Bear Lake Co., Idaho (daughter of Stephen Kellsey and Lydia Snyder, former came to Utah with a contingent of the Mormon Battalion). She was born Feb. 15, 1861, Little Cottonwood, Utah. Their children: Arthur b. Dec. 16, 1878, m. Alice M. Demick; Ida Ann b. July 6, 1881, m. Matthiur Schmidt; Samson William, Jr. b. Dec. 27, 1883, m. Ella Stephens; Rosina b. Sept. 12, 1885; Stephen Henry b. Sept. 12, 1890; George Talmage b. July 27, 1892; Mary Blanch b. Nov. 30, 1894. Family home Dingle, Idaho.

NAYLOR, ROBERT (son of George Naylor and Mary Sefton of Little Budworth, Chestershire, Eng.). Born Oct. 7, 1831, in Chestershire. Came to Utah July 24, 1872.
Married Annie Woodward 1857, Manchester, Lancastershire, Eng., who was born 1841. Their children: George, m. Catherine Thomson; Robert; William, m. Elizabeth Siddoway; Mary Jane, m. Lorenzo S. Briggs; Sarah Ann, m. J. L. Tracy; Amy, died. Family home Manchester, Eng. Farmer. Died September, 1897, in Shasta county, Cal.

NAYLOR, GEORGE (son of Robert Naylor and Annie Woodward). Born Dec. 25, 1858, Manchester, Eng. Came to Utah with parents.
Married Catherine Thomson Aug. 4, 1885, Salt Lake City (daughter of John S. Thomson and Catherine Muir, Fifehire, Scotland, pioneers September, 1866). She was born June 2, 1864. Their children: Ethel K. b. June 26, 1887; George A. b. July 20, 1888; Annie Maude b. Jan. 10, 1891; Clarence R. born Aug. 16, 1895; Lawrence T. b. April 16, 1897; John Quincy b. April 22, 1900; Inez W. b. Feb. 12, 1902; William H. b. Feb. 13, 1904; James E. b. May 11, 1907. Family home, Salt Lake City.
Deacon. County road supervisor. Sheepraiser.

NAYLOR, WILLIAM (son of George Naylor and Mary Sefton of Little Budworth, Chestershire, Eng.). Born Aug. 19, 1835, in Cheshire. Came to Utah 1848, Daniel Spencer company.
Married Annie Wright 1852, Salt Lake City (daughter of Henry Wright and Ruth Nevinson of Crewe, Chestershire, Eng., pioneers 1852, Claudius V. Spencer company). She was born March 31, 1837. Their children: Mary, m. Marcellius Wooley; Abbey R., d. aged 2; Louisa, d. aged 40; William, d. aged 14; Nettie, m. Henry Spencer; George F., m. Bessie Taylor; Joseph Edward, m. Sadie Garnes; Frank Sefton, m. Dora Laird; Howard B. Family home, Salt Lake City.
Member Salt Lake quorum seventies; missionary to Sandwich Islands 3½ years: high priest; second counselor to Bishop Wooley; superintendent Sunday school 15 years. Wheelwright; maker of the Naylor wagon.

NEAL, GEORGE AUGUSTUS (son of Walter Neal, born 1755, died 1822, and Rachel Scammon, born 1754, died 1842, both of Newmarket, N. H., and Cambria, Niagara county, N. Y.). He was born Oct. 3, 1794, Wakefield, Rockingham county, N. H. Came to Utah October, 1852, James Brown company.
Married Asenath Cooley Jan. 30, 1820 (daughter of Samuel Cooley, born Nov. 14, 1775, died Feb. 2, 1843, and Polly Dyke, born Aug. 4, 1781, died Sept. 10, 1838, both of Rutland, Vt.). Their children: Mary Melissa b. July 31, 1824 (d. Jan. 9, 1900), m. Oliver Boardman Huntington Aug. 17, 1845; William Cooley, m. Ann Eliza Dalton. Family home, Salt Lake City.
High priest; missionary in United States 1853-54; president of branch at Cambria, N. Y., 1843-52; block teacher. Called by Brigham Young to go south to locate places for the people on the "Move South" in 1857. One of the earliest pioneer nurserymen to import fruit trees into Utah from New England states. Veteran war of 1812. Farmer; stockraiser; nurseryman; capitalist; philanthropist. Died Oct. 15, 1874.

NEAL, WILLIAM COOLEY (son of George Augustus Neal and Asenath Cooley). Born July 1, 1828, Cambria, N. Y. Came to Utah Oct. 16, 1862, Augustus Canfield independent company.
Married Ann Eliza Dalton June 9, 1852, Cambria, N. Y. (daughter of William Dalton and Ann Eliza Savage of Niagara and Genesee counties, N. Y.), who was born Sept. 2, 1833, Rochester, N. Y., and came to Utah with husband. Their children: Josephine Asenath b. Aug. 28, 1853, m. William H. Schluter Oct. 16, 1876; Ann Eliza b. Nov. 19, 1856, d. Sept. 8, 1869; William Dalton b. Jan. 31, 1869, m. Myra Matilda White; Walter Scammon b. July 17, 1871, killed by O. S. L. train Dec. 8, 1897; Emma Elbertine b. Dec. 18, 1873, d. May 10, 1874. Family home, Salt Lake City.
High priest; missionary to New England states 1869-70, and to Arizona in 1873; block and ward teacher. Started first woolen mills in Ogden. Commissioner under Judge Elias Smith three years. County selectman 1869, and 1870 to 1873; grand juror; justice of peace of third precinct 1882. Served in Andrew Burt's company during Black Hawk Indian war 1866, and received medal for bravery. Farmer; stockraiser; freighter. Capitalist. Died Nov. 11, 1912.

NEAL, WILLIAM DALTON (son of William Cooley Neal and Ann Eliza Dalton). Born Jan. 31, 1869, Salt Lake City (they came to Utah 1876). He was born Feb. 26, 1873. Their children: William White b. Jan. 18, 1900; Lucile Ann b. May 22, 1903; Myra White b. Jan. 27, 1904, d. Jan. 27, 1904; Carrie b. Nov. 4, 1905; George Augustus b. Dec. 26, 1907; Bessie b. Oct. 19, 1909; Frances Dalton b. June 4, 1912. Family home, Salt Lake City.
Member 30th quorum seventies; missionary to Switzerland and Germany 1896-99; president 4th quorum deacons; Sunday school and block teacher; M. I. A. class leader; president Chemutz branch 1898-99. Assistant in United States geological survey of Book Cliff coal regions in Colorado and eastern Utah 1906; chemist for the Amalgamated Sugar Company 1908 in factories at Lewiston, Logan and Ogden. Joined Utah Society, Sons of American Revolution, in 1895; treasurer of same 1904-06; member International Congress of Geologists at St. Petersburg, Russia, 1897; counselor of Utah Academy of Sciences 1909-13; member 12th International Congress of Geologists, Toronto, Canada, August, 1913; member National Geographical Society. Bookkeeper and clerk for Consolidated Wagon and Machine Company 1911. B. S. and M. S., University of Utah; teacher of geology, University of Utah, Salt Lake high school, and Weber State Academy. Charter member Utah Academy of Sciences. Geologist and chemist. Worked at plumbing and gasfitting for David James & Co. 1888-89.

NEBEKER, JOHN (son of George Nebeker and Susannah Meredith of Newcastle county, Del.). Born Aug. 1, 1813, at Newport, Del. Came to Utah Sept. 24, 1847, Abraham Smoot company.
Married Lurena Fitzgerald Oct. 25, 1835, Reily, Butler Co., Ohio (daughter of John Fitzgerald), who was born April 25, 1819. Their children: William Perry, m. Sarah Ivins McKean, m. Phoebe Stafford Tingey; Ira, m. Delia Lano; Aaron, m. Jane A. Smith, m. Jane E. Brunker; Ashton, m. Lucy Pratt; Rosella, m. Christopher Stokes; Samuel; John; Almira Jane, m. Fredrick B. Eldridge; Willey; Precinda, m. Erastus Richards; Laura Lurena, m. Elias A. Smith; Aquila, m. Hortense Haight. Family resided Vermilion, Ill., and Salt Lake City.

Married Mary Woodcock Sept. 12, 1854, Salt Lake City (daughter of William Woodcock and Hannah Stone of Pilleygreen, Yorkshire, Eng.). She was born Sept. 19, 1830, and came to Utah Oct. 14, 1853, Cyrus Wheelock company. Their children: Encora Lurena; William W.; Alfred W., m. Elizabeth Snowball; Sarah Ann, m. Alma Findlay; Susannah Adelia; George W., m. Annie Wilcox; Mary Luella; Zettie May, m. Manasseh Kearl.
President elders quorum; high priest. Justice of the peace; deputy U. S. marshal; member territorial legislature two terms, and of constitutional convention of 1872. Farmer. Died Oct. 25, 1886, Laketown, Utah.

NEBEKER, WILLIAM PERRY (son of John Nebeker and Lurena Fitzgerald). Born Sept. 5, 1836, Reily, Butler Co., Ohio. Came to Utah with parents.
Married Sarah Ivins McKean Oct. 31, 1870, Salt Lake City (daughter of Theodore McKean and Mary Page Gulick of Toms River, Ocean county, N. J., pioneers 1857). She was born April 11, 1849. Their children: Theodore M. b. Aug. 28, 1871; Maud b. Jan. 31, 1874, m. Clarence A. Thompson; Sarah Lurena b. April 20, 1875, m. William L. Emery; William Perry b. Sept. 17, 1876; Laura b. Sept. 17, 1876, m. Milton B. Parks; Mary Page b. Sept. 9, 1878; Ethel b. Feb. 10, 1880. Family home Laketown, Utah.
Married Phoebe Stafford Tingey Feb. 19, 1885, Salt Lake City (daughter of John Tingey and Phoebe Stafford, pioneers Sept. 1, 1852). She was born Dec. 20, 1854. Their children: Charles Stafford; Leo Stokes; Harold Wesley. Family home, Salt Lake City.
Missionary to Germany, France and Switzerland. Member territorial legislature; U. S. census enumerator. Notary public. Died Oct. 16, 1910.

NEBEKER, IRA (son of John Nebeker and Lurena Fitzgerald). Born June 23, 1839, Vermilion, Ill. Came to Utah Sept. 29, 1847, George B. Wallace company.
Married Delia Lane 1861, Salt Lake City (daughter of Hyrum Lane and Naomi Chase of Jamestown, Grant county, Wis., latter a pioneer 1853). She was born June 30, 1845. Their children: John, m. Josephine Wahlstrom; Hyrum, m. Almira Hulme; Frank K., b. May 15, 1870, m. Lillian M. Martineau June 10, 1891; Horace G., m. Florence Gwilliam; Clara, m. Joseph A. Hulme; Naomi, m. W. Z. Terry; Elia, m. H. C. Parker; Effie, m. William Jardine; Laura, m. George Torgeson; Ruby, m. Guy Cardon. Family resided Laketown and Logan, Utah.
Bishop of Laketown 1868-1905. Member board county selectmen several terms. Farmer and stockraiser. Died April 29, 1905, Los Angeles, Cal.

NEBEKER, FRANK K. (son of Ira Nebeker and Delia Lane). Born May 15, 1870, Laketown, Utah.
Married Lillian Martineau June 10, 1891, Logan, Utah (daughter of James H. Martineau and Susan Julia Sherman of Logan; former pioneer July 22, 1850, latter October, 1853). She was born Aug. 13, 1868. Their children: Frank K., Jr., b. July 2, 1892; Marjorie b. April 10, 1896; Laurel M. b. Nov. 27, 1899; Joyce b. Aug. 10, 1901; Delia b. April 26, 1906; Ruth b. May 21, 1909. Family resided Logan and Salt Lake City, Utah.
Instructor of mathematics at Brigham Young College, Logan, Utah. Cache county attorney two terms; district attorney of first judicial district. Lawyer.

NEDDO, ISAAC JAMES (son of Charles Neddo of Monroe, Monroe county, Mich., born March 7, 1812, and Caroline Elizabeth Caldwell of La Salle, Monroe county, born Nov. 3, 1827, in Canada—married in 1849). He was born March 14, 1851, La Salle, Monroe county, Mich. Came to Utah 1853, independent company.
Married Pauline S. Burridge Jan. 8, 1880 (daughter of George Wilcox Burridge and Hannah Jane Shaw—married Nov. 16, 1847, in England—pioneers Oct. 24, 1865, Milo Andrus company). She was born Feb. 26, 1858, Tooele, Utah. Their children: Isaac James b. May 1, 1882, m. Alice Osterhout June 2, 1905; Hannah Pearl b. Aug. 8, 1884, m. Aaron A. Zollinger Nov. 24, 1909; Agnes Elizabeth b. Jan. 6, 1888, m. Archie E. Lloyd June 5, 1907; Ivie Grace b. June 26, 1890, m. Alma Rasmussen May 26, 1909; Charlotte b. July 11, 1892; Ella Pauline b. Jan. 5, 1897; George Willard b. March 6, 1900; Annie Marion b. July 8, 1902. Family home St. John, Tooele Co., Utah.
Veteran Black Hawk war. Brought immigrants to Utah in 1868 under John Gillespie. Missionary to northern states in 1890; president Y. M. M. I. A.; high priest. Farmer and sheepraiser.

NEDDO, ISAAC JAMES, JR. (son of Isaac James Neddo and Pauline S. Burridge). Born May 1, 1882, St. John, Utah.
Married Alice Osterhout June 2, 1905, Logan, Utah (daughter of John Carlos Osterhout, born at Willard, Utah, and Lottie Estella Condit). Their children: Estella Pauline b. Oct. 31, 1906; Isaac James b. March 12, 1908; Milton Le Roy b. May 13, 1910. Family home Malta, Cassia Co., Idaho.
Sunday school superintendent; ward clerk; counselor to president of Y. M. M. I. A. in Malta, Cassia Co., Idaho. President Malta brass band. Farmer and stockraiser.

NEEDHAM, JAMES (son of James Needham and Mary Armitage of Warrington, Eng. Born Aug. 20, 1826, at Warrington. Came to Utah October, 1854.
Married Alice Warburton Jan. 24, 1849, Darsbury, Eng. (daughter of John Warburton and Martha Wilkinson of Darsbury, pioneers 1854), who was born March 10, 1826. Their children: Sophia, d. infant; Mary Alice, m. George C. Lambert; James and John, d. infants; William A., m. Elizabeth Brown; Martha E., m. William T. Rose; George H, d. infant. Family home, Salt Lake City.
Married Martha Barton November, 1857, Salt Lake City (daughter of Thomas Barton and Martha Skinner of Dover, Eng., pioneers 1855). She was born Jan. 25, 1838, in Dover. Their children: Thomas B. b. Feb. 15, 1862; Georgiana B. b. Sept. 10, 1864; Muriel B. b. Sept. 24, 1867; Louisa B. b. Aug. 12, 1871; Frank B. b. Dec. 9, 1873; Albert B. b. Jan. 15, 1876.
Married Elizabeth Snalem March 27, 1858 (daughter of William and Martha Snalem, pioneers 1854), who was born March, 1842, Preston, Eng. Their children: Walter S. b. Oct. 12, 1865, m. Kate Hansen; Nellie S. b. April 23, 1873, m. Benjamin Fullmer.
One of presidents of seventies; missionary to England 1866-69. School teacher. Merchant. Died June 7, 1890, Salt Lake City.

NEEDHAM, JOHN (son of James Needham of Arton, Yorkshire, Eng.). Born April 1, 1819, in Yorkshire. Came to Utah 1850.
Married Martha Millens June 27, 1853, Salt Lake City (daughter of Henry Millens of Arton, who died on plains en route to Utah). She was born Sept. 14, 1833. Their children: Elizabeth T., m. Charles Tuckfield; Amelia J., m. Seth Tingey, m. Fred T. Taylor; Edward H. N., m. Lydia Green; Charles A., d. aged 21; William and Clara, d. infants; Maud L., m. Frank Earl; Claude N. and Seymore, d. infants. Family home, Salt Lake City.
Patriarch; member 13th quorum seventies; missionary to England nine years; block teacher. Manager clothing department Z. C. M. I. many years. Died June, 1901, Logan, Utah.

NEEDHAM, JONATHAN (son of Joseph and Jane Needham of Lancastershire, Eng.). Born Dec. 4, 1836, in Lancastershire. Came to Utah Oct. 20, 1862, Horton D. Haight company.
Married Mary Ann Furniss Jan. 20, 1856, Ashton-Under-Lyne, Lancastershire, Eng. (daughter of Samuel Furniss and Elizabeth Simpson of Yorkshire, Eng., pioneers Oct. 20, 1862, Horton D. Haight company). She was born April 14, 1839. Their children: Martha, d. infant; Joseph B., d. aged 1 year; Lorenzo; Jane E., m. Alexander S. Gillespie; Jonathan, m. Georgina Brown; Charles William, m. Julia F. Donavan; Sarah, died; Francis H., d. aged 1 year. Family home, Salt Lake City.
Elder. Assistant jailer. Laborer. Died May 1, 1873.

NEELEY, ARMENIUS MILLER (son of Lewis Neeley and Elizabeth Miller of Illinois). Born Jan. 7, 1836, in Vermilion county, Ill. Came to Utah in 1849.
Married Susan Potter Dec. 22, 1856 (daughter of William and Betsy Morgan), who was born Dec. 8, 1841. Their children: Armenius Miller b. Sept. 30, 1857, m. Emma A. Mecham .Nov. 25, 1879; Orson D. b. Dec. 23, 1859, m. Mary Shumway Nov. 25, 1880; Dora E. b. June 26, 1861, m. Joseph S. Giedde Dec. 29, 1882; Lauretta G. b. April 14, 1863, m. William Chadwick Nov. 25, 1879; William L. b. May 7, 1865, m. Louisa Foster Dec. 21, 1887; Jonathan J. b. Sept. 2, 1867, m. Elizabeth M. Packer Nov. 25, 1892; Lorenzo H. b. June 8, 1869; Eli Davis b. May 5, 1871; Ezra Elias b. June 6, 1872, m. Eliza F. Lowe; Mary Myrum b. Sept. 19, 1874, m. Amasa Beckstead Nov. 13, 1895; Sarah Jane b. Sept. 14, 1876; Susan b. Dec. 31, 1877, m. Benjamin Dunkley. Family home Franklin, Idaho.

NEELEY, ARMENIUS MILLER, JR. (son of Armenius Miller Neeley and Susan Morgan). Born Sept. 30, 1857, Bingham City, Utah.
Married Emma A. Mecham Nov. 25, 1879 (daughter of Leonidas C. Mecham and Margaret E. Champlain), who was born Nov. 30, 1860, Provo, Utah. Their children: Chloe A. b. Sept. 27, 1880, m. Francis J. Waters April 2, 1903; Leslie A. b. July 15, 1882, m. Mary Evans March 29, 1905; Ira L. b. Jan. 23, 1884, m. Myrtle Greaves Dec. 13, 1905; Asa H. b. Dec. 15, 1885, d. Oct. 30, 1897; Orville b. March 11, 1889, m. Alida Peterson April 27, 1910; Loren b. Jan. 22, 1891, m. Jennie Hymas Nov. 27, 1912; Myrtle b. April 7, 1893; Clarence b. Oct. 6, 1895; Milton b. March 22, 1898; Herschel M. b. April 13, 1899; Lowell M. b. Sept. 13, 1902. Family home Riverdale, Idaho.
Assistant postmaster 21 years. Assistant superintendent Sunday school 15 years. School trustee 18 years.

NEELEY, LEWIS (son of John Neeley and Elizabeth Miller of Ohio). Born Oct. 4, 1805, in Ohio. Came to Utah 1850, Captain Wall company.
Married Elizabeth Miller April 20, 1828, in Ohio (daughter of Armenius Miller, that state), who was born April 4, 1808. Their children: Alanson; William, m. Hellen Carbath; Armenius, m. Susan Morgan; Mary Jane, m. Jonathan C. Wright; Harriet, m. William Strong; Lewis, m. Maud Mary Treseder; John; Hyrum; Elizabeth. Family home, Salt Lake City.
High priest. Farmer. Died Nov. 6, 1856.

PIONEERS AND PROMINENT MEN OF UTAH 1065

NEELEY, LEWIS, JR. (son of Lewis Neeley and Elizabeth Miller). Born Aug. 1, 1841, Vermilion county, Ill. Came to Utah 1850, Captain Wall company.
Married Maud M. Treseder Aug. 3, 1869, Salt Lake City (daughter of Richard D. Treseder and Elizabeth Makay of same place, pioneers 1862, William Godby company). She was born June 20, 1849. Their children: Lewis Richard b. June 7, 1870, m. Elizabeth Hughs: Ada Elizabeth b. Sept. 5, 1873, m. Eli S. Winward; Maud Irene b. June 6, 1876, died; Etna May b. June 30, 1877, m. Thomas Whitman; Harvey LeRoy b. Aug. 20, 1879, m. Hedwig Bills; George Raymond b. Oct. 16, 1881; Willard b. Feb. 3, 1884, m. Hannah Atkinson; Ella Dean b. March 9, 1887, died; Mary Anna, died. Family home Granite, Utah.
High priest. Mail carrier between Sandy and Alta. Farmer. Went to Missouri in 1860 for freight. Drove stage for Ben Halliday 1861. Went to Missouri and Colorado for freight 1863; and to Los Angeles and Montana 1864. Appointed deputy sheriff of Salt Lake City 1883, under John Groesbeck.

NEELEY, WILLIAM N. (son of John Neeley of Ireland and Elizabeth Miller, born Oct. 8, 1808, Miami, Ohio). He was born Aug. 29, 1830, in Dane county, Wis. Came to Utah Oct. 14, 1850, Wilford Woodruff company.
Married Helen Cravath Sept. 19, 1852 (daughter of Austin Cravath and Eliza Doty), who was born Sept. 19, 1835. Their children: Viroqua V., m. Peter Nelson; Lauretta, m. Israel Hunsaker; William, died; Laura, m. Frank Hunsaker; Mary Elizabeth, m. John Smith; Lewis and Horace, died; Arthur C., m. Rose House; Ira J., m. Mr. Loveland; Alferette, m. William Hunsaker. Family home Brigham City, Utah.
Married Mary C. Nelson April, 1862, Salt Lake City (daughter of Neils and Ingabaa Nelson of Denmark). She was born June 17, 1847, Sjelland, Denmark. Their children: John Miller b. Nov. 12, 1864, m. Ellen Johnson; Oliver b. 1866 and Lucy Sophia b. Jan. 24, 1878, died; Amos William b. Dec. 26, 1870, m. Ada M. Natts; Enos Austin b. May 19, 1873, m. Eva Ricks; Elanson Armenmina b. Sept. 10, 1875, and Melleturde Alvira b. June 18, 1877, died; Helen May b. March 9, 1879, m. B. Thomas Morris; Isabella b. March 5, 1881, m. Theodore Daniels; Peter Edgar b. Sept. 3, 1883; Ruben Snow b. March 18, 1885, m. Myrl Heyeslov; Irene b. Sept. 2, 1888, m. David Whitaker; Viola b. Feb. 16, 1891, died. Family home Oneida Co., Idaho.
Bishop of Bear River City ward, Utah, and Neeley ward, Idaho. Founded village of Neeley, Idaho.

NEELEY, PETER E. (son of William Neeley and Mary C. Nelson). Born Sept. 3, 1883, Neeley, Idaho.

NEIBAUR, ALEXANDER (son of Nathan Neibaur and Rebecca Peretz Samuel of Ehrenbreitstein, near Coblenz, Hessen-Nassau, Prussia). Born Jan. 8, 1808, in Ehrenbreitstein. Came to Utah Sept. 20, 1848, Brigham Young company.
Married Ellen Breakell Sept. 16, 1833, Preston, Eng. (daughter of Richard Breakell and Alice Bannister of Preston), who was born Feb. 28, 1811. Their children: Joseph William, m. Elizabeth Cranshaw; Margaret, m. William Miller; Isaac, m. Emily Holland; Samuel, died; Alice, m. Morris Rosenbaum; Bertha, m. Levi Pangburn; Hyrum Smith, m. Jane Spriggs; Leah, m. Adam M. Paul; Sarah Ellen, m. John O'Driscoll; Rebecca Ann, m. Charles W. Nibley; Matilda Isabel, m. William Lorden; Nathan Alexander, m. Georgiana Clyde, m. Lena Borup; Rachel and Mary Esther, died. Family home, Salt Lake City.
Member 5th quorum seventies. Dentist, and original matchmaker in Utah. Died Dec. 15, 1876.

NEILSON, HOGAN (parents lived at Belivella, Sweden). Came to Utah September, 1862, oxteam company.
Married Johanna Larson in Sweden. Their children: Matilda, m. George A. Wilcox; Christina, m. Willard Kofford; Johanna, died; Hyrum, m. Fanny Fisher, m. Malinda Malissa McBride. Family home Mount Pleasant, Utah.

NELSEN, ANDREW. Born March 8, 1834, Velle, Denmark. Came to Utah 1852 by oxteam.
Married Metta Nelsen at Spring City, Utah (daughter of Godfrey Nelsen, of Jutland, Denmark), who was born 1827. Their children: Andrew, m. Annie Lorentzen; Emma, m. John Lemon; August, m. Maggie Brown and Elmina Stevens; Christian, m. Caroline Olsen; Joseph, m. Eleanor Worthen and Annie Sorensen. Family home Manti, Utah.
Married Christina Jensen July 1858, Manti, Utah (daughter of Jens J. Jensen and Anna Lucile Fransen, both of Sjelland, Denmark, pioneers September, 1857, handcart company). She was born March 7, 1840. Their children: James, m. Mary Olsen; Hyrum, m. Artimisia Lowry. Family home Manti, Utah.
Married Camilla Miller 1865, Salt Lake City (daughter of Soren Miller and Anna Christena Hirch, of Roscoe, Denmark, pioneers 1860, last handcart company). Their children: Erastus, m. Celia Olsen; Annie, m. William Geck; Clara, m. James P. Nelson; Franklin, m. Dorothy Calkins Thompson; Julia, d. child; Matilda, d. child. Family home Manti, Utah.
Married Sophia Miller 1865, Salt Lake City (daughter of Soren Miller and Anna Christena Hirch, of Roscoe, Denmark). Their children: Sophus, m. Mary Petty; Maria, m. Thorvald Peterson; Anna Christena, d. infant; Oscar, m. Mary Jane Bearnson; Thorvald, m. Ethel Nelson; Fanny, d. infant; Guy, m. Eunice Madsen; Myrtle. Family home Manti, Utah.
Veteran Black Hawk war. Farmer. Died September, 1909, Manti, Utah.

NELSEN, ANDREW, JR. (son of Andrew Nelsen and Metta Nelsen). Born April 2, 1857, Manti, Utah.
Married Anna L. Lorentzen July 12, 1880, Manti, Utah (daughter of Christen Lorentzen and Dorthea Larsen of Holbek amt, Sjelland, Folleslov, Denmark; came to Utah July 3, 1878). She was born Feb. 15, 1863. Their children: Andrew Lawrence b. March 25, 1881, m. Rhoda L. Smith; Metta Elnora b. Nov. 8, 1882; Lillian D. b. Dec. 21, 1884; Silvia T. b. Nov. 6, 1886; Anna Ethel b. Oct. 16, 1889; Jess R. b. Nov. 29, 1890; Mildred M. b. July 31, 1893; Stanley C. b. Nov. 25, 1895; Linda M. b. July 28, 1899; James Rulon b. May 19, 1901; Ernest Edwin b. May 23, 1904; Emma Margaret b. June 2, 1908. Family home Ferron, Utah.

NELSEN, ERASTUS (son of Andrew Nelsen and Camilla Miller). Born Jan. 29, 1872, Manti, Utah.
Married Celia Olsen March 10, 1897, Ferron, Utah (daughter of Ole Olsen and Christine King, both of Ferron and Spring City, Utah; former a pioneer, handcart company). She was born May 10, 1877. Their children: Celia Edrie b. June 7, 1898; Charles Foster b. Aug. 16, 1900; Gail Elden b. Jan. 3, 1903; Zelma Leita b. Jan. 9, 1905; Lyle O. b. Feb. 11, 1907, d. infant; Vivian b. Jan. 18, 1908. Family home Ferron, Utah.
Farmer and dairyman. Died Nov. 27, 1910.

NELSEN, MADS P. (son of Madson Nelsen of Ephraim). Born Aug. 5, 1835, in Denmark. Came to Utah in 1862, at Lehi, Utah. Came to Utah in 1862. She was born Jan. 11, 1829. Their children: Andrew C. b. Jan. 20, 1864, m. Amanda Jansen; Charles C. b. in 1866, m. Tora Brimholt; Peter C. b. in 1868, m. Hulda Brimholt; Nels P. b. Jan. 16, 1872, m. Amanda Bunnel. Family home Redmond, Utah.
Seventy. School trustee. Teacher; farmer. Died Jan. 29, 1880.

NELSON, ANDREW C. (son of Mads P. Nelsen and Margaret Hansen). Born Jan. 20, 1864, at Ephraim, Utah.
Married Amanda Jansen Aug. 5, 1872, at Redmond, Utah (daughter of John A. Jansen and Andrea Petersen, of Ephraim, Utah; they came to Utah in September, 1863, with the Doms company). She was born March 28, 1863. Their children: Andrew C. b. June 8, 1886, m. Leah Tuttle; Chloe A. b. Nov. 1, 1887, m. Emerson J. Miller; Joseph C. b. Jan. 7, 1891; C. Lamar b. June 9, 1893; Claron b. March 13, 1895; Marion C. b. Jan. 11, 1897; Charles I. b. April 19, 1898; Everett Y. b. Oct. 2, 1900, died; Lloyd C. b. Jan. 26, 1903; Clyde E. b. Sept. 25, 1905; Cleo L. b. Aug. 19, 1907.
Seventy; president T. M. M. I. A.; tithing clerk. County superintendent of schools; state superintendent of schools since 1900 (term expires 1917).

NELSEN, SAREN (son of Christian Nelsen and Christina Peterson, born in Denmark). He was born Jan. 10, 1856, Denmark. Came to Utah 1864, Captain Preston company.
Married Elmyra Purser in 1877 (daughter of Frank Purser and Fannie Enon, pioneers 1861 and 1868). She came to Utah 1864, Captain Preston company. Their children: David b. 1882, m. Olga Fern Topping; Pearl b. 1884, m. Thomas J. Barger; Miriam b. 1888; Frank b. 1890; Glenn b. 1897; Ruby b. 1900; Edith b. 1902; Stanley b. 1904. Family home Treasureton, Idaho.
High priest; bishop's counselor. Farmer; stockraiser.

NELSON, AARON (son of James and Sarah Nelson, Lambley, Eng.). Born March 5, 1823, Lambley. Came to Utah in 1843.
Married Mary Stamford. Only child: William b. April 4, 1844, at Lambley. m. Mary Alice Thompson.
Married Selvia Rulfreyman March 19, 1864, Salt Lake City (daughter of Richard Rulfreyman and Hannah Butler of Denbigh, Eng., pioneers 1862, Captain Hyde company). She was born Sept. 24, 1843. Their children: Hannah, m. Edward H. Snow; James, died; Alice, m. Lafayette Carter; Mary, m. Henry Kemp; Amelia, died; Selma: Alma, m. Rose Reucher; Lettie, m. Heber E. Harrison; Joseph, died; Jennie; Edward, m. Nellie Lamb. Family home St. George, Utah.
High priest. City sexton and marshal; assessor and collector. Shoemaker. Died Oct. 3, 1908.

NELSON, DAVID (son of Jonathan Nelson and Eunice Stone of Shrewsbury, Worcester county, Mass.). Born 1801. Shrewsbury, Mass. Came to Utah Sept. 15, 1852, Thomas Tidwell company.
Married Mary Thompson Miller March 6, 1836, Providence, R. I. (daughter of George and Mary Miller of Providence; latter came to Utah 1873). She was born 1818. Their children: Mary Eunice; James Horace, m. Sarah Ann Pool, m. Annie B. Peterson; Josiah; David George; Samuel Jonathan; Martha Ann. Family home Ogden, Utah.

Married Elizabeth Jane West. Their children: Louis, d. infant; Henry Walker; Guy Brown, m. Alice Cave; Earl, d. infant.
Missionary to eastern states 1872-73; high priest. Justice of peace at Kaysville, Utah. Died September, 1882, Ogden, Utah.

NELSON, JAMES HORACE (son of David Nelson and Mary Thompson Miller). Born March 28, 1839, Jacksonville, Morgan county, Ill. Came to Utah Sept. 16, 1852, Thomas Tidwell company.
Married Sarah Ann Pool Aug. 1, 1859, Ogden, Utah (daughter of William and Elizabeth Pool of Ogden, pioneers 1852, oxteam company). She was born 1844, Nauvoo, Ill. Their children: James Horace b. May 21, 1860; David George b. Nov. 24, 1862; Sarah Elizabeth b. Dec. 30, 1865; Mary Martha b. April 10, 1868; William Francis b. Sept. 21, 1871; Chester Pool b. Feb. 16, 1874; Roscoe Miller b. March 30, 1876; Summer Parker b. June 7, 1879; Maynard Elliott b. Jan. 7, 1882; Leland Kay b. April 6, 1884. Family home Ogden, Utah.
Married Annie B. Peterson Aug. 21, 1876, Salt Lake City (daughter of Jacob Peterson and Petrina Barlak of Ogden, Utah; came to Utah 1875). Their children: Annie Amelia b. July 12, 1877; Clarence Smith b. July 29, 1879; Ella Evaline b. May 22, 1881; Lillie Nicoline b. March 16, 1883; Ellen Josephine b. July 8, 1885; Howard Stanley b. Aug. 5, 1887; Mabel Exila b. Aug. 9, 1889; Horace Jacob b. May 5, 1891; Waldo Petersen b. Aug. 2, 1893; Wilford Leslie b. June 19, 1896; Daniel Stone b. June 1, 1897; Edna Joan b. Aug. 11, 1904.
Missionary to eastern states 1872-73; senior president 53d quorum seventies 25 years. Real estate agent; farmer.

NELSON, EDMOND (son of Thomas B. Nelson and Martha Williams of North Carolina and Illinois). Born Dec. 12, 1799, in North Carolina. Came to Utah Sept. 9, 1850, Thomas Johnson company.
Married Jane Taylor 1828, Mt. Vernon, Jefferson county, Ill. (daughter of Thomas Billington Taylor and Martha Mardgelin of Jefferson county), who was born Jan. 1, 1807. Their children: Pryce Williams, m. Lyda Lake; Hyrum, m. Susan A. Wimmer; William Goforth b. June 10, 1831, m. Elvira Vail; Thomas B. b. May 9, 1833, m. Mary Walker; Joseph Smith b. Dec. 30, 1838, m. Hannah Patten; Edmond, m. Annie Petersen; Mark b. May 6, 1844, m. Orphia Dowdell. Family home Alpine, Utah.

NELSON, WILLIAM GOFORTH (son of Edmond Nelson and Jane Taylor). Born June 10, 1831, Jefferson county, Ill. Came to Utah Sept. 9, 1850, Thomas Johnson company.
Married Elvira Vail Nov. 25, 1855, Alpine, Utah (daughter of Gamaliel Vail, who died June 7, 1844, and Martha Bartholomew of McLean county, Ill., pioneers Sept. 1, 1851, Morris Phelps company—married March, 1830). She was born April 25, 1839, and came to Utah, Morris Phelps company. Their children: William b. Aug. 31, 1856, d. Aug. 16, 1857; Elvira b. Jan. 18, 1858, d. Sept. 23, 1863; Martha b. Oct. 25, 1859, d. April 28, 1891; Luna b. Sept. 18, 1861, m. Charles F. Chadwick; Emmaline b. Sept. 10, 1863, m. Alexander Stalker; George Goforth b. Sept. 25, 1865, m. Eliza Preece; Rhoda b. Oct. 28, 1867, m. William J. Davis; Brigham Young b. July 20, 1869, m. Nancy C. Barley; Gamaliel Vail b. Dec. 8, 1871, m. Emma E. Packer; Angela b. Jan. 11, 1874, m. William T. Packer; Rachel b. Dec. 8, 1876, d. Dec. 23, 1878; Taylor Nelson b. Dec. 23, 1878, m. Susie Hawkes; Ezra b. Sept. 5, 1881. Family resided Alpine, Utah, and Franklin, Oxford and Riverdale, Idaho.
Bishop Oxford, Idaho, Oneida stake, 1864-76; member of Oneida stake high council 12 years. Farmer; stockraiser.

NELSON, HENRY (son of Thomas Nelson and Elizabeth Thompson). Born Sept. 18, 1826, in England. Came to Utah in 1850, oxteam company.
Married Sarah Ann Richmond in 1847 at Nauvoo, Ill. (daughter of Thomas Richmond and Sarah Burrah, both of England), who was born Nov. 20, 1829. Their children: Hy., Thomas, m. Mary Ellen McMillian; Elizabeth Ann, m. Ely Gordon; Jesse Richmond, m. Annie Bonner; William Richard; Wilford, m. Matilda H. Peterson, m. Sadie Morse; Sarah Alice, m. Robert Baird; Merch Jane, m. Henry Moss; Joseph Everett, m. Mary J. Casper; Margaret, m. Thomas J. Vincent; Emmie, died; John Benjamin; Hiram, died; Mary Emily, m. Bartl Gappmayer. Family home Heber City, Utah.
High priest; farmer. Died Sept. 8, 1910, at Burrville, Utah.

NELSON, ISAAC (son of Thomas Nelson and Elizabeth Thompson, both of Westmoreland, Eng.). Born in Westmoreland. Came to Utah 1851, oxteam company.
Married Margaret Weston 1853, Provo, Utah. Their children: Isaac, m. Esther Birch; Elizabeth, m. Edgar Parry; Ann, m. James Fisher; Ellen, m. Jake Young; John, m. Maggie Kirkwood; Mary Eliza, died; Fannie, m. Mervin Bowen; Rose, m. John Vincent; David, m. Annie Skinner; Joseph, died. Family home Provo, Utah.
High priest; ward teacher; Sunday school teacher; block teacher. Farmer. Died at Provo, Utah.

NELSON (NIELSEN), JENS C. (son of Niels Jensen of Denmark). Born Aug. 10, 1830, Denmark. Came to Utah in 1859.

Married Annie Maria Anderson in 1856 at Salt Lake City. She was born June 18, 1837. Their children: Daniel C., m. Mary Sorenson (d. 1896), m. Cecilia Sorenson 1900; Andrew, m. Mena Daniels; Joseph, m. Leonora Smith; Mary, m. Lars Johnson; James C., died; Annie N., m. William Hyler. Family home Moroni, Utah.
Seventy; missionary. Mayor of Moroni. Merchant; farmer.

NELSON, JOSEPH (son of Jens C. Nelson and Annie Maria Anderson). Born Dec. 30, 1862, Moroni, Utah.
Married Leonora Smith June 14, 1893, Salt Lake City (daughter of President Joseph F. Smith and Sarah E. Richards. She was born Jan. 30, 1871. Their children: Joseph S. b. Feb. 22, 1897; George S. b. Oct. 20, 1898; Alvin S. b. Aug. 7, 1900; Alice b. Sept. 27, 1901; Franklin S. b. Sept. 26, 1906. Family home, Salt Lake City.
Early life spent on the farm and in the lumber and tie camps; helped build the Utah Central Railway grade in 1879. Student and school teacher 20 years. President and manager Saltair Beach Company; president and manager Salt Lake & Los Angeles R. R. Engaged in banking 1901-07, and in mining 20 years.

NELSON, JOHN (son of Nels Nelson, Cosalt, Tennesea). Born Oct. 7, 1827, at Tennesea, Eringa Halland Lan, Sweden. Came to Utah Oct. 18, 1864, William B. Preston company.
Married Annetta Benson in 1852 (daughter of Nels Benson, who died in Sweden, and Johannah Johanson, pioneer Sept. 21, 1862, Captain Horne company). She was born Dec. 9, 1832. Their children: Matilda b. 1853; James Peter b. Dec. 13, 1855; Nels August b. May 8, 1857, m. Fidelia Ellen Koffoed Jan. 24, 1884; Josephine b. 1859; Amanda b. 1862; Annetta Josephine b. Nov. 18, 1864, m. Joseph Jonas 1882; Joseph Hyrum b. June 14, 1868, m. Delilah —— ; Jacob and Jacobine (twins) b. 1870; Lottie Abigail b. 1871; Moses b. Oct. 1873. Family home Logan, Cache county, Utah.

NELSON, NELS AUGUST (son of John Nelson and Annetta Benson Nelson). Born May 8, 1857, Eringa, Halland Lan, Sweden.
Married Fidelia Ellen Koffoed Jan. 24, 1884, Salt Lake City (daughter of Paul Ernest Koffoed and Fanny Myrick, who came to Utah 1853, John Forsgren company). She was born April 29, 1858, Ephraim, Utah. Their children: August Levi b. April 27, 1885; Lawrence Egbert b. Nov. 5, 1886; Paul Ernest b. June 13, 1888; James Hyrum b. April 24, 1890; Virgil Homer b. May 15, 1892; Moses Aaron b. June 29, 1894; Fidelia Ellen b. Oct. 12, 1897.
Sunday school superintendent 22 years; ward teacher 24 years; president of Y. M. M. I. A. and other minor offices such as religion class worker committee on finance of L. D. S. U.; high councilor 11 years; member of Sunday school lecture bureau.

NELSON, KNUD CHRESTENSEN (son of Chresten Nelsen and Bergette Chrestensen, of Oppelstrup, Denmark). Born Nov. 24, 1793, Oppelstrup. Came to Utah Sept. 30, 1853, John Forsgren company.
Married Karen Magratte Jenson (daughter of Chresten Jenson and Mette Chrestensen), who was born Nov. 28, 1803. Their children: Christiana b. Jan. 6, 1830, m. Goudy Hogan; Chresten b. Nov. 1831, m. Mary Israelson; Bergette b. Aug. 5, 1833, m. Goudy Hogan; Mette Marie b. May 2, 1835, m. Thomas M. Jeffs Aug. 1854; Ann b. March 17, 1839, m. Goudy Hogan; Jens Christian b. May 8, 1841, m. Eliza S. Bryson Nov. 21, 1869; Nels b. April 19, 1842, m. Karen Marie Larsen March 19, 1865; Christian b. Jan. 24, 1845, m. Charlotte Vienna Call Nov. 21, 1869. Family home Bountiful, Utah.
Joined the church of J. C. of L. D. S., and was baptized Jan. 1, 1851. Crossed the ocean on ship "Foriest Monarck." Arrived in Salt Lake 1853. Moved to Bountiful 1854 and bought a farm of Goudy Hogan. Suffered severely from the grasshopper plague. Helped to bring immigrants from the old country, spending all his surplus money for that purpose. High priest. Died April 11, 1862.

NELSON, JENS CHRISTIAN (son of Knud C. Nelsen and Karen Magratte Jenson). Born May 8, 1841, at Kjelgaarden, Aalborg Amt, Denmark. Came to Utah with parents.
Married Eliza S. Bryson Nov. 22, 1869, at Salt Lake City, Utah (daughter of Samuel Bryson and Sarah Ann Conray, pioneers Oct. 24, 1855, Milo Andrus company). She was born June 13, 1854, in Glasgow, Scotland. Their children: Jens Knud b. Dec. 2, 1870, m. Sarah Jane Duerden; Samuel Roy b. Oct. 4, 1873, m. Zupporal Parker June 25, 1896; David Melvin b. June 7, 1876, m. Hattie E. Hatch April 11, 1900; Sarah b. Dec. 25, 1879, m. John Stoker May 17, 1900; Selvanus b. Dec. 25, 1879, m. Cora Moss May 27, 1908; Eliza b. July 10, 1883, m. W. Walter Barlow Sept. 18, 1902; Hyrum b. July 13, 1885, died; Lawrence Nels b. Sept. 10, 1886, m. Ellen B Hatch April 16, 1909; Clarence Christian b. Sept. 10, 1886, m. Athlinda Snowball Oct. 2, 1908; James Everett b. Dec. 7, 1889, m. Mirtle Willey Nov. 2, 1910; Harold Clyde b. Feb. 18, 1894. Family home Bountiful, Davis county, Utah.
One of the presidents 74th quorum seventies. Settled at Mill Creek 1853, moved to Bountiful 1854, to Salratus Creek, Rich county 1874, returned to Bountiful 1883. Commissioner, Davis county; vice president Deseret Live Stock Co.; farmer and stockraiser. Died Aug. 6, 1910.

NELSON, JENS KNUD (son of Jens Christian Nelson and Eliza S. Bryson). Born Dec. 2, 1870, at South Bountiful, Utah.
Married Sarah J. Duerden (daughter of Richard Duerden and Sarah A. Starkie, pioneers Sept. 15, 1868—who were married February, 1865). She was born July 3, 1874, at South Bountiful, Utah. Their children: Edith Jane b. July 22, 1898; Jens K. b. Nov. 4, 1900; Golda b. Jan 18, 1903; Clarence Merrill b. July 8, 1906; Sarah Alice b. April 17, 1909. Family home Bountiful, Utah.
Missionary to New Zealand 1893-97. City councilman Bountiful; treasurer Davis county.

NELSON, NELS (son of Knud Chrestensen Nelsen and Karen Magratte Jensen). Born April 19, 1842. Came to Utah with parents.
Married Karen Marie Larsen, at Salt Lake City, Utah (daughter of Soren Larsen and Ane Marie Jeppesen; the latter came to Utah October, 1860). She was born Dec. 16, 1843. Their children: Nels K. b. May 24, 1866; Ane Marie b. Aug. 17, 1870; Anton C. b. Dec. 29, 1873; Nephi J. b. Feb. 4, 1876. Family home Bountiful, Utah.
Married Anne Petree Johnson (daughter of John Johnson and Marie Iarelson). Their children: Margrette M. A. b. Sept. 22, 1875; Eliza Sophie Nelsen b. Dec. 18, 1877.
Farmer; stockraiser; mechanic. Died Aug. 26, 1880.

NELSON, CHRISTIAN (son of Knud Chrestensen Nelson and Karen Magrette Jensen). Born Jan. 24, 1845, Kjelgaarden, Denmark. Came to Utah with parents.
Married Charlotte Vienna Call Nov. 22, 1869, Salt Lake City (daughter of Anson Vasco Call and Charlotte Holbrook), who was born Nov. 7, 1853, Willard, Utah. Their children: Christine Sorensen; Emma Patrae Nielsen; Ephraim (who has taken their name) b. Oct. 2, 1884, m. Lula Call Oct. 1904; Olena Jane (adopted and sealed) b. April 14, 1897. Family home Bountiful, Utah.
Missionary to Denmark 1883-85; high priests second counselor later first counselor to Bishop J. A. Tolman. Helped to haul stone for the Temple 1863; helped to bring immigrants across plains 1866; helped settle "Dixie" 1868; then moved to Bountiful; moved to Port Deneuf Valley, Idaho, 1880. While on a mission to Denmark 1883-85, his wife joined him; on their return home visited Hamburg, Paris, London, Bristol and Liverpool. Moved to his present home Bountiful, 1903. Has spent much time on the frontier. Farmer and stockman.

NELSON, LARS P. (son of Peter Nelson and Kiertsti T. Nelson, both of Onnestad, Christianstad, Sweden). Born Aug. 25, 1833, Onnestad, Sweden. Came to Utah Oct. 5, 1854, Captain Olsen company.
Married Mary Magdalene Lovendahl Nov. 26, 1861, Provo, Utah (son of Henry Lovendahl and Anna Monson, both of Horby, Malmo, Sweden). She was born Feb. 17, 1831. Their children: Anna L. b. Feb. 2, 1863, died; Lars L. b. Oct. 1, 1864, m. Eliza Nelson March 26, 1890; Henry L. b. June 18, 1866; Mary Magdalene b. June 2, 1872, last two died. Family home Provo, Utah.
Missionary to Sweden 1878-79; counselor in high priests' quorum of Utah county stake; high priest. Took an active part in guarding against the Indians in early days; assisted in building the fort wall around Alpine for protection against Indians; crossed plains 1861, with John Murdock's company to bring immigrants to Utah.

NELSON, LARS LOVENDAHL (son of Lars P. Nelson and Mary Magdalene Lovendahl). Born Oct. 1, 1864, Provo, Utah.
Married Eliza Nelson March 26, 1890, Manti, Utah (daughter of Jeppa Nelson and Anna Swenson, both of Malmo, Sweden. Came to Utah July 21, 1873). She was born Sept. 16, 1866. Their children: Larence Raymond b. Dec. 1890; Mary Illah b. March 12, 1893; Henry Arthur b. July 28, 1895; Ervin J. b. March 8, 1897; Wilford Karl b. June 26, 1900; Verne Smith b. April 26, 1904; LaGrande Lars b. Nov. 16, 1909. Family home Provo, Utah.
Missionary to Sweden 1890-92; ordained bishop of second ward April 20, 1902; clerk in high council seven years; ward clerk four years; counselor in Y. M. M. I. A.; Sunday school teacher. One of the incorporators of the Provo Building & Loan Association. Provo city recorder 1896-1900; member Provo city council 1900-02; chief deputy county treasurer 1901-09; member Provo city board of equalization 1907-11. Agriculturist.

NELSON, LARS PETER (son of Peter Nelson, born March 4, 1799 and Bodel Olsen of Annclef, born 1804, Sweden). He was born Sept. 9, 1834, at Annclef. Came to Utah Sept. 15, 1864, Captain Preston oxteam company.
Married Bodel Marie Nelson Oct. 9, 1869 (daughter of Christian Nelson, who came to Utah Aug. 6, 1869, Olsen company, and Karny Nelson). She was born Jan. 30, 1849, died Jan. 13, 1875. Their children: Lorenzo Peter b. Oct. 9, 1870, died 1873; Roxie Marie b. Oct. 17, 1872; Lewis P. b. Jan. 8, 1875, died 1881. Family home Bear River City, Utah.
Married Bertha Rasmusen Oct. 13, 1875, Salt Lake City (daughter of Martin Rasmusen, who came to Utah 1874, and Mary Hansen, who came in 1875). She was born Aug. 3, 1847, in Sweden. Their children: Bertha Mary b. July 23, 1876, m. Charles W. Hoones Aug. 12, 1897; Laurence A. b. April 28, 1878; Orson W. b. Feb. 3, 1880; Emma A. b. May 31, 1882, m. James W. Jensen Aug. 5, 1905; Selma b. June

16, 1884, m. Henry L. Gittins Aug. 1912; Evelyn b. July 5, 1887, m. Estus N. Hammond, Jr., Dec. 7, 1910; Joseph A. b. March 10, 1889; Arnold R. b. Sept. 5, 1891.
Ward teacher for 15 years; presided over elders quorum three years; assistant Sunday school superintendent; bishop's counselor. Justice of the peace for two years.

NELSON, SOREN (son of Nels Nelson, of Flada, Denmark). Born March 20, 1803. Came to Utah Sept. 20, 1856, Knud Peterson company.
Married Christiana Hailsen (daughter of Lars Hailsen), who was born March 27, 1804. Came to Utah Sept. 20, 1856, Knud Peterson company. Their children: Nels C. Nelson b. Jan. 26, 1828, m. Catherine Jensen; Christian b. 1838, m. Josephine Evens; Charlotte b. 1841, m. James Peter Krogue; Otana b. 1846, m. James C. Thomas Nov. 20, 1865. Family home Bloomington, Idaho.
Farmer.

NELSON, NELS CHRISTIAN (son of Soren Nelson and Christiana Hailsen). Born Jan. 26, 1828, Flada, Denmark. Married Catherine Jensen Nov. 11, 1855, Alstrup, Denmark (daughter of Jens Jensen), who was born Dec. 5, 1832, Bratteré, Denmark. Their children: Charlotte C. b. Oct. 14, 1857, m. Gilbert Welker; Nels C. b. Feb. 14, 1860, m. Mary Ann Soulsby; James A. b. May 2, 1862, m. Mary E. Arnell; Mary M. b. Aug. 11, 1864, m. Albert B. Dunford; Catherine J. b. April 26, 1867, m. Will Laker; Annie C. b. Sept. 11, 1869, died; Miranda b. Jan. 26, 1872, m. Nelson C. Allred; Warren T. b. March 16, 1875, m. Josephine Jensen. Family home Bloomington, Idaho.
Married Ingar Christina Jensen 1863, at Salt Lake City (daughter of Peter and Mattie Jensen, the latter came to Utah with independent company). She was born April 7, 1845, Noroks, Denmark. Their children: Andrew K. Aug. 5, 1864; Martha b. April 26, 1867, m. Swan Sanderson; Soren C. b. June 20, 1869, m. Effie Pearce; Joseph b. Oct. 16, 1871, m. Daisy Jones; Jacob b. April 3, 1874; Ingar C. b. Dec. 9, 1876, m. Daniel E. Thornock; Mary Allen b. Sept. 9, 1879, m. Joseph Heap; Sarah b. May 26, 1882, m. John Sizemore; John Thomas b. June 3, 1885.
Counselor to Bishop Hulme. Assisted immigrants to Utah.

NELSON, NELS CHRISTIAN JR. (son of Nels Christian Nelson and Catherine Jensen). Born Feb. 14, 1860, in Utah.
Married Mary Ann Soulsby Sept. 22, 1881, Salt Lake City, Utah, Endowment house, who was born Sept. 27, 1863, Northumberland, Eng. Their children: Elenor Ann b. Aug. 16, 1882, m. David Alma Thornock June 17, 1900; Joseph Christian b. July 20, 1885, m. Mary Amanda Johnson April 11, 1907; Edward b. July 19, 1888; James Leo b. Dec. 31, 1891; Jane Dorothy b. May 9, 1894; Jesse Roy b. Dec. 1, 1896; Cardon Phillops b. Dec. 25, 1899; Annie Laura b. July 27, 1903.

NELSON, SWANTY (son of Anna Jacobson). Born October 1853, in Sweden. Came to Utah 1862.
Married Charlotte Johnson, Salt Lake City, Utah Nov. 23, 1874 (daughter of Johannes Johnson and Annie Gabriel, of Sweden, who came to Utah 1871). She was born Nov. 12, 1849. Their children: Alice Josephine b. Sept. 9, 1875, m. Lars P. Larson, d. Sept. 21, 1908; Swanty William b. Feb. 1, 1877, m. Sarah Penelope Bettridge; Caroline b. July 25, 1878, m. Thomas Taylor; Annie Loretta b. Nov. 6, 1880, m. John S. Smith; Jacob Raymon b. Dec. 8, 1882, d. Feb. 11, 1892; Clarence LeRoy b. Oct. 25, 1884; Julia May b. April 29, 1887; Parley Wallace b. Feb. 9, 1889; Pherry Edgar b. April 21, 1891; Estella Louisa b. May 15, 1893; Elva Rachel b. April 20, 1896, d. Nov. 14, 1900. Family home Oakley, Idaho.
Second counselor to Bishop John L. Smith, at Oakley, from July 1888 to May 1900; first counselor to Bishop R. H. Hunter, second ward of Oakley, from May 1900 to Oct. 1909; missionary among the Indians in Tooele county; ward teacher in Oakley, at present county road commissioner, Canyon district, Cassia county. Farmer.

NESLEN, SAMUEL (son of Richard Neslen of Mutford, Suffolk, Eng.). Born Dec. 3, 1808, at Mutford, Eng. Came to Utah Sept. 20, 1853, Claudius V. Spencer company.
Married Eunice Francis (daughter of Robert Francis and Rachel Burgess, Lowestoft, Suffolk, Eng.). She was born June 8, 1809. Their children: Susannah, m. Claude W. Spencer; Samuel F. d. aged 27; Robert F., m. Eleanor Stevens, m. Eliza Savell; Elizabeth D., m. Samuel Tucker; Esther F., m. Samuel Dean; Eunice, m. William H. Foster; Phoebe N., m. George M. Ottinger; William F., m. Eleanor Mitchell, m. Eliza Westerman, m. Mary Evans; Hantah, m. John Sharp Jr. Family home Salt Lake City.
President Lowestoft Branch, Suffolk, Eng. Carpenter and cabinetmaker. Died Aug. 29, 1888.

NESLEN, WILLIAM F. (son of Samuel Neslen, born Dec. 10, 1807, Mutford, Suffolkshire, Eng., and Eunice Francis, born June 1808, Lowestoft, Eng.). He was born Jan. 5, 1841, Lowestoft, Eng. Came to Utah Sept. 20, 1853.
His children: William Samuel; Eunice Mitchell; Samuel Francis; Margaret Grace; Alfred Clements; David Arthur; Eleanor; Charles Frederick; Pearl Westerman; Ruby; Ethel Evans.
Veteran Civil war 1861-62; and Black Hawk war 1866.

NEWBOLD, JOSEPH (son of John Newbold, born 1820 at Castle Donington, Lincolnshire, Eng., and Elizabeth Dakin, born 1829, Castle Donington. both of Draycott, Eng.). He was born April 12, 1858, Breaston, Eng. Came to Utah October, 1873, James J. Hart company.
Married Hanna M. Christensen October, 1882 (daughter of Neils C. Christensen and Bertha M. Sorensen, pioneers 1852, John R. Murdock company). She was born Sept. 22, 1855, Smithfield, Utah. Their children: Joseph N. b. Sept. 29, 1884, m. Jennie M. Cole April 5, 1905; Bertie E. b. Sept. 24, 1886, m. Ole Sonne June 27, 1906; Metta P. b. May 28, 1893; Gertie E. b. Nov. 23, 1896. Family home, Smithfield.
Bishop of fourth ward, Logan. 1906; president 64th quorum seventies; missionary to England 1890-92, and to central states July 12, 1906; assistant superintendent of Sunday school, fourth ward, Logan; chorister Smithfield ward 1876-94; also Logan. fourth ward, 1895-1906. Director in the Cache Valley Banking Company, Logan, Utah. Merchant.

NEWELL, ELLIOT ALFRED (son of Alman Newell and Olive Comstock of Amboy, Oswego county, N. Y.). Born Aug. 2°, 1830, Amboy. Came to Utah October, 1852.
Married Maria Louisa Roberts May 4, 1851, Kanesville, Iowa (daughter of Horace Roberts and Harriett McEvers of Montezuma, Ill., pioneers 1851). She was born Nov. 11, 1829, Montezuma; died Sept. 15, 1904. Their children: Luella Isola, m. Gilbert Oliver Haws; Elliot Alfred, m. Malinda Loveridge; Arthur, m. Caroline Haws; Myron C., m. Alice Smoot; Celia O., m. Zella Wood, m. Ella Clay; Charles Ephraim and Ida Olive, died; Frank Ernest, m. Rebecca Hardy; Maria Louisa. m. Joseph A. Sessions; Lucy Edeth, m. Sidney Harding; George Henry, died.
Member 34th quorum seventies; missionary to New York. Farmer. Died Jan. 14, 1893, Provo, Utah.

NEWEY, JOHN (son of Mathew John Newey and Elizabeth Greenfield of Purbright, Surrey, Eng.). Born Jan. 25, 1806, Worplesdon, Eng. Came to Utah Sept. 7, 1855, Noah T. Guymon company.
Married Leah Welland Aug. 2, 1835, Surrey, Eng. (daughter of John Welland and Ann Swan of Purbright). She was born Feb. 10, 1809, Elstead Parish, Eng. Their children: Jamima Barker; Mary A.; Elizabeth Welsh. Family home Ogden, Utah.
Married Panela Woode. Family home Ogden, Utah.
Married Ann Etherington Heslop (widow of Thomas Heslop) June 2, 1856 (daughter of John and Elizabeth Etherington). She was born Jan. 24, 1830, Durham, Eng. Their children: John Heslop; George Heslop; William; Janie; James L.; Annie E.; Henry Thomas; Effie E.
High priest. Farmer; gardener. Died Aug. 17, 1895, Ogden, Utah.

NEWEY, HENRY (son of John Newey and Ann Etherington). Born April 12, 1865, Ogden, Utah.
Teacher. Employee of the Southern Pacific R. R. for 20 years.

NEWMAN, JOSEPH. Born in England. Came to Utah about 1852.
Married Elizabeth Hughes, pioneer 1852. Their children: John b. Jan. 27, 1838, m. Sarah Marchant Dec. 26, 1859; Ann; Joseph, m. Eliza Moses; James, m. Annette Poulsen; William H.; Thomas, m. Maria Wayman. Family home, Big Cottonwood, Utah.

NEWMAN, JOHN (son of Joseph Newman and Elizabeth Hughes). Born Jan. 27, 1838, in England.
Married Sarah Matilda Marchant Dec. 26, 1859 (daughter of Abraham Marchant and Lydia Johnson, came to Utah in 1854). She was born Sept. 1, 1841, in England. Their children: John Henry b. Oct. 16, 1860, m. Josephine Harmon Oct. 19, 1887; Abraham William b. Sept. 16, 1862, m. Amanda W. Nelson Nov. 18, 1888; Sarah Matilda b. Jan. 7, 1864; Lydia Maria b. March 13, 1865, m. Charles O. Harmon Oct. 19, 1887; Joseph Alma b. Oct. 3, 1866, m. Ellen J. Nelson March 8, 1898; Robert Marchant b. Feb. 24, 1871, m. Violet G. Manning Jan. 12, 1899; James Johnson b. Jan. 11, 1874, m. Ella A. P. Horkley March 5, 1903; Albert Samuel b. Dec. 2, 1874, m. Sarah Julia Anderson Oct. 10, 1900; Amelia Sophia b. July 11, 1878, m. Joseph W. Horkley April 5, 1900. Family resided Peoa, Utah, and Milo, Idaho. Blacksmith. Died July 18, 1902.

NEWMAN, ALBERT SAMUEL (son of John Newman and Sarah Matilda Marchant). Born Dec. 2, 1874, Peoa, Summit Co., Utah.
Married Sarah Julia Anderson (daughter of Neils Anderson and Anne Kristine Paulson, came to Utah in 1863, and Salt Lake City Oct. 19, 1900). She was born July 31, 1874, Goshen, Utah. Their children: Thora b. Dec. 25, 1902; Ralph Fern b. Dec. 10, 1904; Erma Yvonne b. Aug. 15, 1907; Albert Rolph b. May 19, 1909; Arnold Anderson b. April 12, 1911. Family home Milo, Idaho.
Set apart as second counselor to Bishop Parley J. Davis Sept. 23, 1900. Farmer.

NEWSOME, WILLIAM D. (son of George H. Newsome and Sarah Prole of Arklow, County Wicklow, Ireland). Born Feb. 21, 1832, at Arklow. Came to Utah Nov. 10, 1866, Miner G. Atwood company.

Married Catherine E. Morrisey June 12, 1862, Grahamstown, South Africa (daughter of John Morrisey and Kate O'Brien of Kilworth, Aragiyn, County Cork, Ireland). She was born Feb. 7, 1835.
Married Lucy M. Devereaux Nov. 15, 1883, Salt Lake City (daughter of Samuel Devereaux and Lucy Bailey of Wolverhampton. Staffordshire, Eng.). She was born Oct. 27, 1858. Their children: Muzzetta M., m. George Fitt; William A., m. Vivian Hendricson; Claudius; Catherine E.; Fredrick G.; John Lorenzo. Family home, Salt Lake City.
High priest; missionary to England one year; block teacher. Engineer; paperhanger; painter.

NIBLEY, JAMES. Born in 1815, Hunterfield, Scotland. Came to Utah in 1862, Capt. Ross company.
Married Jean Wilson, Edinburgh, Scotland (daughter of Thomas Wilson and Euphamie Chalmers of Hunterfield). Their children: James, m. Elizabeth ——; Mary, m. John Maughan; Margaret, m. William Maughan; Charles W., m. Rebecca Neibaur, m. Ellen Ricks; Henry, m. Amelia Knowles; Euphamie, m. William Maughan. Family home Cache Valley, Utah.
Farmer; merchant. Died August, 1898, Baker City, Ore.

NIBLEY, CHARLES W. (son of James Nibley and Jean Wilson). Born Feb. 5, 1849, at Hunterfield, Scotland. Came to Utah with parents.
Married Rebecca Neibaur March 30, 1869, Salt Lake City (daughter of Alexander Neibaur and Ellen Breakell, Nauvoo, Ill., pioneers Sept. 23, 1848, Brigham Young company). She was born March 30, 1851. Their children: Ellen b. April 21, 1870, died; Charles W. b. April 7, 1872, m. Ollie M. Thatcher; Jean b. May 22, 1874, died; Alexander b. May 7, 1876, m. Constance Thatcher, m. Agnes Sloan; Joseph F. b. March 1, 1880, m. Ada S. Dusenbery; James Oro b. Dec. 21, 1882, m. Emma E. Groesbeck; Merrill b. March 21, 1884, m. Bella Woodmansee; Rebecca b. April 19, 1886, m. Horace B. Whitney; Grover b. June 10, 1888, died; Alice b. April 3, 1890, m. Harold R. Smoot. Family home, Salt Lake City.
Married Ellen Ricks March 30, 1880, Salt Lake City (daughter of Joel Ricks and Sarah A. Fiske, Potsdam, N. Y., pioneers Sept. 14, 1852). Their children: Preston. m. Anne Parkinson; Joel, m. Terressa Taylor; Edna; Florence; Nathan. Family home Logan, Utah.
High priest; missionary to New York 1869; England 1880-82; presiding bishop of the church. Lumberman; merchant.

NICHOLAS, JOHN (son of William Nicholas, Lorestone Parish, Wales). Born Dec. 31, 1839, Lorestone Parish. Came to Utah Sept. 4, 1866, Thomas E. Ricks company.
Married Anne Affleck (Tite) in 1866, Salt Lake City (daughter of Andrew Affleck and Margaret Truitt, Newcastle-on-Tyne, Eng.). She was born March 31, 1840, died Feb. 20, 1885, Ogden, Utah. Their children: George, m. Libbie Wadman; John, m. Martha Cole; Thomas, d. Oct. 19, 1818; Daniel, d. Sept. 3, 1878; Gomer A. b. Dec. 5, 1873, m. Marcia Hinchcliff; Jane A., m. William Pierce. Family home Ogden, Utah.
Elder. Blacksmith. Died Sept. 3, 1878.

NICHOLAS, GOMER A. (son of John Nicholas and Ann Affleck). Born Dec. 5, 1873, Ogden, Utah.
Married Marcia Hinchcliff June 8, 1898, in Ogden (daughter of Charles W. Hinchcliff and Mary Allen of Ogden, both born in Utah). She was born March 28, 1875. Their children: J. Allen b. April 6, 1899; Francis G. b. Dec. 4, 1902; Virginia b. Sept. 14, 1910. Family home Ogden, Utah. Merchant.

NICOL, THOMAS (son of Thomas Nicol and Elizabeth Dryher, Coleton. Scotland). Born Nov. 22, 1824, at Coleton. Came to Utah 1853.
Married Elizabeth Watson 1842, Fifeshire, Scotland, who was born March 10, 1819, and came to Utah 1853; died 1858. Their children: Abraham b. Oct. 1, 1847; Catherine b. Sept. 30, 1848; Thomas b. Jan. 1, 1850; George b. Jan. 3, 1851; Elizabeth b. Dec. 18, 1852; James b. May 20, 1854; Ann b. Feb. 8, 1856; Archibald b. Jan. 23, 1858; all these children died young. Family home Bountiful, Utah.
Married Johanna Christina Handberg March 11, 1858, Salt Lake City (daughter of John Handberg and Christina Traine of Copenhagen, Denmark, pioneers 1857, Christian Christiansen handcart company). She was born March 11, 1830. Their children: Josephine Maria b. Jan. 25, 1859, m. Alva M. Murdock; Thomas Handberg b. Jan. 20, 1861; Johanna Christina b. Dec. 25, 1863, and Jeannette Elizabeth b. Nov. 4, 1864, latter three died in childhood; Rachel Ann b. March 6, 1866, d. young; Sarah Matilda b. April 18, 1868, m. Heber Giles Crook; Adolphus Alexander b. May 9, 1870, d. child; Moroni b. Nov. 9, 1871, d. 1881; Joseph Alma b. Jan. 7, 1873, d. young; Hyrum Chase b. Feb. 9, 1876, m. Isabella Crawford Murdock; Gabriel Blake b. Oct. 29, 1878, m. Estella Duke.
Married Johanna C. Hansen Dec. 14, 1864, Salt Lake City, who came from Denmark. Only child: Dora Elizabeth b. Sept. 29, 1865, m. James S. Murdock. Family home Heber City, Utah.
Married Maria Nelson Dec. 1, 1866, Salt Lake City, native of Denmark. Only child: John Thomas b. Sept. 3, 1867, died. Family home Heber City, Utah.

Missionary in Scotland; high priest. Indian war veteran. In the forefront in Echo Canyon trouble, with Lot Smith company. Located at Bountiful 1854, and in 1858 returned to Salt Lake City. In 1860 moved to Moroni; then to Heber City; fought Indians both places. Pioneered in all the early necessary improvements; made two trips to Missouri river to bring immigrants to Utah. Died Dec. 23, 1909, Heber City, Utah.

NICOL, HYRUM CHASE (son of Thomas Nicol and Johanna Christina Handberg). Born Feb. 9, 1876, Heber City, Utah. Married Isabella Crawford Murdock Sept. 22, 1903, Salt Lake City (daughter of John Murray Murdock and Isabella Crawford of Heber City), who was born Jan. 10, 1876. Their children: Thomas Murdock b. Aug. 26, 1904; Hyrum Chase b. March 19, 1906; Kenneth Crawford b. July 11, 1908; John Murray b. June 20, 1912. Family home Duchesne, Utah.
Member 20th quorum seventies; missionary to New Zealand Jan. 1, 1900, to June 8, 1903; high priest; counselor to Bishop George Victor Billings, Theodore ward, Duchesne stake; Sunday school teacher Heber City and Theodore wards; ward teacher at Theodore. Helped in every possible way the first settlers who came to Uinta reservation May, 1906, and has assisted in all improvements incident to a new country. Rancher. Vice president of Duchesne Irrigation Company; now associated with Pioneer Supply Company; and also engaged in farming.

NIELSEN, AUGUSTINUS (son of Niels Jensen and Maren Jensen, Jutland, Denmark). Born April 14, 1833, in Jutland. Came to Utah Oct. 5, 1854, Hans Peter Olsen company.
Married Ane Benedicta Hansen Engelbrecht Feb. 5, 1854, on ship "Benjamin Adams," on Atlantic ocean (daughter of Hanse Peterson and Hedevig Lucie Engelbrecht of Fyen, Denmark; former died in Denmark, latter came to Utah in 1858). She was born Nov. 6, 1833. Their children: Ephramina B. b. July 11, 1855, m. H. P. Hansen; August b. March 3, 1857, m. Harriet Thurber; Hedevig H. C. b. Oct. 27, 1858, m. Louis Dungar, m. James Crosland; Mary S. b. Nov. 27, 1860, m. Chris. Christiansen; Caroline L. b. Nov. 13, 1862, m. W. E. Thurber; Annie J. b. Nov. 14, 1864, m. Alma Nielsen; Ephraim b. April 10, 1867, m. George Cal'oway; George C. b. June 14, 1869, m. Jessaphine Outzen; Niels Peter b. Oct. 23, 1871, d. in 1889; Joseph b. Dec. 16, 1873, m. Eliza Jane Dell; Clarinda L. b. Aug. 2, 1876, m. Otto S. Dormitzer; LeRoy b. March 9, 1878, m. Bertha Watkins. Family resided South Cotonwood, Ephraim, Mount Pleasant and Richfield, Utah.
Member of high council in Cottonwood; 48th quorum seventies; missionary to Germany 1851. Active pioneer in San Pete and Sevier counties. Farmer; miner; assayer. Died April 4, 1902, at Richfield.

NIELSEN, BENDT (son of Niels Bensen, Christianstad, Sweden). Born May 14, 1796. Came to Utah Oct. 5, 1854.
Married Margrite Eilertsen 1821, Denmark, who was born in 1795. Their children: Niels B., m. Dorthea Margret Jensen, m. Sophia Halvorsen; George, m. Walborg Ericksen, m. Marie Thoreson; Marie; Hans Enoch, m. Nancy Margaret Osborn; Annie; Christine, m. Fredric Nielsen; Andrew B., m. Elizabeth Ericksen, m. Helen McBride. Family home East Weber, Utah.
Married Kisten Knudsen. Their children: Bendt, m. Sarah J. Stanley; Ephraim, m. Annie Petersen; Jacob. Family home East Weber, Utah.

NIELSEN, NIELS B. (son of Bendt Nielsen and Margrite Eilertsen). Born July 14, 1822, Horsholm, Frederiksborg, Denmark. Came to Utah 1856.
Married Dorthea Margret Jensen May 3, 1851, at Horsholm (daughter of Hans Hansen and Greta Yergersen), who was born June 18, 1832. Their children: Margret Christina b. Dec. 20, 1836, m. I. C. Thoresen; Niels Joseph b. May 5, 1859, m. Nancy Anderson, m. Susannah Smuin; Anna Myriah b. Aug. 28, 1861, died; James Henry b. Jan. 16, 1864, m. Lizzie Unsworth; Martha Ann b. July 25, 1866, m. J. F. Nielsen; Ezra Erastus b. July 18, 1868, m. Nora Hansen; Maria Elizabeth b. Sept. 3, 1870, m. Charles Orell; Hans Benjamin b. July 11, 1873, m. Emma E. Jensen Dec. 7, 1898; Emma Micline b. Dec. 14, 1875; Peter Willard; Flora Clamenta; latter three died. Family home Hyrum, Utah.
Married Sophia Halvorsen 1862, Salt Lake City, who was born Sept. 25, 1849, Christiania, Norway. Their children: Elsa Sophia b. Nov. 30, 1868; Pauline b. July 12, 1871; Louis Wilford b. Jan. 22, 1874; Ida Ann b. Nov. 25, 1876; Rhoda V. b. Oct. 8, 1884.
One of the pioneers of Hyrum. Drove the first stakes for the lines of Main street under the direction of Ezra T. Benson. Died March 15, 1913.

NIELSEN, NIELS JOSEPH (son of Niels B. Nielsen and Dorthea Margret Jensen). Born May 3, 1859, Weber Co., Utah.
Married Nancy A. Anderson February, 1883, Salt Lake City (daughter of Andrew Anderson and Alice Brooks), who was born May 12, 1863, Hyrum, Utah. Their children: Joseph A. b. Nov. 12, 1883, m. Ruby Williams Jan. 22, 1907; James b. Sept. 27, 1885; Bessie b. Sept. 14, 1887; Lssie b. Dec. 19, 1891.
Married Susannah Smuin Jan. 9, 1895, Logan, Utah (daughter of George Smuin and Eliza Galsford), who was born

Sept. 28, 1871. Their children: Dora Eliza b. Nov. 24, 1895; Norman L. b. March 24, 1897, died; Dewey H. b. June 16, 1898; Carl George b. Jan. 8, 1901; Ellen Rose b. Sept. 7, 1902; Grant b. April 10, 1904; Norris b. Nov. 21, 1905; Wesley b. Nov. 26, 1907, died; Emery b. Jan. 2, 1910, died; Blaine Loyde b. Jan. 15, 1911. Family home Hyrum, Utah.
Missionary to Nebraska 1891-93; ordained bishop of Hyrum 3d ward Sept. 22, 1901. Farmer; dairyman.

NIELSEN, GEORGE (son of Bendt Nielsen and Margrite Eilertsen of Horsholm, Frederiksborg, Denmark). Born May 1, 1826, at Horsholm. Came to Utah in 1854.
Married Walborg Ericksen.
Married Maria Clara Thoreson Feb. 27, 1866, Hyrum, Utah (daughter of Hans Thoreson and Caroline Nielsen of Christiania, Norway, pioneers Sept. 27, 1863, George Nebeker company). She was born Jan. 10, 1850. Their children: Walborg; Charles Andrew; Caroline Margaret; Clara Elizabeth; George Ilert; Dora Charlotte; Martha Melinda; Lillian Vilate; Leo Conrad; Florella. Family home Hyrum, Utah.
President of high priests quorum. Member of city council. Farmer.

NIELSEN, CHARLES ANDREW (son of George Nielsen and Maria C. Thoreson). Born July 27, 1869, Logan, Utah.
Married Olive Williams Nov. 26, 1890, Logan, Utah (daughter of Thomas Williams and Emily Louisa Allen, Hyrum, Utah), who was born Sept. 14, 1872. Their children: Vinnie Lucinda b. Oct. 18, 1891; Charles Horace b. Aug. 19, 1893; Leora Nielsen b. Sept. 2, 1895; George Marvin b. Aug. 8, 1897; Emily Leta b. June 14, 1900; Thomas Lyman b. Aug. 18, 1903; Rhula Merl b. Nov. 22, 1905; Ceral Arden b. March 12, 1910; Homer Burton b. March 22, 1912. Family home Hyrum, Utah.
Missionary to northern states 1900 to 1902; president of 62nd quorum of seventies; ward chorister. City councilman. Farmer.

NIELSEN, ANDREW B. (son of Bendt Nielsen and Margrite Eilertsen). Born March 24, 1835, Hesterkeb, Frederiksborg, Denmark. Came to Utah Oct. 5, 1854.
Married Elizabeth Ericksen April 1, 1865, Salt Lake City (daughter of Henry Ericksen of Hyrum, Utah, pioneer Oct. 5, 1854), who was born Sept. 28, 1842. Their children: Mary Elizabeth b. March 23, 1866, m. John Swensen; Andrew Henry b. Jan. 5, 1869, m. Anna Johnsen; Annie Melinda b. Sept. 5, 1871, m. Elam Allen; Margaret Marie b. June 5, 1875, m. Silas Allen; Emily Christine b. March 4, 1878, d. July 18, 1885; Joseph Ilard b. Sept. 10, 1882, d. March 29, 1902. Family home Hyrum, Utah.
Married Helen McBride April 9, 1896, who was born Jan. 2, 1872. Their children: Aleda b. March 4, 1897; Rulon Harlum b. Feb. 15, 1899; Harold Mariner b. Jan. 2, 1902. Family home Hyrum, Utah.
Seventy; high priest. Assisted in bringing immigrants to Utah 1864. Pioneer to Hyrum, Utah. City councilman. Farmer; stockraiser. Died Feb. 5, 1913.

NIELSEN, CARL HENDRICK (son of Hendrick Nielsen of Wolstrop, and Anna Margaret Madsen of Stendrup, Denmark). Born Feb. 4, 1846, at Stendrup. Came to Utah Oct. 5, 1867, Leonard G. Rice company.
Married Karen Christina Larsen May 26, 1867, Odense, Denmark (daughter of Hans Larsen, who died in Odense, and Maren Larsen, who came to Utah in early '70s). She was born Nov. 17, 1851. Their children: Alice Christine b. July 29, 1868, m. A. Peter Jensen; Charley Nephi b. Aug. 3, 1870, m. Nora Baker; Clara b. Oct. 27, 1872, m. John Lewis; Martha b. May 26, 1875, m. Lee Isabell; Ammon b. Sept. 17, 1877, d. Sept. 22, 1878; Joseph Alma b. Sept. 19, 1879, m. Caroline Peterson; Eleanor b. Nov. 2, 1881, m. Oluf Anderson; Henry Richard b. June 11, 1885, m. Anna Hansen; Wilford Leo b. Jan. 17, 1888, m. Alta Maria Barrows; Juanita Maralda b. Oct. 3, 1890, m. Joseph Ogden. Family resided at Middleton, Levan, Elsinore and Richfield, Utah.
Elders quorum; missionary to Denmark 1865-67; second counselor to Bishop Raphelson, Elsinore, 1875-77; ward teacher Richfield. Active pioneer in Sevier county. Mason; builder; contractor.

NIELSEN, GUSTAVE (son of Niels Knudson and Ingar Maria Hansen of Christiania, Norway). Born Sept. 30, 1831, Christiania. Came to Utah Sept. 24, 1860, Oscar O. Stoddard company.
Married Christina Nielsen March 11, 1863, Salt Lake City (daughter of Anders Nielsen and Triene Olsen of Sjelland, Denmark; former died in Denmark, latter came to Utah late in 1869). She was born Jan. 23, 1845, and came to Utah Sept. 23, 1862, Ola N. Liljenquist oxteam company. Their children: Mary Josephine b. Feb. 19, 1864, m. Alexander Smith; Emma Christina b. Nov. 10, 1865, m. Isaac Frost; Sarah Tena b. Jan. 16, 1868, m. Charles Henry Baxter; Gustave b. March 10, 1870, m. Gene Jensen; Heber Charles b. Jan. 15, 1872, m. Emily Hicks; Hyrum b. March 25, 1874, m. Garnet Hefir, m. Alwilda Eliza b. Dec. 24, 1876, m. Frank G. Daniels; Annie Lenora Elizabeth m. Jan. 30, 1880, m. George Allan J. Woodruff; George Albert b. July 17, 1882, m. Nettie Mora Barrett. Family home Richfield, Utah.
Seventy; high priest; assistant Sunday school superintendent; ward teacher; missionary in Norway four years. Farmer; stone-mason. Died Nov. 10, 1908.

1070   PIONEERS AND PROMINENT MEN OF UTAH

NIELSEN, HEBER C. (son of Gustave and Christina Nielsen). Born Jan. 15, 1872, Big Cottonwood, Utah.
Married Emily Hicks May 19, 1899 (daughter of John T. R. Hicks and Anna Buhler, who came to Utah with oxteam company). She was born Feb. 9, 1878. Their children: H. Lovell b. Feb. 11, 1900; Ralph H. b. March 8, 1902; Delbert G. b. March 6, 1904; Estella Pearl B. March 4, 1906; Emily Etta b. Nov. 12, 1907. Family home Coltman, Idaho.
Elder. Farmer. Died April 4, 1908.

NIELSEN, GEORGE ALBERT (son of Gustave Nielsen and Christina Nielsen). Born July 17, 1882, Big Cottonwood, Utah.
Married Nettie Mora Barrett Sept. 12, 1903, Salt Lake City, John Henry Smith officiating (daughter of William R. Barrett and Charlotte Herron, Nashville, Tenn., who came to Utah 1891). She was born March 15, 1884. Only child: George Wallace b. May 23, 1904.
Elder. Employed in mailing department of U. S. postoffice.

NIELSEN, HANS J. (son of Niels Jensen and Ingar Hansdatter, Stengade, Tullebolle Sogn, Denmark). Born Nov. 2, 1821, at Stengade. Came to Utah Sept. 22, 1861, Samuel A. Woolley company.
Married Johanna Christena Anderson, in 1840, Skrobetov, Denmark (daughter of Andrew Hansen and Ingar Margretta Larsen, Clausbolle, Denmark). Their children: Jensina Christina, m. Mads Hansel; Ingar, m. Jens Peter Jensen; Dorthea, m. John Riggs; Nieltine, m. William Hjord; Berggitte, m. B. Iversen; Annie Christina, m. Ola N. Liljenquist, who was famed as an immigrant oxtrain captain.
Pioneer. Died Oct. 18, 1911.

NIELSON, HANS (son of Niels Jensen, born 1801, at Oedehadstrup, and Birthe Christofers Dather, born 1809, at Brordrup, both of Sjelland Amt, Denmark). Born Jan. 1, 1833, Brordrup, Sjelland, Denmark. Came to Utah Sept. 15, 1864, William B. Preston company.
Married Maria S. Jonas Iric (widow), Feb. 29, 1860 (daughter of Christoffer Knudsen and Mattie Christensen). She was born Oct. 3, 1827, and had a son by a former marriage, Adolph Hansen, who bore his father's name; both died.
Called to settle on Little Colorado, Ariz., 1876; hauled stone for Salt Lake Temple 1867; assisted in bringing immigrants to Utah. Resided at St. Joseph, Ariz.

NIELSEN, HANS T. Born June 28, 1826, Denmark. Came to Utah Oct. 22, 1866, Abner Lowry company.
Married Nicolina Rasmina Espasen Oct. 4, 1851, in Denmark. She was born Feb. 18, 1827. Their children: Christina b. July 28, 1849, m. Christian Bertlesen; Josephina b. July 29, 1852, d. July 1858; Brighamina Malvina b. Sept. 22, 1854, m. Ole Peter Borg; Catherina b. Sept. 21, 1856, d. April 29, 1858; Fena b. July 29, 1858, m. Ole Peter Borg; Emma b. Feb. 4, 1861, m. Sorn Oleson; Alma b. Jan. 20, 1863, m. Annie Nielsen. Family home Ephraim, Utah.
Conference clerk at Aalborg, Denmark. Tailor. Died Dec. 30, 1887.

NIELSON, JOHANNES (son of Niels Andersen and Inger Pedersdatter, both of Raageleje, Sjelland, Denmark).
Married Ann Petersen. Their children: Annie, m. Lewis C. Jensen; Mary; Christena Marie, m. Peter J. Petersen; Joseph, m. Sarah Eliza Call; John Ephraim, m. Tennie Walker. Family home Mantua, Utah.
Builder, contractor and sawmiller. Died at Mantua, Utah.

NIELSEN, JOSEPH (son of Johannes Nielsen and Ann Petersen). Born Jan. 24, 1876, at Mantua, Utah.
Married Sarah Eliza Call Feb. 2, 1898, Salt Lake City (daughter of Omar Call and Elenor Jones, both of Willard, Utah, pioneers 1849). She was born Feb. 2, 1875. Their children: Elenor Anna b. Jan. 21, 1899, died; Joseph Call b. Aug. 24, 1901; Lyle b. March 11, 1903; Stanley Call b. Jan. 14, 1905; Gwendolyn b. Oct. 12, 1910. Family home Provo, Utah.
President 156th quorum seventies; missionary to Denmark 1898-1900; assistant in Utah stake mutual; counselor to superintendent of Sunday schools Provo, sixth ward. Architect.

NIELSEN, JORGEN CHRISTIAN (son of Hans and Mary Nielsen of Odense, Fyen Amt, Denmark). Born Oct. 6, 1842, Odense, Denmark. Came to Utah Aug. 29, 1863, Captain Murdock company.
Married Anna Kerstine Dorthea Byer June 21, 1865, Provo, Utah, who was born June 21, 1843, Horsena, Denmark, and died April 19, 1881. Their children: Maria Kerstine Dorthea b. March 31, 1866, m. John F. Carter; Emelia Amanda Jorgine b. Oct. 12, 1868; Jorgen Christian b. Dec. 7, 1869, d. Dec. 14, 1869; John Edwill b. Jan. 17, 1871; Dagmar Alfrida b. Oct. 7, 1873; Anna Hansine Antonia b. May 26, 1876, m. W. B. Slick; Dianthe Leonthe b. Feb. 27, 1878, m. William Irvine; m. George Scott; a daughter b. April 20, 1880, and a son b. April 19, 1881, both died. Family home Provo, Utah.
Married Oline Olsen Dec. 15, 1890 (daughter of Annie Olsen of Isvol, Norway), who was born 1852. Only child: Ralph Emanuel b. Feb. 7, 1892.
Elder; ward teacher. Justice of peace at Lake View. Black Hawk Indian war veteran. Farmer and gardener.

NIELSEN, LARS (son of Niels Christensen and Annie Larsen of Denmark). Born March 20, 1828, in Denmark. Came to Utah Sept. 5, 1863.
Married in Denmark May 18, 1853, the daughter of Peter Mekelsen and Bertha Jensen, the former being a pioneer of 1863. She was born March 2, 1826. Their children: Niels Peter b. June 19, 1854, m. Florence Dutsan; Jens Christian b. Feb. 7, 1856, d. Oct. 5, 1863; Annie M. b. March 20, 1858, m. Joseph S. Anderson; August b. Aug. 6, 1860, m. Emmie Overson; Bertha M. b. Aug. 8, 1863, d. Feb. 21, 1866; Louis b. April 18, 1867, m. Mary J. Textorms; Joseph H. b. Oct. 18, 1871, m. Emmie C. Nielson.
Settled at Leamington spring of 1876. Bishop of that ward 1883-1900; presiding priest 1876-83.

NIELSEN, NIELS C. (son of Andrew Nielsen and Magdalena Sorensen of Hjorring Amt, Denmark). Born Aug. 31, 1845, in Hjorring. Came to Utah 1862, Christian A. Madsen independent company.
Married Annie M. Sorensen Jan. 9, 1870, Salt Lake City (daughter of Mikkel Sorensen and Helena Jesperson of Aarhuus Amt, Denmark, pioneers 1864). She was born Nov. 3, 1854. Their children: Niels E., m. Annie Christensen; Angeline, m. Orson E. Armstrong; Mick. m. Nettie Melonson; Helena, m. Christ Thorenson; Maria V., m. Hyrum Danielson; Norah, m. Charles Force; Joseph, m. Arnold J. Arnoldson; Lydia M.; Andrew M.; Ferry L.; Jane; Mary, died; Lillian, died. Family home Moroni, Utah.
Elder; ward teacher; counselor in Y. M. M. I. A. Justice of the peace at Moroni three terms; pound keeper 22 years; watermaster and deputy watermaster 20 years; police officer; city marshal. Black Hawk Indian war veteran. Assisted in bringing immigrants to Utah in 1866. Farmer; stockraiser.

NIELSEN, NIELS CHRISTIAN. Came to Utah 1856, Knud Peterson company.
Married Mary Larsen in Jutland, Denmark. She came to Utah in 1856, Knud Peterson company. Their children: Niels Peter (Tanner), m. Maria Hoggaard; Karen, m. George Frandsen, Sr.
Elder. Located at Kaysville; moved to Mt. Pleasant. Farmer and stockraiser. Died at Mt. Pleasant.

NIELSEN, NIELS PEDER (son of Peder Nielsen and Kirsten Andersen, Norre Orslov, Island of Falster, Denmark). Born Feb. 13, 1847, at Norre Orslov. Came to Utah Oct. 1, 1862, Captain Horne company.
Married Caroline Christensen Dec. 15, 1868, Salt Lake City (daughter of Christen Christensen and Annie Marie Nielsen of Hjorring Amt, Denmark, pioneers 1868 in one of the Church companies). She was born Sept. 5, 1848. Their children: Niels Peter b. Sept. 5, 1869, d. infant; Heber Peter b. March 19, 1872, m. Ida Olivia Larsen June 21, 1899; Hans Frederick b. Aug. 18, 1874, m. Amalie Christenson Nov. 11, 1896; David Waldemar b. Nov. 13, 1876, m. Johnnne Axelsen Nov. 1, 1899; Abel Christian b. Nov. 7, 1878, m. Pearl Riley Oct. 26, 1903; Aurelie Christine b. Aug. 28, 1880, m. Frank Otterstrom Jan. 30, 1909; Aaron Godtfred b. June 24, 1882, m. Ida Beal June 6, 1906; Moses Mariam b. May 26, 1884, m. Ada Johnsen April 6, 1910; Annie Adine Marinda b. Feb. 13, 1886, m. Thomas Jefferson Clark March 4, 1908; Caroline Matilda b. Dec. 26, 1888, m. Ross Andersen Dec. 23, 1909; Ernest Hyrum b. Feb. 6, 1891; Joseph Richard b. Jan. 30, 1893.
Married Caroline Nielsen Nov. 28, 1877 at St. George, Utah (daughter of Christian Nielsen and Karen Harrisen, who were married Jan. 9, 1855, Salt Lake City, pioneers Oct. 24, 1857, Ephraim, Utah. Their children: Carrie Jane b. Sept. 14, 1879, m. Charles Harry Wilson Jan. 4, 1901; Irine Elmine b. April 14, 1894. Families resided Ephraim, Utah.
High priest; missionary to Denmark 1894, where he presided over the Island branch of the Copenhagen conference. Assisted in bringing immigrants to Utah 1868. Sergeant in Black Hawk Indian war.

NIELSEN, HEBER PETER (son of Niels Peder Nielsen and Caroline Christensen). Born March 19, 1872, Ephraim, Utah.
Married Ida Olivia Larsen June 21, 1899, at Ephraim (daughter of Christian A. Larsen and Mary Ann Jensen of same place). Family resided Ephraim and Salt Lake City, Utah.
Graduate University of Utah 1894; school teacher nine years. Sunday school teacher; superintendent religious class. Vice president and secretary McMillin Paper and School Supply company, Salt Lake City.

NIELSEN, NIELSEN JACOB (son of Hans Nielsen and Maren Jacobsen of Odense, Denmark). Born Dec. 13, 1839, Fraugde, Denmark. Came to Utah in 1864, Tom Booth freight train.

Married Christine Peterson March 28, 1866, Provo, Utah. She was born July 30, 1831, Norrkoping, Sweden. Their children: Niels Jacob Christian, m. Agnes Ross; Peter and Henry died; Annie, m. James C. Jensen. Family home Provo, Utah.
Mason.

NIELSEN, PETER (son of Niels Alexsen, Horby Sogn, Holbek Amt, Denmark, and Annie Marie Nielsen, born 1779 in Denmark). He was born April 15, 1836, at Horby Sogn. Came to Utah Nov. 8, 1865, Miner G. Atwood company.
Married Kisten Larsen April 4, 1856, Horby, Denmark (daughter of Lars Larsen and Annie Marie Thomas, both of whom died in Denmark). She was born April 28, 1826. Their children: Lars Nielsen b. June 5, 1857, m. Mary J. Beckstrom; Annie Mary b. Oct. 25, 1859, m. William Vier; Emma b. Nov. 15, 1867, m. Lee Bailey.
Married Nelsine Nielsen Sept. 22, 1872, Salt Lake City (daughter of Niels Christian Nielsen, pioneer Oliver Christiansen handcart company, and Karen Ericksen, pioneer Sept. 13, 1857, Mathias Cowley company). She was born Aug. 29, 1855, Nestgard, Hjorring Amt, Denmark. Their children: Caroline Christine b. Nov. 2, 1874, m. Alfred Hughes 1896; Peter b. Nov. 18, 1876, m. Laura Betts; Joseph Alexander b. July 10, 1878, m. Elsie Barney; William H. b. Jan. 12, 1881, m. Ella Sorensen; Albert C. b. Jan. 19, 1883, m. Mira Holm; Emelie C. b. March 25, 1884; E. Rebecca b. Nov. 30, 1885; Andrew L. b. May 11, 1888, m. Ella Ainge; M. Leoretta b. April 23, 1890; H. Elenora b. Oct. 1, 1892; Annie L. b. Jan. 15, 1895; Elmer F. b. Aug. 24, 1896; Sarah E. b. July 16, 1898; Jemima M. b. March 17, 1900. Families resided Spanish Fork, Utah.
Teacher; elder; high priest. President Co-op. store in Spanish Fork ten years. President of West Field Irrigation company four years.

NIELSEN, SOREN (son of Nels Sorensen of Denmark). Born Nov. 10, 1824, Marsoe, Denmark. Came to Utah Sept. 25, 1868, John G. Holman company.
Married Amelia Berg May 6, 1857, Grenaa, Denmark (daughter of Rasmus Berg and Caroline Tolhoe of Grenaa), who was born Nov. 25, 1833. Their children: Peter Antohn b. Sept. 11, 1865, died Sept. 1, 1885; Mary K. b. Feb. 2, 1867, m. Hyrum Thorpe May 10, 1886; Ane M. b. Nov. 19, 1868, m. Charles Alfred March 18, 1891; Andrew C. b. Dec. 23, 1870, m. Julia E. Christensen and Pauline Christensen; Carl Otto b. Nov. 10, 1872, m. Karen A. Rasmussen; James Lauritz b. Feb. 26, 1875, m. Malinda E. Rasmussen May 13, 1896; Canute b. March 26, 1877, m. Nora M. Bjergard July 6, 1899; Joseph Alma b. Sept. 11, 1879, m. Elizabeth Stevens Dec. 11, 1899; Oscar Wilford b. Oct. 17, 1884, m. Caroline M. Olsen Jan. 24, 1906. Family home Ephraim, Utah.
Married Ellen Gunderson June 10, 1880, Salt Lake City (daughter of Ole Gunderson and Molj Johnson), who was born June 23, 1843, Stordalen, Norway.
High priest; high councilor; first counselor; president high priests quorum South San Pete stake; missionary to Denmark 1881; president Y. M. M. I. A. Farmer; builder; stonecutter.

NIELSON, ANTON (son of Jens Nielson and Annie Christine Hansen, who came to Utah July 24, 1873). He was born Dec. 20, 1866, Almon, Denmark. Came to Utah July 24, 1873.
Married Sarah May Lott Aug. 4, 1897, Salt Lake City (daughter of John W. Lott and Sarah Joan Robison, Kanosh, Utah). Their children: Lenna b. July 23, 1898; Gerald W. b. Nov. 3, 1899; Jens Guy b. April 3, 1902; Roosevelt b. Nov. 1, 1904; Lott b. Oct. 19, 1906; Glen Ford b. May 26, 1909; Paul Robison b. May 1, 1911. Family home Huntington, Utah.
Member 81st quorum seventies; missionary to Denmark 1892-94; bishop Huntington ward 1906. County commissioner two terms; clerk in Utah state senate 1907. Farmer.

NIELSON, AUGUST (son of Lars Nielson, born March 20, 1828, South Orster, and Sidsel Peterson, born March 2, 1826, both of Stubberry, Maribo, Denmark). Born Aug. 6, 1860 at Stubberry. Came to Utah in 1863.
Married Emma Overson April 5, 1884, Salt Lake City (daughter of Christian Overson and Sina Larson), who was born April 23, 1868. Their children: Fred b. March 21, 1886, m. Mary Steedman Oct. 10, 1910; Wells b. March 13, 1888, m. Emily Paxman June 6, 1910; Darta b. July 28, 1890, m. Carl Davis April 2, 1913; Spencer b. March 25, 1893; Lacleud b. Feb. 29, 1896; Shelby b. March 4, 1899; Leroy b. Dec. 3, 1901; Arvilla b. July 26, 1904; Kenneth b. Jan. 28, 1907; Cornel b. May 11, 1910.
President deacons quorum; ward teacher 16 years; seventy; bishop's counselor.

NIELSON, JENS (son of Niels Anderson and Karn Monson of Fener, Sweden). Born June 5, 1826, Fener, Sweden. Came to Utah Sept. 15, 1859, Robert F. Neslen company.
Married Stena Larson 1851, who was born July 29, 1821. Came to Utah with husband. Their children: Brighamena, b. May 13, 1854, m. Peter Estelene; Andrew b. June 26, 1860, d. aged 11. Family home Mt. Pleasant, and Chester, Utah.
Married Cecelia Waldemar April 15, 1860, Fairview, Utah (daughter of Amos Waldemar, pioneer Sept. 15, 1859, Robert F. Neslen company), who was born June 7, 1826 in Sweden. Their children: Hilda C. b. Jan. 19, 1861, m. Hyrum L. Coates March 1, 1880.
Second lieutenant in Black Hawk Indian war, under Captain Fredrick Nelson.

NIELSON, OLE. Born about 1580 in Sweden. Came to Utah September, 1865, Thomas Taylor company.
Married Permelia Baum about 1825 in Sweden (daughter of Niels Baum), who was born 1806 in Sweden. Came to Utah Sept. 5, 1863, John F. Sanders company. Their children: Lizzie, died; Peter, drowned in Green River 1868, going for immigrants; James and two other boys, died; Swen O. b. Jan. 1, 1854, m. Rachel O. Atkin March 14, 1878; Ole; Lars I.; Sina, d. 1863.
Died 1874, Fairview, Utah.

NIELSON, SWEN O. (son of Ole Nielson and Permelia Baum). Born Jan. 1, 1854, in Sweden. Came to Utah Sept. 5, 1863, John F. Sanders company.
Married Rachel V. Atkin March 14, 1878, St. George, Utah (daughter of William Atkin and Rachel Thompson of St. George, pioneers Sept. 4, 1859, George Rowley handcart company). She was born March 14, 1861, Salt Lake City, d. Oct. 26, 1900. Their children: Swen W. b. Jan. 20, 1879; Annie Nellie b. Aug. 3, 1880; Rachel Mable b. July 20, 1882, d. May 23, 1886; Ole Alma b. Sept. 5, 1884, d. March 18, 1884; Sarah Luella b. Jan. 4, 1885; Estella Maud b. Feb. 4, 1887; Sina Christena b. Oct. 6, 1888; Peter Franklin b. Feb. 26, 1891, d. Jan. 27, 1905; Violet Venice b. Aug. 15, 1896, d. Nov. 26, 1896. Family home Fairview, Utah.
Married (Mrs.) Jennie Poulsen June 4, 1902.
Missionary to Sweden. County commissioner two terms; justice of the peace 10 years; constable; marshal; member state board of equalization. Merchant; farmer; stockraiser.

NILSON, NILS (son of Nils Nilson of Simmer Sams, Rorum, born 1771) and Else Olsson, South Rorum, Malmöhus Lan, Sweden; born May 4, 1764, Espinige, Sweden). He was born Dec. 30, 1811, South Rorum, Sweden. Came to Utah Aug. 26, 1859, James B. Brown company.
Married Bocl Tykeson (daughter of John Tykeson and Edna Olas, former born Sept. 20, 1773, Fultofta, Sweden), who was born May 5, 1812, Fultofta, Sweden, and came to Utah Aug. 26, 1859. Their children: Elise b. July 17, 1838, m. Jens N. Christensen; Peter Nilson b. Nov. 18, 1840, m. Svenborg Tufveson October, 1862; Nils b. July 20, 1843, d. 1849; Elna b. May 17, 1846, d. March 1856; Ola b. April 11, 1849, d. Jan. 4, 1874; Bengta b. Aug. 28, 1854, d. Feb. 25, 1856. Family home Smithfield, Utah.
High priest. Farmer. Joined the L. D. S. Church in 1854 at Rorum.

NILSON, PETER (son of Nils Nilson and Bocl Tykeson). Born Nov. 18, 1840, South Rorum, Malmöhus Lan, Sweden. Came to Utah Aug. 26, 1859.
Married Svenborg Tufveson October, 1862, Smithfield, Utah (daughter of Tufve Johnson and Pehrnila Pehrson), who was born Dec. 14, 1833, Osby, Sweden. Their children: Samuel Peter b. July 13, 1863; m. Lorretta L. Miles; Emma Nilson b. April 15, 1865, m. Ed Cazier; James b. May 24, 1867, m. Priscilla Hamilton; John Nephi b. Feb. 6, 1869, d. Aug. 1, 1871; Eliza Nellie b. May 16, 1871; Ella b. June 29, 1873, m. Alma Wright; Zina Matilda b. April 11, 1875, d. Jan. 21, 1877; Daniel b. Feb. 29, 1877, d. Aug. 6, 1878.
Married Minnie Hansen March 13, 1875, Salt Lake City (daughter of Ole and Marie Hansen), who was born Oct. 10, 1858, Odense, Denmark. Their children: Amanda Emelie b. June 13, 1877, m. Frank Miles; Marinda b. March 13, 1879, m. Seth Chambers; Oliver b. Jan. 1, 1882, m. Millicent Low Sept. 1902; Edna b. July 10, 1885, d. Aug. 1887; Ezra b. Jan. 23, 1890, m. Allee Toolson Oct. 1909. Family home Smithfield, Utah.
Married Kierste Jenson Nov. 30, 1882, Salt Lake City (daughter of Peter Jenson and Else Olson), who was born June 16, 1861, Everad, Sweden. Their children: Ida Ellenore b. Oct. 1, 1884, d. Dec. 26, 1905; Amos Carl b. Dec. 24, 1886; Joseph b. May 7, 1890; Elsie Matilda b. Dec. 7, 1891; Parley Franklin b. Oct. 19, 1893; Omer Victor b. Oct. 31, 1897, d. Sept. 23, 1898; Edgar b. Sept. 10, 1899; Milo b. Sept. 10, 1899. Family home Smithfield, Utah.
High priest; performed two missions in Sweden 1880-1888; hauled rock for the Salt Lake temple in 1863; hauled one of the first three loads of rock for the foundation of the tabernacle in 1863.

NIRDEN, THOMAS (son of Thomas Nirden, born at Herefordshire, Eng.). Came to Utah Sept. 19, 1852, Captain Clawson company.
Married Elizabeth Dunn Sept. 19, 1852 (daughter of Joseph and Phoebe Dunn). She was born September, 1832, and came to Utah Sept. 19, 1852, on her wedding day. Their children: Mary Ann b. July 27, 1855, m. William S. Lords,

July 23, 1854; Harriet b. Oct. 12, 1832, m. Thomas Whooley; Phoebe, m. Robert Jones; Elizabeth, m. Albert Harris; Martha, m. George Slough. Family home Pleasant Grove, Utah. Pioneer of Pleasant Grove 1852. Farmer.

NIXON, GEORGE. Born 1818. Came to Utah in 1853, Vincent Schurtliff company.
Married Frances Hart (daughter of William Hart), who was born Feb. 22, 1818, and came to Utah 1853, Vincent Schurtliff company. Their children: George William b. Sept. 26, 1847, m. Elizabeth H. Johnson Oct. 24, 1868; Charlotte b. Dec. 24, 1838, m. William Robins July 7, 1859; Fanny b. Jan. 19, 1851, m. Frank Carling; Stephen Henry b. Feb. 12, 1853, d. Jan. 3, 1910. Family home Holden, Millard Co., Utah.

NIXON, GEORGE WILLIAM (son of George Nixon and Frances Hart). Born Sept. 26, 1847. Came to Utah 1853.
Married Elizabeth H. Johnson Oct. 24, 1868, Salt Lake City (daughter of Richard Johnson and Hussetter Bevan, pioneers 1851, Joseph Horne company). She was born Nov. 1, 1849, Council Bluffs, Pottawattamie Co., Iowa. Their children: Harriet Ellen b. Feb. 1, 1870, m. Benjamin Kenney Sept. 23, 1891; George William b. Feb. 15, 1873, m. Rachel Marinda Stephenson Aug. 28, 1895; Ira Alvin b. Feb. 5, 1875, d. May 14, 1882; Elizabeth H. b. Oct. 2, 1877, d. May 29, 1882; Richard Stephen b. Sept. 12, 1880, m. Sarah Armina Stevens May 16, 1906; Frances Charlotte b. Nov. 9, 1883, m. Alma Stevens Sept. 27, 1905; Marion b. Jan. 19, 1887, d. Feb. 12, 1888; Carl b. May 29, 1889; Flossie b. Oct. 18, 1892. Family home Holden, Millard Co., Utah.
Assisted in bringing immigrants to Utah. Constable two terms; sheriff four years. President, vice president and director of Holden Co-op. store 20 years; director of Holden Irrigation Co. several years.

NIXON, GEORGE W., JR. (son of George William Nixon and Elizabeth H. Johnson). Born Feb. 15, 1873, Holden, Utah.
Married Rachel Marinda Stephenson Aug. 28, 1895, Manti, Utah (daughter of Simeon Stephenson and Rachel Stevens). She was born Aug. 20, 1875. Their children: Neva b. May 26, 1896; Ira b. March 2, 1898; Alda b. Nov. 13, 1902; Marion Albert b. Sept. 29, 1907; Myrl b. June 21, 1911. Family home Holden, Utah.

NOAKES, THOMAS. Born in England. Followed the founders of Utah in all their migrations. Came to Utah 1847.
Married Emma Inkpen at Sussex, Eng. Their children: George, m. Sophia Crowfoot; Thomas; William; John Hubbard, m. Susan Childs. Family home Springville, Utah.
One of Joseph Smith's bodyguards. Died September, 1870, at Springville, Utah.

NOAKES, GEORGE (son of Thomas Noakes and Emma Inkpen). Born Sept. 4, 1811, in England. Came to Utah 1852.
Married Sophia Crowfoot January, 1848, Nauvoo, Ill. (daughter of Benjamin Crowfoot and Samantha Sackett of Saratoga Springs, N. Y.; she came to Utah 1852). She was born Feb. 11, 1818. Their children: George Washington b. Feb. 14, 1849, m. Ann Wintertor, m. Rosina Haney; William Hubbard b. Sept. 25, 1850; Thomas Nephi b. Oct. 10, 1852, m. Neilus Carter; Emma Inkpen b. Dec. 3, 1854, m. John Winterton; Mary Elizabeth b. Oct. 3, 1857; John Hubbard b. March 19, 1859, m. Margeret Priscilla Casper; David E. b. Sept. 9, 1860; Robert Avery b. Sept. 5, 1862. Family home Charleston, Utah.
High priest; ward teacher; bishop; superintendent Sunday school. Veteran Indian war. Farmer.

NOAKES, JOHN HUBBARD (son of George Noakes and Sophia Crowfoot). Born March 19, 1859, Alpine, Utah.
Married Margeret Priscilla Casper May 15, 1889, Manti, Utah (daughter of William Nephi Casper and Agnes McFarland of Charleston, Utah), who was born June 4, 1872. Their children: Mary June b. June 12, 1890, m. John J. Gordon; David Avery b. Sept. 25, 1891; Mable Sophia b. Nov. 1, 1893, m. Frederick Howarth; Gertrude Louisa b. Oct. 9, 1895; William Ruben b. Feb. 13, 1897; Wallace Nephi b. April 4, 1899; Erving Arthur b. Nov. 23, 1900; Beatrice Verga b. Nov. 29, 1902; Vida Luella b. March 10, 1904; Reva Agnes b. Jan. 8, 1906; Margeret Myre b. July 17, 1908.
Elder; ward teacher. Constable; town marshal; road supervisor. Farmer.

NOBLE, JOSEPH B. (son of Ezekiel Noble and Theodocia Bates of Egremont, Mass). Born Jan. 14, 1810, at Egremont. Came to Utah October 2, 1847, Jedediah M. Grant company.
Married Mary Adeline Beman Sept. 11, 1834, Bloomfield, N. Y. (daughter of Alvah Beman and Sally Burtts of Livonia, Livingston county, N. Y.), who was born Jan. 10, 1810. Their children: Meriam; Joseph Heber; Nephi; Louisa; Edward Alvan, m. Jane Peal; Harriet Amelia; Hiram Brigham; Eliza Theodocia. m. Edgar Dalrymple; Benjamin, m. Rachel Lee. Family home Bountiful, Utah.
Members first quorum seventies; missionary to New York; bishop's counselor; bishop; patriarch. Performed the first plural marriage in the L. D. S. church. Miller; farmer; stockraiser. Died Aug. 17, 1901, Wardboro, Idaho.

NOBLE, LUCIAN (son of Silas Noble and Leah Hollenbeck of Ontario county, N. Y.). Born Nov. 26, 1807, East Bloomfield, Ontario county, N. Y. Came to Utah Oct. 6, 1850, William Snow company.

Married Emily Wilcox Jan. 30, 1831, at East Bloomfield, N. Y. (daughter of Smith Wilcox and Martha Turner of that place). Their children: Angeline, m. Ira Nathaniel Hinckley; Adelaide, m. Ira Nathaniel Hinckley; Lucian Gardner, d. child; Theodore Smith, d. child; Emily. Family home, Salt Lake City.
High priest; missionary to eastern states 1872. School teacher. Horticulturist. Died Jan. 20, 1891.

NOBLE, WILLIAM G. (son of Joseph Noble and Ann Hart). Born March 29, 1811, Irchester, Northamptonshire, Eng. Came to Utah Oct. 17, 1862, Henry W. Miller company.
Married Mary Ann Harper Dec. 7, 1830, Irchester, Eng. (daughter of John Harper and Rachel Waterhouse). Their children: Jane Ann b. June 21, 1832, m. Robert W. Fox; Rachel b. Aug. 28, ——, d. infant; Waterhouse Harper b. Sept. 17, 1834 (d. 1856), m. Mary Pearse; Eliza Priscilla b. April 3, 1836, m. R. L. Fishburn; Henrietta b. Aug. 11, 1837, m. George H. Gilbert; Lavinia b. March 20, 1839, m. Benjamin Arkens, m. James Meikle; William Aquilla b. May 4, 1841 (d. Dec. 12, 1880), m. Sarah C. Merrill, m. Sarah F. Smith; Louisa Rock Snow b. Oct. 19, 1842, m. Henry Watts; Zilphah b. April 6, 1844, m. Alonzo P. Raymond; Leonora b. Dec. 21, 1846, m. Samuel Merrill; Laura Matilda b. Feb. 17, 1850, m. R. L. Fishburn. Family home Smithfield, Utah.
High priest; missionary to England. Tailor. Died March 14, 1893.

NOBLE, W. P. (son of William Noble and Jane Payne of Jefferson county, N. Y.). Born Dec. 24, 1847, in Jefferson county, N. Y. Came to Utah Nov. 7, 1883.
Married Margret Holleran 1882, who was born 1848. Their children: Ida J. m. L. C. Robinson; Fred W., m. Mayme Ward; Edith, m. Robert Goldsmith; Mayme. Family home, Salt Lake City.
Police commissioner; Salt Lake City councilman. Engaged in stockraising; banking.

NOE, ABRAM (son of Job Noe and Evaline Tibbets, Cincinnati, Ohio). Born Dec. 18, 1820, Cincinnati, Ohio. Came to Utah October, 1852.
Married Mary Jane Winslow March 1853, Salt Lake City (daughter of Thomas Winslow and Rebecca Tibbets, Cincinnati). She was born Feb. 25, 1830. Their children: Evaline Noe b. Nov. 27, 1852, m. Henry Isaac Bush; Rebecca Jane b. Jan. 26, 1855, m. James Alexander; George Joseph b. Oct. 12, 1859, m. Mary E. Thorne; Emily Losania b. Aug. 4, 1863, m. Lucius Scoville; Edward Prebel b. March 15, 1865, m. Emma Walker.
The children by the second wife were: Eugene Abram b. April 7, 1866; Clarence Winslow b. April 6, 1867; Clarinda Angeline b. April 6, 1867; Charles Lafayette b. March 6, 1868. Family home Springville, Utah.
Veteran Indian wars. Justice of peace 20 years; member constitutional convention.

NORDFORS, PETER. Born Dec. 24, 1805, Farela, Helsenglang, Sweden. Came to Utah Oct. 1, 1862, Joseph Horne company.
Married Margaret Monson, who was born December, 1799. Their children: Cathrina Margaret b. 1830; Andrew M. b. Feb. 29, 1839, m. Cathrine Olson; Carl Constantine b. 1840; Christena Elizabeth b. 1842; Matilda Josephine b. Dec. 2, 1844, m. F. R. Thyberg May 10, 1862; Olov Eric b. 1846. Family resided Beaver City, Fairview, Glenwood and Koosharem, Utah.
Died at latter place 1895.

NORDFORS, ANDREW M. (son of Peter Nordfors and Margaret Monson). Born Feb. 29, 1832, Upsala, Sweden.
Married Cathrine Olson Dec. 1863, Kronge Ade, Ragunda, Sweden (daughter of Jens Olson), who was born Aug. 26, 1832, Holja Lith, Sweden. Their children: Margaret Josephine b. Oct. 13, 1864, m. John W. Jackson Nov. 14, 1883; Cathrine W. b. July 17, 1866, m. James Bunker April 12, 1889; Johan Peter b. Dec. 1871; John Axel b. Sept. 18, 1873, m. Rebecca Roberts 1900; Agnes Rozina b. April 26, 1875, m. Oscar Anderson Feb. 1898; Charles Victor b. July 21, 1877; Emily Matilda b. June 20, 1878; Andrew Leonard b. June 19, 1882. Family resided Bear River City, Glenwood and Annabella, Utah.
High priest; missionary in northern Sweden 1861-62. Blacksmith.

NORTH, LEVI (son of Sidney North and Mary Hawthorne of West Virginia). Born July 17, 1817, in White county, Ill. Came to Utah with Robert Wimmer Sept. 15, 1852.
Married Ariminta Howard (daughter of John and Jane Howard), who was born Feb. 25, 1819, in Madison county (near Detroit), Ill., and came to Utah Sept. 15, 1852, where she died March 12, 1903. Their children: Charles Addison b. Nov. 14, 1838, m. Albertina Silvertia Battleson, who pulled one of the handcarts over the plains, and d. March 12, 1903; Hyrum Bennett. b. Dec. 16, 1840, m. Leah R. Davis and Priscilla Jane Blair; Almyra, m. Ephraim H. Williams; Levi Howard, m. Annie Maria Morgan; Ariminta, m. Amos B. Fuller; Merari, m. Queen Jackson; Mary Jane, m. A. L. Fuller; Malinda Howard, m. William H. Butterworth; Mar-

gery Annie, m. John Price. Family home Mill Creek, Utah. Married Christenia Rassmensen in 1865, who was born in Scandinavia. Their children: John Riley; Rhoda D.; Hulda; Kate; Lula; Maud; James. Missionary to White Mountain. Nev.; ward teacher. Pioneer to Mill Creek. Farmer. Died Feb. 24, 1894.

NORTH, HYRUM BENNETT (son of Levi North and Ariminta Howard). Born Dec. 16, 1840, in Lee Co., Iowa. Came to Utah Sept. 15, 1852, with Robert Wimmer company. Married Leah R. Davis Dec. 31, 1862, Mill Creek, Utah (daughter of John R. Davis and Mary Miles of Ebbwale, South Wales). She was born May 4, 1846, and came to Utah Oct. 15, 1861, with Ira Eldredge company, walking all the way from Florence to Utah. Their children: Levi and Elizabeth, twins, b. Nov. 22, 1863, d. infants; Hyrum Thomas b. Nov. 8, 1864, died; Charles David b. Oct. 5, 1865 and Amos b. April 5, 1866, died; Mary Ariminta b. Aug. 13, 1868, m. Charles Neilson Jan. 29, 1889; Merari Franklin b. Sept. 3, 1870 (d. April 15, 1909), m. Annie Lohr Feb. 20, 1903 (d. June 19, 1909, leaving two children, Leah and Harold); Leah Alwilda b. Sept. 15, 1872, died; Malinda Jane b. Dec. 1, 1873, m. Peter Sorensen; Pheba A. b. Nov. 30, 1875 (d. April 23, 1900), m. G. W. Daybell Nov. 2, 1908; Perry Davis b. May 19, 1877, m. Cynthia Brunsen March 17, 1898; Eunice Ann b. Aug. 26, 1878, died; Martha Almira b. Jan. 29, 1883, m. Robert Daybell. Family home Charleston, Utah.
Married Priscilla Jane Blair April 5, 1869, Salt Lake City (daughter of Harrison Blair and Mary Ann McNutt of Adams county, Ill., pioneers late in 1857 from California). She was born Feb. 13, 1853, in Adams county, Ill. Their children: William Harrison b. May 14, 1870, m. Caroline Steadman; Webster Howard b. July 21, 1872, died; Arthur Mormon b. May 30, 1874, m. Caroline Blinkey; Ashaet Albert b. July 2, 1876, m. Mary Steadman; Milton Blair b. Sept. 27, 1878; Edith Priscilla b. Feb. 16, 1881; Alma b. Jan. 22, 1883; George Addison b. July 23, 1884, and Royal Exile b. Aug. 29, 1886, died; Warren Lyman b. Aug. 22, 1888, m. Hazel Montgomery; Lorin Harvey b. April 4, 1890, m. Zella Lewis.
Ordained a seventy Feb. 25, 1859, Mill Creek, Utah; ward teacher. Member of Utah volunteer cavalry, enrolled April 30, 1862. Farmer and ranchman.

NORTON, ALANSON (son of Allen Norton, Granville, N. Y., and Lucy Wilkinson, born March 3, 1788, in Connecticut). He was born March 26, 1814, at Granville, N. Y. Came to Utah 1851, John G. Smith company.
Married Sallie Maria Freeman (daughter of Silas Freeman and Sallie French), who was born April 24, 1817, and came to Utah with her husband; died 1852, Provo, Utah. Their children: Harriet Emeline b. April 22, 1837, m. Leonard Phillips in 1852; Lucy Ellen b. April 1840, m. Thomas S. Nixon; Mary Eliza b. July 11, 1842, d. infant; Emma Louisa b. March 10, 1844; Martha Elmira b. Sept. 12, 1846, m. Thomas B. Wilde; Althea Maria b. Nov. 1849, m. Isaac Lewis; Sallie Aldura b. Jan. 16, 1852, m. Joseph Southworth 1861. Family home Provo, Utah.
Married Julia Ann Williams in 1856, Salt Lake City (daughter of Andrew B. Williams, died in 1901, McCammon, Idaho, and Abagail Lewis, pioneers 1853). She was born Feb. 24, 1839, Des Moines, Iowa. Their children: Lucena b. 1857, d. infant; Louella Abagail b. April 9, 1860, m. Albert D. Lish 1878; Delinda Amelia b. March 3, 1861, m. Albert J. Lish 1881; Alanson, d. infant; William Andrew b. Aug. 8, 1865, m. Annettie A. Lish Nov. 2, 1886; Erminnie Valettia b. Jan. 1, 1868, m. Hyrum P. Lish Dec. 2, 1885; Ida Elinor b. June 17, 1870, m. James A. Lewis 1888; Annie May b. May 1, 1874, m. Charles A. Romriell 1892; Charles Ethan b. Jan. 6, 1876, m. Alice Evans 1900; George b. 1878, d. infant; Clara Grace b. July 2, 1881, m. James A. Lish Nov. 21, 1896; Lemuel b. May 28, 1883. Family resides Provo, Salt Lake City, Brigham City, Utah, and McCammon, Idaho.
Married Maria Jensen (Cutler) 1872, Salt Lake City (daughter of M. C. Jensen and Maren Hansen), who was born Jan. 28, 1846, in Denmark. Their children: Elvin J. b. Jan. 6, 1877, m. Martha Barron Sept. 13, 1899; Joseph A. b. Feb. 14, 1882, d. March 14, 1902.
Counselor to Bishop Blackburn of Provo; bishop of McCammon ward, Oneida stake, Idaho; patriarch; filled two missions. Provo City councilman; justice of the peace four years. Purchaser machinery for President Lorenzo Snow's woolen mills and operated mills for years; said to have operated first woolen and carding mills in Utah. Died Aug. 1904, McCammon, Idaho.

NORTON, WILLIAM ANDREW (son of Alanson Norton and Julia Ann Williams). Born Aug. 8, 1865, Coleville, Utah.
Married Annettie A. Lish Nov. 2, 1886, Albion, Cassia Co., Idaho (daughter of William Seely Lish and Fairzina C. Cornwell, pioneers 1850). She was born Sept. 12, 1868, Huntsville, Utah. Their children: Alta May b. March 14, 1889, m. Edwin C. Rouse 1904; Annettie Ellen b. April 7, 1891, m. Clifford W. West Feb. 12, 1912; Julia Fairzina b. Sept. 27, 1892, m. H. S. Rodd Sept. 28, 1911; Alanson William b. Feb. 22, 1895; Ethan C. b. Nov. 15, 1896; Hyrum Edmund b. Dec. 19, 1898, d. infant; Joseph Lemuel b. Nov. 8, 1901. Family resided McCammon and Pocatello, Idaho.
President of 88th quorum of seventies; high priest; bishop of McCammon ward, Pocatello stake; president Y. M. M. I. A. Appointed state water commissioner, division 1, April 1, 1912.

NORTON, JAMES WILLEY (son of David Norton and Elizabeth Benafield of Kentucky). Born Aug. 6, 1822, in Wayne Co., Ohio. Came to Utah Sept. 24, 1848, Heber C. Kimball company.
Married Nancy Hammer July 8, 1846, Walnut Grove, Iowa (daughter of Austin Hammer and Nancy Elston, former killed at Haun Mill massacre Oct. 30, 1838). She was born Oct. 14, 1829. Their children: Amanda M. b. April 19, 1847, m. John E. Ross; Nancy P. b. Jan. 1, 1849, m. Sigrue Reynolds; Sarah J. b. April 17, 1852; Rufus W. b. Aug. 14, 1853, m. Cynthia A. Cooper; James R., m. Martha E. Haws; Julia I. b. July 23, 1855; Maryette b. May 29, 1856, m. James N. Southwick; Leander D. b. Feb. 17, 1858, m. Martha E. Cooper Jan. 1, 1886; John F. b. April 27, 1860, m. Margret Williams; Rebecca R. b. Feb. 3, 1862, m. Isaac D. Cooper; Elizabeth A. b. April 20, 1864; Almyra C. b. July 9, 1865, m. John Empy; Alfred S. b. Dec. 31, 1868, m. Ruth Jones. Family home Lehi, Utah.
Married Mary Ann Rolfe in Dec. 1875, Salt Lake City (daughter of Samuel J. Rolfe, born Aug. 26, 1794, Concord, N. H., and Elizabeth Hathaway, born Aug. 29, 1801, Canton Mills, Oxford Co., Maine—married 1819). She was born Feb. 6, 1844, Nauvoo, Ill., and came to Utah. Their children: Samuel Alma b. March 15, 1877; Weltha Ann b. June 27, 1879, m. Canute Ellingson Dec. 22, 1898; Elizabeth Rolfe b. Dec. 31, 1881, m. George Robert Lamb March 11, 1913.
Seventy. Minuteman. Sheriff.

NORTON, LEANDER D. (son of James Willey Norton and Nancy Hammer). Born Feb. 17, 1858, Lehi, Utah.
Married Martha E. Cooper Jan. 1, 1886, Idaho Falls, Idaho (daughter of Isaac Cooper and Mary E. Stuart, American Fork, Utah, pioneers Sept. 19, 1847, Daniel Spencer company). She was born April 7, 1865. Their children: Cynthia U. b. Nov. 4, 1887, m. Maurice Woffenden; Leander C. b. Dec. 3, 1889; Martha S. b. Aug. 23, 1891; Leola N. b. Dec. 18, 1893; Mary E. b. Jan. 23, 1896; Greta I. b. July 10, 1902; Ruel I. b. Jan. 10, 1907. Family home Lincoln, Bonnville Co., Idaho.

NORVILL, GEORGE (son of George Norvill and Elizabeth Gould, Paterson, N. J.). Born June 30, 1800, Paterson. Came to Utah 1851, Alvin Nichols company.
Married Rachel Cook April 23, 1825, Jersey City, N. J., who was born Dec. 5, 1806, and died in New York. Their children: Levi; Rachel A.; Mary E.
Married Catherine Force. Only child: Emma, m. Samuel Dean.
Married Teresa Cragun, who died Jan. 6, 1897.
First shoemaker at Pleasant View, Utah. Died May 1884, North Ogden.

NOWERS, WILLSON GATES (son of Edward Nowers, born Feb. 6, 1781, Brambles Farm, Wye, and Susannah Gates, born Jan. 6, 1794, Dover, Kent, Eng.). Born March 8, 1828, at Dover. Came to Utah Oct. 1, 1851, Orson Pratt oxteam company.
Married Sarah Anderson June 28, 1855 (daughter of Miles Anderson and Nancy Pace, pioneers Oct. 6, 1851, Alfred Cardon company—married Aug. 9, 1821, in Georgia). She was born Dec. 4, 1828, and came to Utah with parents. Their children: Willson Edward b. March 14, 1856, d. Oct. 30, 1860; Nancy Kathleen b. April 22, 1857, m. William Burt; William Gates b. Jan. 27, 1859, m. Catherine Lillywhite; Sarah Susanna b. March 25, 1861, m. Edward W. Thompson; John Alfred b. March 5, 1863, m. Minerva Riddle; James Albert b. Nov. 29, 1864, m. Ella May Wiley; Edwin Lorenzo b. Jan. 26, 1867, d. Dec. 7, 1869; Joseph b. Dec. 15, 1868, d. Dec. 23, 1868. Family home Beaver, Utah.
High priest; member of high council. Took active part in protecting early settlers from Indians. Member of Utah militia. First treasurer of Beaver county; county recorder; justice of peace; city councilman; city recorder. Said to be the only pioneer of this name who ever came to Utah.

NOYES, FRED F. (son of John Henry Noyes and Sarah Burrus, former of Connecticut, latter of St. Augustine, Fla.). Born Dec. 25, 1847, Albany, N. Y. Came to Utah Sept. 25, 1865, Caldwell overland transportation company.
Married Meria Williams Jan. 22, 1869, Salt Lake City (daughter of Gustavious Williams and Meria Andrews, pioneers Sept. 24, 1848, Heber C. Kimball company). She was born June 29, 1849, Salt Lake City. Their children: Gustavious b. June 11, 1870; Diantha b. May 25, 1872, m. John W. Forsyth Sept. 10, 1897; Fred W. b. Sept. 22, 1875, m. Nettie Behanen March 15, 1897; John H. b. March 27, 1877, m. Delia McDougal March 7, 1903; Ada b. March 16, 1879, m. Frank Costburg Dec. 12, 1899; Howard S. b. Jan. 15, 1882, m. May Woolsey Nov. 7, 1905; Emma b. Dec. 28, 1884, m. William H. Heaps June 12, 1907; Frank b. Oct. 11, 1886; Sarah b. Jan. 10, 1888, m. David Rolleyt Sept. 2, 1908; Sylvester b. Dec. 23, 1890; Hyrum b. May 6, 1892. Farmer; carpenter.

NUTTALL, WILLIAM. Came to Utah October, 1852, from Liverpool, Eng.
Married Mary Langhorn. Their children: William; Leonard John b. July 6, 1834, m. Elizabeth Clarkson; Joseph. Family home Provo, Utah.

NUTTALL, LEONARD JOHN (son of William Nuttall and Mary Langhorn). Born July 6, 1834, Liverpool, Eng. Came to Utah October, 1852.
Married Elizabeth Clarkson Dec. 25, 1855, at Provo (daughter of Thomas and Kitty Clarkson), who was born 1835. Their children: Elizabeth Ann b. April 1, 1857, m. George Shumway; Leonard John b. Dec. 5, 1859, m. Christina Little; Thomas Clarkson, m. Harriet Self; Joseph William; Mary Clarkson; Eleanor Clarkson, m. Malin M. Warner; Clara Clarkson, m. Joseph Giles; Wilford Clarkson, m. Delia Lowe. Family home Provo, Utah.
Married Sophia Taylor at Salt Lake City (daughter of John Taylor and Harriet Whitaker of Salt Lake City, pioneers 1847). Their children: William Taylor; Lenora; Mary. Family home, Salt Lake City.
Member 20th quorum seventies; missionary to England 1874-75; high councilor of Utah stake; bishop of Kanab ward 1875-77; president Kanab stake 1877-84; private secretary to President John Taylor 1879-87, and to President Wilford Woodruff 1887-92. Probate judge; county recorder and clerk of Utah county; Provo City recorder; territorial superintendent of schools 1881-87; chief clerk of legislature. Colonel in territorial militia; Black Hawk Indian war veteran. Died Feb. 23, 1905, Salt Lake City.

NUTTALL, LEONARD JOHN, JR. (son of Leonard John Nuttall and Elizabeth Clarkson). Born Dec. 5, 1859, Provo, Utah.
Married Christina Little March 11, 1880, St. George, Utah (daughter of James Amasa Little and Anna Matilda Baldwin, Kanab, Utah, pioneers 1848). She was born Jan. 12, 1863. Their children: Elizabeth Annie b. Oct. 19, 1882; Josephine b. May 30, 1884, died; Leonard John b. July 6, 1887, m. Fannie Burns; Christina b. Nov. 21, 1888; Ethel b. May 19, 1890; James A. b. Aug. 4, 1892; Vernon Malcolm b. Nov. 28, 1893; William b. Dec. 2, 1894, died; Milton Carlos b. Jan. 29, 1896, died; Velma b. April 22, 1899; Rulon b. Dec. 20, 1900; Clarissa b. July 28, 1902; Maurice b. Dec. 19, 1904; Hazel b. Oct. 12, 1907. Family home Lake View, Utah.
Member 123d quorum seventies; president elders and seventies; missionary to England 1884-86 and to central states 1907-10. Justice of peace at Lake View. Farmer.

NUTTALL, THOMAS C. (son of Leonard John Nuttall and Elizabeth Clarkson). Born Oct. 19, 1862, Provo, Utah.
Married Harriet Self Dec. 6, 1883, Salt Lake City (daughter of Anthony and Rebecca Self of England, pioneers 1867). She was born Oct. 27, 1862. Their children: John T. b. Dec. 17, 1886; Blanche b. Sept. 8, 1887, m. Phineas H. Young; Roscoe S. b. Jan. 16, 1891; Clyde b. March 30, 1894, d. infant.
President elders quorum in Pioneer stake; first assistant Sunday school superintendent; Sunday school teacher. President Salt Lake Wire and Iron Works.

NUTTALL, JOSEPH (son of William Nuttall and Mary Langhorn). Born Aug. 31, 1836, in Liverpool, Eng. Came to Utah October, 1852, with company bringing supply of sugar over plains.
Married Emily Isabelle Chesley Provo, Utah (daughter of Emily Haws of Provo, came to Utah Oct. 1852, sugar company). Family home, Provo.
Married Susian Saunsosee Salt Lake City (daughter of Louis Saunsosee and Rebecca Fawcett of Provo, pioneers of 1852). She was born Nov. 28, 1850. Their children: Louis William, m. Laura McEwan; Joseph Charles, m. Mary Williams; Francis Henry, m. Anny Hall. Family home, Provo.
High priest; missionary to Great Britain 1896-97. Crossed the plains seven times. Veteran Indian wars. Farmer; butcher.

NUTTALL, LOUIS WILLIAM (son of Joseph Nuttall and Susian Saunsosee). Born July 11, 1869, Provo, Utah.
Married Laura Saunfah McEwan at Manti, Utah (daughter of Joseph Thompson McEwan and Frenda Naomi Crandall of Provo, pioneers Sept. 1860, J. D. Ross company). She was born Sept. 24, 1871. Their only child: Bertha b. Nov. 20, 1893, m. William F. Abbott. Family home, Provo.
Elder; assistant Sunday school superintendent. Dairyman; fruitgrower.

NYSTROM, THEODORE (son of Peter T. Nystrom, Broby, Sweden). Born Sept. 26, 1870. Came to Utah in 1865.
Married Almira Mae Taylor June 21, 1900, Salt Lake City (daughter of George Hamilton Taylor and Elmina Shepard), who was born Aug. 11, 1871, Salt Lake City.

O

OAKASON, HANS (son of Hans Oakason and Chastie Larson of Woldy, Sweden). Born Sept. 12, 1839, Woldy. Came to Utah Sept. 21, 1861, Heber C. Kimball company.
Married Ingrie Stark.
Married Marie Olsen, Salt Lake City, who was born Jan. 29, 1845, and came to Utah 1862. Their children: Emma Elvira b. July 8, 1866, m. N. J. Harris; Heber b. Feb. 7, 1868, died; Sarah b. July 1, 1871, m. Frank Stewart; Eliza b. Aug. 28, 1873, m. O. L. Witbeck; Albert b. Feb. 26, 1876, m. Lizzie Bergen; Lillian b. Jan. 1, 1879; John b. Aug.

21, 1881; Alice b. July 31, 1884, m. Alfred Hatfield; Mary Ellen b. Dec. 27, 1888, m. M. N. V. Scully.
High priest. Veteran fireman, serving 20 years; veteran of Civil war, California volunteer cavalry, Co. M, 1864-66. Plasterer and builder.

OAKLEY, EZRA. Came to Utah Sept. 30, 1847, John Taylor company.
Married Elizabeth DeGroot 1852 on Staten Island, N. Y. Their children: Henry, m. Mary Baldwin, m. Jannette Racket; John, m. Mary Patterson and Louise Jones; Mary Anne, m. John Taylor; James, m. Anne Cole, Celia Lane, and Fannie Palfryman; Margaret, m. Alfred Best. Family home Long Island, N. Y.
Member of seventy. Farmer.

ODEKIRK, ISAAC (son of Jacob and Katherine Odekirk, both of New York. Born April 1, 1809, in New York; came to Utah 1852.
Married Eliza Dutcher in New York state (daughter of Thomas and Betsey Dutcher, both of New York). She was born Feb. 25, 1814, at Cherry Valley, N. Y. Their children: Betsey, m. James Burrosand; Sarah, m. James Caston; Hannah, m. Charles Dana; Thomas; Heber b. Aug. 5, 1845, m. Hannah Brown; Frank, m. Margaret Dana; John, m. Emma McCann. Family home Ogden, Utah, and Bear Lake, Idaho.
Seventy; teacher. Settled at Ogden, Utah; moved to Bear Lake Valley 1864.

ODEKIRK, HEBER (son of Isaac Odekirk and Eliza Dutcher). Born Aug. 5, 1845, at Nauvoo, Ill. Came to Utah 1852.
Married Hannah Brown June 27, 1870, at Salt Lake City, Utah (daughter of William Brown and Hannah Richardson, both of Salt Lake City). She was born Aug. 15, 1853; came to Utah 1852. Their children: Isaac William b. Aug. 26, 1871, m. Hannah Margaret Pace; Hannah Elizabeth b. April 23, 1873, m. William Stanley Ashton; Mary Adalaid b. Jan. 19, 1875, m. George Julius; Flora b. Sept. 17, 1876; Heber Thomas b. April 29, 1879; Hilda b. Feb. 23, 1881; Franklin b. Dec. 7, 1883; Peter Richardson b. Feb. 9, 1886; Sarah Amy b. May 31, 1888; Wilford LeRoy b. May 15, 1891; Fern b. July 8, 1893; Afton b. Aug. 2, 1895.
Elder; teacher; home missionary; member of Y. M. M. I. A., Garden City, Idaho. Settled at Bear Lake, Idaho, 1864; moved to Ashley Valley 1884. County commissioner. Farmer and stockraiser.

ODEKIRK, ISAAC WILLIAM (son of Heber Odekirk and Hannah Brown). Born Aug. 26, 1871, at Smithfield, Utah.
Married Hannah Margaret Pace Oct. 23, 1890, at Vernal, Utah (daughter of John Alma Lawrence Pace and Susanna Taylor, both of Thistle Junction, Utah). She was born Nov. 11, 1873. Their children: Harvey Eugene b. Sept. 8, 1891, d. in infancy; Heber Lawrence b. Aug. 7, 1894; Isaac Warren b. Oct. 2, 1896, d. at birth; Hyrum b. Sept. 12, 1898; Doris b. Dec. 15, 1899; Preston Pace b. Oct. 27, 1901; Mary Hannah b. March 21, 1903; Cleland Pace b. Sept. 3, 1904; Alma Nichols b. March 19, 1906; John Ford b. July 18, 1908; William Benton b. April 7, 1911. Family home Myton, Utah.
High priest; bishop's counselor; Sunday school superintendent; high councilor. Conducted U. S. forage station one year 1901. Farmer and merchant.

ODELL, THOMAS GEORGE (son of Gregory Fleming Odell and Elizabeth Hopkins of Leighton Buzzard, Bedfordshire, Eng.). Born March 3, 1823, at Leighton Buzzard. Came to Utah Sept. 30, 1861, in the Homer Duncan independent company.
Married Ann Newman 1846 in London, Eng. (daughter of Charles Newman and Sarah Davis of London). Their children: Annie Sarah b. March 27, 1847; George Thomas b. Dec. 4, 1848; Charles b. July 20, 1851; Harry Edward b. Aug. 5, 1860. Family home London, Eng.
Married Mary Ann Cato 1867 at Salt Lake City (daughter of Charles Cato and Ann Higbee of Tring, Herefordshire, Eng., pioneers of 1858, Jesse B. Martin handcart company). She was born Aug. 19, 1833. Only child was Joseph Odell b. March 15, 1870, Ogden, Utah, who married Louise Torgeson May 15, 1895.
City councilman and recorder. Newspaper man in Salt Lake City and Ogden.

ODELL, GEORGE THOMAS (son of Thomas George Odell and Ann Newman). Born Dec. 4, 1848, London, Eng. Came to Utah Sept. 30, 1861.
Married Florence Caroline Grant May 10, 1872, Ogden, Utah (daughter of Joshua Frederick Grant and Louise Marie Goulet of Salt Lake City, pioneers 1847). She was born May 11, 1851, Kanesville, Iowa. Their children: Thomas George b. April 3, 1873; Joshua Frederick b. Aug. 10, 1875; Florence Louise b. June 2, 1878; Adelaide Eugene b. Nov. 11, 1885; Ethel Marie b. June 11, 1892. Family resided at Ogden and Salt Lake City.
Living in London, Eng., until 12 years and 5 months of age, he did everything that a boy of that age could, even to selling papers, when not in school. His education was

obtained through the Home and Colonial school of London, prior to coming to Utah in 1861, with his parents, by oxteam in the Homer Duncan independent company. They located at Ogden. From October, 1861 to 1866, he was employed on a farm, which his father owned. In 1866 he went to Bear River, Boxelder county, to a place called "Hampton's Bridge," a station on the Wells-Fargo Co. stage line, and remained there 2 years. In 1869 moved from Bear River to Corinne. The town was just started and there he engaged with the construction company for the building of the Union Pacific railroad and remained with it until the completion of the lines at Promontory, Utah. He left Promontory on the morning that Governor Stanford, of California, drove the golden spike. From there following the Union Pacific east into the Bitter Creek country, remaining with that company working on bridges until some time in 1871. From early 1871 to 1879 he was a brakeman and conductor on the Central Pacific railroad running between Ogden and San Francisco and worked between Ogden, Toano and Wells, Nev. In 1879 he went the way of most conductors and determined to enter a commercial life, and started in the produce and commission business on 24th street, Ogden, operating there successfully for a little over 2 years. In 1883 he went to Bullionville, Nev., for the Bullionville Smelting Co., whose interests were safeguarded by Messrs. W. H. Godbe and Benjamin Hampton, and remained there until the winter season of 1883 and 1884, at which time their business in Nevada closed down. In the winter season of 1883 and 1884 he came to Salt Lake City and started with the aid of Messrs. Heber J. Grant and Joshua F. Grant the implement and vehicle business under the title of Grant-Odell & Co.; in a little over a year this was changed to Grant-Odell & Co. (Incorporated). In 1885 the business was merged into the Co-operative Wagon & Machine Co. and remained under that title until 1902. In 1902 it was merged with the Consolidated Implement Co., and since 1902 he has been general manager of the Consolidated Wagon & Machine Co., which operates at some 60 points in Utah, Idaho, Wyoming and eastern Nevada, and whose annual sales are about three million dollars. The company's paid up capitalization is two and a half million dollars. He is a director in the Utah State National bank and the Bank of Garland; vice-president and director of the George Romney Lumber Co.; director H. J. Grant & Co., insurance agency; vice-president and director of the board of governors of the Commercial club, Salt Lake City; director of the Pittsburg-Salt Lake Oil Co.; vice-president and director of Rich Lands Irrigation Co.; vice-president and director of the Rexburg Drug Co., Rexburg, Idaho; vice-president and director of the Wright Mercantile Co., Idaho Falls, Idaho; director of the Opex Consolidated Mines Co., of Utah; president and director Odell-Wright Investment Co.; director in the Utah Independent Telephone Co.; director in the Sugar City Hardware & Lumber Co., Sugar City, Idaho; vice-president and member board of directors of the Utah Pioneers Book Publishing Co., and vice-president and director of the Farmers' and Stockgrowers' bank.

Mr. Odell is well known in eastern business circles. He is a member of the Alta and Commercial clubs of Salt Lake City, also a member of Wasatch Lodge No. 1, Free and Accepted Masons and Knights Templar and Shriner.

ODELL, JOSEPH (son of Thomas George Odell and Mary Ann Cato). Born March 15, 1870, Ogden, Utah.
Married Louise Torgeson May 15, 1895, Logan, Utah (daughter of Knud Torgeson and Gurinda Fredrickson of Risor, Norway, pioneers 1863, John Needham company). She was born June 18, 1870. Their children: Joseph Conrad b. May 1, 1896; Florence Louise b. Sept. 23, 1898; Afton b. Nov. 13, 1901; Wesley T. b. Dec. 9, 1906. Family home Logan, Utah.
Printer and publisher; as well as photographer by profession. Chairman of Republican party organization in Cache Valley for many years. Now postmaster at Logan, Utah.

OGDEN, WILLIAM (son of Thomas Ogden, born 1791, and Olive Lumax, born October, 1782, Little Sever, near Bolton, Eng.). He was born Oct. 23, 1820, at Tong, Lancashire, Eng. Came to Utah Sept. 24, 1868, Edward T. Mumford company.
Married Mary Vickers (daughter of William Vickers and Mary Greenhalgh), who was born Oct. 6, 1819, at Hallith Wood, near Bolton. Came to Utah with husband. Their children: James b. Jan. 7, 1845, m. Alice Wray Aug. 24, 1872, m. Betsy Marsh Oct. 13, 1874; Mary Ann b. Dec. 26, 1847, m. William C. B. Orrocks Nov. 1, 1869; Thomas b. Sept. 25, 1849, m. Ann Marsh March 31, 1873, m. Hannah Wells Oct. 3, 1884; Jane b. Jan. 26, 1852, m. Henry D. Dall Oct. 9, 1871; William b. Aug. 25, 1854, m. Emma Fraser Oct. 25, 1877; John b. Jan. 31, 1857, m. Martha M. Outzen Dec. 6, 1882; Joseph b. Aug. 31, 1859, m. Hannah M. Christensen March 25, 1885. Family resided Santaquin and Richfield, Utah.
President of elders quorum; member of high council. City councilman. President of Co-op. store at Richfield.

OGDEN, WILLIAM, JR. (son of William Ogden and Mary Vickers) Born Aug. 25, 1854, Hallith-Wood, Tong, Eng.
Married Emma Fraser Oct. 25, 1877, St. George (daughter of Alexander Fraser and Sarah Scott, pioneers Sept. 16, 1868, John Gillespie company). She was born Oct. 30, 1859, Kirtintilloch, Stirling, Scotland. Their children: Alice Robena b. March 9, 1879, m. Christian P. Christensen Oct. 8, 1903; Junius Francis b. Oct. 18, 1881, m. Alice Jackson June 4, 1909; Daisy May b. Dec. 20, 1883, m. George P. Hansen Oct. 23, 1907; Laura Emma and Lottie Jane (twins) b. Aug. 6, 1887; William George b. Feb. 5, 1893; Violet Rozelle b. -(, 1882; 1895; Owen Miles b. Feb. 17, 1899. Family home Richfield, Utah.
Missionary to England 1889 and to northern states 1907; ward clerk; clerk high council; first counselor to president high priests' quorum; h counselor. County commissioner four years; school trustee 21 years; city councilman; city recorder.

OGDEN, JOSEPH (son of William Ogden and Mary Vickers). Born Aug. 31, 1859, Hallith-Wood, Eng.
Married Hannah M. Christensen March 25, 1885, St. George, Utah (daughter of Hans and Johannah M. Christensen, pioneers 1862, Christian A. Madsen company). Their children: Joseph L. b. Jan. 13, 1886; Rhoda A. b. Oct. 17, 1889, m. George Dobson June 23, 1909; Milo C. b. Nov. 27, 1891; Rodney C. b. Feb. 2, 1898, and Grant b. March 24, 1900, died; Emma M. b. Dec. 31, 1901; Morris D. b. July 6, 1906.
Missionary to Great Britain 1893-94, and 1903-04; president Bristol conference 22 months; clerk of elders' quorum; superintendent of Sunday school; member of high council. Teacher L. D. S. high school one year; county surveyor Sevier county; assistant professor University of Utah two years.

OGILVIE, GEORGE (son of George Byers Ogilvie and Barbara Elizabeth Mattatahl of Halifax, Nova Scotia, Can). Born April 24, 1834, at Halifax. Came to Utah Sept. 7, 1855, Noah T. Guymon company.
Married Eliza Ann Hales March 2, 1857, Big Cottonwood, Utah (daughter of Charles Henry Hales, born June 17, 1817, and Julia Ann Lockwood, born Aug. 10, 1824, both in Canada, pioneers Sept. 29, 1847, Edward Hunter company). She was born Nov. 27, 1840, Quincy, Ill. Their children: Eliza Ann b. April 16, 1858, m. John W. Coons; George William b. March 15, 1860, m. Cosmelia E. Farnsworth; Mary Isabella b. July 17, 1862, m. Raleigh Jones; Charles Henry b. March 13, 1864, d. Feb. 4, 1885; Joseph Smith b. July 1867, d. infant. Family resided Spanish Fork and Richfield, Utah.
Elder; ward teacher. Sheriff of Sevier county 1873-74. Early settler to Sevier and Utah counties. Served as guard in Echo Canyon war; Black Hawk Indian war veteran.

OHLSON, GUSTAVE ADOLPHUS (son of Jepea Ohlson and Bothilda Pramberg of Lund, Sweden). Born Aug. 31, 1828, at Lund. Came to Utah 1863, Enoch Reese company.
Married Elena Anderson 1850, Malmo, Sweden (daughter of Anna Rosequest of Malmo), who was born Dec. 18, 1832. Their children: Arthur Frederick; Hilma Marthina; Thor Wilhelm; William Eave; Emma Gustava, d. infant; Charles Gustaf; Joseph Valdemar, d. aged 12; Ellen Sophrona b. March 2, 1861, m. William Alfred Biddle Jan. 3, 1884; Hyrum, m. Alice Biddle; Anna Loviisa; Oscar Emil; Frithooff; Francis Julius, d. infant; Alfred.
Married Anna Mortensen March 4, 1867, Salt Lake City (daughter of Morton Mortensen and Mariah Larson of Sweden), who was born March 8, 1845, in Sweden. Their children: Anna Rosina b. July 30, 1868; Emma Augusta b. Feb. 2, 1870, m. Thomas H. Carr; Selma Elnora b. Feb. 5, 1872, m. Joseph Cafe; Mary Charlotta b. May 28, 1874, d. aged 5; Ada Cornelia b. April 14, 1876, m. John J. Murphy; Elvira V. b. July 16, 1878, m. Joseph Higginbotham; David H. b. Aug. 5, 1880, d. infant; Evelyn b. Feb. 26, 1882, m. George H. Freecy; John Edgar b. June 1, 1884, d. infant. Family resided Ogden, Utah.
Missionary to Sweden 1865-67; high priest. Tinsmith. Died Dec. 11, 1912, Murray, Utah.

OKERLUND, OLE (son of Jepple Olsen, born April 29, 1803, and Elsie Swensen of Sweden). Born Sept. 16, 1829. Came to Utah Sept. 22, 1861, Samuel A. Woolley company.
Married Bengta Carlson Dec. 20, 1854 (daughter of Pehr Carlson and Kjaiste Johnson, married 1828; former died in Sweden, latter pioneer October, 1863). She was born Aug. 1, 1832. Their children: Charles P. b. May 28, 1856, m. Harriet Blackburn 1881; Hilda b. Feb. 20, 1859, d. in Sweden, Matilda b. Oct. 14, 1860, m. Wilford Vole Nov. 1880; George W. b. Nov. 9, 1862, m. Lydia Hunt May 14, 1890; Lydia b. July 11, 1864, m. Jacob A. Ivie 1882; Hannah b. April 23, 1866, m. Thomas H. Jakeman Nov. 30, 1885; Albertina b. June 15, 1868, m. Ammon Hunt May 11, 1890; Ole A. b. Sept. 17, 1870, m. Katie Oldroyd Aug. 20, 1894; Mary E. b. Feb. 12, 1873, m. Andrew Anderson 1899; Orilla B. b. March 31, 1877, m. Delbert Harris Nov. 1905; Edward b. Sept. 18, 1879, m. Reba Blackburn April 3, 1905. Family resided Mt. Pleasant, Salina, Gunnison, Scipio and Loa, Utah.
Missionary in Sweden four years; superintendent of Sunday school; president of high priests' quorum; home missionary. Veteran Indian wars.

OKERLUND, GEORGE W. (son of Ole Okerlund and Bengta Carlson). Born Nov. 9, 1862, Mt. Pleasant, Utah.
Married Lida Hunt May 14, 1890, Manti, Utah (daughter of Thomas Hunt and Hannah Moon, pioneers Sept. 21, 1861, Samuel Woolley company). She was born April 2, 1866, Monroe, Utah. Their children: Ivan b. May 10, 1891; Ruth b. Jan. 22, 1893; Berta b. Dec. 3, 1895; Dalton Hunt b. Aug.

1076   PIONEERS AND PROMINENT MEN OF UTAH

16, 1897; Loren Clair b. Jan. 17, 1899; Esther b. Jan. 24, 1903; Melvin b. Sept. 7, 1908.
High priest; missionary to Sweden 1901-1903. Worked on Manti temple. Bishop of Loa ward.

OKEY, EDWIN (parents resided at Gloucestershire, Eng.). Came to Utah about 1848.
Married Mary Pitt, Gloucestershire, Eng. Their children: Harriet, m. Jane Green; Elizabeth. m. James Spratty; Sarah Celestia, m. Albert Marsh; Baby, died; Edwin, m. Mary Ellen Clark; Joseph Moroni, m. Synthia Adams. Family resided Kaysville, American Fork and Salt Lake City, Utah.
High priest. Shoemaker. Died about 1855, Salt Lake City.

OKEY, EDWIN, JR. (son of Edwin Okey and Mary Pitt). Born March 10, 1852, Kaysville, Utah.
Married Mary Ellen Clark Jan. 19, 1874, Salt Lake City (daughter of George Clark and Catherine Gascoigne of Pinxton, Derbyshire, Eng., pioneers Oct. 4, 1863, Horton D. Haight company). She was born Sept. 12, 1856. Their children: Harriet Ada b. Nov. 7, 1874, died; Catherine b. Oct. 1, 1876, m. Willard McDaniel; Mary Ruth b. March 15, 1879, m. Frank Devey; Charlotte Ellen b. Oct. 5, 1881, m. William B. Smith; Sarah Adelaide b. Aug. 28, 1884, m. Joseph Devey; George Edwin b. Jan. 19, 1886, died; Lucy Elizabeth b. June 21, 1888, m. Frank Healey; Harvey Clark b. Dec. 6, 1890, m. Zella Cox; Lavina b. Nov. 22, 1892; Martha Hortense b. Jan. 15, 1894, died; Lester Clark b. Dec. 1, 1895. Family home Alpine, Utah.
Member elders' quorum. Pioneer of American Fork 1858, moved to Alpine about 1872. Teamster; farmer. Died Oct. 28, 1904.

OLESON, JORGEN. Born May 10, 1822, Kosteslev, Fyen Amt, Denmark. Came to Utah October, 1868.
Married Kjersten Hansen, who was born Dec. 8, 1820. Their children: Annie C. b. March 4, 1847, m. Henry Hanson; Catherine, m. Christen Christensen; Hans, m. Sena Christensen; Oina, m. Peter P. Hansen.
Died at Spanish Fork.

OLIVER, FRANCIS (son of Frank Oliver and Mariah Batton of England). Born June 12, 1825, Brown Condover, Eng. Came to Utah Sept. 25, 1866, John D. Holladay company.
Married Elizabeth Bailey Feb. 5, 1848, in England (daughter of James and Ann Bailey of same country). Their children: Emily, m. Thomas H. White; Elizabeth b. July 31, 1848, d. Aug. 18, 1866, on plains; Ann. m. James Rice; Francis b. Sept. 2, 1855, d. Dec. 6, 1856; Mary Jane, m. Joseph Hadfield; William F. b. Sept. 2, 1860, d. Nov. 2, 1861. Family home Salina, Utah.
Died Jan. 29, 1905, Riverside, Utah.

OLIVER, HARRISON (son of Samuel N. F. Oliver of Kentucky). Born March 29, 1800. Came to Utah Sept. 23, 1850, Perrigrine Sessions company.
Married Dorothy Martin 1824, Louisville, Ky. (daughter of William Martin and Hannah Adams of same state). She was born in Kentucky, 1804, and died 1828. Their children: Samuel N. F., d. aged 18; William. d. child; Martin, d. aged 21; Sarah, d. infant. Family home Louisville, Ky.
Married Hannah Martin 1832, Louisville, Ky. (daughter of William Martin and Hannah Adams, pioneers 1850, Perrigrine Sessions company). She was born Jan. 27, 1812, at Louisville, and died Jan. 24, 1853. Their children: William T., m. Nancy Lovern; Edward McClelland, d. aged 27; Lamira Jane, m. George Allen and Christopher Tippel; Arabelle, m. James Montague; Dorothy, d. infant. Emily Frances, m. Alexander G. Davis; Polly, d. infant. Family resided Kentucky and Illinois.
Married Rebecca Butler September, 1853, Salt Lake City (daughter of Charles Butler and Lovisa J. Heron of Ogden and Salt Lake City; came to Utah 1850, Perrigrine Sessions company). She was born March 19, 1828. Their children: Hannah M., m. Mr. Reid. m. Mr. Johnson; Harrison; Charles F., m. Lizzie Carter; John; Juliet, d. aged 20. Family home, Salt Lake City.
Bishop. Veteran Indian wars. Farmer and stockraiser.

OLIVER, SAMUEL (son of William Oliver and Susan Fletcher, latter of Barrington, Eng.). Born Dec. 25, 1840, Whaddon, Cambridgeshire, Eng. Came to Utah Sept. 15, 1860, Ira Eldredge company.
Married Fannie Emma Barnes Sept. 5, 1870, Salt Lake City (daughter of J. S. Barnes and Jane Lee). Their children: Minnie Ann b. Aug. 18, 1871. m. John L. Scott; Samuel William b. March 13, 1873, d. 1891; Sarah Jane b. Feb. 15, 1876, d. 1905; Alma A. Morris; Susan Ada b. Dec. 16, 1877, m. Edward A. Gustaveson; Lydia May b. May 19, 1881, died; Mary b. May 21, 1884; Joseph Smith b. Oct. 23, 1886; John Lee b. M---, Nov. 22, 1889. Family home East Mill Creek, Utah.
Patriarch, counselor in the bishopric nearly 35 years. School trustee ten years; justice of the peace ten years. Farmer.

OLLORTON, JOHN (son of Thomas and Betty Ollorton of Croston, Lancashire, Eng.). Born April 20, 1800, at Croston. Started for Utah in Edward Martin "frozen" handcart company, died en route, as did fully one-fourth of this company of 600. The remnant of this family arrived in Salt Lake City Dec. 1, 1856.
Married Alice Dandy 1823, Eccleston, Lancashire, Eng. (daughter of James Dandy and Elizabeth Ogden of Eccleston, Eng.), who died Nov. 20, 1856, near Sandy Creek, Wyo. Their children: Elizabeth, m. James Wilson; Seth. m. Jane Rogerson; Esther, m. Daniel Ashton; John, m. Dinnah Dickerson; Elizabeth; James; Ellen, m. William Howson; Alice and Hannah, died; Jane Ann. m. James R. McPherson; Margret; Henry; Sarah, m. George Eatough.
Elder. Died Nov. 12, 1856, at the "Three Crossings" of the Sweetwater river, which had become a veritable graveyard of those who perished from the hardships of the fateful journey across the frozen desert.

OLSEN, ANDREW (son of Niels Larsen of Denmark). Came to Utah in 1854, Murdock oxteam company.
Married Boletta Larsen 1857, in Denmark (daughter of Niels Larsen). Their children: Cena b. May 30, 1858, m. Charles Swasey; Andrew b. Aug. 20, m. Caroline Johansen; Lewis b. April 7, m. May Westwood; May b. May 24, ———, m. Lewis Halverson; Edward, m. Viola Worthing; Frederick, m. Laura Worthing; George, m. Nancy Hanson. Family home was in Iowa and Moroni, Utah.
Married Jardean Olson, Spring City, Utah (daughter of Martin Olson, later in the Endowment house at Salt Lake City). She was born Oct. 4, 1858. Their children: James, m. Nerve Kofoed; Alfred; Anne, m. Joshua Anderson; Caroline, m. Thomas McGann; Chasta, m. John Teakin; Lena, m. Mr. Peterson; Malle; Eva; Luella, d. aged 2. Family home Castle Dale, Utah.
Member dominant church and was a farmer. Died at Boneta, Uinta county, Utah.

OLSEN, BENGT (son of Ole Bengtson and Ella Svenson of Stora Uppiakrn, Sweden). Born Feb. 5, 1824 at Stora Uppriakra. Came to Utah Sept. 26, 1862, James Wareham independent company.
Married Wilhelmina Petersen (daughter of Paul Pettersen and Badel Anderson of Denmark). She was born Jan. 15, 1823. Their children: Charles F. b. July 25, 1857 (adopted), m. Thurza Ward; Josephine b. March 18, 1860, died; Benjamin F. b. April 13, 1862, m. Emily Clark; Joseph Reuben b. Nov. 7, 1864, m. Mary Frances Jefferies and Josephine C. Josephson; Margrett b. April 24, 1866, m. William John Cawley. Family home Big Cottonwood, Utah.
Farmer and painter. Died December, 1908.

OLSEN, JOSEPH REUBEN (son of Bengt Olsen and Wilhelmina Petersen). Born Nov. 7, 1864, Big Cottonwood, Utah.
Married Mary Frances Jefferies June 19, 1889, Logan, Utah (daughter of William Jefferies and Mary Frances Old of Grantsville, Utah). Their children: Joseph William b. Oct. 24, 1890, m. Erma Crompton; Harold Reuben b. Nov. 5, 1893; Albert Jefferies b. Dec. 13, 1895. Family home Grantsville, Utah.
Married Josephine C. Josephson Sept. 15, 1897, Logan, Utah (daughter of Andrews M. Josephson and Arma Anderson of Brigham City, Utah, pioneers Sept. 5, 1863, John F. Sanders company). She was born Jan. 11, 1877. Their children: Josephine b. Feb. 19, 1899; Joseph Reuben b. July 26, 1900; Mary b. July 12, 1902; Karl L. Grand b. June 5, 1904; Farris Mozart b. June 4, 1907, died; Hard Arma b. Feb. 20, 1910; Lillian Bodel b. Feb. 13, 1912. Family home Brigham City, Utah.
Sheep inspector of Box Elder county three years, and county sheriff since 1911. Farmer and sheepraiser.

OLSEN, CARL STEEN (son of Ole Thorson and Guri Aslaksdater of Risör, Norway). Born Dec. 10, 1830, Risör, Norway. Came to Utah 1866.
Married Maren Marie Wrolsdater Aug. 14, 1858, Risör, Norway (daughter of Wrol Evansen and Karen Thorsdater of Risör, Norway, pioneers 1866). She was born March 25, 1837. Their children: Ole, m. Hanna Kaspara; Wrol Christian, m. Sophie Louise Peterson; Thor Gurnelius, died, and buried at sea; Guro; Karen Olene b. Aug. 23, 1866, d. on plains; Theodore Ephraim; Joseph; Amanda Marie. Family resided Farmington, Utah, and Ovid, Idaho.
Member 14th quorum seventies; high priest. Walked and drove lame oxen all the way across the plains for eight weeks; had 3 yoke of oxen when they started, but had only one yoke when they arrived at Salt Lake.

OLSEN, WROL C. (son of Carl Olsen and Maren Marie Wrolsdater). Born March 7, 1861, Risör, Norway.
Married Sophia Louise Peterson March 19, 1883, Ovid, Idaho (daughter of Henry and Marian Peterson of Ovid, pioneers). She was born Oct. 2, 1864, and died May 24, 1894. Their children: Mary Louisa b. July 2, 1884, d. July 21, 1899; Henry Peterson b. July 21, 1887, m. Retis Cooper; Edna Matilda b. May 12, 1889; Wrolf Christian b. Oct. 6, 1891; Edith b. May 19, 1894, d. May 26, 1894.
Married Ingeborg Holmquist Oct. 11, 1898. Their children: John Fritjof b. Jan. 8, 1900, d. Oct. 21, 1902; Wilford

PIONEERS AND PROMINENT MEN OF UTAH

K. b. Feb. 2, 1903; Henry La Vod b. July 19, 1905; Sarah Geneva b. April 29, 1907. Family home Iona, Idaho. Member 156th quorum seventies; missionary to Norway 1899-1902, and 1907-09.

OLSEN, CHARLES C. (son of Ole and Carrie Olsen of Norway). Born April 2, 1824, Christiana, Norway. Came to Utah 1854.
Married Eveline Benson in 1856, Salt Lake City (daughter of Jerome Benson and Mary Rhodes, pioneers 1850, Ezra T. Benson company). She was born Feb. 28, 1835. Their children: Charles Messenger b. June 27, 1857, died; Mary Caroline b. Aug. 30, 1858, m. Joseph Bartholomew 1883; Oscar Alfred b. Aug. 4, 1860, m. Rachel Weach 1894; Eveline Amelia b. Nov. 28, 1862, m. Austin Evans 1893; Logan N. b. Sept. 22, 1864, d. July 1884; Rosa b. Nov. 26, 1866, d. June 1884; Louie b. June 22, 1868, d. July 1884; Alma b. Feb. 19, 1870, d. Nov. 1870; Vendee b. July 13, 1871, d. April 4, 1875; Elam b. Feb. 26, 1873; Virginia Aurilia b. Feb. 9, 1875, m. Frank Curtis 1901; George Leo b. June 1877, died. Family home Logan, Utah.
Seventy; acting teacher. Cabinet maker and farmer. Died May 12, 1887, Layton, Ariz.

OLSEN, OSCAR ALFRED (son of Charles and Eveline Benson). Born Aug. 4, 1860.
Married Rachel Weach Oct. 1, 1894, Layton, Ariz. (daughter of Joseph Weach and Emma Wilkins). Their children: Joseph Alfred b. July 5, 1895; Emma b. June 24, 1897; Howard b. Dec. 1, 1901; Harry and Harold, twins b. March 27, 1903; Lola b. April 9, 1905; Louis b. July 24, 1909; Glenna b. Aug. 31, 1911.

OLSEN, CHRESTEN J. (son of Jens Olsen and Anne Kjersten of Aalborg, Denmark). Born Aug. 1, 1803, Aalborg, Denmark. Came to Utah Oct. 5, 1854, Hans Peter Olsen company.
Married Anne Nielsen (daughter of Peter Nielsen and Kjersten Nielsen), who was born March 18, 1803. Their children: Mette Kjersten b. Feb. 3, 1830, died on way to Utah; Karen Marie b. May 11, 1832; Chrestine b. Aug. 13, 1834; Nekoline b. April 26, 1836; James b. March 27, 1839; Else Marie b. Feb. 26, 1841; Margrete b. 1843; Chresten b. Oct. 1847. Family home Brigham City, Utah.
High priest. Farmer and stockraiser. Died 1869.

OLSEN, JAMES (son of Chresten J. Olsen and Anne Nielsen). Born March 27, 1839, Aalborg, Denmark. Emigrated from Copenhagen, December, 1852, in first regularly organized company from Scandinavia, arrived in Utah 1853.
Married Marie Petersen Jan. 23, 1862, Brigham City, Utah (daughter of James O. Petersen and Anne Jensen, pioneers 1856, James G. Willie handcart company). She was born Sept. 9, 1846. Their children: James W. b. Dec. 22, 1862; Christian L. b. Feb. 28, 1864; Anne M. b. Dec. 1, 1865; Joseph H. b. Oct. 13, 1867; Hyrum b. Sept. 26, 1869; Lovenus b. Aug. 13, 1871; Alma b. March 3, 1875; Nephi P. b. Dec. 12, 1876; Mary E. b. Aug. 24, 1878; Sarah b. April 19, 1882; Moses b. Aug. 13, 1883; Helana b. July 1, 1888.
President of high priest quorum Box Elder stake. Held civil offices for 20 years in Cache county and precinct.

OLSEN, CHRISTIAN (son of Ole Bartelsen, born about 1781, and Maria Johnson, born Nov. 17, 1782, both of Raade, Norway). Born Jan. 21, 1825, at Raade. Came to Utah Sept. 15, 1859, Robert Nielsen oxteam company.
Married Annie Ellington May 20, 1859 (daughter of Anart and Gubjer Ellington, married 1834, Christiana, Norway). She was born Oct. 27, 1835. Their children: Orson b. Nov. 11, 1860, m. Mary Ann Smith Feb. 24, 1886; Christian b. Sept. 25, 1862, died; Agnes b. April 11, 1864, m. John Maughan Oct. 10, 1881; Annie b. May 12, 1866, m. John Palmer June 21, 1909; Joseph b. March 22, 1868, m. Lorette Smith Jan. 24, 1895; Nephi b. Sept. 20, 1870, m. Katie Hawkins Dec. 12, 1900; Hyrum b. March 17, 1873, died; Martha b. May 7, 1875, m. William Lundquist Jan. 22, 1902; Wilford b. Nov 22, 1877, m. Luella Norton March 17, 1909; Millie b. Sept. 10, 1879, m. Niels Nelsen Dec. 12, 1900.
High priest; missionary to Norway 1886-88; president of Scandinavians, Weston ward; president of ward teachers. Settled in Salt Lake City 1859, moved to Logan 1861, and to Weston in 1869.

OLSEN, FREDERICK. Born in Denmark. Came to Utah Sept. 13, 1857, Chris Christiansen handcart company.
Married Mary Justisen in Denmark (daughter of Lars Justisen of same country), who was born Sept. 1, 1820, in Denmark. Their children: Hannah, died; Ole b. Jan. 19, 1851, m. Elsie L. King; Andrew, m. Stena Nielsen; Lewis and Levi, d. infants; Livy, m. Olive Hitchcock; Mary, d. child; Fredrick, m. Martha Stevens; Diantha, Hannah and Baby, d. infants. Family home Spring City, Utah.
Married Matilda Jensen 1869, Salt Lake City. Their children: Lewis, m. B'yot Hansen; Mary, m. Gustave Iverson; Fredrick Jr., m. Cornelia Rigley, m. Nellie Taylor; Sarah; Deloss, m. Mary Osborne. Family home Spring City and Ferron, Utah.
Veteran Black Hawk war. Seventy; high priest; bishop Monroe ward one and a half years; bishop Spring City ward 14 years; bishop Ferron ward 25 years; patriarch. Assisted in bringing immigrants to Utah. Farmer.

OLSEN, LIVY (son of Frederick Olsen and Mary Justisen). Born Dec. 1, 1856, Copenhagen, Denmark. Came to Utah with parents.
Married Olive M. Hitchcock May 3, 1905, Ferron, Utah (daughter of Franklin Hitchcock and Rosetta Cook of Fillmore, Utah). Their children: Ferrell b. Feb. 15, 1906; Lewis b. Feb. 10, 1908; Justin b. March 20, 1910. Family home Ferron, Utah.
Member 149th quorum seventies; missionary to northern states 1900-02. Acting ward clerk Ferron; sheriff of Emery county two years. Assistant Sunday school superintendent. President town board; president Ferron Creek Canal & Reservoir Co; president Independent Canal & Reservoir Co. Farmer and stockraiser.

OLSEN, OLE (son of Frederick Olsen and Mary Justisen). Born Jan. 19, 1851, in Denmark. Came to Utah with parents.
Married Elsie King, Salt Lake City (daughter of Eleazar King and Mary Caroline Fowler), who was born March 17, 1853, Manti, Utah. Their children: Mary b. Feb. 8, 1872, m. James Nelson; Caroline b. Nov. 14, 1873, m. Christian Nelson; Diantha b. Jan. 25, 1876, m. James Watt; Celia b. May 10, 1877, m. Erastus Nelson; Ole b. June 16, 1879; Hannah b. Sept. 1, 1884, m. Joseph Cameron Jr.; Arthur b. Oct. 1886, m. Della Peterson; Leonard b. Dec. 21, 1888; Ervin b. April 8, 1892, m. Rhoda Worthen; Kenneth b. Dec. 21, 1894. Family resided Spring City and Ferron, Utah.
Seventy; high priest. Black Hawk war veteran. Farmer and stockraiser.

OLSEN, GUSTAVE (son of Olivis Olsen and Kirria Anderson of Swentup, Sweden). Born 1820, in Sweden. Came to Utah 1864, Captain Preston company.
Married Johanna Anderson 1840, Sweden, who was born Feb. 10, 1810. Their children: Mary, m. George Langlois; Stova F., m. D. F. Thomas; Matilda, m. A. Sprague. Family home Huntsville, Utah.
Seventy; president of a branch in Sweden; patriarch. Farmer. Died Dec. 27, 1911, Ogden, Utah.

OLSEN, HANS (son of Lars Olsen). Born May 1, 1800, in Sweden. Came to Utah Sept. 29, 1847, John Taylor company.
Married Chasta Okersen, who was born June 1800. Their children: Benta; Eliza, m. Niels B. Nielsen; Ola; Johanna, m. Wiley P. Alfred; Ingrie, m. Peter Nielsen; Peter b. 1836; Niels; Hannah, m. Orange Seeley. Family home Sweden. Farmer. Died January, 1896, Mt. Pleasant, Utah.

OLSEN, HANS (son of Ole Olsen and Anna Hansen of Wabensted, Maribo, Isle of Laaland, Denmark). Born Dec. 22, 1839, at Wabensted. Came to Utah Sept. 29, 1866, Peter Nebeker company.
Married Hannah Madsen Sept. 29, 1868, Wanship, Utah (daughter of Lars and Taren Madsen of Fuglse, Maribo, Denmark; latter came to Utah 1870). She was born March 4, 1846. Their children: Lewis b. Oct. 23, 1869, m. Hannah E. Lunceford; Carrie Christine b. Feb. 3, 1873, m. Frank Lawrence; Anna Louisa b. April 29, 1874; John Taylor b. Sept. 19, 1879, m. Sina Johnson; Ferdinand Henry b. Sept. 12, 1882, m. Myrel Woodhead.
Married Hannah Oman Sept. 29, 1887, Logan, Utah (daughter of Peter Oman and Annie Christina Andreason of Sköfde, Skaraborg Län, Sweden). Born June 24, 1864. Their children: Karl b. July 1, 1888, died; William Alfred b. Feb. 22, 1890; Ruth Helen b. Sept. 19, 1892; Loren LeRoy b. Nov. 25, 1894; Lillian Belle b. Aug. 15, 1897; Sarah Ellen b. April 26, 1900; Adolph b. Dec. 31, 1907; Paul Oscar b. May 23, 1906. Families resided Lake View, Utah.
High priest; home missionary; presiding elder of branch in Denmark; ward teacher at Wanship. Black Hawk Indian war veteran. Farmer; blacksmith.

OLSEN, JAMES PETER (son of Niels Christian Olsen and Marn Thomasen of Denmark; latter came to Utah 1860). Born June 23, 1851, Skose, Presto Amt, Denmark. Came to Utah Sept. 20, 1860, Oscar O. Stoddard handcart company.
Married Kisten Mary Hansen April 20, 1874, Salt Lake City (daughter of Hans Peter Hansen of Denmark and Kisten Petersen, pioneers 1856). She was born Jan. 29, 1857. Their children: Sarah b. Jan. 7, 1876, died; Mary Lauretta b. April 9, 1878, m. Royal Leo Jensen; Rupert Peter b. July 23, 1881, m. Genevieve Blackburn; Alfred Nels b. Nov. 2, 1883; Anne Cleopha b. Feb. 12, 1886, m. Marcus Hamson; Lewis Hans b. Jan. 22, 1888, died; Hans Peter b. Jan. 16, 1891, died; Daisy Lenora H. b. Feb. 12, 1892, m. Carl Hamson; Leslie John b. Jan. 5, 1895; Norman Alma b. May 24, 1897.
Married Laura Hansen Feb. 23, 1910, Salt Lake City (daughter of Anders Hansen and Anne Kistine Lauritsen of Denmark, who came to Utah Dec. 29, 1890). She was born March 28, 1880. Their children: Lloyde Ireland b. April 21, 1911; Cleon Olean b. Sept. 22, 1912. Family home Brigham City, Utah.
Missionary to Denmark 1888-90; ward teacher; assistant to president of Y. M. M. I. A. Farmer.

OLSEN, SEREN. Born November 1791, in Uland, Denmark. Came to Utah 1853, Lorenzo Snow company.
Married Bertha Peterson in Copenhagen while on way to Utah. She was born May 8, 1821, and came to Utah with husband. Their children: Peter Isaac b. Jan. 6, 1856,

m. Sally Ann Barton; Seren b. Sept. 24, 1860, m. Emily Frances Barton; Joseph b. Sept. 24, 1860, died; Erastus b. April 1, 1863, m. Sarah Cox. Family resided Manti and Rockville, Utah.
Elder; teacher in ward. Helped to build the first canal and roads at Rockville. Died Oct. 8, 1872, at Rockville.

OLSEN, SEREN JR. (son of Seren Olsen and Bertha Peterson). Born Sept. 24, 1860.
Married Emily Frances Barton June 24, 1880, St. George, Utah (daughter of Stephen Smith Barton and Jane Evans, who resided at Lebanon, Ill. and Paragonah, Utah). She was born Nov. 9, 1863. Their children: Bertha Jane b. July 10, 1881, m. Hubbard Warren; Seren Penn b. Oct. 24, 1883; Mary b. June 9, 1885, m. Edward Jones; Frances b. Jan. 10, 1888, (d. Feb. 1909), m. John Allred; Stephen Alvin b. Feb. 6, 1890; Ira Glen b. Nov. 30, 1892; Asael b. Aug. 27, 1895; Fern b. Oct. 2, 1897; Eva b. April 8, 1899; Herald b. Dec. 24, 1901; Leroy Tell b. Jan. 29, 1904; Carl Emron b. Nov. 14, 1906. Family home Price, Utah.
High priest; ward and Sunday school teacher. City councilman at Price. One of the earliest settlers, he planted the first trees on the Price townsite; pioneer. Canal and road builder.

OLSEN, PETER ISAAC (son of Seren Olsen and Bertha Peterson). Born Jan. 6, 1856, Manti, Utah.
Married Sally Ann Barton Jan. 11, 1877, St. George, Utah (daughter of Stephen Smith Barton and Jane Evans of Paragonah, Utah), who was born Sept. 10, 1858, at Paragonah. Their children: Thomas William b. Nov. 22, 1878; William Isaac b. Dec. 27, 1879, Lorenzo b. Dec. 8, 1880, and Erastus b. March 7, 1882, all died infants; Mary Jane b. Oct. 8, 1888, m. Lawrence Rasmussen; Peter Barton b. July 22, 1892; Elvaleene Barton b. Aug. 5, 1894; Stephen Bryan b. Aug. 30, 1896; Viola Penn b. June 20, 1899. Family home Price, Utah.
One of the first settlers of Price, where he located in 1882; helped to build the first canal and wagon roads at that place. Sunday school superintendent 1833-95; ward teacher. Justice of peace.

OLSEN, SHURE (son of Ole and Hannah Maria Olsen, of Skudesnaeshavn, Norway). Born June 23, 1818, Island of Skudess. Came to Utah Oct. 26, 1849, Charles Hopkins company.
Married Elizabeth Jacobs May 19, 1847, Ottawa, Ill. (daughter of Jacob and Bertha Jacobs of Bergen, Norway), who was born June 10, 1823. Their children: Ole, d. aged 20; Gertrude and Elizabeth, died; Maria Hannah, m. Ethan Pettit; Shure D.; Andrew, m. Pauline Hookentumbler; Joseph, m. Annie Hookentumbler. Family home Salt Lake City, Utah.
Married Ellen Jacobs Nov. 30, 1851, Salt Lake City (daughter of Jacob and Bertha Jacobs), who was born Feb. 11, 1830. Their children: Shure D., d. infant; Sarah Ellen, m. Jeremiah E. Langford; Jacob; Minnie, m. William Pickett; Isaac, d. aged 22; Emma F., m. Joseph Evans.
Member of seventy; home missionary; high priest; block teacher. Worked on Tabernacle organ seven years. Carpenter and joiner. Died September, 1900.

OLSON, CARL M. Born May 27, 1836, in Sweden. Came to Utah in 1861.
Married Maria Andersdatter Oct. 4, 1862, Lehi, Utah (daughter of Anders Peterson of Velska Klava, Sweden), who was born Nov. 30, 1831, and came to Utah 1862. Their children: Maria Caroline b. June 22, 1863, m. Joseph S. Larsen; Ole b. March 31, 1865, m. Mary Catherine Pettey; Charles Henry b. March 9, 1867, m. Helen Anderson; Josephine, m. Thomas Jones; Joseph b. Nov. 12, 1870, died; Samuel and Joan, died.
Married Hannah Lindstein 1864, Salt Lake City, pioneer 1862. Their children: James, m. Annie Bolin; Christina, m. Arthur Borang; Hyrum, m. Mary Larson; Anna; Martina; Nora; latter three died.
Married Annie Okelof in 1881, Salt Lake City. She came to Utah in 1880. She was born in 1856. Their children: William, died; Amelia; Ella; Eva; Jennie, m. William Sorensen; Annie; Lillie; Herbert; Alice. Families resided Mayfield, Utah.
Presiding elder; ward teacher. Died May 17, 1910.

OLSEN, OLE (son of Carl M. Olsen and Maria Andersdatter). Born March 31, 1865, Lehi, Utah.
Married Mary Catherine Pettey Nov. 30, 1888, Mayfield, Utah (daughter of Eunice Snow and Heber C. Kimball Pettey of Manti, and Sterling, Utah, pioneers Sept. 24, 1848, Heber C. Kimball company). She was born Jan. 8, 1871, at Manti. Their children: Harold b. Jan. 23, 1899, d. Dec. 1, 1896; Armida b. Dec. 15, 1890, d. Dec. 11, 1896; Glenn C. b. July 25, 1895, d. Feb. 4, 1905; Dewey Lamar b. July 4, 1898; Clinton K. b. June 19, 1901; Eunice Leona b. Aug. 10, 1904. Family home Emery Utah.
Elder. Pioneer of Emery county. Built many roads, irrigation ditches, bridges, etc.; road supervisor Emery county. Farmer; beekeeper.

OLSON, CHRISTOPHER MARINUS. Born in Denmark.
Married Caroline C. Johnson in 1858. Their children: Mary M. b. April 26, 1859, m. David W. Rainey March 24, 1880; Emma, m. T. H. Merrill; Nettie, m. William Merrill; Anna,

m. J. I. Shepard; John, m. Emma Traverler; Julia, m. William Atkin. Family resided Hyrum and Richmond, Utah.
Tithing clerk for the Cache stake for many years. Bookkeeper of Z. C. M. I., Logan, Utah.

OLSON, ERICK ERICKSON (son of Erick Olson, born Jan. 29, 1795, and Ingrid Larson, born April 20, 1804, Wingaker, Sweden). He was born April 26, 1835, Wingaker, Sweden. Came to Utah July 10, 1882.
Married Maria Christina Anderson (daughter of Olof Anderson and Brita Katrina Anderson), who was born Aug. 29, 1834, and came to Utah with husband. Their children: Anna Christina b. Sept. 23, 1859, d. Aug. 1868; Caroline b. Sept. 13, 1861, m. J. P. Jonson; Maria Wilhelmina b. Sept. 22, 1862, d. Sept. 1868; Mathilda b. Sept. 19, 1864, d. Jan. 1866; Louis Erick Erickson b. June 22, 1866, m. Christina Olson Nov. 6, 1890; Charles August b. Feb. 17, 1869, m. Amanda Farnstrom; Hanna Maria b. Jan. 26, 1871, m. Peter S. Olson; Augusta b. May 25, 1874, d. Nov. 1, 1890; Wilhelm b. March 15, 1876, d. March 25, 1877. Family home Wingaker, Sweden.

OLSON, GEORGE DANIEL (son of Daniel Olsen and Maria Jorgensen of Hosterkyob, Denmark). Born Sept. 2, 1835, at Hosterkyob. Came to Utah 1854.
Married Delilah King Nov. 14, 1861, Fillmore, Utah (daughter of Thomas Rice King of New York state and Matilda Robison of Sylvania, Ohio; pioneers 1851, Vincent Shutliff company). She was born July 10, 1841, at Sylvanica. Their children: George Daniel, m. Melissa Russell; Thomas Edmond, m. Emeline Little, m. Drora Moore; Mary Evelyn, m. Alma Greenwood; William Francis, m. Annie May Cluff; Bertha Matilda, m. George M. Hanson; Culbert Levy, m. Kate Jeremy; Emma Eliza, died; Ethel Laverne, m. Dean Bradley; Emmett K. Family home Fillmore, Utah.
Missionary to Denmark 1884-85; high priest. Conducted orchestra which opened Salt Lake theatre. Cabinetmaker and musician.

OLSON, WILLIAM FRANCIS (son of Daniel Olson and Delilah King). Born May 26, 1870, Fillmore, Utah.
Married Annie May Cluff Nov. 27, 1895, Salt Lake City (daughter of William Wallace Cluff and Ann Whipple, of Coalville and Salt Lake City). She was born May 10, 1866. Their children: William Bryan b. Oct. 27, 1896; Evelyn May b. May 13, 1899; Francis Mack b. April 21, 1901; Josephine b. Nov. 20, 1904; Frank Montague b. July 26, 1907.
Missionary to Germany 1895-98; president Y. M. M. I. A.; teacher in Summit stake academy 1902-06. Mayor of Price two terms; organizer and vice president Price Commercial and Savings Bank. Engaged in implement and farm machinery business.

OLSON, ERICK LEHI (son of Lars E. Olson, born June 11, 1841, Wingaker, Sweden, and Anna Petterson, born Dec. 5, 1845, at same place). He was born May 25, 1864, at Wingaker. Came to Utah July 8, 1883.
Married Ingrid Larson April 27, 1893 (daughter of Lars Larson and Ingrid Olson, married at Wingaker; came to Utah July 8, 1883). She was born April 2, 1867, at Wingaker. Their children: Heber L. b. Feb. 23, 1894; Ester Ingeborg b. June 10, 1897; Ella Florence b. Nov. 10, 1899; Anna Evelean b. Aug. 25, 1905; Ingrid Ione b. Nov. 15, 1909. Family home River Heights, Logan, Utah.
Ordained bishop River Heights ward May 4, 1908, by Apostle George F. Richards; president 3d quorum elders of Cache stake 1908. School trustee three years in district No. 12, Providence precinct, Cache county, 1905-08.

OLSON, JAMES C. (son of Ole Jensen and Mary Ann Danielson of Island Falster, Denmark). Born Jan. 25, 1841, on Island Falster. Came to Utah Oct. 1, 1864, William B. Preston company.
Married May Frederikke Jensen May, 1864, who was born October, 1834. Their children: Mary Sophia, m. E. W. Crane; sister of Sophia —— died, aged 1 year.
Married Lara Lund.
Married Anna Lund.
Family home Piute City, Utah.
Missionary to Denmark 1880-83; high priest. Blacksmith. Died October, 1878, Salina, Utah.

OLSON, KNUT (son of Ola Jonson). Born March 4, 1811, at Sandby, Malmo, Sweden. Came to Utah September, 1864, William B. Preston company.
Married Elma Pherson, who was born May 10, 1816; came to Utah with husband. Their children: Anna b. Sept. 20, 1835, m. J. C. Hunt Nov. 1866; Hanna A. b. Feb. 9, 1837, d. May 25, 1840; Hans b. March 15, 1839, m. Elsa Nielson; Hannah B. b. Feb. 24, 1840, d. 1840; Ola b. Dec. 10, 1842, m. Elsa Jonson June 24, 1866; Hanna C. b. Feb. 14, 1845, d. 1845; Anders b. Jan. 23, 1846, m. Mary Jonquist; James b. Aug. 4, 1848, m. Henrietta Sonderberg; Niels K. b. Oct. 12, 1850, d. April 6, 1855; Hanna D. b. Feb. 27, 1853, d. March 3, 1855; Niels b. June 8, 1855, m. Mathilda Johnson; Johana b. July 27, 1857, d. June 13, 1862; Maria b. Feb. 3, 1860, m. W. C. Humphreys; Carl b. March 22, 1862, m. Ida Jongstrom.

OLSON, OLA (son of Knut Olson and Elna Pherson). Born Dec. 10, 1842, in Sweden.
Married Elna Jonson June 24, 1866, on the Atlantic ocean (daughter of Jons Jonson and Elsa Nielson, latter pioneer September, 1866, Peter Nebeker company), who was born June 21, 1847, in Sweden. Their children: George b. Nov. 19, 1868, m. Jean Lishman Jan. 13, 1894; Martin b. Jan. 21, 1870, m. Frances L. Jessop Jan. 22, 1890; James b. March 15, 1872, m. Sarah De Grey Dec. 31, 1902; Helma E. b. Feb. 7, 1875, m. J. W. E. Scott Feb. 11, 1903; Orson b. April 18, 1877, d. May 12, 1878; Olive M. b. Jan. 16, 1880, m. Ernest R. Scott March 2, 1900.
Married Elsa Jonson Oct. 11, 1878, Salt Lake City (daughter of Jons Nielson and Kjarsti Isaacson), who was born Nov. 12, 1852. Their children: Hilding b. Aug. 10, 1879, d. Feb. 24, 1892; Emma Mary b. July 14, 1881, m. James Jenson March 14, 1901; Martha E. b. Nov. 10, 1884.
Filled two missions to Sweden 1876-78, 1886-89 and 1898-1900; member high council of Hyrum stake.

OPENSHAW, JONATHAN E. (son of Job Openshaw and Nancy Beswick of Bolton, Lancashire, Eng. Came to Utah 1874). Born April 17, 1859.
Married Elizabeth Lees Dec. 8, 1881, Salt Lake City (daughter of John Lees, Jr., and Martha Needham, pioneers October, 1855, Milo Andrus company), who was born Dec. 13, 1863, Salt Lake City. Their children: Martha b. Oct. 22, 1882, d. infant; Jonathan E. Jr. b. Oct. 6, 1883, m. Adaline Coalter; Clarence R. b. Aug. 15, 1885, m. Margerite Coalter; Edna b. Sept. 28, 1887, m. Daniel K. Rawlings; Adelbert W. b. April 12, 1890, d. aged 15 months; Melvin b. July 1, 1892, m. Esther Roberts; Ida b. Nov. 19, 1894; Frank M. b. April 5, 1897; Florence b. Aug. 15, 1899; Glenn b. June 14, 1905. Family home, Salt Lake City.

ORD, THOMAS (son of George Ord and Mary Watson, of South Shields, Eng.). Born May 5, 1826, at South Shields. Came to Utah 1856, Edmund Martin handcart company.
Married Eleanor Grant March 4, 1856, Leicester, Eng. (daughter of John Grant and Mary Hall of Leicester), who was born June 14, 1828. Their children: Mary Eleanor; Thomas George; Elizabeth Ann; John William; Isabella Maria; Samuel Grant; Robert James. Family home Nephi, Utah.
High councilor; high priest. Superintendent of schools; county clerk; justice of peace. Lawyer; farmer. Died Oct. 7, 1907.

ORD, JOHN WILLIAM (son of Thomas Ord and Eleanor Grant). Born Oct. 5, 1863, Nephi, Utah.
Married Amelia Hendrickson Sept. 18, 1890, Manti, Utah (daughter of Andrew Hendrickson and Hannah Hansen, of Levan, Utah), who was born May 3, 1867. Their children: Amelia Isabella b. July 29, 1891; John Byron b. May 13, 1894; Eleanor Bernice b. April 22, 1903; Mabel Hannah b. March 30, 1905.
Member 71st quorum seventies; missionary to England 1894-1896; stake superintendent; high councilor. Member school board 2 terms. Farmer; stockraiser.

OREM, ALBERT J. (son of Joshua and Martha Orem of Indiana). Born March 2, 1851, Valparaiso, Porter county, Ind. Came to Utah 1890.
Married Martha A. Leabo 1871, in Ray county, Mo. (daughter of Samuel and Mary Leabo), who was born March 21, 1853. Their children: W. C., m. Mabel Emery; Frank M., m. Orla Mays; Archie J., m. Gertrudee Butter; Mattie, m. H. C. Joy; Mary; Deane. Family home Boston, Mass.
Mining man and railroader.

OREM, W. C. (son of Albert J. Orem and Martha A. Leabo). Born May 23, 1873, in Missouri. Came to Utah 1890.
Married Mabel Emery Dec. 19, 1894, in Iowa (daughter of William W. and Jennie A. Emery of Wapelio, Iowa), who was born Dec. 19, 1871. Their children: William W. b. 1897; Gladys M. b. 1899; Margaret b. 1901; Albert b. 1904; Horace b. 1911. Family home, Salt Lake City.
Mining man and railroader.

ORME, SAMUEL WASHINGTON (son of Samuel Orme of Coalville, Eng., born May 2, 1802, Sliesby, Eng., and Amy Kerby of Leicestershire, Eng., born Jan. 13, 1804, married about 1823). Born July 4, 1832, Mentor, Ohio. Came to Utah Nov. 20, 1856, Edward Martin "Frozen" handcart company.
Married Sarah Cross October, 1857 (daughter of Joseph Cross and Keziah Marshall), who was born March 3, 1833, and came to Utah Sept. 12, 1857, Israel Evans handcart company. Their children: Samuel W. b. Sept. 19, 1858, m. Mary A. Smith Feb. 24, 1886; Joseph Cross b. Aug. 1, 1860, m. Sarah England June 27, 1888; John Kirby b. Oct. 3, 1862, m. Janeta Park Dec. 1, 1887; Silas Cross b. Oct. 26, 1864, m. Emma J. Smith Oct. 11, 1894; Arthur b. Oct. 1867, d. infant; Charles Alvin b. Oct. 21, 1869, m. Ada Dunn Dec. 20, 1899; LaFayette b. March 14, 1872, m. Emily J. Isgreen Sept. 20, 1905; Edwin Marshall b. July 19, 1874, m. Millie McLaws April 24, 1901.
Seventy; superintendent Batesville Sunday school 1876-1879. Mayor of Tooele two terms; school trustee 1882-1889. Settled at E. T. City 1857, moved to Tooele City 1858, and to Lehi same year. Blacksmith and farmer.

ORME, SAMUEL WASHINGTON, JR. (son of Samuel Washington Orme and Sarah Cross). Born Sept. 19, 1858, Tooele, Utah.
Married Mary Agnes Smith Feb. 24, 1886, Logan, Utah (daughter of John A. Smith and Mary Meiklejohn of Tooele, Utah, pioneers 1849, Silas Richards company), who was born Nov. 19, 1865. Their children: Samuel b. Jan. 14, 1887, m. Laura H. Baker; Alberta b. Feb. 17, 1889, m. Eli M. Jorgensen; Milo S. b. May 30, 1892; Joseph R. b. June 3, 1894; Sarah C. b. Oct. 11, 1896; Dean b. Sept. 21, 1898; Luetta b. Nov. 27, 1900; Elva b. April 8, 1904; Reed b. Oct. 15, 1906. Family resided Tooele, Utah, and Wilford, Idaho.
Second counselor to Bishop Thomas Atkin of Tooele ward 2 years; 2nd counselor in Y. M. M. I. A., Wilford ward, 1901; 1st counselor to Bishop George A. Pincock, Wilford ward; ordained bishop of Wilford ward April 24, 1903. Mayor of Tooele 1892-94; county commissioner Fremont county, Idaho, 1909-1910; school trustee three years. Director in Wilford Canal company. Farmer and stockraiser.

ORME, JOSEPH CROSS (son of Samuel Washington Orme and Sarah Cross). Born Aug. 1, 1860, Tooele, Utah.
Married Julia M. Ingree June 27, 1884, Logan, Utah (daughter of John England and Eliza Kennington; former pioneer Sept. 14, 1860, Brigham Y. Young company, latter Sept. 26, 1856, D. D. McArthur company). She was born Oct. 6, 1867, Tooele, Utah. Their children: Joseph Arthur b. June 1, 1889; Gilbert Charles b. Nov. 20, 1891; Ada Marcell b. June 5, 1896; Eliza Luella b. Oct. 3, 1898; Parley b. Aug. 16, 1900; Adrian L. b. Jan. 15, 1903; Julia b. April 16, 1905; Maggie Leona b. April 19, 1908; Sherman M. b. May 8, 1910. Family home Tooele, Utah.
Missionary to southern states 1893-1895; 2nd counselor to Bishop Thomas Atkin; member of high council Tooele stake; 2nd counselor to Tooele stake presidency; ward superintendent of religion classes 1898-1899. City marshal; member of city council 2 terms; county commissioner.

ORME, LAFAYETTE (son of Samuel Washington Orme and Sarah Cross). Born March 14, 1872, Tooele, Utah.
Married Emily J. Ingreen Sept. 20, 1905, Salt Lake City (daughter of Andrew Jens Ingreen and Anna B. Stromberg; former pioneer Aug. 29, 1859, James Brown company, latter Oct. 1, 1862). Their children: Marcellus LaFayette b. Aug. 4, 1906, d. June 29, 1907; Emily Maurine b. Oct. 13, 1908.
President Y. M. M. I. A. 1896-1899; stake aid Y. M. M. I. A. 1900-1906; religion class teacher 1894-1896 and 1899-1900; assistant superintendent Sunday school 1902-1906; seventy; stake secretary Y. M. M. I. A. Business manager of Tooele City Milling company 1903, 1906, 1909 to present time.

ORSER, EVERET. Came to Utah 1856, oxteam company.
Married Mary America Mecham at Provo, Utah. Their children: Frank, m. Mary Rogers; Alice, m. A. N. Billings; Everet, Jr.; Ellen; Laura, m. Joseph A. McKee. Family home Vernal, Utah.
Stockraiser. Died at Vernal.

ORTON, SAMUEL TAYLOR (son of William Orton and Hannah Taylor of Nottinghamshire, Eng.). Born July 1, 1832, Carltonhill, Nottinghamshire, Eng. Came to Utah 1856, Edward Bunker company.
Married Julia Ann Johnson Nov. 29, 1862, Fort Johnson, Utah (daughter of Joel Hills Johnson and Susan Briant of Bellview, Utah, pioneers 1848, Willard Richards company). She was born Feb. 20, 1847. Their children: Julia Ann, m. Elmer W. Johnson; Samuel T., m. Sarah A. Taylor; Oscar J.; Nephi J., m. Alice Benson; Mary A. H.; Charles B.; Joel Hills, m. Eliza J. Warren; Susan A.; Hannah T.; Seth J.; Osman T. b. Jan. 5, 1878; Minnie B. b. April 9, 1879.
Married Esther E. Johnson Dec. 26, 1877, St. George, Utah (daughter of Joel Hills Johnson and Margaret Threlkeld), who was born Dec. 23, 1861. Their children: Mary E. b. March 11, 1880, m. Samuel A. Halterman; Silas T. b. Dec. 10, 1881, m. Mary B. Pendleton; Ernest J. b. Oct. 29, 1883, m. Mary E. Benson; Ellis T. b. Oct. 27, 1885, m. Mary R. Bentley; Donald T. b. Dec. 13, 1887; Rebecca T. b. Nov. 17, 1889, m. Charles C. Smith; William T. b. March 28, 1892; Twenty T. b. May 21, 1894; Maggie J. b. Sept. 2, 1896; Verna M. b. April 14, 1899; Jared J. b. April 2, 1901; Almon H. b. April 1, 1905. Families resided Parowan, Utah.
Counselor to stake President W. H. Dane 1878; counselor to Bishop McGregor 1877; member high council 1881. Marshal, 1872; watermaster, 1873; road supervisor; city councilman, 1880; treasurer, 1888; sexton, 1904; Veteran in Indian wars. Farmer and tanner. Died April 20, 1907.

ORTON, JOEL HILLS (son of Samuel Taylor Orton and Julia Ann Johnson). Born March 4, 1871, Parowan, Utah.
Married Eliza J. Warren July 12, 1892, at Parowan (daughter of William Stockbridge Warren and Ann Fowler, of Parowan; former a pioneer 1854, Amasa M. Lyman company, latter a pioneer in 1863). She was born Feb. 8, 1872. Their children: Lula b. July 4, 1893; Mable W. b. May 22, 1895; Osmond W. b. Feb. 13, 1897; Agnes b. May 26, 1899; Wanda b. April 25, 1902; Virda b. Aug. 10, 1903; Elma b. Dec. 3, 1906; Alva W. b. Dec. 27, 1908; Warren b. Aug. 7, 1911. Family home, Parowan.
Missionary to Southern states 1899-1901; president Y. M. M. I. A. of Parowan stake 1901; bishop's counselor 1892-1912. Deputy sheriff; road supervisor; city marshal; watermaster. Blacksmith.

OSGUTHORPE, JOHN (son of Thomas Osguthorpe and Ann Kitson, of Sheffield, Eng.). Born March 10, 1823, Sheffield, Eng. Came to Utah late in 1853, Charles Wilkin company. Married Lydia Roper about 1844, in Sheffield, Eng. (daughter of Abel and Sarah Roper, of Sheffield). She was born Feb. 4, 1828. Their children: Sarah A., m. Breneman B. Bitner; Emma, died; Priscilla, m. Charles Bolton; Hannah, d. aged 18; John H., m. Mary Garn; Lydia, m. Charles Bolton; Abel, d. aged 3; Thomas. m. Ida Roach; Joseph, m. Luella Russell; Selina, m. Samuel Stillman; Mervin, d. aged 3. Family home East Mill Creek, Utah.
Seventy; block teacher; elder. Lawyer. Died April 13, 1884.

OSMOND, GEORGE. Born 1835, in England. Married Georgena Huckvale 1853. She was born 1835, in England. Their children: Clara, m. Adam Welker; George Anson, m. Alice Hart; Alfred, m. Frances Nelson, m. Annie Lloyd; Ira; Rosa, m. William Ottinger; Ida, m. Oliver Dunford; Ella. m. Louie Newman; Nellie. m. Eugene Hart; Georgena, died; Alice, m. Forest Reed. Family home Bloomington, Idaho.
Married Amelia Jacobson. Their children: Arthur and Archie, died.
Missionary in England 1884-91, where he had charge of the Millennial Star, church paper. Bishop of Bloomington ward, Idaho; counselor to President Budge of Bear Lake stake; president Star Valley stake. Wyoming. Wyoming state senator two terms. Judge and lawyer.

OSMOND, ALFRED (son of George Osmond and Georgena Huckvale). Born Oct. 5, 1862, Willard, Utah.
Married Frances Nelson Dec. 30, 1888, Bloomington, Idaho (daughter of Christian and Josephine Nelson). Their only child was Pearl, born Dec. 23, 1889, died May, 1890.
Married Annie Lloyd June 16, 1897 (daughter of Thomas Lloyd and Susanna Stone, of Logan, Utah, pioneers handcart company). She was born Sept. 7, 1869. Their children: Alfred Wendell b. April 24, 1898; Harvard Reginald b. March 31, 1903; Waldo Lloyd b. Jan. 13, 1904; Constance b. Jan. 7, 1905; Mary Irene b. Sept. 16, 1907; Annie Hermies b. Jan. 27, 1909. Family home Provo, Utah.
Missionary to eastern states 1893-95; president 153d quorum seventies of Provo; president Y. M. M. I. A. of Bear Lake stake. Probate judge; county school superintendent; member Idaho state legislature from Bear Lake county. Professor and head of department of English of B. Y. U. at Provo. Graduate of Harvard University 1903.

OSTENSEN, PETER. Born in Norway. Came to Utah 1858. Married Caroline Anderson. Their children: Parley, died; Mary; Edway Starr; Annie, m. Sim Brady; Clara, m. Daniel Bigelow; Sarah, m. Joseph Fuller; Caroline; Olivia, m. Marlin Cox; Vina, m. Lee Kelsey; Phillip, Ella McNeil. Family home Fairview, San Pete county, Utah.
Seventy. Farmer. Died in June, 1911.

OSTERMANN, JENS CARL DIDDERICK (son of Johan Carl Ostermann and Johanne Jensen, of Copenhagen, Denmark). Born Sept. 17, 1830, Randers, Denmark. Came to Utah Sept. 26, 1868, John G. Holman company.
Married Caroline Marie Berg Nov. 7, 1857, Grenaa, Denmark (daughter of Rasmus Rasmersen Berg and Caroline Marie Tolboe of Grenaa). She was born Aug. 24, 1831. Their children: Johanne C. b. Oct. 3, 1858, m. John T. Thorup; Henriette A. b. Dec. 26, 1859, d. aged 9; Johan C. b. April 21, 1861, d. aged 7; Mary J. b. Jan. 15, 1863, m. Brigham C. Ward; Frederick E. b. March 14, 1865, d. aged 3; Anne M. A. E. b. March 21, 1867, d. infant; Eliza b. May 6, 1870, d. aged 2; James b. May 9, 1874, d. aged 32. Family home, Salt Lake City.
Seventy at Sandy; presiding elder of Grenaa. Denmark. School trustee at Sandy. Shoemaker and general merchant. Died Oct. 20, 1883, Sandy, Utah.

OSTLER, DAVID. Born Sept. 28, 1841, in England. Came to Utah 1861.
Married Anne Beagley on the plains. Their children: Ellen, m. William Watson; Mary, m. William Buttle; Oliver B., m. Ruby Merrill; David J., m. Martha Smiley; Emily, m. Joseph Love; Joseph, m. Pauline Hornbuckle. Family home, Salt Lake City.
Married Ann Scott Nov. 16, 1575, Salt Lake City (daughter of Robert Scott and Jane Martin). Their children: Henrietta, died; Lula Devet b. May 2, 1878, m. Ernest Winn. High priest. Died Sept. 19, 1911.

OSTLER, J. S. (son of John C. and Mary Anne Ostler). Married Hattie Kearns (Goddard) May 25, 1907, Salt Lake City (daughter of Henry H. Kearns and Emma Guymon of Springville, Utah, pioneers 1850). She was born Oct. 12, 1868. Their children: Pruette Kearns Goddard (child by previous marriage adopted); Oleva Ostler, and Lovell Ostler. Family home, Salt Lake City.
Member state board sheep commissioners. Sheepraiser.

OTTERSTROM, JONAS. Born Dec. 9, 1820, Carlsbad, Sweden. Came to Utah Sept. 20, 1856, Knud Peterson company.
Married Marie Kaisa Nielsen (daughter of John Nielsen and Maria Jansen of Carlsbad), who was born Jan. 25, 1825. Their children: Johan, d. child; Stine Marie, m. Orson Hyde; John Henry, m. Lena Olson; Augusta, died; Augusta K.. d. child; Josephine, m. Christopher Cramer; Louisa, m. Lars Peter Oveson; Joseph, d. infant; Caroline, d. child; Brigham, m. Minnie Balson. Family home Ephraim, Utah.
Member 47th quorum seventies; ward teacher. Veteran Black Hawk war. Blacksmith and farmer. Died April 30, 1884.

OTTINGER, GEORGE MARTIN (son of William Ottinger and Elizabeth Martin of Philadelphia, Pa.). Born Feb. 8, 1833, in Montgomery county, Pa. Came to Utah Sept. 12, 1861, Milo Andrus company.
Married Mary Jane McAllister Jan. 9, 1862, Salt Lake City (daughter of William McAllister and Eliza Thompson of Philadelphia, pioneers Sept. 12, 1861). She was born Feb. 2, 1829, and died Dec. 19, 1862. Their only child: William, married Hortense Goddard.
Married Phebe Neslen Dec. 3, 1864, Salt Lake City (daughter of Samuel Neslen and Eunice Francis), who was born Sept. 27, 1839, Lowestoft, Suffolkshire, Eng.; and came to Utah Sept. 20, 1853, Claudius V. Spencer company. Their children: John M. b. April 29, 1866, d. infant; Hannah E. b. Dec. 1, 1867, m. George E. Romney; Esther D. b. Feb. 22, 1873, d. 1876; George N. b. Oct. 17, 1875, m. Dora Lingscog; Sarah Jane b. Jan. 28, 1875; John S. b. Oct. 3, 1876, m. Elvina Parkinson; Rowena b. July 6, 1879, m. Abram Hatch, Jr. Family home, Salt Lake City.
Missionary to England 1879. Adjutant General National Guard of Utah two years. Superintendent waterworks at Salt Lake City; chief engineer in both volunteer and paid fire departments 14 years. Lieutenant-colonel 3d infantry, Nauvoo Legion. President Utah Art Institution; artist in Deseret Dramatic association. Veteran Indian wars of southern Utah. Author of "A Boy's Voyage Around the World," "Leaves from a Log-Book," and "Old America."

OTTOSEN, JENS (son of Otto Nielsen and Kirstine Anders of Denmark). Born June 20, 1813, Bedster, Woognli parish, Ualdborg Amt, Denmark. Came to Utah September, 1858.
Married Anne Jens 1852, in Denmark (daughter of Jens and Johannah Marie Christensen). Their children: Jens b. Dec. 12, 1852, d. Dec. 16, 1856; Niels b Sept. 3, 1855, d. Sept. 9, 1861; Marie b. Dec. 18, 1857, d. Sept. 9, 1858; Emma b. Oct. 10, ——, d. Oct. 28, 1850; Joseph b. Oct. 10, ——, d. Nov. 2, 1859. Family resided Salt City and Goshen, Utah.
Married Johannah Sorensen Nov. 18, 1860, Goshen, Utah (daughter of Niels Sorensen and Anne Marie Jensen, pioneers Sept. 24, 1860, handcart company). She was born Oct. 15, 1839, Aarup, Denmark. Their children: Anne Martina b. Nov. 15, 1861, m. William H. Luke March 14, 1878; Otto b. July 27, 1863, m. Lina Henrie Feb. 4, 1891; Jessie b. Nov. 30, 1866, m. B. D. Seigfus May 11, 1891; Nephi b. April 17, 1870, m. Lizzie Ahlstrom June 6, 1900. Family resided Goshen, Salina and Manti, Utah.
Missionary to Denmark 1854-57. Dead.

OVARD, WILLIAM (son of Thomas Ovard and Anna Stoaks). Born Dec. 23, 1850, in England. Came to Utah Sept. 5, 1866, Samuel D. White company.
Married Phoebe Henefer Jan. 3, 1870 (daughter of James Henefer and Sarah Hulks). She was born April 17, 1852. b. Oct. 27, 1871, m. Thomas Grosse June 4, 1894; George William b. Nov. 14, 1874, died; John Alma b. Nov. 16, 1875, m. Grace Livingston; Thomas b. June 4, 1878, m. Mary A. S. Edgeworth Aug. 9, 1899; Fanny b. June 4, 1881, died; Joe b. March 31, 1883; Rachel Adeline b. July 3, 1884; Sarah A n b. Oct. 3, 1885, and Margret Elizabeth b. Oct. 12, 1886, Linda
Married Bangta Hegg Dec. 26, 1889 (daughter of Andrew Randall Hegg and Anna Jensen). She was born March 25, 1848, Estervan, Sweden. Their child: Anna Rebecca Florence b. Feb. 18, 1894. Family home Henefer, Utah.
Carpenter.

OVARD, THOMAS (son of William Ovard and Phoebe Henefer). Born June 4, 1878, Henefer, Utah.
Married Mary Ann Shill Edgeworth Aug. 9, 1899, Salt Lake City (daughter of Joseph Edgeworth and Prudence Jones, pioneers; former wife joined with Captain White company, latter with Captain Chapman company). She was born Sept. 3, 1877, Henefer, Utah. Their children: Joseph William b. Sept. 14, 1901; George Thomas b. March 21, 1903; Roy b. Nov. 6, 1909. Family home Henefer, Utah.
Teacher. Laborer.

OVERLAID, ANDREW. Came to Utah ahead of Johnston's army, 1857.
Married Caroline ———. Their children: Mary Kristena, m. John Williams; Andreas. m. Andrew Whitlock; Andrew, m. Mary Anderson; Elizabeth, m. Edward Allred; Matilda, m. David Thompson; Josephine, m. Neils O. Anderson, m. Erastus Anderson; Caroline. m. Lehi Peterson Dorcas.
Participated in Black Hawk Indian war. Carpenter. Died about 1890, at Ephraim, Utah.

OVESON, JENS ANDREAS (son of Ove Anderson and Anna Marie Jensen of Ugelt, Hjorring, Denmark). Born Sept. 17, 1816, at Ugelt. Came to Utah Sept. 5, 1863, John F. Sanders company.
Married Kjersten Maria Petersen, at Ugelt, who was born Sept. 14, 1813, and came to Utah with husband. Their children: Ove Christian; Annie Kjerstine, m. Paul Poulsen; Eliza, d. child; Lars Peter, m. Louisa Otterstrom. Family home Ephraim, Utah.
High priest; ward teacher. Carpenter and joiner. Died Jan. 11, 1904.

OVESON, LARS PETER (son of Jens Andreas Oveson and Kjersten Maria Petersen). Born Oct. 25, 1852 at Taars, Hjorring, Denmark. Came to Utah Sept. 5, 1863, John F. Sanders company.
Married Louisa Otterstrom May 18, 1874, at Salt Lake City (daughter of Jonas Otterstrom and Maria Kissa Nielsen, pioneers 1856), who was born Feb. 16, 1858. Their children: Louis Peter b. June 7, 1875, m. May Howard; Parley Parker b. May 14, 1877, d. infant; Aurelia Maria b. April 12, 1878, m. Peter E. Johnson; Urania b. Oct. 31, 1880, d. infant; Louisa Alge Nora b. Nov. 18, 1881, m. Lars Peter Larsen; Geneva b. June 5, 1885, m. Joseph J. Larsen; James and John (twins) b. Nov. 14, 1887, d. infants; Clarence D. b. March 9, 1890, m. Johanna Johnson; Sarah Jane b. Aug. 3, 1893; Moroni Irving b. Dec. 1, 1895; Merrill Mahonri b. Nov. 7, 1900. Family home Cleveland, Utah.
Member 47-81 quorums seventies 1884-1890; missionary to Denmark 1882-84; bishop, Cleveland ward, 1890 to 1910; president Emery stake 1910; county selectman 1892-94. State representative. Veteran Black Hawk war. Farmer and stockraiser.

OVIATT, IRA (son of Benjamin and Frances Oviatt, of Rensselaer county, N. Y.). Born Dec. 8, 1804, in Rensselaer county. Came to Utah Oct. 5, 1851, Kelsey company.
Married Ruth Bennett Jan. 29, 1829 (daughter of John Bennett and Mary Sweet, of New York), who was born Sept. 28, 1808. Their children: John Franklin, m. Mary Jane Whitlock; Henry Herman b. June 17, 1832, m. Sallie Ray Whitlock Feb. 1, 1853; Sarah Jane, Zera, and Willis Murray, d. children; Judith, m. Albert Map, m. James D. Wilcox; Jo, m. Josephine Workman; Lewis, m. Lydia Workman; m. Sarah Hovey; Mary Jane, m. John Jenkins. Family home Farmington, Utah.
High priest; member high council of Council Bluffs, Iowa, 1846-51. Blacksmith and carpenter. Died July 1, 1868.

OVIATT, HENRY HERMAN (son of Ira Oviatt and Ruth Bennett). Born June 17, 1832. Came to Utah Oct. 5, 1851, Captain Kelsey company.
Married Sallie Ray Whitlock Feb. 1, 1853, Spring City, Utah (daughter of Andrew Whitlock and Hannah Allred of Bedford county, Tenn., pioneers September, 1852, Captain Tidwell company). She was born Oct. 9, 1828. Their children: Ormandie b. Oct. 28, 1849, m. Joseph Barney; Henry H. b. Dec. 1, 1853, m. Catherine Madsen; Adelaide b. July 19, 1856, m. Rasmus Rasmussen; Adeline b. July 19, 1856, m. Chris Madsen; Adelbert b. Sept. 7, 1859, m. Melinda Stevens Sept. 22, 1881; Angeline b. Sept. 21, 1861, d. child; Ilernan b. Dec. 12, 1863, m. Sylvia Hill; Agnes b. May 17, 1866, died; George b. Oct. 18, 1868, m. Gena Nielsen; Nora b. May 4, 1871. Family home Ephraim, Utah.
Member 56th quorum seventies; high priest. Settled in Circle Valley 1864. Treasurer Piute county, 1864; Member Ephraim city council 1878-82. Veteran Walker and Black Hawk war. Farmer and stockraiser.

OVIATT, ADELBERT (son of Henry Herman Oviatt and Sallie Ray Whitlock). Born Sept. 7, 1859, at Ephraim.
Married Malinda Stevens Sept. 22, 1881, Gunnison, Colo. (daughter of Henry B. Stevens, and Elizabeth Whitlock, pioneers 1850), who was born Jan. 26, 1866. Their children: Elizabeth Ray b. Sept. 15, 1882, m. Charles Christensen; Marion b. March 31, 1885, d. youth; Newton b. Jan. 30, 1888, d. infant; Maud b. Aug. 18, 1889; Angus b. May 2, 1892; Orley b. Sept. 8, 1895, and Judith b. Dec. 7, 1896, d. young; Olive b. May 26, 1898; Rodney b. Jan. 23, 1901, d. infant; Newel b. May 26, 1902; Helen b. July 24, 1904. Family home Cleveland, Utah.
Elder. Constable at Cleveland 1900-02. Director of Cleveland Canal & Agricultural Co., 1894-1908. Farmer and stockraiser.

OWEN, WILLIAM DAVID (son of David Morgan Owen and Elizabeth Taylor, of London, Eng.). Born June 14, 1810, Paddington, Eng. Came to Utah Sept. 2, 1868, oxteam company.
Married Rhoda Moss in 1842, London, Eng. (daughter of John Moss and Susanna Barber, of Friston, Suffolkshire, Eng.). Their children: William David, m. Marianne Sanders; Mary Ann, m. Thomas R. Jackson; Rhoda, m. Henry Forrest; Horatio, Lavinia, Selina, and Alice Carolina, died; Alvin Cyrus, m. Sarah Naylor; Susanna E., died; Clarissa, m. James Jenkins; Sarah, m. George Luff; Daniel Whitney, m. Maggie Kendall; Rosina, died.
Elder. Sailor in British navy nine years. Died Dec. 23, 1903, Salt Lake City.

OWEN, WILLIAM DAVID, JR. (son of William David Owen and Rhoda Moss). Born Sept. 2, 1843, London, Eng. Came to Utah Oct. 20, 1862, William H. Dames oxteam company.
Married Marianne Sanders Nov. 5, 1866, Salt Lake City (daughter of Simeon Sanders and Frances Waterman of Bishop's Stortford, Hertfordshire, Eng.; latter a pioneer 1864, Warren oxteam company). She was born March 28, 1846. Their children: William S. b. Nov. 11, 1867, m. Lizzie McGee; John David b. April 18, 1869, m. Lucy Whitney; Alice M. b. Oct. 19, 1871, died; Walter James b. Dec. 8, 1872, died; Annie Mabel b. Feb. 6, 1875, m. R. William Roberts; Ernest A. b. June 23, 1878, died; Rulon Moss b. July 13, 1880, m. Eva Hudson; Alma Morgan b. Aug. 7, 1883, died; George Washington b. May 2, 1885, died; Nellie E. b. Dec. 9, 1887, died; Ruby Frances b. Oct. 25, 1891. Family home Salt Lake City.
Married Huldah E. Wilcox Nov. 5, 1880, Salt Lake City (daughter of Walter E. Wilcox and Elizabeth Hawkins). Their children: Huldah Elizabeth b. Oct. 31, 1881, m. Nels Bergeman; Ruth Emma b. April 3, 1883, d. infant; Moroni Orson b. July 24, 1884, m. Dacy Cowart; Ione Josephine b. Sept. 19, 1886, m. Albert Poulsen; Reuben Joseph b. March 14, 1889.
President 4th quorum seventies; Sunday school superintendent 11 years; member Sunday school union board; member Salt Lake Tabernacle choir 40 years. Salesman for Z. C. M. I. since 1869.

OWENS, JOHN E. (son of Edward Owens and Sarah Roberts of Merthyr Tydfil, Wales). Born March 16, 1833, at Merthyr Tydfil. Came to Utah Oct. 10, 1853, John W. Young company.
Married Mary Thomas Feb. 15, 1853, on shipboard (daughter of Richard Thomas and Margret Jones of Merthyr Tydfil, Wales; former died in Wales, latter a pioneer Oct. 10, 1853, John W. Young company). She was born May 6, 1834. Their children: Richard Thomas, m. Susann Thomas, m. Bell Regen; Sarah, m. Dan D. Thomas, m. John R. Thomas; John T., m. Mary Thomas; Edward, m. Ellen Ellis, and Ellen Peabody; Mary Blanch, m. Llewellyn Thomas; Catherine Elizabeth, m. Daniel M. Daniels; Charlotte Jane, m. David S. Jones. Family home Malad, Idaho.
Elder. Farmer. Died Nov. 3, 1895.

OWENS, RICHARD THOMAS (son of John E. Owens and Mary Thomas). Born April 21, 1854, Ogden, Utah.
Married Susann Thomas April 11, 1878, Salt Lake City (daughter of Thomas W. Thomas and Ruth Morgan of Malad, Idaho, pioneers Oct. 10, 1853, John W. Young company). She was born October, 1860. Their children: Ruth Lovina b. Aug. 16, 1879, m. Henry McGee; Richard Evan b. Oct. 23, 1880, m. Sadie Little. Family home Malad, Idaho. Missionary to Wales 1885-87; assistant Sunday school superintendent. County commissioner 1906-08. City councilman 6 years. Merchant.

OWENS, WILLIAM (son of John and Charlotte Owens, of Wales). Born May 1, 1827, in Glamorganshire, Wales.
Married Jenette Lewis (daughter of William and Marie Lewis). She was born Feb. 18, 1836. Their two children, both boys, died infants.
Married Elizabeth Roberts Jan. 20, 1856, Salt Lake City (daughter of Hugh Roberts and Mary Owens, pioneers 1864). She was born March 6, 1835, Little Church, Denbighshire, Wales. Their children: Jennette b. March 24, 1857, m. Walter Henry Shelsey; Elizabeth b. Feb. 9, 1859, m. George W. Hendrickson; William b. July 4, 1861, m. Etta Nelson; John b. June 29, 1863, d. Feb. 14, 1887; Mary b. March 7, 1866, m. Thomas W. Thompson; Charlotte b. March 23, 1868, Nov. 30, 1876; Hannah b. July 28, 1870, d. Nov. 1, 1876. Families resided Salt Lake City, and Henefer, Summit Co., Utah.
Hotel keeper, in Salt Lake City. Rancher at Henefer. Participated in Echo Canyon campaign.

O'DONNEL, EDWARD G. Born March 1, 1865, Limerick, Ireland. Came to Utah July, 1891.
Married Mary Ardean Miller April 19, 1891, San Francisco, Cal. (daughter of Grant Miller and Sadie Monahan, of San Francisco), who was born June 17, 1872. Their children: John E.; Margaret M.; Cornelius Grant; Edmund J., died; Mary Ellen; Edward James; Katherine. Family home, Salt Lake City.
City councilman Salt Lake City. Undertaker.

O'DRISCOLL, JOHN (son of James O'Driscoll and Rachel Knight, of Cape of Good Hope, South Africa). Born Dec. 21, 1845, at Cape of Good Hope. Came to Utah May 13, 1865, Miner G. Atwood company.
Married Sarah Ellen Neibaur Nov. 16, 1867, Salt Lake City (daughter of Alexander Neibaur of Ehrenbreitstein, near Coblenz, Hessen-Nassau, Prussia, and Ellen Breakell, of Salt Lake City, pioneers Sept. 20, 1848, Brigham Young company, former was first surgeon-dentist in Salt Lake City). She was born May 21, 1849. Their children: Rachael b. Jan. 3, 1869, m. William Woolstenhulme; Ellen b. April 6, 1870, m. James Davies; George Alexander b. July 24, 1871; John Hyrum b. March 27, 1873, m. Jeanette Holfeltz; Richard b. Oct. 14, 1874; William Henry b. Dec. 9, 1875; Leslie b. Nov. 5, 1877, m. Irene Cloward; Susie b. May 13, 1880, m. Joseph Edward Wilde; Isaac Breakell b. Nov. 27, 1884, m. Dora Taylor; Nathan Neibaur b. March

23, 1882; Gladys b. Feb. 26, 1888; Jesse Paul b. July 30, 1890, m. Ada May Bowers. Family home Kamas, Utah. Veteran Indian war. Settled at Kamas 1869; moved to the Provo river 1874. Assisted in surveying the South Kamas Irrigating Canal; erected first wire fence in the Kamas valley. Farmer.

O'NEIL, JAMES (son of John O'Neil and Agnes Hair of Delrye, Scotland). Born Nov. 5, 1848, Delrye, Scotland. Came to Utah 1864, with oxteam.
Married Mary Elizabeth Alexander July 12, 1875, Salt Lake Endowment house (daughter of Alvah Jedathan Alexander of Vermont and Elizabeth Soule of Maine, pioneer 1853, oxteam company). She was born Jan. 21, 1855. Their children: James b. Sept. 24, 1876, m. Rachel Jensigne Hards; John Alexander b. Dec. 23, 1877, m. Mary Elizabeth Winn; Mary Annette b. June 9, 1879, m. Robert Forest James; Alvah Alexander b. March 22, 1881, m. Minetta Harriet Hards; Elizabeth b. Dec. 19, 1883, m. James Alfred Winn; Gertrude Debon b. Oct. 28, 1885, m. Einar Johnson; Agnes Ellen b. Jan. 24, 1887, m. David Olius Jacobson; Percy Leroy b. April 2, 1889; George Bonner b. June 4, 1891; Ethel Kate b. Aug. 18, 1893; Dessie Delberta b. June 17, 1898. Family home Vernal, Utah.
Member 97th quorum seventies; ward teacher; Sunday school superintendent. Black Hawk Indian War veteran. Justice of peace at Vernal. School trustee; school teacher. Farmer. Minuteman and guard during early Indian troubles.

O'NEIL, JOHN (son of John O'Neil and Margaret Cummings, of Grey Abbey, County Down, Ireland). Born April 6, 1828, at Grey Abbey. Came to Utah 1864.
Married Agnes Cochran, Delry, Ayrshire, Scotland (daughter of Thomas Cochran and Rachel Ellis of Armagh, Ireland). She was born Jan. 22, 1827 and came to Utah in 1864, Rollins, Warren and Canfield company. Their children: James b. Nov. 15, 1848, m. Mary Elizabeth Alexander; John b. May 21, 1853, d. Oct. 26, 1866; William b. June 22, 1855, m. Susan Matilda Ross; Rachel, m. Louis Coleman; Thomas, Thomas, Samuel and Samuel, dd infants; Samuel, m. Ruth Rockwood; Helen Robertson b. Dec. 22, 1865, m. Levi W. Hancock; George, m. Letta Hordsman; Agnes, m. Samuel Richie.
High priest in Wasatch stake; home missionary. Justice of peace at Mound City. Captain in Black Hawk Indian war. Died June 24, 1880, Midway, Utah.

O'NEIL, WILLIAM (son of John O'Neil and Agnes Cochran). Born June 22, 1855, Delry, Ayrshire, Scotland. Came to Utah with parents.
Married Susan Matilda Ross Dec. 5, 1877, Midway, Utah (daughter of James Jackson Ross and Susan Laverna Roby, of Heber City, Utah). She was born March 22, 1860, Provo, Utah. Their children: William b. Dec. 7, 1878, m. Mary Elizabeth Wardle; Susan b. Feb. 4, 1881, m. Joseph James Hards; Agnes b. Feb. 4, 1883, m. George Fuller; George b. March 20, 1885, m. Lenora Abplanalp; Nancy b. March 30, 1892, m. Louis Wall; Cora b. June 13, 1890, m. Samuel Henry Summerall; Lycurgus b. Jan. 8, 1894; Nellie b. March 4, 1896; Annie b. May 1, 1898; Ross b. Jan. 10, 1900; John Walter b. May 7, 1905. Family home Roosevelt, Utah.
Missionary to Scotland and Ireland 1889-1901; high priest; president Uinta stake Y. M. M. I. A. 1893-96; 1st counselor to Bishop Joseph A. McKee of Glines ward; 1st counselor to S. A. Russell in Cedar View branch; assistant Sunday school superintendent and teacher of Glines ward; home missionary; member high council. Member 3d legislature from Utah county. Secretary and treasurer Cedar View Building Co. Delegate to eleventh national irrigation congress 1903; school trustee and treasurer of Roosevelt school district 1911-12. Veteran Black Hawk Indian war.

P

PACE, GEORGE MILTON (son of Elisha Pace, born in 1801, in Pennsylvania, and Eliza Baldrom, born in 1802, in Ohio). Born Jan. 9, 1837, in Perry Co., Ohio. Came to Utah in 1848, David Pace company.
Married Sarah Alvira Standley (daughter of Alexander S. Standley and Philinda Upson, pioneers 1852, John C. Howell company). She was born in 1844. Their children: Sarah Alvira b. 1860, m. James Prescott 1880; George Milton b. Feb. 16, 1863, m. Elizabeth Lucretia Thomas Nov. 13, 1885; Emily b. 1864, m. William Levi Prescott 1889; Henry Riley b. 1868, m. Emma Jeffs 1892; Freeman Elisha b. 1870, m. Minnie Sweney; James Edwin b. 1872, m. Ellen Tree; Amos Franklin b. 1874, m. Margaret Emma Tree; Ira Alva b. 1877; Philinda b. 1880, m. Thurston Simpson 1898; Eliza b. 1882, m. Daniel Franklin Mitchell; Lettie Jane b. 1884, m. Edward James Tree; Alma b. 1888; Amanda b. 1890.
Bishop of Parley Park ward 1882-97. Veteran Indian wars. Died in 1897.

PACE, GEORGE MILTON, JR. (son of George Milton Pace and Sarah Alvira Standley). Born Feb. 16, 1863, Bountiful, Utah.
Married Elizabeth Lucretia Thomas Nov. 13, 1885, Logan, Utah (daughter of Charles Carter Thomas and Emeline Sessions of Heber City, Utah), who was born Feb. 12, 1866. Their child: Elvira Emeline b. Nov. 29, 1892, m. Leland Attewall Wootton.
Elder; ward teacher. Farmer; rancher; stockraiser.

PACE, JAMES EDWIN (son of George Milton Pace and Sarah Alvira Standley). Born in 1872, Parleys Park, Utah.
Married Ellen Harriet Tree (daughter of Edward William Tree and Julia Holland), who was born in 1882, in England. Their children: Julia Alvira b. 1906; Harvey Edwin b. 1908; Ralph William b. 1910; Henry Alva b. 1912.

PACE, THOMAS (son of John Pace and Ann Barker, of Durham, Eng.). Born Oct. 9, 1827, Durham. Came to Utah Sept. 26, 1862, James Wareham independent company.
Married Mary Jane Blackett March 12, 1854 (daughter of Robert C. Blackett and Ellen Mitchell, pioneers 1861, Samuel A. Woolley company). She was born April 6, 1834. Their children: John Williams b. Sept. 9, 1857, died; Mary Ellen b. May 27, 1859, m. John W. Schofield 1878; Elizabeth Ann b. May 26, 1861, died; Thomas Orson b. Feb. 14, 1863; Frances b. May 28, 1865, m. William I. Norton 1879; Lorenzo b. Oct. 17, 1867, m. Elizabeth Garrett Nov. 2, 1898; Alexander b. Dec. 14, 1869, m. Lizzie Broadhead Dec. 11, 1895; Alfonso b. Oct. 17, 1874, m. Pearl Tidwell Aug. 20, 1900; Walter Blackett b. June 11, 1879, died.
High priest; seventy; worked on St. George and Manti Temples. Early convert in England, having joined the church in September, 1849.

PACE, WILLIAM (son of James Pace born Jan. 23, 1778, in Georgia, and Mary Ann Laven, of Pennsylvania. Born July 3, 1806, in Rutherford county, Tenn.). Came to Utah Sept. 20, 1848, Brigham Young company.
Married Margaret Nichols Oct. 21, 1828 (daughter of Daniel Nichols, and Mary Alexander, of Kentucky, pioneer Brigham Young company). She was born May 30, 1808, and came to Utah with husband. Their children: James B. b. Aug. 12, 1829; Wilson D. b. July 27, 1831, m. Ann M. Redd Aug. 1852; Harvey Alexander b. Oct. 12, 1833, m. Elizabeth Ann Redd Aug. 28, 1853; William F. b. May 19, 1836, m. Caroline Evans; Granvill M. b. Nov. 6, 1838, d. child; John Alma Lawrence b. Feb. 2, 1841, m. Susanna Taylor; Joseph A. R. b. Dec. 24, 1842, d. infant; Parley Pratt b. April 8, 1844, m. Eliza Simmons, who died, m. Annie Thomas; Eli N. b. April 18, 1849, m. Nancy Lee; Mary Ann b. 1852, d. child.
Family home New Harmony, Utah.
Assisted in building fort at Provo 1849; moved to Spanish Fork 1851. Missionary to England in early 50's; bishop of Spanish Fork 1852-56; ward teacher. Member legislature from Utah county 1852-53. Located at New Harmony 1861, and opened first store. Postmaster 1861-75. Veteran Indian wars. Farmer. Died in November, 1875.

PACE, HARVEY ALEXANDER (son of William Pace and Margaret Nichols). Born Oct. 12, 1833, Murfreesboro, Rutherford county, Tenn. Came to Utah with parents.
Married Elizabeth Ann Redd Aug. 28, 1853, Spanish Fork, Utah (daughter of John H. Redd and Elizabeth Hancock of North Carolina, pioneers 1850, James Pace company). She was born Dec. 16, 1831, in North Carolina. Their children: William Harvey b. Nov. 25, 1854 (d. Feb. 15, 1898), m. Hannah Goddard; John Hardison b. Nov. 1, 1856, m. Pauline Ann Bryner; James Franklin b. April 30, 1858, m. Mary Elizabeth Mathis; Margaret Ann b. May 27, 1860; Mary E. b. Feb. 26, 1862, d. March 7, 1863; Marish Jane b. Jan. 12, 1864, m. Albert Bryner; Ann Eliza b. Oct. 31, 1865, d. July 8, 1868; Lemuel Wilson b. May 6, 1867, d. July 8, 1868; Eli Alexander b. March 6, 1869, d. July 21, 1870; Levi B. b. April 16, 1871.
Married Susan E. Keel July 11, 1870, Salt Lake City (daughter of Thomas Keel and Mary Jolly of New Harmony Utah, pioneers 1850). She was born Nov. 3, 1854, Springville, Utah. Their children: Margaret Angeline b. April 27, 1871, m. Joseph Taylor; Susan Evaline b. Oct. 3, 1873, d. June 16, 1874; Nancy Elizabeth b. March 29, 1875, m. George Prince; Henry Alexander b. April 22, 1877, m. Abigail Hammond. Families resided New Harmony, Utah.
High priest; counselor to Bishop Wilson D. Pace of New Harmony ward 15 years; ward teacher; Sunday school superintendent. Justice of peace; constable; school trustee; postmaster three years. Veteran Indian wars. Assisted in bringing immigrants to Utah. Moved from Provo to Spanish Fork 1851, and to New Harmony 1861.

PACE, WILLIAM HARVEY (son of Harvey Alexander Pace and Elizabeth Ann Redd). Born Nov. 25, 1854, Spanish Fork, Utah.
Married Hannah Goddard 1874, New Harmony, Utah (daughter of William R. Goddard and Mary Ann Pace, of Spanish Fork), who was born May 16, 1857. Their children: William H. b. April 7, 1875, m. Kathryn Middleton; Cecil b. 1877, d. infant; Maggie M. b. Dec. 7, 1878, m. Francis Hartley. Family home New Harmony.
Farmer. Died Feb. 15, 1879, Panguitch, Utah.

PACE, WILLIAM H., JR. (son of William H. Pace and Hannah Goddard). Born April 7, 1875, New Harmony, Utah.
Married Kathryn Middleton May 29, 1898, Cedar City, Utah (daughter of John Middleton and Jane Withers, of Cedar City, pioneers 1857). She was born Jan. 27, 1879.

Their children: John William b. Dec. 31, 1899; Carlos M. b. Jan. 8, 1902; Frank b. March 4, 1904; Blythe b. March 17, 1906; Dorothea b. Oct. 13, 1910. Family home, Price, Utah.
Deputy sheriff Emery county 1806-09; deputy treasurer, 1897-98; school trustee Green River, 1895-98. Merchant; manager Eastern Utah Furniture and Undertaking Co.

PACE, JOHN HARDISON (son of Harvey Alexander Pace and Elizabeth Ann Redd). Born Nov. 1, 1856.
Married Pauline Ann Bryner Dec. 25, 1875, New Harmony, Utah (daughter of Hans Ulrich Bryner and Mary Mathis, of New Harmony, pioneers Dec. 24, 1856, handcart company). She was born Dec. 2, 1857. Their children: Elizabeth Mary b. July 1, 1878, d. April 18, 1908; John Albert b. March 12, 1881, m. Ada Cottam: Albertine b. March 12, 1881, d. same day; Harvey Alexander b. Nov. 24, 1882, m. Margaret Moffatt; Edith Ann b. Oct. 1, 1884, m. John W. Prince; Pauline b. Aug. 1, 1886, d. same day; Luray Hardison b. Sept. 18, 1887, m. Natelia Mecham; Francis Marion b. Jan. 24, 1890; Rhoda b. Jan. 4, 1892; Earl b. Jan. 14, 1894; Irene b. Dec. 27, 1895. Family home Price, Utah.
First counselor to President John Insley in New Harmony ward 1875-77; worked on the Manti Temple winter of 1878; called to settle San Juan county with Silas Smith company 1879; assisted in building up the country; took part in Indian troubles; moved to Price, Emery county, 1884; was 1st counselor to Bishop George Frandsen of Price ward, 1886; missionary to southern states 1896-98; 1st counselor to President Reuben G. Miller of Emery stake 1899-1910; senior member of high council of Carbon stake May 1910 —— April 1913; after the reorganization of Carbon stake was chosen 1st counselor to President Arther W. Horsley of Carbon stake. School trustee for 20 years in the Price district. Member 1st corporate board of Price town.

PACE, JAMES FRANKLIN (son of Harvey Alexander Pace and Elizabeth Ann Redd). Born April 30, 1858, Spanish Fork, Utah.
Married Mary Elizabeth Mathis Feb. 21, 1883, St. George, Utah (daughter of Hans Heinrich Mathis and Elizabeth Hoodsmidt of Zurich, Switzerland, pioneers 1862, oxteam company). She was born March 26, 1866. Their children: Franklin b. Sept. 12, 1883, d. infant; Henry Alexander b. Aug. 23, 1884, m. Arabelle Branch; James Levi b. Dec. 29, 1886, m. Caroline Frandsen; Ida Elizabeth b. Jan. 28, 1889; William Ivan b. March 29, 1891; John Mathis b. April 7, 1893; Barbara b. April 30, 1895; Reid b. Aug. 6, 1899; Evangeline b. May 8, 1902; Fern b. Aug. 7, 1906; Fawn b. Aug. 7, 1906. Family resided Price and New Harmony, Utah.
High priest; counselor to Bishop William A. Redd; president Y. M. M. I. A.; Sunday school superintendent; ward teacher. School trustee; constable at New Harmony. Settled at New Harmony in 1861, remaining; moved to Price 1902. Helped to protect property against Indians in early days. Farmer.

PACE, HENRY ALEXANDER (son of James Franklin Pace and Mary Elizabeth Mathis). Born Aug. 23, 1884, New Harmony, Utah.
Married Arabelle Branch Sept. 9, 1910, Salt Lake City (daughter of William Henry Branch and Elia C. Coombs, pioneers Oct. 14, 1850). She was born Dec. 19, 1887. Their only child was Paul Harvey b. March 6, 1912. Family home Price, Utah.
Seventy; missionary to southern states 1906-08; president Y. M. M. I. A.; stake Sunday school superintendent; ward clerk. Farmer; stockraiser.

PACE, JOHN ALMA LAWRENCE (son of William Pace and Margaret Nichols). Born Feb. 2, 1841, in Tennessee. Came to Utah with oxteam company.
Married Susanna Taylor May 30, 1870, Salt Lake City (daughter of Allen Taylor and Hannah Egbert), who was born Sept. 30, 1852. Their children: Mary Ellen, m. Carl E. Lundquist; Hannah Margarith, m. Isaac William Odekirk; William Alma, m. Emma Reynolds; Evaline Corrilla, m. Charles Bennett; Harvey Alexander, d. child; Alfred Pace, m. Sadie Stagg; Effie Lerena. Family home Thistle Junction, Utah.
Elder. Sheepman.

PACKARD, NOAH (son of Noah Packard, born Oct. 3, 1752, Bridgewater, Mass., and Molly Hamblin). Born May 7, 1796, Plainfield, Mass. Came to Utah 1850, Jonathan Foote company.
Married Sophia Bundy June 29, 1820. She was born Jan. 27, 1800, in Southampton, and died Aug. 30, 1858, Springville, Utah. Their children: Noah Jr. b. April 22, 1821, m. Esther Pamella Phippin Oct. 27, 1844; Orren b. Dec. 25, 1822, m. Matilda Stowell; Henry b. May 6, 1825, m. Mary Chase Jan. 16, 1851; Sophia Adelia b. Oct. 1, 1828, m. William Wallace Meneray; Milan b. Oct. 7, 1830, m. Margaret Jane Haymond; Nephi b. July 1, 1832, m. Elizabeth Clucas Nov. 10, 1861; Olive Amelia b. July 5, 1837, m. Charles Jesse Craw.
High priest; bishop's counselor. Captain of the "Silver Grays". Justice of peace; alderman. Surveyor.

PACKARD, MILAN (son of Noah Packard and Sophia Bundy). Born Oct. 7, 1830.
Married Margaret Jane Haymond at Springville, Utah (daughter of Edward Owen Haymond and Margaret Ann Sissel, pioneers 1850, Thomas Johnson company). Their children: Sarah Delilah b. Aug. 21, 1858, m. William Henry Meneray Dec. 9, 1877; Milan Owen b. Oct. 7, 1860, m. Julia Crandall March 2, 1881; Martha Amelia b. Nov. 16, 1862;

Noah Lovell b. Sept. 11, 1864, m. Sarah Crandall Jan. 10, 1886; Jacob Asa b. Feb. 26, 1867, m. Eliza Robinson Feb. 9, 1889; Chillian Fay b. Nov. 8, 1869, m. Phoebe Schuler Nov. 17, 1897; Alpheus Oresta b. April 25, 1872, m. Sarah Groesbeck Sept. 11, 1898; William Melvin b. Nov. 20, 1874, m. Gertrude Harrison July 14, 1904; Ray b. June 2, 1878, m. Edna Allred Aug. 26, 1897; Preal b. March 12, 1884. Family home Springville, Utah.
Veteran Indian wars. Assisted in bringing immigrants and supplies to Utah. Located Pleasant Valley coal fields; organized Utah and Pleasant Valley R. R. Co. (what is now part of D. & R. G. R. R.). Merchant; vice president Springville Banking company.

PACKARD, NEPHI (son of Noah Packard and Sophia Bundy). Born July 1, 1832, Parkman, Ohio. Came to Utah Sept. 17, 1850, Jonathan Foote company.
Married Elizabeth Clucas Nov. 10, 1861 (daughter of Henry Clucas and Elizabeth Martin, pioneers 1855, C. A. Harper company). She was born Sept. 2, 1843, and came to Utah with parents. Their children: Lucy Elizabeth b. Sept. 18, 1862, m. Phillip W. Tukett Sept. 4, 1879; Nephi Henry b. July 15, 1864, m. Clara Jane Sanford Nov. 18, 1885; David Hyrum b. July 26, 1866, d. Jan. 20, 1910; Sophia Amelia b. Jan. 19, 1869; George Washington b. Sept. 8, 1871; William Otto b. April 17, 1874, m. Lucy Clyde Jan. 1, 1896; Pearl Shale b. Aug. 26, 1877, (d. March 24, 1909), m. Hyrum J. Owen June 17, 1902; Ernest Walton b. Aug. 29, 1879, d. Jan. 27, 1880; Jessie Maria b. April 5, 1883, d. Oct. 18, 1887.
Bishop of Springville, Utah 10 years. City councilman two terms. Assayer; carpenter and farmer. Served in the Walker, Tintic and Black Hawk wars.

PACKARD, NEPHI HENRY (son of Nephi Packard and Elizabeth Clucas. Born July 15, 1864, Springville, Utah.
Married Clara Jane Sanford Nov. 18, 1885, Logan, Utah (daughter of Cyrus Sanford and Happylona Clark, former a pioneer Oct. 15, 1850, William Snow company). She was born Oct. 19, 1866, Springville, Utah. Their children: Happy-Iona Flosa b. Sept. 20, 1886; Reuel Nephi b. Sept. 6, 1888; Othel b. March 18, 1890; Marell b. July 24, 1892, m. Clifford Carter Feb. 23, 1909; Wendell Sanford b. Oct. 13, 1894; Rhea b. March 6, 1897; Ira C. b. April 14, 1900; Clara b. May 2, 1905.
First counselor to bishop of Springville 2d ward July 24, 1904. City councilman 1902-04 and 1906-08; mayor of Springville 1907; member of public school board 1908-13.

PACKER, NATHAN W. (son of Moses and Eva Packer of Pennsylvania). Born Jan. 2, 1811, in Jefferson Co., Ohio. Came to Utah in 1848, David Evans company.
Married Elizabeth Taylor, who was born 1812, and came to Utah with husband. Their children: Lewis W. b. March 15, 1831; James b. Oct. 10, 1833, m. Polly Mecham; Isaac H. b. April 27, 1835, m. Lucy Bird; Samuel b. April 29, 1837; William b. May 22, 1838; Nathan T. b. Aug. 8, 1848, m. Mary E. Mecham; Walter M. b. April 23, 1850, m. Elizabeth Ames; Moses b. July 9, 1852; Jonathan b. Jan. 20, 1854; Edson W. b. May 14, 1857, m. Vilda Mecham. Family resided Salt Lake City, American Fork and Lehi, Utah, and Franklin, Idaho.
Married Jane Win. Their children: John and Marrion.
Built grist mill at American Fork 1850; built ferryboat on Bear river and later built first bridge across Bear river in Cache Valley. Millwright.

PACKER, JAMES (son of Nathan W. Packer and Elizabeth Taylor). Born Oct. 10, 1833, Belmont Co., Ohio. Came to Utah 1850.
Married Polly Mecham Feb. 14, 1854, Lehi, Utah (daughter of Moses Mecham and Elvira Derby, pioneers Appleton Harmon company). She was born March 15, 1833, Mercer county, Pa. Their children: Samuel L. b. Jan. 9, 1855; James b. July 21, 1856, m. Celia J. Perkins Dec. 12, 1878; Elvira E. b. March 3, 1858, m. Thomas M. Perkins; Orpha Maria b. Dec. 21, 1859; Ossian Leonidas b. Dec. 10, 1861, m. Annie S. Parkinson Jan. 1, 1885; Ann Eliza b. Dec. 27, 1863; Albert T. b. Sept. 2, 1865; Wilford b. March 10, 1868; Polly S. b. March 1, 1870, m. Andrew Shumway; Walter M. b. May 23, 1872; Josiah George b. June 24, 1874, m. Chase Wallace.
President teachers' quorum and 18th quorum seventies. Justice of peace. Settled at Franklin, Idaho, 1860.

PACKER, JAMES, JR. (son of James Packer and Polly Mecham). Born July 21, 1856, Salt Lake City.
Married Celia J. Perkins Dec. 12, 1878, Salt Lake City (daughter of Joseph Perkins and Margaret Martin, pioneers 1855, Charles A. Harper company). She was born April 20, 1860, Franklin, Idaho. Their children: James Manuel b. Feb. 6, 1880, m. Lonetta Johnson; Luda Celia b. Sept. 26, 1881, m. Albert E. Johnson; Joseph Clement b. June 22, 1884; Philando Perkins b. Nov. 24, 1886, m. H. Veressa Wanward; Laura May b. June 1, 1889, m. Ernest C. Johnson; Lionel b. May 29, 1892; Lizzie Alta b. June 11, 1894, m. B. G. Weaver; twins b. 1897, died; Ila b. Aug. 7, 1905, died. Family home Franklin, Idaho.
Settled at Franklin 1860. President teachers' quorum, elders' quorum and 18th quorum seventies; high priest; missionary to southern states. James and his mother were first white child and woman to set foot on site where Franklin now stands April 13, 1860.

PIONEERS AND PROMINENT MEN OF UTAH

PACKER, OSSIAN LEONIDAS (son of James Packer and Polly Mecham). Born Dec. 10, 1861, Franklin, Idaho.
Married Annie Smart Parkinson Jan. 1, 1885, Logan temple (daughter of Samuel Rose Parkinson and Charlotte H. Smart). She was born Oct. 15, 1867. Their children: Samuel P. b. March 24, 1890, m. Martha Geddes Sutherland; Clyde P. b. Feb. 2, 1892; Anna P. b. Dec. 24, 1893; Edna P. b. Jan. 23, 1896; Grant b. March 12, 1898; Eva P. b. Feb. 1, 1901; Ora P. b. Oct. 17, 1903; Lee P. b. Aug. 25, 1906; James Lyman b. May 14, 1908. Family resided Franklin and Preston, Idaho.
First counselor in Franklin ward Y. M. M. I. A.; first counselor in Oneida stake Y. M. M. I. A.; first counselor to Bishop H. T. Rogers of Preston First ward; first counselor to Bishop John A. Morrison of Preston First ward 1913. Justice of peace, Preston precinct, Oneida Co., Idaho.

PACKETT, CHARLES. Born in France. Came to Utah 1852, oxteam company.
Married Axie Emeterre. Their children: Jane, m. Ervin Wilson; Sarah, d. child; Mary Ellen, m. Andrew Dudley; Martha, m. Egar Houghten; Emily, m. Justus Manville Dudley; Emeline, m. Aaron Gay; Julia, m. David Mickesell; Joseph, m. Elizabeth Boyack. Family home Spanish Fork, Utah.
Seventy. Carpenter; cooper; farmer. Died at Spanish Fork.

PADFIELD, SAMUEL (son of Jeremiah Padfield and Mary Tayton of Somersetshire. Eng.). Born in 1835 in Somersetshire. Came to Utah in 1859.
Married Christina Hutchinson in 1871 at Salt Lake City (daughter of David Hutchinson and Jeanette Crookston), who was born in 1856. Their children: Samuel James b. 1872, m. Catherine Evans; David b. 1879; Thomas b. 1881, m. Alice Pellman; Jessie b. 1883; Mary Jane b. 1885, m. Ira Preston; Amelia b. 1887, m. Towell Larson; Violet b. 1900; George Washington and Daniel, died. Family home American Fork, Utah.

PADFIELD, SAMUEL JAMES (son of Samuel Padfield and Christina Hutchinson). Born in 1872 at American Fork.
Married Catherine Evans (daughter of William Evans). Their children: Pearl b. 1896; James b. 1898; Thelma b. 1900.

PAGE, DANIEL (son of Joseph Page and Sarah Ingram of Newport, Cumberland county, N. J.). Born July 11, 1810, at Newport. Came to Utah September, 1852, Captain Outhouse company.
Married Mary Socwell April 18, 1821, in New Jersey (daughter of Jonathan Socwell and Lorana Whitaker of Dividing Creeks. N. J.). She was born April 26, 1805. Their children: Ruth b. May 1, 1823, m. Samuel H. Rogers; David b. Nov. 17, 1824; Daniel b. June 23, 1827, m. Caroline Pettigrew; Joseph b. Feb. 6, 1830, m. Elizabeth Mills, m. Alice Mills; Lucy Ann b. Sept. 3, 1831, m. George R. Dare; Jonathan S. b. June 4, 1833, m. Mary Leaver; Mary Ellen b. March 1, 1835, m. Edward Davis Wade; George Washington b. Nov. 15, 1836, m. Abby Champion, m. Kate P. Stanger; William Whitaker b. Feb. 15, 1839; Lorana b. Aug. 7, 1843, m. Samuel H. Rogers; Jeremiah Day b. Feb. 21, 1847, m. Deseret Page. Family home Newport, Cumberland county, N. J.
High priest. Indian war veteran. Farmer. Died Aug. 17, 1882, at Mount Pleasant, Utah.

PAGE, JOSEPH (son of Daniel Page and Mary Socwell). Born Feb. 6, 1830, near Newport, N. J. Came to Utah 1852.
Married Elizabeth Mills Aug. 8, 1863, Mt. Pleasant, Utah (daughter of Thomas Mills and Alice Allen of Radcliffe, Lancashire, Eng.). She was born March 16, 1844, d. Jan. 14, 1869. Their children: Joseph Thomas b. June 5, 1864, died; Mary Elizabeth b. Sept. 12, 1866, m. S. H. Freston; Jonathan Socwell b. Jan. 9, 1869, died. Family home, Mt. Pleasant.
Married Alice Mills May 3, 1869, Salt Lake City (daughter of Thomas Mills and Alice Allen of Radcliffe, Lancashire, Eng.). She was born Jan. 2, 1847. Their children: Joseph Ulysesss b. June 23, 1870; Edward C. b. Jan. 29, 1872, died; William T. b. May 11, 1874; Jeremiah I. b. Feb. 21, 1876, m. Ida Jensen; Alice Addie b. April 3, 1878, m. Daniel W. Hancock; Ruth b. May 6, 1880, d. infant; Lorana b. Nov. 13, 1881, m. Joseph Willard Anderson; Samuel R. b. Feb. 12, 1884, m. Lydia Jane McClemonds; Renzie b. Feb. 6, 1886, d. aged 8; Eulalia May b. April 23, 1888, m. Niels S. Nielsen. Family resided at Mt. Pleasant, Orangeville and Roosevelt, Utah.
High priest. Mayor of Mt. Pleasant 10 years; postmaster at Mt. Pleasant 12 years. Assisted in bringing immigrants to Utah 1862. Indian war veteran; member Nauvoo Legion. One of Mt. Pleasant's first school teachers. Farmer; stockraiser; apiarist. Died Jan. 29, 1911, Roosevelt, Utah.

PAGE, SAMUEL R. (son of Joseph Page and Alice Mills). Born Feb. 12, 1884, Mt. Pleasant, Utah.
Married Lydia Jane McClemonds March 21, 1910, Vernal, Utah. (daughter of Samuel McClemonds and Mary Ann Hartle of Vernal, Utah, pioneers 1853). She was born May 8, 1888. Their children: Joseph b. Jan. 28, 1911; Jonathan Samuel b. April 21, 1912. Family home Roosevelt, Utah.
Deacon. Farmer and apiarist.

PAGE, JONATHAN SOCWELL (son of Daniel Page and Mary Socwell). Born June 4, 1833, Newport, N. J. Came to Utah Sept. 3, 1852, with parents and family.
Married Mary Leaver Aug. 12, 1855, Salt Lake City (daughter of Samuel and Mary Ann Leaver of New York, N. Y., formerly of Sheffield, Eng., pioneers Sept. 1852). She was born Aug. 26, 1837. Their children: Jonathan Socwell b. May 14, 1856, m. Lilyus Curtis May 23, 1878; Anna M. b. April 26, 1858, m. Samuel J. Rich; Samuel Leaver b. Nov. 16, 1859, m. Cena Anderson; Mary L. b. Jan. 2, 1862, m. Edward S. Reid; Ruth E. b. March 28, 1864, m. John J. Powell; Hannah Elizabeth b. Jan. 26, 1866, m. George A. Peery; Joseph Edmund b. Feb. 21, 1868, m. Gertrude Thurman; William Henry b. Sept. 22, 1869, m. Lucia Daniels; Nellie Ingram b. Aug. 8, 1872, m. August J. Hanson; George Milton b. Dec. 3, 1874; Hartlett Hall b. Feb. 9, 1877; Ethel A. b. March 7, 1879, m. Thomas Crandall; Cora V. b. March 27, 1881. Family home Payson, Utah.
Bishop's counselor Payson ward; president high priests' quorum Nebo stake; patriarch. Captain cavalry in Walker and Black Hawk Indian wars and in Utah militia; participated in Echo Canyon campaign. Commissioner Utah county 15 years; justice of the peace; alderman and mayor Payson, Utah, 18 years; member state board of equalization; member state legislature—house two terms, senate one term.

PAGE, JONATHAN SOCWELL, JR. (son of Jonathan S. Page and Mary Leaver). Born May 14, 1856, Salt Lake City.
Married Lilyus M. Curtis May 23, 1876, Salt Lake City (daughter of George Curtis, born Oct. 27, 1823, Pontiac, Mich., and Emma Whaley of England, pioneers Oct. 1848). She was born June 10, 1859. Their children: Emma L. b. March 25, 1879, m. Thomas W. Lerwill; Mary Page b. May 3, 1881, m. Laban Harding; Jonathan Socwell b. Nov. 23, 1889, m. Clara Huish; Arza Curtis b. Jan. 7, 1887, m. Ethel A. Taylor; Eva b. March 6, 1889, m. William Wanlass; George W. b. Feb. 19, 1893; Earl Leaver b. April 8, 1897; Anna b. Sept. 29, 1901. Family home Payson, Utah.
Missionary to West Virginia Nov. 1899 to June 1901; bishop of Payson second ward Nov. 1891 to Feb. 1901; ordained president of Nebo stake of Zion Feb. 13, 1901. Justice of the peace one term; recorder for Payson, Utah, three terms; city councilman one term; postmaster at Payson eight years. Merchant; farmer and horticulturist.

PAGE, JAMES. Born Aug. 21, 1815, Wyonondham, Eng. Came to Utah Sept. 13, 1861, Joseph Horne company.
Married Louisa Graves, who was born Dec. 28, 1820, and came to Utah with her husband. Their children: William b. Aug. 4, 1838, m. Mary Ann Clark March 24, 1862; Martha b. June 28, 1840, m. William Waddoups Nov. 27, 1864; Maria b. March 16, 1842, m. Henry Tingey 1862; Thomas b. Dec. 19, 1843, m. Mary Ann Waddoups May 11, 1867; Samuel b. March 12, 1845, died; Louisa May b. April 11, 1847, and Louisa b. Feb. 7, 1849, died; Hyrum b. June 27, 1851, m. Emma Jane Tingey March 21, 1873; Alma b. Oct. 5, 1852, m. Fanney Ashby; Cyrus b. March 10, 1854, m. Susa Ashby March 12, 1875; Orson b. Oct. 14, 1856; Lorenzo b. Dec. 31, 1858, m. Jemima Lewis Feb. 16, 1888; Hannah Bell b. March 15, 1860, died; James b. Feb. 12, 1862, m. Emma Kemp Dec. 12, 1886. Family home Bountiful, Utah.
Farmer.

PAGE, THOMAS (son of James Page and Louisa Graves). Born Dec. 19, 1843, Birmingham, Eng.
Married Mary Ann Waddoups May 11, 1867, Salt Lake City (daughter of Thomas Waddoups and Elizabeth Porter, pioneers August, 1868, Horten Gate company). She was born Jan. 3, 1845, Walgrave on Sow, Eng. Their children: Willard James b. May 22, 1868, m. Lillian E. Thurgood Nov. 16, 1892; Irvin Thomas b. Sept. 27, 1870, m. Martha Jane Smith Oct. 12, 1892; Joseph Hyrum b. Nov. 2, 1873, m. Ada West March 31, 1904; Orson Mark b. Oct. 6, 1876, m. Anna M. Parker April 27, 1904; Porter Elizabeth b. Nov. 27, 1878, died; Louisa May b. Oct. 10, 1881, m. John Ray George April 15, 1904; Hannah Pearl b. Oct. 24, 1884, m. John Wolley Randall Dec. 14, 1910; Annabell b. Oct. 24, 1887. Family home Bountiful, Utah.
Assisted in the construction of the line of the Deseret Telegraph Co.; worked on Utah Central railroad. School trustee district No. 2, Davis county.

PALMER, ABRAM WHITNEY. Born Dec. 14, 1807, New York. Came to Utah in 1847, captain of own company of fifty.
Married Huldah Catherine Hill in 1857 (daughter of Richard Return Hill and Rhoda Wheeler of Missouri, pioneers 1850). She was born Jan. 7, 1842. Their children: Delilah b. 1858, m. William Charles Mellor; Josephine b. 1861, m. William Litchfield; Catherine Althea b. 1863, m. Severin Holger Grundvig; Richard Marcellos b. 1866, m. Amanda Stephens; Mary b. 1869, m. Brigham Pickett; Frank Abram b. 1871, m. Emma Keeneson.
High priest; bishop of Cainesville, Mo.; counselor to Lorin Farr in Weber stake presidency. School teacher. Died May 25, 1875, Fayette, Utah.

PALMER, MIFFLIN (son of Joseph Palmer and Esther Leonard of Pennsylvania). Born June 21, 1813, Chester county, Pa. Came to Utah 1861, Joseph Horne company.
Married Kathrine K. Dolbey Dec. 23, 1837, Chester county,

Pa. (daughter of Abram Dolbey and Katherine King of Chester county). She was born April 6, 1817. Their children: Rebecca W.; Phoebe C.; Selinda D.; Elesia E.; A. Morris; Sarah Bethula, m. John C. Sharp; Laura; Esther. Family home, Salt Lake City. Blacksmith.

PALMER, THOMAS (son of Thomas Palmer). Born Jan. 16, 1820, Windsor, Berkshire, Eng. Came to Utah in 1856. Married Frances Starkins in 1856, Salt Lake City, who was born in England. Their children: William C. b. Nov. 30, 1857, m. Margrett Condie Oct. 13, 1881, m. Emily Jennett Smith March 7, 1900; Thomas. m. Ruth Stewart; Fannie, died; John, m. Eliza Wainwright. Family home Enterprise, Morgan Co., Utah.
Elder; high priest; bishop's counselor Enterprise ward of Morgan stake. Farmer; stockraiser.

PALMER, WILLIAM C. (son of Thomas Palmer and Frances Starkins). Born Nov. 30, 1857, Salt Lake City.
Married Margrett Condie Oct. 13, 1881, Salt Lake City (daughter of Gibson Condie and Elizabeth Robinson), who was born in 1858, American Fork, Utah. Their children: Thomas C. b. Oct. 30, 1882; William G. b. July 16, 1884; Heber C. b. Dec. 23, 1885; Jedediah Morgan b. Dec. 23, 1885; Joseph Earl b. Feb. 16, 1888; John Olive b. Feb. 16, 1888; Maggie Elizabeth b. Nov. 1, 1889.
Married Emily Jennett Smith March 7, 1900, Logan, Utah (daughter of Nathaniel Smith and Sarah Ann Sim, pioneers 1847). Elmer S. b. March 12, 1901; Lulu b. Nov. 29, 1902; Jennie b. Feb. 4, 1905; Leone b. Oct. 23, 1907; Orvil Nathaniel b. July 13, 1908. Family home Preston, Idaho.
High priest; ward teacher. Farmer; stockraiser.

PALMER, ZEMIRA (son of George A. Palmer and Phebe Draper of Canada). Born Aug. 9, 1831. Came to Utah with first detachment Mormon battalion in 1847.
Married Sally Knight Dec. 1, 1851, Salt Lake City (daughter of Newel Knight and Lydia Goldthwait of Kirtland, Ohio). She was born Dec. 1, 1836. Their children: Alma Z., m. Alzada S. Kartchner; Martha and Mary, twins, died; Lydia A., m. John Kartchner; Phebe, m. Mark Elisha Kartchner; James W., m. Mary Ann Black; George A., m. Lucity Stalworthy; Jesse M., m. Amanda Hoyt; Emma, m. Wilford W. Heaton; Newel, m. Lydia Robertson; Joseph, m. Helen Jane Robertson; Chloe.
Married Caroline Jacques in 1856 at Provo, Utah (daughter of Thomas Jacques). Their children: Sarah A., m. Amos Cox; Susan, m. Benjamin Black; George Edw'.., m. Estella MacElprang; Daniel W., m. Violet Walker; Eve m. Theodore Cox; Laura, m. Henry Walker. Families resided at Provo.
Teacher. Veteran Indian war; took part in Echo Canyon trouble. Farmer. Died Oct. 22, 1880, Orderville, Utah.

PAPWORTH, JAMES (son of Richard Papworth and Susan Washington of Cambridge, Eng.). Born Jan. 2, 1826, Cambridge, Eng. Came to Utah Oct. 26, 1864, William Hyde company.
Married Elizabeth Tavener 1847, Cambridge, Eng. (daughter of Osborne Denton Tavener and Ellen Watson of Cambridge, latter pioneer 1866). She was born Jan. 3, 1827. Their children: Susannah b. Dec. 4, 1848, m. George Covell; William. Watson b. Oct. 23, 1850, d. June 20, 1859; Richard b. Feb. 14, 1852, m. Elizabeth Davis; Emma Elizabeth b. Dec. 10, 1853, m. James Kemp; James Robert Hull b. April 8, 1856; Clara b. April 2, 1858, m. Oren Hadlock; Frances Washington b. March 18, 1860, d. March 13, 1865; Mary Ann b. June 19, 1862, d. June 29, 1864; Henry Tavener b. Oct. 24, 1864, d. next day; Osborne Tavener b. Jan. 27, 1866, m. Grace Christy Covey Dec. 24, 1883; George Washington b. Jan. 7, 1869, d. Oct. 19, 1869. Family home Chesterton, Cambridge, Eng.
Died March 23, 1898.

PAPWORTH, RICHARD (son of James Papworth and Elizabeth Tavener). Born Feb. 14, 1852. Came to Utah Oct. 26, 1864, William Hyde company.
Married Elizabeth Davis Oct. 21, 1874, Big Cottonwood, Utah (daughter of John Meeks Davis and America Jane Overland, former pioneer 1854, latter 1856). She was born June 21, 1853, in Beaver Co., Utah. Their children: Florence May b. Dec. 31, 1875, m. Louie Ensign; Richard b. Aug. 22, 1877, m. Miss Llewellyn; Lillian J. b. March 2, 1879, m. William B. Hall; Raymond E. b. Feb. 2, 1881, m. Bertha King; Parley A. b. Feb. 15, 1883, m. Edna Cottrell; Ruby E. b. Jan. 9, 1885, m. John H. Parks; Marvie B. b. Sept. 22, 1887; Charles E. b. Dec. 8, 1889, d. infant; Leroy J. b. Feb. 15, 1892, m. Ethel Duffield; Clyde J. b. Jan. 9, 1895; Wesley G. b. Dec. 29, 1897; Lyle B. b. March 30, 1899. Family home, Salt Lake City.

PAPWORTH, OSBORNE TAVENER (son of James Papworth and Elizabeth Tavener). Born Jan. 27, 1866, Salt Lake City.
Married Grace Christy Covey Dec. 24, 1883 (daughter of Enoch Covey and Jannet Carruth Young of Salt Lake City). She was born May 10, 1865. Their children: Jannet Elizabeth b. July 17, 1885, m. Willard Lancaster; Ethel Grace b. April 27, 1887, m. Thomas J. Call; Osborn Enoch b. March 7, 1889; Elmo William b. Nov. 27, 1890; Leona

PIONEERS AND PROMINENT MEN OF UTAH 1085

May b. Nov. 3, 1892; Stephen Mack b. March 29, 1895; Royle Spencer b. April 4, 1897; Helmar Covey b. June 9, 1899; Lavon Ree b. Feb. 4, 1901; Thelma Mayne b. June 17, 1903; Harold Ray b. Oct. 12, 1905; Roland Covey b. Sept. 12, 1907.

PARCELL, JOHN C., of Wallsburg and Provo, Utah. Came to Utah 1854, Captain Bullock company.
Married Esther Lewis. Their child: Martha Jane b. Dec. 21, 1882, m. Ethan Allen Duke.

PARDEE, JAMES D. (son of William E. Pardee and Helen S. Dickey of Cleveland, Ohio). Born July 27, 1864, Cleveland. Came to Utah Aug. 1, 1891.
Married Daisy S. Taylor April 29, 1902, Salt Lake City (daughter of Levi Taylor and Emaline Owens of Kaysville, Utah). She was born in November, 1876. Family home Salt Lake City.
Attorney-at-law.

PARK, HAMILTON GRAY (son of Samuel Park and Isabell Gray of Kilbarnie, Scotland). Born Nov. 25, 1826, at Kilbarnie. Came to Utah in 1852.
Married Annes Steele at Kilbarnie (daughter of John Steele and Jenette Alexander of that place). Their children: Jenette A., m. Heber Clayton; Hamilton G., d. infant; Marion M., d. aged 5; Isabel G., m. Scipio Kenner; Edwin A., d. aged 7; Agnes S. d. aged 5; John S., d. infant; Edwin A., d. aged 7; Annie, m. Joshua Midgley; Mabel, m. Joseph Thomas. Family home, Salt Lake City.
President high priests' quorum Ensign stake; bishop's counselor 13th ward, Salt Lake City; missionary to Scotland 1869-70. Worked at Z. C. M. I. 32 years. Died May 1, 1912.

PARK, JOHN (son of James Park and Marion Allen of Kent, near Glasgow, Scotland). Born May 11, 1802, Glasgow. Came to Utah Sept. 29, 1847, Edward Hunter company.
Married Louisa Smith March 24, 1840, Plympton, West Ontario, Canada (daughter of William Smith and Mary Ann Staples of Lambton, Ontario, pioneers Sept. 30, 1847, John Taylor company). She was born June 24, 1818, and came to Utah in October, 1847, Edward Hunter company. Their children: Jane, m. Albert Jones; Mary Ann, m. Isaac Brockbank; Marion, m. Daniel Vincent; Louisa, m. Harvey Harper; James William; John Smith, m. Martha M. Parker; Joseph Smith, m. Maria Elizabeth Harding; Martha Ellen, m. Thomas W. Allen; David Smith, m. Epsy Pace; Margaret Naomi, m. John W. Hoover; Andrew Albert, d. aged 18. Family home Provo, Utah.
Elder; high priest. Veteran Echo Canyon campaign. Farmer. Died March 30, 1869.

PARK, JOHN SMITH (son of John Park and Louisa Smith). Born Dec. 30, 1849, Provo, Utah.
Married Martha M. Parker Oct. 26, 1874, Salt Lake City (daughter of Wyman Minard Parker and Martha Simmons of Morgan City, Utah). She was born Oct. 28, 1856. Their children: Johnnie Parker b. Oct. 4, 1875, died; Hugh b. Aug. 12, 1877, m. Nora Fillerup; Nora b. Aug. 29, 1879, died; Albert Andrew b. Sept. 2, 1881, m. Ruth Dilworth; Louisa E. b. June 21, 1883, m. Josiah Howard; William Smith b. Sept. 3, 1885, m. Lizzie Mecham; Eliza Iona b. Aug. 16, 1889, m. Alfred E. Aston; Mary Ann b. May 20, 1893; Uella Jane b. Nov. 6, 1896; Erma Cetris b. June 20, 1899. Family home, Provo.
Member elders' quorum seventies; teacher; ward clerk 1888-1911 Timpanogos ward. Constable two years; justice of peace 14 years; water superintendent. Fruitgrower.

PARK, JOSEPH SMITH (son of John Park and Louisa Smith). Born Aug. 1, 1852, Provo, Utah.
Married Mariah Elizabeth Harding Dec. 21, 1876, Provo (daughter of Samuel Harding and Mary Jeannette Stowe of Provo). She was born Sept. 16, 1858. Their children: John Samuel b. Sept. 19, 1877, m. Mary Hann; Elizabeth Jean b. May 20, 1879, m. Andrew H. Scott; Mary Ellen b. July 28, 1881, m. John Thurgood; Louisa b. May 2, 1883, m. John K. Gilbert; Estella Maud b. March 28, 1885, m. S. Julius Duggins; Lydia Lynn b. April 27, 1887; Edna Florence b. Jan. 26, 1889, m. George Wesley Meyers; Joseph Earl b. March 8, 1891, died; William Vernee b. June 14, 1892, died; Verl Reed b. Dec. 10, 1894; Erma Leree b. Aug. 25, 1897; Vera Lorene b. Dec. 24, 1900; Melba b. Dec. 26, 1904.
High priest. Gardener courthouse grounds. Farmer.

PARK, WILLIAM (son of James Park and Marion Allen, who had emigrated to Ontario, Canada). Born Oct. 26, 1805, Camsiang, Scotland. Came to Utah Sept. 29, 1847, Edward Hunter company.
Married Jane Duncan in 1828 in Canada (daughter of John Duncan and Agnes Thompson of Canada, pioneers, Edward Hunter company). She was born in 1808. Their children: Agnes Thompson b. 1828, m. John Borrowman; James D. b. July 15, 1830, m. Marion Park; John D. b. Jan. 18, 1832, m. Elizabeth Hill; Marion b. 1834, m. James Gordon; Jane b. 1836, m. Alexander H. Hill; William D. b. Sept. 25, 1837, m. Jeanette Gordon; Hugh D. b. Feb. 24, 1840, m. Agnes Hill; Mary b. 1813, m. Peter Sutton; Andrew

1086   PIONEERS AND PROMINENT MEN OF UTAH

Duncan b. March 24, 1845, m. Jane Ann Ellison; Joseph D. b. Aug. 18, 1848, m. Agnes Chappel; Martha Hannah, died. Family resided Salt Lake City and Cottonwood, Utah. Married Janet Finley (no date given). High priest. Farmer and stockraiser. Died March 11, 1890, Mill Creek, Utah.

PARK, ANDREW DUNCAN (son of William Park and Jane Duncan). Born March 24, 1845, in Canada. Came to Utah in 1847 with parents. Married Jane Ann Ellison March 14, 1868, Salt Lake City (daughter of James Ellison and Alice Halliwell of Nephi, Utah, pioneers Oct. 14, 1853, C. H. Wheelock company). She was born in England March 18, 1849. Their children: Alice Ellison b. March 16, 1869, m. Reuben J. Bailey; Martha Jane b. Oct. 26, 1871, m. John Frank Pexton; William Andrew b. June 22, 1874, m. Emma M. Miller; James Henry b. April 9, 1877, m. Sadie B. Flory; Ethel Gertrude b. Nov. 23, 1880, m. William Eugene Watts; Lilly May b. May 11, 1883, m. Jesse Hulse; Amanda Fern b. Jan. 28, 1886, m. Edward J. Mooney; Pearl Lyle b. Nov. 10, 1890, m. James Ernest Neilson; Clive P. S. b. April 29, 1895, m. Elnora C. Draper. Family home Mill Creek, Utah. High priest. School trustee Mill Creek. Farmer.

PARKE, CHARLES (son of Harrison Parke and Hulda Curtis of Albion, Idaho). Born 1834 in Illinois. Came to Utah in 1848. Married Lavinna Coltrin Dec. 13, 1853, Salt Lake City (daughter of Graham Coltrin and Anner Norwood of Ohio, pioneers 1850). She was born in 1832. Their children: William Henry, m. Mary Lucinda Capener; Joseph, m. Elizabeth Harris; Charles Ira, m. Sarah Vaughn; Jane, m. James B. Hitt. Family home Conant, Cassia Co., Idaho. Rancher and sheepraiser. Died May 2, 1902.

PARKE, WILLIAM HENRY (son of Charles Parke and Lavinna Coltrin). Born Dec. 15, 1855, at Bountiful, Utah. Married Mary Lucinda Capener, July 14, 1881, Centerville, Utah (daughter of William Capener and Ellen Rigby of Centerville, pioneers 1852). She was born Aug. 11, 1865. Their children: Clarence W., m. Christie Hatch; William C., m. Alice Arbuckle; Dale H., m. May Rich Taylor; Ellen Lavinna; Ralph G., m. La Verne Mason; Sarah M., m. Edward R. Knerr; Lois I.; Grace E.; Marion. Family home Riverside, Utah. Rancher and sheepraiser. Died Feb. 2, 1907.

PARKE, DALE H. (son of William Henry Parke and Mary Lucinda Capener). Born July 17, 1885, Malta, Idaho. Married May Rich Taylor Dec. 14, 1910, Farmington, Utah (daughter of John W. Taylor and May Leona Rich of Farmington). She was born Oct. 30, 1885. Family home, Salt Lake City. Attorney-at-law. Member law firm of Booth, Lee, Badger, Rich & Parke.

PARKER, ABEL (son of James Parker, a veteran of the War of 1812, and Nancy Fulford of Brockville, Ontario Canada). He was born June 27, 1815, Brockville, Canada. Came to Utah June, 1863. Married Isabel Marshall (Elliott) January, 1838, Brockville (daughter of John Marshall and Mary Wilson of Deanston, Perthshire, Scotland). Their children: James, m. Lucretia Sherry; Nancy, m. George A. Follick; William, m. Bell Gallagher. Family home Middle Canyon, near Tooele, Utah. Child by second marriage: Abel, b. 1874. Member of presidency of high priests' quorum of Tooele stake. President Tooele City Cooperative Mercantile Institution, and of the Tooele County Milling Company. Farmer and w man. Died Jan. 22, 1896, at his home near Tooele mill Isabel Marshall was the widow of George Elliott.

PARKER, HENRY. Born Sept. 26, 1807, Brindle, Lancashire, England. Came to Utah Oct. 13, 1850, Edward Hunter company. Married Ann Comings, Beadle, Yorkshire, Eng. Her father died Sept. 3, 1843 at Nauvoo, Ill. She was born May 22, 1820. Their children: John Parker b. May 1, 1837, died Aug. 15, 1846; William b. Aug. 30, 1843, m. Debora Greer. Married Nancy Riley, who was born May 20, 1817, Lancashire, Eng. Their children: Joseph H. b. Feb. 27, 1845, m. Emaline Jenkins Jan. 13, 1865; Vilate b. June 30, 1847, d. Jan. 28, 1861; Heber T. b. Aug. 30, 1849, m. Sarah Ann Cooper; Ruth b. Jan. 1, 1852, m. Joseph Cooper; Willard b. Oct. 7, 1854, m. Isabel Hendry; Sarah b. Feb. 16, 1857, m. William Murray; Henry A. b. Aug. 11, 1859, d. Jan. 23, 1861; Nancy Ann b. Aug. 11, 1859, d. Feb. 15, 1861. Family home Wellsville, Cache Co., Utah. Married Lucy Burgler who was born Jan. 23, 1828, and died Feb. 8, 1899. No children. Missionary to Great Britain 1878.

PARKER, JOSEPH H. (son of Henry Parker and Nancy Riley). Born Feb. 27, 1845, Nauvoo, Ill. Married Emarine Jenkins Jan. 13, 1865, at Salt Lake City (daughter of William Jenkins and Mary Roebarr, pioneers Oct. 13, 1850, Edward Hunter company). She was born Feb. 12, 1843, St. Louis. Mo. Their children: William J. b. Nov. 26, 1867, m. Alta Hardman Jan. 23, 1907; Sarah b. Jan. 2, 1869, m. Henry Durfee Dec. 13, 1888; Mary J. b. Aug. 22, 1871; Carrie b. Oct. 10, 1873, m. Samuel Miller Oct. 16, 1895; Joseph J. b. March 10, 1876, m. Mary Salversen, Jan. 24, 1907; Nancy b. March 27, 1878, m. Henry Curtis Nov. 14, 1907; Henry J. b. June 12, 1881, m. Emma Redford July 17, 1901; Emma J. b. Feb. 10, 1884, m. John Glenn Feb. 27, 1907; Roy J. b. Nov. 4, 1886, m. Cloe Pearce March 23, 1910; Emma Durfee (granddaughter) b. Oct. 20, 1889, m. O. W. Garrett Dec. 20, 1911, Stella b. May 5, 1902; William b. Jan. 14, 1904; Henry b. Oct. 30, 1905; Reese b. July 1, 1907; Elva b. Dec. 11, 1908; Pearl b. Aug. 14, 1911. Family home Mt. Sterling, Cache Co., Utah. Missionary to Council Bluffs, 1864, for immigrants, and to Arizona, 1876; superintendent of Wellsville and assistant superintendent Mt. Sterling Sunday schools.

PARKER, JOHN. Born Aug. 17, 1775, Chaigley Lane, Eng. Came to Utah Aug. 29, 1852, Captain Parker oxteam company, independent. Married Ellen Heskins, who was born Jan. 23, 1778. Their children: Isabella, m. Thomas Cotton; Ann, m. Thomas Watson; John; Ellen b. July 7, 1817, m. William Corbidge Jan. 1840; Alice, m. Edward Corbidge; William; Mary, m. Samuel W. Richards; Elizabeth b. March 14, 1837, m. John R. Winder Jan. 1, 1857. High priest. Deceased.

PARKER, JOHN DAVIS (son of Abel Parker and Mary Davis of New York). Born Nov. 22, 1799, Saratoga, N. Y. Came to Utah in 1852. Married Almeda Sophia Roundy Feb. 8, 1846, Nauvoo, Ill. (daughter of Shadrach Roundy and Betsy Quimby of Nauvoo, pioneers July 24, 1847). She was born March 7, 1829, at Spafford, N. Y. Their children: Jared Curtis b. Dec. 29, 1847, d. infant; John Davis, Jr., b. April 12, 1849, d. age 19; Malinda b. April 4, 1851; Charles b. Jan. 31, 1853; Mary Ellen b. Oct. 16, 1856; Betsy Jane b. March 21, 1858; Otho b. Nov. 29, 1861; Lauraette b. Feb. 26, 1865; Almeda Sophia b. March 7, 1868; Samantha b. May 27, 1872. Family home Kanarraville, Iron Co., Utah. Member first quorum seventies; missionary; member Zion's camp; high priest. Member of legislature; assessor; collector. Wagonwright; farmer. Died Feb. 27, 1891.

PARKER, JOSEPH F. (son of Thomas Bryant Parker and Martha Ann Nelson of Missouri, former born in Virginia, latter Kentucky). Born April 7, 1841, Marion county, Mo. Came to Utah in July, 1852. Married Mary E. Ross June 30, 1861, Heber City, Utah (daughter of Thomas Ross and Rachel E. Ross Smith), who was born March 4, 1845, in Hancock county, Ill. Their children: Huldah Jane, m. James Leavitt; Joseph William, m. Maggie Neil; Thomas Bryant, m. Ada Gilbert; John Alma, m. Mary C. Gilbert Oct. 9, 1889; Mary Susannah; Anna Elizabeth; Amy Elleanor; Rachel Estella; Ella Minerva; James Marion; Alta Frances. Married Adelia Cooley June 11, 1890, Salt Lake City (daughter of Benjamin Osborne and Frances Rodebach Cooley), who was born March 11, 1874, at Joseph, Utah. Their children: Melvin b. May 27, 1891, m. Brigham Young Baird; Ada Lavern b. Sept. 22, 1893; Oriel F. b. Aug. 21, 1895; Frances Marie b. Oct. 11, 1897; Florence Adelia b. Sept. 17, 1899; Byron Nelson b. Oct. 17, 1901. Bishop of Joseph, Utah, for years.

PARKER, JOSHUA (son of Joshua Parker of New York). Born Nov. 2, 1809, New York City. Came to Utah Sept. 7, 1852, Robert Wimmer company. Married Drucilla D. Hartley in 1844 at Nauvoo, Ill. (daughter of Mary Dickey of Mercer, Pa.). She was born July 23, 1824. Their children: Martin (adopted), m. Nora Robbins; Orson H., m. Effie Minkler; Joshua Jr., and Benjamin, d. infants; Frank W., m. Elizabeth Tuckfield; Melissa M., m. Joseph W. Summerhays; Hannah Jane, m. Fred Ballwinkle; Parley P., m. Rhoda Lee; Fredrick A., m. Mary Thomas; Charles H., m. Ida Aschisson; Ann E., m. Alexander D. Edward; Daniel, m. Annie Morris; Joseph A., m. Fannie Westman. Family home, Salt Lake City. Member 24th quorum seventies; block teacher. Carpenter and cabinetmaker. Died July 17, 1880.

PARKER, FRANK W. (son of Joshua Parker and Drucilla D. Hartley). Born Sept. 2, 1850, Council Bluffs, Iowa. Came to Utah in September, 1852. Married Elizabeth Tuckfield in Oct. 1883 at Ogden, Utah (daughter of James and Elizabeth Tuckfield of England, pioneers 1862). She was born February, 1863. Their children: Bessie, d. aged 6; Birdette b. 1889, m. Mr. Bertosh; Franklin O. b. 1890. Family home, Salt Lake City. Mining engineer.

PARKER, CHARLES H. (son of Joshua Parker and Drucilla D. Hartley). Born March 31, 1861, Salt Lake City. Married Ida Zachrisson March 25, 1885, at Logan, Utah (daughter of Methias Zachrisson and Emma Anderson of Göteborg, Sweden, who came to Utah in 1879). She was born Nov. 5, 1864. Their children: Charles L. b. Aug. 11,

1887; Ida F. b. Oct. 29, 1889, d. aged 1 year; Drucilla M. b. Oct. 8, 1891, m. Edgar Craddock; Alice b. Jan. 31, 1894, m. John Boyd; Theodore and Leo (twins) b. May 19, 1896; Silvia b. April 6, 1899. Family home, Salt Lake City. Elder. Teamster.

PARKER, THOMAS H. G. (son of Thomas Parker, born Sept. 20, 1829, and Mary H. Peake, born April 14, 1834, at Derby, Derbyshire. Eng.; latter died May 26, 1882). He was born May 27, 1861, Derby. Came to Utah in 1863 with mother, who married Thomas Miller.
Married Ellen Lovina Schofield (daughter of Thomas J. Schofield and Sarah Foster), who was born Jan. 14, 1860, and died Dec. 20, 1905. Their children: Mary Ellen b. May 23, 1885; Sarah Ida b. March 27, 1887; Elizabeth Wynona b. March 9, 1890; Thomas Harold; Martha Manerva b. Nov. 14, 1893; William Schofield b. Aug. 8, 1895; Florence Eloise; Rulon Schofield b. May 23, 1900; Flora Louise b. Feb. 10, 1902. Family home Nephi, Utah.
Married Goldie Itha Bigler June 20, 1907 (daughter of Abner Chase Bigler and Elizabeth Tranter), who was born June 20, 1881, Nephi, Utah. Their children: Itha Lovina b. March 27, 1908; Nelda Alice b. April 11, 1910; Vera Dean b. Feb. 21, 1912.
Bishop of second ward. Uephi, Utah; president of deacons quorum; elder; priest; seventy; high priest; missionary to Ohio, Pennsylvania and West Virginia 1887-89. School trustee 1898-1907. Farmer; miner; wheelwright.

PARKER, WILLIAM COPE (son of George Parker, born March 3, 1799, Bickerton, Chestershire, Eng., and Jane Cope, born Feb. 23, 1806, Tattenhall, Chestershire—married about 1826). Born March 21, 1827, Bulkeley, Chestershire. Came to Utah Oct. 28, 1854, Robert Campbell company. He drove an oxteam across the plains for Thomas Bebbington.
Married Sarah Bebbington Edgely May 13, 1855 (daughter of William Edgely of Nantwich, Eng.). She was born Feb. 19, 1835. Came to Utah Oct. 28, 1854, Robert Campbell company. Their children: Sarah Jane b. April 22, 1857, m. Frederick Stimpson Oct. 21, 1876; Thomas b. Dec. 31, 1860, m. Jennett Mitchell July 5, 1883; Joseph b. Aug. 20, 1864, m. Minnie May Elmer Sept. 30, 1886; John b. Oct. 3, 1866, m. Laura Burch June 18, 1890; Edwin b. June 18, 1870, m. Ella Maud Elmer Nov. 27, 1891; Daniel b. April 22, 1877, m. Pearl Taylor April 4, 1900. Family home Riverdale, Weber Co., Utah.
Justice of peace 4 years at Riverdale.
Married Lydia Brewer Dec. 13, 1899, Salt Lake City (daughter of William Brewer and Elizabeth Stratton of Trowbridge, Wiltshire, Eng.), who was born Dec. 17, 1859, at Trowbridge. Their adopted child: Ethel Elizabeth b. Dec. 23, 1897.
Seventy; high priest; missionary to Great Britain 1871; Sunday school teacher; member of Sunday school superintendency 25 years. Miller. President Riverdale Canal Co.; superintendent Davis and Weber Counties Canal Co. Helped to build first railroads in Utah.

PARKER, WYMAN MINER (son of Wyman Parker and Maria Miner). Born April 2, 1828, Franklin, Delaware county, N. Y. Came to Utah in 1850.
Married Eliza Ann Grover Jan. 15, 1860 (daughter of Thomas Grover, pioneer Oct. 2, 1847, Charles C. Rich company, and Caroline Whiting, died in Nauvoo, Ill.). She was born March 13, 1839. Their children: Eliza A. b. March 27, 1961, m. A. L. Stoddard; Julia Maria b. Sept. 30, 1862; Thomas G. b. Sept. 14, 1864, m. Cynthia Smith Jan. 1, 1884; Emeline b. Feb. 1, 1567, m. George Wingar Dec. 16, 1893; Henry M. b. Feb. 5, 1869, d. Jan. 21, 1870; Lionel Parker b. Dec. 26, 1870, m. Laura M. Vaudrey Dec. 24, 1910; Welrose b. Dec. 8, 1872, m. Alice Miller; Joel b. Dec. 31, 1874, d. March 16, 1875; David G. b. Jan. 23, 1878, m. Nettie Dayley; Della b. June 17, 1878, m. John R. Moon; Lucy C. b. March 9, 1880, m. Franklin Oviatt; Albert B. b. June 14, 1882, m. Helen Stoddard. Family resided Morgan, Utah, and Parker, Idaho.
Bishop in Morgan, Utah, and Egin and Parker, Idaho; patriarch. Chairman board of county commissioners Fremont county, Idaho.

PARKER, LIONEL (son of Wyman Miner Parker and Eliza Ann Grover). Born Dec. 26, 1870, Morgan, Utah.
Married Laura M. Vaudrey Dec. 14, 1910, Salt Lake City (daughter of Nephi Vaudrey and Emily Crapo), who was born in Draper, Utah. Family home Parker, Idaho.

PARKIN, JOHN (son of William Parkin and Annie Allen of Loscoe, Derbyshire, Eng.). Born April 12, 1812, Loscoe, Eng. Came to Utah Oct. 4, 1863, Thomas E. Ricks company.
Married Elizabeth Brown Feb. 28, 1838, Duffield church, Derbyshire, Eng. (daughter of John Brown and Ann Wright of Loscoe), who was born March 18, 1821. Their children: William John, m. Eliza Foulds, m. Elizabeth S. Thurgood; George; Harriet. m. Thomas Wardle Matchet; John, m. Mary Ann Lewis; Joseph, m. Eliza S. Cooper; Hyrum, m. Phoebe Stinsley; Heber, m. Roanna Hatch. Family home Woods Cross, Utah.
Elder. School trustee. Farmer. Died Nov. 4, 1886, South Bountiful, Utah.

PARKIN, WILLIAM JOHN (son of John Parkin and Elizabeth Brown of Bountiful, Utah). Born May 19, 1839, Loscoe, Derbyshire, Eng. Came to Utah with parents.
Married Eliza Foulds Aug. 18, 1864, at Bountiful (daughter of James Foulds and Sarah Saxton of Hucknall Torkard, Nottinghamshire, Eng.), who was born Dec. 7, 1839. Their children: Sarah Elizabeth b. May 1865, m. Thomas Hatch; Harriet b. April 1867, m. William Varley; William J. b. Oct. 1869, m. Eliza Birmingham; James Henry b. 1871, died; George b. March 1873, m. Jessie Mann; Stephen b. Oct. 1875 (died), m. Lillie Bell; Zipporah b. April 1878, m. Samuel Nelson; Eliza Jane b. June 1880, m. Charles Yeiter; Grace Hannah b. Oct. 1883, m. Harry Dean; Mary Olive b. May 1886, m. John Davis. Family home Bountiful, Utah.
Married Elizabeth S. Thurgood April 24, 1884, Salt Lake City (daughter of Thomas Thurgood and Sarah A. Banks of London, Eng., pioneers Oct. 6, 1864, William Hyde company). She was born April 29, 1863. Their children: Sarah L. b. Feb. 5, 1885, m. William Hart; Alice E. b. July 9, 1889, m. Joseph Heaps; Thomas C. b. Feb. 21, 1890; Rella A. b. Feb. 3, 1892; Roland T. b. March 24, 1894; Edith L. b. Sept. 5, 1896; Lincoln D. b. Jan. 4, 1899; Carrie L. b. March 14, 1901; Clifford F. b. Feb. 28, 1902; Erma b. Aug. 13, 1906.
High priest; Sunday school superintendent; ward teacher. School trustee. Farmer.

PARKINSON, JAMES. Born Feb. 5, 1811, Rauckliff-on-Wyre, Eng. Came to Utah in September, 1864, John R. Murdock company.
Married Sarah Evans at Liverpool, Eng., who was born July 1, 1815. Their children: William; James, d. infant; Thomas; Sarah E., d. aged 16; John, m. Josephine Osborn; Margret A., d. aged 5; Joseph, d. aged 18; George, m. Margaret Prescott. Family home Milton, Morgan Co., Utah.
High priest; home missionary. Merchant; farmer. Died Feb. 26, 1875.

PARKINSON, GEORGE (son of James Parkinson and Sarah Evans). Born Sept. 26, 1854, Salford, Manchester, Eng. Came to Utah with father.
Married Margaret Prescott March 6, 1884, Bountiful, Utah, Richard E. Egan officiating (daughter of James Prescott and Margaret Westhead of Liverpool, Eng., pioneers 1855). She was born July 30, 1853. Only child: William R. Prescott b. Aug. 7, 1890.
Market gardener; dairyman.

PARKINSON, SAMUEL ROSE (son of William Parkinson, born at Newkirk, Lancashire, Eng., and Charlotte Rose, born 1805 in Kent, Eng.—married 1827 in Kent). He was born April 12, 1831, Barrowford, Lancashire, Eng. Came to Utah May 5, 1854, Captain Field company.
Married Arabella Ann Chandler Jan. 13, 1852 (daughter of George Chandler and Esther Glover, who died in England). She was born Feb. 27, 1824, and came to Utah with husband. Their children: Samuel Chandler b. Feb. 23, 1853, m. Mary Ann Hobbs Dec. 9, 1872; Charlotte Chandler b. Aug. 1, 1855, m. William J. Pratt April 10, 1873 (died), m. Joseph Palmer 1910; William Chandler b. Aug. 2, 1855, m. Ellen Elvira Nash Dec. 12, 1878, m. Louisa Benson Feb. 11, 1887; George Chandler b. July 18, 1857, m. Lucy Maria Doney April 14, 1881; Franklin Chandler b. July 7, 1859, m. Ada Elizabeth Nuttall Jan. 1, 1885; Esther Arabella b. Feb. 2, 1862, m. Henry T. Rogers Oct. 2, 1893; Albert b. Aug. 15, 1863, d. May 23, 1864; Clara Janet Chandler b. April 13, 1865 (died), m. Charles D. Goaslind March 25, 1885; Caroline Matilda Chandler b. Nov. 18, 1866, m. Charles D. Goaslind Feb. 23, 1898. Family resided Kaysville, Utah, and Franklin, Idaho.
Married Charlotte Smart Dec. 8, 1866, Salt Lake City (daughter of Thomas S. Smart and Ann Hater, pioneers 1852). She was born Nov. 6, 1848, at St. Louis, Mo. Their children: Annie Smart b. Oct. 15, 1867, m. O. L. Packer Jan. 1, 1885; Lucy Smart b. Oct. 7, 1869, m. Charles L. Lloyd Dec. 23, 1898; Joseph Smart b. July 15, 1872, m. Ida Maughan Dec. 9, 1900; Frederick Smart b. Jan. 8, 1877, m. Bessie Ann Doney Sept. 2, 1896; Leona Smart b. March 25, 1877, m. Walter P. Monson Nov. 6, 1895; Bertha Smart b. Sept. 24, 1879, m. Nephi Y. Larsen Oct. 7, 1893; Eva Smart b. March 7, 1882, m. Rufus Wood Leigh Sept. 4, 1908; Hazel Smart b. March 31, 1884, m. Peter P. Peterson May 4, 1903; Nettie Smart b. April 9, 1886, m. Isaac Albert Smoot March 31, 1909; Vivian Smart b. Nov. 28, 1893. Family home Franklin, Idaho.
Married Maria Smart Feb. 16, 1868, Salt Lake City (daughter of Thomas S. Smart and Ann Hater), who was born April 24, 1851, at St. Louis, Mo. Their children: Samuel Thomas S. b. March 27, 1869, m. Ellen Binnington Sept. 2, 1891; Luella S. b. Sept. 23, 1871, m. Matthias F. Cowley Sept. 22, 1889; Arabella S. b. Oct. 23, 1873, m. Robert H. Daines May 25, 1898; Sarah Ann S. b. April 22, 1875, m. George T. Marshall March 23, 1892; Olive S. b. May 25, 1877, m. Ezra P. Monson Oct. 14, 1895; Edmond S. b. Feb. 9, 1879, m. Ada West Sept. 11, 1901; Clarence S. b. Dec. 17, 1880, m. Charlotte Wright Oct. 8, 1908; Susa S. b. March 8, 1882, m. Neil P. Nelson June 8, 1904; Hazen S. b. April 1, 1884, m. Lena Allen May 12, 1910; Henry S. b. June 19, 1886, and Chloe b. June 2, 1887, latter two died; Glen S. b. June 20, 1892. Family home Franklin, Idaho.

School trustee. Helped establish mail route between Missouri river and Utah; helped build first schoolhouse in Idaho. Veteran Indian wars. Farmer; stockraiser; dairyman and merchant. General manager Franklin Co-op. 20 years.

PARKINSON, SAMUEL CHANDLER (son of Samuel Rose Parkinson and Arabella Chandler). Born Feb. 23, 1853, St. Louis, Mo. Came to Utah with father.
Married Mary Ann Hobbs Dec. 9, 1872, Salt Lake City (daughter of Charles R. Hobbs and Mary Ann Ems, pioneers 1863). She was born 1855 at Cheltenham, Eng., and died Dec. 21, 1912. Their children: Nessy Estella, m. George Hobbs; Edith Arabella, died; Samuel William, m. Harriett Taylor (died), m. Ina Hatch; Albert Hobbs, m. Eva Monson; May Hobbs; Leonard George, m. Emma Chatterton; Theresa; Raymond Charles; Anita; Bernice Richard; Rowland Hobbs; Myrtle; Roma. Family home Franklin, Idaho.
Missionary to southern states 1884-86, and to northwestern states 1898; high councilor 1886-1907; president high priests' quorum, Oneida stake; ordained bishop of Franklin ward July 7, 1907; president Y. M. M. I. A. four years. Vice-president Idaho State Savings Bank, Preston, Idaho.

PARKINSON, WILLIAM CHANDLER (son of Samuel Rose Parkinson and Arabella Ann Chandler). Born Aug. 2, 1855, Kaysville, Utah.
Married Ellen Elvira Nash Dec. 12, 1878, Salt Lake City (daughter of Isaac Bartlett Nash and Hester Elvira Pool of St. Louis, Mo., pioneers 1849 and 1863). She was born Feb. 17, 1863. Their children: Mary Nash b. Jan. 26, 1883, d. same day; Lillian Nash b. Feb. 3, 1884; Nellie Elvira b. Sept. 13, 1885, m. Alfred L. Kelley; Irene Nash b. March 28, 1887, m. I. Eugene Thoreson; Ray Nash b. March 27, 1889, m. Ralph D. Smuin; William Nash b. Jan. 31, 1891, d. March 14, 1891; Willis Nash b. July 20, 1893; Waldo C. b. July 27, 1895, d. Oct. 25, 1897; Frank L. Feb. 27, 1900; Bartlett Ross b. Dec. 10, 1903; Eda Nash b. March 30, 1907.
Married Louisa Benson Feb. 11, 1887, Logan, Utah (daughter of George T. Benson and Louisa Ballif of Whitney, Idaho, pioneers July 24, 1847, Brigham Young company). She was born March 28, 1869. Their children: Louisa b. July 5, 1889, m. Curtis Y. Clawson; Marie b. Dec. 13, 1891; Charlotte b. July 16, 1894; Clara b. Aug. 8, 1897; George B. b. Oct. 17, 1899; Adeline b. Jan. 2, 1902; Wilbur b. Oct. 10, 1904; Carmen b. Oct. 5, 1907; Evelyn b. March 30, 1910; Wanda b. July 31, 1911. Family home Hyrum, Utah.
Missionary to England 1880-82, and to northwestern states 1898; bishop of Preston ward 1884-98; president Pocatello stake 1898-1901; ordained president Hyrum stake April 30, 1901. Treasurer Cache county 1902-06; justice of peace and school trustee at Franklin, Idaho. Dealer in cattle, sheep, horses, farm produce and lumber. Furnished lumber for the Z. C. M. I. and church assembly hall, Salt Lake City. Freighter between Montana and Corrine 1872-73. Merchant from 1883 to 1901.

PARKINSON, GEORGE CHANDLER (son of Samuel Rose Parkinson and Arabella Ann Chandler). Born July 18, 1857, Kaysville, Utah.
Married Lucy Maria Doney April 14, 1881, Salt Lake City (daughter of John Doney and Ann Temperance George, pioneers Sept. 26, 1856, Edmund Ellsworth handcart company). She was born March 28, 1861, at Franklin. Their children: George Doney b. May 11, 1884; Lucy Ann D. b. Jan. 30, 1886, m. Preston Nibley Sept. 18, 1908; John Leo D. b. Dec. 23, 1887; Vera D. b. Sept. 24, 1889; Parley Samuel D. b. Oct. 16, 1892; Elna D. b. Sept. 7, 1894; Aleida D. b. Oct. 5, 1897; Deanne D. b. Oct. 20, 1899. Family resided at Franklin and Preston, Idaho.
Missionary to southern states and to Great Britain 1881-83; second counselor to William D. Hendricks in presidency of Oneida stake, 1884-87; president Oneida stake 1887-1910; president board of education Oneida stake 1888-1910; president northwestern states mission 1894-97. Superintendent public schools of Oneida county 1884-86; member state senate 1894-96; regent University of Idaho 1895-1907. President Idaho State & Savings Bank 1905-12; general manager Buckhorn Land Co., Salt Lake City; director Beneficial Life Insurance Co.; director Idaho, Western Idaho and Utah-Idaho Sugar companies; president Preston Co-op. Drug Co.; president Preston Commercial Club.

PARKINSON, FRANKLIN CHANDLER (son of Samuel Rose Parkinson and Arabella Ann Chandler). Born July 7, 1859, Kaysville, Utah.
Married Ada Elizabeth Nuttall Jan. 1, 1885, Logan, Utah (daughter of John Nuttall, Jr., and Elizabeth Lawton, who came to Utah in 1890). She was born Oct. 9, 1863, Manchester, Yorkshire, Eng. Their children: Franklin Stuart Nuttall b. Nov. 13, 1885; Harold Nuttall b. Oct. 7, 1887; Florence Nuttall b. Nov. 3, 1889; William Nuttall b. Dec. 20, 1891; Kenneth Nuttall b. Nov. 14, 1893; Edna Nuttall b. Nov. 21, 1895; Sidney Nuttall b. Sept. 11, 1899; Norma Nuttall b. Sept. 6, 1901; Stanley Ross Nuttall b. March 10, 1904; Graham Nuttall b. June 30, 1906. Family home Blackfoot, Idaho.
Bishop of Blackfoot ward. Real estate.

PARKINSON, FREDERICK SMART (son of Samuel Rose Parkinson and Charlotte Smart). Born Jan. 8, 1875, Franklin, Idaho.
Married Bessie Ann Doney Sept. 2, 1896, Logan, Utah (daughter of John Doney and Ann Temperance George), who was born Jan. 28, 1875, at Franklin. Their children: Frederic Doney b. June 26, 1897; Deverge Doney b. Oct. 3, 1898; Ross Doney b. April 17, 1904; Reed Doney b. June 13, 1906; Carroll Doney b. Feb. 14, 1909; Bessie Ann Doney b. Nov. 11, 1910; Keith Doney b. Nov. 1, 1912. Family home, Franklin.
Secretary Y. M. M. I. A. Oneida stake; missionary to northern states 1899-1901 and 1910-12. Moved to Rexburg, Idaho, 1902. Assistant superintendent first ward Sunday school at Rexburg 1904-07; president Y. M. M. I. A. 1907-08; first counselor to President George Hyde Y. M. M. I. A. Fremont stake 1908-10; one of presidents 88th quorum seventies. Manager and secretary Smart & Webster Co.; manager Parkinson Dry Farm at Rexburg. Member advisory board of Pallroade National Forest.

PARKINSON, THOMAS. Born Jan. 1, 1825, Malen, Lancashire, Eng. Came to Utah Oct. 17, 1853.
Married Elizabeth King, who was born Feb. 15, 1823. Their children: John b. Aug. 29, 1847, m. Lulia M. Hall 1875; James b. May 6, 1850, m. Jennetta Harris Nov. 24, 1873; Thomas b. March 27, 1852; Isaac b. March 19, 1855; Mary b. Aug. 9, 1858, m. Daniel B. Harris; Elizabeth b. Oct. 26, 1861, m. Joseph E. Gibbs; Hiram b. 1863; David b. Jan. 30, 1865, m. Annie Young.
Presiding elder over branch in England. Veteran Echo Canyon campaign. Justice of peace. Settled at Salt Lake City 1853; moved to Grantsville, Utah, 1854; Ogden 1856; Wellsville 1859; Portage 1867; back to Ogden 1875.

PARKINSON, JAMES (son of Thomas Parkinson and Elizabeth King). Born Aug. 6, 1850, Wray, Lancashire, Eng. Came to Utah with parents.
Married Jenetta Harris Nov. 24, 1873 (daughter of Robert Harris and Hannah M. Eagle), who was born Aug. 11, 1854. Their children: James Thomas b. Oct. 19, 1874, m. Leona John July 6, 1898; Elizabeth C. b. July 4, 1876, m. William Charles Bell; Mary Ann b. Aug. 7, 1878; Ray b. Aug. 21, 1880; Henrietta b. Dec. 20, 1882, m. Charles W. Yearsley; Sarah Maria b. March 22, 1885, m. Hyrum J. Jones; Jennetta b. Dec. 7, 1886, m. Albert Dopp; John Robert b. Dec. 7, 1888, m. Geneva Southworth Nov. 22, 1911; Vilate b. Dec. 15, 1890, m. Amos Hawks; Laura H. b. Oct. 14, 1893; Chloe b. Aug. 21, 1896. Family home Portage, Utah.

PARR, WILLIAM F. (son of John Parr and Barbara McKechina of Salt Lake City). Born in England. Came to Utah 1868.
In charge of the Deseret Telegraph Co., at Salt Lake City. Died 1881, at Salt Lake City.

PARRISH, EZRA (son of Nathan Parrish and Rebecca Rhodes, the former of Brownville, Jefferson county, N. Y.) Born May 4, 1804, at Brownville. Came to Utah in November, 1850.
Married Susannah Sherwin (daughter of Azariah Procter Sherwin and Sarah Kidder), who was born Sept. 17, 1808. Their children: Charles Edward b. 1828, m. Jane McKenzie; Henry Edwin b. 1829, m. Edna Ladd; Harriet Editha b. Aug. 17, 1831, m. M. L. Shepherd March 9, 1850; Esther Susannah b. 1833, died; Enoch Kidder, m. Susan Merchant; Rebecca Elizabeth m. Elijah Dunlap; Emma Jane, Ezra Azariah and Sarah Elvira, three died; Maryette b. Nov. 29, 1847, m. Alexander Keir Aug. 10, 1869; Alonzo, died; Alonzo Lafayette b. April 2, 1851. Family resided Salt Lake City and Springville, Utah, and in California.
Assisted in building first grist mill at Springville.

PARRY, EDWARD W. (son of Edward Parry and Jane Williams of Llanrwst, Denbigh, Wales). Born May 19, 1825, Llanrwst, Wales. Came to Utah in October, 1852.
Isaac A. Canfield company.
Married Anne Jones Feb. 4, 1860, Brynamman, Wales (daughter of Thomas Jones and Lettaisa Thomas of Brynamman; latter came to Utah in 1878). She was born Jan. 31, 1832. Their children: Owen Jones b. Nov. 25, 1860, m. Janie Holingebry; Anne Jane b. April 6, 1862; Edward J. b. March 15, 1864, died; Thomas B. b. March 30, 1866, m. Mary Hale; Ellen Sept. 29, 1867, m. Elizabeth Showles; William J. b. July 11, 1870, m. Christina Larson; George Walter b. April 15, 1872; Lettaisa Eliza b. Feb. 6, 1875, m. Henry Crabb. Family home, 15th ward, Salt Lake City.
Seventy; high priest; ward teacher. Mechanic. Died May 29, 1907.

PARRY, OWEN JONES (son of Edward W. Parry and Ann Jones). Born Nov. 25, 1860, Brynamman, Wales. Came to Utah with parents.
Married Janie Holingberg Nov. 19, 1892, Salt Lake City (daughter of Carl and Anna Holingberg of Stockholm, Sweden), who was born in November, 1864. Their children: Lawrence b. 1892; Louisa b. July 13, 1893; George b. January, 1895; John b. Sept. 20, 1897; Mary b. April 5, 1900. Family home Idaho Falls, Idaho.
Elder. Engaged with street department Salt Lake City 10 years. Farmer and stockraiser.

PARRY, JOHN (son of John Parry and Winifred Barker of Newmarket, Flintshire, Wales). Born Oct. 20, 1801, Newmarket. Came to Utah Oct. 2, 1856, Edward Bunker handcart company.
Married Elizabeth Parry at Newmarket (daughter of Edward Parry and Mary Faulkes of Newmarket), who

was born Jan. 13, 1809. Their children: Mary E. b. Dec. 21, 1834, m. Elias Morris May 23, 1852; Ann, d. aged 4 years; Winifred b. July 3, 1838, m. Caleb Parry; John b. Nov. 1841, m. Mary Ann Haight; Edward b. Sept. 8, —, m. Margaret Carlett; Elizabeth b. May 12, —, m. William Corry.
High priest. Member city council Cedar City, Utah. Architect and builder. Died at Cedar City.

PARRY, JOHN (son of Bernard Parry, born in 1745 at Newmarket, Flintshire, Wales, died April 16, 1822, and Elizabeth Saunders, born in 1744, died Nov. 1, 1805, at Newmarket—married April 25, 1768). He was born Feb. 10, 1789, at Newmarket. Came to Utah Oct. 27, 1849, George A. Smith company.
Married Mary Williams in 1807, who died in 1849 on way to Utah. Their children: Bernard b. Oct. 9, 1809, d. Nov. 12, 1841, at Birkenhead, Eng.; Elizabeth b. July 21, 1811, d. 1820; Mary b. May 4, 1813, d. Oct. 17, 1893, Mill Creek, Salt Lake Co., Utah, m. John Williams; Sarah b. May 9, 1815, d. 1846, Flintshire, Wales; John b. Oct. 13, 1817, d. May 16, 1882, Logan, Utah, m. Harriet Julia Robert; William b. Oct. 16, 1820, d. April 22, 1893, Ogden, Utah, m. Jane Vaughn; Caleb b. Oct. 9, 1823, m. Catherine Vaughn Evans.
Married Harriet Parry April 2, 1854, Salt Lake City (daughter of William Parry and Ellen Foulkes), who was born Oct. 18, 1822, at St. Asaph, Wales, and came to Utah in 1853, died April 4, 1901, Salt Lake City. Their children: Joseph H. b. Aug. 8, 1855, m. Parthenia Kesler; Bernard L. b. Aug. 10, 1855, d. Oct. 2, 1855; Louisa E. b. Sept. 21, 1857, m. Henry Emery; Edwin F. b. July 11, 1860, m. Margaret Smith; Henry E. b. Feb. 11, 1862, m. Clarissa Woodbury. Families resided at Salt Lake City.
First leader of church choir in Salt Lake City; member of high council. Militiaman. First to introduce lucern into Utah.

PARRY, CALEB (son of John Parry and Mary Williams). Born Oct. 9, 1823, Newmarket, Flintshire, Wales. Came to Utah Oct. 27, 1849, George A. Smith company.
Married Catherine Vaughn Evans Feb. 26, 1849 (daughter of Edward Catherine Vaughn Evans, born at Guildfield, Montgomeryshire, Wales, and Margaret Williams, born at Llanfair, Wales). She was born Dec. 14, 1826, at Trauscoed Hall, Guildfield, Wales, and died Nov. 20, 1893, at Ogden, Utah. Their children: Caleb, Jr., b. Feb. 16, 1850, m. Frances Sophia Marriott; Bernard b. March 1, 1852, m. Anna Marriott; Arthur b. Jan. 9, 1854, d. Sept. 12, 1855; Llewellen b. May 13, d. Nov. 7, 1854; Brigham b. March 14, 1857, d. Sept. 15, 1858; Aneurin b. Feb. 27, 1859, d. Nov. 15, 1867; Leo b. Nov. 9, 1861, m. Ella Jones; Rose Winifred b. April 7, 1864, m. Moroni S. Marriott; Rudolph b. Feb. 2, 1867, m. Mary Ann Hodson. Family home Ogden, Utah.
Married Winifred Parry (daughter of John Parry, born Oct. 20, 1801, Newmarket, Wales, died Oct. 21, 1881, Cedar City, Utah, and Elizabeth Parry, born Jan. 1, 1809, Newmarket, died Oct. 18, 1839, Cedar City—married Sept. 7, 1834, at Newmarket, pioneers 1852, Captain De Lamar company). She was born July 30, 1838, at Newmarket and died October, 1865, at Ogden, Utah. Their children: Gronway b. Aug. 19, 1858, m. Laura Gardner; Mary Frances b. Dec. 19, 1861, d. Oct. 2, 1864; John b. July 25, 1849, on ship "Buena Vista," with 249 Welsh converts, under direction of Dan Jones. They arrived at New Orleans April 19, thence up the rivers to St. Louis and to Council Bluffs, where he joined the George A. Smith company for Utah, arriving at Salt Lake City as above. Master mason on L. D. S. temple 1853-55. Veteran Indian war 1850-55. Member Echo Canyon expedition 1857. Settled in Ogden 1855. Mason on Ogden tabernacle 1856-57. Appointed captain Co. E, 3d battalion, first regiment, first brigade, Nauvoo legion, Feb. 20, 1868 (the militia of the territory of Utah). Missionary to England 1870. Died Sept. 3, 1871, at Birmingham, Eng.

PARRY, CALEB, JR. (son of Caleb Parry and Catherine Vaughn Evans). Born Feb. 16, 1850, Salt Lake City.
Married Frances Sophia Marriott Feb. 18, 1878 (daughter of John Marriott, born March 6, 1817, at Rhodes, Northamptonshire, Eng., died June 10, 1899, at Ogden, Utah, and Elizabeth Stewart, born April 12, 1829, Bedfordshire, Eng., former pioneer 1851). She was born Feb. 22, 1861, at Ogden. Their children: Parley Moroni b. July 18, 1879, m. Otelia Halgren; Lucele b. Sept. 22, 1881; John Harold b. Dec. 11, 1883; Elizabeth Amina b. Feb. 3, 1886, m. Earl A. Stratford Aug. 27, 1908; Willard Ray b. Jan. 15, 1888; Caleb Royal b. March 17, 1890; Myrtle Catherine b. Aug. 16, 1892, m. Henry Brunn; Lillian b. July 22, 1895; Oscar Leland b. July 25, 1897; William Bruce b. Nov. 24, 1901; Ezra Marriott b. Sept. 5, 1903. Family home Marriott ward, Ogden, Utah.
Colonial missionary to Arizona 1867-77. Farmer.

PARRY, PARLEY MORONI (son of Caleb Parry, Jr., and Frances Sophia Marriott). Born July 18, 1879, Ogden, Utah.
Married Otelia Halgren Oct. 15, 1902 (daughter of Truies A. Halgren, born Jan. 5, 1835, at Klorup, Sweden, died Sept. 4, 1902, at Ogden, and Clara Burling, born April 11, 1840, at Kumla, Westmanland, Sweden, died July 3, 1910, at Orden). Their children: Clara Otelia b. Feb. 7, 1904; Varian Parley b. Oct. 20, 1905; Winton Moroni b. Sept. 6, 1908.
Manager of Merchants Light and Power Co. of Ogden.

PARRY, JOSEPH HYRUM (son of John Parry and Harriott Parry). Born Aug. 8, 1855.
Married Lydia Hanks July 19, 1886, Salt Lake City (daughter of Sidney Alvarus Hanks and Mary Ann Cook of Salt Lake City, pioneers July 24, 1847, Brigham Young company). She was born Jan. 21, 1868. Their children: Mary Hanks b. Aug. 8, 1890, m. Seymour B. Curtis; Harriott Eula b. April 8, 1894; Lydia Hanks b. March 25, 1897; Alvarus Hanks b. April 9, 1904. Family home, Salt Lake City.

PARRY, JOSEPH (son of Edward Parry, born in 1769, died Aug. 12, 1842, and Mary Foulke, born in 1777, died Sept. 10, 1838—married at Newmarket, Wales, June 22, 1795). He was born April 4, 1825, at Newmarket. Came to Utah Oct. 3, 1852, William Morgan company.
Married Jane Payne Sept. 1, 1848, at Liverpool, Eng., who died April 19, 1849, at New Orleans, La.
Married Eliza Tunks in April, 1850, at St. Louis, Mo., (daughter of Richard Tunks and Mary Ann Morgan), who was born March 23, 1824, at Leominster, Herefordshire, Eng., and died July 3, 1866, at Ogden, Utah. Their children: Joseph b. Nov. 28, 1850, m. Alice A. Allen July 20, 1874; Edward b. Nov. 19, 1853, d. July 14, 1889; Hyrum b. Nov. 23, 1854; Eliza Jane b. Dec. 5, 1859, m. Joseph Harbertson Dec. 30, 1880; Mary Ann b. March 17, 1862, d. Nov. 21, 1866; Frances b. July 3, 1866, d. same day.
Married Ann Malin in January, 1857, Salt Lake City (daughter of Thomas Malin and Mary Penn), who was born April 10, 1829, in Warwickshire, Eng., and came to Utah Nov. 30, 1856, Edward Martin handcart company. Their child: Ann Henrietta b. Sept. 16, 1857, m. Thomas Greenwood Dec. 18, 1871.
Married Olive Stone Nov. 20, 1866, Salt Lake City (daughter of Amos Pease Stone and Minerva Leantine Jones, former pioneer 1850). She was born April 8, 1847, at Council Bluffs, Iowa. Their children: Brigham b. Dec. 14, 1867, d. Feb. 6, 1868; Chauncey b. Sept. 27, 1869, m. Julia Hutchens Nov. 7, 1894; Olive Ann b. Feb. 26, 1872, d. Jan. 30, 1880; David b. Sept. 28, 1874, d. Jan. 5, 1880; Walter b. April 27, 1877, m. Jeanette Petterson June 24, 1908; Ada b. Dec. 22, 1880, m. Sumner P. Nelson; Lizzie b. Aug. 26, 1882, m. Walter Farr Jan. 14, 1909; Amos b. July 13, 1887, m. Thomas Greenwood Dec. 18, 1871.
Elias b. Feb. 29, 1888.
Married Mrs. Susan A. (Wright) Brown Feb. 22, 1868, Salt Lake City (daughter of Josiah Wright, born Aug. 10, 1805, at Trenton, Conn., died March 21, 1900, at Ogden, Utah, and Susan Buel, born March 29, 1810, died 1883, at Ogden, Utah, pioneers 1854). She was born Sept. 6, 1843, in Connecticut and died Dec. 31, 1903, at Ogden. Their children: Juliett b. Nov. 20, 1868, m. John David Ballanger June 5, 1907; Franklin b. March 16, 1872, d. Jan. 23, 1880; John b. July 28, 1874, m. Pearl Heball; Charles Oliver b. March 27, 1877, m. Ada Crandall Feb. 23, 1897; William b. April 30, 1880, d. Feb. 27, 1894; Albert b. Oct. 9, 1882; Henry Grover b. Oct. 16, 1884.
First counselor to President Lorin Farr of high priests quorum 1896; missionary to Wales 1870; member of high council 1880-1908. City councilman four terms. Veteran Echo Canyon campaign. One of the original 27 settlers of Salmon river district.

PARRY, THOMAS.
Married Ann Roberts. Their children: Mary, m. Morgan Jones; Sarah, m. William Jones; Lea, m. Amos Jones; Edward L, m. Ann ———; Edward R., m. Ellen ———; Joseph; David, m. Margrate Jones; Emma, m. Lucius Billings.

PARRY, EDWARD L. (son of Thomas Parry and Ann Roberts). Born Aug. 25, 1818, in Wales. Came to Utah 1853.
Married Ann ———. Their children: Edward b. Oct. 19, 1859, m. Charlot Edmonds; Mary Ellen, m. Sylvester Coy; John, m. Belle Peacock; Hattie; Bunnard, m. Vilate Harmond; Emma. Family home Manti, Utah.
Died Aug. 27, 1906, Manti, Utah.

PARSONS, GEORGE (son of Stephen and Mary Parsons of Missouri). Born in 1834. Came to Utah in 1854, oxteam company.
Married Lydia R. Fisher (Simmons) in 1853 in Missouri (daughter of Vardis Fisher of New York, pioneer 1854; also the widow of Leven Simmons, pioneer 1852, oxteam company, and by whom she had the following children: Vardis John, m. Jane Steward; Benjamin Franklin, m. Ann Warner; William R., m. Martha Warner; Andrew Jackson, m. Agnes Bellows; Alma Charles, m. Miss Coyle; Lydia Rebecca, d. child; Sarah Elizabeth, m. Charles Forsyth; Fanny E., m. Charles Steward. Family home, Spanish Fork, Utah). She was born Feb. 20, 1837. Their child: Mary Jane, m. William Henry Babcock. Family home Spanish Fork, Utah.
Deceased.

PARTINGTON, RALPH. Came to Utah in 1853.
Married Ann Taylor, who came to Utah with husband. Their children: Catherine, m. Hugh Finley; Ellen, m. John Kay; William, m. Annie Cowley; Sarah, m. Thomas Quayle; Edward, died.
Carpenter and joiner. Died Salt Lake City.

1090   PIONEERS AND PROMINENT MEN OF UTAH

PARTRIDGE, EDWARD (son of Edward Partridge, born Aug. 27, 1793, Painesville, Ohio, and Lydia Clisbee). Born June 25, 1833, Jackson county, Mo. Came to Utah in 1848.
Married Sarah Lucretia Clayton Feb. 4, 1858, Salt Lake City (daughter of William Clayton and Ruth Moon, former pioneer of 1847, latter of 1848). She was born Aug. 1, 1837. Their children: Harriet Parmelia b. Nov. 14, 1858, m. Albert H. Kimball May 15, 1876; Edward b. Dec. 13, 1860, m. Jennie King, m. Dora Davis; William Clayton b. Oct. 2, 1862, m. Sarah Stott; Effie May b. Sept. 2, 1864, and Louis Amasa b. Dec. 27, 1866, d. children; Ernest DeAlton b. June 13, 1869, m. Elizabeth Truman Aug. 16, 1896; Stanley b. Nov. 17, 1871, m. May W. Wright June 19, 1899; Raymond b. Feb. 15, 1875, m. Maud E. Wentz Oct. 16, 1899.
Married Elizabeth Buxton Feb. 16, 1862, Salt Lake City (daughter of John Buxton and Elizabeth Carnel), who was born April 5, 1842. Their children: Emily b. Dec. 1, 1862, m. George A. Black; John C. b. July 29, 1865, and Charles b. June 18, 1867, died; George Arthur b. March 12, 1869, m. Lucy Lyman Nov. 14, 1895; Carlos b. May 14, 1871, m. Nell Darling; Clara b. Aug. 4, 1873, m. David F. Stevens; Frank Harvey b. Aug. 12, 1875, m. Dell Melville, m. Hattie Wicker; Mary Aloha b. Nov. 18, 1877, m. Josiah Wixom; Lydia Maud b. Oct. 13, 1879, m. Clark Kimball. Families resided Fillmore, Utah.
Missionary to Sandwich Islands 1854 and 1882; counselor in presidency Millard stake 1877; counselor in presidency Utah stake 1892; president Utah stake 1895; bishop Fillmore 1869. Manager Co-op. store Fillmore 1869; vice-president Millard County Stockraising Association 1871. Probate judge Millard county 1869; elected to territorial legislature 1873; major Fillmore 1875. Died Nov. 17, 1900.

PARTRIDGE, ERNEST DeALTON (son of Edward Partridge and Sarah Lucretia Clayton). Born June 13, 1869, Fillmore, Utah.
Married Elizabeth Truman Aug. 16, 1896, at Lansing, Mich. (daughter of Abram K. Truman and Gertrude Harrison of Lansing), who was born Jan. 23, 1873. Their children: Ruth Louise b. Dec. 22, 1898; Truman Edward b. July 25, 1903; Ernest DeAlton, Jr. b. Nov. 6, 1906; Gertrude Elizabeth b. Oct. 13, 1909. Family home Provo, Utah.
Bishop 4th ward Provo 1902-07; member high council Utah stake. First principal Murdock Academy Beaver, Utah, 1898-1901; assistant professor mathematics B. Y. U., Provo. Provo city councilman 1904-07.

PASSEY, JOHN (son of Thomas Passey and Margaret Showell of Strensham, Worcestershire, Eng.). Born Dec. 17, 1810, Treyning, Worcestershire. Came to Utah Sept. 13, 1861, Joseph Horne company.
Married Anna New in England and later in Salt Lake City Endowment House (daughter of William New and Elizabeth Colling of England), who was born Oct. 20, 1816. Their children: Thomas, m. Drucilla Theobald; William, m. Asenath Wilcox; Frederick, m. Louie Gray; George, m. Addie Daley; Herbert, died; John, m. Elizabeth Clifton.
Elder. Sawyer and farmer. Died March 21, 1883, at Paris, Idaho.

PASSEY, GEORGE (son of John Passey and Anna New). Born Dec. 14, 1844, in Strensham, Worcestershire, Eng. Came to Utah Sept. 13, 1861, with parents.
Married Addie Daley Sept. 23, 1874, Salt Lake City (daughter of Phineas Daley and Adeline Grover of New York), who was born May 17, 1857. Their children: Ida G. b. Aug. 12, 1875, m. Franklin C. Fuller; Retta b. Aug. 1, 1877, m. Joseph F. Broadbent; George, Jr. b. Aug. 13, 1879, and Ray b. July 15, 1883, died; Roy b. Sept. 13, 1885, m. Sarah M. Harris; Nora b. Jan. 23, 1888, died; Annie b. Jan. 30, 1891, m. Reid Beck; Wilford W. b. Jan. 19, 1893, died; Lorin b. Aug. 15, 1894. Family resided Mesa, Maricopa county, Ariz., and Provo, Utah.
Senior officer of 90th quorum of seventies; missionary to North-Carolina 1880-82; high priest. In 1868 returned to Platte river with church team after immigrants. Merchant.

PATE, ROBERT BURROWS (son of John Pate of Moss End, Lancashire, born Sept. 21, 1769, and Betty Burrows of England). He was born Feb. 27, 1801, Hedge End, Marsden, Lancashire. Came to Utah in 1852.
Married Betty Broughton in 1822, who was born in May, 1802, and died in England May 12, 1838. Their children: Mary b. Aug. 3, 1823; Sarah b. Jan. 3, 1826; Isabelle b. Feb. 17, 1828; Nathan b. June 15, 1830; Rachel b. June 17, 1832; James b. June 28, 1835; Betty b. March 14, 1838.
Married Mary Greenwood March 22, 1840 (daughter of William Greenwood, died Oct. 22, 1842, and Sarah Utly, died Aug. 28, 1842). She was born May 14, 1804, in England. Their children: John G. b. Feb. 17, 1841; Greenwood G. b. March 11, 1842; Ezra G. and Jacob G., twins, b. March 4, 1844, latter m. Ruth J. Still March 3, 1866.
Priest; presided over branch of L. D. S. church at Burnley, Eng. Settled at Union Fort, ten miles south of Salt Lake City. Died Oct. 28, 1875.

PATE, JACOB G. (son of Robert B. Pate and Mary Greenwood). Born March 4, 1844, Hancock county, Ill. Came to Utah with father.
Married Ruth J. Still March 8, 1866, at Union, Salt Lake county (daughter of Andrew J. Still and Mercy Ann Howard, pioneers Utah 1864). She was born Feb. 7, 1844, in Taney county, Mo. Their children: Joseph S. b. Dec. 19, 1866, d. Dec. 29, 1866; Jacob G., Jr., b. Jan. 15, 1868, m.

Rebecca Hunt; Robert B. b. April 7, 1870, m. Frances Honeysett; Ruth b. Jan. 24, 1872, m. John E. Baker; Mercy Ann b. Jan. 12, 1874, d. Sept. 5, 1876; Ezra G. b. Feb. 10, 1876, m. Ada Sharp; William b. Jan. 31, 1878, m. Hazel D. Walker; Mary b. Oct. 18, 1880, d. April 12, 1884; John and Sarah (twins) b. April 25, 1883, John d. March 21, 1884, Sarah m. Samuel Weight; Elizabeth J. b. Dec. 20, 1885, m. Oscar Snarr. Family home, Union.
Ward teacher; member 72d quorum seventies; first Sunday school superintendent Union ward; missionary to northern states 1906; high priest.

PATTEN, THOMAS JEFFERSON (son of John Patten and Hanna Ingersoll of Greene county, Ind.). Born April 10, 1828, in Greene county. Came to Utah 1849, Aaron Johnson company.
Married Joanna Hollister in 1853 at Provo, Utah (daughter of John Hollister and Lovina Clearwater of Marbletown, N. Y.), who was born April 18, 1833. Their children: Vina, m. John Moore; Thomas Jefferson, Jr., m. Isabella Billings; Hannah, m. George Billings; Joanna, m. Joseph Harris; Ida, m. Edward Rawlins; Melissa, m. L. A. Wilson; William, m. Sadie Talmage; Alva, m. Lettie Brown; Phoebe, m. Fred Kropf; David Wyman, m. Menie Williamson.
High priest; counselor to bishop. Veteran Black Hawk war. President Provo Bench Canal Co. Justice of peace. First Sunday school superintendent in Sunday school union. Died Dec. 14, 1910, Provo, Utah.

PATTEN, DAVID WYMAN (son of Thomas J. Patten and Joanna Hollister). Born Nov. 8, 1877, Provo, Utah.
Married Menie Williamson June 5, 1900, at Provo (daughter of John Williamson and Hanna Seward of Lake View, Utah), who was born Nov. 20, 1878. Their children: Scottie Wyman b. Jan. 8, 1901, d. Jan. 22, 1901; Marion John b. Dec. 4, 1902; Paul Williamson b. April 6, 1904; Helen Pauline b. Oct. 26, 1910, d. March 22, 1913.

PATTEN, WILLIAM CORNWELL (son of John Patten, born March 10, 1767, South of Ireland, and Ann Cornwell, born May 20, 1774, in Newcastle county, Del.—married 1796). He was born March 24, 1799, in Chester county, Pa. Came to Utah Oct. 8, 1850, Wilford Woodruff company.
Married Harriet Cooper at Philadelphia, Pa. Only child: Mary Ann.
Married Julianah Bench Dec. 21, 1826 (daughter of Samuel Bench and Ann Townsley), who was born Nov. 10, 1804, and died Jan. 1, 1835. Their children: George b. Oct. 26, 1828, m. Mary Jane Nelson Feb. 20, 1851; Ann, m. Charles S. Peterson.
Married Jane Crouse in 1845, Nauvoo, Ill. Their children: Hannah Jane b. Dec. 6, 1846, m. Joseph S. Nelson; Matilda Rebecca b. Feb. 27, 1848, m. Elijah Nichols Wilson.
Settled at Payson, Utah, 1850.

PATTEN, GEORGE (son of William Cornwell Patten and Julianah Bench). Born Oct. 26, 1828, Cold Rain, Chester county, Pa. Came to Utah with father.
Married Mary Jane Nelson Feb. 20, 1851, Alpine, Utah (daughter of Edmon Nelson and Jane Taylor of Missouri), who was born March 8, 1832, in Jefferson county, Ill. Their children: Joseph Cornwell b. Dec. 17, 1851, m. Rose E. Wright April 29, 1872; George Washinhton b. Jan. 14, 1853, m. Lilian Beckstead July 24, 1871; William Henry b. Sept. 15, 1854, m. Martha M. Patterson April 28, 1873; John Edmon b. Sept. 7, 1856, d. June 9, 1875; Charles Moroni b. April 17, 1858, m. Lucinda Patterson Feb. 19, 1878; Mary Jane b. Jan. 5, 1863, m. C. E. Loose July 20, 1888; Julianah b. Aug. 10, 1867, m. Lachoneas A. Colvin Aug. 19, 1883; Sarah Elizabeth b. March 20, 1870, m. Thomas Wimmer June 1, 1886. Family home Payson, Utah.
High priest. Member Appleton Harmon company, Nauvoo Legion 1844. Appointed major first battalion infantry, 1st regiment, 2d brigade, 2d division Nauvoo Legion April 22, 1866; member police force Payson 1857-66; missionary to The Muddy 1866-71; member city council of Payson 1876-78. Indian war veteran; captain of ten, Homer Duncan company 1856, bringing immigrants to Utah; participated in Echo Canyon trouble. Helped build first telegraph line and first railroad into Payson, also tabernacle and woolen mills at Provo, and all Mormon temples, excepting one at Kirtland, Ohio.

PATTERSON, C. S. (son of William Patterson and Frances M. DeLong of Ohio). Born July 16, 1884, Logan, Iowa (daughter of John Morris and Hannah Clark of Magnolia, Iowa), who was born Dec. 26, 1863.
Member board of commissioners on revenue and taxation. Lawyer.

PAUL, SAMUEL (son of James Paul and Margret Henry of County Londonderry, Ireland). Born Feb. 20, 1836, at Coleraine, Ireland. Came to Utah 1870.
Married Florence Slade Nov. 10, 1874, Salt Lake City (daughter of George Slade and Jane Atwood of Salt Lake City, pioneers 1863), who was born 1861. Their children: Ethel J. b. 1876; Samuel G., m. Elinor Napier; Alice; Lorine N., m. Nellie J. Cooke. Family home Salt Lake City.
Chief supervisor of streets 1890-91; chief of police 1892-93. President and manager Salt Lake Livery & Transfer.

PIONEERS AND PROMINENT MEN OF UTAH 1091

PAUL, WILLIAM (son of Walter Paul and Mary Mitchel of St. Agnes, Cornwall, Eng.). Born May 2, 1803, at St. Agnes. Came to Utah Oct. 1, 1854, Daniel Garn company.
Married Elizabeth Goyne, who was born March 13, 1804. Their children: Mary Jane b. Dec. 17, 1827, m. James Linforth; William b. July 31, 1829, m. Georgeana Burrows; Elizabeth b. March 11, 1832, m. H. W. Naisbitt; Walter b. March 10, 1834, m. Ann Walker Dec. 25, 1856; John b. Feb. 25, 1836, m. Louisa Bourne; Priscilla b. March 25, 1838, m. William Jennings 1855; Edmund b. Feb. 6, 1840, m. Martha Huntington July 16, 1864, who died April 5, 1883, m. Mary Ellen Westover Oct. 11, 1883; Susan R. b. Jan. 27, 1842, m. Philip Brooks.
Married Ann Louder, at Salt Lake City, who was born April 19, 1825, and came to Utah Oct. 24, 1855, Milo Andrus company. Their children: Joseph James Louder b. April 2, 1861; Albert Louder b. Oct. 23, 1863.
Contractor and architect. High priest and Sunday school teacher.

PAUL, WALTER (son of William Paul and Elizabeth Goyne). Born March 10, 1834, Truro, Cornwall, Eng.
Married Ann Walker Dec. 25, 1856, Salt Lake City (daughter of George Walker, pioneer 1851, and Mary Hopkins). She was born Jan. 28, 1840, Grimly, Nottinghamshire, Eng., and died Jan. 14, 1875. Their children: Annie E. b. Dec. 18, 1857, m. Andrew Bigler Nov. 5, 1877; Walter George b. Sept. 24, 1859, m. Kate Painter April 10, 1877; William Henry b. Sept. 30, 1861, m. Lovina Jarvis Feb. 16, 1886; John R. b. Dec. 2, 1863, m. Ardell Hinckley May 20, —; Mary Jane b. March 11, 1866, m. J. K. Whitney Oct. 1, 1884; Priscilla b. Jan. 6, 1868; Edmund Young b. March 22, 1869; Sarah (twin of Edmund Young); Frank Orson b. Sept. 26, 1870, and Minnie Susan b. July 10, 1873, latter five died.
Married Emma Jane Westover March 10, 1877, Logan, Utah (daughter of Edwin Westover and Ann Findly, pioneers 1853). She was born Sept. 3, 1858, Big Cottonwood, Utah, and died Jan. 15, 1897, Rexburg, Idaho. Their children: Oscar S. b. Jan. 18, 1878, m. Emily Randall; Edmund R. W. b. April 10, 1879, m. Sarah Ann Hughes; Louisa Ann W. b. Jan. 18, 1881, m. Edward C. Larsen Dec. 29, 1902; Laura Maud W. b. Sept. 4, 1882, d. April 2, 1891; Clarence W. b. Feb. 28, 1885; Fannie Huddassah W. b. March 26, 1887, m. Charles Ellsworth April 7, 1909; Emma Arminta W. b. Jan. 4, 1889, d. Jan. 21, 1889; Dora Lovina W. b. May 30, 1890; Fremont R. W. b. Jan. 29, 1893, d. Feb. 19, 1893; Elmer Bruce W. b. Jan. 3, 1895; Harold Little W. b. Dec. 30, 1896.
One of presidents 84th quorum seventies. First justice of peace Rexburg, Idaho; first coroner of Fremont county. Organized first home dramatic company, Rexburg. Carpenter; merchant. Postmaster. Echo Canyon war veteran.

PAUL, WALTER GEORGE (son of Walter Paul and Ann Walker). Born Sept. 24, 1859, Salt Lake City.
Married Kate Painter April 10, 1885, Logan, Utah (daughter of George Painter). Their children: Jane Elizabeth b. Dec. 13, 1885, died; Ethel Ann b. Nov. 23, 1886; Joseph Walter b. Oct. 20, 1888, Gilbert George b. Sept. 5, 1890, and Mary Matilda b. Aug. 19, 1892, died; Alfred Henry b. Oct. 3, 1894; Nephi, Emeline, and Priscilla, died. Family resided Mendon and Salt Lake City, Utah, and Rexburg, Idaho.
Missionary to Montana, southern states, England. Undertaker; carpenter.

PAUL, JOHN R. (son of Walter Paul and Ann Walker). Born Dec. 2, 1863, Salt Lake City.
Married Luna A. Hinckley May 20, 1886, Logan, Utah (daughter of Arza E. Hinckley and Mary Hiner of Salt Lake City, pioneers 1847, contingent of Mormon Battalion). She was born March 18, 1867. Their children: J. Leo b. Jan. 31, 1887, m. Isabelle James April 7, 1910; Aldine A. b. May 15, 1888; Earl S. b. Sept. 14, 1889; Frank O. b. March 29, 1891; Bradley H. b. Aug. 22, 1892; Arza W. b. April 13, 1895; Tredgar H. b. Aug. 28, 1898, d. Oct. 8, 1902; Lynn b. June 29, 1898; Mary M. b. April 17, 1900; Mildred b. Sept. 1, 1907. Family home Rexburg, Idaho.
High priest; secretary stake Sunday school; counselor stake Y. M. M. I. A.; second counselor to Bishop T. J. Winter; home missionary; secretary Sunday school at Rexburg; presiding elder Grove branch, Pratt ward. Butcher; farmer.

PAXMAN, WILLIAM (son of James Paxman, born 1802, Suffolk, Eng., and Esther Reynolds, born March 14, 1807, Colchester). He was born Oct. 23, 1835, Hemel Herriated, Eng. Came to Utah Sept. 13, 1851, Joseph Horne company.
Married Ann Rushen Keys March 3, 1855 (daughter of Joseph Keys, came to Utah 1877, and Mary Ann Rushen—married Nov. 4, 1827, Essex, Eng). She was born Sept. 11, 1830, and came to Utah with husband. Their children: William Reed Horizon b. June 3, 1856, m. Urilda Moody Jan. 16, 1879; Edzar Moroni b. Aug. 25, 1857, m. Clara Wrigley Dec. 1, 1880; Emma Tryfena b. Jan. 12, 1859, m. Joseph Miller Jan. 8, 1880; James Walter b. Oct. 12, 1861, m. Julia Sudbury March 1, 1888; George Francis b. April 25, 1863, m. Martha Evans Sept. 18, 1885; Esther Elizabeth b. Feb. 15, 1865, m. Henry M. McCune April 9, 1885; Martha Ellen b. May 2, 1867, m. Isaac C. Gadd April 22, 1887; Joseph Hyrum b. March 26, 1869, d. Nov. 25, 1892; Alice Ann b. Sept. 16, 1870, m. George McCune Sept. 13, 1893; Edwin Washington b. July 4, 1872, m. Emma Jenkins March 27, 1895; Albert Reynolds b. Aug. 9, 1875, m. Margaret Jenkins June 15, 1898. Family resided American Fork and Nephi, Utah.
Married Emily Abel Oct. 11, 1875, Salt Lake City (daughter of Isaac Abel and Ann Methley—married Dec. 25, 1849, Sheffield, Eng.—pioneers 1863, Samuel D. White company). Their children: Emily Ann b. Sept. 21, 1878, d. April 16, 1882; Wilford W. b. March 29, 1881, d. Feb. 17, 1906; Mary Ellen b. Jan. 15, 1883; Ernest b. March 17, 1885, m. Juventa Greenwood; Hattie b. Aug. 4, 1891, m. James Martin; Rebecca A. b. June 3, 1895.
Married Kate Love Oct. 7, 1884, Salt Lake City (daughter of Andrew Love and Sarah M. Humphrey—married April 8, 1854, Salt Lake City—former a pioneer Oct. 4, 1847, Jedediah M. Grant company, latter a pioneer 1850, Lorenzo Hatch company). She was born Dec. 29, 1860, Nephi, Utah. Their children: Sarah J. L. b. Sept. 17, 1885, d. March 10, 1887; Andrew Love b. Jan. 2, 1889; May Love b. May 29, 1891, m. M. K. Hill Nov. 24, 1910; Ezra Love b. Sept. 5, 1893; Douglas Love b. Nov. 5, 1896. Family resided Nephi, Utah, and Alberta, Canada.
Organizer and superintendent of Sunday school, American Fork, 1883; missionary to England 1875-77, presiding over London conference; president New Zealand mission 1886-89, and supervised the translation of the Book of Mormon into the Maori language; acted as agent for Presiding Bishop Hunter; president of Juab stake 1883-97. City alderman. Tinsmith in early days. Delegate to commercial and irrigation congresses. Organizer and superintendent of the Provo Lumber Company until 1883; superintendent of American Fork Co-op. store. Died Oct. 12, 1897.

PAXMAN, JAMES WALTER (son of William Paxman and Ann Rushen Keys). Born Oct. 12, 1861, Salt Lake City.
Married Julia Sudbury March 1, 1888, Logan, Utah (daughter of Samuel John Sudbury and Emma Crossland, pioneers October, 1853, Joseph W. Young company). She was born Oct. 31, 1864, Coalville, Utah. Their children: James Walter, Jr., b. Feb. 12, 1889; Loraine Sudbury b. Dec. 22, 1890, d. Jan. 13, 1909; Clarence b. Aug. 5, 1892; Vera Alice b. May 24, 1894; Samuel George b. Feb. 21, 1896; Julia b. Oct. 29, 1897; Louise Ann b. May 2, 1899; William b. June 29, 1901; Joseph Leland b. June 15, 1903, d. Aug. 10, 1904; Emma b. June 23, 1906. Family home Nephi, Utah.
President of Juab stake December, 1897; counselor in the presidency of Juab stake January, 1887, to December, 1897; missionary to England 1884-86. County clerk Juab county 1887-89. Pioneer dry farmer to Juab Co., Utah. President and director Juab Development Company February, 1907-13; manager of Excelsior Mercantile Company. Cobbler in American Fork from 1875-80. Attended B. Y. U. at Provo.

PAXMAN, ALBERT R. (son of William Paxman and Ann Rushen Keys). Born Aug. 9, 1875, American Fork, Utah.
Married Margaret Grace Jenkins June 15, 1898, Salt Lake City (daughter of James Jenkins and Margaret Grace, the former pioneer, Milo Andrus company). She was born Jan. 19, 1870, Nephi, Utah. Their children: Albert Delos b. June 18, 1899; LeRoy b. Sept. 1, 1901. Family home, Nephi.
Stake superintendent of Sunday schools 1907-11; stake clerk 1901 to date of publication. County treasurer 1911-14; city councilman 1902-05 and 1908-09; school trustee 1910-13. Secretary and director Excelsior Mercantile Company.

PAYNE, EDWARD (son of John Payne and Caroline Arnold of Warminster, Wiltshire, Eng.). Born May 31, 1832, in Wiltshire. Came to Utah Sept. 20, 1854, Joseph S. Rawlins company.
Married Emma Powell Sept. 16, 1854, Dudley, Staffordshire, Eng. (daughter of George Powell and Mariah Mousley of England), who was born March 1, 1838, and came to Utah with husband. Their children: George b. Dec. 4, 1855, m. Mariah Gottfredson; Harry b. Dec. 3, 1857, m. Helen Buchanan; Lucy b. March 16, 1860, m. H. B. Bell; Thomas b. April 10, 1862, d. on the plains; Elizabeth b. Oct. 2, 1864, m. F. H. Bell; Edward William b. April 2, 1867, m. Emily Bean; John Henry b. Aug. 19, 1869, m. Margaret Sampson; Margaret Ann b. Nov. 29, 1871, m. J. L. Fox; Charles Willard b. Feb. 2, 1874, m. Elizabeth Staker; James Heber b. Feb. 27, 1876, died; Emma M. b. June 3, 1877, died; Claud b. Oct. 5, 1878, m. Minnie Jenson; Benjamin Franklin b. Nov. 17, 1881, died. Family home Glenwood, Utah.
High priest; member seventies. Early settler at Heber. Veteran Black Hawk war. Glenwood ward clerk; Glenwood town clerk; trustee Glenwood school. Treasurer Glenwood Irrigation Company; secretary and treasurer Glenwood Co-op.; secretary and treasurer United Order. Farmer.

PEA, JOHN (son of George Pea and Sarah De Armon of York county, S. C.). Born July 11, 1783, in York county. Came to Utah 1853, Orson Pratt company.
Married Elizabeth Knighton June 7, 1804, Crowders Creek, S. C. (daughter of Thomas Knighton and Jane Freeman of Sumpter county, Va.). She was born May 17, 1783, Orange county, Va. Their children: Elizabeth K., m. Abner Herring; John Wesley, d. 1808; Ezekiel, m. Catherine Ann Berry; Nancy Rebecca, d. 1812; Sarah De Armon, m. Charles C. Rich; Messaiah, d. 1819; Thomas K., d. 1836; Jane Freeman, m. William E. Horner.
High priest. Blacksmith. Died April 26, 1875, Salt Lake City, Utah.

PEACOCK, GEORGE (son of Daniel Peacock, died September, 1831, near Marcum, Canada, and Mary Noddings of Hutton, Yorkshire, Eng.). He was born July 22, 1822, at Hutton. Came to Utah Sept. 5, 1850, Thomas Johnson company.
Married Sarah Lowry April 4, 1840, Lee county, Iowa

(daughter of John Lowry of Nashville, Tenn., and Susan Groom of Lee county, Iowa, pioneers Sept. 30, 1847, John Taylor company). Their children: William Henry, m. Mary Snow; Isabelle, m. Edward W. Fox; Sarah, m. O. C. Ornsbey; George D., m. Kezzie Wilson; Susan Rosella, m. James E. Clinton; Alice, m. Frank W. Snow; Charlotte Ann, m. B. T. Young; Jane, m. J. H. Hague.

Married Mary Artimesia Lowry Aug. 5, 1854, Salt Lake City (daughter of John Lowry and Mary Wilcox of Manti, pioneers 1847, John Taylor company). She came to Utah with parents. Their children: John Lowry b. Aug. 5, 1855, m. Serena Evens Moffitt Jan. 29, 1875; George b. March 8, 1857, m. Lucy S. Reid; Brigham James b. Dec. 27, 1858, m. Sarah Eleanor Cox Dec. 1, 1880; Susan L. b. Feb. 19, 1861, m. William Richards; Clarence b. July 27, 1864, m. Margaret Whitlock; Rosebella b. Sept. 6, 1866, died; Ariel Aroldo b. Jan. 7, 1869, m. Retta Allerton; Daniel Movell b. March 5, 1872, m. Clara Madsen: Dell Roy Lynn b. July 18, 1874, m. Orpha Miles; Mary Luella b. Jan. 26, 1879, m. Alexander Tennant.

Married Sarah Bell, Fillmore, Utah (daughter of William Bell and Sarah Brireton). Their children: Warren Snow, m. Elizabeth Ann Parry; Helen Eugenie, m. J. D. Killpack; Lillah Bell, died; William George, m. Margaret C. Crawford; Oliver Cromwell, m. Charlotte Luke; Edmund, died; Sarah Anetta, m. Joseph Larson; Le Roy Durell, died; Olivia, m. J. Milton Burns; Velora, m. Ezra S. Funk.

Married Hannah McCliney. Only child: Willard M. b. March 20, 1860, m. Mary Hoggan. Families resided Manti, Utah.

Member 25th quorum seventies; high priest; counsellor to Bishop Warren Snow seven years; missionary to Europe 1861-63. Assisted in making the first ferryboat, and taking across the Missouri river the first load of immigrants westward-bound. Guard to Joseph and Hyrum Smith while at Nauvoo. Settled at Manti in 1850, where in 1852 he organized San Pete county, by appointing the officers; in 1851 he was appointed constable of Manti; probate judge of San Pete county 1852-1878, excepting 1861-1863; member Utah legislature seven terms beginning 1866. Commander in Utah militia against the Indians. First postmaster of Manti 1853-1878. By request of historical committee of the Utah legislature, wrote historical sketch of settlement of San Pete county. Founded first public library at Manti 1865. Died Sept. 29, 1878.

PEACOCK, JOHN LOWRY (son of George Peacock and Mary Artimesia Lowry). Born Aug. 5, 1855, Manti, Utah.
Married Serena Evens Moffitt Jan. 29, 1875, Salt Lake City (daughter of Andrew Jackson Moffitt and Margaret Easton of Manti). She was born April 20, 1858. Their children: John L. b. April 1, 1877, d. Oct. 17, 1903; Charles Moffitt b. March 14, 1879, m. Weltha O. Whitbeck; Ernest Eugene b. March 22, 1881, m. Emma Christoffersen (who died); m. Augusta Anderson; Leo Cox b. July 19, 1884, m. Effie Whitbeck; George Quince b. Jan. 29, 1886, d. Feb. 18, 1886; Maggie May b. May 10, 1887, m. William H. Bailey; Calvin b. May 6, 1889, m. Asenath Edwards; Clara b. June 14, 1891, m. Albert Anderson; Wendell b. Dec. 1893. Family home Sterling, Utah.
Missionary to Arizona 1876; bishop's counselor 1881-83; bishop of Sterling 1883-92; high priest. Justice of peace. Merchant and farmer.

PEACOCK, BRIGHAM JAMES (son of George Peacock and Mary Artimesia Lowry). Born Dec. 27, 1858, at Manti, Utah.
Married Sarah Eleanor Cox Dec. 1, 1880, St. George, Utah (daughter of Frederick Walter Cox and Jemima Losee of Iowa). She was born Nov. 30, 1859. Their children: Brigham James b. April 8, 1882, m. Lydia Pauline Staker; Minna May b. Dec. 20, 1883, m. James Keele; Edgar Reid b. Nov. 20, 1885, d. infant; Hazel Elvira b. March 16, 1887, m. William Keele; Edward Lynn b. July 17, 1889, m. Mary Johannah Alfred; Ralph Vernon b. June 6, 1891, m. Rosetta Jorgensen; Byron Charles b. March 10, 1893; Eleanor b. July 23, 1896; Wilbur b. June 29, 1899; Riddell b. April 30, 1903. Family home Emery, Utah.
Elder. Settled at Emery 1895; moved to Sterling 1880, and engaged in the sheep business under firm name of B. J. Peacock & Sons. Merchant and farmer.

PEACOCK, WARREN SNOW (son of George Peacock and Sarah Bell). Born Sept. 17, 1857, Manti, Utah.
Married Elizabeth Ann Parry Sept. 11, 1878, St George, Utah (daughter of Edward L. and Ann Parry of Wales, pioneers 1853). She was born March 4, 1858. Their children: Emma Parry b. Nov. 25, 1879, died; Warren Sylvester b. Aug. 13, 1881, m. Elvira Mott; Edward L. b. Dec. 7, 1882, m. Ruth Fox; Ann Elizabeth b. Nov. 6, 1884, died; George b. Nov. 7, 1887, died; Gomer Parry b. Aug. 11, 1888, m. Mabel Brown; Sarah Belle b. Sept. 13, 1891; Nettie b. March 11, 1893; Hattie b. April 3, 1896; Velora b. Nov. 13, 1898; Bernice b. Jan. 4, 1901; Leland b. Dec. 23, 1903. Family home Orangeville, Utah.
Member 91st quorum seventies; missionary to southern states 1888-90. County road commissioner three years.

PEARCE, ALONZO (son of Perry Pearce and Betsey Owen of Beekmantown, Clinton county, N. Y.). Born Oct. 20, 1813, Beekmantown. Came to Utah October, 1852, William McGaugh company).
Married Esther Angel March 5, 1837 (daughter of William Angel, born May 10, 1784, Dewn Ampney, Gloucestershire, Eng., and Esther Coffingbourne, born May 8, 1784, Dintonshire, Eng.). She was born April 10, 1816, in England, and died Dec. 30, 1846. Their children: William Alonzo b. Nov. 29, 1837; John Angel b. Oct. 15, 1839; Walter Amos b. May 18, 1841, died; Sylvester Henry b. March 13, 1843, m. Roseltha Melissa Reynolds; Perry b. Dec. 13, 1846, died.
Married Mary Ann Gardner (Haden) Jan. 30, 1848, who was born Sept. 13, 1822, came to Utah 1852, and died March 20, 1891. Their children: Esther b. May 9, 1849, and Joseph b. July 22, 1850, d. infants; Benjamin, m. Annie Jeppeson; Alfred, m. Fannie Carter; Inez, m. John Love; m. Mr. Hewlett. Family home Provo, Utah.
Farmer. Died Feb. 23, 1898.

PEARCE, SYLVESTER HENRY (son of Alonzo Pearce and Esther Angel). Born March 13, 1843. Came to Utah in 1852 with parents.
Married Roseltha Melissa Reynolds Dec. 25, 1864, Heber City, Utah (daughter of William Peter Reynolds and Melissa E. Bardwell of Michigan, pioneers Oct. 1855, oxteam company). She was born Sept. 13, 1844, Nunda, Livingston county, N. Y., and died June 20, 1906. Their children: Viola b. Oct. 25, 1865, m. Thomas Hatch; Esther Nora b. Sept. 1, 1868, m. Robert L. Tyler; Charles Henry b. Aug. 22, 1871, m. Eliza Noble; Mary Elizabeth b. Nov. 25, 1873, died; Ona Jane b. Jan. 10, 1877, m. Thomas Hatch; William Alonzo b. June 5, 1879, and Martha Ann b. Dec. 11, 1881, d. child; Alice Ermina b. Dec. 8, 1883, m. Emanuel M. Swain; George Albert b. July 5, 1886, m. Ethel Maud Bingham; Clara Bell b. Aug. 19, 1888, m. Lester Weight. Family resided Alpine, Apache county, Ariz., and Provo, Utah.
High priest. Settled in Provo; moved to Alpine 1879; to Vernal, Utah, 1890. Assisted in bringing immigrants to Utah. Home guard during Indian wars. Helped to build Union Pacific, Echo Canyon, Oregon Short Line, and Utah Southern Railways; helped build water system at Woodruff, Ariz.

PEARCE, GEORGE ALBERT (son of Sylvester Henry Pearce and Roseltha Melissa Reynolds). Born July 5, 1886, Alpine, Ariz.
Married Ethel Maud Bingham Aug. 26, 1908, Roosevelt, Utah (daughter of Calvin Perry Bingham and Olive Phelps of Roosevelt and Vernal, Utah). She was born May 25, 1890. Their child: Lamar b. Dec. 25, 1909, Vernal.
Teacher in first school held; secretary in first Y. M. M. I. A., and teacher in first Sunday school organized in Roosevelt; first missionary from Duchesne stake; filled mission in Central states 1910-1912; member 162d quorum seventies; president Y. M. M. I. A.; principal religion class; ward teacher. First clerk of Roosevelt town corporation. Proprietor Cash meat market.

PEARCE, EDWARD (son of Edward Pearce of London and Esther Chidark). Born June 20, 1802, London, Eng. Came to Utah Oct. 19, 1862, Horton D. Haight company.
Married Elizabeth Bennet March 5, 1826 (daughter of Richard and Elizabeth Bennet), who was born August, 1805, and came to Utah with husband. Their children: Elizabeth b. March 10, 1827, m. Charles F. Jennings; Mary b. Oct. 1, 1828, m. Richard Ballantyne; Susan b. Nov. 10, 1830, m. James Giller; Charles b. Feb. 20, 1833, m. Eliza Jane Rodwell; Esther b. Feb. 6, 1835, m. John G. Lindsay; Edward b. Jan. 6, 1837, m. Emaline ——; Eliza b. Jan. 6, 1839, m. Arthur Pickering; William b. Dec. 16, 1841, m. Margaret Jenkins; Richard b. 1843; Sarah b. Nov. 15, 1845, m. John Fowler. Family home Ogden, Utah.

PEARCE, CHARLES (son of Edward Pearce and Elizabeth Bennet). Born Feb. 20, 1833, London, Eng. Came to Utah 1864.
Married Eliza Jane Rodwell (daughter of John Rodwell and Sarah Jane Morgan, pioneers 1863, handcart company). Their children: Eliza Esther b. 1858, m. Jasper Simons 1878; Charles Rodwell b. Oct. 5, 1860, m. Agnes Hogensen Sept. 22, 1882; Nellie b. 1864; Sarah b. 1866, m. Mr. Fisher 1881; Edward; William.
Married Emma Lovesy Sept. 21, 1882, Salt Lake City.

PEARCE, CHARLES RODWELL (son of Charles Pearce and Eliza Jane Rodwell). Born Oct. 3, 1860, London, Eng. Came to Utah with parents.
Married Agnes Hogensen Sept. 22, 1882, Salt Lake City (daughter of Christian Hogensen and Peteria Larsen, pioneers Sept. 4, 1859, George Rowley handcart company). She was born Nov. 9, 1863, Paris, Bear Lake Co., Idaho. Their children: Mary Fredone b. April 6, 1884, died; Nellie Bardelia b. Feb. 6, 1886, m. W. L. Perkins Oct. 5, 1910; Nettie Vera b. Feb. 9, 1888; Mabel b. Aug. 27, 1891; Irene b. July 27, 1894; Jennie b. Sept. 24, 1896; Rulon C. b. Oct. 9, 1898; Ruth b. Nov. 12, 1901; Norman b. June, 1908. Family home Montpelier, Idaho.
Missionary to England 1890-92; high priest; counsellor in bishopric of Wardbrough. Director in two water companies 24 years; and president two years.

PEARCE, ROBERT (son of Thomas Pearce and Mary Snow of Porlock, Somersetshire, Eng.). Born June 13, 1817, at Porlock. Came to Utah Sept. 10, 1863, William B. Preston company.
Married Sarah Brown at Porlock 1844 (daughter of John and Sarah Brown), who was born Dec. 25, 1816. Their children: Elizabeth b. May 16, 1845, m. Edwin T. Pope Sept. 5, 1863; Mary Brown b. Dec. 9, 1846; Sarah b. May 25, 1849;

PIONEERS AND PROMINENT MEN OF UTAH 1093

Robert b. Aug. 24, 1851, m. Annie M. M. Somes Oct. 21, 1872; Mary b. Jan. 3, 1854; Thomas Joseph b. May 28, 1857, m. Mary Alice Davenport Dec. 1, 1881; Charles b. Sept. 6, 1860, m. Harriet Howells Oct. 12, 1882. Family home Paradise, Utah.
Early settler at Paradise, where he assisted in building up the country. High priest. Took active part in protecting settlers against Indians in early days. Shoemaker; gardener; fruitraiser; farmer; stockraiser.

PEARCE, ROBERT (son of Robert Pearce and Sarah Brown). Born Aug. 24, 1851, Cardiff, South Wales. Came to Utah with parents.
Married Annie M. Montierth Somes Oct. 21, 1872 (daughter of Alvin M. Montierth Somes and Harriet West Crapo, married Aug. 1, 1852, Kanesville, Iowa, pioneers 1853, Captain Thorne company). She was born Nov. 15, 1855, Salt Lake City. Their children: Robert Somes b. Nov. 15, 1873, m. Maud Wallace July, 1905; Charles William b. Feb. 7, 1875, m. Elizabeth Housley Dec. 14, 1898; Thomas Lorenzo b. July 20, 1876, m. Emma Nielson Sept. 12, 1900; Ernest Ether b. Jan. 20, 1878, m. Maggie Howells Dec. 11, 1907; Edgar Somes b. July 12, 1879, m. Charlotte Ann Lemmon Feb. 14, 1901; Harriet Ann b. Jan. 20, 1881; Mary Augusta b. March 3, 1882; Alvin Moroni b. June 15, 1883; Joseph Amos b. July 1, 1884, m. Nellie Hall Dec. 9, 1908; Francis Marion b. Sept. 2, 1886; Bertie b. Nov. 27, 1887; Reuben Somes b. March 8, 1889; Chloe b. Nov. 7, 1890, m. Roy J. Parker March 20, 1910; Wilford b. July 8, 1892; Henry b. July 30, 1894; Eva b. Sept. 8, 1896; Franklin b. Oct. 9, 1899. Family home Paradise, Utah.
Sunday school superintendent 19 years; president 62d quorum and later of 118th quorum seventies; choir and band leader; missionary to southern states; president Y. M. M. I. A.; school teacher 30 years. Secretary and treasurer Paradise Irrigation Company. Town clerk of Paradise; school trustee; enumerator of census of 1910. Secretary of Paradise Co-op.; newspaper correspondent. Worked on Central Pacific R. R., and also on Utah Northern. Member local militia. Farmer and stockraiser.

PEARSON, BENJAMIN (son of Ephraim John Pearson and Annie M. Montierth Somes). Born Nov. 15, 1873.
Married Maud Wallace July, 1905, in Arizona, who was born in Montreal, Canada. Their children: Robert b. 1906; Arthur b. July 7, 1907; Charles b. 1909.
Watermaster at Thatcher, Ariz.; canal constructor in Oregon and Arizona. Timber contractor; expert miner and prospector. Member Modern Woodmen of America.

PEARSON, EPHRAIM JOHN (son of Jacob Pearson and Rhoda Ewers of Brookfield, N. Y.). Born Oct. 28, 1825, Brookfield. Came to Utah July 29, 1847, with section of Mormon Battalion under command of Capt. James Brown.
Married Nancy Ann Foutz Dec. 5, 1848, Salt Lake City (daughter of Jacob Foutz and Margaret Munn of Jemper City, Franklin county, Pa.), who was born May 21, 1826. Their children: Ephraim b. Sept. 1, 1849, and Ann Sophia b. Nov. 1, 1850, died; Hyrum b. Jan. 5, 1852; Louisa b. June 10, 1854, m. Joseph Bingham Clark; Phoebe Elizabeth b. Aug. 12, 1855, m. John Albert Robison; Benjamin b. Nov. 29, 1857, m. Sarah Ellis Hawley; George b. March 3, 1859, died; Lewis Heber b. July 6, 1861.
Farmer. Died in California.

PEARSON, BENJAMIN (son of Ephraim John Pearson and Nancy Ann Foutz). Born Nov. 29, 1857.
Married Sarah Ellis Hawley June 30, 1879, Pleasant Grove, Utah (daughter of William John Hawley and Sarah Jane Staker of Pleasant Grove, pioneers 1852). She was born Sept. 10, 1860. Their children: William Benjamin b. May 30, 1882, m. Ida May Driver; Edith Loraine b. Sept. 20, 1884, m. Frank Lyman Jones; Rulian Vance b. July 12, 1886, m. Maude Clytie Lindsay; Stella Beryl b. May 26, 1889, m. Daniel West Neville; Leith St. Clair b. June 24, 1891; Avelan Francis b. Nov. 29, 1893. Family resided Pleasant Grove, Utah, and Colonia Garcia, Mexico.
Sarah Ellis Hawley (Pearson) married Walter Joshua Stevens Nov. 30, 1900. Only child: Grace Hawley Stevens b. Sept. 5, 1901.

PEARSON, WILLIAM BENJAMIN (son of Benjamin Pearson and Sarah Ellis Hawley). Born May 30, 1882, at Pleasant Grove.
Married Ida May Driver March 18, 1909, Ocean Park, Cal. (daughter of William Driver and Charlotte E. Bolter of London, Eng., pioneers 1867). She was born March 24, 1881. Their children: Charlotte Ellice b. Jan. 21, 1910; Marian b. June 18, 1912. Family home, Salt Lake City.
Auditor of accounts.

PEARSON, RULIAN VANCE (son of Benjamin Pearson and Sarah Ellis Hawley). Born July 12, 1886, Pleasant Grove, Utah.
Married Maude C. Lindsay June 10, 1910, Salt Lake City (daughter of Walter J. Lindsay and Adelaide Brunsen), who was born Feb. 8, 1888, Eden, Weber Co., Utah. Only child: Clyde Vance b. Feb. 1, 1912. Family home Ogden, Utah.

Jane b. March 16, 1837, m. Israel Justice Clark; Cassander Malissa b. Nov. 9, 1839; Orson Jesse b. Oct. 25, 1851; Martha Gabreila b. May 5, 1853; James; Benjamin; Libby, m. Mr. Lockyear.
Farmer. Died March 23, 1878, Farmington, Utah.

PEART, JACOB. Born June 3, 1801, Alston, Cumberlandshire, Eng. Came to Utah July 24, 1848, Brigham Young company.
Married Elizabeth Holden at Alston. Their child: Jacob Peart, Jr., b. July 1, 1835, m. Margaret Gray July 20, 1860.
Married Angela Philinda Loss Nov. 22, 1847, who was born Nov. 23, 1826, Corinth, Saratoga county, N. Y. Their children: Benjamin Loss b. June 10, 1849, m. Elizabeth Christiana Ashment; Leander L. b. Aug. 31, 1856.

PEART, BENJAMIN LOSS (son of Jacob Peart and Angela Philinda Loss). Born June 10, 1849. Salt Lake City.
Married Elizabeth Christiana Ashment (daughter of Thomas Ashment and Ann Huggins of Crewkerne, Somersetshire, Eng.). She was born Sept. 23, 1849, and came to Utah Sept. 2, 1868, Simpson M. Molen company: Their children: Sylvia Ann b. Oct. 15, 1870, m. Thomas Allsop Oct. 5, 1888; Meraida b. Dec. 17, 1872, m. Isaac P. Bright Dec. 17, 1895; Joseph b. March 16, 1875, m. Lucina Jane Stoddard Oct. 30, 1901; Leander b. June 21, 1877, m. Estella H. Tripp Dec. 18, 1907; Rhoda b. Sept. 24, 1879, m. John M. Dobson April 20, 1898; Maud b. July 21, 1882, m. Cyrus Bullen July 20, 1904; Ada May b. May 25, 1887, m. Frank W. Traveller June 16, 1910; Olive Melora b. Nov. 7, 1889.
High priest; ward teacher.

PEAY, EDWARD (son of William Peay and Mary Blake of Yapton, Sussex, Eng.). Born May 22, 1829, Phelpham, Sussex. Came to Utah October, 1852, Jedediah M. Grant company.
Married Mary Barnes June 6, 1856, Salt Lake City (daughter of Thomas Barnes and Judith Hibird of Cheshire, Eng.), who was born May 16, 1839. Their children: Edward W., died; George T. B., m. Emily Cook; Peter M., m. Julia Giles; Franklin F., m. Kate Adams; James, died; Mary Ellen, m. Rosell Scott.
Married Amanda Melvina Stubbs March 2, 1867, Salt Lake City (daughter of Richard Stubbs and Eleanor Ware of Cheshire, Eng., pioneers 1852, Jerome Benson oxteam company). She was born Sept. 19, 1846. Their children: Amanda Elizabeth, m. Osborne Samuel Clark; John Edward, m. Ella York; Ida Alice, m. John Durrant; Emma Eliza; Gideon, m. Anetta Ferre; Samuel Stubbs.
Married Rebecca Ann Stubbs May 20, 1874, Salt Lake City (daughter of Richard Stubbs and Elander Ware), who was born May 1, 1853. Their children: Sarah Elnora, m. Brigham Johnson; William Richard, m. Rhoda Buckner; David Wilbert, m. Mary Arrowsmith; Joseph Elvin and Ernest, died. Family home Provo, Utah.
President 34th quorum seventies; missionary to England 1889-90; president teachers quorum of second ward; Sunday school teacher; home missionary for three years. Veteran Black Hawk Indian war; participated in Echo Canyon trouble. Farmer. Died April 25, 1900, at Provo.

PEAY, GEORGE THOMAS (son of William Peay and Mary Blake of Yapton, Sussex, Eng.). Born Jan. 1, 1837, Climpung, Eng. Came to Utah 1852, oxteam company.
Married Anna Margretta Christensen July 4, 1860, Ogden, Utah (daughter of Andrew Chris Christensen and Marie Sophia Pearson of Uland, Denmark, pioneers October, 1857, handcart company). She was born Jan. 19, 1837. Their children: Emily, died; George T., m. Mercy Waters; William W., m. Emma Burton; Frances Elnora and Mary Blake, died; Josephine J., m. Arthur J. Durrant; Edwin A.; Ida Stewart; Ethea Berthelda, m. George E. Ross; James Alfred, died; Ruth Mercy, m. Edward Farrer.
Married Johana C. Pauch 1862, Salt Lake City (daughter of Rodolph Pauch of Germany), who was born 1841. Their children: Anna Margaret, died; Daniel Rodolph b. Jan. 10, 1869, m. Agnus Jean Vincent; Agnus, m. Dan J. Atherley; Gertrude, m. John Rawlings; Parley, m. Emma Poulsen.
Married Marie Sorenson March 2, 1867, Salt Lake City (daughter of Soren Sorenson and Maran Hanson of Denmark), who was born Oct. 1, 1850. Their children: Louisa Alice, m. Anderson McDaniel; Joseph Charles; died; Harriette, m. Albert Bowden; Hortensia, died; Emma, m. William Jacobson; Etta, m. Amory Jacobson; Edwin Lott, m. Rose Lampson. Family home Provo, Utah.
Member 34th quorum seventies; Sunday school, ward and block teacher. City councilman. Farmer.

PEAY, DANIEL RODOLPH (son of George Thomas Peay and Johana C. Pauch). Born Jan. 10, 1869, Provo, Utah.
Married Agnes Jean Vincent Oct. 19, 1899, Salt Lake City (daughter of Daniel Vincent and Mirian Pack of Canada, pioneers 1852, oxteam company). She was born Jan. 9, 1872. Their children: Mirian Vincent b. Jan. 12, 1901; Leslie Rodolph b. Dec. 29, 1903; Albert Earl b. June 22, 1905. Family home, Provo.
Deacon.

born Dec. 23, 1820. Their children: Henry; Elizabeth, died; Ann Maria, m. Alanson Eldredge; Mary Jane, m. Albert Minnerley; Fannie Angier, m. Edwin Elliott; Lyman, m. ——— Bigelow; George, m. Nellie Bryce; Amelia, m. Hyrum Bigelow. Family home, Andover.
Seventy; high priest; missionary to St. George, 1862. Veteran Black Hawk war. Farmer. Died Feb. 8, 1890, Safford, Graham county, Ariz.

PECK, HENRY (son of Charles Peck and Sarah Gosley Q. ——— of Winham, Greene county, N. Y.). Born Feb. 26, 1823, in Greene county, N. Y. Came to Utah 1863, independent company.
Married Julia Everett 1844 (daughter of Jonathan Everett and Rachel Bessell), who was born 1823, in Connecticut. Their children: Dwight A. b. Dec. 1845, m. Martha A. Biddlecome; Frederick b. July 1849, m. Lizzie Leigh; Lenard b. Jan. 7, 1867, m. Sarah Bradburry; Sarah b. April 1852, m. Stanton Fisher; Howard b. Jan. 1855, m. Jane Wooley; Julia b. April 1858, m. William Wesley; Amelia E. b. April 1858, m. William B. Thews; Mary b. Aug. 1860, m. ——— Ellis; Emily b. Feb. 1864, m. William E. Wass; Charles b. Dec. 1866, m. Annie Bywater.
Pioneers of Malad, Idaho, 1864

PECK, DWIGHT (son of Henry Peck and Julia Everett). Born 1845, in Greene county, N. Y.
Married Martha A. Biddlecome 1875, Oxford, Idaho (daughter of Joseph Biddlecome and Martha Ann Cooper of Grantsville, Utah, pioneers 1848, indepndent company). She was born 1857. Their children: Walter H. b. Oct. 3, 1876, m. Margaret Virginia Jones; Edwin b. Sept. 25, 1878; Vera b. Jan. 17, 1894.

PECK, MARTIN H. (son of Ebenezer Peck of Vermont). Came to Utah 1848, Brigham Young company.
Married Susan Cluff 1826, in Vermont. Their children: Edwin, Joseph Augustine, m. Ann Miller; James; William. Family home 17th ward, Salt Lake City.
Seventy; high priest; missionary to eastern states; high councilor. Sealer of weights and measures at Salt Lake City. Blacksmith. Died at North San Juan, Cal.

PECK, JOSEPH AUGUSTINE (son of Martin H. Peck and Susan Cluff). Born April 1830, in Vermont. Came to Utah 1848, Brigham Young company.
Married Ann Miller May 17, 1857, Bishop Thomas Callister officiating (daughter of Thomas and Susan Miller of Manchester, Eng.). She was born Feb. 3, 1837. Their children: Joseph A. b. June 25, 1858, d. infant; Susan Vilate b. Feb. 19, 1860, d. aged 5; Annella M. b. Jan. 30, 1862, d. infant; Herman Adelbert b. Oct. 30, 1863, m. Minnie Ure; Alice Miller b. Nov. 9, 1865, m. Robert M. Thompson; Martha b. March 13, 1868, d. aged 17 months; Mary b. March 13, 1868, d. aged 8; Ellen b. March 27, 1870, d. aged 6; William H. b. Jan. 16, 1872, d. aged 3; Annie May b. Dec. 28, 1876, m. William H. Kingdom; Daisy Pearl b. Aug. 9, 1881, m. Roy J. Bosch, m. Frank Therit.
Seventy; high priest; block teacher; missionary to Sandwich Islands. Sealer of weights for Salt Lake county. Blacksmith.

PECK, THORIT (son of Warren Peck and Hannah Mattison of Cayuga county N. Y.). Born May 30, 1826, in Cayuga county. Came to Utah Oct. 28, 1848, contingent Mormon Battalion.
Married Anna Young January, 1850, Salt Lake City (daughter of James Young and Elizabeth Seely of Ontario, Canada; pioneers 1847, Brigham Young company). She was born Oct. 8, 1834, and died Aug. 3, 1851.
Married Sarah Young 1852 (daughter of James Young and Elizabeth Seely), who was born Oct. 8, 1834, in Upper Canada, township of Whitby. Their children: Alma Mattison b. Sept. 30, 1853, m. Sarah W. Stock Oct. 31, 1871; Thorit Randolph b. Nov. 12, 1854, d. Jan 23, 1859; Anna B. b. Sept. 15, 1857, m. Frederick O. D. Deakin. Family home Pleasant Grove, Utah.
Sheriff of Utah county. Veteran Indian war. Teacher of fencing; lathe turner; farmer. Died at Pleasant Grove Feb. 6, 1858.

PECK, ALMA MATTISON (son of Thorit Peck and Sarah Young). Born Sept. 30, 1853, Pleasant Grove, Utah.
Married Sarah W. Stock Oct. 31, 1871, Salt Lake City (daughter of John Stock and Jane Adams of Salt Lake City, pioneers 1862). She was born July 8, 1854, in South Africa. Their children: Sarah Jane b. Oct. 31, 1872, m. Alonzo R. Teeples; Carlotta b. May 2, 1874, m. Christian Hebertson, m. Hans Hansen; Thorit b. March 28, 1876, m. Sarah Ann Jensen; Alma Mattison b. Jan. 18, 1878, m. Rose Wilkinson; Anna Elizabeth b. Jan. 15, 1880, m. Alva Hatch; Mary Alice b. Dec. 23, 1881, m. Moses Wilkinson; Amy b. Sept. 28, 1883, and Lillian Mary b. July 13, 1885, died; John Stock b. March 5, 1887, m. Hannah Carlietta Singleton; Olive b. Jan. 17, 1890, m. Samuel Wilkinson; Joseph Edwin b. April 26, 1893, m. Vera Gourley. Family resided Mt. Pleasant, Garden City and Vineyard, Utah, and Fish Haven, Idaho.
Elder. Went to Bear Lake 1874, and after several moves finally located in Vineyard ward, where he now resides. General mechanic; inventor; farmer.

PECKTOL, WILLIAM. Came to Utah Sept. 19, 1847, Daniel Spencer company.
Married, and following children composed the family: George, m. Mina Peterson; James, m. Mary Blazzard; Elizabeth; Eunice, m. Robert Brown; Dorothy, m. William Carroll; Jemima, m. Newman Brown; m. John Alma Beal; Eliza, m. Mr. Hutchinson. Family home Manti, Utah.

PEERY, DAVID HAROLD (son of David Peery and Eleanor Harman of Tazewell county, Va.). Born May 16, 1824, in Tazewell county. Came to Utah September, 1864, William Pritchett company.
Married Nancy Campbel Higginbotham (daughter of William Elliott Higginbotham and Louisa Ward of Burke's Garden, Tazewell county, Va.), who was born May 19, 1835, in Tazewell county, and died Sept. 30, 1862. Their children: Thomas Carnahan b. Oct. 9, 1858, d. May 1, 1861; Louisa Letitia o. Oct. 14, 1860, m. Charles Comstock Richards; William Harold b. Sept. 21, 1862, d. Oct. 12, 1862.
Married Elizabeth Letitia Higginbotham April 10, 1865, Salt Lake City (daughter of William Elliott Higginbotham and Louisa Ward), who was born Jan. 13, 1846, Nauvoo, Ill. Their children: David Henry b. April 13, 1866, d. Dec. 6, 1907; Joseph Stras b. Oct. 5, 1868, m. Luacine Hoge, m. Julina Clarissa Smith; Nancy May b. May 2, 1871, d. March 31, 1873; Horace Eldredge b. Nov. 14, 1873, m. Jane Taylor; Eleanor Virginia b. April 29, 1876, d. Jan. 3, 1877; John Harold b. Feb. 19, 1878, m. Hazel Taylor; Margaret Louise b. Feb. 20, 1881, m. Emmett Glen Fulkerson; Simon Francis Higginbotham b. Aug. 18, 1884, m. Florence Carstenson; Lewis Hyrum b. April 11, 1887, m. Mary Scowcroft; Harman Ward b. Aug. 23, 1891.
President 76th quorum seventies; missionary to southern states 1875; president Weber stake 1876-82. Representative to territorial convention at Washington for statehood; member state constitutional convention; mayor of Ogden 1883-87; member Utah legislature 1878-84. Director of Deseret National Bank of Salt Lake and of Thatcher Bros. Bank of Logan; manager Z. C. M. I. at Ogden; president First National Bank at Ogden. Merchant; miller. Died Sept. 17, 1901, Ogden.

PEERY, JOSEPH STRAS (son of David Harold Peery and Elizabeth Letitia Higginbotham). Born Oct. 5, 1868, Ogden, Utah.
Married Luacine Hoge July 20, 1898, Salt Lake City (daughter of Enos Dougherty Hoge and Luacine Williams, Salt Lake City, pioneers July 3, 1865). She was born Sept. 16, 1872, and died April 27, 1908. Their child: Harold Hoge b. Dec. 22, 1903, d. Dec. 22, 1903. Family resided Ogden and Salt Lake City.
Married Julina Clarissa Smith Dec. 23, 1909, Salt Lake City (daughter of Joseph Fielding Smith and Julina Lamson of Salt Lake City). She was born Feb. 10, 1884, Salt Lake City. Their children: Joseph Smith b. Feb. 6, 1911; Luacine b. Dec. 2, 1912. Family home, Salt Lake City.
Member 124th quorum seventies; president 18th ward Y. M. M. I. A., and on board of superintendency of Y. M. M. I. A. of Ensign stake; missionary at bureau of information Temple Grounds, Salt Lake City. Superintendent of schools Weber county, 1891-92; Weber county attorney 1896-97; president Carnegie Public Library at Ogden; president of directors of State Industrial School. Director Pingree National Bank at Ogden. Attorney at law; sheepraiser.

PEIRCE, ROBERT. Came to Utah September, 1847.
Married ———. Their child: Thomas, m. Harriet N. Green 1858.

PEIRCE, ELI HARVEY (son of Robert Peirce and Hannah Harvey of Chester county, Pa.). Born July 29, 1827, in Chester county. Came to Utah July 24, 1847, Brigham Young company.
Married Susannah Neff 1850, Salt Lake City (daughter of John Neff and Mary Barr, pioneers July, 1847). She was born March 26, 1831. Their children: Eli Harvey, Jr., m. Lydia May Snow, m. Henrietta Madson; Mary Barr, m. Oliver G. Snow; Leonidas Thomas, m. Eugenia Snow; Octavia, m. Joseph Hardman. Family home Brigham City, Utah.
Married Emma Zundel 1857, Salt Lake City (daughter of Isaac Zundel and Sarah Forstner of Willard City, Utah, pioneers).
Bishop of Brigham City; high priest; missionary to Europe 1857-58. Built first two-story building in Utah, outside of Salt Lake City. Rescued a company of California goldseekers, who had been lost on Great Desert. Farmer. Died Aug. 12, 1858, Salt Lake City.

PEIRCE, ELI HARVEY (son of Eli Harvey Peirce and Susannah Neff). Born Sept. 27, 1851, Salt Lake City.
Married Lydia May Snow at Salt Lake City (daughter of Lorenzo Snow and Mary E. Houtz of Brigham City, Utah, pioneers). Their children: Pearl Snow b. July 18, 1884, m. Howard Eugene Smith; F. Dolores b. Dec. 12, 1887, m. Walter H. Handin; Ramona May b. June 17, 1892; Elia Harviola b. Jan. 27, 1896. Family home Brigham City, Utah.
Married Henrietta Madson June 20, 1888, Logan, Utah (daughter of Adolph Madson and Mary Wagner of Brigham City and Salt Lake City). She was born Dec. 13, 1863. Their children: Pansy Adina b. Aug. 6, 1893, m. George W. Reddington; Harvey Adolph b. Aug. 27, 1894; Earl Wagner b. July 26, 1896; Mary Henrietta b. Aug. 27, 1905.

High priest; member presidency 59th quorum seventies; missionary to eastern states 1875-77; again in 1878, and was president of that mission; associated with presidency Y. M. M. I. A. of Box Elder stake; home and Sunday school missionary; member tabernacle choir since 1890. Secretary and treasurer Salt Lake Choral Society, organized in the 90s, and chairman board of control of the new choral society, which succeeded the old one in 1905. Stationmaster and operator for Utah & Northern R. R. at Ogden. Engaged in fire insurance.

PEIRCE, THOMAS (son of Robert Peirce).
Married Harriet N. Green 1858, in Pennsylvania, pioneer September, 1847. Their children: Harriet Luna b. 1859, m. William Boyce; Thomas H. b. March 20, 1861, m. Agnes M. Boan; Morris C. b. 1863, d. aged 15. Family home South Cottonwood, Utah.
Elder; missionary to England two years. Farmer; stockraiser. Died 1864, Salt Lake City.

PEIRCE, THOMAS H. (son of Thomas Peirce and Harriet N. Green). Born March 20, 1861, Brigham City, Utah.
Married Agnes M. Boan Nov. 23, 1882, Salt Lake City Endowment House, Daniel H. Wells officiating (daughter of Thomas Boan and Elizabeth McGhie of Mill Creek, Utah). She was born July 15, 1863. Their children: Thomas C. b. 1883, m. Louisa Muir; Elizabeth b. 1885, m. Joseph Leggit; Eva b. Feb. 7, 1887; Emma b. Feb. 7, 1887, m. William Gebhardt; Harriet A. b. 1889, m. Hyrum Brady; Morris E. b. July 16, 1895; Adelbert H. b. July 24, 1899; Elmo b. Aug. 19, 1903; Elmer b. Aug. 19, 1903. Family home South Cottonwood, Utah.
Member 72d quorum seventies; elder; ward teacher. Farmer; stockraiser.

PEIRCE, WILLIAM (son of Robert Peirce and Hannah Harvey). Born April 2, 1833, in Pennsylvania.
Married Jerusha Smith at Salt Lake City (daughter of Hyrum Smith and Jerusha Bardon; former killed in jail at Carthage, Ill., latter died at Nauvoo, Ill.). Their children: Hannah E. b. Sept. 18, 1855, m. Aaron Beckstead; Hyrum R. b. April 9, 1857, m. Nellie Hale; Lovina b. Aug. 26, 1860, m. John Green; Margaret b. Jan. 10, 1863; Sarah M. b. Oct. 20, 1865, m. Josiah Egbert; William H. b. May 26, 1868; Eli T. b. Jan. 27, 1870, m. Maggie Olson; Irene E. b. Jan. 30, 1872, m. Erastus Barnard; Lucy L. b. Jan. 22, 1877.
Built first house erected in Brigham City.

PEIRCE, ELI T. (son of William Peirce and Jerusha Smith). Born Jan. 27, 1870, Brigham City, Utah.
Married Maggie Olson Feb. 14, 1890, Logan, Utah (daughter of Christian Olson and Mary Carlson), who was born Feb. 3, 1871. Their children: Eulalia A. b. July 8, 1891; Leonard E. b. May 14, 1893; Leslie W. b. Jan. 21, 1895; Harvey C. b. Feb. 19, 1897; Hazel M. b. May 22, 1899; Birdie J. b. Feb. 26, 1901; Arnold H. b. Oct. 21, 1903; Asael S. b. Feb. 12, 1906; Clarence F. b. April 1, 1911.
Farmer; stockraiser.

PENDER, JAMES F. (son of Thomas Pender and Marguerite Toelia). Born Nov. 29, 1845, in West Virginia. Came to Utah 1865, in employ of United States government.
Married Sarah Catherine Laub Oct. 24, 1869, in Platte county, Mo. (daughter of John Laub and Matilda Simons of Platte county), who was born May 17, 1850. Their children: Robert E. b. Aug. 26, 1870, m. Ella Harsh; Thomas V. b. Oct. 29, 1872; Olive R. b. Nov. 29, 1872, and Walter b. June 7, 1875, died; Rose M. b. May 14, 1877, m. H. R. Hislop; John A. b. Aug. 1, 1878, m. Fonda Turner; Lulu b. July 18, 1882, m. William R. Swan; James F., Jr., b. Aug. 29, 1883, m. Katherine Swan; E. Craig b. June 21, 1885, m. William R. Hathaway; Mary Alice b. Sept. 12, 1889, m. Richard E. Steuch. Family home Ogden, Utah.
Chief of detectives of Ogden city 20 years.

PENROD, DAVID (son of Lewis and Polly Penrod of Nauvoo, Ill.). Born Jan. 9, 1815, in Union county, Ill. Came to Utah 1850.
Married Temperance Keller (daughter of Abraham and Sally Keller), who was born Nov. 18, 1817, in Rowan county, N. C. Their children: William, m. Polly Ann Riggs; Elizabeth, m. William Wall; Israel, m. Annie Phillips; Christina (Tina), m. James Smith; Abraham, m. Ela Durfee; Minerva Olive, m. George Meldrum; Temperance, m. Joseph Evans; David Nephi, m. Hannah Melissa Baum Oct. 22, 1872; Ephraim b. Jan. 11, 1859, d. Oct. 26, 1865; Amasa Lyman, m. Jemima Wright, m. Hannah Wright. Family home Provo, Utah.
Died Feb. 26, 1872.

PENROD, DAVID NEPHI (son of David Penrod and Temperance Keller). Born Oct. 24, 1850, Second Fort (now Academy Park), Provo, Utah.
Married Hannah Melissa Baum Oct. 22, 1872, Salt Lake City (daughter of George Baum and Hannah Jane Cloward of Provo, Utah, formerly of Pennsylvania—pioneers 1850). She was born Feb. 4, 1856. Their children: Hannah Musetta b. Jan. 19, 1874, d. May 23, 1874; David Nephi b. Dec. 23, 1875, d. June 5, 1879; George b. Oct. 16, 1877, d. Oct. 17, 1877; Wilfred b. Oct. 22, 1878, m. Hattie Fawcett; Lulu Pearl b. Jan. 10, 1881, d. May 10, 1891; William Albert b. Dec. 4, 1882, m.

Zella Stubbs; Ethel Temperance b. Sept. 13, 1885, m. John Nelson; Fern b. March 11, 1886, d. same day; Mary Melissa b. Dec. 24, 1889, m. Fredrick Young.
Elder. Veteran Indian war. Farmer; stockraiser.

PENROD, OLIVER (son of John Penrod, born July 6, 1791, Somerset, Pa., and Barbara Tope, born Oct. 9, 1799, Union, Ill.). Born Sept. 20, 1831, Jackson, Ill. Came to Utah 1853, Richard Ballantyne company.
Married Anna Amelia Hubbard Sept. 19, 1854, Uinta, Utah (daughter of Tilla Hubbard and Hulda Theadotia Parish), who was born 1838. Only child: Hulda Amelia b. Dec. 5, 1855, d. Sept. 11, 1873. Family home, Uinta.
Married Hannahette Mower March 28, 1868, Salt Lake City (daughter of Henry Mower and Mary Amic of Sangamon county, Ill.; former pioneer 1851, Abraham Day company, latter died at Kaysville, Ill.). She was born Oct. 10, 1841, in Sangamon county. Their children: Oliver Allen b. July 31, 1869, m. Ida Alvord, m. Mary Eliza Knighton; Anna A. b. Dec. 4, 1871, d. April 8, 1873; John A. b. July 27, 1875, d. Feb. 4, 1877; Cyrus A. b. Oct. 29, 1877, m. Mary Ann Burt Ge, Nov. 25, 1898; Ida T. b. Dec. 21, 1879, d. Jan. 15, 1880; William C. b. Nov. 3, 1881, m. Martha Hannah Knighton Feb. 18, 1903.
High priest. Farmer; musician. Died Sept. 3, 1908.

PENROD, OLIVER ALLEN (son of Oliver Penrod and Hannahette Mower). Born July 31, 1869, Mt. Green, Morgan Co., Utah.
Married Ida Alvord Dec. 25, 1889, Logan, Utah (daughter of Gideon Alvord and Sarah Shupe of North Ogden, Utah, pioneers 1853, Richard Ballantyne company). She was born May 25, 1872. Their children: Lawrence O. b. Aug. 15, 1890, d. Nov. 15, 1890; William G. b. Oct. 28, 1891, d. Jan. 11, 1892; Sarah S. b. Dec. 5, 1893; Earl T. b. May 29, 1896. Family home Liberty, Utah.
Married Mary Eliza Knighton Feb. 20, 1900, Salt Lake City (daughter of George Knighton and Eliza Johnson of Bountiful, Utah), who was born April 30, 1884. Their children: Oliver H. b. Dec. 5, 1901, d. May 1, 1905; Clyde b. July 27, 1903, d. same day; Ida LaVon b. Dec. 7, 1905; Lloyd Asael b. April 17, 1908; Hulda Elma b. April 8, 1910, d. April 28, 1910; Don Allen b. April 20, 1911.
One of the presidents of 131st quorum seventies; missionary to Indiana 1897-98; Sunday school teacher; instructor in mutual; ward chorister; ward teacher. Justice of peace. Farmer.

PENROSE, CHARLES WILLIAM. Born Feb. 4, 1832, Camberwell, London, Eng. Came to Utah September, 1861, Homer Duncan company.
Missionary in England, before coming to Utah; two years. Settled at Farmington upon his arrival in Utah; moved to Cache Valley in 1864. Missionary to England 1865-68. Engaged in mercantile pursuits at Logan 1868. Moved to Ogden 1870, and took charge of the editorial department of the "Ogden Junction," then a semi-weekly, but later a daily. Member Ogden City council four terms. High priest and member high council Weber stake. Delegate from Weber county to the constitutional convention 1872. Member of the committee appointed to give the state its name, and the memorial to congress. Member legislature from Weber county 1874. In 1877 moved to Salt Lake City and became connected with the "Deseret News," and in 1880 became editor-in-chief of that paper. In 1879, at a special Salt Lake county to fill the vacancy caused by the death of Albert P. Rockwood, and re-elected in 1882. Elected to the constitutional convention, and assisted in framing the constitution of the state of Utah. Second counselor to Angus M. Cannon, president Salt Lake stake 1884; missionary to England 1885. In 1893 became editor-in-chief of Salt Lake "Herald." Sustained a member quorum of twelve apostles Oct. 9, 1904; Dec. 7, 1911, sustained as second counselor to Joseph F. Smith in the first presidency of the Church of Jesus Christ of Latter-day Saints.

PEPPER, JOHN (son of Lawrence Pepper and Mary Ward of Northamptonshire, Eng.). Born Aug. 26, 1836, Northamptonshire. Came to Utah 1861.
Married Anna Mariah Fordham March 7, 1863 (daughter of Elijah Fordham and Anna Boblin Chaffee, pioneers 1850, independent company). She was born May 21, 1844. Came to Utah with parents in 1850. Their children: Anna Mariah Fordham b. Sept. 7, 1864, d. May 21, 1904; m. William P. Rankin; Emily Ann Fordham b. Sept. 15, 1866, d. Dec. 16, 1876. Family home Wellsville, Utah.
Made a trip across the plains for merchandise in 1863; assisted in bringing immigrants to Utah. Blacksmith. Died April 10, 1867, Wellsville, Utah.

PERKES, JAMES (son of James Perkes and Leah Abbot of Wales). Born March 28, 1819, Dudley, Worcestershire, Eng. Came to Utah Oct. 17, 1862, Henry W. Miller company.
Married Eliza Boleson (daughter of Joseph and Sarah Adeliey), who was born March 28, 1819, and came to Utah 1869. Their children: John b. March 30, 1840; Simeon b. Oct. 13, 1843; Reuben b. Aug. 13, 1845, m. Ellen Alfred; Rob b. Nov. 22, 1869, m. Sarah Ann Watkin Dec. 23, 1910; Elizabeth b. Feb. 11, 1847; Leah b. Nov. 1, 1848, m. William Poppleta

1863; Rachel b. Feb. 5, 1852; Ephraim b. Oct. 5, 1853, m. Harriet Clark Nov. 4, 1878.
Married Mary Ann Gibson 1854, in St. Louis, Mo. She was born March 3, 1830, Nottingham, Eng., and came to Utah 1862, Henry W. Miller company. Their children: William Gibson b. March 3, 1856, and Elena b. May 14, 1858, died; Catherine S. b. May 2, 1861, m. William Harry.
High priest.

PERKES, REUBEN (son of James Perkes and Eliza Boleson). Born Aug. 13, 1845, Worcestershire, Eng. Came to Utah with father in 1863.
Married Ellen Allred Nov. 22, 1869, Salt Lake City (daughter of William Allred and Mary Burthwryte; latter pioneer 1868, Simpson Molen company). She was born Dec. 9, 1850, Suffolk, Eng., died June 13, 1908. Their children: James W. b. May 11, 1871, m. Erma Daines Oct. 28, 1896; Reuben Albert b. Feb. 15, 1873, m. Rette Balls Feb. 3, 1891; Kate Sarah b. Aug. 26, 1875, m. Thomas Walker 1892; Arthur b. July 4, 1878; John Alven b. Aug. 24, 1881; Vilda A. b. April 1, 1882, m. Joseph Jones 1900; Thomas W. b. March 18, 1882, m. Roda Jorgesen 1899; Nellie V. b. Oct. 14, 1888, m. Alma Cook Nov. 24, 1909. Family home Hyde Park, Utah.
Married Sarah Ann Watkin Dec. 23, 1910 (daughter of Catherine Wilks, pioneer 1863).
Treasurer Hyde Park town corporation; president Logan and Hyde Park Canal Co.; president Logan, Hyde Park and Smithfield Canal Co.; vice president Farmers' Union Mills Co.

PERKINS, ABSALOM (son of Ute Perkins and Sarah Gant of Macedonia, Hamilton county, Ill.). Born in North Carolina. Came to Utah 1848, Allen Taylor company.
Married Nancy Martin, who came to Utah with husband. Their children: Sarah, m. John Shipley; Ute, m. John Warren Jan. 16, 1835; William Louis b. June 18, 1819, m. Mary Ann Brown June 15, 1842; Hyrum; David M., m. Harriet Brown; Levi b. Dec. 29, 1825, m. Susan Booth Aug. 22, 1858; James; John; Susan, m. Louis Whitesides; Adeline, m. Isaac Carpenter; Francis Marion; George Washington b. May 1, 1836, m. Alice Mellin Jan. 20, 1864; Christopher C. b. 1838, m. Ann Robins.
Presided over a branch of Mormon church in Iowa.

PERKINS, WILLIAM LOUIS (son of Absalom Perkins and Nancy Martin). Born June 18, 1819, in White county, Tenn. Came to Utah Sept. 21, 1850.
Married Mary Ann Brown June 15, 1842, at Macedonia, Ill. (daughter of Alanson Brown and Cynthia Dorcas Hurd, latter pioneer 1850, William Wall company). She was born 1821, in Steuben county, N. Y. Their children: Eliza Ann b. March 14, 1843, m. Edwin Merrill Nov. 2, 1865; George Carlos b. May 15, 1845, m. Isabelle Hunter July 18, 1870; William Thomas b. April 12, 1848, m. Mary Adelaide Lawson Oct. 12, 1878; Hyrum S. b. Oct. 4, 1850. Family home, Salt Lake City.
Married Sarah Jane Richards 1853, Salt Lake City (daughter of John Richards and Sarah Inon of Wales), who was born Jan. 13, 1833, Caermarthenshire, South Wales. Their children: Sarah Jane b. Aug. 27, 1854, m. John Cozzens July 5, 1869; John Absalom b. Sept. 20, 1856, m. Annie Bonney Oct. 11, 1879; William Louis b. July 19, 1858; David Richard b. April 26, 1860, m. Eliza Smith Nov. 19, 1885; Francis Marion b. Feb. 2, 1862, m. Maggie Southworth May 29, 1884; Nancy Adeline b. Jan. 28, 1864, d. same day; Hannah Elizabeth b. Oct. 7, 1865, m. Henry Thomas Hillier June 22, 1887; Jesse Andrew b. Nov. 1, 1867, m. Emily S. Dalrymple July 1, 1891; Isaac Monroe b. Dec. 10, 1869, m. Amy Hancock Sept. 23, 1890; Mary Emma b. March 29, 1872, m. Fredrick Kesler 1892.
Moved from Salt Lake City to Pleasant Green 1889. One of presidents of 30th quorum seventies; high priest. Worked on Salt Lake and St. George temples. Missionary to western states 1869. Died.

PERKINS, GEORGE CARLOS (son of William Louis Perkins and Mary Ann Brown). Born May 15, 1845, Hancock county, Ill. Came to Utah 1850 with parents.
Married Isabelle Hunter July 18, 1870, Salt Lake City (daughter of Adam Hunter and Elizabeth Patterson, pioneers 1552), who was born Oct. 27, 1852, Salt Lake City. Their children: Mary Elizabeth b. Aug. 2, 1871, m. Samuel R. Hall July 17, 1889; George Carlos b. March 28, 1873; Isabelle b. Jan. 30, 1874, m. Peter Hansen Nov. 12, 1891; William b. May 22, 1876, m. Charlotte Law June 3, 1910; Jenett b. May 24, 1879, m. William C. Stephens Aug. 30, 1898; David Hunter b. Aug. 19, 1881, m. Carrie Romina Munk July 7, 1904; Eliza Ann b. March 5, 1884, m. Fredrick Coon Oct. 23, 1901; Ellen b. Oct. 9, 1886, m. David J. Parker Oct. 10, 1906; Louisa b. Jan. 16, 1889, m. John Stephens April 8, 1909; Jessie Myrtle b. May 15, 1892, m. J. A. Artimus Crane June 12, 1912; Lorena Grace b. April 21, 1896. Family resided Salt Lake City, Utah, and Bennington, Idaho.
Moved from Salt Lake City to Bear Lake county, Idaho, 1876. Assistant Sunday school superintendent 29 years; ward teacher 32 years; seventy. Assisted in bringing immigrants to Utah with Horton D. Haight in 1863. Ordained high priest Feb. 4, 1912.

PERKINS, WILLIAM THOMAS (son of William Louis Perkins and Mary Ann Brown). Born April 12, 1848, in Pottawattamie county, Iowa.
Married Mary Adelaide Lawson Oct. 12, 1878, Coalville, Utah (daughter of John Lawson and Margaret Vance), who was born Oct. 7, 1856, at Manti, Utah. Family resided Coalville and St. George, Utah, and Montpelier, Idaho.
Ward teacher; ward clerk; presiding elder; high priest. County commissioner in Idaho 1897-99; sheriff of Washington county, Utah, 1907-09. Temple worker at present. St. George temple.

PERKINS, GEORGE WASHINGTON (son of Absalom Perkins and Nancy Martin). Born May 1, 1836, Macedonia, Ill. Came to Utah 1848 with parents.
Married Alice Mellen Jan. 20, 1864, Salt Lake City, Bishop Kesler officiating (daughter of John Mellen and Jane Ramsden of Salt Lake City, pioneers September, 1848, Brigham Young company). Their children: George Washington, Jr. b. Sept. 10, 1865, m. Catherine Blowers; Mary Alice b. Jan. 28, 1867, m. David Thompson; John Absalom b. April 10, 1870, m. Mary A. Thompson; Nancy Jane b. July 13, 1874, d. aged 36; Ute b. Aug. 23, 1877, m. Etta B. Wilkins; Ray M. b. Jan. 1, 1884, m. Lavina Wolstenholme; May b. Nov. 23, 1889, m. Perry Memmott.
Member 14th quorum seventies; home missionary; ward teacher. Farmer and stockraiser.

PERKINS, AUGUSTUS P. (son of Ezra Perkins and Elizabeth Soule of Marietta, Ohio). Born Feb. 10, 1837, Marietta. Came to Utah May, 1890.
Married Amelia Kullmer 1854, Lafayette, Ind. (daughter of John Kullmer and Amelia Schriner of Lafayette), who was born Aug. 3, 1836. Their children: Walter K., m. Minnie Reese Davies; Winnie S., m. Frank Terry; Percival O., m. Ethelyn R. Frolseth; Mary Belle; Amelia Louise, m. Dr. J. C. Ross. Family home, Salt Lake City.
Grocer. Died Dec. 15, 1911, Salt Lake City.

PERKINS, PERCIVAL O. (son of Augustus P. Perkins and Amelia Kullmer). Born June 12, 1866, Lafayette, Ind. Came to Utah June, 1888.
Married Ethelyn R. Frolseth Sept. 14, 1899, Salt Lake City (daughter of Bernard A. M. Frolseth and Jane Anderson of Washington and New York; came to Utah about 1872). She was born Feb. 23, 1876. Their child: Elizabeth Jane b. June 21, 1905. Family home, Salt Lake City.
County recorder; deputy city treasurer; deputy county auditor. Accountant.

PERKINS, FRANKLIN. Born 1823, in North Carolina. Came to Utah 1848, A. Perkins company.
Married Esther ———— 1825, in Grundy county, Mo., who was born 1833. Their children: Sarah, m. Peter Livingston; Mary, m. Sylvester James; Downey, m. Sylas Sprouse; Ephraim, d. aged 21; Wesely, d. aged 8; Albert, d. aged 3, Manissa and Thomas E., d. infants; Sylvester, m. Martha A. J. Stevens; Charlotte, m. Charles Camble.
Farmer. Died 1878, at Salt Lake City.

PERKINS, JOSEPH (son of Thomas Perkins and Ann Mathews of Wales). Born Sept. 24, 1820, Langher, Glamorganshire, Wales. Came to Utah Oct. 31, 1855, Charles A. Harper company.
Married Margret Martin Dec. 25, 1852 (daughter of Thomas Martin and Gurnefried Williams; former died in Wales, latter came to Utah 1859, Robert F. Neslen company). She was born Dec. 22, 1833. Their children: Thomas b. June 9, 1854, m. E. E. Packer March 14, 1874; Margret b. Sept. 2, 1856, m. Thomas Morrison April 7, 1874; Joseph Mathews b. Sept. 22, 1856; William Daniel b. Aug. 20, 1858; Edward Martin b. Jan. 10, 1860, m. Jane Baird Oct. 18, 1883; Celia Jane b. April 20, 1862, m. James Packer Dec. 12, 1878; Lorenzo Martin b. Nov. 4, 1864, m. Sarah Ann Collon Nov. 9, 1884; Nephi Martin b. May 1, 1867, m. Mary Elvira Mendenhall 1889; David Alma b. Feb. 11, 1870, m. Mary Elizabeth Cullen 1889. Family resided North Ogden, Provo and Franklin, Utah.
Married Harriet Preese Dec. 10, 1873, Salt Lake City (daughter of Richard Preese and Susanah Ritchalt), who was born March 17, 1833, in England. Their children: Joseph Ephraim b. Oct. 31, 1874; Jyram James b. July 26, 1877.
Presiding elder St. Joseph, Idaho. Veteran Indian war; minuteman. Settled at Franklin April 13, 1860.

PERKINS, EDWARD MARTIN (son of Joseph Perkins and Margret Martin). Born Jan. 10, 1860, Provo, Utah.
Married Jane Baird Oct. 18, 1883, Salt Lake City (daughter of Robert Erwin Baird and Jane Hadley, former pioneer July 24, 1847, Brigham Young company). She was born March 28, 1862, Lynn, Utah. Their children: Margret Jane b. Aug. 5, 1884, m. Fred Monson; Orpha Baird b. Feb. 18, 1886; Lettie Baird b. Jan. 29, 1888, m. Rufus C. Long; Edward Erwin b. June 29, 1891; Merlin b. April 27, 1893; Edna b. March 27, 1895; James Aaron b. Feb. 18, 1897; Alta Vivian b. Feb. 22, 1901; Raymond b. Oct. 16, 1903. Family resided Franklin and Mapleton, Idaho, and Cooperville, Utah.
Seventy; high priest; missionary to Great Britain twice; teacher Franklin ward; presiding elder St. Joseph, Idaho; bishop of Mapleton ward.

PERKINS, JOSEPH. Came to Utah by oxteam.
Married Elizabeth Alice Hardman, at Salt Lake City, Brigham Young officiating, who was born 1835, and came to Utah with husband. Their children: Joseph Hyrum;

George Nathan, m. Ellen ———; Nephi Nathaniel, m. Emily Ja e Mead. Family resided Salt Lake City and Ogden, Utah.
Took an active part in protecting the settlers against the Indians in early troubles. Hunter and scout. Deceased.

PERKINS, NEPHI NATHANIEL (son of Joseph Perkins and E Alice Hardman). Born Oct. 24, 1857, Salt Lake City.
Married Emily Jane Mead Nov. 9, 1880, Spanish Fork, Utah (daughter of Orlando Fish Mead and Lydia Aby Presley of Spanish Fork, pioneers with oxteam). She was born March 31, 1864, Spanish Fork. Their children: Nephi Orlando b. Aug. 17, 1881; Emily Alice b. Jan. 8, 1883, d. child; Hyrum Lehi b. May 1, 1885, d. infant; George William b. July 6, 1887; Lydia Aby b. July 23, 1889, m. Harry Ashly Brown; m. Wilber Booker; Samuel Alexander b. June 21, 1891, d. aged 18; Joseph Presley b. Feb. 5, 1893; Franklin Thomas b. Jan. 5, 1895. Family home Price, Utah.
Blacksmith and farmer. Died June 22, 1896, Ogden, Utah.

PERKINS, JOSEPH PRESLEY (son of Nephi Nathaniel Perkins and Emily Jane Mead). Born Feb. 5, 1893, Spring Glen, Utah.
Deacon. Carpenter, plumber and confectioner.

PERKINS, JOHN (son of Samuel Perkins and Rosannah Kitchener of Western Underwood, Buckinghamshire, Eng.). Born Dec. 28, 1821, Western Underwood. Came to Utah 1865.
Married Martha Filer about 1870, Salt Lake City. She was born Dec. 23, 1838. Their children: Ida Jane, d. infant; Ellen M., m. Josiah N. Lees; John S., m. Annie Hopkinson; Ammon M., m. Nevada Turker; Amanda A., d. aged 12. Family home, Salt Lake City.
Seventy; Sunday school and block teacher. Section foreman Utah Central and U. P. R. R. about 17 years. Died May, 1887, Salt Lake City.

PERKINS, REUBEN (son of Ute Perkins of Hancock county, Ill., born Aug. 8, 1760, in Virginia, and Sarah Dant of southern states, born April 22, 1760). Born March 1, 1783, Lincoln county, N. C. Came to Utah from Grundy county, Mo., Oct. 18, 1849, Andrew H. Perkins company.
Married Elizabeth Pittillo June 15, 1802, who was born Nov. 10, 1782. Their children: Ephraim Pittillo b. July 24, 1803, m. Elizabeth Whitson; Wilson Gardner b. March 11, 1807, m. Diana Anderson; Andrew H. b. Dec. 5, 1808, m. Jemima Whitscn; John H. b. July 9, 1813, m. Louisa A. Rhea; James Byron b. Dec. 6, 1815, d. April 19, 1819; Jesse Nelson b. Feb. 19, 1819, m. Rhoda Condra McClellan Jan. 13, 1842; Franklin Monroe b. July 13, 1827, m. Mariah Tuttle.
Married Catherine Wart June 18, 1864, Salt Lake City.
Married Mary Glen July 29, —, Salt Lake City. Family home Bountiful, Utah.
High priest. Farmer. Died Oct. 22, 1871, Bountiful.

PERKINS, WILSON GARDNER (son of Reuben Perkins and Elizabeth Pittillo). Born March 11, 1807, between Chillicothe and Trenton, Grundy county, Mo. Came to Utah in 1849.
Married Diana Anderson at Jackson, Tenn. (daughter of William Anderson and Elizabeth Jones of Grundy county, Mo.), who died 1849, Salt Lake City. Their children: William Anderson and James Monroe, died; John Preston, killed, aged 5; Marion Columbus; Elizabeth Jane b. Feb. 11, 1837, m. Edward Everett Belcher; Mary Ann, m. Joseph Howard; Harvey Huston, m. Helen Colton, m. Sarah Simmons; Louisa Caroline, d. child; Jasper Newton, m. Lucy Garret, m. Lasina Call. Family home Bountiful, Davis Co., Utah.
Elder. Farmer. Died 1849, Salt Lake City.

PERKINS, JESSE NELSON (son of Reuben Perkins and Elizabeth Pittillo). Born Feb. 19, 1819, in Jackson county, Tenn.
Married Rhoda Condra McClelland Jan. 13, 1842, in Mercer county, Mo. (daughter of Josiah McClelland and Rhoda Condra), who was born Oct. 20, 1821, in Monroe county, Ky., and came to Utah Oct. 18, 1849. Their children: John Henderson b. Nov. 9, 1842, m. Louisa Deseret Perkins Nov. 27, 1871; Littleton Lyttle b. Jan. 13, 1847, m. Carrie E. Wood May 30, 1888; Brigham Young b. April 18, 1850, m. Melissa Wallace April 9, 1873; Heber Kimball b. April 12, 1852, m. Martha M. Wallace March 24, 1873; Jesse Nelson, Jr., b. Feb. 28, 1854, m. Mary Lavina Plumb Nov. 25, 1896; Reuben Josiah b. Oct. 14, 1856, m. Eliza Jane Hancock Nov. 2, 1881; Franklin Monroe b. Feb. 26, 1859, m. Sarah C. Hancock March 20, 1889; Rhoda Elizabeth b. March 20, 1862, m. Brigham Young May 17, 1886. Family home Taylor, Ariz.
Married Mariah Tuttle at Salt Lake City. Their children: Franklin Monroe b. July 15, 1867, m. Elizabeth ———; Ellen Elizabeth, m. William Reeves; Martha Mariah, d. infant.
Missionary 1869-70; high priest; member high council of Snowflake stake. Selectman county court of Davis county. Died March 2, 1883, Taylor, Ariz.

PERKINS, BRIGHAM YOUNG (son of Jesse Nelson Perkins and Rhoda Condra McClelland). Born April 18, 1850, Salt Lake City.
Married Melissa Wallace April 9, 1873, Salt Lake City (daughter of George B. Wallace and Melissa King, pioneers), who was born in Salt Lake City Oct. 14, 1853. Only child: Brigham Andrew b. May 25, 1874, m. Frances Barbary Kuhl May 25, 1907. Family home Bountiful, Utah.
Missionary to Little Colorado river, Arizona, 1873. Moved to southern Utah with family 1875, and again to Arizona with father's family 1877. Farmer. Family home Taylor, Ariz.

PERKINS, SAMUEL (son of John Perkins and Elizabeth Letts of Irchester, Eng.). Born Aug. 9, 1832, Irchester. Came to Utah 1856, A. O. Smoot company.
Married Ann Godfrey Feb. 2, 1860 (daughter of Thomas Godfrey and Elizabeth Ainge), who was born Nov. 26, 1832, and came to Utah 1859, George Rowley handcart company. Their children: Ann Elizabeth b. May 27, 1862, m. Egbert Riggs; Mary Alice b. Dec. 9, 1863, m. Job Miller; Samuel John b. Aug. 13, 1866, m. Margaret Glenn Jan. 16, 1890; Thomas Jeffery b. July 27, 1868, d. infant; George Quail b. Aug. 22, 1869, m. Elizabeth Owen Dec. 10, 1890; Ellen Maria b. Jan. 22, 1871, m. John A. Leishman.
Married Elizabeth Chapman July 19, 1871, Salt Lake City (daughter of Isaac B. Chapman and Solona Brown), who was born 1830 in Vermont. Their children: Emily b. Sept. 6, 1872, m. Thomas Maughn Dec. 14, 1892; Louis b. Feb. 13, 1874, m. Charlotte Minnerly Jan. 10, 1894.
Home missionary. Veteran Echo Canyon war. City treasurer four years; city councilman three terms. Settled at Salt Lake City; moved to Wellsville, Cache valley, 1860. Shoemaker in early days. Farmer. Died June 5, 1905.

PERKINS, SAMUEL JOHN (son of Samuel Perkins and Ann Godfrey). Born Aug. 13, 1866, Wellsville, Utah.
Married Margaret Glenn Jan. 16, 1890, Logan, Utah (daughter of Walter Glenn and Elizabeth Stuart, pioneers 1854), who was born July 30, 1867, at Wellsville. Their children: Samuel John b. Sept. 12, 1891; Elizabeth b. July 30, 1893; Margaret b. Dec. 14, 1895, and Earl and Pearl (twins) b. Sept. 9, 1898, d. infants; Walter Philip b. Nov. 29, 1900; Ann b. Oct. 11, 1903; Jennett b. July 26, 1909. Family home, Wellsville.
Missionary to England 1906-07. Farmer.

PERRY, ALEXANDER (son of Matthew Perry and Mary Turner). Born Dec. 21, 1829, Paisley, Scotland. Came to Utah 1853. His brothers and sisters were: James Perry; Malcolm Perry; Matthew; Mary; Elizabeth; Alexander; Robert. All born in Paisley, but came to America in 1852. They conducted a large dye house in New York for several years. Robert, the youngest, fought in the civil war on the side of the North, and although wounded several times lived for years after.
Married Marion Leckie Shanks Dec. 21, 1855, Salt Lake City (daughter of James Shanks and Isabella Dock of North Willard, Utah, pioneers 1855, Charles Harper company). She was born July 19, 1836, and died April 21, 1890. Their children: Isabella Dock b. March 27, 1857, m. James M. Dalton April 5, 1875; Mary Turner b. Jan. 11, 1860, d. Sept. 2, 1872; Marion Elizabeth b. March 29, 1863, m. J. D. Johnson Feb. 1883; Matthew b. April 6, 1865, d. Jan. 8, 1866; James Shanks Sept. 9, 1867, m. Eliza Cordon Sept. 7, 1891; Agnes Jane (twin of James S.), m. Brigham Nebeker July 24, 1888; Lucy Danridge b. Sept. 4, 1871, m. George G. Doyle June 17, 1893. Family resided North Willard and Willard, Utah.
Gardener and farmer. Died Aug. 31, 1889, in Mexico.

PERRY, ASAHEL (son of Abiel Perry, born Dec. 20, 1754, Attleboro, Bristol county, Mass., and Miriam Walcott, born Sept. 19, 1755, Williamsburg, Hampshire county, Mass.). He was born Feb. 26, 1784, Williamsburg. Came to Utah 1850, Captain Bennett company.
Married Polly Chadwick March 6, 1806 (daughter of Isaac Chadwick and Dinah Brewer of Middlebury, Genesee county, (N. Y.), who was born June 24, 1789, Framingham, Mass. Their children: Isaac b. May 4, 1807; Lucy Ann b. Feb. 22, 1809, m. Isaac Story; Willard b. Aug. 3, 1810; William Chadwick b. Jan. 26, 1812, m. Eliza Brown Oct. 1835; Orrin b. May 19, 1814, m. Eliza Marcher; Hiram b. Sept. 29, 1816, m. Eva Nellis 1853; Stephen Chadwick b. Dec. 22, 1818, m. Susanah Calista Hiddon, m. Anna Maria Hewlett, m. Margaret Eleanor Stewart, m. Mary Boggs; Philander Jackson b. Sept. 29, 1821, m. Arvilla Pratt May 27, 1850; Lewis b. Dec. 13, 1825; Polly Maria b. June 16, 1832, m. William Smith May 19, 1850. Family home Springville, Utah.
High priest; missionary in New York 1840; president of Springville branch 1850-51. Judge of election four years; member legislature three years. Farmer. Died Feb. 16, 1869, at Springville.

PERRY, STEPHEN CHADWICK (son of Asahel Perry and Polly Chadwick). Born Dec. 22, 1818, Middlebury, Genesee county, N. Y.
Married Susanah Calista Hiddon Jan. 6, 1840, Middlebury, Genesee county, N. Y.
Married Anna Maria Hewlett (daughter of Charles and Margaret Hewlett), who was born Dec. 11, 1817. Their children: Mahorri Mariancumer; Tryphena Roseltha b. June 19, 1847, m. Leonard J. Whitney Dec. 25, 1866; Lewis Rosalvo b. Dec. 31, 1849, m. Cornelia Whiting; John Sylvester b. March 10, 1852, m. Eva Maud Matson; Colista Ann b. Aug. 10,

1854, m. Francis C. Boyer April 8, 1875; Sarah Elizabeth; Charles Asahel b. Dec. 31, 1858, m. Asenath Melvina Duncan Dec. 23, 1893. Family home Springville, Utah.
Married Margaret Eleanor Stewart Feb. 4, 1854, Salt Lake City (daughter of John Martin Stewart and Nancy King), who was born in Ohio county, Ky. Their children: Harriet Susanna b. Nov. 29, 1855, m. Albert M. Whiting Dec. 22, 1873; Isabel Maria b. Oct. 10, 1857; Martin Stewart b. Aug. 17, 1858, m. Eliza Jane Clark July 3, 1889.
Married Mary Boggs in April, 1857, Salt Lake City (daughter of Francis Boggs and Evaline Martin, pioneers 1847). She was born April 12, 1843, at Nauvoo, Ill. Their children: Francis Martin b. July 14, 1858; Hyrum Boggs b. Aug. 13, 1859, m. Luella Roundy March 24, 1884; George Willard b. Nov. 26, 1861, m. Charlotte Smith Fullmer March 24, 1884; Frances Eveline b. April 26, 1864, m. Edwin M. Snow April 9, 1883; Luella Estella b. Sept. 10, 1866, m. Alonzo S. Fullmer; Lucy Viola b. Sept. 26, 1868, m. John Van Luven Dec. 25, 1890; Edward Harvey b. April 9, 1871, m. Mary Fullmer Feb. 19, 1896; Horace Brigham b. Sept. 12, 1873, m. Ariel Warren Aug. 31, 1895; Parley Pratt b. Nov. 5, 1875, m. Lydia A. Gallup Sept. 8, 1897; Marcus Lafayette b. Nov. 6, 1879, m. Phoebe J. Fullmer June 27, 1900; Marion b. Jan. 11, 1883, m. Clara Larsen. Family resided Springville and Mapleton, Utah.
High priest; missionary to eastern states twice; presiding elder of branch in Utah county; ward teacher at Springville. Early settler to Springville, where he assisted in developing country. Veteran Indian war. Farmer; chairmaker. One of Joseph Smith's bodyguard. Died November, 1888, at Springville.

PERRY, LEWIS R. (son of Stephen Chadwick Perry and Anna Maria Hewlett). Born Dec. 3, 1849, Mt. Pisgah, Iowa.
Married Cornelia D. Whiting Dec. 18, 1871, Salt Lake City (daughter of Edwin Whiting and Almyra Mecham of Springville, Utah, pioneers 1850, Captain Bennett company). She was born June 11, 1851. Their children: Willis Delmar b. June 5, 1873, m. Jessie Porter Jan. 22, 1902; Myra Gertrude b. Sept. 7, 1876, m. Edward A. Killpack Nov. 7, 1894; Erma b. April 29, 1878, m. Hugh Hendrickson Feb. 2, 1910; Leon Lewis b. Nov. 9, 1880, m. Dora Dusten April 10, 1912; Charles Franklin b. March 24, 1884, m. Jessie Henrie Oct. 7, 1909; George W. b. Feb. 22, 1887; Ross Leo b. July 28, 1892. Family home, Springville.
High priest; missionary to eastern states 1897-98; superintendent Sunday school Mapleton ward, 1888-93; member high council of Union stake, Oregon, 1901-06. Farmer; carpenter.

PERRY, JOHN SYLVESTER (son of Stephen Chadwick Perry and Anna Maria Hewlett). Born March 10, 1852, Springville, Utah.
Married Eva Maud Matson Jan. 27, 1873, Salt Lake City (daughter of George Brinton Matson and Mary Jane Guymon of Springville, former pioneer 1847, latter Sept. 7, 1855). She was born March 6, 1857. Their children: Maud b. May 31, 1877, died; Ida Luella b. Aug. 10, 1879, m. Samuel Fullmer Andrew; Edith Estelle b. Dec. 9, 1881, m. Charles Ebon Snow; John Sylvester b. Oct. 10, 1885, died; George Stephen b. Feb. 13, 1888, m. Beula Whiting; Maple b. Nov. 29, 1891; Jesse b. Aug. 3, 1894; Jasper b. Aug. 3, 1894. Family home, Springville.
Missionary to Arizona 1876. Farmer.

PERRY, CHARLES ASAHEL (son of Stephen Chadwick Perry and Anna Maria Hewlett). Born Dec. 31, 1858, Springville, Utah.
Married Asenath Melvina Duncan Dec. 23, 1893, Ferron, Utah (daughter of John Chapman Duncan and Theresa Hayburn of Scotland, Salt Lake City, Cedar City and Ferron, Utah). Their children: Myron Duncan b. Nov. 12, 1894; Ora Belle b. March 23, 1896; Ivan b. Oct. 4, 1897; Stephen Chapman b. March 30, 1899; Arnold Sylvester b. Oct. 29, 1900; Asahel A. b. June 22, 1902; Archie b. Jan. 11, 1904; Rolland b. Jan. 17, 1906; Eunice b. Feb. 15, 1908, d. infant. Family home Vernal, Utah.
Elder; ward teacher. Member town board of Ferron two terms. Farmer.

PERRY, MARTIN STEWART (son of Stephen Chadwick Perry and Margaret Eleanor Stewart). Born Aug. 17, 1858, Springville, Utah.
Married Eliza Jane Clark July 3, 1889, Salt Lake City (daughter of Edward Watkins Clark and Louise Mellor, married Feb. 3, 1857, Salt Lake City; former pioneer Sept. 21, 1852, Orson Hyde company, latter pioneer 1866, "Frozen" handcart company). She was born Nov. 4, 1871, at Santaquin, Utah. Their children: May b. Jan. 28, 1890; Martin Wayne b. April 6, 1892; Edward Clark b. Nov. 9, 1893; Effie b. May 15, 1896; Zena b. Aug. 7, 1898; Myrtle b. March 17, 1900; Louise b. Dec. 11, 1902; Howard Alton b. Sept. 15, 1904; Melvin Stewart b. Aug. 22, 1907; Joseph Francis b. March 29, 1910. Family home, Springville.
Missionary to southern states 1893-95; president Y. M. M. I. A.

PERRY, GEORGE WILLARD (son of Stephen Chadwick Perry and Mary Boggs). Born Nov. 26, 1861, Springville, Utah.
Married Charlotte Smith Fullmer March 24, 1884, Springville (daughter of John S. Fullmer, born in Pennsylvania, and Olive Amanda Smith, born in New York, pioneers 1847). She was born April 3, 1867. Their children: George Othello

m. David W. Dean; Ralph b. Aug. 27, 1890; Leonard D. b. June 15, 1892; Luvell b. Aug. 27, 1894; Clive b. Jan. 15, 1896; Evan b. March 30, 1899; Eldon b. Sept. 20, 1901; Zelia May b. March 24, 1904; Elmer b. May 1, 1907; Jennie Linn b. Oct. 29, 1909. Family resided Ferron, Mapleton and Springville, Utah.
High priest; counselor to Joseph A. McKee of Glines ward, Uintah stake; Hyrum A. Nelson of Ferron ward, Emery stake, and Samuel D. Fullmer of the elders quorum of Mapleton. Director in Ferron Creek Irrigation Company; chairman old folks' committee of Ferron. Emery county school trustee; county commissioner; county road commissioner.

PERRY, STEPHEN (son of Daniel Perry and Sallie Whitmore of Sherburne, Vt.). Born Aug. 12, 1792, Sherburne.
Came to Utah 1850, Thomas Jeremy company.
Married Rhoby Edwards April 12, 1816, Sherburne (daughter of Joseph Edwards and Olive Green of Sherburne), who was born July 23, 1793, Windsor, Vt. Their children: Josiah b. April 5, 1818, m. Lucinda Cole; Susannah b. Aug. 3, 1820, m. William Jones; William Howard b. Aug. 2, 1823, m. Alice Stowell, m. Juliaette Stowell; Sallie S. b. Sept. 1, 1826, m. Daniel Carter; Stephen W. b. Oct. 9, 1829, m. Helen Bishop; Sylvester Lyman b. Jan. 2, 1833, m. Nancy Ann Shaffer; Alonzo O. b. May 17, 1836, m. Jeanette Stowell. Family home Slaterville, Utah.
Missionary to Vermont. Active temple worker. Farmer. Died Dec. 29, 1886, Kanesville, Iowa.

PERRY, WILLIAM HOWARD (son of Stephen Perry and Rhoby Edwards). Born Aug. 2, 1823, in Essex county, N. Y. Came to Utah in 1850, William Clapp company.
Married Alice Stowell Oct. 17, 1851, Lynn, Utah (daughter of A. O. A. Stowell and Mary S. Holmes of New York, latter pioneer 1852). She was born July 19, 1832. Their children: Stephen b. July 16, 1853, m. Mary Ellen Biglow; Cynthia Ernestine b. Feb. 6, 1856, m. William Henry Packard; Joseph b. Sept. 30, 1859, m. Martha Hovey; Hyrum b. Sept. 30, 1859, m. Nora Scott; Don Carlos b. Aug. 19, 1863, m. Martha Bingham; Oren Amos b. Nov. 15, 1867, m. Rose Soth; Mary Alice b. June 5, 1871, m. John Slaugh. Family home Cache Valley, Utah.
Married Juliaette Stowell June 10, 1853, Provo, Utah (daughter of A. O. A. Stowell and Mary S. Holmes), who was born Nov. 29, 1835. Their children: Mary Rhoby b. May 7, 1855, m. Edward Jessup; Susan Caroline b. June 11, 1857, m. George Marler; Alonzo Henry b. Sept. 29, 1859; Heber b. March 23, 1862, d. infant; Harriett b. March 23, 1863, m. David H. Bingham; George William b. April 3, 1866; Juliaette b. Oct. 17, 1868, m. Thomas Caldwell; Minerva Amanda b. Oct. 24, 1873, d. child; Sallie Alvira b. Feb. 20, 1876, m. William Griffin; Rose Czarina b. June 1, 1879, m. Henry Willard Williams. Family home Lynn, Utah.
Missionary to Salmon river 1857-58; bishop's counselor. Farmer. Died Dec. 15, 1904, Vernal, Utah.

PERRY, GEORGE WILLIAM (son of William Howard Perry and Juliaette Stowell). Born April 3, 1866, Huntsville, Utah.
Missionary to central states Nov. 20, 1907, to Jan. 17, 1910; one of seven presidents of the quorum seventies. Farmer; fruitraiser.

PERRY, SYLVESTER LYMAN (son of Stephen Perry and Rhoby Edwards). Born Jan. 2, 1833, Lewis, N. Y. Came to Utah 1850 with father.
Married Nancy Ann Shaffer Jan. 22, 1855, Bingham Fort, Utah (daughter of Henry Shaffer and Eve Beard of Slaterville, Utah, pioneers 1851, Captain Woods company). She was born in Indiana Nov. 14, 1833. Their children: Henry Sylvester b. Dec. 27, 1855, m. Ester N. Price; Mary Jane b. Oct. 24, 1859; William Heber b. June 30, 1862, m. Charlotte Ann Fields; Susan Arrenie b. Oct. 19, 1864, m. John W. Singleton; Sarah Elizabeth b. Oct. 2, 1867, m. John E. Stratton; Nancy Ann b. Aug. 4, 1870, m. James Ross; Margaret Ellen b. April 29, 1874, m. Oliver Henry Bybee. Family home, Slaterville.
Member 60th quorum seventies; teacher; high priest. Farmer. Died July 6, 1908.

PERRY, WILLIAM HEBER (son of Sylvester Lyman Perry and Nancy Ann Shaffer). Born June 30, 1862, Slaterville, Utah.
Married Charlotte Ann Fields Nov. 4, 1886, Logan, Utah (daughter of William Fields and Charlotte Bolt of Slaterville, pioneers 1852). She was born April 1, 1863. Their children: Edward Ernest b. Dec. 9, 1887, d. infant; Ada Ann b. Feb. 7, 1890; Heber LeRoy b. May 23, 1892; Earl Westley b. Aug. 21, 1894; Ray Delwin b. Jan. 28, 1897; Blanch Alta b. March 26, 1899; Irvin Warren b. May 4, 1902.
Elder. Farmer.

PETERS, DAVID (HUGHES) (son of Peter Hughes, born 1771, Merioneth, Wales, and Elizabeth Morris). Born March 10, 1810, in Merioneth. Came to Utah 1849, George A. Smith company.
Married Laura Jones Davis April 11, 1840 (daughter of John Davis and Laura Jones), who was born Feb. 8, 1817; came to Utah with husband. Their children: Sarah b. Feb. 6, 1841, m. Charles P. Squires Sept. 1, 1856; Laura b. March 16, 1842, m. William Woodland; Elizabeth b. June 11, 1845; John David b. May 10, 1851, m. Louisa Bingham Nov. 22, 1869; David b. Oct. 23, 1851; William b. Oct. 20, 1853; Morris Rees b. Nov. 22, 1855, m. Annie Thorn Dec. 11, 1879; Thomas

PIONEERS AND PROMINENT MEN OF UTAH 1099

D. b. Dec. 14, 1857, m. Sarah Thorn Dec. 22, 1887; Peter Hughes b. Nov. 27, 1860, m. Melvina Perry. Family home Three Mile Creek (Now Perry), Utah.
Married Ann Jones Perry Sept. 20, 1851, Salt Lake City (daughter of Edward Jones). Their children: Joseph and Hyrum (twins) b. June 18, 1852; Sarah Ann b. Oct. 7, 1854; Mary b. Feb. 23, 1856, m. John S. Bingham; Richard b. March 3, 1858, m. Orpha Henderson.
Pioneer of Box Elder county 1852. Lived in Brigham City for a few years; moved to Three Mile Creek (now Perry), Utah. Died June 11, 1898.

PETERS, MORRIS REES (son of David Hughes Peters and Laura Jones Davis). Born Nov. 22, 1855, Brigham City, Utah.
Married Annie Thorn Dec. 11, 1879, Salt Lake City (daughter of Richard Thorn and Rebecca Ann Osborn, pioneers 1840), who was born April 16, 1860, Perry, Utah. Only child: Morris William b. March 21, 1881, m. Udessa Elvira Jeppson June 5, 1905.
First counselor to Bishop James Nelsonsen Oct. 25, 1896-1904. Bishop of Perry ward, Utah.

PETERSEN, ANDERS (son of Peder and Anna Andersen of Givskud, Sjaelland, Denmark). Born May 10, 1830, at Givskud. Came to Utah October, 1861.
Married Eliza M. Krough April 12, 1863, Provo, Utah (daughter of Lawrence Krough and Johanna Broe of Heils, Schleswig-Holstein, Germany), who was born July 27, 1838, and came to Utah Sept. 27, 1862, John R. Murdock company. Their children: Andrew P. b. May 20, 1864, died; Annie J. b. May 6, 1866, m. Harry Stone; Peter L. b. Aug. 22, 1868, died; Eliza M. b. April 9, 1870, m. Alfred Anderson; Lawrence P. b. April 12, 1873, m. Minnie Golean Dec. 20, 1899; m. Lucy Aspinall Dec. 1909; Anton M. b. Nov. 1, 1876, m. Millie Wilde Nov. 3, 1905; Mary Ann b. Sept. 26, 1879, m. Arthur Wilde Aug. 1899; Emma Frances Oct. 1902. Family resided at Provo, Utah and Raymond and Barnwell, Alta, Can.
Member 64th quorum seventies. Bought load of telegraph wire from Omaha to Salt Lake Sept. 1861. Settled at Salt Lake City; moved to Provo in 1863, where he resided nearly 40 years, and then moved to Barnwell, Can. Assisted materially in the development of Provo and surrounding country.

PETERSEN, ANDREW (son of Peter Andersen, born 1801, and Annie Petersen of Denmark). Born Dec. 13, 1832, Viborg, Denmark. Came to Utah Oct. 1, 1866, Joseph S. Rawlins company.
Married Caroline D. Dabelstein (daughter of Henry Dabelstein and Christine M. Lytt), who was born Oct. 8, 1835, Holstein, Germany. Their children: Hans P. b. July 21, 1858, m. Mary Rasmussen 1881; James b. Sept. 9, 1860; Annie D. b. April 4, 1863, died; Minnie C. b. July 6, 1865, m. George Brown 1884; Andrew b. Nov. 9, 1867, m. Maud Mills 1892; Adam H. b. Dec. 8, 1869, m. Verdie Post 1905; Emma b. June 16, 1871, m. Richard Redden 1893; Eliza b. Nov. 8, 1872, m. Joshua Bates 1894; George A. b. Jan. 24, 1874, m. Vadie Winters 1899; Eleanor b. Aug. 11, 1867, m. John Williams 1903; Joseph H. b. Jan. 25, 1878, m. Elonora Murdock 1904; Frank b. Oct. 5, 1880, m. Emma Comer 1901.
Married Mary Larsen in 1838, who was born Aug. 13, 1850, in Denmark. Only child: Nephi b. April 24, 1890. Family home Wanship, Utah.
Superintendent Wanship Sunday school 17 years; bishop of Wanship; president high priests quorum; missionary to Denmark and Germany 1898-1900. Veteran Danish-German war 1864-1865; veteran Black Hawk war; guard at penitentiary. Railroad contractor Union Pacific R. R. 1868. Died Nov. 26, 1900, Wanship.

PETERSEN, ANDREW (son of Peder Pedersen and Kirstine Andersdatter of Sjaelland, Denmark). Born Feb. 8, 1829, Jetsmark, Sogn, Denmark. Came to Utah October, 1854.
Married Anna Marie Hansdatter Oct. 15, 1854, Salt Lake City (daughter of Hans Olsen and Tova Knudsdatter of Denmark), who was born March 13, 1822. Their children: Christena, m. Caleb Hartley; Lorenzo, m. Mary Nordstrom; Peter, m. Celestia M. Terry; Mette M., m. Elias A. Terry; Anna Mariah Hancena, m. Louis C. Larsen.
Married Annette Larsdatter (daughter of Lars Andersen and Johanna Larsdatter of Fairview, Utah, pioneers 1863), who was born July 29, 1847. Their children: John T. b. Nov. 19, 1865, m. Sarah E. Taylor; Lewis, m. Sarah E. Bills; Andrew, m. Viola Wilson; James T., m. Malissa Stewart. Families resided Fairview, Utah.
Bishop of Fairview 1863-65. Veteran Black Hawk war. Early settler at Fairview; moved to Mt. Pleasant. Farmer. Died Jan. 20, 1873, at Fairview.

PETERSEN, JOHN T. (son of Andrew Petersen and Annette Larsdatter). Born Nov. 19, 1865, Fairview, Utah.
Married Sarah Elizabeth Taylor Dec. 12, 1884, Logan, Utah (daughter of William Singleton and Phebe Jane Stewart of Fairview, pioneers 1860), who was born Nov. 28, 1868. Their children: Sarah E. b. Aug. 16, 1885, m. Brigham Adelbert Lowe; John A. b. Dec. 26, 1886; Frances E. b. Nov. 8, 1888, m. Ray E. Merkley; Phebe b. Aug. 30, 1890; Lewis S. b. Dec. 4, 1891; Myron b. Nov. 11, 1894; Furn A. b. Dec. 8, 1896; A. La Varre b. June 11, 1899; Alice E. b. Sept. 18,

1901; Ralph b. Dec. 1, 1903; Rose Lee b. Feb. 7, 1906. Family home Fairview, Utah, and Wapello, Idaho.
Sunday school superintendent 1894-1900; president Y. M. M. I. A.; bishop's counselor 1905-07.

PETERSEN, CHRISTIAN (son of Ole Petersen and Annie Christiansen of Denmark). Born Oct. 25, 1824, in Denmark. Came to Utah October, 1860, John W. Young company.
Married Elizabeth Jensen 1847 in Denmark, who was born Sept. 7, 1815. Their children: Ole (adopted) b. Feb. 12, 1840; Rasmus (adopted) b. Feb. 16, 1842, m. Sophia Jensen; Jorgen b. June 3, 1848; Niels b. March 11, 1850; Anne Christiene b. Aug. 21, 1852; Peter b. Jan. 14, 1854; Ellen Marie b. July 12, 1858; Mary b. March 3, 1860, m. Erastus Robert Lark. Family home Brinton, Utah.
Died April 23, 1896.

PETERSEN, FREDERICK A. (son of Powell Frederick Petersen, born Aug. 10, 1800, Copenhagen, Denmark, and Cecelia Alseind, born July 27, 1802, Fyen, Denmark). Born Jan. 28, 1835, at Copenhagen. Came to Utah Aug. 29, 1863, John R. Murdock company.
Married Lelia Olson July, 1863 (daughter of John and Karen Olson, pioneers 1863), who was born 1839 and came to Utah with her husband. Their children: Josephine b. May, 1864; Fredericka b. Jan. 28, 1865, m. James Moss; Powell Frederick b. May 7, 1868, m. Sophrona Smith; Cecelius b. May 8, 1872; Concordia b. Jan. 4, 1873, m. William Brown; Sarah b. Aug. 15, 1874, m. Hans Blomgren; Gusta b. Nov. 1, 1877, m. Charles Dalton; Frederick Alseind b. May 6, 1879; Clara Agneta b. Nov. 26, 1881. Family home Levan, Utah.
High priest. Blacksmith and farmer.

PETERSEN, HANS (son of Peter Larsen of Denmark). Born April 6, 1825, Valloby, Denmark. Came to Utah Sept. 12, 1863, John R. Young company.
Married Doris Lorentzon (daughter of Lorentz Lorentzon and Margaret Jacobson), who was born 1829, Kiel, Germany. Their children: Josephine b. 1843, m. Lars K. Larson; Ernest, m. Elizabeth Benson and Millie Mollen; Lorentz, m. Kristine Nielsen; Hans; Ezra, m. Ella Allen. Family home Hyrum, Utah.
Elder; missionary to Denmark. Took an active part in bringing immigrants to Utah. Settler at Hyrum, Utah.

PETERSEN, LORENTZ (son of Hans Petersen and Doris Lorentzon). Born Feb. 15, 1857, Valloby, Denmark.
Married Kristine Nielsen (daughter of Peter Nielsen and Gundle K. Hansen), who was born March 30, 1859, Gadevang, Denmark. Their children: Lorenzo Carl b. Sept. 9, 1878, m. Javan Jensen; Dora b. Oct. 25, 1880; Waldermar F. b. Sept. 22, 1882, m. F. Flossie Hansen; Willard b. Dec. 12, 1884; Agnes b. April 2, 1878, m. Alma Rasmussen; Eugene b. Jan. 11, 1892; Eva May b. April 29, 1894; Jesse Virio b. Dec. 26, 1899; Verlo b. July 16, 1902.
High priest; missionary to Denmark 1889 and 1906; bishop counselor in second ward, Hyrum, Utah. Resided at Hyrum, Utah.

PETERSEN, WILLARD (son of Lorentz Petersen and Kristine Nielsen). Born December 12, 1884, Hyrum, Utah.

PETERSEN, HANS J. (son of Hans and Mary Petersen of Denmark). Born 1833, Copenhagen, Denmark. Came to Utah May, 1870.
Married Christina Borgesen 1867, at Copenhagen (daughter of Bergo Nilsen and Karren Ryberg of Denmark), who was born May 24, 1829. Their children: Hans T. b. Dec. 9, 1867, m. Selma Sorensen; Mary Helena, m. John H. Snowball; Annie Christina, m. William Corbett; Carrie Maria, m. C. E. Baker. Family home Smithfield, Cache Co., Utah. Manager of Co-operative Shoe Factory at Smithfield, Utah, 1875-1880. Died Sept. 20, 1890.

PETERSEN, HANS T. (son of Hans J. Petersen and Christina Borgesen). Born Dec. 9, 1867, Borup, Copenhagen, Denmark.
Married Selma Sorensen Sept. 20, 1899, Salt Lake City (daughter of Jens Christian Sorensen and Nielsine Isakson of Aarhuus, Denmark, pioneers 1898), who was born June 19, 1880. Their children: Alma Luella b. June 30, 1900; Selma Loverne b. June 29, 1902; Hans Kenneth b. April 10, 1905; Lorin William b. May 29, 1908; Afton Bernice b. June 30, 1910. Family home Smithfield and Trenton, Utah.
Bishop Trenton ward 1907. City recorder, Smithfield, one term; councilman 1900-1904; mayor 1904-1906. Manager Farmers Union Mill 1901-1906; manager Trenton Mill & Elevator Co. 1906. Settled at Smithfield; moved to Trenton 1906.

PETERSEN, JAMES (son of Peter Olsen and Dorthea Petersen of Nyerup, Holbek amt, Denmark). Born Dec. 5, 1847, at Nyerup. Came to Utah Sept. 25, 1868, John G. Holman oxteam company.
Married Mary Sophie Simmonsen Dec. 26, 1878 (daughter of Martin Simmonsen and Mary Petersen), who was born Feb. 26, 1862, Fensmark, Denmark. Their children: James Reuben b. Oct. 11, 1879, m. Morget Olsen 1908; Mary Matilda b. Sept. 29, 1881, m. Joseph Jacobson 1900; Simon Leroy b.

Feb. 15, 1884; Charles Levi b. May 16, 1886; Joseph Melville b. Oct. 16, 1888, m. Tina Maxburn 1907; Martin Benjamin b. June 29, 1892; Clyde Ephraim b. Oct. 21, 1894; Virginia Sophie b. Sept. 29, 1896; Everett Lorenzo b. Feb. 14, 1900; Louis Eugene b. Aug. 25, 1898, d. Aug. 28, 1898; Olive Dorthea b. Aug. 2, 1903; Alice b. April 27, 1906, d. same day; Frederick Irving b. Nov. 7, 1907, d. May 13, 1908. Family resided South Jordan and Riverton, Utah.
One of presidents of 95th quorum seventies; missionary to Denmark 1889-91; to northern states 1907-08; home missionary of Jordan stake two years; acting teacher of South Jordan ward 1877, serving 37 years; had charge of a company of immigrants to Utah 1891. Worked on railroads and in mines for about three years and settled at South Jordan. Merchant; farmer; stockraiser.

PETERSEN, JAMES (son of Rasmus Petersen and Annie Marie Hansen, both of Fyen, Denmark, who died of cholera near Quincy, Ill., while en route to Utah). Born April 28, 1858, at Fyen. Came to Utah September, 1866, Abner Lowry company.
Married Anna Eliza Rasmussen Oct. 16, 1879, Mt. Pleasant, Utah (daughter of Rasmus Rasmussen and Maria Christine Johanstatter of Fyen, Denmark), who was born Jan. 13, 1860. Their children: Elsina Maria b. Sept. 4, 1880; Annie Johanna b. Dec. 8, 1882, m. William E. King; James Erastus b. March 30, 1885, died; Dianthy Sephrona b. May 26, 1887, m. Andrew O. Larson; Parley b. March 30, 1889; Leo Wilford b. May 18, 1891; Delbert b. June 16, 1893; Vern b. Dec. 12, 1895; Myrtle Amanda b. March 12, 1898; Rex b. Oct. 11, 1900; Bienda Irene b. Nov. 14, 1902. Family home Castle Dale, Utah.
High priest; ward clerk; high councilor; member stake board of education; president of town board. School trustee. Merchant; farmer. An early settler at Castle Dale. Has done much to build up Emery county.

PETERSEN, JAMES O. (father from Copenhagen, Denmark, and mother from Sjaelland, Denmark). Born April 8, 1820, at Copenhagen. Came to Utah 1856, James G. Willie handcart company.
Married Anne Jensen about 1843, who was born Sept. 10, 1823 (died 1901), and came to Utah with husband. Their children: Sophia b. Sept. 24, 1844, m. W. Valentine 1858; Marie B. b. Sept. 9, 1846, m. James Olsen Jan. 28, 1862; Hans b. Aug. 1848, m. Marthy Abot; Christ b. Aug. 1850, m. Ellen Nielsen; Peter b. March 14, 1852, m. Mary Andersen; James C. b. Aug. 1854, m. Sarah Hansen; Stene b. Sept 17, 1857, m. Soren Nielsen; Abraham b. Oct. 1859; Annie b. Nov. 1861, m. Christ Nygaard; Isaack b. Nov. 1863, died; Jacob b. Dec. 1865, m. Lene Poulsen; Nephi b. Dec. 1867, m. Louise Arn.
High priest. Cooper; farmer. Died 1900.

PETERSEN, JENS K. Born at Copenhagen, Denmark. Came to Utah 1854.
Married Helena Christina Hansen. Their children: H. C., m. Mary Capson; Anirina C., m. George P. Pectol; Caroline, m. Joseph Hjeerling; James E. b. Nov. 1855, m. Caroline Gottfredson; Joseph, m. Kista Henderickson.
Married Emmie Gourd, Salt Lake City, who was born in Sweden. Their children: Erastus W., m. —— Henderickson; Saphrona; James; Alexander; Melvenia. Family home Ephraim, Utah.

PETERSEN, JAMES EPHRAIM (son of Jens K. Petersen and Helena Christina Hansen). Born Nov. 15, 1858, Ephraim, Utah.
Married Caroline Gottfredson March 8, 1877, St. George, Utah (daughter of Gens Gottfredson and Karen Mileheade, pioneers 1857), who was born Feb. 15, 1859. Their children: Ephraim A. b. Feb. 19, 1878, m. Edna Dalton Nov. 29, 1899; Caroline R. b. Oct. 7, 1879, m. John Whittaker; Virginia b. Feb. 4, 1881, m. Charles R. Dalton Feb. 8, 1899; James L. b. Aug. 26, 1883, m. Irene Dalton June 16, 1909; Vivian M. b. Oct. 21, 1885, m. Joseph Steele June 6, 1906; Le Roy b. Sept. 11, 1887; Maggie Helena b. Sept. 21, 1889, m. J. Dennis Morgan Nov. 9, 1910; Arthur M. b. Feb. 15, 1892; Leonard b. April 20, 1894; Arnold E. b. Sept 1, 1896; Orien b. July 1, 1899; Leda b. June 6, 1901. Family home Circleville, Utah.
Missionary to northern states 1884-85; second counselor in bishopric of Marion ward 1883-85; ordained bishop of Marion ward March 28, 1887. Settled with his parents at Glenwood 1865; moved to Manti. Took part in Black Hawk wars. Moved to Grass Valley 1880, and settled at Circleville. Elected to the state legislature 1904; county commissioner eight years; postmaster; school trustee; notary public.

PETERSEN, EPHRAIM A. (son of James E. Petersen and Caroline Gottfredson). Born Feb. 19, 1878, Glenwood, Utah.
Married Edna Dalton Nov. 29, 1899, Circleville, Utah (daughter of Charles A. Dalton and Sarah J. Wiley), who was born July 26, 1896, at Circleville. Their children: Alvirl Errol b. Sept. 18, 1900; Loretta b. June 18, 1903; Warren D. b. Feb. 9, 1905; Ebert Ray b. Oct. 12, 1907; Hazel b. Jan. 19, 1911. Family home Circleville, Utah.

PETERSEN, LARS PETER (son of Christian Petersen, born Sept. 13, 1789, Aalbek Hjorring amt, Denmark, and Maria Larsen, born Jan. 14, 1780, Voer, Denmark). He was born Nov. 27, 1825, in Aalbek. Came to Utah Sept. 23, 1862, Christian A. Madsen company.

Married Elsie Maria Jensen Nov. 26, 1852 (daughter of Thor Jensen and Johanah Maria Jensen), who came to Utah with husband. Their children: Ane Maria b. May 16, 1853, m. Jens L. Peterson Aug. 3, 1867; James C. b. Dec. 12, 1854, m. Jane Ruth Baker; Mary b. June 12, 1856; Niels Peter b. May 9, 1858, m. Augusta Johnson April 21, 1886; Ole Christian b. June 24, 1859; Christian b. June 17, 1861; Elsie Maria b. Oct. 9, 1862.
Married Maren Andersen Dec. 8, 1862, who was born May 5, 1816, Voer, Denmark.
Married Martha Maria Nielson Aug. 17, 1874, Salt Lake City, who was born Oct. 4, 1843, Sindai, Hjorring, Denmark. Their children: Olena Maria Mogensen (adopted) b. April 25, 1868, m. James Larsen; Carl Peter Christian Mogensen (adopted) b. Sept. 11, 1870.
Counselor to N. M. Peterson; secretary and treasurer immigration fund; one of the head ward teachers; director and treasurer of the Co-Op.

PETERSEN, NIELS PETER (son of Lars Peter Petersen and Elsie Maria Jensen). Born May 9, 1858, in Denmark.
Married Augusta Johnson April 21, 1886, Logan. Utah (daughter of John Backlund and Christina Olsen), who was born July 31, 1866. Their children: John Lester b. March 10, 1888, m. Ellen Oldroyd Sept. 20, 1911; Hanmer B. b. June 13, 1891; Harmel M. b. March 17, 1894; Elsie Christina b. Feb. 13, 1897; Mary b. Nov. 29, 1900; Jerda Aurelia b. Oct. 21, 1903; Lars Eldon Peterson b. Nov. 6, 1906; Niels Marcus b. March 28, 1911. Family home Pleasant Grove, Ephraim, San Pete Co., and Richfield, Utah.
Worked on St. George temple 1874-75; missionary to Denmark 1882-84; alternate high counselor Sevier stake 1894 to 1901, and high counselor 1901 to date. City councilman. Richfield; city supervisor of streets two terms; county road supervisor one term.

PETERSEN, MADS PETER (son of Jens Petersen, born March 4, 1808, and Marie Chrestine Petersen, both of Deiret, Denmark). Born Aug. 13, 1833, at Landborup, Randers Amt, Denmark. Came to Utah Sept. 22, 1861, Samuel A. Woolley company.
Married Louisa Christensen Aug. 21, 1863 (daughter of Christian Christensen and Ane Sophie), who was born Aug. 22, 1845. Their children: Louisa Ane b. Sept. 6, 1864, d. Sept. 13, 1864; Joseph b. July 10, 1865, d. Oct. 1, 1865; Mary Chrestine b. Sept. 24, 1866, m. James P. Hansen 1886; Sarah Sophie b. Feb. 8, 1869, m. Andrew Peterson 1893; James C. b. Feb. 4, 1872, m. Louisa Hansen March, 1899; Sern P. b. March 13, 1874, m. Lena Bower 1907; Ane Sophie b. Aug. 28, 1876, d. Oct. 20, 1888; Ezra P. b. Jan. 8, 1879, d. June 3, 1890; Katie Elizabeth b. Feb. 11, 1882, d. April 11, 1899; Orson Hyrum b. Feb. 23, 1885, m. Louise Mathisen. Family home Newton, Cache Co., Utah.
High priest; ward teacher; ward deacon 6 years. Farmer.

PETERSEN, NIELS MORTEN. Born Nov. 12, 1819, Saeby, Hjorring, Denmark. Came to Utah Sept. 23, 1862.
Married Mette Christene Jensen, who was born Oct. 27, 1824. Their children: James Morten b. April 15, 1850, m. Laura Hansin Christine Hansen; Mattie Christine b. June 15, 1866, m. Lorenzo Nielsen; Josephine b. Feb. 15, 1869, d. Dec. 19, 1886.
Married Hannah Jensen. Their children: Hannah, m. Arthur Beutler; Niels Morten, m. Christene Busk; Joseph Morten, m. Nelda Busk; Jennie Josephine, m. William Christensen. Families resided Richfield, Utah.
High councilor Sevier stake; missionary to Scandinavia.

PETERSEN, JAMES MORTEN (son of Niels Morten Petersen and Mette Christine Jensen). Born April 15, 1850, Donsted, Denmark.
Married Laura Hansin Christine Hansen July 13, 1874, Salt Lake City, Utah. Their children: James Morten b. July 12, 1879, m. Louisiana C. Heppler Nov. 18, 1903; Laurence Morten b. July 17, 1883, m. May Gurr.
Married Sarah Johnson April 15, 1896. Their child: Una Elithe b. July 14, 1897.
Mayor of Richfield, Utah; city councilman; county treasurer; surveyor and assessor. Banker.

PETERSEN, JAMES MORTEN, JR. (son of James Morten Petersen and Laura Hansin Christine Hansen). Born July 12, 1879, Richfield, Utah.
Married Louisiana Carrie Heppler (daughter of Andrew Heppler and Louisiana Seegmiller), who was born July 6, 1882, Glenwood, Utah. Their children: Son b. Feb. 21, 1905, d. Feb. 21, 1905; Madge Heppler b. April 21, 1906; Una Heppler b. May 31, 1908; Leah Heppler b. Aug. 22, 1910; Juana Heppler m. Feb. 10, 1912.
Family home Richfield, Utah.
First counselor to president of Sevier stake. Mayor of Richfield; city councilman; trustee Utah Agricultural college. Cashier James M. Petersen bank; 2d vice president Utah State Bankers association.

PETERSEN, OLE (son of Peter and Anna Andersen, both of Copenhagen, Denmark). Born Oct. 22, 1815, Ballerup, Copenhagen. Came to Utah 1862.
Married Maren Hansen, Copenhagen (daughter of Hans Peters and Kristen Hansen of Copenhagen), who was born Feb. 17, 1823. Their children: Peter, m. Mary Elizabeth

Thurman; Annie, m. Samuel T. Wilcox; Mary, m. Moroni Fisher; Joseph, m. Mary Litster; Inger, m. John Anderson; Laura, d. aged 14; James, m. Eva Smith, m. Lizzia Peterson; Hansen, d. infant; Soren, d. infant. Family home Denmark and Cedar Valley, Utah. High priest. Farmer.

PETERSEN, PETER (son of Ole Petersen and Marn Hansen. Born Feb. 11, 1847, in Denmark. Came to Utah 1862 (with his parents).
Married Mary Elizabeth Thurman (daughter of George William Thurman and Mary Margaret Brown of Kentucky; latter a pioneer 1869). She was born Aug. 25, 1846, died May 1, 1912, Vernal, Utah. Their children: Keturah b. Oct. 8, 1867, m. Nelson Merkley; Alice T. b. July 31, 1871, m. William A. Kone; William Peter b. April 3, 1873, d. infant; Jesse S. b. Feb. 13, 1875, m. Minnie Feuell; James O. b. May 22, 1877, m. Addie Searls; Christie L. b. Aug. 6, 1879, m. John Wardle; David J. b. March 15, 1882, m. Bertha Burgess; Samuel T. b. Feb. 23, 1884, m. Samantha Read; Henry J. b. March 14, 1888, m. Laura Feuell; Franklin H. b. Oct. 6, 1890, d. infant. Family home, Cedar Fort and Vernal.
Bishop's counselor. Justice of the peace. Farmer. Died May 14, 1910, at Vernal.

PETERSEN, PETER C. (son of Peter Petersen and Mary S. Hansen of Denmark). Born June 7, 1835, in Denmark. Came to Utah 1860, Johnson and Peterson company.
Married Christinia Sorensen (daughter of Soren Nielsen and Ingar Mason), who was born Jan. 4, 1838. Their children: Mary b. Jan. 31, 1864, m. A. W. Buchanan Jan. 7, 1882; Josephine b. Aug. 7, 1865, m. T. H. Bell Jan. 21, 1885; Christian b. 1867, m. Mary Williams; Heber b. Jan. 25, 1869, m. Lovina Short Dec. 9, 1903; Hyrum b. April 5, 1870; Brigham b. Feb. 17, 1873, m. Mary Sampson; Sarah b. May 14, 1875, m. P. Heppler Sept. 17, 1897; George b. Oct. 2, 1877, m. Agnes Oldroyd 1901; William b. Dec. 27, 1879, m. Alice Johnson 1901. Family home Glenwood, Utah.

PETERSEN, PETER CHRISTIAN (son of Christian Petersen and Else Nielsen of Denmark). Born Aug. 1, 1823, Hörley, Aalborg, Denmark. Came to Utah 1865, Miner G. Atwood company.
Married Maren Andersen Feb. 25, 1854, in Denmark, who was born April 27, 1828. Their only child: Christian Petersen b. April 28, 1854, m. Mary Sophia Christensen Jan. 12, 1882. Family home Bear River, Utah.
Elder. Carpenter and farmer. Died Jan. 24, 1883, at Bear River.

PETERSEN, CHRISTIAN (son of Peter Christian Petersen and Maren Andersen). Born April 28, 1854, at Hörley, Denmark. Came to Utah with father.
Married Mary Sophia Christensen Jan. 12, 1882, Salt Lake City (daughter of Lars Christensen and Christiane Sophie Christensen of Bear River, Utah; came to Utah Sept. 13, 1859, Christian Christiansen handcart company). She was born Nov. 14, 1862. Their children: Mary Lucinda Petersen b. Nov. 10, 1882; Clara Christiana b. Oct. 19, 1884; Chrest Petersen, Jr. b. Oct. 7, 1886; Edward Raymond b. Jan. 19, 1888; Franklin Reynold b. Nov. 17, 1890; Orsan Sylvester b. Sept. 23, 1893; David Conrad b. June 2, 1895; Dita b. May 17, 1898. Family home Bear River, Utah.
Precinct constable; watermaster; postmaster. Farmer and stockraiser. Died Sept. 18, 1898, Bear River.

PETERSEN, DAVID CONRAD (son of Christian Petersen and Mary Sophia Christensen). Born Jan. 2, 1895, at Bear River, Utah.

PETERSEN, PETER HANSEN (son of Hans Petersen of Fyen, Denmark). Born 1816, Fyen. Came to Utah Aug. 26, 1864, John R. Murdock company.
Married Olene Elizabeth Jorgensen 1838, Fyen, Denmark. Their children: Hans, m. Isabell Ashman; James, m. Annie Tyenson; Johane, m. Lafayett Christopherson. Family home Fillmore, Utah.
Farmer. Died 1896, at Fillmore.

PETERSEN, HANS (son of Peter H. Petersen and Olene E. Jorgensen). Born 1839, Fyen, Denmark. Came to Utah Sept. 29, 1862, John R. Murdock company.
Married Isabell Ashman Sept. 5, 1868, Salt Lake City (daughter of John Ashman and Ann Wild of Manchester, Eng., pioneers Aug. 26, 1864, John R. Murdock company). She was born May 5, 1850. Their children: George Henry b. Oct. 18, 1869; Johnie A. b. Oct. 4, 1870, m. Hattie Sloan; Elizabeth Ann b. April 2, 1873; m. F. F. Merrill; Edward b. April 9, 1876; James b. July 18, 1876, m. Mary Ann Paxton; Mary Alice b. Jan. 12, 1879, m. Bert Mace; Katie b. May 1, 1881; Ellen b. Aug. 4, 1882; Nephi Fillmore b. Jan. 11, 1885; Thomas William b. April 4, 1886, m. Rose Bartholomew. Family home Fillmore, Utah.
High priest. City recorder; city councilman; city marshal; poundkeeper. Farmer.

PETERSEN, SOREN CHRISTIAN (son of Peder Petersen and Cicilia Marie Christensen, of Astrup, Hjorring, Denmark). Born June 13, 1821, Tolne, Hjorring, Denmark. Came to Utah Sept. 10, 1863, William B. Preston company.
Married Mette Marie Larsen, Hjorring, Hjorring Amt, Denmark (daughter of Lars Andersen and Johanna Mikkelsen of St. Olai, Hjorring, Denmark; died at St. Olai). She was born Dec. 4, 1813. Their child: Lars C. b. March 6, 1839, m. Johanna Marie Mouritsen Nov. 25, 1860, m. Mette Johanna Christoffersen, Feb. 14, 1878; m. Thomine Katrine Christensen, March 4, 1887.
Married Else Marie Larsen 1861, Hjorring, Denmark (daughter of Lars Christian Jensen and Mette Christensen; latter a pioneer Sept. 10, 1863, William B. Preston company). She was born March 28, 1828. Their children: Cicilia Matilda b. Jan. 10, 1862, d. Nov. 1862; Soren b. July 4, 1866, m. Annie Elizabeth Scarborough; Theodore b. Feb. 21, 1869, m. Jane Ann Reese; Josephine b. Aug. 9, 1870. Family home Logan, Utah.
High priest. Farmer and stockraiser. Died Oct. 1, 1895, Logan, Utah.

PETERSEN, LARS C. (son of Soren Christian Petersen and Mette Marie Larsen). Born March 6, 1839, Skibby, Hjorring, Denmark. Came to Utah Sept. 15, 1859, Robert F. Neslen company.
Married Johanna Marie Mouritsen Nov. 25, 1860, Salt Lake City, Utah (daughter of Lars Mouritsen and Maren Sorensen of Smithfield, Utah, pioneers Sept. 15, 1859, Robert F. Neslen company). She was born June 17, 1846. Their children: Lorenzo b. Oct. 26, 1862, m. Eliza Balls Dec. 14, 1882; Hannah Marie b. Feb. 3, 1865, m. Lars Christensen April 21, 1881; Lars Christian b. March 15, 1867, d. May 7, 1886; Mary Jane b. Aug. 7, 1869, m. William A. Seamons Sept. 22, 1886; John Samuel b. Dec. 11, 1871, d. Oct. 25, 1872; Martha Elizabeth b. Sept. 11, 1873, d. Nov. 6, 1875; Mette Mariana b. April 2, 1876, d. Jan. 17, 1877; Lettie Lorene b. Feb. 22, 1878, m. Thomas Nilsen March 4, 1896; Arthur Mourits b. June 24, 1880, m. Mary Eliza Seamons Dec. 20, 1890; James Franklin b. May 27, 1883, m. Edith Hawkes Oct. 1, 1903; Parley Ismael b. March 30, 1885, d. June 7, 1886; Cora Dozenda b. Jan. 21, 1888, d. Feb. 18, 1889; Hyrum Edgar b. March 27, 1890. Family home Hyde Park, Utah.
Married Mette Johanna Christoffersen Feb. 14, 1878, Salt Lake City (daughter of Rasmus Christoffersen and Karen Hendricksen; former came to Utah 1879, latter 1880—married at Voldby, Denmark). She was born Oct. 9, 1857, Voldby, died Sept. 22, 1888. Their children: Alfred Christoffersen b. April 18, 1879, m. Charlotte C. Morris July 12, 1905; Emily Caroline b. May 11, 1881, m. Willard Jensen Oct. 18, 1910; Lars Peter b. June 12, 1883, m. Mary Archibold May 27, 1908; John Henry b. Nov. 25, 1885, m. Amy Fallows Nov. 25, 1908; George Edward b. Sept. 13, 1888, d. Oct. 14, 1888. Family home Hyde Park, Utah.
Married Thomine Katrine Christensen March 4, 1887 (daughter of Lars Christensen and Dorthea Marie Back; came to Utah July 23, 1871—married in Denmark). She was born May 28, 1863, Hvorup, Aalborg, Denmark; died Feb. 13, 1904.
Presiding teacher high priests quorum Hyde Park, Utah; ward clerk. Director and clerk United Order, Logan, Utah. Secretary Logan & Hyde Park Canal Co. Dec. 5, 1889; secretary and treasurer Logan, Hyde Park & Smithfield Canal Co. March 19, 1895; secretary and treasurer Logan & Richmond Irrigation district Dec. 5, 1898.

PETERSEN, SOREN LIND (son of Peter Johnsen and Karin Lind of Denmark). Born Feb. 20, 1835, Flestrup, Denmark. Came to Utah 1861, W. W. Cluff company.
Married Anne E. Nielsen en route to America (daughter of Niels Jonasen and Elizabeth Olsdater of Denmark), who was born Feb. 12, 1835. Their children: Anne M. b. April 29, 1862, m. Coe Killgore; Caroline b. July 29, 1864, m. A. P. Renstrom; Emma Louise b. Jan. 7, 1866, m. C. W. Wright; Soren Lind Jr. b. Feb. 7, 1868, m. Mattie Dallimore; Adam Lind b. March 2, 1870, m. Anna M. Petersen; Mary Elizabeth b. March 2, 1870, d. aged 4 months; Matilda b. June 21, 1776; Baby b. June 1879, d. at birth.
Married Katy Lofgreen December, 1869, Salt Lake City (daughter of Paul and Anna Lofgreen, pioneers 1868), who was born Nov. 10, 1842, Hoterp, Sweden. Their children: Josephine b. Dec. 27, 1870, m. Oscar Harris; David b. March 13, 1875, d. 1892; Joseph b. 1881, died; Hyrum b. Oct. 15, 1883.
Married Ella Louisa Petersen 1877, Salt Lake City (daughter of Erland Petersen and Ellen Petersen, who died in Norway). She was born Sept. 11, 1850, in Norway. Their children: Joseph Lind b. July 15, 1878, m. Ida Anderson; Alma Lind b. Feb. 12, 1880, m. Eliza Schade; Olga b. July 2, 1883, m. Miner Wilcox; Canute Thomas b. March 13, 1886, d. May 26, 1908; Ella b. Sept. 21, 1888.
Manager of Co-op. 1870-75; foreign mission; president Christiania conference, Norway, 1875-77; president 75th quorum seventies 1879-1900; first bishop's counselor 1883-1900. Shoemaker, wholesale meat dealer, 1870-1901; stockholder First National Bank; farmer; stockraiser; merchant.

PETERSEN, ADAM LIND (son of Soren Lind Petersen and Anne E. Nielsen). Born March 2, 1870, Huntsville, Utah.
Married Anna M. Petersen May 8, 1888, Salt Lake City (daughter of Christian Petersen and Emma M. Backman, pioneers 1864), who was born March 8, 1870. Their children: Eva Malvina b. Aug. 31, 1889; Ollie May b. Jan. 25, 1892; Ruth Eveline b. March 11, 1895; Vivian Myrtle b. Oct. 18, 1896; Dewey Lind b. Dec. 27, 1898; Bryan Lind b. Jan. 10, 1901; Golden Adam b. March 20, 1905; Eugene Lyman b. Sept. 11, 1907; Lloyd La Mar b. Dec. 23, 1910.
Ward chorister 1887-1902; president Y. M. M. I. A. 1888-1901; member stake Sunday school board 1887-90; assistant Sunday school superintendent 1894-1902; missionary to Scandinavia 1892-94 and 1902-04 to southern Utah, Arizona, New Mexico and Colorado 1907-08; high priest, high counselor. Ogden stake, 1907. Justice of peace three terms. Member J. S. Campbell Co., wholesale grocers, Ogden, Utah. Family home Huntsville, Eden and Ogden, Utah.

PIONEERS AND PROMINENT MEN OF UTAH

PETERSON, ANDREW A. (son of Anders Peterson of Vane, Sweden, and Marna Anderson, both born in Sweden). Born Jan. 13, 1840, Ystad, Sweden. Came to Utah, Sept. 23, 1862, Ola N. Liljenquist company.
Married Mary Ann Earlen Pherson (daughter of Earlen Pherson and Magrata Pherson), who was born June 12, 1844. Came to Utah 1862, Ola N. Liljenquist company. Their children: Leah P. b. Feb. 19, 1864, m. W. L. Hill, June 23, 1885; Andrew b. Dec. 5, 1865, m. Emma Webb Oct. 28, 1891; Mary Ann b. Sept. 6, 1867, m. L. P. Lossee Nov. 14, 1888; Christina b. Aug. 4, 1869, m. W. E. Southwick Jan. 20, 1892; Hannah Elizabeth b. Oct. 15, 1871, died; John Charles b. Jan. 29, 1873, died; Joseph b. April 10, 1874, m. Amanda Andolin Dec. 1897; Hyrum b. Nov. 10, 1876, m. Anna Rogers June 10, 1908; David b. April 22, 1879, m. Maud Smith Nov. 26, 1902; Alma Frederick b. July 16, 1883, died.
Missionary to Sweden 1858-62, one of the presidents of the 68th quorum of seventies; high priest; Sunday school teacher 35 years; president deacons quorum 33 years. Member of the school board, 12 years; member of the water board; city councilman.

PETERSON, CANUTE (son of Peter and Herberg Peterson). Born May 13, 1824, Hardanger, Norway. Came to Utah 1849, Ezra T. Benson company.
Married Sarah Ann Nelson July 2, 1849, while crossing plains (daughter of Cornelius and Carrie Nelson of Illinois), who was born Feb. 16, 1827. Their children: Peter Cornelius b. June 22, 1850, m. Hannah Thompson, m. Louise Amanda Nelson; Sarah Ann, m. Anthon H. Lund; Parley Pratt; Canute Wedeber; Nels; Walber Herbertle Beal; John. Family home Ephraim, Utah.
Missionary to Norway 1852-56 and 1871-73; bishop of Ephraim; president of San Pete stake. Member state legislature several terms. Farmer. Died Oct. 14, 1903, Ephraim, Utah.

PETERSON, PETER CORNELIUS (son of Canute Peterson and Sarah Ann Nelson). Born June 22, 1850, Salt Lake City.
Married Hannah Thompson May 2, 1870, Salt Lake City (daughter of Peter Thompson and Dorothea Petersen of Denmark, pioneers 1854), who was born Oct. 3, 1850. Their children: Sarah Dorothea Jensen b. Feb. 28, 1871; Hannah Lillian Petersen, b. Aug. 10, 1873; Peter Canute b. Feb. 23, 1876. Family home Ephraim, Utah.
Married Louise Amanda Nelson Sept. 30, 1880, Salt Lake City (daughter of Lars Nelson and Botilda Paulson of Sweden, pioneers 1859), who was born Feb. 7, 1861. Their children: Cornelius Nelson Jr.; Anthon Joseph; Lawrence R.; Cornelia; Louise Ann; Florence; Pratt; Olive; Edith. Family home Ephraim, Utah.
Farmer and sheepraiser; quarry owner.

PETERSON, GEORGE (son of Peter Hanson, born Sept. 20, 1782, and Anna Margaret Yorgenson, born Aug. 17, 1787, both of Gothland, Sweden). Born Feb. 9, 1817, Alfta, Gothland. Came to Utah Oct. 1, 1864, John Smith company.
Married Cecilie Lorentena Olafson (daughter of Olof Olson and Brita Mortenson, of Gothland, Sweden), who was born Nov. 26, 1831. Their children: Lars Peter; Anna; Olof; Charles E.; Josephine; Cecilia; Elizabeth; George D. Family resided Richfield, Gunnison and Scipio, Utah.
Assisted in bringing immigrants into Utah. Settled in Richfield, moved to Gunnison, later to Scipio, Utah. Died Aug. 4, 1890, at Scipio, Utah.

PETERSON, LARS PETER (son of George Peterson and Cecilia Lorentena Olafson). Born Feb. 23, 1856, Gothland, Sweden. Came to Utah 1864 with his parents.
Married Elizabeth Brown, Scipio, Utah (daughter of Martin Peter Brown and Anna Hanson, pioneers Sept. 7, 1855, Noah T. Guymon company). She was born Nov. 8, 1861, Gunnison, Utah. Their children: Allen Louis; Loreen Elizabeth; Tessie Ann; Donald M.; George Clifford; Rexton B. Family resided Richfield, Gunnison and Scipio.

PETERSON, GEORGE H. (son of William Peterson). Born in New Jersey. Came to Utah in early days.
Married Eliza Wilde, Salt Lake City (daughter of William Wilde of England). Their children: George; Sophronia; Mary; Charles Henry b. Sept. 1866, m. Mary N. Bruce; Anna B.; Maud; John F.; Thomas Dennis. Family home Coalville, Utah.
Deceased.

PETERSON, CHARLES HENRY (son of George H. Peterson and Eliza Wilde). Born September, 1866, Peterson, Utah.
Married Mary N. Bruce Sept. 22, 1882, Logan, Utah (daughter of James B. Bruce and Isabell Wilson of Scotland). Their children: Eliza May b. May 27, 1887; Isabell May b. May 27, 1887, died; Gertrude b. Oct. 26, 1889; Myrtle Ivy b. March 6, 1891; Afton R. b. May 6, 1896; Rula J. b. Sept. 13, 1898; Charles Newell b. Sept. 2, 1900; Mary Bernice b. June 23, 1902; Fielding Bruce b. Oct. 17, 1905; Harold Franklin b. Oct. 10, 1907; Kimball Wildes b. Sept. 1910. Family home Almy, Wyo.
Member of seventy; Sunday school superintendent; bishop's counselor. County commissioner; school trustee sixteen years. Rancher and merchant.

PETERSON, HANS PETER (son of John Peterson and Annie Peterson of Denmark). Born Sept. 13, 1846, in Denmark. Came to Utah 1867.
Married Julia Emma Cook Jan. 22, 1871, Salt Lake City (daughter of Luke Cook and Louisa Burton of England, pioneers 1852, Captain Shurtliff company). She was born Sept. 19, 1852. Their children: Anne Louisa b. Dec. 11, 1872, d. infant; Eliza Emma b. Aug. 24, 1874, d. 1881; Sarah Jane b. July 11, 1876, m. James Reynolds; Martha Emma b. Sept. 8, 1877, m. Niels Jensen; Bertha Artula b. March 23, 1879, m. James Robinson; Henrietta b. Sept. 22, 1880, d. 1892; Rachael Ida b. Feb. 1, 1882, d. infant; Mary Vernetta b. Nov. 22, 1884, m. William Patton; John H. b. July 20, 1886; George L. b. Aug. 24, 1888, d. infant; Ida May b. May 11, 1890, m. Frank Hider; Priel Geneva b. July 2, 1893. Family home Richfield, Utah.
Missionary to Denmark two years; high priest. Veteran Black Hawk wars. Farmer; stockraiser; mason. Died Feb. 17, 1912, at Richfield.

PETERSON, JOHN HANS (son of Hans Peter Peterson and Julia Emma Cook). Born July 30, 1866, at Richfield. Musician. Farmer.

PETERSON, JENS. Born March 14, 1808, Hals, Denmark.
Married Metta Christena Olsen April 21, 1848, who was born Sept. 16, 1809, and died Feb. 25, 1859, at Ephraim, Utah. He died May 22, 1854, in Kansas.

PETERSON, JOHN AUGUST (son of Johanus Peterson and Anna Olson). Born July 13, 1842, Kolmar, Sweden. Came to Utah Oct. 7, 1866, Andrew H. Scott company.
Married Maria Hansen 1854, at Salt Lake City. Only child: Mary Amanda b. April 10, 1882, m. Ernest Frederick Hale June 19, 1907.
Died May 24, 1912.

PETERSON, JOHN AGUSTUS (son of Peter Peterson and Johana Winburg of Sweden). Born Dec. 3, 1851, in Sweden. Came to Utah 1855.
Married Eliza Hunt Jan. 18, 1877, St. George temple (daughter of Amos Hunt and Rebecca Wiggins of Ogden, Utah). She was born Dec. 10, 1860. Their children: Eliza Ellen b. Aug. 28, 1879, m. James B. Stringham; Josephine b. June 24, 1881, m. William D. Hanks; John E. b. July 9, 1883, m. Grace McClellan; Isabelle b. Sept. 30, 1885; Mary b. Jan. 16, 1887; Bertha b. Aug. 9, 1889, m. James E. Hoyle; Mae b. March 12, 1892; Melvin b. May 21, 1895. Family home Thurber, Wayne Co., Utah.
Moved from Salt Lake City to St. George 1861 and resided there 22 years, helping to build up that city; worked on the St. George temple 18 months; labored as teacher in the St. George ward; acted as guard at the time the Indians were harassing the Saints of southern Utah. Moved from St. George to Thurber, Utah, 1883, where he labored as teacher, assistant superintendent Sunday school and home missionary; helped to build up Thurber and the surrounding country. Moved from Thurber to Nibley, Ore., 1902, where he acted as ward teacher and home missionary, and helped to build up the city of Nibley. From there he moved to Union, Ore., where he was ward teacher.

PETERSON, OLE (son of Per Olsen and Charstena Christensdatter, of Wallby, Sweden). Born Sept. 29, 1810, at Wallby. Came to Utah 1857.
Married Bengta Andersdatter, at Wallby, who was born March 23, 1814, d. July 4, 1881, Ephraim, Utah. Their children: Per Olsen, m. Karna ——; Niels Olsen, m. Karna ——; Berta Olsen, m. August Swenson; Bengta; James Olsen; Kjersty Olsen.
Died Oct. 1, 1857, Little Cottonwood, Utah.

PETERSON, PETER P. (son of Hans Peterson and Margaret Larsen of Denmark). Born Jan. 11, 1841, Bjorup, Falster, Denmark. Came to Utah Sept. 4, 1859, George Rowley handcart company.
Married Ann Powell Dec. 12, 1870, Salt Lake City (daughter of Thomas Powell and Margaret Davis of Wales, pioneers Aug. 20, 1868, Chester Loveland company). She was born June 17, 1850. Their children: Thomas W., m. Lettie Taylor; Peter P., m. Hazel Parkinson; John D., m. Emily Ritchie; Hans C., m. Syrena Keddington; Margaret E., m. Charles L. Green; Mary A. Family home Kanesville, Utah.
Member 75th quorum seventies; bishop of Kanesville ward 22 years. Postmaster at Florence four years.

PETTEGREW, DAVID (son of William Pettegrew born 1752, Woodbury, Conn.). Born July 29, 1791, Chesterfield, Vt. Came to Utah September, 1847, with contingent of Mormon Battalion.
Married Elizabeth Alden (daughter of John Alden), who was born Oct. 14, 1791. Their children: Lucy Ann b. April 26, 1817; David Alden b. March 8, 1819; Betsy Ann b. Feb. 11, 1823; James Phineas b. May 15, 1825; Hyrum King Solomon b. Nov. 22, 1826; Caroline Keziah b. March 22, 1827; Lydia Louisa b. Feb. 16, 1829. Family home Jackson county, Mo., and Nauvoo, Ill.

Married Caroline Cope Feb. 12, 1856, Salt Lake City (daughter of Samuel and Hannah Cope, both died at Nauvoo). She was born Jan. 29, 1840, in England. Their children: Joseph Moroni b. Nov. 9, 1856, m. Annie L. Phippen; Mary Caroline b. Jan. 13, 1858; Josephine b. March 18, 1859; William Helaman b. March 5, 1860, m. Mary E. Lewis; Annie Mariah b. May 12, 1862, m. J. H. Paul. Family home, Salt Lake City.
Bishop 10th ward Salt Lake City 1849-1863; president high priests quorum 1853-56. Captain in Utah militia; master mason 1820; senator in provincial state of Deseret 1849; chaplain house of representatives territory of Utah 1857-58 and 1860-61.

PETTEGREW, WILLIAM HELAMAN (son of David Pettegrew and Caroline Cope). Born March 5, 1860, Salt Lake City.
Married Mary Emma Lewis Dec. 6, 1882, Salt Lake City (daughter of William Lewis and Sarah Leaver), who was born June, 1861, in England. Their children: William Lewis b. Oct. 16, 1883; Mary Estella b. May 2, 1886; Mabel Caroline b. Aug. 29, 1889; Sarah Leah b. April 12, 1890; James Raymond b. March 7, 1893; Annie Paulina b. April 23, 1895; Alma Helaman b. March 23, 1898.
Superintendent Y. M. M. I. A. Juab stake 1892-1898; ordained bishop first ward at Nephi Nov. 24, 1901; missionary to Mississippi 1890-1892. Councilman Nephi City 1892-96 and 1902-04; mayor of Nephi 1904-08.

PETTEY, ALBERT (son of Ebenezer Pettey, born 1737, died Dec. 4, 1814; his mother born 1745, died March 30, 1830, in Kentucky, 25 miles below Cincinnati). Born Aug. 10, 1795, in Bourbon county, Ky. Came to Utah Sept. 24, 1848, Heber C. Kimball company.
Married Catherine Pettey (no relation) June 2, 1829 (parents resided near Dover, Stewart county, Tenn.). She was born Feb. 6, 1803, in Stewart county, and came to Utah with husband. Their children: Eliza Jane, died; William George b. Sept. 3, 1831, m. Susan Lucretia Lowry Dec. 13, 1854, m. Adaline Vorhees; Sarah Geraldine b. March 27, 1833, m. Newman Brown; Lydia Isabel b. July 25, 1835, John Ralph b. April 21, 1837, and Albert Augustus b. Sept. 14, 1839, died; Heber C. Kimball b. Dec. 29, 1840, m. Eunice Snow; Catherine Elizabeth b. May 26, 1844, m. James P. Edwards; Mary Ann b. Oct. 9, 1846, died; Joseph Henry b. June 12, 1848, m. Alveretta Driezett.
Married Lucinda Haggerty (Ayres) June 5, 1853, Salt Lake City (parents lived in Pennsylvania). Their children: Albert b. March 3, 1854, m. Josephine Black; Amanda b. March 3, 1854, died; Frank b. April 26, 1856, m. Jane Brown; John b. June 19, 1859, m. Patrera Brown. Family home Manti, Utah.
Farmer. Died June 10, 1869, Springdale, Kane county, Utah.

PETTEY, WILLIAM GEORGE (son of Albert Pettey and Catherine Pettey). Born Sept. 3, 1831, in Henry county, Tenn. Came to Utah Sept. 24, 1848, Heber C. Kimball company.
Married Susan Lucretia Lowry Dec. 13, 1854, Manti, Utah (daughter of John Lowry and Mary Wilcox, both of Manti, pioneers Sept. 30, 1847, John Taylor company). She was born March 13, 1834, in Clay county, Mo., and died Oct. 21, 1859. Their children: Susan Angeline b. Nov. 19, 1855, m. Walter K. Barton; William George b. Oct. 22, 1857, d. Oct. 25, 1869.
Married Adaline Vorhees Dec. 26, 1859, Manti (daughter of Elisha Vorhees and Nancy Ann Leak, pioneers 1851, Ezra T. Benson company), who was born Aug. 15, 1844, in Hancock county, Ill. Their children: George Albert b. Aug. 4, 1861, m. Clara Ann Barton; Elizabeth Ann b. Dec. 12, 1862, m. Niel C. Christensen; Heber Alonzo b. April 16, 1865, m. Malinda Lowry; John M. b. Sept. 11, 1866, died; Catherine Diantha b. March 27, 1868, m. David H. Jones; Warren Henry b. Nov. 27, 1869, m. Margie Funk; Isaac Adelbert b. July 14, 1871, m. Anena Simeson; Wallace Roundy b. Jan. 21, 1873, m. Winnie Nicholson; James Moroni b. April 16, 1875, died; William Arthur b. Feb. 13, 1877, m. Ada Williams; Franklin b. Aug. 24, 1878, m. Lettie Christensen; Margret b. March 27, 1880, m. Job Oliver; Samuel Rafe b. June 26, 1882, m. Jennie Miller; Susan Jane b. Feb. 29, 1884, m. Parley A. Anderson; Myrtle Adaline b. Nov. 11, 1885, m. Nels Jensen. Family home Emery, Emery Co., Utah.
Member of Manti quorum seventies; missionary among Indians at Moab, Utah 1855; first bishop of Sterling, Utah, six years; set apart as bishop of Emery ward 1890-96. Pioneer to Manti November, 1849; moved to "Dixie" (Rockville) 1862; then to Johnson's Fort where he lived one year; then to Kanarraville where he resided three years; returned to Manti 1871; next resided at Petteyville (Sterling) six years; moved to St. John, Ariz. and then back to Utah; resided at Mayfield several years; then moved to Emery 1888. Participated in the Indian trouble April 3, 1849, at Battle Creek, Utah, also took part in the Walker Indian war 1853; and when the Black Hawk trouble started was in Rabbit valley protecting the settlers from Indian attacks.

PETTEY, HEBER C. KIMBALL (son of Albert and Catherine Petty of Bourbon county, Ky.). Born Dec. 29, 1840, in Missouri. Came to Utah Sept. 24, 1848, Heber C. Kimball company.
Married Eunice Snow, in 1870, Manti, Utah (daughter of George Washington Snow and Mary Wells of Manti; came to Utah with oxteam). She was born Feb. 5, 1850, in Missouri. Their children: Mary Catherine b. Jan. 8, 1871, m.

Ole Olsen; Heber C. b. May 15, 1873, m. Maggie Keele; George W. b. July 1, 1875, m. Zina Williams; Abarintha b. Oct. 28, 1877, m. Charles Thompson; Frank b. Sept. 9, 1880, m. Blanch Jensen; Alexander b. Oct. 19, 1882, m. Maud Bunnel; Sarah Isabell b. Aug. 16, 1884, m. Francis Checketts. Family home Emery, Utah.
Member Emery quorum seventies; missionary to Tennessee 1898-1900; high priest; ward teacher; Sunday school teacher. Road supervisor; farmer and blacksmith. Died Aug. 22, 1902.

PETTIT, EDWIN (son of Jesse and Mary Pettit of Hempstead, N. Y.). Born Feb. 16, 1834, near Hempstead. Came to Utah Sept. 29, 1847, Edward Hunter company.
Married Maria Pettit April 12, 1860 (daughter of James and Phoebe Pettit, pioneers 1848), who was born Feb. 17, 1835. Only child: Alice Maria, b. Feb. 27, 1861, m. Adam Walker, July 24, 1885.
Married Rebecca H. Hill Oct. 29, 1864, Salt Lake City (daughter of Archibald Hill, pioneer Sept. 28, 1847, Newel Whitney company, and Isabel Hood, who died on the plains). She was born April 2, 1845, Nauvoo, Ill. Their children: Mary Isabel b. July 9, 1866, m. Henry Green Dec. 9, 1891; Clara Hannah b. May 6, 1868; Emeline b. Aug. 31, 1870, m. Foster W. Jones Sept. 25, 1901; Edwin b. Feb. 28, 1872, m. Sarah Louise Wickert Dec. 27, 1894; Lillian b. Aug. 5, 1873, m. Benjamin Birkinshaw April 23, 1907; Daisy Elizabeth b. Sept. 18, 1875; Florence b. Jan. 25, 1877; Nellie b. Feb. 10, 1878, m. Thomas F. H. Morton Sept. 6, 1905; Fannie Rebecca b. July 9, 1880; Archibald N. b. June 18, 1882, m. Jennevieve Johnston July 29, 1905; Elsie b. Aug. 15, 1884, m. Victor R. McKnight April 28, 1909; Jesse R. b. July 25, 1886, m. Phyllis Clayton June 16, 1909; Winnifred b. May 3, 1888, m. Bertram Reeves Sept. 7, 1910; William A. b. July 27, 1890.
Went to California 1849 as herd boy for Mr. Pomeroy; worked in gold mines, returning to Salt Lake City 1850 with Charles C. Rich company; went with colony sent by President Young to San Bernardina, Cal., 1850, and there served with "San Bernardino Rangers," returning to Utah six years later. Has crossed desert from Salt Lake City to California twenty times. Member of body guard of Brigham Young and Daniel H. Wells.

PETTIT, ETHAN (son of James Pettit and Mary Seely of Long Island, N. Y.). Born Feb. 14, 1810, Long Island, N. Y. Came to Utah September, 1848, Heber C. Kimball company.
Married Margaret Ellsworth Jan. 4, 1835, Long Island, N. Y. (daughter of Lawrence Ellsworth and Elizabeth Picket of New Jersey). She was born April 16, 1815. Their children: Matilda, m. Levy Reed; Mary, m. Joseph Imlay; Margaret, m. Ira Reed; Ethan, m. Maria H. Olsen; Elizabeth W., m. Thomas E. Jeremy, Jr. Family home, Salt Lake City.
Missionary to Elk Mountain 1857. Farmer and stockraiser. Died April 15, 1884, Salt Lake City.

PETTIT, ETHAN A. (son of Ethan Pettit and Margaret Ellsworth of Hempstead, Long Island, N. Y. Came to Utah 1848). Born Feb. 16, 1852.
Married Maria H. Olsen Feb. 14, 1876, Salt Lake City (daughter of Shure Olson and Elizabeth Jacobs of Salt Lake City, pioneers 1849), who was born May 26, 1853. Their children: Ira O. b. Feb. 14, 1873; Ethan A., Jr. b. Nov. 10, 1876, d. aged 8; Ole Ellsworth b. June 6, 1881, m. Sena Jensen; Elizabeth b. March 31, 1884, m. Herman Kesler; Joseph D. b. Oct. 2, 1886; Ethel b. Dec. 24, 1889; Raymond A. b. Aug. 18, 1892. Family home, Salt Lake City.
Elder. Farmer and stockraiser.

PETTY JOSEPH HENRY (son of Albert Petty of Nebraska). Born June 12, 1848, Loop Fork, Neb., on the Platte river. Came to Utah 1848.
Married Alveretta Duzett 1870, Rockville, Utah (daughter of Edward P. Duzett and Mary Adeline Eweing of Salt Lake City), who was born April 23, 1855. Their children: Joseph A., m. Jane M. DeMill; Mary M., m. David Hirschi; William Wrath, m. May Ballard; Amelia Vilate, m. Daniel Hirschi; Hanmer Duzett; Nathan, m. Adelia DeMill; Zilpha. m. Jesse DeMill.
Second counselor to Bishop Langston and 1st counselor to Bishop David Hirschi. Mechanic. Died March 14, 1912, Kanarra, Utah.

PETTY, ROBERT COWEN. Born Nov. 21, 1812, in Dickson county, Tenn. Came to Utah Oct. 14, 1850, Wilford Woodruff company.
Married Margrate Jefferson Wells, who was born March 22, 1806; came to Utah with husband. Their children: Mary Pryannah b. Jan. 3, 1833; Jane Caroline b. July 8, 1835; Raisia Aibini b. July 8, 1835; Martha Narcissa b. Nov. 8, 1837; Louisa Minerva b. Dec. 29, 1839; Robert Thomas b. Sept. 22, 1842; George Albert b. Feb. 16, 1844; Louis James b. Jan. 11, 1846; John b. March 20, 1848; Margrate Jefferson b. Sept. 13, 1849. Family home, Salt Lake City.

PETTY, LOUIS JAMES (son of Robert Cowen Petty and Margrate Jefferson Wells). Born Jan. 11, 1846.
Married Elvira Hendricks Feb. 8, 1870, Salt Lake City (daughter of William D. Hendricks and Elvira Smett), who was born May 17, 1852, died May 10, 1892. Their children: Lucy b. March 26, 1872; Alvira L. b. Sept. 26, 1874; Margrate b. Feb. 1, 1877; Elsie May b. Sept. 20, 1882;

1104   PIONEERS AND PROMINENT MEN OF UTAH

Louis James b. Nov. 3, 1879; William Peter b. Dec. 17, 1888; Robert Thomas b. July 3, 1888; Joseph Alma b. May 10, 1892. Married Rosabel Pace at Logan, Utah (daughter of Edwin Pace and Mary Jane Atkinson), who was born Nov. 20, 1862. Their children: May Bell b. Nov. 17, 1878; Effie Eugene b. Sept. 5, 1880; Sarah Jane b. May 31, 1882; Rosa Violate b. Jan. 2, 1884; Liley Victory b. Jan. 13, 1886; Thomas Fredric b. Jan. 26, 1888; George Edwin b. Oct. 9, 1889; Albert Lee b. Nov. 21, 1892; Ida Grace b. Feb. 24, 1894; Harold F. b. Nov. 4, 1904.

PHELPS, MORRIS (son of Spencer Phelps). Born Dec. 20, 1805, New York. Came to Utah 1849, oxteam company.
Married Laura Clark. Their children: Paulina, m. Amasa Lyman; Mary, m. Charles C. Rich; Joseph M. b. June 2, 1837, m. Melissa Stevens, m. Eliza Clift, m. Sarah Leggett, m. Margaret Hunter; Harriet, m. James Holmes; Jacob, d. child. Family home Montpelier, Idaho.
Seventy. Stockraiser. Died October, 1887.

PHELPS, JOSEPH M. (son of Morris Phelps and Laura Clark). Born June 2, 1837, Far West, Caldwell Co., Mo. Came to Utah with father.
Married Melissa Stevens Dec. 25, 1857, Alpine, Utah (daughter of Rosewell Stevens, pioneer 1847, and Mariah Vale, of Alpine). She died March 19, 1859.
Married Eliza Clift Jan. 1, 1861, at Alpine, who was born Jan. 25, 1846. Their children: Joseph Morris, m. Mary Osborne; Hyrum Milton; Arthur Marion; Ezra James, m. Jennie Roberts; Caddie Madora, m. William Shupe; Benjamin Franklin; Clara, m. Joseph Raleigh; Pauline, m. Oscar G. Molen; Walter George, m. Ella Holmgren; Hugh Stanley; Heber John, m. Inez Jones.
Married Sarah Leggett Aug. 17, 1867, Salt Lake City, who was born July 25, 1846, in England. Their children: Laura; Eva, m. Enoch Bagley; William, m. Ellen Pearson; Rosetta, m. Ned Bolles; Josephine, m. Randolph H. Groo; Martin Henry, m. Iva Smart; Louise; Lottie A., m. Edward Grosjean; Areta, m. Parley P. George.
Married Margaret Hunter (Groo) May 30, 1880, Salt Lake City, who was born Sept. 30, 1851, Salt Lake City. Their children: Leo Wesley, d. May 19, 1894; Joseph Smith b. March 6, 1883, m. Margaret Wilcox Sept. 30, 1906; Mary Ann, m. William Charles Parker, of Hooper; George Lafayette. Family home Montpelier, Idaho.
Elder; teacher. Assisted in settlement of Alpine City; and with Charles C. Rich helped to settle Bear Lake valley. Assisted in building wagon roads in and around Montpelier, Idaho. Railroad contractor and rancher. Died Sept. 29, 1886, near Cokeville, Wyo.
Margaret Hunter was the widow of Isaac Groo, whom she married Jan. 24, 1870 and mother of: Howard Groo, m. Priscilla Clark; Randolph Groo, m. Josephine Phelps.

PHELPS, JOSEPH SMITH (son of Joseph M. Phelps and Margaret Hunter). Born March 6, 1883, Montpelier, Idaho.
Married Margaret Wilcox Sept. 30, 1906, Montpelier (daughter of Francis Wilcox and Rebecca Ann Brandon of Ohio, pioneers). She was born Oct. 3, 1885. Family home, Montpelier.
Member 79th quorum seventies; missionary to England 1909-12; ward teacher; stake aid in Y. M. M. I. A. Policeman. Plumber and carpenter.

PHELPS, WILLIAM WINES (son of Enon Phelps and Mehitabel Goldsmith, of Hanover, Morris county, N. J., and Nauvoo). He was born Feb. 17, 1792, Hanover, N. J. Came to Utah Sept. 16, 1848, Brigham Young company.
Married Sally Waterman April 28, 1815, Smyrna, N. Y. (daughter of David B. Waterman and Jerusha Bassett of Ohio), who was born July 24, 1797, Franklin, Delaware county, N. Y. Their children: William Waterman, m. Lydia Brewster; Sabrina, m. Joseph K. Bent; Mehitabel, m. Willis Dalis; Sarah, m. Samuel Shaw; Henry Enon, m. Mary Catherine Mickeljohn; James and Jerusha, d. infants; Lydia, m. Jemirah Varney; Mary, and Princetta, d. infants. Family home, Salt Lake City.
Justice of peace; notary public. Speaker house representatives state legislature. Died March 7, 1872.

PHELPS, WILLIAM WATERMAN (son of William Wines Phelps and Sally Westerman). Born Jan. 23, 1823, Homer, Cortland county, N. Y. Came to Utah in 1852.
Married Lydia Brewster (daughter of Charles and Caroline Brewster, pioneers 1852). Their children: Franklin; William Waterman; Clarence; Fredrick; Lydia. Family home Placerville, Cal.

PHELPS, HENRY ENON (son of William Wines Phelps and Sally Waterman). Born Oct. 21, 1828, Canandaigua, N. Y. Came to Utah in 1848.
Married Mary Catherine Mickeljohn Sept. 17, 1863, Salt Lake City (daughter of David Forbes Mickeljohn and Esther Cowen Martin of Glasgow, Scotland), who was born July 28, 1846. Their children: Henry Enon Noah, m. Vina M. Jones; William Wines, m. Letta Roger; Mary Ada, d. child; David Alexander; Pharoah Alfred, m. Lottie Bennett; Clara May, m. Lester R. Rigs; Lillian Almenice, m. Walter Tuhey; Howard Edward, m. Louisa Stokes; Mary Katie, d. child; Joshua Alma b. Sept. 10, 1879; Abraham, d. infant; George Arthur, m. Edna Florence Griggs; Leo, d. infant; Alice Esther, m. Byron Malin. Family home, Salt Lake City.
Missionary to England 1855-57; member historian's office. Merchant. Died March 1, 1901.

PHILLIPS, GEORGE MATHEW DOW (son of David Phillips and Hannah Dow, of New Brunswick, Canada). Born May 23, 1816, in Hampton Parish, County York, New Brunswick, Canada. Came to Utah Sept. 25, 1855.
Married Susan Jacques Dec. 20, 1855, Salt Lake City, (daughter of Thomas Jacques and Sarah Farnsworth, of Aylesford, Nova Scotia, pioneers Oct. 4, 1854, Orson Pratt and Horace S. Eldredge company). She was born Dec. 19, 1832. Their children: Mathew J., m. Elizabeth Woodhead; Arletta, m. Hosea Sterrett; Heber, m. Salena Horton; Alice Maud, m. H. M. Carlow; James Emery, m. Minnie Jensen; Laura A., m. Edward F. Jackman; Luella, died; Flora; James Emery.
Member 45th quorum seventies; president of the church branch in York County, New Brunswick. Settled at Provo, 1855, and assisted in building up that part of the country. Millman and blacksmith. Died Sept. 22, 1893, Provo, Utah.

PHILLIPS, JAMES EMERY (son of George Mathew Dow Phillips and Susan Jacques). Born May 6, 1866, in New Brunswick, Canada. Came to Utah in 1872.
Married Minnie Jensen Dec. 31, 1890, Provo, Utah (daughter of Henrik Peter Jensen of Germany and Johannah Marie Jorgensen of Denmark, former came to Utah 1874, the latter, 1875). She was born April 14, 1870. Their children: Arthur Emery b. Jan. 6, 1892; Virgie Myrle b. June 6, 1893, m. Reed Rudolph Elkins; Leila Mabel b. July 16, 1895; Mathew Dow b. March 4, 1897; Pauline Marie b. May 16, 1901; Etta May b. May 4, 1903; Susan Maurine b. May 27, 1907; James Emery b. Jan. 1, 1909. Family home Provo, Utah.
Farmer and fruitgrower.

PHILLIPS, ISHMAEL (son of Thomas Phillips of Herefordshire, Eng.). Born May 22, 1815, Suttons Lake, West Hyde Parish, Eng. Came to Utah Oct. 4, 1863, John W. Wooley company.
Married Mary Goodsell 1834, Suttons Lake, West Hyde Parish, Eng. (daughter of Susan Bailey), who was born Feb. 14, 1815, and died Dec. 7, 1904. Came to Utah with her husband. Their children: Elizabeth, m. Henry Walker; Thomas, died; Mary Ann, m. John H. Walker. Family home Union ward, Salt Lake county, Utah.
Bishop of Union ward July 1, 1877-1900; ordained patriarch 1900. Farmer. Died Feb. 5, 1905.

PHILLIPS, RICHARD (son of Jacob and Rachel Phillips of American Fork, Utah). Born at Tom's River, Ocean county, N. J.. Came to Utah Sept. 13, 1861, Milo Andrews company.
Married Margaret Luker at Tom's River, N. J. (daughter of Thomas Luker and Mary Ann Rose). Their children: Mary Elizabeth, m. Polar Applegate; Elmira, m. Thomas Allman; Rachael, m. Henry W. Davis; John Wesley, m. Eliza Ann Abbey; Louis Lane, m. Elvira Kenny; Amizon, m. Charlotte Taylor; Emma, m. Oliver Thornton; Thomas, m. Anna Precilla Thornton, m. Suzan Taylor; Sarah, m. Amos Thornton; Richard Ellwood and Benjamin, died. Family home American Fork, Utah.
Married Caroline Hawkins at American Fork, Utah. Their children: Emma; Sidney. Family home, American Fork.

PHILLIPS, JOHN WESLEY (son of Richard Phillips and Margaret Luker). Born June 17, 1843. Came to Utah in 1862.
Married Eliza Ann Eby Feb. 5, 1867, at American Fork, Utah (daughter of John Eby and Elizabeth Pierce, pioneers 1848). Their children: Margarette b. Nov. 1, 1869, m. Harry Glaze; Mary Elizabeth b. Jan. 19, 1871, m. Edwin Barrett; Sylvia b. March 1, 1874, m. George Nichols; John Wesley, Jr. b. Jan. 8, 1877; Roy b. Jan. 22, 1880; Earl b. Feb. 4, 1881; Harriette b. May 27, 1883; Ethel b. June 2, 1885; Priel b. Oct. 27, 1888. Family home American Fork, Utah.
High priest. Marshal 1884-88. Died April 1, 1899.

PHILLIPS, JOHN WESLEY (son of John Wesley Phillips and Eliza Eby), born Jan. 8, 1877, American Fork, Utah.

PHILLIPS, WILLIAM. Born 1809, Monmouth, South Wales. Came to Utah about 1860.
Married Hannah Bognell at Monmouth (daughter of John Bognell and Maria Bock, pioneers 1859). She was born 1814. Only child: Joseph, m. Sarah L. Roundy. Family home Wanship, Summit Co., Utah.
Died Nov. 4, 1881.

PHILLIPS, JOSEPH (son of William Phillips and Hannah Bognell). Born Aug. 15, 1853, Brierly Hill, Staffordshire, Eng. Came to Utah 1864.
Married Sarah L. Roundy Jan. 1, 1876, Wanship, Utah (daughter of Jared Curtis Roundy and Lovisa Jenne, of Wanship; former pioneer July 24, 1847, Brigham Young company). She was born Jan. 17, 1858. Their children: Josephine b. Sept. 19, 1876, m. Eugene Clark; Jennie b. Aug. 4, 1878, m. Lee Chamberlain; Joseph C. b. May 25, 1880, m. Helen M. Lee; Edna Mabel b. Oct. 22, 1883, m. William Newberry; Lula Maud b. March 9, 1886, m. Warren Mecham; Lyle E. b. March 10, 1888; Ernest H. b. Feb. 17, 1891; Blanche b. Feb. 20, 1893; Florence b. Sept. 1, 1895; Evalyn Irene b. March 6, 1898. Family home, Wanship.
Miningman and farmer. Died March 21, 1907, Oakley, Utah.

PHILLIPS, JOSEPH C. (son of Joseph Phillips and Sarah L. Roundy). Born May 25, 1880, Wanship.
Married Helen M. Lee April 7, 1903, at Wanship (daughter of Marquis F. Lee and Ann Lee of Kalamazoo, Mich. Came to Utah 1870). She was born Oct. 10, 1884. Their children: Mark C. b. April 12, 1904; Inez b. Aug. 28, 1908; Fern Lucile b. Feb. 27, 1910. Family home, Wanship.
Farmer.

PICKERING, SIMEON (son of William Pickering of Foster, Yorkshire, and Martha Saunders of Scarborough, Eng.). Born Nov. 10, 1817, Wansford, Eng. Came to Utah Sept. 29, 1868, William S. Seeley company.
Married Ellen Elizabeth Harper Dec. 21, 1839, Driffield, Eng. (daughter of Henry Harper of Yorkshire, and Martha Goltry of Scarborough, Eng.). She was born Aug. 6, 1817, died April 6, 1897. Their children: Ann Elizabeth b. Dec. 17, 1840, d. aged 16; John b. Sept. 23, 1842, m. Naomi ——; Mary b. July 30, 1845, m. Samuel Fifield; Henry Harper b. April 15, 1848, and Martha Ellen b. April 17, 1852, d. infants; Willard Richards b. Sept. 30, 1853, m. Eunice Draker; Heber b. April 25, 1856, d. infant; Franklin Harper b. Dec. 23, 1857, m. Mary Jane Snowball. Family home, Salt Lake City.
Elder. Miller. Died Nov. 22, 1892.

PICKERING, FRANKLIN HARPER (son of Simeon Pickering and Ellen Elizabeth Harper). Born Dec. 23, 1857, Hull, Eng. Came to Utah with parents.
Married Mary Jane Snowball Sept. 6, 1883, Salt Lake City (daughter of Ralph Snowball and Jane Thomas of Salt Lake City, pioneers 1853). She was born Dec. 19, 1866, at Salt Lake City. Their children: Franklin William b. June 13, 1884, d. infant; Jane Elizabeth b. Dec. 12, 1886, m. John Fred Evans; Mary b. Dec. 20, 1888, m. Thomas Bow Brighton.
High priest; ward teacher. Motorman for Utah Light and Railway company at Salt Lake City 23 years.

PICKETT, MORONI (son of Matthew Pickett and Harriett Pocock of England). Born Oct. 16, 1848, Curridge, Berkshire, Eng. Came to Utah Oct. 16, 1862.
Married Frances A. Clegg July 30, 1870, Salt Lake City (daughter of Benjamin Clegg and Elizabeth Dodd, England—pioneers 1849, Daniel Jones company). She was born Sept. 2, 1851. Their children: Hyrum E. b. May 18, 1871, m. Minnie E. Tolman; Oliver B. b. May 10, 1874, m. Ammar E. Marcus; Albert b. July 11, 1877; Rubey P. b. March 13, 1881, m. Judson Mabey; Eugene b. Sept. 22, 1885, m. Emma A. Mabey; Horace R. b. Feb. 15, 1888; Warren L. b. Feb. 13, 1890; Olive E. b. Sept. 5, 1892. Family resided Tooele City, Utah, and Marion, Idaho.
President Y. M. M. I. A. at Tooele 1879; missionary to southern states 1879; counselor to bishop of Tooele 1880; first counselor to president of Cassia stake 1888-90; patriarch. Justice of peace. Died Oct. 16, 1911.

PICKETT, OLIVER B. (son of Moroni Pickett and Frances A. Clegg). Born May 10, 1874, Lake Town, Utah.
Married Ammar E. Marcus Oct. 8, 1896, at Salt Lake City (daughter of William Marcus and Rebecca Malone, both of Junction City, Ark., who came to Utah November, 1885). She was born Aug. 21, 1873. Their children: Leona B. b. July 2, 1897; Hazel A. b. March 6, 1901; Howard O. b. Dec. 13, 1902; Thora A. b. Feb. 22, 1908; Thelma M. b. June 23, 1909. Family resided Marion and Oakley. Idaho.
Counselor to president Y. M. M. I. A. of Marion ward 1890-97; president Y. M. M. I. A.; missionary to northwestern states where he served as president of Seattle conference; ordained bishop of Oakley third ward in 1904. Member state board of education; state bounty commissioner; president Minadoka Woolgrowers' Association. Justice of peace; assessor Cassia Co., Idaho.

PICKUP, GEORGE. Came to Utah Oct. 24, 1848, with a section of Mormon Battalion.
Married Eliza Haws (daughter of Gilbert Haws and Hannah Whitcomb of Pike county, Ill., pioneers 1848, Lorenzo Snow company). The only child was George b. March 8, 1850, m. Mary Olive Durfee. Family resided Salt Lake City and Provo, Utah.
Married Miss Norton, pioneer oxteam company. Their children: Edward; John. Family home Mountainville, Utah.
Member of the church. Died at San Bernardino, Cal.

PICKUP, GEORGE, JR. (son of George Pickup and Eliza Haws). Born March 8, 1850, Salt Lake City.
Married Mary Olive Durfee 1870 at Eden, Utah (daughter Thomas Durfee and Charlotte Sanford of Pike county, Ill., pioneers 1861). She was born Feb. 29, 1852. Their children: Laurania b. Aug. 24, 1871, d. aged 8; George Melvin b. Jan. 20, 1873, m. Edith Keeler; Lola Vilate b. Sept. 29, 1875, m. Joseph Richens; Clarence Ray b. Oct. 10, 1879, m. Vilate Datty; Alton b. Aug. 14, 1884, m. Ada Weight; Lorella b. Oct. 9, 1886. Family resided Provo, Ogden and Roosevelt, Utah.
Elder; ward teacher; home misionary. Veteran Black Hawk war. Assisted in bringing immigrants to Utah. School teacher and school trustee. Farmer and carpenter.

PIDCOCK, WILLIAM HASELGROVE (son of Thomas Pidcock, born at Mansfield, and Martha Haselgrove, born at Hurst, Sussex, Eng.). Born Jan. 18, 1832, Mansfield. Came to Utah Oct. 24, 1854, William A. Empey company.
Married Hannah Blench April 8, 1854, on ship "Marshfield," soon after leaving Liverpool (daughter of Thomas Wheatley Blench and Ann Todner), who was born Sept. 11, 1833, New Castle-on-Tyne, Eng., and died Jan. 20, 1898, Ogden, Utah. Their children: Thomas Wheatley b. Jan. 27, 1855, d. Oct. 23 1855; Jedediah William b. Dec. 9, 1856, m. Roxana Farr March 5, 1877; Ralph b. April 6, 1859, m. Alice Reeves; Joseph b. Nov. 19, 1861, d. May 24, 1885; Hyrum b. Nov. 19, 1861, m. Mary Allen; Martha Ann b. March 27, 1864, m. James A. Wright Aug. 11, 1882; Lorin b. July 9, 1866, d. Jan. 8, 1867; John b. Oct. 29, 1867, d. Jan. 29, 1889; Mary Hannah b. March 16, 1870, m. Dennis Harbaugh; Emeline b. Oct. 20, 1872, m. William Martin; Margaret b. Jan. 24, 1876, d. April 12, 1879. Family resided Ogden and Salt Lake City, Utah.
Married Fannie Branson Aug. 5, 1870, Salt Lake City (daughter of William Branson, born Aug. 5, 1823, in Leicestershire, Eng., died April 27, 1904, at Ogden, Utah, and Elizabeth Bracknock, born June 6, 1828, in England, died Feb. 13, 1897, at Ogden, Utah, who were married September, 1845). She was born July 17, 1849, at Ochnel, Nottinghamshire, Eng. Came to Utah Aug. 5, 1870, Carl G. Maeser company. Their children: Eliza Snow b. July 30, 1871, m. William Hunt May 15, 1888; Edith b. July 23, 1873, m. Harry D. Brighten Sept. 12, 1901; Heber John b. Sept. 19, 1874, d. Oct. 18, 1892; Abraham b. Nov. 13, 1876, d. May 16, 1878; William b. Nov. 13, 1876, d. May 7, 1878; Sarah b. Nov. 6, 1878, m. Benjamin Scrivens Dec. 26, 1899; Zina b. Nov. 1, 1880, d. July 26, 1882. Family home Ogden, Utah.
Married Annie Burton Oct. 31, 1870, at Salt Lake City (daughter of William Burton—born May 5, 1820, Mansfield, Eng., died Sept. 11, 1887, at Ogden, Utah, and Elizabeth Burton—born Dec. 21, 1826, Mansfield. Came to Utah 1873). She was born Sept. 1, 1849, Mansfield, Eng. Came to Utah Oct. 1, 1870, Frank H. Hyde company. Their children: Elizabeth b. Sept. 7, 1875, d. Sept. 2, 1876; Gilbert b. Dec. 7, 1877, m. Ida Hickman May 9, 1902; Willard b. Dec. 26, 1879, m. Blanche Wright 1905; Annie b. May 30, 1882; Samuel T. b. Aug. 29, 1884; Thomas b. Jan. 6, 1890; Emma b. Aug. 15, 1892; Francis b. April 4, 1894. Family home Ogden, Utah.
Married Sarah Burton (daughter of William and Elizabeth Burton), who was born Oct. 10, 1852, Mansfield, Eng., died May 21, 1904, Ogden. Came to Utah July 17, 1872, Eric Peterson company. Their children: Rachel b. Dec. 24, 1874, m. Heber Richens; George Albert b. June 25, 1877, d. Oct. 30, 1904; Charles Innis b. Sept. 1, 1879, d. child; Lucy b. Dec. 2, 1880, d. Feb. 12, 1883; Ada b. Nov. 27, 1882, d. Oct. 6, 1883; William b. Jan. 20, 1885, m. Florence Gibbons Nov. 20, 1904; Family home Ogden, Utah.
Settled at Ogden 1855. Missionary to England 1869-70. Major in Nauvoo Legion. Blacksmith and merchant. Died Nov. 27, 1906, Ogden, Utah.

PIDCOCK, JEDEDIAH WILLIAM (son of William Haselgrove Pidcock and Hannah Blench). Born Dec. 9, 1856, Ogden, Utah.
Married Roxana Farr March 5, 1877, Ogden, Utah (daughter of Lorin Farr and Sarah Giles, the former a pioneer 1847), who was born Feb. 3, 1860, at Ogden, Utah. Their children: Jedediah William b. Dec. 26, 1877, m. Dora M. Moyes Dec. 10, 1908; Roxana b. Aug. 25, 1879, m. Clarence Smith Gunnell Dec. 8, 1903; Lorin Eugene b. Jan. 1, 1882, d. March 3, 1882; Joseph b. June 3, 1883, and Rebecca b. Nov. 22, 1885, both died same day. Family home Ogden, Utah.
Chief clerk of railway offices at Ogden. Merchant. Died April 22, 1886.

PIDCOCK, JEDEDIAH WILLIAM, JR. (son of Jedediah William Pidcock and Roxana Farr). Born Dec. 26, 1877, Ogden, Utah.
Married Dora M. Moyes Dec. 10, 1908 (daughter of Alexander H. Moyes, born March 22, 1851, Hastely, Scotland, and Nancy Marinda Tracy, born Sept. 25, 1861, Ogden, Utah). She was born Oct. 14, 1887, Ogden.
Member Alumni Association of College Physicians and Surgeons at San Francisco; member Weber County Medical Association; member Weber County and State Medical Society. Weber county physician 1909-12.

PIERCE, GEORGE. Born Jan. 20, 1828, in England. Came to Utah August, 1859, James S. Brown company.
Married Nancy Campbell (daughter of Beapitha and Eunice Campbell, former a pioneer, independent company), who was born Jan. 8, 1833. Came to Utah with husband. Their children: Francis Marion b. 1857, m. Elizabeth Jane Lee Jan. 24, 1885; John Keaton b. 1859, d. May 14, 1861. Family home North Ogden, Utah.

PIERCE, FRANCIS MARION (son of George Pierce and Nancy Campbell). Born May 1, 1857, Liberty, Pa.
Married Elizabeth Jane Lee, Menan, Idaho (daughter of Ezekiel Lee and Fannie B. Fisher, pioneers 1855), who was born April 14, 1858, Big Cottonwood, Utah. Their children: Caton W. b. April 2, 1886, m. Louis West, 1909; Fannie Leona b. Aug. 26, 1888, m. Jimmie Nelson, 1912; Nancy May b. May 5, 1890; Ezekiel L. b. Feb. 18, 1892; Lucy Irene b. Jan. 22, 1894; Caroline b. Dec. 20, 1895; George b. Sept. 25, 1898; Eunice Aurilla b. May 22, 1900. Family home Lorenzo, Idaho.
Farmer.

PIERPONT, THOMAS (son of John Pierpont and Anne Fairclough of Lancashire, Eng.). Born Nov. 6, 1836, Rainhill, Lancashire, Eng. Came to Utah Oct. 5, 1864, Captain Lowry company.
Married Naomi King Nov. 2, 1858, in New York (daughter of James King and Mary Bendall of Wiltshire, Eng.), who was born May 27, 1840. Their children: John King b. Dec. 20, 1859, m. Marie Jents; James King b. May 21, 1861, m. Amanda L. Holdaway July 2, 1906; Harry, died; Ruth, m. George H. Naylor; Mary, m. George R. Emery; Annie; Thomas Fairclough, m. Vilate Smoot; Naomi, died; Florence, m. W. W. Taggart; Ella May, m. J. E. Meyer. Family home, Salt Lake City.
Married Javenta Beck 1872, Salt Lake Endowment House (daughter of Thomas Beck and Elizabeth Carlisle, of Lancashire, Eng., pioneers Oct. 5, 1862, Ansel P. Harmon company). She was born April 21, 1855. Their children: George H. b. Oct. 16, 1874, m. Camilla Winberg June 22, 1911; Elizabeth, m. H. J. Young; Anne; Clara; William F.; Margret F.; J. Vera; Albert E.; Mabel; Leah. Family home, Salt Lake City.
Elder. Master mechanic of O. S. L. R. R. President Salt Lake Foundry. Died April 17, 1908.

PIERPONT, JAMES KING (son of Thomas Pierpont and Naomi King). Born May 21, 1861, St. Cathrines, Canada. Came to Utah with father.
Married Amanda Lucinda Holdaway (Young) July 2, 1906, Salt Lake City (daughter of Shadrick Holdaway and Lucinda Haws, of Provo, pioneers Oct. 24, 1848, contingent Mormon battalion. Widow of Almono Leoto Young. Married Dec. 11, 1889 (son of J. W. Young and Lucy Canfield of Salt Lake City, and New York City, at Mantl, Utah. One child was born: Lohelld Young). Amanda Lucinda was born Jan. 17, 1870. Family home Provo, Utah.
Boilermaker and machinist.

PIERPONT, THOMAS FAIRCLOUGH (son of Thomas Pierpont and Naomi King). Born Sept. 16, 1870, Salt Lake City.
Married Vilate Smoot Jan. 4, 1893, Provo, Utah (daughter of A. O. Smoot and Diana Eldredge of Provo, pioneers Sept. 23, 1847, Daniel Spencer company). She was born May 20, 1873. Their children: Pauline b. March 8, 1894; Clifford Smoot b. May 7, 1897; Naomi b. Dec. 26, 1899; Vilate b. Jan. 3, 1902; Margeret b. Nov. 10, 1904; Thomas George b. Dec. 21, 1906; Ruth b. Feb. 28, 1908; John Barney b. June 1, 1910. Family home Provo, Utah.
Manager Provo Foundry and Machine Company, Inc., Provo, Utah.

PIERSON, P. Born in Sweden. Came to Utah with oxteam company.
Married in Denmark. His children: John P., m. Ellen Mathews; Elvina H. Olsen (adopted), m. Isaac E. Black.
High priest. Farmer. Died in 1904, Huntington, Utah.

PIKE, JOHN NIGHTINGALE (son of Edward Pike and Hannah James Baker, of Westholme, near Shepton Mallet, Somersetshire, Eng.). Born Nov. 2, 1846, Pilton, Somersetshire, Eng. Came to Utah Sept. 15, 1868, John Gillespie oxteam company.
Married Elizabeth Rawlings June 21, 1868, Upton Noble, Somersetshire (daughter of James Rawlings and Elizabeth Sharp of Upton Noble, Eng., the former a pioneer Sept. 15, 1869). She was born Sept. 8, 1845. Their children: Elizabeth Ellen b. Aug. 23, 1869, d. Dec. 1, 1876; Edward James b. June 4, 1872, m. Caribel Ridges June 21, 1893; Ethel Hanah Georgeinna b. Sept. 8, 1875, m. Walter L. Holbrook June 28, 1899; Edward Ernest b. June 19, 1877, m. Louise J. England, April 22, 1903; William Albert b. Aug. 5, 1879, d. Jan. 12, 1882; Charles Raymond b. Dec. 4, 1881, m. Beatrice Anderson Sept. 21, 1910; Frederick Rawlings b. Nov. 13, 1884, d. Dec. 9, 1891; Elsie Marian b. Oct. 9, 1890. Family home, Salt Lake City.
Member 30th quorum seventies; high priest; member high council of Liberty stake. Member Salt Lake City board of education.

PIKE, CHARLES RAYMOND (son of John Nightingale Pike and Elizabeth Rawlings). Born Dec. 4, 1881, Salt Lake City.
Married Beatrice Anderson Sept. 21, 1910, Salt Lake City (daughter of Charles L. Anderson and Ellen Ickelberry of Grantsville, Utah). She was born Jan. 15, 1886. Their child: Raymond Anderson, b. April 8, 1912. Family home, Salt Lake City.
Elder; missionary to Germany, 1902-05. Wholesale dealer of bakers' and confectioners' supplies; firm name, Pike Anderson company.

PIMM, JOHN (son of John Pimm, born Jan. 21, 1793, Measham, Derbyshire, Eng., and Ann Martin, born March 20, 1790, Keady, Armagh, Ireland). He was born Sept. 13, 1815, Belistore, Ireland. Came to Utah Sept. 12, 1857, Jesse B. Martin wagon company.
Married Sarah Tabberer (daughter of Henry Milward Tabberer and Sarah Fisher, married at Derby, Derbyshire, Eng.; both died in England). She was born Sept. 5, 1814, and came to Utah with husband. Their children: Henry b. Feb. 28, 1836, d. August, 1857; Isaac b. May 3, 1838, d. April 17, 1841; Sarah Ann b. April 8, 1840, m. James P. Park Oct. 28, 1857; Seth Austin b. June 23, 1842, m. Eliza Jane Dent Nov. 1, 1869; John b. April 15, 1845, d. March 20, 1846; John b. June 13, 1849, d. Feb. 1, 1856. Family resided Salt Lake City, Mill Creek and St. George, Utah.

Married Agnes Donald Feb. 23, 1861, Salt Lake City (daughter of Malcolm Donald and Mary Shaw), who was born Oct. 10, 1834, Blackwood, Scotland. Their children: John D. b. Dec. 1, 1861, m. Eva Dodge Dec. 23, 1888; James D. b. Feb. 21, 1864, died; Mary D. b. Sept. 22, 1865, m. Prescott Lamb June 19, 1885; Agnes D. b. Jan. 1, 1868, m. Sherman Hardy Jan. 17, 1887; Ann D. b. Nov. 24, 1869, m. Ashby Snow; Malcolm D. b. July 14, 1871, m. Elizabeth Gray May 1, 1894; Archibald D. b. July 16, 1873; Jane D. b. Aug. 2, 1874; Charlotte D. b. April 9, 1877; latter three died. Family home St. George, Utah.
Moved to Provo, 1858, in the general move, and returned to Mill Creek in the fall; called to help settle St. George, 1861. President 61st quorum seventies; tithing clerk at St. George 1861, field marshal; city seeton; poundkeeper and city assessor and collector. Postmaster, 1873-1901. Died March 12, 1901, St. George.

PIMM, SETH AUSTIN (son of John Pimm and Sarah Tabberer). Born June 23, 1842.
Married Eliza Jane Dent Nov. 1, 1869, Salt Lake City (daughter of John Dent and Jemima Keeble, former died in England, latter pioneer Sept. 2, 1868, Daniel D. McArthur company). She was born Dec. 29, 1848, Maldon, Essex county, Eng. Family home St. George, Utah.
Missionary to England 1864-66. County clerk and recorder 10 years; assistant postmaster, 1876-1901. School teacher, 15 years. Draftsman in county surveyor's office. Now retired from business.

PINCOCK, JOHN (son of John Pincock and Mary Marsden of Exton, Eng.). Born July 27, 1830, Exton. Came to Utah Aug. 28, 1852, John Parker company.
Married Isabella Douglass Feb. 3, 1851, St. Louis, Mo. (daughter of George Douglass and Ellen Briggs of Downham, Eng., and immigrated to St. Louis, Mo.; former died in Missouri; latter a pioneer Aug. 28, 1852, John Parker company). She was born Nov. 3, 1833. Their children: Mary Ellen b. Nov. 8, 1851, m. Sollman C. Stephens; John Edmond, m. Alice Parker Richard Feb. 27, 1879; Isabell Alice, m. H. B. Forbes June 7, 1873; James Henry, m. Annie E. Garner Nov. 24, 1881; Ann. d. Aug. 20, 1860, d. birth; Charlotte, m. John A. Garner Nov. 24, 1881; Jane b. Nov. 15, 1863, d. Nov. 16, 1863; George Albert, m. Lucinda E. Bingham Oct. 20, 1886; Vilate, m. Charles H. Woodmanser Oct. 26, 1887; Charles, m. Josie Porter Dec. 29, 1893; William Aaron, d. April 13, 1888; Josephine b. Jan. 20, 1874, d. July 22, 1875; Richard Douglass, m. Ethel Jane Fowler Nov. 30, 1905; Wealthy. Family home Ogden, Utah.
High councilor in Weber stake; high priest. Assisted in bringing immigrants to Utah 1863. County commissioner two terms; Ogden city councilman; depot policeman at Ogden for 20 years. Farmer. Died Dec. 16, 1906, Ogden.

PINCOCK, JOHN EDMOND (son of John Pincock and Isabella Douglass). Born Dec. 16, 1853, Kaysville, Utah.
Married Alice Barker Richards Feb. 27, 1879, Salt Lake City (daughter of Samuel W. Richards and Mary Ann Parker of Salt Lake City). She was born Oct. 23, 1857. Their children: John Franklin b. Jan. 15, 1880, m. Susie Blackford June 22, 1910; Mary Alice b. Dec. 22, 1881, m. Charley Nibley Jan. 19, 1905; Henry Dewey b. Dec. 5, 1883, m. May Graham; Richard Parker b. Jan. 21, 1886; Samuel Whitney b. Dec. 31, 1887; William Aaron b. Aug. 8, 1890; Howard b. Nov. 8, 1892; Edith b. July 17, 1895; Carrie Alene b. Feb. 11, 1898; Parley Parker b. Dec. 17, 1900, d. Dec. 29, 1901. Families resided Ogden, Utah, and Wilford, Teton and Sugar City, Idaho.
President quorum Fremont stake; high priest; counselor to bishop of Wilford ward 1888-93; bishop of Teton ward 10 years; high councilor in Fremont stake. Sheriff Fremont county two years; assessor and collector two years; chairman board of county commissioners two years; state grain commissioner two years. Farmer and stockraiser. President and manager of Roxbury Milling company.

PINCOCK, JAMES H. (son of John Pincock and Isabella Douglass). Born Jan. 20, 1858, Ogden, Utah.
Married Annie E. Garner Nov. 24, 1881, Salt Lake City (daughter of Frederick Garner and Ann Horrocks of Ogden, Utah). She was born 1863, Ogden. Their children: Josephine b. Sept. 13, 1882, m. Robert Thomson Jan. 17, 1907; James F. b. Aug. 29, 1884; C. Bert b. April 28, 1889; Annabelle b. March 24, 1891; Alice Pearl b. July 14, 1894; Ida Fern b. May 28, 1900; Rulon D. b. Feb. 26, 1902. Family home Sugar City, Idaho.

PINCOCK, GEORGE A. (son of John Pincock and Isabella Douglass). Born March 1, 1865, Ogden, Utah.
Married Lucinda E. Bingham Oct. 20, 1886, Logan, Utah (daughter of Sanford Bingham and Martha Ann Lewis of Riverdale, Utah, pioneers September, 1847). She was born Nov. 27, 1868. Their children: Martha Isabella b. July 10, 1887; Lottie May b. May 9, 1889; Lucinda Elizabeth b. Oct. 8, 1891; George Sanford b. April 11, 1893; William Albert b. Feb. 21, 1896; Wealtha Jane b. April 9, 1899; Douglass b. Sept. 27, 1900; John Lewis b. Oct. 7, 1902; Lorin b. March 24, 1904; Mark Lavaine b. Sept. 19, 1907, d. May 10, 1912; Grant Bingham b. Sept. 26, 1910. Family home Sugar City, Idaho.
Missionary to southern states 1895-98; counselor to bishop

of Wilford ward 5 years; bishop of Wilford 5 years; alternate member high council and later high councilor; superintendent of religion classes Fremont stake. Representative in Idaho legislature 1911-12. Field superintendent Utah-Idaho Sugar Company. Farmer.

PINGREE, JOB (son of Job Pingree and Charlotte Tyrant of Struntley, Worcestershire, Eng.). Born Nov. 21, 1837, Struntley, Eng. Came to Utah Sept. 12, 1857, Jesse B. Martin company.
Married Esther Hooper Sept. 27, 1861, Salt Lake City (daughter of James Hooper and Susan Hancock of Hallow, Worcestershire, Eng., pioneer Job Pingree company), born Sept. 22, 1839. Their children: James; Annie; William; Esther; Ellen; Elizabeth; Charles; Joseph; Hyrum; Franklin; Pearl. Family home Ogden, Utah.
Missionary to England 1858-61; president eastern states mission 1892-94. City councilman; water-works superintendent; road supervisor; agricultural superintendent of Amalgamated Sugar Company; president of Pingree National bank.

PINGREE, FRANKLIN (son of Job Pingree and Esther Hooper). Born July 15, 1880, Ogden, Utah.
Married Pauline Taggart, Logan, Utah, Jan. 5, 1905 (daughter of George Taggart and Jessie McNiven); born March 28, 1885. Their children: Franklin b. Oct. 5, 1905; Ruth b. June 24, 1907; Paul b. Feb. 4, 1910.
Missionary to Germany March 20, 1901 to May 10, 1904; mayor of Coalville Nov. 1911; president Y. M. M. I. A. Summit stake; president 27th quorum of seventy. Treasurer Summit county 1909-1911.

PITT, JOHN (son of Mathew Pitt and Elizabeth Martin of Willenhall, Staffordshire, Eng.). Born April 9, 1816, Willenhall. Came to Utah September, 1866, Daniel Thompson oxteam company.
Married Caroline Wright February, 1839, St. Peter's church, Wolverhampton, Eng. (daughter of John Wright and Ann Perry of Willenhall). She was born Oct. 18, 1820. Their children: Priscilla, m. Alfred Lunt Dec. 8, 1865; Meshach, m. Alie Price, Jan. 16, 1871; Ann, m. Shadrick Lunt May 27, 1872; Noah b. June 4, 1854, d. June 9, 1857; Hannah, m. Charles Ahlstrom; Caroline, m. C. W. Foote Dec. 10, 1883; John, m. Mary Ann Lund Jan. 14, 1884. Family home Nephi, Utah.
Sunday school worker over 23 years; high councilor. Blacksmith. Died March 25, 1891.

PIXTON, ROBERT (son of George Pixton and Mary Hankinson of England). Born Feb. 27, 1819, Manchester, Lancashire, Eng. Came to Utah Oct. 1, 1848, with Mormon Battalion division.
Married Elizabeth Cooper May 5, 1839, Chesterfield, Derbyshire, Eng. (daughter of John Cooper and Charlotte Hallotte of England), who was born Feb. 8, 1820. Their children: Charlotte b. Feb. 8, 1840, m. William Van Dyke; George b. Sept. 23, 1841, Mary b. Dec. 12, 1844, and John Helaman b. Oct. 3, 1846, d. infants; Robert b. Nov. 6, 1850, m. Amelia M. Atwood; Elizabeth b. Sept. 15, 1852, m. Henry Harker, Sr.; Willard b. Nov. 4, 1854, m. Isabella U. Carter; Sarah b. 1857, d. infant; Joseph C. b. Dec. 18, 1858, m. Emma Ashby; Sariah H. b. Dec. 7, 1862, m. Henry Wheeler. Family home, Salt Lake City.
Married Martha Silcock Jan. 25, 1869, Salt Lake City, who was born April 30, 1852, Tooele, Utah. Their children: Alma b. July 1, 1870, d. July 19, 1870; Nellie b. Sept. 3, 1872, d. Sept. 18, 1874; Seth b. June 20, 1874, m. Emma Weaver; Jane b. March 17, 1879, m. John D. Bowers; Olive b. Jan. 17, 1881, m. Edward H. Eardley.
Missionary to England 1862-66. Farmer. Died Nov. 23, 1881, Taylorsville, Utah.

PIXTON, WILLARD (son of Robert Pixton and Elizabeth Cooper). Born Nov. 4, 1854, Salt Lake City.
Married Isabella U. Carter Jan. 22, 1876, St. George, Utah (daughter of William Carter and Harriette Temperance Utley of St. George, Utah; former pioneer July 24, 1847, Brigham Young company, later pioneer 1852). She was born March 10, 1857. Their children: Willard C. b. April 13, 1877 (d. Dec. 20, 1900), m. Alice Lindsay June 22, 1899; Lafayette C. b. April 21, 1879, d. June 23, 1903; John Edward b. Dec. 9, 1880; Samuel b. Nov. 30, 1882 (d. Oct. 30, 1911), m. Nellie Frampton Aug. 3, 1910; Norton Ray b. Dec. 17, 1884; Hazel Isabella b. April 11, 1888, m. Eugene Paxton Sept. 29, 1909; Grace b. May 8, 1890; Mary Elizabeth b. July 9, 1892, d. Feb. 23, 1905; Robert Carter b. Feb. 28, 1895; Ephraim b. May 24, 1899; George M. b. Aug. 18, 1901. Family home Taylorsville, Utah.
One of the presidents of 115th quorum seventies; missionary to northern states 1894; ward teacher. Farmer.

PLATT, JAMES. Born in England. Came to Utah 1862, oxteam company.
Married Elizabeth ——, who died at Mona, Utah. Their children: Margary, William Much; Johathan, m. Bet Depottle; Elizabeth, m. Thomas Yates; Nancy, m. John Harrison; William, m. Mary Alice Kay; Sarah, m. Hyrum Vest; Marintha, m. William Ostler. Family home, Mona.
Seventy. Veteran Black Hawk war. Farmer. Died at Mona.

PLUMB, JEREMIAH (son of Merlin Plumb and Elizabeth Bellows of Salem, Utah, pioneers 1850). Born Nov. 27, 1860.
Married Sarah Jane Shields Jan. 24, 1870, Salt Lake City (daughter of John F. Shields and Mary Howell, pioneers 1849), who was born Sept. 29, 1854. Their only child was: May E. b. Feb. 6, 1871, m. James R. Davis. Family home Salem, Utah.

POLL, WILLIAM F. (son of William Poll and Jane Long of Norfolk, Eng.). Born June 15, 1823, Norfolk, Eng. Came to Utah November, 1852, Captain Nelson company.
Married Charlotte Long Nov. 3, 1843, Norfolk, Eng. (daughter of John Long of Norfolk). She was born June 29, 1822. Their children: William John, m. Louis Strong; Maria, m. Joseph Gibson; Frederick R., m. Rose Pinock; Jeanette, m. Joseph Earl; Martha A., m. Orson S. Thomson; Maryann, m. William Harrison; Alice, m. George Crabtree; Harriet, m. James Strong; Charles, m. Cora Vine; Joseph, m. Mary Bond. Family home, Salt Lake City.
Presiding teacher. Carpenter. Died Nov. 7, 1896, Salt Lake City.

POMEROY, FRANCIS MARTIN (son of Martin Pomeroy and Sybil Hunt of Somers, Conn.). Born Feb. 22, 1822, at Somers. Came to Utah July 24, 1847, Brigham Young company.
Married Irene Ursula Haskell 1844, Salem, Mass. (daughter of Asabel Green Haskell and Ursula Billings Hastings of Salem and Nauvoo, Ill., pioneers 1847, John Smith company). She was born Nov. 1, 1825, died at Salt Lake City. Their children: Francelle Eugenia, m. Charles Innez Robson; Francis Ashbel, m. Mary A. Rich Jan. 10, 1875; Elijah Pomeroy, m. Mary Annetta Coleman Oct. 16, 1879, m. Lucretia Phelps; John Haskell, m. Emily Hutchinson, m. Clara Drollinger July 13, 1889; Irene Ophelia, m. William M. Newell April 28, 1874; May Isabel; Ella Amelia, m. William L. Rich. Sept. 6, 1877; Emma Adelia, m. Hyrum Grimmitt Oct. 9, 1875. Family home Little Cottonwood, Utah.
Married Sarah Matilda Colborn April 20, 1863, Salt Lake City (daughter of Thomas Colborn, born Aug. 3, 1801, Lyons, Wayne county, N. Y., and Sarah Bowers, born Dec. 30, 1800, Lansing, Tompkins county, N. Y., of Big Cottonwood, Utah, Paris, Idaho and Mesa, Ariz.; latter came to Utah Sept. 24, 1848, Heber C. Kimball company). She was born Nov. 4, 1834. Their children: Mary Ursula b. June 27, 1860, m. Sol. F. Kimball March, 1881; Talmai Emerson b. May 6, 1863, m. Sarah M. Johnson Oct. 13, 1886; William Edley b. March 26, 1866, m. Isabel Robson; Franklin Thomas b. Sept. 15, 1870, m. Isadora Morris March 28, 1893; Sarah Rosina b. March 21, 1873, m. Adam Brewer April 21, 1903; Edward Leslie b. March 19, 1876, m. Serene McGuire July 4, 1892. Family home Mesa City, Ariz.
Married Jassamine Elizabeth Routledge Feb. 27, 1858, Salt Lake City (daughter of Isaac Routledge and Martha Pets of Paris, Idaho, and Mesa, Ariz.). She came to Utah Nov. 30, 1856, Edward Martin handcart company, and died March 19, 1900. Their children: Charles Routledge b. Jan. 26, 1859, d. July 6, 1860; Martin Isaac b. Jan. 16, 1860, m. Mary M. Brizzee Aug. 18, 1884; Eleanor Rosetta b. Nov. 4, 1863, m. Edwin E. Jones June 23, 1891; Gertrude Ophelia b. Feb. 22, 1865, d. June 12, 1888; Henry Austin b. Jan. 6, 1867, d. Oct. 7, 1888; Heber Chase Kimball b. June 6, 1869, m. Cassandra Johnson July 10, 1893.
High priest; missionary to California 1849-50. Justice of Peace at Paris, Idaho and Mesa, Arizona. Engaged in the sawmill, sphinx and lathe machine business. Farmer. Died Feb. 28, 1882, Mesa, Ariz.

POMEROY, FRANKLIN THOMAS (son of Francis Pomeroy and Sarah Matilda Colborn). Born Sept. 15, 1870, Paris, Idaho.
Married Sophia Isadora Morris March 28, 1893, Mesa City, Ariz. (daughter of Hyrum Bowles Morris, born Dec. 23, 1821, Bourbon county, Ky., and Eleanor Crawford Roberts, born Nov. 9, 1830, Morgan county, Mo. both of Quincy, Ill., Kanarah, Rockville, Utah, and Mesa, Ariz., pioneers Aug. 9, 1860, Warren Walling company). She was born April 10, 1873, Kanarah, Utah. Their children: Franklin Ivan b. Jan. 26, 1894; Karl Francis b. Feb. 13, 1899; Adah Eleanor b. March 11, 1902; Gladys b. Dec. 11, 1904; George Hyrum b. Nov. 15, 1907, d. May 7, 1913; Ralph De and Roland Eltweed (twins), b. Sept. 6, 1909, Roland d. Oct. 1, 1910. Family home, Mesa City.
High priest; president Y. M. M. I. A. 1904-05; missionary to southern states 1895-98; president Mississippi conference 33 months; first stake superintendent of religion classes Maricopa stake 1898-1906; senior teacher theological class 13 years; one of the seven presidents 90th quorum seventies; second counselor to John T. Lesueur; president Maricopa stake 1906-11; senior class leader of Y. M. M. I. A. nine seasons; superintendent religion classes 1911. Justice of peace; notary public and city clerk of Mesa City, Ariz. Engrossing and enrolling clerk legislature of 1905. Real estate broker; Persian lamb woolgrower and farmer.

POND, STILLMAN (son of Preston Pond, born Jan. 2, 1779, Wrentham, Mass., and Hannah Rice, born May 13, 1787, Hubbardston, Mass.). Born Oct. 26, 1803, in Worcester county, Mass. Came to Utah Sept. 30, 1847, John Taylor company.
Married Almira Whitemore in Massachusetts, who died. Of five children the three youngest died.
Married Miss Davis. Of six children, all died as did their mother.

1108　　　　PIONEERS AND PROMINENT MEN OF UTAH

Married Abigail Thorn (daughter of Richard Thorn) who was born April 2, 1821, and came to Utah with husband in 1847. Their children: Mary Anna b. Jan. 1, 1850, m. John Buxton; Charles Stillman b. Jan., 1852, died; Brigham b. June 9, 1853, m. Arretta Whittle, m. Catherine Whittle; Lewis Sumner b. Dec. 25, 1854, m. Julia Whittle; Abigail b. Jan. 11, 1857; Joseph Thorn; Martin H.; Zina Adaline. Married (Mrs.) Mountz 1852. Their only child: Martha b. Oct. 6, 1853, m. Walter P. Reed. Married (Mrs.) Christensen 1870. Their children: Lisander; Noah C.; Moses Alonzo. Aaron and Alfonzo, died. Presiding high priest at Richmond. Resided in Salt Lake City until 1856 when, after several moves landed at Richmond, Cache valley in 1860. Took part in Echo Canyon campaign. One of the founders of the Z. C. M. I. at Richmond.

POND, BRIGHAM (son of Stillman Pond and Abigail Thorn). Born June 9, 1853, Salt Lake City. Married Arvetta Whittle (daughter of Thomas L. Whittle and Mary Fulmer, pioneers 1848). She was born Oct. 29, 1857. Their children: Charles; Ruey; Marietta; Bertrand Thorne; Irene; William Leon; Edna; Lewis Vilroy; Mildred. Married Catherine Whittle (daughter of Zera Whittle and Casanda Pope). She was born June 17, 1867. Their children: Rufus Rolland; Zera Whittle; Horace Raymond; Preston; Blanch; George; Edith; Abigail; Howard. Family home Lewiston, Utah.

POND, LEWIS S. (son of Stillman Pond and Abigail Thorn). Born Dec. 25, 1854. Married Julia Ann Whittle (daughter of Casper Whittle and Mary Ann Harris), who was born Jan. 15, 1859. Their children: Lewis Sumner b. Nov. 9, 1880; Casper W. b. Oct. 16, 1852; Flora b. Feb. 3, 1885; Myrtle b. Sept. 18, 1887; Clara b. Dec. 9, 1889; Eugenia b. Aug. 2, 1896; Russell Thorn b. Sept. 7, 1899; Teressa b. March 15, 1901; Abigail b. Sept. 26, 1902. Family home Thatcher, Idaho. Missionary to Southern states 1889-91; Bishop, 1892-98; stake president. County commissioner two terms; county treasurer. Rancher.

POND, MARTIN (son of Stillman Pond and Abigail Thorn). Born May 21, 1862, Richmond, Utah. Married Martha Caroline Harris Dec. 14, 1881, Thatcher, Idaho (daughter of Alexander Harris and Harriet Craner), who was born at Richmond, Utah, Sept. 27, 1862. Their children: Harriet b. Dec. 29, 1882; Hazel b. Aug. 16, 1885; Martin Harris b. Aug. 31, 1887; Alta b. July 17, 1890; Stillman H. b. March 12, 1892; Mary b. July 21, 1894; Alexander Loyal b. Sept. 29, 1897; Gladys b. Dec. 11, 1899; Genevieve b. Aug. 31, 1904; Asael Thorn b. April 25, 1906.

POPE, ROBERT (son of Robert M. Pope and Rebecca Whittaker, of London, Eng.). Born June 16, 1828 in London. Came to Utah, 1858, David Brinton's muleteam company. Married Sarah LeDuke, 1851, at Salt Lake City (daughter of Charles LeDuke of Vermont). She was born Sept. 17, 1834. Their children: Charles Holmea. m. Maria Jane McCann; Hattie Ann. d. infant; Robert Alexander, m. ——; John Theodore, m. Charlotte Stock; George Eugene, m. Margaret Ann Jones; Richard Henry, m. Jane Bennett; William Frank, died age 19; Adeline, m. Edward Longhurst; Sarah Adell, m. Nathan Hunting; Marcellus B., m. Bessie Bruno; Rock, m. Minnie Holdaway. Family home Vernal, Utah. Married Mary Huff Nov. 1, 1869, Salt Lake City (daughter of Joseph Huff and Mary Jane Losee, of Canada, pioneers Sept. 29, 1851, with Joseph W. Young oxteam). She was born March 5, 1852. Their children: Joseph b. Dec. 9, 1870, m. Sarah Jane Anderson; Robert Orlan b. Dec. 20, 1873, m. Harriet Isabell Hunt; Isaac Stephen b. Feb. 26, 1875, m. Sarah Nielsen; Harley Elmer b. June 8, 1877, m. Rozeilly Campbell; Don Carlos b. Nov. 27, 1881, m. Margaret Southam and Amanda Elizabeth Green; Mary Maria b. June 5, 1883, m. William Southam; Mark E. b. March 22, 1886, m. Valda Anderson; Baby b. Sept. 28, 1888, and James b. Aug. 22, 1890, d. infants. Family home, Loa, Utah. Farmer.

POPE, ROBERT ORLAN (son of Robert Pope and Mary Huff). Born Dec. 20, 1873, at Fish Haven, Idaho. Married Harriet Isabella Hunt at Manti, Utah (daughter of Frederick Nephi Hunt and Tomena Larsen, both of Monroe, Utah). She was born Oct. 11, 1875. Their children: Baby, and Robert D., d. infants. Baby and Baby, d. infants; Harriet b. Aug. 31, 1910, d. Sept. 8, 1910; Frederick Leroy b. Nov. 19, 1911, d. Nov. 20, 1911. Family home Vernal, Utah. Elder; deacon; secretary deacon; counselor to Y. M. M. I. A.; missionary. Farmer; freighter; blacksmith; shepherd.

POPE, HARLEY ELMER (son of Robert Pope and Mary Huff). Born June 8, 1878, in Idaho. Married Agnes Rozella Campbell April 24, 1901, Vernal, Utah (daughter of James Heber Campbell and Sara Henry, of Vernal). She was born Dec. 4, 1881. Their children: Elmer Dee, d. infant; Harley Devon b. Dec. 10, 1902; Mary Aloas b. May 14, 1904; Rufus Lynn b. June 8, 1907, died age 4; Hazel; Mark. Family home Roosevelt, Utah. Elder; ward teacher; president Y. M. M. I. A. School trustee. Road builder; farmer; freighter; thresher.

POPE, DON CARLOS (son of Robert Pope and Mary Huff). Born Nov. 27, 1881, Garden City, Utah. Married Margaret Southam Aug. 7, 1900, at Salt Lake City (daughter of George Southam and Katherine Cameron, of Evanston, Wyo. Came to Utah in 1861). She was born Jan. 30, 1882. Their children: Don William b. March 15, 1902; Margaret Eve b. Dec. 19, 1903. Family home Vernal, Utah. Married Amanda Elizabeth Green July 17, 1906, at Vernal, Utah (daughter of Ephraim Green and Sidney Florence Thayne, of Kamas, Utah), who was born Jan. 31, 1885. Their children: Iris Lavaur b. June 12, 1907; Carlos b. Dec. 14, 1910; Baby b. Sept. 15, 1912. Family home, Roosevelt, Utah. Farmer.

PORRITT, THOMAS (son of Thomas Porritt, born Jan. 14, 1817, Stockport, Eng., and Margaret McCann, born 1819, in Ireland). Born Aug. 13, 1849, Stockport. Came to Utah Nov. 30, 1856, Edward Martin handcart company. Married Sarah E. Hampton Nov. 13, 1868 (daughter of Thomas Hampton and Martha R. Bracken, pioneer Edward Martin handcart company). She was born March 13, 1853. Their children: Thomas b. Oct. 14, 1869; Sarah Jane b. May 12, 1872; Martha b. Aug. 30, 1874; George b. Nov. 12, 1878; Margaret b. Sept. 1, 1881; Levi b. Oct. 7, 1884; Nephi N. b. Jan. 27, 1887; John M. b. June 4, 1888; William R. b. April 25, 1891; Bertha b. Oct. 18, 1892; Leola b. Oct. 24, 1894; Rula R. b. Oct. 22, 1896.

PORTER, ABSALOM. Came to Utah, 1847, oxteam company. Married Sarah Ann Holladay, Marion county, Ala., pioneer 1848. Family home, Santaquin, Utah. Missionary to Australia.

PORTER, JARED (son of Nathan Porter of Danby, Rutland county, Vt., and Avisa Salsbery). Born March 23, 1812, Danby, Vt. Came to Utah, 1850. Married Abiah Franklin Feb. 14, 1831 (daughter of Ebenezer Franklin, died Oct. 17, 1841, Nauvoo, Ill., and Esther Hammond, pioneer 1850). She was born Feb. 21, 1815, Northfield, Mass. Only child: Jared (adopted after death of his mother, Cornelia Staker, second wife of Jared Porter), b. Oct. 8, 1848, m. Alice L. Griffin Jan. 1, 1872. Married Cornelia Staker Jan. 1, 1848, Council Bluffs, Iowa. She was born 1811, in Canada, died July 7, 1850, Fort Carney, Neb. Only child: Jared Riley b. Oct. 8, 1848, m. Alice L. Griffin Jan. 1, 1872. Married Harriet Preece Nov. 2, 1852, Salt Lake City (daughter of Richard Preece and Susanna Prichard, married in England; former died on the plains, latter a pioneer 1851). She was born March 17, 1833, in Herefordshire, Eng. Their children: John Henry b. Aug. 21, 1854, m. Mary McNelly Sept. 6, 1884; Benjamin Preece b. July 31, 1857, m. Henrietta Jane Dowdle Dec. 19, 1878; Isaac Arnold b. Oct. 12, 1859, m. Mary Ann Alvy; Andrew Richard b. March 23, 1862, m. Susanna C. Heaps March 8, 1882; Mark Frederick b. Sept. 22, 1864, m. Sarah S. Gregory Dec. 3, 1884; Cecelia Abiah b. Dec. 27, 1867, d. May 19, 1879; Harriet Susanna b. Aug. 7, 1870, m. Preston Howell Jan. 9, 1894. Families resided at Grass Creek, Summit Co., Utah. Settled at Salt Lake City in 1850, moved to Cottonwood in 1852, and after several moves settled at Escalante, Utah, 1881. Counselor to Bishop Elias Aspher of Echo ward; Shoemaker. Died Jan. 2, 1891, at Escalante, Patriarch

PORTER, JARED RILEY (son of Jared Porter and Cornelia Staker). Born Oct. 8, 1848, Pottawattamie Co., Iowa. Married Alice Levina Griffen Jan. 1, 1872, Coalville, Utah (daughter of Charles Griffen and Sarah Smith), who was born March 25, 1852, Salt Lake City. Their children: Sarah Inez b. April 26, 1874, m. Wallace Shirts; Joseph Jared b. Dec. 8, 1877, m. Molly Scow; Emily Cornelia b. April 2, 1880, m. Thomas Alvy; Hyrum Adelbert b. July 28, 1882, m. Alice Roundy; Edith b. Sept. 2, 1884, m. George H. Barney; Alice Hannah b. Sept. 10, 1886; Adelia b. Dec. 28, 1888, m. Albert Roundy; Parley Pratt b. Nov. 2, 1890; Emerson; Leland; Roland. Family home Escalante, Utah.

PORTER, BENJAMIN PREECE (son of Jared Porter and Harriet Preece). Born July 31, 1857, South Cottonwood, Utah. Married Henrietta Jane Dowle Dec. 19, 1878 (daughter of Robert H. Dowle and Henrietta Miservy; married March 29, 1858, Santaquin, Utah; former a pioneer 1849, Kinghad and Livingston company, latter, Oct. 17, 1853, Joseph Young company). She was born July 25, 1861, Franklin, Idaho. Their children: Benjamin Jerome b. Oct. 1, 1879, m. Ida Maud Durrant Dec. 23, 1903; Henrietta Adelia b. Dec. 25, 1812, m. Alma Olsen March 7, 1906; Sarah Ada b. June 9, 1885, m. William Lewis Larsen Dec. 4, 1907; Parley Milton b. June 27, 1891; Ina b. Dec. 25, 1893; Verna b. April 16, 1898; Wilford Dowdle b. April 23, 1900. Family home Franklin, Idaho. High priest; superintendent of Sunday school, 1897; assistant superintendent Sunday school of Oneida stake 1898. Member village board several terms, and chairman one term; trustee of village school board; ward teacher, 25 years. Farmer; carpenter; thresher.

PORTER, SANFORD (son of Nathan Porter and Susannah West). Born March 7, 1790, Brimfield, Mass. Came to Utah October 2, 1847, Charles C. Rich company. Married Nancy Warriner Jan. 1, 1812, in Orange county, Vt. (daughter of Reuben Warriner and Sarah Colton), who was born July 29, 1791. Their children: Chauncy Warriner b. Oct. 20, 1812, m. Amy Sumner, 1833; Malinda b. 1814, m. Ezra Chipman; Sarah b. 1816, m. David Willard. August, 1839; John President b. July 28, 1818, m. Nancy Rich Feb. 5, 1843, m. Mary P. Graves; Nathan Tanner b. July 10, 1820, m. Rebecca Cherry Nov. 12, 1848, m. Eliza Ford; Reuben b. May, 1822, d. infant; Sanford b. June 25, 1823, m. Emma Ensign, m. Malinda Porter July 25, 1852; Nancy Areta b. Aug. 8, 1825, m. Edward Stevenson; Justin Theodore b. 1828. killed by a falling horse. 1841; Lyman Wight b. May 5, 1833, m. Electa Kilbourn March 5, 1852.

Soon after coming to Utah he settled at Mill Creek, Salt Lake county; in 1849, moved to Centerville, Davis county. Presiding elder, over Centerville branch, and in 1852, upon organization of a ward at that place, became its first bishop. Original pioneer of Porterville, Morgan county, where, in 1860, he built the first house. Farmer and sawyer. Died Feb. 7, 1873, at Porterville.

PORTER, CHAUNCY WARRINER (son of Sanford Porter and Nancy Warriner). Born Oct. 20, 1812, Holland, Erie county, N. Y. Came to Utah October, 1848.

Married Amy Sumner 1833, Independence, Mo., who was born Feb. 22, 1815. Their children: Alma b. Dec. 15, 1834, m. Minerva Duell; Malinda Ann b. July 9, 1836, m. Sanford Porter; William b. Nov. 5, 1838, died; Sarah Angeline b. Sept. 14, 1841, m. George Leavitt; Nancy Areta b. March 15, 1845, m. Nelson Mattice; Hyrum S. b. March 15, 1845, died; Joseph and Benjamin (twins) b. Dec. 11, 1846, died next day. Family resided, Mill Creek, Centerville and Porterville, Utah.

Married Lydia Ann Cook, March 1846 (daughter of Ahaz and Mercy Cook), who was born Aug. 6, 1830, Peoria. Ill., and died Dec. 20, 1882. Their children: Warriner Ahaz b. May 20, 1848, m. Mary Malinda Norwood Oct. 5, 1867, m. Martha Norwood July 22, 1873, m. Rachel Aun Black April 23, 1879; Cynthia Caudness b. June 22, 1850, m. Evan Jones; Amy Zenora b. May 4, 1851, m. John P. Porter; Justin Rocksford b. Oct. 18, 1853, m. Mary Mariah Porter; Nancy Arena b. Sept. 20, 1855, m. Sanford Chipman; Mary Ziona b. April 25, 1857, d. 1857; Edson Darias b. April 12, 1859, m. Catherine Carling, m. Phoebe Carling; Omni Lehi b. Jan. 27, 1861, d. Nov. 22, 1873; Annie Ozina b. April 27, 1863, m. Benjamin D. Black; Abinadi b. March 28, 1865, m. Annie Louisa Jensen; Arvel Marion, died; Lydia Bereft b. Jan. 21, 1868, died.

Married Priscilla Strong Feb. 10, 1847, Winter Quarters, Neb. (daughter of Ezra Strong and Mary Lowell, former pioneer 1848). She was born Dec. 11, 1830. Their children: Chauncy Union b. March 16, 1850, m. Parvette Rich; Daniel Dorath b. June 27, 1851, died; Printha Priscilla b. Aug. 29, 1852, m. Charles Simpson; Francis Lysander b. July 4, 1854, m. Mariah Hoyt; Mary Etta b. July 5, 1856, m. Edward Crofts; Melvin Omer b. June 11, 1858, d. June 10, 1879; Carmi Nephi b. Oct. 31, 1860, m. Hannah E. Hoyt; David Nathaniel b. Feb. 23, 1862, died; Wilford Woodruff b. Feb. 22, 1864; Olive Martha, died; Ezra Solomon b. Dec. 1, 1867, m. Mattie Turman.

High priest; presiding elder over East and West Porterville. Millwright, sawyer and carpenter. Died March 3, 1868, Centerville, Utah.

PORTER, WARRINER AHAZ (son of Chauncy Warriner Porter and Lydia Ann Cook). Born May 20, 1848, Florence, Neb.

Married Mary Malinda Norwood Oct. 5, 1867, Salt Lake Endowment hou (daughter of Richard Smith Norwood and Elizabeth Stevenson of Salt Lake City, pioneers Oct. 12, 1848), who was born Nov. 1, 1851. Their children: Warriner Eugene b. Sept. 17, 1868, d. Oct. 28, 1889; Walter Alvin b. Feb. 3, 1870, m. Ablone Black; Mary Elizabeth b. Sept. 9, 1872, m. Walter J Stimer; Orvei Wallace b. April 19, 1875, m. Elizabeth Carroll; Effa Vilate b. July 23, 1877, m. Lorenzo Rowley; Lydia Ellen b. Nov. 21, 1879, m. Morley L. Black; Jesse Smith b. Aug. 13, 1882; Hyrum Edward b. June 6, 1885, m. Lucy Carroll; Jennie Arvena b. Oct. 13, 1887, d. July 12, 1889; Milla Maud b. Nov. 28, 1891; Mabel Amelia b. Dec. 31, 1894. Family resided Porterville and Orderville, Utah, and Colonia Pacheco, Chihuahua, Mexico.

Married Martha Norwood July 22, 1873, Salt Lake Endowment house (daughter of Richard Smith Norwood and Elizabeth Stevenson), who was born July 27, 1856, Big Cottonwood, Utah; died Aug. 31, 1893. Their children: Martha Luella b. Aug. 10, 1874, m. John E. Steiner; Ann Eliza b. June 30, 1878, m. William L. Young; Emma Zenora b. June 1, 1881, d. March 9, 1882; Cyntha Jane b. April 9, 1885, m. Abel W. Hardy; Ahaz Abinadi b. March 30, 1889.

Married Rachel Ann Black April 23, 1879, St. George temple (daughter of William M. Black and Mariah Hanson), who was born March 8, 1863, died May 5, 1906. Their children: Ann Mariah b. April 27, 1880, m. Aaron B. Hardy; Morley b. Aug. 16, 1882; Joseph Henry b. April 14, 1885, m. Hannah James; David Sanford b. May 13, 1887, d. July 8, 1887; Myrtle Drucilla b. June 4, 1888, m. Herbert H. Redd; Hatty Hortense b. Dec. 2, 1890, d. Aug. 30, 1910; Katie Marinda b. Jan. 3, 1893, d. Jan. 23, 1893; Ablone b. Feb. 24, 1894; Minnie Minerva b. June 12, 1896; Warren Snow b. July 4, 1898, d. Aug. 10, 1898; Rachel Maletta b. July 25, 1899; Roxey Gertrude b. Oct. 2, 1901; Margery Arreta b. Sept. 18, 1903; Blanch b. April 27, 1906, d. next day. Missionary to Mexico 1899-1912; seventy; high priest. Constable of Kane county. Machinist; lumber dealer; sawyer; cabinet maker; farmer.

PORTER, JOHN PRESIDENT (son of Sanford Porter and Nancy Warriner). Born July 28, 1818, Plymouth, N. Y.

Married Nancy Rich Feb. 5, 1843, Nauvoo, Ill. (daughter of Joseph Rich and Nancy O'Niel of Indiana and Kentucky; pioneers Oct. 2, 1847, Charles C. Rich company). She was born Dec. 5, 1821. Their children: Joseph Rich b. March 29, 1844, m. Eliza Jane Bratton, m. Electa E. Porter; Sanford C. b. Dec. 26, 1845, m. Olive Kilbourn; John P. b. Sept. 4, 1847, m. Zenora Porter; Nancy b. March 16, 1851, d. May 7, 1851. Family resided Salt Lake City, Centerville and Porterville, Utah.

Married Mary P. Graves, born Sept. 13, 1818, Concord, Essex county, Vt. Their children: Charles G. b. April 3, 1854, m. Bessie White, July, 1876; Sarah b. Feb. 8, 1860, m. Frederick White.

Pioneer to Porterville 1861 and Centerville 1850, where he was a leader in making roads, building school houses and canals. School trustee, and water commission many years. Died May 28, 1895.

PORTER, JOSEPH RICH (son of John President Porter and Nancy Rich). Born March 29, 1844, Charleston, Lee county, Iowa.

Married Eliza Jane Bratton Jan. 4, 1868, Salt Lake City (daughter of George Washington Bratton and Mary Palmer Graves, of Council Bluffs, Ia.; latter pioneer 1852). She was born March 6, 1845. Only child: Eliza B. b. Feb. 19, 1870, m. Alva S. Porter.

Married Electa E. Porter May 8, 1876, Salt Lake City (daughter of Lyman W. Porter and Electa Mariah Kilbourn of Porterville; pioneers 1848, Charles C. Rich company). She was born 1858, Centerville. Their children: Marlow Rich b. May 8, 1877, m. Emily Araminta Hooper; Nellie E. b. Aug. 17, 1879, d. April 17, 1881; May. b. May 23, 1882, d. May 30, 1882; Bertha M. b. Nov. 25, 1883, m. Arthur Rich; Nancy Athena b. June 5, 1886; Nathaniel V. b. Nov. 11, 1888; Joseph Irvine b. Jan. 23, 1894; Mary Viola b. Sept. 29, 1897. Families resided Porterville, Utah.

Missionary to Illinois and Kentucky 1875-77; bishop of Porterville ward 1877-97; high councilor Morgan stake 1908-12. County commissioner and superintendent district schools 1870-74; prosecuting attorney 1878-82 and 1910-12; probate judge 1882-86; commissioner 1886-92, all in Morgan Co., Utah; member house of representatives 1889-91 and 1908-10; chaplain 1903-05. School teacher 1862-1902.

PORTER, SANFORD (son of Sanford Porter and Nancy Warriner). Born June 25, 1823, Vienna, Trumbull Co., Ohio. Came to Utah from California Oct. 16, 1847, contingent Mormon battalion.

Married Emma Ensign July 25, 1852, Salt Lake City (daughter of Zophar Ensign and Priscilla Billings, latter a pioneer). She was born March 4, 1833, Spafford, Onondaga county, N. Y. Their children: Emma Priscilla b. Sept. 23, 1853, m. Thomas Spencer April 2, 1877; Sanford Marius b. Aug. 5, 1855, m. Nina M. Leavitt Sept. 4, 1879; Jared Ensign b. Oct. 22, 1857, d. May 13, 1869; Cevilla Ann b. Nov. 5, 1859; Sarah Lavera b. April 2, 1861, d. July 22, 1861; Marion Marcellus b. Oct. 1, 1862, d. Oct. 13, 1885; Aaron Milton b. Aug. 13, 1866, m. Cylvia VanBeet; Mary Arizona b. March 27, 1870, m. David Jenkins; Warren b. Nov. 18, 1872, d. Dec. 13, 1872; Ensign Moses b. Dec. 21, 1873, m. Matilda Stratford. Family resided at Centerville and Porterville, Utah.

Married Malinda Ann Porter July 25, 1852, Salt Lake City (daughter of Chauncey Warriner Porter and Amy Sumner), who was born July 9, 1836. Their children were: Nathan Theodore b. May 27, 1853, m. Mary Emma Bond; Samuel Uriah b. Oct. 21, 1855, m. Mary Minerva Porter; Amy Arena b. Dec. 23, 1857, m. Charles Whiting; William Ira b. Jan. 28, 1859, m. Adeline Porter; Alva b. Feb. 8, 1862, m. Elizabeth Shelley; Alma b. Feb. 8, 1862, d. infant; Edith b. April 18, 1864, m. Thomas Brockbank; Joseph Isaiah b. June 24, 1866, m. Maud Shelley; Hyrum Jeremiah b. June 24, 1866; Benoni; Moroni; latter three d. infants; Nancy Angeline b. Jan. 24, 1872, m. David Cluff; Chauncy Warriner, died. Family resided at Porterville, Utah, and Sunset, Ariz. Member of Mormon battalion Company E. Built first sawmill in Morgan Co., Utah, 1854, in Hardscrabble Canyon, carrying the necessary machinery on pack mules over the Wasatch mountains from Centerville, Davis county. Assisted in settling The Muddy in southeastern Nevada in 1868. In 1877 made a visit to the valley of the Little Colorado river in northern Arizona; and in 1880 moved one of his families there, settling at Sunset in what is now Navajo county.

PORTER, SANFORD MARIUS (son of Sanford Porter and Emma Ensign). Born Aug. 5, 1855, Centerville, Davis Co., Utah.

Married Nina Malinda Leavitt Sept. 4, 1879, Salt Lake City (daughter of George Leavitt and Sarah A. Porter), who was born Nov. 25, 1861, Richville, Morgan Co., Utah. Their children: Marius Earl b. July 8, 1880, d. Aug. 10, 1881; Rulon Ensign b. Feb. 8, 1882; Emma Ethel b. April 24, 1884, m. Edwin S. Westover Oct. 8, 1903; Adah Janet b. March 23, 1886, m. J. Clark Owens; Aaron Bond b. Aug. 23, 1887, m. Jane Rogers; Mirai Adrian b. Feb. 15, 1889, d. June 27, 1889; Mamie Teresa b. April 3, 1890; Sarah Abline b. Feb. 1, 1892, m. Jesse S. Bushman; Liona Ordell b. Feb. 6, 1894, d. Nov. 19, 1902; Myron Leavitt b. May 13, 1896, d. Nov. 3, 1902; Leo Fenton b. Feb. 24, 1898; Sanford Emil b. May 4, 1900; Nina Areta b. June 12, 1901; Thora b. Oct. 15, 1902.

Moved from Porterville, Utah, to Sunset, Ariz., 1880, and to St. Joseph, Ariz., in 1884. Constable of St. Joseph precinct 1887-90; school trustee. High priest; member Snowflake stake high council. Farmer and stockraiser.

PORTER, AARON BOND (son of Sanford Marius Porter and Nina Malinda Leavitt.) Born Aug. 23, 1887, St. Joseph, Ariz.
Married Jane Rogers Oct. 7, 1909, Salt Lake City (daughter of Davis Rogers and Minnie Woolley of Snowflake, Ariz.). She was born Oct. 7, 1888, at Snowflake. Their child: Glenda b. June 15, 1911. Family home St. Joseph, Ariz.
Farmer; stockman; rancher.

PORTER, WILLIAM F. (son of John Porter of England and Mary Ann Bryant, born May 13, 1826, Kent, Eng.). Born Jan. 6, 1845, New Castle, New South Wales, Australia. Came to Utah 1859.
Married Margret L. Benson June 27, 1868 (daughter of Joseph W. Benson and Mary C. Lee, who were married 1843, in Graves county, Ky., pioneers Aug. 19, 1868, John R. Murdock company). She was born May 14, 1847, pioneer Aug. 19, 1868, John R. Murdock company. Their children: William J. b. April 21, 1870, m. Malissa Thurston Dec. 16, 1891; John F. b. Jan. 3, 1873; Thomas Leroy b. Dec. 21, 1874; Margret Lillian b. March 4, 1876; Samuel Arthur b. April 1, 1879; Ruben Victor Penson b. June 8, 1885; Rheuben.
First counselor to Bishop Greenwood of central ward 1882-95. Moved from Beaver to Sevier county 1877.

POTTER, GARDNER GODFREY (son of Thomas Potter and Wealthy Weiller of Essex, N. Y.). Born 1820 at Essex. Came to Utah Dec. 22, 1848.
Married Emily Allen, Essex, N. Y., who died without issue.
Married Evelina Maria Hinman December, 1844, Iowa River, Iowa (daughter of Lyman Hinman and Aurelia Lewis, married Aug. 16, 1819, New Lebanon, N. Y., pioneers 1848). She was born Aug. 8, 1829, West Stockbridge, Mass. Their children: Melvin Lyman b. Sept. 1, 1850, m. Asenith Glover, 1871; Earnest Henry b. Aug. 3, 1854, m. H. Priscilla Bourne Oct. 11, 1875; Monica Amelia b. Sept. 2, 1856, m. Jacob M. Secrist 1879. Family home Farmington, Utah.

POTTER, ERNEST HENRY (son of Gardner Godfrey Potter and Evelina M. Hinman). Born Aug. 3, 1854, Springville, Utah.
Married Hannah Priscilla Bourne Oct. 11, 1875, Salt Lake City (daughter of Charles Bourne and Jane Alder, pioneers Sept. 14, 1853, Claudius V. Spencer company), who was born Sept. 21, 1854, Salt Lake City. Their children: William Ernest b. Aug. 20, 1876, m. Olive L. Moon March 15, 1905; Horace C. b. Aug. 28, 1878; Alice M. b. Oct. 22, 1881; Wallace b. May 31, 1886; Vernon Leo b. Feb. 18, 1890; Inez Aureta b. May 6, 1892. Family home Farmington, Utah.

POTTER, WILLIAM ERNEST (son of Ernest Henry Potter and Hannah Priscilla Bourne). Born Aug. 20, 1876, Farmington, Utah.
Married Olive Lelia Moon March 15, 1905, Salt Lake City (daughter of Henry Moon and Temperence Westwood; married March 18, 1856, Salt Lake City, pioneers Oct. 5, 1850, latter Sept. 11, 1853, Jesse W. Crosby company). She was born Oct. 15, 1874, Farmington, Utah. Their children: Herman E. b. May 3, 1906; Helen Louise b. July 18, 1908; Lucile b. June 13, 1911. Family home Riverside, Utah.

POTTER, RANSOM R. (parents lived at Waterbury, Conn.). Born March 4, 1807.
Married Rhoda E. Ferrell Sept. 25, 1825, who was born Jan. 10, 1807, at Waterbury, Conn. Their children: Rhoda Emeline, m. William Miller; Ransom Robert, died; Isaac S., m. Mary Ford; Benjamin F., m. Eliza Demmick. Family home Springville, Utah.
Farmer. Died Nov. 15, 1884, Albion, Idaho.

POTTER, ISAAC S. (son of Ransom Potter and Rhoda E. Ferrell). Born April 19, 1833, in Loraine Co., Ohio.
Married Mary Ford, Salt Lake City. Their child: Isaac M., m. Lucy Williams.
Married Asenith Lawrence, Salt Lake City (daughter of Aaron Lawrence). Their children: Emily M. b. Nov. 19, 1858, m. John A. Warner; James b. April 19, 1857, m. Jennie Peck; Rhoda b. Dec. 13, 1859, m. James F. Clyde; Rosalia b. Nov. 7, 1861, m. John Ferry; Bertha b. Jan. 13, 1863, m. David W. Holdaway; Christina b. Oct. 25, 1865, m. Tryphene Burrs.
Married Amelia Brown, Salt Lake City. Their children: Charles; Emeline, m. Charles Lyons; Annie. Families resided Springville, Utah.
Stockraiser. Died Aug. 1, 1867, Coalville, Utah.

POTTER, WILLIAM GEORGE. Came to Utah Sept. 19, 1847, Daniel Spencer company.
Married Sarah Ann Whitney. Their children: William George, m. Atimishia Minerva Washburn; Elijah, m. Sarah Jolley; Sarah Ann, m. Walter Winsor; Weltha, m. Joseph Scott. Family home Fort Ephraim, Utah.
Elder. Farmer. Killed during Black Hawk war.

POTTER, WILLIAM GEORGE, JR. (son of William George Potter and Sarah Ann Whitney). Born about 1839 in Ohio.
Came to Utah with father.
Married Artimishia Minerva Washburn about 1865, Fort Ephraim, Utah (daughter of Daniel Abraham Washburn and Tammer Washburn, of Monroe, Utah, pioneers). She was born June 17, 1849, in Nebraska. Their children: Artimishia Minerva, m. Joseph Burnett; Sarah Ann, m. Samuel B. Shumway; William George, m. Mary Brown; m. Parley Church (Hart); Elija John, died; Tammer Jane, died; Daniel Abraham, m. Sophia Jensen; Thomas Gardner, m. Agnes Hughes; Stephen and Susan, died; Almeda, m. John Burnham; Essa, m. Knude Jensen. Family home Mesquite, Nevada.
Made three trips across plains for immigrants and freight. Hauled the tithing grain from San Pete county to Salt Lake City.

POULSEN, ANDREW (son of Peter Jensen Poulsen of Weiby, Denmark). Born June 8, 1843, at Weiby. Came to Utah Oct. 6, 1862, Christian A. Madsen company.
Married Caroline Hansen Oct. 18, 1866 (daughter of Jorgen L. and Annie Hansen, pioneers handcart company). She was born 1848; came to Utah with parents. Their children: Caroline b. Nov. 28, 1867, m. Peter Nielson; Andrew Peter; Andrew b. Oct. 18, 1870, m. Cloe Parish; George C. b. March 11, 1875. Family home Richfield, Utah.
Married Annie Christina Andersen (daughter of Chresten Andersen and Christina Marie Sorensen, former a pioneer, Jensen handcart company). She was born Feb. 1, 1853. Their children: Peter C. b. March 21, 1875; Marie b. Jan. 11, 1879; Joseph F. b. Nov. 30, 1880; Ellen Nora b. Jan. 24, 1883.
High councilor 25 years; teacher 40 years.

POULSEN, JENS (son of Poul Nielsen, born 1792, Valby, Denmark, and Kirstina Katrine Elim, born 1801, Sorslev, Denmark). Born Oct. 28, 1831, Kirkestillinge, Denmark. Pioneer Oct. 1, 1862, Joseph Horne company.
Married Kirsten Nielsen November, 1851, in Denmark (daughter of Jens and Kirsten Nielsen, both died in Denmark). She was born Aug. 17, 1832, died 1862 while crossing Atlantic ocean. Their children: Frederika Marie b. Sept. 15, 1857, James Peter b. May 9, 1859, and Poul b. May 8, 1862, died. Family home, Denmark.
Married Maren Kirstina Arff June, 1862, Florence, Neb. (daughter of Peter Soren Arff, who died in Denmark). She was born Aug. 17, 1836, at Dyereng, Denmark. Their children: James S. b. May 3, 1864, m. Grace Price, m. Harriet Humphreys; Mary Caroline b. Jan. 1866, m. Hyrum H. Wooley; Sophia b. Jan. 22, 1868, m. Robert Shepherd; Joseph F. b. Dec. 4, 1870, m. Elizabeth Strauthaar; Julia M. b. 1872, m. Hyrum H. Hymas; Lena b. July 22, 1874, m. Henry Passey; Charles C. b. Jan. 26, 1876, d. 1897. Family home Liberty, Idaho.
Married Mary Humphreys Feb. 15, 1870, Salt Lake City (daughter of David Humphreys and Mary Matthews, both died in Wales). She was born Feb. 4, 1848, in Wales. Their children: Hyrum Smith b. Jan. 25, 1871, m. Sarah Ann Hymas; David Moroni b. Feb. 1, 1873, d. 1899; William Eli b. April 22, 1875, m. Sarah Ann Johnson; Mary Ann b. March 28, 1877; Klim b. Dec. 4, 1878, m. Martha Nelson; Margaret Elizabeth b. Nov. 10, 1880, m. Simpson Rich; Alma Matthews b. Oct. 12, 1882, m. Laura Toomer; Amelia Ann b. Sept. 14, 1884, m. Wesley Collins; George Lorenzo b. Nov. 22, 1886, m. Susan Smith; Walter b. Nov. 22, 1888; Elonora b. May 13, 1892; Edgar b. April 5, 1895; Kenneth b. May 26, 1897. Family home Liberty, Idaho.
Married Trine Jensen July 26, 1885, at Salt Lake City, who was born in Denmark. Their children: Christian Nelson (adopted), Karl Nelson (adopted).
High priest; missionary to Denmark 1859-62 and 1887-90 bringing 22 relatives to Utah; home missionary 15 years. Trustee. Farmer.

POULSEN, JAMES SHRYNE (son of Jens Poulsen and Maren Kristina Arff). Born May 8, 1864, Paris, Idaho.
Married Grace Price Oct. 18, 1888, Logan, Utah (daughter of Robert Price and Matilda Raley, pioneers, Milo Andrus company). She was born Sept. 1, 1871, at Paris. Their children: Ezra James b. Dec. 26, 1889; Henry Benjamin b. Oct. 14, 1891; Grace Ellen b. Dec. 10, 1901.
Married Harriet Humphreys July 19, 1904, Logan, Utah (daughter of George Humphreys and Sarah Ann Eaton, pioneers). She was born Aug. 4, 1882, at Paris. Their children: Leraine b. June 21, 1906; Ruth b. Oct. 30, 1907; Louis b. May 21, 1910. Families resided at Paris.
Bishop of second ward, Paris, Idaho.

POULSEN, JOSEPH F. (son of Jens Poulsen and Maren Kristina Arff). Born Dec. 4, 1870, Ovid, Idaho.
Married Elizabeth Straubhar Nov. 2, 1892, Logan, Utah (daughter of Jacob Straubhaar and Anna Elizabeth Strahm, who came to Utah 1883). She was born May 22, 1870, in Canton Bern, Switzerland. Their children: Joseph Archie b. Nov. 6, 1893; Etta Elizabeth b. Aug. 18, 1895; Gladys Kirstina b. March 3, 1898; Charles Hubert b. Dec. 14, 1901; Nola b. Dec. 23, 1904; Clarence b. Jan. 11, 1908; Lawrence b. March 21, 1910. Family home Raymond, Idaho.

POULSEN, PAUL (son of Peder Jensen Poulsen, born Feb. 24, 1816, at Lokken, Denmark, and Sidsel Kathrine Andersen, born Sept. 7, 1815; Weiby, Denmark—married July, 1839). Born Sept. 10, 1845, at Weiby. Came to Utah Sept. 23, 1862, Christian A. Madsen independent company.
Married Annie Marie Christensen Aug. 24, 1872 (daughter of Jens Christensen and Maren Andersen), who was born

PIONEERS AND PROMINENT MEN OF UTAH

Feb. 6, 1850. Their children: James P. b. July 15, 1875, m. Mary Ann Ogden Dec. 22, 1897; Ammon W. b. July 3, 1879, m. Mathilda Christensen Dec. 14, 1899; Elida C. b. May 12, 1881, m. Frank Olson Oct. 10, 1905; Arthur M. b. Dec. 21, 1883, m. Diantha L. Barrows Feb. 8, 1905. Family home Richfield, Utah.

Married Oliana Martina Olsen Oct. 2, 1879, Salt Lake City (daughter of Ole Larsen and Karen Andrea Olsen, who was born July 4, 1852, Aalesund, Norway. Their children: Henry O. b. July 31, 1881, m. Elizabeth M. Brady Sept. 1910; Joel Milton b. Oct. 15, 1883; Clara Annetta b. April 29, 1886, m. Stephen Perry Abbott July 20, 1905; Ezra Exile b. Sept. 27, 1888.

Married Mary Davidson March 11, 1887, Logan, Utah (daughter of David Culdbransen and Maren Kirstina Johansen), who was born Feb. 6, 1867, Idswold, Norway. Their children: Prudence b. April 2, 1891; Byron O. b. July 25, 1897; Erma D. b. Feb. 17, 1900; Dorthella L. b. April 27, 1902; Ellen b. April 13, 1906; Silven R. b. March 28, 1908.

Was baptized Jan. 28, 1862. Started for Utah April 4, 1862, with his mother, brothers and a sister; his father, sister and youngest brother not coming. They walked the entire distance from the Missouri river to Salt Lake City. Moved to Pleasant Grove in fall of 1862, to Gunnison, San Pete county, April, 1863. Raised a crop and hauled wheat to Camp Floyd for U. S. soldiers on contract of President Brigham Young. This paid their immigration transportation. Moved to Richfield March, 1866. 128 claims of 20 acres each were distributed among the settlers, and they surveyed and built with spade and shovel a canal, nine miles long and nine to twelve feet wide, to irrigate this land; the first water reached Richfield March 22d. Food was very scarce, the nearest grist mill being at Manti, so wheat was ground in a hand mill. Tea was $15 per pound and money almost unknown, taxes and salaries being paid in produce. In 1866 the Indians started their depredations, killed many settlers, drove the people in from Glen Cove and other outlying settlements, necessitating placing the town under guard, as also the herds, and men had to work together in squads for protection. In April, 1867, Richfield was abandoned, and the settlement moved to Fountain Green.

Missionary to Denmark in 1871, and visited his father. Had charge of Hjorring branch of the church at Osth; traveling elder in Aalborg. Returned to Richfield June 2, 1872, bringing with him his youngest brother. Set apart first counselor to William H. Seegmiller April, 1877; ordained bishop of first ward July 25, 1877, by Erastus Snow, remaining bishop until 1894, when the wards were united, and he was set apart as first counselor to Bishop Theodore Brandley, which position with that of acting bishop he held until March 25, 1899, when he was ordained high councilor, until Sept. 18, 1910. He was made patriarch Sept. 24, 1899; member prayer circle 28 years; superintendent Sunday school first ward three years, released on account of polygamous prosecution; arrested for unlawful cohabitation May 24, 1888, sentenced to four months in state penitentiary and a fine of $200; again arrested August, 1892, and discharged; again on Oct. 11, 1894, sentenced to 30 days in penitentiary; again Oct. 21, 1899, and fined $150 by Judge W. M. McCarty; all of these offenses were for "unlawful cohabitation." Is the father of 22 children, 14 of whom are living and appear in this genealogy. Was city councilman three years, school trustee two years, treasurer of Sevier stake tabernacle, disbursing $27,000 in its construction. Connected with many co-operative institutions.

POULSON, CHRISTIAN (son of Peder Jensen Poulson, born Feb. 24, 1816, Lokken, Denmark, and Sidsel Kathrine Andersen, born Sept. 7, 1815, Welby, Hjorring Amt, Denmark—married July, 1839). He was born 1848 at Welby, Denmark. Came to Utah Sept. 23, 1862, Christian A. Madsen company.

Married Anna Kathrine Oletzen May 25, 1874, Salt Lake City (daughter of Jens Christian and Martha Marie Oletzen of Richfield, Utah). She was born March 31, 1857, died April 16, 1888. Their children: Henry C. b. April 11, 1876; Martha K. b. April 2, 1875; Parley Peter b. April 7, 1878; Augusta M. b. June 21, 1881; E. W. b. May 5, 1885; Anna E. b. Feb. 27, 1887.

Married Annie Macelia Jessen Jan. 20, 1892, Manti, Utah (daughter of Mads Peter and Anna A. Jensen, of Mt. Pleasant, Utah, pioneers 1857). She was born Jan. 4, 1863. Their children: Jesse W. b. Sept. 24, 1893; Agnes C. b. April 8, 1895; Ephraim L. b. Dec. 11, 1896; Rulon Grant b. March 20, 1903.

Missionary to Denmark 1882-85; home missionary eight years. Assisted in leveling the present site of the Manti temple. Veteran Indian wars.

POULSON, JOHN CHRISTIAN (son of Christian Abel Poulson, born July 8, 1813, at Flyngborg, Denmark, and Jensine Axelline, born Jan. 10, 1813, Orsø, Denmark). Born Feb. 21, 1841, in Hjorring Amt, Denmark. Came to Utah Oct. 22, 1866, Abner Lowry company.

Married Eliza Thompson 1866 (daughter of Thomas Madson and Mary Ann Peterson), who was born June 11, 1842. Their children: Frederikke b. Oct. 18, 1867, m. Frank F. Merrill 1897; John C. b. Nov. 3, 1868, m. Edna Earl Hawley March 25, 1897; Pauline, m. Henry Hughes; George Alma, m. Zilla Johnson.

POULSON, JOHN C. (son of John Christian Poulson and Eliza Thompson). Born Nov. 3, 1869, Holden, Millard Co., Utah.

Married Edna Earl Hawley March 25, 1897, Manti, Utah (daughter of William P. Hawley and Violate Snow), who was born March 25, 1873, Provo, Utah. Their children: Edna Lorene b. Dec. 17, 1897; Myrl b. Aug. 19, 1899; John Stanley b. June 28, 1901; Alton Melrose b. May 17, 1903; Winford Pierce b. Sept. 29, 1906; Spencer Earl b. March 23, 1910. Family home Holden, Utah.

POULTER, WILLIAM (son of Thomas Poulter and Sarah Davis). Born March 3, 1820, Moulsey, Surrey, Eng. Came to Utah Sept. 29, 1854, Joseph Field company.

Married Caroline Strubell in Surrey, Eng. (daughter of Richard Strubell and Mary Ann Davis of Moulsey). She was born Jan. 23, 1820, Surrey, and died Nov. 7, 1887, Ogden, Utah. Their children: William b. March 19, 1845, died; George b. Nov. 25, 1846, m. Mary E. Jackson Feb. 9, 1874; Sarah Jane b. Oct. 1851, died; Ephraim b. March 11, 1849, d. April 1879; Thomas b. July 19, 1853; Moroni Strubell b. Jan. 6, 1856, m. Hannah Burton Sept. 5, 1878, m. Alice Snell Maw Oct. 4, 1887; Rachel b. Sept. 23, 1858, m. Asa Farley Sept. 5, 1878; Joseph b. 1860, died. Family home Ogden, Utah.

Settled at Ogden 1855; moved to Salt Lake City 1858; returned to Ogden 1865. Member of first brass band of Ogden, which accompanied the militia in the Echo Canyon campaign. One of the committee to induce President Brigham Young to build the Salt Lake theater. Member first theatrical company that played in Salt Lake theater March 8, 1862; was an associate of Phil Margretts, Harry Bowring, McEwan, and was in the Mechanics Dramatic association. Accidentally killed by a falling tree in Ogden Canyon March 7, 1869.

POULTER, GEORGE (son of William Poulter and Caroline Strubell). Born Nov. 25, 1846, London, Eng. Came to Utah 1854 with parents.

Married Mary E. Jackson Feb. 9, 1874, Salt Lake City (daughter of Aaron Jackson, born Sept. 30, 1823, Eyne, Derbyshire, Eng., died Oct. 20, 1856, while crossing the plains, and Elizabeth Horrocks, born Aug. 5, 1826, Macclesfield, Chestershire, Eng., pioneer Nov. 30, 1856, Edward Martin handcart company, died Oct. 17, 1908, Ogden, Utah). She was born July 22, 1851, at Macclesfield and came to Utah with mother and family. Their children: George Aaron b. Nov. 12, 1874, m. Lillie Obern April 1901; Grace Elizabeth b. March 5, 1877, d. May 24, 1893; Claude Jackson b. Nov. 4, 1879, d. Oct. 8, 1891; William Richard b. Aug. 30, 1882, m. Matilda Hancock June 23, 1909; Martha Caroline b. Nov. 3, 1885; Mary Frances b. Aug. 17, 1888, m. George Burton June 14, 1911. Family home Ogden, Utah.

Missionary to England 1890-92. Assisted in plastering the Salt Lake theater and took part in the first play at the opening March 8, 1862. Plastering contractor.

POULTER, MORONI STRUBELL (son of William Poulter and Caroline Strubell). Born Jan. 6, 1856, Ogden, Utah.

Married Hannah Burton Sept. 5, 1878, Salt Lake City (daughter of William Walton Burton, born March 23, 1833, Bradford, Yorkshire, Eng., and Rachel Fielding, born June 27, 1839, Preston, Eng., former pioneer Sept. 23, 1854, Job Smith company, latter 1848 with her parents). She was born Jan. 14, 1859, at Mill Creek, Utah. Their children: Rachel May b. June 3, 1879, d. April 13, 1880; Clara Burton b. March 12, 1881, m. Joseph J. Hancock Sept. 29, 1909; Hannah Ellen b. Sept. 14, 1883, m. Albert H. Krumperman Aug. 23, 1911; Moroni Carl b. Nov. 4, 1885, m. Mary J. Peterson June 26, 1907; Florence Carrie b. March 31, 1888, m. Isaac S. Hunt Jan. 17, 1912; Ruby Isabel b. March 21, 1890, d. May 27, 1892; Ina Roseltha b. Oct. 6, 1893; William Irvin b. Nov. 10, 1895; Glenn Minerva b. May 25, 1898. Family home Ogden, Utah.

Married Alice Snell Maw Oct. 4, 1887, at Salt Lake City (daughter of Edward Maw, born Feb. 19, 1800, in England, died Aug. 16, 1893, Ogden, Utah, and Christina Snell, born March 16, 1831, died Nov. 7, 1861, at Hull, Eng.; married Aug. 16, 1855, former pioneer Oct. 19, 1862, Horton D. Haight company). She was born May 29, 1859, at Hull, Yorkshire, Eng. Came to Utah Oct. 19, 1862, Horton D. Haight company. Their children; Lawrence b. May 18, 1890, m. Lucy S. Moyes Oct. 9, 1912; Ephraim b. Sept. 30, 1893; Alice Lamont b. Dec. 24, 1897; Marvel Lucile b. June 13, 1904. Family home Salt Lake City and Ogden, Utah.

First counselor to Joseph A. West, president of the first Y. L. M. I. A. and organized in Mormon church; first president of Y. M. M. I. A. of the 4th ward, in 1878, Ogden.

POWELL, JAMES (son of Abraham and Elizabeth Powell of North Carolina). Born 1809 in North Carolina. Came to Utah Oct. 13, 1852, Robert Wimmer oxteam company.

Married Jamima Wimmer 1834 in Indiana (daughter of Peter and Elizabeth Wimmer, both of Indiana, pioneers 1850, oxteam company). She was born March 14, 1814, in Ohio. Their children: Elizabeth, d. aged 3; Peter, d. infant; Robert A., m. Rachel J. Davis; Simion Comfort, m. Lydia Hawley; m. Edith Canaday; John A., m. Matilda Snyder; Malinda, m. Caleb Rhodes, m. Josephus Gammage; Martha E., m. Frederick E. Grames; James, d. aged 14 months; Abraham, killed by a grizzly bear on Mt. Nebo, Utah, aged 23. Family resided at Ogden, Mill Creek, Springville, Provo and Kamas, Utah.

Elder. Farmer and stockraiser. Drowned in Weber river July 19, 1857.

1112 PIONEERS AND PROMINENT MEN OF UTAH

POWELL, ROBERT A. (son of James Powell and Jamima Wimmer). Born Oct. 13, 1839, Adams county, Ill. Pioneers Oct. 13, 1852. Brought an oxteam company.
Married Rachel J. Davis Aug. 17, 1872, at Diamond City, Utah (daughter of George Preston Davis and Elizabeth Lewis, both of Logan, Utah). She was born Oct. 23, 1855. Their children: John Riley b. Sept. 18, 1873, d. infant; Robert Wimmer b. Aug. 18, 1874, m. Estella Hall; Martha Ellen b. Sept. 2, 1876, m. Charles McKendrick; Sarah Elizabeth b. Oct. 13, 1878, m. Benjamin G. Wyther; Betsy Jamima b. Sept. 18, 1880, m. Charles Honick; Simion Comfort b. May 14, 1882; James Abraham b. July 10, 1884; George Preston b. Nov. 8, 1886; Joseph b. March 8, 1889; Lucy Malinda b. Dec. 23, 1891, m. Tony Malino; Hyrum b. Jan. 28, 1893, d. March 20, 1893; Ransom Peter b. Feb. 2, 1894; David b. April 1, 1896, d. Sept. 14, 1897; Jaroma A. b. Feb. 23, 1898. Family resided at Salem and Carbonville, Utah.
Elder. School trustee. Farmer and stockraiser.

POWELL, JOHN AMON (son of James Powell and Jamima Wimmer). Born Nov. 27, 1844. Came to Utah 1850.
Married Hannah Matilda Snyder January, 1864, at Kamas, Utah (daughter of Robert and Hannah Snyder of Payson, Utah, pioneers 1848). She was born Feb. 23, 1846. Their children: John A. Jr., b. Oct. 14, 1864, m. Hanna Halverson; Maria b. May 18, 1867, m. William Warren; Elmeda Matilda b. Sept. 29, 1869, died; James b. March 14, 1872; Leah b. Aug. 23, 1874, m. Raymond Madison, m. George Rand; Robert b. Jan. 4, 1877, m. Emma Eugals.
Married Sarah Jane Plumb (Shields) Jan. 6, 1872, Salt Lake City (daughter of John F. Shields and Mary Howell of Salem, Utah, pioneers 1847). She was born Sept. 29, 1854. Their children: Sarah Jane b. Dec. 13, 1874, m. Eben Snow; Lot b. April 14, 1876, m. Mary Jane Burgess; Florence b. Sept. 30, 1878, m. John Johnson, m. George Sawyer; Martha b. Dec. 1, 1880, d. infant; Abraham b. March 6, 1882, m. Pearl Leonard; Joseph F. b. Feb. 1, 1884, and Pearl b. Nov. 24, 1885, d. children; Zoe E. b. Dec. 6, 1887, m. Leo Leonard; Franklin Irvin b. Nov. 12, 1894, d. child. Family home Price, Utah.
Married Rose Altha Allred Jan. 10, 1882, at Salt Lake City (daughter of Green W. Allred and Amy Howse of San Pete Co., Utah). She was born March 7, 1863. Their children: William R. b. May 21, 1883, m. Jennie Luke; Maud M. b. Aug. 23, 1885, m. John Safley; Dora A. b. Dec. 6, 1887, m. George Spencer; Elmer W. b. March 5, 1890, m. Gertrude Roberts; Clarence H. b. May 31, 1892; Ethel N. b. Sept. 7, 1894; Sheridan R. b. Sept. 13, 1896; Earl H. b. Nov. 9, 1898; Ada J. b. May 21, 1901; Grant b. Sept. 21, 1903. Family home Price, Utah.
Elder. Served in Black Hawk war. Farmer and stockraiser.

POWELL, JOHN AMON, JR. (son of John Amon Powell and Hannah Matilda Snyder). Born Oct. 4, 1864, Lambs Canyon, Utah.
Married Hannah Fredericka Halverson April 2, 1885, Price, Utah (daughter of Frederick Halverson and Hannah Nielsen of Copenhagen, Denmark. Came to Utah 1872). She was born March 16, 1868. Their children: Hannah Matilda b. May 30, 1887; Verner Amon b. Oct. 22, 1889; John Frederick b. Oct. 28, 1891; Clarence b. April 11, 1894; May b. May 1, 1896.
Married Margarette Catherina Johnson Oct. 3, 1906, at Salt Lake City (daughter of Halldor Johnson and Gertrude Berenson of Cleveland, Utah. Came to Utah 1881). She was born Aug. 12, 1882. Their children: Parley Grant b. Aug. 5, 1908; Gertrude and Geneva (twins) b. Sept. 18, 1910.
Elder; ward teacher. Settled at Wellington 1893, where he assisted in building up the country. Farmer; miner; stockraiser

POWELL, JAMES Q. Born Nov. 7, 1807, in Pennsylvania. Came to Utah 1848, Zera Pulsipher company.
Married Mary Jane Cooper 1841, Lancaster, Lancaster county, Pa., who was born Oct. 17, 1810, and came to Utah with husband. Their children: Isaac b. Aug. 2, 1842, d. Jan. 1848; Naomi b. Aug. 16, 1844, m. Norman Wines Dec. 25, 1863; James b. June 15, 1846, d. Jan. 1848; Augustus N. b. Aug. 1, 1851, m. Sarah Losee July 7, 1872; Thaddeus b. Sept. 30, 1854, m. Esther Ann Ashton Jan. 24, 1883.
Married Hannah Anderson 1854, Salt Lake City (daughter of Andrew Anderson), who was born March 7, 1818, Denmark. Their children: Susan b. 1860, m. Charles C. Trane April 12, 1888; Benjamin b. March 7, 1867, m. Mary Anne Southwick.
Pioneer in sheep and cattle business; from his sheep the greater part of the clothing worn in the neighborhood of Lehi 1855-72 was made.

POWELL, THADDEUS (son of James Q. Powell and Mary Jane Cooper). Born Sept. 30, 1854, Salt Lake Co., Utah.
Married Esther Ann Ashton Jan. 24, 1883, Lehi, Utah (daughter of Thomas Ashton and Arminta Lawrence, pioneers Morris Phelps company). Their children: Thaddeus A. b. March 27, 1884, m. Nicoline E. Schow Oct. 30, 1905; Eugene b. Nov. 11, 1885, m. Mable Snider Jan. 8, 1909; Leland b. July 24, 1887, m. Grace Comer Feb. 15, 1910; Hazel May b. May 1, 1889; T. J. b. April 2, 1893. Family home Lehi, Utah.
City councilman Lehi two years. Owner of the Mulliner mill property, which was sold to the Utah Sugar Co. 1890. Director Lehi Commercial & Savings Bank 1893-1900.

POWELL, JOHN (son of John Powell and Ann Belfield, both of London, Eng.). Born Oct. 31, 1822, St. Sepulchres parish, London, Eng. Came to Utah 1856.
Married Fanny Chamberlin. Their children: Mary Ann b. Sept. 16, 1843, m. Jacob Croft; Fanny Louisa b. July 16, 1845, m. Lee Cropper; John b. Sept. 14, 1847; Jessie b. June 3, 1849, m. Peter Huntsman; Mercy b. May 15, 1852; Samuel b. April 20, 1855; Ephraim b. Oct. 13, 1856; Bessy b. Nov. 5, 1858, m. Heber J. Mitchell; Alice Jane b. June 18, 1864.
Married Henrietta Seaton Blyth June 18, 1864 (daughter of Charles Blyth and Isabella Brown, former pioneer Captain Clark company 1856). She was born June 6, 1831, Dalkeith, Scotland. Their children: Sarah b. April 13, 1865, m. John Broadhead; Annie b. Sept. 8, 1866, m. Joseph Beckwith; Henrietta b. Aug. 15, 1868; Lilly b. March 29, 1870, m. Willard Rogers; Alma b. Jan. 13, 1872, m. Margret Burt; May b. May 7, 1873, m. Lars Rasmussen; Ellen b. April 1, 1875, m. James A. Kelley.
Married Martha Ashby March 20, 1885. Their children: John Franklin b. July 22, 1886; Jessie Truman b. April 11, 1888; Nathaniel b. Feb. 15, 1891.
Took active part in Echo Canyon campaign. Pioneer of Fillmore. Died June 3, 1902, Fillmore.

POWELL, THOMAS (son of Joseph Powell and Anna Crocker of Yorkshire, Eng., who came to Utah September, 1886). Born May 27, 1857. Came to Utah 1864.
Married Emma Maria Warburton Dec. 10, 1884, Salt Lake City (daughter of Joseph Warburton and Emma Maria Whatnough), who was born Dec. 1, 1863, Salt Lake City. Their children: Albert T. b. Sept. 25, 1885, m. Irene Braby; Florence E. b. Feb. 27, 1888, m. Augusta Brown; Lawrence R. b. March 1, 1892; Clyde J. b. July 17, 1897; Vera b. Dec. 15, 1903. Family home, Salt Lake City.

POWELL, WILLIAM JAMES (son of Thomas Powell).
Married Mary Ann Simson. Their children: Mary Jane, d. child; Martha Ann, m. Thomas Rhoads; Elvira, m. Lars J. Marsing; Sarah Elizabeth, m. Hans Peter Marsing; William James, Jr., m. Rachel Ann Hadden; Dan Thomas b. Jan. 26, 1871, m. Emma Lozzetta Higby; Joseph Hyrum, m. Ada Hadden; Francis Lyman, m. Lucy Stilson; Orson Mark, m. Lorena Jensen; Lucy Fidelia, m. Martin Luther Marsing; John Taylor, m. Mary Smith. Family home Castle Dale, Emery Co., Utah.

POWELL, DAN THOMAS (son of William James Powell and Mary Ann Simson). Born Jan. 26, 1871, St. Thomas, Lincoln county, Nev.
Married Emma Lozzetta Higby May 6, 1891, Castle Dale, Utah (daughter of William Higby and Emma Maria Lancer of Castle Dale). She was born Sept. 1, 1873. Their children: Nellie May b. Nov. 23, 1892, m. Paul G. Cluff Oct. 6, 1911; Arthur Enos b. March 17, 1896; Clara Grace b. Aug. 25, 1897; William Lee b. Sept. 2, 1899; Emma Pearl b. Feb. 8, 1903; Ray Elizabeth b. July 30, 1906. Family home Theodore, Utah.
High priest counselor to Manassa J. Blackburn of Deseret, Lake ward, Emery county; ward and Sunday school teacher. Moved to St. Joseph with parents, then to Kanab, to Richfield, to Huntington where he was small; to Castle Dale ward with first settlers; moved to Deseret lake among first settlers, and assisted in building canals, wagon roads and homes, and in reclaiming the land; from here he went to Uinta Indian reservation Dec. 20, 1905, and in 1906 began building the canal at Moffatt, finishing it that summer; in August of 1906 he located at Duchesne, took up a homestead, and resides there at the present time. School trustee. Farmer and stockman.

POULTON, THOMAS (son of Richard Poulton and Margaret Hand of England). Born April 10, 1834, in England. Came to Utah Sept. 12, 1861, Milo Andrus company.
Married Mary Hand Dec. 4, 1857, in England (daughter of John Hand), who was born 1837. Their children: William b. Nov. 3, 1858, m. Sarah Ann Birch; Thomas b. 1869, died; Ira Eldredge b. Aug. 23, 1861, m. Emma V. Grover. Family home Coalville, Utah.
Married Zeruah M. Grover April 17, 1884, Salt Lake City (daughter of Thomas Grover and Elizabeth Walker of Farmington, Utah; former pioneer 1847, latter Sept. 26, 1856, Edmond Ellsworth company).
High priest; missionary to England 1895; pioneer in building up Goose Creek valley. Moved to Oakley, Idaho. Died April 21, 1912.

PRATT, JONATHAN BLACKMORE (son of William Pratt of Virginia and Isabell Hall of Ireland). Born Jan. 18, 1807, Greenville, Tenn. Came to Utah 1857.
Married Susannah Halbert (daughter of William Halbert and Susannah Taylor), who came to Utah with husband. Their children: William Halbert b. May 8, 1844, m. Ann Burgess Jan. 19, 1864; Rebecca, m. Mr. Jones; Martha, m. James Worthington; Isabell, m. William Martindale; Mary, m. Claborn Elder; Frances, m. Claborn Elder. Family home Duncan's Retreat, Washington Co., Utah.
Earlier settler to "Dixie," Utah.

PRATT, WILLIAM H. (son of Jonathan Blackmore Pratt and Susannah Halbert). Born May 8, 1844.
Married Ann Burgess June 19, 1864, Virgin City, Utah (daughter of Thomas Burgess and Elizabeth Isaac, pioneers 1854, Nelson Empey company). She was born June 11, 1843,

Badmington, Eng. Their children: Elizabeth S. b. April 3, 1865, m. Hyrum F. Wright; William F. b. April 27, 1867, m. Elizabeth E. Tolbert Nov. 23, 1892; Jonathan B. (3rd bishop of Hinckley, Utah) b. June 28, 1869, m. Emma Alldredge Nov. 23, 1892; Thomas H. b. Dec. 3, 1873, m. Jane Harmon Oct. 8, 1903; James b. Oct. 29, 1876, died. Family home Hinckley, Utah.
First bishop of Hinckley ward, Millard stake.

PRATT, WILLIAM F. (son of William H. Pratt and Ann Burgess). Born April 27, 1857, Duncan's Retreat, Utah. Married Elizabeth E. Tolbert (daughter of William Tolbert, pioneer 1859, and Sarah Pack, born 1848, Salt Lake City). She was born Aug. 27, 1875, Kamas, Utah. Their children: Rosette E. b. Nov. 8, 1894; Wilford F. b. Nov. 6, 1897; Golda b. Dec. 25, 1899; Lawrence b. June 19, 1902; Nora and Olive b. Dec. 19, 1904, Olive d. same day; Eva Ann b. Sept. 1, 1908; Parnell b. Dec. 3, 1910. Family home Hinckley, Utah.
Bishop Hinckley ward, Millard stake.

PRATT, ORSON (son of Jared Pratt and Charity Dickinson of Hartford, Washington county, New Lebanon and Canaan, Columbia county, N. Y.). Born Sept. 19, 1811, Hartford, Washington county, N. Y. Came to Utah July 21, 1847, Brigham Young company.
Married Sarah Marinda Bates July 4, 1836, Henderson, Jefferson county, N. Y. (daughter of Cyrus and Lydia Bates of Henderson, N. Y.). She was born Feb. 5, 1817. Their children: Orson, Jr. b. July 11, 1837, m. Susan Snow Oct. 1, 1854, d. Dec. 6, 1903; Lydia b. Dec. 17, 1838, d. Aug. 13, 1839; Celestia Larissa b. May 10, 1842, m. Albert P. Tyler Jan. 4, 1858, d. Jan. 6, 1905; Sarah Marinda b. Oct. 27, 1844, d. July 26, 1845; Vanson b. Jan. 23, 1846, d. July 22, 1847; Laron b. July 10, 1847, m. Ethelwynn Clarissa Brown June 27, 1869, d. Aug. 21, 1908; Marion b. Oct. 13, 1848, d. Sept. 4, 1849; Marintha Althera b. Dec. 31, 1849, d. March 24, 1851; Harmel b. Aug. 21, 1851, m. Mary Elizabeth Cullen Nov. 18, 1873, d. Dec. 20, 1907; Arthur b. March 12, 1853, m. Agnes Ellen Caine Dec. 25, 1872; Herma Ethna b. May 16, 1856, m. William F. Beiding Feb. 18, 1874, d. Dec. 26, 1877; Loila Menella b. Oct. 22, 1858, d. Sept. 21, 1860.
Married Charlotte Bishop 1844, Nauvoo, Ill. (daughter of John Fitch Bishop and Lucy Goff), who was born March 1824, Crown Point, Essex county, N. Y.
Married Adelia Ann Bishop Dec. 13, 1844, Nauvoo, Ill. (daughter of John Fitch Bishop and Lucy Goff of Crown Point, N. Y.). She was born Nov. 5, 1826, Crown Point. Their children: Lucy Adelia b. Sept. 15, 1847, m. Ashton Nebeker March 9, 1865; Zina Bishop b. Feb. 26, 1851, m. Francis M. Bishop Jan. 24, 1873, d. May 16, 1902; Lorum b. Dec. 18, 1852, m. Frances Lane Theobald May 17, 1878; Lorus b. Nov. 27, 1855, m. Eizina Wheeler Nov. 27, 1879; Eltha b. Dec. 12, 1858, m. John Stephen Edwards Aug. 2, 1880; Orthena b. Oct. 31, 1863, m. John Askie Silver Nov. 5, 1880.
Married Mary Ann Merrill March 27, 1845, Nauvoo, Ill. (daughter of Voluntine Merrill and Lydia Sisson of Southhold and Greenport, Long Island, N. Y.). She was born June 2, 1819, Southhold; came to Utah with husband in 1851, died Dec. 12, 1903. Their children: Marian Agnes b. Feb. 16, 1853, d. Oct. 17, 1853; Larinda Marissa b. Dec. 15, 1855, m. Willard E. Weihe July 10, 1876; Milson Ross b. Nov. 4, 1859, m. Jemima G. Vincent Kilgore March 14, 1888, (d. 1893); m. Mary Frances Tuttle Kimball March 29, 1894; Irintha b. July 5, 1862, m. James Henry Douglas Jan. 12, 1882; Ray Ross b. Feb. 14, 1871, m. Mulvie McCloed 1898; Ruby b. Feb. 20, 1874, m. Alvin Augustus Beesley May 24, 1894.
Married Sarah Louisa Lewis June 21, 1853, Birmingham, Eng., who was born July 7, 1831, Old Radnor, Hereford, Eng.; came to Utah September, 1854, died Sept. 27, 1855, Salt Lake City. Only child: Willow Lewis b. Sept. 8, 1854, d. Oct. 27, 1854.
Married Juliaett Phelps Dec. 14, 1855, Fillmore, Utah (daughter of Alva Phelps, who died in service Mormon Battalion, and Margaret Phelps). She was born April 19, 1839. Their children: Alva Phelps b. Jan. 31, 1859, m. Cassie Allen, d. Feb. 18, 1906; Clomenia b. Jan. 29, 1861, m. Frank Larsen; Ortherus F. b. Oct. 26, 1863, m. Emma Louise Taysum Oct. 28, 1885, m. Kittie Evelyn Eagan June 27, 1906; Margaret b. Oct. 5, 1868, m. Mr. Armstrong; Rella b. Jan. 16, 1872, m. Mr. Farrington; Neva b. July 27, 1874, m. William Lyman Shiverick Aug. 6, 1908; Julius F. b. May 12, 1877, m. Etta D. Boucher Sept. 8, 1900. First eight families resided Salt Lake City.
Married Eliza Crooks July 24, 1857, Islington, Liverpool, Eng., who was born July, 1829, Monaghan, Glastock, Ireland; came to Utah Jan. 9, 1869, Tooele City, Utah. Their children: Lerius Crooks b. April 9, 1858, d. June 17, 1862; Dora b. March 23, 1860, m. Willard Snow May 14, 1882; Jared b. July 15, 1862, killed by snowslide March 11, 1877; Onthew b. Dec. 30, 1864, d. same day; Samuel b. Nov. 24,

1868, killed by falling into a hot spring in Nevada, Oct. 4, 1888. Family home Tooele, Utah.
Married Margaret Graham Dec. 28, 1868, Salt Lake City (daughter of William Graham and Jane Ross of Edinburgh, Scotland, latter pioneer 1865). She was born Jan. 20, 1852, Edinburgh, Scotland, pioneer with mother in 1865. Their children: Orion Graham b. Sept. 14, 1869, m. Amy Williamson; Pearl b. May 2, 1872, m. James S. Morgan; Royal b. June 3, 1874. Family home, Salt Lake City.
Member first apostles quorum; missionary in United States, Great Britain and Austria 1830-81; high councilor; church historian. Regent University of Deseret. Member legislature and speaker of the house of representatives; city councilman. Established the Great Salt Lake Base & Meridian, S. E. corner temple block (topographical survey); topographical engineer for the general staff, with the rank of colonel, of the territorial militia. Scientist; mathematician; translator; author, etc. Died Oct. 3, 1881, Salt Lake City.

PRATT, MILANDO (son of Orson Pratt and Mary Ann Merrill). Born Sept. 30, 1848, Harris Grove, Pottawattamie Co., Iowa. Came to Utah Oct. 7, 1851, Orson Pratt company.
Married Elizabeth Rich May 16, 1870, Salt Lake City (daughter of Charles Coulson Rich and Sarah DeArmon Pea of Kirtland, Ohio, pioneers 1847, Charles C. Rich company). She was born Oct. 6, 1849, Salt Lake City. Their children: Viola Bell b. Oct. 7, 1871, m. George H. Gillett Sept. 12, 1896; Milando, Jr., b. Dec. 8, 1873; Charles Rich b. March 1, 1876, m. Zina Mowrey Nov. 10, 1897; Orson Merrill b. Aug. 19, 1878; Leonie DeArmon b. July 18, 1882, m. George Douglas Bergenet Feb. 25, 1905; Benjamin Rich b. Feb. 10, 1888, d. Oct. 12, 1912; Frederick Earl b. March 19, 1891, m. Edna V. Saunders June 28, 1911. Family home, Salt Lake City.
High priest; missionary to eastern states 1876-77; high councilor Salt Lake stake of Zion 1873-1911; then patriarch. Member of the church bureau of information, Temple Block, since its organization. Served in legislature. Among his various activities he was railroad contractor, farmer, merchant and mining man.

PRATT, PARLEY PARKER (son of Jared Pratt and Charity Dickinson). Born April 12, 1807, Burlington, N. Y. Came to Utah Sept. 28, 1847, John Taylor and Perrigrine Sessions company.
Married Thankful Halsey (Hand) Sept. 9, 1827, Canaan, N. Y., who was born March 18, 1797. Only child: Parley Parker, Jr. b. March 25, 1837 (d. Aug. 26, 1897), m. Esther Romania Bunnell Feb. 23, 1859, m. Brigamena Nealeon Jan. 18, 1877, m. Susan Pulley. Family home, Salt Lake City.
Married Mary Ann Frost (Stearns) May 9, 1837, Kirtland, Ohio (daughter of Aaron Frost of Bethel, Oxford Co., Maine, pioneer 1852). She was born Jan. 14, 1809, Nauvoo, Ill.; Olivia b. June 2, 1841, d. Aug. 28, 1844, at Nauvoo; Moroni L. b. Dec. 7, 1844 (d. April 18, 1913), m. Caroline Mabel Beebe Sept. 5, 1870, who died March 27, 1913. Family home Pleasant Grove, Utah.
Married Elizabeth Brotherton July 24, 1843, who was born March 27, 1816, Manchester, Eng., and died May 9, 1897.
Married Mary Wood Sept. 9, 1844, who was born June 18, 1818, Glasgow, Scotland, and died March 5, 1898, Forest Dale, Utah. Their children: Eleanora b. July 31, 1846, m. Emeline V. Billings July 25, 1868, m. Dorothy Wilkin, m. Miss Wilkin; Cornelia b. Sept. 5, 1848, m. Apollos G. Driggs Oct. 5, 1867, died; Mary W. b. Sept. 14, 1853, m. Royal Barney Young, died; Mathoni W. b. July 6, 1856, m. Elizabeth Leaver Sheets Nov. 17, 1880. Family home, Salt Lake City.
Married Hannahette Snively 1844 (daughter of Henry and Mary H. Snively), who was born Oct. 2, 1842, and died Feb. 17, 1893, Salt Lake City. Their children: Alma b. July 21, 1846 (d. Nov. 13, 1902), m. Rebecca Beebe Jan. 10, 1876, who died Sept. 1, 1886; Lucy b. March 9, 1848, m. Samuel Russell Feb. 4, 1869; Henrietta b. Dec. 26, 1851, m. Samuel Russell Nov. 14, 1877.
Married Belinda Marden Nov. 20, 1844, who was born Dec. 24, 1820, Chichester, Merrimack county, N. H., and died Feb. 19, 1894, Salt Lake City. Their children: Nephi Pratt b. Jan. 1, 1846 (d. April 29, 1910), m. Lizzie Warren April 13, 1867, m. Hannah Phillips Feb. 20, 1871, m. Alice Jerome Ray Nov. 25, 1872, m. Sarah Melissa Callister; Belinda b. May 8, 1848 (d. Dec. 10, 1893), m. Heber M. Stenhouse Nov. 28, 1863, m. Henry J. Smith Jan. 9, 1871, m. Amos Milton Musser Sept. 4, 1872; Abinadi b. May 8, 1848; Lehi b. June 9, 1851 (d. Aug. 15, 1905), m. Sarah Ann Mitchell Nov. 21, 1870, m. Nora Athilda, m. Emma Dalley Jan. 3, 1878; Isabel Elenor b. Sept. 1, 1854 (d. April 24, 1913), m. Franklin Alonzo Robison April 10, 1872. Family resided Salt Lake City and Fillmore, Utah.
Married Sarah Huston Oct. 15, 1845, Nauvoo, Ill., who was born Aug. 3, 1823, Starke Co., Ohio, and died May 26, 1886, Coyote, Garfield Co., Utah. Their children: Julia b. April 1, 1847, m. John Gardener June 1, 1860; Mormon b. Jan. 8, 1850, d. Nov. 19, 1850; Teancum b. Nov. 15, 1851 (d. Sept. 8, 1900), m. Annie Eliza Mead Oct. 10, 1872, m. Sarah Eliza Ewell Oct. 25, 1875; Sarah Elizabeth b. May 31, 1856 (died), m. Culbert King. Family home, Salt Lake City.
Married Phoebe Soper Feb. 8, 1846, Winter Quarters, Neb., who was born July 8, 1823, Hempstead Harbor, Queens county, Long Island, N. Y., and died Sept. 17, 1887, Provo, Utah. Their children: Mosiah b. Feb. 26, 1850, m. March

26, 1850; Omner b. Nov. 30, 1851, d. Jan. 7, 1852; Phoebe Soper b. May 19, 1853. m. William Shadrach Holdaway Sept. 11, 1872. Family home, Salt Lake City.
Married Martha Monks April 28, 1847, who was born April 28, 1825, Raynor, Chestershire, Eng., and came to Utah with husband. Only child: Ether b. Jan. 30, 1849, d. Feb. 22, 1849. Family home, Salt Lake City.
Married Ann Agatha Walker April 28, 1847, Winter Quarters, Neb. (daughter of William Gibson Walker and Mary Goodwin of Manchester, Eng.). She was born June 11, 1829, Leek, Staffordshire, Eng., and came to Utah with husband. Their children: Agatha b. July 7, 1848. m. Joseph Harris Ridges Jan. 21, 1866; Malona b. April 15, 1850, m. Elnathan Eldredge, Jr., Nov. 11, 1870; Marion b. Nov. 28, 1851, d. Oct. 6, 1852; Moroni Walker b. Oct. 10, 1853. m. Mary Chugg. m. Mary Owens; Eveline b. Aug. 8, 1856, m. Francis G. Woods. Family home, Salt Lake City.
Married Keziah Downes Dec. 27, 1853. Salt Lake City, who was born May 10, 1812, Raynor, Chestershire, Eng., and died Jan. 11, 1876, Salt Lake City.
Married Elenor J. McComb Nov. 14, 1855, Salt Lake City, who was born Dec. 29, 1817, Wheeling, W. Va., and died Oct. 24, 1874, Salt Lake City.

PRATT, MORONI WALKER (son of Parley Parker Pratt and Ann Agatha Walker). Born Oct. 10, 1853, Salt Lake City.
Married Mary Chugg. Their children: Ellis, m. Frank Cole; Mary Louie, m. Truman J. Cole; Francis Moroni, m. Myrtle Grace Young; Evelyn Vilate, m. George A. Griffeth; Cora Agatha; Mabel Elizabeth, m. Willard Leroy Van Orden; Hazel; Florence. Family resided Meadowville, Utah, Malad and Fairview, Idaho.
Married Mary Owens Nov. 7, 1894, Logan, Utah (daughter of William Owens, pioneer 1854, and Elizabeth Roberts, pioneer 1855. Seth M. Blair company—married Jan. 28, 1856, Salt Lake City). She was born March 7, 1866, Henefer, Summit Co., Utah. Their children: Esther b. Aug. 8, 1895; Laura b. Jan. 29, 1897; Viola b. Jan. 26, 1899; Vida b. Feb. 22, 1901; Parley Owens b. Dec. 14, 1903, died; Athleen b. Feb. 21, 1904; Ruth b. March 30, 1906; Milton O. b. Nov. 5, 1908; Harold O. b. Dec. 13, 1910. Family resided Fairview and Preston, Idaho.
Bishop of Fairview ward 16 years; bishop's counselor at Meadowville; stake president of high priests quorum several years; high councilor; missionary to Indiana. Trustee Oneida Stake Academy. Poet. Died June 28, 1911, Salt Lake City.

PRATT, WILLIAM DICKINSON (son of Jared Pratt and Charity Dickinson). Born Sept. 3, 1802, Worcester, Otsego county, N. Y. Came to Utah Oct. 7, 1851, with Orson Pratt, who was returning from the European mission.
Married Hannah Ward Jan. 1, 1837, Kirtland, Ohio, who was born Feb. 26, 1808, Chester, Windsor county, Vt., and died Sept. 20, 1840, Nauvoo, Ill. Their child: Sarah Jane b. Feb. 19, 1838, d. Oct. 1838.
Married Wealthy Shumway (widow) March 1, 1841. Their children: Martha b. Dec. 13, 1841, d. Oct. 15, 1847; William Jared b. June 22, 1844 (d. June 16, 1909), m. Alice Smart Dec. 1, 1862; Stephen b. 1847, d. infant; Mirza Lyona b. 1849, d. 1851.
The third and fourth wives bore no children.
Married Jane Holley (O'Bannion). Only child: Alice b. Aug. 23, 1856, m. Orson Merrill Dec. 28, 1878. Family home, Salt Lake City.
The sixth wife bore no children.
Married Azubah Cox July 27, 1867, Salt Lake City, who was born Nov. 5, 1850, Lehi, Utah. Only child: Joseph Milando b. April 6, 1870, d. child. Residue of all these families resided in Salt Lake City.
Seventy. Took part in Echo Canyon and Indian wars. School teacher. Died Sept. 15, 1870.

PREATOR, RICHARD (son of William Preator and Mary Jones). Born Feb. 24, 1826, Chalford Hill, Gloucestershire, Eng. Came to Utah with handcart company.
Married Mary Harper Sept. 2, 1847 (daughter of Thomas Harper of Eastrombs, Gloucestershire), who was born Sept. 1824. Their children: Fred Thomas, d. in England; Mary Salome, m. Hyrum Egan; Lora, d. on the plains; Richard Lorenzo, m. Florenzo McIntosh; Elizabeth, m. Edward Wallace Guymon; Joseph William. Family home Richmond, Utah.
Married Ruth Harper Salt Lake City (daughter of Thomas Harper). Only child: Rosa Lilly, m. George McCormick.
Member of seventy; choir leader Providence; bandmaster and choir leader Richmond, Utah. Carpenter and joiner; farmer. Died March, 1911, Independence, Mo.

PREECE, JOHN. Born Nov. 26, 1811, Lancashire, Eng. Came to Utah Sept. 24, 1848, Heber C. Kimball company.
Married Elizabeth Jenkins in England (daughter of Thomas Jenkins, pioneer 1848, Heber C. Kimball company). Their children: Heber, m. Isadora Jameson; Annie, m. Reuben Fuller; Alma, died; William, m. Eliza Jacobs (Snyder); Moroni, m. Mamie Atwood; Mary Ann, m. George Taylor. Family home, Salt Lake City.
Married Ann Overend 1856 Salt Lake City (daughter of James Overend and Mary Woolyard of Sutton, Eng.). She was born Feb. 21, 1830. Their children: Albert, m. Margaret Thorne; Nephi, m. Sarah Ellingston; Margrett, m.

ork, Utah; pioneers Nov. 10, Edward Hunter company), he was born May 1, 1856. Their children: Emeline b. Oct. 6, 875, m. William Sykes; Els b. Aug. 20, 1880, m. Max Colman; James b. Sept. 2, 18!, d. aged 14; Frederick b. Feb. 8, 1885, m. May Padfield; Hen b. April 6, 1887, m. Benjamin ". Moffett; William b. Ma: 2, 1889; Anna b. June 1891; 'earl b. Nov. 27, 1895.
City councilman three ters 1893-99; mayor of American 'ork 1899-1901; watermasterone term and substitute watermaster two terms. Farmer ad stockraiser.

PRESTON, SAMUEL (son f John Preston and Elizabeth Laycock of Wycalder, Larastershire, Eng.). Born Nov. 5, 1825, at Wycalder. Com to Utah Sept. 2, 1868, Simpson M. Molen company.
Married Louisa Coe Nov 5, 1848, England (daughter of John Coe and Mary Kemp f Sussex, Eng.), who was born April 1827. Their children John A. b. March 26, 1850, m. Agnes Fife; William b. Fb. 10, 1860, m. Annie Clarke; Thomas b. Jan. 16, 1865, r Evelyn Clarke. Family home Weston, Idaho.
High priest; Sunday scbol superintendent. Justice of peace. Weaver; spinner ar farmer. Died July 1906.

PRESTON, WILLIAM (son of Samuel Preston and Louisa Coe). Born Feb. 10, 186 Norwood, Peterboro, Ontario, Canada. Came to Utah wit father.
Married Annie Clarke Oc 10, 1882, Salt Lake City (daughter of John H. Clarke and Elizabeth Heaver of Weston, Idaho), who was born Ma 12, 1862. Their children: Lorin W. b. July 31, 1883; Elizaeth L. b. April 9, 1886. Family home Weston, Idaho.
President 88th quorum seventies; missionary to England 1903-05; secretary, assistnt superintendent and superintendent of Sunday school; d counselor bishopric of Weston ward, and aid in Y. M. M. A., Beaver River stake. Farmer and merchant.

PRESTON, THOMAS (son of Samuel Preston and Louisa Coe). Born Jan. 16, 186! in Ontario, Canada.
Married Emeline H. Clrke April 26, 1888, Logan, Utah (daughter of John H. larke and Elizabeth Heaver of Weston, Idaho). She die June 11, 1888.
Married Evelyn H. Crke Dec. 5, 1890, Logan, Utah (daughter of John H. Crke and Elizabeth Heaver, born Aug. 24, 1870). She died ct. 12, 1905. Their children: May Evelyn b. July 5, 1892; Ira Louisa b. May 10, 1896; Herbert Thomas b. Jan. 13, 190 Vera Emeline b. Dec. 5, 1902; Hortense Emily b. Sept. 4, 1905, d. Oct. 14, 1906. Family home Weston, Idaho.
Missionary to northwetern states July 1897 to October 1899; 1st counselor to ishop 1902-05; superintendent of Sunday school 1909-12. epresentative from Oneida county, Idaho 1902; senator fra Oneida county, 1908 and 1910. Merchant.

PRESTON, WILLIAM BWKER (son of Christopher Preston and Martha Mitchel Claytor, of Franklin county, Va.). Born Nov. 24, 1830, near Staunton, Augusta (then Franklin) county, Va. Came to tah from California Jan. 1, 1858, Henry G. Boyle compan;
Married Harriett Anr Thatcher Feb. 24, 1858, Salt Lake City (daughter of Hezeiah Thatcher and Alley Kitchen, Berkeley county, Va.; pringfield, Ohio; Springfield and Nauvoo, Ill.; and Wintrs Quarters, Iowa; pioneers Sept. 19, 1847, Daniel Spenc- company). She was born Feb. 11, 1839. Their childre: Alfred b. May 27, 1861; Ailey b. March 2, 1863; Willin Bowker b. Aug. 25, 1864, m. Katherine Dollinger Pyer May 20, 1885; May b. May 30, 1869. Family resided Lgan and Salt Lake City, Utah.
Married Bertha Ande'on, who was born July 5, 1849, and died Oct. 4, 1889. The children: Lee b. May 16, 1873, m. Amy D. Davidson; Steen b. May 28, 1876, d. April 1878; Nephi b. June 14, 187 d. infant; Samuel A. b. Oct. 11, 1881; Mary A. b. Marc! 7, 1885.
One of the founder and first bishop of Logan, Utah, 1859. Surveyed and 1d out Logan City and its first irrigation system, the ogan and Hyde Park canal, with Jesse W. Fox. Captai immigration trains 1862 and 1863. Representative of stat legislature 1862-63, and ensuing two sessions ending 1865. Issionary to Denmark 1867-68; president Newcastle and urham conferences 1865; Liverpool, 1865-68, on the "Millnial Star," Liverpool, and in charge of immigration. Reosentative to state legislature 1868-83, continuously. Fender, vice-president and superintendent of constructic of the Utah Northern railroad. In charge of all Cache lley settlements from the death of Peter Maughn until ache stake was organized 1869-77. First counselor to Mss Thatcher, the first president of Cache stake 1877. Dctor and vice-president of the Brigham Young college f Logan for many years. Mayor of Logan City, March ? 1870 to March 1882. President of Cache stake 1879-84. 'residing bishop of the church 1884-1907. Died Aug. 2, 1)8.

PRESTON, WILLIAM BOWKER (son of William Bowker Preston and Harriett Ann Thatcher). Born Aug. 25, 1864.
Married Katherine ollinger Pyper May 20, 1885, at Logan (daughter of Alexan r Cruickshanks Pyper and Catherine ... City), who was born Jan. 6, 1862.

Amussen; Alexander Pyper b. Nov. 16, 1887; Verne Monroe b. April 22, 1892; Claytor b. Feb. 12, 1894; George Dollinger b. Feb. 24, 1897; Katherine b. Nov. 5, 1906. Family home, Logan.
Seventy; missionary to Germany 1888-91; second counselor to bishop of first ward, Logan. Merchant. Died Aug. 13, 1907, Cache Junction, Utah.

PRESTON, WILLIAM BOWKER (son of William Bowker Preston and Katherine Dollinger Pyper). Born Aug. 2, 1886, at Logan.
Married Mable Amussen June 18, 1912, Salt Lake City (daughter of Carl Cristensen Amussen and Barbara McIsaac Smith—former of Kjoge, Sjaelland, Denmark, latter of Lake View, Tooele Co., Utah, pioneers 1865, Thomas Taylor company). She was born May 19, 1890. Family home, Salt Lake City.
Missionary to Germany 1906-09. Physician.

PRESTWICH, WILLIAM (son of Abraham and Sarah Prestwich of Lancastershire, Eng.). Born May 9, 1816, Odenshaw, Eng. Came to Utah Oct. 19, 1861.
Married Jane Lanshaw Feb. 14, 1835, Lancastershire, Eng. (daughter of George Lanshaw, born in Wigan, Lancastershire, moved to Ireland). Their children: Elizabeth, m. (daughter of John H. Clarke); Caroline, m. Robert Mallinson; Jane, m. David Atchison; William, m. Jennett Harvey; Cyrus H. W., m. Lacy Morley; George, m. Julah N. Draper; Mary Ann, m. Moses H. Draper. Family home Timpanagas ward, Provo, Utah.
High priest; home missionary. Farmer. Died Dec. 8, 1892, Moroni, Utah.

PRESTWICH, CYRUS HERBERT WHEELOCK (son of William Prestwich and Jane Lanshaw). Born June 20, 1852, Lancastershire, Eng. Came to Utah Oct. 19, 1862, Horton D. Haight company.
Married Lucy Amanda Morley Oct. 11, 1874, Salt Lake City (daughter of Isaac Morley and Abah Bradley), who was born Dec. 20, 1867. Their children: Cyrus Eugene b. Sept. 8, 1875, m. Eleanor Roseltha Bunnell; Adelaide b. Sept. 17, 1877, m. Christen Larson; Abraham b. Feb. 8, 1880; Sarah b. Feb. 8, 1880; Orsen b. Nov. 15, 1881, m. Sarah Crandell; Leonard b. Sept. 16, 1883, m. Ethel Jackman; Eva b. Sept. 29, 1885; Edith b. Oct. 31, 1887, m. Samuel Kitchen Feb. 15, 1913; Amanda b. July 21, 1890, m. Barny Biglow; Jane Abia b. Oct. 12, 1892; William Morley b. Sept. 27, 1894; Horace Emerson b. Dec. 24, 1896; Ormeido b. Feb. 7, 1900; Ora Viola b. March 21, 1902.
High priest. School trustee. Fruitgrower.

PRESTWICH, CYRUS EUGENE (son of Cyrus Herbert Wheelock Prestwich and Lucy Amanda Morley). Born Sept. 8, 1875, Moroni, Utah.
Married Eleanor Roseltha Bunnell Dec. 1, 1897, Provo, Utah (daughter of Daniel Kimball Bunnell and Mary Mulh, Heber, Utah), who was born Aug. 12, 1878. Their children: Merlin Eugene b. Sept. 5, 1898; Elvin b. Sept. 18, 1900; Elner R. b. Nov. 17, 1902; Leland Kimball b. March 10, 1905; Ferne b. Sept. 20, 1908; Mary Claudia b. March 22, 1911. Family home Sharon ward, Provo, Utah.
Elder. Fruitgrower.

PRICE, EDWARD (son of William Price and Jane Roden). Born Sept. 29, 1811, Tentenhall, Eng. Came to Utah Oct. 19, 1862, Horton D. Haight company.
Married Matilda Lawrence, Birmingham, Eng. (daughter of John Lawrence and Letesa Longstrom), who was born Feb. 13, 1821, Broxgrove, Eng. Their children: Matilda, m. Claudius Spencer; Lorenzo, m. Annie Buckley; Isabell, m. Frank Smith, m. Saul Kunkle; Agnes, m. Elias Price (not related); Walter L., m. Esther Bird; Arlinda, m. Addison Hurd, m. William Woodard; Ell L., m. Georgie Needham; William L. All born in England. Family home, Salt Lake City.
Merchant. Died August 1874, Salt Lake City.

PRICE, LORENZO (son of Edward Price and Matilda Lawrence). Born May 27, 1846, Birmingham, Eng. Came to Utah Oct. 19, 1862, Horton D. Haight company.
Married Annie Buckley Nov. 27, 1866, Salt Lake City (daughter of James Buckley of Oldham, Lancashire, Eng., who died en route to Utah, but his family came on to their destination Oct. 4, 1854, Captain Nebeker company). She was born Nov. 27, 1844, and came to Utah with mother. Their children: Lorenzo, Jr., m. Emma Handley; Edward, m. Artie Smith; Harry, m. Miss Burnett; Matilda, m. Mr. Edmonds; Florence, m. George L. Hardy; Bessie, m. Harry K. Downing; Lawrence, m. Leona Christensen, m. Gladys Stifler; James Nelson. Family home, Salt Lake City.
Cabinet-maker.

PRICE, LORENZO, JR. (son of Lorenzo Price and Annie Buckley). Born May 10, 1868, Salt Lake City.
Married Emma N. Handley June 26, 1890, Salt Lake City (daughter of George Handley and Elizabeth Clark of Cambridgeshire, Eng., pioneers Oct. 6, 1853, Cyrus H. Wheelock company). She was born Oct. 17, 1867. Their children: George B. b. Aug. 20, 1891, m. Bessie Sadley; Inez b. May 6, 1894, m. George W. Morse; Lorenzo V. b. Dec. 20, 1897; Blanche b. Jan. 20, 1900; Ona ... ct. 12, 1902; Evans b. July 14, 1906, d. aged 18 month ... lyna b. May 20, 1909.

26, 1850; Omner b. Nov. 30, 1851, d. Jan. 7, 1852; Phoebe Soper b. May 19, 1853, m. William Shadrach Holdaway Sept. 11, 1872. Family home, Salt Lake City.
Married Martha Monks April 28, 1847, who was born April 28, 1825, Raynor, Chestershire, Eng., and came to Utah with husband. Only child: Ether b. Jan. 30, 1849, d. Feb. 22, 1849. Family home, Salt Lake City.
Married Ann Agatha Walker April 28, 1847, Winter Quarters, Neb. (daughter of William Gibson Walker and Mary Goodwin of Manchester, Eng.). She was born June 11, 1829, Leek, Staffordshire, Eng., and came to Utah with husband. Their children: Agatha b. July 7, 1848, m. Joseph Harris Ridges Jan. 21, 1866; Malona b. April 15, 1850, m. Elnathan Eldredge, Jr., Nov. 11, 1870; Marion b. Nov. 28, 1851, d. Oct. 6, 1852; Moroni Walker b. Oct. 10, 1853, m. Mary Chugg, m. Mary Owens; Eveline b. Aug. 8, 1856, m. Francis G. Woods. Family home, Salt Lake City.
Married Keziah Downes Dec. 27, 1853, Salt Lake City, who was born May 10, 1812, Raynor, Chestershire, Eng., and died Jan. 11, 1876, Salt Lake City.
Married Elenor J. McComb Nov. 14, 1855, Salt Lake City, who was born Dec. 29, 1817, Wheeling, W. Va., and died Oct. 24, 1874, Salt Lake City.

PRATT, MORONI WALKER (son of Parley Parker Pratt and Ann Agatha Walker). Born Oct. 10, 1853, Salt Lake City.
Married Mary Chugg. Their children: Ellis, m. Frank Cole; Mary Louie, m. Truman J. Cole; Francis Moroni, m. Myrtle Grace Young; Evelyn Vilate, m. George A. Griffeth; Cora Agatha; Mabel Elizabeth, m. Willard Leroy Van Orden; Hazel; Florence. Family resided Meadowville, Utah, Malad and Fairview, Idaho.
Married Mary Owens Nov. 7, 1894, Logan, Utah (daughter of William Owens, pioneer 1854, and Elizabeth Roberts, pioneer 1855, Seth M. Blair company—married Jan. 28, 1856, Salt Lake City). She was born March 7, 1866, Henefer, Summit Co., Utah. Their children: Esther b. Aug. 8, 1895; Laura b. Jan. 29, 1897; Viola b. Jan. 26, 1899; Vida b. Feb. 22, 1901; Parley Owens b. Dec. 14, 1903, died; Athleen b. Feb. 21, 1904; Ruth b. March 30, 1906; Milton O. b. Nov. 5, 1908; Harold O. b. Dec. 13, 1910. Family resided Fairview and Preston, Idaho.
Bishop of Fairview ward 16 years; bishop's counselor at Meadowville; stake president of high priests quorum several years; high councilor; missionary to Indiana. Trustee Oneida Stake Academy. Poet. Died June 28, 1911, Salt Lake City.

PRATT, WILLIAM DICKINSON (son of Jared Pratt and Charity Dickinson). Born Sept. 3, 1802, Worcester, Otsego county, N. Y. Came to Utah Oct. 7, 1851, with Orson Pratt, who was returning from the European mission.
Married Hannah Ward Jan. 1, 1837, Kirtland, Ohio, who was born Feb. 26, 1808, Chester, Windsor county, Vt., and died Sept. 20, 1840, Nauvoo, Ill. Their child: Sarah Jane b. Feb. 19, 1838, d. Oct. 1838.
Married Wealthy Shumway (widow) March 1, 1841. Their children: Martha b. Dec. 13, 1841, d. Oct. 15, 1847; William Jared b. June 22, 1844 (d. June 16, 1909), m. Alice Smart Dec. 1, 1862; Stephen b. 1847, d. infant; Mirza Lyona b. 1849, d. 1851.
The third and fourth wives bore no children.
Married Jane Holley (O'Bannion). Only child: Alice b. Aug. 23, 1856, m. Orson Merrill Dec. 28, 1878. Family home, Salt Lake City.
The sixth wife bore no children.
Married Azabah Cox July 27, 1867, Salt Lake City, who was born Nov. 5, 1850, Lehi, Utah. Only child: Joseph Milando b. April 6, 1870, d. child. Residue of all these families resided in Salt Lake City.
Seventy. Took part in Echo Canyon and Indian wars. School teacher. Died Sept. 15, 1870.

PREATOR, RICHARD (son of William Preator and Mary Jones). Born Feb. 24, 1826, Chalford Hill, Gloucestershire, Eng. Came to Utah with handcart company.
Married Mary Harper Sept. 2, 1847 (daughter of Thomas Harper of Eastrombs, Gloucestershire), who was born Sept., 1824. Their children: Fred Thomas, d. in England; Mary Salome, m. Hyrum Egan; Lora, d. on the plains; Richard Lorenzo, m. Florenzo McIntosh; Elizabeth, m. Edward William Guymon; Joseph William. Family home Richmond, Utah.
Married Ruth Harper Salt Lake City (daughter of Thomas Harper). Only child: Rosa Lilly, m. George McCormick.
Member of seventy; choir leader Providence; bandmaster and choir leader Richmond, Utah. Carpenter and joiner; farmer. Died March, 1911, Independence, Mo.

PREECE, JOHN. Born Nov. 26, 1811, Lancashire, Eng. Came to Utah Sept. 24, 1848, Heber C. Kimball company.
Married Elizabeth Jenkins in England (daughter of Thomas Jenkins, pioneer 1848, Heber C. Kimball company). Their children: Heber, m. Isadora Jameson; Annie, m. Reuben Fuller; Alma, died; William, m. Eliza Jacobs (Snyder); Moroni, m. Mamie Atwood; Mary Ann, m. George Taylor. Family home, Salt Lake City.
Married Ann Overend 1856 Salt Lake City (daughter of James Overend and Mary Woolyard of Sutton, Eng.). She was born Feb. 21, 1830. Their children: Albert, m. Margaret Thorne; Nephi, m. Sarah Ellingston; Margrett, m. David McKenzie; Louise, m. Wilford Smith; Oliver; Joseph, m. Minnie Sperry. Family home, Salt Lake City.
Missionary to Salmon River, Ariz., 1859-61; bishop's counselor. Died Oct. 1, 1887, Salt Lake City.

PREECE, WILLIAM (son of John Preece and Elizabeth Jenkins). Born Feb. 11, 1856, Salt Lake City.
Married Mary Eliza Jacobs (Snyder) Dec. 5, 1880, Vernal, Utah (daughter of Norton Jacobs and Emily Eaton of Salt Lake City and Woods Cross, Utah, pioneers July 24, 1847, Brigham Young company). She was born Dec. 25, 1849, at Woods Cross and had previously married Robert Hyrum Snyder Dec. 12, 1874, Salt Lake City (son of Samuel Cornwell Snyder and Maria Stockwell of Snyderville, Utah, who was born March 19, 1852, and was father of Mary Ida Snyder b. Sept. 16, 1875; Robert Ashley Snyder b. May 12, 1878, the first white child born in Ashley Fork, Utah, but who died March 22, 1881). The Preece children were: William Rowland b. July 2, 1881; Margaret May b. Feb. 27, 1884, m. Lafayette Richardson; Nellie Elizabeth b. Sept. 27, 1886; Clarence Jacobs b. Feb. 3, 1889; Vera b. Nov. 16, 1891.
Came to Park City in 1871 and was the first white boy to stay overnight in Park City; in the fall of 1878 he came to Ashley Ford and wintered on the Duchesne river with cattle. Freighter between Vernal, Salt Lake and Rock Springs ten years. Sheriff. Worked for the government. Farmer.

PREECE, JOSEPH H. (son of John Preece and Ann Overend). Born May 10, 1869, Salt Lake City.
Married Minnie E. Sperry Nov. 24, 1897, Salt Lake City (daughter of Harrison Sperry and Susan Mosley of Salt Lake City, pioneers 1847). She was born March 18, 1871. Their children: John Lamont b. Aug. 29, 1898; Sherman J. b. July 13, 1900; Minnie S. b. June 27, 1906; Louise Ann b. Oct. 23, 1912. Family home, Salt Lake City.
Seventy; missionary to California 1910-11; Sunday school superintendent. City councilman. Merchant.

PREECE, MARK (son of Richard Preece, born Oct. 21, 1806, and Susannah Pritchard, born May 15, 1806, both of Herefordshire, Eng.). He was born Sept. 1, 1839, Rollaton, Herefordshire. Came to Utah 1852, Thomas Tidwell company.
Married Ellen Comish Nov. 21, 1865 (daughter of William Comish and Elizabeth Kegg, pioneers Sept. 3, 1855, John Hindley company—married January, 1831, Douglas, Isle of Man). She was born Dec. 30, 1840. Their children: Susanna Elizabeth b. Oct. 19, 1863, m. Andrew B. Allen Jan. 6, 1881; Mark Henry b. Nov. 26, 1865, m. Charlotte M. Gregory May 20, 1885; William Frederick b. Nov. 19, 1867; Francis Chase b. Oct. 24, 1869, m. Nina Peck May 15, 1894; Isabell Ellen b. Nov. 11, 1871. Family resided Franklin, Idaho, and Coveville, Utah.
Married Octavia Elener Braley June 3, 1885, Logan, Utah (daughter of John Braley and Nancy Melvina Stowe, latter came to Utah Nov. 25, 1883). She was born Dec. 1, 1851, Linden, Perry Co., Tenn. Their children: Elener Vilate Braley b. Aug. 20, 1886, m. Alonzo J. W. Henson July 12, 1904; Freeman Braley b. Oct. 12, 1888. Children adopted by them: Byron E. Braley b. Sept. 1, 1869, m. Thomas W. Comish Nov. 28, 1888; Harriett L. Braley b. Feb. 17, 1872; Beulah B. Braley b. Dec. 20, 1874, m. John W. Biggs July 11, 1894; John W. Braley b. Dec. 19, 1878. Family home Coveville, Utah.

PREECE, MARK HENRY (son of Mark Preece and Ellen Comish). Born Nov. 26, 1866, Franklin, Idaho.
Married Charlotte M. Gregory May 20, 1885, Logan, Utah (daughter of Robert Gregory and Selena Marshall; former came to Utah Oct. 18, 1862, Horton Haight company, latter with Ellsworth handcart company). She was born Feb. 1, 1868, Franklin, Idaho. Their children: Ellen Selena b. March 6, 1886, m. George F. Bowman Nov. 28, 1905; Robert W. b. Oct. 26, 1887, m. Mary J. Bair Oct. 30, 1907; Aaron H. b. May 5, 1890; Charlotte Phebe b. Feb. 1, 1892, m. Elmor D. Bailey Feb. 28, 1911; Lula G. b. Dec. 21, 1897; Lona G. b. March 21, 1900; Mark Golden b. Jan. 25, 1902; Estey Geneva b. Dec. 2, 1903; Hylda G. b. May 22, 1907; Norris G. (adopted) b. Feb. 11, 1911. Family home Coveville, Utah.

PRESTON, JAMES WHITMORE (son of Richard Preston of Salem, Mass.). Born Oct. 7, 1822, at Salem. Came to Utah 1851.
Married Emeline Houston 1851 in Vermont (daughter of Isaac Houston and Theodosia E. Keyes, both of Vermont; pioneers 1851). She was born Feb. 28, 1834. Their children: Theodosia, m. William Brown; James Whitmore, m. Annie Conder; Richard, m. Bessie Chipman; Emeline, d. child; Mary Ann, m. William Henry; Isaac H., m. Eliza Bishop; Washburn C., m. May Huish; William A., m. Elsie Goff; Minawell, m. Ephraim Nash; Charles Henry, m. Dalla Cutis; Harriet A., m. John Vier. Family home American Fork, Utah.
Member of 67th quorum seventies; missionary to Boston, Mass., 1880-82. School trustee at American Fork for 12 years. Assisted in the building of all canals about American Fork. Alpine and Provo, Utah. Farmer; sheepman and stockman.

PRESTON, JAMES WHITMORE, JR. (son of James Whitmore Preston and Emeline Houston). Born Jan. 7, 1854, Alpine, Utah.
Married Annie Conder Nov. 14, 1874, Salt Lake City, Utah (daughter of Edward Conder and Helen Pierce of American

PIONEERS AND PROMINENT MEN OF UTAH

Fork, Utah; pioneers Nov. 1850, Edward Hunter company). She was born May 1, 1856. Their children: Emeline b. Oct. 6, 1875, m. William Sykes; Ellis b. Aug. 20, 1880, m. Max Holman; James b. Sept. 2, 1882, d. aged 14; Frederick b. Feb. 18, 1885, m. May Padfield; Helen b. April 6, 1887, m. Benjamin F. Moffett; William b. May 2, 1889; Anna b. June 1891; Pearl b. Nov. 27, 1895.
City councilman three terms 1893-99; mayor of American Fork 1899-1901; watermaster one term and substitute watermaster two terms. Farmer and stockraiser.

PRESTON, SAMUEL (son of John Preston and Elizabeth Laycock of Wycalder, Lancastershire, Eng.). Born Nov. 5, 1825, at Wycalder. Come to Utah Sept. 2, 1868, Simpson M. Molen company.
Married Louisa Coe Nov. 5, 1848, England (daughter of John Coe and Mary Kemp of Sussex, Eng.), who was born April 1827. Their children: John A. b. March 26, 1850, m. Agnes Fife; William B. Feb. 10, 1860, m. Annie Clarke; Thomas b. Jan. 16, 1865, m. Evelyn Clarke. Family home Weston, Idaho.
High priest; Sunday school superintendent. Justice of peace. Weaver; spinner and farmer. Died July 1906.

PRESTON, WILLIAM (son of Samuel Preston and Louisa Coe). Born Feb. 10, 1860, Norwood, Peterboro, Ontario, Canada. Came to Utah with father.
Married Annie Clarke Oct. 10, 1882, Salt Lake City (daughter of John H. Clarke and Elizabeth Heaver of Weston, Idaho), who was born May 12, 1862. Their children: Lorin W. b. July 31, 1883; Elizabeth L. b. April 9, 1886. Family home Weston, Idaho.
President 88th quorum seventies; missionary to England 1903-05; secretary, assistant superintendent and superintendent of Sunday school; 2d counselor bishopric of Weston ward, and aid in Y. M. M. I. A., Beaver River stake. Farmer and merchant.

PRESTON, THOMAS (son of Samuel Preston and Louisa Coe). Born Jan. 16, 1865, in Ontario, Canada.
Married Emeline H. Clarke April 25, 1888, Logan, Utah (daughter of John H. Clarke and Elizabeth Heaver of Weston, Idaho). She died June 11, 1888.
Married Evelyn H. Clarke Dec. 5, 1890, Logan, Utah (daughter of John H. Clarke and Elizabeth Heaver, born Aug. 24, 1870). She died Oct. 12, 1905. Their children: May Evelyn b. July 5, 1892; Ines Louisa b. May 10, 1896; Herbert Thomas b. Jan. 13, 1901; Vera Emeline b. Dec. 5, 1902; Hortense Emily b. Sept. 24, 1905, d. Oct. 14, 1906. Family home Weston, Idaho.
Missionary to northwestern states July 1897 to October 1899; 1st counselor to bishop 1902-05; superintendent of Sunday school 1909-12. Representative from Oneida county, Idaho 1902; senator from Oneida county, 1908 and 1910. Merchant.

PRESTON, WILLIAM BOWKER (son of Christopher Preston and Martha Mitchell Clayton, of Franklin county, Va.). Born Nov. 24, 1830, near Staunton, Augusta (then Franklin) county, Va. Came to Utah from California Jan. 1, 1858, Henry G. Boyle company.
Married Harriett Ann Thatcher Feb. 24, 1858, Salt Lake City (daughter of Hezekiah Thatcher and Alley Kitchen, Berkeley county, Va.; Springfield, Ohio; Springfield and Nauvoo, Ill.; and Winters Quarters, Iowa; pioneers Sept. 19, 1847, Daniel Spencer company). She was born Feb. 11, 1839. Their children: Alfred b. May 27, 1861; Alley b. March 2, 1863; William Bowker b. Aug. 25, 1864, m. Katherine Dollinger Pyper May 20, 1885; Mary b. May 30, 1869. Family resided Logan and Salt Lake City, Utah.
Married Bertha Anderson, who was born July 5, 1849, and died Oct. 4, 1889. Their children: Lee b. May 16, 1873, m. Amy D. Davidson; Stephen b. May 28, 1876, d. April 1878; Nephi b. June 14, 1879, d. infant; Samuel A. b. Oct. 11, 1881; Mary A. b. March 7, 1885.
One of the founders and first bishop of Logan, Utah, 1859. Surveyed and laid out Logan City and its first irrigation system, the Logan and Hyde Park canal, with Jesse W. Fox. Captain immigration trains 1862 and 1863. Representative of state legislature 1862-63, and ensuing two sessions ending 1865. Missionary to Europe 1865-68; president Newcastle and Durham conferences 1866; Liverpool, 1865-68, on the "Millenial Star," Liverpool, and in charge of immigration. Representative to state legislature 1868-83, continuously. Founder, vice-president and superintendent of construction of the Utah Northern railroad. In charge of all Cache valley settlements from the death of Peter Maughn until Cache stake was organized 1869-77. First counselor to Moses Thatcher, the first president of Cache stake 1877. Director and vice-president of the Brigham Young college at Logan for many years. Mayor of Logan City, March 7, 1870 to March 1882. President of Cache stake 1879-84. Presiding bishop of the church 1884-1907. Died Aug. 2, 1908.

PRESTON, WILLIAM BOWKER (son of William Bowker Preston and Harriett Ann Thatcher). Born Aug. 25, 1864, at Logan.
Married Katherine Dollinger Pyper May 20, 1885, at Logan (daughter of Alexander Cruickshanks Pyper and Catherine Dollinger of Salt Lake City), who was born Jan. 5, 1862.

Amussen; Alexander Pyper b. Nov. 16, 1887; Verne Monroe b. April 22, 1892; Claytor b. Feb. 12, 1894; George Dollinger b. Feb. 24, 1897; Katherine b. Nov. 5, 1906. Family home, Logan.
Seventy; missionary to Germany 1888-91; second counselor to bishop of first ward, Logan. Merchant. Died Aug. 13, 1907, Cache Junction, Utah.

PRESTON, WILLIAM BOWKER (son of William Bowker Preston and Katherine Dollinger Pyper). Born Aug. 2, 1886, at Logan.
Married Mable Amussen June 18, 1912, Salt Lake City (daughter of Carl Cristensen Amussen and Barbara McIsaac Smith—former of Kjoge, Sjaelland, Denmark, latter of Lake View, Tooele Co., Utah, pioneers 1865, Thomas Taylor company). She was born May 19, 1890. Family home, Salt Lake City.
Missionary to Germany 1906-09. Physician.

PRESTWICH, WILLIAM (son of Abraham and Sarah Prestwich of Lancastershire, Eng.). Born May 9, 1816, Odenshaw, Eng. Came to Utah Oct. 19, 1861.
Married Jane Lanshaw Feb. 14, 1835, Lancastershire, Eng. (daughter of George Lanshaw, born in Wigan, Lancastershire, moved to Ireland). Their children: Elizabeth, m. Arrin Hardy; Sarah, m. John Killett; Caroline, m. Robert Mallinson; Jane, m. David Atchison; William, m. Jennett Harvey; Cyrus H. W., m. Lacy Morley; George, m. Julah N. Draper; Mary Ann, m. Moses H. Draper. Family home Timpanogas ward, Provo, Utah.
High priest; home missionary. Farmer. Died Dec. 8, 1892, Moroni, Utah.

PRESTWICH, CYRUS HERBERT WHEELOCK (son of William Prestwich and Jane Lanshaw). Born June 20, 1852, Lancastershire, Eng. Came to Utah Oct. 19, 1861, Horton D. Haight company.
Married Lucy Amanda Morley Oct. 11, 1874, Salt Lake City (daughter of Isaac Morley and Abah Bradley), who was born Dec. 20, 1867. Their children: Cyrus Eugene b. Sept. 8, 1875, m. Eleanor Roseltha Bunnell; Adelaide b. Sept. 17, 1877, m. Christen Larson; Abraham b. Feb. 8, 1880; Sarah b. Feb. 8, 1880; Orsen b. Nov. 15, 1881, m. Sarah Cran (dell; Leonard b. Sept. 16, 1883, m. Ethel Jackman; Eva b. Sept. 29, 1885; Edith b. Oct. 31, 1887, m. Samuel Kitchen Feb. 15, 1913; Amanda b. July 21, 1890, m. Barny Biglow; Jane Abia b. Oct. 12, 1892; William Morley b. Sept. 27, 1894; Horace Emerson b. Dec. 24, 1896; Ormeldo b. Feb. 7, 1900; Ora Viola b. March 21, 1902.
High priest. School trustee. Fruitgrower.

PRESTWICH, CYRUS EUGENE (son of Cyrus Herbert Wheelock Prestwich and Lucy Amanda Morley). Born Sept. 8, 1875, Moroni, Utah.
Married Eleanor Roseltha Bunnell Dec. 1, 1897, Provo, Utah (daughter of Daniel Kimball Bunnell and Mary Muth, Heber, Utah), who was born Aug. 12, 1878. Their children: Merlin Eugene b. Sept. 5, 1898; Elvin b. Sept. 18, 1900; Elner R. b. Nov. 17, 1902; Leland Kimball b. March 10, 1905; Ferne b. Sept. 20, 1908; Mary Claudia b. March 22, 1911. Family home Sharon ward, Provo, Utah.
Elder. Fruitgrower.

PRICE, EDWARD (son of William Price and Jane Roden). Born Sept. 29, 1811, Tentenhall, Eng. Came to Utah Oct. 19, 1862, Horton D. Haight company.
Married Matilda Lawrence, Birmingham, Eng. (daughter of John Lawrence and Letesa Longstrom), who was born Feb. 13, 1821, Brosgrove, Eng. Their children: Matilda, m. Claudius Spencer; Lorenzo, Jr., m. Annie Buckley; Isabell, m. Frank Smith, m. Saul Kunkle; Agnes, m. Elias Price (not related); Walter L., m. Esther Bird; Arlinda, m. Addison Bluford, m. William Woodard; Eli L., m. Georgie Needham; William L. All born in England. Family home, Salt Lake City.
Merchant. Died August 1874, Salt Lake City.

PRICE, LORENZO (son of Edward Price and Matilda Lawrence). Born May 27, 1846, Birmingham, Eng. Came to Utah Oct. 19, 1862, Horton D. Haight company.
Married Annie Buckley Nov. 27, 1866, Salt Lake City (daughter of James Buckley of Oldham, Lancashire, Eng., who died en route to Utah, but his family came on to their destination Oct. 4, 1854, Captain Nebeker company). She was born Nov. 27, 1844, and came to Utah with mother. Their children: Lorenzo, Jr., m. Emma Handley; Edward, m. Artie Smith; Harry, m. Miss Burnett; Matilda, m. M. Edmonds; Florence, m. George L. Hardy; Bessie, m. Hardy K. Downing; Lawrence, m. Leona Christensen, m. Gladys Stifler; James Nelson. Family home, Salt Lake City.
Cabinet-maker.

PRICE, LORENZO, JR. (son of Lorenzo Price and Annie Buckley). Born May 10, 1868, Salt Lake City.
Married Emma N. Handley June 26, 1890, Salt Lake City (daughter of George Handley and Elizabeth Clark of Cambridgeshire, Eng., pioneers Oct. 6, 1853, Cyrus H. Wheelock company). She was born Oct. 17, 1867. Their children: George B. b. Aug. 20, 1891, m. Bessie Sadley; Inez b. May 6, 1894, m. George W. Morse; Lorenzo V. b. Dec. 20, 1897; Blanche b. Jan. 20, 1900; Ona b. Oct. 12, 1902; Evana b. July 14, 1906, d. aged 18 months; Alyna b. May 20, 1909. Family home, Salt Lake City.

1116 PIONEERS AND PROMINENT MEN OF UTAH

PRICE, JAMES (son of James Price and Ann Danks of Ludlow, Salopshire, Eng.). Born May 17, 1837, Salopshire. Came to Utah in September, 1864, Joseph S. Rawlins company.
Married Ann Powell March 28, 1857, at Ludlow (daughter of George Powell and Maria Mausley of Blockwitch, Staffordshire, Eng., pioneers 1864, Joseph S. Rawlins company). She was born June 2, 1840. Their children: Ann b. June 21, 1854, m. William Daybell; George b. Jan. 6, 1861, m. Mary Hannah Daybell; James, Jr., b. Feb. 12, 1863, died on the plains; Maria Rawlins b. Aug. 22, 1864, m. Charles E. Thacker; Sarah Jane b. Dec. 28, 1866, m. Fred Thacker; John H. b. May 22, 1869, m. Sarah Ellen Wintertor; Emma b. June 10, 1871, m. John Penfold; Charles E. b. Oct. 1, 1873, m. Sarah Collins Bethers; Rachel Mary b. Dec. 18, 1875, m. Al Penfold; James William b. Dec. 31, 1877, m. Martha McAffee; Margaret b. April 18, 1879, m. James Casper; Lottie R. b: Aug. 16, 1881, died; Maybell b. Nov. 5, 1883, m. George Walker. Family home Charleston, Utah.
High priest; assistant Sunday school superintendent; counselor Y. M. M. I. A. School trustee. Settled at Heber City, Utah, 1864. Farmer.

PRICE, GEORGE (son of James Price and Ann Powell). Born Jan. 6, 1861, Tipton, Staffordshire, Eng. Came to Utah with parents.
Married Mary Hannah Daybell Nov. 29, 1883, Salt Lake City (daughter of Robert Daybell of Sheffield, Eng., and Agnes Ann Bancroft of Breaston, near Barrows Hill, Derbyshire, Eng., pioneers Sept. 1866, Samuel White company). She was born Jan. 9, 1866, at Breaston. Their children: James Robert b. April 3, 1885, m. Mabel Alexander; George Finity b. June 28, 1886, m. Effie May Wagstaff; Theresa b. June 28, 1888, m. Stephen A. Simmons; Ray Levi b. March 4, 1890; Franklin Daybell b. June 12, 1892; Fern b. Sept. 27, 1894; Rintha b. Feb. 4, 1897; Willard Powell b. Sept. 11, 1898; Rodney Daybell b. Aug. 20, 1901; Ruby b. May 3, 1903; Mabel b. May 9, 1905, died; Ernest b. Oct. 19, 1907, and Winnette b. Dec. 7, 1908, latter three died; Wendell Bancroft b. Dec. 7, 1908. Family home Charleston, Wasatch Co., Utah.
High councilor; president Y. M. M. I. A.; second counselor to Bishop William Daybell, Charleston ward 1899-1904. President Charleston town board 1902-05. Member of firm of Price Bros., merchants, Charleston. Director in Charleston and the Midway Irrigation Companies.

PRICE, JOHN I. (son of John Price and Ann Cook of Glastry, Radnorshire, Eng.). Born May 10, 1830, Glastry. Came to Utah in 1862, William Keywood freight train.
Married Mary Ann Wingrove (daughter of Richard Wingrove and Margaret Parker). Only child: Isaac T. b. Oct. 26, 1855, m. Ann Maria Reed Sept. 26, 1877. Family home, Wanship, Summit Co., Utah.
Married Ellen Hick in December, 1864, at Wanship (daughter of Thomas Hick and Sarah Roberts, former a pioneer, Captain Snow company). She was born at Birmingham, Eng. Only child: John Thomas b. May 3, 1866, m. Mary Ellen Allen Dec. 7, 1888.
Settled at Wanship 1864. Moved to Laketown, Utah, 1872.

PRICE, ISAAC T. (son of John I. Price and Mary Ann Wingrove). Born Oct. 26, 1855, Cincinnati, Ohio. Came to Utah with father.
Married Ann Maria Reed Sept. 26, 1877. Their children: Alice A. b. Nov. 14, 1879, m. Arthur Smith Oct. 11, 1898; Elizabeth E. b. Dec. 23, 1881, m. Joseph H. Astle June 13, 1906; Mary A. b. June 2, 1884, m. Joseph Stucki April 6, 1904; Isaac Elvin b. Jan. 29, 1887; Ezra Luther b. Feb. 12, 1890, m. Alzina Tingey Nov. 23, 1910; Franklin Jesse b. May 21, 1892; Wilford Marion b. May 8, 1895; Myrtle H. b. May 22, 1898; Laverne R. and Melverne W. b. June 30, 1900; Leslie Lyman b. June 18, 1901; Asael Woodruff b. Dec. 23, 1904. Family home Round Valley, Utah.
Bishop of Round Valley 1893.

PRICE, ROBERT (son of Simon Price, born March 1, 1808, and Mary Stamers, born April 12, 1807). He was born June 19, 1835, in England. Came to Utah Sept. 12, 1861, Milo Andrus company.
Married Matilda Louisa Kelsey Oct. 13, 1855 (daughter of Edward Kelsey), who was born 1832. Their children: Matilda Mary b. Jan. 3, 1857, m. George Sparks 1877; Robert Henry b. Nov. 2, 1858, m. Ellen Croft Oct. 2, 1884; Welcome William b. July 8, 1860, m. Lottie Imes 1886; Ellen Louisa b. Feb. 25, 1863, m. Henry Athay Oct. 2, 1884. Family home Paris, Idaho.
Married Susannah Juchaw March 2, 1864, Salt Lake City (daughter of Charles Daniel Juchaw and Susannah Deighton, pioneers 1861, Milo Andrus company). Their adopted children: Violet b. June 1, 1905; Pearl b. July 3, 1907; Gwendolyn b. March 17, 1909.
Married Christine Shepherd Sept. 1, 1879 (daughter of William and Ann Shepherd).
Married Wilhelmina Grey Feb. 6, 1887.

PRICE, WILLIAM S. (son of Charles Price of Coleton, Leicestershire, Eng.). Born in 1808, Coleton. Came to Utah in 1853.
Married Ann Platts at Coleton, who was born in Sept. 1808. Their children: Charles; Jane; Herbert, m. Sarah Howcroft. Family home, Salt Lake City.
Shoemaker. Died October, 1890.

PRICE, HERBERT (son of William S. Price and Ann Platts). Born Sept. 17, 1848, Coleton, Leicestershire, Eng. Came to Utah with father.
Married Sarah Howcroft Sept. 7, 1874, Salt Lake City (daughter of John Howcroft and Mary Holland of Farnsworth, Lancashire, Eng.; came to Utah in 1870, Captain Mumford company). She was born Nov. 1, 1853. Their children: Mary Ann b. July 18, 1875, m. David O. Willey; Sarah Jane b. June 6, 1877; Herbert, Jr., b. July 24, 1880; Gertrude Alice b. Dec. 27, 1882, died; Charles William b. Nov. 19, 1887, m. Edna Hampton. Family home, Salt Lake City.
Farmer and stockraiser. Died August, 1909.

PRICE, CHARLES WILLIAM (son of Herbert Price and Sarah Howcroft). Born Nov. 19, 1887, Salt Lake City.
Married Edna Hampton April 7, 1910, Salt Lake City (daughter of Brigham Young Hampton and Mary Jane Robinson of Sunderland, Durham, Eng., pioneers Sept. 1, 1868, Captain Murdock company). She was born Jan. 3, 1891. Their child: Charles Hampton b. March 2, 1911. Family home, Salt Lake City.
Clerk in general passenger department of Oregon Short Line at Salt Lake City for last ten years.

PRIESTLEY, JOHN (son of John Priestley and Jane Adamson of Bradford, Yorkshire, Eng.). Born Feb. 25, 1843, Bradford. Came to Utah Oct. 19, 1862, Houtz and Bringhurst company.
Married Margaret D. F. McMaster Oct. 31, 1863, Salt Lake City (daughter of William A. McMaster and Margaret Drummond Ferguson of Dunfermline, Fifeshire, Scotland, pioneers Oct. 1, 1854, Daniel Garn company). She was born Jan. 15, 1845. Their children: Margaret Jane b. Sept. 24, 1864; John William b. March 8, 1866; Grace Lillian b. Dec. 10, 1871; Annie Elizabeth b. April 22, 1874; Mary Emily b. July 12, 1877; Alex Athol b. Nov. 1, 1878; Sarah McMaster b. Aug. 8, 1881; Donald A. S. b. March 19, 1886; Virginia Irene b. May 5, 1889; Thomas Bruce b. Dec. 28, 1890. Family home, Salt Lake City.
Member 6th quorum seventies. Printer on Deseret News for 25 years.

PRITCHETT, LEONIDAS ALFRED (son of James Pritchett). Born Dec. 14, 1838, Rich Valley, Va. Came to Big Cottonwood, Utah, in 1864.
Married Elizabeth Ann Heningar in Virginia (daughter of Philip Heningar). Their children: Cathern C.; Elizabeth Ann, m. Parley P. Carver Nov. 27, 1889; Rose Ellen; Alfred Leonidas; Margaret C.; Matilda P.; Nancy M. Family resided at Harrisville and Eden (Ogden valley), Utah.
Seventy; Sunday school superintendent. Justice of peace. Carpenter. Died June 9, 1889, at Eden.

PROBST, JOHN ULRICH (son of John Ulrich Probst and Anna Barbara Hess of Lützelflüh, Canton Bern, Switzerland). Born April 23, 1838, Lützelflüh. Came to Utah July 4, 1872.
Married Anna Barbara Kiener Oct. 16, 1857, at Herzogenbuchsee, Canton Bern, Switzerland (daughter of Christian Kiener and Rosina Hofer of Boltigen, Canton Bern, Switzerland). She was born June 17, 1831. Their children: John Gottlieb; John Ulrich, m. Susannah Gertsch; Frederich; Jacob, m. Mary Magdalena Huber; Ernest, m. Emma Kohler; Emil; John; Edward August, m. Margaret Watkins; Emma Elizabeth. Family home Midway, Wasatch Co., Utah.
President 96th quorum seventies; missionary to Switzerland 1888-90. Tailor; farmer.

PROBST, JACOB (son of John Ulrich Probst and Anna Barbara Kiener). Born Jan. 3, 1864, Habstetten, Canton Bern, Switzerland. Came to Utah July 4, 1872.
Married Mary Magdalena Huber Sept. 23, 1891, Manti, Utah (daughter of John Huber and Mary Magdalena Munz of Midway, Utah, pioneers 1863, Peter Nebeker company). She was born Oct. 15, 1869. Their children: Karl Lorenzo b. June 7, 1895; Vernon Huber b. Jan. 17, 1897; Leah Huber b. May 19, 1899; Estella Huber b. Dec. 10, 1901; Stanley Huber b. April 2, 1905. Family home Midway, Wasatch Co., Utah.
Missionary to Switzerland and Germany 1891-94; president 96th quorum seventies; president Y. M. M. I. A. 1897-98; high councilor 1900-1903; bishop of second ward Midway since 1903. County commissioner; county assessor; justice of peace; city councilman. Farmer and stockraiser.

PROVIS, RICHARD S. (son of John Provis and Grace Williams). Born July 15, 1825, Cornwall, Eng. Came to Utah Oct. 5, 1859, Nephi Johnson oxteam train.
Married Dorothy L. Langeviid Nov. 1, 1851, Cape Town, South Africa (daughter of Phillip Langeviid and Wilhelmena Barchfeld). Their children: Grace, m. Henry W. DeSpain of Joseph City, Ariz.; Annie L. Family home, Salt Lake City.

Left England May 19, 1849, for South Africa. Converted L. D. S. April 5, 1853. High priest; seventy; block teacher; Sunday school superintendent. Gardener. Died Sept. 3, 1908.

PROVOST, LUKE (son of Luke Provost and Catharine Henon of Pompton, N. J.). Born Jan. 2, 1809, at Pompton. Came to Utah Dec. 18, 1856, William B. Hodgett company.
Married Julia Ann Wheeler in July, 1832, Newark, N. J., who was born Sept. 23, 1815. Their children: Julia, m. David Van Wagenen; Charles Baldwin, died; James W., m. Clara Love; David, m. Clara Van Wagenen; Luke, m. Alice Hofelts; Sarah, m. James Ross. Family home Provo, Utah.
President of branch at Newark. Died March 1866, St. Marys, Iowa.

PROWS, WILLIAM COOK (son of Thomas and Elenor Prows). Born June 11, 1827, in Indiana. Came to Utah with division Mormon battalion.
Married Modeska Ann Roberts in 1852 (daughter of Thomas Roberts, pioneer 1850). Their children: John Thomas, m. Mary Manhard and Lovina Cooley; William, d. infant; Joseph, m. Caroline Christensen; Francis, d. infant; Martha Elenor, m. William Perry Miller; Hyrum, m. Annie May Howlett; Elizabeth, died; Margaret Ann, m. Charles Bement; Lovina, m. Osborn Cooley; Sarah, m. Arthur Howlett; George, died. Family resided in California and at Deseret and Kanosh, Utah.
Married Louisa M. R. James at Salt Lake City (daughter of Abraham James and Elizabeth Jane Ragsdale of Little Rock, Ark., pioneers 1867, independent company). She was born May 22, 1847. Their children: Josephine, m. James L. Memmott; Thomas Abraham, d. aged 6; James Calvin, m. Nancy E. Humphrey; David Alvin, m. Mary Ann Davis; Elizabeth Jane, m. Joseph Orson Barney; Charles Aaron and Lorin Edward, died; Leslie Webster. Family home Clawson, Utah.
Seventy and high priest. Farmer. Died April 29, 1893, Juarez, Mexico.

PROWS, JAMES CALVIN (son of William Cook Prows and Louisa M. R. James). Born Oct. 11, 1872, Kanosh, Utah.
Married Nancy Elmina Humphrey at Juarez, Chihuahua, Mexico (daughter of Charles Humphrey of Mill Creek, Utah). Their children: Charles William b. June 20, 1896; Elmina b. May 3, 1899; Morrel; Baby, d. infant. Family resided Music Mountains, Ariz., Kanosh, Utah, and in Mexico.
Married Lilly Alice Wayman at Clawson, Utah (daughter of Charles Wayman of Ferron, Utah), who died April 22, 1908, Clawson, Utah. Their child: Ovid Fay b. April 5, 1908. Family home Clawson, Utah.
Elder. Farmer.

b. May 5, 1848, m. Sarah Augusta Pulley; Joseph Henry b. Dec. 9, 1849, m. Alice E. Moon; David Alexander b. July 9, 1852, m. Lydia Moon; Alice Jane b. Jan. 18, 1855, m. Joseph Henry Moon.
Married Lydia Esther Hall May 11, 1874, Salt Lake City (daughter of Daniel Hall of England), who was born April 23, 1854. Their children: Edward Parley, m. Miss Rodgers; Shadrach, m. Nettie Aliquist; Chester Charles, m. Minnie Martin; Noah Malanda, m. Rebecca Goat; Esther, m. Hans Nielson; Elsie, m. Lewis Nielson; Ether; Leviri; Lydia Marie. Families resided American Fork, Utah.
High priest; home missionary. Took active part in Morrisite war. Farmer. Died Dec. 14, 1906, at American Fork.

PULLEY, JAMES FRANKLIN (son of James Pulley and Alice Moon). Born May 5, 1848, Alton, Ill. Came to Utah with father.
Married Sarah Augusta Pulley March 15, 1875, Salt Lake City (daughter of Joseph Pulley and Annah Chandney of Ayton, Herefordshire, Eng., the latter a pioneer 1873). She was born Jan. 25, 1848. Their children: Ophelia b. April 13, 1877; Leonidas b. June 17, 1879; Edith b. Sept. 22, 1881; Luella b. Oct. 29, 1887; Armond b. Dec. 23, 1889. Family home American Fork, Utah.
Elder; ward teacher. Veteran Black Hawk Indian war. Farmer.

PULLEY, CHESTER CHARLES (son of James Pulley and Lydia Esther Hall). Born Feb. 8, 1883, American Fork, Utah.
Married Minnie Martin Jan. 13, 1909, Salt Lake Temple (daughter of James Martin and Mary A. Lysons of Low Valley, Yorkshire, Eng., pioneers 1904). She was born April 9, 1890. Their children: Wilford b. Nov. 20, 1909; Ray b. Oct. 17, 1911. Family home, Pleasant Grove.
High priest; second counselor to James T. Gardner of first ward, American Fork; missionary to southern states 1903-05; president Y. M. M. I. A. of first ward, American Fork, and teacher of second intermediate and theological classes; second assistant Sunday school superintendent. Farmer.

PULSIPHER, ORSON HYDE (son of Elias Pulsipher, born Nov. 12, 1805, Newbury, Vt., and Polly Chubbuck, born March 26, 1809, Londonderry, Vt.). He was born May 9, 1835, Kirtland, Ohio. Came to Utah in 1852.
Married Susannah Rasmussen, who was born June 14, 1839. Their children: Orson Henry b. Aug. 26, 1863, m. Martena Olsen; Susannah b. Jan. 27, 1865, m. Oliver F. Davis Sept. 17, 1884; Ephraim; William b. June 15, 1868, m. Carrie Wight Nov. 19, 1892; Asenath; Polly Ann; Eliza J.; Elias.

1118   PIONEERS AND PROMINENT MEN OF UTAH

PUZEY, HENRY (son of William Puzey and Jane Briar of Alton, Hampshire, Eng.). Born Aug. 7, 1828. Came to Utah in 1866.
Married Ann Selina Earney in Nov. 1867, Salt Lake City (daughter of Arthur Earney and Harriett Hodges, of Hale, Hampshire; pioneers 1866, William Henry Chipman company). She was born Jan. 11, 1841. Their children: Frank E., m. Jane Todd; Mary Ena, m. James Loyn; Edwin Arthur, m. Alta Mae Chugg. Family home, Salt Lake City.
High priest; bishop's counselor; block teacher. School trustee. Blacksmith and wheelwright. Died May 8, 1896, Salt Lake City.

PUZEY, EDWIN ARTHUR (son of Henry Puzey and Ann Selina Earney). Born Sept. 12, 1878, Salt Lake City.
Married Alta Mae Chugg June 2, 1909, Salt Lake City (daughter of John Chugg and Catherine Jones of Salt Lake City), who was born Feb. 12, 1886. Their child: Alta Catherine b. May 30, 1910. Family home, Salt Lake City.
Deacon. Draftsman Oregon Short Line R. R.

PYPER, JOHN (son of Alexander Pyper of Fife, born in 1784, and Catherine Munro, born in 1796, of Ross, Scotland). He was born June 17, 1820, Kilmuir, Ross, Scotland. Came to Utah Oct. 15, 1849, Allen Taylor company.
Married Madaline Gardner April 24, 1846 (daughter of James Gardner and Mary Noble, pioneers Oct. 15, 1849, Allen Taylor company). She was born Oct. 12, 1830. Their children: James Monroe b. July 14, 1847, m. Mary Anna Barton Dec. 22, 1865; m. Nancy J. Caldwell June 29, 1879; Alexander G. b. March 15, 1849, m. Harriet A. Grace; Mary Madaline b. Feb. 23, 1851; John, Jr. b. March 24, 1853; William b. July 17, 1855; Catherine Agnes b. July 14, 1857; Robert b. May 19, 1859, m. Martha Ann Jones Jan. 1, 1885; Madaline Chapman b. April 2, 1861, m. Mark Bigler Dec. 18, 1879; Joseph b. April 18, 1863; Margaret Ellen b. April 24, 1865; George Edward b. March 18, 1867; Edward Noble b. Jan. 6, 1869, m. Ellen Frances Goldborough June 19, 1889; Charles John b. Feb. 16, 1871, m. Clara J. Gunderson July 25, 1899; Arthur Liddell b. May 24, 1873.
Missionary to Scotland 1871; high priest. County recorder 1873-81.

PYPER, JAMES MUNRO (son of John Pyper and Madaline Gardner). Born July 14, 1847, St. Louis, Mo.
Married Mary Anna Barton Dec. 22, 1866, Salt Lake City (daughter of Thomas Barton and Martha Skinner), who was born Aug. 16, 1848, Dover, Kent, Eng. Their children: Mary Alice b. Sept. 21, 1867; Rose Ellen b. Jan. 1, 1870; John Barton b. May 7, 1872; Sarah Elizabeth Johnson Feb. 20, 1895; Clara Ann b. April 14, 1875, m. Heber Peter Johnson Dec. 14, 1892; James Thomas b. April 2, 1877, m. Clarissa Van Wagener Feb. 1900.
Married Nancy Jane Caldwell June 29, 1879, Nephi, Utah (daughter of Matthew Caldwell, pioneer 1846, and Nancy Butler). She was born Dec. 14, 1855, Spanish Fork, Utah. Their children: George C. b. May 31 1880, m. Sarah E. Giles June 12, 1901; Charles M. b. April 25, 1882; Alex L. b. March 3, 1885, m. Anne E. Thomason Dec. 2, 1908; William W. b. Aug. 20, 1888; Jennie M. b. April 20, 1891; Matthew C. b. Feb. 24, 1893; Donald M. b. Feb. 18, 1895; Arthur G. b. July 6, 1897; Walter S. b. July 14, 1899. Family resided Fairview and Taylorville, Canada, and Nephi, Utah.
Elder.

PYPER, CHAS. JOHN (son of John Pyper and Madaline Gardner). Born Feb. 16, 1871, Nephi, Utah.
Married Clara J. Gunderson July 25, 1899, Santaquin, Utah (daughter of Mathias Gunderson and Marie Cristson).

Q

QUAYLE, JAMES (son of Robert Quayle, born in 1804, at Kirkmichael, Isle of Man, and Catharine Shimmon, of Isle of Man). Born July 16, 1831, at Kirkmichael. Came to Utah Oct. 14, 1853, Cyrus H. Wheelock company.
Married Elizabeth Saxton Gillions (daughter of William Gillions, who died May 17, 1854, Quarantine Island, and Elizabeth Saxton, who died on the plains). She was born Feb. 23, 1830, and came to Utah Oct. 24, 1854, William A. Empey company. Their children: James William b. June 5, 1856, m. Adelia Bird; m. Gundheil Rurd; John b. Jan. 8, 1858, m. Emma H. Thorp; Christian b. Jan. 24, 1860; Philip b. June 29, 1861, m. Almeda Hymas; m. Mary Ellen Thornton.
Married Margaret Hodson Clegg, Logan, Utah, who was born in England and came to Utah Sept. 25, 1863, Peter Nebeker company.
Married Sarah Ann Bull in March 1867, at Logan (daughter of Lovell Bull, pioneer Nov. 2, 1864, Warren S. Snow company).
Married Betty Larsen May 1, 1893, at Logan.
Vice-president Logan temple 15 years. Mayor of Logan City. Vice-president First National bank, Logan. Master mechanic.

QUAYLE, PHILIP (son of James Quayle and Elizabeth Saxton Gillions). Born June 29, 1861, Logan, Utah.
Married Almeda Hymas Jan. 27, 1897, Logan (daughter of Benjamin Hymas and Hannah Thurston), who was born Nov. 7, 1873, Hyde Park, Utah, and died July 6, 1902.

Married Mary Ellen Thornton Jan. 10, 1906, Logan (daughter of James Thornton and Elizabeth Fowler), who was born Oct. 23, 1875, Clayton-le-Moors, Lancastershire, Eng. Their children: Doris Almeda b. Nov. 2, 1907; Mona Elizabeth b. Jan. 19, 1908; Philip Douglass b. June 30, 1910; Melba b. April 26, 1912. Family home Perry, Box Elder Co., Utah.
Bishop of Treasureton ward four years; missionary to England 1898-1901; member high council of Box Elder stake. Farmer and fruitgrower.

QUAYLE, JOHN (son of John Quayle and Ann Cowley). Born June 24, 1801, Ramsa, Isle of Man. Came to Utah in September, 1847, John Taylor company.
Married Catherine Killip (daughter of Thomas and Eleanor Killip), who was born in 1813, and died Nov. 6, 1850. Their children: John, Jr. b. 1833, killed 1853, by Indians; Thomas b. March 1835, m. Sarah Partington; Catherine b. 1837, m. John Carson; William b. 1839, m. Jane Cook; Joseph R. b. 1841; Charles b. 1842; Eleanor b. 1843; James b. 1844; Maria b. 1845; Henry b. 1846; Mary Ann b. 1848, latter seven died. Sarah b. 1849 (d. Jan. 5, 1892), m. John Cook. Family home, Salt Lake City. Died Jan. 5, 1892.

QUAYLE, THOMAS (son of John Quayle and Catherine Killip). Born in 1835, Isle of Man. Came to Utah with father.
Married Sarah Partington, Salt Lake City (daughter of Ralph Partington and Ann Taylor, pioneers 1853). She was born Dec. 17, 1840, Preston, Lancastershire, Eng. Their children: Catherine Elia b. Jan. 13, 1859, m. Waldemar Van Cott; Henry b. Sept. 28, 1860, m. Frances Free; John R. b. Sept. 28, 1862, d. Jan. 15, 1868; Ida b. Sept. 24, 1864, m. Oscar Van Cott; Ernest b. Nov. 1866, m. Julie A. Young; Byron b. Feb. 7, 1870 (d. July 20, 1899), m. Persis G. Young; Willard b. May 16, 1872, d. Dec. 13, 1882; Laurence b. July 28, 1874, m. Persis Young; Charles b. July 18, 1876, m. Coral Senior; Bert Leroy b. Nov. 15, 1878, m. Eleanor Quayle; Thomas Ray b. April 17, 1881 (d. May 28, 1913), m. Hazel Osborn; Mortimer b. Jan. 11, 1886 (d. Oct. 21, 1910), m. Mary Fish.
Freighter from Utah to West 1858-60, between Utah and Missouri river 1866-67. Rancher in Utah county 1855-67; farmer 1870-90. Owner real estate Salt Lake City and Oakland, Cal. Capitalist.

R

RADDATZ, E. J. (son of Otto C. Raddatz and Wilhelmine Lange of Wentzville, Mo.). Born Oct. 5, 1857, Stettin, Germany. Came to Utah in 1887.
Married Emma Guth June 4, 1890, St. Louis, Mo. (daughter of Joseph and Elizabeth Guth of St. Louis). She was born Sept. 14, 1865. Their children: Pearl; Flora; Eunice; Harold: Lucille. Family home, Salt Lake City.
Mayor of Stockton, Utah; state representative from Tooele county, 1906. Miningman; president and treasurer of the Tintic Standard Mining Co.

RADMALL, HENRY B. (son of William John Radmall and Ann Butler both of Nottinghamshire, Eng.). Born Oct. 23, 1814, at Nottinghamshire, Eng.; came to Utah 1853, with independent company.
Married Caistine Severn 1844 in England (daughter of James Severn and [Miss] McDermot), who was born Sept. 28, 1825. Their children: Elizabeth Ann, m. Nathan Hunting; Samuel Daniel, m. Emma M. White, m. Caroline Levan, m. Annie Catherine Anderson; Alma, m. (Miss) Larson; Henry James, m. Annie Richards; Joseph A., m. Victoria Anderson; Zera D.; Mary Jane, m. Thomas Ainsworth; Caroline W., m. George Woodtread.
Bishop. Donated land for Pleasant Grove Park to the city. Farmer and stockraiser.

RADMALL, SAMUEL DANIEL (son of Henry B. Radmall and Ann Butler). Born July 21, 1852, at St. Louis, Mo.; came to Utah 1853, with independent company.
Married Emma M. White May 15, 1876, at Salt Lake City (daughter of Roswell White and Myrah Leader—pioneers 1860, the Handcart company). She was born March 3, 1858. Their children: Samuel Henry b. March 24, 1877, m. Forman Hodback; Eroswas B. b. Aug. 4, 1881, m. Ida Bennett; James Servin b. Sept. 1, 1883, m. Annie Damer; Caroline Myrah b. Aug. 19, 1888, m. Albert Williams. Family home Pleasant Grove, Utah.
Married Annie (Barrett) Anderson (daughter of Hans C. Anderson and Myria Overtson, both of Fountain Green, Utah). She was born July 15, 1874. Their children: Elhaline b. April 9, 1894, m. Sterling Vickers; George Clifford b. Feb. 16, 1896; Joseph Samuel b. Feb. 16, 1896; Elva M. b. June 25, 1902; Claude Marvel b. Feb. 19, 1904; Zera D. b. June 2, 1908. Family home Pleasant Grove, Utah.
Counselor elders quorum. Pioneer of Pleasant Grove 1862. Farmer. School teacher. Horticulturist.

RAINEY, DAVID PINKNEY (son of David and Nancy Rainey of Tennessee). Born Feb. 1, 1815, in Tennessee. Came to Utah in 1856 with a detachment of Mormon battalion, first corporal, Co. B.
Married Dorothy Jane Dennis Feb. 9, 1857 (daughter of William Taylor Dennis and Tabitha Bankhead, pioneers 1855, Gilbert I. Gavin company). She was born June 16, 1840, and came to Utah with parents. Their children: David William b. Jan. 6, 1858, m. Mary Maria Olsen March 24, 1880; Margaret M. b. Sept. 15, 1869, m. W. S. Hendricks; Joseph P. b. Sept. 19, 1861, d. child; Mary E. b. Aug. 25, 1863, m. William E. Fisher; George W. b. Oct. 2, 1865, m. Emma Robinson; James A. b. Feb. 2, 1867, m. Mamie Merrill; Frederick H. b. Oct. 29, 1868, m. Maud Tibbetts; Emma C. b. Aug. 9, 1870, m. J. P. Griffin; Tabitha D. b. Sept. 18, 1873, m. Fred Kearns; Chloe E. b. Dec. 7, 1875, m. William Harrison; Jennie B. b. June 23, 1879, m. John Campbell; Inez L. b. Jan. 26, 1882, m. Albert Jenkins. Family home Richmond, Utah.
Bishop of Salem (Pondtown); missionary to California and southern states. Died Nov. 6, 1888.

RAINEY, DAVID WILLIAM (son of David P. Rainey and Dorothy Jane Dennis). Born Jan. 6, 1858, Provo, Utah.
Married Mary Maria Olsen March 24, 1880, Richmond, Utah (daughter of Christopher M. Olsen and Caroline C. Johnason), who was born April 26, 1859, South Weber, Utah. Their children: Florence May b. May 8, 1881, m. Lionel Farrell May 8, 1896; Iva I. b. Feb. 22, 1884, m. Wilford F. Burton Dec. 22, 1910; Claudine b. Aug. 9, 1886; David W., Jr. b. July 4, 1888; Ruby M. b. April 14, 1891; Christie J. b. Nov. 18, 1893; Lucile b. March 6, 1896; Josephine b. Jan. 26, 1899; Ralph b. Aug. 11, 1902.

RALPHS, THOMAS (son of Benjamin and Mary Ralphs). Born July 22, 1819, Shropshire, Eng. Came to Utah in 1849.
Married Sarah Johnson May 10, 1842, in Missouri (daughter of Joseph and Margaret Johnson), who was born Feb. 3, 1821, in Ireland, and died April 14, 1896, Brigham City, Utah. Among their children were: Ephraim; Mary Frances. Family home Brigham City, Utah.
Settled at Brigham City 1855. Died June 11, 1859.

RALPHS, WILLIAM B. (son of Benjamin and Mary Ralphs of Shropshire, Eng.). Born May 6, 1816, Shropshire, Eng. Came to Utah with oxteam.
Married Elizabeth Brooks of Staffordshire, Eng., May 10, 1841, who was born March 30, 1819. Their children: Mary Elizabeth b. Oct. 22, 1842, m. William Hunter; Sarah b. May 12, 1845, d. child; William b. June 6, 1847, d. child; Joseph b. July 10, 1849, m. Amanda Jensen; Thomas B. b. Nov. 9, 1851, d. child; Emily b. March 23, 1855, m. Mark Tanner; Parley P. b. July 25, 1858, m. Hannah Hansen; John Heber b. March 24, 1860, m. Ede Hansen. Family resided Nauvoo and Burlington, Ill., and Salt Lake City and South Cottonwood, Utah.
Married Mary Ann Johnson, at American Fork, Utah, who was born Oct. 17, 1870. Their child: William Benjamin b. May 17, 1872. Family home American Fork.
Seventy. Enlisted and served in Echo Canyon trouble. Shoemaker. Died April 29, 1900, American Fork.

RALPHS, JOSEPH (son of William Ralphs and Elizabeth Brooks). Born July 10, 1849, Burglington, Ill. Came to Utah with father.
Married Ann Cable, at American Fork (daughter of William Cable of Pleasant Grove, pioneer oxteam company). Their children: Mary, m. David Meldrum; Baby, d. infant. Family home American Fork.
Married Amanda Jensen, at Manti, Utah (daughter of Christian and Albertina Jensen of Manti, Utah). Family home Ferron, Utah.
Priest. Farmer.

RANDALL, ALFRED (son of Jason Randall and Martha Thompson). Born June 13, 1811, Bridgewater, N. Y. Came to Utah in 1848.
Married Emerette Davis Jan. 8, 1834. Their children: Charles Franklin b. Feb. 8, 1835, m. Ellen Jane Duncan; Sarah L., died; Alfred Jason b. Jan. 8, 1845, m. Ruth Campkins; Emerette J., Levi L., Alizon R., Davis R., and Charlotte A., latter five died; Martha J. m. Edward S. Luty.
Married Margaret Harley Jan. 31, 1848. Their children: Orrin H.; Melvin H.; Mary E.; Margaret Ellen b. March 31, 1858, m. James Hyrum Baird; Thurza A.; Alice; Emily.
Married Mildred E. Dickinson May 30, 1860. Their children: Francis; Eli B.
Married Hannah S. Severn March 7, 1863. Their children: James E.; Ann S.; David E.; Heber J.; George E.; Lucy S.; Samuel; Esther.
Married Elsie Anderson May 13, 1865. Their children: Jared A.; Isaac L.; Joseph H.
Missionary to Sandwich islands twice. Carpenter and farmer. Died March 19, 1891, North Ogden, Utah.

RANDALL, CHARLES FRANKLIN (son of Alfred Randall and Emerette Davis). Born Feb. 8, 1835, Munson, Ohio. Came to Utah with parents.
Married Ellen Jane Duncan Jan. 14, 1857 (daughter of Chapman Duncan), who was born Jan. 10, 1840, Lee Co., Iowa, and died Nov. 4, 1876, Ogden, Utah. Their children: Sarah P., m. William H. Brereton; Charles C., m. Harriet Woodhead; Ellen E., m. Robert E. Fisher; John A., m. Esther Smout; Rebecca, died; Franklin A., m. Rosebell Bronson; Harvey P., m. Minnie I. Horrocks; Homer A., m. Annie Westergard; Otis A., and Orval A., latter two died.
Married Sarah Ann Smith Nov. 13, 1878, Ogden, Utah, who was born Dec. 31, 1856, Leicester, Eng. Their children: William J.; Joseph B.; Edward S.; Robert E.; Clarence D.; Rhoda E.; Cora M.; Lester S.
Died June 27, 1904.

RANDALL, JOHN A. (son of Charles Franklin Randall and Ellen Jane Duncan). Born April 10, 1864, Virgin, Utah.
Married Esther Smout May 7, 1891 (daughter of Edwin W. Smout and Leah Oakley), who was born April 12, 1862, Ogden, Utah. Their children: J. William b. Sept. 23, 1892; E. Laura b. March 21, 1894; Ellen J. b. Jan. 23, 1896; Edwin C. b. Aug. 7, 1900. Family home Ogden, Utah.

RANDALL, HARVEY P. (son of Charles Franklin Randall and Ellen Jane Duncan). Born Oct. 22, 1870, Harrisville, Utah.
Married Minnie I. Horrocks March 15, 1906, Ogden, Utah (daughter of Edward Gregory Horrocks and Ida Johnson), who was born Oct. 5, 1879, Ogden. Their children: Myrtle I. b. Dec. 30, 1906; Viola I. b. Jan. 29, 1908; Estella M. b. May 13, 1910; Tressie L. b. Sept. 8, 1911. Family home Ogden.
City councilman two terms 1902-05; member state legislature 1907-10. Lumber and coal dealer.

RANDALL, ALFRED JASON (son of Alfred Randall and Emerette Davis). Born Jan. 8, 1845, Nauvoo, Ill. Came to Utah with parents.
Married Ruth Campkins, at St. Louis, Mo. Their children: Annie E.; Alfred B.; Emeretta; Walter; Frank; Burt; Harry; Howard.
Missionary to Sandwich islands. Settled at Salt Lake City 1848. Carpenter and farmer. Died Sept. 26, 1907.

RANDALL, LEVI L. (son of Alfred Randall and Emerette Davis). Born Nov. 18, 1860, Salt Lake City.
Married Emma Burton Jan. 14, 1879 (daughter of William and Elizabeth Burton of Mansfield, Eng.). Their children: Nora L.; Edward L.; Verna L.; Hazel L. Family home Ogden, Utah.
Died Nov. 10, 1893.

RANDALL, JOSEPH HENRY. Born March 17, 1822. Came to Utah in 1853.
Married Anne Burdette, who was born Dec. 9, 1825, and died Feb. 11, 1878. She was a widow and had one child by former husband, viz.: Oscar Isaac b. June 15, 1854 (d. Feb. 11, 1878), m. Annie C. Reed Jan. 1876. Their children: Annie Burdett b. Dec. 1, 1857, m. Joseph W. Carpenter Feb. 4, 1875; Clara Jane b. Feb. 23, 1859 (d. 1882), m. Haden Wells Church Jan. 11, 1875; Joseph H. b. May 23, 1860, m. Rebecca Ann Lewis; John William b. June 24, 1867. Family resided St. George and Spanish Fork, Utah.
Missionary to "Dixie" 1874. Went to meet first handcart company that came to Utah. Policeman at Spanish Fork nine years. Minuteman Black Hawk war. Worked in stone quarry at St. George. Janitor St. George temple 1878-1909. Died March 1, 1909, St. George.

RANDS, JOSEPH (son of Isaac Rands and Sarah Short of Suffolk, Eng.). Born Aug. 27, 1827, Hampstead, Eng., moved to Cape Town, South Africa, 1843. Came to Utah October, 1868, John Gillespie company.
Married Sarah Anderson 1847 in England (daughter of William Anderson and Ann Cowley of Middlesex, Eng.). She was born April 12, 1829. Their children: Sarah Rodia, m. John Leigh; Joseph William, m. Louise Sadler; Lydia Jane, m. Barney Weyland; Hyrum, m. Sarah Winters; Jessie Lovina, m. James Maxwell; Elizabeth, m. Hyrum Larsen. Family home, Salt Lake City.
18th gardener for President Brigham Young. Died Oct. 11, 1890.

RANDS, HYRUM (son of Joseph Rands and Sarah Anderson). Born July 1, —, Cape Town, South Africa.
Married Sarah Winters, at Salt Lake City (daughter of Bishop and Myra Winters).

RAPPYLEYE, TUNIS (son of John R. Rappleye and Margaret Tillie of New Jersey). Came to Utah July 24, 1847, Brigham Young company.
Married Louisa Cutler at Kirtland, Ohio (daughter of John Alphens Cutler and Lois Lathrop of New York). Their children: Emily Jane b. Dec. 21, 1836, died; John Olpheus b. Aug. 22, 1838, died; Lauraette b. March 23, 1840, m. George Staples; Clarissa b. March 23, 1842, m. John Lott; Ammon L. b. Sept. 23, 1844, m. Sophia Larson; David F. M. b. June 22, 1849, m. Laura A. Morris; Harriet F. M. b. June 22, 1849, died; Ezra Tunes, m. Jane Black; Edwin R., m. Alice Black. Family resided in Ray county, Mo., and in Illinois.
Missionary to eastern states. Assisted in bringing immigrants to Utah. Veteran Indian war. Farmer.

RASBAND, THOMAS (son of John and Mary Rasband of Lincoln, Eng.). Born Dec. 21, 1818, Hinckley, Warwickshire, Eng. Came to Utah August, 1856.
Married Elizabeth Giles Jan. 25, 1847, Lincoln, Eng.

1120 PIONEERS AND PROMINENT MEN OF UTAH

(daughter of William Giles and Sarah Hutchinson, pioneers Aug. 1856). She was born April 11, 1826. Their children: John, died in England; Emily b. June 30, 1849, m. Orson Hicken Jan. 1, 1869; William Giles b. Dec. 24, 1852, m. Maria Ann Carlisle Nov. 29, 1877; Frederick B. Sept. 2, 1856, m. Mary Elizabeth Hawkins Sept. 28, 1879; Thomas Heber b. Jan. 15, 1859, m. Sarah Jane Murdock Nov. 28, 1879; George Westey, d. infant; James Franklin b. Aug. 6, 1862, m. Josephine Booth Feb. 18, 1888; Joseph A. b. March 17, 1867, m. Eliza Jeffs Dec. 3, 1890; Charles b. July 21, 1870, m. Emily Esther Hawkins May 27, 1891. Family home Heber City, Utah.
Ordained bishop of Heber east ward July 18, 1877, and remained until his death. Veteran Black Hawk Indian war. Died July 24, 1884, Heber, Utah.

RASBAND, WILLIAM GILES (son of Thomas Rasband and Elizabeth Giles). Born Dec. 24, 1852, Quincy, Ill. Came to Utah August, 1856.
Married Maria Ann Carlisle Nov. 29, 1872, Salt Lake City (daughter of George Carlisle and Laura Ann Giles of Heber City, Utah). She was born June 3, 1858. Their children: William Franklin, m. Sarah Ellen White; Elizabeth Ann b. July 9, 1881, m. Henry Baird; Mary Levina b. Oct. 5, 1883, m. Vernon Wickham; George Thomas b. May 31, 1886, m. Catharine Hicken; Edwin Giles b. June 24, 1889; Viva Blanche b. Aug. 4, 1893; Don Alfred b. July 30, 1887; Muriel b. Jan. 16, 1900, d. infant; Ida b. Feb. 18, 1902.
Member 20th quorum seventies; high priest. Farmer.

RASBAND, FREDERICK (son of Thomas Rasband and Elizabeth Giles). Born Sept. 2, 1856, Provo, Utah.
Married Mary Elizabeth Hawkins Sept. 29, 1882, Salt Lake City (daughter of John Bemet Hawkins and Sarah Moulton, latter pioneer, Martin S. Lyles handcart company). Their children: Sarah Elizabeth b. May 4, 1885, m. Earl J. Slade Sept. 11, 1907; Ethel May b. Jan. 31, 1890, m. William J. Lewis Oct. 26, 1910; Della b. May 10, 1895. Family resided Heber and Park City, Utah.
First bishop Park City ward; ordained Aug. 18, 1901, serving until Nov. 1, 1909, when he moved to Provo. State senator 1904; member state legislature from 5th district, comprising Summit and Wasatch counties, two terms.

RASMUSSEN, ANDREW (son of Rasmus and Moren of Sjaelland, Denmark). Born Jan. 22, 1834. Came to Utah in 1860, Wideborg company.
Married Severna Maria Madsen Oct. 12, 1862, West Jordan, Utah. Bishop Gardner officiating (daughter of Mads Sorensen and Johanna Jensen of Linderum Hjorring, Denmark, pioneers 1862, Christian Augusta Madsen and John Van Cott company). She was born Aug. 21, 1836. Their children: Andrew, m. Sarah Barnes; Amasa, m. Sarah Elizabeth Stewart; Nephi, m. Annie Elizabeth Lawhorn; Jacob, m. Sarah Rebecca Howell; Mary Johanna, m. Elias Adolphus Terry and Otis Lysander Terry. Family home Fairview, Utah.
Senior president 26th quorum seventies; missionary to Denmark 1856-60. Farmer. Died February, 1903.

RASMUSSEN, JENS (son of Rasmus Hansen and Magdalene Larsen of Vallöby, Denmark). Born Jan. 31, 1815. Came to Utah Sept. 12, 1863, John R. Young company.
Married Bendta Nielsen Nov. 20, 1846, at Vallöby (daughter of Lars Nielsen and Mary Larsen of Monge, Denmark, former a pioneer Sept. 12, 1863, John R. Young company, latter died in Denmark). Their children: Rasmus, died; Mada, m. Mary C. Jorgenson; Sena, died; Laurine, m. Harold Liljenquist. Family home Hyrum, Utah.
Elder; high priest. Farmer. Died Feb. 18, 1902.

RASMUSSEN, JORGAN (son of Rasmus Jensen and Boal Jensen, both born at Borgense Fen, Ellesborro Fen, Denmark). He was born Feb. 26, 1814, at Ellesborro. Came to Utah Oct. 2, 1864, John Smith company.
Married Hansena M. Hansen December, 1847 (daughter of Lars Peter Hansen and Anna Elizabeth Hansen), who was born May 9, 1817. Their children: Julius N. and Petria B., d. infants; Dorcas Julia b. Aug. 5, 1857, m. Thomas Dyer Nov. 1877; William E. b. April 12, 1859, m. Trena Jensen Feb. 17, 1885. Family resided Council Bluffs, Iowa; Omaha, Neb.; Ogden and Butler, Utah.

RASMUSSEN, WILLIAM E. (son of Jorgan Rasmussen and Hansena Maria Hansen). Born April 12, 1859, Omaha, Neb.
Married Trena Jensen Feb. 17, 1885, Holiday, Salt Lake Co., Utah (daughter of Soren P. Jensen and Jensena M. Jensen), who was born March 17, 1868, in Denmark. Their children: W. Edward b. Sept. 8, 1886; J. Frank b. March 19, 1888; Albert l. b. Oct. 22, 1889, d. infant; H. Dellas b. Feb. 27, 1891; Ivan J. b. May 25, 1895; Pearl E. b. Dec. 9, 1898. Family home Butler, Salt Lake Co., Utah.

RASMUSSEN, JORGEN HANSTED (son of Rasmus Anderson and Cecelia Peterson Anderson of Hansted, Denmark). Born April 8, 1837, at Hansted. Came to Utah 1867.
Married Sine M. Mortensen (daughter of Andrew P. Mortensen and Ingerborg Peterson). Their children: Jorgine Cecelia: Anna N.; Jorgen P.; Andrew C.; Amelia I.; Mary E.; Elvena M.

RASMUSSEN, LARSE. Born Dec. 30, 1844, Denmark. Came to Utah 1866, oxteam company.
Married Christane Sorensen Salt Lake City, who was born July 9, 1850. Their children: Mary Lucy, m. Charles A. Winn; Christane, m. Erastus Sorensen; Larse Brady, d. aged 4; Karen Metthea b. June 2, 1875, m. Frank A. Young. Family home Richfield, Utah.
Farmer. Died August, 1873.

RASMUSSEN, MORTEN (son of Rasmus and Maria Rasmussen). Born Oct. 27, 1834, Brendekilde, Fyen, Denmark. Came to Utah Oct. 5, 1854, Hans Peter Olsen company.
Married Karen Marie Christiansen April 1, 1859, Ephraim, Utah (daughter of Christian N. Christiansen and Anne Margaret Jensen, of Assens, Fyen, Denmark, pioneers Sept. 13, 1857, Chr. Christiansen company). She was born July 26, 1842. Their children: Morten, Jr., m. Nicoline Christensen, May 27, 1880; Maria Sophia, m. Lars P. Madsen Oct. 10, 1881; Lars Christian, m. Cecelia Johansen Oct. 9, 1890; John, m. Albertine Christensen Dec. 30, 1884; Mary, died; Anna Margaret, m. Robert Kenner Oct. 15, 1893; Henry, died; Erastus, m. Emma Winkleman Nov. 14, 1893; Daniel, m. Annie Jane Jorgensen July 30, 1902; George, died; Wilford W., m. Matilda Winkelman April 9, 1902; Hyrum, died. Family home Mt. Pleasant, Utah.
Member 66th quorum seventies; missionary to Denmark 1881-83. City councilman at time of death. Farmer. Died June 28, 1885.

RASMUSSEN, DANIEL (son of Morten Rasmussen and Karen Mai Christiansen). Born Feb. 25, 1876, Mt. Pleasant, Utahe
Married Annie Jane Jorgensen July 30, 1902, Manti, Utah (daughter of Jens Jorgensen and Kirsten Bertelsen), who was born April 13, 1867. Their children: D. Irvine b. May 21, 1903; Mary b. Sept. 24, 1905; Lester Paul b. Sept. 19, 1907; James Howard b. Aug. 21, 1909; Esther b. March 25, 1912. Family home Mt. Pleasant, Utah.
President 66th quorum seventies; missionary to New England 1899-1901; bishop Mt. Pleasant North ward 1904-09. City recorder; school teacher and principal. Family resides Cedar City, Utah.

RASMUSSEN, NIELS (son of Henrik Rasmussen and Rebekka Hansen of Maderup Fyen, Denmark). Born May 29, 1846. Came to Utah Oct. 1866, Abner Lowry company. (Nearly half this ill-fated company, including Rasmussen's mother and eldest brother, had died from privations and hardships before they were met, about 400 miles east of Salt Lake City, by a mule relief train of 10 wagons, which had been sent to convey the orphans and survivors. The first detachment of the company arrived Oct. 8, 1866, in charge of Arza E. Hinckley, the main body under Lowry arriving Oct. 22.)
Married Laura A. M. Thorup Sept. 11, 1879, Salt Lake City (daughter of Herman A. Thorup and Mary C. Christensen of Copenhagen, Denmark, pioneers 1869). She was born Feb. 10, 1854. Their children: Niels Moroni b. July 13, 1880, d. aged 4; Alma Emmanuel b. Aug. 1, 1882, m. Agnes M. Peterson; Laura M. R. b. Aug. 19, 1884; Sarah Josephine b. Feb. 25, 1886; Annie Eliza b. Dec. 25, 1888; Rhoda Constance b. Sept. 21, 1890.
Married Christine V. Thorup Nov. 21, 1885, Salt Lake City (daughter of Herman A. Thorup and Mary Christine Christensen of Copenhagen, Denmark, pioneers 1869). She was born Nov. 3, 1868. Their children: Ellen C. b. Nov. 26, 1886, m. George W. Poulson; Clara Veronica b. Dec. 8, 1888, d. aged 20; May Catherine b. May 13, 1891; Esther Olive b. Nov. 25, 1893; David Leroy b. June 26, 1896; Adeline b. Sept. 30, 1899; Florence Geneve b. Dec. 27, 1906.
Missionary to Nebraska 1878-79; high priest; counselor in 1st quorum elders; Sunday school superintendent of 1st ward 15 years; 2d counselor to bishop of 1st ward 12 years; active worker in Y. M. M. I. A. and Sunday school of Liberty stake. Bookkeeper in presiding bishop's office 40 years. Farmer.

RASMUSSEN, PETER (son of Rasmus Miller). Born at Mots, Jutland, Denmark. Came to Utah 1859.
Married Karen Peterson 1859 (daughter of Sern Peterson and Ane Margritte Peterson, latter pioneer 1860). Their child: Joseph Solon b. May 7, 1869; Anna.
Settled in Morgan county, moved to Bear Lake, Idaho, then to Uinta Co., Utah.

RASMUSSEN, JOSEPH SOLON (son of Peter Rasmussen and Karen Peterson). Born May 7, 1869, Farmington, Utah.
Married Susie Hughes June 18, 1892, Morgan City, Utah (daughter of George Hughes and Anna Elizabeth Welch, both died at Salem, Ohio). She was born Feb. 28, 1867, in Franklin county, Pa. Their children: Eva; Nancy; Thelma; George J.; Gilbert H.
Seventy; first counselor Y. M. M. I. A.

RASMUSSEN, SOREN. Born July 12, 1818, in Denmark. Came to Utah in 1862, George Stringhaus company.
Married Anne Hogensen in Denmark, who was born May 15, 1813. Their children: Rasmus, m. Mrs. Sophia Smith Nielson; Susanna m. Orson Pulsipher; Emma, m. Martin F. Martinson; Soren, died; Soren H.; Drighamina,

died; Larsine, m. Richard Loynd. Family home Copenhagen, Denmark, and Utah.
Missionary in Denmark before coming to Utah. Farmer. Died Dec. 16, 1870, Richfield, Utah.

RAVSTEN, BENGT MATHIS (son of Mathis Ravsten, born July 17, 1796, Olstorp, Sweden, and Boel Matson, born 1755, both of Sweden). Born Aug. 29, 1838, Saxtorp, Malmö Län, Sweden. Came to Utah Aug. 6, 1869.
Married Betty Johanson May 9, 1870, Salt Lake City (daughter of Johan Jensen), who was born May 4, 1837, and came to Utah with husband. Their children: John b. Feb. 17, 1871, m. Eliza B. Christensen March 18, 1896; Allen b. March 2, 1873, died; Bennie b. April 8, 1875, m. Clara Christensen Dec. 10, 1902; Frank b. Sept. 14, 1877, m. Josephine Christensen March 6, 1901; Anna Sophia b. Sept. 28, 1879, died. Family resided Logan and Clarkston, Utah.
Missionary to Sweden, where he served as president of Malmö conference 1894-96; presiding elder of Trenton ward four years; president 7th quorum seventies; high priest.

RAVSTEN, JOHN (son of Bengt Mathis Ravsten and Betty Johanson). Born Feb. 17, 1871, Logan, Utah.
Married Eliza B. Christensen March 18, 1896, Logan, Utah (daughter of James Christensen and Trena Benson, who came to Utah 1880). She was born Feb. 9, 1875, died April 23, 1913. Their children: Betty Eliza b. Aug. 23, 1902; Leah b. May 22, 1906; Amy b. June 28, 1907; John Byron b. Aug. 10, 1908; Ida b. Jan. 9, 1910; Ivin Oliver b. June 24, 1911.
Counselor in elders quorum; missionary to northern states 1897-99; president 7th quorum seventies 1900-02; ordained bishop of Clarkston ward Aug. 24, 1902. President Clarkston water works.

RAWLINGS, EBER B. (son of John B. Rawlings and Mariah Hunt of Eydon, Northamptonshire, Eng.). Born June 24, 1826, at Eydon. Came to Utah Oct. 8, 1862, James Wareham company.
Married Ann Skinner Dec. 31, 1850, in England (daughter of John Skinner and Ann Beeby of Daventry, Eng., pioneers 1862). She was born Sept. 13, 1828. Their children: Henry E., m. Sarah A. McLauslin; Zeda Emma, m. E. S. Lund; George P., m. Kate Gatherum; Annie M., m. A. Holman; William S., m. Margaret Gillespie; Kate Estella, m. John T. Pyne; Ernest. Family resided Alton, Ill., and Provo, Utah. President of branch at Alton. Lived at Alton 1850-61.

RAWLINS, JAMES (son of Charles Rawlins, veteran of the Revolutionary war, and Eustacie Gregory, both of Pitt county, N. C.). Born Jan. 6, 1794. Came to Utah 1848, Andrew Cunningham company.
Married Jane Sharp (daughter of James Sharp), who was born March 22, 1794, and came to Utah with husband. Their children: Sarah b. March 3, 1817, died; Lucinda b. March 12, 1819, m. Andrew Cunningham; Elizabeth b. Feb. 27, 1821, died; Joseph Sharp b. April 9, 1823, m. Mary Frost; Harvey McGalyard b. Feb. 14, 1825, m. Margaret Eliza Frost Dec. 3, 1846; Leah b. Sept. 19, 1827, m. Henry Day Dec. 1, 1859, d. Millie Jane b. July 16, 1831, m. David Carson July 31, 1853; Elva A. b. Jan. 6, 1834, m. George Carson July 31, 1853; Charlotte Melvina b. Feb. 9, 1837, m. Jasper Lemons Feb. 1858. Family home Big Cottonwood, Utah.
Married Mrs. Harriet Wheat at Salt Lake City.
Moved from Big Cottonwood to Draper in 1852; to Spring City in 1865; then to Richmond, and from there to Lewiston in 1871. High priest. Farmer.

RAWLINS, HARVEY McGALYARD (son of James Rawlins and Jane Sharp). Born Feb. 14, 1825, in Greene county, Ill.
Married Margaret Elzira Frost Dec. 3, 1846, Fremont Co., Iowa (daughter of McCaslin Frost and Penina Smith, pioneers 1856). She was born April 28, 1830, in Knox county, Tenn. Their children: Margaret Eliza b. April 30, 1848, m. Robert Marion Kerr March 28, 1863; James McCaslin b. July 3, 1850, d. infant; Harvey McGalyard, Jr., b. Dec. 13, 1851, m. Rebecca Lewis Dec. 28, 1877; Samuel Lafayette b. July 17, 1854, m. Sarah E. Van Orden Feb. 16, 1882; Franklin Archibald b. Jan. 22, 1857, m. Leona Leavitt Dec. 18, 1879; Penina Jane b. April 6, 1859, m. James B. Leavitt May 5, 1881; Mary Eslyn b. Nov. 19, 1861, m. Joseph Wire Leavitt May 4, 1882; Joseph William b. March 4, 1864, m. Mary Ann Pope June 24, 1885; Alma Frost b. Oct. 23, 1866, m. Lauretta Huff March 26, 1890; Elva Arminta b. Jan. 14, 1869, m. Goudy A. Hogan Nov. 9, 1892; Jasper Alphonzo b. Feb. 1, 1872, m. Cora May Burbank March 5, 1902; Nancy Ellen b. Aug. 1, 1874, m. Edwin Murray Stocks Dec. 4, 1894.
High priest. Farmer.

RAWLINS, HARVEY McGALYARD (son of Harvey M. Rawlins and Margaret Elzira Frost). Born Dec. 13, 1851, Big Cottonwood, Utah.
Married Rebecca Lewis Dec. 28, 1877 (daughter of William Hendricks Lewis and Martha N. Petty—married 1856 Fort Herriman, Utah, former a pioneer 1851, latter Oct. 14, 1850, Wilford Woodruff company). She was born Nov. 1, 1859, Richmond, Utah. Their children: William Harvey b. Oct. 13, 1878; Lina Dean b. Sept. 9, 1882, d. May 21, 1888; Clement Lewis b. Aug. 12, 1885, m. Gertrude O. Smith June 28, 1911; Fern b. May 20, 1889; Lorenzo Kimball

b. Sept. 4, 1896, d. June 2, 1898; Elmina b. July 12, 1899, d. April 19, 1903. Family home Lewiston, Utah.
Married Louisa Waddoups June 5, 1884, Logan, Utah (daughter of William Waddoups and Martha Page—married Nov. 27, 1864, Bountiful Utah, former a pioneer Oct. 13, 1863, Rosel Hyde company, latter 1862, Captain Thorne company). She was born Aug. 13, 1865, Bountiful, Utah. Their children: Burnes b. June 12, 1887, d. April 20, 1903; Ila Rene b. March 16, 1892; Alvira b. March 1, 1902. Family home, Lewiston.
Moved from Big Cottonwood to Draper, then to Spring City and to Richmond, finally settling at Lewiston. Home missionary; second counselor Y. M. M. I. A. of Lewiston ward 1877-80; president of same 1880-84; one of presidents of 39th quorum seventies; missionary to Indian Territory 1891-95; superintendent religion class Lewiston ward 1895-1901, and Benson stake 1902-08; high priest; member high council of Benson stake. Constable of Lewiston precinct 1879-83; school trustee; member town board 1904-06.

RAWLINS, FRANKLIN ARCHIBALD (son of Harvey M. Rawlins and Margaret Elzira Frost). Born Jan. 22, 1857, Draper, Utah.
Married Leona Leavitt Dec. 18, 1879 (daughter of George Leavitt and Janette Brinkerhoff, pioneers 1847, former Jedediah M. Grant company, latter Ira Eldredge company). She was born Sep. 25, 1860, Centerville, Utah. Their children: George F. b. Dec. 4, 1880, m. Nellie D. Lambert June 17, 1908; Elzira J. b. July 13, 1882; James b. Feb. 23, 1884, died; Alpheus L. b. Feb. 10, 1886, m. Mabel Lloyd Dec. 23, 1908; Merle L. b. Nov. 22, 1887; William b. Feb. 23, 1889, and Roy b. Aug. 25, 1891, died; Edith b. Feb. 19, 1893; Zeddie b. March 28, 1895, died; Reuel L. b. Sept. 22, 1896; Aurili b. Aug. 7, 1903, died. Family home Lewiston, Utah.
High priest; counselor to Bishop William Waddoups; member high council of Benson stake. Farmer and dairyman.

RAWSON, HORACE STRONG (son of Daniel Rawson and Polly Strong of New York). Born July 15, 1799, Oneida county, N. Y. Came to Utah Oct. 16, 1850, Wilford Woodruff company.
Married Elizabeth Coffin Oct. 9, 1825, who was born in 1807. Their children: Mary Ann Olive b. Oct. 8, 1826, m. John Garner; Daniel Berry b. Dec. 16, 1827, m. Nancy Boss; Samantha Priscilla b. April 26, 1830, m. Charles Hancock; William Coffin b. Jan. 13, 1832, m. Eliza Jane Cheney; Oriah b. March 15, 1834, d. young; Sariah b. March 15, 1834, m. James Owens; Chloe Ann b. Aug. 15, 1836, m. C. B. Hancock; Caleb Linsey b. March 5, 1839, d. young; Arthur Morrison b. June 17, 1840, m. Margret Pace; Sariah Urinda b. Feb. 8, 1844, m. Orvil R. Child; Cyrus b. June 15, 1846, m. Mary Dixon; Horace Franklin b. Oct. 9, 1848, m. Malinda Hancock; Elizabeth b. Aug. 21, 1853, m. Myron Butler. Family home Ogden, Utah.
Member high council of Weber stake. Weber county selectman; member Ogden city council; justice of peace 7 years. Died Oct. 10, 1882.

RAWSON, WILLIAM COFFIN (son of Horace Strong Rawson and Elizabeth Coffin). Born Jan. 13, 1832, in Randolph county, Ind. Came to Utah with father.
Married Eliza Jane Cheney Oct. 12, 1856, Farmington, Utah (daughter of Nathan Cheney and Eliza Ann Rohe of Kirtland, Ohio, Missouri, Illinois and Davis Co., Utah, pioneers Oct. 6, 1850, William Snow company). She was born Aug. 29, 1837. Their children: Eliza Jane, m. Aaron Jackson Jan. 26, 1877; William Franklin, m. Mary Alice Wilson; Olive Ann, m. William N. McEntyre; Zenia Venetie, m. Joseph Chugg; Sarah Emily, m. John Prichett; Nathan Cheney, m. Minnie Allred; Elizabeth Rebecca, m. Elsberry Garlic.
Member 40th quorum seventies; missionary 1875; Sunday school superintendent; ward teacher; bishop's counselor. Worked for George A. Lowe company. Materially aided in building roads and canals and otherwise improving the adjacent country. Died April 26, 1891, Far West, Weber Co., Utah.

RAY, JOHN ALEXANDER (son of John Ray, born at Shelby, Miss., and Elizabeth Nuttall). Born in Mississippi 1817. Came to Utah Sept. 4, 1853, Moses Dailey company.
Married Mary Wingo Young 1841 in North Carolina (daughter of William Calvin Young, and General Miller Warr, and Mary Hayes, pioneers Whitmore McIntire, Johnson and McCullah company). She was born in North Carolina in 1820 and died April 20, 1890. Their children: Ellen Barton, m. John Vickers; Martha Jane, m. Sims Matheny; Hester, m. W. W. Dameron; Mary Virginia, m. Orson Holbrook; William Alexander, m. Minerva Hinckley; Joseph Edward, m. Mary Emily Warner; Alice Jerome, m. Nephi Pratt; Melissa Hayes, m. W. S. Smith; John A., died; Eleanor, m. Alonzo Huntsman; Ann Wingo, died. Family home Fillmore, Utah.
Settled at Fillmore, Utah, early in 1854. First government Indian agent in that section, receiving his appointment 1858; also first probate judge; member territorial legislature. Missionary to England, where he was associate editor of the "Millennial Star"; president Millard stake 4 years. Merchant; farmer. Died July 4, 1862.

RAY, JOSEPH EDWARD (son of John Alexander Ray and Mary Wingo Young). Born Jan. 7, 1851, Waike, Madison Co., Texas. Came to Utah with father.
Married Mary Emily Warner Dec. 25, 1870, Fillmore,

Utah (daughter of Orange Warner and Mary E. Tyler, pioneers October, 1851, with Shurtliff part of the way, the remainder alone). She was born July 13, 1852. Their children: Ruby b Aug. 5, 1872, m. Albert W. Davis; Raymond E. b. Dec. 26, 1874, m. Ruby Collister; Clinton Dewitt b. Oct. 22, 1876, m. Sarah Jessie Whitaker; Claude Calvin b. Nov. 10, 1878; Josephine b. June 14, 1884, m. S. A. Greenwood; William Alonzo b. Dec. 25, 1886; John A. b. June 21, 1891, died. Family home Fillmore, Utah.

John A. Ray and family arrived in Fillmore, Utah, in the spring of 1854, where they found about 20 families who had built a mud wall 10 feet high around 50 acres of ground for the protection of their families against Indians. These Indians were known at that time as the Walker band. After the death of Walker, however, the notorious Black Hawk dominated the tribes for many years. These Indians were very numerous and committed many depredations, stealing stock and killing many people. John A. Ray was the first Indian agent in this part of the country, getting his appointment in 1858. This gave his son, Joseph E. Ray, a splendid opportunity to learn the ways of the red man. He became at a very early date an expert with the bow and arrow and sported with them in all their pastimes; in fact, almost lived with them until he was 15 years of age. He developed into a splendid shot and a good horseman; in fact, was as wild as the Indians themselves. Later he joined the state militia and continued in the service for four years and until honorably discharged.

During these early days the white boys and Indian papooses had many battles, using slings for weapons. That with his early experience with the bow and arrow, associated with a natural inclination to the use of firearms, was responsible for the fact that he developed into an expert shot, and in later years he killed a great amount of game of all kinds; probably 3,000 deer.

As a young man he was engaged in the cattle business, and he made two trips: one to Abilene, Kansas, in 1870, the other to Cheyenne, Wyo., in 1877.

After he grew to manhood he assisted greatly in ridding the country of many outlaws, among whom were the "Ney" and "Ben Tasker" gangs. Following closely upon the days of Indian outbreaks came a period when the early settlers had nearly as much trouble with the white outlaws. Among some of the thrilling experiences in which he figured conspicuously was the capture of eight highwaymen about Jan. 20, 1883. These outlaws had held up a Southern Pacific train at Montello, Utah, about 100 miles west from Ogden. They first captured the station, stampeding eight Chinese section men who fled into the hills and froze to death. This was one of the coldest periods in the history of the state, the thermometer reaching 40 degrees below zero. These highwaymen flagged the incoming express train and undertook to rob it. The messenger, however, barricaded himself in his car, fought several hours holding the robbers at bay, while they were riddling his car with bullets. When the incoming train came in sight they retreated in a southerly direction. The next day they were pursued by the sheriff with a posse, who were waylaid and captured by the robbers and their horses and firearms, etc., taken away, and they were privileged to return home afoot. On their retreat through the country the robbers committed a number of other crimes. At Deep Creek they robbed the Devine store, and also entered a woman's house and robbed her, who soon after died from fright.

About this time, J. E. Ray was making a farm at Deseret. One day six men, heavily armed, rode into the town of Deseret, and from their general demeanor it was immediately assumed by the citizens that there was something unusual in their visit. W. A. Ray, an older brother, who at that time running a store in the small settlement, and he informed his brother Joseph that these strangers were buying large quantities of cartridges, and that this was on their part looked very suspicious. These men made arrangements with the people of Deseret, by which they were to take care of their horses on the range. This, however, was only a ruse, and given for the purpose of hiding their identity. It developed later that they had prepared a strong fortification in the top of the mountain range which lay to the northwest of this community. John Sharp was a leading railroad man in the territory, and knowing that J. E. Ray and G. W. Crapper had at different times captured outlaws, wired them to be on the alert, and described these strangers. Messrs. Ray and Crapper knew immediately that he had reference to the suspicious men in question. They at once organized a party to go out and intercept them or attack them in their mountain fortification.

This party left Deseret at one o'clock on the morning of Jan. 20, 1883, and rode about 70 miles in a northwesterly direction. As they approached the mountains they stopped and sent two of their men, Edward Craft and Charles Webb, on a scouting expedition. These scouts were captured by the outlaws and held until the next day, when they were relieved by a rescuing party. "The party" traveled until sunset in a northerly direction when they saw two men riding up a long draw or hollow. Upon the first sight of these men they dropped back under cover, hitched their horses and cautiously slipped over the hills to a point of advantage. As "the party" came to the hill top they looked down into the hollow below, and at a distance of 250 yards again saw these two men. The pursuing party was then directly south from, and above them. They called to them to throw up their hands. Instead of surrendering, however, they slipped off their horses, dropped their guns across the saddles and opened fire. There was a lively exchange of shots for a few minutes, the result being that both robbers were badly wounded and their horses killed. At this juncture two more

outlaws came in sight, and they also were captured. The posse was then about seven miles from the fortification, and the weather extremely cold, it being 20 degrees below zero. They could not make a fire, for fear the four uncaptured men now in the stronghold might see the smoke and escape. They waited until twelve o'clock at night for a detachment from their party, to get a wagon and return so that the wounded men might be sent to the railroad. At three o'clock in the morning, the pursuing party was reenforced by 15 other fighting men from all over the country. They then proceeded to the fortification, seven miles distant, and there they captured the remainder of the gang. These men were all sent to Carson City prison for from 12 to 15 years.

He was one of the pioneer movers in the opening up of lands by means of reservoir irrigation systems, and took an active part in purchasing and cultivating large tracts of dry farm land. He has also assisted in developing mines at Rico, Colo., and in other places.

RAYMOND, GRANDISON (son of Lemuel Raymond and Catherine Woodbeck, the latter of New York). Born May 25, 1818, Liberty, Sullivan county, N. Y. Came to Utah 1852. Married Celia Hall Aug. 12, 1849 (daughter of Bradley and Elizabeth Hall), who was born April 20, 1825 (d. Oct. 29, 1893), and came to Utah in 1852 with husband. Their children: Martha b. June 21, 1850, m. Samuel Walter Hart Feb. 20, 1880; Emma b. May 23, 1852, m. Henry Evans; Alice b. Jan. 17, 1854, d. Dec. 26, 1865; Assenath b. Nov. 11, 1855, m. Albert Bomar; Grandison b. Sept. 29, 1857 (d. Aug. 1, 1909), m. Elizabeth Tunks; David b. Jan. 21, 1860, d. Feb. 25, 1882; Walter b. Oct. 9, 1861; Bradley Lemuel b. Dec. 4, 1863, d. Jan. 4, 1866; Elizabeth b. April 6, 1865, m. Joseph Openshaw; Celia b. April 1, 1868, m. George H. Hall. Family home Kaysville, Utah.

Missionary to New York. Settled at Bountiful 1853. Assisted in bringing immigrants to Utah. Moved to Kaysville 1855. Died Feb. 10, 1898.

READ, WILLIAM SMITH (son of William Read and Sarah Brimley). Born Dec. 1, 1816, North Crawley, Buckinghamshire, Eng. Came to Utah Oct. 16, 1852.

Married Elizabeth Simmons April 30, 1852, St. Louis, Mo., who was born June 14, 1825, London, Eng.; came to Utah with husband, and died May 11, 1904, at Ogden. Their children: Sarah Ann b. May 21, 1853, d. Jan. 2, 1862; William Simmons b. June 26, 1855, m. Elizabeth Mary Taylor; Joseph Reform b. Aug. 30, 1857, d. Oct. 13, 1857; Josiah George b. Jan. 2, 1859, m. Mary Rodelpha Thomas; Tryphena Maria b. March 30, 1861, m. Albert John Aland Oct. 11, 1880; Annie Rebecca b. June 10, 1864, m. Frank Weston Coburn April 5, 1890, m. Edwin Dix July 26, 1905; Oscar Isaac b. Feb. 19, 1867, m. Elizabeth Mackay Treseder. Family home, Ogden.

Missionary to England 1884. Died Dec. 3, 1891.

READ, WILLIAM SIMMONS (son of William Smith Read and Elizabeth Simmons). Born June 26, 1855, at Ogden.

Married Elizabeth Mary Taylor May 29, 1878, at Ogden (daughter of Joseph Taylor and Elizabeth Mary Collier, latter pioneer 1853). Their children: William Royal b. Jan. 8, 1881, d. July 29, 1892; Lewis Josiah b. Nov. 28, 1882, m. Mattie Rushton May 8, 1907; Joseph Oscar b. Sept. 30, 1884, m. Elberta Moore May 6, 1907; Albert Eugene b. Nov. 8, 1886, m. Harriet Ann Jones Feb. 14, 1912; Viola Mary b. March 5, 1890, m. Preston Badger Feb. 21, 1912; Edith Grace b. Aug. 24, 1893; Melba Mae b. April 28, 1896. Family home, Ogden.

Member J. G. Read & Bros. Harness Company.

READ, JOSIAH GEORGE (son of William Smith Read and Elizabeth Simmons). Born Jan. 2, 1859, Slaterville, Utah.

Married Mary Rodelpha Thomas March 11, 1887, Ogden, Utah (daughter of James Moroni Thomas and Mary Holroyd), who was born Feb. 28, 1865, Ogden. Their children: Bertie Josiah b. March 19, 1888, d. July 6, 1888; Lionel Thomas b. Aug. 1, 1890; William Earl b. Oct. 9, 1892; Mary Elizabeth b. May 30, 1895; Walter Thomas b. Jan. 24, 1897. Family home, Ogden.

President J. G. Read Bros. Harness Company since 1883.

READ, OSCAR ISAAC (son of William Smith Read and Elizabeth Simmons). Born Feb. 19, 1867, Ogden, Utah.

Married Elizabeth Mackay Treseder Oct. 16, 1890, Logan, Utah (daughter of Richard Mackay Treseder, born March 9, 1838, Davenport, Eng., and Jane Edmunds, born May 15, 1841, Glasgow, Scotland, latter pioneer 1855). She was born Sept. 25, 1870. Their children: Oscar Leland b. Oct. 8, 1891; Marian Treseder b. Nov. 21, 1896; Donald Treseder b. Nov. 7, 1908, d. Feb. 7, 1909. Family home, Ogden.

Member of Read Bros. Harness and Saddlery Company of Ogden.

READER, JAMES (son of Herbert and Mary Reader). Born 1830, Dorsetshire, Eng. Started for Utah in 1857, but died on the way.

Married Honor Welch Sept. 3, 1851 (daughter of Job Welch and Charlotte Rawlins) of South Cottonwood, Utah,

pioneers). She was born Nov. 8, 1829, and came to Utah with children, who were: John Henry b. Jan. 2, 1855, m. Mary Malinda Erekson, m. Marie Vorden; Charlotte, m. Frederick Fowks.
Priest. Tailor. Died July 15, 1857, crossing the plains. Honor Welch Reader afterward married James Gallyer.

READER, JOHN HENRY (son of James Reader and Honor Welch). Born Jan. 2, 1855, Alton, Ill. Came to Utah with mother and sister in 1857 with handcart company.
Married Mary Malinda Erekson Jan. 12, 1882, South Cottonwood, Utah (daughter of Peter Erekson and Maria Crumpton, pioneers 1847, settlers of American Fork; also lived at South Cottonwood). Their children: Stella b. Jan. 29, 1884, died same day; Ray b. Oct. 30, 1886, m. Olive Beers; Leon b. Dec. 13, 1888; Herald b. April 20, 1892; Shirley b. June 2, 1894, died. Family home Vernal, Utah.
Married Marie Vorden (Voight) July 24, 1905, Vernal, Utah (daughter of Henry Vorden and Rosina Blaser of Montagny, Switzerland; came to Utah 1890. Fred Inebent company). She was born March 13, 1859. Her child by a former marriage to Vincent Voight: Louis Vincent Voight b. Dec. 21, 1879, Neufchatel, Switzerland, d. Nov, 1910.
Elder. Cattle and sheepman. Uinta county commissioner; postmaster at Vernal. Banker; president sheep association; stockholder in many corporations throughout the state. Apiarist.

READING, WILLIAM (son of William Reading of Stonelagh, Eng., and Sarah S. Kelsher of Cublington, Eng.). Born April 16, 1808, Bubbenhall, Eng. Came to Utah 1863.
Married Elizabeth Mansfield of Hunningham, Eng. Their children: John b. Aug. 24, 1834, m. Annie Brown May 29, 1856; William b. April 26, 1843; Job b. 1847; Joseph, died.

READING, 'OHN (son of William Reading and Elizabeth Mansfield). Born Aug. 24, 1834, Bubbenhall, Eng. Came to Utah Sept. 13, 1861, Joseph Horne company.
Married Annie Brown May 29, 1856 (daughter of William and Fannie Brown of Leamington, Eng.). Their children: Annie b. Aug. 8, 1857; Frances J. b. May 20, 1859, m. Roscoe E. Savage 1878; Eliza G. b. May 7, 1862, m. W. F. Williams 1882; Sarah L. b. Feb. 10, 1864, m. Rollo Taysum 1883; Ann G. Feb. 28, 1866; William J. b. Feb. 17, 1867, m. Nellie Crane 1888; John B. b. Feb. 5, 1869; Daniel M. b. April 16, 1871; Charles J. b. Dec. 9, 1873, m. Ella Meears; Elbert O. b. June 22, 1875, m. Lula Evans.
Married Eliza Isom 1868, at Salt Lake City (daughter of David Isom and Charlotte Morris of Ashoine, Eng., the latter came to Utah 1864 or 65, Thomas Taylor company). Their children: David, died; Charlotte, m. Samuel Rierce; Annette, m. Hyrum Hubbard; May, died. Family home, Salt Lake City.
Missionary to England 1885-86. Volunteer fireman; member police 1867. Served in Black Hawk Indian war in Captain Burt's company, 1866. Salt Lake County constable; justice of peace at Centerville four years. First to introduce the Lombard poplar tree in Utah 1862; built first greenhouse in Utah, at Salt Lake City.

REDD, JOHN H. (son of Whitaker Redd of Spanish Fork, Utah). Born Dec. 27, 1799, in North Carolina. Came to Utah September, 1850, James Pace company.
Married Mary Hardison March 2, 1826, in North Carolina (daughter of Zebedee Hancock, pioneer 1850, James Pace company). She was born Jan. 25, 1798. Their children: Ann b. July 26, 1830, m. Wilson D. Pace; Elizabeth Ann b. Dec. 16, 1831, m. Harvey A. Pace; Mary C. b. Jan. 4, 1834, m. Wilson D. Pace; Lemuel H. b. July 31, 1836, m. Keziah Butler; Edward W. b. Jan. 31, 1838, d. child; John H. b. June 13, 1837, died; Benjamin J. b. Jan. 20, 1842, m. Clarissa Taylor. Family home, Spanish Fork.
Died 1858.

REDDEN, RETURN JACKSON (son of George Grant Redden, born Nov. 8, 1790, in New Jersey, and Adelia Higley, born in New York). He was born Sept. 26, 1817, in Hiram, Portage Co., Ohio. Came to Utah July 23, 1847, Brigham Young company.
Married Laura Troske. Their children: Marion b. Aug. 30, 1841, m. James McBride; Charles b. Sept. 11, 1843, d. child.
Married Martha Whiting.
Married Naomi Eliza Murray Feb. 16, 1847, Winter Quarters, Neb. (daughter of William E. Murray and Mary Springer), who was born July 9, 1830, Victor, N. Y. Their children: William Carlos b. April 5, 1849, m. Margaret Fletcher; Adelbert Jackson b. May 20, 1853, m. Kate Eskelson; George Grant b. June 15, 1854, m. Elizabeth Ann Wilson; Eliza Naomi b. Oct. 5, 1855, m. William H. Kimball March 27, 1891; Vilate Murray b. Feb. 30, 1856, m. Eli Saxton; Heman Murray b. June 25, 1859, m. Kate Eskelson; John Henry b. Sept. 28, 1861, m. Martha Cloward; Murray Carlos b. Oct. 11, 1863, m. Julia Olsen; Carlos Murray b. Oct. 11, 1863, m. Amelia Cloward; Richard Edmond b. Aug. 29, 1866, m. Emma Peterson; Heber Roswell b. April 11, 1869, d. infant.
It has always been claimed and tacitly acknowledged by authorities, that he was really the first of the advance party of "Mormon" pioneers to gaze upon the beauties of the great Salt Lake Valley, on the 23d day of July, 1847. He was hunting for some of their driving stock that had strayed away during the night. Arriving on the top of the mountain, which afterward was called Little Mountain, he beheld that strange and wonderful body of water, Great Salt Lake. On looking back toward the camp, he is said to have discerned Orson Pratt coming up toward his view-place on the crest of the mountain. When Pratt came up, the two stood and gazed upon and admired the exquisite panorama spread out in a marvelous scenic expanse. He then went on and drove in the stock, and with them returned to camp. He afterward found that Pratt had had Thomas Bullock record him as the first to see the valley. The characteristic of the man was duty before glory or notoriety, and the incident seemed forgotten, as proper credit was never rendered. It was always said that Heber Chase Kimball acknowledged that Redden was the first of the advance company of "Mormons" to see the valley.
He staked and laid the overland route from Salt Lake City to California, and the Overland Stage Company "got away" with the road, but retained the same names he had christened the rivers, creeks, peaks, hills, fords and loitering places in that vast overland expanse until then practically unknown. The commerce of a great nation now rolls over this highway. He was at one time justice of the peace in Tooele county, and three times at Summit county. He was U. S. deputy marshal under Leonard Phillips and was known in all the pioneer camps as a bold and fearless man. He possessed and exhibited those traits of character which were essential to his being — or performing the miracle of reclamation now greeting the tired eye of the traveler. He was a member of the 35th quorum seventies at the time of his demise, and had joined the church when very young. He was private detective and bodyguard to Joseph Smith, saving him from many serious and threatened troubles. He returned in 1847 to Winter Quarters. Justice of the peace in Tooele county, and in Summit county, Utah; deputy marshal under Leonard Phillips. Died Aug. 30, 1891, Hoytsville, Utah.
[The foregoing resume furnished by the Editor of this volume.]

REDDEN, GEORGE GRANT (son of Return Jackson Redden and Naomi Eliza Murray). Born June 15, 1854, at Salt Lake City.
Married Elizabeth Ann Wilson at Salt Lake City (daughter of John Wilson and Margaret Molyneaux; former pioneer Jacob Gates company 1853; the latter of Richard Ballantyne company 1855). She was born Feb. 7, 1857, at Salt Lake City. Their children: George C. b. April 24, 1875, m. Lorena Yeager Mousley; John J. b. April 13, 1877, m. Ethel Hobson; Elizabeth N. b. May 8, 1879, d. 1879; Maggie b. May 5, 1880, d. 1894; William A. b. April 18, 1883, d. 1894; Maude E. b. March 22, 1885, m. Bert Eldredge. Family home Coalville, Utah.
Home missionary; president Y. M. M. I. A. 1898-1899. Justice of the peace at Wanship, Utah, 1889; city councilman at Coalville 1901-1905. Lives at Coalville.

REDDEN, RICHARD EDMON (son of Return Jackson Redden and Noami Eliza Redden). Born Aug. 29, 1866, at Coalville.
Married Emma Petersen Oct. 26, 1893, Wanship, Utah (daughter of Andrew Peterson and Caroline Dabelstein, pioneers Oct. 1, 1866, Joseph S. Rawlins company). She was born June 16, 1871, Kamas, Utah. Their children: Irene Elsie b. Sept. 1, 1894; Richard Edmon b. Jan. 3, 1897; Mabel Caroline b. Oct. 7, 1898; Nita Althea b. Sept. 24, 1900. Family home Hoytsville, Utah.

REDFIELD, LEVI HARLOW (son of — Redfield of Connecticut). Born North Madison, Conn., Sept. 23, 1801. Came to Utah Sept. 8, 1850, Aaron Johnson company.
Married Alpha L. Foster 1835, in Connecticut (daughter of Orin Foster and Rachel Stone of Connecticut, pioneers 18551. She was born May 12, 1816. Their children: Rachel, m. Edward Bovier; Susan R., m. Albert C. Lyon: Alfred, d. infant; Chloe A., m. Horace S. Eldridge; Adelaide, d. aged 6; Amelia, d. infant; Eva J., m. Joseph Grow; Edward M., d. aged 8; William H., d. infant. Family home, Salt Lake City.
High priest; block teacher. Farmer and fruit-grower. Died August, 1866, Salt Lake City, Utah.

REDINGTON, JOHN (son of Joseph Redington, born May 29, 1804, and Elizabeth Littlechild, born 1810, of Harlow, Essex, Eng.). He was born Oct. 23, 1835, Wazin, Essex. Came to Utah Aug. 29, 1863, John R. Murdock company.
Married Marian Brown Dec. 2, 1860 (daughter of Francis Brown and Marian Hays), who was born 1837, and came to Utah with husband. Their children: Marian Elizabeth b. Sept. 4, 1861, d. 1863; Kate Emily b. Nov. 29, 1863, m. Benjamin B. Robinson; John Walter b. Feb. 26, 1868, m. Anne M. Robinson; Annie Sarah b. July 21, 1866, d. 1867; George Robert b. June 11, 1873, d. 1874; Alice Maud b. April 17, 1875, m. Sylvester Pierce. Family resided Payson and Fayette, Utah, and Oxford, Idaho.
First settled at Salt Lake City; moved to Payson 1864; to Dover 1879, and to Oxford, Idaho, 1903. Member Utah militia in Indian troubles 1865-66. School teacher. Farmer.

REDINGTON, JOHN WALTER (son of John Reddington and Marian Brown). Born Feb. 26, 1868, Payson, Utah.
Married Annie Maria Robinson Jan. 15, 1890, Manti temple (daughter of William Robinson and Elizabeth Nealy). She

was born Nov. 4, 1870, Fayette, Utah. Their children: Ray William b. Dec. 5, 1892; George Arthur b. July 17, 1895; Frank Edward b. Oct. 8, 1897; Annie Ruth b. Sept. 21, 1900; Burton Joseph b. April 7, 1903; Agnes Grace b. June 29, 1906; Glenn b. Sept. 29, 1908. Family resided Dover and Fayette, Utah, and Oxford, Idaho.
Farmer.

REED, LEVI W. (son of John Reed of Cleveland, Ohio). Born Nov. 15, 1831, at Cleveland. Came to Utah 1849.
Married Matilda Pettit 1852, Salt Lake City (daughter of Ethan Pettit and Margaret Ellsworth of Long Island, N. Y.). She was born April 4, 1839. Their children: Matilda E., m. George Baldwin; Mary R., m. Orson Rudy; Ira A., m. Katherine Rudy; Elizabeth R. d. aged 12; Caroline A., m. William E. Langford; Levi A., m. Elizabeth Alford; Harriet A., m. Charles Erickson; Tamson R. d. aged 5; Clarica R., m. Otto Larson; Rachael R., m. William Larson; Laura R., m. John P. Evans. Family home, Salt Lake City.
High priest; bishop North Point ward 16 years; teacher. Farmer; stockraiser. Died Nov. 30, 1893.

REEDER, FRANCIS HUBBARD (son of Edward Reeder, born 1763, Maxtoke, Eng., died Nov. 25, 1842, and Frances Hubbard, born 1800, in Warwickshire, Eng., died Nov. 30, 1851). He was born Oct. 13, 1830, in Warwickshire. Came to Utah Oct. 6, 1853.
Married Elizabeth Maria Hemming Jan. 4, 1852, Trinity Church, London, Eng. (daughter of George Hemming, born 18 ' in England, and died July 3, 1863, and Ambrosia Haynes, born in England May 7, 1807, and died April 5, 1851). She was born April 30, 1830, Coventry, Eng., came to Utah with husband, and died Sept. 19, 1885, Ogden, Utah. Their children: Francis George Edward b. April 14, 1854, d. Oct. 13, 1855; Jane Ambrosia b. Oct. 22, 1855, m. Robert Crawshaw, m. Peter McBride; William Henry b. Oct. 26, 1857, m. Elizabeth Bachmann Nov. 15, 1879; Emily Eliza b. Nov. 13, 1859, m. William S. Hill, d. Oct. 11, 1896; Leo Jesse Charles b. Aug. 12, 1861, m. Jennie Morrison; Elizabeth Maria b. June 5, 1863, d. Jan. 10, 1865; Franklin Samuel b. June 16, 1865, m. Birdie Armstrong; Chauncey Bickington b. Oct. 1, 1867, m. Mary Keenan.
Married Jane Ambrosia Hemming Feb. 8, 1857, Salt Lake City (daughter of George Hemming and Ambrosia Haynes), who was born March 22, 1835, Coventry, Eng., came to Utah Dec. 2, 1856, "Frozen" handcart company, died Aug. 21, 1876, Wellsville, Utah. Their children: Ann Collingwood b. Nov. 17, 1859, m. Washington Jenkins; Frances Hannah b. April 28, 1862, m. George Reader; Thomas Hemming b. May 29, 1864, m. Cordelia Smith; Arthur b. May 2, 1866, d. July 22, 1866; Harriet b. Dec. 18, 1867, d. Feb. 5, 1868; Sarah b. April 3, 1870, d. April 9, 1870; Edwin Furgus b. April 19, 1871, m. Margaret Minnoch, m. Phoebe Wharton; John Alma b. Jan. 12, 1874, m. Hannah Hayes. Families resided Wellsville and Ogden, Utah.
Candy merchant; tailor; farmer. Used first candy-making machinery brought to Utah.

REEDER, WILLIAM HENRY (son of Francis Hubbard Reeder and Elizabeth Maria Hemming). Born Oct. 26, 1857, Salt Lake City.
Married Elizabeth Bachmann Nov. 15, 1879, Salt Lake City (daughter of Jacob Bachmann and Elizabeth Sutter of Switzerland, former born April 26, 1830, pioneer 1863, died Dec. 19, 1907, Ogden, Utah; latter died Nov. 18, 1866, Eden, Utah—married Dec. 3, 1852). She was born March 14, 1860, in Switzerland. Their children: Elizabeth Maria b. Aug. 6, 1881; William Henry, Jr., b. April 27, 1884, m. Birdie Farr Wotherspoon Sept. 22, 1909; Francis Hubbard Hemming b. May 8, 1886, m. Madeline Chatelain July 27, 1905; Herbert Thaddeus b. Sept. 9, 1889, d. July 5, 1909; Annetta Grace b. Jan. 21, 1892, m. Ray G. Blaketey July 17, 1912; Earl Arthur b. March 14, 1895; Rowena Lenora b. Feb. 1, 1897. Family resided Ogden, Utah, and Rose Fork, Idaho.
Indian agent at Fort Hall. Carpenter and builder. Elder.

REES, EDMUND (son of Morgan Rees, born 1737, Merthyr Tydfil, Wales). He was born Feb. 7, 1814, Cardiff, Wales. Came to Utah Sept. 22, 1859, Captain Beebe company.
Married Margaret Ellis 1842 (daughter of Thomas Ellis and Jane Rees), who was born April 18, 1824, and came to Utah with husband. Their children: David b. Nov. 30, 1847, m. Jane Crompton Sept. 12, 1870; Ellis b. Aug. 18, 1850, m. Rachel Frisbee 1876; Mary b. Jan. 28, 1853, m. David Moore Nov. 1870; Thomas b. Nov. 5, 1855, m. Charlott Addy Oct. 3, 1883; Edmund b. May 1, 1858, m. Hannah Chappel Jan. 7, 1882; Sarah J. b. Feb. 11, 1861; Morgan b. Dec. 27, 1863; Ruth A. b. May 22, 1866, m. Buriah Wilkins Feb. 1882. Family home Coalville, Utah.

REES, DAVID (son of Edmund Rees and Margaret Ellis). Born Nov. 30, 1847, Abberpengan, Wales.
Married Jane Crompton Sept. 12, 1870, Salt Lake City (daughter of William Crompton and Hannah Hobson, pioneers September, 1866, Captain Thompson company). She was born July 19, 1853, Kearfley, Eng. Their children: Phoebe J. b. June 20, 1874; Minnie M. b. Feb. 10, 1876; David, Jr. b. Dec. 22, 1879, m. Lillian Clayton Aug. 11, 1906; William b. Dec. 4, 1881, m. Pearl L. Porter Nov. 20, 1907; Elinor b. Sept. 6, 1883, m. Benjamin Gunn Nov. 20, 1907; Edmund C. b. May 12, 1886, m. Lottie N. Fulkerson Oct. 19, 1907; Raymond b. June 14, 1889, m. Lois Porter March 15, 1911; Lois b. Jan. 27, 1893; Clarice b. May 25, 1895; Ralph M. b. Jan. 1, 1900. Family home Castle Rock, Utah.
Presiding elder of Castle Rock; bishop of same place; assistant Sunday school superintendent at Coalville. Town trustee; city councilman. Rancher and stockraiser.

REES, WATKIN (son of Thomas Rees, born Sept. 1, 1807, and Mary Jones, born Sept. 10, 1808, both of Merthyr Tydfil, Wales—married 1829). He was born Jan. 23, 1830, at Merthyr Tydfil. Came to Utah Oct. 5, 1854, Daniel Garn company.
Married Jane Williams Dec. 25, 1852 (daughter of John Williams and Elizabeth Davies, married about 1829, Dowlais, Glamorganshire, Wales, and died there). She was born April 23, 1836, and came to Utah with husband. Their children: Alice b. Nov. 15, 1853, d. child; Elizabeth b. Nov. 24, 1855, m. Henry Emerson 1874; John W. b. Nov. 20, 1856, d. Oct. 23, 1874; Thomas Henry b. Dec. 9, 1860, m. Anna Rees Jan. 1, 1882; Watkin William b. May 22, 1863, m. Izabel Smith 1885; Jacob b. Oct. 17, 1865, m. Grace Williams 1887; Rees Hyrum b. March 9, 1868, m. Frances Young Nov. 1899; Matthew David b. May 18, 1870; Jane Griffith (adopted) b. Jan. 12, 1873, m. Jacob Timor 1900; Edwin b. July 12, 1873, m. Mary Elizabeth Lymb 1899; Willard Arthur b. Jan. 27, 1876, m. Elizabeth Pearce 1899. Family resided Fillmore, Cedar, Beaver, Minersville, Greenville and Adamsville, Utah.
High priest; counselor in bishopric of Adamsville ward 1876-99; missionary. Justice of peace at Adamsville; school trustee 1890-99.

REESE, ENOCH (son of John Reese and Susanna Owen of Montgomeryshire, Wales). Born May 25, 1813, Whitestown, N. Y. Came to Utah 1849.
Married Hannah Harvey Sept. 5, 1843, Buffalo, N. Y. Their children: Enoch M. b. July 14, 1844, m. Zina D. Eldredge; David b. Aug. 27, 1846, James H. b. Aug. 11, 1848, Hannah A. b. Aug. 16, 1851, latter three died; Isaac G. b. Feb. 13, 1856, d. May 15, 1912.
Married Sarah E. McKinley June 22, 1850, Salt Lake City (daughter of John McKinley and Elizabeth Dixon of Sackville, N. B., pioneers 1849, Ezra T. Benson company). She was born March 10, 1831, and came to Utah 1849. Their children: John H. b. April 18, 1851, m. Frances E. Fox, m. Eleanor Edler; Enoch L. b. July 9, 1855, d. Feb. 25, 1911, m. Mary Ellen Knowlton.
Married Anne Dunlap April 18, 1856, Salt Lake City (daughter of Joseph and Alice Dunlap of Ireland, latter pioneer 1849, Ezra T. Benson company). She was born Nov. 25, 1822. Their children: Ruth Amelia b. Sept. 27, 1857, and Alice, died; Mary Ellen b. Dec. 5, 1859, m. Edward Loven-

Jan. 17, 1853, Salt Lake City. Their children: Enoch Moroni b. Sept. 23, 1871, m. Rachel Davis; Isaac W. b. Dec. 29, 1874, m. Dora Crockwell; Chase Harvey b. Aug. 14, 1877, d. aged 13 months; Nora b. Sept. 13, 1881; Luna and Leona b. July 3, 1884 (twins), d. infants; Myrtle Edna b. June 28, 1885; Zina b. July 21, 1890. Family home, Salt Lake City. Missionary to Virginia one year. Pioneer to Carson Valley, Nev. Freighter; contractor; stockraiser.

REESE, JOHN H. (son of Enoch Reese and Sarah E. McKinley). Born April 18, 1851, Salt Lake City. Married Frances E. Fox Jan. 3, 1875, Salt Lake City (daughter of Jesse W. Fox and Eliza Gibbs of Salt Lake City, pioneers 1848). She was born 1856. Their children: John Roy b. Nov. 13, 1875, died; Enoch William b. Nov. 13, 1879, m. Ruth A. Dalquist.
Married Eleanor Edler Dec. 31, 1889, Salt Lake City (daughter of Carl Edler and Mary Jensen of Tooele, Utah, pioneers 1866). She was born 1869. Their children: Sarah E. b. Oct. 19, 1890; Clarence E. b. Dec. 27, 1891; Carl E. b. Dec. 16, 1893; first three died; Margaret E. b. April 29, 1897; Francis E. b. Nov. 26, 1898, died; John Heber b. April 27, 1905; Richard E. b. Aug. 15, 1912.
In early life followed freighting to Idaho, Montana and Nevada. Began civil engineering 1879, which occupation he followed for 10 years on the Utah Central and other southern Utah railroads. In 1882 began railroad contracting and canal building; built railroads in Spanish Fork Canyon, Colorado and southern Utah; also canal for Caraboo Mining Company, and the Lucerne irrigation canal between Utah and Wyoming. Built the first macadamized wagon road in Utah at Fort Douglas, and has followed contracting and mining until the present time.

REESE, CHARLES W. (son of Enoch Reese and Amy Whiteman). Born April 8, 1869, Payson, Utah. Married Lillian G. Christensen Nov. 20, 1901, Salt Lake City (daughter of Peter Christensen of Denmark and Annie M. Dunsdon of England, pioneers). She was born Aug. 31, 1879. Their children: Estella L. b. May 28, 1903; Wyma M. b. Nov. 11, 1904; Charles Wayne b. March 8, 1907; Kenneth D. o. July 13, 1911; Ruth E. b. Jan. 6, 1913. Family home, Salt Lake City.
High priest; bishop's counselor; missionary to eastern states. Surveyor Juab county four years. Miningman; real estate dealer.

REID, JOHN P. (son of John Reid and Fanny White of Belfast, Ireland). Born Feb. 25, 1825, in County Down. Came to Utah 1871, family follow 1872.
Married Margaret Kirkwood Oct. 10, 1844, in Ireland (daughter of Edward and Mary Kirkwood of Ireland). She was born March 14, 1826. Their children: Edward, died; William K., m. Jane Leathem; John Kirkwood, m. Elizabeth Jackson Jan. 5, 1869; Eliza, m. Hugh Smith; Margaret, m. Hugh Sloan; Alexander, m. Ann Macky; Agnes, m. James Tooth; Lucy S., m. George Peacock, m. Alexander Tennent; Robert, m. Mae Leathem; Sarah, m. H. G. Folsom; Thomas, died. Family home Belfast, Ireland.
Elder. Farmer and gardener.

REID, JOHN KIRKWOOD (son of John P. Reid and Margaret Kirkwood). Born Dec. 22, 1850, Edinburgh, Scotland. Came to Utah Sept. 27, 1862, John R. Murdock company, accompanying his uncle, William L. Reid and family.
Married Elizabeth Jackson Jan. 5, 1869, Payson, Utah (daughter of Thomas Jackson and Alice Crompton of Manchester, Eng., pioneers August, 1856, Captain Groesbeck company). She was born Jan. 17, 1851. Their children: Margaret b. March 2, 1870, m. Ben F. Jewkes; John Thomas b. April 6, 1871, m. Edna Niel; Alice b. July 14, 1872; Elizabeth b. Nov. 9, 1873, died; Edward J. b. June 23. 1875, m. Clara J. Gentry; Minnie b. Dec. 31, 1876, m. Jesse D. Jewkes; Milly May b. May 7, 1878, m. Quimby Lamplaugh; Eliza Jane b. Feb. 6, 1880, m. O. M. English; William J. b. Dec. 14, 1881, m. Olive Gentry; Robert b. Aug. 5, 1884, m. Cora Stutt; Lucy b. April 1, 1886, died; Joseph Royal b. July 15, 1888, died; Alexander Terrance b. Nov. 29, 1890, m. Kate Fox; Clairmont J. b. May 4, 1892; Rhea b. May 6, 1894, m. Bryant A. Moffitt.
High priest; bishop's counselor Orangeville, Emery Co., Utah, 11 years. Justice of peace six years; first treasurer; postmaster 11 years; notary public; admitted to the bar of the Seventh judicial district court June 1901; prosecuting attorney Emery county nine years. First settler Castle Dale, named Orangeville, and originated the name of Castle Dale November, 1878. Pioneer of Emery county 1878.

REID, JOHN WHIRK (son of George Reid and Elizabeth Whirk). Born July 12, 1831, Wigtown, Scotland. Came to Utah Oct. 26, 1864, William Hyde company.
Married Agnes Western April 24, 1865 (daughter of Samuel Western and Ann Wingborough, married April 9, 1836, at Tiverton, Devonshire, Eng.). She was born May 30, 1841, and came to Utah Nov. 2, 1864, Warren S. Snow company. Their children: George b. Feb. 11, 1866, d. same day; Ann Marie b. Jan. 27, 1867, d. Feb. 14, 1869; John William b. Jan. 14, 1869, m. Phoebe Debora Black; Agnes Emma b. Jan. 4, 1871, m. George Davis; Elizabeth Ann b. Dec. 29, 1873, m. James F. Thompson; Samuel Western b. May 6, 1875, d. July 11, 1895; Mary Jane b. May 6, 1875, m. Samuel George Dye; Thomas George b. April 30, 1877, m. Edith M. Haynes;

PIONEERS AND PROMINENT MEN OF UTAH 1125

Ada Adelaide b. Jan. 17, 1879, m. Julius K. Thompson; David Oscar b. Sept. 1, 1880. Family resided Mt. Carmel and Oasis, Utah.
Died July 22, 1910.

REID, PETER (son of Peter Reid and Annie Campbell of Argyleshire, South End parish, Scotland). Born Aug. 14, 1826, South End parish. Came to Utah Oct. 24, 1855, Milo Andrus company.
Married Diana Davidson July 22, 1856, Salt Lake City, Thomas Bullock performing ceremony (daughter of James Davidson and Margaret Armstrong, pioneers 1866). She was born Dec. 22, 1832. Their children: Peter J. b. May 30, 1857, m. Janet Alice Spencer; David, m. Mary Rockwell; Alfred C., m. Eliza Jacobs; George A., m. Eliza Garrick; Walter S., m. Jane Edith Spencer; Helen M., m. Archibald S. Geddes. Family home, Salt Lake City.
Senior president 24th quorum seventies; missionary to England 1878-80; Sunday school superintendent. Captain in state militia; master carbuilder for Union Pacific R. R. Carpenter; contractor and builder; stage carpenter Salt Lake Theatre for 25 years. Died April, 1902.

REID, PETER J. (son of Peter Reid and Diana Davidson). Born May 30, 1857, Salt Lake City.
Married Janet Alice Spencer Dec. 29, 1879, at Pleasant Green, Bishop Kessler performing ceremony (daughter of Hiram Theron Spencer of Nauvoo, Ill., and Mary B. Young of Scotland, pioneers, former came 1847, latter 1848). She was born March 28, 1860. Their children: Mary Diana (adopted) b. Oct. 21, 1880, m. Ernest C. Sutton; Ray S. b. July 1, 1882, d. infant; Scott S. (adopted) b. Jan. 21, 1883, d. 1900. Family home Pleasant Green, Utah.
Deacon. Deputy sheriff and assessor of Nye county, Nev., two years; postmaster at Fish Springs five years. Miner; farmer; stockraiser.

REID, WALTER S. (son of Peter Reid and Diana Davidson). Born Oct. 17, 1866, Salt Lake City.
Married Jane Edith Spencer May 25, 1893, Pleasant Green, Utah, by Bishop Spencer (daughter of Hiram Theron Spencer of Nauvoo, Ill., and Mary B. Young of Scotland; former came to Utah 1847, latter 1848). Their children: Walter Spencer b. July 15, 1894; Glen W. b. July 1, 1896; Merl Y. b. Aug. 24, 1898; Diana b. Nov. 19, 1900; Edith b. Aug. 6, 1903. Family home Pleasant Green, Utah.
Postmaster and mining recorder of Fish Springs mining district five years; deputy statistician of Juab county one year; deputy assessor Salt Lake county two years; deputy sheriff Salt Lake county four years; road supervisor Salt Lake county 10 years. Farmer.

REID, WILLIAM TAYLOR (son of John Reid and Fanny White of Ireland). Born July 21, 1830, at County Down, Ireland. Came to Utah September, 1862, John Murdock company.
Married Jane McEwan of Scotland (daughter of Henry McEwan and Jane Thompson, Edinburgh, Scotland). Their children: John, m. Isabella Wilkins; Jane, m. E. H. Cox; Henry McEwan, m. Harriet L. Cox; Francis, died; Fanny, died; William Francis, m. Diantha Lowary; Eliza, m. Steven Vorhees; Edward E., m. Izenna Anderson. Family home Manti, Utah.
Married Adelaide Cox, Salt Lake City (daughter of Frederick Walter Cox and Jemima Losee), who was born Aug. 28, 1848. Their children: Clair William, m. Miss Lowry; Edgar, m. Miss Farrenworth; Alice, m. Doctor Bird.
Bishop. County clerk, Manti; county superintendent of schools for several years. Farmer; stockraiser. Dead.

REID, HENRY McEWAN (son of William Taylor Reid and Jane McEwan). Born Dec. 18, 1853, at Edinburgh, Scotland. Came to Utah Sept. 27, 1862, John Murdock company.
Married Harriet Lenora Cox Jan. 31, 1876, Salt Lake City (daughter of Frederick W. Cox and Emeline Whiting of New York state). She was born Feb. 6, 1855. Their children: Henry McEwan b. Oct. 24, 1876, died; Howard Marion b. Jan. 14, 1879, m. Celia Jenson; Ernest Edward b. April 29, 1881, m. Nettie Huntington; Fredrick Walter, b. Oct. 10, 1883, m. May Poulsen; Jane b. Sept. 9, 1886, m. Lincoln Grant Kelly; William Taylor b. Sept. 22, 1890; Jessie b. Nov. 15, 1893; Lanora b. Dec. 2, 1896. Family home Orangeville, Utah.
Missionary to Ireland 1886-88; bishop for six years; teacher of ward for 20 years; town clerk for six years; member school board for six years. Farmer.

REISER, HENRY (son of Henry Reiser and Susannah Ottiker, both of Fischenthal, Canton Zurich, Switzerland). Born July 29, 1832, at Fischenthal, Canton Zurich. Came to Utah Oct. 5, 1860, William Budge company.
Married Susannah Rupp June 14, 1856, Canton Bern, Switzerland. She was born Aug. 10, 1834, at Sigriswell, Canton Bern, and died Jan. 1, 1874, Salt Lake City.
Married Magdalena Schneider May 9, 1861, Salt Lake City. She was born Nov. 27, 1836, Almendingen, Canton Bern, Switzerland, and died Aug. 3, 1893. Their children: Josephine Johanna b. Jan. 8, 1866, m. Daniel McIntosh; Albert Schneider b. March 1, 1871, m. Nellie Hamer; Mary Magdalena b. Nov. 20, 1875, m. John Gallacher.
Married Catherine Auer Feb. 16, 1866, Salt Lake City. She was born July 19, 1850, Sennwald, Switzerland. Their chil-

dren: Henry Alma b. Oct. 6, 1872; Sidonia b. April 3, 1875, d. May 5, 1900, m. Edwin Halverson; Arnold b. July 5, 1876, m. Hazel Hawlins; Theodore George b. Dec. 17, 1877, m. Ellen Forsieth; Paul David b. March 24, 1883, m. Nellie Jacobson; Selina May b. Aug. 11, 1886, m. William Ormond.
Married Margaret Von Bergen July 26, 1875, Salt Lake City (daughter of Johannes Von Bergen, born July 15, 1815, died Dec. 8, 1898, Schattenhalb, Switzerland, and Barbara Kleck, born Nov. 1, 1818, at Thaingen, Switzerland, died Dec. 29, 1894, Unterstock, Switzerland). She was born Jan. 11, 1852, Meiringen, Switzerland, and came to Utah July 8, 1875. Their children: Alice b. Sept. 12, 1876, m. Burgess Miller; Susette b. June 16, 1878, m. George Leslie; Olga Isabel b. Feb. 5, 1882; Cora Adeline b. April 4, 1884; Lily Josephine b. Aug. 2, 1888; Marguerite N. b. Aug. 5, 1890, m. Howard Paskett; Ruby Pearl b. Feb. 12, 1894. Family home, Salt Lake City.
Member 2d quorum seventies. Died Aug. 29, 1904.

REISER, ALBERT S. (son of Henry Reiser and Magdalena Schneider). Born March 1, 1871, Salt Lake City.
Married Nancy Ellen (Nellie) Hamer Feb. 20, 1895, Salt Lake City, John R. Winder officiating (daughter of Samuel Hamer and Sarah Openshaw of Salt Lake City, former pioneer October, 1851). She was born Aug. 20, 1871. Their children: Ellen Magdalena b. Nov. 23, 1895; Albert Hamer b. Aug. 31, 1897; Ruth b. Dec. 17, 1900; Evelyn b. Jan. 16, 1902; Henry Hamer b. Nov. 9, 1904; Sarah Geneva b. Sept. 14, 1906; Naomi b. April 12, 1909; Orsen Franklin b. March 15, 1911. Family home, Salt Lake City.
Member 100th quorum seventies; missionary to Switzerland 1887-90; high priest. City auditor four years; deputy recorder two years; general delivery clerk at Salt Lake City postoffice four years. Jeweler. Died July 9, 1911.

REMINGTON, JEROME NAPOLEON (son of Joseph Remington, born 1780, and Sallie Fuller, born May 15, 1791, White Hall, Md., both of Pennsylvania. Illinois, and Council Bluffs, Iowa). He was born Feb. 27, 1819, New York State. Came to Utah 1850.
Married Lydia Ripley Chamberlain Badger Jan. 22, 1848, Council Bluffs, Iowa (daughter of John Badger of Vermont, and Lydia Chamberlain. born March 16, 1831, of Nauvoo, Ill., pioneers 1851). She was born March 16, 1831, died May 9, 1906. Their children: Ernest, died; Lydia Eugenia, m. Jerome Merrill; Jerome Eugene, m. Elizabeth Sarah Jackson; Harriette Amelia, m. Porter William Merrell; Rodney Badger, m. Eliza Oldham; Helen Marie, m. Frank Davenport; Joseph Fuller, m. Amanda Rasmussen; Nancy Roxana, m. Christopher Iverson; Marion Vilate, m. George Leonard Goodrich; John Bradley, d. infant; Phoeba, died; Violet, died; Laura Ellen, died. Family resided Salt Lake City and Paradise, Utah.
Settled at Paradise 1860, where he assisted in the developing of the country. Took part in Echo Canyon trouble. Seventy. Died Dec. 10, 1877, Paradise.

RENBURG, CHARLES JENSEN (son of Jens Sorensen and Mary Ann Larsen of Eling, Hjorring, Denmark). Born July 4, 1839, Eling, Denmark. Came to Utah 1855.
Married Maren Jensen, in mid-Atlantic (daughter of Jens Neilsen and Johane Kjerstine of Roaberg, Hjorring amt, Denmark). She was born Aug. 23, 1843. Their children: Charles Jensen, m. Christina Gunderson; Jennie Jensen, m. James P. Gunderson; Joseph Jensen, m. Margaret Bristol. Family home Mt. Pleasant, Utah.
High priest; missionary to Denmark. Black Hawk Indian war veteran, in which he was killed June 18, 1865, at Mt. Pleasant, Utah. Farmer.
Maren Jensen (Renburg) married Soren Christensen Oct. 25, 1866, Salt Lake Endowment house. Their children: Christina, m. Mr. Dalton; Soren, d. infant; Hyrum, m. Millie Christensen; Eliza, Almy, Amos and Nephi, d. in childhood; Hannah, m. James Garrett. Family home Mt. Pleasant.

REYNOLDS, GEORGE (son of George Reynolds and Julia Ann Loutz of London, Eng.). Born Jan. 1, 1842, in Marylebone, London, Eng. Came to Utah July 5, 1865, Independent company.
Married Mary Ann Tuddenham in 1865, Salt Lake City Endowment house (daughter of John Tuddenham and Mary Anne Pumble of London, Eng., pioneers 1864). She was born Sept. 9, 1846. Their children: George, died; Amelia Emily, m. Charles T. Martin; Alice L.; Annie T., m. George Donaldson; Julia, died; Elinor Elizabeth, m. William Harmer; John L., m. Belva Fisher; Harold G., m. Mildred Howarth; Heber T., died; Herbert B., died. Family home, 343 Wall St., Salt Lake City.
Married Amelia Schofield Aug. 3, 1874, Salt Lake City (daughter of John Schofield and Suzana Hewett of Manchester, Eng.). She was born December 1853. Their children: Sidney S., m. Maude Davis; Alberta Russel, m. John Russel; May, m. Charles Wilfington; Charlie, died; George, m. Ellinor Jenson; Carl Wilford, m. Eva Pyper; Nephi, m. Hertha Hardy; Ethel, m. Joseph F. Smith Jr.; Josephine Broford; Gertrude.
Married Mary Goold in 1885, Salt Lake City (daughter of John Goold and Elizabeth Merridith of South Malin, pioneers May 1880). She was born Sept. 16, 1859. Their children:

Geogia Anne, m. Frank Gibson; Philip C.; Gwenlyn; Rosalie T.; Julia A.; George Gordan; Olanthe Reed; Clifford M.
Held many positions of honor in the church. Died Aug. 11, 1909.

REYNOLDS, HAROLD G. (son of George Reynolds and Mary Anne Tuddenham). Born Nov. 18, 1883, Salt Lake City.
Married Ann Amelia Howarth June 23, 1311, Salt Lake City (daughter of Nephi Howarth and Amelia Price), who was born Nov. 30, 1884. Only child: Elizabeth B. June 24, 1912. Family home, Salt Lake City.
Missionary to Germany and England 1903-1906; member of Deseret Sunday school union and secretary of missionary committee. Engaged in clerical work; manager of hotel Utah Souvenir Co.

REYNOLDS, LEVI BURT (son of James Burkley Reynolds and Eliza Ann Lawrence of Maryland). Born Feb. 22, 1831, Fayette, Ind. Came to Utah 1851.
Married Hannah Johnson Sept. 4, 1853, Pleasant Grove, Utah (daughter of William and Elizabeth Johnson of Lye, Worcestershire, Eng., who came to Utah 1850). She was born Jan. 5, 1832. Their children: Hanna E., m. Don Carlos Seely; Charlotte L., m. William H. Seely; Levi B., m. Emilie Rosenlund; Harriet Anna, m. Henry Spencer; James E., died; Francis M., m. Diantha Andersen; Rosa May, m. Moroni Farnsworth; George Willard, m. Augusta Lewis; Fritz Earl, m. Nellie Moore; Jesse B., m. Emilie Petersen. Family home Mt. Pleasant, Utah.
President 66th quorum of seventies; missionary to Kentucky 1881-83. Miller and carpenter. Died July 1, 1903.

REYNOLDS, JESSE BERKLEY (son of Levi Burt Reynolds and Hannah Johnson). Born July 30, 1874, Mt. Pleasant, Utah.
Married Emilie Petersen Sept. 20, 1900, at Mt. Pleasant (daughter of Charles C. E. Petersen and Johanna A. Christensen, former came to Utah 1880, latter 1891). She was born June 3, 1882. Their children: Jessie Pearl b. July 12, 1901; Leonard B. b. July 24, 1903; Royal Willard b. April 6, 1906; Bolde Eugene b. December, 1908; Crysta H. b. Nov. 14, 1910; Ruby E. b. Nov. 28, 1912. Family home Mt. Pleasant, Utah.
Farmer.

REYNOLDS, WILLIAM GEORGE BARDWELL (son of William Peter Reynolds and Melissa Bardwell of Michigan). Born Nov. 19, 1847, in Michigan. Came to Utah 1855, by oxteam.
Married Elizabeth Maria Peterson Jan. 6, 1872, Heber City, and later in Endowment house, Salt Lake City (daughter of Mr. Peterson and Anna Boletta Larson of Norway, pioneers 1867, Captain Kimball company). She was born May 23, 1855. Their children: Roseltha Melissa b. Jan. 23, 1874, m. Joseph Hyrum Hardy; George Bardwell b. Nov. 22, 1875; Agnes Matilda b. May 29, 1878, m. George La Lonel Alice Melvina b. Nov. 18, 1880, m. Lorin C. Caldwell; William Clark b. Jan. 29, 1884, d. child; Emma Joan b. Aug. 5, 1886, m. Jesse Winn; Della Mildred b. April 2, 1889, m. Frederick Anderson; Raymond b. July 2, 1891; Essie Pearl b. Nov. 14, 1893; Inez Elizabeth b. Sept. 14, 1898. Family home Maeser ward, Vernal, Utah.
Elder. First located at Heber City, moved to Provo, and returned to Heber City and was the miller for the Abram Hatch Milling Co. In 1879 moved to Ashley Valley, at which place, during the winter the people nearly starved to death; he took stones and made burrs for the grinding of what grain they had; the horses and cattle nearly all died of starvation, and those that were living were so weak they could not work, so the men pulled the sweep that turned the burrs for the grinding of flour and thus prevented starvation. He was the pioneer miller at Vernal, which he conducted until 1911. He was one of the original locators of the mineral veins at Park City, Utah. Black Hawk Indian war veteran.

RHEES, CHARLES HORATIO (son of Horatio Nelson Rhees, born July 3, 1802, and Sarah Ann Green, born July 25, 1798, both at Bath, Somersetshire, Eng.). He was born Feb. 27, 1833, at Bath. Came to Utah Oct. 1, 1854, Daniel Garn company.
Married Elizabeth Budd May 21, 1863 (daughter of William Budd and Mary Ann Watts), who was born Sept. 17, 1837, and came to Utah Sept. 23, 1863, Daniel Garn company. Their children: Rufus b. Oct. 17, 1869, m. Ellen Rose Dec. 9, 1891; Lorenzo b. March 6, 1872, m. Sarah Vanderhoof; Alice E. b. March 29, 1876, m. George Lanford April 14, 1897; Amy b. Feb. 18, 1878, m. Emery A. Scott June 29, 1904; Helen b. March 16, 1879, m. Alexander Fife Oct. 8, 1902.
Married Eliza Parratt Dec. 8, 1866, Salt Lake City, Utah (daughter of John Parratt and Jane Body, who were married at Bath, Somersetshire, Eng.). She was born Jan. 13, 1848, London, Eng. Their children: Reuben T. b. Nov. 18, 1867, m. Mary R. Tucker Feb. 8, 1894; Charles Herbert b. May 3, 1869, m. Eliza Parratt Jan. 3, 1894; Chauncey W. b. Dec. 8, 1870, m. Sarah Shaw. Family home Pleasant View, Utah.
Served in Echo Canyon war 1857-58. Filled three missions to England, first April 6, 1860 to Sept. 23, 1863; second Oct. 17, 1882 to Aug. 30, 1884; third Feb. 27, 1886 to June 22, 1889; officer in Sunday school and the Young Men's Mutual Improvement Association. Pleasant View ward.

RHEES, REUBEN THOMAS (son of Charles H. Rhees and Eliza Parratt). Born Nov. 18, 1867, Ogden, Utah.
Married Mary Rebecca Tucker Feb. 8, 1894, Logan, Utah (daughter of George Tucker and Emma Hurst, former pioneer James Snow company, latter Captain Jepson company). She was born May 18, 1874, Fairview, Utah. Their children: Lucille E. b. July 26, 1896; Mary E. b. Jan. 16, 1900; Helen E. b. Oct. 17, 1901; Flora G. b. April 10, 1903; Reuben G. b. Feb. 2, 1905; Earl J. b. May 26, 1906; Mildred b. Nov. 5, 1907; Pearl b. April 27, 1909. Family home Pleasant View, Utah.
Bee inspector in Weber Co. 1889-1890; secretary Utah Beekeepers Association, afterwards vice president until April 1911. Justice of the peace of Pleasant View from Jan. 1, 1907 to Dec. 31, 1912; school trustee. Officer in Sunday school and Y. M. M. I. A.; president 38th quorum seventies June 24, 1900 to Feb. 24, 1901; bishop's counselor Feb. 24, 1901 to July 26, 1908; high councilor in Ogden stake; missionary to the eastern states October 1896 to December 1898; Y. M. M. I. A. missionary to Wasatch stake 1899-1900.

RHEAD, JOSIAH (son of Josiah Rhead, born March 14, 1794, and Sarah Bourne, born March 4, 1796, both in England). He was born April 26, 1831, Longport, Staffordshire, Eng. Came to Utah Sept. 23, 1861, Joseph A. Young company.
Married Eliza Lewis (Beach) (daughter of Thomas Lewis and Mary Astberry), who was born Nov. 4, 1824, and came to Utah with husband. Their children: Edward Henry b. Jan. 3, 1851, m. Susan Alvira Huffman Jan. 27, 1873; Eliza Persis b. May 9, 1855, m. Joseph Farnsworth; James Bourne b. March 17, 1858, m. Maria W. Hortin; William George b. July 30, 1860, m. Annie Williamson Hodson; Sarah Ann b. Dec. 22, 1862, m. Alexander C. Salmon; Josiah Lewis b. May 8, 1868, m. Delila Davis, (who died), m. Margaret Carruth.
President council 27th quorum seventies and first elders' quorum of Summit stake. Made first crockery ware in Summit county 1863. Died Nov. 21, 1887, Coalville, Utah.

RHEAD, JAMES BOURNE (son of Josiah Rhead and Eliza Lewis). Born March 17, 1858, Des Moines, Iowa. Came to Utah Sept. 10, 1861, Joseph A. Young company.
Married Maria W. Hortin June 21, 1896, Salt Lake City (daughter of John Hortin and Maria Wilkinson, former pioneer Aug. 28, 1860, independent company, latter Sept. 20, 1864, Joseph S. Rawlins company). She was born Jan. 17, 1869. Their children: Fiametta b. April 3, 1897; Hortense b. Jan. 25, 1899; LaVon b. Sept. 25, 1901; Josiah Lafayette b. May 21, 1903; James Orison b. June 10, 1908. Family home Coalville, Utah.
Member high council; missionary to Sandwich Islands 1881-84; high priest. Member Coalville city council and city recorder. Director in Coalville Co-op.; rancher and stockraiser. Died Jan. 23, 1911, South Fork, Utah.

RHEAD, WILLIAM GEORGE (son of Josiah Rhead and Eliza Lewis). Born July 30, 1860, Des Moines, Iowa.
Married Ann Williamson Hodson Jan. 30, 1889, Logan, Utah (daughter of William Hodson and Isabella Williamson, pioneers September 1863). She was born Feb. 7, 1864, Coalville, Utah. Their children: William Elmo b. Feb. 5, 1890, m. Margaret Hazel Skeen Feb. 8, 1911; Guy Lewis b. Feb. 6, 1894; Claude Embleton b. April 6, 1902. Family home Plain City, Utah.
Farmer.

RHOADES, THOMAS (son of Daniel Rhoades, who fought in the Revolutionary war, of Danielson, Conn., and which was named after him). Came to Utah 1846, with trappers and fur hunters en route to the hunting grounds of California.
Married Elizabeth Foster. Their children: Thomas died; Kate; Caleb Baldwin, m. Malinda Powell; Lucinda, m. J. Clawson, m. Mr. Dodge. Family home Danielson, Conn.
Seventy. Assisted in rescuing the Donner party in the Sierra Nevada mountains in 1846. Trapper and scout. Farmer, prospector and stockraiser. Indian interpreter. Died 1868.

RHOADES, CALEB BALDWIN (son of Thomas Rhoades and Elizabeth Foster). Born April 4, 1836, in Edgar county, Ill. Came to Utah 1846.
Married Malinda Powell Oct. 12, 1862 (daughter of James Powell and Jemima Wimmer), who was born Oct. 13, 1847, in Iowa. Their children: Malinda b. Dec. 23, 1863, m. George Williams, m. William Morgan; Caleb B. Jr. b. Jan. 22, 1865, d. aged 6; Martha Ellen b. Sept. 14, 1868, m. Samuel Mann; James Thomas b. Aug. 1, 1871, d. aged 2; William Henry b. May 23, 1873, m. Annie ———. Family home Uintic, Utah.
First man to convey water through Pioneer Water Company canal from Price river. Second counselor to Bishop George Fransden; high priest. Treasurer Emery stake; school trustee. Trapper and prospector. Died June 2, 1904, near Price, Utah.

RHODEHOUSE, JOHN WILLIAM (son of William H. Rhodehouse and Mary Truscott of Oxford, Idaho). Born Aug. 11, 1882, at Oxford.
Married Lettie A. Smith Jan. 1, 1907, Parker, Idaho (daughter of James Franklin Smith and Martha Alice French of Pounding Mill, Va). She was born April 24, 1887. Only child: Ferrold W.
Missionary to California 1904-06; bishop of Elgin ward, Yellowstone stake. Farmer.

RHODES, ALONZO D. (son of Erie Rhodes and Eunice Wright). Born Sept. 2, 1824, in Trumbull Co., Ohio. Came to Utah September, 1851, James Allred company.
Married Barbara Kearns Sept. 14, 1843 (daughter of Henry Kearns and Barbara Pickle, pioneers 1851, James Allred company). She was born Aug. 20, 1824, and came to Utah with husband. Their children: Lamyra Amanda b. Dec. 23, 1844; Julia Ann b. Sept. 20, 1846; Henry Erie b. Sept. 4, 1848; Alverana Barbara b. Aug. 20, 1851, m. Hyland D. Wilcox Dec. 15, 1867; Ellen Maria b. July 8, 1853, m. Jacob Nelson Jan. 8, 1872; Adeline Malisia b. Oct. 11, 1855, m. Mathias Peterson Jan. 1, 1872; Sarah Lavina b. March 8, 1857, m. Henry Houre Feb. 8, 1875; Clarissa Elizabeth b. Sept. 2, 1859; Ross Bell b. Dec. 21, 1861, m. Theodore Green; Lagrand b. May 13, 1863.
Married Sarah Ann Bushman May 25, 1852, Salt Lake City (daughter of Martin Bushman and Elizabeth Degen, pioneers September, 1851, James Allred company). She was born Jan. 9, 1833, in Lancaster county, Pa. Their children: Alonzo D. b. April 17, 1853, m. Harriet E. Stewart April 19, 1875; Elizabeth Emira b. April 10, 1855, m. Joseph Barnes Jan. 19, 1871; Sarah Ann b. March 4, 1857, m. Ephraim Empey April 19, 1875; Martin Elmer b. Feb. 8, 1859, m. Louisa E. Childs March 20, 1888; Alva Benjamin b. Feb. 26, 1861; John Franklin b. April 12, 1863, m. Mary E. Ashton Jan. 21, 1881; Elsie Marie b. March 12, 1865, m. George Briggs March, 1883; Lois Ladelia b. Aug. 4, 1867, m. Joseph Briggs May 1, 1887; Marcellus Albert b. Aug. 6, 1869, m. Amanda Hodge Feb. 1, 1892; Bertha Salome b. Oct. 27, 1872, m. William H. Neiber July 19, 1892; Lorena b. Sept. 9, 1875, m. John M. Smith Dec. 24, 1895; Jacob Wilson b. May 24, 1881. Family home Lehi, Utah.
First marshal of Lehi city; constable. Indian war veteran. One of first to help build bridges, dig canals, and make roads thereabouts. Assisted in bringing immigrants to Utah.

RHODES, ALONZO D. (son of Alonzo D. Rhodes and Sarah Ann Bushman). Born April 17, 1853, Lehi, Utah.
Married Harriet E. Stewart April 19, 1875, Salt Lake City (daughter of John Stewart and Lydia Balf, former pioneer 1849, latter 1847). She was born June 11, 1856. Their children: Lydia Ann b. March 9, 1876, m. David Prior; Alva Alonzo b. Dec. 26, 1877, m. Ida Barnard; John Glenn b. Jan. 26, 1881, m. Emma Barnard; Julian b. March 25, 1884, m. Elmer Beck; William Jasper b. July 11, 1885, m. Ellen Capener; Prudence b. July 10, 1887; Maggie Marvel b. Jan. 18, 1889; Samuel Jesse b. July 31, 1893; Clifton b. July 16, 1895; Hugh Ralph b. 1897; Hulda b. 1899.
Elder. Farmer; overseer for Utah Sugar Company.

RHODES, THOMAS. Born July 13, 1785, in Kentucky. Came to Utah 1857.
His child: Lucinda, m. John Clawson, m. William Dodge.
Married Cecelia Johnson 1854, Salt Lake City, who was born March 5, 1818. Their children: Olive; Josephine, m. John Walker Williams; Nephi, m. Kate Higbey; John Joseph, m. Mary Ann Horsley. Family home Minersville, Utah.
Married B. Johnson. Their children: Thomas, m. Martha Powell; Anna, m. William Hodson; Enoch, killed by Indians on Uinta reservation.
Trapper; miner; farmer; stockraiser. Died Feb. 20, 1865.

RHODES, JOHN JOSEPH (son of Thomas Rhodes and Cecelia Johnson). Born March 6, 1863, Rhodes Valley, Utah.
Married Mary Ann Horsley March 27, 1884, Ferron, Utah, later in temple at Salt Lake City (daughter of John P. Horsley and Frances Jane Mills of Ferron and Joseph City, Utah, pioneers 1860, oxteam company). She was born July 1, 1867. Their children: Olive Ann b. April 29, 1885, m. James S. Westonskow; John Joseph, Jr., b. Dec. 3, 1887; Charles Edward b. Nov. 6, 1890; Florence Eva b. May 28, 1894; Jennie Emma b. June 11, 1897; Frances Ivella b. May 1, 1900; William Arthur b. May 23, 1905; Zelma Ethel b. Jan. 29, 1908. Family home Ferron, Utah.
Seventy; treasurer of the Sunday school at Price, Utah. Farmer; horticulturist; bookkeeper.

RICE, IRA (son of Titus Rice, born Feb. 4, 1745, Wallingford, Conn., and Lois ——— of Vermont). He was born Oct. 27, 1793, Berkshire, Franklin county, Vt. Came to Utah Sept. 29, 1847, Bishop Edward Hunter company.
Married Minerva Saxton in 1814, who was born in 1796, died 1824. Their children: Acepis b. 1820, m. Mary Hall, m. Louisa Hall; William Kelsey b. Oct. 27, 1822, m. Lucy Witter Gear Oct. 8, 1845, m. Ann Rose Oct. 25, 1855; Maryette, m. Orson Cook; Juliett; Ira, died.
Married Sarah Harrington in 1826, New York state (daughter of Benjamin and Ruth Harrington), who was born Jan. 30, 1800, died in the east. Their children: Harriet, m. Henry Lameraux; Benjamin, a child; Henriette; Delia, d. infant; Adeline, m. Jonathan Bowen March 15, 1844; Leonard, m. Elizabeth Babbitt, m. Margaret Duckwater March 18, 1849, m. Lucy Stevens; Oscar North, m. Jane Miller, m. Margaret Matthews Dec. 6, 1899; Ephraim, drowned trying to save companion in 1859; Adelbert, m. Jane Cottrell; Henriette; Sarah Ann; Hyrum, m. Olive Smith; Caroline, m. John McGuire.
Married Elizabeth Ann Buttler (widow) in 1863, Providence, Cache Co., Utah.
First bishop of North Ogden ward. Moved to Providence and thence to St. George, Utah. Died 1869, near St. George.

RICE, WILLIAM KELSEY (son of Ira Rice and Minerva Saxton). Born Oct. 27, 1822, Manchester, Ontario county, N. Y. Came to Utah Sept. 29, 1847, Edward Hunter company.
Married Lucy Witter Gear Oct. 25, 1845, Nauvoo, Ill. (daughter of Moses Gear and Sally Thomas), who was born Feb. 23, 1824, Ashtabula Co., Ohio. Their children: Ellen Maria b. Sept. 13, 1846, m. Joseph Glover Dec. 26, 1868; William Kelsey b. Aug. 22, 1848, m. Ada Clawson Sept. 1871; Lucy Augusta b. March 5, 1850, m. Timothy B. Clark Nov. 23, 1867; Sarah Minerva b. Oct. 10, 1852, m. Caleb Lyons Oct. 12, 1869; Kelsey b. Aug. 1859, m. Margret Edward Jan. 1888; Elizabeth Adelaide b. March 15, 1856, m. David R. Bybee Oct. 6, 1874; Maryette b. Feb. 14, 1858, m. Solomon Harris, m. Michael Stanley; Juliette b. 1860, and Ira, d. children; John b. Sept. 19, 1865, m. Elsie Allen Dec. 22, 1892; Ardella b. Oct. 23, 1867, m. Joseph Albertson April 16, 1891.
Married Ann Victoria Rose Oct. 25, 1855, Salt Lake City (daughter of Abraham and Catharine Almira Rose, pioneers 1853). She was born June 4, 1832, in Steuben county, N. Y. Their children: Ann Victoria b. Jan. 4, 1856, m. Lysander Brown; Catharine Almira b. Dec. 9, 1858, m. Charles Duncan Dec. 25, 1876; Orson Abraham b. Nov. 1860, d. child; Martha Deseret b. March 3, 1862, m. George Higgins July 13, 1881; Olive Jane b. Aug. 6, 1863, m. Archibald Duncan Aug. 21, 1880; Leonard Ira b. Aug. 26, 1865, died; Harriet Maria b. June 1, 1867, m. William Birks; Emma Sariah b. Jan. 10, 1869, m. George A. Davis; Rachael Sylvia b. Sept. 12, 1870, m. Lysander Brown; William Warren b. May 3, 1873; Charles Fanelyn, m. Lilly Hill; May Lavilla, m. Samuel Davis Sept. 18, 1893.
Missionary to Iron Co., Utah. 1851. Participated in Echo Canyon trouble. Pioneer, Farmington, 1. 19-1908. Resides Centerville, Utah.

RICE, OSCAR NORTH (son of Ira Rice and Sarah Harrington). Born Oct. 19, 1835, in Michigan.
Married Jane Clarissa Miller April 25, 1859, Farmington, Utah (daughter of Daniel Miller and Clarissa Pond, pioneers 1847, Henry Miller company). She was born in Adams county, Ill. Their children: Alice M. b. Feb. 3, 1860, m. Nicolas W. Crookston Nov. 8, 1883; Clara b. Nov. 13, 1861, m. Fred G. Benson Sept. 29, 1889; Eva R. b. May 25, 1864, m. Charles F. Martineau Jan. 20, 1886; Henriette b. Aug. 10, 1867, m. Daniel Crookston; Oscar Franklin b. March 17, 1870, m. Charlotte Pickett June 30, 1897; Abbie H. b. Nov. 22, 1872, m. Joseph R. Kimball 1894; Sarah Ann b. June 8, 1875, m. Hyrum S. Benson Jan. 6, 1888. Family home Logan, Utah.
Seventy; missionary to Salmon river. Pioneer Cache county 1859. Veteran Indian war.

RICE, OSCAR FRANKLIN (son of Oscar North Rice and Jane Clarissa Miller). Born March 17, 1870, Providence, Utah.
Married Charlotte Pickett June 30, 1897 (daughter of John W. Pickett and Charlotte R. White, former pioneer 1862, latter 1849, Ezra T. Benson company). She was born Jan. 17, 1874, Tooele, Utah. Their children: Oscar Le-Grand b. March 24, 1898; Inez b. Aug. 29, 1899; Jane b. April 9, 1905; Joseph Allen b. Oct. 24, 1910; Mahlon F. b. Dec. 1911.
Missionary to eastern states 1908-10; bishop 6th ward, Logan, Feb. 23, 1910.

RICH, ERNEST H. (son of Edwin E. Rich and Mary Ann Porter of Trowbridge, Eng.). Born Dec. 13, 1866, Trowbridge. Came to Utah Sept. 15, 1886.
Married Claudia Edith Tucker Aug. 1, 1894, Salt Lake City (daughter of Samuel B. Tucker and Elizabeth B. Neslen, latter came to Utah Sept. 20, 1853, with brother, former in 1860). She was born Jan. 8, 1872. Their children: Ida Leona b. May 30, 1895; Bertha Claudia b. Jan. 22, 1898; Gilbert Tucker b. Aug. 29, 1899; Ernest Herbert b. Feb. 13, 1902. Family home, Salt Lake City.
Meat dealer; stockman; rancher.

RICH, JAMES JOHN (son of John Peter and Johannah Rich of Middelfart, Denmark). Born Oct. 17, 1817, at Middelfart. Came to Utah August, 1857, James Brown company.
Married Karoline Nielsen Dec. 24, 1844, Denmark (daughter of Henry and Johannah Nielsen of Melby, Fyen, Denmark). She was born April 18, 1819, and came to Utah with husband in 1857. Their child: Henry John b. Feb. 17, 1846, m. Julia Ann Julander. Family resided Salt Lake City and Monroe, Utah.
High priest; missionary in Denmark; tithing clerk at Odense, Denmark, and Fairfield, Iowa. Indian war veteran. Early settler in San Pete and Sevier counties. Died June 23, 1889, at Monroe.

RICH, HENRY JOHN (son of James John Rich and Caroline Nielsen). Born Feb. 17, 1846, Fyen, Denmark. Came to Utah with father.
Married Julia Ann Julander March 20, 1870, Scipio, Utah (daughter of Jacob Julander and Johannah Christina Vacht of Denmark, pioneers August, 1857, handcart company). She was born May 15, 1855, and came to Utah with parents. Their children: James b. April 26, 1871, m. Florence Almira Golding; Henry Jacob b. Sept. 27, 1873, m. Eliza Losee; Julia Christina b. Nov. 18, 1875, m. Aaron Asay; William b. Nov. 27, 1877, m. Ruth Losee; Elizabeth b. Jan. 23, 1880, m. Squire Siddall; Orissa b. Dec. 29, 1881, d. July 16, 1889; Martin b. April 14, 1885; Orvel b. Dec. 20, 1887, d. Aug. 24, 1889; Jesse b. June 3, 1890; Earl b. May 27, 1892; Sidney b. July 31, 1895, d. Aug. 23, 1895; Le Roy b. Sept. 9, 1896, d. Oct. 29, 1896; Caroline Yetta b. April 21, 1898, d. April 24, 1898. Family home Monroe, Utah.
Member 2d quorum elders; ward teacher. Settled at Monroe 1871. Assisted in bringing immigrants to Utah 1863 and 1868. Black Hawk war veteran. Farmer.

RICH, JOHN JAMES (son of Henry John Rich and Julia A. Julander). Born April 26, 1871, Monroe, Utah.
Married Florence Almira Golding Jan. 5, 1892, Manti, Utah (daughter of Sebron Johnson Golding and Nannie E. McNiece of Wellington, Utah, came to Utah 1877). She was born Sept. 27, 1875. Their children: Vida b. Feb. 25, 1893; John Kelvien b. March 10, 1895; Thora b. April 9, 1897; Orven b. Jan. 15, 1900; Tressie b. Nov. 20, 1902; Deleel b. Oct. 1, 1903, d. June 2, 1904; Delile b. Oct. 1, 1903, d. Nov. 20, 1903; Rulon b. Nov. 27, 1906; Ferral b. Nov. 14, 1908; Glen b. May 26, 1910. Family home Wellington, Utah.
High priest; counselor to Lyman Smith Beach of Molen ward 1906-07; ward teacher Wellington ward. Marshal Wellington, 1910-11; justice of peace Molen, and also Cainesville. First white child born in Monroe, Utah. Carpenter; builder; farmer.

RICH, JOHN HENRY (son of James Rich, born 1790, Rhoade, Somersetshire, Eng., and Jemima Halliday, born 1790, Earl Stoke, Wiltshire, Eng.—married 1816). He was born Sept. 1, 1831, Trowbridge, Wiltshire. Came to Utah Sept. 29, 1853, Moses Dalley independent company.
Married Lydia Pond December, 1852, at Trowbridge (daughter of Thomas Pond and Ann Garrett, who died in England). She was born Oct. 9, 1834. Their children: Franklin John b. Aug. 24, 1853, m. Sarah Ann Rawle Dec. 28, 1874; James Thomas b. Jan. 1, 1855, m. Emma Elizabeth Hemming Dec. 27, 1877; William Henry b. Sept. 4, 1857, m. Flora Kate Rawle Jan. 8, 1880; Lydia Melissa b. Oct. 31, 1859, m. Frank Eli Whitesc March 1879; Louisa Ann b. Jan. 7, 1862, d. 1864; Lucy Jane b. Nov. 12, 1864, m. Joseph Henry Florence Jan. 24, 1889. Family resided Centerville, Richville and Morgan City, Utah.
High priest July 1, 1877; high councilor, Morgan stake July 1, 1877; first counselor to stake president of elders quorum two years; missionary two years. County commissioner Dec. 31, 1877, to March 1883. Helped to organize and support Z. C. M. I. and Fry Mercantile Co., Morgan Mill. Moved to Payson 1857, and in July of same year to Centerville, Davis county; April 6, 1861, moved to Weber Valley (now Richville), Morgan county.

RICH, FRANKLIN JOHN (son of John Henry Rich and Lydia Pond). Born Aug. 21, 1853, in Nebraska.
Married Sarah Ann Rawle Dec. 23, 1974, Salt Lake City (daughter of Richard Rawle and Sarah Ann Sweetland, former a pioneer John I. Hart company). She was born March 8, 1834, at Bristol, Eng. Their children: Franklin John b. Oct. 14, 1875; James Richard b. Nov. 9, 1876, m. Jenna Brough Nov. 27, 1901; Albert Fredrick b. Jan. 9, 1879, m. Eliza Dickson Nov. 27, 1905; George Raymond b. May 16, 1880, m. Lulla Neuberger March 30, 1907; Arthur Rawle b. March 20, 1883, m. Bertha Porter 1904; Flora May b. Jan. 24, 1884; Clarence Edgar b. Jan. 29, 1888, m. Mae Martha Dickson Oct. 5, 1910. Family home Morgan City, Utah.

RICH, JAMES RICHARD (son of Franklin John Rich and Sarha Ann Rawle). Born Nov. 9, 1876, Morgan Co., Utah.
Married Jenna Brough Nov. 27, 1901, Salt Lake City, Utah (daughter of William George Brough and Emily Jane Cotterell of Poterville, Morgan Co., Utah). She was born July 25, 1882. Their children: James Lavaun b. Jan. 16, 1903, Lona Ann b. March 3, 1905; Nelda Jane b. Oct. 29, 1907; Franklin Brough b. May 29, 1910. Family resided Richville and Morgan City, Utah.
Secretary of Sunday school 1900; superintendent 1901. Moved to Morgan City from Richville 1901.

RICH, JOSEPH (son of Thomas Rich and Ann Pool of Kentucky). Born April 16, 1786, in Maryland. Came to Utah 1847, Charles C. Rich company.
Married Nancy O'Neal, who was born in Ireland. Their children: Charles C. b. Aug. 21, 1809, m. Sarah D. Pea, Eliza Graves, Mary Ann Phelps, Sarah Peck, Emeline Grover and Harriett Sargent; Jane Ann b. 1813, m. Harvey Green; Minerva b. 1815, m. Asa Earl; Nancy b. 1819, m. John Porter. Family resided Centerville, Utah, and Paris, Idaho.
High priest; patriarch. Died at Paris.

RICH, CHARLES COULSEN (son of Joseph Rich and Nancy O'Neal). Born Aug. 21, 1809, in Campbell county, Ky. Came to Utah Oct. 2, 1847, Charles C. Rich company.
Married Sarah Dearmon Pea Feb. 11, 1838. Their children: Charles C.[2] b. Sept. 8, 1844, m. Jane Susanna Stock; Benjamin E. b. Nov. 27, 1851, m. Diana Farr.
Married Mary Ann Phelps Jan. 6, 1845 (daughter of Morris Phelps and Laura Clark, who were married July 1827, in Illinois, the former came to Utah 1851, himself captain of a company, the latter died 1841, in Illinois). She was born Aug. 6, 1828. Their children: Laura b. Sept. 25, 1849, d. 1849; Mary Ann b. May 15, 1850, m. Aabbel Pomroy Jan. 10, 1875; William L. b. Aug. 9, 1852, m. Ella Pomroy Sept. 6, 1877; Morris b. Aug. 7, 1854, d. June 4, 1855; Minerva b. Oct. 7, 1884, m. Hyrum S. Woolley Oct. 5, 1873; Amasa M. b. Oct. 25, 1856, m. Mary Jacobs Sept. 29, 1880; Paulina b. April 21, 1829, d. Oct. 8, 1860; Ezra C. b. Aug. 18, 1864, m. Annie Lowe

June 29, 1893; Edward I. b. April 29, 1868, m. Almyra Cozzens April 9, 1893; Jacob b. Sept. 4, 1876, d. Sept. 4, 1876.
Married Emeline Grover Feb. 2, 1846 (daughter of Thomas Grover and Caroline Whitney, married 1828, at Whitehall, N. Y., the former a pioneer October, 1847, latter died in 1841). She was born July 30, 1831. Their children: Thomas Grover b. Dec. 30, 1849, m. Elizabeth McKay Pugmire Feb. 1877; Caroline Whitney b. Jan. 22, 1852, m. Hyrum Humphries Oct. 7, 1873; Nancy Emeline b. Feb. 19, 1854, m. Vincent McKay Perrigrine Oct. 7, 1873; Landon Jedediah b. March 11, 1858, m. Dora Wanlers; Samuel Joseph b. May 1, 1860, m. Anne Page; Heber Charles Chase b. Aug. 8, 1862, m. Edna Shepherd; Joel Hezekiah b. March 17, 1865, m. Luella Arnold; George Quayle b. March 17, 1869, m. Lettie Nancy. Families resided Paris, Idaho.

RICH, CHARLES COULSON (son of Charles Coulson Rich and Sarah Dearmon Pea). Born Sept. 8, 1844, Nauvoo, Ill. Came to Utah 1847, C. C. Rich company.
Married Jane Susanna Stock Aug. 27, 1865, Paris, Idaho (daughter of John Stock of South Africa and Jane Adams of England, pioneers 1860, Nephi Johnson company). She was born Aug. 21, 1846. Their children: Charles Coulson b. July 26, 1866, m. Elizabeth Hatch, m. Docia Clark; Don Carlos b. March 30, 1868, died; Joseph Edwin b. Feb. 13, 1870, m. Louisa Pool Hatch; Sarah D. b. Jan. 24, 1872, m. George Young; John b. Jan. 27, 1874, m. Annie Andrews; Libby b. Nov. 27, 1875, m. James Sobey; Arthur b. Oct. 12, 1877, m. Gertrude McCarrel; Ada b. March 24, 1880, m. Clarence Irwin Johnson.
Elder. Early settler at Bear Lake, Idaho, 1864; moved to Ashley Valley 1884. County attorney; school teacher. Merchant. Died June 8, 1890, Vernal, Utah.

RICH, CHARLES COULSON (son of Charles Coulson Rich and Jane Susanna Stock). Born July 26, 1866, Paris, Idaho.
Married Elizabeth Hatch Jan. 1, 1886, Vernal, Utah (daughter of Alva Alexander Hatch and Mary Nelson of Vernal). She was born 1869. Their children: Charles Coulson b. Dec. 18, 1887; Sarah D. Armond b. April 16, 1889, m. Andrew Jevins; Essy b. Jan. 1, 1891, m. Jesse Hiatt; Alvah Alexander b. April 4, 1893, d. infant.
Married Theadocia Clark Jan. 2, 1898, Vernal, Utah (daughter of John E. Clark and Theadocia Hatch of Vernal). She was born June 13, 1882. Their children: Clarence b. March 28, 1899; Lawrence Coulson b. Jan. 13, 1901; Jeremiah b. May 18, 1903; Edwin Earl b. Feb. 1, 1905; John Bean b. May 12, 1907; Theadocia Pear b. Dec. 19, 1908; Arbun Mariolo b. June 20, 1911. Family home Roosevelt, Utah.

RICH, JOSEPH EDWIN (son of Charles Coulson Rich and Jane Susanna Stock). Born Feb. 13, 1870, at Paris, Idaho.
Married Louisa Pool Hatch March 7, 1889, at Vernal, Utah (daughter of Alvah Alexander Hatch and Mary Elizabeth Nelson, both of Vernal, Utah, pioneers 1847). She was born Sept. 11, 1873. Their children: Joseph Edwin b. July 22, 1890, m. Flossie Gardner; Leora b. July 12, 1895; Elizabeth b. April 16, 1897; Elva Fern b. Jan. 25, 1899, died; Jane Susanna b. Jan. 28, 1900; Alvah Alexander b. Oct. 11, 1902; John Arvil b. March 4, 1905; Reed S. b. Jan. 21, 1907; Homer Valoy b. March 21, 1912. Family home Vernal, Utah.
Elder; ward teacher. Settled at Ashley Fork 1884, where he has assisted in building up the country. Farmer and merchant.

RICH, BENJAMIN E. (son of Charles Coulson Rich and Sarah Pea). Born Nov. 27, 1857, Salt Lake City.
Married Diana Farr (daughter of Lorin Farr and Nancy Chase of Ogden, Utah, pioneers Sept. 20, 1847, Daniel Spencer company). She was born April 5, 1858. Their children: Benjamin Leroy b. Oct. 18, 1878, m. Dora Anna Clegg Aug. 1900; Lorin, m. Ruth Blair; Fred, m. Eva Evans; Homer Erastus, m. Ethel Watkins; Ida, m. Alvin C. Strong; Don O'Neill; Andrea, m. Vivian Watkins; Frank Cannon. Family home Centerville, Utah.
Missionary to England 1881-84; president southern states mission 1897-1907; and of eastern states 1907 to date. Editor of Rexburg "Press," "Silver Hammer" and Rexburg "Standard." Merchant at Ogden 1884-93.

RICH, BENJAMIN LEROY (son of Benjamin E. Rich and Diana Farr). Born Oct. 18, 1878, Ogden, Utah.
Married Dora Anna Clegg Aug. 29, 1900, Salt Lake temple (daughter of Isaac Clegg and Dora Jackman of Rexburg, Idaho, pioneers 1860). She was born Jan. 16, 1878. Family home, Salt Lake City.
Member of seventies; missionary to southern states 1898-99; and to northern states 1899-1900. Graduate from Columbian University; member Kappa Sigma fraternity. Lawyer, practicing at Salt Lake City, Utah.

RICH, WILLIAM LYMAN (son of Charles Coulson Rich and Mary A. Phelps). Born Aug. 9, 1852, San Bernardino, Cal.
Married Ella Amelia Pomeroy June, 1877 (daughter of Francis M. Pomeroy and Irene Haskell, former pioneer July 24, 1847, Brigham Young company). She was born June 17, 1859. Their children: William Lafayette b. June 17, 1878, m. Elizabeth Jenett Smith Sept. 15, 1909; Zula b. Sept. 3, 1880, m. Lesslie Cole June 1908; Jesse P. b. April 1883, m. Louise Rogers Oct. 1908; Mabel b. Feb. 14, 1885, m. Rich Sutton Oct. 1904; Gertrude b. May 13, 1888, m. Fred Price Jan. 4, 1911; Hazel b. Sept. 22, 1890, m. Lesslie Shepheard Aug. 26, 1910; Thales b. March 24, 1895, died March 27, 1895. Family resided Montpelier and Paris, Idaho.
Married Llmyra Holmes Oct. 5, 1887, Salt Lake City (daughter of James Holmes and Harriet Phelps, married at Kanesville, Iowa, pioneers 1851, Morris Phelps company).

She was born Aug. 12, 1864, Montpelier, Idaho. Their children: Iris b. Nov. 23, 1889; Lyman b. May 12, 1894.
Married Emily Matthews July 1, 1896 (daughter of Samuel Matthews and Elizabeth Keetch). Their children: Clarence b. July 21, 1898; Naoma b. Aug. 26, 1901; Lois b. April 3, 1904; Rolla b. Sept. 17, 1905; Edith b. Aug. 29, 1908; Lyle b. Oct. 29, 1911.
Mayor of Paris, Idaho, five terms; stage senator; county assessor, commissioner and treasurer of Bear Lake county.

RICH, WILLIAM LAFAYETTE (son of William Lyman Rich and Ella Amelia Pomeroy). Born June 17, 1878, Montpelier, Idaho.
Married Elizabeth Jenett Smith Sept. 15, 1909, Salt Lake City (daughter of William Henry Smith and Mary Magdelina Garn), who was born March 16, 1888, Park City, Utah. Their child: Odes Osler b. Aug. 31, 1910. Family home Garland, Utah.
Served as interne of the Washington University hospital, St. Louis, Mo., one year; physician for the Utah-Idaho sugar factory; health officer of Garland three years; health officer of District No. 2, Box Elder county, four years. Member auxiliary legislative committee, American Medical Association.

RICH, AMASA MASON (son of Charles C. Rich and Mary Ann Phelps). Born Oct. 25, 1856, San Bernardino, Cal.
Married Mary E. Jacobs Sept. 30, 1880, Salt Lake City (daughter of Daniel Jacobs and Mary Hains, pioneers Sept. 1, 1859, Horton Haight company). She was born at Grantsville, Utah. Their children: Amasa Marion b. Oct. 26, 1881, d. July 7, 1894; Daniel Coulson b. March 31, 1884, m. Annie Stucki July 18, 1906; Myrtle b. July 12, 1890; Errol b. June 12, 1895, d. June 12, 1895; Charles O'Neal b. Dec. 16, 1897; Spencer Hains b. Dec. 22, 1899; Reed Jacobs b. Jan. 12, 1903. Family home Paris, Idaho.
President 11th quorum seventies; elder; missionary to southern states 1887-88. Sheriff of Bear Lake Co., Idaho, 1896-97; assessor and collector Bear Lake county 1909-10; mayor of Paris, Idaho, 1911.

RICH, EDWARD ISRAEL (son of Charles C. Rich and Mary Ann Phelps). Born April 9, 1868, Paris, Idaho.
Married Almira Cozzens April 9, 1894, Salt Lake City (daughter of John Cozzens and Emily Merill, the former pioneer Oct. 3, 1856, handcart company). Their children: Oertel; Cleone; Junior Edward; Avon; Thair Cozzens; Myrene; Mary Almire. Family home Ogden, Utah.
Physician and surgeon.

RICH, HEBER CHARLES CHASE (son of Charles Coulson Rich and Emeline Grover). Born Aug. 8, 1863, Centerville, Utah.
Married Edna Matilda Shepherd July 11, 1888, Manti, Utah (daughter of Marcus DeLafayette Shepherd and Harriet Editha Parrish; former pioneer 1849, contingent Mormon Battalion). She was born Oct. 12, 1869, Payson, Utah. Their children: Heber Charles Chase b. Oct. 12, 1889; Edna Clara b. Aug. 14, 1891; Oral b. Dec. 29, 1892; Lafayette Shepherd b. Sept. 28, 1894; Dean Shepherd b. Sept. 19, 1896; Arretta b. March 8, 1899, d. June 7, 1899; Terrell Shepherd b. March 22, 1903; Don Carlos b. June 28, 1905; Editha Emeline b. July 15, 1908. Family resided Paris and Rich, Idaho, and Logan, Utah.
Missionary to southern states 1886-88. Moved from Logan, Utah, to Paris, Idaho; from there to Rich, Idaho, 1905. Member high council Bingham stake; 2d counselor in stake presidency. Assessor and collector of Bingham county; first city attorney of Logan, Utah. Attorney.

RICH, GEORGE Q. (son of Charles Coulson Rich and Emeline Grover). Born March 17, 1869, Paris, Idaho.
Married Lettie B. Hancey (daughter of James Hancey and Louise Purser of Hyde Park, Utah, former pioneer 1860, the latter 1863). Their children: Portia; George Q.; Emeline G.; Lettie; Russell; Moses; Virginia Louise.
Attorney at law.

RICHARDS, JOHN (son of John Richards of Hamilton, Scotland, born May, 1769, and Mary Angelica Kenny of Toronto, Home District, Canada, born 1782, Quebec, Canada). He was born May 16, 1806, at Quebec. Came to Utah September, 1851, Lyman Shurtliff company.
Married Agnes Hill 1831, Lanark, Canada (daughter of Alexander Hill and Agnes Currey Hill, who came to Utah 1851, James Allred company). She was born June 6, 1808, Johnston, Scotland. Their children: Elizabeth b. Jan. 13, 1832, d. 1834; Elizabeth Angelica b. July 22, 1835, m. Manning Rowe July 23, 1854; Mary b. May 14, 1837, m. James Terry March 1, 1855; John Hill b. June 2, 1839, d. Sept. 2, 1861; Joseph Hill b. Dec. 5, 1841, m. Mary Willie Nov. 9, 1867; Agnes b. Nov. 1, 1843, m. George Baker Jan. 18, 1861; Rachel b. July 27, 1846, m. Jarvis Baker Dec. 25, 1864; Hyrum T. H. b. March 22, 1849, m. Agnes Muir April, 1876; Alexander W. H. b. Nov. 10, 1851, m. Sena Sorensen April, 1876; Daniel B. H. b. Nov. 14, 1853, m. Mariah Sorensen 1883.
Assisted in building Nauvoo temple. Died Nov. 15, 1889.

RICHARDS, JOSEPH HILL (son of John Richards and Agnes Hill). Born Dec. 5, 1841, Toronto, Canada. Came to Utah 1851.
Married Mary Willie Nov. 9, 1867, Salt Lake City (daughter of James G. Willie and Elizabeth Ann Pettit, who came to Utah 1847). She was born May 31, 1850, Salt Lake City.

Their children: Joseph Parley b. April 24, 1869, m. Melvina Freeman Oct. 8, 1896; James Willie b. April 13, 1871, m. Mary Westover Oct. 10, 1900; John Ezra b. Nov. 29, 1872, m. Cora Cross Oct. 14, 1896; Emma Elizabeth b. Aug. 21, 1876, m. Joseph Facer Nov. 7, 1902; Mary Amelia b. Feb. 6, 1879, d. Nov. 24, 1893; Hyrum Enos b. May 7, 1881; Anna Dell b. July 9, 1883, m. Wilford W. Freeman Oct. 1905; George Elmer b. July 16, 1885; Letty Pearl b. April 19, 1889. Family resided Millcreek and Mendon, Utah, and St. Joseph, Ariz.
Married Martha Ann Quinn Dec. 11, 1878, St. George, Utah (daughter of John and Sarah Ann Quinn), who was born Dec. 22, 1861, and died Jan. 8, 1880. Their children: Martha Ann b. Jan. 6, 1880, d. Jan. 18, 1880; Sarah Jane b. Jane 8, 1880, d. Jan. 8, 1880.
Bishop for 10 years; stake president three years; high councilor and patriarch. Postmaster 28 years; county commissioner and treasurer. Captain of militia.

RICHARDS, ALEXANDER WILLARD HILL (son of John Richards and Agnes Hill). Born Nov. 10, 1851, Mill Creek, Utah.
Married Seny Sorensen April 10, 1876, Salt Lake City (daughter of Nicholia Sorensen and Malina Olsen), who was born March 2, 1854, Hagrup, D-nmark. Their children: Alexander W. R. b. March 22, 1877, m. —— Jan. 1907; John Eugene b. March 30, 1879, m. Pearl Thompson Jan. 16, 1907; Nicholas Leo b. April 25, 1881, m. Hannah Jeffs May 27, 1903, m. Nancy Parker Jan. 8, 1913; Isaac Elmer b. April 20, 1883; Joseph Raymond b. Oct. 16, 1885; Malena Agnes b. April 9, 1888; Ireta b. June 21, 1890; Enoch b. Oct. 28, 1894; Daniel Brigham b. Aug. 6, 1896. Family home Mendon, Cache Co., Utah.
Missionary to southern states Feb. 24, 1883, to January, 1885; president of elders quorum 1885 to 1907; president first Y. M. M. I. A. in Mendon ward; high priest. Helped to build St. George temple. Justice of the peace; city marshal; city councilman for five terms; school trustee for 18 years.

RICHARDS, PHINEAS (son of Joseph Richards and Rhoda Howe of Hopkinton, Mass.). Born Nov. 15, 1788, at Hopkinton. Came to Utah Oct. 19, 1848, F. D. Richards company.
Married Wealthy Dewey Feb. 24, 1818, at Richmond, Berkshire county, Mass. (daughter of the 3d Samuel Dewey and Milley McKee of Hopkinton, Mass., pioneers Oct. 19, 1848, Franklin D. Richards company). She was born Sept. 6, 1786. Their children: Abraham; Moses; Betsy; Franklin Dewey, m. Jane Snyder Dec. 18, 1842; George Spencer, d. Oct. 30, 1838 (shot by border ruffian and buried in the well at Haun's Mill, Mo.); Samuel Whitney, m. Mary Haskin Parker Jan. 29, 1846; Maria Wealthy, m. Walter Eli Wilcox Dec. 10, 1844; Joseph William, d. near Pueblo, Colo., Nov. 19, 1846, from exposure while serving in the Mormon Battalion; Henry Phineas, m. Margaret Minerva Empey Dec. 30, 1852. Family home, Salt Lake City.
High priest. State senator; representative to legislature. Carpenter and joiner. Died Nov. 25, 1874.

RICHARDS, FRANKLIN DEWEY (son of Phineas Richards and Wealthy Dewey, Salt Lake City). Born April 2, 1821, at Richmond, Mass. Came to Utah Oct. 19, 1848.
Married Jane Snyder Dec. 18, 1842, Job Creek, Ill. (daughter of Isaac Snyder and Lovisa Comstock of Nauvoo, Ill.; the mother, Lovisa, also lived at Winter Quarters, Iowa, and Salt Lake City, pioneers Oct. 19, 1848, Franklin D. Richards company). She was born Jan. 31, 1823. Their children: Wealthy Lovisa b. Nov. 2, 1843, d. Sept. 14, 1846; Isaac Phineas b. July 23, 1846, d. July 23, 1846; Franklin Snyder b. June 20, 1849, m. Emily S. Tanner; Josephine b. May 25, 1853, m. Joseph A. West; Lorenzo Mazer b. July 5, 1857, d. Dec. 21, 1883, m. Mary M. Dunford; Charles Comstock b. Sept. 16, 1859, m. Louisa Letitia Peery. Family resided Nauvoo, Ill., Winter Quarters, Iowa, Salt Lake City and Ogden, Utah.
Married Mary Thompson March 6, 1857, Salt Lake City (daughter of John Thompson and Phoebe Robson of Nauvoo, Ill.). She was born Oct. 21, 1827. Their children: Myron John b. May 22, 1858, m. Julia Anna Peterson; Wealthy b. March 22, 1861, m. Edward B. Clark; Mary Alice b. July 5, 1863, m. Joseph E. Stevenson; Wilford Woodruff b. May 8, 1866, m. Emily Randell.
Seventy; high priest; ordained one of the 12 apostles Feb. 12, 1849; president of the 12 apostles 1898-99; church historian and recorder 1889-99. Probate judge of Weber county 1869-83; member territorial legislature; regent University of Deseret; brigadier general Nauvoo legion; member constitutional convention. Died Dec. 9, 1899, Ogden, Utah.
Mary Thompson was the widow of Willard Richards; mother of Phoebe Amelia b. June 7, 1851, m. Jacob Peart; Jennetta b. Oct. 22, 1854, d. Sept. 23, 1855.

RICHARDS, JOSEPH T. (son of Franklin S. and Emily S. Tanner). Born Dec. 8, 1871, Ogden, Utah.
Married Mattie Sells. Their children: Martha; Josephine; Edward. Family home, Salt Lake City.
Member of the law firm of Richards, Moyle & Richards; and of Richards & Richards he was the junior member; in 1898 he became a member of the firm of Bennett, Harkness, Howat, Bradley & Richards, and in 1900 upon the dissolution of that firm became the senior member of the firm of Richards & Ferry, which later changed to Richards, Richards & Ferry. Assistant United States attorney for the territory of Utah 1893. Mining man. Member Alta Club, Commercial and Country clubs.

RICHARDS, CHARLES COMSTOCK (son of Franklin Dewey Richards and Jane Snyder). Born Sept. 16, 1859, Salt Lake City.
Married Louisa Letitia Peery Dec. 18, 1877, Salt Lake City (daughter of David Harold Peery and Nancy Campbell Higginbotham of Burk's Garden, Tazewell county, Va., former came to Utah about Sept. 1, 1864, William Pritchett company, latter died in Virginia). She was born July 14, 1860. Their children: Letitia Jane b. Feb. 2, 1879, m. Robert L. Burton; Charles Comstock b. May 29, 1881, m. Beatrice Finn; Mabel Clare b. May 12, 1884, d. Oct. 22, 1892; Jesse Snyder b. April 11, 1887, m. Kathryn Coughnet; Harold Peery b. Nov. 6, 1889; Laurence William b. Dec. 4, 1892; Lorenzo Mazer b. Jan. 10, 1896; Franklin Dewey b. Nov. 11, 1969. Family home Ogden, Utah.
Elder; seventy; high priest; member Weber stake Sunday school board 1905-08; alternate high councilor in Weber stake in 1908; 1st counselor in Ogden stake presidency since July 26, 1908. County recorder of Weber county 1881-84; county attorney for Weber county 1884-90; county clerk of Weber county 1883-88; representative in territorial legislature 1888; councilor in territorial legislature 1890; member constitutional convention 1887; regent University of Deseret 1888-90; member territorial board of equalization 1888-92; trustee territorial reform school 1888-92; secretary and acting governor of the territory of Utah 1893-96. Attorney at law.

RICHARDS, MYRON JOHN (son of Franklin Dewey Richards and Mary Thompson). Born May 22, 1858, Provo, Utah.
Married Julia Anna Peterson July 3, 1879 (daughter of Charles S. Peterson and Ann Patten), who was born June 8, 1862. Their children: Mary Ann b. Nov. 4, 1880, d. Feb. 18, 1884; Myron John b. Aug. 29, 1882, m. Alla M. Vandeet; Mabel b. June 27, 1884, d. June 5, 1888; Ralph C. b. April 14, 1886, m. Ethel May Ford.
Married Isabella Mary Young May 29, 1885, at Logan, Utah (daughter of Thomas C. and Mary Young), who was born at Perry, Utah. Their children: Hyrum Y. b. Aug. 5, 1886; Maggie b. May 26, 1888, m. George Franklin Wood; Elmer T. b. Aug. 31, 1891; Florence b. Nov. 3, 1896; Eden b. Feb. 17, 1899; Legrand b. Nov. 10, 1901, d. Nov. 10, 1901.
Bishop for 27 years. Assisted in building Plymouth, Fielding and Riverside wards. School trustee for six years; county commissioner for two years; county treasurer four years.

RICHARDS, WILFORD WOODRUFF (son of Franklin Dewey Richards and Mary Thompson). Born May 8, 1866, Farmington, Utah.
Married Emily Randall March 28, 1888, Logan, Utah (daughter of Alfred J. Randall and Margaret Harley of Salt Lake City, Ogden and Centerville, Utah, came to Utah 1848, Heber C. Kimball company). She was born April 8, 1869. Their children: Laura b. March 31, 1890; Wilford Woodruff, Jr., b. June 5, 1891; Clyde R. b. Oct. 17, 1894; Mary b. March 30, 1896; Melvin Ross b. Jan. 5, 1898; Ruth b. March 15, 1900; Ireta b. March 3, 1902; Carol b. Dec. 25, 1903; Pearl b. Dec. 29, 1905; Franklin D. b. Aug. 7, 1908; Margaret Iva b. July 21, 1910; Helen b. Oct. 31, 1912. Family resided Farmington, Utah, and Georgetown and Paris, Idaho.
Bishop of Georgetown, Idaho, June, 1901, to June, 1906; member of the Bear Lake stake presidency June, 1906, till death; missionary to old Virginia Dec. 28, 1891, to Dec. 20, 1893. Mayor of Paris, Idaho, 1906-10; justice of the peace for two terms; commissioner of Bear Lake county for one term; Idaho state representative one term. Farmer; stockraiser. Died Sept. 6, 1912, Paris, Idaho.

RICHARDS, HENRY PHINEAS (son of Phineas Richards and Wealthy Dewey). Born Nov. 30, 1831, Richmond, Berkshire county, Mass. Came to Utah Oct. 19, 1848, F. D. Richards company.
Married Margaret Minerva Empey Dec. 30, 1852, Salt Lake City (daughter of William and Mary Ann Empey of same place, pioneers 1847, Brigham Young company). She was born April 19, 1831. Their children: Henrietta b. June 11, 1854 (d. May 24, 1904), m. Phillin Margetts; Mary Ann b. Sept. 5, 1856, m. Alonzo Young; Joseph Henry b. Sept. 2, 1860, d. May 16, 1896; Minerva b. Oct. 17, 1862, m. Richard W. Young; William Phineas b. March 12, 1865, d. Oct. 18, 1908; Nelson Alonzo b. Sept. 7, 1867, d. Dec. 22, 1874; Henry Willard b. Oct. 21, 1869, d. July 2, 1892; Emma Woodruff b. July 20, 1872, d. Aug. 22, 1878. Family home, Salt Lake City.
President 8th quorum seventies; missionary to Hawaiian Islands 1854-57; high councilor. Oil inspector and sealer of weights and measures. Merchant.

RICHARDS, THOMAS (son of William Richards of South Wales and Elizabeth Bowen). Born May 5, 1846, at Neath, Abbey, South Wales; came to Utah October, 1862, Horton Haight company.
Married Adalaide Rose March 22, 1868 (daughter of Ralph Rose and Manerva Clothier). She was born Nov. 9, 1849. Their children: Thomas W. b. Feb. 2, 1869, m. Elizn Bird Jan. 3, 1893; William R. b. Nov. 10, 1870, m. Salina Hathaway Oct. 23, 1896; Elizabeth b. Oct. 22, 1872, m. Charles Dayton July 28, 1891; George R. b. May 26, 1875, m. Mina Wilson April 1, 1901; Ellen b. Dec. 13, 1877, m. Don C. Dayton Feb. 5, 1896; Reese b. May 28, 1880, m. Pearl b. Aug. 4, 1883, m. Alonzo Waldrum Jan. 14, 1905; Minerva b. May 15, 1886, m. Kenneth Molen Feb. 14, 1907; Ester A. b. July 21, 1889; Daisy b. Sept. 2, 1892. Family home St. Anthony, Idaho.
High priest; bishop's counselor at Twin Groves ward.

PIONEERS AND PROMINENT MEN OF UTAH 1131

RICHARDS, THOMAS, Jr. (son of Thomas Richards and Adalaide Rose). Born Feb. 2, 1869 at Malad, Idaho.
Married Eliza Bird (daughter of Martin Bird and Emma Gardiner). She was born Feb. 2, 1877. Their children: Grace b. March 26, 1895; Aita b. —; Louis b. —; Albert b —; Ella b. Aug. 25, 1903; Emma b. March 16, 1905; Ronald b. Nov. 5, 1907; Wayne b. Dec. 3, 1910. Family home Palisade, Idaho.
Bishop's counselor; elder at Palisade, Idaho.

RICHARDS, WILLARD (son of Joseph Richards and Rhoda Howe of Massachusetts). Born June 24, 1804, in Massachusetts. Came to Utah July 24, 1847, Brigham Young company.
Married Nannie Longstroth (daughter of Stephen Longstroth and Ann Gill of Iron Clift, Lancastershire, Eng., pioneers 1848, Brigham Young company). She was born April 15, 1828. Their children: Alice Ann, m. Lott Smith; Mary Absena, m. Joel F. Grover; Stephen Longstroth b. July 29, 1853, m. Emma Louise Stayner. Family home, Salt Lake City.
Married Rhoda Harriett Foss Nov. 30, 1851, Salt Lake City (daughter of Calvin Foss, Saco, Me., and Sarah Bracket Carter, Saco, Me., and Salt Lake City; she was a pioneer Oct. 14, 1850, Wilford Woodruff company). She was born April 19, 1830, and came to Utah with mother. Only child: Calvin Willard b. Oct. 7, 1852, m. Emma Irene Walker, m. Martha Louise Madsen. Family home, Salt Lake City. Died March 11, 1854.

RICHARDS, STEPHEN LONGSTROTH (son of Willard Richards and Nannie Longstroth). Born July 29, 1853, Salt Lake City.
Married Emma Louise Stayner Aug. 25, 1878, Salt Lake City (daughter of Arthur Stayner and Emma Turner of Island Guernsey, Eng.; former came to Utah 1855, latter 1854). She was born Dec. 5, 1858. Their children: Stephen Longstroth b. June 18, 1879, m. Irene B. Merrill; Alice b. Sept. 20, 1880, died; Claud b. June 14, 1882, m. Mary C. Taylor; George Gill b. Sept. 5, 1883, m. Florence Lott Farnsworth, Stayner b. Dec. 20, 1885, m. Jennie Foot Taylor; Willard b. Sept. 30, 1887; Russell b. July 18, 1889; Arthur b. Feb. 3, 1891, d. child; Nannie b. March 31, 1893, d. child; Grace b. March 15, 1895.
Elder; missionary to England 1876-78; treasurer of Y. M. M. I. A. Physician and surgeon.

RICHARDS, GEORGE GILL (son of Stephen Longstroth Richards and Emma Louise Stayner). Born Sept. 5, 1883, Salt Lake City.
Married Florence Lott Farnsworth Sept. 3, 1912, Salt Lake City (daughter of Philo T. Farnsworth and Julia Murdock, pioneers, oxteam company).

RICHARDS, CALVIN WILLARD (son of Willard Richards and Rhoda Harriett Foss). Born Oct. 7, 1852, Salt Lake City.
Married Emma Irene Walker Dec. 24, 1872, at Salt Lake City (daughter of Lorin Walker and Lavina Smith, both of Farmington, Utah, pioneers 1860, John Smith company). She was born July 28, 1854. Their children: Calvin Willard b. April 28, 1874, m. Faney Snow; Effie Irene b. Feb. 13, 1876, m. Joseph H. Welling; Sarah Bracket b. March 10, 1878, m. Milton H. Welling; Rhoda Harriett b. Nov. 6, 1879, m. William H. Stayner; Hyrum Smith b. Dec. 23, 1882, d. Dec. 29, 1905; Ezra Carter b. Oct. 9, 1884, m. Blanch Laub; Bertie Loren b. Nov. 4, 1886, m. Ella Chamberlin; Ruby Lovina b. Sept. 6, 1888, m. Leo Farnsworth; Horace Leroy b. Nov. 1, 1891. Family resided Farmington and Fielding, Utah.
Married Martha Louise Madson Jan. 16, 1901, Salt Lake City (daughter of Adolph Madson and Mary Wagner of Brigham City, Utah, pioneers 1860). She was born Feb. 12, 1866. Their children: Melvin Madson b. April 23, 1902; Lorenzo Adolph b. April 24, 1904; Mathias Cowley b. Dec. 7, 1907; Sterling J. b. March 24, 1909. Family home Brigham City, Utah.
High priest; missionary to England 1904-06. Commissioner of Box Elder county. Farmer.

RICHARDS, WILLIAM. Born 1797, Glamorganshire, Wales. Came to Utah Oct. 1, 1854, Daniel Garn company.
Married Alice Howells, who died in Wales. Their children: Kathryne, m. James Radford Millard; William; Cecilia; Morgan.

RICHARDSON, SHADRACH (son of Shadrach Richardson of Cumberland county, Ky.). Born Nov. 21, 1816, in Cumberland county, Ky. Came to Utah 1852, Truman Tryon company.
Married Lavina Stewart about 1841 (daughter of Philander B. Stewart and Sarah Scott, former died in Ohio, latter a pioneer 1850). She was born June 8, 1824. Came to Utah 1852, Truman Tryon company. Their children: Shadrach M. b. March 11, 1848, m. Keturah Hand June 14, 1875; William W. b. Nov. 9, 1851, m. Sarah J. Hone Oct. 1879. Family home Payson, Utah.
Married Sarah Haskell in 1860, at Payson, Utah (daughter of James Miles and Sarah Haskell, former came to Utah with a contingent of Mormon Battalion). Their children: Thomas b. Feb. 2, 1861, m. Eunice L. Hickman 1884; Richard b. Aug. 18, 1862; Lavina b. Aug. 16, 1864, m. Isaac Hansen 1882; David b. April 1866, m. Eliza J. Betts 1899.
Member 17th quorum seventies.

RICHARDSON, SHADRACH M. (son of Shadrach Richardson and Levina Stewart). Born March 11, 1848, in Mills Co., Iowa.
Married Keturah Hand June 14, 1875, Salt Lake City (daughter of James Hand and Sarah Simpkins). Born Dec. 11, 1858, Yorkshire, Eng. Their children: Shadrach W. b. April 13, 1876; George M. b. Dec. 12, 1877; James I. b. Jan. 26, 1880; Sarah K. b. June 7, 1882; Adaline b. Aug. 12, 1884, m. William Hone Sept. 11, 1901; Nellie b. Feb. 6, 1887, m. J. H. Schaerrer Feb. 14, 1906; Ivy b. May 7, 1889, m. J. A. Francorom March 15, 1911; Lexia b. Nov. 16, 1891; Delilah b. March 13, 1893, m. C. A. Fugal June 21, 1911; Joseph Woodruff b. Aug. 26, 1896; Teresa b. June 22, 1899; Orion Franklin b. Nov. 5, 1901. Family home Benjamin, Utah.
Elder 1875; high priest; alternate high councilor, Nebo stake. Constable Benjamin precinct, Utah county, one term; justice of peace three terms; appointed U. S. deputy surveyor June 15, 1883.

RICHARDSON, THOMAS (son of Thomas Richardson, born Feb. 18, 1779, Manchester, Eng. Came to Utah July 29, 1847, James Brown's detachment of the Mormon Battalion.
Married Mary M. Mallalu 1824, at Preston, near Manchester, Eng. She died October, 1845, Nauvoo, Ill. Their children: Jane, died; Mary, m. Mr. Latronch; John b. July 21, 1835 (d. March 10, 1906), m. Lola Tyler; Robert, m. Sarah Taylor; Susan, m. George Hutchins; m. Howard Bratton; Violet, m. James Steed; Benjamin and Sarah, died; Thomas Jr. b. April 9, 1844, m. Merab Stone 1864.
Married Annie (Owen) Clark February, 1846, Nauvoo, Ill. Resided at Farmington 1852, and later moved to Kaysville; moved to Ogden 1854, and to Kaysville 1856. The seventh convert in England to be baptized into L. D. S. church; became a high priest and presided over Gadfield Elm conference, England. First president of Slaterville stake, 1864-77. Died Nov. 3, 1886, Richmond, Utah.

RICHARDS, THOMAS (son of Thomas Richardson and Mary M. Mallalu). Born April 9, 1844, Montrose, Iowa. Came to Utah 1852.
Married Merab Stone in 1864 at Slaterville, Utah (daughter of Amos Pease Stone and Amelia Bishop, pioneers 1850). She was born Sept. 26, 1845, New Haven, Conn, and died b. Oct. 5, 1865, d. same day; Thomas Ives b. Nov. 30, 1866, m. Kate Bratton June 18, 1885, m. Ellen Lance Feb. 8, 1890, b. Oct. 17, 1875, m. James Albert b. Sept. 15, 1870, d. Dec. 26, 1875; John b. Feb. 20, 1873, m. Fannie Francis June 22, 1898; George b. Oct. 14, 1875, d. same day; Merab Violet b. Oct. 17, 1876 (d. June 14, 1901), m. Edward T. Morgan 1893; Emily b. April 2, 1879 (d. Jan. 9, 1907), m. Heber Dillie 1899; Minerva b. May 6, 1881, m. Andrew Sorenson, m. Houghton Weaver 1908; Nathan b. June 9, 1883, d. same day; Robert b. Jan. 17, 1884, m. Dora Hunt Oct., 1909; Anna b. May 14, 1887, d. same day.
Missionary among Indians at Washakee, Box Elder county, Utah, 1876-77. First pioneer settler of Pocatello, Idaho, moving there Sept. 10, 1881. Farmer.

RICHARDSON, THOMAS IVES (son of Thomas Richardson and Merab Stone). Born Nov. 30, 1865, Slaterville, Utah.
Married Kate Bratton Jan. 13, 1885, American Falls, Idaho, who was born 1869, San Diego, Cal.
Married Ellen Lance Feb. 8, 1890 (daughter of Lewis Temperance Lance), who was born Jan. 12, 1874, America Fork, Utah. Their children: Thomas Lewis b. Feb. 1, 1901; Howard Robert b. Sept. 28, 1892, m. Eva Barron Dec. 13, 1911; Myrtle Ellen b. July 12, 1894, m. Floyd Pope Aug. 16, 1912; Lizzie Temperance b. July 31, 1896; Grace Merab b. Nov. 1897; Frank George b. Oct. 1899; Ida Alice b. March 9, 1901; Frank George b. 1902; Hattie May b. May 20, 1903; Richard Lance b. Feb. 5, 1907. Family home Neeley, Idaho.
Married Hattie Knapp April 29, 1908, Brigham City, Utah (daughter of William Knapp and Eliza Cole), who was born April 9, 1876, Chestertown, Warren county, N. Y. Their children: Ralph Lee b. Jan. 19, 1909; Ella Pearl b. April 5, 1910; Ona Maude b. March 24, 1911; Edward Francis b. March 15, 1912.
Member 124th quorum seventies; missionary to New York 1902-04. Farmer; sheepraiser.

RICHARDSON, WILLIAM (son of William Richardson and Isabell Richardson of Tole Cross, Lanarkshire, Scotland). Born June 18, 1829, Park Head, Glasgow, Scotland. Came to Utah Oct. 17, 1863, Captain Rawlins company.
Married Joannah Fotheringham Walker June 20, 1851, Park Head, Lanarkshire, Scotland (daughter of Francis Walker and Jeanette Fotheringham of Tole Cross, Scotland). She was born Dec. 11, 1827, at Tole Cross. Their children: Jeanette R. b. April 8, 1852, d. infant; William, b. April 4, 1854, m. Jane Muir; John b. April 13, 1856, m. Isabell Muir; James b. June 16, 1858, d. infant; Harriett R. b. Dec. 20, 1860, m. Thomas Todd; Robert b. Sept. 1862, d. infant; Archibald Ogilvie b. Oct. 1, 1863, m. Sarah Ann Horrocks; David Fisher b. Oct. 1, 1865, m. Lydia Moon, m. Helen Merrels; Isabell b. March 17, 1868, m. Adolphus Sessions; Annie b. March 27, 1868, m. John Stimpson. Family home Heber City, Utah.
Bishop. Settler of Heber City 1863. Farmer. Died Aug. 9, 1904. Jensen, Uintah Co., Utah.

PIONEERS AND PROMINENT MEN OF UTAH

RICHARDSON, WILLIAM (son of William Richardson and Joanna Fotheringham Walker). Born April 4, 1854, in Scotland. Came to Utah Oct. 17, 1863, Captain Rawlins company.
Married Jane Muir Jan. 1, 1874, Heber City, Utah (daughter of George Muir and Margaret Howe of Heber City, pioneers 1856, Captain McCurdy handcart company). She was born July 5, 1854. Their children: Margaret Ann b. Aug. 19, 1874, m. William, J. Kirk; Jeanet b. Oct. 2, 1876, m. Joseph Lindsey; Walter R. b. Oct. 17, 1879, m. Vernie Ohlwiler; James William b. Aug. 9, 1881; Rose Halladay b. April 23, 1885, m. George Walker; Kate b. Dec. 20, 1888, m. Ernest Ast; George Muir b. April 23, 1892; Archie L. b. Jan. 4, 1895, died; Ralph b. June 26, 1897, died. Family home Pleasant Grove, Utah.
High priest; Sunday school superintendent. Farmer and stockraiser.

RICHARDSON, JOHN THORNTON (son of William Richardson and Joanna Fotheringham Walker). Born April 13, 1856, at Pittaton, Pa. Came to Utah Oct. 1, 1863, Isaac C. Haight oxteam company.
Married Isabella Muir Dec. 24, 1878, Heber City, Utah (daughter of George Muir and Margaret Hannah of Kilmarnia, Scotland; came to Utah September, 1856, handcart company). She was born June 21, 1860, Wales, San Pete Co., Utah. Their children: Joan b. July 27, 1879, died Aug. 3, 1879; Leroy H. b. July 16, 1881; John Thornton b. April 8, 1884, m. Pearl Timothy; Maggie Bell b. Nov. 3, 1886, m. Henry Moroni Moon; William M. b. May 8, 1891, m. Clara Collier; George Francis b. Feb. 13, 1895. Family resided Heber City and Jensen, Utah.
Constable of Jensen, Utah, 5 years. Clerk of the school district 5 years. Carpenter; farmer and apiarist.

RICHARDSON, ARCHIE SQUIRES (son of William Richardson and Joanna Fotheringham Walker). Born Oct. 11, 1863, Heber City, Utah.
Married Sarah Ann Horrocks Sept. 11, 1889, Manti, Utah (daughter of Roger Horrocks and Sarah Ann Taylor, pioneers 1866). She was born Dec. 22, 1869. Their only child was Sarah Ann b. July 29, 1906.
Missionary to southern states 1895-96; to central states 1904; to Scotland 1905-06; counselor to Bishop Benjamin Cluff, center ward, Wasatch stake; bishop of Jensen ward August, 1908; president of Y. M. M. I. A. Wasatch county. School trustee Jensen county; commissioner Uinta county 1903-04. Located in Jensen June, 1899. Farmer; cattle and sheep raiser.

RICHEY, WILLIAM. Came to Utah 1848.
Married Margaret Ann Adair (daughter of Mrs. Belden). Their children: James; Jane; William B., m. Johanna Maria Hougaard.
Member 48th quorum Seventies. Missionary to Cherokee Nation. Patriarch and high priest. Died at Parowan, Utah.

RICHEY, WILLIAM B. (son of William Richey and Margaret Ann Adair). He was born May 17, 1838, in Mississippi.
Married Johanna Maria Hougaard 1867, Manti, Utah (daughter of Rasmus H. Hougaard and Mary Magdaline, both of Falster, Denmark—pioneers 1848). She was born Jan. 1, 1849. Their children: Margaret Ann b. Nov. 3, 1868, m. Jens. J. Hansen; Mary M., died aged 9; Jeannetta J. b. July 25, 1871, m. Jens J. Hansen; Emily Jane b. June 19, —, died aged 7; Sarah Bell b. Nov. 19, —, m. Dr. Frank Tinges; Julia Dean, m. Adolph Hansen; Nellie L. b. Feb. 5, —, m. Joseph A. Young; Jennie Lynn b. Oct. 27, —, m. Fred Risley; Will Ina b. Oct. —. m. Leo Foster; William b. Sept. 21, 1883, m. Martha Braithwaite; John B. b. April 20, 1885, m. Mabel Kennedy; Benjamin B. Apr. —. Family home Manti, Utah.
Road Supervisor. Freighter and farmer. Died May 9, 1911, Manti, Utah.

RICHINS, EDWARD (son of Richard Richins and Priscilla Wager, of Gloucestershire, Eng.). Born April 16, 1835, Sheepcombe, Eng. Came to Utah Nov. 7, 1855, William H. Hooper company.
Married Caroline Ellen Tipper Dec. 25, 1862, Henefer, Utah (daughter of Harriet Tipper of Nettleton, Gloucestershire, Eng.). She was born Feb. 20, 1846. Their children: Albert Edward b. 1863, died; Alma Ether b. Dec. 3, 1867, m. Hattie Richins.
Married ———. She was born April 30, 1849. Their children: Sarah Ellen b. Oct. 6, 1869, m. Alexander Calderwood; Heber Charles b. Dec. 25, 1871, m. Ruth Ralph; Moroni b. April 3, 1873, m. Laura Bull; Carolina Lavenia b. Nov. 12, 1874, m. Alexander Steele; Nephi b. Sept. 25, 1896, m. Sarahann Banks; Ebenezer b. April 9, 1878, m. Lilly Ralph; Joseph Elijah b. Feb. 28, 1880, m. Eva Richins; Willard Richard and Wilford Thomas (twins) b. Nov. 25, 1882, both died same day; Jared b. April 6, 1894, m. Ethel Ralph; George Edward b. April 4, 1886, m. Myrtle Ralph; Florence Precilla b. July 16, 1891, m. Walter B. Wilson. Families resided Echo, Utah.
High priest; missionary to England 1889-90; bishop of Echo ward four years. Veteran Echo Canyon campaign; selectman at Coalville, Utah. Farmer and stockraiser.

RICHMAN, JOHN (son of Matthew Richman and Elizabeth Tagg of England). Born Jan. 14, 1828, Molton Egate, Eng. Came to Utah Oct. 17, 1862, Henry W. Miller company.
Married Sarah Ann Stephenson (daughter of Simon and Mary Ann Sims), who was born April 21, 1826, and came to Utah Oct. 17, 1862, Henry W. Miller company. Their children: Hyrum S. b. June 5, 1851, m. Rhoda Ann Smith 1875; John W., m. Jane Sinfield; George H. b. 1861, m. Mary W. McKinley; Elizabeth b. 1864, m. Charles Haws; Mary Ellen b. 1868, m. John Henderson. Family home Paradise, Cache Co., Utah.

RICHMAN, HYRUM S. (son of John Richman and Sarah Ann Stephenson). Born June 5, 1851, in England.
Married Rhoda Ann Burrows, Bottsford, Lincolnshire, Eng.). (daughter of John Smith and Elizabeth Chapman), who was born Dec. 24, 1858, Salt Lake City. Their children: Hyrum John b. Sept. 22, 1876, m. Rosella Acock Aug. 17, 1898; Isaac S. b. June 30, 1878, m. Nettie McKinley Nov. 11, 1903; Thomas G. b. Nov. 19, 1852, m. Elizabeth May Butt Oct. 2, 1908; Elizabeth S. b. April 18, 1884, m. John R. George April 1, 1903; Parley S. b. Jan. 24, 1888, m. Clara Elizabeth Stewart Sept. 22, 1910; Louis Orar b. Sept. 21, 1892. Family home Teton, Fremont Co., Idaho.

RICHMOND, JOSEPH BURROWS (son of Thomas Richmond and Sarah Ann Burrows, Bottsford, Lincolnshire, Eng.). Born May 16, 1841, Nauvoo, Ill. Came to Utah September, 1852.
Married Emma Orton May 3, 1863, Provo, Utah (daughter of William Reed Orton, Des Moines, Iowa, pioneer 1852). She was born Dec. 9, 1842. Their children: Polly Ann b. Feb. 6, 1864, m. Richard Smith; Almeda b. June 25, 1865, m. Jabez Waters; Emma Jane b. Jan. 31, 1867, m. George Meldrum; Sonoma b. Aug. 25, 1868, m. Joseph Meldrum; Joseph Thomas b. May 22, 1870, died; William Reed b. Nov. 20, 1871; Evert Burrows b. Dec. 25, 1873, m. Carrie Ellen Martin; Maud b. Sept. 16, 1875, m. E. Swarts; Harriet Rebecca b. March 29, 1877, m. Frank Speckert; Jessie b. Feb. 27, 1879; Florence b. Jan. 29, 1899, m. William Crethers; Fred Garfield b. Nov. 1, 1882, m. —— Naylor; Ray b. Dec. 7, 1884, died.
Married Francis Jane Lawrence (Martin) May 25, 1909, Manti, Utah (daughter of Joseph Lawrence and Rachel Burcham of Illinois), who was born July 25, 1861. Family home Provo City, Utah.
Elder. Councilman from 4th precinct, Provo. Farmer.

RICHTER, ADOLPH (son of John and Ernestine Richter of Germany). Born Aug. 10, 1859, in Germany. Came to Utah 1892.
Married Lucy A. Deakin May 2, 1893, Salt Lake City (daughter of Robert and Hannah Deakin, St. Paul, Minn). Family home, Salt Lake City.
Real estate, insurance and loans.

RICKS, JOEL (son of Jonathan Ricks, born Feb. 18, 1772, Nash county, N. C., and Temperance Edwards, born Jan. 23, 1883, Nash county—were married 1796). He was born Feb. 18, 1804, on the Donaldson Creek farm, Trigg Co., Ky. Came to Utah September 24, 1848, Heber C. Kimball company.
Married Eleanor Martin May 1, 1827, who came to Utah with husband. Their children: Thomas Edwin b. July 21, 1828, m. Tabitha Hendricks Aug. 18, 1853; Lewis b. Dec. 25, 1830, m. Ammorette Allen Dec. 25, 1859; Sally Ann b. Dec. 28, 1832, died; Clarinda b. Jan. 10, 1835, died; Temperance b. Jan. 4, 1837, m. Arza E. Hinckley February, 1857; Jonathan, b. Jan. 23, 1841, m. Eliza Zymon; Mary b. June 19, 1843, m. William R. Smith April 23, 1857; Josiah b. May 27, 1845, m. Lucy A. Merrill; Joel Martin b. Oct. 15, 1850, died; Nathan b. Jan. 17, 1853, m. Sarah A. Taylor Nov. 13, 1879. Family home Logan, Utah.
Married Sarah B. Fisk (Allen) Oct. 26, 1852 (daughter of Varnum Fisk and Sally Eams). She was born Sept. 22, 1819, Potsdam, St. Lawrence Co., N. Y. Their children: Ezra Varnum b. July 13, 1853, m. Lois J. Clark Oct. 24, 1888; Sarah Seriah b. Jan. 17, 1856, died; Ellen b. March 30, 1856, m. Charles W. Nibley March 30, 1858; Joel b. July 21, 1858, m. Susette Cardon Jan. 13, 1881; Adelia b. Oct. 24, 1860, died; Esther Adeline b. Oct. 28, 1862, m. Joseph E. Wilson Aug. 17, 1888.
In connection with others he built the first saw mill and grist mill in Logan. Treasurer Cache county more than 30 years. He was also interested in many other industries. He was a very energetic worker in the church.

RICKS, THOMAS E. (son of Joel Ricks and Eleanor Martin). Born July 21, 1828, Donaldson Creek, Trigg Co., Ky. Came to Utah with father.
Married Tabitha Hendricks Aug. 18, 1853, who was born Sept. 30, 1830, and came to Utah Sept. 24, 1848, Heber C. Kimball company. Their children: Sarah C. b. June 4, 1854, m. James R. Turman Oct. 19, 1874; Thomas Edwin Jr. b. Dec. 3, 1855, m. Mary Ann Hibbard Oct. 1, 1878; Joseph b. June 7, 1857, m. Margaret Charles Oct. 20, 1876; Hyrum b. July 24, 1858, m. Martha Bitter April 1, 1880; Heber b. April 27, 1860, m. Mary Ann Nelson Jan. 13, 1881; Brigham b. April 27, 1864, m. Clara Josephine Larson Jan. 13, 1881; Mary Elizabeth b. Aug. 19, 1861; William b. Sept. 25, 1868, m. Sarah Ellen Harris April 14, 1886; Alice b. Aug. 20, 1866; James b. Dec. 14, 1867, m. Lucretia H. Arrowsmith Oct. 3, 1894; Samuel b. Feb. 20, 1870, m. Ada Turner 1897; George b. Jan. 7, 1876, m. Hattie Secrist March 15, 1899. Family resided Centerville, Farmington, Logan, Utah, and Rexburg, Idaho.
Married Tamer Loader March 27, 1857, who was born Sept.

PIONEERS AND PROMINENT MEN OF UTAH 1133

8, 1833, in England. Their children: Amy Eliza b. Dec. 11, 1858, m. Alpha Loader Jaques March 1, 1876; Sarah Eleanor b. Feb. 6, 1861, m. John Dalling June 27, 1877; Joel b. Feb. 12, 1863, died; Ann b. Nov. 17, 1864, died; Moriah b. Aug. 23, 1867, m. John T. Smallie; Clarinda b. Feb. 15, 1872, died; Lamelia b. Nov. 24, 1874, died.
Bishop Cache Valley stake several years; president Fremont stake, which position he held to his death. He was the founder of academy at Rexburg, Idaho, which was afterward named Ricks Academy in memory of its founder.

RICKS, THOMAS EDWIN (son of Thomas Edwin Ricks and Tabitha Hendricks). Born Dec. 3, 1855, Centerville, Utah.
Married Mary Ann Hibbard Oct. 11, 1878 (daughter of George Hibbard and Hannah Williams). She was born May 19, 1858, Salt Lake City. Their children: Silas Edward b. June 21, 1879, died; Thomas Edwin, III b. June 6, 1882, m. Maude E. Dayhell; Floretta b. Sept. 23, 1886, m. James Webster; George Abraham b. May 5, 1889; Joel b. July 28, 1892; Preston b. Oct. 21, 1898. Family resided Centerville, Farmington and Logan, Utah, and Rexburg, Idaho.
Bishop first ward Rexburg. City councilman and mayor Rexburg. Public-spirited, and prominent in all things for advancement and progress.

RIDDLE, ISAAC (son of John Riddle and Elizabeth Stewart). Born March 22, 1830, in Boone county, Ky. Came to Utah Sept. 15, 1850, Richard Sessions company.
Married Mary Ann Eagles Aug. 29, 1863 (daughter of Elias and Mary Eagles of England, pioneers). She was born Nov. 5, 1845, in England. Their children: Lydia A.; Safrona; Lillie C.; Wallace M.; Charles E.; John E.; Andrew I., died. Family home Beaver, Utah.
Missionary to Georgia; bishop's counselor. Missionary among the Indians 10 years. Miller and stockraiser. Died Sept. 1, 1906.

RIDGES, JOSEPH HARRIS (son of Edward Ridges of Tottenham, Hampshire, Eng.). Born April 27, 1827, at Tottenham. Came to Utah September, 1857, Charles C. Richards company.
Married Adelaide Whitley 1852, in London, Eng. (daughter of William Whitley and Nancy Johnson of London), who was born in 1830. Their children: Alfred J. m. Mary A. Morris; Adelaide, m. George Wood; Annie, m. David Williams; Alma, d. aged 8; Ernest E., m. Ella Beesley; May E., m. Josiah Sees. Family home, Salt Lake City.
Married Emma Smith in 1858, Salt Lake City, Utah, who was born 1823. Their only child: Mary, m. Mr. Perry.
Married Agatha Pratt January 11, 1866, Salt Lake City (daughter of Parley P. Pratt and Ann Agatha Walker, of Salt Lake City), who was born July 7, 1848. Their children: Florence, m. Joseph H. Dean; Milton, m. May Foster; Claribel, m. John E. Pike; Aggie Louise, m. George E. Carpenter; Beatrice, m. Thomas J. Jones; Berenice, m. Alonzo J. Haddock; Joseph P., m. Viola Brimm; Sidney P., d. aged 2.
High priest; builder of tabernacle organ; built first organ in Australia, brought it to Utah and placed it in the old Adobe Tabernacle. Organ builder and contractor.

RIGBY, WILLIAM (son of Edward Rigby and Susanna Hartliff, of Lancastershire, Eng.). Born Aug. 8, 1838, Gayland, Lancastershire, Eng. Came to Utah in September, 1847.
Married Catherine Glover March 18, 1859, Salt Lake City (daughter of William Glover and Jane Cowan, of Scotland, pioneers fall of 1849). She was born Feb. 10, 1842. Their children: William Seth, m. Agnes Walker; Edward; Jane; Joseph Edward; Catherine Elizabeth, m. Chas. Mageets; John Alma; George Frederick, m. Chessie Bouregard; Vinnie May. Family home, Salt Lake City.
Member quorum seventies; block teacher. Farmer and stockraiser. Veteran Indian wars, 1864-66. Died Dec. 24, 1903.

RIGBY, WILLIAM FREDRICK (son of Joseph Rigby and Margarett Littlewood, of Saddleworth, Yorkshire, Eng.). Born Jan. 29, 1833, Saddleworth, Eng. Came to Utah Oct. 5, 1853, Brown and Harmon company.
Married Mary Clark Aug. 9, 1852, Blockport, Eng. (daughter of John Clark and Elizabeth Brodbury), who was born Sept. 8, 1831. Their children: John, died; Mary Jane b. June 28, 1857, m. Samuel Roskelly March 2, 1874; William Fredrick, Jr. b. Oct. 9, 1859, m. Sarah Clarke April 28, 1881; George C. b. Feb. 23, 1863, m. Mary C. Clarke March 1, 1883; Margarett b. Feb. 12, 1864, m. Samuel Roskelly March 11, 1882; Lavina b. Feb. 28, 1866, m. Charles Oea Card Dec. 1855; Marlin b. May 23, 1868, m. Annie F. Rigby; Sarah b. July 26, 1871, died. Family home Newton, Utah.
Missionary to Great Britain 1887-89; bishop; representative to the legislature from Fremont Co., Idaho. Died March 13, 1901, at Logan.

RIGBY, GEORGE C. (son of William Fredrick and Mary Clark). Born Feb. 23, 1862, Wellsville, Utah.
Married Mary C. Clarke March 1, 1883, Salt Lake City, Utah (daughter of Amos Clarke and Ann Johnston of Rhollanerchingog, Wales). She was born May 27, 1864. Their children: Mary Ann b. Oct. 18, 1884, m. Horace Jenkins Nov. 15, 1905; Amos b. Aug. 11, 1886, m. Ann Christensen Jan. 27, 1910; Moses W. b. Aug. 11, 1888, m. Iva Nelsen Dec. 21, 1911; Mariam b. Aug. 11, 1888; Ejiner C. b. March 13, 1890; Ida L. b. Jan. 27, 1892; Orella E. b. March 7, 1894; Harrold E. b. Aug. 5, 1896; Golden H. b. Sept. 14, 1898; Liberty L. b. July 4, 1900; Sterling C. b. June 7, 1903; Milton and Murland (twins) b. June 4, 1905; Gwendolin b. Oct. 9, 1908. Family home Newton, Utah.
Missionary to Great Britain 1893-95; presided over Massachusetts conference 1894-95; president Y. M. M. I. A. County sheriff Cache county, 1900-04; justice of peace; constable. Assisted in organizing Danielsen Manufacturing Co., at Logan, Utah; vice president and director of that company, 1897-1908; director of Danielsen Plow Co., Independence, Mo., 1908-13; assisted in organizing Farmers Banking Co., at Cache Junction, 1910, and made president in 1910.

RIGBY, GEORGE AMOS (son of George C. Rigby and Mary C. Clarke). Born Aug. 17, 1886, Newton, Utah.
Married Ann Christensen Jan. 27, 1910, Salt Lake City (daughter of James Christensen, pioneer 1864, and Caroline Jensen, who came to Utah July 24, 1873, of Denmark). She was born Dec. 25, 1880. Their child: Lucile b. Sept. 19, 1911. Family home Newton, Utah.
Elder. Farmer.

RIGGS, DR. JOHN (son of Major Gideon Riggs and Susan Pitcher of Connecticut and Kirkland, Ohio). He was born Dec. 20, 1812, at Oxford, New Haven county, Conn. Came to Utah Sept. 5, 1851, with Captain McPherson, No. 10 church train.
Married Jane Kilton Bullock Oct. 8, 1843 (daughter of Benjamin Bullock and Dorothy Kimball; the former died crossing the plains July, 1852, latter came on to Utah). She was born Sept. 4, 1819. Their children: Susan Jane Riggs, d. 1857; Mary Ruth, d. 1847; Dorothy Melissa, m. Andrew J. Stewart, Jr.; Julia Maria, d. Aug. 1854; Martha Adaline, m. P. M. Beesley; John Gideon Benjamin, d. 1857; Marritte, m. W. O. Beesley; Jane Kilton, d. 1864.
Married Adelia Ann Philips April 2, 1856 She was born April 9, 1843, in New Brunswick.
Married Minnie Ann Cook Sept. 24, 1867, at Salt Lake City. Family home Provo, Utah.
Member 5th quorum seventies; missionary to Illinois, Indiana and Ohio 1840. Worked on the Kirkland Temple and attended its dedication. Was present at the battle of Crooked River when Apostle David Patten was mortally wounded. Began study of medicine 1838 under Dr. F. G. Williams and finished at Quincy, Ill. Was surgeon in Walker war and rated as captain, belonging to the general staff. Died in March, 1892.

RIGGS, WILLIAM SEARS (son of John Riggs and Mary Gillman of Indiana). Born March 19, 1830, in Putnam county, Ind. Came to Utah July, 1850.
Married Sarah Reeves Feb. 7, 1855, at Cedar City, Utah (daughter of William Reeves and Frances Long of England). She was born Sept. 28, 1837. Their children: Sarah m. E. W. Littlefield; Mary Elizabeth, m. David C. Wixom; Melissa Ann, m. Joseph S. Ingram; Caroline Jane; Emma Lovina, m. George E. Griffin; William Reeves b. May 22, 1865, m. Priscilla S. Barnhurst; Andrew Jackson, m. Christena Henrie; Amanda Ellen, m. Ernest A. Griffin; Malinda Isabelle, m. William H. Bryce; Rosella, m. Frank Ahlstrom. Family resided Kanarra and Panguitch, Utah.
High councilor of Panguitch stake 1879-91; bishop's counselor of Henrieville ward 1892. Carpenter.

RIGGS, WILLIAM REEVES (son of William Sears Riggs and Sarah Reeves). Born May 22, 1865, Cedar City, Utah.
Married Priscilla S. Barnhurst Jan. 17, 1886, Cedar City, Utah (daughter of Samuel Barnhurst and Anna Marie Jensen of Cedar City), who was born May 6, 1863. Their children: William Reeves b. Dec. 5, 1886; Sarah Annie b. Aug. 19, 1888, m. Thomas J. Barney; Samuel Barnhurst b. Oct. 17, 1890, m. Effel Burrow; Andrew Franklin b. Jan. 19, 1893; Priscilla Josephine b. Dec. 19, 1895; Mary Emma b. Sept. 20, 1896; Vilate Irene b. Feb. 9, 1899; John Sears b. Nov. 11, 1900; Joseph Ernest b. July 16, 1903; Orlas James b. July 13, 1906. Family resided Henrieville and Hatch, Utah.
Bishop's counselor 1897-1913. County assessor. Farmer; merchant.

RILEY, WILLIAM L. (son of Jonathan Riley and Frances M. Johnson of Nottingham, Eng.). Born March 15, 1829, Nottingham. Came to Utah Oct. 13, 1863, Rosel Hyde company.
Married Mary Ann Clark May, 1851, Nottingham (daughter of John and Mary Clark of Nottingham; latter a pioneer Oct. 13, 1863, Rosel Hyde company). She was born June 4, 1830. Their children: Arthur, m. Sarah Goodfellow; Frances M., m. William Rooch; Emma, m. John Goodfellow; Elizabeth, d. aged 5; William, d. aged 2; Eliza Ann, m. Cyrus Tolman; Clarisa, m. Alexander Laird, m. Morgan Knapp; Fredrick R., m. Emma Tolman. Family home East Bountiful, Utah.
Married Jane Osborne Dec. 21, 1887, Logan temple, President Merrill officiating (daughter of William Osborne and Mary George of Ilkeston, Derbyshire, Eng.), who was born Nov. 18, 1848. Only child: Mary Ann b. Jan. 10, 1829, d. infant. Family home Bountiful, Utah.
Member 70th quorum seventies; high priest; Sunday school teacher. Janitor of Bountiful tabernacle. Wood finisher and polisher.

1134   PIONEERS AND PROMINENT MEN OF UTAH

RIRIE, JAMES (son of David Ririe, born 1778, in Aberdeenshire, Scotland, and Isabell Shariss of Arbroath, Scotland, born 1789—married 1809). Born Jan. 24, 1827, at New Castle, Frazer, Scotland. Came to Utah September, 1853, Jacob Gates oxteam company.
Married Ann Boyack Nov. 23, 1855 (daughter of James Boyack, born Jan. 3, 1806, in Scotland, died Feb. 1, 1888, and Elizabeth Mealmacker of Spanish Fork, Utah—married in 1827, at Strid Martin, Scotland, pioneers Sept. 1853, Captain Gates oxteam company). She was born May, 1830, and came to Utah Oct. 24, 1855, Milo Andrus company. Their children: Margrett Ann b. Feb. 26, 1857, m. William G. Hogge June 23, 1876; James Boyack b. Oct. 22, 1858, m. Elizabeth A. Morgan 1881; David b. Nov. 21, 1860, m. Leah Ann Lovell 1892; William; Alexander b. Oct. 24, 1863, m. Elizabeth J. McBride Jan. 5, 1887; George; Elizabeth b. Oct. 25, 1865, m. James A. Farrell Nov. 30, 1887; Isabell b. Feb. 25, 1870, m. Joseph P. Stallings Jan. 28, 1891; Mary; Joseph b. Feb. 27, 1872, m. Anna Farrell Oct. 20, 1898; Hyrum b. Feb. 27, 1872, m. Maggie Farrell March 21, 1898; Agnes b. March 27, 1874, m. David Burnett June 23, 1897. Family resided Springville, North Ogden and West Weber, Utah.
Missionary to Scotland 1849-51. Farmer and stockraiser. Died June 17, 1905.

RIRIE, ALEXANDER (son of James Ririe and Ann Boyack). Born Oct. 24, 1863, West Weber, Utah.
Married Elizabeth J. McBride Jan. 5, 1887, Logan, Utah (daughter of Heber R. McBride and Elizabeth Ann Burns; former a pioneer with Morten and Taylor handcart company). She was born April 30, 1869. Their children: Myrtle E. b. May 14, 1888, m. Clarence M. Baker Feb. 24, 1909; Lavina A. b. Jan. 13, 1890; Ethel E. b. Nov. 27, 1891, m. Howard Nelsen April 28, 1907; Mable M. b. Oct. 13, 1893; Elda E. b. Jan. 6, 1897; Sylvin A. b. March 19, 1899; Olin H. b. May 7, 1902; Afton J. b. Dec. 15, 1904; Floyd H. b. Oct. 4, 1906; Zelma McBride b. Nov. 21, 1910; Lois Elenor b. Sept. 11, 1912. Family resided Ogden and Eden, Utah.
Farmer and stockraiser.

RISHTON, EDWARD (son of Henry Rishton, born April 4, 1810, in England, and Mary Blaud, born May 9, 1815, in England, and married 1833 in England, both residents of Council Bluffs, Iowa). He was born Jan. 4, 1834, Acorington, Eng. Came to Utah Sept. 14, 1852, 12th Company, Captain Cuillo.
Married Mary Ann Slater April 23, 1855 (daughter of James Slater and Mary Ramsbolton, pioneers 1854). She was born April 27, 1840. Their children: Edward b. Jan. 27, 1857, m. Helen Houston 1883; Mary E. b. May 18, 1860, m. James Paxman 1882; William b. July 29, 1862, m. Laura Nell 1885; Thomas b. Feb. 2, 1866, m. Mary Judd; Maria b. Sept. 19, 1864, m. Almo Silcock; James b. March 28, 1869; Bland b. June 28, 1871; David b. Oct. 31, 1873, m. Maka Bennion; Blanche b. Nov. 28, 1876, m. Edward Bowen. Family home Riverton, Utah.
Assisted in bringing immigrants to Utah; crossed plains six times by horse and oxteam.

RITCHIE, JOHN (son of James and Agnes Ritchie of Glasgow, Scotland). Born Oct. 28, 1844. Came to Utah in 1863.
Married Sarah McAffee (daughter of John Smith McAffee and Ann Sparks of Glasgow). Their children: John McAffee b. Oct. 30, 1867, m. Sarah Elizabeth Wright; Sarah Ann, m. Wilford David Wright; James, m. Anna Tressa Wilson; Agnes, died; Jane, m. Joseph Smith Wright; Mary, m. James Wagstaff; Phoebe, m. George Baum Wright; William, m. Annie Frisbie, died; Ella.
High priest. Pioneer road and canal builder; farmer.

RITCHIE, JOHN McAFFEE (son of John Ritchie and Sarah McAffee). Born Oct. 30, 1867, Heber City, Utah.
Married Sarah Elizabeth Wright Nov. 3, 1889, Manti, Utah (daughter of William Wright and Jemima Dands of Provo, Utah, pioneers 1852). She was born Aug. 27, 1869, Provo, Utah. Their children: Mable Jamima b. Aug. 17, 1893; Joseph William b. May 24, 1894; Lacy b. Oct. 18, 1895; Vera Josephine b. March 26, 1901; Elden LaMar b. Jan. 23, 1903; Clyde b. Nov. 12, 1904; Horace J. b. July 5, 1907; Verdell W. b. Oct. 23, 1910. Family home Charleston, Utah.
Missionary to Australia 1897-99; bishop of Charleston ward; bishop's counselor to N. C. Murdock 1898-99; counselor to Bishop William Daybell 1899-1904; president Y. M. M. I. A. 6 years; member of school board. Farmer and thoroughbred stock breeder.

RITTER, GEORGE M. (son of Adam Ritter and Nancy Ward of Burkes Garden, Va.). Born Feb. 19, 1840, Burkes Garden. Came to Utah late in 1862, independent company.
Married Louise J. Thompson in 1870 at Burkes Garden, Va. (daughter of John Thompson and Lydia Ward of Burkes Garden). She was born Aug. 27, 1832. Their only child was John T. b. May 2, 1875, m. Martha Lewis. Family home Riverdale, Utah.
Farmer.

RITTER, JOHN THOMPSON (son of George M. Ritter and Louise Thompson). Born May 2, 1875, Riverdale, Utah.
Married Martha Lewis April 29, 1896, Riverdale (daughter of John Lewis and Jane Crismon of Mesa City, Ariz., pioneers July 24, 1847, Brigham Young company). She was born June 1, 1875, Coalville, Utah. Only child: George Max b. Jan. 17, 1911.
Justice of peace 1909-13. Dairyman and farmer.

RITTER, JOHN (son of Michael Ritter, born Jan. 13, 1784, and Phoebe Ritter, born Jan. 10, 1788, of Bingen-on-the-Rhine, Germany). Born Dec. 30, 1820. Came to Utah late in 1849 with contingent Mormon Battalion.

ROBB, WILLIAM. Born in Scotland. Came to Utah in 1857, from Australia.
Married Ellen Bell in Scotland, who came to Utah with husband. Their children: James, d. child; William Jr., m. Ellen Stones; Ellen, m. William Anderson; Ann, m. William Edwards; Thomas, m. Alice Benson; John, m. Mary Santon, m. Sarah Edseo; Alexander, m. Ellen Benson; Adam, m. Sarah Hollyhock; George, m. Caroline Jones; Caroline, d. child.
Married Susan ———. Their children: Samuel, m. Amanda Daly; Belle, m. William Wilson; Lyda, m. Hyrum Barton; Jane, m. Joseph J. Jones. Families resided Paragonah, Utah.
Called to help settle Harrisburg; moved to Paragonah, 1858, where took active part in early Indian troubles. Assisted bringing immigrants to Utah. Died 1891, Paragonah.

ROBB, GEORGE (son of William Robb and Ellen Bell). Born Sept. 23, 1857, Sidney, New South Wales. Came to Utah 1857.
Married Caroline Jones Jan. 8, 1876, St. George, Utah (daughter of William Jones and Mary Jones, of South Wales, pioneers 1854, James Brown company). She was born Sept. 8, 1861. Their children: Mary b. Sept. 1, 1878, m. James S. Mathis; Ellen b. Feb. 3, 1881, m. John B. Pesette; George, Jr. b. April 20, 1883, d. child; William Jones b. May 30, 1885; Ada b. May 6, 1887, m. Joseph Naylor; Vesta b. May 27, 1890; Blanche b. April 24, 1892; Earl Peer b. March 14, 1895; Arlin b. July 2, 1897; Angus John b. Dec. 15, 1904. Family home Price, Utah.
Member 101st quorum seventies. Called to San Juan to settle that country, 1882. Worked on Manti temple, 1875. Counselor Y. M. M. I. A.; ward teacher. Settled at Price, 1883, where he assisted in building canals and wagon roads. Farmer and stockraiser.

ROBBINS, ISAAC R. (son of Antrim Robbins and Lydia Rogers of Chesterfield, Burlington county, N. J.) Born March 24, 1805, at Chesterfield. Came to Utah 1848, Sam Brandon company.
Married Ann Shinn Burtis March 21, 1838, Chesterfield, N. J. (daughter of Abner Burtis and Rachel Shinn of Chesterfield). Their children: Joseph Reeves, died; Wesley, m. Caroline Larson; Margaret, m. Joseph E. Beck; Isaac Rogers, m. Celia Dudley.
Married Abiah R. Carter Nov. 16, 1851, Salt Lake City (daughter of William F. Carter and Sarah York of Bethel, Oxford county, Me., pioneers Oct. 12, 1850, Joseph Young company). She was born Aug. 21, 1834. Their children: William Carter, m. Betsy Taylor; Lydia Ann Rogers; Antrim Zeezram, m. Luna Holliday; Charles Beniah, died; Abiah Russell, m. Hiram Beckstead; Joseph Eleson, m. Martha Stout; Mary Antrim, died; Hester Ann, m. Peter B. Johnson; George Albert, m. Nellie D. Thompson; John Carter, m. Ella Frank; Alvin Carter, m. Arimenta Jimison.
Married Hannah Libby Carter March 24, 1855, Provo, Utah (daughter of William F. Carter and Sarah York), who was born March 25, 1841. Their children: Mary Celestine, died; Sarah Drusilla, m. William Harding; John Rogers, died; Aaron Rogers, m. Elizabeth Swensen; Lyman Carter; Hanna Libby, m. William Hodson; Ferlsberry Carter and Lavan Carter, died; Elizabeth Ann, m. Abraham H. Jones; Emma Carter, m. Abraham H. Jones. Families resided Provo, Utah.
High priest; first counselor to Bishop Bird, of 2nd ward, Provo. Farmer. Died Jan. 4, 1883, Provo.

ROBBINS, JOHN ROGERS (son of Antrim Robbins and Lydia Rogers of New Jersey). Born Sept. 11, 1809, New Jersey. Came to Utah late in 1853.
Children by first wife: Charles Burtis, m. Adeline Young; Zilphia, d. infant.
Married Phoebe A. Wright Dec. 26, 1837, in Burlington county, N. J. (daughter of Mahlon Wright and Ann Wilgus, of Jacobstown, N. J.), who was born Feb. 27, 1812. Their children: George E., and John F., d. infants; Georgiana Pacific, m. Clarence Barrett; Mary F., d. infant; Emma L., m. O. H. Riggs; Sarah F., d. infant. Family home, Salt Lake City.
Member of the School of the Prophets; high priest. Farmer; sawmill man. Died Feb. 1, 1873, Salt Lake City.

ROBERTS, DAVID GILES (son of Robert Roberts, born Jan. 4, 1794, Mallwyd, North Wales, and Pane Giles, born Jan. 1, 1794, of Machynlleth, North Wales, married June 9, 1820). He was born March 18, 1826, Machynlleth. Came to Utah in 1866.
Married Mary Morgan Dec. 26, 1866 (daughter of Thomas

Morgan and Margaret Jones; former born June 17, 1815. Kyrhym Pembrey, Caermarthenshire, South Wales, pioneer 1868, John Seeley company, d. Aug. 18, 1872, Malad, Idaho). She was born May 10, 1834. Came to Utah in 1863; died Aug. 3, 1912. Their children: David Morgan b. Oct. 2, 1867, m. Emma K. Aegerter Oct. 4, 1906; Margaret J. b. March 16, 1869, m. Oliver Hartman Jan. 1, 1891; Robert M. b. Sept. 16, 1870; Thomas C. b. March 23, 1872; Mary A. b. April 3, 1874, m. John T. Harrison Dec. 31, 1903; John M. b. Aug. 11, 1876, m. Agnes McDonald June 29, 1899.
Settled at Brigham City, Utah, moved to Malad 1865. Died June 18, 1893.

ROBERTS, DAVID MORGAN (son of David Giles Roberts and Mary Morgan). Born Oct. 2, 1867, Malad, Idaho.
Married Emma K. Aegerter Oct. 4, 1906, Paris, Idaho (daughter of Frederick Aegerter and Katherine Lehman, who came to Utah in 1889). She was born Aug. 29, 1884, Bern, Switzerland. Their children: David F. b. Sept. 12, 1907; Gladys b. Dec. 1, 1910; Thomas V. b. Sept. 14, 1912. Family home Malad, Idaho.

ROBERTS, DAVID ROBERT (son of Robert Roberts, born Jan. 18, 1775, at Cae Glas, Clynnogfawr, Caernarvonshire, Wales, and Elizabeth Edwards, married Feb. 3, 1805, Beddgelert, Wales). He was born April 3, 1814, Meirionethshire, Nanmor, Wales. Came to Utah Oct. 2, 1856, Edward Bunker company.
Married Catherine Richard at Llanfrothen, Wales, 1836 (daughter of Thomas Richard and Ann Morris, of Creua, Maur, Wales). She was born June 25, 1807, died Oct. 17, 1892, Logan, Utah. Their children: Robert David b. Sept. 21, 1837, m. Hannah Roberts June 6, 1870; Thomas David b. July 6, 1840, m. Margaret Goodman Feb. 24, 1881; Daniel b. Sept. 8, 1842, m. Sarah A. Hughes March 29, 1875; Ann b. Dec. 19, 1844, m. William Hopkins; Elizabeth b. Nov. 13, 1846, m. Talusen Hughes; Jane b. Jan. 11, 1850, m. Gcmar Hughes. Family home Farmington, Utah.
Settled at Farmington. Died Nov. 9, 1858.

ROBERTS, DANIEL (son of David Robert Roberts and Catherine Richard). Born Sept. 8, 1842, Llanfrothen, Wales. Came to Utah with parents.
Married Sarah A. Hughes March 29, 1875, Salt Lake City (daughter of James Hughes and Mary Jones; latter died Dec. 5, 1858, Kaysville, St. Clair county, Ill.; former a pioneer 1858). She was born Oct. 21, 1856, Pottsville, Pa.; came to Utah 1858. Their children: Catherine; Margaret; Ida; Anna; Mary; Irene, died; Daniel H. Family home Ogden, Utah.

ROBERTS, EDWARD GILES (son of Robert Roberts, born Jan. 4, 1794, at Mallwyd, North Wales, and Susan Giles of Dinas, Merthyr, North Wales). Born Dec. 8, 1825, at Dinas. Came to Utah Oct. 2, 1866, James Chipman company.
Married Elizabeth Lewis Nov. 14, 1851 (daughter of Robert and Jane Lewis, of Dinas), who was born March 5, 1827, and died Feb. 28, 1909. Came to Utah Oct. 2, 1866, James Chipman company. Their children: Jane Lewis b. Aug. 23, 1854, m. David Davis Thomas Feb. 6, 1874; Margarett Elizabeth b. Aug. 11, 1857, m. Charles Bolingbroke Sept. 8, 1876. Superintendent Sunday schools 23 years. Farmer; weaver. Settled at Malad City, Idaho, 1866. Died Jan. 2, 1894.

ROBERTS, EDWARD KILLICK (son of John W. Roberts of Leeds Co., Upper Canada, born June 19, 1800, at London, Eng., and Mary Gilchrist, born Feb. 7, 1804, Canada; married Jan. 2, 1822). He was born April 14, 1823, in Leeds county. Came to Utah Sept. 23, 1849, William Miller company.
Married Emeline Mathews Sept. 24, 1850 (daughter of Anson Mathews and Elizabeth Burges, pioneers 1848). She was born Feb. 7, 1833, Macomb, McDonough county, Ill., died April 17, 1867. Their children: Eliza Emeline b. Aug. 2, 1851, m. Jeremiah Bingham March, 1869; Susannah b. June 5, 1853, m. Calvin Pendleton May, 1870; Julia S. b. Oct. 17, 1854, m. Joseph Asay, 1872; William Edward b. Nov. 19, 1856, died; Elizabeth E. b. Aug. 14, 1858; Joseph Samuel b. Aug. 31, 1860; Mary A. b. April 28, 1863, m. Joseph Asay, 1877; George Hannibal m. Feb. 13, 1865, m. Almina Malinda Lewis Sept. 27, 1883; John Henry b. April 17, 1867. Family home Payson, Utah.
Married Hannah Gleave April 19, 1869, Salt Lake City (daughter of John Gleave and Jane Brindly, married May 1, 1843, at Wilmslow, Chestershire, Eng., pioneers Aug. 20, 1868, Chester Loveland company). She was born Oct. 23, 1846, Stockport, Eng. Their children: Hannah J. b. May 15, 1870; Killick Elton b. June 23, 1871, m. Edna M. Gardner; Lucy A. b. May 9, 1873; Boretta b. Oct. 8, 1874, m. Hyrum P. Thurston; Walter b. June 23, 1876, m. Millie Lekeker; Rebecca b. Jan. 1, 1878, m. John Nordfoese Dec. 1900; Bertha b. Jan. 2, 1880; Thomas Wilburn b. Aug. 13, 1881, m. Jennie Gleave Oct. 4, 1909; Herbert Franklin b. Sept. 7, 1883, m. Rosa Davis Jan. 22, 1908; Sabra S. b. Feb. 1, 1885, m. J. Davis Sept. 22, 1905; Ammon b. Aug. 6, 1888, m. Susia E. Adams Jan. 27, 1909. Family home Annabella, Sevier Co., Utah.
Married Ann Sophia Rollins April 19, 1869, Salt Lake City (daughter of Enoch P. Rollins of Cache Valley, Utah, and Sophia W. Philbrook, married at Bangor, Penobscot county, Me., pioneers 1852; and widow of Sidney Beckstead, by whom she had the following children: Sarah Ann, m. Henry Elmer; Sabra Jane, m. George B. Rust, m. Geo. A. Hatch; Lillian, m. George W. Patten; Mary Emily, m. Joseph Jackson; Rosa, d. child; Cordelia Loretta, d. infant. Family home West Jordan, Utah). She was born March 25, 1832, at Bangor, died May 10, 1884; pioneer 1852. Their children: Melinda Elvina b. Feb. 12, 1870, m. George B. Rust. 1888; Sidney Enoch b. Nov. 5, 1871, m. Marilla Hooper June 10, 1903. Family home, Annabella.
Presiding elder Annabella ward; high priest; member 29th quorum seventies; teacher. Assisted bringing immigrants to Utah. Black Hawk war veteran. Farmer; timberman.

ROBERTS, GEORGE HANNIBAL (son of Edward Killick Roberts and Emeline Mathews). Born Feb. 13, 1865.
Married Almira Malinda Lewis Sept. 27, 1883, Salt Lake City (daughter of Falton Lewis, pioneer 1848, and Almira Ferguson, born 1851, Big Cottonwood, Utah). She was born Aug. 24, 1867. Their children: George W. b. June 26, 1884; Mary Almira b. Aug. 1, 1886; Eugenia b. June 16, 1889, m. George M. Hunt May 5, 1910; Dorothy Eliza b. Sept. 20, 1890; Rebecca b. June 27, 1892, m. James Cook Jan. 3, 1911; Edward Killick b. March 16, 1894; Ray b. Feb. 1, 1896; Sarah Leland b. June 8, 1899; Ora b. Aug. 26, 1900; Shirden b. Jan. 28, 1902; Lewis Earl b. Feb. 1, 1904; Oren b. Nov. 3, 1906; Lora S. b. May 31, 1909. Family home Annabella, Utah.

ROBERTS, GEORGE (son of Edward Roberts, born in London, and Eliza Maynard, born Kent, Eng.). Born Sept. 21, 1833, London. Came to Utah in December, 1857.
Married Susan Gallard in May, 1857 (daughter of Mathew Gallard, who died in Australia, and Frances A. Smith, pioneer Alex Carr company). She was born May 3, 1840, and came to Utah with husband. Their children: George Edward b. July 13, 1858, m. Eliza Bradshaw Oct. 11, 1880; Frances Rosina b. Oct. 17, 1860, m. Frank R. Rollins Nov. 18, 1885; Emma Eliza b. Dec. 7, 1862, m. Will Albert Zabresice Aug. 6, 1884; Frank Edwin b. March 14, 1865, m. Jane Rollins April 5, 1883; William Henry b. July 21, 1867, m. Frances M. Smith Aug. 11, 1895; Walter b. Oct. 4, 1869, m. Alice Cuderback Jan. 17, 1895; Mark b. March 2, 1872, m. Susia McKnight March 27, 1896; Lydia Ann b. Dec. 30, 1872, m. James Eyre Jan. 17, 1894; Edith Elizabeth b. Feb. 5, 1878, m. James Heber Myers Oct. 17, 1894. Family home Minersville, Beaver Co., Utah.
Settled in Parowan, Utah; moved to Minersville 1860. School teacher; ward clerk. Farmer.

ROBERTS, HORACE. Born in 1801. Came to Utah in 1851.
Married Harriet McEvers at Montezuma, Pike county, Ill. Their children: Maria Louisa, m. Elliott Alfred Newell. Jr.; Charles, died; Jane, m. Thomas Wheeler, m. James E. Snow; Susan, m. Alva Zabriskie; Ephraim, m. Emma Bell; Gerulges; Laura, m. Watson Bell. Family home Provo, Utah. Potter.

ROBERTS, JOHN (son of John and Mary Roberts of Merthyr Tydfil, Wales). Born in 1821, Wales. Came to Utah in 1863, Thomas E. Ricks company.
Married Adelaide Ford in 1848, in England, who was born in June 1832. Their children: John, Jr., m. Alice Taylor, m. Mary Cutler, m. Emma J. Evans; Robert, d. infant; Joseph, m. Esther Taylor; James, m. Eldora Smith; Mary, m. Wheeler Whipple; Jane, m. Thomas Shaw, m. Louis Sinclair; Hyrum, m. Julia Ashton; David, m. Lydia Brown; Emily, m. George Martin; Lily, m. Frank Stanfast; Edwin. Family home Lehi, Utah.
Seventy; high priest; missionary to Wales two years. Farmer and stockraiser. Died in 1896.

ROBERTS, JOHN DUNN (son of David Roberts and Ann Powell of Merthyr Tydfil, Glamorganshire, South Wales). Born May 26, 1824, Merthyr Tydfil. Came to Utah in October, 1856, Edward Bunker handcart company.
Married Ann Powell in 1843, Merthyr Tydfil (daughter of Jacob Powell and Mary Walters, Merthyr Tydfil), who was born in March, 1822, and died in November, 1904. Their children: Jacob Roberts b. 1848, d. 1872; John Powell; Mary Ann, d. Oct. 4, 1900; David; Madoc; Mary. Family home Perry, Box Elder Co., Utah.
Missionary in South Wales 12 years; high priest. Settled in Brigham City, where he resided until 1862. Water master 11 years. Miner and farmer. Died Oct. 17, 1904, Perry.

ROBERTS, JOHN POWELL (son of John Dunn Roberts and Ann Powell). Born July 17, 1856, in Pottawattamie county, Ia. Came to Utah with parents.
Married Jeannette Holton Nov. 11, 1903, Salt Lake City (daughter of Isaiah R. Holton and Sarah Janet Brittain of Northamptonshire, Eng.), who came to Utah. Families resided Perry, Box Elder Co., Utah.
Member 59th quorum seventies; missionary to eastern states 1898-1900; second counselor to bishop. Justice of peace. Farmer.

ROBERTS, LEVI (son of Samuel and Mary Margret Roberts of Deerhurst, Gloucestershire, Eng.). Born Feb. 26, 1815, Deerhurst. Came to Utah in 1850, Captain Pearson independent company.

1136 PIONEERS AND PROMINENT MEN OF UTAH

Married Harriet Ann Hefford, at Deerhurst (daughter of Thomas Hefford and Mary Ann Ellis of Deerhurst, pioneers 1850, Captain Pearson independent company). She was born May 16, 1819. Their children: Henry b. June 16, 1836, m. Mary Ellen Wardrop; Caroline b. Oct. 1, 1837, m. James Oliverson; Phebe Ann b. Jan. 22, 1843, m. Allen Taylor; Marinda, m. John Doney; Harriet Ann b. Sept. 8, 1849, m. Robert Bodily; Mary Jane b. Dec. 13, 1851, m. Christopher Layton; Matilda b. Jan. 2, 1854. m. Edwin Bodily; Lucy Ellen, m. William Bennett. Family home Kaysville, Utah. Member Joseph Smith's bodyguard; member Mormon Battalion. Died Jan. 22, 1894.

ROBERTS, HENRY (son of Levi Roberts and Harriet Ann Hefford). Born June 16, 1836, Deerhurst, Eng. Came to Utah with father.
Married Mary Ellen Wardrop in 1870, Kaysville, Utah (daughter of Robert Wardrop and Margret Owen of Wellsville, Utah, pioneers 1849, George A. Smith company). She was born Aug. 10, 1852. Their children: Henry Levi b. July 6, 1871, m. Millie Stoddard; Walton Anthony b. March 17, 1873, m. Olive Elizabeth Corbridge; Mark Owen b. Oct. 27, 1874, m. Eva Ruth Jones; Vida Margret b. Sept. 25, 1876, m. George J. Stafford; Harriet Ann b. Sept. 16, 1878, m. Archie Wardsworth; Mary Ellen b. May 1, 1880, m. Marvin Thornley; Phebe b. March 8, 1882; William Robert b. Jan. 20, 1884, m. Julia Louise Steed; Jane Caroline b. March 16, 1888, m. George Jones.
Freighter in Nevada and Montana. Did much in upbuilding Davis county and surrounding country.

ROBERTS, WALTON ANTHONY (son of Henry Roberts and Mary Ellen Wardrop). Born March 17, 1873, Kaysville, Utah.
Married Olive Elizabeth Corbridge March 14, 1900, Salt Lake City (daughter of William Henry Corbridge and Olive Cordelia Sessions of Bountiful, Utah, pioneers in August, 1852, John Parker independent company). She was born April 3, 1881. Their children: Arvilla b. Dec. 4, 1900; Gwendola b. Dec. 1, 1902; Welden C. b. Jan. 30, 1905; Snoden H. b. Aug. 21, 1907; Evadna b. March 8, 1910; Zora b. Oct. 24, 1912. Family home Kaysville, Utah.
Presiding elder Spring Coulie branch, Alta, Canada, 1902; 1st counselor in bishopric Frankburg ward, Alta, 1904-09.

ROBERTS, MARK OWEN (son of Henry Roberts and Mary Ellen Wardrop). Born Oct. 27, 1874.
Married Eva Ruth Jones (daughter of Samuel Lane Jones, born April 14, 1828, Worcestershire, Eng., and Martha Simmons, born July 17, 1851, Bristol, Eng., pioneers 1847 and Sept. 13, 1861, respectively). She was born Sept. 14, 1878, Kaysville, Utah. Their children: Bernice b. May 23, 1900; Harmond H. b. April 17, 1902; Howard J. b. Oct. 26, 1905; Wilda Virginia b. July 13, 1910. Family home Layton, Utah.

ROBERTS, ORVILLE CLARK (son of Daniel Roberts and Eliza Aldula Clark of Keokuk, Iowa). Born Sept. 1, 1833, Manchester, Morgan county, Ill. Came to Utah in 1850, Milo Andrus company.
Married Mary Coray July 24, 1868, Provo, Utah (daughter of Howard Coray and Martha Jane Knowlton of Provo, pioneers 1850, John Sharp company). Their children: Orville Clark b. Oct. 24, 1869, m. Persis Young; Howard Daniel b. July 10, 1871, m. Mary Young; Harriet Virginia b. April 7, 1873, m. Charles Milton; Steele; Mary Eliza b. Aug. 13, 1876, m. Frank L. Noel; Martha Jane b. June 15, 1878, m. Jens P. Nielson; Frank Homer b. April 10, 1880, m. Evaline Taylor; Daphne b. Dec. 3, 1882, m. Robert P. Cooper; Don Carlos b. June 12, 1885, m. Claire Poyer; Louis Dermont b. Sept. 17, 1889. Family home Mancos, Colo.
Member 70th quorum seventies. Settled a Provo 1851. Crossed plains 13 times. Minuteman at Provo under Colonel Peter Conover. Took active part in protecting settlers against Indians in early days, was wounded while carrying express July 24, 1854. Moved to southern Colorado 1880, and in 1912 to San Diego, Cal. Freighter; mail carrier; farmer and stockraiser. Died Dec. 12, 1912, Le Mesa, Cal.; buried in San Diego.

ROBERTS, OWEN (son of Evan Roberts and Ellen Tydir, of Llandegwan Parish, Merionethshire, North Wales). Born Jan. 21, 1828, in Wales. Came to Utah October, 1849, first company of Welsh saints.
Married Sarah Treharne May 26, 1855, Salt Lake City (daughter of William Treharne and Ann Richards, of Llangendyrn, Carmarthenshire, South Wales), who was born Feb. 14, 1830, and came to Utah 1852, Capt. Green company. She died Nov. 1, 1898. Family home, Salt Lake City. Stonecutter for Salt Lake theater 30 years. Died Sept. 17, 1892.

ROBERTS, PETER (son of John Roberts, born at Thanasa, Flintshire, North Wales, and Ann Pool of Newmarket, North Wales). Born March 5, 1830, at Thanasa. Came to Utah in 1864, Joseph S. Rawlins company.
Married Harriet Jones 1844 (daughter of Robert and Ann Jones). She died in 1859, in England. Their children: Ann, d. infant; John b. May 20, 1850, m. Persis McKee Dec. 24, 1878.
Married Phoebe Richardson 1860 (daughter of Peter Richardson and Jane Warmouth, former a pioneer 1864, Joseph S. Rawlins company). She died in 1870, Goshen, Utah. Their children: Jane b. 1861, d. child; Mary Ann b. 1862, m. Willard Cole; Peter b. 1864, d. child; Nicholas W. b. Dec. 25, 1865, m. Annie Mortison Nov. 3, 1892; Ann b. 1870, d. infant.

Married Sarah Price Jones April 15, 1870, who was born in England.
High priest; member high council. Nebo stake. Settled at Coalville; moved to Kamas and then to Goshen, where he last resided.

ROBERTSON, JAMES. Born Sept. 22, 1827, Faulds, Glenisla, Forfar, Scotland.
Married Matilda Graham, May 4, 1855. Their children: Matilda Elizabeth b. May 5, 1856, m. William Alexander Chesley; Christina Jane b. Dec. 6, 1857, d. Nov. 11, 1867. Lucy b. Feb. 12, 1860, m. Joseph E. Green; Grace Darling b. Nov. 19, 1861, m. John T. Beck, divorced, then married Henry Matley; Anna Laura b. Sept. 13, 1863, d. April 13, 1864; Flora MacDonald b. March 14, 1865, m. George H. Brimhall; Clara b. July 31, 1867, d. Aug. 17, 1867; Elizabeth Edward b. Aug. 16, 1868, m. Jacob H. Schwartz. Family home, Spanish Fork, Utah.
Married Mary Cox, Logan, Utah. Only child: Arthur b. Nov. 19, 1886.
High priest; counselor to Bishop A. K. Thurber; president high priests' quorum at Spanish Fork. Died at Spanish Fork.

ROBEY, JEREMIAH (son of Jeremiah Robey and Mary Ogden, of Shinnston, W. Va.). Born April 14, 1808, in Harrison county, W. Va. Came to Utah August, 1852, David Wood company.
Married Ruth Tucker Nov. 7, 1833 in West Virginia (daughter of Jeremiah Tucker and Ruth Ashcroft, of Shinnston), who was born June 26, 1816, and died Jan. 17, 1892, Midway, Utah. Their children: Theophilus, m. Sarah Mathews and Maria Ralph Field; Mary Jane, m. S. H. Epperson; James Allison; Maria and Sophia, died; Susan Luvernia, m. James Ross; Jeremiah Albert, m. Martha Dowdle; Matilda, m. Nathan C. Springer; Theodore and Theodric, died.
High priest; missionary to West Virginia 1876-71. Settled at Midway, Utah, 1859. School trustee thirteen years. Mining recorder, Snake Mining district. Carpenter and cabinetmaker; farmer; bee keeper and fruit raiser. Died Nov. 22, 1903.

ROBEY, JEREMIAH ALBERT (son of Jeremiah Robey and Ruth Tucker). Born March 12, 1845 in Hancock county, Ill. Came to Utah in 1858. Travelled with father.
Married Martha Jane Dowdle, Midway, Utah (daughter of Absalom Porter Dowdle and Sarah Ann Holliday, both of Marion county, Ala.), who was born in 1848, Salt Lake City. Their children: Mary Jane, m. Joseph Tietjen; Electa Ruth, m. Harold F. Heninger; Jeremiah Jr., m. Emma Larsen; Matilda, m. James Dahl; Sidney Theophilus, m. Ethel Whitmore; Henrietta, m. Adam Ludwig; Mary Sophia, m. Jonathan Smith. Family home Midway, Utah.
Veteran Black Hawk war; minute man. Farmer; carpenter; stockraiser.

ROBINS, EDMUND. Born at Cheltenham, Eng. Came to Utah in 1854.
Married Elizabeth Welch in England, who came to Utah with husband. Their children: Edmund Jr., m. Ann Douglas; William; Thomas; Joseph; Ann; Ellen.

ROBINS, EDMUND (son of Edmund Robins and Elizabeth Welch, of Cheltenham, Eng.). Born Feb. 27, 1828, Cheltenham. Came to Utah Aug. 28, 1852, John Parker independent company.
Married Ann Douglas June 21, 1848, St. Louis, Mo. (daughter of George Douglas and Anna Briggs, of Dawnham Lane, Eng., pioneers Aug. 28, 1852, John Parker independent company). She was born Oct. 4, 1831. Their children: Elizabeth Ann, m. William Sewell; Edmund John, m. Rose Groo; Frederick William; Richard Douglas, m. Ellen Currie; George Douglas; Ellen Vilate, m. Richard Leek; Mary Alice, m. Frederick V. Dankuski; Capitola Isabella, m. John Pingree; Lillie Mary, m. James E. Halverson; Emily Leonora; Susan Jeannette, m. Robert Prandfit. Family home Ogden, Utah.
Bishop; counselor; high priest; seventy. Officer state militia. Died May 25, 1889.

ROBINS, WILLIAM (son of Shadrick Robins and Alice Eaton of Culeston, Bedfordshire, Eng.). Born Feb. 25, 1839.
Married Ann Nighton Wooley (daughter of John Wooley and Mary Nighton, of Wenwick, Huntingdonshire, Eng.), who came to Utah in 1858. Their children: Thomas b. Dec. 16, 1861, m. Sara Staugh; Arthur, b. May 2, 1863, died; Emily b. July 29, 1865, m. James Gillin; Elizabeth b. April 16, 1867, died; Annie b. June 21, 1871, m. James Wright; Martha b. 1873, m. Andrew Nelson; William John b. Oct. 16, 1875, m. Elizabeth Harris; Charles Wooley b. Dec. 11, 1877, died. Family home Pleasant Grove, Utah.
Elder. Aided in building up community. Farmer and stockraiser.

ROBINS, WILLIAM JOHN (son of William Robins and Ann Nighton Wooley). Born Oct. 16, 1875, Pleasant Grove, Utah. Married Elizabeth Ann Harris in 1898, Salt Lake City (daughter of Albert Harris and Elizabeth Nerden of Pleasant Grove), who was born Feb. 11, 1879. Their children: Charles Albert b. March 1, 1899; Harold Wooley b. Aug. 28, 1901; Erral b. Sept. 9, 1903; Lucile b. Aug. 9, 1905; Anna Elizabeth b. Aug. 20, 1907; Lola b. Jan. 2, 1909. Family home, Pleasant Grove.

ROBINSON, ANDREW. Came to Utah 1856. Married Sarah Yates. Their children: Herbert; Richard; Eliza; Charles, m. Maria Howick; Jane.

ROBINSON, CHARLES (son of Andrew Robinson and Sarah Yates). Born March 26, 1847, Shropshire, Eng. Came to Utah October, 1872. Captain Dobson company.
Married Maria Howick April, 1873, Salt Lake City (daughter of Andrew Robinson and Charlotta Howick of Shropshire), who was born April, 1845. Their children: Annie, died: Attie, m. David Williams; Millie, m. Frank Thomas. Family home Winter Ward, Salt Lake City.
Elder; high priest. Farmer and stockraiser.

ROBINSON, EDWARD (son of James Robinson of Little Sutton, Eng.). Born Oct. 16, 1807, Chestershire, Eng. Came to Utah Oct. 28, 1849, Ezra T. Benson company.
Married Mary Smith 1828, Manchester, Eng. who was born in 1809. Their children: Richard, m. Elizabeth Wootten; John, m. Mary Ann Clements; Mary and Martha, d. children; Elizabeth, m. Morgan Phelps; Edward, Jr., m. Sarah Harrington; William Smith, m. Orpha E. Adams; Mary Jane, m. Oscar Wood; Joseph, d. child. Family home, Manchester.
Married Ann Wootten 1845, Nauvoo, Ill., who was born 1809. Their children: George Heber, m. Delia Smith, m. Margaret Crystal; Alfred, d. child.
Helped build first railway and was guard on first train from Manchester to Liverpool 1830. High priest. Farmer. Died April, 1896, American Fork, Utah.

ROBINSON, WILLIAM SMITH (son of Edward Robinson and Mary Smith). Born July 29, 1840, Manchester, Eng. Came to Utah 1849 with father.
Married Orpha E. Adams Dec. 27, 1865, American Fork, Utah (daughter of Arza Adams and Sabina Clark of Canada, pioneers October, 1849). She was born Oct. 23, 1849. Their children: William b. Sept. 28, 1866, m. Jane Chipman; Sabina b. Jan. 25, 1869, m. Darius Allen; Richard b. April 25, 1871, d. infant; Mary b. Dec. 26, 1872, m. John Halliday; Arza b. April 22, 1875, d. infant; Margret Blanche b. Dec. 18, 1876, m. Joseph J. Jackson; Nathan b. April 14, 1879, m. Caroline Mogg; John H. b. June 2, 1881, m. Leah Bigler; Olive b. Oct. 14, 1884, m. Roy Gardner; Florence May b. May 26, 1886, m. Frank Ehrbar; Ida b. Oct. 1888, m. Ira Mann; Millie b. Jan. 5, 1892, m. Reuben Howard. Family home, American Fork.
President Y. M. M. I. A.; high priest. Member city council of American Fork for several years. Farmer; stockraiser and sheepman.

ROBINSON, GEORGE. Born Jan. 4, 1800, in Derbyshire, Eng. Came to Utah Sept. 30, 1852, Captain Burbank company.
Married Sarah Holt 1824, Manchester, Eng. (daughter of William Holt and Sarah Massa of England), who was born March 8, 1804. Their children: John, died; Joseph, m. Elizabeth Hobson; Eliza, m. Daniel Peet; William, m. Miss Wood; Elizabeth, m. Joseph Shelley; James. Family home American Fork, Utah.
High priest. Farmer. Died June 27, 1883.

ROBINSON, JOSEPH (son of George Robinson and Sarah Holt). Born Sept. 25, 1827, Ribbleton. Eng. Came to Utah Sept. 30, 1852, Captain Burbank company.
Married Elizabeth Hobson Feb. 3, 1850, St. Louis, Mo. (daughter of William and Sarah Hobson, of Yorkshire, Eng.) who was born March 27, 1830. Their children: Joseph H., died; Sarah H., m. Moroni Jackson; William H-m. Annie Shaw; Mary H., m. Charles Poppleton; George H. and John H., died; Eleanor H., m. James Smith; Samuel, died; Joshua, m. Mary Moore; Samuel m. Emanda Tempest; Martha. Family home American Fork, Utah.
Member 69th quorum seventies; president teachers' quorum in St. Louis 1848. Cabinet maker.

ROBINSON, JAMES (son of Samuel Robinson and Mary Price of Nottingham, Eng.). Born Dec. 28, 1829, Nottingham. Came to Utah in early days.
Married Mary Pollid at Nottinghamshire (daughter of Robert Pollid and Ann Veneson of Nottinghamshire), who was born Oct. 6, 1831. Their children: Sussanher b. Dec. 15, 1851, m. Fredrick Birch; Elizabeth b. Dec. 29, 1853, m. William Foulger; Sarriah b. Jan. 15, 1856, m. John F. Wilde; James b. March 8, 1858, m. Mary Moore; Samuel m. Emanda Chandler; Mary H., m. Edwin Wilde; Emmanuel, m. Alice McKlin; Annie m. Henry Cox; Fredrick, m. Florence Farnsworth; Emma, m. Eli Robinson.
President of a branch in Nottinghamshire, Eng. Opened up coal mines at Coalville, Utah. Died March 30, 1898.

ROBINSON, JOHN (son of N. Robinson). Born Feb. 14, 1825, Bury, Lancasterhire, Eng. Came to Utah 1855.
Married Ann Gregson (daughter of Thomas and Jacosa Gregson) of Lancastershire). Their children: Jacosa Jane b. July 21, 1852, m. Frank Whitehead; Franklin Gregson b. Oct. 18, 1854, m. Ellen Salina Griffen Feb. 1, 1877; Elizabeth Ann b. March 19, 1857, m. Parley P. Walton; John, Jr. b. Aug. 18, 1859, m. Merelda Peart; James b. Sept. 3, 1861, m. Effie Swain; William Paxton b. Aug. 7, 1863, m. Emily Whittle; Sarah Emmeline b. May 6, 1866, m. Franklin C. Christensen; Willard b. Jan. 4, 1869, m. Mary Abigail Allen; Emma b. Nov. 13, 1870, m. George Rainey.
President London conference. Settled at Salt Lake City, moved to Willard and to Richmond in 1860. Farmer.

ROBINSON, FRANKLIN GREGSON (son of John Robinson and Ann Gregson). Born Oct. 18, 1854, London, Eng. Came to Utah with parents.
Married Ellen Salina Griffin Feb. 1, 1878 (daughter of Thomas Griffin and Amanda Ellen Perkins; former a pioneer Sept. 23, 1854, Job Smith independent company, latter 1850). She was born July 26, 1857. Their children: Franklin Griffin b. Nov. 21, 1878, m. Bertha Blake June 26, 1901; Thomas Arnold b. Sept. 30, 1880, m. Nettie Johnson Dec. 31, 1907; Anna Ellen b. Dec. 7, 1882, m. Joseph Palmer Sharp Feb. 8, 1906; Nellie b. Sept. 28, 1885; Earl G. b. Oct. 25, 1887; Leone Irene b. Aug. 20, 1889, m. John Mather April 5, 1911; Julian LeRoy b. July 3, 1891, m. Laverna V. Stoddard June 4, 1903; Verna Lodicy b. April 25, 1893; John Marlan b. March 3, 1895. Family home Richmond, Utah.
City councilman 12 years. Director in irrigation company at Richmond 12 years. Farmer and stockraiser; merchant and manufacturer. Died.

ROBINSON, FRANKLIN GRIFFIN (son of Franklin Gregson Robinson and Ellen Salina Griffin). Born Nov. 21, 1878, Richmond, Utah.
Married Bertha Blake June 26, 1901, Salt Lake City (daughter of James Blake and Elizabeth Beckstead), who was born March 12, 1883, West Jordan, Utah. Their children: Vera Naomi b. Nov. 21, 1902; Marguerite b. July 18, 1904; E   b. Oct. 4, 1905; Gayle b. Feb. 1, 1907; Lyal b. Dec. 6, 1910.11a

ROBINSON, JOSEPH LEE (son of Nathan Robinson, born April 22, 1764, and Mary Brown, born 1775—married Feb. 21, 1802). He was born Feb. 18, 1811, at Shaftsbury, Vt. Came to Utah 1848.
Married Maria Wood July 23, 1832 (daughter of Zephaniah Wood and Anna Carpenter), who was born Jan. 5, 1806. Their children: Oliver Lee b. July 8, 1833, m. Lucy Miller Nov. 26, 1854; Ebenezer Jay b. Oct. 19, 1835, m. Chloe Young; Anna Maria b. June 8, 1838, m. James D. Wilcox Nov. 26, 1854; Joseph b. Oct. 31, 1840; Zephaniah W. b. Sept. 21, 1843, and Mary Elizabeth b. Jan. 12, 1845, latter three died young; Joseph Elijah b. Feb. 2, 1849, m. Dorothy Watson March 2, 1874. Family home Farmington, Utah.
Married Susan McCord Jan. 31, 1846, Nauvoo, Ill. (daughter of James McCord and Elizabeth Barnet), who was born Dec. 14, 1808, Christian, Ky. Their children: Susan Aseneth b. Nov. 16, 1846, d. child; Mary Jane b. Oct. 24, 1848, m. John A. West May 25, 1865; Solomon b. Aug. 27, 1851, m. Albertene Smith Sept. 11, 1876.
High priest; counsellor in bishopric of 9th ward Nauvoo; bishop of 7th ward Winter Quarters 1846-47; bishop of North Cottonwood ward; member high council Davis stake; patriarch. Justice of peace. In connection with George A. Smith and others selected and located towns of Parowan and Fillmore.

ROBINSON, OLIVER LEE (son of Joseph Lee Robinson and Maria Wood). Born July 8, 1833, Boonville, N. Y.
Married Lucy Miller Nov. 26, 1854, Salt Lake City (daughter of Henry W. Miller and Almira Pond), who was born Jan. 10, 1837, in Adams county, Ill. Their children: Joseph Oliver b. Oct. 13, 1855, d. child; Lucy Maria b. Nov. 22, 1866, m. Joseph S. Clark Jan. 17, 1877; Loren Jay b. Feb. 3, 1859, m. Sarah Richards Jan. 26, 1882; Oliver LeGrand b. Oct. 28, 1860, m. Alice Smith March 6, 1884; Eugene Delacy b. Aug. 11, 1862, m. Sarah France Dec. 13, 1883; Alice Almira b. May 14, 1864, m. George F. Richards March 9, 1882; James Henry b. Nov. 8, 1865, m. Rumina C. Chaffin Dec. 18, 1889; Sarah Jane b. Nov. 25, 1867, m. William Dunn; Anna Amelia b. April 8, 1870, m. Frank D. Steed; Helen A. b. July 23, 1872, d. child; Lillian Estelle b. Sept. 1876, m. Hyrum Lee. Family home Farmington, Utah.
President 74th quorum seventies; alternate high councilor of Davis stake; missionary to eastern states 1876; to Salmon River 1857; and to "the Muddy" 1868.

ROBINSON, JAMES HENRY (son of Oliver Lee and Lucy Miller). Born Nov. 8, 1865, Farmington, Utah.
Married Rumina C. Chaffin Dec. 18, 1889 (daughter of Darwin E. Chaffin and Elizabeth V. Wilson), who was born Nov. 3, 1866, Farmington. Their children: Henry Harald b. Feb. 3, 1891, m. Hazel Thatcher April 6, 1910; Edward C. b. Aug. 30, 1892; Alta b. Feb. 22, 1894; Sherman C. b. April 27, 1896; Filbert C. b. Jan. 24, 1898; Glen b. Oct. 7, 1899; Preston b. June 25, 1903; Afton b. Jan. 31, 1907; Naoma b. March 29, 1909. Family home, Farmington.
President deacons', elders' and seventies quorums; Sunday school superintendent 4½ years; ordained bishop Farmington ward Nov. 27, 1906. First marshal of Farmington; member city council; mayor 1904-08; school trustee. Manager Farmington C. M. Co.

ROBISON, ALEXANDER. Came to Utah in 1860 Daniel Robinson company.
Married Nancy Walderman. Among their children was William, whose genealogy follows.

1138   PIONEERS AND PROMINENT MEN OF UTAH

ROBISON, WILLIAM (son of Alexander Robison and Nancy Walderman). Born April 18, 1829, in Franklin county, Pa. Came to Utah Sept. 22, 1860, Daniel Robinson company. Married Margaret Smith, in Franklin county (daughter of Daniel Smith and Catherine Guseman of Franklin county, pioneers Daniel Robinson company). She was born Dec. 23, 1834. Their children: Daniel Alexander b. July 18, 1853, m. Mary Morris Aug. 31, 1873; Jaben S., m. Harriet Clawson; Malissa, m. Henry Robinson; William Jr., m. Eva Robinson; George Franklin, m. Flora Fry; Rachel Sabina, m. Curtis Rogers; Margaret Catherine, m. Charles Tonks; Nancy Lavina, m. Edward Wadsworth; Lehi Nephi, David and Annie Elizabeth, latter three died. Family home Morgan, Utah.
Elder. Died Nov. 19, 1897.

ROBISON, DANIEL ALEXANDER (son of William Robison and Margaret Smith). Born July 18, 1853, in Franklin county, Pa. Came to Utah with parents.
Married Mary Morris Aug. 31, 1873, Morgan, Utah (daughter of Isaac C. Morris and Elizabeth Williams of Morgan county, pioneers 1853). She was born Oct. 25, 1855. Their children: Margaret Elizabeth b. April 13, 1875, m. David John Richards; May Inez b. Jan. 4, 1877, and William Alexander b. Nov. 12, 1880, died; George Alvin b. Nov. 23, 1882, m. Millie Lamb; Charles Conway b. Feb. 21, 1885, m. Lillie Voss; Lottie May b. Dec. 16, 1886, m. James P. Grover; Lucy Prescilla b. Jan. 18, 1889, m. Christian Jensen; Lillian, died; Leland b. Feb. 14, 1895; Vivian b. Feb. 14, 1895, died.
Married Louisa Winnetta Grover Aug. 31, 1899, Salt Lake City (daughter of Thomas Grover and Louisa Picton of Morgan, Utah, pioneers July 24, 1847, Brigham Young company). She was born April 26, 1880. Their children: Roscoe Bryant b. June 29, 1900; Harold Leon b. Oct. 23, 1903; Roland and Ruland (twins) b. May 27, 1896; Maurine b. Oct. 1, 1909; Ivy b. June 26, 1912. Family resided at Morgan.
Seventy; ward clerk, 30 years; stake clerk, 7 years. County and office clerk of district court; city recorder; road supervisor. Farmer; carpenter.

ROBISON, DAVID (son of Alexander Robison in Pennsylvania and Nancy Walderman). Born April 2, 1827, Harrisburg, Pa. Came to Utah Sept. 27, 1860, Charles Rich company.
Married Mary E. Grover (daughter of Thomas Grover and Caroline Whiting, former a pioneer, Charles Rich company, latter died at Nauvoo, Ill). She was born April 13, 1833, Cattaraugus county, N. Y. Their children: David Jr. b. Oct. 14, 1861; Emma Jane b. March 2, 1863; and Thomas b. Dec. 17, 1865, all died; Heber C. b. Nov. 20, 1866, m. Sophia Foss; Emeline b. May 15, 1878, m. Enoch Henson; Caroline b. May 27, 1869; Charles b. Feb. 16, 1871, died; Eliza Ann b. Feb. 2, 1874, m. Joseph Butler; Joel b. Nov. 13, 1876, m. Mamie Cutler.
Married Johana F. J. Kofvelstrom in May, 1872, Salt Lake City (daughter of Jonas J. Kofvelstrom and Anna Britta Farley), who was born July 4, 1848, Lestrop, Gerdham, Sweden. Their children: Moroni b. March 14, 1873, m. Dora C. Sharp Dec. 10, 1895; George V. b. March 16, 1875, died; James A. b. Jan. 9, 1877, m. Chloe Wilcox; Effie S. b. Oct. 5, 1879, m. Criss Jensen; Anna J. b. Jan. 3, 1882, died; Ivan Oscar b. March 27, 1886. Family home Lyman, Idaho.
Patriarch. Deceased.

ROBISON, MORONI (son of David Robison and Johana F. J. Kofvelstrom). Born March 14, 1873, Morgan, Utah.
Married Dora C. Sharp Dec. 10, 1895, Lyman, Idaho (daughter of Francis Sharp and Dortha Gill), who was born March 29, 1878, Smithfield, Utah. Their children: Jesse M. b. Sept. 30, 1896; Wilma Dortha b. April 6, 1899; Estella Hannah b. Dec. 30, 1900; Florence Effie b. Nov. 4, 1902; Lawrence G. b. Nov. 8, 1903; David Lee b. March 23, 1906; Hugh Francis b. May 20, 1909. Family home Lyman, Idaho.

ROBISON, GEORGE H. (son of Henry and Mira Robison of Akron, Ohio). Born 1862, at Akron. Came to Utah 1892. Married Matty Hutchinson 1888, in Ohio. Their children: Mabel; Florence. Family home, Salt Lake City.
Manager Drum Lymmun Mining company; manager Mammoth mine and of all Dellamar property. Mining engineer. Died July 4, 1903, New York.

ROBISON, PETER. Born April 27, 1817, in Pennsylvania. Came to Utah 1850.
Married Selina Chaffee. Their children: Maryette b. Aug. 24, 1841, d. aged 6; David Peter b. Sept. 17, 1846; Cornelia b. Sept. 17, 1848, m. Gilbert Furbush; Charles b. Aug. 23, 1850, m. Mary Lott; Joseph Millard b. March 29, 1852, m. Sarah Louisa Staples, Dec. 25, 1875; Lucy Matilda b. April 2, 1854, m. Carl Young; Sarah Johanna b. July 18, 1856, m. John Lott; James H. b. May 27, 1859, m. Emma Gandy; George Samuel b. Nov. 18, 1860, m. Emma Meacham. Family resided Fillmore and Petersburg, Utah.
Married Mary Ashly (daughter of —— Ashly). Their children: Elizabeth b. April 29, 1859, m. Brigham Young; John b. Aug. 4, 1853, died; Hyrum Peter b. Jan. 25, 1855, m. Annie Pack; William Henry b. Jan. 6, 1857, m. Rosetta Pack; Elsie Rosetta b. May 1, 1859, m. Alexander Gonder; Jacob Thomas b. Oct. 29, 1861, m. Ina Callister; Margaret Retta b. Nov. 7, 1863, m. William Gregory; Lura Delila b. May 24, 1866, m. Mr. Fowler; Edmund B. b. Dec. 5, 1870, m. Mary Ramsey; Almon Dewitt b. May 5, 1873; Lester Jerome b. Aug. 13, 1875, m. —— Rowland.
Presiding elder Petersburg branch of Millard stake, 1859-62; missionary to England 1857-59.

ROBISON, JOSEPH MILLARD (son of Peter Robison and Selina Chaffee). Born March 29, 1852, Fillmore, Utah.
Married Sarah Louisa Staples Dec. 25, 1875, Petersburg, Utah (daughter of George Staples and Lauretta Rappley, latter a pioneer). She was born Jan. 18, 1858. Their children: Dora May b. Nov. 29, 1876, m. John Black Jr., Oct. 8, 1894; Laverna Lazetta b. May 11, 1878, m. Leslie George Dec. 19, 1900; Laura Selina b. April 1, 1880; Clara Malissa b. Feb. 23, 1882, m. Haden W. Church, Jr. Jan. 29, 1902; Ethel Valeria b. May 23, 1889, m. Rufus Liston Dec. 29, 1906; Wina Louisa b. Feb. 4, 1895. Family resided Kanosh and Hatton, Utah.
President Y. M. M. I. A. 1896-98; high councilor in Millard stake; Sunday school superintendent at Boulder, Utah; second counselor to Bishop C. F. Christensen, 1898-08.

ROCKWOOD, ALBERT PERRY (son of Luther Rockwood, born Jan. 7, 1780, and Ruth Perry, of Holliston, Mass., married Dec. 27, 1801). Born June 9, 1805, at Holliston. Came to Utah July 24, 1847, Brigham Young company.
Married Nancy Haven April 3, 1827 (daughter of John Haven, pioneer 1849). She was born June 13, 1805. Only child: Ellen Ackland b. March 23, 1829, m. Brigham Young.
Married Elvira Teeples Wheeler, whose father was an 1849 pioneer). She was born Nov. 11, 1810, La Harpe, N. Y. Their children: Mary Ann b. Oct. 15, 1847, m. Joseph L. Card Dec. 20, 1878; Charles Welcome b. March 2, 1850, m. Anna B. Starr Nov. 27, 1872.
Married Angeline Horne, who came to Utah in 1849. Their children: Nancy Angeline; Moses Perry b. Nov. 13, 1852, m. Mary D. Balem Dec. 24, 1876. Family home, Salt Lake City.
Married Juliane Sophia Olsen April 11, 1862, Salt Lake City. Their children: Nancy Matilda b. Jan. 27, 1863; Luther b. Dec. 31, 1863; Timothy b. Feb. 20, 1865; Mary Emma b. May 4, 1868; Samuel b. May 21, 1870, m. Esther Larsen; Ole Olsen b. Dec. 28, 1873; Frederick b. Aug. 12, 1875; Julius Apollos b. March 5, 1878, m. Mary Ellen Hill Dec. 11, 1901.
Married Susannah Cornwall Jan. 6, 1870, Salt Lake City. Their children: Ruth b. Nov. 13, 1872, m. Samuel O'Niel; Alpheus b. Dec. 28, 1874, m. Emily D. North; Thomas b. May 20, 1877; Franklin b. Oct. 20, 1872.
One of the first seven presidents of seventies, 1845-79. Captain, drill officer and general of Nauvoo legion. Acting adjutant of company of horsemen that aided in rescue of Joseph Smith when kidnaped at Dixon, Ill., 1843. Municipal officer at Nauvoo; warden territorial penitentiary, 1851-1879. First fish commissioner of the territory. Director of Deseret Agricultural and Manufacturing Society. Died Nov. 25, 1879, in Sugar House ward, Salt Lake City.

ROCKWOOD, CHARLES WELCOME (son of Albert Perry Rockwood and Elvira Teeples Wheeler). Born March 2, 1850, Salt Lake City.
Married Anna B. Starr Nov. 27, 1872, Salt Lake City (daughter of Jared Starr and Anna Barr, pioneers 1849), who was born Feb. 3, 1850, Salt Lake City. Their children: Anna Lulu b. Oct. 15, 1873, m. Hubert L. Hall Dec. 4, 1891; Martha Starr b. Dec. 17, 1875, m. John Witt Telford Dec. 22, 1900; Eva Starr b. Dec. 3, 1877, m. Darwin E. Chaffin May 11, 1898; Charles Barr b. Sept. 7, 1880; Albert Jared b. June 25, 1882, m. Mary Amelia Mulliner Nov. 5, 1902; James Warren b. Aug. 11, 1885, m. Melissa Rushton Dec. 22, 1904; Ella b. April 18, 1888; Bryant Nixon b. Feb. 2, 1895. Family home Iona, Idaho.
Bishop of Iona ward, Iona; ward teacher, 1880; second counselor to superintendency North District Sunday school of Centerville; president theological class; counselor in Y. M. M. I. A.; missionary to northern states, 1890-91; presided over Indiana conference; organized first Sunday school at Robinson, Greene county, Ind.; president 106th quorum seventies. Moved to Poncah, 1859. Member of Utah militia, company C. Veteran Black Hawk war. Helped build the settlement on The Muddy, Nevada, 1874; once a guard at Utah penitentiary. Chairman of Acreage committee of Sugar Beet Contracts for erection of the factory at Lincoln (then Iona ward), Idaho; field superintendent eight years for factory. Director of Farmers Progress Canal Co., 1908.

RODEBACK, CHARLES (son of Charles Rodeback and Sarah Quaintance of Chester county, Pa.). Born June 8, 1811, in Pennsylvania. Came to Utah, 1852, independent company.
Married Jane Morgan in Pennsylvania (daughter of Benjamin Morgan and Mary Fisher). Their children: Mary Ann b. June 30, 1839, m. Samuel Malin Oct. 21, 1855; Sarah Jane b. Aug. 18, 1842, m. Oliver N. Harmon Oct. 18, 1857; Frances I. b. Oct. 11, 1846, m. Osborn B. Cooley November 16, 1861; Charles L. b. Nov. 29, 1851, m. Mary Ann Clayton Oct. 16, 1872. Family home, Salt Lake City.
High priest. Indian war veteran. Farmer. Pioneer to Hoytsville, Utah.

RODEBACK, CHARLES L. (son of Charles Rodeback and Jane Morgan). Born Nov. 29, 1850, Kanesville, Iowa. Came to Utah with parents.
Married Mary Ann Clayton Oct. 16, 1872 (daughter of Al-

bert Clayton and Fannie Higginbotham of Sheffield. Eng.), who was born Jan. 30, 1855. Their children: Charles A. b. Aug. 8, 1873, m. Tabitha Layton; Mary L. b. Nov. 12, 1874, m. John R. Smith; Elizabeth b. Oct. 9, 1876, m. H. B. Barrett; David b. Jan. 26, 1879, m. Elizabeth Lee; Clara b. April 14, 1881, m. William Merritt; Nora b. Aug. 13, 1883, m. Edward Hunter; James b. Feb. 16, 1886, m. Pearl Cobley; Edmond b. March 17, 1888, m. Vilate Smith; John William b. Oct. 13, 1890; Beatrice b. Oct. 21, 1892, m. Albert Smith; George b. Dec. 11, 1894; Fern b. Dec. 5, 1896; Noah b. March 31, 1900. Family home Pleasant Grove, Utah.
High priest. Veteran Black Hawk war. Built irrigation ditches. Farmer; stockraiser.

RODEBACK, JAMES (son of Charles Rodeback and Margaret Quaintance of Chester county, Pa.). Born May, 1807, in Chester county. Came to Utah 1852, Uriah Curtis company.
Married Phoebe Beagle, 1832 (daughter of Henry Beagle and Sarah Evans), who was born June, 1811, and came to Utah with husband. Their children: Edward H. b. May, 1833, m. Elizabeth McMichael 1855; Phoebe A. b. Nov. 1836, m. David Crafts 1855; Lorenzo Barnes b. March 11, 1843, m. Mary E. Bassett June 7, 1875; Rebecca H. b. May 1846, m. William Cook 1875; Catherine A. b. Nov. 1848, m. George W. Thurman 1864; James, Jr., b. Feb. 1853, m. Lourana Weeks 1874. Family home Cedar Valley, Utah.
Bishop's counselor; president high priests quorum; superintendent Sunday school. Justice of peace Cedar Fort 1856-75; postmaster 1854-75; assessor; collector Cedar county 1858-61

RODEBACK, LORENZO BARNES (son of James Rodeback and Phoebe Beagle). Born March 11, 1843, Nauvoo, Ill.
Married Mary E. Bassett June 7, 1875, Salt Lake City (daughter of Charles H. Bassett and Mary Knight), who was born June 9, 1854, Salt Lake City. Their children: Lester Barnes b. July, 1876, m. Mary E. Lewis 1904; Milton H. b. Sept. 1877; Douglas F. b. July, 1880; Myra M. b. Nov. 1881, m. Henry Rillingsly 1904; Charles Howard b. Feb. 1883; Mary Esther b. Aug. 1884, m. Ray S. Davis 1907; Ruby B. b. June, 1888. Family resided Cedar Fort, Utah, 1854-98, and Lago, Bannock Co., Idaho, 1898-1912.
Deputy sheriff; constable Utah county 1864-75; postmaster Cedar Valley 1875-98.

ROGERS, ALMA DENTON (son of Isaac Rogers and Susan Mills). Born June 18, 1836, Geneseo, Livingston county, N. Y. Came to Utah 1862, independent company.
Married Mary Jane Collins June 13, 1861, Fort Smith, Ark. (daughter of John Collins and Polly Minerva Chapman of Fort Smith), who was born June 15, 1837. Their children: Sallie Columbia Ann; Alma Hermando; Laura Etta; Adolphus Dion; Theron Aspacio; Astolpho Dio. Family home Sugar House, Utah.
Elder. Deputy marshal. School teacher; dentist.

ROGERS, ELISHA HENRY. (Seventh son of Noah Rogers, born March 17, 1797, in Connecticut, who after having been the first known missionary to circumnavigate the globe, died in the flower of manhood May 31, 1846, at Mt. Pisgah, Iowa, while preparing to come to Utah. He had married Eda Hollister, born Aug. 19, 1800, in Connecticut, pioneer 1849, with their children: Russell b. May 17, 1820; Theodore b. Feb. 3, 1824, m. Hannah Jones; Washington B. b. Sept. 16, 1826, m. Mary Ann Owens; David b. May 24, 1828, m. Mary Ann Mayers; Chauncy F. b. Aug. 23, 1829, m. Ellen Kelcy; Henrietta b. May 30, 1832, m. Henry Standage; Elisha Henry b. March 27, 1836, m. George Taggart; Nephi b. March 10, 1838, m. Elizabeth Payne July 24, 1859). Came to Utah 1849.
Married Susannah Julie Rogers Oct. 9, 1871, Salt Lake City (daughter of Freeman Rogers and Sarah Dowell of Rochester, N. Y., pioneers Sept. 13, 1861, Joseph Horne company). She was born Jan. 17, 1855. Their children: Nellie b. Jan. 21, 1873, Julia Clarissa b. June 19, 1874, and Elisha Freeman b. Jan. 15, 1876, died; Noah Henry b. Jan. 19, 1879, m. Lila Chapman; Sophronia H. b. Oct. 8, 1881, m. Oliver Hoppie; Lucy Ann b. July 20, 1884, Ellen Velate b. May 10, 1891, died. Family resided Bear Lake, Idaho, Richmond and Lewiston, Utah.
Married Emily Clarissa Clarkson Oct. 12, 1882, Salt Lake City (daughter of Robert Clarkson and Sarah Dowell [Rogers], who were married April 1862, Salt Lake City; latter pioneer Sept. 13, 1861, Joseph Horne company). She was born Jan. 24, 1863, Salt Lake City. Their children: Sarah Ada b. July 31, 1883, m. Fredrick C. Hoppie, Jr.; Delila Emily b. Jan. 18, 1886, m. Heber Wood; Amanda Jane b. Dec. 31, 1889, m. Luther Fellows; Horlick Dowell b. Dec. 31, 1891, died; Vica May b. July 17, 1895; Elmer Hollister b. Oct. 9, 1898; Iraley Slaten b. Jan. 28, 1902. Family home Lewiston, Utah.
High priest; missionary and trader among the Indians. Minuteman. Hauled rock with oxteams for Salt Lake temple; made three trips across plains for immigrants; located at Brigham City and after several changes finally settled at Lewiston, Utah. Died Dec. 9, 1906.

ROGERS, ISAAC, JR. (son of Isaac Rogers and Mary Maranda White, both pioneers Sept. 19, 1847, Daniel Spencer company). Born Sept. 5, 1845, at Middletown, N. J. Came to Utah Sept. 19, 1847, Daniel Spencer company.
Married Eunice Lestra Stewart Oct. 11, 1869, at Salt Lake City (daughter of Andrew J. Stewart of Monroe Co., and Eunice Pease Hawes of Marietta, Ohio, pioneers Sept. 15, 1850, independent company). She was born Feb. 1, 1853, at Payson, Utah. Their children: Eunice Lestra b. Aug. 15, 1870, m. William W. Phelps; Mary Maud Elson b. June 30, 1872, m. Thomas Nicholls Taylor; Florence Stewart b. Jan. 9, 1875, m. J. Frederick Fechser; Isaac Lynne b. Nov. 10, 1876, d. 1877; Ethel Melissa b. Jan. 9, 1879, m. Ruben Percy Greenwood; Nellie Stewart b. Jan. 9, 1881, m. Edgar H. Reeves.
Deacon. First settler in Payson Oct. 20, 1850. Drummer boy Daniel H. Wells company in Indian wars. Farmer. Died Aug. 25, 1901, Salt Lake City.

ROGERS, NEPHI (son of Noah Rogers born March 17, 1797, Connecticut, and Eda Hollister born Aug. 19, 1800, Connecticut). Born March 10, 1838, Daviess county, Mo. Came to Utah 1849.
Married Elizabeth Payne July 24, 1859 (daughter of Samuel Payne and Mary Barnes of England), who was born May 30, 1844. Their children: Nephi Noah b. Sept. 16, 1860, m. Charlotte A. Van Orden; Mary Elizabeth b. Nov. 10, 1862; Eda Ann b. Oct. 6, 1865, m. Joseph R. Peunningham; Isabella Catherine b. April 8, 1868; Philemon Aaron b. May 7, 1870; Sarah Emily b. June 2, 1873, m. W. A. Elmer; Samuel Russel b. March 23, 1876, m. Ida Hougaard Sept. 28, 1904. Family home Bloomington, Idaho, and Lewiston, Utah.
One of the first settlers of Logan, Cache Co., Utah, settling there in 1859; moved to Richmond 1871, then to Lewiston, Utah. Veteran Indian war. Ward teacher at Richmond, Utah.

ROGERS, NEPHI NOAH (son of Nephi Rogers and Elizabeth Payne). Born Sept. 16, 1860, Logan, Utah.
Married Charlotte Amelia Van Orden, Logan, Utah (daughter of Peter Edmond Van Orden and Sarah Ellen McFerson; latter pioneer Oct. 6, 1861, Isaac Allred company). She was born Sept. 29, 1878, Lewiston, Utah. Their children: Verlin Dell b. Feb. 2, 1905; Dorrel Nephi b. Oct. 28, 1906; Nile Edmond b. Feb. 23, 1909; Ellen b. May 12, 1911. Family home Lewiston, Utah.
Member of seventy; ward teacher; missionary to northern states 1894-96.

ROGERS, RUEL MILLS. Born Jan. 19, 1835, in New York.
Married Hannah C. Nelson, 1868, Salt Lake City (daughter of Levi Nelson), who was born March 17, 1851, Alton, Ill. Came to Utah 1857, handcart company. Their children: Victoria Maria b. March 10, 1870, died; Mary Effie b. Nov. 1872, m. William P. Blanchard 1889; Rufus Milan b. July 8, 1875, m. Mary Venter 1896; Ruella Pearl b. Oct. 30, 1878, m. Thomas King, Jr., 1897; Lilly May b. March 28, 1881, m. Darwin Mecham 1899; Katie Naomi b. Jan. 19, 1883, m. Clyde Metcalf 1906; Randolph Murcer b. March 29, 1885, m. Lizzie Nibley 1906. Family resided at Pleasant Grove, Utah, and Afton, Wyo.
Physician.

ROGERS, THEODORE (second son of Noah Rogers and Eda Hollister). Born Feb. 3, 1824, in Ohio. Came to Utah 1849 with mother.
Married Hannah Jones, who was born July 14, 1831. Came to Utah with Willard Richards family. Their children: Willard b. Feb. 21, 1853, m. Lilly Powell; John b. Aug. 26, 1854, m. Mina Sorenson; Mary Amelia b. Aug. 23, 1856, m. James Woodiard; Hannah L. b. Oct. 30, 1858, m. Thomas Cropper; Theodosia b. Feb. 4, 1861; Henry b. Jan. 20, 1863, m. Lizzie Lay; James Noah b. Sept. 28, 1871, m. Alice Chrichley; Washington b. July 4, 1865, m. Margaret Sorton. Missionary to Ohio in 1875. Pioneer of Fillmore, Utah, in 1853. Died May 21, 1901.

ROGERS, WILLARD (son of Theodore Rogers of Ohio and Hannah Jones). Born Feb. 21, 1853, Provo, Utah.
Married Lilly Powell (daughter of John Powell and Henriette Blyth), who was born at Meadows, Utah. Their children: Willard Theodore and Sarah. Family home Fillmore, Utah.
County surveyor Millard county for several years. Rancher and farmer.

ROGERS, THOMAS (son of John Rogers and Martha Reece of East Lake, Pembroke, Wales). Born April 5, 1830, in Wales. Came to Utah 1859, John Brown company.
Married Ann Evans 1851, while crossing the ocean, who was born July 3, 1830. Their children: John, William, Thomas and Mary Jane, died; Elizabeth Ann; Henry T. b. Jan. 19, 1862; Celestia M.; Martha M.; Markis E.; George Charles, died. Family home Benson ward, Utah.
Member of seventy; high priest. Postmaster. Farmer and stockraiser. Died Nov. 5, 1891, Benson.

ROGERS, HENRY T. (son of Thomas Rogers and Ann Evans). Born Jan. 19, 1862, Hyde Park, Utah.
Married Rebecca J. Williams Feb. 8, 1884 (daughter of John and Rebecca Williams, pioneers), who died. Their

children: William b. Jan. 24, 1885, died; Annie Rebecca b. May 11, 1886, m. William Hawkes. Family home Tooele, Utah.
Married Ahigal B. Marble Dec. 5, 1888 (daughter of Henry Marble and Mary Burbank, pioneers), who died. Their children: Thomas Henry b. Feb. 3, 1890, died; Lydia M. b. April 7, 1892. Family home Deweyville, Utah.
Married Esther C. Parkinson Oct. 2, 1893 (daughter of Samuel R. Parkinson and Arrabella Chandler, pioneers). Their children: Alice P. b. March 4, 1895; Lucile P. b. Sept. 1896; Clara P. b. March 23, 1898, died; Henry F. b. Jan. 19, 1900; Ruland P. b. Oct. 8, 1906, died; George Leonard b. Aug. 27, 1911. Family home Franklin, Idaho.
Member of seventy; bishop's counselor; bishop. Farmer and stockraiser.

ROLFE, SAMUEL JONES (son of Benjamin Rolfe and Mary Sweet of Massachusetts). He was born Aug. 26, 1794, Concord, N. H. Came to Utah September, 1847, A. H. Smoot company.
Married Elizabeth Hathaway March 4, 1818, Maine. She was born Aug. 29, 1801. Their children: Gilbert H. b. 1820; Benjamin W. b. 1822; Tallman H. b. 1824; Ianthus J. b. 1826; Weltha, b. 1828; Lydia b. Dec. 26, 1831; Horace C. b. Jan. 4, 1834; Samuel J. b. Jan. 3, 1836; William J. b. Dec 8, 1839; Mary Ann b Feb. 6, 1843; David L. b. 1846.
Member high priests quorum; bishop at Winter Quarters, Neb., 1846-47. County treasurer San Bernardina, Calif. House carpenter and joiner. He died July, 1867, at Lehi, Utah.

ROLFE, WILLIAM JASPER. Born Dec. 8, 1839. Came to Utah 1847.
Married Ellen Wilkshire at Lehi, Utah. She was born April 2, 1842. Their children: William Jasper, m. Hannah Jacobs; Ann Elizabeth, m. Gursbalda Gamble; Lydia M., m. James M. Shaffer; Samuel J., m. Hattie Crandall; Ellen, d. child. Family home Lehi, Utah.

ROLFSEN, JACOB (son of Bent and Gertrude Marie Rolfsen of Resor, Norway). Born 1828. Came to Utah Sept. 22, 1861, Samuel A. Woolley company.
Married Margaret Christinia Kjelson May, 1852, at Resor (daughter of Niels Kjelson and Helga Olsen, pioneers 1861, Samuel A. Woolley company). She was born Nov. 4, 1828. Their children: Nicholine, m. Nils H. Jensen; Bent; Maria, m. Otto Lylia; Niels, m. Annie Frandsen; Helga Sophia, m. George G. Frandsen; Jacobina, m. Clarence Winchester; Jacob; Annie Helen, m. William A. C. Bryan. Family home Mt. Pleasant, Utah.
High priest; missionary to Norway 1877-79; ward teacher. Worked on St. George and Manti temples. Settled at Ephraim 1861; moved to Mt. Pleasant 1863. Carpenter. Died Oct. 21, 1883, Mt. Pleasant.

ROLLINS, HENRY (son of Austin Rollins and Betsy Wells of Lincolnshire, Eng.). Born August, 1790, at Lincolnshire. Came to Utah 1848.
Married Ann Witherogg (daughter of Thomas Witherogg and Ann Witherogg of Hingle, Lincolnshire, who came to Utah 1851). She was born Dec. 21, 1799. Their children: Nancy; Austin; Alice, m. Ruben Flickner; Jane, m. Thomas Tomkins; Henry; John; Betsy, m. Edward Burrel; Isaac; Steuben b. June 15, 1832, m. Amanda M. France. Family home Steuben county, N. Y.
Died June 9, 1865.

ROLLINS, STEUBEN (son of Henry Rollins and Ann Witherogg). Born June 15, 1832, in Steuben county, N. Y.
Married Amanda M. France Feb. 10, 1855, Salt Lake City (daughter of Joseph France and Betsy Card of Allegany county, N. Y., pioneers 1849, William Hyde company). Their children: Steuben Oscar b. Dec. 10, 1855, m. Susan J. Whitaker; Joseph H. b. May 15, 1857, m. Georgana Cleveland; Moroni b. Feb. 4, 1859; Franklin b. April 9, 1860; William D. b. March 6, 1861, m. Lizzie Morris; Thomas A. b. May 14, 1863; Charles O. b. Aug. 23, 1865, m. Viola Chase; Alice E. b. Nov. 21, 1867, m. John W. Ford; George W. b. Sept. 20, 1869, m. Elizabeth Rampton; Amanda M. b. Oct. 26, 1871, m. Phillip Ford; Roda E. b. Jan. 2, 1874, m. James Savage; Blanch b. Sept. 3, 1876, m. Phillip A. Weaver. Family home Centerville, Davis Co., Utah.
Sunday school superintendent. Veteran Echo Canyon campaign.

ROLLINS, STEUBEN OSCAR (son of Steuben Rollins and Amanda M. France). Born Dec. 10, 1855, Centerville, Davis Co., Utah.
Married Susan J. Whitaker Jan. 21, 1887, Logan, Utah (daughter of Thomas Whitaker and Elizabeth Mills, both of Centerville, who was born March 21, 1866. Their children: Oscar Whitaker b. Nov. 19, 1887, m. Zina Pearl Bybee; Louise W. b. April 8, 1890, m. Edwin C. Warner; Enid W. b. Dec. 8, 1893, m. Walter A. Fernelius; Thelma W. b. Jan. 17, 1897; Josephine W. b. Nov. 28, 1899. Family home, Centerville.

ROLLINS, OSCAR WHITAKER (son of Steuben Oscar Rollins and Susan J. Whitaker). Born Nov. 19, 1887, Centerville, Utah.
Married Zina Pearl Bybee Jan. 10, 1910, Salt Lake City (daughter of Byram L. Bybee and Jane Robinson of Uinta, Utah), who was born March 30, 1889. Their children: Viola Bybee b. Aug. 5, 1910; Lee Bybee b. Dec. 5, 1911.

ROMRELL, FRANCIS (son of Francis Romrell, born 1760, and Jane Hutton, born 1770, of Isle of Jersey, Eng.). Born Aug. 18, 1799, St. John, Isle of Jersey. Came to Utah 1854, Charles Harper company.
Married Mary Billot, who was born April 18, 1807, Isle of Jersey, Eng. Their children: Mary b. May, 1828, m. Richard Carnish; Francis b. July 21, 1829, m. Christina Anderson; George b. Oct. 14, 1832, m. Patience Swingewood Sept. 29, 1861; Jane V. b. Feb. 22, 1838, m. George Pierce Sept. 18, 1864; Fannie A. b. April 26, 1840, m. Charles Singleton July, 1874; Ann b. Sept. 29, 1841, died; Abraham Charles b. May 18, 1843, m. Mary Marley 1865; Sophia Jane b. 1845, m. Milan Russell. Family home Ogden, Utah.
High priest. Moved from Salt Lake City to Ogden about 1858.

ROMRELL, GEORGE (son of Francis Romrell and Mary Billot). Born Oct. 14, 1832, Isle of Jersey, Eng. Came to Utah Sept. 15, 1861, Ira Eldredge company.
Married Patience Swingewood Sept. 29, 1861, Ogden, Utah (daughter of John Swingewood, died June 14, 1849, on way to Utah, and Jemima Baker of Stourbridge, Eng., pioneer 1869). She was born Sept. 29, 1841, at Stourbridge. Their children: William H. and Anna E. (twins) b. 1862, d. infants; George Heber b. June 21, 1863, m. Louisa M. Smithes Oct. 1889; Mary J. b. Sept. 27, 1865, d. May 15, 1880; Patience E. b. Jan. 7, 1868, m. August Ossmen May, 1887; Joseph E. b. March 8, 1870, m. Esther Burbank 1895; Alfred b. Feb. 13, 1872, m. Alba Burbank Oct. 20, 1898; Fannia A. b. Aug. 6, 1874, m. Ole C. Oleson Nov. 30, 1901; Charles H. b. Jan. 22, 1877, d. infant; Lorenzo J. b. Dec. 30, 1877, m. Emma Eggerty April 5, 1905; Hyrum J. b. March 31, 1880, m. Ruby Taylor Dec. 10, 1902; Josephine D. b. Nov. 17, 1883, m. Richard Mills March 8, 1905.
High priest. Settled at Ogden 1861, where he built a molasses mill. Died Dec. 31, 1912.

ROOT, EMERSON FRANK (son of Alonzo and Emeretta Root). Born Nov. 1, 1858, Hartford, Wis. Came to Utah Nov. 1, 1890.
Married Emma Kind Sept. 21, 1882, in Nebraska (daughter of John Kind), who was born June 2, 1863. Their children: Louise, m. A. J. Eakins; Frank, m. Emma St. Claire.
Married Kathleen Wallace. Family home, Salt Lake City.
Physician and surgeon.

ROPER, HENRY (son of William Roper and Susanna Smith, Lincolnshire, Eng.). Born Feb. 9, 1836, Tornton Bridge, Lincolnshire. Came to Utah Sept. 24, 1848, Heber C. Kimball company.
Married Charlotte Elizabeth Mellor Feb. 4, 1857, Provo, Utah (daughter of James Mellor and Mary Ann Payne of Leicester, Eng., pioneers November, 1856, Edward Martin handcart company). She was born Jan. 16, 1842. Their children: Henry Hutchinson b. Aug. 25, 1858, d. infant; Susanna b. July 23, 1859, m. James Case; William B. Feb. 2, 1861, m. Maria Wimmer; Salena b. Nov. 23, 1862, m. George Bartholomew; Sarah b. March 13, 1865, m. David Dimmick; Mary Ann b. Feb. 23, 1867, m. John Wesley Guyman; Clara Althara b. Oct. 15, 1869, m. James Lake; Charlotte Elizabeth b. March 4, 1872, m. Olaf Nielsen; Charles Henry b. Jan. 10, 1874, m. Hope Dack; George Albert b. Feb. 8, 1876, m. Charlotte Lewis; Benjamin Franklin b. Sept. 8, 1878; James Leo b. Dec. 29, 1881, m. Maria Wilasted; Oliver Marian b. May 13, 1884, m. Leurie Fowler. Family home Lawrence, Utah.
Married Amy Salina Matthews (Shaw) June 5, 1881, Manti, Utah (daughter of William Matthews and Maria Payne of Wittlesey, Cambridge, Eng.), who was born Jan. 27, 1850.
Member 52d and 32d quorums seventies; high priest; superintendent of Sunday school at Gunnison and later at Lawrence. Settled in Emery county. Indian war veteran. Farmer; apiarist; rancher. Families resided Lawrence, Utah.

ROSE, ABRAHAM (son of Abraham Rose, born April 1, 1767, Manchester, Vt., and Rachel Haws. born Aug. 3, 1769, of Burlington, Vt.—married April 10, 1791). Born Oct. 5, 1803, Utica, N. Y. Came to Utah Sept. 17, 1853, John W. Cooley company.
Married Catherine Nicholson March 7, 1830 (daughter of Jonathan Nicholson and Betsy Swingle—married July 4, 1804, Hornellsville, N. Y.). She was born Dec. 22, 1804. Their children: Adaline b. Dec. 2, 1831; William Warren b. May 6, 1833, m. Lorinda Garner Dec. 4, 1853; Betsey Elizabeth b. July 17, 1835, m. Nathaniel Underwood May 18, 1852; Orson Hyde b. March 25, 1837; Ann Victoria b. June 4, 1839, m. William K. Rice Oct. 5, 1857; Alley Stephen March 6, 1841, m. Alvira E. Smith April 12, 1863; Martha

b. May 5, 1843, m. Allen Burk; Erastus Francisco b. Aug. 26, 1847, m. Josephine Robinson Jan. 4, 1868. Family home Farmington, Utah.
President high priest quorum 30 years; ward teacher. Died Sept. 9, 1884.

ROSE, ALLEY STEPHEN (son of Abraham Rose and Catherine Nicholson). Born March 6, 1841, at Carthage, Athens Co., Ohio.
Married Alvira E. Smith April 12, 1863, at Farmington, Utah (daughter of Thomas S. Smith and Polly Clark, pioneers 1848), who was born Dec. 16, 1846, Council Bluffs, Iowa. Their children: Adaline, m. Oscar S. Rice Oct. 26, 1893; Leon Alley b. Aug. 27, 1865, m. Elvira Welling March 14, 1889; Ursel Stephen b. May 6, 1867, m. Nellie Burns Feb. 17, 1897; Armond Thomas b. Oct. 20, 1869, m. Clara L. Sanders June 1, 1899; Inez Evalette b. March 29, 1873, m. John W. Haws March 3, 1897; Theresa Florence b. March 5, 1876, m. Arthur J. Barber March 8, 1905; Charles Edwin b. Sept. 1, 1878, m. Cecellia Larsen Oct. 8, 1902; Almy Genette b. March 21, 1881, m. Edward S. Rice April 10, 1901; Henry Smith b. March 23, 1883, m. Olive M. Barlow Oct. 10, 1906; Lorette Helen b. Nov. 26, 1885, d. Dec. 23, 1895. Family home Farmington, Utah.
President 56th quorum seventies 34 years; Sunday school superintendent 36 years; missionary to New York 1876; high priest 1905; president Y. M. M. I. A. 4 years. County commissioner 3 years.

ROSE, ANDERS PETER (son of Thomas Petersen Hansen Rose and Gjertrude Oisen, of Vejle, Vejle Amt, Denmark). Born Nov. 8, 1828, at Vejle. Came to Utah September, 1861, Captain Porter company.
Married Mette Marie Johnsen February, 1861, Vejle (daughter of John Christiansen and Ane Marie Invardsen, of Greis, Denmark), who was born Oct. 25, 1834. Their children: Gjertrude Marie b. April 11, 1862, m. Lauritz P. Hendriksen; Ane Katrine Magrethe b. April 3, 1864, d. young; Thomas Jinny Peter b. July 31, 1866, m. Elise Williams; Antonie Kjeistine Petrea b. Sept. 23, 1868, m. Alvin McBride; Ane Marie Juditha b. Feb. 14, 1871, m. Peter O. Hansen; Joseph Bernando b. Sept. 20, 1874, d. young; Peter Parley b. July 20, 1876, m. Elisa Eliasen. Family resided at Salt Lake City and Hyrum, Utah.
Married Jensine Kjerstine Jensen Bager. Their children: Francis Peter; Florance Jensine Bager; Ferdinando Jacobus Bager; Emma Chrestiane Bager; Jens Vernon Bager.
President 62d quorum seventies; assistant Sunday school superintendent several years; missionary to Denmark 1878-80; tithing clerk; also superintended the building of several church buildings at Hyrum. Councilman and mayor of Hyrum. Farmer.

ROSE, FREDERICK W. Born July 16, 1835, London, Eng. Came to Utah Oct. 3, 1854, Orson Pratt company.
Married Elizabeth E. Domville Dec. 25, 1856, Salt Lake City, Bishop Perkins officiating (daughter of Thomas Domville and Mary Peters of Liverpool, Eng., pioneers Oct. 4, 1851, Morris Phelps company). She was born June 23, 1838. Their children: William T., m. Martha Needham; Mary A., d. infant; Emma C.; Lillian S., m. Walter Lewis; Frederick W., m. Amelia Horsley; Maria I., d. aged 10; Charles E., m. Florence Rawlings; James E., m. Annie Clark; Walter, d. aged 5; Arthur and Albert, d. infants. Family home, Salt Lake City.
Member 8th quorum seventies; high priest; block teacher. Carpenter and builder. Died Jan. 2, 1908, Salt Lake City.

ROSE, CHARLES EDGAR (son of Frederick W. Rose and Elizabeth E. Domville). Born Dec. 9, 1871, Salt Lake City.
Married Florence Rawlings May 30, 1900, Salt Lake City (daughter of William Rawlings and Mary A. Carpenter of Somerset, Eng., pioneers 1869). She was born May 30, 1875. Their children: Donald b. March 15, 1902; Gordon b. Feb. 3, 1904; Eveline b. Jan. 13, 1909, d. infant. Family home, Salt Lake City.
Member 10th and 105th quorum seventies; missionary to England 1896-98; assistant Sunday school superintendent 1st ward; block teacher; counselor to president of Y. M. M. I. A., Forest Dale ward; home missionary at Salt Lake stake 2 years; member tabernacle choir 15 years. In charge of job presses of Deseret News Printing Co.

ROSEBERRY, CHARLES. Born Aug. 22, 1825, Malmo, Sweden. Came to Utah Sept. 1, 1859, George Rowley handcart company.
Married Helena Erickson April 7, 1849, at Malmo (daughter of Peter and Hannah Erickson of Sweden), who was born Oct. 11, 1822, Scona, Sweden. Their children: Caroline Helena b. Aug. 1, 1850, and Anna Augusta b. Jan. 2, 1853, d. infants; Anna Maria b. Sept. 2, 1855, m. Oscar B. Young; Niels Joseph b. Sept. 10, 1858, m. Lucretia Keeler; Emma Carolina b. Sept. 10, 1858, m. Jens L. Jensen; Hannah Helena b. Oct. 2, 1861, m. George Larson; Charles b. Oct. 2, 1861, m. Lydia Dodge; Ellen Augusta, Louisa Charlotte and Helena (triplets) b. Dec. 26, 1864; Helena and Augusta, died; Louisa Charlotte, m. Joseph Rogers; Elizabeth b. March 8, 1867, m. Jack Loving. Family home Moroni, Santaquin, Richfield, Utah.
Early settler in San Pete and Utah counties; veteran Black Hawk war. Killed while working on railroad in Weber Canyon Nov. 15, 1868. Carpenter.

ROSKELLEY, SAMUEL (son of Thomas Roskelley and Ann Kitt, both of Devonport, Devonshire, Eng.). Born Jan. 1, 1837, at Devonport. Came to Utah Oct. 16, 1853; Appleton Harmon company.
Married Rebecca Hendricks, July 22, 1858, Salt Lake City, Utah (daughter of James Hendricks and Druzilla Dorris of Simpson county, Ky., pioneers 1847), who was born Nov. 2, 1835. Their children: Rebecca b. April 22, 1859, m. Thomas Hillyard; Charlotte b. Oct. 7, 1860, d. child; Zina Y. b. March 18, 1862, m. Don C. Hyde; Samuel b. Aug. 11, 1863, m. Agness E. Thyberg; James b. Jan. 10, 1865, m. Frances A. Emery; William H. b. May 4, 1866, m. Agness Wieldman; Joseph b. June 5, 1868, m. Frances A. Hinckley.
Missionary to Wales 1857-58; presided over Cardiff conference in Wales; bishop of Smithfield ward 1862-80; patriarch; filled another mission to England and presided over London conference from 1880 until 1881; and with wife labored as a missionary at St. George, Utah; recorder of Logan temple 1884-1911. Superintendent of common schools for Cache Co., Utah, 6 years; major of 4th Battalion, 1st Regiment Infantry, Cache valley Brigade, three years during Indian troubles, and afterwards captain of brigade under Brig. Gen. William Hyde.

ROSS, DANIEL. He was born in Scotland. Came to Utah 1851, oxteam company.
Married Agnes McKella of Dumbartonshire, Scotland; she came to Utah 1852, with her husband. Their children: Archibald; Alexander; Mary, m. Robert Henry; Jeanette, m. Benjamin Tooksbury; Daniel, m. Francis Peay, m. Hannah Adams; Agnes, m. Walter Thompson; Duncan; Katherine, m. John Gillespie; Joan, m. John McClaus; Hugh, died. Family home Hillensbury, Scotland, and Salt Lake City.
Farmer. Died at Salt Lake City.

ROSS, DANIEL JR. (son of Daniel Ross and Agnus McKella of Dumbarton, Scotland). Born Jan. 22, 1827, Halensburg, Scotland. Came to Utah 1851, oxteam company.
Married Frances Peay Oct. 12, 1852, Salt Lake Endowment house. She was the daughter of William Peay and Mary Blake of Climping, Sussex, Eng.; pioneers Oct. 3, 1852, Harmon Cutler oxteam company. She was born Sept. 15, 1833. Their children: Daniel, m. Ida A. Frisby; William P., m. Annie Johnson; Nephi, m. Mary Delilah Stubbs; Hugh m. Kathaline Alice Farrer; Mary, m. John Hallen Ceck; Johan, died; Elizabeth, m. Abraham Johnson; George E., m. Bertha Peay; Agnes, m. Nels N. Nelson. Family home South Weber, Utah.
Married Hannah Adams April, 1865, Salt Lake Endowment house, whose parents lived in Northampton, Eng. She was born 1839. Their children: Thomas A., m. Mary Hardy; John, m. Elizabeth Smith; James, m. Annie Perry.
Minuteman in Walker and Battle Creek troubles. Farmer. Died Sept. 5, 1901, at Hooper, Utah.

ROSS, NEPHI (son of Daniel Ross and Frances Peay). Born Dec. 19, 1858, in Iron Co., Utah.
Married Mary Delilah Stubbs July 22, 1891, Provo City, Utah (daughter of Richard Stubbs and Elender Ware of Provo), who was born Dec. 19, 1862. Their children: Elender D. b. Dec. 5, 1892, died; Daisan N. b. May 14, 1893; Edith F. b. Feb. 27, 1895; Grace R. b. Jan. 10, 1897; Silva A. b. Oct. 27, 1899; Jennie V. b. Jan. 6, 1905. Family home Provo, Utah.
Member of first city council, Provo, divided on party lines. Farmer and miner.

ROSS, HUGH (son of Daniel Ross Jr. and Frances Peay). He was born Jan. 25, 1861, South Weber, Utah.
Married Catherine A. Farrer March 25, 1896, Provo, Utah (daughter of William Farrer and Elizabeth Ann Kerry, both of Brigstreer, Westmoreland, England—pioneers 1847, Captain Taylor company). She was born Sept. 15, 1865. Their children: Hugh S. b. Jan. 17, 1897; William Kenneth b. Sept. 20, 1899; Elizabeth F. b. Oct. 18, 1901; Thelma Lucile b. Sept. 28, 1903, died; Alma D. b. Jan. 14, 1907; Catherine A. b. March 1, 1909. Family home Provo, Utah.
Mason; contractor and builder.

ROSS, JAMES JACKSON (son of Melvin Ross and Rebecca Smith, of Heber City and Vernal, Utah). Born Nov. 23, 1837. Came to Utah 1850, Aaron Johnson company.
Married Susan Laverna Roby 1857, Salt Lake City (daughter of Jeremiah Roby and Ruth Tucker of Provo and Midway, Utah), who was born April 14, 1838, died 1862. Their children: Sarah Jane b. Jan. 7, 1858, m. Henry Miles Alexander; Susan Matilda b. March 22, 1860, m. William O'Neil; Laverna Virginia b. April 14, 1862, m. Hyrum Gould. Family home Heber City, Utah.
Married Sarah Provost 1874, Heber City, Utah (daughter of Luke Provost, of Midway, pioneer, oxteam company), who was born January, 1855. Their children: Emma, died; James Isaac, m. Jane Young. Family home Vernal, Utah.
Took part in Echo Canyon trouble. Veteran Indian war. Farmer and stockraiser. Died May 2, 1909, Vernal, Utah.

ROSS, STEPHEN WEEKS. Born May 2, 1855.
Married Jane Stevenson of New York state. Their children: John E., m. Amanda Norton; Stephen Weeks, Jr., m. Ginevre E. Molen; Sarah Elizabeth, m. James Lamb; Adrian, died. Lived at Newark, N. J.
Marble engraver and merchant.

1142   PIONEERS AND PROMINENT MEN OF UTAH

ROSS, STEPHEN WEEKS, JR. (son of Stephen Weeks Ross and Jane Stevenson). Born April 12, 1841, Newark, N. J. Came to Utah fall of 1855, Jefferson Tidwell oxteam company.
Married Ginevra Ellen Molen Dec. 25, 1866, Lehi City, Utah (daughter of Jesse Molen and Lurany Huffaker of Illinois; pioneers 1847; Jedediah M. Grant company). She was born April 16, 1845. Their children: Lurany Jane, m. P. Palvin Duke; Stephen M., m. Margaret Wardle; Michael A., m. Hulda Perry; Jesse Edgar, died; John W., d. infant; William Simpson, m. Myrtle Whiteman; Francis A., m. Etta Wardle; Perlettie L., m. John Eaton; Margaret L., m. Henry Abplanalp; Forrest M., m. Josephine Mitchell; Warren L., m. Bernett Sprouse; Ginevra, d. infant.
High priest; president 4th quorum elders; constable of Vernal; deputy sheriff Utah county. Veteran Black Hawk war. Farmer and stockraiser.

ROSS, MICHAEL ADRIAN (son of Stephen W. Ross and Ginevra Ellen Molen). Born Sept. 7, 1872, at Lehi, Utah.
Married Hulda Perry June 5, 1901, at Salt Lake City, Utah (daughter of Alonzo Orson Perry and Anjeanette Abigail Stowell), who was born July 30, 1874. Their children: Helen Mar b. April 8, 1902; Ainona b. Jan. 17, 1904; Perry Adrian b. Feb. 16, 1910. Family home Vernal, Utah.
Missionary to West Virginia 1898-1900; school superintendent; ward teacher; president Y. M. M. I. A. Road supervisor. Farmer. Died at Vernal.

ROSS, THOMAS. Born Sept. 15, 1814, in Gilbert county, N. C. Came to Utah Sept. 6, 1850, Lije Everett's fifty, Aaron Johnson company.
Married Rachel Smith, who was born Aug. 22, 1813; came to Utah with her husband. Their children: James A. b. Sept. 20, 1836, m. Sarah Ann Smith b. March 6, 1857; Margaret Ann b. March 3, 1839, m. Sidney R. Carter March 6, 1857; Lucinda b. Feb. 14, 1842, m. Sidney R. Carter March 6, 1857; Mary E. b. March 4, 1845, m. Joseph F. Carter; Nancy Jane b. Dec. 11, 1848, m. Albert McMillen April 15, 1869; Thomas W. b. Jan. 25, 1851, m. Margaret Ann Harvey; Robert F. b. Oct. 18, 1853, m. Mary Evelyn Gay Dec. 25, 1879; John Franklin b. May 15, 1856.
Married Margaret Maria Meacom (daughter of Lewis and Lydia Meacom). Their children: Mary Ann b. Oct. 19, 1858, m. Culbert L. King; George Lewis b. April 30, 1862, m. Mary Ann Anderson May 13, 1885; Joshua b. Oct. 2, 1864; Lydia Lucinda b. Oct. 13, 1865, m. George Charlesworth; Joshua Josiah b. June 3, 1867; Daniel Thomson b. Nov. 8, 1868, m. Elizabeth Ann King; Maria Emeline b. April 24, 1871, m. Volney H. King; Samantha Matilda b. Feb. 13, 1873, m. Horton Haight; Sarah Luticia.
Settled Provo, Utah, 1851. Veteran Black Hawk, Walker and Tintic Indian wars. Farmer.

ROSS, JAMES ANDREW (son of Thomas Ross and Rachel Smith). Born Sept. 20, 1836, in Gibson county, Tenn. Came to Utah with parents Sept. 6, 1850.
Married Sarah Ann Smith March 6, 1857, Salt Lake City (daughter of Richard Smith and Diana Brazwell, pioneers 1857). She was born in Gibson county, Tenn.
Married Catherine Elnora Anderson May 25, 1879, Meadow Creek, Utah (daughter of Hoken and Mary Ann Anderson, pioneers Sept. 12, 1861, John R. Murdock company). She was born Jan. 9, 1856, Copenhagen, Denmark.
Assisted in bringing immigrants from the Missouri river to Utah, and was one of the relief party rescuing the "frozen" handcart company December, 1856, Indian war veteran, serving in the Walker war 1853-54, in the Tintic war 1854-55, and in the Black Hawk war 1865-67. Helped build the Union Pacific R. R. through Echo canyon, 1868. High priest; missionary to Tennessee 1876-77, and 1883-84. President and director Canal and Otter Creek Reservoir Co.; vice president Richfield Commercial & Savings Bank.

ROSSITER, WILLIAM A. (son of William A. Rossiter, born in London, and Mary Smith, born in Wentworth, Eng.). Born Feb. 26, 1843, in London. Came to Utah Oct. 29, 1862, W. H. Dame church freight train, the last that year.
Married Eliza A. Crabtree Dec. 27, 1863 (daughter of Charles Crabtree, pioneer 1857, James Brown company), who was born Aug. 5, 1842. Their children: Phoebe Ellen b. Dec. 17, 1865, m. Henry O. Baddley Sept. 9, 1885; William Herbert b. Sept. 14, 1867, m. Maria Baddley Jan. 1, 1896; Alice b. 1870; Elizabeth b. March 18, 1872, m. David M. Campbell May 9, 1894; Frederick Charles b. April 7, 1874, m. Sarah A. Shannon Nov. 14, 1900; Edith May b. Jan. 29, 1876, m. William H. Lovesy June 14, 1869; George Alfred b. Jan. 31, 1878, m. Nettie Boyle Feb. 23, 1900; Lucy b. Aug. 26, 1880, m. William C. Evans Oct. 7, 1901; Ernest C. b. Oct. 16, 1882, m. Venus Robinson June 28, 1911; Elmer Dean b. May 13, 1886. Family home Salt Lake City.
Married Shamira Young Oct. 9, 1877, Salt Lake City (daughter of Brigham Young and Lucy A. Decker, latter a pioneer 1848). She was born March 21, 1853, Salt Lake City. Their children: Clifford Y. b. Dec. 21, 1878, died; Lillian b. May 10, 1880; Russell Y. b. Aug. 26, 1881, m. Leah Farr Aug. 9, 1911.
Member of seventy. President Brigham Young's coachman five years; general superintendent of President Young's business affairs 1872-77; after the president's death agent of the estate. Banking.

ROSSITER, FREDERICK CHARLES (son of William A. Rossiter and Eliza A. Crabtree). Born April 7, 1874, Salt Lake City, Utah.
Married Sarah A. Shannon Nov. 14, 1900, Salt Lake City (daughter of William Shannon and Jennie Harding), who was born Feb. 14, 1880, San Francisco, Cal. Their children: Ruth Mary b. Sept. 22, 1901; Frederick Shannon b. Dec. 28, 1902; William Algenier b. April 1, 1904; Afton Eliza b. Nov. 16, 1905; Lawrence Campbell b. June 13, 1907; Adfred Harding and Sadie Lucille (twins) b. Nov. 14, 1909. Family resided Salt Lake City and Providence, Utah.
Member of seventy; missionary to Society Islands 1893-1898. Horticulturist.

ROSSITER, WILLIAM H. (son of William A. Rossiter and Eliza Crabtree). Born Sept. 14, 1867, Salt Lake City.
Married Maria Baddley Jan. 1, 1896, Salt Lake City (daughter of George Baddley and Charlotte DeGray of England, pioneers 1853), who was born Oct. 16, 1866. Their children: Edith b. Aug. 30, 1897; Bryant b. Aug. 31, 1899; Eliza b. May 10, 1901; William b. March 5, 1904; Frank b. May 10, 1907. Family home, Salt Lake City.
Plumber.

ROUNDY, SHADRACH (son of Uriah Roundy of New York). Born Jan. 1, 1789, in Windham county, Vt. Came to Utah July 24, 1847, Brigham Young company.
Married Betsy Quimby. Their children: Lauren Hotchkiss b. May 21, 1815, m. Joanna Carter 1843, m. Jane Ann Koyle; Julia Rebecca b. 1817; Lorenzo Wesley b. June 18, 1819, m. Susan Wallace; Laura b. 1822, m. David Beck; Samantha b. 1824, m. John D. Parker; Jared Curtis b. Jan. 5, 1827, m. Lovisa Jenne; Almeda Sophia b. March, 1829, m. John D. Parker; William Felshaw b. 1831; Nancy Jane b. 1833, m. Calvin Foss; Malinda b. 1835. Family home, Salt Lake City.
Bishop of 16th ward, Salt Lake City. Veteran Indian war. Member of Joseph Smith's bodyguard. Farmer. Died July 4, 1872.

ROUNDY, LAUREN HOTCHKISS (son of Shadrach Roundy and Betsy Quimby). Born May 21, 1815, Spafford, Onondaga county, N. Y. Came to Utah September, 1847, handcart company.
Married Joanna Carter 1843, Nauvoo, Ill. (daughter of John S. Carter of Nauvoo, Ill., pioneer September, 1847), who died at Winter Quarters, Iowa. Their children: Byron Donalvin b. Jan. 29, 1844; William Heber b. Feb. 5, 1846, m. Malinda Parker Aug. 20, 1872. Family home, Illinois.
Married Jane Ann Koyle, Salt Lake City (daughter of John Koyle of Mallahide, Canada), who was born Sept. 5, 1831. Their children: Julia b. 1849, d. in 1852; Jared Washington b. Feb. 22, 1851, m. Louise Taylor; Hyrum Koyle b. Dec. 12, 1854, m. Ann Chase; Laurette b. May 12, 1860, m. Thomas Nelson; John b. May 18, 1864, m. Eleanor McEwan; Lilly b. Dec. 25, 1866, m. Oliver Gallup; Charles b. Dec. 25, 1866, d. infant. Family resided Centerville and Springville, Utah.
Married Martha Edmondson. She died. Their children: Luella, m. Hyrum Perry; Mary Ann, m. Abner Dee Miner; Adelbert.
Member bishopric of Spanish Fork; high councilor. Indian war veteran. Farmer. Died March, 1900, Knightsville, Utah.

ROUNDY, WILLIAM HEBER (son of Lauren Hotchkiss Roundy and Joanna Carter). Born Feb. 5, 1846, Nauvoo, Ill. Came to Utah with parents.
Married Malinda Parker Aug. 20, 1872, Salt Lake City (daughter of John Davis Parker and Almeda Sophia Roundy of Upper Kanab, Utah, pioneers 1847). She was born April 4, 1851. Their children: Marian, d. infant; William Heber, d. aged 22; John Davis; Middie May; Lauren Hotchkiss, d. aged 22; Maud Samantha; Sophia; Quimby; Joanna Malinda; Otho. Family home, Upper Kanab Ranch (now Alton, Utah).
Elder. Assessor and collector. Farmer and rancher. Died July 23, 1899.

ROUNDY, JOHN (son of Lauren Hotchkiss Roundy and Jane Ann Koyle). Born May 18, 1864, at Springville, Utah.
Married Eleanor McEwan Feb. 14, 1889, at Provo, Utah (daughter of John H. McEwan and Amanda Higbee, of Provo), who was born Oct. 10, 1869. Their children: Nellie b. May 14, 1891, m. Julian F. Greer; John McEwan b. Sept. 24, 1894; Amanda Ione b. April 13, 1899; Clayton b. Oct. 2, 1900; Fern b. April 30, 1903; Bert Lincoln b. Feb. 12, 1906; Loren b. March 2, 1909, d. March, 1909. Family resided Provo and Knightsville, Utah.
Bishop of Knightsville 1900-09; president Y. M. M. I. A. at Knightsville 1897-1900. Mining man; merchant.

ROUNDY, JOHN DAVIS (son of William Heber Roundy and Malinda Parker). Born Nov. 3, 1876, Upper Kanab, Utah.
Member 85th quorum seventies; missionary to eastern states 1899-1901; member bishopric. Farmer and stockraiser.

ROUNDY, JARED CURTIS (son of Shadrach Roundy and Betsy Quimby). Born Jan. 5, 1827, in Ohio. Came to Utah July 24, 1847, Brigham Young company.
Married Louisa Jenne at Salt Lake City (daughter of

PIONEERS AND PROMINENT MEN OF UTAH 1143

Benjamin Jenne and Sarah Snyder, pioneers 1849), who was born June 15, 1832. Their children: Evelyn H. b. Nov. 23, 1852, m. Lucius Peck; Jared Curtis b. March 13, 1855. m. Alice Apgood; Saran Louisa b. Jan. 17, 1858, m. Joseph Phillips; Shadrach b. Feb. 9, 1860, m. Sarah A. Edgel; George Snyder b. Oct. 10, 1862; Ida May b. Oct. 14, 1864, m. John Snyder; Roseanna b. Dec. 22, 1867, m. George Gibbons; Frank Spencer b. Oct. 3, 1870; Maud S. b. July 7, 1875, m. John Thompson. Family home Wanship. Bishop of Wanship ward 1875-84. Commander of soldiers in Black Hawk Indian war. Farmer. Died May 22, 1895, St. David, Ariz.

ROWAN, MATHEW (son of James Rowan, born July 10, 1799, Renfrew, Scotland, and Margaret Miller). Born April 12, 1827, Renfrew, Scotland. Came to Utah Oct. 28, 1855. Married Jane Martin June 6, 1853 (daughter of Barnabas and Sarah Martin), who was born Jan. 31, 1827, Norwich, Eng. Their children: Ammon b. April 27, 1854; Emma b. March 15, 1856, m. Alexander McGhie June 13, 1881; Mathew Martin b. Aug. 28, 1859, m. Hannah Swenson.
Married Annie Olsen Feb. 23, 1862, South Cottonwood, Utah. She was born June 8, 1839, in Sweden. Their children: Annie Jane b. Dec. 7, 1862, m. Mathew Ellison; Sarah Ellen b. Sept. 23, 1865, m. Francis Beckstead.
Second counselor to Bishop Cahoon, South Cottonwood; ward clerk; school teacher South Cottonwood.

ROWE, WILLIAM H. (son of James W. Rowe of Portsmouth, Eng.). Born Feb. 14, 1841, in England. Came to Utah 1873.
Married Anna Frances Bates May, 1858, Birmingham, Eng. (daughter of George Bates and Anna Wild of England), who was born March 1, 1835. Their children: Minnie, m. Edward Smith; Amy, m. Julian Houtz; Louise, m. Roland Green; Lorenzo W., m. Ada Gilbert; Effie, m. Walter E. Maddison; William H.; Nellie; Mabel; Alice; Arthur. Family home Salt Lake City, Utah.
Seventy. State road commissioner. President of Bear River Canal Co.; shoe manufacturer Z. C. M. I. Died Jan. 28, 1913, Salt Lake City.

ROWLAND, BENJAMIN (son of Edward Rowland and Mary Williams of Dowells, Glamorgan, Wales). Born Sept. 30, 1837, Dowells. Came to Utah autumn of 1853, Daniel Jones company.
Married Elizabeth Williams May 18, 1862, Salt Lake City (daughter of William and Emma Williams of Denbigh, Wales, pioneers Sept. 13, 1861, Homer Duncan company). She was born Dec. 21, 1843. Their children: Benjamin William; Morgan W. and John Thomas, died; Emma Elizabeth, m. Albert Love; Margaret Clara; Rosella; Roy Ephraim, m. Martha Wiesman; Annie Pearl, m. Dean Richmond; Parley. Family home, Salt Lake City.
Member of seventy; block teacher. Guard in early Indian wars, in Iron county. Hauled rock with oxteam for Salt Lake temple; worked on Salt Lake temple 3 years. Died June 23, 1910.

ROWLAND, ROY EPHRAIM (son of Benjamin Rowland and Elizabeth Williams). Born Oct. 21, 1880, at Salt Lake City.
Married Martha Wiesman Sept. 16, 1903, Salt Lake City (daughter of Charles Williams and Elizabeth Wiesman). Only child: Elizabeth Ellen b. March 29, 1904.
Commission merchant.

ROWLAND, GEORGE (son of Ephraim Rowland, born Jan. 13, 1808, Nottinghamshire, Eng., and Mary Drabble, born Feb. 25, 1807, Gresley, Nottinghamshire). He was born April 18, 1840, at Gresley. Came to Utah Sept. 30, 1862, Joseph Horne company.
Married Martha Boot Feb. 25, 1864 (daughter of Joseph Boot and Elizabeth Sudberry—married at Mansfield, Eng.). She was born Aug. 28, 1838, at Mansfield; came to Utah 1863. Their children: George Ephraim b. Jan. 30, 1865, m. Rhoda Daniel Mills Sept., 1885; Mary Elizabeth b. March 14, 1867, m. H. C. Santmyers; Edwin b. June 14, 1870, m. Nellie Strong. Family home Springville, Utah.
Married Amy Naylor May 18, 1874, at Salt Lake City (daughter of William Naylor and Fanny Knighton), who was born May 4, 1860, at Gresley, Eng. Their children: Eliza b. April 13, 1875, m. W. J. Russell March 10, 1897; Fanny b. May 16, 1876; Ida b. May 8, 1878, m. Lorenzo Weight Dec. 30, 1903; Amy b. May 8, 1878, m. T. A. Worthen Jan. 24, 1900; Louisa b. Sept. 5, 1880; John Scott b. June 21, 1882, m. Alma Hansen Nov., 1905; William Owen b. June 21, 1882, m. Ella Brannon June, 1907; Enos b. April 22, 1884, m. Agnes Thomas June, 1902; Martha b. May 18, 1886, d. Aug. 20, 1887; Hannah b. Oct. 18, 1888; Ettie b. May 7, 1890, d. Feb. 15, 1891; Seth b. Dec. 28, 1891; Grace b. April 21, 1896. Family home Springville, Utah.
High priest; president elders' quorum 1863-83. Veteran Indian war.

ROWLEY, GEORGE (son of Richard Rowley of Nethersfield, Yorkshire, Eng.). Born 1827 in England. Came to Utah Nov. 16, 1855.
Married Ann Brown in England (daughter of John Brown of Nethersfield, Yorkshire, Eng.). Their children: Rachel, died; William, m. Emily Green; Joseph Smith, m. Lydia Young Morse; Alma, m. Emily Amelia Shipley. Family home American Fork, Utah.
Married Sarah Tuffey. Their child: Sarah, m. Isaac Wagstaff. Family home American Fork, Utah.
High priest; missionary to South Wales. Wool spinner. Died Dec. 14, 1907, American Fork, Utah.

ROWLEY, JOSEPH SMITH (son of George Rowley and Ann Brown). Born May 17, 1849, at Yorkshire, Eng.
Married Lydia Young Morse March 13, 1879, St. George, Utah (daughter of Francis Y. Morse and Elizabeth Thomas of Boston, Mass., pioneers 1859, Peter Nebeker company). She was born June 11, 1860. Their children: Eva Elizabeth b. Jan. 30, 1880, m. Frank Hanson; Laura Ann b. March 13, 1882, m. Moroni Peck; Joseph Francis b. Aug. 29, 1885, m. Ruby Pratt; Lydia Lenora b. Dec. 14, 1887, m. Thomas Carrol; Elva Ray b. Sept. 3, 1890, m. Don Carlos Wadsworth; Leah Wilda b. April 21, 1893; Marlow Morse b. March 18, 1895; Jedediah Young b. Nov. 5, 1897; Isaac Monroe b. Aug. 20, 1901; David Aaron b. July 30, 1905. Family home American Fork, Utah.
Elder. Fruit grower. Resided at American Fork, Utah.

ROWLEY, RALPH NEPHI (son of John Rowley and Sarah Wright of Handley, Stafford, Eng.). Born April 1, 1824. Came to Utah 1852, Abraham O. Smoot company.
Married Mary Ann Thompson Oct. 30, 1843, Glasgow, Scotland (daughter of Hugh Thompson of Glasgow, Scotland, pioneer 1852, Isaac C. Haight company). She was born July 14, 1824, died June 13, 1886. Their children: Mary Ann, m. Ira Lyman; John Thompson b. Nov. 7, 1847, m. Jane Paul, m. Mary Jane Smith; Hugh T. and Ephraim George, died; Walter T., m. Lena Peterson; Ralph Nephi, died; Elizabeth Ann, m. Ira D. Lyman; Moroni; Georga. Family home Meadow, Millard Co., Utah.
Missionary and president of a branch in Glasgow, Scotland; high priest; head teacher at Fillmore; ward teacher. Farmer; mason and builder. Veteran Black Hawk war.

ROWLEY, JOHN THOMPSON (son of Ralph Nephi Rowley and Mary Ann Thompson). Born Nov. 7, 1847, Glasgow, Scotland. Came to Utah with his father.
Married Jane Paul May 22, 1868, Salt Lake City (daughter of Nicholas Paul and Harriett May of Fillmore, Utah, pioneers 1856, independent company). Their children: John T.; Harriet Ann, m. Curtis Galloway; Elizabeth Jane, m. William Day; Ralph Nephi, m. Larinda Jorgensen; Hugh; Royal; Lyda May; Clara and William Wallace, died.
Married Mary Jane Smith June 23, 1880, at St. George, Utah (daughter of Silas Smith and Elizabeth Orton of Stockholm, St. Lawrence county, N. Y., pioneers 1852). She was born July 17, 1853. Their children: John Henry (filled mission Australia 1907-10) b. Feb. 10, 1882; David (filled mission southern states) b. Aug. 28, 1883, m. Sarah Noyes; Silas (filled mission in New Zealand 1907-11) b. Oct. 28, 1885; Mary Ann b. Dec. 6, 1887, m. William E. Jones; Franklin Irvin b. Jan. 1, 1890; Ephraim b. Oct. 14, 1893, died; George Albert b. Nov. 27, 1894. Family home Spring Glen, Utah.
High priest; presiding bishop of Spring Glen ward 1903-10. Veteran Black Hawk war; school trustee 22 years. Charcoal manufacturer; farmer and merchant.

ROWLEY, SAMUEL (son of William Rowley and Ann Jewell, Suckley parish, Worcester, Eng.). Born Oct. 29, 1842, in Suckley parish. Came to Utah Nov. 9, 1856, James G. Willie handcart company.
Married Ann Taylor April 23, 1865, Parowan, Utah (daughter of George Taylor and Mary Franks of Nottingham, Eng., pioneers 1864). She was born April 24, 1846, died Jan. 14, 1901. Their children: Mary Ann b. March 6, 1866, m. Willard R. Guymon; Samuel James b. Jan. 12, 1868, m. Margaret E. Black; Hannah Eliza b. Jan. 20, 1870, m. M. E. Johnson; Sarah Jane b. July 15, 1872, m. William Hartford Avery; Alice Louisa b. Oct. 11, 1874, m. J. H. Leonard; George Walter b. June 25, 1877, m. Jane Howard; John Taylor b. Sept. 1, 1879, d. child; Maggie Elizabeth b. Dec. 27, 1881, m. George W. Collard; Ida May b. Feb. 23, 1885, m. Francis M. Brasher; Thomas Jewell b. May 2, 1887, m. Myrtle Gardner; Richard Edwin b. Aug. 22, 1889, d. child. Family home, Huntington.
Married Julia Ann Westover Dec. 17, 1903, Manti, Utah (daughter of Charles Westover and Mary E. Shumway of Huntington, Utah, pioneers 1847). She was born Feb. 28, 1860.
President 81st quorum seventy 16 years; high priest; missionary to San Juan 1879-80. First constable of Bluff, Utah. Farmer and stockraiser.

ROWLEY, SAMUEL JAMES (son of Samuel Rowley and Ann Taylor). Born Jan. 12, 1868, at Parowan, Utah.
Married Maggie E. Black March 13, 1889, Manti, Utah (daughter of William Black and Amy Jane Washburn), who was born Jan. 10, 1869. Their children: Ellen Jane b. Jan. 26, 1890, d. infant; J. Alphonzo b. April 29, 1891; Amelia b. Oct. 10, 1893, d. infant; Orson b. Nov. 7, 1895; Leona b. Jan. 10, 1897; Merrill b. Feb. 25, 1900, d. infant; Clara b. March 31, 1901; Lila b. Oct. 26, 1904; Cyril b. May 5, 1906, d. infant; Edna b. July 26, 1908, d. infant; Samuel A. b. Sept. 20, 1911. Family home, Huntington.
Elder; ward teacher. Farmer. Died Feb. 12, 1910, Huntington.

ROWLEY, JAMES ALPHONSO (son of Samuel James Rowley and Maggie E. Black). Born April 29, 1891, at Huntington. Member 81st quorum seventies; ward teacher. Farmer and liveryman.

ROYLANCE, JOHN. Born Nov. 20, 1807, in Chester, Eng. Came to Utah October, 1850, with Jonathan Foote company. Married Mary Ann Oakes (daughter of Randall Oakes of England), who was born June 22, 1810. Their children: Henry, m. Elizabeth Bell: Ann, m. William Bird; Thomas, m. Philinda Cuttler; William, m. Lucy Clucas; Elizabeth, m. William M. Bromley; Alma, m. Emma Mendenhatt; Mary Francis, m. John Nelson; Sarah Jane, m. Fred M. Houtz; Olive, m. Cyrus Daley. Family home Springville, Utah. Farmer. Director of Co-op.

ROYLANCE, HENRY (son of John Roylance and Mary Ann Oakes). Born May 21, 1821, Chester, Eng. Came to Utah 1850, Captain Foote company.
Married Elizabeth Bell Dec. 25, 1853, Springville, Utah (daughter of William Bell and Sarah Brereton of Liverpool, Eng., latter pioneer Sept. 1852, Captain Tidwell company). She was born March 13, 1837, Liverpool, Eng. Their children: Sarah Ann b. Oct. 4, 1854, died; Henry b. Aug. 21, 1856, m. Martha Sanford, m. Frances Hewlett; William B. b. Sept. 2, 1858, m. Caroline Ellis; Marian E. b. Aug. 25, 1860, m. John R. Menary; John b. May 4, 1862, m. Sylvia Scovill; Eveline b. Dec. 13, 1863, m. Charles S. Lively; Clarabelle b. Jan. 26, 1866, died; Elizabeth b. Jan. 21, 1868, died; Prunella b. Nov. 10, 1869, m. John Wallace Storrs; Leon b. Jan. 6, 1872, m. Gertie Holmes, who died May 17, 1913; Richard b. Feb. 4, 1874, died; Bruce b. April 15, 1876, m. Effie Wheeler; Milton b. July 14, 1878. Family home Springville, Utah.
Member 51st quorum seventies. Deputy marshal. Farmer.

ROYLANCE, WILLIAM (son of John Roylance and Mary Ann Oakes). Born April 1, 1840, in Chester, Eng. Came to Utah October, 1850, with Jonathan Foote company.
Married Lucy Clucas (daughter of Henry Clucas of the Isle of Man, and Elizabeth Martin of England, pioneer 1850, lived at Springville, Utah). She was born July 1843. Their children: William Martin b. March —, m. Laura Ann Turner and May Zabriskie; John H.; Elizabeth; Nephi, died; Archie W.; Thomas S.; Nell; Frank E.; Lillie. Family home Springville, Utah.
President elders' quorum. Merchant; stockraiser and railroad contractor. Died April 2, 1903.

ROYLANCE, WILLIAM M. (son of William Roylance and Lucy Clucas). Born March 31, 1865, Springville, Utah.
Married Laura Ann Turner Dec. 23, 1885, Logan, Utah (daughter of John W. Turner and Sarah L. Faucett of Provo, Utah; came to Utah 1851 with Roswell Stevens company). She was born Oct. 22, 1863. Their children: Hazel T. b. Dec. 18, 1886, died; Martin Wesley b. March 26, 1889; Merline b. April 26, 1894; Enid and Ellis (twins) b. March 26, 1901; Ellis, d. Sept. 1901.
Married Mary Zabriskie (widow of C. E. Young) Aug. 6, 1902, at Salt Lake City (daughter of Alma M. Zabriskie and Emma Brain of Provo, Utah). She was born Dec. 18, 1876. Their children: Charles Edward Young b. Jan. 5, 1900 (son of C. E. Young); William Clucas b. Sept. 7, 1908. Family home Provo, Utah.
Elder. City recorder and councilman at Springville; mayor of Provo 1904-5; member Utah state legislature 1897-1900; speaker of house 1899-1900; chairman Democratic state committee 1901. Merchant 27 years; one of the incorporators and directors of the Springville Banking Co.

ROYLANCE, WILLIAM J. (son of George Roylance of Peover, Chester, Eng.). Born April 19, 1819, at Lower Peover. Came to Utah August, 1852, Orson Spencer company.
Married Mary Yarwood (daughter of Samuel Yarwood), who was born 1807. Their children: Hyrum b. July 4, 1844, m. Isabell Newby May 4, 1868; James b. Nov. 30, 1849, m. Georgena Barrett; Rachel, m. John Woodfield May 16, 1865. Family home North Ogden, Utah.
Married Martha Janet Smith Oct. 4, 1860, Salt Lake City (daughter of Aaron Smith of Pennsylvania), who was born Aug. 12, 1837, in Pennsylvania. Their children: Aaron b. Aug. 9, 1861, m. Charlotte Elnora Berry June 25, 1891; William George b. Oct. 9, 1863, m. Rosie Snyder June 7, 1897; Alma Thomas b. March 1, 1865, m. Irene Daniels May 1891; Mary Janet b. Feb. 28, 1867, m. Parley P. Hill; Heber C. b. March 30, 1869, m. Alice Jane Ward Sept. 15, 1892; Harvey b. Jan. 17, 1871, m. Eliza M. Ward 1893. Family home Springville, Utah.
Settled at North Ogden 1863; moved to Springville; later to Snake River valley. High priest. Pioneer; surveyor. Conducted tannery, shoe and harness shop 1889 at Springville. Farmer. Died June 29, 1895, Salem, Idaho.

ROYLANCE, JAMES (son of William Roylance and Mary Yarwood). Born Nov. 30, 1849, Burlington, Iowa. Came to Utah 1852, Orson Spencer company.
Married Georgena Barnett Oct. 9, 1871, Salt Lake City (daughter of George Barnett and Mary Ann Mathews, both of Steeple Ashton, Wiltshire, Eng., pioneers 1864, John M. Kay company). She was born June 6, 1854. Their children: Mary Ann b. Sept. 3, 1873, m. Frank Blodget Dec. 5, 1894; James H. b. Jan. 17, 1874, m. Annie Maggie Hawkins Oct. 11, 1898; George W. b. Nov. 14, 1876, m. Alice Campbell March 15, 1900; Alma b. Feb. 14, 1880, m. Ada Pearl Pickford Oct. 9, 1902; Mariah b. April 1, 1882, m. Fred E. Garner Aug. 24, 1903; John b. March 15, 1884, m. Mary Shipley Nov. 19, 1912; Rachel b. May 5, 1886; Rosena Virtue b. July 5, 1888, d. Nov. 18, 1907; Heber T. b. March 10, 1891, m. Rebecca Asper Dec. 13, 1912; Sarah Serena b. April 27, 1893, m. Joseph Harrop Nov. 27, 1912; Edna I. b. June 25, 1896, m. Richard Chapple June 22, 1912; Myrtle Elizabeth b. May 25, 1901. Family home North Ogden, Utah. High priest. Farmer.

ROYLANCE, AARON (son of William J. Roylance and Martha Janet Smith). Born Aug. 9, 1861, North Ogden. Utah.
Married Charlotte Elnora Berry June 25, 1891, Manti, Utah (daughter of Charles S. Berry and Eliza Jane Harmer), who was born Nov. 30, 1872, Springville, Utah. Their children: Kenneth Glend b. May 11, 1893; Dorthea b. March 21, 1896; Ireta b. Sept. 5, 1898; Lucretia b. March 23, 1901; Freida Eliza b. Jan. 4, 1904.

ROYLANCE, HEBER C. (son of William J. Roylance and Martha Janet Smith). Born March 30, 1869, Springville.
Married Alice Jane Ward Sept. 15, 1892, Logan. Utah (daughter of George P. Ward and Jane Ashworth of Hyrum, Utah. Came to Utah 1873). She was born Dec. 14, 1874. Their children: William Heber b. Sept. 1, 1893; George Edmund b. Jan. 27, 1896; Nellie Jane b. April 20, 1898; Alva Janet b. Sept. 1, 1900; Milan b. Nov. 25, 1903; Vera b. Aug. 4, 1905; Elva Cora b. Sept. 28, 1908; Gladys b. March 4, 1911. Family home, Salem.

ROYLE, HENRY. Born in England. Came to Utah 1848.
Married Ann Capstick at St. Louis. Mo., who came to Utah with husband. Their children: Sarah Ann b. Sept. 22, 1849, m. Loren Almstead 1865; Henry Moroni b. June 22, 1851, m. Harriette Abigail Zimmerman Jan. 7, 1872, m. Mary Curtis Fawsett June 11, 1894 Family home Lehi, Utah.
Missionary in England. Farmer. Died July 1852.
Ann Capstick Royle married John Mercer Nov. 9, 1852. Only child, Martha, was born Oct. 9, 1853, m. James Kirkham.

ROYLE, HENRY MORONI (son of Henry Royle and Ann Capstick). Born June 22, 1851, Lehi, Utah.
Married Harriette Abigail Zimmerman Jan. 7, 1872, Lehi, Utah (daughter of John Zimmerman and Harriet Lamb of Lehi, pioneers 1849). She was born Oct. 6, 1853, died March 19, 1892. Their children: Henry Moroni b. Feb. 25, 1873, m. Alice Sandering (Barr) Jan. 21, 1903; Polly Emmeline b. April 15, 1875, m. Hyrum Webb Feb. 10, 1897; Harriette Abigail b. Oct. 1, 1880, m. Noal West March 1, 1905; Sarah Ann b. Oct. 20, 1882, m. James Toddard Oct. 1, 1903; James Freeman b. Dec. 9, 1884, m. Lavina McAllister March 2, 1910; Rawsen b. Dec. 5, 1886, died; Myrtle b. July 2, 1889, m. William McEwan March 1, 1911.
Married Mary Curtis Fawsett June 11, 1894, at Lehi, who was born 1852. Only child: Hyrum Alvin b. June 17, 1895. Families resided Lehi, Utah.
High priest; block teacher. Was first white male child born at Lehi. Builder of canals, irrigating ditches and bridges. Farmer and stockraiser.

ROYLE, JAMES FREEMAN (son of Henry Moroni Royle and Harriette Abigail Zimmerman). Born Dec. 9, 1884.
Married Lavinia McAllister March 2, 1910, St. George Utah (daughter of Joseph Warrington McAllister and Mary Ann Miller of St. George). She was born Feb. 4, 1885. Their child: Homer Freeman b. April 14, 1911.
Missionary to southern states.

ROYLE, WILLIAM. Born 1820 at Staley Bridge, Yorkshire, Eng. Came to Utah on Sept. 13, 1861, with Homer Duncan company.
Married (second wife) Anne Rasmussen (daughter of Rasmus Anderson and Nette Nielson) Nov. 9, 1882, Salt Lake City. She was born Dec. 24, 1843, at Fensmark, Sjaelland, Denmark. Their child: William Royle b. Aug. 13, 1884.
Elder; member seventies; ward teacher. Assisted in constructing first canal to irrigate arid lands near West Weber, Weber county. Farmer.

RUFF, GEORGE (son of James Ruff and Eliza Mealock of Dillington, Huntington, Eng.). Born Jan. 18, 1850, at Dillington. Came to Utah Oct. 5, 1879.
Married Sarah Elizabeth Grayson 1871, in parish church. Sheffield, Eng. (daughter of Henry Grayson and Mary Jones of Rotherham, Yorkshire, Eng., latter came to Utah May 5, 1879). She was born April 25, 1851. Their children: Mary Jane, m. Joseph Jones; George Henry b. Oct. 10, 1876, m. Nettie Calderwood; John James, m. Alice Dunster; William Edward b. May 24, 1881, m. Margaret Morgan; Joseph Heber b. Oct. 1, 1884, m. Ida W. Bowley; Wilford, m. Elizabeth Blackham. Her home Moroni, San Pete Co., Utah; his Coalville, Utah.
Married Mary Hood (Johnstone) Aug. 4, 1909, Salt Lake City (daughter of Nicol Hood and Angelina O'Nell of Bathgate, Scotland). She was born June 4, 1854.
Ordained bishop July 19, 1902, by Hyrum M. Smith; president first quorum elders of Summit stake; missionary to Sheffield and Nottingham, Eng., 1898-1900; home missionary in Summit stake 1883-98. President Scofield town board;

city councilman at Scofield two terms; member Scofield school board two terms; justice of peace at Coalville 1896-97. Blacksmith.
Mary Hood was the widow of Samuel Johnstone, married June 26, 1878, at Glasgow, Scotland. Their children: Agnes b. April 16, 1880, m. Alfred Newneen; Francis b. March 12, 1882, m. Willard Stillman; Andrew H. b. May 14, 1884, d. youth. Family home, Scofield.

RUSHTON, EDWIN (son of Richard Rushton and Lettace Johnson of Leek, Stafford. Eng.). Born June 1, 1824, Leek, Eng. Came to Utah Sept. 28, 1851, John Brown company.
Married Mary A. Fowell Jan. 31, 1842, Liverpool, Eng. (daughter of John Fowell and Elizabeth Regars of Leek, Eng.). She was born April 23, 1823. Their children: Edwin J., d. infant; Francis E., d. aged 2; Martha S., d. aged 3; Edwin J. R., m. Sarah Cheever; Mary A., m. Daniel Clays; Henritta, m. Hyrum H. Evans; Fortune, d. infant; Fortunate.
Member 22d quorum seventies; 1st counselor in bishopric of 6th ward, Salt Lake City; block teacher; high priest. Millman; farmer and stockraiser. Died Dec. 28, 1904, at Salt Lake City.

RUSS, NELSON DANIEL (son of John Russ, born Jan. 9, 1819, and Abbie Kenyon, both of Alabama, Genesee county, N. Y.) He was born March 14, 1846, at Alabama. Came to Utah November, 1865, a soldier in Co. L, 1st regiment Michigan cavalry.
Married Ellen Agnes Flygare July, 1867 (daughter of Nils Flygare and Anna Nelson), who was born Aug. 30, 1837. Their children: Anna May b. May 26, 1868, m. Charles A. Gordon July 20, 1891; Mary Jane b. Aug. 6, 1870, m. B. Herbert Dec. 15, 1907; John Daniel b. April 4, 1875, m. Blanche King Feb. 12, 1910; Albert Nelson b. May 20, 1878, d. Aug. 10, 1878.
Married B. Christenia (Peterson) Jorgensen (widow of Rasmus Christian Jorgensen, who died June 23, 1886, by whom she had had two children, viz.: Eli Moroni Jorgensen b. Sept. 16, 1884, m. Alberta Orme at Salt Lake City June 25, 1909; Eliza Christina Jorgensen b. Sept. 30, 1886, d. April 1, 1889), July 17, 1892, at Bear River City, Box Elder Co., Utah (daughter of Nels and Elizabeth Peterson). She was born May 2, 1855, Island of Faeno, Denmark. Family home Wilford, Idaho.
High priest; missionary to eastern states March 31, 1898, to Oct. 1, 1898; Sunday school superintendent East Wilford, ten years.

RUSSELL, JONATHAN (son of Daniel Russell). Born May 11, 1783. Came to Utah Sept. 24, 1852, Benjamin Gardner company.
Married Nancy Wilson (daughter of Stebben Wilson). Their children: Gennett b. March 29, 1804, m. Allen Twist; George b. Sept. 6, 1806, d. aged 14; Annie b. Aug. 6, 1808, m. Jonathan Trumble Walton; Daniel b. March 8, 1811, m. Harriet Egliston; Martin b. May 7, 1813, m. Louisa Mours; Loman b. April 17, 1815, d. young; Lyman b. June 11, 1817, m. Nancy Bird, m. Amanda Eldredge; Mary b. Oct. 16, 1819, m. John Allen; Nancy b. Aug. 3, 1822, m. James Caldwell; Allen b. Nov. 1, 1824, m. Harriet Massina Hutchens; Horace b. March 10, 1831, m. Lydia Ann Hobson; Sally b. March 9, 1827, m. Finley Page. Family home Genesee county, N. Y. Died July 27, 1855, Fillmore, Utah.

(daughter of Jesse Hobson and Catherine Dougherty of North Pigeon, Pottawattamie Co., Iowa, pioneers Sept. 1852, Benjamin Gardner company). She was born Jan. 1, 1838. Their children: Lydie C., m. George W. Bryan; Lewey R., m. Elizabeth Dewitt; Horace Jesse; Henry L., m. Harriet L. Brewer; Daniel C., m. Sarah Jane Hunt; William R.; Ada C.; Alma L., m. Lillie M. Willis. Family home Fillmore, Millard Co., Utah.
Minuteman, guarded the settlers against the Indians. Farmer. Died June 6, 1901, Fairview, New Mexico.

RUSSELL, DANIEL C. (son of Horace Russell and Lydia Ann Hobson). Born July 10, 1865, Fillmore, Utah.
Married Sarah Jane Hunt May 17, 1900, Fairview, New Mexico (daughter of Joel Hunt and Matilda E. Moore of Perryville, Perry county, Tenn.; came to Colorado 1883). She was born June 19, 1853. Their children: Fenton B. b. March 1, 1903; Ada E. b. June 10, 1906.
Presiding elder of Fairview branch, San Louis stake, Colo. 1880-85; missionary to St. Johns, Ariz. 1885. Defended the settlers against the lawless whites and Mexicans.

RUSSELL, SAMUEL (son of Isaac Russell and Mary Waltom of Toronto, Canada). Born June 7, 1835, Toronto. Came to Utah Sept. 13, 1861, Homer Duncan company.
Married Lucy Pratt Feb. 4, 1869, Salt Lake City (daughter of Parley P. Pratt and Hannahette Snively of Salt Lake City). She was born March 9, 1848. Their children: Jacob Parley, m. Daisy Clark; Francis J.; Henrietta Hope, m. Francis Platt; Ellen.
Married Henrietta Pratt June 14, 1877, St. George, Utah (daughter of Parley P. Pratt and Hannahette Snively of Salt Lake City, pioneers Sept. 1847, Parley P. Pratt company). She was born Oct. 26, 1851. Their children: Samuel b. April 14, 1878; Isaac, m. Althea Farr; Lucy; Christopher P.; Jared; Mary; Sarah Eliza. Family home, Salt Lake City.
Member 2d quorum seventies; special missionary to Canada 1882. Captain in militia. Indian war veteran. Manager Armstrong & Bagley Lumber Co. Died April 20, 1896, Salt Lake City.

RUSSELL, SAMUEL, JR. (son of Samuel Russell and Henrietta Pratt). Born April 14, 1878, Salt Lake City.
Lawyer.

RUSSELL, WILLIAM GREENWOOD (son of William Greenwood Russell). Born at Liverpool, Eng. Came to Utah Oct. 3, 1852, Isaac Bullock company.
Married Louise Jones 1839 in New York City. Their children: George W., m. Elizabeth Pierce; Eliza Ann, m. Isaac James Caldwell. Family home Tooele City, Utah.
Married Elizabeth Vickery 1848, Buffalo, N. Y. (daughter of William Vickery and Mary Holland of Buffalo, pioneers 1852). She was born 1827. Their children: William G. b. July 4, 1852, m. Minnie Beathel, m. Margaret Clark; Brigham Y. b. March 1854, d. aged 18; John T. b. Jan. 24, 1856, m. Agnes Charles; Joseph S. b. Dec. 23, 1858, m. Margaret Charles; Heber C. b. Nov. 1860, m. Elizabeth Orr; Hyrum b. Dec. 1861; Elizabeth b. Oct. 1863, m. William Bracken, m. Mr. McCloud; Annie b. Dec. 1865, m. Albert MacIntosh; James b. 1867, d. infant. Family residence, Tooele county.
Presiding elder at Rush Valley and Kamas. Farmer and stockraiser. Died 1870, Rush Valley, Utah.

1146 PIONEERS AND PROMINENT MEN OF UTAH

Missionary to eastern states 1854-56; bishop in Wayne stake 1879; called to work in Manti temple 1901; member high council in Utah county. Veteran Walker and Black Hawk Indian wars. Discovered the Eureka mine at Tintic 1870. Member Payson city council 1870-78. Settled at Payson 1858, and moved to Grass Valley 1878. Located the town of Burrville. Farmer; stockraiser and miner.

RUST, GEORGE B. (son of George Smith Rust and Eliza S. Brown). Born Oct. 31, 1856, Spanish Fork, Utah.
Married Melinda Elvina Roberts Dec. 21, 1887, Logan, Utah (daughter of Edward Killick Roberts and Ann Sophia Rollins of Salt Lake City, Payson and Annabella, Utah). She was born Feb. 12, 1870, at Payson. Their children: Genevieve b. Feb. 21, 1889, m. Alma L. Potter; Rand O. b. Jan. 2, 1891, m. Evaline Rachel Davies Nov. 20, 1912; Eliza Ann b. Jan. 11, 1893, m. Glen Seager; Ethel b. April 26, 1895; Alva George b. Dec. 16, 1897; Elton Roberts b. April 21, 1900; Mary b. Aug. 14, 1902; Sarah b. Dec. 19, 1904, d. infant; Ella b. Oct. 10, 1906; Nora b. Dec. 12, 1911. Family home Caineville, Utah.
Married Eliza Jane Smith Dec. 21, 1887, Logan, Utah (daughter of Absalom Smith and Mary Ann Jenson of Draper, Utah). Only child: Baby b. July 16, 1889, d. infant.
High priest; counselor to Bishop Walter E. Hanks 17 years; counselor in presidency of Y. M. M. I. A.; Sunday school superintendent; ward teacher. Constable at Burrville, Utah. Fruit tree inspector, Wayne county; director board of health, Wayne county; treasurer of Caineville Irrigation Co. Farmer and stockraiser.

RYSET, FRANCIS FREDRICK. Born in Germany. Came to Utah 1857.
Married Nancy Jane Radford at Deseret, Millard Co., Utah (daughter of John W. and Leah Radford of Deseret). She was born 1847. Their children: Maranda Jane b. 1862; Sarah Ellen b. 1864; Francis Daniel b. 1866, m. Priscilla Morgan; Melvin b. 1868. Family home Deseret, Millard Co., Utah.

RYSET, FRANCIS D. (son of Francis Fredrick Ryset and Nancy Jane Radford). Born 1866, Deseret, Utah.
Married Priscilla Morgan 1888, Leamington, Utah (daughter of Edward Morgan and Sarah West, both of Oak City, Millard Co., Utah, pioneers 1853, Joseph Young company). She was born 1872. Their children: Nora b. 1889, m. George Moore; Violet Viola b. 1891; Francis E. b. 1893; Thomas C. b. 1896; Zella Priscilla b. 1899; Sarah Jane b. 1901; Mary Vileto b. 1903; Ellen b. 1905; Leona b. 1908; Janie b. 1910. Family home Prospect, Idaho.

S

SABEY, JAMES (son of Tingey Sabey). Born 1834. Came to Utah 1856, handcart company.
Married Jane Bower in England, who came to Utah with husband. Their children: Joseph, m. Emily Clark; Sarah Jane, m. John Jacobs; m. Marion Walker; John, m. Amanda Bushman; William, m. Sarah Evans. Family home Lehi, Utah.
Married Eliza McCollun of Scotland. Their children: Mary Hannah b. Jan. 18, 1866, m. Brigham Timothy; Thomas, m. Jane Hatch; Ann, m. George Young; James, Jr. b. Jan. 20, 1872, m. Libbie Jane Rich; Ephraim, d. child; Charles, m. Miss Evans; Moroni, m. Julia Walters; m. Miss Jacklin; Eugene, m. May Wilcox. Family resided Lehi and Charleston, Utah.
Settled at Lehi; moved to Charleston where he assisted in building canals, roads, and in developing the country. Farmer and sheepraiser. Died April 1910, Wallsburg, Utah.

SABEY, JAMES (son of James Sabey and Elizabeth McCollun). Born Jan. 20, 1872, Charleston, Utah.
Married Libbie Jane Rich July 24, 1893, Vernal, Utah, Bishop Joseph Black officiating (daughter of Charles Coulson Rich and Jane Susannah Stock of Port Elizabeth, South Africa, latter a pioneer Oct. 1860, Nephi Johnson company). She was born Nov. 27, 1875. Their children: Jay b. Feb. 16, 1894, d. May 1906; Afton b. Jan. 31, 1899; Arthur b. Feb. 14, 1907, died; Arvin b. Aug. 22, 1908; Thora b. Nov. 24, 1910. Family home Roosevelt, Utah.
Settled at Vernal 1890; moved to Keystone ranch, Route county, where he engaged in the cattle business; moved to Roosevelt 1905. Interested in Dry Gulch Irrigation Co., and Page Lateral Ditch. Farmer and stockraiser.

SADIN, ARA WILLIAM (son of Salmon B. Sabin, born Dec. 24, 1795, in Otsego county, N. Y., and Sarah S. Miller, born May 11, 1791, in Saratoga county, N. Y.). He was born Aug. 4, 1822, in Steuben county, N. Y. Came to Utah September, 1850, Philo Dibble company.
Married Nancy Ann Hanes in May 1850 (daughter of Azariah Hanes and Polly Ann Newman), who was born Nov. 12, 1828. Their children: Ara William b. Feb. 17, 1851, m. Amanda Gardner; Flora Ann, m. James Wrathall; Eri Deson; Bertha Blanche b. Jan. 14, ——, m. Jesse Carter;

Eugene Morton b. Feb. 20, ——, m. Lily Shaw; Lily Ernestine b. July 15, 1862, m. Heber Robinson; Harriet Eurilda b. Aug. 27, 1867, m. John S. Lee; Lula May b. May 3, 1870, m. Andrew G. Benson.

SABINE, JAMES (son of Moses Sabine and Sarah Woodman of Wiltshire, Eng.). Born Feb. 21, 1821, in Wiltshire. Came to Utah Sept. 2, 1868, Simpson M. Molen company.
Married Jane Holder Oct. 9, 1853, Corsham, Wiltshire, Eng. (daughter of Daniel Holder and Marie Wheatland, same place). She was born Nov. 6, 1825. Their children: Albert, d. infant; Selina J., m. John A. Maynes; James, m. Mary L. Fairbourne. Family home, Salt Lake City.
Elder. Builder and contractor. Died Jan. 24, 1911.

SAINSBURY, JOHN H. Came to Utah in the early days.
Married Laura Wiscombe Nov. 1871, at Salt Lake City (daughter of James Wiscombe and Mary Ann Fleet of England; they came to Utah in Nov. 1871). She was born June 14, 1850. Their children: Ellen Maria, m. Alma N. Timothy; James William; Charles Holland.

SALISBURY, O. K. (son of Pehr Salisbury and Hannah Oredson). Born Nov. 17, 1836, Sonasslof, Sweden. Came to Utah Sept. 13, 1857, Christian Christiansen handcart company.
Married Elizabeth Catherine Iverson (daughter of Heppe and Anna Christina Iverson). Their children: Olenia; Hannah and Elenia Christina (twins); Amanda Malinda; Anna Maria; Elizabeth Catherine; Oke; Ellen; Jeppe Israel; Joseph Elijah; Cornelius: Aaron; Celesta. Family resided in "Dixie" and afterward Richfield, Utah.
Married Mary Jane Gold (daughter of Robert F. and Emma Gold). Their children: Robert Franklin; Samuel William. Family resided "Dixie" and Richfield, Utah.
High priest. Farmer.

SALISBURY, JOSEPH M. (son of Joseph Salisbury). Born Feb. 13, 1852, Birmingham, Eng. Came to Utah 1856, with his parents.
Married Miranda Ramsden (daughter of John Ramsden, pioneer 1863), who was born March 15, 1851, Bradford, Eng. Their children: Hattie, m. Dimond Loosli; Morris J., m. Bertha Johnson; William J., m. Cleo McRay; Rosella, m. Otto Johnson; George, died; Henry; Alice.
Carpenter and farmer. Died April 22, 1898, Granger, Utah.

SALISBURY, ORANGE J. Came to Utah in 1868.
Married Margaret B. Walker. Their children: Stella J., m. L. B. McCornick; Orange J., Jr., m. Marian McGilvray; Robert W. b. Dec. 27, 1883, m. Genevieve McCornick Nov. 17, 1909; Blaine G., died. Family home, Salt Lake City. Member state board of equalization. National Republican committeeman. Capitalist. Died June 18, 1907, New York City.

SALISBURY, ROBERT W. (son of Orange J. Salisbury and Margaret B. Walker). Born Dec. 27, 1883, Salt Lake City.
Married Genevieve McCornick Nov. 17, 1909, Salt Lake City (daughter of W. S. McCornick and Hannah Keogh of Canada). Their children: Evelyn E. b. Sept. 1910; Margaret B. b. Nov. 6, 1912. Family home, Salt Lake City. Member state board of equalization. President Salisbury Co. Capitalist.

SANDBORG, JOHN S. (son of Swen Sanderson and Anna Jepson of Nosabe, Sweden). Born Nov. 2, 1836, Nosabe, Sweden. Came to Utah 1869, O. C. Oleson company.
Married Anna Louisa Oleson May, 1861, Stockholm, Sweden (daughter of Ole Oleson and Anna Katrina Anderson of East Jutland, Sweden; came to Utah 1871). She was born Dec. 15, 1839. Their children: Anna Sophia, m. John Johnson; John, m. Nellie Clawson; Selma; Carl Ludwig, m. Estella Jacobs; Oscar K., m. Esther Connell. Family home Salt Lake City.
Shoemaker.

SANBORN, GEORGE B. (son of Isaac Sanborn and Sarah Jane Cobb of Bangor, Penobscot Co., Maine; came to Utah 1873). Born Nov. 14, 1858. Came to Utah with his parents.
Married Sarah Jane Smith Nov. 16, 1875, Salt Lake endowment house, Daniel H. Welis officiating (daughter of William Smith and Jane Rawlings of Paradise, Utah, pioneers 1856). She was born April 1, 1856, in Iowa. Their children: Sarah J. b. Nov. 21, 1876, m. William Mikesell; George B., Jr., b. July 6, 1878, m. Amy Haywood; Laura E. b. Sept. 28, 1880, m. Mark Haywood; William b. July 7, 1882; Joseph b. May 11, 1884; Eva b. April 11, 1885, d. infant; Mary Ann b. Dec. 15, 1887, m. Frank Hove, m. Charles Helms; Henry b. Sept. 2, 1889, m. Blanch Quigley; John W. b. Sept. 11, 1891, m. Henrietta Gall; Ella b. Nov. 30, 1893, m. John Kellerher; Gladys b. Sept. 5, 1895, d. aged 1 year; Jennings b. Sept. 15, 1896. Family home, Salt Lake City.
Elder; ward teacher at Pocatello, Idaho. Blacksmith.

SANBORN, GEORGE B., JR. (son of George B. Sanborn and Sarah Jane Smith). Born July 6, 1876, Paradise, Utah.
Married Amy Haywood June 22, 1898, Salt Lake City (daughter of George Haywood and Sarah Archer of 15th ward, Salt Lake City; came to Utah 1850). She was born in Oct. 1876. Their children: Harold G. b. Jan. 25, 1899; Clarence H. b. Aug. 23, 1902; Stella May b. Jan. 4, 1905; Albert b. Nov. 2, 1907; Ruth b. April 19, 1910. Family home 15th ward, Salt Lake City.
Deacon. Foreman of blacksmith shops of the Denver & Rio Grande Railway, Salt Lake City.

SANBORN, WILLIAM (son of George B. Sanborn and Sarah Jane Smith). Born July 7, 1882, Paradise, Utah.
Blacksmith. Home in 15th ward, Salt Lake City.

SANBORN, JOHN W. (son of George B. Sanborn and Sarah Jane Smith). Born Sept. 11, 1891, Salt Lake City.
Married Henrietta Gall July 25, 1911, Ogden, Utah, (daughter of Wesley Gall and Dora Eilander of Ogden. Came to Utah April 1905). She was born April 16, 1893. Their children: Dora Jane b. July 24, 1912. Family home, Salt Lake City.
Deacon. Blacksmith.

SANDERS, DAVID A. (son of William Sanders and Elizabeth Hunt, pioneers 1850). Born July 14, 1848. Came to Utah with parents.
Married Lucy Grover Jan. 4, 1868, Salt Lake endowment house (daughter of Thomas Grover and Lodoiska Tupper of Farmington, Utah, pioneers 1847, C. C. Rich company). She was born Jan. 7, 1849, Farmington, Utah, and was first white child born in Davis county. Their children: Lucy Elizabeth b. Oct. 6, 1869, m. George A. Hess; Clara Lodoiska b. Jan. 20, 1871, m. Armond T. Rose; David Albert b. Feb. 6, 1873, d. aged 2; Mary Ann b. Sept. 20, 1875, m. George M. Leonard; Frances Eveline b. Feb. 3, 1877, m. Charles J. Steed; Thomas Grover b. Aug. 4, 1878, d. infant; Horace Edward b. Oct. 11, 1880, d. infant; Pearl Adelle b. March 30, ——, m. Milton L. Lee; Dowe Clarence b. April 12, m. Laurette Burton; Frank Thatcher b. Dec. 17, 1895; Asenath b. Nov. 9, d. infant; Nellie b. July 11, m. Clarence Dawson. Family home Farmington, Utah.

SANDERS, ELLIS M. (son of Ellis Sanders and Hannah Mendenhall of Delaware). Born Dec. 5, 1808, Newcastle, Del. Came to Utah Sept. 24, 1848, Heber C. Kimball company.
Married Rachel B. Roberts July 9, 1830, in Delaware (daughter of John Roberts and Elizabeth Broom of Baltimore, Md.). She was born Oct. 1808. Their children: Annie, m. Spencer Willbanks; Elizabeth, m. Leonard Conger; Hannah M., m. Oliver Huntington; Rachel, m. Schuyler Everet; Sarah Jane, m. Nelson Merkley; Ellis, m. Mary Ann Smith; Ellen, m. Joseph Cunningham. Family resided Delaware; Nauvoo; Salt Lake City and St. George, Utah.
High priest. Assessor and collector; road supervisor; city water master. Farmer. Died Jan. 15, 1873, St. George, Utah.

SANDERS, WILLIAM (son of Simeon Sanders and Frances Waterman of Bishop's Stortford, Hertfordshire, Eng.). Born Oct. 7, 1836, at Bishop's Stortford. Came to Utah Nov. 2, 1864, Warren Snow's company, after a five months' journey from London with father's family.
Married Naomi Orchard Oct. 20, 1866, Salt Lake City (daughter of James Orchard and Susannah Harding of Bulkington, Wiltshire, Eng.). She was born Nov. 21, 1842, and came to Utah in Sept. 1866, d. Aug. 4, 1912. Their children: Edith Naomi b. Oct. 5, 1867, d. June 6, 1871; Alice Maud b. Aug. 6, 1869, m. Albert S. Horn June 25, 1896; William H. O. b. Sept. 30, 1871, m. Pearl Schreck Oct. 22, 1901; Clara Anna b. March 1874, m. Harold P. Jenning Feb. 27, 1896; Frederick L. b. June 27, 1876, d. Sept. 27, 1877; Laura Josephine b. June 28, 1878, m. Robert L. Campbell Oct. 16, 1902; Lester James b. March 9, 1885, m. Florence Lee Nov. 6, 1906. Family home, Salt Lake City.
Missionary to Kent, Eng., 1859-64; president of conference one year; member of his priests' quorum of Salt Lake City; member tabernacle choir since 1865. Employed at the Z. C. M. I. from its start and still with it. He was their first traveling salesman.

SANFORD, ALLEN TILGHMAN (son of Allen Sanford and Catherine Elizabeth Hartman of Amber, Jones Co., Iowa). Born May 13, 1870, at Amber. Came to Utah in October, 1895.
Married Helen Edith Sheehan July 1, 1896, Anamosa, Iowa (daughter of Jeremiah Lord Sheehan and Laura Rawlins of Anamosa). She was born March 24, 1872.
Graduate State University of Iowa and law department of Harvard University. Lawyer.

SANT, JOHN (son of Abel and Margaret Sant of Middlewich, Chestershire, Eng.). Born Jan. 11, 1811, at Middlewich. Came to Utah August, 1861, Job Pingree company.
Married Mary Shaw Dec. 12, 1831, at Middlewich (daughter of Richard Shaw and Elizabeth Pocelles of Middlewich,

pioneers 1861, Job Pingree company). She was born Jan. 2, 1814. Their children: George, m. Margaret Mustard; John, m. Martha Ellen Roscoe; Hannah, m. John Millington; Betsey, m. Thomas McCann; Margaret, m. Charles William; Jane, m. Nathan Smith; William, m. Adah Clifford; Eliza, m. Edmund Hepworth; Thomas, m. Lizzie Truscot, m. Jane Winterbottom. Family resided Smithfield, Utah, and Clifton, Idaho.
High priest. Farmer. Died Oct. 15, 1887, Clifton, Idaho.

SANT, GEORGE (son of John Sant and Mary Shaw). Born Dec. 15, 1833, Middlewich, Eng. Came to Utah Sept. 3, 1855, John Hindley company.
Married Margaret Mustard Oct. 3, 1858 (daughter of David Mustard and Margaret Kay, pioneers Sept. 3, 1852, Abraham O. Smoot company). She was born March 9, 1842. Their children: Mary Ellen b. Sept. 10, 1859, m. Preston Thomas Dec. 31, 1876; George b. Jan. 31, 1862, m. Sarah J. Clifford Nov. 9, 1884; William R. b. Feb. 9, 1864, m. Rosa A. Clifford Nov. 2, 1897; Margaret Kay b. July 3, 1866, m. William Smith Oct. 25, 1883; James b. Aug. 31, 1868, d. March 21, 1870; Lizzie b. March 3, 1870, d. Sept. 15, 1887; Eliza b. June 19, 1874, m. Charles Johnson Aug. 24, 1892; Mary b. Oct. 29, 1877, m. Alma Johnson Jan. 17, 1899; David b. Oct. 2, 1882, m. Elizabeth Cole Jan. 18, 1905; Edmund b. Sept. 22, 1884, d. Aug. 4, 1887. Family resided Smithfield, Utah, and Treasureton, Idaho.
High priest.

SAUNDERS, WILLIAM GILBERT (son of Charles Saunders and Mary Ann Leavitt of Soham, Cambridgeshire, Eng.). Born Jan. 10, 1819, at Soham. Came to Utah in 1854.
Married Phoebe Marrill in England (daughter of John and Mary Marrill of England). She was born June 7, 1817, Little Port, Eng. Their children: Mary Ann, m. Richard Mathews; William G.; Charles and Caroline, d. infants; Caroline Eliza, m. Andrew Miller; James M.; Phoebe, m. Richard Oram; John M., m. Tillie Garmer. Family home Collinston, Utah.
Missionary to England 1878; also missionary U. S. Wagon maker. Died at Ogden, Utah.

SAUZA, WILLIAM. Born in London, Eng. Came to Utah in September, 1853, Jacob Gates company.
His wife, Amy, was a pioneer, coming to Utah with him in 1853. Their children: Frederick; Charles: Harriett, m. James Vaughn; Eliza Sarah, m. William Joseph Killpack; James; Clara. Family home Manti, Utah.
Elder. Farmer and manufacturer of umbrellas. Died at Manti, Utah.

SAVAGE, DAVID (son of Roger Savage and Phoebe Stevens). Born July 25, 1810, Johnstown, Leeds Co., Canada. Came to Utah Sept. 24, 1847, Parley P. Pratt company.
Married Theodocia Finch 1834 in Canada, who was born in 1811. Only child: Amanda b. Aug. 23, 1836, m. Phineas W. Cook Dec. 17, 1853. Family home, Salt Lake City.
Married Mary Abigail White Oct. 17, 1841, Nauvoo, Ill. (daughter of John White and Lucy Bailey, pioneers Oct. 1847, Perrigrine Sessions company). She was born May 30, 1823, in St. Lawrence county, N. Y. Their children: John Roger b. Dec. 1842, d. 1843; Elizabeth b. 1844, d. 1844; Mary Theodocia b. Feb. 28, 1847, m. John D. Wilcox Aug. 16, 1865; David William b. July 11, 1849, m. Julia Merrill 1877; Sarah Miranda b. April 24, 1850, m. Amasa C. Linford June 29, 1867; Anna Eliza b. Dec. 17, 1856, m. Henry Teeples 1875; Agnes Belzora b. June 29, 1861, m. John Whitton 1879; Ellen Maria b. May 1863; Lucy Estell b. Dec. 8, 1865, m. John Lundquist.
Married Mary Ward in 1858 (daughter of George and Isabella Ward, pioneers 1851, Vincent Shurtliff company). She was born Dec. 6, 1830, and came to Utah 1851, Vincent Shurtliff company. Their children: Isabella Elicia b. Oct. 28, 1859, m. Thomas Edwin King Jan. 16, 1878; David Edward b. Nov. 29, 1862, m. Caroline King; William Albert b. Dec. 29, 1865, m. Caroline Clark; Parley Franklin b. Dec. 31, 1868, m. Clair Bell McCullough; Barbara Alice b. Apr. 1, 1872, m. William Sudweeks.
Married Margaret Evans in 1859. Their children: Margaret b. July 28, 1860, m. N. Karchner; Laura b. Aug. 1863, m. C. Stratton; Charles R. b. Dec. 1866, m. Ella Hall; Gomer b. Oct. 1869.
Married Susan Black in 1878.
Missionary to Michigan 1843; to Canada 1873; and to the Indians on the Salt River at Mesa, Ariz. Worked on Nauvoo temple. Assisted in bringing immigrants to Utah. Settled at Lehi 1850; one of first settlers of Bear Lake valley; lived at various places, finally settling at Snowflake, Ariz. Freighted between Salt Lake City and California. Mail carried between Salt Lake City and Cedar Fort, Utah. Brought first threshing machine to Salt Lake City 1860. Died in Arizona.

SAVAGE, LEVI (son of Daniel Savage, born Feb. 28, 1762, and Sally Savage, born Feb. 28, 1762, latter of Hebron, N. Y.). He was born Aug. 25, 1790, Hebron, Washington county, N. Y. Came to Utah in 1848.
Married Polly Haines, who was born Aug. 11, 1799, and died in 1847. Their children: Levi b. March 23, ——; Polly b. June 24, 1818; Alonzo b. Jan. 22, 1825; Emeline b. Jan. 22, 1825, m. Benjamin Waldron 1849; Matthew b. June 3,

1837, m. Emily Mitchell; Hannah M. b. Jan. 10, 1832, m. Ira Eldredge; Moroni E. b. July 22, 1843; John b. Oct. 6, 1829; Daniel Nathaniel b. Feb. 18, 1834; David b. Aug. 23, 1839; Phoebe b. March 6, 1841.
Died 1874 at Willard City, Box Elder Co., Utah.

SAWLEY, EDWARD (son of William Sawley, born May 26, 1823, and Margaret Hartley, born July 24, 1820, of Colne, Lancastershire, Eng.). He was born March 12, 1854, Burnley, Lancastershire. Came to Utah Sept. 16, 1887.
Married Sarah Ann Stokes (daughter of Joseph and Ellen Stokes), who was born April 19, 1857. Came to Utah Sept. 16, 1887. Their children: Margaret Ellen b. April 27, 1876, m. Joseph E. Wright; Sarah b. Sept. 19, 1877, m. Frank P. O'Neill; Mary b. May 20, 1880 d. child; Jane b. June 16, 1882, m. Joseph H. Wilde; Joseph b. June 30, 1884; William b. July 4, 1886; Martha b. Oct. 9, 1888, m. Robert Wilson; Florence b. April 19, 1890, m. R. G. Stone; Edward b. April 6, 1892. Family home Coalville, Utah.
Bishop of Grass Creek; ward of Summit stake.

SAXTON, SOLOMAN (son of William Saxton and Catherine Hemenway of Nottinghamshire, Eng.). Born Feb. 21, 1825, Leicestershire, Eng. Came to Utah Sept. 9, 1861, John Murdock company.
Married Matilda Dexter Oct. 26, 1848, in England (daughter of John Dexter and Lydia Wardell of Nottinghamshire). She was born Feb. 5, 1827. Their children: Brigham, Catherine, Hannah, Lydia A., and Victoria; first five d. infants; Sarah E., m. William Staley; John S., m. Andria Johanson; Charles D., m. Sarah Harris; William S., m. Annie Johanson; Maud S., m. John W. Mumford. Family home Coalville, Summit Co., Utah.
High priest; first counselor in bishopric 15 years; block teacher. Mining man; farmer and stockraiser. Died Feb. 19, 1903.

SCHADE, CHRISTIAN F. (son of Frederick Ludvick Schade, born Feb. 18, 1773, Skandavorg, Denmark, and Margrette Marie Ravn, born Sept. 23, 1792, Kornum, Denmark—married 1815). He was born April 27, 1827, in Denmark. Came to Utah Sept. 30, 1864, John Smith independent company.
Married Abelone Thorstensen Aug. 15, 1856 (daughter of Evan Christian Thorstensen and Magdaline Christensen—married 1831 in Denmark). She was born April 3, 1835, and came to Utah with husband. Family home Huntsville, Utah.
Married Mary Sophia Heder Sept. 15, ———, Salt Lake City (daughter of John Heder and Christine Erickson—married 1849 in Dahlsland, Sweden, pioneers Sept. 5, 1863, John F. Sanders company). She was born Dec. 20, 1850, Vennersborg, Sweden. Their children: Marie Abelone b. Nov. 10, 1871, d. 1878; C. Fred b. March 20, 1876, m. Mary C. Wangsgard June 20, 1900; A. Wilhart b. Sept. 5, 1878 (missionary to Sweden 1907; president of Sundsvall conference; counselor to Bishop Halls, Huntsville, Utah), m. Lillie Jensen June 15, 1910; Martha Eliza b. April 2, 1881, m. Alma Petersen April 16, 1902; Mary Elizabeth b. June 21, 1884, m. L. H. Peterson June 22, 1904. Family home Huntsville, Utah.
President Aarhuus conference, Denmark, 1872-74; counselor to Bishop David McKay, Huntsville ward, 1885-1901; ward treasurer several years. School trustee 1877-81.

SCHADE, C. FRED (son of Christian F. Schade and Mary Sophia Heder). Born March 20, 1876, Huntsville, Utah. Came to Utah September, 1860, James D. Ross company.
Married Mary C. Wangsgard June 20, 1900, Salt Lake City (daughter of Christian C. Wangsgard and Anna Anderson, former pioneer 1866, Peter Nebeker company, latter 1869). She was born Aug. 15, 1878, at Huntsville. Their children: Kenneth F. b. Oct. 24, 1901; Della May b. July 7, 1903; Marion Frederick b. Aug. 22, 1905; Melva Rae b. Oct. 27, 1907. Family resided Huntsville and Logan, Utah.
Missionary to Norway 1897-99; secretary Christiania conference 18 months; assistant superintendent Y. M. M. I. A. of Ogden stake 1909-10; chorister and member board Y. M. M. I. A., Cache stake.

SCHAERRER, HENRY (son of John Jacob Schaerrer of Schoenenberg, Canton Zurich, Switzerland, born November, ?782, and Barbara Staub of Richterswell, Canton Zurich, born 1781). He was born May 13, 1813, at Schoenenberg. Came to Utah September, 1860, James D. Ross company.
Married Anne Goetz July 1843 (daughter of Jacob Goetz and Elizabeth Peter), who was born Dec. 17, 1819, and came to Utah with husband. Their children: John Jacob b. Dec. 28, 1845, m. Lamecia Ann Taylor, m. Mary Ott; Annie E. Louisa b. Oct. 1851, m. John Jacob Walser. Family resided Bingham's Fort and St. George, Utah.
Married Paulina Ott Nov. 1879, St. George, Utah. Their child: Mary b. March 24, 1880, m. August Martin Peterson.
Located at St. George, Utah, 1861, where he assisted in building up the country; moved to Payson 1868 and resided there until his death. High priest.

SCHAERRER, JOHN JACOB (son of Henry Schaerrer and Anne Goetz). Born Dec. 28, 1845, Hegi, Canton Zurich, Switzerland.
Married Lamecia Anna Taylor May 9, 1870, Salt Lake City (daughter of Benjamin Taylor and Ann J. Hiatt, pioneers, Henry G. Boyle company). She was born June 18, 1846,

in Surry county, N. C. Their children: Jacob Henry b. March 19, 1871, d. March 17, 1885; Rosaline b. Feb. 17, 1873, d. Oct. 1885; Adelia Ann b. Sept. 2, 1875, m. Charles C. F. Dixon; Emma Frances b. Sept. 23, 1880, d. Dec. 9, 1895; George Albert b. June 22, 1882, m. Geneva Stewart June 16, 1909; Ada Matilda b. Oct. 28, 1893, m. Raymond H. Clayton; Alma Benjamin b. July 2, 1888. Family home Payson, Utah.
Married Mary Ott July 1880, Salt Lake City (daughter of John Jacob Ott and Magdalena Bear), who was born March 10, 1846, Colbrun, Canton Zurich, Switzerland. Their children: Franklin Edward b. Dec. 24, 1881, m. Alice Loveless; Clara Mathilda b. June 8, 1883, m. Byron Gleason; John Henry b. Oct. 6, 1885, m. Nellie Richardson.
Settled at St. George 1861. Called to drive teams to the Missouri river for immigrants 1864. Missionary to Switzerland and Germany 1877 and 1891; president Swiss and German mission 1891-94; senior president 46th quorum seventies, Payson, Utah; home missionary, high councilor and member church board of education of Nebo stake. Farmer and stockraiser.

SCHEIB, JOHN PIERRE (son of Henry F. Scheib and Anna Maria English). Born Oct. 12, 1802, Sobernheim, Coblenz, Rhenish Prussia. Came to Utah Sept. 20, 1852, Captain McGaw company.
Married Catharina Weinmann May 17, 1835 (daughter of Christopher Weinmann and Elizabeth Joiner, latter born March 12, 1740). She was born July 17, 1809, and died Feb. 26, 1866. Came to Utah with husband. Their child: Sabina b. March 28, 1839, m. James Henry Hart May 4, 1861.
Married Susannah Deck. Their children: John F. b. Aug. 26, 1879, m. Annie A. Colclough March 20, 1901; Emilie b. Sept. 17, 1880, Conrad b. Dec. 20, 1881; Samuel b. May 14, 1883; Alma Moroni b. Feb. 9, 1885; latter four d. infants.
Died Feb. 16, 1886, Salt Lake City.

SCHMUTZ, JOHN (son of John Schmutz and Marie Gostoli of Vechingen, Canton Bern, Switzerland). Born July 19, 1818, at Vehingen. Came to Utah June 15, 1874.
Married Elizabeth Leman of Wattenwyl, Canton Bern. Their children: Anna Maria Christian; Lena; John; Rosetta; Jacob; Eliza; Gottlieb; Bertha.
Helped build temple at St. George, Utah.

SCHMUTZ, GOTTLIEB (son of John Schmutz and Elizabeth Leman). Born April 28, 1861, Bolligen, Canton Bern, Switzerland.
Married Amelia Neiderer April 28, 1887, St. George, Utah (daughter of John Neiderer). Their children: Andrew G.; Donald; Anna Bell; Eldon L.; Rosalia; George C.; Victor L.; Ethel.
Bishop New Harmony ward, Parowan stake; missionary to Switzerland and Germany, 28 months.

SCHNEITTER, CHARLES (son of John Schneitter and Susannah Beütler of Canton Bern, Switzerland). Born Dec. 11, 1837, in Canton Bern. Came to Utah Sept. 1861, Joseph W. Young company.
Married Mary Karwinsky June 10, 1860, New York City (daughter of Florian Karwinsky and ——— Achtelik of Poland). She was born July 21, 1823. Family home, Salt Lake City.
Member 16th and 21st quorum seventies; missionary to Switzerland 1880-82; to Germany and Belgium 1889-91; high priest. Farmer and miner.

SCHOENFELD, FREDERICK WILLIAM (son of Frederick William Schoenfeld and Sophia Krebs of Magdeburg, near Leipzig, Germany). Born Feb. 14, 1831, Edenburg, Prussia. Came to Utah Sept. 15, 1864, with William B. Preston company.
Married Wilhelmine Henriette Lohmann May 10, 1859, Church of St. Thomas, at Leipzig (daughter of John Christian Lohmann and Henriette Leopoldine Wald of Eythra, near Leipzig). She was born Oct. 27, 1830. Their children: Amanda Mary b. Jan. 31, 1860, d. child; Camilla A. b. April 16, 1862, d. infant at sea; Joseph Frederick Platt b. July 22, 1864, m. Emma Boss; John Edward b. Jan. 26, 1867, m. Eleanor L. Jones; Mary Edgar b. July 16, 1868, d. Aug. 28, 1895; Huldah Elizabeth b. Oct. 1, 1871, m. Mathias E. Hansen; Hertha Amelia b. Oct. 1, 1873, m. Robert Maw. Family home Brighton ward, Utah.
Seventy; missionary to Switzerland and Germany 1883-88; president Swiss and German mission four years; bishop Brighton ward July 29, 1877 to March 13, 1912, when he was ordained patriarch by President Joseph F. Smith; revised translation of the Book of Mormon and Doctrine and Covenants into German Language. Justice of peace, 10 years, Brighton precinct.

SCHOENFELD, JOHN EDWARD (son of Frederick William Schoenfeld and Wilhelmine Henriette Lohmann). Born Jan. 26, 1867, Brighton, Utah.
Married Eleanor Louisa Jones Nov. 19, 1892, Manti, Utah (daughter of Mark Jones and Ellen Herridge, former pioneer 1866, William Henry Chipman company). She was born

Dec. 31, 1874. Their children: John Raymond b. Aug. 6, 1893; Eleanor Edith b. Sept. 17, 1894, m. Charles R. North; Laura Estrella b. March 20, 1896; Mark Levarr b. Aug. 4, 1897; Frederick Wilford b. Feb. 14, 1902; Parley Harold b. Nov. 19, ——; Arthur James b. Jan. 19, ——; Violet and Viola (twins) b. Oct. 9, 1907; Alvin Russel b. July 21, 1910. Family home Brighton, Utah.

SCHOENFELD, EMIL EDGAR (son of Frederick William Schoenfeld and Wilhelmine Henriette Lohmann). Born Oct. 1, 1869, Brighton, Utah.
Married Magdalene Boss Aug. 28, 1895, Salt Lake City (daughter of Johannas Boss and Marianna Gertsch of Gundlischwand, Canton Bern, Switzerland). She was born July 14, 1872, and came to Utah June 1891. Their children: Clarence Emil b. Aug. 24, 1896; Florence Magdalene b. Sept. 3, 1899; Allen Clyde b. March 16, 1902; Lester Theodore b. Dec. 3, 1903; Irene Elizabeth b. June 21, 1906; Elmer John b. March 7, 1908; Olive Rosetta b. Nov. 14, 1909. Family home Brighton, Utah.
Elder. Stockraiser.

SCHOFIELD, JOHN (son of Jonah Schofield and Elizabeth Jackson of Droylesden, near Manchester, Eng.). Born Feb. 3, 1826, at Droylesden. Came to Utah October, 1882.
Married Susannah Hewitt Dec. 21, 1852, at Droylesden (daughter of James Hewitt and Amelia Savage of Clitheroe, Yorkshire, Eng., died at St. Louis on way to Utah). She was born Aug. 3, 1828. Their children: Amelia J., m. George Reynolds; John C., m. Nellie Reed, m. Isabel Price; Nephi Y., m. Ellen V. Romney; Charles Heber, m. Elizabeth Swift; Joseph Hyrum, d. infant; Hyrum Smith, m. Grace Appleby. Family home, Salt Lake City.
Member 13th quorum seventies; president of the Manchester, Starley, Bridge, Ashton-Under-Lyne, Oldham and Rochdale branches in England. Curator Deseret museum. Real estate dealer. Died Aug. 28, 1899.

SCHOW, HANS SORENSON (son of Soren Epsen Schow, born 1798, Vamdrup, Ribe Amt, Denmark, and Annie Marie Hansen, born 1800, at Sjogard, Denmark). Born Sept. 22, 1825, at Vamdrup. Came to Utah Sept. 13, 1857, Chr. Christiansen handcart company.
Married Mary Nielsen Nov. 3, 1853 (daughter of Anders Nielsen and Celia Marie Hansen, latter died June 30, 1906, Huntsville, Utah). She was born March 29, 1826, Peste, Veile Amt, Denmark, and came to Utah with husband. Their children: Maria b. Aug. 28, 1854, d. 1866; Hyrum Smith b. Sept. 15, 1856, d. Sept. 26, 1857; Soren Anderson b. Oct. 1, 1858, d. 1880; Celia b. Dec. 30, 1860, m. Niels Mortensen, d. Oct. 18, 1890; Andrew b. Feb. 5, 1863, d. 1866; Marion b. March 17, 1865, m. William H. Eccles March 17, 1883; Hans b. April 3, 1867, d. May 3, 1879; Sarah S. b. March 31, 1870, m. Philip L. Orth Dec. 23, 1904. Family resided Salt Lake City 1857-64, then at Huntsville, Utah.

SCOTT, ANDREW HUNTER (son of Joshua Scott, born Sept. 17, 1785, and Ann Keen, born Oct. 19, 1788, both in Bucks county, Pa.). He was born Aug. 21, 1815, Middleton, Bucks county. Came to Utah Sept. 26, 1851, Morris Phelps company.
Married Sarah L. Sleeper Feb. 1838, who was born July 21, 1816. Their children: George C. b. July 8, 1840, m. Cornelia E. Kennedy Dec. 25, 1861; Mary Emma b. Feb. 21, 1843, m. George W. Ivins; Hyrum Smith b. April 1, 1845, d. June 17, 1852; Ann Eliza and Ann Margaret (twins) b. March 8, 1849. Family home Bristol, N. J.
Married Sarah Ann Roe Jan. 12, 1851, Kanesville, Iowa (daughter of George Humphrey Roe, died 1847, Philadelphia, Pa., and Abby Jane Weldon—married in 1831, Philadelphia—latter pioneer with son, George W., Sept. 26, 1851, Morris Phelps company). She was born Sept. 26, 1832, at Philadelphia. Their children: Franklin b. Dec. 1, 1851, m. Sarah Ellen Stubbs; m. Eliza Stubbs; Sir Walter b. March 17, 1853, m. Martha J. Taylor; m. Harriet Broadhead; Anna b. March 2, 1855, m. John A. Wilkens; Andrew Hunter b. Nov. 27, 1856, m. Winifred Taylor; m. Myrtle Warwood; Mary Emma b. Sept. 14, 1858, m. Jesse Harding; Canby b. Oct. 28, 1860, m. Eliza B. Cook; Sarah Ann b. June 7, 1862, m. W. J. Hardy; Abby Jane b. Jan. 30, 1864, m. William Joseph Taylor; Howard b. March 23, 1866, m. Eunice L. Stubbs; Roselle Eugene b. May 18, 1868, m. Mary L. Peay; Francelle b. Feb. 6, 1871, m. Walter Sorensen. Family home Provo, Utah.
Married Martha Ann Norton April 1, 1856, Provo (daughter of John Westley Norton, and Dorotha Osburn, who came to Utah 1854). She was born Sept. 28, 1840, Limestone, Ala. Their children: William Norton, m. Marietta Clark; Lois D.; General W.; Milton; Flora; Dallas L.
Settled at Provo 1851. Bishop 1861-74. Superintendent of construction of fort wall around city 1854. Built first schoolhouse in second ward; first Utah county courthouse 1867-78; Provo meeting house 1861-62, and Provo Woolen Mills 1870-74. Also constructed canyon roads, bridges and dams on the Provo river. Conducted an oxtrain of 48 wagons across the plains 1866. One of the organizers and president of the Utah County Agricultural & Home Manufacturing society. Nurseryman; fruit and seedsman. City recorder; assessor and councilman; mayor of Provo six years.

SCOTT, GEORGE COMB (son of Andrew Hunter Scott and Sarah Lee Sleeper). Born July 8, 1840, Vincent, N. J. Came to Utah Sept. 1851, with Morris Phelps company.
Married Cornelia Elmina Kennedy Dec. 25, 1861, Provo, Utah (daughter of Charles Kennedy and Elvira Clark of Provo, Utah, pioneers Sept. 23, 1848, Brigham Young company). She was born Nov. 4, 1844. Their children: Anna Eliza b. Oct. 3, 1862, died; Frances Cornelia b. Dec. 4, 1863, m. Mads Peter Madsen; George Combe, Jr. b. Feb. 12, 1866, m. Josephine Jacobsen; Hulda Elvira b. Oct. 15, 1868, m. Charles Nelson; Susan Elmina b. Oct. 13, 1870, m. Joseph Madsen; Sarah May b. May 6, 1873, m. Lars Jacobsen; Hyrum Clark b. Aug. 30, 1875, m. Emily Jacobsen; Mary Emma b. Dec. 11, 1877, m. Frank Hopkins; Charles Kennedy b. Dec. 10, 1880, m. Lula Dilatouch; Lula Belle b. Jan. 25, 1885, m. David Lee; Anthony b. July 21, 1887, died. Family home Lake View, Utah.
Member 34th quorum seventies; ward and Sunday school teacher. Farmer; rancher; miner. Indian war veteran, also in Johnston army trouble, Echo Canyon.

SCOTT, GEORGE COMB, JR. (son of George Comb Scott and Cornelia Elmina Kennedy). Born Feb. 12, 1866, Provo, Utah.
Married Josephine Jacobsen Jan. 2, 1890, Manti, Utah (daughter of Lars Jacobsen, Sr., and Inger Andres Thompson of Lake View, Utah, pioneers 1857, with Chr. Christiansen handcart company). She was born April 11, 1867. Their children: Frances Fern b. Oct. 7, 1890; Johanna b. Oct. 3, 1892; Josephine b. July 16, 1895; Delivar b. Jan. 21, 1898; Delilile b. March 4, 1900; George Combe b. June 24, 1903; Orthedila b. Jan. 25, 1906; Effie b. May 2, 1909. Elder. Constable of Provo. Dairyman; farmer.

SCOTT, SIR WALTER (son of Andrew Hunter Scott and Sarah Ann Roe). Born March 17, 1853, Provo, Utah.
Married Martha Jane Taylor Dec. 15, 1873, Salt Lake City (daughter of William Joseph Taylor and Mary Bowering, pioneers 1853). She was born March 30, 1856, Provo, Utah. Their children: Mary b. Sept. 5, 1874, d. infant; Walter Taylor b. Dec. 25, 1875, m. Lillie F. Peay; Martha b. Oct. 14, 1877, d. infant.
Married Harriet Broadhead April 9, 1880, Salt Lake City (daughter of David Broadhead and Harriet Betta, pioneers 1853). She was born Nov. 16, 1853, Salt Lake City. Their children: Seth b. March 7, 1881, m. Isabelle Harrison; Reed b. March 7, 1883, m. Mary Jennings; Harriet b. Aug. 22, 1884; Lexia b. Feb. 25, 1886; David b. Aug. 22, 1887, m. Margaret F. Cooke; Bird b. Dec. 12, 1888; Kate b. April 13, 1890, m. Ernest J. Mangum; Oran b. Nov. 4, 1891; Clarence b. April 25, 1894; Zina b. July 25, 1896; True b. March 22, 1898. Family home Provo, Utah.
Farmer.

SCOTT, ANDREW HUNTER (son of Andrew Hunter Scott and Sarah Ann Roe). Born Nov. 27, 1856, Provo, Utah.
Married Winifred Taylor at Provo (daughter of William Joseph Taylor and Mary Bowering of Provo). She was born Nov. 26, 1862. Their children: Andrew H. b. Feb. 27, 1877, m. Jennie Parks; Lewis Canby b. April 9, 1880, m. Zina Jorgenson; William Joseph b. May 6, 1883, died; Winnifred b. April 3, 1887, m. Arthur D. b. Sept. 18, 1885, m. Hattie Vincent; Clyde b. March 22, 1888, m. Nellie Roby; Norman b. Oct. 9, 1890, m. Martha Parkins; L. Vera b. Nov. 29, 1895; Lamar b. Aug. 25, 1899, Provo, Utah.
Married Myrtle Warwood June 16, 1904, Provo, Utah (daughter of John Warwood, Jr., and Eliza Taylor of Nephi, Utah). She was born Oct. 30, 1885. Their children: Winnifred b. March 3, 1905; Fern b. July 23, 1907; Virginia b. March 22, 1909.
Elder; Sunday school teacher. Farmer. Family home Provo, Utah.

SCOTT, CANBY (son of Andrew Hunter Scott and Sarah Ann Roe). Born Oct. 28, 1860, Provo, Utah.
Married Eliza B. Cook Nov. 29, 1883, Salt Lake City (daughter of Luke Cook and Louisa Burton of Wales, pioneers 1853, Vincent Shurtliff oxteam company). She was born April 22, 1856. Their children: Lorin b. Nov. 29, 1884, died; Ethel Daisy b. Aug. 30, 1886, m. Henry Clay Spencer; Eliza Louise b. Dec. 3, 1887, m. Carlyle C. Cochran; Verna Grace b. Oct. 3, 1891; Inez Silvia b. Feb. 28, 1893; Irvine Leslie b. Aug. 15, 1896. Family home Provo, Utah.
City councilman, Provo. Farmer.

SCOTT, HOWARD (son of Andrew Hunter Scott and Sarah Ann Roe). Born March 23, 1866, Provo, Utah.
Married Eunice Lester Stubbs Dec. 10, 1890, Manti, Utah (daughter of Richard Stubbs and Eleanor Ware of Chestershire, Eng., pioneers 1852, Jerome Benson oxteam company). She was born Dec. 21, 1865. Their children: Howard Arvil b. Nov. 17, 1891; Wayne b. July 14, 1894; Morris Stubbs b. Oct. 14, 1899; Elva Fawn b. May 31, 1901; Ruby Ellen b. July 1, 1904; William Delose b. Aug. 30, 1906. Family home Provo, Utah.
Elder. Farmer.

SCOTT, JOHN (son of Jacob Scott and Sarah Warnock of Toronto, Canada). Born May 6, 1811, Armagh, Ireland. Came to Utah 1848, John Scott company.
Married Elizabeth Meneary 1836 (daughter of William Meneary and Catherine McMillin), who was born Sept. 10, 1815, Dublin, Ireland. Their children: Isaac b. Feb. 15, 1837, m. Martha Moor; Matilda b. Nov. 1, 1838; Louisa b. March 20, 1840, m. Edward Morgan; Ephraim b. June 6, 1842, m. Sarah Ellen Smithies; John W. b. Nov. 6, 1844, m. Fanny Mariah Ellis, m. Marinda V. Weaver; Elizabeth b. March 15,

1847, m. Robert Smithies; Heber M. b. Nov. 1, 1849, and Sarah C. b. July 4, 1852, died; Josiah b. Aug. 20, 1854, m. Mary E. Walton; Sophia b. Aug. 20, 1857, m. Edward Morgan; Alfonzo b. Jan. 28, 1859, m. Caroline E. Pratt; Alvina b. Jan. 28, 1859, m. Thomas H. Ellis. Family home Mill Creek, Utah.
Married Mary Pugh 1844, Nauvoo, Ill. (daughter of Edward Pugh of Sussex, Eng.). Their children: Hyrum b. July 15, 1846, m. Amelia Morgan; Mary E. b. May 22, 1849, and Eliza A. b. Oct. 20, 1852, m. Peter S. Barson; Lucy J. b. April 19, 1855; Vilate b. May 12, 1861, m. Fred Fowler.
Married Sarah A. Willis 1846, who was born Feb. 4, 1825. Their children: Joseph L. b. April 16, 1847, m. Sarah J. Hemsley; Rebecca A. b. March 25, 1849; Simeon W. b. Aug. 25, 1851, m. Martha Ellis; Zebulon b. Dec. 22, 1853; William R. b. Dec. 25, 1855, m. Mary L. Green; Hannah M. b. March 2, 1859, m. John G. Morgan; Martha L. b. July 19, 1861, m. —— McDonald; Sarah M. b. Feb. 3, 1864, m. Winslow F. Walker; Benjamin F. b. Aug. 7, 1868, m. Rebecca Hemsley.
Married Esther Yeates 1860 (daughter of George Yeates and Mary Chance), who was born April 4, 1843, in Worcestershire, Eng., and came to Utah 1859, handcart company. Their children: Brigham b. April 22, 1861, m. Sarah Stoddard; Mary L. April 1863; George T. b. Aug. 20, 1865, m. Esther Lishman; Sarah M. b. Nov. 22, 1867, m. Henry Bair; Esther A. b. Dec. 23, 1869, m. Joseph Bindrup; Fredrick W. b. July 27, 1872, m. Frances Rothrock.
Married Angeline Keller (daughter of Alva Keller). Their children: Winfield M. b. April 4, 1872; Mary B. 1874; Jacob F. b. Feb. 19, 1876.
Settled at Salt Lake City 1848; moved to Mill Creek 1852; senior president 61st quorum seventies; missionary to Ireland 1854-57. Member Joseph Smith's bodyguard; colonel in Nauvoo Legion. Indian war veteran. Died 1876, Millville, Utah.

SCOTT, EPHRAIM (son of John Scott and Elizabeth Meneary). Born June 6, 1842.
Married Sarah Ellen Smithies Nov. 9, 1567, Salt Lake City (daughter of James Smithies and Nancy Knowles, pioneers Sept. 1847, Abraham O. Smoot company). She was born July 5, 1846, in Nebraska. Their children: Sarah Melvina b. Aug. 29, 1868, m. Elias S. Merrill 1889; Mary Marinda b. June 13, 1870, m. Ephraim Lawson 1888; Ann Eliza b. Jan. 19, 1872; Ephraim Moroni b. Sept. 11, 1873, m. Hannah Sophia Ostram 1907; James Heber b. Oct. 6, 1875, m. Maud Bybee 1901; John Robert b. Oct. 25, 1877, m. Luella Campbell 1901; Louisa Delia b. Oct. 31, 1879, m. Daniel O. Neville 1905; Isaac Clarence b. Dec. 5, 1881, m. Nettie May Poole 1906; Alice May b. May 22, 1884, m. Pleasant W. Dabelle 1903; Josiah Alfonzo b. Dec. 6, 1887; Sophia Mabel b. Oct. 31, 1890, m. Clarence McMurtrey 1909. Family home Menan, Idaho.

SCOTT, JOHN W. (son of John Scott and Elizabeth Meneary). Born Nov. 6, 1844, Nauvoo, Ill.
Married Fanny Mariah Ellis Jan. 12, 1874, Salt Lake City (daughter of John E. Ellis and Hannah Barber, latter pioneer 1868, Captain Hyde company). She was born July 19, 1849, in England. Their children: John W. E. b. Jan. 3, 1875, m. Hilma Olsen; Earneat R. b. Oct. 8, 1876, m. Olive Olsen; Fanny M. b. Aug. 5, 1878; Rose E. b. June 30, 1879; Arthur L. b. Dec. 27, 1881, m. Esther Malm 1900; David M. b. March 11, 1884; Harold S. b. Dec. 17, 1885.
Married Marinda V. Weaver March 31, 1897 (daughter of Franklin Weaver and Sarah Holmes, latter pioneer 1847). She was born July 31, 1864, Millville, Utah. Their children: Newel E. b. Feb. 27, 1898; Warren C. b. Dec. 30, 1900; Wilma b. June 10, 1902; Lucile b. July 15, 1904; Franklin W. b. Sept. 8, 1906. Family home Blackfoot, Idaho.

SCOVILLE, HORATIO BARDWELL (son of Ebenezer R. Scoville and Sally Bassett of Ohio). Born Nov. 12, 1832, Meridith, N. Y. Came to Utah in 1868 with company of miners.
Married Maria Goodale Oct. 25, 1867, Salt Lake City (daughter of Isaac Newton Goodale and Maria Louisa Bingham of Ogden, Utah). She was born Nov. 26, 1849. Their children: William Horatio, died; Clara Maria; Alice G., died; Francis Louis; Lester Seely; Horatio Bardwell; Alva LeRoy; Joseph Goodale; Walter Bassett. Family home Ogden, Utah.
High priest; president elders quorum. Ogden city councilman. Broom manufacturer. Died July 29, 1893.

SCOVILLE, LUCIUS N. Came to Utah 1847, Brigham Young company.
Married Alice —— at Liverpool, Eng. Their children: William; Hyrum; Loretta, m. Rodney Swasey. Family home Provo, Utah.
Seventy; missionary to England. Farmer. Died in 1906 at Springville, Utah.

SCROWTHER, WILLIAM (son of William Scrowther, born May 27, 1827, Perth, Scotland, and Mary Ann Moon, born June 5, 1815, at Perth, both of Dundee, Scotland—married June 27, 1843). He was born Nov. 5, 1854, Dundee. Came to Utah Sept. 10, 1863, William B. Preston company.
Married Sirbina A. Aiken July 24, 1881 (daughter of Benjamin B. Aiken and Lavina Noble, former pioneer 1848, independent company, latter Sept. 22, 1861, S. A. Woolley company—married 1861, Smithfield, Utah). She was born Oct. 1, 1864. Their children: William b. April 17, 1884, m. Deloris Rucker March 20, 1906; Ann b. Nov. 10, 1885; Leslie b. Oct. 20, 1887, m. Millie Covey Feb. 12, 1907; Almeada b. Oct. 10, 1889; Aldaray b. July 22, 1891, m. Carl A. Anderson Sept. 20, 1911; Venna b. July 3, 1893; Melvin Aiken b. April 8, 1895; Mary b. April 2, 1897; Katie Lazell b. Oct. 29, 1899; Zilpha Ethel b. Aug. 21, 1902; Verner Legrand b. Sept. 26, 1904. Family home, Smithfield.
Farmer.

SEAMAN, JOHN (son of Jasper Seaman and Dyan Reed of Ithaca, N. Y.). Born Dec. 18, 1832, Ithaca. Came to Utah Aug. 4, 1854, Bartlett Brown company.
Married Susannah Stevens Brown April 4, 1855, Salt Lake City (daughter of Bartlett Brown and Joanna Austin Leach of Centerville, Utah). She was born April 15, 1838, and died April 22, 1913, at Ogden. Their children: Mary Susannah, m. Charles W. Taggart; John William, d. March 10, 1863; Andrew Jerome, d. Oct. 11, 1864; Joanna Dyan, m. Wiley G. Cragun; George Alexander, m. Charlotte J. Fox; Harriet Josephine.
Pioneer in Morgan county in 1862. Member 6th quorum seventies; missionary to New York 1876-77; presiding elder at Richville; second counselor in bishopric of Pleasant View ward. School superintendent Morgan county; assessor and collector of Morgan county 1876-76; county commissioner of Weber county 1897-98; justice of peace, Canyon Creek precinct; school trustee at Richville and Pleasant View; state senator from Weber and Box Elder counties 1894. Farmer and lumber merchant.

SEAMONS, ELIJAH (son of William Seamons of Chediston, Suffolk, Eng., born at Allsaints, Eng., and Elizabeth King of St. Michaels, Suffolk). He was born Feb. 14, 1836, Chediston, Eng. Came to Utah Oct. 14, 1853, Cyrus H. Wheelock company.
Married Emma Lyons (daughter of William and Mary Lyons, who came to Utah Oct. 1, 1862, Joseph Horne company). She was born Sept. 12, 1840.
Married Sarah Balls in 1873, Salt Lake City (daughter of John Balls and Sarah Baxter), who was born Sept. 5, 1865, Linstead, Suffolk, Eng. Their children: Laura L. b. Dec. 13, 1873, m. Herbert Elwood 1890; Emma E. b. July 20, 1877, m. John Kirby Dec. 1897; William D. b. March 26, 1879, m. Annie Jackson April 10, 1907; Joseph E. b. April 13, 1882, m. Lucy Jackson Dec. 4, 1907; John R. b. Oct. 4, 1884, m. Hannah Lund March 10, 1909; Sarah b. March 10, 1887; Elvira b. July 31, 1892; Henry S. b. Dec. 17, 1890; Ruby H. b. Aug. 1, 1896. Family home Hyde Park, Utah.
Elder; high priest. Veteran Indian war; assisted in bringing immigrants to Utah 1861 and 1862.

SEAMONS, HENRY (son of Henry Seamons and Mary King of Suffolk, Eng.). Born Sept. 27, 1835, in Suffolk. Came to Utah Aug. 28, 1860, Franklin Brown independent company, stopping off at Rockport, Summit county, while the company arrived at Salt Lake City Sept. 4, 1860.
Married Emma Horton in May 1860, at Omaha, Neb. (daughter of Edmund Horton and Maria Meade of Leamington, Eng., pioneers Sept. 4, 1860, Franklin Brown company). She was born in May 1842. Their children: Henry, d. infant; James Allan, d. aged 13; George Edmund, m. Cora Stembridge. Family home Rockport, Utah.
Married Catherine Blake April 9, 1866, Salt Lake City (daughter of William Blake and Sarah Borro of Northmolton, Devonshire, Eng.; former died on the plains, the latter came to Utah Sept. 25, 1866, John D. Holladay company). She was born March 24, 1841. Their children: Samuel John, d. infant; Henry E., m. Mary A. Staker; Catherine, m. Thomas Chappell; Alfred, m. Clara S. Yates; David E., m. Johannah Sutherland; Jesse E., m. Mary Sutherland; Stephen J.; Ruben A. Family resided, Rockport and Salt Lake City.
Bishop of Rockport ward 10 years; choir leader at Rockport 30 years. Veteran Black Hawk Indian war. School trustee 20 years. Postmaster at Rockport 40 years. Blacksmith and farmer.

SEAMONS, ALFRED (son of Henry Seamons and Catherine Blake). Born March 24, 1872, Rockport, Utah.
Married Clara S. Yates March 16, 1904, Salt Lake City (daughter of John M. Yates and Samantha Young of Mona, Utah). She was born Nov. 29, 1885. Their children: Clara Opal b. Nov. 22, 1906; William Arian b. July 25, 1909. Family home Mona, Utah.

SEAMONS, SAMUEL (son of Henry Seamons, born May 5, 1809, Rumborough, Suffolk, Eng., died at Omaha, Neb., and Mary King, born March 5, 1801, St. Michaels, Suffolk, Eng.). He was born June 7, 1845, Allsaints, Suffolk, Eng. Came to Utah 1860.
Married Louisa E. Griffeth April 25, 1870 (daughter of Pattison D. Griffeth and Elizabeth Carson—married 1845 in Illinois, pioneers 1851, William Critchlow company). She was born Sept. 19, 1851. Their children: Emma L. b. April 18, 1871, m. Edgar D. Hale Oct. 1, 1890; Elizabeth A. b. July 26, 1872, m. Aroet C. Hale Oct. 15, 1893; Mary Emily b. Oct. 15, 1875, d. June 2, 1877; Samuel G. b. Dec. 10, 1877, m. Janette Nyman June 13, 1900; Elva A. b. March 31, 1880, m. Arthur Bennette Oct. 17, 1900; William D. b. Aug. 8, 1883;

Wilford L. b. June 4, 1886; Janette M. b. April 10, 1889, m. William m T. Merrill June 7, 1911; Ivan V. b. Nov. 19, 1894. Family home Hyde Park, Utah.
Married Sarah Hurren May 25, 1875, Salt Lake City (daughter of James Hurren and Eliza Reeder pioneers Nov. 9, 1856, James G. Willie handcart company). She was born March 23, ——, in Suffolk, Eng. Their children: Henry H. b. Sept. 15, 1876, m. Maria Bennette April 19, 1900; James W.; m. Lenora Waite Sept. 29, 1900; Mary E. b. July 22, 1880, m. Arthur Peterson Dec. 20, 1900; Rhoda L. b. April 28, 1882, d. June 15, 1889; George D. b. Dec. 22, 1884, m. Susie Wardle; Grace E. b. Oct. 20, 1886, d. June 23, 1889; Orson L. b. Nov. 16, 1888, d. Dec. 20, 1892; Loran B. b. Jan. 27, 1890, d. Feb. 5, 1891; Delbert K. b. Oct. 19, 1892, d. Dec. 20, 1900; Harvey N. b. Nov. 8, 1895.
Ward and Sunday school chorister, Hyde Park ward; assisted in bringing immigrants from the Missouri river to Utah 1864; hauled rock for the temple at Salt Lake. Secretary of Co-op. store and member of martial band for a number of years. Member of Utah militia, and served as home guard during Indian troubles in Cache county.

SEARLE (GRANDFATHER). Came to Utah in 1852.
His children: John C., m. Jerusha Hill and Mariah Hill; Rebecca, m. William Cloward; Joseph; Charles D., m. Jane Adair; Adelbert, m. Jane Cloward; Philo, m. Jane Davis; Anna, m. Frank Huish. Family home Payson, Utah.
Farmer. Died at Payson.

SEARLE, CHARLES D. Born Oct. 26, 1834, in Mississippi.
Married Jane Adair 1855, at Payson. She was born June 23, 1836, and came to Utah with a handcart company. Their children: Jane, m. Thomas Price; Sarah b. May 25, 1868, m. David Bills; Charles, m. Julia Wilson; Newton, m. Julia Taylor; Joseph, died; George, m. Zina Alexander; John, m. Julia Adams; James, m. Mary Alexander; Charlotte b. Oct. 29, 1874, m. George Murry, m. Clarence Bird; Alonzo, died. Resided at Payson.
Veteran of Black Hawk war. Farmer. Died Aug. 24, 1908, at Dry Fork, Utah.

SEARS, JOHN. Born in England. Came to Utah 1864.
Married Sarah Wagstaff 1843 in England (daughter of William Wagstaff of England). Their children: Septimus W., m. Anne Chission. m. Mary Ann Needham. m. Isabel M. Whitney; Isaac, m. Sarah Jane Gailey; Neaham, m. M. Wilson; Mariah Anne, m. Edward Little; Heber John, m. Isabel Farr; Anna, m. Joseph A. Wells; John, m. Maidie Hyde. Family home, Salt Lake City.
Seventy; Teacher.

SEARS, SEPTIMUS W. (son of John Sears and Sarah Wagstaff). Born March 8, 1844, Caidecot, Eng. Came to Utah 1866.
Married Anne Chission, who died.
Married Mary Ann Needham.
Married Isabel M. Whitney April 1869, Salt Lake City (daughter of Newel Kimball Whitney and Emeline B. Woodward, pioneers 1848). She was born Nov. 2, 1848. Their children: Sidney W. and Herbert W., died; Isabel, m. C. W. Bucholz; Septimus W., Jr.; Lucile L.; Emilie, m. J. G. Roberts; Eugene S., m. Eleanor Rhein; Brenton M. Family home, Salt Lake City.
Superintendent Utah State Fair Association. Member state legislature 1894. Manager Z. C. M. I. several years. In 1879 he chartered the ship "Ivy" and shipped a cargo of Utah wheat to Europe. In San Francisco, London and Salt Lake City he was called the "Utah Wheat King." Died April 7, 1903, Salt Lake City.

SEARS, ISAAC (son of John Sears and Sarah Wagstaff). Born Dec. 2, 1845, at Caldecot, Eng. Came to Utah 1863.
Married Sarah Jane Gailey Sept. 28, 1867, Salt Lake City (daughter of John Gailey and Anne Groves of England, pioneers 1848). She was born Aug. 20, 1849, m. Arthur Simmons; Isaac J. b. April 3, 1871, died; William G. b. Feb. 17, 1873, m. Agnes McMuir; Sarah Lucilla b. Dec. 20, 1874, m. John F. Howard; Etta May b. Dec. 1, 1876, m. Heber Pitt; Jessie b. Aug. 28, 1878, m. Royal Hintze; Ida b. Aug. 22, 1880, and Harold E. b. Aug. 10, 1882, died; Albert E. b. March 5, 1884, m. Edith Lungren; Milton Henry b. April 9, 1886, m. Ida Racine; Ethel Irene b. May 24, 1888, m. Henry Hintze; Afton b. Nov. 30, 1892. Family home, Salt Lake City.
Seventy; missionary to Norwich 1888-90; ward teacher. Proprietor of grain store; also salt business. Died Oct. 3, 1912, Salt Lake City.

SECRIST, JACOB F. (son of Solomon Secrist and Polly Fautz of Tomstown, Franklin county, Pa.). Born 1820 in Franklin county, Pa. Came to Utah 1849.
Married Ann Eliza Logan of Tomstown, Pa. Their children: Louisa b. Nov. 9, 1846, m. Charles Parker; Mary Elizabeth b. Jan. 15, 1848, m. Emory W. Soule; Jacob Moroni b. Aug. 15, 1850, m. Polly Estella Smith; Heber Nephi b. 1852, m. Florence Adelia Smith. Family home Farmington, Davis Co., Utah.
Missionary to Germany 1852-55. Farmer. Died July 2, 1855, on Ketchum Creek, near Fort Kearney, Neb.

SECRIST, JACOB MORONI (son of Jacob F. Secrist and Ann Eliza Logan). Born Aug. 15, 1850, at Salt Lake City.
Married Polly Estella Smith June 1870, Salt Lake City (daughter of Thomas S. Smith and Polly Clark of Farmington, Utah). Their children: Jacob Moroni, Jr., b. Feb. 9, 1871, m. Ruth Barber; Thomas Edwin b. May 6, 1872, m. Lillian Blanche Wood Feb. 4, 1891; Polly Estella b. April 24, 1874, m. Franklin D. Welling; Charles Albert b. Aug. 19, 1875, m. Hattie Hess; Annie Louisa b. June 27, 1879, m. George C. Layton; Mary Elizabeth b. June 27, 1879, d. infant; Horace b. Oct. 9, 1881, m. May Alexander. Family home Farmington, Utah.
High priest; bishop of Farmington ward for 25 years. Commissioner. Farmer. Died Nov. 6, 1906, at Farmington.

SECRIST, THOMAS EDWIN (son of Jacob Moroni Secrist and Polly Estella Smith). Born May 6, 1872, at Farmington.
Married Lillian Blanche Wood Feb. 4, 1891, Logan, Utah (daughter of Jonathan David Wood and Catherine Blanche Bird of Farmington). She was born Nov. 9, 1872. Their children: Edwin Thomas b. March 5, 1893; Sterling Wood b. May 6, 1896; Wallace LeGrande b. Oct. 30, 1899; Herscheil Moroni b. Dec. 9, 1900; Blanche Estella b. April 26, 1904; Alice b. March 16, 1906; Grant J. b. Jan. 7, 1913. Family home Garland, Utah.
High priest; missionary to Kentucky 1908-10; first counselor to bishop. Town trustee for eight years. Farmer.

SECRIST, HEBER NEPHI (son of Jacob F. Secrist and Ann Eliza Logan). Born Sept. 28, 1852, Salt Lake City.
Married Florence Adelia Smith (daughter of Thomas S. Smith and Polly Clark), who was born Oct. 5, 1855, and died April 1895. Their children: George Nephi b. Jan. 19, 1872, m. Henrietta Miller; Jesse Edwin b. Oct. 28, 1873; Thomas b. Jan. 26, 1876, d. July 3, 1883; Effie Abigail b. Feb. 1, 1878, m. Arnold D. Miller; Hattie b. Feb. 13, 1880, m. George Ricks; Albert Emery b. Oct. 29, 1883, m. Vera Stoddard; Lawrence Moroni b. Nov. 26, 1885; Adelia b. April 10, 1900, m. Cleveland Powell; Vernon Logan b. Nov. 20, 1901.
Moved from Farmington, Utah, to Parker, Idaho, Oct. 1884. Teamster; farmer and guide. Died Dec. 28, 1905.

SEELY, WILLIAM STEWART (son of Justice Azel Seely and Mehitable Burnett). Born May 18, 1812, in Connecticut. Came to Utah 1847, John Taylor company.
Married Elizabeth DeHart. Their children: Elizabeth, m. William Stevens; Emily, m. George Coats; Moroni, m. Alice Barton; Emeline, m. Oscar Barton; Joseph Nephi, m. Cecelia Winters; Lucinda, m. Author James Jeffs.
Married Ellen Carter. Salt Lake Endowment house. Their children: Justice Leigh, m. Maggie Jensen; William Stewart, m. Jennett Merrick. Family home Mt. Pleasant, Utah.
Married Ann Watkins 1851, Salt Lake Endowment house (daughter of Thomas Watkins). Their children: Alford, m. Sarah Bomen; Annie, m. Jess Petersen. Family home Mt. Pleasant, Utah.

SEEGMILLER, ADAM F. (son of Adam Seegmiller, born Aug. 24, 1807, Reischweiler Rhenish, Bavaria, Germany, and Anna Eva Knechtel, born Nov. 13, 1815, Zweibrucken, Bavaria, later of Stratford, Ontario, Canada—married Aug. 24, 1834). He was born June 29, 1839, Goderich, Canada. Came to Utah September 1861, William H. Hooper company.
Married Laura Quarm 1867 (daughter of Robert Quarm and Sarah Littlejohn, pioneers Sept. 25, 1866, John D. Holladay company). She was born 1872 on Isle of Jersey. Came to Utah Oct. 8, 1866, Andrew H. Scott company.

SEEGMILLER, DANIEL (son of Adam Seegmiller, born Aug. 24, 1807, Reischweiler, Rhenish, Bavaria, Germany, and Anna Eva Knechtel, born Nov. 13, 1815, Zweibrucken, Bavaria, later of Stratford, Ontario, Canada—married Aug. 24, 1834). He was born Dec. 6, 1836, Preston, Canada. Came to Utah 1861, William H. Hooper company.
Married Ellen Smith May 10, 1862 (daughter of Joseph Smith and Sarah Sailor), who was born May 7, 1846, pioneer 1860. Their children: Daniel b. Oct. 1, 1863, d. child; Charles b. July 29, 1865, m. Ida M. Morris April 17, 1891; Maggie b. Dec. 26, 1866, m. John G. McQuarrie Dec. 10, 1887; Ellie b. Jan. 12, 1869, m. F. B. Woolley, Jr., Sept. 29, 1886; Rose b. Oct. 26, 1870, m. John P. Fuller June 1, 1895; Anna Eva b. Jan. 23, 1874, m. David H. Frost Dec. 17, 1892; Artimesia Snow b. Nov. 1, 1874, m. W. T. Stewart, Jr., Dec. 27, 1901; William West b. Oct. 16, 1876, m. Ada Pratt July 31, 1899. Family resided Salt Lake City and St. George, Utah.
Married Artimesia Snow Woolley April 16, 1873, Salt Lake City (daughter of Erastus Snow and Artimesia Beman, former a pioneer July 24, 1847, Brigham Young company, the latter in 1849).
Married Emma Carroll (daughter of Charles N. Carroll and Keziah Giles), who was born Oct. 6, 1868, Heber City, Utah. Their children: Daniel George b. July 14, 1891; Sterling b. May 21, 1893; Adam b. June 1, 1895; Flora b. Sept. 8, 1897; Paul Carroll b. March 14, 1899.
Second counselor to E. D. Woolley in the presidency of the Kanab stake 1885. Member of police force of Salt Lake City; chief of police at St. George and also sheriff of Washington county. Went east with team and assisted immigrants across the plains 1862. Died July 23, 1899.

1152   PIONEERS AND PROMINENT MEN OF UTAH

SEEGMILLER, WILLIAM WEST (son of Daniel Seegmiller and Ellen Smith). Born Oct. 16, 1876, St. George, Utah.
Married Ada Pratt July 31, 1899, Kanab, Utah (daughter of Lorum Pratt, born Dec. 18, 1853, and Frances Theobald, born Jan. 24, 1859, both of Salt Lake City). She was born May 19, 1881, at Toquerville, Utah. Their children: Zona b. May 1, 1902; Olva b. Sept. 13, 1904; Larue b. Oct. 28, 1905; Lorna b. April 21, 1907; West W. b. Jan. 1, 1909; Jenor b. Nov. 20, 1910; Pratt D. b. Nov. 21, 1912. Family home Kanab, Utah.
President of Kanab stake Dec. 3, 1910; bishop of ward Sept. 3, 1905; missionary to Germany 1899-1902.

SEEGMILLER, WILLIAM HENRY (son of Adam Seegmiller, born Aug. 24, 1807, Reischweiler, Rhenish, Bavaria, Germany, and Anna Eva Knechtel, born Nov. 13, 1815, Zweibrucken, Bavaria, later of Stratford, Ontario, Canada). Born Dec. 19, 1843, at Baden, Waterloo Co., Canada. Came to Utah Sept. 13, 1861, Homer Duncan independent company.
Married Mary Ellen Laidlaw Nov. 2, 1867, Salt Lake City (daughter of Francis Laidlaw and Jane Ferguson Graham of Liverpool, Eng.; former died en route, and latter came to Utah 1854). She was born Feb. 10, 1852. Their children: William Adam b. Feb. 21, 1869, m. Mary S. Harmon; Dan b. Sept. 1, 1870, d. Oct. 5, 1871; Chariton b. Feb. 5, 1872, m. Mary Jane Orrock; Clara Jane b. Dec. 28, 1873, m. John J. Toronto; Frank K. b. Aug. 20, 1875, m. Henrietta Baker; Derondo Charles b. Oct. 2, 1877, m. Inez Clark; Lizzie Belle b. Aug. 7, 1879, m. G. T. Olsen; Junius b. April 15, 1881, m. Serinda Jorgenson; Amelia b. July 4, 1883, m. Abram F. Acord; Louisiana b. July 22, 1885, m. R. T. Thurber; Call b. March 11, 1887, d. March 15, 1887; Irene b. June 3, 1888; Marion b. Nov. 1, 1889, m. Pearl Johnson; Ferry Lavar b. July 21, 1892, d. Aug. 24, 1892; Mary b. Sept. 15, 1893, d. April 28, 1898.
Married Sarah Jane Stewart Jan. 12, 1874, at Salt Lake City (daughter of William A. Stewart and Jane Neil Browning), who was born Jan. 10, 1855, and died Feb. 12, 1882. Their children: Joseph Watson b. Dec. 2, 1874, m. Mary Ann Enice; Rulon Henry b. Oct. 29, 1876, m. Martha Williams; Minnie Neal b. June 5, 1879, m. J. L. Quiet; Sarah Mabel b. Feb. 7, 1882, m. Harvey Ross. Family home Richfield, Utah.
Missionary to Canada 1879; bishop of Richfield 1873-77; second counselor to President Franklin Spencer 1877-87; first counselor to President A. K. Thurber 1887-88; president Sevier stake 1888-1910; president Y. M. M. I. A. Member territorial legislature 1888; member of senate 1890; member board of directors of the B. Y. U. at Provo; director of Snow Academy of Ephraim; speaker of the house of representatives 1892; mayor of Richfield two terms; treasurer of Sevier county; selectman; school trustee; superintendent of schools; member board of university land commission. Farmer and stockraiser.

SEELY, JUSTUS AZEL (son of Justus Seely of Canada). Born Nov. 17, 1779, in Connecticut. Came to Utah Sept. 29, 1847, John Taylor company.
Married Mehitable Bennett 1800, Luzerne, Pa. She was born Nov. 17, 1779. Their children: Rachel b. Sept. 1801, m. Parlin Webb; John, died; Elizabeth, m. James Young; Mary b. Jan. 24, 1810, m. John Hemmenway; William Stewart b. May 18, 1812, m. Elizabeth DeHart; Justus Wellington b. Jan. 30, 1815, m. Clarissa Jane Wilcox, m. Sarah Jane McKinney; Sarah b. Aug. 27, 1817, m. Asa McGann; David b. Oct. 12, 1819, m. Mary Pettit. Family home in Canada.
High priest. Built the first cooperahop in Salt Lake. Cooper; sailor and lumberman. Died April 1, 1859, Pleasant Grove, Utah.

SEELY, JUSTUS WELLINGTON (son of Justus Azel Seely and Mehitable Bennett). Born Jan. 30, 1815, Pickering, Canada. Came to Utah September, 1847, John Taylor company.
Married Clarissa Jane Wilcox March 10, 1842, Charleston, Iowa (daughter of Hazard Wilcox, Jr. and Sarah Seely of Charleston, Iowa, pioneers Sept. 29, 1847, John Taylor company). She was born Oct. 1, 1821; came to Utah with husband in 1847. Their children: Orange b. Feb. 20, 1843, m. Hannah Olsen; Sarah b. April 10, 1844, m. W. J. Tidwell; Don Carlos b. Jan. 4, 1846, m. Hannah E. Reynolds; Hyrum b. March 29, 1848, m. Mary E. Goldsbrough; Justus Wellington b. June 25, 1850, m. Annie E. Reynolds; William Hazard b. Oct. 25, 1852, m. Charlotte Reynolds; John Henry b. April 29, 1856, m. Margaret Peel Jan. 15, 1880; Mary Miranda b. June 25, 1857, m. Christian F. Peel; Joseph b. March 30, 1862, m. Sarah H. Allen; Stuart Randolph b. Feb. 16, 1865, m. Millie Nielsen.
Married Sarah Jane McKinney Nov. 17, 1873, Salt Lake City (daughter of William McKinney and Sarah Wilcox), who was born Dec. 23, 1837, in Lewis county, Mo. Only child: Eva Rebecca b. Dec. 6, 1874, m. Jens Christian Christensen. Family home Mt. Pleasant, Utah.
Settled at Mt. Pleasant 1859. Justice of peace at Mt. Pleasant 20 years; member city council 1877-81 and 1883. Member ward bishopric 20 years. Farmer. Died April 28, 1894, at Mt. Pleasant.

SEELY, ORANGE (son of Justus Wellington Seely and Clarissa Jane Wilcox). Born Feb. 20, 1843, Nashville, Iowa.
Married Hannah Olsen July 24, 1863, Mt. Pleasant, Utah (daughter of Hans Olsen and Chasty Okersen of Sweden, pioneers Oct. 20, 1867). She was born Nov. 27, 1842. Their children: Emma Jane b. Oct. 30, 1864, m. Christian Grice Larsen; Hanna b. Sept. 19, 1866, m. Nad Olsen; Orange b. Dec. 29, 1869, m. Trena Hansen; Sarah b. Feb. 7, 1871, m. Samuel H. Larsen; Chasty b. June 9, 1873, m. Heber Frandsen; Henry Alonzo b. Dec. 2, 1875; Mary Bertrude b. April 3, 1878; Ethel Ingre b. Sept. 16, 1880, died; David Randolph b. Jan. 15, 1882, m. Elva Singleton. Family home Castledale, Utah.
Bishop of North ward, Mt. Pleasant, 1877-79; also bishop of Castle Valley ward 1879-83. First counselor to President C. G. Larsen 18 years. President of town board two terms. Member legislature 1894.

SEELY, DON CARLOS (son of Justus Wellington Seely and Clarissa Jane Wilcox). Born Jan. 4, 1846, in Iowa.
Married Hannah Elizabeth Reynolds March 28, 1875, Mt. Pleasant, Utah (daughter of Levi Bert Reynolds and Hannah Johnson), who was born Feb. 24, 1855. Their children: Don b. Jan. 7, 1876, died; Lottie Sybil b. Sept. 23, 1877, m. Joseph Jones; James Bert b. Sept. 28, 1879, died; Marion Carlos b. Oct. 23, 1881, m. Laura Hansen; George Willard b. May 17, 1884; Levi Earl b. April 29, 1887, m. Mertha Moore; Azael b. Aug. 28, 1890. Family home Castle Dale, Utah.
Elder. Crossed the plains twice. Deputy sheriff three years and jailer six years. Farmer and stockraiser.

SEELY, JOHN H. (son of Justus Wellington Seely and Clarissa Jane Wilcox). Born April 29, 1855, San Bernardino, Cal.
Married Margaret Peel Jan. 15, 1880, Salt Lake City (daughter of Peter Madsen Peel and Christiana Folkman, pioneers 1854, John Jorsgren company). She was born March 7, 1858, at Lehi, Utah. Their children: Ethel Alberta b. Oct. 7, 1880, m. O. E. McGahen Oct. 18, 1905; Zella Gertrude b. Dec. 6, 1882, m. Albert Merrill April 18, 1906; Earl Henning b. Dec. 10, 1884, m. Louie M. Miner May 21, 1910; John b. Aug. 4, 1887, m. Edna Lucile Ralph Oct. 6, 1910; Leonard Joseph b. June 15, 1890; Arbrella Clarissa b. Sept. 19, 1892; Lucretia Vern b. Jan. 26, 1895; Chesley Peel b. March 20, 1898; Margaret Rae b. Sept. 27, 1900; Oliver Dwight b. April 27, 1902. Family home Mt. Pleasant, Utah.
Deputy constable 1882-83; member city council 1891-93; mayor of Mt. Pleasant 1900-01; state senator 1906-10; member board of directors of Utah State Fair association; vice-president Utah Woolgrowers association; president American Rambouillet Sheep Breeders association three years. Farmer and stockraiser.

SELCK, JOHANN HEINRICH (son of Johann Ditlef Selck and Charlotte Welhelmine Knall of Borbye, near Eckernforde, Schleswig-Holstein, Germany). Born Oct. 31, 1812, Eckernforde. Came to Utah Aug. 29, 1863, John Murdock company.
Married Alicia Withicar Hitchenson in 1842, Copenhagen, Denmark (daughter of Ralph Hitchenson and Marianne Withicar of Birmingham, Eng., who went to Denmark to introduce silver-plating in 1805). She was born June 2, 1813. Died on the plains a half day's journey east of Laramie, Wyo. Their children: Carl Andreas, died; William Waldemar b. Oct. 26, 1845, m. Anna Chrestine Sorensen Nov. 23, 1867; Marianne, died.
Painter and artist. Died 1890, Provo, Utah.

SELCK, WILLIAM WALDEMAR (son of Johann H. Selck and Alicia Withicar Hitchenson). Born Oct. 26, 1845, Copenhagen, Denmark. Came to Utah Sept. 4, 1863, Captain Patterson company.
Married Anna Chrestine Sorensen Nov. 23, 1867, Provo, Utah (daughter of Jorgen Sorensen and Karen Rasmusdatter of Kamsas, Utah, who came to Utah in 1873). She was born Jan. 5, 1847. Their children: Clarissa Eliza b. Sept. 18, 1868, m. Thomas H. Boyce; William Walter b. Jan. 31, 1870, m. Sarah Elizabeth Myler; John Henry, d. child; Irene Eleonora, m. Robert Gilchrist; Ernest Allen, d. child; Henry Ernest; John Wallace, d. child.
Member 63d, 67th and 130th quorum seventies; clerk of Bannock stake 1887-89; and of Rigby stake from its organization, 1907, to present date. Clerk of town board of Lewisville, Idaho 1906-10. Notary public; fruit grower.

SELCK, WILLIAM WALTER (son of William Waldemar Selck and Anna Chrestine Sorensen). Born Jan. 31, 1870, Kansas, Utah.
Married Sarah Elizabeth Myler Nov. 23, 1892, Salt Lake temple (daughter of Orrin M. and Elizabeth Myler of Lewisville, Idaho). Their children: William Archy; Millie; Chrestine; Leith Lavon. Family home, Lewisville.
Member 130th quorum seventies; missionary to southern states; member council of 130th quorum seventies; 2d counselor in presidency of Rigby stake. Member town board. Farmer.

SELLEY, WILLIAM (son of William Selley and Grace Partridge of Devonshire, Eng.). Born March 18, 1833, in Devonshire. Came to Utah Sept. 25, 1866, John Holladay company.
Married Sarah Lake 1858, in Devonshire (daughter of William Lake and Emma Court of Devonshire, pioneers Sept. 25, 1866, John Holladay company). She was born June 29, 1834. Their children: Hannah, m. Stephen J. Newman; ² William, m. Lucinda Humpheries; Joshua, m. Elizabeth Crismon; Sarah Jane, m. Morgan James; John Henry, m. Trenna Cotter; Emily Grace, m. Edwin Fletcher. Family home, Salt Lake City.
Seventy; high priest; block teacher. Gardener.

PIONEERS AND PROMINENT MEN OF UTAH 1153

SELLEY, WILLIAM (son of William Selley and Sarah Lake). Born Oct. 19, 1847, Salt Lake City.
Married Lucinda Humpheries Dec. 29, 1886, Logan, Utah, President Merrill officiating (daughter of John Humpheries and Hannah Baugh of Lancastershire. Eng., pioneers 1854). She was born April 26, 1869. Their children: William J. b. Oct. 24, 1887, m. Ethel Leischman; Harvey L. b. Aug. 24, 1889; Lucinda b. Jan. 10, 1892; Alice V. b. Aug. 24, 1893, d. aged 9; Elmer b. Sept. 7, 1896, d. aged 12; Joseph C. b. Oct. 24, 1898, d. aged 6; Emily L. b. Dec. 17, 1900, d. infant; Mabel Ione b. Oct. 10, 1902; Sarah L. b. Aug. 14, 1912. Family home 16th ward, Salt Lake City.
Member 24th quorum seventies; elder and block teacher. Builder and contractor.

SELMAN, MORMON VERNON (son of Isaac Selman and Margaret Giles of Whitchurch, near Cardiff, Wales). Born July 4, 1855, Bath, Whitchurch, Wales. Came to Utah Oct. 2, 1866, Joseph Rawlins company.
Married Louisa Jane Daniels April 23, 1877, St. George, Utah (daughter of Thomas D. Daniels of Payson, Utah). Their child: Inez, m. Ernest Menlove.
Married Lavinia Elizabeth Williams Nov. 30, 1878, Salt Lake City (daughter of George Williams and Mary Baldwin of Birmingham, Eng., pioneers 1864, Captain Patterson company). She was born Feb. 16, 1859. Their children: Rachael Elizabeth, died; Martha Ann, m. Ephraim Jefferson; George Vernon, m. Alla Theria McEwan; Joseph Hiram, m. Maggie Roach; Levina Jane, m. John D. Park; Sophia, m. Edwin Ostler; Isaac Selman; Alma Giles, died; Robert William; Abner Oliver; Mary.
Elder 1879-1910; high priest; home missionary 22 years; missionary among Ute Indians at Indianola, Utah; Sunday school superintendent; ward clerk. Postmaster three years; justice of peace. Fruit grower.

SESSIONS, ²DAVID (son of ¹David Sessions and Ann Hall of Newry, Oxford Co., Maine). Born 1793, Newry. Came to Utah Sept. 24, 1847, Perrigrine Sessions company.
Married Patty Bartlett 1813 at Bethel, Maine (daughter of Enoch Bartlett and Lydia Nelson of Bethel). She was born 1795. Their children: Perrigrine b. June 15, 1814, m. Julia Ann Killgore Sept. 21, 1834; m. Lucina Call Jan. 28, 1845; m. Mary Call June 28, 1845; m. Fanny Emmerette Loveland Sept. 13, 1852; m. Sarah Crossley March 2, 1861; m. Betsy Birdenow March 25, 1865; m. Sarah Ann Bryson Sept. 29, 1866; m. Esther Mabey Nov. 23, 1873; Sylvanus; Anna; Asa; Annie; Sylvia, m. Windsor Lyon; ²David, m. Phoebe Carter Foss. Family home, Salt Lake City.
Married Harriet Worthing at N:uvoo, Ill. (daughter of James Worthing and Harriet Tibbets of Nauvoo, pioneers Sept. 24, 1847, Perrigrine Sessions company). Only child: James. Family home, Bountiful, Utah.
Elder. Successful farmer. Died 1850, Salt Lake City.

SESSIONS, PERRIGRINE (son of ¹David Sessions and Patty Bartlett). Born June 15, 1814, Newry, Maine. Came to Utah Sept. 24, 1847, with company of which he was captain.
Married Julia Ann Killgore Sept. 21, 1831, Newry (daughter of Phineas F. Killgore and Ann York of Newry). She was born June 24, 1815. Their children: Martha Ann, m. William Smoot; Carlos Lyon b. July 16, 1842, m. Elizabeth Wintle April 2, 1864. Family home Bountiful, Utah.
Married Lucina Call Jan. 28, 1845, Nauvoo, Ill. (daughter of Cyril Call and Sally Tiffany of Mentor, Ohio, pioneers Sept. 1850, Chester Loveland company). Their children: Perrigrine, Jr., d. young; Keplar b. Dec. 3, 1856, m. Ann Call Jan. 25, 1876; Harvey; Lucina, d. young. Family home Bountiful, Utah.
Married Mary Call June 28, 1845, Nauvoo, Ill. (daughter of Cyril Call and Sally Tiffany), who may have been Mrs. Perrigrine's children: Julius, m. Thompson Parks; Byron, m. Ida Twombly; Cyril, died; Zina, m. Thomas Burningham; Perry, m. Esther Tolman. Family home Bountiful, Utah.
Married Fanny Emerette Loveland Sept. 13, 1852, Salt Lake City (daughter of Chester Loveland and Fanny Call of Ohio, pioneers September, 1850, Chester Loveland company). She was born Dec. 13, 1838. Their children: Fanny E., m. James Baird; Alice, died; Chester, m. Isabell Corbridge; Agnes, m. John R. Stoddard; Sylvanus, m. Lavina Hall; Lucina, m. John Wait; Sylvia, died; Orson, m. Mary Burningham; Samantha, m. David Smith; Perrigrine, Jr., m. Jennie Engebretsen; Chancy, m. Mattie Cloughin. Family home, Bountiful.
Married Sarah Crossley March 2, 1861, Salt Lake City (daughter of James Crossley and Mary Jarvous of Lancashire, Eng., pioneers Nov. 25, 1856, Edward Martin handcart company). She was born Jan. 29, 1843. Their children: James, m. Selena Holt; Elvira, m. David Briggs; Mary, m. Walter Scott; Joseph, m. Mary Ann Pearson; Wallace O., m. Elizabeth Holt; William Westley, died; Liliac C., m. Willard Eagan; Hannah Ann, died; Phoebe Olive, m. Clarence Evans; Hannah L., m. Heber Burningham. Family home, Bountiful.
Married Betsy Birdenow March 25, 1865, Salt Lake City (daughter of John Birdenow and Zibiah McCarley of Jackson Co., Ohio). She was born Sept. 18, 1861, Captain Brown company.
Married Sarah Ann Bryson Sept. 29, 1866, Salt Lake City (daughter of Samuel Bryson and Sarah Ann Conray of Glasgow, Scotland, pioneers 1848, Milo Andrus company). She was born Aug. 21, 1849. Their children: Samuel, m. Ellan Wood; Alice, m. George Freestona; Hyrum, m. Laura

Thompson; Jedediah, m. Ella Moss; Eliza, m. Henry Armstrong; Patty O., m. Wilder Hatch; Sarah Ann, m. Eugene Clark; Heber John, m. Artulus Holbrook; Olivia, m. William Waddoups; LeRoy, m. Tessie Cook; Calvin, m. Ruth Hess. Family home, Bountiful.
Married Esther Mabey Nov. 22, 1873, Salt Lake City (daughter of Thomas Mabey and Esther Chalker of Dorchester, Eng., pioneers Oct. 5, 1862, Captain Hammond company). She was born July 4, 1850. Their children: Thomas, m. Julia Burningham; David E., Jane M., and Presley, latter three died; Parley P., m. Bessie Goddard; Susan G., m. Thomas Neatte; Ezra T., m. Nellie Goodfellow; Linnie, m. Samuel LeRoy Hepworth; Walter, died; Alvin.
President high priests' quorum of Davis stake; counselor to Bishop John Stoker of North Canyon ward; spent 15 years and $50,000 in missionary work, traveling over 25,000 miles; made large donations for building of L. D. S. temples and meeting and schoolhouses. Bodyguard to Joseph Smith and Brigham Young. First settler in Bountiful, where he built first house. Member of Nauvoo police force; postmaster at Bountiful 1871-77; school trustee. Engaged in milling business with Heber C. Kimball. Farmer and stockraiser.

SESSIONS, CARLOS LYON (son of Perrigrine Sessions and Julia Ann Killgore). Born July 16, 1842, Nauvoo, Ill. Came to Utah Sept. 24, 1847, Parley P. Pratt company.
Married Elizabeth Wintle April 2, 1864, Salt Lake City Endowment House, Heber C. Kimball officiating (daughter of George Wintle and Elizabeth Sewell of Yarmouth, Eng., pioneers 1863, John Hart company). She was born March 20, 1848. Their children: Patty B. b. March 25, 1865, m. William B. Bitton; David C. b. Aug. 13, 1867, d. aged 2; George P. b. Jan. 7, 1870, m. Lillie Bruce; Barney W. b. Sept. 8, 1873, m. Sarah C. Wood; Joseph W. b. May 7, 1876, d. aged 8; Harvey W. b. Aug. 6, 1879, m. Laura Burningham; Julia B. b. Feb. 24, 1882, m. August Wallin; Oscar B. b. Oct. 27, 1884, m. Harriett Brown; Hannah L. b. Sept. 27, 1887, m. George Simpson; Nannie M. b. July 6, 1889, m. Marion G. Boyd. Family home Bountiful, Utah.
Married Sallie L. Hill March 1882, Salt Lake City Endowment House, Heber C. Kimball officiating (daughter of James Hill and Melicia Hadlock of Davis Co., Utah, pioneers 1852). She was born in 1862.
Married Mary Rakestraw May 15, 1911, Bountiful, Utah, who was born April 27, 1814, and came to Utah April 27, 1911.
Member 70th quorum seventies; missionary to Colorado and Arizona two years; elder; high priest. Sheriff of Davis county; marshal; special policeman of Bountiful; estray poundkeeper; school trustee. Carpet weaver and sawmiller.

SESSIONS, KEPLAR (son of Perrigrine Sessions and Lucina Call). Born Dec. 3, 1856, Bountiful, Utah.
Married Ann Call Jan. 25, 1876, Salt Lake City (daughter of Anson Call and Emma Summers, pioneers 1859, handcart company). She was born March 20, 1858. Their children: Keplar b. Jan. 12, 1878, m. Eva Alsop; Perrigrine b. March 26, 1880; Lucina b. June 24, 1883, m. Carlos Gustavson; Ivan b. Dec. 12, 1885; Emma b. March 25, 1887, m. Edwin Reese; Austin b. Aug. 9, 1889; Anson b. March 14, 1892; Ella b. May 27, 1895; Ann b. Nov. 25, 1898; Bergretta T. b. Dec. 24, 1900. Family home Chesterfield, Idaho.
High priest; missionary to North Carolina 1891-94; high councilor of Bannock stake; member Sunday school union. Farmer and stockraiser.

SESSIONS, CHESTER (son of Perrigrine Sessions and Fanny Emmerette Loveland). Born May 29, 1859, Bountiful, Utah.
Married Isabell Corbridge Oct. 2, 1879, Salt Lake City (daughter of Edward Corbridge and Alice Parker of Bountiful). She was born March 28, 1862. Their children: Chester b. July 5, 1880, m. Urinda Dewey; Edward b. Aug. 25, 1882, m. Effie U. Child; Laura Bell b. Jan. 4, 1885, died; Roy b. June 10, 1886, m. Chloe Welker; Willey R. b. Nov. 13, 1888, m. Jennie Harrison; Alice May b. May 14, 1891, m. Hyrum Roose; Russ H. b. Feb. 15, 1894, m. Lucy Bleavard; Delbert b. Sept. 29, 1896; Loal b. Aug. 29, 1899; Fannie V. b. July 2, 1902; Hilda b. Jan. 17, 1905; Ruby b. Sept. 28, 1907. Family home Bountiful, Utah.
Member 100th quorum seventies; missionary to Arizona 1884-85; first counselor in elders' quorum; bishop's counselor. Road supervisor. Farmer.

SESSIONS, ²DAVID (son of ²David Sessions and Patty Bartlett). Born May 5, 1823, Newry, Maine. Came to Utah July 1850.
Married Phoebe Carter Foss in Dec. 1852, Salt Lake City (daughter of Calvin Foss and Sarah B. Carter of Scarboro, Maine; latter came to Utah 1850, Wilford Woodruff company, and settled at Bountiful). She was born in 1831 at Scarboro and came to Utah with mother. Their children: Sarah Phoebe b. Nov. 26, 1853, m. Joseph Moss Dec. 18, 1872; Cerdinia Estell b. Jan. 30, 1856, m. Arthur Burnham Feb. 1873; ²David b. Jan. 9, 1888, m. Lettie Rawson May 22, 1912; Olive Cordelia b. Dec. 16, 1859, m. William Corbridge 1888; Fabian C. b. July 22, 1862, m. Elizabeth Moss Feb. 1892; Darius b. Oct. 2, 1864, m. Charlotte Chipin June 5, 1892; Calvin F. b. Oct. 24, 1866, died; Elizabeth b. May 25, 1869, m. William Lewis Nov. 23, 1888; Rhoda Harriet b. Oct. 3, 1871, died; Annie Sylvia b. April 30, 1875, m. George Neville June 22, 1899.
Member Nauvoo legion. One of Joseph Smith's bodyguards. Farmer and harness maker. Died April 19, 1896, Bountiful.

1154 PIONEERS AND PROMINENT MEN OF UTAH

SESSIONS, RICHARD (son of Saulmon Sessions and Mary Hargraves of Logan county, Ky., and Wayne county, Ill.). Born April 28, 1799, Logan county, Ky. Came to Utah 1847. Contingent Mormon battalion.
Married Lucretia Haws 1820, White county, Ill. (daughter of Jacob Haws and Hannah Nail), who was born Nov. 22, 1802. Their children: John b. Aug. 22, 1821, m. Emeline Sessions July 1846; Sarah Ann and Richard, Jr., died; William Bradford b. Jan. 23, 1827, m. Cathrine Yeger; Daniel Alexander b. Jan. 11, 1829, m. Janette Baum; Mary, died; Louisa b. July 26, 1833, d. 1891; Eliza Jane, died; Melissa b. March 11, 1836, m. Isaac Baum; Emeline b. May 1, 1840, m. Charles Carter Thomas; Elizabeth b. Aug. 31, 1842, m. David Condon; Hannah b. Jan. 19, 1846, m. William Gallagher.
Seventy. Counselor to Bishop Terry of Mosquito Creek, Iowa; 2d counselor to Bishops Fawsett and William Wall of Provo. Member of 30th regiment. 1st brigade Illinois mounted volunteers in the Illinois Black Hawk Indian war. Farmer and stockraiser. Died March 1879, Heber, Utah.

SESSIONS, DANIEL ALEXANDER (son of Richard Sessions and Lucretia Haws). Born Jan. 11, 1829.
Married Janette Baum. Their children: Rachael b. 1861, m. Thomas G. Clagg; Adolphus b. May 13, 1862, m. Rachael Hickens; m. Mary J. Nelson; Dolphy b. May 13, 1862, m. Rachael Neil; m. Isabelle Richardson; William; Jane, m. Andrew Nelson; Alfred, m. Matilda Poulson; Agnes, m. Joseph Fratillio.
Farmer and cattleman. Died Sept. 1905, Heber, Utah.

SESSIONS, ADOLPHUS (son of Daniel Alexander Sessions and Janette Baum). Born May 13, 1862, at Heber, Utah.
Married Rachael Hickens, July 1892, Heber, Utah (daughter of Thomas Hickens and Margret Powell, of Heber City, Utah). Their child: Charles, b. Oct. 13, 1899.
Married Mary J. Nelson Dec. 26, 1900, Heber, Utah (daughter of Henry T. Nelson and Mary E. McMillan of Heber). Their children: Cordon b. Oct. 21, 1901; Chloe Ellen b. Jan. 29, 1903; Ella Janette b. Jan. 22, 1905; Bernal Alex b. Aug. 1, 1906; Agnes Larna b. Aug. 24, 1908; Irwin b. Dec. 11, 1910. Families resided Heber, Utah.
Farmer and cattleman.

SEVERE, HARRISON (son of James Severe and Polly Harris of Knox county, Ohio). Born Sept. 17, 1820, in Knox county. Came to Utah Oct. 30, 1850, Joseph Young company.
Married Dorcas McBride Dec. 31, 1839, in Adams county, Ill. (daughter of Thomas McBride and Cathrine Johns), who was born Aug. 15, 1822. Their children: Lyman W. b. Aug. 31, 1840, m. Malinda McIntosh; Ann J. b. Dec. 6, 1844, m. George Whittle; Arminta b. Aug. 6, 1849, m. John Craner; Hyrum H. b. Feb. 6, 1852, m. Leonora Eastham; Deseret b. May 13, 1856, m. F. M. Cummins; Don C. b. Oct. 6, 1868; Emily b. May 19, 1865, m. James F. Walker. Family home Grantsville, Tooele Co., Utah.
Captain in Nauvoo legion; pony express rider; bodyguard of President Brigham Young. Died Dec. 1901.

SEVERE, HYRUM H. (son of Harrison Severe and Dorcas McBride). Born Feb. 6, 1852, Grantsville, Utah.
Married Leonora Eastham July 18, 1870, Salt Lake City (daughter of John Eastham and Jane Huntington, pioneers Nov. 1864, Captain Walker company). She was born Jan. 9, 1853. Their children: Hyrum H., Jr. b. June 10, 1871, m. Nellie Smith; John G. b. Nov. 26, 1872, m. Mary Wixom; James R. b. Jan. 5, 1876, m. Grace Cummins; George H. b. Sept. 18, 1877, m. Bertha Bates; Dorcas J. b. May 11, 1879, m. Edward Hunter; Joseph W. b. Sept. 25, 1880, m. Lillie Briggs; Lyman C. b. Feb. 11, 1882, m. Retta Grant; m. Myrtle Hunter; Jane L. b. July 11, 1874, m. Samuel Poulton; Emma L. b. May 22, 1885, m. Cyrus Hunter; Althera b. Nov. 12, 1893, d. May 7, 1897.
First child born in Grantsville. High priest; high councilor at Cassia stake.

SEVERN, WILLIAM (son of Enoch Severn and Ann Allen of Hucknall Torkard, Nottinghamshire, Eng.). Born Oct. 4, 1836, Hucknall Torkard. Came to Utah Dec. 1, 1856, Martin and Tyler handcart company.
Married Mary Astle May 29, 1856, on ship Orrizon (daughter of Frank Astle and Fleischa Raynor of Hucknall Torkard, pioneers Oct. 1861, Joseph Horne company). She was born March 16, 1837, and died Aug. 6, 1898.
Married Ann Baguley May 16, 1870, Salt Lake City (daughter of Thomas Baguley and Grace Wayne of Derbyshire, Eng., who came to Utah 1874). She was born Nov. 10, 1850. Their children: Mary Ann, m. J. S. Robinson; William Thomas, m. Bertha Myer; Enoch Daniel, died; Elizabeth Sarah, m. J. J. Jones; Harry Allen, m. May Hoff; Daniel Enoch, m. Flora Lewis. Family home Montpelier, Idaho. This wife deserted him.
Married Marie Kowallis July 11, 1899, Logan, Utah (daughter of Otto Kowallis and Pauline Worbs of Berlin, Germany; latter came to Utah June 24, 1890). She was born Aug. 10, 1872. They have one child, Pauline.
Missionary to Sioux Falls, S. D., 1887-90; high priest; ward teacher. Farmer.

SEWELL, JOSEPH (son of Thomas Sewell, born 1758, and Ann Bacchus, born 1750, both of England). He was born Jan. 2, 1796, Essex, Eng. Came to Utah in September, 1862.
Married Sarah Stevens Jan. 10, 1814, Norfolk, Eng. (daughter of Barnard Stevens and Elizabeth Rivett), who was born April 9, 1797, and died Oct. 16, 1881. Their children: Elizabeth b. June 13, 1815, m. George Wintle; Sarah b. Dec. 19, 1817; Joseph, Jr. b. Nov. 13, 1819, m. Emily Ellett Jan. 17, 1841; Barnard b. March 18, 1821. Family home Woods Cross, Utah.
Left without a father at an early age, he helped to support his mother and a large family, but married at 18 years of age. By insistent economy became the owner of two small sailing vessels, which were used for fishing expeditions. These, with his other belongings, he sold, and with the funds he and his wife came to America to become a part in building up the Church of Jesus Christ of Latter-day Saints, which faith they had embraced, having previously been allied with the Presbyterian sect. Immediately after arriving in Salt Lake he located in Davis county, where he lived until March 24, 1880, dying at the age of 84.

SEWELL, JOSEPH (son of Joseph Sewell and Sarah Stevens). Born Nov. 13, 1819, Norfolk, Eng. Came to Utah Sept. 8, 1861.
Married Emily Ellett Jan. 17, 1841, at Yarmouth, Eng. (daughter of James Ellett and Esther Balls), who was born May 18, 1816, at Yarmouth. Their children: Emily b. Jan. 23, 1842; Joseph B. b. Oct. 5, 1843; George B. b. Nov. 22, 1845; Mary Ann b. Sept. 26, 1847; William b. Feb. 1, 1850, m. Elizabeth Ann Robins Aug. 29, 1871; Edward b. Jan. 27, 1856; Sarah Ann b. Feb. 4, 1858. Family home Weber Co., Utah.
Began working as apprentice in shipyard at fifteen years of age after having received common school education and continued at this trade seven years. His father had preceded him to America and he, likewise, turned his all into money and on March 21, 1860, set sail for New York City. Reached St. Louis May 15, 1861. Joined a company of immigrants who were starting to Utah, arriving in Salt Lake City Sept. 8, 1861, and locating at Ogden the same year. There, after much hard labor, with the characteristic energy for which he was noted, he placed his family in comfortable circumstances. Soon after arriving there he decided the teachings and principles of the Mormon faith were so entirely contrary to his idea and belief that he withdrew from this church and never had anything further to do with it. However, he took an active part in developing and building up that section of the west. He took up a homestead just west of Ogden, making this his permanent home. Helped to erect the first schoolhouse built in this section, and labored incessantly in the upbuilding of the industrial life of Ogden. He died in September, 1894, and his wife passed away four years later. His son, George B. Sewell, was drowned Nov. 30, 1861, while fording the Weber river with a yoke of oxen. Of the three remaining sons none ever had any connection with the Mormon church, and like their father, were opposed to the teachings of that faith.

SEWELL, WILLIAM (son of Joseph Sewell and Emily Ellett). Born Feb. 1, 1850, Yarmouth, Eng.
Married Elizabeth Ann Robins Aug. 29, 1871, Salt Lake City (daughter of Edmund Robins and Ann Douglas), who was born Nov. 30, 1854, Kaysville, Utah. Their children: Frederick George b. Jan. 16, 1874, m. Sarah E. Cole June 6, 1900; Rosa Bell b. Feb. 8, 1876, m. F. K. Smith Sept. 1, 1904; Mary Ella b. May 3, 1879, m. F. D. Hyland June 15, 1905; Clara Emily b. May 10, 1881; Henry William b. Oct. 10, 1883; Charles Barnard b. April 21, 1886. Family home Weber Co., Utah.
Attended school at St. Louis, but grew up in Weber county and has resided permanently on the old homestead ever since. He has taken an active part in the industrial and political development of that part of the state, having filled many important positions of trust by appointment.

SEWELL, FREDERICK GEORGE (son of William Sewell and Elizabeth Ann Robins). Born Jan. 16, 1874, Ogden, Utah.
Married Sarah E. Cole June 6, 1900, Logan, Utah (daughter of George Cole and Mary Painter), who was born Oct. 20, 1876, at Logan.
Assayer and chemist.

SHAFER, JOHN O. (son of Johan Shafer and Hannah Rossa). Came to Utah October, 1849.
Married Hannah Casto (daughter of Abel Casto and Mary Galland). Their children: Orson W. b. Dec. 2, 1846, m. Elizabeth Kingdom; Mary A. b. Nov. 19, 1848 (deceased), m. Jacob Hunter; John H. b. March 1851; Eliza b. Oct. 22, 1853, m. John William Snell July 21, 1873; Oliver b. Nov. 2, 1855, m. Mary Coon; James A. b. March 1857, m. Elizabeth Hagel; Frank b. Oct. 30, 1859, m. Emma J. Cooper; Charles b. Sept. 1862, d. aged 30; Mabel b. Aug. 12, 1867, m. W. R. Smith. Family home, Salt Lake City.

SHAFFER, HENRY (son of Jacob Shaffer). Came to Utah 1858.
Married Eve Beard, who came to Utah 1858 and died at Ogden. Their children: John Isaac, m. Nancy Hill; Joseph Russell, m. Gilleed Taylor; George Henry, m. Esther Ann Jessop; Elizabeth, m. John Rolph; Nancy, m. Sylvester Perry; William, m. Mary Ann Bradshaw; Abigail, m. Levi Dougherty. Family resided Ogden, Slaterville and Millville, Utah.
Elder. Farmer. Died about 1869 at Millville.

PIONEERS AND PROMINENT MEN OF UTAH 1155

SHAFFER, JOSEPH RUSSELL (son of Henry Shaffer and Eve Beard). Born March 31, 1830, in Virginia. Came to Utah 1858.
Married Gillead Taylor, who was born May 3, 1840. Came to Utah 1858. Their children: Mary Ellen, m. Richard Jessop; George Henry, d. aged 20; Margarett Eve, m. Thomas Jessop; Joseph Kinnion, m. Helen Weaver; William Heber; John Franklin, m. Elizabeth Buckley; Jeanette Larona, m. Richard Jessop; James Marion, m. Lydia M. Rolfe; Isaac Newton, m. Ellen McKowen; Louisa Esther, m. John F. Sessions; Martin Luther, m. Matilda Hunt; Samuel Lafayette, m. Irene Jackson; Laura Elphy, died.
High priest; ward teacher. Justice of peace 15 years. Died June 23, 1901, Millville, Utah.

SHAFFER, JAMES MARION (son of Joseph Russell Shaffer and Gillead Taylor). Born Jan. 7, 1861, Slaterville, Utah.
Married Lydia Mandania Rolfe March 31, 1884, Vernal, Utah (daughter of William Jasper Rolfe and Ellen Wilkshire of Vernal, Utah). She was born March 22, 1865. Their children: Marion Kinnion b. Dec. 5, 1884, m. Susan Stringham; Estella b. March 23, 1887; Ethel b. April 24, 1889, m. Clifford Hatch; Ellen b. Aug. 25, 1891; Ernest b. Jan. 5, 1894; Barth Cannon b. Jan. 19, 1896; William Jasper Rolfe b. Feb. 22, 1898, d. April 22, 1898, at Lehi, Utah; Pearl b. June 5, 1900; Corilla b. Nov. 12, 1902; Joseph Alden b. Sept. 12, 1904; Newell Waldo b. Dec. 5, 1907. Family home Vernal, Utah.
Ordained bishop of Naples ward May 17, 1891, and was honorably released Dec. 29, 1909; counselor to Bishop Thomas J. Caldwell of Naples ward 1887-91; superintendent Sunday school; ward teacher; secretary to Y. M. M. I. A.; member high council. Treasurer Uinta county 1910-12. President Ashley Central Irrigation Co., 1897-1902. Clerk Ashley Co-op., Vernal, 6 years.

SHANKS, JAMES (son of James Shanks and Marion Leckie of Paisley, Renfrewshire, Scotland). Born Aug. 31, 1810, at Paisley. Came to Utah Oct. 29, 1855, Charles H. Harper company.
Married Isabella Dock 1832 (daughter of Robert and Euphemia Dock of Paisley), who was born 1809 and came to Utah with husband. Their children: James Dock b. Nov. 29, 1833, m. Isabella Muir Dec. 21, 1855, m. Eva Erickson March 10, 1875, m. Caroline M. Homan Nov. 16, 1899; Marion b. July 19, 1836, m. Alexander Perry Dec. 21, 1855; Isabella; William D. b. Feb. 10, 1840. Family resided at Paisley, Scotland; St. Louis, Mo., and Salt Lake City, Utah.
Elder. Pattern setter. Crossed plains sixteen times. Died Jan. 22, 1866, St. Louis, Mo.

SHANKS, JAMES DOCK (son of James Shanks and Isabella Dock). Born Nov. 29, 1833, Paisley, Scotland. Came to Utah September, 1853, Jacob Gates company.
Married Isabella Muir Dec. 21, 1855, at Salt Lake City (daughter of James Muir, born at Muchling, and Mary Muney of Kilmarnock, Ayrshire, Scotland, pioneers Oct. 9, 1853, Appleton Harmon company). She was born Aug. 15, 1837. Their children: Mary E. Shanks b. Oct. 8, 1856, m. Gustave Wodberg March 25, 1880; Isabella b. Feb. 18, 1859; James M. b. Jan. 16, 1861; William b. April 20, 1863; Marion b. Aug. 12, 1865, m. William J. Doyle July 19, 1888; Elizabeth b. Sept. 10, 1867, m. William Fister Aug. 20, 1895; John M. b. Nov. 23, 1869; Archibald b. March 29, 1872, m. Lilly Buke; Margaret b. Aug. 3, 1874, m. Mr. McEwan; George Albert b. Jan. 1, 1878.
Married Eva Erickson March 10, 1875, at Salt Lake City (daughter of Eric Erickson and Fredericka Carlson of Upland, Sweden, who came to Utah by railroad). She was born Nov. 27, 1845, Upland, Sweden. Their children: Catrina Amelia b. May 1, 1876; Joseph b. Sept. 29, 1877, m. Mary Jacobs Dec. 24, 1902; Louise b. Sept. 29, 1879; Josephine b. July 10, 1881, m. C. M. Gorin Dec. 29, 1910; Hyrum b. March 29, 1884; Evelyn b. July 1, 1887; Fredericka b. March 11, 1889, d. June 27, 1891.
Married Caroline M. Homan Nov. 16, 1899, at Salt Lake City (daughter of Andrew Homan and Sophia Esing of Latdrof, Germany), who was born Oct. 19, 1848.
High priest; home missionary; superintendent Sunday school at Riverdale. Assisted in building wall around Salt Lake for protection from Indians. Veteran Black Hawk war.

SHARP, ADAM (son of John Sharp and Mary Hunter, both of Scotland). Born in Scotland. Came to Utah Dec. 18, 1850.
Married Elizabeth Cook 1848 (daughter of David Cook and Mary Pattersen, both of Scotland, pioneers Dec. 18, 1850). She was born April 6, 1828. Their children: John A., m. Rebecca Bennion; David, m. Emma S. Ajax; Elizabeth, m. Samuel Bennion; Mary Anna, m. Joseph Bennion; Jennett, died; Jennett 2d, m. Israel Bennion; Adam, Joseph, Agnes and Isabella, latter four died; Adam 2d. Family home, Salt Lake City.
Elder. Cattleman. Died March 8, 1890.

SHARP, JOHN A. (son of Adam Sharp and Elizabeth Cook). Born June 27, 1850, at South Platte, Neb. Came to Utah Dec. 18, 1850.
Married Rebecca Bennion Dec. 23, 1872, Salt Lake City (daughter of Samuel Bennion and Mary Bushel of Taylorsville, Utah, pioneers Oct. 5, 1847, John Taylor company). She was born March 17, 1853. Their children: Mary Emma b. Dec. 5, 1875, m. George A. Sand; Jesse B. March 6, 1887, m. Minnie Creer; Clyde b. May 9, 1889, died; June b. Jan. 17, 1892; Leo b. June 18, 1894; Ira b. Oct. 30, 1896; Willey b. Jan. 30, 1898. Family home, Salt Lake City.
Seventy. Cattleman and sheep raiser.

SHARP, FRANCIS (son of Michael Pearson Sharp of Wellington and Jane Armstrong born Aug. 19, 1811, both in Biggsmain, Northumberlandshire, Eng.—married Sept. 15, 1833). He was born Jan. 24, 1834. Came to Utah Oct. 19, 1862, Francis M. Lyman company.
Married Dorothy Gill October, 1855 (daughter of William Gill, pioneer Oct. 19, 1862, Francis M. Lyman company, and Mary Chicken). She was born April 21, 1840. Their children: Mary Jane b. Sept. 5, 1856, d. Nov. 22, 1857; Ann b. July 20 1858, m. Edward A. Galbraith Feb. 8, 1875; Elizabeth b. Dec. 16, 1860, d. 1867; Jane b. Sept. 24, 1865, m. John C. Reid Dec. 24, 1880; John Gill b. Feb. 10, 1866, m. Lydia Millgate; Francis, Jr. b. Feb. 17, 1868, m. Lydia Ann Pilkington Nov. 14, 1887, m. May Seymour Neff Jan. 7, 1903; Michael Pearson b. May 7, 1870; William Thomas b. April 10, 1872, m. Adeline Farrell; Isaac Gill b. March 30, 1874, d. next day; Mary b. Feb. 6, 1876, m. William J. Young; Dora Clarissa b. March 29, 1878, m. Moroni Robison; Sarah b. Nov. 24, 1880, Married Mary Jane Watson May 30, 1870, Salt Lake City (daughter of William Watson, pioneer 1862, Francis M. Lyman company), who was born May 26, 1853, Marley Hill, Durham, Eng. Their children: Robert b. April 7, 1873, died; George Armstrong b. July 13, 1874, m. Maud Zimmerman June 1911; Henry Watson b. Dec. 26, 1876; James William b. March 27, 1879; Margaret Chloe b. March 30, 1881, and Frances b. Oct. 19, 1882, latter four died; Hugh b. Dec. 26, 1884; Estelle Pearl b. April 20, 1887; Ruby Isabel b. Sept. 15, 1889. Family resided Smithfield, Utah, and Lyman, Idaho.
High priest. Ward clerk many years under Bishop Samuel Roskelly and Bishop Ferrell. Justice of the peace of Smithfield several terms. Ordained patriarch May 5, 1889, at Logan. Died February, 1891.

SHARP, FRANCIS (son of Francis Sharp and Dorothy Gill). Born Feb. 17, 1868, Smithfield, Cache Co., Utah.
Married Lydia Ann Pilkington Nov. 14, 1887, Smithfield, Utah (daughter of William and Lydia Pilkington, who came to Utah 1876). She was born Nov. 22, 1866, in England. Their children: Francis, Jr. b. Oct. 26, 1888; William Cahoon; Kate, m. Parley L. Williams; Adam; Agnes, m. Abram W. Caine; Secelia; Elizabeth Alice, m. Harry Nesbit. Family home, Salt Lake City.
Bishop of 20th ward for 30 years. Manager of the Temple Stone quarries. Police captain. Member of city council; superintendent public works; member of legislature. Railroad contractor and builder. Died Dec. 23, 1901.

SHARP, JOHN (son of John Sharp and Jane Patterson). Born Dec. 28, 1841, in Clackmannanshire, Scotland. Came to Utah Sept. 1, 1850, John Sharp company.
Married Hannah Neslen Sept. 8, 1856, at Salt Lake City (daughter of Samuel Neslen and Eunice Francis, both of Salt Lake City, pioneers Sept. 20, 1853, C. Spencer company). She was born June 1, 1844. Their children: Eunice Jane b. Sept. 29, 1867, d. child; John N. b. June 11, 1869, m. Margaret E. Miles. Family home, Salt Lake City.
Member of high council. State fish and game commissioner 11 years. Mining man; capitalist.

SHARP, JOHN N. (son of John Sharp and Hannah Neslen). Born June 11, 1869, at Salt Lake City.
Married Margaret E. Miles November, 1892, at Salt Lake City (daughter of Orson Miles and Margaret Lawrence, of Salt Lake City, pioneers 1850). She was born December, 1872, died Jan. 7, 1912. Their children: Phylis M. b. 1893; John N. b. 1899. Family home, Salt Lake City.
City councilman 1906-08. Representative of Selby Smelting & Lead Co.

SHARP, JAMES (son of John Sharp and Jane Patterson). Born Nov. 18, 1843, in Scotland.
Married Lizzie Rogers Oct. 31, 1864, Salt Lake City (daughter of Francis and Jemima Rogers of England, pioneers 1856, Edward Martin handcart company). She was born Sept. 13, 1847. Their children: Lizzie b. Sept. 24, 1865, m. Ben R. Eldredge; Kate b. June 11, 1870, m. Ern R.

1156 PIONEERS AND PROMINENT MEN OF UTAH

Eldredge; Celia b. July 7, 1872, m. M. M. Young; Aggie b. April 14, 1876, m. James R. Hay; John Francis b. May 2, 1878, m. Luella Ferrin; Heber Chase b. Feb. 10, 1880, m. Vera Cannon; Joseph Hyrum b. Sept. 5, 1882, m. Maud Shirley; Chloe b. Jan. 2, 1888; William Hooper b. April 3, 1884. Family home, Salt Lake City.
House representative. Mayor of Salt Lake City 1884. Chairman board of regents University of Utah. Died May 7, 1904.

SHARP, JOHN FRANCIS (son of James Sharp and Lizzie Rogers). Born May 2, 1878, at Salt Lake City.
Married Luella Ferrin Sept. 18, 1903, at Salt Lake City (daughter of Josiah M. Ferrin and Martha Brunson, both lived in Ogden Valley, Utah; former pioneer 1856, latter 1847). She was born May 12, 1877. Their children: Denner Francis b. June 23, 1904; Marion b. May 2, 1906; Harlow Brooks b. March 29, 1909; Martha b. Feb. 27, 1912. Family home, Salt Lake City.
Physician and surgeon.

SHARP, JOSEPH (son of John Sharp of Clackmannanshire, Scotland). Born in 1817, in Clackmannanshire, Scotland. Came to Utah Aug. 28, 1850, independent company.
Married Janet Condie 1849, St. Louis, Mo. (daughter of Thomas Condie and Janet Sharp of Clackmannanshire, Scotland, pioneers 1855). She was born Jan. 30, 1851. Their children: John C. b. May 28, 1850, m. Sarah Bethula Palmer; Helen; Mary Jane, m. Joseph J. Daynes; Margaret Ann, m. H. T. McCune; Janet, m. E. A. Senroot. Family home, Salt Lake City.
Married Margaret Condie at Salt Lake City (daughter of Thomas Condie and Janet Sharp). Their children: Celia, m. F. E. Barker; Joseph C., m. Jane Bennett.
Elder. Furnished stone for Salt Lake temple. Freighter. Died Sept. 5, 1864, Sweetwater, Wyo.

SHARP, JOHN C. (son of Joseph Sharp and Janet Condie). Born May 28, 1850, Kaw River, Kansas. Came to Utah 1850 with parents.
Married Sarah Bethula Palmer Feb. 12, 1872, Salt Lake City (daughter of Mifflin Palmer and Katherine K. Dolbey of Salt Lake City, pioneers 1851). She was born Jan. 30, 1851. Their children: Joseph P. b. Sept. 5, 1874, m. Emma Irene Merrill; James P. b. Aug. 17, 1876, m. Olive Sausman. Family home, Salt Lake City.
Bishop of Vernon, Tooele county; member high council. Trustee of State Agricultural college. Stockraiser and capitalist.

SHARP, JOSEPH C. (son of Joseph Sharp and Margaret Condie). Born Dec. 17, 1864, Salt Lake City.
Married Jane Bennett June, 1893, Salt Lake City (daughter of Richard Bennett and Mina Foster of Salt Lake City, pioneers 1867). Their children: J. Clyde; Lavon. Family home, Salt Lake City.
Member 13th quorum seventies; missionary to Scotland 1890-92. Sheriff of Salt Lake county 1909-13. General foreman of Utah Central shops.

SHARP, JOSEPH S. (son of James R. Sharp, born June 20, 1809, and Martha Griffin, born Aug. 7, 1820, of Tennessee). Born July 17, 1840, in Calhoun county, Ill. Came to Utah with his own company.
Married Rebecca Higby March 13, 1862, in Tooele Co., Utah (daughter of Truman and Lucy A. Higby). Their children: Joseph b. 1864, m. Elsie Lamb 1887; James Ervin b. 1866, m. Melissa Ellsworth; William F. b. 1868, m. Miss Smith; Anna R. b. 1870, died; Lucy Ellen b. 1872, m. Isaac Packer; John Henry b. 1876, died; Arminta E. b. 1877, m. William Packer; George A. b. 1884; Daniel H. b. 1887, died; Emily Zet b. 1887, m. Elif Hoglin. Family home Preston, Idaho.

SHARP, JOSEPH TRUMAN (son of Joseph S. Sharp and Rebecca Higby). Born Sept. 4, 1864, Tooele, Utah.
Married Elsie Lamb April 1, 1887, Logan, Utah (daughter of Suel Lamb and Elizabeth Zimmerman), who was born 1888, m. Hugh Kid Nov. 14, 1906; Alvin Joseph b. March 17, 1891; Clarence John b. July 20, 1893; Vernon T. b. Dec. 20, 1895; Elmer A. b. May 10, 1900; Elizabeth b. May 2, 1904; Delbert b. March 15, 1907. Family home Preston, Idaho.
Married Annie Woodhead Nov. 10, 1910 (daughter of Albert Woodhead and Sarah Fast), who was born Jan. 1887, Heddersfull, Eng.

SHAW, ABRAHAM (son of Abram Shaw and Nancy Hartley of Ruthie, Lancastershire, Eng.). Born Dec. 8, 1808, Ruthie, Eng. Came to Utah Sept. 22, 1852, Isaac Bullock company.
Married Margaret Thornber 1828 (daughter of Richard and Hannah Thornber), who was born Aug. 9, 1811, and came to Utah with husband. Their children: Richard Hartley b. Aug. 15, 1829, d. Oct. 1833; Leah Jane b. Sept. 17, 1831, m. Abner Eldredge Keeler. Family resided Provo and Salt Lake City.
Married Jane Lawrenson Dec. 2, 1856 (daughter of William Lawrenson and Ann Quick, pioneers 1856, handcart company). She was born Oct. 9, 1838. Their children: Margret Ann b. May 4, 1858, m. Seth Wareham; Abraham b. Jan. 11, 1860, m. Selina Ann Wall Nov. 28, 1883; Eliza Jane b. March 13, 1862, m. T. E. Jackson Dec. 9, 1877; William Hartley b. Jan. 8, 1864, died; Alice b. Jan. 7, 1866, m. James Ainsworth; Richard H. b. March 5, 1868, m. Ada Ainsworth; Nancy b. July 8, 1871, m. Worthington Bills Feb. 17, 1888;

Mary b. Oct. 21, 1874, m. Joseph Cowley; Fredrick b. Oct. 7, 1877, m. Annie Van Dyke; Thomas Q. b. June 30, 1889, m. Carrie Godfreyson; Harriet b. Feb. 20, 1881, m. Roy Larsen.
Veteran Black Hawk war. Settled in Provo, later moved to Glenwood. Watermaster in Eastfield Irrigation Co.

SHAW, ABRAHAM, JR. (son of Abraham Shaw and Jane Lawrenson). Born Jan. 13, 1860, Provo, Utah.
Married Selina Ann Wall Nov. 28, 1883, St. George, Utah (daughter of Joseph L. Wall, pioneer Nov. 1856, and Selina Stevens). She was born Oct. 6, 1865, at Glenwood, Utah. Their children: Abraham Joseph b. Aug. 25, 1884, m. Lenore Crosland March 24, 1908; William Hartly b. April 5, 1886, m. Mary Harding April 5, 1907; Emeron Henry b. June 19, 1888, m. Blanche Ashby May 11, 1910; Earl b. Aug. 14, 1889; Estella Lavine b. Nov. 4, 1891; Sylvia b. June 10, 1894; Fredrick Doyle b. Oct. 7, 1896; Selina Jane b. Oct. 30, 1898; Glen Thomas b. Dec. 22, 1900; Lawrence W. b. Dec. 23, 1902; Melba b. Jan. 12, 1904; Levar b. Jan. 24, 1906; Richard Lynn b. July 28, 1908; Della b. Nov. 9, 1910.

SHAW, ELIJAH. Born Feb. 15, 1822, at Cincinnati, Ohio. Came to Utah 1853.
Married Martha Ann Thomas 1849, Nauvoo, Ill. (daughter of Jacob Thomas, pioneer 1853, handcart company), who was born Nov. 20, 1824. Their children: William O. b. 1850, m. Phoebe Ann Rose Jan. 20, 1872; Martha Ellen b. 1852, m. Hyrum Rose 1868; Edmund Riley b. 1855, m. Elizabeth Rose 1871; Lorna b. 1857, m. Willard Cragun 1871; Elijah b. 1859, m. Louise Chadwick 1879; Amelia b. 1861, m. Jessie Hiatt 1879; John b. 1864, m. Mary Brown 1886; George b. 1866, m. Mary Storey 1885; Samuel b. 1869, m. Harriet Parker 1891. Family home North Ogden, Utah.
Elder and ward teacher. Farmer.

SHAW, WILLIAM ORSON (son of Elijah Shaw and Martha Ann Thomas). Born 1850 at Council Bluffs, Iowa. Came to Utah 1853.
Married Phoebe Ann Rose 1872 at Ogden (daughter of Wesley Rose and Maria Gates of Nauvoo, Ill., pioneers 1850). She was born 1856. Their children: Maria b. 1876; Elizabeth Ann b. 1878; Zella b. 1881; Rachel b. 1885; Mable Irene b. 1892. Family home Liberty, Utah.
High priest; missionary 1891-1911. Farmer; stockraiser.

SHAW, JAMES FERGUSSON (son of Alexander Shaw and Elizabeth Fergusson, Garnkirk, Scotland). Born Feb. 21, 1847, Garnkirk Cottage, Scotland. Came to Utah September, 1868, Captain Gillespie company.
Married Margaret Robertson Sept. 5, 1870 (daughter of James Robertson and Sarah Colter, who came to Utah 1869), who was born July 24, 1848, and died Nov. 20, 1909. Their children: Alexander b. Aug. 17, 1871, m. Etta Hamton; Joseph F. b. Nov. 26, 1873, m. Nanie Broadbent; Margaret R. b. Dec. 1, 1875, d. May 27, 1879; Robert Milton b. March 28, 1878, d. May 18, 1878; Agnes R. b. Aug. 30, 1882, m. Miland Hutchings; Franklin S. b. July 11, 1886, m. Ella Rebecca Woods; Thomas D. b. Jan. 3, 1888; John Roy b. May 27, 1880, m. Bertha May Gulbransen. Family home Elsinore, Utah.
Settled at Coalville 1868, moved to Richfield 1875 and to Elsinore 1881. Choir member and also member brass band. School trustee 15 years. Member bishopric.

SHAW, JOHN (son of Job Shaw and Lucy Sherman of Windsor county, Vt., born Oct. 25, 1765). He was born June 30, 1790, Bridgewater, Windsor county, Vt. Came to Utah Sept. 20, 1848, Lorenzo Snow company.
Married Polly Maria Fox Jan. 1, 1812, Victor, Ontario county, N. Y. (daughter of Jeremiah and Olive Fox), who was born Jan. 1, 1790, in Sheffield, Mass., died January, 1873, North Ogden, Utah. Their children: Myrtillo b. Aug. 1, 1814, m. Harriet Aurelia Austin Sept. 16, 1838; John L. b. May, 1816, m. Tryphenia Merrill 1842; Sylvester b. 1818, m. Amelia Noble; Harvey T. b. Jan. 1, 1820, m. Jane Waldron 1846; Zebediah b. Aug. 5, 1822, m. Betsie Starks 1847; Ambrose b. Sept. 12, 1824, m. Pamelia Dunn June 22, 1846, m. Minerva P. Stone Jan. 1, 1875; William b. Sept. 8, 1826, m. Diana Chase 1848; Polly Maria b. Feb. 28, 1830, m. Lorin Dunn 1846, m. Lafayette Williams 1856; Olive b. 1833, m. Benjamin Cazier 1848.
Settled at Salt Lake City 1848; moved to Ogden 1850. Died July 5, 1880, at Ogden, Utah.

SHAW, AMBROSE (son of John Shaw and Polly Maria Fox). Born Sept. 12, 1824, Victor, Ontario county, N. Y. Came to Utah September, 1847.
Married Pamelia Dunn June 22, 1846, near Mt. Pisgah, Iowa (daughter of James Dunn and Sally Barker), who was born July 28, 1830, in Michigan, died March 21, 1871, at Ogden, Utah.
Married Minerva Pease Stone Jan. 1, 1875, North Ogden, Utah (daughter of Amos Pease Stone and Minerva Leantine Jones, pioneers Sept. 30, 1850, Joseph Young company). She was born Nov. 29, 1851, Bountiful, Utah. Their children: Ambrose Amos b. Nov. 4, 1876, m. Mary Elizabeth Dee Dec. 9, 1903; Ernest b. Oct. 3, 1877, m. Grace Vanderhoof July 14, 1901; Eva Pamelia b. Jan. 23, 1880, d. March 3, 1886; Cordelia b. Dec. 12, 1881, d. Oct. 10, 1883; Merlin b. June 14, 1885, m. Irma Douglass Aug. 26, 1908; Olive Theresa b. March 9, 1889, m. William Gordon Aug. 10, 1906. Family home Ogden, Utah.

Assisted in constructing first irrigation ditches in Weber county and near Cottonwood Creek 1847; raised first crop of corn in Weber county 1849. Settled at Ogden in 1849. Veteran Indian war. Assisted in bringing immigrants to Utah. Died Jan. 15, 1906.

SHAW, WILLIAM (son of John Shaw and Polly Maria Fox). Born Sept. 8, 1826, Bennington, N. Y.
Married Diana Chase Jan. 1, 1849, Ogden, Utah (daughter of Ezra Chase and Tirza Wells, pioneers 1848), who was born July 21, 1827, Criston, Addison county, Vt. Their children: Rosabell b. Oct. 13, 1849, m. John Hubbard Oct. 8, 1868; Manley b. Dec. 28, 1851, died; Geneva b. Feb. 5, 1854, m. Frederick Miller Oct. 21, 1870; William Dudly b. May 15, 1855, m. Anna Rosina Cardon Dec. 29, 1878; Ambrose b. Aug. 31, 1857, m. Rosetta Childs Dec. 25, 1878; Romania b. Sept. 26, 1859, m. Isaac Clark Dec. 2, 1877; Annis b. March 6, 1861, m. Orsen Badger Sept. 26, 1879; Ine b. Dec. 22, 1862, m. Samuel Drake; Frank b. May 2, 1865, m. Caroline Stanger; Clarence b. March 15, 1870. Family resided Salt Lake City and Ogden, Utah.
Farmer.

SHAW, WILLIAM DUDLY (son of William Shaw and Diana Chase). Born May 15, 1855, Ogden, Utah.
Married Anna Rosina Cardon Dec. 29, 1878 (daughter of John Cardon and Anna Furrer, pioneers 1853 and 1856, respectively—married 1856, Salt Lake City). She was born Feb. 14, 1858, Ogden, Utah. Their children: William Alben b. Feb. 23, 1880, m. Constance M. Minna Aug. 25, 1904; Rosina Diana b. June 23, 1882, m. Lawrence W, Sherner June, 1902; Ariel Ruben b. June 10, 1884, died; Joseph Daniel b. Jan. 15, 1888, died; David John b. Jan. 28, 1890; Mary Anna b. Aug. 2, 1892; Martha Lily b. June 23, 1895; Lucy Leahona b. June 30, 1910. Family resided Ogden and Logan, Utah.
Seventy; Sunday school superintendent; ward teacher; missionary to eastern states 1896-1898. Merchant.

SHAW, AMBROSE AMOS (son of Ambrose Shaw and Minerva Pease Stone). Born Nov. 4, 1875, Ogden, Utah.
Married Mary Elizabeth Dee Dec. 9, 1903, Ogden, Utah (daughter of Thomas Duncombe Dee, born Nov. 10, 1844, Llanelly, Carmarthenshire, Wales, and Annie Taylor, born Nov. 4, 1852, at Lostockgralen, Chestershire, Eng.—married April 10, 1871, Salt Lake City). She was born Jan. 27, 1878, Ogden, Utah. Their child: Elizabeth Dee b. April 30, 1905. Family home, Ogden.
Engaged in the coal business at Ogden.

SHAW, MYRTILLO (son of John Shaw and Polly Maria Fox). Born Aug. 1, 1814, Victor, N. Y.
Married Harriet Aurelia Austin Sept. 16, 1838, town of Vermont, Wyoming county, N. Y. (daughter of Robert R. Austin and Harriet Rhodes), who was born Feb. 3, 1820, Bennington, N. Y. Their children: Francis b. July 1, 1841, m. Ophelia Farley; Harriet Aurelia b. Feb. 23, 1843, m. Cornele Stevens; Robert R. b. April 15, 1845, m. Ninnetta Caziah June 14, 1869; Polly Maria b. Feb. 6, 1848, m. Alfred Folker; John b. Feb. 17, 1850, m. Julia Gaido; James Henry b. Feb. 9, 1852, m. Mary Williams; Pyrmelia b. Dec. 8, 1853, d. Oct. 16, 1855; Jedediah M. b. Nov. 24, 1855, m. Mary Hannah Burchel; Myrtillo b. March 29, 1858, m. Anna H. Cardon Sept. 25, 1879; Wilber b. Feb. 20, 1860; Welcome Austin b. Oct. 29, 1863, d. Nov. 11, 1881; Crandle b. Feb. 19, 1866, d. April 9, 1866. Family home Ogden, Utah.

SHAW, MYRTILLO (son of Myrtillo Shaw and Harriet Aurelia Austin). Born March 29, 1858, at Ogden, Utah.
Married Anna Hermina Cardon Sept. 25, 1879 (daughter of John Cardon and Anna R. Furrer), who was born Jan. 23, 1861, at Ogden. Their children: David Myrtillo b. Nov. 6, 1881, m. Gwendolyn Williams June 11, 1907; Austin Herman b. April 9, 1884, m. Eva B. Brown June 22, 1909; Hermina Nettie b. July 28, 1887, m. Elbert P. Drumiler June 3, 1908; Rozina Pearl b. June 21, 1890, m. Lester I. Perry June 14, 1911; Lester Moses b. Oct. 12, 1894, d. Dec. 16, 1894; Bertha Mary b. Jan. 23, 1896; Lillian Aurelia b. Oct. 12, 1900. Family home Ogden, Utah.
Missionary to southern states 1886. Member city council of Ogden 1898-99. Merchant.

SHAW, JOSEPH. Came to Utah 1854.
Married Mary Ann Taylor 1857, Salt Lake endowment house, Salt Lake City (daughter of John Taylor and Margerite Baster of Staffordshire, Eng.). She was born March 1, 1821, Liverpool, Eng. Their children: John T. b. July 30, 1858; Thomas B. b. Sept. 25, 1860, m. Jane Roberts and Daisy Vanetti; Edward b. Aug. 11, 1862, d. infant; Eliza A. b. March 4, 1865, m. Thomas Bult. Family home, Salt Lake City.

SHAW, LUKE (son of William Shaw and Ellen Collins of Stockport, Lancashire, Eng.). Born Feb. 27, 1847. Came to Utah 1868.
Married Nancy Westwood Jan. 4, 1869, at Salt Lake City, Daniel H. Wells performing ceremony (daughter of Thomas Westwood and Martha Lomax of Berry, Lancashire, Eng., pioneers 1863). She was born Oct. 31, 1847. Their children: Luke, Jr., m. Jessie Pugh; Joseph, d. aged 2; Lily M., d. infant; Thomas N., m. Elsie Williams; John S., m. Mary Adams; Elizabeth, d. aged 6; Herbert, d. aged 10; B… m. Henry F. Hanson; James T. Family home, Salt Lake City.
Elder; block teacher 40 years. Raised first celery in Utah. Gardener and florist.

SHAW, OSMOND B. (son of Simeon Shaw and Mary Broad of Staffordshire, Eng.). Born 1821. Came to Utah 1851.
Married Eliza Wilding (daughter of William Wilding of Staffordshire, Eng., came to Utah 1871). She was born Feb. 22, 1822. Their children: William, d. aged 6; Harriett; Osmond W., m. Ann Atwood; Rose E., m. William Winegar; James A., m. Elizabeth Atwood; Louis C., m. Sarah Ann Lambert; John W., d. aged 2. Family home, Salt Lake City.
Missionary to England 1869-71; block teacher. Painter and decorator. Died Jan. 2, 1888.

SHAW, LOUIS C. (son of Osmond B. Shaw and Eliza Wilding). Born May 4, 1860, Salt Lake City.
Married Sarah Ann Lambert Aug. 30, 1883, Salt Lake City (daughter of Charles Lambert and Mary Alice Cannon, both of Nauvoo, Ill., pioneers Oct. 15, 1849, Allen Taylor company). She was born Nov. 1, 1861. Their children: Louis C. b. May 17, 1884, m. Jessie Morrison; Sarah Eiline b. Feb. 13, 1886, m. Moroni C. Woods; Hazel L. b. March 18, 1888, d. infant; Mary Alice b. Aug. 19, 1889, m. Rushby C. Midgley; Clarence L. b. Sept. 3, 1891; Harold L. b. Oct. 2, 1893; Ronald L. b. March 31, 1896; Dorothy L. b. March 6, 1898; Era L. b. Sept. 28, 1899; George W. b. Feb. 22, 1903.
Assistant Sunday school superintendent; block teacher; stake missionary. Builder and contractor.

SHEEN, JAMES. Came to Utah Sept. 28, 1856, Edmund Ellsworth company.
Married Maria Loverage in Gloucestershire, Eng., who died at Florence, Neb. Their children: Robert, m. Miss Taylor; James, m. Mary Jeans; Anna, m. John Forbes; Harriet, m. John Tranter; Emma, m. John Parsons; Ellen, m. Joseph Hill.
Died in fall of 1856, from exposure on the trip to Utah.

SHEETS, ELIJAH FUNK (son of Frederick Sheets of Germany and Hannah Page of Charleston, Pa.). Born March 22, 1821, at Charleston. Came to Utah Sept. 22, 1847, Perrigrine Sessions company.
Married Margaret Hutchinson Jan. 16, 1846, in England, who was born July 3, 1819, Prestelgn, Radnorshire, Eng. Died Feb. 1, 1847, Winter Quarters, Neb.
Married Susannah Musser April 6, 1847, Winter Quarters, Neb. (daughter of Samuel Musser and Anna Barr), who was born Sept. 2, 1827, and died May 11, 1861. Their children: Anna M.; Elijah M.; Nephi M.; Moroni M.; Amos M.; Susannah M.; Martha M. b. May 3, 1861, m. David F. Davis. Family home, Salt Lake City.
Married Elizabeth Leaver Feb. 8, 1857, Salt Lake City (daughter of Samuel Leaver and Mary Ann Hartlett), who was born Aug. 31, 1834, New York City; died July 26, 1892, Salt Lake City. Their children: Samuel L.; Elizabeth L.; Mary Ann L.; Frederick L.; Edward L.; Ellen L.; Brigham L.; Milton L.; Eva L.; Joseph L. Family home, Salt Lake City.
Married Emma Spencer Dec. 7, 1861, Salt Lake City (daughter of Edwin Spencer and Hannah Wardle), who was born Sept. 23, 1845, Arnold, Nottingham, Eng.; died May 25, 1900, Salt Lake City. Their children: Jedediah S.; Emma S.; William S.; Heber S.; Elijah S.; Edwin S.; Blanch S.; Eliza S.; Bertha S.; Ray S. Family home, Salt Lake City.
Bishop of 8th ward 48 years; traveling bishop 1871; assistant trustee-in-trust of the Mormon church. Assessor and collector of Utah county 1870; railroad contractor. U. P. R. R. 1869-70; stockbreeder and agriculturist. Died July 3, 1904.

SHEETS, NEPHI MUSSER (son of Elijah Funk Sheets and Susannah Musser). Born Aug. 24, 1850, Salt Lake City.
Married Ellen McAllister Jan. 1, 1873, Salt Lake City (daughter of John T. D. McAllister and Ellen Handley), who was born Jan. 26, 1853, Salt Lake City. Their children: Roy M.; Ella M.; Florence M.; Rene M.; Scott M.; Louis M.; Bon M.; Kate M. Family home, Salt Lake City.
Worked in U. P. R. R. in Echo Canyon 1869-70. Prominent agriculturist and sheepraiser. Shot to death by highwaymen Dec. 28, 1905.

SHEETS, EDWIN SPENCER (son of Elijah Funk Sheets and Emma Spencer). Born Jan. 23, 1875, Salt Lake City.
Married Alice Taylor Dec. 27, 1899 (daughter of James Taylor and Martha Hurst), who was born Oct. 29, 1876, West Vale, Eng. Their children: Walter T. b. Nov. 2, 1902; Alice T. b. Oct. 19, 1907. Family home, Salt Lake City.
Missionary to northern states 1896-98; bishop of 31st ward at Salt Lake City 1902-08 and also of 33d ward 1911. Graduate of University of Chicago, law department; instructor in Commercial English, L. D. S. Business College 1907-08; principal L. D. S. Business College night school 1910-1913; and principal of L. D. S. Missionary Correspondence school 1912-1913. Attorney and counselor at law.

SHELLEY, JAMES (son of James Boyer Shelley and Elizabeth Bourbon of Claverley, Eng.). Born May 14, 1828, Claverley, Shropshire, Eng. Came to Utah Oct. 3, 1851.
Married Mary Lee Oct. 29, 1852, American Fork, Utah (daughter of Thomas Lee and Mary Hurbace of Oxfordshire, Eng., pioneers Oct. 3, 1852). She was born May 1, 1827. Their children: James M., d. infant; Mary E., m. Charles H. Roberts; Sarah H., m. Amman Mercer; Leo T.,

m. Melissa J. King; Alma G., d. infant; Harriet M., m. Moroni A. Wild; John H., m. Deborah Clements.
Member 144th quorum seventies. Shoemaker. Died Jan. 21, 1907, American Fork, Utah.

SHELLEY, JAMES BOYER. Born Jan. 7, 1792, Claverly, Shropshire, Eng. Came to Utah 1851, Alfred Cardon company.
Married Elizabeth Bourbon at Claverly, Eng. Their children: William, m. Jane Dunn; Thomas, m. Charlotte Elsmore; Martha; James, m. Mary Lee; John, m. Ellen Gibson; Joseph, m. Elizabeth Robinson; Sarah, m. Edward Conder, m. Jacob Varney.
Sawed the first log in American Fork, Utah; lumberman and farmer. Died Nov. 19, 1870, American Fork.

SHELLEY, THOMAS (son of James B. Shelley and Elizabeth Bourbon of Claverley, Eng.). Born April 7, 1822, Claverley. Came to Utah Oct. 3, 1852.
Married Charlotte Elsmore Jan. 18, 1851, at Claverley (daughter of George Fredrick and Elizabeth Elsmore of American Fork, pioneers Oct. 3, 1853). She was born Oct. 3, 1828. Their children: James Edward, m. Margret Hunter; Elizabeth, d. infant; Charlotte, m. Henry J. Buich; Thomas Ammon, m. Jennett Crystal; Emma, d. infant; John Franklin, m. Theodocia Chipman; Mary Ellen, m. George Edward Abel; George Fredrick, m. Mary Ann Jacklin.
High priest. Farmer. Died Sept. 8, 1903, American Fork, Utah.

SHELLEY, STEPHEN (son of William Shelley and Jane Dunn, former born in Parish Cheatton, Shropshire, Eng., and the latter born at Avley, Shropshire, Eng.). He was born Feb. 14, 1849, Bobbington, Eng. Came to Utah Aug. 13, 1852, independent company.
Married Sarah Clegg Feb. 21, 1870, Salt Lake City (daughter of Thomas Clegg and Susannah Redman of Sagerfold, Lancastershire, Eng., pioneers Oct. 8, 1866, Andrew H. Scott company). She was born Aug. 21, 1851. Their children: Eliza Ann, m. Joseph W. G. Wild; Sarah Jane, m. John Thornton; June, m. Arthur Wright; Amy; Stephen T.
Watermaster 22 years. Farmer.

SHELTON, ROBERT (son of George Shelton of England). Born Jan. 5, 1832, in England. Came to Utah October, 1865.
Married Margaret Slother May 20, 1853, in England, who was born May 19, 1834. Their children: Margaret, m. William Heath; Isabelle, m. Samuel Tucker; George, m. Caroline Britain; Sarah, m. Henry F. Heath. Family home, Salt Lake City.
Shoemaker. Died Dec. 4, 1906, Salt Lake City.

SHELTON, STEPHEN, came to Utah 1850, Melvin Ross ox-team company.
Married Abigail Harris, Nauvoo, Ill. Their children: John, m. Mary Martin; Elizabeth, d. infant; Martha Jane, m. James B. Hamilton; Joseph, d. aged 21; Hyrum, m. Emma Sultzer; Stephen, m. Maggie Bonner; Abigail, m. Delbert Hullinger. Family home Provo, Utah.
Seventy. Body guard of the Prophet Joseph Smith. Sealed to the Prophet's family. Farmer. Died 1853, Provo.

SHEPHERD, SAMUEL (son of David Shepherd, born 1759, in Catskill county, N. Y., and Diodama Hopkins). He was born Nov. 10, 1788, in Vermont. Came to Utah Oct. 2, 1847, C. C. Rich company.
Married Roxalana Ray (daughter of William Ray), who died before coming to Utah. Their children: Sarah Adaline b. 1821, m. Charles Garrowtle; Lucelia L. b. 1822, died; Marcus DeLafayette b. Oct. 10, 1824, m. Harriet E. Farnsworth March 9, 1851; Fanny Jane b. June, 1829; Julia Ann b. 1829, m. Sidney Tanner; Rollin Carlos b. Dec. 8, 1830, m. Sarah Smitheon 1851; William Ray, died. Family resided Illinois, Salt Lake City, Utah, and California.
Married Charity Bates 1835 in Jackson county, Mo. (daughter of Walter and Elizabeth Bates, former pioneer 1847). Their only child: Lydia b. Sept. 15, 1836, m. James Jackson Davidson 1851.
Fought in war of 1812.

SHEPHERD, MARCUS DALAFAYETTE (son of Samuel Shepherd and Roxanna Ray). Born Oct. 10, 1824, at Wiloughty, Cuyahoga Co., Ohio. Came to Utah 1849, with a division of Mormon Battalion.
Married Harriet Editha Parrish March 9, 1851, Salt Lake City (daughter of Ezra Parrish and Susannah Sherwin, pioneers November, 1850). She was born Aug. 17, 1831, Brownville, Jefferson county, N. Y. Their children: Charles Henry b. Aug. 10, 1852, died; Mary Elizabeth b. March 24, 1854, m. William Ashworth May 26, 1873; Lyman Andrew b. Feb. 9, 1856, m. Sarah A. Stoney Dec. 4, 1878; Harriet Susannah b. March 26, 1858, m. William H. Farnsworth Aug. 4, 1879; Sarah Caroline b. July 5, 1860, m. Reinhard Maeser 1882; Marcus DeLafayette, Jr. b. Oct. 18, 1862, died; Edna Matilda b. Feb. 29, 1864, m. Heber C. C. Rich; Samuel Ezra b. April 12, 1867, died; Julia Esther b. April 22, 1870,

m. Hyrum Johnson 1873; Henrietta Edith b. June 11, 1872, died. Family home Beaver, Utah.
Married Cedarissa Cartwright Dec. 13, 1869 (daughter of Thomas Henry Cartwright, born in England, and Jane Allen, born in Dublin, Ireland). She was born May 9, 1852, at Cedar City, Utah. Their children: Thomas Oscar b. Nov. 14, 1872; Rhoda Jane b. June 18, 1877, m. Joseph Alma Harris Oct. 10, 1900; Warren b. June 3, 1880, m. Sorepta Bell Leroy June 3, 1904; Carlos b. March 29, 1882; Precinda b. May 23, 1885; Martha Adaline b. Sept. 4, 1889; Willard b. Aug. 25, 1891. Family home Beaver, Utah.
Member Mormon Battalion; bishop of 1st ward in Beaver, Utah; stake counselor in Beaver stake. Mayor of Beaver city.

SHEPHERD, WILLIAM (son of Nathaniel John Shepherd and Mary Andrews). Born May 9, 1827, London, Eng. Came to Idaho September, 1877.
Married Mary Ann Tracey (daughter of Richard Tracey and Sarah Lane), who was born Jan. 5, 1831. Their children: Angelina Emma b. Dec. 27, 1850, m. John Norton; Christina b. Nov. 6, 1852, m. Robert Price; William Nathaniel Budge b. Sept. 18, 1854, m. Emily M. Phippa; Constance Tracey b. July 27, 1856, d. Aug. 21, 1857; Lorenzo Tracey b. July 15, 1858, m. Sarah Clifton; Henry Robert b. May 16, 1860, m. Sophia Poulsen; Edward Tracey b. Feb. 27, 1862, m. Harriet Humpherys, d. June 10, 1911; Joseph Russell b. March 18, 1865, m. Rose Budge; Frederick Tracey b. March 22, 1867, m. Lizzie Morgan; Ernest Arthur Tracey b. May 1, 1870, m. Eliza Lewis; Mary Elizabeth b. Dec. 1, 1871, m. Frank Lewis.
Married Sarah Ellen Humpherys June 22, 1887 (daughter of John J. Humpherys, pioneer John Banks company, 1856, and Hannah Bocock, pioneer March 24, 1856). She was born April 6, 1865. Their children: Leonora May b. July 29, 1888, m. Ezra Jacobson; Estella Victoria b. Aug. 22, 1890, m. John Jaussi June 8, 1911; Alvin Edmund b. March 24, 1892; Vinnie Althura b. Dec. 29, 1893; Edwin Henry b. Dec. 18, 1895; Annie Haines b. Sept. 21, 1897. Family home Paris, Idaho.

SHEPHERD, JOSEPH RUSSELL (son of William Shepherd and Mary Ann Tracey). Born March 18, 1865, Brockenhurst, Eng.
Married Rose Budge Sept. 25, 1884, Logan, Utah (daughter of William Budge and Eliza Jones), who was born June 22, 1866, Providence, Utah. Their children: Joseph Russell, m. Lottie Nye; Alfred William; Clarence, m. Amida Bowen; David, m. Ivy Ford June 12, 1912; Eva Rosselle; Harold; Earl; Louise; Celia; Ruth. Family home Paris, Idaho.
Missionary to California 1895-96; superintendent of Sunday schools Bear Lake stake; president of Bear Lake stake. County commissioner, Bear Lake county, 1906; member of the board of trustees of Academy of Idaho; senator from Bear Lake Co., Idaho, 1913.

SHERMAN, ALBEY LYMAN (son of Lyman Royal Sherman and Delsena Johnson of New York state). Born Oct. 30, 1832. Came to Utah in 1856.
Married Mary Elvira Swan Jan. 10, 1854, Woodriver Center, Iowa (daughter of George Swan and Elizabeth Warrenden of Scotland), who was born Dec. 15, 1835. Their children: Elkinah b. April 29, 1855, died; Mary Elvira b. June 7, 1856, m. Elias H. Cox; Abbey William b. June 4, 1859, m. Annie Eliza Pugson; Lyman Royal b. Dec. 22, 1860, m. Martha E. Jones; Delsena Elizabeth b. May 22, 1862, m. Peter Thomas Furlong; Ellen Viola b. Nov. 23, 1863, m. Elias H. Cox; George Alphonso b. July 23, 1865, m. Temperance Eliza Brasher; Don Franklin b. Sept. 6, 1867; Susia Julia b. May 6, 1869, m. Miller Snow Black; Anlo Lionel b. Jan. 5, 1871, m. Agnes Gorden; David Edgar b. Aug. 28, 1872; Gertrude Estell b. Oct. 18, 1874, m. Robert James Gorden; Joel Elmer b. June 19, 1876, m. Martha Maria Robins; Ada C. b. Aug. 15, 1879, m. Elum L. Jones.
High priest and missionary. Farmer and stockgrower. Died Sept. 18, 1910, at Huntington.

SHERMAN, GEORGE ALPHONSO (son of Albey Lyman Sherman and Mary E. Swan). Born July 23, 1865, Fountain Green, Utah.
Married Temperance Eliza Brasher July 23, 1891, Huntington, Utah (daughter of John L. Brasher and Eliza Chuser of Kentucky), who was born Nov. 14, 1892, died; Stella Eliza; Vida Mearl. Family home Huntington, Utah.
Missionary to Georgia 1904-06; ward teacher 15 years; counselor to superintendent of Y. M. M. I. A.; counselor to conference president in Georgia. Stockgrower and fruitraiser.

SHIELDS, GEORGE (son of James Shields and Elizabeth Blackburn of Paisley, Scotland, former came to Utah 1874). Born Aug. 15, 1828, Paisley. Came to Utah Oct. 6, 1853, Appleton Harmon company.
Married Jane Carday 1848, Johnston, Scotland (daughter of Albert Carday and Margaret Craig, former died in Scotland, latter pioneer 1853, Appleton Harmon company, died of Johnston, Scotland). She was born May 17, 1828. Their children: James, m. Elizabeth Dow; Martha Soffe; Margaret and George, died; Elizabeth, m. Joseph A. Beckstead; Margaret J., m. James A. Abbott; William John, m. Elizabeth Huskey; Sarah B., m. William Soffe; David A., m. Sarah Beckstead, m. Elizabeth Shepick; George W., m. Mary

E. Stocking; Isabell J., m. Ensign Woodruff; Joseph A., died; three children died before being named. Family home West Jordan, Utah.
Paid for bringing 33 immigrants from the old country; made four trips across the plains for immigrants. Weaver; farmer; sheepraiser. Died April 19, 1908, Salt Lake City.

SHIELDS, GEORGE W. (son of George Shields and Jane Carday). Born Oct. 27, 1865, West Jordan, Utah.
Married Mary E. Stocking September, 1888, West Jordan (daughter of Ensign Israel Stocking and Elizabeth Ellen Arnold, former of Springfield, Mass., latter of Herefordshire, Eng., pioneers 1850). She was born June 15, 1869. Their children: Wallace b. 1889, m. Clema Gardner; Jennie b. 1891, m. Donald Gardner; Leonard b. 1898; Claudia b. April, 1901; Arnold b. 1903; Gladys b. 1907, died; Utahna b. 1910. Family home South Jordan, Utah.
Farmer; sheepraiser. Died Feb. 1, 1912, Salt Lake City.

SHIELDS, JOHN (son of Robert Shields, born June 22, 1781, in Scotland, and Mary Melvin). Born April 3, 1805, Renfrewshire, Scotland. Came to Utah Oct. 12, 1852.
Married Primrose Cunningham, who was born Sept. 17, 1805. Their children: Mary b. Oct. 29, 1827, m. James Bevan; Annie b. July 11, 1827; Robert b. March 16, 1831, m. Mary Jenkins; Archibald b. Aug. 16, 1833, m. Helen Gillespie; John b. March 10, 1835, and Primrose b. May 21, 1837, died; Primrose b. July 7, 1840, m. Thomas Lee; John b. Jan. 22, 1842, m. Jane Meiklejohn.

SHIELDS, JOHN F. (son of Samuel Shields of Beaver county, Pa.). Born Feb. 3, 1823, in Beaver county, Pa. Came to Utah 1849.
Married Mary Howell July 1, 1847, Springfield, Ill. (daughter of Samuel and Mary Howell of Springfield), who was born June 21, 1825. Their children: James F. b. Jan. 11, 1850, d. child; John T. b. May 7, 1852; Sarah Jane b. Sept. 29, 1854, m. Jeremiah Plumb; m. John A. Powell; Louis b. Aug. 22, 1856, m. Annie White; Rhoda b. June 2, 1859. m. David Taylor; Martha b. Nov 19, 1863, m. Horace Jones; Mary Eliza b. April 27, 1866, m. Charles McKendrick; Rachel M. b. Nov. 12, 1869, m. Samuel T. Gardener. Family home Salem, Utah.
Married Eliza Ann 1870, at Salt Lake City. Their children: Faithful, m. Mr. Mathis; Brigham; Franklin. Family home Gila River, Ariz.
Presiding elder at Salem, Utah. Veteran Black Hawk Indian war. Justice of peace several years. Farmer and apiarist. Died Nov. 9, 1908, Puyma, Ariz.

SHIRTS, PETER (parents resided at Nauvoo, Ill.). Born Aug. 6, 1800, in Pennsylvania. Came to Utah Aug. 1, 1850, oxteam company.
Married Margaret Cameron (parents resided in Pennsylvania), who was born in 1810. Their children: George b. May 13, 1832, m. Elizabeth Barney; Derias b. July 8, 1833; Moroni b. Nov. 30, 1834, died; Don Carlos b. July 27, 1836, m. Mary Lee, m. Elizabeth Barney; Sariah b. Dec. 27, 1838, m. William McDonald; Elizabeth Ann b. Feb. 15, 1849, m. William McDonald.
Married Belaney White. Their children: Elsa b. Dec. 6, 1854, m. Reese Richards; Peter b. March 27, 1856, m. Belle Reynolds; Eliza b. April 15, 1858.
One of the leaders of the Nauvoo Legion. Helped build the Nauvoo Temple and was closely associated with Joseph Smith. Brigham Young and other leaders of the church. Appointed by Brigham Young to locate different parts of the country suitable for settlement and where agriculture was good.

moreland county, Pa. Their children: Sarah Ann; Nancy Jane; Manda Maria; Margaret Eliza, m. Mr. Clement; Alexander Morain; Miriam Elizabeth; Heber Taylor; Margeory America. Family home Plain City, Utah.
Farmer. Died April 20, 1872.

SHORT, WILLIAM JOHN (son of Stephen Short and Miss Adams of Devonshire, Eng.). Came to Utah 1864.
Married Elizabeth Curtis Oct. 27, 1834, St. Mary's Parish, Islington, Eng. (daughter of William Curtis and Elizabeth Dobney Holt—married 1802, in London, latter pioneer Sept. 4, 1863, Captain Patterson company). She was born Aug. 8, 1807. Their children: William Sephen, m. Fannie Swift; Elizabeth Dobncy, m. Philander Brown; Charles, m. Ann Krestine Nielesen; Samuel Joseph, m. Isabelle Clayton; Mary Ann, m. Joseph Bull, m. J. M. Palmer. Family home, Salt Lake City.
Elder. Butcher. Died April 30, 1878.

SHULDBERG, WILLIAM ANDERSON (son of Peter Adolph Sköldberg, born Feb. 19, 1844, and Anna Anderson, born March 16, 1837, of Munkfors, Mestman Lan, Sweden—married February, 1865). He was born Dec. 1, 1873, Munkfors, Sweden.
Married Sarah Jane Hansen June 22, 1898 (daughter of Hans Peter Hansen, pioneer 1864, John Smith company, and Cecilia Maria Thompson, married Nov. 25, 1872, Salt Lake City). She was born June 22, 1879. Their children: Leroy b. April 3, 1899; Linney b. April 11, 1901; William b. April 7, 1904; Anna b. Oct. 29, 1906; Elva b. May 1, 1909; Haward b. Jan. 31, 1912. Family home Winder, Idaho.
Bishop's counselor; bishop of Winder ward. President Winder Telephone Co.; director and president of reservoir and canal company.

SHUMWAY, CHARLES (son of Samuel and Polly Shumway of Sturbridge, Worcester county, Mass.). Born Aug. 1, 1806, Oxford, Mass. Came to Utah July 24, 1847, Brigham Young company.
Married Julia Ann Hooker, at Sturbridge (daughter of Samuel Hooker and Polly Nichols of Sturbridge, pioneers July 24, 1847, Brigham Young company). She was born Nov. 28, 1807. Their children: Andrew P., m. Amanda Graham; Mary E., m. Charles Westover; Charles Samuel, d. infant; Harriet, d. child. Family home, Salt Lake City.
Married Louisa Minerly 1845, Nauvoo, Ill. Their children: Catherine, d. infant; Charles M., m. Sarah Jardine. m. Agnes Jardine; Robert; Peter; Joseph, d. infant; Louisa Adalisa, d. infant; Levi. Family home Shumway, Navajo county, Ariz.
Married Henrietta Bird, Salt Lake City (daughter of Charles and Mary Ann Bird of Cottonwood and Mendon, Utah, pioneers 1850). Their children: George A., m. Elizabeth Ann Nuttall; Mormon Bird, m. Sarah Ann Evert; David Spencer Bird, m. Lizzie Ann Baker; Hyrum Bird, m. Annie P. Johnson; Brigham Bird, d. infant; Samuel Bird, m. Sarah Ann Potter; Charles Bird, m. Eliza Johnson; Jedediah Grant, m. Elizabeth Robison; Bradford, died; William, m. Lilly Glazier. Family home Kansb, Kane Co., Utah.
Married Elizabeth Jardine October, 1861, Salt Lake City. Their children: Julia Ann, m. Nephi Johnson; James; Richard, m. Miss Johnson; Howard; Melinda, m. Mr. Johnson. Family home Shumway, Ariz.
Missionary to Massachusetts twice; high priest. Member first legislature of Utah. Carpenter; farmer. First emigrant from Nauvoo to cross Mississippi river. Died May 21, 1898.

SHUMWAY, ANDREW P. (son of Charles Shumway and Julia Ann Hooker). Born Feb. 20, 1833, Millbury, Worcester county, Mass. Came to Utah July 24, 1847, Brigham

SHUMWAY, CHARLES MENDON (son of Andrew P. Shumway and Mary Ann Christian). Born 1872, Mendon, Utah. Married Caroline Hymas September, 1898, Logan, Utah (daughter of Benjamin Hymas and Hanna Thurston), who was born Nov. 20, 1877, Hyde Park, Utah. Their children: Hattie b. Oct. 8, 1899; Earl H. b. Dec. 3, 1901; Quentin H. b. June 24, 1904; Annoria b. Sept. 29, 1906; Nettie b. July 20, 1909; Kermit b. Dec. 31, 1911. Ordained bishop 1910. Farmer; stockraiser.

SHUMWAY, SAMUEL BIRD (son of Charles Shumway and Henrietta Bird). Born June 30, 1856, Little Cottonwood, Utah. Married Sarah Ann Potter Feb. 3, 1885, Kanab, Kane Co., Utah (daughter of William George Potter and Artemishia Minerva Washburn of Kanab). She was born Nov. 9, 1866. Their children: Henrietta Pearl b. Jan. 27, 1886, m. Andrew Anderson June 14, 1907; Samuel Douglas b. March 8, 1888; Beatrice b. Oct. 14, 1890, m. Norman Draper June 10, 1908; Bradford b. Dec. 10, 1892; William b. July 22, 1894; Artemishla b. July 30, 1898; Melvin b. Nov. 7, 1906; Afton b. March 8, 1908. Family home Vineyard, Utah. Road supervisor at Vineyard. Farmer; stockraiser.

SHURTLEFF, EMERSON (son of Vincent Shurtleff and Elizabeth Loomis). Born 1839, Westfield, Mass. Came to Utah 1847, Brigham Young company. Married Mary Ann Tribe 1858, Salt Lake City (daughter of George Tribe and Sarah Ann Mates of Ogden), who was born Aug. 24, 1842. Their children: Annie, m. Edwin Williams; Lettie, m. John Douglas; Emerson, m. Ida Burton; Sarah Elizabeth, d. aged 6. Family home Salt Lake City. Freighter. Died Aug. 16, 1868, Salt Lake City.

SHURTLEFF, VINCENT (son of E. Shurtleff and Susan Gorham of Russell Hampden county, Mass., born 1776, at same place). Born May 14, 1814. Came to Utah 1847. Married Elizabeth Loomis Oct. 27, 1836, at Russell, Mass. (daughter of Mr. Loomis and Patience Root), who was born March 19, 1816. Their children; Lucy Avirea S. b. Jan. 8, 1838, died; Emmerson Davis b. July 29, 1839, m. Mary Ann Trilie; Harrison Tuttle b. Jan. 1, 1841, m. Nellie Smith 1863; Hyrum Chester b. Nov. 29, 1845, m. Ellen Cressmon 1867; Buson b. April 15, 1847, died; Albert Dewey b. May 25, 1849, m. Ofidia Stoddard April 11, 1872; Mary Elizabeth b. Dec. 18, 1851, died; Laura Celistia b. Aug. 25, 1855, m. Gilbert Webb Jr. Oct 16, 1874; Vincent Haswell b. Sept. 2, 1859, m. Elizabeth Cory Hickerson Aug. 10, 1890. Married Mary Hadlock Brockway Oct. 22, 1847, Salt Lake City, who was born Nov. 2, 1821, Waterford, Caledonia county, Vt. Their children: Lyman Elisha b. Sept. 2, 1848, d. Jan. 20, 1883; Luther Gorham b. Dec. 11, 1849, d. Nov. 10, 1850; Martha Maria b. April 2, 1852, m. Melvin Miller Feb. 12, 1872; Brigham Young b. Oct. 2, 1854, m. Mary Augusta Clinton Nov. 20, 1877; Vincent b. Aug. 20, 1857, m. Sarah E. Brinton Jan. 17, 1881; Mary Emma b. June 19, 1860, d. Oct. 12, 1865; George Washington b. April 6, 1862, m. Alice Elvira Cook July 3, 1888. Married Elizabeth Tophan Dec. 4, 1850, Salt Lake City (daughter of John Tophan and Jane Tophan, latter pioneer 1848, Bishop Evans company). She was born June 10, 1833, Eden Saken, Bedfordshire, Eng. Their children: Sarah Jane b. Nov. 23, 1851, m. Charles A. Smith Dec. 25, 1874; Emily b. Feb. 27, 1856, m. Philip Goffney; Heber Rimbek b. Aug. 5, 1854; Frank b. April 19, 1855; Eliza Alvira b. March 3, 1860; John Tophan b. Dec. 26, 1861; Harrold Bexter b. Dec. 8, 1862; last five died; Hannah b. Oct. 2, 1864, m. William Johnston Sept. 11, 1893; William b. Dec. 3, 1866, m. Annie Williams April 12, 1889; John b. Aug. 1869, d. Feb. 10, 1875. Family home Mill Creek, Salt Lake county. Married Lydia Amanda Shurtliff Dec. 9, 1854, Salt Lake City (daughter of Luman Shurtliff), who was born Aug. 1, 1838, Far West, Caldwell county, Mo. Their children: Louis Vincent b. July 23, 1857, m. Alice Harriet Casto Jan. 29, 1881; Haskell b. Feb. 18, 1862, d. Nov. 23, 1864; Charles H. b. Dec. 30, 1868, m. Florence Odekirk Dec. 13, 1893. Family home, Salt Lake City. Missionary to England 1851. School trustee in Mill Creek; helped to build first adobe school houses. Farmer and stockraiser.

SHURTLEFF, HARRISON TUTTLE (son of Vincent Shurtleff and Elizabeth Loomis). Born Jan. 1, 1841, Russell, Hampden county, Mass. Came to Utah 1847 with parents. Married Nellie Smith Feb. 14, 1863, Salt Lake City (daughter of Noah Smith, born April 14, 1803, and Mary DeForest, born Feb. 20, 1816, pioneers 1862, Ansel P. Harmon company). She was born Feb. 13, 1843, New Conard, Conn. Their children: Nellie Elizabeth b. Sept. 4, 1864, m. Joseph Morgan Jan. 12, 1881; Harrison Smith b. Dec. 7, 1867, m. Rachael Park Oct. 17, 1889; Edgar DeForest b. April 23, 1870, m. Josephine Sinclair July 25, 1892; Mary Ella b. Sept. 22, 1874, m. Charles Bell Nov. 28, 1895; Le Roy b. Oct. 10, 1878; Arthur Thomas b. April 20, 1882, m. Marian Ellen Hamilton June 15, 1910. Missionary. At the age of six years drove two yoke of oxen throughout the entire journey en route to Utah. School trustee for 17 years. Assisted in bringing immigrants to Utah.

SHURTLIFF, LUMAN ANDRUS (son of Noah Shurtliff and Lydia Brown of Ravenna, Portage Co., Ohio). Born March 13, 1807, Montgomery, Hampden county, Mass. Came to Utah Sept. 27, 1851, captain his own company. Married Eunice Baggs Gaylord, Ravenna, Portage Co., Ohio (daughter of John Gaylord and Joanna Baggs of Portage Co., Ohio). Their children: Elcemina Imogene, m. Haskell V. Shurtliff; Marcy Eliza, m. Pleasant G. Taylor; Lewis Warren, m. Louisa C. Smith; m. Emily M. Wainwright; Lydia Ann; Lydia Manda, m. Vincent Shurtleff; Jane Narcissus, m. Pleasant G. Taylor; Elizabeth Hatch, m. Isaiah L. Steward. Family home Harreville, Utah. Married Altamira Gaylord, who was born Aug. 7, 1816, Westfield, Mass. and died July 30, 1883. Their children: Noah Luman b. Nov. 25, 1846, d. June 19, 1892; Ellen Cordelia b. March 14, 1849; Francis Marion b. Jan. 23, 1851; m. Alta Priscilla Hancock; m. Betsy Jane Hancock; Lucy Ann b. Sept. 16, 1853, d. Jan. 13, 1866; Charles Vinson b. Jan. 26, 1856; Samuel Darwin b. March 9, 1858, d. March 9, 1858. Family resided Springville and Ogden, Utah. Home missionary in Weber county. Member state legislature. Settled in Weber county. Farmer; brickmason. Died at Harrisville, Utah.

SHURTLIFF, LEWIS WARREN (son of Luman Andrus Shurtliff and Eunice Baggs Gaylord). Born July 24, 1835, Sullivan, Ashland Co., Ohio. Came to Utah Sept. 27, 1851, with father. Married Louisa Catherine Smith Jan. 4, 1856, at Salmon River Colony (daughter of Addison Smith, and adopted daughter of David and Susan Moore, who were pioneers 1849, Allen Taylor company). She was born 1841, and died 1866. Their children: Laura Jane b. Dec. 27, 1858, m. Franklin D. Richardson; Lewis Chester b. Aug. 19, 1860, m. Almeda Raymond; Haskell Heber b. Jan. 27, 1863, m. Annie Folkman; Louisa Catherine A. b. May 8, 1866, m. Myron Richardson. Married Emily Moorfield Wainwright April 10, 1872, Salt Lake City (daughter of William B. Wainwright and Eliza Moorfield of Mansfield, Nottinghamshire, Eng., former pioneer 1869, latter came to Utah 1873). She was born Dec. 16, 1851. Their children: Louie Emily b. June 16, 1876, m. Joseph F. Smith, Jr.; John W. b. Sept. 5, 1881, m. Lillian Gundy Anderson; Luman Andrus b. March 27, 1883; William M. b. Sept. 8, 1885; Frank E. b. Jan. 13, 1892. Families resided Ogden, Utah. Settled in Weber county. Lieutenant in cavalry minute company. Moved in 1855 to the Salmon river mission. Assisted in bringing immigrants to Utah 1863. Member 60th quorum seventies; missionary to Great Britain 1866; bishop of Plain City ward 1868-83; president Weber stake 1883. Commissioner of Weber county 1872-86; member constitutional convention, and also of the territorial legislature 1886; probate judge of Weber county; county commissioner 1889-94; served in the upper house of the state legislature 1896 and 1898. Closely connected with the Trans-Mississippi Commercial Congress, and also the National Irrigation Congress. Postmaster of Ogden 1909-13.

SHURTLIFF, FRANCIS MARION (son of Luman Andrus Shurtliff and Altamira Gaylord). Born Jan. 23, 1851, Springville, Pottawattamie Co., Iowa. Married Alta Priscilla Hancock Nov. 22, 1872, Salt Lake City (daughter of Charles B. Hancock and Samantha P. Rawson of Payson, Utah, pioneers 1847). She was born Dec. 23, 1853. Their children: S. Eva b. May 22, 1874, m. A. J. Bell; Franklin M. b. Feb. 16, 1876, m. Marie A. Halbert; Asel E. b. March 14, 1878, m. Olive Halverson; Edith V. b. July 17, 1880, m. W. Frank Owens; Arnold R. b. Oct. 24, 1882, m. Ruth Richardson; Perry L. b. July 30, 1885; Lorenzo J. b. Jan. 5, 1887; Alta E. b. March 18, 1891. Married Betsy Jane Hancock Nov. 14, 1878, Salt Lake City (daughter of George W. Hancock and B. J. Fackrell, Salt Lake City and Payson, Utah, pioneers October, 1849). She was born Feb. 22, 1851, Woods Cross, Utah. Their children: George Luman b. Oct. 19, 1879; Leo Earl b. Jan. 10, 1881, m. Ann Janet Stowell; Charles Lewis b. April 6, 1884, m. Julia Larson; Daniel Ray b. Sept. 3, 1886, m. Myrtle Ballard; Francis Wayne b. Dec. 28, 1887, m. Jeanett Davidson; David Vernon b. Feb. 19, 1891. Families resided Logan, Utah.

SILCOCK, NICHOLAS THOMAS (son of John Silcock of Handley, Staffordshire, Eng., born April 2, 1772, Marsden, Montgomery, Derbyshire, Eng., and Ann Cook of Blythafield, Staffordshire, born July 14, 1779, Blythsfield—married Dec. 29, 1800). He was born Sept. 29, 1819, at Handley. Came to Utah Oct. 4, 1850, Bishop Edward Hunter company. Married Jane Heath April, 1841 (daughter of John Heath, who died in Handley 1841, and Barbara Hulme, who died at Winter Quarters 1846). She was born Nov. 6, 1826, and came to Utah with husband. Their children: Alma b. Feb. 6, 1842, m. Mary Ann Hudson Aug. 2, 1863; Elizabeth J. and Barbara Ann, died; Thomas b. Dec. 4, 1849, m. Annie Oasther April 1877; Martha b. April 30, 1852, m. Robert Pinton Jan. 1869; Esther b. March 25, 1854, m. Joseph Draper Dec. 1873; Rosena b. Jan. 27, 1856, m. Robert Dansie 1875; Almira b. April 4, 1858, m. Alice Henderson 1874; Sarah b. Nov. 5, 1859, m. William Bowlden 1883; Paulina b. Oct. 4, 1861, m. Robert Dansie 1880; John Walter b. Aug. 17, 1863, d. Nov. 1881; Nina D. b. July 25, 1865, m. C. N. Dansie; Nicholas Henry b. Aug. 13, 1867, m. Minnie Brown 1903; William Hulme b. Sept. 8, 1869, m. Margret Dansie 1893; Samuel Ephi b. Sept. 5, 1871, d. 1881. Married Harriet Bebington April, 1855, Salt Lake City

(daughter of Thomas Bebington and Martha Reed), who was born Feb. 1, 1814, Bulkley, Chestershire, Eng., and came to Utah in 1854. Family home Riverton, Utah.
Assisted in construction of South Jordan canal; raised first crop of grain 1867; pioneer Salt Lake and Tooele counties.

SILCOCK, NICHOLAS HENRY (son of Nicholas Thomas Silcock and Jane Heath). Born Aug. 13, 1867.
Married Minnie Brown (Calient) June 10, 1903, Riverton, Utah (daughter of Henry and Elizabeth Ann Brown), who was born in 1879. Their children: Thomas Calient b. 1897 (adopted); Estella Calient b. 1900 (adopted); Eva Jane b. April 27, 1904; Farrell Henry b. June 25, 1909; Ella b. Aug. 1911. Family home, Riverton.
Farmer.

SILL, JOHN (son of John Sill and Edith Dennis of New Egypt, N. J.). Born Jan. 19, 1816, New Egypt. Came to Utah Sept. 29, 1856, oxteam.
Married Sarah Morris 1851, at New Egypt (daughter of Abraham Morris and Hannah Johns of New Egypt), who was born April 8, 1826. Their children: Elizabeth Ann b. March 13, 1853, m. Joseph E. Hodson; Edith b. 1855, died; Maria b. June 22, 1857, m. Lorenzo Dow Imlay; John Heber and Daniel Rush (twins) b. March 5, 1859; Daniel Rush, died; John Heber, m. Martina Anderson; Howard Ivins b. Dec. 14, 1863, died.
Married Elizabeth Kirkham Feb. 27, 1864, Salt Lake City (daughter of Thomas Kirkham and Elizabeth Duerden of Preston, Lancastershire, Eng., pioneers Aug. 29, 1852, Lewis Brunson company). She was born April 2, 1845. Their children: William Henry b. May 25, 1865; Joseph Albert b. Jan. 11, 1867, m. Marietta Welling; Mary Elizabeth b. Feb. 4, 1869; Robert Wilford and Ann Eliza (twins) b. Nov. 1, 1870; David Morris b. Dec. 23, 1871, m. Rose E. Webster; George b. Jan. 27, 1875; Charles b. Sept. 15, 1876, m. Mary E. Nalder; Jesse b. Aug. 3, 1878, m. Minnie Lundberg; Arthur Thomas b. March 18, 1881; Daniel Ephraim b. April 11, 1883. Family home Kaysville, Utah.
High priest. Farmer; stockraiser; fruitgrower. Died Oct. 25, 1906.

SILL, JOSEPH ALBERT (son of John Sill and Elizabeth Kirkham). Born Jan. 11, 1867, Kaysville, Utah.
Married Marietta Welling Aug. 29, 1894, Salt Lake City (daughter of Job Welling and Marietta Holmes of Farmington, Utah, pioneers Sept. 29, 1856, Edmund Ellsworth and Daniel D. McArthur handcart companies). She was born April 5. 1875. Their children: Joseph Ralph b. July 17, 1895; Mabel b. March 23, 1898; Marietta b. Feb. 9, 1901; Sterling W. b. March 31, 1903; Russell W. b. Aug. 24, 1905; Marguerite and Genevieve (twins) b. Nov. 5, 1908; Laura b. Feb. 15, 1912. Family home Layton, Utah.
Elder and high priest. School teacher 11 years. Farmer and orchardist. Attended college and University of Utah; now studying medicine.

SILVER, WILLIAM JOHN (son of William Wright Silver, born Feb. 23, 1802, Yarmouth, and Miriam Healley Ives, born April 19, 1800, Yarmouth; moved to London, Eng.). He was born Sept. 1, 1832, in London. Came to Utah Sept. 16, 1859, Edward Stevenson company.
Married Mary Askie Dec. 5, 1852, in London, later in Endowment House. Salt Lake City, Brigham Young officiating (daughter of William John Askie and Rosannah Bagger of London). She was born Oct. 22, 1829, and died June 2, 1862. Their children: William A. b. Dec. 8, 1853, d. Oct. 2, 1855; John A. b. Aug. 7, 1855, m. Orthena Pratt; Joseph A. b. July 13, 1857, m. Ellen Watson; Hyrum A. b. April 25, 1859, m. Elenora K. Benzon; Mary A., d. Nov. 12, 1863.
Married Hannah Sims (Swetman) Aug. 2, 1862, Salt Lake City (daughter of George Sims and Mary Wilkinson of Lancastershire, Eng.). She was born Oct. 24, 1825, and died in 1878.
Married Elizabeth Price Sept. 28, 1863, Salt Lake City (daughter of Thomas Price and Mary Ann Platts of Coalkolton, Worcestershire, Eng.). She was born June 11, 1835, and died Sept. 1, 1869. Their children: Elizabeth F., d. child; Mariam P., d. aged 23; Mary Ann, m. Roll Harding.
Married Althea Jones Sept. 7, 1867, Salt Lake City (daughter of Henry Jones and Caroline Brooks of Upper Housel, Worcestershire, Eng., pioneers Nov. 4, 1855, Milo Andrus company). She was born Sept. 3, 1851. Their children: Althea J., m. John Sheets; William J., d. aged 1 year; George J., m. Maria Meredith; Francis J., m. Alice Godfrey; Josephine J., d. aged 13; Caroline J., m. Alma Bachman; Henry J., d. aged 1 year; Laura J., m. William Bachman.
Married Mary Louisa Pile Oct. 12, 1870, Salt Lake City (daughter of Alexander Pile and Sarah Clark of Medford, Somerset, Eng.). She was born July 27, 1836, and died May 11, 1912. Their children: William P., m. Miss Pratt; Mary P., drowned aged 1 year. Families resided Salt Lake City.
Married Ann Brookes March 19, 1880, Salt Lake City (daughter of George Brookes and Mary Arminger of Leigh Parish, Worcestershire, Eng.). She was born May 3, 1834.

SILVER, JOHN A. (son of William John Silver and Mary Askie). Born Aug. 7, 1855, on the Atlantic ocean.
Married Orthena Pratt Nov. 25, 1880, Salt Lake City (daughter of Orson Pratt and Adelian Bishop, pioneers July 21, 1847, Brigham Young company). She was born Oct. 31, 1863. Their children: John Raymond, died; Eugenie, m. Quayle Cannon; Orson Pratt and Orthena Pratt, died; Glenn; Algina: Edith; Leland.
Married Nellie Clawson (Brown) (daughter of Hirum Bradley Clawson and Emily Augusta Young, former came to Utah, latter born in Salt Lake City). She was born May 19, 1872, Salt Lake City. Their children: William John b. April 1, 1905; Mary Askie b. Jan. 20, 1907, died; Hirum Clawson b. July 21, 1908; John Clawson b. Feb. 23, 1911.
Member 109th quorum seventies. Vice-president and general manager Lethbridge Iron Works, Limited. Prominent farmer. Engineer; mechanic.
By a former marriage Nellie Clawson became the mother of these children: Leigh Richmond Brown and Nellie Louine Brown b. Dec. 4, 1892, latter died; Thedora Beatty b. Jan. 10, 1895.

SILVER, HYRUM A. (son of William John Silver and Mary Askie). Born April 25, 1859, Brooklyn, N. Y.
Married Elenora K. Benzon Nov. 6, 1879, Salt Lake City (daughter of Andrew B. Benzon of Denmark and Kathrine Wickle of Pennsylvania). Their children: Nova, m. Robert Runswick; Hyrum B.; Kathrine. m. Melvin B. Johnson; May; Rene; Eleanor K., d. Feb. 10, 1896. Family home, Salt Lake City.
Married May McAllister at Salt Lake City (daughter of John D. L. McAllister and Matilda C. Nielsen). Their children: Amy; Walter; Theodore; Helen; Jean.
High priest. President and manager H. A. Silver Foundry & Machine Company; formerly part owner and vice-president of Silver Brothers' Iron Works.

SIMKINS, CHARLES. Born March 25, 1798, in Lancastershire, Eng. Came to Utah 1850, Abraham O. Smoot merchandise train.
Married Rachel Hawthorne in Staffordshire, Eng. (daughter of William Hawthorne of Staffordshire). Their children: James; Daniel; Charles, Jr.; Hezekiah; William; Rosten; Isaiah; Eliza Charlotte; Joseph. Family home Beaver, Utah.
Seventy. Carpenter; farmer. Died March 13, 1875, at Beaver.

SIMKINS, JOSEPH (son of Charles Simkins and Rachel Hawthorne). Born Dec. 4, 1842, in Lancastershire, Eng. Came to Utah with father.
Married Charlotte Elena Lundblad Oct. 18, 1867, Beaver, Utah (daughter of Hans Lundblad and Karstie Mortenson of Beaver, pioneers September, 1855, first oxtrain company). She was born May 12, 1851. Their children: Emma Elizabeth b. Oct. 25, 1869, m. Joseph Neilson; Rachel Charlotte b. Jan. 26, 1872, died; Joseph Charles b. Jan. 21, 1874, m. Ida Hardy; Rosten Lundblad b. March 24, 1876, m. Ella Veater (died), m. Mae Dailey; James Willard b. June 21, 1878, m. Clara Gillies; Marion Andrew b. Oct. 9, 1881, m. Nora Dailey; Daniel H. b. Jan. 5, 1883, m. Annie Wiley; Augus Le Roy b. Oct. 17, 1886; Ellen Vilate b. March 7, 1889, m. Otto Roundy; Edgar L. b. Sept. 11, 1891; Vern and Vera b. Nov. 13, 1894, died; Clarence b. June 9, 1896. Family resided Beaver and Circleville, Utah.
Sunday school superintendent; first counselor to Bishop J. E. Peterson. Farmer.

SIMMONS, LEVEN. Born Aug. 1, 1812, in Mead county, Ky. Came to Utah 1847, Captain Howell oxteam company.
Married Harriet Bradford (daughter of George and Sarah Bradford), who was born March 30, 1821, in Jefferson county, Ill. Their children: Samuel b. 1838, m. Guiety Hilman; Sarah Jane b. 1840, m. William J. Warren 1853; Jonathan b. 1842, m. Betsy Sumerville; Leven, Jr., b. 1844, m. Luna Spencer; Matthew b. 1846, m. Lyda C. Butler; Levi b. 1848, m. Mary Powell; Lizzie b. 1850, m. Pratt Pace; Harriet b. 1854, m. Hubard Tuttle 1872; Mariah b. 1857, m. Andrew Ferguson; Ammon b. 1860, m. Elizabeth Thomas 1885; Albert b. Sept. 11, 1866.
Married Lydia Fisher, Spanish Fork, Utah, in 1856. Their children: Vard John, m. Jennie Steward; Benjamin F., m. Ann Warner; William R., m. Martha Warner; Andrew J., m. Aggie Bellos; Almond Charles, m. Miss Coyle; Sadie E., m. Charles Forsyth; Fannie E., m. Charles Steward. Families resided Spanish Fork.
Indian war veteran. Served in Echo Canyon war. Died at Spanish Fork.

SIMMONS, AMMON (son of Leven Simmons and Harriet Bradford). Born in 1860.
Married Elizabeth Thomas Feb. 5, 1885, at Spanish Fork (daughter of William and Betsey Thomas), who was born in 1860. Their children: David G. b. Nov. 13, 1885; Albert T. b. Jan. 20, 1887; Lucy b. Jan. 16, 1888; Dorley b. Apr. 13, 1889; Ethel b. April 2, 1892; Mary Ann b. Dec. 2, 1893; Caroline b. March 28, 1895; Samuel b. Dec. 13, 1897; Cora b. Aug. 13, 1899; Ruth b. June 27, 1902.

Married Martha Dixon Oct. 11, 1846 (daughter of Charles Dixon, who died at Rock Island, Ill., in 1854, en route to Utah, and Elizabeth Humphrey—married Oct. 13, 1799, Sackville, N. B.). She was born June 27, 1825, and came to Utah with husband. Their children: Ada A. and Ida F. b. June 20, 1847; Elizabeth A. b. June 26, 1849, m. Thomas A. Wimmer April 21, 1866; Edward b. Oct. 22, 1854, m. Julia Collett Oct. 11, 1874; Orrawell, Jr., b. Dec. 27, 1859, m. Mary F. Brewerton Sept. 4, 1884; Martha b. March 10, 1862, m. Lyman Kappie Nov. 10, 1881; Albert Lee b. Aug. 15, 1863, m. Elizabeth Knight July 4, 1884; Enos Wells b. Jan. 20, 1866, m. Elizabeth Pickering Sept. 1, 1886; Major Gustavus b. Sept. 16, 1867, d. child.
Married Jane Tenney, who was born Dec. 7, 1824. Their children: Emma Jane, d. child; Grant.
Married Kate Baldwin July 2, 1864, Salt Lake City (daughter of David Baldwin and Elizabeth Cole, latter pioneer 1861, John Murdock company—married 1821, Birmingham, Eng.). She was born May 31, 1847, at Birmingham. Their children: Ruth Elversa b. March 24, 1867, m. David Brewerton March 11, 1885; Kate b. Feb. 25, 1869, m. George Williams April 3, 1887; Viola Lucile b. July 25, 1870; Hyrum Greely b. April 25, 1872; Charles Buell b. March 13, 1874; Minnie Jane b. Jan. 8, 1876; Frank b. Dec. 4, 1879; Ezra Ord b. Oct. 13, 1882, m. Effie Mary Madison Sept. 13, 1904; Omer b. Nov. 24, 1885.
Families resided Payson, Utah.
High priest; counselor to Bishop John B. Fairbanks; acting bishop of Payson ward 1871. City councilman of Payson 1861-62; mayor of Payson 1867-74. Built two flour mills.

SIMONS, EDWARD (son of Orrawell Simons and Martha Dixon). Born Oct. 22, 1854, Spanish Fork, Utah.
Married Julia Collett Oct. 11, 1874, Payson, Utah (daughter of Robert Collett and Caroline Pickles, pioneers 1851, Captain Hooper company). She was born Feb. 10, 1855, at Payson. Their children: Edward b. July 14, 1875; Robert Orrawell b. May 18, 1877, m. Clara Oberhansly April 7, 1897; Pearl b. Dec. 19, 1879, died; Delpha b. June 15, 1882; Lynn b. June 4, 1886; Ruby b. April 5, 1889; Iliff b. Oct. 19, 1891; Guy b. Sept. 9, 1895. Family home, Payson.

SIMONS, ROBERT ORRAWELL (son of Edward Simons and Julia Collett). Born May 15, 1877, Payson, Utah.
Married Clara Oberhansly April 7, 1897 (daughter of Ferdinand Oberhansly and Mary Staheli), who was born April 13, 1878, Payson, Utah. Their children: Daisy b. May 3, 1899; Maxine b. Dec. 1, 1903; Pearl b. Sept. 25, 1905; Geneva b. Nov. 28, 1906; Boyd b. Sept. 13, 1910. Family home, Payson.

SIMPER, THOMAS WILLIAM. Born Aug. 5, 1818, Stowell Park, Eng. Came to Utah 1865, Thomas Taylor company.
Married Elizabeth Massey, Chedworth, Gloucestershire, Eng., who came to Utah with husband. Their children: Reuben b. July 30, 1846, died; Daniel b. April 30, 1848; Mary Jane b. May 23, 1850; Caroline H. E. b. April 4, 1854; Dorcas b. July 30, 1860, died; Thomas William b. Oct. 27, 1857.

SIMPER, DANIEL (son of Thomas William Simper and Elizabeth Massey). Born 1848, Chedworth, Gloucestershire, Eng. Came to Utah with father.
Married Mary A. Panter in 1874, Salt Lake City (daughter of William Panter and Sarah Lane of Compton Abdale, Eng.). She was born in 1851. Their children: Ernest b. Oct. 6, 1875; Rosella b. June 6, 1877; George W. b. Dec. 2, 1878; Raymond b. Jan. 31, 1880; Mary A. b. Nov. 10, 1882; Thomas R. b. April 26, 1884; Pearl b. Feb. 4, 1885; Kate b. Sept. 25, 1887; Ethel b. Oct. 6, 1891. Family home South Cottonwood, Utah.
High priest.

SIMPSON, THURSTON. Born Dec. 11, 1808, in Norway. Came to Utah Sept. 24, 1848, Heber C. Kimball company.
Married Mary Sophia Barlin 1841, in Iowa (daughter of Hans Barlin of Norway), who was born March 7, 1818. Only child: John b. Jan. 12, 1842, m. Mary Christensen 1861. Family resided Salt Lake City and Kamas, Utah.
Missionary to Wisconsin 1855; seventy. Farmer. Died May 2, 1889.

SIMPSON, JOHN (son of Thurston Simpson and Mary Sophia Barlin). Born Jan. 12, 1842, Lee Co., Iowa. Came to Utah with father.
Married Mary Christensen 1861, Salt Lake City (daughter of J. Christensen and Sophia Peterson), who was born April 6, 1844. Their children: Joseph John b. March 25, 1862, m. Alice Murphy 1901; Mary Sophia b. Dec. 17, 1863, m. Leonard Osborn; George B. b. Sept. 1, 1866, m. Alice Woolstenhulme; Thurston b. May 29, 1869, m. Philinda Pace 1898, m. Angeline Turnbow; Edward L. b. Dec. 23, 1872, m. Mary Ann Broadhead, divorced May 1908; James b. July 1, 1875; Sady b. April 18, 1878, m. Elias Burbidge 1898; Ella Laminda b. Feb. 2, 1883, m. Ebenezer Johnston 1907.
Married Elizabeth McNorton 1911, Salt Lake City (daughter of James McNorton and Elizabeth Shaw, pioneers 1853, Appleton Harmon company.)
High priest. Veteran Black Hawk war. Farmer and stockraiser.

June 11, 1843, m. John Heaton 1859; William b. Jan. 21, 1846, m. Mary Hoskin; m. Mary Heaton; m. Malinda Hall.
President elders quorum several years previous to 1876; high councilor of Malad stake a few years before death. Pioneer to Portage, where he assisted in making canals and wagon roads in early days. Died Jan. 21, 1892.

SINNETT, GEORGE (son of George Sinnett and Mary Lewis, the former of Angol, Pembrokeshire, South Wales). Born Oct. 9, 1816, at Angol. Came to Utah Dec. 10, 1856, William B. Hodgett and John A. Hunt company.
Married Martha Walkins (daughter of John and Nannie Walkins), who was born Aug. 10, 1810. Came to Utah with husband. Family home Spanish Fork, Utah.
Married Kjerstine Nielsen June 6, 1863, Salt Lake City (daughter of Jens Nielsen Bryger and Mette Katrine Larsen, pioneers Oct. 5, 1862, Ansel P. Harmon company). She was born Feb. 22, 1832, Slimstrup, Aalborg Amt., Denmark.
Assisted in bringing immigrants to Utah, John R. Murdock company, in 1863.

SIRRINE, THEODORE CURTIS (son of Mephibosheth Sirrine and Marie Wheeler of Cold Springs, N. Y.). Born Oct. 27, 1840, at Cold Springs. Came to Utah 1852, Captain Foote company.
Married Laura Holmes Nov. 14, 1869, Montpelier, Idaho (daughter of James and Harriet Holmes of Alpine, Utah, pioneers 1851, Morris Phelps company). She was born June 15, 1852. Their children: Harriet b. Aug. 14, 1870; Delilah b. July 2, 1872, m. Marland G. Richins; George b. Sept. 27, 1874; Mary E. b. Sept. 2, 1877, m. James A. Holmes; James Curtis b. March 24, 1880, m. Olive Ethel Fullmer; Morris C. b. Oct. 24, 1882; Mittie A. b. Oct. 8, 1886, m. Ammon L. Johnson; Seth E. b. Feb. 2, 1890; Wilford W. b. July 19, 1892; Samuel M. b. Dec. 21, 1895. Family home Mesa, Ariz.
Elder. Assisted in building canals.

SIRRINE, JAMES CURTIS (son of Theodore Curtis Sirrine and Laura Holmes). Born March 24, 1880, Mesa, Ariz.
Married Olive Ethel Fullmer Dec. 13, 1905, Raymond, Alberta, Canada (daughter of Edwin and Ada Fullmer of Springville, Utah). She was born Sept. 16, 1884. Their children: Theodore b. Feb. 27, 1908; Lawrence b. Dec. 23, 1909; Dean Lamar b. Sept. 22, 1912. Family home Union, Ore.
Missionary to southwestern states 1899-1902; seventy.

SKANCHY, ANTHON LORENZO (son of Elling Lorenson Schanksy and Mina Olson Amajon of Trondhjem, Norway). Born Sept. 17, 1839, Trondhjem, Norway. Came to Utah Sept. 15, 1868, Horton D. Haight company.
Married Christiana Jacobson 1867, Christiana, Norway, who came to Utah 1868. Their children: Anthon, Orson, Elias, Emalie, all died. Family home Logan, Utah.
Married Caroline Flygare 1872 (daughter of Swen Flygare of Sweden, who came to Utah 1871). Their children: Lorenzo Oliver b. Sept. 8, 1873, m. Lena Marie Sorensen July 7, 1897; Willard Richards b. Nov. 19, 1875, m. Alice Wray Sept. 30, 1900; Mina Christina b. Dec. 31, 1877, d. July 1908; Carl Norman b. Nov. 19, 1884.
Married Sigrid Landgaard Nov. 20, 1885. Their children: Zigne b. Sept. 1, 1886, died; Fritzjof Nansen b. March 27, 1894; Clara B., died; Lillian Sophia b. June 8, 1900; Sigrid Antonia b. Sept. 11, 1907.
Married Caroline Bergh.
Bishop of 6th ward, Logan, Utah, 25 years. Lumber merchant.

SKELTON, ROBERT (son of Thomas Skelton of Carlisle, Cumberland county, Eng.). Born 1824 in Carlisle. Came to Utah in 1849, Ezra T. Benson company.
Married Eliza Angeline Gollaher February, 1857, at Tooele, Utah (daughter of William Colbertson Gollaher and Elizabeth Orton of Adams county, Ill., pioneers 1849, Ezra T. Benson company). She was born Feb. 20, 1841. Their children: Elizabeth, m. George Rimington; Adelia, m. Andrew Russell; Robert, m. Sarah Gee; James Patrick, m. Eliza Bevan; William C.; Oren, m. Luella Herwood; Thomas, died; Polly, m. Joseph Lee; Mary, m. Frank Whitehead; Pamelia; Alma; Olive, died. Family home, Tooele.
Seventy; missionary to India 1852-56; bishop's counselor Tooele ward 1895. Mayor; councilman; assessor; member state legislature 1856-57. Farmer and stockraiser. Died Feb. 2, 1895.

SKELTON, ROBERT, JR. (son of Robert Skelton and Eliza Angeline Gollaher). Born May 31, 1863, Tooele, Utah.
Married Sarah Gee May 20, 1891, Logan, Utah (daughter of Lysander Gee and Theresa Bowley of Tooele, pioneers 1849). She was born Sept. 16, 1868. Their children: Paul Theresa b. Oct. 2, 1895; Edgar Almon b. Dec. 9, 1897; Gerald b. Jan. 14, 1899; Lucy b. Sept. 19, 1901; Joel b. Sept. 15, 1903; Philip b. Sept. 16, 1907. Family resided Provo and Salt Lake

PIONEERS AND PROMINENT MEN OF UTAH 1163

SKIDMORE, HENRY B. (son of Henry and Harriet Skidmore of Philadelphia, Pa.). Born December, 1830, Philadelphia. Came to Utah September, 1851, John Smith company.
Married Sarah Ann Elliott in April, 1855, at Philadelphia (daughter of Daniel Elliott of Philadelphia, pioneer Sept. 3, 1855, John Hindley company). She was born April 30, 1834. Their children: Harriett, m. Silas Knapp; Mary, m. Martin Garn; Sarah Ann, m. George Hardy; Elizabeth, m. Jesse W. Hardy; Clara, m. Moroni Hodson; Josephine and Henry, died; Edward, m. Maud Hackett; Frederick, Charles a d Oliver, latter three died; Lucy, m. William Ashton; Elva, died.
High priest; counselor in bishopric of East Mill Creek ward. Saw manufacturer.

SKIDMORE, WILLIAM LOBARK (son of Charles Brett Skidmore, born 1805, Sheffield, Eng., and Harriet Henrietta Shrader, born 1808, Philadelphia, Pa.). He was born Sept. 22, 1844, at Philadelphia. Came to Utah Sept. 3, 1855, John Hindley company.
Married Sarah Armina Knapp March 28, 1868 (daughter of Albert Knapp and Rozina Shepard, pioneers 1847, contingent Mormon Battalion—married in Utah). She was born Feb. 10, 1853, Farmington, Utah. Their children: William Alonzo b. April 27, 1869, m. Ellen Ma nda Monson; Harriet Armina b. April 15, 1871, m. Hyrum Lester Baer; Justin Albert b. May 6, 1873, m. Agnes Emmeret Stoddard; Judson Alvin b. May 6, 1873, d. May 7, 1873; Charles Henry b. July 23, 1875, m. Anna Louisa Wangsgaard; George Willis b. Aug. 25, 1877, m. Mary Louise Burnham; John Samuel b. Feb. 25, 1880, d. Dec. 20, 1902; Joseph Francis b. Oct. 22, 1882, d. Jan. 31, 1890; Malinda Ray b. March 1, 1885; Rozina Marinda b. April 14, 1887; Earl Doback b. Oct. 18, 1889; Edna Mary b. Oct. 17, 1891, d. March 9, 1892. Family home Richmond, Utah.
Married Charlotte Wilhelmina Pearson Feb. 19, 1886, Logan, Utah (daughter of Jonas Pearson and Charlotte Olsen, former came to Utah in 1884). She was born Nov. 24, 1857, Sodermanland, Sweden. Their children: Charlotte Ann b. April 25, 1886, d. Aug. 18, 1889; Edwin Wilbur b. Feb. 9, 1858; Elsie Lucina b. May 19, 1894; Ada Louise b. March 17, 1896; Elmer Gustave b. April 29, 1897; Cyrus Randolph b. Feb. 10, 1900. Family home Richmond, Utah.
Assisted in bringing immigrants to Utah; superintendent Richmond Sunday school 1876-79; counselor to President A. U. Hobson of first Y. M. M. I. A. in Richmond ward 1875-78; bishop of Richmond ward; ordained patriarch 1905 by Apostle C. W. Penrose. Minuteman; justice of peace 1876-78; member of city council November, 1901-05; senior member high council Benson stake 1901-05; president high priest quorum from 1905 to date. Hauled rock and lumber for Logan temple 1878-79.

SLACK, WILLIAM (son of Joseph Slack and Dorothy Greatorece of Middleton, Derbyshire, Eng.). Born Feb. 5, 1827, Middleton. Came to Utah 1859, Fred Kesler company.
Married Eliza Frost Jan. 21, 1847, Middleton (daughter of Jacob Frost and Betty Nefton of Middleton), who was born May 27, 1825. Their children: Thomas; William; Eliza Cornelia, m. George Cottrell; Joseph Abraham, m. Lear Ferrimond. Family home Kaysville, Utah.
of 55th quorum seventies. Farmer. Died Dec. 3, 18Clerk

SLADE, WILLIAM RUFUS. Born July 2, 1811, in Washington county, N. Y.
Married Julia Higganbotham in Louisiana. Their children: William, m. Nancy Katherine Holt; Martha, d. 1835; Jefferson, m. Sarah M. Chestnut; Margiana, d. 1840; Albert, d. 1853; Clara; Benjamin, d. 1847; John, d. 1853; Henry; Alice, d. 1853; James McGaw, d. 1870. Family home Opelousas, La. Died Nov. 28, 1872, Panaca, Nev.

SLADE, JEFFERSON (son of William Rufus Slade and Julia Higganbotham). Born Sept. 25, 1836, Opelousas, La. Came to Utah 1849.
Married Sarah M. Chestnut in 1861 (daughter of William and Johanna Chestnut). Only child: Jefferson C. b. April 11, 1862, m. Maria M. Ter Bruggen June 25, 1887. Family home Ogden, Utah.
Member of Slade Transfer Company.

SLADE, JEFFERSON C. (son of Jefferson Slade and Sarah M. Chestnut). Born April 11, 1861, Ogden.
Married Sarah Barker (daughter of James and Mary Barker). Their children: Pauline; James Jefferson.
Married Maria M. Ter Bruggen June 25, 1887, Ogden (daughter of Hermann Ter Bruggen and Maria Bakker of Ogden, who came to Utah in September, 1879, Mormon missionary company). She was born Nov. 5, 1868. Their children: Anna M.; Ada M.; Jefferson; Marie; Louise; Edward; Althea; Marjorie. Family home, Ogden.
Member Slade Transfer Company of Ogden.

SLATER, JOHN (son of Thomas Slater and Elizabeth Wombsley of Ashton-under-Lyne, Lancastershire, Eng.). Born Oct. 14, 1822, Lancastershire. Came to Utah 1868, John Gillespie company.
Married Jane Booth in 1841 at Lancastershire (daughter of who was born in 1821.

Their children: Thomas, d. infant; Mary, d. aged 2; Charles, d. infant; Eliza, m. Richard Moyse; Elizabeth, m. Charles T. Husbands; John C., m. Martha Griffith; Mary Jane, m. Mr. Moytz, m. Richard Moyse; Cordelia, d. aged 2; Joseph, m. Edith Clark. Family home Beaver, Utah.
Elder. Stonecutter. Died July, 1871, Malad, Idaho.

SLATER, RICHARD (son of Thomas Slater and Elizabeth Wombsley of England). Born Feb. 2, 1812, Lancastershire, Eng. Came to Utah Sept. 13, 1852, Thomas Howell company.
Married Ann Corbridge 1834 (daughter of William Corbridge and Ellen Bolton—married in 1811 at Clipping, Lancastershire). She was born Nov. 15, 1812, and came to Utah with husband. Their children: Thomas b. June 14, 1836, m. Mary Broadbent Sept. 22, 1859; Mary b. Aug. 11, 1838, m. John Read May 20, 1856; Priscilla b. Aug. 16, 1840, m. James Cowan March 15, 1857; Margaret b. Sept. 20, 1844, m. Buford A. Bybee Nov. 19, 1863; Rachel b. Jan. 8, 1847, m. Fred L. Foy Dec. 25, 1863; Richard b. Oct. 12, 1849, m. Sarah Allen May 13, 1885; Ann b. Oct. 12, 1849, m. Charles Read May 21, 1891; Lizzie b. May 14, 1852, m. Amasa S. Condon June 18, 1889; John b. Feb. 6, 1854, m. Margaret Howell May 15, 1875; James A. b. April 11, 1856, m. Mary E. Allred Dec. 28, 1877. Family home Slaterville, Utah.
Farmer.

SLATER, THOMAS (son of Richard Slater and Ann Corbridge). Born June 14, 1836, in Lancastershire, Eng.
Married Mary Broadbent Sept. 22, 1859, Provo, Utah (daughter of Znoeth Broadbent and Keturah Lund, pioneers 1852, Captain Outhouse company). She was born Sept. 11, 1842, Lincolnshire, Eng. Their children: Thomas b. July 2, 1860, d. aged 30; John b. Nov. 30, 1861, m. Mary Hannah Stanger Nov. 30, 1881; Mary b. Nov. 14, 1863, m. William Stanger Jan. 16, 1882; Keturah L. b. March 1, 1865, m. Alfred J. Palmer April 8, 1886; William J. b. July 9, 1867, m. Casstina Wayman Jan. 27, 1892; Richard A. b. Jan. 30, 1869; Anna A. b. Feb. 11, 1871, m. Harry Sharp March 6, 1906; Nellie b. Dec. 24, 1872, m. Ezra Richardson May 19, 1892; James E. b. March 4, 1876. m. Ella Heap Jan. 4, 1902; Charles E. b. Sept. 23, 1878, m. Hazel Brown Jan. 2, 1905; Pearl b. Oct. 24, 1880, m. Harry Clay Lyon June 14, 1905; Edna b. March 25, 1883, m. Eli Heap Sept. 14, 1904. Family home Slaterville, Utah.
Farmer and stockraiser.

SLAUGH, GEORGE JACOB (son of George Jacob Slaugh and Margaret Hammon of Philadelphia, Pa.). Born March 31, 1828, Philadelphia. Came to Utah 1862, Captain Hyde company.
Married Mary Ivory Nov. 19, 1850, Kensington, Pa. (daughter of Isaac Ivory and Rachel Smith of Philadelphia). She was born April 1, 1828. Their children: John Henry, m. Ellenor Bacus; Sarah, m. Edward Harris; Isaac Ivory b. Oct. 29, 1857, m. Annie Culmer Jan. 3, 1884, m. Sarah Ellen Johnson Sept. 26, 1894; Mary, m. Frederick Fage; Benjamin, m. Rachel Smuin. Family home Pleasant Grove, Utah.
High priest; teacher. Died December, 1905.

SLAUGH, ISAAC IVORY (son of George Jacob Slaugh and Mary Ivory). Born Oct. 29, 1857, Philadelphia, Pa. Came to Utah Sept. 28, 1868, James Brown company.
Married Annie Culmer Jan. 3, 1884, Salt Lake City (daughter of Alfred and Sopha Culmer), who was born April 16, 1866. Their children: Etta Viola b. Sept. 11, 1886, and Hazel Sopha b. Oct. 19, 1889, d. infants; Emma b. June 1, 1892, m. John Smuin.
Married Sarah Ellen Johnson Sept. 26, 1894, Salt Lake City (daughter of Benjamin Franklin Johnson and Mary Eliza Williams of Salt River, Ariz.). She was born Oct. 22, 1875. Their children: Frederick Eleas b. June 30, 1895; Idella b. April 23, 1897; Arla M. b. Aug. 10, 1899; Henry Ivory b. Sept. 19, 1901; Joseph b. April 20, 1903; Gilbert Willard b. April 16, 1906; Mary Vanola b. Oct. 5, 1907; Wilda Minnetta b. Feb. 12, 1910. Family home Naples, Utah.
Elder; ward and Sunday school teacher 30 years; Sunday school superintendent, Naples ward. 19 years. School trustee three years. Pioneer road builder.

SLAUGH, JOHN JACOB (son of John Slaugh and Margaret Hommann of Philadelphia, Pa.). Born Feb. 15, 1819, Philadelphia. Came to Utah 1861, Carl G. Maeser company.
Married Matilda Smuin Jan. 2, 1864, Salt Lake City (daughter of Thomas Smuin, pioneer 1863). Their children: John Jacob, Jr., m. Mary Alice Perry; Sarah Ellen; George Alfred; Ada Halena; Florence Matilda; Elmer Warren; Dorah Elizabeth. Family resided Pleasant Grove and Vernal, Utah.
Seventy; president of branch of church, Philadelphia. Pleasant Grove city councilman. Stonemason. Died April 22, 1903, at Vernal.

SLAUGH, JOHN JACOB (son of John Jacob Slaugh and Matilda Smuin). Born Nov. 17, 1864, Salt Lake City.
Married Mary Alice Perry Jan. 1, 1886, Vernal, Utah (daughter of William Howard Perry and Alice Evelyn Walcot of Plain City, Utah). She was born June 5, 1871, Millville, Utah. Their children: Richard John b. Oct. 11, 1887, m. Alberta Green; Elizabeth Ivoy b. Oct. 2, 1889, m. Lewis Chivers; Forrest Stephen b. May 8, 1892; Edward Curtis b. Nov. 10, 1894; Letha Pearl b. March 19, 1897; Kimball

George b. May 4, 1899; Leona Mary b. Sept. 1, 1901; Bessie Lenora b. Dec. 19, 1904; William Henry b. June 3, 1906.
Missionary to New Zealand 1897-98; elder; Sunday school superintendent and teacher; ward teacher. Moved to Ashley Valley 1885, where he assisted in building up country. Road supervisor; school trustee. Director Ashley Upper Irrigation Co.

SLAUGHTER, CHARLES MERRIWEATHER (son of William Slaughter of Charleston, W. Va.). Born May 2, 1819. Came to Utah Sept. 4, 1860, Franklin Brown company.
Married Fannie Piety Kenner in 1853 (daughter of Robert John Kenner and Hannah Stubblefield of Russellville, Logan county, Ky., pioneers 1860, Franklin Brown company). She was born Feb. 17, 1836, in Kentucky. Their children: Cora Minnie b. Aug. 25, 1857, died; Frank Thomas b. July 13, 1858, m. Annie Terry; Charles Kenner b. Dec. 13, 1860, died; Rosa Hannah b. Sept. 11, 1863, m. Edward Hanmer Duzett; Robert Erastus b. Nov. 30, 1866, m. Sarah Farns; Fannie b. Nov. 26, 1869, m. George W. Terry; Missouri Tennessee b. March 30, 1875, died. Family home Rockville, Utah.
Elder; working missionary to Dixie. Located at Rockville, and assisted in developing country. Farmer. Died April, 1883.

SLAUGHTER, SAMUEL NATHANIEL (son of Edward Slaughter and Catherine Cronk of Sandwich, Eng.). Born Oct. 16, 1840, Uitenhage, South Africa. Came to Utah Oct. 5, 1860, Nephi Johnson company.
Married Annie E. Huey June 4, 1860, Florence, Neb. (daughter of Robert Huey and Clara W. Thomas of Port Elizabeth, South Africa). She was born Feb. 19, 1844, and came to Utah with husband. Their children: Emma Jane, m. James Hall; Edward Huey, m. Mary Winchester; Samuel C., m. Martha Glanfield; Clara E., m. Robert A. Coleman, m. James L. Griffeths; William H., m. Ella Rasmussen; Catherine M., m. George W. Woodhouse; Robert, d. aged 4½ years; Edith Ellen, m. Frank L. Osborn; Sarah S., m. John P. James; Annie, m. Hugh B. Sackett; Evelyn, m. Carl Madsen; John L., m. Nellie Barnes; Walter, m. Ella Olsen. Family home, Salt Lake City.
Block teacher; elder; high priest. Assessor and collector Beaver county 11½ years; school trustee six years; county commissioner Beaver county two years; postmaster Frisco, Utah, five years. Tanner since 1883; merchant.

SLEIGHT, THOMAS (son of Richard Sleight and Ann Lamb of Swineshead, Lincolnshire, Eng.). Born Sept. 25, 1833, Swineshead. Came to Utah Aug. 9, 1860, Warren Walling company.
Married Marianne Reynolds Smith in 1857, Florence, Neb. (daughter of Joseph Reynolds of Limonton, Berkshire, Eng.). She was born in 1823.
Married Mary M. Wixom, who was born April 7, 1853, Cottonwood, Utah. Their children: Thomas George; Mary Frances Bunn; Hannah Ann Grimmett; Marianne Alice; Joseph Henry; John Orson; Richard S.; Olive Irene Baxter; Viola J. Family home Paris, Idaho.
Elder; missionary to England 1884-86. Lieutenant-captain of cavalry in Nauvoo Legion. Farmer.

SMART, ABEL (son of William Smart, born 1819, Minety, Wiltshire, Eng., and Jane Stockham of Lea, Wiltshire, Eng.). He was born Jan. 30, 1848, Lea, Wiltshire. Came to Utah September, 1868, Simeon Alvord company.
Married Sarah Gittins Sept. 20, 1869, at Salt Lake City (daughter of James Gittins and Mary Powell, pioneers, Daniel D. McArthur company). She was born Dec. 23, 1850, and came to Utah with parents. Their children: Abel b. June 9, 1870; William b. Dec. 7, 1871, died; James b. May 21, 1873, m. Nora Jensen; Sarah b. June 3, 1875, m. Joseph Hebden; Mary b. April 14, 1877, m. John McDonald; Jane b. June 20, 1879, m. Rutherford Hayes; Lottie b. Dec. 2, 1881, m. Alma H. Hayes; Maud b. March "8, 1884, m. Charles Black; Frederick b. May 6, 1886, m. Esther Hayes; Ezra b. April 13, 1889, died; Parley b. Aug. 4, 1891, m. Emma McCammon; Hazel b. Oct. 29, 1893. Family resided Smithfield, Utah, and Georgetown, Idaho.
Married Emma Irene Staley Feb. 11, 1885, Logan, Utah (daughter of John Staley and Sarah Wilde), who was born Aug. 22, 1868, Coalville, Utah. Their children: Emma b. Nov. 7, 1885, m. Harrison Hess; John A. b. March 29, 1887, d. April 14, 1887; Grace b. Jan. 14, 1889, m. Wilbur Bacon; Joseph A. b. Jan. 13, 1891, d. Feb. 28, 1891; Ada b. June 29, 1892; Wilford Willard b. Nov. 8, 1894; Ida b. Sept. 26, 1896, d. Sept. 8, 1902; Vernal b. Aug. 7, 1878; Edith b. May 22, 1900; Annie b. July 21, 1902; Ray Staley b. Dec. 10, 1904; Edna b. May 27, 1907; Irene b. Sept. 30, 1909; Iva b. April 1, 1913. Family resided Ovid and Georgetown, Bear Lake Co., Idaho.
Married Annie Christena Jensen Nov. 14, 1888, at Logan (daughter of Peter and Boleta Marie Jensen), who was born Aug. 10, 1867, Ovid, Bear Lake Co., Idaho. Their children: George b. Dec. 3, 1889, m. Margaret Murray; Hannah b. July 27, 1893; Jesse b. July 15, 1895; Lyman b. June 1, 1898; Charles Orrin b. March 23, 1901, d. 1916. Family home Ovid and Georgetown, Bear Lake Co., Idaho.
Clerk of high priest quorum of Cache stake 1878-84; ward

Came to Salt Lake City; later to Promontory; thence to Wellsville, 1869; leaving there for Smithfield in 1870, where he resided until 1887; moved to Ovid, Bear Lake Co., Idaho; moved to Georgetown 1886, where now resides.

SMART, NEPHI (son of Thomas Smart, born April 8, 1798, at Leicester, Leicestershire, Eng., and Elizabeth Bailis, born July 8, 1798, in Kidderminster, Eng., both of Leicester—married June 11, 1818). He was born Aug. 18, 1840, at Leicester. Came to Utah 1868 with the independent company.
Married Ellen Woodburn (daughter of Simon and Elizabeth Woodburn—married 1866 in Somersetshire, Eng.). She was born March 29, 1840, and came to Utah 1868 with the independent company. Their children: Cicil Thomas b. Aug. 6, 1866, m. Martha P. Rowland; Lorenzo Woodburn b. May 16, 1865, m. Lucy Peterson; Ethel Alice b. Dec. 22, 1870, m. Martin R. Ivie. Family home East Mill Creek, Utah.
Married Amelia Higgins Sept. 7, 1874, Salt Lake City (daughter of William Higgins and Charlotte Nivis, pioneers 1877—married 1837 at London, Eng.). She was born Jan. 16, 1844, in England. Their child: Herber Higgins b. May 6, 1866.
High priest; missionary to England for four years; bookkeeper and accountant in the tithing office. Worked in tannery. Farmer at Mill Creek, Utah.

SMART, THOMAS SHARRATT (son of William Smart and Mary Maria Sharratt of Stonewall, Staffordshire, Eng.). Born Sept. 14, 1823, at Stonewall. Came to America 1845, and to Utah Sept. 4, 1852, captain of company of 20 families.
Married Ann Hayter in Endowment House June 3, 1856 (daughter of Henry Hayter, born 1789, and Kezzia Denison of Portsmouth, Hampshire, Eng.). She was born Sept. 18, 1822, at Portsmouth. Their children: Mary Ann b. Nov. 5, 1842, m. Andrew Morrison; Alice b. Jan. 1, 1845, m. William Pratt; Louisa b. Oct. 11, 1846, m. Thomas Mendenhall; Charlotte Elizabeth b. Nov. 6, 1848, m. Samuel R. Parkinson; Maria b. April 29, 1851, m. Samuel R. Parkinson; Thomas b. Dec. 16, 1853, m. Catherine Alvenia Hatch; Sarah Ann b. Oct. 24, 1856, m. Joshua Hawks; Eliza b. Nov. 1, 1857, m. Leonidas A. Mecham; Frances Ann b. 1860, d. infant; William Henry b. April 6, 1862, m. Anna Haines; Mary Jane b. Feb. 15, 1866, m. James W. Webster.
Married Minnie Shrives at Salt Lake City (daughter of Edwin Shrives and Elizabeth Holton of Stanwick, Northamptonshire, Eng.). She was born Dec. 12, 1860, Stanwick. Their children: Leslie Edwin b. July 14, 1880, m. May Hess; Vernon b. May 9, 1882; Iva Lilla b. Dec. 18, 1886, m. Martin Henry Phelps; Melvin Shrives b. May 30, 1889. Families resided Franklin, Idaho.
Settled at American Fork, and after several moves located at Franklin, Idaho. First president of branch, and later member bishopric at Franklin; high councilor; missionary to England 1886. School trustee at Franklin several terms. Made a number of trips bringing immigrants to Utah. Active participant in early Indian troubles. Farmer; stockraiser; brick manufacturer. Died April 18, 1901.

SMART, THOMAS (son of Thomas Sharratt Smart and Ann Hayter). Born Dec. 16, 1853, American Fork, Utah.
Married Catherine Alvenia Hatch Jan. 11, 1875, Salt Lake City, Daniel H. Wells officiating (daughter of Lorenzo Hill Hatch and Catherine Karren of Franklin, Idaho). She was born Feb. 14, 1859. Their children: Catherine Ann, m. Ezra C. Foss; Thomas Delbert, d. child; Carl L., m. Julia Hendricks; Zella Cloe; Meda, m. Jonathan Powell; Lorenzo; Uarda Georgia; Junius; Hellen.
Counselor in presidency of Uinta stake. Resided at Franklin, Idaho, 1860-92; moved to Logan, Utah. President and director of First National Bank of Logan; assisted in organizing the City National Bank and Farmers' and Stockgrowers' Bank of Salt Lake City, and in each of which he is a director; one of incorporators of Beneficial Life Insurance Company, and has been a member of the board of directors since its organization. Appointed trustee of Utah Agricultural College by Governor John C. Cutler, and reappointed by Governor Spry in 1909 and 1913; member of executive and building committees of the college board of trustees; donated $10,000 toward the gymnasium at Logan, which was named the "Thomas Smart" gymnasium, made a liberal donation to the pioneer monument at Franklin, Idaho, 1910. Member Republican state central committee of Utah. Engaged in farming and sheepraising.

SMART, WILLIAM HENRY (son of Thomas Sharratt Smart and Ann Hayter). Born April 6, 1862, at Franklin.
Married Anna Haines Oct. 3, 1888, Logan, Utah (daughter of Isaac David Haines and Elizabeth Highfield of Zanesville, Ohio, came to Utah October, 1854, independent company). She was born Oct. 11, 1867. Their children: Elizabeth b. Nov. 1, 1889; William Haines b. Sept. 8, 1891; Thomas Lawrence b. Dec. 5, 1893; Edna b. Dec. 24, 1895; Joseph Heber b. Nov. 12, 1900; Anna b. Aug. 25, 1903; Ruth b. Aug. 23, 1909. Present family home Roosevelt, Utah.
Member 18th quorum seventy; missionary to England 1886, with his father, collecting family genealogy; assisted in and supervised first vicarious work for his relatives in Logan and Salt Lake temples; missionary to Turkey and England 1889-90; missionary to eastern states 1898-1900, being its president during latter part; president Wasatch

stake; president Uinta stake; president Duchesne stake. School teacher at Brigham Young College of Logan six years; two years principal of public schools of Franklin, Idaho. Director in Beneficial Life Insurance Company. One of the founders of Smart & Webster Live Stock Company of Rexburg, Idaho, and its first president and general manager; one of the organizers of the Heber City Bank and its first president; one of the organizers of Heber Mercantile Company and its first president; assisted in the organization of the Wasatch Wave Pub. Co., and its first president; director of Utah National Bank of Salt Lake City; one of the organizers and directors of Salt Lake Knitting Works; one of the organizers and first president Uinta State Bank; one of the organizers of Roosevelt Realty Company and Roosevelt Mercantile Corporation; organizer and chief proprietor of Duchesne Record Publishing Co.

SMITH, ADAM (son of Michael Smith and Katherine Avenger, of Highland, Germany). Born May 6, 1825, in Germany. Came to Utah 1857, Captain Walker company.
Married Melissa M. Hendry Pew 1849, in Wood county, Va. (daughter of Joseph Few and Rachel Hendry, pioneers 1848, independent company). She was born July 11, 1827. Their children: Elsone b. July 16, 1850, m. William Judah; Octaves b. April 29, 1852, m. Clara Bradley; Joseph M. b. July 17, 1855, m. Josephine Anderson; Josephine b. Feb. 20, 1858, m. James E. Togg; Ellington b. Feb. 17, 1860, m. Louise Wilson; Edaline b. Aug. 27, 1862, m. John Farnes; Rozeia b. July 21, 1864, m. Wells Cheney; Rosetta b. Dec. 30, 1866, m. Thomas Williams; Zora N. b. Nov. 7, 1870, m. Thomas Smith. Family home Hyrum, Utah.
High priest. Settled at Bountiful, Utah, 1857, moved to Cache Valley. Participated in Echo Canyon war. Farmer and stockraiser.

SMITH, JOSEPH M. (son of Adam Smith and Melissa M. Hendry Pew). Born July 17, 1855, in Iowa.
Married Josephine Anderson Dec. 25, 1878, Hyrum, Utah (daughter of Peter Anderson and Caroline Jeppson, of Sweden, pioneers 1860). She was born Oct. 20, 1860. Their children: Joseph E. b. Oct. 12, 1879, m. Hilda Jensen; Sylvia b. Oct. 22, 1881, m. Walter Fife; Ida b. May 15, 1884, m. Francis Olsen; Roy b. June 1, 1886; William b. Sept. 4, 1889, m. Lillian Liljenquist; Hazel b. Feb. 11, 1892; Nelton b. Sept. 29, 1894; Beatrice b. Aug. 22, 1896; Rusell b. Jan. 5, 1900; Glenn b. April 1, 1904. Family home Hyrum, Utah.
Member of 62d quorum seventies; high councilor and officiator in Logan Temple 1902. Marshal; justice of peace; city councilman. Farmer.

SMITH, ALBERT (son of David Smith and Deborah Smith, of Ashfield, Franklin county, Mass.). Born Nov. 18, 1804, in Franklin county, Mass. Came to Utah with discharged Mormon Battalion soldiers 1847.
Married Esther Dutcher May 19, 1826 (daughter of Thomas and Betsy Dutcher), who was born Jan. 25, 1811. Their children: Azariah; Emily; Candace; Joseph; Esther.
Married Rhoda Gifford Oct. 17, 1856, who was born April 28, 1827, in New York. Their children: Albert; Deborah; Anna.
Married Sophia W. Clown, born August 17, 1824, in Denmark. Their children: Albertena; Louisa; Albert; Esther; David; Hirum; Charlotte.
Sergeant and quartermaster in Mormon Battalion.

SMITH, AZARIAH (son of Albert Smith and Esther Dutcher). Born Aug. 1, 1828, Darlston, Oswego county, N. Y. Came to Utah Sept. 28, 1848.
Married Camilla Augusta Taylor April 10, 1849, Salt Lake City (daughter of Stephen Taylor), who was born Jan. 28, 1833. Their children: Camilla; Stephen Azariah; Samuel.
Married Joanne Maria Christensen Oct. 7, 1871, who was born Jan. 7, 1817, in Denmark, and died Jan. 27, 1903.
Married Sevilla Stay Mitchell Aug. 1, 1903, who was born July 17, 1832.
Was working at the Sutter's Fort mill race, California, when gold was first discovered there. Located at Salt Lake City, later moved to San Pete Valley, where he has resided since.

SMITH, ARTHUR S. (son of John Smith and Elizabeth Pye of Shropshire, Eng.). Born Jan. 31. 1818, in Shropshire. Came to Utah October, 1854, James Brown company.
Married Elizabeth Logue May, 1840, Liverpool, Eng. (daughter of James Logue and Nancy Campbell of Glasgow, Scotland). She was born Jan. 1, 1813. Their children: Mary Ellen, m. Hugh Findlay, m. W. D. Major; Jared, d. aged 20; Jane Ann, m. Aaron Nebeker; Elizabeth, m. Joseph Arnold. Family home, Salt Lake City.
High priest; worked as steward for Brigham Young nine years. Tailor. Died Dec. 12, 1878, Laketown, Utah.

SMITH, BENJ. F. (son of Conrad Smith and Ann Elizabeth Geeseman, of Tomstown, Franklin county, Pa.). Born Feb. 22, 1846, Tomstown. Came to Utah Sept. 3, 1860, James D. Ross company.
Married Mary Ann Simmons Jan. 26, 1874, Salt Lake City (daughter of George Simmons and Mary Ann Ford. of Brighton, Eng., pioneers 1855). She was born July 18, 1853. Their children: Annie; George; Mina; Frank; Delia;

Charles; William; Walter; Lloyd; Archie. Family home Morgan. Utah.
Assisted in bringing immigrants, and brought first telegraph wire to Utah; in 1869 went to Laramie City for freight. Elder. Laborer.

SMITH, GEORGE YOUNG (son of James Smith and Ann George of Dundee, Scotland). Born Dec. 5, 1835, at Dundee. Came to Utah Nov. 3, 1862, Jacob Gates company.
Married Johann Luckie Dec. 29, 1854, Forfarshire. Dundee, Scotland (daughter of John Luckie and Sarah Forgenson of Dundee, Scotland), who was born Jan. 16, 1836. Their children: Sarah Forgenson, m. William A. Noble; Annie George, m. Edwin R. Miles Jr.; Margaret Young, d. aged 19; Mary Jane, m. William A. Noble Jr.; Johann Elizabeth, d. aged 13; George Young, m. Savira Green; James John; Alexander Clarence; William Allen; Agnes; latter four d. infants.
Secretary elders quorum; Sunday school teacher. Notary public and justice of peace at Smithfield. Utah. Manager Smithfield Co-op., and of Thomas Richardson's mercantile business. Died Aug. 29, 1903, at Smithfield.

SMITH, GEORGEN (son of Christian A. Smith. born Aug. 15, 1782, Sterndrope, Prussia, and Mary J. Swan born Jan. 1, 1785, Rurop, Prussia). Born May 28, 1823, Fadested, Prussia.
Married Christina Berkidile, born April 11, 1825. Their children: Mary Smith b. July 28, 1851; Christen M. b. Feb. 6, 1853; Bertil b. Sept. 18, 1855; Mariah b. March 20, 1857; Susana b. May 30, 1859; John b. Sept. 13, 1862, m. Sarah S. Durfey, April 12, 1887; Christina M. b. March 22, 1864, m. James Nielson; Wilhelmina b. May 11, 1865, m. John F. Haws Feb. 17, 1862; Caroline b. May 11, 1865; Joseph b. June 6, 1867, m. Stella Holt Dec. 25, 1888.
Married Maria Johnson (daughter of Johnson Willson and Anna Krestina Christensen), who was born June 3, 1841, Norholm, Denmark. Their children: William Smith b. Jan. 3, 1864, m. Mary Moss; Maria b. April 28, 1865, m. Joseph Woolcock; Anna C. b. Nov. 2, 1866; Mary b. Oct. 22, 1867, m. Andrew Box; James A. b. March 17, 1870, m. Nellie Croutier; Evardine M. M. b. Dec. 17, 1871, m. Charles Mulford; Ane Laurine b. Nov. 14, 1873, m. Leo Holt; Adelaide b. April 7, 1874, m. William Willson; Eliza b. Feb. 11, 1876; Catrine Lizzie b. Nov. 4, 1877, m. Jeremiah Mott; John Christian b. March 3, 1881; Condy b. Aug. 7, 1884, m. Charlotte Dimic.

SMITH, JOHN (son of Georgen Smith and Christina Berkidile). Born Sept. 13, 1862, Fountain Green, Utah.
Married Sarah S. Durfey April 12, 1887, Thurber, Utah (daughter of Alma Durfey, pioneer 1852, and Amanda M. Haws). She was born April 20, 1872, Salem. Utah. Their children: John F. b. Feb. 16, 1888; Charles W. b. Feb. 14, 1890; Amanda M. b. April 11, 1891; Artie J. b. March 17, 1893, m. Luther Dee Taft, June 13, 1911; George b. Jan. 10, 1895; Joseph Alma b. Dec. 12, 1895; Eda Bell b. March 3, 1898; Jayson L. b. Sept. 17, 1900; Merin b. Jan. 13, 1903; Ardella C. b. Oct. 29, 1905; Norma and Norman b. April 22, 1908; Franklin D. b. Sept. 18, 1910.

SMITH. J. FEWSON (son of Robert Smith and Mary Fewson, of Preston, Eng.). Born Jan. 1, 1834, at Preston. Came to Utah Oct. 4, 1863, Horton D. Haight company.
Married Christiana Venobles Vernon April 27, 1863, Hull, Yorkshire, Eng. (daughter of Joseph Venobles Vernon and Margaret Senior, of Hull. Former came to Utah 1852, President John Taylor company, to establish first sugar factory, Sugar House ward). Their children: J. Fewson, Jr., m. Alice E. Steers; Joseph Vernon, m. Agnes H. Timms; Marea M. V., d. infant; Reinold Vernon, m. Lena M. White. Family home was 136 I St., Salt Lake City.
High priest. Ensign stake. Was prominent in politics in Salt Lake City and in railroad building in western United States and Mexico.

SMITH. JOSEPH VERNON (son of J. Fewson Smith, and Christiana Venobles Vernon). He was born March 8, 1867, Salt Lake City.
Married Agnes H. Timms June 10, 1891, at Logan. Utah (daughter of William J. A. Timms and Harriet Sisam of Salt Lake City, pioneers 1866, Captain Wheeler's mule teams). She was born Jan. 9, 1868. Their child: Irene Vernon Smith b. Aug. 22, 1892. The family home was 118 I St., Salt Lake City, Utah.
Was prominent in church affairs and was a railroad man and later a life insurance salesman.

SMITH, JAMES HENRY (son of James Smith, of Newark, N. J.). Born March 16, 1805. Came to Utah Sept 12, 1847, Jedediah M. Grant company.
Married Hannah Van Wagoner April 4, 1833, Pompton Plains. N. J. (daughter of Halma Van Wagoner), who was born April 4, 1815. Their children: Halma b. March 31, 1834, m. Annie Bolton. m. Elizabeth Dyke; Josiah b. April 3, 1836; Hyrum b. April 2, 1838, m. Julia Holdaway; John V. b. April 6, 1840, m. Julia Bowen; Sarah Ann b. Sept. 11, 1842, m. Enoch Clark; Emma b. May 21, 1845, m. Alfred Conover; Joseph Van b. Dec. 11, 1847, m. Isabell Pace; Eunice b. Jan. 8,

1166   PIONEERS AND PROMINENT MEN OF UTAH

1851, m. John Croft; James H. b. 1853; Henry b. May 19, 1855, m. Retta Conover; Edwin P., m. Rosetta Conover.
High priest; counselor to President John Nebeker's elders quorum; first leader of Salt Lake choir. Farmer. Died in California.

SMITH, HALMA (son of James Henry Smith and Hannah Van Wagoner). Born March 31, 1834.
Married Annie Bolton, 1859, Salt Lake City (daughter of Curtis E. Bolton and Mary Bunker of Long Island, N. Y.), who was born August, 1840. Their children: Gertrude A. b. 1860, m. David Loveless; Halma, m. Rena Clark; Rebecca, died; Edwin, m. Millie Curtis; Luella, m. Daniel Kellogg; John, died; Alphus, m. Zella Gardner; Edith, m. William Taylor; Charles, died.
Married Elizabeth Duke (Mecham) May 8, 1907, at Provo, Utah (daughter of Jonathan Oldham Duke and Sarah Thompson, of Provo), who was born May 9, 1864. Families resided Provo, Utah.
Elizabeth Duke was the widow of Jonathan James Mecham, whom she married Oct. 26, 1881, at Provo. Their children: Lewis; Jonathan O., m. Eva Adams; Estella, m. Wilford Poulson; Leo, m. Edith Liddard; Wells; Edith Lloyd Singleton; Rowley; Ethel; Amy; Fred D.
Seventy. Teacher; pioneer irrigationist and orchardist; manufacturer of musical instruments.

SMITH, JOSEPH VAN (son of James Henry Smith and Hannah Van Wagoner). Born Dec. 11, 1847, Salt Lake City, Utah.
Married Isabell Pace May, 1881, Provo. Utah (daughter of William Pace and Epsy Williams of Provo, pioneers 1848), who was born Dec. 6, 1856, and died Nov. 6, 1906. Their children: Edna b. July 22, 1882, died; Joseph W. b. Nov. 17, 1884, m. Ivy Mae Cowan; James H. b. Sept. 13, 1886, m. Jennie Hardy; Frank b. Jan. 19, 1888; Bella Nora b. March 29, 1890, m. Lester Bates; Ralph b. Aug. 1892, died.
Pioneer builder and lumberman; musician; farmer and horticulturist.

SMITH, JESSE (son of George Smith and Mary Flower of Pensford, Somerset, Eng.). Born May 14, 1836, Pensford. Came to Utah Sept. 15, 1866, William Henry Chipman company.
Married Mary A. Price September, 1861, Newport, Monmouthshire, Eng. (daughter of Charles Price and Ann Harris of Pontypool, Eng.), who was born Jan. 20, 1838. Their children: Jesse b. Feb. 12, 1866; Charles b. June 1, 1868; George A. b. Sept. 11, 1869, m. Clara Anderson, m. Emma Fenton; John T. b. Jan. 30, 1872, m. Emmerette Cutler; Sara Ann b. May 9, 1874, m. A. C. Pearson; Mary Rachel b. April 18, 1876, m. German E. Ellsworth; Joseph Frederick b. Sept. 26, 1878, m. Genevieve Teasdale; Jesse Norman b. June 28, 1881, m. Melissa Boley. Family home Lehi, Utah.
Married Sarah A. Teillbery Oct. 10, 1906, Salt Lake City (daughter of Thomas John Teillbery and Sarah Ann Jarratt, of Portsmouth, Hampshire, Eng.), who was born May, 1857. Family home Lehi. Utah.
Senior president 127th quorum seventies. Member city council two terms; road supervisor 15 years.

SMITH, JOB (son of Thomas Smith and Ann Taylor of Deerhurst, Gloucestershire, Eng.). Born Dec. 2, 1828, at Deerhurst. Came to Utah Sept. 25, 1848, Brigham Young company.
Married Adelaide Fowles Jan. 5, 1852, Bedford, Eng. (daughter of Henry Fowles and Ann Sheffield of Bedford), who was born Sept. 8, 1830. Their children: Georgiana b. Feb. 6, 1855, m. John Olsen; Job Fowles b. July 9, 1859, m. Eliza Scott; Albert Henry b. Sept. 29, 1861, m. Emma Felsted; Rachel b. July 27, 1865, m. Frank Glenn; Lola Allie b. Nov. 13, 1869, m. Richard Alliston.
Married Jane Fowles March 14, 1855, Salt Lake City (daughter of Henry Fowles and Ann Sheffield), who was born Aug. 26, 1825. Their children: Mormon J. (Henry), m. Elizabeth Barkdull, m. Edith Jorgensen, m. Amy Pauley; Lucy, m. William Pyott, m. Alvira Dunn; Wilford, m. Louie Preece; George T., m. Hattie Winters; Francis H., m. Eunice Fuller.
Married Sarah Punter May 25, 1874, Salt Lake City (daughter of Abraham Punter and Sarah Smith of Hemel Hempstead, Eng., latter came to Utah 1874). She was born April 21, 1855. Their children: Jane Ann b. Aug. 26, 1875, d. April 23, 1913; Adelaide b. May 27, 1880, m. William Thompson; Sarah Ellen b. Feb. 15, 1883, m. David Harwood; Willard R. b. Oct. 6, 1887, d. aged 10; Mary E. b. Aug. 5, 1892.
Married Charlotte Sophronia Slinger Dec. 1, 1885, Logan, Utah. Only child: Annie Sophronia b. Sept. 23, 1888, m. William Mitchell. Families resided Salt Lake City.
Seventy; missionary to England 1849; president of the Bedfordshire branch for five years. On return to Utah, was captain of company of immigrants and whenever confronted by painted and hostile Indians, made peace with them by feeding instead of fighting them. Basketmaker in Salt Lake 1860-90.

SMITH, JOHN (son of Asael Smith and Mary Duty). Born July 16, 1781, Derryfield, N. H. Came to Utah 1847, Brigham Young company.
Married Clarissa Lyman Sept. 11, 1815 (daughter of Richard and Philomela Lyman of Lebanon, N. H., pioneers Sept. 23, 1847). She was born June 27, 1790. Their children: George Albert b. June 26, 1817, (see marriages below); Caro-
line b. June 6, 1820, m. Thomas Callister; John Lyman b. Nov. 17, 1823, m. Augusta B. Cleveland. Family home, Salt Lake City.
High priest; presiding patriarch 1849.

SMITH, GEORGE ALBERT (son of John Smith and Clarissa Lyman). Born June 26, 1817, Potsdam, St. Lawrence county, N. Y. Came to Utah July, 1847, Brigham Young company.
Married Bathsheba W. Bigler 1841, Nauvoo, Ill. (daughter of Mark Bigler and Susannah Ogden, of Harrison county, W. Va.), who was born May 3, 1822. Their children: George Albert b. July 7, 1842, d. Nov. 2, 1860; Bathsheba, m. Clarance Merrill, Jan. 3, 1861; John, d. infant. Family home, Salt Lake City.
Married Lucy M. Smith Nov. 29, 1844, who was born Feb. 9, 1817, Newry, Maine. Their children: Don Carlos b. Aug. 11, 1846, died; Joel b. Aug. 6, 1850, died.
Married Nancy Clements Feb. 1, 1845 (daughter of Thomas and Betsy Clements), who was born Oct. 31, 1815, Dryden, N. Y. Their child: Nancy Adelia b. March 22, 1846, died.
Married Zilpha Stark March 8, 1845 (daughter of John Stark and Lovisa Stockwell), who was born July 3, 1818. Their children: Zilpha A., m. March 21, 1846; Joseph, b. Jan. 12, 1850; Mary A. b. Feb. 14, 1852, m. Peter Wimmer June 1, 1865.
Married Sarah Ann Libby Nov. 20, 1845, Nauvoo, Ill. (daughter of Nathaniel Libby and Tirzah Lord, of Ossipee, N. H.), who was born May 7, 1818. Their child: John Henry b. Sept. 18, 1848, m. Sarah Farr, m. Josephine Groesbeck.
Married Hannah W. Libby Nov. 20, 1845 (daughter of Nathaniel Libby and Tirzah Lord), who was born June 29, 1828, Ossipee, N. H. Their children: Charles W. b. Jan. 16, 1849, m. Isabelle Martin, m. Esther Martin; Sarah M. b. Jan. 16, 1849, m. Byron O. Colton; Eunich Albertine b. March 6, 1850, died; George A. b. April 7, 1862, died.
Married Susan E. West Oct. 28, 1857, Salt Lake City (daughter of Samuel West and Margaret Cooper, pioneers 1851, Captain Walton company). She was born Dec. 4, 1833, in Benton county, Tenn. Came to Utah 1851, Captain Walton company. Their children: Clarissa W. b. April 21, 1859, m. William N. Williams; Margaret b. Dec. 6, 1862, m. Edwin F. Parry; Elizabeth b. Sept. 28, 1866, m. Thomas H. Cartwright; Priscilla b. June 11, 1869, m. George S. Taylor; Emma F. b. April 19, 1871, d. Oct. 6, 1905. Families resided Salt Lake City.
Member first quorum seventies; missionary to eastern states 1835; ordained an apostle April 26, 1839; first counselor to Brigham Young. Member of senate of provisional state of Deseret. Historian. Died Sept. 1, 1875, Salt Lake City.

SMITH, JOHN HENRY (son of George Albert Smith and Sarah Ann Libby). Born Sept. 18, 1848, Kanesville, Iowa. Came to Utah Oct. 27, 1849, with father.
Married Sarah Farr Oct. 20, 1866, Salt Lake City (daughter of Lorin Farr and Nancy Chase of Salt Lake City, pioneers July 1847, Brigham Young company). She was born Oct. 30, 1849. Their children: John Henry b. Feb. 28, 1868; George Albert b. April 4, 1870, m. Lucy E. Woodruff; Lorin b. April 22, 1872; Don Carlos b. March 13, 1874, m. Esther Shields; Ezra Chase b. Sept. 21, 1876, m. Elizabeth Shields; Charles Warren b. Aug. 3, 1879; Winslow Farr b. Jan. 19, 1881, m. Emily Whitney; Nathaniel Libby b. June 19, 1883, m. Leah Whitehead; Nancy Claribell b. Jan. 22, 1886; Tirzah Priscilla b. June 11, 1888, m. William Langton; Elsie Louise b. Oct. 19, 1891.
Married Josephine Groesbeck April 4, 1877, St. George, Utah (daughter of Nicholas Groesbeck, born Sept. 5, 1819, Buskirk Bridge, Rensselaer county, N. Y., and Elizabeth Thompson, born Aug. 16, 1820, of Salt Lake City, pioneers Oct. 2, 1856, John Banks company). She was born Oct. 13, 1857, Salt Lake City. Their children: Sarah Ann b. Oct. 22, 1878, m. Moses A. Pond; Nicholas G. b. June 20, 1881, m. Florence Gay; Joseph H. b. Dec. 17, 1884, m. Sarah McKinnon; Lucy b. Dec. 24, 1887, d. Aug. 24, 1900; Elizabeth b. Jan. 30, 1890, m. Samuel Rex; Glenn b. Sept. 19, 1893; Arzella b. Nov. 5, 1895; Josephine b. Jan. 3, 1898. Families resided Salt Lake City.
Bishop of 17th ward, Salt Lake City; missionary to Great Britain 1874-75; apostle; second counselor to president of church. Member city council six years; president of convention 1895. Died Oct. 13, 1911, Salt Lake City.

SMITH, GEORGE ALBERT (son of John Henry Smith and Sarah Farr). Born April 4, 1870, Manti, Utah.
Married Lucy Emily Woodruff May 25, 1892, Salt Lake City (daughter of Wilford Woodruff, Jr., and Emily Jane Smith of St. Thomas, Nev., Randolph and Salt Lake City, Utah, the former a pioneer Oct. 14, 1850, the latter Sept. 28, 1851). She was born Jan. 10, 1869, St. Thomas, Nev. Their children: Emily b. Nov. 19, 1895; Edith b. Nov. 10, 1899; George Albert b. Sept. 10, 1905. Family home, Salt Lake City.
Member third quorum seventies; missionary to southern states 1892-94; Sunday school superintendent; superintendent Y. M. M. I. A. of Salt Lake City stake 1901; ordained apostle Oct. 6, 1893. Receiver of U. S. land office under appointment of Presidents McKinley and Roosevelt. Associated with Z. C. M. I. and Co-op, W. & Machine Co., Utah National Bank, Heber J. Grant & Co.

SMITH, JOHN (son of William Smith of Ludington, Huntingdonshire, Eng.). Born Aug. 4, 1795, Ludington. Came to Utah 1861, Thomas Wooley company.
Married Hannah Sutton 1820 (daughter of Robert Sutton),

PIONEERS AND PROMINENT MEN OF UTAH 1167

who was born March 10, 1801. Came to Utah Sept. 15, 1861, with husband. Their children: Sarah b. April 27, 1821, m. Thomas Cobbley; Robert Sutton b. June 8, 1823; Ann b. May 8, 1825, m. William Brudnall; Hannah b. July 1, 1827, m. Thomas Wooley; Charlott b. March 2, 1830, m. John Wright; James b. March 18, 1833; Jane b. Oct. 7, 1834, m. James Skinner; Harriet E. b. Sept. 2, 1837, m. Ruben V. Harrison; John b. May 30, 1843. Family home in Huntingdonshire, Eng.

SMITH, JOHN A. (son of James Smith of Glasgow, Scotland). Born 1814, Glasgow. Came to Utah 1848 with first mail.
Married Annie Anderson (daughter of John Anderson and Catherine Brown), who came to Utah 1849, Captain Richards company. Their children: Catherine A. b. March 8, 1836, m. James Croslan; James A. b. May 31, 1838, m. Jane Burnett; John A. b. March 7, 1840, m. Mary Meiklejohn; Mary A. b. March 2, 1842, m. John Wamble; William A. b. Jan. 17, 1844, m. Mary Marsden; Emma A. b. Jan. 11, 1847, m. Frank Carpenter; Joseph H. b. March 16, 1849, m. Annie Blomquist; Janet A. b. March 6, 1851, m. Warren Vose; Brigham A. b. Feb. 19, 1853, m. Jane Burnett Smith—brother's widow; Sarah A. b. Nov. 22, 1854, m. Frank Paxton; Heber A. b. Dec. 20, 1856, m. Agnes Stewart. Family resided Cottonwood and Tooele, Utah.
Counselor to Bishop Miller of Mill Creek ward 1854-1859. Moved from Mill Creek to Tooele 1859. Lumberman. Died in 1853.

SMITH, JOHN A. (son of John A. Smith and Annie Anderson). Born March 7, 1840, in Canada. Came to Utah with parents.
Married Mary Meiklejohn at Tooele, Utah (daughter of Robert Meiklejohn and Mary McLackin), who was born 1843, Dumbartonshire, Scotland. Their children: John M. b. June 4, 1864; Mary Agnes b. Nov. 19, 1865, m. S. W. Orme Feb. 24, 1886; Janet b. Dec. 20, 1867, m. E. M. Atkin; Emma J. b. May 26, 1870, m. S. C. Orme; William John; Luetta; Luella; Robert b. July 23, 1878, m. Mary A. Birch; Katy. Family home Tooele, Utah.

SMITH, JOHN B. (son of Adam Smith and Martha Browning of Ayrshire, Scotland). Born Jan. 19, 1829, in Ayrshire. Came to Utah 1852.
Married Margaret Gibson April 15, 1851, Council Bluffs, Iowa (daughter of John Gibson of Scotland, pioneer 1852). She was born March 13, 1825. Their children: Adam G. b. Feb. 14, 1852, m. Martha S. Martin, m. Eliza Shields; m. Esther Jones: Mary b. Sept. 5, 1853, d. child; John G. b. Jan. 25, 1855, m. Esther Simms; Margaret G. b. Sept. 19, 1856, m. Charles Y. Taggart; Martha G. b. Nov. 22, 1859, m. Adam S. Sagera; George G. b. Nov. 3, 1861, m. Eva H. Martensen; Ellen G. b. April 24, 1864, m. Neil S. Larson; James G. b. June 11, 1866, m. Irene Brown; Marion G. b. Feb. 10, 1869, d. child. Family home Tooele, Utah.
Married Agnes M. Love Aug. 10, 1869, Salt Lake City (daughter of John Maine of Tooele, Utah, pioneer 1868). She was born Aug. 12, 1840. Their children: Agnes M. b. April 16, 1870, m. Charles Fritchie; Joseph M. b. June 24, 1871, m. Louie Knight; Jane M. b. Nov. 17, 1872, m. George M. Garvin; Isabell M. b. April 13, 1874, d. child; Hyrum M. b. Oct. 24, 1875, m. Sarah Shields; Don Carlos M. b. May 16, 1878, and Jedediah M. b. July 7, 1877, d. children.
Counselor to Bishop Moses Martin at Pine Canyon for several years. Participated in Echo Canyon trouble.

SMITH, ADAM G. (son of John B. Smith and Margaret Gibson). Born Feb. 14, 1852, Council Bluffs, Iowa.
Married Martha S. Martin Nov. 4, 1872, Tooele, Utah (daughter of Moses Martin and Isabell Gillispie of Tooele, Utah, pioneers Sept. 13, 1853). She was born Aug. 20, 1852. Their children: Adam M. b. April 26, 1873, d. April 27, 1873; Moses M. b. April 29, 1874, m. Lucina Sessions; George M. b. Jan. 22, 1876, d. Jan. 24, 1876. Family resided Tooele, Utah. and Marion, Idaho.
Married Eliza Shields April 17, 1877, Tooele, Utah (daughter of Robert Shields and Ann Jenkins of Tooele, Utah, pioneers 1852). She was born Dec. 24, 1856. Their children: Margaret b. Feb. 14, 1878, m. William C. Whittle; Robert b. Oct. 12, 1879, m. Edna L. Whittle; John b. Aug. 31, 1881, m. Rettie Nelson; Joseph b. May 14, 1883, m. Mae De La Mare; George A. b. Dec. 7, 1885; James E. b. Oct. 21, 1887, m. Marian Whittle; Hyrum b. Jan. 2, 1894, died; Wilford A. b. Sept. 8, 1898. Family home Marion, Idaho.
Married Esther Jones Dec. 4, 1901, Salt Lake City (daughter of Evan Jones and Margaret Davis of Elba, Idaho). She was born May 20, 1878. Their children: Alma G. b. Nov. 22, 1902; Evan J. b. Feb. 17, 1904; Esther J. b. Dec. 5, 1905; Marion J. b. Nov. 13, 1907; Lyman J. b. Sept. 15, 1909; Hermoine L. b. Sept. 9, 1911.
Bishop of Marion ward, Idaho, Nov. 21, 1887, to June 13, 1911. Commissioner of Cassia Co., Idaho, six years. Died June 13, 1911.

SMITH, MOSES (son of Adam G. Smith and Martha S. Martin). Born April 29, 1874, Tooele, Utah.
Married Lucina Sessions Oct. 4, 1898, Woodruff, Utah (daughter of Harvey Sessions and Alice Bryson, both born at Marion, Idaho). She was born Sept. 12, 1880, Woodruff, Utah. Their children: Martha Lucina b. March 9, 1900; Golden K. b. Jan. 29, 1902; Ada b. Jan. 3, 1904; Ruth b. Oct. 1, 1906; Oleen b. Sept. 21, 1908; Arwyn G. b. May 6, 1910; Max Leroy b. March 29, 1912. Family home Marion, Idaho.
First counselor to Bishop Harvey Sessions 1911; missionary to southern states April 13, 1904. Assessor and collector of Cassia county 1907-08.

SMITH, JOHN PEARSON (son of Amos Smith, born Dec. 20, 1785, Buckingham, Bucks county, Pa., and Charity Kitchen, born April 13, 1787, Tinicum, Bucks county). He was born Aug. 21, 1812. Came to Utah 1851.
Married Jane H. Opdyke Aug. 27, 1835 (daughter of Joseph Opdyke and Martha Merrick), who was born March 4, 1815. Their children: Albert b. Aug. 24, 1837, m. Josephine Roe; Theodore b. Sept. 18, 1839, m. Amy Hemenway; Mary Frances b. April 2, 1842; George O. b. Sept. 21, 1844, m. Nellie Creer; Ella b. Sept. 15, 1847; Ellwood b. Oct. 2, 1850; John Pearson, Jr., b. Dec. 5, 1855, m. Eliza A. Stratford. Family home, Salt Lake City.

SMITH, JOHN PEARSON (son of John Pearson Smith and Jane H. Opdyke). Born Dec. 5, 1855, Salt Lake City.
Married Eliza A. Stratford Oct. 10, 1878, Salt Lake City (daughter of Edwin Stratford and Marianna Crabb), who was born Jan. 23, 1859, in Iowa. Their children: Maud M. b. July 27, 1879, m. B. J. Griffin March 21, 1906; Effie E. b. July 25, 1881, m. H. F. Barrows June 19, 1907; John P. b. Aug. 15, 1883, m. Clara Jones Aug. 3, 1903; Ivy L. b. Oct. 13, 1885; Ella F. b. April 25, 1888, m. O. O. Roskelley June 15, 1910; Edwin S. b. July 11, 1890; Jesse E. and Leslie A. b. Aug. 23, 1892; Orita b. Dec. 3, 1894; Percy E. b. Feb. 11, 1898. Family home Logan, Utah.

SMITH, JOHN SIVIL (son of William Smith, born 1770, Muchmotal, Hereford, Eng., and Mary Sivil, born 1778, Berns, Worcestershire, Eng.). He was born March 10, 1809, in Worcestershire, Eng. Came to Utah. William Snow company.
Married Jane Wadley (daughter of Michael Wadley and Jane Ennis), who was born Jan. 2, 1814. Came to Utah, William Snow company. Their children: Anna b. Jan. 6, 1839, m. Norman Brown Dec. 20, 1858; Ellen Smith b. Feb. 17, 1842, m. John Q. Knowlton March 17, 1862; Elizabeth (daughter of Edwin Dilworth Woolley and Ellen Wilding), Stevenson March 21, 1867; William C. b. Jan. 1, 1852, m. Mary E. Smith Jan. 18, 1882; Joseph T. b. June 27, 1853, d. aged 42; George M. b. April 11, 1855, m. Mary E. Woolley Jan. 13, 1881; Harriet E. b. April 9, 1857, m. Jesse M. Smith Feb. 19, 1880.

SMITH, GEORGE MICHAEL (son of John Sivil Smith and Jane Wadley). Born April 11, 1855, Draper, Utah.
Married Mary Ellen Woolley Jan. 13, 1881, Salt Lake City (daughter of Edwin Dilworth Woolley and Ellen Wilding), who was born Dec. 1, 1858, Salt Lake City. Their children: Edna May b. Nov. 2, 1881; George Sivil b. March 3, 1883, m. Ethel Egbert Feb. 17, 1909; Ernest Heber b. April 29, 1885, m. Cecelia L. Short June 17, 1908; Elmer Wilding b. Oct. 25, 1887; Hyrum Wendell b. Aug. 7, 1890; Michael Paul b. Feb. 9, 1893; Edwin Parley b. May 22, 1896; Luella b. Sept. 1, 1898; Joseph Harold b. Sept. 21, 1900. Family resided Kaysville, Utah, and Thatcher, Idaho.

SMITH, JOHN X. (son of John Smith, born March 25, 1796, Rands, Northamptonshire, Eng., and Sarah Smith, born 1797, Great Cathworth, Northamptonshire). He was born Sept. 9, 1827, in Northamptonshire.
Married Margaret Patterson July 24, 1855, Cedar City (daughter of Andrew Patterson, pioneer Aug. 14, 1852, Captain Higby company). She was born Dec. 1, 1838, and came to Utah Aug. 14, 1852, John Higby company. Their children: John Andrew b. June 9, 1856, m. Charlotte Swindlehurst April 26, 1878; Joseph Anthony b. Feb. 26, 1858, m. Amelia Swindlehurst Sept. 19, 1883; Margaret b. Nov. 4, 1859, m. John Ashworth Nov. 27, 1878; Sarah b. Feb. 22, 1861, m. Ebenezer Gillis Oct. 29, 1880; Robert Hyrum b. Feb. 22, 1861, m. Caroline Carlow Feb. 1900; Mary Ann b. May 26, 1863, m. James Farer April 26, 1881; Richard H. b. Feb. 13, 1865; Susan Jane b. Oct. 25, 1866, m. John Murdoch; Thomas Ekin b. March 21, 1868; Emma E. b. March 7, 1870, m. Wilford Robinson June 4, 1890; William Edward b. April 29, 1873, m. Elsie Eyre Jan. 24, 1894; Catherine P. b. Dec. 21, 1874, m. Thomas Bennet Sept. 18, 1893; Nettie b. Aug. 17, 1876, m. John Stoney Feb. 25, 1895; Clara Ellen b. Nov. 11, 1878.
Bishop of 2d ward of Beaver stake 1877-88.

SMITH, JOHN ANDREW (son of John X. Smith and Margaret Patterson). Born June 9, 1856, Cedar City, Utah.
Married Charlotte Swindlehurst April 26, 1878, St. George, Utah (daughter of John Swindlehurst and Rachild Rothwell, pioneers 1868, Daniel D. McArthur company). She was born March 4, 1857, Baxenden, Lancashire, Eng. Their children: John Thomas b. May 10, 1880, m. Elizabeth A. Bradshaw Oct. 28, 1903; Ida b. Aug. 28, 1882, m. James Riley June 3, 1903; Mary b. May 14, 1885, m. Heber Atkin Sept. 11, 1907; Ettie b. Dec. 25, 1887, m. Jedediah Atkin Dec. 25, 1907; Edwin b. June 8, 1891; Albert b. Aug. 31, 1895; Gilbert b. Aug. 31, 1895; Leroy b. Nov. 3, 1897. Family home Beaver City, Utah.
Alternate member high council Beaver stake.

SMITH, JOSEPH FIELDING (son of Hyrum Smith [the patriarch], born Feb. 9, 1800, Tunbridge, Vt., and Mary Fielding [daughter of John and Rachel Fielding], born July 21, 1801, Honeydon, Bedfordshire, Eng., died Sept. 21, 1852, Salt Lake City—married in 1837). He was born Nov. 13, 1838, Far West, Caldwell county, Mo. Came to Utah with mother Sept. 23, 1848, Heber C. Kimball company.
Married Levira A. C. Smith April 4, 1859 (daughter of Samuel Harrison Smith and Levira Clark), who was born April 29, 1842, Nauvoo, Ill.
Married Julina Lambson May 5, 1866 (daughter of Alfred B. Lambson and Melissa J. Bigler), who was born June 18, 1849, Salt Lake City. Their children: Mercy Josephine b. Aug. 14, 1867, d. June 6, 1870; Mary Sophronia b. Oct. 7, 1869, m. Alfred W. Peterson Dec. 17, 1901; Donnette b. Sept. 17, 1872, m. Alonzo P. Kesler Dec. 26, 1900; Joseph Fielding, Jr., b. July 19, 1876, m. Louie E. Shurtliff April 26, 1898, who died March 30, 1908, m. Ethel Reynolds Nov. 2, 1908; David Asael b. May 24, 1879, m. Emily Jenkins Jan. 24, 1901; George Carlos b. Aug. 14, 1881, m. Lillian Emery Oct. 29, 1903; Julina Clarissa b. Feb. 10, 1884, m. Joseph S. Peery Dec. 23, 1909; Elias Wesley b. April 21, 1886, m. Edith Eleanor Patrick Dec. 14, 1910; Emily b. Sept. 11, 1888; Rachel b. Dec. 11, 1890; Edith b. Jan. 3, 1894.
Married Sarah Ellen Richards March 1, 1868 (daughter of Willard Richards and Sarah Longstroth), who was born Aug. 24, 1850, Salt Lake City. Their children: Sarah Ellen b. Feb. 5, 1869, d. Feb. 11, 1869; Leonora b. Jan. 30, 1871 (d. Dec. 23, 1907), m. Joseph Nelson June 14, 1893; Joseph Richards b. Feb. 22, 1873; Heber John b. July 3, 1876, d. March 3, 1877; Rhoda A. b. July 20, 1878, d. July 6, 1879; Minerva b. April 30, 1880, m. Matthew Miller April 25, 1902; Alice b. July 27, 1882, d. April 29, 1901; Willard Richards b. Nov. 20, 1884, m. Florence Grant Feb. 3, 1910; Franklin Richards b. May 12, 1888; Jeannetta b. Aug. 25, 1891; Asenath b. Dec. 28, 1896.
Married Edna Lambson Jan. 1, 1871 (daughter of Alfred B. Lambson and Melissa J. Bigler), who was born March 3, 1851, Salt Lake City. Their children: Hyrum Mack b. March 21, 1872, m. Ida Bowman Nov. 15, 1895; Alvin Fielding b. Aug. 7, 1874, m. Millie Atkins June 29, 1903; Alfred Jason b. Dec. 13, 1876, d. April 6, 1877; Edna Melissa b. Oct. 6, 1879, m. John F. Bowman Jan. 27, 1903; Albert Jesse b. Sept. 16, 1881, d. Aug. 25, 1883; Robert b. Nov. 12, 1883, d. Feb. 4, 1886; Emma b. Aug. 21, 1888; Zina b. Oct. 11, 1890, m. Ambrose Greenwell Dec. 12, 1910; Ruth b. Oct. 21, 1893, d. March 17, 1898; Martha b. May 12, 1897.
Married Alice Kimball Dec. 6, 1883 (daughter of Heber C. Kimball and Anna Gheen), who was born Sept. 6, 1858, Salt Lake City. Their children: Lucy Mack b. April 14, 1890; Andrew Kimball b. Jan. 6, 1893; Jesse Kimball b. May 21, 1896; Fielding Kimball b. April 9, 1898.
Married Mary Taylor Schwartz Jan. 13, 1884 (daughter of William Schwartz and Agnes Taylor), who was born April 30, 1865, Holliday, Utah. Their children: John S. b. Aug. 20, 1888, d. Aug. 3, 1889; Calvin S. b. May 29, 1890; Samuel S. b. Oct. 26, 1892; James S. b. Nov. 13, 1894; Agnes b. Nov. 3, 1897; Silas S. b. Jan. 3, 1900; Royal S. b. May 21, 1906.
His early training was amid the scenes and vicissitudes incident to his father's martyrdom and the driving of the Latter-day Saints to the Rocky mountains from Nauvoo, Ill. With his mother he left Nauvoo in 1846 when only 8 years old and drove an oxteam across the state (then territory) of Iowa to Council Bluffs. The following year he drove an oxteam from the Missouri river to Salt Lake valley, enduring all the hardships of the journey over the plains and barren country intervening, and performing much labor that was required of the men. His opportunities for schooling were limited, and his early education was chiefly acquired from his mother. She left him an orphan at the age of 14 years. In 1854 he went to the Hawaiian Islands on a mission for the Church of Jesus Christ of Latter-day Saints, where he remained four years, mastering the native tongue. After returning in 1858 he officiated as sergeant-at-arms in the Utah territorial legislature (1858-59), and upon its adjournment went to England with his cousin, Samuel H. B. Smith, there laboring in the ministry. In 1864, after his return from England, he again went to Hawaii and continued his ecclesiastical labors. Upon returning to Utah he served as a member of the Salt Lake City municipal council and as a member of the territorial legislature, and in 1882 was president of the legislative council. He presided over the constitutional convention held in Utah in 1882, but was debarred as a legislator by the Edmunds law. He served eight years as a clerk in the historian's office and was active in church work, serving as a missionary for the church and in various positions in Davis and Salt Lake stakes of Zion. He went on a second mission to Great Britain in 1874, and on a third mission in 1877. He was ordained an apostle July 1, 1866, and became a member of the council of the twelve in 1880. He was chosen to be second counselor to President John Taylor and also served as counselor to President Wilford Woodruff and later to President Lorenzo Snow. Following the death of the latter he was sustained as president of the church, which office he now holds.

SMITH, JOSEPH II. (son of John Smith of Dudley, Worcestershire, Eng.). Born Aug. 23, 1819, at Dudley. Came to Utah in September, 1855, Milo Andrus company.
Married Maria Stanford 1842 (daughter of Richard and Latitia Stanford of Shaterford, Worcestershire). She was born Nov. 12, 1809, and came to Utah with husband. Their children: Emma; Mary Ann; Joseph Stanford.
One of presidents of seventies' quorum. Farmer.

SMITH, JOSEPH STANFORD (son of Joseph H. Smith and Maria Stanford). Born June 23, 1850, Tipton, Staffordshire, Eng. Came to Utah with father.
Married Jane Arabella Coombs Oct. 23, 1871, Cedar City, Utah, who was born Dec. 28, 1853. Their children: Ellen b. Sept. 29, 1872; Ida Olive and Ada Olevia b. Jan. 24, 1874; Joseph Elroy b. Sept. 14, 1876; George Abraham b. June 8, 1879; Mabel b. Dec. 30, 1882. Family home Cedar City, Utah. High priest; bishop's counselor.

SMITH, JOSEPH JOHNSON (son of William Smith, born in December, 1799, at Bedford, Eng.). He was born April 8, 1821, Kempston, Eng. Came to Utah Sept. 17, 1850, David Evans company.
Married Mary Ann Smart, who was born Nov. 5, 1823, m. William Skein.
Married Ann Coleman Jan. 1, 1850, Maryville, Mo. (daughter of Prime Coleman and Sarah Thornton, pioneers, David Evans company). She was born Oct. 2, 1833, at Odhusten, Lehi City, Utah. Their children: Sarah Ann b. Nov. 10, 1850, m. Samuel Southwick, d. 1870; Joseph William b. Oct. 20, 1852, m. Julia McCracklin; Hyrum b. March 20, 1856, m. Eliza A. Fowler; m. Amy D. Devey; Aldrira b. Jan. 14, 1858, m. James Roberts/Julia Elizabeth b. Dec. 16, 1859, m. James Taylor; Samuel A. b. Sept. 17, 1863, m. Harriet A. Webb; John Franklin b. Aug. 17, 1865, m. Sarah A. Yates; David b. July 30, 1869; Albert b. Aug. 20, 1871, m. Maud Thomas; Moroni Alma b. June 27, 1873, m. Blanch Beck.
Married Sarah A. Liddiard Feb. 10, 1866, who was born Oct. 16, 1831, and died Sept. 25, 1909. Their only child was Florence Sophia b. Oct. 1, 1866, m. J. Edward Cotter.
Seventy. Assisted in bringing immigrants to Utah. Made the first plow and the first nails at Lehi, Utah. Built several mills at Lehi, making of wagon tires the parts necessarily made of iron. Took part in clearing the first fields at Lehi. Indian war veteran. Blacksmith; farmer and stockraiser. Died Aug. 6, 1902, Lehi, Utah.

SMITH, HYRUM (son of Joseph Johnson Smith and Ann Coleman). Born March 20, 1856, Lehi, Utah.
Married Eliza A. Fowler April 3, 1879, at Lehi, Utah (daughter of Thomas Fowler and Jane Kemishe), who was born Nov. 4, 1861, at West Jordan, Utah; died March 1, 1897, Lehi City, Utah. Their children: Hyrum Eugene b. Jan. 25, 1880, m. Louie Singleton; Charles Henry b. Nov. 15, 1881, m. Ada Dughey; Isaac William b. Feb. 22, 1886, m. Elizabeth Davis Sept. 12, 1913; Lillian Edna b. April 28, 1888, m. Ambrose G. Reese Dec. 29, 1906; Jennie Eveline b. Feb. 7, 1890, m. Ambrose Fotheringham; Joseph Earl b. March 26, 1894; Elizabeth A. b. Feb. 17, 1897. Family home Lehi, Utah.
Married Amy D. Devey Jan. 16, 1907, Salt Lake City, who was born Nov. 8, 1876, Alpine, Utah. Their children: Douglas C. b. Feb. 16, 1908; Amy Damarus b. Jan. 5, 1910.
Member 68th quorum seventies. Farmer and stockraiser.

SMITH, LOT.
Married Lydia McBride in 1851, Salt Lake City (daughter of Robert McBride of Farmington, Utah). Their children: Samuel b. 1852; Robert b. 1862, m. Oma Smith.
Married Jane Walker Feb. 14, 1852, Salt Lake City (daughter of John Walker and Lydia Holmes of Peacham, Caledonia county, Vt., pioneers 1848, Heber C. Kimball company). She came to Utah with parents. Their children: Rhoda J. b. Sept. 26, 1853, m. Jacob Flynn Hutchinson; William Lot b. Sept. 12, 1855, m. Mary Jenkins; Jedediah Heber b. Aug. 29, 1857, m. Sylvia Stoddard; Emily Abigail b. Sept. 8, 1859, m. Moroni Hess; Annetta b. March 9, 1863, m. Joseph Udy; Alice b. Nov. 11, 1865, m. Oliver LeGrand Robinson; Margaret Agnes b. Aug. 15, 1868, m. George Parmer; Lucy Effie b. Nov. 13, 1874, m. Nephi Parmer. Family home Farmington, Utah.
Married Julian P. Smith Nov. 25, 1855, Salt Lake City (daughter of Ira Smith and Louise Chapin of Iowa, pioneers 1848). She was born March 6, 1837. Their children: Phoebe Vilate b. Sept. 30, 1857, m. Edward Steed, m. Mr. Smith; Marie Louise b. Dec. 15, 1861, m. Edward Stoddard, m. Bart Krumkerman; Julia Adelaide b. Sept. 14, 1863, and Sarah Theresa b. July 6, 1866, died; Hyrum Burton b. July 10, 1869; Julia Amanda b. Jan. 4, 1875. Family home, Farmington.
Married Laura Burdick 1857, Salt Lake City (daughter of Bryons Burdick), who was born 1838. Their children: Helen b. 1861, m. Mr. Vance; Lillian b. 1865; Abiah b. 1867, m. Samuel Nelson; Laura b. 1869; Alden b. 1872.
Married Alice Ann Richards May 30, 1868, Salt Lake City (daughter of Willard Richards and Nannie Longstroth). Their children: Nannie A. b. Feb. 10, 1869, m. James Ashcroft; Willard R. b. July 31, 1872, m. Melissa Parker; George A. b. Sept. 9, 1874, died; Lot b. June 30, 1827, m. Sarah Bingham; Wilford W. b. 1879, died; Joseph H. b. April 21, 1882, m. Bertha Jensen; Rhoda b. June 1834, and Rexey b. June 1886, died; George Albert b. Aug. 14, 1889, m. Samantha Willie. Family home, Farmington.

Married Alice Baugh April 29, 1872, Salt Lake City (daughter of George Thomas Baugh and Elizabeth Ann Ferenough). Their children: Elizabeth Jane b. March 1873; Mary Melissa b. Feb. 19, 1875, m. Robert C. Carr; Brigham b. Jan. 22, 1878, m. Belle Hawkinson; Diantha b. April 12, 1880, m. William M. Wilson; Franklin D. b. April 5, 1882, m. Rosetta Pearl Huntsman; Jesse N. b. March 27, 1884; Martha b. 1886, m. Alexander J. Schott; Charles R. b. Nov. 27, 1888; Kate b. Dec. 1, 1891, m. William K. Fleischmann.
Married Mary Garns. Their children: Lorenzo; Samuel; Emily; Heleman; Francis.
Married Diantha Mortensen. Their children: Charlott; Hyrum; Diantha; Nephi; Edward; Baby, died.
Officer of the Deseret militia; defended settlers at Provo against Indians; major of the Utah militia and in charge at the burning of Johnston's army provision trains on their way to Echo Canyon, Utah.

SMITH, NOAH (son of William Smith and Polly Whitney of Long Ridge, Stamford, Conn.). Born 1803, Stamford, Conn. Came to Utah Oct. 5, 1862, Ansel P. Harmon company.
Married Mary De Forest at Stamford (daughter of Samuel De Forest and Elizabeth Chapman of Pound Ridge, Conn). She was born Feb. 20, 1816. Their children: Henry, m. Annie Ross; Mary Eliza, m. James Sanderson; Sarah Elizabeth, died; Harriet Emily, m. Theodore Bellwood; Cornelia Frances, m. Harrison Tuttle Shurtliff; Melissa Alice, m. John Malin; Charles Albert, m. Sarah Jane Shurtliff; George Edward; Cora Elizabeth; Ida Louisa, latter three died; Ella Ethelina, m. George Laney.
Shoemaker. Died 1863, Salt Lake City.

SMITH, RICHARD (son of James Smith, born Sept. 20, 1784, Musselburgh, Scotland, and Euphemia Adams, born 1784, Tranent, Scotland—married 1807). Born April 29, 1821, Arneston, Scotland. Came to Utah Sept. 22, 1866, William Henry Chipman company.
Married Helen Hogg 1841 (daughter of George Hogg and Isabell Willson, married 1804). She was born July 3, 1822, and came to Utah with husband. Their children: James b. June 11, 1842, m. Marian McNeil; Isabell b. Oct. 14, 1844, m. William McNeil; George H. b. Jan. 21, 1847, m. Agnes Park; Robert H. b. Aug. 26, 1849, m. Mary Thompson; John H. b. March 5, 1852, m. Margaret Nielsen; Euphemia b. May 26, 1854, m. Nephi Andrews; Cathrine b. April 5, 1857, m. George McCulloch; Jenet b. June 25, 1860, m. Charles McCulloch; Richard H. b. Jan. 14, 1863, m. Agnes McCulloch April 10, 1890; William b. March 4, 1865.

SMITH, RICHARD H. (son of Richard Smith and Helen Hogg). Born Jan. 14, 1863, Scotland. Came to Utah with parents.
Married Agnes McCulloch April 10, 1890, at Rexburg, Idaho. Their children: James A. b. Oct. 18, 1891, m. Edna Arnold Dec. 21, 1910; Leora Eva b. May 2, 1894; Vera Calanthe b. June 25, 1903; Kenneth Echlo b. April 1, 1910.
Lived at Logan, Utah until 1884 when he moved to Rexburg, Idaho. Sunday school superintendent; president seventies; counselor to president Y. M. M. I. A., Fremont stake; bishop of Rexburg 3d ward; missionary to England 1907-08. Probate judge of Fremont Co., Idaho, 1901-02; Fremont county commissioner.

SMITH, RICHARD (son of Joseph Smith of England). Born in England. Came to Utah 1852, with oxteam.
Married Diana Brasell, in Pennsylvania (daughter of John Brasell of Scotland). Their children: Phillip, m. Eliza Ann Frampton; James, m. Christena Penrod; m. Janie Duke; William, m. Mariah Parry; Thomas, m. Sarah Frampton; Ephraim, m. Nancy Bethers; Nancy, m. Andrew Ross; Elizabeth, died; Rachel, m. John Ross; Lare. Family resided Heber and Provo, Utah.
Seventy. Farmer. Died at Provo.

SMITH, PHILLIP (son of Richard Smith and Diana Brasell). Born Dec. 27, 1821, in Tennessee. Came to Utah 1852.
Married Eliza Ann Frampton March 4, 1849, Mt. Pisgah, Iowa (daughter of David Frampton and Elizabeth Huff of Iowa, latter came to Utah). She was born July 14, 1830. Their children: David Frampton b. Feb. 27, 1850, died; Richard b. April 21, 1852, m. Sarah Ann Lee; Phillip A. b. Aug. 16, 1854, died; Melissa Ann b. July 17, 1856, m. Samuel Lee; Eliza Lovisa b. Feb. 23, 1859, m. Joseph Ford; Sarah Carlista b. Sept. 20, 1861, m. Herbert Clegg; Ida Victoria b. Dec. 14, 1863, m. Joseph Johnson; Alonzo b. Dec. 4, 1865, and Adelbert b. Nov. 4, 1867, died; Effie Armenta b. June 8, 1869, m. Ephraim Haws; Charlie (adopted) b. Dec. 6, 1873, m. Malinda Smith. Family home Heber, Utah.
Seventy. Sheriff of Wasatch county. Veteran Black Hawk and Walker Indian wars; took part in Echo Canyon trouble. School trustee. Farmer.

SMITH, RICHARD (son of William Smith and Mary Pierce of Yorkshire, Eng.). Born Aug. 2, 1829, in Yorkshire. Came to Utah 1855, oxteam company.
Married Tabitha Holroyd Oct. 30, 1861, American Fork, Utah (daughter of Seth and Mary Holroyd of Yorkshire, who came to Utah in 1869). She was born Jan. 14, 1837, and came to Utah in 1861. Their children: Richard Lorenzo b. Oct. 13, 1862, m. Henrietta Augusta Hill; Mary Ellen b.

April 6, 1864, m. Aneurin Zim Marshall; Seth William b. March 7, 1866, m. Ida J. Lund; Thomas b. April 14, 1868, died; Martha Jane b. June 11, 1869, m. Edgar Hunt Thayn; Joseph b. Sept. 4, 1871, died; Sarah b. Dec. 7, 1873, m. Brigham Hunt Thayn; John Pierce b. April 12, 1877, m. Violet Saville; Anna May b. May 26, 1882, m. Ervin Branch.
High priest. Shoemaker. Died Aug. 5, 1904, Beaver, Utah.

SMITH, SAMUEL (son of Samuel Smith of Castle Hedingham, Essex, Eng.). Born 1805, at Castle Hedingham. Came to Utah Sept. 29, 1866, Daniel Thompson company.
Married Elizabeth Cheek 1832, at West Hanningfield, Essex, Eng. (daughter of Samuel Cheek and Rachel Mead of that place). She was born June 6, 1809. Their children: Samuel, m. Jane Ellison; Emma, m. Rolia Butcher; Frances, m. John Winch; Joseph Daniel, b. May 6, 1846, m. Mary Ann Frampton, m. Adeline Brunson.
Farmer. Died Sept. 27, 1866, Wanship, Utah.

SMITH, JOSEPH DANIEL (son of Samuel Smith and Elizabeth Cheek). Born May 6, 1846, Margaretting Tye, Essex, Eng. Came to Utah with father.
Married Mary Ann Frampton July 16, 1866, in Wyoming (daughter of James Frampton and Mary Boosey of Stanford Le Hope, Eng., who came to Utah 1870). She was born Feb. 19, 1849. Their children: Elizabeth b. Dec. 18, 1868, m. Mary Jackson; Charles Daniel b. Jan. 6, 1873, m. Mary Greenhaigh; James Hyrum b. Sept. 20, 1875, drowned; Arthur John b. March 13, 1878, died; Lois Josephine b. Aug. 13, 1882, m. Earl Viele; Francis b. Oct. 8, 1884, m. John Rowley. Family home Fillmore, Utah.
Married Adeline Brunson Oct. 7, 1880, Salt Lake City (daughter of Lewis Brunson and Eliza Park of Fillmore, Utah). She was born Jan. 3, 1862. Their children: Lewis b. Jan. 31, 1882, m. Eva Beckstrand; William b. Jan. 3, 1884, died; Peter Lorenzo b. April 7, 1888; David b. Oct. 14, 1889; John b. Aug. 20, 1891, m. Jetta Burnett; Ephraim Park b. March 5, 1893; Daniel Zebulon b. Jan. 9, 1895; Albert b. Sept. 7, 1897, died; Addie Victoria b. May 24, 1899; Myrtle b. Dec. 7, 1901. Family home Fillmore, Utah.
Missionary to England and Ireland 1886-87; high councilor; bishop; patriarch; Sunday school superintendent. Treasurer, assessor and collector Millard county; alderman and mayor Fillmore city. Farmer; merchant; traveling salesman; miller; dairyman.

SMITH, SAMUEL (son of Daniel Smith and Sarah Wooding of Sherrington, Buckinghamshire, Eng.). Born May 22, 1818, at Sherrington. Came to Utah Sept. 5, 1850, Aaron Johnson company.
Married Mary Ann Lines Oct. 12, 1837, at Hemel Hempstead, Hartfordshire, Eng. (daughter of Michael Lines and Hannah Abley of Hemel Hempstead, pioneers Sept. 5, 1850, Aaron Johnson company). She was born June 17, 1811. Their children: Mary Ann b. July 23, 1839, d. June 22, 1840; Mary Ann b. April 19, 1841, d. Aug. 23, 1843; Samuel Lorenzo b. July 17, 1843, m. Amanda J. Tibbets Feb. 4, 1864, m. Eunice Tibbets 1873; Sarah Ann b. Nov. 20, 1845, d. Sept. 19, 1846; Eliza Jane b. Nov. 20, 1845, d. Nov. 4, 1846; Hyrum James b. Oct. 31, 1847, m. Sarah A. Fosgreen Oct. 10, 1870, m. Cornelia E. Walker Dec. 30, 1878; Marette b. Sept. 9, 1850, m. Dr. O. C. Ormsby Oct. 11, 1869; Hannah Lines b. Oct. 10, 1852, d. Oct. 15, 1861; David John b. Feb. 15, 1855, d. July 12, 1855.
Married Sarah Jane Ingraham 1853, Salt Lake City (daughter of William Ingraham and Susannah Griffith, of Worcester, Worcestershire, Eng.). She was born Oct. 10, 1836. Their children: Thyrsa Ann b. Nov. 20, 1853, m. Huber C. Tippets Oct. 1872; Daniel William b. Nov. 5, 1855, ... Sept. 8, 1873; Isaac b. Dec. 31, 1857, m. Harriet C. Ensign Dec. 28, 1876, m. Anna Elizabeth Carlisle, m. Elizabeth Fuhrimann; Sarah Eliza b. Jan. 13, 1860, m. David P. Evans Sept. 8, 1881; John Woodlng b. May 12, 1862, m. Mary Neeley Jan. 1880; Susannah b. May 24, 1864, m. Thomas B. Evans Oct. 18, 1881; Frances Mary b. Jan. 9, 1867, m. Eli Fosgreen Oct. 23, 1885; Franklin Richard b. Aug. 20, 1869, d. Aug. 6, 1870; Alice Rozella b. July 18, 1871, m. William Impy Dec. 25, 1888.
Married Frances Ann Ingraham July 31, 1856, Salt Lake City (daughter of William Ingraham and Susannah Griffith), who was born Jan. 23, 1840. Their children: Charles Fosgreen Oct. 18, 1876; Priscilla b. Jan. 14, 1860, m. Elias Jensen June 16, 1886; Elias J. b. Oct. 7, 1861, d. Aug. 13, 1862; Mary E. b. Nov. 8, 1863, d. Oct. 12, 1864; Olivia J. b. July 22, 1865, m. John T. Kelly Jan. 3, 1887; Phoebe E. b. Nov. 18, 1867, d. May 23, 1874; Roxey A. b. Feb. 6, 1870, d. May 5, 1874; Viola May b. Feb. 25, 1872, d. Oct. 18, 1874; Eliza Beatrice b. Sept. 29, 1875, m. Joseph H. Weeks Aug. 15, 1894; Warren Samuel b. Sept. 22, 1877, m. Esther Coleman Jan. 3, 1900; Everet b. April 7, 1880, m. Lillie J. Fishburn Sept. 9, 1901; Wm. Rufus b. Dec. 7, 1881, m. Miriam Miles June 10, 1903, m. Hannah McClain Jan. 12, 1908; Phosa b. Feb. 4, 1884, m. Rast Larsen Sept. 6, 1901.
Married Janett Maria Smith June 7, 1857, Salt Lake City (daughter of George Smith and Caroline Harrison, pioneers Sept. 5, 1850, Aaron Johnson company). She was born Jan. 20, 1839. Their children: Abraham b. April 20, 1858, m. Laura M. Fishburn Dec. 3, 1880; Letitia b. May 3, 1860, m. Charles Oscar Dunn Oct. 18, 1878; Thomas b. Oct. 22, 1862, m. Frances Van Noy Dec. 29, 1881; James George b. Nov. 3, 1865, m. Louisa Gilbert Nov. 18, 1885; Leslie b. April 21,

1869, d. Nov. 18, 1869; Lester b. Sept. 7, 1870, d. April 1874; Earnest Charles b. Aug. 18, 1875, m. Annie Laughton Nov. 5, 1902; Charles Eli b. March 11, 1879, m. Lillie Laurensen.
Married Caroline Smith June 7, 1857, Salt Lake City (daughter of George Smith and Caroline Harrison), who was born Nov. 5, 1841. Their children: Delina Caroline b. June 23, 1859, m. Gordon E. Beckstead Sept. 27, 1877; Jacob Smith b. March 18, 1861, m. Sophia Jensen Dec. 24, 1878; Rose Emma b. June 27, 1863, d. Oct. 1864; Eliza M. b. July 5, 1865, d. March 1878; Netta b. July 17, 1867, d. March 1, 1874; Lorenzo D. b. July 10, 1869, d. Jan. 1874; Cynthia b. Nov. 12, 1871, d. March 8, 1874; Vilate b. Nov. 13, 1873, m. Ralph B. Wiggins Feb. 12, 1894; Edessia b. Oct. 8, 1875, m. Arthur D. Hamsen July 24, 1894; Janett Laura b. Jan. 20, 1878, d. Dec. 12, 1890; Theodore b. July 13, 1880, d. Dec. 6, 1889; Tobias Chancy b. Jan. 28, 1883, d. Dec. 18, 1889. Family home Brigham City, Utah.
High priest; family patriarch; high councilor, Box Elder stake, 1855-77. Vice-president and assistant superintendent of the Brigham Co-op. Judge. Box Elder county; mayor, March 3, 1879, to March 14, 1883; postmaster 1855-82, of Brigham City; Farmer; manufacturer; railway builder. Died Oct. 2, 1896, Smithfield, Utah, and was buried at Brigham City.

SMITH, ISAAC (son of Samuel Smith and Sarah Jane Ingraham). Born Dec. 31, 1857, Brigham City, Utah.
Married Harriet Camilla Ensign Dec. 28, 1876, Salt Lake City (daughter of Martin Luther Ensign and Mary Dunn of Brigham City, pioneers 1847, Ira Eldredge and Brigham Young companies). She was born April 24, 1859. Their children: Isaac Samuel b. Dec. 4, 1878, m. Lulu Yates June 2, 1904; Martin Luther b. Aug. 20, 1881, d. April 7, 1884; William Richard b. March 21, 1884, m. Zina Crouch July 28, 1910; Mary Camilla b. June 14, 1886, d. Sept. 20, 1899; Wesley Ensign b. Dec. 9, 1888, m. Lucy Lishman Sept. 22, 1909; m. Alta Pond March 20, 1913; Sarah Ann b. Nov. 1, 1891, m. Dow Lewis June 29, 1910; Theron Ensign b. Dec. 13, 1893; Leona Ensign b. Dec. 25, 1895; George Ensign b. March 24, 1898; Malcolm Woodruff b. Feb. 20, 1911; Theodore Roosevelt b. Sept. 20, 1903, d. July 19, 1904; Ruby Ensign b. Nov. 5, 1905.
Married Anna Elizabeth Carlisle Sept. 15, 1885, Logan, Utah (daughter of John G. Carlisle and Margaret Kewley of Logan, Utah; former pioneer 1854, Hooper and Eldredge merchandise train, latter Nov. 1856, Edward Martin handcart company). She was born Jan. 18, 1860, died Sept. 17, 1886. No children.
Married Elizabeth Fuhrimann June 2, 1894 (daughter of Jacob Fuhrimann and Barbara Loosle of Providence, Utah, pioneers 1860). She was born June 9, 1872. Their children: Jacob Isaac b. Sept. 18, 1895; Joseph Fuhrimann b. July 18, 1897; Welland b. Feb. 19, 1899; Ingraham b. March 21, 1901; Elva b. Oct. 22, 1904; Oliver b. Oct. 6, 1908. Family home Logan, Utah.
Missionary to Great Britain and Channel Islands 1878; bishop seventh ward, Logan 1884-90; counselor in presidency 1890-1906, and president 1906-11 Cache stake; ordained a patriarch May 3, 1913. Manager Brigham City lumber yard 1880-82; manager Logan Z. C. M. I. 1891-97; merchandise, produce, cold storage and ice business.

SMITH, SILAS (son of Asael Smith and Elizabeth Shilling of Stockholm, St. Lawrence county, N. Y.). Born June 6, 1822. Came to Utah 1853.
Married Elizabeth Norton in Pennsylvania (daughter of William and Elizabeth Norton of Clinton Co., Iowa). She was born June 1, 1826. Their children: Silas Marion b. April 17, 1845, in Lee Co., Iowa, m. Alvira Partridge; Julia Elizabeth, m. Melvin Ross; Frederick Asael; Mary Jane b. June 17, 1853, m. John Thompson Rowley; Henry, m. Catherine Saunberg; Franklin, m. Rose Ann Gallaway; Vienna, died; Martha E., m. John Byrne. Family home Provo, Utah.
Missionary to Sandwich Islands 1854; bishop at Provo, Utah. Farmer; lawyer. Died June 11, 1892.

SMITH, SILAS SANFORD (son of Silas Smith, born Oct. 1, 1779, Derryfield, Hillsboro county, N. H., and Mary Aikens, born Aug. 13, 1797, Barnard, Vt.—married March 4, 1828). Born Oct. 26, 1830, Stockholm, St. Lawrence county, N. Y. Came to Utah 1847, Perrigrine Sessions company.
Married Clarinda Ricks July 9, 1851 (daughter of Joel Ricks and Eleanor Martin—married May 1, 1827, in Trigg county, Ky., pioneers September, 1848, Heber C. Kimball company). She was born July 10, 1833, and came to Utah with parents. Their children: Silas Sanford, Jr., b. July 10, 1853, m. Betsy Williamson Nov. 3, 1873; Jesse Joel b. Nov. 4, 1857, m. Margaret A. Haskell April 6, 1884; Leonora A. b. Oct. 22, 1859; Stephen Augustus b. Nov. 1, 1861, m. Elizabeth J. Elledge Dec. 20, 1882; Ella C. b. March 9, 1864, m. Benjamin F. Boice Dec. 20, 1882.
Married Sarah Ann Ricks March 17, 1853 (daughter of Joel Ricks and Eleanor Martin), who was born Dec. 28, 1832, in Madison county, Ill. Their children: John Aikens b. March 19, 1854, m. Emily J. Bennett June 1, 1877; Mary E. b. Sept. 26, 1857, m. Edward M. Owens; Hortense b. Oct. 14, 1859, m. Aaron S. Hawkins March 25, 1885; Hyrum b. June 16, 1864.
Married Martha Eliza Bennett July 19, 1865 (daughter of Hiram B. Bennett and Martha Smith, pioneers 1851). She was born Jan. 24, 1850, Kanesville, Iowa. Their children: Sarah Ann b. July 11, 1868; Martha E. b. March 17, 1870, m. Thales H. Haskell Oct. 8, 1897; Curtis B. b. Oct. 23, 1871, m. Ursula P. Harrison June 1, 1898; Elias Austin b. March 4, 1874, m. Jessie Black June 15, 1898; Emma Jane b. April 4, 1876, m. Edwin C. Dibble June 15, 1900; George Essex b. Sept. 24, 1878, m. May Rogers Aug. 1, 1901; Erastus Snow b. Aug. 18, 1881; Hiram A. b. Sept. 15, 1883, m. Rebecca Hodson; Lucy Edith b. Aug. 12, 1886; Joseph F. b. April 7, 1889; C. Estella b. Aug. 4, 1891; Verlie D. b. Oct. 14, 1894. Families resided Parowan and Paragonah, Utah.
Settled at Salt Lake City 1847; moved to Grover Creek 1849; to Parowan 1851; and to Paragonah 1857. Major in Indian war 1853. Missionary to Sandwich Islands 1854-56; bishop of Paragonah several years; ordained patriarch Aug. 26, 1899. Member Utah legislature 20 years; U. S. deputy marshal; probate judge and prosecuting attorney Iron county. Led an exploring expedition to southeastern Utah for the purpose of selecting locations for settlements, locating the site of Bluff City; and later led a company of settlers into the San Juan Valley. President San Luis stake 1883-92. Settled at Layton 1901. Died Oct. 11, 1910, at Layton.

SMITH, SILAS SANFORD, JR. (son of Silas Sanford Smith, Jr., and Clarinda Ricks). Born July 10, 1853, Parowan, Utah.
Married Betsy Williamson Nov. 3, 1873, Salt Lake City (daughter of James Williamson and Ann Aldread, latter pioneer Nov. 30, 1856, Martin and Tyler handcart company). She was born Jan. 13, 1853, in England. Their children: Clarinda A. b. May 2, 1876, d. Oct. 4, 1893; Silas Sanford b. Oct. 4, 1878, d. July 16, 1899; Betsy L. b. Sept. 25, 1883, m. John S. Knight Dec. 17, 1902; John William b. Sept. 26, 1886; James Albert b. May 26, 1889; Don Samuel b. Sept. 16, 1894. Family home Manassa, Colo.
President Y. M. M. I. A. at Paragonah 1875-78. Called to assist Jesse N. Smith in colonizing Arizona 1878, returning to San Juan Co., Utah, in 1879. Counselor in presidency Y. M. M. I. A. of Manassa ward; bishop's counselor 1881; clerk Manassa ward eight years; high councilor; missionary to southern states 1900-02. Moved to Rexburg, Idaho, 1906, where he served as U. S. commissioner, police judge and city clerk. Died Jan. 19, 1911, Rexburg, Idaho.

SMITH, JOHN WILLIAM (son of Silas Sanford Smith, Jr., and Betsy Williamson). Born July 26, 1886, Manassa, Colo. Secretary Y. M. M. I. A., Rexburg, first ward, 1909-11; secretary and treasurer elders quorum; secretary and treasurer of Fremont stake Sunday school 1911; second counselor presidency elders quorum; president elders quorum. U. S. commissioner 1911.

SMITH, WARREN (son of Warren Smith). Born near Nashville, Tenn. Came to Utah in September, 1850, captain of his own company.
Married Lydia Alexander 1830, Weakley county, Tenn. (daughter of Randall and Maria Alexander, pioneers 1855). Their children: Melissa, m. Stephen Mott; Eldredge, m. Sarah Dudley; Benjamin Mark, m. Agnes E. Wood; Martha, m. Henry Chipman; Abinadi, m. Docia Wheeler.
Married Amanda Barnes May 1840, Nauvoo, Ill. (widow of another Warren Smith. Children: Alma L.; Willard; Hortensia; Artemena). She was born Feb. 22, 1809, and came to Utah with husband. Their children: Amanda, d. child; Warren Barnes b. Dec. 20, 1844, m. Elizabeth Echo Mercer; Sarah b. Sept. 1846, m. George Burnham.
Married Rachel Blackburn. There were two children.
Married Mahala Dudley. Their children: Hyrum; Lydia; Carson; Agnes. Families resided Salt Lake City.
Went to Carson. Nev., where he lived 20 years, returning to Utah 1874. Died May, 1884, American Fork, Utah.

SMITH, BENJAMIN MARK (son of Warren Smith and Lydia Alexander). Born 1834, Nashville, Tenn. Came to Utah, Warren Smith company.
Married Agnes Elizabeth Wood 1855, American Fork, Utah (daughter of David Wood and Catherine Krietz of American Fork, pioneers 1850, David Wood company). She was born 1836 in Osnabruck, Canada. Their children: Winifred Catherine b. 1856, m. Sylvania C. Waddell; Martha Ann b. 1858, m. Charles I. Branson; Amanda Agnes b. 1861, m. Casper Sulser; David Warren, b. 1863, m. Mary Jane Jones; Mark Alexander b. 1865, m. Margret Taylor; Stephen Hiram b. 1868, m. Anna Hasler; Charles William b. 1871, m. Emma Barlow; Lydia Melissa b. 1873, m. Simon S. Epperson; Carson Orear b. 1875, m. Ellen Springer. Family home Midway, Wasatch Co., Utah.

SMITH, DAVID WARREN (son of Benjamin Mark Smith and Agnes Elizabeth Wood). Born Oct. 2, 1863, Sacramento, Cal.
Married Mary Jane Jones 1887 (daughter of Richard Jones and Mary Cummings of Heber City, Utah). She was born 1867. Their children: Ada Saphrona b. 1887; Leonard b. 1888; Richard W. b. 1889; Wallace Warren b. 1894; Nettie b. 1901. Family home Heber City, Utah.
Bishop's counselor. Farmer.

SMITH, WARREN BARNES (son of Warren Smith and Amanda Barnes). Born Dec. 20, 1844, Nauvoo, Ill. Came to Utah with father.
Married Elizabeth Echo Mercer Oct. 11, 1865, American Fork, Utah (daughter of John Mercer and Nancy Wilson

of Chadburn, Eng., pioneers 1848). She was born Oct. 11, 1848. Their children: Amanda, m. William Henry Steele; Margaret, died; Warren; John M., m. Larene Rhodes; Melissa, m. Lawrence Hutchings; Nancy, died; Alma; Leah, m. William Moyle; Margery, m. David Peterson; Florence, m. Stephen Willis.
Married Mary Emeline Tyrrell February, 1873, Salt Lake City (daughter of Asahel Tyrrell, born Sept. 23, 1802, Bridgeport, Conn., and Lucretia Webster, born Oct. 30, 1805, Tyringham, Mass., latter came to Utah 1871). She was born 1845. Their children: Telitha, m. Stanley Dallon; Asahel T., m. Ella Tyring; Ortentia. m. William Rose; Estella, m. Erin Tollman; Mary, m. George Toone; Junius. Family home American Fork, Utah.
Married Harriet A. Harrington Nov. 15, 1885, Salt Lake City (daughter of Leonard E. Harrington and Harriet F. Noon of American Fork, Utah). She was born March 16, 1860, died March 14, 1901. Their children: Leonard and Willard H., died; Leslie A.; Ida F.; Alvira, died; Hattie V.; Iona A.; Sarah M. Family home American Fork, Utah.
Married Emma Crompton (Rushton) May 29, 1907, Salt Lake City (daughter of John Crompton b. July 6, 1829, and Hannah Hardy b. June 10, 1815, both of Bolton and Oldham, Lancastershire, Eng., pioneers 1853). She was born July 21, 1853, in Nebraska.
Member 67th quorum seventies; missionary to England 1877-79, and to southern states 1887-89; member presidency seventies quorum, Utah county, 1880-84, when all seventies were under one presidency. Settled at American Fork 1857. Counselor to Bishop William M. Bromley 1887; set apart bishop 4th ward July 14, 1898; superintendent Sunday schools 15 years, and choir leader 30 years; senior member high council, Alpine stake. Member American Fork city council. Member brass band at American Fork.

SMITH, ALMA L. (son of Warren Smith and Amanda Barnes of Marion, Ohio). Born Dec. 16, 1833, at Marion. Came to Utah 1848, Joseph Young company.
Married Telitha Free March 1855, Salt Lake City (daughter of Absalom Free and Betsy Strait of St. Clair county, Ill., pioneers 1848, Joseph Young company). She was born Oct. 5, 1835. Their children: Alma L., m. Marguerite Black, m. Annie Roberts; Willard F., m. Cora A. Fisher; Hammer, d. aged 2; Florence, d. aged 4; Cora, m. John Hodson; Rosa, d. child; Julian F., m. Pearl Colton; Betsy, d. aged 25. Family home, Salt Lake City.
Missionary to England two years; to Sandwich Islands ten years; high priest; bishop of Coalville three years; high counselor of Summit stake. County recorder Summit county six years. Bookkeeper; contractor. Died June 1887 at Coalville, Utah.

SMITH, WILLARD F. (son of Alma L. Smith and Telitha Free). Born Feb. 3, 1860.
Married Cora A. Fisher May 5, 1886, Logan, Utah (daughter of Joseph A. Fisher and Sarah L. Harris), who was born March 25, 1865, Coalville, Utah. Their children: Willard C. b. July 16, 1887; Erschel F. b. Dec. 26, 1888; Ray L. b. Dec. 3, 1890; Leah A. b. May 28, 1893; Carol F. b. July 8, 1895; Helen L. b. April 4, 1898, d. aged 2; Joseph A. b. Jan. 18, 1901, d. infant; Kenneth H. b. June 6, 1903; Gale D. b. Nov. 28, 1908. Family home, Salt Lake City.
Missionary to England two years; high priest; superintendent Sunday school and president Y. M. M. I. A. at Coalville, Utah; home missionary ten years. Mining promoter.

SMITH, WILLIAM (son of Richard Smith and Dianah Brazzell Smith). Born Sept. 3, 1831, Gibson county, Tenn. Came to Utah 1850, Captain Bennett company.
Married Polly Marie Perry May 19, 1850, Mt. Pisgah, Iowa. She was born June 16, ——, Middlebury, Genesee county, N. Y. (daughter of Asahel and Polly Chadwick Perry, who came to Utah in 1850). Their children: William Riley b. April 24, 1851; Mary Louisa b. Nov. 6, 1852; Sarah Ellen, b. June 29, 1855; James R. b. Feb. 12, 1858; Flora J. b. May 29, 1860; Henrietta I. b. Dec. 19, 1862; Lucy M b. Dec. 20, 1864; George A. b. May 2, 1867; Andrew R. b. Feb. 3, 1869; Elizabeth A. b. Aug. 25, 1871; Calista M. b. Nov. 6, 1872.
Married —— Dec. 8, 1860, Salt Lake City, who was born Sept. 3, 1844, Nauvoo, Ill. Their children: Julia Charlotte b. Oct. 9, 1861; William H. b. Feb. 12, 1863; Joseph C. b. April 7, 1864; Rachel L. b. Jan. 28, 1866; John W. b. Feb. 24, 1868; Albert T. b. Jan. 14, 1872; George P. b. April 11, 1873; Jordan b. April 19, 1875; Amasa b. Oct. 10, 1877; Frank b. Sept. 3, 1880, Ralph b. Oct. 17, 1883; Elial b. Sept. 3, 1885.
Farmer; blacksmith. Indian interpreter.

SMITH, WILLIAM (son of John and Sarah Smith of Herefordshire, Eng.). Born June 4, 1806, in Herefordshire. Came to Utah 1856.
Married Jane Rawlings 1849, in Herefordshire (daughter of William and Jane Rawlings of same place, pioneers 1856). She was born March 8, 1820. Their children: William, d. aged 8; Joseph, m. Louisa Obery; Thomas, m. Emma Obery; Sarah Jane b. April 1, 1856, m. George B. Sanborn Nov. 16, 1875; Hyrum, m. Syrepta Davis; Martha A., m. Neils Hendrickson; Ellen, m. Edward Howells; John, d. aged 11; Emma L., d. aged 6. Family home Paradise, Utah.
Seventy; high priest; block teacher. Farmer and stockraiser. Died April, 1888, Paradise.

SMITH, WILLIAM JOSEPH (son of William Smith, born at Ruthland, Lincolnshire, Eng., and Sarah Atkinson, born at Rippingale, Eng.). Born April 26, 1820, Gosberton, Risgate, Lincolnshire. Came to Utah Sept. 23, 1849, Orson Spencer company.
Married Mary Ann Frier 1845 (daughter of Samuel Frier and Roseline Walker), who was born May 18, 1821, Pinchback, Lincolnshire. Their children: William Smith b. Feb. 20, 1846; Samuel Frier b. Sept. 7, 1847; Joseph b. May 18, 1849, m. Eliza Bean; Moses and Ann (twins) b. June 23, 1851; Rachel b. July 4, 1852, m. William A. McMaster; Hyrum b. Feb. 22, 1854, m. Susan Garret; Jacob b. March 27, 1856, m. Kate Hampton; Mary Ann b. Jan. 19, 1860; Margaret Roseline b. Jan. 16, 1862, m. William Woodard. Family home, Salt Lake City.
Missionary to England 1855; first councilor to Bishop Lytle of 11th ward, Salt Lake City, 1852; patriarch.

SMITH, JOSEPH (son of William Joseph Smith and Mary Ann Frier). Born May 18, 1849, Council Bluffs, Iowa. Came to Utah with parents.
Married Eliza Bean Jan. 18, 1869, Salt Lake City (daughter of Joseph Bean and Sarah Beanland, pioneers Sept. 16, 1869, Edward Stevenson company). She was born at Bradford, Yorkshire, Eng. Their children: Eliza Lavina b. Jan. 26, 1870, m. Charles Livingston; Joseph b. July 13, 1872, m. Minnie Lloyd; William Parley b. Jan. 4, 1875; Edwin Frier b. March 11, 1877; Ernest Welcome b. March 5, 1879, m. Sabina Smith; Sarah Beanland b. March 9, 1882, m. August Anderson; Milton and Mable b. April 18, 1890; Benjamin Harrison b. March 20, 1892, m. Hattie Isabella Rupp. Family home, Salt Lake City.
Helped to build Deseret telegraph lines. Black Hawk Indian war veteran. Sheepraiser; woolgrower; business man and capitalist.

SMITHIES, JAMES (son of Richard Smithies and Mary Robinson of Downham, Lancastershire, Eng.). Born Oct. 29, 1807, at Downham; pioneer September, 1847, Geo. B. Wallace company, a part of Daniel Spencer's 100.
Married Nancy Knowles in Lancastershire, Eng. (daughter of Robert Knowles and Ann Parker of Downham, Eng., pioneers September, 1847, George B. Wallace company). She was born Aug. 2, 1809. Their children: Mary b. Oct. 7, 1836, m. Heber C. Kimball; Robert b. Oct. 5, 1839, m. Elizabeth Scott; Joseph Richard b. May 31, 1842; James A. b. Oct. 11, 1845; Sarah E. b. July 5, 1847, m. Ephraim Scott; Alice A. b. Dec. 5, 1850, m. Nelson Beebe. Family home, Salt Lake City.
Married Hannah Crowther 1857, Salt Lake City. Their children: Joseph Heber b. Aug. 9, 1857; Elizabeth b. Sept. 29, 1859; John James b. March 6, 1862; Miriam b. April 23, 1865; Leah b. May 11, 1868; Lucy b. Oct. 12, 1870; Melvina b. Nov. 27, 1872.
Member 13th quorum seventies; organized the first choir in Salt Lake City. Farmer. Died June 26, 1882, at Salt Lake City.

SMITHIES, ROBERT (son of James Smithies and Nancy Knowles). Born Oct. 5, 1839, in Lancastershire, Eng. Came to Utah with father.
Married Elizabeth Scott April 11, 1865, Salt Lake City (daughter of John Scott and Elizabeth Meneary of England, pioneers 1848, John Scott company). She was born March 15, 1847. Their children: Elizabeth A. b. May 21, 1866, m. Theodore Beck; Sarah M. b. Sept. 12, 1867, m. C. E. Rostan; Louisa M. b. Aug. 23, 1869, m. G. H. Romrell; Robert A. b. March 9, 1872; Alfonzo F. b. Dec. 22, 1873, m. L. A. Gibson; Isaac W. b. Nov. 30, 1875, m. Eliza Stucker; Mary A. b. Sept. 24, 1877, m. Aaron Harrot; Etta S. b. Sept. 1, 1879, m. Charles Byington. Family home, Salt Lake City.
Member 13th quorum seventies. Road supervisor. Farmer.

SMOOT, A. O. (son of George Washington Smoot and Ann Rowlett of Prince Edward county, Va.). Born Feb. 17, 1815, in Owen county, Ky. Came to Utah Sept. 24, 1847, A. O. Smoot company.
Married Diana Eldredge May 6, 1855, Salt Lake City (daughter of Ira Eldredge and Nancy Black of Indianapolis, Ind., pioneers Sept. 19, 1847, Daniel Spencer company). She was born March 28, 1837. Their children: Abraham Owen, m. Electa Bullock; Nancy, m. David R. Beebe; Olive, m. J. W. Bean; Elizabeth m. Milton H. Hardy; Leanora; Joseph; Ella, m. Dr. George E. Robison; Arthur; Vilate, m. Thomas F. Pierpont; Parley, m. Helen Condur; Alma, m. Edna Stubbs; William, m. Florence Kimber.
Married Annie Kristina Morrisen, Salt Lake City (daughter of Neils Morrison of Aålå, Frederickstad, Norway). She was born Dec. 20, ——. Their children: Annie Christina, m. George S. Taylor; Alice, m. Myron C. Newell; Reed, m. Allie Eldredge; George Morrison, m. Mary Ann Larsen; Agnes May, m. Charles Albert Glazier; Brigham, m. Margerette Nesbit; Ida Mauline, m. George A. Dusenberry. Family home Provo, Utah.
High priest; missionary in United States and England 1840-54; president of Utah stake. Mayor of Salt Lake City ten years, and of Provo fourteen years. President of two banks in Provo. Super lumber yard, Provo woolen mills, B. Y. University, Provo Co-op. flour mill, and a number of other concerns. Died March 6, 1896.

1172   PIONEERS AND PROMINENT MEN OF UTAH

SMOOT, A. O. (son of A. O. Smoot and Diana Eldredge). Born March 11, 1856, Sugar House ward, Salt Lake City.
Married Electa Bullock Oct. 30, 1878, Salt Lake City (daughter of Isaac Bullock and Electa Wood of Provo, Utah, former pioneer September, 1852, Isaac Bullock company, and the latter September, 1848, Gideon D. Wood company). She was born March 6, 1859. Their children: Abraham Owen b. Sept. 9, 1879, m. Phoebe Campbell; Isaac Albert b. Nov. 3, 1880, m. Nettie Parkinson; Allie b. April 3, 1882, m. Jacob Coleman; Electa b. Sept. 25, 1884, m. LeRoy Dixon; Fern b. March 23, 1885, m. Wells L. Brimhall; Ethel b. April 7, 1887. Family home, Provo.
High counselor; missionary to England 1875-77. County assessor and collector; city councilman; state senator; secretary state insane asylum and U. S. commissioner. Manager lumber company. Died May 20, 1911.

SMOOT, ISAAC ALBERT (son of A. O. Smoot and Electa Bullock). Born Nov. 3, 1880, at Provo, Utah.
Married Nettie Parkinson March 31, 1909, Salt Lake City (daughter of Samuel R. Parkinson and Charlotte Smart of Preston, Idaho, pioneers May 5, 1854, Captain Field company). Only child: Ruth P. b. June 24, 1910. Family home, Provo.
Elder; missionary to England 1903-06; assistant superintendent Utah state Sunday school board. Clerk in the state senate. District manager of the Mountain States Telephone Co. County assessor Utah county.

SMOOT, GEORGE MORRISON (son of Abraham Owen Smoot and Annie Kristina Morrison). Born Jan. 9, 1864, Salt Lake City.
Married Mary Ann Larsen Dec. 20, 1888, Manti, Utah (daughter of Neils Larsen, of Salem, Utah, and Bangta Flygare, pioneers). She was born April 1, 1866. Their children: Zella b. April 5, 1890, died; Mary Erma b. Dec. 5, 1893; Margrette b. Dec. 20, 1896. Family home, Provo.
Missionary to Scandinavia; bishop of Vineyard 1906-07; high priest; bishop's counselor Lake View, Utah, 1901-06. President of Smoot Investment Co., dealers in lumber and building materials. Farmer; miningman; investor; real estate dealer.

SMOOT, WILLIAM COCHRAN ADKINSON (adopted son of Abraham Owen Smoot and son of Margett T. Adkinson). Born Jan. 30, 1828, Roan county, Tenn. Came to Utah July 24, 1847, Brigham Young company.
Married Martha Ann Sessions Jan. 29, 1852. Their children: William Cochran Adkinson, Jr.; Martha Ann; Abraham Owen; Margarett T.; Eliza E.; Josephine; Lucina; Albert C.; Louisa T.; Lima A.; Sarah E. Perregrine; Parley W.; Phila P.
Married Margrett Freeman 1857. Their children: John W., m. Mahala Garns 1875; Rhode; Wilford; Willie.

SMOUT, EDWIN WARD (stepson of John Smout and son of Esther Ward of Dudley, Staffordshire, Eng.). Born May 21, 1823, Tipton, Eng. Came to Utah August, 1854, independent company.
Married Leah Oakley Feb. 16, 1847, Dudley, Staffordshire, Eng. (daughter of Samuel Oakley and Mary Adelington), who was born May 5, 1823, Dudley, Eng. Their children: Felix; Parley; William b. 1850, m. Sarah Moore April 24, 1871; Sarah J.; Mary A.; Edwin W.; Leah O.; Esther b. April 12, 1862, m. John A. Randall May 7, 1891; Sophia; Samuel b. Aug. 6, 1866, m. Clara M. Crowther Oct. 25, 1905; Lois. Family resided Ogden and Slaterville, Utah.
Bishop's counselor. Settled at Ogden 1854. Tailor. Died Jan. 16, 1900.

SMOUT, WILLIAM O. (son of Edwin W. Smout and Leah Oakley). Born 1850 in Pennsylvania. Came to Utah 1854.
Married Sarah Moore April 24, 1871, Salt Lake City (daughter of James Moore and Alice Young, both of Riverdale, Utah, pioneers Oct. 4, 1863, Thomas Hicks company). She was born June 20, 1849. Their children: William E. b. July 29, 1872; Winslow T. b. July 29, 1872; James M. b. Nov. 16, 1874; Sadie b. Feb. 16, 1876; John b. Oct. 1, 1878; Nora b. March 10, 1881; Joseph b. Oct. 18, 1884; Ella b. July 18, 1886. Family home Slaterville, Utah.

SMOUT, SAMUEL (son of Edwin Ward Smout and Leah Oakley). Born Aug. 6, 1866, Slaterville, Utah.
Married Clara M. Crowther Oct. 25, 1905 (daughter of David Crowther and Josephine Koltgrain, former pioneer 1863, Captain Rollings company, latter came 1871, Captain Reece company). Annie Jane. m. Joseph Atwood; Effie Matilda b. Aug. 9, 1883, m. Levi Cyrus Kendall; Ellina Elizabeth, died; Minnie Eliza, m. John Robbins. Family home Vernal, Utah.
Elder. Settled at Oxford, Idaho, 1876; moved to Vernal 1881. Died Aug. 20, 1911.

SMUIN, DAVID (son of Thomas Smuin of Battle Creek, Utah). Born Sept. 6, 1850. Came to Utah 1868.
Married Emma Robison of England Aug. 16, 1870, who was born Jan. 16, 1849. Their children: George, m. Edna Loder; William Bradford, m. Eliza Ann Kendall; Rachel Syntha, m. Benjamin C. Slough; Rosa May, m. Findlay Odam; Annie Jane, m. Joseph Atwood; Effie Matilda b. Aug. 9, 1883, m. Levi Cyrus Kendall; Ellina Elizabeth, died; Minnie Eliza, m. John Robbins. Family home Vernal, Utah.
Elder. Settled at Oxford, Idaho, 1876; moved to Vernal 1881. Died Aug. 20, 1911.

SMUIN, GEORGE (son of Thomas Empey and Susanah Smuin of Eatonbray, Bedfordshire, Eng.). Born Nov. 11, 1844, at Eatonbray. Came to Utah Dec. 6, 1864, Brigham H. Young company.
Married Eliza Gaisford April 11, 1869, Salt Lake City (daughter of Isaac Gaisford and Ellen Rex of Bath, Eng., pioneers April 7, 1852). She was born June 29, 1853. Their children: Susanah, m. N. J. Nielsen; Rose, m. Robert Burk; Lillie, m. John F. Lifgren; Ellen; Myrtle; Viola; Horace; Ruth; George Joseph, died; Mabel Blanche, died; Henry, m. Florence Griffin; Richard, m. Laura Wansgaard; Ralph, m. Ray Parkinson. Family home Ogden, Utah.
Bishop of Lynne ward 1891-1908; president Y. M. M. I. A. City councilman two terms. Horticulturist. Died Jan. 22, 1913.

SMUIN, THOMAS (son of Joseph Smuin and Hannah Pearce). Born Dec. 6, 1816, Radley, Berkshire, Eng. Came to Utah in 1869.
Married Sarah Hook in England (daughter of Richard Hook and Mary Tredwell), who was born Sept. 22, 1816. Came to Utah 1861. Their children: Matilda, m. John J. Slaugh; Eliza, m. Michael Clark; Rachel; Thomas; David. Farmer. Died Oct. 26, 1889, Kaysville, Utah.

SNEDAKER, JOHN FREDERICK (son of John Frederick Snedaker and Clara Claymore of Salt Lake City). Born March 28, 1831, Essen, near Hanover, Germany. Came to Utah in 1847, Jedediah M. Grant company.
Married Elizabeth Rock 1859 (daughter of Henry Rock and Catherine Mentzer of St. Louis, Mo., latter a pioneer Henry Brown company). She was born Nov. 7, 1836, and came to Utah with mother. Their children: Clara Elizabeth b. Dec. 1, 1860, m. John Philip Carlisle; Frederick b. Oct. 1861, m. Clara Capsen; Catherine b. Feb. 8, 1863, m. Orson Bennion Calder; Joseph b. 1864, died; Reuben b. Oct. 22, 1866; Mary b. April 7, 1868, d. aged 18; Louisa b. Sept. 6, 1869, m. William N. Hill; Ellen, m. William Gabbot; Rebecca, David, Parley, Claymore and Bathsheba, latter five died.
Married Sarah Ann Thurston (Grant), Salt Lake City (daughter of Thomas Jefferson Thurston and Rosetta Bull of Centerville, Utah; pioneers October, 1847, Jedediah M. Grant company). She was born May 23, 1835. Their children: Charles Alma, Rosetta Alice, Laura Elizabeth and Minnie Jenette, all four died; Rosalia Vilate, m. Wilford C. McMurray; Willard Jefferson, died; Jedediah LeRoy. Families resided Mill Creek, Utah.
Member 81st quorum seventies; high priest; missionary to Pennsylvania 1855-56; counselor to Bishop Hamilton; Sunday school superintendent, Mill Creek ward. Justice of peace. Farmer and dairyman. Worked on U. P. R. R. in Utah. Died January, 1890.

SNEDAKER, JEDEDIAH LeROY (son of John Frederick Snedaker and Sarah Ann Thurston (Grant). Born Sept. 4, 1878, Mill Creek, Utah.
Member 2d quorum elders; missionary to Germany 1906-09; member Sunday school superintendency, Logan 4th ward. Employed in street railway service.

SNEDAKER, MORRIS JACKSON (son of Derrick Snedaker and Lucinda Bowker of Lansing, N. Y.). Born Dec. 16, 1818, at Lansing. Came to Utah Sept. 21, 1847, Daniel Spencer company.
Married Ann Earl in 1844, at Kalamazoo, Mich.
Married Elizabeth Mobbs, at Salt Lake City. Their children: Ellen Lucinda b. Nov. 2, 1860; Laura Ann b. Nov. 27, 1864, m. Lee Clinton Snedaker; Elizabeth Permilda Mobbs b. March 16, 1868, m. George Playter, m. Fred B. Gillett. Family home, Salt Lake City.
First salt manufacturer in Salt Lake City. Merchant and mining man. Died Dec. 12, 1882.

SNELL, JOHN WILLIAM (son of William Snell of Devonshire, Eng., and Margaret Earl of eastern Canada). He was born March 2, 1842, La Harpe, Hancock county, Ill. Came to Utah September, 1857, James H. Hart company.
Married Luemma Elizabeth Laub in 1864, St. George, Utah (daughter of George Laub and Mary Ellen McGinnis of St. George, pioneers 1852). She was born December, 1849. Their child: John William, m. Elizabeth Lund.
Married Eliza Shafer July 21, 1872, Salt Lake City (daughter of John Shafer of Wayne county, N. Y., and Hannah Casto of Indiana, pioneers Oct. 1849). She was born Oct. 22, 1853.

SNELL, JOHN WILLIAM (son of John William Snell and Luemma E. Laub). Born in 1866 at Salt Lake City. It is said he could trace his genealogy back to the time of the famous "King-Killer" MacGinness.
Married Elizabeth Lund June 8, 1889, at St. George, Utah (daughter of Robert C. Lund and Miss Romney of St. George). Their children: John W. b. May 12, 1900; Robert; George Henry. Family home, Salt Lake City.
Elder. Practiced law in New York and Utah. Died May 3, 1907, Salt Lake City.

SNIDER, JOHN (son of Marlin Snider and Sarah Armstrong of Eglington, Canada). Born Feb. 11, 1800, New Brunswick, Nova Scotia. Came to Utah 1850, Lorin W. Babbitt company.
Married Mary Heron Feb. 28, 1822, who was born Nov. 10, 1804. Their children: Harriet, m. Joseph E. Johnson; Edgerton, m. Mary J. McBride: John, Jr., m. Martha L. Babbit; m. Susan E. Allen; m. Mary Hooper. Family home Toronto, Canada.
Married Sylvan Meacham March 11, 1855, Salt Lake City. Their children: Martin H., d. aged 9; John H., m. Annie Brown.
High priest; missionary to England. Bricklayer. Died Dec. 19, 1875, Salt Lake City.

SNIDER, JOHN (son of John Snider and Mary Heron). Born May 2, 1828, Toronto, Canada. Came to Utah 1851.
Married Martha L. Babbitt Feb. 22, 1853, Salt Lake City, who was born April 7, 1832. Their children: Don L. b. Jan. 29, 1854, and Harriet A. b. April 8, 1858, d. infant. Family home, Salt Lake City.
Married Susan E. Allen Sept. 20, 1863, Salt Lake City, who was born Aug. 28, 1834. Their children: Frank L. b. Aug. 6, 1864, m. Louisa D. Peck; Rosalie b. Nov. 30, 1865, m. Ernest M. Cummings; John E. b. Aug. 29, 1867, m. Jennie E. Taylor. Family home, Salt Lake City.
Married Mary Hooper Dec. 25, 1875, Salt Lake City (daughter of Thomas Hooper and Elizabeth Brooks of Herefordshire, Eng.). She was born Jan. 20, 1841.

SNOW, BERNARD (son of Garry and Edna Snow). Came to Utah 1851, oxteam company.
Married ———. Their only child: Bernard, died in childhood.
Married Alice Smith, Salt Lake City (daughter of Stephen and Mary Smith of Barry, Eng., latter a pioneer, oxteam company). Their children: Alice, m. Ira W. Gardner; Bernard, m. Nancy Killion; Verona. m. Charles Whiting; Herman, m. Lydia Bingham; Eben b. Dec. 26, 1863, m. Sarah Jane Powell. Family resided Mt. Pleasant, Fountain Green, Springville, Hoytsville and Salt Lake City.

SNOW, EBEN (son of Bernard Snow and Alice Smith). Born Dec. 26, 1863, Ephraim, Utah.
Married Sarah Jane Powell Dec. 13, 1891, Salem, Utah Co., Utah (daughter of John A. Powell and Sarah Jane Shields of Salem, pioneers 1847, oxteam company). She was born Dec. 13, 1874. Their children: Justus Forrest b. Oct. 1, 1892; Florence Hazel b. Feb. 7, 1895; Asel Gale b. Jan. 12, 1900; Violate Wave b. Sept. 10, 1903; Thora Fantella b. July 14, 1905; Bernard Eben b. April 18, 1908; Irene b. April 27, 1911, d. May 5, 1911. Family home Roosevelt, Utah.
Elder, Constable of Jensen, Utah. Farmer and stockraiser.

SNOW, ERASTUS (son of Levi Snow and Lucina Streeter). Born Nov. 8, 1818, St. Johnsbury, Vt. Came to Utah July 24, 1847, Brigham Young company.
Married Julin Josephine Spencer April 11, 1856, Salt Lake City (daughter of Mathias F. Spencer and Mary Brown of Nauvoo, Ill.). She was born April 9, 1837, New York City. Their children: Edward H., m. Hannah Nelson; William S., m. Emily E. Eyring; Amelin S.; Joseph S., m. Olive Black; Mary B., died; Maude R. Family home St. George, Utah.
Apostle in L. D. S. church. Member legislature. Died May 18, 1888, Salt Lake City.

SNOW, EDWARD H. (son of Erastus Snow and Julin Josephine Spencer). Born June 23, 1865, St. George, Utah.
Married Hannah Nelson Sept. 24, 1885, St. George (daughter of Aaron Nelson and Selvia Rulfreyman of St. George, pioneers 1862, Captain Hyde company). She was born March 27, 1865. Their children: Edward Vernon b. Feb. 16, 1889, m. Lucille Forsyth; Dilworth b. Aug. 1, 1891; Karl N. b. Jan. 17, 1894; Laura b. March 9, 1897; Rulon b. May 31, 1902; Olive b. March 12, 1904; Irma b. Nov. 2, 1909. Family home, St. George.
High priest; missionary to southern states 1886-88; and to eastern states 1889-1901. Member constitutional convention and of first state senate; county superintendent of schools; St. George city recorder. President Bank of St. George and Co-op. store.

SNOW, GARDINER. Came to Utah in 1848.
Married Sarah Hasting. Among their children were James Chauncy and George Washington. Family home Manti, Utah.

SNOW, JAMES CHAUNCY (son of Gardiner Snow and Sarah Hasting). Born Jan. 11, 1817, Chesterfield, N. H. Came to Utah Oct. 9, 1852, at head of own company.
Married Eliza Ann Carter in 1836 at Kirtland, Ohio (daughter of Hanna Libby of Newry, Maine). Born Sept. 28, 1818. Their children: Sarah Jane, m. Marshall Kinsman; John C., m. Harriet Baker, m. Ester Chidester; Don Carlos, m. Mary Hallett: Eliza, m. Caleb Haws; James Erastus, m. Josephine Ferre; Richard C., m. Mary Day; Dominicus C., m. Hannah Harrison; Mary Ellen, died; Arletta Colista. Family home Provo, Utah.
Missionary to New England states 1836; seventy. Member of Nauvoo Legion. Legislator 1856. Farmer and surveyor. Died April 30, 1884, Pettyville, Utah.

SNOW, JOHN C. (son of James C. Snow and Eliza Ann Carter). Born June 28, 1840, Lima, Ill. Came to Utah with parents.
Married Harriet Baker, Salt Lake City (daughter of John and Mary Ann Baker of Herefordshire, Eng., pioneers 1856, Edward Bunker handcart company). She was born Oct. 15, 1844. Their children: Harriet Ann b. Sept. 5, 1861, m. James Fielding Dunn; John C., m. Sarah Ellison; Erastus Warren, m. Maud Wallworth; Joseph Howard, died; Ernest Alfred, m. Ester Shaw; Reed. died.
Married Ester Chidester (Pulsipher) 1883, Salt Lake City. Their children: Lapreal; Myrtle, m. James Sumner; Arletta. Families resided Provo, Utah.
Priest; elder; ward and block teacher. Pioneer in making roads and canals. Second lieutenant Co. A, state militia. Died July 10, 1909.

SNOW, RICHARD C. (son of James Chauncy Snow and Eliza Ann Carter). Born Oct. 5, 1848.
Married Mary Bay Jan. 1, 1871 (daughter of James Willard Bay and Lucinda Sprague). Their children: Mary Ellen, died; Lucinda, m. Pleasant C. Turnbow; Amelia. m. Charles W. Carlile; Ella Pearl; Eliza Barbara, m. Milo J. Morrill; Myrtle Dawn, died. Family home Provo, Utah.
High priest. Farmer.

SNOW, GEORGE WASHINGTON (son of Gardiner Snow and Sarah Hasting of Manti, Utah). Came to Utah with oxteam.
Married Mary Wells at Nauvoo, Ill. Their children: Mary, m. William Henry Peacock; Eunice b. Feb. 5, 1850, m. Heber C. Kimball Pettey; Sarah. m. Alexander Tennant; Gardiner, m. Hannah Larsen. Family home, Manti.
Member Manti quorum seventies; high priest. Lawyer; cooper; agent for George A. Lowe Hardware Company. Died in 1905.

SNOW, LORENZO (son of Oliver Snow and Rosetta L. Pettibone of Mantua, Portage Co., Ohio). Born April 3, 1814, Mantua. Came to Utah Sept. 20, 1848, captain of second hundred in Brigham Young company.
Married Charlotte Merrill (daughter of Charles Merrill and Charlotte Smith Squires), who was born Nov. 19, 1825, Bainbridge, Geauga Co., Ohio, and died Sept. 25, 1850, Salt Lake City. Their children: Leonora Charlotte b. Jan. 23, 1847, d. June 1847; Roxcy Armatha b. Dec. 14, 1849, m. Elijah Arnold.
Married Mary Adaline Goddard (daughter of Dan Goddard and Percy Amanda Pettibone), who was born March 8, 1812, Hartford, Conn. Their children: Rosetta Adaline b. Nov. 7, 1846, m. Chester Loveland; Oliver Goddard b. Feb. 20, 1849, m. Mary B. Peirce; Isadore Percy b. Feb. 24, 1855, m. Homer S. Woodworth.
Married Sarah Ann Prichard (daughter of John Prichard and Polly Tillotson of Massachusetts). She was born Nov. 29, 1826, Nelson, Portage Co., Ohio. Their children: Eliza Sarah b. Nov. 30, 1847, m. George Dunford; Sylvia b. Jan. 16, 1850, m. Chauncey West; Lorenzo, Jr., b. July 7, 1853, m. Huldah Jensen; Parintha b. Oct. 5, 1855; Laurin Alvirus L. Dec. 2, 1863.
Married Harriet Amelia Squires (daughter of Aaron and Elizabeth P. Squires), who was born Sept. 13, 1819, Aurora, Geauga Co., Ohio. Their children: Abigail Harriet b. July 16, 1847, m. Thomas Caldwell; Lucius Aaron b. Dec. 10, 1849, m. Elizabeth Wilson; Alonzo Henry b. Feb. 15, 1854, m. Amelia Henrietta b. Feb. 15, 1854, d. Oct. 30, 1854; Celestia Armeda b. Dec. 2, 1856, m. Brigham Morris.
Married Eleanor Houtz (daughter of Christian and Susan Pauling Houtz), who was born Aug. 14, 1831, in Pennsylvania. Their children: Amanda Eleanor b. April 19, 1850, d. Oct. 21, 1850; Ida b. Jan. 2, 1854, m. George Francis Gibbs; Eugenia b. July 5, 1856, m. Leonidas Thomas Pierce; Alphonso Houtz b. Oct. 13, 1858; Susan Imogene b. May 4, 1861, d. Oct. 16, 1864; Roxey Lana b. Oct. 22, 1863; Hortensia b. July 17, 1867; Chauncey Edgar b. July 8, 1870.
Married Caroline Horton, who was born Dec. 25, 1828, in England, and died Feb. 1857, Brigham City, Utah. Their children: Clarissa Caroline b. July 19, 1854, m. John Archibald McAllister; Franklin and Sarah Augusta b. Feb. 3, 1857, latter d. Feb. 17, 1857.
Married Mary Elizabeth Houtz (daughter of Jacob and Lydia M. Houtz), who was born May 19, 1840, Penn's Town, Union county, Pa., and died March 31, 1906. Their children: Lydia May b. Jan. 21, 1860, m. Eli Harvey Peirce, Jr.; Jacob E. Fitzroy b. Oct. 31, 1862, d. Dec. 2, 1862; Virginia M. Marian b. Jan. 30, 1864; Mansfield Lorenzo b. Sept. 5, 1866; Mortimer Joseph b. Nov. 19, 1868; Flora Bell Birdie b. July 9, 1871.
Married Phebe Augusta Woodruff at Salt Lake City (daughter of Wilford Woodruff and Phebe Whittemore Carter of Salt Lake City, pioneers 1847. Brigham Young company). She was born March 4, 1842, Nauvoo, Ill. Their children: Mary Amanda b. Sept. 4, 1860, d. Sept. 6, 1860; Leslie Wilford Woodruff b. Feb. 6, 1862, m. Ida Daynes; Orion b. Sept. 6, 1866, m. Marintha Reeves; Milton Woodruff b. Feb. 7, 1869, m. Villette Eardley; Florence Augusta Woodruff b. Aug. 2, 1870, m. John Q. Critchlow; Families resided at Brigham City and Salt Lake City, Utah.
Married Minnie Jensen (daughter of J. P. Jensen and Sarah Clawson of Denmark and Germany). She was born Oct. 10, 1853, Brigham City, Utah, and died Jan. 2, 1908. Their children: Clarence Leroi b. Aug. 26, 1876; Minnie Mabel b. May 23, 1879; Cora Jeane b. Feb. 16, 1883, d. Aug. 11, 1883; Lorenzo; Lucile. Family home, Brigham City.

1174　　　PIONEERS AND PROMINENT MEN OF UTAH

Colonized Box Elder county. Missionary to Italy and Great Britain; member twelve apostles. Member legislature. President Church of Jesus Christ of Latter-Day Saints. Died Oct. 10, 1901, Salt Lake City.

SNOW, LESLIE WILFORD WOODRUFF (son of Lorenzo Snow and Phebe Augusta Woodruff). Born Feb. 6, 1862, Salt Lake City.
Married Ida Daynes June 11, 1901, Salt Lake City (daughter of John Daynes and Rebecca Bushby of Salt Lake City, pioneers October, 1862). She was born March 6, 1872. Their children: Leslie Lyndon Daynes b. Dec. 3, 1906.
President T. M. M. I. A., 14th ward, Salt Lake City. President Salt Lake County Medical Society; vice-president Utah State Medical Association. City physician at Logan, Utah. Physician and surgeon; oculist.

SNOW, WILLARD (son of Levi Snow and Lucina Streeter). Born May 6, 1811, St. Johnsbury, Vt. Came to Utah Sept. 22, 1847, Ira Eldredge company.
Married Melvina Harvey 1837 (daughter of Joel Harvey and Betsy Bowen, pioneers 1847. Ira Eldredge company). She was born Dec. 16, 1811. Their children: Amanda Melvina b. March 18, 1838, m. Willard Bingham June 28, 1859; Leonidas b. 1840 and Eugene b. March 10, 1841, died; Willard Lycurgus b. March 8, 1842, m. Sarah A. Bowyer April 15, 1865, m. Flora Lewis Mousley; Almira b. 1846, and Helen b. Feb. 8, 1848, died; Ellen b. Feb. 8, 1848 (first twins born in Utah), m. Henry Smith 1867; William b. 1850, died. Family home, Salt Lake City.
Married Susan Harvey 1846 (daughter of Joel Harvey and Betsey Bowen). Their child: Susan b. Jan. 25, 1848, m. Benjamin T. DeLong.
Member state legislature. Member first quorum seventies organized in L. D. S. church; counselor to Daniel Spencer in first organization of town of Salt Lake; member perpetual emigration fund committee; missionary to Scandinavia 1851-52. Died and buried at sea Aug. 25, 1852, 80 miles from Hull, Eng.

SNOW, WILLARD LYCURGUS (son of Willard Snow and Melvina Harvey). Born March 8, 1842, in Lee Co., Iowa.
Married Sarah A. Bowyer April 15, 1865, Salt Lake City (daughter of Joshua Bowyer and Maria Wadle, former pioneer 1860, Joseph W. Young company, latter came to Utah 1874). She was born July 20, 1844, Philadelphia, Pa. Their children: Sarah Ellen b. Jan. 10, 1866, m. Samuel Moore Oct. 18, 1888; Maria b. Dec. 15, 1867, d. infant; Ada May b. Sept. 25, 1869, m. Norman Boyle July 3, 1893; Willard b. Dec. 1, 1871, m. Hulda Holmes June 19, 1903; Minnie Melvina b. Feb. 28, 1874, m. David Bernhisel Dec. 14, 1905; Joseph Raymon b. May 21, 1879; Fannie b. July 21, 1881, m. Doyle Christensen; Mary Elizabeth b. June 1, 1876, m. Andrew J. Day; Lillian b. Dec. 4, 1883, m. Harold Lessinger 1908; Ethel J. b. Dec. 17, 1886, m. Jerald W. Bills March 27, 1907.
Married Flora Lewis Mousley April 13, 1874, Salt Lake City (daughter of William P. Mousley and Elizabeth Craig, former pioneer 1868). She was born Nov. 24, 1856, Newcastle, Del. Their children: Frank M. b. March 30, 1876, m. Mary E. Sullivan June 2, 1906; Ernest Leroy b. Nov. 12, 1878, m. Jane Cottrell Feb. 10, 1904; Louis Henry b. April 10, 1880, m. Hazel Poulsen Oct. 12, 1910; Alice b. Dec. 24, 1881, m. Roy T. Fitzgerald Dec. 10, 1909; Flora b. Sept. 16, 1884, m. Charles Cox Jan. 4, 1909; Eva b. Jan. 14, 1890, died; Emma b. July 9, 1891; Althia b. Nov. 19, 1895; Nellie Ione b. May 30, 1899. Families resided Draper, Utah.
Member old folks' stake committee 10 years and one of the central committee of the Draper ward of the old folks' committee. Black Hawk Indian war veteran.

SNOW, FRANK M. (son of Willard Lycurgus Snow and Flora Lewis Mousley). Born March 30, 1876.
Married Mary E. Sullivan May 2, 1906, Salt Lake City (daughter of David D. Sullivan, pioneer December, 1865, and Caroline C. Calkins, pioneer 1852). Their only child was Mary Helen b. May 11, 1907. Family home Turner, Idaho.
Missionary to eastern states 1901-03; assistant Sunday school superintendent Grace ward 1907; bishop of Turner ward May 23, 1910.

SNOW, WILLIAM (son of Levi Snow of St. Johnsbury, Vt.). Born Dec. 14, 1806, St. Johnsbury. Came to Utah Oct. 6, 1850, at head of own company.
Married Hannah Miles Sept. 21, 1832, Charleston, Vt., who died March 30, 1841. Their children: Levi b. June 1834, d. infant; Lucina b. Feb. 1835, died; Abigail D. b. Nov. 5, 1847.
Married Lydia Adams in August, 1842, who died Jan. 9, 1847. Their children: Sarah H. b. July 28, 1843; Levi William b. July 1846, d. infant.
Married Sally Adams in January, 1846 at Nauvoo, Ill. (daughter of James Adams and Elizabeth Leavitt, former pioneer 1852). She was born May 29, 1825, and came to Utah with husband. Their children: Julia M. b. Feb. 20, 1849, m. Joseph D. Cox Jan. 1, 1867; Sarah S. b. March 4, 1852, m. George Forsyth Oct. 31, 1870; Emma L. b. July 6, 1856, m. Harrison J. Burgess Nov. 17, 1874; Chloe L. b. Jan. 12, 1859, m. Royal J. Gardner Nov. 22, 1876; Lucy A. b. March 25, 1861, m. Reuben Gardner Dec. 10, 1879; Mariette b. Oct. 14, 1863, m. M. Osro Gardner Dec. 28, 1883; William J. b. April 19, 1869, m. Hattie Marie Thornton May 10, 1899. Family resided Salt Lake City, Lehi and Pine Valley, Utah.

Married Jane Maria Shearer Oct. 13, 1850, Salt Lake City. Their children: William, Jr., b. Aug. 28, 1851; Maria S. b. Feb. 25, 1853, m. W. B. Sargent; Mary L. b. Jan. 3, 1860, m. James Rencher; Mason L. b. Jan. 27, 1862, m. Betty Mason.
Married Ann Rogers March 12, 1853, Salt Lake City. Their children: Willard, m. Melissa Meeks; Celestia, m. John A. Gardner; Jeter, m. Alice Gardner; Charles, m. Sarah May Coleman; Frank, m. Effie M. Harrison; Bernella E., m. R. B. Gardner; Orrin H., Ella M. Burgess, m. Vilo Redd; George. Family home Pine Valley, Utah.
Married Roxana Leavitt March 12, 1853, Salt Lake City. Their children: John L., m. Anne Eastmond; Melissa, m. Jacob Greenwood.
Member territorial legislature at Fillmore several sessions; probate judge of Washington county. Bishop of Pine Valley ward 1867-79.

SNOW, WILLIAM J. (son of William Snow and Sally Adams). Born April 19, 1869, Lehi, Utah.
Married Hattie Marie Thornton May 10, 1899, St. George, Utah (daughter of Amos G. Thornton and Mary Whittaker, the former pioneer 1852, latter 1851). She was born Dec. 2, 1875. Their children: William J., Jr.; Emma; Ronald Thornton; Claud Shipley. Family home, Provo.
Associate professor of history in Brigham Young University, Provo. Justice of peace and superintendent of schools of Washington county; school teacher. Superintendent Sunday schools; missionary to eastern states 1899-1901. President Y. M. M. I. A.

SNOWBALL, RALPH. Born July 25, 1844, England. Came to Utah 1853.
Married Jane Thomas March 18, 1867, Salt Lake City (daughter of Thomas F. Thomas of Merthyr Tydfil, Wales, pioneer 1853). She was born May 7, 1848, in Wales. Their children: Mary Jane, m. Franklin Harper Pickering; Julia, m. William Ringwood; Ralph, m. Estella Woolley; John, m. Mary Peterson; Thomas, m. Louise Snyder; Maud Eliza, m. Thomas Hadder; Nettie May, m. John S. Ferrington; Estella Harriet, m. Francis A. Vincent; Pearl, d. infant; James; Bird, m. Chester C. Zinger.
Elder. Veteran Black Hawk war. Teamster. Died June 13, 1908, Salt Lake City.

SNYDER, GEORGE G. (son of Isaac Snyder and Lovisa Comstock). Born June 12, 1819, Jefferson county, N. Y. Came to Utah 1849.
Married Sarah Hatch (daughter of Wilden Hatch of Nauvoo, Ill., pioneer 1850). She was born Nov. 2, 1820. Their children: Robert and Parley Pratt, died; Emily, m. Orvil Thompson; Lucy, m. William Tanner; George W., died; Lovisa, m. Charles M. Alexander; Wesley, Sarah and Isaac, latter three died.
Married Elsie Jacobs in 1852 at Nauvoo, Ill. (daughter of Norton Jacobs). Their children: Wilson, m. Sypha Brown; m. Lizzie Welle; Cora, m. George Evans; Norton and Maryette, died; Grant, m. Evelyn Kenney; Bismarck, m. Maraynette Snell.
Married Caroline Kylfoyl in 1856, Salt Lake City. Their children: Ortla; Luna, m. Bridgam Bowman; Frank Richards, m. Nina Williams; Olive, died; Zina, m. Murry Shepard; Giddian, m. Pearl Wilkinson; May, died; Brigham, m. Ester Carrol; Horace Greeley, m. Ada Sylvester; Croyton Chambers.
Married Martha Kylfoyl. Their children: Louis, m. Jennette Gray; Nellie, m. Edward Thiriot; Willard, m. Dora Walker.
Married Roda Orchard. Their children: Lillie, m. Edward Evans; Sylva, m. Chance McMendrick; Kimball, m. Lovisa Hamilton; Sherman; Ruby, m. Mr. Brown; Rose, m. Mr. De Workman. Families resided Park City, Utah.
Bishop of Wanship, Utah, many years; missionary to England 1858-59. Probate judge number of years. Stockraiser. Died March 11, 1887.

SNYDER, JAMES C. (son of Henry Snyder and Elizabeth Tartar of Roxbury, Pa.). Born Jan. 8, 1820, Philadelphia, Pa. Came to Utah Sept. 13, 1861, Milo Andrus independent oxteam company.
Married Mary Ann Onimus April 22, 1845, at Philadelphia (daughter of Mathias Onimus and Mary Magdaline Develin of Philadelphia). She was born Aug. 14, 1821, and died June 12, 1851. Only child: Edward C. b. Oct. 22, 1851, d. July 29, 1852. Family home, Philadelphia.
Married Jane B. Forsyth Sept. 14, 1861, Salt Lake City (daughter of John I. Forsyth and Sarah F. Barker of Carlisle, Cumberland, Eng., pioneers Sept. 11, 1861, Milo Andrus independent oxteam company). She was born April 29, 1842. Their children: Mary E. b. Aug. 17, 1862, d. Aug. 28, 1864; Sarah Jane b. Nov. 30, 1864, m. Graham L. Daley; James Edwin b. March 7, 1867, m. Leila Meacham; Simon F. b. June 13, 1869, m. Edith Wall; John Forsyth b. April 27, 1872, m. Martha Rosetta Fausett; Theodore A. b. April 21, 1875, m. Aurelia Clyde. Family home Provo, Utah.
Secretary and treasurer branch, Philadelphia, Pa.; elder; member 62nd quorum seventies. By request of Brigham Young he planned and staked out meeting houses and public buildings; planned main canal on Provo bench. Architect and builder. Died Aug. 1, 1906.

SNYDER, JOHN FORSYTH (son of James C. Snyder and Jane B. Forsyth). Born April 27, 1872, Provo, Utah.
Married Martha Rosetta Fausett Dec. 16, 1901, Provo (daughter of Joseph Smith Fausett and Rosetta Glazier of Hancock county, Ill., and Call county, Mo., pioneers 1854, Alexander Stevens oxteam company). She was born Oct. 27, 1873. Their children: James Clyde b. Sept. 15, 1902, died; Claud F. b. July 26, 1904. Family home, Provo.
Counselor in elders quorum; block teacher. Carpenter and mining engineer.

SNYDER, MARTIN L. (son of Henry Snyder and Elizabeth Tartar of Philadelphia, Pa.). Born at Philadelphia. Came to Utah in September, 1856, oxteam company.
Married Lydia C. Yeager at Philadelphia. Their children: Jacob; James Henry, m. Mary E. Hoover, m. Ellen Barton; John G., m. Pearl D. ——. Family home Provo, Utah.
Member 45th quorum seventies. Carpenter and farmer. Died March 2, 1892.

SNYDER, JAMES HENRY (son of Martin L. Snyder and Lydia C. Yeager). Born Feb. 14, 1857, Provo, Utah.
Married Mary E. Hoover at Salt Lake City (daughter of John Whitmar Hoover and Mary Elizabeth Corsa of Pennsylvania). She was born May 1, 1859, Springville, Utah. Their children: James Whitmer, m. Natalia Leveridge; Martin Leslie, died; Florence Maud, m. George A. Christensen; Elvin, m. Elizabeth Wright; Mary E.; Waldo, died; Karl. Family home, Provo.
Married Ellen Barton March 6, 1912, Salt Lake City (daughter of William Fleming Barton and Ann Rigby of Deane, Lancastershire, Eng.; came to Utah July 18, 1879). She was born Oct. 11, 1867.
Member 45th quorum seventies; missionary to eastern states 1903-05; counselor Y. M. M. I. A.; Sunday school, ward and block teacher; bishop's counselor. Carpenter; contractor and builder.

SNYDER, ROBERT (son of Jacob Snyder and Hannah Anderson of Red Bank, N. J.). Born March 5, 1910, Red Bank. Came to Utah 1848, Brigham Young company.
Married Almeda Melissa Livermore April 3, 1841, Nauvoo, Ill. (daughter of Benjamin and Matilda Livermore of Vermont). She was born Sept. 20, 1815, and died April 8, 1896, Payson, Utah. Their children: Mary Ann, m. John Fosgren; Gideon and Samuel Hyrum, both died; Hannah Matilda (died), m. John A. Powell; Robert A., m. Sarah Lusina Curtis Feb. 10, 1881.
High priest; member Nauvoo legion. Early settler of Payson and Provo, Utah. Gardener. Died Dec. 26, 1901, Payson.

SNYDER, ROBERT A. (son of Robert Snyder and Almeda Melissa Livermore). Born March 23, 1854, Payson, Utah.
Married Sarah Lusina Curtis Feb. 10, 1881, Salt Lake City (daughter of Lyman Curtis and Sarah Wells Hartley of Salem, Mass., pioneers July 24, 1847, Brigham Young company). She was born May 22, 1863. Their children: Sarah M. b. Jan. 21, 1882, m. David S. Anderson; Robert W. b. June 22, 1883, m. Elva Hill; Iris V. b. Jan. 29, 1885, m. William L. Jesson; Royal C. b. April 12, 1886, m. Mary E. Tidwell; Ethel R. b. Oct. 8, 1887; Carlottie b. Jan. 2, 1890, John Baptiste; Litizsette Lilly b. Aug. 22, 1891; Mabel b. May 26, 1893; Lizzie b. Jan. 12, 1895; Asa Lyman b. Nov. 4, 1896; Edwin C. b. Sept. 27, 1898; Frank L b. Dec. 9, 1901; Albert b. Jan. 28, 1904, d. March 11, 1905; Agnes G. b. Feb. 11, 1906.
High priest; bishop's counselor; assistant superintendent Sunday school. School trustee; road supervisor. Farmer and stockraiser.

SNYDER, SAMUEL COMSTOCK (son of Isaac Snyder and Lovisa Comstock of New York). Born Feb. 14, 1808, New York. Came to Utah Oct. 10, 1848, Willard and Levi Richards company. Levi came as far as Winter Quarters, and from there departed on a mission to England.
Married Henrietta Maria Stockwell in March, 1826, in New York (daughter of Ephraim Stockwell of New York, pioneer 1848, Willard and Levi Richards company). She was born Sept. 4, 1810. Their children: Parmelia, m. Meltiar Hatch; Betsy Ann, m. Jesse Johnson; Ephraim Stockwell, m. Susannah Fullmer; Amy, m. John Brown; Jane S., m. James Dickinson; Laura, m. Franklin D. Richards; Goerge, d. aged 11 years; Mary Ann, m. Hyrum Williams; Isaac, d. aged 61 years; Henrietta M., m. William Page; Robert H., m. Mary Jacobs. Family resided Salt Lake City and Ashley, Utah.
Seventy at Salt Lake City. Pioneer March 21, 1887, to Parley P. Pratt, where he established first saw mill in Utah; also established grist mill at same place, and another in 19th ward, Salt Lake City; established turning and lathing machine at Parley's Park. He had to scatter the lumber, sawed at his mill in Parley's Park, over the field to prevent the Indians from burning it. Built the first road through Parley's Canyon to Park City. Farmer, stockraiser and sheep man. Died April 8, 1866, Salt Lake City.

SNYDER, EPHRAIM STOCKWELL (son of Samuel Comstock Snyder and Henrietta Maria Stockwell). Born Oct. 27, 1831, New York. Came to Utah Oct. 10, 1848, with father.
Married Susannah Fullmer Oct. 27, 1861, Salt Lake City (daughter of David Fullmer and Rhoda Ann Marvin), who was born Nov. 25, 1844, Nauvoo, Ill. and came to Utah Oct. 14, 1850, with parents. Their children: Ephraim George b. Nov. 17, 1862, m. Lou Lillian Ashcraft; Sextus Fullmer b. March 24, 1865, m. Mary Peterson Dec. 24, 1887; David Stockwell b. April 1, 1867; Rhoda Mariah b. July 5, 1869, m. Orlando Johnson; Bertram Octavius b. March 15, 1872, m. Isabell Dennis; Robert Wesley b. April 14, 1874, d. infant; Wealthy b. Aug. 15, 1875, m. William J. Wabel; Wilford Woodruff b. May 2, 1878, m. Rose Lincoln; Susannah Pearl b. April 29, 1880; Amy Elvira b. Feb. 3, 1883, d. aged 2 years; Don Vernon Eugene b. July 30, 1886.
Married Elizabeth McNaughton June 20, 1863, Salt Lake City (daughter of James William McNaughton and Elizabeth Shaw, former came to Utah, later died in Scotland). She was born Oct. 2, 1847. Their children: James William McNaughton b. Nov. 25, 1864, m. Isabel Blaisdell; Amelia Elizabeth b. Oct. 26, 1866, m. Elijah Chapman; Isaac Lorenzo b. Feb. 7, 1869, m. Sarah Stewart; Lucy Thompson b. Nov. 24, 1870, m. Theodore Johnson; Samuel b. Oct. 25, 1872, m. Elizabeth ——; Benjamin Comstock b. Dec. 11, 1874, m. Mitt Maxwell; Miriam b. Dec. 14, 1879, d. aged 6 years; Gilla Ann b. April 29, 1882; Newell K. Whitney b. Feb. 9, 1885, m. Kate Tribley. Families resided Parley's Park, Utah.
Seventy; presiding elder of Parley's Park. Sent team to Missouri river with provisions for poor immigrants. Minuteman during Indian troubles. While on trip to Fort Bridger, Wyo., he was often forced to keep the mules moving all night so they would not freeze to death; they had eaten the blankets off one another because of scarcity of food. Died Oct. 11, 1905, Parley's Park, Utah.

SOLOMON, WILLIAM H. Born Feb. 6, 1828, Truro, Cornwall, Eng. Came to Utah in October, 1862, John R. Murdock company.
Married Elizabeth H. Drew Oct. 13, 1851, in Truro, who was born Nov. 14, 1825. Their children: Elizabeth E., m. Samuel J. Brown; Mary Louisa, m. Alfred Solomon; William, d. aged 2; William H., d. child; Hilda. m. James H. Lewis; Ellen A., d. infant; Edwin D., m. Effie Knight, m. Elnora Jennings; Eliza, d. aged 16 months. Family home, Salt Lake City.
Seventy; patriarch. Farmer and stockraiser; shoemaker.

SOMERVILLE, WILLIAM (son of Andrew Somerville and Margaret Fuller of Lanarkshire, Scotland). Born April 4, 1817, near Lanark, Lanarkshire. Came to Utah 1852, O. M. Allen company.
Married Eliza Smith Feb. 3, 1847, Keg Creek, —— (daughter of Walter Smith and Mary Trunkey of Vernon, Trumbull Co., Ohio). She was born Feb. 18, 1816. Their children: Mary; Eliza; Margaret, m. James Jerman; William, m. Rosannah Stewart; Sarah, m. Orson Williams; Emma, m. George W. McConkle. Family resided Spanish Fork and Mona, Utah.
Member 5th quorum seventies; missionary to Canada 1842-43. Farmer and stockraiser. Died April 25, 1878, Mona, Utah.

SONNEDECKER, N. W. (son of Josephus Sonnedecker and Sophia Peters of Ohio). Born Dec. 16, 1856, Ohio. Came to Utah Nov. 1, 1891.
Married Fannie H. Rivers Jan. 15, 1889, Kendall, Kan. (daughter of Albert L. Rivers and Martha C. Myers, who came to Utah in 1890). She was born Dec. 9, 1866. Their children: Josephine Alberta; Helen Louise; Martha; Ada. Family home. Salt Lake City.
Attorney-at-law.

SORENSEN, MADS. Born March 29, 1830, at Vive, Aalborg, Denmark. Came to Utah July, 1874.
Married Kirsten Larson, who was born March 8, 1827, and came to Utah with husband. Their children: Soren Christian b. Jan. 6, 1854, d. infant; Jacob b. Feb. 15, 1854; Nels Miller b. Sept. 23, 1857; Soren Christian b. Feb. 16, 1859; Sine b. Sept. 16, 1861; Hans Christian b. Nov. 30, 1864; Kirsten Maria b. Jan. 12, 1868; Eliza b. Jan. 5, 1871.

SORENSEN, HANS CHRISTIAN (son of Mads Sorensen and Kirsten Larson). Born Nov. 30, 1864, Dastrup, Aalborg amt. Denmark.
Married Miranda Esplin March 18, 1890, St. George, Utah (daughter of John Esplin and Margret Webster), who was born Jan. 25, 1873, Mt. Carmel, Utah. Their children: Binnie H. b. Jan. 25, 1891; Kirsten b. Jan. 20, 1892; Evelen b. Feb. 3, 1893; David b. April 23, 1895; Earl John b. June 8, 1897; Loyd b. Nov. 13, 1900; Marie b. Oct. 26, 1903; Vilate b. Sept. 22, 1905; Joseph b. June 26, 1908. Family home. Mt. Carmel.
Missionary to Scandinavia May 21, 1887, to Aug. 13, 1889; bishop of Mt. Carmel ward since Aug. 15, 1900.

SORENSEN, PETER (son of Nicolai Sorensen and Malena Olsen). Born Oct. 10, 1832. Came to Utah with father, Captain Cowley company.
Married Rikke Andersen Oct. 17, 1857, who was born Feb. 14, 1835. Came to Utah Sept. 15, 1857, Mathias Cowley company. Their children: Peter Andrew b. Sept. 1858; Willard b. May 9, 1860, m. Agnes Duncan; Marie b. Oct. 18, 1863, m. D. B. Richards; Carrie M. b. Sept. 11, 1865, m. Matthew M. Forster; George N. b. April 23, 1867; Rebecca

b. Dec. 23, 1869, m. Peter Hansen; Philip b. Nov. 5, 1871, m. Maria Bird; Anna M. b. Dec. 13, 1873. Family home Mendon, Cache Co., Utah.
Prominent in church affairs in the Mendon ward. Died Oct. 21, 1874.

SORENSEN, PETER ANDREW (son of Peter Sorensen and Rikke Anderson). Born Sept. 12, 1858.
Missionary to Norway 1899-1901; member of high council of Hyrum stake of Zion 1901-10. Mayor of Mendon City for twelve years; school trustee.

SORENSEN, NICOLAI (son of Soren Abrahamsen, born in 1762 at Fjenneslov [his mother was born July 6, 1764, at Soro], Soro amt. Denmark). He was born June 23, 1799, at Fjenneslov. Came to Utah Sept. 15, 1857, Mathias Cowley company.
Married Malene Olsen July 6, 1830 (daughter of Ole Pedersen and Ingeborg Sorensen, Fjenneslov, Soro amt, Denmark; came to Utah Sept. 15, 1857, Mathias Cowley company). She was born March 21, 1807, died March 30, 1887. Their children: Cathrine Sophie b. May 7, 1831, m. Andrew Andersen 1857; Peter Sorensen b. Oct. 10, 1832, m. Rikke Andersen Oct. 17, 1857; Soren b. April 24, 1834, d. 1846; Christine b. Jan. 18, 1836, m. James H. Hill 1859; Abraham b. Nov. 18, 1837, m. Mary Jensen 1858; Isaac b. Feb. 24, 1840, m. Mary Jacobsen 1869; Mary or Marie b. June 25, 1843, m. William H. Hill 1859; Jacob b. Sept. 29, 1844, m. Susan Hancock; Christian b. Dec. 1, 1846, m. Jennie Hill and Caroline Halverson; Henry b. May 21, 1851. m. Marie Andersen; Seng b. March 2, 1854, m. A. H. Richards.
Settled at Mill Creek, Utah at the time of the great "move" south; went to Pondtown (Salem), Utah. Pioneer to Cache county 1859. High priest. Mechanic; farmer. Died March 30, 1887, and buried with wife in one grave.

SORENSEN, ISAAC (son of Nicolai Sorensen and Malene Olsen). Born Feb. 24, 1840, Hangerup, Soro amt, Denmark. Came to Utah with father, Captain Cowley company.
Married Mary Jacobsen Nov. 15, 1869, Salt Lake City (daughter of Jacob Christensen and Bertha Hansen; came to Utah 1862, Captain Liljenquist company). She was born May 18, 1850. Their children: William Isaac b. Sept. 19, 1870, m. Rhoda Key Feb. 16, 1898; Malene b. Sept. 13, 1872, m. David Hill Oct. 11, 1900; Hannah S. b. Sept. 20, 1874, m. Herbert Whitney Dec. 14, 1898; Bertha b. Dec. 7, 1876, m. Alexander Buest Feb. 1, 1906; Alma b. March 3, 1879; Mary Eva b. June 2, 1881, m. John A. Gardner July 19, 1906; Joseph C. b. April 5, 1884, m. Alice Laddie June 22, 1910; Henry C. b. Feb. 6, 1886; Ina b. May 22, 1888; Eulalia b. April 1, 1890; Olive b. Feb. 14, 1894.
Missionary to Denmark 1879-81; Sunday school superintendent for 40 years; chorister; high councilor. Member of the home militia; took part in the Echo Canyon trouble. City councilman for a number of years; school trustee for 12 years. At the time of the "move" went to Pondtown; in 1859 went to Mendon. Cache Valley, Utah. In 1862 drove oxteam to Florence, Neb.

SORENSEN, WILLIAM ISAAC (son of Isaac Sorensen and Mary Jacobsen). Born Sept. 19, 1870, at Mendon.
Married Rhoda Key Feb. 16, 1898, Logan Temple (daughter of Thomas Key and Sarah Riley, Rawcliffe, Yorkshire, Eng.). Their children: Alice b. Nov. 23, 1898; Hilda b. April 14, 1900; Rhoda b. Jan. 31, 1903; Isaac b. Jan. 24, 1905; Thomas Key, b. Oct. 17, 1909. Family home Mendon, Cache county.
Member high priest quorum seventies; missionary to Denmark 1894-96; Sunday school superintendent. Deputy assessor several times; mayor four years; recorder number of years. Farmer and mechanic.

SORENSEN, PETER HANSON (son of Soren Monson and Anna Maria Peterson). Born Aug. 14, 1809, Bornholm, Denmark. Came to Utah in September, 1857.
Married Anna Maria Peterson (daughter of Ole Peterson of Bornholm). Their children: Maria Caroline, m. Christian Grice Larsen; Peter, died. Family home Ephraim, San Pete Co., Utah.
Died at Ephraim.

SORENSEN, RASMUS (son of Soren Rasmussen and Maren Sorensen of Randers, Denmark). Born Jan. 26, 1517, Sjaelland, Denmark. Came to Utah in 1862, C. C. Rich company.
Married Maren Chresteson of Denmark. Their children: James Julius b. Jan. 28, 1854, m. Elizabeth Byington 1878; Erick b. Dec. 26, 1856, m. Hannah Oleson 1873; Anna Maria b. 1858, d. 1880; Christian b. 1863, m. Jeneta Boringor; Inoch, died. Family home Brigham City, Utah.

SORENSEN, JAMES J. (son of Rasmus Sorensen and Maren Chresteson). Born Jan. 28, 1854, in Sjaelland, Denmark. Came to Utah with father.
Married Elizabeth Byington Dec. 9, 1878, Richmond, Utah (daughter of Joseph H. Byington and Nancy M. Avery of Oxford, Idaho, pioneers 1847, Heber C. Kimball company). She was born June 27, 1861. Their children: L. L. b. Sept. 11, 1882, m. Effie Ellis Aug. 14, 1906; James W. b. Aug. 22, 1885, m. Hazel Rudeen 1910; Millie A. b. Aug. 15, 1888, m. Frank Moench Sept. 20, 1907; Ina D. b. Aug. 1890, m.

Daniel Pack 1910; Mina D. b. Aug. 29, 1891; Archie T. b. Aug. 18, 1892; Ethel E. b. June 2, 1899. Family home Neely, Idaho.
Member high priests' quorum seventies; missionary to southern Utah 1872-74; Sunday school superintendent. Justice of the peace. Farmer; miner.

SORENSON, KNUD (son of Soren Madsen and Ann Madsdaughter of Denmark). Born June 23, 1817, Denmark. Came to Utah October, 1862.
Married Mette C. Jensen Feb. 25, 1849 (daughter of Mads H. Sorenson and Johanna Dahlsdaughter), who was born Nov. 11, 1827. Their children: Ann b. Dec. 22, 1849, m. Bartlett Nielsen Sept. 1863; Johannah b. Nov. 29, 1855, m. Erick Nielsen, spring 1873; James b. Jan. 23, 1858, m. Ane F. Thompson April 28, 1881; Electric Sophia b. May 31, 1862, m. Charley Christiesen; Soren b. Oct. 10, 1864, m. Mary J. Butler.
Mason; plasterer; farmer.

SORENSON, JAMES (son of Knud Sorenson and Mette C. Jensen). Born Jan. 28, 1858, Aardestrup, Denmark. Came to Utah October, 1862.
Married Annie F. Thompson April 28, 1881 (daughter of Anders Thompson and Mary Ann Jenson), who was born June 1, 1861. Their children: James b. Dec. 23, 1881, m. Effie E. Nelson Oct. 18, 1905; Hannah Almira b. July 31, 1883, m. George Boice March 7, 1906; Annie Elnora b. Sept. 11, 1885, m. William H. Nelson Dec. 18, 1901; Mary Ann b. Jan. 4, 1888, m. David H. James Oct. 18, 1909.
Railroad man; farmer.

SORENSON, JAMES JR. (son of James Sorenson and Annie F. Thompson). Born Dec. 23, 1881, Spanish Fork, Utah.
Married Effie E. Nelson Oct. 18, 1905, Salt Lake City (daughter of Andrew V. Nelson and Harriet E. Hales), who was born Jan. 16, 1887. Their children: Harriet Eliza b. Aug. 15, 1906; Mary Annie, b. Nov. 19, 1907; James Andrew b. Oct. 29, 1909.
Sunday school teacher in theological department 1900-02; assistant Sunday school superintendent Palmyra 1902-07. Railroadman. Farmer.

SORENSON, JULIUS (son of Peter Olson and Bodil Kirstine Larsen of Denmark; latter born Feb. 4, 1829, Haarsley, Odense amt, Fyen, Denmark). He was born Dec. 25, 1854, Odense. Came to Utah Sept. 29, 1866, Peter Nebeker company.
Married Hannah Ackerman, Sovestad, Sweden (daughter of Ole Ackerman and Ingra Jensen), who was born Nov. 27, 1859, in Sweden. Their children: Orson Julius b. Sept. 19, 1881; Lovina Christine b. Dec. 30, 1883; William Gilbert b. Oct. 17, 1886; Anna Laura b. Nov. 16, 1889.
Married Caroline Christensen Feb. 20, 1896, Logan, Utah (daughter of Nels Peter Christensen and Martha M. Jenson of Wellinio, Hjorring amt, Denmark; former pioneer 1867). She was born Sept. 19, 1876, Bear River City, Utah. Their children: Mary C. b. May 11, 1897; Hannah Violla b. July 17, 1900; Alonzo Julius b. June 4, 1902; Alma Peter b. Jan. 5, 1905; Elva Myrtle b. July 4, 1907; Elias Herbert b. Feb. 12, 1911. Families resided Hyrum, Utah.
Elder.

SORENSON, WILLIAM GILBERT (son of Julius Sorenson and Hannah Ackerman). Born Oct. 17, 1886, Hyrum, Utah.
Married Florence James in 1906 at Logan, Utah (daughter of David James and Fannie Webb), who was born at Paradise, Utah. Their children: Fannie; Harold.

SORENSON, MARTIN (son of Soren Mortensen and Meta Maria Rasmussen of Thorslunde Bye, Holbek amt, Denmark). Born Oct. 31, 1831, at Thornslunde. Came to Utah Sept. 13, 1857, Christian Christiansen handcart company.
Married Christena Wicklund July 19, 1852 (daughter of Olof Wicklund and Ella Johnson—married 1844, Firilia parish, Sweden, pioneers Nov. 15, 1856, James G. Willie handcart company). She was born Feb. 5, 1848, and came to Utah with parents. Their children: Ellen C. b. March 28, 1866, m. William Moon Dec. 12, 1892; Martha Maria b. Nov. 15, 1868, m. Orson Hutchinson Dec. 5, 1889; Amanda Clara b. Jan. 5, 1876, m. William Bertieson Nov. 6, 1901; Ida V. b. Feb. 15, 1878, m. Martin Christiansen April 26, 1899; Nels M. b. March 19, 1882, m. Laura Winget May 1, 1912; Lionel W. b. April 6, 1885, m. Clara Larsen Jan. 17, 1905; Ethel M. b. May 16, 1888, m. Levi Mortensen Oct. 2, 1907.

SOULE, EMORY WATSON (son of Isaac Soule, born 1796, Banroor, Me., died 1874, and Elizabeth Harrison Smith of Ottobine, Rockingham county, Va., born 1805, Harrisburg, Pa., died 1875). He was born in 1836 in Ottobine. Came to Utah Oct. 5, 1859, independent company.
Married Mary Elizabeth Secrist April 12, 1864. Farmington, Utah (daughter of Jacob F. Secrist and Ann Eliza Logan of Farmington, pioneers 1847). She was born Jan. 15, 1848. Their children: Emory Moroni, died; Annie Lucretia; Orson Pratt, m. Hannah Hanson; Henry Watson, m. Alice Steed; Lawrence Jacob; Frank LeRoy, m. Mary Ann Christensen;

Eva Louisa, m. Horace Van Fleet; Mae Elizabeth, m. Herbert Sturdefant; Hugh Logan, died; Grant Wirt.
High priest; missionary to southern states 1882. Justice of peace. Farmer.

SOUTH, JOHN (son of William South and Marguerite Buins of England). Born Aug. 31, 1835. Bluetown, Kent, Eng. Came to Utah Nov. 9, 1866, Captain Walker company.
Married Kate Thurgood April 20, 1867, Salt Lake City (daughter of Thomas Thurgood and Catherine Jenkins of Tirling, Essex, Eng., pioneers Oct. 1867, William Godbe company). She was born April 2, 1845. Their children: John William, d. child; Amelia, d. aged 20; Marguerite Burns, m. Albert Van Cott; Eleanor, m. John Danvers; Jessie, m. Thomas Bytheway; Sarah Ann, d. child; Samuel, d. child; Kate, m. George McDonald. Family home, Salt Lake City.
Missionary to England 1879-80; member 30th quorum seventies; ordained priest Aug. 18, 1860; elder; ward clerk; Sunday school clerk. Veteran Black Hawk war 1866. Bookkeeper and salesman.

SOWLES, MELVIN B. (son of Stephen B. Sowles and Lurancy Reynolds, of Alburg, Vt.). Born May 27, 1844, Alburg, Vt. Came to Utah Dec. 25, 1875.
Married Clara L. Bowen July 31, 1873, Moira, Franklin county, N. Y. (daughter of Nason C. Bowen and Clarissa Stevens, of New York). She was born Oct. 13, 1851. Their children: Arthur N., died; Myra, m. G. H. Roberts; Melvin H., m. Constance Dininny; Lewis W., m. Mary Halloran; Clara, m. Forrest Walden; Ruth L. Family home, Salt Lake City.
Member of city council; member of state board of equalization; member of agricultural college board; general manager of Utah Nursery Co.; member of state board of correction eight years.

SPAFFORD, WILLIAM NELSON (son of Horace Spafford and Martha Stiles). Born Jan. 23, 1827, in Canada. Came to Utah in 1850.
Married Emma M. Johnson (daughter of Aaron Johnson and Polly Zerviah Kelsey), who was born Sept. 13, 1836, at Haddam, Conn. (deceased). Their children: Minerva Z.; Emma M.; Azalia M.; William N.; Lillian T.; Horace; Willis K.; Laura; Weltha; Con C.; Ida LaPrele.
Came to Utah 1850, settled at Springville, Utah. Served in the Mexican war 1849. Now dead.

SPAFFORD, WILLIAM N. (son of William Nelson Spafford and Emma M. Johnson). Born May 26, 1859, at Springville, Utah.
Married Estella Huntsman Sept. 4, 1880, Richfield, Utah (daughter of Isaiah Huntsman and Rebecca Ames). Their children: Emma; William Earl; Estella R.; Azalia M.; Elmer; Carl Y.; Willis I.; Vera M. Family home Annabella, Utah.
Bishop's counselor for 26 years. Game warden of Sevier county.

SPAFFORD, WILLIS K. (son of William Nelson Spafford and Emma M. Johnson). Born May 17, 1866, at Springville, Utah.
Married Ann E. Stubbs Jan. 7, 1891, Manti, Utah (daughter of Peter Stubbs and Ann Wride). Their children: Willis Earl; Annie; Marie; Emma; Harold S.; Reed; Jesse White; Louise. Family home Provo, Utah.
Second counselor to Bishop O. H. Berg, First ward, Provo. Has been associated with Reed Smoot for 20 years in coal business.

SPARKS, ALFRED (son of George Sparks and Hannah Lake of England). Born March 7, 1835, at Hollow, Worcestershire, Eng. Came to Utah in 1853, Cyrus H. Wheelock company.
Married Jane Ann Fowler Jan. 30, 1853, while crossing the Atlantic (daughter of Samuel Fowler and Ann Linton of Daughton, Worcestershire, Eng., and who came to Utah in 1877). She was born Nov. 27, 1835. Their children: George S. b. Sept. 29, 1854, m. Matilda Mary Price Sept. 29, 1876; Alfred W. b. Jan. 21, 1857, m. Sarah J. Grimmett Aug. 21, 1878; Mary Ann b. Feb. 6, 1859, m. W. H. Bird Oct. 11, 1875; Thomas F. b. April 7, 1861, m. Elisa J. Wilcox Oct. 16, 1884; Laura J. b. Sept. 9, 1863, d. infant; Alice M. b. Nov. 21, 1865, m. George Cook Oct. 11, 1883; John H. b. Feb. 20, 1870, m. Henerette Dayton Oct. 24, 1890; Caroline H. b. Feb. 17, 1872, m. J. Henry Dayton Oct. 24, 1890; Ann b. March 1, 1867, d. infant.
Married Ruth Slater March 14, 1863, at Salt Lake City (daughter of James Slater, who came to Utah June 4, 1838, at Bedfordshire, Eng. Their children: James H. b. Sept. 21, 1865, m. Rose Nate Oct. 3, 1888; Hannah b. March 28, 1864, m. Thomas Lindsay; Frances b. May 17, 1869, m. Frank Smedley Oct. 1, 1878; Joseph b. May 17, 1869; William b. Apr. 13, 1870; Henry b. June 11, 1872. Families resided Salt Lake City, Fort Herriman, Lehi, Utah, and Paris and Dingle, Idaho.
Elder and ward teacher. Veteran Echo Canyon war. School trustee. President Dingle Irrigation Co.

SPARKS, GEORGE SAMUEL (son of Alfred Sparks and Jane Ann Fowler). Born Sept. 29, 1854, Salt Lake City.
Married Matilda Price Sept. 25, 1876, Salt Lake City (daughter of Robert Price and Matilda Kelsey), who was born Jan. 1, 1856, St. Joseph, Ariz. Their children:

Bertran b. Aug. 29, 1879, m. Luella Dimmick Oct. 22, 1906; Beatrice b. Aug. 29, 1879, died; Sarah I. b. March 8, 1881, m. Elina Dayton; John A. b. June 8, 1883, died; George H. b. Dec. 31, 1884, m. Myrtle Cook April 24, 1906; Rose Annie b. March 19, 1887, died; Caddia A. b. June 24, 1889, m. Grantley Wilcox; Alice G. b. Sept. 2, 1893, m. Corneil Nate Sept. 28, 1911; Magdeline b. July 8, 1897; Margery F. b. Sept. 25, 1899.

SPAULDING, IRA N. (son of Stephen Spaulding and Susan Drake of Uinta, Utah). Born December, 1808. Came to Utah July 24, 1847, Brigham Young company.
Married Elizabeth Morris 1830, at Council Bluffs, Iowa, who was born 1815. Their children: Eli D., m. Eliza Wardsworth; Lucinda, m. George L. Corey; Ida S., m. Phoebe France; Stephen, m. Rhoda Nichols; Julius C., m. Lotta Nichols; Nathan. Family home Uinta, Utah.
Married Elizabeth Wright 1855, at Salt Lake City (daughter of Silas Wright of Michigan). She was born Sept. 6, 1818. Their children: Ira, m. Elizabeth Young; Joseph, m. Joseph Russell.
Missionary to Ohio 1871-72; bishop of Mt. Green ten years and at Uinta until death. Farmer. Died Dec. 21, 1883.

SPAULDING, IRA (son of Ira N. Spaulding and Elizabeth Wright). Born Aug. 6, 1856, Uinta, Utah.
Married Rebecca Stimpson Nov. 28, 1879, Ogden, Utah (daughter of William Stimpson and Edna Hinscliff of Riverdale, Utah, pioneers handcart company). She was born Feb. 24, 1861. Their children: Coral b. Aug. 31, 1881; Alta b. June 30, 1884, m. William Bowman; Ruby b. June 30, 1887, m. J. C. Hutchins; Lula b. April 30, 1890, m. Robert Loper; Lloyd b. April 6, 1897. Family home Birch Creek, Utah.
Foreman Utah Construction Co.

SPAULDING, CORAL (son of Ira Spaulding and Rebecca Stimpson). Born Aug. 31, 1881, Uinta, Utah. Machinist.

SPEIRS, GEORGE (son of William Speirs, born Nov. 16, 1788, at Tarbolton, Ayrshire, Scotland, and Agnes Tomson, born July 18, 1787, at Kilmarnock, Ayrshire). He was born Jan. 6, 1827, Tarbolton, Ayrshire, Scotland. Came to Utah Jan. 30, 1860, J. D. Murphy company.
Married Janet Lyon 1848 (daughter of John Lyon and Janet Thomson, Kilmarnock, Ayrshire), who came to Utah with husband. She was born Jan. 5, 1829. Their children: William H. June 19, 1849, m. Mary Walters; Janet b. May 30, 1851, m. William Dunn; John b. Jan. 28, 1853, d. Jan. 29, 1853; Agnes b. June 28, 1854, d. 1864; George b. June 15, 1856, d. 1858; Thomas b. May 31, 1859, m. Ann Bevan; Mary Ann b. Dec. 14, 1861, d. May 12, 1880; Lillias b. Sept. 15, 1863, m. William Tanner; Christinia b. Sept. 1, 1865, John Park; Ellen b. June 7, 1867, m. William Stewart; Matthew b. May 6, 1870, m. Maud Hardy. Family resided Salt Lake City and Tooele, Utah.
Member 43d quorum seventies; high priest; patriarch. Came to Utah 1860; moved to Tooele 1861.

SPEIRS, THOMAS (son of Adam Speirs of Edinburgh, Scotland). Born July 14, 1804, in Scotland. Came to Utah 1848.
Married Mary Cochran Dec. 20, 1829, Pittsburgh, Pa., who was born Sept. 30, 1804. Their children: Adam b. July 7, 1834, m. Charlotte Clark Dec. 3, 1854; Mary, m. John Pendieton; George b. Nov. 6, 1837, m. Adeline Harris 1862; Orson, m. Elizabeth Dye; Harrison, m. Bessie Hedger. Family home 10th ward, Salt Lake City.
Member seventy. Blacksmith. Died July 8, 1877, Salt Lake City.

SPEIRS, ADAM (son of Thomas Speirs and Mary Cochran). Born July 7, 1834, Pittsburgh, Pa. Came to Utah Oct. 17, 1848, Amasa M. Lyman company.
Married Charlotte Clark Dec. 3, 1854, Salt Lake City Endowment House (daughter of John Clark and Mary Noddings of England and Canada, pioneers Sept. 1850). She was born Nov. 12, 1834. Their children: Thomas, d. infant; Mary, m. Gilbert A. McLean; Adam C., m. Alice Alder; George Alfred, m. Ida Baddley; Arthur, d. aged 9; Ernest b. Jan. 10, 1865; Effie, m. George W. Spokes; Edna C., d. aged 7; Edgar Franklin. Family home, Salt Lake City.
High priest; teacher; bishop's counselor; bishop of 21st ward, Salt Lake City. City councilman; police judge at Salt Lake. Indian war veteran. Blacksmith and merchant. Died June 2, 1908, Salt Lake City.

SPEIRS, ERNEST (son of Adam Speirs and Charlotte Clark). Born Jan. 10, 1865, Salt Lake City.
Deacon. Dealer in merchandise.

SPEIRS, GEORGE (son of Thomas Speirs and Mary Cochran). Born Nov. 6, 1837, in Pennsylvania. Came to Utah 1847.
Married Adeline Harris 1862, Salt Lake City (daughter of William Harris of England). Their children: Adeline, m. David Felt; George, m. Minnie Squires; Mary, m. David Rich; Thomas, m. Clara Young; Lucy, m. Clyde Ward; Annie, m. Earnest Gregory; Jessie, m. George Howarth; William H., m. Melissa Cooley. Family home 10th ward, Salt Lake City.
Member seventy; missionary to Sandwich Islands 4 years. Blacksmith. Died March 6, 1911, Salt Lake City.

1178 PIONEERS AND PROMINENT MEN OF UTAH

SPEIRS, WILLIAM H. (son of George Speirs and Adeline Harris). Born Dec. 26, 1880, Salt Lake City. Married Melissa Cooley March, 1901, Salt Lake City (daughter of Andrew Cooley and Jane Jenkins of Brighton ward, Salt Lake). She was born Sept. 18, 1878. Their children: William Leigh b. Oct. 25, 1901; Adeline Jane b. Feb. 3, 1904; Jessie Ione b. May 25, 1906. Family home 23d ward, Salt Lake City. Miner and farmer.

SPENCER, DANIEL (son of Daniel Spencer and Chloe Wilson). Born July 20, 1794, West Stockbridge, Mass. Came to Utah in September, 1847, captain of his company. Married Emily Thompson of Hartford, Conn. Their children: Emma, m. Adam S. Patterson; John D., m. Clarissa H. Young; Jared, died; Josephine. Family home, Salt Lake City. President Salt Lake stake. Rancher and merchant. Died in December, 1868, Salt Lake City.

SPENCER, ORSON (son of Daniel Spencer and Chloe Wilson). Born March 14, 1802, West Stockbridge, Berkshire county, Mass. Came to Utah 1849, captain of his company. Married Catherine Curtis April 13, 1830 (daughter of Samuel Curtis and Patience Smith, latter died March 12, 1846, Indian Creek, Keosauqua, Iowa). She was born March 21, 1811. Their children: Catherine b. Oct. 6, 1831; Ellen b. Nov. 21, 1832, m. Hiram B. Clawson March 18, 1850; Aurelia b. Oct. 4, 1834, m. Thomas Rogers March 27, 1851; Catherine b. Oct. 2, 1836, m. Brigham Young, Jr. Nov. 15, 1856; Howard Orson b. June 16, 1838, m. Louise Cross April, 1860; George Boardman b. Feb. 21, 1840, m. Leonora T. Horne Nov. 10, 1867; Lucy b. Oct. 9, 1842, m. George W. Grant Jan. 2, 1867; Chloe b. July 26, 1844. Married Martha Knight. Their children: Martha Emma b. Jan. 30, 1848, m. Samuel Woodward; Albert James b. June 24, 1850; William Collinson b. Dec. 10, 1851, d. aged 1; June Knight b. June 28, 1854, m. Ellsworth Daggett. Married Jane Davis. Their child: Luna Spencer b. Dec. 6, 1856, m. Levin Simons 1873. Residded West Stockbridge and Middlefield, Mass., Nauvoo, Ill., and other places. Missionary to Great Britain 1848; to Prussia 1852; to United States 1854. Chancellor University of Deseret 1850. Died Oct. 15, 1855, St. Louis, Mo.

SPENCER, GEORGE BOARDMAN (son of Orson Spencer and Catherine Curtis). Born Feb. 21, 1840, at Middlefield, Hampshire county, Mass. Married Leonora Taylor Horne Nov. 10, 1867, Salt Lake City (daughter of Joseph Horne and Mary Isabella Hales; came to Utah Oct. 6, 1847, Edward Hunter company). She was born Jan. 16, 1849, Salt Lake City. Their children: Lucy Isabella b. July 4, 1869, d. Jan. 16, 1870; Leonora Horne b. March 27, 1871; Lilian b. Sept. 19, 1873, m. Ezra T. Budge June 12, 1895; George Boardman b. Feb. 7, 1876, m. Adeline Horsley Sept. 5, 1900; Joseph Horne b. April 20, 1878, m. Netta Poulton March 4, 1908; Howard and twin sister, b. Dec. 19, 1880, both d. at birth; Mary Ellen b. April 7, 1882, d. March 6, 1883; Orson b. Dec. 10, 1883, d. Jan. 17, 1888; Herbert Leo b. June 11, 1886; Seymour Horne b. July 16, 1888; Edwin b. June 5, 1893. Family resided Salt Lake City, Utah, and Paris, Idaho. Helped settle the Muddy. Missionary to Switzerland 1864-66; alternate high councilor Salt Lake stake; bishop 1st ward Paris, Idaho. Settled in Idaho 1874. Bear Lake county sheriff several years; probate judge two years; county treasurer two terms; road supervisor and school trustee.

SPENCER, CLAUDIUS V. (son of Daniel Spencer and Sophronia Eliza Pomeroy of West Stockbridge, Berkshire county, Mass.). Born April 2, 1824, at West Stockbridge. Came to Utah Sept. 23, 1847, Daniel Spencer company. Family home, Salt Lake City. Farmer. Chosen member of the territorial assembly 1856; member city council Salt Lake City; supervisor of streets without remuneration. Active and influential in church work; filled two missions to Great Britain and two in the United States. Patriarch. At time of death, March 5, 1910, Salt Lake City, his posterity numbered 20 children, 38 grandchildren and 6 great-grandchildren.

SPENCER, DANIEL S. (son of Claudius V. Spencer and Susannah Frances Neslen). Born June 12, 1857, at Salt Lake City. Married Margaret Louise Crismon Nov. 9, 1887, at Logan, Utah (daughter of George Crismon and Mary Louise Tanner of Salt Lake City). Their children: Margaret Louise b. May 21, 1889; Daniel Francis b. Feb. 2, 1891; Dorothy Dean b. April 23, 1897; Kathryn b. Jan. 3, 1901; David Crismon b. Oct. 29, 1905. Family home, Salt Lake City. Assistant general passenger agent Oregon Short Line Railroad Co.

SPENCER, JOHN D. (son of Daniel Spencer and Emily Thompson). Born June 27, 1858, Provo, Utah. Married Clarissa H. Young Jan. 19, 1882, Salt Lake City (daughter of Brigham Young and Lucy Decker), who was born July 23, 1860. Their children: John Allan b. July 1, 1885, m. Lula Young; Jean b. June 16, 1888, m. Morrill N. Farr; Renan b. April 15, 1890; Daniel T. b. Dec. 11, 1893; Helen Y. b. Nov. 9, 1896. Family home, Salt Lake City. County treasurer. Aide to Governor Heber M. Wells during first term. Engaged in life insurance business.

SPENCER, ISAAC. Born July, 1851, in Iowa. Came to Utah 1875. Married Mary E. Burmingham March 4, 1879, Salt Lake Endowment House (daughter of Thomas Burmingham and Ellen Hook of Bountiful, Utah, pioneers 1860). Their children: Asa L. b. Sept. 23, 1881, d. aged 2; Isaac W. b. Jan. 14, 1883, d. infant; Mary L. b. Jan. 23, 1885, m. Smith Clark; Luella b. July 20, 1887; Clarence b. April 9, 1889, d. infant; Lillie P. b. May 2, 1891, m. Edgar Tuttle; Harvey Earl b. May 2, 1891; Jennie and Glen (twins) b. Dec. 22, 1893; Ralph b. Dec. 16, 1895; Warren E. b. March 31, 1907, d. infant; Vera b. April 2, 1909, d. infant. Missionary to England 1909-11; member 6th quorum elders; Sunday school superintendent; home missionary. Farmer and truck gardener.

SPENCER, HARVEY EARL (son of Isaac Spencer and Mary E. Burmingham). Born May 2, 1891, Bountiful, Utah.

SPENDLOVE, JOHN. Came to Utah 1863, Daniel D. McArthur company. Married Elizabeth Harrison. Their children: Alfred, m. Harriet Winspear; John, Jr., m. Mary Davis; Emma, m. John Hinton; Mary, m. George St. Clair; Rebecca; William, m. Lydia Mathews. Family home Virgin City, Utah. Elder; ward and block teacher. Shoemaker. Died Virgin City, Utah.

SPENDLOVE, JOHN (son of John Spendlove and Elizabeth Harr ——). Born at Birmingham, Eng. Came to Utah with father. Married Mary Davis, Birmingham, Eng. (daughter of Benjamin Davis and Elizabeth Brooks of Stackpool Park, Wales). Their children: John Alfred b. Dec. 16, 1864, m. Eleanor Jepson; Lorenzo James b. June 12, 1865, m. Ellen Isom; William W., m. Alice Isom; Arthur D., died; Mary Elizabeth b. Dec. 16, 1871, m. Nephi J. Workman; Emma A., died; Mary Jane, m. John E. Wright; Clara, died; Fannie, m. John Sanders; Ada, m. Wilson Imley; Walter, m. Nettie Sanders. Family home Virgin City, Utah. Elder; Sunday school superintendent; ward and block teacher. Railroader; mason; farmer.

SPENDLOVE, JOHN ALFRED (son of John Spendlove and Mary Davis). Born Dec. 16, 1864, Virgin City, Utah. Married Eleanor Jepson Sept. 19, 1886, St. George, Utah (daughter of James Jepson and Eleanor Nightingale of Dalton, Eng., latter a pioneer 1849, oxteam company). She was born Sept. 1, 1858, and died Oct. 3, 1909. Their children: Joseph A. b. June 11, 1887, m. Sarah Jane Jones; James Jepson b. Sept. 13, 1888; Janus Alburn b. July 9, 1891; John A. b. Dec. 21, 1893; Mary Eleanor b. Feb. 11, 1895; Leonard b. Nov. 23, 1898; Wealthy b. Aug. 11, 1899; Baby b. April 20, 1904. Family home Virgin City, Utah. Married Addie Henline May 3, 1911, Salt Lake City (daughter of Sylvester Henline and Mary C. Privett of Bluff City, Mo.; came to Utah 1906). She was born May 1, 1880. Their child: ——b. April 23, 1912. High priest; missionary to southern states 1888-90; Sunday school superintendent; president Y. M. M. I. A.; ward and block teacher. Carpenter.

SPERRY, CHARLES (son of Joy Sperry, born Feb. 9, 1785, and Mary Lamont, born Nov. 29, 1789, both in New York state—married April 26, 1810). He was born June 30, 1829, Mecca, Trumbull Co., Ohio. Came to Utah October, 1847, Jedediah M. Grant company. Married Emily L. Miller Feb. 21, 1848 (daughter of Josiah Miller and Mary Morgan, pioneers 1847, J. B. Noble company). Their children: Philand Amanda b. Nov. 18, 1848, m. Alvins Sap Jan. 31, 1868; Charles Henry b. Oct. 15, 1850, m. Caroline Webb Nov. 13, 1871; Sarah Elizabeth b. Aug. 18, 1852, m. Charles E. Abbott May 30, 1870; Mary Emily b. Oct. 9, 1854, m. James R. Black Sept. 21, 1874; Miles Harrison b. March 27, 1857, m. Sarah Edmunds April 30, 1885; Clarissa Lorett b. Feb. 9, 1859, m. Dwight C. Sparks May 9, 1875; Maren Olive b. April 4, 1861, m. William C. Wheeler Feb. 17, 1881; William J. b. July 29, 1863, m. Augusta Taylor Oct. 27, 1885; John Alvins b. Feb. 22, 1865, d. March 17, 1870; Vilate b. June 7, 1870, d. same day. Bishop of Nephi, second ward; counselor to President Joel Grover, Juab stake; patriarch Feb. 21, 1888. Sheriff Juab Co., Utah; county commissioner one term.

SPERRY, HARRISON (son of Joy Sperry and Mary Lamont of Mecca, Trumbull Co., Ohio). Born March 24, 1832, in Trumbull county. Came to Utah Oct. 2, 1847, Jedediah M. Grant company. Married Mary Mosley Oct. 27, 1852, Salt Lake City (daughter of William Mosley and Mary Beardmore of England, the latter pioneer 1848). She was born March 21, 1835. Their children: Mary Ann, d. aged 17; Henry, d. child; Hannah E., d. infant. Family home, Salt Lake City. Married Susan Mosley Feb. 17, 1861, Salt Lake City (daughter of William Mosley and Mary Beardmore), who was born Oct. 11, 1845. Their children: George H., m. Sarah Weight, m. Jersey Beardmore; Charles A., m. Sarah Ager; William A., m. Ann Eardley, m. Lillian May Foster; Harrison S., m. Miss Titcomb; Minnie E., m. Joseph Priest;

Mary, d. aged 9; Ermie, m. David Walker; Byron, m. Edith Luelan; Walter, d. infant; Ralph B., m. —— Williams.
Married Ellenor M. Butterworth Dec. 15, 1873 (daughter of William Butterworth and Mary Rose), who was born Aug. 22, 1857. Their children: William O., m. —— Stout; Elizabeth Jane, m. Harvey Stout; Milton, d. aged 2; Mary E., d. infant; Correll and Harrell (twins), d. infants; Naomi, m. Rudolph Holmes; Edmond; Melba, d. aged 7.
Bishop 31 years; patriarch; bishop's counselor 15 years. Member city council two terms. Farmer; stockraiser.

SPRAGUE, S. L. Came to Utah 1848.
Married Mary Woodard, who came to Utah with her husband. Their child: Samuel Linzey b. March 23, 1843, m. Anna Marian Kimball.
Was the first doctor to arrive in Salt Lake City. Planted the first flower garden, the bulbs and seeds being brought from Boston by himself.

SPRAGUE, SAMUEL LINZEY (son of S. L. Sprague and Mary Woodard). Born March 23, 1843, Salem, Mass. Came to Utah with father.
Married Anna Marian Kimball 1868 (daughter of William H. Kimball, the pioneer stage line owner). Their children: Linzey E.; Mrs. Percy Sadler; Mrs. Herman A. Prosser of New York city; Milton S. of San Francisco; Mable V., d. aged 4.
Freighter between Missouri river and Salt Lake City, Utah. Developer of several mining claims. Member of Colonel Hodge's surveying party, which surveyed for the Union Pacific railroad through Utah and Nevada 1867. Deputy United States marshal 1871-90. Died May 11, 1900.

SPRINGALL, ARTHUR D. (son of James Springall and Sarah Sharp of Liverpool, Eng.; came to Utah on railroad). Born July 27, 1860. Came to Utah in early days.
Married Katherine Knox Dec. 19, 1882, Salt Lake City (daughter of William Knox and Kate Tearn of Salt Lake City, pioneers Sept. 3, 1855). She was born April 4, 1868, Logan, Utah. Their children: William A. b. Dec. 6, 1886, m. Geneva Mina Brandley; Fredrick E. b. June 22, 1896. Family home, Salt Lake City.

SPRINGER, NATHAN CHATMOND (son of John S. Springer and Eliza Manchester of New Bedford, Mass). Born June 26, 1843, Providence, R. I. Came to Utah 1863, freight train for California.
Married Matilda Robey Nov. 2, 1867, Midway, Utah (daughter of Jeremiah Robey and Ruth Tucker of Harrison county, W. Va., pioneers Aug. 1, 1852, David Wood company). She was born Dec. 13, 1849, Honey Creek, Pottawatamie Co., Iowa. Their children: Emily Matilda b. Sept. 6, 1868, m. Henry T. Coleman; Laila Ruth b. Aug. 25, 1870, m. Charles E. Alexander; Ellen Malissa b. July 30, 1872, m. Carson O. Smith; Nathan Chapman b. July 1, 1874; Franklin Theophilus b. Aug. 30, 1876, died; Jeremiah Robey b. Nov. 17, 1878, m. Lydia Rosetta Bigler; Ida May b. Sept. 1, 1880, and Lethe Belle b. July 17, 1883, died.
Elder. Veteran Black Hawk war; civil war veteran. Miner; promoter. Died Nov. 16, 1888, Bluefield, Nicaragua, Central America.

SPRINGER, JEREMIAH ROBEY (son of Nathan Chatmond and Matilda Robey). Born Nov. 17, 1878, Midway, Utah.
Married Lydia Rosetta Bigler Nov. 9, 1904, Heber City, Utah (daughter of Jacob A. Bigler and Pauline Ott of Mount Pleasant, Utah). She was born June 12, 1881. Their children: Jay Reed b. Nov. 8, 1905; Lydia Pauline b. July 19, 1907; Beryl Ott b. Feb. 16, 1909; Lowell Franklin b. April 16, 1912. Family home Midway, Utah.
Elder; ward teacher at Midway, Utah. Marshal of Midway. Blacksmith; farmer.

SPRY, WILLIAM (son of Philip Spry and Sarah Field). Born Jan. 11, 1864, Windsor, Berkshire, Eng. Came to Utah 1875 with his father, mother and two brothers, George H. and Samuel, and an adopted sister, reaching Salt Lake City June 2. In October, 1885, was called to southern states on a mission, and remained there until the fall of 1891. Was president of the mission during the last four years of his service.
Married Mary Alice Wrathall of Grantsville July, 1890. Their children: Mary A.; Lita M.; James W.; two other children d. young.
Located at Tooele 1893, where he engaged in farming and stockraising. County collector of Tooele county 1894; member of legislature from Tooele county 1902-04; state chairman of the Republican party; president state land board 1905-06; United States marshal for the district of Utah Feb. 15, 1906; elected governor of Utah 1909-13; re-elected 1913-17. President of the Farmers' and Stockgrowers' Bank; director of other banks and mercantile institutions; director of the Utah Pioneers Book Publishing Company.

SQUIRE, JOHN P. (son of Aaron Squire, born Sept. 19, 1795, and Elizabeth Squire, born April 26, 1796, of Ohio). Born March 30, 1824, in Ohio. Came to Utah 1848, Lorenzo Snow company.
Married Adelia Demill Dec. 31, 1851 (daughter of Freeborn and Annie Demill). Their children: Orpha E. b. Nov. 31, 1852; Harriet A. b. Dec. 2, 1854; John P. b. Oct. 9, 1856; Aaron D. b. May 6, 1858; Annie M. b. Jan. 23, 1860; Adelia L. b. Sept. 3, 1862; Eliza R. b. Feb. 1, 1865; Oliver E. b. Feb. 26, 1867.
Seventy. School teacher; farmer.

SQUIRE, JOHN P., JR. (son of John P. Squire and Adelia Demill). Born Oct. 9, 1856, Manti, Utah.
Married Ansil Farrie 1888, Manti, Utah (daughter of Ludvig and Christena Farrie), who was born May 7, 1868, Provo, Utah, and died Nov. 5, 1895. Their children: Leona b. Feb. 4, 1889; Gilbert L. b. July 30, 1891; John L. b. July 30, 1892, d. March 10, 1893; Ruth b. Oct. 24, 1895, d. Sept. 3, 1896.
Married Christena H. Kenney Jan. 8, 1897, Manti, Utah, who was born Jan. 12, 1879. Their children: Lorin D. b. Jan. 2, 1898; Canna Mary b. Jan. 5, 1900; Adrien A. b. June 27, 1902.

SQUIRES, CHARLES PORTER (son of Charles Merrill Squires and Charlotte Smith). Born March 22, 1827, Newbury, Geauga Co., Ohio. Came to Utah 1848, Lorenzo Snow company.
Married Sarah Peters Sept. 1, 1856 (daughter of David Peters and Laura Davis, married April 11, 1840, in North Wales, pioneers 1849, George A. Smith company). She was born Feb. 6, 1841, in North Wales. Their children: Charles Morgan b. July 13, 1857, m. Luna C. Nichols June 21, 1898, d. March 31, 1911; m. Elizabeth Sarah Hunt Jan. 6, 1913; David Merrill b. Nov. 18, 1859, m. Margaret Jane Burt Dec. 27, 1883; John Albin b. Jan. 1, 1861, d. Oct. 19, 1864; William Porter b. Oct. 13, 1864, m. Zilpah E. Young; Charlottie Laura b. Feb. 6, 1867, m. Charles Tillotson; Laurence Calvin b. Dec. 3, 1869, m. Maud Wilcox; Porter Huse b. Sept. 29, 1872.
High priest; missionary to eastern states 1869-70; high councilor Box Elder stake. Drove team across plains for President Snow. Died 1872.

SQUIRES, DAVID MERRILL (son of Charles Porter Squires and Sarah Peters). Born Nov. 18, 1859, Brigham City, Utah.
Married Margaret Jane Burt Dec. 27, 1883, Salt Lake City (daughter of John Davidson Burt and Elizabeth Paterson), who was born Dec. 9, 1858, Brigham City, Utah. Their children: David P. b. Oct. 13, 1884, m. Sarah Florence Fowler Feb. 28, 1910; Laura Jane b. Sept. 21, 1887, m. Clyde Gillespie June 17, 1909.
Married Anna Belle Tillotson Nov. 18, 1903, Salt Lake City (daughter of Ephraim Tillotson and Ruth Collinson, married Sept. 30, 1856, St. Louis, Mo., came to Utah 1877). She was born June 22, 1870, St. Louis, Mo. Only child: Merrell Charles b. Oct. 26, 1905.
High priest.

SQUIRES, GEORGE B. Born Sept. 25, 1844, Pittsfield, Mass. Came to Utah 1889.
Married Ruth Jones Feb. 22, 1904, Salt Lake City (daughter of Dan and Elizabeth Jones of that place), who was born September, 1849. Family home, Salt Lake City.
Deputy secretary of state; first county statistician; warden state prison; held seat in state constitutional convention; first state insurance commissioneer. Expert accountant. Died Sept. 30, 1910, Salt Lake City.

SQUIRES, HENRY AUGUSTUS (son of Thomas Squires and Sarah Patnoster of Herefordshire, Eng). Born Feb. 22, 1825, Hartford, Eng. Came to Utah Nov. 27, 1856, Edward Martin handcart company.
Married Sarah Minnie Cattlin March, 1847, at Wellin, Hartfordshire, Eng. (daughter of William Cattlin and Sarah Bigg of Wellin). She was born Nov. 16, 1826. Their children: Sarah Augusta, m. Charles T. Toone; Mary Emily, m. John Bowker; Catherine Harriet, m. Clements Horsley; Clara Annie, m. Thomas Allen; Rosetta Agnes, m. George William Huntington; Echo Levinia, m. Ruben Kirkham; Celestia Angelica, m. Preston Free; Grace Alice, m. Albert Edwards; Ida Philla, m. William Smith; Henrietta Ellen, m. Frederick Caterer; Thomas Henry; Florence Adelade, m. Bert Griffin. Family resided Salt Lake City, Utah, and London, Eng.
Seventy; block teacher. Captain home guard. Merchant.

STAHLE, JOHN (son of Joachim Stahle, died at Florence, Neb., en route to Utah, and Catherine Kreis, died at Santa Clara, Utah 1863, of Amriswil, Thurgau, Switzerland). Born July 25, 1830, Amriswil. Came to Utah Oct. 31, 1862, Captain Baliff company.
Married Susan Baumann (daughter of Rudolph Baumann, of Wadensweil, Canton Zurich, Switzerland, and Anna Katharina Grafiin of Steckborn, Thurgau, Switzerland). She was born Sept. 27, 1838. Their children: Sophia, d. Oct. 7, 1863; John Jr., m. Cora E. Stayner June 4, 1902; Mary, d. Sept. 11, 1887; Emma, m. David Stoker Jr. Dec. 24, 1891; Henry W., m. Elizabeth A. Cook Sept. 24, 1902; Selena, d. Aug. 9, 1873; Susie F., m. Frank Wright May 24, 1905; Minnie A., m. Andrew Weaver March 27, 1902; Bertha M., m. Alma H. Hardy May 24, 1905. Family home Bountiful, Utah.
Seventy; high priest; ward teacher at Bountiful 40 years. Farmer and gardener. Died Dec. 18, 1910, Bountiful.

STAHLE, HENRY W. (son of John Stahle and Susan Baumann). Born July 6, 1875, Bountiful, Utah.
Married Elizabeth A. Cook Sept. 24, 1902, Salt Lake City (daughter of David Cook and Hannah H. Holt of Bountiful;

came to Utah Oct. 16, 1853, Jacob Gates company). Their children: Therice H. b. Jan. 24, 1904; LaVoun b. June 7, 1907; Dale Cook b. April 4, 1911. Family home, Bountiful. President 100th quorum seventies; missionary to southern states Jan. 18, 1896, Nov. 25, 1899; Sunday school superintendent at Bountiful, Utah. Davis county clerk six years; and county attorney two years; city councilman; city treasurer and city attorney at Bountiful. Manager Security Investment company, bookkeeper and accountant.

STAINES, WILLIAM C. (son of William Staines and Blanche Potter of Bedfordshire. Eng., pioneers fall of 1848).
Married Lillias Lyon Oct. 3, 1854, Salt Lake City (daughter of John Lyon and Janet Thompson, pioneers Sept. 26, 1853, Jacob Gates company). She was born Aug. 22, 1836, at Kilmarnock, Scotland.
Immigration agent for the Mormon church at New York City.

STAKER, NATHAN (son of Nathaniel and Cornelia Staker of Pickering, Canada). Born 1801 at Pickering. Came to Utah November, 1852, Henry Miller company.
Married Jane Richmond 1827 at Pickering (daughter of David Richmond of Pickering), who was born 1810. Their children: John, m. Mary Ann Wiggins; William, m. Catherine Parsons; Sarah, m. Vance Shafer, m. Mr. Holly; Alma, m. Elizabeth Young; Nathaniel, Nathan and Aaron, died; Lydia, m. Solon Robison; Mary, m. Alonzo Farnsworth; Joseph, m. Sarah Brown.
Married Mrs. Eliza Burton 1857, Pleasant Grove, Utah, who was born 1825. Their children: James Benjamin, m. Elizabeth Fisher; Eliza Jane, m. Ezeriah Day; Phoebe, m. Hyrum Farnsworth; Ellis, m. George Day. Families home Mount Pleasant, Utah.
Missionary to Canada 1842-44; president high priests quorum at Mount Pleasant, Utah. Farmer. Died.

STAKER, ALMA (son of Nathan Staker and Jane Richmond). Born June 15, 1837. Came to Utah with father.
Married Elizabeth Young Feb. 7, 1856, Pleasant Grove, Utah (daughter of James Young and Elizabeth Seeley of Canada). She was born March 29, 1837. Their children: William Alma b. Jan. 7, 1857, m. Hilma Egberg; Elizabeth Jane b. Aug. 1858, m. Abraham Day; Martha b. 1861, m. Christian Miller; Annie b. 1863, d. child; Mary b. 1865, d. infant; Luna May b. 1867, d. infant; Elnora b. 1869, m. Alma Fillmore; Hettie b. 1871, m. Alvin Johnson; Joseph Ether b. 1876, m. Matilda Stalworthy. Family home Mount Pleasant, Utah.
High priest; member United Order. Minuteman in Black Hawk Indian war; served in Walker war. Sawyer; carpenter; farmer.

STAKER, WILLIAM ALMA (son of Alma Staker and Elizabeth Young). Born Jan. 7, 1857, at Pleasant Grove, Utah.
Married Hilma Egberg March 7, 1877, Mount Pleasant, Utah (daughter of Carl and Clara Egberg), who was born May 3, 1860. Their children: William Heleman b. Jan. 18, 1878, m. Elizabeth Lewis; Lawrence Raymond b. June 26, 1880, m. Amy Howard; Lona May b. Dec. 23, 1882, m. Nelson Day; Clara Elizabeth b. Feb. 1, 1885, m. Alfred Wilstead; Victor Nathan b. Sept. 16, 1887, d. youth; Katy Marinda b. March 20, 1890, m. James Osmond Elliott; Alden Orlando b. April 28, 1892, m. Annie Thomas; Annie Louisa b. June 29, 1897; Bertha Ellis b. April 25, 1902. Family home Lawrence, Utah.
Elder; Sunday school superintendent at Lawrence 1892. School trustee at Lawrence several years. Member United Order. Farmer; stockraiser. Came to Lawrence as a pioneer in 1879.

STANDLEY, ALEXANDER SCHOBY (son of Richard Standley, born Feb. 14, 1777, and Elizabeth Staltz, born 1786, of Ohio). He was born May 12, 1800, New Brunswick, Middlesex county, N. J. Came to Utah Sept. 15, 1852.
Married Philanda Upson March 19, 1829 (daughter of Freeman Upson and Sally Culver—married March 17, 1810, Portage Co., Ohio). She was born Aug. 1, 1814. Their children: Eliza b. April 16, 1830, died; Franklin b. Aug. 19, 1831, m. Sarah Ann Haig April 5, 1857; Ellen b. April 8, 1833, m. Thomas Jefferson Osborn Sept. 14, 1851; Martha b. Sept. 20, 1834, died; Alexander Henry b. April 28, 1836, m. Adelia Ann Brown Oct. 27, 1856, m. Jemima Cregar; Elizabeth b. March 7, 1838, m. Thomas Jefferson Osborn Jan. 24, 1854; Cyrene b. May 1, 1840, m. Merriner Wood Merrill June 6, 1856; Philanda b. March 19, 1842, m. Wallace Kendell Burnham Nov. 30, 1856; Sarah Alvira b. May 26, 1844, m. George Milton Pace March 7, 1860; Lydia b. Dec. 13, 1846, m. Wallace Kendell Burnham April 11, 1865; Michael b. May 7, 1849, m. Naomi Ann Kemp Feb. 27, 1879, m. Maryette Rice Dec. 31, 1885. Family home Suffield, Portage Co., Ohio.
Assisted in bringing immigrants to Utah. Died Dec. 30, 1854.

STANDRING, EDWIN (son of James Standring and Mary Howell of Oldham, Lancashire, Eng.). Born April 27, 1828, at Oldham. Came to Utah in 1852, A. Melton Musser company.
Married Rebecca Smith (daughter of William Smith and Charlota Ford, pioneers 1857). She was born Feb. 20, 1828. Their children: Edwin H. b. Sept. 1867, died; Mary Eliza-

beth b. Nov. 1878, d. 1879; John Edwin b. Feb. 24, 1881, m. Mary Jane Hurly Jan. 21, 1903.
Missionary in U. S. 1876. Assisted in bringing immigrants to Utah 1862. Chief clerk in People's Co-Operative Company in Lehi for many years. Died Nov. 20, 1888.

STANDRING, JOHN EDWIN (son of Edwin Standring and Rebecca Smith). Born Feb. 24, 1881.
Married Mary Jane Hurley Jan. 21, 1903. Their children: Mildred Viola b. Aug. 31, 1903; Elsie May b. Aug. 23, 1905; Edwin Louis b. June 26, 1907; Frances Owen b. Feb. 1, 1910. Family home Lehi, Utah.

STANFORD, JOSEPH (son of Thomas Stanford and Elizabeth Barnett of Southwick, Sussex, Eng.). Born Aug. 16, 1834, at Southwick. Came to Utah Sept. 13, 1861, Joseph Horne company.
Married Elizabeth Young May 20, 1859, at Southwick (daughter of Thomas Young and Margaret Martin of England). She was born Dec. 26, 1836. Their children: Joseph, d. Sept. 4, 1861; Thomas Y., m. Laura D. Horr; Elizabeth M., m. Hyrum H. Goddard; Amelia, m. Benjamin F. Gwilliams; Marian N., m. Joseph Wilcox; Rachel Y., d. Sept. 3, 1869; Eva, d. Sept. 5, 1870; Ida Laura, d. July 12, 1873; Josephine, d. March 21, 1878; Alice B., d. July 1, 1875; George Y., m. Florence O'Neil. Family home Ogden, Utah.
Missionary to England 1852-61; high priest; member Weber stake high council. County recorder for Weber county 1878-82; also 1889-91; county commissioner 1900-04; Ogden city alderman three terms; city councilman 10 years; school trustee; member territorial legislature 1894-98. Merchant. Died Feb. 11, 1909.

STANFORD, STEPHEN (son of Thomas Stanford and Elizabeth Barnett of Southwick, Eng.). Born Dec. 6, 1832, Southwick. Came to Utah Sept. 13, 1861, Joseph Horne company.
Married Louisa Foreman May, 1855, Dover, Kentshire, Eng. (daughter of James and Mary Ann Foreman of Dover, pioneers, Captain Smith company). She was born Dec. 26, 1832. Their children: Cyrus J. b. Jan. 31, 1856, m. Ella Philpin; Louisa C. b. Dec. 12, 1858, m. Albert S. Ure; Harriett Esther b. on plains Aug. 16, 1861, m. William Shill; Caroline S. b. Sept. 20, 1864, m. Charles Hyde; Thomas C. b. Sept. 24, 1866, m. Ida Ivey; Stephen A. b. Oct. 20, 1868, m. Martha Finch; Ruth M. b. Nov. 20, 1870, m. Charles Cromer; Charlotte Eliza b. Oct. 10, 1872, died; Albert B. b. Aug. 30, 1874, m. Edith Rawson; James E. b. Nov. 20, 1876, died.
Married Jennie Barker Feb. 9, 1892, Logan, Utah (daughter of John Henry H. Barker and Anna Dunlap of Southampton, Eng.). She was born Jan. 19, 1850, and came to Utah 1890. They resided at Logan and Salt Lake City, Utah.
Missionary in England 1850-52. - In charge of L. D. S. Immigration in Boston for several years. Member Utah State Fair Association. Florist. Died Dec. 14, 1909, Salt Lake City.

STANGER, GEORGE (son of James Stanger and Isabella Thompson of Faceby, Yorkshire, Eng.). Born Nov. 5, 1832, at Faceby. Came to Utah 1855, Richard Ballantyne company.
Married Mary Etherington Feb. 13, 1855, Stocksley, Eng. (daughter of John Etherington and Elizabeth Emsley of Faceby, pioneers 1855, Secrist and Guymon company). She was born Jan. 12, 1834. Their children: George W. b. Nov. 8, 1856; Alfred J. b. April 4, 1859; James b. Nov. 29, 1860; Thomas E. b. Dec. 4, 1862; Mary A. b. Dec. 31, 1865; Joseph E. b. March 18, 1866; Hyrum T. b. Jan. 25, 1868; Sarah E. b. March 7, 1870; Albert E. b. March 13, 1872; Charles H. b. June 21, 1874; Isabella J. b. Aug. 1, 1876; Susan b. Nov. 29, 1878. Family home Slaterville, Utah.
Member 60th quorum seventies; bishop's counselor. Farmer.

STANGER, GEORGE W. (son of George Stanger and Mary Etherington). Born Nov. 8, 1856, Ogden, Utah.
Married Sarah Ellen Knight Nov. 8, 1877, at Ogden (daughter of John Knight and Sarah E. Taylor of Slaterville, Utah). She was born Sept. 26, 1860. Their children: Sarah Ellen b. March 21, 1879; George Oscar b. March 28, 1880; Mary Millie b. Jan. 11, 1882; Annie Ethel b. March 19, 1885; Georgiana b. Aug. 24, 1883; John Rudcer b. Oct. 15, 1888; Edward Marion b. Oct. 6, 1890; Don Carlos b. Feb. 16, 1892; Lula Althea b. March 21, 1894; James Cecil b. Jan. 28, 1897; Elsie Elizabeth b. Oct. 10, 1900. Family home Neeley, Idaho.
Missionary to southern states 1886-88; high priest; deacon; bishop's counselor. Constable; road supervisor. Farmer; stockraiser.

STANGER, THOMAS (son of James Stanger and Isabella Thompson of Faceby, Yorkshire, Eng. Came to Utah 1869). Born July 8, 1830, Faceby. Came to Utah Sept. 25, 1855, Richard Ballantyne company.
Married Jane Wilson July 8, 1853, at Faceby (daughter of John Wilson and Ann Irwin, who died at Swainby, Eng.). She was born April 21, 1832. Their children: Annie E. b. April 28, 1854, m. Adolph Layman Jan. 13, 18?3; Thomas James b. Oct. 4, 1856, m. Hannah Williams June 28, 1875;

PIONEERS AND PROMINENT MEN OF UTAH 1181

John W. b. April 30, 1858, m. Ellen Hutchins Oct. 5, 1882; William R. b. June 16, 1860, m. Mary Slater Aug. 8, 1883; Isabella Jane b. Dec. 1, 1861, m. Hugh McLain June 15, 1882; Mary H. b. April 20, 1863, m. John Slater Nov. 30, 1881; George E. b. March 19, 1865, m. Jane Sharp Jan. 7, 1891; David H. b. Dec. 3, 1866, m. Caroline Wilson March 8, 1886; Caroline R. b. June 19, 1869, m. Frank Shaw July 22, 1890; Charles M. b. April 30, 1871, m. Mary Laughlin June 28, 1893; Reuben E. b. April 3, 1873, m. Mrs. Mary Stanger May 17, 1892. Family home Marriott, Utah.
Member 56th quorum seventies. Farmer.

STANWORTH, SAMUEL. Born 1836, Lancashire, Eng. Came to Utah with oxteam.
Married Nancy Stanworth. They had nine children. Family home Hinckley, Utah.
Worked as machinist for Joseph Smith at Nauvoo. Assisted in bringing immigrants to Utah. Indian war veteran. Called to assist in settling Clary, near St. George; and later to Grafton. Died 1864, Grafton.

STANWORTH, SAMUEL (son of Samuel and Nancy Stanworth). Born March 21, 1864, Duncan's Retreat.
Married Ellen Elders 1885 (daughter of Claybourn Elders), who was born June, 1869. They have six children. Family home Hinckley, Utah.
Assisted financially in building St. George and Salt Lake temples. Farmer and rancher.

STAPLES, JAMES (son of Henry Staples and Anne Staples of England). Born Jan. 18, 1810. Came to Utah 1852.
Married Sarah Limerick, England (daughter of Richard Limerick, pioneer 1852), who was born Aug. 14, 1804. Their children: Anne b. April 3, 1831, m. Andrew Hooper; George b. June 8, 1834, m. Lauraette Rappleye; Elizabeth b. Jan. 8, 1837, m. Simon Baker; James b. Feb. 14, 1840; Henry b. Dec. 11, 1843, m. Mary Duncanson. Family home, Salt Lake City. Veteran Indian war. Brick and stone mason. Died April 8, 1875.

STAPLES, GEORGE (son of James Staples and Sarah Limerick). Born June 8, 1834, Red Morley, Worcestershire, Eng. Came to Utah 1852.
Married Lauraette Rappleye Nov. 15, 1854, Salt Lake City (daughter of Tunis Rappleye, pioneer July 24, 1847, Brigham Young company, and Louisa Cuttler of New York, latter came to Utah 1852, Bryant Jolley company). She was born March 23, 1840. Their children: George A. b. Jan. 1, 1856, m. Susan Hawley; Sarah Louisa b. Jan. 18, 1858, m. Joseph M. Robinson; James Tunis b. April 29, 1860, m. Ruthette Gardner; Lauraette Jand b. June 7, 1862, m. Elias Gardner; Joseph Levi b. June 22, 1864, m. Matilda Anderson; William Henry b. Dec. 25, 1866, m. Mary Ella Crane; Clara Samantha b. June 27, 1869, m. Odis Rogers; Mary Sophia b. May 21, 1872, m. Peter Christensen; Ammon Franklin b. July 25, 1874, m. Caroline Johnson; Aleveretta Augusta b. Oct. 4, 1876, m. Charles J. Engar; Rachel Alice Dora b. April 12, 1879, m. Niels C. Poulson; Moroni Andrew Alexander b. April 11, 1881, m. Caroline Thueson; Eliza Roxi b. March 15, 1884, m. Lafayette Hill.
Missionary among the Indians; veteran Black Hawk and Walker wars. Farmer; stockraiser. Family resided Salt Lake City and Sevier Co., Utah. Died Oct. 31, 1890, Elsimore, Utah.

STAPLES, JOSEPH L. (son of George Staples and Lauraette Rappleye). Born June 22, 1864, Kanab, Utah.
Married Matilda Anderson March 16, 1904, Salt Lake City (daughter of Niels Anderson and Anna Christensen of Denmark; came to Utah 1882). She was born Feb. 13, 1882. Their children: Erwin L. b. April 15, 1905; Anna Laura b. Oct. 6, 1907; George W. b. July 26, 1909. Family home Elsimore, Utah.
High priest; president Y. M. M. I. A. Elsimore class teacher; elder quorum; bishop in Elsimore ward 1911. Member city council six years; president town board at Elsimore four years. Farmer; stockraiser.

STAPLEY, CHARLES (son of Charles Stapley, born March 17, 1800, Kent, Eng., and Sarah Bryant, born May 22, 1802, at Kent). Born Nov. 28, 1824, at Kent. Came to Utah 1856, Sterling Driggs company.
Married Sarah Parkinson July 24, 1854 (daughter of James Parkinson and Elizabeth Chattle), who was born May 24, 1831; came to Utah with husband. Their children: Harriet E. b. July 1, 1855, m. John Batty; Charles H. b. March 27, 1858, m. Jane Adams; Jane E. b. July 5, 1860, m. Halinton Wallace; Mary J. b. Feb. 11, 1865, m. William A. Dringhurst Dec. 18, 1884; James C. b. Sept. 1867, m. Tresa Magee; Emma E. b. Nov. 3, 1869, m. Henry Tanner; Adelaide b. Nov. 22, 1872; Seymour T. b. June 22, 1878. Family home Toquerville, Utah.
Missionary in Australia 1853-54; bishop's counselor 1860-1901; assistant Sunday school superintendent; choir leader. Justice of peace; constable.

STARBUCK, I. J. (son of Guayer Starbuck and Cynthia A. Shaw). Born June 20, 1849, in Ohio. Came to Utah 1888.
Married Eva E. Weygint June 12, 1883 (daughter of William Weygint and Sophronia Blanchard of Salt Lake City). Only child: Jay G. b. Oct. 1, 1890, d. 1900.
Deputy food commissioner; real estate and mining man.

STARK, DANIEL (son of John Stark and Sarah Mann of Halifax, Nova Scotia). Born June 29, 1820, Boston, Mass. Came to Utah Feb. 1858, Joseph Mathews company.
Married Ann Cooke Dec. 1, 1844, Boston, Mass., who was born June 4, 1825. Their children: John D. b. Sept. 18, 1845, m. Clarissa Amelia Webb; Annie Frances b. Feb. 19, 1848, m. Charles B. Oliver; James T. b. April 26, 1850, m. Evaline Browning, died; Mary Ellen b. April 23, 1855, died; Elizabeth Bird (adopted) b. Dec. 31, 1845, m. H. N. Howell. Family resided San Francisco, San Jose and San Bernardino, Cal.
Married Betsy Baldwin March 22, 1862, Salt Lake City (daughter of David Baldwin and Elizabeth Cutler of Birmingham, England, pioneers October, 1861, Daniel Stark company). She was born June 24, 1843. Their children: Sarah Ellen b. Feb. 4, 1863, m. John Van Wagoner; Joseph D. b. Dec. 25, 1863, m. Maggie Mardin; David b. Sept. 25, 1865, m. Martha Ramsey; Alice b. Feb. 14, 1870, m. Justin A. Loveless; Samuel b. March 12, 1868, m. Lizzie Worsencroft; William B. b. Oct. 14, 1871, m. Rosetta Baker; Kate Matilda b. Oct. 8, 1874, m. George Van Wagoner; George b. Feb. 6, 1877, died; Elizabeth b. Dec. 4, 1879, m. David Holiday; Louie b. March 6, 1884, m. Garry Conk.
Married Priscilla Berkenhead March 16, 1867, Salt Lake City (daughter of Isaac Birkenhead of Payson, Utah, pioneer October, 1861, Daniel Stark company). She was born Nov. 29, 1849. Their children: Harriet b. Sept. 23, 1868, m. Lewis Wride; Charles Henry b. Nov. 28, 1870, m. Sarah Kay; Ernest Albert b. Oct. 1, 1874, m. Sarah Douglass; Franklin b. Aug. 16, 1879, m. Theresa Todd; Isaac Walter b. Jan. 23, 1882; Mabel b. March 12, 1884. Family home Payson, Utah.
Bishop. City and county surveyor in Payson and Utah county. Assisted in bringing immigrants to Utah. Farmer; joiner and builder. Died April 23, 1907, at Payson, Utah.

STARK, JOHN DANIEL (son of Daniel Stark and Ann Cooke). Born Sept. 18, 1845, Boston, Mass. Came to Utah February, 1858, Joseph Mathews company.
Married Amelia Webb Dec. 21, 1868, Salt Lake City (daughter of Pardon Webb and Clarissa J. Lee of Payson, Utah). She was born Oct. 22, 1850. Their children: Minnie b. Oct. 24, 1869, m. Samuel J. Robinson; James Warren b. Oct. 24, 1873, m. Malissa Taylor; Lee Cook b. April 8, 1876, m. Ivy McClellan; Lula b. Sept. 6, 1880, m. John C. Wecksworth; Mary b. April 15, 1882, m. Rey L. Pratt; Anna b. Oct. 12, 1884, m. Orla E. McClellan; Lesslie Webb b. June 24, 1888, m. Roxy Cador; Zina b. April 16, 1892, m. Jesse A. Smithwaite; Jane b. Jan. 3, 1895. Family home Payson, Utah.
Assisted in collecting and establishing Payson Sunday school library; member of Philomathean society; Sunday school teacher; ward clerk. City recorder for Payson City three years. Bookkeeper; telegrapher and storekeeper; in band and orchestra.

STARK, PAUL (son of Martin Stark, born July 4, 1792, Tofta, Malmohus Lan, Sweden and Anna Dunner, born Dec. 3, 1794, Saxtorp, Malmohus Lan, Sweden, both of Landskrona, Sweden). Born Jan. 5, 1830, Sodra Moinge, Saxtorp Socken, Malmohus Lan, Sweden.
Married Mari Miner Oct. 22, 1858, in Landskrona, Sweden (daughter of Andrew Miner, pioneer 1861, Captain Woolley company, and Ingrid Jenson, who married 1838, Landskrona, Sweden, pioneer Sept. 13, 1861, John Murdock company). She was born Dec. 8, 1838, in Saby Malmohus Lan, Sweden. Their children: Elvira Martina b. Feb. 27, 1859, in Landskrona, Sweden, d. infant; Martin b. Jan. 7, 1861, m. Christena Jenson 1883; David b. Oct. 3, 1864; Maria Sophia b. April 25, 1865, d. 1866; Ellen Jane b. May 2, 1866, m. Willie Jones 1887; Hilda Biata b. May 2, 1866, m. Phynias Reese 1886; Paul Andrew b. Nov. 6, 1868, d. 1869; Lilly Ann b. March 12, 1873, d. 1875; Helen Elizabeth b. Aug. 3, 1870 (d. 1904), m. Nels Carlson 1889; Sarah Ingebor b. May 13, 1876, d. 1900; Norman Mineer b. Jan. 12, 1880, m. Bessie Blight 1911; Eva Constance b. Dec. 15, 1882, m. Lyman James Matlock 1906.
Married Helena Johanna March 1, 1869, Salt Lake City (daughter of Andrew Mineer and Ingar Jenson, pioneers, Sept. 13, 1861, John Murdock company). She was born July 21, 1847, at Landskrona, Sweden. Their children: Franklin Emelius b. Dec. 30, 1869, m. Mari Orme 1897; Edgar Immanuel b. March 31, 1872, m. Mamie Feldstedt 1909; Sylvia Pauline b. March 28, 1874, m. Charley Arthur Finn 1904; Louise Minerva b. May 20, 1876, m. Benjamin Franklin Boothe 1897; Lorenzo Bordeen b. Aug. 9, 1878, d. 1881; Reginald Mineer b. Sept. 1881, d. 1891; Raymond Mineer b. 1882; Inga Elida b. Jan. 31, 1885, m. Eugene Levy 1908; Vega Grace b. Aug. 17, 1887, m. Charles C. Maddux 1911; Helen b. April 25, 1890, m. Eugene A. Terry 1913. Family home Brigham City.
Ward teacher; high priest. Minute man. Veteran Black Hawk Indian war. Worked in Co-op store at Brigham City, Utah. Butcher; farmer; stockraiser.

STARK, SOREN PEDERSEN (son of Peter Sorensen Pederstrup and Annie Elizabeth Venkel). Born Sept. 5, 1829, Sorup Sogn, Viborg, Denmark. Came to Utah Sept. 23, 1862, Madsen and Lillianquist company.
Married Ane Sophia Pedersen April 16, 1862, on Atlantic ocean, who was born Jan. 5, 1838. Their children: Soren Pedersen, Soren Peter Pedersen, Ane Sophia P., latter three died; Moroni P., m. Dec. 10, 1897; Inner Elizabeth P., died; Alma P., m. March 30, 1898; Nephi P.; Joseph P., died. Died May 15, 1881, at Spanish Fork, Utah.

PIONEERS AND PROMINENT MEN OF UTAH

STARK, MORONI P. (son of Soren P. Stark and Ane Sophia Pedersen). Born Oct. 11, 1869, at Spanish Fork, Utah.
Married Sarah C. Hanson Feb. 10, 1897, at Salt Lake City (daughter of Henry Hanson and Annie C. Oleson of Spanish Fork), who was born Nov. 9, 1871. Their children: Anna E. b. Nov. 30, 1897; Henry M. b. March 28, 1900; Grant S. b. Aug. 27, 1902; Mark H. b. Oct. 6, 1904; Elenor Sophia b. Aug. 29, 1906. Family home Spanish Fork, Utah.
President 129th quorum seventies; missionary to northern states 1899-1901; member stake board religion classes. Farmer.

STARLEY, JAMES (son of John Starley and Sarah Lindfield, former of Boburg, Sussex, Eng.). Born Aug. 5, 1817, Sussex, Eng. Came to Utah Nov. 17, 1855, Hooper and William freight train company.
Married Caroline Mitchel (daughter of Thomas Mitchel and Elizabeth Sears), who was born Dec. 21, 1820, and died Jan. 18, 1855, on Mississippi river. Their children: Jane b. May 16, 1842, m. Anthony Martin; Julia b. Feb. 29, 1852, d. Jan. 16, 1855.
Married Mary Jupp June 1857, Salt Lake City (daughter of Thomas Jupp, pioneer, handcart company), who was born April 29, 1821. Their child: John J. b. March 3, 1858, m. Elizabeth Payne.
Filled a ten-year mission at Fillmore, Utah. Teacher.

STARLEY, JOHN J. (son of James Starley and Mary Jupp). Born March 3, 1856.
Married Elizabeth Payne (daughter of James Payne).

STARTUP, WILLIAM D. (son of William Startup and Selina Morris of England). Born Sept. 8, 1846, Widcombe. Came to Utah October, 1868.
Married Hager Hick Nov. 14, 1868, Salt Lake City (daughter of James Hick and Elizabeth Stiles of Worcestershire and Birmingham, Eng.; came to Utah in 1873). She was born Dec. 27, 1844. Their children: William James b. Sept. 6, 1869, m. Dena Nelson; Minnie Alice b. Oct. 12, 1871, m. Charles Thornburg; Harry Walter b. Sept. 5, 1874, m. Artemisia Harris; George Albert b. Jan. 31, 1877, m. Emma May Dunn. Family resided Salt Lake City and Provo, Utah. Elder. Merchant. Died Jan. 28, 1878.
Hager Hick (Startup) subsequently married Albert Singleton Oct. 18, 1883, Salt Lake City. The three children of this marriage were: Alberta b. Nov. 12, 1886; Hazel b. Nov. 26, 1888; Cossette b. Aug. 27, 1894.

STAUFFER, CHRISTIAN. Born at Bern, Switzerland. Came to Utah 1860.
Married Maria Moser. Their children: Christian; Samuel; Johannes; Susanna; Ulrich; Elizabeth; Friederich. Family home Willard, Utah.
Elder. Farmer. Died Sept. 27, 1870.

STAUFFER, ULRICH (son of Christian Stauffer and Maria Moser). Born March 21, 1838, Redunbergh, Switzerland. Came to Utah 1861.
Married Verena Brechbiehl August, 1876, Salt Lake City (daughter of Peter Brechbiehl and Verena Ashbeacher, who came to Utah 1876). She was born Aug. 15, 1858. Their children: Henry A. b. Nov. 20, 1879, m. Claudia E. Hughs; Oliver Wilford b. April 15, 1883, m. La Vourn Hudson; Olive Rozilla b. June 8, 1885, m. Joseph Bench; David b. Nov. 1889, m. Pauline Hompson; Adella b. Aug. 20, 1887; Verena Louise b. Jan. 5, 1892, m. Charles Whitworth; Mabel A. b. July 9, 1895; Ernest Lloyd b. May 9, 1897; Ven Royal b. Aug. 11, 1899. Family home Willard, Utah.
High priest; missionary to Switzerland. Farmer; stockraiser.

STAUFFER, HENRY ALFRED (son of Ulrich Stauffer and Verena Brechbiehl). Born Nov. 20, 1879, Willard, Utah.
Married Claudia Elizabeth Hughs Aug. 20, 1904, Salt Lake City (daughter of John Hughs and Emma Willie of Mendon, Utah). She was born Jan. 3, 1882. Their children: Lynn b. Feb. 1, 1906; Henry Clair b. July 25, 1908; John Clifford b. Nov. 4, 1909; Faun Elizabeth b. Aug. 16, 1911. Family home Riverdale, Utah.

STAUFFER, JOHN (son of Christian Stauffer). Born Eggiwiyl, Switzerland. Came to Utah 1862.
Married Elizabeth Nussli 1864, Willard City, Utah. Their children: Bertha; Frederick, m. Mary Leaver; Emma, m. George B. Barker; Susannah, m. Jacob Schiess. Family home, Willard City.
Elder. Died 1875.

STAUFFER, FREDERICK (son of John Stauffer and Elizabeth Nussli). Born Oct. 24, 1866, Willard City, Utah.
Married Mary Leaver June 22, 1892, Salt Lake City (daughter of Samuel H. Leaver and Mary Spriggs of Salt Lake City, pioneers 1850). She was born July 28, 1869. Their children: Fred Leaver b. May 18, 1893; John Harold b. Oct. 12, 1895. Family home, Salt Lake City.
Seventy; missionary to Turkey 1889-91, and president of the mission: superintendent 18th ward Sunday school. Mayor of Eureka, Utah, 1898-99. Physician and surgeon; eye, ear, nose and throat specialist.

STAYNER, THOMAS JOHN (son of Thomas Colly Stayner and Elizabeth Pill). Born June, 1828. Came to Utah 1852.
Married Rosa Ann Orrell 1852. Their children: Thomas Orrell b. 1854, d. 1870; Rosa Emily b. Dec. 11, 1856, m. A. V. Call Oct. 1, 1883.
Died 1909.

STEADMAN, GEORGE (parents resided Sussex, Eng.). Came to Utah 1860.
Married Elizabeth Wilkins in 1861, at Salt Lake City (mother came to Utah 1860, her father died at sea on way to America). She was born Feb. 14, 1834. Their children: Jane Elizabeth b. Feb. 16, 1863, m. William Mariott Winterton April 13, 1892; Caroline, m. William North; Sarah Ann, m. John Hartle; James, m. Miss Winder; George; Mary, m. Albert North; Edward, m. Louisa ——.
Farmer.

STECK, CHRISTENSEN PETER (son of Andreas Steck of Germany and Anna Christena Peterson of Denmark). Born July 25, 1800, Germany. Came to Utah Sept. 27, 1862, John R. Murdock company.
Married Marie Sophia Was (daughter of William Was and Anna Hanson), who was born June 12, 1806. Their children: Wilkelomine b. Jan. 1, 1826, m. S. E. Houson 1856; Anna Christena b. 1828 and Andreas b. 1829, died; William Peter b. April 14, 1831; Jens Fredrik b. Jan. 28, 1833, m. Petria Bergethi Mickelsen June, 1861, m. Inger Hanson Dec. 1867; Johanna M. b. 1835; Peter C. b. 1837; Anna Elizabeth; Anna Bergethi b. Jan. 8, 1840, m. Soren Christofferson; Anna Lizzie b. March 6, 1842, m. Eric Ludvigsen; Carl M. b. Feb. 2, 1845; Andreas b. Ju'y, 1846, died; Stephena b. March 28, 1848, d. Jan. 20, 1900.
Married Jane Reid March 28, 1894, Manti, Utah (daughter of Chancellor and Betty Reid—married at Ballycone, County Down, Ireland). Family resided Bristen, Veile, Denmark. and Manti, Utah.

STECK, JENS FREDRIK (son of Christian Peter Steck and Marie Sophia Was). Born Jan. 28, 1833, Bristen, Veile, Denmark.
Married Inger Hansen December, 1867, Salt Lake City (daughter of Hans Henrick and Anna Hansen), who was born Feb. 6, 1841. Their children: Maria F. b. Oct. 23, 1868, m. George Thurgood Dec. 17, 1883; Petrea b. March 3, 1870, m. David Shond; Mary b. Nov. 17, 1871, m. J. G. Reese; James T. b. March 2, 1874, m. Retha Dickensen; Heber C. b. July 4, 1876, m. Clara R. Anderson; Joseph Smith b. Aug. 19, 1877, m. Amelia Deunison; Hyrum b. Aug. 19, 1877, m. Lillian America; Auna b. Sept. 23, 1879, d. May 22, 1880; Eirina Inger b. April 25, 1881, m. William Thomas. Family home Manti, Utah.

STECK, JENS. Came to Utah oxteam company.
Married Mariah Vosse. Their children: Jens, Jr.; Mena. m. Soren Christoffersen; Anna, m. Eric Ludvigsen; Bregeta. m. Soren Christoffersen; Stophena, m. Mr. Johansen; Andrea, m. Andrew Poulsen; Hannah, m. Mr. Nelsen. Family resided in Denmark and Manti, Utah.
Died at Manti.

STEELE, JAMES EPHRAIM (son of James Steele and Elizabeth Wylie of American Fork, Utah). Born June 22, 1852, Manchester, Eng. Came to Utah December, 1856, Edward Martin handcart company.
Married Elvira Crompton Dec. 23, 1880, Salt Lake City (daughter of John Crompton and Hannah Hardy of South Cottonwood, Utah, pioneers 1853). She was born Nov. 15, 1855. Their children: James H.; William; Hannah E.; Oscar W.; Robert S.; Emma M.; Bruce B.; Laura E. Family home Iona, Idaho.-
President Bingham stake 1895-1908; bishop Iona ward; second counselor to President Thomas E. Ricks five years. State representative one term; state senator one term. President and manager Iona Mercantile Company; president Anderson Bros.' Bank, Rigby, Idaho; president Idaho World's Fair Commission at St. Louis; president Eagle Rock & Willow Creek Canal Company 22 years; member Idaho State Insane Asylum Board 1907-10.

STEELE, JESSE PIERCE (son of John Steele and Susanah Jackson of Illinois). Born Sept. 9, 1828, Washington county, Ill. Came to Utah in 1853.
Married Nancy Evaline Alexander Oct. 4, 1853, Salt Lake City (daughter of Horace Alexander, pioneer 1847 with a division of the Mormon Battalion, and Nancy Walker, died 1847, Winter Quarters, Neb.). She was born Sept. 1, 1836. Their children: Horace A. b. Sept. 9, 1854, m. Catherine Martin; Jesse Fielding b. Oct. 2, 1856, m. Mina D. Ivie; Louisa D. b. Nov. 8, 1858, m. John Carter; Nancy E. b. Sept. 26, 1861, m. Roswell Bird; Sarah C. b. Feb. 22, 1864, m. John Biggs; Daniel W. b. July 5, 1866, m. Mod Doo; Adarn D. b. Feb. 7, 1869, m. Anna ——; Mary J. b. March 1, 1871, m. Eleanor Taylor; Joseph W. b. July 6, 1873; John P. b. Sept. 12, 1876, m. Mary Fay; Cora G. b. Feb. 11, 1879. Family resided Salt Lake City and Springville, Utah.
Married Mary Ann Sornsen May 27, 1876, Salt Lake City (daughter of Peter and Anna Sornsen), who was born Dec. 28, 1850, in Denmark. Their children: Joel P. b. Feb. 22, 1877; Luella b. Sept. 6, 1879, m. Mr. Young; Henry b. April

12, 1882; Susanah b. Oct. 11, 1885, m. Mr. Lillie; Walter b. Aug. 19, 1889. Family home Salina, Sevier Co., Utah.
Married Emma M. Buettner Oct. 14, 1908, Manti, Utah (daughter of Eberhardt Buettner and Louisa Reiss, former of Germany and latter of Illinois—married April 2, 1878). She was born March 16, 1881, Belleville, Ill.
Presiding elder Springville, Utah; first counselor to bishop; superintendent first Sunday school organized in Utah county, at Springville; president LaPlatta branch in New Mexico. First lieutenant in Walker Indian war 1853; colonel of Nauvoo Legion; captain of the minutemen, the Springville company, in Black Hawk war.

STEELE, JESSE FIELDING (son of Jesse Pierce Steele and Nancy Evaline Alexander). Born Oct. 2, 1856, Salt Lake City.
Married Mina D. Ivie Oct. 16, 1880, Glenwood, Sevier Co., Utah (daughter of James Ivie and Sarah West Willeys, former pioneer 1849, latter 1856, handcart company). Their children: Minnie V. b. July 26, 1881, m. Claud Allred; Eva S. b. March 22, 1884, m. James Peters; Pearl b. Oct. 4, 1885; Mary M. b. Sept. 6, 1887; Chloe V. b. Nov. 12, 1889, m. Alfred Evans; Ellee J. b. Oct. 22, 1891; Roswell b. Sept. 19, 1893; Glenn b. June 12, 1895; Linn b. Aug. 3, 1897; Dean b. Aug. 6, 1899; Franklin b. Oct. 18, 1901; Harry b. Oct. 16, 1903; Valgene b. Oct. 20, 1909. Family home Salina, Sevier Co., Utah.
Elder; teacher first ward Salina.

STEELE, JOHN (son of John Steele, born 1768, Ireland, and Nancy Kennedy, born Oct. 15, 1790, Holywood, Ireland). He was born March 21, 1821, Holywood. Came to Utah July 29, 1847, division Mormon Battalion.
Married Catherine Campbell (daughter of Michael Campbell and Mary Knox), who was born Nov. 16, 1816, Belfast, Ireland. Their children: Mary Campbell b. Dec. 23, 1840, m. Joseph Fish; John b. June 2, 1842, and Margaret b. June 17, 1844, d. infants; Young Elizabeth b. Aug. 9, 1847, m. James Stapley; Mahonri Moriancumer b. May 1, 1849, m. Emily Bunker April 19, 1869, m. Mary Ellen Jepson May 11, 1874; Susann Adams b. April 28, 1851, m. William A. Bringhurst; John Alma b. April 6, 1853; Jane Catherine b. April 26, 1855, m. Peter Jensen; Robert Henry b. Sept. 1, 1857, d. infant. Family resided Toquerville and Kanarra, Utah.
High priest; missionary to Las Vegas 1854-56, and to Europe 1877-78; first counselor to President J. C. L. Smith of Parowan stake. Major of infantry in Iron Military district; marshal of Parowan 1851; mayor of Parowan 1853; judge of Iron county; Iron county recorder; justice of peace at Toquerville several years; postmaster 15 years. Worked on Nauvoo temple. Died Dec. 31, 1903, Kanarra.

STEELE, MAHONRI MORIANCUMER (son of John Steele and Catherine Campbell). Born May 1, 1849, Salt Lake City.
Married Emily Bunker April 19, 1869, Salt Lake City (daughter of Edward Bunker and Emily Abbott, the former pioneer 1847, division Mormon Battalion, latter 1850, Aaron Johnson company). She was born March 1, 1849, in Iowa. Their children: Mahonri Moriancumer, Jr., b. Feb. 2, 1870, m. Charlotte Moore Lefevre; John Edward b. Sept. 24, 1872, m. Zephyr L. Deuel; Arthur b. July 16, 1877, d. May 18, 1891; Parley Bunker b. July 23, 1890.
Married Mary Ellen Jepson May 11, 1874, Salt Lake City (daughter of James Jepson and Eleanore Nightengale), who was born Nov. 1, 1851, in St. Louis. Their children: Alice Eleanore b. Nov. 10, 1875, m. William A. Lee; Mary Ellen b. Sept. 23, 1879, m. James Marshall 1905; Catherine b. Nov. 10, 1881, m. Job Riding Dec. 23, 1900; James b. Aug. 31, 1883, m. Almina Wiltshire; Joseph b. Sept. 1, 1885, m. Vivian Maud Petersen June 6, 1906; Emily b. May 18, 188·, m. Alvin M. Jensen Oct. 3, 1906. Family resided Parowan, Toquerville and Panguitch, Utah.
Missionary to Europe 1877-78. Captain in Nauvoo Legion; Indian war veteran. Superintendent of schools; clerk of Garfield county; deputy sheriff Iron county; member state land board 1909. Assisted in bringing immigrants to Utah 1868. Counselor in Panguitch stake presidency 1879-08; stake tithing clerk and historian 20 years; patriarch.

STEELE, MAHONRI MORIANCUMER, JR. (son of Mahonri Moriancumer Steele and Emily Bunker). Born Feb. 2, 1870, Toquerville, Utah.
Married Charlotte Moore Lefevre Oct. 2, 1889, St. George, Utah (daughter of William Lefevre and Frances Banks), who was born March 24, 1873, Panguitch, Utah. Their children: Lindsay b. Aug. 3, 1890; Frances Fern b. April 1, 1893; Abigail b. March 5, 1895; Harold L. b. Jan. 29, 1898; Doyle L. b. Dec. 23, 1899; Faymetta b. May 23, 1902; Lila b. Sept. 13, 1904; Mahonri Arthela b. Sept. 8, 1908; Irene b. Feb. 26, 1910. Family home Panguitch, Utah.
Garfield county recorder four years; Garfield county clerk six years; chief clerk Utah legislature 1901; postoffice inspector six years.

STEPHENS, ABRAHAM (son of Jacob Stephens and Eliza Symons). Born Sept. 30, 1840, Phillack, Cornwall, Eng. Came to Utah 1866, independent company.
Married Eliza Edwards Jan. 13, 1863, Bristol, Eng. (daughter of Richard Edwards and John Palmer of Bristol). She was born Dec. 14, 1840. Their children: Oscar E. b. Nov. 20, 1863, m. Florence Tribe; Ida b. July 10, 1868, m. John W. Wilcox; Ernest E. b. Oct. 3, 1869, m. Mary E. Cole.
Elder. Foreman blacksmith. Died Aug. 4, 1886, Tulare, Cal.

STEPHENS, DANIEL MONROE (son of John Stephens, born March 31, 1811, in Davidson county, N. C., and Elizabeth Briggs, born May 9, 1812, North Carolina—married Aug. 1, 1833, settled at Ogden, Utah). He was born Oct. 4, 1842, Nauvoo, Ill. Came to Utah Oct. 4, 1851, Captain Bates company.
Married Mary Ann Clark Dec. 21, 1868, Salt Lake City (daughter of Alfred Clark and Hannah Waterfield—married Jan. 1, 1844, in Leicestershire, Eng.—pioneers Sept. 5, 1866. Effie Estella Staker Sept. 12, 1900; John Taylor b. June 8, 1880, died; Joseph Franklin b. Oct. 13, 1883, m. Nettie L. Carden Nov. 8, 1905; Samuel Lehi b. May 5, 1886, m. Lillian Eames Dec. 20, 1905; Walter Clark b. July 14, 1889; Aldo Briggs b. Nov. 2, 1890, m. Laura Eames Jan. 11, 1911. Family home Ogden, Utah.
Missionary in U. S. A. 1881-82. School trustee Riverdale, 1890; judge of election at Ogden three times. Carpenter; farmer.

STEPHENS, JAMES MONROE (son of Daniel Monroe Stephens and Mary Ann Clark). Born July 11, 1870, Weber county, Utah.
Married Elizabeth Crump July 15, 1891, Logan, Utah (daughter of Henry C. Crump and Nancy Cragg, pioneers missionary company). She was born July 19, 1869, in North Carolina. Their children: James Monroe b. May 17, 1892; Robert Henry b. March 19, 1897, and Sarah Elizabeth b. April 20, 1900, both died; Nancy May b. April 30, 1907; Pearl An. b. Jan. 16, 1911. Family home Ogden, Utah.
Second counselor in bishopric of Riverdale ward. Road supervisor Riverdale ward, 1913. Farmer.

STEPHENS, FRANK BRAY (son of Edwin Fessenden Stephens and Sally Berry Ricker of Turner, Me.). Born Oct. 14, 1856, Turner. Came to Utah June 8, 1868.
Married Lunette Stebbins Dec. 5, 1883, Crete, Neb. (daughter of Daniel Willard Stebbins and Sarah Reynolds of Ottumwa, Iowa). She was born Jan. 7, 1861. Their child: Harold Montell, m. Virginia Bush. Family home, Salt Lake City.
President Salt Lake City Y. M. C. A. President Utah Society, Sons of Revolution. Assistant United States attorney; member board of police and fire commissioners Salt Lake City, 1894-96; city attorney Salt Lake City, 1901-02; regent of State University; aide to Gov. John C. Cutler at first convention of governors called by President Roosevelt. Lawyer.

STEPHENS, JOHN (son of Alexander Stephens and Mary Daily of Davis county [afterward called Rowan county], N. C.). Born March 3, 1811, in Rowan county. Came to Utah Oct. 14, 1851, captain of 10 in Orson Pratt company.
Married Elizabeth Briggs 1831 in Brown county, Ill. (daughter of John Briggs and Constance Peacock of Rowan county). She was born March 14, 1812. Their children: James O., m. Mary Stubblefield; m. Martha Wilson; m. Dorthula C. Shupe; David H., m. Albertine Peterson; m. Sophia L. Cannon; Daniel M., m. Harriet O. Shaw; Almira C. m. William Baker; Alexander N., m. Sarah Geen; m. Amina Raymond; David M., m. Mary Clark; Elizabeth J.; Thomas J., m. Susan Shupe; Constance A. m. Orson Eggleston; m. Ether McBride; Solomon C., m. Mary E. Pincock; m. Zilpha J. Heninger; William J. and George W. (twins), died.
High priest. Resided at Nauvoo, Ill.; later at Council Bluffs, Iowa, where he had a farm. Built first reservoir in Weber Co., Utah, in 1856. Died Dec. 3, 1870, at Ogden, Utah.

STEPHENS, SOLOMON C. (son of John Stephens and Elizabeth Briggs). Born Sept. 1, 1850, Kanesville, Iowa. Came to Utah with parents.
Married Mary E. Pincock Feb. 1, 1878, Salt Lake City (daughter of John Pincock and Isabella Douglas of Ogden). She was born March 8, 1851, at St. Louis, Mo. Their children: Lottie M. b. March 3, 1879; Isabella D. b. May 3, 1882, m. Heber Colman; Solomon C. b. May 7, 1884, m. Olive Stephens; John P. b. Aug. 21, 1886; William P. b. Dec. 29, 1888; Eliza beth J. b. Aug. 22, 1892; Pearl and Ruby (twins) b. March 4, 1895. Family home Ogden, Utah.
Seventy; high priest; missionary to Georgia 1879-81. Farmer; real estate dealer. Built about 500 houses in Ogden. Author of "The Philosophy of the Earth and Man."

STEPHENS, JOHN B. (son of Bartholomew Stephens and Mary Alingham of Ireland). Born Jan. 3, 1846, in Ireland. Came to Utah in May, 1873.
Married Julia Mullin Feb. 7, 1875, Pioche, Nev. (daughter of Thomas Mullin and Mary Neylon of Ireland). She was born Jan. 14, 1855. Their children: Dr. Minnie Holstein; William J.; Mamie E., m. Willard Hamer; Rose J.; Alfred and Arthur, died; Mabel; Julia; Francis; Harry; Bernon; Lawrence, died. Family home, Salt Lake City.
School trustee at Bingham, Utah. Mining.

STEPHENS, THOMAS D. (son of Lewis Stephens and Sarah Daniels of Liverpool, Eng.). Born January, 1837, in Wales. Came to Utah Sept. 1, 1860, John Smith company.
Married Mary Ann Webb July 6, 1857, in Pennsylvania (daughter of Joseph Webb and Mary Evans of Monmouth, Eng.). She was born Nov. 30, 1834. Their children: Thomas, d. aged 8; William, d. aged 10; Joseph, d. aged 4; Elizabeth, d. infant; Alice, m. Henry Davis; Henry, d. infant; Louis, d. aged 8.
Seventy. Worked in church office at Liverpool, Eng.; worked on Salt Lake temple. Farmer and dairyman; contractor and builder.

STEPHENSON, FRANCIS MARION (son of Isaac Henderson Stephenson, born 1808, Jefferson county, Tenn., and Mary Pugh, born May 9, 1806, Knoxville, Tenn.). He was born Jan. 3, 1841, Knoxville. Came to Utah October, 1851, Milo Andrus company.
Married Sarah Ann Bright Jan. 13, 1864, Richmond, Utah (daughter of John Bright, died at Council Bluffs, Iowa, and Susan Pugh, pioneer Sept. 15, 1852, Isaac Stewart company). She was born April 1, 1847. Their children: Susan Eliza b. July 27, 1865, m. James M. Anderson Nov. 23, 1887; Francis Marion, Jr., b. Sept. 26, 1867, m. Louisa Wheeler Oct. 19, 1892; Sarah Matilda b. Jan. 3, 1870, d. March 19, 1891; George Quincy b. April 28, 1872, m. Olive Talbot Dec. 20, 1899; Alwilda b. June 2, 1874, d. March 27, 1891; Alnora b. June 2, 1874, d. Jan. 25, 1891; William Parley b. June 13, 1876, d. Feb. 21, 1878; John Henderson b. Oct. 25, 1878, d. March 4, 1891; Chester Preston b. Sept. 6, 1880, d. Feb. 7, 1881; Joseph b. April 12, 1882, d. April 3, 1891; Henry b. Jan. 21, 1885, d. Feb. 1, 1891; Effie b. Sept. 12, 1887, m. Asahel Cheney Jan. 8, 1913. Family resided Richmond and Lewiston, Utah.
Married Orpha Elvira White June 10, 1891, Logan, Utah (daughter of John S. White, born Feb. 15, 1818, died June 5, 1907, and Ann Eliza Adalide Everett, born Aug. 30, 1832, and died April 19, 1904, former a member of Mormon Battalion). She was born Sept. 3, 1862. Their children: Schuyler Wesley b. Aug. 13, 1892, d. April 18, 1908; Lawrence Leslie b. Oct. 31, 1893, d. March 28, 1899; Linnie May b. June 14, 1895; Blanche Nevella b. Sept. 15, 1897; Vincent Edward b. Feb. 14, 1899; Millie Leone b. April 13, 1901; Lola Bell b. March 15, 1904. Family home Lewiston, Utah.
Member 39th quorum seventies; missionary to northern states 1895; high priest; teacher. Member Utah militia.

STEPHENSON, FRANCIS MARION, JR. (son of Francis Marion Stephenson and Sarah Ann Bright). Born Sept. 26, 1867, Richmond, Utah.
Married Louisa Wheeler Oct. 19, 1892, Logan, Utah (daughter of George W. Wheeler and Hannah Humphreys, latter pioneer, handcart company). She was born Dec. 16, 1874. Their children: Verda Lucille b. Aug. 20, 1893; Esther Luella b. June 12, 1895; Heber Francis b. July 2, 1897; Ora b. June 13, 1899; Ralph Lamoin b. March 9, 1901; Edgar Laverne b. July 20, 1903; Walter Shannon b. Aug. 18, 1904; George Owen b. Feb. 22, 1907; Lois b. April 17, 1909; Milford Wheeler b. Aug. 23, 1911. Family home Lewiston, Utah.
President 117th quorum seventies; missionary to southern states 1896-97; ward and Sunday school teacher.

STEPHENSON, THOMAS CHRISTIAN (son of Stephen Peterson, born 1788, Jerslev, Hjorring, Denmark, and Anne Thompson, born 1788, Hellested, Denmark). Born June 14, 1825, Jerslev. Came to Utah Sept. 23, 1862, Christian A. Madsen independent company.
Married Maren Simons in 1846 (daughter of Jensen Simons and Mettie Johanna Jensen, married 1822, in Jerslev). She was born Oct. 8, 1823, and died Feb. 11, 1862. Their children: Stephen Peter b. April 8, 1847, d. Dec. 23, 1856; Anne b. Dec. 12, 1848, m. Edward Stevens Dec. 14, 1868; Simon b. Aug. 27, 1850, m. Rachel Stevens; Anthony b. April 5, 1852, m. Mary Ann Bennett March 9, 1874; James Jasper b. Aug. 7, 1853, m. Jane Bennett; Andrew b. March 27, 1855, m. Sarah Jane McKee; Peter b. Dec. 23, 1856, m. Jane Stringham; Anne Thornene b. Dec. 1, 1858, d. at Florence June 25, 1862; Marthene b. Sept. 26, 1860, d. at Florence June 17, 1862. Family resided Deseret and Holden, Utah.
Died May 22, 1912, Halden Millard Co., Utah.

STEPHENSON, SIMON (son of Thomas Christian Stephenson and Maren Simons). Born Aug. 27, 1850, Jerslev, Hjorring, Denmark. Came to Utah Sept. 23, 1862 with father.
Married Rachel Stevens Dec. 16, 1872, Salt Lake City (daughter of Albert Stevens and Lettie McKee), who was born Oct. 28, 1855. Their children: Simon Thomas b. Oct 26, 1873, m. Emma Louisa Ashby; Rachel Marinda b. Aug. 20, 1875, m. George W. Nixon; Lettie Armina b. Sept. 15, 1878, m. LeRoy Stevens; Joseph Albert b. Feb. 2, 1880, m. Ruby Johnson; James Edward b. June 28, 1883, d. April 8, 1883; Elsie Maud b. Jan. 14, 1886, m. John Elmer Stevens; Mabel b. April 18, 1888, m. Heber J. Webb; Martha Lavern b. March 2, 1890; Bruce Stevens b. June 9, 1892; Hazel Anne b. Nov. 30, 1896; Joan b. May 29, 1898. Family home Holden, Utah.

STEPHENSON, ANTHONY (son of Thomas Christian Stephenson and Maren Simons). Born April 5, 1852, in Denmark. Came to Utah with brother.
Married Mary Ann Bennett March 9, 1874, Salt Lake City (daughter of John Bennett and Jane Roberts, pioneers Oct. 15, 1863, Samuel D. White company). She was born June 27, 1855. Their children: John Bennett b. April 19, 1875, died; Jane Marinda b. April 16, 1877, m. Rodney Badger Ashby Sept. 29, 1898; Anthony Edward b. March 24, 1879, m. Ussier Johnson April 12, 1900; Mary Elizabeth b. Sept. 17, 1881, m. Joseph Anderson Nov. 7, 1906; James Abner b. Feb. 13, 1884, m. Josephine Badger March 22, 1906; Emily Ann b. Dec. 30, 1886, d. March 24, 1888; Catherine Amanda b. Feb. 15, 1889; Ormus William b. Feb. 2, 1892; Eva Ruth b. Nov 17, 1894; Joseph Mabben b. Oct. 18, 1897; Clara Emeline b. Jan. 27, 1901. Family home Holden, Utah.

STEPHENSON, ANDREW (son of Thomas Christian Stephenson and Maren Simons). Born March 27, 1855, in Denmark.
Married Sarah Jane McKee Dec. 13, 1877, St. George, Utah (daughter of James McKee and Matilda Sweat of Holden, Utah). She was born Oct. 6, 1856. Their children: Sarah Matilda b. Sept. 26, 1878, m. Ephraim Dastrup May 3, 1899; Amy Armina b. Sept. 14, 1880; Clarissa Ann b. Nov. 28, 1882; David Andrew b. April 23, 1886, d. Nov. 10, 1886; Mercy b. Sept. 13, 1888. Family home Holden, Utah.
President 111th quorum of seventies 1897-1909; high priest, missionary to Denmark 1905-1907. Worked on St. George Temple 1875-1877; carpenter. Died Aug. 26, 1912.

STEVENS, CHARLES HENRY ROBINSON (son of Thomas Stevens and Johannah Robinson of Cheltenham, Gloucestershire, Eng.). Born Aug. 16, 1837, at Cheltenham. Came to Utah August, 1854, Van Etten freight train.
Married Fanny Hannah Paskett Aug. 25, 1864, Henefer, Utah (daughter of James Pope Paskett and Charlotte Buckingham of Tedperry, Gloucestershire, pioneer 1868). She was born Oct. 21, 1841. Their children: Charlotte Ann b. July 3, 1865 (d. Oct. 15, 1884), m. Richard Wickel, Jr.; Sarah Jane b. April 1, 1867, m. Charles Henry Anderton; Charles Henry Robinson b. May 7, 1869; Salina Johannah R. b. July 25, 1871, m. James Keppin; Thomas James R. b. May 25, 1874, m. Virginia Jones; John Paskett R. b. Dec. 21, 1876, m. Gertrude Wright; Caroline Elizabeth b. Aug. 7, 1878, m. George Ackerman; William Tunley R. b. Nov. 16, 1880, m. Emily P. ——; Norah Buckingham R. b. Jan. 13, 1883, d. April 2, 1902; Fanny May b. May 1, 1885, m. Thomas R. Porter. Family home Henefer, Utah.
Member 23d and 27th quorums seventies. Went to Denver with Major Russell's flour train 1860, continued to Omaha 1861; went to Missouri with Jacob Gates and Claudius Spencer, where they bought stock for immigrant teams to be used crossing the plains. Brought the Wright train of freight with a few families to Utah 1861; went to Weeping Willow for immigrants 1864. First lieutenant of cavalry in Black Hawk Indian war 1865-67; scouted against Bannock Indians 1862. Road supervisor two terms; watermaster; registration officer; judge of election; deputy assessor.

STEVENS, HENRY B. Came to Utah 1850.
His children: Henry B., m. Elizabeth Whitlock; Chloe, m. Andrew Jackson Allred; James; Elisha, m. Miss Lamb. Family home San Pete, Utah.
High priest. Farmer and peddler. Died August, 1906, Ephraim, Utah.

STEVENS, HENRY B. (son of Henry B. Stevens). Came to Utah 1850.
Married Elizabeth R. Whitlock 1854, at Ephraim (daughter of Andrew Whitlock and Hannah Allred, former pioneer September 1862, Thomas Tidwell company). She was born 1834. Their children: Helen, m. Christian Anderson; Olive; Lula, m. Parley Christensen; Malinda b. Jan. 26, 1866, m. Adelbert Oviatt. Family home Ephraim, Utah.
Elder. Farmer. Died Aug. 1, 1909, at Ephraim.

STEVENS, LYMAN. Came to Utah 1847, contingent of Mormon Battalion.
Married Martha Durfee (daughter of Edmund Durfee and Miss Pickle). Their children: John, d. aged 2; Reuben L., m. Lydia Gribble; Hyrum S., m. Deborah Lemmon; Edmond, d. aged 1; Joseph S., m. Abigail M. King; Amos H., m. Elmina Belnamin; Ezra W., m. Edith Lemmon; Charles F., m. Olive DeMill. Family home Cedar Fort, Utah.
Married Elizabeth Lucina, Salt Lake City. Only child: Nathan Henry. Family home Tooele, Utah.
Married Mariah Perkins, Ephraim, Utah. Only child: Olive, m. Joseph Crofts. Family home Ephraim, Utah.
Seventy; bishop's counselor, Holliday ward and Camp Floyd; high priest. Walker war veteran. Farmer. Died April 1886, Ferron, Utah.

STEVENS, HYRUM (son of Lyman Stevens and Martha Durfee). Came to Utah with oxteam company.
Married Deborah Lemmon (daughter of James Lemmon). Their children: Wallace, m. Olive Strong; Mira Louisa, m. F. W. Cox 3d; Martha, m. Thomas Marker; Heber, m. Lucy ——; Vilate, m. William Lamb; m. Lincoln Gray. Family home Ferron, Utah.
Married Anna Warde, who was born 1861. Their children: Joseph; Rose; Deby; John; Zial; Nettie; Ira; Frank; Bertha.
Seventy. Veteran Black Hawk Indian war. Sheriff Iron county, Utah. Farmer.

PIONEERS AND PROMINENT MEN OF UTAH 1185

STEVENS, JOSEPH S. (son of Lyman Stevens and Martha Durfee). He was born March 12, 1845, Yellroom, Hancock county, Ill. Came to Utah 1849, oxteam company.
Married Abigail M. King Aug. 12, 1865, Circleville, Utah (daughter of Eleazer King and Mary Caroline Fowler), who was born Sept. 16, 1849. Their children: Martha Caroline b. April 30, 1866, m. Fred Olsen; Abigail M. b. March 25, 1868, d. aged 12; Joseph S. b. May 11, 1870, m. Clara Wrigley; George W. b. Jan. 19, 1873, m. Catherine Richards; Mary Jane b. March 25, 1875, m. David O. Morgan; Charles F. b. June 2, 1877, d. aged 10; John E. b. Jan. 7, 1880, m. Annie Swenson; James L. b. Sept. 28, 1882, m. Effie Petty; Huldah L. b. April 20, 1885, m. William Stringham; Lillie J. b. March 21, 1890, m. Melvin Petty. Family resided Ephraim and Ferron, Utah.
Veteran Walker and Black Hawk wars. Constable at Mayfield one term and at Ferron two terms. Farmer; stockraiser; apiarist.

STEVENS, SIDNEY (son of James Stevens, born Feb. 5, 1797, Nunney, Somersetshire, and Hannah Martin, born January 1797, Liverpool, Eng., married about 1821). Born June 18, 1839, Nunney, Somersetshire. Came to Utah Oct. 3, 1863, Daniel D. McArthur company.
Married Mary Jane Thick May 22, 1863, Liverpool, Eng. (daughter of William Thick and Lydia Savery of Hammon, Eng., married about 1829). She was born May 13, 1838, and came to Utah with husband. Their children: Sidney Orson b. Aug. 28, 1864, m. Tyra Yates March 10, 1903; Frank Joseph b. Feb. 10, 1866, m. Mary Priscilla West April 23, 1888 (died); m. Aggie Herrick June 5, 1895; Alice Mary b. Nov. 16, 1867, m. Walter Thomas Warren Dec. 22, 1886; Bessie Roxanna b. Sept. 18, 1869, m. Gideon T. Alvord Jan. 20, 1889; Nettie Rozina b. Sept. 18, 1869, m. Frank H. DePuy Feb. 8, 1903; Sarah Kate b. Sept. 9, 1871, m. Augustus V. Curby May 27, 1903; Charles Henry b. Aug. 18, 1873, m. Mary E. Harrington Sept. 11, 1901; Lillian Eva b. July 21, 1875, m. Hyrum Adolph Sodenberg Nov. 5, 1911; James William b. Aug. 13, 1877, m. Lillian Foulger June 5, 1912; Elizabeth Emeline b. July 31, 1879, m. Edward Paul Jones June 16, 1902; Albert Ulman Samuel b. Nov. 26, 1881; Walter Frederick b. May 30, 1883, m. Amanda Sidonia Alsten June 22, 1910. Family home 2562 Adams ave., Ogden, Utah.
Assistant Sunday school superintendent at North Ogden 1869; counselor in bishopric of North Ogden ward 1875; home missionary. Postmaster at North Ogden several terms. Established tannery yard and leather manufactory and later engaged in lumber, grain, implement and vehicle business, extending his business to Logan, Utah, and Preston and Montpelier, Idaho. Erected the first three-story business block in Ogden 1878. Was prominent in club life and business and municipal affairs at the time of his demise at Ogden, May 21, 1910.

STEVENS, SIDNEY ORSON (son of Sidney Stevens and Mary Jane Thick). Born Aug. 28, 1864, Kaysville, Utah.
Married Tyra Yates March 10, 1903, Millville, Utah (daughter of Frederick and Sarah M. Yates, former pioneer 1857, Jacob Officer company, latter came to Utah October 1873). She was born March 4, 1882, Millville, Utah. Their children: Helen Yates b. Jan. 29, 1904; Sidney Yates b. Feb. 17, 1905; Max DePuy b. April 25, 1907; Margaret Elizabeth b. Aug. 10, 1909; Eleanor b. Jan. 21, 1912. Family resided North Ogden, Ogden City and Logan, Utah.
Manager Sidney Stevens Mercantile Co. at North Ogden 1884-90, and also of the same company at Logan 1894. City councilman Logan, two terms.

STEVENS FRANK JOSEPH (son of Sidney Stevens and Mary Jane Thick). Born Feb. 10, 1866, at North Ogden, Utah.
Married Mary Priscilla West April 23, 1888, at Ogden, Utah (daughter of Chauncy W. West and Sarah Covington, both of Ogden, pioneers Sept. 1862, Captain Smoot company). She was born April 3, 1870, died Aug. 25, 1893. Their children: Ada Adelia b. Jan. 18, 1889, m. Walker B. Scoville; Frank Joseph b. June 7, 1892. Family home Ogden, Utah.
Married Aggie Herrick June 5, 1895, at Ogden, Utah (daughter of Lester J. Herrick and Agnes McQuarrie, both of Ogden, Utah, pioneers September 1850, Jesse B. Martin company). She was born Nov. 15, 1870. Their children: Lester James b. Oct. 7, 1897; Sidney Alan b. June 17, 1899; Agnes b. Sept. 29, 1901; Virginia b. Oct. 29, 1903. Family home Ogden, Utah.
Engaged in agricultural implement-business with the Sidney Stevens Implement Company 1887; vice president and general manager of the Sideny Stevens Implement Company.

STEVENS, CHARLES HENRY (son of Sidney Stevens and Mary Jane Thick). Born Aug. 18, 1873, at North Ogden, Utah.
Married Mary Emeroy Harrington Sept. 11, 1901, at Ogden, Utah (daughter of Charles Harrington and Helen Emeroy Craigue, both of Ogden, Utah, since 1890). She was born Jan. 11, 1880. Their children: Charles Sidney b. Feb. 29, 1904; Helen Emeroy b. Dec. 28, 1906. Family home Ogden, Utah.
Secretary of the Sidney Stevens Implement Company; engaged in the agricultural implement business for about 20 years.

STEVENS, WALTER F. (son of Sidney Stevens and Mary Jane Thick). Born May 30, 1883, at North Ogden, Utah.
Married Amanda Sidonia Olsten June 22, 1910, at Manti,
75

Utah (daughter of William H. Olsten and Lodicy A. Griffin), who was born Aug. 22, 1886. Their children: Walter Herbert b. April 1, 1911; Helen Sidonia b. March 17, 1913.

STEVENS, WILLIAM (son of Thomas Stevens and Ann Lock of Somersetshire, Eng.). Born Dec. 23, 1819, in Somersetshire. Came to Utah 1860.
Married Emma Crowden 1845, Bridgwater, Somersetshire (daughter of Isaac Crowden and Charlotte Brewer of Somersetshire), who was born June 27, 1825. Their children: Sarah Ann, m. Hyrum Mecham; William Henry, m. Eliza Horton; Ellen Christene, m. John Neel; Emeline Augusta, m. Daniel Bigelow; Simon Percival, d. aged 45; Thomas Isaac, m. Emma Wooley; Franklin Theophilus, d. aged 19; Abigail Charlotte, m. Charles T. Watterson. Family resided Wanship and Oakley, Utah.
Member seventies. Blacksmith and farmer. Died March 1900, at Oakley.

STEVENS, WILLIAM (son of Roswell Stevens of New York and Sibbell Spencer of Pennsylvania, and Upper Canada, moved to Hancock county, Ill.). Born Oct. 1, 1799, Herkimer county, N. Y. Came to Utah Oct. 4, 1850, William Snow company.
Married Marinda Thomas Sept. 2, 1827, Mount Pleasant, Upper Canada (daughter of David Thomas of Mount Pleasant, Upper Canada). She was born June 27, 1809; died June 27, 1848. Their children: Albert b. Dec. 16, 1829, m. Lettie McKee 1852; Walter b. Jan. 17, 1831, m. Abigail Holman 1854; William b. Feb. 14, 1832, m. Elizabeth Seley 1854; Elanor b. July 26, 1833, d. 1844; Rachel b. Dec. 1, 1834, m. John Holman 1857; Jonathan b. July 2, 1836, d. Feb. 1838; Sarah Anna b. Aug 24, 1338, m. Matthew McCuen 1855; David Riley b. Nov. 21, 1839, m. Caroline Felshaw 1861; Edward b. Aug. 26, 1841, m. Annie Stephenson 1868; Eliza b. 1843, d. 1848; Amos b. 1846, d. 1847; Alma b. 1848, d. Aug. 1848.
Member high priest quorum. Member territorial legislature in 1856-57. Farmer and stockraiser. Died Feb. 5, 1877, Hoden Utah.

STEVENS, ALBERT (son of William Stevens and Marinda Thomas). Born Dec. 16, 1829.
Married Lettie McKee, Salt Lake City, Utah (daughter of Thomas McKee, Holden, Utah). Their children: Albert Jr. b. Sept. 27, 1853, m. Sept. 3, 1883; Rachel; Mary; David; James; George; Martha; Lettie. Family home Holden, Utah.
Farmer. Died March 6, 1910, Holden, Utah.

STEVENS, EDWARD (son of William Stevens and Marinda Thomas). Born Aug. 26, 1841, in Illinois. Came to Utah 1850 with father in William Snow company.
Married Annie Stephenson Dec. 14, 1868, Salt Lake City, Utah (daughter of Thomas C. Stephenson and Marilda Simenmon, pioneers, C. M. Madison company). She was born Dec. 12, 1848, in Denmark. Their children: Marinda b. Oct. 20, 1870; Edward F. b. Nov. 14, 1874, m. Emma M. Robins 1898; Sarah Armina b. June 17, 1876, m. Mary R. S. Nixon 1906; William T. b. Dec. 7, 1877; J. A. Stevens b. Dec. 10, 1879; Bertha E. b. June 18, 1883; Florence A. b. Aug. 4, 1885; Clara M. b. Feb. 27, 1889. Family home Millard county, Utah.
Member elder quorum. Assisted in bringing immigrants to Utah; missionary to Virginia 1879-1881. County commissioner of Millard Co., Utah; school trustee. Farmer and stockraiser. Living at Holden, Millard Co., Utah.

STEVENSON, EDWARD (son of Joseph Stevenson and Elizabeth Stevens of Gibralter, England). Born May 1, 1820. Gibralter. Came to Utah Sept. 2, 1847—he was captain of ten in C. C. Rich's company.
Married Nancy Areta in 1844, Nauvoo, Ill. (daughter of Sanford Porter and Nancy Warriner of Nauvoo, latter a pioneer Oct. 2, 1847, C. C. Rich company). She was born Aug. 8, 1825, Trumbull county, Ohio. Their children: Nephi P., m. Louisa Stewart; Eliza, m. John R. Stewart; Edward A., m. Emeline Stewart; Nancy, d. infant; Joseph E., m. Mary A. Richards. Family home 14th ward, Salt Lake City.
Married Emily E. Williams 1857, Salt Lake Endowment House, Daniel H. Wells officiating (daughter of Daniel R. Williams and Electa C. Briggs of Nauvoo, Ill., pioneers September 1852, Henry Miller company). She was born Sept. 23, 1841. Their children: Electa M., m. George Manwaring, m. Frederick Stiner; Henry R., m. Hannah R. Buckwalter; William O., d. aged two; Emily Rosella, m. Francis McDonald; Daniel W., d. infant; John W., m. Sarah Perry; Eugene E., m. Etta Staples; Lester A., m. Bertha Starley; Hyrum S., m. Mary Slaughter; Ernest E., m. Emma Walker; Harriet L., m. Franklin Walker. Family home Brerlton ward, Big Cottonwood, Utah.
Member first council of seventies, 1894-97; high priest; home missionary in Utah, Idaho and Arizona twelve years; senior president 30th quorum seventies; missionary to the States, 1857-58 and 1869-70; to Canada in 1872; to southern states 1877-78; in United States and Canada, 1883-84; and in United States and Europe in 1886; crossed the plains nineteen times, and the Atlantic ocean nine times, doing missionary work; organized branch of the church at Gibralter, Spain, in 1852. Took part in Echo Canyon trouble; chaplain in militia. Tinsmith, apiarist, manufacturer and farmer. Died Jan. 27, 1897.

STEVENSON, JOSEPH ECHO (son of Edward Stevenson and Nancy Porter). Born Oct. 1, 1857, fourteenth ward, Salt Lake City.
Married Mary Alice Richards Dec. 8, 1881, Salt Lake Endowment House, Franklin D. Richards officiating (daughter of Franklin D. Richards and Mary Thompson of Nauvoo, Ill., who came to Utah Oct. 19, 1848, captain of his own company). She was born July 5, 1863. Their children: Joseph W. b. Oct. 23, 1887, d. infant; Orson b. March 2, 1889, d. infant; Frank J. b. April 22, 1891; Clarence C. b. March 14, 1893; Merlon L. b. Oct. 18, 1895; Dewey W. b. Jan. 2, 1898; Roy S. b. May 22, 1900. Family home Holliday, Utah.
Member 35th quorum seventies at Morgan City. County superintendent of schools of Morgan county. Morgan city councilman. Rancher and miner.

STEVENSON, JAMES (son of Joseph Stevenson of Leicestershire, Eng., and Elizabeth Stevens of London, Eng.—married June 28, 1812). Born Aug. 12, 1830, at Albany, N. Y. Came to Utah 1848, Amasa M. Lyman company.
Married Sarah Elnora White (daughter of Joseph White and Ruby Searns White, pioneers 1849). She was born Nov. 18, 1831. Their children: James Ira b. Aug. 2, 1853, d. infant; William Henry b. Dec. 12, 1854, m. Jane E. Bourne; Mary Elnora b. 1856 and Lenora Estella b. 1858, died; Ruby Annetta b. Nov. 15, 1860, m. Herbert Hayner; Charles Joseph b. March 28, 1863, died; Edward Delros b. Oct. 2, 1867; Ezra Clark b. Jan. 22, 1867, died; Wilford Albert b. April 11, 1871, m. Andrew Johnson; Alfred Frank b. Dec. 22, 1874; Orson Leo b. Jan. 1876.
Elder; high priest; missionary among the Indians.

STEVENSON, JAMES. Born July 26, 1815, England. Came to Utah October, 1857, Captain Hoffines company.
Married Martha Charles June 16, 1835, in England (daughter of John Charles of England). She was born Jan. 29, 1815. Their children: Sarah Ann, m. J. S. Fullmer; John Charles, m. Sarah Goff; Emma and Joseph, died; Lucy, m. Thomas Terry; Agnes, m. Peter Haze; Emma Jane, m. George Williams; Esther, m. Samuel Grange. Family home Springville, Utah.
High priest. Served as guard in Black Hawk Indian war. Tailor. Died Dec. 24, 1882.

STEVENSON, THOMAS PAUL (son of William Stevenson and Mary Maud of Hull, Eng.). Born March 20, 1832, Pocklington, Yorkshire, Eng. Came to Utah Sept. 25, 1855, Richard Ballantyne company.
Married Jane Cobb Oct. 12, 1852, at Hull (daughter of Robert Cobb and Mary Selby of Pocklington), who was born Sept. 20, 1833. Their children: Joseph, died; Thomas William, m. Alice Maud West; Robert Cobb, m. Mary Ann Warner; Mary Jane, Mary Ettie and John Henry, latter three died; Susan, m. Alfred Stanbridge; Priscilla, m. James Madsen; Charles Edward, m. Lizzie Peterson; David Cobb, m. Minnie West; Eliza Jane; Harry. Family home Nephi, Utah.
Teacher; high priest. Farmer. Died March 20, 1907.

STEWART, ANDREW JACKSON (son of Philander Barrett Stewart and Sally Scott of Williamstown, Mass.). Born Sept. 13, 1819, Jackson township, Monroe Co., Ohio. Came to Utah Oct. 20, 1850.
Married Eunice Pease Haws Quimby Jan. 1, 1844, Keosauqua, Van Buren Co., Iowa (daughter of Ephraim Quimby and Catherine Pease Quimby Haws of Van Buren county, pioneers 1851). She was born July 12, 1825. Their children: Sarah Catherine b. Dec. 17, 1844, died; Andrew Jackson b. Aug. 8, 1846, m. Melissa Riggs; Samuel Silvester b. Aug. 18, 1848, Silvia Caroline b. April 6, 1850, and Birdwell Fountain b. May 5, 1851, latter three died; Eunice Listra b. Feb. 1, 1853, m. Isaac Rogers, m. George Morrison; Elon Levara b. July 28, 1855, m. Charles August Allen. Family resided Payson, Provo and Benjamin, Utah.
Married Caroline Nickerson Hubbard Grover Feb. 22, 1851, Salt Lake City (daughter of Freeman Nickerson and Hulda Chapman of Provo, Utah, pioneers 1850). Only child was Moses Carlos b. Jan. 1, 1852, who died young.
Married Mariah Mary Judd July 26, 1852, Salt Lake City (daughter of Philo Judd and Nancy Eames, pioneers 1850). She was born June 3, 1828. Their children: Preston Thomas b. May 8, 1853, m. Christina Hannah Bidmore; Philo Jackson b. Sept. 28, 1855, d. in California; Benjamin Franklin b. Aug. 24, 1859, m. Mary C. Huntsman; John Oscar b. 1861, died; Aaron Ashbel b. March 15, 1864. Family home Provo, Utah.
Married Catherine Holden (daughter of Wiley and Abigail Holden), who was born in 1848. Their children: David Wiley b. April 30, 1865, m. Emily Hidden; Mary Abigail b. 1867, died. Family home Provo, Utah.
Married Mary Eliza Weir Aug. 5, 1863, Salt Lake City (daughter of Thomas Weir and Elizabeth Clark of Ogden, Utah). She was born Dec. 20, 1846. Their children: John Clark b. Sept. 27, 1865, died; Eva Elizabeth b. June 22, 1868, m. Ora B. Haynes; Nancy Lucinda b. July 1, 1871, m. C. U.

Losander; Maggie May b. May 24, 1874, died; Otto Ren b. May 29, 1878, m. Millicent Tallstrup; Lulu Rachel b. June 6, 1881, m. Robert E. Corless.
Clerk of Payson branch 1850; missionary to Australia 1855, and served as president of that mission. Territorial surveyor 1850; assistant attorney-general 1860; deputy clerk of supreme court 1861. President Utah Stock Association 1884. Died Dec. 12, 1911.

STEWART, ANDREW JACKSON, JR. (son of Andrew Jackson Stewart and Eunice Pease Quimby Haws). Born Oct. 8, 1846, in Pottawattamie Co., Iowa.
Married Melissa Riggs Jan. 25, 1868, Salt Lake City (daughter of Dr. John Riggs and Jane Kilton Bullock of Provo, Utah, pioneers Sept. 20, 1851, Captain McPherson company). She was born Jan. 21, 1849. Their children: Melissa Jane b. May 23, 1869, m. William Clements Horsley; Julia Kimball b. Aug. 1870, died; Addie Lavaria b. June 28, 1871, died; Andrew Jackson b. April 10, 1873, m. Helena Roseberry Young; Ida Christmas b. Dec. 25, 1874, m. Edwin Arthur Peay; Scott Pease b. June 10, 1876, m. Myrtle Marben; John Riggs b. Jan. 20, 1878, m. Esther Call. Family resided Provo and Benjamin, Utah.
Married Mary Eliza Smith Sept. 2, 1885, Logan, Utah (daughter of John Glover Smith and Margaret Allen of Mill Creek, Smithfield and St. George, Utah, pioneers September, 1852, Captain Foote company). She was born May 8, 1865. Their children: Addie b. Jan. 2, 1887; Quimby b. Oct. 27, 1888; Eunice Lucile b. July 26, 1891; Marguerite b. Oct. 7, 1893; Theresa Arlena b. Sept. 30, 1895; Allen Glover m. May 16, 1898; Paul Barrett b. Jan. 23, 1900; Elon May b. Feb. 3, 1903; Robert Wilson b. Dec. 24, 1904; James Olander b. Aug. 23, 1907; Samuel Elwood b. April 7, 1909. Family home Provo, Utah.
Assisted in bringing immigrants to Utah 1866. Taught school at Provo and Salt Lake City 1869-70. U. S. deputy surveyor 1872-1902. Assisted in making ditches and developing the country around Benjamin 1862-65. Missionary to California 1907.

STEWART, ANDREW J. (son of Andrew Jackson Stewart and Melissa Riggs). Born April 10, 1873, Provo, Utah.
Married Helena Roseberry Young Oct. 1, 1901, Salt Lake City (daughter of Oscar B. Young and Anna Marie Roseberry of Provo and Salt Lake City, former pioneer 1848, the latter 1857). She was born July 30, 1876. Their children: Helena b. July 5, 1903; Burr Young b. Aug. 4, 1905; Dorothy b. Sept. 26, 1908.
Missionary to Germany 1896-99. U. S. deputy surveyor 1903-05. Graduated from College of Physicians and Surgeons of Baltimore, Md., 1904. Practicing physician Salt Lake City.

STEWART, CHARLES (son of Nicholas Stevens Stewart and Lucy Kilborn of Denmark, Lewis county, N. Y.). He was born May 14, 1814, at Denmark, N. Y. Came to Utah October, 1852, Captain Snow company.
Married Sarah Ann Roberts in 1836 at Denmark, N. Y. (daughter of James Roberts and Lois Chapin of Oswegatchie, St. Lawrence county, N. Y.). She was born in February, 1820. Their children: Mary Priscilla, m. John Burriston, m. Era Hawley; William Henry, m. Elizabeth Davis; Jane Eveline; Sarah Ellen, m. Elisha Davis; Olive Ann; Charles Echo; Emma Maria, m. Charles Samuel White; Lois Adeline, m. Heber Clark; James Stevens; Lucy Adelaide, m. Alexander Gray.
Married Fannie Eliza Hunt 1870, Salt Lake City (daughter of William Hunt and Fannie Matilda Stewart, Dianna, N. Y.). She was born Sept. 7, 1848. Their children: Etta Estella; Louise; Fannie Luella; Clara, m. Edward Watkins; Blanche. Families resided Pleasant Grove, Utah.
Missionary to New York 1869-70. Farmer. Died Jan. 18, 1879, Pleasant Grove, Utah.

STEWART, WILLIAM HENRY (son of Charles Stewart and Sarah Ann Roberts). Born Dec. 3, 1842, Oswegatchie, N. Y. Came to Utah October, 1852, Captain Snow company.
Married Elizabeth Davis January, 1871, Salt Lake City (daughter of John Catlin Davis and Phoebe Oxenbauld. Handsworth, Staffordshire, Eng., came to Utah 1859, Edward Stevenson company). She was born Nov. 20, 1852. Their children: Sarah Ann b. Aug. 26, 1872, d. Aug. 28, 1872; William Davis b. Nov. 17, 1873, m. Alice Spratley; Lois Elizabeth b. Oct. 8, 1875, m. Alvin West; Sylvia Jane b. Aug. 26, 1877, m. William Atwood; Charles Stoddart b. Dec. 13, 1879, m. Margaret Gaines; John Henry b. Dec. 1, 1881, m. Flora Gaines; Caddie Lyle b. Nov. 4, 1884, m. Charles Santford Jones; Rua Francis b. Aug. 22, 1887; Alfred Duane b. March 1, 1890; Walter Roberts b. April 23, 1893, d. Aug. 26, 1893. Family home Pleasant Grove, Utah.
Member high priests' quorum seventies. Assisted immigrants to Utah 1866, Henry Chipman company. Farmer. Died Aug. 28, 1912, Pleasant Grove.

STEWART, ISAAC MITTON (son of Beakley Stewart, of Burlington, N. J., and Alice Hopkins, born 1781 in New Jersey). He was born March 18, 1815, Burlington, N. J. Came to Utah 1852, captain of his own company.
Married Matilda Jane Downs (daughter of Ezekiel Downs and Chalotte Rawlins, latter a pioneer 1848). She was born Oct. 1, 1817, and came to Utah with husband. Their children: James Zebulon b. Oct. 31, 1844, m. Julia Ann Wads-

worth Fitzgerald Dec. 27, 1869; Mary Emily b. 1848; Maranda Jane b. Oct. 1852, m. William L. Allen; Isaac John b. Sept. 29, 1855, m. May Crossgrove, m. Eva Hepler, m. Jennie Parish. Family home Draper, Utah.
Married Elizabeth White March 8, 1857, Salt Lake City (daughter of William White and Mary Ann Syer—married in London, Eng.—latter came to Utah Dec. 10, 1856, with John A. Hunt company). She was born Feb. 22, 1838, London, Eng., and came to Utah with mother. Their children: Mary Ann b. March 4, 1858, m. R. A. Ballantyne Dec. 27, 1875; William Mitton b. Sept. 5, 1859, m. Sarah Vincent Dec. 17, 1884; Alice Caroline b. Feb. 16, 1862, m. Richard H. Stringfellow May 5, 1885; Elizabeth b. Sept. 3, 1863, m. William W. Fife Dec. 7, 1882; Eliza Jane b. Aug. 27, 1865, m. John D. Fife Feb. 20, 1889; Samuel White b. May 21, 1867, m. Ella M. Nebeker Sept. 19. 1894; Charles Beakley b. July 20, 1870, m. Kate Romney Sept. 30, 1896; Joseph Barnard b. Jan. 13, 1873, m. Leonora Cannon Sept. 13, 1889; Luella Evaline b. Dec. 5, 1875, m. Marian Lindsay Oct. 5, 1898; Nettie Priscilla b. Sept. 11, 1879, m. Alfred Taylor June 11, 1902; Orson Richard b. 1881, d. 1886. Family resided Draper and Salt Lake City, Utah.
Married Emma Baynum (Lloyd). Only child: Joshua Baynum b. 1868, m. Mary Jane Fitzgerald Dec. 7, 1885.
Bishop of Draper ward 38 years. County selectman 16 years. A promoter of educational institutions—University of Utah and Draper public schools. Farmer; stockraiser. Died March 15, 1890, Draper, Utah.

STEWART, JAMES ZEBULON (son of Isaac Mitton Stewart and Matilda Jane Downs). Born Oct. 31, 1844, near Carthage, Ill.
Married Julia A. Fitzgerald Dec. 27, 1869, Salt Lake City (daughter of Perry Fitzgerald and Agnes Wadsworth, former a pioneer July 24, 1847). She was born March 24, 1854, Draper, Utah. Their children: James Zebulon b. March 6, 1871, m. Hanna Kotter; Isaac Perry b. Dec. 13, 1872, m. Rebecca Evans; Carrie Julia b. Oct. 1, 1874, m. Thomas H. Humphreys; Ida May b. Aug. 23, 1878, m. Joseph M. Anderson; Ernest Israel b. June 8, 1882, m. Sarah Walters; Agnes Matilda b. May 2, 1884, m. James C. Allen; Willie Helaman b. April 9, 1886, m. Mabel Richards; Royal Angus b. Nov. 19, 1887; Eugene Fitzgerald b. July 23, 1891; Jessie Fitzgerald b. May 22, 1893. Family home Logan, Utah.
President of faculty of Brigham Young College at Logan several years. Located Mormon colonies in Colorado. Member high council of Cache stake 25 years; filled three missions to old Mexico. In collaboration with M. G. Trejo, translated Book of Mormon into Spanish.

STEWART, JAMES ZEBULON, JR. (son of James Zebulon Stewart and Julia Ann Fitzgerald). Born March 6, 1871, Draper, Utah.
Married Hanna Kotter (daughter of Heinrich Herman Ludwig Kotter and Henrietta Bozrup, former came to Utah from Germany). She was born March 8, 1872, Brigham City, Utah. Their children: LeGrande b. Jan. 3, 1902; Vera b. July 11, 1903; James Zebulon b. Oct. 24, 1904; Kingsley Heinrich b. July 9, 1906; Velois b. May 6. 1908; Gracia Henrietta b. June 19, 1910; Miriam Hannah b. July 24, 1912. Family home Logan, Utah.
Has served as president of Brooklyn, N. Y. conference; Sunday school superintendent; member religion class board. City attorney of Logan.

STEWART, DR. WILLIAM MITTON (son of Isaac Mitton Stewart and Elizabeth White). Born Sept. 5, 1859, Draper, Utah.
Married Sarah E. Vincent Dec. 17, 1884, Salt Lake City. She was a young woman of strong character, with a remarkable educational insight, and one who has been a great factor in his educational career.
He spent his early boyhood working on his father's farm, and while the plow was being guided by his youthful hands upturning the fertile soil, his thoughts soared upward in primitive aspirations toward an ethical ideal of life and education.
He attended the University of Deseret at the age of 29 and came in direct and intimate contact with some of Utah's pioneers of education—Karl G. Maeser, John R. Park, J. B. Toronto and others. Graduating in 1883, he took up the profession of teaching and his school became noted throughout the state. Instrumental in organizing literary societies, he finally accumulated an enormous library. Elected county superintendent of schools in 1885, which then included the schools of Salt Lake City.
In 1888 he became a member of the Utah University faculty, and for 25 years his labors were untiring in building up its departments of education. He had the utilitarian idea of education and worked it out in his everyday life. Regent of the university four years, he later was placed at the head of the normal school and it became the School of Education. Under his deft direction the training school became world-famed and the prominent educators of the country have marveled at its thoroughness and the material it has turned out of its halls.
In 1899 he did post-graduate work at the University of Chicago, working with Dr. John Dewey, Colonel Parker and Dr. Harper. While there he presented many papers that received marked recognition.
In 1897 the University of Utah conferred upon him the degree of Master of Didactics, a title well-earned by his devotion to the university and his marked ability.
Having traveled throughout the United States, attending the meetings of the National Education Association, delivering lectures and presenting papers before national conventions and meetings of the national superintendents, he was just completing a new course of study and had worked out an entirely new scheme of industrial work for Utah, when his exemplary life closed June 26, 1913, mourned by thousands throughout the United States.

STEWART, SAMUEL W. (son of Isaac M. Stewart and Elizabeth White). Born May 21, 1867, Draper, Utah.
Married Ella M. Nebeker Sept. 19, 1894, Salt Lake City (daughter of George Nebeker and Maria Delwith of Salt Lake City, pioneers 1847). She was born Oct. 7, 1867. Family home, Salt Lake City.
Member third state legislature; judge in third judicial district court four years. Practicing attorney.

STEWART, CHARLES BEAKLEY (son of Isaac M. Stewart and Elizabeth White). Born July 20, 1870, Draper, Utah.
Married Katherine Romney Sept. 30, 1896, Salt Lake City (daughter of George Romney and Margaret Thomas, pioneers), who was born March 18, 1875. Their children: Charles B. b. Aug. 7, 1898; Margaret A. b. Oct. 5, 1899; Katherine R. b. Jan. 4, 1902; Elizabeth W. b. July 19, 1894; Isaac M. b. Dec. 30, 1906; Josephine R. b. Aug. 30, 1907; George R. b. June 7, 1908; Romney b. Feb. 13, 1913. Family home, Salt Lake City.
Worked on farm and attended public schools during winter months. Student at University of Deseret (now University of Utah), and a graduate of the law department of the University of Michigan (at Ann Arbor) June, 1893. Admitted to the bar of the state of Michigan June. 1893, and to the supreme court of the United States Feb. 23, 1912. Taught in the Utah public schools for two years. Commenced the practice of law in Salt Lake City June. 1895, with the law firm of Stewart, Stewart & Stewart (brothers) until 1908, when he became the senior member of the law firm of Stewart, Bowman & Morris. Elected justice of peace for fourth precinct Salt Lake City, one term, served as assistant city attorney for Salt Lake City, two terms. Was director in Salt Lake & Jordan Mill & Elevator Co., the Summit County Mercantile Company, Western Wyoming Land & Livestock Co., Stewart Harding Sheep Company, Utah Coal & Supply Co. of Park City, Stewart Ranch Company, Birdseye Marble Company. President of University Investment Company. He in connection with J. C. McAllister organized the Farmers' & Stockgrowers' Bank and is first vice president, director and member of the executive committee of that bank. Director Utah Pioneer Book Publishing Company. Sheepraiser and farmer. Secretary Utah Sheepman's Association.

STEWART, BARNARD J. (son of Isaac M. Stewart and Elizabeth White). Born Jan. 13, 1873, Draper, Utah.
Married Leonora M. Cannon Sept. 13, 1899, Salt Lake City (daughter of Angus M. Cannon and Sarah Mousley of England, pioneers 1851). She was born Oct. 12, 1874. Their children: Madeline C. b. March 1, 1901; Ruth b. May 18, 1903; Barnard J. b. Dec. 31, 1906; William M. b. July 2, 1909; Leonora C. b. June 14, 1911.
Practices law in Salt Lake City.

STEWART, JAMES WESLEY (son of George Stewart, born Jan. 29, 1796, Cumberland, N. C., and Ruth Baker, born Jan. 24, 1807, Clark county, Ga., both of Fayette county, Ala.). Born May 19, 1825, in Fayette county. Came to Utah July 24, 1847, Brigham Young company.
Married Jane Grover in Southern California (daughter of Thomas Grover and Caroline Whiting of Farmington, Utah, pioneers). Their children: Mary Jane, m. John Bourne; Ruth Caroline, m. Alexander Tubbs; Eliza Ann, m. John S. Barrett; James Wesley, Jr., m. Lavinia Jane Stewart; Luella Lorena, m. Frank Goddard; Cynthia Emeline, m. James Barron; Hannah, m. George Munns; George Thomas; Isaiah Joshua, m. Esther Mellinger; Samuel Spaulding; Margaret E. Family home Farmington, Utah.
High priest. Died March 22, 1913, Cokeville, Wyo.

STEWART, JAMES W. (son of James W. Stewart and Jane Grover). Born Aug. 9, 1857, San Bernardino, Cal.
Married Lavinia Jane Stewart Jan. 1, 1880, Salt Lake City (daughter of George Rufus Stewart and Nancy Browning of Ogden, Utah, pioneers 1847, second company), who was born March 7, 1859. Family home Morgan, Utah.
High priest; high councilor; superintendent Sunday school and president Y. M. M. I. A. City councilman and county commissioner. Farmer.

STEWART, GEORGE RUFUS (son of George Stewart). Born July 29, 1827, Tuscaloosa, Ala. Came to Utah September, 1847.
Married Barbara Jane Stewart Nov. 26, 1833 (daughter of Johnathan Browning and Elizabeth Stallcup of Ogden, Utah). Only child: James Rufus, d. Oct. 12, 1887. Family home, Ogden.
Married Nancy Lovinia Browning April 1, 1856, who was born Jan. 13, 1842, in Illinois, died June 22, 1875, Ogden, Utah. Their children: Lovinia Jane b. March 7, 1859, m. James Wesley Stewart Jan. 1, 1890; George Johnathan b. Aug. 13, 1861, m. Mary Ellen Heinner; Barbara Malvina b. Oct. 27, 1863, m. Frank E. Lloyd; Martha Malinda b. Dec. 13, 1865, m. Fredric R. Kramer; Rutha Elizabeth b. March 16, 1867, m. Thomas Palmer; John Virgil b. June 1, 1870, m. Mary Devine; William Henry b. June 5, 1875. Family home Ogden, Utah.
Seventy; home missionary; ward teacher. Died Jan. 20, 1891.

1188   PIONEERS AND PROMINENT MEN OF UTAH

STEWART, JOHN (son of James Stewart and Harriet Glen). He was born Sept. 27, 1827, at Chester, Kent county, Md. Came to Utah 1849.
Married Lydia M. Rolfe Feb. 12, 1851, Salt Lake City, Utah (daughter of Samuel J. Rolfe and Elizabeth Hathaway). She was born Dec. 26, 1831, in Oxford Co., Maine, came to Utah September, 1847. Their children: Arthur M. b. Jan. 26, 1852; James b. Feb. 16, 1854; Harriet E. b. June 11, 1856, m. A. D. Rhodes, Jr.; Julianna b. Feb. 10, 1859, m. Edward Karren; John b. Feb. 25, 1862, m. Henrietta Ashton; Henry T. b. Jan. 1, 1864; Charles T. b. Oct. 11, 1866, m. Cora Brown; Harry J. b. May 2, 1869, m. Victoria Bone; Margret b. June 3, 1871; Benjamin b May 12, 1873, m. M. E. Hindmarsh; Samuel Stewart b. April 2, 1875, m. Nellie Enloe. Family home Lehi, Utah.
Carpenter and builder. Died July 12, 1895, Lehi, Utah.

STEWART, ARTHUR M. (son of John Stewart and Lydia M. Rolfe). He was born Jan. 26, 1852, at San Bernardino, Cal. Came to Utah 1858.
Married Sarah P. Thomas July 4, 1871, Lehi, Utah (daughter of Daniel S. Thomas and Martha P. Jones, Lehi, Utah, came to Utah 1849). She was born Feb. 3, 1849. Their children: A. M. b. March 7, 1872, m. Ella Herron; Owen T. b. Feb. 8, 1874, m. Geneva Evans; Sarah J. b. Nov. 20, 1875, m. William Vaughn; Paul J. b. June 20, 1878, m. Annie Burns; Malinda b. June 15, 1880. m. Samuel Hammer; Leon J. b. Sept. 13, 1882; Lola D. b. Sept. 19, 1884, m. M. Copenhaver; Martha L. b. April 12, 1886, m. M. Prestrich; Maggie Ferole b. Aug. 30, 1892. Family home Lehi, Utah.

STEWART, NEIL M. (son of William Stewart, born March 15, 1828, Edinburgh, Scotland, and Elizabeth Murdock, born Dec. 18, 1822, Fifeshire, England—married Nov. 18, 1850, both of Edinburgh, Scotland). He was born April 15, 1855, Peoria, Ill. Came to Utah December, 1856, Captain Hunt company.
Married Hannah Fisher Nov. 20, 1880 (daughter of James Fisher and Hannah Stott of Meadow, Millard Co., Utah, pioneers October, 1852, Isaac Bullock company). She was born March 21, 1860, and came to Utah with parents.
Member 47th quorum seventies; missionary to Scotland 1898 to 1900. Moved to Meadow at the age of 14 years. High priest; high councilor; president Y. M. M. I. A.; bishop's counselor; bishop of Meadow ward 9 years. County commissioner. Farmer.

STEWART, WILLIAM LYLE (son of Archabald Stewart and Esther Lyle, Glasgow, Scotland). Born Nov. 19, 1846, Glasgow, Scotland. Came to Utah 1854, Daniel Garn company.
Married Sarah Jane Thomas Jan. 29, 1872 (daughter of Daniel E. Thomas and Jane Gaither, pioneers 1850, Seth M. Blair company). She was born Dec. 21, 1852. Their children: Nellie Elizabeth; William Thomas; Daniel Clarberm; Archabald; Nellie; Esther; John Franklin; Mary; Effie; Ruth. Family resided Plain City, Warren and Corinne, Utah.
Member quorum seventies; missionary to Great Britain 1898 to 1900; member Sunday school board Plain City, 10 years; superintendent Plain City Sunday school from 1882 to 1888 and from 1893 to 1896; bishop Warren ward 1896-1909. Representative to sixth legislature, Utah. Constable and justice of peace, Plain City.

STEWART, URBAN VAN (son of William Stewart, born 1766, Overton, Tenn., and Elizabeth Van Hooser, born 1772, of Overton). He was born Nov. 9, 1817, at Overton. Came to Utah September, 1847.
Married Lydia Gage Iacobs 1837, in Caldwell county, Mo., who was born 1822, and came to Utah with husband. Their children: Edna A. b. May, 1840, m. Robert McDonald April 18, 1855; Henry b. 1842, d. infant; Urban Jacob b. May 13, 1846, m. Emily ——. Family home, Salt Lake City.
Married Elizabeth Luck May 21, 1854, Parowan, Utah, who was born Nov. 7, 1827, in Buckinghamshire, Eng. Their children: Joseph Stewart b. Nov. 9, 1852 (adopted); Van b. April 16, 1855, d. Feb. 14, 1864; Levi b. March 4, 1857, d. April 21, 1864; Elizabeth b. March 18, 1859, m. Samuel B. Ward March 21, 1875; Rosanna E. b. Sept. 12, 1861, m. Jason D. Webb May 24, 1876; Sarah V. b. Sept. 27, 1863, m. Albert Bird Nov. 12, 1878; Eunice A. b. Aug. 21, 1868, m. George W. Valentine March 15, 1885. Family home Beaver, Utah.
Married Mary Ann Jones March 11, 1860 (daughter of William B. and Mary Jones), who was born Feb. 8, 1845. Their children: Mary Jane b. Nov. 18, 1861, m. John Limb Feb. 6, 1878; Liza Ann b. Dec. 15, 1863, d. July 6, 1865; Martha Ellen b. June 21, 1866, m. John E. Cox Dec. 27, 1882; William Urban b. Oct. 10, 1868, m. Rosa B. Adams Nov. 14, 1890; Daniel Jones b. Feb. 25, 1871, m. Ellen S. Adams June 19, 1895; Margret Caroline b. Nov. 26, 1873, m. John D. Adams Dec. 30, 1891; Robert Charles b. April 7, 1876, d. July 23, 1901; George Heber b. March 30, 1879, m. Lydia C. Covington June 5, 1901; Lewis Jenkins b. Sept. 18, 1881, d. Jan. 20, 1907; Clara Bell b. March 25, 1884. Family home Beaver, Utah.
Married Ellen Adams July 14, 1865, Salt Lake City (daughter of David B. Adams and Mary Cook, who were married 1834, former came to Utah, latter died in Missouri). She was born May 10, 1848, Northumberland, Pa. Their children: Mary Ellen b. July 20, 1867, m. Walter F. Hanks April 15, 1887; David James b. Sept. 25, 1869, m. Fanny Simmons Dec. 22, 1892; Urban Van b. Oct. 6, 1871, m. Margret Franklin Dec. 21, 1897; John Ruly b. Aug. 27, 1873, m. Cornelia Covington Aug. 14, 1903; Lydia Catherine b. Nov. 3, 1875, d. Feb. 1, 1877; Andrew Adams b. March 5, 1877, d. July 10, 1882; Rosa May b. June 14, 1880, m. Moroni Lazenby Oct. 14, 1898; Levi b. Oct. 31, 1882, d. Feb. 10, 1892. Effie Elizabeth b. Feb. 17, 1886, m. William J. Covington; Walter Ernest b. Sept. 27, 1888. Family resided Beaver and Adamsville, Utah.
Married Keziah Jones (daughter of William and Mary Jones), who was born July 16, 1855. Their children: Margret, m. Mr. Valentine; Edward, m. May Pace; Susan, m. Lars Frandson.
Seventy; high priest; presiding elder of Grover, Teasdale branch; missionary to southern Illinois, 1843; and also to the White mountains. He assisted in putting in the crops in Clover valley. Farmer. Died Dec. 25, 1899, Grover, Utah.

STEWART, JOHN RILLY (son of Urban Van Stewart and Ellen Adams). Born Aug. 27, 1873, Beaver, Utah.
Married Ellen Cornelia Covington Aug. 14, 1903, Salt Lake City (daughter of John Covington and Elizabeth Adams), who was born Dec. 10, 1884, Orderville, Utah. Their children: Ellen Elizabeth b. April 26, 1904; John Rilly, Jr. b. Oct. 28, 1905; Golda b. Dec. 21, 1907; Cecil Van b. March 7, 1910; Harold William b. March 21, 1911. Family home Loa, Utah.
Missionary to northwestern states 1897-1900; presiding elder and assistant Sunday school superintendent of Grover ward; bishop Torrey ward five years; second counselor to G. S. Bastian, president of Wayne stake, 1906-10; and first counselor to Joseph Eckersley, president same stake.

STEWART, WILLIAM (son of James Stewart, born Aug. 12, 1796, Blairothel, Scotland, and Helen Young, born 1796, St. Andries, Scotland. Family home Edinburgh, Scotland). He was born March 15, 1828, at Edinburgh. Came to Utah December, 1856, John A. Hunt company.
Married Elizabeth Murdock Nov. 13, 1850, Newcastle, Northumberland, Eng. (daughter of James Murdock and Elizabeth Salter), who was born Dec. 18, 1822, and came to Utah with husband. Their children: James Murdock b. Sept. 22, 1851, m. Mary J. Duncan Dec. 22, 1873; William b. Oct. 7, 1853, d. Aug. 19, 1854; Neil M. b. April 15, 1855, m. Hannah Fisher Nov. 20, 1880; Elizabeth b. Oct. 23, 1856, d. Oct. 26, 1856. Family resided Goshen and Meadow, Utah.
Married Ruth Carans Sept. 22, 1857, Salt Lake City, who was born April 13, 1905, in Scotland.
Married Jane Jenkins 1864, at Salt Lake City (daughter of James Jenkins and Jenet Lard of Scotland, pioneers 1864). Their children: Jennett b. Sept. 8, 1865, m. Peter Greenhaigh; Elizabeth b. Aug. 25, 1867, m. James E. Fisher; Isabell b. Jan. 8, 1870, m. Edwin Stott, Jr.; Jane b. May 9, 1872, d. May 24, 1872; William b. Aug. 16, 1873, d. Aug. 15, 1873; Enoch b. Nov. 8, 1874, m. Laura Greenhalgh; Ellen b. April 17, 1877, m. Lester W. Stott; James J. b. July 8, 1879, m. Mary Church; May b. May 1, 1882, m. John Williams; George b. June 6, 1885, m. Raymond Stott; Myrtle b. March 26, 1892, m. Philip Borup.
Served in Echo Canyon and Black Hawk wars. Moved from Spanish Fork to Goshen and then to Meadow in 1869. Worked on St. George temple. Carpenter and farmer. Died Dec. 2, 1892 at Meadow.

STEWART, JAMES M. (son of William Stewart and Elizabeth Murdock). Born Sept. 22, 1851, St. Louis, Mo. Came to Utah December, 1856, with father.
Married Mary J. Duncan Dec. 22, 1873, Salt Lake City (daughter of James Duncan and Jennett Snedden, pioneers September, 1852, John Higby company). She was born April 15, 1854, at Fillmore, Utah. Their children: James W. b. Jan. 19, 1875, d. Oct. 9, 1878; Nephi R. b. Feb. 6, 1877, m. Hilman Pearson; Mary E. b. June 13, 1879, m. Heber W. Beckstrand; Duncan b. Sept. 6, 1882, m. Signa Christensen Dec. 1910; Christina b. April 12, 1887, m. William Davis May 11, 1910; George Lile b. Feb. 22, 1889, m. Laura Walker Oct. 1812; Ephraim b. Sept. 8, 1892; Clifford b. Oct. 27, 1894; Jacob b. March 13, 1897. Family home Meadow, Utah.
Married Elizabeth Duncan Dec. 21, 1883, St. George, Utah (daughter of James Duncan and Jennett Snedden, pioneers September, 1852, John Higby company). She was born Feb. 8, 1866, Meadow, Utah. Their children: Emma J. b. Nov. 8, 1884, m. Matry A. Gulic Sept. 25, 1907; Nell M. b. Feb. 10, 1887, m. Ada Stott Sept. 30, 1908; Ruth b. Aug. 24, 1889, m. Albert Eli Bennett Sept. 5, 1911; Isaac b. Sept. 25, 1892; Zina b. July 8, 1895; Violet b. Jan. 2, 1898; Grace b. July 28, 1901; Blanche b. Oct. 17, 1903; Golden b. March 7, 1906. Family home Meadow, Utah.
Ward teacher thirty years; missionary to Eastern states; one of the presidents of 42d quorum seventies; member high council Millard stake. Black Hawk Indian war veteran. Farmer.

STEWART, WILLIAM (son of William and Mary Stewart of Greenock, Scotland). Born May 12, 1817, at Campbelltown, Scotland. Came to Utah October, 1864.
Married Sarah Thompson (daughter of Sam Thompson). Their children: Anna; William; Samuel; Elizabeth; Hugh; Thompson; Sarah; Martha. Family home Clarkston, Utah. He died at Clarkston.

STEWART, SAMUEL (son of William Stewart and Sarah Thompson). Born April 9, 1834, Greenoch, Scotland. Came to Utah Oct. 27, 1862, Ansel P. Harmon company.
Married Mary Ann Clark April 16, 1864, Salt Lake City (daughter of Joseph Clark and Ann Clark of Sugar House ward, Salt Lake City—married Oct. 3, 1844, pioneers 1857, Captain Merrell company). She was born Aug. 24, 1847, Cambridge, Eng. Their children: Samuel C. b. Feb. 19, 1865, m. Salma Dahle Feb. 19, 1890; Joseph William b. March 19, 1868, m. Sady Godfrey Aug. 24, 1893; James Edward b. Jan. 30, 1870, m. Emily Jane Basset Dec. 1890; Julia Ann b. March 2, 1872, m. James Clark Feb. 11, 1892; Angahne Vilat b. June 30, 1874, m. Charles Buttars May 18, 1892; George b. Oct. 22, 1876, m. Leong Birgh Oct. 17, 1892; Sarah b. Oct. 15, 1878, m. Joseph W. Black July 20, 1898; Mary Ann b. Dec. 17, 1880, m. James T. Birch March 11, 1898; Andrew b. Jan. 11, 1883, m. Elizabeth Bagley Aug. 19, 1907; Hugh b. May 18, 1885, m. Adeline Greenhalm Dec. 19, 1907; Benjamin Isaac b. Sept. 28, 1887, m. Caroline Birch May 3, 1910; Clara Elizabeth b. Feb. 27, 1891, m. Parley Richmond Sept. 22, 1910.

STEWART, SAMUEL C. (son of Samuel Stewart and Mary Ann Clark). Born Feb. 19, 1865, Salt Lake City.
Married Salma Dahle Feb. 19, 1890, Logan, Utah (daughter of John Dahle and Janettie Ingerman of Logan, Utah), who was born Nov. 14, 1877, Logan, Utah. Their children: Jannettie b. May 17, 1891, m. Claud Rackham, m. Olau Rackham Nov. 13, 1907; Lettie b. April 26, 1894; Samuel Leroy b. July 2, 1896; Amy May b. Aug. 12, 1901; John Dahle b. Oct. 25, 1904.

STEWELL, DAN. Came to Utah in fall of 1847.
Married Louisa Barnum in St. Joe county, Ind. Their children: William; Harriet, m. William Stewell; George, m. Jane Bybee; Mary, m. Alonzo Perry; Anjeanette Abigail, m. Alonzo Orson Perry; Louisa, d. infant. Family home Ogden, Utah.
Merchant.

STEVENS, ALBERT (son of William and Marinda Stevens, both of Canada). Born Dec. 16, ——. Came to Utah 1852, oxteam company.
Married Lette McKee (daughter of David and Mary McKee, of Iowa). Their children: Albert, m. Elsie McClellan; Rachael, m. Simeon Stevenson; Mary, m. George Badger; James, died; David Edward, m. Kate Kenney; George Thomas, m. Cynthia McClellan; Martha Ann, m. Harden Ashby; Lette, died. Family home Holden, Utah.
Black Hawk Indian war veteran. Settled at Pleasant Grove, moved to Holden, Utah. Farmer. Died March 6, 1910, at Holden, Utah.

STEVENS, DAVID EDWARD (son of Albert Stevens and Lette McKee). Born Dec. 9, 1860, Holden, Utah.
Married Kate Kenney March 29, 1881, Salt Lake City, Utah (daughter of John Kenney of Ireland and Elizabeth Bennet of England, former pioneer 1858, latter 1860). Their children: Elizabeth A. b. May 11, 1883, m. E. W. Crane; Wilford b. April 12, 1886; LaVern b. Dec. 19, 1889, m. John Earl Pickett; Vivien b. July 11, 1892; George b. Jan. 21, 1895; Ruth b. Feb. 19, 1897; Austin b. Sept. 11, 1899; Kate b. Aug. 7, 1903. Family resided Holden, Salina and Aurora, Utah.
Elder. Constable of Holden two years. Sheepraiser and farmer.

STILLMAN, CHARLES. Born June 1, 1834. Came to Utah 1848.
Married Elizabeth Neff, Salt Lake City. Their children: Mary Elizabeth, m. Mores Ross Porter; John F.; Harriet Seymore, m. Eli Curtis; Della Barr, m. John Fagg; Charles Franklin, m. Mariah Neff; Samuel Sermore, m. Selina Osguthorpe; Forest Neff, m. Elizabeth Ellis; Frances Minerva, m. Andrew H. Bagley; Cyrus Neff, m. Eliza Hippler; Letitia Bower, m. Joseph Moss; Brigham Jason; Barbara Matilda, m. George P. Taylor; Joseph Julian, m. Emma Osguthorpe; Susanna Ethel, m. H. Albert Wagstaff.
Farmer; stockraiser. Died July 16, 1905, East Mill Creek, Utah.

STILLMAN, CHARLES FRANKLIN (son of Charles Stillman and Elizabeth Neff).
Married Mariah Neff, Logan, Utah (daughter of Bishop John Neff and Eliza Benedittee, East Mill Creek, Utah, pioneers 1847). Their children: Kenneth Vere; Charles Neff; Wayne; Franklin; John; Wilmer; Jene; June. Family home, East Mill Creek.
President Y. M. M. I. A.; superintendent Sunday school. Farmer; stockraiser.

STIMPSON, WILLIAM (son of William Stimpson and Mary Smith, Stalham, Norfolk, Eng.). Born June 15, 1821, Hempstead, Norfolk, Eng. Came to Utah Nov. 30, 1856, Edward Martin handcart company.
Married Rebecca Loubbuck Nov. 19, 1848, East Ruston, Norfolk, Eng. (daughter of James Loubbuck and Susan Hewett), who was born March 31, 1826, and died on the plains. Their children: Frederick, m. Sarah Jane Parker, m. Lizzie Ellen Davis; William B., d. on plains.
Married Edna Hinchcliff in 1858, Ogden, Utah (daughter of Elijah Hinchcliff and Hannah Field, pioneers 1854, Captain James Brown company). She was born March 24, 1828, Yorkshire, Eng. Their children: William b. April 27, 1859, m. Rebecca A. Bybee; Eliza Ann b. Feb. 24, 1861, m. Frank Wadsworth; Ann Rebecca b. Feb. 24, 1861, m. Ira E. Spalding; Robert P. b. May 14, 1863, m. Adeline Gale; Sarah b. Aug. 7, 1865, m. William Drysdale; Edna b. July 27, 1867, m. Hyrum E. Gale.
Married Ann Mary Christensen in 1868, at Salt Lake City, who was born July 23, 1840. Their children: Mary Ann b. Aug. 7, 1869, m. Thomas Story; Martha b. Dec. 16, 1871; Elizabeth b. Aug. 7, 1873, m. Clarence E. Porter; Margaret b. Feb. 8, 1876; John b. Oct. 2, 1878, m. Annie E. P. Gale; George Q. b. Feb. 29, 1884, died; Joseph H. b. June 12, 1885.
Families resided Riverdale, Weber Co., Utah.
Second counselor to Bishop Bingham of Riverdale for 30 years. Served in Echo Canyon war 1857-8. Farmer. Died Jan. 12, 1907.

STIMPSON, FREDERICK (son of William Stimpson and Rebecca Loubbuck). Born June 15, 1852, at Ridlington, Norfolk, Eng. Came to Utah Nov. 30, 1856, with father.
Married Sarah Jane Parker Oct. 21, 1876, Salt Lake City (daughter of William C. Parker and Sarah B. Edgeley, West Jordan, Salt Lake county, pioneers 1854, Robert L. Campbell company). She was born April 22, 1857. Their children: Frederick, Jr., b. Dec. 13, 1877; Sarah Jane b. Dec. 19, 1879, d. 1880; William b. March 1, 1881, d. 1881; John b. Aug. 17, 1882, m. Sarah E. Singleton; Rebecca b. April 18, 1885, m. Albert J. Thompson; James L. b. April 3, 1887, d. 1888; Mary E. b. Feb. 17, 1889; Eliza A. b. April 24, 1891, m. Charles C. Murri; George; Robert E. b. Oct. 25, 1897, d. 1897; Margaret b. Dec. 18, 1899; Martha b. June 4, 1902, d. 1903.
Married Lucy Ellen Davis March 11, 1885, Logan, Utah (daughter of George Davis and Elizabeth M. Hammon, East Weber, Utah, pioneers 1851, Alford Cardon company). She was born Feb. 9, 1864. Their children: Lucy E. b. Feb. 16, 1886, m. Charles C. Murri; Sarah E. b. Nov. 14, 1887, m. G. P. Parson. Families resided South Hooper, Utah, and St. Anthony, Idaho.
Member 76th quorum seventies; Sunday school worker, 35 years; ward chorister same length of time. School trustee, 15 years. Farmer.

STINGER, JOHN HENRY (son of Adam Stinger and Anna Mary Rode, of Alsenua, Germany). Born April 23, 1839, Zanesville, Ohio. Came to Utah Sept. 13, 1861, Joseph Horne company.
Married Elizabeth Hollist Oct. 1, 1859, Florence, Neb. (daughter of Henry Hollist and Elizabeth Chandler, pioneers 1861, Joseph Horne company). She was born Feb. 14, 1842. Their children: John William, m. Gwenilon Marley; Jane Elizabeth, d. Oct. 29, 1883; Henry Hollist, m. Elizabeth E. Gittins; Mary Deborah, m. Joseph Marley; Frances Mindwell, d. Feb. 9, 1868; Rosanna, d. Feb. 14, 1871; Lillie Adelaide, m. Addison L. Long; Harriett Ann, m. William H. Esler; Florence, m. Henry W. Nelson; Alice Emily, m. Samuel Blundell; Rhoda Pearl, m. E. Louis Saunders; Ada May, m. Aaron Headlee; Fanny Gwenlion, m. Orson P. Merrell.
Settled in Ogden in 1861; following year went to Toquerville as pioneer, and later returned to Ogden, where he went into bakery business; built first bakery oven in that city in 1869. Worked for Utah Northern railway in 1878; settled in Pocatello where he operated a bakery and finally settled in McCammon, where for four years he was justice of peace.

STOCK, JOHN (son of Robert Stock and Susan Pierce of Kent, Eng.). Born Oct. 12, 1820, Bathurst, South Africa. Came to Utah Oct. 1, 1860, William Budge company.
Married Jane Adams Feb. 13, 1841, Port Elizabeth, South Africa (daughter of Poyntz Adams and Mary Staines of Port Elizabeth), who was born Aug. 27, 1822. Their children: Mary Ann b. Sept. 27, 1842, m. William Stokes 1859; John William Edwin b. Dec. 20, 1844, m. Harriet E. Steed Oct. 23, 1871; Jane Susan b. Aug. 21, 1846, m. Charles C. Rich, Jr., Aug. 27, 1865; Elizabeth b. Sept. 21, 1848, m. Hyrum Rich June 23, 1867; Richard Poyntz b. Aug. 27, 1850, m. Rosetta Gardner June 14, 1881; Robert Wallace b. Aug. 1, 1852, m. Annie Isabel Findlay Sept. 28, 1874; Sarah Wilkinson b. July 8, 1854, m. Alma Peck Oct. 23, 1871; Jessie Ester b. Oct. 6, 1856, m. Horace F. Nelson Sept. 28, 1874; Maria Josephine b. Sept. 3, 1858, m. Medwin Allred May 31, 1875; Ephraim b. Jan. 4, 1861, m. Susan Nelson; Claudia Ellen b. Oct. 12, 1864, m. Seymour L. Alland June 21, 1883. Family resided Port Elizabeth, South Africa, and Fish Haven, Idaho.
Married Frances Gillison Gibbs Dec. 7, 1861, Salt Lake City (daughter of William Gillison and Charlotte King, pioneers Sept. 18, 1859, and widow of Richard Gibbs, who died Sept. 23, 1859; twin son Heber b. Nov. 1, 1858). She was born Jan. 15, 1837, Long Clauson, Leicestershire, England. Their children: Charlotte Ann b. Dec. 30, 1862, m. John T. Pope April 12, 1882; Mary Frances b. June 24, 1866, m. John Louis Gardner Oct. 22, 1884; Charles C. b. April 18, 1869, m. Sophia Thompson Aug. 30, 1893; Grace Maud b. April 24, 1870, m. Charles C. Shirley Sept. 12, 1888; John R. b. April 24, 1874, m. Charlotte Croft Galloway Sept. 11, 1895; William King b. June 6, 1876, died; Joseph P. b. Dec. 11, 1878, m. Annie J. Cottle June 7, 1902; Lydia b. Nov. 2, 1880, died. Family home Fish Haven.
Missionary to South Africa 1862-1863; bishop Fish Haven ward 1882-1893; patriarch. Postmaster Fish Haven 1868-1893. Carpenter; farmer.

STOCK, JOHN WILLIAM EDWIN (son of John Stock and Jane Adams). Born Dec. 20, 1844, Port Elizabeth, South Africa.

Married H. Henrietta Teeples Oct. 23, 1871, Salt Lake City (daughter of George B. Teeples and Huldah Colby of Holden, Utah, pioneers 1850). She was born May 1, 1852. Their children: Emma Jane b. Oct. 4, 1872; Bertha Henrietta b. Sept. 1, 1874; Alice Luella b. June 11, 1876; Edwin Ephraim b. March 15, 1879, m. Florence Bee Sept. 18, 1907; Louisa Effie b. Oct. 27, 1881, m. Abraham Tyson June 7, 1905; John William b. April 10, 1884, m. Aurelia Martineau July 1, 1911. Family home Fish Haven, Idaho.
Married Clara Victoria Olsen Oct. 10, 1894, Logan, Utah (stepdaughter of Andrus Olsen and Christina Neilsen of Sweden), who was born Aug. 12, 1874, in Sweden. Their children: Sidney Richard b. Dec. 18, 1895; Bernice Clara b. Feb. 24, 1898; Wesley Karl b. March 21, 1900; Fern Edna b. July 17, 1902; Owen Ray b. Jan. 4, 1905; Russel Blaine b. March 22, 1907; Eldon Mark b. March 9, 1909.
President of Y. M. M. I. A. 11 years; bishop's counselor 1882 to 1904; ordained bishop of Fish Haven ward 1904.

STOCK, ROBERT WALLACE (son of John Stock and Jane Adams). Born Aug. 1, 1852, Port Elizabeth, South Africa. Came to Utah with parents.
Married Annie Isabel Findlay Sept. 28, 1874, Salt Lake City (daughter of Hugh Findlay and Catherine Partington), who was born 1857, Salt Lake City. Their children: Robert Ernest b. Aug. 12, 1875, m. Annie Young 1896; Wallace Findlay b. April 13, 1878, m. Emma Hilt 1902; Catherine Isabel b. Sept. 24, 1881, m. Hyrum Michealson 1904; Harold J. b. June 2, 1884, m. May Eggleston 1905; Maud Ethel b. Oct. 4, 1887, m. Daniel Nield 1911; Lawrence Rattery b. June 24, 1892. Family home Fish Haven, Idaho, and Afton, Wyo.
High priest.

STOCK, JOHN R. (son of John Stock and Frances Gillson Gibbs). Born April 24, 1874, Fish Haven, Idaho.
Married Charlotte Croft Galloway Sept. 11, 1895 (daughter of Curtis Galloway and Harriet Annie Rowley). Their children: Reuben Galloway b. April 24, 1897; Rachel Charlotte b. May 13, 1900; Viola Frances b. Dec. 13, 1903; Heber Devine b. Feb. 20, 1911. Family home Fish Haven.

STOCK, JOSEPH P (son of John Stock and Frances Gillson Gibbs). Born Dec. 11, 1878, Fish Haven, Idaho.
Married Annie J. Cottle June 7, 1902, Logan, Idaho (daughter of Thomas E. Cottle and Flora England, pioneers 1860, Homer Duncan company). She was born Dec. 30, 1881, Plain City, Utah. Their children: La Priel b. May 7, 1903; Glenn J. b. July 23, 1906; Margery b. June 16, 1908.
President of deacons' quorum; assistant secretary Y. M. M. I. A.; Sunday school teacher. Business man and sportsman.

STOCKING, ENSIGN ISRAEL (son of John J. Stocking and Mary Ensign of England, and Springfield, Mass.). Born Sept. 6, 1837, at Springfield. Came to Utah 1850.
Married Elizabeth Ellen Arnold in 1866 at Herriman, Utah (daughter of Henry Arnold and Elizabeth James of Herefordshire, Eng., pioneers 1850). She was born June 19, 1844. Their children: Ensign, m. Isabell Shields; Mary Ellen, m. George W. Shields; John, m. Georgianne Wright; Jeremiah, m. Ellis King; Emma, m. Joseph Holt; Lucy, m. Royal Soffe; Joseph; Hyrum, m. Orvell Beckstead. Family home, Herriman.
Missionary to Great Britain 4 years; seventy; high priest. Farmer and stockraiser. Died July 11, 1883.

STOCKS, HENRY (son of Thomas Stocks of England). Born Aug. 17, 1821, Derbyshire, Eng. Came to Utah March, 1855, John S. Fullmer company.
Married Mary Halley (daughter of James Halley and Isabella Murry of Glasgow, Scotland—married 1843, in England). She was born July 21, 1820. Their children: Angus Murry b. April 12, 1844, m. Elizabeth Faubush; Moroni b. Oct. 21, 1845, m. Sarah Heward Jan. 21, 1865, m. Nancy Amanda Cahoon; Simeon Carter b. 1846; Mary b. March, 1848; Isabella; Henry Jr. b. Aug. 6, 1851, m. Murilla Draper; Louisa Jane b. Sept. 21, 1855, m. James T. Wilkins; William; Eliza Ellen b. April 30, 1862, m. George W. Terry. Family resided Salt Lake City, Manti, Gunnison and Rockland, Utah.
High priest. Farmer. Died May 25, 1911, Lewiston, Utah.

STOCKS, MORONI (son of Henry Stocks and Mary Halley). Born Oct. 21, 1845, Lancastershire, Eng. Came to Utah 1855, Milo Andrus company.
Married Sarah Heward Jan. 21, 1865, Rockville, Utah (daughter of John Heward and Elizabeth Terry, Draper, Utah, pioneers October, 1848, Zera Pulsipher company). She was born March 4, 1848, Mosquito Creek, Pottawattamie Co., Iowa. Their children: Moroni Heward b. Dec. 2, 1866, m. Flora Bright Jan. 2, 1890; Sarah Rachel b. Nov. 26, 1867, m. Albert Blair Oct. 27, 1886; Wallace Hunter b. Jan. 29, 1870, m. Emma Sandberg May, 1907; Mary Elizabeth b. June 30, 1872, m. Robert Fife April 16, 1891; Edwin Murry b. Feb. 1, 1875, m. Ella Rawlins Dec. 12, 1894; James Halley b. March 14, 1877, m. Lettie H. Thompson Jan. 4, 1905; John Carter b. April 23, 1879, m. Mary Argyle in March, 1904; Henry b. March 24, 1881, m. Vinnie Dopp Dec. 26, 1906; Luella b. June 18, 1883, m. Edward J. Watkins April 29, 1903; Williamson b. March 23, 1885, m. Maud Williamson Dec. 6, 1906; Effie b. Feb. 11, 1887, m. George Villett Jan. 16, 1907; Glenchora b. April 23, 1889, m. Rufus Pond Aug. 24, 1910; Eva b. Nov. 10, 1891, m. Zera Pond March 22, 1913.

Married Nancy Amanda Cahoon at Logan, Utah (daughter of Daniel Cahoon, born 1822, and Martha Spencer, born 1831). She was born May 21, 1848, Council Bluffs, Iowa. Only child: Charles Reynolds b. Dec. 7, 1886.

STOKES, HENRY. Came to Utah 1862, Henry Miller company.
Married Elizabeth Stokes. Among their children was Elizabeth, m. Orrin Myler.
Crossed the plains on foot to Salt Lake City; went to Mendon with his teamster, Isaac Sorenson; lived in Cache county 20 years; helped to settle the Snake River country, and lived there 30 years; now resides at Logan, Utah.

STODDARD, CHARLES (son of Curtis Stoddard, who died in Knoxville, Ill., Aug. 29, 1840, and Pamelia West, who died in Council Bluffs, Iowa, June 27, 1849). He was born May 8, 1820, Norton, Medina Co., Ohio. Came to Utah Oct. 16, 1852, Uriah Curtis company.
Married Lucetta Jane Murdock, May 27, 1843, Walnut Grove, Knox county, Ill. (daughter of John Murdock and Sophia Trask of Council Bluffs, Iowa, pioneers 1852, Uriah Curtis company). She was born Aug. 2, 1814, and died in September, 1886. Their children: Curtis Charles b. March 17, 1844, m. Mary Ann Hardy Jan. 1, 1866; Marian Eliza b. Aug. 20, 1847, m. George Franklin Stoddard; Hyrum Franklin b. Nov. 29, 1849, m. Alice Wise. m. Eva Cleveland; John Francis b. Sept. 14, 1852, m. Isidara Belnap. Family home Uinta. Weber Co., Utah.
Elder. School trustee; justice of peace. Water master; farmer. Died April 29, 1891.

STODDARD, CURTIS CHARLES (son of Charles Stoddard and Lucetta Jane Murdock). Born March 17, 1844, Walnut Grove, Knox county, Ill. Came to Utah with parents.
Married Mary Ann Hardy Jan. 1, 1866, Uinta, Weber Co., Utah (daughter of Zachariah Hardy, Council Bluffs, Iowa, who died in Nauvoo July 20, 1846, and Eliza Philbrook, pioneer 1852, Benjamin Gardner's company). She was born Feb. 8, 1846. Their children: Curtis Charles Jr. b. Aug. 6, 1865, m. Margret Valentine Robinson April 5, 1890; William Henry b. Jan. 29, 1868, m. Mariah Farrow July 27, 1889; Hyrum Franklin b. March 25, 1870; Joseph Francis b. March 21, 1872, m. Margret V. Stoddard April 10, 1903; John Warren b. Sept. 21, 1875, m. May Wadsworth Oct. 31, 1902; Mary Lucetta b. March 24, 1878, m. Biran Bybee May 20, 1903; Eliza Jane b. Sept. 28, 1881, m. Birtie Wadsworth Aug. 1, 1903; Thomas Parley b. June 23, 1883, d. Feb. 11, 1884; Orson Pratt b. April 1, 1885, m. Alice Wadsworth Oct. 27, 1904; Wilford David b. April 3, 1888; Lymond b. March 17, 1891. Family home, Uinta.
Bishop's counselor; home missionary. School trustee; constable.

STODDARD, CHARLES HENRY (son of Israel Stoddard and Sarah Woodward, of Nauvoo, Ill., and Philadelphia, Pa.). Born April 21, 1827, Newark, N. J. Came to Utah in 1851, Harry Walton company.
Married Anna Telford Feb. 22, 1851, Bountiful, Utah (daughter of John and Jane Telford, of Nauvoo, pioneers 1851, Harry Walton company). She was born Nov. 22, 1827. Their children: George Henry b. Oct. 25, 1852, m. Hannah E. Bowman Jan. 19, 1874; John Robert, m. Agnes Sessions Sept. 26, 1876; Charles Witt, m. Alice Weaver; William Israel, m. Fannie Gibbs; Mary Rebecca, m. Brigham A. Hendricks; Jane Telford, m. Hyrum Leavitt; Joseph Smith, m. Susan E. Thomas; Anna Victora, m. Charles E. Merrill. Family resided Bountiful and Richmond, Utah.
Married Matilda Ann Duncan 1858, Salt Lake City (daughter of James and Hulda Duncan of Bountiful), who was born in 1838. Their children: Sarah Hulda, m. Edward Thomas; James Duncan, m. Genebra Curtice; Susan E., m. James Wood.
Member 9th quorum seventies; missionary in San Pete county 1852-53; acting ward teacher; bodyguard of Brigham Young. Carried food and messages to and from Prophet Joseph Smith, while in hiding, during the trouble in Nauvoo. Took part in Echo Canyon campaign; veteran Indian war. Farmer and thresher. Died Sept. 2, 1907, Richmond.

STODDARD, GEORGE HENRY (son of Charles Henry Stoddard and Anna Telford). Born Oct. 25, 1852, Bountiful, Utah.
Married Hannah E. Bowman Jan. 19, 1874, Salt Lake City (daughter of Hyrum W. Bowman and Hannah Wilson of Richmond), who was born Oct. 19, 1855. Their children: Hannah Rebecca b. Dec. 1874, m. Edwin L. Larson; Anna Victora b. May 19, 1876, m. Carl A. Olson; William Henry b. Nov. 13, 1880, m. Cathrine Coffin; Flossie Dean b. Feb. 12, 1882, died; Joseph Duncan b. Aug. 10, 1884, m. Maud E. Fox; George Brigham b. Oct. 5, 1885, m. Grace Van Leuven; John Telford b. Jan. 9, 1887, m. Edna Crockett; Jennie Vene b. June 23, 1889, m. Charles A. Royter; Charles b. Nov. 18, 1891; Mary; Edith, died. Family home Richmond, Utah.
High priest; ward teacher. Farmer.

STODDARD, WILLIAM HENRY (son of George Henry Stoddard and Hannah E. Bowman). Born Nov. 13, 1880, Richmond, Utah.
Married Cathrine Coffin Aug. 29, 1901, Pocatello, Idaho

PIONEERS AND PROMINENT MEN OF UTAH 1191

(daughter of William Coffin and Sephrona Hunt of Cambridge, Idaho), who was born July 5, 1882. Their children: Telford S. b. July 7, 1902; Estella M. b. Nov. 22, 1903; Leone S. b. Sept. 11, 1905; George H. b. Sept. 2, 1907; Roscoe b. April 25, 1909; David W. b. Aug. 11, 1911. Family home Grant, Idaho.
Bishop's counselor. Farmer.

STODDARD, JUDSON LYMAN (son of Lyman Stoddard). Born April 13, 1823, at Bastard, Canada. Came to Utah 1848, Brigham Young company.
Married Rhoda Chase in Kirtland, Utah (daughter of Issac Chase, pioneer 1848). She was born Sept. 29, 1830. Their children: Judson Lyman Jr.; Marion L.; Elanthropy; Lewis Arden. Family home Farmington, Utah.
Veteran Black Hawk Indian war; brought first news to Brigham Young of coming of Johnston's army. County attorney 1858. Died Jan. 10, 1869.

STODDARD, JUDSON LYMAN (son of Judson Lyman Stoddard and Rhoda Chase). Born May 22, 1849, Salt Lake City. Married Alice Cottrell Jan. 1, 1869, Farmington, Utah (daughter of Samuel Cottrell and Elenor Taylor of Farmington, pioneers 1853), who was born Feb. 5, 1851. Their children: Judson H. b. Oct. 24, 1869; Samuel b. Sept. 6, 1871; Alice Lena b. Nov. 14, 1873; Rhoda H. b. Jan. 28, 1875; Chloe b. Oct. 3, 1878; Sheldon U. b. Nov. 14, 1882; Elias b. July 27, 1885; Phoebe A. b. Aug. 19, 1893; Clara b. Oct. 24, 1897. Family home, Farmington.
Member 84th quorum seventies; missionary to Montana 1898. Farmer.

STOKER, JOHN (son of John Stoker, of Doncaster, Yorkshire, Eng., who was born June 15, 1815). Born Aug. 4, 1856, Doncaster, Yorkshire, Eng. Came to Utah August, 1893.
Married Clara Swaby Aug. 4, 1882, Normanton, Eng. (daughter of George Swaby and Elizabeth Bean Swaby). Their children: John William, m. Ruby Davis; Harry S., m. Janette Gilchrist; Dorothy E., m. Hanmer J. White; Olive M., m. Ebben R. Speer; Clara L. Family home Lehi, Utah.
Ordained bishop of Lehi fourth ward 1903. Lehi city treasurer, 1909-1911. Farmer.

STOKER, WILLIAM (son of David Stoker and Barbara Graybill of Ohio). Born March 26, 1819, in Jackson Co., Ohio. Came to Utah in 1852, Isaac Stewart company.
Married Almira Winegar 1838, in Missouri (daughter of Samuel Winegar and Rhoda Cummins of Palmyra and Spanish Fork, Utah, pioneers 1852, Isaac Stewart company). She was born Feb. 27, 1818. Their children: Samuel D., m. Elizabeth Jones; William A., m. Martha Larsen; Susan A., m. Thomas Riley; Michael, m. Almira J. Wilson; Sarah, d. infant; Emily J., m. Robert M. Boyack; Almira, m. Warren E. Davis; John S., m. Mary E. West. Family home Spanish Fork, Utah.
President 50th quorum seventies 20 years. City councilman two terms. Farmer. Died May 19, 1892.

STOKES, CHRISTOPHER (son of John Stokes and Rachel Rogers of Trowbridge, Wiltshire, Eng.). Born Dec. 19, 1830, at Trowbridge. Came to Utah 1853, John Daily company, which brought paper for "Deseret News."
Married Rosella Nebeker Nov. 4, 1864. Salt Lake City (daughter of John Nebeker and Lurena Fitzgerald of Vermilion county, Ill., pioneers Sept. 26, 1847, George B. Wallace company). She was born Oct. 3, 1845, and came to Utah with parents. Family home, Salt Lake City.
High priest; elder; block teacher; missionary to Ireland, 1552-53. Veteran Echo Canyon campaign with militia. Freighter, worked at the Godbe Pitts Drug Co. 17 years.

STOKES, JEREMIAH (son of William and Elizabeth Stokes, Heath, Eng.). He was born Nov. 9, 1819, Bolsover, Derbyshire, Eng. Came to Utah 1859, James Brown company.
Married Fanny Walker in 1836, Bolsover, Eng. (daughter of Robert and Elizabeth, who came to Utah with husband). She was born March 15, 1819. Their children: Robert, m. Ann Wilson; John, died; Thomas, m. Ellen L. Canfield; Elizabeth; Tamer, m. Robert Rawlins of Wiltshire, Eng.; and Eliza-infant; Jeremiah, m. Josephine Olsen; Fanny; Alvin Sylvester, d. infant; Sarah Ann, m. Lewis Andrus. Family home Draper, Utah.
Member high priests quorum seventies; president lesser priesthood at Draper. Farmer. Died July 1, 1875.

STOKES, THOMAS (son of Jeremiah Stokes and Fanny Walker). Born Nov. 13, 1842, at Belsover, Eng.). Came to Utah Aug. 29, 1859, James Brown company.
Married Ellen L. Canfield Sept. 6, 1870, Salt Lake City (daughter of Cyrus C. Canfield and Clarissa L. Jones, former pioneer, contingent Mormon Battalion 1849; latter with Heber C. Kimball's company, 1848). She was born September 2, 1850. Their children: Thomas Justin b. Sept. 6, 1871; Clara Viola, b. Jan. 28, 1873; Eugene Canfield b. Oct.

14, 1874; Fanny Mellissa b. Aug. 8, 1877; last four died; Royal Wells b. May 4, 1879, m. Mary Boberg; Joseph Franklin b. Sept. 5, 1881, m. Sadie Jenkins; Marie Louisa b. Jan. 15, 1884, m. Howard Phelp; Archibald Legrand b. July 24, 1886, m. Mary Heward; Marcus Albert b. Nov. 1, 1888, m. Florence Meyers; Orson Arnold b. June 5, 1890; Bertha Anetta b. Feb. 19, 1893. Family home Draper, Utah.
Member 73rd quorum seventies; missionary to England 1905; high priest; superintendent Draper Sunday school 1906-08. Veteran Black Hawk war. Assisted immigration to Utah 1866. Farmer.

STONE, JOSEPH ADAMS (son of Calvin Gideon Stone and Jane Elizabeth King, Pilot Mountain, Surry county, N. C.). Born Nov. 30, 1853, at Pilot Mountain. Came to Utah 1873, independent company.
Married Phoebe Belinda Taylor Oct. 15, 1871, Surry county, N. C. (daughter of James Taylor and Nancy Hiatt, who came to Utah 1873, independent company). She was born May 1, 1854. Their children: Nancy Jane, m. Henry Sabin; Charles Walter, Daisy M. Gardner; Joseph Oliver, m. Emma Christena Larson; James Calvin, m. Lucy Dredge Roberts; Robert Henderson, m. Lillian Allred; Effie Ann, m. James Christensen; Maggie Angeline, m. Frank Jones; Wesley Ervin.
Married Mary Johnson March 12, 1902, Salt Lake City, Utah (daughter of Ole C. and Nellie Johnson, of Berg, Norway, came to Utah September, 1878, independent company). She was born April 25, 1884. Their children: Lynn Adams; Zella May; Nora Mary. Families resided Salem, Utah.
Married Caroline Augusta Johnson Jan. 11, 1893, Manti, Utah (daughter of Nellie Larsen, Berg, Norway; came to Utah September, 1878, independent company). She was born May 10, 1870. Their children: Phebe Minerva; Nellie Elizabeth; Laura Augusta; Louisa Viola.
Member seventies; missionary to southern states 1899-1900. Ward teacher; school trustee. Director canal board; member Salem town board. Farmer and fruit grower.

STONE, JOSEPH OLIVER (son of Joseph Adams Stone and Phoebe Belinda Taylor). Born Nov. 7, 1876, Salem, Utah.
Married Emma Christena Larson Jan. 19, 1898, Salt Lake City (daughter of Niels Larson and Bangta Flygare, latter pioneer 1862). Born July 21, 1875. Their children: Arvil Oliver b. Nov. 20, 1898; Clonide Morris b. May 4, 1902; Harry Melvin b. March 7, 1905. Family home Vineyard, Utah Co., Utah.
Bishop's counselor; superintendent Sunday school; bishop; ward clerk; president M. I. A. Corporal Idaho National Guards. School trustee. President Union Dairy Co. and Vineyard Amusement Co.

STONE, AMOS PEASE (son of Amos Sheldon Stone, born July 21, 1777, North Madison, Conn., died Nov. 28, 1836, Stockbridge, Mass., and Rachel Pease, born Sept. 9, 1780, Canaan, Columbia county, N. Y., died May 17, 1851, Richmond, Mass., married April 19, 1801, at Canaan). Born March 18, 1815, Canaan, N. Y. Came to Utah Sept. 30, 1850, Joseph Young company.
Married Amelia Bishop March 30, 1838, North Haven, Conn. (daughter of Azariah Bishop, born April 20, 1783, died Feb. 23, 1884, at North Haven, Conn., and Content Blakeslee, born Sept. 24, 1793, died Dec. 20, 1848, at North Haven, married April 2, 1809). She was born June 19, 1819, North Haven, Conn., died Dec. 29, 1845, at New Haven. Their children: Emily Amelia b. Jan. 4, 1839, m. Newton Tuttle April 7, 1855; Charles Amos b. Dec. 27, 1840, d. March 24, 1842; Harman b. July 3, 1843, d. Jan. 13, 1844; Merab b. Sept. 26, 1845, m. Thomas Richardson 1864.
Married Minerva Leantine Jones Feb. 1, 1846, Hamden, Conn. (daughter of Merlin Jones, born May 16, 1795, North Haven, Conn., died Dec. 4, 1879, Ogden, Utah, and Roxana Ives, born April 17, 1799, at Wallingford, Conn., died Aug. 5, 1866, at Ogden, married Aug. 17, 1820, at Wallingford; former, pioneer 1852). She was born June 4, 1822, at Wallingford, and died Aug. 17, 1867, at Ogden. Their children: Olive Ann b. April 8, 1847, m. Joseph Parry Nov. 20, 1866; Amos Ives b. Sept. 1, 1849, m. Emilar Webb Nov. 26, 1876; Minerva Pease b. Nov. 29, 1851, m. Ambrose Shaw Jan. 1, 1875; Merlin Jones b. Nov. 26, 1853, m. Maria Baker Jan. 17, 1878; Cordelia Hotchkiss b. May 21, 1856, d. Feb. 15, 1858; Sylvia b. July 11, 1859, m. Irvin T. Alvord Nov. 18, 1885; Friend b. Jan. 5, 1862, (d. Sept. 25, 1907), m. Josephine Johnson April 29, 1883; Vincy Rice b. Jan. 16, 1864, m. James John Barker May 16, 1888.
Married Dinah Rawlins Dec. 31, 1852, Salt Lake City (daughter of Robert Rawlins of Wiltshire, Eng., and Elizabeth Moody, born Feb. 14, 1877, at Lanford, Wiltshire). She was born July 26, 1816, in Wiltshire, and died May 28, 1893, at Ogden, Utah. Their children: Elizabeth b. Sept. 27, 1855, m. David M. Moore Dec. 3, 1871; Julia Ann b. Oct. 16, 1855, d. May 7, 1858; Lewis Pease b. Nov. 13, 1857, m. Amelia L. Smith Feb. 14, 1881.
Married Sarah Spencer Sept. 18, 1865, Salt Lake City (daughter of John Spencer, born May 7, 1810, Whittlebury, and died Sept. 16, 1887, Stanion, Northamptonshire, Eng., and Sarah Chapman, born Nov. 19, 1818, and died 1888, at Bridgstock, Eng.). She was born Dec. 8, 1844, Stanion, Eng., and came to Utah Oct. 4, 1863, John W. Woolley company. Their children: Laura Jane b. April 13, 1867, m. Henry Tribe, June, 1897; Bernard Spencer b. Sept. 3, 1869, m. Mary Maria Newman Oct. 12, 1896; Clarence John b.

July 1, 1872, m. Edith Rolstone Burt August, 1897; Matilda May b. Sept. 6, 1875, d. June 16, 1877. Family home Ogden, Utah.
Settled at Bountiful 1850, moved to Ogden 1857. First president of the Mound Fort ward at Ogden. Blacksmith; farmer and fruitgrower. Died March 17, 1890.

STONE, BERNARD SPENCER (son of Amos Pease Stone and Sarah Spencer). Born Sept. 3, 1869, Ogden, Utah.
Married Mary Maria Newman Oct. 12, 1896, Salt Lake City (daughter of Henry James Newman, born July 22, 1853, in London, Eng., and Josephine Brown, born Jan. 8, 1858, Ogden, Utah; pioneers Nov. 9, 1856, Abraham O. Smoot company). She was born Jan. 1, 1877, Ogden, Utah. Their children: Grace b. May 12, 1900; Hazel May b. Jan. 12, 1903; Bernard Amos b. July 5, 1911. Family home Ogden, Utah.
Wholesale and retail dealer in coal and ice.

STONE, WILLIAM GILLARD (son of John Stone and Anna D. Gillard. Castlecary, Somersetshire, Eng.). Born Jan. 29, 1821, Castlecary. Came to Utah Sept. 15, 1866, William Henry Chipman company.
Married Jane Stride May 15, 1841, Castlecary, Eng. (daughter of Samuel Stride and Jane Rochester of Ditchet, Somersetshire, Eng.). Their children: William Sidney b. Jan. 21, 1842, m. Emma Biddle; Mary Jane b. Dec. 27, 1844, m. Joseph H. Gough; Henry John b. Dec. 15, 1846, m. Larson Louisa Stratton; Samuel Seth b. April 20, 1849, m. Alice Wiscome; Joseph Paul b. Dec. 2, 1851, m. Mary Kilburn; Edgar Dewer b. April 8, 1855, m. Ann Eliza Gale; Nephi Napper b. March 6, 1858, d. May 8, 1860; Cyrus Herbert b. Jan. 21, 1861, m. Augusta E. Peterson; Frederick G. b. Sept. 10, 1865, m. Hester Hutchings. Family resided at Salt Lake City and Ogden, Utah.
Worked on first railway coming to Utah. Carpenter and foundryman.

STONE, HENRY JOHN (son of William Gillard Stone and Jane Stride). Born Dec. 15, 1846, Bristol, Eng., pioneers Oct. 4, 1853, Edward Woolley company.
Married Susan Louisa Stratton March 22, 1868 (daughter of James Stratton and Frances Clarke, Salt Lake City, pioneers 1852). She was born March 21, 1853. Their children: Louisa Jane b. Dec. 3, 1868, d. Dec. 16, 1868; William Henry b. Nov. 17, 1869, m. Cora Wardle Dec. 18, 1892; Effie May b. May 19, 1872, m. A. C. Emert July 6, 1893; Sidney b. April 16, 1874, d. April 26, 1874; James Fredrick b. April 11, 1875, m. Bessie Smith 1897; John Franklyn b. March 21, 1877, m. Mabel T. Crandell; Wallace Birt b. May 2, 1879, m. Julia R. Walton Jan. 12, 1892; George Edgar b. March 15, 1882; Joseph Orrin b. Jan. 8, 1885, d. June 25, 1885; Ernest b. Oct. 22, 1886; Nellie Grace b. Dec. 11, 1888, m. Marion LaFayette Harris Dec. 24, 1907; Mary Edna b. March 13, 1891; Olive b. April 16, 1893; David Ray b. Sept. 27, 1895; Cora b. Sept. 27, 1897.
Sunday school superintendent 14 years; member of bishopric; high councilman. Justice of peace.

STORRS, GEORGE (son of Joseph Storrs, born January, 1799, and Mary Scott, born 1800, of Yorkshire, Eng.). Born Jan. 31, 1825, Missen, Yorkshire, Eng. Baptized April 19, 1849, by Henry Stevenson at Skelio, Eng. Came to Utah October, 1851, J. W. Cummings company on ship, and Ernest Bates company crossing plains.
Married Eliza Fincher Layton August, 1852.
Married Lydia Mary Kindred June 29, 1861, Salt Lake City (daughter of Edmond Henry Harriet Kindred, of Farthingham, Suffolk, Eng., pioneers Oct. 24, 1855, Milo Andrus company). She was born April 11, 1844. Their children: George A. b. July 5, 1863, m. Sarah Corcelia Oakley; Lydia Amelia b. September, 1864, died; Lavina b. Jan. 10, 1866, m. Spicer W. Bird; Joseph Henry b. Aug. 25, 1867, m. Rosella Arvilla Harrison; John Wallace b. June 25, 1869, m. Prunella Roylance; Lillian b. May 8, 1871, d. aged 8; William Scott b. May 10, 1873, m. Julia Kirkman; Eliza May b. Sept. 4, 1875; Harriett Luella b. Jan. 4, 1877; Charles Arthur b. Dec. 29, 1879, m. Almeda Stringham; Mary, d. infant. Family home Springville, Utah.
President seventies at Springville; high priest; Sunday school and ward teacher. Settled at Springville 1855. Miller. Died Sept. 1, 1901, American Fork, Utah.

STORRS, JOSEPH HENRY (son of George Storrs and Lydia Mary Kindred). Born Aug. 25, 1867, Springville, Utah.
Married Rosella Arvilla Harrison Oct. 24, 1888, Mantl, Utah (daughter of George Harrison and Rosella Damon White, of Springville, Utah). She was born Oct. 20, 1867. Their children: Joseph" Bertrand b. April 12, 1891; Rosella b. Sept. 20, 1892; Duane b. June 6, 1895, died; Norven Lloyd b. Feb. 3, 1898; Myrie b. Nov. 17, 1899; Wilford Leon b. March 21, 1904; Betha b. Jan. 21, 1909. Family home American Fork, Utah.
Bishop of 2d ward American Fork; president Y. M. M. I. A., Springville, Utah, 1892-98, and of American Fork 1900-01, Springville city councilman; secretary and treasurer of Springville six years; superintendent Co-op. and director of Peoples State Bank, American Fork; director Belgium horse association.

STORRS, JOHN WALLACE (son of George Storrs and Lydia Mary Kindred). Born June 25, 1869, Springville, Utah.

Married Prunella Roylance Oct. 13, 1889, Provo, Utah (daughter of Henry Roylance and Elizabeth Bell, of Springville). She was born Nov. 10, 1869. Their children: Wallace Glen b. March 8, 1891; Mabel b. Sept. 4, 1893; Lawrence Edmond b. Feb. 12, 1895; Norman b. July 6, 1901. Family home American Fork, Utah.
Priest; block teacher. American Fork city recorder 1905-06; manager Studebaker Bros. Company, of American Fork, 1905-13; secretary of American Fork Commercial Club 1905-10. Railroad station agent and telegrapher 1905-06.

STOTT, WILLIAM (son of John and Susan Stott of Greenacres, Lancastershire, Eng.). Born April 15, 1803, Soyland, Yorkshire, Eng. Came to Utah October, 1852, Isaac Bullock company.
Married Sarah Lees 1823, Yorkshire (daughter of James and Sarah Lees of Rushworth, Yorkshire), who was born Aug. 23, 1800. Their children: Hannah Lees, m. James Fisher; James, d. young; William Henry, m. Alice Nield, m. Hannah Nield; Thomas Fenton. d. infant; Edwin, m. Sarah Jane Holden, m. Elizabeth Paul; Emma, m. Isaac Bullock. Family home Meadow, Utah.
High priest. Member first city council of Fillmore. Farmer. Died Nov. 3, 1883.

STOTT, EDWIN (son of William Stott and Sarah Lees). Born Nov. 5, 1836, Greenacres. Lancastershire, Eng. Came to Utah October, 1852, Isaac Bullock company.
Married Sarah Jane Holden November, 1863, Fillmore, Utah, who was born August, 1846. Their children: Mary Elizabeth b. Oct. 5, 1864, m. John A. Beckstrand; Sarah Jane b. Sept. 2, 1866, m. William Clayton Partridge; Edwin b. May 11, 1869, m. Isabelle Stewart; Raymond b. Aug. 23, 1872, m. Georgie Stewart.
Married Elizabeth Paul Feb. 18, 1876, Salt Lake City (daughter of Nicholas Paul and Harriet May of Holden, Utah, pioneers October, 1860, Oscar Stoddard company). She was born Nov. 3, 1851. Their children: Paul Edward b. December, 1875, m. Elizabeth A. Robison; Arthur Lees b. May 10, 1878; Evelyn May b. Nov. 7, 1880; Amy Laura b. April 15, 1884; William Edwin b. Sept. 10, 1887; Mabel Ann b. Sept. 10, 1891. Family home Meadow, Utah.
Member 43d quorum seventies: superintendent Sunday school at Meadow, 10 years. Veteran Indian war. Farmer. Called to Missouri River 1864, to take charge of cattle of incoming immigration.

STOUT, ALLEN JOSEPH (son of Joseph Stout and Anna Smith, of North Carolina). Born Dec. 5, 1815, Mercer, Ky. Came to Utah 1851, Alfred Cardon company.
Married Elizabeth Anderson July 19, 1843.
Married Amanda Melvina Fisk April 30, 1848, Winter Quarters, Nebraska (daughter of Alfred Fisk and Mariah Sagers of Kirtland, Ohio). She was born June 12, 1832. Their children: Lydia Maria, m. Norman I. Bliss; Hosea F., m. Martha Sherrell, m. Clarinda Langston; Rebecca A., m. John Dennett; Amanda. m. Lewis Stout; Orlando F., died; Don Carlos, died; Huldah L., m. Nathan Terry, m. Charles Rawlinson; Anna S., died; Marion F., m. Caroline Larson, m. Mary Crawford; Alfred Fisk, m. Mary E. Langston; David F., m. Henrietta Sadie; m. Julia Cox; m. Mary J. Terry; Allen J., m. Sarah Ann Sullivan; John H., m. Anna S. Hall; Milton F., m. Adelaide Smith. Family home Rockville, Utah.
Member 19th quorum seventies. Bodyguard of Joseph Smith and Brigham Young. Aide-de-camp in Nauvoo Legion. Farmer. Died Dec. 18, 1889.

STOUT, ALFRED FISK (son of Allen Joseph Stout and Amanda Melvina Fisk). Born March 9, 1851, Kanesville, Iowa.
Married Mary Emma Langston March 7, 1872, Rockville, Utah (daughter of John Langston and Clearinda Phillips of Missouri, pioneers 1854). She was born Feb. 15, 1859. Their children: Mary Clearinda b. Sept. 12, 1873, m. Henry Hirschi; Martha and Dorthay (twins) b. March 21, 1875, died; Alfred Fisk Jr. b. Nov. 1, 1876, m. Dora M. M. Hall; Louisa Melvina b. Aug. 28, 1879, died; Anna Laura b. April 14, 1881, m. Philetus D. Jones; Minerva b. March 16, 1884, died; Lionel Langston b. June 22, 1886, died; Elmer b. March 22, 1889; Sylvia b. Jan. 11, 1892, m. Richard R. Carey; Ernest Franklin b. July 24, 1894, m. Clothiel Free; Victor b. Dec. 27, 1896, died; Clinton Tracy b. Feb. 23, 1899; Homer Bryan b. Jan. 29, 1901; Hosea Afton b. Nov. 7, 1903. Family home Rockville, Utah.
Elder. School trustee and deputy constable. Lumberman.

STOUT, ALFRED FISK JR. (son of Alfred Fisk Stout and Mary Emma Langston). Born Nov. 1, 1876, Rockville, Utah.
Married Dora M. Hall March 24, 1898, St. George, Utah (daughter of John C. Hall and Keziah DeGrey of England, pioneers August, 1857, Jesse B. Martin company). She was born Jan. 8, 1878. Their children: Myron b. June 28, 1903; Erma b. 1908; Verle b. Oct. 7, 1911, died; Baby b. March 7, 1913. Family home Hurricane, Utah.
Elder; ward teacher and chorister. Carpenter.

STOWELL, WILLIAM RUFUS RODGER (son of Augustus Stowell, Chautauqua county, N. Y.). Born in Chautauqua, N. Y. Came to Utah 1852, oxteam company.
Married Hannah Toppins, Salt Lake City, Utah.

Married Cynthia Jane Parks, Salt Lake City. Their children: Brigham, m. Olive Bybee; Amanda, m. Myron Butler; Maranda, m. Myron Butler; Rufus, d. aged 2; Heber John, m. Ellen Lavenia Thompson; Matilda, m. Myron Butler; Cynthia, m. James Pingree; Francis. Family home Provo, Utah.
Married Sophrona Kelley, Salt Lake City, Utah. Their children: Elvira, m. William Wallace; Martha, m. John Hill; Mariah, m. Evan Evans; David, m. Ruth Birch; Alexander, m. Ellen Dalton; Mary, m. Joseph Jackson.
Married Harriet Stowell, Salt Lake City, Utah. Their children: Louisa, m. Alburn Allen; Ephraim; Harriet, m. Mr. Hyde; William Barnum, m. Merril Session; George, d. infant; Israel, d. aged 4; Jeanette; Vesta, m. Mr. Kingston. Families resided Ogden, Utah.
Seventy; Sunday school superintendent many years. Veteran Echo Canyon and Black Hawk wars. Farmer. Died 1901, at Juarez, Utah.

STOWELL, HEBER JOHN (son of William Rufus Rodger Stowell and Cynthia Jane Parks). Born July 14, 1860, Ogden, Utah.
Married Ellen Lavenia Thompson Feb. 8, 1888, Manti, Utah (daughter of William Henry Thompson and Jane Frisby of Birmingham, Eng.; came to Utah 1883). She was born April 13, 1869. Their children: Stella Lavenia b. Feb. 8, 1889, d. June 12, 1891; Clarence Heber b. March 8, 1891, d. Oct. 19, 1904; Mabel Viola b. Dec. 28, 1893; Eston Earl b. Jan. 25, 1896; Urbon Elmo b. Dec. 2, 1898; Gardie Elizabeth b. Dec. 2, 1900; Elvin James b. Feb. 26, 1902; Cynthia Ellen b. Jan. 5, 1904; Dell Clifton b. March 5, 1906; Gladys Jane b. April 4, 1908; John Arthur b. July 15, 1910. Family home Spring Glen, Utah.
Elder; seventy; high priest; bishop, Spring Glen, Utah. School trustee; justice of peace, Carbonville, Utah. Farmer; coal miner. Died Spring Glen, Utah.

STRADLING, WILLIAM (son of Obadiah Stradling and Martha Shadrick, of Wellington, Eng.). Born Sept. 10, 1824, at Wellington. Came to Utah 1854, oxteam company.
Married Sophia Bush October, 1856, Pleasant Grove, Utah (daughter of James Bush and Sophia Humphries, of Pleasant Grove), who was born May 10, 1831. Their children: Mary Ann, m. George E. Cook; Selener, m. Arthur Marott; Albert. and John Henry, died; Joseph O., m. Sina Thompson; Sarah Ann, m. Albert A. Haws; Rose Vilate, m. Arba Lambson; James William, died; Ephraim, m. Elizabeth J. Williams; Susie, m. Soren Thompson; Owen, died. Family home Provo, Utah.
Member 77th quorum seventies; missionary to St. Johns, Ariz., 1880-90; high priest. Farmer.

STRATFORD, EDWIN (son of George Stratford, born Nov. 7, 1807, and Eliza Barwell, born Oct. 5, 1809, of Malden, Eng.). He was born Feb. 6, 1833, at Malden. Came to Utah Sept. 15, 1861, Homer Duncan company.
Married Marianna Crabb Dec. 25, 1855, Chelmsford, Essex, Eng. (daughter of Jesse Crabb and Ann Chapman), who was born Dec. 6, 1831, and came to Utah with husband. Their children: Edwin A. b. Oct. 17, 1856, m. Mary M. Coates Bergstrom Feb. 6, 1879; Eliza A. b. Jan. 23, 1859, m. John P. Smith July 1878; Jesse G. b. May 4, 1861, m. Roseltha Ballantyne; Charles H. b. Sept. 17, 1863, m. Ida Lynham; Francis W. b. Dec. 6, 1865, m. Lizzie Farley; Lilliam M. b. Feb. 26, 1868, m. Peter H. Baird; Albert E. b. Jan. 6, 1870, m. Georgie Chandler; Egbert C. b. March 10, 1872, m. Edna P. Eldredge; Horace B. b. Aug. 1, 1875, m. Kate Haines. Family resided Farmington, Providence and Ogden, Utah.
Bishop, fourth ward, Ogden, 20 years. Member of legislature; city councilman, Ogden. President board trustees, school for deaf and blind. Furniture dealer. Died Oct. 1, 1899, at Ogden.

STRATFORD, EDWIN A. (son of Edwin Stratford and Marianna Crabb). Born Oct. 17, 1856, Tarrytown, N. Y. Came to Utah with parents.
Married Mary M. Coates Bergstrom Feb. 6, 1879, Salt Lake City (daughter of Andrew and Isabella Coates of Port Glasgow, Scotland, pioneers Sept. 10, 1863, William B. Preston company), who was born Sept. 6, 1860. Their children: Ethel I. Stratford b. Dec. 9, 1879, m. J. D. Skeen; Earl A. b. Feb. 2, 1883, m. Mina Parry; Alfred E. b. Aug. 29, 1886; Howard J. b. Jan. 6, 1891; Mary M. b. Aug. 26, 1896; Edmund Carl b. March 20, 1899. Family resided Farmington, Logan, Providence, and Ogden, Utah.
Missionary to Great Britain 1891 to 1893. Conducted collection agency.

STRATFORD, FRANCIS WILLIAM (son of Edwin Stratford and Marianna Crabb). Born Dec. 6, 1865, Providence, Utah.
Married Lizzie Farley Oct. 20, 1885, Logan, Utah (daughter of Winthrop Farley and Mary Hastings of Ogden, Utah, pioneers 1850, latter died Feb. 20, 1891). She was born March 3, 1866. Their children: Francis W. b. Feb. 14, 1891, m. Albert Bingham; Francis W. b. Feb. 14, 1891.
Married Minnie Clara Battle May 31, 1893, Manti, Utah (daughter of George W. Battle and Olive Baker, of Wilson Lane, Ogden, Utah, came from Georgia to Utah 1888). She was born Oct. 13, 1874. Their children: George Edwin b. March 20, 1894, m. Melva Olson; William Eugene b. Feb. 29, 1896; Lizzie Olive b. Dec. 2, 1899.

Member 77th quorum seventies; missionary to southern states 1886-88; high priest; 2d counselor to bishop John Rockham of Wilson ward, 6 years; bishop of Wilson ward 2 years; 2d counselor to President James Wotherspoon of North Weber stake. Water commissioner 4 years. Chairman of county board of education ten years. Farmer and merchant.

STRATTON, ANTHONY JOHNSON (son of Calvin Stratton and Gabrilla Johnson, both supposedly of Pottawattamie Co., Iowa). Born Jan. 11, 1824, Bedford county, Tenn. Came to Utah 1849, believed to have come in Captain Smoot company.
Married Martha Jane Layne April 3, 1845, in Hancock county, Ill. (daughter of David Layne and Lucinda Biby—probably of Kentucky), who was born July 26, 1827. Their children: Emeline, died; Martha Jane, died; Gabrilla, m. William Wesley Willis, Jr.; Mary, died; Rozilpha; Anthony Wayne, died; Lucinda. died; Calvin Layne; William Ellis; Ja Marion; Artemisia. Family home Salt Lake City, Utmes
Bishop's counselor at Virgin City, Utah; school teacher; 1st lieutenant, Company C, Battalion of Infantry. Farmer. Died Nov. 29, 1887, Snowflake, Ariz.

STRATTON, WILLIAM ELLIS (son of Anthony Johnson Stratton and Martha Jane Layne). Born Jan. 28, 1862, Virgin City, Utah.
Married Minnie Kartchner Oct. 20, 1886, St. George, Utah (daughter of William D. Kartchner and Elizabeth Gale, of Snowflake, Ariz.), who was born Dec. 26, 1870. Their children: Mabel b. Feb. 16, 1888; Zella b. March 25, 1890; William Raymond b. March 24, 1892; Leo Wayne b. March 11, 1894, died; Lena b. Sept. 18, 1895; Minnie and Vinnie b. May 27, 1898, both died; Mary b. March 25, 1902; Elsie b. April 11, 1904, died: Irene b. March 18, 1907; Lorum Ellis b. March 22, 1910; Leona b. Sept. 18, 1912.
Member 33d quorum seventies; missionary to southern states 1899-01. Farmer and stockraiser.

STRATTON, EDWARD (son of Samuel Bailey Stratton, born Aug. 10, 1781, Somersetshire, Eng., and Ann Stratton, born Aug. 3, 1789, Westwood, Wiltshire, Eng.) He was born March 10, 1831, Freshford, Somersetshire. Came to Utah Sept. 29, 1853, Moses Daly company.
Married Adele DeSaules June 21, 1863 (daughter of Fredrick Louis and Adele DeSaules), who was born June 21, 1847, and came to Utah 1859. Their children: John b. Aug. 28, 1864, d. Oct. 14, 1864; Edward b. Jan. 2, 1867, drowned May, 1871; William b. Aug. 22, 1870, m. Sarah Firth May 2, 1895; A. b. Jan. 5, 1873, m. Adam Aranthon Bingham Nov. 14, 1889; Elizabeth b. Aug. 4, 1874, m. Jesse A. Child Oct. 21, 1891; Adele b. May 18, 1878, m. John B. Fife December, 1897; Sophia b. June 3, 1880, m. S. James Bingham June 26, 1901. Family home Riverdale, Weber Co., Utah.
Member 76th quorum seventies; drove an oxteam loaded with paper across the plains. Wool carder at Riverdale, Utah; miller. Died Nov. 18, 1880.

STRATTON, JAMES (son of Barton Stratton, born March 27, 1794, North Minns, Eng., died Nov. 30, 1862, and Susan Vyse, born February, 1793, died Jan. 26, 1865). He was born Dec. 22, 1824, Parish Ware, Herefordshire, Eng. Came to Utah Aug. 21, 1852.
Married Frances Clark 1851, in England (daughter of Benjamin Thomas Clark, born Feb. 20, 1799, died Sept. 4, 1867, and Ann Shukers, born June 19, 1810, died June 24, 1848). She was born April 3, 1828, and died August, 1904. Their children: Louisa Susan, m. Henry J. Stone; Maria Jane, m. Philip Ryan; James Barton, m. Mary Smith; Charles William, died.
Married Eliza Briggs, Salt Lake City, Utah. Their children: Ruth B., m. John Handley; Sarah Ann, m. W. F. Handley; John Henry, m. Emma Evans; Joseph, died; Eliza, m. Newel J. Knight; David Thomas, m. Caroline Mary Dittmore; Samuel, and Alfred James, died. Family home, Cedar Valley, Utah.
High priest; missionary to The Muddy; Indian war veteran. Died March 23, 1907, Provo, Utah.

STRATTON, DAVID THOMAS (son of James Stratton and Eliza Briggs). Born Dec. 19, 1866, Provo, Utah.
Married Caroline Mary Dittmore Sept. 20, 1894, Salt Lake City (daughter of Henry Dittmore and Rachel Smuin of Pleasant Grove, Utah), who was born Feb. 21, 1867. Their children: Ann Artell b. July 26, 1895; Rhoda b. May 23, 1898; Miralda b. Dec. 12, 1899; Mabel b. April 6, 1901; Martin David b. June 11, 1903; Furel Henry b. Feb. 12, 1905; James Reed b. May 6, 1907. Family home Sharon ward, Utah.
Elder; assistant superintendent of Sunday school, Timpanogos ward; president of deacons quorum; ward teacher. Fruitgrower and horticulturist.

STRICKLEY, JOHN (son of Joseph Strickley of Birmingham, Eng.). Born 1843, at Birmingham. Came to Utah June, 1868, Captain Hunter company.

Married Ellen Brindle December, 1864, at Brimingham (daughter of Benjamin Brindle and Sarah Ponney of that place, pioneers 1867), who was born Aug. 30, 1844. Their children: William J., m. Mary E. Cooper; Ellen E. E., m. John G. Gray; Mariam Z. A., m. E. W. Mason; Joseph B., m. Marie Hale; Laura B., m. H. W. Gray; George F., m. Gertrude Penfold; Albert B., d. infant; Frank H., m. Lula Armstrong; James G.; Blanche H. Family home, Salt Lake City. General merchant.

STRICKLEY, JOSEPH B. (son of John Strickley and Ellen Brindle). Born Feb. 18, 1870, Salt Lake City.
Married Marie Hale Dec. 21, 1896, Salt Lake City, S. S. Geddes officiating (daughter of Joseph Hale and Elizabeth Williams of Wales, pioneers 1865). She was born June 27, 1872. Family home, Salt Lake City.
Contractor.

STRINGFELLOW, GEORGE (son of Joseph Stringfellow and Lucy Tagg of Hucknall, Nottingham, Eng.). Born 1834, at Hucknall. Came to Utah 1864, Joseph S. Rawlins company.
Married Grace E. Wilkinson April 1, 1867, Salt Lake City (daughter of Luke Wilkinson and Ann Barker). Their children: Joseph W., m. Fannie Maria Little; Erastus W., m. Etta Bennion; Alonzo W.; Junius R.; Grace E. Family home Salt Lake City, Utah.
Missionary to England. City councilman and member board of public works. Merchant and president Utah Casket company.

STRINGFELLOW, JOSEPH W. (son of George Stringfellow and Grace E. Wilkinson). Born Jan. 15, 1874, Salt Lake City.
Married Fannie Maria Little Sept. 19, 1909, Salt Lake City (daughter of James T. Little of Salt Lake City), who was born Aug. 7, 1885. Family home, Salt Lake City.
Seventy. Lawyer.

STRINGHAM, GEORGE. Born in New York State. Came to Utah 1849.
Married Polly Hendrickson 1829, in New York state. Their children: Briant, m. Susie Ann Ashby; m. Harriet Ashby, m. Martha Ashby, m. Nancy Badger; Sabra; Jeremiah, m. Sallie Bove, m. Mary Brinkerhoff; Benjamin Joseph, m. Emma Ashby; George, m. Mary Ashby; Meda, m. Appleton Harmon. Family home Salt Lake City, Utah.
Butcher. Died at Salt Lake City.

STRINGHAM, BRIANT (son of George Stringham and Polly Hendrickson). Born 1830, in New York state. Came to Utah July 24, 1847, Brigham Young company.
Married Susan Ann Ashby 1848, Salt Lake City. Their children: Susan b. Dec. 25, 1849, m. Sheridan Jacobs; Briant b. Dec. 25, 1851, m. Jessie Eldredge; James b. 1853, d. youth; Philip b. July 14, 1856, m. Caroline Ann Crouch, m. Mary Hall; Lucy b. 1858, m. Heber J. Grant; Jacob b. 1860, d. youth; Julia b. 1862, m. Albert Woolley; Ashby b. 1864; William b. 1866, m. Lucy Ferron; John b. 1868, m. Ettie Penrose. Family home, Salt Lake City.
Married Harriett Ashby, at Salt Lake City. Their children: Maria, m. Thomas Stephens; Harriett, m. Brigham Nowlen; Polly; Rozilla, m. Frank Grant; Henry, m. Fannie ———; George, m. Miss Freeze. Family home Salt Lake City, Utah.
Married Martha Bucklan Ashby, at Salt Lake City. Their children: Martha, m. Joseph Edmonds; Chloe, m. Hyrum Johnson; Theresa; Jeremiah; Richard. Family home, Salt Lake City.
Married Nancy Badger (Garr). Their children: Jane, m. ———, Staveson. Family home, Salt Lake City.
High priest; bishop's counselor; in charge of tithing stock of Utah, 15 years, and of commissary during Indian wars. Died August, 1870, Salt Lake City.

STRINGHAM, PHILIP (son of Briant Stringham and Susan Ann Ashby). Born July 14, 1856, Salt Lake City.
Married Caroline Ann Crouch Feb. 12, 1873, Salt Lake City (daughter of William Crouch and Caroline Baker of London, Eng. who came to Utah 1875). She was born Feb. 7, 1855. Their children: Caroline Clair b. Nov. 3, 1874, m. Joseph P. Hacking; Ethelwynn b. July 25, 1876, m. Sylvenus Collet; Grace b. Aug. 26, 1878, m. Don B. Colton; Mary Fontela b. Feb. 28, 1881, m. Mark M. Hall; Philip Crouch b. Feb. 19, 1883, m. Ella Jane Wimmer; Susan b. Feb. 18, 1885, m. Marion Shaffer; Zina Roxana b. March 14, 1887, m. Hyrum Lorenzo Reed; Briant b. April 2, 1889, m. Delpha Rolfe, m. Katherine Chipman; Gertrude b. June 2, 1891, d. child; William Sterling b. July 25, 1892; Irvin b. Oct. 26, 1895; Beatrice b. Sept. 8, 1898. Family home Vernal, Utah.
Married Mary Bingham (Hall) Dec. 21, 1907, Salt Lake City (daughter of Thomas Bingham, Sr., and Karen Holliday of Ogden, Utah, pioneers 1848, contingent Mormon Battalion; widow of Mark Moroni Hall, whom she married Jan. 12, 1877, Huntsville, Utah. Children of this former marriage: Mary Maria b. Aug. 17, 1878, m. Don B. Colton; Chloe Louisa b. Sept. 15, 1879, d. child; Mark Moroni b. Jan. 2, 1881, m. Mary Fontella Stringham; Thomas Edwin b. March 20, 1886. Family home Vernal, Utah). She was born Sept. 18, 1852.
High priest: Sunday school superintendent; president Y. M. M. I. A. of Uinta stake. Superintendent schools of Uinta county; county recorder three terms; county clerk. Farmer and sheep raiser.

STRINGHAM, JEREMIAH (son of George Stringham and Polly Hendrickson). Came to Utah 1863, John R. Young company.
Married Sallie Bovee in eastern states, who came to Utah with husband. Their children: Benjamin; George, m. Emily Billings; William, m. Annie Cameron; Mary, m. Joseph Colby; Jacob, m. Anna Harmon; Jeremiah, m. Martha Keel; Zina, died. Family resided Salt Lake City, Manti and Nephi, Utah.
Married Mary Brinkerhoff at Salt Lake City (daughter of George Brinkerhoff of Long Valley, Utah). Their children: Sallie, m. ——— King; Jeanette; James; Lillian, m. Mr. Grundy; David; Thomas. Family home Thurber, Utah.
Active pioneer in San Pete and Juab counties. Guard during Black Hawk Indian war. Farmer and stockraiser. Died 1904, Manti, Utah.

STRINGHAM, JACOB (son of Jeremiah Stringham and Sallie Bovee). Born Oct. 3, 1862, in Missouri.
Married Anna Harmon Oct. 4, 1884, Salt Lake City (daughter of Ansel P. Harmon and Roseline Chandler of Holden, Utah). She was born Nov. 11, 1862, and died Oct. 26, 1910. Their children: Ethel b. Jan. 30, 1885, m. Ole Dastrup; Roseline b. Sept. 5, 1887; Marion b. Feb. 1, 1890; Zina b. Dec. 28, 1892; Ansel b. Aug. 26, 1895; Ruby b. Oct. 19, 1898, died; Alta b. Feb. 4, 1901; Sarah b. May 15, 1904; Anna b. Sept. 5, 1908. Family home Vermillion, Utah.
High priest; counselor in bishopric and assistant Sunday school superintendent Vermillion ward. Farmer and stockraiser.

STRINGHAM, BENJAMIN JOSEPH (son of George Stringham, born March 16, 1790, Long Island, N. Y., and Polly Hendrickson, born April 3, 1803, in Broom county, N. Y., married Aug. 17, 1820). He was born March 16, 1839. Came to Utah September, 1848, Heber C. Kimball company.
Married Emma Smith Ashby Oct. 26, 1861 (daughter of Nathaniel and Susan Ashby), who was born March 14, 1843. Only child: Benjamin Ashby b. May 22, 1863, m. Mary Charlotte Probert.
Married Olive Ann Johnson Sept. 16, 1880, Salt Lake City (daughter of Richard Johnson and Frances Hart (Nixon). She was born May 3, 1862, Holden, Utah. Their children: Joseph Ray b. July 24, 1881, m. Mary Edna Mitchell Oct. 25, 1905; Emma b. Feb. 14, 1883, m. John E. Anderson April 5, 1906; Polly Eimeda b. Nov. 13, 1884, m. James Henry Ramsey March 8, 1911; Elmer Taylor b. Jan. 2, 1887; Louis b. May 15, 1889, m. David W. Duncan Oct. 3, 1907; Viola b. Feb. 13, 1891, m. Alex Trimble June 5, 1909; Platte b. Nov. 26, 1894; Minerva b. Aug. 14, 1897; Alonzo Kimball b. Dec. 29, 1899, died; Bryant b. May 19, 1901; Zina Bernice b. Aug. 13, 1903. Family home Holden, Millard Co., Utah.
Missionary to England April 13, 1863, to Sept. 1, 1866. Called to preside over Harrisburg, and organize and colonize Leeds, Washington Co., Utah, Dec. 1, 1867. President high priests quorum at Holden, July 1, 1878 to June 23, 1905. Ordained patriarch Feb. 19, 1899 by President Francis M. Lyman. Justice of peace at Holden 1881 to 1890.

STRINGHAM, BENJAMIN ASHBY (son of Benjamin Joseph Stringham and Emma Smith Ashby). Born May 22, 1863, Salt Lake City.
Married Mary Charlotte Probert, Manti, Utah (daughter of William Probert and Mary Ann Johnson). Their children: Rulon Ashby; Evan; Veda Emma; Sanzas; Forest; Maline. Family resided Provo, Utah and Tabor, Alberta, Canada.
Missionary to southern states. Pioneer in Tabor and Raymond, Canada.

STRONG, JACOB (son of James Strong and Catherine Howard, former of Strongstown, Pa., the latter of York county, Pa). Born Oct. 9, 1799, in York county, Pa. Came to Utah October, 1849, Silas Richard company.
Married Sarah Hill Feb. 28, 1822 (daughter of James Hill and Barbara Emerkeizer), who was born Sept. 1, 1806. Their children: Sarah, m. William Wilson; Susan Strong, m. Henry Mower; William, m. Martha Alvord; Lucinda; John Albert; James Thomas, m. Eliza Swaner; Hyrum, m. Mary I. Newton. Married Alice Fish March 5, 1857, Salt Lake City, who was born April 16, 1829, in Lancashire, Eng. Their children: Lucinda b. March 10, 1859, m. Scott Campbell; William Jacob b. Aug. 13, 1863, m. Emma Duncan; Alma Ester, m. Lizzie Underwood. Family home, Salt Lake City.

STRONG, HYRUM (son of Jacob Strong and Sarah Hill). Born Sept. 28, 1846, Nauvoo, Ill. Came to Utah October, 1849, with father.
Married Mary Isabella Newton Feb. 1, 1868, Salt Lake City (daughter of James L. Newton and Elizabeth Blackburn, pioneers 1853, John Brown company). She was born April 3, 1849. Their children: Hyrum Albert b. Jan. 8, 1871, d. Dec. 17, 1878; Elizabeth Irene b. July 17, 1874, d. Jan. 8, 1879; Irvin Jacob b. Oct. 9, 1877, m. Hannah Maud Harris; Myrtle Belle b. Sept. 6, 1880, m. Arthur F. Galley; Ralph James b. Aug. 11, 1883, m. Cynthia Blamires; May b. Dec. 17, 1886; Daisy b. Oct. 13, 1890. Family resided Salt Lake City and Kaysville, Utah.

STRONG, JOHN (son of John Strong, Sr., and Mary Hewett of Westmoreland, Eng.). Born Sept. 3, 1805, Danton, Cumberland, Eng. Came to Utah 1855, Milo Andrus company.
Married Agness Miller September, 1828, Kendal, Westmoreland, Eng. (daughter of John Miller and Agnes Dean of Clapham, Yorkshire, Eng., pioneers 1855, Milo Andrus com-

PIONEERS AND PROMINENT MEN OF UTAH 1195

pany). She was born May 26, 1809. Their children: John b. Aug. 13, 1829, m. Maria Nelson; George b. Jan. 28, 1832, died; Mary b. Jan. 22, 1835, m. Thomas Farrer; Agnes b. Oct. 3, 1837, m. Roger Farrer; William b. Jan. 25, 1840, m. Celestia Young; Hannah b. July 22, 1842, m. Caleb H. Davis; Joseph S. b. Aug. 23, 1844, m. Matilda Young; Eleanor M. b. Jan. 30, 1847, m. William H. Gray; Elizabeth A. b. July 9, 1849, m. Robert Boardman; Miles b. Nov. 2, 1852, m. Maria Jensen. Family home Provo, Utah.
Seventy; high priest. Blacksmith. Died Dec. 21, 1862, Provo.

STUART, DANIEL (son of John Stuart and Margrite Nelson of Rimphin, Scotland). Born May 20, 1820, Kindle, Eng. Came to Utah Oct. 10, 1850, Milo Andrews company.
Married Agness Huddleston in 1845 (daughter of John Huddleston and Margerett Huddleston), who was born Aug. 11, 1821. Their children: George Stewart b. Feb. 27, 1846, m. Mary Evans 1866; Mary Ann b. May, 1847, d. 1847; Elisa Anna M. b. June 4, 1851, m. C. E. Pomroy; Zina A. b. 1853, m. William Lambaum. Family home, Salt Lake City.
Veteran of Echo Canyon campaign and Black Hawk Indian war. Early settler to Carson Valley. Shoemaker.

STUART, GEORGE (son of Daniel Stuart and Agness Huddleston). Born Feb. 27, 1845. Came to Utah with parents.
Married Mary Evans in 1866, Salt Lake City (daughter of Thomas E. Evans and Jane Davis), who was born 1841 in Wales. Their children: Jane Agnes b. June, 1868, d. 1868; Eva Eveline b. Oct. 6, 1869, m. George Richardson 1887; Mary Margrett b. Oct. 1871, m. James McKay; George Daniel b. 1873, died; Ammie b. 1874; George S. b. March 1875, m. Rebecca Williams; Benjamin b. Nov. 22, 1875, m. Sally Jones.
Missionary to Scotland 1894-96; bishop; member of Nauvoo Guard. Telegraph operator.
Married Jemima Evans April 8, 1874, Salt Lake City (daughter of Thomas L. Evans and Jane Davis, former pioneer 1868, Captain Gillett company, latter 1866, same captain). She was born April 1, 1850, in Glamorganshire, Wales. Their children: Thomas b. Jan. 1875, m. Annie Jones; William A. b. June 1877, m. Mary Ann Thomas; Ivan b. Aug. 22, 1879, m. Mary Williams; Sarah b. Sept. 13, 1882, m. William Follace; Zina b. Sept. 18, 1886, m. Frank Robert; Agness b. May 21, 1889, m. Davy Burnett; Jemima b. Nov. 18, 1891; Daniel W. b. 1899.

STUCKI, JOHN U. (son of Johannes Stucki and Elizabeth Sauter of Neunforn, Thurgau, Switzerland). Born Jan. 8, 1837, Neunforn, Thurgau, Switzerland. Came to Utah Aug. 30, 1860, Jesse Murphy company.
Married A. Margaret Huber Aug. 19, 1859, Mettendorf, Thurgau, Switzerland (daughter of Hans Heinrich Huber and Anna Maria Schneider of Mettendorf). She was born Feb. 20, 1835. Their child: John Henry, d. Oct. 25, 1877.
Married Jane Butler Feb. 1, 1870, Salt Lake City (daughter of Thomas Butler and Dinah David of Bridge End, South Wales, who came to Utah June 2, 1875, by rail). She was born Nov. 8, 1851, St. Brides, Wales. Their children: Charles Thomas b. Aug. 11, 1872, m. Caroline Pink; Caroline Elizabeth b. Feb. 4, 1874, d. Sept. 2, 1880; Maria Jane b. April 22, 1877, m. Charles Cole; William B. b. Aug. 21, 1880, m. Marie Lehr; Hyrum David b. Oct. 17, 1882, d. Nov. 30, 1882; Joseph Smith b. June 1, 1884, m. Mary Ann Price; Annie b. Aug. 26, 1886, m. Daniel Rich; Margaret b. Aug. 15, 1891; Erastus Woodruff b. March 19, 1894.
Married Anna Clara Spori September. 1890, Salt Lake City (daughter of Jacob Spori and Susannah Katherine Bochlen of Oberwyl, Bern, Switzerland). She was born Sept. 21, 1859, at Oberwyl. Their children: Elfrieda S. b. April 29, 1893; Ezra S. b. Feb. 25, 1895.
Member 62d quorum seventies; missionary to Switzerland and Germany 1874-76 and 1888-90; high councilor; stake clerk; president high priests quorum; patriarch; bishop's counselor; second counselor to president of stake. Mayor of Paris, Idaho; member board of education Academy of Idaho; justice of peace; county auditor and recorder; county treasurer; notary public; school trustee.

STUBBS, RICHARD (son of Samuel Stubbs and Sarah Shaw of Norwich, Cheshire, Eng.). Born July 30, 1823, Norwich. Came to Utah October, 1852, Jerome Benson cowteam company.
Married Eleanor Ware June 21, 1843, Busher Branch, Lee Co., Iowa (daughter of Abishai Ware and Delilah Rogers of Frederick, W. Va., pioneers 1852, Jerome Benson oxteam company). She was born Dec. 1, 1825. Their children: Amana Melvina, m. Edward Peay; Samuel, died; Sarah Ellen, m. Franklin Scott; Rebecca Ann, m. Edward Peay; Heber William, m. Blanche Whipple; Eliza R., m. Franklin Scott; John R., m. Temperance Goodman; Mary D., m. Nephi Ross; Eunice Lester, m. Howard Scott; Hannah D., m. Walter Gale; Joseph A., m. Phillipa Moyle. Family home Provo, Utah.
High priest; ward and Sunday school teacher. Farmer. Died July 25, 1902, Provo.

STUBBS. JOHN RODHOM (son of Richard Stubbs and Eleanor Ware of Provo, Utah). Born July 2, 1860, at Provo, Utah.
Married Susannah Temperance Goodman Dec. 22, 1881, Salt Lake City (daughter of John Richardson Goodman and Sarah Lee of Provo, Utah, pioneers 1852). She was born Jan. 12, 1863. Their children: John William b. April 24, 1883, m. Margret Ritchie; Jesse Goodman b. Jan. 9, 1885, m. Annie Loveless; Zella Temperance b. Sept. 14, 1886, m. William A. Penrod; Maud Ellen b. April 4, 1888, m. Charles Ashton; Wilford Richard b. April 6, 1890, m. Pearl Penrod; David Alfonso b. June 9, 1892, d. March 12, 1903; Albert Owen b. May 5, 1896; Leona b. May 27, 1903. Family resided Pleasant View and Provo, Utah.
High priest; bishop's counselor; missionary to Great Britain May 26, 1899 to 1901; Sunday school superintendent; ward teacher. Farmer and horticulturist.

STUMPF, TRAUGOTT (son of John Stumpf and Elizabeth Fehr of Buchakern, Canton Thurgau, Switzerland, latter a pioneer 1863). Born Jan. 2, 1840, Buchakern, Switzerland. Came to Utah 1861, Jabez Woodard independent oxteam train.
Married Elizabeth Turner 1867, Salt Lake City (daughter of William Turner and Ann Turner of Chilvers Coten, Warwickshire, Eng., pioneers 1850). She was born Sept. 5, 1829, Warwickshire, Eng. There were no children.
Married Jane Buist March 13, 1884, Logan, Utah (daughter of David Buist and Isabella Mathers of Arbroath, Scotland; former came to Utah 1883). She was born Jan. 9, 1855, at Arbroath, and came to Utah with father. Their children: Isabella Jane b. Nov. 28, 1886; Elizabeth Ann b. May 17, 1888, m. Oscar Junies Barratt.
High priest. Brought immigrants to Utah from the terminals of railroads, Laramie and Fort Benton, 1868. Farmer.

SULLIVAN, DAVID D. (son of James T. Sullivan of Nashville, Ind., and Annie Weddell of Valiska, Iowa). Born Jan. 21, 1845, Nashville, Ind. Came to Utah December, 1865, freighting outfit.
Married Caroline C. Calkins 1827 in New York City (daughter of Israel Calkins and Lavina Wheeler, pioneers 1852). She was born Jan. 7, 1851, Council Bluffs, Iowa. Their children: Julia Melvina b. Nov. 19, 1869, m. Guy Hartley Greene Nov. 29, 1909; Indemora b. March 20, 1874, m. Thorber Johnson Nov. 5, 1909; Helen Amelia b. Feb. 8, 1877, m. Theodore Dewey Jan. 2, 1900; Minnie Martha b. Dec. 18, 1878; David Dolen b. Sept. 6, 1880, m. Maud Buckland March 20, 1902; Mary Elizabeth b. Sept. 12, 1882, m. Frank Mousley Snow June 20, 1906; Caroline b. July 4, 1886; Walter Scott b. Feb. 24, 1889; Irene b. April 21, 1891, m. Harry Westenfelder Feb. 17, 1908; Gladys b. Aug. 17, 1893.
Civil war veteran. Postmaster at Grace, Idaho, 13 years. Died March 30, 1911.

SULLIVAN, GEORGE MILTON (son of David Linn Sullivan and Rebecca Morris of Troy, Davis Co., Iowa). Born March 13, 1866, Van Buren Co., Iowa. Came to Utah August, 1899.
Married Margaret McReynolds May 7, 1892, Hot Springs, S. D. (daughter of Robert C. McReynolds of Alliance, Neb.). She was born 1872. Their children: Fern D. b. April 12, 1893, m. Earl F. Hiller; Wilma Floy b. Oct. 20, 1894; Glenn b. Aug. 7, 1896, d. child.
Married Daleth Pearl Kelley Oct. 1, 1902, Colorado Springs, Colo. (daughter of James E. and Margaret Kelley of Bloomington, Neb.). She was born Sept. 22, 1872.
Admitted to the bar May, 1890, in the state of Nebraska. Member board of education of Salt Lake City. Lawyer.

SULZER, CASPER (SULSER) (son of Peter and Ann Sulzer of Switzerland). Born Oct. 17, 1821, in Switzerland. Came to Utah in October, 1861, Joseph W. Young company.
Married Kathryn Steidler 1839 in Switzerland (daughter of Ulrich Steidler and Maragrete Abblanalp of Switzerland). She was born March 28, 1819. Their children: Kathryn and Maragrete, died; John, m. Mary M. Keller; Casper and Jacob, twins, died; Casper, m. Amanda Smith; Maragrete, m. George Henry Bumell; Susianna, m. Sidney McCarrel; Emma, m. Hiram Shelton; Amelia, m. Christen Burgener; Elizabeth, m. Joseph McCarrel. Family home, Meyringer, Switzerland.
Elder. Veteran Black Hawk war. Stockraiser; farmer. Died Oct. 12, 1891, Midway, Utah.

SULZER, JOHN (son of Casper Sulzer and Kathryn Steidler). Born March 28, 1846, in Switzerland. Came to Utah 1861, Joseph W. Young company.
Married Mary Margaret Keller at Heber, Utah (daughter of Adam Keller and Anna Barbara Enz of Switzerland). She was born Oct. 10, 1859. Their children: John Albert b. May 16, 1878, m. Mary E. Burgener; Mary Alice b. Aug. 1, 1880, m. Frederick Raymond; Elizabeth Bertha b. Nov. 17, 1882, m. John B. Fowers; Nephi b. June 10, 1885, m. Annie Simmins; Eliza b. Oct. 28, 1896, died; Kathryn Niccle b. Feb. 27, 1889, m. Thomas J. Baird; Della b. June 24, 1892, m. Clifford John Phillips; Lillie b. April 16, 1895; Ella Edna b. Nov. 4, 1897; Owen b. Sept. 5, 1900, died; Anna Ina b. Dec. 23, 1902; Dean Glade b. April 4, 1907, died. Family home Midway, Utah.
High priest; ward teacher since 1865. Veteran Black Hawk war. stockgrower; farmer.

SUMSION, DANIEL (son of Samuel Sumsion and Jane Jones of Colerne, Eng.). Born Dec. 21, 1810, Colerne, Wiltshire. Came to Utah 1852, Woodhouse company.

Married Ellen Spender (daughter of George Spender and Eleanor Davis), who was born May 15, 1816. Their children: William, m. Christean Mary Alleman, m. Sarah Ann Cranmer; George, m. Ann Elizabeth Bird; Daniel, died; James Henry, m. Talmer Ann Bird.

SUMSION, WILLIAM (son of Daniel Sumsion and Ellen Spender). Born Jan. 7, 1837, Colerne, Wiltshire, Eng. Came to Utah 1852. Woodhouse company.
Married Christean Mary Alleman Feb. 3, 1858, Springville, Utah (daughter of John Alleman and Christean Stentz of Nauvoo, Ill., pioneers 1852, Walker company). She was born Oct. 15, 1840, Nauvoo, Ill. Their children: Mary Ellen b. Dec. 6, 1858, m. George Lyman McKenzie; William b. Feb. 19, 1861, m. Celestia Alexander; Emma b. July 30, 1863, m. Joseph Cranmer; Emily b. July 30, 1863, m. David A. Crandall; John b. Oct. 12, 1866, m. Celia E. Bramall; Daniel b. Sept. 27, 1869, m. Phoebe Loretty Oakley; Nellie b. July 20, 1872; Willis b. Dec. 19, 1875, m. Phoebe Milinda Singelton; Frank b. March 25, 1878, m. Pearl Bartlett; Anna b. Oct. 31, 1880, m. Arch Hailey Bird; Jesse b. Aug. 16, 1883, m. Lillie May Clinger; Christean b. April 27, 1888, d. April 1888.
Married Sarah Ann Cranmer Nov. 5, 1890, of Logan, Utah (daughter of William Cranmer and Sarah Ann Nightengale of Springville, Utah; former pioneer 1855, latter 1856, Wheelock handcart company). She was born Nov. 17, 1866, Springville, Utah. Their children: Lee Grand b. Dec. 6, 1891; Donna b. July 11, 1893; Lois b. Feb. 16, 1896; Elmo b. Jan. 15, 1899; Edna b. April 27, 1901; Melba Sarah Ann b. Nov. 30, 1903; Louise b. Nov. 1, 1907. Families resided Springville, Utah.

SUTHERLAND, JOHN (son of Gilbert Sutherland and Bruce Morrison of Shetland Island). Born Oct. 12, 1832, Brough Nesting parish, Shetland Islands. Came to Utah Sept. 1, 1859, Haight company.
Married Ellen Catherine Nicholson in 1859 at Florence, Neb. (daughter of Magnus Nicholson and Catherine Danoldson of Shetland Islands). She was born Jan. 1, 1832. Their children: William John, m. Josephine Hansen; Joseph, m. Cecelia Samules; Hyrum B.; Isaiah; Jonah, m. Jane Dagoo; Mary Ellen, m. David Crystal; Catherine E.; Zenobia Jane, m. George Harper. Family home Big Cottonwood, Utah. Worked hauling rock for Salt Lake temple. Served in the Black Hawk war.

SUTHERLAND, THOMAS (son of Alexander Sutherland, born in Scotland, and Elizabeth Lawlor of New Castle, Eng.). He was born 1804. Came to Utah in 1851.
Married Mary Ann Timmings 1828 in London (daughter of Thomas Timmings of London). Their children: Eliza b. Dec. 18, 1831, m. William Dallin; Mary Ann. m. John Gleason; Thomas H., m. Annie Tunbridge; Alexander George, m. Fannie Slater; Catherine, Ellen, William and Catherine Ellen, died. Family home Springville, Utah.
Farmer and gardener; baker and confectioner. Died Oct. 1890, Provo, Utah.

SUTHERLAND, ALEXANDER GEORGE (son of Thomas Sutherland and Mary Ann Timmings). Born Aug. 23, 1838, New Castle, Eng. Came to Utah Oct. 5, 1863, Captain Haight company.
Married Fannie Slater March 30, 1861, Stony Stratford, Buckinghamshire, Eng. (daughter of James Slater and Anna Pratt, both of Bedford, Eng.). She was born June 5, 1835, and came to Utah 1872. Their children: George b. March 25, 1862, m. Rose Lee; Fannie b. Feb. 10, 1864, m. Ephraim Davis Sutton; Thomas b. Oct. 1, 1865, died; Henry E. b. Sept. 4, 1867, m. Sophia Sutton; James b. Dec. 25, 1869, m. Clara Williamson; Frederick b. Jan. 5, 1872, m. Della Allen. Family home Springville, Utah.
Missionary to England. Locomotive engineer; freighter; blacksmith; storekeeper; school teacher. Postmaster; justice of the peace; recorder for U. S. land office. Died July 30, 1911, at Provo.

SUTHERLAND, GEORGE (son of Alexander George Sutherland and Fannie Slater). Born March 25, 1862, Stony Stratford, Eng.
Married Rose Lee June 16, 1883, Beaver, Utah (daughter of John P. Lee and Eliza Foscue of Beaver, pioneers). She was born July 16, 1865. Their children: Emma b. Nov. 14, 1884, m. Charles Lawrence; Philip b. March 6, 1886, died; Edith b. Jan. 4, 1888, m. Robert Elmore.
Member U. S. congress 1901-03; U. S. senator since 1905. Lawyer.

SWANN, EPHRAIM (son of Ephraim Swann of Fenbury and Elenor Broome of Leicester, Eng.). Born May 24, 1824, Fenbury, Eng. Came to Utah 1857, Jesse B. Martin company.
Married Fanny Jones Aug. 15, 1848 (daughter of Edward Jones and Hannah Went), who was born May 26, 1825, and came to Utah with husband. Their children: Hannah, m. Thomas Condie; Ephraim, died; Elizabeth, died Elenor b. April 7, 1857, m. L. L. Toone; Fanny Eliza b. Oct. 3, 1861, m. John M. McQueen; Edward William b. Oct. 15, 1863, m. Marie D. Ericksen; James E. b. Nov. 2, 1846, died; Mary Ellen b. Nov. 6, 1869, m. Richard C. Toone.
Settled in Ogden until 1861; moved to Morgan county, where he resided until 1864; moved to Croydon, Utah; in 1884 moved to Preston, Oneida Co., Idaho, where he remained until his death. Died Sept. 13, 1896.

SWANN, EDWARD W. (son of Ephraim Swann and Fanny Jones). Born Oct. 15, 1863, Milton, Morgan Co., Utah.
Married Marie D. Ericksen March 16, 1892, Logan, Utah

(daughter of Bengt J. Ericksen af Ellen C. D. Johansen), who was born April 3, 1871, BearRiver City. Their children: Edward Harrold b. Jan. 16 1893, d. April 11, 1898; Ephraim b. Dec. 31, 1894; Fanny Iarie b. June 15, 1897; Ben Ericksen b. April 25, 1899; obert Glen b. Jan. 14, 1902; Ellen b. March 29, 1904; William Lee b. Aug. 6, 1906.
Missionary to Great Britain Nr. 13, 1886, to June 6, 1890; Sunday school superintendent; bishop's counselor. Farmer and stockman.

SWASEY, FRANCIS. Born in low; Married Mary Dow in Iowa City, Iowa, where they resided before coming to Utah. Their children: Rodney, m. Loretta Deoville; George, died; Mor Ann, m. Simon Martin. Family resided Nephi and Mot, Utah. Died 1896.

SWASEY, RODNEY (son of Franci.Swasey and Mary Dow of Iowa). Born 1831. Came to Uta 1847, Brigham Young oxteam company.
Married Loretta Scoville in Salt Lce City in 1849 (daughter of Lucius Scoville of Provo). T-ir children: Charles b. Oct. 24, 1850, m. Cena Olson; Sidne m. Mary Rowe: Hannah, m. Allen Rowe; Joseph, m. Ma McDonald; Rodney, m. Eva Miles: Livia. m. Pondos Rome; Lcius, m. Netta Brotherson; Frank. m. Ema Olson. Family ome Mona. Utah.
Married Martha Carter at Salt Lae temple (daughter of William Carter of Provo). Their children: Mary Ann. m. Patrick Condon: Sarah. m. Henry III: Luna. m. Ephraim Ellison; Marcella; Estella. m. Alber Slade; Pearl. m. Marcello Jones; Rodney, m. Miss Kay Family home Mona, Utah.
Veteran of the Walker and Blac Hawk wars. Helped to settle up the California country. Stockraiser. Died in Provo, Utah, Dec. 25, 1899.

SWASEY, CHARLES (son of Rodne Swasey and Loretta Scoville). Born Oct. 24, 1850. Eldora) county, Cal.
Married Cena Olson Aug. 11, 1878, Iona. Utah (daughter of Andrew Olson and Boletta Larsorof Denmark, pioneers 1854, John R. Murdock company). he was born May 30, 1859. Their children: Charles Andrv b. Jan. 1, 1885, m. Alice Hambrick; Rodney; Moretta b. April 2, 1895. Family home Castle Dale, Utah.
Veteran of Black Hawk war. Mu; raiser.

SWEETEN, ROBERT (son of George Sweeten and Mary Gardner, the latter came to Utah 1th her son. Robert. and died at Spanish Fork, Utah. uring Johnson army trouble). Born Dec. 14, 1840, Brck, Ontario, Canada. Came to Utah Sept. 21, 1847, John Telor company.
Married Amanda Hogle Feb. 24, 158, in Ontario, Canada. while there settling his fathes estate. She came to Utah with her husband in 1870. Teir children: Martha E., m. Heber A. Holbrook; Robert 1 m. Althea Morgan; Mary A., m. Melvin Atkinson; Georgs G., m. Sarah Evans; Susan I., m. Wallace Cragun; Color H.; Warren H., m. Lilla Howard; Alice A., m. Elbert Baow; Chloe.
Seventy. Settled in Salt Lake City; noved to Mill Creek, Salt Lake county, 1848, and to Medon. Cache county, 1859. Member Medon city council 20 ars. Director Mendon Co-op. store 15 years. Moved to olbrook, Idaho, 1898. Justice of the peace; city marshal mayor two terms. Farmer.

SWENSON, AUGUST (son of Sven ndersen, born 1792, Trynge, Halland, Sweden, and Brita nderson, born 1791, Smoland, Sweden). Born Aug. 7, 1831 Stafsinge, Hallande, Sweden. Came to Utah Sept. 19, 185, Canute Petersen company.
Married Bertha O. Petersen Jan. 3 1859 (daughter of Ole Petersen and Bengta Andersen. oneer* 1857). She was born June 14, 1841. Their childr: Peter b. Dec. 10, 1859, d. Dec. 20, 1859; John O. b. Feb.), 1861, m. Priscilla Lewis Jan. 2, 1890; Emma b. March 2 1863. m. Joseph C. Hansen March 24, 1881; Alfred b. Feb. 0, 1865. d. Sept. 14, 1867; Oliver b. Oct. 14, 1866, m. Maggi S. Nielsen Feb. 24, 1892; Mary b. Dec. 7, 1868, m. George hristensen Feb. 18, 1894; Hyrum b. Nov. 25, 1870; Albert . Dec. 16, 1872, m. Sina D. Nielsen Feb. 9, 1898; Maggie . b. Nov. 26, 1874, m. Daniel Williams Jan. 26, 1898; Josph A. b. Dec. 23, 1876, m. Cornelia Nielsen June 19, 190 James H. b. Jan. 13, 1886.
Married Bergitha Johnson Nov. 14, 188. Salt Lake City (daughter of Hans Peter Johnson and nna Dorthea Jensen, pioneers 1866—married 1842). She was born Feb. 2, 1849, at Blands, Sjelland, Denmark. Their hildren: Hans Peter b. June 23, 1875; George b. Aur 7, 1886: Olivia b. Dec. 27, 1891; Wilford b. Feb. 19, 1594, d Sept. 2, 1894.
Married Sarah P. Hansen April 1?, '48, St. George, Utah (daughter of James Hansen and Karer Petersen, pioneers 1854—married Feb. 13, 1853, Salt Lake C y). She was born April 29, 1860, at Spanish Fork. Their children: William H. b. Feb. 3, 1881, d. March 10, 1882; arah Ann b. Jan. 21, 1883, m. Charles Hayes April 27, 904; Isaac b. Oct. 27, 1885; Nephi E. b. March 2, 1890; Ina B. b. Oct. 23, 1893; Carrie Myrtle b. April 2, 1898, d. an. 25, 1907; Levi Earl b. March 1, 1903. Family home Spaish Fork. Utah.
Counselor to president of elders quorum: member of presidency of 50th quorum of seventies high priest; bishop's counselor; missionary to Sweden 18-1884; high councilor. Vice-president of Spanish Co-operative Institution. Farmer and stockraiser.

SWENSEN, KND (CANUTE) (son of Svend Larsen and Annie Petersen, both of Weiby, Hjorring, Vendsyssel, Denmark). Born April 11, 1827, Weiby, Denmark. Came to Utah July 10, 1853, Horace Eldredge company.
Married Johanah Maria Peterson June 24, 1861, Salt Lake City (daughter of Hans Peterson of Maigard and Johannah Jens; of Hoisier, Denmark). She was born Sept. 13, 1838, heir children: Annie, m. Ezra F. Walker; Swen L., m. Sue Brown; Maria, died; Mary M., m. George Kelley; John Cnute, m. Margaret Davis; Hannah Eliza; Henson P. and Croline, died. Family home Pleasant Grove, Utah.
Counselor to Bishop John Brown 1877-90 at Pleasant Grove; bishop f third ward at Pleasant Grove 1890-99. School trustee 5 years; city councilman and treasurer several years. Farmer. Died March 14, 1902, at Pleasant Grove.

SWENSEN, JON CANUTE (son of Knud Swensen and Johannah Mar. Peterson). Born Feb. 4, 1869, Pleasant Grove, Utah.
Married Mararet Davis June 21, 1899, Salt Lake City (daughter of Jeph W. Davis and Maria Williams of Panguitch, Utah, pioneers July 1852). She was born Sept. 2, 1877. Their children: John Starr b. March 27, 1900; Carl Davis b. Aug. , 1901; Reed Knud b. Feb. 16, 1903; Alice b. May 14, 19(died; Margaret b. May 29, 1906; Frances McLean b. Jun 29, 1908; Louise b. March 24, 1910. Family resided Pleasa: Grove and Provo, Utah.
High council Utah stake. Graduate Stanford University 1898. Dean of he B. Y. U. of Provo 1902-09; professor of history and social science 1902-12; professor of economics and sociology 912; principal of Panguitch Stake Academy 1890-92; princial of Fillmore public schools 1893-94.

SWINDLE, GDRGE (son of George Swindle, born Oct. 10, 1794, died Sept. 24, 1854, and Elizabeth Miller, born Sept. 11, 1792, lied Sept. 26, 1854, both of Durham, Eng.). He was born ct. 29, 1824, Walker, Durham, Eng. Came to Utah 1857, ose Martin company.
Married An Hopper (daughter of John and Mary Hopper), who wa born July 14, 1843, and died Jan. 27, 1900. Came to Uta 1857, Jesse Martin company. Their children: George March 3. 1849; Mary b. Jan. 27, 1851, John b. Dec. 27, 185 John b. Dec. 24, 1854, John b. June 15, 1856, and Elizabeth, Sept. 3, 1858, died; David b. Nov. 14, 1860, d. Nov. 4, 189 Charles b. Nov. 18, 1864, m. Emma Folett and Sorena Shnmin. Family resided Spanish Fork, Lewiston. Richheld nd Monroe, Utah.
Married Mar Maddeline Witzig March 4, 1872, Salt Lake City (daughter of John Witzig and Doritha Goasoure), who was born Ma 29, 1843, Horgen, Switzerland. Their children: Amanda b. pril 1, 1873, m. Cyrus Winget; Heber b. Nov. 28, 1875, m. mma Warnock 1901; Joseph A. b. July 24, 1878, m. Etta odges; Ellen D. b. April 19, 1881, m. William Goold. Famil home Monroe, Utah.
Justice of te peace. Farmer. Died June 28, 1882.

SYLVESTER, JAMES (son of Joshua Sylvester and Ann Webb of She'eid, Eng.). Born Dec. 4, 1815, Pitsmay, Eng. Came to Utah September, 1852, James Jepson company.
Married Recca Nicholson in 1837, Sheffield, Eng. (daughter of Willia Nicholson and Mariah Cakkwell of Thorne, Eng.). She was born March 10, 1819. Their children: Ann Mariah and ebecca, died; Joshua William, m. Christena Christenson; ary Elizabeth, m. Joseph Birch; Emma, James and Eliza, d: Lavina, m. William Berry; Rozinia, m. George F. rvis; Althea, m. Andrew Gregerson; Joseph, m. Jane Hans. Family home Springville, Utah.
Elder; predent of the church branch at Sheffield, Eng. Farmer and lacksmith. Died May 19, 1888, at Bellevue.

SYLVESTER JOSHUA WILLIAM (son of James Sylvester and Rebecca Richolson). Born Feb. 5, 1843, Sheffield, Eng. Came to Utah with Parents.
Married Christina Christensen Jan. 1862, Gunnison, Utah (daughter o Jens Christensen and Margaret Krensen of Denmark, pioeers 1861, John R. Murdock company). She was born 18 . Their children: James William b. Aug. 31, 1864, m. Malna Bell; Eliza b. Nov. 4, 1866; Rebecca b. Dec. 13, 1869, m. Christian Johnson; Joshua b. June 18, 1872, m. Anna Jolson; Rosina b. Oct. 30, 1875, m. James Sorenson; Ralph, June 1878; Emma b. April 19, 1880. Family home Elainor, Utah.
Married Croline Christensen May, 1873, Salt Lake City (daughter o Jens Christensen of Denmark, pioneer 1861, John R. Mudock company). She was born 1853. Their children: Ad m. Greely Snyder; Altheria, m. Christo Nydahl; Elizah, m. Walter Jensen; George, m. Jennie Dall; Arthur; Don and Caroline, died; Agnes; Woodruff; Eleanor, died; Herma; Claudius and Curtis, died.
Married Cra Woodbury Barlew April 14, 1908, St. George, Utah (daugter of Orin Woodbury and Ann Cannon of St. George, piorers 1847). She was born Nov. 30, 1875. Their children: race Greeley; Margaret. Family home Mesquite, Nev.
High prie: bishop. County commissioner; school trustee. Farme and stockraiser.

SYLVESTE JAMES WILLIAM (son of Joshua William Sylvester at Christina Christensen). Born Aug. 31, 1864, Mona, Utah.
Married Ahala Bell March 12, 1884, St. George (daughter of Thoas Bell of England and Henrietta Lundquist of Sweden, ioneers). She was born Oct. 5, 1866, in Glen-wood. Utah. Their children: Leonard W. b. Aug. 19, 1886, m. Zion Smith; Hessie b. Dec. 29, 1888, m. George Joos; Mabel b. Oct. 11, 1890; Lorin b. Oct. 19, 1892; Roy C. b. Feb. 19, 1895; Dea T. b. April 4, 1897; Tell Joshua b. Jan. 22, 1899; Faun W. b. Oct. 23, 1901; Clinton R. b. Sept. 17, 1903; Merrill b. March 28, 1905, d. Oct. 10, 1907; Jay G. b. Sept. 21, 1908; Ronald b. May 13, 1909. Family home Elsinore, Utah.
Elder. Member of Elsinore town board three terms. Farmer and stockraiser.

SYME, HUGH (son of William Syme and Margaret Wimly of Burnt Island, Fifeshire, Scotland). Born July 7, 1826, Fifeshire. Came to Utah September, 1853.
Married Margaret Farrer (daughter of Roger Farrer and Mary Stubbs), who was born Sept. 17, 1859. Their children: Margaret Ann, died; Hugh Leslie, m. Rachael A. Loveless, m. Emma Ettie White. Family home Provo, Utah.
Married Elizabeth Buckley, Salt Lake City, who was born Sept. 17, 1829, Lancastershire, Eng. Their children: William Alexander; Margeret Jane, m. Richard J. Nuttall; Fannie Elizabeth, m. George W. Giles. Family home Provo, Utah.
Member 7th quorum seventies. Carpenter; wheelwright; cooper. Died May 23, 1877, at Provo, Utah.

SYME, HUGH L. (son of Hugh Syme and Margeret Farrer). Born July 16, 1861, Provo, Utah.
Married Rachael A. Loveless Dec. 16, 1887, at Logan, Utah (daughter of James W. Loveless and Josephine Caldwell, both of Provo, Utah). She was born June 4, 1866. Their child: James Hugh b. Sept. 24, 1899. Family home Provo, Utah.
Married Emma Ettie White Nov. 16, 1904, at Salt Lake City (daughter of Henry White and Emma Saunders, both of Provo, Utah). She was born Feb. 7, 1871. Their children: George Leslie b. Oct. 3, 1907; Margeret b. Feb. 14, 1909; Edward Farrer b. Nov. 30, 1911. Family home Provo, Utah.
High priest. Carpenter; machinist.

SYMONS, NATHANIEL. Born Aug. 21, 1805. Came to Utah Aug. 20, 1863, John Seeley company.
Married Susannah M. Olivere (daughter of Peter Olivere), who was born Aug. 10, 1822 (deceased). Their children: Benjamin b. Feb. 23, 1840, m. Sarah Cater 1869; Joseph b. Dec. 1845, m. Louise Proctor 1880; Nathaniel, m. Mr. Sheen (died); Providence b. May 9, 1850 (died), m. Daniel Verrip (died); Mercy, m. John C. Munter (died); Hepzebah b. April 16, 1858, m. Charles Jones (died) Nov. 25, 1874; Naomi Grace b. March 12, 1860, m. George Augustus Tyler (died) Oct. 7, 1880; Rebecca Omega b. Oct. 20, 1862, m. Edgar Graham; John W. b. March 5, 1867, m. Mary Elizabeth Lunn Oct. 8, 1896; James Emanuel b. Aug. 25, 1869, m. Florence Johnson. Family home, Salt Lake City.
Embraced the gospel in England 1854. Was presiding elder over the Deptford, Walworth Common, Lambeth and Greenwich branches in 1862. Died Jan. 21, 1883.

SYMONS, JOHN W. (son of Nathaniel Symons and Susannah Mary Olivere). Born March 5, 1867, at Salt Lake City.
Married Mary Elizabeth Lunn Oct. 8, 1896, at Salt Lake City (daughter of John Lunn and Harriet Cookson), who was born April 24, 1873, at Salt Lake City. Their children: Harriet Susannah D. b. Jan. 31, 1898, d. Sept. 9, 1899; John William b. Oct. 24, 1900; George Daniel b. Jan. 2, 1903; Joseph Nathaniel b. June 5, 1905; Mary Elizabeth b. Sept. 22, 1910; Walter Thomas b. Dec. 1, 1911. Family home Lava, Bannock Co., Idaho.
Was a pioneer of Lava, having arrived here when it was first settled in the year 1889. President of Y. M. M. I. A. in Dempsey ward in 1899; superintendent of Dempsey ward Sunday school for three years; bishop's counselor of Dempsey ward from Dec. 10, 1905, up till the present time.

T

TAGGART, CHARLES Y.
Married Margaret G. Smith (daughter of John B. Smith and Margaret Gibson of Tooele, Utah, pioneers 1852). She was born Sept. 19, 1856. Their children: Henry C. b. June 10, 1882, m. Ellen Nibley; John N. b. Feb. 17, 1885, m. Dora Stringfellow; Orson P. b. May 26, 1887, d. infant; Margaret H. b. Jan. 13, 1889; Joseph S. b. Oct. 24, 1891; Milton H. b. July 8, 1896, d. infant. Family home, Salt Lake City.

TAGGART, GEORGE WASHINGTON (son of Washington Taggart and Susan Law of Petersborough, N. H.). Born Nov. 6, 1816, at Petersborough. Came to Utah 1848 with a contingent of the Mormon Battalion.
Married Harriet Atkins Bruce (daughter of Peter and Eliza Bruce of Petersborough, N. H.). She was born March 20, 1821, and died at Nauvoo, Ill. Only child: Eliza Ann b. Jan. 28, 1844, m. George Albert Goodrich. Family home Richville, Utah.
Married Clarissa M. Rogers about 1860 at Brigham City (daughter of Washington Rogers of Nauvoo, Ill., pioneer 1848). She was born 1833. Their children: Clarissa M., m. W. B. Parkinson; Sarah Jane, m. George Hiner; Reuben, d. infant; Albert N., m. Sarah Kingston; Julia M., m. W. H.

Married Ellen Spender (daughter of George Spender and Eleanor Davis), who was born May 15, 1816. Their children: William, m. Christean Mary Alleman, m. Sarah Ann Cranmer; George, m. Ann Elizabeth Bird; Daniel, died; James Henry, m. Talmer Ann Bird.

SUMSION, WILLIAM (son of Daniel Sumsion and Ellen Spender). Born Jan. 7, 1837, Colerne, Wiltshire, Eng. Came to Utah 1852, Woodhouse company.
Married Christean Mary Alleman Feb. 3, 1858, Springville, Utah (daughter of John Alleman and Christean Stentz of Nauvoo, Ill., pioneers 1852, Walker company). She was born Oct. 15, 1840, Nauvoo, Ill. Their children: Mary Ellen b. Dec. 6, 1858, m. George Lyman McKenzie; William b. Feb. 19, 1861, m. Celestia Alexander; Emma b. July 30, 1863, m. Joseph Cranmer; Emily b. July 30, 1863, m. David A. Crandall; John b. Oct. 12, 1866, m. Celia E. Bramall; Daniel b. Sept. 27, 1869, m. Phoebe Loretty Oakley; Nellie b. July 20, 1872; Willis b. Dec. 19, 1875, m. Phoebe Milinda Singleton; Frank b. March 25, 1878, m. Pearl Bartlett; Anna b. Oct. 31, 1880, m. Arch Hailey Bird; Jesse b. Aug. 16, 1883, m. Lillie May Clinger; Christean b. April 27, 1888, d. April 1888.
Married Sarah Ann Cranmer Nov. 5, 1890, of Logan, Utah (daughter of William Cranmer and Sarah Ann Nightengale of Springville, Utah; former pioneer 1855, latter 1856, Wheelock handcart company). She was born Nov. 17, 1866, Springville, Utah. Their children: Lee Grand b. Dec. 6, 1891; Donna b. July 11, 1893; Lois b. Feb. 16, 1896; Elmo b. Jan. 15, 1899; Edna b. April 27, 1901; Melba Sarah Ann b. Nov. 30, 1903; Louise b. Nov. 1, 1907. Families resided Springville, Utah.

SUTHERLAND, JOHN (son of Gilbert Sutherland and Bruce Morrison of Shetland Island). Born Oct. 12, 1832, Brough Nesting parish, Shetland Islands. Came to Utah Sept. 1, 1859, Haight company.
Married Ellen Catherine Nicholson in 1859 at Florence, Neb. (daughter of Magnus Nicholson and Catherine Danoldson of Shetland Islands). She was born Jan. 1, 1832. Their children: William John, m. Josephine Hansen; Joseph, m. Cecelia Samules; Hyrum B.; Isaiah; Jonah, m. Jane Bagoo; Mary Ellen, m. David Crystal; Catherine E.; Zenobia Jane, m. George Harper. Family home Big Cottonwood, Utah. Worked hauling rock for Salt Lake temple. Served in the Black Hawk war.

SUTHERLAND, THOMAS (son of Alexander Sutherland, born in Scotland, and Elizabeth Lawlor of New Castle, Eng.). He was born 1804. Came to Utah in 1851.
Married Mary Ann Timmings 1828 in London (daughter of Thomas Timmings of London). Their children: Eliza b. Dec. 18, 1831, m. William Dallin; Mary Ann, m. John Gleason; Thomas H., m. Annie Tunbridge; Alexander George, m. Fannie Slater; Catherine, Ellen, William and Catherine Ellen, died. Family home Springville, Utah.
Farmer and gardener; baker and confectioner. Died Oct. 1890, Provo, Utah.

SUTHERLAND, ALEXANDER GEORGE (son of Thomas Sutherland and Mary Ann Timmings). Born Aug. 23, 1838, New Castle, Eng. Came to Utah Oct. 5, 1863, Captain Haight company.
Married Fannie Slater March 30, 1861, Stony Stratford, Buckinghamshire, Eng. (daughter of James Slater and Anna Pratt, both of Bedford, Eng.). She was born June 5, 1835, and came to Utah 1872. Their children: George b. March 25, 1862, m. Rose Lee; Fannie b. Feb. 10, 1864, m. Ephraim Davis Sutton; Thomas b. Oct. 5, 1865, died; Henry E. b. Sept. 4, 1867, m. Sophia Sutton; James b. Dec. 25, 1869, m. Clara Williamson; Frederick b. Jan. 5, 1872, m. Della Allen. Family home Springville, Utah.
Missionary to England. Locomotive engineer; freighter; blacksmith; storekeeper; school teacher. Postmaster; justice of the peace; recorder for U. S. land office. Died July 30, 1911, at Provo.

SUTHERLAND, GEORGE (son of Alexander George Sutherland and Fannie Slater). Born March 25, 1862, Stony Stratford, Eng.
Married Rose Lee June 16, 1883, Beaver, Utah (daughter of John F. Lee and Eliza Foscue of Beaver, pioneers). She was born July 16, 1865. Their children: Emma b. Nov. 14, 1884, m. Charles Lawrence; Philip b. March 6, 1886, died; Edith b. Jan. 4, 1888, m. Robert Williams.
Member U. S. congress 1901-03; U. S. senator since 1905. Lawyer.

SWANN, EPHRAIM (son of Ephraim Swann of Fenbury and Elenor Broome of Leicester, Eng.). Born May 24, 1824, Fenbury, Eng. Came to Utah 1857, Jesse B. Martin company.
Married Fanny Jones Aug. 15, 1848 (daughter of Edward Jones and Hannah Went), who was born May 25, 1825, and came to Utah with husband. Their children: Hannah; m. Thomas Condie; Ephraim, died; Elenor b. April 7, 1857, m. L L Toone; Fanny Eliza b. Oct. 3, 1861, m. John M. McQueen; Edward William b. Oct. 15, 1863, m. Marie D. Ericksen; James E. b. Nov. 2, 1866, died; Mary Ellen b. Nov. 6, 1869, m. Richard C. Toone.
Settled in Ogden until 1861; moved to Morgan county, where he resided until 1864; moved to Croydon, Utah; in 1884 moved to Preston, Oneida Co., Idaho, where he remained until his death. Died Sept. 13, 1896.

SWANN, EDWARD W. (son of Ephraim Swann and Fanny Jones). Born Oct. 15, 1863, Milton, Morgan Co., Utah. Married Marie D. Ericksen March 16, 1892, Logan, Utah (daughter of Bengt J. Ericksen and Ellen C. D. Johansen), who was born April 3, 1871, Bear River City. Their children: Edward Harrold b. Jan. 16, 1893, d. April 11, 1895; Ephraim b. Dec. 31, 1894; Fanny Marie b. June 15, 1897; Ben Ericksen b. April 25, 1899; Robert Glen b. Jan. 14, 1902; Ellen b. March 29, 1904; William Lee b. Aug. 6, 1906.
Missionary to Great Britain Nov. 13, 1886, to June 6, 1890; Sunday school superintendent; bishop's counselor. Farmer and stockman.

SWASEY, FRANCIS. Born in Iowa.
Married Mary Dow in Iowa City, Iowa, where they resided before coming to Utah. Their children: Rodney, m. Loretta Deoville; George, died; Mary Ann, m. Simon Martin. Family resided Nephi and Mona, Utah. Died 1896.

SWASEY, RODNEY (son of Francis Swasey and Mary Dow of Iowa). Born 1831. Came to Utah 1847, Brigham Young oxteam company.
Married Loretta Scoville in Salt Lake City in 1849 (daughter of Lucius Scoville of Provo). Their children: Charles b. Oct. 24, 1850, m. Cena Olson; Sidney, m. Mary Rowe; Hannah, m. Allen Rowe; Joseph, m. May McDonald; Rodney, m. Eva Miles; Livia, m. Pondos Rome; Lucius, m. Netta Brotherson; Frank, m. Ema Olson. Family home Mona, Utah.
Married Martha Carter at Salt Lake temple (daughter of William Carter of Provo). Their children: Mary Ann, m. Patrick Condon; Sarah, m. Henry Bell; Luna, m. Ephraim Ellison; Marcella; Estella, m. Albert Slade; Pearl, m. Marcello Jones; Rodney, m. Miss Kay. Family home Mona, Utah.
Veteran of the Walker and Black Hawk wars. Helped to settle up the California country. Stockraiser. Died in Provo, Utah, Dec. 25, 1899.

SWASEY, CHARLES (son of Rodney Swasey and Loretta Scoville). Born Oct. 24, 1850, Eldorado county, Cal.
Married Cena Olson Aug. 11, 1878, Mona, Utah (daughter of Andrew Olson and Boletta Larson of Denmark, pioneers 1854, John R. Murdock company). She was born May 30, 1859. Their children: Charles Andrew b. Jan. 1, 1885, m. Alice Hambrick; Moretta b. April 2, 1895. Family home Castle Dale, Utah.
Veteran of Black Hawk war. Mule raiser.

SWEETEN, ROBERT (son of George Sweeten and Mary Gardner, the latter came to Utah with her son, Robert, and died at Spanish Fork, Utah, during Johnson army trouble). Born Dec. 14, 1840, Brook, Ontario, Canada. Came to Utah Sept. 21, 1847, Captain John Taylor company.
Married Amanda Hagle Feb. 24, 1868, in Ontario, Canada, while there settling his father's estate. She came to Utah with her husband in 1870. Their children: Martha E., m. Heber A. Holbrook; Robert L., m. Althea Morgan; Mary A., m. Melvin Atkinson; George G., m. Sarah Evans; Susan I., m. Wallace Cragun; Colon H.; Warren H., m. Lilla Howard; Alice A., m. Elbert Barlow; Chloe.
Seventy. Settled in Salt Lake City; moved to Mill Creek, Salt Lake county, 1848, and to Mendon, Cache county, 1859. Member Mendon city council 20 years. Director Mendon Co-op. store 15 years. Moved to Holbrook, Idaho, 1898. Justice of the peace; city marshal; mayor two terms. Farmer.

SWENSON, AUGUST (son of Sven Andersen, born 1792, Trynge, Halland, Sweden, and Brita Anderson, born 1791, Smoland, Sweden). Born Aug. 7, 1836, Stafsinge, Halland, Sweden. Came to Utah Sept. 19, 1856, Canute Petersen company.
Married Bertha O. Petersen Jan. 31, 1859 (daughter of Ole Petersen and Bengta Andersen, pioneers 1857). She was born June 14, 1841. Their children: Peter b. Dec. 10, 1859, d. Dec. 20, 1859; John O. b. Feb. 19, 1861, m. Priscilla Lewis Jan. 2, 1890; Emma b. March 3, 1863, m. Joseph C. Hansen March 24, 1881; Alfred b. Feb. 10, 1865, d. Sept. 14, 1867; Oliver b. Oct. 14, 1866, m. Maggie S. Nielsen Feb. 24, 1892; Mary b. Dec. 7, 1868, m. George Christensen Feb. 18, 1891; Hyrum b. Nov. 25, 1870; Albert b. Dec. 16, 1872, m. Sina D. Nielsen Feb. 9, 1898; Maggie J. b. Nov. 26, 1874, m. Daniel Williams Jan. 26, 1898; Joseph A. b. Dec. 28, 1876, m. Cornelia Nielsen June 19, 1907; James H. b. Jan. 10, 1879, m. Hanna G. Snell May 1, 1907; Clara A. b. March 13, 1886.
Married Bergitha Johnson Nov. 14, 1868, Salt Lake City (daughter of Hans Peter Johnson and Anna Dorthea Jensen, pioneers 1866—married 1842). She was born Feb. 2, 1849, at Blands, Sjelland, Denmark. Their children: Hans Peter b. June 23, 1875; George b. Aug. 7, 1886; Olivia b. Dec. 27, 1881; Wilford b. Feb. 19, 1894, d. Sept. 2, 1894.
Married Sarah P. Hansen April 12, 1878, St. George, Utah (daughter of James Hansen and Karen Petersen, pioneers 1854—married Feb. 3, 1855, Salt Lake City). She was born April 29, 1860, at Spanish Fork. Their children: William H. b. Feb. 3, 1881, d. March 10, 1882; Sarah Ann b. Jan. 31, 1883, m. Charles Hayes April 27, 1904; Isaac b. Oct. 27, 1886; Nephi E. b. March 2, 1890; Edna B. b. Oct. 23, 1893; Carrie Myrtle b. April 2, 1898, d. Jan. 25, 1907; Levi Earl b. March 1, 1903. Family home Spanish Fork, Utah.
Counselor to president of elders quorum; member of presidency of 50th quorum of seventies; high priest; bishop's counselor; missionary to Sweden 1883-1884; high councilor. Vice-president of Spanish Co-operative Institution. Farmer and stockraiser.

SWENSEN, KNUD (CANUTE) (son of Svend Larsen and Annie Petersen, both of Weiby, Hjorring, Vendsyssel, Denmark). Born April 11, 1827, Weiby, Denmark. Came to Utah July 10, 1858, Horace Eldredge company.
Married Johannah Maria Peterson June 24, 1861, Salt Lake City (daughter of Hans Peterson of Maigard and Johannah Jensen of Hoisler, Denmark). She was born Sept. 13, 1838. Their children: Annie, m. Ezra F. Walker; Swen L., m. Susie Brown; Maria, died; Mary M., m. George Kelley; John Canute. m. Margaret Davis; Hannah Eliza; Henson P. and Caroline, died. Family home Pleasant Grove, Utah.
Counselor to Bishop John Brown 1877-90 at Pleasant Grove; bishop of third ward at Pleasant Grove 1890-99. School trustee 15 years; city councilman and treasurer several years. Farmer. Died March 14, 1902, at Pleasant Grove.

SWENSEN, JOHN CANUTE (son of Knud Swensen and Johannah Maria Peterson). Born Feb. 4, 1869, Pleasant Grove, Utah.
Married Margaret Davis June 21, 1899, Salt Lake City (daughter of Joseph W. Davis and Maria Williams of Panguitch, Utah, pioneers July 1852). She was born Sept. 2, 1877. Their children: John Starr b. March 27, 1900; Carl Davis b. Aug. 3, 1901; Reed Knud b. Feb. 15, 1903; Alice b. May 14, 1905, died; Margaret b. May 29, 1906; Frances McLean b. June 29, 1908; Louise b. March 24, 1910. Family resided Pleasant Grove and Provo, Utah.
High council Utah stake. Graduate Stanford University 1898. Dean of the B. Y. U. of Provo 1902-09; professor of history and social science 1902-12; professor of economics and sociology 1912; principal of Panguitch Stake Academy 1890-92; principal of Fillmore public schools 1893-94.

SWINDLE, GEORGE (son of George Swindle, born Oct. 10, 1794, died Sept. 24, 1854, and Elizabeth Miller, born Sept. 11, 1792, died Sept. 26, 1854, both of Durham, Eng.). He was born Oct. 29, 1824, Walker, Durham, Eng. Came to Utah 1857, Jesse Martin company.
Married Ann Hopper (daughter of John and Mary Hopper), who was born July 14, 1843, and died Jan. 27, 1900. Came to Utah 1857, Jesse Martin company. Their children: George b. March 3, 1849; Mary b. Jan. 27, 1851, John b. Dec. 27, 1852, John b. Dec. 24, 1854, John b. June 15, 1856, all Elizabeth b. Sept. 3, 1858, died; David b. Nov. 14, 1860, d. Nov. 4, 1895; Charles b. Nov. 18, 1864, m. Emma Folett and Sorena Shimmin. Family resided Spanish Fork, Gunnison, Richfield and Monroe, Utah.
Married Mary Maddeline Witzig March 4, 1872, Salt Lake City (daughter of John Witzig and Doritha Goasoure), who was born May 29, 1843, Horgen, Switzerland. Their children: Ann b. April 1, 1873, m. Cyrus Winget; Heber b. Nov. 28, 1875, m. Emma Warnock 1901; Joseph A. b. July 24, 1878, m. Etta Hodges; Ellen D. b. April 19, 1881, m. William Goold. Family home Monroe, Utah.
Justice of the peace. Farmer. Died June 28, 1882.

SYLVESTER, JAMES (son of Joshua Sylvester and Ann Webb of Sheffield, Eng.). Born Dec. 4, 1815, Pitsmay, Eng. Came to Utah September, 1852, James Jepson company.
Married Rebecca Nicholson in 1837, Sheffield, Eng. (daughter of William Nicholson and Mariah Calkwell of Thorne, Eng.). She was born March 10, 1819. Their children: Ann Mariah and Rebecca, died; Joshua William, m. Christena Christenson; Mary Elizabeth, m. Joseph Birch; Emma, James and Eliza, died; Lavina, m. William Berry; Rozinia, m. George F. Jarvis; Althea, m. Andrew Gregerson; Joseph, m. Jane Hanks. Family home Springville, Utah.
Elder; president of the church branch at Sheffield, Eng. Farmer and blacksmith. Died May 19, 1888, at Bellevue.

SYLVESTER, JOSHUA WILLIAM (son of James Sylvester and Rebecca Nicholson). Born Feb. 5, 1843, Sheffield, Eng. Came to Utah with parents.
Married Christina Christensen Jan. 1862, Gunnison, Utah (daughter of Jens Christensen and Margaret Krensen of Denmark, pioneers 1861, John R. Murdock company). She was born 1847. Their children: James William b. Aug. 31, 1864, m. Malaha Bell; Eliza b. Nov. 4, 1866; Rebecca b. Dec. 13, 1869, m. Christian Johnson; Joshua b. June 18, 1872, m. Anna Johnson; Rosina b. Oct. 30, 1875, m. James Sorenson; Ralph b. June 1878; Emma b. April 19, 1880. Family home Elsinore, Utah.
Married Caroline Christensen May, 1873, Salt Lake City (daughter of Jens Christensen of Denmark, pioneer 1861, John R. Murdock company). She was born 1853. Their children: Ada, m. Greely Snyder; Altheria, m. Christo Hyldahl; Elizabeth, m. Walter Jenson; Georgia, m. Jennie Dall; Arthur; Dora and Caroline, died; Agnes; Woodruff; Eleanor, died; Herman; Claudius and Curtis, died.
Married Clara Woodbury Barlow April 14, 1908, St. George, Utah (daughter of Orin Woodbury and Ann Cannon of St. George, pioneers 1547). She was born Nov. 30, 1875. Their children: Horace Greeley; Margaret. Family home Mesquite, Nev.
High priest; bishop. County commissioner; school trustee. Farmer and stockraiser.

SYLVESTER, JAMES WILLIAM (son of Joshua William Sylvester and Christina Christensen). Born Aug. 31, 1864, Mona, Utah.
Married Mahala Bell March 12, 1884, St. George (daughter of Thomas Bell of England, and Henrietta Lundquist of Sweden, pioneers). She was born Oct. 5, 1586, in Glenwood, Utah. Their children: Leonard W. b. Aug. 19, 1886, m. Zion Smith; Hessie b. Dec. 29, 1888, m. George Joos; Mabel b. Oct. 11, 1890; Lorin b. Oct. 19, 1892; Roy C. b. Feb. 19, 1895; Dea T. b. April 4, 1897; Tell Joshua b. Jan. 22, 1899; Faun W. b. Oct. 23, 1901; Clinton R. b. Sept. 17, 1903; Merrill b. March 28, 1905, d. Oct. 10, 1907; Jay G. b. Sept. 21, 1908; Ronald b. May 13, 1909. Family home Elsinore, Utah.
Elder. Member of Elsinore town board three terms. Farmer and stockraiser.

SYME, HUGH (son of William Syme and Margaret Wimly of Burnt Island, Fifeshire, Scotland). Born July 7, 1826, Fifeshire. Came to Utah September, 1853.
Married Margaret Farrer (daughter of Roger Farrer and Mary Stubbs), who was born Sept. 17, 1859. Their children: Margaret Ann, died; Hugh Leslie, m. Rachael A. Loveless, m. Emma Ettie White. Family home Provo, Utah.
Married Elizabeth Buckley, Salt Lake City, who was born Sept. 17, 1829, Lancastershire, Eng. Their children: William Alexander; Margeret Jane, m. Richard J. Nuttall; Fannie Elizabeth, m. George W. Giles. Family home Provo, Utah.
Member 7th quorum seventies. Carpenter; wheelwright; cooper. Died May 23, 1877, at Provo, Utah.

SYME, HUGH L. (son of Hugh Syme and Margeret Farrer). Born July 16, 1861, Provo, Utah.
Married Rachael A. Loveless Dec. 16, 1887, at Logan, Utah (daughter of James W. Loveless and Josephine Caldwell, both of Provo, Utah). She was born June 4, 1866. Their child: James Hugh b. Sept. 24, 1899. Family home Provo, Utah.
Married Emma Ettie White Nov. 16, 1904, at Salt Lake City (daughter of Henry White and Emma Saunders, both of Provo, Utah). She was born Feb. 7, 1871. Their children: George Leslie b. Oct. 3, 1907; Margeret b. Feb. 14, 1909; Edward Farrer b. Nov. 30, 1911. Family home Provo, Utah.
High priest. Carpenter; machinist.

SYMONS, NATHANIEL. Born Aug. 21, 1805. Came to Utah Aug. 20, 1863, John Seeley company.
Married Susannah M. Olivere (daughter of Peter Olivere), who was born Aug. 10, 1822 (deceased). Their children: Benjamin b. Feb. 23, 1840, m. Sarah Cater 1869; Joseph b. Dec. 1845, m. Louise Proctor 1880; Nathaniel, m. Mr. Sheen (died); Providence b. July 9, 1850 (died), m. Daniel Verrip (died); Mercy, m. John C. Munter (died); Hepzebah b. April 16, 1858, m. Charles Jones (died) Oct. 25, 1874; Naomi Grace b. March 12, 1860, m. George Augustus Tyler (died) Oct. 7, 1880; Rebecca Omega b. Oct. 20, 1862, m. Edgar Graham; John W. b. March 5, 1867, m. Mary Elizabeth Lunn Oct. 8, 1896; James Emanuel b. Aug. 25, 1869, m. Florence Johnson. Family home, Salt Lake City.
Embraced the gospel in England 1854. Was presiding elder over the Deptford, Walworth Common, Lambeth and Greenwich branches in 1862. Died Jan. 21, 1883.

SYMONS, JOHN W. (son of Nathaniel Symons and Susannah Mary Olivere). Born March 5, 1867, at Salt Lake City.
Married Mary Elizabeth Lunn Oct. 8, 1896, at Salt Lake City (daughter of John Lunn and Harriet Cookson), who was born April 24, 1873, at Salt Lake City. Their children: Harriet Susannah D. b. Jan. 31, 1898, d. Sept. 9, 1899; John William b. Oct. 24, 1900; George Daniel b. Jan. 2, 1903; Joseph Nathaniel b. June 5, 1905; Mary Elizabeth b. June 22, 1910; Walter Thomas b. Dec. 1, 1911. Family home Lava, Bannock Co., Idaho.
Was a pioneer of Lava, having arrived here when it was first settled in the year 1889. President of Y. M. M. I. A. in Dempsey ward in 1899; superintendent of Dempsey ward Sunday school for three years; bishop's counselor of Dempsey ward from Dec. 10, 1905, up till the present time.

T

TAGGART, CHARLES Y.
Married Margaret G. Smith (daughter of John B. Smith and Margaret Gibson of Tooele, Utah, pioneers 1852). She was born Sept. 19, 1856. Their children: Henry C. b. June 10, 1882, m. Ellen Nibley; John N. b. Feb. 17, 1885, m. Dora Stringfellow; Orson F. b. May 26, 1887, d. infant; Margaret H. b. Jan. 13, 1889; Joseph S. b. Oct. 24, 1891; Milton H. b. July 8, 1896, d. infant. Family home, Salt Lake City.

TAGGART, GEORGE WASHINGTON (son of Washington Taggart and Susan Law of Petersborough, N. H.). Born Nov. 6, 1816, at Petersborough. Came to Utah 1848 with a contingent of the Mormon Battalion.
Married Harriet Atkins Bruce (daughter of Peter and Eliza Bruce of Petersborough, N. H.). She was born March 20, 1821, and died at Nauvoo, Ill. Only child: Eliza Ann b. Jan. 28, 1844, m. George Albert Goodrich. Family home Richville, Utah.
Married Clarissa M. Rogers about 1860 at Brigham City (daughter of Washington Rogers of Nauvoo, Ill., pioneer 1848). She was born 1833. Their children: Clarissa M., m. W. B. Parkinson; Sarah Jane, m. George Hiner; Reuben, d. infant; Albert N., m. Sarah Kingston; Julia M., m. W. H.

1198 PIONEERS AND PROMINENT MEN OF UTAH

Lewis; Markus. m. Florence Bright; James. m. Baleria Laird; Alice J., m. J. W. Bright; Henry M., m. Mary Laird; Fredrick, m. Eulalia Leavitt.
High priest. Carpenter; millwright and farmer. Died June 3, 1893.

TAGGART, HENRY MILTON (son of George W. Taggart and Clarissa M. Rogers). Born March 9, 1875, Richville, Utah.
Married Alice M. Bright in October, 1896, Logan, Utah (daughter of John Bright and Miss Smith of Lewiston, Utah). She was born 1875.
Married Mary Laird Nov. 20, 1898, Salt Lake City (daughter of Edward Laird and Valeria Fling; former of Edinburgh, Scotland, and a pioneer, the latter of Salt Lake City). She was born Oct. 3, 1875. Their children: Milton H. b. Aug. 3, 1899; Edward L. b. Jan. 20, 1902; Leonard L. b. Dec. 24, 1905; Renold L. b. Aug. 7, 1909.
Seventy; missionary to southern and eastern states; block teacher; home missionary. Lumber merchant.

TALBOT, HENRY (son of John Talbot and Priscilla Percil of England). Born Oct. 16, 1813, London, Eng. Came to Utah Sept. 28, 1861, Homer Duncan company.
Married Ruth Sweetnam in 1833 (daughter of Thomas Sweetnam and Jennie Barton), who was born Feb. 4, 1817. Their children: Henry J., m. Lovina Wall; John J., m. Jane Hunter; Thomas B., m. Margaret A. Wiggell; Charles S., m. Rosanna M. Wiggell; Priscilla J., m. Jeremiah F. Wiggell; Hannah; Sarah, m. William Bodley; Albert J., m. Della Richards; Richard; Walter G., died; Edward W., m. Pennetta Partridge; Susannah, m. Lee Heward; Stephen B., m. Roeletta Brownell; Eliza, m. Mr. Moore; Hyrum P., m. Ellen Bennett; Ruth, m. Teyankum Heward.
Married Agnes Goddard in 1868, Salt Lake City. Their children: Sarah, m. William Ellis; Heneretta, m. George Tubbs; Henry W., m. Florence Stinger; George R., m. Huldah Adams; Alfred; Ester, m. William Bennett. Families resided Layton, Davis Co., Utah.
One of the first pioneers going to South Africa from England.

TALBOT, THOMAS B. (son of Henry Talbot and Ruth Sweetnam). Born March 25, 1838, Graham Town, South Africa.
Married Margaret A. Wiggell June 13, 1861, at Florence, Neb. (daughter of Eli Wiggell and Susannah Bentley of Winterburg, South Africa, pioneers Sept. 28, 1861, Homer Duncan independent company). She was born Oct. 11, 1843. Their children: Henry N. b. July 7, 1862, d. 1863; George E. b. Oct. 27, 1863, m. Sarah Alldredge Jan. 18, 1891; Harriet b. Oct. 16, 1865, m. Brigham Lovell Oct. 9, 1884; Arthur J. b. Oct. 24, 1868, m. Clara E. Theobald May 13, 1896; Thomas E. b. Dec. 25, 1870, m. Hannah Johnson Sept. 7, 1893; Joseph E. b. Jan. 29, 1873, died; Margaret Alice b. June 30, 1875, died; Sarah E. b. March 20, 1880, died; Lydia Ruth b. July 17, 1884, m. Charles Theobald Dec. 7, 1903. Family home Millard Co., Utah.
Ward teacher. Farmer.

TALMAGE, JAMES E. (son of James Joyce Talmage and Susannah Preater of England). Born Sept. 21, 1862, Hungerford, Berkshire, Eng. Came to Utah June 14, 1876.
Married Mary May Booth of Alpine, Utah county, June 14, 1886 (daughter of Richard Thornton Booth and Elsie Edge). Their children: Sterling Booth b. May 21, 1889; Paul B. b. Dec. 21, 1891; Zella b. Aug. 3, 1894, d. April 27, 1895; Elsie b. Aug. 16, 1896; James Karl b. Aug. 29, 1898; Lucile b. May 29, 1900; Helen May b. Oct. 24, 1902; John Russell b. Feb. 1, 1911.
High priest; member quorum seventies; member Deseret Sunday school union board 1901; ordained an apostle in Mormon church Dec. 8, 1911. Received baccalaureate degree from Lehigh University 1891; degree of Ph. D. from the Illinois Wesleyan University 1896; degree of D. Sc. D. from Mormon church. Professor of chemistry and geology of the Brigham Young Academy, Provo, 1884-88; president L. D. S. College of Salt Lake City 1888-93; president of the University of Utah and Deseret; professor of geology therein 1894; resigned presidency in 1897, retaining chair of geology; resigned professorship of geology July 1907; has since been consulting geologist and mining engineer. In 1891 was appointed curator of the Deseret Museum and later became its director, which position he still holds. Delegate from the Royal Society of Edinburgh to the seventh international geological congress held in Russia in 1897; fellow of the Royal Microscopical Society of London; fellow of the Geological Society of London; fellow of the Royal Society of Edinburgh; fellow of the Royal Scottish Geographical Society; fellow of the American Society for the Advancement of Science; life associate of the Philosophical Society of Great Britain.

TALL, GEORGE (son of George Tall and Sarah Proutt of North Devonshire, Eng.). Born July 25, 1826, Emington, St. Marys Parish, Eng. Came to Utah Sept. 27, 1853, Jacob Gates company.
Married Elizabeth Ormond July 3, 1856, Endowment House, Salt Lake City (daughter of John Ormond and Elizabeth Codd of Pembrokeshire, South Wales, former a pioneer Sept. 19, 1852, Joseph Outhouse and James Lloyd company). She was born June 22, 1839. Their children: Mary Jane b. March 14, 1857, m. John W. Keddington; George Samson b. Dec. 15, 1858, m. Emily Fulmer; John William b. Jan. 17, 1861, m. Matilda Ball; infant b. March 28, 1863, d. same day; Elizabeth Ellen b. Feb. 3, 1864; Charles Henry b. Feb. 22, 1866, d. Nov. 17, 1868; Sarah Ann b. Sept. 13, 1868, m. Heber H. Davis; David Samuel b. March 6, 1871, m. Lillian Eddington; James Alma b. Oct 14, 1873, m. Mae Houton; Albert Charles b. May 16, 1875, d. 1876; Joseph Tobias b. Dec. 6, 1877; Orson Francis b. Nov. 27, 1880, d. Dec. 18, 1880; Richard b. Nov. 27, 1880, d. next day; Alice Letisha b. March 31, 1882, m. Alois Price. Family home Salt Lake City.
Member 6th quorum elders; high priest; assistant superintendent Sunday school. Special police officer. Blacksmith.

TANNER, JOHN (son of Joshua Tanner and Thankful Tefft of New York). Born Aug. 15, 1778, Hopkinton, R. I. Came to Utah Oct. 17, 1848, Amasa M. Lyman company.
Married Tabitha Bently in Jan. 1800, Greenwich, N. Y. (daughter of Elisha Bently, pioneer Oct. 17, 1848, Amasa M. Lyman company). She was born Aug. 23, 1780, died April 1, 1801. Only child: Elisha Bently b. March 23, 1801.
Married Lydia Stewart in 1801 at Greenwich, Washington county, N. Y. (daughter of William Stewart and Amy Hunton), who was born 1783. Their children: William Stewart b. Oct. 27, 1802; Matilda b. Sept. 14, 1804, d. April 27, 1888; Willard b. Oct. 29, 1806, d. Aug. 12, 1807; Sidney b. April 1, 1809 (d. Dec. 5, 1895), m. Louisa Conlee; m. Julia Ann Shepherd; m. Rachel Neyman; John Joshua b. Dec. 19, 1811, d. Sept. 9, 1897; Romelia b. April 1, 1814, d. April 16, 1814; Nathan b. May 14, 1815; Edward b. Oct. 3, 1817, d. Oct. 21, 1817; Edwin (twin of Edward b. Oct. 3, 1817, d. Oct. 8, 1817; Maria Louisa b. Nov. 28, 1818, m. Amasa M. Lyman (died); Martin Henry b. March 21, 1822; Albert Miles b. April 4, 1825, d. July 16, 1879.
Married Eliza Beswick 1825, Bolton, Warren county, N. Y. (daughter of Everton Beswick and Anna Lamb), who was born Nov. 28, 1803, at Bolton, and died June 8, 1890, Payson, Utah. Their children: Myron b. June 7, 1826; Seth Benjamin b. March 6, 1828; Freeman Everton b. Jan. 3, 1830; Joseph S. b. June 11, 1833, m. Elizabeth Hawer m. Jannette Hamilton; Philomelia b. March 10, 1835, d. May 28, 1838; David Dan b. Feb. 8, 1838; Sariah b. July 19, 1840, d. March 12, 1853; Francis b. March 10, 1843, d. June 5, 1844. Family home Payson, Utah.

TANNER, SIDNEY (son of John Tanner and Lydia Stewart). Born April 1, 1809, Bolton, Warren county, N. Y.
Married Louisa Conlee March 1, 1830, Bolton, N. Y. who was born Feb. 6, 1811. Their children: Allen Benedict b. March 2, 1831, m. Elizabeth Jane Mathews; Lydia b. Nov. 3, 1832, m. Charles Allen Burk; Emma Smith b. June 1, 1835, m. Nathan Swarthout; Mary Louisa b. Sept. 4, 1837, m. George Crismon; Elsie Elizabeth b. May 14, 1840, m. Newton Chase; Sidney, Jr., b. March 6, 1842, James Monroe b. July 30, 1844, and Mason Lyman b. July 1, 1846, latter three d. infants. Family home, New York.
Married Julia Ann Shepherd in 1847, Bolton, N. Y. (daughter of Samuel Shepherd and Roxie Laney Ray of Vermont, pioneers, 1848, Amasa M. Lyman company). She was born March 24, 1829. Their children: Julia Ann b. June 10, 1849, m. Charles T. Tyler; Albert Myles b. March 5, 1850, m. Charlotte Banks; Henry Martin b. June 11, 1852, m. Eliza E. Parkinson; m. Emma E. Stapley; Naomi Ruth b. July 17, 1854, m. George Theobald; Samuel E. b. June 4, 1857, d. infant; Shepherd Leroy b. April 12, 1859, m. Olive Oakden; Rollin Ray b. Sept. 9, 1861, m. Rhoda Hales; Walter Wate b. Nov. 30, 1863, m. Hattie Fotheringham.
Married Rachel Neyman (daughter of William and Jane Neyman). Their children: William Neyman b. Jan. 8, 1860; Edith Idelia b. July 4, 1862, and Howard Harper b. Jan. 4, 1864, died; Rachel Adelia b. Sept. 4, 1866, m. Barlow Ferguson; North Sillman and Cyrus Livingstone, died. Families resided Beaver, Utah.
Called to San Bernardino, Cal., 1849, and returned 1857. Member high council of Beaver stake; counselor in bishopric Beaver ward. Died Dec. 5, 1895, Beaver, Utah.

TANNER, HENRY M. (son of Sidney Tanner and Julia Ann Shepherd). Born June 11, 1852, San Bernardino, Cal.
Married Eliza Parkinson Jan. 25, 1877, St. George, Utah (daughter of Thomas Parkinson and Mary Ann Bryant of Beaver, pioneers 1858). She was born Sept. 8, 1857. Their children: Martin Ray b. Jan. 22, 1878, m. Prudence Miller; Thomas William b. Jan. 25, 1880, m. Marian Miller; Julia Alice b. March 4, 1882, m. John L. Fish; Mary Ida b. Feb. 25, 1884, m. Jesse H. Rogers; Rollin C. b. Sept. 9, 1886, m. Anna Harbracht; Hazel b. Aug. 5, 1888, m. Harbert Cooper; Marion Lyman b. Aug. 7, 1890; Arthur b. Sept. 19, 1892; Leroy Shepherd b. Jan. 12, 1895; George Parkinson b. Jan. 26, 1897; Donnette b. March 31, 1899.
Married Emma E. Stapley March 24, 1886, St. George, Utah (daughter of Charles Stapley of Toquerville, Utah, pioneer 1858). She was born Nov. 30, 1862. Their children: Eva b. Oct. 29, 1891; Horace b. Aug. 2, 1894; Clifford b. Sept. 23, 1896; Golden J. b. Dec. 29, 1899; Charles Stapley b. Jan. 10, 1890, d. March 14, 1896; Francis Sidney b. May 23, 1904. Families resided St. Joseph, Ariz.
Missionary to England 1888-90; superintendent of Sunday schools, Arizona, 1889-97; member bishopric of St. Joseph ward since 1878.

TANNER, JOHN J. (son of John Tanner and Lydia Stewart). Born Dec. 19, 1811, Bolton, Warren county, N. Y. Came to Utah in 1852.
Married Rebecca A. Smith (daughter of William Smith

and Jane Calkins), who was born March 17, 1816. Their children: Lydia Jane b. Nov. 28, 1836, m. Luke Titcomb; William Smith b. March 28, 1839, m. Clarissa J. Moore Jan. 19, 1868; m. Susan Burgess Nov. 3, 1909; Marquis D. b. Oct. 1, 1840, m. Emily Ralphs Sept. 4, 1871; Edward Orlando b. Jan. 20, 1843, m. Mary E. Grigg Feb. 24, 1870; Cynthia Maria b. March 12, 1845; John Henry b. March 10, 1847, m. Mary Melissa Colvin Nov. 21, 1869; Elsie b. Sept. 22, 1849; m. David Lant April 5, 1869; Esther b. Jan. 4, 1853. Family home Cottonwood, Utah.
Married Mary Anna Neyman.
Married Mahala Jane Chase March 13, 1856, Salt Lake City. Their children: Albert Joshua b. Dec. 14, 1859; Nathan Chauncy b. Feb. 8, 1865; Mahala b. March 31, 1867.
Married Augusta Ferguson March 13, 1856, Salt Lake City (daughter of Isaac Ferguson and Almera Foote). Their children: Almira Artimisia b. Dec. 13, 1860; Isaac William b. Jan. 19, 1863; Warren Foote b. Dec. 8, 1864; Rebecca Augusta b. Oct. 21, 1866; Freeman Everton b. Feb. 22, 1869; Horace Greeley b. Nov. 22, 1872; Ona Eugene b. July 17, 1876; Clarence Leverne b. July 3, 1878; Ethel May b. May 2, 1882; Arthur Lyman b. June 18, 1887.
Died Sept. 9, 1897.

TANNER, WILLIAM SMITH (son of John J. Tanner and Rebecca A. Smith). Born March 28, 1839, New Liberty, Adams county, Ill. Crossed plains to Utah 1851, Isaac Allred company.
Married Clarissa Jane Moore Jan. 19, 1868, Payson, Utah (daughter of John Harvey Moore and Clarissa J. Drollinger), who was born Oct. 7, 1849, in Pottawattamie Co., Iowa. Their children: Delos Franklin b. Nov. 5, 1868, m. Armina Ellsworth March 6, 1890; William Frederick b. Jan. 2, 1873, m. Minnie Inez Winward Jan. 2, 1901; Julia Louisa b. May 10, 1871; Nellie Geneva b. Sept. 25, 1874, and Annie Estella b. July 10, 1876, died; Leone Smith b. April 9, 1878, m. Jessie Graham Dec. 21, 1898; Owen Emery b. June 25, 1880, m. Leree Viiate Hjorth March 13, 1902; Ezra Lyle b. March 16, 1882, m. Etta Goddard Dec. 4, 1912; Clarissa Jane b. Oct. 4, 1884, died; Mabel Rebecca b. Feb. 5, 1886, m. Nephi Stewart Nov. 28, 1906; Emma Elena b. Dec. 18, 1888, m. William Madsen Feb. 5, 1913; Harold K. b. July 8, 1890, m. Myrtle Monk Nov. 16, 1910; Kenneth J. b. Jan. 12, 1892; Olive Augusta b. Aug. 16, 1894. Family home Payson, Utah.
Married Susan Burgess Nov. 3, 1909, Salt Lake City (daughter of Horace Burgess and Almira Pulsipher), who was born Oct. 5, 1846, Florence, Douglass Co., Iowa.
Ordained elder March 31, 1867; missionary to Great Britain 1882-83; president high priests quorum 1874; high councilor; ordained a patriarch Oct. 20, 1890.

TANNER, WILLIAM FREDERICK (son of William Smith Tanner and Clarissa Jane Moore). Born Jan. 2, 1873.
Married Minnie Inez Winward Jan. 2, 1901 (daughter of Peter Winward and Lucinda Bingham, former a pioneer 1847, A. O. Smoot company, latter 1848—married 1854 at Payson, Utah). She was born Aug. 25, 1875, Payson. Their children: Inez Lucinda b. Sept. 24, 1902; Winward Fred b. Nov. 16, 1903; Nelda Jane b. April 28, 1907; William Sterling b. March 10, 1911.
President 46th quorum seventies; missionary to southern states 1895-98. President district school board 1908; member Payson city council 1910. Director Payson Exchange & Savings Bank.

TANNER, NATHAN (son of John Tanner and Lydia Stewart). Born May 14, 1815, Greenwich, Washington county, N. Y. Came to Utah 1848, Amasa M. Lyman company.
Married Rachel Winter Smith June 30, 1836 (daughter of William Smith and Ja.ie Colkins), who was born May 1, 1818, Bolton, N. Y. Came to Utah with husband. Their children: Romelia b. April 15, 1837, d. infant; Lydia Jane b. Jan. 27, 1838, m. James Stephens Brown; Helen Alcy b. Dec. 18, 1839, m. Elijah H. Maxfield; John William b. Nov. 6, 1841, m. Sarah Kent, m. Lucy Snyder; Nathan, Jr., b. Oct. 27, 1845, m. Margaret Harrington; m. Annie Pingree; m. Jane Hamilton; Rachel Winter b. Feb. 7, 1848, m. George G. Snyder, m. Charles E. Winegar; Emily Sophie b. May 13, 1850, m. Franklin S. Richards; Matilda Maria b. March 5, 1852, m. Joseph Lingo; Stewart Tefft b. June 4, 1856, m. Jessie Coates; Juliette b. Feb. 16, 1858, d. July 3, 1861; Franklin Smith b. Dec. 15, 1861, d. April 30, 1863.
Married Mary Rosina Baker Dec. 16, 1847, Winter Quarters, Iowa (daughter of Benjamin Baker, pioneer Oct. 19, 1848, Amasa M. Lyman company). She was born March 12, 1824, Albion, Oswego county, N. Y.
Married Persis Tippets April 10, 1849, Salt Lake City, who was born March 15, 1821, in New York. Their children: Alva Amasa b. Dec. 25, 1849, m. Mary Van Valkinberg; Martin Henry b. April 26, 1852, m. Emeline A. Barrus Jan. 7, 1879; Harriet Persis b. June 10, 1856, m. Daniel Gibson Oct. 28, 1875; m. John Ort; m. John Watson; Abigail L. b. March 18, 1858, m. Frederick C. Thompson Dec. 23, 1872.
Married Sarah Littley. Their child: Sarah Littley b. Jan. 28, 1859.
Married Mary Augusta Benbow. Their children: Rosetta b. Oct. 12, 1866, d. Nov. 28, 1866; Isabella b. Jan. 28, 1869.
Member Zion's camp; president 4th quorum seventies; missionary.

TANNER, NATHAN (son of Nathan Tanner and Rachel Winter Smith). Born Oct. 27, 1845, near Montrose, Lee Co., Iowa. Came to Utah 1848, Amasa M. Lyman company.
Married Margaret G. Harrington March 21, 1868, Salt Lake City (daughter of Thomas Harrington and Mary Greenwell of Salt Lake City, pioneers 1848). She was born Jan. 4, 1848, Winter Quarters, Iowa. Their children: Nathan Amasa b. Jan. 14, 1870, m. Ellen Hinchcliffe; Margaret Bently b. Jan. 19, 1873, d. Aug. 26, 1873; Rachel Emily b. Nov. 9, 1875, m. William M. Thomas; Francis Marion b. April 14, 1877, m. Rhoda Wolfinger; William Joseph b. Feb. 28, 1879, m. Inga K. Andreason; Thomas Harrington b. April 27, 1881, d. April 12, 1901; Benjamin Franklin b. March 4, 1883, m. Evelyn Jensen; Lyman Greenwell b. Aug. 27, 1888; Mary Ann b. April 28, 1891; Clarence b. Dec. 26, 1892, d. June 17, 1893. Families resided South Cottonwood and Ogden, Utah.
Married Annie Pingree June 7, 1890, Paso del Norte, Old Mexico (daughter of Job Pingree and Esther Hooper), who was born April 18, 1865, Ogden, Utah. Their children: Earl Pingree b. Oct. 16, 1891; Lydia b. Oct. 1, 1893; Frank Byron b. Feb. 2, 1896.
Married Jane Allen Hamilton June 12, 1898, Ogden, Utah (daughter of Henry Hamilton and Janet Johnston, pioneers 1856, handcart company). She was born Jan. 25, 1876, Provo, Utah.
President of the 72d and later of the 76th quorum of seventies; missionary to southern states 1884. Member constitutional convention of the proposed state of Utah 1882. Deputy probate clerk; Ogden city alderman; city attorney.

TANNER, NATHAN AMASA (son of Nathan Tanner and Margaret G. Harrington). Born Jan. 14, 1870, Salt Lake City.
Married Ellen Hinchcliffe March 4, 1891, Logan, Utah (daughter of Mathias Hinchcliffe and Catherine Russell, former a pioneer Sept. 10, 1861, Milo Andrus company). She was born Nov. 17, 1866, in Weber Co., Utah. Their children: Mathias C. b. Dec. 4, 1891; Amasa Thomas b. March 20, 1894; Nathan Russell b. June 14, 1895; Margaret b. Sept. 7, 1897; Ruth b. Nov. 28, 1898; Martha b. March 23, 1901; John Horace b. Aug. 13, 1902; Helen b. Dec. 13, 1904; Emma b. Feb. 19, 1913. Family home Ogden, Utah.
Member 76th quorum seventies; counselor in bishopric of 1st ward of Ogden. Trustee and treasurer of Utah State Industrial School. Vice-president and manager Watson-Tanner Clothing Co.

TANNER, JOSEPH SMITH (son of John Tanner and Elizabeth Beswick). Born June 11, 1833, in New York. Came to Utah 1848.
Married Elizabeth C. Haws Feb. 17, 1860, Salt Lake City (daughter of Elijah Haws and Catherine Clark), who was born 1843. Their children: Mary E., m. Henry Nebeker; Annie S., m. Hiram White; Joseph E., died; Henry S. b. Feb. 15, 1869, m. Laura L. Woodland; Lois A. b. 1867, m. Frank Fairbanks; Nathaniel H., m. Mary Wilkins.
Married Jannette Hamilton (daughter of Henry Hamilton and Jannette Johnson). Their children: John Sidney, m. Orilla Wolf; George Wilford; Hyrum; Jannette Fern; Beatrice, died; Sarah Agnes; Leland Scott; Jennie Mabel; Arnold Franklin; Iona; Clarice; Lucile, died. Families resided Payson, Utah.
Bishop of Payson 20 years. Mayor of Payson; member city council. Business manager church herds. Veteran Black Hawk war. Farmer and stockraiser. Died Feb. 28, 1910.

TANNER, HENRY S. (son of Joseph S. Tanner and Elizabeth C. Haws). Born Feb. 15, 1869, Payson, Utah.
Married Laura L. Woodland March 5, 1890, Logan, Utah (daughter of William Woodland and Laura Peters of Marsh Valley, Idaho, pioneers 1848). She was born June 10, 1867, Their children: Henry B. b. Aug. 19, 1891; Vella E.; Laura M. b. Aug. 9, 1895; LaFond b. 1897; DeOnge W. b. 1899; Merlyn; Clarice; Konda; Joseph E.; Katherine. Family home. Salt Lake City.
Missionary to southern states 1890-92; high priest. City judge at Salt Lake. Lawyer.

TANNER, GEORGE WILFORD (son of Joseph Smith Tanner and Jannette Hamilton). Born Jan. 7, 1885, Payson, Utah.
High priest; missionary to New Zealand 1905-09; bishop of 2d ward at Payson. Farmer.

TATTON, JOHN CHARLES (son of William Tatton). Born Aug. 4, 1818, in England. Came to Utah in October, 1853.
Married Caroline Webb (daughter of Ralph Webb and Miss Akenbottom), who was born Jan. 5, 1820. Their children: Eliza b. Jan. 27, 1840, Hannah Mary b. Dec. 24, 1844, Frances Ann b. Nov. 16, 1843, Charles b. Aug. 3, 1845, and Ann b. Feb. 1847, all died; John Charles b. Jan. 18, 1851; Martha Ann b. Oct. 16, 1854, m. Joseph Hyrum Taylor; Joseph b. Jan. 9, 1857; William and Caroline (twins) b. Aug. 9, 1859, died.
Seventy. Farmer. Died March 4, 1889, Manti, Utah.

TAYLOR, ALLEN (son of William Taylor and Elizabeth Patrick, born March 21, 1787, and Dec. 9, 1793, respectively, both in Kentucky). He was born Jan. 17, 1814, Bowling Green, Ky. Came to Utah Oct. 15, 1849, Allen Taylor company.
Married Sarah Louisa Allred Sept. 5, 1833 (daughter of Isaac Allred and Mary Calvert, pioneers Oct. 15, 1849, Allen Taylor company—married March 22, 1811, in Kentucky). She was born Nov. 14, 1817, and came to Utah with husband. Their children: Isaac Moroni b. June 29, 1834, d. June 3, 1836; Mary Elizabeth b. March 8, 1837, m. Francis M. Owen May 28, 1854; William Riley b. Feb. 12, 1839, m. Margaret J. Ellison Sept. 27, 1857; Sarah Jane b. Feb. 2, 1841, m. Robert Richardson Sept. 21, 1856; Joseph Allen b. May 25, 1844, d. May 11, 1845; Nancy Melvina b.

May 30, 1846, m. George Bennett Aug. 25, 1861; Clarissa Elvira b. Oct. 3, 1849, m. Benjamin Redd June 20, 1865; Orissia Angelia b. Oct. 13, 1851, m. Briant Heber Jolley Dec. 25, 1869; Independence b. July 4, 1854, m. Aner J. Taylor; Jedediah b. May 13, 1857, m. Catherine Woolsey; Louisa Jennett b. May 12, 1860, m. Willard Pace Feb. 15, 1877.
Married Hannah Egbert Jan. 1, 1850, Salt Lake City (daughter of John Egbert and Susana Cardhan, pioneers 1848, Allen Taylor company). She was born May 27, 1829, in Pennsylvania. Their children: John Taylor b. Oct. 25, 1851, m. Mary Kelsey Aug. 1869; Susana b. Sept. 30, 1853, m. Alma Pace May 1870; Liberty b. Oct. 8, 1854, m. Joseph Brundage 1875; Jeremiah b. May 7, 1857, m. Sarah Kelsey Oct. 1880; Crillia b. Aug. 16, 1859, m. William Goddard Jan. 1, 1877; Alfred Allen b. Dec. 15, 1862, m. Margaret Frost June 10, 1890.
Married Elizabeth Dirdle 1856, Salt Lake City, who was born 1822 in England. Their child: Annie D. b. April 22, 1858, m. Peter Neilson April 22, 1874, St. George, Utah.
Married Phoebe Ann Roberts April 1857, Salt Lake City (daughter of Levi and Harriet Roberts). Their children: Harriet Ann b. Oct. 31, 1859, m. Jacob Bastian March 22, 1877; Mary Ann b. Dec. 4, 1862, m. Joseph Cook Dec. 1879; Julia C. b. Feb. 22, 1864, m. Newton Searls Sept. 5, 1880; Mandy Melvina b. Aug. 11, 1866, m. Alma Young Sept. 1885; Levi Allen b. July 1, 1869, m. Rhoda C. Jameson Oct. 28, 1890; James Henry b. March 3, 1872, d. Nov. 29, 1871; Phoebe V. b. June 10, 1873, d. July 7, 1876; Allen, Jr., b. May 4, 1876, m. Lule Jameson May 8, 1901; Louisa b. July 12, 1878, m. Heber Blackburn Dec. 20, 1898; Amy b. July 5, 1880, d. Oct. 10, 1902: Wilford Woodruff b. April 14, 1883; Matilda b. June 26, 1886, m. Frank Edwards Dec. 23, 1903.
On arrival at Salt Lake City settled at mouth of Mill Creek canyon. Moved to Kaysville, Davis county, 1850, and was chosen bishop there 1854. Moved to St. George, Utah, 1862, and from there to Loa, Wayne county, in 1883. Died at Loa Dec. 5, 1891.

TAYLOR, WILLIAM RILEY (son of Allen Taylor and Sarah Louisa Allred). Born Feb. 12, 1839, in Caldwell county, Mo. Came to Utah Oct. 15, 1849.
Married Margaret J. Ellison Sept. 27, 1857, Kaysville, Utah (daughter of John Ellison and Alice Pilling, pioneers Sept. 13, 1852, Thomas Howell company). She was born Aug. 11, 1842, Nauvoo, Ill. Their children: William Allen b. April 19, 1859, m. Della Ivie April 1, 1884; m. Elizabeth A. Allred July 9, 1889; John Henry b. Jan. 4, 1861, m. Augusta E. Stevenson May 15, 1894; Joseph Ephraim b. Dec. 24, 1862, m. Annie Sophia Brian Jan. 30, 1894; David Moroni b. March 30, 1865, d. Nov. 29, 1878; Thomas Alvin b. May 20, 1867, m. Hannah Frederson Aug. 3, 1888; Sarah Alice b. July 17, 1869, m. Daniel H. Allred Jan. 1, 1894; James E. b. April 2, 1872, d. March 17, 1890; Isaac Harvey b. March 25, 1874, m. Zona Jeffery Sept. 5, 1900; Loren Independence b. May 15, 1878, m. Elizabeth Grundy June 5, 1901; Lorenzo Jedediah b. April 30, 1881, m. Jennie Grundy June 8, 1904; Heber Calvert b. July 21, 1883, m. Chloe Willliams July 1892; George Irvin b. May 29, 1885, m. Catherine Butler Nov. 30, 1894; Susannah Jennette b. June 4, 1887, m. Alma James Lee Feb. 19, 1908.
Served as bishop's counselor at Kaysville from 1878 to 1881; he then moved to Loa, where he acted as ward teacher for 31 years.

TAYLOR, WILLIAM ALLEN (son of William Riley Taylor and Margaret J. Ellison). Born April 19, 1859, Kaysville, Utah.
Married Della Elizabeth Ivey April 1, 1884 (daughter of Frank Ivey and Jane Young, former came to Utah about 1850). She was born April 1, 1865, Scipio, Utah. Their children: Mary Violet b. April 8, 1885, m. Ole Ernston April 6, 1904; William Franklin b. July 26, 1886, m. Irene Lewis July 17, 1911; Ella May b. May 13, 1888, m. Axel Ernston Oct. 22, 1907; James Calvert b. Oct. 28, 1890; Ada Matilda b. Aug. 8, 1892, m. William Blackwell July 19, 1910; Thomas Riley b. July 16, 1894; Iven Ellison b. Sept. 17, 1897; Maude I. b. June 8, 1901; Wilford Otto b. Dec. 8, 1903.
Married Elizabeth Ann Allred July 9, 1889 (daughter of Isaac Allred and Chloe Stevens), who was born May 9, 1872. Their children: Chloe I. b. Feb. 2, 1892, d. same day; Della A. b. May 25, 1893, m. Lewis Nielson Dec. 20, 1912; Joseph and Hyrum (twins) b. Nov. 7, 1894, Joseph d. same day, Hyrum d. March 2, 1895; Rose B. b. May 26, 1897; Susie A. b. Oct. 20, 1899; Nettie E. b. Nov. 5, 1901; Luven D. b. Oct. 31, 1904; Tressie O. b. Feb. 11, 1907; Zelma O. b. July 8, 1909; Daniel A. b. Dec. 12, 1912.
Missionary to England; ward teacher; bishop's counselor and member of the high council. School trustee; watermaster. County commissioner two terms.

TAYLOR, CYRNUS HENRY. Born July 30, 1826. Came to Utah 1848.
Married Emily Smith, who was born Jan. 26, 1832. Their children: Cyrnus Almon b. March 5, 1849; Emily Melissa b. May 1, 1850, m. George C. Johnston; Joseph Hyrum b. Oct. 23, 1853, m. Martha Ann Tatton; Esther b. Jan. 25, 1855, m. Joseph Breathweight; Albert b. Jan. 25, 1855, m. Eliza Wollsey, m. Eliza McFarlane.
First county clerk, Manti, Utah. Carpenter. Died Nov. 15, 1851, Manti, Utah.

TAYLOR, JOSEPH HYRUM (son of Cyrnus Henry Taylor and Emily Smith. Born Oct. 22, 1852, Manti, Utah.
Married Martha Ann Tatton Nov. 25, 1872, Manti, Utah (daughter of John Charles Tatton and Caroline Webb,

pioneers 1853), who was born Oct. 16, 1854. Their children: Ida Caroline b. Sept. 28, 1873, m. Anthon VanBuren; William Henry b. April 10, 1876, m. Arimilin Laenick; John Henry b. Feb. 1, 1879, m. Susie Woodward; Harold b. Feb. 28, 1883, m. Elma Anderson; Emily b. Oct. 7, 1885, m. Francis Dennison; George Lee b. Jan. 11, 1888, m. Francis Woodward; J. Leroy b. Feb. 8, 1890. Family home Orangeville, Utah.
High priest; ward teacher 30 years; Sunday school superintendent 5 years. Member town board; school trustee. Farmer and stockraiser.

TAYLOR, ELMER (son of Benjmain F. Taylor and Ann Mennell). Born Nov. 4, 1831, Grafton, Lorain Co., Ohio. Came to Utah 1850, William Wall cqmpany.
Married Weltha Ann Spafford (daughter of Horace Spafford and Martha Stiles, pioneers 1850, William Wall company). She was born Oct. 31, 1831. Their children: Martha b. Nov. 17, 1851, died; Horace F. b. May 28, 1854, m. Annie Peterson Nov. 18, 1887; Weltha b. Feb. 2, 1857, died; Olive U. b. April 26, 1858, m. Daniel Whitbeck Dec. 13, 1877; Helen b. Feb. 22, 1861, died; James E. b. Feb. 20, 1864, m. Almira Ollerton Nov. 12, 1885; Irinda b. June 1, 1868, m. Joseph J. Miller Jan. 17, 1888; Pattie b. Feb. 2, 1871, m. W. V. Osborn May 5, 1891; Minerva b. Aug. 22, 1873, m. N. J. Schow Aug. 2, 1894.
Bishop of Levan ward 1871; bishop of Juab ward at time of death. Merchant and county commissioner. Died April, 1896.

TAYLOR, JAMES E. (son of Elmer Taylor and Weltha Ann Spafford). Born Feb. 20, 1864, Springville, Utah.
Married Almira Ollerton Nov. 12, 1885, who was born April 7, 1868, Farowan, Utah. Their children: Ann Mennell b. Nov. 8, 1886; Joel E. b. Oct. 4, 1888; Vinnie J. b. April 1, 1890, m. Ivan C. Dalby Dec. 22, 1909; Frank S. b. Nov. 21, 1894; May Josephine b. Feb. 22, 1897; James O. b. Nov. 11, 1901; Weltha Eva b. Nov. 9, 1903; Olive b. Feb. 22, 1910.
Bishop of Levan, Utah; missionary to England 1895-98. School trustee; constable; commissioner; health officer.

TAYLOR, FRED T. (son of John Taylor of London, Eng.). Born March 11, 1854.
Married Amelia J. Needham July 11, 1892, Logan, Utah (daughter of John Needham and Martha Millens, pioneers 1850), who was born Sept. 11, 1857, at Salt Lake City. Their child: Lenessa N. b. March 11, 1894.

TAYLOR, GEORGE (son of Thomas Taylor, born June 13, 1800, Woodboro, Nottinghamshire, Eng., and Hannah Nichols, born 1802, Arnold, Nottinghamshire). He was born March 16, 1830, Woodboro. Came to Utah Oct. 16, 1853, Appleton M. Harmon company.
Married Mary Ann Quinn May 27, 1859 (daughter of William Quinn and Mary Ann Hosking, pioneers 1860, Andrew J. Moffatt company). She was born July 19, 1834. Came to Utah Nov. 29, 1856, Edward Martin company. Their children: Mary Ann b. April 2, 1860, m. Joseph Thorp; Harriet b. Nov. 10, 1861, m. Peter Jasteson; George b. Dec. 23, 1863; Minnie Frost; Elizabeth b. Jan. 16, 1863, m. Niels Kjeldsen; Zina b. Jan. 29, 1867, m. Andrew Hansen; Thomas b. Sept. 14, 1868, m. Hannah Whitcock; Presindia b. April 26, 1870, m. Thomas L. Thorp; Hannah b. Aug. 14, 1874. Family home Ephraim, Utah.
Married Charlotte E. Leggett June 1881, Salt Lake City, who was born 1837, in Illinois.
Bishop's counselor 1867-94. Member legislative assembly 1866-70; mayor of Ephraim City 1868-74. Member South San Pete stake high council from organization of stake until date. Veteran Black Hawk Indian war 1865-67.

TAYLOR, GEORGE (son of Edward Taylor and Ann Nichols of Gloucestershire, Eng.). Born April 6, 1830, Kensal Green, Eng. Came to Utah Oct. 3, 1862, Homer Duncan company.
Married Louisa Gwyther November 1853, in England (daughter of Thomas Kwyther and Louisa Palmer of Bristol, Eng.), who was born Jan. 15, 1827. Their children: Emma Louisa b. Aug. 13, 1854, m. John Laird Jenkins; Hattie Jane, m. William T. Higrinson; George Milo, m. Martha liowlse; Lucy Palmer, m. Zachariah S. Taylor; Alice Ann, died. Family home Goshen, Utah.
Secretary elders quorum; traveling elder and president of the branch at Cheltenham, Eng. Supervisor of road, bridge and canal construction. Blacksmith, farmer and mechanic.

TAYLOR, GEORGE (son of Thomas Taylor and Ann Hill of Birmingham, Eng.). Born March 25, 1838, at Birmingham. Came to Utah October 1863, John W. Wooley company.
Married Eliza Nicholls July 4, 1857, at Birmingham (daughter of Thomas Ashford Nicholls and Harriett Ball), who was born April 29, 1838. Came to Utah with husband. Their children: Hattie C. b. June 25, 1858, m. James F. McClellan Nov. 1, 1890; Emma b. May 13, 1860; Parley G. b. Aug. 4, 1862; George b. Aug. 31, 1864, m. Sarah E. Thomas Dec. 23, 1884; William b. July 2, 1866; Thomas N. b. July 23, 1868, m. Maud Rogers; Arthur N. b. March 2, 1870, m. Maria L. Dixon May 9, 1895; Walter G. b. Sept. 25, 1873, m. Agnes McKinley Sept. 28, 1892; Ashsted b. Sept. 22, 1875, m. Kate Strebel April 11, 1900.
Married Henrietta Sawyer 1865, at Salt Lake City (daughter of Joseph Sawyer and Henrietta Tranman), who was born 1846, Isle of Jersey, Eng. Their children: Nettie b.

Oct. 6, 1867, m. George A. Kerr Dec. 14, 1887; Mary Ann b. Feb. 14, 1869, m. William D. Roberts, Jr., June 20, 1894; John T. b. 1872, m. Edna Pulsipher Jan. 3, 1900; Ella b. Oct. 4, 1875.

Member Provo City council. Founder of Taylor Bros. Co.; president and director of Provo Commercial and Savings Bank.

TAYLOR, THOMAS NICHOLLS (son of George Taylor and Eliza Nicholls). Born July 28, 1868, Provo, Utah.

Married Maud Rogers Sept. 18, 1889, Manti, Utah (daughter of Isaac Rogers and Eunice Stewart), who was born June 30, 1872. Their children: Thomas S. b. July 4, 1890; Ethel b. April 26, 1892; Lester R. b. Nov. 24, 1893; Vesta b. June 28, 1895; Aldon R. b. June 1, 1897; Marion R. b. July 10, 1899; Victor b. Sept. 3, 1902; Maud b. June 28, 1906. Family home Provo, Utah.

Mayor of Provo 1900-04. Manager Taylor Bros. Co.; president Farmers & Merchants Bank; president Provo Building and Loan Society; president Taylor Investment Co.; president Malben Glass and Paint Co. Ordained bishop of 3d ward of Provo in 1900.

TAYLOR, GEORGE HAMILTON (son of Samuel Taylor and Lydia Osgood of West Bloomfield, N. J.). Born Nov. 4, 1829, West Bloomfield, N. J. Came to Utah in September 1859.

Married Elmina Shepard Aug. 31, —, in New York state (daughter of David Shepard and Rozella Bailey of Madison, Wis. Came to Utah 1871). She was born Sept. 12, 1830. Their children: George S. m. Christine Smoot; Frank D., m. Phebe Clawson; Rozella, d. aged 3; Minnie M., d. infant; Clarence W., m. Nellie Rogers; Almira Mae, m. Theodore Nystrom; Eugene A., d. infant. Family home Salt Lake City, Utah.

Bishop 14th ward 25 years; superintendent Sunday school; trustee L. D. S. college; missionary to England 1878-80. President Taylor, Romney and Armstrong Lumber Co. Died April 11, 1907.

TAYLOR, JOHN (son of James and Agnes Taylor of Hale, Westmorelandshire, Eng.). Born Nov. 1, 1808, Milnthorpe, Eng. Came to Utah Oct. 5, 1847, captain of his company.

Married Leonora Cannon Jan. 28, 1833, Toronto, Canada (daughter of George Cannon of Peel, Isle of Man). Among their children was: John W. b. Dec. 17, 1834, m. Jane Tenant; m. Mary Young.

Married Mary Ann Oakley. Among their children was: Henry Edgar b. Dec. 26, 1849.

At the age of fourteen he became a cooper's apprentice in Liverpool, and subsequently learned the turner's trade at Penrith, in Cumberland. He received his first schooling at the village of Hale, Westmorland, where his parents lived on a small estate bequeathed to the head of the house by an uncle. In 1830 he emigrated to America, following his parents, who were then residing at Toronto, Upper Canada. He was baptized into the Mormon Church May 9, 1836, at Toronto, Canada, and ordained an elder by Apostle Parley P. Pratt; shortly afterward he was set apart to preside over the Church in Upper Canada. In March, 1837, he visited Kirtland, where he first met the Prophet Joseph Smith, and was his guest while sojourning there. He attended a meeting in the temple, at which Warren Parrish made a violent attack upon the Prophet. Elder Taylor defended the absent Prophet and endeavored to pour oil upon the troubled waters. He was ordained a high priest Aug. 31, 1837. In 1838 he removed to Kirtland, proceeding thence in the general exodus of the Saints to Missouri. At DeWitt, Carroll Co., Mo., he and his party, numbering twenty-four, were confronted by an armed mob of one hundred and fifty, led by Abbott Hancock and Samuel Bogart, the former a Baptist, the latter Presbyterian minister, who, after some parleying, retired and permitted them to continue on to Far West. He was a witness to the outrages perpetrated by the Missourians upon the new settlers, and a participant in the scenes of peril and disaster ending in the imprisonment of the Prophet and other leaders and the expulsion of the Mormon community from the state. That he bravely and unflinchingly bore his part of the general burden of sorrow and trial we may be sure. John Taylor knew no fear, and shirked no responsibility or sacrifice that his duty entailed. In the fall of 1837 he was told by the Prophet that he would be chosen an apostle, and at a conference in Far West, October, 1838, it was voted that he fill the vacancy occasioned by the apostasy of John S. Boynton. The High Council at Far West took similar action on the 19th of December, and on that day John Taylor was ordained an apostle by Brigham Young and Heber C. Kimball. He was one of the committee appointed to memorialize the Missouri Legislature for redress of grievances, and was also appointed with Bishop Edward Partridge to draft a similar petition to the general government. He assisted President Young to superintend the exodus of the Saints from Missouri, and was with him and others of the Twelve when they made their famous ride from Quincy to Far West, prior to starting upon their mission to Great Britain. He started upon this mission Aug. 8, 1839. At Nauvoo he was joined by Wilford Woodruff, and these two were the first of the Twelve to sail. They landed at Liverpool on Jan. 11th, 1840, and at a council held at Preston, it was decided that John Taylor should labor in Liverpool, with Elder Joseph Fielding. He was appointed a member of the committee to select hymns and compile a hymn book for the Latter-Day Saints. In July, 1840, he passed over to Ireland, and preached in the court house at Newry, County Down. This was the introduction of Mormonism in the Emerald Isle, the first convert being Thomas Tate. He next went to Glasgow, and after preaching to the Saints in that city, returned to Liverpool and delivered a course of lectures at the music hall in Bold street. On September 16th, he, with elders Hiram Clark and William Mitchell, sailed for the Isle of Man. He delivered a course of lectures, baptized a goodly number, organized a branch, and then returned to Liverpool. He returned to America with President Young and other apostles, arriving at Nauvoo, July 1, 1841.

At Nauvoo he was a member of the city council, one of the Regents of the University, Judge Advocate with the rank of Colonel in the Nauvoo Legion, associate editor and afterwards chief editor of the "Times and Seasons." He was also editor and proprietor of the "Nauvoo Neighbor," in the columns of which paper, in February, 1844, he nominated Joseph Smith for the Presidency of the United States.

He, with Willard Richards, voluntarily shared the imprisonment with the Prophet and Patriarch. While in prison he sang a hymn to raise their drooping spirits, and soon after the jail was assaulted by the mob who shot to death the Prophet and Patriarch. In the midst of the melee the apostle stood at the door with a heavy walking stick, beating down the muskets of the assassins that were belching deadly volleys into the room. After Joseph and Hyrum were dead, he, himself was struck by a ball in the left thigh, while preparing to leap from the window whence the Prophet had fallen. Another missile, from the outside, striking his watch, threw him back into the room, and this was all that prevented him from descending upon the bayonets of the mob. In his wounded state he dragged himself under a bedstead that stood near, and while doing so received three other wounds, one a little below the left knee, one in his left hip, and another in the left fore-arm and hand. The Prophet's fall from the window drew the murderers to the yard below, which incident saved the lives of John Taylor and Willard Richards, the latter the only one of the four prisoners who escaped unharmed. As soon as practicable Apostle Taylor, who had been carried by Doctor Richards for safety into the cell of the prison, was removed to Hamilton's hotel in Carthage, and subsequently to Nauvoo.

He accompanied the exodus, February 16, 1846, to Council Bluffs, from where he was sent with Parley P. Pratt and Orson Hyde to set in order the affairs of the British mission. After accomplishing their purpose they returned, arriving in 1847. Apostle Taylor brought with him a set of surveying instruments, with which Orson Pratt, a few months later, laid out Salt Lake City.

After the departure of President Young and the pioneers, in April, Parley P. Pratt and John Taylor exercised a general superintendency over the affairs at Winter Quarters, and with Isaac Morley and Newel K. Whitney organized the immigration that crossed the plains that season. It was about the 21st of June when these apostles, with six hundred wagons and upwards of fifteen hundred souls, began the journey from the Elk Horn. John Taylor's division arrived at Salt Lake City Oct. 5, 1847.

In 1849 he was called to head a mission to France, and in company with Lorenzo Snow, Erastus Snow and Franklin D. Richards, who were on their way to Italy, Denmark and England, respectively, he set out on the 19th of October to re-cross the plains. After a very successful mission, where he organized a branch and made arrangements for translating the Book of Mormon into the Gallic tongue, he returned, arriving at Salt Lake City Aug. 20, 1852. He brought with him the machinery for the beet sugar plant, manufactured in Liverpool at a cost of twelve thousand five hundred dollars; also the busts of Joseph and Hyrum Smith, prepared under his personal direction by one of the first artists of England. Two years later he was called to preside over the Eastern States mission and to supervise the emigration. Resigning as a member-elect of the legislature, he, accompanied by his son, George J. Taylor, and by Elders Jeter Clinton, Nathaniel H. Felt, Alexander Robbins and Angus M. Cannon, set out in the fall of 1854 for New York City, where the first number of "The Mormon" was issued Feb. 17, 1855. In 1857, at the outbreak of the "Utah War," John Taylor returned to Salt Lake City.

He was a member of the Utah legislature 1857-76, and for the first five sessions of that period, speaker of the house. From 1868 to 1870 he was probate judge of Utah county. In 1869 he held his celebrated controversy with Vice-President Colfax through the columns of the New York press, and from 1871 to 1875 he published a series of letters in the "Deseret News," reviewing the situation in Utah, denouncing territorial government as un-American and oppressive, but warning the people against violent resistance to Judge McKean's high-handed and exasperating course. In 1877 he was elected territorial superintendent of schools, and served as such for several years.

The next important event in his history was his elevation to the Presidency of the Church, to which he virtually succeeded at the death of President Young, August 29, 1877. He had been for some years President of the Twelve Apostles. He continued to act in that capacity until October, 1880, when the First Presidency was again organized, with John Taylor, George Q. Cannon and Joseph F. Smith as its personnel.

President Taylor's last appearance in public was on Sunday, Feb. 1, 1885, when he preached his final discourse in the tabernacle at Salt Lake City. He had just returned from Mexico and California, after a tour through the settlements of the Saints in Arizona. That night he went into retirement and was never again seen in life except by a few trusted friends. He died July 25, 1887, at the home of Thomas F. Rouche, in Kaysville, Davis Co., Utah. His funeral was held four days later, at the tabernacle in Salt Lake City.

1202   PIONEERS AND PROMINENT MEN OF UTAH

TAYLOR, JOHN W. (son of John Taylor and Leonora Cannon). Born Dec 17, 1834, Newham buildings, Eng. Came to Utah Oct. 6, 1863, Thomas Ricks company.
Married Jane Tenant, who died in Eng. Their children: Elizabeth b. Nov. 2, 1855; Mary Ann b. Jan. 23, 1857; Margarett b. March 17, 1858; Jane T. b. Dec. 27, 1859. Family home Northumberland, Eng.
Married Mary Young May 5, 1862, Woolen, Eng. (daughter of Thomas Young and Isabell Wallace of Northumberland, Eng.), who was born Jan. 17, 1833, Whinney Hill, Eng., came to Utah with husband. Their children: Isabell b. Sept. 6, 1864, m. John A. Hill; John Thomas b. Nov. 6, 1866; George b. March 17, 1869; William b. Feb. 22, 1872, m. Eliza May Badger; Rachel b. June 16, 1874.
Missionary to England 1887-89; ward teacher; Sunday school teacher; high priest. Street commissioner, Weber county, 1880-82; street supervisor Ogden, 1882-86. Sub contractor for the Union Pacific R. R. Plumber and lime manufacturer.

TAYLOR, WILLIAM (son of John W. Taylor and Mary Young). Born Feb. 22, 1872, Ogden, Utah.
Married Eliza May Badger Oct. 17, 1894, Salt Lake City (daughter of Orson Pratt Badger pioneer 1848, and Eliza Jane Gay, pioneer 1851, John Brown company). She was born Jan. 11, 1875, Ogden, Utah. Their children: Eldred Orson b. June 4, 1895; May b. March 2, 1897; Gerald William b. May 17, 1900; Franklyn John b. Aug. 17, 1902; Lowell Badger b. May 31, 1906. Family home Ogden, Utah.
Ward teacher; Sunday school librarian eight years; counselor in presidency deacon's quorum. Warehouse foreman for Denver & Rio Grande R. R. Co. at Ogden, Utah.

TAYLOR, HENRY EDGAR (son of John Taylor, born Nov. 1, 1808, Milnthorpe, Westmoreland, Eng., and Mary Ann Oakley, born March 20, 1826, Flat Lands, Long Island, N. Y., married April, 1845, Nauvoo, Ill.). He was born Dec. 26, 1849, Salt Lake City.
Married Hariet A. Weaver Aug. 6, 1875 (daughter of William Weaver and Ann Watkins, came to Utah 1869, Captain Parry company). She was born March 15, 1859. Their children: Lawrence b. Jan. 1, 1879, m. Pearl Pingree Aug. 16, 1905; Ida May b. April 5, 1876, m. Alma T. Flinders April 8, 1899; Henry E. b. Sept. 5, 1882; Mary Ann b. Feb. 9, 1886, m. E. Norman Freeman Dec. 5, 1906; Ernest Weaver b. Nov. 24, 1891. Family resided Salt Lake City and Ogden, Utah.
Missionary to eastern states 1894-96. Worked on Assembly Hall organ from start to finish, and on the Tabernacle organ during reconstruction.

TAYLOR, LAWRENCE (son of Henry Edgar Taylor and Hariet A. Weaver). Born Jan. 1, 1879, Seventh ward, Salt Lake City.
Married Pearl Pingree Aug. 16, 1905, Salt Lake City (daughter of Job Pingree and Ester Hooper, former came to Utah Aug. 12, 1857, Jesse Martin company, latter September, 1861). She was born July 7, 1883. Their children: Lawrence, Jr. b. June 1, 1906; Phyllis b. Oct. 9, 1907; Inez b. July 4, 1909. Family home Ogden, Utah.

TAYLOR, JOHN. Born Dec. 7, 1812. Came to Utah 1853.
Married Eleanor Burkett, who was born July 2, 1815. Their children: Alma and Eleanor (twins) b. March 6, 1834, former m. Celia A. Keyes; Teancum, m. Mary Jane Hiat; Joseph M.; Sarah Elizabeth; Mary Ellanor; John Amon; Hyrum; Eliza Jane; Minerva; William; James Henry; Amanda. Family home Ogden, Utah.
Farmer. Died 1896, Ogden.

TAYLOR, ALMA (son of John Taylor and Eleanor Burkett). Born March 6, 1834, in Clay county, Mo. Came to Utah August 1853.
Married Celia Anzinette Keyes Dec. 3, 1856, Fort Supply, Utah (daughter of Elisha Barrus Keyes and Joanna Case Worden, pioneers Oct. 27, 1852, Eli B. Kelsey company). She was born May 10, 1841. Their children: Charles Alma b. July 22, 1858, d. infant; Sarah Anzinette b. Sept. 27, 1859, died; Mary Eleanor b. Sept. 11, 1861, m. Patten Huffaker; Joanna Rosealia b. Dec. 22, 1863, m. John Steinaker; Clara Louise b. Jan. 31, 1867, m. Lee Cover; Hyrum Henry b. June 27, 1870, m. Eliza Jane Bird; Amy May b. May 19, 1872, m. James C. Gardiner; Ermina Isabell b. April 9, 1874, m. Harry Meadows; Inis Pearl b. April 7, 1876, m. Jake Workman; Lola Lucy b. April 22, 1879, and Rebecca Jane b. Feb. 21, 1881, d. infant; James Anson b. Oct. 6, 1882, d. Nov. 9, 1905; Minnie Viola b. March 2, 1888, m. Frank Croxford. Family home Vernal, Utah.
Married Martha Keyes 1864 (daughter of Elisha Barrus Keyes and Joanna Case Worden). Four children were born.
Married Cornelia Congdon 1864. Five children were born by this marriage.
Missionary to Fort Supply 1855. Settled at Ogden 1856. A pioneer to Franklin, Idaho. Farmer. Died Aug. 10, 1910, at Vernal, Utah, from injuries received in a runaway.

TAYLOR, HYRUM HENRY (son of Alma Taylor and Celia Antinette Keyes). Born June 27, 1870, Ogden, Utah.
Married Eliza Jane Bird July 24, 1892, Vernal, Utah (daughter of Taylor R. Bird and Alice Stokes of St. George, Utah, pioneers 1852). She was born July 13, 1876. Their children: Violet b. April 27, 1893; Clarence b. Oct. 17, 1894; Eliza May b. May 19, 1896; Hyrum Henry b. July 27, 1894, d. infant; Ida b. Aug. 31, 1899; Lola Isabella b. Jan. 13, 1902; Alma Reaves b. Sept. 9, 1904; James Ernest b. Sept. 10, 1906; Alice Celia b. July 25, 1908, d. Aug. 6, 1910; Minnie b. Aug. 23, 1911; Joseph b. March 25, 1913, d. May 29, 1913. Family home Mesa, Ariz.
Member seventy. Farmer.

TAYLOR, JOSEPH came to Utah with a contingent of the Mormon Battalion.
Married Jane Lake. Their children: Joseph Allan; Elizabeth Bachman; Jonnie Bird; Frank.

TAYLOR, JOSEPH (son of William Taylor, born 1793, at Chelford, Chestershire, Eng., died 1840, at Lostockgralen, and Nancy Postals. He was born March 15, 1833, at Lostockgralen, Chestershire, Eng. Came to Utah Sept. 4, 1863, Captain Patterson company.
Married Elizabeth Mary Collier July 15, 1855, at Presbury, Chestershire, Eng. (daughter of James Collier, born September 1802, and Sarah Goodfellow). She was born May 9, 1826, at Macclesfield, Chestershire, Eng. Came to Utah with her husband. Their children: James Henry, d. infant; Elizabeth Mary b. April 2, 1858, m. William S. Read Jan. 29, 1878; Joseph Ezra b. June 23, 1860, m. Sarah Ellen Barker Sept. 13, 1883; Sarah Jane b. Sept. 30, 1861, died; Lucy and Marion (twins) b. 1864, d. infants; Julia Grace b. Sept. 23, 1865, m. Franklin Moore Oct. 29, 1882; George William b. April 6, 1868, m. Sarah Ann Connell June 1, 1890; Annie Margarette b. Sept. 21, 1870, m. Alfred Robert Folker June 29, 1892, m. Thomas C. Loveren May 9, 1900; William Goodfellow b. Feb. 15, 1873, m. Louisa Edwards Taylor Dec. 14, 1898; David Josiah b. June 24, 1875, d. April 13, 1911, m. Eva Bailey Jan. 1900; Clara b. 1877, d. youth; Israel b. 1879, d. youth; Florence Maud b. Jan. 11, 1881, m. Gustavus A. Horne Feb. 14, 1899, m. Lee Robert Cain March 16, 1910.
Missionary to England 1855-56; president of mission at Iowa City 1860-63. Tailor.

TAYLOR, GEORGE WILLIAM (son of Joseph Taylor and Elizabeth Mary Collier). Born April 6, 1868, Salt Lake City.
Married Sarah Ann Connell June 1, 1890, Ogden, Utah (daughter of William Samuel Connell, born June 3, 1850, Lancasterhire, Eng., and Emma Maria Wright, born Sept. 29, 1852, Manchester, Eng.—married Sept. 25, 1870, Salt Lake City, Utah, pioneers Nov. 30, 1856, Edward Martin handcart company). She was born Aug. 22, 1871, Nephi, Utah. Their children: George Leonard b. Dec. 15, 1892; Alfred Leslie b. July 23, 1897; Cora Myrth b. May 2, 1901.

TAYLOR, JOSEPH. Born April 24, 1800. Came to Utah October 1853, Cyrus Wheelock company.
Married Harriet Barnes in Lancastershire, Eng., who was born Oct. 9, 1805. Their children: Joseph, m. Hariet Barnes; John, drowned in Platte river; Martha, m. John Phillips; Levi Mary, m. Alfred Moss; Samuel B., m. Eliza Jane West; Jane, d. young; Harriet. Family home. Salt Lake City.
Seventy. Weaver and gardener. Died June, 1879, Salt Lake City.

TAYLOR, SAMUEL B. (son of Joseph Taylor and Harriet Barnes). Born Oct. 16, 1841, Lancastershire, Eng. Came to Utah 1853, with parents.
Married Eliza J. West June 1865, Salt Lake City (daughter of John West and Rachel Keeling, pioneers 1851), who was born April 20, 1847, Derbyshire, Eng. Their children: Mary Jane b. March 4, 1866, d. infant; John W. b. April 28, 1867, m. Mary E. Burns; Harriet Littlefair; Lillian, m. Joseph S. Richards; Eleanor, m. D. A. Engler; Edward T., m. Fannie Mulholland; Annie R., m. Daniel Higgins; Alvin V., m. Blanch Powers; Elizabeth, m. Benjamin J. Beer; Josephine, m. William F. Beer; Jennie, m. Edward Snyder. Family home, Salt Lake City.
Assisted in bringing immigrants to Utah 1862-63. Elder; block teacher. Died November, 1885.

TAYLOR, JOSEPH E. (son of George Edward Groves Taylor and Ann Wicks of Horsham, Sussex county, Eng.). Born Dec. 11, 1830, Horsham. Came to Utah Sept. 5, 1852, Joseph Outhouse company.
Married Louisa R. Capener 1855, Salt Lake City (daughter of William R. Capener and Sarah Verender of Cleveland, Ohio, pioneers 1850). She was born 1835. Their children: Joseph William, m. Margret Littlefair; Lillian, m. Joseph S. Richards; Eleanor, m. D. A. Engler; Edward T., m. Fannie Mulholland; Annie R., m. Daniel Higgins; Alvin V., m. Blanch Powers; Elizabeth, m. Benjamin J. Beer; Josephine, m. William F. Beer; Jennie, m. Edward Snyder. Family home, Salt Lake City.
Married Jane Capener. Their children: Jane, m. George Alexander; Margret Wicks, m. Fred Cluff.
Married Lisadore Williams at Salt Lake City. Their children: Samuel M., m. Lucile Badger; Alma O.
Married Clara Sudberry. Their children: Ruth, m. August Tohmstorff; Lisadore, m. William Campbell; Joseph E., died; Mahonri M., m. Cora Platt; Clara; Ida; George; Eugene.
Married Harriett A. Woolley.
Member 31st quorum seventies; missionary to central states 1875-76; high councilor; 2d counselor to president of Salt Lake stake 28 years; counselor in bishopric of 11th ward; patriarch. City sexton many years. Member 2d state legislature. Undertaker and casket manufacturer. Died Feb. 17, 1913, Salt Lake City.

TAYLOR, ALVIN V. (son of Joseph E. Taylor and Louisa R. Capener). Born Feb. 25, 1865, Salt Lake City.
Married Blanche Powers March 31, 1892, Salt Lake City (daughter of John Powers and Sarah Capener of Baraboo,

Wis., came to Utah 1902). She was born 1870. Their children: Gerald b. 1893, died; Margret b. 1895; Florence b. 1898, died; Alvin V. b. 1901. Family home, Salt Lake City.
Member 1st state legislature. Attorney at law; graduate Columbian University (law school) class '91.

TAYLOR, SAMUEL MOORE (son of Joseph E. Taylor and Lisadore Williams). Born March 11, 1880, Salt Lake City.
Married Lucile Badger April 15, 1903, Salt Lake City (daughter of Rodney C. Badger and Harriet Ann Taylor of Salt Lake City). She was born July 6, 1881. Their children: Harold Badger b. Jan. 18, 1904; Dorothy b. July 3, 1906, died; Marion b. March 22, 1910; Virginia b. July 30, 1911. Family home, Salt Lake City.
Missionary to Great Britain 1898-1901; member 8th quorum seventies; counselor in bishopric of wards. President and manager S. M. Taylor & Co., undertakers and embalmers.

TAYLOR, ISAIAH (son of John Taylor and Esther Wilson of Stockport, Eng.). Born Sept. 17, 1836, Stockport, Chestershire, Eng. Came to Utah Sept. 15, 1861, Ira Eldredge company.
Married Mercy Veater March 14, 1868 (daughter of James Veater, Sr., and Dina Frances Baber, latter pioneers 1862). She was born March 21, 1849. Came to Utah 1862. Their children: Harriet b. Feb. 25, 1870; George Nephi b. April 15, 1871; William James b. April 8, 1873; Charles Owen b. March 17, 1876; Albert Isaiah b. March 23, 1878; Esther Frances b. Oct. 12, 1880, m. Phillip Orwin June 12, 1901; Ella b. Nov. 20, 1882, m. Orrin Phillips June 28, 1905; Ray Wilson b. Dec. 10, 1884; Clyde Baber b. Oct. 4, 1886, m. Amelia Edwards May 28, 1908; Heber b. Nov. 19, 1889, m. Myrtle Bird July 20, 1911. Family home Beaver City, Utah.
Married Emeline J. Hutchings 1869, Salt Lake City (daughter of William W. Hutchings and Ruth C. Chase, who were married at Nauvoo, Ill., pioneers 1851). She was born Feb. 10, 1849, in Platte county, Mo.
Drove an oxteam across plains in Horace S. Eldredge company 1861. High priest; Sunday school librarian 38 years; Sunday school treasurer 6 years; ward teacher 30 years. Sent to St. George to fill a mission. Moved to Beaver 1868.

TAYLOR, CLYDE BABER (son of Isaiah Taylor and Mercy Veater of Beaver City, Utah). Born Oct. 4, 1886, Beaver City.
Married Amelia Edwards May 28, 1908, Buckhorn, Iron Co., Utah (daughter of Aaron Edwards and Fanny Farnsworth), who was born May 10, 1888, Beaver City. Their child: Amelia Babera b. Nov. 5, 1910. Family home Buckhorn, Utah.
Elder and counselor to president of Y. M. M. I. A. Died Nov. 5, 1910, four hours prior to birth of child.

TAYLOR, JABEZ THOMPSON (son of William Taylor, born 1803, died Claycross, Derbyshire, Eng., latter pioneer 1867). He was born April 26, 1840, Belper, Derbyshire, Eng. Came to Utah September 1864, James Miller company.
Married Ann Fisher Dec. 26, 1860, Chesterfield, Eng. (daughter of John Fisher of Man-of-Wood, Yorkshire, Eng.), who was born May 10, 1840, and died at Brampton, near Chesterfield, Eng. Their child: Edwin Arthur A.
Married Marian Brewer February 1867, Salt Lake temple (daughter of James Brewer and Margaret Wall of Beccles, Suffolk, Eng., pioneers 1862, independent company). She was born Jan. 2, 1837. Their children: Jabez William b. July 23, 1867, died; Ezra James b. April 14, 1870, died; George Francis b. March 13, 1872, m. Lelia Anderson, m. Mattie Johnson; Miriam b. April 16, 1874, m. Nugent Williams; Louise Maud b. Feb. 25, 1878, m. Leslie Hodgson; Jessie b. May 23, 1880, m. Ray D. Simons (died), m. Feramore Clawson.
Married Anna Peterson Nov. 25, 1896, Salt Lake temple (daughter of Charles Peterson and Wilhelmina Kroll of Copenhagen, Denmark, pioneers 1861). She was born Aug. 8, 1866. Their children: Ruby Violet (adopted) b. Nov. 6, 1884, m. Israel S. Kirkwood; Alleen Virginia b. Oct. 7, 1897; Melvin Marion b. July 30, 1900; Beatrice b. Sept. 27, 1902; Ray b. March 17, 1905; Eugene Fred b. Sept. 14, 1907, died. Families resided, Salt Lake City.
Member 16th and 57th quorum seventies; missionary to England 1876-78; to Ohio and Kentucky 1889-91; and to northwestern states; high priest. Veteran Black Hawk Indian war under Major Burt. Volunteer fireman about 20 years; special police officer several years. Appointed special representative to the World's Congress that was auxiliary to World's Columbian Exposition at Chicago. Physician about 35 years.

TAYLOR, STEPHEN W. (son of George Taylor and Catherine Broadbent of Yorkshire, Eng.). Born Dec. 25, 1835, in Yorkshire. Came to Utah Oct. 12, 1848, Brigham Young company.
Married Harriet Seely March 14, 1857, Salt Lake City (daughter of William Seely and Lucy Decker Young, pioneers 1847), who was born Oct. 5, 1838. Their children: Stephen; Catherine B., m. Thomas McClelland; Fanny, m. Ray Decker; George, m. Ollie Green; Amy, m. Fred E. Green; Florence, m. Oliof Parsons; Daniel A. and Nellie M., died; Hanmer D. b. July 9, 1870. Family home, Salt Lake City.
Married Mary Evans Dec. 2, 1872, Salt Lake City (daughter of William Evans and Sarah Keel of Worcester, Eng., came to Utah September 1871). She was born Sept. 16, 1851. Their children: Sidney W., m. Elsie Reilly; Lavenia, m. Fred G. Ford; Samuel D.; Jay James, m. Maud E. Dover;

Delmer Lee; William E.; Royal E.; Alice M.; Maud Incatze; Kenneth.
High priest; missionary to England 1869-71; went from Salt Lake City to Devils Gate in 1856 to assist Edwin Martin's handcart company on journey to Utah. In 1867, was with a company of gold seekers up to the Strawberry on the Sweetwater, when 506 were killed by Indians. Was in military service for brief periods, as follows: Under Colonel George A. Smith, Nauvoo Legion in expedition against Utah Indians July 22 to Aug. 25, 1853; under Colonel William H. Kimball in expedition against Indians from Aug. 25 to Sept. 10, 1853; under Captain James W. Cummings cavalry of Nauvoo Legion in expedition against Indians from Sept. 6 to Oct. 9, 1855; under Major Robert T. Burton with detachment of Life Guards against the Shoshone Indians from Oct. 12 to 26, 1855; under Captain R. T. Burton mounted men of Utah militia, protecting overland mail, east of Salt Lake City from April 25 to June 2, 1862. Sheriff of Summit county 1867-68; policeman at Salt Lake City 1874-76; messenger in territorial legislature 1850. Farmer and stockraiser.

TAYLOR, WILLIAM ANDREW (son of Joseph Taylor and Mary Moore, both of Kanesville, Iowa). Born May 15, 1850, at Kanesville, Iowa. Came to Utah Sept. 5, 1850, Captain Hawkins company.
Married Philomela Lake April 26, 1869, Salt Lake City (daughter of Bailey Lake and Sarah Jane Marler, both American born, pioneers Sept. 5, 1850, Captain Hawkins company). She was born Aug. 9, 1853. Their children: William Andrew, Jr., m. Annie E. Holley March 23, 1892; Bailey, Millie Almeda and George Lorin, latter three died; Mary Ellen, m. David Lee April 2, 1902; Ida, m. Moroni Chugg Jan. 23, 1900; Eliza Ann, m. John Lee Feb. 6, 1900; Aner, m. Joseph Shurtliff Jan. 9, 1907; Riley Edmund, m. Bessie Kinghorn Feb. 17, 1908; Iraminda, m. Clarence Stephenson May 16, 1912; Icivinda. Family home Harrisville, Utah.
Member 60th quorum seventies; missionary to central states 1887-89; first bishop of Farr West ward. Member school board five years. Farmer. Died March 6, 1892, Farr West, Utah.

TAYLOR, WILLIAM ANDREW (son of William Andrew Taylor and Philomela Lake). Born July 12, 1870, Harrisville, Utah.
Married Annie Edith Holley March 23, 1892, Logan, Utah (daughter of Henry and Ann Hutchins of England, the former pioneers Dec. 27, 1856, the latter 1855). She was born Dec. 19, 1868. Their children: William Russell b. Nov. 12, 1893; Annie Edith b. July 15, 1895; Blanche Ursula b. Nov. 24, 1897; Buell b. Sept. 7, 1899; Orin Helley b. Nov. 2, 1902; Norma Ann b. Oct. 16, 1904; Mildred Jane b. June 20, 1907; Junior Ivin b. April 15, 1910. Family home Farr West, Utah.
One of the presidents 60th quorum seventies 12 years; member of the superintendency of Sunday school 14 years; member high council of North Weber stake. Member school board 7 years. Justice of peace. Farmer.

TAYLOR, WILLIAM JOSEPH (son of William Taylor and Winifred Ferris of Trowbridge, Eng.). Born July 7, 1832, Trowbridge, Eng. Came to Utah Sept. 27, 1853, oxteam company.
Married Mary Bowring Jan. 30, 1853, Liverpool, Eng. (daughter of Joseph Bowring and Jane Cook of Wanmouth, Eng.). She was born Aug. 5, 1827. Their children: Mary Eliza b. June 7, 1854, m. John Warwood, Jr.; Martha Jane b. Sept. 23, 1856, m. Walter Scott; Ellen Ann b. March 3, 1858, m. John Warwood, Sr.; William Joseph, Jr. b. Nov. 23, 1859, m. Abby Jane Scott; Winifred b. Nov. 26, 1861, m. Andrew H. Scott; Walter Henry b. March 9, 1864, m. Rachel Broadhead; Lydia b. Dec. 29, 1866, m. John K. Allen; Jane b. Sept. 13, 1868, died.
Married Rebecca Harris, at Salt Lake City (daughter of Emer Harris). Their children: Emer Harris; Rebecca. Families resided Provo, Utah.
Home missionary; ward teacher; member 34th quorum seventies. Constable at Provo. Assisted in organization of Provo Woolen Mills. Veteran Black Hawk Indian war. Died May 18, 1869, Provo, Utah.

TAYLOR, WILLIAM JOSEPH (son of William Joseph Taylor and Mary Bowring). Born Nov. 23, 1859, at Provo, Utah.
Married Abby Jane Scott Aug. 3, 1882, at Salt Lake City (daughter of Andrew Hunter Scott and Sarah Ann Roe, of Provo, Utah, pioneers September, 1851, Morris Phelps oxteam company). She was born Jan. 30, 1864. Their children: William Weldon b. Dec. 9, 1883, m. Nora Johnson; Mary b. Oct. 8, 1885, m. C. Asal Dahlquist, Jr.; Andrew Scott, b. April 11, 1887, m. Clara Madsen; Joseph Hyrum b. Jan. 27, 1889; Ruth Elva b. Dec. 13, 1890, m. August J. Johnson; Golden b. Jan. 15, 1893; Frank Rouselle b. March 8, 1895; Glenn Lee b. July 24, 1897; Della Scott b. Nov. 8, 1899; Ruby b. Jan. 4, 1902; Karl Rowe b. Dec. 4, 1904. Family home Provo, Utah.
Missionary to southern states 1888-90; member 34th quorum seventies; high priest; counselor to Bishop S. P. Eggertsen; Sunday school superintendent; president Y. M. M. I. A. Justice of peace at Lake View. Farmer and dairyman.

TERRY, OTIS (son of John Terry and Sarah Ramsdell of Massachusetts). Born Feb. 28, 1796, in Worcester county, Mass. Came to Utah in October, 1850, Warren Foote company.
Married Syntha Ruggles of Massachusetts, who died.

Their children: Otis Lysander, m. Fanny Marilla Loveridge, m. Levee Terissa Dancy, m. Jane Hart, m. Sarah Vail, m. Martha Jane Van Valkenburg; Charles Alphonzo, m. Syntha Philinda Loveridge; Henry Algernon, m. Mary Ann Fotheringham; Horace Melvin and Edwin Delos, died. Family home Union ward, Salt Lake Co., Utah.
Married Philinda Marsh Loveridge.
High priest; acting bishop of Honey Creek and Kanesville, Iowa. Farmer and gardener. Died Oct. 31, 1887, Fairview, Utah.

TERRY, OTIS LYSANDER (son of Otis Terry and Syntha Ruggles). Born March 12, 1818, Worcester, Mass. Came to Utah in October, 1850, captain of one hundred in the Warren Foote company.
Married Fanny Marilla Loveridge Oct. 18, 1842, in Michigan (daughter of Ambrose Loveridge and Philinda Marsh of Pleasant Valley, Oakland county, Mich.), who was born July 8, 1825, and came to Utah with husband. Their children: Orson Merritt b. Jan. 25, 1845, m. Margaret Housekeeper; Elizabeth Ann b. June 15, 1847, died; Emma Jane b. Dec. 19, 1849, m. John R. Bennion; Otis Lysander, Jr., b. Jan. 6, 1852, m. Sarah Lovenia Howell, m. Lydia Ann Butterfield (Middleton), m. Mary Johanna Rasmussen; Alvin Delos b. Dec. 4, 1854, m. Salina Marinda Stewart. Family resided Mill Creek and Union Fort, Utah.
Married Levee Terissa Dancy July 6, 1851, Salt Lake City, who was born Sept. 30, 1830, in Upper Canada. Their children: Hulda Content, m. Charles Wilford Terry, m. August A. Hjorth; Obadiah, died; Levee Terissa, m. Edmond Stewart; Syntha Phylinda, m. Ole Lasson; Lois Almeda, m. Amaas Tucker; John Alexander, m. Ruth Daniels; Ira Judd, died; Emily Anna, m. Hyrum Partridge. Family resided Union and Fairview, Utah.
Married Jane Hart Nov. 16, 1851, Salt Lake City. Their children: Mary Jane, died; Elias Adolphus, m. Metta Mary Peterson, m. Mary Johanna Rasmussen.
Married Sarah Vail (Howell) Jan. 27, 1853, Salt Lake City (daughter of Edward Vail of Long Island, N. Y.) who was born June 24, 1818. Their children: Edmond Lysander, m. Rebecca Tucker; Fanny Marilla, died; Charles Alfonzo, m. Margerett A. Anderson; Celestia Melissa, m. Peter Peterson.
Married Martha Jane Van Valkenburg Nov. 30, 1856, Salt Lake City (daughter of Peter Van Valkenburg), who was born Dec. 7, 1839. Their children: Parley Pratt, died; Margerett Ann, m. Heber Barber; David Elias, died; Eugenie Gertrude, m. Isaac Allred; William Henry, m. Selena Beswick; m. Lillie A. Searls Barker; Andrew Burdell, m. Burnetta Taylor; Wilford Alonzo, m. Emma Hansen.
Families resided Union Fort 1851; North Ogden 1855, during which winter they nearly abandoned; Fairview, San Pete county, 1860, where he was choir leader, officer high priests quorum, ward teacher, president Y. M. M. I. A. six years; mayor and city councilman. Built canals, wagon roads, saw mills; operated a flour mill many years; grew the first apples; raised first cows, horses and sheep; did extensive farming, and in building up the community. Died Nov. 16, 1899, Fairview. His posterity number 382 persons. The posterity of Sarah V. H. Terry number 428 persons.

TERRY, OTIS LYSANDER (son of Otis Lysander Terry and Fanny Marrilla Loveridge). Born Jan. 6, 1852, Mill Creek, Salt Lake Co., Utah.
Married Sarah Lovenia Howell, Feb. 28, 1876, Salt Lake City (daughter of Elias Willis Howell and Martha Jane Rigby of Salt Lake City, pioneers 1852). She was born Jan. 3, 1859. Their children: Otis Lysander b. Dec. 21, 1876, died; Philinda b. July 17, 1880, m. Peter Nielsen; Willis Elias b. Jan. 28, 1882, m. Pearl Ekins; Martha Lovenia b. Sept. 5, 1883, m. Ivern Pyne; Charles Delos b. Oct. 22, 1885, m. Mary Ann Hurst; Fanny b. July 7, 1887; Roselee b. July 8, 1889, m. Robert Lynn Cook; Oscar b. Aug. 14, 1892; Walter b. Nov. 12, 1893; Emma Jane b. Nov. 12, 1895, died.
Married Lydia Ann Butterfield (Middleton) April 14, 1881, Salt Lake City (daughter of Jacob and Sarah Butterfield, of Taylorsville, Salt Lake county), who was born in 1862. Their children: Olive Lovina b. Nov. 16, 1883, m. Frank Humphries; William Edwin b. Feb. 25, 1886, m. Miss Ballard; Emma Jane b. May 17, 1889, m. William Dody.
Married Mary Johanna Rasmussen (Terry) Jan. 3, 1900, Salt Lake City (daughter of Andrew Rasmussen and Severtine Marie Madsen, pioneers in 1860 and 1862 respectively). She was born Dec. 26, 1863. Their children: Amasa Vivian b. Feb. 21, 1901; Andrew Severn b. Jan. 31, 1905; Otis Merlin b. Oct. 15, 1908.
Superintended Sunday school; president Y. M. M. I. A.; 2nd counselor to Bishop Phillips at Mill Creek, 1887. Moved to Fairview 1887; back to Mill Creek 1889; to Provo bench, 1901. Bishop of Timpanogos ward, 1903. Farmer and sheepraiser. Has 13 living children and 27 grandchildren.
Lydia Ann Butterfield first married Thomas Middleton. Their children were: Mary, Thomas and Eliza.
Mary Johanna Rasmussen first married Elias Adolphus Terry, May 17, 1883, Salt Lake Endowment House (son of Otis Lysander Terry and Jane Hart of Fairview, Utah). He was born March 2, 1854 and died Nov. 9, 1895. Their children: Mary Jane b. Oct. 1, 1885, m. Carl Farley; Elias Milton b. July 23, 1894, died. Family home Fairview, Utah. He was a farmer and sawmill owner.

TERRY, PARSHALL (son of Parshall Terry and Amy Stevens, of New York). Born Sept. 30, 1778, Fort Niagara, N. Y. Came to Utah Oct. 15, 1849, Allen Taylor company.
Married Hannah Terry March 16, 1802 (daughter of Joshua Terry and Elizabeth Parshall), who was born Oct. 8, 1786,
Goshen, N. Y., and came to Utah with husband, died Oct. 4, 1877, Rockville, Utah). Their children: Stevens b. Aug. 19, 1803, m. Sarah Bryant; Jacob E. b. July 4, 1805, m. Catherine Brown, m. Mary Urena Riley, m. Clarissa Williams, m. Ellen Reed; Dency b. July 20, 1807, m. Samuel Hackett; Clark b. Sept. 19, 1809, d. child; Joel b. May 23, 1812, m. Maria Anderson, m. Hannah Shelton, m. Jane Hacken, m. Rowena Garner; Elizabeth b. Nov. 17, 1814, m. Francis Kirby, m. John Huard; David b. April 17, 1817, m. Elizabeth Washburn, m. Mary Ann Cunningham; Jane b. May 21, 1819, m. George Tarbox, m. George Young; Amy b. June 5, 1821, m. Zemira Draper Jan. 30, 1842; Marilla b. July 2, 1823, m. John Crawford, m. Nelson Hanson; Joshua b. Aug. 11, 1825, m. Ann Greasewood; Mary Emma Reid (Johnson) b. Jan. 20, 1857; Deborah b. Dec. 25, 1827, d. child; James Parshall b. Jan. 1, 1830, m. Mary Richards (died May 17, 1902) Nov. 2, 1856; m. Sarah K. Brown. Family home South Willow Creek, Utah.
Toll-gate keeper Red Butte Canyon road. Salt Lake county, 1849. Moved to Lehi 1851 and to Draper 1853. Kept toll-gate at bridge over Jordan river at Lehi 1856, and in Provo Canyon 1858. Died Oct. 8, 1861, at Terry's Mound, Draper ward, Utah.

TERRY, JOSHUA (son of Parshall Terry and Hannah Terry). Born Aug. 11, 1825, Albion, Ontario, Canada. Came to Utah Sept. 26, 1847, George B. Wallace company.
Married Ann Greasewood in 1852, at Fort Bridger, Wyo. (an Indian girl), who was born in Wyoming. Their children: George b. Feb. 1, 1853, m. Kate Einis; Jane b. April 26, 1855, m. John Rideout.
Married Mary Emma Reid (Johnson) Jan. 20, 1857, Salt Lake City (daughter of John Reid and Sarah Corter, pioneers 1852, Warren Snow company). She was born June 7, 1840, at Golden Point, Hancock county, Ill. Their children: William Johnson (adopted) b. Feb. 18, 1856; Mary Ann b. Nov. 1857, m. Amelia Charles; Sarah Ann b. Dec. 3, 1861, m. Winfield Scott Ballard Dec. 15, 1881; Hunter b. Oct. 1, 1863, m. Harriet Brown; Hannah L. b. Aug. 17, 1865, m. David Brown 1885; Deborah b. July 4, 1867, died; Emma b. Aug. 3, 1869, m. Hyrum Brown 1889; Elisha T. b. Oct. 7, 1871; Joseph H. b. April 28, 1873; Porter M. b. July 21, 1875; Valeria P. b. Jan. 18, 1877; Deney M. b. Jan. 14, 1879; and Mayra b. Jan. 3, 1880; latter six died; Redell S. b. Jan. 7, 1882, m. Eliza Henderson 1903.
High priest; patriarch. Assisted in building Fort Bridger. Indian interpreter; spending fifteen years among the tribes. Drove first wagon into Davis county, Box Elder county, and into the Bear River country, and was a pioneer into many other parts of Utah.

TERRY, JAMES PARSHALL (son of Parshall and Hannah Terry). Born Jan. 1, 1830, Albion, Ontario.
Married Mary Richards Nov. 2, 1856, Mill Creek, Utah (daughter of John Richards and Agnes Hill), who was born May 14, 1837, in Home District and died May 17, 1902, Canada. Their children: Mary Jane b. Sept. 26, 1857, m. David F. Stout; George Washington b. May 21, 1859, m. Eliza E. Stocks 1878, m. Fannie L. Slaughter; James Parshall, Jr. b. Feb. 5, 1861; Hannah Agnes b. Feb. 17, 1863, m. Frank I. Slaughter June, 1878; Marilla b. Jan. 5, 1866, m. William H. Beebe March 10, 1888; John Richards b. July 10, 1868, m. Fannie Melvina Bliss March 20, 1890; David Parshall b. Dec. 5, 1870, m. Phebe Daly; Deney Elizabeth b. Dec. 5, 1872, d. July 15, 1892; Sarah Maria b. June 27, 1875, d. April 30, 1886; Joseph Clark b. Sept. 21, 1878; L. Daniel b. May 15, 1883; Richard Surprise b. Nov. 16, 1887. Family home Rockville, Utah.
Married Sarah K. Brown, a widow, who is the mother of Richard Surprise.
Member of bishopric of Rockville ward fifteen years. Moved to Rockville 1863, and to Hinckley in 1899. School trustee; road supervisor; Washington county selectman two terms, beginning 1883. Veteran of Walker and Black Hawk wars.

TERRY, PARSHALL PETER (son of Timothy P. Terry and Adella May of Upper Canada). Born Aug. 29, 1832, Upper Canada. Came to Utah July 24, 1847, Brigham Young company.
Married Rosina Hadlock Nov. 25, 1852, Salt Lake City (daughter of Chauncey and Jane Hadlock of Ogden, Utah, pioneers 1848, Brigham Young company). She was born Nov. 15, 1832, died Oct. 3, 1884. Their children: Sarah Ann b. Sept. 25, 1854, m. John Roof; Parshall S. b. July 6, 1856, m. May Bennett; Rosina E. b. Jan. 1, 1859, m. John Mallen; Durbin H. b. Nov. 11, 1861, m. Jane Barnette; George A. b. Aug. 5, 1862, d. Oct. 20, 1863; Orin A. b. March 15, 1865; Emily L. b. Nov. 11, 1866, d. aged 16; Ellen E. b. Oct. 6, 1867, m. Charles Conklin; Eliza Adella b. Aug. 16, 1870, m. John Miles; Almeda b. Jan. 16, 1872, m. Walter Hudson; Coquille b. April 26, 1874, m. William Glenn.
Married Esther Hadlock June, 1856, Salt Lake City (daughter of Chauncey and Jane Hadlock), who was born Feb. 12, 1841. Their children: Timothy b. Nov. 17, 1859, m. Mary Ann Joyce; Henretta A. b. Feb. 24, 1862, m. William J. Hodson; John b. Nov. 4, 1866, d. aged 14; Caroline b. 1868, d. infant; Ida b. Nov. 11, 1869, m. Preston S. Blair; Symon b. 1871, d. infant.
Married Jane Bond Jan. 8, 1890, at Ogden, Utah, Frank Burnette officiating (daughter of Henry Bond [died], and Emily Osborn of England). She was born March 30, 1868, in England. Their children: Gertrude H. b. Aug. 8, 1895; Loretta J. b. July 26, 1898. Families resided Plain City, Utah.
Member 70th quorum seventies; missionary to "Dixie" 1859-61. Justice of peace; school trustee. Farmer; blacksmith and machinist. Died Dec. 16, 1912.

PIONEERS AND PROMINENT MEN OF UTAH 1205

TERRY, WILLIAM REYNOLDS (son of Moses Terry of Exeter, R. I., and Sarah Reynolds). Born June 2, 1812, Exeter. Came to Utah 1852, at head of own company.
Married Mary A. Phillips (daughter of John Phillips and Polly Allen of Wakefield, R. I.). She was born March 11, 1815, Wakefield, and came to Utah with husband; died Oct. 9, 1898. Their children: Albina b. Oct. 5, 1836, m. John R. Young; Darcus b. April 13, 1838, m. Ostin Farnsworth; Mary Abbie b. July 12, 1840, m. William Frampton; Joseph b. June 6, 1842, m. Margaret M. Allen Dec. 4, 1864, m. Annie M. Garfield (Ennis) Feb. 3, 1892; Benjamin F. b. April 15, 1845, m. Mary Lay; Sarah M. b. Oct. 9, 1848, m. Richard White; Leah Avon b. Dec. 13, 1852, m. Marlow Andrus; Rose Annah b. July 7, 1856, m. Laron Andrus; Menerva Deseret b. March 22, 1859, m. Willard Andrus. Family home Draper, Utah.
Served as first counselor to bishop of Draper, and was the first school teacher in that town. Moved to St. George, Utah, 1860. Died May 31, 1868.

TERRY, JOSEPH (son of William Reynolds Terry and Mary A. Phillips). Born June 6, 1842, Van Buren county, Iowa. Came to Utah with parents.
Married Margaret M. Allen Dec. 4, 1864, Draper, Utah (daughter of James and Nancy Allen, pioneers 1862, independent company). Their children: Joseph A. b. Nov. 29, 1865, m. Hannah Rawlins; Lisadora b. Nov. 6, 1867, m. Franklin Walker; William R. b. Sept. 20, 1869; Mary A. b. March 3, 1875, m. Hyrum Peterson; Alma b. Jan. 9, 1878, m. Annie E. Ennis.
Married Annie M. Garfield (Ennis) Feb. 3, 1892. Their children: Henry Clyde b. Dec. 6, 1892; James Garfield b. April 26, 1897.
Served as ward teacher for over 50 years. Active in settling of Draper. Went to Arizona in 1872-73, afterward moving to St. George, later returning to Draper.

TEW, THOMAS (son of Joseph Tew of Burbage, Leicestershire, Eng., born May 1, 1777, Bubbenhall, Warwickshire, Eng., died Oct. 23, 1847, and Elizabeth Billing, born 1779 at High Cross, Leicestershire, died Sept. 6, 1822). He was born March 1, 1804, Burbage. Came to Utah Oct. 24, 1855, Milo Andrus company.
Married Hannah Smith (daughter of William and Catherine Smith), who was born April 29, 1811, Birmingham, Eng., and came to Utah with husband; died Feb. 11, 1882. Their children: Thomas, Jr. b. June 27, 1833, m. Rebecca Bird Jan. 22, 1856; Ann b. July 18, 1835, m. Levi W. Hancock; Sarah, m. Josiah Hancock; Samuel H. b. Jan. 20, 1842, m. Nancy E. Mayberry; Emma, d. child; William, d. infant; Emily b. Aug. 18, 1847; Eliza b. Feb. 6, 1851, m. Albert Wartnan Sept. 25, 1870; Mary Ann, d. infant; Ellen Amelia b. Sept. 4, 1856, m. Loran E. Harmer Sept. 27, 1875.
Died Dec. 24, 1888.

TEW, THOMAS (son of Thomas Tew and Hannah Smith). Born June 27, 1833, Birmingham, Eng. Came to Utah Aug. 30, 1851, independent company.
Married Rebecca Bird Jan. 22, 1856, Springville, Utah (daughter of John Bird and Ann Russen, pioneers 1855, Richard Ballantyne company). She was born Oct. 28, 1838, Yardley, near Birmingham, Eng. Their children: Eliza Rebecca b. March 23, 1857, m. John Mendenhall April 24, 1879; William Thomas b. Feb. 2, 1859, m. Clara Elizabeth Snow Jan. 31, 1884; Lorinda Ann b. July 11, 1861, m. Joseph Alonzo Reynolds Jan. 15, 1880, d. Nov. 9, 1890; Julia Adelade b. March 24, 1864, d. infant; Annie Belle b. July 24, 1865, m. Charles D. Evans Feb. 9, 1887; John Henry b. May 11, 1868, m. Emma Leona Bulkley Jan. 2, 1890; Cora Ellen b. Feb. 22, 1871, m. John P. Anderson Jan. 7, 1901, d. March 25, 1908; Melvina b. Feb. 14, 1874, m. John S. Smith Nov. 7, 1912; Erma Dell b. Sept. 24, 1880, m. Arville Leroy Titus Feb. 9, 1901.
Missionary to England 1882-84. Veteran Walker Indian war. Mechanic. Settled at Springville 1852; moved to Paris, Idaho, 1865; to Richmond, Cache county, 1868; to Springville 1872. Died Aug. 6, 1906, Springville.

TEW, WILLIAM THOMAS (son of Thomas Tew and Rebecca Bird). Born Feb. 2, 1859, Springville.
Married Clara Elizabeth Snow Jan. 31, 1884, Salt Lake City (daughter of Gen. Warren S. Snow and Sarah E. Whiting). Their children: William Thomas, Jr.; Sarah Rebecca; Warren Snow; Monroe Bird; Bryan; Burton Edwin; Melba.
Bishop. Farmer; mechanic. Town official. Director of the Strawberry Valley Water Users association.

TEW, WILLIAM THOMAS, JR. (son of William Thomas Tew and Clara Elizabeth Snow). Born Jan. 2, 1885, Springville, Utah.
Married Jennie M. Houtz June 18, 1913, Mapleton, Utah (daughter of Christian W. Houtz and Esther Waters).
Missionary among New Zealand natives 1905-08; Sunday school worker. Farmer.

TEXTORIUS, BENGT PERSON (son of Per Anderson, born Aug. 1, 1816, Gustaf, Malmohus, Län, Sweden, and Gertrude Anderson, born July 3, 1819, at Hyby, Malmohus, Sweden—married 1839). Born Aug. 11, 1845, Sturup, Malmö Län, Sweden. Came to Utah July 17, 1872, Eric Peterson company.
Married Josephine Hendrickson Aug. 9, 1873 (daughter of Sven Hendrickson and Nilia Borg, both died in Landskrona, Sweden). She was born March 19, 1848, and came to Utah July 24, 1873, David O. Calder company. Their children: Mary Josephine b. Sept. 6, 1874, m. Louis Nielson Feb. 13, 1895; John Ephraim b. May 6, 1876, d. July 8, 1878;

Albert Bennet b. Oct. 28, 1877, m. Phebe Jane Dutson Sept. 15, 1897; Maggie Elizabeth b. Sept. 17, 1879, m. Wyly Strange Jan. 26, 1900; Bertha Edith b. Sept. 2, 1881, m. Bert Kinney Dec. 16, 1898; Joseph Alexander b. Dec. 16, 1883, d. Nov. 12, 1886; Nellie Jane b. Sept. 11, 1885, m. Emil Anderson May 10, 1905; Meda Gertrud b. Jan. 1, 1888, d. Sept. 11, 1888; Henry Burton b. Jan. 4, 1889, d. Sept. 14, 1890; Josiah b. June 21, 1899. Family resided Salt Lake City, Alta, Sandy, Leamington, Holden, and again Leamington, Utah.
Missionary and elder in Sweden 5 years, 1867-72, before emigrating; and again 1900-02. Sunday school assistant superintendent and teacher; bishop's counselor. School trustee; election judge.

TEXTORIUS, ALBERT BENNET (son of Bengt Person Textorius and Josephine Hendrickson). Born Oct. 28, 1877, Sandy, Utah.
Married Phebe Jane Dutson (daughter of John Dutson and Fannie Johnson Nixon). Their child: Marvin b. Dec. 21, 1898. Family home Leamington, Utah.

THACKER, WILLIAM (son of Aaron Thacker and Leah Horton of Staffordshire, Eng.). Born June 6, 1823, Darlington, Staffordshire, Eng. Came to Utah 1861, Joseph Horne company.
Married Rachel Tonks 1844, in England (daughter of Firnaiby and Ann Tonks). She died 1893. Their children: Leah b. Sept. 13, 1845, died; Hannah b. March 22, 1847, m. James Shorten; Lida b. Aug. 25, 1848, died; Anna Maria b. Nov. 1, 1849, m. Joseph Myler; Elizabeth b. May 24, 1851, m. John Penfold; William Timothy b. Nov. 7, 1854, m. Sarah Tonks; James Moroni b. Nov. 2, 1856, and Eliza Jane b. Nov. 1, 1856, died; Isabell b. July 12, 1858, m. John E. Moulton; Sarah Ann b. Jan. 7, 1861, died; Charles E. b. Aug. 18, 1862, m. Maria Price; John b. June 7, 1863; Frederick A. b. Oct. 22, 1864, m. Sarah J. Price; George Nephi Hughes (adopted) b. March 23, 1852.
Married Mary Ann Brown Oct. 25, 1899.
Worked in Brigham Young's blacksmith shop making nails for the Salt Lake theatre. Moved to Cache Valley in early pioneer days and from there to Peoa and lastly to Heber, where he now resides.

THACKER, WILLIAM TIMOTHY (son of William Thacker and Rachel Tonks). Born Nov. 7, 1854, Staffordshire, Eng.
Married Sarah Tonks Dec. 7, 1875, Salt Lake City (daughter of Jacob Tonks and Elizabeth Rooker), who was born Dec. 11, 1848, in England. Their children: Sarah b. Sept. 30, 1876; William Raymon b. Oct. 26, 1877; Mary L. b. Dec. 14, 1879; Fredrick R. L. b. Aug. 26, 1881; Rosy Nellie May b. Nov. 19, 1883, m. Hans P. C. Hanson; John M. E. M. b. May 7, 1885, m. Jane Ann Bell; Maybell Y. G. b. April 10, 1891, m. Lewis F. D. Massey. Family home Heber, Utah.
Stonecutter and mason.

THACKERAY, GEORGE (son of Robert Thackeray, born March 28, 1798, and Elizabeth Jackson, born 1797, York, Yorkshire, Eng.—married 1820). He was born April 18, 1836, at York. Came to Utah Jan. 7, 1853.
Married Helen Condie May 12, 1855 (daughter of Thomas Condie and Helen Sharp, pioneers Sept. 12, 1852, Isaac Bullock company—married Aug. 21, 1830, Clackmanan, Scotland). She was born July 24, 1837, and came to Utah Sept. 20, 1852, Joseph Russell company. Their children: Helen Elizabeth b. Feb. 21, 1856, m. R. P. Stokes Jan. 10, 1876; Martha b. Nov. 23, 1857, m. George Chapman Oct. 16, 1879; George Robert b. June 29, 1860, m. Anne E. London April 5, 1883; Thomas b. March 1, 1862, d. Sept. 30, 1892, m. Magdalen Allison Oct. 15, 1891; Margret Ann b. March 12, 1865, m. Ruben Paradise May 1, 1899; Joseph b. Sept. 20, 1867, d. Feb. 3, 1899; Eliza b. Feb. 20, 1870, m. J. D. Murdoch Nov. 14, 1898; Mary Jane b. Sept. 22, 1874; Howard Alma b. Feb. 26, 1877, m. Ada Jackson Jan. 11, 1899; Adeline b. Dec. 1, 1879. Family home Croydon, Morgan Co., Utah.
Justice of peace 1872-85; county commissioner two terms. Died March 25, 1890.

THACKERAY, GEORGE ROBERT (son of George Thackeray and Helen Condie). Born June 29, 1860, Salt Lake City.
Married Anne E. London April 5, 1883, Salt Lake City (daughter of John London and Hannah E. Smith, former pioneer 1862, Homer Duncan company, latter pioneer 1863, Horton D. Haight company). She was born Sept. 9, 1864, Echo, Utah. Their children: Laura Annie b. Dec. 1, 1884, m. Jesse C. Little Nov. 27, 1907; Ada Blanche b. Sept. 5, 1886; m. Joseph E. Rees June 6, 1906; Thomas Royal George b. April 1, 1888; Zina b. March 23, 1890; Mark b. July 4, 1892; Parley Allen b. Feb. 20, 1895, died; Elsie b. July 12, 1899; Horace Emanuel b. April 28, 1904; John b. Jan. 27, 1910, died. Bishop Croydon ward eight years. County commissioner one term. A prominent rancher and business man.

THATCHER, HEZEKIAH (son of James Thatcher and Mary Gano of Martinsburg, Berkeley county, W. Va.). Born Aug. 25, 1809, Martinsburg. Came to Utah Sept. 23, 1847, Daniel Spencer company.
Married Alley Kitchen in 1829, near Martinsburg (daughter of Joseph Kitchen and Catherine Ghulic of Martinsburg). Their children: Joseph Wycoff b. Aug. 10, 1829, m. Hannah Morrison; Abraham b. 1830; Catherine Mary b. July 28, 1831; Mary Ellen b. March 14, 1833; John Bethewel b. Oct. 22, 1834, m. Rachel Hanna Davis, m. Sarah Maria Davis; Aaron Dunham b. April 25, 1836, m. Marie Baliff; Harriett Ann b. Feb. 1839, m. William

1206　　　PIONEERS AND PROMINENT MEN OF UTAH

Bowker Preston; George Washington b. Feb. 1, 1840, m. Luna Young, m. Fannie Young; Moses b. Feb. 2, 1842, m. Letitia Ann Farr; Sarah; Hyrum b. Nov. 25, 1844; Hezekiah b. 1846; Virginia b. March 7, 1851. Family resided Sacramento, Cal., and Logan, Utah.
Married Jane Amy Baugh Oct. 5, 1869, Salt Lake City (daughter of George G. Baugh and Elizabeth Furneaux), who was born Nov. 25, 1851, Birmingham, Eng. Their children: Evangeline and Ada, twins, b. Oct. 22, 1870, died; Samuel B. b. Jan. 11, 1872, m. Verna Lufkin, m. Maud Bowen; Wilford Woodruff b. Feb. 17, 1874; Orson Pratt b. Aug. 19, 1876, m. Nettie E. Reeder.
Seventy; missionary to Sweetwater 1848, to bring immigrants. Indian war veteran. Built first mill in Cache county. Merchant; banker; stockman; miller. Philanthropist. Died April 23, 1879, Logan.

THATCHER, JOHN BETHEWEL (son of Hezekiah Thatcher and Alley Kitchen). Born Oct. 22, 1834, Springfield, Ohio.
Married Rachel Hanna Davis March 9, 1858, Salt Lake City (daughter of Nathan Davis and Miss Woolley), who was born March 5, 1836. Their children: John Bethewel, Jr.; Hezekiah; Katie; Eva; Milton Herbert; Nathan Davis; Lula; Letta; Howard; Gilbert; Henry.
Married Sarah Maria Davis (daughter of Nathan Davis and Miss Woolley). Their children: Frank Davis; Roy; Sarah; Raymond; Martha; Ethel; Kingsley; Alice; Wallace.

THATCHER, GEORGE W. (son of Hezekiah Thatcher and Alley Kitchen). Born Feb. 1, 1840, Springfield, Ill. Came to Utah August, 1847, 2nd company Mormon Battalion.
Married Luna C. Young April 4, 1861, Salt Lake City (daughter of Brigham Young and Mary Ann Angel, pioneers July 24, 1847). She was born Aug. 20, 1842. Their children: Virginia Mary, m. July, 1881; Alice Young, d. infant; Nellie May June, 1888; George W., Jr., m. Emma Jean Crismon, Feb., 1892; Nettie Young, m. Dec. 1887; Brigham Guy, m. June, 1891; Kathryn, m. Sept. 1891; Luna A., m. July, 1897; Constance, m. June, 1902; Phylis, m. 1909. Family home Logan, Utah.
High priest; missionary to England 1873-74; president Brigham Young College board. Mayor 1888. Pony express rider. Banker; mill owner. Contractor on Utah & Northern R. R. Died December, 1902, Logan, Utah.

THATCHER, GEORGE W. (son of George W. Thatcher and Luna C. Young). Born Aug. 9, 1866, Salt Lake City.
Married Emma Jean Crismon February, 1892, Logan, Utah (daughter of George Crismon and Mary Louise Tanner of Salt Lake City, pioneers September, 1847, third company Mormon Battalion). She was born Dec. 15, 1869. Family home Logan, Utah.
Seventy; high priest. County treasurer. Professor at Utah Agricultural College. Musician.

THATCHER, MOSES (son of Hezekiah Thatcher and Alley Kitchen). Born Feb. 2, 1842, Sangamon county, Ill. Came to Utah with father.
Married Lettie A. Farr April, 1861, Salt Lake City (daughter of Aaron F. Farr and Persis Atherton of Salt Lake City), who was born Jan. 3, 1844. Their children: Ida b. May 5, 1863, m. Seth A. Langton; Emma b. May 2, 1865, m. Siverine Jepeson; Moses Jr. b. May 18, 1869, m. Sarah Catherine Hopkins; George F. b. July 11, 1871; Leonidas b. July 25, 1874, m. Mary Eliza Kimball; Lettie Vida b. March 14, 1884, m. William Alonzo Squires; Preston A. b. Sept. 24, 1877, m. Etta Murdock. Family home Logan, Utah.
Member quorum Twelve Apostles of Church of Jesus Christ of Latter-day Saints; missionary to England 1868; and to Mexico. Died Aug. 21, 1909, Logan.

THATCHER, MOSES, (son of Moses Thatcher and Lettie A. Farr). Born May 18, 1869, Logan, Utah.
Married Sarah Catherine Hopkins Dec. 17, 1890, Logan, Utah (daughter of William T. Hopkins and Ann Roberts of Logan). She was born April 14, 1868. Their children: Lettie A. b. Sept. 20, 1891; Leora b. May 12, 1894; Helen C. b. June 20, 1897; Martha E. b. March 26, 1900; Ida L. b. April 8, 1904; Moses, III. b. June 9, 1906. Family home Logan.
Elder; missionary to England 1891-92. City councilman. Manager Thatcher Livery & Transfer Co. and Thatcher Coal Company.

THATCHER, NATHAN DAVIS (son of John Bethewel Thatcher and Rachel Hanna Davis). Born Oct. 3, 1867.
Married Rachel Serena Faulkman May 18, 1892 (daughter of Jeppa George Faulkman of Bjornsholm, Denmark, and Anna Serena Anderson of Christiansand, Norway—married 1861, Salt Lake City). She was born Aug. 20, 1871, Plain City, Utah. Their children: Nathan Davis, Jr. b. March 29, 1893; George Basel b. April 5, 1894; Rachel Hannah b. May 27, 1896; Eulalia Serena b. March 15, 1898; John Kenneth b. Dec. 10, 1899; Reginald Henry b. June 14, 1902; Bethewel Floyd b. Jan. 27, 1905; Fleda b. April 3, 1908; Lavar Winole b. April 22, 1908; Donetta b. April 30, 1910; Alton Vear b. June 14, 1912. Family home Thatcher, Idaho.
Missionary to southern states 1893-95; one of the presidents of 108th quorum seventies. Bishop at Thatcher since 1907. In 1901 moved to Thayne, Wyo., where he built its first creamery and mercantile business; returned to Thatcher 1904.

THATCHER, ORSON PRATT (son of Hezekiah Thatcher and Jane Amy Baugh). Born Aug. 19, 1876, Logan, Utah.
Married Nettie E. Reeder May, 1903, Salt Lake City (daughter of Robert Reeder and Ellen Flatt, former pioneer 1856, James G. Willie company, latter pioneer 1868, Simpson M. Molen company). She was born Sept. 9, 1877, Hyde Park, Utah. Their children: Virginia May b. May 30, 1904; Orson Reeder b. May 20, 1904; Ray Alden b. June 8, 1906; Philip Elliot b. Sept. 1, 1909; Ruth Ellen b. May 5, 1911. Family home Logan, Utah.
Seventy; missionary to northwestern states; Sunday school teacher; second assistant in Y. M. M. I. A. Farmer.

THAYN, JOHN JOHNSON (son of Ebenezer Thayn and Jane Lockhead of Glasgow, Scotland). Born Nov. 11, 1825, Glasgow. Came to Utah 1861.
Married Sidney Boyer, who was born July 16, 1824, in Pennsylvania. Their children: Mary Ann b. Aug. 30, 1849, m. Mr. Moon; Nephi b. Nov. 1850; John Lehi b. July 8, 1852, m. Annabell Read; Ellen Jane b. March 3, 1854, m. James Lewis; Emma b. Sept. 10, 1855, m. Jeter Edward Jones, m. George Milner; Fanny Elizabeth, m. John C. Vance, m. William Turner; Eliza Catherine b. July 28, 1858, m. Elisha Allen Jones; Sidney Florence, m. Ephraim Green; Hyrum, died; Amanda Louisa b. Sept. 5, 1865, died.
Married Elizabeth Hunt 1862, Salt Lake City (daughter of William Hunt and Fannie Woodman of Newport, Monmouth, Eng., pioneers 1861). She was born Aug. 19, 1839. Their children: Joseph Hunt, d. Nov. 8, 1863; William Alvin Hunt b. April 13, 1865, m. Sarah Sorenia Tidwell; Brigham Hunt b. May 25, 1867, m. Sarah Smith; Edgar Hunt b. March 7, 1869, m. Martha Jane Smith; Ebenezer Hunt b. Aug. 30, 1874, m. Rosilla Branch. Family home, Salt Lake City.
High priest; missionary to Canada, United States and England 1878-89; ward teacher; assisted in bringing immigrants to Utah. Justice of peace. Settled at Salt Lake City; moved to Kamas 1875; to Wellington 1886. Died May 21, 1910, Wellington, Utah.

THAYN, WILLIAM ALVIN (son of John Johnson Thayn and Elizabeth Hunt). Born April 13, 1865, Salt Lake City.
Married Sarah Sorenia Tidwell Jan. 29, 1889, Wellington, Utah (daughter of Jefferson Tidwell and Sarah Seely of Lee Co., Iowa, pioneers 1852, John Tidwell company). She was born Feb. 7, 1865. Their children: David Alvin b. Dec. 9, 1889; George Lester b. Jan. 8, 1892; William Azell b. Dec. 7, 1893; Della Sorenia b. Oct. 23, 1895, died; Elizabeth Sarah b. June 23, 1898; Horace b. June 7, 1901; Albert b. March 11, 1904.
Missionary to England 1895-97; Sunday school teacher; ward teacher. First surveyor of Carbon county 1892-94-96; first town clerk of Wellington four years; road supervisor; school trustee; assistant postmaster. Farmer and merchant.

THAYN, EDGAR HUNT (son of John Johnson Thayn and Elizabeth Hunt). Born March 7, 1869, Salt Lake City.
Married Martha Jane Smith Aug. 3, 1893, Beaver, Utah (daughter of Richard Smith and Tabitha Holroyd, pioneers 1855). She was born June 11, 1869. Their children: Mabel b. June 5, 1894; Myrtle b. Jan. 29, 1896; Joseph Kenneth b. July 16, 1898; Edith b. Feb. 4, 1902; Edgar Ward b. April 3, 1906; Wilford Wallace b. Oct. 7, 1909.
High priest; bishop's counselor, Wellington ward; bishop, Wellington ward; president Y. M. M. I. A.; Sunday school teacher; teacher in Y. M. M. I. A.; home missionary. School trustee 12 years; county commissioner 1897-98 and 1906-08. Farmer.

THAYN, EBENEZER HUNT (son of John Johnson Thayn and Elizabeth Hunt). Born Aug. 30, 1874, Salt Lake City.
Married Rosilla Branch Sept. 20, 1900, St. George, Utah (daughter of Eugene Elisha Branch and Jane Blake of St. George and Wellington, Utah). She was born June 11, 1879. Their children: Ida b. July 27, 1901; Irene b. Dec. 18, 1902; Homer b. Sept. 27, 1904; John Johnson b. July 17, 1907; Alta b. March 11, 1909; Eugene Elisha b. Sept. 27, 1911.
Missionary to eastern states 1907-08; counselor Y. M. M. I. A.; president deacons quorum; Sunday school teacher; ward teacher; ward clerk. Farmer.

THEOBALD, WILLIAM (son of John Theobald of Kent, Eng., and Elizabeth Dore of Isle of Wight). Born March 31, 1812, Freshwater, Isle of Wight. Came to Utah Oct. 4, 1851, John R. Murdock company.
Married Martha Lane on Isle of Wight (daughter of William Lane and Ann Parish), who was born Oct. 18, 1814, and came to Utah with husband. Their children: Drucilla b. Oct. 22, 1842, m. Thomas Passey 1860; Arthur b. June 1, 1844, m. Jane Burgess Sept. 4, 1864; Clara b. June 15, 1846, m. Loren Shaw 1863; George b. May 22, 1848, m. Naomi R. Tanner March 18, 1874; Ruth b. Sept. 1, 1850, m. Joseph Gibson 1867; Martha b. Jan. 20, 1853; John b. Feb. 11, 1855; Elizabeth b. Jan. 24, 1857, m. Mr. Jackson; Frances b. Jan. 24, 1858, m. Lorum Pratt 1877. Family resided Isle of Wight, Eng., and Salt Lake City and Toquerville, Utah.
Married Elizabeth Uren, Salt Lake City (daughter of Thomas Uren and Mary Enude, former pioneer 1860, Oscar O. Stoddard company). She was born in Cornwall, Eng. Their children: Ann b. June 20, 1862, m. Mr. Richards; Mary b. March 23, 1863, m. John Baker; Amelia b. Feb. 9, 1867, m. Martin Slack; William b. Feb. 21, 1869, m. Lorena Jackson; Charles b. Aug. 4, 1870; Lenora b. Aug. 12, 1873, m. Harry Jackson. Family home, Toquerville.
Elder Duncan Retreat four years. Commissioner two years; policeman; postmaster. Carpenter. Died Feb. 15, 1895, at Toquerville.

THEOBALD, ARTHUR (son of William Theobald and Martha Lane). Born June 1, 1844, Isle of Wight, Eng. Came to Utah with parents.
Married Jane Burgess Sept. 4, 1864, Dalton, Kane Co., Utah (daughter of Thomas Burgess and Elizabeth Isaacs, pioneers Nelson Empey company). She was born Sept. 22, 1848. Their children: William Arthur b. June 27, 1865, d. same day; Ernest Burgess b. July 18, 1867, m. Susie Alldredge; Martha Lizette b. Aug. 7, 1869, m. William Alldredge; Nellie Jane b. Dec. 6, 1871, m. Nathan Badger; Thomas George b. March 28, 1874, m. Etta Elder; Charles b. May 17, 1877, m. Alba Whitehead; Clara Elizabeth b. March 24, 1880, m. Arthur Talbot; Emma Naomi b. Sept. 18, 1883, m. Joseph E. Spendlove. Family home Hinckley, Utah.
Elder. Assisted in bringing immigrants to Utah. Helped build road to Colorado river. Carpenter. Died March 3, 1890, Provo, Utah.

THEOBALD, ERNEST BURGESS (son of Arthur Theobald and Jane Burgess). Born July 18, 1867, Duncan's Retreat, Utah.
Married Susie Alldredge Nov. 23, 1892, Manti, Utah (daughter of Isaac Alldredge and Susannah Evans of Lehi, Utah, pioneers Oct. 17, 1853, John Brown company). She was born Nov. 7, 1874. Their children: Inez b. Oct. 6, 1893; Evan b. Aug. 22, 1896; Arthur b. March 29, 1900; Elwin b. Feb. 1, 1902; Susie b. Aug. 22, 1903; Desa b. Dec. 11, 1905; Leo b. Nov. 13, 1907. Family home Hinckley, Utah.
Missionary to northern states 1895-96; senior president of seventies. Civil engineer.

THEOBALD, GEORGE (son of William Theobald and Martha Lane). Born May 22, 1848, Newport, Isle of Wight, Eng.
Married Naomi R. Tanner March 18, 1874, Beaver, Utah (daughter of Sidney Tanner and Julia A. Shepard, pioneers Oct. 19, 1848, Amasa M. Lyman company). She was born July 17, 1854, San Bernardino, Cal. Their children: Julia b. Dec. 10, 1874, m. Thomas Herbert June 30, 1897; George, Jr. b. Aug. 8, 1876, d. Nov. 14, 1878; William Sidney b. Feb. 16, 1879, d. July 9, 1879; Martha b. March 31, 1881, m. George Gabbitas Nov. 7, 1901; Edgar b. Nov. 11, 1883, d. April 19, 1884; Rollin b. Feb. 8, 1885, d. March 6, 1887; Harriet b. March 30, 1887, m. Norman I. Bliss April 1, 1908; Lafayette b. April 24, 1889; John b. March 1, 1892, d. March 7, 1892; Nettie Mae b. May 25, 1893; Iva Naomi b. Nov. 11, 1896, d. June 21, 1897; Myron Lane b. Feb. 7, 1898. Family home Duncan's Retreat and Hinckley, Utah.
Veteran Indian wars. Watermaster 24 years.

THEURER, JOHN (son of Michael Theurer and Barbara Hariocher of Switzerland). Born Sept. 1, 1837, in Switzerland. Came to Utah Sept. 12, 1857, Israel Evans company.
Married Barbara Wehrli Nov. 4, 1860, Providence, Utah (daughter of Jacob and Magdelana Wehrli of Switzerland). She was born May 19, 1841. Their children: Magdelana and Mary, died; Emily, m. A. C. Ellsworth; Anna, m. Heber Chekette; Ida, m. Joseph Quinney; Laura, m. William Wilson; Sophia, m. H. Thorp; John, died; Adelina, m. E. Mathews; Clara, m. A. Feller; Verana, m. M. Tibbets. Family home, Providence.
High priest; missionary to Germany 1878-80; home missionary. School trustee; member town board. Farmer.

THOMAS, CHARLES. Born April, 1811, in Herefordshire, Eng.
Married Elizabeth Carter, born March 28, 1811, in England. Their children: Elisha b. Aug. 2, 1834, m. Jane Balm; Emma b. Jan. 24, 1837; Charles b. Sept. 16, 1839, Emeline Sessions; John b. Dec. 12, 1843, m. Emma Ross; Jacob b. July 27, 1845, m. Mariam Woodward; Joseph b. Nov. 12, 1848, m. Margaret Watson; James W. b. Nov. 21, 1850, m. Larrah Lee; Sarah E. b. Jan. 30, 1853, m. Aaron Beach; George b. Oct. 5, 1856, m. Nellie Allen. Family home, Salt Lake City.

THOMAS, CHARLES CARTER (son of Charles Thomas, born April 11, 1811, Herefordshire, Eng., and Elizabeth Carter, born March 28, 1811, Worcester, Eng.). Born Sept. 16, 1839, in Herefordshire. Came to Utah Sept. 9, 1852, Bryant Jolley company.
Married Emeline Sessions Dec. 25, 1860, at Heber City (daughter of Richard Sessions and Lucretia Haws—married February, 1821—former came with the first portion of the Mormon Battalion. 1847, latter 1850. Richard Sessions company). She was born May 1, 1840, and came to Utah 1850, James Pace company. Their children: Charles Richard b. Jan. 1, 1862, m. Agnes Jane Yates Dec. 25, 1882; William Jacob b. June 17, 1863, d. Oct. 6, 1864; Elizabeth Lucretia b. Feb. 12, 1866, m. George Milton Ince Nov. 15, 1885; John Alexander b. Jan. 8, 1868, m. Mary Jane Hughes June 1890; Helen Louisa b. Nov. 15, 1870, m. George Henry Prescott Feb. 1892; James Earlton b. Aug. 2, 1872; Ada Emeline b. April 5, 1875, d. Feb. 14, 1882; George Bradford b. April 1, 1877 (d. April 17, 1912), m. Betsy Prescott July 1, 1899; Eliza Melissa b. July 21, 1879. Family home Heber City, Utah.
Member Nauvoo Legion; took part in Echo Canyon trouble. Early settler to Heber City. Veteran Indian war.

THOMAS, CHARLES RICHARD (son of Charles Carter Thomas and Emeline Sessions). Born Jan. 1, 1862, Heber City, Utah.

Married Agness Jane Yates Dec. 25, 1882, Wallsburg, Utah (daughter of Agness Murry), who was born in Rothsie, Scotland. Their children: Richard b. Aug. 26, 1884, d. same day; William Carter b. Oct. 6, 1885, m. Amelia Lewis Jan. 14, 1909; John Franklin b. Dec. 6, 1888, d. June, 1886; Robert b. 1889, d. 1889; Agness Emeline b. Aug. 25, 1891, d. Feb. 25, 1907; Ada Elizabeth b. Nov. 16, 1893, m. Fredric Sellers; Fredric b. 1895; Alice b. Jan. 4, 1898; Rothsie Clyde b. Oct. 6, 1902.

THOMAS, JOSEPH (son of Charles Thomas and Elizabeth Carter of Worcestershire, Eng.). Born Nov. 12, 1848, in Iowa. Came to Utah Sept. 9, 1852, Bryant Jolley company.
Married Margaret Watson Jan. 7, 1867, Heber, Utah (daughter of James Watson and Jennett Campbell of Edinburgh, Scotland, pioneers 1852, Bryant Jolley company). She was born July 17, 1850. Their children: Joseph William b. Dec. 4, 1867, m. Eliza R. Lindsay; James Whittington b. May 1, 1869, d. Jan. 22, 1885; Agnes Irinda b. March 9, 1871, m. George L. Muir; Sarah Elizabeth b. May 9, 1873, m. John E. Austin; Jennett Campbell b. Nov. 11, 1874, m. George Coleman; Margaret Eleanor b. Jan. 9, 1897, m. William H. Lindsay; Jessup W. b. Oct. 6, 1878, m. Eunice S. Lindsay Oct. 26, 1899; Maude b. July 3, 1880, m. Albert Smith; Edward Monroe b. June 12, 1882, d. Aug. 30, 1884; John Ernest b. Nov. 1883, m. Lizzie Clyde; Harold b. Oct. 29, 1885, m. Blanche Huffaker. Family home Center Creek, Heber, Utah.
Seventy. Farmer and stockraiser. Died March 4, 1886.

THOMAS, JESSUP WATSON (son of Joseph Thomas and Margaret Watson). Born Oct. 6, 1878, Center Creek, Heber, Utah.
Married Eunice S. Lindsay Oct. 26, 1899, at Heber (daughter of Robert Lindsay and Sarah A. Murdock, of that place, former pioneer 1862, Homer Duncan company, latter born in Utah). She was born April 6, 1879. Their children: Eliza Alta b. Oct. 27, 1900; Jessup Roland b. Sept. 24, 1903; Ora M. b. Aug. 23, 1906; Robert Daryl b. May 4, 1912. Family home Heber, Utah.
Sheepman and farmer.

THOMAS, DANIEL CLAYBORN (son of Joseph Thomas). Born Dec. 12, 1815, in North Carolina. Came to Utah Sept. 8, 1850, Aaron Johnson company.
Married Jane Gaither (daughter of Forest Gaither), who was born in 1821 and came to Utah with husband. Their children: Daniel Clayborn b. July 14, 1850, m. Elizabeth Sharp; Sarah Jane b. Dec. 21, 1852, m. William L. Stewart; James Madison b. Aug. 18, 1855, m. Mary Geddes Sept. 18, 1879. Family resided Lehi, Cedar Fort, Smithfield and Plain City, Utah.
One of the first five families to settle at Lehi; also an early settler to Cedar Fort; moved to Smithfield 1861, and in 1863 went to Plain City where he lived until his demise, 1890.

THOMAS, JAMES MADISON (son of Daniel Clayborn Thomas and Jane Gaither). Born Aug. 18, 1855, Cedar Fort, Utah.
Married Mary Geddes Sept. 18, 1879, Salt Lake City (daughter of William and Martha Geddes), who was born Sept. 18, 1861, Plain City, Utah. Their children: Mary Melvina b. July 4, 1880, m. George W. Wayment May 20, 1903; Elizabeth b. June 23, 1882; James Madison b. Aug. 2, 1884; William Preston b. April 8, 1887; Lois Laurietta b. Sept. 19, 1890; Elvin Daniel b. March 26, 1893; Luella Martha b. Nov. 21, 1896. Family home Plain City, Utah.
Farmer and stockraiser.

THOMAS, DANIEL FRANCIS (son of David Thomas, born Aug. 2, 1775, Carmarthenshire, South Wales, and Hannah Williams, born in March 1796, at Carmarthenshire, South Wales). He was born April 13, 1826, in Carmarthenshire. Came to Utah in 1855, Captain Jones company.
Married Mary Langlois Nov. 29, 1856 (daughter of Samuel Langlois and Mary Ann Merchant, pioneers 1855, Dan Jones company). She was born 1834; came to Utah with parents. Their children: David F. b. Dec. 6, 1861; Mary Ann b. Feb. 18, 1858, m. Peter Peterson Dec. 15, 1880; Elizabeth Jane b. Feb. 18, 1858, m. S. T. Whitaker Dec. 15, 1880; Hannah Nancy b. March 30, 1860, m. Phillip Dixon Oct. 27, 1885; Harriet b. Sept. 26, 1863, m. Edward Horrop Dec. 30, 1883. Family resided South Cottonwood and Lynn, Utah.
Married Stova Fredricka Olsen Jan. 15, 1866, at Lynne, Utah (daughter of Gustave Olsen and Johanna Anderson of Sweden, pioneers Sept. 15, 1864, William B. Preston company). She was born March 21, 1849, at Sweets, Sweden. Their children: Margrete Ann b. May 14, 1867; Charlotte b. Jan. 30, 1869; Rachel b. Feb. 26, 1871; Ineze b. Aug. 27, 1878; Percy Albert b. March 4, 1876; Albert Augustus b. Nov. 23, 1879; Walter Leo b. Jan. 28, 1881; Rose May b. May 28, 1883; Daniel Francis, Jr. b. April 13, 1886. Family home Lynne, Utah.
Bishop's counselor; bishop of Lynn ward 1875-90. Justice of peace at Lynn, Utah, 1874. Died 1890.

THOMAS, DANIEL W. (son of David Thomas and Ann Jones, of Gill Green, and latter of Carmarthenshire, South Wales). He was born June 16, 1817, Gill Gren, Wales. Came to Utah Sept. 3, 1852, Abraham O. Smoot's first company to come by P. E. Aid Fund.

Married Margeret Davis in 1840 (daughter of Daniel Davis and Sarah Davis, of Carmarthenshire, Wales). She died before the family left Wales. Their children: David Davis b. June 7, 1841, m. Jane Lewis Roberts Feb. 6, 1874; Hannah b. May 20, 1843, m. David Daniels; m. Robert Caldwell.
Married Mary Jones 1844, Gili Gren, Carmarthenshire, Wales (daughter of Louis Jones and Ellen Lewis, of that place). She was born May 14, 1819, at Gili, and died September, 1899. Their children: Henry b. March 27, 1846, d. 1854; Daniel b. Aug. 7, 1847, m. Sarah Jones Dec. 9, 1874; John b. April 1, 1850, m. Mary Jane Evans 1876; Benjamin b. Oct. 13, 1853, m. Rachael Jones; m. Elizabeth Evans; Joshua Lewis b. July 21, 1857, m. Anne Williams.
School trustee 1874. Settled southwest of Salt Lake; then moved to Brigham City 1854; then to Malad, Idaho, 1864. Farmer. Died Sept. 1897, Malad.

THOMAS, DAVID DAVIS (son of Daniel W. Thomas and Margeret Davis). Born June 7, 1841, Gili Gren, Wales.
Married Jane Lewis Roberts Feb. 6, 1874, Malad, Idaho (daughter of Edward Giles Roberts and Elizabeth Lewis, pioneers Oct. 2, 1866). She was born Aug. 23, 1854, Dinas Mowddwy, South Wales. Their children: Daniel Henry b. April 11, 1875, m. Mary Roberts Thomas Aug. 23, 1894; Edward Joshua b. Dec. 16, 1877; Mary Louise b. July 24, 1880, m. William Henderson March 5, 1897; David Oliver b. June 12, 1883; Margarette Elizabeth b. Dec. 15, 1885, m. Charles Bowcutt Nov. 5, 1898; John Charles b. July 11, 1888, m. Margeret Elizabeth Bennett Dec. 5, 1898; Robert Lewis b. June 28, 1892; Mabel Jane b. Oct. 12, 1896. Family home Malad, Idaho.
From Utah he moved to Nevada in 1859, then to Malad, Idaho, 1871. Farmer.

THOMAS, JOSHUA LEWIS (son of Daniel William Thomas and Mary Jones). Born July 21, 1857, Brigham City, Utah.
Married Anna Ellen Williams March 26, 1888, Malad, Idaho (daughter of John Haines Williams and Sarah Davis, pioneers Oct. 7, 1861). She was born April 11, 1860, Petersburg, Pa. Their children: John W. b. Dec. 16, 1889, d. Dec. 24, 1889; Joshua W. b. July 27, 1892; Daniel W. b. July 13, 1895.
Farmer and stockraiser.

THOMAS, ELISHA (son of Charles and Betsy Thomas). Born Aug. 2, 1834, Herefordshire, Eng. Came to Utah in September, 1852.
Married Jane Harris Baum in 1853, Provo, Utah (daughter of Jacob Baum and Agnes Nancy Harris of Provo, Utah, pioneers 1852). She was born July 2, 1832. Their children: Sarah; Elizabeth, m. James Richardson; Ellen, m. James Adams; Elisha, Jr., m. Josephine Snow; Eliza, died; Rachel, m. Thaddeus H. Cluff; Charles, died. Family home Provo, Utah.
Married Elizabeth Lee, at Provo, Utah (daughter of John and Sarah Lee, handcart pioneers). She was born 1846, in England. Their children: Elizabeth; Sarah; Rozilla; Elisha John b. June 7, 1873, m. Eliza J. Hancock May 8, 1895; Mollissie; Chancy W.; Phoebe; Delina, died. Family home Farr West (Harrisville), Utah.
High priest; seventy. Made two trips across the plains for immigrants. Veteran Black Hawk Indian war and Echo Canyon trouble. Farmer.

THOMAS, ELISHA, JR. (son of Elisha Thomas and Jane Harris Baum). Born Aug. 26, 1861, Heber City, Utah.
Married Josephine Snow Nov. 7, 1889, Provo, Utah, by Judge Edge Booth (daughter of James E. Snow and Josephine Ferry of Provo). She was born Sept. 17, 1872. Their children: Myrtle b. Sept. 8, 1890; Florence b. Nov. 1, 1892; Lora b. April 2, 1897, died; Pearl b. Nov. 1, 1898; Bryan b. March 12, 1900; Lillian b. Sept. 14, 1901; Arden b. Nov. 9, 1903; Ruby b. May 4, 1906; Elva b. Aug. 10, 1908. Family home Pleasant View ward, Provo.
Elder; block teacher. Farmer and fruitgrower.

THOMAS, ELISHA JOHN (son of Elisha Thomas and Elizabeth Lee). Born June 7, 1873, Farr West, Utah.
Married Eliza J. Hancock May 8, 1895, Logan, Utah (daughter of Charles B. Hancock and Chloe A. Rawson of Payson and Harrisville, Utah, pioneers 1849, Wilford Woodruff company). She was born April 22, 1875. Their children: Raymond John b. April 17, 1896; Leo Lenord b. Nov. 5, 1899; Desmond Lyle b. Jan. 7, 1903; Chloe Ilah b. Sept. 29, 1905; Eliza Fawn b. Dec. 20, 1907; Laverdia Fern b. Sept. 26, 1909. Family resided Farr West, Utah, and also in Idaho.
Missionary to western states 1909-10; president Y. M. M. I. A.; secretary in Sunday school; bishop's counselor; ward chorister. School trustee. Farmer and stockraiser.

THOMAS, HARRISON AYERS (son of Joseph and Mary Ann Thomas, both of North Carolina; latter born 1810). He was born April 5, 1837, Summerville, Kemper county, Miss. Came to Utah 1851, John Brown company.
Married Ann Morehead Feb. 12, 1858 (daughter of James Madison Morehead and Elizabeth Turner Thomas, former died en route to Utah, latter came Sept., 1850, Aaron Johnson company—married 1836). She was born March 20, 1841, and came to Utah with mother. Their children: Mary Ann b. Jan. 11, 1859; Joseph Harrison b. Dec. 24, 1861, m. Agnes Meikle Nov. 13, 1889; Daniel Preston b. Sept. 12, 1866, m. Ida Dobbs Nov. 1892; James Madison b. Oct. 13, 1866, m. Minnie Allen Nov. 13, 1889; John Franklin b. Nov. 8

1868; Nellie Elizabeth b. Sept. 25, 1870, m. Joseph Johnson June 30, 1909; Fanny Frances b. Jan. 6, 1872; Cordelia Jane b. Jan. 8, 1874; Fensetta b. Dec. 9, 1876, m. Bryant Mecham Nov. 1901; Howard Lafayette b. Aug. 13, 1879, m. Anna Turner Dec. 20, 1903. Family resided Lehi, Cedar Fort, American Fork and Smithfield, Utah, and Preston, Idaho.
Counselor to Samuel Roskelly, bishop of Smithfield ward. Took part in Echo Canyon trouble; guard in Indian wars. Road supervisor. Owner first sawmills in Cache county and southern Idaho. Engaged in making ties for Utah Northern R. R. Farmer.

THOMAS, HUGH WILLIAM (son of David Thomas and Elizabeth Williams). Born Jan. 29, 1830, Pembrey, Carmarthenshire, South Wales. Came to Utah Aug. 29, 1868, William S. Seeley company.
Married Mary Ann Sparrey (daughter of Thomas and Sarah Sparrey, former of Carmarthenshire). She also came with William S. Seeley company. Their children: George Sparrey, m. Hannah Adelia Dredge; Sarah; David Sparrey, m. Alice Dredge; Elizabeth, died on the plains. Family h Pembrey, Carmarthenshire, Wales, before coming to Uanlo

THOMAS, DAVID SPARREY (son of Hugh William Thomas and Mary Ann Sparrey). He was born Sept. 23, 1862, Pembrey, Wales, as also were his brothers and sisters.
Married Alice Dredge April 13, 1888, Logan, Utah (daughter of Jesse Richard Dredge and Ellen Rhees, pioneers Sept. 13, 1861, Joseph Horne company). She was born Dec. 7, 1868, Malad City, Idaho. Their children: David Dredge b. April 28, 1889; Jesse Dredge b. July 28, 1891; William b. June 7, 1894; Alice Adelia b. Dec. 7, 1896; Herbert Dredge b. May 15, 1900; Liza b. Feb. 2, 1905.

THOMAS, JAMES MORONI (son of Nathaniel Thomas, died in 1841, at Nauvoo, Ill., and Susan Luce, of Mount Pisgah, Iowa). He was born July 27, 1841, Rochester, Sangamon county, Ill. Came to Utah Sept. 15, 1850, James Pace company.
Married Mary Hebden Holroyde March 12, 1862, Ogden, Utah (daughter of Thomas E. Holroyde and Dinah Williams of England, Philadelphia and Omaha, pioneers Sept. 13, 1861, Joseph Horne company). She was born Nov. 9, 1846. Their children: Nathaniel J., m. Elizabeth Brown Dec Jan. 12, 1887; Mary Rodelphia, m. Josiah G. Read March 11, 1887; Moroni Holroyde, m. Katie Fitzgerald Nov. 9 38; Dinah Elizabeth, m. Albert J. Johnson July 17, 18⁹⁰ oert William, died; Ellen Hebden; Edwin Martin, di _, Crissie Ann, died; Chester Holroyde. Family home Ogden, Utah.
High priest. Went to Omaha in 1862 for immigrants. Merchant.

THOMAS, JAMES WYLIE (son of James Sands Thomas and Mary Morrow of Mississippi). Born Sept. 7, 1834, Dallas county, Ala. Came to Utah Oct. 2, 1847, Jedediah M. Grant company. His step-father, Washington Norwood Cook, accompanied him.
Married Mary Elizabeth Koyle in December, 1855, Spanish Fork, Utah (daughter of John H. Koyle and Nancy Macurdy of Illinois, pioneers 1852, Edward Hunter company). She was born May 30, 1840. Their children: Mary Elizabeth b. Dec. 25, 1856, m. Samuel Brockbank; Wylie Edward b. Aug. 3, 1858, m. Mary Ann Banks; Hyrum Franklin b. Aug. 28, 1860, m. Jane Hawkes; James Madison b. Aug. 18, 1862; Andrew Perry b. Dec. 10, 1864, m. Vina Fuller; Julia Adelaid b. Sept. 6, 1866; John Albert b. Nov. 8, 1869, m. Celia Jones; George b. Oct. 20, 1870; Nancy Armelia b. Oct. 5, 1871, m. David Davis; Harriet Evaline b. Aug. 29, 1875, m. James Hanson; David Heber b. Sept. 11, 1880. Family home Spanish Fork, Utah.
One of first settlers of Spanish Fork 1851. City councilman and marshal at Spanish Fork. One of presidents of the 50th quorum seventies.

THOMAS, JENKYN (son of Jenkyn Thomas and Anne David of Wales). Born July 25, 1831, Brigend, Wales. Came to Utah July 18, 1878, Lorenzo D. Young company.
Married Joanna T. Brennan 1858, Neath, Wales (daughter of Edward Albert Brennan and Miss Flemming of Ireland). She was born May 30, 1830. Their children: Jenkyn, m. Ellen P. Kessler; David, m. Eleanor Pyper; Mathoninah, m. Angeline A. Smith; Albert Edward, Cyrus and Ella, latter three died. Family resided Farmington and Salt Lake City, Utah.
Member 56th quorum seventies; missionary to Wales 1886-88; high priest. Shoemaker. Died Dec. 7, 1896, Farmington, Utah.

THOMAS, MATHONIHAH (son of Jenkyn Thomas and Joanna T. Brennan). Born July 20, 1872, Aberdare, Glamorganshire, South Wales. Came to Utah when 6 years of age.
Married Angeline A. Smith Sept. 22, 1897, Salt Lake City (daughter of Elias Smith and Amy Jane King of Salt Lake City, pioneers 1850). She was born July 11, 1869. Their children: David Smith b. July 1, 1898; Brennan Smith b. March 30, 1901; Mathonihah Smith b. Sept. 15, 1902; Edwin Smith b. Oct. 5, 1904; Philip Smith b. May 10, 1907, d. Aug. 25, 1907; Walter Smith b. July 25, 1908. Family home, Salt Lake City.

Member 56th quorum seventies; missionary to Virginia 1894-96; high priest; alternate high councilor of Ensign stake; first counselor in Salt Lake stake. Member board of education 8 years; trustee of agricultural college; chief clerk of house of representatives 1897. Superintendent Y. M. M. I. A. of Davis and Ensign stakes. President Utah educational association 1910.

THOMAS, JOSEPH MOREHEAD. Came to Utah in 1851. Married Mary Ann Thomas. Their children: Frances Ann, m. Joel White; Daniel, d. young man; Harrison Ayers, m. Ann Morehead; Emily, died; James Clayborne, m. Teana Nelson.

THOMAS, JAMES CLAYBORNE (son of Joseph M. and Mary Ann Thomas). Born March 10, 1843, in Kemper county, Miss. Came to Utah 1851, Preston Thomas company. Married Teane Nelson Nov. 20, 1865, Bloomington, Idaho (daughter of Soren Nelson and Christiania Hansen of Mosbjerg, Hjörring amt, Denmark, pioneers Sept. 20, 1856, Knud Peterson company). She was born Nov. 20, 1846, and came to Utah with parents. Their children: Mary Jane b. Oct. 23, 1866, m. Josiah Taylor Oct. 9, 1883; James Clayborne, Jr., b. March 13, 1868, m. Mariah E. Haddock Oct. 23, 1890; Frances Amelia b. Oct. 22, 1869, m. Franklin Grenhalgh Nov. 4, 1893; Joseph Harrison b. Dec. 21, 1871, d. Oct. 11, 1893; Daniel Preston b. Aug. 25, 1873, m. Nellie Bromley Feb. 1904; Burton Lewis b. Aug. 9, 1876, m. Mary Stevenson March 22, 1905. Family home Bloomington, Idaho. Elder. Early-day mail carrier. Stockraiser and farmer.

THOMAS, JAMES CLAYBORNE, JR. (son of James Clayborne Thomas and Teane Nelson). Born March 13, 1868, Bloomington, Idaho. Married Mariah E. Haddock Oct. 23, 1890, Logan, Utah (daughter of John Haddock and Margaret Pennson, pioneers 1860, Milo Andrus company). She was born May 30, 1869, Bloomington, Idaho. Their children: Leo Milton b. Aug. 16, 1891; James Rollo b. May 6, 1894; LaRue Marguerite b. June 3, 1896; Verona Geneva b. June 25, 1900; Ramona b. July 26, 1904.

THOMAS, BURTON LEWIS (son of James Clayborne Thomas and Teane Nelson). Born Aug. 9, 1876, Bloomington, Idaho. Married Mary Stevenson March 22, 1905, Logan, Utah (daughter of Thomas Stevenson and Zelinora Weaver of Preston, Idaho, pioneers). She was born June 10, 1887. Their children: Hazel Audrey b. Dec. 19, 1905; Ariel Lewis b. May 20, 1908; Burton Elmo b. Jan. 25, 1910. Family home Bloomington, Idaho. Elder. Farmer and stockraiser.

THOMAS, ROBERT T. (son of Henry Thomas). Came to Utah July 24, 1847, Brigham Young company. Married Mary Ann Turner, Provo, Utah (daughter of Chauncy Turner and Hannah Redfield, pioneers July 24, 1847, Brigham Young company (Aaron Farr). Their children: Robert Henry, m. Sarah Ellen Cluff; Ann; Maria, died; Chauncy E., m. Mary Jane Farrer; Sylvania, m. Christina Olsen. Family home Provo, Utah.

THOMAS, CHAUNCY E. (son of Robert T. Thomas and Mary Ann Turner). Born Sept. 25, 1855, Provo, Utah. Married Mary Jane Farrer Sept. 16, 1876, Salt Lake City (daughter of Thomas Farrer and Mary Strong of Provo). She was born Sept. 6, 1857. Their children: Jennie May b. March, 1878, m. Robert Steel; Edna F. b. Feb., 1881; Mary b. Dec. 1884, m. George Monson; Emma b. May, 1888, m. Benjamin Georgerson; Chauncy b. Nov. 1891; Robert b. April 1896; Ellwood b. May 1901. Counselor to Bishop Warnick of Pleasant Grove, Utah. Marshal Pleasant Grove 1912. Farmer.

THOMAS, SAMUEL (son of Daniel and Sarah Thomas of Caermarthenshire, South Wales). Born Feb. 3, 1812, in Caermarthenshire. Came to Utah Oct. 27, 1849, Dan Jones division of George A. Smith company. Married Ann Jones at Sale Lake City March 19, 1819. (daughter of Thomas Jones and Sarah Jeremy of Carmarthenshire). She was born July 19, 1818. Their children: Sarah, m. John Florzcy, m. Ludwig Bohling; Samuel J., d. aged 45; Hannah, m. Joseph James; Ann, m. George James; Thomas J., m. Ellen Cumberland; Mary J., m. Michael S. Katz. Family home 15th ward, Salt Lake City. Married Mary Darknell Oct. 13, 1873, Salt Lake City (daughter of William Henry Darknell and Mary Longest of Carmarthenshire, who came to Utah June, 1882). She was born Aug. 23, 1847. Their children: Sarah Jane, m. William Matthews, m. John A. Johnson; William H. D., m. Lavina Steck; Mary Ann, d. infant; Mary Elizabeth, m. Oliver A. Jones. Family home 15th ward, Salt Lake City. High priest. Farmer, stockraiser and butcher. Died Nov. 21, 1893.

THOMAS, THOMAS W. (son of William Henry Thomas and Ann Williams, former born 1790, in Winvow Parish, South Wales, latter 1795, at same place). He was born Feb. 8, 1833, in Winvow Parish. Came to Utah October 10, 1853, Joseph A. Young company. Married Ruth Morgan Oct. 10, 1855 Provo, Utah (daughter of Evan Morgan and Mary Jones, pioneers Oct. 10, 1853, Joseph A. Young company). She was born Feb. 24, 1839, and came to Utah with parents. Their children: Thomas M. b. March 8, 1857, m. Rachel Rees Jan. 3, 1884; Llewelyn M. b. Nov. 14, 1858, m. Mary B. Owens March 15, 1883; Susan b. Oct. 9, 1860, m. R. T. Owens April 11, 1878; Mary Jane b. Sept. 12, 1862, m. John T. Owens Oct. 10, 1882; Evan M. b. Aug. 17, 1864; Wiliam H. b. Feb. 12, 1866, m. Anne E. Reynolds March 13, 1886; Ruth Lavina b. Feb. 25, 1868; Jacob b. Dec. 29, 1870. Family resided Brigham City, Utah, and Malad City, Idaho. Went out and met immigrants in 1855, and assisted them into their zion, and to the settling points further down the country. Served through the Echo Canyon difficulty. He was one of the early settlers of Malad City, going there in April, 1866.

THOMAS, THOMAS MORONI (son of Thomas W. Thomas and Ruth Morgan). Born March 8, 1857, Brigham City, Utah. Married Rachel Rees Jan. 3, 1884, at Brigham City (daughter of John D. Rees and Mary Morgan, pioneers September 1852, Captain Morgan company). She was born May 1, 1866, at Brigham City. Their children: Thomas Moroni b. Dec. 8, 1884; Seth b. Aug. 26, 1886, m. Julia Peck June 16, 1909; John R. b. Feb. 20, 1888, m. Edith Davis Dec. 30, 1908; Pearl b. Nov. 3, 1889; David b. March 1, 1898. Family home Malad City, Idaho. Was one of the first merchants of Malad City starting in business in 1879. Died Nov. 8, 1905.

THOMAS, SETH (son of Thomas Moroni Thomas and Rachel Rees). Born Aug. 26, 1886, Malad City, Idaho. Married Julia Peck June 16, 1909 (daughter of Fred Peck, born July 21, 1849, in Greene county, N. Y., pioneer Oct. 15, 1863, Samuel D. White company, and Lizzie Leigh, born July 3, 1854, Brigham City, Utah). She was born Jan. 26, 1888, at Malad City, Idaho. Only child: Carol b. June 29, 1910. Family home Malad City, Utah. Manager of the mercantile firm of T. M. Thomas Sons, Malad City.

THOMAS, WILLIAM. Came to Utah about 1852. Married Elizabeth David (daughter of Morgan and Mary David), who was born July 7, 1830. Their children: John b. Nov. 26, 1851, m. Ellen James; Mary Jane b. Jan. 19, 1854, m. Llewellyn Thomas; Caroline b. Jan. 16, 1856, m. William Ferguson; Morgan W. b. Jan. 23, 1858, m. Alice Malcolm; Elizabeth A. b. April 28, 1860, m. Ammon B. Simmons; Rachel H. b. Dec. 12, 1862, m. John J. Banks; Margret Helen b. Dec. 9, 1864, died; Emma b. Jan. 1, 1867, m. Andrew Prior; David G. b. May 27, 1870, m. Kathrine Davis; Ophelia M. b. March 4, 1873, m. Albert Rockhill; Lucy b. Oct. 27, 1876, m. Nathan Rockhill.

THOMAS, JOHN (son of William Thomas and Elizabeth David). Born Nov. 26, 1851, St. Louis, Mo. Married Ellen James at Spanish Fork, Utah (daughter of Howel James and Mary ———). Their children: Elizabeth, m. Benjamin Lloyd; William, m. Minnie Tew; John H., m. Isabella Beckstrom; Reese, died; Arthur, m. Ione Brown; Ella, m. Charles Davis; Lenora, m. Carl Corbett; Annie Laurie; Francis. Family home Spanish Fork, Utah.

THOMAS, WILLIAM C. (son of John Thomas and Ann Price of Llanelly, South Wales). Born Jan. 27, 1827, at Llanelly. Came to Utah Oct. 9, 1850. Married Margrett Phillps Aug. 7, 1850 (daughter of Benjamin Phillips and Sarah Owens), who was born June 6, 1817. Their children: Mary Ann b. May 23, 1853, m. Oran C. Brown June 13, 1870; Margaret b. June 1, 1855, m. James T. Dunn Feb. 1876; David Price b. Feb. 17, 1858, m. Maud Mary Frost Dec. 21, 1881; Caroline b. June 25, 1860, m. James C. Armstrong 1882. Family home Brigham City, Box Elder Co., Utah. Missionary to Europe 1867-68. Kept the first hotel at Brigham City; agent for Wells-Fargo Stage Company; pioneer merchant in northern Utah. Early settler in Park Valley and Grouse Creek, Utah.

THOMAS, DAVID PRICE (son of William C. Thomas and Margrett Phillips). Born Feb. 17, 1858, Brigham City, Utah. Married Maud Mary Frost Dec. 21, 1881, Corinne, Utah (daughter of Edward Frost and Maud Mary Scottorn, the latter a pioneer, Israel Evans company). Only child: Maud Mary b. June 10, 1890, m. Ezra Clark June 12, 1907. Family resided Brigham City, Park Valley, Grouse Creek, Utah, and Oakley, Idaho. Bishop of 4th ward Oakley, Idaho. Member of village board; president Farmers Commercial & Savings Bank of Oakley, Idaho. Stockraiser. Furniture and lumber merchant.

THOMASON, GUSTAF (son of Andreas Thomason, born July 1, 1793, Saxareby, Dahlsland, Sweden, and Mari Pehrson, born Jan. 9, 1809, Artimwick, Sweden). Born Aug. 3, 1837, at Billingsfors, Dahlsland, Sweden. Came to Utah Aug. 7, 1869. Married Andrina Christine Olsen Oct. 4, 1861 (daughter of Jens Olsen, born Feb. 27, 1805, Ida Sogn, Norway, and Annie Dorthea Johnson, born 1804, at Berg Sogn, Norway). She was born July 29, 1833; came to Utah with husband.

1210 PIONEERS AND PROMINENT MEN OF UTAH

Their children: Carl Johan Furdenant b. Feb. 26, 1863, died; Rickard Theodor b. Feb. 28, 1865, died; Christine Elizabeth b. Aug. 14, 1869, m. Adolph Ljellstrim Jan. 2, 1889; Charles Rickhard b. March 18, 1869, m. Maren Henge June 30, 1897; Mathilda b. Oct. 18, 1871; Gustaf b. Sept. 12, 1873; Yara b. Sept. 13, 1875; latter three died.
Married Jula Farsberg Jan. 16, 1879, Salt Lake City (daughter of Jan Magnus Farsberg and Christine Nystrom, who came to Utah July 1873). She was born Feb. 5, 1852, Christena, Dahlsland. Their children: Jennie Victoria b. Dec. 1, 1879, m. Leonard Handy; Mari b. Aug. 24, 1881, d. July 10, 1891; Ludvig b. April 23, 1883; Mose b. July 20, 1885; David b. Sept. 27, 1887, d. Nov. 10, 1909; Annie b. Nov. 10, 1898.
Married Martha Hansen July 1, 1885, who was born March 9, 1851, Haegelund, Norway.
Missionary to Sweden 1902-04; missionary in Nebraska; president Goteborg Branch, Sweden; high priest; bishop's counselor.

THOMASON, CHARLES R. (son of Gustaf Thomason and Andrina Christine Olsen). Born March 18, 1869, Goteborg, Sweden. Came to Utah 1869.
Married Marie K. Hentze June 30, 1897. She was born Sept. 26, 1873. Their children: Hazel M. b. May 18, 1899; Gladys V. b. Nov. 9, 1900; Mabel A. b. June 9, 1903; Viola b. Nov. 9, 1905; Jennie b. March 3, 1908; Charles G. b. Feb. 11, 1910.
Missionary to Samoan Islands 1892-95; president Y. M. M. I. A., Burton, 1898-1900; high councilor 1900-08; bishop 1908.

THOMPSON, GEORGE, of Hull, Yorkshire, Eng. Came to Utah 1853.
Married Jane Thompson, who came to Utah in 1856. Their children: Charles; Mary m. John Burkett; Sarah, m. Jonathan Oldham Duke; William, m. Sarah Fenn; Martha, m. Jonathan Oldham Duke. Family home Heber City, Utah.
High priest. Farmer. Died at Heber City.

THOMPSON, WILLIAM (son of George Thompson and Jane Thompson). Born Dec. 19, 1829, Hull, Yorkshire, Eng. Came to Utah in 1853.
Married Sarah Fenn in 1856 (daughter of William and Sarah Fenn), who was born Aug. 3, 1842, and died March 15, 1888. Their children: Sarah Jane m. Andrew Lindsay; Martha, died; George, m. Elizabeth Brady; Mary Ann, m. Andrew Mair; Eliza, m. Alexander Mair; Emma, m. Peter Howarth; William, m. Nancy Baines; Elizabeth, m. Frank Lake; Charles, m. Elizabeth Jordon; Marintha, m. Joseph Ritson; Ellen, died; Franklin; Maggie, m. Hyrum Winterton; Andrew Alexander, died; Frederick, died.
Elder. Veteran Indian war. Farmer. Settled in Heber City 1859. Died Dec. 27, 1894, Heber City, Utah.

THOMPSON, JAMES LOUIS (son of John David Thompson of Chautauqua county, N. Y.). Born Jan. 22, 1818, Pomfort, Chautauqua county, N. Y. Came to Utah in November, 1852, Isaac Bullock company.
Married Matilda Willis at Nauvoo, Ill. (daughter of John Willis and Jane Kirkpatrick of Kentucky). She was born Feb. 16, 1819. Their children: John Orson b. Aug. 8, 1844, m. Lucy Maria Groves; James Brigham b. Oct. 12, 1848, m. Anne Jenette Bryce; Mary Matilda b. June 7, 1850; Lydia Dolly b. April 8, 1853; Margaret Elizabeth b. Jan. 7, 1865; William Samuel b. Jan. 26, 1856, m. Sarah Louisa Thompson; Joseph Enoch b. July 25, 1859, m. Phoebe Jane Thompson. Family home Spanish Fork, Kanarraville and Henrieville, Utah.
Member of Zion's camp and Co. C Mormon Battalion. Died March 25, 1891.

THOMPSON, JOHN ORSON (son of James Louis Thompson and Matilda Willis). Born Aug. 8, 1844, Nashville, Lee Co., Iowa.
Married Lucy Maria Groves Dec. 27, 1863, Kanarraville, Iron Co., Utah (daughter of Elisha M. Groves and Lucy Simmons, pioneers 1848, Brigham Young company). She was born May 7, 1848, Winter Quarters, Ia. Their children: John Orson b. Feb. 21, 1866, m. Amanda Mead; Brigham Samuel b. Oct. 25, 1868; James Elisha b. Oct. 17, 1870, m. Cyrena Young; Joseph Wallace b. Feb. 23, 1872, m. Helen G. Pratt Sept. 20, 1901; m. Rachel Wilson July 3, 1913; William Llewellyn b. Oct. 12, 1874, m. Adelaide Smith 1899; Lucy Matilda b. Feb. 14, 1877; Sarah Jane b. Oct. 17, 1879, m. George C. Mead 1902; George Franklin b. May 1, 1882; Arthur Alonzo b. Oct. 29, 1884; Mary Frances b. Nov. 27, 1887, m. George Avrett 1908. Family resided Henrieville and Duchesne, Utah.
Farmer.

THOMPSON, JOSEPH WALLACE (son of John Orson Thompson and Lucy Maria Groves). Born Feb. 23, 1872, Helper, Utah.
Married Helen Grace Pratt (daughter of Teancum Pratt and Ann Eliza Mead, natives of Utah). She was born July 6, 1885, Helper, Utah. Their children: Wayne Pratt b. April 29, 1905; Anthon Reed b. Jan. 28, 1907; Joseph Barr b. April 27, 1909. Family home Duchesne, Wasatch Co., Utah. He was divorced May 7, 1912.
Married Rachel Wilson July 3, 1913 (daughter of George H. Wilson and Mary Julia Johnson), who was born April 7, 1886, Hillsdale, Utah.
Missionary to the southern states 1897; religious class superintendent. Justice of the peace. Farmer.

THOMPSON, JAMES BRIGHAM (son of James Louis Thompson and Matilda Willis). Born Oct. 12, 1848, Council Bluffs, Iowa.
Married Anne Jenette Bryce Nov. 22, 1877, St. George, Utah (daughter of Ebenezer Bryce and Mary Ann Park of Salt Lake City, Tooele, St. George and Pine Valley, former a pioneer Sept. 16, 1800, James Pace company). She was born Jan. 19, 1857. Their children: Annie Matilda b. Aug. 17, 1878, m. Charles Thomas Smith; Barbara Ellen b. Nov. 21, 1879, m. Samuel Iven Goulding; Jessie Jane b. May 11, 1881, m. John Thomas Messervy; James Brigham b. Dec. 25, 1882; Lenore b. Nov. 12, 1884, m. Edwin Thompson; Mary Jenette b. April 20, 1885, m. George Cramer; David Ebenezer b. May 18, 1888; Lorenzo Bryce b. Dec. 23, 1891; Maggie Josephine b. Jan. 30, 1894; Alma b. Oct. 28, 1898. Family resided Henrieville, Utah, and Idaho Falls, Idaho.

THOMPSON, JOHN C. (son of Larkin Thompson and Elizabeth Crow). Born May 15, 1821, in Tazewell county, Va. Came to Utah Oct. 16, 1847.
Married Anne Broy Clark March 20, 1845 (daughter of John Clark and Eliza Santifer), who was born Oct. 6, 1821. Their children: Elizabeth Jane, died; Larkin Santifer; John C., m. Mary Sanders; Ann Eliza; Sarah Ellen, m. L. F. Pritchett; Mary Louise, m. Austin W. Child; Amanda America, m. John A. West; Joseph Matthew, m. Mary Jones; Linzy Clark; William L., m. Lillie Brown. Family home Ogden, Utah.
Missionary to Arizona 1874-76; presiding elder and counselor to Sanford Bingham 20 years at Riverdale, Utah. Member Co. A, Mormon Battalion. Farmer. Died Nov. 11, 1900, at Ogden.

THOMPSON, JOHN S. (son of James Thompson and Margaret Strang of Fifeshire, Scotland). Born Jan. 26, 1831, in Fifeshire. Came to Utah September, 1866.
Married Catherine Muir July 4, 1851, Fifeshire (daughter of Thomas Muir and Christina Smyth of Fifeshire; came to Utah 1873). Their children: John M., m. Jane Curtis; Thomas; Archibald; Joseph; Robert M., m. Alice Peck; James M., m. Nora Staker; Catherine, m. George Naylor; Margaret S.; William H., m. Vivian Hendricsen; Christinia M., m. Frank M. Dorrington; Adam, m. Josephine Lindsay.
Postmaster at Sugar House station eight years.

THOMPSON, JOSEPH (son of Joseph Thompson and Agnes Hirst of Lancastershire, Eng.). Came to Utah 1852.
Married Ann Grayson 1850, in Sheffield, Eng. (daughter of William Grayson of Sheffield). She came to Utah 1852. Their children: John G. b. 1851, m. Minnie Huber; Joseph, m. Libbie Brady; Agnes, m. Samuel Robert Bennion; Hannah, m. Albert Brown; Ann Elizabeth, m. Simeon Walker; Lucy; Lucy Ellen, Martha and Mary—latter four died.
High priest. Stonecutter, Salt Lake temple; stonemason. Died Sept. 10, 1911, South Cottonwood, Utah.

THOMPSON, JOSEPH LEWIS. Born Feb. 8, 1815, Birmingham, Warwickshire, Eng. Came to Utah Sept. 27, 1862, John R. Murdock company.
Married Penelope Thompson 1835, Birmingham, Eng. Their children: Susannah, m. Michael Clark; William Henry, m. Matilda Young; Eliza, m. Joseph Coacher; Joseph, m. Hannah Crompton; Jane, m. James G. Bleak; Ann, m. James Clark; John; Richard; Harry; James Godson; Benjamin; Samuel. Family home Clarkston, Cache Co., Utah, and he died there Feb. 15, 1875.

THOMPSON, WILLIAM HENRY (son of Joseph Lewis and Penelope Thompson). Born May 1, 1838, Birmingham, Warwickshire, Eng. Came to Utah Sept. 15, 1861, Ira Eldredge company.
Married Matilda Young May, 1859 (daughter of Henry Young), who was born May 31, 1835; came to Utah with husband. She died in February, 1865. Their children: Emily Adelaide b. April 21, 1860; Matilda Irene b. Dec. 27, 1861, m. James G. Blake; Amelia Young b. April 17, 1864, m. Franklin Pendleton; William Henry b. Feb. 9, 1866.
Married Emma Cottam Nov. 20, 1868, Salt Lake City (daughter of Thomas Cottam and Caroline Smith, who were married Oct. 9, 1847). She was born June 27, 1850, at St. Louis, Mo., and died at St. George, Utah, in April 1901. Their children: Emma Cottam b. Aug. 21, 1869, m. John M. Squire; Penelope Caroline b. Sept. 15, 1871, m. Robert P. Woodbury; William Alma b. Oct. 27, 1874; Mary Elizabeth b. Aug. 29, 1877, m. Joseph Webb; Joseph Smith b. Nov. 14, 1880, m. Mae Jones; George Thomas b. Aug. 13, 1883, m. Martha Baker; Ezra Cottam b. April 25, 1887, m. Rose Jarvis; Samuel b. June 8, 1891, m. Lucy Hatch. Families resided St. George, Utah.
Married Agnes Elizabeth Perkes in February, 1878, St. George, Utah (daughter of Henry Perkes and Charlotte Lowe), who was born Feb. 23, 1840, Dudley, Warwickshire, Eng. Their children: Hyrum Smith b. Dec. 27, 1880, m.

Flora Schmutz; Wilford Woodruff b. Aug. 27, 1883, m. Kate Judd.
Carpenter; was an overseer in the erection of the St. George temple, where he has since employed his time as engineer and assistant ordinance worker.

THOMPSON, MATTHEW (son of Matthew Thompson and Margaret Malarkey, born in County Antrim, Ireland). Born Aug. 21, 1832, Lurgan, County Armagh, Ireland. Came to Utah Oct. 19, 1862, David P. Kimball oxteam company.
Married Alice Liddard December, 1874, Salt Lake City (daughter of Robert Liddard of Tooele and Provo, Utah). She was born 1857. Only child: Joseph b. Sept. 1878. Family home Tooele, Utah.
Married Eliza Wiley Aug. 25, 1875, Salt Lake City (daughter of Alexander Wiley and Mariah Alexander of County Antrim, Ireland). She was born Oct. 27, 1838. Their child: Matthew Chamas b. July 16, 1876. Family home Wallsburg, Utah.
High priest. Cut stone for the Salt Lake temple and tabernacle 1862. Worked on Union Pacific railway 1869; also on the Utah Southern. Weaver; miner; farmer.

THOMPSON, PETER P. (son of Peter Petersen Skytte and Johannah Petersen of Breining, Isle of Falster, Denmark). Born Jan. 15, 1808, Breining. Came to Utah Oct. 5, 1854, Hans Peter Olsen company.
Married Dorthea Andersen Oct. 20, 1837, Horbelev, Isle of Falster, Denmark (daughter of Anders Larsen Buck and Karen Rasmussen Belling of Verket, Isle of Falster). She was born Oct. 13, 1808. Their children: Andrew Thompson (a son by a former husband); Mary Petersen; Thomas Peter; Caroline, m. Joseph S. Black; Niels; Johannah. Family home Falkerslev, Denmark, before immigrating to Utah. High priest. Farmer. Died Feb. 25, 1875, Ephraim, Utah.

THOMPSON, SOREN (son of Jorgen Thompson, born March, 1804, and Anna Catherine Sorenson, born July 21, 1803, both of Jutland, Denmark—married 1835). He was born June 11, 1837, at Jutland. Came to Utah October, 1864, Soren Christoffersen company.
Married Annetta Marie Swenson April 19, 1869 (daughter of Swen Swensen and Bengta Pearson, the latter coming to Utah Oct. 4, 1862, Joseph Horne company—married Dec. 12, 1843, Nefjing, Sweden). She was born Nov. 8, 1850, in Sweden, and came to Utah with mother. Their children: Helen Catherine b. Oct. 22, 1871, m. Charles C. Wilson Sept. 23, 1900; Anna William b. June 18, 1873; Sylvia Betilla b. Sept. 9, 1875; Alvin Theodore b. Jan. 8, 1878; Jueniva b. Feb. 25, 1880, m. Victora Anderson May 24, 1904; Edward Christian b. Feb. 7, 1882, m. Emma Nelson Nov. 5, 1909; William S. b. July 5, 1884, m. Minerva Keele Dec. 30, 1904; Ephraim b. April 23, 1888; Eunice Floresa b. Jan. 17, 1890, m. George A. Clark Sept. 15, 1910. Family home Bear River City, Box Elder Co., Utah.
Filled a mission to Denmark 1885-87; served as ward teacher for 25 years; high priest. Pioneer of the Bear River valley.

THOMPSON, THOMAS W. (son of Robert Thompson, born Feb. 14, 1829, Alston, Cumberland, Eng., and Elizabeth Hillyard, born Jan. 1, 1837, Waddington, Denbighshire, Eng.—married July 16, 1859). He was born Feb. 26, 1860, Salt Lake City.
Married Cordelia Theresa Ainscough (daughter of William and Mary Ainscough—married at Salt Lake City). Their children: William and two daughters, died. Family home Smithfield, Utah.
Married Mary Owens June 19, 1889, Logan, Utah (daughter of William Owens, pioneer 1854, and Elizabeth Roberts, who came to Utah 1855, both N. Blair company—married Jan. 28, 1856, Salt Lake City). She was born March 7, 1866, Henifer, Summit Co., Utah. Their child: Mildred b. July 17, 1890.
Seventy; school teacher; president of Smithfield Y. M. M. I. A. Died May 12, 1890.

THOMPSON, WILLIAM. Came to Utah in October, 1851, Harry Walton company.
Married Elizabeth McCeruley. Their children: David, m. Mary Thompson; Daniel; William, Jr., b. Jan. 12, 1836, m. Mary Ellen Isaacson; Maria, m. Orin Hatch; Orville, m. Emily Snyder. Family home Bountiful, Utah.
Married Mrs. Hale.

THOMPSON, WILLIAM (son of William Thompson and Elizabeth McCeruley). Born Jan. 12, 1836, in Canada.
Married Mary Ellen Isaacson June 1, 1868, Salt Lake City (daughter of Neils Isaacson and Bertha Catherine Ogis, pioneers Sept. 13, 1863). She was born Nov. 21, 1851, Christiania, Norway. Their children: William Orville b. Nov. 24, 1869, m. Ada Lawrence Dec. 7, 1892; Daniel Isaac b. March 24, 1871, m. Lettie Hendricks March, 1901; Walter George b. Feb. 6, 1873, m. Caroline Lawrence March, 1901; Mary Florence b. Jan. 13, 1875, m. Parley N. Nelson Sept. 30, 1896;

PIONEERS AND PROMINENT MEN OF UTAH 1211

Francis Ira b. Feb. 22, 1877, m. Etta Webb Nov. 15, 1900; Bertha Estella b. June 6, 1879, m. William M. Whittle Dec. 21, 1901; Albert Henry b. Oct. 28, 1881, m. Amy Packer Dec. 21, 1903; Neils Oliver b. Feb. 27, 1884, m. Elizabeth Smith March 11, 1908; Nellie Maria b. June 19, 1886, m. Sansom Webb June 14, 1911; Melvin Edward b. June 21, 1889; Raymond Junius b. June 21, 1891; Inez Evelyn b. March 30, 1894; Ivan Cyril b. June 9, 1896. Family home Richmond, Utah.
Assisted in bringing immigrants to Utah in 1861 and 1868. Early settler in Richmond, Utah.

THOMPSON, WALTER GEORGE (son of William Thompson and Mary Ellen Isaacson). Born Feb. 6, 1873, Richmond, Utah.
Married Caroline Lawrence March, 1901 (daughter of Elisha Randolph Lawrence and Mary Ann Ratcliff), who was born May 24, 1875, Preston, Idaho. Their children: Louisa Caroline b. Nov. 1, 1900; Paulina b. May 21, 1902; Alverta b. Aug. 5, 1904; Walter Iver b. May 5, 1906; Fontella b. Aug. 31, 1908; Millie b. May 14, 1910.

THOMSON, ORSON S. Born April 28, 1855.
Married Martha A. Poll April 13, 1878, Salt Lake City (daughter of William F. Poll and Charlotte Long, pioneers November, 1852, Captain Nelson company). She was born Jan. 5, 1857, Salt Lake City. Their children: Charlotte I. b. April, 1879, m. Albert Clisold; Alice S. b. Oct. 5, 1883, m. Ernest Herridge; Orson Leroy b. June 5, 1886, m. Hettie Turnboe; Alvin b. Feb. 9, 1888, m. Josephine Clawson; William F. b. June 5, 1889; Ruby b. Oct. 29, 1891; Raymond C. b. Jan. 17, 1893; Nellie R. b. Aug. 10, 1900; Norman J. b. Dec. 13, 1910. Family home, Salt Lake City.

THORN, ASHAEL (son of Richard Thorn and Mary Ann Armstrong of Pennsylvania). Born Sept. 16, 1808, in Pennsylvania. Came to Utah in 1853, Joseph Thorn company.
Married Sarah Lester 1829 in Pennsylvania (daughter of John and Nancy Lester of New York). She was born June 14, 1809, in New York state. Their children: William b. March 17, 1830, m. Trollie Wilcox; Elizabeth Lucretia b. March 24, 1832, m. Calvin Bingham; Mary Ann b. Feb. 11, 1834, m. Augustus Bingham; Sarah b. Feb. 12, 1836, m. Alonzo Bingham; Richard b. Feb. 20, 1838, m. Rebecca A. Osborne; Isaac b. Jan. 30, 1840, m. Elizabeth Walker; Nancy b. Oct. 24, 1842, m. David Osborne; Lydia Saphronia b. June 30, 1843, m. Henry Perry, m. William Hall; Abigail b. July 14, 1845, m. Alexander Robertson; Barbara Ann b. Jan. 20, 1847, m. Dan W. Walker.
Settled in Uinta, Utah, later moving to Three-Mile Creek, Box Elder county, where he presided over the branch there. Moved to Willard, Utah, 1885. Died Feb. 10, 1897.

THORN, RICHARD (son of Ashael Thorn and Sarah Lester). Born Feb. 20, 1838, Summerhill, Pa. Came to Utah 1853, Joseph Thorn company.
Married Rebecca A. Osborne Dec. 25, 1858, East Weber, Uinta Co., Utah (daughter of David Osborne and Cynthia Butler of Hancock county, Ill., pioneers of 1852, Captain Howell company). She was born Oct. 15, 1842. Their children: Annie b. April 16, 1860, m. Morris Peters; Cynthia Marie b. Sept. 4, 1864, m. John Forsgren, d. Nov. 14, 1901; William Richard b. Oct. 27, 1866, d. Sept. 29, 1888; Sarah Lester b. March 11, 1869, m. Thomas Peters; David Ashael b. Aug. 22, 1871, d. Jan. 14, 1889; Hyrum b. Feb. 10, 1874, m. Jane Davis; Barbara Adeline b. Nov. 16, 1876, m. Brigham Nelson; Milton Jefferson b. April 16, 1879, m. Elmerta Nelson; Margaret Estella b. July 18, 1881, d. Aug. 1, 1881; Rebecca Jane b. Sept. 3, 1882, d. Sept. 14, 1882.
Married Eunice Jane Perry Feb. 15, 1884, Salt Lake City (daughter of Henry Perry and Elizabeth Zablaski of Perry, Utah). She was born Nov. 18, 1854. Their children: Edith Luella b. Nov. 9, 1886, m. Ellis Wood; Henry Leslie b. Feb. 5, 1888, m. Anetta Johnson. Family home Perry, Utah.
Served as missionary to southern states 1887-88; member of bishopric of Three-Mile Creek, Box Elder Co., Utah. Assisted in bringing immigrants to Utah 1864.

THORNBURG, BEARNT FREDERICK (son of Fire Thorne). Born Dec. 28, 1831, Falkastra, Christianstad, Sweden. Came to Utah Nov. 28, 1858.
Married Anna Johnson Nov. 26, 1859, who came to Utah in 1859, John R. Murdock handcart company. Their children: Mary Ann; Alma Frederick; William Fire; Emma Jennetta; Nora Rebecca; Margaret Rosetta; Ella; Pearl. Family home, Salt Lake City.
Drove team for United States government from Fort Leavenworth to Salt Lake City.

THORNE, DAVID (son of Peter Thorne of Kensal Green, Middlesex county, Eng.). Born 1800, at Kensal Green. Came to Utah Oct. 6, 1851, Alfred Cardon company.
Married Elizabeth Reeves, at Kensal Green. Their children: Charles; John; Sarah; George, m. Mary Rebecca Rogers; Frederick, m. Margaret Harmsted; Robert, m. Cordelia Walker; David, m. Anna Harmsted; Joseph, m. Elizabeth Holman; James, m. Harriet Farnsworth Brown; Emma, m. James Cobbley. Family home Pleasant Grove, Utah.
High priest; teacher. Farmer. Died 1876.

THORNE, GEORGE (son of David Thorne and Elizabeth Reeves). Born Feb. 1, 1840, at Kensal Green, Eng. Came to Utah with parents.
Married Mary Rebecca Rogers Feb. 12, 1865, Pleasant Grove, Utah (daughter of William Rogers of Birmingham, Eng.). She was born May 7, 1831. Their child: Alice Rebecca b. Aug. 15, 1868, m. James Bralford. Family home Pleasant Grove, Utah.
High priest. Watermaster. Farmer. Assisted immigrants to Utah 1864.

THORNLEY, JOHN (son of Robert Thornley and Jane Welsh of Ulneswalten, Lancastershire, Eng.). Born March 4, 1801, at Ulneswalten. Came to Utah 1865.
Married Helen Langton 1827, Eccles, Lancashire, Eng. (daughter of Ralph Langton and Mary Rigby of Eccles). Their children: Alice b. 1827, m. Thomas Swift; Robert b. 1830, m. Annie Brighton; John b. 1832, m. Margaret Stringfellow; Mary b. 1834, d. infant; Thomas b. 1837; Mary b. 1842, m. Thomas Carr. Family home was in England until they came to Utah. Died May 18, 1893.

THORNLEY, ROBERT (son of John Thornley and Helen Langton). Born June 3, 1830, Leyland, Lancastershire. Eng. Came to Utah Oct. 1, 1855. John Hindley company.
Married Annie Brighton March 24, 1858 (daughter of Robert Brighton and Elizabeth Stewart), who was born in 1840, and came to Utah in October 1857, with the Israel Evans handcart company. Their children: Robert Brighton b. Dec. 11, 1861, m. Annie G. Teer April 8, 1891; John Stewart b. Jan. 8, 1864, m. Liddy Baker Nov. 1895; William b. Jan. 26, 1866, m. Emma Clark June 6, 1894; Helen b. June 29, 1868, m. W. J. Timmins June 24, 1891; Annie b. July 13, 1870, m. Walter White Aug. 29, 1894; Seth b. Oct. 1, 1872, m. Alice Glazier July 20, 1904; Thomas b. Oct. 29, 1877, m. Pearl Gammon; James b. May 16, 1877, m. Mary Smith May 23, 1900; George b. March 18, 1880; Samuel b. July 20, 1882, m. Etta Barnet Nov. 28, 1906. Family home Smithfield, Cache Co., Utah, and all are living (1913).
High priest; Sunday school and ward teacher for 31 years; missionary. Member of Utah militia. One of the first nine families settled at Smithfield, where he helped to survey and lay out the city. Worked on the tabernacle and temple at Logan.

THORNLEY, ROBERT B. (son of Robert Thornley and Annie Brighton). Born Dec. 11, 1861, Smithfield, Utah.
Married Annie Teer April 8, 1891, Logan (daughter of John and Jane Teer). Their children: Annie b. Aug. 25, 1892; Jane b. Aug. 25, 1892.

THORNLEY, JOHN (son of Thomas Thornley and Miss Bolton of Leyland, Lancashire, Eng.). Born June 25, 1822, Leyland. Came to Utah 1854.
Married Martha Seed Nov. 25, 1843, Preston, Eng. (daughter of Thomas and Elizabeth Seed of Preston). She was born Sept. 22, 1819. Their children: William G. b. Aug. 18, 1848; Elizabeth Ann b. June 24, 1851, m. Daniel D. Harris; Mary Ellen b. June 8, 1853, m. William Mocker; Martha Seed b. Dec. 11, 1857, m. Benjamin B. Heywood; John W. b. May 19, 1859, m. Josephine King; Alice b. Dec. 7, 1860, m. Charley Cox; Jane b. June 13, 1862, m. Harry Aldous. Family home Kaysville, Utah.
Senior president of seventies 1857-92; high priest; ordained patriarch by George Teasdale Dec. 12, 1896. Pioneer dry farmer. Settled on Kay's Creek in 1855, and from there moved to Kaysville. Died Dec. 1, 1907.

THORNTON, HORACE (son of Ezra Thornton and Harriet Goodrich of Hinsdale, Cattaraugus county, N. Y.). Born May 7, 1822, Hinsdale. Came to Utah Sept. 8, 1850, Aaron Johnson company.
Married Elizabeth Wimmer March 17, 1851, Ogden, Utah (daughter of John Wimmer and Elizabeth Hendricks of Indiana, pioneers 1850, Stephen Markham company). She was born in 1831 in Indiana. Family resided at Springville and Parowan, Utah.
Member 20th quorum seventies and president of 69th quorum. Worked in Manti and St. George temples. Miller.

THORNTON, OLIVER (son of Joseph Thornton and Lucretia Calkins of Pickering, Lower Canada and later of New York). Born Sept. 6, 1806, in Canada. Came to Utah 1852, John Wimmer company.
Married Mary Griswold in 1827, a Pickering, Canada (daughter of Amos Griswold and Eleanor Stotts of Pickering, Canada, and American Fork, Utah, pioneers 1852). Their children: Lydia Meacham b. Oct. 19, 1830, m. Edmund Butler; m. Joshua Adams; Amos Griswold b. Dec. 30, 1832, m. Mary Whittaker; Thomas Ephraim, m. Priscilla Covington; Edward Hotchkiss b. 1836; Alice b. Sept. 28, 1839, m. Stephen Mott; Applos Griswold b. 1841; Eleanor hood; Oliver Evans b. May 14, 1848, m. Emeretta Davis Phillips (b. Nov. 19, 1850); Joseph Smith b. June 29, 1853, Singleton; Edmund B. b. Nov. 28, 1855, m. Sarah Lecey Christensen; Nathan M. b. Nov. 28, 1855, m. Sarah High priest. Early settler to American Fork, Utah. Member city council. Farmer. Died Jan. 21, 1891, American Fork.

THORNTO, AMOS G. (son of Oliver Thornton and Mary Griswold). Born Dec. 30, 1832, Pickering, Ontario county, Canada.
Married Mary Whittaker Dec. 15, 1856, Cedar City, Utah (daughter of James Whittaker and Rachel Taylor of Cedar City—pioneers 1852). She was born Nov. 15, 1838. Their children: Mary Alice b. July 29, 1859; Amos Whittaker b. Oct. 10, 1861; Lydia Meacham b. Aug. 22, 1862, m. James G. Knell; Oliver Griswold b. Nov. 15, 1864; Rachel G. b. April 6, 1867; Elm Lunt b. Feb. 18, 1870, m. J. Granville Pace; Sarah May. May 1, 1873, m. Joseph D. Cox, Jr.; Hattie Maria b. Dec. 2. 1875, m. William J. Snow; James Whittaker b. Dec. 9, 1884, m. Matilda Grace Green; m. Nellie Schofield. Family home Pinto, Utah.
Married Charity Butler (Wallace) 1862, Salt Lake City (daughter of John Butler and Caroline Skeen of Spanish Fork, Utah-pioneers 1852). Their children: William L. b. Aug. 3, 1864, died; James Apollos b. Dec. 23, 1866; Amos Edmund T. b. Jan. 5, 1867, m. Jennie Cox Sept. 22, 1886; Lydia Adele b. Jan 19, 1870, m. Hezekiah L. Dunn Sept 3, 1895; Aimesia b. Oct. 6, 1871; Taylor Butler b. March 1, 1873. Family home Pinto, Utah.
Called to southern Utah 1854. Presiding elder of Pinto ward seven years. Veteran Walker Indian war. Died April 5, 1906.
Charity Ityler was the widow of Mr. Wallace. The two children of her first marriage were: Caroline M., m. Dag. bert Whipl; Hamilton Monroe, m. Jane Stapley.

THORNTON OLIVER EVANS (son of Oliver Thornton and Mary Griswold). Born May 12, 1848, Des Moines, Iowa. Came to Utah 1852, John Wimmer company.
Married Everetts Davis Phillips Feb. 15, 1873, Salt Lake City (daughter of Richard A. Phillips and Margaret Lucker of Toms River, N. J.;—pioneers 1861, Captain Martindale company). She was born Dec. 25, 1854. Their children: Oliver S. b. Oct. 2, 1873, d. infant; Richard A. b. Feb. 6, 1873, d. infant; Rett May b. May 25, 1877, m. Thomas J. Crook, ston; Ira Jan b. Sept. 30, 1879, m. Belle Norton; Alice Menety b. Q. 15, 1882, m. George Holman; Evy Elzety b. Dec. 15, m. Thomas Wilson; Mary Delcia b. Sept. 12, 1887, d. infant; Edmund Owen b. Dec. 14, 1888, m. Alice Peterson; Sylvia Ann b. Sept. 5, 1893.
Assisted in building the first canal across Provo Bench; assisted in building the first telegraph line; worked on U. P. lumber elders quorum. Farmer, fisherman and orchardist.

THORUP, HERMAN AUGUST (son of Christian Larsen Thorup and Johanne Catrine Holm of Copenhagen. Denmark). Born Aug. 11, 1826, Copenhagen. Came to Utah Aug. 8, 1869.
Married Mie Christine Christensen Feb. 25, 1848, Copenhagen (daughter of Christen Hansen and Ellen Kirstine Hansen of Fyrup Gaard, Sjelland, Denmark). She was born Sept. 8, 1824. Their children: Herman F. F., m. Sophie G. Johnson; m. Annie C. Anderson; m. Jessine Jensen; Laura EE. d. child; Laura A. M., m. Niels Rasmusson; John Theoba, m. Johanne Caroline Osterman, m. Hansine Enceline Anrea Berg; Christine V., m. Niels Rasmusson; Maria, d. child; Hyrum E., m. Nette Nelsen; Joseph, m. Clara Romney. Family home, Salt Lake City.
High priest. Carpenter and joiner. Died Aug. 20, 1907, Salt Lake City.

THORUP, HERMAN F. F. (son of Herman August Thorup and Marie Cristine Christensen). Born April 19, 1849, Copenhagen, Denmark. Came to Utah with father.
Married Sophie G. Johnson May 28, 1872, Salt Lake City (daughter of Johnson of Sweden). She was born Dec. 12, 1847. Their children: Maria J. b. July 10, 1873; Albert M. b. Nov. 5, 1874; Christine b. July 1876, and Sophie C. b. Sept 16, 1878, all fir died. Family home, Salt Lake City.
Married Ane C. Anderson Sept. 29, 1881, Salt Lake City (daughter of Anders Rasmusson and Anne Petersen of Denmark). She was born Dec. 16, 1857. Their children: Annie C. b. Sept. 18, 1882, d. child; Herman F. b. Feb. 10, 1884, m. Caroline Alisen; Joseph F. b. Nov. 1, 1885; Eliza A. b. Oct. 30, 1887, m. Axel L. Fikstad; William W. b. Jan. 21, 1891, m. Esther Norberg.
Married Jesine Jensen Dec. 21, 1882, Salt Lake City (daughter of Leis Peter Jensen and Bertha Rasmusson of Denmark). She was born July 17, 1861. Their children: Bertha J. b. Nov. 1, 1883, m. William Lindstrom; Anne M. b. Jan. 23, 1885, d. infant; Reb ca E. C. b. Oct. 31, 1887, m. Leonard Mitchell; Nephi F. b. M ch 31, 1889, d. infant; Nephine M. b. June 14, Andrv W. Rowley; Zina F. A. b. March 10, 1892; Lizzie H. b. M ch 16, 1894; Henry J. b. March 9, 1896; Lawrence S. b. Apl 10, 1898; Francis E. b. April 11, 1903; Gertrude P. b. v. 27, 1905.
President 13 h quorum seventies; missionary to Denmark 1879-81; home missionary five years; block teacher. Florist and nurseryman.

THORUP, JOHN THEOBALD (son of Herman August Thorup and Marie Christine Christensen). Born May 1856, Copenhagen, Denmark. Came to Utah with father.
Married Johanne Caroline Osterman Aug. 24, 1882, Caroline Marieberg of Grenaa, Denmark, pioneers 1868, John G. Elman company). She was born Feb. 6, 1859. Their children: John M. b. May 19, 1883, m. Karen Caroline M. L., May 7, 1886, m. Sanford S. Stevens.

E. b. Sept. 24, 1888; Rachel H. b. Mr 29, 1892; Ruth O. b. Dec. 12, 1894; Martha O. b. Oct. 28, 18?; Naomi O. b. Aug. 2, 1901. Family home, Salt Lake City.
Married Hansine Engeline Andre Berg April 11, 1887, Salt Lake City (daughter of Andres Berg and Hansine Engeline Petersen of Grenaa, Denmark, who came to Utah June 7, 1885). She was born Jan. 18, 1868. Their children: Alvin T. b. Jan. 8, 1888; Franklin J. b. March 24, 1891, d. infant; Grover A. b. June 11, 1893; Iva B. b. Sept. 4, 1895; Edna B. b. Aug. 14, 1898; Abrahar B. b. Sept. 23, 1901; James B. b. May 7, 1906; Levi B. b. March 2, 1909.
Member 16th quorum seventies; missionary to Denmark 1879-81; 2d counselor 1887-97; 1st counselor 1897-1910 to Bishop Joseph Warburton of 1st ward member high council of Liberty stake 1910 to date; president Y. M. I. A.; block teacher. Graduate of Brigham Young University of Provo 1872. School trustee. Vice-president Freeze Mercantile Company 1890-1900; manager 13th ward store of Provo 1900-06. Carpenter and builder; general merchant.

THURGOOD, THOMAS (son of Wilam Thurgood of Terling, Essex county, Eng.). Born Ju, 1807, Terling. Came to Utah 1867, William Godbe company.
Married Catherine Jenkins 1839 a Terling (daughter of Ephraim Jenkins of Hatfield, Essex Eng.). She was born in 1803. Their children: Joseph, aged 4; Thomas, d. aged 16; Kate, m. John South; George, m. Elizabeth Edwards, m. Mariah Slack; Abraham, r Annie Frick. Family home, Salt Lake City.
Laborer. Died July 1, 1883.

THURMAN. SAMUEL R. (son of Wilam T. Thurman and Margaret Brown of Louisville, Ky. Born May 6, 1850, Louisville. Came to Utah October, 170.
Married Isabell Karren May 6, 187 Lehi, Utah (daughter of Thomas Karren and Ann Ratcliff f Liverpool, Eng., pioneers July 24, 1847, Brigham Your company). She was born Jan. 1, 1856. Their children: chard B., m. Elizabeth C. Ayton; Mabel, m. Moses C. Davis Margaret, m. Dr. Ray Irvine; Lydia C., m. C. W. Reed; Wiiam T., m. Pearl Taft; Samuel D., m. Henrietta Young; Victor E., m. Vaughn Christianson; Allen G. Family resid Provo and Salt Lake City, Utah.
Seventy; missionary to England 1f0-92. County attorney for Utah county; mayor of Lehi; mober of territorial legislature and of both constitutional conventions; assistant U. S. district attorney under last Cleveland administration; one of first Democratic nominees f supreme bench after statehood of Utah. Lawyer.

THURMAN, RICHARD B. (son of Smuel R. Thurman and Isabell Karren). Born Nov. 7, 1873, Lehi, Utah Co. Utah.
Married Elizabeth C. Ayton Sep 7, 1898, Laytonsville, Montgomery county, Md. (daughter f James Edward Ayton and Frances Evelyn King of Laytonsville). She was born Aug. 22, 1872. Their children: Jnes Ayton b. Feb. 27, 1900; Samuel Richard b. Oct. 26, 102; Frances Isabell b. Jan. 18, 1905. Family resided Pro and Salt Lake City, Utah.
Lawyer.

THRELKELD, JOHN (son of Isaac nd Margaret Threlkeld of Carlisle, Cumberland, Eng.). Bor March 4, 1814, Carlisle, Eng.
Married Elizabeth Barker 1840, rlisle, Eng. (daughter of John Darker and Margaret Freand, of Carlisle, latter died on plains, on route to Utah). She was born Dec. 17, 1810, Glasgow, Scotland, and died Ic. 19, 1870, at Carlisle. Their children: Margaret, m. Joe H. Johnson; Thomas; Mary Jane, m. Henry Coleman; Harah, m. Herbert Harris; Joseph; Sarah Ann, m. Peter O'Brie; Mary Elizabeth, died; John, m. Eliza Davis. Family hon Carlisle, Eng.
Died 1875, at Carlisle.

THURSTON. JAMES (son of Stephe Thurston and Frances Raynor of Rumburg, Suffolk. E., former born about 1770). He was born May 1, 1829, t Rumburgh. Came to Utah Sept. 9, 1860, Franklin Brown company.
Married Mary Seamons April 6. 54 (daughter of Henry Seamons and Mary King, pioneers Sept. 9, 1860, Franklin Brown company—married January 1832, in Suffolk, Eng.). She was born March 17, 1833, St. Michaels, Suffolk, Eng., and came to Utah with husband. heir children: Hannah b. June 17, 1855, m. Benjamin Hyas Jan. 28, 1869; Mary Castelena b. March 23, 1856, d. July 1, 1856; Sarah Elizabeth b. Oct. 22, 1857, m. John Dake 187; Stephen b. Aug. 25, 1859, m. Eliza Marietta Hurren Ap 7, 1884; Edith Mariam b. Sept. 4, 1861, m. Walter Hawks Ja. 14, 1880; Frances Lucy b. Nov. 9, 1863, m. James Dalls Jn 24, 1884; Eliza Marette b. Jan. 14, 1866, m. D   Hyr s Nov. 15, 1884; Phebe Ann   1868,   Lai) Dec. 12, 1888; Simpson Ben   rch 2   el Follett March 26, 1890; Ima   172,   'si Ju   9 1897; Tracy b.   hn   sta b. March 18   1r   rk, Cache
                          'e City
                          pio-
                          ol-
                          t

9, 1869; Emma b. Dec. 1, 1871, m. Ezra J. Seamons Sept. 24, 1891; Ellen Elizabeth b. March 17, 1877, m. Alma J. Hancey Dec. 16. 1897; Frederic Graham b. May 13, 1881, d. April 24, 1889; Edella Emily b. Oct. 7, 1886, d. Feb. 17, 1888. Families resided Hyde Park, Cache Co., Utah.
Watermaster many years. Farmer; stockraiser; horticulturist, being the first in these lines in Hyde Park. Died Dec. 12, 1907.

THURSTON, STEPHEN (son of James Thurston and Mary Seamons). Born Aug. 25, 1859, Omaha, Neb.
Married Eliza Marietta Hurren April 7, 1884, Salt Lake City (daughter of James Hurren and Eliza Reeder, pioneers July 15, 1856, James G. Willie handcart company). Their children: Mary Eliza b. Feb. 19, 1885, m. Joseph W. Waite 1903; Dessie b. Feb. 20, 1887, m. Andrew Nyman 1909; Lydia b. Oct. 17, 1889, m. Orvin Nyman 1909; Phebe b. Nov. 25, 1891, m. George F. Ashcroft 1912; Vera and Veda (twins) b. Aug. 8, 1894; Stephen James b. July 11, 1899; Myrle b. Feb. 2, 1903; Wanda b. Dec. 23, 1905.
Sunday school teacher; missionary to England 1899-1901. Chairman old folks' committee. Watermaster Hyde Park Canal Company seven years; trustee of same company ten years. Member stake board of education since 1905; member incorporated town board of Hyde Park. Farmer; stockraiser.

THURSTON, THOMAS JEFFERSON (son of Peter Thurston and Hannah Butler of Granville, Licking Co., Ohio). Born Feb. 12, 1809, Fletcher, Vt. Came to Utah Oct. 6, 1847, Jedediah M. Grant company.
Married Rosetta Bull March 28, 1828, Granville, Ohio (daughter of Smith Bull and Sarah Burr of Manchester, Vt., pioneers Oct. 6, 1847, Jedediah M. Grant company). She was born April 25, 1809, and died July 29, 1880. Their children: Harriet Elizabeth b. Jan. 27, 1829, m. William Washington Potter; George Washington b. Nov. 1, 1830, m. Sarah Lucina Snow March 28, 1858; Smith Butler, m. Mary Garn; Sarah Ann, m. Jedediah M. Grant, m. J. F. Snedaker; Hannah Maria; Reuben Johnson; Julia Rosetta, m. Joseph Bates Nobles; Caroline Rozalia, m. John James Fry; Huldah Cordella, m. Willard G. Smith; Thomas Jefferson; Peter Franklin, m. Mary Ann Spendlove. Family home Centerville, Utah.
Married Elizabeth Smith at Salt Lake City (daughter of John Smith and Mary Johnson of Lancaster, Eng.). She was born Feb. 27, 1835, and died in 1899. Their children: Rozetta, m. Mr. Bryan; Elizabeth, m. Jedediah Grant Little; John, m. Alice Josephine Little; Clara, m. George Leonard Little; Mary, m. Andrew Laden; William Henry, m. Katie Nemp; Frederick; Jedediah Morgan; Edward; Leah Helen; Rebecca, m. Ephraim Whittier; Leroy, m. Ada J. Anson; Harris, m. May Peterson.
Married Helen Maria Davis (daughter of Eliakim Spooner Davis and Orpha Hopkins of Lowell, Mass.). She was born in 1845; died.
Counselor to Bishop Hickenlooper of 6th ward, Salt Lake City, 1847; acting bishop of Morgan county for many years; president high council of Morgan stake. He was sent by Brigham Young on the first exploring expedition in Cache valley in 1848, and later moved to Centerville, where he took up 80 acres of land and engaged in farming. He, together with Charles S. Peterson and their sons, built the first road through Weber canyon, and they were among the first settlers of Weber valley. Moved to St. George, William W. Potter, himself and others built the first boat and made the first known trip on Salt Lake, exploring all the islands. The boat was named "Mud Hen." While on the lake they were overtaken by a storm in which they almost lost their lives. He also established the first ferry on Bear river. Farmer. Died May 4, 1885, St. George, Utah.

TIBBITTS, BENJAMIN (son of Richard Tibbitts and Mary Sandals of Kidderminster, Worcestershire, Eng.). Born Sept. 8, 1826, at Kidderminster. Immigrated to America in 1848 and came to Utah Sept. 25, 1856, John D. Holladay company.
Married Eliza Moody 1852, Thompsonville, Conn. (daughter of Henry Moody of Kidderminster, Eng.). Born April 21, 1831. Their children: George Henry b. Feb. 25, 1853, m. Dec. 29, 1877; James b. July 22, 1854, d. Feb. 5, 1896; Emeline b. March 15, 1856, m. April 21, 1876; Lorenzo Edwin b. Aug. 7, 1861 (d. Dec. 27, 1911), m. Dec. 2, 1885; Eliza Jane b. Dec. 22, 1867, m. July 21, 1886; Benjamin Richard b. July 27, 1870, m. Dec. 30, 1891; Edgar b. July 16, 1872, m. Oct. 10, 1896; Mira b. Nov. 2, 1874, d. Dec. 17, 1874. Family home Providence, Cache Co., Utah.
Ward teacher many years. Farmer. Died March 22, 1902.

TIBBITTS, GEORGE HENRY (son of Benjamin Tibbitts and Eliza Moody). Born Feb. 25, 1853, Roxbury, Mass. Came to Utah with father.
Married Mary Harriet Holt Dec. 29, 1877, Salt Lake City (daughter of Samuel Holt and Selina Deston of Salt Lake City). She was born Oct. 5, 1860. Their children: George S. b. Dec. 9, 1878, m. May 20, 1903; Selina b. Jan. 29, 1880, m. Dec. 19, 1900; Ernest H. b. Dec. 8, 1882; Edwin B. b. Feb. 29, 1884, m. June 27, 1906; Marion Benjamin b. Feb. 13, 1887, m. Dec. 13, 1911; Elmer M. b. March 18, 1890; Ira James b. July 11, 1892; Mary Lavern b. July 8, 1896; Frances Veda b. Nov. 21, 1902. Family home Providence, Utah.
Member 32d quorum seventies; ward teacher; high priest. School trustee two terms. Farmer.

THORNE, GEORGE (son of David Thorne and Elizabeth Reeves). Born Feb. 1, 1840, at Kensal Green, Eng. Came to Utah with parents.
Married Mary Rebecca Rogers Feb. 12, 1865, Pleasant Grove, Utah (daughter of William Rogers of Birmingham, Eng.). She was born May 7, 1831. Their child: Alice Rebecca b. Aug. 15, 1868, m. James Bralford. Family home Pleasant Grove, Utah.
High priest. Watermaster. Farmer. Assisted immigrants to Utah 1864.

THORNLEY, JOHN (son of Robert Thornley and Jane Welsh of Ulneswalten, Lancastershire, Eng.). Born March 4, 1801, at Ulneswalten. Came to Utah 1865.
Married Helen Langton 1827, Eccles, Lancashire, Eng. (daughter of Ralph Langton and Mary Rigby of Eccles). Their children: Alice b. 1827, m. Thomas Swift; Robert b. 1830, m. Annie Brighton; John b. 1832, m. Margaret Stringfellow; Mary b. 1834, d. infant; Thomas b. 1837; Mary b. 1842, m. Thomas Carr. Family home was in England until they came to Utah. Died May 18, 1893.

THORNLEY, ROBERT (son of John Thornley and Helen Langton). Born June 3, 1830, Leyland, Lancastershire, Eng. Came to Utah Oct. 1, 1855. John Hindley company.
Married Annie Brighton March 24, 1858 (daughter of Robert Brighton and Elizabeth Stewart), who was born in 1840, and came to Utah in October 1857, with the Israel Evans handcart company. Their children: Robert Brighton b. Dec. 11, 1861, m. Annie G. Teer April 8, 1891; John Stewart b. Jan. 8, 1864, m. Liddy Baker Nov. 1895; William b. Jan. 26, 1866, m. Emma Clark June 6, 1894; Helen b. June 29, 1868, m. W. J. Timmins June 24, 1891; Annie b. July 13, 1870, m. Walter White Aug. 29, 1894; Seth b. Oct. 1, 1872, m. Alice Glazier July 20, 1904; Thomas b. Oct. 29, 1874, m. Pearl Gammon; James b. May 16, 1877, m. Mary Smith May 23, 1900; George b. March 18, 1880; Samuel b. July 20, 1882, m. Etta Barnet Nov. 28, 1906. Family home in Smithfield, Cache Co., Utah, and all are living (1913).
High priest; Sunday school and ward teacher for 31 years; missionary. Member of Utah militia. One of the first nine families settled at Smithfield, where he helped to survey and lay out the city. Worked on the tabernacle and temple at Logan.

THORNLEY, ROBERT B. (son of Robert Thornley and Annie Brighton). Born Dec. 11, 1861, Smithfield, Utah.
Married Annie Teer April 8, 1891, Logan, Utah (daughter of John and Jane Teer). Their children: Annie b. Aug. 25, 1892; Jane b. Aug. 25, 1892.

THORNLEY, JOHN (son of Thomas Thornley and Miss Bolton of Leyland, Lancashire, Eng.). Born June 25, 1822, Leyland. Came to Utah 1854.
Married Martha Seed Nov. 25, 1843, Preston, Eng. (daughter of Thomas and Elizabeth Seed of Preston). She was born Sept. 22, 1819. Their children: William G. b. Aug. 18, 1848; Elizabeth Ann b. June 24, 1851, m. Daniel B. Harris; Mary Ellen b. June 8, 1853, m. William Mocker; Martha Seed b. Dec. 11, 1857, m. Benjamin B. Heywood; John W. b. May 19, 1859, m. Josephine King; Alice b. Dec. 7, 1860, m. Charley Cox; Jane b. June 13, 1862, m. Harry Aldous. Family home Kaysville, Utah.
Senior president of seventies 1857-92; high priest; ordained patriarch by George Teasdale Dec. 12, 1896. Pioneer dry farmer. Settled on Kay's Creek in 1855, and from there moved to Kaysville. Died Dec. 1, 1907.

THORNTON, HORACE (son of Ezra Thornton and Harriet Goodrich of Hinsdale, Cattaraugus county, N. Y.). Born May 7, 1822, Hinsdale. Came to Utah Sept. 8, 1850, Aaron Johnson company.
Married Elizabeth Wimmer March 17, 1851, Ogden, Utah (daughter of John Wimmer and Elizabeth Hendricks of Indiana, pioneers 1850, Stephen Markham company). She was born in 1831 in Indiana. Family resided at Springville and Parowan, Utah.
Member 20th quorum seventies and president of 69th quorum. Worked in Manti and St. George temples. Miller.

THORNTON, OLIVER (son of Joseph Thornton and Lucretia Calkins of Pickering, Lower Canada and later of New York). Born Sept. 6, 1806, in Canada. Came to Utah 1852, John Wimmer company.
Married Mary Griswold in 1827, at Pickering, Canada (daughter of Amos Griswold and Eleanor Stotts of Pickering, Canada, and American Fork, Utah, pioneers 1852). Their children: Lydia Meacham b. Oct. 19, 1830, m. Edmund Butler; m. Joshua Adams; Amos Griswold b. Dec. 30, 1832, m. Mary Whittaker; Thomas Ephraim, m. Priscilla Covington; Edward Hotchkiss b. 1836; Alice b. Sept. 28, 1839, m. Stephen Mott; Applos Griswold b. 1841; Eleanor b. 1843, and Mary b. Oct. 7, 1845, latter three died in childhood; Oliver Evans b. May 12, 1848, m. Emeretta Davis Phillips (b. Nov. 19, 1850); Joseph Smith b. June 29, 1850, m. Lecy Christensen; Nathan M. b. Nov. 28, 1855, m. Sarah Singleton; Edmund B. Family home American Fork, Utah.
High priest. Early settler to American Fork. Member city council. Farmer. Died Jan. 21, 1891, American Fork.

THORNTON, AMOS G. (son of Oliver Thornton and Mary Griswold). Born Dec. 30, 1832, Pickering, Ontario county, Canada.
Married Mary Whittaker Dec. 18, 1856, Cedar City, Utah (daughter of James Whittaker and Rachel Taylor of Cedar City—pioneers 1852). She was born Nov. 18, 1838. Their children: Mary Alice b. July 29, 1858; Amos Whittaker b. Oct. 10, 1860; Lydia Meacham b. Aug. 22, 1862, m. James G. Knell; Oliver Griswold b. Nov. 15, 1864; Rachel G. b. April 6, 1867; Ellen Lunt b. Feb. 18, 1870, m. J. Granville Pace; Sarah May b. May 1, 1873, m. Joseph D. Cox, Jr.; Hattie Maria b. Dec. 2, 1875, m. William J. Snow; James Whittaker b. Dec. 9, 1883, m. Matilda Grace Green; m. Nellie Schofield. Family home Pinto, Utah.
Charity Butler (Wallace) 1862, Salt Lake City (daughter of John Butler and Caroline Skeen of Spanish Fork, Utah—pioneers 1852). Their children: John L. b. Aug. 3, 1863, died; James Apollos b. Dec. 23, 1864; Amos; Edmund T. b. Jan. 8, 1867, m. Jennie Cox Sept. 22, 1896; Lydia Adeline b. Jan 19, 1870, m. Hezekiah E. Duffin Sept. 22, 1896; Artimesia b. Oct. 6, 1871; Taylor Butler b. March 3, 1873. Family home Pinto, Utah.
Called to southern Utah 1854. Presiding elder of Pinto ward several years. Veteran Walker Indian war. Died April 5, 1901.
Charity Butler was the widow of Mr. Wallace. The two children of her first marriage were: Caroline M., m. Dagbert Whipple; Hamilton Monroe, m. Jane Stapley.

THORNTON, OLIVER EVANS (son of Oliver Thornton and Mary Griswold). Born May 12, 1848, Des Moines, Iowa. Came to Utah 1852, John Wimmer company.
Married Emeretta Davis Phillips Feb. 15, 1873, Salt Lake City (daughter of Richard Phillips and Margaret Lucker of Toms River, N. J.—pioneers 1861, Captain Martindale company). She was born Dec. 25, 1854. Their children: Oliver S. b. Oct. 29, 1873, d. infant; Richard A. b. Feb. 6, 1875, d. infant; Retty May b. May 25, 1877, m. Thomas J. Crookston; Ira John b. Sept. 30, 1879, m. Belle Norton; Alice Menesty b. Oct. 15, 1882, m. George Holman; Evy Eltety b. Dec. 15, 1884, m. Thomas Wilson; Mary Delcia b. Sept. 17, 1887, d. infant; Edmund Owen b. Dec. 14, 1888, m. Alice Peterson; Silvia Ann b. Sept. 5, 1893.
Assisted in building the first canal across Provo Bench; assisted in building the first telegraph line; worked on U. P. R. R. Member elders quorum. Farmer, fisherman and orchardist.

THORUP, HERMAN AUGUST (son of Christian Larsen Thorup and Johanne Catrine Holm of Copenhagen, Denmark). Born Aug. 11, 1826, Copenhagen. Came to Utah Aug. 8, 1869.
Married Marie Christine Christensen Feb. 25, 1848, Copenhagen (daughter of Christen Hansen and Ellen Kirstine Hansen of Myrup Gaard, Sjelland, Denmark). She was born Sept. 19, 1824. Their children: Herman F. F., m. Sophie G. Johnson; m. Annie C. Anderson; m. Jensine Jensen; Laura E. E., d. child; Laura A. M., m. Niels Rasmusson; John Theobald, m. Johanne Caroline Osterman, m. Hansine Engeline Andrea Berg; Christine V., m. Niels Rasmusson; Maria, d. child; Hyrum E., m. Nette Nelsen; Joseph, m. Clara Romney. Family home, Salt Lake City.
High priest. Carpenter and joiner. Died Aug. 20, 1907, Salt Lake City.

THORUP, HERMAN F. F. (son of Herman August Thorup and Marie Christine Christensen). Born April 19, 1849, Copenhagen, Denmark. Came to Utah with father.
Married Sophie G. Johnson May 28, 1872, Salt Lake City (daughter of G. Johnson of Sweden). She was born Dec. 12, 1847. Their children: Maria J. b. July 10, 1873, Albert M. b. Nov. 5, 1874, Christine b. July 1876, and Sophie C. b. Sept. 16, 1878, all four died. Family home, Salt Lake City.
Married Annie C. Anderson Sept. 29, 1881, Salt Lake City (daughter of Anders Rasmusson and Anne Petersen of Denmark). She was born Dec. 16, 1857. Their children: Annie C. b. Sept. 18, 1882, d. child; Herman F. b. Feb. 10, 1884, m. Caroline A. Nelsen; Joseph F. b. Nov. 1, 1885; Eliza A. b. Oct. 30, 1887, m. Axel L. Fikstad; William W. b. Jan. 21, 1891, m. Esther Norberg.
Married Jensine Jensen Dec. 21, 1882, Salt Lake City (daughter of Niels Peter Jensen and Bertha Rasmusson of Denmark). She was born July 17, 1861. Their children: Bertha J. b. Nov. 1, 1883, m. William Lindstrom; Anne M. b. Jan. 23, 1885, m. Paul K. Nielson; Emily S. b. April 12, 1886, d. infant; Rebecca E. C. b. Oct. 31, 1887, m. Leonard Mitchell; Nephi F. b. March 31, 1889, d. infant; Nephine M. b. June 14, 1890, m. Andrew W. Rowley; Zina F. A. b. March 19, 1892; Lizzie H. b. March 16, 1894; Henry J. b. March 15, 1896; Lawrence S. b. April 10, 1898; Francis E. b. April 11, 1903; Gertrude F. b. Nov. 27, 1905.
President 138th quorum seventies; missionary to Denmark 1879-81; home missionary five years; block teacher. Florist and nurseryman.

THORUP, JOHN THEOBALD (son of Herman August Thorup and Marie Christine Christensen). Born May 13, 1856, Copenhagen, Denmark. Came to Utah with father.
Married Johanne Caroline Osterman Aug. 24, 1882, Salt Lake City (daughter of Jens Carl Didderick Osterman and Caroline Marie Berg of Grenaa, Denmark, pioneers Sept. 26, 1868, John G. Holman company). She was born Oct. 3, 1858. Their children: John M. b. May 19, 1883, m. Kate Wilson; Caroline M. L. b. May 7, 1886, m. Sanford S. Stevens; Mabel

PIONEERS AND PROMINENT MEN OF UTAH 1213

E. b. Sept. 24, 1888; Rachel H. b. May 29, 1892; Ruth O. b. Dec. 12, 1894; Martha O. b. Oct. 28, 1897; Naomi O. b. Aug. 2, 1901. Family home, Salt Lake City.
Married Hansine Engeline Andrea Berg April 11, 1887, Salt Lake City (daughter of Andreas Berg and Hansine Engeline Petersen of Grenaa, Denmark, who came to Utah June 7, 1885). She was born Jan. 18, 1868. Their children: Alvin T. b. Jan. 8, 1888; Franklin A. b. March 24, 1891, d. infant; Grover A. b. June 11, 1893; Eva B. b. Sept. 4, 1895; Edna B. b. Aug. 14, 1898; Abraham B. b. Sept. 23, 1901; James B. b. May 7, 1906; Levi B. b. March 2, 1909.
Member 16th quorum seventies; missionary to Denmark 1879-81; 2d counselor 1887-97; 1st counselor 1897-1910 to Bishop Joseph Warburton of 1st ward; member high council of Liberty stake 1910 to date; president Y. M. M. I. A.; block teacher. Graduate of Brigham Young University of Provo 1872. School trustee. Vice-president Freeze Mercantile Company 1890-1900; manager 13th ward store of Provo 1900-06. Carpenter and builder; general merchant.

THURGOOD, THOMAS (son of William Thurgood of Terling, Essex county, Eng.). Born July, 1807, Terling. Came to Utah 1867, William Godbe company.
Married Catherine Jenkins 1839 at Terling (daughter of Ephraim Jenkins of Hatfield, Essex, Eng.). She was born in 1803. Their children: Joseph, d. aged 4; Thomas, d. aged 16; Kate. m. John South; George, m. Elizabeth Edwards, m. Mariah Slack; Abraham, m. Annie Frick. Family home, Salt Lake City.
Laborer. Died July 1, 1883.

THURMAN, SAMUEL R. (son of William T. Thurman and Margaret Brown of Louisville, Ky.). Born May 6, 1850, Louisville. Came to Utah October, 1870.
Married Isabell Karren May 6, 1872, Lehi, Utah (daughter of Thomas Karren and Ann Ratcliff of Liverpool, Eng., pioneers July 24, 1847, Brigham Young company). She was born Jan. 1, 1856. Their children: Richard B., m. Elizabeth C. Ayton: Mabel, m. Moses C. Davis; Margaret, m. Dr. Ray Irvine; Lydia C., m. C. W. Reed; William T., m. Pearl Taft; Samuel D., m. Henrietta Young; Victor E., m. Vaughn Christianson; Allen G. Family resided Provo and Salt Lake City, Utah.
Seventy; missionary to England 1890-92. County attorney of Utah county; mayor of Lehi; member of territorial legislature and of both constitutional conventions; assistant U. S. district attorney under last Cleveland administration; one of first Democratic nominees for supreme bench after statehood of Utah. Lawyer.

THURMAN, RICHARD B. (son of Samuel R. Thurman and Isabell Karren). Born Nov. 7, 1873, Lehi, Utah Co., Utah.
Married Elizabeth C. Ayton Sept. 7, 1898, Laytonsville, Montgomery county, Md. (daughter of James Edward Ayton and Frances Evelyn King of Laytonsville). She was born Aug. 22, 1872. Their children: James Ayton b. Feb. 27, 1900; Samuel Richard b. Oct. 26, 1902; Frances Isabell b. Jan. 18, 1905. Family resided Provo and Salt Lake City, Utah.
Lawyer.

THRELKELD, JOHN (son of Isaac and Margaret Threlkeld of Carlisle, Cumberland, Eng.). Born March 4, 1814, Carlisle, Eng.
Married Elizabeth Barker 1840, Carlisle, Eng. (daughter of John Barker and Margaret Freeland, of Carlisle, latter died on plains, en route to Utah). She was born Dec. 17, 1810, Glasgow, Scotland, and died Dec. 19, 1870, at Carlisle. Their children: Margaret, m. Joel H. Johnson; Thomas; Mary Jane, m. Henry Coleman; Hannah, m. Herbert Harris; Joseph; Sarah Ann, m. Peter O'Brien; Mary Elizabeth, died; John, m. Eliza Davis. Family home Carlisle, Eng.
Died 1875, at Carlisle.

THURSTON, JAMES (son of Stephen Thurston and Frances Raynor of Rumburgh, Suffolk, Eng., former born about 1770). He was born May 1, 1829, at Rumburgh. Came to Utah Sept. 9, 1860, Franklin Brown company.
Married Mary Seamons April 6, 1854 (daughter of Henry Seamons and Mary King, pioneers Sept. 9, 1860, Franklin Brown company—married January, 1832, in Suffolk, Eng.). She was born March 17, 1833, St. Michaels, Suffolk, Eng., and came to Utah with husband. Their children: Hannah b. June 17, 1855, m. Benjamin Hymas Jan. 28, 1869; Mary Castelena b. March 23, 1856, d. July 31, 1856; Sarah Elizabeth b. Oct. 22, 1857, m. John Dake 1877; Stephen b. Aug. 25, 1859, m. Eliza Marietta Hurren April 7, 1884; Edith Mariam b. Sept. 4, 1861, m. Walter Hawks Jan. 1, 1880; Frances Lucy b. Nov. 9, 1863, m. James Dalls Jan. 24, 1884; Eliza Marette b. Jan. 14, 1866, m. Benjamin Hymas Nov. 15, 1884; Phebe Ann b. Feb. 23, 1868, m. Suel E. Lamb Dec. 12, 1888; Simpson Benjamin b. March 26, 1870, m. Belle Follett March 26, 1890; Ima b. April 3. 1872, m. Nellie Nelson June 9, 1897; Tracy B. June 22, 1874, m. John Lamb March 5, 1896; Augusta b. March 8, 1878, d. Aug. 29, 1878. Family home Hyde Park, Cache Co., Utah.
Married Jane Sinclair Graham Aug. 4, 1866, Salt Lake City (daughter of Frederic Graham and Elizabeth Swan, pioneers 1859, Horton D. Haight company—married at Woolwich, Kentshire, Eng.). She was born April 20, 1848, at Woolwich. Their children: George b. Feb. 27, 1869, d. Sept.

9, 1869; Emma b. Dec. 1, 1871, m. Ezra J. Seamons Sept. 24, 1891; Ellen Elizabeth b. March 17, 1877, m. Alma J. Hancey Dec. 16, 1897; Frederic Graham b. May 13, 1881, d. April 24, 1889; Edella Emily b. Oct. 7, 1886, d. Feb. 17, 1888. Families resided Hyde Park, Cache Co., Utah.
Watermaster many years. Farmer; stockraiser; horticulturist, being the first in these lines in Hyde Park. Died Dec. 12, 1907.

THURSTON, STEPHEN (son of James Thurston and Mary Seamons). Born Aug. 25, 1859, Omaha, Neb.
Married Eliza Marietta Hurren April 7, 1884, Salt Lake City (daughter of James Hurren and Eliza Reeder, pioneers July 15, 1856, James G. Willie handcart company). Their children: Mary Eliza b. Feb. 19, 1885, m. Joseph W. Waite 1903; Dessie b. Feb. 20, 1887, m. Andrew Nyman 1909; Lydia b. Oct. 17, 1889, m. Orvin Nyman 1909; Phebe b. Nov. 25, 1891, m. George F. Ashcroft 1912; Vera and Veda (twins) b. Aug. 8, 1894; Stephen James b. July 11, 1899; Myrle b. Feb. 2, 1903; Wanda b. Dec. 23, 1905.
Sunday school teacher; missionary to England 1899-1901. Chairman old folks' committee. Watermaster Hyde Park Canal Company seven years; trustee of same company ten years. Member stake board of education since 1905; member incorporated town board of Hyde Park. Farmer; stockraiser.

THURSTON, THOMAS JEFFERSON (son of Peter Thurston and Hannah Butler of Granville, Licking Co., Ohio). Born Feb. 12, 1805, Fletcher, Vt. Came to Utah Oct. 6, 1847, Jedediah M. Grant company.
Married Rosetta Bull March 28, 1828, Granville, Ohio (daughter of Smith Bull and Sarah Burr of Manchester, Vt., pioneers Oct. 6, 1847, Jedediah M. Grant company). She was born April 25, 1809, and died July 29, 1880. Their children: Harriet Elizabeth b. Jan. 27, 1829, m. William Washington Potter; George Washington b. Nov. 1, 1830, m. Sarah Lucina Snow March 28, 1858; Smith Butler, m. Mary Garn; Sarah Ann, m. Jedediah M. Grant, m. J. F. Snedaker; Hannah Maria; Reuben Johnson; Julia Rosetta, m. Joseph Bates Nobles; Caroline Rozalia, m. John James Fry; Huldah Cordelia, m. Willard G. Smith; Thomas Jefferson; Peter Franklin, m. Mary Ann Spendlove. Family home Centerville, Utah.
Married Elizabeth Smith at Salt Lake City (daughter of John Smith and Mary Johnson of Lancaster, Eng.). She was born Feb. 27, 1835, and died in 1899. Their children: Rozetta, m. Mr. Bryan; Elizabeth, m. Jedediah Grant Little; John, m. Alice Josephine Little; Clara, m. George Leonard Little; Mary, m. Andrew Laden; William Henry, m. Katie Nemp; Frederick; Jedediah Morgan; Edward; Leah Helen; Rebecca, m. Ephraim Whittier; Leroy, m. Ada J. Anson; Harris, m. May Peterson.
Married Helen Maria Davis (daughter of Eliakim Spooner Davis and Orpha Hopkins of Lowell, Mass.). She was born in 1845; died.
Counselor to Bishop Hickenlooper of 6th ward, Salt Lake City, 1847; acting bishop of Morgan county for many years; president high council of Morgan stake. He was sent by Brigham Young on the first exploring expedition in Cache valley in 1848, and later moved to Centerville, where he took up 80 acres of land and engaged in farming. He, together with Charles S. Peterson and their sons, built the first road through Weber canyon, and they were among the first settlers of Weber valley. Moved to St. George. William W. Potter, himself and others built the first boat and made the first known trip on Salt Lake, exploring all the islands. The boat was named "Mud Hen." While on the lake they were overtaken by a storm in which they almost lost their lives. He also established the first ferry on Bear river. Farmer. Died May 4, 1885, St. George, Utah.

TIBBITTS, BENJAMIN (son of Richard Tibbitts and Mary Sandals of Kidderminster, Worcestershire, Eng.). Born Sept. 8, 1826, at Kidderminster. Immigrated to America in 1848 and came to Utah Sept. 25, 1866, John D. Holladay company.
Married Eliza Moody 1852, Thompsonville, Conn. (daughter of Henry Moody of Kidderminster, Eng.). She was born April 21, 1831. Their children: George Henry b. Feb. 25, 1853, m. Dec. 29, 1877; James b. July 22, 1854, d. Feb. 5, 1896; Emeline b. March 16, 1856, m. April 21, 1876; Lorenzo Edwin b. Aug. 7, 1861 (d. Dec. 27, 1911), m. Dec. 2, 1885; Eliza Jane b. Dec. 22, 1867, m. July 21, 1886; Benjamin Richard b. July 27, 1870, m. Dec. 30, 1896; Edgar b. July 16, 1872, m. Oct. 10, 1896; Mira b. Nov. 2, 1874, d. Dec. 17, 1874. Family home Providence, Cache Co., Utah.
Ward teacher many years. Farmer. Died March 22, 1902.

TIBBITTS, GEORGE HENRY (son of Benjamin Tibbitts and Eliza Moody). Born Feb. 25, 1853, Roxbury, Mass. Came to Utah with father.
Married Mary Harriet Holt Dec. 29, 1877, Salt Lake City (daughter of Samuel Holt and Selina Beston of Salt Lake City). She was born Oct. 5, 1860. Their children: George S. b. Dec. 9, 1878, m. May 20, 1903; Selina b. Jan. 29, 1880, m. Dec. 19, 1900; Ernest H. b. Dec. 8, 1882; Edwin B. b. Feb. 29, 1885, d. June 27, 1906; Marion Benjamin b. Dec. 13, 1887, m. Dec. 13, 1911; Elmer M. b. March 18, 1890; Ira James b. July 11, 1892; Mary Lavern b. July 8, 1896; Frances Veda b. Nov. 21, 1902. Family home Providence, Utah.
Member 32d quorum seventies; ward teacher; high priest. School trustee two terms. Farmer.

1214 PIONEERS AND PROMINENT MEN OF UTAH

TIDWELL, JOHN (son of William Tidwell, born in Shelby county, Ky., and Sarah Goben, born in Clay county, Ind., both of Henry county, Ky.). He was born Jan. 14, 1807, in Shelby county, Ky. Came to Utah Sept. 15, 1852, captain of his own company.
Married Jane Smith Dec. 18, 1828, in Clark county, Ind., who was born June 5, 1812, and died May 20, 1893. Their children: James Harvey, m. Elizabeth Harvey, m. Emma Sanderson; William Nelson, m. Mary Elizabeth Reynolds; Mary Jane, m. Benjamin Johnson; Jefferson, m. Sarah Seely; Lyman and Nancy Ann, died; Martha, m. John Lusk; Margeret, m. Albert Zabriskie; Sarah, m. Bent Johnson; John, Jr.; Emma Jane, died; Emeline Mariah, m. Isaac Smith.
Member 1st quorum seventies and president of seventies at Provo. Located at Pleasant Grove 1852, and moved to Mount Pleasant 1859. Built a fort for protection against the Indians. Died Jan. 24, 1887, at Mount Pleasant.

TIDWELL, JEFFERSON (son of John Tidwell and Jane Smith). Born Oct. 7, 1835, in Clark county, Ind. Came to Utah 1852 with father.
Married Sarah Seely 1859, Mount Pleasant, Utah (daughter of Justus W. Seely and Clarissa Jane Wilcox, pioneers 1847, John Lowry company). She was born April 10, 1844, in Lee Co., Iowa. Their children: William Jefferson b. Oct. 8, 1861, m. Emma Clarissa Jones; Clarissa, died; Sarah Sorena, m. William Alvin Thayn; Frank, m. Eva Rumgue; Hyrum, m. Mary Grundvig; Joseph Randolph b. Oct. 3, 1872; Maranda, m. Samuel Strong; Orange b. Oct. 1876; David A., m. Carlie Clegg; Hannah, m. Albert Barnes; Beatrice, died.
Member 101st quorum seventies; bishop of Indianola. San Pete county; presiding elder at Wellington ward; Sunday school superintendent several years. Assisted in bringing immigrants to Utah. Early settler at Wellington. Indian war. veteran. School trustee. One of the rescuers of the "Frozen" handcart company. Farmer.

TIDWELL, WILLIAM JEFFERSON (son of Jefferson Tidwell and Sarah Seely). Born Oct. 8, 1861, Mount Pleasant, Utah.
Married Emma Clarissa Jones Dec. 25, 1889, Wellington. Utah (daughter of Jeter E. Jones and Emma Thayn of Salt Lake City, pioneers 1848). She was born Jan. 8, 1874. Their children: William Leroy b. June 7, 1891; Sarah Clarissa b. April 9, 1893; Pearl b. Nov. 24, 1895; Jennie Moranda b. Oct. 14, 1897; John Leslie b. Sept. 8, 1899; Stewart Randaugh b. Dec. 15, 1901; Justus Chesley b. May 16, 1903; Jeter Edward b. June 29, 1905; Joseph Rulon b. May 13, 1907; Ida May b. May 12, 1909; Emma Clarine b. Oct. 12, 1911.
Member 101st quorum seventies; Sunday school and ward teacher. Surveyor Emery county 1902-03; assessor Carbon county 1898-99 and 1906-09. Settled at Wellington with father in 1879. Assisted in building Tidwell canal and improving country around Wellington. Pioneer school teacher of Carbon county. Graduated June 2, 1882, University of Deseret.

TIDWELL, JOSEPH RANDOLPH (son of Jefferson Tidwell and Sarah Seely). Born Oct. 3, 1872, Mount Pleasant, Utah.
Settled at Wellington in 1884 with parents, where he assisted in building up country. Helped also to build the Pioneer monument at Mount Pleasant.

TIDWELL, THOMAS (son of Absalom Tidwell and Elizabeth McBride). Born July 8, 1826, in Illinois. Came to Utah July, 1854, with mother.
Married Elizabeth Jane Henderson, who was born July 4, 1830. Their children: James Absalom b. July 12, 1848, died; Celestia Annie b. Nov. 18, 1849, m. Mr. Jackson; Elizabeth Alice b. Dec. 7, 1851, m. Cyrus Foote; Thomas Jasper b. Aug. 12, 1853, died; Mary Adlai b. July 23, 1855, m. Warren Brady; Lenora b. Aug. 23, 1857, m. Matt Boulger; Nancy Elvina b. April 1, 1859, m. Walter Jenkins; Sarah Esther b. Aug. 9, 1861, died; Clara Ethel b. Feb. 12, 1865; Martha Irena b. Nov. 14, 1866; Anna Rosetta b. Dec. 4, 1869.
Married Louisa Tyler. Their children: Louanda Jennette, m. D. B. Miller; Thomas Philemon, m. Elizabeth Jenkins; Francis Marion, m. Teby J. Burdick; Liona Lovette, m. Aldin Burdick, m. C. Mayerfield; Lola Lucinda, m. Alonzo Smith; Alphretta Williametta, died; David Absalom, m. Sarah Elizabeth Robison; Louise, m. Harry Anderson; Rolland, m. Lena Phillips; Elizabeth, m. Don Burdick; Lulu Pearl, died; Sarah Jane, m. Grant Farr. Families resided Nephi, Utah.
Married Mary Abie Eakle Nov. 23, 1897, American Fork. Utah (daughter of Henry Kennedy Eakle and Mary Jane Johnson of Virginia), who was born Aug. 24, 1858. Their child: Mildred Maria b. Jan. 4, 1900. Family home, American Fork.
Married Mary Murphy Jan. 4, 1909, American Fork (daughter of William Murphy and Katherine Murphy of Cumberland, Eng.), who was born May 17, 1879. Their child: Martha Elmira b. Sept. 22, 1910.
Died June 17, 1912, American Fork.

TIDWELL, DAVID ABSALOM (son of Thomas Tidwell and Louisa Tyler). Born Dec. 23, 1866, Nephi, Utah.
Married Sarah Elizabeth Robison in 1888 (daughter of J. N. Robison of Georgia), who was born in 1868. Their children: David Roy b. Dec. 19, 1889; Hazel Elizabeth b. July 11, 1893; Rolland b. Aug. 10, 1895; Robert b. Oct. 10, 1897. Family home Salina, Utah.
Farmer.

TIMMS, JOHN W. A. (son of William Timms and Mary Ann Avery of Kingston, Eng., who came to Utah Aug. 16, 1871, Lott Smith company). He was born Jan. 14, 1856.
Married Sarah Ann Latimer Jan. 11, 1878, Salt Lake City (daughter of Thomas Latimer and Ann Hardy), who was born April, 1857, Salt Lake City. Their children: John H. b. Nov. 22, 1879, d. aged 7½; Thomas L. b. May 1, 1881, m. Arminta Roberts; Eugene b. May 14, 1883, d. infant; Clarence A. b. Sept. 30, 1885, d. aged 19; William H. b. Feb. 3, 1890, d. aged 17; Sarah b. June 22, 1892, m. Bertrand W. Clayton; Lucile b. Oct. 23, 1896; Robert J. b. Feb. 25, 1899. Family home Salt Lake City, Utah.

TIMOTHY, JOHN GRIFFITHS (son of David Timothy and Esther Griffiths of Cardiganshire, Wales). Born March 12, 1825, Grigwin, Cardiganshire, Wales. Came to Utah 1862, David Jones company.
Married Martha Davis 1853, at Cardigan (daughter of David Davis and Martha Lewis). Their children: David b. March 6, 1854, m. Martha Elvira Hawes; John b. Feb. 18, 1855, m. Emily Hawes, m. Margaret Ann Hall (Price); Joshua b. Aug. 10, 1856, died; Alma Nephi b. Dec. 9, 1857, m. Ellen Mann Sainsbury; Brigham b. June 21, 1859, m. Mary Hannah Sabey; Heber b. April 2, 1861, m. Esther Elizabeth Vernon; Martha b. Aug. 3, 1862, m. Charles Alma Gardener, m. J. P. Rudy; Hyrum b. Oct. 18, 1863, m. Rose Clark; Joseph b. Oct. 2, 1865, m. Lucy Jane Thomas; Mary b. June 23, 1867, died; Eleanor b. Aug. 27, 1868; Jedediah b. March 7, 1870, m. Jane Vilate Wamsley.
Died April 18, 1900, Vernal, Utah.

TIMOTHY, DAVID (son of John Griffiths Timothy and Martha Davis). Born March 6, 1854, in Wales. Came to Utah with parents.
Married Martha Elvira Hawes Oct. 11, 1878, Salt Lake City (daughter of William Hawes and Emily Mecham of Provo, Utah, who came to Utah with oxteam company). She was born May 7, 1860, died Jan. 26, 1905. Their children: Mary Pearl b. Sept. 7, 1879, m. Hyrum L. Larson; Martha Ilse b. Dec. 30, 1880, m. Andrew Theodore Johnson; Emily b. Dec. 15, 1882, m. Hugh M. Woodward; David John b. Dec. 23, 1884; Alice b. Dec. 20, 1886, m. Thomas R. Todd; Leah b. Sept. 29, 1888, m. Jacob Wilford Bastian; Amber b. Jan. 19, 1890; Lamar b. May 15, 1892; Golden b. March 11, 1894, d. May 7, 1904; Ada Fern b. March 2, 1896; Celestia b. Feb. 18, 1899, d. April 11, 1900; Rulon Lavelle b. Aug. 31, 1901; Lucile b. Jan. 26, 1904, d. July 8, 1904. Family home Jensen, Utah.
High priest; ward teacher at Wallsburg. Settled at Jensen 1885. Sunday school superintendent 18 years and chorister 26 years. Assisted in developing country around Vernal. School trustee; road supervisor. One of the foremost in education in Uinta county.

TIMOTHY, JOHN (son of John Griffiths Timothy and Martha Davis). Born Feb. 18, 1855, South Wales. Came to Utah with parents.
Married Emily Hawes June 27, 1875, Salt Lake City (daughter of William Hawes and Emily Mecham of Provo, Utah). Their children: Emily Myrtle; John William, m. Margaret Ann Price; Mary Elvira, m. James Johnson; Oren Leo, m. Mame Walmsley; Jedediah, d. child; Martha Pearl, m. Thornton Richardson.
Married Margaret Ann Hall (Price) May 31, 1899, Maeser, Utah (daughter of Joseph Hall and Margaret Hill of Fairview, Utah, pioneers 1847; she was also the widow of Daniel Price of Measer, whom she married in 1883, at Fairview, her children by marriage being: Daniel Leroy b. April 2, 1884, m. Martha Allen; Margaret Ann b. Dec. 12, 1885, m. William Timothy; Carolina b. Feb. 5, 1888, m. Wallace Oakes; Rhoda b. Jan. 16, 1890, m. Loren Hatch; Joseph Charles b. March 21, 1892; Absalom b. Feb. 13, 1894). She was born Dec. 2, 1865. Their children: Charles Earl b. Aug. 5, 1900; Carrie Wilder b. Aug. 26, 1904. Families resided Maeser.
Elder. Guard in Black Hawk war. Settled at Heber 1864, and in Ashley Valley 1886. Farmer and stockraiser.

TIMOTHY, ALMA NEPHI (son of John Griffiths Timothy and Martha Davis). Born Dec. 9, 1857, Tredegar, Monmouthshire, Wales. Came to Utah with parents.
Married Ellen Maria Sainsbury Oct. 1, 1890, Manti, Utah (daughter of John Sainsbury and Laura Wiscomb of Springville, Utah), who was born June 22, 1874. Their children: John Alma b. May 7, 1892, d. infant; Laura b. Oct. 1, 1893; Joshua b. July 25, 1896; LeRoy b. May 3, 1900; Elmer b. Aug. 13, 1902; Arvilla b. April 18, 1904; Martha b. Sept. 8, 1906; Golden b. Nov. 10, 1908; Owen b. Oct. 8, 1910.
Member 97th quorum seventies; missionary to southern states 1887-89, and to Great Britain 1904-05; home missionary; ward and Sunday school teacher; high priest. School trustee. Coal dealer; miner; proprietor of Timothy coal mine. Settled in Ashley Valley, 1884, where he assisted in building up country.

TIMOTHY, HEBER (son of John Griffiths Timothy and Martha Davis). Born April 2, 1861, Swansea, Caermarthenshire, Wales. Came to Utah with parents.
Married Esther Elizabeth Vernon May 17, 1890, Vernal, Utah (daughter of William Vernon and Cynthia Moody Cordial of Caswell, Va.), who was born Oct. 20, 1867, Blain. Lawrence county, Ky., and came to Utah in 1889. Their children: Heber Vernon b. Jan. 24, 1891; Louis Andrew b. Oct. 1, 1893; Weston b. July 1, 1896; Parley b. July 8, 1898; Evan b. Aug. 22, 1900; Presley b. Oct. 6, 1902; Mardin b.

June 29, 1904; Esther b. Aug. 13, 1906; Lynne b. March 25, 1909; Telyntha b. Feb. 5, 1912. Family home Roosevelt, Utah. Farmer.

TIMOTHY, JOSEPH (son of John G. Griffiths Timothy and Martha Davis). Born Oct. 2, 1865, Heber, Utah. Married Lucy Jane Thomas Feb. 2, 1887, Vernal, Utah (daughter of Joseph Maddison Thomas and Louisa Arella Houghton of Spanish Fork and Vernal. Utah, pioneers 1847. Brigham Young company). She was born July 25, 1767. Their children: Joseph, Jr., b. Dec. 8, 1887, m. Lillian Wardle; Franklin Wile, m. Nellie Searle; Orin William, m. Nellie Johnston; Maddison Earl; Ethel Jane; Delbert; Bertha; Chloe; Leland. Family home Roosevelt, Utah. High priest; counselor in bishopric of Glines ward; counselor in presidency of Y. M. M. I. A. of Glines ward; superintendent Sunday school Crescent ward 3 years. Moved to Vernal 1885 with parents, where he assisted in building up country. School trustee; constable six years; deputy sheriff 4 years; road supervisor 4 years. Delegate to eleventh National Irrigation Congress. Farmer and stockraiser.

TIMPSON, GEORGE WILLIAM (son of William B. Timpson and Elizabeth Fordham Smith of Northamptonshire, Eng., pioneers 1868, Chester Loveland company). Born Sept. 20, 1856, Oundle, Northamptonshire. Came to Utah August 1868, with parents. Married Sarah Elizabeth Strickland Jan. 1, 1883, Salt Lake City (daughter of Alvin B. Strickland of Franklin Co., Ohio, pioneer 1854, and Sarah Boughey Elkin of Staffordshire, Eng., pioneer 1854, Captain Fielding company). She was born Dec. 6, 1861, San Pete Co., Utah. Their children: George W. b. Jan. 16, 1884, died; Joseph Elkin b. Jan. 6, 1885, m. Isabel Fitzgerald of San Francisco, Cal.; Leila Celestine b. April 12, 1888, m. Alexander D. Edgar; Moroni Boughey b. July 23, 1890, m. Nora P. Hansen; Ella Louise b. Jan. 16, 1893; Austin LeRoy b. June 30, 1895; Melba b. June 1, 1897; Vera Edora b. Jan. 22, 1901, died. High priest; principal of religion class of 16th ward; member tabernacle choir 25 years; leader of 16th ward choir nine years. President Western Association of Adult Blind 1912-13. Member Alert Hose Company No. 3 of volunteer fire department, Salt Lake City. Secretary and aided in construction of old Utah Southern railroad. Shoe salesman with Z. C. M. I. and other firms 28 years.

TINGEY, LEHI (son of John Tingey and Phoebe Stafford of Staffordshire, Eng.). Born July 23, 1852. Married Amelia J. Needham Nov. 1, 1882, Salt Lake City (daughter of John Needham and Martha Millens, pioneers 1850). She was born Sept. 11, 1857, Salt Lake City. Their children: Lehi N. b. Oct. 22, 1883, m. Gertrude Smith; Ralf N. b. Sept. 14, 1885, d. aged 5. Family home, Salt Lake City.

TIPPETS, WILLIAM P. (son of John Tippets and Abagail Percy). Born June 26, 1812. Came to Utah 1850, Captain Hunt company. Married Sophia B. Mead Jan. 1, 1842 (daughter of Ezra Mead and Elizabeth Wilcox, pioneers 1850, Captain Hunt company). She was born July 12, 1812. Their children: Alice Jeanette b. March, 1844, m. Joseph M. Tippets Jan. 1, 1860; Emma Ann b. Jan. 1846, m. William Ferry 1867; Mary Ellen b. Dec. 1848, m. Hyrum Tippets; Eliza Abagail b. Jan. 1850, m. Brigham Tippets; Rebecca Moon b. June 2, 1852; Delia Sophia b. March 28, 1854, m. Hyrum S. Dudley March 30, 1874; Caroline Matilda b. Dec. 1856; William Plummer b. 1858; Walter Henry b. March, 1860, m. Maria Stokes 1878. Family home Perry, Utah, of which town he was a pioneer.

TITCOMB, JOHN (son of William and Annie Titcomb of Berkshire, Eng.). Born in Berkshire. Came to Utah September, 1850, William Wall company. Married Mary Atkins of Berkshire, who was born 1810. Their children: Luke, m. Lydia Jane Tanner; Naomi, m. Philander Bell; John, Jr., m. Susan Walpall; Ruth, m. Preston Free; Mary, m. Preston Free. Family resided Lehi and Cottonwood. Utah. High priest; teacher. Settled at Lehi 1853; moved to Cottonwood 1858. Shoemaker; farmer. Died 1858 at Cottonwood.

TITCOMB, LUKE (son of John Titcomb and Mary Atkins). Born March 3, 1832, Berkshire, Eng. Came to Utah Oct. 31, 1849, Ezra T. Benson company. Married Lydia Jane Tanner May 26, 1854, Cottonwood, Utah (daughter of John Joshua Tanner and Rebecca Smith of Cottonwood). She was born Nov. 28, 1836. Their children: Mary Jane b. Dec. 31, 1854, m. Thomas Gray; Joseph Luke b. Jan. 10, 1856, m. Sarah Larsen; Rebecca Maria b. Aug. 29, 1857, m. Thomas Jones; John Francis b. March 1, 1859, died; Naomi Sophie b. Feb. 23, 1863, m. Thomas Powers; Sarah Eunice b. July 6, 1864, m. Lott Russen; Helen Elsie b. July 11, 1866, m. Heber Commer; Mahonri b. April 6, 1869, m. Susan Mower; Preston Freeman b. Oct. 13, 1870; Lillie Ruth b. May 18, 1871, m. John Jackson; Lydia Louisa b.

PIONEERS AND PROMINENT MEN OF UTAH 1215

Feb. 15, 1873, and Edward Smith b. Nov. 30, 1874, died; Florence May b. June 15, 1878, m. Alma Berg; Annie S. b. June 14, 1880, died. High priest; block teacher; Sunday school superintendent. Settled in Lehi 1854. Veteran Indian war. Freighter; shoemaker; farmer.

TODD, THOMAS (son of John Todd and Marian Lorimer of Dumfrieshire, Scotland). Born Jan. 28, 1821, Penpont, Dumfrieshire. Came to Utah 1854, Daniel Garn company. Married Margaret Shankland Jan. 25, 1850, in Dumfrieshire (daughter of James Shankland of Dumfrieshire and Margaret Cummings of Thornhill). She was born Nov. 12, 1826, and came to Utah with husband. Their children: John b. Dec. 1850, d. child; James, d. infant; Thomas, Jr., b. Feb. 18, 1856, m. Harriet Richardson; Margaret b. Nov. 22, 1858, m. David Nathaniel Murdock; Marian Jane b. March 19, 1861, m. John Campbell March 19, 1890; Isabel Ellen b. March 17, 1863, m. John Henry Hicken; Sarah Ann b. March 15, 1865, m. John A. Simpson; John Murray, d. child; David Alexander b. Dec. 4, 1868, m. Josephine Moulton. Family resided Salt Lake City and Heber, Utah. President elders quorum; high priest; counselor to Bishops Rasband and Dickes. Veteran Black Hawk and Echo Canyon wars. Chairman of county commissioners; road supervisor; school trustee. Farmer. Died Oct. 5, 1909, Heber.

TODD, THOMAS (son of Thomas Todd and Margaret Shankland). Born Feb. 18, 1856, Salt Lake City. Married Harriet Richardson Dec. 16, 1880, Salt Lake City (daughter of William Richardson and Joanna Fotheringham of Rutherglen, Scotland, pioneers 1862, osteam company). She was born Dec. 20, 1859. Their children: Hattie May b. Dec. 5, 1881, m. Frank Horrocks; Thomas R. b. Aug. 1, 1883, m. Alice Timothy; Joanna b. Sept. 26, 1885, m. John Franklin Watkins; Margaret b. Jan. 22, 1887, d. aged 3; Ellen b. Feb. 14, 1890; William Russell b. May 1, 1892; Sarah b. Dec. 12, 1894; Elva b. Nov. 28, 1897, d. aged 4; Florence b. Dec. 1, 1900; Francis Squire b. Oct. 12, 1906. Family resided Heber City, Jensen, and Roosevelt, Utah. Elder; counselor elders quorum; counselor to President Y. M. M. I. A.; secretary Y. M. M. I. A. Secretary Wasatch Irrigation Company; vice-president Burns Bench Irrigation Company. Water commissioner. Farmer; stockraiser.

TOLLEY, WILLIAM FISHER (son of Roger Tolley, born 1792, and Susan Fisher, born 1798, both of Devonshire, Eng.). He was born Nov. 23, 1824, South Molton, Devonshire. Came to Utah Sept. 16, 1859, Edward Stevenson company. Married Sarah Warren Aug. 1, 1848 (daughter of William Warren and Ann Hobbs), who was born June 24, 1825, and came to Utah with husband. Their children: Samuel b. June 20, 1849, m. Sarah Jane Picton; Maria b. Oct. 1, 1851, m. Jabez Nowlin; Emma b. Nov. 12, 1853, m. Joseph Bryan; Charles b. Sept. 28, 1855, d. 1856; Charles William b. Dec. 7, 1857, m. Mary Melvina Christenson; George b. Sept. 3, 1860, m. Esther F. Christenson; Sarah Jane b. Feb. 7, 1863, m. Edward Jones 1881; Elizabeth Ann b. March 27, 1865, m. William Jones 1883; Susan b. Sept. 7, 1867, m. John R. Downs; Hyrum Warren b. May 10, 1870, m. Bessie Whittaker. Family home Nephi, Utah. Married Sarah Gadd (daughter of Samuel and Eliza Gadd), who was born Sept. 8, 1850, Cambridge, Eng. Their children: Samuel b. Nov. 1, 1869; William, died; Lovina E. b. Jan. 4, 1871, m. Harry Downs; Joseph F. b. May 13, 1872, m. Etta Herring; Isaac B. b. Nov. 24, 1875, m. Violet Herring; Louie R. b. Oct. 13, 1877, m. Miss Crowley; Edith b. Dec. 8, 1879, m. William Cook; Alfred C. b. June 10, 1880, died; Albert b. July 4, 1882; Mary L. b. April 6, 1884, m. Christopher Peterson; Leah C. b. April 2, 1886; Eugene b. in 1891; Ruth Amy b. in 1894. High priest; counselor to Bishop Charles Sperry. Judge of Juab county. Farmer; railroad contractor. Died Feb. 13, 1906, at Nephi.

TOLLEY, CHARLES WILLIAM (son of William Fisher Tolley and Sarah Warren). Born Dec. 7, 1857, in New York. Came to Utah with parents. Married Mary Melvina Christenson May 6, 1880, at Nephi (daughter of Peter Christenson and Maria Dunstan), who was born Dec. 1, 1862, Moroni, Utah. Their children: Charles Roscoe b. June 17, 1881, m. Sarah S. Sperry; Emma Florence b. Feb. 21, 1883, m. Henry C. Parkins Dec. 12, 1900; Leah Elizabeth b. Jan. 15, 1885, d. Feb. 2, 1885; Katie W. b. Jan. 29, 1886, m. Edward Shephard July 13, 1902; Claud Murll b. March 7, 1888; Sarah Maria b. Oct. 30, 1890, m. Evan E. Harris; Adelia b. Oct. 15, 1892; Lee Douglas b. Oct. 3, 1894; James Elmer b. Sept. 15, 1896; Ella Dorthie b. Sept. 6, 1898, d. Sept. 7, 1902; Loran Burdette b. Jan. 2, 1902; Rex Leland b. Dec. 31, 1903; William Norman b. Oct. 31, 1907, d. Nov. 3, 1907.

TOLMAN, JUDSON (son of Nathan Tolman, born Oct. 4, 178_, Waldo Co., Maine, and Sarah Hemett, born March 17, 1789, Co., Maine, married in 1812). He was born July 14, 1826, Kennebec Co., Maine. Came to Utah Sept. 20, 1848, Brigham Young company. Married Sarah L. Holbrook Jan. 12, 1845 (daughter of Joseph Holbrook and Nancy Sampson, former pioneer 1848, Brigham Young company). She was born Jan. 21, 1832, and came to Utah with husband. Their children: Sarah M. b. March 28, 1847, d. April 12, 1847; Nancy J. b. Feb. 4, 1848,

1216 PIONEERS AND PROMINENT MEN OF UTAH

m. Wallace W. Willey Oct. 20, 1862; Judson A. b. Feb. 25, 1850, m. Mary A. Howard Dec. 23, 1872; Joseph H. b. July 17, 1851, m. Belle Wood Feb. 1871; Jaren b. April 18, 1853, m. Emma Biggs June 1, 1874; Sarah L. b. April 7, 1855, m. Joseph T. Mabey March 13, 1871; Hannah A. b. Aug. 24, 1856, d. Dec. 20, 1862; Lamoni b. March 17, 1858, m. Agness Call Dec. 28, 1880; Charlotte b. Dec. 9, 1859, d. Oct. 29, 1860; Catherine B. Sept. 13, 1861, m. Alma Stuber Oct. 1879; Alice b. Aug. 27, 1863, m. Adam Yancy Oct. 1880; Cyrus b. Feb. 13, 1865, m. Lizzie A. Riley; Wallace b. April 13, 1867, m. Annie Huffine; Lucretia b. Feb. 1869, d. infant. Family resided Tooele and Bountiful, Utah.
Married Sophia Merrell. Their children: Samuel; Esther, m. Perry Sessions June 6, 1891; Nathan; Elna.
Married Jane Z. Staker April 5, 1869, Salt Lake City (daughter of John Staker and Jane McDonnal, pioneers 1848, Lorenzo Snow company). She was born May 21, 1847, in Pottawattamie Co., Iowa. Their children: Martha b. Jan. 1, 1870, m. Samuel Thurgood Nov. 27, 1888; Mary J. b. June 24, 1872; Julia b. Aug. 9, 1874, m. Brigham Hartly Oct. 1891; Ella A. b. April 7, 1877, m. George Dihle Aug. 1, 1908; Lilly R., Sept. 23, 1879, m. John Robinson Oct. 10, 1900; David R. b. Dec. 5, 1881, m. Maude Baulton June 23, 1909; Alma R. b. Dec. 5, 1881, d. June 5, 1898; Mira A. b. June 19, 1884, m. Alexander Patterson June 10, 1903; Justin b. April 10, 1889. Family resided Tooele and Bountiful, Utah.
High priest; patriarch; president high priests' quorum; missionary to Maine 1877. First settler in Tooele county and city. Indian war veteran; member Nauvoo Legion; minuteman. Descendants now number more than five hundred.

TOLMAN, JUDSON A. (son of Judson Tolman and Sarah L. Holbrook). Born Feb. 25, 1850, Tooele, Utah.
Married Mary Ann Howard Dec. 23, 1872, Salt Lake City (daughter of Joseph Howard and Ann Shelton, former pioneer 1863, Rosel Hyde company, latter died on the plains). She was born March 11, 1851, Birmingham, Eng. Their children: Sarah Ann b. Feb. 15, 1874, m. Fredrick Neils Bergeson; Dora Matilda b. March 12, 1876, m. Nathan Barlow; Mary Emma b. Jan. 10, 1878, m. William H. Garner Nov. 13, 1895; Clara Elizabeth b. Jan. 20, 1880, m. Benjamin D. Jensen Nov. 13, 1893; Alice Elnora b. Dec. 12, 1881, m. Peter Anderson Sept. 28, 1898; Charlotte Mary b. Nov. 28, 1883, m. Leonidas S. Mecham Dec. 5, 1900; Judson Adoniram b. Jan. 14, 1886, m. Jennie Call Sept. 3, 1902; Hannah Lucretia b. April 6, 1888, m. Elbert V. Call Aug. 4, 1902; Myrtie Lavern b. May 6, 1891; Howard Milton b. March 3, 1893; Lloyd Wilber b. May 7, 1895. Family home Chesterfield, Idaho.
Assisted in bringing immigrants to Utah 1868. Moved to Chesterfield, Idaho, 1872; and then to Preston. Second counselor in bishopric of Chesterfield ward 1890; ordained bishop of Chesterfield ward Oct. 26, 1891, and served in that capacity 13 years; high councilor five years.

TOOMER, JAMES (son of James Toomer and Jane Carpenter of Salisbury, Eng.). Born June 8, 1827, Salisbury. Came to Utah Oct. 1, 1854, Daniel Garn company.
Married Mary Jane Cook March, 1854, Southampton, Eng. (daughter of Thomas Cook and Mary Ann Harris of Southampton). She was born July 7, 1830. Their children: Sarah Jane b. Aug. 11, 1855, m. Eberezer Crough Oct. 11, 1873; James b. Oct. 10, 1857, m. Agness Parker: John Thomas and Joseph William, latter b. March 19, 1861, died; Charles Herbert b. May 10, 1864, m. Maude Richards Jan. 5, 1887; Emeline Eliza b. Sept. 10, 1866, m. Richard R. Fry March 24, 1887; Lydia Ann b. June 10, 1869, m. William T. Passey Aug. 19, 1888; David Richard b. Sept. 20, 1871, m. Eliza Matthews June 21, 1894. Family resided Farmington, Payson and Morgan, Utah, and Lanark, Idaho.
Seventy; leader of choir at Morgan. Member Farmington and Morgan brass bands. Captain of police at Morgan 1868-72. Died Jan. 31, 1894.

TOONE, JOHN (son of John Toone and Elizabeth Masters of Leamington, Warwickshire, Eng.). Born March 10, 1813, Birmingham, Eng. Came to Utah October, 1852, Captain Howell company.
Married Emma Prosser in 1836 at Leamington, Eng. (daughter of James Prosser and Mary Ann Morgan of Peterchurch, Herefordshire, Eng.). She was born April 29, 1819. Their children: Mary Elizabeth b. April, 1840, m. John Lyon; William H. b. March 4, 1842, m. Hannah Webb; Charles J. b. March 17, 1844, m. Sarah Augusta Squires: John P. b. Feb. 19, 1854, m. Emma Black. Family home, Salt Lake City. Missionary to England 1854. Played an instrument in the first orchestra in the Salt Lake Theatre. Guard on the pioneer mail routes. Died Aug. 31, 1893.

TOONE, WILLIAM HENRY (son of John Toone and Emma Prosser). Born March 4, 1842, Leamington, Eng. Came to Utah 1861.
Married Hannah Webb March 4, 1865, Salt Lake City (daughter of Thomas Webb and Sarah Hunt of Liddington, Cambridgeshire, Eng., pioneers 1869). She was born March 25, 1845, and came to Utah 1863 in the "Dixie" company. Their children: Sarah Emma b. July 9, 1866, m. Marcus Hollins; Jessie Georgina b. Aug. 26, 1868, m. Charles E. Condie; Hannah Elizabeth b. May 11, 1870, m. G. A. Wilde; William Henry b. June 2, 1872, m. Inez Grover; Charles J. b. April 24, 1874, m. Jessie Walker; Nettie b. Aug. 4, 1876,

George H. Wilde; John Wilford b. Dec. 14, 1878, m. Hattie Grover; George Ernest b. March 28, 1881, m. Bessie Mulholland; Lyda Maud b. March 7, 1883; Ida May b. May 1, 1885; James Malvin b. Sept. 13, 1887; Lawrence Webb b. Aug. 30, 1889. Family home Croydon, Utah.
Drove teams both to California and to the Missouri river for freight 1861-63. Settled at Morgan, Utah, 1865. Morgan county commissioner 14 years, two of which he acted as chairman. Member of Croydon bishopric 13 years; missionary to England 1897; bishop of Croydon ward. U. S. mail carrier to Montana 1864. Sergeant Utah militia.

TOONE, CHARLES J. (son of John Toone and Emma Prosser of England). Born March 17, 1844. Came to Utah in 1852.
Married Sarah Augusta Squires Oct. 26, 1865, Salt Lake City (daughter of Henry Augustus Squires and Sarah Cattlin), who was born March 8, 1848, at Welling, Herefordshire, Eng. Their children: Charles S. b. Sept. 2, 1866, m. Clara Jones; George H. b. June 4, 1869, m. Mary A. Smith; Augusta Alice b. Jan. 28, 1871, m. Arthur Gilbert; Clara A. b. Nov. 29, 1872, m. John S. Jones; John William b. Feb. 28, 1875, m. Margerite Stone; Clement Freal b. March 29, 1877, m. Ada Rock; Sarah M. C. b. April 8, 1879; Mary Agnes b. March 13, 1881, m. George Stone; Rachel Lovinia b. Aug. 27, 1883, m. John Clayton; Ivy Dora b. Dec. 4, 1887, m. O. G. Brough; Josia Celesti b. Jan. 14, 1899. Family home Morgan, Utah.

TOPHAM, JOHN. Came to Utah Oct. 2, 1847, Jedediah M. Grant company.
Married Jane Thornton (daughter of William Thornton of Bedfordshire, Eng., pioneer 1850). Their children: John, m. Elizabeth Baker; William, m. Malinda Balding; Hannah, m. Joseph Clark; Sarah J., m. Joseph Clark; Elizabeth, m. Vincent Shurtliff; Thomas, m. Sarah Carter; Jane and Rebecca, died; Susannah, m. Alma Parker. Family home, Salt Lake City.

TORGERSON, EVAN (son of Torger Evanson of Sigdal, Buskerud amt, Norway). Born August, 1819. Came to Utah 1863, Captain Nebeker company.
Married Olena Reiersen, at Sigdal, Norway, who came to Utah with husband. Their children: Gunild, m. John F. F. Dorius; Gurine, m. Leonard G. DeLong; Matilda, m. Mr. Sorenson; Charles Edward, m. Teckla Schaugaard; m. Jane Lettie Williams. Family home Ephraim, Utah.
Died August, 1884, Koosharem, Utah.

TORGERSON, CHARLES EDWARD (son of Evan Torgerson and Olena Reiersen). Born Sept. 18, 1855, Sigdal, Norway. Came to Utah with parents.
Married Teckla Schaugaard May 25, 1887, St. George, Utah (daughter of Niels Christian and Chrestina Schaugaard of Christiana, Norway; came to Utah 1876). She died 1884. Their children: Clara, Willard and Joseph, died.
Married Jane Lettie Williams Jan. 25, —, Logan, Utah (daughter of Stephen William and Emma Jane Hillyard (Hillard) of Ditchett, Eng., pioneers 1854). She was born Sept. 3, 1866. Their children: Charles Alvin; Iva Olena, m. John Albert Maxfield; Ferry Conrad: Samuel Lavern; Ethen Rull; Leah Orveta; Sheldon Ordell; Edward Vaun; Vada Jane; Orville. Family home Emery, Utah.
High priest. Postmaster. Carpenter and builder.

TOWNSEND, JAMES FOSS (son of Jacob Townsend, born 1752, and Abigail Elden, born August, 1785, both of Buxton, York Co., Maine). He was born Feb. 20, 1808, Buxton. Came to Utah Aug. 12, 1852, John M. Higby company.
Married Susan Davis (daughter of John Davis and Hannah Fletcher), who was born at Saco, Maine, and came to Utah with husband. Their children: Mary Jane b. Aug. 24, 1827, m. Thomas Denton Pitt; James F. b. Aug. 25, 1830, m. Elizabeth John Dunn; Martha A. b. March 2, 1832, m. George W. Lufkin; Susan M. b. June 10, 1834, m. William Sloan. Family home, Salt Lake City.
Married Elizabeth Murray in England.
Seventy; counselor to Bishop Woolley, 13th ward, Salt Lake City. Built the first hotel in Utah, and sold it, 1864.

TOWNSEND, JAMES F., JR. (son of James Foss Townsend and Susan Davis). Born Aug. 25, 1830.
Married Elizabeth I. Dunn 1851, St. Joseph, Mo. (daughter of John Dunn and Sophia McNeal), who was born in Alabama.
Elder. Minuteman in Walker Indian war. Took part in Echo Canyon campaign. Missionary to "Dixie" ten years.

TRACY, MOSES (son of Caleb Tracy of Vermont and Susannah Colvin, born 1787 in Vermont). He was born April 11, 1810, at Ellsburg, Jefferson county, N. Y. Came to Utah Sept. 12, 1850, Thomas Johnson company.
Married Nancy N. Alexander July 15, 1832 (daughter of Aaron Alexander and Betsy Johns), who was born May 14, 1816, in Jefferson county, N. Y., and came to Utah with husband. Their children: Eli A. b. Nov. 25, 1833, m. Eliza Ann Sprague Dec. 25, 1853; Lachoneus M. b. Oct. 21, 1835, d. child; Moses M. b. 1837; William F. b. 1839, and Theodore F. b. 1842, d. children; Austin W. b. 1845, m. —— Wilson; Helen

H. b. 1847, m. Emma Burdett; David S. b. 1850, m. Elizabeth Marriot; Charles A. b. 1852, m. Agnes McLane. Family home Weber Co., Utah.
Member first high council of Weber stake.

TRACY, ELI A. (son of Moses Tracy and Nancy N. Alexander). Born Nov. 25, 1833, in Jefferson county, N. Y. Came to Utah with father.
Married Eliza Ann Sprague Dec. 25, 1853, at Ogden, Utah (daughter of Richard D. Sprague and Lousia Rose, pioneers 1849, Captain Clark company). She was born March 12, 1837, in Broome county, N. Y. Their children: Eliza Ann b. Feb. 3, 1857, m. Orson Hall 1877; Eli M. b. Jan. 29, 1862, m. Mary E. Homes 1887; Charles A. b. Nov. 26, 1869, d. Nov. 1891; David F. b. Jan. 11, 1879, m. Emma Peterson Dec. 20, 1895. Family home Huntsville, Utah.
Missionary to southern states 1891; missionary among the Indians.

TRAVELLER, CORNELIUS (son of Thomas Traveller, born 1789, and Jane Moore, born 1787, both at London, Eng.). Born Sept. 29, 1820, at London. Came to Utah Sept. 1, 1860, John Smith company.
Married Ann Eliza Atkins 1840, who was born June, 1820, and died at London. Their children: Sarah Ann b. Oct. 19, 1811, m. James Coult; Cornelius John b. Feb. 26, 1844, d. Aug. 1848; Jane Caroline b. Nov. 11, 1846, m. Peter Christensen; Mary b. Oct. 1, 1849, d. Feb. 1850; Amy b. Nov. 16, 1851, d. May, 1854.
Married Frances Hobbs Dec. 25, 1854, at London (daughter of Joseph Hobbs and Caroline Noyse), who was born March, 1834, in Somersetshire, Eng. Their children: Lorenzo T. b. Feb. 19, 1856, d. June 25, 1858; Frances Lucy b. Oct. 31, 1857, m. James W. Hendricks Jan. 13, 1876; Franklin Hobbs b. Dec. 6, 1859, m. Mary Ann Webb March 15, 1882; Emily Elizabeth b. Nov. 28, 1862, m. W. H. Hendricks Dec. 11, 1878; Walter James b. Feb. 24, 1866, d. Jan. 13, 1867; Reuben Cornelius b. Feb. 7, 1870, m. Maggie Hogan Oct. 16, 1901; Mildred Caroline b. Dec. 25, 1873, m. John C. Olsen Oct. 16, 1895.
Settled at Richmond, Utah. High priest; ward teacher. City treasurer and city sexton a number of years. Minuteman. Cabinetmaker. Died Jan. 8, 1904, at Richmond.

TRAVELLER, FRANKLIN HOBBS (son of Cornelius Traveller and Frances Hobbs). Born Dec. 6, 1859, Philadelphia, Pa.
Married Mary Ann Webb March 15, 1883, Salt Lake City, Utah (daughter of Simon Webb and Elizabeth Rowsell, pioneers, Henry Miller company). She was born Feb. 10, 1864, at Richmond, Utah. Their children: Mary Elva b. Nov. 11, 1884, m. Jan. 13, 1886; Franklin Webb b. Nov. 9, 1886, m. Ada May Peart June 15, 1909; Frances Elizabeth b. May 14, 1889; Lester Elmo b. Oct. 5, 1891, m. Sadonie Plowman Feb. 7, 1912; Harriet Irene b. Dec. 31, 1894; Ariel Cornelius b. Feb. 15, 1903. Family home Richmond, Utah.
Ordained high priest Dec. 17, 1905; ward teacher a number of years.

TREHARNE, WILLIAM (son of William Treharne and Ann Richards of Llangendyrn, Caermarthenshire, Wales). Born July 14, 1838, at Llangendyrn. Came to Utah 1852, Captain Green company.
Married Ann Hughes March 26, 1864, Salt Lake City (daughter of John Hughes and Sarah Jones of Denbighshire, Wales, pioneers September, 1860, John Smith company). She was born April 1, 1845. Their children: Sarah Ann, m. Warren M. Lowry; William H., m. Mary Cooper; John H., m. Anne Chugg; Alice H. Family home, Salt Lake City.
High priest; missionary to Wales 1894-96. Veteran Echo Canyon and Indian wars. Died Jan. 27, 1907.

TREHARNE, WILLIAM H. (son of William Treharne and Ann Hughes). Born May 3, 1867, Salt Lake City.
Married Mary Cooper Nov. 14, 1892, Salt Lake City (daughter of Samuel Cooper and Catherine Crane of Duniden, New Zealand), who came to Utah 1884). She was born Feb. 20, 1869. Their children: William R. b. Oct. 5, 1893; Alma Cooper b. July 17, 1897; Vera b. Feb. 23, 1900; June b. June 26, 1902; Ina Mary b. April 10, 1906; Glen b. Oct. 8, 1911. Family home, Salt Lake City.
Teacher in 15th ward. Foreman with Ashton Bros., contractors.

TRESEDER, RICHARD D. (son of Richard Treseder and Charlotte Douty of Devonport, Eng.). Born March 1, 1818, at Devonport. Came to Utah Oct. 15, 1862, Benjamin Hampton company.
Married Elizabeth Mackay (daughter of Thomas Mackay and Elizabeth Holland), who was born Nov. 19, 1812. Their children: Charles M.; Richard M.; George; Emma M.; Ellen; Phoebe Ellen; Charlotte; Elizabeth M.; Maud Mary; Moroni; Emily M.; Frank M. Family home, Salt Lake City.
Merchant tailor. Died Sept. 25, 1881.

TRESEDER, RICHARD M. (son of Richard D. Treseder and Elizabeth Mackay). Born March 31, 1851, Devonport, Eng. Came to Utah 1855, Milo Andrus company.
Married Jane Edmunds Dec. 31, 1881, Salt Lake City (daughter of James Edmunds and Marian Carmichael of Glasgow, Scotland, latter pioneer with family Sept. 2, 1852, Abraham O. Smoot company). She was born May 15, 1841. Their children: Marian E. b. Oct. 18, 1862, m. William

F. Burton; Richard W. b. Jan. 26, 1865, m. Ida Packard; Franklin E. b. Jan. 18, 1869, died one week later; Elizabeth M. b. Sept. 25, 1870, m. Oscar I. Read; Lorenzo D. b. Oct. 20, 1875, m. Anna Mildred Sisk; Albert C. b. Jan. 5, 1882, m. Ma— C. Stallings. Family resided Salt Lake City and Ogden, Utah.
Member of the first artillery company organized in Utah. Assisted in firing the cannon on the temple block, welcoming Governor Cummings, first governor of Utah sent out by the president of the U. S. Contractor.

TRESEDER, ALBERT C. (son of Richard M. Treseder and Jane Edmunds). Born Jan. 5, 1882, at Ogden, Utah.
Married Mary C. Stallings June 15, 1910, at Salt Lake City (daughter of Charles A. Stallings and Mary Farrell of Eden, Utah), who was born May 4, 1884. Their children: Jenive Lucile b. June 15, 1911; Janet b. June 2, 1912. Family home Ogden, Utah.
Sunday school and Mutual Improvement Association worker. Clothing merchant.

TRIM, HYRUM PENDLETON (son of John Trim and Mary Pendleton of Belfast, Me.). Born Nov. 16, 1815, in Maine. Came to Utah October, 1861, Captain Hansie company.
Married Maria Argent (Goodwin) October, 1861, Salt Lake City (daughter of John Argent and Mary Griddley of Somersetshire, Eng., pioneers Oct. 1, 1866, Joseph S. Rawlins company). She was born Oct. 14, 1831, died June 5, 1909. Their children: Solomon Pendleton b. July 25, 1863, m. Lois Ann Workman; Amanda Maria b. Oct. 18, 1865, m. Newell Green; Eunice b. Sept. 22, 1867, m. Samuel Egbert; Lois b. Jan. 2, 1869, d. Aug. 4, 1872; Rosetta b. Oct. 9, 1871, m. Jacob Killian; Israel D. b. Aug. 22, 1876, m. Mattie Greenlee. Family home, Salt Lake City.
High priest; ward teacher. Justice of peace, Snyderville, Utah, to which place he moved in 1861, to cut timber for court house in Salt Lake City. Died Jan. 25, 1892, Vernal, Utah.

TRIM, SOLOMON PENDLETON (son of Hyrum Pendleton Trim and Maria Argent (Goodwin)). Born July 25, 1863, Parley's Park, Utah.
Married Lois Ann Workman July 16, 1890, Vernal, Utah (daughter of Jacob Reader Workman and Maria Amity Johnston of Vernal, pioneers 1847). She was born Sept. 25, 1873, Snyderville, Utah. Their children: De Los Pendleton b. May 24, 1891; Lois Maria b. Feb. 2, 1893; Gertrude Estella b. Dec. 5, 1894; Virtu Neften b. April 6, 1897; Jerrold Q. b. Aug. 2, 1898, d. Jan. 19, 1900; Iona b. Dec. 4, 1900; Phila Phrene b. Dec. 6, 1902; Madge b. Sept. 7, 1904; Ethel Winnie b. June 23, 1906; Alta Eunice b. Dec. 15, 1908; Jacob Solomon b. Oct. 19, 1911, d. same day.
Farmer Salt Lake county; moved to Vernal, Utah, 1888, where he engaged in sheep business with his father until 1902. Then engaged in mercantile and undertaking business, later giving up former but continuing latter. Member of city council.

TRIMBLE, EDWARD (son of Robison Trimble and Mary Jefferson of Gatarigg, Cumberlandshire, Eng.). Born April 2, 1815. Eastwoodside, Cumberlandshire. Came to Utah October, 1865.
Married Elizabeth Lennox in Cumberlandshire (daughter of William Lennox and Elizabeth Sanderson of Penrith, Eng., pioneers October, 1865). She was born May 9, 1816, May 9, 1839; William b. Oct. 3, 1842; Susan b. Nov. 27, 1843, m. George Erminson; John b. May 31, 1846, m. Emma Lock; Robison b. March 8, 1849; Jefferson b. Oct. 28, 1851, m. Maggie Fortie; Joseph b. June 5, 1854, m. Malissie Davis; Mary Elizabeth b. Oct. 28, 1856. Family home Fillmore, Utah.

TRIMBLE, JOHN (son of Edward Trimble and Elizabeth Lennox). Born 1846, near Carlisle, Eng. Came to Utah October, 1865, Kimball and Lawrence company.
Married Emma Lock (daughter of Joseph Lock and Eliza Tayney, the latter pioneer Sept. 5, 1866, Samuel D. White company). She was born in 1848, Ashwood Bank, Cumberland, Eng., and came to Utah with mother.
Settled at Fillmore 1865. Black Hawk Indian war veteran. Worked on U. P. R. R.; also on St. George and Manti temples; assisted in surveying Deseret Telegraph line to St. George, Utah.

TRUMBO, JOHN K. (son of Isaac Trumbo and Elizabeth Keithley of Bath county, Ky.). Born Nov. 14, 1821, in Bath county. Came to Utah 1855, John Reese company.
Married Mary M. Reese Nov. 29, 1857, Genoa, Utah (daughter of John Reese and Catherine Miles of New York state, pioneers 1849 and 1857, respectively). She was born Oct. 15, 1838. Their children: Isaac, d. aged 51; William M. Ormsby, d. aged 30; John D. Winters; Jacob Wayman, d. aged 28; George; Andrew J.; Howard; Catherine M., m. Edward McGurrin. Family home, Salt Lake City.
Auctioneer. Died June 19, 1885, in Bath county, Ky.

TUCKER, CHARLES (son of John Tucker of Highbray, Devonshire, Eng., born 1805, and Susan Blackmore of Kentisbury, Devonshire, born 1809). He was born Jan. 14, 1842, at Eastdown, Devonshire. Came to Utah Sept. 25, 1863, Peter Nebeker company.
Married Betsy Rawle July 23, 1863, at Florence, Neb.

(daughter of John Rawle and Nancy Blackmore), who was born July 9, 1832. Family home Morgan, Utah.
Married Mary Smith 1882, Salt Lake City (daughter of William and Grace Smith), who was born 1832, in England. Family home Milton, Morgan Co., Utah.
Married Annie Hardman Dec. 12, 1884, Logan, Utah (daughter of John Hardman and Ann Seddon), who was born Aug. 30, 1866, Haydock, Eng. Their children: Ann and Susan (twins) b. June 24, 1886; Charles J. b. July 16, 1889; Janet Pearl b. March 30, 1891; Olive Jane b. April 9, 1893; Moroni James b. Oct. 19, 1898; Harold Nephi b. Dec. 29, 1909. Family home Milton, Morgan Co., Utah.
Assisted in building the first stage and mail route through Morgan county, 1865; worked on first transcontinental railroad, 1867; answered the call for volunteers to commence the building of St. George temple. One of the presidents of 35th quorum seventies, 1889; filled mission to England, returning in 1901. Agriculturist and horticulturist.

TUCKER, SAMUEL STARKEY (son of William Tucker and Elizabeth Starkey of Cannington, Somersetshire, Eng.). Born Oct. 16, 1828, at Cannington. Came to Utah 1860.
Married Emma Cotter Sept. 8, 1849, Parish church of St. James, Bristol, Eng. (daughter of Adam Cotter and Jemima Pullen of Cannington, Eng.). She was born May 2, 1824. Their children: Emma Elizabeth and Samuel, died; Fanny Amelia, m. W. F. Stoker Aug. 21, 1870; Isabel Martin, m. O. L. Marsh Jan. 2, 1889; Matilda, died; Jemima Cerelia, m. Isaac Blair Dec. 25, 1880; Alice Rosena, m. Samuel Blair; William Charles, m. Annie Reed Aug. 20, 1887. Family home Ogden, Utah.
Married Elizabeth Burgess Neslen (Wheelock) April 10, 1871, Salt Lake City (daughter of Samuel Neslen and Eunice Francis of Lowestoft, Suffolk, Eng., pioneers Sept. 20, 1853, Claudius V. Spencer company). She was born June 4, 1835. Their children: Claudia Edith b. Jan. 8, 1872, m. Ernest H. Rich Aug. 1, 1894; George Maurice b. March 7, 1874, m. Minnie Skelton March 7, 1905; Hannah Neslen b. Feb. 4, 1876, m. Clarence O. Brunner Aug. 14, 1901; Ray Starkey b. Oct. 11, 1878, and Walter Roy b. May 6, 1881, died. Family home, Salt Lake City.
Member 47th quorum seventies. Carpenter. Died Feb. 28, 1893, Salt Lake City.
Elizabeth Burgess Neslen was the widow of Cyrus H. Wheelock. Their children: Elizabeth Edna b. March 8, 1855, m. Henry T. Gingell Aug. 5, 1875; Samuel Francis b. Dec. 19, 1859, m. Isabelle Shelton July 29, 1881; Ida Beatrice b. June 15, 1864, m. George J. Suess Nov. 19, 1884.

TUCKETT, JOHN (son of Charles Tuckett, born about 1800, Riverton, Devonshire, Eng., and Dunn Tuckett of Devonshire). Born April 26, 1834, London, Eng. Came to Utah Sept. 28, 1855, Moses Thurston company.
Married Sarah Ann Gee April 7, 1862 (daughter of Noah Gee and Mary Ann Moor—married at Philadelphia—pioneers October, 1852, Eli B. Kelsey company). She was born Aug. 18, 1844, and came to Utah October, 1852, Eli B. Kelsey company. Their children: Sarah Ann Jane b. June 2, 1863, m. Nicklos Iverson; Caroline b. Sept. 9, 1867, m. B. Y. Johnson; Lelia b. June 8, 1871, m. Oscar Whiting Dec. 4, 1889; John b. Jan. 8, 1874, m. Marian Mendenhall Jan. 8, 1873; Josephine b. Sept. 19, 1876, m. Adelbert Roundy; Charles Noah b. June 27, 1880, m. Eveline Bird; Luella b. March 23, 1884, m. R. G. Smith July 8, 1908. Family home Springville, Utah.
Drove three yoke of oxen across plains to Utah. Veteran Echo Canyon war. Hauled timber for first cotton mill in Utah. Indian missionary 1856; bishop; Sunday school superintendent; presiding teacher fifth district; first counselor to C. Berrie in presidency Y. M. M. I. A.; senior teacher in parents' class. City councilman.

TUDDENHAM, JOHN (son of Dennis Tuddenham and Amy Durrant). Born Feb. 17, 1811, Gooderstone, Norfolk, Eng. Came to Utah Nov. 2, 1864, Warren Snow company.
Married Mary Rumbell 1838 (daughter of William Rumbell and Mary Ann Rolfe), who came to Utah with husband, and died Oct. 23, 1899. Their children: Elizabeth Ann b. March 13, 1840, m. George W. Reed 1866; John b. June 23, 1842, d. infant; Mary Ann b. Sept. 19, 1846, m. George Reynolds July 22, 1865; William John b. May 27, 1848, m. Mary Ann Read July 22, 1872. Family home Salt Lake City, Utah.
High priest, Salt Lake stake; missionary to England 1867-68. Contractor and builder. Died April 6, 1885, at Salt Lake City.

TUDDENHAM, WILLIAM JOHN (son of John Tuddenham and Mary Rumbell). Born May 27, 1848, London, Eng. Came to Utah with parents.
Married Mary Ann Read July 22, 1872 (daughter of John Read and Mary Ann Barnham, pioneers 1866, Captain Thompson company). She was born Sept. 4, 1850, Cambridge, Eng., and came to Utah 1866 with parents. Their children: Mary Evelyn b. May 1, 1873, m. A. B. Needham Sent. 14, 1910; William John b. Feb. 24, 1876, m. Alice M. Calder Oct. 17, 1901; Joseph Rolfe b. June 20, 1879, m. Bertha O. Atkins Jan. 18, 1906; Florence Emma b. Dec. 6, 1883, m. J. E. Langford, Jr., Oct. 14, 1908; John Charles b. Nov. 11, 1886; Read b. July 24, 1890, d. infant. Family home, Salt Lake City.
High priest. Supervisor of streets and public improvements; member of Salt Lake City municipal council five terms of two years each.

TUFT, HANS N. (son of Niels Hansen Tuft of Jutland, Denmark). Born September, 1807, Veile, Denmark. Came to Utah Sept. 5, 1863, John F. Sanders company.
Married Ann Tompsen 1840, who was born 1820, in Denmark, and there died March 21, 1862. Their children: Christine, d. child; Neils Carl, d. in king's service; Thomas; Ole Nielsen b. Dec. 6, 1849, m. Laura Annie Day 1873; Hans Christian b. June 1, 1851, m. Josephine Wicklund 1872; Jacob A. b. March 4, 1854, m. Mary Ellen Kearnes; Christian b. Oct. 1856, m. Emma Birtch 1882; Christiana, d. infant. Family home Gunnison, Utah.
Presiding elder at Mayfield, Utah; high priest. Veteran Black Hawk wars. Farmer. Died 1894, Monroe, Utah.

TUFT, OLE NIELSEN (son of Hans N. Tuft and Ann Tompsen of Denmark). Born Dec. 6, 1849, Jutland, Denmark. Came to Utah with father.
Married Laura Annie Day Jan. 5, 1873, Mt. Pleasant, San Pete Co., Utah (daughter of Abraham Day and Elmira Buckley of Kanesville, Iowa, former pioneer contingent Mormon Battalion). She was born June 6, 1853. Their children: Joseph Alfred b. Nov. 22, 1873, and Annie Elmira b. May 24, 1875, d. children; Laura Estella b. Dec. 7, 1876, m. Hans E. Jensen; Jenette b. June 5, 1878, and Ole William b. March 17, 1880, d. children; Dora Amelia b. Dec. 26, 1881, m. John P. Hansen; Arlington b. Sept. 12, 1883, d. child; Flavilla Josephine b. July 22, 1884, m. Edgar M. Barton; Bertha b. April 19, 1887, d. infant; Abraham Summers b. April 1, 1889; Hans Alfred b. Feb. 9, 1891; Calvin F. b. Feb. 6, 1893; Ivan Ira b. March 7, 1895, and Roy b. Nov. 22, 1896, d. infants. Family home Lawrence, Utah.
Bishop of Lawrence ward April 30, 1912; Sunday school superintendent 1906-10. Member board of directors of Huntington Canal and Reservoir Association; road supervisor several years; school trustee. Farmer and stockman.

TUFT, JACOB A. (son of Hans N. Tuft and Ann Tompsen). Born March 4, 1854, in Denmark. Came to Utah 1863.
Married Mary Ellen Kearnes Dec. 31, 1877, Gunnison, Utah (daughter of Hamilton H. Kearnes and Mary Mendenhall), who was born Sept. 23, 1859, Springville, and died, Centerville, May 14, 1913. Their children: Anna b. Feb. 13, 1879, and Alster F. b. Jan. 15, 1881, died; Mida b. July 15, 1885; Hannah b. Aug. 31, 1888; John W. b. July 19, 1891; Byard K. b. June 8, 1894; Clyde H. b. Jan. 31, 1897; Thomas b. Sept. 16, 1901; Mary E. b. April 8, 1902. Families resided Gunnison and Centerfield, Utah.
Director and president of Gunnison Co-operative Mercantile Institution 4 years. County commissioner San Pete county 1896-98.

TURLEY, THEODORE. Born April 10, 1800. Came to Utah 1849.
Married Frances A. Kimberly Nov. 27, 1821, Birmingham, Eng., who was born June 22, 1800, and died Aug. 22, 1844, Florence, Neb. Their children: Theodore b. 1822, (d. 1825); Frances Ann b. 1824, (d. 1833); Mary Ann b. July 13, 1827 (d. 1904), m. John Cook; Priscilla b. June 1, 1829 (d. 1904), m. Amasa M. Lyman; Frederick b. May 23, 1832, d. 1875; Sarah Elizabeth b. Sept. 24, 1835, m. Stephen Franklin; Isaac b. Nov. 22, 1837, m. Sarah and Clara Dalton; Charlotte b. April 15, 1840 (d. Nov. 1, 1899), m. Jacob Bushman March 2, 1857.
Married Sarah Greenwood at Beaver, Utah.
Died Aug. 22, 1872, at Beaver.

TURNBOW, SAMUEL. Born 1814. Came to Utah Sept. 24, 1847, Abraham O. Smoot company.
Married Sophia Hart 1836, in Alabama, who was born 1820. Their children: John G., m. Sarah Elizabeth Horn; Robert Franklin, m. Sarah A. Smith; Adeline, d. aged 13; Sophia, m. William Carter; Milton, m. Mary Mitchell, m. Sophia Carter; Joseph S., d. aged 10; Margaret Ann, m. Moroni Mitchell. Family home, Salt Lake City.
Counselor bishopric of 14th ward, Salt Lake City; high priest; block teacher. Farmer. Died August, 1890.

TURNBOW, ROBERT FRANKLIN (son of Samuel Turnbow and Sophia Hart). Born Dec. 11, 1840, in Alabama. Came to Utah Sept. 24, 1847, Abraham O. Smoot company.
Married Sarah Ann Smith Dec. 29, 1860, Salt Lake City (daughter of Samuel Smith and Martisa Smoot of same place, pioneers Oct. 14, 1850, Wilford Woodruff company). She was born Dec. 14, 1842. Their children: Luella A. b. Nov. 21, 1861, m. Henry S. Harrow; Herme b. Nov. 3, 1863, d. infant; Robert F. b. Dec. 25, 1864, m. Caroline Hackwell; Joseph A. b. March 8, 1866, m. Lenny Lyons; Lillian B. b. Nov. 27, 1868, d. aged 3; Wilford S. b. April 1, 1870, d. aged 2; Parley W. b. Jan. 16, 1872, m. Minnie ———; Tersia A. b. Dec. 27, 1874, m. Benjamin Brown; Gertrude A. b. Nov. 3, 1876, m. Alonzo Libbey; Hette P. b. Oct. 23, 1888, m. Roy Thompson; LaGrande b. Jan. 16, 1889, m. Mary P. Collett. Family home, Salt Lake City.
High priest; counselor in bishopric of Farmers ward; ward teacher, Teamster.

TURNER, BENJAMIN GODFREY (son of David Turner, born June 3, 1819, at Leeds, Yorkshire, Eng., and Rose Collier, born Jan. 16, 1821, in Yorkshire; married April, 1839). Born Aug. 18, 1855, at Glenham, Dutchess county, N. Y. Came to Utah Sept. 12, 1861, John R. Murdock company.
Married Susan Auld Sept. 25, 1879 (daughter of Emanuel Auld and Elizabeth Uran), who was born April 14, 1857, and came to Utah, handcart company. Their children: Susan Rozella b. July 8, 1877; Marion and Miriam (twins) b. Feb. 6, 1879, d. infants; Benjamin Godfrey b. Dec. 27, 1879, b. Annie White Jan. 6, 1902; Mary Elizabeth b. Dec. 20, 1881, m. Stephen Farnsworth Aug. 1898; Altha Elnorah b. Nov. 21, 1883, m. Enoch Holt Jan. 14, 1903; Ray Emanuel b. Jan. 28, 1886; Ida b. March 1, 1888, m. Byron Cook March 25, 1908; David Ernest b. Oct. 21, 1891; James Collier b. Dec. 19, 1893; Veltha b. Dec. 16, 1895; Artenca b. Jan. 7, 1899.
Family resided Deseret, Holden and Lyman, Utah.
Early settler in Millard and Wayne counties. High priest; councilor; home missionary

TURNER, CHAUNCEY (son of Thomas Turner and Betsy Bishop of New York and Michigan). Born May 19, 1800, in New Hampshire. Came to Utah in 1847, George A. Smith and Orson Pratt company.
Married Hanna Franklin Redfield (daughter of Zina Redfield of New York). Their children: Mary Ann, m. Robert Thomas; John Wesley, m. Sarah L. Fausett; Harriet Maria, died; Julia Ann. m. Thaddius Fleming; Charles and Henry Moroni, died. Family home Provo, Utah.
Seventy. Farmer. Died September, 1870.

TURNER, JOHN WESLEY (son of Chauncey Turner and Hanna Franklin Redfield). Born Nov. 21, 1832, Avon-on-Hudson, New York. Came to Utah with father.
Married Sarah L. Fausett Dec. 1, 1852, at Provo (daughter of William Fausett of Kentucky and Matilda Bucher, of West Virginia, pioneers September, 1851, Rosewell Stevens company). She was born Feb. 15, 1835. Their children: Sarah L. b. Sept. 11, 1854, m. Silas Allred; John Franklin b. Jan. 9, 1856, died; George William b. March 2, 1859, died; Charles Henry b. Aug. 8, 1861, m. Eliza Haws; Laura Ann b. Oct. 22, 1863, m. William M. Roylance; Harriet Maria b. Oct. 10, 1865, m. Alvin Brinton; Chirissa Matilda b. Dec. 2, 1867, m. John Stubbs; Willard Chauncey b. Oct. 15, 1870, and Eugene F. b. June 13, 1873, and Eva Diantha b. April 17, 1874, last three died. Family home Provo, Utah.
Member 42nd quorum seventies; missionary to Canada, 1855-57, and Las Vegas, 1857-58. Sheriff of Utah county 16 years, 1884-1900; city marshal; U. S. deputy marshal. Farmer; merchant. Died Jan. 20, 1895.

TURNER, JOHN (son of John Turner and Mary Ann Newman of London, Eng.). Born February, 1801, Exeter, Devonshire, Eng. Came to Utah August, 1861, Homer Duncan company.
Married Mary Ann Newman at London, Eng. Their children: Elizabeth. m. John Gray; Charles; Frederick, m. Elvira Hyde; m. Caroline Deseret Hyde; m. Sarah Ann Cardon. Family resided at Hyde Park. Utah, and Montpelier, Idaho.
High priest. One of founders of Montpelier, Idaho. Built first frame house in Logan. Builder and architect. Died 1868, at Montpelier.

TURNER, FREDERICK (son of John Turner and Mary Ann Newman). Born Aug. 17, 1847, Camdentown, London, Eng. Came to Utah with father.
Married Elvira Hyde Oct. 5, 1869, Salt Lake City (daughter of William Hyde and Sallie Allred of Hyde Park, Utah, pioneers 1847 with a contingent of the Mormon Battalion). She was born Dec. 31, 1834. Only child: Frederick William b. Sept. 11, 1870, d. aged 1 year. Family home, Logan, Utah.
Married Caroline Deseret Hyde (daughter of William Hyde and Sallie Allred, pioneers 1847, contingent Mormon Battalion). She was born May 3, 1855. Their children: Sallie Elvira b. Oct. 16, 1874, d. April 18, 1877; Frederick Hyde b. July 7, 1876; Mary Ann b. Aug. 28, 1878; John Henry b. Jan. 15, 1881; Oliver Charles b. Aug. 24, 1883; Jennie Vera b. May 19, 1885; Simpson Montgomery b. Dec. 20, 1887; Lyman b. Dec. 25, 1889; George Cleveland b. March 8, 1898; Lettie b. March 4, 1895; Grace b. Jan. 18, 1897; Clara Marie b. Oct. 8, 1901.
Married Sarah Ann Cardon June 25, 1884, Logan, Utah (daughter of Paul Cardon and Susannah Gouldin, pioneers 1852). She was born Nov. 30, 1862. Their children: Franklin David b. Jan. 24, 1886; Susette b. March 11, 1888, m. Hyrum E. Crockett Sept. 6, 1911; Lucy b. July 12, 1890, m. Charles Jenkins Sept. 18, 1912; Lee Cardon b. Aug. 16, 1897; Marriner Cardon b. Aug. 1, 1902; Lapriel b. Jan. 28, 1908. Family home Logan, Utah.
High priest; acting bishop of Logan, sixth ward. Cache county sheriff four years; county commissioner four years; city councilman at Logan, four years. Manager Implement Houses at Logan and Ogden, six years. Built Uncle Sam Cleanser factory at Salt Lake City.

TURNER, WILLIAM W. (son of Benjamin Turner and Elizabeth Cot. of Lewes, Sussex, Eng.). Born Jan. 22, 1842, at Lewes. Came to Utah Sept. 4, 1864, Kimball and Lawrence freight train company.

Married Sarah Brown March 6, 1864, Brighton, Sussex, Eng., who was born June, 1840, and died July, 1864, Antelope Springs, Wyo.
Married Anne Williams May 6, 1865, Salt Lake City (daughter of Morris Williams and Mary Lloyd, of Caernarvon, Caernarvonshire, Wales. Their child (adopted): Mabel Juliet b. July 9, 1885, m. E. L. Rottman.
Married Joanna Williams May 17, 1912, Salt Lake City (daughter of George M. Williams and Lucy Ball, both of Jo Daviess county, Ill.). She was born Oct. 28, 1855.
Member of 131st quorum seventies; missionary to England 1879-81; missionary eastern states 1895. Veteran Black Hawk wars, with Major Bert company. Carpenter and builder.

TURPIN, JESSE (son of James Turpin and Nancy Ann Taltum, of Tennessee). He was born June 22, 1816, Stewart county, Tennessee. Came to Utah Sept. 20, 1848, Brigham Young company.
Married Jane Smith April 16, 1846, Nauvoo, Ill. (daughter of Daniel Smith and Sarah Wooding, of London, Eng., pioneers Sept. 20, 1848, Brigham Young company). She was born Aug. 15, 1827. Their children: Jesse R., m. Joan Jennetta Litzon, m. Maria Decker; Sarah Jane, m. George Budd April 7, 1872; Nancy Ann, m. Daniel L. Higley. Family home, Salt Lake City.
Member seventies; missionary to eastern states 1840, and to West Indies 1852-54. Saddle and harness maker.
Died June 22, 1854, near Ft. Leavenworth, Kansas.

TUTTLE, ELANSON (son of Jeremiah Tuttle and Clarrissa Powell of Upper Canada). Born Sept. 18, 1807, in Matilda township, Upper Canada. Came to Utah fall 1850.
Married Mary Ann Taylor Merritt, widow of John Thomas Merritt, June 29, 1861, Salt Lake City, Utah (daughter of Edward Taylor and Mary Tarrant, of London, Eng.; came to Utah 1848). She was born Sept. 9, 1831. Their children: Elanson; Mary Frances, m. Washington M. Kimball; Julia Ann; Reuben M., m. Maria Wixey; Amelia Jane, m. Heber Bouck. Family home Salt Lake City, Utah.
Block teacher. Member Mormon Battalion. Sawmiller.
Died Feb. 17, 1879, at Salt Lake City.

TUTTLE, LUTHER T. (son of Terry Tuttle and Ellen Mills of New York City). Born Nov. 19, 1852, at New York City. Came to Utah 1863, Captain Crayton freight train.
Married Abigail Haws July 18, 1846, near Council Bluffs, Iowa (daughter of Peter Haws of Montreal, Canada, pioneer Sept. 9, 1853, Daniel A. Miller company). She was born June 15, 1828. Their child: Louisa, m. Delia Atwood Family home Manti, Utah.
Married Lola Ann Haws Jan. 17, 1850, Council Bluffs, Iowa (daughter of Peter Haws of Montreal, Canada, pioneer Sept. 9, 1853, Daniel A. Miller company). She was born Jan. 11, 1833. Their children: Luther and Charlotte E., d. young; Albert, m. Lucia Cox; Luther T., d. young; Frank P., m. Orlette Cox; John H., d. young; Louis E.; Lola A., m. James B. Tatton; Lily B., m. William Hosford; Ethelfa C., m. Edwin Hosford; Alpheus, d. young.
Member 20th quorum seventies; high councilor. Member of Mormon Battalion, leaving Council Bluffs July 20, 1846, for Mexico. Mayor of Manti; member legislature two terms. Merchant; banker.

TUTTLE, NEWTON (son of Zerah P. Tuttle and Maria Todd of North Haven, Conn.). Born April 13, 1825, North Haven. Came to Utah 1854, Captain Grow company.
Married Emily A. Stone April 7, 1855, Salt Lake City, Heber C. Kimball performing ceremony (daughter of Amos P. Stone and Amelia Bishop of New Haven, Conn., former pioneer Sept. 10, 1850, Joseph Young company). She was born Jan. 4, 1839. Their children: Emily L., m. David Dille; Rachel A., m. David Briggs; Newton Z.; Edgar A., m. Cynthia E. Jones; Clara M., m. Samuel Smith, m. Henry Bartholomew; Wilford b. March 7, 1867, m. Sarah A. Howard Jan. 23, 1889; Francis, m. Alzina Bateman; Franklin O., d. aged 17; Jesse P., m. Martha Dover, m. Martha Cypher; Horace, m. Hannah Gifford. Family home East Bountiful, Utah.
Member 13th quorum seventies; missionary to Connecticut one year; high priest. Blacksmith. Died Feb. 13, 1905.

TUTTLE, NEWTON ZERAH (son of Newton Tuttle and Emily A. Stone). Born Dec. 1, 1863, East Bountiful, Utah.

TUTTLE, WILFORD (son of Newton Tuttle and Emily A. Stone). Born March 7, 1867.
Married Sarah A. Howard Jan. 23, 1889, Logan, Utah (daughter of Thomas Howard and Mary Love of Bountiful, Utah, pioneers Oct. 7, 1861). She was born Feb. 3, 1871, at Bountiful. Their children: Mary E. H. b. Nov. 21, 1889, m. Lawrence Corbridge; Lucinda H. b. Sept. 5, 1891, m. F. A. Richards; Christa H. b. Sept. 4, 1893; Wilford H. b. Sept. 12, 1895, d. infant; Joseph H. b. Oct. 19, 1896; Florence H. b. Oct. 11, 1898; Fearnley H. b. Oct. 21, 1902, d. infant; Eva H. b. Dec. 10, 1903; Thoral H. b. Jan. 3, 1906; Ida H. b. Dec. 9, 1907, d. infant; Lilly H. b. July 14, 1909; Charles H. b. July 8, 1911, d. infant. Family home Bountiful, Utah.
President 100th quorum seventies; missionary to England 1899 to 1901; member of the Sunday school union board. City councilman Bountiful 1893 to 1899 and 1911. Market gardener; director of the Market Gardeners Ass'n. Died Dec. 27, 1911.

PIONEERS AND PROMINENT MEN OF UTAH

TWELVES, CHARLES (son of Robert Twelves and Ann Williams, both of Lincolnshire, Eng.). Born May 19, 1819, in Lincolnshire. Came to Utah Nov. 30, 1856, Edward Martin's "second" handcart company.
Married Ann Elizabeth Henrietta Gunn, May 24, 1841, at Manchester, Eng. (daughter of Samuel Gunn and Elizabeth Bridge, of Lincolnshire). She was born April 27, 1820. Their children: Charles, d. on plains; John R., m. Eliza Angela Daniels; Ann E. Henrietta; Orson, m. Sophronia Martin; Brigham and Mary Jane, died; Emma Jemima, m. William C. Pitts. Family home Provo, Utah.
Seventy. Merchant and gardener. Died May 12, 1896.

TWELVES, ORSON (son of Charles Twelves and Ann E. H. Gunn). Born Oct. 31, 1850, Gazberton, Eng. Came to Utah Nov. 30, 1856, Edward Martin handcart company.
Married Sophronia Lillian Martin Jan. 4, 1875, Salt Lake City (daughter of Jesse E. Martin and Sophronia Moore of Eaton, Utah, pioneers July 22, 1847, contingent Mormon Battalion). She was born July 4, 1858. Their children: Eliza Isabella b. May 1, 1876, m. Lyon Paul; m. Iver Lawson; Ida Henrietta b. Sept. 13, 1878; Alice Merinthe b. June 4, 1881; Flora Elizabeth b. Feb. 21, 1884, m. James Creighton Brown; Walter Orson b. Jan. 15, 1886; John Glendon b. Nov. 4, 1889; Lucella Sophronia and Leland Jesse (twins) b. Feb. 26, 1892; Rowland Van b. Aug. 9, 1895; Hollis Martin b. March 13, 1897.
Elder. Farmer.

TWITCHELL, EPHRAIM. Born in Vermont. Came to Utah 1858, Ezra Chase company.
Married Malissa Knight. Their children: Ancell (member Mormon Battalion), m. Eliza Hitchcock; Celestia, died; Unis, m. James Porter; James, m. Margaret Moore and Fannie Markham; Edwin b. May 22, 1836, m. Vesta Lucetta Bishop; Orrin, m. Elizabeth Smith; Amanda, m. Joseph Hoops; Joshua, m. Emma Maggum; Sarah, m. William Manhart. Family home Beaver, Utah.
Married Sarah Jane Hader, at Salt Lake City. She was born at Portswan, Utah. Their children: Maruria, m. John Long; Sanford; Lorenzo; Ephraim; Rosetta; Delora.
Died at Beaver, Utah.

TWITCHELL, EDWIN (son of Ephraim Twitchell and Malissa Knight). Born May 22, 1836, in McDonough county, Ill.
Married Vesta Lucetta Bishop Feb. 24, 1860, Fillmore, Utah (daughter of William B. Bishop and Eliza Pratt). She was born May 16, 1842, in Hancock county, Ill. Their children: Eliza Juliette b. Nov. 24, 1860, and Edwin b. Jan. 12, 1862, died; Beatrice b. Oct. 24, 1864, m. Willard Heaps Cox, d. 1886; Adelbert b. Feb. 11, 1866, m. Lucy Cottam Nov. 12, 1890; Monroe b. Dec. 2, 1867, m. Violate Heaps Dec. 24, 1889; William Henry b. Sept. 27, 1870, m. Nancy Openshaw Sept. 4, 1891; Sarah Elizabeth b. Nov. 9, 1872, m. Nelbeth Allen Oct. 31, 1895; James Nelson b. July 4, 1875, d.; Vesta Lucetta b. Dec. 2, 1876, m. Perry J. Shirts, d.; Joshua Lafayette b. June 9, 1880; Ancell Knight b. 1882, d. died.
Missionary to The Muddy, Nev., six years; bishop's counselor; also 1st counselor to Bishop A. P. Schow of Escalante for 15 years. Died Sept. 8, 1907, Escalante, Utah.

TWITCHELL, ADELBERT (son of Edwin Twitchell and Vesta Lucetta Bishop). Born Feb. 11, 1866, Overton, Lincoln county, Nev.
Married Lucy Ann Cottam Nov. 12, 1890, Manti, Utah (daughter of William Cottam and Eveline Allen). Their children: Ruby b. Aug. 6, 1891, m. Joseph Osborn Sept. 11, 1910; Milton b. Dec. 5, 1895; Leland b. Oct. 2, 1897; Adelbert Monroe b. Feb. 12, 1899; Grant b. Dec. 18, 1901; Blain b. Nov. 6, 1903. Family home Escalante, Utah.
Missionary to Samoan Islands.

TWITCHELL, WILLIAM B. Born Oct. 1, 1829, at Portland, Maine. Came to Utah 1851.
Married Augusta Hawkins March 17, 1854 (daughter of Benjamin Hawkins, pioneer 1848, contingent Mormon Battalion, and Rhoda Cleaviand). She was born Jan. 9, 1836, in Oneida county, N. Y., and came to Utah 1848, Captain Tanner company. Died June 28, 1879. Their children: William H. b. Jan. 30, 1855, m. Emma Jimmet; Benjamin H. b. Aug. 29, 1856, m. Luela Busenbark; Charles Edwin b. June 16, 1859, m. Elizabeth Fannie Simmons; m. Susan Pearl Elmer; Peter; Alice M. b. May 1, 1865, m. Joseph B. Moore; Eli Earlier b. April 15, 1867, m. Mary Tesmond 1901. Family home, Salt Lake City.
Missionary to Canada 1857; elder. School teacher. Carpenter.

TWITCHELL, CHARLES EDWARD (son of William B. Twitchell and Augusta Hawkins). Born June 16, 1859, at Salt Lake City.
Married Elizabeth Fannie Simmons June 14, 1883, at Salt Lake City (daughter of George Simmons and Eliza Barrie). She was born Dec. 20, 1863, Haywards Heath, Sussex, Eng. Their children: Charles Edward, Jr. b. May 9, 1886; Frederick William b. Feb. 13, 1889; Lizzie May b. July 25, 1891; Alice U. b. Sept. 15, 1893; Ester b. Aug. 15, 1896.
Married Susan Pearl Elmer June 8, 1905, Logan, Cache Co., Utah (daughter of Charles Jackson Elmer and Susan Katherine Thornton, who were married Dec. 31, 1882, Providence, Utah). She was born Dec. 5, 1885, at Newley, Idaho.

Their children: Eli Lavan b. March 27, 1906; Irvan, April 11, 1908; Libbie b. Nov. 12, 1910. Family home Bear Dam, Box Elder Co., Utah.
Missionary to northwestern states 1899-1900; first counselor in Sunday school and ward teacher 14 years; second counselor to Bishop Francullo Durfey 1901; first counselor to Bishop R. A. Johnson 1907.

U

UDALL, DAVID (son of Jesse Udall and Ann Dra bridge of Goudhurst, Kent, Eng.). Born Jan. 18, 1829, a Goud. hurst. Cam- to Utah Sept. 3, 1852, independent company.
Married Eliza King Dec. 2, 1850, Hammersmith, London, Eng. (daughter of Charles King and Ann Anderson Waltham, Berkshire, Eng.), who was born Dec. 30, 1826, d died March 15, 1863, at Nephi, Utah. Their children: David King, m. Eliza Luella Stewart, m. Ida Frances Hunt; illiam Jesse, d. child; Eliza Ann, m. Ammon M. Tenney; Ma Ann. m. William Thomas Stewart; Charles, d. child; Joh b. m. Emma Goldsbrough. Family home Nephi, Juab Co. I th.
Married Elizabeth Rowley April 5, 1857, Salt Lal City, who was born Dec. 14, 1838, Sucley, Worcestershir Eng. and died June 24, 1907, Nephi, Utah. Their children: illiam David and Emily, died; Elizabeth Ann, m. James D. Farlane; Sarah Jane, m. William J. Schofield; Edwir died; Louisa Melissa (died), m. John Stephen Ostler; Al, m. John Edghiel; George Albert, m. Maud Stewart; mma Keturah and Willie Richard, died; Kate Eveline, n Wil. liam Dailey; Alvin Jewel, m.
Married Eliza Rebecca May July 2, 1864, at Neph who was born Oct. 6, 1840, Liverpool, Eng., and died Jan. 9 1911, Alamo, Nev.
Bishop; patriarch; member 49th quorum seventies missionary to England. Served in Black Hawk war. F mer. Died Nov. 14, 1910, Nephi, Utah.

UDALL, DAVID KING (son of David Udall and Eliza ing). Born Sept. 7, 1851, St. Louis, Mo. Came to Utah with ar. ents.
Married Eliza Luella Stewart Feb. 1, 1875, Salt Lak ity (daughter of Levi Stewart and Margery Wilkerson, pioners 1848, Brigham Young company), who was born M 21, 1855. Their children: Pearl b. June 20, 1880; Erma b. ept. 11, 1882, m. William Sherwood; Mary b. July 5, 10, d. child; Luella b. Jan. 18, 1886, m. Garland H. Pace; vid King, Jr. b. May 26, 1888; Levi Stewart b. Jan. 20, 191 Paul b. Dec. 2, 1894, and Rebecca May b. Sept. 1, 1897, d. sil-dren. Family home St. Johns, Apache county, Ariz.
Married Ida Frances Hunt May 24, 1882, St. George, tah (daughter of John Hunt and Lois Barnes Pratt of Bever, Utah, pioneers 1847 with others of the Mormon Batta n). She was born March 8, 1858. Their children: Pauli n. March 26, 1885, m. Asahel H. Smith; Grover Cleveland b. Feb. 24, 1887, m. Dora Sherwood; John Hunt b. Aug 23, 1889, m. Ruth Kimball; Jesse Addison b. June 24, 1893; il-bert Douglas b. May 13, 1895; Don Taylor b. July 20, 19 1875-1877; president Y. M. M. I. A.; bishop of St. John's w'd president St. John's stake. Member legislature of Ariz a. Farmer.

UDY, JAMES (son of Hart Udy and Ann Birkenshire, th born at Lanlivery, Cornwall, Eng.—married 1815). Born Aug. 16, 1820, Lanlivery. Came to Utah 1852.
Married Mary Ann Trengrove, who was born in June, and died in 1850 at St. Louis, Mo. Their children: William Henry b. 1845; James Jr. b. 1848; John b. 1849.
Married Isabella Ann Cowley 1849, Council Bluffs, I a (daughter of James Cowley), who was born 1832 on e of Man, Eng. Their children: Elizabeth Ann b. Novem 1852, m. Edwin Smith; Mathias Cowley b. July 9, 1854, Emily R. Hess; Hart b. Aug. 27, 1856, m. Alice Vand; Joseph b. July 4, 1859, m. Annett Smith; Thomas Jame, Oct. 13, 1861, m. Rowane Moon; Nephi Royal b. Nov. 1863; Esther Isabella b. April 28, 1865; Mary Alice b. (b. 1866, m. George L. C. Hess; Eleanor b. Oct. 18, 1870, m. Jl Hess; George L. C. b. Sept. 28, 1874, m. Evaline Mc Family home Farmington, Davis Co. Utah.
Married Mary Sophia Hansen in March, 1863, Salt L City (daughter of Hans Christian Anderson and Cather Larsen, former Pioneer Oct. 15, 1852, Joseph Horne c pany). She was born Feb. 11, 1842, at Falster, Denma and came to Utah with father. Their children: Mr Emelia b. Aug. 3, 1864; Charles Albert b. April 29, 1866, Adeline Hess Aug. 16, 1887; Alnet b. Feb. 4, 1868; A Lorenzo b. Jan. 16, 1870, m. Arenath Edna Potter June 1895; Nancy M. b. Oct. 19, 1872, m. John Garn Nov. 17, 18 James Henry b. Nov. 9, 1874; Hyrum b. Nov. 25, 1878, Rhumine Earl April, 1900; Gertrude b. July 21, 1881, Charles Hess Nov. 6, 1901. Family home Farmington, U.
Helped make first plows, harrows, wagons, threshi machines, etc., manufactured in Utah. Expert blackami

UDY, MATHIAS COWLEY (son of James Udy and Isabel Ann Cowley). Born July 9, 1854, Bountiful, Utah.
Married Emily R. Hess Jan. 20, 1875, Salt Lake, C (daughter of John W. Hess, pioneer July 29, 1847, Jam Brown company, and Emily Card). She was born June 1854, Farmington, Utah. Their children: Jessie Emily

PIONEERS AND PROMINENT MEN OF UTAH 1221

Jan. 3, 1876; Mathias C. Jr. b. Nov. 7, 1877, m. Mary Lessey; James Raleigh b. Oct. 10, 1879, m. Lona Sanders; Frank H. b. March 27, 1882, m. Ethel Brown; Charlotte b July 19, 1884, m. Henry Secrist; Julia Irene b. July 17, 1887, m. Delbert E. Wilcox; Hazel Bell b. Oct. 12, 1889; Marvin J. b. Feb. 19, 1892; William Hart b. Sept. 25, 1894.
Elder; ward teacher. City councilman Farmington, 4 years; deputy sheriff, Davis county, 2 years; superintendent Haight Bench Irrigation company, 10 years; school trustee, Davis county, 15 years.

UDY, ANES LORENZO (son of James Udy and Mary Sophia Hansen). Born Jan. 16, 1870, Farmington, Utah.
Married Arenath Edna Potter June 27, 1895, at Fielding, Box Elder Co., Utah (daughter of Melvin L. Potter, born Sept. 1, 1850, and Arenath Glover, born Aug. 8, 1852, both of Salt Lake City). She was born Nov. 16, 1872, at Farmington. Their children: Melvin Anes b. April 25, 1896; Gardner L. b. Sept. 4, 1898; Clifton James b. Oct. 23, 1901; Eugene S. b. Feb. 15, 1905; Clem E. b. Oct. 8, 1907; Oscar Marvin b. March 2, 1911. Family home Plymouth, Box Elder Co., Utah.
Elder; priest; teacher. Farmer and stockraiser.

UNSWORTH, JAMES (son of William Unsworth, born in Bolton, Lancastershire, Eng., 1816, and Elizabeth Tong, born Aug. 19, 1815, at Bolton—married 1834). Born Dec. 25, 1838, Bolton. Came to Utah Sept. 22, 1861, Samuel A. Woolley company.
Married Alice Cockshott Aug. 25, 1860, at Bolton (daughter of John and Alice Cockshott), who was born 1840, and came to Utah with husband. Their children: Betsy b. June 1, 1861, d. Oct. 18, 1861; Alice b. Dec. 1, 1862, m. Charles Sorenson; Elizabeth Ellen b. Jan. 7, 1866, m. James H. Neilsen; Mary Ann b. Oct. 3, 1867, m. C. F. Olsen; Eva M. b. Feb. 13, 1870, m. Soren Hanson; Ella b. March 1, 1872, m. Albert P. Ellis; Lillian b. March 16, 1874, d. Jan. 31, 1875; James b. Aug. 5, 1875, d. Feb. 19, 1877; William b. Dec. 1, 1880; Maud b. Nov. 1882; Samuel b. March 14, 1886. Family home Hyrum, Utah.
Married Wilhelmina A. Orell March 3, 1873, Salt Lake City (daughter of Charles Frederick Orell and Johanna Charlotte Granne, latter pioneer Sept. 29, 1866, Peter Nebeker company—married 1851, in Sweden). She was born Feb. 2, 1855, at Norrköping, Sweden. Their children: Charlotte b. Oct. 11, 1875, d. March 24, 1882; Ida Augusta b. March 27, 1877, d. March 27, 1882; Charles Clarence b. March 7, 1881, m. Agnes Liljenquist; Edna Ione b. March 27, 1883, m. Alma Allen; Joseph b. May 1, 1885, m. Josephine Crookston; Bertrand Tong b. June 24, 1893, d. March, 1894; Leon Grand b. April 11, 1895, d. Sept. 1896; Gihon Kenneth b. April 11, 1895; Felicia Hortense b. Dec. 11, 1897, d. Dec. 15, 1901.
Ordained high priest 1876; bishop's counselor; missionary to England 1885-87; high counselor in Hyrum stake at its organization. Pioneer merchant of Hyrum 1867. Manager secretary and treasurer of Hyrum Co-op. for twenty-five years. Farmer and merchant.

URE, JAMES (son of James Ure, born 1791, at Greenock, and Janet McCale, born in 1790 at Bridge of Weir, Scotland). Born June 11, 1817, at Bridge of Weir. Came to Utah Oct. 27, 1849, George A. Smith company.
Married Janet Scott in October, 1845, in Scotland (daughter of James Scott and Catherine Laing), who was born April 18, 1818, and came to Utah with husband. Their children: Catherine b. July 4, 1846; James William b. Oct. 31, 1847, m. Lucinda Ann Cunningham June 6, 1868; m. Mary Jane Carson Oct. 17, 1879; Janet Scott b. May 27, 1850, m. Thomas C. Griggs Feb. 1870; Alma Scott b. Nov. 15, 1851; Albert Scott b. March 31, 1853, m. Louisa Stanford Dec. 16, 1885; John Alexander b. April 6, 1855; Robert Alvin b. Nov. 25, 1859, m. Leonora Bullock Aug. 20, 1884. Family home, Salt Lake City.
Married Agnes Jones Oct. 17, 1866, Salt Lake City, who was born May 15, 1831, at Renton, Dumbartonshire, Scotland.
Married Elizabeth Jones Oct. 17, 1866, Salt Lake City (daughter of William Jones and Mary Schill, of Brimsfield, Gloucestershire, Eng., pioneers 1868), who was born Jan. 6, 1844. Their children: William Jones b. July 21, 1869, m. Ellen Watstenholme; Agnes b. Nov. 4, 1870; Heber Jones b. April 14, 1872, m. Myrtle Pack; James Jones b. Jan. 9, 1876. Family home Kamas, Utah.
High priest; missionary to Europe 1856-58 and 1864-67; first counselor in presidency of Tooele stake; patriarch. Veteran Indian war.

URE, JAMES WILLIAM (son of James Ure and Janet Scott). Born Oct. 31, 1847, Louth, Lincolnshire, Eng.
Married Lucinda Ann Cunningham June 6, 1868, Salt Lake City (daughter of Andrew Cunningham and Lucinda Rawlins, pioneers Oct. 13, 1848, Amasa M. Lyman company). She was born March 29, 1852, Salt Lake City. Their children: Lucinda Ann b. June 22, 1869, m. W. J. Kemp June 24, 1896; James William Jr. b. March 31, 1874, m. Isabell Ball June 26, 1895; Janet Scott b. July 14, 1874; Andrew Cunningham b. May 7, 1876, m. Eliza A. Burrows June 24, 1896; Clarissa Eustacia b. April 1, 1897, m. John M. Miller March 1, 1900; Isabell Scott b. July 2, 1881, m. Horace E. Garner Oct. 28, 1903; Bertha L. b. Aug. 10, 1884, m. George

Q. Moss Nov. 25, 1903; Samantha C. b. Oct. 5, 1887; Clarence Cunningham b. May 14, 1890.
Married Mary Jane Carson Oct. 17, 1879, Salt Lake City (daughter of David Carson and Millie Jane Rawlins of Draper, Utah, pioneers 1848, Amasa M. Lyman company). She was born June 30, 1854. Their children: David Carson b. Jan. 20, 1882; John Alma b. Oct. 29, 1883; Albert Carson b. May 1, 1886. Families resided, Salt Lake City.
President 5th elders quorum in Salt Lake stake; member general Sunday school board; high priest; high councilor in Salt Lake stake. School trustee.

URE, ALBERT SCOTT (son of James Ure and Janet Scott). Born March 31, 1853, Salt Lake City.
Married Louisa Stanford Dec. 16, 1885, Salt Lake City (daughter of Stephen Stanford and Louisa Foreman of Logan, Utah, pioneers September, 1862), who was born Dec. 12, 1858, Boston, Mass. Their children: Louisa S. b. Oct. 29, 1886; Scott S. b. Dec. 2, 1887, died; Albert Raymond b. Nov. 3, 1888; Geneva S. b. Jan. 6, 1890, m. Marion Heaps; Irene S. b. July 10, 1891 Family home, Salt Lake City.
Deputy sheriff of Salt Lake county; police officer of Salt Lake City. Fireman for Inland Salt company of Garfield, Utah. Carpenter; plumber.

UTLEY, GABRIEL MARION (son of Samuel Utley, born Oct. 28, 1790, and Maria Barry, born Jan. 21, 1812, both of Perry county, Ala.). He was born July 27, 1844, in Perry county. Came to Utah 1852, Captain Wimmer company.
Married Sophia Minerva Burgess (daughter of Harrison Burgess and Amanda Hammon), who was born in February, 1855. Their children: Harrison J. b. 1870; Harriet b. 1872, m. William J. Stewart; Mary J. b. 1874, m. Edward Gardner; Gabriel M. b. 1876, m. Verona Gardner 1902; Samuel b. 1878, m. Rosetta Bridges 1902; Willard b. 1880, m. Ida Skinner; Benjamin b. 1882, m. Ella Levie; Amanda b. 1884, m. Harry Bairline 1902; John b. 1886, m. Theba Mackey; Ethel b. 1888, m. Ray Hunt; Myrtle b. 1890, m. Debert Robinson 1907; Ray and Roy (twins) b. 1892; Earl Ernest b. 1894; Vera b. 1896.
High priest; bishop's counselor Mesquite ward, Lincoln county, Nev. Constable of Pine Valley three years. Settled at Salt Lake City 1852; moved into Nevada, where he labored several years and returning to Utah, settled in "Dixie." Called to help settle the Mesquite, on Virgin River, where he lived three years and then settled at Annabella. Blacksmith and farmer.

UTLEY, L. J. Born Feb. 1, 1806, Mobile, Ala. Came to Utah Sept. 23, 1849, Orson Spencer company.
Married Elizabeth Rutlidge. Their children: William J.; Martha Ann; Helen Elizabeth; Margaret Eliza; L. J. Rutlidge; Sarah Matilda; James Milton; Abraham Gray; Sapphronia Jane; Mary Agnes; Mildred Caroline.
Married Deborah White. Their children: Samuel Smith; William H.; Lafayette.

V

VALENTINE, AUGUST (son of Wallantine Wallantinson and Engel Margret Kofod). Born Aug. 27, 1837, m. Bornholm, Denmark. Came to Utah Sept. 30, 1853, John Forsgren company.
Married Mary Huston in April, 1861, Brigham City (daughter of John and Christina Huston of Iowa; latter came to Utah). She was born July, 1842. Their children: August, Jr. b. 1862, m. Fatinna Knudson; Mary Ellen, d. aged 16; Carlos Holmes; Bernice, m. Hans Jensen; m. Ambrose Jensen; William Jensen; Christopher Columbus, m. Lovina Petersen; Argenta, m. C. Wixum; Winnie, m. Lee Holst. Family home Brigham City.
Married Sophy C. Hansen Egesen 1885, Salt Lake City (daughter of R. Hansen Egesen and Anna Christensen of Copenhagen, Denmark), who was born 1863. Their children: Leon Augustus b. Jan. 1888, m. Hannah Pett; Florence Elizabeth b. Sept. 1893; Harland Alexander b. Jan. 1895; Holger Alonzo b. April, 1899. Mildred Isabella b. 1903.
Seventy; missionary to Denmark 1883-85; bishop. Stockraiser.

VAN BUREN, ANDREW CHENEY (son of Cheney Garrett Van Buren and Lucy Phillips, of Garden Grove, Iowa). Born Feb. 9, 1840, in Missouri. Came to Utah 1853, James Snow company.
Married Lovina Emeline Cox Dec. 1, 1866, Salt Lake City (daughter of Frederick Walter Cox and Cordelia Calista Morley, of Oswego county, N. Y., pioneers Oct. 4, 1852). Their children: Laurett b. Oct. 25, 1867, m. Thomas Fullmer; Arthur A. b. Nov. 13, 1869, m. Ida Taylor; Vernoa b. Oct. 30, 1872, d. 1895; Chester G. b. March 15, 1875; Kate Leone b. Dec. 6, 1880, m. Charles Killion; Frederick b. Sept. 26, 1883, m. Celia Pendleton; Clyde Vernon b. Feb. 13, 1886, m. Ila Mangum. Family home Orangeville, Utah.
Member of city council Manti eight years; president of Orangeville town board six years. Farmer.

1220　　　　PIONEERS AND PROMINENT MEN OF UTAH

TWELVES, CHARLES (son of Robert Twelves and Ann Williams, both of Lincolnshire, Eng.). Born May 19, 1819, in Lincolnshire. Came to Utah Nov. 30, 1856, Edward Martin "frozen" handcart company.
Married Ann Elizabeth Henrietta Gunn, May 24, 1841, at Lincolnshire, Eng. (daughter of Samuel Gunn and Elizabeth Bristow of Lincolnshire). She was born April 27, 1820. Their children: Charles, d. on plains; John R., m. Eliza Louella Daniels; Ann E. Henrietta; Orson, m. Sophronia L. Martin; Brigham and Mary Jane, died; Emma Jemima, m. William C. Foote. Family home Provo, Utah.
Seventy. Merchant and gardener. Died May 12, .896.

TWELVES, ORSON (son of Charles Twelves and Ann E. H. Gunn). Born Oct. 22, 1850, Gasberton, Eng. Came to Utah Nov. 30, 1856, Edward Martin handcart company.
Married Sophronia Lillian Martin Jan. 4, 1875, Salt Lake City (daughter of Jesse B. Martin and Sophronia Moore of Scipio, Utah, pioneers July 29, 1847, contingent Mormon Battalion). She was born July 4, 1853. Their children: Edna Isabelle b. May 2, 1876, m. Logon Paul; m. Iver Lawson; Ida Henrietta b. Sept. 12, 1878; Alice Merinthe b. June 4, 1881; Flora Elizabeth b. Feb. 17, 1884, m. James Creighton Brown; Walter Orson b. Jan. 15, 1886; John Glendon b. Nov. 6, 1889; Louella Sophronia and Leland Jesse (twins) b. Feb. 24, 1891; Rowland Van b. Aug. 9, 1895; Hollis Martin b. March 15, 1897.
Elder. Farmer.

TWITCHELL, EPHRAIM. Born in Vermont. Came to Utah 1858, Ezra Chase company.
Married Malissa Knight. Their children: Ancell (member Mormon Battalion), m. Eliza Hitchcock; Celestia, died; Unis, m. James Puffer; James, m. Margaret Moore and Fannie Manhart; Edwin b. May 23, 1836, m. Vesta Lucetta Bishop; Orrin, m. Elizabeth Smith; Amanda, m. Joseph Hoops; Joshua, m. Elmina Mangum; Sarah, m. William Manhart. Family home Beaver, Utah.
Married Sarah Jane Haden at Salt Lake City. She was born at Parowan, Utah. Their children: Maruria, m. John Lott; Sanford; Lorenzo; Ephraim; Rosetta; Delora.
Died at Beaver, Utah.

TWITCHELL, EDWIN (son of Ephraim Twitchell and Melissa Knight). Born May 23, 1836, in McDonough county, Ill.
Married Vesta Lucetta Bishop Feb. 24, 1860, Fillmore, Utah (daughter of William H. Bishop and Eliza Pratt). She was born May 15, 1843, in Hancock county, Ill. Their children: Eliza Juliette b. Nov. 24, 1860, and Edwin b. Jan. 12, 1862, died; Beatrice b. Oct. 24, 1864, m. Willard Heaps Oct. 27, 1880; Adelbert b. Feb. 11, 1866, m. Lucy Cottam Nov. 12, 1890; Monroe b. Dec. 2, 1867, m. Violate Heaps Dec. 24, 1889; William Henry b. Sept. 27, 1870, m. Nancy Openshaw Sept. 6, 1908; Sarah Elizabeth b. Nov. 27, 1872, m. Nelson Cottam Nov. 1892; Augustus b. Dec. 8, 1874, m. Elizabeth Allen Oct. 31, 1895; James Nelson b. July 2, 1878, died; Vesta Lucetta b. Dec. 2, 1876, m. Perry M. Shirts Oct. 9, 1901; Joshua Lafayette b. June 9, 1880; Anceil Knight b. Oct. 24, 1882, died.
Missionary to the Muddy, Nev., six years; bishop's counselor; also 1st counselor to Bishop A. P. Schow of Escalante for 25 years. Died Sept. 8, 1907, Escalante, Utah.

TWITCHELL, ADELBERT (son of Edwin Twitchell and Vesta Lucetta Bishop). Born Feb. 11, 1866, Overton, Lincoln county, Nev.
Married Lucy Ann Cottam Nov. 12, 1890, Manti, Utah (daughter of William Cottam and Eveline Allen). Their children: Ruby b. Aug. 8, 1891, m. Jasper Osborn Sept. 11, 1910; Milton b. Dec. 8, 1895; Leland b. Oct. 6, 1897; Adelbert Monroe b. Feb. 12, 1899; Grant b. Dec. 18, 1901; Blain b. Nov. 5, 1903. Family home Escalante, Utah.
Missionary to Samoan Islands.

TWITCHELL, WILLIAM B. Born Oct. 1, 1829, at Portland, Maine. Came to Utah 1851.
Married Augusta Hawkins March 17, 1854 (daughter of Benjamin Hawkins, pioneer 1848, contingent Mormon Battalion, and Rhoda Cleavland). She was born Jan. 9, 1836, in Oneida county, N. Y., and came to Utah 1848, Captain Tanner company. Died June 28, 1879. Their children: William H. b. Jan. 30, 1855, m. Emma Jimmet; Benjamin H. b. Aug. 20, 1856, m. Luela Busenbrek; Charles Edward b. June 16, 1859, m. Elizabeth Fannie Simmons; m. Susan Pearl Elmer; Mary Alice M. b. May 1, 1865, m. Joseph B. Moore; Eli Ezarier b. April 15, 1867, m. Mary Tesmond 1901. Family home Salt Lake City.
Missionary to Canada 1857; elder. School teacher. Carpenter.

TWITCHELL, CHARLES EDWARD (son of William B. Twitchell and Augusta Hawkins). Born June 16, 1869, at Salt Lake City.
Married Elizabeth Fannie Simmons June 14, 1893, at Salt Lake City (daughter of George Simmons and Eliza Barrie), who was born Dec. 20, 1863, Haywards Heath, Sussex, Eng. Their children: Charles Edward, Jr. b. May 9, 1886; Frederick William b. Feb. 13, 1889; Lizzie May b. July 25, 1891; Alice U. b. Sept. 15, 1893; Ester b. Aug. 15, 1896.
Married Susan Pearl Elmer June 8, 1905, Logan, Cache Co., Utah (daughter of Charles Jackson Elmer and Susan Katherine Thornton, who were married Dec. 31, 1882. Providence, Utah). She was born Dec. 5, 1885, at Neeley, Idaho.

Their children: Eli Lavan b. March 27, 1906; Irvan b. April 11, 1908; Libbie b. Nov. 12, 1910. Family home Beaver Dam, Box Elder Co., Utah.
Missionary to northwestern states 1898-1900; first counselor in Sunday school and ward teacher 14 years; second counselor to Bishop Francillo Durfey 1901; first counselor to Bishop R. A. Johnson 1907.

U

UDALL, DAVID (son of Jesse Udall and Ann Drawbridge of Goudhurst, Kent, Eng.). Born Jan. 18, 1829, at Goudhurst. Came to Utah Sept. 3, 1852, independent company.
Married Eliza King Dec. 2, 1850, Hammersmith, London, Eng. (daughter of Charles King and Ann Anderson of Waltham, Berkshire, Eng.), who was born Dec. 30, 1826, and died March 15, 1863, at Nephi, Utah. Their children: David King, m. Eliza Luella Stewart, m. Ida Frances Hunt; William Jesse, d. child; Eliza Ann, m. Ammon M. Tenney; Mary Ann, m. William Thomas Stewart; Charles, d. child; Joseph, m. Emma Goldsbrough. Family home Nephi, Juab Co., Utah.
Married Elizabeth Rowley April 5, 1867, Salt Lake City, who was born Dec. 14, 1838, Sucley, Worcestershire, Eng., and died June 24, 1907, Nephi, Utah. Their children: William David and Emily, died; Elizabeth Ann, m. James D. McFarlane; Sarah Jane, m. William J. Schofield; Edwin, died; Louisa Melissa (died), m. John Stephen Ostler; Alice, m. John Edghiel; George Albert, m. Maud Stewart; Emma Ketumah and Willie Richard, died; Kate Eveline, m. William Bailey; Alvin Jewel, m. ——.
Married Eliza Rebecca May July 2, 1864, at Nephi, who was born Oct. 6, 1840, Liverpool, Eng., and died Jan. 7, 1913, Alamo, Nev.
Bishop; patriarch; member 49th quorum seventies; missionary to England. Served in Black Hawk war. Farmer. Died Nov. 14, 1910, Nephi, Utah.

UDALL, DAVID KING (son of David Udall and Eliza King). Born Sept. 7, 1851, St. Louis, Mo. Came to Utah with parents.
Married Eliza Luella Stewart Feb. 1, 1875, Salt Lake City (daughter of Levi Stewart and Margery Wilkerson, pioneers 1848, Brigham Young company), who was born May 21, 1855. Their children: Pearl b. June 20, 1889; Erma b. Sept. 16, 1882, m. William W. Sherwood; Mary b. July 5, 1884, d. child; Luella b. Jan. 13, 1886, m. Garland H. Pace; David King, Jr. b. May 26, 1888; Levi Stewart b. Jan. 20, 1891; Paul b. Dec. 2, 1894, and Rebecca May b. Sept. 1, 1897, d. children. Family home St. Johns, Apache county, Ariz.
Married Ida Frances Hunt May 24, 1882, St. George, Utah (daughter of John Hunt and Lois Barnes Pratt of Beaver, Utah, pioneers 1847 with others of the Mormon Battalion). She was born March 8, 1858. Their children: Pauline b. March 26, 1885, m. Asahel H. Smith; Grover Cleveland b. Dec. 28, 1887, m. Dora Sherwood; John Hunt b. Aug. 23, 1889, m. Ruth Kimball; Jesse Addison b. June 24, 1893; Gilbert Douglas b. May 13, 1895; Don Taylor b. July 20, 1897. Member 49th quorum seventies; missionary to England 1875-77; president Y. M. M. I. A.; bishop of St. John's ward; president St. John's stake. Member legislature of Arizona. Farmer.

UDY, JAMES (son of Hart Udy and Ann Birkenshire, both born 1788, at Lanlivery, Cornwall, Eng.—married 1807). Born Aug. 16, 1820, Lanlivery. Came to Utah 1852.
Married Mary Ann Trengrove, who was born in June, 1820, and died in 1850 at St. Louis, Mo. Their children: William Henry b. 1845; James Jr. b. 1848; John b. 1849.
Married Isabella Ann Cowley 1849, Council Bluffs, Iowa (daughter of James Cowley), who was born 1832 on Isle of Man, Eng. Their children: Elizabeth Ann b. November, 1852, m. Edwin Smith; Mathias Cowley b. July 4, 1854, m. Emily R. Hess; Hart b. Aug. 27, 1856, m. Alice Vanfleet; Joseph b. July 4, 1859, m. Annett Smith; Thomas James b. Oct. 13, 1861, m. Rowane Moon; Nephi Royal b. Nov. 14, 1863; Esther Isabella b. April 28, 1865; Mary Alice b. Oct. 8, 1866, m. Joseph L. Hess; Eleanor b. Oct. 18, 1870, m. John T. Hess; George L. C. b. Sept. 28, 1874, m. Evaline Moon. Family home Farmington, Davis Co. Utah.
Married Mary Sophia Hansen in March, 1863, Salt Lake City (daughter of Hans Christian Anderson and Catherine Larsen, former pioneer Oct. 15, 1862, Joseph Horne company). She was born Feb. 11, 1842, at Palster, Denmark, and came to Utah with father. Their children: Mary Emelia b. Aug. 3, 1864; Charles Albert b. April 29, 1866, m. Adeline Hess Aug. 16, 1887; Annie b. Feb. 4, 1863; Anes Lorenzo b. Jan. 16, 1870, m. Arenath Edna Potter June 27, 1895; Nancy M. b. Oct. 19, 1872, m. John Garn Nov. 17, 1897; James Henry b. Nov. 9, 1874; Hyrum b. Nov. 25, 1878, m. Rhumina Earl April, 1900; Gertrude b. July 21, 1881, m. Charles Hess Nov. 6, 1901. Family home Farmington, Utah.
Helped make first plows, harrows, wagons, threshing machines, etc., manufactured in Utah. Expert blacksmith.

UDY, MATHIAS COWLEY (son of James Udy and Isabella Ann Cowley). Born July 9, 1854, Bountiful, Utah.
Married Emily R. Hess Jan. 20, 1875, Salt Lake City (daughter of John W. Hess, pioneer July 29, 1847, James Brown company, and Emily Card). She was born June 26, 1854, Farmington, Utah. Their children: Jessie Emily b.

PIONEERS AND PROMINENT MEN OF UTAH 1221

Jan. 3, 1876; Mathias C. Jr. b. Nov. 7, 1877, m. Mary Lessey; James Raleigh b. Oct. 10, 1879, m. Lona Sanders; Frank H. b. March 27, 1882, m Ethel Brown; Charlotte b. July 19, 1884, m. Henry Secrist; Julia Irene b. July 17, 1887, m. Delbert E. Wilcox; Hazel Bell b. Oct. 12, 1889; Marvin J. b. Feb. 19, 1892; William Hart b. Sept. 25, 1894.
Elder; ward teacher. City councilman Farmington, 4 years; deputy sheriff, Davis county, 2 years; superintendent Haight Bench Irrigation company, 10 years; school trustee, Davis county, 15 years.

UDY, ANES LORENZO (son of James Udy and Mary Sophia Hansen). Born Jan. 16, 1870, Farmington, Utah.
Married Arenath Edna Potter June 27, 1895, at Fielding, Box Elder Co., Utah (daughter of Melvin L. Potter, born Sept. 1, 1850, and Arenath Glover, born Aug. 8, 1852, both of Salt Lake City). She was born Nov. 16, 1872, at Farmington. Their children: Melvin Anes b. April 25, 1896; Gardner L. b. Sept. 4, 1898; Clifton James b. Oct. 23, 1901; Eugene S. b. Feb. 15, 1905; Clem E. b. Oct. 8, 1907; Oscar Marvin b. March 2, 1911. Family home Plymouth, Box Elder Co., Utah.
Elder; priest; teacher. Farmer and stockraiser.

UNSWORTH, JAMES (son of William Unsworth, born in Bolton, Lancastershire, Eng., 1816, and Elizabeth Tong, born Aug. 19, 1815, at Bolton—married 1834). Born Dec. 25, 1838, Bolton. Came to Utah Sept. 22, 1861, Samuel A. Woolley company.
Married Alice Cockshott Aug. 25, 1860, at Bolton (daughter of John and Alice Cockshott), who was born 1840, and came to Utah with husband. Their children: Betsy b. June 1, 1861, d. Oct. 18, 1861; Alice b. Dec. 1, 1862, m. Charles Sorenson; Elizabeth Ellen b. Jan. 7, 1866, m. James H. Neilsen; Mary Ann b. Oct. 3, 1867, m. C. F. Olsen; Eva M. b. Feb. 13, 1870, m. Soren Hanson; Ella b. March 1, 1872, m. Albert P. Ellis; Lillian b. March 15, 1874, d. Jan. 31, 1875; James b. Aug. 5, 1875, d. Feb. 19, 1877; William b. Dec. 1, 1880; Maud b. Nov. 1882; Samuel b. March 14, 1886. Family home Hyrum, Utah.
Married Wilhelmina A. Orell March 3, 1873, Salt Lake City (daughter of Charles Frederick Orell and Johanna Charlotte Granne, latter pioneer Sept. 29, 1866, Peter Nebeker company—married 1851, in Sweden). She was born Feb. 2, 1855, at Norrköping, Sweden. Their children: Charlotte b. Oct. 11, 1875, d. March 24, 1882; Ida Amanda b. June 27, 1877, d. March 27, 1882; Charles Clarence b. March 7, 1881, m. Agnes Liljenquist; Edna Ione b. March 27, 1883, m. Alma Allen; Joseph b. May 1, 1885, m. Josephine Crookston; Bertrand Tong b. June 24, 1893, d. March, 1894; Leon Grand b. April 11, 1895, d. Sept. 1896; Gihon Kenneth b. April 11, 1895; Felicia Hortense b. Dec. 11, 1897, d. Dec. 19, 1901.
Ordained high priest 1876; bishop's counselor; missionary to England 1885-87; high counselor in Hyrum stake at its organization. Pioneer merchant of Hyrum 1867. Manager secretary and treasurer of Hyrum Co-op. for twenty-five years. Farmer and merchant.

URE, JAMES (son of James Ure, born 1791, at Greenock, and Janet McCale, born in 1790 at Bridge of Weir, Scotland). Born June 11, 1817, at Bridge of Weir. Same to Utah Oct. 27, 1849, George A. Smith company.
Married Janet Scott in October, 1845, in Scotland (daughter of James Scott and Catherine Lang), who was born April 18, 1818, and came to Utah with husband. Their children: Catherine b. July 4, 1846; James William b. Oct. 31, 1847, m. Lucinda Ann Cunningham June 6, 1868; m. Mary Jane Carson Oct. 17, 1879; Janet Scott b. May 27, 1850, m. Thomas C. Griggs Feb. 1870; Alma Scott b. Nov. 15, 1851; Albert Scott b. March 31, 1853, m. Louisa Stanford Dec. 16, 1885; John Alexander b. April 6, 1855; Robert Alvin b. Nov. 25, 1859, m. Leonora Bullock Aug. 20, 1884. Family home, Salt Lake City.
Married Agnes Davis in April, 1856, Salt Lake City, who was born May 15, 1831, at Renton, Dumbartonshire, Scotland.
Married Elizabeth Jones Oct. 17, 1866, Salt Lake City (daughter of William Jones and Mary Schill, of Brimsfield, Gloucestershire, Eng., pioneers September, 1868), who was born Jan. 6, 1844. Their children: William Jones b. July 21, 1869, m. Ellen Watstenholme; Agnes b. Nov. 4, 1870; Heber Jones b. April 14, 1872, m. Myrtle Pack; James Jones b. Jan. 9, 1876. Family home Kamas, Utah.
High priest; missionary to Europe 1856-58 and 1864-67; first counselor in presidency of Tooele stake; patriarch. Veteran Indian war.

URE, JAMES WILLIAM (son of James Ure and Janet Scott). Born Oct. 31, 1847, Louth, Lincolnshire, Eng.
Married Lucinda Ann Cunningham June 6, 1868, Salt Lake City (daughter of Andrew Cunningham and Lucinda Rawlins, pioneers Oct. 13, 1848, Amasa M. Lyman company). She was born March 29, 1852, Salt Lake City. Their children: Lucinda Ann b. June 22, 1869, m. W. J. Kemp June 24, 1896; James William Jr. b. March 31, 1872, m. Isabell Ball June 26, 1895; Janet Scott b. July 14, 1874; Andrew Cunningham b. May 7, 1876, m. Eliza A. Burrows June 24, 1896; Charissa Eustacia b. April 1, 1879, m. John M. Miller March 7, 1900; Isabell Scott b. July 2, 1881, m. Horace E. Garner Oct. 28, 1903; Bertha L. b. Aug. 10, 1884, m. George Q. Moss Nov. 25, 1903; Samantha C. b. Oct. 5, 1887; Clarence Cunningham b. May 14, 1890.
Married Mary Jane Carson Oct. 17, 1879, Salt Lake City (daughter of David Carson and Millie Jane Rawlins of Draper, Utah, pioneers 1848, Amasa M. Lyman company). She was born June 30, 1854. Their children: David Carson b. Jan. 20, 1882; John Alma b. Oct. 29, 1883; Albert Carson b. May 1, 1886. Families resided, Salt Lake City.
President 5th elders quorum in Salt Lake stake; member general Sunday school board; high priest; high councilor in Salt Lake stake. School trustee.

URE, ALBERT SCOTT (son of James Ure and Janet Scott). Born March 31, 1853, Salt Lake City.
Married Louisa Stanford Dec. 16, 1885, Salt Lake City (daughter of Stephen Stanford and Louisa Foreman of Logan, Utah, pioneers September, 1862), who was born Dec. 12, 1858, Boston, Mass. Their children: Louisa S. b. Oct. 29, 1886; Scott S. b. Dec. 2, 1887, died; Albert Raymond b. Nov. 3, 1888; Geneva S. b. Jan. 6, 1890, m. Marion Reaps; Irene S. b. July 10, 1891 Family home, Salt Lake City
Deputy sheriff of Salt Lake county; police officer of Salt Lake City. Fireman for Inland Salt company of Garfield, Utah. Carpenter; plumber.

UTLEY, GABRIEL MARION (son of Samuel Utley, born Oct. 28, 1790, and Maria Barry, born Jan. 21, 1812, both of Perry county, Ala.). He was born July 27, 1844, in Perry county. Came to Utah 1852, Captain Wimmer company.
Married Sophia Minerva Burgess (daughter of Harrison Burgess and Amanda Hammon), who was born in February, 1855. Their children: Harrison J. b. 1870; Harriet b. 1872, m. William J. Stewart; Mary J. b. 1874, m. Edward Gardner; Gabriel M. b. 1876, m. Verona Gardner 1902; Samuel b. 1878, m. Rosetta Bridges 1902; Willard b. 1880, m. Ida Skinner; Benjamin b. 1882, m. Ella Levie; Amanda b. 1884, m. Harry Bairline 1902; John b. 1886, m. Theba Mackey; Ethel b. 1888, m. Ray Hunt; Myrtle b. 1890, m. Debert Robinson 1907; Ray and Roy (twins) b. 1892; Earl Ernest b. 1894; Vera b. 1896.
High priest; bishop's counselor Mesquite ward, Lincoln county, Nev. Constable of Pine Valley three years. Settled at Salt Lake City 1852; moved into Nevada, where he labored several years and returning to Utah, settled in "Dixie." Called to help settle the Mesquite, on Virgin River, where he lived three years and then settled at Annabella. Blacksmith and farmer.

UTLEY, L. J. Born Feb. 1, 1806, Mobile, Ala. Came to Utah Sept. 22, 1849, Orson Spencer company.
Married Elizabeth Rutlidge. Their children: William J.; Martha Ann; Helen Elizabeth; Margaret Eliza; L. J. Rutlidge; Sarah Matilda; James Milton; Abraham Gray; Sapphronia Jane; Mary Agnes; Mildred Caroline.
Married Deborah White. Their children: Samuel Smith; William H.; Lafayette.

V

VALENTINE, AUGUST (son of Wallantine Wallantinson and Engel Margret Kofod). Born Aug. 27, 1837, m. Bornholm, Denmark. Came to Utah Sept. 30, 1853, John Forsgren company.
Married Mary Huston in April, 1861, Brigham City (daughter of John and Christina Huston of Iowa; latter came to Utah). She was born July, 1842. Their children: August, Jr. b. 1862, m. Fatinna Knudson; Mary Ellen, d. aged 16; Carlos Holmes; Bernice, m. Hans Jensen; Ambrose Jensen; Clara, m. William Jensen; Christopher Columbus, m. Lovina Petersen; Argenta, m. C. Wixum; Winnie, m. Lee Holst. Family home Brigham City.
Married Sophy C. Hansen Egesen 1885, Salt Lake City (daughter of R. Hansen Egesen and Anna Christensen of Copenhagen, Denmark), who was born 1863. Their children: Leon Augustus b. Jan. 1888, m. Hannah Pett; Florence Elisabeth b. Sept. 1893; Harland Alexander b. Jan. 1895; Holger Alonzo b. April, 1899. Mildred Isabella b. 1903.
Seventy; missionary to Denmark 1883-85; bishop. Stockraiser.

VAN BUREN, ANDREW CHENEY (son of Cheney Garrett Van Buren and Lucy Phillips, of Garden Grove, Iowa). Born Feb. 9, 1840, in Missouri. Came to Utah 1853, James Snow company.
Married Lovina Emeline Cox Dec. 1, 1866, Salt Lake City (daughter of Frederick Walter Cox and Cordelia Calista Morley, of Oswego county, N. Y., pioneers Oct. 4, 1852). Their children: Laurett b. Oct. 25, 1867, m. Thomas Fullmer; Arthur A. b. Nov. 13, 1869, m. Ida Taylor; Vernos b. Oct. 30, 1872, d. Dec. 25, 1885; Chester G. b. March 15, 1875, Kate Leone b. Dec. 6, 1880, m. Charles Killion; Frederick b. Sept. 26, 1883, m. Celia Pendleton; Clyde Vernon b. Feb. 13, 1886, m. Ida Mangum. Family home Orangeville, Utah.
Member of city council Manti eight years; president of Orangeville town board six years. Farmer.

VANCE, JOHN (son of James Vance, born Sept. 30, 1761, and Margaret Reno, both of Tennessee). He was born Nov. 8, 1794, in Tennessee. Came to Utah Oct. 2, 1847, Jedediah M. Grant company.
Married Sarah Perkins Feb. 10, 1817, Jackson (now Putnam) county, Tenn. (daughter of Ute Perkins and Sarah Gant of Tennessee), who was born Jan. 11, 1801. Their children: Isaac Y.; Margaret. m. John Lawson; William P., m. Ann Hidson; m. Hannah Richardson; Nancy Ann, m. William Wordsworth; James; three boys d. childhood; John, Jr., m. Miss Bunting.
Married Elizabeth Campbell March 7, 1837, McDonough county, Ill. (daughter of Ezekiel and Jane Campbell of McDonough county, former a pioneer Oct. 2, 1847, Jedediah M. Grant company). She was born Jan. 25, 1800. Their children: Martha Jane b. Sept. 25, 1839, m. William H. Kimball; Mary Elizabeth b. Nov. 2, 1844, m. John Thornton Gilmer; Lehi Moroni, d. child. Family home Salt Lake City.
Bishop at Winter Quarters. Assisted in bringing immigrants to Utah. Counselor to Bishop Perkins of 7th ward, Salt Lake City; high councilor; visiting teacher of 7th ward. School commissioner and justice of peace. Farmer. Died Jan. 24, 1882.

VANCE, WILLIAM P. (son of John Vance and Sarah Perkins). Born Oct. 20, 1822, Jackson (now Putnam) county, Tenn. Came to Utah July 22, 1847, Brigham Young company.
Married Ann Hidson March 10, 1865, who was born March 18, 1837, and came to Utah Oct. 16, 1863, Rosel Hyde company. Died Jan. 28, 1900.
Married Hannah Richardson Oct. 19, 1874, who was born June 21, 1855, and came to Utah Oct. 16, 1863, Rosel Hyde company. Their children: Sarah Mahala; Joseph Amos; William Abner; John Moroni; Ann Elizabeth; Lenora, died; Agnes Minerva.
Missionary in the east. Judge of Summit county.

VAN COTT, JOHN (son of Losee Van Cott and Lovina Pratt of Canaan, Columbia county, N. Y.). Born Sept. 7, 1814, Canaan. Came to Utah Sept. 25, 1847.
Married Lucy L. Sackett Sept. 15, 1835, in New York (daughter of Calvin P. Sackett and Hannah Douglas of New York), who was born July 17, 1815. Their children: Martha b. Feb. 29, 1838 (d. March, 1908); m. William Price; Lucy b. Dec. 16, 1839, d. Sept. 9, 1843; John Jr. b. Jan. 15, 1842, d. Nov. 16, 1843; Mary b. Feb. 2, 1844 (d. Jan. 5, 1884), m. Brigham Young; Losee B. April 18, 1850, m. A. F. McDonald; Byron b. March 2, 1852, d. Nov. 19, 1853.
Married Jemima Morris May 2, 1849, Salt Lake City. Their child: Morris b. March 14, 1851, d. March 16, 1851.
Married Caroline Pratt Feb. 2, 1857, Salt Lake City (daughter of Anson Pratt and Sarah Barber). Their children: Viola, m. Joseph Madson; Oscar M., m. Ida Quayle; Marlon, m. Sarah Gabbott; Edith, m. Ezra T. Palmer; Harold, m. Ella Sheets; Lavina, m. Mr. White; Orson and Anson, d. children. Family home, Salt Lake City.
Married Laura Lund Feb. 2, 1857, Salt Lake City (daughter of Lars Peter Lund and Magdalena Olsen of Copenhagen, Denmark, pioneers 1856). She was born Feb. 27, 1843. Their children: Agnes Lund b. May 9, 1858, d. Jan. 16, 1859; Waldemar b. Dec. 11, 1859, m. Ella Quayle; Frank Victor b. Aug. 7, 1863, m. Annie Mary Anderson; Lucy May; Roy b. Jan. 12, 1873, d. 1877; Ernest b. Dec. 18, 1875, m. May Siddoway. Family home, Salt Lake City.
Married Lena Erickson Nov. 22, 1862, Salt Lake City (daughter of Eric Erickson of Sweden, pioneer 1862). She was born July 17, 1833. Their children: Selma b. Nov. 12, 1863, m. William W. Taylor; Nephi b. Feb. 25, 1865, d. 1865; Albert b. Dec. 25, 1868, m. Margaret South; Enoch b. Jan. 7, 1873, m. Clara Bailey; Olivia b. April 27, 1875, m. Thomas Davis. Family home, Salt Lake City.
Missionary to England 1852-53; president Scandinavia mission 1853-56, also 1859-62; one of the presidents of seventies. Member of house of representatives 1864-65; street supervisor. Farmer. Died Feb. 18, 1883, Salt Lake City.

VAN COTT, FRANK VICTOR (son of John Van Cott and Laura Lund). Born Aug. 7, 1863, Salt Lake City.
Married Annie Mary Anderson Feb. 8, 1905, Salt Lake City (daughter of Ole Anderson and Minnie Neilsen of Pleasant Grove, Utah; came to Utah June 29, 1884). She was born Nov. 12, 1882. Their children: Frank Anderson b. Feb. 20, 1906; Helen May b. April 18, 1908; John Waldemar b. June 24, 1911; Byron Le Roy b. July 1, 1913.
Ward teacher; missionary to Samoan Islands 1891-94.

VAN DYKE, WILLIAM (son of Nicholas Van Dyke and Lydia Okie of Philadelphia, Pa.). Born Dec. 11, 1830, Philadelphia. Came to Utah, spring of 1849.
Married Charlotte Pixton March 6, 1857, Salt Lake City (daughter of Robert Pixton and Elizabeth Cooper of Taylorsville, Utah, pioneers 1849). She was born Feb. 8, 1840.
Their children: William David b. March 2, 1858, m. Martha Ellen Evans; Robert Pixton b. Feb. 26, 1860, m. Eliza Wareing; Charlotte E: b. March 23, 1862, m. Paul F. Shaeffer; McGaw b. Nov. 12, 1864, m. Louisa Howell; Don Carlos b. Jan. 16, 1866, m. Kate Underwood; Lydia b. Nov. 5, 1868, m. Chase L. Ashton; Eugenia b. March 15, 1870, m. Ernest Parish; Louis B. b. Nov. 17, 1872, m. Sophia Beck; Maude b. Nov. 15, 1875, m. William G. Sadler; Alfred O. b. April 18, 1879, m. Vera Hardy. Family resided Ogden and Salt Lake City, Utah.
Member of seventy. One of the founders of Lehi and Plain City, Utah. Produce merchant. Died Jan. 18, 1901.

VAN DYKE, WILLIAM DAVID (son of William Van Dyke and Charlotte Pixton). Born March 2, 1858, Lehi, Utah.
Married Martha Ellen Evans Sept. 26, 1878, Salt Lake City (daughter of George Evans and Sarah Twigg of Wales), who was born July 14, 1859. Their children: William David Jr. b. Aug. 17, 1879, m. Lelia V. Bingham; Robert W. b. Sept. 26, 1881, d. Oct. 25, 1884; Lawrence A. b. Jan. 11, 1886, m. Alice Dinsdale; Elies N. b. Sept. 20, 1887, m. Ella Jorgensen; Leslie H. b. Jan. 12, 1891; Verna b. April 8, 1893. Family home Ogden, Utah.
Missionary to eastern states 1902 and 1904. High councilor in North Weber stake. For twenty-three years was in service of Southern Pacific Railway company, and is now in the employ of John Scowcroft & Sons Co., at Ogden.

VAN DYKE, WILLIAM DAVID, JR. (son of William David Van Dyke and Martha Ellen Evans). Born Aug. 17, 1879, Ogden, Utah.
Married Leila V. Bingham Sept. 26, 1900, Salt Lake City (daughter of Willard Bingham, Jr., and Cyntha Shurtliff of Ogden, both born in Utah). She was born Feb. 19, 1881, and died Jan. 6, 1906. Their children: Derrah B. b. May 25, 1901; Arleen b. Oct. 2, 1902, d. Nov. 24, 1902.
Married Julia D. Anderson June 27, 1912. Family home Ogden, Utah.
Missionary to northern states 1907-09; member high council of North Weber stake; ordained bishop of Ogden 2d ward Jan. 1, 1911. Deputy city clerk of Weber county 1905-07; auditor of Ogden city 1912-1913.

VAN FLEET, ELIAS (son of Lanson Van Fleet and Sylva Chaso of Sparta, Livingston county, N. Y.). Born 1839 in Livingston county. Came to Utah October, 1848, Brigham Young company.
Married Lucy Adams May 10, 1860, Centerville, Utah (daughter of James Adams and Betsy Levitt of Lee county, Ill., pioneers 1850, James Allred company). She was born Feb. 4, 1839. Their children: Mary Alice, m. Hart Udy; Elias Judson; Rosebell, m. Lemuel Rogles; Sylvia, m. C. H. Bourne; Zina, m. R. H. Peck; Jessie; Horace, m. Eva Louise Soul; Lucy. Family home Farmington, Utah.
Senior president 74th quorum seventies; missionary to "Dixie" 1870-71. Deputy sheriff of Davis county. Superintendent Co-op. Davis county. Lieutenant in Black Hawk war. Farmer and stockraiser.

VAN LEUVEN, CORNELIOUS. Born Aug. 23, 1805, on shore of Lake Erie near Canadian boundary. Came to Utah 1852, Captain Wimmer company.
Married Lovina Draper (daughter of Thomas Draper), who was born March 6, 1807, and came to Utah with husband; died Jan. 14, 1867. Their child: Dunam b. Jan. 13, 1838, m. Anna Hannah Larson.
Married Margaret Stuart July, 1867, Springville, Utah. Their children: Marticia, m. Edward Johnson; Zina, m. George Robinson; Anson, m. —— Beardell; Catherine, m. Mell Clark.
Settled at Springville 1852; moved to Cottonwood 1853, and returned the same year to Springville, where he made his permanent home. Died July 12, 1886.

VAN LEUVEN, DUNAM (son of Cornelious Van Leuven and Lovina Draper). Born Jan. 13, 1838, Kirtland, Ohio.
Married Anna Hannah Larson Nov. 30, 1864, Springville, Utah (daughter of Andrew Larson and Caroline Andrews, pioneers Sept. 13, 1857, Christian Christiansen company). She was born Nov. 30, 1849, Malmö, Sweden. Their children: Anna Lovina b. June 20, 1866; Dunam Pulver b. Nov. 20, 1867; m. Hannah Turner; m. Carrie Humphrey; Caroline Luveria b. March 10, 1870, m. Van Orden Fullmer; Neuman Duveria b. March 17, 1870, m. Ida May Robinson; Delina Jane b. June 27, 1872, m. Reuben Newell Kendall; Mary Malinda b. March 29, 1875; Andrew Lewis b. Jan. 24, 1876, m. Ida Estell Jackson; Hannah Matilda b. Jan. 6, 1878; Ida May b. July 31, 1879, m. Joseph William Jackson; Fannie Roselia b. March 10, 1881, m. Albert Newell Kendall, m. Wiliam Kingsford; Rhoda Lucinda b. May 30, 1883, m. John William Russel; Sarah Edith b. Aug. 29, 1885, m. Milton Fullmer; Ralph Cornelious b. Dec. 29, 1887; Seth Alvin b. Oct. 19, 1889.

VAN LEUVEN, NEUMAN DUVERIA (son of Dunam Van Leuven and Anna Hannah Larson). Born March 10, 1870, Levan, Utah.

Married Ida May Robinson (daughter of James Robinson and Mary Morgan), who was born March 7, 1870, Galveston, Texas. Their children: Grace b. Sept. 8, 1891; Mabel b. May 10, 1893; Silas Emil b. Nov. 3, 1895; Cyrus Elmo b. Sept. 7, 1898; Mattie b. May 23, 1902; Adelbert b. Nov. 22, 1904; Arthur b. March 6, 1907.

VAN LEUVEN, RANSOM (son of John Van Leuven and Mary Pulver of North Ogden and St. Thomas, Utah, and Clifton, Idaho). Born April 25, 1810, Gananoque, Ontario, Canada. Came to Utah October, 1852.
Married Lucinda Harvey (daughter of Louis Wiswell), who was born Aug. 12, 1813. Their children: Matilda A., m. John C Sperry; Mary L., m. John Clifford; Seth; Leveret, m. Janett Wilson; Charles, d. child; Eliza Jane, m. John Merrill; William E., m. Julia Lake; Sarah E., m. William Billingsley; Harriet L., m. Orson Henderson; Ransom Carlos, m. Sarah L. Lake.
High priest. Farmer. Died Feb. 18, 1899, Lewiston, Utah.

VAN LEUVEN, RANSOM CARLOS (son of Ransom Van Leuven and Lucinda Harvey). Born Nov. 18, 1858, North Ogden, Utah.
Married Sarah L. Lake Oct. 30, 1879, Clifton, Idaho (daughter of Barney and Lucy Jane Lake of Clifton, pioneers). She was born May 3, 1861. Their children: Nellie b. Sept. 17, 1880, m. Jess C. Kent; Etta b. Aug. 12, 1883, m. Jabus M. Harris; Ethel b. March 24, 1885, m. C. O. Henderson; Lois b. March 22, 1887, m. Aivirus Dustin; Alta b. Dec. 28, 1890, m. Adelbert H. Henderson; Ransom C. b. March 28, 1893; Marvin George b. Aug. 12, 1895; Verna b. April 23, 1898; Herbert b. July 3, 1901. Family home, Clifton.
Member of seventies; missionary to southern states 1888-90; ward teacher; Sunday school teacher; assistant Sunday school superintendent 1886-7; counselor Y. M. M. I. A. Farmer.

VAN ORDEN, CHARLES L (son of Everett C. Van Orden and Elizabeth Harris). Born May 30, 1880, Lewiston, Utah.
Married Rose Tucker Nov. 8, 1900, Morgan, Utah (daughter of James Tucker and Betsy Lerwill of Morgan). She was born June 28, 1878. Their children: Sylvin L. b. Aug. 17, 1901; Betsy O. b. July 9, 1903; Leora M. b. March 13, 1908; Everett A. b. Aug. 25, 1910.
Farmer.

VAN ORDEN, PETER (son of William Van Orden and Julia Ann Haight, of New York state). Born Jan. 27, 1830, in Cayuga county, N. Y. Came to Utah in 1860.
Married Sarah E. McFerson Oct. 10, 1870, Salt Lake City (daughter of Dimon McFerson and Mary Ann Neas of Kaysville, Utah—pioneers, October, 1853, Isaac Allred company). She was born Oct. 20, 1846, died July 17, 1871, m. Eva Lucile Chiley; David H. b. Dec. 31, 1873, m. Martha Waddoups; Sarah Ann b. Feb. 5, 1876; Charlotte A. b. Sept. 29, 1878, m. Nephi N. Rogers; Miriam b. Dec. 4, 1880, m. Christopher F. Burton; Keturah b. March 23, 1883, died Nov. 7, 1887; Abner b. April 28, 1885.
Member Nauvoo Legion; worked on Nauvoo Temple; helped to build Winter Quarters; assisted in bringing immigrants to Utah 1856; first settler at Lewiston. Died Sept. 25, 1911.

VAN TASSELL, HENRY (son of John and Sarah Van Tassell). Born May 26, 1816, New York City. Came to Utah Oct. 5, 1862, Ansel P. Harmon company.
Married Emily L. Street, who was born Oct. 24, 1821, and came to Utah with husband. Their children: George H. b. Nov. 27, 1840, m. Sarah Frances Bean April 23, 1860; William B. Nov. 4, 1842, m. Amelia Bapp Sept. 1, 1861; James D. b. May 12, 1845, m. Jane E. Swift Nov. 14, 1867; Frances L. b. June 5, 1849, m. George E. Hill; Annie M. b. April 18, 1852, m. Barnabas L. Adams; Henrietta b. Sept. 29, 1857, m. David Dowding Dec. 8, 1872.

VAN WAGENEN, JOHN H. (son of Halma Van Wagenen and Miss Van Houten of Pompton Plains, N. J.). Born Sept. 1, 1811, Pompton Plains. Came to Utah 1848, oxteam company.
Married Eliza Smith at Pompton Plains (daughter of Mr. Smith of Newark, N. J., pioneer 1848, oxteam company). She was born in September, 1815, and came to Utah with husband. Their children: David, m. Julia Provost; Mary, m. Alfred Newell.
Married Clarissy Tappon at Pompton Plains (daughter of Mr. Tappon of Pompton Plains, pioneer 1848, oxteam company). She was born Nov. 24, 1824. Their children: Ephraim, m. Catherine Hamilton; John, m. Margarett Tossett; Ann, m. Joseph Bagley; Cyntha, m. Everett Bronson; Clara, m. David Provost; George, m. Eva Bunnell. Families resided Provo, Utah.
Member high priests quorum. Millwright; carpenter and wagonmaker. Died September, 1886.

VAN WAGENEN, DAVID (son of John H. Van Wagenen and Eliza Smith). Born July 18, 1836, at Pompton Plains, N. J. Came to Utah 1852, oxteam company.
Married Julia Provost March 25, 1857, Salt Lake City (daughter of Luke Provost and Julia Ann Wheeler of

---

PIONEERS AND PROMINENT MEN OF UTAH 1223

Newark, N. J., pioneers 1856, William B. Hodgett company). She was born March 2, 1834. Their children: Eliza b. Dec. 18, 1857, m. T. Eppson; David, Jr., b. Nov. 20, 1860, m. Avis Bronson; John b. Feb. 13, 1862, m. Eliza Smith; Wilford b. Dec 6, 1863, m Rachel Hofelt; Edwin b. Sept. 19, 1865, m. Alice Bronson; George b. March 5, 1869, m. Katie Stark; Emily b. Feb. 19, 1871, m. David Murdock; Alma b. Oct. 21, 1872, m. Bertie Gray; Lettie b. June 25, 1874, m. George Bronson; Minnie J. b. Sept. 16, 1878, m. John Benroyd. Family home Provo, Utah.
High priest; bishop of Midway 16 years. Selectman and justice of peace; postmaster 35 years. Merchant. Died Sept. 13, 1906.

VARLEY, WILLIAM (son of Thomas Varley and Marie Slater of Chesterfield, Eng.). Born June 11, 1837, Sheffield, Eng. Came to Utah September, 1861.
Married Mary Ellen McDuff Feb. 24, 1861, at Chesterfield (daughter of John McDuff and Ellen Hancock of England; former pioneer September, 1861, Captain Warren company). She was born April 5, 1840. Their children: William, Jr., b. Dec. 11, 1861, m. Harriet Parkin; John b. Feb. 21, 1864, m. Catherine Durbridge, m. Rillie Wingar; Charles Abraham b. May 10, 1866, m. Clara Mantle; Ada Alice b. July 30, 1868, died; Ellen b. June 3, 1871, m. Stephen W. Walker; Marrie b. May 26, 1873; Sarah Jane b. Dec. 3, 1875, died; Thomas b. Nov. 12, 1877, m. Charlotte Driggs; Franklin Malcolm b. Sept. 2, 1879, m. Mabel Edgar; Catherine b. Aug. 16, 1881, m. John Aston.
Assistant Sunday school superintendent South Bountiful ward; ward teacher. School trustee. Limeburner and quarryman. Died Nov. 23, 1908, Salt Lake City.

VARLEY, WILLIAM (son of William Varley and Mary Ellen McDuff). Born Dec. 11, 1861, Bountiful, Utah.
Married Harriet Parkin Oct. 16, 1886, Logan, Utah (daughter of William John Parkin and Eliza Foulds of Bountiful, Utah). She was born April 15, 1867, at Bountiful, Utah. Their children: Eliza Irene b. March 19, 1888, m. William A. Wright; Florence b. Sept. 30, 1889, m. Allen Duke; Sarah Ellen b. Dec. 18, 1890; Ethelene Foulds b. Sept. 17, 1892; Zipporah b. March 31, 1696; Vanza Grace b. March 19, 1899; Lowell Pratt b. July 22, 1903; Beulah b. Nov. 25, 1906. Family home Vineyard, Utah.
Sunday school superintendent; bishop's counselor; filled a mission in northwestern states 1903-04. Farmer and dairyman.

VARNEY, JACOB (son of William Varney and Charlotte Tyso of Horley, Oxfordshire, Eng.). Born Aug. 7, 1831, Horley. Came to Utah September, 1856, Knud Peterson company.
Married Caroline Lee in December, 1850, at Banbury, Eng. (daughter of Thomas Lee and Mary Burbage of Banbury, pioneers September, 1852, Thomas Howell company). She was born May 3, 1832. Their children: Sarah Amelia b. Sept. 7, 1852, and Isabelle b. Dec. 27, 1853, d. infants; Mary Jane b. Jan. 8, 1856; Caroline Elizabeth b. April 1, 1858, and Jacob William b. Jan. 22, 1861, all three died children; George Alma b. Jan. 4, 1863, m. Elizabeth Chipman; Ezra Thomas b. May 20, 1865, m. Cynthia Mullner; Harriet Amy b. Aug. 1867, d. child; James b. Oct. 16, 1869, m. Rose Darton; Charlotte Maud b. March 1871 and John Willard b. Oct. 1873, d. children.
Married Sarah (Conder) Shelley Oct. 9, 1906, Salt Lake City (daughter of James Boyer Shelley and Elizabeth Bray of Claverly, Shropshire, Eng., pioneers 1851, Alfred Cardon company). She was born July 14, 1841, in Shropshire. Families resided American Fork, Utah.
Member 44th quorum seventies. Black Hawk war veteran. Farmer.

VAUDREY, NEPHI (son of Thomas Vaudrey, born April 10, 1827, Macclesfield, and Hannah Bruff of Sandbach, both of Chestershire, Eng.). Born May 9, 1858, Sandbach. Came to Utah 1861.
Married Emily F. Crapo Feb. 23, 1887 (daughter of Jonathan C. Crapo and Emily F. Burnham, pioneers—married March 20, 1859, Draper, Utah). She was born Sept. 29, 1866. Their children: Corala Hannah b. Oct. 31, 1887, m. F. F. Oviatt Dec. 21, 1908; Anna b. July 24, 1889; Edna b. Jan. 9, 1891; Laura b. Nov. 23, 1892, m. Lionel Parker Dec. 14, 1910; Raymond b. May 25, 1897; Vilda b. March 18, 1901; Elden b. June 17, 1905. Family resided Draper, Utah, and Parker, Idaho.

VERNEY, JEREMIAH (son of Nicolas and Sarah Verney of Saco, Maine). Born May 16, 1820. Came to Utah 1852.
Married Lydia Phelps, Salt Lake City (daughter of William Wines Phelps and Sally Waterman), who was born March 15, 1835, in Clay county, Mo. Their children: James Leroy; Princetta, m. Joseph Elias Hutchins; Annie, m. William Thomas Curtis; Sarah Delilah, m. Edwin John Allen; Lydia, m. Philip Spry; Henry F., m. Kate Case. Laborer. Died 1869.

VERNON, FRANCIS. Born July 12, 1813, Derbyshire, Eng. Came to Utah 1868.
Married Elizabeth Cotrell Jan. 8, 1848, in Derbyshire (daughter of James Cotrell and Martha Taylor, pioneers

PIONEERS AND PROMINENT MEN OF UTAH

1868). She was born Sept. 22, 1827. Their children: Ann, m. William Davis; Martha, m. George Robinson; Mary, m. John Beard; Jane, m. Thomas Birch; Francis, Jr., m. Phinniah Stewart; James, m. Emma Marie Staker; Joseph, m. Sarah E. Malin; Ellen; Annice, d. Jan. 9, 1895. Family home Rockport, Summit Co., Utah.

VERNON, JAMES (son of Francis Vernon and Elizabeth Cotrell of Derbyshire, Eng.). Born April 18, 1862, Derbyshire. Came to Utah with parents.
Married Emma Marie Staker Jan. 1, 1886, Rockport, Utah (daughter of William Henry Staker and Sarah Marchant), who was born Dec. 21, 1864, and died Aug. 18, 1908. Their children: James Alvin b. Jan. 16, 1887; Francis b. Feb. 24, 1888, d. infant; Sarah Edna b. Oct. 17, 1889, m. Frank Melvin Judd; Earl b. June 4, 1891; Anice La Prelle b. Sept. 3, 1893; Edward b. Jan. 28, 1895; Nathaniel Lloyd b. Oct. 30, 1896; Richard Lynn b. May 21, 1899; Ray Staker b. Oct. 23, 1902; Paul b. April 10, 1905, d. infant; Lionel Joseph b. Nov. 25, 1907.
Married Mary Jane Hodgson Sept. 15, 1910, Salt Lake City (daughter of Henry Swift Hodgson and Annie Gardiner of Yorkshire, Eng.). She was born Sept. 6, 1874. Their children: Agnes Annie, d. infant; Dorothy b. Nov. 18, 1912.
President Y. M. M. I. A. of Rockport ward; bishop Rockport ward. School trustee. Director Wanship, Rockport and Hoytsville Live Stock Co. Lumberman; sheep and cattle raiser.

VERNON, JOSEPH VENOBLES (son of Thomas Vernon of Winsford, Chestershire, Eng.). Born Feb. 16, 1806, Winsford. Came to Utah Aug. 20, 1852, with President John Taylor, who was returning from the English mission with $12,500 worth of sugar-making machinery.
Married Margaret Senior in May, 1829, Liverpool, Eng. (daughter of Thomas Senior and Elizabeth Jackson of Northwich, Eng.). She was born Oct. 24, 1805. Their children: Christiana Venobles, m. John Fewson Smith; Thomas, died; Eliza Brerton, m. Henry Schutt; John and Edward Venobles, died; Emily Anne, m. John Jackson; Horatio Venobles. Family home Hull, Yorkshire, Eng.
Was a very active worker in the church. Left Utah for Honolulu, where he died.

VINCENT, DANIEL. Born 1803, Wiltshire, Eng. Came to Utah Sept. 9, 1852, Bryant Jolley oxteam company.
Married Elizabeth Mills at Cardiff, Wales, who was born in 1800. Their children: Charles, m. Catura ——; Harriet, m. Sidney Bailey; Thomas, m. Mary Latreel; Eliza and Edward, died; Daniel, Jr., m. Marian Park. Family home Provo, Utah.
High priest. Farmer. Died 1887.

VINCENT, DANIEL (son of Daniel Vincent and Elizabeth Mills). Born April 11, 1841, Cardiff, Glamorganshire, Wales. Came to Utah with parents.
Married Marian Park Feb. 22, 1867, Provo, Utah (daughter of John Park and Louisa Smith of Ontario, Canada, pioneers 1847, Edward Hunter company). She was born April 6, 1845. Their children: Charles Albert b. Oct. 6, 1867, and Louisa Elizabeth b. Sept. 26, 1868, died; Daniel Park b. Feb. 4, 1870, m. Mary Ann Birkin; Agnes Jean b. Jan. 9, 1872, m. Daniel R. Peay; Marian Kate b. Oct. 4, 1878, m. Chris Anderation; Harriet Allie b. Feb. 13, 1885, died. Family home Provo.
Elder; missionary to Arizona 1881-82; ward and block teacher. Veteran Black Hawk war; took part in Echo Canyon trouble. Farmer.

VINCENT, JAMES (son of William Vincent, born 1790, Salehouse, Norfolk, Eng., and Mary Arnup, born 1803, Rackheath, Eng.—married 1824). He was born March 7, 1829, Rackheath. Came to Utah Oct. 9, 1864, John M. Kay company.
Married Mary Holmes in 1850 (daughter of Charles Holmes and Elizabeth Alexander, married 1820, Crostwick, Norfolk, Eng.). She was born June 12, 1829, and came to Utah with husband. Their children: Charlotte b. Jan. 27, 1851, m. Stephen Shingleton June 27, 1874; Mary Ann b. Jan. 6, 1853; Sarah b. April 16, 1854; Emma b. May 21, 1856; Matilda b. July 7, 1858; Willard James b. March 20, 1864, m. Eliza Standley Nov. 24, 1886; Elizabeth Ellen b. Aug. 8, 1867, m. Joseph John Crump Nov. 12, 1890; William Charles b. July 14, 1870; Walter Henry b. July 13, 1873. Family home Spanish Fork, Utah.
Settled at Spanish Fork 1864. Veteran Indian war. Farmer.

VIRGIN, AMOS MOSES (son of George Thompson Virgin and Mary Ann Barker of Marston Mariton, Bedfordshire, Eng.). Born Jan. 23, 1854, Marston. Came to Utah Oct. 19, 1862, Horton D. Haight company.
Married Sarah F. Merkley Sept. 27, 1875, Salt Lake City (daughter of Christopher Merkley and Xarissa Fairbanks of Salt Lake City, pioneers 1851, independent company). She was born May 19, 1857, Salt Lake City. Their children: Sarah Frances b. July 22, 1876, m. James F. Shirley; Alice Xarissa b. March 31, 1879, m. Hans C. Hansen; Linda Rose b. Nov. 24, 1880, d. Aug. 6, 1882; Mary Ann b. Oct. 10, 1882, m. Walter B. Muir; George Amos b. Sept. 5, 1885, d. Aug.

19, 1903; Eugenie b March 8, 1889; Jessie b. Jan. 28, 1892, m. James Willis; Zalia Louise b. Nov. 20, 1894, m. Augustus M. Brown; Alicia Naomi b. Feb. 6, 1897; Heber Harold b. May 31, 1899. Family home Salem, Idaho.
High priest.

VORHEES, ELISHA. Parents lived in Pennsylvania. Born about 1786. Came to Utah 1851, Ezra T. Benson company.
Married Nancy Ann Leak of Pennsylvania, who was born Feb. 22, 1799, died Feb. 15, 1891, Manti, Utah. Came to Utah with husband. Their children: William, went to California, never heard from; Mary Ann, m. Warren S. Snow; Cornelius, died; Sabra, m. John Tuttle; Elmyra, m. Louis D. Bunce; Isaac, m. Eliza Lewis; Moroni, m. Susan Carter; Margaret, m. James Hardin Whitlock; Matilda, died; Arthur Perry, died; Sarah, m. William Beal; Adaline, m. William George Pettey. Family home Manti, Utah.
High priest. Farmer. Died Aug. 10, 1856.

W

WADDOUPS, THOMAS (son of Thomas Waddoups and Elizabeth Porter of Sowe, near Coventry, Warwickshire, Eng.). Born April 11, 1850. Came to Utah 1866, Horton D. Haight company.
Married Mary Call 1874 in Salt Lake City (daughter of Anson Call and Margaretta Clark of Bountiful, Utah). Their children: Thomas Anson, m. Myra Willey; William M., m. Olevia Sessions; Cyral, died; Ezra, m. Ethel Moss; Royal, m. Olive England; Mary, Bertha and Ida Elizabeth, died; Ralph; Omer; Mabel.
One of presidents 70th quorum seventies; missionary to England 1883-84; high priest. Farmer.

WADDOUPS, THOMAS ANSON (son of Thomas Waddoups and Mary Call). Born Dec. 24, 1875, Bountiful, Utah.
Married Myra Willey Feb. 20, 1901, Salt Lake City (daughter of Parley Pratt Willey and Sarah Jane Pace of Bountiful, Utah). She was born 1877. Their children: Clyde A. b. March 2, 1902; Bernice b. Sept. 4, 1903; Irma b. Sept. 4, 1904; Edna b. March 9, 1907.
Member 100th quorum seventies; missionary to Hawaiian Islands 1897-1900. President colony at Iosepa, Tooele Co., Utah, since March 1901. Manager Iosepa Agriculture and Stock Company.

WADE, MOSES. Born in Allegany county, N. Y. Came to Utah 1850, contingent Mormon Battalion, Company C.
Married Mary Bundy. Their children: Mary; Sarah Maria, m. James Monroe Elliott; Edward D., m. Belinda Hickenlooper; Minerva, m. William Hickman. Family home, Salt Lake City.
Married Mrs. Armstrong at Salt Lake City. Their child: Jane Wade, m. ———— Chaffon.
Died 1865, Salt Lake City.

WADE, EDWARD D. (son of Moses Wade and Mary Bundy). Born in Allegany county, N. Y.
Married Belinda Hickenlooper 1849, at Salt Lake City (daughter of William H. Hickenlooper and Jane Hawkins of Pennsylvania, former pioneer 1847). She was born March 4, 1830, in Pennsylvania. Their children: Edward W. b. Oct. 1850, m. Julia Ellis Dec. 1872; James M. b. Feb. 15, 1852, m. Isabelle Crandall Jan. 24, 1875; Charles F. b. Dec. 8, 1853, m. Sarah Bidwell Dec. 28, 1874; Sarah Jane b. 1855, m. Dennis Quinlan 1878; John A. b. 1857, m. Olive F. Ferrin 1875; Moses A. b. 1859, m. Sarah J. Lyster Dec. 1888; Joseph D. b. 1861, m. Maud Frodsham 1895; Andrew b. 1863, m. Lillie Rose Dec. 14, 1889; George b. 1865, m. Mary A. Barnett 1892; Clarence B. b. about 1867, m. Marian Driscoll 1893. Family home North Ogden, Utah.
Married Mary Ellen Page (daughter of Daniel and Mary E. Page). Their children: Daniel D.; Mary E.; Henry E.; Isaac; Minerva L.; Lucy; George; Ruth; Jeremiah D.
Member Mormon Battalion. Died 1880, Pleasant View, Utah.

WADE, JAMES MONROE (son of Edward D. Wade and Belinda Hickenlooper). Born Feb. 15, 1852, Salt Lake City.
Married Isabelle Crandall Jan. 24, 1875 (daughter of Myron Crandall and Mary Jane Hurst), who was born Feb. 11, 1858. Their children: Ida S. b. Jan. 23, 1877; Melbourne M. b. Dec. 14, 1878; Elsie M. b. Feb. 28, 1881, m. William Wayment Feb 5, 1908; Myron C. b. April 19, 1883; Albert F. b. April 17, 1885; Louie L. b. May 15, 1887; Lester A. b. July 8, 1889; Herbert C. b. Oct. 11, 1891; Hazel F. b. Aug. 5, 1893; Don C. b. Oct. 6, 1895; Ardelia Belinda b. Oct. 20, 1897; Vera Crandall b. Sept. 3, 1899; Earl Crandall b. April 9, 1901. Family home Pleasant View, Utah.
Married Ellen Stevenson Feb. 14, 1884, Salt Lake City (daughter of, Walter Stevenson and Jane Wickham), who was born May 17, 1861, in England. Their children: Iva b. May 16, 1885, m. Walter Wayment Oct. 1905; Louis James; Alfred.
Bishop's counselor Liberty ward 11 years; also bishop's counselor in Warren ward five years.

WADE, CHARLES F. (son of Edward D. Wade and Belinda Hickenlooper). Born Dec. 8, 1853, Salt Lake City.
Married Sarah Bidwell Dec. 28, 1874, Salt Lake City (daughter of Joseph Bidwell and Hannahette Mower), who was born May 23, 1859, North Ogden, Utah. Their children: Anna Elizabeth b. Dec. 1, 1875, d. infant; Charles Ezra b. Oct. 11, 1877, m. Minerva Allred; Hannahette b. March 11, 1880, m. Walter A. Lindsay; Josephine b. May 21, 1882, d. infant; Adella Belinda b. Nov. 9, 1885, d. infant; Alvin Franklin b. July 1, 1888; Cora Jane b. July 20, 1891, m. Edward Gunderson; Edith Amanda b. March 7, 1894; George b. July 21, 1896, d. infant.
Married Mary Gosling Oct. 11, 1904, who was born in England Oct. 22, 1867. Their children: Nellie Elizabeth b. Sept. 19, 1905; Mary Viola b. Dec. 28, 1906, d. infant; Sadie Lucille b. Feb. 12, 1910.
Bishop of Liberty ward.

WADE, CHARLES E. (son of Charles F. Wade and Sarah E. Bidwell). Born Oct. 11, 1877, North Ogden, Utah.
Married Minerva Allred Nov. 19, 1902, Salt Lake City (daughter of James Allred and Kate Jones of Lehi, Utah). She was born July 21, 1879. Their children: Kate b. Jan. 13, 1904; Morris Franklin b. Feb. 24, 1906; Hugh Allred b. May 19, 1903; James Wallace b. Oct. 31, 1910; Charles Forest b. Dec. 25, 1912. Family home Lehi, Utah.
Member 167th quorum seventies; missionary to southern states 1900-01; president Y. M. M. I. A. Liberty ward 1902; ward teacher; choir leader; one of seven presidents seventies North Weber stake; Sunday school teacher. Carpenter and contractor.

WADLEY, JOSEPH (son of Edward Wadley and Ann Reynolds of Newent, Gloucestershire, Eng.). Born Dec. 23, 1830, at Newent. Came to Utah fall 1853.
Married Hannah Dorney 1856, Pleasant Grove, Utah (daughter of John Dorney and Mary Davis; former died in England, latter pioneer 1856, handcart company). She was born Oct. 6, 1830. Their children: Joseph Daniel, m. Rozilla Jane Enniss; Hannah Mary Emily, m. Willard B. Enniss. Family home Pleasant Grove, Utah.
Married Emily Dee 1861 at Pleasant Grove, who was born Dec. 9, 1833, Westbury, Gloucestershire, Eng.
Missionary to England 1872, again in 1881; high priest. Crossed plains seven times and ocean five times in response to ecclesiastical calls. Farmer and fruitgrower. Died July 28, 1904, Linden, Utah.

WADLEY, WILLIAM (son of Edward Wadley and Ann Reynolds of Newent, Gloucestershire, Eng.). Born Oct. 8, 1825. Came to Utah Sept. 28, 1853, Vincent Shurtliff company.
Married Mary Chandler July, 1854, Salt Lake City (daughter of William Chandler of Brighton, Eng., pioneer October, 1853, Cyrus H. Wheelock company). She was born 1806. No children.
Married Isabell McKay April, 1860, Salt Lake City (daughter of William McKay and Ellen Oman of County Caithness, Scotland, pioneers 1859, James Brown company). She was born August, 1842. Their children: David Benjamin; Mary Ellen; William Washington, m. Margaret Ladel; Edward Franklin, m. Pearl Halliday; Isaac Joseph, m. Tarset West; Emily Agnes, m. Etrick Miller; Richard David, m. Ellen Olsen; John Emer, m. Martha Bullock; Daniel McKay, m. Nettie Wilson; Jeanett Isabell, m. Wilford Warnick; Helena and Thomas, died. Family resided Manila and Pleasant Grove, Utah.
Married Mary Byard 1869, Salt Lake City (daughter of John and Mary Byard of Newent, Gloucestershire, Eng.). Their children: Julia Ann, m. James Allen; Elizabeth, m. Arthur R. Winters; Solomon, died; Nephi, m. Jessie Robertson; John, died.
High priest; missionary to England 1889. Moved to Ogden 1853; pioneer to "Dixie" 1862; called by President Young; released and moved to Pleasant Grove 1872. Farmer and fruitgrower; one of the first to raise fruit in Ogden.

WADSWORTH, THOMAS SHORE (son of Jonathan Wadsworth, born 1808, and Ann Shore, born Jan. 11, 1813, both of Halifax, Eng.). He was born Oct. 6, 1838, Bradford, Yorkshire, Eng. Came to Utah Sept. 15, 1853, David Wilkins company.
Married Catherine Moore (daughter of Jacob Moore and Catherine Jarmon, pioneers October, 1864, Captain Ricks company). She was born Oct. 24, 1847. Their children: T. J. b. Oct. 21, 1865, m. Rose Taylor; Lenora b. Sept. 4, 1870, m. John A. Eddington; Martha Jane b. Dec. 18, 1875, m. Thomas Quinn; Edward Morris b. April 5, 1879, m. Lavina Robison; Kate b. April 9, 1881, m. Joseph G. Littlefield; Luty b. June 24, 1884, m. James C. Clark; Ann b. April 11, 1886, m. Charles Stuart; Primrose b. April 10, 1889, m. Earl C. Ball; Christmas b. Dec. 25 1890, m. Varsal Ballyntine.
Captain of artillery of Nauvoo Legion under General Chauncey W. West 1862; served in Echo Canyon war under Captain Switzler 1857-8. Sheriff of Morgan county in 1890; justice of peace for eight years in Morgan county; juvenile judge of Morgan county since 1907; county court bailiff since 1908.

WAGSTAFF, H. ALBERT (son of William Wagstaff and Jane E. Radford). Born Oct. 31, 1879.
Married Susanna Ethel Stillman June 10, 1908, Salt Lake City (daughter of Charles Stillman and Elizabeth Neff), who was born April 14, 1882, Mill Creek, Utah. Their children: Mary Leona b. June 7, 1909; Albert Stillman b. July 6, 1910; Elizabeth b. April 10, 1912.

WAGSTAFF, WILLIAM (son of Isaac Wagstaff and Mary Gillions of Caldicote, Bedfordshire, Eng.). Born July 13, 1809, at Caldicote. Came to Utah September, 1853, Claudius V. Spencer company.
Married Mary Rock July 13, 1833, in England (daughter of John and Hannah Rock of England). She was born May 18, 1815. Their children: Isaac, d. aged 17; James, d. aged 14; John, d. infant; Mary, d. aged 13. Family home Caldicote, Eng.
Married Mary Gilby November, 1839, at Caldicote (daughter of Joseph and Mary Gilby of Eaton, Eng.). She was born Dec. 31, 1816. Their children: Newman and Jacob, d. infants; Daniel, d. aged 4; Rachel, d. aged 2; Susannah, d. aged 1 year.
Married Martha Pack January, 1851, St. Louis, Mo., who was born May 6, 1808, and died June, 1851.
Married Martha Chitty 1853, Salt Lake City (her parents resided at Chertsey, Surrey, Eng.). Their child: Isaac W., d. infant.
Married Maria Stubbs May, 1854, Salt Lake City (daughter of Thomas Stubbs and Elizabeth Hall of Warwickshire, Eng.). She was born Jan. 31, 1825. Their children: Mary Rachel, m. Lorenzo S. Clark; Maroni W., m. Rebecca Ann Rance; Hyrum, m. Eliza Jane Fowler; Lucillia M., m. William B. Kelly; Nephi, m. Margaret J. Bates.
Married Matilda Emily Limb Jan. 20, 1857, Salt Lake City (daughter of William Limb and Sarah Wilkinson of Markpool, Derbyshire, Eng.). She was born Oct. 20, 1831. Their children: Willard R., d. aged 6; Martha Ellen, d. aged 4; Joseph A., m. Matilda Jane Staker; Alma W., m. Lucina Smoot, m. Esther Hunsaker; Matilda E., m. Nathan H. Staker; Susannah M., m. James McGee; Lorena, m. William S. Sorenson; Sally E., m. Leander N. Butler; Rachel, m. Ole H. Sonne. Family home Salt Lake City.
Married Elizabeth Wheeler May 25, 1866, Salt Lake City (daughter of Thomas Wheeler of Humblestone, Worcestershire, Eng.). She was born May 12, 1847. Their children: Emily E., m. John D. Crow; Maria, d. infant; Alexander, m. Annie M. Salzner; Frederick, m. Lucy J. Seaman, m. Mary Worley; Isabella, d. infant; William H., m. Anna W. Jonas; Abraham, d. infant; Leroy A., m. Margaret W. Stewart; Sarah S., m. Clarence Mabey. Family home, Salt Lake City.
Member Salt Lake quorum seventies; counselor to Bishop Weiler number of years; high priest. Nurseryman and seedsman. Died May 24, 1897.

WAITE, JOHN A. (son of John Waite and Jane Caldwell of Cincinnati, Greene county, Ind.). Born April 16, 1838, Cincinnati, Ind. Came to Utah Sept. 15, 1848, Brigham Young company.
Married Margret Barnes Oct. 26, 1861, Salt Lake Endowment House, Daniel H. Wells officiating (daughter of George Barnes and Jane Howard of Manchester, Eng., latter pioneer Nov. 30, 1856, Edward Martin "frozen" handcart company). She was born Oct. 9, 1840. Their children: John, m. Lasina Sessions; George, m. May Read; Margret, m. Henry Smedley; Mary Jane; William L., m. Edith Waddoups; Ira, m. Stella Moss. Family home Bountiful, Utah.
Member 25th quorum seventies; missionary to central states 1897-99; elder; high priest. Farmer.

WAKEFIELD, JOHN. Born in England. Came to Utah 1868, wagon train.
Married Caroline R. Wilson 1854, London, Eng., who was born September, 1828, and died on way to Utah. Their child: Caroline R., m. George Fitt.
Warehouse clerk and stenographer.

WALDRON, BENJAMIN. Born March 29, 1795, Bellbroughten, Eng. Came to Utah 1852.
Married Ann Crochett. Their child: Frederick b. Feb. 1821.
Married Mary A. Day. Their children: Jane b. Aug. 9, 1826; Martha L. b. Sept. 27, 1828; Byron b. Aug. 15, 1830.
Married Sally Laphain, who was born April 27, 1793. Their children: Thomas T. b. Oct. 5, 1834; Gillispie W. b. Aug. 15, 1836, m. Ann Dewhurst Sept. 13, 1857; Orson H. b. Oct. 1838.
Married Emeline Savage 1849. Their children: Levi Savage b. July 7, 1850, m. Davinah Elizabeth C. Roderick Jan. 11, 1875; Benjamin b. Aug. 18, 1853, m. Axie Cheeny June 7, 1908; Emeline Eliza b. Oct. 9, 1856, m. Charles Rowland Thomas Jan. 5, 1874; Sarah Ann b. Feb. 27, 1859.
Missionary to eastern states and Idaho. Shoemaker; farmer. Died Oct. 11, 1882, Uinta, Utah.

WALDRON, GILLISPIE WALTER (son of Benjamin Waldron and Sally Laphain). Born Aug. 15, 1836, at Castille, Wyoming county, N. Y. Came to Utah 1851, James Allred company.

1226 PIONEERS AND PROMINENT MEN OF UTAH

Married Ann Dewhurst Sept. 13, 1857 (daughter of James Dewhurst and Elizabeth Fielding—married 1834, Blackburn, Lancastershire, Eng., latter pioneer Oct. 24, 1854, William A. Empey company). She was born Sept. 20, 1840. Their children: Joseph Theodore b. Sept. 10, 1859, m. Maryette Rich Dec. 16, 1882; Ann Elizabeth b. Aug. 31, 1862, m. Charles R. Clark Nov. 24, 1886; Walter Gillispie b. Nov. 4, 1864, m. Elizabeth Chapin Sept. 28, 1887; James Benjamin b. Feb. 22, 1867, m. Phoebe Rose Oct. 24, 1900; Thomas Orson b. Oct. 4, 1871, m. Agnes Bowen June 1, 1904; Esther Lucina b. March 6, 1873; Harriet Eliza b. Sept. 15, 1874, m. Robert C. Harris Feb. 2, 1898; Mary Maria b. March 18, 1877, m. Joseph D. Harris May 1898; Levi Elias b. June 30, 1879, m. Helena Newberger May 23, 1900; Lucy Emeline b. Aug. 13, 1881, m. John Everton June 25, 1902; Hulda Lovisa (adopted) b. July 10, 1896. Family home Richville, Morgan Co., Utah.
President Richville branch 1873-75; first counselor to Bishop Dickson of Richville ward 1875-1907. School trustee 6 years. Road supervisor 4 years.

WALDRON, JOSEPH THEODORE (son of Gillispie Walter Waldron and Ann Dewhurst). Born Sept. 10, 1859, Centerville, Utah.
Married Maryette Rich Dec. 16, 1882, Salt Lake City (daughter of Thomas Rich and Henrietta Peck, pioneers Sept. 30, 1850, Joseph Young company). She was born Dec. 10, 1861, Richville, Utah. Their children: Mabel b. July 19, 1884, m. George Abbott Dec. 4, 1907; Joseph Rich b. Nov. 23, 1885; Bessie Ann b. Aug. 29, 1887; Josephine b. Aug. 22, 1891; Esther b. May 10, 1893; Ernest Theodore b. March 3, 1895; Alice Vera b. April 19, 1897; Walter Burdett b. June 22, 1899; Thomas Landon b. Nov. 1, 1901; Lewis Dewhurst b. July 4, 1909. Family home Morgan, Utah.
One of seven presidents 35th quorum seventies; missionary to New Zealand 1887-90. Assessor and collector; deputy sheriff; justice of peace 1902-04; city councilman of Morgan 5 years.

WALDRON, LEVI SAVAGE (son of Benjamin Waldron and Emeline Savage). Born July 7, 1850, Pottawattamie, Iowa. Came to Utah 1852 with parents.
Married Davinah Elizabeth C. Roderick Jan. 11, 1875, Salt Lake City (daughter of David Roderick and Hannah Spencer, who came to Utah 1869 by rail). She was born June 5, 1859, in Wales. Their children: Hannah Elizabeth b. Nov. 8, 1875, m. Alfred Atkinson Feb. 18, 1896; Levi Gillispie b. March 10, 1878, m. Eliza Thomas July 2, 1900; Emeline Janette b. Dec. 28, 1879, m. John H. Richard 1899; Mary Ann b. Feb. 28, 1882, m. David James Hughes 1901; David Roderick b. Feb. 7, 1884; Benjamin Haines b. June 5, 1886, m. Mervilla Gill Nov. 8, 1911; Charles Edward b. Jan. 7, 1891; William Spencer b. Dec. 24, 1891; Walter Andrew b. March 25, 1893; Thomas John b. Sept. 4, 1895; Nathaniel Acie b. Feb. 4, 1898; Ernest Savage b. March 19, 1900; Lewis Roderick b. July 19, 1904. Family resided in Idaho.
Oldest pioneer of Malad Valley, Idaho. Farmer and stockraiser.

WALDRON, LEVI GILLISPIE (son of Levi Savage Waldron and Davinah Elizabeth C. Roderick). Born March 10, 1878, Samaria, Idaho.
Married Eliza Thomas July 2, 1900, Samaria, who was born June 5, 1859, in Glamorganshire, Wales. Their children: David b. Jan. 2, 1902; Elizabeth b. Dec 17, 1903; Frederick b. Aug. 21, 1904; Levi b. April 19, 1906; John b. Nov. 6, 1907; Ruth b. Oct. 22, 1909; Edith b. Jan. 13, 1911. Family home Malad, Idaho.
Farmer and rancher.

WALKER, DAVID F. (son of Mathew Walker and Marcy Long of England). Born April 19, 1838, Yeadon, Yorkshire, Eng. Came to Utah Sept. 20, 1852.
Married Emeline Holmes May 18, 1859, Salt Lake City. Their children: Emeline, died; Sarah Ann, m. A. Paul; David F., Jr., m. Minnie Gilmer; Henry W., m. Grace Putman; Maud; Stella May, m. A. C. Ellis, Jr.
Married Althea Hunt Oct. 25, 1883, at New York. Their children: Althea M.; Clarence H.
Merchant.

WALKER, HENRY W. (son of David F. Walker and Emeline Holmes). Born Feb. 12, 1868, Salt Lake City.
Married Grace Putman June, 1890, in California (daughter of Jefferson Putman and Cornelia Norton of California). She was born July 11, 1872. Their children: Erminie b. Feb. 19, 1892; Ralph b. Dec. 25, 1893; Ethelene b. June 16, 1897; Natalie b. Nov. 11, 1900; Vern b. June 6, 1902; Carlton b. Dec. 11, 1905. Family home, Salt Lake City.
President and general manager Keith O'Brien Co. department store.

WALKER, HENRY (son of Thomas Walker of Upper Bullingham, Eng.). Born Dec. 9, 1806, at Upper Bullingham. Came to Utah Sept. 20, 1853, Claudius V. Spencer company.
Married Ann Preece (daughter of Thomas Preece, who died at Callow, Eng.). She was born 1799 and came to Utah with husband. Their children: Caroline, d. in England; Ann, m. Thomas A. Wheeler; Eliza, m. Thomas P. Smith; Sarah, m. Joseph Henry Gough; Mariah, m. William Burston; Elizabeth and Ellen, d. in England; Selina, m. John E. Hammond; John Henry b. Sept. 6, 1843, m. Mary Ann Phillips Aug. 28, 1864. Family home Union, Utah.
Early settled at Union, Utah. High priest. Shipbuilder; carpenter; cooper; farmer.

WALKER, JOHN HENRY (son of Henry Walker and Ann Preece). Born Sept. 6, 1843, Upper Bullingham, Eng.
Married Mary Ann Phillips Aug. 28, 1864, Union, Utah (daughter of Ishmael F. Phillips and Mary Goodsell, pioneers 1863, Edward Woolley company). She was born Sept. 16, 1840, West Hyde, Herefordshire, Eng. Their children: Selina Elizabeth b. June 9, 1865, d. 1867; Frederick William b. Sept. 14, 1866, m. Elizabeth Walker; John Henry b. March 9, 1868, m. Mary Alice Graham; Reuben Ishmael b. Jan. 11, 1870, m. Lillie Morton; Helen Udora b. Nov. 25, 1872, m. Francis James Proctor; Clara Elvina b. July 3, 1876, m. Charles Francis Cole; Henry b. July 5, 1879, m. Kindness Ann Gibson March 1, 1900; Mary Ann b. July 19, 1882, m. Willard Charles Burgon. Family home Union, Utah.
President Y. M. M. I. A. at Union; superintendent Sunday school; missionary to England 1895-97. Veteran Wahshakie Indian war 1862 in Capt. Lot Smith's company. Justice of peace at Union 1898; constable 1887-95.

WALKER, HENSON (son of Henson Walker and Matilda Arnold of Michigan). Born March 13, 1820, Manchester, N. Y. Came to Utah July 24, 1847, Brigham Young company.
Married Elizabeth Foutz April 24, 1845, Nauvoo, Ill. (daughter of Jacob Foutz and Margaret Mann of Pennsylvania, pioneers September, 1847). She was born Sept. 13, 1827. Their children: Henson Walker, m. Caroline Farmworth; Lewis Heber; Victorine, m. Joseph Eaton; Appollos Benjamin, m. Jane Holman; John Young, m. Christina Holman; Eveline, m. Christopher Iverson; Sanford, m. Nettie Shipley.
Married Margaret Foutz. Their child: Ezra.
Married Sophrona Clark at Pleasant Grove. Their children: Martha Jane, m. Austin S. Mayhew; Cordelia, m. Robert Thorne; Medora, died; Lewis, died.
Married Mary — at Pleasant Grove. Their children: William; Cassie, m. —— West; Delbert; Emma; Perry, died.
Families resided Pleasant Grove, Utah.
First bishop and first mayor Pleasant Grove. Veteran Indian war. Died Jan. 24, 1894.

WALKER, APPOLLOS BENJAMIN (son of Henson Walker and Elizabeth Foutz). Born Nov. 4, 1855, Pleasant Grove, Utah.
Married Jane Holman April 24, 1876, Salt Lake City (daughter of James Holman and Sarah Mathis, pioneers October, 1852, Charles C. Rich company). Their children: Benjamin Santaquin, Utah, June 13, 1858. Their children: Benjamin b. March 17, 1877, m. Ruth Keetch; James Henson; Idella Cobbley; Jennie, m. John V. Johnson; Margaret, m. Leicester West; Lawrence, m. Dahlia Radman; Jesse M., m. Fern Adamson; Robert, m. Mae Richards. Family home Pleasant Grove, Utah.
Member of 44th quorum seventies; missionary to Indiana 1892-93; served as a president for several years; high councilor. Member board of county commissioners and of town board several terms. Died Feb. 8, 1910.

WALKER, JAMES HENSON (son of Appollos Benjamin Walker and Jane Holman). Born Oct. 12, 1878, Pleasant Grove, Utah.
Married Idella Cobbley May 20, 1879, Pleasant Grove (daughter of Charles A. Cobbley and Emma Davis, same place). Their children: Charles B. b. July 5, 1897; Leo R. b. July 25, 1898; Zola b. Sept. 5, 1900; Roena b. Dec. 1, 1902; Thomas b. July 5, 1904; LeGrande b. June 7, 1906; Calvin; Edna; Myron; Jane. Family home Pleasant Grove, Utah.
Bishop of third ward Pleasant Grove; member of 44th quorum seventies; counselor to Bishop S. L. Swenson two years. Superintendent of Pleasant Grove school district nine years; principal Pleasant Grove high school.

WALKER, WALTER (son of John Walker and Elizabeth Coleman of Cheltenham, Eng.). Born Sept. 17, 1835, at Cheltenham. Came to Utah Sept. 20, 1864, Joseph S. Rawlins company.
Married Sophia Woodcock Sept. 14, 1856, at Cheltenham (daughter of Thomas Woodcock), who was born Jan. 6, 1836. Their children: John Thomas, m. Elizabeth Hill; Walter Emanuel, m. Rose C. Smith; Franklin Joseph, m. Louisa Earl; Horace Lional; Ernest George, m. Inez Hess; Fredrick Hyrum. Family resided Bloomington, Idaho, and Farmington, Utah.
Seventy; presided over branch of church at Flintshire, Wales, 1863-64. Shoemaker; merchant.

WALKER, FRANKLIN JOSEPH (son of Walter Walker and Sophia Woodcock). Born Feb. 14, 1862, Birmingham, Eng. Came to Utah 1863, Captain Ellsworth company.
Married Louisa Earl Jan. 3, 1884, Farmington, Utah (daughter of John Earl and Rheumina Wilson of Farmington). She was born Oct. 22, 1862. Their children: Rheumiton b. Jan. 30, 1887, m. Dewey Leroy Earl; Eva b. Oct. 6, 1889, m. Albert W. Burns; Edith b. Aug. 14, 1891; Louisa b. March 17, 1894; Rhoda b. March 13, 1896; Frank Earl b. Feb. 4, 1898; Leland Walter b. June 16, 1900; Milton Wilson b. June 10, 1902; Harold b. Oct. 6, 1904; Clifton b. Jan. 28, 1907. Family home Fielding, Utah.
Missionary to Nevada and California 1898-99; secretary

PIONEERS AND PROMINENT MEN OF UTAH 1227

and treasurer of Sunday school; secretary Y. M. M. I. A.; home missionary; ward teacher; choir leader; superintendent religion class; high councilor; president high priests quorum Bear River stake. School trustee; justice of peace 4 years. Shoemaker; carpenter; builder; farmer; merchant.

WALKER, WILLIAM HENRY (son of James Walker of Dogan county, Ky., and Mary Coon of Miami Co., Ohio). Born March 14, 1836, near Dubuque, Iowa. Came to Utah Sept. 9, 1852, Bryant Jolley company.
Married Lydia Ann Horn 1851, Fort Supply, Wyo. (daughter of Moses and Angeline Horn; former killed at Nauvoo, Ill., latter pioneer 1847). She was born July, 1835; came to Utah with mother. Their children: William Henry b. Nov. 22, 1858, m. Ella Woolstenhulme; Nancy Angeline b. March 28, 1860, d. 1867; Mary Ellen b. March 30, 1862, m. Edward Dillon; James Moses b. April 17, 1864, m. Tillie Anderson Oct. 30, 1893; Dora b. March 19, 1866, m. Willard F. Snyder, d. Feb. 1907; Sydney b. June 21, 1868, m. Lydia Moore; Lydia Ann Violate b. Nov. 5, 1870, m. William Graham Sept. 15, 1896, d. March 10, 1904; Josephine b. Sept. 4, 1872, d. July 14, 1879; Sarah b. Dec. 18, 1874, d. July 9, 1879; Rosa May b. Feb. 20, 1878, m. Harrison Sperry Nov. 1900.
Married Ada Louisa Phippen Aug. 1, 1870, Salt Lake City (daughter of Isaac Phippen and Ada Stewart—married Oct. 9, 1818, in Ohio, pioneers Oct. 3, 1852, Harmon Cutler company). She was born Sept. 2, 1842, Nauvoo, Ill. Their children: J. Morgan b. July 13, 1871, m. Sylena Giles June 5, 1894; Sirus Eugene b. Jan. 29, 1874, d. Nov. 27, 1874; Murry Kimball b. Nov. 19, 1875, d. July 7, 1879; Ada Eugenie b. April 10, 1878, d. Feb. 18, 1882; Henerstta Clare b. March 14, 1881, m. Heber H. Giles March 15, 1899; Victor Roy b. March 31, 1883, m. Alice Sweat Sept. 26, 1906. Families resided Heber, Utah.
Seventy; missionary to Fort Supply 1856. Drum major in Black Hawk war; captain of 50 in Echo Canyon trouble. Assisted in bringing immigrants to Utah 1856.

WALKER, VICTOR ROY (son of William Henry Walker and Ada Louisa Phippen). Born March 31, 1883, Elkhorn, Utah.
Married Alice Sweat Sept. 26, 1906, Salt Lake City (daughter of Lewis Sweat, born September, 1859, Provo, Utah, and Elizabeth Broadhead, born October, 1866, Heber, Utah). She was born Sept. 24, 1889, Center, Utah.
Seventy; assistant Sunday school superintendent 3d ward, Heber; Sunday school teacher.

WALL, JOSEPH L. (son of William Wall, born October, 1813, and Sarah Sanson, born Sept. 20, 1815, both of Horsley, Gloucester, Eng.). He was born July 2, 1838, at Worcester, Eng. Came to Utah Nov. 30, 1856, Edward Martin "frozen" handcart company.
Married Selina Stevens March 7, 1863 (daughter of John Stevens and Martha Stevens of England). She was born April 29, 1840. Their children: Joseph S. b. May 30, 1864, m. Ella Cowley Dec. 3, 1885; Selena Ann b. Oct. 6, 1865, m. Abraham Shaw, Jr., Nov. 28, 1883; Rose Etta b. March 30, 1867, m. William John b. July 13, 1868, m. Sena Folster Dec. 17, 1890; Francis Henry b. July 28, 1870, and Franklin b. Dec. 11, 1871, died; Sarah Prenpa b. Feb. 24, 1873, m. John Wilson March 20, 1895; Dora b. June 30, 1876, m. Lorenzo Christensen March 7, 1900. Family home Glenwood, Utah.
Built the first grist mill in Sevier county. Pioneer to Glenwood.

WALL, ROBERT WILLIAM WILSON (son of Robert Wall and Anna Sweetman, both of South Africa). Born April 15, 1842, in South Africa. Embarked from Port Elizabeth, South Africa, Feb. 28, 1861; crossed plains to Utah with Homer Duncan company, arriving Oct. 1, 1861.
Married Belinda J. Bair Oct. 29, 1866, Kaysville, Utah (daughter of John Bair and Lucinda Owen, pioneers February, 1850). She was born 1848, Garden Grove, Iowa. Their children: Augusta Bell b. Sept. 26, 1867, m. J. W. Ellis; Robert William b. Jan. 3, 1869, m. Anne Wiggill; Mary Ann b. Nov. 21, 1870; Belinda Jane b. Nov. 15, 1872; Thomas Holwell b. Aug. 30, 1874, m. Florence Jaques; Henry Dinnis b. April 29, 1878, m. Mary Ann Summers; Jennie Leona b. June 29, 1880; Owen Allen b. Aug. 12, 1882, m. Jannett Bruce; Charles Katin b. April 21, 1885, m. Elizabeth Jones; Besse Lavina b. March 1, 1889.
Settled in Kaysville in 1861. Stockraiser and farmer.

WALL, WILLIAM. JR. (son of William Wall of Horsley, Eng.). Came to Utah 1862, Thomas Ricks company.
Married Sarah Sampson, who was born Sept. 30, 1814, at Horsley and came to Utah 1862. Their children: David Laban, m. Celina Stevens; Emily, m. William Cowley; Fannie Mariah, m. Samuel Whitney; Dorcas, m. F. R. Cantwell; Celia, m. William Francom; Francis George, m. Mary Bench; Emron and Rose, died; Henrietta, m. Isaac K. Wright. Family home Glenwood, Utah.
Early Glenwood settler. Veteran Black Hawk Indian war. Mason and architect. Died at Venice, Utah

WALL, FRANCIS GEORGE (son of William Wall, Jr., and Sarah Sampson). Born May 3, 1846, Horsley, Eng. Came to Utah 1862 with father.
Married Mary Bench June 24, 1872, Salt Lake City (daughter of William Bench and Ann Longman of England, pioneers 1852). She was born Oct. 20, 1847, Southampton, Eng. Their children: Frank E. b. Sept. 24, 1873, m. Maggie May Jackson; Minnie Ann b. Oct. 20, 1875, m. Joseph Curtis Cowley; Henrietta b. July 10, 1878, m. George M. Haws; Jessie b. Oct. 15, 1880; George B. May 18, 1883, died; Ella b. Sept. 5, 1885; Clara b. April 28, 1887, died. Family resided Venice, Utah, and Colonia, Juarez, Mexico.
Married Susie E. Bench August, 1888, Logan, Utah (daughter of John L. Bench and Mariah Kirby of England, pioneers 1852). She was born Oct. 19, 1864, Manti, Utah. Their children: John Edward b. Feb. 13, 1890; Myrtle b. May 20, 1892, and Clyde b. July 12, 1894, died; Angus b. Dec. 5, 1895; May b. Feb. 6, 1897, and Mabel b. Feb. 6, 1897, died; George Milne b. Sept. 13, 1900; Leah b. Feb. 29, 1904; Dora b. Oct. 12, 1907. Family home Colonia, Juarez, Mexico.
High priest. Early settler at Glenwood, Utah; moved to Juarez, Mexico. Veteran Black Hawk Indian war. Merchant and farmer.

WALL, WILLIAM MADISON (son of Isaac and Nancy Wall). Born Sept. 30, 1821, Rockingham county, N. C. Came to Utah September, 1850, in company of which he was captain.
Married Nancy Haws. Their children: Mary, m. George Bean; Isabel, m. Jesse Fuller; William Madison, Jr., m. Martha Mecham; Eliza, m. Nathaniel Williams; Josephine, m. Joseph Rogers; Isaac, m. Annie Glenn; Juliette, m. William G. Nuttall; Bathsheba, m. Alma Kirby; George A., m. Hannah Maria Clark. Family resided Provo and Wallsburg, Utah.
Married Elizabeth Penrod, Salt Lake City (daughter of David Penrod and Temperance Keller of Illinois, pioneers 1850, oxteam company). She was born Sept. 9, 1836. Their children: Olive, m. James Davis; David, d. infant; Susan Malinda, m. Elijah Davis; William, d. infant; John, m. Susan Davis; Joseph P., m. Emily Workman; Temperance, m. William Jasper Boren, Jr., Sept. 6, 1883; Abraham, m. Valeria Rogers.
Married Emma Ford Jan. 23, 1858, at Salt Lake City (daughter of William Ford and Lucy Mayo of Chautauqua county, N. Y.). She was born Dec. 6, 1834. Their children: Emma Adelia, died; William Adelbert, m. Mary Ann Davis; Rosalie, m. William L. Davis; Charles F., m. Nettie Hardy; Martin Ford, died.
Married Susan Gurr (daughter of Enoch and Ruth Gurr of England). Their children: Elijah, d. infant; Susanna, m. A. J. B. Stewart; William Peter, m. Maud Nebeker; Louisa, m. James Twitchell.
Married Sarah Gurr (daughter of Enoch and Ruth Gurr). Their children: Ruth, m. William Steward; Alice, m. John Hone; William James, m. Lorana Boren. Families resided Wallsburg, Utah.
Bishop of Provo, Heber, and Wallsburg, Utah. Member legislature from Wasatch county. Farmer and stockraiser. Died Sept. 18, 1869, Provo, Utah.

WALL, WILLIAM MADISON, JR. (son of William Madison Wall and Nancy Haws). Born Oct. 19, 1847, in Iowa. Came to Utah with father.
Married Martha Jane Mecham Nov. 25, 1869, Provo, Utah (daughter of Lewis Mecham and Lydia Knight Wells of Garden Grove, Iowa). She was born Jan. 29, 1852. Their children: Eva Mabel b. Jan. 10, 1871, m. John Abplanalp; Nancy Isabel b. Oct. 28, 1872, m. David Meeks; Eliza Helen b. Oct. 31, 1874, m. George Dickson; Willmarth Lemoca b. Dec. 29, 1876, m. Hon Dole; William Madison b. Dec. 25, 1877, d. infant; Susan Vilate b. March 4, 1880, m. George Hislop; Lewis b. Oct. 28, 1882, m. Nancy O'Neil; Emma Elizabeth b. Oct. 30, 1883, m. Frank Mecham; Amasa Marion b. May 21, 1886; Mary Jane b. Nov. 1, 1887, m. George Powell; Nettie b. Oct. 17, 1890, m. Frank Teter; Isaac Wallace b. Oct. 10, 1892; Marjorie b. Jan. 8, 1894. Family home Vernal, Utah.
Veteran Black Hawk wars. Farmer and cattleman.

WALL, LEWIS (son of William Madison Wall, Jr., and Martha Jane Mecham). Born Oct. 28, 1882, Wallsburg, Utah.
Married Nancy O'Neil Aug. 7, 1905, Vernal, Utah (daughter of William Walter O'Neil and Susan Matilda Ross of Park City, Utah). She was born March 30, 1888. Their children: Lewis Lereari b. Feb. 4, 1906; Nancy Isabel b. May 11, 1908; Helen Fern b. Feb. 10, 1910; Anna Laura b. May 29, 1912. Family home Vernal, Utah.
Member of Mormon church. Farmer and cattleman.

WALLACE, GEORGE B. (son of John Wallace and Mary True of Epsom, Merrimac county, N. H.). Born Feb. 16, 1817, at Epsom. Came to Utah Sept. 29, 1847, George B. Wallace division of Abraham O. Smoot company.
Married Martha Davis Oct. 15, 1852, Salt Lake City (daughter of Edward Davis and Sarah Drabble of London, Eng., came to Utah Sept. 2, 1852, Abraham O. Smoot company). She was born Jan. 9, 1836. Their children: Martha M., m. Heber Perkins; Lucy D., m. James McIntyre; Mary E., m. James Garrett; George B., m. Mary J. Hodgett; Lois W., m. William Watson; William D., m. Faney Naylor; Alzono, m. Carolina Naylor; Zina, m. Edwin Little; Henry,

m. Susan Ellie; Arthur, m. Cora Martin; Maud, m. George Barratt. Family home, Salt Lake City.
High priest; president Salt Lake stake; counselor to Daniel Spencer. Builder and contractor; nurseryman. Died Jan. 31, 1900.

WALLACE, GEORGE B. (son of George B. Wallace and Martha Davis). Born July 24, 1853.
Married Frances Emily Folsom Oct. 20, 1873, Salt Lake City (daughter of William H. Folsom and Zerviah E. Clark, pioneers Oct. 3, 1860, Joseph W. Young company). She was born Sept. 29, 1853, Keokuk, Iowa. Their children: Harriet b. Sept. 7, 1874, m. Oscar A. Peterson; Edward b. Dec. 1, 1877, m. Lucy Cox; Emma b. July 26, 1880; Stuart b. May 12, 1884, m. Alice Douglas; George B. b. Feb. 17, 1887; Richard b. Sept. 25, 1889; Rhea b. July 9, 1892; Ruby b. May 30, 1895; Lewis b. July 30, 1899. Family home, Salt Lake City.

WALLACE, GEORGE Y. (son of George Y. Wallace, born 1776, Ackworth, N. H.). Born Oct. 27, 1844, Brandywine Mills, Ohio. Came to Utah 1868.
Married Inez C. Belden Jan. 9, 1868 (daughter of Seymour Belden and Rebecca Pfouts), who was born Oct. 16, 1847. Their children: Grace Dean b. Jan. 1870, m. George M. Tuttle 1899; George Y. b. June 1876, m. Jessie Alley 1908.
At the time of the incorporation of the Rocky Mountain Bell Telephone Company 1883, when it absorbed four other local companies, one in Wyoming, and one each in Ogden and Park City, Utah, Mr. Wallace was elected a member of the board of directors of that company and later became its president. Capitalist.

WALLACE, HENRY (son of John Wallace and Elizabeth Ashley of Frome, Somersetshire, Eng.). Born April 27, 1840, at Frome. Came to Utah Oct. 5, 1862, Ansel Harmon company.
Married Elen Harper Feb. 7, 1863, Salt Lake City (daughter of John Harper and Mary Hetherington of Newcastle, Eng.). She was born May 22, 1837. Their children: Henry John, m. Josephine Winchester; William Ross, m. Annie McChrystal; Howard Ashley, m. Margaret Groves Little; Rosetta Elizabeth, m. John Foster Bennett; George Hetherington, m. Anne Neve; Mary Elen; Walter Alexander, m. Lulu Penrose; Mabel Katherine, m. Frederick William Reynolds; Ashley Harper, m. Claribel Woods. Family home, Salt Lake City.
President 23d quorum seventies; bishop's counselor 7th ward, Salt Lake City; member high council Pioneers stake. School trustee; city councilman. Manager National Biscuit Co. Confectioner and baker 1865-75.

WALLACE, WILLIAM R. (son of Henry Wallace and Elen Harper). Born Dec. 10, 1865, Salt Lake City.
Married Annie McChrystal March 7, 1890, Salt Lake City (daughter of John McChrystal and Sarah Ann Hancock of Houghton, Mich., who came to Utah 1873). She was born Feb. 4, 1863. Their children: Helen b. Oct. 22, 1891, died; John M. b. Dec. 14, 1894; Henry A. b. Feb. 22, 1896; William R. b. Aug. 14, 1899; Alexander b. Sept. 23, 1900. Family home, Salt Lake City.
Manufacturer and dealer in paint, oil and glass. Bank director; capitalist. Chairman Democratic state central committee 1912. Mining.

WALLANTINSON, WALLANTINE (son of Wallantine Peterson of Banholm, Denmark). Born May 28, 1813, at Banholm. Came to Utah Oct. 4, 1854, Hans Peter Olsen company.
Married Engel Margret Kofoed 1836, who was born March, 1816, and came to Utah with husband. Their children: August b. Aug. 27, 1837, m. Mary Huston; Peter Christian Kofoed b. Oct. 21, 1841, m. Elizabeth Caldwell April 3, 1861; Charles b. May 1845, m. Sophia Loveland; daughter died of cholera, buried on banks of Mississippi river, near St. Louis, Mo.
Married Sophia Petersen 1859, Salt Lake City (daughter of James O. Petersen), who was born 1847. Their children: Lena; Anna; James; Celia.
Married Hannah ———. Their children: Nephi; Joseph; Antonious; Hyrum; Louis; Alice. Families resided Brigham City, Utah.
Officer and drillmaster in home guard militia. Among first to settle outside fort in Brigham City. Assisted financially in bringing immigrants to Utah; captain of ten wagons in Hans Peter Olsen company. Shoemaker; farmer. Died 1877.

WALLANTINSON (WALLANTINE) PETER CHRISTIAN KOFOED (son of Wallantine Wallantinson and Engel Margret Kofoed). Born Oct. 21, 1841, Banholm, Denmark. Came to Utah with parents.
Married Elizabeth Caldwell April 3, 1861, Brigham City, Utah (daughter of William Caldwell and Margret Ann McPhail, latter pioneer Nov. 9, 1856, James G. Willie handcart company). She was born May 8, 1844, in Scotland. Came to Utah with her mother, had her feet frozen, losing toes from one foot. Their children: Christian William b. Feb. 18, 1852, m. Elthura Oakey 1889; Charles Antonious b. March 15, 1884, m. Elizabeth Brown 1894; Margret Ann b. April 16, 1866, m. Rebert Kelsey 1886; Thomas Caldwell b. July 24, 1868, m. Mary Ellen Pain 1891; Robert Walles b. Oct. 21, 1871, m. Emily Davis 1893; Clara b. Dec.

4, 1874, m. Silvester Caldwell 1905; Elizabeth b. Dec. 2, 1880, m. Ezra Allred 1900; Mabel Agnes b. Nov. 18, 1884, m. John Welks 1905; Nathaniel Roy b. May 26, 1887.
Settled at Brigham City, Utah, 1854; moved to Paris, Idaho, 1864, where he built the first frame house with shingle roof. Director in Paris Co-operative Institution several years; one of organizers of Bear Lake State Bank and is a director and one of its auditing committee. Twice elected sheriff of Bear Lake county, 1878-80. Missionary to northern states two years, 1881-83. Elected county commissioner and chairman of board 1892; twice representative from Bear Lake county to legislature, 1896-98; temporary speaker house of representatives 1898. Author of bill equalizing property valuation. Prompt and fearless in his duty to public interests, honest and upright in his own affairs and a leader in the upbuilding of Idaho.

WALSH, JOSEPH C. (son of Cornelius J. Walsh of Torrington, Devonshire, Eng.). Born March 4, 1843, at Torrington. Came to Utah 1866, Patrick Moss company.
Married Mary S. Moss 1869, Salt Lake Endowment House (daughter of Patrick Moss of Decatur Co., Iowa, pioneer 1849). She was born 1855. Their children: Lulu and Myrtle, d. infants; Lavina, m. John Nash; Amelia, m. William Shepherd; Joseph C., Jr., b. Sept. 28, 1879, m. Margaret Miller May 16, 1900. Family home Kaysville, Utah.
Elder. Market gardener and fruitgrower.

WALSH, JOSEPH C., JR. (son of Joseph C. Walsh and Mary S. Moss). Born Sept. 28, 1879, Kaysville, Utah.
Married Margaret Miller May 16, 1900, Salt Lake City (daughter of Ernest Miller and Frances Barriswill of Bestin, Germany, who came to Utah 1885). She was born Feb. 3, 1881. Family home Holliday ward, Salt Lake City.
Musician and music teacher.

WANGSGAARD, CHRISTEN (son of Christen Wangsgaard and Dorthea Jensen, former of Snedsted, Denmark). Born Feb. 4, 1820, at Hvidbjerg, Denmark. Came to Utah Sept. 29, 1866, Peter Nebeker company.
Married Kirstine Petersen 1846 (daughter of Peter Skrivers and Kirstine Krabe), who was born May 24, 1824, and came to Utah with husband. Their children: Peter b. Jan. 21, 1847, m. Karen Jensen Aug. 9, 1866; Dorthea b. April 19, 1848, m. Niels Knudsen April 1867; Mads b. Nov. 8, 1849, m. Kirstine Christensen May 9, 1876; Christen C. b. April 26, 1851, m. Anna Anderson Oct. 23, 1876; Jens b. March 23, 1855, m. Bergite Johansen May 24, 1875; Peter Skaarup b. Aug. 25, 1858, m. Kirstine Emmersen June 1880; Kirstine b. May 21, 1860, m. Joseph Harrop 1883; Dusine b. May 31, 1863, m. Edgar Staples July 1888; Christine b. April 21, 1865, d. 1866; Christian b. Oct. 24, 1867, m. Louisa E. Hall Dec. 25, 1891. Family home Huntsville, Utah.

WANGSGAARD, CHRISTEN C. (son of Christen Wangsgaard and Kirstine Petersen). Born April 28, 1851, at Snedsted, Denmark.
Married Anna Anderson Oct. 23, 1876, Salt Lake City (daughter of Gustaf Anderson and Mary C. Johansson), who was born Sept. 2, 1858, at Kinne Klefva, Sweden. Their children: Mary C. b. Aug. 15, 1877, m. C. Fred Schade June 20, 1900; Anna L. b. Feb. 29, 1880, m. C. H. Skidmore June 3, 1903; Christen W. b. Dec. 22, 1881, m. Lillie Jorgensen Feb. 21, 1912; Gustave Edwin b. March 6, 1884; David b. Dec. 16, 1886; Louis B. b. Oct. 26, 1888, m. Ione Maughan Dec. 20, 1912; Ernest b. March 3, 1891; Ruby Edna b. Nov. 25, 1895. Family home Huntsville, Utah.
School trustee 1894-1900; city councilman 1907-09; health officer 1901-13.

WARBURTON, JOHN. Born in Lancastershire, Eng. Came to Utah in 1856, handcart company.
His child by first wife: Edward, m. Alice Richens. Family resided in England.
Married Sarah Williams (Green) at Pleasant Grove, Utah. Their children: Lizzie Ann, m. Almon Drown; John, d. infant; James. m. Flo Foutz; Abram b. March 1, 1870, m. Annie Hay. Family home Pleasant Grove, Utah.
Watchmaker and farmer. Died at Pleasant Grove, Utah. Sarah Williams was the widow of a Mr. Green. The children of this marriage were: Mary, m. Hyrum Cooper; Lorenzo, d. aged 16; Sarah Jane, m. Hyrum Cooper. Family home Pleasant Grove, Utah.

WARBURTON, ABRAM (son of John Warburton and Sarah Williams). Born March 1, 1870, Pleasant Grove, Utah.
Married Annie Hay, Pleasant Grove, Utah (daughter of Robert Hay and Mary Haley of Glasgow, Scotland). She was born Sept. 18, 1872. Their children: LeRoy b. Dec. 11, 1893; Lola May b. Nov. 1, 1895; Stella Fern b. Jan. 6, 1900; Abram Floyd b. Sept. 5, 1903; Anna Laura b. July 11, 1908; Earl Lewain b. Dec. 3, 1911. Family home Vernal, Utah.
Carpenter and farmer.

WARBURTON, JOSEPH (son of James and Sarah Warburton of Lancaster, Eng.). Born Sept. 21, 1831, Radcliffe, Eng. Came to Utah September, 1860, Jesse Murphy company.
Married Emma Whatnough June 4, 1854, at Radcliffe

(daughter of William Whatnough and Ann Butterworth of Radcliffe). She was born April 9, 1834. Their children: Sarah Ann, m. Jasper Fletcher; Ellen, m. George Kinghorn; Joseph C., m. Rebecca Stay; Emma Maria, m. Thomas Powell; Mary Jane, m. Thomas B. Shannon; William H., d. infant; William H., m. Lizzie Golding; Joshua E., m. Molly Trump; Samuel E., d. infant; Samuel E., m. Maggie Miller, m. Nettie Burrow. Family home, Salt Lake City. Bishop 1st ward of Salt Lake City 48 years; patriarch. Brickmaker and merchant. Died March 18, 1911.

WARD, GEORGE P. (son of John Ward of Eye, Northamptonshire, Eng., and Ann Woods of North Lufnaham, Rutlandshire, Eng.). Born Jan. 1, 1828, at Newboro, Northamptonshire, Eng. Came to Utah Sept. 14, 1861, Ira Eldredge company.
Married Sarah Ann Plant March 28, 1849. Their children: Elizabeth Ann b. Jan. 7, 1850; Mary Ellen b. April 1, 1852; George V. b. Aug. 20, 1854; Sarah Ann b. Sept. 10, 1856. Family resided Wellsville and Hyrum, Utah, and Salem, Idaho.
Married Martha Monks July 21, 1860, Bolton, Lancastershire, Eng. (daughter of John and Alice Monks), who was born Sept. 14, 1839, at Bolton. Their children: Martha Ann M. b. Oct. 6, 1862, m. Erastus Jensen Nov. 25, 1880; John M. b. Aug. 20, 1864; Joseph M. b. June 26, 1891; Henry M. b. Aug. 26, 1867; Clements George M. b. Oct. 14, 1868, m. Alice Linsenmann July 29, 1901; William Albert M. b. Jan. 29, 1871, m. Cordellia Lutz April 14, 1897; Charles Heber M. b. Aug. 29, 1873, m. Mabel Knapp Jan. 19, 1899; Eliza M. b. Aug. 17, 1876, m. Harvey Roylance Nov. 15, 1893; Lucy Ann M. b. March 15, 1879, m. Ely Curtis Jan. 22, 1900; Ester May M. b. May 20, 1882. Family resided Wellsville and Hyrum, Utah, and Salem, Idaho.
Married Senie Neilson Aug. 18, 1866, who was born Sept. 25, 1846. Their children: Sarah b. Sept. 25, 1867; Lorenzo N. b. July 18, 1869, m. Luth R. Jones Dec. 2, 1891; Henry Alfred N. b. Jan. 8, 1872, m. Mary Ann Woods Dec. 16, 1909; Willard N. b. May 15, 1874, m. Ethel Jacobs Oct. 10, 1900; Mary Ann N. b. Sept. 16, 1876, m. William Aaron Judy Oct. 27, 1897; James M. b. Sept. 30, 1879; Minnie L. N. b. Oct. 29, 1882, m. Allan T. Pugmire March 23, 1903; Rosina N. b. Oct. 1, 1885; David C. N. b. Sept. 8, 1888. Family resided Wellsville and Hyrum, Utah, and Salem, Idaho.
Married Jane Ashworth March 30, 1874, who was born Oct. 4, 1853. Their children: Alice Jane A. b. Dec. 14, 1874, m. Heber Roylance Sept. 15, 1892; Edmund A. b. Jan. 10, 1877, m. Ida May Cherry Oct. 9, 1901; Hyrum Enos A. b. Sept. 13, 1879, m. Jennie Bennington Nov. 12, 1903; Martha Ellen A. b. Feb. 5, 1882, m. George Parritt May, 1901.
Elder; missionary in Great Britain 1853-60 and 1871-72; president teachers' quorum 1854; member 64th quorum seventies; member of the school of prophets; secretary quorum seventies. Moved from Hyrum to Randolph 1878; then to Midvale; finally settled at Meadowville, Idaho, 1883.

WARD, CLEMENTS GEORGE M. (son of George P. Ward and Martha Monks). Born Oct. 14, 1868, Hyrum, Cache Co., Utah.
Married Alice Linsenmann July 29, 1901, St. Anthony, Fremont Co., Idaho (daughter of Charles Linsenmann and Emma Boardman), who was born Dec. 22, 1883, St. Louis, Mo. Their children: Charles C. b. June 7, 1902; Melba Alice b. Jan. 6, 1906; Bernice b. Jan. 23, 1909.
Priest 1888; church detective 1887-90. Farmer and stockraiser.

WARD, GEORGE WELTON (son of John Ward and Susan Welton of Leiston, Suffolkshire, Eng.). Born Sept. 12, 1814, at Leiston. Came to Utah Oct. 9, 1852.
Married Ann Trulock Jan. 24, 1812, parish of St. George, Bloomsbury, Middlesex. Eng. (daughter of William and Elizabeth Trulock of London, Eng.). She was born May 13, 1816. Their children: William, m. Rachel Ann Cordon; George, m. Eunice Alice Nichols; Richard T., m. Lizzie Sabie; Alfred b. April 18, 1849, m. Mary Ellen Lowe Nov. 6, 1871; Moroni. m. Eliza Voss Nov. 18, 1872, m. Phoebe Mariah Zundle Sept. 25, 1884; John Joseph, m. Mary Ellenor Owens; Ann Elizabeth, m. John Lowe; Charles Robert, m. Margret Ellen Mason. Family home Willard, Utah.
Married Mary Hankinson in 1857, at Salt Lake City (daughter of James Hankinson and Ann Waich of Didsbury, Lancastershire, Eng.). She was born Jan. 12, 1840, and died March 1, 1882, Willard, Utah. Came to Utah Oct. 29, 1855, C. A. Harper company. Their children: Mary Ann, m. Robert Wake; David Henry, m. Cyntha Zundel; Sarah Ellen, d. Dec. 6, 1863; Joseph Welton, m. Julia Holland; James Albert, d. July 15, 1868; Eliza Jane, d. Aug. 27, 1869; Hyrum Hankinson, m. Maggie Wickle. Family home Willard, Utah.
High priest; counselor to Bishop A. Cordon of Willard, Utah, 1857-71; acting bishop of Willard ward 1871-77; ordained bishop Sept. 9, 1877, and continued until Aug. 18, 1882. Selectman of Box Elder county 1857-82; Estray poundkeeper 1864-65; mayor of Willard City 1870-82. Served in Echo Canyon war 1857-58. Farmer and stockraiser. Died Aug. 18, 1882, Willard, Utah.

WARD, ALFRED (son of George W. Ward and Ann Trulock). Born April 18, 1849, Southampton, Hampshire, Eng. Came to Utah Oct. 9, 1852.
Married Mary Ellen Lowe Nov. 6, 1871, Salt Lake City (daughter of John Lowe and Mary Wilgoose of Wigan,

PIONEERS AND PROMINENT MEN OF UTAH 1229

Eng., pioneers 1853, Cyrus H. Wheelock company). She was born Feb. 11, 1855. Their children: John Alfred b. Sept. 11, 1872, m. Marian Dalton Sept. 14, 1898; Jarvis Welton b. Nov. 10, 1873, d. Nov. 10, 1873; May Ann b. Sept. 10, 1874, d. Sept. 10, 1874; Martha Armeda b. Aug. 19, 1875; James b. March 8, 1878, d. March 9, 1878; Alice Trulock b. March 15, 1879, m. Robert H. Morgan June 25, 1902; Elmer Henry b. Feb. 15, 1881, d. April 13, 1881; George Eli b. Feb. 18, 1882, d. June 16, 1883; Sarah Ellen b. March 26, 1884, m. A. M. Benedict March 23, 1908; Ida Irene b. Feb. 2, 1887, m. Henry B. Baird Dec. 14, 1907; David Charles b. Feb. 1, 1889; Ethel Lavern b. Jan. 26, 1891; Vernon Leroy b. Nov. 11, 1894; Lester Lowe b. Oct. 4, 1897. Family home Willard, Utah.
Member 59th quorum seventies; president elders' quorum; ward teacher; high priest; missionary in Box Elder stake. Precinct justice of peace 1893-94 and 1899-1900; assessor 1905-06; city recorder 1870-82; city councilman 1888-90; assessor and collector 1890-91; city justice of peace 1896-97. School teacher. Stockholder and director Willard Mercantile Co. Merchant; farmer and stockraiser.

WARD, JAMES. Born in 1793, in Staffordshire, Eng. Came to Utah Oct. 15, 1863, Samuel D. White company.
Married Elizabeth Taylor, who was born April 18, 1805, and came to Utah with husband. Their child: Edwin J., m. Mary Alice Backhouse. Family home Pleasant Grove, Utah.
High priest. Brickmaker. Died in 1866, at Pleasant Grove.

WARD, EDWIN J. (son of James Ward and Elizabeth Taylor). Born July 28, 1842, in Nottingham, Eng. Came to Utah Oct. 17, 1862, W. S. Godbe freight train.
Married Alice Backhouse Feb. 11, 1864, Pleasant Grove, Utah (daughter of James Backhouse and Jane Williams of Lancastershire, Eng., pioneers September, 1861, Horace S. Eldredge company). She was born March 14, 1848. Their children: Edwin James b. Nov. 14, 1865, died; Charles Henry b. May 27, 1867, m. Martha Brereton; Joseph Orson b. May 2, 1869, m. Mary Boardman; Mary Ellen b. April 12, 1871, m. Hyrum L. Clark; Willard B. b. March 11, 1873, m. Noama Beck; Eliza Jane b. March 31, 1875, m. William O. Ramshaw; Alice b. March 26, 1877, m. Claudius Flemming; Edith b. Feb. 12, 1879, died; Eva b. March 4, 1881, m. Thomas Harry Heal; John Franklin b. Dec. 20, 1884, m. Bessie McEwan; Cora b. Jan. 21, 1886, m. William Frisby; Grace b. March 14, 1889. Family home Pleasant Grove, Utah.
Special elder; missionary to England 1909. Settled at Pleasant Grove 1862, moved to Provo 1889. City councilman at Provo; judge of elections; registration officer. Carpenter and builder. Member E. G. Ward & Sons Lumber Company.

WARD, JAMES (son of William Ward and Sarah Brown). Born June 12, 1840, Pewsey, Wiltshire, Eng. Sailed from Liverpool in the clipper ship "Underwriter" April 23, 1861, with 623 converts, arriving at New York, May 21. Came to Utah Oct. 1, 1861, Charles William Penrose company. Milo Andrus and Homer Duncan having preceded this contingent of English immigrants, arriving Sept. 12 and 13, with Captains John Murdock and Joseph Horne, respectively.
Married Harriet Brown March 16, 1861, Wiltshire, Eng (daughter of John Brown and Sarah Mundy of West Lavington, Wiltshire, Eng., pioneers Oct. 10, 1863, William Bramwell company). She was born Oct. 5, 1838. Their children: Sarah Jane b. Dec. 20, 1861, m. Edmund R. Shaw; Elizabeth Ward b. July 13, 1863, m. Charles Storey; James H. b. Aug. 22, 1865, m. Minnie Love; William Ward b. Sept. 4, 1867, m. Celestia Bailey; John Ward b. Dec. 3, 1869, m. Kate Brown; Albert George b. Dec. 15, 1871, m. Charlott Woodfield; Cyrus b. Dec. 29, 1873, m. Juliet Wade; Joseph Edward b. Nov. 25, 1875, m. Mary E. Garner; Lorenzo b. Feb. 14, 1877, m. Mary E. Barker; Harriet E. b. April 13, 1880, m. Lyman Barker; Hyrum H. b. Oct. 6, 1882, d. Dec. 12, 1889. Family home North Ogden, Weber Co., Utah.
Bishop's counselor 13 years; bishop of North Ogden ward 16 years, and still in that position (1911). Helped to build the first transcontinental telegraph line through the west, 1861; helped to build the first river canal in Weber county in 1866.

WARD, JAMES H. (son of James Ward and Harriet Brown). Born Aug. 22, 1865, North Ogden, Weber Co., Utah.
Married Minnie Love 1890, Logan, Utah (daughter of Caton Love and Susan Rowley, who came to Utah 1878). Their child: Henry A. b. April 16, 1906. Family home Liberty, Utah.
Counselor to Bishop Joseph E. Ward in the Liberty ward.

WARD, WILLIAM (son of William Ward and Sarah Brown of England). Came to Utah Oct. 1, 1850, Stephen Markham company.
Married Sarah Latham of Spanish Fork, Utah, who also came to Utah with Stephen Markham company. Their children: Kate, m. Mr. Lloyd; Hannah, m. Thomas Ashby; Phoebe; Sarah, m. Thomas Draper; William.
Lived in England. Took part in early Indian troubles at Spanish Fork, Utah. Died there.

1230 PIONEERS AND PROMINENT MEN OF UTAH

WARDLE, GEORGE. Born at Leak, Staffordshire, Eng. Came to Utah July 24, 1847, Brigham Young company.
Married Fannie Ruston at Leak (parents lived at that place). Their children: Edwin Ruston, m. Louisa Thompson (Merkley); Heber George, m. Amanda Fausett; Fannie Lucretia, m. John Morton; Jedediah b. May 4, 1857, m. Elizabeth Abplanalp; Lucy Ann, m. John Bell; Lielie, d. aged 4. Family resided Salt Lake City, Provo, Midway, Glenwood and Vernal, Utah.
Married Lucy ———— at Salt Lake City. Their children: Alice and Ida, d. children; Alfonzo, m. Lottie Waite. Family home Provo, Utah.
Married Caroline Fisher at Salt Lake City. Their children: Eliza, m. William Tucker; Baby, d. infant; Cora, m. William Stone; Edith, m. Robert Hair, m. William Reed; Etta, m. Francis Ross; Hattie, m. Allie Pickup. Family home Vernal, Utah.
Seventy; chorister at Vernal. Taught Presidents Brigham Young and Heber C. Kimball how to dance. Veteran Walker and Black Hawk Indian wars. Music teacher; farmer; wheelwright. Died at Vernal, Utah.

WARDLE, JEDEDIAH (son of George Wardle and Fannie Rusten). Born May 4, 1857, Provo, Utah.
Married Elizabeth Abplanalp at Salt Lake City (daughter of Peter Abplanalp and Margaret Eckler of Switzerland, pioneers 1861, oxteam company, settled at Midway, Utah). She was born Aug. 27, 1859, at New York City. Their children: Alonzo, d. aged 22; Jedediah, m. Isabella Holfeltz; Elizabeth, m. Frank Davis; Margaret, m. Lorenzo Finn; Lillie, m. Joseph Tirrothy; Ezra, d. infant; Fannie Louis; Flora Bell; Bertha; Austin; Elsie Olive. Family home Roosevelt, Utah.
High priest; counselor to Bishop Peter Abplanalp, Vernal, Utah; ward teacher; president Y. M. M. I. A.; teacher of Sunday school theological class at Vernal; missionary to Birmingham, Eng., 1889-90. Farmer and stockraiser.

WARDLE, ISAAC JOHN (son of John Wardle and Mary Kinston, the former of Ravenstone, Eng., the latter of Snayson, Leicestershire, Eng.). Born June 14, 1835, at Ravenstone. Came to Utah Nov. 30, 1856, Edward Martin "frozen" handcart company.
Married Martha A. Egbert April 17, 1859 (daughter of Samuel Egbert and Maria Beckstead, pioneers 1849), who was born March 1, 1844, and came to Utah with parents. Their children: Isaac John b. Oct. 31, 1862, m. Alice Robinson; Samuel b. Feb. 4, 1864, d. March 26, 1864; Crella Marie b. Oct. 13, 1864, m. Zachariah Butterfield; Araminta b. April 25, 1868, m. Daniel Densely; Joseph Smith b. Sept. 13, 1870, m. Sabina Ann Beckstead; Hyrum Smith b. May 26, 1873, d. July 26, 1873; Silas D. b. July 16, 1875, m. Emeline Orgill; Junius F. b. June 9, 1879; Etney May b. May 15, 1882, m. John William Palmer; Edgar R. b. May 15, 1882, d. Sept. 3, 1882. Family home South Jordan, Utah.
Married Mary Ann Ashton, 1868, Salt Lake City (daughter of William Ashton, pioneer 1856, Edward Martin "frozen" handcart company). She was born at Oldham, Lancastershire, Eng. Their child: William H. b. April 5, 1869, m. Annie Sorenson.
Married Sophia Meyers July 26, 1869, Salt Lake City (daughter of Charles F. Meyers and Annie Jacobson, pioneers Oct. 1, 1862, Joseph Horne company). She was born Sept. 11, 1849, in Denmark. Their children: Charles M. b. Dec. 18, 1870, m. Harriet Rhodehouse; Hannah M. b. March 13, 1873, m. Robert N. Holt; Atheamer M. b. Sept. 3, 1881, m. Rosa Powell; Wilford Woodruff b. Oct. 6, 1883, d. Aug. 7, 1887.
Took an active part in the Echo Canyon trouble. Missionary to England 1879; superintendent South Jordan Sunday school 1879-97; home missionary; ward teacher; high priest. Moved from South Jordan, Utah, to Parker, Idaho, 1900.

WARDLE, WILLIAM H. (son of Isaac J. Wardle and Mary Ann Ashton). Born April 5, 1869, South Jordan, Utah.
Married Annie Sorenson Aug. 27, 1890, Logan, Utah (daughter of Jens and Ane Sorenson of Murray, Utah, who came to Utah August, 1869, Jens Johnson company). She was born Feb. 19, 1871. Their children: James Wilford b. Nov. 2, 1891; William Leroy b. Jan. 13, 1894; Mary Ann b. March 14, 1896; Leo Isaac b. Dec. 17, 1897; Vernal Haston b. Jan. 26, 1900; Delilah Sarah b. Jan. 10, 1902; Reed Smoot b. Sept. 2, 1904; Elbirdie Christina b. Oct. 18, 1906; Norval Junius b. March 21, 1909; Norman Andrew b. March 18, 1912. Family home Victor, Idaho.
Sunday school teacher South Jordan stake eight years; member of board of Y. M. M. I. A. Teton stake two years. District assessor of Salt Lake county, Utah; member school board five years. Rancher and sheepraiser.

WARDLEIGH, HENRY C. (son of James H. Wardleigh and Elizabeth Hanserd). Born Oct. 31, 1843, Frampton, Eng. Came to Utah July, 1860, William Camp company.
Married Elizabeth C. Whitaker Aug. 23, 1864, Willard, Box Elder Co., Utah (daughter of James W. Whitaker and Nancy Woodland of Willard, pioneers 1851), who was born May 24, 1849. Their children: James Henry b. Nov. 15, 1869; William Clarence b. April 2, 1871; Reed Hanserd b. March 24, 1872; Lillie Elizabeth b. Oct. 11, 1873; Daisy Ellen b. June 9, 1875; Porter Anderson b. April 14, 1878;

Leroy Whitaker b. Aug. 28 1879; Robert McLaren b. Aug. 7, 1881; Foster Ellsworth b. Jan. 22, 1883; Otis Ransford b. Jan. 14, 1885; Claude Ernest b. June 17, 1887. Family home Ogden, Utah.
Justice of peace 17 years. Member city council two terms. Dealer in musical merchandise. School teacher.

WARDROP, JOHN. Born in Glasgow, Scotland. Came to Utah Sept. 10, 1852, Bryant Jolley company.
Married Lucy McIntosh in Glasgow. Their children: Mary, m. Levi Abrahams, m. William Fotherington; Emily, died; Lucy, m. Abraham Reister Wright; Isabell, m. Josiah Rogerson; James, m. Amelia Woolley; John, m. Ella Rumell; Abraham, m. Mary Ann Chevrill.
Carpenter. Died at family home, Salt Lake City.

WAREHAM, JAMES (son of Philip and Elizabeth Wareham of Bradford county, Pa.). Born July 2, 1813, in Bradford county. Came to Utah October, 1852, William Wood company.
Married Harriet Adams Aug. 13, 1835, West Milton, Montgomery Co., Ohio (daughter of Edmund and Rachel Adams of that place). She was born May 22, 1818, in Montgomery Co., Ohio, and died Sept. 1, 1867, Manti, Utah. Their children: Philip Edmund b. Feb. 28, 1837, d. July 17, 1839; Mary Elizabeth b. June 9, 1838, d. Aug. 3, 1842; Susan Caroline b. Jan. 13, 1842, d. May 3, 1844; Seth b. March 30, 1845, m. Margaret Ann Shaw. Family home Manti, Utah.
Married Rebecca Attwood Feb. 20, 1868, Salt Lake City. Bishop of Glenwood; missionary to Ohio and Pennsylvania 1860-62; member high council; counselor to President Chapman, Manti, Utah. Assisted in bringing immigrants to Utah 1863; captain of independent company 1862. Farmer; wool-carder and spinner. Died June 21, 1898.

WAREHAM, SETH (son of James Wareham and Harriet Adams). Born March 30, 1845; came to Utah with father.
Married Margaret Ann Shaw April 15, 1872, Manti, Utah (daughter of Abraham Shaw and Jane Lawrenson of Glenwood, Utah), who was born May 4, 1858. Their children: James Edmund b. Oct. 11, 1873; George Abraham b. Sept. 28, 1875; Harriet b. June 20, 1878, m. George Henry Reid; Clair b. Feb. 2, 1881, m. Rachel Burgess; Lester b. May 27, 1883, m. Hazel Swasey; Victor Adams b. Sept. 1, 1885; Hartley Orlando b. April 18, 1888, m. Lacorn Wrigley; Jane b. Sept. 2, 1890, m. Rosco Pettey; Orson b. April 27, 1893, d. Aug. 10, 1895. Family home Ferron, Utah.
Settled at Manti 1854, moved to Glenwood 1864, returning to Manti 1867; again moved to Glenwood 1870, and then to Manti 1875; settled at Ferron 1879. Indian war veteran; took active part in protecting settlers from Indians in early days.

WAREHAM, JAMES EDMUND (son of Seth Wareham and Margaret Ann Shaw). Born Oct. 11, 1873, Glenwood, Utah.

WARNER, JOHN E. Born November, 1817. Came to Utah Sept. 24, 1848, Heber C. Kimball company.
Married Eunice B. Billings April 4, 1849, Salt Lake City, Utah (daughter of Titus Billings and Diantha Morley of Manti, Utah, pioneers 1848, Heber C. Kimball company). She was born Jan. 3, 1830, in Cuyahoga Co., Ohio. Their children: Eunice and Diantha, died; John Adelbert, m. Emily M. Potter; Samuel D., m. Lucinda Pierce. Family resided Manti and Provo, Utah.
Seventy. Walker Indian war veteran. Carpenter; millwright; miller. Died 1853, Manti Canyon, Utah.

WARNER, JOHN ADELBERT (son of John E. Warner and Eunice B. Billings). Born Oct. 24, 1852, Manti, Utah.
Married Emily M. Potter Feb. 16, 1874, Salt Lake City, Utah (daughter of Isaac S. Potter and Aseneth Lawrence of Springville, Utah), who was born Nov. 19, 1855. Their children: Leo A. b. Dec. 7, 1874, m. Lizzie McKinley; Earl Ray b. Aug. 7, 1877, d. March 30, 1880; Ray b. Dec. 24, 1887, d. July 2, 1910; Eva b. March 1, 1891, d. April 5, 1901. Family home Provo, Utah.
Elder. Superintendent West Union Canal, Provo, Utah, for 15 years. Farmer and fruitgrower.

WARNER, ORANGE (son of Orange Warner and Julia Brezee of Syracuse, N. Y.). Born June, 1815, at Syracuse. Came to Utah September, 1851, Luman Shurtliff company.
Married Lovina Robison (daughter of Joseph William Robison). Only child: Byron, m. Ann S. Tyler.
Married Delilah Robison. Their children: Holstein, m. Ann Dewsnup; Dorus, m. Cordelia Webb; Mortimer, m. Christine Brown; Cornelia, m. Joseph Prisbrey; Orange H., m. Lovina Stewart.
Married Mary E. Tyler. Their children: Cyrus A., m. Abazail Tyler; Mary Emily, m. Joseph F. Ray; Rhoda E., m. DeWitt Tyler; Jedediah M., m. Julia Russell; Orson J.; Levi M., m. Abigail Rowley; Eliza Ann, m. John Fitzgerald.
High priest. Farmer. Indian war veteran; helped build first wall around Fillmore to protect settlers against Indians.

WARNER, WILLIAM (son of William Warner and Margret Anderson of Glooson, Leicestershire, Eng.). Came to Utah Nov. 1, 1855, Isaac Allred company.
Married Keziah Goodman Dec. 2, 1854, at sea, who was born July 16, 1826. Their children: William G. b. Aug. 14, 1856, m. Minnie A. Candland: Job b. May 11, 1858, m. Margret Ann Chappel; Heber b. Jan. 20, 1861, m. Jane Sprunt; Margret, m. Hyrum Williams.. Family home Ogden, Utah.
Pioneer. Died July 14, 1863.

WARNER, WILLIAM GOODMAN (son of William Warner and Keziah Goodman). Born Aug. 14, 1856, Ogden, Utah.
Married Minnie A. Candland May 11, 1879, Ogden, Utah (daughter of David Candland and Katherine Jost of Mount Pleasant, Utah), who was born Oct. 12, 1859. Their children: William David b. April 30, 1880, m. Anna Nelson; Jesemine Keziah b. March 3, 1882, m. Benjamin Fife; Cora Allena b. July 15, 1883, m. Thomas D. Perrier; Laura Alice b. July 25, 1885, died; Edwin Candland b. June 21, 1886, m. Louise Rollins; Ralph b. 1888, m. Katherine Freestone; Frank Candland b. Jan. 23, 1889, m. Hazel Williams; Harry Candland b. June 2, 1893; Homer Candland b. Dec. 11, 1896; Minnie Edna b. Sept. 25, 1900.

WARNICK, CHARLES PETER (son of Anders Peter Warnick and Anna Lena Anderson of Vestergotland, Sweden). Born April 5, 1850, near Skofde, Sweden. Came to Utah Oct. 22, 1866, Abner Lowry company.
Married Christina Marie Larson March 14, 1874, Salt Lake City, Utah (daughter of Lars C. Larson and Maren Bartleson of Pleasant Grove, Utah, pioneers Sept. 10, 1863, W. B. Preston company). She was born Nov. 15, 1855. Their children: Charles Louis, m. Angie Webb; Howard B., m. Maud May Gardner; Wilford W., m. Jeanett Wadley; Effie Christina; Cora Augusta, m. Lawrence Atwood; Adena Hanna, m. Helge Swensen; Adolphus Peter, m. Geneva West; Joseph T.; Reed Whitney; Merrill Newell.
High priest; missionary to Sweden 1880-1882; bishop Manilla ward; counselor Y. M. M. I. A. Member city council, Pleasant Grove, two terms. Helped build U. P. Railway through Echo and Weber canyons.

WARNICK, CHARLES LOUIS (son of Charles P Warnick and Christina Marie Larson). Born April 13, 1875, Pleasant Grove, Utah.
Married Angie Webb June 11, 1902, Salt Lake City (daughter of George Webb and Mary Ann Ward of Lehi, Utah, pioneers Nov. 2, 1864, Warren Snow company). She was born June 11, 1875. Their children: Louis Ward b. April 3, 1903, died; Blaine b. May 22, 1904; Angelyne Mary b. Jan. 4, 1908; Miriam b. July 30, 1910. Family home Idaho Falls, Idaho.
Senior president 146th quorum seventies 1909; missionary to Samoa 1897-01; superintendent of Bingham stake Sunday schools 1909. Representative to legislature of Idaho 1910-12.

WARNICK, HOWARD BENJAMIN (son of Charles P. Warnick and Christena Marie Larson). Born April 13, 1877, Pleasant Grove, Utah.
Married Maud May Gardner Sept. 18, 1901, Salt Lake City (daughter of Elias Harvey Gardner and Caroline Ada Jackman of Salem, Utah), who was born April 30, 1883. Their children: Howard G. b. June 30, 1902; Ruth May b. Jan. 27, 1905; Melva Vervene b. Aug. 29, 1908; David Owen b. Jan. 30, 1911.
Bishop Manila ward; Sunday school superintendent 1900-1907; member of presidency of Y. M. I. A.; home missionary. Farmer and stockraiser.

WARREN, WILLIAM J. (son of William Z. Warren and Mary Woods). Born March 11, 1830, Pigsbee, Mo. Came to Utah with Matthew Caldwell oxteam.
Married Sarah Jane Simmons, Spanish Fork (daughter of Levi and Harriet Simmons of Missouri, and Spanish Fork, Utah, pioneers with Matthew Caldwell oxteam). She was born July 8, 1840. Their children: Mary Jane, m. John Morrison; William Z., m. Mariah Powell; Samuel, d. aged 3; Joseph, d. aged 2; Franklin D., m. Ellen Hamilton; Lewis, m. Sarah Blaine; Parley P., m. Sarah Blaine; Sarah Jane, m. John Milburn; Deseret, m. James Rooney; Hubbard, m. Bertha Olson; Rawlins, d. aged 1. Family home, Spanish Fork.
Seventy; elder. Veteran Black Hawk Indian war. Merchant and farmer. Died Nov. 11, 1899, Argyle Creek, Utah.

WARREN, FRANKLIN D. (son of William J. Warren and Sarah Jane Simmons). Born June 25, 1864, Spanish Fork.
Married Ellen Hamilton Dec. 31, 1889, Price, Utah (daughter of David F. Hamilton and Martha Ellen Bennett of Springfield, Utah, pioneers 1867). She was born Sept. 4, 1873. Their children: Violet Ellen b. Oct. 24, 1890, m. Frank McElheny; Franklin b. Jan. 22, 1893, d. same day; Deseret b. Nov. 8, 1893, d. same day; Vernal b. Nov. 2, 1894; Sarah Jane b. July 7, 1897, d. July 24, 1897; Lewis Melvin b. Oct. 19, 1899; Ernest Lynn b. June 30, 1902; Mary Ruth b. Oct. 21, 1904, d. Aug. 5, 1908; Bernice and Berneal b. March 1, 1907; William Demont b. Aug. 20, 1909. Family resided Price and Spring Glen, Utah.
Deacon; ward teacher. Farmer, stockraiser and freighter.

PIONEERS AND PROMINENT MEN OF UTAH 1231

WARRICK, THOMAS (son of Blackman Warrick). Born Jan. 2, 1818, in Pike county, Ala. Came to Utah 1847, Abraham O. Smoot company.
Married Louisa Taylor April 4, 1841, who was born Oct. 31, 1823, in Barbour county, Ala., and came to Utah with husband. Their children: Calysta W. b. Feb. 15, 1843, m. R. John Strickland; Thomas b. Dec. 2, 1849, m. Mary Ann Taylor Feb. 1881; Veda b. November, 1906.
Upon arriving in Salt Lake City, he settled in South Cottonwood and engaged in farming. The following year, 1848, he went to California to work in the mines, where he died.

WARRICK, THOMAS, JR. (son of Thomas Warrick and Louisa Taylor). Born Dec. 2, 1849, South Cottonwood, Utah.
Married Mary Ann Taylor Feb. 3, 1881, Salt Lake City, Utah (daughter of James C. Taylor and Sarah M. Hyde, pioneers 1849), who was born 1860, Kaysville, Utah. Their children: Meda b. Nov. 3, 1906.
Seventy; missionary to southern states 1887-89; high priest. Farmer and stockman.

WARWOOD, JOHN (son of — Warwood and Mirah Harwood). Born in England. Came to Utah 1852, oxteam company.
Married Rachel Hunt 1852, in England (daughter of Elias Hunt of England), who was born Oct. 3, 1824, and came to Utah with husband. Their children: John, m. Eliza Taylor; Ellen, m. Zenos Whittaker; Rachel, died. Family home Nephi, Utah.
Railroad engineer. Died June, 1904.

WARWOOD, JOHN, JR. (son of John Warwood and Rachel Hunt). Born at Nephi, Utah.
Married Eliza Taylor. Their child: Myrtle, m. Andrew Hunter Scott.

WASDEN, THOMAS (son of William Wasden and Mary Ann Peniston, of England). Born June 29, 1821, in Loughton, Eng. Came to Utah Sept. 16, 1859, Edward Stephenson company.
Married Mary Coucorn 1841 (daughter of John Coucorn), who was born April 25, 1816. Came to Utah with husband. Their children: Alice Peniston b. Aug. 29, 1842, m. Jacob F. Hutchinson June 9, 1861; John B. b. May 12, 1844, m. Nancy R. Herring 1864; Frederick b. May 22, 1846, m. Anna M. Esklund Oct. 18, 1865; Ellen b. July 15, 1848, m. Theodore R. Brown Aug. 2, 1875; Willard b. July 12, 1851; Sarah Ann b. June 7, 1854; Mary b. June 7, 1856, m. Titus Christenson 1878; Thomas Nephi b. May 22, 1859; Eliza M. b. Oct. 13, 1861, m. Charles Weiser July 25, 1883. Family home Gunnison, Utah.
High priest; ward teacher; home missionary. Settled at Provo 1859; moved to Ephraim 1860, and later to Gunnison; assisted in bringing immigrants to Utah; took an active part in Black Hawk war; moved to Scipio 1868; returned to Gunnison 1881, where he died.

WASDEN, ORSON (son of Thomas Wasden and Mary Coucorn). Born Sept. 27, 1850, Aston, Yorkshire, Eng.
Married Annie M. Brown Aug. 2, 1875, Salt Lake City (daughter of Martin P. Brown and Annie Hansen, pioneers Eric Hogan company). She was born Jan. 22, 1857, Ephraim, Utah. Their children: Annie Arrilla b. Feb. 28, 1877, m. Charles Memmott Nov. 3, 1898; Mary Elizabeth b. May 8, 1879, m. David Evans Jan. 22, 1901; Ellen C. b. March 9, 1882; Orson Earl b. April 25, 1885, m. Mamie Bradfield Jan. 22, 1906; Elner b. April 2, 1887, m. Ethelyn Ivie Oct. 18, 1907. Family home Scipio, Utah.
Veteran Black Hawk Indian war; ward teacher; priest; justice of peace. Farmer and stockherder.

WASHBURN, ABRAHAM (son of Daniel Washburn of Mt. Pleasant, Westchester county, and Ann Wright of Bedford county, N. Y.). He was born March 17, 1805, Essing, N. Y. Came to Utah 1848, Captain Musser company.
Married Tamar Washburn March 16, 1824, Mt. Pleasant, Westchester county, N. Y. (daughter of Jesse Washburn and Susannah Tompkins of Mt. Pleasant). She was born July 4, 1805, died Oct. 10, 1882, Nephi, Utah. Their children: Daniel b. July 23, 1826, d. Dec. 6, 1837; Mary Ann b. Nov. 15, 1828, m. Edwin Whiting; Emma Jane b. July 28, 1830, m. Charles Morley Black March 13, 1851; Daniel A. b. Sept. 13, 1837, m. Ann Price; Sarah Elizabeth b. Aug. 16, 1839, d. 1841; John E. b. April 13, 1842, d. 1842; Susannah b. June 23, 1843, m. Thomas Bowles Jan. 27, 1859; Joseph Bates b. July 20, 1845, d. 1845; Artemisia Minerva b. June 17, 1847, m. George Potter May 5, 1864. Family resided New York, Nauvoo, Ill., and Winter Quarters, Neb.
Married Flora Clarinda Gleason February, 1849, Salt Lake City (daughter of Joel Gleason and Philena Williams of Tolland, Berkshire county, Mass.). She was born in Tolland Aug. 2, 1819. Their children: Almeda Mariah b. Nov. 22, 1849, m. Alphonso Winget; Louisa N. b. Sept. 29, 1851, m. William Morley Black; Hyrum Smith b. July 20, 1853, m. Caroline Christiansen; Philena b. April 6, 1855, m. Hyrum Forbush, m. W. A. Warnock; Parley Pratt b. July 25, 1857, m. Maria Gregeson; Lorena Eugenia b. Jan. 10, 1860, m. Bent Larsen; Orson Pratt b. Nov. 7, 1862, m. Zina Higgs and Mary Thueson. Family home Manti and Monroe, Utah.
Early settler in San Pete and Sevier counties. Patriarch;

1232   PIONEERS AND PROMINENT MEN OF UTAH

first Sunday school superintendent of Manti; first counsellor to Bishop Bates Noble at Winter Quarters, Neb. Veteran Indian war. Member first city council of Manti one term. Shoemaker; farmer. Died June 17, 1895.

WASHBURN, PARLEY PRATT (son of Abraham Washburn and Flora Clarinda Gleason). Born July 13, 1857, Manti, Utah.
Married Maria Gregson June 19, 1878, St. George, Utah (daughter of N. P. Gregson and Maria Smith of Denmark, pioneers 1863). She was born Oct. 12, 1856. Their children: Rosetta b. April 15, 1879, d. same day; Parley Franklin b. March 4, 1829, d. April 11, 1881; Oliver b. July 5, 1882; Peter A. M. Aug. 4, 1884, m. Eliza Lower; Mattie b. Feb. 7, 1886, d. Nov. 18, 1886; Anna M. b. Nov. 25, 1887; Jesse D. b. April 19, 1889; Anna b. Nov. 12, 1890; Eva b. Oct. 20, 1892, m. Carlos Anderson; Grace b. Nov 21, 1894; Irwin b. Feb. 7, 1895; Joel Washburn was last child born. Family home Monroe, Utah.
Elder. Member Monroe town council. Farmer, fruitgrower and stockraiser.

WATKINS, EDWARD JOHN (son of Richard Watkins, born July 24, 1792, Banwell, Somersetshire, Eng., and Ruth Hamlin, born November, 1792, Clevedon, Eng., the former of Wrington and latter of Clevedon, Somersetshire). He was born March 4, 1829, at Wrington. Came to Utah Oct. 3, 1863, Daniel McArthur company.
Married Elizabeth Lawrence Nov. 2, 1850 (daughter of William Lawrence and Hester Whitnell, married 1850, Bridgewater, Eng.). She was born April 6, 1832, and came to Utah with parents. Their children: Joseph Hyrum b. Aug. 13, 1851, m. Mary Ann Doxey and Mary Ann Ellis April 23, 1879; Hester Alice Alexia b. Sept. 12, 1565, m. James C. Thomas May 1, 1882; Franklin Richard b. March 18, 1868, m. Hannah E. Newman Oct. 1, 1890; Bessie Ada Ellena b. Sept. 12, 1871, m. Thomas Boxey, Jr., April 30, 1889. Family home Ogden, Utah.
Married Gertrude M. Boserup July 22, 1880, Logan. Utah (daughter of Christian Redile Boserup and Kristine Mogensdatter, married 1824, Thved, Denmark). She was born Nov. 14, 1828, Tillerup, Randers Amt. Denmark.
High priest. Boot and shoe business Twenty-fifth street, Salt Lake City, for 30 years. On this location, assisted by his son Joseph H., he built first two-story brick business block on that street, which was used as city postoffice.

WATKINS, JOSEPH HYRUM (son of Edward John Watkins and Elizabeth Lawrence). Born Aug. 13, 1851, Street, Somersetshire, Eng.
Married Mary Ann Doxey April 30, 1879, Salt Lake City (daughter of Thomas Doxey and Ann Elizabeth Hunt, pioneers Oct. 5, 1852, Appleton Harmon company). She was born Aug. 28, 1856, Ogden, Utah. Their children: Lilly May b. Feb. 17, 1880, died same day; Hyrum Lawrence b. Feb. 13, 1881, m. Mary Elizabeth Clark DeLouche June 2, 1902; Mary Elizabeth b. June 11, 1883, m. Marcus B. Farr April 17, 1912; Thomas Doxey b. Oct. 26, 1884, m. Mildred May Carter June 14, 1911; Ruby May b. Nov. 9 1886, m. Arthur Middleton Dec. 18, 1909; John Franklin b. Nov. 6, 1888; Joseph Hyrum b. Sept. 17, 1890; Mabel Rozelta b. Sept. 6, 1892; David Hunt b. Nov. 5, 1894, d. Dec. 9, 1894; Ellis Doxey b. Jan. 15, 1896, d. Oct. 13, 1908; Pearl Viola b. Dec. 5, 1897; Eva b. Jan. 25, 1900, d. same day; Jane b. Feb. 17, 1901, d. same day; Rollo Edward b. March 25, 1903. Family home Ogden, Utah.
High priest; teacher; superintendent Sunday school; ward teacher; ward clerk; missionary to Arizona November, 1879, to June, 1882. Assistant foreman and foreman of the fire department of Ogden; was honored by appointment as chief Feb. 21, 1879, but did not accept. Justice of peace, first precinct; city sanitary inspector.

WATKINS, HYRUM LAWRENCE (son of Joseph Hyrum Watkins and Mary Ann Doxey). Born Feb. 13, 1881, St. Johns, Apache county, Ariz.
Married Mary Elizabeth Clark DeLouche June 2, 1902, Ogden, Utah (daughter of Howard DeLouche, born Aug. 27, 1857, Martinsburg, Lewis county, N. Y., and Alfaretta Clark, born Nov. 28, 1858, Ogden, Utah). She was born April 16, 1880, St. George, Utah. Their children: Hyrum Lawrence b. April 15, 1903; Nina b. Nov. 14, 1904; Lorenzo Clark b. Jan. 14, 1908. Family home Ogden, Utah.

WATKINS, FRANKLIN RICHARD (son of Edward John Watkins and Elizabeth Lawrence). Born March 18, 1868, Ogden, Utah.
Married Hannah E. Newman Oct. 1, 1890, Logan. Utah (daughter of Henry James Newman and Maria Louise Penn of Ogden, Utah, pioneers November, 1856). She was born April 21, 1868. Their children: Franklin R. b. Aug. 28, 1891; Henry James b. May 3, 1892; Horace Edward b. July 9, 1895; Inez Louise b. May 9, 1900; Heber Lewis b. July 30, 1902; Alvin Eugene b. July 21, 1908; Josephine Annie b. June 22, 1911; Joseph Elbert b. June 23, 1911. Family home Ogden, Utah.
High priest; counselor 11th ward, Ogden, Utah. Merchant.

WATKINS, JOHN (son of Thomas Watkins of Rainham, Kent, Eng.). Born April 13, 1834, at Rainham. Came to Utah 1856, Martin Harris handcart company.
Married Margaret Akerst 1851, Sheer Nast on the Sea,

Kent. Eng. (daughter of Edward Akerst), who was born Sept 18, 1832). Their children: Elizabeth b. 1851, m. Charles Edward Ellen; John Thomas b. Oct. 29, 1854, m. May Clift; Edward b. Oct. 27, 1857, m. Margaretha Abplanalp; Samuel Richard, d. infant; Mary, m. William Andrew; Alfred, m. Lenora Lewis; Charles and Frederick, d. infants.
Married Harriett Steele 1859, Salt Lake City (daughter of John Steele and Maria Woods of Stafford, Eng.). She was born 1841, died March 10, 1884, Midway, Utah. Their children: Henry m. Jane Alder; Arthur, m. Della Gerber; Laura. m. John Clift; William, m. Mary Busby; Minnie Maria, m. John Martin; Frank b. Dec. 21, 1873, m. Isabell McKowen; Albert Ernest, m. Miss Harrison; Sylvanius. m. Daisy Dean; Archie; Eva; David James, Lorenzo John, and Harriet Amy, all d. infants. Family home Midway, Wasatch Co., Utah.
Bishop 17 years. Veteran Echo Canyon campaign and Indian wars. Early settler at Midway. Died Dec. 23, 1902.

WATKINS, EDWARD (son of John Watkins and Margaret Akerst). Born Oct. 27, 1857, Provo. Utah.
Married Margaretha Abplanalp Oct. 28, 1880, Salt Lake City (daughter of Peter Abplanalp and Margaretha Eggler, both of Midway, pioneers 1861). She was born April 4, 1859, in New York; came to Utah with parents. Their children: Edward b. Aug. 7, 1881, m. Clara Bell Stewart; John b. Nov. 22, 1882, m. Lenora Karren; Margaretha b. Aug. 18, 1884, m. Clarence J. Collett; William b. Sept. 1, 1886, m. Amanda Cobb; Pearl b. Sept. 5, 1888, m. Charles Jenkins; Lorenzo b. Aug. 1, 1890, m. Jennie Cobb; Charles b. Aug. 1, 1890, d. infant; Peter b. June 27, 1894, d. infant; Viola b. Nov. 25, 1896; Leona b. Aug. 31, 1899.
Missionary to England 1899-1901; high priest; ward and Sunday school teacher; counselor in Y. M. M. I. A. Moved to Ashley Valley 1885, to Vernal 1886. Farmer and stockraiser.

WATKINS, FRANK (son of John Watkins and Harriet Steele). Born Dec. 21, 1873, Midway, Utah.
Married Isabell McKowen March 10, 1897, at Vernal (daughter of Phillip McKowen and Mary Hughes of Vernal, who came to Utah 1884). She was born June 6, 1875. Their children: Phillip b. Dec. 26, 1897; Isabell b. Aug. 20, 1900; Duane b. Dec. 12, 1901; Gerald b. May 17, 1904; Orlin b. July 2, 1906; Burnell b. Dec. 2, 1908; Winona b. March 6, 1913. Family home Vernal, Utah.
Elder; ward teacher. Farmer; merchant; butcher.

WATKINS, ROBERT. Came to Utah 1852.
Married Mary Smallman. Their children: Rhoda, m. Ezekiel Price; Sarah Ann, m. John R. McDaniel; Mary Matilda, m. Ephraim Healey; Martha, m. John R. McDaniel; Joseph, m. Tiera Beck; James, m. Fannie Nielson.
High priest. Farmer. Died March, 1869, Alpine, Utah.

WATSON, ALEXANDER (son of Robert Watson and Mary Miller of Glasgow, Scotland). Born May, 1835, Glasgow.
Married Margarett Miller (daughter of Charles Miller and Mary Magowan of Rutherglen, Scotland), who was born May 18, 1836, and came to Utah with John Sharp company. Their children: Alexander, m. Elizabeth Linell; Mary Jane, Allan b. Dec. 22, 1862, m. Annie Shand; George Allan b. June 14, 1864, died; Margaret Jean b. Dec. 21, 1865, m. Alva N. Murdock; James Snarr; Margarett Ellen, m. Thomas Condey; Robert William, died; James David. m. Celia Golden; Sarah Elizabeth, died; John Robert; William Childs, died; Hugh; Agnes, m. Robert Booth. Family home 474 South 3d West, Salt Lake City.
Seventy; missionary to "Dixie" 1872-74. General contractor. Died March, 1901.

WATSON, ANDREW (son of James Watson and Janet Rumgay of Kirtle Bridge, Scotland). Born Oct. 13, 1832, at Kirtle Bridge. Came to Utah Nov. 9, 1856, James G. Willie handcart company.
Married Jean Allan Oct. 16, 1860, Provo, Utah (daughter of George Allen and Margaret Matheson of Arbroath, Scotland). She was born Aug. 29, 1830, d. March 21, 1882. Their children: Janet Watson b. July 30, 1861, died; Andrew Allan b. Dec. 22, 1862, m. Annie Shand; George Allan b. June 14, 1864, died; Margaret Jean b. July 5, 1867, died; Mary Jane Blo Watson (adopted) b. Aug. 4, 1861, m. John Harvey Allsad.
Married Maragaret Purvis January, 1881, Salt Lake City (daughter of George Purvis and Margaret Alexander of Aberdeen, Scotland), who was born March 5, 1832. They adopted one child: Isabell Watson b. May 11, 1879, m. John W. Anderson. Families resided at Provo, Utah.
Member of 45th quorum seventies; missionary to Scotland 1877-79; ordained high priest June 20, 1877; first counselor to Bishop John E. Booth. 4th ward, Provo; ordained a patriarch by Apostle Reed Smoot June 24, 1902. Stationary engineer and wool-carder. Died Sept. 24, 1908, Lethbridge, Canada.

WATSON, HIRAM ABIFF (son of Nathan Whitney Watson and Electa Phillips of Chicago, Ill.). Born Aug. 22, 1828, in New York. Came to Utah 1850, with company en route to California.
Married Rebecca Hendricks June 23, 1852, Salt Lake City (daughter of James Hendricks and Drusilla Dorris of Salt

Lake City). She was born Nov. 2, 1835. Their children: Hiram Abiff, Jr., m. Lovina Hyer. Family home, Salt Lake City.
Carpenter. Died May 2, 1908, Minneapolis, Minn.

WATSON, HIRAM ABIFF, JR. (son of Hiram Abiff Watson and Rebecca Hendricks). Born April 8, 1853, Salt Lake City.
Married Lovina Hyer May 11, 1874, Salt Lake City (daughter of Christian Hyer and Lovina Hogan of Richmond, Utah), who was born March 4, 1855. Their children: Hiram Abiff b. June 30, 1875; Lovina Rebecca b. Oct. 18, 1876; Harriet Caroline b. Oct. 15, 1878, m. John Morris; Electa b. Oct. 4, 1880, m. Robert A. Tempest; Zina b. Dec. 14, 1882; Elizabeth b. Aug. 8, 1884, m. Dennis Farnsworth; Ira b. March 31, 1887, m. Anna Edwards; Cyrus H. and Cyral A. (twins) b. Sept. 11, 1889; Irving b. April 5, 1894; Oliver b. Dec. 23, 1900. Family home La Grande, Ore.
Married Addie Jane Wildman Oct. 14, 1885, Logan, Utah (daughter of Edward Wildman and Jane Baxter, pioneers Sept. 2, 1868, Simpson M. Molen company). She was born Jan. 4, 1864. Their children: Glenn b. Jan. 11, 1886; Addie b. Nov. 2, 1888, m. Theodore Chambers, Jr.; Iniz b. March 19, 1890, m. Fred Lewis; Eniz b. March 19, 1890; Joseph b. June 8, 1893; Alfonzo b. July 23, 1895; Maggie b. Aug. 14, 1898. Family home Smithfield, Utah.

WATSON, JOSEPH M. (son of Robert Watson and Barbara Morcles of Northumberland, Eng.). He was born July 7, 1846, Byldon, Northumberland, Eng. Came to Utah 1857, Robert Neslen company.
Married Annie M. Thompson March 30, 1861, Salt Lake City (daughter of Edward Thompson and Marine Rutherford of Warkworth, Eng., pioneers 1863). She was born 1841. Their children: Joseph W. and Annie M., d. infants.
Married Annie M. Davis April 20, 1881, at Salt Lake City (daughter of Charles Davis and Elizabeth Morehouse, who came to Utah Nov. 12, 1876). She was born Nov. 8, 1843, Stockfort, Lancastershire, Eng. Families resided Salt Lake City.
City councilman for two terms. Assisted in building Fort Douglas. Contractor; builder. Died Dec. 14, 1885.

WATSON, ROBERT. Lanackshire, Scotland. Came to Utah 1850.
Married Mary Cowan. Their children: Agnes, m. Alexander Burt; Robert, m. Harriet Hatfield; James Cowan, m. Mary Condie; Mary, m. Mr. Austin; Alexander, died; Hugh, m. Sarah J. Williams; Jeanette, m. Peter S. Condie; John, m. Maria Litley; William R., m. Helen Ostler. Family home, Salt Lake City.
High priest. Contractor and first miner in Bingham canyon. Died January, 1882.

WATSON, HUGH (son of Robert Watson and Mary Cowan). Married Sarah J. Williams in Salt Lake City (daughter of Evan V. Williams and Sarah Jane Jeremy of Wales), who was born 1852. Their children: Hettie Ann. m. George Bowers; Hugh Cowan; Robert, d. aged 10; Sarah, d. aged 4; Mary, m. Christopher Covitt; Evan D.; Nugent W. Family home, Salt Lake City.
Married Mary H. Chapuis (daughter of Louis Chapuis and Johanna A. Bertoch, who was born Dec. 11, 1826, Piedmont, Italy, and came to Utah Oct. 24, 1854, William A. Empey company). She was born Jan. 2, 1862. Their children: Sarah J. b. Sept. 3, 1857, m. Gustave E. Johnson; Louis R. b. Feb. 5, 1890; Hugh W. b. Feb. 22, 1894; Alma C. b. June 14, 1896; M. Helene b. Sept. 5, 1899; John W. b. April 27, 1901, d. infant; Daniel B. b. Oct. 10, 1902; Elizabeth A. b. May 16, 1908.
Married Esther H. Davey, in Salt Lake City (daughter of Charles Davey and Louisa Maddox, of England, pioneers Sept. 16, 1859, Edward Stevenson company). She was born Aug. 1, 1864. Their children: Louisa M. b. June 17, 1889, m. George Kendall; Jessie T. b. Feb. 18, 1892; Robert H. b. Jan. 2, 1895; E. Katherine b. April 17, 1897; M. Norma b. Jan. 13, 1900; Elva H. b. June 4, 1903; Isabel F. b. Nov. 15, 1905. Families resided Salt Lake City.
Married Elizabeth A. Chapuis, in Salt Lake City (daughter of Louis Chapuis and Johanna A. Bertoch), who was born Dec. 12, 1864.
Member 7th quorum seventies; missionary to Scotland two years; elder; high priest; counselor to President McKenzie. Member state legislature; city councilman. Transfer man. Died April 10, 1910.

WAYLETTE, GEORGE D. (son of George Waylette and Mary Dowsett b. Feb. 14, 1890, former of Essex, Eng.). Born June 7, 1830, in Essex, Eng. Came to Utah Sept. 11, 1857, Israel Evans handcart company.
Married Martha A. King Jan. 28, 1863 (daughter of John King and Hannah Halls, of England). She was born April 16, 1838, at Hockley, Essex, Eng. Came to Utah Oct. 19, 1862, Horton Haight company. Their children: George D. b. Dec. 7, 1863, m. Edith M. Garnett Sept. 16, 1891; Annie M. b. Jan. 20, 1866, m. William Gray June, 1891; John Samuel b. Nov. 20, 1868, d. May 4, 1869; Herbert K. b. April 12, 1870, m. Effie Van Blaricom Jan. 18, 1897; Stanley W. b. Aug. 29, 1872, m. Belle Jamison Nov. 26, 1895; Edwin R. b. Feb. 2, 1875, d. April 20, 1901; Joseph b. June 9, 1878 (d. Feb. 17, 1910), m. Elmina Dye Dec. —, 1900; Harry Octavius b. Oct. 29, 1880, m. Ella Ellis July 8, 1909.

Elder. Assisted in bringing immigrants to Utah in 1861. Resided in San Pete county a number of years; during Indian troubles assisted in building forts; later removed to Cache county, and from there to Montana, where he died Oct. 2, 1898. His home was always a home for the missionaries.

WAYMAN, JOHN (son of Thomas Wayman and Sarah Wool, of Doddington, Cambridgeshire, Eng.). Born June 3, 1825. Doddington. Came to Utah Aug. 24, 1859, Captain Beebe company.
Married Sarah Wool Oct. 11, 1843. She was born Nov. 23, 1820. Came to Utah with husband. Family home, Salt Lake City.
Married Sarah Jane Connell Oct. 29, 1885, Logan, Utah (daughter of Thomas Connell and Jane Cross, who were married on Isle of Man, Eng.). She was born Feb. 18, 1848, Onchan, Isle of Man. Their children: Sarah Wool b. Nov. 23, 1884; John Thomas b. Aug. 14, 1887; Ernest Henry b. Aug. 8, 1889; Frank William b. July 3, 1892; Edgar Wool b. March 29, 1894; John b. Feb. 3, 1905; Ernest H. b. Nov. 8, 1896; John T. b. Oct. 23, 1909. Family home Centerville, Utah.
First counselor to Jacob Weiler 1871; ward clerk 1871-87. Director of Davis County bank 1892-05.

WAYMENT, JOSEPH (son of William Wayment and Martha Brown, former born May 14, 1822, Whaddon, Cambridgeshire, Eng., latter born May 26, 1823, Bassingbourn, Eng.—married Dec. 25, 1841). He was born Feb. 7, 1844, at Whaddon. Came to Utah Oct. 3, 1863, "Dixie" company.
Married Ann Reed Aug. 7, 1874 (daughter of James Reed and Sarah East—married 1837, at Whaddon). She was born Jan. 1, 1852. Their children: Sarah b. Oct. 29, 1875, m. Joseph E. Hansen April 14, 1897; Martha Ann b. June 2, 1877, m. Louis A. Hansen Nov. 23, 1898; Leonard J. b. Sept. 12, 1878, m. Sarah N. Hodson Dec. 12, 1902; Mary Jane b. May 8, 1880, m. Samuel B. Willis Sept. 18, 1901; Walter H. b. Nov. 14, 1881, m. Iva Wade Oct. 5, 1905; Hannah A. b. Aug. 23, 1883, m. Leroy White April 8, 1902; Amelia B. b. July 29, 1890.
Served as missionary to central states; superintendent West Warren Sunday school. Road supervisor and justice of peace.

WAYMENT, SAMUEL (son of William Wayment, born May 26, 1822, at Whaddon, Cambridgeshire, Eng., and Martha Brown, born May 28, 1846, at Whaddon. Came to Utah Sept. 15, 1868, John Gillespie company.
Married Castina Chapman March 11, 1868 (daughter of Jonathan Chapman and Julia Smith), who was born April 11, 1850. Came to Utah Sept. 15, 1868, with husband. Their children: Julia F. b. Dec. 13, 1868, m. Joseph Knight Dec. 7, 1888; Samuel J. b. Aug. 17, 1870, m. Ellen Hulls; Castina b. Oct. 22, 1872, m. William Slater Jan. 27, 1892; Benjamin b. Aug. 30, 1875, m. Ida Foy Fox Dec. 23, 1903; William C. b. Sept. 10, 1877, m. Elizabeth Walker Sept. 21, 1895; Alma E. b. March 13, 1879, m. Mary J. Slater Nov. 30, 1905; Ethel R. b. June 25, 1881, m. D. C. Stewart Dec. 12, 1900; Edith P. b. Aug. 12, 1885. Family home Warren, Utah.
High priest; 1st counselor to bishop of Warren ward 1894; missionary to Great Britain 1893-95. Justice of peace 1908-11. Took charge of the Corrine saw mill and water works 1871; installed the machinery for Slaterville creamery, also for the Plain City and North Ogden canning factories.

WAYMENT, ALMA E. (son of Samuel Wayment and Castina Chapman). Born March 13, 1879, Plain City, Utah.
Married Mary Jane Slater Nov. 30, 1904, Logan, Utah (daughter of John Slater and Mary Stanger, of Slaterville, Utah). She was born Sept. 26, 1882. Their children: Fern b. Oct. 9, 1905; Byron Slater b. June 20, 1907; Grant Slater b. Feb. 1, 1911. Family home, Plain City.
Seventy; missionary to England 1902-04. Deputy sheriff; road supervisor; constable 4 years. Farmer.

WAYMENT, WILLIAM THOMAS (son of William Wayment and Martha Brown, of Whaddon, Cambridgeshire, Eng.). Born April 29, 1858, at Whaddon. Came to Utah June 3, 1878.
Married Maud Mary Bullock Feb. 20, 1884, Logan, Utah (daughter of Thomas H. Bullock and Mary Ann Wagstaff; the former a resident of Nauvoo, Ill., a pioneer 1847, the latter of Cambridge, Eng., pioneer 1863). She was born July 16, 1867, died Nov. 18, 1900. Their children: Horace W.; Albert B., m. Alice Ury 1909; Mary Bell; Theodore; Myrtle I.; Chester W.; Vernal.
Married Elsie Wade Feb. 6, 1908, Salt Lake City (daughter of James M. Wade and Isabell Crandel, both born in Utah). She was born Feb. 28, 1881. Their children: Thora; Russel Wade; Blaine Wade. Family home Warren, Weber Co., Utah.
Bishop; missionary eastern states 1897-99; Sunday school superintendent 1882-97; president Y. M. M. I. A. Warren ward 1900 to 1908. Farmer.

1234   PIONEERS AND PROMINENT MEN OF UTAH

WATTS, ROBERT HARRIS (son of John Watts and Lucy Dalton, of Albemarle county, Va.). Born Sept. 5, 1801, Albemarle county. Came to Utah Sept. 8, 1850, Aaron Johnson company.
Married Elizabeth Heath 1830, near Raymond, Hinds county, Miss. (daughter of John Heath of Hinds county), who was born Dec. 8, 1815. Their children: Bauldwin Harvey, m. Barbara Jane Levie and Emma Wheadon; Elizabeth; Franklin Moroni; Hyram Smith; Lucy; John; Robert; Phoeba; James; Eliza Ann, m. Joseph Watts. Family home South Weber, Utah.
Member 11th quorum seventies. Farmer and stockraiser. Died March 23, 1879.

WATTS, BAULDWIN HARVEY (son of Robert Harris Watts and Elizabeth Heath). Born April 10, 1835, near Raymond, Hinds county, Miss. Came to Utah with parents.
Married Barbara Jane Levie Oct. 26, 1856, North Ogden, Utah (daughter of Frederick and Julia Ann Levie of North Ogden, pioneers 1852). She was born July 24, 1837, Toronto, Ontario, Can. Their children: Bauldwin Henry b. Aug. 15, 1857, and Juliette b. March 15, 1860, died; Charles William b. Jan. 9, 1862, m. Mary Ann Hopkins June 9, 1881; Barbara Jane b. Dec. 2, 1864, m. Jacob Hopkins; Charlotte Ann b. Jan. 9, 1868, died; Harvey Franklin b. Jan. 17, 1870, m. Betsy Hunter; Ettie Elizabeth b. March 21, 1872, m. Lewis Barney.
Married Emma Wheadon April 10, 1876, Salt Lake City (daughter of John Wheadon and Jane Seal, Broad Windsor, Dorsetshire, Eng.; came to Utah 1879). She was born Sept. 29, 1860, and came to Utah 1876. Their children: John A. b. April 20, 1877, m. Alice Dame; Emma Jane b. Nov. 15, 1879, m. Erastus Iverson; Robert b. Oct. 15, 1881, m. Florence S. Bowen; Jeremiah b. Dec. 6, 1883, m. Lutie Walker; Eliza Elizabeth b. Oct. 15, 1885, and Lucy Myrtle b. July 21, 1887, died; Ruby Exile b. Feb. 4, 1891, m. Hyrum Iverson. Families resided Kanosh, Utah.
Member 11th quorum seventies; missionary to England 1874-75; missionary among Salmon River Indians 3 years; Sunday school superintendent about 5 years. President Corn Creek Irrigation Co. 5 years; Kanosh Co-op. 25 years. Farmer and stockraiser.

WATTS, CHARLES WILLIAM (son of Bauldwin Harvey Watts and Barbara Jane Levie). Born Jan. 9, 1862, near Huntsville, Utah.
Married Mary Ann Hopkins June 9, 1881, at Kanosh, Utah (daughter of Charles Hopkins and Mary Edds of Kanosh), who was born June 9, 1863. Their children: Charles William b. March 15, 1882, m. Margret Ann Bird; Reta Ann b. June 6, 1884, and Mary Jane b. June 1, 1887, died; Ida Etelka b. Feb. 9, 1890; Jean b. April 1, 1894, m. Winford Paxton; Cleon Levie b. April 22, 1898, died; Leah Marie b. Sept. 6, 1904. Family home Kanosh, Utah.
Member 42d quorum seventies; missionary to England 1891-93; Sunday school superintendent. Millard county commissioner 1901-03. Representative from Millard county in state legislature 1903-05. Farmer and stockraiser.

WATTIS, EDMUND (son of Edmund Wattis and Hannah Crumpton, of London, Eng., and Nauvoo, Ill.). Born Jan. 20, 1828, in London. Came to Utah 1849, Porter Rockwell company.
Married Mary Jane Corey June 27, 1852, Uinta, Utah (daughter of Lyman Lafayette Corey and Elizabeth Wright, of Council Bluffs, Iowa, pioneers Sept. 28, 1851, Harry Walton company). She was born July 28, 1835. Their children: Mary Jane, m. Joseph Fretwell; Edmund Orson, m. Martha Ann Bybee; George Lyman, m. Addie Scott; William Henry, m. Marie D. Stander; Eunice Elvira, m. Archie Bowman; Warren Lafayette, m. Veda Kay Littlefield; Frank Archie, d. child. Family home Uinta, Utah.
Bishop. Farmer.

WATTIS, WILLIAM HENRY (son of Edmund Wattis and Mary Jane Corey). Born Aug. 15, 1859, Uinta, Utah.
Married Marie D. Stander Jan. 9, 1888. Their children: Estella Hope b. Oct. 3, 1889, m. D. E. Rhivers; Florence Louise b. Nov. 11, 1891, died; Mary Jane b. July 8, 1894; Edmund b. Aug. 19, 1896, died. Family home Ogden, Utah.
President Utah Construction Co.; director various sugar companies and Ogden Rapid Transit Co.; Vineyard Land & Livestock Co., etc.

WEAVER, GILBERT (son of Edward Weaver and Martha Raimer, of Scio, Allegany county, N. Y.). Born March 2, 1835, Conneaut, Crawford county, Pa. Came to Utah 1848.
Married Sarah E. Conover (daughter of Peter Wilson Conover and Eveline Golden, former pioneer Sept. 24, 1848, Heber C. Kimball company). She was born June 31, 1834. Their children: Gilbert Edward b. April 24, 1857, m. Mary Ann Gamble Jan. 1, 1877; Peter Wilson b. Nov. 15, 1858, m. Mary Jane Davis Dec. 3, 1884; Christina b. Sept. 22, 1860, died; Zerelda Eveline b. Nov. 14, 1861, m. Frank Kite Aug. 18, 1878; Sarah Janet b. May 22, 1864, m. Liberty Hunt May 5, 1885; Alice America b. April 22, 1866, m. W. Amos Wright May 6, 1885; Dora Mae b. July 1, 1870, m. Daniel Davis Oct. 29, 1890; Catharine Ann, m. Morris Holmes Sent. 4, 1889; Alpheus b. Nov. 3, 1874, m. Olive Clark Oct. 29, 1896; Rachel Ida b. Nov. 28, 1876, m. John Frederic Haycock Oct. 29, 1896; Houghton b. Sept. 22, 1879, m. Minerva Richardson Jan. 25, 1907.

Active church worker. Called by Brigham Young to help settle Bear Lake district. Veteran of Indian wars. Sheriff Cache Co., Utah, several years. Died at Whitney, Idaho, March 13, 1910.

WEAVER, GILBERT EDWARD (son of Gilbert Weaver and Sarah E. Conover). Born April 24, 1857, Provo, Utah.
Married Mary Ann Gamble Jan. 1, 1877, at Logan, Utah (daughter of Daniel Gamble and Sarah Yates, former pioneer 1861, latter 1857). She was born Jan. 27, 1855. Their children: Gilbert Daniel b. Nov. 22, 1878, m. Olive Clark Jan. 12, 1910; Sarah Virginia b. July 7, 1880, m. Robert Holt Oct. 22, 1900; Pearl b. May 19, 1882, m. Ralph Gayman Dec. 29, 1907; Sylvan Gamble b. March 9, 1884, m. Harriet Maughn July 28, 1909; Allabel b. Aug. 1, 1887, m. LeRoy Hull June 1, 1910; Mary Setira b. April 16, 1888; Earl b. June 22, 1890; Baldia b. April 5, 1892; St. Chir b. April 14, 1894; Vivian b. Feb. 23, 1897; Eva b. Jan. 28, 1900; Lillian b. Aug. 13, 1902; Gerald b. Jan. 18, 1904.

WEAVER, FRANKLIN (son of Edward Weaver and Martha Raimer, of Scio, Allegany county, N. Y.). Born May 29, 1828, at Scio. Came to Utah 1847, contingent Mormon Battalion.
Married Christianna Rachel Reed 1847 (daughter of John H. Reed and Christianna Gregory—married at Millville, N. J.). She was born Dec. 1, 1830. Their children: Franklin Edward b. Dec. 22, 1848, m. Christianna Graham Jan. 18, 1868; Christianna M. b. July 11, 1850, m. Joseph O. Henry Jan. 18, 1874; Elmina A. b. May 10, 1852, m. George W. Birch; Mary Jane b. Dec. 15, 1854, m. Henry Hulse; John Reed b. May 29, 1856, died; Francie Cecelia b. Feb. 19, 1858, m. Timothy Cummings; Hyrum b. May 31, 1860, d. 1863; George Gregory b. June 17, 1862 (d. July 10, 1910), m. Myram Davis; James Dart b. Dec. 14, 1865, d. 1867; Horace b. Aug. 28, 1868, m. Adelaide Wright; Hannah Maud b. Sept. 19, 1872, m. Wells Davis.
Married Sarah Elizabeth Holmes May 9, 1856, Salt Lake City (daughter of Jonathan H. Holmes and Marietta Carter of Kirtland, Ohio, pioneers 1847, contingent Mormon Battalion). She was born Jan. 24, 1838. Their children: Miles Franklin b. Nov. 11, 1857, m. Sarah Elizabeth Lindsay; Marietta b. Nov. 17, 1860, m. Enoch T. Hargraves; Marinda V. b. July 31, 1864, m. Alexander Hargraves; Jonathar. H. b. Sept. 21, 1867, m. Estella Curtis; Gilbert O. b. Oct. 11, 1870, m. Hannah Irene Steers; Sarah Jane b. Nov. 3, 1875, d. Oct. 20, 1894; David b. May 8, 1878, d. Feb. 13, 1904; Phebe May b. June 21, 1881, m. Edward Smith. Families resided Millville, Utah.
Took active part in Echo Canyon war; member Mormon Battalion; Indian war veteran. Had charge of church cattle on Jordan river. Died June 12, 1884, Bennington, Idaho.

WEAVER, FRANKLIN EDWARD (son of Franklin Weaver and Christianna Rachel Reed). Born Dec. 23, 1848, Salt Lake City.
Married Christianna Graham Jan. 18, 1868, Salt Lake City (daughter of James Graham and Hannah Tucker Reed, pioneers 1848, Samuel Brannan company), who was born June 15, 1850, Ogden, Utah. Their children: Wallace Watson b. Feb. 27, 1884, m. Ida Jane Sleight Nov. 29, 1911, (latter died May 28, 1912); Eliza King b. Feb. 26, 1893; Rachel Hill b. Oct. 21, 1902.

WEAVER, MILES FRANKLIN (son of Franklin Weaver and Sarah Elizabeth Holmes). Born Nov. 11, 1857, Farmington, Utah.
Married Sarah Elizabeth Lindsay Feb. 26, 1884, Salt Lake City (daughter of William B. Lindsay and Sarah Henderson of Paris, Idaho), who was born March 8, 1862. Their children: Alexander b. Jan. 10, 1885, d. same day; Sarah Jane b. Feb. 2, 1886, m. Andrew Gregory Sorenson; Miles Franklin Jr. b. Oct. 3, 1887, d. Oct. 11, 1891; William Jasper b. May 5, 1889; Lula b. Jan. 8, 1891, d. same day; Zula b. Aug. 28, 1892, d. June 25, 1895; Idelia b. July 9, 1893; Nathaniel Holmes b. July 1, 1898; Marietta b. Dec. 5, 1900; Melba Vilate b. Nov. 14, 1903; Herriman Lindsay b. Dec. 17, 1906, d. same day; Joseph Smith b. Dec. 26, 1909, d. Dec. 28, 1909. Family home Bennington, Idaho.
Missionary to northern states 1894-96; Sunday school superintendent of Bennington ward; senior president 111th quorum seventies. Farmer and stockraiser.

WEAVER, WILLIAM. Born in England. Came to Utah 1856.
Married (Mrs.) Catharine Beck Johnson (daughter of John Frederick and Christina Maria Beck), who was born Oct. 27, 1828, in Denmark and came to Utah 1863. Their children: George Henry, m. Annie D. Morrill; Joseph, m. Addie L. Morrill; Willis (Johnson) b. Nov. 4, 1868, m. Emma Phedora Morrill; Sarah b. August, 1870, m. Heber D. Wiley. Children took name of mother's first husband—Johnson. Family resided Ogden and Circleville, Utah.
Farmer and gardener.

WEBB, PARDON (son of James and Hannah Webb of Hanover, Chautauqua county, N. Y.). Born Dec. 26, 1818, at Hanover. Came to Utah 1848.
Married Clarissa J. Lee Jan. 7, 1844, Kalamazoo, Mich. (daughter of Ezekiel and Elizabeth Lee of Clarendon, Orleans county, N. Y.), who was born Aug. 19, 1823, and came

to Utah with husband. Their children: Adelaide E. b. April 11, 1845, m. Warren Dusenberry; Adolpha D. b. Dec. 9, 1847, m. Althea Loveless; Clarissa A. b. Oct. 22, 1850, m. John D. Stark; Helen A. b. March 20, 1853, m. Parley O. Loveless; Martha Jane b. Dec. 19, 1855, d. same day; Pardon Jr. b. Dec. 22, 1856, d. July 5, 1863; Mary Alice b. June 1, 1859, m. Isaac Bullock Jr.; James Henry b. Dec. 23, 1861, m. Jane Austin; Zella Lee b. July 14, 1864, d. Sept. 28, 1887. Family home Payson, Utah.
Assisted in bringing immigrants to Utah. Early settler at Payson, pioneer to Arizona. Counselor to Bishop C. B. Hancock and city councilman at Payson. Farmer; carpenter and builder. Died July 29, 1892, Lehi, Ariz.

WEBB, SIMON (son of Samuel Webb, born April 6, 1789, and Ann Furzer, born April 6, 1787, both at Axminster, Eng.; they resided in Somersetshire, Eng.). Born Aug. 3, 1831, Crewkerne, in Somersetshire. Came to Utah Oct. 17, 1862, Henry W. Miller company.
Married Elizabeth Rowsell Sept. 8, 1851 (daughter of Robert Rowsell and Susan Perry), who was born Jan. 11, 1831, and came to Utah with husband. Their children: Eli b. July 23, 1852, m. Elena Ashment May 6, 1872; John Robert b. March 3, 1859, m. Mary Arabel Laurence May 10, 1879; Thomas William b. Aug. 15, 1861, d. June, 1862; Mary Ann b. Feb. 10, 1864, m. Franklin Hobbs Traveler March 15, 1883; Harriet Elizabeth b. May 26, 1866, m. William R. Lawrence, Nov. 16, 1887; Joseph b. June 7, 1869, m. Cora Jane Hendricks Feb. 13, 1895; Simon Jr. b. May 2, 1872, d. Dec. 1, 1873. Family home Richmond, Cache Co., Utah.
Married Harriet Brooks Skidmore Aug. 3, 1882, Salt Lake City (daughter of Henry Britt Skidmore and Rachel Brooks, former pioneer Sept. 3, 1855, John Hindley company—married 1850, Philadelphia, Pa.). She was born Aug. 10, 1851, in Newcastle county, Del. Their children: Henry Sansom b. May 25, 1883, m. Nellie Thompson June 14, 1911; Charles Edward b. Aug. 14, 1885, m. Eliza Wilcox Jan. 15, 1907; Edith Louisa b. April 24, 1889; Jesse Ernest b. March 7, 1891; Esther Elizabeth b. March 21, 1893; Lucy Grace b. Aug. 18, 1896.
High priest. City councilman four years. Died Oct. 31, 1912.

WEBB, ELI (son of Simon Webb and Elizabeth Rowsell). Born July 23, 1852, Crewkerne, Eng.
Married Elena Ashment May 6, 1872, Salt Lake City (daughter of Thomas Ashment and Ann Huggins), who was born Jan. 19, 1852, at Crewkerne. Their children: Charles Eli b. Jan. 13, 1874, d. Nov. 12, 1878; Laura Estella b. April 12, 1876, d. June 21, 1876; William Henry b. May 1, 1877, d. July 28, 1887; George Oliver b. July 24, 1878, m. Ethel Bullen Dec. 8, 1903; Franklin Augusta b. July 12, 1881, d. Feb. 6, 1883; Elizabeth Elena b. Feb. 27, 1884, m. Lafayette Hendricks Sept. 18, 1907; Joseph Eugene b. Aug. 6, 1886; James Walter b. Sept. 11, 1888, m. Alice LaPreal Buxton Nov. 29, 1911; Floasie Mildred b. Dec. 30, 1890; Lucy Irene b. Feb. 2, 1894; Florence Viola b. Nov. 4, 1897. Family home Richmond, Utah.
Clerk 9th quorum elders four years; clerk high priest quorum April 26, 1885, to present time; assistant superintendent Sunday school Richmond ward 20 years. Assessor and collector of Richmond eight years; road supervisor nine years; city councilman eight years; justice of peace four years; member irrigation board 13 years.

WEBB, WILLIAM (son of William Webb of Cambridgeshire, Eng.). Born Aug. 6, 1806, Drayton, Cambridgeshire. Came to Utah Nov. 2, 1864, Warren S. Snow company.
Married Emma Stokes, who was born 1811, Whipsnade, Eng. Their children: John Stokes b. Nov. 20, 1831, m. Hannah Grace; Ann b. April 17, 1833; Mark b. July 27, 1835, died; George b. May 6, 1839, m. Julia Cushing, m. Mary Ann Ward; William Jr. b. Aug. 6, 1843, m. Harriet Grace; Edwin b. Aug. 17, 1846, died. Family home Studham, Bedfordshire, Eng.

WEBB, GEORGE (son of William Webb and Emma Stokes). Born May 6, 1839, Studham, Eng.
Married Julia Cushing at Shipdham, Eng., who died on the plains.
Married Mary Ann Ward May 31, 1865, Lehi, Utah (daughter of Robert Ward and Isabella Watford), who was born Oct. 24, 1840. Their children: Thomas (adopted) b. 1858; George Arthur b. March 1, 1868, d. infant; Walter Lorenzo b. March 20, 1869, m. Martha Lovina Francom (b. Jan. 3, 1869); Laura Isabella b. Dec. 1871; Angeline Ellen b. June 1, 1874; Bernard Graham b. Dec. 4, 1876; Eva Maud b. July 4, 1879; Arthur Folthrop b. Jan. 21, 1882; Dulcie May b. May 9, 1885.
One of the seven presidents of 127th quorum of seventies seven years; assistant Sunday school superintendent Utah stake three years, and Lehi ward seven years. Delegate to three constitutional conventions; Lehi city attorney two terms; alderman two terms; mayor one term; justice of peace three terms; member of legislature 1884-86; member of school board 19 years; county commissioner Utah county 1902-04. President Lehi Irrigation Co., ten years.

WEBB, WILLIAM (son of William Webb and Emma Stokes). Born Aug. 6, 1843, Studham, Bedfordshire, Eng. Came to Utah Nov. 2, 1864, Warren S. Snow company.
Married Harriet Grace May 9, 1881 (daughter of John Grace and Sarah Matthews, who was born June 29, 1841,

PIONEERS AND PROMINENT MEN OF UTAH 1235

and came to Utah with husband. Their children: William David b. March 14, 1866; Sarah Emma b. May 31, 1869, m. Andrew Peterson Oct. 28, 1891; John Hyrum b. May 31, 1869, m. Emma Royal Feb. 10, 1897; Heber C. b. Feb. 22, 1873, m. Minnie Evans Jan. 12, 1898; Jesse G. b. May 28, 1875, m. Tyresha Kirkham 1897; Frederick N. b. April 27, 1877, m. Jennie Allred March 4, 1903; Eli J. b. March 17, 1879, m. Daisy Austin April 29, 1903; Eden Eugene b. Sept. 26, 1881, m. Annie Smith Feb. 22, 1905; Harriet Pearl b. Dec. 14, 1883; Ernest N. b. Aug. 9, 1835, m. Annie Loveridge June 19, 1909; Eleazer G. b. April 8, 1887. Family home Lehi, Utah Co., Utah.

WEBBER, THOMAS G. (son of Thomas B. Webber and Charlotte Burgh). Born Sept. 17, 1836, Exeter, Eng. Came to Utah 1863, independent company.
Married Mary E. F. Richards May 25, 1867, Salt Lake City (daughter of Franklin D. Richards and Charlotte Fox of Salt Lake City, pioneers Oct. 10, 1848, Willard Richards company). She was born June 30, 1850. Their children: Charlotte b. April 3, 1869, m. James L. Franken; Georgina b. Nov. 25, 1870; William b. Aug. 15, 1872, died; Ethelyn b. Nov. 8, 1873, m. George L. Nye; Shirley b. May 14, 1876; Mildred b. July 4, 1893, died. Family home, Salt Lake City.
High priest; missionary to Germany 1876-78. City councilman; alderman. General manager Z. C. M. I., Salt Lake City.

WEBSTER, GEORGE (son of William Webster and Hannah Day of Bedfordshire, Eng.). Born May, 1836, in Bedfordshire. Came to Utah, Milo Andrus company.
Married Christiannah Elliott 1859, Salt Lake City (daughter of Luke Elliott, pioneer independent company), who was born 1821. Their children: George W. b. June 2, 1861, m. Anna M. Green 1886; John Alfred b. Oct. 24, 1865, m. Fannie Barnes 1888.
Married Annie Latimer 1895, Salt Lake City, who was born 1848, in Ireland.
One of the first to promote irrigation in Utah. Church worker. Farmer and stockraiser. Died 1909.

WEBSTER, JOHN ALFRED (son of George Webster and Christiannah Elliott). Born Oct. 24, 1865, Kaysville, Utah.
Married Fannie Barnes 1888, at Kaysville (daughter of William J. Barnes and Mary Simmons, pioneers), who was born Nov. 8, 1866, Kaysville. Their children: Mary Edna b. May, 1889; Wilford Henry b. Aug. 7, 1891; Lola Christiannah b. Sept. 1893; Josie Junitia b. Dec. 6, 1895; Jemima b. March 23, 1899; Golden J. b. Sept. 18, 1901; Maggie E. b. Dec. 2, 1903.
Farmer and stockraiser.

WEBSTER, JOHN (son of James Webster born April 15, 1792, Careston, Forfarshire, Scotland, and Isabella Duncan of Lochlee, Forfarshire). Born Oct. 17, 1830, at Lochlee. Came to Utah Sept. 27, 1867, George Dunford company.
Married Mary Ann Wright July 15, 1858 (daughter of William Wright and Charlotte Rouse, who were married April 6, 1832, at Pointon, Lincolnshire, Eng., pioneers Oct. 17, 1862, Henry W. Miller company). She was born Sept. 17, 1838, and came to Utah with husband. Their children: Isabella C. b. July 11, 1859, m. William H. Haigh July 10, 1884; Mary A. b. Oct. 14, 1860, m. Charles E. Smith July 7, 1881; John W. b. June 15, 1862, m. Jessie Bringhurst Oct. 15, 1896; Frances E. b. April 8, 1864, m. James S. W. Frame Feb. 16, 1887; Helen b. Oct. 26, 1866, d. Jan. 18, 1867; Samuel H. b. Nov. 20, 1868, d. Nov. 21, 1868; Georgiana b. March 9, 1870; Minnie b. Feb. 3, 1872, m. Archie Frame, Jr. Nov. 23, 1892; Emma Jane b. April 7, 1874; Alice b. April 1, 1876, d. April 3, 1876; James A. b. Jan. 30, 1878; George W. b. Aug. 5, 1880, m. Elsie Duncan Feb. 23, 1906; Rachel b. Jan. 29, 1883, m. Alice Grether April 25, 1906. Family resided Genesee, Wis.; Salt Lake City and Taylorsville, Utah.
Came to America, 1855; settled at Taylorsville 1868. Member 14th quorum seventies; high priest; Sunday school superintendent 1870-84. School trustee 12 years; justice of peace eight years. Postmaster of Taylorsville 1875-89.

WEBSTER, JOHN WILLIAM (son of John Webster and Mary Ann Wright). Born June 15, 1862, Genesee, Waudesha county, Wis.
Married Jessie Bringhurst Oct. 15, 1896, Salt Lake City (daughter of John B. Bringhurst and Emma Tripp), who was born July 22, 1876, Taylorsville, Utah. Their children: John D. b. Sept. 24, 1897; Mary E. b. June 29, 1900; Rulon b. June 27, 1903; Myles b. Jan. 17, 1906; Samuel b. April 3, 1908, d. June 27, 1908; Ruth b. May 24, 1909; Mark b. Sept. 8, 1911.

WEBSTER, WILLIAM M. (son of Frederick Webster, born 1825, in Yorkshire, Eng., and Sarah Moorhouse, born 1829, in New Jersey—married in 1848; the former of Glenham, Dutchess county, N. Y., the latter of Vanderville Mills, N. J.). Born Jan. 29, 1850, at Vanderville Mills. Came to Utah Sept. 12, 1861, John R. Murdock company.
Married Margaret Mathews May 14, 1876 (daughter of John Mathews and Ann Evans—married 1832, Mt. Nashy, Wales). She was born April 12, 1858. Their children: Sarah b. Feb. 8, 1877, m. Isaac Blackburn Nov. 30, 1894; Rosa b.

Dec. 11, 1878, m. James Berry Dec. 27, 1904; Frederick b. Oct. 3, 1881, m. Amy Cedina Carrell June 23, 1906; Elizabeth b. Feb. 11, 1884, m. Elijah Maxfield Aug. 4, 1904; Daniel b. Dec. 3, 1886. Family home Loa, Utah.
Married Kate Frederickson July 17, 1889, Manti, Utah (daughter of James Frederickson and Ellen Nielsen, who were married 1808, in Sweden, the latter came to Utah 1873). She was born May 30, 1859, Westrup, Sweden. Their children: James b. Aug. 11, 1890; Alice b. May 19, 1892; Mabel b. Sept. 25, 1895; Attella b. June 13, 1897; Loren b. Sept. 15, 1900; Pearl b. Nov. 19, 1902.
Elder. Settled at Deseret 1861, moved to Holden 1868; to Fremont Valley 1877; and later to Loa.

WEBSTER, FREDERICK (son of William M. Webster and Margaret Mathews). Born Oct. 3, 1881, Loa, Utah.
Married Amy Cedina Carrell June 23, 1896, Loa, Utah (daughter of John F. Carrell and Olive Foy, born in Utah). She was born June 25, 1886, Giles, Utah. Their child: Maud b. Jan. 21, 1911. Family home Loa, Utah.

WEEDING, HANS O. (son of Christen Weeding, born at Satten, Nordland Amt., Norway, and Rachel Greghusdatter, born at Qvejford, Tromsö Amt., Norway). Born Sept. 12, 1814, at Dahle, Qvejford, Tromso, Norway. Came to Utah Oct. 8, 1862.
Married Karren Norum Berg in Norway (daughter of Elert Berg and Randine Pedersdatter, of Norway, pioneers Oct. 8, 1862). She was born Aug. 14, 1825; came to Utah with husband. Family home Hyrum, Utah.
Married Jensine Nielsen Frogner Nov. 15, 1869, at Salt Lake City, Utah (daughter of Niels Hansen Frogner and Gunlil Kerstene Jensdatter). Their children: Caroline Jensine b. Sept. 4, 1870, m. John H. Hansen March 10, 1907; Emma Christine b. July 11, 1872, m. Hiram A. Nielsen Dec. 20, 1899; Hans Richard b. April 27, 1874, m. Jessie Poppleton Sept. 23, 1902; Randine Amelia b. May 28, 1877; Nephi Theodore b. Dec. 19, 1879; Agnes Sophia b. May 16, 1882; Charles Gideon b. Sept. 9, 1884, m. Wanda H. Salverson June 5, 1908; Lovella Marie b. Sept. 21, 1888. Family home Hyrum, Utah.
High priest; ward teacher, and also traveling priest. Fisherman; farmer. Died May 24, 1899, at Hyrum.

WEEDING, HANS RICHARD (son of Hans O. Weeding and Jensine Nielsen Frogner). Born April 27, 1874, Hyrum, Utah.
Married Jessie Poppleton Sept. 23, 1902, Wellsvlle, Utah (daughter of Thomas and Mary Poppleton, of Wellsville, Utah), who was born Sept. 13, 1883, at Wellsville. Their children: Hans O. b. Dec. 31, 1903; Lovella M. b. Dec. 27, 1905; Russel b. Dec. 16, 1908; Jessie b. Jan. 21, 1911, d. Feb. 21, 1911. Family home Hyrum, Utah.
Farmer.

WEGGELAND, DANQUART ANTHON (son of Aanen Samuelson Weggeland and Annie Norman of Christiansand, Norway). Born March 31, 1827. Came to Utah Oct. 17, 1862, Henry Miller company.
Married Andrine M. Holm Feb. 5, 1865, Salt Lake City (daughter of Andrew Holm and Astried Knudsen of Norway), who was born Dec. 2, 1839; came to Utah with Captain Eldredge company. Their children: Annie, m. William Cockren; D. Norman, m. Annie Jensen; William A., m. Sophia Jones; George A., m. Pearl Shannon; Henry N., m. Nina Tollhurst; Ada, m. Henry Reimers; Samuel O., m. Dala Swenson; Alma T., d. infant. Family home, Salt Lake City.
Married Maritt Poulson Sept. 30, 1905, Salt Lake City (daughter of Jacob Telefason and Ingjor Olson of Norway, who came to Utah Sept. 13, 1882). She was born July 15, 1836.
Member 10th quorum seventies; missionary to England 1856-57; high priest; block teacher; ward secretary 20 years; home missionary. Artist and decorator in Manti, St. George, Salt Lake and Logan temples.

WEIGHT, FREDRICK (son of James Weight, born Feb. 28, 1758, Bowbridge, Eng., and Ann Foukes, born June 24, 1791, Voxam, Wiltshire, Eng.). He was born June 18, 1828, Stroud, near Bristol, Eng. Came to Utah Sept. 15, 1851, Captain Howell company.
Married Charlotte Burgum Aug. 18, 1849 (daughter of Henry Burgum), who was born October, 1828, and died October, 1851. Only child: Martin b. Jan. 9, 1851, m. Eliza Ann Brown, m. Jennie Gee. Family resided in Sevier Co., Utah.
Married Mary Milnes Jan. 7, 1853, Salt Lake City (daughter of Edward Milnes), who was born Dec. 31, 1834, Bradford, Eng. Their children: Joseph H. b. Sept. 25, 1855, m. N. Reuhama Johnson; Mary Charlotte b. May 9, 1859, m. John F. Averett; Fredrick H. b. Dec. 10, 1861, m. Hattie Whittaker; Sarah E. b. Aug. 18, 1864, m. George Sperry; James E. b. March 13, 1867, m. Annabelle Johnson; Maria E. b. October, 1871, m. Joseph Chamberlain.
Married Elizabeth Bocock July 1, 1865, Salt Lake City (daughter of William Bocock and Sarah Brough, former pioneer Sept. 12, 1857, Jesse B. Martin company), who was born May 11, 1837, Tinsley, Yorkshire, Eng. Their children: Alfred William b. April 7, 1866, m. Eunice A. Noakes; George Albert b. April 28, 1868, m. H. Lenora Childs; Wallace Fredrick b. Jan. 22, 1870, died; Amelia Ann b. Sept. 20, 1871; Arthur Burgum b. April 3, 1873; Alice Cora b. Nov. 23, 1874;

Samuel Eugene b. Aug. 26, 1876; latter three died; Claude Francis b. March 3, 1879, m. Bertha I. Harmer; Ralph Brough b. March 25, 1882, m. Minerva Bryan.
High priest; member Salt Lake tabernacle choir; chorister at Springville 25 years, and organist for many years. Played in first brass band at Salt Lake City. Drum major in Nauvoo Legion. One of the first members of Salt Lake Theatrical company. Home guard in Black Hawk Indian war. Died Dec. 15, 1901.

WEIGHT, CLAUDE F. (son of Fredrick Weight and Elizabeth Bocock). Born March 3, 1879, Springville, Utah.
Married Bertha I. Harmer June 19, 1907, Salt Lake City (daughter of Lorin Harmer and Ellen Tew of Springville), who was born March 7, 1885. Their children: Lewis F. b. May 25, 1908; Reed Leroy b. Aug. 28, 1909; Bert Howard b. Nov. 22, 1911. Family home Springville, Utah.
Member 51st quorum seventies; missionary to Virginia 1904-06; chorister at first ward, Springville. Piano tuner.

WEILER, JACOB. Born March 14, 1808, in Chester county, Pa. Came to Utah July 24, 1847, Brigham Young company.
Married Anna Maria Malin in Pennsylvania (daughter of Elijah Malin and Catherine Essick, of Chester county, pioneers 1848, John Gleason company). She was born March 28, 1802. Their children: Joseph, m. Mary A. Chaffin; Catherine, m. Hector C. Haight; Elijah M., m. Emily P. Crismon; Lydia A., m. Joseph S. Horne. Family home Salt Lake City, Utah.
Bishop of third ward, Salt Lake City, 40 years; patriarch. Farmer. Died March 25, 1896, Salt Lake City.

WEILER, JOSEPH (son of Jacob Weiler and Anna Maria Malin). Born Nov. 17, 1836, in Chester county, Pa. Came to Utah 1848.
Married Mary A. Chaffin Oct. 26, 1861, Salt Lake City (daughter of Louis Rice Chaffin and Sarah Maria Cositt of St. Louis, Mo.—pioneers October, 1852, Henry Miller company), who was born Dec. 27, 1843. Their children: Mary A. b. Dec. 12, 1864, m. Heber S. Cutler; Joseph L. b. Oct. 17, 1868, m. Catherine Curtis; Annie M. b. July 4, 1869, d. infant; Sarah E. b. Feb. 13, 1871, d. aged 4; Edith L. b. Jan. 1, 1872, d. 1897; Jacob M. b. Jan. 2, 1874, m. Lily S. Nicholson; Gearda B. b. Sept. 24, 1876, m. E. A. Lambourne; Lydia A. b. Sept. 16, 1878, m. Frank W. Brazier; Darwin L. b. Jan. 28, 1881, d. aged 4. Family home, Salt Lake City.
Missionary to Holland 1864-68; seventy; Sunday school superintendent fourth ward. Translator. Dairyman. Died Aug. 4, 1885, Salt Lake City.

WELCH, CHARLES (son of John Welch and Maria Butler, former of Leir, Leicestershire, Eng.). Born May 18, 1828, at Leir. Came to Utah in 1853.
Married Sophia Parkins December, 1854, Salt Lake City (parents resided in England). She was born Nov. 2, 1832. Their child: Katherine b. Sept. 26, 1855, m. Charles Bogart. Family home Ogden, Utah.
Married Elizabeth Newey (daughter of John Newey and Leah Weland, former pioneer, Captain Secrist company, the latter died in England—married at Purbright, Surrey). She was born Aug. 18, 1839, Cove, Hampshire, Eng., and came to Utah with her father. Their children: Charles John b. March 14, 1858, d. aged 14; Leah Newey b. Feb. 28, 1860, m. John Friend Aug. 7, 1882; Samuel b. June 10, 1863, m. Jenny Grose July, 1900; Annie Elizabeth b. Feb. 26, 1865, m. Lorenzo Jackson May 18, 1887; James b. Feb. 26, 1867, m. Julia Winger Nov. 20, 1899; Jane b. Jan. 10, 1869, m. Edward Jude March 11, 1894; William H. b. Jan. 21, 1871, d. Feb. 4, 1871; Nettie b. Jan. 6, 1872, m. Joseph Firth Aug. 1897; Charles b. May 4, 1874, died; George b. Feb. 2, 1877, m. Hyacinth Covington Dec. 24, 1906; Ethel E. b. March 2, 1879, m. M. J. Cullen Jan. 4, 1901; Maud J. b. June 29, 1881, m. C. E. Monagan June 17, 1903. Family home Ogden, Utah.
Married Hannah Stephensen November, 1862, Salt Lake City (daughter of James Stephensen, pioneer Sept. 24, 1862, wagon company). She was born in Derbyshire, Eng. Their children: Mary b. Oct. 10, 1863, m. W. A. Clark; Sarah Jane b. Sept. 17, 1865, m. James Wardleigh; Fannie; Hannah b. Feb. 24, 1867, m. John Day; Alvin b. Oct. 7, 1870, d. Nov. 3, 1906; Alma b. Oct. 7, 1870, d. Nov. 9, 1873.
Member of high council 20 years; ordained elder June 19, 1851; missionary in England before leaving; missionary to England April, 1860-62; counselor to Lorn Farr in quorum of high priests of Weber stake for many years. Street supervisor of Ogden for many years. Died Jan. 13, 1902, Ogden.

WELCH, THOMAS R. G. (son of Robert Welch, born May 11, 1805, Shepton, Mallet, Somersetshire, Eng., and Isabella Friday, born 1815, of Shepton—married at Salisbury, Wiltshire, Eng.). He was born July 10, 1835, at Shepton. Came to Utah Sept. 12, 1857, Jesse B. Martin company.
Married Harriet Nash Aug. 27, 1858 (daughter of Charles Nash and Mary Davey), who was born April 17, 1831. Came to Utah with husband. Their children: Thomas Friday b. July 25, 1856, m. Martha J. Tonks April 10, 1879; Emily Louisa b. Oct. 20, 1858, died; Charles Arthur b. April 10, 1860, m. Mary L. Hinckley April 5, 1883; James Nash b. Nov. 12, 1863, m. Sarah C. Hiner Feb. 25, 1885; Isabella Lizzie b. Oct. 29, 1865, m. Joseph E. Butters Nov. 29, 1883; Robert Hyrum b. April 11, 1867, m. Emily Fry Nov. 19, 1888;

Joseph Smith b. Dec. 30, 1868, m. Sarah V. Bull Aug. 26, 1891; William Frederic b. April 4, 1871, died. Family home Morgan, Utah.

Married Mary Jane Cook (Toomer) September, 1869 (daughter of Thomas Cook and Mary Ann Harris, widow of James Toomer), who was born July 7, 1829, in Hampshire, Eng. Family home Morgan, Utah.

High council of Morgan stake 1877-1906; president elders quorum 1874-77; secretary of church association of Morgan stake 1886-94; member board of education of Morgan stake and secretary and director six years; appointed committeeman with W. W. Cluff to select officers of Morgan stake. Member Nauvoo Legion. Went south with the "move" and returned to Salt Lake City 1860. Postmaster at Morgan 1862-68; clerk and recorder of Morgan county 1864-71; assessor and collector of Morgan county 1867-74; county road commissioner 1869-72; county superintendent of schools six years. Drew plans and superintended the erection of Morgan city and county building; fruit, tree and bee inspector for two years; city recorder 1868-84; member committee on municipal laws 16 years; chairman of the county Republican committee and member of the state committee 1892-98; officer of first state legislature 1896. Associated with Richard Fry in contract for construction of a portion of the Union Pacific Railroad through Morgan city and county, and was bookkeeper for the company. Assessor and collector for the South Morgan school district six years. Tithing clerk 1864-1900.

WELCHMAN, ARTHUR PENDRY (son of Edward Welchman, born May 11, 1773, Kineton, Warwickshire, Eng., and Jemima Williams, both of Rugby, Eng.). Born April 20, 1834, at Kineton. Came to Utah in September, 1854, Preston Thomas oxteam company, driving 5 yoke of oxen.

Married Joanna Murray Bee Oct. 13, 1860, Salt Lake City (daughter of George Bee, who died in Scotland, and Janette Achison, pioneer 1851, and married to Joseph Dobson in 1851, at Salt Lake City; the latter was a member of Company B, Mormon Battalion). She was born Oct. 14, 1828, and came to Utah in Morris W. Phelps company; died Jan. 14, 1913, Grover, Lincoln county, Wyo.

Married Sarah Lucretia Kershaw March 16, 1867, Salt Lake City (daughter of George Frederick Watkins Kershaw, who died aboard ship in 1865, and Eliza Byard). She was born Nov. 1, 1850, Graham's Town, South Africa. Their children: Sarah Eliza b. April 10, 1868, m. Joseph Crow Dec. 13, 1890; Charles Arthur b. June 19, 1870, m. Annie E. Christensen Oct. 16, 1899; Frederick Richard b. Sept. 1, 1873, d. Jan. 19, 1879; Edward Walter b. March 18, 1876, d. March 1, 1877; Emma Joanna b. March 21, 1878, m. Olof Julius Hokanson Nov. 6, 1895; George William b. Oct. 29, 1880, m. Clara May Lake Dec. 3, 1905; Alvin Joseph b. March 8, 1883, m. Ida Bull June 14, 1912; Mary Fortuna b. June 17, 1885; Louisa Isabel b. Oct. 18, 1890, m. Martin LeRoy Bee Oct. 18, 1911; David Samuel b. Nov. 8, 1892. Family home Grover, Lincoln county, Wyo.

Seventy; high priest; missionary to eastern states 1854-56; acting teacher and ward clerk and choir member; clerk in high priests quorum; Sunday school teacher. School teacher; ranchman.

WELKER, JAMES WILBURN (son of James Welker, born Aug. 19, 1803, in Rowan county, N. C., and Elizabeth Holbrook, born Feb. 28, 1800, in Ashe county, N. C.). He was born Jan. 17, 1825, in Jackson Co., Ohio. Came to Utah 1853, Isaac Stewart company.

Married Annie Pugh Feb. 17, 1845, in Pottawattamie Co., Iowa (daughter of Isaac and Martha Pugh, latter pioneer 1853, Isaac Stewart company). She was born Jan. 31, 1821. Came to Utah with husband. Their children: Alfred b. July 22, 1847, m. Eliza Madsen; Harriety Emeline b. Nov. 7, 1848, m. Alvero Dunn; Orlena b. Jan. 4, 1850, m. Journal A. Palmer; James Albert b. July 6, 1851, m. Inger Madsen; Adam b. Feb. 4, 1853, m. Clara Osmond Feb. 1, 1878; Gilbert b. Aug. 24, 1855, m. Charlotte Nelson; Wilbern b. Sept. 10, 1857, m. Hannah Solsby; Ephraim b. Feb. 3, 1860; Rebecca Ann b. Jan. 24, 1864, m. Peter Greenhalgh. Family resided Willard, Utah, and Bloomington, Idaho.

Married Susan Caroline Stevenson, who was born June 29, 1833. Their children: Isabel Jane b. Nov. 9, 1864, m. Walter Ackroyd; Susan Eveline b. March 19, 1866, m. Warren Lindsay; Sarah b. Jan. 28, 1868, and Francis Marion b. Jan. 23, 1870, d. children; Harris Alexander b. Nov. 17, 1872; Abraham b. May 7, 1875; Catherine Almira and Caroline Alvina b. Dec. 22, 1876, d. children. Family home Bloomington, Idaho.

Bishop; alternate high councilor. Member of Nauvoo Legion. Settled at Alpine 1853; moved to Willward, Utah, and later to Bear Lake Valley, Idaho. Blacksmith. Erected one of first sawmills at Bloomington.

WELKER, JAMES ALBERT (son of James Wilburn Welker and Annie Pugh). Born 1851, in Pottawattamie Co., Iowa.

Married Ingar Mary Madison Feb. 25, 1875, Bloomington, Idaho (daughter of Jacob Madison and Dortha Christina Jensen, pioneers 1857, Maryland company). She was born 1854, in Denmark. Their children: Clara b. Aug. 27, 1877, m. Thomas Stephens Jan. 3, 1899; Arthur b. Sept. 29, 1879; Ada b. Feb. 1, 1881, m. Ambrose Merrell June 7, 1898; Mary b. April 22, 1883, m. Norman Bourne Sept. 5, 1906; Melvin b. Feb. 5, 1885; Dortha b. Nov. 28, 1889, m. John Van Orman June 9, 1909; Rozelta b. Jan. 15, 1889, m. William Roberts June 22, 1910; Geneva b. Jan. 8, 1891; Delilah b. Feb. 27, 1893; Fern b. April 14, 1899. Family resided Bloomington and Bennington, Idaho.

High priest; bishop's counselor. Farmer and rancher.

WELKER, ADAM (son of James Wilburn Welker and Annie Pugh). Born Feb. 4, 1853, Alpine, Utah.

Married Clara Osmond Feb. 1, 1878, Bloomington, Idaho (daughter of George Osmond and Georgina Huckvale, pioneers 1855, Hooper and Williams company), who was born Dec. 4, 1856. Their children: Roy Anson b. Nov. 9, 1878, m. Lizzie Hoge June 7, 1906; Raymond b. Sept. 19, 1880, m. Libbie Wright Nov. 9, 1904; Georgina b. Feb. 9, 1883, m. Milton Floyd June 27, 1906; Rosa b. Feb. 9, 1886; George Adam b. April 18, 1888, d. June 24, 1899; Nina b. Sept. 5, 1891; Pearl b. Aug. 4, 1896; Clara b. March 6, 1903. Family home Bloomington, Bear Lake Co., Utah.

Active church worker. Settler in Willard, Utah; moved to Bloomington 1864. Mail carrier two years between Bloomington and Franklin.

WELKER, GILBERT (son of James Wilburn Welker and Annie Pugh). Born Aug. 24, 1855, Willard, Utah.

Married Charlotte Nelson Jan. 1, 1874, Bloomington, Idaho (daughter of Nels Christian Nelson and Catherine Johnson, pioneers handcart company 1857). She was born Oct. 14, 1857, Provo, Utah. Their children: C. Olive b. Sept. 21, 1875, m. Daniel Harvey; Catherine Ann b. Sept. 27, 1877, and Gilbert Anthon b. Oct. 16, 1879, died; Alla Rebecca b Nov. 10, 1881, m. Melvin Loveland Nov. 30, 1899; Mary Susan b. Feb. 18, 1884, m. J. G. Watson Oct. 19, 1907; James Lawrence b. Sept. 21, 1887, m. Beatrice Christenson Oct. 17, 1909; Luelia b. May 25, 1886, died; Albert Wesley b. Nov. 12, 1889, m. Ethel Bacon June 5, 1910; Bardella Jane b. Jan. 10, 1895, m. Charles Rasmusson April 8, 1910; Carson Nelson b. Jan. 24, 1893; Alfred Nelson b. April 8, 1895; Laura b. June 18, 1898; Elga Darrell W. b. Nov. 8, 1901. Family home Bloomington, Bear Lake Co., Idaho.

WELLING, JOB (son of John Welling of Andlam, Chestershire, Eng.). Born Jan. 9, 1833, Andlam. Came to Utah Sept. 26, 1856, Edmond Ellsworth company.

Married Frances E. Yeoman 1853, Southampton, Eng. Their children: J. Y., d.; Marion and John. d. infants; Willard K. b. March 16, 1859, m. Alice Leonard; Annie M. b. March 19, 1864, m. Orland Dalton.

Married Marietta Holmes May 12, 1866, Farmington, Utah (daughter of Jonathan H. Holmes and Elvira Cowles, former pioneer contingent of Mormon Battalion). She was born July 17, 1849. Their children: Franklin D. b. Dec. 20, 1868, m. Estella Secrist May 15, 1890; Joseph H. b. June 21, 1870, m. Effie I. Richards; Jonathan H. b. April 1, 1873, died; Marietta b. April 5, 1875, m. Joseph A. Sill; Arthur b. Dec. 18, 1877, m. Phoebe McCloughlin; Rhoda b. Nov. 19, 1880, m. John W. Taylor; Edward H. b. June 16, 1883; Charles R. b. Nov. 18, 1885.

Married Phoebe L. Holmes Dec. 21, 1868, at Farmington (daughter of Jonathan Holmes and Elvira Cowles), who was born Feb. 5, 1851, at Farmington. Their children: Zina Elvira b. Sept. 29, 1869; Elvira A. b. May 2, 1871, m. Leon A. Rose; Job A. b. Aug. 16, 1873, m. Lena Wood; George A. b. Nov. 11, 1875, m. Judith Oviatt; Sarah E. b. May 14, 1878, m. Eberhart Zundel; Wilford A. b. Nov. 19, 1880, m. Alice Lyman; Hyrum S. b. July 25, 1883; Leonard Henry b. Aug. 29, 1886, died.

Married Emma L. Holmes April 28, 1875 (daughter of Jonathan H. Holmes and Elvira Cowles), who was born Feb. 1, 1856, at Farmington. Their children: Milton H. b. Jan. 25, 1876, m. Sarah B. Richards Dec. 26, 1900; Emma L. b. July 8, 1878, m. Wilson Earl; Eliza Roxla b. July 18, 1880, m. John W. Taylor; Reuben b. July 3, 1883; Alice Belva b. March 9, 1886, m. Israel Barlow. Families resided Farmington, Utah.

Missionary to Australia 1875-76; bishop's counselor. Superintendent Farmington Co-operative Store.

WELLING, FRANKLIN DAVID (son of Job Welling and Marietta Holmes). Born Dec. 20, 1868, Farmington, Utah.

Married Estella Secrist May 15, 1890, Logan, Utah (daughter of Jacob Moroni Secrist and Estella Smith of Farmington). She was born April 24, 1874, died Feb. 1, 1909. Their children: Franklin Moroni; Ray Secrist; Emery Job; Estella; Ralston David.

Married Emelia Marie Madsen June 1, 1911, Salt Lake City (daughter of Peter F. and Emelia D. Madsen of Brigham City, Utah).

Seventy; high priest; second counselor to Bishop W. L. Grover of Garland ward eight years; superintendent Y. M. M. I. A. of Bear River stake 1908-12. Connected with the early settlement of Bear River valley.

WELLING, JOSEPH H. (son of Job Welling and Marietta Holmes). Born June 21, 1870, Farmington, Utah.

Married Effie Irene Richards Feb. 5, 1896, Logan, Utah (daughter of Calvin Willard Richards and Emma Irene Walker of Farmington, Utah). She was born Feb. 13, 1876. Their children: Herald J. b. Feb. 16, 1897; Tracy Richards b. Oct. 25, 1898; Karl G. b. Jan. 30, 1901; Ruby b. Jan. 5, 1904, d. Jan. 8, 1904; Leslie b. July 15, 1905; Lawrence Daniel b. May 27, 1906; Mabel b. May 7, 1909. Family home Riverside, Utah.

Missionary to eastern states 1901-02 and in 1912; first counselor in bishopric of Riverside ward 13 years; ordained bishop of Riverside Feb. 18, 1911.

PIONEERS AND PROMINENT MEN OF UTAH

WELLING, MILTON H. (son of Job Welling and Emma L. Holmes). Born Jan. 25, 1876, Farmington, Utah.
Married Sarah B. Richards Dec. 26, 1900, Salt Lake City (daughter of Calvin W. Richards and Emma I. Walker), who was born March 10, 1878, d. March 14, 1905. Their children: Emma Irene b. Jan. 21, 1902; Virginia b. May 29, 1904. Family home Fielding, Utah.
Married Alice Sylvia Ward May 17, 1906, Salt Lake City (daughter of Moroni Ward and Eliza Voss of Willard, Utah, pioneers October, 1863, Daniel Miller company). She was born July 13, 1879. Their children: Ward Holmes b. March 12, 1908; Lysle b. Dec. 30, 1910.
Missionary to southern states 1896-98; president Malad stake 1902-08. State legislator. Graduate of University of Utah.

WELLS, DANIEL HANMER (son of Daniel Wells, born at Wethersfield, Conn., and Catherine Chapin). He was born Oct. 27, 1814, Trenton, N. Y. Came to Utah Sept. 20, 1848, Brigham Young company, captain of a division.
Married Eliza Robinson 1835 at Commerce, Ill. (daughter of Lewis Robinson of Salt Lake City). Only child: Albert E.
Married Louisa Free in 1849, Salt Lake City (daughter of Absalom Pennington Free and Betsy Strait of Bellville, St. Clair county, Ill., pioneers 1848). She was born Aug. 9, 1824. Their children: Daniel Hanmer, Jr., b. Nov. 24, 1849, m. Geneva Price; Frances Louisa b. March 13, 1852, m. George Naylor; Rulon Seymour b. July 7, 1854, m. Josephine Eliza Beatie; Emeline Young b. April 13, 1857; Eliza Free b. Oct. 3, 1859; Clara Ellen b. Oct. 23, 1862, m. William S. Hedges; Melvin Dickenson b. July 31, 1867, m. Elizabeth Ann Young.
Married Martha Harris in 1849. Their children: Martha Deseret, m. Charles Read: Emily, m. Heber Jeddy Grant; Heber Manning, m. Elizabeth Beatie, m. Theresa Clawson, m. Emily Katz; Joseph Smith, m. Annie Sears, m. Mary Lovell; Edna, m. Thomas W. Sloan; Briant Harris, m. Mary Jennings.
Married Lydia Ann Alley in 1852 (daughter of George Alley and Ann Symons). Their children: Catherine; Lucy Ann; Wilford; Arthur D.; Mary Minerva, m. Orson F. Whitney; Louis Robison, m. Inga Hansen.
Married Susan H. Alley in 1852 (daughter of George Alley and Ann Symons). Their children: Annette, m. H. L. A. Culmer; George A.; Stephen; Charles H., m. Susan Riter.
Married Hannah C. Free (daughter of Absalom Pennington Free and Betsy Strait). Their children: Abbie C., m. Seymour B. Young; Junius Free b. June 1, 1854, m. Helena Forbes; Gershom Britain Finley b. Nov. 1864, m. Nellie Sheets, m. Maud Freeze; Victor Pennington; Luna Pamela, Brigham, Ephraim and Preston, d. children.
Married Emmeline B. Woodward (Whitney) in 1852. Their children: Emmie b. Sept. 10, 1853, d. 1877; Annie, m. John Q. Cannon; Louie, d. aged 18.
Emmeline B. Woodward married Newell K. Whitney (first husband). Their children: Isabel, m. Septimus A. Sears; Melvina, m. Maj. William W. Woods.
In the organization of the provisional government was attorney-general and later chief justice of Deseret; member first territorial legislative council many terms; member constitutional convention; mayor of city of Salt Lake 1866-76; member city council until 1882, when he was disfranchised by the Edmunds law. In 1848 appointed superintendent public works; acted in that capacity in laying cornerstone of the temple 1853; superintended building of old council house, which was used as a courthouse and as the home of the University of Deseret; which institution he was chancellor 1869-78. Apostle and second counselor to President Brigham Young 20 years, becoming counselor to twelve apostles at the death of President Young. Associated with the military from the battle of Nauvoo, Ill., till disbandment of Nauvoo Legion. He, with Charles C. Rich, organized the Utah militia, and was elected major-general by the state assembly May 26, 1849, receiving the rank of lieutenant-general; under the territorial militia law was re-elected lieutenant-general April 6, 1857, and the forces under him opposed General Johnston's advance into Salt Lake valley during that and the ensuing year. During the Indian troubles in Utah and San Pete counties he took the field in defense of the settlers. Missionary to Liverpool 1864-65, and presided over the European mission. Succeeded Heber C. Kimball in charge of the Endowment House at Salt Lake City. Directed organization of settlements in Utah and Arizona. In December, 1884, was sent to preside over European mission, which position he held till 1887. President Manti temple 1888. Present at the dedication of St. George, Logan and Manti temples.
First to develop coal mines in Summit county; operated lumber mills in Cottonwood canyon; manager Salt Lake nail factory; established Salt Lake City gas works, and was interested in many other business and industrial institutions. Died March 24, 1891, Salt Lake City.

WELLS, RULON SEYMOUR (son of Daniel Hanmer Wells and Louisa Free). Born July 7, 1854, Salt Lake City.
Married Josephine Eliza Beatie Jan. 18, 1883, Salt Lake Endowment House (daughter of Hampden Sidney Beatie and Marion Thankful Mumford of Salt Lake City). She was born Feb. 10, 1857. Their children: Josephine Louisa b. Feb. 18, 1884, m. David Douglas Moffat; Rulon Seymour, Jr. b. Oct. 5, 1885; Sidney Beatie b. Oct. 3, 1887; Elizabeth b. Sept. 14, 1890; Lillian b. Oct. 2, 1894; Helen b. June 16, 1896; Dorothy Marion b. Nov. 25, 1899. Family home, Salt Lake City.
Missionary; one of seven presidents of seventies. Associated with the Heber J. Grant Co. Insurance.

WELLS, JONATHAN SAWYER (son of Judah and Sarah Wells). Born June 3, 1805, in Grafton county, N. H. Came to Utah 1850, Captain Johnson company.
Married Margret Gardner June 23, 1829, in Erie county, Pa. (daughter of Nathaniel B. Gardner and Hannah Briggs), who was born Sept. 15, 1811. Their children: Lyman Briggs b. June 12, 1830, m. Bethiah Fordham; Hannah Swanthy b. Oct. 7, 1831, m. John Memorial McCrary; Otis Nathaniel b. July 1, 1833, m. Victoria Fordham; Erastus Nelson b. Feb. 18, 1835, m. Nancy Malinda Whitaker, d. July 28, 1900; Huldah Mariah b. June 11, 1837, m. Timothy Lish; Sarah Matilda b. April 15, 1843, m. Richard Drake; Julia Ann and Judah Smith (twins) b. Oct. 26, 1846, latter married Ada Lish; Margret Ann b. June 11, 1851, m. David Pinny Wells.
Member of seventy; counselor in bishopric of Willard ward. Justice of peace at Willard. Veteran Indian war. Farmer. Died July 27, 1867, in Harrison Co., Iowa.

WELLS, ERASTUS NELSON (son of Jonathan Sawyer Wells and Margret Gardner). Born Feb. 18, 1835, in Erie county, Pa. Came to Utah with parents.
Married Nancy Malinda Whitaker Jan. 4, 1855, Willard, Utah (daughter of James Whitaker and Nancy Woodland of Willard, pioneers 1850). She was born Oct. 11, 1838, in Davies county, Mo., died Nov. 9, 1909. Their children: Erastus Nelson b. Aug. 10, 1856, m. Mary Moon; James Oscar b. Aug. 14, 1859, m. Rowena Moon; Clara Malinda b. Dec. 21, 1862, m. Benjamin Moon; William Carman b. March 1, 1866, d. same day; Margret Marinda b. Feb. 20, 1868, m. Manasah Moon, m. Hance Knudsen; Jonathan Sawyer b. April 12, 1870; Nancy Myrtle b. May 5, 1875; Lawrence Ray b. Nov. 4, 1878, m. Annie Bell. Family home Woodruff, Idaho.
Member seventy at Willard, Utah. Justice of peace; trustee at Woodruff. Farmer. Died July 28, 1900, Woodruff, Idaho.

WELLS, JONATHAN SAWYER (son of Erastus Nelson Wells and Nancy Malinda Whitaker). Born April 12, 1870, Woodruff, Idaho.
School trustee Woodruff, Idaho. Assisted in building the Farmers' Telephone in Malad Valley, Idaho.

WELLS, LAWRENCE RAY (son of Erastus Nelson Wells and Nancy Malinda Whitaker). Born Nov. 4, 1878, Woodruff, Idaho.
Married Annie Arbella Bell Nov. 21, 1907 (daughter of Robert Bell and Lizzie John). Born Jan. 10, 1888, Malad, Idaho. Their children: Laura Bell b. Oct. 22, 1908; Erastus Nelson b. Nov. 30, 1910.

WEST, CHAUNCEY WALKER (son of Alva West, born June 21, 1795, and Sally Benedict, born Oct. 19, 1800, of Lee and Lenox, Mass.). He was born Feb. 6, 1827, in Orange township, Erie county, Pa. Came to Utah 1847.
Married Mary Hoagland May 1, 1846 (daughter of Abraham L. Hoagland and Margaret Quick—married Nov. 24, 1825). She was born Feb. 11, 1829, and died Aug. 27, 1870. Their children: Margaret b. Sept. 1847, died; Chauncey Walker b. Aug. 3, 1849, m. Sylvia Snow Nov. 9, 1868; Joseph Alva b. Sept. 12, 1851, m. Josephine Richards March 4, 1873; John Abraham b. June 25, 1856, m. Amanda A. Thompson Oct. 25, 1876; Josephine b. 1861, died. Family resided Salt Lake City and Ogden, Utah.
Ordained a seventy in 1845; bishop of first ward at Ogden May 29, 1855, and later was presiding bishop of Weber county for many years. Member house of representatives several terms. Colonel in Weber military district; brigadier-general in Nauvoo Legion. Member legislative convention of the inchoate state of Deseret. Missionary to Siam in 1852; to England 1863, where he was president of the European mission. Died Jan. 9, 1870.

WEST, JOSEPH ALVA (son of Chauncey Walker West and Mary Hoagland). Born Sept. 12, 1851, Salt Lake City.
Married Josephine Richards March 4, 1873, Salt Lake City (daughter of Franklin D. Richards and Jane Snyder), who was born May 25, 1853, Salt Lake City. Their children: Jane b. Dec. 29, 1873, m. John L. Herrick June 11, 1894; Joseph Walker b. Oct. 1, 1875, m. Mary E. Littlefield June 1, 1894; Willard Alva b. Jan. 11, 1878. d. Feb. 10, 1880; George Edward b. Aug. 5, 1880, d. Sept. 10, 1882; Ray Benedict b. Oct. 21, 1882, m. Mary Morrell; Franklin Lorenzo b. Feb. 1, 1885, m. Gladys Spencer Aug. 19, 1904; Mary Josephine b. Feb. 11, 1888, m. Reuben T. Evans Nov. 4, 1909; Charles Henry b. Sept. 22, 1890. Family home Ogden, Utah.
Married Sylvia A. Child Feb. 24, 1888 (daughter of Warren G. Child and Martha Elmer), who was born April 11, 1869, Ogden, Utah. Their children: Sylvia Valencia b. Feb. 1, 1890, d. July 17, 1904; Howard Alva b. Sept. 4, 1891, d. Nov. 3, 1892; Martha Rosetta b. Dec. 31, 1893; Chauncey Warren b. Jan. 27, 1897; John Francis b. June 1, 1899; Darell Grant b. June 4, 1901; Clarence Vivian Le Roy b. July 24, 1903; Joseph Franklin b. July 1, 1905, d. Dec. 23, 1908; Pearl Marie b. Sept. 23, 1907; Fred b. March 1, 1909.

Regimental adjutant in Utah militia 1868, and in 1870 made major of cavalry. Deputy territorial surveyor 1868; member lower house of Utah legislature 1885; Ogden city councilman 1878. Went on a mission to England in 1882; member presidency of 76th quorum seventies; high priest; member high council of Weber stake and later of Box Elder stake; counselor to president of Y. M. M. I. A. Had charge of the preliminary surveys of the Union Pacific Railway 1880 and 1889. One of the organizers of the Sumpter Valley Railway in Oregon 1870 and was made successively secretary, chief engineer, general freight and passenger agent and superintendent. In 1898 he built the Utah and Western from Milford to Uvada and after its completion became its superintendent; built the Mt. Hood Railway from Hood river in Oregon to Dee and was for a time its superintendent and also its general freight and passenger agent. Built the Ogden Rapid Transit Company's Ogden Canyon and Brigham City extensions. He has constantly been occupied in railroad engineering and construction. Engineer on Utah Central Railroad between Ogden and Salt Lake City in 1870.

WEST, FRANKLIN LORENZO (son of Joseph Alva West and Josephine Richards). Born Feb. 1, 1885, Ogden, Utah. Married Gladys Spencer Aug. 19, 1904, Salt Lake City (daughter of Edmund Burke Spencer and Virginia Thatcher of Logan). She was born May 7, 1883. Their children: Virginia Gladys b. Nov. 12, 1905; Marjorie b. Jan. 12, 1909. Family home Logan, Utah.
Received Ph. D. degree from University of Chicago 1911. Professor of physics and director school of general science at Utah Agricultural College.

WEST, DAVID (son of William West, born March 24, 1787, and Hannah Winterton, born 1789, of Oakbrook, Derbyshire, Eng.). He was born June 26, 1824. Came to Utah Sept. 27, 1853, Moses Dailey company.
Married Amelia Hooley July 5, 1844, in England (daughter of John Hooley and Mary White), who was born July 3, 1825. Their child: Charles Henry b. May 14, 1846, m. Frederikke Claudina Jacobsen. Family home Pleasant Grove, Utah.
Justice of the peace; councilman and alderman Pleasant Grove.

WEST, CHARLES HENRY (son of David West and Amelia Hooley). Born May 14, 1846, in Derbyshire, Eng. Came to Utah 1851.
Married Frederikke Claudina Jacobsen Aug. 17, 1867, Salt Lake City (daughter of Willhelm Waldemar Alaphelt of Copenhagen, Denmark). She was born Jan. 12, 1847. Came to Utah 1860. Their children: Charles Henry, died; Annie Amelia, m. Andrew Thompson; Hensen J., died; David Waldemar, m. Elva Vilate Adams; Leicester Gay, m. Margaret Foutz Walker; Minnie and Heber C., died; Alroy Hooley, m. Eva Marrott; Mary Ellen, Nellie Elmira, William and Frank, latter four died; Archie C. Family resided Linden Ward, Pleasant Grove, Utah.

WEST, LEICESTER GAY (son of Charles Henry West and Frederikke Claudina Jacobsen). Born Jan. 2, 1876, Pleasant Grove, Utah.
Married Margaret Foutz Walker June 29, 1904, Salt Lake City (daughter of Appollis Benjamin Walker and Sarah Jane Holman of Pleasant Grove, Utah). She was born July 20, 1882. Their children: Leo Berry b. April 7, 1905; Burnell Gay b. May 24, 1907; Ray Walker b. Sept. 21, 1909; Rulon Lester b. April 12, 1912.
Missionary to South Carolina 1900-02; teacher in Sunday school. Miner; electrician; farmer and fruitgrower.

WEST, JESSE (son of William West and Hannah Winterton of Burnswick, Eng.). Born March 30, 1827. Came to Utah in 1850.
Married Isabella Windley, who was born April 9, 1828. Their children: Sarah Ann; Caroline; Isabella Ruth; Emma Selenia, m. William Evans; Jesse, Jr., m. Cathrine Alice Johnson; Alma Henry, m. Adelaide Fullmer; Hannah C., m. Heber M. Hawkes; Orson Moroni, m. Annie Williams; Nephi Thomas, m. Nettie Hunter; Alice M., m. Thomas Steveson; Matilda, m. Burton S. Rupp; Eliza, m. John Fenton; Nellie May, m. William Foster, Jr., m. John Waterhouse.
Bishop's counselor 6th ward 40 years; patriarch nine years. Was captain of a company that fought Indians in 1863. Builder and contractor. Died Dec. 24, 1906, Salt Lake City.

WEST, JESSE (son of Jesse West and Isabela Windley). Born Feb. 20, 1854, Salt Lake City.
Married Catherine Alice Johnson Oct. 10, 1877, Salt Lake City (daughter of Daniel Johnson and Catherine Webb of Toms River, N. J., pioneers September, 1853, Israel Ivins company). She was born May 29, 1858. Their children: Martha b. June 27, 1878, m. J. W. Vincent June 27, 1900; Jesse Leroy b. Sept. 21, 1879, m. Elizabeth H. Snerr Oct. 5, 1904; Carl Henry b. April 18, 1881, m. Lucy Priest July 3, 1906; Catherine Isabelle b. Oct. 30, 1882, m. Llewellyn Shurtliff May 27, 1905; Laverne b. Aug. 4, 1884, m. Edward Cuthbert Aug. 1, 1903; Eunice Edna b. March 8, 1887, m. Carl Schneiter May 16, 1908; Lois b. Oct. 2, 1888, m. Caton W. Pierce Jan. 6, 1910. Family home, Salt Lake City.
Missionary to Arizona. Contractor and builder. Died Nov. 16, 1888, Salt Lake City.

WEST, CARL HENRY (son of Jesse West and Catherine Alice Johnson). Born April 18, 1881, Hyde Park, Utah.
Married Lucy Priest July 3, 1906, Union, Fremont Co., Idaho (daughter of Edward Priest and Mary Beus of Ogden, Utah; former pioneer Oct. 6, 1862, Ansel P. Harmon company, latter 1856, Edmund Ellsworth company). She was born Jan. 14, 1886. Their children: Bently Irvine b. May 15, 1907; Spencer Leroy b. Nov. 9, 1908; Mary b. Dec. 26, 1910.
President deacons' quorum of 26th ward when first organized. Printer by trade; later occupation farmer.

WEST, SAMUEL (son of John West and Sarah Walker of Benton county, Tenn.). Born March 30, 1894, in South Carolina. Came to Utah Sept. 25, 1851, Harry Walton company.
Married Margaret Cooper Jan. 29, 1829 (daughter of John Cooper and Esther Fletcher of Tennessee). She was born December, 1804. Their children: Sarah E., m. William Barton; John A., m. Betsy J. Fish, m. Mary J. Robinson; Iles Marion, d. infant; Susan E., m. George A. Smith; Emma S., m. Jesse N. Smith; Margaret Fletcher, m. Jesse N. Smith; Lyda C., m. Columbus Freeman; William Moroni, m. Tryphenia Hobbs; Nancy M., m. John H. Rollins; Samuel W., d. infant. Family home Parowan, Iron Co., Utah.
High priest; high councilor of Parowan stake. Farmer and stockraiser. Died 1873 in Washington Co., Utah.

WEST, THOMAS (son of Thomas West and Harriet Moore). Born Oct. 1, 1852, St. Joseph, Mo. Came to Utah 1853.
Married Emma M. Allred March 11, 1876, Mt. Pleasant, Utah (daughter of Isaac Allred and Emma Dewy of Mt. Pleasant, pioneers 1856). She was born Oct. 15, 1857. Their children: Grace, m. Rasmus L. Madsen; Thomas Wilford, m. Louise Jordan; Stella, m. Charles A. Hyde; Zella, m. Myron Turfrue; Ray Adelbert. Family home Mt. Pleasant, Utah.
Missionary to England 1898-1900; high priest; bishop's counselor; tithing clerk. City councilman. Farmer and miner.

WESTENSKOW, HANS (son of Ole Hansen Westenskow and Maren Hansdatter of Ulslev, Falster, Denmark). Born Sept. 17, 1835, at Ulslev. Came to Utah Sept. 5, 1863, John F. Sanders company.
Married Karen Jorgensen Petersen Oct. 18, 1860, Stubberup, Denmark (daughter of Peter Jorgensen and Ane Petersen of Stubberup, both died in Denmark). She was born March 21, 1839, at Stubberup. Their children: Ole Peter b. Oct. 18, 1861, d. July 2, 1863; Peter H. b. June 16, 1863, m. Annie Keller; Mary b. March 12, 1865, m. Leonard Billings; Hannah b. Jan. 27, 1867, m. William Henrie; Hans Larvett b. 1869, m. Christina Anderson; Louis H. b. Oct. 15, 1871, d. May 16, 1872; Caroline b. April 13, 1873, m. James Henrie; Annie Christina b. Feb. 6, 1875, m. Louis Jensen; Maria b. March 17, 1877, d. Nov. 19, 1879; Magdalina b. March 17, 1877, m. William Worthing; William Henry b. May 28, 1879, m. Matilda A. Bodden; Sarah b. April 22, 1881, m. Joseph Heningson.
Married Karen E. Hansen April 18, 1869, Salt Lake City (daughter of Nikolai Hansen and Birthe Maudatther of Bjorup, Denmark, both died in Denmark). She was born March 2, 1852. Their children: John b. Dec. 1, 1871, m. Suexen Chesses; James Peter b. Oct. 5, 1874, m. Olive Bodden; Margeret B. b. April 8, 1877, m. Isaiah Thomas. Families resided Manti, Utah.
Ordained high priest Sept. 7, 1890; seventy April 25, 1857; bishop's counselor 1888-1900; ward teacher 1865-75; head ward teacher 1875-88. Leader of Manti brass band and orchestra 20 years; also played for the tabernacle choir 20 years. Farmer.

WESTENSKOW, PETER H. (son of Hans Westenskow and Karen Jorgensen Petersen). Born June 16, 1863, Albany, N. Y.
Married Anna Keller Oct. 22, 1886, St. George, Utah (daughter of Jacob Keller and Annie R. Hemman of Switzerland, pioneers 1864). She was born Dec. 8, 1868. Their children: Annie Zelma b. Aug. 21, 1887, m. William A. Funk; Alvin b. May 27, 1889; Peter Daniel b. April 14, 1891; Jacob LeMar b. Jan. 22, 1893; Wilford b. March 26, 1895; Ethel b. Oct. 30, 1898; Florence b. Aug. 7, 1903. Family resided Manti, Utah, and Imbler, Ore.

WESTERN, SAMUEL R. (son of John Western and Elizabeth Durham of Tiverton, Devonshire, Eng.). Born March 17, 1817, at Tiverton. Came to Utah 1868.
Married Ann Winsborough April 9, 1836, Tiverton (daughter of Robert Winsborough and Mary Copp of Tiverton). She was born Oct. 6, 1814. Their children: Emma; Eliza-phram O.; Hannah M.; Adah A. Family home Deseret, Utah.
Elder; missionary to England. Farmer and wire drawer in England. Died Jan. 25, 1904, Deseret, Utah.

WESTERN, SAMUEL WINSBOROUGH (son of Samuel R. Western and Ann Winsborough). Born Dec. 4, 1843, Tiverton, Eng. Came to Utah Sept. 13, 1861, Homer Duncan company.
Married Sarah Ann Wood Jan. 29, 1866, Berryville, Washington Co., Utah (daughter of John Wood and Ellen Smith

of Lehi, Virgin City and Grafton, Utah, pioneers 1853, Cyrus H. Wheelock company). She was born May 8, 1850. Their children: Samuel W. b. May 10, 1867, m. Clara M. Phillips; John Henry b. March 13, 1869, m. Musetta Palmer; Sarah Ann b. Aug. 28, 1871, m. Isaac Alldredge, Jr.; Eliza Ellen b. March 10, 1874, m. Thomas L. Cropper; Lucy Jane b. Dec. 24, 1876, m. Joseph B. Dewsnup; Joseph Franklin b. Nov. 27, 1879, m. Jennie B. Palmer; Ernest b. July 21, 1882, died; Ruth b. Sept. 11, 1884, m. J. H. Durbin; Francis M. b. Dec. 15, 1887, m. Eva D. Black; Mary A. b. July 23, 1895, died. Family home Deseret, Utah.
Married Mary Alice Hutchinson May 24, 1884, Salt Lake City (daughter of James Hutchinson and Ellen Redmond), who was born April 26, 1866, Deseret. Their children: Sarah Alice b. July 1, 1885, d. March 7, 1890; Clarence Levi b. March 27, 1887, d. May 4, 1887; Alma b. Aug. 8, 1888, m. Nancy Stamworth; Jessie W. b. July 29, 1892; Myron L. b. Sept. 10, 1894; Ellen Gladys b. July 1, 1896; James H. b. May 1, 1898; Elizabeth b. Jan. 18, 1900; Mary Gertrude b. Feb. 9, 1901; Bernice b. June 29, 1903; Samuel Ray b. July 30, 1907; Mina Ann b. April 30, 1909. Family home, Deseret.
Missionary to England 1889-91, where he served as president of Birmingham conference; high priest; ward teacher; counselor to Bishop J. S. Black of Deseret; conductor of ward and Sunday school choirs 35 years; president Y. M. M. I. A. Drove team for Thomas G. Odell in Homer Duncan's company across the plains. Settled at Deseret 1877, where he has resided ever since.

WESTMAN, PETER ERICK (son of Peter Oluf Olsen and Margarite Ramnell of Sweden). Born Oct. 9, 1829, Westmanland, Sweden. Came to Utah July 17, 1872, Erick Petersen company.
Married Christina Johnson in Sweden, who was born July 26, 1825, and died Sept. 6, 1864. Their children: Emma Christina b. Jan. 18, 1856, m. Anders Anderson, m. John Anderson; Carl August b. Nov. 19, 1859, d. March 15, 1862. Family home in Sweden.
Married Johanna Mathilda Berge Nov. 1, 1866, in Sweden (daughter of Anders Gustave Berge and Margarite Johnson of Sweden). She was born Oct. 17, 1840, and came to Utah with husband. Their children: Agusta b. April 12, 1871, d. Jan. 5, 1886; Annie M. b. Aug. 28, 1876, m. William Gardner; Elizabeth b. Nov. 21, 1878, m. David Hansen; Peter Alma b. Aug. 21, 1880, m. Anna Axelson. Family home Richfield, Utah.
Counselor in presidency of high priests quorum 1883; member high council; member Sevier stake Sunday school board; home missionary. Worked on St. George temple as stone mason 1874-75. Superintendent city waterworks. Farmer and merchant. Died May 12, 1912.

WESTMAN, PETER ALMA (son of Peter Erick Westman and Johanna Mathilda Berge). Born Aug. 21, 1880, Richfield, Utah.
Married Anna Axelson April 10, 1907, Salt Lake City (daughter of Axel Axelson and Anna Ervall of Sweden). She was born June 25, 1879. Their children: Lillian b. Jan. 3, 1909; Margarite b. Sept. 11, 1910. Family home Richfield, Utah.
Missionary to Sweden 1901-04; member 76th quorum seventies; member general board of Y. M. M. I. A. of Sevier stake. Produce merchant.

WESTON, GEORGE GIFFORD (son of Nehemiah Weston, born July 19, 1820, West Harptree, and Roseanna Gifford, born Feb. 24, 1821, Fairwood [Wellow], both in Somersetshire, Eng., later of Rich Co. Utah—married Sept. 29, 1845). He was born Sept. 9, 1848, at Coley (Woolley), East Harptree, Somersetshire. Came to Utah Sept. 2, 1868, Simpson M. Molen company.
Married Emma Robinson Oct. 26, 1874 (daughter of George Robinson, born May 15, 1824, and Sarah Craven, born April 29, 1830—married 1849, Bradford, Yorkshire, Eng.; both came to Utah in October, 1873). She was born at Clayton, Yorkshire, Eng., Jan. 10, 1852, died April 24, 1898. Came to Utah with parents. Their children: Lovinia b. Sept. 3, 1875, m. Rose Linjenquist Dec. 23, 1908; John Henry b. Jan. 4, 1878, m. Bessie E. Barker Sept. 12, 1906; Emma Sarah b. Aug. 30, 1879, m. Clarence E. Cheney Sept. 12, 1906; Albert Robinson b. Dec. 16, 1880; Lydia Ann b. Sept. 9, 1882, m. DeWitt Johnson June 6, 1906; Elizabeth Anna b. April 21, 1884; Thomas Gifford b. July 18, 1885, m. Ethel Kearl June 6, 1906; Ella Sylvia b. Aug. 9, 1892; Eva Loretta b. Sept. 20, 1895; Lucy R. b. April 24, 1898. Family home, Laketown, Utah.
Worked on U. P. and C. P. Railroads in 1868-69. Settled at Laketown 1869. School trustee; director in two irrigation companies. High priest; ward teacher.

WESTON, SAMUEL (son of Nehemiah Weston and Roseanna Gifford and younger brother of George Gifford Weston). He was born Jan. 27, 1865, Woolley, Somersetshire, Eng. Came to Utah in August, 1870, with parents.
Married Lillian Estella Kearl (daughter of James Kearl and Fanny Martin—April, 1862, Salt Lake City; former a pioneer 1854, latter came to Utah Aug. 25, 1855, Richard Ballantyne company). She was born Jan. 8, 1873, Laketown, Utah. Their only child was John Weston Hodges (adopted) born Aug. 22, 1896.

Missionary to England 1891-93; ordained bishop of Garden City ward June 20, 1897. Representative from Rich county to the seventh session (1907) Utah State Legislature.

WESTOVER, CHARLES (son of Alexander Westover and Electa Beal of Licking, Muskingum Co., Ohio). Born Nov. 25, 1827, Licking, Ohio. Came to Utah 1853, Captain Snow company.
Married Eliza Ann Haven at Salt Lake City, who was born May, 1829. Their children: Charles, m. Ellen Parker; Oscar F., m. Ann Robinson; Eliza, m. Lemuel Redd; Harriett, m. Charles Gracy; Maria, m. Charles Knell; Artemesia, m. Leonard Congor; John, d. infant; William; Lewis, m. Eliza Funk; Minnie, m. Arthur Paxman; Clara Ellen, d. infant. Family home Washington, Utah.
Married Mary E. Shumway Sept. 1, 1856, Salt Lake City (daughter of Charles Shumway and Julia Ann Hooker of Sturbridge, Worcester county, Mass., former pioneer July 24, 1847, Brigham Young company). She was born Oct. 27, 1835. Their children: Andrew Jerome b. Feb. 2, 1858, d. infant; Julia Ann b. Feb. 28, 1860, m. Samuel Rowley; Charles Edwin b. May 4, 1863, m. Ziporah Jones; George Henry b. Oct. 25, 1865, m. Alice Leonard; Alberto b. Jan. 9, 1868; Mary Louisa b. Oct. 7, 1870, m. Lewis Johnson; Arthur Adelbert b. Nov. 2, 1876, d. infant. Family home Huntington, Utah.
High priest; ward teacher. Settled at St. George, Utah, 1861. Farmer and thresher.

WESTWOOD, THOMAS (son of Charles Westwood and Margarite Taylor of Edgworth Lancastershire, Eng.). Born Jan. 5, 1822, at Edgworth. Came to Utah 1868.
Married Martha Lomax 1841, Bolton, Lancastershire (daughter of Charles and Betsy Lomax of Bolton). She was born May 23, 1822. Their children: Sarah Ann, d. infant; Nancy, m. Luke Shaw; John, d. aged 17; Nephi M., d. infant; Joseph, m. Catherine C. Holder; Elizabeth, m. Joseph Wright, m. William Maxwell; Thomas, d. infant. Family home 16th ward, Salt Lake City.
Elder. Gardener. Died Jan. 16, 1892, 10th ward, Salt Lake City.

WESTWOOD, JOSEPH (son of Thomas Westwood and Martha Lomax). Born Feb. 28, 1855, Berry, Lancastershire, Eng. Came to Utah with parents.
Married Catherine C. Holder June 23, 1881, Salt Lake City, Daniel H. Wells officiating (daughter of Thomas G. Holder, and Caroline Allington of Karori, New Zealand; came to Utah Sept. 7, 1870). She was born June 7, 1860. Their children: Joseph C. b. March 17, 1882, m. Edith A. Holley; Albert G. b. April 11, 1883, m. Edith M. Sharer; Nephi J. b. Aug. 11, 1885, m. Clara Hopkinson; Maud H. b. April 29, 1891, m. Fredrick W. G. Hansen; Emma b. Feb. 24, 1893, m. James B. Williams. Family home 29th ward, Salt Lake City.
Elder. Blacksmith.

WHEELER, GEORGE WALTON (son of Levi Wheeler, born July 5, 1812, and Mary Ann Arnold of Augusta, Maine—married 1833). He was born March 30, 1844, at Augusta. Came to Utah 1854, Perrigrine Sessions company.
Married Hannah Humphreys in August, 1863 (daughter of George Humphreys and Harriet Harden, pioneers 1856, second handcart company—married 1829). She was born Dec. 28, 1846; came to Utah 1856, second handcart company. Their children: George Edwin b. Jan. 18, 1865, m. Ida Wood Dec. 5, 1888; Mary Ann b. Jan. 28, 1866, m. Joseph Ransom Oct. 30, 1883; Simon b. April 24, 1869, m. Jane Mills Oct. 26, 1892; Richard b. March 25, 1871; Harriet b. June 15, 1872, m. Joseph Hutchinson April 8, 1891; Louisa b. Dec. 16, 1874, m. F. M. Stephenson, Jr., Oct. 19, 1892; William b. Dec. 16, 1877, m. Mary Eliza Talbot Feb. 21, 1906; Arthur b. Sept. 21, 1880, m. Alice Ann Stephenson Jan. 28, 1903; Isabella b. April 25, 1882; Walter b. Dec. 6, 1884, m. Alice Blair Jan. 8, 1908; James b. May 24, 1887, m. Della Rigby Dec. 21, 1910; Dora b. Dec. 28, 1891. Family home Lewiston, Utah.

WHEELER, WILLIAM (son of George Walton Wheeler and Hannah Humphreys). Born Dec. 16, 1877, Lewiston, Utah.
Married Mary Eliza Talbot Feb. 21, 1906, Logan, Utah (daughter of Henry James Talbot and Livinia Ann Wall, pioneers 1861, Homer Duncan company). She was born Dec. 7, 1879, at Lewiston. Their children: Fontella b. Dec. 16, 1906; Thora b. April 29, 1909.

WHEELER, JOHN (son of John Wheeler, born Aug. 10, 1768, Harvestly, Eng., and Mary Fisher, born April 6, 1780, in England). He was born Sept. 13, 1804, Gravely, Cambridgeshire, Eng. Came to Utah Sept. 6, 1857, William Walker company.
Married Elizabeth Gillings (daughter of William Gillings and Sarah Marns), who was born in October, 1807, and came to Utah with husband. Their children: Mary b. May 8, 1831 (d. Nov. 8, 1912), m. Abram Chadwick; Joseph b. March 9, 1833, m. Nancy C. Bratton Jan. 15, 1865; John b. Sept. 13, 1834, m. Sarah E. Stone July 1866; Sarah b. Oct. 21, 1840, m. Thomas Etherington March 9, 1858; William b. Sept. 4, 1842, m. Martha L. Howell Dec. 15, 1861; Eliza b. April 11, 1846, m. George J. Linford Feb. 1, 1868.

WHEELER, WILLIAM (son of John Wheeler and Elizabeth Gillings of England). Born Sept. 4, 1842, Gravely, Cambridgeshire, Eng.
Married Martha L. Howell Dec. 15, 1861, Ogden, Utah (daughter of William Howell and Louisa Thomas, pioneers 1861, Captain Duncan company). She was born Nov. 21, 1843, Pembrokeshire, Wales. Their children: Susan M. b. Dec. 27, 1862, m. Joseph Bidwell March 8, 1889; William b. Sept. 21, 1864, m. Jane D. Dorney Oct. 9, 1889; John b. Jan. 11, 1867, m. Emma S. Manning June 13, 1894; Louisa b. Sept. 7, 1869, m. Orson Hudman May 19, 1889; Arthur b. May 30, 1872, d. June 25, 1912; Martha L. b. Sept. 10, 1874, d. Nov. 21, 1888; David b. Sept. 10, 1874, m. George Millard April 7, 1894; David b. Feb. 6, 1877, d. July 12, 1908; Andrew b. April 29, 1880; Jerome b. April 21, 1883. Family home Slaterville, Utah.

WHEELER, JOSEPH (son of Edward Wheeler of Whitburne, Herefordshire, Eng., and Ann Wood of Martley, Eng.; former born Jan. 22, 1804, latter April 5, 1800). He was born Oct. 27, 1828, at Whitburne. Came to Utah in 1853, oxteam company.
Married Alice Reede Dec. 11, 1855, Ogden, Utah, who was born Nov. 4, 1832, Newton, Lancastershire, Eng. Only child: Joseph Edward b. Aug. 22, 1856. Family home Ogden, Utah.
Married Sarah Ann Wood Oct. 3, 1858, American Fork, Utah (daughter of John B. and Mary Wood, pioneers Nov. 30, 1856, Edward Martin "frozen" handcart company). She was born March 2, 1827, Stockport, Eng. Their children: Frederick b. Sept. 30, 1859, m. Martha Knight March 1, 1883; Alice b. May 10, 1861, Thomas b. March 23, 1862; Hyrum b. May 29, 1863, latter three died; Sarah Ann Mariah b. Oct. 22, 1865, m. Hans Peterson. Family home Plain City, Utah.

WHEELER, FREDERICK (son of Joseph Wheeler and Sarah Ann Wood of Whitelawn, Eng.). Born Sept. 30, 1859, Ogden, Utah.
Married Martha Knight March 1, 1883, at Ogden (daughter of Alonzo Knight and Martha Sanders), born Oct. 11, 1861, at Plain City, Utah. Their children: Martha Pearl b. Nov. 30, 1883, m. Thomas Walker; Frederick Martin b. Nov. 10, 1886, m. Ruth Hodson; Irene b. July 13, 1889; Alonzo b. Oct. 21, 1892; Millie Enis b. March 5, 1896; Joseph Edward b. July 13, 1901; Adora Merea b. Oct. 4, 1903. Family home Ogden, Utah.

WHEELER, WALTER (son of Joseph Wheeler, born Feb. 27, 1817, Cheltenham, Gloucestershire, Eng., and Ann Buckingham, born Aug. 1, 1814, Twinton, Eng.). He was born May 22, 1844, at Charlton Kings, Cheltenham. Came to Utah Sept. 15, 1861, Milo Andrus company.
Married Ellen Maria Childs July 28, 1873 (daughter of Thomas Childs and Tabitha Milnes—married March 27, 1847, Bradford, Eng., pioneers Sept. 2, 1852, Abraham O. Smoot company). She was born in Liverpool, Eng., and came to Utah with parents. Their children: Walter b. May 9, 1874, d. June 23, 1887; Ellen Maria b. Jan. 20, 1876, m. Jesse O. Reynolds June 23, 1896; Tabitha Ann b. Jan. 29, 1878, d. Aug. 23, 1878; Joseph Thomas b. Aug. 9, 1879, m. Edith M. Hutchinson Sept. 25, 1901; Alma Young b. Feb. 10, 1882, m. Dorothy M. Stoker Sept. 23, 1903; Mary Matilda b. June 3, 1884, m. Cyrus G. Sanford; Emma Bell b. Nov. 1, 1886, m. Dimmick Childs; Hilda Elizabeth b. Sept. 16, 1889, m. Amyot W. Cherrington June 9, 1909; Kate Milnes b. Jan. 9, 1892, m. Andrew B. Olsen Aug. 1, 1911. Family home Springville, Utah.
Made several trips across the plains for immigrants and merchandise. Took active part in protecting the settlers against the Indians. Worked on Union Pacific and Central Pacific railroads, and as mason of Provo woolen mills. Undertaker and embalmer at Springville.

WHEELER, JOSEPH THOMAS (son of Walter Wheeler and Ellen Maria Childs). Born Aug. 9, 1879.
Married Edith M. Hutchinson Sept. 25, 1901, Springville, Utah (daughter of Robert A. Hutchinson and Harriet Elizabeth Hall), who was born May 26, 1881, Springville, Utah. Their children: Joseph Walter b. Aug. 10, 1904; Robert b. Nov. 19, 1906; Beatrice b. April 9, 1910.

WHERRY, ELI J. (son of James Wherry and Elizabeth Patterson, Scenery Hill, Washington county, Pa.). Born March 1, 1843, Scenery Hill. Came to Utah 1901.
Married Frances Ann Weaver Sept. 1, 1866, Mt. Vernon, Ohio (daughter of William Henry Weaver and Nancy Hill of Scenery Hill). She was born June, 1844. Their children: Jennie, m. C. W. Jewett; Emery, died; Curtis A., m. Eva Young; Styles W., m. Cornelia V. Zimmerman; Pearl, died; Arthur C., m. Daisy P. Smith; Linnie P., m. Maud Roberts; Lee O., died.
Farmer and contractor.

WHERRY, CURTIS A. (son of E. J. Wherry and Frances Ann Weaver). Born Dec. 18, 1872, De Soto, Kan. Came to Utah April 4, 1899.
Married Eva Young Sept. 18, 1900, Marshall, Mo. (daughter of George Young and Virginia F. Gillham of Marshall). She was born Jan. 17, 1876. Their children: Virginia F. b. Dec. 9, 1902; Curtis A., Jr., b. Jan. 2, 1905; George Y. b. April 5, 1907; Jack L. b. Jan. 30, 1909.

WHIPPLE, NELSON WHEELER (son of Daniel Whipple and Mary Tiffany, Sanford, Broom county, N. Y.). Born July 7, 1818, at Sanford. Came to Utah 1848.
Married Susan Jane Bailey Aug. 6, 1843, Elysia, Lorain Co., Ohio, who was born March 9, 1828. Their children: Meranda Jane, m. Henry Code; Mary, m. Richard Waddems; George Nelson; Edson, m. Mary Beck; Harriet Emily, d. infant; Annie Bard.
Married Rachel Keeling West of Derbyshire, Eng., March 12, 1855, Salt Lake City, who was born March 19, 1818. Their children: Daniel, m. Ellen Hearst; Cynthia, d. infant; Wheeler b. April 15, 1859, m. Mary Roberts Feb. 1, 1881.
Married Susan Ann Gay Feb. 9, 1857, Salt Lake City (daughter of Alexander Gay and Martha Covington, De Kalb, Kemper county, Miss.; former died at Mt. Pisgah, Iowa, on the way to Utah, latter pioneer 1850). She was born June 13, 1841, and came to Utah 1851, John Brown company. Their children: Martha Ellen, m. Jacob Kesler; Nelson Gay, m. Susanah Wanless; Sylvia, m. Fred B. Margetts; Susan Ann, m. Archer W. Clayton; Alexander, m. Sarah Vannotta; Robert John, m. Susan Winn; Amy Jane, m. John H. Evans; Ida, m. Ezra O. Taylor; Annor. Families resided Salt Lake City.
Seventy; block teacher. Lumberman; made first shingles for the tabernacle. With army that met Johnston in Echo Canyon. Policeman. Died July 5, 1884.

WHIPPLE, WHEELER (son of Nelson Wheeler Whipple of Ohio and Rachel Keeling of Derbyshire, Eng.). Born April 15, 1859.
Married Mary Roberts Feb. 1, 1881, Lehi, Utah (daughter of John Roberts and Adelaide Ford of Lehi, pioneers 1864, Captain Ricks company). She was born July 15, 1857, Merthyr Tydfil, Wales; came to Utah with parents. Their children: John W. b. Oct. 19, 1881, m. Clara McMillan; Mabel b. July 4, 1883, m. Leo Jones; Rachel b. Dec. 20, 1885, d. infant; Nelson b. March 13, 1887, d. infant; Adelaide b. May 5, 1888, d. aged 10; Lawrence b. Sept. 24, 1891; Lillie b. May 6, 1894; Leslie b. Oct. 1, 1897. Family home 28th ward, Salt Lake City.

WHITAKER, JAMES (son of William and Mary Canada Whitaker, former born Nov. 22, 1772, in Davidson county, N. C., latter Oct. 27, 1772, in Halifax county, N. C.). He was born May 14, 1805, in Buncombe county, N. C. Came to Utah 1850, William Snow company.
Married Milinda Fishel February, 1824, Fairview, Buncombe county, N. C., who was born Feb. 13, 1806, in Stokes county, N. C. Their children: Louisa b. Feb. 28, 1825, m. Harmon D. Pierson Aug. 16, 1848; Solomon b. Aug. 21, 1826, m. Mary Sanford; Martha b. Jan. 8, 1828, m. John Woodworth; Rozilla b. Dec. 12, 1829, m. Mathew M. Dalton Dec. 15, 1850; Margret b. Feb. 28, 1831, m. Thomas Woodland Feb. 8, 1849; David b. Nov. 8, 1832, m. Naomi Jinkins, Nancy Woodland in 1838 (daughter of John Woodland and Celia Steepleford, pioneers 1850, William Snow company). She was born Dec. 13, 1820. Their children: Nancy M. b. Oct. 11, 1838, m. Erastus Vella Jan. 4, 1855; James W. b. May 7, 1841, m. Mary J. McMinn Dec. 6, 1859; Leander J. b. Jan. 15, 1844 (d. Jan. 5, 1912), m. Ann E. Mitchell; William D. b. Dec. 6, 1846, died; Elizabeth C. b. May 24, 1849, m. H. C. Wardleigh; Celia M. b. Aug. 27, 1851, m. S. S. Sadoris Feb. 5, 1869; John N. b. Nov. 3, 1853, m. Sarah J. Malory Feb. 18, 1877; Hyrum P. b. Oct. 30, 1855; Mary A. b. Dec. 11, 1857, m. Henry Call March 22, 1879; Jerusha L. b. March 10, 1860, m. J. W. Smith March 22, 1879; Henry M. b. March 10, 1862, m. Viola Savage; Marriam H. b. March 10, 1862, m. D. J. Costley Oct. 5, 1889. Family home Willard City, Utah.
High priest; missionary to southern states 1876. Died in 1892.

WHITAKER, LEANDER J. (son of James Whitaker and Nancy Woodland). Born Jan. 15, 1844, in Hancock county, Ill.
Married Ann Eliza Mitchell June 12, 1864, Willard, Utah (daughter of T. Mitchell and Rebecca Huff), who was born April 23, 1849, in Chickasaw county, Miss. Their children: L. T. b. Feb. 13, 1867, m. Mary A. Parsons Nov. 1890; Rebecca A. b. Feb. 10, 1870, m. E. Hunt Feb. 1888; Nancy V. b. Dec. 14, 1870, m. Marcho Peterson 1887; James S. b. Aug. 6, 1873, m. Sarah Low 1901; Martha M. b. Jan. 23, 1876; Parley H. b. March 9, 1879, m. Ellan Erickson; Lorah J. b. Jan. 22, 1881, m. Samuel M. Newbold 1902; Henry S. b. Aug. 3, 1882. Family home Downey, Idaho.

WHITAKER, L. T. (son of Leander J. Whitaker and Ann Eliza Mitchell). Born Feb. 13, 1867, Richmond, Utah.
Married Mary A. Parsons Nov. 20, 1890, Logan, Utah (daughter of James Parsons, born Jan. 26, 1836, and Mary A. Catt, born May 26, 1836, of Newton, Cache Co., Utah). She was born June 20, 1872, Sussex, Eng. Their children: Violet b. Sept. 14, 1891, d. Oct. 8, 1912; Guy T. b. Jan. 23, 1893; Claude M. b. Sept. 11, 1894; Essie b. Sept. 29, 1896; Zelpha b. Sept. 11, 1898; Lorine G. b. Jan. 27, 1900; James J. b. Aug. 24, 1902; Cecil b. Aug. 5, 1904, d. Feb. 4, 1905; Preston P. b. Dec. 6, 1905; Karma b. Oct. 14, 1907; Randa b. Jan. 17, 1910; Wendell b. Nov. 2, 1912. Family home Downey, Bannock Co., Idaho.

WHITAKER, JOHN N. (son of James Whitaker and Nancy Woodland). Born Nov. 3, 1853, Willard, Utah.
Married Sarah J. Malory 1876, Willard, Utah (daughter of Elisha Malory and Emma Zundle), who was born 1860 at Willard. Their children: James J. b. Nov. 27, 1877;

Sarah M. b. Dec. 29, 1878, m. Lewis Wight; William E. b. Nov. 19, 1880, m. Emily Palmer; John H. b. Feb. 19, 1883; Udalia b. May 7, 1884; Lewis E. b. Dec. 6, 1885, m. Emma C. Cole; Don J. b. Nov. 29, 1887, m. Florence Ottly; Elwood L. b. Oct. 1, 1889; Andy S. b. June 12, 1891; Clara A. b. Sept. 21, 1892, m. Thor Lund; Ira B. b. Aug. 19, 1894; Ercy U. b. April 17, 1897; Adelia J. b. Nov. 29, 1898; Terteilian B. b. June 17, 1900; Reuben L. b. Feb. 2, 1902; Cecy F. b. Feb. 17, 1904. Family home Almo, Idaho.
Ward teacher.

WHITAKER, LEWIS E. (son of John N. Whitaker and Sarah J. Malory). Born Dec. 6, 1885, Almo, Idaho.
Married Emma C. Cole March 6, 1911, Ogden, Utah (daughter of Thomas R. Cole and Emma E. Lowe of Willard, Utah). She was born 1890 at Willard. Their child: John E. b. Oct. 9, 1911.
Priest.

WHITBY, WINWARD. Born Oct. 16, 1831, Cheltenham, Eng. Came to Utah 1853, Cyrus H. Wheelock company.
Married Martha Antell in 1853, Salt Lake City. Their child: Thomas, d. child.
Married Anne Jane McCowan Feb. 17, 1856, Salt Lake City (daughter of Robert McCowan and Elizabeth Skeleton of Liverpool, Eng., pioneers Oct. 10, 1853, John Brown company). She was born Sept. 27, 1839. Their child: James b. Nov. 30, 1856, m. Harriet Lee. Family home Nephi, Utah. Member 49th quorum seventies; elder. Farmer. Died May 7, 1880.

WHITBY, JAMES (son of Winward Whitby and Anne Jane McCowan). Born Nov. 30, 1856, Nephi, Utah.
Married Harriet Lee Dec. 18, 1879, Salt Lake City (daughter of Thomas Lee and Primrose Shields of Tooele, Utah, pioneers Oct. 5, 1852, Philemon C. Merrill company). She was born Nov. 6, 1858. Their children: James Leroy b. Jan. 7, 1883, d. child; Thomas W. b. Jan. 14, 1885, m. Clara Burgess; Primrose b. Feb. 27, 1887, m. Frank De La Mare; Le Nora b. June 27, 1889, m. Rudolph Olson; Melvin b. Feb. 28, 1892, Eveline b. Dec. 30, 1894, and Lee Milton b. Sept. 18, 1897, latter three died children; Leo Lavora b. 1899. Family home Marion, Idaho.
Elder. School trustee; constable of Marion. Farmer.

WHITE, JOHN CHAMBERS (son of John and Mary Ann White of Birmingham, Warwickshire, Eng.). Born June 1, 1832, at Birmingham. Came to Utah Sept. 20, 1853, Claudius V. Spencer oxteam company.
Married Mary Ann Ingram March 9, 1863, Spanish Fork, Utah (daughter of Edward Ingram and Ann Smith of Newbold, Warwickshire, Eng., pioneers 1869). She was born April 20, 1841. Their children: John Edward b. June 24, 1864, d. aged 3; Elizabeth Ann b. Dec. 24, 1866, m. Edward C. Abbott; Levi C. b. March 5, 1868, m. Bertha Giles; Oscar Thomas b. April 2, 1870, m. Ann Baxendale; Rosetta b. Aug. 7, 1872, m. Elijah W. Mayhew; Lilly Ann b. June 14, 1874, m. Sol Parker; Hyrum b. April 17, 1876, d. infant; Mary Ann b. Feb. 10, 1878, d. infant; John Henry b. June 30, 1883, m. Annie Ekker. Family home Levan, Juab Co., Utah.
High priest; ward teacher. Hauled first rock for Salt Lake temple. Called to help settle The Muddy. Veteran Indian war. Farmer and gardener.

WHITE, OSCAR THOMAS (son of John C. White and Mary Ann Ingram). Born April 2, 1870, Levan, Utah.
Married Ann Baxendale Dec. 16, 1903, Manti, Utah (daughter of John Baxendale and Lydia Blackledge of Chorley, Lancastershire, Eng.; latter came to Utah). She was born Dec. 5, 1880. Their children: Pearl b. Dec. 9, 1904; May b. Jan. 20, 1907; Evaline b. March 6, 1909, d. infant; Leona B. b. March 6, 1910; Harold b. Dec. 2, 1911. Family home Duchesne, Utah.
Missionary to England 1900-02; seventy; ward teacher; Sunday school teacher. Farmer.

WHITE, JOHN S. (son of Andrew White of Middleton, N. J., born Sept. 15, 1791, in Monmouth county, N. J., and Jane Tunis, born in 1792, in same county and state). He was born Feb. 15, 1818, Keyport, N. J. Came to Utah September, 1848, Company C. Mormon Battalion.
Married Ann Eliza Everett April 5, 1849 (daughter of Addison Everett and Eliza Ann Elting—former pioneer 1847, Captain Grant company, latter died in New York City). She was born Aug. 30, 1832, and came to Utah 1847, Jedediah M. Grant company. Their children: Mary Jane b. April 5, 1853, m. Henry L. Hinman; Medora b. April 9, 1855, m. Israel Call; Margret Mariah b. June 9, 1857, m. James M. Andersen; Eliza Ann b. July 8, 1860, m. Peter Christensen; Orpha Elvira b. Sept. 3, 1862, m. Marion F. Stephenson; Elizabeth b. April 24, 1864, m. James H. Hess; John S., Jr., b. March 16, 1867, m. Ethellynn Rice; Adelaide b. Dec. 13, 1868, m. Willard Call; Schuyler E. b. Oct. 2, 1870, m. Ruth Talbot; Henry Addison b. Dec. 22, 1872, died; James Monroe b. April 16, 1875, died. Family home Farmington, Utah.
Member of Colonel Scott's artillery in Illinois in 1846; enlisted as private in Iowa volunteers at Council Bluffs July 16, 1846, and started west the same year, going to California, and was foreman of Captain Sutter's shoe factory at the time gold was discovered in California; he left this position to pan gold for himself. Came to Utah in the fall of 1848.

WHITE, JOHN S., JR. (son of John S. White and Ann Eliza Everett). Born March 16, 1867, Farmington, Utah.
He married Ethellynn Rice Jan. 10, 1890, Logan, Utah (daughter of Leonard G. Rice and Lucy Jane Stevens; latter came to Utah with Brigham Young, Jr.). She was born Oct. 13, 1872, Farmington, Utah. Their children: Gertrude b. March 29, 1892; John Leonard b. March 8, 1894; James Leroy b. May 22, 1895. Family resided Bear River City and Farmington.
Established the Reflex Publishing Co., September, 1909; editor "Weekly Reflex." Served six years as city councilman; six years as president Farmington school board. Farmer; horticulturist; publisher.

WHITE, JOSEPH (son of Jonathan White, born Nov. 11, 1809, Tealby, Lincolnshire, Eng., and Elizabeth Dodd, born Aug. 1, 1813, Dillingga, Lincolnshire—married Nov. 3, 1835). He was born Dec. 26, 1840, Yorkshire, Eng. Came to Utah Oct. 28, 1849, Ezra Taft Benson company.
Married Samantha Gollaher May 7, 1865 (daughter of William and Elizabeth Gollaher), who was born January, 1847. Their children: Jonathan b. April 6, 1866; Joseph b. Aug. 1869, m. Elizabeth Tanner 1894. Family home Tooele, Utah.

WHITE, SAMUEL STEPHEN (son of Henry White and Rebecca Smith of Vermont). Born April 8, 1821, in Chittenden county, Vt. Came to Utah late in 1848 with members of Co. A, Mormon Battalion, and an independent company.
Married Catherine Foutz Sept. 27, 1849, Salt Lake City (daughter of Jacob Foutz and Margeret Mann of Nauvoo, Ill., pioneers Oct. 1, 1847, Edward Hunter company). She was born Dec. 25, 1831. Their children: Charles Samuel b. Sept. 27, 1850; Jacob Hanmer b. 1852; Henry Edgar b. Jan. 9, 1855; Clarissa b. July 25, 1857; Mary Abigail b. May 3, 1859; Isaac Harvey b. Nov. 6, 1861; Margeret Emeretta b. Aug. 4, 1864; Alma F. b. March 13, 1867; Evelyn b. April 22, 1869; Caroline b. Nov. 6, 1871. Family home Pleasant Grove, Utah.
School trustee; constable. Farmer and stockraiser. Died Oct. 15, 1900.

WHITE, CHARLES SAMUEL (son of Samuel Stephen White and Catherine Foutz). Born Sept. 27, 1850, in Cottonwood. Salt Lake county.
Married Emma M. Stewart (daughter of Charles Stewart and Sarah A. Roberts), who was born Dec. 19, 1853, Pleasant Grove, Utah. Their children: Samuel Charles b. Feb. 27, 1882, died; Lorena b. Jan. 29, 1885; Stewart LeGrande b. Jan. 1, 1887; William Vordy b. Aug. 28, 1889, died.
Farmer and stockman.

WHITE, THOMAS HENRY (son of George White and Mary Rivers of Calne, Wiltshire, Eng.). Born Nov. 25, 1846, Chalcutt, Eng. Came to Utah Sept. 25, 1863, Peter Nebeker company.
Married Emily Oliver Feb. 5, 1867, Salt Lake City (daughter of Francis Oliver and Elizabeth Bailey of Crabgutter, Eng., pioneers 1866, Patterson Holliday independent company). She was born April 10, 1848. Their children: Mary Emily b. Jan. 13, 1868, d. infant; Lucy Agnes b. April 19, 1869, m. Sidney Alexander Pace; Katie Rosabell b. Sept. 25, 1870, m. Thomas E. T. Doman; Lily May b. May 28, 1872, d. infant; Amelia Janet b. Nov. 9, 1873, m. Arthur Henry Ellis; Thomas Henry, Jr., b. Oct. 5, 1875, m. Leticia Pearl Cloward; Jennie Isabella b. Aug. 30, 1877, m. Alexander O. Barnett; George Francis b. Oct. 21, 1879, m. Emily Swaby Baggs; Elizabeth Jane b. Dec. 25, 1882, m. Tracy Bronson; Millie Ann b. Dec. 12, 1886, m. William Wallace Woodard; Myrtle Myra b. Sept. 24, 1891. Family resided Salt Lake City, Ogden, Farmington and Layton, Utah.
Married Mary Ann Jones Nov. 2, 1874, Salt Lake City (daughter of Jeremiah Jones and Ann Johnson of Norfolk, Yorkshire, Eng., and came to Utah in 1872). She was born April 15, 1858. Their children: Joseph Elijah b. Dec. 30, 1875, m. Diantha E. Pace (died), m. Ethel I. Hodson; Emily Ann b. June 13, 1877, m. John W. Lefler; Mary Elizabeth b. May 28, 1879, d. infant; Pleasants Maud b. June 20, 1880, m. Thomas Lewis; Jacob Jeremiah b. Oct. 14, 1882, m. Nellie Potts; John Ray b. Feb. 28, 1885, m. Ascenith Bodon; Malinda b. July 8, 1887, m. Nephi Moon; James William b. Oct. 20, 1889, and Orabell b. May 29, 1891, d. infants; Archie Thomas b. Jan. 5, 1897.
High priest; missionary to Green River 1881. Assisted in bringing immigrants to Utah in 1866. Did all the blacksmithing on the Utah stake tabernacle; worked on the temple and tabernacle and on various other buildings in the state. Blacksmith.

WHITE, WILLIAM (son of William White and Martha Griffith, both of Wales). Born Sept. 21, 1826, Fishguard. Wales. Came to Utah 1876.
Married Anne Thomas, Haverford, Wales (daughter of David Thomas and Elizabeth Nash, same country, pioneers Oct. 23, 1862). She was born Feb. 21, 1832. Their children: John H., m. Clara Feveryear; Sarah Jane, died; William L.

m. Croilla Louise Egbert; David H., m. Harriet Lawson; Martha Jane; Elizabeth Ann. m. Robert B. T. Taylor; Benjamin, Mary Ann, James Thomas. latter three died; Joseph Parley. m. Isabell Barrett; Mira Matilda. m. William Dalton Neal; Thomas Charles, m. Edith May Margetts; Ada Maria, m. Reed T. Cannon.
Member 3d quorum seventies; patriarch. Wholesale dealer meats. Died Dec. 11, 1905. Salt Lake City.

WHITE, J. PARLEY (son of William White and Ann Thomas). Born Jan. 21, 1871, Neyland, Wales. Came to Utah 1876.
Married Isabell Barrett Dec. 21, 1893, Salt Lake City (daughter of Clarence and Hannah Barrett of same place, pioneers 1568). She was born Dec. 6, 1876. Their children: Vivian Parley b. Sept. 12, 1896; Leslie Barrett b. July 7, 1898. Family home, Salt Lake City.
Elder, Chief deputy sheriff ten years. Director Farmers & Stockgrowers Bank. Cattle and sheep raiser.

WHITE, JOHN H. (son of William White and Anne Thomas). Born Aug. 24, 1855, Haken, Wales. Came to Utah 1876.
Married Clara Feveryear Jan. 18, 1883, Salt Lake City (daughter of Robert Feveryear and Mary Ann Welton of Norwich, Eng., who came to Utah April, 1883). She was born June 11, 1861, came to Utah November. 1882. Their children; William Henry b. Nov. 2, 1883, m. Gertrude Kelly; Thomas Charles b. June 12, 1885; Ada Irene b. Feb. 12, 1887; John Harrison b. March 4, 1889, died; Chancy L. b. April 8, 1891; Hazel Ann b. March 19, 1893; Cornelius George b. April 16, 1895; Mira b. Oct. 27, 1896; Byron L. b. May 6, 1899; Mabel Clara b. May 13, 1902; Gertrude B. Jan. 11, 1905. Family home, Salt Lake City.
Member 3d quorum seventies; missionary to England 1879-82. Vice-president State Fair Association. Wholesale meat dealer; breeder of cattle and buffaloes; one of the owners of Antelope Island. Died July 12, 1910.

WHITEHEAD, WILLIAM (son of Robert and Alice Whitehead of England). Born July 3, 1816, Lancastershire, Eng. Came to Utah 1852, Captain Howell company.
Married Jane Hardman. Nauvoo, Ill., who was born Sept. 1, 1816, and died 1848, at Nauvoo. Only child: Joseph Samuel b. April 1, 1845, m. Delia P. Curtis. Family home Payson, Utah.
Married Anne Spencer, Council Bluffs, Iowa. Their children: Mary Alice, m. William Depew; Martha Jane, m. Delbert Simons; William Henry, m. Ruth Oyler; Elizabeth Anne, m. John Sturgis; Hannah Mariah, m. Gus Royer; Reuben Hyrum; Matilda Anne, m. Niel Daley. Family home Payson, Utah.
High priest; bishop of Payson ward 20 years. One of early settlers of Payson. Veteran Black Hawk war. Payson city marshal. Mason and farmer. Died Nov. 5, 1885.

WHITEHEAD, JOSEPH SAMUEL (son of William Whitehead and Jane Hardman). Born April 1, 1845, Nauvoo, Ill. Came to Utah 1852, Thomas Howell company.
Married Delia Presendia Curtis July 24, 1869, Payson, Utah (daughter of Joseph Curtis and Sarah Reed of same place, pioneers Oct. 12, 1848), who was born Dec. 9, 1849. Their children: Presendia Adelma b. April 23, 1870, m. J. Ian Taylor; Joseph William b. March 14, 1872, m. Alzina Swart; James Franklin b. March 3, 1874, d. May 11, 1876; Ann Alma b. Feb. 4, 1876, d. Feb. 9, 1878; Sarah Jane b. March 2, 1878, m. James M. Rigby; George Eli b. March , 1881, m. Bertha Anderson; Alice Zobedia b. June 15, 83, m. R. H. Barney; Emma Sophia b. Oct. 26, 1886, m. avid S. Sanderson; Frederick Adolphus b. Aug. 17, 1889; Mary Ethel b. Sept. 27, 1892; Orie T. Fillison b. June 3, 1895. Family resided Burrville and Annabella, Utah.
High priest; bishop of Burrville ward four years; counselor to Bishop Cloward of Burrville ward ten years. Veteran Black Hawk war. Assisted in bringing immigrants to Utah 1864. Settled in Grass Valley 1878. Farmer and stockraiser.

WHITESIDES, LEWIS (son of James Whitesides). Born March 26, 1828, Chester county, Pa. Came to Utah 1852, John Walker company.
Married Susannah Perkins, who was born April 5, 1830, and came to Utah with husband. Their children: Elizabeth A.; Ann Deseret; Joshua Harris; James Lewis; Marion Mark; Mary Susan; Edward Morris; Nancy. m. Joseph S. Free; John Absolam; William Wilford. Family home Kaysville, Davis Co., Utah.

WHITING, EDWIN. Born Sept. 9, 1809, in Lee county, Mass. Came to Utah 1849, Captain Morley company.
Married Elizabeth Tilotson. Only child: Louisa M. b. May 17, 1850. m. Aaron Johnson, Jr. Oct. 8, 1871. Family home Springville, Utah.
Settled at Manti 1849. Missionary to Ohio two years. Member Utah legislature from Manti 1859-60; mayor of Manti. Moved to Springville 1862. Nurseryman. Died Dec. 8, 1890.

WHITLOCK, ANDREW. Came to Utah in September, 1853, Captain Tidwell company.
Married Hannah Allred (daughter of James and Betsy Allred, Tennessee, pioneers Oct. 5, 1851, Captain Kelsey company). Their children: Sallie Ray b. Oct. 9, 1828, m.

Henry H. Oviatt Feb. 1, 1853; Charles, m. Matilda King; Mary Jane, m. John Franklin Oviatt; Hardin. m. Margaret Vorse; Elizabeth R., m. Henry B. Stevens 1854; Maria, m. William Beal; Andrew H., m. Andrea Overlade; Thursa, m. Louis Larsen. Family home Ephraim, Utah.
Elder. Hatter; farmer. Died in 1865.

WHITMORE, JAMES MONTGOMERY (son of George Whitmore of Tennessee). Born September, 1822, in Tennessee. Came to Utah in 1857, Homer Duncan company.
Married Mary Elizabeth Carter in 1852 (daughter of Richard and Elizabeth Carter of Texas), who was born in 1826.
Their children: George C. b. Jan. 26, 1853, m. Mary Elizabeth Hague; James Montgomery b. June 5, 1855, m. Hannah Nixon; Joseph b. 1857, died; Brigham b. 1859, m. Eva Perkins; Samuel M. b. 1864, m. Elizabeth Grange; Tasy b. Dec. 1865, m. William Grace. Family home St. George, Utah.
Seventy. Killed by Indians Jan. 6, 1866, Pipe Springs, Utah.

WHITMORE, JAMES MONTGOMERY, JR. (son of James Montgomery Whitmore and Mary Elizabeth Carter). Born June 5, 1855, Waxahachie, Texas. Came to Utah with parents.
Married Hannah Maria Nixon Dec. 25, 1883, St. George, Utah (daughter of James W. Nixon and Hannah Nixon, of Wisconsin, pioneers 1860). She was born Nov. 16, 1865. Their children: Mary E. b. April 19, 1886, died; Junius Leo b. May 13, 1888; Arthur Lawrence b. March 19, 1890, m. Ada Shinen; Virnie Ray b. March 14, 1892; Leland b. March 25, 1895; George Lacelle b. July 7, 1897. Family home Price, Utah.
President First National Bank of Price; president board trustees of Price for seven years; member of city council. Stockraiser.

WHITNEY, ORSON F. (son of Horace K. Whitney, a pioneer of 1847 and the eldest son of Newel K. Whitney, who was Presiding Bishop of the Church of Jesus Christ of Latter-day Saints, and Helen Mar Kimball, eldest daughter so to speak, he r.esented his church, by appointment of the Heber C. Kimball, one of the original Twelve Apostles of Deseret, and at the time of his death a member of the First Presidency). He was born July 1, 1855, Salt Lake City.
Married Zina Smoot December, 1879 (daughter of President A. O. Smoot). She was the mother of nine children. She died May, 1900.
Married May Wells (daughter of Daniel Hammer Wells and Lydia Ann Alley). She is the mother of two children.
"Elder 1873; seventy 1876; ordained a high priest and set apart as Bishop of the Eighteenth ward July 14, 1878; member of the council of the twelve apostles of the Church of Jesus Christ of Latter-day Saints; missionary to eastern states October, 1876-78; to Europe 1881-83. Main founder and first president of the Wasatch Literary Association. Clerk, collector and city editor of the 'Deseret News' 1878 City councilman 1880—his first civic office. Helped to organize, and was president of the Home Dramatic Club. Associate editor of the 'Millennial Star' at Liverpool, Eng. City treasurer 1883-1890. Chancellor of the University of Deseret, succeeding Hon. George Q. Cannon. Chief clerk of the House of Representatives 1888. First elder to hold Sabbath services at the Penitentiary. The town of Whitney, Idaho, was named for him. One of the three framers of the 'Declaration of Grievances and Protest,' and the reader of that document at the great Tabernacle mass meeting May, 1885, and a year later he delivered the address of welcome to Governor Caleb W. West, on his arrival at Salt Lake City. At the General Conference in October, 1890, he was called to read President Woodruff's 'Manifesto' to the Congregation. In May, 1890, Bishop Whitney began the History of Utah. He was the choice for this work, of the most prominent men and women in the community and was employed by the publishing company organized by Dr. John O. Williams, an experienced book man from the east, who was the main owner of the enterprise. The Bishop's duties were purely literary; at no time did he have anything to do with the business management. Served the public gratuitously in various ways. At a Unitarian conference held in the Jewish Synagogue at Salt Lake City in 1892, at which ministers of various denominations were invited First Presidency. His address was pronounced by the Rabbi the most impressive one delivered on the occasion. He was prominent at peace and charity meetings and other gatherings of a public character. In the fall of 1894, Mr. Whitney engaged in his first political campaign. Up to this time he had never made a political speech, nor had he united with either of the new organizations which had superseded the People's and the Liberal parties. His predilections were for Democracy. Never an office-seeker, and shunning rather than courting public life, at the solicitation of Democratic leaders, he became a candidate for the Constitutional Convention, and was elected by the largest majority cast in his precinct. The part played by him in the convention—notably in the great woman's suffrage debate—is well known. He served upon various important committees, and was one of the special committee that revised the constitution prior to its transmission to Washington. In January, 1896, accepted a professor's chair in the Brigham Young College at Logan, and for the next eighteen months was a resident of that town, and an in-

structor in Theology and English. In the Pioneer Jubilee, Bishop Whitney played a prominent part, beginning with the reading for President Woodruff, who was too feeble to speak, of the dedicatory prayer at the unveiling of the pioneer monument. He compiled for the Jubilee Commission the 'Book of the Pioneers' for the state archives, and contributed to the literature of the period a poem, 'The Lily and the Bee,' an allegory of the founding of Utah. His 'Ode to the Pioneers,' adapted from one of his earlier poems, and set to music by Professor Evan Stephens, was sung with thrilling effect by the Tabernacle choir during the five days' celebration. Since the opening of 1899, Bishop Whitney has been connected with the Church Historian's Office. For several years he has presided over the State Historical Society. In literature he shines conspicuously, but all his previous efforts are eclipsed by his latest production, 'Elias, an Epic of the Ages.' It is lofty, massive, grand, exhibiting fertility of thought, expansive research and wonderful constructive ability. The great theme that it embodies—Eternal Truth—has probably never before been treated so comprehensively in a poetic way. Along with his devotion to literature, he retains his early affection for music and the drama, and makes it a point to see and hear the most gifted artists, as also the best preachers and lecturers."

WHITNEY, SAMUEL ALONZO (son of Alonzo Wells Whitney, born Dec. 27, 1818, Canandaigua, Ontario county, N. Y., and Henrietta Keys, born Dec. 25, 1821, in Pike Co., Ohio). Born Nov. 10, 1840, Palmyra, Union Co., Ohio. Came to Utah Sept. 29, 1847, John Taylor company.
Married Fannie Mariah Wall September, 1862 (daughter of William Wall, who came to Utah September, 1863, Thomas E. Ricks company). She was born Feb. 13, 1842. Their children: Fannie Louisa b. Sept. 23, 1864, m. Robert Burns 1886; Laura Ann b. May 10, 1866, m. Louis Reynolds Sept. 25, 1885; Harriet Mariah b. April 23, 1867, m. Fritz Jensen May 5, 1888; Ada Henrietta b. July 2, 1869, m. Percy Chandler Feb. 16, 1888; Margaret Melissa b. Feb. 15, 1871, m. Henry Chandler Sept. 1, 1889; Mary Elvira b. April 14, 1873, m. George Stringham; Samuel Alonzo b. April 14, 1873, m. Edna Hulse Aug. 7, 1893; Sarah Vilate b. Feb. 12, 1875, m. Frank Cowley Sept. 8, 1893; William Wells b. June 29, 1877, m. Nellie Fox April 29, 1901; Zalnora Adell b. Aug. 7, 1879, m. George Chandler. Family home Millville, Cache Co., Utah.
Married Pauline Ann Campbell Aug. 8, 1878, Salt Lake City (daughter of Samuel and Rebecca Campbell, latter pioneer 1847, Brigham Young company). Their children: Don Carlos b. Dec. 15, 1879, d. infant; Almira May b. April 28, 1881, m. Harvey Fisher Jan. 1, 1897.
Sunday school teacher. Minuteman; veteran Indian wars. Indian interpreter for Cache county since 1861. Called to herd cattle on Promontory, Box Elder county, three winters, 1860-62. Carried first mail out of Cache county 1862. Lost an arm in 1856 and a foot in 1890, but still remained an active and successful farmer.

WHITNEY, SAMUEL ALONZO (son of Alonzo Whitney and Fannie Mariah Wall). Born April 14, 1873, Millville, Utah.
Married Edna Hulse, Millville, Utah (daughter of Charles Wesley and Ann Smith Hulse, pioneers 1862), who was born Feb. 8, 1874, at Millville. Their children: Wills Alonzo b. May 6, 1894; Edna L. b. Jan. 24, 1896; Forest Ann b. Sept. 26, 1897; Myrtle b. Nov. 3, 1899; Leon b. Jan. 23, 1902; Mervin b. May 22, 1905; Merlin b. Aug. 27, 1907; Varsel b. Aug. 6, 1910. Family home Millville, Utah.

WHITTAKER, ISAAC. Born in England. Came to Utah 1847.
Married Betsy Gallant, at Salt Lake City, who was born May 8, 1833. Their children: David, m. Mary Smith; Isaac N. b. Dec. 1, 1861, m. Mary Curl; Zenus, m. Nellie Warwood, m. Ida Wright; Joseph, m. Nessie Winn; Martha, m. George Manwarring, m. Lon Reynolds; Rachel, m. Francis T. Bailey. Family home, Salt Lake City.
Member seventy. Served in Echo Canyon campaign. Farmer. Died at Salt Lake City.

WHITTAKER, ISAAC NATHANIEL (son of Isaac Whittaker and Betsy Gallant). Born Dec. 1, 1861, Salt Lake City.
Married Mary Curl, Salt Lake City (daughter of Archibald Curl), who was born Aug. 1, 1866. Their children: Louisa E. b. May 19, 1881, m. William Fleet Wiscombe; Samuel C., m. Jennie Dalton; Archibald C.; Mary, m. Morris Gray; Isaac, m. Lizzie Hunter; Earl; Lester. Family home, Salt Lake City.
Married Kate Fisher, Salt Lake City, who was born 1870. Their children: Norman b. Dec. 28, 1905; Armenia b. July 26, 1907. Family home Lake Shore, Utah.
Elder. Farmer and real estate dealer.

WHITTLE, THOMAS L. (son of Thomas Whittle). Born May 21, 1812, in Upper Canada, Montreal, Canada. Their Pulsipher company.
Married Mary Fullmer 1833, Montreal, Canada. Their children: Olive, m. Aroet Hale; Casper, m. Mary Ann Harris; Mary, m. Asro Eastman; George, m. Janette Sevier; Zera, m. Casan Pope; Emeline, m. William Harris; Thomas William, m. Adelia Hendricks; Aroetta, m. Brigham Pond.

Family resided Salt Lake City, Fort Harriman, Grantsville and Richmond, Utah.
Married Mary Jane Butterfield. Their children: Manerva, m. Andrew Allen; Edwin, m. Adeline Doty; Almond; Mary, m. Mr. Jensen.
Missionary to Sandwich Islands 1849-51; 1st counselor to Bishop M. W. Merrill. Farmer. Died July 3, 1865, Richmond, Utah.

WHITWORTH, GEORGE (son of Francis Whitworth and Dorothy Watkinson of Temple Normanton, Derbyshire, Eng.). Born July 15, 1831, at Temple Normanton. Came to Utah Sept. 12, 1861, Milo Andrus company.
Married Mary Wheatley Dec. 18, 1854, Grassmore, Eng. (daughter of John and Sarah Wheatley of Grassmore), who was born Dec. 25, 1837. Their children: Joseph, m. Catherine Arhman; Sarah Florence, m. W. E. Loveland; George Albert, m. Catherine A. Griffeths; Charlotte Maria, m. Alphaius Johnson; Herbert, m. Ida Werner; Michael Wheatley, m. Lucy Emily Kelly; Martha, m. Edwin Francis Kelly; John Thomas, m. Catherine Muir; Francis, m. Jennie Steely; Elias; William; Dorothy Ann; Mary Ellen; Ruth. Family home Calls Fort, Box Elder Co., Utah.
Bishop's counselor; high priest. Farmer.

WHITWORTH, JOHN THOMAS (son of George Whitworth and Mary Wheatley). Born Sept. 27, 1877, Calls Fort, Utah.
Married Catherine Muir June 15, 1904 (daughter of Moses Muir and Mary Call, of Bountiful, Utah). Their children: Frances; John Milton; Edgar Lee; George; Mary Vashti; Janie.
Farmer.

WICKEL, HARMON (son of Harmon Wickel, of Earl township, Lancaster county, Pa.). Born 1798. Came to Utah Sept. 26, 1862, James Wareham company.
Married Elizabeth Rickard in Earl township (daughter of Christian Rickard of Earl township), who was born 1805. Their children: Henry, d. infant; Harrison; John, m. Nellie Brighist; Richard, m. Louisa Weaver; Lemuel, m. Margaret Buckwater; Catherine, m. Andrew Beck Benzon. Family home, Salt Lake City.
High priest; missionary to eastern states seven years; block teacher; chief of commissary at Nauvoo, Ill. Merchant. Died 1872, Salt Lake City.

WICKLAND, OLOF (son of Jacob and Kerstin Olsen). Born Oct. 31, 1825, Storbyn, Finlla parish, Sweden. Came to Utah Nov. 9, 1856, James G. Willie handcart company.
Married Ella Johnson in 1846 (daughter of Jonas Stener Esbjornson and Ella Mechelson of Copenhagen, Denmark), who was born Nov. 7, 1825, and came to Utah with husband. Their children: Christena b. Dec. 5, 1848, m. Sorenson July 19, 1868; Jonas b. Dec. 30, 1849, m. Rachel A. Gifford Feb. 1, 1877; Sarah J. b. Aug. 3, 1852, m. Fredrick B. Gould March 20, 1874; Josephine b. Oct. 24, 1854, m. Hans Tuf Aug. 20, 1872; Jacob b. Oct. 16, 1856, m. Estella Patten Ju' 24, 1882, m. Fannie Hansen Feb. 13, 1902.

WICKLAND, JONAS (son of Olof Wickland and Ella Jo' son). Born Dec. 30, 1849, Finlla parish, Sweden.
Married Rachel A. Gifford Feb. 1, 1877, Monroe. U' (daughter of Moses Gifford and Sarah Price, former pion. July 21, 1847, Erastus Snow company, latter pioneer 15? She was born Feb. 25, 1858, Manti, Utah. Their childr Clarence b. Oct. 18, 1880, m. Ethel Gardner Dec. 10, 19 Elmer G. b. Nov. 3, 1882; Leroy O. b. Dec. 15, 1884, m. Gert Johnston June 10, 1908; Ervin A. b. Sept. 21, 1888; Leste b. Oct. 3, 1891; Harold T. b. Sept. 23, 1894. Family home Monroe, Utah.

WIGGELL, ELI. Came to Utah Sept. 28, 1861, Homer Duncan company, having been one of the pioneers of South Africa.
Married Susannah Bentley, of Winburg, South Africa, who came to Utah with husband. Their children: John W. b. Dec. 7, 1832, m. Margaret Buckley; Sarah Ann b. Oct. 14, 1834, died; Jemima b. Jan. 27, 1837, m. George Ellis; Jeremiah F. b. May 12, 1839, m. Priscilla J. Talbot; Sarah Ann Susannah b. Oct. 13, 1841, m. Charles Staples; Margaret Alice b. Oct. 11, 1843, m. Thomas B. Talbot; Rosannah M. b. Aug. 31, 1846, m. Charles S. Talbot; Frances A. b. May 6, 1849, m. William Lowe; Joseph Elijah Talbot b. Nov. 3. 1852, m. Mary Whitesides. Family resided and children were born at Grahamstown, Bachuist, Tabo Nchu, Winburg, Post Retief and Kaal Hock, South Africa.

WIGHT, EPHRAIM (son of Daniel Wight and Mary Randal' Hewitt of Centerville, Allegany county, N. Y.). Born March 13, 1926, at Centerville. Came to Utah Oct. 13, 1850, Edward Hunter company.
Married Harriet Elizabeth Pulsipher April 9, 1859. Mill Creek, Salt Lake Co., Utah (daughter of Elias Pulsipher and Polly Chubbuck of Vermont), who was born April 7, 1841. Their children: Ephraim Hewitt, m. Emma Watkins. Henry, m. Ellen Jensen; Harriet E., m. Thaddeus Wight; Mary Maria, m. Brigham Y. Hamson; Lucinda. m. Alma Jensen; Marvin; Arvilla. Family home Brigham City, Utah. Married Sarinh Pulsipher 1871.

PIONEERS AND PROMINENT MEN OF UTAH 1245

Married Sarah Wight Cutler 1872. Their children: William b. May 8, 1874; Alice b. April 14, 1876, m. J. Kimble Haws.
High priest; missionary to Elk Mountains, Utah; member high council. Justice of peace; city councilman; chief of police. Mechanic. Died Aug. 8, 1902, Brigham City.

WIGHT, LEWIS (son of William Wight, born March 2, 1783, Centerville, Allegany county, N. Y., and Abigail Cudworth, born 1787, Openheim, N. Y.—married Oct. 19, 1806). He was born Dec. 11, 1807, at Openheim. Came to Utah Oct. 13, 1850, Edward Hunter company.
Married Nancy Elliot 1827 at Centerville, N. Y. (daughter of Thaddeus Elliot and Sarah Lathe), who was born March 18, 1809. Their children: Lyman b. Sept. 24, 1829, m. Harriet Bateman, m. Christina Olsen; Charles b. March 28, 1831, m. Sarah Ellen Lovelass; Sarah b. May 28, 1833, m. Sheldon Bela Cutler, d. Jan. 20, 1891; Samuel b. Aug. 6, 1838, and Elizabeth b. Sept. 5, 1841, died; Joseph M. b. June 18, 1844, m. Mary Herren Oct. 5, 1864; William L. b. March 22, 1850, m. Melissa Watkins Nov. 16, 1874.
Baptized Feb. 21, 1843, in Allegany county, N. Y.; had charge of church cattle for several years in early fifties. Moved to Brigham City in fall of 1856. Had charge of public works getting out timber for courthouse.

WIGHT, LYMAN (son of Lewis Wight and Nancy Elliot). Born Sept. 24, 1829, Centerville, N. Y.
Married Harriet Bateman in Augusta, Ohio (daughter of Thomas Bateman and Mary Street), who was born Nov. 4, 1830, Manchester, Eng. Their children: Harriet Amelia b. Nov. 4, 1849, m. Ralph Jenkins Feb. 1, 1866; Lyman, Jr., b. Feb. 23, 1851, and Thomas Lewis b. Feb. 22, 1852, died; Thaddeus b. April 14, 1854, m. Harriet Elizabeth Wight April 9, 1883; Mary Elizabeth b. Oct. 6, 1856, m. Stephen Wight; Betsy Ann b. May 17, 1859, and Nancy b. Oct. 31, 1861, died; Pheba Ann b. Nov. 25, 1863, m. William Walker; William b. Sept. 29, 1865, and James Henry b. Nov. 27, 1866, died; Samuel Moroni b. March 4, 1869, m. Minnie Miller; Margret May b. July 28, 1871, m. Nephi Ipsen; Charles Alma b. Sept. 28, 1874, m. Emeline Thomas.
Married Christina Olsen January, 1858, Salt Lake City (daughter of Christian Olsen of Brigham City, Utah, pioneers Sept. 13, 1857, Chr. Christiansen handcart company). She was born Aug. 13, 1834. Their children: Almon Lyman b. Feb. 15, 1859; Roxy b. May 4, 1860; Adeline b. Dec. 8, 1862; Christina b. Oct. 15, 1864; Charlotte b. Aug. 21, 1865; Lewis b. June 26, 1867; Edgar b. March 21, 1878; Aaron b. April 23, 1882. Families resided Brigham City, Utah.
Operated Neff's grist mill; built first sawmills in Brigham City. Elected adjutant of First Battalion March 8, 1864; elected major of battalion April 28, 1866; alternate high councilor of Box Elder stake Nov. 7, 1891.

WIGHT, THADDEUS (son of Lyman Wight and Harriet Bateman). Born April 14, 1854, West Jordan, Utah.
Married Harriet Elizabeth Wight April 9, 1883 (daughter of Ephraim Wight and Harriet Elizabeth Pulsipher, pioneers 1850, Edward Hunter company—married April 9, 1859, Mill Creek, Utah). She was born Sept. 6, 1863, Brigham, Utah. Their children: Arvilla b. Feb. 13, 1884, m. William Orme Dec. 25, 1907; Thaddeus Theon b. Oct. 27, 1885; Lillian b. March 24, 1888; Ephraim Emery b. June 5, 1890; Harriet Kathleen b. June 18, 1892; Mary Amelia b. Sept. 7, 1894; Clinton Lyman b. Dec. 5, 1896. Family home Harper ward, Box Elder stake.
Missionary to southern states November, 1897, to Dec. 20, 1899; first counselor to Bishop Thomas Yates Dec. 24, 1899, to 1904; high councilor Box Elder stake 1907; set apart bishop Harper ward May 28, 1910.

WIGHT, ALMON LYMAN (son of Lyman Wight and Christina Olsen). Born Feb. 15, 1859, Brigham City.
Married Mary Ann Nelson Jan. 17, 1884, Salt Lake City (daughter of James and Marie Nelson). Born Jan. 12, 1862. Their children: Almon N. b. April 19, 1885; Sylvester b. Nov. 28, 1887; Eva M. b. Oct. 16, 1888; Sylvia C. b. March 10, 1891; Elery J. b. Nov. 24, 1893; Lyman V. b. Feb. 2, 1897; Erma M. b. Sept. 20, 1899; Reed J. b. Jan. 31, 1903; Hortence b. May 2, 1905. Family home Perry, Utah.
Missionary to eastern states 1909-10. Member of town board Perry, Utah. Farmer.

WIGHT, LEWIS (son of Lyman Wight and Christina Olsen). Born June 26, 1867, Brigham City, Utah.
Married Sarah Matilda Whitaker Oct. 11, 1898, Salt Lake City (daughter of John Whitaker and Josephine Mallory of Willard, Utah), who was born Dec. 29, 1879. Their children: Lewis Silvester b. Aug. 1, 1899; Leland Nelson b. Feb. 28, 1902; Thelma Vodas b. July 22, 1905; Elva Josephine b. Feb. 19, 1907; Norma Matilda b. Oct. 8, 1909; Ruth May b. Aug. 28, 1911.
Missionary to eastern states 1898 to 1901.

WIGHT, STEPHEN (son of Daniel Wight, born Jan. 23, 1785, and Mary Randall Hewitt, born Aug. 10, 1780, both of Centerville, Allegany county, N. Y.—married Nov. 18, 1810). He was born May 7, 1820, Montgomery, N. Y. Came to Utah Sept. 13, 1852, Thomas Howell company.
Married Pheba Ann Gates April 5, 1845, who died shortly afterward.
Married Lucy E. Waterbery Jan. 29, 1850 (daughter of Solomon Waterbery and Charlotte Post), who was born Oct. 15, 1825, in New York. Their children: Rachel J. b. Nov. 27, 1851, m. John Thorpe; Stephen, Jr., b. April 1, 1854, m. Mary Wight Sept. 4, 1876; Daniel b. May 31, 1856, died; Sarah D. b. Nov. 6, 1858, m. Thomas Thorpe; Lucy E. b. July 24, 1862, m. David J. Davis Dec. 20, 1885; Alvin Luies b. April, 1864, died; Charlotte L. b. July 15, 1866, m. William Jenkins Oct. 29, 1880; Marreta A. b. Dec. 3, 1871, m. Frederick W. Simmons; Charles E. b. Jan. 22, 1873.
Married Abigail Emma Pulsipher April 20, 1856 (daughter of Elias Pulsipher and Polly Chubbuck), who was born Oct. 3, 1839, Island Grove, Sangamon county, Ill. Their children: Levi b. Aug. 16, 1859, died; Asenath b. April 30, 1862, m. Lorenzo Pitt; Wilford b. Oct. 17, 1864, m. Lucy Ann Davis; Mary Ann b. April 14, 1867, m. Nathan D. Yearsley; Melvin b. Aug. 21, 1869, died; Hattie b. Nov. 12, 1871; Emma Jenett b. Aug. 16, 1873, m. Frank May; Phoebe Ann b. April 12, 1876; Wesley b. March 9, 1879, m. Sylva Bott Wight.
Bishop's counselor 11 years; bishop three years. Surveyor Box Elder county 20 years. Farmer; machinist.

WIGNALL, WILLIAM. Born at Preston, Eng. Came to Utah Nov. 30, 1856, Edward Martin frozen handcart company.
Married Grace Slater. Their children: Joseph, m. Elizabeth Kendall; Mary, m. William Sidwell; James, m. Harriet Burt; Jane, m. William Thomas; Grace, d. aged 38; William Henry, m. Matilda Jane Loveless; John T., m. Clarissa Patterson; Margaret, m. Marian Lucy.
Married Jane Winsby, Salt Lake City. Their child: Alice, d. aged 2. Families resided Payson, Utah.
Home missionary; Sunday school superintendent; choir leader. Veteran Black Hawk and Echo Canyon wars. Farmer; limeburner.

WIGNALL, WILLIAM HENRY (son of William Wignall and Grace Slater). Born Feb. 9, 1856, in England. Came to Utah with parents.
Married Matilda Jane Loveless Feb. 7, 1881, Payson, Utah (daughter of Joseph Loveless and Sarah Jane Scriggins of Payson), who was born Aug. 7, 1863. Their children: Edith, m. Frank Searle; William Nelson, m. Havel Barr; James E.; Wells, m. Goldie Tanner; John; Beulah May; Maggie V.; Allen R. b. Aug. 21, 1898; Sargent; Dean; Irene, d. infant.
Teacher; elder. Farmer. Died at Payson.

WILCOX, ELISHA (son of Francis Wilcox). Born Oct. 24, 1809, in Delaware county, Pa. Came to Utah in 1847.
Married Anna Pickle Jan. 15, 1835 (daughter of Minard Pickle and Barbara Farley). Their children: Miner, m. Julia Alrad; Polly, m. Alma Bennett; Francis, m. Becca Brandon; Margaretta, m. W. W. Brandon; Emma and Sally, died; Joseph, m. Cansus B. Roe; Hyrum, m. Sarinda Aired; Elisha, m. Lucinda Oliver; George Albert, m. Matilda Nielson; Asa, m. Sarah Davison. Family home Pleasant Grove, Utah.
High priest. Farmer.

WILCOX, GEORGE ALBERT (son of Elisha Wilcox and Anna Pickle). Born Sept. 10, 1853, Pleasant Grove, Utah.
Married Matilda Nielson (daughter of Hogan Nielson and Johanna Larson of Mt. Pleasant, Utah, pioneers September, 1862, oxteam company). She was born Oct. 10, 1853. Their children: Hannah Matilda b. Sept. 25, 1873, m. Laural Peterson; George Albert b. Nov. 15, 1875, died; Annie b. March 12, 1878, m. Joseph B. Peterson; Hyrum b. July 13, 1880, died; Alma b. July 14, 1882; Francis Elisha b. July 15, 1885, m. Ethel Maud Handley; Andrew H. b. Nov. 3, 1888. Family home Provo, Utah.
Elder; president teachers' quorum. Deputy sheriff Carbon county 1903-10. Fruitgrower and farmer.

WILCOX, JAMES DAVID (son of Henry Wilcox, born Jan. 16, 1792, Hillsdale, N. Y., and Susan Miller, born March 2, 1800, Lexington, N. Y., married Feb. 19, 1819). He was born Jan. 17, 1827, Lexington, N. Y. Came to Utah Sept. 23, 1852, Henry W. Miller company.
Married Anna Maria Robinson Nov. 26, 1854, Salt Lake City (daughter of Joseph Lee Robinson, pioneer 1849, captain of own company, and Maria Wood, who came to Utah with husband). She was born June 8, 1838. Their children: James Henry b. Oct. 7, 1855, m. Mary Magdalene Wood Nov. 28, 1878; Joseph Dorvil b. Aug. 15, 1857, d. Oct. 14, 1857; Ebenezer Orlando b. Feb. 5, 1859, m. Abigail Alvina Abbott, April 26, 1883; Julia Maria b. March 14, 1861, m. Walter W. Steed, Sept. 16, 1880; Lucy Annella b. Sept. 2, 1863, d. Sept. 30, 1864; Oliver Leroy b. Sept. 6, 1865, m. Lucy Evaline Clark Nov. 23, 1892; Annabelle b. Feb. 13, 1867, d. Sept. 15, 1867; Margaret Ruth b. Sept. 30, 1869, m. David Eli Manning April 11, 1888; David Eugene b. April 3, 1872, m. Elizabeth Layne Dec. 20, 1894; William Arnold b. Nov. 27, 1874, d. Jan. 3, 1875; George Wallace b. March 11, 1876, m. Nettie Jane Barber Nov. 16, 1898; Mary Helen b. Feb. 5, 1879, d. April 13, 1880; Orson Charles b. Oct. 15, 1881, m. Adeline Rosa Fehr March 26, 1908. Family home Farmington, Utah.
Married Judith Oviatt Feb. 15, 1862, Salt Lake City (daughter of Ira Oviatt and Ruth Bennett, pioneers 1851, Isaac Allred company, married Jan. 29, 1829, Berton, Rensselaer county, N. Y.) She was born March 22, 1841, Kirkland, Ohio. Their children: Ruth Angelia b. Jan. 11, 1863, d. Oct. 23,

1864; Mary Evelyn b. Sept. 6, 1865, d. Sept. 15, 1867; Clara Orliva b. June 28, 1868, m. Edward Alvin Steed Dec. 14, 1887; Thomas Feris b. July 14, 1870, m. Eliza Criddle Nov. 28, 1894; Susan Olive b. Sept. 6, 1872, m. William John Hardy; Cynthia Orilla b. Feb. 23, 1875, m. William Edward Criddle Feb. 13, 1895; Ira Herman b. April 5, 1877, d. Sept. 27, 1897; Lewis Oviatt b. Aug. 30, 1879; Orrin Miller b. Dec. 13, 1881; Ruby Lovena b. May 29, 1887, m. John Sheppard Sept. 1907. Family home Farmington, Utah.
Missionary to Salmon River October, 1857, to April, 1858. Ordained a patriarch April 15, 1901.

WILCOX, JAMES HENRY (son of James David Wilcox and Anna Maria Robinson). Born Oct. 7, 1855, Farmington, Utah.
Married Mary Magdalene Wood Nov. 28, 1878, Salt Lake City (daughter of John Wood and Fanny Goble, pioneers October, 1855, Moses Thurston company). She was born April 15, 1857, Farmington, Utah. Their children: William Henry b. Sept. 20, 1879, m. Emily Barber Dec. 14, 1904; Delbert Eben b. Oct. 12, 1881, m. Julia Irene Udy June 16, 1909; Joseph Edward b. March 20, 1883, m. Leona Jane Hatch Dec. 6, 1905; Mary Estella b. Sept. 4, 1885; Fanny Alice b. March 1, 1888, m. Amasa Merlin Steed Nov. 24, 1909; Clyde Harley b. Nov. 28, 1889; Luella b. Jan. 8, 1892; Ruth b. Dec. 15, 1893; Blanche b. Nov. 9, 1896. Family home Farmington, Utah.
Missionary to eastern states Jan. 16, 1897. Appointed assessor and collector Davis county March 15, 1882, Aug. 6, 1883, Aug. 4, 1884, Aug. 2, 1886; county recorder Davis county Aug. 4, 1884; county clerk Aug. 6, 1888, Aug. 4, 1890; first mayor of Farmington City Nov. 8, 1892, and elected again Nov. 7, 1893; prosecuting attorney Davis county Nov. 6, 1894. By virtue of his being assessor and collector of Davis county he was a member of the board that chose the site for the Agricultural College. Admitted to the bar March 4, 1906.

WILCOX, WILLIAM HENRY (son of James Henry Wilcox and Mary Magdalene Wood). Born Sept. 20, 1879, Farmington, Utah.
Married Emily Barber Dec. 14, 1904 (daughter of David Barber and Esther French; came to Utah July 3, 1877, married June 4, 1879, Salt Lake City). She was born Nov. 13, 1884, Centerville, Utah. Their children: David Henry b. Oct. 8, 1905; Hugh Barber b. Feb. 17, 1907; Harold b. Sept. 5, 1908; Elmer b. May 5, 1910. Family home Syracuse, Utah. Missionary to southern states Aug. 23, 1900.

WILCOX, SAMUEL ALLEN (son of Silas Wilcox and Margrett Allen of St. Lawrence county, N. Y.). Born March 21, 1819, in St. Lawrence county. Came to Utah Oct. 7, 1861, David H. Cannon company.
Married Martha Parker July 16, 1838, Province of Ontario, Canada (daughter of Joseph Parker and Lucy Boyd—they resided in Ontario, Nauvoo, Ill., Fremont county, Iowa, and Cedar Fort, Utah—pioneers Oct. 7, 1861, David H. Cannon company). She was born Jan. 23, 1820, and died Jan. 23, 1912. Their children: John Dingman b. April 23, 1843, Nauvoo, Ill., m. Mary T. Savage 1865; Malinda b. 1838, m. Isaac Pugh, m. James Cook; Sarah Jane b. Oct. 24, 1841, Nauvoo, Ill., m. William Allred, m. Newtin Austin; Adam b. Feb. 11, 1847, in Iowa, m. Eunice Dalrymple, m. Octavia Cheney; Asenath Viola b. April 1, 1845, m. William Passey; Samuel Allen b. March 9, 1850, in Iowa; Julia Lochlin; Joseph b. Nov. 30, 1851, in Iowa, m. Ermina A. Hiatt; Silas b. 1854 in Iowa; Phoebe Roselthe b. Sept. 29, 1856, in Iowa, m. John Berry, m. Louis G. Christie; Boyd Extine b. Sept. 1860, m. Mary Sophrona Dayton; David Almearn b. Oct. 11, 1862, m. Florence Cook, m. Martha Hansen. Family home Cedar Fort, Utah.
Married Annie C. Peterson Oct. 21, 1872, Salt Lake City (daughter of Ole Peterson and Mari Hansen of Cedar Fort, Utah, pioneers 1862). She was born March 18, 1856, in Denmark. Their children: James Alford b. Oct. 10, 1877, m. Bertha Mathews 1911; Anna Laura b. Jan. 18, 1874, m. Fred Colton; Margret Marn b. Dec. 11, 1875, m. John Brems Jan. 4, 1893; Bertha Charlotte b. Oct. 8, 1879, m. Samuel Anderson Oct. 18, 1897; Martha Cordelia b. Dec. 25, 1882, m. Joseph M. Stephens July, 1903; May Inger b. March 19, 1884, m. Eugene Saby May 20, 1903, m. Joseph Calton; Ross Ernest b. April 13, 1886; Helen Mar b. Sept. 8, 1888, m. John H. Yates Sept. 1907; Ole Able b. Nov. 23, 1911. All born at Cedar Fort. Families resided Cedar Fort, Utah.
Missionary to Canada 1868; seventy; member of bishopric of Cedar Fort, Utah. Farmer and stockraiser.

WILCOX, JOHN DINGMAN (son of Samuel Allen Wilcox and Martha Parker). Born April 23, 1843, Nauvoo, Ill. Came to Utah Aug. 16, 1861, David H. Cannon company.
Married Mary T. Savage Aug. 23, 1865, Paris, Idaho (daughter of David Savage, born July 25, 1814, and Mary Abigail White, born March 30, 1823, pioneers 1847, P. P. Pratt company—they died in Snowflake, Ariz.). She was born Feb. 28, 1847, en route to Utah. Their children: John Elbert b. Aug. 23, 1866, m. Helen Mar McCullough; David Oswel b. Sept. 13, 1870, m. Francis Melissa McCullough; Samuel Orris b. Oct. 19, 1872; Lucy Abigail b. Nov. 3, 1874, m. John P. Burr; Martha Elnora b. Aug. 6, 1877, m. Henry Hacking; Joseph Ezra b. March 11, 1880, d. April 6, 1881; Adam Vernile b. Aug. 3, 1882, d. April 27, 1909; Mary Melinda b. Jan. 3, 1885, m. Ezra Liljenquist; Leo Boyd b. Feb. 24, 1889, d. March 25, 1889. Family home Grass Valley, Piute Co., Utah.
High priest; presiding elder Wilmot branch. Justice of the peace 1883-84. Family home Sunny Dell, Idaho.

WILCOX, WALTER ELI (son of William Wilcox and Huldah Lucas, of Hartford, Conn.). Born April 11, 1821, Dorchester, Mass. Came to Utah 1852.
Married Maria Wealthy Richards (daughter of Phineas Richards). Their children: Cynthia Maria, m. Henry Arnold; William Wallace, m. Nellie Partridge; Ellen Amelia, m. Alonzo E. Hyde; Adelaide Adelia, m. William Osper; Walter, d. aged 14; George Albert, m. Marion ——; Charles Frederick b. Feb. 23, 1859, m. Elizabeth Stevenson; Franklin Alonzo, m. Annie Jenkins; Edwin Eli b. April 28, 1865, m. Florence Burton.
Married Elizabeth Hawkins Sept. 4, 1853, Salt Lake City. Their children: Emma Louisa, died; Huldah E., m. William Owings; Moroni Ed., m. Ella U. Decker; Fredricks Spain, died; John William, m. Ida May Stephens; Joseph Walter, m. Marian N. Stanford.
Married Matilda M. Watmough April 7, 1858, Salt Lake City (daughter of William Watmough of Boston, Mass., pioneer 1862). She was born May 14, 1843. Their children: Matilda S., m. Charles H. Bliss; Amanda W., died.
Married Melinda Wood at Salt Lake City (daughter of Moses Wood and Melinda Wilcox of Boston, Mass.), who was born 1825. Only child: Walter Franklin.
Married Amanda Hillam May 9, 1860, Salt Lake City (daughter of Abraham Hillam and Hannah Hellivell of Yorkshire, Eng., pioneers Sept. 16, 1859, Edward Stevenson company). She was born Feb. 10, 1843. Their children: Arthur H., m. Maria Jensen; Joseph E., and Amy E., died; Rodney E., m. Margaret Fairclough, m. Hannah Fairclough; Ralph Leo, m. Amy A. Anakin; Hannah M., m. Samuel L. Hoover, m. George J. Dupont; Alvin Abraham, died; Ernest L., m. Mary Alice Shelton; Lily May, m. Peter Fairclough; Walter S., m. Mary Corias; Albert G., died; Charles H., m. Bessie Jerrard; Flora Lucy, m. Milton Trenam. Families resided Salt Lake City.
Worker in Salt Lake temple since 1897.

WILCOX, CHARLES FREDERICK (son of Walter Eli Wilcox and Maria Wealthy Richards). Born Feb. 23, 1859, Salt Lake City.
Married Elizabeth Stevenson Dec. 25, 1884, Salt Lake City. Franklin D. Richards officiated (daughter of Edward Stevenson and Elizabeth DuFresne, of New Jersey, former born on Rock of Gibraltar, pioneers Sept. 19, 1847, Daniel Spencer company). She was born March 18, 1859. Their children: Charles Frederick b. Sept. 22, 1885; Ramona Stevenson b. April 8, 1887; Edward Stevenson b. March 18, 1890; Claire Augusta b. Aug. 16, 1892; Ramon Stevenson b. April 27, 1894; Mary Stevenson b. June 15, 1900. Family home, Salt Lake City.
President 57th quorum seventies; missionary to England 1880-82; ward teacher; Sunday school superintendent. Assistant surgeon state militia four years; health commissioner of Salt Lake City; surgeon of L. D. S. hospital; graduate medical department of University of New York, 1890. Principal 14th district school six years. Physician and surgeon.

WILCOX, JOHN WILLIAM (son of Walter Eli Wilcox and Elizabeth Hawkins). Born Jan. 23, 1864, Salt Lake City.
Married Ida Stephens November, 1889, Logan, Utah (daughter of Abraham Stephens and Eliza Edwards of Ogden, pioneers 1866, Independent company). She was born July 10, 1868, Santa Clara b. Sept. 28, 1890; Mabel b. Nov. 23, 1891; Lucile b. Nov. 19, 1893; Milton b. May 20, 1895; Sidney b. March 1, 1899; Ellsworth b. Oct. 8, 1900. Elder. Member legislature, 1912. Grocer.

WILD, JOSEPH (son of John Wild of Bury, Lancastershire, Eng.). Born May 1, 1834, at Bury, Lancastershire.
Married Mary Shuttleworth 1854 (daughter of William Shuttleworth and Mariam Reese, of Lancastershire, Eng.). d. infant; Joseph W. S., m. Eliza Shelley; Edwin J., m. Margaret Lee, m. Lilly Kelley; Moroni A., m. Maud Shelley; John T. and Mary M., died; Sarah E., m. William Currie; Heber D., m. Matilda Neilson; Walter J., m. Nettie Lewis. Family home American Fork, Utah.
Married Hannah Binns (Singleton) Jan. 11, 1868, Salt Lake City (daughter of John Binns of England). Their children: Eliza, m. John Buckwalter; Ernest, m. Mary A. Taylor; Susanna, m. William Miller.
Married Jane Crowther in January, 1904, Salt Lake City. High priest; member 67th quorum seventies; missionary to England 1882-84. Town marshal. Died March 23, 1911, Ogden, Utah.

WILD, JOSEPH WILLIAM SHUTTLEWORTH (son of Joseph Wild and Mary Shuttleworth). Born Oct. 2, 1860, Salt Lake City.
Married Eliza A. Shelley March 16, 1892, American Fork, Utah (daughter of Stephen Shelley and Sarah Clegg of American Fork). Family home American Fork, Utah.
High priest; president of elders quorum, 1902-1909; counselor to Sunday school superintendent 1903-10; block teacher.

WILDE, WILLIAM. Born 1807, in Hampshire, England. Came to Utah Sept. 6, 1859, George Raleigh handcart company.
Married Eliza Phillips in Hampshire. Their children: John b. April 12, 1831, m. Mary Reyhec; Henry b. May 14, 1832, m. Jane Batchelor, m. Marman Frost; Fredrick b. Oct. 8, 1834, m. Louise Farnsworth, m. Jemima Clark; Thomas b.

Jan. 12, 1842, m. Fanny Gunn; Eliza, m. George Peterson; Mary, died; Sarah b. Feb. 18, 1832, m. Heber Stallings. Family home Coalville, Utah.
High priest. Assisted in building railroads through Echo Canyon, from Echo to Coalville. Died Dec. 12, 1886.

WILDE, JOHN (son of William Wilde and Eliza Phillips). Born April 12, 1831, at Fair Oak, Bishop stake, Eng. Came to Utah September, 1854.
Married May Reybec November, 1857, Salt Lake City (daughter of Mr. Reybec and Cecelia Parsons, of Malma, Sweden, pioneers September, 1857). She was born Nov. 13, 1836. Their children: Cecelia M. b. Sept. 30, 1858, d. July 14, 1875; Clara b. Dec. 15, 1860, m. William Welsh; John E. b. Nov. 24, 1863, m. Eliza Hurst; Joseph H. b. March 23, 1865; Amelia E. b. March 16, 1867, m. George Hollands; Daniel W. b. May 1, 1870, m. Lucy Callis; Matilda b. May 14, 1872, m. William H. Beech.
Seventy. City councilman 1874. Died March 3, 1886.

WILDE, DANIEL WILLIAM (son of John Wilde and Mary Reybec). Born May 1, 1870, Coalville, Utah.
Married Lucy Callis July 13, 1892, Logan, Utah (daughter of John Callis and Charlotte Quilliam, of Liverpool, Eng.; came to Utah November, 1876). She was born Nov. 8, 1873. Their children: Rodney Charles b. April 27, 1893; Daniel Lester b. Aug. 1, 1894; Orville John b. Oct. 17, 1896; Eldred Joseph b. Feb. 14, 1898; Lucille b. Dec. 22, 1899; Paul Pollts b. April 17, 1905; Sheldon Edward b. Dec. 5, 1907. Family home Park City, Utah.
Sunday school superintendent; elder.

WILDE, HENRY (son of William Wilde and Eliza Phillips). Born May 16, 1822, in Hampshire, Eng.
Married Jane Batchelor, in Hampshire (daughter of Benjamin Batchelor of Hampshire, pioneer Sept. 6, 1859, Captain Raleigh handcart company). She was born Dec. 11, 1833. Their children: John F. b. May 16, 1853, m. Sarriah Robinson; Mary b. May 27, 1855, m. Joseph Barber; Heber b. Sept. 9, 1859, m. Martha Moore; Sarrah b. Aug. 19, 1861, m. William Frost; William b. Feb. 9, 1864, m. Nancy Shaw; Walter H. b. May 11, 1866, m. Mary Cherry; Emma M. b. April 21, 1868, m. John E. Pettie; Emanuel b. Aug. 19, 1870, m. Annie Howard; Joseph T. b. Oct. 1, 1873, m. Annie Boothe; Jarne b. Jan. 26, 1875, died; Benjamin b. Aug. 21, 1876, m. May Weltch. Family home Coalville, Utah. Died June 4, 1899.

WILDE, JOHN FREDERICK (son of Henry Wilde and Jane Batchelor). Born May 16, 1853, in Hampshire, Eng.
Married Sarriah Robinson June 14, 1875, Salt Lake City (daughter of James Robinson and Mary Pollid, of Coalville, Utah). She was born Jan. 15, 1856. Their children: John W. b. Feb. 25, 1876, m. Hannah Holt; Mary J. b. Dec. 13, 1878, m. Benjamin Meadow; James F. b. Feb. 7, 1880; Oswald S. b. Jan. 6, 1882, m. Louisa Claxton; Samuel C. b. Oct. 22, 1883, and Elizabeth S. b. March 6, 1886, died; Lebbie H. b. June 30, 1884, m. William Robinson; Violet R. b. Jan. 15, 1890; Gladdys A. b. Sept. 20, 1897. Family home Coalville, Utah.
Bishop of Coalville ward; Sunday school superintendent four years; president Y. M. M. I. A. two years. Road supervisor. Worked on railroad through Echo Canyon.

WILDE, THOMAS (son of William Wilde and Eliza Phillips). Born Jan. 12, 1842, Fair Oak, Bishop stake, Hampshire, Eng.
Married Fanny Gunn 1865, Coalville, Utah (daughter of William and Emma Gunn, of Hoytsville, Utah, pioneers 1857). She was born Nov. 11, 1846. Their children: Emma Eliza b. Feb. 24, 1866, m. John Reese, m. Joseph Pyrah; Thomas b. Oct. 6, 1867, m. Elizabeth Chappel; George W. b. May 20, 1869, m. Mary Anna Clark; Edwin b. Nov. 1, 1871, m. Mary Hannah Robinson; Fanny Priscilla b. May 3, 1874, m. John Boothe; Richard b. March 18, 1876, m. Ella Stalley; Joseph H. b. July 9, 1878, m. Jane Sawley; Gilbert b. April 8, 1880, m. Joan Brinton; Silvester b. Dec. 29, 1881, m. Mary E. Randall; Emily b. Dec. 30, 1884, m. Thomas E. Moore; Lois Rebecca b. Oct. 2, 1885, m. Joseph H. Boyer; Ernest b. Aug. 20, 1887, m. Della Nix; Lorenzo b. March 13, 1889, d. Nov. 19, 1900; Mary b. July 26, 1890, d. infant. Family home Coalville, Utah.
Veteran Black Hawk war. Counselor in bishopric of Coalville ward 1906-08.

WILDING, GEORGE (son of David Wilding and Alice Adkinson, of England). Born Nov. 9, 1829, Preston, Eng. Came to Utah Sept. 24, 1852, Benjamin Gardner company.
Married Mary Elizabeth Layne, June 30, 1850, Council Bluffs, Iowa (daughter of David Layne, who died in Indiana, and Lucinda Bybee, a resident of Iowa; latter pioneer Sept. 24, 1852, Benjamin Gardner company). She was born Dec. 24, 1832. Their children: George b. June 5, 1851, m. Sarah Brown; David b. May 6, 1853, d. Oct. 12, 1854; Mary Alice b. Nov. 3, 1854, m. William Widdson; Roselpha b. March 4, 1857, m. George R. Emery; Elizabeth Ann b. Jan. 4, 1859, m. Joseph Burdett; Jermerha b. Oct. 26, 1860, m. Oak Polton; Preston b. Nov. 9, 1862, d. Oct. 21, 1863; Elenor b. Aug. 28, 1864, m. Steven Love; Maggie b. Aug. 21, 1866, m. Nephi Timpean; Henry David b. Oct. 15, 1868, m. Eliza Ann Oldham; Eve Wilding b. Dec. 31, 1870, m. Charles Tibbetts; Olive b. June 16, 1873; Walter b. Oct. 10, 1875, m. Vivian Little.
Married Leoni Leoti Winner Aug. 29, 1875, Salt Lake City (daughter of James Winner, killed in Civil war, and Isabella Lambert—came to Utah 1874). She was born July 15, 1857.

Their children: Alice Isabella b. June 12, 1876, m. George Fox; Anna b. May 21, 1878, died; Mary Latilla b. Aug. 21, 1879, m. William Hadfield; Jenny Leonie b. Nov. 7, 1881, m. Walter Rushton; Elvira Naomi b. Oct. 15, 1883, m. Ira E. Hayden; Rhoda Lambert b. March 23, 1886, m. Albert Reed; George Lambert b. May 14, 1888, m. Emma Peterson; Elizabeth Jeffs b. May 1, 1891, d. Oct. 9, 1903; Emma Estella b. Oct. 4, 1893; Clara Cornelia b. Nov. 7, 1895; Leoni Leoti b. May 11, 1896; Evelyn Winner b. Feb. 22, 1901.
Ward teacher; choir leader. Mason.

WILKINS, CHARLES (son of Charles Wilkins and Jane Rixon of Berkshire, Eng.). Born Dec. 28, 1828, Berkshire, Eng. Came to Utah 1854.
Married Elizabeth Drinkwater (daughter of James Drinkwater). Only child: Lillian b. May 9, 1852, m. Daniel Weaverling Feb. 14, 1878.
Married Ury Welch (daughter of Job Welch and Charlotte Rawlins, pioneers 1854), who was born May 5, 1842, in Dorsetshire, Eng. Their children: Clarissa b. Oct. 11, 1857, m. Herbert Manwaring May 23, 1876; Ury H. b. Dec. 18, 1859, m. Andrew Severson 1877; Charles A. b. Dec. 14, 1861, m. Ida Smith 1881; Heber C. b. Feb. 7, 1864; Nephi b. March 18, 1866; Eli b. March 18, 1866; Jesse b. Feb. 15, 1868, m. Fanny J. Burton 1897; Charlotte A. b. April 7, 1870, m. George Victor 1888; William H. b. July 9, 1872, m. Hannah M. Butler 1901; Mary J. b. Oct. 21, 1874, m. Hans Hanson 1894; Reuben b. Jan. 31, 1877, m. Mary Sorenson 1902; Andrew b. Feb. 13, 1879, m. Vida L. Cole 1903; Stephen J. b. June 18, 1881; Lydia L. b. Dec. 13, 1882; Nettie L. b. July 25, 1885, m. Charles A. Randall 1903. Family home South Cottonwood, Utah.

WILKINS, JESSE (son of Charles Wilkins and Ury Welch). Born Feb. 15, 1868, South Cottonwood, Utah.
Married Fanny J. Burton Sept. 29, 1897, Irwin, Idaho (daughter of Charles Burton and Hannah Skilton), who was born April 3, 1875, Grantsville, Utah. Their children: Ida b. Aug. 24, 1898; Charles H. b. March 26, 1900; Nettie L. b. April 11, 1902; Jesse L. b. Oct. 22, 1904; Clarissa M. b. May 26, 1907; James R. b. Feb. 25, 1909. Family home Coltman, Idaho.

WILKINS, GEORGE W. (son of Abraham and Mary Emmons Wilkins). Born Oct. 28, 1822, Peterboro, N. H. Came to Utah Oct. 12, 1849.
Married Catherine Augusta Lovett, July 4, 1846. Their children: Augusta b. July 5, 1851, m. John W. Snell; George A. b. Feb. 18, 1853, m. Elizabeth Mayer; Charles b. Dec. 18, 1854, died; Alsina E. b. May 7, 1856, m. George H. Brimhall; Lucy A. b. March 14, 1858, m. Carl A. Marcusen; Joseph E. b. October 23, 1860, m. Arminta Wilson; Albert W. b. May 11, 1863, m. Mary E. Duly. Family home, Spanish Fork.
Married Mary M. Myer Sept. 17, 1886. There were four children of this marriage in family.
President high priest's quorum; second counselor to Bishop John L. Butler; first counselor Bishop A. K. Thurber; patriarch; missionary to England 1871; president Bedford and Norwich conference; missionary New England states, 1876. Assisted in bringing immigrants to Utah. Pioneer settler at Spanish Fork, Utah, 1855. Member city council, Spanish Fork. Second vice-president and Board of Directors Spanish Fork Co-op. two years.

WILKINS, JOHN GANSWORTH (son of John Wilkins and Jane McGray of Saratoga, N. Y.). Born July, 1800, Saratoga county, N. Y. Came to Utah 1850, Captain Cooley company.
Married Nancy Kennedy 1830, at Saratoga, N. Y. (daughter of Charles and Mary Jane Kennedy of Canada, pioneers 1850, Captain Cooley company). She was born 1808. Their children: Edward, died; Alexander, m. Alice Melena Barney; Susan Jane, m. Charles Shelton; Oscar, m. Mary Jane McEwan; John Austin, m. Anna Scott; Nancy Adaline, m. Sterling Colton. Family home Provo, Utah.
High priest; president Bluff City branch. Settled at Provo, 1851, where he assisted in building canals, wagon roads, sawmills, and in developing the country. Sent ox-teams at two different times for immigrants 1860. First supervisor of Provo City. Farmer and stockraiser. Died 1890, Provo.

WILKINS, JOHN AUSTIN (son of John G. Wilkins and Nancy Kennedy). Born May 24, 1850, in Illinois. Came to Utah 1851.
Married Anna Scott December 22, 1872, Provo, Utah. Charles Smith officiating (daughter of Andrew Hunter Scott and Sarah Ann Humphrey Roe of Philadelphia, Pa., pioneers 1851). She was born March 21, 1855, at Provo. Their children: Charlotte May b. 1873, m. Cyrus H. Wilson; Andrew Austin b. 1875, m. Freda Rhodes; Anna Margrett b. 1877, m. William Wadkins; Susan Jane b. 1879, m. John Clark; Charles Shelton b. 1882, died; Eugene b. 1888, m. Ella Jones. Family home Provo, Utah.
Elder. Went to the Missouri River for freight, crossing the plains with six yoke of oxen. Took active part in the early Indian troubles. Watermaster; road supervisor; peace officer. Has done much in the upbuilding of the country in and around Provo. Farmer.

WILKINS, OSCAR (son of John G. Wilkins and Nancy Kennedy). Born May 7, 1845.
Married Mary Jane McEwan 1864 (daughter of John T. McEwan and Amanda Highby, of Provo, Utah), who was born Nov. 17, 1846. Their children: Ellen, m. Frank Rosell; Oscar, m. Lillian Deal; Minerva Melvina, m. J. Warren Johnson, m. Merton Karren; Mary, m. Nathaniel Tanner; Zina, m. Perry Fuller; Ada, m. William Evans; Robert.
High priest. Miner.

WILKINS, OSCAR (son of George Wilkins and Hannah Stoneham (Gillet) of Tetbury, Gloucestershire, Eng.). Born Feb. 14, 1851, at Tetbury, Eng.
Married Elizabeth Durrah Oct. 17, —, Salt Lake Endowment house (daughter of Henry Durrah and Jane Donely of Scotland), who was born Jan. 1, 1852, and came to Utah with Arthur and Elizabeth Maxwell, her adopted parents. Their children: Emma Jane, m. Edwin Francis Palmer; Hannah Elizabeth, m. Henry Miles; Clara Ellen, m. George G. Stevens; George Edgar b. Nov. 1, 1876, m. Zina Estella Miles; Sarah Janet, m. Abraham M. Lyons; Oscar William, m. Ella C. Moyle; Arthur Harbert, died; Mary Alice, m. Parley P. Walker; Albert, m. Myrtle Marchant; Ruben Ralph; Pearl, m. Joseph McIntyre; Edith.

WILKINS, GEORGE EDGAR (son of Oscar Wilkins and Elizabeth Durrah). Born Nov. 1, 1876, Peoa. Utah.
Married Zina Estella Miles Jan. 30, 1901, Salt Lake City (daughter of Benjamin Franklin Miles and Rachel Emily Shippen of Peoa, Utah). She was born Sept. 2, 1878. Their children: George Victor b. Oct. 22, 1902; Edgar Wesley b. Aug. 10, 1906; Margaret Leon b. June 2, 1908; Grant b. May 29, 1912.
Member 22d quorum seventies; missionary to southwestern states 1898-1900, to Great Britain 1903-05; high councilor; stake Y. M. M. I. A. superintendent, Summit; Sunday school superintendent; bishop 2d ward, Vernal, 1911. Moved from Peoa to Vernal 1909, where he is engaged in farming, and is a pioneer to that place.

WILKINSON, ALLEN (son of Joseph Wilkinson). Born Oct. 20, 1818, at Ondley, Yorkshire, Eng. Came to Utah 1849.
Married Mary A. Morris. She was born Nov. 16, 1818. Their children: Fannie b. Sept. 1840; Francis b. Sept. 19, 1841, m. Isaac Morley; John b. Jan. 1, 1843, m. Johanna Mortinson Jan. 28, 1866; Joseph Smith, b. Dec. 15, 1844; Mary Ann b. Dec. 1845, m. Orson Taylor; Sarah b. Dec. 12, 1848, m. John Buchanan. Family resided in England, at Manti and Richfield, Utah.
Married Harriet Mackey Jan. 16, 1853, at Manti, Utah (daughter of Samuel Mackey and Phebe Wilkinson—pioneers Oct. 29, 1852, Isaac Stewart company). She was born Nov. 22, 1836, Canistoga, Pa. Their children: Joseph b. Dec. 12, 1853, m. Florence Jones; Allen b. Jan. 8, 1856, m. Martene Nielson; Levi A. b. Jan. 16, 1858, m. Carrie Peterson; Phebe b. Oct. 16, 1859, m. Erastus Jensen; Hannah b. Nov. 11, 1861, m. Andraes Jensen; Eleanor A. b. Oct. 28, 1863, m. Fred Bentler; Samuel b. May 17, 1866, m. Malissa Winn; Walter b. July 29, 1868, m. Harriet Howath; Jared b. April 24, 1870, m. Louise Farnsworth; Harriet b. March 8, 1872, m. Frank Winn; Benjamin b. Feb. 12, 1874, m. Effie Knight; Inez b. April 16, 1876, m. Louis Gore; Eunice b. Feb. 15, 1878, m. Hans Peterson.
Worked on Nauvoo Temple; member Nauvoo Legion. Moved from Salt Lake City to Manti in 1850, where he worked in stone quarry and assisted in building a fort for protection against the Indians. Went to Richfield 1872, where he engaged in farming. Veteran Indian wars.

WILKINSON, JOHN (son of Allen Wilkinson and Mary Ann Morris). Born Jan. 1, 1843, in Chestershire, Eng.
Married Johanna Mortison Jan. 28, 1866, Richfield, Utah (daughter of Dedrick Mortison and Mary Jensen—pioneers Sept. 13, 1857, Christian Christiansen handcart company). She was born Oct. 18, 1844, in Jutland, Denmark. Their children: Roxie J. b. March 28, 1867; Mary Ann b. Aug. 17, 1869, m. Joseph Jackson 1887; Emma C. b. Dec. 30, 1871, m. Clifton Bunker; John b. Feb. 9, 1873; William H. b. Nov. 12, 1876; James M. b. March 30, 1879, m. Orilla Dickinson Sept. 16, 1903; George W. b. Sept. 20, 1882. Family resided Richfield and Annabella, Utah.
Ward teacher. Assisted in bringing immigrants to Utah 1863 and 1864. Veteran Black Hawk war. Settled at Richfield 1864, but was forced to leave and move to San Pete county on account of the Indians. After moving several times he finally settled at Annabella in 1885.

WILKINSON, CHARLES (of Bradford, Yorkshire, Eng.). Came to Utah 1862, Henry W. Miller company.
Married Sarah Merser. Their children: William, m. Sarah M. Brown: Moses b. Feb. 13, 1837, m. Mary J. Richardson Jan. 11, 1869; Sarah, m. Joseph E. Morris; Mary, m. Charlie Smith; Martha, m. Samuel McKay; John, m. Lottie Moore; Joseph, m. Martha Mills; Samuel, died. Family home, Hoytsville, Utah.
Seventy; chorister of East Mill Creek ward thirty years. Farmer. Deceased.

WILKINSON, MOSES (son of Charles Wilkinson and Sarah Merser). Born Feb. 13, 1837, at Bradford, Eng. Came to Utah 1862, Henry W. Miller company.
Married Sarah Ann Butterworth January, 1858 at Lawrence, Mass. (daughter of James and Susan Butterworth, both of Lawrence, Mass., the former came to Utah with Henry W. Miller company). She was born Nov. 18, 1840. Their children: Mary J. b. Nov. 21, 1859, m. Peter Midwed; Etty H. b. Aug. 14, 1861, m. David Broadhurst; Emily b. Jan. 12, 1864, m. Carl Lund; Lovenia b. Jan. 14, 1866, m. Julius Jensen; Martha Ann b. Oct. 14, 1867, d. aged 11; Roseatta b. Oct. 13, 1869, m. Nuten Brown; Moses b. Oct. 3, 1871, m. Alice Peck; Ella May b. June 14, 1873, d. aged 6; Laura Isabella b. March 28, 1875, m. Henry Lidyard; James A. b. Sept. 30, 1876, m. Clyde Boyal; Ernest E. A. b. March 28, 1879, m. Cora Midwed; Forest Butterworth b. Nov. 8, 1880; Alvin M. b. Sept. 27, 1882. Family home East Mill Creek, Utah.
Married Mary Ellen Bircumshaw Jan. 11, 1869, at Salt Lake City (daughter of Joseph Bircumshaw and Rosetta Plackett, both of Taghill, Ena, Derbyshire, Eng.—pioneers August. 1865, Captain Atwood company). She was born Aug. 13, 1851. Their children: Alma b. July 16, 1870, m. Jennie M. Decker; Drucilla b. Feb. 21, 1873, died; John Willard b. Aug. 12, 1875; Joseph Albert b. April 19, 1878, m. Maggie Gilless; Rosa Hanna b. Sept. 5, 1880, m. Alma M. Peck; Amelia May b. May 17, 1883, m. Thomas Reese; Charles Henry b. Nov. 20, 1885; Samuel Bircumshaw b. Nov. 23, 1887, m. Olive Peck. Family home Mill Creek, Utah.
Seventy; chorister of East Mill Creek ward 30 years. Farmer. Died Jan. 11, 1899, at East Mill Creek, Utah.

WILKINSON, ALMA (son of Moses Wilkinson and Mary E. Bircumshaw). Born July 16, 1870, at Salt Lake City.
Married Jennie Maud Decker Dec. 24, 1894, at East Mill Creek, Utah (daughter of Charles Frank Decker and Margaret Jane Maxfield, both of Salt Lake City—pioneers July 24, 1847, Brigham Young company). She was born Oct. 10, 1876. Their children: Henry Lawrence b. Sept. 17, 1895; Jay C. b. Feb. 9, 1898; Grace Marie b. March 26, 1900; Elmo Rae b. Nov. 5, 1902; Alma LeRoy b. Oct 10, 1904; Zelda May b. Nov. 5, 1906; Thomas Nolan b. May 10, 1908; Russell K. b. Aug. 10, 1910. Family home Vineyard, Utah.
Deacon. Farmer and fruitraiser.

WILLCOX, JOHN HENRY (son of Hazzard Willcox and Sarah Seely of Arkansas). Born Feb. 14, 1824. in Arkansas. Came to Utah 1847.
Married Mary Young March 14, 1848, Salt Lake City (daughter of James Young and Elizabeth Seely of Canada, pioneers 1847). She was born June 6, 1831. Their children: Hazzard, m. Tilda Westwood; Elizabeth, m. Philip Hurst; Sarah, m. Wesley Bills; James Henry, m. Harrett Day; m. Ellis Staker; John Carlos, m. Violet Westwood; Mary Mehitable, m. Richard Clark; Clarissa Jane, m. Peter Melling; Ellen (Sabray), m. John Oliver; Hannah, m. Joseph Corison; Martha A., m. Richard D. Westwood; Justice Azel, m. Selma Corison. Family home Mt. Pleasant, Utah.
Farmer. Died Nov. 21, 1909, Mt. Pleasant, Utah.

WILLCOX, JAMES HENRY (son of John Henry Willcox and Mary Young). Born Nov. 10, 1855, North Ogden, Utah.
Married Charlott Day Oct. 27, 1880, Mt. Pleasant, Utah (daughter of Abraham Day and Charlot Doroming, pioneers September, 1847, contingent Mormon Battalion). She was born Dec. 27, 1864. Their children: James b. Oct. 25, 1881; died; Harrett b. Dec. 11, 1882, m. Charles Dorius; Ephraim b. Feb. 15, 1884, m. Edna Smith; George b. Sept. 9, 1887, died; Henry b. May 8, —, m. Edna Beach; Edgar b. June 15, 1892; Hazzard b. Oct. 13, 1894; Quintin b. April 23, 1897; Pearl and Ruby b. Jan. 28, 1901; Annie b. Sept. 29, 1902. Family home Castle Dale, Utah.
Married Elizabeth Ellis Staker April 7, 1904, Salt Lake City (daughter of Nathan Staker and Eliza Cusworth of Canada, pioneers September, 1847, Captain Hunter company). She was born Feb. 4, 1866. Their children: Truman Ambrose b. Jan. 10, 1905; Arden James b. July 6, 1907; Olive Louine b. July 31, 1909. Family home Castle Dale, Utah.
Member 91st quorum seventies; missionary to northern states 1899-99. Town board member two terms. Farmer and stockraiser.

WILLEY, JEREMIAH (son of Isaiah Willey, born 1760, and Sarah Daniels, born 1762, both of Northfield, N. H.). He was born Nov. 6, 1804, at Northfield. Came to Utah Sept. 16, 1851, John G. Smith company.
Married Samantha Call April 28, 1839, Warsaw, Ill. (daughter of Cyril Call and Sally Tiffany). Their children: William Wallace b. Oct. 20, 1841, m. Nancy Tolman, m. Martha Jane Tuttle; Jeremiah Bussie b. Feb. 17, 1847, m. Annie Roberts; David Orson b. Sept. 26, 1849, m. Mary A. Barlow; Parley Pratt b. Dec. 17, 1854, m. Sarah Jane Pace; Willard Cyril b. June 10, 1857, d. infant; Joseph b. May 17, 1859, m. Amy Maude Thurgood; Armena Elizabeth; Samantha Ellen. Family home Bountiful, Davis Co., Utah.
Married Sarah Ann Sanders. Their child: Alfonso.
Participated in exodus of Mormons from Kirtland, Ohio, also from Missouri and Illinois. Member Mormon Battalion, Company A; member escort of General S. F. Kearney from California to Ft. Leavenworth, Kansas, in 1847, having Colonel John C. Fremont in custody, on his way to Washington to answer a charge of insubordination for refusing to recognize Kearney's authority as military commandant of California. President of seventies. Chaplain first Utah territorial legislature, which convened Sept. 22, 1851.

PIONEERS AND PROMINENT MEN OF UTAH 1249

WILLEY, WILLIAM WALLACE (son of Jeremiah Willey and Samantha Call). Born Oct. 20, 1841, Warsaw, Ill.
Married Nancy Tolman Dec. 23, 1862, Salt Lake City (daughter of Judson Tolman and Sarah Lucretia Holbrook, pioneers Sept. 20, 1848, Brigham Young company). She was born in Pottawattamie county, Iowa, Feb. 4, 1848. Their children: Nancy Samantha b. Nov. 3, 1863, d. infant; Sarah Eldora b. Jan. 27, 1865, m. Charles Lyon; Effie b. Nov. 15, 1866, m. Walter Holt; Maraldia b. Feb. 26, 1868, m. Emanuel Hanks; Ellen b. Feb. 28, 1870, d. infant; Alice b. Aug. 9, 1871, m. Janthus H. Barlow; William Wallace, Jr. b. May 8, 1874, m. Melinda Adams; Catherine b. Nov. 29, 1876, m. George W. Pearson; Vasco b. May 22, 1882, m. Millie Reading; Rosco b. May 22, 1882, m. Jude Chealis; Archer b. Jan. 13, 1884, m. Fannie Tuttle; Rudger b. March 16, 1886, m. Bird McClaren; Edna b. Nov. 18, 1889, m. Roy Tribe. Family home Bountiful, Utah.
Married Martha Jane Tuttle Nov. 7, 1871, Salt Lake City (daughter of Norton Ray Tuttle and Elizabeth Utley), who was born Jan. 15, 1854, at Tooele, Utah. Their children: Gertrude Elizabeth b. Nov. 7, 1872, m. Robert Anderson; Martha Emily b. Aug. 18, 1874, m. Albert Brown; Norton Ray b. Feb. 26, 1877, m. Mrs. Brown; Theodore William b. Sept. 23, 1891. Family home Bountiful, Utah.
Missionary to England 1879; alternate high counselor. Worked on Salt Lake Temple at different times for 40 years. Assisted in bringing immigrants to Utah. Veteran Black Hawk war. Farmer.

WILLEY, DAVID ORSON (son of Jeremiah Willey and Samantha Call). Born Sept. 26, 1849, in Pottawattamie Co., Iowa. Came to Utah with parents.
Married Mary A. Barlow in 1868, Salt Lake City (daughter of Israel Barlow and Elizabeth Haven, pioneers 1848, Brigham Young company). She was born in 1850 at Bountiful, Utah. Their children: David Orson, Jr.; Jeremiah; Israel E.; Mary P.; Flora E.; Clarence; Earl; Charles L.; Silva; Willard H.; Thatcher H. Family home, Bountiful.
High counselor to Davis stake. Sheriff Davis county; mayor of Bountiful.

WILLIAMS, ALEXANDER. Born in Georgia. Came to Utah in 1848, Brigham Young company.
Married Isabella Gill in Tennessee. Their children: Francis, m. Martha Frazier; Thomas, m. Albina Merrill; Cyntha, died; Epsey, m. Byrom Pace; Clinton, m. Martha Porter; Nathaniel, m. Eliza Helen Wall; Alma, m. Sarah Jane Applegate; Archibald, m. Eliza Armstrong; Alexander, Jr. m. Vira Whipple; Seth; Joseph, died. Family home Provo, Utah.
Counselor to Bishop Elias Blackburn of Provo. Sheriff of Utah county. Died at Independence, Mo.

WILLIAMS, NATHANIEL (son of Alexander Williams and Isabella Gill). Born Feb. 26, 1835, Galland Point, near Nauvoo, Ill. Came to Utah Oct. 2, 1847, Jedediah M. Grant company.
Married Eliza Helen Wall Oct. 26, 1862, Provo, Utah (daughter of William Madison Wall and Nancy Haws of Provo, pioneers 1852). She was born Sept. 26, 1843. Their children: Isabella b. Aug. 14, 1865, m. James G. Haws; Viola b. Aug. 31, 1867, m. Charles Fausett; William Alvah b. Dec. 9, 1869, m. Elizabeth Choules; Dora Vlate b. March 13, 1871, m. James Orlin Fausett; Don Carlos b. May 24, 1874, m. Milessa Bunnell; George Albert b. Dec. 13, 1876, m. Winefred Colman; Helen b. March 7, 1882, m. John Gulick. Family home Provo, Utah.
Furnished much of the lumber for ties and bridges for early railroads in Utah. Sawmill owner and lumberman.

WILLIAMS, WILLIAM ALVAH (son of Nathaniel Williams and Eliza Helen Wall). Born Dec. 9, 1869, Provo, Utah.
Married Elizabeth Choules Sept. 30, 1891, Manti, Utah (daughter of George Choules, of Provo, who came to Utah 1882). She was born July 18, 1870. Family home, Provo.
Missionary to Sandwich Islands 1897-1901 and 1905-06; second counselor to bishop of fifth ward Provo, 1908-12. Plumber and contractor.

WILLIAMS, CHARLES (son of James Williams and Catharine Price, of England). Born Sept. 1, 1831, Sutton, Herefordshire, Eng. Came to Utah Sept. 26, 1857, William G. Young company.
Married Margaret Sant in October, 1861 (daughter of John Sant and Mary Shaw), who was born Feb. 20, 1844. Their children: Charles, Jr. b. June 28, 1863, m. Elizabeth J. Clements November, 1886; Mary Jane b. Aug. 4, 1865, m. John P. Clifford 1884; Fannie E. b. March 1, 1868, m. William H. Paskins 1896; Margaret b. March 14, 1870, m. John F. Morton 1886; Catherine b. March 13, 1872, m. Reuben Howell 1893; Elizabeth b. Feb. 6, 1874, m. Edward A. Ward 1891; Thomas James b. April 12, 1876, m. Mary Alice Sant July 8, 1897, m. Rosa Belle Standfill Jan. 27, 1909; Martha E. b. July 21, 1878, m. James W. Southwick 1899. Family resides in Logan.
High priest. Served in Echo Canyon trouble. Moved to Smithfield and in 1864 to Bear Lake, Idaho.

WILLIAMS, THOMAS JAMES (son of Charles Williams and Margaret Sant). Born April 12, 1876, Clifton, Idaho.
Married May Alice Sant July 8, 1897, at Logan, Utah (daughter of George Sant and Ann Treasurer, of Treasureton, Idaho, pioneers 1854). She was born Feb. 19, 1879, died Feb. 2, 1905. Their children: Jennie V. b. Sept. 22, 1899; Thomas Odell b. April 26, 1901; Charles b. Jan. 12, 1903.
Married Rosa Belle Standfill Jan. 27, 1909, at Logan, Utah (daughter of Partor Standfill and Florence McCleod, of Card, Ark.), who was born Aug. 2, 1879. Their children: Paul Eugene b. Dec. 14, 1909; Alice Rose b. April 16, 1911.
Elder. Constable. Farmer and stockraiser.

WILLIAMS, CHRISTOPHER (son of Ichabod Williams and Sybil Clark, of Prattsville, N. Y.). Born March 7, 1789, at Prattsville. Came to Utah 1848, Orson Pratt company.
Married Mellicent Vannostrand (daughter of James Vannostrand and Sarah Vannostrand), who was born Aug. 27, 1802, and died in Iowa. Their children: James V. b. Dec. 13, 1830, m. Eda Pearson July 8, 1866; Cornelius b. Dec. 11, 1832, m. Sarah George; Catharine b. June 6, 1836, m. Iver N. Iverson Jan. 19, 1854. Family home, Salt Lake City.
Married Jacobina Wells Patton 1856, Salt Lake City, who was born 1813, at Kilmarnock, Scotland. Their child: Mellicent Sophia b. Sept. 12, 1856, m. Joseph Golightly.
Bishop third ward, Salt Lake City. Carpenter; farmer.

WILLIAMS, JAMES V. (son of Christopher Williams and Mellicent Vannostrand). Born Dec. 13, 1830, near Toronto, Canada.
Married Eda Pearson July 8, 1866, Richfield, Utah (daughter of Pere Knudsen and Hannah Swenson, both died in Sweden). She was born Sept. 8, 1836, Onslunda, Sweden. Their children: James Isaac b. April 15, 1867, m. Nicholena Jensen Dec. 28, 1892; Christopher Peter b. May 29, 1869, d. Feb. 14, 1870; Moses Elias b. Dec. 11, 1871, m. Etta Hyatt Oct. 12, 1902; Ida Meillicent b. Dec. 3, 1873, m. Christian Anderson June 29, 1898. Family home Monroe, Utah.
Member of Mormon Battalion. Farmer and sheepherder.

WILLIAMS, JAMES ISAAC (son of James V. Williams and Eda Pearson). Born April 15, 1867, Glenwood, Utah.
Married Nicholena Jensen Dec. 28, 1892 (daughter of Christian Jensen and Christiana Nielsen. Came to Utah by train, 1877). She was born Jan. 3, 1873, in Denmark. Their children: James Clarence b. May 13, 1894; Eda Sylva b. Aug. 11, 1896; Ernest Naveil b. Nov. 13, 1898, d. Nov. 20, 1905.

WILLIAMS, DANIEL J. (son of William W. Williams, born May 7, 1829, in South Wales, and Mary Hodge). He was born April 14, 1856, in Pennsylvania. Came to Utah in October, 1861.
Married Margret Morse Jan. 11, 1874, Samaria, Idaho (daughter of Richard Morse and Maria Jones of Samaria), who was born July 1, 1859. Their children: Daniel M. b. Dec. 27, 1874, m. Lucy A. Thorpe; Rebecca b. Aug. 29, 1877, m. George Stuart; Rachel b. Aug. 20, 1880, m. Benjamin Williams; Richard M. b. April 20, 1883, m. Rachel Powell; Mary Jane b. Feb. 12, 1886, m. Samuel Mansfield; Maria b. July 20, 1889, m. Thomas Luak; William M. b. Dec. 4, 1892; Margret b. Nov. 29, 1896; Ernest b. Sept. 4, 1899; Sarah b. July 21, 1904. Family home, Samaria.
Farmer.

WILLIAMS, DANIEL M. (son of Daniel J. Williams and Margret Morse). Born Dec. 27, 1874, Samaria, Idaho.
Married Lucy A. Thorpe Oct. 16, 1894, Logan, Utah (daughter of John Thorpe and Rachel Wight of Samaria, Idaho), who was born Jan. 13, 1876, and died Aug. 25, 1912. Their children: Harold b. April 21, 1896; Alice b. Sept. 19, 1897; Rose b. Dec. 15, 1899; Daniel Lloyd b. Oct. 3, 1904; Sylvia b. Aug. 11, 1909; John Gilbert b. Aug. 24, 1912.
Member 52d quorum seventies; Sunday school superintendent; president Y. M. M. I. A. Farmer.

WILLIAMS, DANIEL R. (son of Daniel Williams and Vina Hovey, of Wales). Born Aug. 7, 1802, Lima, Livingston county, N. Y. Came to Utah Sept. 25, 1852, Henry W. Miller company.
Married Electa Caroline Briggs in 1838, Nauvoo, Ill. (daughter of Allen and Elizabeth Caroline Briggs of Michigan), who was born Jan. 26, 1805. Their children: Alma A., m. Sophia Katz; Emily E., m. Edward Stevenson; Elizabeth C., m. James Montgomery. Family home Farmington, Utah.
Member 10th quorum seventies; high priest. Died October, 1882.

WILLIAMS, ELIAS WILLARD. Born June 26, 1818, Whitinsville, Mass. Came to Utah Aug. 1, 1854, independently, with his family and that of A. Snell.
Married Lucy Hendricks. Their children: Ellen, m. Asa Bartlett York; Mary, m. Benjamin Franklin Johnson, m. Isaac McDonald Kolb; Elias Willard, Jr. b. April 19, 1858, m. Ida Jane Bascom; Charles Oson Sibley (adopted) b. Feb. 15, 1848. Family resided Salt Lake City, Springville, Provo and Mona, Utah.
Seventy. Settled at Salt Lake City, moved to Springville, to Grafton, to Provo, to Mona, thence to Vernal, Utah. Worked on Salt Lake City Temple. Justice of peace, Mona, for several years. Painter, cabinetmaker and ironworker. Oldest man in county when he died April 30, 1905 (in his eighty-seventh year).

WILLIAMS, ELIAS WILLARD (son of Elias Willard Williams and Lucy Hendricks). Born April 19, 1858, Springville, Utah.
Married Ida Jane Bascom at Mona, Utah (daughter of Joal Almon Bascom and Alice Jane Bell, of England, later of Vernal, Utah). She was born Feb. 8, 1860. Their children: Willard Henry b. Sept. 27, 1876, m. Rose Perry; John Elias b. Nov. 2, 1878, m. Mary Lords; Joal Orson b. March 31, 1881; Charles Almon b. Oct. 4, 1883, m. Jessie Green; Levi b. Feb. 5, 1885, m. Eliza Green; Alice Nora b. June 15, 1888, m. Vergil Burke; Ira Kimball b. Dec. 3, 1891, m. Pearl Anderson; Lyman Leroy b. Feb. 23, 1893; Ida May b. July 21, 1895; Lucy b. Jan. 14, 1898; Lorn b. May 3, 1900; Elva b. Sept. 4, 1903.
Deacon. Settled in Ashley valley 1889. Farmer and sheepman.

WILLIAMS, EVAN (son of William Williams of Caermarthenshire, Wales). Born June 15, 1805, in Wales. Came to Utah 1861.
Married Sarah Jeremy at Caermarthenshire (daughter of Thomas Jeremy and Sarah Evans of Caermarthenshire), who was born Aug. 10, 1817. Their children: Thomas J., m. Ellen Eccles; Mary, m. Louis Howell; William N., m. Clarissa Smith; Sarah J., m. Hugh Watson; David J., m. Annie Ridges; Esther C., m. Robert H. Hastam. Family home, Salt Lake City.
Block teacher. Gardener and farmer. Died in 1893.

WILLIAMS, WILLIAM N. (son of Evan Williams and Sarah Jeremy). Born March 17, 1851, in Wales. Came to Utah with father.
Married Clarissa Smith July 17, 1877, Salt Lake City (daughter of George A. Smith and Susan E. West, of Salt Lake City, pioneers July 24, 1847, Brigham Young company). She was born April 21, 1859. Their chilren: Clarissa b. Aug. 6, 1880, m. Earl G. Van Law; Sarah b. June 29, 1885, m. Robert N. Wilson; Josephine b. July 21, 1887; Hetty b. March 30, 1889, died; Eva b. July 21, 1890; Georgia b. June 20, 1892; George A. b. June 26, 1894; Bathsheba b. Aug. 3, 1896; Lyman S. b. March 22, 1899. Family home, Salt Lake City.
Seventy; missionary to Wales 1877-79; high counselor. Member legislature seven terms. President and general manager Co-op. Furniture Co. Merchant.

WILLIAMS, EVAN AUSTIN (son of Noah Williams, born March 13, 1795, and Jane Austin, born Oct. 9, 1798, both at Llantrisant, Wales—married 1821). He was born Oct. 29, 1822, at Llantrisant. Came to Utah September, 1853, Joseph A. Young company.
Married Mary Ann Tomkins Feb. 29, 1848 (daughter of William Tomkins and Marie Nutting), who was born Aug. 26, 1825, and came to Utah with husband. Their children: Mariemtha Althera b. Feb. 1850; Noah Mormon b. Sept. 19, 1851, m. Harriet Cordelia Lindsay Dec. 8, 1872; Mary Jane b. Feb. 2, 1855, m. Albert Dalton; Evan Llewellyn b. Dec. 1, 1856, m. Emman Bird May 25, 1885; William Morgan b. Dec. 4, 1858, m. Josephine Anderson June 4, 1882; Thomas Henry b. Nov. 8, 1850, m. Lezetta Bunn June 26, 1893; Sarah b. Dec. 7, 1862; Ellen Maria b. Aug. 22, 1864, m. Philip Chugg May 16, 1900; Chester Ensol b. March 27, 1867, m. Mary Haddock Nov. 1888; George Albert b. May 25, 1898, m. Mary Ann Skinner Sept. 19, 1894. Family home Paris, Bear Lake Co., Idaho.
Tithing clerk and priest at Willard, Utah; first superintendent of Sunday schools at Paris. Moved from Willard, Utah, to Paris, Idaho, in Aug. 1864. Blacksmith. Died at Paris.

WILLIAMS, NOAH MORMON (son of Evan Austin Williams and Mary Ann Tomkins). Born Sept. 19, 1851, Briton Ferry, Wales.
Married Harriet Cordelia Lindsay Dec. 8, 1872, Paris, Idaho (daughter of William B. Lindsay and Permelia Blackman, pioneers October, 1852, Captain Walker company). She was born Feb. 1, 1851, in Pottawattamie Co., Iowa. Their children: Mary Ann b. Sept. 10, 1873, m. Alexander Stovell Feb. 9, 1894; Permelia b. May 24, 1875, m. William Skinner Aug. 19, 1897; William Mormon b. Feb. 22, 1877, m. Marie Nelson June 7, 1897; Evan b. Nov. 15, 1879; Philemon b. Oct. 13, 1882; Oliver b. Dec. 28, 1883, m. Hannah Johnson Sept. 23, 1902; Cora b. Dec. 28, 1885, m. Herman W. Hodges June 5, 1905. Family home Nounan, Bear Lake Co., Idaho.

WILLIAMS, EZRA GRANGER (son of Frederick Granger Williams, born Oct. 28, 1787, Suffield, Conn., and Rebecca Swain, born Aug. 3, 1798, Loyalsock, Northumberland Co., Pa., and died Sept. 25, 1861, Smithfield, Utah). He was born Nov. 17, 1823, Warrensville, Cuyahoga Co., Ohio. Came to Utah Oct. 28, 1849, Ezra T. Benson company.
Married Henriette Elizabeth Crombie Aug. 15, 1847, St. Louis, Mo. (daughter of John Crombie, born Nov. 17, 1800, Chester, N. H., and Elizabeth Pope Philips, born Aug. 18, 1804, Boston, Mass.). She was born Sept. 27, 1827, in Boston. Their children: Lucy Ellen b. Sept. 30, 1848, m. W. R. Godfrey Oct. 10, 1867; Mary Elizabeth b. Feb. 2, 1851, Salt Lake City, m. Joseph Smith Gardner March 15, 1869; Frederick Granger b. March 29, 1853, m. Amanda Burns Jan. 24, 1876; Ezra Henry Granger b. April 16, 1855, m. Sarah Ann Hickenlooper Dec. 28, 1874; Joseph Swain b. March 10, 1858, d. Oct. 24, 1860; John Albert b. April 13, 1860, d. Nov. 20, 1870; Brigham Young b. May 18, 1862, and Heber Chase Kimball (twins) b. May 18, 1862, d. infants; Frances Henrietta Maria b. May 24, 1864, m. Thomas Budge Dec. 16, 1880. Family resided Kanesville, Iowa, Salt Lake City, Smithfield, Pleasant View and Ogden, Utah.
Married Electa Jane Barney Feb. 19, 1857, Salt Lake City (daughter of Royal Barney, pioneer, and Sarah Esterbrook). She was born Aug. 23, 1840, Freeport, Ind., died Jan. 25, 1883, Ogden, Utah. Only child: Hyrum Royal b. April 3, 1858, m. Della Huffaker April 3, 1879. Family resided Salt Lake City and Ogden, Utah.
His father was appointed second counselor to Joseph Smith March, 1832, the first in that office, and was president of first high council 1834. Ezra Granger was baptized by Joseph Smith and confirmed by Hyrum Smith; member 3d quorum seventies; missionary to White Mountains, Ariz., and Smithfield, Utah, during Indian troubles. Practicing physician. Died Aug. 1, 1905.

WILLIAMS, FREDERICK GRANGER (son of Ezra Granger Williams and Henriettaa Elizabeth Crombie). Born March 29, 1853, Salt Lake City.
Married Amanda Burns 1876, Salt Lake City (daughter of Enoch Burns of Eden, Utah, pioneer). Their children: Amanda Elizabeth b. Feb. 23, 1877, m. Heber Erastus Farr; Frederick Ezra b. Jan. 11, 1879, d. Nov. 14, 1879; Sarah Josephine b. Oct. 1, 1880, m. Francis Gee Johnson; Frederick Enoch b. Nov. 11, 1882, d. June 8, 1883; Alonzo b. April 11, 1884, d. May 15, 1886; Flora May b. Dec. 20, 1886; Joseph b. Oct. 15, 1888; Nathena Hazel b. Oct. 21, 1890; Leonard B. b. Nov. 21, 1893; Vernal b. Nov. 2, 1895; Ivan; Clyde; Rolla. Family resided Pleasant View, Utah, Ashley, Idaho, and Dublin, Mexico.
Died at Tucson, Ariz.

WILLIAMS, EZRA HENRY GRANGER (son of Granger Williams and Henriette Elizabeth Crombie). Born April 16, 1855, Salt Lake City.
Married Sarah Ann Hickenlooper Dec. 28, 1874, Salt Lake City (daughter of John T. Hickenlooper, born July 7, 1836, in Pennsylvania, and Elvira Martha Fullmer, born Oct. 14, 1839, Nauvoo, Ill.). She was born May 25, 1857, Salt Lake City. Their children: John Ezra b. Oct. 4, 1876, m. Harriet Rhoda Miller Feb. 22, 1905; Charles Orson b. Sept. 14, 1878, m. Emma Louisa Built Aug. 15, 1900; Frederick David b. May 28, 1880, m. Nettie Mae Farley Nov. 26, 1902; Joseph Henry b. March 23, 1882, m. Miriam Gertrude Chandler Feb. 4, 1903; Annie Rebecca b. Nov. 19, 1883, m. Sarah Melvina b. July 5, 1887; Bessie Elizabeth Elvira b. Sept. 19, 1889, m. Joseph Lawrence Millard April 3, 1913. Family resided Salt Lake City, Smithfield, Pleasant View and Ogden, Utah.
Senior president of 53d quorum seventies; missionary eastern states 1907-08; second assistant superintendent religion class North Weber stake board.

WILLIAMS, GEORGE (son of James and Elizabeth Williams). Born Dec. 4, 1858, Des Moines, Iowa. Came to Utah 1870.
Married Malinda Rhoades July 4, 1881, Salt Lake City (daughter of Caleb Baldwin Rhoades and Malinda Powell), who was born Dec. 23, 1863. Their children: James Caleb, m. Sarah Scoville; Malinda Elizabeth, m. Dell Rowland Family resided Provo and Scofield, Utah.
Died Jan. 3, 1902, Springville, Utah.

WILLIAMS, GEORGE (son of Robert and Jane Williams of Wiltshire, Eng.). Born Oct. 13, 1828, in Wiltshire. Came to Utah 1864, Erastus Snow company.
Married Harriet Sumdrel in Wiltshire, Eng., who was born March 22, 1828, and came to Utah with husband. Their children: George Enia b. May 22, 1853, died; George Hyrum b. July 25, 1855, m. Sophia Franson; George Roland b. July 31, 1860, m. Sarah Burbank Oct. 25, 1883; James Edwin b. Aug. 8, 1863, died; Eliza J. (Adline) b. Sept. 26, 1865; Ellie b. Sept. 17, 1869, m. Maggie Pope. Family home Brigham City, Utah.

WILLIAMS, GEORGE ROLAND (son of George Williams and Harriet Sumdrel). Born July 31, 1860, Wiltshire, Eng.
Married Sarah S. Burbank Oct. 25, 1883, Salt Lake City (daughter of Daniel M. and Sarah S. Burbank, former pioneer Oct. 6, 1852). She was born July 31, 1866, at Brigham City, Utah. Their children: Roland B. b. Nov. 24, 1885, m. Sophia Georgesen Dec. 18, 1907; Sarah B. b. March 11, 1888, m. Charles Kofoed Nov. 21, 1904; Rose B. b. Jan. 4, 1890, m. George Kofoed Jan. 13, 1910; Elvira B. b. July 31, 1894; Chloe B. b. March 7, 1897; Bessie B. b. Feb. 9, 1900; Jennie B. b. Oct. 17, 1903; Lenoa B. b. Jan. 14, 1907; Georgia B. b. Feb. 9, 1910. Family home Weston, Idaho.

WILLIAMS, ROLAND B. (son of George Roland Williams and Sarah S. Burbank). Born Nov. 24, 1885, Brigham City, Utah.
Married Sophia Georgesen (daughter of Nels Georgesen, born Jan. 17, 1834, at Koster, Rjob, Denmark and Catherine —— born May 6, 1859, Lilkelong, Denmark). She was born March 25, 1888, at Oxford, Idaho. Their children: Gladys b. Oct. 20, 1908; Lavon b. Oct. 8, 1911. Family home Weston, Idaho.
Elder; ward teacher.

PIONEERS AND PROMINENT MEN OF UTAH 1251

WILLIAMS, JOHN JONES (son of Daniel Williams, born 1747, and Ruth Jones, born 1794; former of Brecknockshire, Wales, latter of Lladnaymid parish, Wales). He was born Aug. 12, 1823, Black Thorne, Brecknockshire. Came to Utah Oct. 17, 1853, Christopher Arthur company.
Married Jane Merriefield Feb. 14, 1852 (daughter of Uriah Merriefield, born May 2, 1799, and Jane Denning, born April 11, 1793). She was born Nov. 4, 1834, and came to Utah with husband. Their children: Elvira A. b. Feb. 28, 1853, m. James P. Harrison Dec. 13, 1869; John Uriah b. Jan. 9, 1855, m. Margret Pugh Dec. 10, 1878; Ephraim M. b. Jan. 9, 1857, d. Jan. 9, 1899; Sarah Jane b. March 21, 1859, m. Nephi Lewis Dec. 30, 1880; Daniel M. b. March 9, 1861, d. Oct. 1861; Priscilla M. b. Sept. 8, 1862, d. March 1863; Samuel M. b. Oct. 24, 1864, m. Matilda Gleed Jan. 28, 1886; Hyrum M. b. Feb. 23, 1867, m. Eva Perkins Feb. 22, 1893; Elizabeth M. b. Feb. 2, 1869. d. Aug. 22, 1871; Arthur M. b. July 18, 1872, m. Mary P. Thomson April 13, 1888; Reuben M. b. Nov. 5, 1874, m. Maria Tippets Nov. 4, 1895.
Married Mary Jones March 6, 1857, Salt Lake City (daughter of Thomas Jones and Ruth Thomas, pioneers Oct. 2, 1856, Edward Bunker handcart company). She was born Jan. 12, 1837, Hansouil, Wales. Their children: Ozariah F. Jones b. Dec. 20, 1857, m. Elizabeth Denning March 4, 1885; Roseanna b. Dec. 13, 1859, m. James H. Denning Dec. 21, 1874; Ruth E. b. April 1861, m. Josiah A. Richardson March 22, 1883; Lodemina Louisa b. March 15, 1863, d. Oct. 15, 1863; Mary Ellen b. July 9, 1864, m. David Evans Oct. 29, 1885; Clara Vilate b. March 27, 1867, d. Nov. 1867; Thomas Oliver b. March 11, 1870, m. Mary E. Gleed Feb. 27, 1890, d. Oct. 9, 1897, m. Elizabeth Evans April 1899; Victoria b. March 3, 1872, m. Hyrum D. Davis Dec. 19, 1894; George Albert Jones b. April 5, 1874, m. Nellie Griffin Aug. 4, 1895; Martha May b. Feb. 23, 1876, d. Nov. 1876; Annie S. b. Dec. 28, 1877, m. James Westergard Dec. 4, 1902; Hannah Adell b. Aug. 8, 1879, d. June 29, 1880. Families resided Brigham City, Utah, and Malad City, Idaho.
Baptized January, 1850, in Wales. Ordained elder 1851; high priest 1860; counselor to Bishop George Stuart 1884-90. Blacksmith and farmer. Died Jan. 10, 1899.

WILLIAMS, AZARIAH F. JONES (son of John Jones Williams and Mary Jones). Born Dec. 20, 1857, Brigham City, Utah.
Married Elizabeth M. Denning March 4, 1885, Logan, Utah (daughter of James Denning and Sarah Merriefield, former pioneer Oct. 2, 1856, Christopher Arthur company). Their children: Azariah D. b. Sept. 25, 1886; Elizabeth D. b. Oct. 15, 1889; Mary D. b. June 3, 1892; Saraelia D. b. May 15, 1896; James D. b. Dec. 25, 1898, d. Feb. 2, 1899; John J. b. Feb. 16, 1902; Ruth D. b. July 11, 1905. Family resided Malad and Idaho Falls, Idaho.
Ordained elder Dec. 10, 1872. Farmer; stockraiser; dairyman.

WILLIAMS, JOHN ROWLAND (son of Evan and Catherine Rowland of Denbighshire, Wales). Born Dec. 15, 1802, Denbighshire. Came to Utah October, 1855, Thomas Jeremy company.
Married Mary Roberts at St. Asaph, Wales, who was born Jan. 19, 1801. Their children: Thomas Lloyd, m. Elizabeth Rowland; John P., m. Elizabeth Davis; Elizabeth, m. Isaac Morris. Family home Ogden, Utah.
Williams was his adopted name. Elder. Farmer and miller. Died Aug. 25, 1884.

WILLIAMS, THOMAS LLOYD (son of John Rowland Williams and Mary Roberts). Born March 31, 1826, St. Asaph, Wales. Came to Utah October, 1855, Thomas Jeremy company.
Married Elizabeth Rowland April, 1851, St. Asaph, Wales (daughter of Thomas Rowland and Margaret Williams of Newbridge, near Denbighshire, Eng.). She was born March 20, 1835. Their children: Thomas R. b. Oct. 21, 1852, m. Clara E. Ballinger; John R. b. Oct. 8, 1857, d. Aug. 30, 1886; Caroline b. Aug. 14, 1860, m. L. G. Tisman; Mary H. b. Dec. 21, 1862, m. Winslow Farr; Frank R. b. April 14, 1865, m. Lucy Frost; Maggie b. March 4, 1867, m. David Farr; Elizabeth b. Jan. 27, 1869, d. infant; James R. b. Jan. 25, 1871, m. Sarah Frye; William Henry b. June 29, 1873, m. Ethel Payne; Clem b. Oct. 10, 1875, m. Adelaide Proudfort; Frederick b. April 1, 1878, m. Eva Greenwood. Family home Ogden, Utah.
Farmer and miller. Died Feb. 24, 1889.

WILLIAMS, WILLIAM HENRY (son of Thomas Lloyd Williams and Elizabeth Rowland). Born June 29, 1873, Ogden, Utah.
Married Ethel Payne June 29, 1909, at Ogden (daughter of Joseph R. Payne and Sarah Purdy of Ogden). Only child: Ruth b. Oct. 1, 1911.
Member board of education. Candy merchant.

WILLIAMS, JOSHUA (son of James Williams and Sarah Folland of England). Born March 23, 1838, in Wales. Came to Utah November, 1862.
Married Annie Coy at Liverpool, Eng., in 1856. She was born in September, 1836. Their children: Jessie b. Oct. 17, 1858, m. J. B. Green; Edwin b. June 17, 1860, m. Annie Shurtliff; James b. Sept. 23, 1863, m. Brit. Frances Milford b. Oct. 3, 1865, m. Sarah Burgoyne; Annie b. March 17, 1869, m. William Shurtliff; Emily b. Nov. 17, 1870, m. Zachariah Cheeney; Laura b. Feb. 17, 1872, m. William Rene. Family resided in Morgan county, later at Ogden, Utah.
Receiver of timber Union Pacific Railroad. Chief Ogden fire department 1875; prosecuting attorney Morgan county 1896-1900. Died November, 1901.

WILLIAMS, EDWIN (son of Joshua Williams and Annie Coy). Born June 17, 1860, Liverpool, Eng. Came to Utah with parents.
Married Annie Shurtliff Nov. 7, 1878, Ogden, Utah (daughter of Emerson Shurtliff and Mary Ann Tribe of Ogden). She was born Nov. 6, 1860. Their children: Walter b. March 29, 1880, m. Helen Reeder; Frederick E. b. June 17, 1881, m. Nellie Driver; Pearl b. Aug. 9, 1883, m. Ashby Newman; Floy b. Aug. 9, 1887, m. LeRoy Seager; Blanche b. Dec. 30, 1890; Howard b. Aug. 20, 1895. Family home Ogden, Utah.
Merchant.

WILLIAMS, MILFORD (son of Joshua Williams and Annie Coy). Born Oct. 3, 1865, in Morgan Co., Utah.
Married Sarah Burgoyne in Bear Lake Co., Idaho, June 1, 1899 (daughter of Edward Burgoyne and Mary A. Eynon, pioneers 1864). She was born May 23, 1865. Their children: Genevieve b. Aug. 11, 1890; Gwendolyn b. May 8, 1896; Venus b. Jan. 22, 1899; Lois b. Sept. 17, 1901; Edward and Roma (twins) b. Nov. 21, 1904; Mary b. Aug. 22, 1907. Family resided Montpelier, Idaho, and Ogden, Utah.
Missionary to Great Britain 1895-97. Mayor Montpelier, Idaho, 1903-06.

WILLIAMS, OWEN (son of John Williams and Ann Davis of Eglwys Bach, Denbigshire, Wales). Born April 3, 1804, Eglwys Bach, Wales. Came to Utah September, 1860, Captain Horne company.
Married Ann Thomas 1835 at Llafyllin, Montgomery, Wales (daughter of John Thomas and Cathren Vaughn). Their children: John O., m. Ellen ———; Maria, m. Joseph C. Davis. Elder. Died Oct. 29, 1875, Panaca, Lincoln county, Nev.

WILLIAMS, ROBERT (son of Robert Williams of London, Eng.). Born August, 1815, London. Came to Utah 1849.
Married Emma N. Hocken Feb. 24, 1854, Southwork, Eng. (daughter of Edward Hocken and Catherine Crowl of London). She was born Sept. 7, 1834. Their children: Robert E.; William J., d. aged 2; Annie D., m. Alma Caffal; John, d. aged 2; Nellie, m. Charles Lutz; George E., m. Emma Wilcken; Catherine, m. Ernest Tullidge; Eliza, m. Samuel Glass; Edwin S., m. Nellie Tullidge; Alice B., m. William B. Clemment. Family home, Salt Lake City.
Missionary. Tailor. Died Jan. 1, 1882.

WILLIAMS, SAMUEL D. (son of Daniel Williams and Ruth Jones of South Wales; former born 1761, latter 1759). He was born April 10, 1826, Brecknockshire, Wales. Came to Utah Aug. 24, 1868, Horton D. Haight company.
Married Ann Price in November, 1850 (daughter of Daniel Price), who was born April 10, 1826, and died in Wales. Their children: Daniel b. Feb. 3, 1853; Mary b. Aug. 25, 1854, m. John Jenkins Nov. 1, 1875; Ruth b. March 27, 1857, m. Jeremiah Hodge Williams Dec. 29, 1875; Samuel John b. May 2, 1865, m. Fanny Williams Dec. 14, 1898.
Married Elizabeth Powell Nov. 25, 1866, Llandilo, Caermarthenshire, Wales (daughter of John Perry and Mary Powell), who was born May 1, 1845, at Llandilo. Their children: Elizabeth b. March 22, 1868, m. B. Y. Mansfield Feb. 6, 1883; Margarett b. May 18, 1870, m. William M. Caldwell Jan. 1, 1889; Sarah Jane b. Aug. 23, 1871, m. William Thomas Co. S, 1892; William Reece b. Feb. 13, 1873, d. Aug. 13, 1775; Joan b. Nov. 20, 1874, m. Gomer Thomas March 17, 1895; John b. April 23, 1876, m. Zina Landon Feb. 13, 1901; Brigham b. Oct. 24, 1877; Ezriah b. Feb. 23, 1880, m. Agness Anthony Dec. 27, 1902; Hannah b. Aug. 13, 1881, m. David B. Evans July 6, 1898; Ann b. July 8, 1884, m. David G. Huntsman Aug. 6, 1902; Oliver b. Dec. 30, 1886. Families resided Samaria, Idaho.
First presiding elder for Samaria ward 1869-80.

WILLIAMS, SAMUEL JOHN (son of Samuel D. Williams and Ann Price). Born May 2, 1865, Topglass, South Wales.
Married Fannie Williams Dec. 14, 1898, Samaria, Idaho (daughter of John Haines Williams and Sarah Jane Davis, pioneers Oct. 7, 1860). Their child: Ann Eunella b. Oct. 1, 1903.
Sheepraiser and farmer.

WILLIAMS, STEPHEN. Came to Utah Sept. 30, 1854, Darwin Richardson company.
Married Emma Jane Hilyard at Bristol, Eng. (daughter of Andrew Hilyard, born Nov. 30, 1799, and Mary Higgins, both of Ditchett, Somersetshire, Eng., pioneers Sept. 30, 1854, Darwin Richardson company). She was born March 30, 1826, died June 27, 1897. Their children: John, m. Mary Christina Overlaid; Stephen, died; Thomas Andrew, m. Elizabeth Anderson; Emma Jane, m. William Brown; Joseph Alma, died; Samuel Moroni, m. Etta Milo; Nephi, m. Amelia Stalson; Mary, m. Charles Dorius; George Edward, m. Elvina Long; Sarah Elizabeth, m. Andrew C. Anderson; Charles Heber, m. Sarah Shiner; Jane Lettie, m. Charles Edward Torgerson; Stephen, m. Hannah Anderson.
Died Jan. 8, 1897, at Ephraim, Utah.

1252   PIONEERS AND PROMINENT MEN OF UTAH

WILLIAMS, JOHN (son of Stephen Williams and Emma Jane Hilyard). Born Nov. 9, 1841, Bristol, Eng. Came to Utah with parents.
Married Mary Christina Overlaid March 16, 1863 (daughter of Andrew and Caroline Overlaid), who was born Nov. 20, 1845. Their children: David Henry b. May 31, 1872, m. Anna M. Sorensen; Elizabeth C. b. May 10, 1875, m. Hans C. Christensen; John S. b. Feb. 8, 1877, died; Mary A. b. Oct. 31, 1880, m. John T. Edwards; Carry M. b. July 28, 1882, m. Neils C. Hansen; Ervin Kimball b. April 10, 1887, m. Ingry Lucinda Bunderson; Edward E. b. March 20, 1889, died. Family home Emery, Utah.
Married Annie Kristena Larson Aug. 18, 1881, Salt Lake City. Their children: Ann Rhodelia b. June 8, 1882, m. William F. Edwards; Ella Andrear b. Oct. 2, 1885. Family home Mayfield, Utah.
High priest; counselor to Bishop Parley Christiansen of Mayfield ward; superintendent Sunday school at Mayfield. Worked on St. George and Manti temples. First lieutenant in cavalry in Black Hawk war. Constable of Ephraim 12 years. Assisted in bringing immigrants to Utah. Manager of Co-op. Store at Mayfield. Moved to Emery 1894, where he acted as marshal and school trustee. Freighter and miller.

WILLIAMS, ERVIN KIMBALL (son of John Williams and Mary Christina Overlaid). Born April 10, 1887, Ephraim, Utah.
Married Ingry Lucinda Bunderson June 22, 1910, at Manti, Utah (daughter of Peter Victor Bunderson of Sweden and Sena Nielson of Denmark, who came to Utah in 1872). She was born Oct. 14, 1888. Their child: Dorris b. July 2, 1911. Family home Emery, Utah.
Member 149th quorum seventies; assistant Sunday school superintendent; home missionary. Mayor of Emery. Farmer and stockraiser.

WILLIAMS, THOMAS (son of Thomas Williams, born 1800, and Sarah Pearson, both of Bedworth, Eng.). He was born Nov. 12, 1837, Bedworth, Warwickshire, Eng. Came to Utah Sept. 15, 1861, Ira Eldredge company.
Married Jane Fawson June 27, 1859 (daughter of Abraham Fawson and Ann Hodrienne, latter died May 18, 1864, on the way to Utah). Their children: Priscilla Jane b. Feb. 2, 1861, m. H. P. Parkinson; Sarah Ann S. b. Feb. 6, 1863, m. Harrison Matthews; Thomas Arich b. Sept. 28, 1865, m. Anna Bell; George b. 1867, died; James b. July 12, 1870, m. Merlin Ann Ratcliffe; Esther Helen b. Sept. 13, 1872, m. Chester Rydalch; Louisa Hannah b. April 17, 1875, m. Charles Jenkins.
Married Emma Fairless Brown (daughter of David Brown and Emma Fairless), who was born Nov. 28, 1865, Salford, Yorkshire, Eng. Their children: John Leslie b. Aug. 19, 1883, d. Aug. 26, 1891; Alexander T. b. May 5, 1886, d. same day; Charles Guy b. Dec. 21, 1890, d. same day; Clyde b. Aug. 21, 1899, m. Anna Judd Dec. 20, 1911; Ruth Leonora b. Dec. 9, 1892.
Assistant clerk of Tooele stake; tithing clerk. Clerk of Grantsville ward 38 years; city and county assessor and collector.

WILLIAMSON, JAMES. Born Dec. 19, 1804, Bufford, Lancastershire, Eng. Came to Utah in 1850.
Married Ann Allred (daughter of John Allred), who was born Feb. 4, 1808, and came to Utah Nov. 30, 1856, Edward Martin "frozen" handcart company; died Dec. 21, 1892. Their children: Elizabeth b. Aug. 8, 1831, d. April 27, 1850; Ellen b. Jan. 17, 1833, m. Benjamin Watts Jan. 1, 1857; John b. Dec. 7, 1834, d. Oct. 30, 1840; Ann b. Oct. 22, 1836, m. Mr. Jose March 1, 1857; Mary b. March 13, 1839, m. William Barton Aug. 23, 1857; Martha b. Jan. 23, 1841, d. same day; William b. March 23, 1842, m. Martha Knowles April 15, 1865; John b. Sept. 6, 1844, d. April 27, 1886; James b. Aug. 10, 1848, d. July 13, 1850; Betsy b. Jan. 15, 1853, m. Silas S. Smith, Jr., Nov. 3, 1873. Family home Paragonah, Utah.

WILLIAMSON, NIELS (son of William and Bertha Blum of Brevik, Norway). Born in 1821 in Stavanger, Norway. Came to Utah Oct. 8, 1866, Andrew H. Scott oxteam company.
Married Pernelia Peterson at Brevik, Norway, who was born May 12, 1814. Their children: John, died; Marten, m. Inger Anderson; Mary Paulina, m. James Henry Clinger; John, m. Hannah Sward. Family home Brevik, Norway. Sailor; farmer; miner.

WILLIAMSON, MARTEN (son of Niels Williamson and Pernelia Peterson). Born Aug. 26, 1844, Brevik, Norway. Came to Utah Oct. 8, 1866, Andrew H. Scott company.
Married Inger Anderson July 23, 1868, Salt Lake City (daughter of Paul Anderson and Chartay Hoganson, both of Daredorm, Sweden, pioneers 1862, oxteam company). She was born April 10, 1849. Family home Lake View, Utah.
High priest; ward teacher; missionary to Norway 1897-99. Worked on Salt Lake and St. George temples; assisted in construction of railroad into Utah. Early settler at Lake View. Farmer and stockraiser.

WILLIES, IRA JONES (son of Eleazar Willies and Achsa Jones of New York). Born Jan. 21, 1812, in New York. Came to Utah 1847 with advance party of Mormon Battalion.
Married Melissa Lott (Smith) May 18, 1849, Salt Lake City (daughter of Cornelius P. Lott and Permelia Darrow, widow of Joseph Smith). She was born Jan. 9, 1824, on Luzerne Plains, N. Y., and came to Utah 1848. Their children: Ira Pratt and Achsa Permelia, died; Cornelius John, killed Dec. 5, 1863; Polly Melissa, m. William Wheeler Clark; Lyman Benjamin, m. Sarah Ann Munn; Steven Eleazer, m. Matilda Hall; m. Sopha Clark; m. Malinda Shelton; Sarah Amanda, m. Albert King Mulliner. Family home Lehi, Utah.
Elder. Farmer. Died Dec. 5, 1863.

WILLIS, JOSHUA THOMAS (son of Merrill Willis and Margaret Cherry, former of North Carolina). Born Dec. 12, 1818, in Gallatin county, Ill. Came to Utah in September, 1847, captain of ten in John Taylor company.
Married Sarah Melissa Dodge (daughter of Erastus and Melissa Dodge), who was born June 7, 1827, and came to Utah Sept. 29, 1847, Edward Hunter company. Their children: Joshua T. b. Nov. 3, 1849, m. Mariah Duffin May 31, 1870; Merrill E. b. Jan. 28, 1851, m. Cedenia Bagley May 31, 1870; Sarah M. b. May 27, 1852, m. Fred Mullens 1872; Mary D. b. Aug. 2, 1853; Mary H. b. Aug. 14, 1854; Henry T. b. Oct. 21, 1855, m. Kathleen Dykes 1876; Joseph S. b. Oct. 23, 1856; Martha E. b. Oct. 13, 1857, m. Mathew Batty 1874; John M. b. Dec. 13, 1858; Lavina L. b. May 18, 1860, m. Joseph Rodgers 1876; Maria M. b. July 25, 1861; Mary Agnes b. Dec. 31, 1862; Irena Rebecca b. May 22, 1864; Roseliah b. May 26, 1865; Rozilpha b. Oct. 19, 1867; George Albert b. Aug. 11, 1870.
Married Dosha Cherry 1841, who died 1845. Their only child died.
Married Ellen Oldridge 1864, Salt Lake City, who was born Feb. 1, 1830, in Berkshire, Eng. Their children: Hyrum A. b. April 12, 1865, m. Lola Peirce; Richard M. b. Jan. 3, 1867, m. Adelia Buchanan 1889; Franklin J. b. March 18, 1869, m. Elizabeth Kay.
Settled at Provo, Utah, 1849, where he later served as sheriff; moved to Cedar City 1853; founded Toquerville 1858. Set apart bishop of that ward Nov. 18, 1861; counselor to Bishop Isaac Higbee. Veteran Walker, Black Hawk and Navajo Indian wars. Moved to Arizona 1879.

WILLIS, MERRILL E. (son of Joshua T. Willis and Sarah Melissa Dodge). Born Jan. 28, 1851, Provo, Utah.
Married Cedenia Bagley May 31, 1870 (daughter of Daniel Bagley and Mary Wood), who was born Nov. 22, 1854, Grantsville, Tooele Co., Utah. Their children: Merrill E. b. Aug. 18, 1871, m. Sarah C. Kay 1889; Thomas H. b. Dec. 8, 1873; Samuel B. b. Aug. 13, 1876, m. Mary J. Wayment 1901; Mary b. June 25, 1880; Lily b. Sept. 1881, m. A. L. Russell 1896; Cedenia b. Sept. 24, 1885, m. C. Wayment 1905; Daniel B. b. Nov. 15, 1889, m. Viola Brown 1909; Joseph E. b. July 29, 1893; Emanuel B. b. July 6, 1896.
Ordained teacher April 25, 1866; priest Feb. 2, 1869; elder May 31, 1870; bishop Taylor ward, Arizona, 1882; seventy Dec. 14, 1881; high priest Nov. 16, 1885; superintendent of Sunday school and president of Y. M. M. I. A. for several years. Went with parents to Cedar City, Iron Co., Utah, 1853; moved to Toquerville 1858; to Arizona 1878; to New Mexico 1894; returned to Warren, Weber Co., Utah. Minuteman in Indian wars under Col. J. D. L. Peirce.

WILLIS, MERRILL E., JR. (son of Merrill E. Willis and Cedenia Bagley). Born Aug. 18, 1871, Toquerville, Utah.
Married Sarah C. Kay Oct. 30, 1889, St. George, Utah (daughter of William Kay and Katherine Jones), who was born in 1870. Their children: Melissa b. Dec. 24, 1890; Arthur W. b. Sept. 23, 1892; Boyd M. b. Jan. 18, 1895; Grace b. Jan. 14, 1897; Katherine b. Feb. 9, 1899; Hazel b. Sept. 24, 1901; Dora C. b. Aug. 25, 1903; Clifford T. b. Aug. 9, 1905; Josephine b. July 13, 1907; Gladius b. May 5, 1910. Family resided Utah, Arizona and New Mexico.

WILLIS, WILLIAM WESLEY (son of Merrill Willis and Margaret Cherry of Hamilton county, Ill.). Born Aug. 16, 1811, in Hamilton county. Came to Utah July 29, 1847, James Brown contingent of Mormon Battalion.
Married Jane Willis 1833 in Hamilton county, Ill. (daughter of John Willis of Hamilton county). She was born Aug. 17, 1812. Their children: Ann C. m. Willis Young; John H., m. Frances Reeves; Mary Lucretia, m. J. T. Brown; Lemuel M., m. Eliza Webb; Thomas Tillman, m. Ann Louisa Pratt; Josephine, m. William J. Cox; William Wesley, m. Gabrilla Stratton; George Albert; Margaret Jane. Family home Big Cottonwood, Utah.
Missionary to Iron county 1853-58. Mayor Cedar City. Millwright; farmer. Died April 8, 1872, Beaver City, Utah.

WILLIS, WILLIAM WESLEY (son of William Wesley Willis and Margaret Jane Willis). Born May 14, 1846, Nashville, Iowa. Came to Utah Sept. 28, 1847, John Nebeker company.
Married Gabrilla Stratton March 22, 1870, Virgin City, Washington Co., Utah (daughter of Anthony J. Stratton and Martha Jane Lane of Virgin City, pioneers 1849). She was born Oct. 18, 1850. Their children: Delilah Jane b. Jan. 28, 1871, m. Alma R. Turley; Frances Ann b. June 12, 1872; William Wesley b. April 16, 1873; Anthony Lorum b. June 29, 1874; George Ramey b. Dec. 14, 1875; Sixtus Ellis b. Jan. 14, 1877; Mary Josephine b. Feb. 10, 1879, m. Stephen H. Duncan; Martha Augusta b. April 20, 1881, m. William E. Stratton; Ida b. April 4, 1883, m. Alvin

PIONEERS AND PROMINENT MEN OF UTAH 1253

Despain; Joseph S. b. March 2, 1885, m. Willmirth Flake; Altha Gabrilla b. April 28, 1887, m. Asburn H. Douglas; John Irvin b. May 1, 1889; Lucretia D. b. Nov. 8, 1891; Leo Adison b. July 8, 1894. Family home Snowflake, Ariz. Missionary to North Carolina 1885-86; member Snowflake stake high council. Justice of peace; selectman in Virgin City, Utah; justice of peace at Snowflake. Farmer and brickmaker.

WILSON, BENJAMIN (son of Robert Wilson, born 1773 in County Down, Ireland, died 1843, and Jennie Ryan of Scotland). He was born Jan. 1, 1810, in County Down, Ireland. Came to Utah Sept. 2, 1868.
Married Mary Bell July 12, 1844, Kilmaurs, Scotland (daughter of Stuart Bell and Catherine McPhail), who was born Oct. 31, 1820, in Ayrshire, Scotland; died Sept. 23, 1886, Ogden, Utah. Their children: Robert Bell b. Sept. 23, 1845, m. Henrietta Almeda Emmet May 15, 1871; Helen b. in 1847; Jane, died; William Gibson b. May 6, 1850, m. Mary Wahlen April 26, 1881; Isaac, died; John Lyon b. Oct. 20, 1853, m. Ellen Moore; James, died; Isaac 2d b. May 6, 1858, m. Elizabeth Baird; Andrew Hunter b. Oct. 23, 1859 (died March 5, 1880), m. Mary Ann Chase Oct. 11, 1885.
Died March 5, 1880, Ogden, Utah.

WILSON, WILLIAM GIBSON (son of Benjamin Wilson and Mary Bell). Born May 6, 1850, Burlford, Ayrshire, Scotland. Came to Utah Sept. 2, 1868, with father.
Married Mary Wahlen April 26, 1881, Ogden, Utah (daughter of Michael Wahlen b. 1834 in Germany; died May 12, 1889, Globe, Ariz., and Mary Ternes, born April 7, 1836, daughter of Peter Ternes and Margaret Sherf). She was born March 4, 1861, Ogden, Utah. Their children: Mary Bell and Emily, drowned April 26, 1889; William; Robert; Hattie; Flora.
Was present at the great celebration held at Promontory Hill, Utah, at completion of Union Pacific railroad, which made railroad connection from Atlantic to the Pacific. Commissioner Weber county 1895-96 and 1900-06. Built "The Hermitage," a summer hotel in Ogden Canyon, one of the largest log buildings in America.

WILSON, GEORGE CLINTON (son of Bradley B. Wilson and Polly Gill of Vermont). Born Aug. 23, 1800, in Vermont. Came to Utah Aug. 29, 1853, Daniel A. Miller company.
Married Elizabeth Kinney in 1826 (daughter of Aaron Kinney and Mary Pearce—married Jan. 29, 1792). She was born 1805; came to Utah with husband; died Jan. 13, 1892, Hooper, Utah. Their children: Emily b. April 6, 1827; Lewis Kinney b. April 10, 1828, m. Emily Reval 1849; Polly b. Nov. 24, 1829; Thomas Jefferson b. March 25, 1832, m. Mary Ann Sewell 1869; Patty b. March 25, 1832, m. Hyram Kempton 1858; Aaron C. b. Nov. 15, 1834, m. Mary Johnson; Nancy Jane b. July 7, 1835, m. A. J. Hunt; Bradley B. b. May 1, 1837, m. Elizabeth Western 1873; Whitford Gill b. April 1, 1839, m. Hannah Wardsworth and Jane Mathews; Bushrod W. b. Dec. 5, 1840; Avra Elizabeth b. Feb. 19, 1843; William b. Oct. 21, 1847, m. Mary Ann Western 1873.
Assisted in bringing immigrants to Utah. School teacher. Died May 9, 1874, Ogden, Utah.

WILSON, THOMAS JEFFERSON (son of George Clinton Wilson and Elizabeth Kinney). Born March 25, 1832, in Richland Co., Ohio. Came to Utah Aug. 28, 1853, Daniel Miller company.
Married Mary Ann Sewell April 19, 1869 (daughter of Joseph Sewell and Emily Elliott—married January, 1841, Yarmouth, Eng., pioneers Sept. 15, 1861, Job Pingree company). She came to Utah with parents. Their children: Thomas Jefferson, m. Elizabeth Hunter; Martha Jane, m. M. F. Moore; Emily Florence, m. C. B. Tracy; George Clinton; Charles Edward.
First settlers to Wilson ward. Assisted in bringing immigrants to Utah. School trustee 14 years at Wilson ward. Donated one acre of land and acres of land for a schoolhouse. Road supervisor and justice of peace. First assistant Sunday school superintendent of Wilson ward and donated land for meeting house.

WILSON, JAMES T. (son of Thomas Wilson and Jane Ellis of Ireland). Born Oct. 7, 1828, in Ireland. Came to Utah Sept. 3, 1852, Abraham O. Smoot company.
Married Isabella Ross Nov. 16, 1855, Salt Lake City (daughter of David Ross and Rossana Prunta of Scotland). She was born Feb. 26, 1836, and came to Utah October, 1854. Their children: James Brigham, m. Maragrette Powell; Thomas Ross, m. Susannah Sheets; David John, m. Maggie Willett; Isabella, m. Jacob P. Olson; William Walter, m. Elizabeth Bailey Coleman; m. Bertha Sonderegger; Jarrod, d. infant. Family home, Salt Lake City.
Married Emily Mallissia Handcock (daughter of L. W. Handcock), who was born Sept. 24, 1850. Their children: Levi Ward b. Aug. 6, 1867, and Emily Mallissia b. Dec. 20, 1869, and Elizabeth Clayburn b. Jan. 15, 1871, died. Family home, Salt Lake City.
Married Annie Walker Feb. 8, 1877, Salt Lake City (daughter of William Walker and Annie McGuire of Scotland). She was born April 30, 1856. Their children: George

Walker b. March 3, 1878, died; Daniel Hanmer b. May 10, 1880; Joseph Fielding b. Aug. 29, 1883, m. Belle Gibbons; Rachel b. Aug. 16, 1886, m. William Buhler; Ellen Marianna b. March 10, 1889; Charles Innes b. Sept. 6, 1891; Ruth b. Jan. 13, 1894, died; Cordelia b. Aug. 23, 1895. Family home Midway, Utah.
Married Margeret Walker Dec. 19, 1877, Salt Lake City (daughter of William Walker and Annie McGuire of Scotland). She was born 1851. Their children: Annie Terresa b. Nov. 8, 1878, m. James Ritchie; Margeret Walker b. Jan. 14, 1881, m. James L. Wright; Mary Ellis b. May 15, 1883, m. Murray Davis. Family home Midway, Utah.
Farmer and stockraiser. Died at Midway Sept. 26, 1905.

WILSON, JAMES BRIGHAM (son of James T. Wilson and Isabella Ross). Born Oct. 22, 1856, Carson City, Nev.
Married Maragrette Powell Sept. 29, 1881, Salt Lake City (daughter of Reese Powell and Maragrette Morgan of Wales). She was born Sept. 2, 1858. Their children: James Brigham b. July 12, 1882, m. Lota Eliza Huffaker; Maragrette Edna b. April 22, 1884, m. William G. Young; David John b. Oct. 27, 1887; Isabella Ethyl b. Dec. 11, 1889; Reese Arthur b. Jan. 13, 1896; Elizabeth Edith b. May 22, 1898. Family home Midway, Utah.
High priest; member of bishopric; first counselor to Bishop Probst; ward teacher. Mayor 5 terms; senator 1 term, and representative 2 terms. Farmer and stockraiser.

WILSON, WILLIAM WALTER (son of James T. Wilson and Isabella Ross). Born Sept. 22, 1863, Salt Lake City.
Married Elizabeth Bailey Coleman March 21, 1894, Salt Lake City (daughter of William Coleman and Mary Clotworthy of England). She was born in 1873. Their children: Mable b. Jan. 13, 1895, died; William Rondo b. March 1, 1896; Cecil b. May 4, 1899; Elizabeth Isabella b. Jan. 20, 1901. Family home Midway, Utah.
Married Bertha Sonderegger Dec. 23, 1903, Salt Lake City (daughter of John Sonderegger and Bertha Buhler of Salt Lake City). She was born June 22, 1880. Their children: Evelyn Bertha b. Nov. 6, 1904; Amos Milton b. Oct. 3, 1906; Grant Ellis b. Dec. 31, 1910.
Teacher of theology; missionary to central states 1908-10; high priest. Member town board; constable; secretary Midway waterworks. Farmer and stockraiser.

WILSON, DANIEL HANMER (son of James T. Wilson and Annie Walker). Born May 10, 1880, Midway, Utah. Deacon. Engaged in mining. Resided at Midway.

WILSON, LEWIS DUNBAR (son of Bradley B. Wilson and Polly Gill of Nauvoo). Born June 2, 1805, Chittenden, Vt. Came to Utah Sept. 9, 1853, Daniel A. Miller and Sept. 17, John W. Cooley company.
Married Nancy Waggoner July 11, 1830 (daughter of David and Therma Waggoner), who was born in 1810, died in 1851. Their children: Lovina b. July 15, 1831, m. John Brown Feb. 25, 1854; Lemuel Green b. Oct. 22, 1832; Oliver Granger b. July 1, 1836, died; Almeda b. April 19, 1838, m. James Dailey; Lewis Dunbar, Jr. b. Sept. 21, 1840, m. Catherine Wiggins Dec. 31, 1862; David b. June 21, 1842, m. Maria Drake; Mary Malinda b. Jan. 21, 1845, died; Malissa b. Feb. 2, 1847, m. Joseph Sewell; George Miles b. May 13, 1849; Samuel b. July 19, 1851, m. Eliza Racham.
High councilor in Nauvoo at time of Joseph Smith's death; high councilor Ogden.

WILSON, LEWIS DUNBAR (son of Lewis Dunbar Wilson and Nancy Waggoner). Born Sept. 21, 1840, in Nauvoo, Ill.
Married Catherine Wiggins Dec. 31, 1862, Ogden (daughter of Ebenezer Fairchild Wiggins, pioneer, 1852, Henry Miller company, and Elenor Moore, pioneer). She was born April 13, 1845, Crooked Creek, Ill. Their children: Catherine Rozilla b. Oct. 15, 1863, m. Brigham H. Bingham Jan. 17, 1884; Jennie b. April 18, 1865, m. Elijah Bingham Jan. 17, 1884; Martha Vilate b. Feb. 22, 1867, m. Daniel J. Murdock Sept. 16, 1885; Mary Elizabeth b. Sept. 27, 1868, m. George B. Wintle Nov. 1885; Sarah Lettie b. Dec. 11, 1870, m. John Lingreen June 21, 1895; William Lewis b. Nov. 26, 1872, died; Ezra Dunbar b. Oct. 30, 1873, m. Rebecca Davis Jan. 30, 1901; Elveretta Annie b. Jun. 22, 1877, m. John Isaac Watson April 12, 1899; Pearl Ellen b. Dec. 4, 1879, m. Ulysses Fay Campbell Oct. 8, 1903; Arthur Ebenezer b. April 6, 1884.
Married Eliza Eleanor Hunt March 10, 1873, Salt Lake City (daughter of William Bradford Hunt and Eleanor Wiggins), who was born Aug. 29, 1856, Ogden, Utah. Their children: Rosella May b. June 12, 1874, m. John S. Bowker Nov. 27, 1895; Enoch Albert b. Sept. 14, 1876, m. Effie Williams Nov. 27, 1901; Joseph Linord b. Dec. 21, 1878, m. Lucy Dean Feb. 28, 1906; Lola Eleanor b. May 8, 1881, m. Andrew C. Jensen Nov. 19, 1902; Ethel Rebecca b. Dec. 15, 1883, m. E. Leroy Harrison June 1, 1909; Maude Ross b. Sept. 4, 1886, m. A. Rowley Babcock Dec. 18, 1912. Families resided at Ogden, Utah, and at Riverside, Idaho.
Counselor to the bishop of Blackfoot 4 years; counselor to president high priests quorum Blackfoot stake, Idaho. Assisted immigrants to Utah with Harry Miller company in 1862.

WILSON, EZRA DUNBAR (son of Lewis Dunbar Wilson and Catherine Wiggins). Born Oct. 30, 1873, Ogden, Utah.
Married Rebecca Davis Jan. 30, 1901, Logan, Utah (daughter of Jarrold M. Davis and Harriet Jane Osborn), who was born June 17, 1879, Montpelier, Idaho. Their chil-

dren: Erma Rebecca b. Nov. 12, 1901; Ione Harriet b. May 25, 1904; Vaughn Rebecca b. Aug. 6, 1906; Wane Ezra b. June 20, 1908; Var D. b. April 22, 1911.
Ordained a seventy in Salt Lake City 1898; missionary to northeastern states in 1898.

WILSON, LYCURGUS (son of Guy C. Wilson, born 1805 in New York, and Elizabeth Hunter, both of Richland Co., Ohio). He was born Feb. 27, 1828, in Richland Co., Ohio. Came to Utah June 27, 1851, Benjamin Holladay company.
Married Lois Ann Stevens Dec. 29, 1849 (daughter of Arnold Stevens and Lois Coon of Ontario, Canada; former pioneer 1847, contingent Mormon Battalion, Co. "D," latter a pioneer 1852). She was born Dec. 15, 1835, and came to Utah with husband. Their children: Lycurgus Arnold b. Nov. 7, 1856, m. Alice Tucker Oct. 9, 1876; Lois Elizabeth b. March 1, 1859; Ellen Adelia b. Oct. 11, 1861, m. Philip H. Hurst; Guy C. b. April 10, 1864, m. Elizabeth Hartspurg Sept. 25, 1885; Justin b. Sept. 19, 1866; Mary Mehitable b. May 14, 1869, m. Philip H. Hurst; Viola b. Nov. 27, 1871, m. Andrew Peterson; Lucy Arabella b. Oct. 23, 1874, m. Thomas Anderson. Family home Fairview, Utah.
High priest. Postmaster at Fairview 13 years; justice of peace 1872-74 and 1876-78. Veteran Indian wars.

WILSON, ROBERT (son of William Wilson and Catherine Davis of Overton, Flintshire, Wales). Born April 29, 1819, Lightwoodgreen, Flintshire, Wales. Came to Utah 1849.
Married Mary Ann Point June 23, 1843, New Portage, Summit Co., Ohio (daughter of Nathan and Eleanor Point of Ohio, pioneers 1849). She was born Jan. 14, 1816. Their children: Catherine b. May 7, 1844; William G. b. Sept. 8, 1845; Phoebe Ann b. Sept. 25, 1847; Robert b. Oct. 1, 1850; Robert H. b. Dec. 31, 1851. Family home, Ohio.
Married Mary Ann Boldwine 1849, Salt Lake City (daughter of Caleb Boldwine), who was born March 9, 1823. Their children: Robert C. b. Aug. 17, 1849, m. Lena Lay; Richard E. b. July 23, 1853; Mary Ann A. b. Nov. 16, 1854, m. Joseph Lay; Leonora A. b. June 8, 1856; George B. b. Dec. 8, 1858; Heber J. b. Aug. 28, 1860. Family home Kaysville, Utah.
Married Ann Blood June 26, 1853, Salt Lake City (daughter of William Blood and Mary Stretten of Nauvoo, Ill., pioneers 1849, Horton D. Haight company). She was born Aug. 13, 1837. Their children: William H. b. Dec. 11, 1854, m. Margret Cook; James D. b. Nov. 12, 1856; Robert L. b. Jan. 11, 1859, m. Olive E. Dahlquist; Mary A. b. June 20, 1861, m. William F. Rawson; Ann Wilson b. Dec. 4, 1863, m. Ephraim W. Bird; Ellen M. b. Jan. 29, 1866; Jane W. b. Feb. 16, 1868, m. Lewis A. Critchfield; Margret A. b. Jan. 11, 1871; Benjamin F. b. July 15, 1872, m. Rebecca H. Hawkins; Alfred b. Sept. 12, 1874, m. Nora McMurry; Daniel B. b. Nov. 16, 1876, m. Edith Clark; Olive V. b. Feb. 1, 1879, m. William T. Harper; Rosetta Wilson b. May 16, 1881. Family home Harrisville, Utah.
Married Mary Blood April 3, 1857, Salt Lake City (daughter of William Blood and Mary Stretten of Nauvoo, Ill., pioneers 1849, Horton D. Haight company). She was born May 29, 1842. Their children: Robert S. b. March 11, 1860, m. Charlotte Cole; Joseph W. b. Dec. 26, 1861, m. Emily Stronberg; John S. b. March 31, 1864; Charles R. b. May 27, 1866, m. Josephine Samuelson; Ether L. b. May 10, 1868, m. Clara Critchfield; Hyrum b. April 11, 1870; Willard b. March 29, 1872; Lorin B. b. Aug. 31, 1872, m. Elizabeth McMurry; Mary E. b. Nov. 20, 1874, m. Joseph McBride; Jessie b. Dec. 12, 1876; Florence M. b. May 4, 1879, m. Joseph Permer; David b. April 26, 1881; Parley b. June 7, 1882, m. Phoebe McMurry; Lillian b. Oct. 28, 1885, m. Raymond McMurry. Family home, Harrisville.
Missionary to eastern states and England; patriarch; high councilor in Weber stake. Pioneer to Oakly, Idaho. Died Sept. 18, 1895, in Idaho.

WILSON, WELLINGTON PAUL (son of Deliverance Wilson and Lovina Fairchild of Vermont and Ohio). Born Feb. 1, 1814, near Burlington, Vt. Came to Utah Oct. 4, 1864, William Warren company.
Married Elizabeth Boardman Smith Dec. 13, 1836, Kirtland, Ohio (daughter of Ira, pioneer Oct. 4, 1864, William Warren company, and Philomela Smith, who afterward was the wife of James Lake and came to Utah with him 1849, both of Ontario, Canada). She was born Jan. 27, 1817. Their children: Stephen F. b. Sept. 27, 1837, m. Hester Brown, m. Sarah Jane Brown; Wellington Paul b. Oct. 28, 1838, died; Sidney Smith b. Dec. 7, 1839 (died 1909), m. Nancy Brisendine; Maryette b. Sept. 18, 1841, d. 1856; Elizabeth b. Oct. 9, 1843, d. 1864; Serah Alice b. Jan. 27, 1846, d. 1864; Clarissa Jane b. April 4, 1848, d. 1864; Ira Lyman b. June 4, 1852, m. Lavina Shurtliff, m. Roxey Ballard; Oliver Cowdery b. April 15, 1855 (d. 1876), m. Anetta Clifford; Joseph Ellis b. May 2, 1858, m. Lerona A. Monroe Martin, m. Esther A. Ricks. Family resided in Ohio, Illinois, Iowa and Utah.
Married Rebecca McBride 1846 (daughter of Amos and Kezia McBride of Iowa and Grantsville, Utah, pioneers Oct. 4, 1864, William Warren company). She was born April 14, 1828, and came to Utah with husband. Their children: Esther Evaline b. Aug. 25, 1848, m. Levi W. Hancock, Jr.; Ellen b. Nov. 2, 1850, m. Albert A. Steele; Martha b. July 1852, d. 1864; Marcus b. Feb. 26, 1854, d. 1864; Emma Catherine b. Feb. 28, 1856 (d. July 1900), m. Orrin Barrus; Almira b. March 25, 1858, m. Elisha Hubbard; Fanny b. May 1860, d. 1864; Lavina B. Nov. 1861, d. 1864; Grace b. 1864, d. 1865; Mabel b. 1866, died; Rebecca b. Sept. 1868, m. Mr. Wilson. Family home Hillsdale, Utah.
Missionary to New England 1869-70. Settled at St. Thomas, Nev., 1865. School teacher. Died May 29, 1896.

WILSON, JOSEPH ELLIS (son of Wellington Paul Wilson and Elizabeth Boardman Smith). Born May 2, 1858, Monroe Co., Iowa.
Married Lerona A. Monroe Martin, July 22, 1877, Clifton, Idaho (daughter of Marion Monroe Martin and Lucinda Busenbark of Ogden and Providence, Utah, and Clifton, Idaho; former pioneer 1855, latter 1850). She was born Feb. 23, 1862, near Huntsville, Utah. Their children: Joseph Ellis b. June 15, 1878, m. Annie Izatt; Amy Elizabeth b. Nov. 19, 1881; Eva Lerona b. Jan. 21, 1883, m. Charles M. Izatt; Effie Lucinda b. Jan. 21, 1883, m. Irvin M. Allred; Abigail b. Dec. 26, 1884, m. Walter R. Sant; Mabel b. Dec. 25, m. C. William Hadley; Kate b. March 26, 1889, m. John M. Thorup; George Albert b. Feb. 19, 1891; Wellington Paul b. March 20, 1894; Virginia b. Sept. 8, 1896; Marion Lyman b. Oct. 26, 1898; Bathsheba b. Jan. 24, 1901. Family resided Logan and Salt Lake City.
Married Esther Adeline Ricks Aug. 22, 1888, Logan, Utah (daughter of Joel Ricks and Sarah Beriah Fisk of Logan). She was born Oct. 28, 1862. Their children: Esther b. July 8, 1891; Ida b. May 9, 1893; Ellis Ricks b. Sept. 23, 1896; Jean b. Feb. 23, 1898; Joel Ricks b. March 10, 1900. Family home Logan, Utah.
Counselor in bishopric of Clifton ward 1877-79; president Y. M. M. I. A. of 1st ward, Logan, 1882-84; missionary to Colorado 1902-04; counselor in bishopric of Logan, 1st ward, 1884-98; clerk of Cache stake 1896-1907. City recorder Logan 1884 and 1888-90. Secretary of A. C. U. 1897-1900. Founder of the Keister Ladies Tailoring College in Utah.

WILSON, JOSEPH ELLIS, JR. (son of Joseph Ellis Wilson and Lerona Abigail Monroe Martin). Born June 15, 1878, Clifton, Idaho.
Married Annie Izatt Nov. 27, 1901, Logan, Utah (daughter of Alexander Izatt and Elizabeth Boyle of Logan, pioneers Oct. 4, 1864, William Warren company). She was born Feb. 7, 1879. Their children: Joseph Ellis b. April 11, 1905; Alexander Izatt b. March 7, 1907; Royal Guy b. Oct. 19, 1908; Luther Edmund b. June 22, 1911. Family home Logan, Utah.
Counselor in bishopric of Logan, 1st ward, 1907 to the present time; missionary to northern states 1897-99. Contractor in cement and concrete work. Second vice-president Farmers and Merchants Savings Bank.

WIMMER, PETER. Born 1776. Came to Utah 1850.
Married Elizabeth Shirley, who was born in 1780 and died in 1862, Springville, Utah. Their children: Jacob; Robert; John; Peter, Jr.; Polly; Jamima; Susan; Martha; Elizabeth; Ellen. Family resided in Ohio, Indiana, California and Ogden and Mill Creek, Utah.
Farmer. Died 1864 Springville.

WIMMER, ROBERT (son of Peter Wimmer of Germany and Elizabeth Shirley). Born Dec. 11, 1805, Pennsylvania. Came to Utah 1852 at head of own company.
Married Elizabeth Wilkerson (daughter of Thomas Wilkerson of Kentucky), who was born in 1812. Their children: William Jas., m. Elizabeth Funnel; John Pr., m. Sarah Moores; Eliza J., m. Albert Dimick; Susan, m. Henry Boyce; Thomas G., m. Elizabeth Simons. Family resided Cottonwood and Payson, Utah.
Member Payson quorum seventies. Farmer and fruitraiser. Died 1893, Payson.

WIMMER, THOMAS G. (son of Robert Wimmer and Elizabeth Wilkerson). Born May 10, 1847, Harris Grove, Harrison Co., Iowa. Came to Utah with father.
Married Elizabeth Simons April 21, 1866, Salt Lake City (daughter of Orra Simons and Martha Dixon, pioneers Oct. 12, 1854). She was born June 26, 1849. Their children: Thomas G., Jr., b. June 12, 1867, m. Sarah C. Patten; Emily E. b. May 25, 1869, m. Andrew J. Shores; Orra, died; Robert S. b. Oct. 31, 1872, m. Anna N. Douglas; Martha L. b. Oct. 29, 1874, m. Silas F. Johnson; Ethel G. b. April 3, 1876, m. Charles W. Spaulding; William L. b. Jan. 17, 1878, m. Edith Dramer; Susan L. b. Dec. 6, 1879; Wayne b. March 3, 1884; Ina b. March 5, 1886, died; Hazel b. May 13, 1887, m. Fred Bennion; Reed B. July 7, 1890; Remus b. Dec. 24, 1891, died. Family resided Payson and Salt Lake City.
Elder. Farmer and stockraiser.

WIMMER, THOMAS G., JR. (son of Thomas G. Wimmer and Elizabeth Simons). Born June 12, 1867, Payson, Utah.
Married Sarah E. Patten June 1, 1886, Payson, Utah (daughter of George Patten and Mary Nelson of Payson). She was born 1869. Their children: Lloyd P. b. March 3, 1887, m. Ida Kirk; Andy J. b. Feb. 26, 1889; Laura b. 1890; Marguerite b. 1898; Edwin b. Nov. 1900. Family resided Green River, Payson and Salt Lake City, Utah.
Postmaster at Green River. Farmer and stockraiser.

PIONEERS AND PROMINENT MEN OF UTAH

WINBERG, ANDERS W. (son of Swen Winberg and Helen Nelson of Sweden). Born April 13, 1830. Came to Utah 1854. Married Andrine W. Friese Feb. 4, 1854, on board steamer "Benjamin Adams" (daughter of Edward Bernhert Friese and Louisa Karata Knudson of Vordingborg, Denmark). She was born Sept. 5, 1831. Their children: Wilhelmina L., m. Samuel Newton; m. Francis Tate; Eliza M., m. Joseph J. Snell; Anders William, m. Josephine Poulson; Andrine J., m. Joseph Knight; Sarah, m. Bernhert Friese, m. Wilford Hancock; Eva, m. Charles Cummings, m. Simon P. Creagh. Family home, Salt Lake City.
High priest; member 49th quorum seventies; missionary to Scandinavia six years; patriarch. Publisher Scandinavian paper. Died August, 1909.

WINDER, JOHN REX (son of Richard and Sophia Winder of Beddington, Kent, Eng.). Born Dec. 11, 1821, Beddington. Came to Utah Oct. 10, 1853, John W. Young company. Married Ellen Walters Nov. 24, 1845, London, Eng. (daughter of William and Ellen Walters of Liverpool, Eng.). Their children: Ellen b. Jan. 31, 1847, d. March 17, 1848; John R. b. Sept. 19, 1848; Alma W. b. June 27, 1850, d. July 1851; Martha W. b. July 7, 1852, m. N. W. Kimball; Mary W. b. July 7, 1852, m. Charles W. Carrington; Emily W. b. Aug. 20, 1854, d. Aug. 15, 1855; Lizzie b. July 2, 1856, m. Joshua Eldridge; Eliza Ann b. Feb. 13, 1858, m. John G. Midgley; Frederick William b. April 18, 1860, d. May 1860; Susan Sophia b. Nov. 10, 1861, m. T. A. Williams. Family home, Salt Lake City.
Married Elizabeth Parker Jan. 11, 1857, Salt Lake City (daughter of John and Alice Parker), who was born March 14, 1837. Their children: William Charles b. Sept. 30, 1858, m. Rose Taylor; Alice b. Sept. 1, 1860, m. William Bradford; Richard b. July 31, 1862, m. Mary Emma Cahoon; Mary Ann b. April 28, 1865, m. James Stedman; Edwin Joseph b. June 8, 1867, m. Ada B. Calder; Matilda Edna b. Dec. 9, 1871, m. Reuben S. Hamilton; Ella May b. Jan. 14, 1875, m. Walter S. Mackay; Gertrude b. Aug. 23, 1877, m. Mark Y. C. Cannon; Rex Parker b. Sept. 9, 1879, m. Reuhannah E. Fisher; Luella b. Sept. 27, 1870, m. James Giles.
Married Mira Burnham Oct. 27, 1893, Salt Lake City (daughter of Luther C. Burnham and Matilda Barnett of Salt Lake City). She was born Sept. 30, 1869.
Associated with the Liverpool branch until February, 1853; first counselor to the President of the Church from Oct. 17, 1901, to time of death; in April, 1892, was selected by the first presidency to have special charge of the completion of the Salt Lake Temple; first assistant to Apostle Lorenzo Snow, in the presidency of the Temple; second counselor to William B. Preston, presiding bishop; seventy 1854; high priest 1872; one of the 12th quorum of seventies; subsequently acting bishop of 14th ward, Salt Lake City; counselor in bishopric of 14th ward, Salt Lake City, April, 1872; member of the high council of Salt Lake stake. Captain of a company of lancers during the Echo Canyon war; with General George D. Grant on an Indian expedition in Tooele Valley March, 1858; served in the Black Hawk war 1865 to 1867 and collected and made up the accounts of the expenses of that strife; lieutenant-colonel of cavalry in the militia. Assessor and collector for Salt Lake City 1870-84; city councilman three terms; city watermaster 1884-87; United States gauger, in the internal revenue department. President for many years of Deseret Agricultural and Manufacturing Society. Member of the early constitutional conventions. Shoe manufacturer and tanner; director of Utah Iron Manufacturing Company, Z. C. M. I., Deseret National Bank, Deseret Savings Bank, Zion's Saving Bank and Trust Co., and the Utah-Idaho Sugar Company; president of the Deseret Investment Company; vice-president of the Utah Light and Power Company. Died April 27, 1910.

WINDER, JOHN R. (son of John Rex Winder and Ellen Walters). Born Sept. 19, 1848, Liverpool, Eng. Came to Utah Oct. 10, 1853, with parents.
Business man.

WINDER, EDWIN JOSEPH (son of John Rex Winder and Elizabeth Parker). Born June 8, 1867, Mill Creek, Utah. Married Ada Bennion Calder Nov. 23, 1898, Salt Lake City (daughter of George Calder and Mary Bennion, of Salt Lake City and Vernal, Utah), who was born May 25, 1872. Their children: Mary Elizabeth b. May 22, 1900; John Rex b. Oct. 23, 1904; George Calder b. March 31, 1907; Edwin Joseph, Jr. b. Aug. 12, 1909; William Wallace b. July 3, 1912. Family home Vernal, Utah.
Member of 61st and 97th quorums seventies; missionary to Great Britain 1894-96; high priest; alternate member of high council; counselor to Bishop George E. Wilkins, Bishop Frederick G. Bringham and Bishop David Bennion, second ward, Vernal, Utah; stake superintendent of Sunday schools 1907-09; missionary to Uinta Indian reservation 1907. Moved to Vernal July 24, 1901. Merchant; farmer; stockraiser. Member of the firm of Winder & Bingham, later the Acorn Mercantile Co. Taught school three years at Jensen, Union and Vernal, Utah.

WINEGAR, ALVIN (son of Samuel and Rhoda Winegar of Chenango county, N. Y.). Born May 13, 1816, in Chenango county. Came to Utah 1852, Benjamin Gardner company. Married Mary Judd Aug. 29, 1837, Chenango county, N. Y. (daughter of John and Rhoda Judd of North Carolina), who was born July 26, 1817. Their children: John, m. Grace Jane Mellen; Samuel (Thomas), m. Rachel Kilfoyle; m. Elizabeth Deshazo; m. Alice Robinson; Alvin Jr., m. Louisa Druce; Margeret Ann, m. Peter Howell; William, m. Eliza Stewart; m. Rose Shaw; Louisa, m. Zadock Mitchell; Sarah, m. Delancy Harmon; m. Alexander Brown. Family home 6th ward, Salt Lake City.
Member 5th quorum seventies; elder; high priest. Stonecutter for Salt Lake Temple. Died June 12, 1874.

WINEGAR, JOHN (son of Alvin Winegar and Mary Judd). Born Sept. 28, 1838, Clay county, Mo. Came to Utah with father.
Married Grace Jane Mellen in 1858, Salt Lake City (daughter of John Mellen and Jane Ramsden of Bolton Lancastershire, Eng., pioneers 1848). She was born Aug. 27, 1840. Their children: Mary Jane b. Jan. 25, 1859, m. Samuel Mills; Lucinda E. b. Jan. 16, 1861, m. Able J. Flint; Alice b. Feb. 3, 1863, m. John Franklin Frost; Annie Laura b. Jan. °4, 1866, m. William Brown; Susan b. March 16, 1868, d. aged 16; John J. Alvin b. June 20, 1873, m. Rosabell Walker; Rosina b. April 18, 1875, m. Joseph Parkins; Grace b. June 4, 1878, m. Samuel Hepworth; Lawrence L. b. Sept. 5, 1880, m. Silvia Stoddard; Chloe b. Sept. 21, 1883, m. John Bolt. Family home South Bountiful, Utah.
Member 5th quorum seventies; elder; high priest; highway school superintendent South Bountiful ward .11 years. Farmer and stockraiser. Famous duck hunter.

WING, JOHN WILLIAM (son of Mathias Wing and Elizabeth Chenaworth, of Illinois; former born Nov. 22, 1813, latter 1820). He was born May 25, 1845, Pike county, Ill. Came to Utah Aug. 29, 1862, Lewis Bronson company.
Married Martha Goates Oct. 11, 1868 (daughter of William Goates and Susan Raynor, pioneers Sept. 3, 1852, Abraham O. Smoot company). She was born June 12, 1848. Their children: John William, Jr. b. July 28, 1870, m. Rachel Evans Sept. 7, 1898; Rosalinda b. April 17, 1872, m. James E. Ross; George Hyrum b. March 31, 1874, m. Harriet Jacob June 19, 1895, m. Martha Ann Fox Dec. 5, 1900; Norman Arthur b. Sept. 23, 1876, m. Marian Boley Sept. 7, 1898; Emma Jane b. Oct. 11, 1878; Samuel Joseph b. Feb. 15, 1882, m. Barbara Marie Bush; Charles Rodolph b. Nov. 2, 1884, m. Violet Taylor; Alva b. July 17, 1887.
High priest; member of high council of Heber City ward. Went to Missouri River in 1863 to assist immigration; also made five trips across plains for freight. Soldier in Black Hawk war in Sant Pete county. Early settler of Heber City. Farmer; freighter; contractor. Furnished Utah Sugar Co. with its lime rock for ten years.

WING, JOHN WILLIAM, JR. (son of John William Wing and Martha Goates). Born July 28, 1870, Lehi, Utah. Married Rachel Evans Sept. 7, 1898, Salt Lake City (daughter of Bishop David Evans, pioneer 1850, in his own company, and Margaret C. Holm, pioneer 1857, with Christian Christiansen company). Their children: Elden William b. June 23, 1899; Velma b. Dec. 5, 1901; Leia Race b. Jan. 22, 1908; Arva Deborah b. Nov. 10, 1912.
Missionary to England 1905-1907; one of the seven presidents of 68th quorum of seventies.

WINGET, CYRUS (son of William Winget and Sarah Lindley of Pennsylvania). Born Jan. 22, 1815, Pennsylvania. Came to Utah Oct. 3, 1847, Charles C. Rich company.
Married Catharine Hulet April 7, 1841, Nauvoo, Ill. (daughter of Charles Hulet and Margaret Noah of Nelson, Portage Co., Ohio, pioneers September, 1850). She was born March 12, 1820. Their children: Zenos, m. Huetta Johnson; Malvina, m. Elias De Mills; Alphonzo, m. Almeda Mariah Washburn; Fidelia, m. Oliver De Mills; Cyrus, Jr., m. Adelia Squires; Elvira D., m. James Locks; Catharine E., m. Jergen Jergensen. Family resided Nauvoo, Ill., and Springville, Utah.
Elder. Settled in Iron county, 1853, Indian war veteran. Choir leader at Springville. Cooper; farmer. Died Jan. 14, 1854, Cedar City, Utah.

WINGET, ALPHONZO (son of Cyrus Winget and Catharine Hulet). Born Jan. 5, 1846, Nauvoo, Ill. Came to Utah with parents.
Married Almeda Mariah Washburn Jan. 5, 1866, Manti, Utah (daughter of Abraham Washburn and Clarinda Gleason of New England, pioneers 1848, Captain Musser company). She was born Nov. 22, 1849, Manti, Utah, being the first white child born in San Pete county. Their children: Alphonzo, Jr. b. June 24, 1867, died; Lucian Zenos b. Dec. 19, 1868, m. Mary Ellen Lisonbee; Cyrus Abraham b. March 24, 1871, m. Annie Swindle; Civilia Almeda b. March 18, 1873, m. Alma Mageley; Alonzo b. April 5, 1875, m. Lula Lorena b. Sept. 22, 1877, died; Parley b. Feb. 11, 1880, m. Frances Jolley; John Frederick b. Dec. 5, 1881, m. Clara Lewis; Maud b. May 15, 1885, m. Charles Arnold; Printha b. Sept. 11, 1887, m. Charley Foutin; Claudius b. April 26, 1890; Grover Cleveland b. Nov. 8, 1892, m. Lilly Brown. Family home Monroe, Utah.
Missionary to southern states 1889; high priest. Early settler at St. George, Utah. Active pioneer in Utah, San Pete and Sevier counties. Black Hawk war veteran. Member Monroe town board eight years; marshal at Monroe five years; school trustee of Monroe three years. President Monroe Irrigation Co., 1890-91; watermaster Monroe Irrigation Co. ten years; watermaster South Bend Canal Co., 1905-12. Farmer and apiarist.

PIONEERS AND PROMINENT MEN OF UTAH

WINKLESS, JOSEPH (son of Thomas Winkless and Mary Palmer) of St. Louis, Mo.). Born Jan. 31, 1847, at St. Louis. Came to Utah 1850, Bishop Edward Hunter company.
Married Sarah Ann Pridy July 25, 1868, Salt Lake City (daughter of Samuel Pridy and Mary James of London, Eng., pioneers 1861). She was born Feb. 8, 1854. Their children: Sarah Elizabeth b. Sept. 28, 1870, m. John Wilkins; Mary Emily b. Sept. 8, 1872, m. E. C. Nelson; Lilly May b. Jan. 7, 1875, m. G. F. Watson; Hattie Florence b. Jan. 11, 1878, m. C. C. Carstensen; Ray b. Nov. 4, 1880, m. Arch H. Pett; Mabel b. Oct. 11, 1885, m. M. S. Saville; Adel b. June 22, 1887, m. Gordon Cain; Mattie b. Sept. 16, 1890; Dora b. April 14, 1893; Joseph Thomas b. May 18, 1895. Family home, Salt Lake City.
Elder. Superintendent of construction for Walker & McCormick; built Grand Theater and other large buildings.

WINN, DENNIS GEORGE (son of John Winn and Susan Spaulding of Lincolnshire, Eng.). Born Aug. 8, 1831, Lincolnshire. Came to Utah Oct. 10, 1853, John W. Young company.
Married Hannah Crossley 1859 (daughter of John and Mary Crossley, pioneers 1858). Their children: Latitia, m. Robert Siley; George; Ephraim; Annie; William; Bertha, m. Mr. Johns. Family home St. Charles, Idaho.
Married Alice Cunliffe April, 1866, Salt Lake City (daughter of John and Alice Cunliffe, of Liverpool, Eng., pioneers October, 1865). She was born July 12, 1846. Their children: John b. July 6, 1867, died; Elizabeth b. March 14, 1869, m. Albert Beutler; Thomas C. b. March 7, 1871, m. Elsie Pitt; Robert b. March 12, 1873, m. Annie Jensen; Eden b. March 19, 1875, m. Carrie Brimhall; Ernest b. Aug. 6, 1877, m. Lula Davet Ostler; Georgiana b. Nov. 5, 1879, m. George Worthington; David b. Sept. 22, 1883, m. Jennie Cooper. Family home Nephi, Utah.
Miller. Died Aug. 17, 1910, St. Charles, Idaho.

WINN, ERNEST (son of Dennis George Winn and Alice Cunliffe). Born Aug. 6, 1877, Bountiful, Utah.
Married Lula Davet Ostler Jan. 11, 1899, Salt Lake City (daughter of David Ostler and Ann Scott [Foster] of Nephi, Utah), who was born May 2, 1878. Their children: Ernest Raymond b. Jan. 1, 1900; Leroy b. Dec. 13, 1903, d. same day; Evelyn b. April 14, 1905; Carlyle b. July 28, 1908; Erma b. Nov. 30, 1911. Family home American Fork, Utah.
President religion class work Jaub stake; chorister Nephi first ward Sunday school; high council Juab stake; president T. M. M. I. A.; chorister and superintendent Sunday school 22nd ward, Salt Lake City; assistant superintendent Sunday school second ward, American Fork; high priest. Salesman.

WINN, MINER. Came to Utah in 1847.
Married Nancy Wilson. Their children: Dennis Wilson; John, m. Elizabeth Pugh; James and Elias, died; Thomas, m. Phoebe Norton; Alma, m. Catharine McDonald; Jane, m. Ezra Beckstead; Mary. Family home, Salt Lake valley.
Seventy. Indian war veteran. Farmer. Died at Richfield, Utah.

WINN, DENNIS WILSON (son of Miner Winn and Nancy Wilson of Mobile, Ala.). Born Dec. 11, 1826, Mobile. Came to Utah 1848, contingent Mormon Battalion.
Married Margaret Bateman Jan. 2, 1849, Salt Lake City (daughter of Joseph Bateman and Margaret Turner of Bolton, Lancastershire, Eng., pioneers 1848, Lorenzo Snow company). She was born Jan. 5, 1831. Their children: Dennis Alma, m. Emma Bair; John, m. Lottie Fluett; James, m. Angeline Thomas; Elizabeth, m. Henry Meyer; Margaret; Joseph, m. Lou Crawl; Elias, m. Nancy Winn; Mary, m. Charles Alonzo McCarrel; Sarah, m. Mark Jessup Golightly; William, m. Elizabeth Eaton; Tessie, d. child. Family resided Richmond and Preston, Idaho, and Vernal, Utah.
High priest. Indian war veteran. Built first house in Preston. Farmer. Died Jan. 23, 1907, at Vernal.

WINN, DENNIS ALMA (son of Dennis Wilson Winn and Margaret Bateman). Born Dec. 21, 1849, Salt Lake City.
Married Emma Bair June 5, 1869, Salt Lake City (daughter of John Batr and Lucinda Owen of Nauvoo, Ill., pioneers with oxteams). She was born Feb. 14, 1854, Kaysville, Utah. Their children: Dennis Evermont b. April 2, 1870, d. aged 5; Charles Franklin b. April 28, 1872, m. Effie Weeks; William Lafayette b. Feb. 28, 1874, m. Susanna Campbell; John b. May 7, 1876, m. Fannie Weeks; Henry b. June 15, 1878, m. Ida Rupie, m. Effie Snow; Emma Lillian b. May 18, 1880, m. Vincent Faler; Ella b. July 5, 1884, d. aged 2; Joseph b. Oct. 31, 1885, m. Elsie Orcutt; Elsie Vivian b. Jan. 23, 1887, m. Ralph Faier; Jesse Ray b. Feb. 20, 1889, m. Jean Reynolds. Family resided Vernal and Roosevelt, Utah.
Ward teacher. Indian war veteran. Freighter and farmer.

WINN, CHARLES FRANKLIN (son of Dennis Alma Winn and Emma Bair). Born April 28, 1872, Richmond, Idaho.
Married Effie Weeks Sept. 14, 1894, Vernal, Utah (daughter of Edward G. Weeks and Elizabeth Hadlock), who was born Aug. 7, 1875. Their children: Alto Marie b. Aug. 11, 1896; Morris Alton b. July 14, 1898; Marvel Frances b. Aug. 12, 1900; Gladys May b. June, 1902; Jessie b. Sept. 20, 1904; Frank b. April, 1906; Emma b. Jan. 1908; Georgia b. March 1910; Owen b. May 1912. Family home Cedarville, Utah.
Deacon; ward teacher. Miner; farmer; lumberman.

WINN, JESSE RAY (son of Dennis Alma Winn and Emma Bair). Born Feb. 20, 1889, Vernal, Utah.
Married Jean Reynolds Feb. 28, 1912, Vernal, Utah (daughter of William H. Reynolds of Vernal), who was born Aug. 5, 1885. Family home Roosevelt, Utah.
Farmer.

WINN, THOMAS GRIFFIN (son of John Winn, born February, 1804, Mohawk county, N. Y., and Christena Finch, born Jan. 25, 1792, Goshen, Orange county, N. Y., both of Lehi, Utah). He was born Dec. 20, 1829, Blakely, Luzerne county, Pa. Came to Utah in 1850.
Married Elizabeth Hatch, who was born Jan. 19, 1837. Their children: Elizabeth C. b. Sept. 7, 1855, m. Jeremiah Hatch; Adaline b. Dec. 8, 1857, m. Lorenzo Hatch. Family resided Lehi and Smithfield, Utah.
Married Elizabeth Nelson, who was born in May, 1839. Their children: Julia B. Nov. 7, 1861, m. William Peirce; Martha b. Aug. 31, 1864, m. Welby Huffaker; William L. b. Oct. 13, 1866, m. Edith Weeks; Silvia L. b. Dec. 23, 1868, m. Andrew Peirce; Mary L. b. March 7, 1871, m. David J. Weeks; George H. b. May 2, 1873.
Missionary to New York 1871. Captain of minutemen of northern Cache county. Assisted in defending settlers against Johnston's army. City marshal at Smithfield 14 years.

WINN, WILLIAM L. (son of Thomas Griffin Winn and Elizabeth Nelson). Born Oct. 13, 1866, Smithfield, Utah.
Married Edith Weeks Nov. 14, 1888, Logan, Utah (daughter of David Weeks and Hannah Riches, latter pioneer 1861, Ira Eldredge company). She was born Sept. 5, 1870, Smithfield, Utah.
Missionary to northern states 1898-99; superintendent Sunday school of Smithfield seven years; president 17th quorum seventies; bishop of Smithfield 2d ward. City councilman 1895; city marshal 1903.

WINSOR, ANSON P. (son of Abraham Winsor, born at Providence, R. I., and Sophia Bigelow, born in Connecticut; the former of Jamestown, N. Y.). He was born Aug. 19, 1818, Ellicottville, N. Y. Came to Utah Sept. 20, 1852, James McGaugh company.
Married Emeline Z. Brower (daughter of John Brower and Deligh Smith), who was born March 21, 1824, and came to Utah with husband. Their children: Walter J. b. Nov. 30, 1844, m. Sarah Potter June 28, 1866; Ida R. b. May 9, 1847, d. May 21, 1850; Margaret E. b. May 9, 1852, d. May 11, 1873; Anson P. Jr. b. Oct. 9, 1854, m. Sarah L. Terry March 9, 1877; Samuel A. b. Jan. 20, 1857, m. Ella Westover March 9, 1877; Emeline Z. b. Jan. 7, 1859, m. Eleazar Asay Sept. 15, 1879; Phoebe D. b. Nov. 11, 1861, d. May 29, 1873; Lucy T. b. Sept. 7, 1868, m. David Hatch Feb. 9, 1892. Family home Provo, Utah.
Married Mary Nelson in 1855, Provo, Utah (daughter of Peter Nelson), who was born in Denmark. Their children: Joseph F. b. Feb. 18, 1864, m. Effie Hunt Dec. 22, 1897; Andrew N. b. Feb. 15, 1866, m. Agnes McFarland; Mary J. b. June 6, 1868, m. Theodora Asay July 4, 1883.
Settled at Provo, 1852. Wagon master of Young's Express Company, 1857. In charge of company on march to Fort Leavenworth, Kansas, May 1, 1857, where he sent the first word of the formation of Johnston's army to President Young. Was placed in charge of 300 men to guard against the invaders. Moved to "Dixie" 1861; ordained bishop of Grafton ward, 1863. Colonel of 3d regiment militia under General Erastus Snow, 1864. Was in charge of church cattle at Pipe Springs. Called to St. George to assist in preparation of temple for ordinance work, and is still engaged as an ordinance worker therein. Took active part in Indian wars, helping to build a fort for the protection of the settlers.

WINTERS, OSCAR F. (son of Hiram Winters and Rebecca Burdick). Born Feb. 7, 1825, Jamestown, Ohio. Came to Utah 1852.
Married Mary Ann Stearns Aug. 25, 1852, on plains while on way to Utah. Their children: Delia Ina b. March 16, 1854, m. John Edge Booth; Huldah Augusta b. July 7, 1856, m. Heber J. Grant; Susan Marian b. June 25, 1859, m. Heber Bennion; Mary Ann b. Jan. 3, 1862 (d. Oct. 14, 1900), m. William H. Freeman; Oscar Lycortez b. Sept. 9, 1864; Nathan Stearns b. Feb. 10, 1867, d. Oct. 16, 1867; Arthur Ray b. May 15, 1871; Helen May b. Sept. 24, 1873 (d. June 7, 1906), m. A. O. Woodruff. Family home Pleasant Grove, Utah.
Died Jan. 22, 1903, Provo, Utah.

WINTERTON, WILLIAM HUBBARD (son of John Winterton and Ann Hubbard, of Nottingham, Nottinghamshire, Eng.). Born Nottingham. Came to Utah 1863, John R. Murdock company.
Married Sarah Marriott in 1842 (daughter of George Marriott of Nottingham, Eng.), who was born Feb. 14, 1824, and died Feb. 19, 1902, at Nottingham. Their children: John b. May 16, 1844, m. Emma Noaks; William M. b. May 6, 1846, m. Ellen Widdison; m. Jane E. Steadman; John. m. George Noaks; Thomas, m. Fannie Boardman; Sarah, m. Arthur Parker.
Home missionary; teacher in England. Tollgate keeper in Parley's Canyon. Died Salt Lake City.

WINTERTON, WILLIAM M. (son of William Hubbard Winterton and Sarah Marriott). Born May 6, 1846, Carlton, Nottinghamshire, Eng. Came to Utah with father.
Married Ellen Widdison Feb. 21, 1870, Salt Lake City (daughter of William Widdison and Ellen Stafford, of Nottingham, Eng.), who was born Sept. 11, 1849. Came to Utah 1869 and died March 8, 1889. Their children: Sarah Ellen b. Dec. 10, 1870, m. John H. Price; Eliza Ann b. Oct. 9, 1872, m. John Thacker; William Heber b. Oct. 4, 1874, m. Agnes Webster; John Joseph b. Aug. 31, 1876, d. Oct. 4, 1882; Hyrum Shurtliff b. Aug. 16, 1878, m. Sarah Van Wagener; Ralph Stafford b. Sept. 27, 1880, m. Louisa Ririe; Moroni b. Sept. 28, 1882, m. Mabel Giles; Baby b. Oct. 26, 1884; Thomas Frederick b. Aug. 14, 1886, m. Sheila Carlile; Alice Malissa b. July 31, 1888, m. George Thomson.
Married Jane E. Steadman April 13, 1892, Manti, Utah (daughter of George Steadman and Elizabeth Wilkins of Sussex, Eng., pioneers 1860). She was born Feb. 16, 1864, Mill Creek, Utah. Their children: Carrie Elizabeth b. May 5, 1893; Nettie Rachel b. May 7, 1895; Edward Marriott b. Sept. 16, 1897; Valeo James b. Oct. 10, 1900. Family home Mill Creek, Utah.
High priest; teacher in ward; president deacons quorum; moved to Charleston, Wasatch county, 1865. He and John C. Parcell named the town of Charleston. He with others constructed the first irrigation canal, known as the Charleston Canal. Worked on railroad in Echo Canyon and on Provo Canyon wagon road. Member of the guard at Provo, under the leadership of Edward Pea, to defend the community against Indian depredations. Farmer; stockman.

WINTLE, GEORGE (son of Jacob Wintle, born 1783, and Elizabeth Lee, who after death of husband lived in London, Eng.). He was born April 17, 1812, Isle of Helgoland, off coast of Germany, near Hamburg. Came to Utah Sept. 2, 1861, Job Pingree company.
Married Elizabeth Sewell July 9, 1835, Yarmouth, Norfolk, Eng. (daughter of Joseph Sewell born Jan. 2, 1796, died March 24, 1880, at Ogden, Utah, and Sarah —— born April 16, 1793, died Oct. 16, 1881, at Ogden; pioneers 1857). She was born June 13, 1814, at Yarmouth, and died April 15, 1882, Bountiful, Utah. Their children: George J. b. March 9, 1837, m. Emily Dungee; Sarah b. March 25, 1839 (d. Sept. 27, 1907), m. John Bitton; Joseph Barney b. Feb. 29, 1840, m. Sarah Jane Evans, m. Mary Marinda Wilson; Charlotte b. 1844; Hannah b. Jan. 29, 1846, m. Ianthus Barlow; son, d. young; Elizabeth b. March 9, 1849, m. Carlos L. Sessions. All born at Yarmouth.
Married Sarah Janette Ogden Aug. 6, 1884.
Sailor in Queen of England's service 27 years. Moved to Bountiful, Utah, 1863. Died there Feb. 11, 1897.

WINTLE, JOSEPH BARNEY (son of George Wintle and Elizabeth Sewell). Born Feb. 29, 1840, Yarmouth, Eng. Came to Utah 1857, James Brown company.
Married Sarah Jane Evans in September, 1862, at West Weber, Utah, who was born April 24, 1843, in England and drowned in Weber River Feb. 12, 1863.
Married Mary Marinda Wilson April 2, 1863, at West Weber (daughter of Bradley Barlow Wilson born Oct. 11, 1806, died Jan. 12, 1874, at Wilson, Utah, and Agnes Hunter, died Feb. 7, 1886, at Ogden, Utah; pioneers 1853, John W. Cooley company). She was born May 15, 1842, Nauvoo, Ill.; died Nov. 11, 1911, Ogden, Utah. Their children: Agnes b. May 9, 1864, m. A. T. Waidram Oct. 2, 1884; George B. b. Oct. 6, 1865, m. Elizabeth Wilson Nov. 18, 1885; Elizabeth b. July 5, 1867, d. March 15, 1869; Joseph C. b. Dec. 10, 1868, m. Nora Rex March 16, 1892; John Wesley b. May 20, 1870, m. Daisy Louella Stone Aug. 5, 1908; Adeline b. April 22, 1872, d. June 28, 1873; Mary A. b. Feb. 22, 1874, m. Charles Malan May 27, 1891; Sarah b. Feb. 6, 1876, d. Aug. 23, 1876; Ellen M. b. July 19, 1877, m. Orson Covington; Clarence and Lawrence (twins) b. Oct. 17, 1879, d. Nov. 10, 1879; Maud E. b. July 20, 1881, m. John Wykes Nov. 21, 1901; Austin T. b. Oct. 17, 1883, m. Hazel Spiers July 31, 1909; Grace b. July 29, 1886, m. Thomas R. Doran Nov. 6, 1909.
Assisted immigrants to Utah from the Missouri River 1861. Pony express rider from Fort Carney on the South Platte River to Cottonwood Springs, a distance of 110 miles, being the first to carry west news of Abraham Lincoln's election. Resided at Wilson 1863-70; at Hooper 15 years, then returned to Wilson; thence in 1902 to Ogden.

WINTLE, JOHN WESLEY (son of Joseph Barney Wintle and Mary Marinda Wilson). Born May 20, 1870, Wilson, Weber Co., Utah.
Married Daisy Louella Stone Aug. 5, 1908, Salt Lake City (daughter of Merlin J. Stone born Nov. 26, 1853, at Bountiful, Utah, and Maria Baker born Nov. 8, 1860, Salt Lake City—married Jan. 17, 1878, Richmond, Utah). She was born Dec. 9, 1878, at Ogden.
Missionary to Germany 1898. School teacher in public schools of Weber county two years; teacher and principal in Ogden city schools 11 years. Attended University of Utah and graduated from Weber Academy at Ogden, Utah.

WINWARD, PETER (son of Thomas Winward and Betty Silcock of Warrington, Lancastershire, Eng.). Born Dec. 22, 1832, Warrington. Came to Utah 1847, Charles Shumway company.
Married Lucinda Bingham May 7, 1855, Payson, Utah (daughter of Jeremiah Bingham and Abigail Harrington of Lake Erie, Canada, pioneers 1848). She was born Sept 24, 1837. Their children: Lucinda Abigail, m. F. M. Ballard Sept. 17, 1878; Sarah Elizabeth, m. Heber Curtis May 10, 1881; Peter William, died; Lucretia Melvina, m. George Cloward; Lola Ann, m. David Mitchell; John Albert, m. Matilda Haskel; Charles Andrew, m. Florence Sargent; Perry Augustus, died; Minnie Ines, m. William Frederick Tanner Jan. 2, 1901; Mary Naomi, m. John C. Taylor June 24, 1903; Ella Melissa, m. Brigham Stone; Iva. Family home Payson, Utah.
Member 46th quorum seventies; missionary to England 1884-85; elder; high priest. Water overseer. Policeman. Farmer. Died May 30, 1909, Payson, Utah.

WIRTHLIN, LEOPOLD (son of Stephen Wirthlin and Teresia Goder of Möhlin, Canton Aargau, Switzerland; the former born Dec. 27, 1786; the latter in 1787, both at Möhlin —married June 6, 1814). He was born Dec. 3, 1832, Möhlin. Came to Utah Nov. 28, 1864, Horton D. Haight company.
Married Anna Hirschi Jan. 8, 1865 (daughter of John Hirschi and Magdalene Kernen—married March 6, 1824, Reutigen, Canton Bern, Switzerland). She was born July 8, 1842, and came to Utah Nov. 28, 1864, Horton D. Haight company. Their children: Josephine; Joseph; Paul; Leopold, Jr.; William Henry; John Edward. Family resided Salt Lake City, Payson and Eureka, Utah.
Elder; seventy. Called on mission April 10, 1876.

WIRTHLIN, JOSEPH (son of Leopold Wirthlin and Anna Hirschi). Born Oct. 6, 1867, Salt Lake City.
Married Emma Hillstead July 25, 1892, Salt Lake City (daughter of John Hillstead and Charlotte Gray), who was born April 19, 1868. Their children: Joseph L.; Emma; Ellis; Verginia; LeRoy; Edith; Earl H. Family home, Salt Lake City.
Deacon.

WISCOMBE, JAMES. Came to Utah by rail a number of years after the arrival of his son, William Fleet Wiscombe.
Married Mary Ann Fleet (daughter of William Fleet of England). Their children: Elizabeth, m. William Bramhall; Martha, m. John Sainsbury; Emma; William Fleet, m. Sarah Newland; Laura, m. John Sainsbury, m. William Hunting; Ellen, m. William Bringhurst. Family home Springville, Utah.
High priest. Gardener. Died in August, 1892.

WISCOMBE, WILLIAM FLEET (son of James Wiscombe and Mary Ann Fleet). Came to Utah Sept. 20, 1864, Joseph S. Rawlins company.
Married Sarah Newland at Salt Lake City. Their children: Emma, m. Albert H. Walsh; Mary Frances, m. L. John Hansen; William Fleet, Jr. b. July 14, 1877, m. Loula E. Whittaker; James, m. Nellie Weight; Amelia, d. child; Sarah; George, d. young; John, m. Margaret E. Miller; Leonard; Arthur; Lucile, d. aged 9. Family home Springville, Utah.
Sunday school superintendent; president priests quorum; chorister. Made several trips across the plains for immigrants. Horticulturist. Died Nov. 27, 1896.

WISCOMBE, WILLIAM FLEET (son of William Fleet Wiscombe and Sarah Newland). Born July 14, 1877, Springville, Utah.
Married Louia E. Whittaker June 15, 1904, Salt Lake City (daughter of Isaac Nathaniel Whittaker and Mary Curl, of Boston, Mass.). She was born May 19, 1881. Their children: Loleta b. June 12, 1905; Ralph W. b. March 14, 1907; Myra b. Feb. 13, 1909; William Morris b. Sept. 11, 1911. Family home Roosevelt, Utah.
Missionary to California 1901-03; high priest; president Y. M. M. I. A.; superintendent Sunday schools; chorister; Sunday school teacher; ward superintendent religion class; bishop's counselor. Member town board of Mapleton. Farmer and stockraiser.

WIXOM, SOLOMON (parents lived at Log Creek, Caldwell county, Mo.). He came to Utah in 1850.
Married Miss Avery. Among their children were: Justin C. b. Dec. 3, 1838, m. Annie Jackson; Joseph M.

WOOD, CHARLES (son of Samuel Wood and Sarah Steadwell, of Berlin, Huron Co., Ohio). Born June 9, 1837, at Berlin. Came to Utah 1848.
Married Alice Horrocks March 31, 1858, Ogden, Utah (daughter of Edward Horrocks and Alice Houghton, of Macclesfield, Chestershire, Eng., former pioneer 1857, Jesse B. Martin company). She was born March 3, 1841. Their children: Alice Ann, m. W. A. Moffett; Charles Samuel, m. Emma E. Mortensen; Mary Elizabeth, m. James S. Carver; Sarah Eliza, m. Marius Madsen; Joseph, m. Amelia Olsen; Catherine Moiselle, m. Jessie Meisner; Frederick William, m. Charlotte Durrant; Laura Pearl, m. Arthur McCarty; Benjamin Franklin, m. Olevia Felt; Chloe Adel, m. George R. Doxey; Edward Warren, Martha Emma, Minnie Mabel, James Silvester, all died. Family home Huntsville, Utah.
Member 75th quorum seventies; missionary to Indians at Fort Supply 1854-66. Settled at Lewiston 1876, where he assisted in building up the country. Farmer. Died August, 1905, Provo, Utah.

WOOD, CHARLES SAMUEL (son of Charles Wood and Alice Horrocks). Born July 11, 1861, Ogden, Utah.
Married Emma Elizabeth Mortensen Dec. 11, 1884, Logan, Utah (daughter of Niels Christian Mortensen and Mariana Christensen of Denmark, pioneers 1864, John Smith independent company). She was born Dec. 29, 1865. Their children: Minnie Mabel b. Oct. 11, 1885, m. William J. Wood; Mary Elizabeth b. March 14, 1888, m. Ezra Bingham; Charles Warren b. March 31, 1891, m. Martha E. Andersen; Viola Lucretia b. July 25, 1893, m. Lorin M. Grove; Elvira Lillian b. July 25, 1893; Selma Amelia b. Nov. 2, 1895; Rulon Samuel b. April 11, 1898; Ruth Elvina b. Sept. 1, 1900; Alice Emma b. May 20, 1904; Mark Silvester b. Nov. 2, 1907. Family home Huntsville, Utah.
President 75th quorum seventies; missionary to southern states 1888-90; bishop's counselor 1900 and 1905. Farmer.

WOOD, CHARLES (son of Benjamin Wood born April 11, 1778, London, Eng., and Ann Elizabeth Apps born Dec. 23, 1793, Kingsworth, Eng.—married Aug. 14, 1814). Born April 22, 1825, at London. Came to Utah Oct. 5, 1860, William Budge oxteam company.
Married Ann Day June 11, 1848 (daughter of George Day and Sarah Honeysett), who was born 1829 and came to Utah with husband. Their children: Charles b. Feb. 21, 1849, m. Sophia Dame March 31, 1872; William b. March 12, 1855, m. Eliza Stevens Feb. 18, 1881; Elizabeth b. Aug. 8, 1857, m. Edward Bennett March 2, 1887; Jesse b. April 3, 1860; Richard b. June, 1863; John b. April 8, 1866, m. Nina Ashby Sept. 12, 1888; Edward b. Nov. 5, 1868, m. Ada Ashby Nov. 8, 1893; Sarah Ann b. Aug. 16, 1871, m. David McKell Jan. 18, 1899. Family home Holden, Utah.
Postmaster at Holden 25 years.

WOOD, CHARLES (son of Charles Wood and Ann Day). Born Feb. 21, 1849.
Married Sophia Dame March 31, 1872 (daughter of Janvarin Hayes Dame). Their children: George C. b. Feb. 1, 1873, m. Julia Cazier Nov. 2, 1899; William b. May 27, 1875; Lovina Ann b. Aug. 24, 1877, m. R. M. Cropper Sept. 10, 1903; Richard b. June 25, 1880, m. Pearl Duval May 8, 1903; Benjamin b. March 1, 1883; Rebecca Ellen b. July 10, 1885, m. Frank Shaw Dec. 27, 1907; Jane b. Feb. 21, 1888, m. Thomas Hicks Jan. 29, 1909; Joseph Ezra b. July 3, 1890; Rulon Wells b. Dec. 21, 1893; Gertrude Sophia b. Sept. 16, 1897; George Cazier b. Oct. 10, 1900; Charles b. April 5, 1902; John Vivian b. Jan. 18, 1904. Family home Holden, Utah.

WOOD, DANIEL. Came to Utah Sept. 20, 1848, Brigham Young company.
Married Mary Snyder. Their children: Rebecca b. May 11, 1826, m. John Moss; Henry b. June 9, 1828, d. 1845; John b. April 10, 1830; Harriet b. Dec. 21, 1834; Elizabeth b. Dec. 30, 1839; Cathrine and Mary b. Aug. 25, 1842.
Married Peninah S. Cotton. She was born March 12, 1824, Vienna, Johnson county, Ill. Their child: Daniel C. b. Jan. 27, 1847, m. Elizabeth Waddoups. Family home Bountiful, Utah.

WOOD, DANIEL C. (son of Daniel Wood and Peninah S. Cotton). Born Jan. 27, 1847.
Married Elizabeth Waddoups Feb. 18, 1869, Salt Lake City (daughter of Thomas and Elizabeth Waddoups, former pioneer 1868, Horton D. Haight company), who was born June 28, 1853, in Warwickshire, Eng. Their children: Daniel T. b. Oct. 8, 1870, m. May Walton; Joseph W. b. Oct. 4, 1874, m. Agnes Brion Oct. 13, 1898; William b. Jan. 22, 1876, m. Etta Merrill; Franklin D. b. April 14, 1879, m. Martha Brion; Parley P. b. Aug. 20, 1881; Elizabeth May b. May 27, 1883, m. George Parrish Nov. 6, 1902; Sylvia Irene b. Sept. 29, 1885, m. Peter Hansen May, 1909; Victoria Everline b. Oct. 24, 1887, m. Albert Hodson Jan. 26, 1909; Clarence Ray b. June 15, 1890; Florence Elvia b. Dec. 26, 1891, m. John Sorenson May 30, 1909.
Married Margaret Ann Edwards Oct. 30, 1895, Logan, Utah (daughter of Ellis Edwards and Mary Roberts; came to Utah Sept. 11, 1895). She was born March 26, 1876, Pendleton, Lancastershire, Eng. Their children: Milton E. b. Aug. 30, 1897; Mary Edna b. Nov. 11, 1898; Andrew E. b. Nov. 13, 1900.
Missionary to England 1902-03. Helped settle Arizona 1873. Assisted in bringing immigrants to Utah 1868.

WOOD, DAVID (son of Jonah Wood of Osneburg, Canada). Came to Utah 1851.
Married Catherine Critis of Osneburg. Their children: Benjamin; Margaret, m. Levi Empey; Sarah Catherine, m. Hyrum Oakes; David, died; Catherine, d. infant; Amanda, m. Jesse McCarl; Delilah, d. child; William, m. Eliza Kettle; Agnes, m. Mark Smith; Oscar Alexander, m. Mary Jane Robinson and Linnah F. Harrison. Family home Osneburg, Canada.
Missionary to the Indians. High priest. Assisted in building Nauvoo Temple. Carpenter and cabinetmaker. Died Midway, Utah.

WOOD, OSCAR ALEXANDER (son of David Wood and Catherine Critis). Born Sept. 30, 1838, Osneburg, Canada. Came to Utah with father.
Married Mary Jane Robinson Nov. 5, 1860, American Fork, Utah (daughter of Edward Robinson and Mary Smith, of Manchester, Eng., pioneers Oct. 9, 1849, Ezra T. Benson company). She was born March 6, 1842.
Married Linnah F. Harrison Dec. 19, 1879, St. George, Utah (daughter of Richard Harrison and Jane Fryer, of Liverpool, Eng., pioneers 1849, Ezra T. Benson company). She was born Dec. 19, 1860. Their children: David Hyrum b. Dec. 10, 1880, m. Ada McElprang; Lena Maggie Jane b. Feb. 22, 1883, m. William W. Smith. Family home Pinto, Utah.
Member high priests quorum; missionary to "Dixie" 1866; member high council Emery stake. Commissioner Emery county 1897-98. Farmer and carpenter. Died Oct. 9, 1901, Huntington, Utah.

WOOD, DAVID HYRUM (son of Oscar Alexander Wood and Linnah F. Harrison). Born Dec. 10, 1880, Pinto, Utah.
Married Ada McElprang June 7, 1905, Manti, Utah (daughter of Samuel William McElprang of Cedar City, Utah, and Adelia Terry, of Washington Co., Utah). She was born Jan. 8, 1887. Their children: Oscar Neldon b. April 14, 1906; Lina Neoma b. May 1, 1908; David Randal b. Aug. 24, 1910. Family home Huntington, Utah.
Member 81st quorum seventies; missionary to New Zealand 1901-04 and in 1912. Surveyor Emery county 1904-12. Civil engineer.

WOOD, JAMES DAVID (son of Jeptha Wood, Sullivan county, Mo.—pioneer, and Marcia Cassandra Fowler of Virginia and Tennessee). Born Aug. 27, 1841, Sullivan county, Mo. Came to Utah 1864.
Married Catherine E. Murphy (Hagenbarth) 1884, Challis, Idaho (daughter of Wilhelm Veit), who was born in 1843, Vienna, Austria. Their children: Hugh Charles (adopted); Cassandra. Family resided in Salt Lake City and at their ranch home in Idaho.
Engaged in livestock business between Missouri and Chicago, and later in Idaho with Virginia City, Beartown and Blackfoot, Mont. Moved to Leesburg, Idaho, 1866, resided there until 1878; moved to Custer and later to Fremont county, and again engaged in mining. Established Wood Livestock Co., in Idaho, which is the largest in that state, giving him renown as the "sheep king" of Idaho; also principal owner of one of the largest ranches in the world, near Chihuahua, Mex. Established Wood Grocery & Produce Co., Salt Lake City; was president Inter-Mountain Ice Co., and vice-president Daly-West Mine, Park City. Took an active part in the early Indian and outlaw troubles. Was accidently killed in the passenger depot yards in Salt Lake City 1890.
Catherine E. Murphy first married (1863) Frank J. Hagenbarth, who died in 1871; there were two sons, one of whom was adopted by Mr. Wood, the eldest being Frank J. Hagenbarth, a prominent business man of Salt Lake City. The other son, Hugh, took the name of his adoption.

WOOD, JOHN (son of Henry Wood of Wigan, Lancashire, Eng.). Born 1819. Came to Utah 1853, Cyrus H. Wheelock company.
Married Ellen Smith at Wigan, Eng., who came to Utah with husband. Their children: Sarah Ann, m. Samuel Winsbrow Western; Ellen, m. Isaac D. Brown; John W., m. Sarah Gibson; George Henry, m. Emily Hastings; Emily, m. George Gibson.
Farmer. Died May, 1911, Hurricane, Utah.

WOOD, JOHN (son of David Wood and Sarah Linghan, of Eng.). Born March 14, 1811, Adlam, Sussex, Eng. Came to Utah in October, 1855, Moses Thurston company.
Married Fannie Goble April 21, 1840, in England (daughter of William Goble and Harriet Johnson, of England). She was born Oct. 9, 1815. Their children: Fannie b. Oct. 11, 1841, m. Michael Garn; Ellen b. Sept. 6, 1843, m. Edwin Pierce; John William b. Oct. 30, 1845, died; Harriet Ann b. June 11, 1847, m. William Hardy; Jonathan David b. April 29, 1849, m. Cathleen Blanche Bird; m. Eliza Hess; Edward Augustus b. Nov. 7, 1851, died; Oliver b. Oct. 26, 1853, m. Selena Rogers; Mary Magdalene b. April 15, 1857, m. James Henry Wilcox; Phillip James b. April 10, 1860, died. Family home Farmington, Davis Co., Utah.
High priest; teacher. Merchant. Died Jan. 25, 1896.

WOOD, JONATHAN DAVID (son of John Wood and Fannie Goble). Born April 29, 1849, in England.
Married Cathleen Blanche Bird Oct. 9, 1871, Salt Lake City (daughter of James Bird and Harriet Goble, of Nephi, Utah, pioneers in November, 1864). She was born July 4, 1852. Their children: Lillian Blanche b. Nov. 9, 1872, m. Thomas Edwin Secrist; Jonathan David b. June 20, 1875, m. Phoebe Gleason; Phillip James b. March 13, 1878, m. Elizabeth Johnson; Elizabeth Ann b. July 1, 1880, m. Edwin Whitaker; Charles William b. Aug. 24, 1882, m. Clara Leviatt; George Franklin b. Nov. 13, 1884, m. Maggie Richards; Willard Learnard b. Feb. 12, 1887, m. Electa Hall; Allace Myrtle b. Jan. 21, 1889, m. John Wilkensen; Wallace Harry b. July 18, 1891; Geneva Bird b. Sept. 23, 1894; Clifton B. and Afton G. (twins) b. March 12, 1899.
Married Eliza Hess Oct. 26, 1882 (daughter of John W. Hess and Mary Ann Steed, of Farmington, Utah, pioneers), who was born July 4, 1864. Their children: John Henry,

PIONEERS AND PROMINENT MEN OF UTAH 1259

m. Agusta Gallop; Edward A., m. Millie Gallop; Lewis, Clarence B. and Hyrum H., died; Kenneth J.; Gladys Ellen; Dorah; Herman L. Families resided Farmington, Davis Co., Utah.
Bishop's counselor; high councilor. Merchant.

WOOD, JONATHAN DAVID (son of Jonathan David Wood and Cathleen Blanche Bird). Born June 20, 1873, Farmington, Utah.
Married Phoebe Gleason Sept. 9, 1903, Salt Lake City, Utah (daughter of Alvirus Horn Gleason and Meady Maria Lane, of Farmington, Utah). She was born Sept. 12, 1878. Their children: David G. b. July 27, 1904; Earn b. Aug. 16, 1905, died; Ross C. b. March 18, 1907; Roxie b. Dec. 4, 1909.
Family home Fielding, Box Elder Co., Utah.
Ward teacher; Sunday school teacher; member of seventy. Farmer.

WOOD, JOHN P. Born in 1817, in England. Came to Utah in 1852.
Married Ann L. ——.

WOOD, JOSIAH (son of John P. and Ann L. Wood). Born in 1846 at Galena, Ill.
Married Clara A. Woodhead in 1874, Salt Lake City (daughter of George Woodhead and Caroline Lane), who was born in 1858, at North Ogden. Their children: Caroline Ann b. Dec. 8, 1876, m. Levi C. Ward; George E. b. June 25, 1878, m. Nancy Jane Woodland; Uriah b. Sept. 13, 1881; William J. b. Oct. 31, 1883, died; Charles E. b. July 3, 1886, m. Syvella Brown; Jennie R. b. May 7, 1888, m. Joseph Cutler; James C. b. June 9, 1891; Charlotte E. b. Oct. 1, 1895.
Elder; high priest. Farmer; stockraiser.

WOOD, GEORGE J. (son of Josiah Wood and Clara Woodhead). Born June 25, 1878.
Married Nancy Jane Woodland in 1899, Brigham, Utah (daughter of Daniel Woodland and Sofronia Davis), who was born Dec. 17, 1882. Their children: Rella b. Feb. 5, 1900; Leona b. Feb. 3, 1905; Merlan G. b. Dec. 5, 1906; Dallas H. b. Sept. 18, 1911.

WOOD, WILLIAM (son of John Wood and Ann Lawrence, both of Herefordshire, Eng.). Born 1823, in Herefordshire. Came to Utah in 1848, independent company.
Married Lucy Babcock 1849 (daughter of Dolfus Babcock and Jarusia Rowley, pioneers 1847, John Taylor company), who was born 1832. Came to Utah with parents. Their children: Lucy Ann b. 1849, m. Benjamin Ayer Jan. 7, 1868; William B. b. 1851, m. Mary J. Clements; Mary G. b. 1853, m. H. A. Walker; Eliza Frances b. 1855; John Albert b. 1856; Alice S. b. 1858, m. Samuel Bradshaw; Abraham b. 1860, m. Mary A. Baker; Frances Permelia b. 1862, m. William Hamlen; Celestia Ann b. 1863. Family resided San Bernardino, Cal., and Minersville, Utah.
Married Ann Eyre Banks March 7, 1865, Minersville, Utah (daughter of Joseph and Charlotte Banks, pioneers, independent company), who was born in Australia June 15, 1845. Their children: Joseph b. 1866, m. Susie Gillins; Milisia b. 1867, m. John Turby; Barbara b. 1868, m. Pearl Grisman; John L. b. 1870, and Ann L. b. 1872, died; Charlotte N. b. 1874, m. Tom Gray; Emma C. b. 1875, m. William Banks; Willard A. b. 1877, m. Eva Berd; Thomas H. b. 1879, m. Jennie Tanner; Bertha L. b. 1881, m. Vine Evans; Nellie M. b. 1883, m. Edward Erickson; Hannah M. b. 1885; David b. 1886; George F. b. 1888.

WOOD, WILLIAM B. (son of William Wood and Lucy Babcock). Born May 18, 1851, Centerville, Utah.
Married Mary Jane Clements, 1872, Minersville, Utah (daughter of Joseph Clements and Mary Donaldson, pioneers 1855, independent company). She was born 1854, in Johnson county, Ind.
Missionary 1886-89; high priest; member high council; Sunday school superintendent; bishop's counselor. Farmer and stockraiser.

WOOD, WILLIAM (son of William Wood born May 12, 1811, Mountnessing, Essex, Eng., and Elizabeth Gigseey born Sept. 29, 1812, Ostend. Burnham, Essex, Eng.—married 1836). Born May 1, 1837, Ostend, Burnham. Came to Utah Oct. 18, 1862, D. P. Kimball freight train.
Married Elizabeth Gentry Nov. 1, 1862 (daughter of Samuel Gentry and Elizabeth Davis, pioneers Oct. 3, 1867, W. R. Smith company), who was born Oct. 18, 1845, and came to Utah with James S. Brown independent company. Their children: William b. Nov. 10, 1863, m. Ellen Goddard Aug. 3, 1891; Joseph b. June 13, 1865, m. Sarah Lees, Oct. 11, 1889; Edward James b. Oct. 27, 1866, m. Mary Ann Solomon Sept. 27, 1892; Arthur George b. Oct. 29, 1868; Barnabas b. Aug. 1870; Elizabeth Mary b. Jan. 4, 1872, m. Charles Trealease April 5, 1894; Henry Barnabas b. Aug. 1, 1874; Mary Eva b. Sept. 11, 1876, m. Byard Smith Oct. 1902; Albert Lorenzo b. June 21, 1878, m. Eva Probert May 24, 1904; Susan Rebecca b. Jan. 31, 1880, m. Frank A. Rose April 5, 1901; Benjamin James b. Oct. 1, 1883, m. Fern Bigelow Jan. 9, 1907; August John b. May 18, 1885; Frederick John b. March 2, 1887.
Married Susan Parker, who was born 1850, in England.
Married Eliza Whytock Sept. 26, 1888, Logan, Utah (daughter of James Whytock and Jessie Larkie, who married Dec. 29, 1853, Glasgow, Scotland). Their children:

Harold b. June 28, 1889, m. Ida Stacy Sept. 30, 1910; Grace b. Sept. 14, 1891; Virginia b. Feb. 21, 1894; Le Roy b. June 19, 1896; Gordon b. Oct. 22, 1898; Jean b. Dec. 19, 1900; Ruth b. May 3, 1903; Miriam b. Feb. 28, 1908.
In British navy, 1856-60, where he assisted in laying the first submarine cable in the Red Sea to Aden. Missionary to The Muddy, Ariz.; called to Eagle Valley, 1872; returned in 1880 to Salt Lake City; missionary to England 1880 to 1882. Settled in Canada in 1892.

WOOD, WILLIAM, JR. (son of William Wood and Elizabeth Gentry). Born Nov. 10, 1863, at Salt Lake City.
Married Ellen S. Goddard Aug. 9, 1893, at Salt Lake City (daughter of George Goddard). Their children: Raphael b. Sept. 20, 1894; Don Carlos b. May 3, 1896; George G. b. Dec. 5, 1897; Allan Gentry b. May 21, 1900; Myron Douglas b. May 6, 1903; Mary b. Oct. 5, 1908.
Bishop of 24th ward of Salt Lake City.

WOODARD, CHARLES NORTHROP (son of Jedediah Stark Woodard and Emily Northrop of Kirtland, Ohio, and Nauvoo, Ill.). Born Sept. 15, 1827, Baneston, Franklin county, Mass. Came to Utah 1847, Jedediah M. Grant company.
Married Margaret Ann Malin 1857, Salt Lake City (daughter of Elijah Malin and Sarah McGuckin, of Chester county, Pa.; former died on way to Utah, latter came in 1847). She was born Feb. 14, 1835. Their children: Charles Northrop, Jr., m. Samantha Jane Russell; Margaret Ann, m. John C. Lambert; John Franklin, m. Minerva McCornick; Jedediah, m. Evaline Vilate Russell; Sarah Emily, m. M. N. Pack; Catherine: Emma, m. Heber Garfield; Anna, m. James H. Evans; James, m. May Taylor. Family home Kamas, Utah.
Member seventy. Crossed plains five times for immigrants. Mail carrier in early days. Rancher and farmer. Died Jan. 5, 1912, Salt Lake City.

WOODARD, CHARLES NORTHROP (son of Charles Northrop Woodard and Margaret Ann Malin). Born Aug. 3, 1857, Salt Lake City.
Married Samantha Jane Russell July 5, 1877, Kamas, Utah (daughter of Charles L. Russell and Samantha Jane Buckland, of Kansas), who was born May 7, 1858. Their children: Charles N., d. infant; Samantha Jane; Lonzo Russell; Margare Ann, d. infant. Family resided Kamas and Woodland, Utah.
Member seventies. Farmer.

WOODARD, JEDEDIAH (son of Charles Northrop Woodard and Margaret Ann Malin). Born Jan. 2, 1863, Salt Lake City.
Married Evaline Vilate Russell Feb. 9, 1880, Rockport, Summit Co., Utah, and later in Salt Lake temple (daughter of Charles Russell and Samantha Jane Buckland of Kamas, Utah, pioneers). She was born Sept. 6, 1863, Kamas, Utah. Their children: Jedediah Jr. b. 1881, m. Franty Rose; Calvin, m. Millie Swift; William W., m. Millie White; Leory; Lillie Gertrude; Edith May; James Clifford; Peril Vilate; Walter Ray; Charles Alphard. Family home Kamas, Summit Co., Utah.
Missionary to southern states 1901-03; high priest; second counselor to bishop of Park City ward; high councilor, Summit stake. County commissioner, Summit county. Farmer. Merchant.

WOODBURY, JEREMIAH (son of John Woodbury and Mary Ward of Massachusetts). Born March 9, 1791, Leverett, Mass. Came to Utah Sept. 26, 1847, Abraham O. Smoot company.
Married Elizabeth Bartlett June 20, 1815, Montague. Franklin county, Mass. (daughter of Daniel Bartlett and Hannah Woodbury of Montague), who was born April 24, 1794. Their children: William Hamilton, m. Clarissa Howe; Joseph Jeremy, m. Mary Lindsay; Thomas Hobert, m. Katherine R. Haskell; John Stillman, m. Martha Alice Parker; Orin Nelson, m. Ann Cannon; Susan Elizabeth; Hannah Maria, m. Thomas Haskell. Family home New Salem, Franklin county, Mass.
Sunday school superintendent; patriarch. Farmer. Died Oct. 8, 1883, Salt Lake City.

WOODBURY, THOMAS HOBERT (son of Jeremiah Woodbury and Elizabeth Bartlett of Massachusetts). Born July 4, 1822, in Massachusetts. Came to Utah Sept. 29, 1847, George B. Wallace company.
Married Katherine R. Haskell May 8, 1842, New Salem, Mass. (daughter of Samuel Haskell and Elizabeth Reynolds of New Salem), who was born July 6, 1816. Their children: Elizabeth b. 1843, d. infant; John H. b. Sept. 11, 1845, Nauvoo, Ill.. m. Alexina Bray May 10, 1870; Catherine b. June 1850, d. infant; Thomas H. b. June 3, 1852, m. Mary Alice Lambert June 10, 1872; Mary C. b. March 29, 1857, m. Joseph H. Stay May 8, 1877. Family home, Salt Lake City.
Married Harriet Miller in 1850. Their children: Elizabeth b. May 30, 1852, died as result of accident 1866; William J. b. Nov. 25, 1857, m. Louisa Stay Nov. 28, 1878.
Missionary to "Dixie" 1861; bishop's counselor; in charge of deacons quorum. Postmaster at Grafton, Utah. President Horticultural Society several years. Nurseryman and farmer. Died June 6, 1898, Salt Lake City.

WOODBURY, THOMAS H. (son of Thomas H. Woodbury and Katherine R. Haskell). Born June 3, 1852, Salt Lake City.
Married Mary Alice Lambert June 10, 1872, Salt Lake City (daughter of Charles Lambert and Mary Alice Cannon of Salt Lake City, pioneers 1849). She was born July 14, 1852. Their children: Thomas L. b. April 5, 1873, m. Maud Bowring; Maria L. b. Nov. 9, 1874, m. Ed. J. Liddle, m. Thomas W. Ross; Mary Alice b. Dec. 6, 1876, d. infant; Charles b. Jan. 4, 1879, m. Sarah Peart; George b. Jan. 16, 1881, d. infant; Ella F. b. March 20, 1883, m. Richard Osborne; Katherine b. July 31, 1885; Loretta b. April 25, 1887, m. Eli B. Rogers; Richard b. Feb. 22, 1889, d. infant; Myrtle b. April 11, 1891, m. Reinhold Doelle; Irene b. Feb. 6, 1893, d. April 30, 1906; Annie b. March 22, 1895; Elias b. April 3, 1898. Family home, Salt Lake City.
Member 123d quorum seventies; high priest and visiting high priest. Farmer.

WOODBURY, JOHN STILLMAN (son of Jeremiah Woodbury and Elizabeth Bartlett). Born Nov. 20, 1825, New Salem, Mass. Came to Utah with father.
Married Martha Alice Parker Dec. 27, 1864, Beaver, Utah (daughter of Robert Parker and Ann Hartley of Beaver, pioneers October, 1856, Daniel D. McArthur handcart company). She was born May 22, 1846. Their children: John S. b. Nov. 16, 1865, m. May Higbee July 17, 1895; Martha A. b. Aug. 16, 1867; Franklin J. b. Oct. 9, 1868, m. Vivien M. Watson; Arthur H. b. Jan. 5, 1871, m. Harriet Pickett; Robert P. b. Jan. 17, 1873, m. Penelope Thompson; Ada E. b. April 21, 1875, m. George R. Scott; Max W. b. June 13, 1877, m. Kate Forsha; Nellie b. June 16, 1881, m. Lorenzo Bringhurst; Charles T. b. Oct. 7, 1883; Ann R. b. Feb. 8, 1886, m. Rudger Amundson; S. Camilla b. Dec. 23, 1887, m. John A. Judd. Family home St. George, Utah.
Joined Church of L. D. S. Aug. 27, 1841, at New Salem, Mass. Went to Nauvoo, Ill., summer of 1842, where he participated in tribulations of his people. Ordained an elder in the summer of 1844 and at October conference Oct. 8, 1844, was ordained a seventy. Left Nauvoo in spring of 1846, journeying to Council Bluffs and thence across the plains to Salt Lake City. Missionary to Hawaiian Islands, 1851-56, 1857-58, and 1877-79. Assisted in developing southern Utah; settled near St. George, where he engaged in farming, horticulture and fruit-tree nursery business. Home missionary, St. George stake; high priest; member high council, St. George stake; patriarch. Served in the militia, standing guard during trouble with the Indians.

WOODFIELD, JOHN (son of Thomas Woodfield and Ann Hasson of Warwickshire, Eng.; former died in 1859, latter in 1897). He was born near Birmingham, Warwickshire, Eng. Drove oxteam to Utah 1862, Kimball and Lawrence company.
Married Rachel Roylance 1825 (daughter of William Roylance and Mary Yarwood of Ogden). Their children: Mary Ann, m. James Dudman; Jane, m. William A. Chadwick; Rachel, d. aged 18; Charlotte, m. Albert Ward; Elizabeth; John A., m. May Chadwick; Thomas A. d. aged 30; Isabel; Emily, m. Ward Fisher; Rosene, m. William McEntire; William G.; Harriet E., m. Norton Bowns. Family home North Ogden, Utah.
Elder. Settled at North Ogden 1865. Watermaster for the Cold Water Creek Irrigation Co.; director and president North Ogden Irrigation Co. Breeder of thoroughbred stock; farmer; holds many prizes for the excellence of his wheat and barley; an exhibit of his seeds having received honorable mention at the World's Columbian Exposition 1893, in Chicago.

WOODHEAD, WILLIAM (son of Richard Woodhead and Grace Wheater of Gowdle, Yorkshire, Eng.). Born May 19, 1805, at Gowdle. Came to Utah October, 1855, Milo Andrus company.
Married Charlotte Spencely 1819, Grimsby, Lincoln, Eng. (daughter of Thomas Spencely and Ann Wright of Grimsby), who was born June 13, 1802. Their children: Grace b. July 1830, d. infant; George Thomas b. 1831, m. Caroline Lane; Richard b. 1833, d. 1834; Sarah Ann b. 1835, m. Robert G. Berrett; Charlotte E. b. Oct. 19, 1837, m. James Lofthouse; Richard Spencely b. 1840, d. 1844. Family home Paradise, Utah.
High priest. Farmer. Died Dec. 10, 1885.

WOODHOUSE, CHARLES CHAMBERS (son of Charles Woodhouse, born Aug. 13, 1806, and Ann Long, born Oct. 6, 1807, of England—married Oct. 6, 1829). He was born March 5, 1832, at Adwick Lee Street, Mexborough, Yorkshire, Eng. Came to Utah Sept. 10, 1852, Hyrum Jepson company.
Married Sophia Kershaw March 15, 1855 (daughter of Abram Kershaw and Alice Buckley, married 1815, Whitefield, Lancastershire, Eng., pioneers Sept. 17, 1850, David Evans company). She was born Aug. 24, 1834, and came to Utah with parents. Their children: Alice Ann b. March 30, 1856, m. James R. Lindsay; Charles Chambers, Jr., b. Feb. 14, 1858, m. Belle Wiley; Ida Sophia b. Feb. 4, 1863, m. John B. Gehr; Fredrick b. Aug. 27, 1865; Florence Nightingale b. July 1867, m. George Cockett; George Washington b. Sept. 27, 1871, m. Catherine M. Slaughter Aug. 22, 1890; Mary b. 1873, died; Emily Gertrude b. Sept. 20, 1876, m. Thomas W. Forrester. Family home Beaver, Utah.
Elder. Veteran Indian war. Assisted in bringing immigrants to Utah. Postmaster. Freighter. Merchant and tailor.

WOODHOUSE, GEORGE WASHINGTON (son of Charles Chambers Woodhouse and Sophia Kershaw). Born Sept. 27, 1871.
Married Catherine M. Slaughter Aug. 22, 1890, Beaver, Utah (daughter of Samuel N. Slaughter and Annie Huey, pioneers 1860, Nephi Johnson company). She was born April 10, 1871, Beaver, Utah. Their children: Katherine Sophia b. Feb. 29, 1891; George Ambrose b. Aug. 21, 1894; Anthony Forrester b. Oct. 15, 1899; Nathaniel Charles b. Aug. 30, 1901; Ida Evangeline b. Sept. 30, 1904; Alden Le Roy b. Nov. 28, 1907; Clara, b. June 3, 1911.
President elders quorum; choir director. Leader Beaver brass band; instructor of band and orchestra at Murdock 1904-1910. Proprietor of saddlery and implement business 1890-1910.

WOODHOUSE, JOHN (son of Charles Woodhouse, born Aug. 13, 1806, Adwick Lee Street, Mexborough, Yorkshire, Eng., and Ann Long, born Oct. 6, 1807, Mexborough—married Oct. 6, 1829). He was born July 21, 1830, Adwick Lee Street, Mexborough. Came to Utah Sept. 10, 1852, Hyrum Jepson company.
Married Emma Smith Thomas (daughter of Daniel S. Thomas and Martha P. Jones, pioneers 1849, Redick Allred company—married in Kentucky). She was born Oct. 21, 1836, and came to Utah with parents. Their children: Morgan T. b. March 31, 1855, m. Matilda House Nov. 2, 1874; John D. b. June 17, 1859, m. Rosabel Karren February 1882; Wilford b. March 14, 1861, m. Mary Jane Moian Jan. 19, 1881; Charles b. Jan. 19, 1864, m. Rosalie Carter Jan. 21, 1890; Isaac b. Aug. 5, 1868, m. Matilda Wines March 18, 1891; Arzie b. Sept. 7, 1870; Harden b. Oct. 14, 1874, m. Iseline Bray Jan. 17, 1900.
Bishop's clerk Cedar City, Iron Co., Utah, 1854-55; ordained priest in England June 1, 1849; missionary to Indians, Iron county, Utah; ordained a seventy 1854; missionary to Las Vegas, N. M., 1856; called to White Mountain mission; went to Missouri river with John R. Murdock company 1862 as clerk, commissary and general assistant to the captain; missionary to England Sept. 9, 1874; appointed to preside over the Leeds conference Sept. 15, 1875; was then transferred to and made president of the Bristol conference; appointed to take company of immigrants to Utah May 24, 1876, arriving in Salt Lake City June 14, 1876. Went to Provo November, 1852; to Cedar City 1853; and from there to Beaver, July 1858. Probate and county clerk Beaver City, Beaver Co., Utah, 1858-62, also county recorder of Beaver county; justice of peace at Lehi, Utah, 1865-69; city alderman at Lehi 1867-70; justice of peace at Lehi 1891-92 and one more term; deputy assessor and collector four years. Secretary and treasurer of Lehi Irrigation Co. 23 years. Saltpeter manufacturer 1859.

WOODLAND, JOHN (son of John Woodland and Mary Brown of Virginia). Born March 27, 1772, Norfolk, Va. Came to Utah October, 1850, Gardner Snow company.
Married Celia Steepleford in 1818 in Illinois (daughter of Noah Steepleford and Molly Sanders of Barren county, Ky.). Their children: Polly, m. John Wakley; Nancy, m. James Whitaker; James; Elizabeth; John, Jr.; Noah; William W.; Celia; Henry H.; Solomon A.; Thomas; Lucinda; Martha Jane; Daniel B. Family home Willard, Utah.
High priest. Farmer. Died Nov. 8, 1868.

WOODLAND, WILLIAM WEST (son of John Woodland). Born 1830. Came to Utah in 1848.
Married Laura Peters, who came to Utah in 1848. Their children: William W.; Laura L., m. Henry S. Tanner; Celia, m. Dimic Cooper; Dicey, m. B. W. Henderson; Thomas M., m. Mamie Anderson; Lilian, m. James T. Henderson; Polly, m. John Henderson; Mary; Daniel P.; Charlotte, m. Jesse Reader; Pearl, m. C. Chadwick. Family home Oneida, Idaho.
High priest. Farmer and stockraiser. Died at Salt Lake City.

WOODMANSEE, CHARLES (son of James Woodmansee, born Dec. 17, 1793, died March 8, 1849, Burlington, Iowa, and Sarah Terrill, born April 4, 1804, died 1848, Burlington). He was born March 4, 1828, Highland Co., Ohio. Came to Utah in 1853, Joel Terrill company.
Married Harriet Eleanor Porter Sept. 4, 1864, Salt Lake City (daughter of Abram Porter, born Feb. 3, 1807, Livingston county, N. Y., died June 19, 1885, Ogden, Utah, and Marcia Maria Bisbee, born Oct. 24, 1805, Cummington, Hampshire county, Mass., died Nov. 22, 1867, Ogden, Utah, pioneers Oct. 7, 1863, Augustus Canfield company). She was born Oct. 16, 1848, Livingston county, N. Y., and came to Utah with her parents. Their children: Minnie b. July 27, 1865, m. Lorenzo Farr March 2, 1882, m. S. S. Smith Nov. 1, 1900; Charles Henry b. June 4, 1867, m. Vilate Pincock Oct. 26, 1887; Marcia Annis b. Nov. 10, 1869, d. April 5,

1883; Henrietta b. Dec. 11, 1871, m. John Douglass Watson June 17, 1891; Samuel Porter b. June 6, 1874, m. Arminta Little April 4, 1893, m. Alice Amelia Ashley May 30, 1897; James Albert b. Aug. 19, 1876, m. Elizabeth Ann Moyes Dec. 31, 1895; Joan Adelle b. Dec. 9, 1878, m. Walter Rollo Emmett Oct. 10, 1900; Sarah Maria b. Nov. 24, 1881; Winifred b. March 28, 1884, m. Walter John Poulton April 24, 1907; Belva b. Sept. 20, 1886, m. Merrill Nibley April 27, 1909. Family home, Ogden.
Settled at Salt Lake City, where he engaged in the mercantile business with his brothers under the firm name of Woodmansee Bros.; in 1854 he moved to Ogden, where he continued in the mercantile business. In 1870 he established the Woodmansee theater at Ogden. After a successful course of 13 years he closed the theater and remodeled the building into a business house. He then engaged in agriculture, horticulture and improved his realty holdings. Died March 24, 1894, Ogden, Utah.

WOODMANSEE, CHARLES HENRY (son of Charles Woodmansee and Harriet Eleanor Porter). Born June 4, 1867, Ogden, Utah.
Married Vilate Pincock Oct. 26, 1887, Logan, Utah (daughter of John Pincock, born July 27, 1830, Lancastershire, Eng., died Dec. 15, 1905, Ogden, Utah, and Isabel Douglass, born Nov. 1, 1833, Lancastershire—married Feb. 5, 1856, pioneers Aug. 27, 1852, John Parker company). She was born Aug. 24, 1867, Ogden, Utah. Their children: Grace b. Dec. 20, 1888, m. Eamer Beasley Dec. 22, 1912; Pearl b. Sept. 11, 1890, d. Oct. 16, 1890; Charles Raymond b. Oct. 21, 1891, d. May 24, 1911; Clyde b. Oct. 25, 1893; Ethel b. May 27, 1896, d. infant; Glenn Douglass b. May 1, 1897; Henry and Harvey (twins) b. June 3, 1899; Marion b. Oct. 18, 1901; John b. Sept. 5, 1905. Family resided Ogden, Utah, and Rexburg, Idaho.
Counselor to the stake president Thomas E. Bassett; member academy board of directors. Commissioner Fremont county, Idaho. One of the incorporators and president First National Bank of Rexburg. Farmer.

WOODMANSEE, SAMUEL PORTER (son of Charles Woodmansee and Harriet Eleanor Porter). Born Aug. 6, 1874, Ogden, Utah.
Married Arminta Little April 4, 1893, Ogden, Utah (daughter of William Henry Little, born 1843, Augusta, Ga., and Elizabeth Inglett, born 1544, Augusta, who came to Utah 1891). She was born April 3, 1870, Augusta. Their children: Lucile b. April 20, 1894, m. Andrew P. Gallacher Sept. 18, 1912; Blanch b. Sept. 5, 1895; Ima b. March 15, 1897. Family resided Ogden, Utah, and Rexburg, Idaho.
Married Alice Amelia Ashley May 30, 1897, Ogden, Utah (daughter of Albert Flower Ashley, born June 15, 1849, Somersetshire, Eng., and Sarah Elizabeth Parker, born Feb. 7, 1845, Redford, Nottinghamshire, died May 30, 1891, Worksop). She was born May 12, 1874, Worksop, Eng. Came to Utah Oct. 25, 1889. Their children: Thelma b. Feb. 5, 1898; Ruth b. May 12, 1900. Family home Ogden, Utah.
Moved to Rexburg, Idaho, 1894, and engaged in farming and stockraising. He returned to Ogden, Utah. 1896, where he engaged in the building and contracting business.

WOODMANSEE, JAMES ALBERT (son of Charles Woodmansee and Harriet Eleanor Porter). Born Aug. 19, 1876, Ogden, Utah.
Married Elizabeth Ann Moyes Dec. 31, 1895, Ogden, Utah (daughter of Robert Hutchison Moyes, born Jan. 1, 1844, Paisley, Scotland, and Lucy Agnes Wilson, born Nov. 20, 1855, Wilson, Weber Co., Utah, died Oct. 28, 1889, Ogden, Utah—married Dec. 31, 1872, in Ogden, pioneers Sept. 22, 1868, Edward T. Mumford company). She was born May 5, 1878, Ogden, Utah. Their children: James Albert b. 1896; Carl Moyes b. Nov. 15, 1898; Charles Thurman b. April 2, 1901; Robert Irving b. May 20, 1903; LeRoy b. Feb. 5, 1905; Lucy b. March 1, 1907; Alice b. Aug. 7, 1909; Eleanor b. June 2, 1912. Family resided at Ogden, Utah, and Rexburg, Idaho.
Moved to Rexburg, Idaho, 1900, where he is engaged in farming.

WOODRUFF, APHEK (son of Eldad Woodruff and Dina Woodford, both of Farmington, Hartford county, Conn.). Came to Utah 1847.
Married Beulah Thompson. Their child: Wilford, m. Phoebe Whitmore Carter.

WOODRUFF, WILFORD (son of Aphek Woodruff and Beulah Thompson). Born March 1, 1807, West Avon, Conn. Came to Utah July 24, 1847, Brigham Young company.
Married Phoebe Whittemore Carter April 13, 1837, Scarboro, Me. (daughter of Ezra Carter and Sarah Fabyan of Scarboro). She was born March 8, 1807. Their children: Sara Emma. d. infant; Wilford, Jr., m. Emily Jane Smith Oct. 12, 1867; Phoebe Amelia, m. Lorenzo Snow; Susan Cornelia, m. Robert Scholes; Joseph, Ezra and Sarah Carter, latter three d. infants; Beulah Augusta, m. H. S. Beatie; Aphek, d. infant. Family home, Salt Lake City.
Married Emma Smith March 13, 1852, Salt Lake City (daughter of Samuel Smith and Martishia Smoot of Salt Lake City, pioneers Oct. 14, 1850, Wilford Woodruff. company). She was born March 1, 1838. Their children: Hyrum Smith b. Oct. 4, 1857, d. Nov. 24, 1858; Emma M. b. July 4, 1860 (deceased), m. Henry Woodruff; Asahel Hart b. Feb. 3, 1863, m. Naomi Abbott Butterworth; Ann Thompson b. April 10, 1867, d. April 11, 1867; Clara Martisbia b. July 22, 1869, m. O. C. Beebe; Abraham Owen b.

Nov. 23, 1872 (deceased), m. Helen May Winters; Mary Alice b. Jan. 1, 1879, m. William McEwan.
Married Sarah Brown March 13, 1853, Salt Lake City (daughter of Henry Brown, killed at Lexington, Mo., April 9, 1852, on his way to Utah, and Rhoda North, who lived near Cleveland, Ohio, latter a pioneer 1852). She was born Jan. 1, 1834, and died at Salt Lake City. Their children: David Patten b. April 4, 1854, m. Arabelle J. Hatch; Brigham Young b. Jan. 18, 1857, drowned June 16, 1877; Phoebe Arabella b. May 30, 1859, m. Jesse T. Moses; Sylvia Melvina b. Jan. 14, 1862, m. Heber John Thompson; Newton b. Nov. 3, 1863, m. Millie Partington; Mary b. Oct. 26, 1867; Charles Henry b. Dec. 5, 1870; Edward Randolph b. Feb. 2, 1873. Family resided Salt Lake City and Randolph, Utah.
Married Sarah Delight Stocking July 31, 1857, at Salt Lake City (daughter of John J. Stocking and Catherine Ensign of Connecticut, pioneers 1848). She was born July 26, 1838, and died at Salt Lake City. Their children: Marion, m. Bertha Christian Stephenson; Emeline, m. David C. Burrows; Ensign, m. Isabell Shields; Jeremiah, died; Rosanna; John J., m. Annie Neilson; Julia Delight S., m. John Rubin Park. Family home, Salt Lake City.
Assisted in laying out Salt Lake City, in building the "Old Fort," and in exploring the valley of the Great Salt Lake; returned to the Missouri river autumn of 1848 with President Brigham Young. Missionary to eastern states 1848-50. Agriculturist. First president Utah Horticultural Society, which was organized in 1855; also president of Deseret Agricultural and Manufacturing Society. In 1881 succeeded Orson Pratt as church historian, holding this position until he became president of the Mormon church. Became president of the St. George temple at time of its dedication 1877. Ordained an apostle April 26, 1839, and in October, 1880, was sustained president of the quorum of twelve apostles; and was sustained president of the Church of Jesus Christ of Latter Day Saints April 9, 1889. The famous "Manifesto" discontinuing the practice of plural marriage in the church was issued by him Sept. 24, 1890; and was accepted by the church at the general conference held at Salt Lake City the following October. President Z. C. M. I., Utah Sugar Company and Zion's Savings Bank and Trust Company. Died Sept. 2, 1898, San Francisco, Cal.

WOODRUFF, WILFORD, JR. (son of Wilford Woodruff and Phoebe Whittemore Carter). Born March 22, 1840, at Montrose, Iowa. Came to Utah Oct. 14, 1850, Wilford Woodruff company.
Married Emily Jane Smith Oct. 12, 1867, Salt Lake City (daughter of Elias A. Smith and Lucy Brown of Salt Lake City). She was born Oct. 28, 1850. Their children: Lucy Emily b. Jan. 10, 1869, m. George Albert Smith; Wilford Smith b. Sept. 25, 1871, m. Fannie M. Carrington; Elias S. b. Dec. 15, 1873, m. Nellie Davies; Asahel b. March 30, 1876, died. Family home, Salt Lake City.
Missionary to England 1863-66; member presidency of high priest Liberty stake. Worked in Salt Lake temple. Farmer and general workman.

WOODRUFF, ASAHEL H. (son of Wilford Woodruff and Emma Smith). Born Feb. 3, 1863, at Salt Lake City.
Married Naomi Abbott Butterworth Dec. 14, 1887, Salt Lake City (daughter of William Butterworth and Mary Rose of Mill Creek, Utah, pioneers 1873). She was born March 21, 1864. Their children: Roxie Norma b. Oct. 26, 1888; Beulah b. Sept. 3, 1890, m. Lawrence G. Naylor; Asahel Hart b. Feb. 13, 1893; Douglas Owen b. Jul 10, 1895; Emma Rose b. Oct. 6, 1899; Kenneth Claud b. Nov. 9, 1905. Family home, Salt Lake City.
Bishop Waterloo ward. Manager Z. C. M. I. wholesale dry goods department 1893; director Zion's Savings Bank 1905; director Deseret Building Society.

WOODRUFF, DAVID PATTEN (son of Wilford Woodruff and Sarah Brown). Born April 4, 1854, at Salt Lake City.
Married Arabelle Jane Hatch Feb. 19, 1877, Logan, Utah (daughter of Jeremiah and Louisa Alexander Hatch of Lehi, formerly of Nauvoo, Ill., pioneers September, 1850). She was born April 2, 1859. Their children: Sarah Amy b. Dec. 10, 1877, m. John E. Bennion; Phoebe A. b. Sept. 20, 1879, m. Peter E. Fleming; David Patten b. Aug. 24, 1881, m. Alice Hinman; Wilford L. b. Aug. 3, 1883, m. Gertrude Atkins; Willard C. b. Aug. 3, 1883, m. Martha Perry; Hatch b. Oct. 23, 1885, m. Tura Newby; Louisa A. b. Nov. 20, 1887, m. Olive H. Caldwell; Mary b. Sept. 14, 1889, m. Arthur Vickery; Emma A. b. May 7, 1891, m. Ellsworth Bevans; Torrey B. N. b. Nov. 15, 1894; Beulah A. b. Oct. 1, 1896. Family reside Smithfield and Vernal, Utah, Burlington, Wyo., Cardston and Alberta, Canada.
Bishop's counselor; high councilor Big Horn stake. Assessor and collector Uintah Co., Utah, 1891-92; treasurer Big Horn county, Wyo., 1896-1900.

WOODRUFF, ENSIGN (son of Wilford Woodruff and Sarah Delight Stocking). Born Dec. 23, 1865, Salt Lake City.
Married Isabell Shields Oct. 15, 1889, Salt Lake City (daughter of George Shields and Jane Craig, pioneers 1853, Captain Harmon company). She was born Oct. 25, 1867, West Jordan, Utah. Their children: Jane Isabell b. Jan. 7, 1891, d. Jan. 8, 1891; George Ensign b. March 3, 1892; Sarah Lenora b. Jan. 22, 1896; Vera Elizabeth b. Oct. 1, 1898; Joseph Wilford b. Sept. 16, 1901; Etta Shields b. March 11, 1906; Delifford Albert b. Oct. 6, 1908; Olive Shield b. Dec. 16, 1911. Family home Brinton, Utah.
President 14th quorum elders Granite stake Oct. 29,

1899, to Feb. 12, 1911, when he was ordained a high priest and set apart a counselor in the bishopric of the Brinton ward; Sunday school officer and worker. School trustee 37th district two terms. Farmer; carpenter.

WOODRUFF, WILFORD S. (son of Wilford Woodruff, Jr. and Emily Jane Smith). Born Sept. 25, 1871, Salt Lake City. Married Fannie M. Carrington Feb. 5, 1896, Salt Lake City (daughter of Charles Carrington and Mary Winder of Salt Lake City). Their children: Wilford Charles b. Aug. 10, 1896; Josephine b. Dec. 14, 1900. Family home Salt Lake City. Salesman.

WOODRUFF, ELIAS S. (son of Wilford Woodruff, Jr., and Emily Jane Smith). Born Dec. 15, 1873, at Randolph, Utah. Married Nellie M. Davis June 20, 1901, at Salt Lake City (daughter of Edwin W. Davis and Elizabeth Derrick of Salt Lake City). She was born March 5, 1872. Their children: Nellie b. Nov. 3, 1902; Asahel Davis b. Oct. 25, 1904; Margaret b. Sept. 22, 1906; Elias Laurence b. April 24, 1908, d. Aug. 29, 1909; Mildred Jennie b. May 23, 1912. Family home, Salt Lake City.
He was a member of the 3d quorum of seventies; missionary to southern states from 1895 to 1898; president of the 3d quorum of seventies and a member of the high council of S. L. stake; bishop of the 14th ward of Salt Lake City.

WOODS, FRANCIS L. (son of Francis Charles Woods and Evelyn Pratt; former came to Utah on train, latter daughter of Parley P. Pratt and Agatha Walker). Born Aug. 7, 1874, at Salt Lake City.
Married Elizabeth L. Gibbons June 26, 1901, Salt Lake City (daughter of Thomas Gibbons and Ann Caroline Evans of Huntsville and Ogden, Utah, latter came to Utah October, 1854, Thomas E. Ricks company). She was born June 10, 1879, and died Aug. 26, 1907. Their children: Francis William b. Sept. 10, 1902; Anntonette b. June 5, 1904; Nell Evelyn b. April 4, 1906.
Married Jennie Groberg Aug. 19, 1908, Salt Lake City (daughter of John Groberg and Johanna Larson of Farr West, Utah, pioneers). She died Nov. 14, 1909. Only child: Lowell Groberg b. Aug. 26, 1909. Family home at Ogden, Utah.
Married Myrtle Stephenson May 18, 1910, Salt Lake City (daughter of Joseph Stephenson and Dorthea Lee of Farr West, Utah, pioneers). Their children: Vellys b. Dec. 12, 1910; Parker James b. Oct. 14, 1912. Family home Marriott, Utah.
Member 53d quorum seventies; missionary to southwestern states 1899-1901; Sunday school teacher; assistant Sunday school superintendent; member W. S. S. board; assistant ward clerk; high councilor. Served in battery "B" of Utah first artillery three years. Architect and mechanical engineer.

WOODS, JAMES (son of James Woods, born Nov. 9, 1802, and Harriet Hart, born July 21, 1809, of Chobham, Surrey, Eng.). He was born Sept. 13, 1839, at Chobham. Came to Utah Sept. 15, 1859, Robert F. Nelsen company.
Married Fanny Croswellar May 5, 1864 (daughter of David Croswellar and Harriet Brown, latter a pioneer Oct. 4, 1863, Horton D. Haight company). She was born Jan. 6, 1842, and came to Utah with mother. Their children: Harriet S. b. Jan. 10, 1866, m. James I. Gallacher Oct. 18, 1899; James C. b. April 23, 1869, m. Edith G. Shelly Oct. 8, 1897; William H. b. Jan. 29, 1871; Arthur H. b. Oct. 27, 1872; John D. b. April 11, 1874; Ernest B. b. May 2, 1875; Emma F. b. Sept. 19, 1877, m. John C. Bryan Dec. 12, 1900.
Married Charlotte Howell July 18, 1870, Salt Lake City (daughter of James Howell and Sarah Marshall of Essex, Eng., pioneers Oct. 5, 1862, Ansel P. Harmon company). She was born April 24, 1853, Essex, Eng. Their children: Sarah H. b. July 8, 1871; Annie C. b. Nov. 11, 1872; Vernon H. b. Feb. 15, 1875; George M. b. May 1, 1877; girl, born and died Dec. 1878; Dora Emily b. June 23, 1880, m. Fred Bryan April 16, 1902; Hazel Ella b. Oct. 2, 1884, m. Oliver M. Shields Nov. 29, 1905; Roy Owen b. Aug. 21, 1886. Families resided Salt Lake City.
One of the seven presidents of the 43d quorum seventies in 1892-97; Sunday school superintendent 9th ward 1880-82 and in Tooele 1889-97; superintendent religion class. One of the 25 sent to Laramie at the request of the government under Gen. Robert J. Burton to protect mail service against Indians. Died 1897 in Tooele county.

WOODWARD, JAMES. Born in Minnesota. Came to Utah 1851.
Married Nancy McCurdy 1844 in Minnesota (daughter of James McCurdy of Minnesota). Their children: George and Charles, d. child; Enoch, m. Annie McKee; James Comfort, m. Eliza Barentson; William Andrew, m. Mary Guyman; Nancy, m. William James; Benjamin Franklin, m. Carrie Hails. Family home Spanish Fork, Utah. Missionary to Wisconsin; high priest. Worked on St. George and Manti temples. Coroner of Emery county. Justice of peace at Huntington. Veteran Black Hawk and Walker Indian wars. One of first settlers at Spanish Fork. Farmer and cooper. Died at Huntington, Utah.

WOODWARD, JAMES COMFORT (son of James Woodward and Nancy McCurdy). Born Nov. 3, 1852, Spanish Fork, Utah.
Married Eliza Barentson Dec. 14, 1873, Salt Lake City (daughter of Andrew Marcus Barentson and Maria Erickson of Denmark, pioneers 1861, oxteam company). She was born Nov. 18, 1859. Their children: James Franklin b. March 17, 1876, m. Martha Tatton; Robert Calvin b. Aug. 5, 1878, m. Minnie Tatton, m. Golda McKee; Susanna Eliza b. Feb. 13, 1881, m. John Taylor; Gertrude b. April 13, 1884, d. infant; Mary Adlinda b. Aug. 28, 1886, m. Joseph Denison; Katie Verona b. May 16, 1890, m. Samuel Cowley; Frances b. June 16, 1892, m. George Taylor; Edward Ray b. Oct. 8, 1896; Glenn Ivan b. Jan. 19, 1899; Grant M. b. Jan. 23, 1907. Family home Sunnyside, Utah.
Member 101st quorum seventies; ward teacher; superintendent of Sunday schools of Orangeville; counselor in Y. M. M. I. A. of Sunnyside; president first Y. M. M. I. A. of Emery stake 1879-82. First white child born at Spanish Fork. Veteran Black Hawk Indian war. Early settler at Orangeville, where he assisted in developing country. Constable at Orangeville 1900-02, at Sunnyside 1910-11; school trustee at Orangeville 1883-89.

WOODWARD, WILLIAM. Born Jan. 4, 1833, Bushey, Herefordshire, Eng. Came to Utah in September, 1851, Captain Horner company.
Married Harriet Howgan Feb. 1, 1857, Salt Lake City. Only child: Marinda, m. Orin Hatch.
Married Sarah Davis Sept. 20, 1857, Salt Lake City. Their children: Ellen, m. James Frew; Argo, m. Emma Densmore; Zina, m. Alexander Stalker, Jr.; St. Leon, m. Rachel Thomas; Oscar, m. Margaret McAlpine; Lucy, m. Joel Hinckley; Beatrice and Annie, died; Sarah. Family home Franklin, Idaho.
Married Rebecca Wright June 14, 1869, Salt Lake City. Their children: Deborah; Phoebe, m. Ed. J. Smith; Jane, m. Fred Rallison; Ruth, m. George Foster; Ivan, m. Rose Hart; Winifred, d. young; Cecil, m. Bertha Crandall; Garnet, m. Alice Porter; Fabius and Mina, d. young. Family home Franklin, Idaho.
Member 19th and president 18th quorum seventies; high priest; missionary to England 1853-56. Postmaster; justice of peace and city councilman. School teacher at Franklin, Idaho. Member legislature. Farmer. Died Nov. 22, 1908, Franklin.

WOOLEY, JOHN, of Wenwick, Eng. Came to Utah in fall of 1858.
Married Mary Nighton of England. Their child: Ann Nighton, m. William Robins.

WOOLF, JOHN ANTHONY (son of John Anthony Woolf and Phoebe Weeks of Westchester county, N. Y.). Born July 31, 1805. Came to Utah Oct. 6, 1847, Edward Hunter company.
Married Sarah Ann Devoe 1831 in Westchester county, N. Y. (daughter of John Devoe and Sarah Weeks of Pelham, Westchester county). She was born April 10, 1814, and came to Utah with husband. Their children: Absalom, m. Harriet Brown; John, m. Lucy Hamilton; Sarah Ann, m. Homer Brown; James, m. Malinda Bradley, m. Emma Hurren; Hannah Eliza, m. Homer Brown; Isaac, m. Ellen M. Hyde, m. Melissa Ashcraft; John Anthony, m. Mary Lucretia Hyde, m. Celia Ann Hatch; Andrew; William Henry, died; Phoebe Elizabeth, m. William Gibson; Harriet, m. William Gibson; Homer, m. Loila Bates; Wallace, died. Family resided Salt Lake City, Mona, Nephi and Hyde Park, Utah.
Married Mary Ann Atkins in 1872, Salt Lake City (daughter of William Atkins and Lucy Heert), who was born Dec. 20, 1815, Hockley, Essex, Eng. Came to Utah Sept. 26, 1852, James Wareham company.
Member 49th quorum seventies; counselor to Bishop William Hyde of Hyde Park; president of branch in New Rochelle, N. Y., in 1842; ordained president 49th quorum of seventies of Nephi 1855. Justice of peace Hyde Park, Utah. Farmer and stockraiser. Died Nov. 7, 1881, Hyde Park.

WOOLF, JOHN ANTHONY (son of John Anthony Woolf and Sarah Ann Devoe). Born Feb. 27, 1843, Pelham, Westchester county, N. Y. Came to Utah with parents.
Married Mary Lucretia Hyde Dec. 21, 1866, Salt Lake City (daughter of William Hyde and Elizabeth Howe Bullard of Salt Lake City, Lehi and Hyde Park, Utah, pioneers 1849, Samuel Gulley company). She was born Dec. 23, 1848. Their children: Sarah Elizabeth b. Nov. 24, 1867, died; John William b. Nov. 27, 1869, m. Lucinda M. Layne; Willard b. Sept. 11, 1871, died; Jane Eliza b. Aug. 8, 1873, died; Ormus Ernest Bates; Arthur Hyde b. June 25, 1875, died; Mary Lula b. April 25, 1877, m. Robert Bey; Simpson Melvin b. Oct. 22, 1879, m. Harriet Stotard; Wilford b. Oct. 1, 1882, m. Pearl Wright; Milton Howe b. May 25, 1885, m. Iretta France; Zina Alberta b. Dec. 17, 1887; Grace Myrtle b. Aug. 2, 1889; Charles Oliver b. July 9, 1891. Family resided Hyde Park and Logan, Utah, and Cardston, Canada.
Married Celia Ann Hatch April 10, 1876, Salt Lake City (daughter of Lorenzo Hill Hatch and Catherine Kerren, resided at Franklin, Idaho, and Woodruff, Ariz., St. George, Lehi and Logan, Utah, pioneers 1850, David Evans company). She was born March 19, 1856, Lehi City, Utah. Their children: Catherine b. Nov. 10, 1878, m. Horton H.

Hammond Jan. 9, 1901; Derttie Aldura b. Sept. 24, 1880, m. John Lake July 14, 1901; Ethel b. Nov. 17, 1883, m. Alma John Balls June 7, 1905; Eva Savona b. Dec. 3, 1885.

Ordained a seventy 1871; missionary to New York City, Iowa, and Nebraska 1876-77; high priest; superintendent Sunday school; second counselor to Bishop Daines of Hyde Park, Utah; bishop of Cardston, Canada, 1888; counselor to President C. O. Card of Alberta stake 1895; ordained patriarch 1901. Mayor of Cardston two terms; postmaster of Cardston nine years. Farmer and stockraiser.

WOOLLEY, EDWIN DILWORTH (son of John Woolley, born Aug. 17, 1779, and Rachel Dilworth, born Aug. 10, 1782, both of Chester county, Pa.). He was born June 28, 1807, in Chester county, Pa. Came to Utah in 1848, Brigham Young company.

Married Mary Wickersham (daughter of Amos and Annie Wickersham), who was born Nov. 4, 1808, and came to Utah with husband. Their children: John W. b. Dec. 30, 1831; Franklin D.; Rachel Emma; Henrietta; Samuel W. b. April 2, 1840, m. Maria Angell; Edwin Dilworth b. April 30, 1845; Mary Louisa; Marsellus. Family home, Salt Lake City.

Married Louisa Chopin Gordon Feb. 6, 1846, Nauvoo, Ill., who was born Feb. 28, 1820, at Williamson, N. Y. Their only child was Edwin Gordon Woolley.

Married Ellen Wilding, who was born April 8, 1822, at Leon, Eng. Their children: Sarah; Joseph; Hyrum Smith; Edwin Thomas; Mary Ellen. Family home, Salt Lake City.

Married Ann Olpin. Their children: Henry Alberto; Amelia; Orson; Ruth; Olive; Fannie; George; Carlos.
Married Betsy Ann Jackman. One son: Oceolo.
Married Elizabeth Jackman.

WOOLLEY, SAMUEL WICKERSHAM (son of Edwin Dilworth Woolley and Mary Wickersham). Born April 2, 1840, at Nauvoo, Ill. Came to Utah in 1848 with Heber C. Kimball.

Married Maria Angell 1858 at Salt Lake City (daughter of Truman Angell and Polly Johnson of Nauvoo, pioneers July 24, 1847, Brigham Young company). She was born March 23, 1841, at Nauvoo. Their children: Samuel Edwin, m. Alice Rowterry; Eugene Freeman, m. Annie E. Clark; Leo Carlos, m. Annie M. Anderson; Horace Wickersham, m. Annie L. Bates; Rachel Emma; Walter Dee, d. child; Mary Louisa; Alice May; Nellie Vilate, m. Arthur G. Burrett; Sarah Viola; Franklin Edgar and Fanny Leone, died. Family resided Grantsville and Salt Lake City, Utah.

Married Rachel Cahoon, Salt Lake City (daughter of Andrew and Jeanett Cahoon of Cottonwood, Murray, Utah). Their children: Jeanett Maria, m. John W. Taylor; Maggie Elizabeth, m. Leroy Anderson; Phebe Ann, m. J. W. Jeffs; Andrew Dilworth, m. Hattie Schoenfeldt. Family home Grantsville, Utah.

Married Polly Tolman, Salt Lake City (daughter of Benjamin Tolman of Brigham City, Box Elder Co., Utah). Their children: Alonzo Hewet; Lucy; Lenora. Family home Grantsville, Utah.

High priest; high councilor; patriarch; seventy; missionary to Ohio 1872-73. Selectman several years; justice of the peace. Minuteman and veteran Indian war; participated in Echo Canyon campaign. President Co-op. at Grantsville. Farmer and stockraiser. Died Jan. 28, 1908.

WOOLLEY, SAMUEL EDWIN (son of Samuel Wickersham Woolley and Maria Angell). Born Dec. 22, 1859, Salt Lake City.

Married Alice Rowberry May 6, 1885, Logan, Utah (daughter of John Rowberry and Harriet Frances Golliher of Grantsville, Utah). She was born Aug. 6, 1861. Their children: Ralph Edwin b. March 4, 1886; John Franklin b. March 3, 1888; Leone b. Jan. 19, 1890; Moroni Rowberry b. April 6, 1892; Ethel b. March 30, 1895; Joseph Rowberry b. Sept. 13, 1898, Hawaiian Islands; Samuel Ray b. Nov. 15, 1900, Sandwich Islands. Family home Grantsville, Utah.

In early boyhood he moved with his parents from Salt Lake City to Grantsville, Tooele county, where he grew up under the guidance and influence of his father, who instructed him in the duties and work of the ranch. He attended school a few months each year when he could be spared from his place in the saddle on his father's ranch. In his teens he was ordained a deacon and acted as one of the presidents of a quorum. Was appointed missionary to Sandwich Islands by President John Taylor and left three days later for his post, accompanied by his uncle, Henry A. Woolley, after being ordained an elder by Joseph F. Smith.

After three and one-half years in the Sandwich Islands he returned 1884 to Utah and was appointed home missionary of Tooele stake and became also a seventy and member of the 31st quorum at Grantsville. Later he was made alternate high councilor of the stake and was ordained a high priest by Heber J. Grant; presided over the Y. M. M. I. A. of Tooele stake. In 1890 was called by President Woodruff to a mission in the Iosepa colony and from there was called by President Joseph F. Smith to take charge of the Hawaiian mission. Taking his wife and four children with him, he sailed on Aug. 31, 1895, for the post, whence he returned in 1902 to bring home his wife, whose health was failing. Went back to his mission, where he went on with the work which he and his wife so earnestly commenced and where he succeeded in building up the church membership to over 8,500 souls.

WOOLLEY, HORACE WICKERSHAM (son of Samuel Wickersham, Woolley and Maria Angell). Born Dec. 9, 1864, Grantsville, Utah.

Married Annie Bates Dec. 26, 1889, Logan, Utah (daughter of Ormes Eaton Bates and Sarah Weir of Rush Valley, Tooele Co., Utah). She was born March 23, 1866. Their children: Horace Walter b. Nov. 4, 1890; Leah b. Feb. 19, 1893; Howard Bates b. Feb. 21, 1895; Iona b. April 6, 1897; Marguerett b. April 16, 1899; Samuel Bates b. Jan. 13, 1901; Erma b. Jan. 16, 1903; Muriel b. March 13, 1905; Maud b. May 13, 1908; Arthur Bates b. April 6, 1910. Family home Vernal, Utah.

Member 47th quorum seventies; missionary to Great Britain 1891-1893; high priest; ward teacher; superintendent Sunday schools; counselor to stake superintendent of the Mutuals; clerk of Uintah stake 1896-1902; member of the high council. Engrossing clerk of the legislature 1896. Farmer; stockraiser; sheepman. Settled at Grantsville; moved to Vernal 1896.

WOOLLEY, EDWIN DILWORTH (son of Edwin Dilworth Woolley and Mary Wickersham). Born April 30, 1845, Nauvoo, Ill.

Married Emma Bentley March 11, 1867, Salt Lake City (daughter of Richard Bentley and Elizabeth Price, pioneers 1852, Henry W. Miller company). She was born May 11, 1847, at Kanesville, Iowa. Their children: Mary Elizabeth b. Dec. 23, 1867, died; Mary Elizabeth b. Jan. 31, 1870; Edwin Dilworth b. Jan. 11, 1873, died; Olive Geneva b. June 22, 1874, died; Joseph Anthony b. June 24, 1876, m. Margret Holt July 12, 1904; Royal Bentley b. Sept. 3, 1878, m. Viola Barney April 24, 1903; Radel Henrietta b. Dec. 2, 1880, m. Julius S. Dailey May 2, 1912; Ruth b. Nov. 24, 1882, m. David D. Rust May 27, 1903; Ella b. Oct. 3, 1884, m. Israel H. Chamberlain Oct. 4, 1905; Grace b. May 2, 1887, m. Othello C. Bowman June 23, 1909.

WOOLLEY, EDWIN DILWORTH, JR. (son of Edwin Dilworth Woolley, Sr., and Mary Wickersham Woolley). Born April 30, 1845, Nauvoo, Ill.

Married Florence Snow April 12, 1877, at St. George, Utah (daughter of Erastus Snow and Elizabeth Ashby), who was born June 16, 1856, Salt Lake City. Their children: Florence Evlyn b. Aug. 26, 1878, died; Erastus Dilworth b. Dec. 22, 1880, m. Alice Snow Sept. 9, 1903; Hurbert Elliot b. May 19, 1883, m. Perscinda Ballentyne Sept. 6, 1911; Elizabeth b. March 11, 1885, m. Albert R. Day Aug. 31, 1904; Le Grande b. April 3, 1887, m. Alida Snow Aug. 2, 1911; Arthur Snow b. May 12, 1889; Marion b. April 2, 1895; Pruda b. July 7, 1902. Family resided Salt Lake City and Kanab, Utah.

Justice of peace; sheriff of Washington county 1879. Served in Black Hawk war 1865. Constable of St. George. President of Kanab stake June 9, 1884, to Dec. 2, 1910.

WOOLLEY, JOSEPH ANTHONY (son of Edwin Dilworth Woolley and Emma Bentley). Born June 24, 1876, at St. George, Utah.

Married Margret Holt July 12, 1904, St. George, Utah (daughter of John Roskell Holt and Sophia Ashworth), who was born Feb. 22, 1881, at Manchester, Eng. Their children: Rachel b. March 18, 1906; Joseph Anthony, Jr., b. July 21, 1908; Anna b. May 26, 1912.

WOOLLEY, JOHN MILLS (son of John Woolley, born Aug. 19, 1779, and Rachel Dilworth, born Aug. 10, 1782, both of Chester county, Pa.). Born Nov. 20, 1822, at New Lynn, Pa. Came to Utah Sept. 26, 1847, George B. Wallace company.

Married Maria Lucy Dewey Jan. 9, 1846 (daughter of Ashbel Dewey, who died August, 1846, and Harriet Adams, pioneers Sept. 26, 1847, George B. Wallace company—married 1819). She was born Aug. 3, 1823. Their children: John Dewey b. Dec. 30, 1846, died; Ashbel Dewey b. June 1, 1850, m. Ida Ann Bird Dec. 12, 1878; Harriet Arabell b. March 27, 1853, m. George E. Taylor Sept. 5, 1889; Frank Albert b. May 4, 1856, m. Eliza Kimball May 14, 1880; William Dewey b. Feb. 25, 1858; Vilate Annabell b. Aug. 21, 1860, d. Oct. 13, 1867; Marion Dewey b. June 28, 1862, d. Dec. 19, 1888. Family home, Salt Lake City.

Married Caroline Patience Harrar Jan. 25, 1857, Salt Lake City (daughter of John Harrar and Mary Law), who was born Feb. 20, 1832, Philadelphia, Pa. Their children: Lorenzo Harrar b. Jan. 12, 1858, d. Nov. 1859; Taylor Harrar b. March 29, 1860, m. Caroline Louise Ahlstrom May 19, 1881, who died Aug. 4, 1889, m. Florence Belle Garrard Jan. 23, 1891; Albaroni Harrar b. April 2, 1862, at Salt Lake City, m. Josephine L. Groo Oct. 22, 1884; Laura Virginia b. Feb. 5, 1864, Salt Lake City, m. Theodore Tobiason Oct. 21, 1885.

Missionary; bishop's counselor; bishop. Built first house in 9th ward Salt Lake City. Sawmill owner and lumberman.

WOOLLEY, ALBARONI HARRAR (son of John Mills Woolley and Caroline Patience Harrar). Born April 2, 1862, Salt Lake City.

Married Josephine L. Groo Oct. 22, 1884, Logan, Utah (daughter of Isaac Groo and Eliza Lyons), who was born Feb. 3, 1865, Salt Lake City. Family home 9th ward, Salt Lake City.

First counselor to Bishop Jabez W. West 9th ward, Salt Lake City, 1899-1909; bishop of 9th ward since 1909; missionary to New York and Pennsylvania 1888-89. Manager and buyer grocery department Z. C. M. I.

1262 PIONEERS AND PROMINENT MEN OF UTAH

1899, to Feb. 12, 1911, when he was ordained a high priest and set apart a counselor in the bishopric of the Brinton ward; Sunday school officer and worker. School trustee 37th district two terms. Farmer; carpenter.

WOODRUFF, WILFORD S. (son of Wilford Woodruff Jr. and Emily Jane Smith). Born Sept. 25, 1871, Salt Lake City. Married Fannie M. Carrington Feb. 5, 1896, Salt Lake City (daughter of Charles Carrington and Mary Winder of Salt Lake City). Their children: Wilford Charles b. Aug. 10, 1896; Josephine b. Dec. 14, 1900. Family home Salt Lake City.
Salesman.

WOODRUFF, ELIAS S. (son of Wilford Woodruff, Jr., and Emily Jane Smith). Born Dec. 15, 1873, at Randolph, Utah. Married Nellie M. Davis June 20, 1901, at Salt Lake City (daughter of Edwin W. Davis and Elizabeth Derrick of Salt Lake City). She was born March 5, 1872. Their children: Nellie b. Nov. 3, 1902; Asahel Davis b. Oct. 25, 1904; Margaret b. Sept. 22, 1906; Elias Laurence b. April 21, 1908, d. Aug. 29, 1909; Mildred Jennie b. May 23, 1912. Family home, Salt Lake City.
He was a member of the 3d quorum of seventies; missionary to southern states from 1895 to 1898; president of the 3d quorum of seventies and a member of the high council of S. L. stake; bishop of the 14th ward of Salt Lake City.

WOODS, FRANCIS L. (son of Francis Charles Woods and Evelyn Pratt; former came to Utah on train, latter daughter of Parley P. Pratt and Agatha Walker). Born Aug. 7, 1874, at Salt Lake City. Married Elizabeth L. Gibbons June 26, 1901, Salt Lake City (daughter of Thomas Gibbons and Ann Caroline Evans of Huntsville and Ogden, Utah, latter came to Utah October, 1854, Thomas E. Ricks company). She was born June 10, 1879, and died Aug. 26, 1907. Their children: Francis William b. Sept. 10, 1902; Anntonette b. June 5, 1904; Nell Evelyn b. April 4, 1906.
Married Jennie Groberg Aug. 19, 1908, Salt Lake City (daughter of John Groberg and Johanna Larson of Farr West, Utah, pioneers). She died Nov. 14, 1909. Only child: Lowell Groberg b. Aug. 26, 1909. Family home at Ogden, Utah.
Married Myrtle Stephenson May 18, 1910, Salt Lake City (daughter of Joseph Stephenson and Dorthea Lee of Farr West, Utah, pioneers). Their children: Vellys b. Dec. 12, 1910; Parker James b. Oct. 14, 1912. Family home Marriott, Utah.
Member 53d quorum seventies; missionary to southwestern states 1899-1901; Sunday school teacher; assistant Sunday school superintendent; member W. S. S. S. board; assistant ward clerk; high councilor. Served in battery "B" of Utah first artillery three years. Architect and mechanical engineer.

WOODS, JAMES (son of James Woods, born Nov. 9, 1802, and Harriet Hart, born July 21, 1809, of Chobham, Surrey, Eng.). He was born Sept. 13, 1839, at Chobham. Came to Utah Sept. 15, 1859, Robert P. Nelsen company.
Married Fanny Crosweller May 5, 1864 (daughter of David Crosweller and Harriet Brown, latter a pioneer Oct. 4, 1863, Horton D. Haight company). She was born Jan. 6, 1842, and came to Utah with mother. Their children: Harriet S. b. Jan. 10, 1866, m. James I. Gallacher Oct. 18, 1899; James C. b. April 23, 1869, m. Edith G. Shelly Oct. 8, 1897; William H. b. Jan. 29, 1871; Arthur H. b. Oct. 27, 1872; John D. b. April 11, 1874; Ernest B. b. May 2, 1875; Emma F. b. Sept. 19, 1877, m. John C. Bryan Dec. 12, 1900.
Married Charlotte Howell July 18, 1870, Salt Lake City (daughter of James Howell and Sarah Marshall of Essex, Eng., pioneers Oct. 5, 1862, Ansel P. Harmon company). She was born April 24, 1853, Essex, Eng. Their children: Sarah H. b. July 8, 1871; Annie C. b. Nov. 11, 1872; Vernon H. b. Feb. 15, 1875; George M. b. May 1, 1877; girl, born and died Dec. 1878; Bryan April 16, 1902; Hazel Ella b. Oct. 2, 1884, m. Oliver M. Shields Nov. 29, 1905; Roy Owen b. Aug. 21, 1886. Families resided Salt Lake City.
One of the seven presidents of the 43d quorum seventies in 1892-97; Sunday school superintendent 9th ward 1880-82 and in Tooele 1889-97; superintendent religion class. One of the 25 sent to Laramie at the request of the government under Gen. Robert J. Burton to protect mail service against Indians. Died 1897 in Tooele county.

WOODWARD, JAMES. Born in Minnesota. Came to Utah 1851.
Married Nancy McCurdy 1844 in Minnesota (daughter of James McCurdy of Minnesota). Their children: George and Charles, d. child; Enoch, m. Annie McKee; James Comfort, m. Eliza Barentson; William Andrew, m. Mary Guyman; Nancy, m. Carrie Hails. Family home Spanish Fork, Utah.
Missionary to Wisconsin; high priest. Worked on St. George and Manti temples. Coroner of Emery county. Justice of peace at Huntington. Veteran Black Hawk and Walker Indian wars. One of first settlers at Spanish Fork. Farmer and cooper. Died at Huntington, Utah.

WOODWARD, JAMES COMFORT (son of James Woodward and Nancy McCurdy). Born Nov. 3, 1852, Spanish Fork, Utah.
Married Eliza Barentson Dec. 14, 1873, Salt Lake City (daughter of Andrew Marcus Barentson and Maria Erickson of Denmark, pioneers 1861, oxteam company). She was born Nov. 18, 1859. Their children: James Franklin b. March 17, 1876, m. Martha Tatton; Robert Calvin b. Aug. 5, 1878, m. Minnie Tatton, m. Golda McKee; Susanna Eliza b. Feb. 13, 1881, m. John Taylor; Gertrude b. April 13, 1884, d. infant; Mary Adlinda b. Aug. 28, 1886, m. Joseph Denison; Katie Verona b. May 18, 1890, m. Samuel Cowley; Frances b. June 16, 1892, m. George Taylor; Edward Ray b. Oct. 8, 1896; Glenn Ivan b. Jan. 19, 1899; Grant M. b. Jan. 23, 1907. Family home Sunnyside, Utah.
Member 101st quorum seventies; ward teacher; superintendent of Sunday schools of Orangeville; counselor in Y. M. M. I. A. of Sunnyside; president first Y. M. M. I. A. of Emery stake 1879-82. First white child born at Spanish Fork. Veteran Black Hawk Indian war. Early settler at Orangeville, where he assisted in developing country. Constable at Orangeville 1900-02, at Sunnyside 1910-11; school trustee at Orangeville 1883-89.

WOODWARD, WILLIAM. Born Jan. 4, 1833, Bushey, Herefordshire, Eng. Came to Utah in September, 1851, Captain Horner company.
Married Harriet Howgan Feb. 1, 1857, Salt Lake City. Only child: Marinda, m. Orin Hatch.
Married Sarah Davis Sept. 20, 1857, Salt Lake City. Their children: Ellen, m. James Frew; Argo, m. Emma Densmore; Zina, m. Alexander Stalker, Jr.; St. Leon, m. Rachel Thomas; Oscar, m. Margaret McAlpine; Lucy, m. Joel Hinckley; Beatrice and Annie, died; Sarah. Family home Franklin, Idaho.
Married Rebecca Wright June 14, 1869, Salt Lake City. Their children: Deborah; Phoebe, m. Ed. J. Smith; Jane, m. Fred Rallison; Ruth, m. George Foster; Ivan, m. Rose Hart; Winifred, d. young; Cecil, m. Bertha Crandall; Garnet, m. Alice Porter; Fabius and Mina, d. young. Family home Franklin, Idaho.
Member 19th and president 18th quorum seventies; high priest; missionary to England 1853-56. Postmaster; justice of peace and city councilman. School teacher at Franklin, Idaho. Member legislature. Farmer. Died Nov. 22, 1908, Franklin.

WOOLEY, JOHN, of Wenwick, Eng. Came to Utah in fall of 1858.
Married Mary Nighton of England. Their child: Ann Nighton, m. William Robins.

WOOLF, JOHN ANTHONY (son of John Anthony Woolf and Phoebe Weeks of Westchester county, N. Y.). Born July 31, 1805. Came to Utah Oct. 6, 1847, Edward Hunter company.
Married Sarah Ann Devoe 1831 in Westchester county, N. Y. (daughter of John Devoe and Sarah Weeks of Pelham, Westchester county). She was born April 10, 1814, and came to Utah with husband. Their children: Absalom, m. Harriet Wood, m. Lucy Hamilton; Sarah Ann, m. Homer Brown; James, m. Malinda Bradley, m. Emma Hurren; Hannah Eliza, m. Homer Brown; Isaac, m. Ellen M. Hyde, m. Melissa Ashcraft; John Anthony, m. Mary Lucretia Hyde, m. Celia Ann Hatch; Andrew; William Henry, died; Phoebe Elizabeth, m. William Gibson; Harriet, m. William Gibson; Homer, m. Loila Bates; Wallace, died. Family resided Salt Lake City, Mona, Nephi and Hyde Park, Utah.
Married Mary Ann Atkins in 1872, Salt Lake City (daughter of William Atkins and Lucy Heert), who was born Dec. 20, 1815, Hockley, Essex, Eng. Came to Utah Sept. 26, 1862, James Wareham company.
Member 49th quorum seventies; counselor to Bishop William Hyde of Hyde Park; president of branch in New Rochelle, N. Y., in 1842; ordained president 49th quorum of seventies of Nephi 1855. Justice of peace Hyde Park, Utah. Farmer and stockraiser. Died Nov. 7, 1881, Hyde Park.

WOOLF, JOHN ANTHONY (son of John Anthony Woolf and Sarah Ann Devoe). Born Feb. 27, 1843, Pelham, Westchester county, N. Y. Came to Utah with parents.
Married Mary Lucretia Hyde Dec. 21, 1866, Salt Lake City (daughter of William Hyde and Elizabeth Howe Bullard of Salt Lake City, Lehi and Hyde Park, Utah, pioneers 1849, Samuel Gulley company). She was born Dec. 23, 1848. Their children: Sarah Elizabeth b. Nov. 24, 1867, died; John William b. Nov. 27, 1869, m. Lucinda M. Layne; Willard b. Sept. 11, 1871, died; Jane Eliza b. Aug. 8, 1873, died; Mary Lula b. April 25, 1877, m. Robert Ibey; Simpson Melvin b. Oct. 22, 1879, m. Harriet Stotard; Wilford b. Oct. 1, 1882, m. Pearl Wright; Milton Howe b. May 25, 1885, m. Iretta France; Zina Alberta b. Dec. 17, 1887; Grace Myrtle b. Aug. 2, 1889; Charles Oliver b. July 9, 1891. Family resided Hyde Park and Logan, Utah, and Carbonton, Canada.
Married Celia Ann Hatch April 10, 1876, Salt Lake City (daughter of Lorenzo Hill Hatch and Catherine Kerren, resided at Franklin, Idaho, and Woodruff, Ariz., St. George, Lehi and Logan, Utah, pioneers 1850, David Evans company). She was born March 19, 1856, Lehi City, Utah. Their children: Catherine b. Nov. 10, 1876, m. Horton H.

Hammond Jan. 9, 1901; Derttie Aldura b. Sept. 24, 1880, m. John Dake July 14, 1901; Ethel b. Nov. 17, 1883, m. Alma John Balls June 7, 1905; Eva Savona b. Dec. 3, 1885.
Ordained a seventy 1871; missionary to New York City, Iowa, and Nebraska 1876-77; high priest; superintendent Sunday school; second counselor to Bishop Daines of Hyde Park, Utah; bishop of Cardston, Canada, 1888; counselor to President C. O. Card of Alberta stake 1895; ordained patriarch 1901. Mayor of Cardston two terms; postmaster of Cardston nine years. Farmer and stockraiser.

WOOLLEY, EDWIN DILWORTH (son of John Woolley, born Aug. 17, 1779, and Rachel Dilworth, born Aug. 10, 1782, both of Chester county, Pa.). He was born June 28, 1807, in Chester county, Pa. Came to Utah in 1848, Brigham Young company.
Married Mary Wickersham (daughter of Amos and Annie Wickersham), who was born Nov. 4, 1808, and came to Utah with husband. Their children: John W. b. Dec. 30, 1831; Franklin B.; Rachel Emma; Henrietta; Samuel W. b. April 2, 1840, m. Maria Angell; Edwin Dilworth b. April 30, 1845; Mary Louisa; Marsellus. Family home, Salt Lake City.
Married Louisa Chopin Gordon Feb. 6, 1846, Nauvoo, Ill., who was born Feb. 28, 1820, at Williamson, N. Y. Their only child was Edwin Gordon Woolley.
Married Ellen Wilding, who was born April 8, 1822, at Leon, Eng. Their children: Sarah; Joseph; Hyrum Smith; Edwin Thomas; Mary Ellen. Family home, Salt Lake City.
Married Ann Olpin. Their children: Henry Alberto; Amelia; Orson; Ruth; Olive; Fannie; George; Carlos.
Married Betsy Ann Jackman. One son: Ocelo.
Married Elizabeth Jackman.

WOOLLEY, SAMUEL WICKERSHAM (son of Edwin Dilworth Woolley and Mary Wickersham). Born April 2, 1840, at Nauvoo, Ill. Came to Utah in 1848 with Heber C. Kimball.
Married Maria Angell 1858 at Salt Lake City (daughter of Truman Angell and Polly Johnson of Nauvoo, pioneers July 24, 1847, Brigham Young company). She was born March 23, 1841, at Nauvoo. Their children: Samuel Edwin, m. Alice Rowberry; Eugene Freeman, m. Annie E. Clark; Leo Carlos, m. Annie M. Anderson; Horace Wickersham, m. Annie L. Bates; Rachel Emma; Walter Dee, d. child; Mary Louisa; Alice May; Nellie Vilate, m. Arthur G. Burrett; Sarah Viola; Franklin Edgar and Fanny Leone, died. Family resided Grantsville and Salt Lake City, Utah.
Married Rachel Cahoon, Salt Lake City (daughter of Andrew and Jenett Cahoon of Cottonwood, Murray, Utah). Their children: Jeanett Maria, m. John W. Taylor; Maggie Elizabeth, m. Leroy Anderson; Phebe Ann, m. J. W. Jeffs; Andrew Dilworth, m. Hattie Schoenfeldt. Family home Grantsville, Utah.
Married Polly Tolman, Salt Lake City (daughter of Benjamin Tolman of Brigham City, Box Elder Co., Utah). Their children: Alonzo Hewet; Lucy; Lenora. Family home Grantsville, Utah.
High priest; high councilor; patriarch; seventy; missionary to Ohio 1872-73. Selectman several years; justice of the peace. Minuteman and veteran Indian war; participated in Echo Canyon campaign. President Co-op. at Grantsville. Farmer and stockraiser. Died Jan. 28, 1908.

WOOLLEY, SAMUEL EDWIN (son of Samuel Wickersham Woolley and Maria Angell). Born Oct. 22, 1859, Salt Lake City.
Married Alice Rowberry May 6, 1885, Logan, Utah (daughter of John Rowberry and Harriet Frances Goliher of Grantsville, Utah). She was born Aug. 6, 1861. Their children: Ralph Edwin b. March 4, 1886; John Franklin b. March 3, 1888; Leone b. Jan. 19, 1890; Moroni Rowberry b. April 6, 1892; Ethel b. March 30, 1895; Joseph Rowberry b. Sept. 13, 1898, Hawaiian Islands; Samuel Ray b. Nov. 15, 1900, Sandwich Islands. Family home Grantsville, Utah.
In early boyhood he moved with his parents from Salt Lake City to Grantsville, Tooele county, where he grew up under the guidance and influence of his father, who instructed him in the duties and work of the ranch. He attended school a few months each year when he could be spared from his place in the saddle on his father's ranch. In his teens he was ordained a deacon and acted as one of the presidents of a quorum. Was appointed missionary to Sandwich Islands by President John Taylor and left three days later for his post, accompanied by his uncle, Henry A. Woolley, after being ordained an elder by Joseph F. Smith.
After three and one-half years in the Sandwich Islands he returned 1884 to Utah and was appointed home missionary of Tooele stake and became also a seventy and member of the 31st quorum at Grantsville. Later he was made alternate high councilor of the stake and was ordained a high priest by Heber J. Grant; presided over the Y. M. M. I. A. of Tooele stake. In 1890 was called by President Woodruff to a mission in the Iosepa colony and from there was called by President Joseph F. Smith to take charge of the Hawaiian mission. Taking his wife and four children with him, he sailed on Aug. 31, 1895, for the post, whence he returned in 1902 to bring home his wife, whose health was failing. Went back to his mission, where he went on with the work which he and his wife so earnestly commenced and where he succeeded in building up the church membership to over 8,500 souls.

WOOLLEY, HORACE WICKERSHAM (son of Samuel Wickersham, Woolley and Maria Angell). Born Dec. 9, 1864, Grantsville, Utah.
Married Annie Bates Dec. 26, 1889, Logan, Utah (daughter of Ormes Eaton Bates and Sarah Weir of Rush Valley, Tooele Co., Utah). She was born March 22, 1866. Their children: Horace Walter b. Nov. 4, 1890; Leah b. Feb. 19, 1893; Howard Bates b. Feb. 21, 1895; Iona b. April 6, 1897; Marguerett b. April 16, 1899; Samuel Bates b. Jan. 13, 1901; Erma b. Jan. 16, 1903; Muriel b. March 13, 1905; Maud b. May 13, 1908; Arthur Bates b. April 6, 1910. Family home Vernal, Utah.
Member 47th quorum seventies; missionary to Great Britain 1891-1893; high priest; ward teacher; superintendent Sunday schools; counselor to stake superintendent of the Mutuals; clerk of Uintah stake 1896-1902; member of the high council. Engrossing clerk of the legislature 1896. Farmer; stockraiser; sheepman. Settled at Grantsville; moved to Vernal 1896.

WOOLLEY, EDWIN DILWORTH (son of Edwin Dilworth Woolley and Mary Wickersham). Born April 30, 1845, Nauvoo, Ill.
Married Emma Bentley March 11, 1867, Salt Lake City (daughter of Richard Bentley and Elizabeth Price, pioneers 1852, Henry W. Miller company). Born May 11, 1847, at Kanesville, Iowa. Their children: Emma Lavinia b. Dec. 23, 1867, died; Mary Elizabeth b. Jan. 31, 1870; Edwin Dilworth b. Jan. 11, 1873, died; Olive Geneva b. June 22, 1874, died; Joseph Anthony b. June 24, 1876, m. Margret Holt July 12, 1904; Royal Bentley b. Sept. 3, 1878, m. Viola Barney April 24, 1903; Radel Henrietta b. Dec. 2, 1880, m. Julius S. Dailey May 2, 1912; Ruth b. Nov. 24, 1882, m. David D. Rust May 27, 1903; Ella b. Oct. 3, 1884, m. Israel H. Chamberlain Oct. 4, 1905; Grace b. May 2, 1887, m. Othello C. Bowman June 23, 1909.

WOOLLEY, EDWIN DILWORTH, JR. (son of Edwin Dilworth Woolley, Sr., and Mary Wickersham Woolley).
Married Florence Snow April 12, 1877, at St. George, Utah (daughter of Erastus Snow and Elizabeth Ashby), who was born June 16, 1856, Salt Lake City. Their children: Florence Evlyn b. Aug. 26, 1878, died; Erastus Dilworth b. Dec. 2, 1880, m. Alice Snow Sept. 9, 1903; Robert Elliot b. May 19, 1883, m. Perscinda Ballentyne Sept. 6, 1911; Elizabeth b. March 11, 1885, m. Albert R. Day Aug. 31, 1904; Le Grande b. April 3, 1887, m. Alida Snow Aug. 2, 1911; Arthur Snow b. May 12, 1889; Marion b. April 2, 1895; Pruda b. July 7, 1902. Family resided Salt Lake City and Kanab, Utah.
Justice of peace; sheriff of Washington county 1879. Served in Black Hawk war 1865. Constable of St. George. President of Kanab stake June 9, 1884, to Dec. 2, 1910.

WOOLLEY, JOSEPH ANTHONY (son of Edwin Dilworth Woolley and Emma Bentley). Born June 24, 1876, at St. George, Utah.
Married Margret Holt July 12, 1904, St. George, Utah (daughter of John Roskell Holt and Sophia Ashworth), who was born Feb. 22, 1881, at Manchester, Eng. Their children: Rachel b. March 18, 1906; Joseph Anthony, Jr., b. July 21, 1908; Anna b. May 26, 1912.

WOOLLEY, JOHN MILLS (son of John Woolley, born Aug. 19, 1779, and Rachel Dilworth, born Aug. 10, 1782, both of Chester county, Pa.). Born Nov. 20, 1822, at New Lynn, Pa. Came to Utah Sept. 26, 1847, George B. Wallace company.
Married Maria Lucy Dewey Jan. 9, 1846 (daughter of Ashbel Dewey, who died August, 1846, and Harriet Adams, pioneers Sept. 26, 1847, George B. Wallace company—married 1819). She was born Aug. 3, 1823. Their children: John Dewey b. Dec. 30, 1846, died; Ashbel Dewey b. June 1, 1850, m. Ida Ann Bird Dec. 12, 1878; Harriet Arabell b. March 27, 1853, m. Joseph E. Taylor Sept. 5, 1889; Frank Albert b. May 2, 1856, m. Eliza Kimball May 14, 1880; William Dewey b. Feb. 25, 1858; Vilate Annabell b. Aug. 21, 1860, d. Oct. 19, 1867; Marion Dewey b. June 28, 1862, d. Dec. 19, 1888. Family home, Salt Lake City.
Married Caroline Patience Harrar Jan. 25, 1857, Salt Lake City (daughter of John Harrar and Ann Law), who was born Feb. 20, 1832, Philadelphia, Pa. Their children: Lorenzo Harrar b. Jan. 12, 1858, d. Nov. 1859; Taylor Harrar b. March 29, 1860, m. Caroline Louise Ahlstrom May 19, 1881, who died Sept. 4, 1889, m. Florence Belle Garrard Jan. 23, 1891; Albaront Harrar b. April 2, 1862, at Salt Lake City, m. Josephine L. Groo Oct. 22, 1884; Laura Virginia b. Feb. 15, 1864, Salt Lake City, m. Theodore Tobiason Oct. 21, 1885.
Missionary; bishop's counselor; bishop. Built first house in 9th ward Salt Lake City. Sawmill owner and lumberman.

WOOLLEY, ALBARONI HARRAR (son of John Mills Woolley and Caroline Patience Harrar). Born April 2, 1862, Salt Lake City.
Married Josephine L. Groo Oct. 22, 1884, Logan, Utah (daughter of Isaac Groo and Eliza Lyons), who was born Feb. 3, 1865, Salt Lake City. Family home 9th ward, Salt Lake City.
First counselor to Bishop Jabez W. West 9th ward, Salt Lake City, 1899-1909; bishop of 9th ward since 1909; missionary to New York and Pennsylvania 1888-89. Manager and buyer grocery department Z. C. M. I.

WOOLSEY, HYRUM (son of Hyrum Woolsey and Rachel Mitchell of Missouri). Born February, 1826. Came to Utah July 24, 1847, Brigham Young company.
Married Lucinda Jameson in 1846 at Council Bluffs, Iowa (daughter of Charles Jameson and Mary Shadrick of Scotland and Pennsylvania, pioneers 1847). She was born June 16, ——. Their children: Eliza Jane, m. Edward McLatchie; Mary Ann, m. Johnson McGinnis; Amanda, m. Isaac Thomas; Joseph; Agnes, died; Margarette Evelyn, m. John Hemmelwright, m. John Newberry, m. Jehu Blackburn; Glades Elwilda. m. George Kelley, m. Thomas Allen; William Franklin, m. Maggie Baum; Rosabell, m. William Johnson. Family home Harmony, Utah.
Elder. Took part in Echo Canyon trouble. Indian war veteran. Farmer. Died in 1886 at Beaver Bottoms, Beaver Co., Utah.

WOOLSTENHULME, JAMES (son of John Woolstenhulme, born March 24, 1814, and Alice Mellor, born April 27, 1815, both of Oldham, Lancastershire, Eng.). He was born March 24, 1837, at Oldham. Came to Utah Nov. 11, 1852, Philip De La Mar's sugar company.
Married Mary Love Page April 23, 1858 (daughter of William Page, who died at Council Bluffs, Iowa, Feb. 21, 1851, and Hephzibah Whitney Pierce—married June 27, 1837, Hancock, Hillsboro county, N. H.). She was born Nov. 1, 1840, and came to Utah Oct. 11, 1852, Captain Hicks company. Their children: Elva Eudora b. Jan. 3, 1859, m. Richard Franklin Lambert April 14, 1889; Laura Amelia b. July 1, 1870, m. Daniel Lewis July 6, 1892; Reuben Allen b. March 5, 1872, m. Sarah Ellen Sorensen Oct. 15, 1903; Charlott Elizabeth b. Aug. 18, 1874, died; Ellen Mellor b. Nov. 5, 1876, m. William J. Ure; Hephzibah Alice b. Oct. 11, 1879, m. John G. Turnbow Nov. 9, 1904. Family home Marion, Summit Co., Utah.
Married Julia Mary Ann Duhamel Feb. 15, 1863, Bountiful, Utah (daughter of John Duhamel, who died in 1851 on Isle of Jersey, and Mary L. Greeley, pioneer 1854, Captain Taylor company). She was born Jan. 15, 1844, Isle of Jersey. Their children: James Albert b. Nov. 24, 1863. m. Mary Jane Evans Sept. 11, 1893; Valina Olympia b. Aug. 24, 1865, m. John Larsen Dec. 27, 1888; William Edward b. Sept. 22, 1867, d. infant; Mary Alice b. June 30, 1868, m. George F. Simpson June 30, 1889; Martha E. b. May 23, 1870, m. Marion L. Corbett Jan. 15, 1890; John b. Sept. 21, 1871, d. infant; Joseph b. Nov. 30, 1872, d. aged 4 years; Thomas Ephraim b. July 10, 1876, m. Thyrza Pack Dec. 25, 1909; Hannah Amelia b. Jan. 14, 1879, m. John A. Lewis March 14, 1900; John Hardman b. Oct. 21, 1881, m. Jennett Lynn Pack May 23, 1911; Royal Walter b. April 6, 1885, m. Hazel Leonard Dec. 18, 1907. Family home Marion, Utah.
High priest; president 22d quorum seventies; missionary to Great Britain. Justice of peace; county commissioner Summit county. Joined church April 13, 1851, on board ship Olympus, en route to America. Settled at Bountiful, Utah; moved to Provo, 1858; returned to Bountiful, 1860; to Kamas 1863, where he took an active part in building up the community. Has had two golden weddings and is said to have the only polygamous family in Summit county.

WOOLSTENHULME, JAMES ALBERT (son of James Woolstenhulme and Julia Mary Ann Duhamel). Born Nov. 24, 1863, Bountiful, Utah.
Married Mary Jane Evans Sept. 11, 1893, Kamas, Utah (daughter of Joseph Evans), who was born Sept. 27, 1873, at Ramsbottom, Eng. Their children: Cecil Lillian b. June 5, 1896, d. June 16, 1896; Cereal James b. Nov. 25, 1898; Ada b. Oct. 11, 1900; Joseph b. March 5, 1902; Julia Violet b. March 5, 1913, d. March 21, 1913. Family home Marion, Utah.
Member seventies; missionary to central states; president 22d quorum seventies; high councilor Summit stake; now first counselor to bishop in Marion ward.

WOOTTON, JOHN (son of John Wootton of Staffordshire, Eng.). Born May 15, 1842, at Staffordshire, Eng. Came to Utah Oct. 28, 1849, Ezra T. Benson company.
Married Sarah Amelia Britton Oct. 30, 1868, Salt Lake City (daughter of Richard Britton and Elizabeth Lee of Oxfordshire, Eng., pioneers 1851, William Howell company). She was born April 4, 1844. Their children: John b. Dec. 5, 1865, m. Ada Dilworth; Joseph Attewall b. Oct. 1, 1874, m. Nellie King; Sarah b. Aug. 29, 1878. m. Willis M. Bromley; Clara Ann b. Jan. 23, 1884; Gilbert Lesley b. March 27, 1887, m. Mary Elizabeth Hansen. Family home American Fork, Utah.
High priest. Marshal. Farmer.

WORDSWORTH, WILLIAM (son of Catherine Morgan). Came to Utah July 24, 1847, Brigham Young company.
Married Nancy Ann Vance (daughter of John Vance, Salt Lake City, pioneer 1847—mother of Hannah, born at Winter Quarters by a previous marriage). Their children: Eliza Jane b. 1850, m. Moroni Fuller; John b. 1852, m. Sarah Warren; Mary Elizabeth, m. George James.

WORKMAN, JACOB LINDSAY (son of John A. Workman and —— Bellew, said to be a sister of former President James A. Garfield's mother, both of Overton county, Tenn., later of Nauvoo, Ill.). He came to Utah in 1847, Brigham Young company.
Married Nancy Reader in Tennessee in 1832. She died at Mt. Pisgah, Iowa, on the way to Utah. Their children: Thomas James, m. Lucy ——; William; Jacob Reader b. Aug. 19, 1836, m. Maria Amity Johnstun; Samuel; Alma, m. Adelia Delilah Pierce; Hyrum, m. Marinda Merrill; Josephine, m. Dee Oviatt.
Helped build Nauvoo, St. George and Salt Lake City temples. Died 1882, Virgin City, Utah.

WORKMAN, JACOB READER (son of Jacob Lindsay Workman and Nancy Reader). Born in Overton county, Tenn., Aug. 19, 1836. Came to Utah in 1848, Lorenzo Snow company.
Married Maria Amity Johnstun Dec. 9, 1864, at Snyderville, Utah (daughter of Jessie Walker Johnstun and Betsy Ann Snyder of Snyderville). She was born Jan. 12, 1849, St. Joseph, Mo. Their children: Jacob Jesse b. Sept. 21, 1865, d. infant; Don Alma b. May 18, 1867, m. Catherine Odekirk; William James b. June 25, 1869, m. Emma Alpblanalp; Dee Albert b. June 28, 1871, m. Elizabeth Cook; Lois Ann b. Sept. 25, 1873, m. Solomon P. Trim; Samuel b. Oct. 3, 1875, d. infant; Gilbert Van b. Nov. 19, 1876; Jared Roundy b. March 24, 1879, d. boyhood; Josephine b. July 15, 1881, m. William Andrews; Joseph Nimrod b. Dec. 4, 1883, m. Elvira Beddo; Amy Rosetta b. March 10, 1886, m. Orin Griffin; Vernal Ambrose b. May 8, 1888, m. Estella Gurr; Oltha b. Feb. 13, 1893, d. infant.
Sunday school and ward teacher; president Y. M. M. I. A. Assisted in building Ben Holladay stage road. Helped build wall that was to surround Salt Lake City. Met Johnston's army under Ephraim Hanks and Lot Smith and took active part in Echo Canyon trouble in the various dangerous raids and stampedes. Brought first sawmill into Ashley valley and built first shingle-roofed house, first dance hall, erected first flagpole and fired first salute on 4th and 24th of July, at that place.

WORKMAN, JOHN A. (son of John A. Workman and Adelia D. Pierce). Born May 27, 1860. Came to Utah in 1862.
Married Susan Catherine Barben at Snyderville, Utah (parents lived in Germany). Their children: John Alma b. Nov. 4, 1887, m. Laura America McKee Oct. 1, 1908; Joseph William; Jacob Franklin; Susan Lillie; Edgar Ray; Florence Adelia, d. infant; Barben; Reuben; Eugene; Jessie. Family home Vernal, Utah.
Seventy; missionary to Texas 1898-90; bishop and teacher Glines ward; chorister. Farmer. Now resides Alberta, Canada.

WORKMAN, JOHN ALMA (son of John A. Workman and Susan Catherine Barben). Born Nov. 4, 1887, Vernal, Utah.
Married Laura America McKee Oct. 1, 1908, Salt Lake City (daughter of Joseph McKee and Laura Orser of Jensen, Utah). She was born Dec. 10, 1888. Their children: Joseph Alma b. Jan. 24, 1910; Laura b. June 4, 1911. Family home Vernal, Utah.
Elder; counselor in Y. M. M. I. A. Farmer.

WORKS, JAMES MARKS (son of Asa Works and Abigail Marks of Bennington, Vt.). Born Oct. 5, 1821, Aurelius, Cayuga Co., N. Y. Came to Utah in 1847.
Married Phoebe Jones April 15, 1858, at Salt Lake City (daughter of John and Mary Jones), who was born Nov. 14, 1825, and came to Utah with Captain Jones company. Their children: James Marks, Jr., b. April 6, 1859, d. Jan. 1, 1888; Edwin Mosiah b. Dec. 28, 1861, m. Margret Maria Munk, m. Hannah Cordelia Munk, m. Matilda Lindberg; Mary A. A., m. Nels Benson. Family home Manti, Utah.
Missionary to Great Britain 1860-64; high priest; patriarch.

WORLTON, JAMES TIMBRIL (son of John Worlton and Mary Parsons of London, Eng.). Born March 20, 1821, Walcot, Bath, Eng. Came to Utah in September, 1855, Richard Ballantyne company.
Married Elizabeth Bourne Dec. 3, 1848, London, Eng. (daughter of James Bourne and Sarah Clare of Bath, Eng.). She was born Dec. 18, 1827. Their children: Martha b. Sept. 14, 1849, m. Martin Bushman; Flora b. May 9, 1851, m. Elisha P. Hardy; Emily b. April 13, 1853, m. John Oboin; James C. b. April 26, 1855. Family home Lehi, Utah.
Presided over branch at Marshfield, Eng., in 1849; superintendent of Sunday school Morgan, Utah, about 8 years immediately preceding his death. Died Feb. 6, 1885.

WORTHEN, SAMUEL (son of Richard Worthen and Mary Worthen of England). Born Dec. 21, 1825, at Northwich, Chestershire, Eng.
Married Sarah Hallam. Their children: Joseph S., m. Mary Heaps; William H., m. Nancy E. Keele; Sarah Jane, died; Samuel, Jr., m. Sarah Jane Craigen; Mary Ann, m. John Sullivan; Charles R., m. Mary Ann Sullivan; Esther Louisa, m. Samuel Miles; George W., m. Leonora Woodbury; Hyrum, died; Alice M., m. Alexander Milne. Family home St. George, Utah.

Married Maria L. Grow April 27, 1856, at Salt Lake City (daughter of Henry and Mary Grow of Pennsylvania). She was born Sept. 10, 1838. Their children: James A., m. Mary Ann Lee; Robert R., m. Julia A. Montague; Eliza, m. Samuel Judd; Almina, m. John F. Chideater; Mary E., died; Henry Grow, m. Laura Cameron; Sarah Louisa, m. John Henrie; Maria, m. Ernest Hancock. Family home Panguitch, Utah.
Married Jane Osborn Feb. 4, 1865, at Salt Lake City (daughter of Elizabeth Osborn of England). Their children: John Franklin, m. Rosella Montague; Frederick, m. Minerva Reynolds; Osborn, died; Elizabeth S.; Ruth, died; Rhoda, m. John Lee; Millie J., m. Brandon Shakespeare. Family home, Panguitch, Utah.
Veteran Echo Canyon campaign. Stone and brickmason; farmer. Died Feb. 2, 1888, Panguitch, Utah.

WORTHEN, WILLIAM H. (son of Samuel Worthen and Sarah Hallam). Born Dec. 24, 1847, St. Louis, Mo. Came to Utah in 1850.
Married Nancy E. Keele Dec. 25, 1868, New Harmony, Utah (daughter of Thomas Keele and Mary A. Jolly, pioneers 1852, oxteam company). She was born Jan. 15, 1853. Their children: Sarah b. Dec. 21, 1869, m. Wyatt Bryan; Mary L. b. Sept. 9, 1871, d. aged 3; Susan E. b. May 12, 1873, m. Joseph Nelson; William S. b. Feb. 17, 1875, m. Magdalene Westenskow; Frances Britanna b. Dec. 8, 1876, m. Charles Alldridge; Nancy Viola b. Nov. 25, 1878, m. Edward Olsen; Laura A. b. Sept. 25, 1880, m. Fred Olsen; Joseph R. b. Sept. 8, 1882, m. Minnie Petersen; Alice b. July 2, 1884, m. Hyrum Bernsen; Maud b. May 18, 1886, m. Thomas Thompson; Thomas b. March 17, 1888; Rhoda b. Feb. 17, 1890, m. Ervin Olsen; Kata b. Aug. 1, 1894.
High priest; Sunday school superintendent; president Y. M. M. I. A. 12 years; Sunday school teacher 30 years; president elders quorum six years. Veteran Indian war. Justice of peace 8 years; president town board; treasurer town board 6 years; school trustee 9 years.

WRIDE, EVAN (son of Thomas Wride and Ann James of Monachdy Farm, near Cardiff, Wales). Born Feb. 17, 1843, at Llantrissant. Bach. Wales. Came to Utah Sept. 2, 1868, William B. Preston company.
Married Martha Ann Jones June 29, 1868, at Llantrissant Church, Llantrissant, Wales (daughter of Benjamin Jones and Margarette Davies of Cardiff, Wales). She was born Dec. 31, 1839. Their children: Thomas William, m. Rosetta Peay; Evan David, John Henry and Margarette Jane, three died; Mary, m. Edwin Ankerw; Benjamin, m. Sarah Jepperson; Angus, m. Harriet Clinger.
Married Phoebe Truelove Ward Feb. 16, 1887, Logan, Utah (daughter of Thomas Ward and Mary Monk of Provo, Utah, who came to Utah in October, 1890). She was born Sept. 1, 1860. Their children: James Alfred, died; Ernest, m. Sylvia Shepard; Martha Elizabeth, m. Henry Peter Anderson; Fern; Barrington; Elwyn; Evan, died; Ann; Sarah. Families resided Provo, Utah.
Member 34th quorum seventies; missionary to Wales 1879-80; superintendent Sunday school; first counselor to Bishop Loveless; high councilor Provo stake; upon the death of Loveless was made bishop of the ward; special missionary in Springville three months.

WRIGHT, ABRAHAM REISTER (son of William E. Wright and Mary Kite of Philadelphia, Pa.). Born Aug. 18, 1811, Philadelphia. Came to Utah Nov. 2, 1856, Smoot and Eldredge company.
Married Mary Ann Brockerman Nov. 14, 1833, Philadelphia, Pa. (daughter of William Brockerman and Catherine Rudy of Philadelphia). She was born March 18, 1816. Their children: William, m. Emma Yearsley; Amanda M., m. Charles H. Bassett; Hannah A., m. David Candland; Abraham Reister, Jr., m. Lucy Wardrop; John R., m. Susan Bethel; Isaac K., m. Henriette Wall; Charles H., m. Annie Galloway; George W., m. June Welch. Family home, Salt Lake City.
Member 30th quorum seventies; president of seventies 13th quorum; missionary to Pennsylvania; ward clerk; block teacher. Freighter; photographer; merchant. Died July 1, 1889.

WRIGHT, ABRAHAM REISTER, JR. (son of Abraham Reister Wright and Mary Ann Brockerman). Born July 10, 1842, Philadelphia, Pa. Came to Utah with father.
Married Lucy Wardrop June 7, 1862, at Salt Lake City (daughter of John Wardrop and Lucy MacIntosh of Nauvoo, Ill., pioneers Sept. 10, 1852, Bryant Jolley company). She was born Dec. 10, 1843. Their children: John R. b. March 24, 1863, d. aged 17; Charles H. b. Feb. 6, 1865, m. Alice V. Phillips; James W. b. April 13, 1867, m. Jennette Gibson; Joseph b. Aug. 9, 1869, d. aged 11; Edwin b. Aug. 7, 1871, m. Katie A. Pettitt; Lucy M. b. Sept. 25, 1873; Alma B. b. Nov. 22, 1875, m. Alice M. Hooper; William W. b. Oct. 13, 1877, d. infant; Samuel D. b. April 3, 1879, d. aged 19; Mary A. b. Sept. 30, 1881, m. James S. Noall; Thomas b. Sept. 13, 1883, d. infant; Clarence A. b. Aug. 21, 1886, m. Rachel L. Terry. Family home, Salt Lake City.
Missionary to eastern states 1893-94; president 30th and 13th quorums seventies; high priest; block teacher. Member Nauvoo Legion. Member volunteer fire department 10
80

years. Assistant architect on Salt Lake temple 3 years. Builder and contractor.

WRIGHT, JONATHAN C. (son of Peter Wright and Elizabeth Shead of Rome, Oneida Co., N. Y.). Born Nov. 29, 1808, Rome. Came to Utah Oct. 13, 1850, Edward Hunter company.
Married Cynthia Martin (Nicholls) Dec. 23, 1850, Salt Lake City (daughter of James Martin and Miss Mosher of Oswego county, N. Y.). She was born in 1818. Their children: Willard, killed by Indians, aged 16; Cynthia, m. Amasa M. Lyman, Jr.; Henry Nicholls (son by first marriage). Family home Brigham City, Utah.
Missionary to eastern states 1842; first counselor to Lorenzo Snow; president Box Elder stake. Probate judge; county clerk; county recorder; prosecuting attorney; member territorial legislature 21 years. Farmer. Died Nov. 8, 1880.

WRIGHT, JOSEPH (son of John Wright and Grace Shephard of Bubwith, Yorkshire, Eng.). Born Dec. 25, 1817, Bubwith. Came to Utah Sept. 23, 1849, Orson Spencer company.
Married Mary Ann Fryer of Lincolnshire, Eng., Jan. 4, 1857, Salt Lake City (daughter of William Fryer and Ann Colton). Their children: John M. b. Jan. 21, 1861, m. Emma Hinton June 16, 1885; Anna M. b. March 8, 1863; Hyrum F. b. Oct. 27, 1865, m. Elizabeth S. Pratt Dec. 28, 1887; George W. b. Feb. 23, 1867, m. Laura J. Morris Jan. 23, 1889; Zina F. b. Oct. 9, 1869, m. Daniel A. Morris Dec. 20, 1893; Edwin F. b. March 26, 1872, m. Cora C. Peterson Nov. 7, 1894. Family home Duncan, Utah.
Member 22d quorum seventies.

WRIGHT, JOHN M. (son of Joseph Wright and Mary Ann Fryer). Born Jan. 21, 1861, Mill Creek, Utah.
Married Emma Hinton June 16, 1885, St. George, Utah (daughter of John N. Hinton and Emma Spendlove), who was born at Virgin City, Utah, May 27, 1868. Their children: Wallace Hinton b. April 24, 1886; Joseph Moroni b. Nov. 27, 1887; Mary Ann b. April 14, 1889; John William b. Dec. 25, 1890; Spencer Hinton b. Dec. 7, 1892; Genevieve b. July 4, 1894; Zina b. Feb. 20, 1896; Mina b. Feb. 26, 1898; Ianthus b. Aug. 2, 1899; Bernard B. b. Oct. 21, 1901, m. infant; Vernell b. June 12, 1906; Chester E. b. Oct. 29, 1906; Lawrence Leone b. Feb. 22, 1909; Glade Mervin b. Oct. 15, 1911.
One of seven presidents of 21st quorum of seventies. Farmer and stockraiser.

WRIGHT, JOSIAH ATWELL (son of Martin Wright and Dolly Benjamin). Born Aug. 10, 1805, Trenton, Middlesex county, Conn. Came to Utah in September, 1852, Joseph Outhouse company.
Married Susan Buell April 6, 1830, Westbrook, Conn. (daughter of Oliver Buell and Polly Wilcox of Westbrook). She was born March 29, 1810. Their children: Albert Atwell; Wilson Andrew, m. Aurelia Stoddard; Henry Alexandria; Susan Eliza; Gilbert Josiah, m. Annie S. Odell; Adeline Amanda, m. Chauncy W. West; Susan A., m. Frank Brown, m. Joseph Parry; Hyrum Smith b. Nov. 10, 1849, m. Jeanette Kay, m. Mary Ann Fidler; Juliette. Family home Clayton, Utah.
High priest; ward teacher. Taught school in Kaysville ward. Moved to Ogden 1855. Farmer. Died Aug. 4, 1896.

WRIGHT, GILBERT JOSIAH (son of Josiah Atwell Wright and Susan Buell). Born May 14, 1838, Horse Hill, Conn. Came to Utah with father.
Married Annie S. Odell Jan. 1, 1866, Ogden, Utah (daughter of Thomas George Odell and Ann Newman of London, Eng., pioneers Sept. 13, 1861, Homer Duncan company). She was born March 27, 1847. Their children: Gilbert George b. Sept. 28, 1866, m. Matilda E. Baily; Annie Isabelle b. Nov. 27, 1870; Eugene b. Aug. 5, 1872, m. Caroline E. Smith; Lester Thomas b. Jan. 10, 1875, m. Edith Wallace; Adeline b. Nov. 2, 1878, m. Cleney St. Clair; Geneva Odell b. Nov. 4, 1888, m. Orson Arnold Snow. Family home Ogden, Utah.
Member 60th quorum seventies; ward teacher; assistant Sunday school superintendent. Member Ogden school board. Assisted in publishing first edition of first daily newspaper in Ogden. Called to Salmon River to assist in protecting the settlers against Indians; major on staff of Chauncy W. West in Utah militia. Worked on Southern Pacific railroad with his teams and was present at the uniting of the Union Pacific and Central Pacific. Early settler in Snake River valley, Idaho. Merchant. Died March 25, 1908, at Idaho Falls.

WRIGHT, HYRUM SMITH (son of Josiah Atwell Wright and Susan Buell). Born Nov. 10, 1849, Clinton, Conn. Came to Utah with father.
Married Jeanette Kay.
Married Mary Ann Fidler Dec. 28, 1882, Ogden, Utah (daughter of Samuel Fidler and Ann White of Arnold, Nottinghamshire, Eng.). She was born Aug. 5, 1862. Their children: Wallace Albert b. Oct. 7, 1883, died; Annette

1266　　PIONEERS AND PROMINENT MEN OF UTAH

Monvilla b. Jan. 7, 1885, m. E. J. Bradshaw; Edna Buell b. June 21, 1887, m. Nelson Wright; Harriet Casette b. Oct. 30, 1889, m. C. Q. Wilson; John Birguet b. March 30, 1891, m. Jessie Andrews; Lizzie Marie b. Oct. 25, 1893; Walmer Atwell b. Dec. 5, 1895; Aldemar Arnold b. Sept. 14, 1898, died; Mary Finis b. Jan. 5, 1901; Robert Linton b. March 8, 1903. Family home Ogden, Utah.
Member 76th quorum seventies. Musician. Railway employee.

WRIGHT, THOMAS D. (son of Andrew Wright and Sarah Ann Brett of Manchester, Eng.). Born Oct. 24, 1851. Came to Utah Nov. 30, 1856, Martin and Tyler handcart company.
Married Mary Jane Clough April 6, 1871, Nephi, Utah (daughter of Samuel Clough and Martha Carter), who was born Oct. 17, 1839, and came to Utah August, 1871. Their children: Sarah E., m. James Prince; Thomas C.; Rosebelle, m. Christian Petersen; Lillie M., m. Clarence Moler.
Member 138th quorum seventies; block teacher. Librarian at Cedar City, Utah. Expressman.

WRIGHT, WILLIAM (son of William Wright and Margaret Ashbridge of Cumberland, Eng.). Born Oct. 5, 1832, Cumberland. Came to Utah in 1852.
Married Jemima Dands April 8, 1856, Salt Lake City (daughter of Thomas Dands and Mary Hinds of Cumberland, Eng., latter pioneer 1856). She was born March 10, 1833. Their children: William T., m. Ellen Charlotte Murdock; Jemima A., m. A. L. Penrod; Margaret, m. Joseph R. Murdock; Wilford D., m. Sarah A. Ritchie; James L., m. Nellie Nuttall (died), m. Maggie Wilson; Joseph S., m. Jane Ritchie; Hannah R., m. A. L. Penrod; Sarah E., m. John M. Ritchie; Hyrum S., d. infant.
Married Mary Jane Baum Oct. 31, 1871, at Salt Lake City. Their children: George Baum, m. Phoebe Ritchie; Eliza Jane, m. Lauritz Jacobson; Mary Isabel, m. Elmer Penrod; Owen Uria, m. Matilda Casper; Wallace, m. Clara Bills; John Elmer, m. Phoebe Casper; Charles, m. Julia Mecham; Stella Mellisa, m. John Mason; Elbart, died; May Pearl, m. Don Ivie; David Nephi, died; Zora, m. Gordon Bills; Zella; Edna, died; Leora; Leoran Atkinson.
Missionary to Great Britain 1883-84; high priest; ward clerk. Justice of peace; school trustee. Tollgate keeper. Farmer. Died Nov. 11, 1903, Charleston, Utah.

WRIGHT, WILLIAM (son of Benjamin Wright and Frances Seward). Born Jan. 30, 1800, Suffolk, Eng. Came to Utah October, 1862, Captain Miller company.
Married Charlotte Rouse April 6, 1832, Pointon, Lincolnshire, Eng. (daughter of John Rouse and Elizabeth Gibson of Sutterton, Lincolnshire, Eng.). She was born Dec. 25, 1812. Their children: William b. Jan. 24, 1833, m. Mary Roberts May 12, 1857; Samuel b. March 12, 1835, m. Elizabeth Hodget; Mary Ann b. Sept. 17, 1838, m. John Webster July 15, 1858; Sarah Jane b. Feb. 22, 1840, m. Charles M. Plant; John G. b. Oct. 11, 1842, m. Ruth Mitchell; m. Aditha Harrison; Benjamin b. Sept. 12, 1844, m. Eliza Darton; m. Mahala Darton; m. Bessie Nichols; Charles R. b. Feb. 9, 1847, m. Margaret Mackay; Frances E. b. March 16, 1851, m. William Harker. Family home Taylorsville, Utah.

WRIGHT, WILLIAM H. (son of William S. Wright and Esther Camm of Birmingham, Eng.). Born March 11, 1827, Birmingham. Came to Utah Aug. 18, 1859, James S. Brown company.
Married Emma Taylor Sept. 9, 1846, Birmingham, Eng (daughter of Thomas Taylor and Jane Clark of Birmingham), who was born June 15, 1829. Their children: Julia Ann, m. Thomas Petty; William H., Jr.; Jane Taylor, m. Luke Crawshaw; Angus Taylor, m. Martha Middleton; Parley Taylor, m. Anna M. Halgren; Brigham Taylor; Charles E., m. Clara Scoville; Joseph E., m. Kathryne Lyon; William C., m. Edith Dinwoody; Frank L., m. Martha Brown; Florence E., m. A. J. Brown, m. H. W. Dunn. Family home Ogden, Utah.
High priest; missionary to England 1882-84; Sunday school superintendent. City councilman. Merchant. Died Dec. 29, 1897.

WRIGHT, PARLEY TAYLOR (son of William H. Wright and Emma Taylor). Born Sept. 29, 1861, Richmond, Utah.
Married Anna M. Halgren March 9, 1887, Logan, Utah (daughter of T. A. Halgren and Clara Bjuling of Stockholm, Sweden, pioneers 1864, Isaac Canfield company). She was born in March, 1868. Their children: Lillian Magdaline b. Oct. 7, 1892; Ellen Clara b. Sept. 25, 1894; Marion Ottilia b. Aug. 9, 1898; Annie Lucile b. May 20, 1901; Pauline Theresa b. Aug. 11, 1904. Family home Ogden, Utah.
Member 77th quorum seventies; missionary to California 1885-87; high priest; member Weber stake mutual board; member bishopric. Merchant.

WRIGLEY, JOSEPH (son of Thomas Wrigley and Grace Mary Wilkinson of Manchester, Eng.). Born Feb. 24, 1841, Manchester. Came to Utah in 1850, St. Louis company.
Married Ada Steele (daughter of Edward Steele). Their child: Edward.
Married Ann Singleton Nov. 1, 1869,. Salt Lake City (daughter of John Singleton and Catherine Creer of Manchester, Eng., pioneers 1848). She was born Aug. 18, 1853. Their children: Mary Ellen b. Jan. 16, 1871, m. Jexreel Fugate; Thomas, died; Clara, m. Joseph S. Stevens.

Jr.; Cornelia, m. James F. Olsen; Joseph Alma; Wellington; Catherine P., m. Lars Peter Thompson; Lacoran, m. Orlando W. Werham; Osborn;· Llewellen. Family home Ferron, Utah.
Married Dinah Stoddard (Crookston) in 1880 (daughter of Robert Stoddard and Margarette McCelvin of Carlisle, Cumberlandshire, Eng., latter pioneer 1856, first handcart company). She was born March 16, 1850. Their children: Marion, James Owen, Mary Grace and Stephen Roy, first four died; Marintha b. Aug. 2, 1887, m. George Angus; Blanche b. Oct. 2, 1891, m. Reuben Jesse Jacobs.
High priest; Sunday school teacher. Settled at Ferron 1878. Assisted in bringing immigrants to Utah. Died May 5, 1911.

Y·

YANCEY, HYRUM.
Married Harriett Wood (daughter of Daniel Wood and Mary Snyder, former a pioneer July 24. 1847, Brigham Young company). Their children: John H. b. March 25, 1856; Parley P. b. Nov. 5, 1857, d. infant; Adam b. April 6, 1859, m. Alice Tolman Oct. 2, 1879.

YANCEY, ADAM (son of Hyrum Yancey and Harriett Wood). Born April 6, 1859, Bountiful, Utah.
Married Alice Tolman Oct. 2, 1879, Salt Lake Endowment House (daughter of Judson Adoniram Tolman and Sarah Lucretia Holbrook), who was born Aug. 29, 1863, Bountiful, Utah. Their children: Adam Adoniram b. Aug. 9, 1880, d. Sept. 2, 1892; Orville b. Sept. 12, 1882, m. Mary Keeler; James Henry b. July 24, 1884, m. Effie Cobbley; Emron b. July 25, 1886, m. Dorthy Dean; Bertha Lucretia b. Aug. 21, 1888, m. Joseph F. Jensen; Cyrus b. Dec. 3, 1890; Allice b. Oct. 8, 1892; Daniel b. Feb. 24, 1895; Sylvia May b. May 1, 1897; Mary b. Sept. 3, 1898, d. Sept. 24, 1898; Nathan Orlie b. July 23, 1900; Sarah Luella b. Jan. 2, 1903; William b. Feb. 24, 1909.

YARDLEY, JOHN. Born July 24, 1817, Staffordshire, Eng.
Married Mary Shean. Their children: John b. June 1852; Sarah b. Dec. 3, 1854, m. Thomas Cartwright March 20, 1873; William Edward b. Nov. 8, 1859, m. Janet Levi April 1, 1885, m. Jane E. Gower; James Heber b. Jan. 21, 1862, m. Harriet J. Anderson Dec. 22, 1886; Daniel Alfred b. Dec. 6, 1865, m. Emma Jane Robinson. Family home Beaver, Utah.
Died Oct. 10, 1885.

YARDLEY, WILLIAM EDWARD (son of John Yardley and Mary Shean). Born Nov. 8, 1859, Beaver, Utah.
Married Janet Levi April 1, 1885, St. George, Utah (daughter of David Levi and Ann Gillespie of Beaver, Utah). She died Jan. 14, 1888. Their children: William Ray b. Jan. 18, 1886, d. Oct. 29, 1905; Janet Levi b. Jan. 5, 1888, m. George Thomas Price Nov. 8, 1906. Family home, Beaver.
Married Jane Elizabeth Gower Nov. 12, 1889 (daughter of Thomas Gower and Martha Ann Stockdale, pioneers in October, 1854, Joseph Field company, and widow of James M. Hamilton). She was born May 12, 1858. Their children: Sarah Inez b. Sept. 10, 1890; Mary Violet b. Dec. 25, 1892; Gladys b. Sept. 10, 1894; Grace b. Sept. 10, 1894. Family home Beaver, Utah.
Has attained the ordination of elder.

YATES, JOHN. Born in 1802 in Warwickshire, Eng. Came to Utah in 1852, John Tidwell company.
Married Lucy Holick, who was born in 1805 and died in June, 1850, at Council Bluffs, Iowa. Their children: Henry b. March 4, 1827, m. Ann —— ; William b. 1830; John b. 1833; Ann b. 1836, m. John Clark 1853; Harriet b. 1838, m. Andrew Quigley 1856; Thomas b. May 17, 1840, m. Jane Baty March 1866; Joseph b. March 16, 1845, m. Elizabeth Wilson Baty Nov. 17, 1873. Family home Farmington, Utah.
High priest.

YATES, JOSEPH (son of John Yates and Lucy Holick). Born March 16, 1845, at Warwick, Eng.
Married Elizabeth Wilson Baty Nov. 17, 1873, Salt Lake City (daughter of Thomas and Ann Baty, pioneers in 1861, Sextus Johnson company). She was born Nov. 23, 1852, in Shropshire, Eng. Their children: William b. Oct. 26, 1875, died; Esther Annie b. April 2, 1877, m. Orson J. Olsen; Thomas John b. Oct. 3, 1879, died; Henry b. June 8, 1881, m. Effie Moss 1903; Jane Wilson b. May 21, 1883, m. Norman Hanson 1902; Lucy b. June 14, 1886, m. Joseph A. Orme, 1906; Katherine b. March 19, 1888, Harriet b. June 12, 1889, Joseph b. March 20, 1891, and Willard Dobson b. Feb. 5, 1893, last four died. Lived at Calls Fort, Box Elder county.
High priest; missionary to England 1883; went across plains for company of immigrants in 1862. Justice of peace; school trustee.

YATES, HENRY (son of Joseph Yates and Elizabeth Wilson Baty). Born at Calls Fort, Utah.
Married Effie Moss Oct. 8, 1903, Salt Lake City (daughter of Nephi Moss and Rhoda Pace), who was born Dec. 13, 1886, at Chesterfield, Idaho. Their children: Joseph b. June 19, 1904; Effie La Von b. July 27, 1905; Elsie Elizabeth Nov. 20, 1906; Willard b. March 30, 1908; La Rue b. Aug. 4, 1909; Wynn Del b. March 20, 1912.
Elder; Sunday school teacher.

YATES, WILLIAM (son of Thomas Yates and Violet Owen of Wortley, Lancastershire, Eng.). Born Oct. 31, 1832, Wortley, Eng. Came to Utah in 1863.
Married Mary Partington 1860, Upholand, Lancastershire, Eng. (daughter of Thomas Partington and Marguerite Otten of England, pioneers 1863). She was born Sept. 18, 1840. Their children: Marguerite, m. William C. Bouck; Mary E., m. Henry Player, m. John Kirkwood, m. Clarence Mentor; Martha A., m. Samuel Lufkin, m. Clarence Hendershot; William T., m. Mary Evans; John O., m. Lucile Zimmermann; Amanda, m. Albert Kirkwood; Stephen E., m. Sabina Chidester; Bertha A., m. Walter C. Brown; Hattie, m. Benjamin Richards; Carrie, m. Henry Harmon, m. Stephen Dangerfield.
Seventy at Mona, Utah; elder; choir leader. Veteran Black Hawk war. Farmer. Dead.

YEAMAN, THOMAS (son of John W. Yeaman and Martha Yeaman). Born Toronto, Canada, Sept. 7, 1836.
Married Anne Garner, Huntsville, Utah (daughter of David and Eliza Garner). Their children: John W. b. Feb. 6, 1859, m. Anne Garner; Storing b. May 4, ——, m. Maria Grow; Thomas, Jr., b. April 21, 1875, m. Etta Brow; Michael b. Dec. 29, 1877, m. Edith Meacham; George W. b. Feb. 22, 1881, m. Mary Roberts.

YEARSLEY, NATHAN (son of David Yearsley and Mary Ann Hoops of West Chester, Pa.). Born Nov. 8, 1835, in West Chester. Came to Utah in 1848.
Married Ruthinda E. Stewart in January, 1865, Salt Lake City (daughter of Mr. Stewart and Ruth Baker). She came to Utah with parents 1847. She was born 1844. Their children: Nathan D., m. Mary Ann Wight; Emma L., m. Joseph A. Vance; May Elizabeth, died; Annie Ruthinda, m. Henry Bowring; James Heber, m. Rosy J. Howell; Hores Calvin, died; Charles William, m. Henrietta Parkinson; Minnie Jenetta, m. George Nichols. Family home Brigham City, Utah.
High priest; presiding elder Promontory 1885-89. Participated in Echo Canyon campaign in 1857; made two trips across plains for immigrants. Farmer and stockraiser. Died Oct. 28, 1910.

YEARSLEY, NATHAN D. (son of Nathan Yearsley and Ruthinda E. Stewart). Born Oct. 13, 1865, Ogden, Utah.
Married Mary Ann Wight Jan. 31, 1888, Brigham City, Utah (daughter of Stephen Wight and Emma Pulsipher of Brigham City). She was born 1867, died Dec. 22, 1903. Only child: Nathan Melvin b. April 10, 1889. Family home Woodruff, Idaho.
Married Julia Ann Gibbs Dec. 21, 1905, Logan, Utah (daughter of William H. Gibbs and Lettia John, who were married Feb. 5, 1872, Salt Lake City, latter pioneer 1862). She was born Dec. 22, 1875, West Portage, Utah. Their children: Clifford L. b. Aug. 1, 1907; Carl G. b. Oct. 2, 1909; Ruthinda G. b. Jan. 15, 1911; Alta L. b. April 10, 1912.
High priest; bishop's counselor 16 years; Sunday school superintendent Woodruff ward, Malad stake, six years. Pioneer dry farmer and stockraiser.

YEATES, GEORGE (son of John and Mary Yeates of Worcestershire, Eng.). Born April 28, 1814, at Broad parish, Hampton. Came to Utah in 1861.
Married Mary Chance (daughter of Thomas Chance and Sarah Oliver), who was born Oct. 10, 1816. Their children: Sarah Yeates b. May 26, 1836, m. Daniel Gamble; Frederick b. Jan. 11, 1838, m. Sarah Webb Nov. 9, 1862; Thomas b. Nov. 3, 1840; Esther b. April 4, 1843, m. John Scott; Ann b. June 18, 1846. Family home Millville, Cache Co., Utah.

YEATES, FREDERICK (son of George Yeates and Mary Chance of Hampton parish, Worcestershire, Eng.). Born Jan. 11, 1838, in Broad parish. Came to Utah Sept. 21, 1857, Jacob Hoffines company.
Married Sarah Webb Nov. 9, 1862 (daughter of Anthony Webb and Elizabeth Humphries), who was born Jan. 3, 1840. Their children: Frederick Thomas b. July 31, 1863, m. Annie Frances Jessop Dec. 16, 1885; Eva Annie b. Sept. 28, 1864, m. Frederick Eliason; Mary Elizabeth b. Oct. 26, 1865, m. James Jessop; Ephraim b. March 3, 1867, m. Cathrine Wright June 1, 1888; Eliza Ann b. June 4, 1868, m. James B. Cantwell; George Anthony b. Nov. 25, 1869; Mart-a-More b. July 8, 1871, m. Joseph S. Jessop; John b. March 19, 1873, m. Elizabeth Bailey; Esther Phoebe b. Oct. 15, 1874, m. Joseph Eliason; Israel b. July 24, 1876, m. Marietta Hargraves; Sylvia Chance b. Feb. 7, 1878, m. Ephraim Jessop; Alma b. May 31, 1881. Family home Millville, Cache Co., Utah.
Married Sarah Maria Spackman April 13, 1874, Salt Lake City (daughter of Henry Spackman and Ann Bond), who was born May 10, 1859, at Burbidge, Wiltshire, Eng. Their children: James b. May 18, 1875, died; William b. May 10, 1876, died; Allie b. April 3, 1877; Sarah Olive b. Oct. 12, 1879, m. Ralph Mitchell; Roxana Stahia b. March 4, 1882, m. Sidney O. Stevens; Lula Annie b. Sept. 6, 1884, m. Isaac Samuel Smith; Josephine b. April 29, 1887, m. Roy Rudolph; Joseph Ruthford b. Sept. 4, 1890. Lived in Millville, Cache Co., Utah.
High priest; seventy. Held many positions of trust. Is now working in the Logan temple.

YEATES, FREDERICK THOMAS (son of Frederick Yeates and Sarah Webb). Born July 31, 1863, in Salt Lake county.
Married Annie Frances Jessop (daughter of Thomas Jesson and Eliza Jane Humphries) in the Logan temple. Their children: Walter Yeates b. Dec. 12, 1886; Frederick Eugene b. July 17, 1888; Nina b. Feb. 25, 1891, m. Niels Orson Olson June 8, 1910; Thomas Leo b. Feb. 24, 1893; Mary Marvel b. Oct. 3, 1895; Eulalia b. Nov. 7, 1897; Annie Reva, b. Feb. 12, 1902; Eliza Elva b. March 8, 1904. Family home Millville, Utah.

YOUNG, BRIGHAM (son of John Young and Nabie Howe, the former a Revolutionary soldier, serving under the immediate command of Washington). He was born June 1, 1801, Whittingham, Windham county, Vt. He was one of ten children, and the youngest but one of five brothers, named in their order as follows: John, Joseph, Phineas, Brigham and Lorenzo. His sisters were Nancy, Fanny, Rhoda, Susan and Nabbie. The first four married and became respectively Mrs. Kent, Mrs. Murray, Mrs. John P. Greene, and Mrs. James Little. Nabbie died in her girlhood. In religion, the family were Methodists. Brigham's early avocations were those of carpenter and joiner, painter and glazier. He came to Utah July 24, 1847, as captain of the first company of immigrants.
Married Miriam Works Oct. 8, 1824, who died September, 1832. Their children: Vilate, m. Charles Franklin Decker; Elizabeth Y., m. Edmund Ellsworth.
Married Mary Ann Angell February, 1834. Among their six children were: Brigham, Jr. b. Dec. 1836, m. Katherine Spencer Nov. 15, 1855; Luna C. b. Aug. 20, 1842, m. George W. Thatcher April 4, 1861.
Married Lucy Decker (daughter of Isaac and Hannah Decker, pioneers 1847, Brigham Young company), who was born May 17, 1821. Among their children were: Shamira b. March 21, 1853, m. William J. Rossiter Oct. 9, 1877; Clarissa H. b. July 23, 1860, m. John D. Spencer Jan. 19, 1882.
Married Clarissa C. Decker (daughter of Isaac and Hannah Decker), who was born July 22, 1828. Among their children was: Nabbie b. March 22, 1852 (d. 1894), m. Spencer Clawson Feb. 15, 1876.
Married Sarah Malin April 18, 1848 (daughter of Elijah and Hannah Malin of Chester county, Pa.), who was born Jan. 10, 1804.
Married Ellen Ackland Rockwood (daughter of Albert Perry Rockwood and Nancy Haven), who was born March 23, 1829.
Married Clarissa Ross (daughter of William Ross and Phoebe Ogden of New York), who was born June 16, 1814. Their children: Mary, m. Mark Croxall; Clarissa Maria, m. William B. Dougall; Willard, m. Harriet Hopper; Phoebe L. b. Aug. 1, 1854, m. W. J. Beatie Jan. 7, 1872.
Married Mary Jane Bigelow (eldest daughter of Nahum Bigelow and Mary Gibbs, pioneers 1850, William Snow oxteam company).
Married Lucy Bigelow (daughter of Nahum Bigelow and Mary Gibbs).
Married Mary Van Cott (daughter of John Van Cott, born Sept. 7, 1814, Canaan, N. Y., and Lucy L. Sackett, born July 17, 1815, pioneers Sept. 25, 1847—married Sept. 15, 1835, in New York). She was born Feb. 2, 1844, and died Jan. 5, 1884.
Married Eliza Babcock (daughter of Adolphus Babcock and Jerusha Jane Rowley of New York, pioneers 1847, oxteam company).
Married Harriet Amelia Folsom (daughter of William H. Folsom and Zerviah E. Clark of New Hampshire and Massachusetts).
Married Emmily Dow Partridge. Their children: Mary Eliza b. June 8, 1847, m. Mark Croxall; Caroline b. Feb. 1, 1851, m. Mark Croxall 1868; Joseph Don Carlos b. May 6, 1855, m. Alice Naomi Dowden Sept. 22, 1861.
Married Elizabeth Robison (daughter of Peter Robison and Mary Ashly, pioneers 1850), who was born April 29, 1850. Family home Millville, Utah.
Married Sarah Ann McDonald (daughter of William McDonald and Seriah Shirts of Crawford, Burn, County Down, Ireland). She was born March 3, 1856.
There were other wives, whose genealogies are not printed here.
Whitney's History says of Brigham Young:
It was at Aurelius, Cayuga county, N. Y., in 1824 that he first saw the Book of Mormon, a copy of which had been left at the house of his brother Phineas, in the neighboring town of Victor, by Samuel H. Smith, a brother to Joseph Smith, the Prophet. Deeply impressed with the principles of Mormonism, he, in company with Phineas and his friend Heber C. Kimball, visited a branch of the church at Columbia, Bradford county, Penn., from which state had previously come several Mormon elders, preaching the doctrines of their faith in and around Mendon. Subsequently proceeding to Canada, where his brother Joseph was laboring in the Methodist ministry, Brigham presented to him the claims of Mormonism. He then returned with him to Mendon, where they both joined the Church of Jesus Christ of Latter-day Saints.
He was baptized on the 14th of April, 1832, by Elder Eleazer Miller, who confirmed him at the water's edge and ordained him an elder the same evening. About three weeks later his wife Miriam was baptized.
His first meeting with the founder of Mormonism was in the fall of the same year, when he visited Kirtland, Ohio,

the headquarters of the Latter-day Saints. Joseph Smith, it is said, prophesied on that occasion that Brigham Young would yet preside over the church. A year later he removed to Kirtland.

He was chosen one of the Twelve Apostles—the council or quorum second in authority in the Mormon church—Feb. 14, 1835, and forthwith he entered upon his eventful and wonderfully successful career. With his quorum he traversed the eastern states and Canada, making proselytes to the faith and gathering funds for the completion of the Kirtland Temple and the purchase of lands in Missouri, where Mormon colonies from Ohio and the East were settling. When disaffection arose and persecution threatened the existence of the church and the lives of its leaders, he stood staunchly by the Prophet, defending him at his own imminent peril. Finally the opposition became so fierce, that he as well as the Prophet was compelled to flee from Kirtland.

He next appears at Far West, Mo., the new gathering place of the Saints, where after the apostasy of Thomas B. Marsh and the death of David W. Patten (his seniors among the Apostles), he succeeded to the presidency of the Twelve. This was in the very midst of the mob troubles that culminated in the expulsion of the Mormon community from that State. In the absence of the first presidency, composed of the Prophet, his brother Hyrum Smith, and Sidney Rigdon, who had been thrown into prison, President Young, though not then in Missouri, directed the winter exodus of his people, and the homeless and plundered refugees—twelve to fifteen thousand in number—fleeing through frost and snow by the light of their burning dwellings, were safely landed upon the hospitable shores of Illinois.

His next notable achievement was in connection with the spread of Mormonism in foreign lands. As early as July, 1838, he and his fellow Apostles had been directed by the Prophet to take a mission to Europe, and "the word of the Lord" was pledged that they should depart on a certain day from the Temple lot in Far West. This was before the mob troubles arose, before the Mormons had been driven, and before there was any prospect that they would be. But all was now changed, the expulsion was an accomplished fact, and it was almost as much as a Mormon's life was worth to be seen in Missouri. The day set for the departure of the Apostles from Far West (April 26, 1839) was approaching, but they were far away, and apostates and mobocrats were boasting that the revelation pertaining to that departure would fail. Before daybreak, however, on the morning of the day appointed, Brigham Young and others of the Twelve rode into the town, held a meeting on the Temple lot, and started thence upon their mission, their enemies meanwhile wrapped in slumber, oblivious of what was taking place. Delayed by the founding of their new city, Nauvoo, in Hancock county, Ill., and by an epidemic of fever and ague that swept over that newly settled section, they did not cross the Atlantic until about a year later, and even then this indomitable man and his no less indomitable associates arose from sick beds, leaving their families alive and almost destitute, to begin their journey.

Landing at Liverpool penniless and among strangers, April 6, 1840—Mormonism's tenth anniversary—they remained in Great Britain a little over a year, during which time they baptized between seven and eight thousand souls and raised up branches of the church in almost every noted city and town throughout the United Kingdom. They established the periodical known as "The Millennial Star," published five thousand copies of the Book of Mormon, three thousand hymn books and fifty thousand tracts, emigrated a thousand souls to Nauvoo, and founded a permanent shipping agency for the use of future emigration. The British Mission had previously been opened, but its foundations were now laid broad and deep. The first foreign mission of the Mormon church, it still remains the most important proselyting field for the energetic elders of this organization.

Brigham Young, soon after his return from abroad, was taught by the Prophet the principle of celestial or plural marriage, which he practiced as did others while at Nauvoo. He married among other women, several of the Prophet's widows. It was not until after the settlement of Utah, however, that "polygamy" was proclaimed.

Brigham Young was in the eastern states, when Joseph and Hyrum Smith were murdered in Carthage jail, June 27, 1844. The business which had taken him and most of the Apostles from home was an electioneering mission in the interests of the Prophet, who was a candidate for the presidency of the United States. As soon as they heard the awful tidings of the assassination, they hurried back to Nauvoo.

Their return was timely. The Saints, grief-stricken at the loss of their leaders, needed the presence of the Apostles, but not merely as a means of consolation. Factions were forming and a schism threatened the church. Sidney Rigdon, who had been the Prophet's first counselor in the first presidency, was urging with all his eloquence—for he was an eloquent and a learned man—his claim to the leadership, contending that he was Joseph's rightful successor; notwithstanding that for some time he had absented himself from Nauvoo and the society of the Saints, manifesting a disposition to shirk the trials patiently borne by his much suffering associates. Brigham Young, with little learning and less eloquence, but speaking straight to the point, maintained the right of the Twelve Apostles to lead the church in the absence of the first presidency, basing his claim upon the teachings of the martyred Seer, who had declared: "Where I am not, there is no first presidency over the Twelve." He had also repeatedly affirmed that he had rolled the burden of the "Kingdom" from his own shoulders upon those of the Twelve.

The great majority of the people sustained President Young, and followed him in the exodus from Illinois, leaving Elder Rigdon and other claimants at the head of various small factions which have made no special mark in history. Brigham, by virtue of his position in the quorum of the Twelve, was now virtually president of the church, though he did not take that title until nearly two years later, when the first presidency was again organized. The exodus began in February, 1846.

Expelled from Nauvoo across the frozen Mississippi, armed mobs behind them, and a savage wilderness before, the homeless pilgrims, with their oxteams and heavily loaded wagons, halted in their westward flight upon the Missouri river, where, in the summer of the same year they filled a government requisition for five hundred men to serve in the United States in its war against Mexico. Thus originates the famous Mormon Battalion, whose story is told in another place.

President Young and his associates, after raising the Battalion and witnessing its departure for the West, set about preparing for the journey of the pioneers to the Rocky Mountains. This company, including himself, numbered one hundred and forty-three men, three women and two children, meagerly supplied with wagons, provisions, firearms, plows, seed-grain and the usual camp equipment. Leaving the main body of their people upon the Missouri, with instructions to follow later, the pioneers started from Winter Quarters (now Florence, Neb.), early in April, 1847. Traversing the trackless plains and snow-capped mountains, they penetrated to the very heart of the "Great American Desert," where they founded Salt Lake City, the parent of hundreds of cities, towns and villages that have since sprung into existence as Brigham Young's and Mormonism's gift to civilization. The date of their arrival in Salt Lake Valley was July 24, a day thenceforth "set among the high tides of the calendar."

Flinging to the breeze the stars and stripes, these Mormon colonizers took possession of the country, which then belonged to Mexico, as in the name of the United States, and after the treaty of Guadalupe Hidalgo, by which, in February, 1848, the land was ceded to this nation, they organized, pending the action of Congress upon their petition for a State government, the Provisional State of Deseret, of which Brigham Young was elected governor, March 12, 1849. They thoroughly explored the surrounding region, placated or subdued the savage tribes (President Young's policy was to feed the Indians rather than fight them), battled with crickets, grasshoppers and drouth, instituted irrigation, redeemed arid lands, built cities, established newspapers, founded schools and factories, and made the whole land hum with the whirring wheels of industry. They were emphatically what they styled themselves, "the busy bees of the hive of Deseret."

There was but one branch of industry that they did not encourage. It was mining. In the midst of one of the richest metal-bearing regions in the world, their leader discountenanced mining, advising his people to devote themselves primarily to agriculture. "We cannot eat gold and silver," said Brigham Young. "We need bread and clothing first. Neither do we want to bring in here a roving, reckless frontier population to drive us again from our hard-earned homes. Let mining go for the present, until we are strong enough to take care of ourselves, and meantime let us devote our energies to farming, stock-raising, manufacturing, etc., those health-giving pursuits that lie at the basis of every State's prosperity." Such, if not his precise language, was the substance of his teachings upon this point. It was the premature opening of the mines, not mining itself, that he opposed.

Congress denied Deseret's prayer for Statehood, but on the 9th of September, 1850, organized the Territory of Utah, of which Brigham Young became governor, by appointment of President Millard Fillmore, after whom the grateful Mormons named the county of Millard and the city of Fillmore, originally the capital of the Territory. Governor Young served two terms, and was succeeded in 1858 by Governor Alfred Cumming, a native of Georgia, Utah's first non-Mormon executive.

Just prior to Governor Cumming's installation occurred the exciting but bloodless conflict known as "The Echo Canyon War," but officially styled "The Utah Expedition." It was the heroic crisis of Brigham Young's life, when, on the 15th of September, 1857, he, as governor of Utah, proclaimed the Territory under martial law, and forbade the United States army then on our borders (ordered here by President Buchanan to suppress an imaginary Mormon uprising) to cross the confines of the commonwealth. His purpose was not to defy the national authorities, but to hold in check Johnston's troops (thus preventing a possible repetition of the anti-Mormon atrocities of Missouri and Illinois) until the government—which had been misled by false reports—could investigate the situation and become convinced of its error. Governor Young, backed by the Utah militia, fully accomplished his design and the affair was amicably settled.

Though no longer governor of Utah, Brigham Young remained president of the Mormon church, and as such was the real power in the land. Under his wise and vigorous administration the country was built up rapidly. The settlements founded by him and his people on the shores of the Great Salt Lake formed a nucleus for western civilization, greatly facilitating the colonization of the vast arid plateau known as the Great Basin. Idaho, Montana, the Dakotas, Colorado, Wyoming, Nevada (once a part of

Utah), Arizona and New Mexico, owe much in this connection to Utah and her founders.

It was presumed by many that the opening of the great conflict between the northern and the southern states, would find Brigham Young and his people arrayed on the side of secession and in arms against the Federal government. What was the surprise, therefore, when, on the 18th of October, 1861, at the very threshold of the strife, with the tide of victory running in favor of the Confederacy, there flashed eastward over the wires of the Overland Telegraph line, just completed to Salt Lake City, the following message signed by Brigham Young: "Utah has not seceded, but is firm for the constitution and laws of our once happy country." At this time also the Mormon leader offered to the head of the nation the services of a picked body of men to protect the mail route on the plains, an offer graciously accepted by President Lincoln. Early in 1862, Utah applied for admission into the Union.

The prevailing prejudice, however, was too dense to be at once dispelled. Hence, notwithstanding these evidences of loyalty, springing not from policy but from true patriotism, a body of Government troops—the California and Nevada Volunteers, commander by Colonel Patrick E. Connor—were ordered to Utah and assigned the task of "watching Brigham Young and the Mormons," during this period of national peril. The insult implied by the presence of the troops—who founded Fort Douglas on the bench east of Salt Lake City—was keenly felt, and considerable friction arose, though no actual collision occurred between the soldiers and the civilians in general. Gradually the acerbities wore away and friendly feelings took their place. In after years, when President Young was summoned to be tried before Chief Justice McKean, who should offer to become one of his bondsmen but General Patrick Edward Connor, ex-commander at the Fort, who was then engaged extensively in mining, of which industry he was Utah's pioneer.

It was twenty-two years after the settlement of Salt Lake Valley when the shriek of the locomotive broke the stillness of the mountain solitudes, and the peaceful settlements of the Saints were thrown open to the encroachment of modern civilization. A new era then dawned upon Deseret. Her days of isolation were ended. Population increased, commerce expanded and a thousand and one improvements were planned and explained. Telegraphs and railroads threw a net-work of steel and electricity over a region formerly traversed by the slow-going oxteam and lumbering stage coach. The mines, previously opened, were developed, property of all kinds increased in value, and industry on every hand felt the thrill of an electric reawakening. Tourists from East and West began flocking to the Mormon country, to see for themselves the "peculiar people" and their institutions, trusting no more to the wild tales told by sensational traducers.

In the midst of it all, Brigham Young remained the master mind and leading spirit of the time. He had predicted the transcontinental railroad and marked out its path while crossing the plains and mountains in 1847, and now, when it was extending across Utah, he became a contractor, helping to build the Union Pacific grade through Echo and Weber canyons. Two and a half years earlier he had established the Deseret Telegraph line, a local enterprise constructed entirely by Mormon capital and labor under his direction. In the early "seventies" he with others built the Utah Central and Utah Southern railroads, the pioneer lines of the Territory, and of the first-named road he was for many years the president.

But while in sympathy with such enterprises and anxious to forward them, he was not to be caught napping by the changes that he knew would follow. Just before the coming of the railroad he organized Zion's Co-operative Mercantile Institution, a mammoth concern designed to consolidate the commercial interests of his people. In this and in other ways he sucessfully met the vigorous and in many respects unfriendly competition that surged in from outside.

With the increase of the Gentile population came the formation of rival political parties, the first that Utah had known. Non-Mormon churches and newspapers also multiplied, religious and political agitators made the air sulphurous with their imprecations against "the dominant power," and Congress at regular intervals was asked to exterminate the remaining "twin relic of barbarism." Still, Mormonism, personified in Brigham Young, continued to hold its own.

Under the anti-polygamy statute enacted by Congress in July, 1862, but one attempt was made to prosecute the Mormon leader. This was in March, 1863, when a plot was said to be forming to arrest him by military force and run him off to the States for trial. He forestalled the success of the scheme—if such a scheme existed—by surrendering to the United States Marshal and going before Chief Justice Kinney in chambers, where he was examined and held to bail, but subsequently discharged, there not being sufficient evidence to justify an indictment. The charge in this case was that of marrying a plural wife, the only act made punishable by the law of 1862, which was silent as to the maintenance of polygamous relations. Thenceforth that law remained a dead letter, no attempt being made to enforce it, the Mormons regarding it as unconstitutional, as it trenched upon a principle of their religion, and many non-Mormons, including noted editors, jurists and statesmen, sharing the same view. In 1874 a test-case was instituted, under President Young's sanction, to secure a decision from the Supreme Court of the United States, but that decision, sustaining the law's constitutionality, was not rendered until eighteen months after his death.

But while measurably safe from prosecution under the anti-polygamy act, the Mormon leader and his compeers were not free from judicial harassments. In the fall of 1871 President Young and others were prosecuted before Chief Justice McKean under a local law enacted by the Mormons themselves against the social evil, adultery and other sexual sins, and never intended to apply to polygamy or association with plural wives, which was the head and front of their offending. These prosecutions, with others, were stopped by the Englebrecht decision of April, 1872, in which the court of last resort held that the grand jury which had found the indictments was illegal.

A few years later Judge McKean had the Mormon leader again in the toils. Under his fostering care had arisen the case of Ann Eliza Young vs. Brigham Young, in which the plaintiff, one of the defendant's plural wives, sued him for divorce and alimony. The judge in his zeal went so far as to give Ann Eliza the status of a legal wife, deciding against all law and logic that the defendant should pay her alimony pendente lite, to the amount of nearly ten thousand dollars. Failing to promptly comply with this demand—which set the whole country in a roar—the venerable founder of Utah was imprisoned by order of court in the Utah penitentiary. Sentence was passed upon him March 11, 1875—the term of imprisonment being twenty-four hours—and just one week later the storm of censure resulting from this act culminated in McKean's removal from office.

In the autumn of the same year President Grant visited Utah, the first executive of the nation to set foot within the Territory. The most interesting incident of his visit was a cordial interview between him and President Young, who with a party welcomed the chief magistrate at Ogden and rode in the same train with him and his suite to Salt Lake City. This was the first and only time that Brigham Young met a president of the United States.

The closing labors of President Young's life, following a vigorous and partly successful effort to re-establish the "United Order" (a communal system introduced by the Prophet Joseph Smith), comprised the dedication in January and April, 1877, of the St. George Temple—the first Temple erected by the Saints since leaving Nauvoo; also a reorganization of the Stakes of Zion, beginning with St. George Stake on April 7th, and ending with Box Elder Stake on August 19th of that year. To effect the latter organization, he made his final trip beyond the limits of Salt Lake City.

President Young died at his residence, the historic Lion House, August 29, 1877. He left an estate valued at two and a half million dollars, most of which was divided among the members of his family. These were numerous, but their number, for sensational effect, has been grossly exaggerated. His children at his death numbered about forty. Six of his widows survive. The majority of his families dwelt in the Lion and Bee-hive houses, where each wife with her children had separate apartments, and where, contrary to facetious reports, all dwelt together in amity. The Gardo House, a handsome and stately modern mansion, surnamed by non-Mormons the "Amelia Palace," and pointed out to tourists as the "home of the favorite wife" was in reality the president's official residence, erected mainly for the entertainment of distinguished visitors.

The best known of President Young's sons are Brigham Young, president of the Twelve Apostles; Hon. Joseph A. Young, (deceased); John W. Young, once a member of the first presidency, now a noted business man, and Colonel Willard Young, of the United States Army, who commanded a regiment of volunteer engineers during the war with Spain. Among the president's grandsons are Laurence H. Young, well known as a business man. Major Richard W. Young (like his Uncle Willard a graduate of West Point) who recently won laurels in the Philippines. He commanded the Utah Light artillery at the capture of Manila, and was subsequently one of the judges of the supreme court at that place. Another grandson, Brigham S. Young, is a member of the Salt Lake Board of Education; another is John Willard Clawson, the painter; and still another, George W. Thatcher, Jr., musician. Elder Seymour B. Young, of the First Council of Seventy; Judge LeGrange Young; Brigham Bicknell Young, vocalist; Dr. Harry A. Young, killed in the Philippines, and Private Joseph Young, who died in the same cause, are among the president's nephews. Corporal John Young, slain in battle near Manila, was his grand-nephew. Two of President Young's daughters have been mentioned. In addition might be named Mrs. Luna Thatcher, Mrs. Emily Clawson, Mrs. Caroline Cannon, Mrs. Zina Card, Mrs. Maria Dougall; Mrs. Phebe Beatie, Mrs. Dora Hagan, Mrs. Eva Davis, Mrs. Nettie Easton, Mrs. Louisa Ferguson, Mrs. Susa Gates, Mrs. Mira Rossiter, Mrs. Clarissa Spencer, Mrs. Miriam Hardy, Mrs. Josephine Young, Mrs. Fannie Clayton and others. The most noted grand-daughter is Emma Lucy Gates, the singer.

Brigham Young, like Joseph Smith, was a warm friend of education. Among the monuments left to perpetuate his memory are two noble institutions of learning, namely the Brigham Young academy and the Brigham Young college, the former at Provo, 50 miles south, and the latter at Logan, 100 miles north of Utah's capital. He also projected the Young university at Salt Lake City, but died before perfecting his plans concerning it. Believing that man, in order to be fully educated, must be developed mentally, physically, morally and spiritually, he provided that religion and manual training should be included in the curriculum of the institutions he founded. In the trust deed endowing the Brigham Young college with 10,000 acres of land (worth now about $200,000) it was prescribed that no text book should be used which misrepresented or spoke lightly of "the divine mission of our Savior or of the Prophet Joseph Smith." The founding of these institutions was not the sum of President Young's labors in the cause of education. The entire school system of the state, crowned with the University of Utah, is largely the result of his zealous efforts in this direction.

Among the president's many talents was a genius for architecture, some of the evidences of which are the St. George, Logan, Manti and Salt Lake temples, and the Salt Lake tabernacle. As early as 1862 he built the Salt Lake theatre, at the time of its erection the finest temple of the drama between St. Louis and San Francisco. The Brigham Young memorial building, one of a group of structures belonging to the Latter-day Saints university, founded by the church at Salt Lake City, was erected with means raised from the sale of lands whereon he proposed placing the Young university; said lands being donated by his surviving heirs for that purpose.

A mere sketch, this, of the life and character of Utah's illustrious founder. You who would peruse him more fully, pore over the annals of Mormonism during its first half century; you who would witness his works, look around you—they are manifest on every hand. He was not only a Moses, who led his people into a wilderness, but a Joshua who established them in a promised land and divided to them their inheritance. He was the beatitude heart, the thinking brain, the directing hand in all the wondrous work of Utah's development, and to a great extent the development of the surrounding states and territories, transformed by the touch of industry from a desert of sagebrush and sand, into an Eden of fertility, a veritable "Garden of the Lord," redolent of fruits and blossoming with flowers. Brigham Young needs no monument of marble or bronze. His record is imperishably written upon the minds and hearts of many tens of thousands to whom he was a benefactor and friend. His name and fame are forever enshrined in the temple of history, in the Pantheon of memory, in the Westminster Abbey of the soul.

"In regard to the Mountain Meadow Massacre, Brigham Young testified that he knew nothing of it until some time after it occurred, and then only by a floating rumor. The first official report was from John D. Lee, two or three months after it occurred."

"He personally donated $1,000 for the relief of the people left destitute by the fire in Chicago in 1871. And with donations from the Salt Lake City corporation, the receipts tendered by the management of the Salt Lake theatre, and personal donations, the amount aggregated about $20,000."

"At the annual conference of the church in April, 1873, he resigned the office of trustee-in-trust, which he had held for about 25 years, and George A. Smith was chosen to succeed him. At this conference he chose five additional counselors to aid him in the presidency of the church. They were: Lorenzo Snow, Brigham Young, Jr., Albert Carrington, John W. Young and George Q. Cannon."

"His last public address was Sunday afternoon, Aug. 19, 1877, at Brigham City. The occasion was the organization of Box Elder stake."

Died Aug. 29, 1877, at Salt Lake City.

YOUNG, BRIGHAM, JR. (son of Brigham Young and Mary A. Angell of Nauvoo, Ill.). Born December, 1836. Came to Utah July 24, 1847, with father.
Married Katherine Spencer Nov. 15, 1855, at Salt Lake City (daughter of Orson Spencer and Katherine Curtis of Nauvoo, latter died on plains en route to Utah, children came 1843). She was born Oct. 6, 1836. Their children: Alice, m. Charles Hopkins; Brigham, m. Lottie Claridge, m. Marie Johanson; Howard O., m. Jennie Moore; Lawrence H., m. Eliza Brinton; Mabel, m. Charles T. Held; Joseph A., m. Ella Lewis; George S., m. Martha Rigby; Florence, m. Robert S. Bradley; Eugene H., m. Eva Little; Katherine, m. H. L. Jennings; Cora, m. James Rogers. Family home, Salt Lake City.
Seventy; president quorum of Twelve Apostles of Church of Jesus Christ of Latter-day Saints; missionary. Deceased.

YOUNG, LAWRENCE H. (son of Brigham Young, Jr., and Katherine Spencer). Born Aug. 17, 1861, Salt Lake City.
Married Eliza Brinton May 6, 1886, Salt Lake City (daughter of David Brinton and Harriet Dilworth of Brinton, pioneers 1848). She was born March 30, 1864. Their children: Louise b. April 7, 1888, m. Joseph C. Jack; Lawrence H., Jr. b. Sept. 13, 1891; Hebe Brinton b. March 8, 1893; Katherine b. Feb. 3, 1900; Francis b. July 31, 1903. Family home, Salt Lake City.
Missionary to England 1884-86. Engaged in real estate and insurance.

YOUNG, JOSEPH DON CARLOS (son of Brigham Young, Sr., and Emily Dow Partridge). Born May 6, 1855, Salt Lake City.
Married Alice Naomi Dowden Sept. 22, 1881, Salt Lake City (daughter of Edwin Dowden and Naomi Debenham of Salt Lake City). Their children: Don Carlos, Jr. b. Aug. 5, 1882, m. Teckla Louise Hagman; Kirtland Dowden b. Sept. 6, 1885; Naomi, m. J. Lesley Spence; Constance, m. F. C. Smith; Katie Clair; Gladys; George Cannon; Edward Partridge; Edwin Dowden; Sydney. Family home, Salt Lake City.
Missionary to southern states 1895-97; high priest. Architect.

YOUNG, DON CARLOS, JR. (son of Joseph Don Carlos Young and Alice Naomi Dodwen). Born Aug. 5, 1882, Salt Lake City.
Married Teckla Louise Hagman June 27, 1912, Salt Lake City (daughter of John Hagman of Salt Lake City). She was born May 7, 1883. Family home, Salt Lake City.
Member 10th quorum seventies; missionary to Switzerland and Germany 1909-11. Architect.

YOUNG, LE GRANDE (son of Joseph Young and Jane Adeline Bicknell). Born Dec. 27, 1840, Nauvoo, Ill. Came to Utah September, 1850, Captain Snow company.
Married Grace Hardie April 18, 1863, Salt Lake City (daughter of John Hardie and Janet Downey of Edinburgh, Scotland, pioneers September, 1856, McArthur company). She was born Dec. 14, 1842, Edinburgh, Scotland. Their children: Joseph Hardie, m. Katherine Lawrence; Grace, m. Kenneth Kerr; Lucille, m. William Reid; Afton; Marcus Le Grande, m. Fern Scott; Jasmine, m. Lester J. Freed. Family home, Salt Lake City.
Member 3d quorum seventies; missionary to New York and Illinois 1869-70; high priest. City councilman 2 terms. Judge 3d district court. Lawyer.

YOUNG, LEVI EDGAR (son of Seymour B. Young and Ann Elizabeth Riter). Born Feb. 2, 1874, Salt Lake City.
Married Valeria Brinton June 18, 1907, Salt Lake City (daughter of David Brinton and Susan Huffaker of Cottonwood, Utah, pioneers 1847, Jedediah M. Grant company). She was born Dec. 13, 1876. Their children: Harriet Wollerton b. July 17, 1909; Jane Seymour b. May 16, 1911. Family home. Salt Lake City.
Seventh president 1st council seventies; missionary to Germany 1901-04; and president Swiss and German mission 1902-04. Professor of history in University of Utah. Representative from the state of Utah to the International convention on school hygiene held at Nuremberg, Germany, 1904. Graduate University of Utah, and did advance work at Harvard university, Columbia college of New York City; and holds degrees of B. S. and M. A.

YOUNG, EBENEZER RUSSEL (son of Ebenezer Russel Young and Margaret Lockwood of Richmond county, N. Y.). Born at Port Richmond, N. Y., Nov. 14, 1814. Came to Utah Oct. 1, 1858, E. R. Young company.
Married Margaret Holden at Westport, Conn., May 1, 1836 (daughter of Robert Holden, Westport, Conn., and Martha Shaltcross, Manchester, Eng.). She was born April 17, 1813. Their children: Margaret, m. John Taylor; Mary, m. W. I. Appleby; Ebenezer Russel, m. Matilda Wikoff Shreve; John W., m. Ida C. Harter; Esther E., died; Esther A., m. L. H. King; Robert, m. Anne Taylor Shreve; George W., m. Mary Leota Gibson. Family home Paterson, N. J.
Missionary. Miller; lumberman; merchant. Died Nov. 23, 1890, at Wanship, Utah.

YOUNG, ROBERT (son of Ebenezer Russel Young and Margaret Holden). Born June 25, 1851, at Paterson, N. J. Came to Utah Oct. 1, 1858, E. R. Young company.
Married Anne Taylor Shreve Jan. 21, 1877, at Wanship, Utah (daughter of Edwin Agustus Shreve and Elizabeth Homes Wikoff of Hornestown, N. J., who came to Utah Sept. 9, 1861, Martindale company). She was born Sept. 5, 1856. Their children: Robert S. b. Oct. 25, 1877; Anne Ray b. Sept. 22, 1882, m. Nathan F. Vernon; Elizabeth S. Young b. Aug. 18, 1887; William S. Young b. June 20, 1890; Edwin Russel Young b. Oct. 4, 1893. Family home Wanship, Utah.
Railroad construction contractor.

YOUNG, JAMES. Came to Utah July 24, 1847, Brigham Young company.
Married Elizabeth Seeley. Their children: Mary, m. Henry Wilcox; Annie, m. Thorit Peck; John, m. Susannah Wishaw; Sarah, m. Thorit Peck; Hannah, m. Joseph Moore; Elizabeth, m. Alma Staker. Family resided Salt Lake City and Pleasant Grove, Utah.
Died, aged 96.

YOUNG, JAMES (son of George Young and Ann Willshire, both of Northill Beds, Eng.). Born Sept. 23, 1848, at Caldecota Beds.
Married Francesca Campkin June 4, 1877, at Brigham City, Utah, Apostle Lorenzo Snow conducting ceremony, received endowment at Salt Lake endowment house (daughter of Isaac Campkin and Martha Webb, of Bedfordshire, Eng., former died in St. Louis, Mo., latter pioneer 1858, Marchant company). She was born Oct. 1, 1850. Their children: Lilly Annedia b. July 4, 1878, m. Oluf Johnson Jan. 11, 1899; Fanny Maud b. Nov. 10, 1880, m. John G. Watt Nov. 1906; Wilford James b. Dec. 31, 1881, m. Sarah Shipley June 18, 1908; Harvey George b. Nov. 15, 1883; Elizabeth Ann b. April 19, 1886, m. Almon N. Wight Feb. 1908; Isaac Albert b. Sept. 11, 1887; Henry Leslie b. May 13, 1889; Lawrence Alfred b. April 5, 1891; Joseph Thomas b. March 20, 1893. Family resided Harrisville, Hainsville, Brigham City and Perry, Utah, and Preston, Idaho.
High priest; choir leader. Justice of peace; notary public; school trustee.

PIONEERS AND PROMINENT MEN OF UTAH 1271

YOUNG, JOHN (son of John Young and Nabbie Howe of Hopkinton, Middlesex county, Mass.). Born May 22, 1791, Hopkinton, Mass. Came to Utah in September, 1847, in command of four companies.
Married Theodocia Kimball 1813. Their children: Charlotte; Caroline, m. Martin Harris; Louisa, m. Lyman O. Littlefield; Clarissa; Candace.
Married Mary Ann Guernsey 1847.
Married Sarah McCleve October, 1853, Salt Lake City (daughter of John McCleve and Nancy Jane McFern of Belfast, Ireland). Their children: Lydia Ann b. Nov. 7, 1854, m. Marion Merrill; John McCleve b. Aug. 7, 1856, m. Chloe Louise Spencer; Joseph b. June 23, 1859, d. March 8, 1865.
Married Ann Oliver 1857, Salt Lake City.
Missionary in Pennsylvania, Ohio and New York, 1834-36; president high priests quorum; president Kirtland stake. Farmer. Died April 27, 1870.

YOUNG, JOHN McCLEVE (son of John Young and Sarah McCleve). Born Aug. 7, 1856, Salt Lake City.
Married Chloe Louise Spencer Aug. 7, 1883, Salt Lake City (daughter of Daniel Spencer and Elizabeth Funnel of Salt Lake City). She was born March 16, 1866. Their children: John Groo b. July 31, 1884; Spencer b. Sept. 7, 1886; Sarah Irene b. Dec. 18, 1888; Dorothy b. Aug. 20, 1897; Waldemar Van Cott b. March 21, 1905.
Missionary to Australia 1875-77 and to England 1909-11; president Y. M. M. I. A.; member 16th quorum seventies. City marshal 1890; member legislative council 1888. Clerk.

YOUNG, JOHN R. Came to Utah Oct. 21, 1847.
Married Albina Terry (daughter of William Reynold Terry and Mary Phillips). Their children: Frank A. b. Jan. 6, 1861, m. Karen Metthea Rasmussen; Silas Smith, m. Mary Ann Young; Ferra Little, m. Nancy Loella Green; William R., m. Lydia Bradley; J. Royal, m. Elizabeth Wilcox; Joseph W., m. Loella Zufelt. Family resided Orderville and Lyman, Utah, and Fruitland, N. M.

YOUNG, FRANK A. (son of John R. Young and Albina Terry). He was born Jan. 6, 1861, Payson, Utah.
Married Karen Metthea Rasmussen Oct. 23, 1891, Manti, Utah (daughter of Larse Rasmussen and Christane Sorensen, of Jordan, Utah). She was born June 2, 1875. Their children: John Alvin b. Dec. 17, 1892; Fern Albina b. April 15, 1894; Sidney Coons b. March 29, 1896; Melvin LeRoy b. Feb. 18, 1898; Iven Wayne b. Jan. 26, 1900; Lee Erastus b. June 12, 1901; Mary Metthea b. July 26, 1903; Ella Christane b. March 27, 1905; George Earl b. July 14, 1907; Floyd Rasmussen b. Jan. 22, 1910. Family home Huntington, Utah.
Ward teacher; counselor elders quorum. Counselor Y. M. M. I. A., Orderville, Utah. School trustee. Farmer.

YOUNG, JONATHAN. Came to Utah 1851.
Married Sarah Toomer 1851, at Portsmouth, Eng. She was born July 26, 1816. Came to Utah in 1851. Their children: Brigham J. b. Dec. 23, 1853, m. Sarah Ann McDonald; Sarah Ann b. 1855, m. Robert Montgomery; David b. 1857, m. Mary McDonald; Fannie b. 1859, m. John Clyde. Family resided Salt Lake City and Payson, Utah.
High priest. Sailor; gardener. Died October, 1866, Heber City, Utah.

YOUNG, BRIGHAM J. (son of Jonathan Young and Sarah Toomer). Born Dec. 23, 1853. Came to Utah 1851.
Married Sarah Ann McDonald April 11, 1875, at Heber City, Utah—in Endowment House three months later (daughter of William McDonald and Sarliah Shirts of County Down, Ireland, pioneers). She was born March 3, 1855. Their children: Sarah Sarliah b. Dec. 18, 1875, m. John H. Duke; Brigham D. b. Dec. 8, 1877, m. Sarah McMullin; Margeret b. Aug. 4, 1879, m. John Van Wagenen; Fannie b. April 30, 1851, m. Joseph Peterson; Mary b. March 11, 1883, and Eliza b. March 11, 1883, died; William G. b. April 22, 1884, m. Edna Wilson; Blanche b. March 11, 1886, m. Moroni McAffee; Bernice b. Nov. 27, 1888, m. Hyrum Anderson; Cloe Violet b. Jan. 7, 1890, m. Adolphus Sessions; Angeline b. Nov. 25, 1892, m. Augustus Johnson; Ray b. Nov. 8, 1894, died; Arthur b. June 6, 1896, died; Walter b. April 7, 1898; Alma b. Sept. 21, 1901, died. Family home Heber City, Utah.
High priest; ward teacher; superintendent Sunday schools, Riverdale ward, four years. Road supervisor 1894-1902. Settled in Wasatch county 1864, where he assisted in building up the country. Farmer and cattle raiser.

YOUNG, JOSEPH (son of John Young and Nabbie Howe, of Quincy, Ill., where former died 1839). He was born April 7, 1779, Hopkinton, Mass. Came to Utah in September, 1850, with Wilford Woodruff company.
Married Jane Adeline Bicknell, at Kirtland, Ohio, 1834 (daughter of Calvin Bicknell and Chloe Seymour, both of Geneseo, Ohio, where they died). She was born August 14, 1814. Their children: Jane Adeline, m. Charles B. Robins; Joseph, d. 1858; Seymour B. m. Elizabeth Ann Riter, m. Abbie C. Wells; Le Grand, m. Grace Hardy; John Calvin and Mary Lucrecia, died; Vilate J. A.; Chloe, m. Francis Denton Benedict; Rhoda, m. Thomas J. McIntosh; Henriette; Brigham B., m. Alisa Muzzacotta. Family home, Salt Lake City.
Married Lucinda Allen in 1846, at Nauvoo, Ill., who was born 1824 and came to Utah 1848, Brigham Young company. Their children: Josephine, m. Oliver Free; Phineas Howe; John C., m. Cyntha Chrismon; Willard L., m. —— Shurtliff.
Married Lydia Flemming (widow) 1846, at Nauvoo, Ill. Their children: Isaac, m. —— Neff; Caroline, m. William Statie.
Married Mary Ann Burnham (widow) 1846, at Nauvoo, Ill. Their children: Elmyra, m. Robert Russell Clarentine, m. Jasper Conrad.
Married Sarah Jane Kinsman (widow) 1868, at Salt Lake City Endowment house (daughter of James Snow of Provo, Utah). Their children: Edward; Sarah Kinsman, died.
Senior president all quorums of seventies, Church of J. C. of L. D. S.; missionary to eastern states 1844; minister of Gospel. Died July 16, 1881.

YOUNG, SEYMOUR B. (son of Joseph Young and Jane Adeline Bicknell). Born Oct. 3, 1837, Kirtland, Ohio. Came to Utah 1850, Wilford Woodruff company.
Married Elizabeth Ann Riter, April, 1867, at Salt Lake City Endowment house (daughter of Levi E. Riter and Rebecca Dalworth, of Chester county, Pa., pioneers Oct. 2, 1847, Jedediah M. Grant company). She was born 1847, at Winter Quarters, in Nebraska. Came to Utah with parents. Their children: Seymour B., m. Louine Clawson; Lillie, m. Melvin D. Wells; Florence Pearl; Joseph B., died; Ada L., m. Thomas J. Lambert; Louis C., died; Elma; Levi Edgar, m. Valina Brinton; Clifford Earl, m. Edith Grant; Bernice, m. Orson Rogers; Irene; Hortense C.
Married Abbie C. Wells April, 1884, at Salt Lake City Endowment house (daughter of Daniel E. Wells and Hannah C. Free, of Salt Lake City, pioneers in 1848, Daniel H. Wells company). She was born in September, 1852. Their children: Hannah L., m. Allen Clark; Alice, died.
Senior president first council of seventies; missionary to Great Britain 1857 and in 1870. City health officer Salt Lake City four years; veteran Union army 1862; corporal, Lot Smith company, in Black Hawk war, and at Western Tooele and Cedar Mountains. Physician and surgeon.

YOUNG, LORENZO DOW (son of John Young of New Hampshire). Born Oct. 9, 1807, Hillsboro, N. H. Came to Utah July 24, 1847, Brigham Young company.
Married Persis Goodally (daughter of Noel Goodall and Mary Swain, of England). She was born March 15, 1806. Their children: William Goodall, m. Delia Clark; Joseph Watson, m. Katy ——, m. Loretta Eldredge, m. Julia T. Adams; Harriet Maria, m. Joseph Gurnsey Brown; John R.; Perry Le Grand, m. Abbina Terry, m. Tamar Jane Black; Franklin Wheeler, m. Nancy Leonard Green, m. Anna ——; Lorenzo Sabisky, m. Sarah Amelia Black. Family home, Salt Lake City.
High priest; bishop 18th ward, Salt Lake City, 1850. Farmer; stock and wool grower. Died October, 1895.

YOUNG, LORENZO SABISKY (son of Lorenzo Dow Young and Persis Goodall). He was born March 9, 1841, Winchester, Ill. Came to Utah July 24, 1847, Brigham Young company.
Married Sarah Amelia Black July 15, 1872, Salt Lake City (daughter of William Black and Emma Jane Washburn, of Illinois, pioneers in 1849). She was born July 13, 1854. Their children: Joseph Watson b. Jan. 22, 1873, m. Delight McConnel; Persia Amy b. Oct. 15, 1874, m. Orville Claud Roberts; Lorenzo Dow b. May 18, 1877, m. Rose Bassell; Howard William b. Feb. 2, 1880, m. Lucy Thomas; Sabisky Grant b. April 16, 1882, d. aged 19; Gurnsey Brown b. Jan. 3, 1884; Charles Ray b. Sept. 1, 1886, m. Christina Gilbert; Benjamin Franklin b. May 17, 1889; Angus b. April 14, 1891; Tamar b. Dec. 1, 1893; Chillas b. Aug. 18, 1897; Orville Harry b. Jan. 26, 1900. Family home Huntington, Utah.
Early settler in "Dixie" country. High priest. Farmer.

YOUNG, PERRY LE GRAND (son of Lorenzo Dow Young and Hannah Hewitt). Born Nov. 1, 1858, Salt Lake City.
Married Elinor Telle Young Feb. 1, 1883, at Salt Lake City (daughter of Phineas Young and Elinor Maria James, of Salt Lake City, pioneers July 24, 1847, Brigham Young company). She was born Oct. 4, 1858. Their children: Lorenzo Clifford b. Jan. 20, 1884, m. Susie Colton; Lyle Le Grand b. Feb. 16, 1886; Brigham Willard b. Nov. 5, 1888; Dallas Huber b. Jan. 6, 1892. Family home Vernal, Utah.
High priest. Deputy marshal Vernal, Utah; postmaster at Vernal three years. Farmer; stockraiser; contractor.

YOUNG, H. PHINEAS (son of John Young and Abigail Howe, Hopkinton, Middlesex county, Mass.). Born Feb. 15, 1799, Hopkinton. Came to Utah July 24, 1847, Brigham Young company.
Married Clarissa Hamilton Sept. 28, 1818, at Auburn, N. Y. Their children: Brigham H., m. Cedenia Clark; Abigail. Family home Auburn, N. Y.
Married Lucy Cowdery. Their children: Harriet, m. Edwin C. Williamson; Adelaide, m. Abner Bevan; Phineas and Sarah, d. young. Family home Nauvoo, Ill.
Married Phoebe Clark. Their children: Cedenia, d. infant; Celeste, m. James Pack; Virgini, m. James Carrigan; Seraph, m. Henry White; Julia, m. Frederick Chandler; Phineas, m. Helena ——; Seymour, d. young; William, m. Margret Stanley.
Married Elinor Maria James 1856, at Salt Lake City

(daughter of William James and Mary Williams, of Lugwardine, Herefordshire, Eng., latter pioneer). She was born Nov. 27, 1827. Their children: Elinor Tillie, m. Perry La Grande Young; Marian Ross, m. Alonzo Mitchell; Emeline Free, m. Leon Pack; May Isobel, m. Dan Lambert. Last two families resided Salt Lake City.
Bishop of 2nd ward at Salt Lake City; missionary to England and Canada. Early printer in Salt Lake City; mail contractor and saddler. Died Oct. 10, 1876.

YOUNG, ROBERT D. (son of Archibald M. Young of Kirkintolloch, born 1822, and Mary Graham of Glasgow, Scotland, born 1832, at Glasgow). Born July 24, 1867, at Kirkintolloch. Came to Utah 1872.
Married Mary S. Parker Oct. 28, 1891 (daughter of Joseph E. Parker and Mary Ross, former pioneer 1851, latter 1852). She was born Aug. 18, 1872, at Kanosh, Utah. Their children: Robert Orval b. Oct. 30, 1892; Rodney Dixon b. June 6, 1894; Mary Velma b. March 25, 1896; Archibald Bryant b. Feb. 26, 1899; Lauretta b. Feb. 16, 1901; Beatrice Sonoma b. Sept. 28, 1906; Huldah Isabell b. July 27, 1908; Joseph Llewellyn b. Nov. 21, 1910.
Missionary to Australia. 1901-03; counselor to stake president; stake president. City councilman three terms. Superintendent Western Construction Co.; manager Richfield Implement Co.

YOUNG, THOMAS CUNNINGHAM (son of Robert Young and Catherine Cunningham of Renfrew, Scotland). Born Oct. 31, 1825, at Renfrew. Came to Utah August, 1852, Captain Jepson company.
Married Mary Hay Oct. 8, 1856, Salt Lake City (daughter of William Hay and Margaret Frazer of Paisley, Scotland), who was born April 21, 1821. Their children: Thomas b. Sept. 14, 1857, m. Emma Susannah Bowen; William Hay b. Dec. 31, 1858; Margaret b. Nov. 22, 1860, m. D. J. Bowen; Catherine b. March 9, 1862; Robert Cunningham b. July 25, 1863 (d. Nov. 10, 1901), m. Bianca Osborne, m. Selma Danielson; Isabella Mary b. Feb. 25, 1865 (d. Nov. 10, 1901), m. Myron John Richards. Family home Perry, Utah.
Elder. Died May 6, 1868.

YOUNG, THOMAS CUNNINGHAM, JR. (son of Thomas Cunningham Young and Mary Hay). Born Sept. 14, 1857, Perry, Utah.
Married Emma Susannah Bowen July 10, 1884, Logan, Utah (daughter of David Bowen and Annie Shackleton, of Salt Lake City, Utah. Father came to Utah Sept. 26, 1856, Edmund Ellsworth handcart company). Their children: Ernest Thomas b. May 11, 1885; Le Roy Bowen b. April 19, 1887; Annie b. Feb. 25, 1892, d. infant; Mary b. Feb. 22, 1894; Stella b. Feb. 12, 1897; Ora Ellen b. Aug. 23, 1899, d. infant; David Bowen b. Dec. 11, 1903, d. infant Family home Perry, Utah.
Elder; seventy; missionary to New Zealand May 26, 1888-91; president Houraki district of that mission.

YOUNG, WILLIAM LOWE (son of Benjamin and Sarah Lowe Young, of England). Born Feb. 4, 1830. Came to Utah, Sept. 1, 1860, John Smith company.
Married Helen Bunting Sept. 30, 1850 (daughter of James and Ann Bunting, former died in England, latter pioneer 1860, John Smith company). She was born Sept. 6, 1827. Family resided Spanish Fork, Salt Lake City, Kaysville and Preston, Utah.
Married Julia Widdisen Reeves Aug. 8, 1870, at Salt Lake City (daughter of Abraham Reeves and Bessie Widdisen, pioneers 1868). Their children: William Francis Lowe b. July 23, 1871, d. April 10, 1878; Eunice Elizabeth b. Nov. 23, 1872, m. James D. Dawson Oct. 1900 (d. Jan. 15, 1910); George b. March 10, 1874, m. Rosetta Barfus May 15, 1901; Urban b. Oct. 17, 1875, m. Annie Michelson Dec. 31, 1908; Ernest b. May 17, 1877 (d. in Windsor, Can.), m. Mary Draper; Nathan b. June 4, 1879, d. Sept. 14, 1880; Julia b March 28, 1881, d. Aug. 16, 1881; William Henry b. Feb. 4, 1883. Family resided Kaysville, Utah, and Preston, Idaho.
Veteran Black Hawk war. Helped survey townsite of Preston, Idaho. Helped build first railroad in Utah.

Z

ZABRISKIE, LEWIS (son of Christian Zabriskie and Elizabeth Morgan, of Hackensack, N. J.). Born March 8, 1796, in New York. Came to Utah in 1849.
Married Amelia Burton Sept. 9, 1822. Their children: William b. June 29, 1823, died; Alva b. March 26, 1825, m. Susan Roberts; Elizabeth b. Sept. 9, 1827, died; Sarah b. Jan. 19, 1830, m. Dr. Dennis; Susanna b. Nov. 29, 1832; Amy b. May 5, 1835, died.
Married Jane Porter Reed Sept. 3, 1835. Their children: Julian and Cynthia Ann (twins) b. Feb. 24, 1843; Phoebe b. Feb. 2, 1846; Arvilla b. April 14, 1848; Lucinda Jane b. Feb. 19, 1850; Lewis John b. July 2, 1852; Emily b. March 12, 1855; Oran b. Nov. 27, 1857; Charles William b. Aug. 1, 1860.
Married Elizabeth Wise Oct. 26, 1872. Families resided Provo, Utah.
Farmer. Died April 7, 1884, McCloud, Kan.

ZABRISKIE, ALVA (son of Lewis Zabriskie and Amelia Burton). Born March 25, 1825. Came to Utah in 1849.
Married Susan Roberts June 25, 1854, Provo, Utah (daughter of Horace Roberts and Harriet McEvers, of Provo, pioneers 1851, Gordon Grove company). She was born Feb. 16, 1834. Their children: Alva Marcellus b. Feb. 17, 1855, m. Emma Hooper; George Albert b. Nov. 15, 1856, m. Annie Christina Jensen; Horace Ephraim b. May 15, 1858, m. Della Snow. Family home Provo, Utah.
Member 70th quorum seventies. Early settler in Provo. Veteran Black Hawk Indian war. Farmer. Died Jan. 8, 1860.

ZABRISKIE, ALVA MARCELLUS (son of Alva Zabriskie and Susan Roberts). Born Feb. 17, 1855, Provo, Utah.
Married Emma Brain, at Provo, Utah (daughter of John Brain and Susan Sinctrom, of 'Bath, Eng.), who was born June 16, 1857. Their children: Alva Marcellus, Jr.; May, m. William Martin Roylance; George; Irwin, m. Maud Daniels; Emma; Walter; Arnold. Family home, Provo. Machinist.

ZABRISKIE, GEORGE ALBERT (son of Alva Zabriskie and Susan Roberts). Born Nov. 15, 1856, Provo, Utah.
Married Annie Christina Jensen April 12, 1882, Fairview, Utah (daughter of Peter Christian Jensen, of Milburn, Utah, pioneer 1853). She was born Nov. 6, 1855. Their children: George Alva b. Feb. 1, 1883, m. Mary Breckenridge; Mary Christine b. Nov. 1, 1884, m. Henry W. Sanderson, Jr.; Susan Cecelia b. Sept. 19, 1886, died; Maud b. Oct. 4, 1888, m. Thomas H. Robinson; John Peter b. Oct. 24, 1890, m. Violet Harding; Bytha Mabel b. Sept. 12, 1892, died; Claudius b. June 24, 1894; Arvilla Cerena b. Nov. 13, 1896; Albert Morley b. Oct. 3, 1898; Olive b. Sept. 2, 1900; Zella Monetah b. Jan. 4, 1903; Coral Ruby b. Feb. 25, 1905. Family home Vineyard, Utah.
High priest; ward teacher; ward clerk; home missionary; 2d counselor in bishopric of Vineyard ward; superintendent of Sunday schools, Milburn, Utah, 1885-98. Justice of peace, Milburn; school trustee. Farmer and fruitgrower.

ZIMMERMAN, GEORGE GOTTLAB, of Franklin, Pa. Born July 23, 1781, Wurtemberg, Germany. Came to Utah in 1851.
Married Julia Ann Hoke, who was born Nov. 27, 1798, at Wurtemberg. Their children: Jacob b. Dec. 24, 1816, d. Dec. 14, 1891 Chrestena, m. Abraham Stevens, m. Ezekiel Hopkins; John, m. Harriet Laura Lamb; Mary; Emanuel; Catherine; Julia Ann, m. Charles Horatio Drury, m. William Clark; Elizabeth, m. Suel Lamb; Fredricca, m. John Brown; Rosannah, m. John C. Naegle; Susan, m. John Naegle, m. William A. Terry. Family home Lehi, Utah.
Superintendent Sunday school, Lehi. First keeper of toll bridge over Jordan river; school teacher; shoemaker. Died June 17, 1866.

ZIMMERMAN, JOHN (son of George Gottlab Zimmerman and Julia Ann Hoke of Franklin, Pa.). Born Oct. 3, 1820, in Washington county, Md. Came to Utah in 1852.
Married Harriet Laura Lamb Sept. 21, 1850, Garden Grove, Iowa (daughter of Erastus Lamb and Abigail Jackson, of Wayne county, N. Y.), who was born Dec. 2, 1830, and died Feb. 22, 1899. Their children: George Erastus, m. Mary Ann Clark; Harriet Abigail, m. Henry Moroni Royle; Louisa Emeline, m. Abel John Evans; Margaret, m. Albert Bushman; Polly Ann, m. David Lossie; Elizabeth, m. Isaac Fox; Juliann, m. George Southwick; Saul, m. Flora Bushman; John, Jr.; Jacob Henry, and Robert Wilson, died.
Member 66th quorum seventies; high priest; block teacher. Major in Nauvoo legion; veteran Indian wars; city councilman. Farmer and sheepraiser. Died November, 1908, Lehi, Utah.

ZIMMERMAN, GEORGE ERASTUS (son of John Zimmerman and Harriet Laura Lamb). Born June 22, 1851, Garden Grove, Iowa. Came to Utah with parents.
Married Mary Ann Clark Aug. 31, 1874, Salt Lake City (daughter of William Clark of England, and Jane Stephens of Newark, N. J., pioneers 1853). She was born March 8, 1859. Their children: Mary Abigail b. June 16, 1875, m. Charles A. Turner; George Erastus, Jr. b. Dec. 8, 1877, died; John William b. Jan. 26, 1881, m. Christena Soleborg; Laura Jane b. Dec. 9, 1883, died; James Erie b. Aug. 22, 1885; Viola b. Aug. 7, 1887, m. Ervin Henry; Valarious b. Oct. 18, 1891; Saul Stephen b. Oct. 13, 1892; Lester b. Jan. 28, 1895; Zeltha May b. May 8, 1899; Warren Clark b. Sept. 4, 1904.
Member 127th quorum seventies; high priest; block teacher 25 years; president deacons quorum second ward; city councilman Lehi, 1898-99. Member of Nauvoo Legion, in company of Capt. Joseph Thomas. Pioneer road builder. Farmer and stockman.

ZOLLINGER, JOHN (son of Heinrich Zollinger, born Jan. 4, 1750, and Barbara Bram b. April 30, 1752, of Urdorf, Canton Zurich, Switzerland). He was born June 4, 1796, at Urdorf. With his family, left his home in Switzerland in April, 1862, spent nine weeks on the ocean. Came to Utah Nov. 2, 1862, William H. Dame company.
Married Elizabeth Usteri in 1829 (daughter of — Usteri and Catherine Irminger), who was born July 4, 1809, Zurich, Switzerland, and came to Utah with husband. Their chil-

dren: Ferdinand Johann b. Oct. 18, 1829, m. Louisa Meyer; Anna b. Nov. 11, 1831, m. John N. Haderli; Johannes b. Oct. 25, 1833, died; Anna Barbara b. Jan. 27, 1835, m. Conrad Meyer; Elizabetha b. Oct. 18, 1837, m. Jacob Neser; Dorothea b. Feb. 3, 1841, m. Daniel Law; Jacob b. July 3, 1845, m. Rosetta Loosli May 9, 1870. Family home Zurich, Switzerland.
Settled at Providence, Utah, where he resided until his death Feb. 18, 1875.

ZOLLINGER, FERDINAND JOHANN (son of John Zollinger and Elizabeth Usterli). Born Oct. 18, 1829, Flunten, Switzerland. Came to Utah in same company with father.
Married Louisa Meier May 12, 1862 (daughter of Jacob Meier and Barbara Knecht), who was born Oct. 18, 1829, and came to Utah with husband. Their children: Louisa b. Jan. 24, 1864, m. John Nuffer October, 1886; Ferdinand b. Jan. 24, 1866, m. Emma Fuhriman Oct. 27, 1892; Bertha b. Aug. 3, 1867, m. William John Chugg Jan. 9, 1889; Mary Elizabeth b. March 3, 1870, m. James Bullock Dec. 31, 1890; Sarah b. July 26, 1875, m. Lorenzo McAllister March 29, 1894.

ZOLLINGER, JACOB (son of John Zollinger and Elizabeth Usterli). Born July 3, 1845, Urdorf, Switzerland.
Married Rosetta Loosli May 9, 1870, Salt Lake City (daughter of Ulrich Loosli and Magdalena Aashlmann, pioneers Sept. 3, 1860, James D. Ross company). She was born June 16, 1851, Durrenroth, Switzerland. Their children: Jacob Ezra b. May 30, 1871, m. Bertha Aikeli Feb. 27, 1901; William Richard b. May 4, 1873, m. Bertha Rosa Furrer June 3, 1903; John David b. Jan. 17, 1875, m. Jenny Pearce Dec. 24, 1901; Joseph Hyrum b. Sept. 27, 1877, m. Laura Alkeli Feb. 14, 1905; Rosetta Amelia b. Oct. 17, 1879, m. John Stauffer Feb. 26, 1908; Henry Moroni b. Oct. 8, 1881, m. Eliza Stirland Feb. 24, 1910; Aaron Arthur b. Oct. 8, 1883, m. Hannah Pearl Nedda Nov. 24, 1909; Mary Magdalena b. Nov. 27, 1885; Elizabeth b. May 3, 1888, d. Nov. 1892; Oliver Herman b. Oct. 15, 1892; Anna Gertrude Geneva b. Aug. 12, 1895; Daniel Lawrence b. May 20, 1898; Evelyn Zina Otilia b. Nov. 21, 1900. Family home Providence, Utah.
Went to Missouri River for immigrants 1866; railroad builder 1868-1869; built meeting houses. Missionary to Switzerland 1889-1891; active church worker. Farmer; dairyman.

ZOLLINGER, WILLIAM RICHARD (son of Jacob Zollinger and Rosetta Loosli). Born May 4, 1873, Providence, Utah.
Married Bertha Rosa Furrer June 3, 1903, Salt Lake City (daughter of Christian Furrer and Elizabeth König), who was born Aug. 1, 1878, Kiesen canton, Bern, Switzerland. Their children: Homer William b. June 9, 1904; Ruth Elizabeth b. Dec. 31, 1905; Rachel Rosetta b. May 3, 1908; Jessie Jacob b. Oct. 26, 1911.
Officer in Y. M. M. I. A. 1884-1897; missionary to Switzerland 1897-1900; ward clerk 1901-1909; secretary 32d quorum seventies 1907-1909; high priest; bishop's counselor. Member town board; town clerk. Director in several corporations.

ZUNDEL, JACOB (son of Eberhart Zundel and Julia Ann Pfluger, of Germany). Born Aug. 28, 1796, Wertheim, Wurtemberg, Germany. Came to Utah in October, 1852, David Wood company.
Married Sarah Forstner (daughter of George Forstner and Mariah Zoll), who was born Jan. 8, 1809, Old Harmony, Pa. Their children: Melena b. Nov. 1833, m. Noah Brimhall, m. John Miller; Abraham b. Jan. 25, 1836, m. Abigail Abbott, m. Mary Elenor Ingram; Emma Mariah b. Aug. 28, 1838, m. Eli Harvey Pierce, m. Elisha Meilroy, m. Elihu Pettingill; Isaac David Eberhart b. Nov. 17, 1840, m. Elizabeth Jane Harding, m. Philene Hall, m. Almira Hall, m. Iduna Hunsaker; Jacob, Jr. b. Feb. 10, 1843, d. Oct. 10, 1843; Matilda Josephine b. Jan. 16, 1845, m. Charles Harding; Daniel b. July 25, 1849, m. Betsy Hill.

ZUNDEL, ABRAHAM (son of Jacob Zundel and Sarah Forstner). Born Jan. 25, 1836, Phillipsburg, Pa. Came to Utah with parents.
Married Abigail Abbott Feb. 13, 1857, Ogden, Utah (daughter of Stephen Abbott and Abigail Smith; former died at Nauvoo, Ill., latter pioneer Oct. 27, 1849, George A. Smith company). She was born Feb. 3, 1842, Perry, Pike county, Ill. Their children: Abigail Lucina b. Jan. 9, 1859, m. Fred O. Beecher Jan. 9, 1879; Cyntha Matilda b. Jan. 1, 1861, m. David H. Ward Feb. 5, 1880; Abraham Eberhart b. March 20, 1864, m. Sarah Elizabeth Welling Jan. 9, 1895; Sarah Emily b. Feb. 21, 1867, m. Joseph Josephsen May 2, 1888; Mariah Estelle b. Nov. 8, 1869; Limhi Forstner b. Sept. 24, 1872, m. Evelyn Gibbs, May 9, 1892; Jacob Abbott b. March 3, 1875, m. Minnie Hockins Nov. 15, 1896; Stephen Louis b. Oct. 3, 1877; Joseph M. b. Dec. 23, 1881, m. Kate Bench Dec. 23, 1903; John Henry b. Jan. 6, 1880, m. Clarissa Mariah Pettingill Feb. 8, 1904 (latter died Dec. 12, 1909), m. Ida Christena Dagmer Sorensen Sept. 4, 1912.
Married Mary Elenor Ingram Sept. 3, 1884, Logan, Utah (daughter of James Ingram and Charlotte Holland), who was born Jan. 21, 1866, at Three Mile Creek (now Perry), Box Elder county, Utah. Their children: George Lorenzo b. Dec. 23, 1885, m. Rose Mae Bell Sept. 14, 1910, Logan, Utah; Fanny Louise b. March 10, 1890, d. Sept. 27, 1901; Ruth b. April 16, 1893, d. Sept. 22, 1894; Mary Ellenor b. Dec. 21, 1894; Asenath b. Jan. 21, 1897, d. April 2, 1906; Oliver b. Feb. 21, 1900, d. Feb. 22, 1900; Theodore Roosevelt b. March 31, 1901, d. May 5, 1901.

Filled a mission to Salmon River in 1855; bishop's counselor to Bishop George Ward and George Facer, of Willard ward 20 years; bishop of Willard Ward for four years; first counselor to President Hockins of Malad stake, four years; Indian missionary eight years. State senator from Box Elder and Tooele counties, first Utah legislature; mayor of Willard City two years; justice of peace, Willard three terms. Carried mail from Utah Salmon River 1855-57, summer and winter.

ZUNDEL, ISAAC DAVID EBERHART (son of Jacob Zundel and Sarah Forstner). Born Nov. 17, 1840, Nauvoo, Ill. Came to Utah with parents.
Married Elizabeth Jane Harding Sept. 30, 1865, Salt Lake City (daughter of Dwight Harding and Phoebe Holbrook, pioneers in September, 1851, John Smith company). She was born Oct. 23, 1840, at Quincy, Ill. Came to Utah with parents. Their children: Phoebe M. b. Aug. 12, 1866, m. Moronia Ward Sept. 25, 1884; Isaac David b. Sept. 18, 1868, m. Julia B. Hall April 11, 1889; Jacob Eberhart b. Dec. 19, 1871, m. Uphana Welker Sept. 19, 1895; Dwight Harding b. Sept. 3, 1873, d. May 13, 1874; Elizabeth Sarah b. April 9, 1876, m. William H. Gibbs Dec. 16, 1896; Moses Abraham b. Sept. 28, 1878, m. Lena Walner Oct. 23, 1907; Joseph b. Aug. 22, 1881, d. Aug. 25, 1881; George Alma b. March 11, 1883, m. Irene Morris June 1, 1911. Family resided Plymouth, Utah, and Woodruff, Idaho.
Married Philene Hall July 14, 1881, Salt Lake City (daughter of David Hall and Jane Hale—married July 23, 1850, near Franklin, Iowa, pioneers Aug. 2, 1862, Captain Brun company). She was born Aug. 26, 1863, Little Cottonwood, Utah. Their children: Philene Jane b. Nov. 30, 1882, died; Leona b. Oct. 26, 1884.
Married Almira Hall.
Married Iduma Hunsaker.
Missionary among Indians 14 years; acting bishop Washakie ward; bishop of Thatcher, Ariz. ward three years; now high councilor of Lagrand stake, Oregon; first bishop in Mormon Church ordained to preside over an Indian ward.

ZUNDEL, ISAAC DAVID (son of Isaac David Eberhart Zundel and Elizabeth Jane Harding). Born Sept. 18, 1868, Willard, Utah.
Married Julia B. Hall April 11, 1889, Logan, Utah (daughter of David Hall and Jane Hale), who was born Oct. 16, 1869, Crescent, Iowa. Their children: David Leo b. Jan. 29, 1890, d. March 12, 1891; William Sylvester b. Sept. 3, 1891; Sarah Bell b. June 18, 1893; Dwight Hall b. Feb. 27, 1896; Jane Hall b. Nov. 20, 1897; Vera Harding b. April 22, 1901; Verga Hale b. April 22, 1901; Afton b. Feb. 18, 1903; Reed b. March 14, 1905; Leona b. April 20, 1907, d. Nov. 6, 1907; Verium b. Aug. 31, 1908; Gladys b. Feb. 21, 1911. Family home Woodruff, Idaho.
Missionary to northern states in 1897; released August, 1900; bishop of Woodruff ward June 25, 1905.

ZUNDLE, JOHN (son of John Zundle of Nauvoo, Ill.). Born in 1791, Wurtemberg, Prussia. Came to Utah Oct. 1, 1852, David D. Wood company.
Married Chrestina Lauttenslager in 1832 (daughter of John Lauttenslager of Rheibach, Darmstadt, Germany), who was born July 31, 1811, at Darmstadt, and came to Utah with husband. Their children: John, Jr., m. Fannie Fry; Thomas, m. Josephine Hartly; Gideon, Henry, Margaret, and Justina, latter four died; Julia Ann, m. John Couch; Joseph, m. Julia Copland; Amelia, m. John Wesley Keele; Christina, m. Joseph Crook; Mary Ann, m. Mr. Cocahanse; William.
High priest. Wheelwright. Dead.

ZUNDLE, THOMAS (son of John Zundle and Chrestina Lauttenslager). Born March 16, 1836, Allegheny county, Pa. Came to Utah with parents.
Married Josephine (Lucy Smith) Hartly May 25, 1862, Mona, Utah (daughter of Samuel Hartly and Eliza Gill, of Sheffield, Yorkshire, Eng.), who was born April 11, 1846, and came to Utah in 1856.
High priest. Settled at Grantsville 1852; moved to Ogden 1855, to Payson 1857, and to Salem 1862; thence to Leamington and Rabbit Valley; returned to Salem and finally settled at Wellington in 1882. Assisted in digging canals and building wagon roads; also in bringing immigrants to Utah. Farmer and freighter.

ZWAHLEN, JOHN. Born Aug. 14, 1851, in Switzerland. Came to Utah 1874.
Married Mary Shultless October, 1874, Richfield, Utah, who was born April 6, 1850. Their children: Mary, m. Joseph Henry Behunin; John, died; Joseph, m. Viola Petersen; Hyrum, m. Emma Rapley; Frederick; Samuel; Emma; David, d. aged 17 months. Family home Ferron, Utah.
High priest; missionary to Germany 1895-97. Farmer and apiarist.

ZWEIFEL, JACOB (son of John Zweifel and Barbara Martin of Linthal, Canton Glarus, Switzerland). Born in 1840, in Canton Glarus. Came to Utah 1861, independent company.
Married Elizabeth Smid in 1882, Salt Lake City (daughter

of Davit Smid of Switzerland), who was born in 1851. Their children: Jacob Josef, died; John Hyrum b. 1885, m. Hermina Feligs 1902; Cathrina Emma; Lisie Sarah. Family resided in Utah and Idaho.

ZWEIFEL, JOHN HYRUM (son of Jacob Zweifel and Elizabeth Smid). Born in 1885, Rexburg, Idaho. Married Hermina Feligs in 1902 at Rexburg.

ZWEIFEL, JOHN (son of John Zweifel and Barbara Martin of Linthal, Canton Glarus, Switzerland). Born Dec. 24, 1845, in Canton Glarus. Came to Utah Oct. 24, 1864, Bishop Hyde oxteam company.

Married Susan Kummer in April, 1868, Providence, Utah, and later at Salt Lake Endowment house (daughter of Johan Kummer and Elizabeth Bigler, of Bern, Switzerland). She was born in 1839. Their children: Susan b. April 11, 1869, died; Mary b. June 27, 1870, m. A. P. Springer; John b. Oct. 26, 1872, died; Elizabeth b. Nov. 5, 1874, m. Roy Bagley; Albert b. Jan. 25, 1876; William b. Jan. 19, 1879, died; Annie b. winter of 1881, d. infant; Eliza b. Feb. 19, 1883, m. Chriss Burgi; Frank b. March 19, 1885. Family home Providence and Midway, Utah.

Married Elizabeth Feuz Oct. 10, 1911, Salt Lake City daughter of John Feuz and Anna Abegglen), who was born Dec. 12, 1862. Family home Midway, Utah.

High priest; missionary to Missouri. Indian fighter. Farmer.

CHURCH CHRONOLOGY AND HISTORY

Historical events leading up to the beginning, foundation and organization of the Church of Jesus Christ of Latter-day Saints, for which this publication is indebted to the "Church Chronology," compiled by Andrew Jensen, assistant Church Historian, "The Doctrine and Covenants of the Church of Jesus Christ of Latter-day Saints," "Containing the Revelations Given to Joseph Smith, Jr., The Prophet, for the Building Up of the Kingdom of God in the Last Days," divided into verses by Orson Pratt, Sr., "The Pearl of Great Price," "a Selection from the Revelations, Translations and Narrations of Joseph Smith, Jr.," divided into chapters and verses by James E. Talmage, and the "History of Utah," by Orson F. Whitney.

Note:—These historical facts are presented in connection with this work to show why Utah was settled at the time it was; to show the spirit that imbued these pioneers to suffer the privations, hardships, sacrifices and deaths they did, that they might have a home and country where they could worship God according to the dictates of their conscience and in accord with their religious creed.

AUTHOR.

During the two first decades of the Nineteenth Century a number of men who were destined to take a most active part in the ushering in of the new gospel dispensation were born. Chief among these was the Prophet Joseph Smith.
1805.—December 23.—Joseph Smith, the Prophet, was born in Sharon, Windsor Co., Vt.
Among the men, older than the Prophet, who became intimately associated with him in establishing the Latter-day work, were the following:
Joseph Smith, Sr., born July 12, 1771, in Topsfield, Essex Co., Mass.
Martin Harris, born May 18, 1783, in Easttown, Saratoga Co., N. Y.
Sidney Rigdon, born Feb. 19, 1793, in St. Clair, Allegheny Co., Pa.
Edward Hunter, born June 22, 1793, in Newtown, Delaware Co., Pa.
Edward Partridge, born Aug. 27, 1793, in Pittsfield, Berkshire Co., Mass.
Newel K. Whitney, born Feb. 5, 1795, in Marlborough, Windham Co., Vt.
Lyman Wight, born May 9, 1796, in Fairfield, Herkimer Co., N. Y.
John E. Page, born Feb. 25, 1799, in Trenton, Oneida Co., N. Y.
Thomas B. Marsh, born Nov. 1, 1799, in Acton, Middlesex Co., Mass.
Hyrum Smith, born Feb. 9, 1800, in Tunbridge, Orange Co., Vt.
David W. Patten, born about 1800, in the State of New York.
Brigham Young, born June 1, 1801, in Whitingham, Windham Co., Vt.
Heber Chase Kimball, born June 14, 1801, at Sheldon, Franklin Co., Vt.
Willard Richards, born June 24, 1804, at Hopkinton, Middlesex Co., Mass.
David Whitmer, born Jan. 7, 1805, near Harrisburg, Dauphin Co., Pa.
Orson Hyde, born Jan. 28, 1805, in Oxford, New Haven Co., Conn.
Oliver Cowdery, born October, 1805, in Wells, Rutland Co., Vt.
1806.—Wm. E. McLellin was born this year in Tennessee.
1807.—March 1.—Wilford Woodruff was born in Farmington, Hartford Co., Conn.
April 12.—Parley Parker Pratt was born in Burlington, Otsego Co., N. Y.
November 3.—Luke S. Johnson was born in Pomfret, Windsor Co., Vt.
1808.—November 1.—John Taylor was born in Milnthorpe, Westmoreland, England.
1809.—August 21.—Charles Coulson Rich was born in Campbell County, Mass.
1811.—February 22.—Ezra Taft Benson was born in Mendon, Worcester Co., Mass.
March 13.—Wm. Smith was born in Royalton, Windsor Co., Vt.
September 19.—Orson Pratt was born in Hartford, Washington Co., N. Y.
September 20.—John F. Boynton was born in Bradford, Essex Co., Mass.
October 24.—Lyman Eugene Johnson was born in Pomfret, Windsor Co., Vt.
1813.—January 8.—Albert Carrington was born in Royalton, Windsor Co., Vt.
March 30.—Amasa M. Lyman was born in Lyman, Grafton Co., N. H.
1814.—April 3.—Lorenzo Snow was born in Mantua, Portage Co., Ohio.
October 27.—Daniel Hanmer Wells was born in Trenton, Oneida Co., N. Y.
1815.—Joseph Smith, Sr., removed with his family from Vermont to Palmyra, Wayne Co., N. Y.
1816.—February 21.—Jedediah Morgan Grant was born in Windsor, Broome Co., N. Y.
1817.—June 26.—George Albert Smith was born in Potsdam, St. Lawrence Co., N. Y.

1818.—November 9.—Erastus Snow was born in St. Johnsbury, Caledonia Co., Vt.
1820.—The Baptists, Methodists and Presbyterians held protracted revival meetings in and about Palmyra, N. Y., which resulted in great contention among the preachers and members of the different sects who sought to influence the new converts to join their respective churches. Joseph Smith, Jr. (then about fourteen years old), being unable to decide which of all the sects was right, and being deeply impressed with the promise in James 1, 5: "If any of you lack wisdom, let him ask of God that giveth to all men liberally, and upbraideth not; and it shall be given him," retired to a grove near his father's house, early in the spring of the year, where he sought the Lord in earnest prayer. While thus engaged, he beheld two glorious beings wrapped in a brilliant light, standing above him in the air. One of them spoke to him, calling him by name, and said (pointing to the other), "This is my beloved Son, hear Him." Joseph then asked the personages, standing above him in the light, which of the sects was right and which he should join. He was answered that he must join none of them, for they were all wrong. The person speaking said further that all their creeds were an abomination in his sight and that "those professors were all corrupt." "They draw near to me with their lips, but their hearts are far from me; they teach for doctrine the commandments of men, having a form of godliness; but they deny the power thereof."
1821.—April 2.—Franklin Dewey Richards was born in Richmond, Berkshire Co., Mass.
1823.—September 21.—Joseph Smith, Jr., while engaged in earnest prayer in his father's house in Manchester, near Palmyra, N. Y., saw the room in which he had retired for the night filled with light surpassing that of noonday; in the midst of which stood a person dressed in white, whose countenance was as lightning, and yet full of innocence and goodness. This was the angel Moroni (sometimes erroneously called Nephi), who informed Joseph that God had a work for him (Joseph) to do, and that his "name should be had for good and evil among all nations." The angel quoted many passages of Scripture, and told Joseph that the native inhabitants of America were a remnant of Israel who had anciently enjoyed the ministry of inspired men, that records engraved on plates of gold, containing their history and also the fulness of the everlasting Gospel had been preserved and were buried in a neighboring hill. While conversing with the angel, a vision was opened to Joseph's view, so that he could see the place where the plates were deposited, and he was told by the angel that he should obtain them at some future day, if he was faithful. After imparting many instructions, the angel disappeared, but returned twice during the night, and repeated what he had said on his first visit; he also gave further instructions.
September 22.—Joseph Smith, Jr., was again visited by the angel Moroni and received further instructions. He related what he had seen and heard to his father, who believed his words, and advised him to do as he had been instructed. He then went to the hill (Cumorah) that he had seen in his vision the previous night, and soon found the spot where the plates containing the ancient records were buried in a stone box. He lifted the lid of the box and beheld "the plates, the Urim and Thummim and breastplate, as stated by the angel." While attempting to "take them out," the angel informed him "that the time for bringing them forth had not yet arrived, neither would, until four years from that time."
1824.—September 22.—Joseph Smith, Jr., again visited the hill Cumorah, according to previous commandment, and there received further instructions from the angel. On the same day of the two following years he made similar visits to the hill, receiving instructions from the angel each time.
1827.—January 11.—George Quayle Cannon was born in Liverpool, Lancashire, England.
January 18.—Joseph Smith, Jr., married Emma Hale, a daughter of Isaac Hale, while in the employ of Josiah Stoal, in Chenango County, N. Y.
September 22.—The angel Moroni delivered to Joseph Smith, Jr., the ancient records, or the plates of the Book

1275

ommanding them to ordain each other. But they were to wait for this ordination till the others who had been baptized assembled together.

1830.—March.—Martin Harris was commanded by revelation through Joseph Smith, Jr., at Manchester, N. Y., to repent of his sins. (Doc. and Cov., Sec. 19.)

April.—An important revelation on Priesthood and Church government in general was given through Joseph Smith, Jr. and again, by way of commandment to the church concerning the manner of baptism.

All those who humble themselves before God, and desire to be baptized and come forth with broken hearts and contrite spirits, and witness before the church that they have truly repented of all their sins, and are willing to take upon them the name of Jesus Christ, having a determination to serve him to the end, and truly manifest by their works that they have received of the Spirit of Christ unto the remission of their sins, shall be received by baptism into his church.

The duty of the elders, priests, teachers, deacons, and members of the church of Christ.

An apostle is an elder, and it is his calling to baptize.
And to ordain other elders, priests, teachers, and deacons.
And to administer bread and wine—the emblems of the flesh and blood of Christ—
And to confirm those who are baptized into the church, by the laying on of hands for the baptism of fire and the Holy Ghost, according to the scriptures;
And to teach, expound, exhort, baptize, and watch over the church;
And to confirm the church by the laying on of the hands, and the giving of the Holy Ghost.
And to take the lead of all meetings.

The elders are to conduct the meetings as they are led by the Holy Ghost, according to the commandments and revelations of God.

The priest's duty is to preach, teach, expound, exhort, and baptize, and administer the sacrament.
And visit the house of each member, and exhort them to pray vocally and in secret, and attend to all family duties;
And he may also ordain other priests, teachers, and deacons.
And he is to take the lead of meetings when there is no elder present;
But when there is an elder present, he is only to preach, teach, expound, exhort, and baptize,
And visit the house of each member, exhorting them to pray vocally and in secret, and attend to all family duties.
In all these duties the priest is to assist the elder if occasion requires.

The teacher's duty is to watch over the church always, and be with and strengthen them.
And see that there is no iniquity in the church—neither hardness with each other—neither lying, backbiting, nor evil speaking;
And see that the church meet together often, and also see that all the members do their duty;
And he is to take the lead of meetings in the absence of the elder or priest—
And is to be assisted always, in all his duties in the church, by the deacons, if occasion requires;
But neither teachers nor deacons have authority to baptize, administer the sacrament, or lay on hands:
They are, however, to warn, expound, exhort, and teach and invite all to come unto Christ.

Every elder, priest, teacher, or deacon, is to be ordained according to the gifts and callings of God unto him; and he is to be ordained by the power of the Holy Ghost, which is in the one who ordains him.

The several elders, composing this church of Christ are to meet in conference once in three months, or from time to time as said conferences shall direct or appoint;

And said conferences are to do whatever church business is necessary to be done at the time.

The elders are to receive their licenses from other elders, by vote of the church to which they belong, or from the conferences.

Each priest, teacher, or deacon, who is ordained by a priest may take a certificate from him at the time, which certificate when presented to an elder, shall entitle him to take a license, which shall authorize him to perform the duties of his calling, or he may receive it from a conference.

No person is to be ordained to any office in this church, where there is a regularly organized branch of the same, without the vote of that church;

But the presiding elders, traveling bishops, High Counsellors, High Priests, and elders, may have the privilege of ordaining, where there is no branch of the church that a vote may be called.

Every President of the High Priesthood (or presiding elder), bishop, High Counselor, and High Priest, is to be ordained by the direction of a High Council or general conference.

The duty of the members after they are received by baptism.

The elders or priests are to have a sufficient time to expound all things concerning the church of Christ to their understanding, previous to their partaking of the sacrament and being confirmed by the laying on of the hands of the elders, so that all things may be done in order.

And the members shall manifest before the church, and also before the elders, by a Godly walk and conversation, that they are worthy of it, that there may be works and faith agreeable to the Holy Scriptures—walking in holiness before the Lord.

Every member of the church of Christ having children, is to bring them unto the elders before the church, who are to lay their hands upon them in the name of Jesus Christ, and bless them in his name.

No one can be received into the church of Christ, unless he has arrived unto the years of accountability before God, and is capable of repentance.

Baptism is to be administered in the following manner unto all those who repent:—

The person who is called of God, and has authority from Jesus Christ to baptize, shall go down into the water with the person who has presented him or herself for baptism, and shall say, calling him or her by name—Having been commissioned of Jesus Christ, I baptize you in the name of the Father, and of the Son, and of the Holy Ghost. Amen.

Then shall he immerse him or her in the water, and come forth again out of the water.

It is expedient that the church meet together often to partake of bread and wine in the remembrance of the Lord Jesus;

And the elder or priest shall administer it; and after this manner shall he administer it—he shall kneel with the church and call upon the Father in solemn prayer, saying—

O God, the eternal Father, we ask thee in the name of thy Son, Jesus Christ, to bless and sanctify this bread to the souls of all those who partake of it, that they may eat in remembrance of the body of thy Son, and witness unto thee, O God, the eternal Father, that they are willing to take upon them the name of thy Son, and always remember him and keep his commandments which he has given them, that they may always have his Spirit to be with them. Amen.

The manner of administering the wine. He shall take the cup also, and say—

O God, the eternal Father, we ask thee in the name of thy Son, Jesus Christ, to bless and sanctify this wine to the souls of all those who drink of it, that they may do it in remembrance of the blood of thy Son, which was shed for them; that they may witness unto thee, O God, the eternal Father, that they do always remember him, that they may have his Spirit to be with them. Amen.

Any member of the church of Christ transgressing, or being overtaken in a fault, shall be dealt with as the scriptures direct.

It shall be the duty of the several churches composing the church of Christ, to send one or more of their teachers to attend the several conferences held by the elders of the church,

With a list of the names of the several members uniting themselves with the church since the last conference, or send by the hand of some priest, so that a regular list of all the names of the whole church may be kept in a book by one of the elders, whoever the other elders shall appoint from time to time;

And also if any have been expelled from the church, so that their names may be blotted out of the general church record of names.

All members removing from the church where they reside, if going to a church where they are not known, may take a letter, certifying that they are regular members and in good standing, which certificate may be signed by any elder or priest, if the member receiving the letter is personally acquainted with the elder or priest, or it may be signed by the teachers or deacons of the church.—Doc. and Cov. 20:37-84.

Tues. 6.—The Church (afterwards named by revelation the Church of Jesus Christ of Latter-day Saints) was organized according to the laws of the State of New York, in the house of Peter Whitmer, Sr., at Fayette, Seneca Co., N. Y., with six members, namely, Joseph Smith, Jr., Oliver Cowdery, Hyrum Smith, Peter Whitmer, Jr., Samuel H. Smith and David Whitmer. Joseph Smith, Jr., and Oliver Cowdery ordained each other Elders—the first Elders in the Church—according to commandment from God. They then laid hands on all the baptized members present, "that they might receive the gift of the Holy Ghost and be confirmed members of the Church." The Holy Ghost was poured out upon them "to a very great degree." Some prophesied and "all praised the Lord and rejoiced exceedingly."

The rise of the church of Christ in these last days, being one thousand eight hundred and thirty years since the coming of our Lord and Saviour Jesus Christ in the flesh, it being regularly organized and established agreeable to the laws of our country, by the will and commandments of God, in the fourth month, and on the sixth day of the month which is called April;

Which commandments were given to Joseph Smith, Jr., who was called of God, and ordained an apostle of Jesus Christ, to be the first elder of this church;

And to Oliver Cowdery, who was also called of God, an apostle of Jesus Christ, to be the second elder of this church, and ordained under his hand.—Doc. and Cov. 20:1-3.

The Church was commanded by revelation to keep a record, and Joseph Smith, Jr., was named by the Lord a Seer, a Revelator, a Prophet, an Apostle of Jesus Christ, etc. (Doc. and Cov., Sec. 20.)

Behold there shall be a record kept among you, and in it thou shalt be called a seer, a translator, a prophet, an apostle of Jesus Christ, an elder of the church through the will of God the Father, and the grace of your Lord Jesus Christ.

From Revelation to Joseph Smith, Jr., given at Fayette, New York, April 6, 1830. (See Doc. and Cov. 21:1.)

Continuation of Church Chronology and History on page 1286.

of Mormon; also the Urim and Thummim, with which to translate them, and the breastplate.

When it became known that Joseph Smith, Jr., had obtained the plates, severe persecutions arose against him and his father's family, and every effort was made to rob him of the sacred treasure.

December.—Owing to persecutions Joseph Smith, Jr., removed from Manchester, N. Y., to Harmony, Susquehanna Co., Pa., but there also persecution awaited him. During this and the following month he translated some of the characters of the plates.

1828.—February.—Martin Harris visited Joseph Smith, Jr., at Harmony, Pa., and took some of the characters, which had been transcribed, and the translation of them, to New York City, where he showed them to Professor Charles Anthon and Doctor Mitchell.

April.—Martin Harris returned from New York City and commenced to write for Joseph Smith, Jr., who continued to translate from the plates until June 14th.

June.—Martin Harris lost the manuscript which he had obtained contrary to the will of the Lord. It consisted of 116 written pages translated from the plates by Joseph Smith, Jr., and has never since been recovered.

July.—Joseph Smith, Jr., having returned to Harmony, Pa., from a visit to his father's family in Manchester, N. Y., enquired of the Lord through the Urim and Thummim and received the first revelation published in the Book of Doctrine and Covenants. (Doc. and Cov., Sec. 3.)

1829.—February.—Joseph Smith, Jr., was visited by his father, Joseph Smith, Sr., at Harmony, Pa., and received a revelation addressed to him. (Doc. and Cov., Sec. 4.)

March.—The revelation known as Section 5 of the Doctrine and Covenants was given at Harmony.

April. Sun 5.—Joseph Smith, Jr., and Oliver Cowdery met for the first time.

Tues, 7.—Joseph Smith, Jr., resumed the translation of the Book of Mormon, assisted by Oliver Cowdery as scribe, at Harmony.

Later in April, Oliver Cowdery was called by revelation to assist Joseph Smith, Jr., in his labors and stand by him in his difficulties. Oliver was also promised the gift of translating like Joseph, if he desired it.

Therefore be diligent, stand by my servant Joseph, faithfully, in wh tsoe e difficult circumstances he may be for the word's sake. a v f

Admonish him in his faults, and also receive admonition of him. Be patient; be sober; be temperate; have patience, faith, hope and charity. * *

And, behold, I grant unto you a gift, if you desire of me, to translate even as my servant Joseph.—Doc. and Cov. 6:18, 19, 25.

The Lord revealed to Joseph Smith, Jr., that John, the beloved Disciple was given power over death, that he might live and bring souls to Christ and to prophesy before nations, kindreds, tongues and people until the coming of Christ in his glory. (Doc. and Cov., Sec. 7.)

Translated from parchment, written and hid up by himself (John).

And the Lord said unto me, John, my beloved, what desirest thou? For if ye shall ask, what you will, it shall be granted unto you.

And I said unto him, Lord, give unto me power over death, that I may live and bring souls unto thee.

And the Lord said unto me, Verily, verily, I say unto thee, because thou desirest this thou shalt tarry until I come in my glory, and shalt prophesy before nations, kindred, tongues and people.—Doc. and Cov. 7:1-3.

Oliver Cowdery was instructed by revelation through Joseph Smith, Jr., to exercise great faith, that he might know the mysteries of God, translate and receive knowledge from ancient records. (Doc. and Cov., Sec. 8.)

Ask that you may know the mysteries of God, and that you may translate and receive knowledge from all those ancient records which have been hid up, that are sacred, and according to your faith shall it be done unto you.—Doc. and Cov. 8:11.

As Oliver Cowdery did not translate, according to his former desire, he was commanded to write for Joseph Smith, Jr., until the translation of the Book of Mormon was finished.

Behold, I say unto you, my son (Oliver Cowdery), that because you did not translate according to that which you desired of me, and did commence again to write for my servant Joseph Smith, Jr., even so I would that ye should continue until you have finished this record, which I have entrusted unto him.—Doc. and Cov. 9:1.

May.—A revelation concerning the alteration of the forepart of the Book of Mormon was given to Joseph Smith, Jr., at Harmony. (Doc. and Cov., Sec. 10.)

Verily, I say unto you, that I will not suffer that Satan shall accomplish his evil design in this thing. *

For, behold, he has put it into their hearts to get thee to tempt the Lord thy God, in asking to translate it over again;

And then, behold, they say and think in their hearts, we will see if God has given him power to translate, if so, he will also give him power again:

And if God giveth him power again, or if he translates again, or in other words, if he bringeth forth the same words, behold, we have the same with us, and we have altered them:

Therefore, they will not agree, and we will say that he has lied in his words, and that he has no gift, and that he has no power. * *

And now, because the account which is engraven upon the plates of Nephi is more particular concerning the things which, in my wisdom, I would bring to the knowledge of the people in this account;

Therefore, you shall translate the engravings which are on the plates of Nephi, down even till you come to the reign of king Benjamin, or until you come to that which you have translated, which you have retained;

And behold, you shall publish it as the record of Nephi, and thus I will continued those who have altered my words.—Doc. and Cov. 10:14-18; 40-42.

—Joseph Smith, Jr., was visited by Joseph Knight, Sr., from Broome Co., N. Y., who brought him provisions, Mr. Knight being anxious to know his duty in relation to the work of God, Joseph Smith, Jr., enquired of the Lord and received a revelation.

Now, as you have (Joseph Knight, Sr.) asked, behold, I say unto you, keep my commandments, and seek to bring forth and establish the cause of Zion.

Behold, I speak unto you, and also to all those who have desires to bring forth and establish this work.

And no one can assist in this work, except he shall be humble and full of love, having faith, hope, and charity, being temperate in all things, whatsoever shall be intrusted to his care.—Doc. and Cov. 12:6-8.

Fri. 15—While Joseph Smith, Jr., and Oliver Cowdery were engaged in prayer in the woods, near Harmony, John the Baptist descended as a messenger from heaven in a cloud of light and ordained them to the Priesthood of Aaron and commanded them to baptize and ordain each other. This they did the same day. Immediately after being baptized, the Holy Ghost fell upon them in great measure and both prophesied. (See History of Joseph Smith.)

Words of the Angel, John, (the Baptist,) spoken to Joseph Smith, Jr., and Oliver Cowdery, as he (the angel) laid his hands upon their heads and ordained them to the Aaronic Priesthood, in Harmony, Susquehanna County, Pennsylvania, May 15th, 1829.

Upon you my fellow servants, in the name of Messiah, I confer the Priesthood of Aaron, which holds the keys of the ministering of angels, and of the gospel of repentance, and of baptism by immersion for the remission of sins; and this shall never be taken again from the earth, until the sons of Levi do offer again an offering unto the Lord in righteousness.—Doc. and Cov. Sec. 13.

Mon. 25.—Samuel Harrison Smith, who had come to visit his brother Joseph at Harmony, was baptized by Oliver Cowdery.

A few days later Hyrum Smith visited Harmony to make enquiries about the work of God, and received through his brother Joseph a revelation, calling him to assist in the work.

Now, as you (Hyrum Smith) have asked, behold, I say unto you, keep my commandments, and seek to bring forth and establish the cause of Zion.—Doc. and Cov. 11:6.

June.—Joseph Smith, Jr., removed from Harmony, Pa., to the home of Peter Whitmer, Sr., at Fayette, Seneca Co., N. Y., where he resided while finishing the translation of the Book of Mormon. The Whitmer family was very kind to Joseph, and John Whitmer rendered efficient aid as a scribe.

—David Whitmer, John Whitmer and Peter Whitmer, Jr., being very desirous to know their respective duties, besought Joseph Smith, Jr., to "enquire of the Lord concerning them." He did so through the Urim and Thummim, and received the revelations known as Sections 14, 15 and 16 of the Doctrine and Covenants.

—Hyrum Smith, David Whitmer and Peter Whitmer, Jr., were baptized in Seneca lake, near Fayette.

—As Joseph Smith, Jr., progressed with the work of translation, he ascertained that three special witnesses "were to be provided by the Lord" to see the plates and bear record of the same. (Ether. 5:2-4.) Oliver Cowdery, David Whitmer and Martin Harris, being very desirous to "be these three special witnesses", received the promise by revelation through Joseph Smith, Jr., that they should "have a view of the plates, and also of the breastplate, the sword of Laban, the Urim and Thummim and the miraculous directors."

Revelation given through Joseph, the Seer, to Oliver Cowdery, David Whitmer, and Martin Harris, in Fayette, Seneca County, New York, June, 1829, given previous to the viewing the plates containing the Book of Mormon.

Behold, I say unto you, that you must rely upon my word, which if you do, with full purpose of heart, you shall have a view of the plates, and also of the breastplate, the sword of Laban, the Urim and Thummim, which were given to the brother of Jared upon the mount, when he talked with the Lord face to face, and the miraculous directors which were given to Lehi while in the wilderness, on the borders of the Red Sea;

And it is by your faith that you shall obtain a view of them, even by that faith which was had by the prophets of old.

And after that you have obtained faith, and have seen them with your eyes, you shall testify of them, by the power of God;

And this you shall do that my servant, Joseph Smith, Jr., may not be destroyed, that I may bring about my righteous purposes unto the children of men in this work.

And ye shall testify that you have seen them, even as my servant Joseph Smith, Jr., has seen them, for it is by my power that he has seen them, and it is because he had faith;

And he has translated the book, even that part which I have commanded him, and as your Lord and your God liveth it is true.

Wherefore you have received the same power, and the same faith, and the same gift like unto him;

And if you do these last commandments of mine, which I have given you, the gates of hell shall not prevail against you: for my grace is sufficient for you, and you shall be lifted up at the last day.

And I, Jesus Christ, your Lord and your God, have spoken it unto you, that I might bring about my righteous purposes unto the children of men. Amen.—Doc. and Cov. 17.

—A few days later an angel showed the plates of the Book of Mormon to the Three Witnesses.

—Soon afterwards the plates were shown by Joseph Smith, Jr., to Christian Whitmer, Jacob Whitmer, Peter Whitmer, Jr., John Whitmer, Hiram Page, Joseph Smith, Sr., Hyrum Smith and Samuel H. Smith, who subsequently gave their testimony as the Eight Witnesses to the Book of Mormon.

—A revelation was given to Joseph Smith, Jr., Oliver Cowdery and David Whitmer, "making known the calling of Twelve Apostles in these last days," and containing "instructions relative to building up the Church of Christ, according to the fulness of the gospel." (Doc. and Cov. Sec. 18. See "Council of Twelve Apostles.")

Joseph Smith, Jr., and Oliver Cowdery being desirous to obtain the Melchisedek Priesthood which had been promised them by John the Baptist, engaged in "solemn and fervent prayer," at Fayette, when "the word of the Lord came," commanding them to ordain each other. But they were to wait for this ordination till the others who had been baptized assembled together.

1830.—March.—Martin Harris was commanded by revelation through Joseph Smith, Jr., at Manchester, N. Y., to repent of his sins. (Doc. and Cov., Sec. 19.)

April—An important revelation on Priesthood and Church government in general was given through Joseph Smith, Jr. And again, by way of commandment to the church concerning the manner of baptism.

All those who humble themselves before God, and desire to be baptized and come forth with broken hearts and contrite spirits, and witness before the church that they have truly repented of all their sins, and are willing to take upon them the name of Jesus Christ, having a determination to serve him to the end, and truly manifest by their works that they have received of the Spirit of Christ unto the remission of their sins, shall be received by baptism into his church.

The duty of the elders, priests, teachers, deacons, and members of the church of Christ.

An apostle is an elder, and it is his calling to baptize.

And to ordain other elders, priests, teachers, and deacons.

And to administer bread and wine—the emblems of the flesh and blood of Christ—

And to confirm those who are baptized into the church, by the laying on of hands for the baptism of fire and the Holy Ghost, according to the scriptures;

And to teach, expound, exhort, baptize, and watch over the church;

And to confirm the church by the laying on of the hands, and the giving of the Holy Ghost.

And to take the lead of all meetings.

The elders are to conduct the meetings as they are led by the Holy Ghost, according to the commandments and revelations of God.

The priest's duty is to preach, teach, expound, exhort, and baptize, and administer the sacrament.

And visit the house of each member, and exhort them to pray vocally and in secret, and attend to all family duties;

And he may also ordain other priests, teachers, and deacons.

And he is to take the lead of meetings when there is no elder present;

But when there is an elder present, he is only to preach, teach, expound, exhort, and baptize.

And visit the house of each member, exhorting them to pray vocally and in secret, and attend to all family duties.

In all these duties the priest is to assist the elder if occasion requires.

The teacher's duty is to watch over the church always, and be with and strengthen them.

And see that there is no iniquity in the church—neither hardness with each other—neither lying, backbiting, nor evil speaking;

And see that the church meet together often, and also see that all the members do their duty;

And he is to take the lead of meetings in the absence of the elder or priest—

And is to be assisted always, in all his duties in the church, by the deacons, if occasion requires;

But neither teachers nor deacons have authority to baptize, administer the sacrament, or lay on hands;

They are, however, to warn, expound, exhort, and teach and invite all to come unto Christ.

Every elder, priest, teacher, or deacon, is to be ordained according to the gifts and callings of God unto him; and he is to be ordained by the power of the Holy Ghost, which is in the one who ordains him.

The several elders composing this church of Christ are to meet in conference once in three months, or from time to time as said conferences shall direct or appoint;

And said conferences are to do whatever church business is necessary to be done at the time.

The elders are to receive their licenses from other elders, by vote of the church to which they belong, or from the conferences.

Each priest, teacher, or deacon, who is ordained by a priest may take a certificate from him at the time, which certificate when presented to an elder, shall entitle him to a license, which shall authorize him to perform the duties of his calling, or he may receive it from a conference.

No person is to be ordained to any office in this church, where there is a regularly organized branch of the same, without the vote of that church;

But the presiding elders, traveling bishops, High Counselors, High Priests, and elders, may have the privilege of ordaining, where there is no branch of the church that a vote may be called.

Every President of the High Priesthood (or presiding elder), bishop, High Counselor, and High Priest, is to be ordained by the direction of a High Council or general conference.

The duty of the members after they are received by baptism.

The elders or priests are to have a sufficient time to expound all things concerning the church of Christ to their understanding, previous to their partaking of the sacrament and being confirmed by the laying on of the hands of the elders, so that all things may be done in order.

And the members shall manifest before the church, and also before the elders, by a Godly walk and conversation, that they are worthy of it, that there may be works and faith agreeable to the Holy Scriptures—walking in holiness before the Lord.

Every member of the church of Christ having children, is to bring them unto the elders before the church, who are to lay their hands upon them in the name of Jesus Christ, and bless them in his name.

No one can be received into the church of Christ, unless he has arrived unto the years of accountability before God, and is capable of repentance.

Baptism is to be administered in the following manner unto all those who repent:—

The person who is called of God, and has authority from Jesus Christ to baptize, shall go down into the water with the person who has presented him or herself for baptism, and shall say, calling him or her by name—Having been commissioned of Jesus Christ, I baptize you in the name of the Father, and of the Son, and of the Holy Ghost. Amen.

Then shall he immerse him or her in the water, and come forth again out of the water.

It is expedient that the church meet together often to partake of bread and wine in the remembrance of the Lord Jesus;

And the elder or priest shall administer it; and after this manner shall he administer it—he shall kneel with the church and call upon the Father in solemn prayer, saying—

O God, the eternal Father, we ask thee in the name of thy Son, Jesus Christ, to bless and sanctify this bread to the souls of all those who partake of it, that they may eat in remembrance of the body of thy Son, and witness unto thee, O God, the eternal Father, that they are willing to take upon them the name of thy Son, and always remember him and keep his commandments which he has given them, that they may always have his Spirit to be with them. Amen.

The manner of administering the wine. He shall take the cup also, and say—

O God, the eternal Father, we ask thee in the name of thy Son, Jesus Christ, to bless and sanctify this wine to the souls of all those who drink of it, that they may do it in remembrance of the blood of thy Son, which was shed for them; that they may witness unto thee, O God, the eternal Father, that they do always remember him, that they may have his Spirit to be with them. Amen.

Any member of the church of Christ transgressing, or being overtaken in a fault, shall be dealt with as the scriptures direct.

It shall be the duty of the several churches composing the church of Christ, to send one or more of their teachers to attend the several conferences held by the elders of the church.

With a list of the names of the several members uniting themselves with the church since the last conference, or send by the hand of some priest, so that a regular list of all the names of the whole church may be kept in a book by one of the elders, whoever the other elders shall appoint from time to time;

And also if any have been expelled from the church, so that their names may be blotted out of the general church record of names.

All members removing from the church where they reside, if going to a church where they are not known, may take a letter, certifying that they are regular members and in good standing, which certificate may be signed by any elder or priest, if the member receiving the letter is personally acquainted with the elder or priest, or it may be signed by the teachers or deacons of the church.—Doc. and Cov. 20:37-84.

Tues. 6.—The Church (afterwards named by revelation the Church of Jesus Christ of Latter-day Saints) was organized according to the laws of the State of New York, in the house of Peter Whitmer, Sr., at Fayette, Seneca Co., N. Y., with six members, namely, Joseph Smith, Jr., Oliver Cowdery, Hyrum Smith, Peter Whitmer, Jr., Samuel H. Smith and David Whitmer. Joseph Smith, Jr., and Oliver Cowdery ordained each other Elders—the first Elders in the Church—according to commandment from God. They then laid hands on all the baptized members present, "that they might receive the gift of the Holy Ghost and be confirmed members of the Church." The Holy Ghost was poured out upon them "to a very great degree." Some prophesied and "all praised the Lord and rejoiced exceedingly."

The rise of the church of Christ in these last days, being one thousand eight hundred and thirty years since the coming of our Lord and Saviour Jesus Christ in the flesh, it being regularly organized and established agreeable to the laws of our country, by the will and commandments of God, in the fourth month, and on the sixth day of the month which is called April;

Which commandments were given to Joseph Smith, Jr., who was called of God, and ordained an apostle of Jesus Christ, to be the first elder of this church;

And to Oliver Cowdery, who was also called of God, an apostle of Jesus Christ, to be the second elder of this church, and ordained under his hand.—Doc. and Cov. 20:1-3.

The Church was commanded by revelation to keep a record, and Joseph Smith, Jr., was named by the Lord a Seer, a Revelator, a Prophet, an Apostle of Jesus Christ, etc. (Doc. and Cov. 20.)

Behold there shall be a record kept among you, and in it thou shalt be called a seer, a translator, a prophet, an apostle of Jesus Christ, an elder of the church, through the will of God the Father, and the grace of your Lord Jesus Christ.

From Revelation to Joseph Smith, Jr., given at Fayette, New York, April 6, 1830. (See Doc. and Cov. 21:1.)

Continuation of Church Chronology and History on page 1286.

THE ANCESTRY OF THE PROPHET

The Lineal Ancestry of Joseph Smith Jr., Prophet, Seer and Revelator, and Hyrum Smith, Patriarch of the Church of Jesus Christ of Latter-day Saints

ROBERT SMITH immigrated in the year 1638 from England; the exact location is unknown. He married Mary French and settled in that part of Rowley, in Essex County, Mass., which afterwards became the township of Boxford. He was the father of ten children.

SAMUEL, the fifth child and third son of Robert, was born January 26, 1666. He moved to Topsfield where he became an influential citizen. He married Rebecca Curtis, daughter of John Curtis. They had nine children. He died July 12, 1748.

SAMUEL, the third child and oldest son of Samuel was born in Topsfield January 26, 1714. He married Priscilla Gould, daughter of Zaccheus Gould. They had five children. He was known as Captain Samuel Smith and served his country during the Revolutionary war. He was also a delegate to the Provincial Congress in 1774 and again in 1775 and was chairman of the tea committee in 1773. In 1764-70 and in 1772, '77· '78 and '81· he was representative to the General Court and served on the Committee of Safety for a number of years.

ASAEL, the youngest child and second son of Samuel², was born in Topsfield March 7, 1744; died October 31, 1830 in Stockholm, N. Y. He had eleven children and was the father of Joseph Smith the first Presiding Patriarch of the Church. He served in the American army during the Revolutionary war. He married Mary Duty.

JOSEPH, third child and second son of Asael, was born in Topsfield, July 12, 1771. He moved to Tunbridge, Vt., in 1791. In 1816, he moved to New York and settled in Manchester. He was one of the six original members of the church of Jesus Christ of Latter-day Saints, organized April 6, 1830. In 1833, he was called to the office of Presiding Patriarch of the Church. He married January 24, 1796, Lucy Mack, daughter of Solomon and Lydia (Gates) Mack. They had ten children, seven sons, three daughters, and were the parents of the Prophet Joseph and Patriarch Hyrum Smith.

HYRUM, second son of Joseph, Sr., was born February 9, 1800 and was martyred with his brother Joseph Smith the Prophet at Carthage, Ill., June 27, 1844. He married (first Jerusha Barden and (second) Mary Fielding.

Issue by first marriage: Lovina, b. Sept. 16, 1827; d. Oct. 8, 1876; m. Lorin Walker. Mary, b. June 27, 1829, d. May 29, 1832. John, b. Sept. 22, 1832, d. Nov. 6, 1911; m. Helen Fisher. Hyrum, b. April 27, 1834; d. Sept. 21, 1841. Jerusha, b. Jan. 13, 1836; m. William Pierce. Sarah, b. Oct. 2, 1837, d. Nov. 1876; m. Charles E. Griffin.

Issue by second marriage: Joseph Fielding (subject of this sketch), b. Nov. 13, 1838. Martha Ann, b. May 14, 1841; m. William J. Harris. Married Catherine Phillips (daughter of Thomas Denner Phillips and Sarah Godshall) Aug. 1843, Nauvoo, Ill. She was born Aug. 1, 1819, Philadelphia, Pa.

Joseph Fielding Smith's Genealogy, page 1168.

SMITH, JOSEPH, Jr., (Son of Joseph Smith and Lucy Mack.) Born Dec. 23, 1805, Sharon, Windsor Co., Vermont. Married Emma Hale Jan. 18, 1827, at South Bainbridge, Chenango Co., N. Y. (daughter of Isaac Hale of Harmony, Susquehanna Co., Pa.) Their children: Joseph; Frederick G. W.; Alexander; Don Carlos; David H. The last named was born about five months after the assassination of his father.

Married Helen Mar Kimball (daughter of Heber Chase Kimball and Vilate Murray). The authority for this statement is on page 339 of the "Life of Heber C. Kimball," by Orson F. Whitney. This author says, "Soon after the revelation (see revelation on celestial marriage, written July 12, 1843, page 1304. * * * Helen Mar, the eldest daughter of Heber Chase and Vilate Murray Kimball, was given to the Prophet in the holy bonds of celestial marriage."

In 1905, there was issued from the press of the Deseret News at Salt Lake City, Utah, a publication entitled "Blood Atonement and the Origin of Plural Marriage." In the first part of this publication, is the "Correspondence between Elder Joseph F. Smith, Jr., of the Church of Jesus Christ of Latter-day Saints, and Richard C. Evans, second counselor in the Presidency of the 'Reorganized' Church." Following this correspondence on page 81 under the heading "Introduction of Celestial and Plural Marriage," are a number of affidavits, among them, those of Lorenzo Snow, Elizabeth Ann Whitney, Sarah A. Kimball, Catherine Phillips Smith, Martha McBride Kimball, and Melissa Lott Willes, setting forth the following marriages of Joseph Smith, Jr.

Married Louisa Beaman, April 5, 1841, at Nauvoo, Ill.
Married Sarah Ann Whitney, July 27, 1842, at Nauvoo, Ill. (daughter of Newell K. and Elizabeth Ann Whitney).
Married Martha McBride, 1842.
Married Rhoda Richards, June 12, 1843, at Nauvoo, Ill.
Married Almira W. Johnson, 1843 (daughter of Ezekiel Johnson and Julia Hills).
Married Lucy Walker, May 1, 1843.
Married Melissa Lott, Sept. 20, 1843 (daughter of Cornelius P. Lott).
Married Eliza R. Snow (sister of Lorenzo Snow, fifth president of the Church of Jesus Christ of Latter-day Saints).
Married Eliza Partridge.
Married Emily Partridge.
Married Maria Lawrence.
Married Sarah Lawrence.

The "Life of Heber C. Kimball" by Orson F. Whitney (see page 431 of that book) is the authority for the following marriages of Joseph Smith, Jr.

Married Prescinda Huntington
Married Mary Houston.
Married Sylvia P. Sessions.
Married Nancy Maria Smith.
Married Sarah Scott.

On page 81 of "Blood Atonement and the Origin of Plural Marriage," the following statement is made: "One hundred or more affidavits in relation to the introduction of celestial and plural marriage are on file in the Historian's office, Salt Lake City, and are expressions of eye and ear witnesses, who know that the Prophet Joseph Smith introduced and taught celestial and plural marriage. Most of these witnesses are members of the Church, but some of them are not, and have not been connected with the Church from before the martyrdom of the Prophet and Patriarch."

JOSEPH SMITH.
Son of Joseph Smith and Lucy Mack (the daughter of Solomon Mack and Lydia Gates). Born Monday, Dec. 23, 1805, Sharon, Windsor Co., Vermont. Prophet and founder of the Church of Jesus Christ of Latter-day Saints. Martyred with his brother Hyrum Smith at Carthage, Ill., June 27, 1844.

HYRUM SMITH.
Son of Joseph Smith and Lucy Mack (the daughter of Solomon Mack and Lydia Gates). Born Feb. 9, 1800. Martyred with his brother Joseph Smith the Prophet at Carthage, Ill., June 27, 1844. Father of Joseph Fielding Smith, president of the Church of Jesus Christ of Latter-day Saints.

CHURCH ORGANIZATION

The Church of Jesus Christ of Latter-day Saints was organized with six members, April 6, 1830, at a meeting held at Fayette, Seneca Co., N. Y.

The general authorities of the Church consists of (1) The First Presidency; (2) The Council of Twelve Apostles; (3) Presiding Patriarch; (4) The First Council of Seventies; (5) The Presiding Bishopric; (6) Church Historians.

THE FIRST PRESIDENCY

Joseph Smith the Prophet, "who was called of God and ordained an Apostle of Jesus Christ, to be the first Elder of this Church" was the first President of the Church of Jesus Christ of Latter-day Saints. For nearly three years after its organization he acted without Counselors, but close by his side and associated with him in nearly all his administrations, stood Oliver Cowdery, "who was called of God, an Apostle of Jesus Christ, to be the second Elder of this Church, and ordained under his (Joseph's) hand."

"Which commandments were given to Joseph Smith, Jr., who was called of God, and ordained an apostle of Jesus Christ, to be the first elder of this church; and to Oliver Cowdery, who was also called of God, an apostle of Jesus Christ, to be the second elder of this church, and ordained under his hand."—Doc. and Cov. 20:2-3.

March 18, 1833, agreeable to a revelation given March 8, 1833, the Prophet Joseph ordained Sidney Rigdon to be his first, and Frederick G. Williams to be his second, Counselor.

"And again, verily I say unto thy brethren, Sidney Rigdon and Frederick G. Williams, their sins are forgiven them also, and they are accounted as equal with thee in holding the keys of this last kingdom."—Doc. and Cov. 90:6.

Prior to this, at a Conference held at Amherst, Lorain Co., Ohio, Jan. 25, 1832, Joseph the Prophet had been acknowledged as President of the High Priesthood. A similar action was taken at a General Council, held April 26, 1832, at Independence, Jackson Co., Mo.

At an important Conference held at Far West, Caldwell Co., Mo., Nov. 7, 1837, Frederick G. Williams was rejected as a Counselor to Pres. Smith, charges having previously been made against him at a Conference held at Kirtland, Ohio, Sept. 3, 1837. On the same occasion Hyrum Smith was appointed his successor by unanimous vote. Hyrum Smith filled his position with honor and ability, until some time after the demise of his father, Joseph Smith, Sr. who died at Nauvoo, Ill., Sept. 14, 1840.

In a revelation given through Joseph the Prophet at Nauvoo, Jan. 19, 1841, Hyrum Smith was called to take the office of Patriarch to the Church, as his father's successor[1]. In the same revelation William Law was called to succeed Hyrum Smith[2] as second Counselor to Pres. Joseph Smith. William Law occupied this position until April 18, 1844, when he, together with others, who like himself had apostatized, were excommunicated from the Church.

"And again, verily I say unto you; Let my servant William (Law) be appointed, ordained, and anointed, as a counselor unto my servant Joseph, in the room of my servant Hyrum, that my servant Hyrum may take the office of Priesthood and [2]Patriarch, which was appointed unto him by his father, by blessing and also by right."—Doc. and Cov. 124:91.

"Let him assist my servant Joseph; and also let my servant William Law assist my servant Joseph, in making a [3]solemn proclamation unto the kings of the earth, even as I have before said unto you."—Doc. and Cov. 124:107.

Joseph the Prophet was martyred at Carthage, Ill., June 27, 1844, when the responsibility of presiding over the Church fell upon the Twelve Apostles. They constituted the presiding Council of the Church till Dec. 5, 1847, when an important council meeting was held at the house of Apostle Orson Hyde. On this occasion Brigham Young was unanimously elected President of the Church, with authority to choose his Counselors, which he did by naming Heber C. Kimball for his first and Willard Richards for his second Counselor. The following Apostles attended this council meeting: Brigham Young, Heber C. Kimball, Orson Hyde, Willard Richards, Wilford Woodruff, Geo. A. Smith, Amasa M. Lyman and Ezra T. Benson. These transactions on the part of the Twelve

were ratified by the Church at a conference held in the Log Tabernacle, at Council Bluffs, Iowa, Dec. 27, 1847, and at the general conference held in Great Salt Lake valley, Oct. 8, 1848.
Counselor Willard Richards died of dropsy in Great Salt Lake City, March 11, 1854. At the general conference, held April 6, 1854, Jedediah M. Grant was called to fill the vacancy thus created.
Counselor Jedediah M. Grant died Dec. 1, 1856, and Daniel H. Wells succeeded him as second Counselor to Pres. Brigham Young, being ordained and set apart to that position, Jan. 4, 1857. Daniel H. Wells acted in that capacity till the death of Pres. Young.
Counselor Heber C. Kimball died June 22, 1868, in Salt Lake City. The vacancy occasioned thereby was filled by the appointment of George A. Smith to the position of first Counselor in the First Presidency. He served in that capacity until his death, which occurred in Salt Lake City, Sept. 1, 1875. John W. Young succeeded him as first Counselor, being sustained as such by the general conference held Oct. 8, 1876.
Pres. Brigham Young died in Salt Lake City, Aug. 29, 1877, after which the Twelve Apostles again presided over the Church, continuing to do so for three years, or until the general conference held in Salt Lake City in October, 1880, when the First Presidency was organized, for the third time, by the appointment of John Taylor as President, with Geo. Q. Cannon as his first and Joseph F. Smith as his second Counselor.
Pres. John Taylor died at Kaysville, Davis Co., Utah, July 25, 1887, after which the Twelve Apostles presided over the Church till the general conference, held in Salt Lake City, in April, 1889, on which occasion a First Presidency was again organized, consisting of Wilford Woodruff, President; Geo. Q. Cannon, first Counselor; and Joseph F. Smith, second Counselor.
Pres. Wilford Woodruff died in San Francisco, Cal., Sept. 2, 1898. At an important council meeting of the Apostles

FREDERICK G. WILLIAMS

held in Salt Lake City, Sept. 13, 1898, the First Presidency was once more organized, as follows: Lorenzo Snow, President; Geo. Q. Cannon, first Counselor; Joseph F. Smith, second Counselor.
Counselor George Q. Cannon died April 12, 1901, at Monterey, California; and on Oct. 7th of the same year, Joseph F. Smith was sustained as first and Rudger Clawson as second Counselor to President Snow.
President Lorenzo Snow died at Salt Lake City Oct. 10, 1901; and on the 17th of the same month, the First Presidency was reorganized with Joseph F. Smith as President, and John R. Winder, first, and Anthon H. Lund, second Counselors.
Counselor John R. Winder died March 27, 1910, at Salt Lake City and on the 7th of the next month, John Henry Smith was chosen second Counselor—Anthon H. Lund becoming first Counselor—to President Joseph F. Smith.
Counselor John Henry Smith died Oct. 13, 1911, at Salt Lake City; and Charles W. Penrose was chosen to succeed him as second Counselor in the First Presidency Dec. 7, 1911.
By the foregoing it will be seen that six Apostles, namely, Joseph Smith, Brigham Young, John Taylor, Wilford Woodruff, Lorenzo Snow and Joseph F. Smith, have filled the exalted position of President of the Church; seven (Sidney Rigdon, Heber C. Kimball, Geo. A. Smith, John W. Young, Geo. Q. Cannon, Joseph F. Smith and Anthon H. Lund) have acted as first Counselors; and ten (Frederick G. Williams, Hyrum Smith, William Law, Willard Richards, Jedediah M. Grant, Daniel H. Wells, Joseph F. Smith, Rudger Clawson, John Henry Smith and Chas. W. Penrose) as second Counselors in the First Presidency, since the first organization of the Council in 1833.

COUNCIL OF TWELVE APOSTLES

In a revelation, given through Joseph the Prophet, in June, 1829, at Fayette, Seneca Co., N. Y., the Lord made known that Twelve Apostles should be called in this dispensation.

"And now, behold, there are others who are called to declare my gospel, "both unto Gentile and unto Jew;
"Yes, even Twelve, and the Twelve shall be my disciples, and they shall take upon them my name; and the Twelve are they who shall desire to take upon them my name with full purpose of heart;
"And if they desire to take upon them my name with full purpose of heart, they are called to go into all the world to preach my gospel unto every creature.
"And now, behold, I give unto you Oliver Cowdery, and also unto David Whitmer, that you shall search out the Twelve, who shall have the desires of which I have spoken;
"And by their desires and their works you shall know them.—Doc. and Cov. 18:26-28; 37-38.

Nearly six years later, on Feb. 14, 1835, at a special meeting, held at Kirtland, Ohio, Joseph the Prophet, in accordance with that revelation, blessed Oliver Cowdery, David Whitmer and Martin Harris, the Three Witnesses to the Book of Mormon, to select twelve men who should constitute the Council of Twelve Apostles. They were chosen by the Three Witnesses in the following order: Lyman E. Johnson, Brigham Young, Heber C. Kimball, Orson Hyde, David W. Patten, Luke S. Johnson, Wm. E. McLellin, John F. Boynton, Orson Pratt, William Smith, Thos. B. Marsh and Parley P. Pratt. Most of these brethren the previous year (1834) had proved their faithfulness and integrity to the Church as members of Zion's Camp, which journeyed from Kirtland, Ohio, to Missouri and back, subject to much suffering and many privations. They were ordained to the Apostleship by Joseph Smith, Oliver Cowdery, David Whitmer and Martin Harris as follows: Lyman E. Johnson, Brigham Young and Heber C. Kimball on Feb. 14, 1835; Orson Hyde, David W. Patten, Luke S. Johnson, Wm. E. McLellin, John F. Boynton and William Smith on the following day, Feb. 15th; Parley P. Pratt on Feb. 21st; and Thomas B. Marsh and Orson Pratt, who had been absent on missions, in April, 1835. At a grand council, held at Kirtland, Ohio, May 2, 1835, at which the First Presidency was in attendance, the Twelve were arranged according to their age, after which they stood as follows, commencing with the eldest: Thomas B. Marsh, David W. Patten, Brigham Young, Heber C. Kimball, Orson Hyde, William E. McLellin, Parley P. Pratt, Luke S. Johnson, William Smith, Orson Pratt, John F. Boynton and Lyman E. Johnson.

In 1837 and 1838 four of the Twelve apostatized, namely, John F. Boynton, disfellowshipped Sept. 3, 1837, at Kirtland, Ohio; Lyman E. Johnson and Luke S. Johnson, excommunicated April 13, 1838, at Far West, Missouri; and Wm. E. McLellin, excommunicated May 11, 1838, at Far West.
July 8, 1838, John Taylor, John E. Page, Wilford Woodruff and Willard Richards were called by revelation to fill the places of those who had fallen. Elders Page and Taylor were ordained Dec. 19, 1838; Wilford Woodruff April 26, 1839, at Far West, Missouri; and Willard Richards April 14, 1840, at Preston, England.
In the meantime other vacancies occurred. David W. Patten was killed in the Crooked River battle, in Missouri, Oct. 25, 1838, and Thos. B. Marsh was excommunicated for apostasy, March 17, 1839, at Quincy, Ill. To fill the two vacancies occasioned thereby, George A. Smith (ordained April 26, 1839, at Far West, Mo.) and Lyman Wight (ordained April 8, 1841, at Nauvoo, Ill.), were chosen.
William Smith was rejected as an Apostle, at the general conference held at Nauvoo, in October, 1845, and finally excommunicated from the Church, Oct. 12, 1846. John E. Page was disfellowshipped, Jan. 9, 1846, at a council meeting held at Nauvoo, Ill. Amasa M. Lyman, who had been ordained an Apostle, Aug. 20, 1842, at Nauvoo, and Ezra T. Benson, ordained July 16, 1846, at Council Bluffs, Iowa, were chosen to fill the vacancies.
The reorganization of the First Presidency in December, 1847, with three of the Apostles (Brigham Young, Heber C. Kimball and Willard Richards), and the excommunication of Lyman Wright for apostasy, Feb. 12, 1849, made four vacancies in the Council of the Twelve. These were filled Feb. 12, 1849, at an important council meeting held in the "Old Fort," Great Salt Lake City, when Elders Charles C. Rich, Lorenzo Snow, Erastus Snow and Franklin D. Richards were ordained Apostles.
The next vacancy occurred May 13, 1857, when Parley P. Pratt was assassinated near Van Buren, Arkansas. George Q. Cannon was chosen to fill the vacancy, being ordained an Apostle Aug. 20, 1860, Great Salt Lake City, Utah.
In October, 1867, Amasa M. Lyman was dropped from the Council of the Twelve; and Joseph F. Smith, who had previously been ordained to the Apostleship, was chosen to fill the vacancy, Oct. 6, 1867, at a general conference.
Geo. A. Smith was chosen as first Counselor to Pres. Brigham Young, after the demise of Heber C. Kimball in 1868. Elder Brigham Young, Jr., who previously had been ordained an Apostle, was chosen to fill the vacancy, being sustained as a member of the Council of the Twelve at the general conference held Oct. 9, 1868.
Elder Ezra T. Benson died Sept. 3, 1869, at Ogden, Utah. Albert Carrington was chosen to fill the vacancy, and was ordained an Apostle, July 3, 1870, in Salt Lake City.
Orson Hyde, who had acted as president of the Twelve Apostles, from the reorganization of the First Presidency in 1847, to October, 1875, died Nov. 28, 1878, at Spring City, Sanpete Co., Utah. At the annual conference, held April 7, 1879, Elder Moses Thatcher was chosen to fill the vacancy.
After the death of Pres. Brigham Young, in 1877, the Twelve Apostles presided over the Church nearly three years. Daniel H. Wells and John W. Young, who had acted as Pres. Brigham Young's Counselors, were sustained by the Church as Counselors to the Twelve.
Another reorganization of the First Presidency took place, Oct. 10, 1880, at the general conference held in Salt Lake City, three of the Apostles (John Taylor, Geo. Q. Cannon and Joseph F. Smith) being chosen to constitute said Presidency. This caused three vacancies in the Council of the Twelve, two of which were filled Oct. 27, 1880, by the ordination of Francis M. Lyman and John Henry Smith to the Apostleship.

PIONEERS AND PROMINENT MEN OF UTAH

Orson Pratt, the last surviving member of the first Council of Twelve Apostles, died in Salt Lake City, Utah, Oct. 3, 1881. The vacancy occasioned by his demise, and the vacancy left since October, 1880, was filled by the calling of George Teasdale and Heber J. Grant to the Apostleship. These brethren were called by direct revelation, through Pres. John Taylor, and were ordained in Salt Lake City, Oct. 16, 1882.

Charles C. Rich died at Paris, Bear Lake Co., Idaho, Nov. 17, 1883, and the vacancy caused thereby, in the Council, was filled by the ordination of John W. Taylor to the Apostleship Oct. 16, 1883.

After the death of Pres. John Taylor, July 25, 1887, the Twelve Apostles acted as presiding Council of the Church for about one year and nine months, during which time Geo. Q. Cannon and Joseph F. Smith occupied their former positions as members of the Council of Twelve Apostles.

At the general conference, held in April, 1889, the First Presidency was reorganized, with Wilford Woodruff as President. The vacancy in the Council of the Apostles caused thereby, as well as that occasioned by the excommunication of Albert Carrington, in November, 1885, and a third vacancy caused by the demise of Erastus Snow, May 27, 1888, were filled at the general conference, held in October, 1889, by the calling of Marriner W. Merrill, Anthon H. Lund and Abraham H. Cannon to the Apostleship.

Abraham H. Cannon died in Salt Lake City, July 19, 1896, and Moses Thatcher was dropped from his position as one of the Twelve Apostles, Nov. 19, 1896. The two vacancies thus occasioned were filled at the general conference held in Salt Lake City, in October, 1897, when Matthias F. Cowley and Abraham Owen Woodruff were sustained as members of the Council of Twelve Apostles.

After the death of Pres. Wilford Woodruff, Sept. 2, 1898, the Twelve Apostles once more became the presiding Council of the Church, and Geo. Q. Cannon and Joseph F. Smith were returned to their former positions among the Twelve Apostles. But the Apostles only retained the presidency a few days, Sept. 13, 1898, the First Presidency was organized the fifth time since the organization of the Church. Lorenzo Snow, Geo. Q. Cannon and Joseph F. Smith being the three Apostles chosen to form the new Presidency. This caused a vacancy in the Council of the Apostles, which was filled at the general conference, held in Salt Lake City, Oct. 9, 1898, when Rudger Clawson was sustained as one of the Twelve Apostles.

Franklin D. Richards, President of the Twelve Apostles, died at Ogden, Utah, Dec. 9, 1899; and the vacancy thus caused in the quorum was filled April 8, 1900, when Reed Smoot was sustained as one of the Twelve Apostles.

Hyrum M. Smith was ordained to the Apostleship Oct. 24, 1901, following the promotion of Apostle Anthon H. Lund to the position of second Counselor in the First Presidency, which had occurred on the 17th of the same month.

Rudger Clawson became second Counselor to President Lorenzo Snow Oct. 7, 1901; but the death of the President three days later released him from the First Presidency, and he again took his position in the quorum of the Twelve Apostles.

Brigham Young, Jr., died at Sugar House Ward, Salt Lake County, Utah, April 11, 1903; and on the 6th of the next October, George A. Smith was sustained in the Apostleship to fill the vacancy. On the same date Francis M. Lyman was sustained as the successor of Brigham Young, Jr., in the presidency of the quorum.

Abraham Owen Woodruff died June 20, 1904, at El Paso, Texas; and on the 7th of the following month, July, Charles W. Penrose was ordained an Apostle to complete the quorum.

Marriner W. Merrill died at Richmond, Utah, Feb. 6, 1906, and on April 8, 1906, George B. Richards, Orson F. Whitney, and David O. McKay were sustained as members of the quorum of Twelve Apostles, to fill the vacancies caused by the death of Apostle Merrill and by the removal of John W. Taylor and Matthias F. Cowley from the quorum.

A vacancy caused by the death of George Teasdale was filled Oct. 6, 1907, when Anthony W. Ivins was sustained in the Apostleship.

Joseph F. Smith, Jr., was chosen an Apostle April 10, 1910 to complete the quorum after the promotion of John Henry Smith to the position of second Counselor in the First Presidency.

James E. Talmage was ordained to the Apostleship Dec. 8, 1911, to fill a vacancy occasioned by the promotion of Charles W. Penrose to the position of second Counselor to Joseph F. Smith, President of the Church.

The Council of the Twelve Apostles now (1913) stands as follows: Francis M. Lyman, president. Heber J. Grant, Rudger Clawson, Reed Smoot, Hyrum M. Smith, George A. Smith, George F. Richards, Orson F. Whitney, David O. McKay, Anthony W. Ivins, Joseph F. Smith, Jr., and James E. Talmage.

PRESIDING PATRIARCHS

Joseph Smith, Sr., father of the Prophet Joseph Smith, was the first Patriarch in the Church. He was ordained to that high and holy calling, Dec. 18, 1833, at Kirtland, Ohio, under the hands of the Prophet Joseph, Oliver Cowdery, Sidney Rigdon and Frederick G. Williams. Father Smith continued as Patriarch until his death, which occurred at Nauvoo, Ill. Sept. 14, 1840. In an important revelation, given through the Prophet Joseph, Jan. 19, 1841, Hyrum Smith, Father Smith's eldest living son, who then acted as second Counselor in the First Presidency, was called to succeed his father as Patriarch.

"And again. Verily I say unto you: Let my servant William (Law) be appointed, ordained, and anointed, as a counselor unto my servant Joseph, in the room of my servant Hyrum, that my servant Hyrum may take the office of Priesthood and Patriarch, which was appointed unto him by his father by blessing and also by right.—Doc. and Cov. 124:91.

Hyrum Smith "received" the office, Jan. 24, 1841, and kept it until his martyrdom in Carthage Jail, Ill., June 27, 1844. His brother William Smith, who was also a member of the Council of Twelve Apostles, succeeded him by virtue of his birthright, or age, but he apostatized. At the general conference, held in October, 1845, he was rejected as an Apostle and as a Patriarch. He was finally excommunicated from the Church, Oct. 12, 1845.

After the rejection of William Smith, the Patriarchal office, according to the hereditary order, belonged to Asahel Smith (a brother of Joseph Smith, Sr.), who had been ordained a Patriarch at Nauvoo in 1844; but his health being poor, he is not known to have magnified his office as a Patriarch. Soon afterwards (July 20, 1848) he died at Iowaville, Wapello Co., Iowa.

John Smith, another brother of the late Joseph Smith, Sr., who had previously been ordained a Patriarch at Nauvoo, was ordained presiding Patriarch in the Church, Jan. 1, 1849, at Great Salt Lake City, under the hands of Brigham Young and Heber C. Kimball. He had been sustained as a "Patriarch in the Church" as early as the general conference, held at Winter Quarters, April 6, 1847.

Uncle John Smith, as he was familiarly called, died May 23, 1854, in Great Salt Lake City. John Smith, eldest son of the martyred Hyrum Smith, to whom the Patriarchal Priesthood descended direct from his father, was chosen as his successor. At the time of his father's death he was too young to receive the office. He was ordained presiding Patriarch, Feb. 18, 1855, in Great Salt Lake City, by Pres. Brigham Young.

John Smith died Nov. 6, 1911, at Salt Lake City; and on April 6, 1912, his son Hyrum G. Smith was chosen to succeed him as Presiding Patriarch of the Church.

FIRST COUNCIL OF SEVENTIES

The organization of the first quorum of Seventy was commenced at Kirtland, Ohio, Feb. 28, 1835. Nearly all the first members consisted of men who had distinguished themselves for their faithfulness as members of Zion's Camp. When the quorum was fully organized the following were chosen to act as its seven presidents: Hazen Aldrich, Joseph Young, Levi W. Hancock, Leonard Rich, Zebedee Coltrin, Lyman Sherman and Sylvester Smith.

Questions arose among some of the brethren in regard to the corresponding grades of the Seventies and High Priests, and it was ascertained that five or six of the seven presidents had previously been ordained High Priests. The Prophet Joseph Smith, in a meeting held in the Kirtland Temple, April 6, 1837, counseled these brethren, namely, Hazen Aldrich, Leonard Rich, Zebedee Coltrin, Lyman Sherman and Sylvester Smith, to join the High Priests' quorum, which five of them did, and the following named Elders were chosen to fill the vacancies thus created in the First Council of the Seventies: John Gould, in place of Hazen Aldrich; James Foster, in place of Leonard Rich; Daniel S. Miles, in place of Zebedee Coltrin; Josiah Butterfield, in place of Lyman Sherman; Salmon Gee, in place of Levi W. Hancock, and John Gaylord, in place of Sylvester Smith.

In the summer of 1837 it was ascertained that Levi W. Hancock, who was in Missouri at the time of the April meeting, was not a High Priest, and he was therefore received back into his former position as one of the First Seven Presidents of Seventies, at an important meeting held at Kirtland, Ohio, Sept. 3, 1837. John Gould, one of the newly appointed presidents, was asked by the Prophet Joseph to join the High Priests, which he did. After these changes the First Council of Seventies stood as follows: Joseph Young, Levi W. Hancock, James Foster, Daniel S. Miles, Josiah Butterfield, Salmon Gee, and John Gaylord.

Jan. 13, 1838, John Gaylord, together with many others, was excommunicated from the Church by the High Council at Kirtland, Ohio, for rising up in rebellion against the Church authorities. Elder Henry Herriman was called and ordained Feb. 6, 1838, to fill the vacancy in the First Council of Seventies.

In a meeting of the Seventies, held at Kirtland, Ohio, March 6, 1838, the council withdrew their fellowship from Salmon Gee for neglect of duty and other causes. Elder Zera Pulsipher was chosen and ordained to fill the vacancy the same day. The foregoing information about the Seventies is obtained from the original record of Seventies kept at Kirtland, Ohio.

After these two changes the council stood unchanged until the Church had removed to Nauvoo, Ill. It appears that James Foster, instead of gathering with the Saints, settled at Jacksonville, Morgan Co., Ill., and had no direct communication with his brethren. Prior to the October conference, 1844, he was dropped from his position by the council of the Seventies. In the following spring (1845), Albert P. Rockwood was called to fill the vacancy caused by the removal of Foster.

Josiah Butterfield retained his standing as one of the seven Presidents until a misunderstanding arose between the Prophet Joseph and him, and he was finally cut off from the Church, Oct. 7, 1844, at the general conference held at Nauvoo, for neglect of duty, etc. The vacancy was filled the same day by the appointment of Jedediah M. Grant as one of the council of the Seventies, but he was not ordained until some time afterwards.

Elder Daniel S. Miles died a faithful man in the early part of 1845, in Hancock County, Ill., and the vacancy occasioned by his death was filled by Elder Benjamin L. Clapp, in April, 1845. Elder Albert P. Rockwood, Benjamin L. Clapp and Jedediah M. Grant were ordained to the positions to which they had been elected Dec. 2, 1845.

After the demise of Willard Richards in 1854, Elder Jedediah M. Grant was selected by President Brigham Young to fill the office of second Counselor in the First Presidency, thus leaving another vacancy in the council of Seventies. Elder Horace S. Eldredge was called, at the October conference, 1854, to fill that vacancy, and was ordained about the same time in Great Salt Lake City.

Elder Benjamin L. Clapp, after living some years in Great Salt Lake City, removed his family to Ephraim, Sanpete Co., where he had some difficulty with Bishop Warren S. Snow. After investigation before the Council of Seventies, he was dropped from his position in the council, and finally excommunicated from the Church at the general conference, held in Great Salt Lake City, April 7, 1859. Elder Jacob Gates was called to fill the vacancy at the April Conference, 1860, but, being absent on a mission to Europe, he was not ordained until October, 1862, some time after his return home.

Elder Zera Pulsipher transcended the bounds of the Priesthood in the ordinance of sealing, for which he was cited to appear before the First Presidency of the Church, April 12, 1862. It was there voted that he be rebaptized, reconfirmed and ordained to the office of a High Priest, or go into the ranks of the Seventies. Subsequently he was ordained a Patriarch. Elder John Van Cott was called to fill the vacancy in the council of the Seventies, at the October conference, 1862.

Albert P. Rockwood died in Sugar House Ward, Salt Lake Co., Nov. 26, 1879, and at the April conference, 1880, Elder Wm. W. Taylor was called to fill the vacancy and soon afterwards ordained one of the First Seven Presidents of Seventies.

The vacancies caused by the death of Pres. Joseph Young, July 16, 1881, and of Levi W. Hancock, June 10, 1882, were filled by the ordination of Abraham H. Cannon as one of the First Seven Presidents, Oct. 9, 1882, and Seymour B. Young as another, Oct. 16, 1882.

Elder John Van Cott died Feb. 18, 1883. Christian Daniel Fjeldsted was called to fill the vacancy. He was ordained April 23, 1884, after his return from a mission to Scandinavia. The demise of Elder Wm. W. Taylor, Aug. 1, 1884, caused another vacancy, which was filled Oct. 7, 1884, by the ordination of John Morgan as one of the First Seven Presidents. Horace S. Eldredge died in Salt Lake City, Sept. 6, 1888, and the vacancy caused thereby was filled by the calling of Brigham H. Roberts to act as one of the council, at the October conference, 1888.

Abraham H. Cannon having been ordained an Apostle in October, 1889, George Reynolds was sustained as one of the First Seven Presidents of Seventies, at the April conference, 1890.

Elder Henry Herriman died at Huntington, Emery Co., Utah, May 17, 1891. Elder Jacob Gates died at Provo, Utah Co., April 1, 1892. The vacancies caused by the demise of those two veteran members were filled by the selection of Jonathan G. Kimball and Rulon S. Wells as members of the First Council of Seventies. The former was sustained at the general conference, held in October, 1892, and the latter at the general conference, held in April, 1893.

Elder John Morgan died at Preston, Idaho, Aug. 14, 1894. At the following October conference, Edward Stevenson was chosen to fill the consequent vacancy in the council.

Elder Edward Stevenson died in Salt Lake City, Jan. 27, 1897; and at the general conference of the Church, held in Salt Lake City, in October, 1897, Joseph W. McMurrin was chosen to fill the vacancy. He was ordained by Apostle Anthon H. Lund in Liverpool, England, Jan. 21, 1898.

Christian D. Fjeldsted died Dec. 23, 1905, in Salt Lake City; and, at the general conference of the Church, held at Salt Lake City April 6, 1906, Charles H. Hart was chosen to fill the vacancy thus caused in the council.

George Reynolds died Aug. 9, 1909, and at the next general conference, Oct. 6, 1909, Levi Edgar Young was chosen to complete the council.

The council now (1913) stands as follows: Seymour B. Young, Brigham H. Roberts, Jonathan G. Kimball, Rulon S. Wells, Joseph W. McMurrin, Charles H. Hart, and Levi Edgar Young.

PRESIDING BISHOPRIC

Edward Partridge, the first Bishop of the Church, was called to that position Feb. 4, 1831, by revelation.

"And again, I have called my servant Edward Partridge, and give a commandment, that he should be appointed by the voice of the church, and ordained a bishop unto the church, to leave his merchandise and to spend all his time in the labors of the church."—Doc. and Cov. 41:9.

Later, when other Bishops were ordained, he became known as the first or presiding Bishop. June 6, 1831, in solemn meeting, held at Kirtland, Ohio, Isaac Morley and John Corrill were ordained and set apart as counselors to Bishop Partridge.

In a letter written by the First Presidency at Kirtland, Ohio, to Wm. W. Phelps and others, in Missouri, under date of June 25, 1833, the following occurs: "Let Brother Isaac Morley be ordained second Bishop in Zion, and let Brother John Corrill be ordained third. Let Brother Edward Partridge choose as counselors in their place, Brother Parley P. Pratt and Brother Titus Billings, ordaining Brother Billings to the High Priesthood."

Owing to the persecutions which befell the Saints in Missouri, these appointments were not made; but at a meeting held at Far West, Mo., Aug. 1, 1837, Titus Billings was elected Bishop's counselor, in place of John Corrill; and at a conference held at the same place, Nov. 7, 1837, Edward Partridge "was nominated to still act as Bishop"; after which he nominated Isaac Morley and Titus Billings for his counselors, and they "were unanimously chosen."

These three constituted the head Bishopric of the Church during the lifetime of Bishop Partridge.

Bishop Edward Partridge filled his responsible position faithfully, in the midst of the most severe persecutions, until his death, which occurred at Nauvoo, Ill., May 27, 1840.

In a revelation given through Joseph the Prophet, Jan. 19, 1841, George Miller was called to the position of Bishop, in place of Edward Partridge, deceased.

"I therefore say unto you, I send upon his head the office of a bishopric, like unto my servant Edward Partridge, that he may receive the consecrations of mine house, that he may administer blessings upon the heads of the poor of my people, saith the Lord. Let no man despise my servant George Miller, for he shall honor me."—Doc. and Cov. 124:21.

In the same revelation (Doc. & Cov., 124:141), the Lord says: "I give unto you, Vinson Knight, Samuel H. Smith and Shadrach Roundy, if he will receive it, to preside over the Bishopric."

From the documents at our command at present, we are unable to learn whether or not the above named brethren officiated in the callings whereunto they were called; but at the general conference, held in October, 1844, at Nauvoo, Ill., Newel K. Whitney (who had been called by revelation to act as Bishop at Kirtland, Ohio, Dec. 4, 1831, was sustained as "first Bishop," and George Miller as "second Bishop" in the Church.

"And the duty of the bishop shall be made known by the commandments which have been given, and the voice of the conference. "And now, verily I say unto you, my servant Newel K. Whitney is the man who shall be appointed and ordained unto this power. This is the will of the Lord your God, your Redeemer."—Doc. and Cov. 72:7-8.

From that time till his death Newel K. Whitney was recognized, and after April, 1847, sustained by the voice of the general conference, as presiding Bishop of the Church. He had no regularly appointed Counselors; but recognized Brigham Young and Heber C. Kimball as his chief counselors and advisers.

Bishop Newel K. Whitney died in Great Salt Lake City, Sept. 23, 1850. At the general conference of the Church, held in April, 1851, Edward Hunter, who had been ordained a Bishop in Nauvoo in 1844, was sustained as presiding Bishop. It appears, however, that he was not ordained and set apart to that position till a year later. Like his predecessor, he received immediate advice from Presidents Brigham Young and Heber C. Kimball, and chose no other counselors until October, 1856, when, at the general conference, held in Great Salt Lake City, Leonard W. Hardy was sustained as first and Jesse C. Little as second counselor to Bishop Edward Hunter.

Counselor Jesse C. Little resigned his position as counselor. At the general conference held in Salt Lake City, in October, 1874, Robert T. Burton was sustained as second counselor to Bishop Hunter. He was ordained and set apart to this position, Sept. 2, 1875, after his return from a mission to England.

Bishop Edward Hunter died in Salt Lake City, Oct. 16, 1883. At the general conference, held in April, 1884, Wm. B. Preston, who had previously presided over the Cache Stake of Zion, was sustained as presiding Bishop, with Leonard W. Hardy as his first and Robert T. Burton as his second counselor.

Counselor Leonard W. Hardy died in Salt Lake City, July 31, 1884. At the general conference, held in April, 1884, Robert T. Burton was sustained as first and John Q. Cannon as second counselor to Bishop Wm. B. Preston.

Counselor John Q. Cannon, because of transgression, was released from his position. At the general conference, held at Provo, Utah Co., in April, 1886, John R. Winder was sustained as second counselor in the Presiding Bishopric.

Counselor John R. Winder was chosen first Counselor to President Joseph F. Smith at the re-organization of the First Presidency of the Church, Oct. 17, 1901; and on the 24th of the same month, Orrin P. Miller was chosen to succeed him as second Counselor to Bishop William B. Preston.

Counselor Robert T. Burton died at Salt Lake City Nov. 11, 1907.

Bishop William B. Preston was honorably released from his position Dec. 6, 1911; and on the 11th of the same month, the Presiding Bishopric was re-organized with Charles W. Nibley as Bishop, and Orrin P. Miller, first, and David Smith, second Counselors.

CHURCH HISTORIANS AND RECORDERS.

The office of Church Historian and Recorder was provided for by direct revelation, given April 6, 1830, immediately after the organization of the Church. In that revelation the Lord says, "Behold, there shall be a record kept among you," etc. (Doc. and Cov. 21:1). Oliver Cowdery, who had acted as a scribe for the Prophet Joseph, while translating the Book of Mormon, received the appointment as the first Church Recorder.

March 8, 1831, John Whitmer, one of the Eight Witnesses to the Book of Mormon, was called by revelation to the position of Church Historian. "Behold, it is expedient in me," said the Lord, "that my servant (John Whitmer) should write and keep a regular history," and "It shall be appointed unto him to keep the Church record and history continually, for Oliver Cowdery I have appointed to another office." (Doc. and Cov., Sec. 47.) John Whitmer removed to Missouri in the winter of 1831-32, and he was consequently unable to attend to his duties as Historian and Recorder at the headquarters of the Church, which were still at Kirtland. Hence, at a meeting of the Presidency of the Church and the High Council, held at Kirtland, Ohio, Sept. 14, 1835, Oliver Cowdery was again appointed "Recorder for the Church."

At a conference of the authorities of the Church and of the Saints, held in the Kirtland Temple, Sept. 17, 1837, Geo. W. Robinson was elected General Church Recorder, in place of Oliver Cowdery, who had removed to Missouri.

At a general conference, held at Far West, Mo., April 6, 1838, John Corrill and Elias Higbee were appointed Church Historians, "to write and keep the Church history"; and Geo. W. Robinson was sustained as General Church Recorder and clerk to the First Presidency.

John Corrill apostatized during the Missouri persecutions, and was excommunicated from the Church, at a conference, held at Quincy, Ill., March 17, 1839.

Elias Higbee was selected to accompany the Prophet Joseph to Washington, D. C., as a delegate from the Church to the Federal Government, and later was chosen as a member of the committee appointed to superintend the building of the Nauvoo Temple. Owing to these additional responsibilities, he was unable to devote much of his time to the writing of Church history. He finally died at Nauvoo, June 8, 1843.

At the general conference of the Church, held at Nauvoo, Ill., Oct. 3. 1840. Robert B. Thompson was appointed General Church Clerk, in place of George W. Robinson, who intended to remove to Iowa.

Elder Thompson entered upon the duties of his office faithfully, but took suddenly sick and died at Nauvoo, Aug. 27, 1841.

Oct. 2, 1841, at a general conference, held in the Grove at Nauvoo, Ill., James Sloan was elected General Church Clerk, in place of Robert B. Thompson, deceased.

At a special meeting, held at Nauvoo, July 30. 1843, Elder Willard Richards was appointed General Church Recorder, succeeding James Sloan, who had left Nauvoo on a mission to Ireland.

Elder Richards returned from his mission to England in August, 1841. Dec. 13, 1841, he was appointed by Joseph Smith to act as Recorder for the Temple, and also as private secretary and general clerk to the Prophet. He entered immediately upon the duties of his office, and continued the labors connected therewith till June 28, 1842, when he committed the business of the office to Wm. Clayton, and left Nauvoo, July 1, 1842, on a visit to the New England States. From this visit he returned Oct. 20, 1842. Dec. 21, 1842, the Prophet Joseph again appointed him private secretary and historian, while Wm. Clayton was retained as Temple Recorder and clerk of the Prophet's temporal business.

At the general conference of the Church, held at Nauvoo, in October, 1845, President Brigham Young remarked that "about three years ago, Elder Willard Richards was appointed by Pres. Joseph Smith as historian for the Church and General Church Recorder." The Saints had previously acted on his appointment as recorder, but not as historian. He therefore moved that "the Church receive the appointment of Brother Joseph, and that we continue and sustain Elder Richards as Historian for the Church and General Church Recorder." The motion was carried unanimously. Since that time the double office of Church Historian and General Church Recorder has been vested in the same person.

Willard Richards filled the office faithfully until his death, which occurred in Great Salt Lake City, March 11, 1854. At the general conference, held in Great Salt Lake City in April, 1854, Geo. A. Smith was chosen and sustained as Church Historian and General Church Recorder.

As the Church grew and increased in numerical strength and importance, the labors of the Church Historian increased proportionately, and it became necessary to appoint assistants to the Church Historian. Accordingly, Apostle Wilford Woodruff was sustained as assistant Church Historian, at the general conference, held in Salt Lake City, in October, 1856. Elder Woodruff was the first Elder sustained in that capacity by a general conference of the Church.

Apostle Geo. A. Smith, having been chosen as First Counselor to Pres. Brigham Young, was released from his position as Church Historian. At the general conference, held in April, 1871, Apostle Albert Carrington was sustained in that position, with Wilford Woodruff as his assistant.

Apostle Orson Pratt succeeded Albert Carrington as Church Historian and General Church Recorder, being sustained as such at the general conference, held in Salt Lake City, May 9, 1874. With Wilford Woodruff as his assistant, he filled the position till his death, which occurred in Salt Lake City, Oct. 3, 1881.

At the semi-annual conference, held in October, 1883. Apostle Wilford Woodruff was sustained as Church Historian and General Church Recorder, and at the next general conference, held in April, 1884, Franklin D. Richards was sustained as Assistant Church Historian.

At the general conference, April 7, 1889, Wilford Woodruff was chosen and sustained as President of the Church, and Franklin D. Richards was appointed his successor as Church Historian and General Church Recorder. At the next general conference, held in October, 1889, Elder John Jaques was sustained as assistant Church Historian. Elder Charles W. Penrose was sustained in a similar capacity at the general conference, held in April, 1896; and Elder Andrew Jenson at the general conference held in April, 1898.

Franklin D. Richards died at Ogden, Utah, Dec. 9, 1899; and on July 26, 1900, Apostle Anthon H. Lund was chosen to succeed him as General Church Historian.

THE HOLY PRIESTHOOD

The Church, which was established on the earth by Jesus Christ and his Apostles anciently, ceased in course of time to exist, through the martyrdom of many of its chief representatives and the final "falling away" of the remnant of its members, as predicted by the Apostles Paul (2 Thess. 2:3), and Peter (2 Pet. 2:1), and others.

In the present century the gospel of Christ, with its ancient powers and blessings, has been restored to earth anew, through the administration of heavenly messengers. Early in the spring of 1820, God the Father and his Son Jesus Christ appeared to Joseph Smith and revealed the true spiritual condition of the world. About three years later the angel Moroni appeared to him and subsequently visited him periodically for several years, imparting important instructions. On Sept. 22, 1827, he gave into the hands of Joseph Smith the plates on which was inscribed the history of the early inhabitants of America.

While Joseph Smith and Oliver Cowdery were engaged in translating the Book of Mormon, from the plates, at Harmony, Susquehanna Co., Pa., they went into the woods to enquire of the Lord respecting baptism for the remission of sins. While thus employed, on the 15th of May, 1829, a messenger from heaven descended in a cloud of light. Having laid his hands upon them, he ordained them, saying: "Upon you, my fellow servants, in the name of Messiah, I confer the Priesthood of Aaron, which holds the keys of the ministering of angels, and of the gospel of repentance and of baptism by immersion for the remission of sins; and this shall never be taken again from the earth, until the sons of Levi do offer again an offering unto the Lord in righteousness." (Doc. and Cov., 13.)

The heavenly messenger told Joseph Smith and Oliver Cowdery that the "Aaronic Priesthood had not the power of laying on of hands for the gift of the Holy Ghost," but that this should be conferred on them later. He then commanded them "to go and be baptized," and directed that Joseph Smith should baptize Oliver Cowdery, after which he should baptize Joseph.

The messenger told them "that his name was John, the same that is called John the Baptist in the New Testament, and that he acted under the direction of Peter, James and John, who held the keys of the Priesthood of Melchisedek," which Priesthood he said should in due time be conferred on them (Joseph and Oliver).

In accordance with the commandment aforesaid, Joseph Smith baptized Oliver Cowdery, who then baptized Joseph. Joseph Smith then laid his hands upon the head of Oliver Cowdery and ordained him to the Aaronic Priesthood. Finally Oliver laid his hands on Joseph and ordained him to the same Priesthood.

Soon after these important events, Joseph Smith and Oliver Cowdery "became very anxious" to receive the Melchisedek Priesthood, which John the Baptist had promised them, if they continued faithful. They had for some time made this matter a subject of humble prayer, and at length they met "in the chamber of Mr. Whitmer's house," at Fayette, Seneca Co., N. Y., one day in June, 1829. They engaged in solemn and fervent prayer, when the word of the Lord came to them in the chamber commanding that Joseph Smith "should ordain Oliver Cowdery to be an elder in the Church of Jesus Christ," and that Oliver should ordain Joseph to the same office. After that, they were to ordain others, as it should be made known unto them from time to time. However, they were commanded to defer these ordinations until "such times as it should be practicable to have their brethren, who had been and who should be baptized, assemble together."

This commandment was complied with April 6, 1830, the day on which the Church was organized. On that occasion Joseph Smith laid his hands upon Oliver Cowdery and ordained him an Elder in the Church, after which Oliver ordained Joseph to the office of an Elder. Next, they administered the Sacrament, and then laid their hands on each individual member of the Church present, that they might receive the Holy Ghost and be confirmed members of the Church.

The exact date of the ordination of Joseph Smith and Oliver Cowdery to the Melchisedek Priesthood by Peter, James and John is not stated, but it is generally believed to have taken place in June or July, 1829. In proof of the ordination we have the word of the Lord Jesus Christ, in a revelation, given to Joseph Smith at Fayette, N. Y., in September, 1830, as follows: "Listen to the voice of Jesus Christ, your Lord, your God, and your Redeemer, whose word is quick and powerful. * * * The hour cometh that I will drink of the fruit of the vine with you on the earth, with Moroni, whom I have sent unto you to reveal the Book of Mormon, containing the fullness of my everlasting gospel. * * * And also John, the son of Zacharias, * * * which John I have sent unto you, my servants, Joseph Smith, Jr., and Oliver Cowdery, to ordain you unto this first Priesthood, which you have received, that you might be called and ordained even as Aaron. * * * And also with Peter and James and John, whom I have sent unto you, by whom I have ordained you and confirmed you to be Apostles and especial witnesses of my name, and bear the keys of your ministry, and of the same things which I revealed unto them." (Doc. and Cov., 27:1, 5, 7, 8, 12.)

In a revelation on Church Government, given through Joseph Smith, the Prophet, in April, 1830, the following passage occurs: "Commandment was given to Joseph Smith, Jr., who was called of God and ordained an Apostle of Jesus Christ, to be the first Elder of this Church; and to Oliver Cowdery, who was also called of God, an Apostle of Jesus Christ, to be the second Elder of this Church, and ordained under his (Joseph's) hand." (Doc. and Cov., 20:2, 3.)

In the light of the foregoing it is plain that none among the children of men at the present time possess the holy Priesthood, with divine authority to administer in the ordinances of the gospel, except those who have received their ordinations through the laying on of hands by men whose commissions rest upon the divine calling of Joseph the Prophet. This being the case, it is desirable that every Apostle, Prophet, Patriarch, High Priest, Seventy, Elder, Bishop, Priest, Teacher and Deacon in the Church should be able to trace the Priesthood they hold back to the Prophet Joseph.

For the benefit of the brethren who are endeavoring to make proper records of these things, we publish the subjoined biographical notes, which contain the ordinations of nearly all the Elders who have been sustained at the present time as being sustained as the general authorities of the Church.

ALDRICH, Hazen; ordained a Seventy Feb. 28, 1835, under the hands of Joseph Smith and others.

BENSON, Ezra Taft; born Feb. 22, 1811; baptized July 19, 1840, at Quincy, Ill.; ordained a High Priest Oct. 25, 1840, by Hyrum Smith; ordained an Apostle July 16, 1846, by Pres. Brigham Young; died Sept. 3, 1869.

BILLINGS, Titus; born March 25, 1793, at Greenfield, Franklin Co., Mass.; baptized at Kirtland, Ohio, in November, 1830, by Parley P. Pratt; ordained a High Priest and counselor to Bishop Edward Partridge, Aug. 1, 1837, under the hands of Edward Partridge and Isaac Morley; died Feb. 6, 1866, at Provo, Utah.

BOYNTON, John Farnham; born Sept. 20, 1811; baptized in September, 1832, by Joseph the Prophet; ordained an Elder in 1832, by Sidney Rigdon; ordained an Apostle, Feb. 15,

1835, under the hands of Oliver Cowdery, David Whitmer and Martin Harris; died Oct. 20, 1890.

BURTON, Robert Taylor; born Oct. 25, 1821, in Amersburgh, Ontario, Canada; ordained a High Priest and Bishop and set apart as second counselor to Bishop Edward Hunter, Sept. 2, 1875, by Edward Hunter assisted by Brigham Young and Daniel H. Wells.

BUTTERFIELD, Josiah; ordained and set apart as one of the First Council of Seventies, April 6, 1837, under the hands of Sidney Rigdon and Hyrum Smith.

CANNON, Abraham Hoagland; born March 12, 1859; baptized March 12, 1867, by his father Geo. Q. Cannon; ordained an Elder July 7, 1875, by Geo. Q. Cannon; ordained a Seventy by ; ordained an Apostle Oct. 7, 1889, by Joseph F. Smith, assisted by Wilford Woodruff and George Q. Cannon and nearly all the Apostles; died July 19, 1896.

CANNON, George Quayle; born Jan. 11, 1827; baptized in June, 1840, by John Taylor; ordained an Elder at Nauvoo, by John Taylor; ordained a Seventy Feb. 9, 1845, by Arza Adams; ordained an Apostle Aug. 26, 1860, by Pres. Brigham Young, assisted by his Counselors and ten of the Apostles.

CANNON, John Q.; born April 19, 1857, at San Francisco, Cal.; baptized April 19, 1865, by his father, George Q. Cannon; ordained an Elder by Geo. Q. Cannon; ordained a Seventy Aug. 8, 1881, by Joseph F. Smith; ordained a High Priest and set apart as second counselor to Bishop Wm. B. Preston in October, 1884, by Pres. John Taylor.

CARRINGTON, Albert; born Jan. 8, 1813; baptized in July, 1841, by Wm. O. Clark; ordained an Apostle July 3, 1870, by Pres. Brigham Young; died Sept. 19, 1889, in Salt Lake City, Utah.

CLAPP, Benjamin L.; born Aug. 19, 1814, in Alabama; ordained and set apart as one of the presidents of the 8th quorum of Seventy, Oct. 20, 1844, under the hands of Joseph Young and Levi W. Hancock, set apart as one of the First Council of Seventies Dec. 2, 1845, under the hands of Apostles Brigham Young, Heber C. Kimball, Orson Hyde, Parley P. Pratt and George A. Smith; died in California about 1860.

CLAWSON, Rudger; born March 12, 1857, in Salt Lake City, Utah; baptized when about eight years old; ordained a Seventy March 7, 1875, by Hiram B. Clawson, who was ordained a Seventy Feb. 2, 1845, by Joseph Young; ordained a High Priest Feb. 12, 1888, by Lorenzo Snow; ordained an Apostle Oct. 10, 1898, by Lorenzo Snow, assisted by his Counselors, and all the Apostles.

CORRILL, John; ordained a High Priest and set apart as second counselor to Bishop Edward Partridge, June 6, 1831, under the hands of Edward Partridge and others.

COLTRIN, Zebedee; ordained a Seventy Feb. 28, 1835, under the hands of Joseph Smith and others; died July 21, 1887, at Spanish Fork, Utah Co., Utah.

COWDERY, Oliver; born in 1805; ordained to the Aaronic Priesthood in connection with Joseph Smith, May 15, 1829, by John the Baptist; baptized and reordained by Joseph Smith the same day; later in 1829, together with Joseph Smith, ordained to the Melchisedek Priesthood by Peter, James and John; confirmed a member of the Church and reordained an Elder, April 6, 1830, by Joseph Smith; together with David Whitmer and Martin Harris, he was "blessed by the laying on of the hands of the Presidency" (Joseph Smith, Sidney Rigdon and Fred. G. Williams) to select twelve Elders to constitute the Council of Twelve Apostles, Feb. 14, 1835; died March 3, 1850.

COWLEY, Matthias Foss; born Aug. 25, 1858, in Salt Lake City, Utah, baptized in 1866 by Samuel Turnbow; ordained an Elder Dec. 28, 1874, by Oluf F. Due; ordained a Seventy Oct. 11, 1880, by Joseph Young; ordained a High Priest Oct. 25, 1884, by Francis M. Lyman; ordained an Apostle Oct. 7, 1897, by Geo. Q. Cannon.

ELDREDGE, Horace S.; born Feb. 26, 1816, at Brutus, Cayuga Co., N. Y.; baptized June 4, 1836, by Libbeus T. Coon; ordained a Seventy Oct. 13, 1844, by Joseph Young; chosen one of the First Seven Presidents of Seventies in 1854; died Sept. 6, 1888, in Salt Lake City.

FIELDSTED, Christian Daniel; born Feb. 20, 1829, in Sundbyvester, Amager, Copenhagen Amt, Denmark; baptized Feb. 20, 1852, by Chr. Samuel Hansen; confirmed by Ole U. C. Monster; ordained an Elder July 25, 1853, by Peter O. Hansen, who was ordained a Seventy Nov. 17, 1844, by Joseph Young; ordained a Seventy Feb. 5, 1859, by Wm. H. Walker, who was ordained a Seventy Nov. 24, 1844, under the hands of Harrison Burgess, who was ordained a Seventy Feb. 28, 1835, by Sidney Rigdon; set apart as one of the First Council of Seventies, April 28, 1884, by Wilford Woodruff.

FOSTER, James; ordained and set apart as one of the First Seven Presidents of Seventies April 6, 1837, under the hands of Sidney Rigdon and Hyrum Smith.

GATES, Jacob; born March 9, 1811, at St. Johnsbury, Caledonia Co., Vt.; baptized June 17, 1833, by Orson Pratt; ordained a Seventy in 1838, under the hands of Sidney Rigdon and Joseph Smith; set apart as a president of the 4th quorum of Seventy Oct. 8, 1844; chosen as one of the First Council of Seventies in 1862; died April 14, 1892.

GAYLORD, John; ordained a Seventy December 20, 1836, by Hazen Aldrich, and set apart as one of the First Seven Presidents of Seventies April 6, 1837, under the hands of Sidney Rigdon and Hyrum Smith.

GEE, Salmon; ordained and set apart as one of the First Seven Presidents of Seventies April 6, 1837, under the hands of Sidney Rigdon and Hyrum Smith.

GOULD, John; ordained and set apart as one of the First Seven Presidents of Seventies April 6, 1837, under the hands of Sidney Rigdon and Hyrum Smith.

GRANT, Heber J.; born Nov. 22, 1856; baptized June 2, 1864; ordained a High Priest Oct. 31, 1880, by Pres. John Taylor; ordained an Apostle by Geo. Q. Cannon Oct. 16, 1882.

GRANT, Jedediah Morgan; born Feb. 21, 1816, baptized March 21, 1833, by John F. Boynton; ordained a Seventy Feb. 28, 1835, under the hands of Joseph Smith and others; set apart as one of the First Council of Seventies, Dec. 2, 1845, under the hands of Apostles Brigham Young, Heber C. Kimball, Orson Hyde, Parley P. Pratt and George A. Smith; ordained an Apostle and set apart as second Counselor in the First Presidency in 1854, under the hands of Brigham Young and others; died Dec. 1, 1856.

HANCOCK, Levi W.; born April 17, 1803, in Massachusetts; baptized Nov. 16, 1830; ordained a Seventy Feb. 28, 1835, under the hands of Joseph Smith and others; soon afterwards chosen as one of the First Seven Presidents of Seventies; died June 10, 1882.

HARDY, Leonard Wilford; born Dec. 31, 1805, in Bradford, Essex County, Mass.; baptized Dec. 2, 1832, by Orson Hyde; ordained an Elder soon afterwards; ordained a Seventy March 8, 1851; ordained a High Priest and Bishop of the 12th Ward, Salt Lake City, April 7, 1856; set apart as first counselor to Bishop Edward Hunter, Oct. 12, 1856; died July 31, 1884.

HARRIS, Martin; born May 18, 1783; baptized in 1830; ordained a High Priest June 6, 1831, by Lyman Wight; blessed Feb. 14, 1835, together with Oliver Cowdery and David Whitmer, under the hands of Joseph Smith, Sidney Rigdon and Frederick G. Williams, to select and ordain the Twelve Apostles; died July 10, 1875.

HERRIMAN, Henry; born June 9, 1804, in Rowley, Essex Co., Mass.; baptized in 1832, by Orson Hyde; ordained a Seventy in March, 1835, under the hands of Joseph Smith and Sidney Rigdon; set apart as a member of the First Council of Seventy, Feb. 6, 1838, under the hands of Joseph Young, James Foster and Josiah Butterfield; died May 17, 1891.

HIGBEE, Elias; born Oct. 23, 1795, in Galloway, Gloucester Co., N. J., baptized in 1832; ordained an Elder Feb. 20, 1833, by his brother, Isaac Higbee; ordained a High Priest by Amasa M. Lyman, about 1835; died June 8, 1843, at Nauvoo, Ill.

HUNTER, Edward; born June 22, 1793; baptized Oct. 8, 1840, by Orson Hyde; ordained a High Priest and Bishop Nov. 23, 1844, at Nauvoo, Ill., by Brigham Young, assisted by Heber C. Kimball and Newel K. Whitney; called and sustained as presiding Bishop of the Church at the general conference held in April, 1851; ordained and set apart to that position April 11, 1852, by Willard Richards, assisted by Heber C. Kimball; died Oct. 16, 1883.

HYDE, Orson; born Jan. 8, 1805; baptized Oct. 31, 1830, by Sidney Rigdon; ordained a High Priest about 1831; ordained an Apostle Feb. 15, 1835, under the hands of Oliver Cowdery, David Whitmer and Martin Harris; died Nov. 28, 1878.

JAQUES, John; born Jan. 7, 1827, at Market Bosworth, Leicestershire, England; baptized in the fall of 1845 by Thos. B. Ward; ordained an Elder Jan. 9, 1848, under the hands of John Fidoe, Thos. Stevenson and Wm. Cartwright; ordained a Seventy Feb. 3, 1857, by Wm. Burgess, who was ordained a Seventy Oct. 8, 1844, by Daniel S. Miles; ordained a High Priest Dec. 21, 1898, by Angus M. Cannon.

JENSON, Andrew; born Dec. 11, 1850, in Torslev, Hjorring Amt, Denmark; baptized and confirmed Dec. 2, 1859, by Carl W. J. Hecker; ordained an Elder April 10, 1873, by William H. Folsom, who was ordained a High Priest Oct. 7, 1862, by Pres. Brigham Young; ordained a Seventy May 4, 1873, by Geo. Q. Cannon.

JOHNSON, Luke S.; born Nov. 3, 1807; baptized May 10, 1831, by Joseph Smith; ordained a High Priest Oct. 25, 1831, by Joseph Smith; ordained an Apostle Feb. 15, 1835, under the hands of Oliver Cowdery, David Whitmer and Martin Harris; died Dec. 9, 1861.

JOHNSON, Lyman Eugene; born Oct. 24, 1811; ordained an Elder and subsequently a High Priest in 1831, by Joseph Smith; ordained an Apostle Feb. 14, 1835, under the hands of Oliver Cowdery, David Whitmer and Martin Harris; died Dec. 20, 1856.

KIMBALL, Heber Chase; born June 14, 1801; baptized in April, 1832, by Alpheus Gifford; ordained an Elder in 1832, by Joseph Young; ordained an Apostle Feb. 14, 1835, under the hands of Oliver Cowdery, David Whitmer and Martin Harris; died June 22, 1868.

KIMBALL, Jonathan Golden; born June 8, 1853, in Salt Lake City, Utah; ordained a Seventy July 21, 1886, by Chr. D. Fjelsted; set apart as one of the First Seven Presidents of Seventies, April 8, 1892, by Apostle Francis M. Lyman.

LAW, William; called by revelation, Jan. 19, 1841, to "be ordained, ordained and anointed as a Counselor" to Joseph the Prophet (Doc. and Cov., 124:91); soon afterwards he was ordained and set apart as second Counselor in the First Presidency, under the hands of Joseph the Prophet and others.

LITTLE, Jesse Carter; born Sept. 26, 1815, at Belfast, Maine; ordained a High Priest April 17, 1845, by Parley P. Pratt; ordained a Seventy and set apart as second counselor to Bishop Edward Hunter, in 1856; died Dec. 26, 1893.

LUND, Anthon Henrik; born May 15, 1844; baptized May 15, 1856, by Jacob Julander; ordained an Elder a few years later; ordained a Seventy March 23, 1864, by Peter Madsen Peel, who was ordained a Seventy Nov. 21, 1862, by John Tidwell; ordained an Apostle Oct. 7, 1889, by Geo. Q. Cannon.

LYMAN, Amasa Mason; born March 30, 1813; baptized April 27, 1832, by Lyman E. Johnson; confirmed the following day by Orson Pratt; ordained an Elder Aug. 23, 1832, by Joseph Smith; ordained a High Priest Dec. 11, 1832, by Lyman E. Johnson, assisted by Orson Pratt; ordained an Apostle Aug. 20, 1842, by Brigham Young, assisted by Heber C. Kimball and Geo. A. Smith; died Feb. 8, 1877.

LYMAN, Francis Marion; born Jan. 12, 1840, at Good Hope, McDonough Co., Ill.; baptized in the Elkhorn river, Neb. and confirmed July 1, 1849, by Amasa M. Lyman; ordained an Elder in 1856, at San Bernardino, Cal., by Amasa M. Lyman; ordained a Seventy Jan. 7, 1860, at Farmington, Davis Co., Utah, by John S. Gleason, who was ordained a

PIONEERS AND PROMINENT MEN OF UTAH 1285

Seventy Oct. 30, 1843, by Pres. Brigham Young, ordained a High Priest March 13, 1869, at Fillmore, Millard Co., Utah, by Thomas Callister, who was ordained a High Priest and Bishop Sept. 17, 1855, in Great Salt Lake City, Utah, by Edward Hunter; ordained one of the Twelve Apostles Oct. 27, 1880, in Salt Lake City, Utah, by John Taylor, assisted by his Counselors and nearly all the Apostles.

MARSH, Thomas Baldwin; born Nov. 1, 1799; baptized in September, 1830, by David Whitmer; ordained a High Priest June 6, 1831, by Lyman Wight; ordained an Apostle April 26, 1835, under the hands of Oliver Cowdery, David Whitmer and Martin Harris; died about 1866, at Ogden, Utah.

McLELLIN, William E.; born 1806, baptized, confirmed and ordained an Elder in 1831, under the hands of Samuel H. Smith and Reynolds Cahoon; ordained an Apostle Feb. 15, 1835, under the hands of Oliver Cowdery, David Whitmer and Martin Harris; died April 24, 1883.

McMURRIN, Joseph William; born Sept. 5, 1858, at Tooele, Tooele Co., Utah; baptized in 1866, by Henry W. Lawrence; ordained a Seventy April 21, 1884, by Royal Barney, who was ordained a Seventy in 1835, under the hands of Joseph Smith and Sidney Rigdon; ordained a Seventy Jan. 21, 1898, by Apostle Anthon H. Lund in Liverpool, England.

MERRILL, Marriner Wood; born Sept. 25, 1832; baptized April 6, 1852, by John Skerry; ordained an Apostle Oct. 7, 1889, by Wilford Woodruff, assisted by his Counselors and most of the Apostles.

MILES, Daniel S.; ordained a Seventy April 6, 1837, by Hazen Aldrich; set apart as one of the First Seven Presidents of Seventies April 6, 1837, under the hands of Sidney Rigdon and Hyrum Smith.

MORGAN, John; born Aug. 8, 1842, near Greensburgh, Decatur Co., Ind.; baptized Nov. 26, 1867, in Salt Lake City, Utah, by Robert Campbell; ordained an Elder Oct. 23, 1868, by Wm. H. Folsom, who was ordained a High Priest Oct. 7, 1862, by Pres. Brigham Young; ordained a Seventy Oct. 8, 1875, by Joseph Young; died Aug. 14, 1894.

MORLEY, Isaac; born March 11, 1786, in Montague, Hampshire Co., Mass.; baptized in November, 1830, at Kirtland, Ohio, by Parley P. Pratt; ordained a High Priest June 6, 1831, by Lyman Wight, and on the same day set apart as a counselor to Bishop Edward Partridge; ordained a Patriarch at Far West, Mo., Nov. 7, 1837, under the hands of Joseph Smith, Sidney Rigdon and Hyrum Smith; died June 24, 1865.

PAGE, John E.; baptized Aug. 18, 1833, by Emer Harris; ordained an Elder in September, 1833, by Nelson Higgins; ordained an Apostle Dec. 19, 1838, under the hands of Brigham Young and Heber C. Kimball; died near Sycamore, De-Kalb Co., Ill., in the fall of 1867.

PARTRIDGE, Edward; born Aug. 27, 1893; baptized Dec. 11, 1830, by Joseph the Prophet; ordained an Elder Dec. 5, 1830, by Sidney Rigdon; called by revelation to be the first Bishop of the Church, and ordained and set apart to that position Feb. 4, 1831, by Sidney Rigdon; ordained a High Priest, June 6, 1831, by Lyman Wight; died May 27, 1840.

PATTEN, David W.; born 1800; baptized June 15, 1832, by John Patten; ordained an Elder June 17, 1832, by Elisha H. Groves; ordained an Apostle Feb. 15, 1835, under the hands of Oliver Cowdery, David Whitmer and Martin Harris; died Oct. 25, 1838.

PENROSE, Charles William; born Feb. 4, 1832, in London, England, baptized May 14; 1850, by John Hyde, Sr.; ordained an Elder Jan. 6, 1851, by Geo. B. Wallace; ordained a Seventy Oct. 27, 1861, by Truman Leonard; later ordained a High Priest.

PRATT, Orson; born Sept. 19, 1811; baptized Sept. 19, 1830, by Parley P. Pratt; ordained an Elder Dec. 1, 1830, by Joseph Smith; ordained a High Priest Feb. 2, 1832, by Sidney Rigdon; ordained an Apostle April 26, 1835, under the hands of David Whitmer and Oliver Cowdery; died Oct. 3, 1881.

PRATT, Parley Parker; born April 12, 1807; baptized, confirmed and ordained an Elder by Oliver Cowdery, in September, 1830; ordained a High Priest June 6, 1831, by Joseph Smith; ordained an Apostle Feb. 21, 1835, by Joseph Smith; died May 13, 1857.

PRESTON, William Bowker; born Nov. 24, 1830, at Halifax, Franklin Co., Va.; baptized in February, 1857, by Henry G. Boyle; ordained an Elder by Geo. Q. Cannon; ordained a High Priest and Bishop Nov. 14, 1859, by Orson Hyde; set apart as Presiding Bishop of the Church in 1884, by Pres. John Taylor.

PULSIPHER, Zera; born June 24, 1789, in Rockingham, Windham Co., Vt.; baptized and ordained to the ministry in 1832; ordained and set apart as one of the First Seven Presidents of Seventies March 6, 1838, under the hands of James Foster and Joseph Young; died Jan. 1, 1872.

REYNOLDS, George; born Jan. 1, 1842, in London, England; baptized May 4, 1856; ordained a Seventy March 18, 1866, by Israel Barlow, who was ordained a Seventy in 1835, by Sidney Rigdon; set apart as one of the First Seven Presidents of the Seventies, April 10, 1890, by Lorenzo Snow.

RICH, Charles Coulson; born Aug. 21, 1809; baptized April 1, 1832, by Geo. M. Hinkle; ordained an Elder May 16, 1832, under the hands of Zebedee Coltrin and Solomon Wixom; ordained a High Priest in April, 1836, under the hands of Hyrum Smith and Uncle John Smith; ordained an Apostle Feb. 12, 1849, by Pres. Brigham Young; died Nov. 17, 1883.

RICH, Leonard; ordained a Seventy Feb. 28, 1835, under the hands of Joseph Smith and others.

RICHARDS, Franklin Dewey; born April 2, 1821; baptized June 3, 1838, by Phinehas Richards, at Richmond, Berkshire Co. Mass.; confirmed June 10, 1838, by Gibson Smith; ordained a Seventy April 9, 1840, at Nauvoo, Ill., by Joseph Young; ordained a High Priest May 17, 1844, at Nauvoo, Ill., by Brigham Young; ordained an Apostle Feb. 12, 1849, in the "Old Fort," Great Salt Lake City, by Heber C. Kimball.

RICHARDS, Willard; born June 24, 1804; baptized Dec. 31, 1836, by Brigham Young; ordained an Elder March 6, 1837, by Alma Beeman; ordained a High Priest April 1, 1838,

under the hands of Heber C. Kimball and others; ordained an Apostle April 14, 1840, by Brigham Young; died March 11, 1854.

RIGDON, Sidney; born Feb. 19, 1793; baptized, confirmed and ordained an Elder late in 1830, under the hands of Oliver Cowdery, Parley P. Pratt, Peter Whitmer, Jr., and Ziba Peterson. Subsequently he was ordained a High Priest by Joseph the Prophet, and on March 18, 1833, he was ordained and set apart as first Counselor in the First Presidency by Joseph Smith; died July 14, 1876.

ROBERTS, Brigham Henry; born March 13, 1857, in Warrington, Lancashire, England; baptized in 1867, by Seth Dustin; ordained a Seventy March 8, 1877, by Nathan T. Porter, who was ordained a Seventy Oct. 6, 1844, by Joseph Young; set apart as one of the First Council of Seventies in October, 1889, by Lorenzo Snow.

ROCKWOOD, Albert P.; born June 5, 1805, in Holliston, Middlesex Co., Mass.; baptized in 1833; ordained a Seventy Jan. 5, 1839, under the hands of Joseph Young, Zera Pulsipher, Henry Harriman and Levi W. Hancock; set apart as one of the First Council of Seventies Dec. 2, 1845, under the hands of Apostles Brigham Young, Heber C. Kimball, Orson Hyde, Parley P. Pratt and Geo. A. Smith; died Nov. 26, 1879.

SHERMAN, Lyman; ordained a Seventy Feb. 28, 1835, at Kirtland, Ohio, under the hands of Joseph Smith and others.

SLOAN, James; born at Donaghmore, Tyrone Co., Ireland; ordained a High Priest Feb. 18, 1838, under the hands of Joseph Smith, Sr.

SMITH, Asahel, son of Asahel Smith and Mary Duty; born May 21, 1773, at Windham, Rockingham Co., N. H.; baptized June 29, 1835, at Stockholm, Lawrence Co., N. Y., by Lyman E. Johnson; ordained a High Priest in 1836, by Don Carlos Smith; ordained a Patriarch Oct. 7, 1844, at Nauvoo, Ill., under the hands of the Twelve Apostles.

SMITH, George Albert; born June 26, 1817; baptized Sept. 10, 1832, by Joseph H. Wakefield; ordained a Seventy March 1, 1835, by Sidney Rigdon; ordained an Apostle April 26, 1839, by Heber C. Kimball; died Sept. 1, 1875.

SMITH, Hyrum; born Feb. 9, 1800; baptized by Joseph Smith in Seneca Lake, N. Y., in June, 1829; ordained a High Priest June 6, 1831, by Joseph Smith; chosen as second Counselor in the First Presidency Nov. 7, 1837; ordained a Patriarch Jan. 28, 1841, under the hands of Joseph the Prophet and others; died June 27, 1844.

SMITH, John, familiarly known as Uncle John Smith; born July 16, 1781, in Derryfield, Rockingham Co., N. H.; baptized, confirmed and ordained an Elder Jan. 9, 1832, by his brother Joseph Smith, Sr.; ordained a High Priest June 6, 1833, by Sidney Rigdon; ordained a Patriarch Jan. 10, 1844, by Joseph Smith; ordained Presiding Patriarch Jan. 1, 1849, under the hands of Brigham Young and Heber C. Kimball; died May 23, 1854.

SMITH, John, eldest son of Hyrum Smith; born Sept. 22, 1832, at Kirtland, Ohio; baptized in 1841, by John Taylor; ordained Presiding Patriarch in the Church Feb. 18, 1855, by Pres. Brigham Young.

SMITH, John Henry; born Sept. 18, 1848; baptized Sept. 18, 1856, by Geo. A. Smith; ordained an Elder Jan. 16, 1864, by Samuel L. Sprague; ordained a High Priest and Bishop Nov. 22, 1875, by Pres. Brigham Young; ordained an Apostle Oct. 27, 1880, by Wilford Woodruff.

SMITH, Joseph, the Prophet, born Dec. 23, 1805; ordained to the Aaronic Priesthood May 15, 1829, by John the Baptist; baptized and reordained the same day by Oliver Cowdery; later, perhaps in June or July, 1829, he and Oliver Cowdery were ordained to the Melchisedek Priesthood by Peter, James and John, three of the ancient Apostles, who held the keys of that Priesthood; confirmed a member of the Church and ordained the first Elder in the Church April 6, 1830, by Oliver Cowdery; died June 27, 1844.

SMITH, Joseph, Sr.; born July 12, 1771; baptized April 6, 1830; ordained a High Priest June 6, 1831 by Lyman Wight; ordained a Patriarch Dec. 18, 1833, under the hands of Joseph Smith, Oliver Cowdery, Sidney Rigdon and Frederick G. Williams; died Sept. 14, 1840.

SMITH, Joseph Fielding; born Nov. 13, 1838; baptized in 1850 or 1851 by Heber C. Kimball; ordained an Elder in May, 1854, by Geo. A. Smith; ordained a Seventy March 20, 1858, by George Meyer, who was ordained a Seventy July 13, 1845, by Jesse P. Harmon, who was ordained a Seventy Oct. 8, 1844, by Brigham Young; ordained a High Priest Oct. 16, 1859; ordained an Apostle July 1, 1866, by Pres. Brigham Young, and set apart as one of the Twelve Apostles Oct. 8, 1867, by Pres. Brigham Young, assisted by all the members of the Council of Twelve Apostles.

SMITH, Sylvester; ordained a Seventy Feb. 28, 1835, at Kirtland, Ohio, under the hands of Joseph Smith and others.

SMITH, William; born March 13, 1811; ordained a High Priest June 6, 1833, by Sidney Rigdon; ordained an Apostle Feb. 15, 1835, under the hands of Oliver Cowdery, David Whitmer and Martin Harris; died Nov. 13, 1893.

SNOW, Erastus; born Nov. 9, 1818; baptized Feb. 3, 1833; ordained an Elder Aug. 16, 1835, by Luke S. Johnson; ordained a High Priest in October, 1839; ordained an Apostle Fb. 12, 1849, by President Brigham Young; died May 27, 1868.

SNOW, Lorenzo; born April 3, 1814; baptized June. 1836, by John F. Boynton; confirmed by Hyrum Smith; ordained an Elder in the winter of 1836-37 by Alva Beeman; ordained a High Priest July 17, 1840, by Joseph Young; ordained a High Priest July 18, 1840, by Don Carlos Smith; ordained an Apostle Feb. 12, 1849, by Heber C. Kimball.

STEVENSON, Edward; born May 1, 1820, at Gibraltar, Spain; baptized in 1834, by Jared Posdick; ordained a Seventy May 1, 1845, under the hands of Joseph Young and others; set apart as one of the First Council of Seventies, Oct. 5, 1894, by Apostle Brigham Young; died Jan. 27, 1897.

TAYLOR, John; born Nov. 1, 1808; baptized, confirmed and ordained an Elder in 1836, by Parley P. Pratt; ordained an

Apostle, Dec. 19, 1838, under the hands of Brigham Young and Heber C. Kimball; died July 25, 1887.

TAYLOR, John Whittaker; born May 18, 1858, at Provo, Utah Co., Utah; ordained an Elder March 13, 1876, by Wm. J. Smith; ordained an Apostle April 9, 1884, by John Taylor, assisted by his Counselors and most of the Apostles.

TAYLOR, William W.; born Sept. 11, 1853, in Salt Lake City, Utah; baptized by his father, John Taylor; ordained a Seventy Oct. 11, 1875, by Orson Pratt, and chosen as one of the First Council of Seventies in 1880; died Aug. 1, 1884.

TEASDALE, George; born Dec. 8, 1831, in London, England; baptized Aug. 8, 1852, by Robert Till; ordained an Elder April 30, 1854, by John Tuddenham; ordained a Seventy Oct. 18, 1875, by Joseph Young; ordained a High Priest July 9, 1877, by Pres. Brigham Young; ordained an Apostle Oct. 16, 1882, by John Taylor.

THATCHER, Moses; born Feb. 2, 1842, in Sangamon County, Ill.; baptized and confirmed Dec. 25, 1856, by Henry G. Boyle; ordained an Elder March 23, 1857, by Henry G. Boyle; ordained a Seventy by Brigham Young; ordained a High Priest and set apart to preside over the Cache Stake of Zion in 1877, by Pres. Brigham Young; ordained an Apostle April 9, 1879, by John Taylor.

THOMPSON, Robert Blashel; born Oct. 1, 1811, in Great Driffield, Yorkshire, England; baptized and confirmed in May, 1836, in Canada, by Parley P. Pratt; ordained an Elder July 22, 1836, by John Taylor; died Aug. 27, 1841.

VAN COTT, John; born Sept. 7, 1814, at Canaan, Columbia Co., N. Y.; baptized in September, 1845, by Parley P. Pratt; ordained a Seventy Feb. 25, 1847, by Joseph Young; died Feb. 18, 1883.

WELLS, Daniel Hanmer; born Oct. 27, 1814; baptized Aug. 9, 1846, by Almon W. Babbitt, at Nauvoo, Ill.; ordained an Apostle and set apart as second Counselor in the First Presidency Jan. 4, 1857, by President Brigham Young; died March 24, 1891.

WELLS, Rulon Seymour; born July 7, 1854, in Salt Lake City, Utah; baptized about 1862, by Daniel H. Wells; confirmed by John V. Long; ordained an Elder Aug. 15, 1866, by Wm. J. Smith; ordained a Seventy Oct. 22, 1875, by Pres. Brigham Young; set apart as one of the First Seven Presidents of Seventies April 5, 1893, by George Q. Cannon.

WHITMER, David; born Jan. 7, 1805; baptized in June, 1829, by Joseph Smith; confirmed April 6, 1830; ordained an Elder soon afterwards, and subsequently ordained a High Priest; set apart in 1834 by Joseph Smith to preside over the Saints in Missouri; "blessed by the laying on of hands of the Presidency" (Joseph Smith, Sidney Rigdon and Frederick G. Williams), in connection with Oliver Cowdery and Martin Harris, Feb. 14, 1835, to choose the Twelve Apostles, in accordance with revelation (Doc. and Cov. 18:37); died Jan. 25, 1888.

WHITMER, John; born Aug. 27, 1802; baptized and ordained an Elder at an early day; ordained a High Priest June 6, 1831, at Kirtland, Ohio, by Lyman Wight; died July 11, 1878.

WHITNEY, Newel K.; born Feb. 5, 1795; baptized late in 1830; called by revelation Dec. 4, 1831, to the office of a Bishop; died Sept. 23, 1853.

WIGHT, Lyman; born May 9, 1796; baptized in 1830, by Oliver Cowdery; ordained a High Priest June 6, 1831, by Joseph the Prophet; ordained an Apostle April 8, 1841, by Joseph Smith; died March 31, 1858.

WILLIAMS, Frederick Granger; born Oct. 28, 1787, in Suffield, Hartford Co. Conn.; baptized, confirmed and ordained an Elder in November, 1830, under the hands of Oliver Cowdery, Parley P. Pratt, Peter Whitmer, Jr., and Ziba Peterson; called by revelation to "be a High Priest" and a Counselor to Joseph t e Prophet in March, 1832; ordained and set apart by Joseph Smith as his second Counselor, March 18, 1833; died Oct. 25, 1842, at Quincy, Ill.

WINDER, John Rex; born Dec. 11, 1820, in Biddenden, County of Kent, England; baptized Sept. 20, 1848; ordained a Seventy in 1854; ordained a High Priest March 4, 1872, by Edward Hunter; ordained a Bishop and set apart as second counselor to Bishop Wm. B. Preston in 1886, by Franklin D. Richards, assisted by George Q. Cannon.

WOODRUFF, Abraham Owen; born Nov. 23, 1872, near Salt Lake City, Utah; baptized May 3, 1881, by Henry Fowler; ordained an Elder Jan. 8, 1894, by Samuel H. Harrow; ordained a Seventy June 19, 1894, by Wilford Woodruff; ordained an Apostle Oct. 7, 1897, by Wilford Woodruff.

WOODRUFF, Wilford; born March 1, 1807; baptized by Zera Pulsipher Dec. 31, 1833; ordained an Elder by Warren Parrish in 1835; ordained a Seventy May 31, 1836, under the hands of David W. Patten and Warren Parrish, ordained an Apostle April 26, 1839, by Brigham Young; died Sept. 2, 1898.

YOUNG, Brigham, born June 1, 1801; baptized, confirmed and ordained an Elder April 14, 1832, by Eleazer Miller; ordained an Apostle Feb. 14, 1835, under the hands of Oliver Cowdery, David Whitmer and Martin Harris; died Aug. 29, 1877.

YOUNG, Brigham, Jr.; born Dec. 18, 1836; baptized in 1845, by his father, Brigham Young; ordained a Seventy; ordained an Apostle Nov. 22, 1855, by Brigham Young, and admitted into the Council of Twelve Apostles Oct. 9, 1868, being set apart by Brigham Young.

YOUNG, John W.; born Oct. 1, 1844, ordained an Apostle Nov. 22, 1855, by Pres. Brigham Young, but has never been admitted into the Council of Twelve Apostles.

YOUNG, Joseph; born April 7, 1797, in Hopkinton, Middlesex Co., Mass.; baptized April 6, 1832, by Daniel Bowen; ordained an Elder in 1832, by Ezra Landen; ordained a Seventy Feb. 28, 1835, under the hands of Joseph Smith and others, and soon afterwards chosen as one of the seven Presidents of Seventy; died July 16, 1881.

YOUNG, Seymour Bicknell; born Oct. 3, 1837, at Kirtland, Ohio; baptized in 1848, at Carterville, Ohio, by Ezekiel Lee; ordained an Elder in the Endowment House, Salt Lake City, Utah, April 15, 1856, by Samuel L. Sprague; ordained a Seventy Feb. 18, 1857, by Edmund Ellsworth, who was ordained a Seventy March, 8, 1843, by Joseph Young.

Continuation of Church Chronology and History (1830) from page 1277

Soon after the organization of the Church the Prophet's parents (Joseph Smith, Sr., and Lucy Smith), Martin Harris and A. Rockwell were baptized.

Some persons who had been baptized in the sectarian denominations desired to join the Church without further baptism, but the Lord, by revelation through the Prophet Joseph, instructed them to enter in at the gate, as He had commanded, and not seek to counsel God.

Revelation to the Church of Christ, which was established in these last days, in the year of our Lord one thousand eight hundred and thirty, given through Joseph, the Seer, in Manchester, New York, April, 1830, in consequence of some desiring to unite with the Church without rebaptism, who had previously been baptized.

Behold, I say unto you, that all old covenants have I caused to be done away in this thing, and this is a new and an everlasting covenant, even that which was from the beginning.

Wherefore, although a man should be baptized an hundred times, it availeth him nothing, for you cannot enter in at the straight gate by the law of Moses, neither by your dead works;

For it is because of your dead works, that I have caused this last covenant and this church to be built up unto me, even as in days of old.

Wherefore, enter ye in at the gate, as I have commanded, and seek not to counsel your God. Amen.—Doc. and Cov. Sec. 22.

Oliver Cowdery, Hyrum Smith, Samuel H. Smith and Joseph Knight being anxious to know their respective duties in relation to the work of God, Joseph the Prophet enquired of the Lord and received a revelation. (Doc. and Cov. Sec. 23.)

Sun. 11.—Oliver Cowdery preached the first public discourse delivered by any of the Elders in this dispensation. The meeting was held in the house of Peter Whitmer, Sr., at Fayette. Hiram Page, Catherine Page, Christian Whitmer, Annie Whitmer, Jacob Whitmer and Elizabeth Whitmer were baptized by Oliver Cowdery, in Seneca lake.

Sun. 18.—Peter Whitmer, Sr., Mary Whitmer, Wm. Jolly, Elizabeth Jolly, Vincent Jolly, Ziba Peterson and Elizabeth Anne Whitmer were baptized by Oliver Cowdery in Seneca lake.

Late in April the Prophet Joseph visited Joseph Knight, at Colesville, Broome Co., N. Y., where, under the Prophet's administration, the first miracle was wrought in this dispensation, viz.: Casting out devils.

May.—Newel Knight visited Joseph Smith, Jr., at Fayette and was baptized by David Whitmer.

June.—The Church held its first conference, at Fayette. Several of the brethren were ordained to the Priesthood; the Holy Spirit was poured out in a miraculous manner; many of the Saints prophesied and Newel Knight and others had heavenly visions.

—Later in June David Whitmer baptized Wm. Smith, Don Carlos Smith, Catherine Smith and six others in Seneca lake.

—Joseph Smith, Jr., returned with his family to his own home at Harmony, Pa.

—Joseph Smith, Jr., Oliver Cowdery, John Whitmer and David Whitmer visited Colesville, N. Y., where they held meeting, notwithstanding the mob, and baptized thirteen persons, among whom were Emma Smith and Joseph Knight. Joseph Smith, Jr., was arrested, charged with setting the country in an uproar by his preaching, tried and acquitted in South Bainbridge, Chenango Co., N. Y. Immediately afterwards he was again arrested, tried and acquitted at Colesville.

—Joseph Smith, Jr., and Oliver Cowdery again visited Colesville, but were driven away by a mob.

—An important revelation (Words of Moses) was given to Joseph Smith, Jr. (Pearl of Great Price, page 1.)

—Joseph Smith, Jr., and Oliver Cowdery again visited Colesville and confirmed the newly baptized members.

July.—Joseph Smith, Jr., was commanded by revelation to devote all his time to the interest of the Church, but in temporal labors he should "not have strength."

And thou shalt continue in calling upon God in my name, and writing the things which shall be given thee by the Comforter, and expounding all scriptures unto the church; * * *

For thou shalt devote all thy service in Zion; and in this thou shalt have strength. * *

And in temporal labors thou shalt not have strength, for this is not thy calling. Attend to thy calling and thou shalt have wherewith to magnify thine office, and to expound all scriptures, and continue in laying on of the hands and confirming the churches. —Doc. and Cov. 24:5, 9.

—Emma Smith, the Prophet's wife, was called by the Lord to expound scriptures, exhort the Church, and make a selection of sacred hymns for the use of the Saints.

Hearken unto the voice of the Lord your God, while I speak unto you, Emma Smith, my daughter, for verily I say unto you, all those who receive my gospel are sons and daughters in my kingdom. * * *

For he shall lay his hands upon thee, and thou shalt receive the Holy Ghost, and thy time shall be given to writing, and to learning much. * * *

And it shall be given thee, also, to make a selection of sacred hymns, as it shall be given thee, which is pleasing unto me, to be had in my church. * * * —Doc. and Cov. 25:1, 8, 11.

—The Lord commanded that "all things" in the Church should "be done by common consent."
And all things shall be done by common consent in the church, by much prayer and faith, for all things you shall receive by faith.—Doc. and Cov. 26:2.

—Oliver Cowdery returned to Fayette where he and the Whitmer family became disaffected because of a paragraph in one of the revelations (Doc. and Cov., 20:37. See revelation on Priesthood and Church government, April, 1830, above); but Joseph the Prophet paid them a visit and set matters right.

August.—Newel Knight and wife visited Joseph Smith, Jr., at Harmony, Pa., which gave occasion for the appearance of a heavenly messenger and a revelation on the Sacrament. (Doc. and Cov., Sec. 27, and History of Joseph Smith.)

* * * It mattereth not what ye shall eat, or what ye shall drink, when ye partake of the sacrament, if so be that ye do it with an eye single to my glory; remembering unto the Father my body which is laid down for you, and my blood which was shed for the remission of your sins:

Wherefore, a commandment I give unto you, that you shall not purchase wine, neither strong drink of your enemies:

Wherefore, you shall partake of none, except it is made new among you; yea, in this my Father's kingdom which shall be built up on the earth.—Doc. and Cov. 27:2-4.

—Joseph Smith, Jr., and others visited the branch of the Church at Colesville, N. Y., where they barely escaped mob violence.

—Joseph the Prophet removed with his family to Fayette, N. Y., on account of the persecutions prevailing against them at Harmony. At Fayette, Hiram Page had obtained possession of a stone by means of which he received false revelations.

September.—In a revelation, given through Joseph the Prophet to Oliver Cowdery, the Lord said that "those things" which Hiram Page had written from the stone were not of God, and that none could receive commandments and revelations for the Church except Joseph Smith, Jr.

And again, thou shalt take thy brother, Hiram Page, between him, and thee alone, and tell him that those things which he hath written from that stone, are not of me, and that Satan deceiveth him;

For, behold, these things have not been appointed unto him, neither shall anything be appointed unto any of this church contrary to the church covenants.

For all things must be done in order, and by common consent in the church, by the prayer of faith.—Doc. and Cov. 28:11-13.

—In a revelation given through Joseph the Prophet in the presence of six Elders at Fayette, N. Y., the Lord spoke of the gathering of the Saints, the end of the world, the reward of the righteous, the punishment of the wicked, etc. (Doc. and Cov., Sec. 29.)

—The second conference of the Church, which was continued three days, was held at Fayette, N. Y. After considerable discussion, Hiram Page and the whole Church renounced the stone and all things connected therewith, after which the power of God was made manifest. David Whitmer, Peter Whitmer, Jr., John Whitmer and Thos. B. Marsh were called by revelation to preach the gospel. (Doc. and Cov., Sec. 30 and 31.)

October.—Oliver Cowdery, Parley P. Pratt, Peter Whitmer, Jr., and Ziba Peterson were called by revelation to preach the gospel to the Lamanites.

Revelation given through Joseph, the Seer, to Parley P. Pratt and Ziba Peterson, October, 1830.

And now concerning my servant Parley P. Pratt, behold, I say unto him, that as I live I will that he shall declare my gospel and learn of me, and be meek and lowly of heart;

And that which I have appointed unto him is, that he shall go with my servants Oliver Cowdery and Peter Whitmer, Jr., into the wilderness among the Lamanites;

And Ziba Peterson, also, shall go with them, and I myself will go with them and be in their midst; and I am their advocate with the Father, and nothing shall prevail.

And they shall give heed to that which is written and pretend to no other revelation, and they shall pray always that I may unfold them to their understanding;

And they shall give heed unto these words and trifle not, and I will bless them. Amen.—Doc. and Cov. Sec. 32.

—Oliver Cowdery, Parley P. Pratt, Peter Whitmer, Jr., and Ziba Peterson started westward as the first missionaries to the Lamanites. On their journey they established a large branch of the Church at Kirtland, Geauga Co., Ohio. Among those baptized by Parley P. Pratt was Sidney Rigdon.

—A revelation calling Ezra Thayre and Northrop Sweet to the ministry was given through Joseph Smith, Jr., at Fayette.

November. Thurs. 4.—Orson Pratt, then nineteen years old, was called to the ministry by revelation through Joseph Smith, Jr. Brother Pratt was visiting the Prophet at Fayette.

My son Orson, hearken and hear and behold what I, the Lord God, shall say unto you. * * *

And blessed are you because you have believed;

And more blessed are you because you are called of me to preach my gospel,

To lift up your voice as with the sound of a trump, both long and loud, and cry repentance unto a crooked and perverse generation, preparing the way of the Lord for his second coming: * * *

Wherefore lift up your voice and spare not, for the Lord God hath spoken; therefore prophesy, and it shall be given by the power of the Holy Ghost; * * * —Doc. and Cov. 34:1, 4-6, 10.

December.—Sidney Rigdon and Edward Partridge, from Ohio, visited Joseph Smith, Jr., at Fayette, N. Y. Sidney Rigdon was called by revelation to assist Joseph in his labors, and both he and Edward Partridge were commanded to preach the gospel.

Behold, verily, verily, I say unto my servant Sidney, I have looked upon thee and thy works. I have heard thy prayers, and prepared thee for a greater work.

Thou art blessed, for thou shalt do great things. Behold thou wast sent forth, even as John, to prepare the way before me, and before Elijah which should come, and thou knewest it not.

Thou didst baptize by water unto repentance, but they received not the Holy Ghost;

But now I give unto thee a commandment, that thou shalt baptize by water, and they shall receive the Holy Ghost by the laying on of the hands, even as the apostles of old. * * *

And a commandment I give unto thee, that thou shalt write for him; and the Scriptures shall be given, even as they are in mine own bosom, to the salvation of mine own elect;

And now I say unto you, tarry with him, and he shall journey with you; forsake him not, and surely these things shall be fulfilled.—Doc. and Cov. 35:3-6, 20, 22.

Thus saith the Lord God, the Mighty One of Israel, Behold, I say unto you, my servant Edward, that you are blessed, and your sins are forgiven you, and you are called to preach my gospel as with the voice of a trump;

And I will lay my hand upon you by the hand of my servant Sidney Rigdon, and you shall receive my Spirit, the Holy Ghost, even the Comforter, which shall teach you the peaceable things of the kingdom;

And you shall declare it with a loud voice, saying, Hosanna, blessed be the name of the most high God.—Doc. and Cov. 36:1-3.

—The prophecy of Enoch was revealed to Joseph the Prophet. (See Pearl of Great Price.)

—The Saints in the State of New York were commanded by revelation to gather to Ohio.

Sat. 11.—Edward Partridge was baptized by Joseph Smith, Jr., in the Seneca river.

1831

January. Sun. 2.—The third conference of the Church was held at Fayette, Seneca Co., N. Y., and a revelation given through Joseph Smith, Jr., in which the Lord promised the Saints a land of inheritance.

And I hold forth and deign to give unto you greater riches, even a land of promise, a land flowing with milk and honey, upon which there shall be no curse when the Lord cometh:

And I will give it unto you for the land of your inheritance, if you seek it with all your hearts:

And this shall be my covenant with you, ye shall have it for the land of your inheritance, and for the inheritance of your children forever, while the earth shall stand, and ye shall possess it again in eternity, no more to pass away.—Doc. and Cov. 38:18-20.

Wed. 5.—James Coville, a Baptist minister, who had come to visit Joseph at Fayette, was commanded by revelation through Joseph the Prophet to receive the fullness of the gospel. (Doc. and Cov., Sec. 39.)

As James Coville rejected the word of the Lord and returned to his former doctrines and people, the Lord gave a revelation explaining why he did so. (Doc. and Cov., Sec. 40.)

In the latter part of this month, Joseph Smith, Jr., and wife, in company with Sidney Rigdon and Edward Partridge, left Fayette, N. Y., for Kirtland, Geauga Co., Ohio, where they arrived about the first of February.

—Oliver Cowdery and fellow-missionaries arrived in Jackson County, Missouri, where they commenced their mission among the Lamanites on its western border.

February. Fri. 4.—Edward Partridge was called by revelation to leave his merchandise and be ordained the first Bishop of the Church.

And again, I say unto my servant Edward Partridge, and give a commandment, that he should be appointed by the voice of the church, and ordained a bishop unto the church, to leave his merchandise and to spend all his time in the labors of the church;

To see to all things as it shall be appointed unto him, in my laws in the day that I shall give them.—Doc. and Cov. 41:9-10.

—The first revelation given through Joseph the Prophet at Kirtland, Ohio.

Wed. 9.—In the presence of twelve Elders, the Lord gave through Joseph Smith, Jr., an important revelation on Church government and how transgressors should be dealt with. The Elders were commanded to go out two and two to preach the gospel.

Revelation given through Joseph, the Seer, at Kirtland, Ohio, February 9th, 1831.

Hearken, O ye elders of my church, who have assembled yourselves together in my name, even Jesus Christ the Son of the living God, the Saviour of the world: inasmuch as they believe on my name and keep my commandments.

Again, I say unto you, hearken and hear and obey the law which I shall give unto you;

For verily I say, as ye have assembled yourselves together according to the commandment wherewith I commanded you, and are agreed as touching this one thing, and have asked the Father in my name, even so ye shall receive.

Behold, verily I say unto you, I give unto you this first commandment, that ye shall go forth in my name, every one of you, excepting my servants Joseph Smith, Jr., and Sidney Rigdon.

And I give unto them a commandment that they shall go forth for a little season, and it shall be given by the power of my Spirit when they shall return;

And ye shall go forth in the power of my Spirit, preaching my gospel, two by two, in my name, lifting up your voices as with the voice of a trump, declaring my word like unto angels of God;

And ye shall go forth baptizing with water, saying—Repent ye, repent ye, for the kingdom of heaven is at hand.

And from this place ye shall go forth into the regions westward; and inasmuch as ye shall find them that will receive you, ye shall build up my church in every region.

Until the time shall come when it shall be revealed unto you from on high, when the city of the New Jerusalem shall be prepared, that ye may be gathered in one, that ye may be my people and I will be your God.

And again, I say unto you, that my servant Edward Partridge shall stand in the office wherewith I have appointed him. And it shall come to pass, that if he transgress, another shall be appointed in his stead. Even so. Amen.

Again, I say unto you, that it shall not be given to any one to go forth to preach my gospel, or to build up my church, except he be ordained by some one who has authority, and it is known to the church that he has authority, and has been regularly ordained by the heads of the church.

And again, the elders, priests, and teachers of this church shall teach the principles of my gospel, which are in the Bible and the Book of Mormon, in the which is the fullness of the gospel;

And they shall observe the covenants and church articles to do them, and these shall be their teachings, as they shall be directed by the Spirit;

And the Spirit shall be given unto you by the prayer of faith, and if ye receive not the Spirit, ye shall not teach.

And all this ye shall observe to do as I have commanded concerning your teaching, until the fullness of my scriptures is given.

And as ye shall lift up your voices by the Comforter, ye shall speak and prophesy as seemeth me good;

For, behold, the Comforter knoweth all things, and beareth record of the Father and of the Son.

And now, behold, I speak unto the church. Thou shalt not kill; and he that kills shall not have forgiveness in this world, nor in the world to come.

And again, I say, thou shalt not kill; but he that killeth shall die.

Thou shalt not steal; and he that stealeth and will not repent shall be cast out.

Thou shalt not lie; he that lieth and will not repent, shall be cast out.

Thou shalt love thy wife with all thy heart, and shalt cleave unto her and none else;

And he that looketh upon a woman to lust after her, shall deny the faith, and shall not have the Spirit, and if he repents not he shall be cast out.

Thou shalt not commit adultery; and he that committeth adultery, and repenteth not, shall be cast out;

But he that has committed adultery and repents with all his heart, and forsaketh it, and doeth it no more, thou shalt forgive;

But if he doeth it again, he shall not be forgiven, but shall be cast out.

Thou shalt not speak evil of thy neighbor, nor do him any harm.

Thou knowest my laws concerning these things are given in my scriptures; he that sinneth and repenteth not, shall be cast out.

If thou lovest me, thou shalt serve me and keep all my commandments.

And behold, thou wilt remember the poor, and consecrate of thy properties for their support that which thou hast to impart unto them with a covenant and a deed which cannot be broken;

And inasmuch as ye impart of your substance unto the poor, ye will do it unto me, and they shall be laid before the bishop of my church and his counselors, two of the elders, or High Priests, such as he shall or has appointed and set apart for that purpose.

And it shall come to pass, that after they are laid before the bishop of my church, and after that he has received these testimonies concerning the consecration of the properties of my church, that they cannot be taken from the church agreeable to my commandments; every man shall be made accountable unto me, received by consecration, inasmuch as is sufficient for himself and family.

And again, if there shall be properties in the hands of the church, or any individuals of it, more than is necessary for their support, after this first consecration, which is a residue to be consecrated unto the bishop, it shall be kept to administer to those who have not, from time to time, that every man who has need may be amply supplied, and receive according to his wants.

Therefore, the residue shall be kept in my storehouse, to administer to the poor and the needy, as shall be appointed by the High Council of the church, and the bishop and his council.

And for the purpose of purchasing lands for the public benefit of the church, and building houses of worship, and building up of the New Jerusalem which is hereafter to be revealed.

That my covenant people may be gathered in one in that day when I shall come to my temple. And this I do for the salvation of my people.

And it shall come to pass, that he that sinneth and repenteth not, shall be cast out of the church, and shall not receive again that which he has consecrated unto the poor and the needy of my church; or in other words, unto me;

For inasmuch as ye do it unto the least of these, ye do it unto me;

For it shall come to pass, that which I spake by the mouths of my prophets, shall be fulfilled; for I will consecrate of the riches of those who embrace my gospel among the Gentiles, unto the poor of my people who are of the house of Israel.

And again, thou shalt not be proud in thy heart; let all thy garments be plain, and their beauty the beauty of the work of thine own hands;

And let all things be done in cleanliness before me.

Thou shalt not be idle; for he that is idle shall not eat the bread nor wear the garments of the laborer.

And whosoever among you are sick, and have not faith to be healed, but believe, shall be nourished with all tenderness, with herbs and mild food, and that not by the hand of an enemy.

And the elders of the church, two or more, shall be called, and shall pray for and lay their hands upon them in my name; and if they die they shall die unto me, and if they live they shall live unto me.

Thou shalt live together in love, insomuch that thou shalt weep for the loss of them that die, and more especially for those that have not hope of a glorious resurrection.

And it shall come to pass that those that die in me, shall not taste of death, for it shall be sweet unto them;

And they that die not in me, woe unto them, for their death is bitter.

And again, it shall come to pass that he that hath faith in me to be healed, and is not appointed unto death, shall be healed;

He who hath faith to see shall see;

He who hath faith to hear shall hear;

The lame who hath faith to leap shall leap;

And they who have not faith to do these things, but believe in me, have power to become my sons; and inasmuch as they break not my laws, thou shalt bear their infirmities.

Thou shalt stand in the place of thy stewardship;

Thou shalt not take thy brother's garment; thou shalt pay for that which thou shalt receive of thy brother;

And if thou obtainest more than that which would be for thy support, thou shalt give it into my store-house, that all things may be done according to that which I have said.

Thou shalt ask, and my Scriptures shall be given as I have appointed, and they shall be preserved in safety;

And it is expedient that thou shouldst hold thy peace concerning them, and not teach them until ye have received them in full.

And I give unto you a commandment that then ye shall teach them unto all men; for they shall be taught unto all nations, kindreds, tongues and people.

Thou shalt take the things which thou hast received, which have been given unto thee in my Scriptures for a law, to be my law to govern my church;

And he that doeth according to these things shall be saved, and he that doeth them not shall be damned, if he continues.

If thou shalt ask, thou shalt receive revelation upon revelation, knowledge upon knowledge, that thou mayest know the mysteries and peaceable things—that which bringeth joy, that which bringeth life eternal.

Thou shalt ask, and it shall be revealed unto you in mine own due time where the New Jerusalem shall be built.

And behold, it shall come to pass that my servants shall be sent forth to the east and to the west, to the north and to the south;

And even now, let him that goeth to the east, teach them that shall be converted to flee to the west, and this in consequence of that which is coming on the earth, and of secret combinations.

Behold, thou shalt observe all these things, and great shall be thy reward; for unto you it is given to know the mysteries of the kingdom, but unto the world it is not given to know them.

Ye shall observe the laws which ye have received and be faithful.

And ye shall hereafter receive church covenants, such as shall be sufficient to establish you, both here and in the New Jerusalem.

Therefore, he that lacketh wisdom, let him ask of me, and I will give him liberally and upbraid him not.

Lift up your hearts and rejoice, for unto you the kingdom, or in other words, the keys of the church have been given. Even so. Amen.

The priests and teachers shall have their stewardships, even as the members;

And the elders, or High Priests who are appointed to assist the bishop as counselors in all things, are to have their families supported out of the property which is consecrated to the bishop, for the good of the poor, and for other purposes, as before mentioned.

Or they are to receive a just remuneration for all their services, either a stewardship or otherwise, as may be thought best or decided by the counselors and bishop.

And the bishop, also, shall receive his support, or a just remuneration for all his services in the church.

Behold, verily I say unto you, that whatever persons among you, having put away their companions for the cause of fornication, or in other words, if they shall testify before you in all lowliness of heart that this is the case, ye shall not cast them out from among you;

But if ye shall find that any persons have left their companions for the sake of adultery, and they themselves are the offenders, and their companions are living, they shall be cast out from among you.

And again, I say unto you, that ye shall be watchful and careful, with all inquiry, that ye receive none such among you if they are married;

And if they are not married, they shall repent of all their sins, or ye shall not receive them.

And again, every person who belongeth to this church of Christ, shall observe to keep all the commandments and covenants of the church.

And it shall come to pass, that if any persons among you shall kill, they shall be delivered up and dealt with according to the laws of the land; for remember that he hath no forgiveness, and it shall be proven according to the laws of the land.

And if any man or woman shall commit adultery, he or she shall be tried before two elders of the church, or more, and every word shall be established against him or her by two witnesses of the church, and not of the enemy; but if there are more than two witnesses it is better.

But he or she shall be condemned by the mouth of two witnesses, and the elders shall lay the case before the church, and the church shall lift up their hands against him or her, that they may be dealt with according to the law of God.

And if it can be, it is necessary that the bishop is present also.

And thus ye shall do in all cases which shall come before you.

And if a man or woman shall rob, he or she shall be delivered up unto the law of the land.

And if he or she shall steal, he or she shall be delivered up unto the law of the land.

And if he or she shall lie, he or she shall be delivered up unto the law of the land.

And if he or she do any manner of iniquity, he or she shall be delivered up unto the law, even that of God.

And if thy brother or sister offend thee, thou shalt take him or her between him or her and thee alone; and if he or she confess, thou shalt be reconciled.

And if he or she confess not, thou shalt deliver him or her up unto the church, not to the members, but to the elders. And it shall be done in a meeting, and that not before the world.

And if thy brother or sister offend many, he or she shall be chastened before many.

And if any one offend openly, he or she shall be rebuked openly, that he or she may be ashamed. And if he or she confess not, he or she shall be delivered up unto the law of God.

If any shall offend in secret, he or she shall be rebuked in secret, that he or she may have opportunity to confess in secret to him or her whom he or she has offended, and to God, that the church may not speak reproachfully of him or her.

And thus shall ye conduct in all things.—Doc. and Cov. Sec. 42.

Mon. 14.—Oliver Cowdery, Parley P. Pratt, Ziba Peterson, Peter Whitmer, Jr., and Frederick G. Williams (who had joined the mission at Kirtland, Ohio) held a council at Independence, Mo., and decided that Parley P. Pratt should return to the East to report their labors to the heads of the Church.

A woman, who pretended to receive commandments, laws and other "curious matters," visited Joseph Smith, Jr., who inquired of the Lord and received a revelation in which God said that none but Joseph would be appointed to receive revelations and commandments, as long as he lived and remained faithful.

For behold, verily, verily, I say unto you, that ye have received a commandment for a law unto my church, through him (Joseph Smith, Jr.) whom I have appointed unto you, to receive commandments and revelations from my hand.

And this ye shall know assuredly that there is none other appointed unto you to receive commandments and revelations until he be taken, if he abide in me.

But verily, verily, I say unto you, that none else shall be appointed unto this gift except it be through him, for if it be taken from him, he shall not have power except to appoint another in his stead;

And this shall be a law unto you, that ye receive not the teachings of any that shall come before you as revelations or commandments;

And this I give unto you that you may not be deceived, that you may know they are not of me.

For verily I say unto you, that he that is ordained of me shall come in at the gate and be ordained as I have told you before, to teach those revelations which you have received, and shall receive through him whom I have appointed.—Doc. and Cov. 43:2-7.

A revelation instructing the Elders who had gone on missions to assemble at Kirtland in June following was given to Joseph Smith, Jr., and Sidney Rigdon, at Kirtland. (Doc. and Cov., Sec. 44.)

March. Mon. 7.—An important revelation concerning the salvation of man and the calamities of the last days was given through Joseph Smith, Jr., at Kirtland. The Saints were also commanded to gather means wherewith to purchase a land of inheritance on which to build a New Jerusalem. (Doc. and Cov., Sec. 45.)

Wherefore I, the Lord, have said, gather ye out from the eastern lands, assemble ye yourselves together ye elders of my church; go ye forth into the western countries, call upon the inhabitants to repent, and inasmuch as they do repent, build up churches unto me;

And with one heart and with one mind, gather up your riches that ye may purchase an inheritance which shall hereafter be appointed unto you,

And it shall be called the New Jerusalem, a land of peace, a city of refuge, a place of safety for the saints of the most High God; * * * —Doc. and Cov. 45:64-66.

Tues. 8.—A revelation was given through Joseph Smith, Jr., at Kirtland, relative to the gifts of the Holy Ghost, and John Whitmer was called by revelation to be Church Historian. (Doc. and Cov., Sec. 46.)

Revelation to Joseph Smith, Jr., and John Whitmer, given in Kirtland, Ohio, March 8th, 1831.

Behold, it is expedient in me that my servant John should write and keep a regular history, and assist you, my servant Joseph, in transcribing all things which shall be given you, until he is called to further duties.

Again, verily I say unto you, that he can also lift up his voice in meetings, whenever it shall be expedient.

And again, I say unto you, that it shall be appointed unto him to keep the church record and history continually, for Oliver Cowdery I have appointed to another office.

Wherefore it shall be given him, inasmuch as he is faithful, by the Comforter, to write these things. Even so. Amen.—Doc. and Cov. Sec. 47.

Later in March, the Saints were commanded by revelation to save their money to purchase land for an inheritance; and Sidney Rigdon, Parley P. Pratt and Lemon Copley were called by revelation to preach the gospel to the Quakers. (Doc. and Cov., Sec. 48 and 49.)

Revelation given through Joseph, the Seer, at Kirtland, Ohio, March, 1831.

It is necessary that ye should remain for the present time in your places of abode, as it shall be suitable to your circumstances;

And inasmuch as ye have lands, ye shall impart to the eastern brethren;

And inasmuch as ye have not lands, let them buy for the present time in those regions round about as seemeth them good, for it must needs be necessary that they have places to live for the present time.

It must needs be necessary, that ye save all the money that ye can, and that ye obtain all that ye can in righteousness, that in time ye may be enabled to purchase land for an inheritance, even the city.

The place is not yet to be revealed, but after your brethren come from the east, there are to be certain men appointed, and to them it shall be given to know the place, or to them it shall be revealed.

And they shall be appointed to purchase the lands, and to make a commencement to lay the foundation of the city; and then shall ye begin to be gathered with your families, every man according to his family, according to his circumstances, and as is appointed to him by the Presidency and the bishop of the church, according to the laws and commandments which ye have received, and which ye shall hereafter receive. Even so. Amen.—Doc. and Cov. Sec. 48.

Hearken unto my word, my servants Sidney, and Parley, and Lemon, for behold, verily I say unto you, that I give unto you a commandment that you shall go and preach my gospel which ye have received, even as ye have received it, unto the Shakers.—Doc. and Cov. 49:1.

April.—Joseph Smith, Jr., continued to translate the Scriptures.

May.—As a number of Elders did not understand the different spirits which manifested themselves at the time, Joseph Smith, Jr., inquired of the Lord and received a revelation. (Doc. and Cov., Sec. 50.)

—The Saints from the State of New York and other places commenced to gather to Kirtland, Ohio, and vicinity; and Edward Partridge was appointed by revelation through Joseph Smith, Jr., to locate them for a short time at Thompson, Geauga Co., Ohio, agreeable to the principles of the United Order.

Revelation given through Joseph, the Seer, in Thompson, Geauga County, Ohio, May, 1831.

Hearken unto me, saith the Lord your God, and I will speak unto my servant Edward Partridge, and give unto him directions, for it must needs be that he receive directions how to organize this people;

For it must needs be that they be organized according to my laws—if otherwise, they will be cut off;

Wherefore let my servant Edward Partridge, and those whom he has chosen, in whom I am well pleased, appoint unto this people their portion, every man equal according to their families, according to their circumstances, and their wants and needs.

And let my servant Edward Partridge, when he shall appoint a man his portion, give unto him a writing that shall secure unto him his portion, that he shall hold it, even this right and this inheritance in the church, until he transgresses and is not accounted worthy by the voice of the church, according to the laws and covenants of the church, to belong to the church;

And if he shall transgress and is not accounted worthy to belong to the church, he shall not have power to claim that portion which he has consecrated unto the bishop for the poor and needy of my church; therefore, he shall not retain the gift, but shall only have claim on that portion that is deeded unto him.

And thus all things shall be made sure, according to the laws of the land.

And let that which belongs to this people be appointed unto this people;

And the money which is left unto this people, let there be an agent appointed unto this people, to take the money to provide food and raiment, according to the wants of this people.

And let every man deal honestly, and be alike among this people, and receive alike, that ye may be one, even as I have commanded you.

And let that which belongeth to this people not be taken and given unto that of another church;

Wherefore, if another church would receive money of this church, let them pay unto this church again according as they shall agree;

And this shall be done through the bishop or the agent, which shall be appointed by the voice of the church.

And again, let the bishop appoint a storehouse unto this church, and let all things both in money and in meat, which is more than is needful for the want of this people, be kept in the hands of the bishop.

And let him also reserve unto himself for his own wants, and for the wants of his family, as he shall be employed in doing this business.

And thus I grant unto this people a privilege of organizing themselves according to my laws:

And I consecrate unto them this land for a little season, until I, the Lord, shall provide for them otherwise, and command them to go hence:

And the hour and the day is not given unto them, wherefore let them act upon this land as for years, and this shall turn unto them for their good.

Behold, this shall be an example unto my servant Edward Partridge, in other places, in all churches.—Doc. and Cov. 51:1-18.

June. Mon. 6.—The fourth conference of the Church was held at Kirtland, Ohio, on which occasion several brethren were called by revelation to the office of High Priests. This was the first occasion in which this office in the Priesthood was fully revealed and conferred upon any of the Elders in this dispensation.

Tues. 7.—Joseph Smith and about thirty other Elders were called by revelation to go to Missouri and preach the gospel by the way. (Doc. and Cov. Sec. 52.)

Later in June a revelation was given through Joseph Smith, Jr., at Kirtland, to Algernon Sidney Gilbert. (Doc. and Cov., Sec. 53.)

The Saints in Thompson, Ohio, were commanded by revelation to remove to Missouri. (Doc. and Cov., Sec. 54.)

Wherefore, go to now and flee the land, lest your enemies come upon you; and take your journey, and appoint whom you will to be your leader, and to pay monies for you.

And thus you shall take your journey into the regions westward, unto the land of the Missouri, unto the borders of the Lamanites.

And after you have done journeying, behold, I say unto you, seek ye a living like unto men, until I prepare a place for you.—Doc. and Cov. 54:7-9.

The Elders, in obedience to revelation, began to take their departure for the western country two and two.

About the middle of the month, Wm. W. Phelps arrived at Kirtland with his family. He was commanded by revelation to receive the fullness of the gospel, and then to assist in writing and printing for the Church, and also accompany the Prophet Joseph and Sidney Rigdon to Missouri.

And again, you (William W. Phelps) shall be ordained to assist my servant Oliver Cowdery to do the work of printing, and of selecting, and writing books for schools in this church, that little children also may receive instruction before me as is pleasing unto me.

And again, verily I say unto you, for this cause you shall take your journey with my servants Joseph Smith, Jr., and Sidney Rigdon, that you may be planted in the land of your inheritance to do this work.—Doc. and Cov. 55:4-5.

Thomas B. Marsh and others were commanded by revelation through the Prophet Joseph to go to Missouri. (Doc. and Cov., Sec. 56.)

Sun. 19.—Joseph Smith, Jr., Sidney Rigdon, Martin Harris, Edward Partridge, Wm. W. Phelps, Joseph Coe and A. S. Gilbert and wife left Kirtland, Ohio, for Missouri.

July.—About the middle of this month Joseph Smith, Jr., and his companions arrived at Independence, Jackson Co., Mo. The first Sabbath after their arrival Wm. W. Phelps preached to a western audience, over the boundary line of the United States. The following week the Colesville branch arrived. The Lord revealed the location of the New Jerusalem and the spot upon which the Temple was to be built. (Doc. and Cov., Sec. 57.)

And thus saith the Lord your God, if you will receive wisdom, here is wisdom. Behold, the place which is now called Independence, is the center place, and a spot for the temple is lying westward, upon a lot which is not far from the court house; * * * —Doc. and Cov. 57:3.

August. Mon. 1.—A revelation, directing the Saints how to locate in the land of Zion, was given in Jackson County. (Doc. and Cov., Sec. 58.)

Let no man break the laws of the land, for he that keepeth the laws of God hath no need to break the laws of the land:

Wherefore, be subject to the powers that be, until He reigns whose right it is to reign, and subdues all enemies under his feet.

Behold, the laws which ye have received from my hand are the laws of the church, and in this light ye shall hold them forth. Behold, here is wisdom. * * *

And also, this is a law unto every man that cometh unto this land, to receive an inheritance; and he shall do with his monies according as the law directs.

And it is wisdom also, that there should be lands purchased in Independence, for the place of the store-house, and also for the house of the printing. * * *

And let there be an agent appointed by the voice of the church, unto the church in Ohio, to receive monies to purchase lands in Zion.

And I give unto my servant, Sidney Rigdon, a commandment that he shall write a description of the land of Zion, and a statement of the will of God, as it shall be made known by the Spirit unto him;

And an epistle and subscription, to be presented unto all the churches to obtain monies, to be put into the hands of the bishop to purchase lands for an inheritance for the children of God, of himself or the agent, as seemeth him good or as he shall direct.

For, behold, verily I say unto you, the Lord willeth that the disciples, and the children of men should open their hearts, even to purchase this whole region of country, as soon as time will permit.

Behold, here is wisdom. Let them do this lest they receive none inheritance, save it be by the shedding of blood.—Doc. and Cov. 58:21-23; 36-37; 49-53.

Tues. 2.—The Saints commenced erecting houses in Jackson County, the first log being laid in Kaw Township, twelve miles southwest of Independence. The log was carried and placed in position by twelve men, in honor of the twelve tribes of Israel. On that occasion the land of Zion was consecrated and dedicated by Elder Rigdon for the gathering of the Saints.

Wed. 3.—The spot for the Temple, a short distance west of Independence, was dedicated in the presence of eight brethren, among whom were Joseph Smith, Jr., Sidney Rigdon, Edward Partridge, Wm. W. Phelps, Oliver Cowdery, Martin Harris and Joseph Coe.

Thurs. 4.—The fifth conference of the Church, and the first in the land of Zion, was held at the house of brother Joshua Lewis, in Kaw Township, Jackson Co., Mo.,

Sun. 7.—Polly Knight, wife of Joseph Knight, Sr., died in Jackson County, Mo. This was the first death among the Saints in that land. On the same day Joseph the Prophet received a revelation about the Sabbath. (Doc. and Cov., Sec. 59.)

But remember that on this the Lord's day, thou shalt offer thine oblations and thy sacraments unto the Most High, confessing thy sins unto thy brethren, and before the Lord.

And on this day thou shalt do none other thing, only let thy food be prepared with singleness of heart that thy fasting may be perfect, or, in other words, that thy joy may be full.

Verily, this is fasting and prayer; or in other words, rejoicing and prayer.

And inasmuch as ye do these things with thanksgiving, with cheerful hearts and countenances; not with much laughter, for this is sin, but with a glad heart and a cheerful countenance * * * —Doc. and Cov. 59:12-15.

Mon. 8.—A revelation, directing some of the brethren to return to the East, was given through Joseph Smith, Jr., in Jackson County.

But verily, I will speak unto you concerning your journey unto the land from whence you came. Let there be a craft made, or bought, as seemeth you good, it mattereth not unto me, and take your journey speedily for the place which is called St. Louis.

And from thence let my servants Sidney Rigdon, and Joseph Smith, Jr., and Oliver Cowdery, take their journey for Cincinnati;

And in this place let them lift up their voice and declare my word with loud voices, without wrath or doubting, lifting up holy hands upon them. For I am able to make you holy, and your sins are forgiven you.

And let the residue take their journey from St. Louis, two by two, and preach the word, not in haste, among the congregations of the wicked, until they return to the churches from whence they came.

And all this for the good of the churches; for this intent have I sent them.

And let my servant Edward Partridge impart of the money which I have given him, a portion unto mine elders who are commanded to return; * * * —Doc. and Cov. 60:5-10.

Tues. 9.—Joseph the Prophet, in company with ten Elders, left Independence, Mo., in sixteen canoes, on their return to Kirtland, Ohio.

Thurs. 11.—The returning Elders reached McIlwair's Bend (of the Missouri river) where Wm. W. Phelps "saw in open vision, by daylight, the Destroyer in his most horrible power ride upon the face of the water; others heard the noise, but saw not the vision."

Fri. 12.—A revelation was given through Joseph Smith, Jr., at McIlwair's Bend, about the cursing of the waters in the last days. (Doc. and Cov., Sec. 61.)

Sat. 13.—Joseph Smith, Jr., and company met several of the Elders on their way to the land of Zion. A revelation was given to them through Joseph Smith, Jr., on the bank of the Missouri river. (Doc. and Cov., Sec. 62.)

Sat. 27.—Joseph Smith, Jr., Sidney Rigdon and Oliver Cowdery arrive dat Kirtland, Ohio, from their visit to Missouri.

Late in August, the Saints were commanded by revelation, through Joseph the Prophet, to purchase lands in Jackson County, Mo., and the future persecutions of the Church were foreshadowed. (Doc. and Cov., Sec. 63).

Verily, I say unto you, there are those among you who seek signs, and there have been such even from the beginning;

But, behold, faith cometh not by signs, but signs follow those that believe. * * *

Nevertheless, I give commandments, and many have turned away from my commandments and have not kept them. * * *

Nevertheless, I, the Lord, rendereth unto Caesar the things which are Caesar's:

Wherefore, I the Lord, willeth that you should purchase the lands that you may have advantage of the world, that you may have claim on the world, that they may not be stirred up unto anger;

For Satan putteth it into their hearts to anger against you, and to the shedding of blood:

Wherefore the land of Zion shall not be obtained but by purchase or by blood, otherwise there is none inheritance for you.

And if by purchase, behold you are blessed;

And if by blood, as you are forbidden to shed blood, lo, your enemies are upon you, and ye shall be scourged from city to city, and from synagogue to synagogue, and but few shall stand to receive an inheritance.—Doc. and Cov. 63:8, 9, 13, 26-31.

September. Sun. 11.—The Saints were commanded by revelation through Joseph Smith, Jr., to forgive one another; and the Lord, in speaking of the present time, said it was a day of sacrifice and a day of tithing for His people. (Doc. and Cov., Sec. 64.)

Mon. 12.—Joseph Smith, Jr., removed with his family from Kirtland to Hiram, Portage Co., Ohio, about thirty miles from Kirtland, where he continued the translation of the Bible.

Ezra Booth, formerly a Methodist minister, came out as an apostate.

A conference was held in Hiram, at which Wm. W. Phelps was instructed to purchase a press and type, at Cincinnati, Ohio, for the purpose of establishing and publishing a monthly paper at Independence, Jackson Co., Mo., to be called the Evening and Morning Star.

October.—Early in this month the revelation on prayer was given. (Doc. and Cov., Sec. 65.)

Tues. 11.—A conference was held at Father John Johnson's house, in Hiram, at which the Elders were instructed about the ancient manner of holding meetings.

Tues. 25.—An important conference was held at Orange, Cuyahoga Co., Ohio. Wm. E. McLellin and Samuel H. Smith were called by revelation through Joseph the Prophet to preach the gospel. (Doc. and Cov., Sec. 66.)

November. Tues. 1.—At a special conference held at Hiram, Oliver Cowdery was appointed to go to Independence, Jackson Co., Mo., with the revelations which Joseph the Prophet had received up to that time and get them printed. The revelation known as the Preface to the Doctrine and Covenants was given. (Doc. and Cov., Sec. 1.)

Some of the brethren having criticised the language used in some of the revelations, given through Joseph the Prophet, the Lord gave the wisest among the Elders permission to write a revelation like the least of those the Prophet had received, on certain conditions. (See Doc. and Cov., Sec. 67.)

Wm. E. McLellin, as the "wisest man in his own estimation," failed in his attempt to write a revelation. (See History of Joseph Smith.)

Thurs. 3.—The revelation called the Appendix was given through Joseph Smith, Jr. (Doc. and Cov., Sec. 133.)

In a revelation given through Joseph Smith, Jr., at Hiram, to Orson Hyde, Luke S. Johnson, Lyman E. Johnson and Wm. E. McLellin, the Lord explained the nature and authority of the Aaronic Priesthood, the duties of parents towards their children, etc. (Doc. and Cov., Sec. 68.)

There remaineth hereafter, in the due time of the Lord, other bishops to be set apart unto the church, to minister even according to the first;

Wherefore they shall be High Priests who are worthy, and they shall be appointed by the First Presidency of the Melchisedek Priesthood, except they be literal descendants of Aaron.

And if they be literal descendants of Aaron, they have a legal right to the bishopric, if they are the firstborn among the sons of Aaron;

For the firstborn holds the right of the presidency over this priesthood, and the keys of authority of the same.

No man has a legal right to this office to hold the keys of this priesthood, except he be a literal descendant and the firstborn of Aaron;

But as a High Priest of the Melchisedek Priesthood has authority to officiate in all the lesser offices, he may officiate in the office of bishop when no literal descendant of Aaron can be found, provided he is called, and set apart and ordained unto this power under the hands of the First Presidency of the Melchisedek Priesthood.

And a literal descendant of Aaron, also, must be designated by this Presidency, and found worthy, and anointed, and ordained under the hands of this Presidency, otherwise they are not legally authorized to officiate in their priesthood;

But by virtue of the decree concerning their right of the priesthood descending from father to son, they may claim their anointing, if at any time they can prove their lineage, or do ascertain it by revelation from the Lord under the hands of the above named Presidency.

And again, no bishop or High Priest who shall be set apart for this ministry, shall be tried or condemned for any crime, save it be before the First Presidency of the church;

And inasmuch as he is found guilty before this Presidency, by testimony that cannot be impeached, he shall be condemned;

And if he repents he shall be forgiven, according to the covenants and commandments of the church.

And again, inasmuch as parents have children in Zion, or in any of her Stakes which are organized, that teach them not to understand the doctrine of repentance, faith in Christ the son of the living God, and of baptism and the gift of the Holy Ghost by the laying on of the hands when eight years old, the sin be upon the heads of the parents;

For this shall be a law unto the inhabitants of Zion, or in any of her Stakes which are organized;

And their children shall be baptized for the remission of their sins when eight years old, and receive the laying on of the hands.

And they shall also teach their children to pray and to walk uprightly before the Lord.—Doc. and Cov. 68:14-28.

John Whitmer was called by revelation to accompany Oliver Cowdery to Missouri, and to travel among the different branches of the Church in order to obtain information in his capacity as Church Historian.

Wherefore, I the Lord will that my servant, John Whitmer, should go with my servant Oliver Cowdery;

And also that he shall continue in writing and making a history of all the important things which he shall observe and know concerning my church;

And also that he receive counsel and assistance from my servant Oliver Cowdery and others.

And also my servants who are abroad in the earth, should send forth the accounts of their stewardships to the land of Zion;

For the land of Zion shall be a seat and a place to receive and do all these things;

Nevertheless, let my servant, John Whitmer, travel many times from place to place, and from church to church, that he may the more easily obtain knowledge;

Preaching and expounding, writing, copying, selecting, and obtaining all things which shall be for the good of the church, and for the rising generations, that shall grow up on the land of Zion, to possess it from generation to generation, for ever and ever. Amen.—Doc. and Cov. 69:2-8.

Joseph Smith, Jr., Martin Harris, Oliver Cowdery, John Whitmer, Sidney Rigdon and Wm. W. Phelps were appointed by revelation "to be stewards over the revelations and commandments" which had been given.

Behold, and hearken, O ye inhabitants of Zion, and all ye people of my church, who are far off, and hear the word of the Lord which I give unto my servant Joseph Smith, Jr., and also unto my servant Martin Harris, and also unto my servant Oliver Cowdery, and also unto my servant John Whitmer, and also unto my servant Sidney Rigdon, and also unto my servant William W. Phelps, by the way of commandment unto them;

For I give unto them a commandment; wherefore hearken and hear, for thus saith the Lord unto them—

I, the Lord, have appointed them, and ordained them to be

stewards over the revelations and commandments which I have given unto them, and which I shall hereafter give unto them.— * * * —Doc. and Cov. 70:1-3.

Oliver Cowdery and John Whitmer started for Missouri with the revelations, after which Joseph the Prophet, assisted by Sidney Rigdon as scribe, resumed the translation of the Scriptures.

December. Thurs. 1.—Joseph Smith, Jr., and Sidney Rigdon were called by revelation to go out and preach the gospel.

Behold, thus saith the Lord unto you my servants, Joseph Smith, Jr., and Sidney Rigdon, that the time has verily come, that it is necessary and expedient in me that you should open your mouths in proclaiming my gospel, the things of the kingdom, expounding the mysteries thereof out of the scriptures, according to that portion of Spirit and power which shall be given unto you, even as I will.

Verily, I say unto you, proclaim unto the world in the regions round about, and in the church also, for the space of a season, even until it shall be made known unto you.—Doc. and Cov. 71:1-2.

Sat. 3.—Joseph Smith, Jr., and Sidney Rigdon went to Kirtland in obedience to revelation.

Sun. 4.—Joseph Smith, Jr., and a number of other Elders and members of the Church assembled at Kirtland to learn their duties. Newel K. Whitney was called by revelation to act as Bishop in Kirtland, and the duties of that calling were made known. (Doc. and Cov., Sec. 72.)

And the duty of the bishop shall be made known by the commandments which have been given, and the voice of the conference.

And now, verily I say unto you, my servant Newel K. Whitney is the man who shall be appointed and ordained unto this power. This is the will of the Lord your God, your Redeemer. Even so. Amen.

The word of the Lord, in addition to the law which has been given, making known the duty of the bishop which has been ordained unto the church in this part of the vineyard, which is verily this:—

To keep the Lord's storehouse; to receive the funds of the church in this part of the vineyard;

To take an account of the elders as before has been commanded; and to administer to their wants, who shall pay for that which they receive, inasmuch as they have wherewith to pay;

That this also may be consecrated to the good of the church, to the poor and needy;

And he who hath not wherewith to pay, an account shall be taken and handed over to the bishop of Zion, who shall pay the debt out of that which the Lord shall put into his hands;

And the labors of the faithful who labor in spiritual things, in administering the gospel and the things of the kingdom unto the church, and unto the world, shall answer the debt unto the bishop in Zion. * * * —Doc. and Cov. 72:7-14.

1832

January.—Joseph Smith, Jr., preached in Shalersville, Ravenna and other places in Portage County, Ohio.

Tues. 10.—The Elders were commanded by revelation to continue their preaching till the next conference. (Doc. and Cov., Sec. 73.)

Later in the month, a revelation, explaining 1 Cor. 7:14, was given to Joseph Smith, Jr., at Hiram. (Doc. and Cov., Sec. 74.)

Wed. 25.—A conference was held at Amherst, Loraine Co., Ohio, at which a number of Elders were called by revelation on special missions and to preach the gospel in different parts of the country. (Doc. and Cov., Sec. 75.) [In this revelation, William E. McLellin, Luke Johnson, Major N. Ashley and Burr Riggs were called to preach in the "south country"; Orson Hyde, Samuel H. Smith, Lyman Johnson and Orson Pratt, in the "eastern countries"; and Asa Dodds and Calves Wilson, in the "western countries."—Ed.]

February. Thurs. 16.—The revelation known as the "Vision" was given at Hiram, in which the beautiful doctrine of the three glories was explained. In this vision Joseph Smith, Jr., and Sidney Rigdon "beheld the glory of the Son on the right hand of the Father," and "saw the holy angels and they who are sanctified before His throne." And after the many testimonies which had been given of the Son, they, last of all, gave this testimony, that he lived, for they "saw him, even at the right hand of God," and "heard the voice bearing record that he is the Only Begotten of the Father."

We, Joseph Smith, Jr., and Sidney Rigdon, being in the Spirit on the sixteenth of February, in the year of our Lord, one thousand eight hundred and thirty-two,

By the power of the Spirit our eyes were opened and our understandings were enlightened, so as to see and understand the things of God—

Even those things which were from the beginning before the world was, which were ordained of the Father, through his Only Begotten Son, who was in the bosom of the Father, even from the beginning,

Of whom we bear record, and the record which we bear is the fullness of the gospel of Jesus Christ, who is the Son, whom we saw and with whom we conversed in the heavenly vision;

For while we were doing the work of translation, which the Lord had appointed unto us, we came to the twenty-ninth verse of the fifth chapter of John, which was given unto us as follows.

Speaking of the resurrection of the dead, concerning those who shall hear the voice of the Son of Man, and shall come forth:

They who have done good in the resurrection of the just, and they who have done evil in the resurrection of the unjust.

Now this caused us to marvel, for it was given unto us of the Spirit;

And while we meditated upon these things, the Lord touched the eyes of our understandings and they were opened, and the glory of the Lord shone round.

And we beheld the glory of the Son, on the right hand of the Father, and received of his fullness;

And saw the holy angels, and they who are sanctified before his throne, worshiping God, and the Lamb, who worship him for ever and ever.

And now, after the many testimonies which have been given of him, this is the testimony last of all, which we give of him, that he lives;

For we saw him, even on the right hand of God, and we heard the voice bearing record that he is the Only Begotten of the Father—

That by him and through him, and of him the worlds are and were created, and the inhabitants thereof are begotten sons and daughters unto God.

And this we saw also, and bear record, that an angel of God who was in authority in the presence of God, who rebelled against the Only Begotten Son, whom the Father loved, and who was in the bosom of the Father—was thrust down from the presence of God and the Son,

And was called Perdition, for the heavens wept over him—he was Lucifer, a son of the morning.

And we beheld, and lo, he is fallen! is fallen! even a son of the morning.

And while we were yet in the Spirit, the Lord commanded us that we should write the vision, for we beheld Satan, that old serpent—even the devil—who rebelled against God, and sought to take the kingdom of our God, and his Christ.

Wherefore he maketh war with the saints of God, and encompasses them round about.

And we saw a vision of the sufferings of those with whom he made war and overcame, for thus came the voice of the Lord unto us.

Thus saith the Lord, concerning all those who know my power, and have been made partakers thereof, and suffered themselves, through the power of the devil, to be overcome, and to deny the truth and defy my power—

They are they who are the sons of perdition, of whom I say that it had been better for them never to have been born,

For they are vessels of wrath, doomed to suffer the wrath of God, with the devil and his angels in eternity;

Concerning whom I have said there is no forgiveness in this world nor in the world to come,

Having denied the Holy Spirit after having received it, and having denied the Only Begotten Son of the Father—having crucified him unto themselves, and put him to an open shame.

These are they who shall go away into the lake of fire and brimstone, with the devil and his angels,

And the only ones on whom the second death shall have any power;

Yea, verily, the only ones who shall not be redeemed in the due time of the Lord, after the sufferings of his wrath;

For all the rest shall be brought forth by the resurrection of the dead, through the triumph and the glory of the Lamb, who was slain, who was in the bosom of the Father before the worlds were made.

And this is the gospel, the glad tidings which the voice out of the heavens bore record unto us,

That he came into the world, even Jesus, to be crucified for the world, and to bear the sins of the world, and to sanctify the world, and to cleanse it from all unrighteousness;

That through him all might be saved whom the Father had put into his power and made by him.

Who glorifies the Father, and saves all the works of his hands, except those sons of perdition, who deny the Son after the Father has revealed him;

Wherefore, he saves all except them: they shall go away into everlasting punishment, which is endless punishment, which is eternal punishment, to reign with the devil and his angels in eternity, where their worm dieth not, and the fire is not quenched, which is their torment;

And the end thereof, neither the place thereof, nor their torment no man knows,

Neither was it revealed, neither is, neither will be revealed unto man, except to them who are made partakers thereof:

Nevertheless I, the Lord, show it by vision unto many, but straightway shut it up again:

Wherefore the end, the width, the height, the depth, and the misery thereof, they understand not, neither any man except them who are ordained unto this condemnation.

And we heard the voice, saying, Write the vision, for lo! this is the end of the vision of the sufferings of the ungodly!

And again, we bear record, for we saw and heard, and this is the testimony of the gospel of Christ, concerning them who come forth in the resurrection of the just;

They are they who received the testimony of Jesus, and believed on his name and were baptized after the manner of his burial being buried in the water in his name, and this according to the commandment which he has given,

That by keeping the commandments they might be washed and cleansed from all their sins, and receive the Holy Spirit by the laying on of the hands of him who is ordained and sealed unto this power,

And who overcome by faith, and are sealed by the Holy Spirit of promise, which the Father sheds forth upon all those who are just and true.

They are they who are the church of the first born.

They are they into whose hands the Father has given all things—

They are they who are Priests and Kings, who have received of his fullness, and of his glory,

And are Priests of the Most High, after the order of Melchisedek, which was after the order of Enoch, which was after the order of the Only Begotten Son:

Wherefore, as it is written, they are Gods, even the sons of God—

Wherefore all things are theirs, whether life or death, or things present, or things to come, all are theirs and they are Christ's and Christ is God's,

And they shall overcome all things;

Wherefore let no man glory in man, but rather let him glory in God, who shall subdue all enemies under his feet—

These shall dwell in the presence of God and his Christ for ever and ever.

These are they whom he shall bring with him, when he shall come in the clouds of heaven, to reign on the earth over his people.

These are they who shall have part in the first resurrection.

These are they who shall come forth in the resurrection of the just.

These are they who are come unto Mount Zion, and unto the city of the living God, the heavenly place, the holiest of all.

These are they who have come to an innumerable company of angels, to the general assembly and church of Enoch, and of the firstborn.

These are they whose names are written in heaven, where God and Christ are the judge of all.

These are they who are just men made perfect through Jesus the mediator of the new covenant, who wrought out this perfect atonement through the shedding of his own blood.

These are they whose bodies are celestial, whose glory is that of the sun, even the glory of God, the highest of all, whose glory the sun of the firmament is written of as being typical.

And again, we saw the terrestrial world, and behold and lo, these are they who are of the terrestrial, whose glory differs from that of the church of the firstborn, who have received the fullness of the Father, even as that of the moon differs from the sun in the firmament.

Behold, these are they who died without law.

And also they who are the spirits of men kept in prison, whom the Son visited, and preached the gospel unto them, that they might be judged according to men in the flesh.

Who received not the testimony of Jesus in the flesh, but afterwards received it.

These are they who are honorable men of the earth, who were blinded by the craftiness of men.

These are they who receive of his glory, but not of his fullness.

These are they who receive of the presence of the Son, but not of the fullness of the Father;

Wherefore they are bodies terrestrial, and not bodies celestial, and differ in glory as the moon differs from the sun.

These are they who are not valiant in the testimony of Jesus; wherefore they obtain not the crown over the kingdom of our God.

And now this is the end of the vision which we saw of the terrestrial, that the Lord commanded us to write while we were yet in the Spirit.

And again, we saw the glory of the telestial, which glory is that of the lesser, even as the glory of the stars differs from that of the glory of the moon in the firmament.

These are they who received not the gospel of Christ, neither the testimony of Jesus.

These are they who deny not the Holy Spirit.

These are they who are thrust down to hell.

These are they who shall not be redeemed from the devil, until the last resurrection, until the Lord, even Christ the Lamb shall have finished his work.

These are they who receive not of his fullness in the eternal world, but of the Holy Spirit through the ministration of the terrestrial;

And the terrestrial through the ministration of the celestial;

And also the telestial receive it of the administering of angels who are appointed to minister for them, or who are appointed to be ministering spirits for them, for they shall be heirs of salvation.

And thus we saw in the heavenly vision, the glory of the telestial, which surpasses all understanding,

And no man knows it except him to whom God has revealed it.

And thus we saw the glory of the terrestrial, which excels in all things the glory of the telestial, even in glory, and in power, and in might, and in dominion.

And thus we saw the glory of the celestial, which excels in all things—where God, even the Father, reigns upon his throne for ever and ever;

Before whose throne all things bow in humble reverence and give him glory for ever and ever.

They who dwell in his presence are the church of the firstborn, and they see as they are seen, and know as they are known, having received of his fullness and of his grace;

And he makes them equal in power, and in might, and in dominion.

And the glory of the celestial is one, even as the glory of the sun is one.

And the glory of the terrestrial is one, even as the glory of the moon is one.

And the glory of the telestial is one, even as the glory of the stars is one, for as one star differs from another star in glory, even so differs one from another in glory in the telestial world;

For these are they who are of Paul, and of Apollos, and of Cephas.

These are they who say they are some of one and some of another—some of Christ and some of John, and some of Moses, and some of Elias, and some of Esaias, and some of Isaiah, and some of Enoch;

But received not the gospel, neither the testimony of Jesus, neither the prophets, neither the everlasting covenant.

Last of all, these all are they who will not be gathered with the saints, to be caught up unto the church of the firstborn, and received into the cloud.

These are they who are liars, and sorcerers, and adulterers, and whoremongers, and whosoever loves and makes a lie.

These are they who suffer the wrath of God on the earth.

These are they who suffer the vengeance of eternal fire.

These are they who are cast down to hell and suffer the wrath of Almighty God, until the fullness of times when Christ shall have subdued all enemies under his feet and shall have perfected his work.

When he shall deliver up the kingdom, and present it unto the Father spotless, saying—I have overcome and have trodden the wine-press alone, even the wine-press of the fierceness of the wrath of Almighty God.

Then shall he be crowned with the crown of his glory, to sit on the throne of his power to reign for ever and ever.

But behold, and lo, we saw the glory and the inhabitants of the telestial world, that they were as innumerable as the stars in the firmament of heaven, or as the sand upon the sea shore.

And heard the voice of the Lord, saying—these all shall bow the knee, and every tongue shall confess to him who sits upon the throne for ever and ever;

For they shall be judged according to their works, and every man shall receive according to his own works, his own dominion, in the mansions which are prepared.

And they shall be servants of the Most High, but where God and Christ dwell they cannot come, worlds without end.

This is the end of the vision which we saw, which we were commanded to write while we were yet in the Spirit.

But great and marvelous are the works of the Lord, and the mysteries of his kingdom which he showed unto us, which surpasses all understanding in glory, and in might, and in dominion.

Which he commanded us we should not write while we were yet in the Spirit, and are not lawful for man to utter;

Neither is man capable to make them known, for they are only to be seen and understood by the power of the Holy Spirit, which God bestows on those who love him, and purify themselves before him;

To whom he grants this privilege of seeing and knowing for themselves;

That through the power and manifestation of the Spirit, while in the flesh, they may be able to bear his presence in the world of glory.

And to God and the Lamb be glory, and honor, and dominion for ever and ever. Amen.—Doc. and Cov. 76:11-119.

March.—A key to John's Revelation was given to Joseph Smith, Jr., at Hiram. (Doc. and Cov., Sec. 77.)

—The order of the Lord in relation to the poor was revealed. (Doc. and Cov., Sec. 78.)

For verily I say unto you, the time has come, and is now at hand; and behold, and lo, it must needs be that there be an organization of my people, in regulating and establishing the affairs of the storehouse for the poor of my people, both in this place and in the land of Zion.—Doc. and Cov. 78:3.

—Jared Carter, Stephen Burnett and Eden Smith were called by revelation to preach the gospel, and Frederick G. Williams to be a Counselor to Joseph Smith, Jr. (Doc. and Cov., Sec. 79, 80 and 81.)

Verily, verily I say unto you my servant Frederick G. Williams, listen to the voice of him who speaketh, to the word of the Lord your God, and hearken to the calling wherewith you are called, even to be a High Priest in my church, and a counselor unto my servant Joseph Smith, Jr.—Doc. and Cov. 81:1.

Sun. 25.—Joseph Smith, Jr., and Sidney Rigdon were mobbed and nearly killed at Hiram.

April. Sun. 1.—Joseph Smith, Jr., left Hiram, Ohio, to make a second journey to Missouri, accompanied by Newel K. Whitney, Peter Whitmer, Jr., and Jesse Gause to fulfill a revelation. (See Doc. and Cov., Sec. 78:9.)

Sat. 14.—Brigham Young was baptized by Eleazer Miller at Mendon, Monroe Co., N. Y.

Tues. 24.—Joseph Smith, Jr., and company arrived at Independence, Jackson Co., Mo.

Thurs. 26.—At a general council, held in Jackson County, Mo., Joseph Smith, Jr., was acknowledged the president of the High Priesthood.

A revelation "showing the order given to Enoch and the Church in his day" was given. (Doc. and Cov., Sec. 82.)

And you are to be equal, or in other words, you are to have equal claims on the properties, for the benefit of managing the concerns of your stewardships, every man according to his wants and his needs, inasmuch as his wants are just;

And all this for the benefit of the church of the living God, that every man may improve upon his talent, that every man may gain other talents, yea, even an hundred fold, to be cast into the Lord's storehouse, to become the common property of the whole church.—Doc. and Cov. 82:17-18.

Mon. 30.—A revelation concerning the rights of women and children in the Church was given through Joseph Smith, Jr., at Independence, Mo.

Verily, thus saith the Lord, in addition to the laws of the church concerning women and children, those who belong to the church, who have lost their husbands or fathers.

Women have claim on their husbands for their maintenance, until their husbands are taken, and if they are not found transgressors they shall have fellowship in the church;

And if they are not faithful, they shall not have fellowship in the church; yet they may remain upon their inheritances according to the laws of the land.

All children have claim upon their parents for their maintenance until they are of age.

And after that they have claim upon the church, or in other words upon the Lord's storehouse, if their parents have not wherewith to give them inheritances.

And the storehouse shall be kept by the consecrations of the church, and widows and orphans shall be provided for, as also the poor. Amen.—Doc. and Cov. Sec. 83.

May. Tues. 1.—At a council, held at Independence, it was decided to print 3,000 copies of the "Book of Commandments."

Sun. 6.—Joseph Smith, Jr., Sidney Rigdon and Newel K. Whitney left Independence, Mo., for Ohio. On the journey Bro. Whitney broke his leg and was miraculously healed. Joseph was poisoned by his enemies, but was restored in an instant.

June.—Joseph Smith, Jr., arrived at Kirtland, Ohio, and recommenced the translation of the Scriptures; thus he spent most of the summer.

—The first number of the "Evening and Morning Star" was issued at Independence, Mo. "The Upper Missouri Advertiser" a newspaper, was commenced about the same time in connection with the Star.

September. Sat. 22 and Sun. 23.—An important revelation on Priesthood was given through Joseph Smith, Jr., at Kirtland, Ohio, as the Elders began to return from their missions to the Eastern States. (Doc. and Cov., Sec. 84.)

November. Tues. 6.—Joseph Smith returned home from a rapid journey to Albany, New York and Boston. On the day of his return his son Joseph was born.

Tues. 27.—Joseph Smith, Jr., wrote an encouraging letter and revelation to the Saints in Jackson County, Mo. (Doc. and Cov., Sec. 85.)

December. Thurs. 6.—A revelation, explaining the parable of the wheat and tares, was given through Joseph Smith, Jr., at Kirtland. (Doc. and Cov., Sec. 86.)

Tues. 25.—Joseph Smith, Jr., prophesied about the civil war between the North and the South which commenced about twenty-eight years afterwards. (Doc. and Cov., Sec. 87.)

Revelation and Prophecy, given through Joseph, the Seer, on War. Given December 25th, 1832.

Verily, thus saith the Lord, concerning the wars that will shortly come to pass, beginning at the rebellion of South Carolina, which will eventually terminate in the death and misery of many souls.

The days will come that war will be poured out upon all nations, beginning at that place;

For behold, the Southern States shall be divided against the Northern States, and the Southern States will call on other nations, even the nation of Great Britain, as it is called, and they shall also call upon other nations, in order to defend themselves against other nations; and thus war shall be poured out upon all nations.

And it shall come to pass, after many days, slaves shall rise up against their masters, who shall be marshalled and disciplined for war.—Doc. and Cov. 87:1-4.

Thurs. 27.—The revelation known as the "Olive Leaf" was given through Joseph Smith, Jr. at Kirtland, Ohio. It contains grand and glorious principles and tells of important future events. The saints were commanded to build a House of the Lord at Kirtland and to open a school for the benefit of the Elders to be known as the School of the Prophets. (Doc. and Cov., Sec. 88.)

Joseph Smith, Jr., spent the winter of 1832-33 translating the Scriptures, attending the School of the Prophets and sitting in conferences.

1833

January. Tues. 22.—Joseph Smith, Jr., Sidney Rigdon, Frederick G. Williams, Newel K. Whitney, Hyrum Smith, Zebedee Coltrin, Joseph Smith, Sr., Samuel H. Smith, John Murdock, Lyman E. Johnson, Orson Hyde, Ezra Thayer, Levi W. Hancock and William Smith assembled in conference at

Kirtland, Ohio. On this occasion the Prophet Joseph, Zebedee Coltrin and Wm. Smith spoke in tongues, "after which the Lord poured out his spirit in a miraculous manner, until all the Elders and several members, both male and female, spoke in tongues." Praises were sung to God and the Lamb, and speaking and praying in tongues occupied the conference until a late hour at night. (See History of Joseph Smith.)

Wed. 23.—The conference was continued at Kirtland. "After much speaking, singing, praying and praising God, all in tongues," the brethren "proceeded to the washing of feet, as commanded of the Lord," according to the practice recorded in John 13:4-15. (See History of Joseph Smith.)

February. Sat 2.—Joseph Smith, Jr., completed the translation of the New Testament.

Wed. 27.—The revelation known as the "Word of Wisdom" was given through Joseph Smith, Jr., at Kirtland.

A Word of Wisdom, for the benefit of the Council of High Priests, assembled in Kirtland, and church; and also the saints in Zion.

To be sent greeting—not by commandments or constraint, but by revelation and the word of wisdom, showing forth the order and will of God in the temporal salvation of all saints in the last days.

Given for a principle with promise, adapted to the capacity of the weak and the weakest of all saints, who are or can be called saints.

Behold, verily, thus saith the Lord unto you, in consequence of evils and designs which do and will exist in the hearts of conspiring men in the last days, I have warned you, and forewarn you, by giving unto you this word of wisdom by revelation.

That inasmuch as any man drinketh wine or strong drink among you, behold it is not good, neither meet in the sight of your Father, only in assembling yourselves together to offer up your sacraments before him.

And, behold, this should be wine, yea, pure wine of the grape of the vine, of your own make.

And, again, strong drinks are not for the belly, but for the washing of your bodies.

And again, tobacco is not for the body, neither for the belly, and is not good for man, but is an herb for bruises and all sick cattle, to be used with judgment and skill.

And again, hot drinks are not for the body or belly.

And again, verily I say unto you, all wholesome herbs God hath ordained for the constitution, nature, and use of man.

Every herb in the season thereof, and every fruit in the season thereof; all these to be used with prudence and thanksgiving.

Yea, flesh also of beasts and of the fowls of the air, I, the Lord, have ordained for the use of man with thanksgiving; nevertheless they are to be used sparingly;

And it is pleasing unto me that they should not be used only in times of winter, or of cold, or famine.

All grain is ordained for the use of man and of beasts, to be the staff of life, not only for man but for the beasts of the field, and the fowls of heaven, and all wild animals that run or creep on the earth;

And these hath God made for the use of man only in times of famine and excess of hunger.

All grain is good for the food of man, as also the fruit of the vine, that which yieldeth fruit, whether in the ground or above the ground.

Nevertheless, wheat for man, and corn for the ox, and oats for the horse, and rye for the fowls and for swine, and for all beasts of the field, and barley for all useful animals, and for mild drinks, as also other grain.—Doc. and Cov. 89:1-17.

March. Fri. 8.—A revelation concerning the keys of the kingdom and the oracles of God was given to Joseph Smith, Jr., at Kirtland. (Doc. and Cov., Sec. 90.)

Sat. 9.—Joseph Smith, Jr., was commanded by revelation not to translate the Apocrypha. (Doc. and Cov., Sec. 91.)

Fri. 15.—A revelation concerning Frederick G. Williams was given through Joseph Smith, Jr., at Kirtland. (Doc. and Cov., Sec. 92.)

Mon. 18.—Sidney Rigdon and Frederick G. Williams were appointed and set apart by President Joseph Smith to be his Counselors in the Presidency of the Church, according to the revelation given March 8th. On the same occasion "many of the brethren saw a heavenly vision of the Savior and concourses of angels." (See History of Joseph Smith.)

Sat. 23.—A committee was appointed to purchase lands for the Saints at Kirtland.

Tues. 26.—An important council was held by the High Priests in Jackson County, Mo., in which some misunderstanding in regard to the presiding authorities in that land was amicably settled.

April.—In this month the first mob gathered at Independence, Jackson Co., Mo., to consult upon a plan for the removal or immediate destruction of the Church in that county.

Sat. 6.—About eighty official and some unofficial members of the Church met at the ferry on Big Blue river, near the western boundary of Jackson County, Mo., and, for the first time, celebrated the birthday of the Church.

May. Sat. 4.—Hyrum Smith, Jared Carter and Reynolds Cahoon were appointed a committee to obtain subscriptions for building a house for the Priesthood at Kirtland.

Mon. 6.—A revelation on the pre-existence of man was given through Joseph Smith, Jr., at Kirtland, and on the same date the Saints were commanded by revelation to build a House to the Lord at Kirtland. (Doc. and Cov., Sec. 93 and 94.)

Man was also in the beginning with God. Intelligence, or the light of truth, was not created or made, neither indeed can be.

All truth is independent in that sphere in which God has placed it, to act for itself, as all intelligence also, otherwise there is no existence.

Behold, here is the agency of man, and here is the condemnation of man, because that which was from the beginning is plainly manifest unto them, and they receive not the light.

And every man whose spirit receiveth not the light is under condemnation.

For man is spirit. The elements are eternal, and spirit and element, inseparably connected, receiveth a fullness of joy;

And when separated, man cannot receive a fullness of joy.

The elements are the tabernacle of God; yea, man is the tabernacle of God, even temples; and whatsoever temple is defiled, God shall destroy that temple.

The Glory of God is intelligence, or, in other words, light and truth;

Light and truth forsaketh that evil one.

Every spirit of man was innocent in the beginning, and God having redeemed man from the fall, men became again in their infant state, innocent before God.—Doc. and Cov. 93:29-38.

And again, verily I say unto you, my friends, a commandment I give unto you, that ye shall commence a work of laying out and preparing a beginning and foundation of the city of the Stake of Zion, here in the land of Kirtland, beginning at my house;

And behold it must be done according to the pattern which I have given unto you.

And let the first lot on the south, be consecrated unto me for the building of an house for the Presidency, for the work of the Presidency, in obtaining revelations; and for the work of the ministry of the Presidency, in all things pertaining to the church and kingdom.

Verily I say unto you, that it shall be built fifty-five by sixty-five feet in the width thereof and in the length thereof, in the inner court;

And there shall be a lower court and a higher court, according to the pattern which shall be given unto you hereafter;

And it shall be dedicated unto the Lord from the foundation thereof, according to the order of the Priesthood, according to the pattern which shall be given unto you hereafter: * * * Doc. and Cov. 94:1-6.

June. Sat. 1.—The Lord gave further instructions to Joseph the Prophet about the Temple to be built at Kirtland.

Yea, verily I say unto you, I gave unto you a commandment that you should build an house in the which house I design to endow those whom I have chosen with power from on high; * * *

Therefore let it be built after the manner which I shall show unto three of you, whom ye shall appoint and ordain unto this power.

And the size thereof shall be fifty and five feet in width, and let it be sixty-five feet in length, in the inner court thereof;

And let the lower part of the inner court be dedicated unto me for your sacrament offering, and for your preaching, and your fasting, and your praying, and the offering up your most holy desires unto me, saith your Lord.

And let the higher part of the inner court be dedicated unto me, for the school of mine apostles, saith Son Ahman; or, in other words, Alphus; or, in other words, Omegus; even Jesus Christ your Lord.—Doc. and Cov. 95:8, 14-17.

Tues. 4.—A revelation, showing the order of the Kirtland Stake of Zion, was given to Joseph Smith, Jr. (Doc. and Cov., Sec. 96.)

Thurs. 6.—A conference of High Priests held at Kirtland, O., instructed the committee for building the House of the Lord to proceed at once in obtaining material for its construction.

Sun. 23.—Doctor P. Hurlburt, afterwards connected with the spurious Spaulding story, was excommunicated from the Church for adultery.

Tues. 25.—An explanation of the plat of the city of Zion was sent to the brethren in Jackson County, Mo. (See History of Joseph Smith.)

July.—By this time about twelve hundred Saints, including children, had gathered to Jackson County, Mo.

Tues. 2.—Joseph the Prophet finished the translation of the Bible.

Sat. 20.—The printing office belonging to the Saints at Independence, Jackson County, Mo., was destroyed by a mob, who also tarred and feathered Bishop Edward Partridge and a Brother Allen.

—Orson Pratt preached in Patten, Canada. This is supposed to be the first discourse preached by a Latter-day Saint Elder in The Dominion.

Tues. 23.—The Saints at Independence, Mo., made a treaty with the mob and consented to leave Jackson County. Oliver Cowdery was dispatched as a special messenger to Kirtland, Ohio, to consult with the First Presidency.

—The corner stones of the Lord's House at Kirtland, O., were laid.

August. Fri. 2.—In a revelation given through Joseph Smith, Jr., at Kirtland, the Lord commanded that a house be built to Him in the land of Zion by the tithing of His people.

Verily, I say unto you, that it is my will that an house should be built unto me in the land of Zion, like unto the pattern which I have given you;

Yea, let it be built speedily, by the tithing of my people.—Doc. and Cov. 97:10-11.

Tues. 6.—The Saints were commanded by revelation to observe the constitutional laws of the land, to forgive their enemies and cultivate a spirit of charity toward all men. Their rights of self-defense were also made clear.

And now, verily I say unto you concerning the laws of the land, it is my will that my people should observe to do all things whatsoever I command them;

And that law of the land which is constitutional, supporting that principle of freedom in maintaining rights and privileges, belongs to all mankind, and is justifiable before me;

Therefore, I, the Lord, justify you, and your brethren of my church, in befriending that law which is the constitutional law of the land;

And as pertaining to law of man, whatsoever is more or less than these, cometh of evil. * * *

Now I speak unto you concerning your families; if men will smite you, or your families, once, and ye bear it patiently and revile not against them, neither seek revenge, ye shall be rewarded;

But if ye bear it not patiently, it shall be accounted unto you as being meted out a just measure unto you.

And again, if your enemy shall smite you the second time, and you revile not against your enemy, and bear it patiently, your reward shall be an hundred fold.

And again, if he shall smite you the third time, and ye bear it patiently, your reward shall be doubled unto you four fold;

And these three testimonies shall stand against your enemy if he repent not, and shall not be blotted out.

And now verily I say unto you, if that enemy shall escape my vengeance, that he be not brought into judgment before me, then ye shall see to it that ye warn him in my name, that he come no more upon you, neither upon your family, even your children's children unto the third and fourth generation;

And then if he shall come upon you, or your children, or your children's children unto the third and fourth generation; I have delivered thine enemy into thine hands.

1294 PIONEERS AND PROMINENT MEN OF UTAH

And then if thou wilt spare him, thou shalt be rewarded for thy righteousness; and also thy children and thy children's children unto the third and fourth generation;

Nevertheless thine enemy is in thine hands, and if thou reward him according to his works, thou art justified, if he has sought thy life, and thy life is endangered by him, thine enemy is in thine hands and thou art justified.

Behold, this is the law I gave unto my servant Nephi, and thy fathers Joseph, and Jacob, and Isaac, and Abraham, and all mine ancient prophets and apostles.—Doc. and Cov. 98:4-7 23-32.

A few days later John Murdock was called to the ministry by revelation. (Doc. and Cov., Sec. 99.)

September. Wed. 11.—It was decided in council to establish a printing press at Kirtland, and publish a paper to be called the "Latter-day Saints' Messenger and Advocate;" also that the "Evening and Morning Star," formerly published in Jackson County, Mo., should be published at Kirtland.

—Bishop Edward Partridge was acknowledged as the head of the Church in Zion, and ten High Priests were appointed to watch over the ten branches of the Church there.

October.—Orson Hyde and John Gould arrived in Jackson County, Mo., as messengers from Kirtland; and the Church in Zion dispatched Wm. W. Phelps and Orson Hyde to Governor Daniel Dunklin at Jefferson City, with a petition from the Saints.

Sat. 5.—Joseph Smith, Jr., in company with Elders Sidney Rigdon and Freeman Nickerson, left Kirtland on a visit to Canada.

Tues. 8.—Wm. W. Phelps and Orson Hyde presented to Governor Daniel Dunklin, of Missouri, the petition from the Saints in Jackson County.

Sat. 12.—In a revelation given at Perrysburg, N. Y., Joseph Smith, Jr., and Sidney Rigdon were commanded to continue their missionary labors in the East. (Doc. and Cov., Sec. 100.)

Sat. 19.—In answer to the petition from the Saints in Jackson County, Gov. Dunklin, of Missouri, wrote a letter to the leading men of the Church in that county, promising to enforce the laws.

Sat. 26.—Joseph Smith, Jr., preached and baptized twelve persons at Mount Pleasant, Upper Canada.

Thurs. 31.—A mob attacked a branch of the Church, west of the Big Blue, in Jackson County, Mo., destroyed ten houses, and beat several of the brethren in a most brutal manner.

November. Fri. 1.—The Saints at Independence were attacked by a mob, and Gilbert & Whitney's store was partly destroyed, besides many private dwellings.

Sat. 2.—The mob attacked the Saints on the Big Blue, Jackson County, and beat David Bennett severely.

Mon. 4.—A skirmish took place between a company of Saints and a mob, several miles west of the Big Blue, in Jackson County. Andrew Barber, one of the Saints, was mortally wounded, two of the mob were killed, and several others wounded on both sides.

—Joseph Smith, Jr., returned to Kirtland, O., from his mission to Canada.

Tues. 5.—Col. Thos Pitcher, commanding the mob militia, in Jackson County, demanded that the Saints should give up their arms, which order was reluctantly complied with. During the following night and the next day the mob drove the Saints from their homes at the point of the bayonet. The exiles were thereby exposed to the most severe sufferings from cold and hunger.

Thurs. 7.—On this and the following day the exiled Saints were busy crossing the Missouri river from Jackson to Clay County, Mo., where the inhabitants received them with some degree of kindness.

Others of the Saints found temporary shelter in Ray, Van Buren, Lafayette and other counties.

Wed. 13.—A grand meteoric shower or "falling of the stars" was witnessed throughout the land, which cheered the Saints and alarmed their enemies.

December.—Persecution raged against the Saints who had fled to Van Buren County, Mo.

—Oliver Cowdery and Bishop Newel K. Whitney arrived at Kirtland, O., with a new printing press.

Fri. 6.—The Saints in Clay County, Mo., sent another petition to Gov. Dunklin, praying for redress.

Mon. 16.—Joseph Smith, Jr., received a revelation at Kirtland, Ohio, in which the Lord said that he had allowed afflictions to come upon the Saints in Missouri because of their transgressions, but that he in His own due time would permit the pure in heart to return to their inheritances. This was illustrated by a parable. (Doc. and Cov., Sec. 101.)

Verily I say unto you, concerning your brethren who have been afflicted, and persecuted, and cast out from the land of their inheritance,

I, the Lord, have suffered the affliction to come upon them, wherewith they have been afflicted, in consequence of their transgressions; * * *

Zion shall not be moved out of her place, notwithstanding her children are scattered;

They that remain, and are pure in heart, shall return, and come to their inheritances, they and their children, with songs of everlasting joy, to build up the waste places of Zion. * * * —Doc. and Cov. 101:1-2, 17-18.

Wed. 18.—The printing office at Kirtland, O., was dedicated and the publication of the "Evening and Morning Star" recommenced with Oliver Cowdery as editor.

—Joseph Smith, Sr., was ordained Patriarch to the whole Church.

Thurs. 19.—Wm. Pratt and David W. Patten left Kirtland, Ohio, for Missouri, bearing a message from the First Presidency to the exiled Saints.

Mon. 23.—Four aged families, living near Independence, Mo., whose penury and infirmities, incident to old age, forbade a speedy removal, were driven from their houses by a mob.

Fri. 27.—The printing press and materials, taken from the Saints at Independence, Mo., were disposed of by the mob to Davis & Kelley, who removed them to Clay County, and there commenced the publication of the "Missouri Enquirer."

Tues. 31.—Wilford Woodruff was baptized at Richland, N. Y., by Zera Pulsipher.

1834

January. Wed. 1.—A conference of the scattered Saints in Clay County, Mo., resolved to send Lyman Wight and Parley P. Pratt as special messengers to the First Presidency at Kirtland, O.

February. Mon. 17.—The first High Council of the Church was organized at Kirtland. The members were Joseph Smith, Sr., Joseph Smith, Joseph Coe, John Johnson, Martin Harris, John S. Carter, Jared Carter, Oliver Cowdery, Samuel H. Smith, Orson Hyde, Sylvester Smith and Luke S. Johnson. Joseph Smith, Jr., Sidney Rigdon and Frederick G. Williams were acknowledged as presidents by the voice of the council.

Minutes of the Organization of the High Council of the Church of Christ of Latter-day Saints. Kirtland, February 17, 1834.

This day a general council of twenty-four High Priests assembled at the house of Joseph Smith, Jr., by revelation, and proceeded to organize the High Council of the Church of Christ, which was to consist of twelve High Priests, and one or three Presidents, as the case might require.

The High Council was appointed by revelation for the purpose of settling important difficulties which might arise in the church, which could not be settled by the church or the bishop's council to the satisfaction of the parties.

Joseph Smith, Jr., Sidney Rigdon, and Frederick G. Williams, were acknowledged Presidents by the voice of the council; and Joseph Smith, Sr., John Smith, Joseph Coe, John Johnson, Martin Harris, John S. Carter, Jared Carter, Oliver Cowdery, Samuel H. Smith, Orson Hyde, Sylvester Smith, and Luke Johnson, High Priests, were chosen to be a standing Council for the church, by the unanimous voice of the Council.

The above-named counselors were then asked whether they accepted their appointments, and whether they would act in that office according to the law of heaven: to which they all answered that they accepted their appointments, and would fill their offices according to the grace of God bestowed upon them.

The number composing the council, who voted in the name and for the church, in appointing the above-named counselors were forty-three, as follows:—Nine High Priests, seventeen elders, four priests, and thirteen members.

Voted: that the High Council cannot have power to act without seven of the above-named counselors, or their regularly-appointed successors are present.

These seven shall have power to appoint other High Priests, whom they may consider worthy and capable to act in the place of absent counselors.

Voted: that whenever any vacancy shall occur by the death, removal from office for transgression, or removal from the bounds of this church government, of any one of the above-named counselors, it shall be filled by the nomination of the President or Presidents, and sanctioned by the voice of a general council of High Priests, convened for that purpose, to act in the name of the church.

The President of the church, who is also the President of the council, is appointed by revelation, and acknowledged in his administration, by the voice of the church:

And it is according to the dignity of his office that he should preside over the Council of the church; and it is his privilege to be assisted by two other Presidents, appointed after the same manner that he himself was appointed.

And in case of the absence of one or both of those who are appointed to assist him, he has power to preside over the Council without an assistant: and in case that he himself is absent, the other Presidents have power to preside in his stead, both, or either of them.

Whenever an High Council of the church of Christ is regularly organized, according to the foregoing pattern, it shall be the duty of the twelve counselors to cast lots by numbers, and thereby ascertain, who of the twelve shall speak first, commencing with number one, and so in succession to number twelve.

Whenever this Council convenes to act upon any case, the twelve counselors shall consider whether it is a difficult one or not: if it is not, two only of the counselors shall speak upon it, according to the form above written.

But if it is thought to be difficult, four shall be appointed: and if more difficult, six; but in no case shall more than six be appointed to speak.

The accused, in all cases, has a right to one half of the Council, to prevent insult or injustice:

And the counselors appointed to speak before the Council, are to present the case after the evidence is examined, in its true light before the Council, and every man is to speak according to equity and justice.

Those counselors who draw even numbers, that is 2, 4, 6, 8, 10, and 12, are the individuals who are to stand up in behalf of the accused, and prevent insult or injustice.

In all cases the accuser and the accused shall have a privilege of speaking for themselves before the Council after the evidences are heard, and the counselors who are appointed to speak on the case, have finished their remarks.

After the evidences are heard, the counselors, accuser and accused have spoken, the President shall give a decision according to the understanding which he shall have of the case, and call upon the twelve counselors to sanction the same by their vote.

But should the remaining counselors, who have not spoken, or any one of them, after hearing the evidences and pleadings impartially, discover an error in the decision of the President, they can manifest it, and the case shall have a re-hearing;

And if, after a careful re-hearing, any additional light is shown upon the case, the decision shall be altered accordingly;

But in case no additional light is given, the first decision shall stand, the majority of the Council having power to determine the same.

In cases of difficulty, respecting doctrine or principle, (if there is not a sufficiency written to make the case clear to the minds of the Council,) the President may inquire and obtain the mind of the Lord by revelation.

The High Priests, when abroad, have power to call and organize a council after the manner of the foregoing to settle difficulties when the parties, or either of them shall request it:

And the said council of High Priests shall have power to appoint one of their own number, to preside over such council for the time being.

It shall be the duty of said council to transmit immediately, a copy of their proceedings, with a full statement of the testimony accompanying their decision, to the High Council of the seat of the First Presidency of the church.

Should the parties, or either of them be dissatisfied with the decision of said council, they may appeal to the High Council of the seat of the First Presidency of the church, and have a re-hearing, which case shall there be conducted, according to the former pattern written, as though no such decision had been made. This council of High Priests abroad, is only to be called on the most difficult cases of church matters; and no common or ordinary case is to be sufficient to call such council.

The traveling or located High Priests abroad, have power to say whether it is necessary to call such a council or not.

There is a distinction between the High Council of traveling High Priests abroad, and the traveling High Council composed of the Twelve apostles, in their decisions.

From the decision of the former there can be an appeal, but from the decision of the latter there cannot.

The latter can only be called in question by the general authorities of the church in case of transgression.

Resolved, that the President or Presidents of the seat of the First Presidency of the church, shall have power to determine whether any such case, as may be appealed, is justly entitled to a re-hearing, after examining the appeal and the evidences and statements accompanying it.

The twelve counselors then proceeded to cast lots or ballot, to ascertain who should speak first, and the following was the result, namely:

1 OLIVER COWDERY.
2 JOSEPH COE.
3 SAMUEL H. SMITH.
4 LUKE JOHNSON.
5 JOHN S. CARTER.
6 SYLVESTER SMITH.
7 JOHN JOHNSON.
8 ORSON HYDE.
9 JARED CARTER.
10 JOSEPH SMITH, Sr.
11 JOHN SMITH.
12 MARTIN HARRIS.

After prayer the conference adjourned.

OLIVER COWDERY, } Clerks.
ORSON HYDE,   }
—Doc. and Cov. Sec. 102.

Wed. 19.—The first case brought before the High Council was tried at Kirtland.

Thurs. 20.—Lyman Leonard, who had returned from Van Buren County, Mo., and Joseph Summer and Barnet Cole were severely beaten with clubs by a mob in Jackson County, Mo.

Mon. 24.—A revelation concerning the redemption of Zion was given through Joseph Smith, Jr., at Kirtland, Ohio. (Doc. and Cov., Sec. 103.)

And let all the churches send up wise men with their moneys, and purchase lands even as I have commanded them; * * *

Let my servant Lyman Wight journey with my servant Sidney Rigdon.

Let my servant Hyrum Smith journey with my servant Frederick G. Williams.

Let my servant Orson Hyde journey with my servant Orson Pratt, whithersoever my servant Joseph Smith Jr., shall counsel them, in obtaining the fulfilment of these commandments which I have given unto you, and leave the residue in my hands.—Doc. and Cov. 103:23, 35-40.

Wed. 26.—Joseph Smith, Jr., commenced to obtain volunteers for the redemption of Zion, in obedience to the revelation given on the 24th.

March. Fri. 28.—Joseph Smith, Jr., returned to Kirtland from his trip to the State of New York, whither he went to get volunteers for the expedition to Missouri.

April. Wed. 9.—Dr. P. Hurlburt, the apostate, who had threatened the life of Joseph, the Prophet, was put under $300 bonds in Chardon, Ohio.

Thurs. 10.—The United Order at Kirtland was dissolved.

The Saints, who had been expelled from Jackson County, Mo., wrote a petition to the President of the United States, asking for redress.

Wed. 23.—A revelation was given through Joseph Smith, Jr., g the order of Enoch. (Doc. and Cov., Sec. 104.)concernin

The covenants being broken through transgression, by covetousness and feigned words:

Therefore, you are dissolved as an United Order with your brethren, that you are not bound only up to this hour unto them, only on this wise, as I said, by loan as shall be agreed by this order in council, as your circumstances will admit and the voice of the council direct. Doc. and Cov. 104:52-53.

Thurs. 24.—On this and the following six days the mob burned about one hundred and fifty houses belonging to the Saints in Jackson County, Mo.

May. Thurs. 1.—Over twenty men with four baggage wagons left Kirtland, Ohio, for Missouri and traveled to New Portage, about fifty miles distant, where they waited for the rest of the company from Kirtland.

Sat. 3.—At a conference of Elders, held at Kirtland, the Church was first named "The Church of Jesus Christ of Latter-day Saints."

Mon. 5.—Joseph Smith, Jr., left Kirtland with the remainder of the company, which was being organized for the relief of the suffering Saints in Missouri.

Wed. 7.—The Prophet's company of volunteers, known in the history of the Church as Zion's Camp, was partly organized, consisting of over one hundred and fifty men with twenty baggage wagons.

Thurs. 8.—The organization of Zion's Camp was completed, and it traveled twelve miles.

June. Wed. 4.—On this and the following day Zion's Camp crossed the Mississippi river into Missouri. Sylvester Smith rebelled against the order of the camp.

Sun. 8.—Zion's Camp was strengthened by a company of volunteers led by Hyrum Smith and Lyman Wight. It then numbered two hundred and five men and twenty-five baggage wagons.

Mon. 16.—A large meeting of the citizens of Clay County, Mo., held at the Liberty court house, failed to adjust the difficulties between the Saints and the Jackson County people. From the meeting Samuel C. Owens, James Campbell and about thirteen other mob-leaders started for Jackson County to raise a mob, in which, however, they failed, as Mr. Campbell and six others were drowned in attempting to cross the Missouri River.

Thurs. 19.—Notwithstanding the threats of enemies, Zion's Camp passed through Richmond, Mo., and camped at night between two branches of Fishing river. A mob, numbering over three hundred men, who had arranged to concentrate that night to attack them, were prevented from crossing the river by a terrible storm.

Sun. 22.—An important revelation was given to Joseph Smith, Jr., on Fishing river, in which the Lord told his Saints that the time for the redemption of Zion had not yet come. (Doc. and Cov., Sec. 105.)

I speak not concerning those who are appointed to lead my people, who are the first elders of my church, for they are not all under this condemnation;

But I speak concerning my churches abroad—there are many who will say, Where is their God? Behold, he will deliver them in time of trouble, otherwise we will not go up unto Zion, and will keep our moneys.

Therefore, in consequence of the transgression of my people, it is expedient in me that mine elders should wait for a little season for the redemption of Zion. * * * —Doc. and Cov. 105:7-9.

Mon. 23.—Zion's Camp arrived at a point near Liberty, Clay Co., Mo.

Tues. 24.—The cholera, which during several preceding days had attacked some of the brethren, broke out in its most terrible form in Zion's Camp. It continued its ravages about four days; sixty-eight of the Saints were attacked and thirteen died, among whom was A. Sidney Gilbert, a prominent man in the Church; he expired on the 26th.

July. Tues. 1.—In company with a few friends, Joseph Smith, Jr., visited Jackson County, Mo., secretly.

Thurs. 3.—The High Priests of Zion assembled in Clay County, Mo., and organized a High Council with David Whitmer as president and Wm. W. Phelps and John Whitmer as counselors. The members of the council were: Christian Whitmer, Newel Knight, Lyman Wight, Calvin Bebee, Wm. E. McLellin, Solomon Hancock, Thos. B. Marsh, Simeon Carter, Parley P. Pratt, Orson Pratt, John Murdock and Levi Jackman.

Wed. 9.—Joseph Smith, Jr., started on his return journey to Kirtland, where he arrived in the latter part of the month.

October.—The first number of the "Latter-day Saints' Messenger and Advocate" was published at Kirtland, Ohio, taking the place of the "Evening and Morning Star," suspended.

Thurs. 16.—Joseph Smith, Jr., and other Elders left Kirtland to visit the Saints in Michigan, from which trip they returned in the latter part of the month.

November. Tues. 25.—Warren A. Cowdery was called by revelation to preside over the Saints at Freedom, N. Y., and the regions round about. (Doc. and Cov., Sec. 106.)

Sat. 29.—Joseph Smith, Jr., and Oliver Cowdery covenanted with the Lord to pay their tithing.

1835

February.—"The Northern Times," a weekly newspaper supporting democracy, was commenced by the Saints at Kirtland, Ohio.

Sat. 14.—At a special meeting held in Kirtland twelve Apostles were chosen by the Three Witnesses to the Book of Mormon according to revelation (Doc. and Cov., Sec. 18:37), namely: Thos. B. Marsh, David W. Patten, Brigham Young, Heber C. Kimball, Orson Hyde, Wm. E. McLellin, Parley P. Pratt, Luke S. Johnson, Wm. Smith, Orson Pratt, John F. Boynton and Lyman E. Johnson. Brigham Young and Heber C. Kimball were ordained and blessed the same day.

And now, behold, I give unto you Oliver Cowdery, and also unto David Whitmer, that you shall search out the Twelve, who shall have the desires of which I have spoken;

And by their desires and their works you shall know them; * * * —Doc. and Cov. 18:37-38.

Sun. 15.—Orson Hyde, David W. Patten, Luke S. Johnson, Wm. E. McLellin, John F. Boynton and Wm. Smith were ordained Apostles.

Sat. 21.—Parley P. Pratt was ordained to the Apostleship. Thos. B. Marsh and Orson Pratt, who were absent on missions, were not ordained until their return in April.

Sat. 28.—The organization of the First Quorum of Seventy was commenced at Kirtland.

March. Sat. 28.—An important revelation concerning the order of the Priesthood was given to Joseph Smith, Jr., at Kirtland. (Doc. and Cov., Sec. 107.)

A Revelation through Joseph, the Prophet, given at Kirtland, Ohio, on Priesthood; the fore part, or the first fifty-eight verses, being given March 28th, 1835; the other items were revealed at sundry times.

There are, in the church, two Priesthoods, namely, the Melchisedek, and Aaronic, including the Levitical priesthood.

Why the first is called the Melchisedek Priesthood, is because Melchisedek was such a great High Priest.

Before his day it was called the Holy Priesthood after the order of the Son of God;

But out of respect or reverence to the name of the Supreme Being, to avoid the too frequent repetition of his name, they, the church, in ancient days, called that Priesthood after Melchisedek, or the Melchisedek Priesthood.

All other authorities or offices in the church are appendages to this Priesthood;

But there are two divisions or grand heads—one is the Melchisedek Priesthood, and the other is the Aaronic, or Levitical priesthood.

The office of an elder comes under the Priesthood of Melchisedek.

The Melchisedek Priesthood holds the right of Presidency, and has power and authority over all the offices in the church in all ages of the world, to administer in spiritual things.

The Presidency of the High Priesthood, after the order of Melchisedek, have a right to officiate in all the offices in the church.

High Priests after the order of the Melchisedek Priesthood, have a right to officiate in their own standing, under the direction of the Presidency, in administering spiritual things; and also in the office of an elder, priest, (of the Levitical order,) teacher, deacon, and member.

An elder has a right to officiate in his stead when the High Priest is not present.

The High Priest and elder are to administer in spiritual things, agreeable to the covenants and commandments of the church; and they have a right to officiate in all these offices of the church when there are no higher authorities present.

The second priesthood is called the priesthood of Aaron, because it was conferred upon Aaron and his seed, throughout all their generations.

Why it is called the lesser priesthood, is because it is an appendage to the greater or the Melchisedek Priesthood, and has power in administering outward ordinances.

The bishopric is the presidency of this priesthood and holds the keys or authority of the same.

No man has a legal right to this office, to hold the keys of this priesthood, except he be a literal descendant of Aaron.

But as a High Priest of the Melchisedek Priesthood has authority to officiate in all the lesser offices, he may officiate in the office of bishop when no literal descendant of Aaron can be found, provided he is called and set apart and ordained unto this power by the hands of the Presidency of the Melchisedek Priesthood.

The power and authority of the Higher or Melchisedek Priesthood, is to hold the keys of all the spiritual blessings of the church—

To have the privilege of receiving the mysteries of the kingdom of heaven—to have the heavens opened unto them—to commune with the general assembly and church of the first born, and to enjoy the communion and presence of God the Father, and Jesus the Mediator of the new covenant.

The power and authority of the lesser, or Aaronic priesthood, is to hold the keys of the ministering of angels, and to administer in outward ordinances, the letter of the gospel—the baptism of repentance for the remission of sins, agreeable to the covenants and commandments.

Of necessity there are presidents, or presiding offices growing out of, or appointed of or from among those who are ordained to the several offices in these two priesthoods.

Of the Melchisedek Priesthood, three Presiding High Priests, chosen by the body, appointed and ordained to that office, and upheld by the confidence, faith, and prayer of the church, form a quorum of the Presidency of the church.

The Twelve traveling counselors are called to be the Twelve apostles, or special witnesses of the name of Christ in all the world: thus differing from other officers in the church in the duties of their calling.

And they form a quorum, equal in authority and power to the three Presidents previously mentioned.

The seventy are also called to preach the gospel, and to be especial witnesses unto the Gentiles and in all the world. Thus differing from other officers in the church in the duties of their calling;

And they form a quorum equal in authority to that of the Twelve special witnesses or apostles just named.

And every decision made by either of these quorums, must be by the unanimous voice of the same: that is, every member in each quorum must be agreed to its decisions, in order to make their decisions of the same power or validity one with the other.

(A majority may form a quorum, when circumstances render it impossible to be otherwise.)

Unless this is the case, their decisions are not entitled to the same blessings which the decisions of a quorum of three Presidents were anciently, who were ordained after the order of Melchisedek, and were righteous and holy men.

The decisions of these quorums, or either of them, are to be made in all righteousness, in holiness, and lowliness of heart, meekness and long-suffering, and in faith, and virtue, and knowledge, temperance, patience, godliness, brotherly kindness and charity;

Because the promise is, if these things abound in them, they shall not be unfruitful in the knowledge of the Lord.

And in case that any decision of these quorums is made in unrighteousness, it may be brought before a general assembly of the several quorums, which constitute the spiritual authorities of the church, otherwise there can be no appeal from their decision.

The Twelve are a traveling presiding High Council, to officiate in the name of the Lord, under the direction of the Presidency of the church, agreeable to the institution of heaven; to build up the church, and regulate all the affairs of the same in all nations: first unto the Gentiles, and secondly unto the Jews.

The seventy are to act in the name of the Lord, under the direction of the Twelve or the traveling High Council, in building up the church and regulating all the affairs of the same in all nations—first unto the Gentiles and then to the Jews;

The Twelve being sent out, holding the keys, to open the door by the proclamation of the gospel of Jesus Christ—and first unto the Gentiles and then unto the Jews.

The standing High Councils, at the Stakes of Zion, form a quorum equal in authority, in the affairs of the church, in all their decisions, to the quorum of the Presidency, or to the traveling High Council.

The High Council in Zion, form a quorum equal in authority, in the affairs of the church, in all their decisions, to the Councils of the Twelve at the Stakes of Zion.

It is the duty of the traveling High Council to call upon the seventy, when they need assistance, to fill the several calls for preaching and administering the gospel, instead of any others.

It is the duty of the Twelve, in all large branches of the church, to ordain evangelical ministers, as they shall be designated unto them by revelation. * * *

It is the duty of the Twelve, also, to ordain and set in order all the other officers of the church, agreeable to the revelation which says:

To the church of Christ in the land of Zion, in addition to the church laws respecting church business—

Verily, I say unto you, says the Lord of hosts, there must needs be presiding elders to preside over those who are of the office of an elder:

And also priests to preside over those who are of the office of a priest:

And also teachers to preside over those who are of the office of a teacher; in like manner, and also the deacons:

Wherefore, from deacon to teacher, and from teacher to priest, and from priest to elder, severally as they are appointed, according to the covenants and commandments of the church.

Then comes the High Priesthood, which is the greatest of all:

Wherefore it must needs be that one be appointed of the High Priesthood to preside over the Priesthood, and he shall be called President of the High Priesthood of the church:

Or, in other words, the Presiding High Priest over the High Priesthood of the church.

From the same comes the administering of ordinances and blessings upon the church, by the laying on of the hands.

Wherefore the office of a bishop is not equal unto it: for the office of a bishop is in administering all temporal things:

Nevertheless a bishop must be chosen from the High Priesthood, unless he is a literal descendant of Aaron:

For unless he is a literal descendant of Aaron he cannot hold the keys of that priesthood

Nevertheless, a High Priest that is after the order of Melchisedek, may be set apart unto the ministering of temporal things, having a knowledge of them by the Spirit of truth.

And also to be a judge in Israel, to do the business of the church, to sit in judgment upon transgressors upon testimony as it shall be laid before him according to the laws, by the assistance of his counselors, whom he has chosen, or will choose among the elders of the church.

This is the duty of a bishop who is not a literal descendant of Aaron, but has been ordained to the High Priesthood after the order of Melchisedek.

Thus shall he be a judge, even a common judge among the inhabitants of Zion, or in a Stake of Zion, or in any branch of the church where he shall be set apart unto this ministry, until the borders of Zion are enlarged, and it becomes necessary to have other bishops or judges in Zion, or elsewhere;

And inasmuch as there are other bishops appointed they shall act in the same office.

But a literal descendant of Aaron has a legal right to the presidency of this priesthood, to the keys of this ministry, to act in the office of bishop independently, without counselors, except in a case where a President of the High Priesthood, after the order of Melchisedek, is tried, to sit as a judge in Israel.

And the decision of either of these councils, agreeable to the commandment which says,

Again, verily, I say unto you, the most important business of the church, and the most difficult cases of the church, inasmuch as there is not satisfaction upon the decision of the bishop or judges, it shall be handed over and carried up unto the Council of the church, before the Presidency of the High Priesthood;

And the Presidency of the Council of the High Priesthood shall have power to call other High Priests, even twelve, to assist as counselors; and thus the Presidency of the High Priesthood and its counselors shall have power to decide upon testimony according to the laws of the church.

And after this decision it shall be had in remembrance no more before the Lord; for this is the highest Council of the church of God, and a final decision upon controversies in spiritual matters.

There is not any person belonging to the church who is exempt from this Council of the church.

And inasmuch as a President of the High Priesthood shall transgress, he shall be had in remembrance before the common council of the church, who shall be assisted by twelve counselors of the High Priesthood;

And their decision upon his head shall be an end of controversy concerning him.

Thus, none shall be exempted from the justice and the laws of God, that all things may be done in order and in solemnity before him, according to truth and righteousness.

And again, verily I say unto you, the duty of a president over the office of a deacon is to preside over twelve deacons, to sit in council with them, and to teach them their duty—edifying one another, as it is given according to the covenants.

And also the duty of the president over the office of the teachers is to preside over twenty-four of the teachers, and to sit in council with them, teaching them the duties of their office, as given in the covenants.

Also the duty of the president over the priesthood of Aaron is to preside over forty-eight priests, and sit in council with them, to teach them the duties of their office, as is given in the covenants.

This president is to be a bishop; for this is one of the duties of this priesthood.

Again, the duty of the president over the office of elders is to preside over ninety-six elders, and to sit in council with them, and to teach them according to the covenants.

This presidency is a distinct one from that of the seventy, and is designed for those who do not travel into all the world.

And again, the duty of the President of the office of the High Priesthood is to preside over the whole church, and to be like unto Moses.

Behold, here is wisdom; yea, to be a seer, a revelator, a translator, and a prophet, having all the gifts of God which he bestows upon the head of the church.

And it is according to the vision, showing the order of the seventy, that they should have seven Presidents to preside over them, chosen out of the number of the seventy;

And the seventh president of these presidents is to preside over the six;

And these seven presidents are to choose other seventy besides the first seventy, to whom they belong, and are to preside over them;

And also other seventy, until seven times seventy, if the labor in the vineyard of necessity requires it.

And these seventy are to be traveling ministers unto the Gentiles first, and also unto the Jews;

Whereas other officers of the church, who belong not unto the Twelve, neither to the seventy, are not under the responsibility to travel among all nations, but are to travel as their circumstances shall allow, notwithstanding they may hold as high and responsible offices in the church.

Wherefore now let every man learn his duty, and to act in the office in which he is appointed, in all diligence.

He that is slothful shall not be counted worthy to stand, and he that learns not his duty and shows himself not approved, shall not be counted worthy to stand. Even so. Amen.—Doc. and Cov. 107: 1-39, 58-100.

May. Sat. 2.—Elders Brigham Young, John P. Greene and Amos Orton were appointed to preach the gospel to the Lamanites.

Mon. 4.—The Twelve left Kirtland on their first mission as Apostles.

July. Fri. 3.—Michael H. Chandler arrived at Kirtland to exhibit four Egyptian mummies and some rolls of papyrus, covered with hieroglyphic figures and devices. They were afterwards purchased by some of the Saints, and Joseph the Prophet translated some of the characters on the rolls. One was found to contain the writings of Abraham, subsequently published in the Pearl of Great Price; another the writings of Joseph in Egypt.

August. Mon. 17.—At a general assembly of the Church, held at Kirtland, the Book of Doctrine and Covenants was approved, and thus became a law of faith and practice to the Church.

September. Mon. 14.—Oliver Cowdery was appointed to act as Church Recorder, and Emma Smith to make a selection of sacred hymns, according to revelation.

From revelation to Joseph Smith, Jr., given at Fayette, New York, April 6, 1830. (See Doc. and Cov. 21:1.)

Behold there shall be a record kept among you, and in it thou shalt be called a seer, a translator, a prophet, an apostle of Jesus Christ, an elder of the church through the will of God the Father, and the grace of your Lord Jesus Christ.

October. Sun. 25.—The Twelve returned to Kirtland from their mission to the East.

Thurs. 29.—Joseph Smith, Jr., was abused by his brother William in a council meeting, held at Kirtland.

November. Fri. 27.—Christian Whitmer, one of the Eight Witnesses to the Book of Mormon, died in Clay County, Mo.
December. Wed. 16.—Wm. Smith became enraged in a debating school, held at Kirtland, and used violence upon the person of his brother, Joseph Smith, Jr., and others.
Sat. 26.—Joseph Smith, Jr., with other Elders, commenced studying the Hebrew language, having previously commenced reading Greek. Mr. Seixas, a competent professor of languages, was subsequently employed as teacher.
—A revelation concerning Lyman Sherman, was given through Joseph Smith, Jr., at Kirtland. (Doc. and Cov., Sec. 108.)

1836

The Kirtland Temple was dedicated, and the Savior, Moses, Elias and Elijah the Prophet appeared to the Elders in that building and committed the keys of their respective dispensations to the Prophet Joseph Smith. The Saints who had resided temporarily in Clay County, Mo., removed to another location on Shoal Creek, which was organized into Caldwell County.
January. Fri. 1.—Wm. Smith received forgiveness of his brother Joseph, and a general family reconciliation took place in the house of the latter, at Kirtland, Ohio.
Wed. 6.—At a council meeting, held at Kirtland, the High Council of Zion (Missouri) was reorganized.
Thurs. 7.—A sumptuous feast, to which the lame, the halt and the blind were invited, was held in Bishop Newel K. Whitney's house, at Kirtland.
Sat. 16.—In a council of the Twelve Apostles, held at Kirtland, President Joseph Smith said: "The Twelve are not subject to any other than the First Presidency. * * * Where I am not, there is no First Presidency over the Twelve." (See History of Joseph Smith.)
Sun. 17.—Joseph the Prophet organized the several councils of the Priesthood at Kirtland, on which occasion the Lord poured out His Spirit in a great measure upon the brethren, who confessed their faults to each other; the congregation was overwhelmed in tears and the spirit of tongues came upon them "like the rushing of a mighty wind." (See History of Joseph Smith.)
Thurs. 21.—The Presidency of the Church, and the councils of Kirtland and Zion, met in the evening in the Lord's House, at Kirtland, and attended to the ordinance of anointing with oil and blessing each other. The visions of heaven were opened, angels ministered to them, and the house was filled with the glory of God. Joseph the Prophet "beheld the celestial kingdom of God and the glory thereof," the "transcendent beauty of the gate through which the heirs of that kingdom will enter, the throne of God whereon was seated the Father and Son," and the beautiful streets of the kingdom. He also saw Fathers Adam and Abraham. On seeing his brother Alvin, who died before the Church was organized, the Prophet marveled, but the voice of the Lord told him that all who had died without a knowledge of the gospel, who would have received it if they had been permitted to tarry, should be heirs of the celestial kingdom of God. (See History of Joseph Smith.)
Fri. 22.—The Twelve Apostles, the Presidency of the Seventy and others were blessed and anointed in the Lord's House, at Kirtland.
Thurs. 28.—The leading authorities of the Church administered in the Lord's House at Kirtland, on which occasion angels again appeared to the brethren, and other great manifestations of the power of God were witnessed. (See History of Joseph Smith.)
February. Sun. 7.—The organization of the second quorum of Seventy was commenced at Kirtland.
Mon. 22.—The sisters at Kirtland met in the Lord's House to commence their work of making the veil for that building.
March. Sun. 27.—The Lord's House, at Kirtland, afterwards known as the Kirtland Temple, was dedicated. It is a rock building, 80 feet long and 60 feet wide; its walls are 50 feet and the tower 110 feet high. (For dedicatory prayer, see Doc. and Cov., Sec. 109.)
Tues. 29.—On this and the following day the ordinance of the washing of feet was attended to in the Kirtland Temple.
April. Sun. 3.—Joseph Smith, Jr., and Oliver Cowdery saw and heard the Savior in the Kirtland Temple. Moses also appeared before them and committed unto them "the keys of the gathering of Israel from the four parts of the earth, and the leading of the Ten Tribes from the land of the north." Then Elias appeared and committed the dispensation of the gospel of Abraham, and finally Elijah the Prophet "stood before them" and committed to them the keys of turning "the hearts of the fathers to the children, and the children to the fathers." (See History of Joseph Smith and Doc. and Cov., Sec. 110.)
Mon. 4.—The Elders began to spread abroad from Kirtland into all parts of the land, preaching the gospel.
May. Tues. 17.—Mary Smith, aged 93 years, and grandmother of Joseph the Prophet, arrived at Kirtland from the East.
June.—Warren Parrish and other Elders were mobbed and arrested in Tennessee for preaching the gospel, and subsequently compelled to leave the country.
Wed. 29.—A large meeting of citizens held at Liberty, Clay County, Mo., passed resolutions to expel the Saints from Clay County.
July. Fri. 1.—In a large meeting of Elders, held in Clay County, Mo., it was agreed that the Saints should leave the county, agreeably to the request of the older settlers.
Mon. 25.—Joseph Smith, Jr., left Kirtland for a trip to the Eastern States.
August.—Joseph Smith, Jr., arrived at Salem, Mass., where he, on August 6th, received a revelation, in which the Lord said He had many people in that city. (Doc. and Cov., Sec. 111.)
September.—Joseph Smith returned to Kirtland from his trip to the East.

.—The Saints in Missouri began to remove from Clay County to their newly selected location on Shoal Creek (later known as Far West), in the territory attached to Ray County. That part of the State of Missouri was at that time almost uninhabited, but in the following December it was organized under the name of Caldwell County.
Thurs. 22.—Peter Whitmer, Jr., one of the Eight Witnesses to the Book of Mormon, died near Liberty, Clay County, Mo.
November. Wed. 2.—Preparations were made for organizing a banking institution at Kirtland, Ohio, to be called the "Kirtland Safety Society."
December. Sun. 18.—Brigham Young, Jr., was born at Kirtland.
Sat. 31.—Dr. Willard Richards was baptized at Kirtland, by Brigham Young.

1837

April. Thur. 6.—An important Priesthood meeting was held in the Kirtland Temple, in which new presidencies were ordained to preside over the Seventies, as some of the former presidents were High Priests.
April. Fri. 7.—The city plat of Far West, Caldwell County, Mo., having been surveyed, the sale of town lots was left to Wm. W. Phelps, John Whitmer and Edward Partridge. Jacob Whitmer, Elisha H. Groves and Geo. M. Hinkle were appointed a building committee for the erection of a house of the Lord at Far West.
May.—A spirit of apostasy and speculation, affecting every quorum of the Church, more or less, became very prevalent at Kirtland.
June.—Early in this month Apostles Heber C. Kimball and Orson Hyde were set apart by the First Presidency of the Church to go on a mission to England. This was the first foreign mission of the Church. A few days later Willard Richards was called to accompany them.
Tues. 13.—Apostles Heber C. Kimball and Orson Hyde and Elders Willard Richards and Joseph Fielding left Kirtland, O., on their missions to England.
July. Sat. 1.—Apostles Heber C. Kimball and Orson Hyde and Elders Willard Richards and Joseph Fielding, accompanied by three brethren from Canada, namely, John Goodson, Isaac Russell and John Snider, sailed from New York on the ship "Garrick." They arrived in Liverpool, England, on the 20th.
Mon. 3.—Ground was broken at Far West, Mo., for the foundation of a Temple, which, however, was not built, on account of persecutions.
Sun. 23.—A revelation concerning the Twelve Apostles was given through Joseph, the Prophet, at Kirtland. (Doc. and Cov., Sec. 112.)
—The gospel was first preached by Latter-day Saint Elders in England, in the church of the Rev. James Fielding, at Preston.
Thur. 27.—Joseph, the Prophet, was persecuted with a vexatious lawsuit at Painesville, Ohio.
Sun. 30.—Nine persons were baptized in the river Ribble, at Preston, England, as the first converts to the fullness of the gospel in England. Geo. D. Watt was the first person baptized.
August.—In the latter part of this month Joseph Smith, Jr., returned to Kirtland, Ohio, from a mission to Canada, on which he had started July 27th.
September. Sun. 3.—At a conference, held at Kirtland, Oliver Cowdery, Joseph Smith, Sr., Hyrum Smith and John Smith were appointed assistant counselors to the First Presidency. Luke S. Johnson, Lyman E. Johnson and John F. Boynton, three of the Twelve Apostles, were disfellowshipped.
Sun. 10.—Luke S. Johnson, Lyman E. Johnson and John F. Boynton made confessions and were received back into fellowship.
Sun. 17.—Geo. W. Robinson was elected General Church Recorder, in place of Oliver Cowdery, who had removed to Missouri.
Wed. 27.—Joseph Smith, Jr., and Sidney Rigdon left Kirtland, Ohio, to establish other places of gathering for the Saints, and to visit with the Saints in Missouri, where they arrived in the latter part of October.
About this time the "Voice of Warning" was published in New York City by Parley P. Pratt.
October.—The first number of the "Elders' Journal," edited by Joseph Smith, Jr., and published at Kirtland, Ohio, bears date of this month. It was published instead of the "Messenger and Advocate," which had been discontinued.
Fri. 13.—Jerusha F. Smith, Hyrum Smith's wife, died at Kirtland.
November. Tues. 7.—An important conference was held at Far West, Mo., Joseph Smith, Jr., having arrived from Kirtland. Frederick G. Williams was rejected as a counselor to Pres. Joseph Smith, and Hyrum Smith appointed in his stead. David Whitmer, John Whitmer and Wm. W. Phelps were sustained as the presidency of Far West, and a High Council was reorganized consisting of John Murdock, Solomon Hancock, Elias Higbee, Calvin Bebee, John M. Hinkle, Thos. Grover, Simeon Carter, Lyman Wight, Newel Knight, Geo. M. Hinkle, Levi Jackman and Elisha H. Groves.
Fri. 10.—At a general meeting held at Far West it was voted that the town of Far West "be enlarged so as to contain two square miles."
December.—The printing office at Kirtland was destroyed by fire, and the publication of the "Elders' Journal" ceased.
—Joseph Smith, Jr., arrived at Kirtland, Ohio, from Missouri. During his absence a number of prominent men, including Warren Parrish, John F. Boynton, Luke S. Johnson and Joseph Coe, had united together for the overthrow of the Church at Kirtland.
Fri. 22.—Apostle Brigham Young left Kirtland on account of the fury of the mob, who threatened to kill him because he would proclaim publicly and privately that he knew by the Holy Ghost that Joseph Smith, Jr., was a Prophet of the Most High God.

Mon. 25.—The first general conference by Latter-day Saints in England was held in the "Cock Pit," at Preston. The Church in England numbered already about one thousand members. At this conference the "Word of Wisdom" was first publicly taught in England.
Apostasy, persecution, confusion and mobocracy reigned in Kirtland, Ohio, at the close of the year.

1838

January. Fri. 12.—Joseph Smith, Jr., and Sidney Rigdon left Kirtland, Ohio, on horseback to escape mob violence. They traveled toward Missouri.
February. Mon. 5.—In a general assembly of Saints at Far West, Mo., David Whitmer, John Whitmer and Wm. W. Phelps were rejected as the presidency of the Church in Missouri because of transgression.
Sat. 10.—Thomas B. Marsh and David W. Patten were appointed presidents pro tem. of the Church in Missouri, until the arrival of Joseph Smith, Jr., or Sidney Rigdon from Kirtland.
March.—Answers to certain questions on Scripture, principally the 11th chapter of Isaiah, were given by revelation through Joseph Smith, Jr. (Doc. and Cov., Sec. 113.)
Sat. 10.—Wm. W. Phelps and John Whitmer were excommunicated from the Church by the High Council at Far West, Mo. Some time afterwards Wm. W. Phelps was received back into the Church by baptism.
Wed. 14.—Joseph the Prophet, arrived at Far West, Mo., with his family, accompanied by Apostle Brigham Young and others.
April. Fri. 6.—The Saints in Missouri met at Far West to celebrate the anniversary of the organization of the Church and transact business. John Corrill and Elias Higbee were appointed historians and Geo. W. Robinson General Church Recorder and clerk to the First Presidency. Thomas B. Marsh was sustained as president pro tem. in Missouri, with Brigham Young and David W. Patten as assistant presidents.
Sat. 7.—On this and the following day, the Church held its first quarterly conference at Far West.
John Whitmer refused to give up the records of the Church in his possession to the newly appointed Church clerk and recorder.
Thur. 12.—Oliver Cowdery was excommunicated from the Church by the High Council at Far West, Mo. The following day David Whitmer and Lyman E. Johnson were cut off.
Tues. 17.—Apostle David W. Patten was called by revelation through Joseph the Prophet, at Far West, Mo. to "make a disposition of his merchandise," and prepare for a mission.
Verily thus saith the Lord, it is wisdom in my servant David W. Patten, that he settle up all his business as soon as he possibly can, and make a disposition of his merchandise, that he may perform a mission unto me next spring, in company with others, even Twelve, including himself, to testify of my name, and bear glad tidings unto all the world; * * * —Doc. and Cov. 114:1.
Fri. 20.—Apostles Heber C. Kimball and Orson Hyde sailed from Liverpool, England, for America on the ship "Garrick." They arrived in New York May 12th, and at Kirtland, O., May 22nd.
Thurs. 26.—A revelation was given through Joseph Smith, Jr., at Far West, Mo., concerning the building up of that place and the Lord's House. (Doc. and Cov., Sec. 115.)
Let the city, Far West, be a holy and consecrated land unto me, and it shall be called most holy, for the ground upon which they standest is holy:
Therefore I command you to build an house unto me, for the gathering together of my saints, that they may worship me:
And let there be a beginning of this work, and a foundation, and a preparatory work, this following summer; * *
And again, verily I say unto you, it is my will that the city of Far West should be built up speedily by the gathering of my saints. * * * Doc. and Cov. 115:7-9, 17.
May. Fri. 11.—Wm. E. McLellin was excommunicated from the Church, at Far West.
Sat. 19.—Joseph Smith, Jr., Sidney Rigdon and others visited a place on the north side of Grand river (about twenty-five miles north of Far West) called by the Saints Spring Hill, which by revelation was named Adam-ondi-Ahman, because "it is the place where Adam shall come to visit his people of the Ancient of Days shall sit, as spoken of by the Prophet Daniel." (Dan. 7:9-14; Doc. and Cov. Sec. 116.)
June. Thurs. 28.—A Stake of Zion called Adam-ondi-Ahman was organized in Daviess County, Mo., with John Smith as president and Reynolds Cahoon and Lyman Wight as his counselors. A High Council was also organized with John Lemon, Daniel Stanton, Mayhew Hillman, Daniel Carter, Isaac Perry, Henry Harrison Sagers, Allanson Brown, Thomas Gordon, Lorenzo D. Barnes, George A. Smith, Harvey Olmstead and Ezra Thayer as members.
July.—The third number of the "Elders' Journal" was published at Far West, Mo. The first two numbers had been published at Kirtland, Ohio.
Wed. 4.—The corner stones of the House of the Lord, at Far West, Mo., were laid, agreeable to a commandment of the Lord, given April 26th, 1838.
Fri. 6.—Five hundred and fifteen Saints left Kirtland, Ohio, for Missouri, under the direction of the Seventies.
Sun. 8. — Wm. Marks, Newel K. Whitney and Oliver Granger were commanded by revelation to leave Kirtland, Ohio, and remove to Missouri. (Doc. and Cov., Sec. 117.)
—John Taylor, John E. Page, Wilford Woodruff and Willard Richards were called by revelation to the Apostleship, "to fill the places of those who had fallen." (Doc. and Cov., Sec. 118.)
Let my servant John Taylor, and also my servant John E. Page, and also my servant Wilford Woodruff, and also my servant Willard Richards, be appointed to fill the places of those who have fallen, and be officially notified of their appointment.—Doc. and Cov. 118:6.
—In answer to the question, "O Lord, show unto thy servants how much thou requirest of the properties of the people for a tithing," the Lord gave a revelation on tithing. (Doc. and Cov., Sec. 119.)
Wed. 18.—A revelation making known the disposition of property tithing was given through Joseph the Prophet, at Far West.

Revelation given through Joseph, the Prophet, at Far West, Missouri, July 8th, 1838, in answer to the question, O Lord, show unto thy servants how much thou requirest of the properties of the people for a tithing?

Verily, thus saith the Lord. I require all their surplus property to be put into the hands of the bishop of my church of Zion,
For the building of mine house, and for the laying of the foundation of Zion and for the Priesthood, and for the debts of the Presidency of my church;
And this shall be the beginning of the tithing of my people;
And after that, those who have thus been tithed, shall pay one-tenth of all their interest annually; and this shall be a standing law unto them for ever, for my holy Priesthood, saith the Lord.
Verily I say unto you, it shall come to pass, that all those who gather unto the land of Zion shall be tithed of their surplus properties, and shall observe this law, or they shall not be found worthy to abide among you.
And I say unto you, if my people observe not this law, to keep it holy, and by this law sanctify the land of Zion unto me, that my statues and my judgments may be kept thereon, that it may be most holy, behold, verily I say unto you, it shall not be a land of Zion unto you;
And this shall be an ensample [example] unto all the Stakes of Zion. Amen.—Doc. and Cov, Sec. 120.

August.—During this month the Saints at DeWitt, Carroll County, Mo., were threatened by a mob.
Mon. 6.—The Missourians opposed the voting of the Saints at Gallatin, Daviess County, and a skirmish occurred, in which about twelve brethren gained a victory over about one hundred and fifty mobbers. Some of the brethren took their families into the hazel brush and guarded them during the night, through fear of the mob.
Wed. 8.—Joseph Smith, Jr., and others called on Adam Black, a justice of the peace in Daviess County, Mo., and had a friendly conversation with him about the trouble in Gallatin.
Thurs. 30.—Gov. Lilburn W. Boggs, of Missouri, ordered out a part of the State militia to quell the civil disturbances in Caldwell, Daviess and Carroll Counties. The whole upper Missouri was in an uproar and state of confusion about the "Mormons."
September. Mon. 3.—A great number of mobbers had collected in Daviess County, Mo, with headquarters at Millport.
Tues. 4.—Joseph Smith, Jr., and Sidney Rigdon commenced to study law, under the instructions of Generals David R. Atchison and Alexander W. Doniphan.
Fri. 7.—Joseph Smith, Jr., and Lyman Wight appeared before Judge Austin A. King, in Daviess County, they and others having been falsely accused of threatening Adam Black's life on their visit to his house, Aug. 8th.
Sun. 9.—Captain William Allred, of Far West, frustrated the plans of the mob, by arresting three men who were bringing guns and ammunition from Richmond, Ray County, Mo., to the mobbers in Daviess County.
October. Mon. 1.—As the militia, under Generals Atchison, Doniphan and Parks, had succeeded in restoring temporary peace in Daviess County, the mobbers went to DeWitt, Carroll County, and attacked the Saints there.
Thurs. 4.—The Kirtland Camp arrived at its destination, Adam-ondi-Ahman.
Sat. 6.—Joseph the Prophet arrived at DeWitt, Carroll County, Mo., whither he went to assist the brethren who were trying to defend themselves against an overwhelming mob force.
Thurs. 11.—After several days' bombardment, the mob succeeded in driving the Saints from DeWitt. During the siege some of them had perished from starvation, and their sufferings had been very great.
Fri. 12.—The exiles from DeWitt arrived at Far West.
Mon. 15.—The brethren at Far West organized for self-defense.
—The mobbers renewed their depredations in Daviess County, by burning the houses of the Saints, driving off their stock, etc. Col. Lyman Wight, agreeable to an order from General Parks, organized a company in self-defense. This frightened the mobbers, who fled from the neighborhood, after burning some of their own houses, of which they wickedly accused the Saints.
Tues. 23.—The Saints were fleeing from the smaller settlements into Far West for safety, the mobs increasing in numbers all around. The most wicked lies were circulated about the Saints, and their movements in self-defense were by the State authorities construed into treason.
Thurs. 25.—A battle was fought between a mob and about seventy-five brethren on Crooked river, Ray County, Mo., in which Gideon Carter was killed and eleven others wounded, among these were Apostle David W. Patten and Patterson O'Banion who died soon afterwards.
Sat. 27.—Apostle David W Patten was buried at Far West.
—Gov. Lilburn W. Boggs issued his famous exterminating order, which gave the Saints the choice between banishment from Missouri and death.
About this time Sampson Avard, an apostate, secretly organized a company called Danites. The Church used all proper means to expose and counteract his schemes.
Tues. 30.—A mob under the leadership of Col. Wm. O. Jennings attacked a little settlement of Saints at Haun's Mill, Caldwell County, Mo., and killed and mortally wounded Thomas McBride, Levi N. Merrick, Elias Benner, Josiah Fuller, Benjamin Lewis, Alexander Campbell, Warren Smith, Geo. S. Richards, Wm. Napier, Austin Hammer, Simon Cox, Hiram Abbott, John York, John Lee, John Byers, Sardius Smith and Charles Merrick. Others were severely wounded, but recovered. Among these were Alma L. Smith, who was healed in a most miraculous manner, through prayers and faith.

—The mob-militia, about two thousand strong, under command of Samuel D. Lucas, arrived near Far West, and the citizens prepared for their own defense.

Wed. 31.—Joseph Smith, Jr., Sidney Rigdon, Parley P. Pratt, Lyman Wight and Geo. W. Robinson were betrayed by Col. George M. Hinkle and made prisoners in the camp of the mob-militia.

November. Thurs. 1.—Hyrum Smith and Amasa M. Lyman were brought as prisoners into camp. A court martial was held, and the prisoners were sentenced to be shot the following morning; they were, however, saved through the interference of General Doniphan.

On demand of Gen. Samuel D. Lucas, the citizens of Far West were forced to give up their arms, after which the mob-militia pillaged the town, ravished women, and committed other acts of barbarity.

Fri. 2.—Joseph Smith, Jr., and fellow-prisoners were taken to Far West under a strong guard and permitted to see their families, from whom they then were rudely torn and started under a strong guard, commanded by Generals Samuel D. Lucas and Robert Wilson, for Independence, Jackson County, where they arrived on the 4th.

Sun. 4.—Gen. John B. Clark arrived at Far West with about two thousand troops, and the following day he made most of the brethren prisoners.

Tues. 6.—John B. Clark delivered an insulting speech to the brethren at Far West, in which he advised the Saints to scatter abroad and never again organize with bishops, presidents, etc. Of the leaders of the Church, who had been imprisoned, he said their fate was fixed, their die cast, and their doom sealed, and that they would never be seen by their friends again.

The brethren were compelled to sign deeds of trust for paying the expense of the mob. About sixty men were retained as prisoners, and the remainder of the Saints ordered to leave the State, according to the exterminating order of Governor Boggs.

Thurs. 8.—General Wilson placed guards around Adamondi-Ahman, took all the men prisoners and put them under guard. A court of inquiry was organized, with Adam Black on the bench, which resulted in the acquittal of the prisoners.

Fri. 9.—Joseph Smith, Jr., and fellow-prisoners arrived at Richmond, Ray County, Mo., where they were put in chains and much abused by their guards. On one occasion the Prophet Joseph rebuked the wicked guard with the power of God, and stopped the foul conversation with which the prisoners were being tantalized.

Sat. 10.—General Wilson ordered every family to be out of Adam-ondi-Ahman in ten days, with permission to go to Caldwell County and tarry till spring, then to leave the State under pain of extermination.

Tues. 13.—Joseph Fielding Smith was born at Far West, Mo.

—A mock trial, which lasted sixteen days, was commenced at Richmond, and nearly sixty of the brethren were brought before Judge Austin A. King, charged with treason, murder, burglary, arson, robbery and larceny. Up to that date about thirty of the brethren had been killed and many wounded since the hostilities commenced the previous August.

Sat. 24.—Twenty-three of the Far West prisoners were discharged at Richmond, Mo., as nothing could be found against them.

Wed. 28.—The remaining prisoners in Richmond were released, or admitted to bail, except Joseph Smith, Jr., Lyman Wight, Caleb Baldwin, Hyrum Smith, Alex. McRae and Sidney Rigdon, who were sent to jail in Liberty, Clay County, to await their trial for treason and murder, of which they were falsely accused; and Parley P. Pratt, Morris Phelps, Luman Gibbs, Darwin Chase and Norman Shearer were confined in the Richmond jail to stand their trial on a similar charge.

December. Wed. 19.—John Taylor and John E. Page were ordained Apostles, at Far West, Mo.

—A petition from the Saints in Caldwell County was presented to the Missouri legislature, causing much warm debate, but the petition was finally laid on the table, which meant that the legislature would do nothing for the suffering Saints.

Thurs. 27.—Anson Call was brutally whipped by a mob, near Elk Horn, Ray County, Mo.

1839

January. Tues. 29.—The Elders met at Far West to complete measures for the removal of the poor from Missouri, and pledged themselves to assist each other until all were removed.

February. Thurs. 14.—Brigham Young, President of the Twelve, left Far West, Mo., for Illinois, on account of persecution.

Sat. 23.—Many of the fugitive Saints having arrived at Quincy, Adams County, Ill., the citizens of that place met to adopt measures for their relief.

About this time Sidney Rigdon was released from prison in Liberty jail, Mo., on bail.

March. Sun. 17.—Thomas B. Marsh, formerly President of the Twelve, Wm. W. Phelps, Frederick G. Williams, George M. Hinkle and others were excommunicated from the Church at a conference held at Quincy, Ill.

Fri. 20.—Joseph Smith, Jr., who was still imprisoned in Liberty jail, Mo., wrote an excellent epistle "to the Saints at Quincy, Ill., and scattered abroad," in which was embodied a most fervent prayer in behalf of the suffering Saints, and words of prophecy. (See Doc. and Cov. Sec. 121, and History of Joseph Smith.)

A few days later the Prophet Joseph continued his epistle and wrote among other beautiful gems that which constitutes Sections 122 and 123 of the Doctrine and Covenants.

April. Fri. 5.—A company of about fifty men in Daviess County, Mo., swore that they would never eat or drink until they had murdered Joseph the Prophet.

Sat. 6.—Joseph Smith, Jr., and fellow-prisoners were started from Liberty jail, to Gallatin, Daviess County, Mo., where they arrived on the 8th, and were again subjected to a mock trial before a drunken court and jury.

Thurs. 11.—Ten mobbers made an unsuccessful attempt to kill Stephen Markham in Daviess County, Mo., because he had testified truthfully in the case of the prisoners.

Sun. 14.—The committee for the removal of the Saints from Missouri moved thirty-six families into Tenney's Grove, about twenty-five miles from Far West.

Mon. 15.—Joseph Smith, Jr., and fellow-prisoners, started from Daviess towards Boone County, Mo., under a change of venue.

Tues. 16.—The guard being drunk, Joseph Smith, Jr., and fellow-prisoners made their escape. After a severe journey they arrived at Quincy, Ill., on the 22nd.

Sat. 20.—The last of the Saints left Far West. Thus a whole community, numbering about fifteen thousand souls, were expelled from their homes on account of their religion.

Wed. 24.—Parley P. Pratt and fellow-prisoners were brought before the grand jury of Ray County, at Richmond. Darwin Chase and Norman Shearer were dismissed after having been imprisoned for six months.

Thurs. 25.—Joseph Smith, Jr., and others visited Iowa for the purpose of finding a location for the Church. Commerce, Hancock Co., Ill., was finally selected as a gathering place for the Saints.

Fri. 26.—Early in the morning a conference was held on the Temple site at Far West, Mo., in fulfilment of the revelation given July 8, 1838. Among those present were Apostles Brigham Young, Heber C. Kimball, Orson Pratt, John E. Page and John Taylor, who ordained Wilford Woodruff and George A. Smith Apostles, "to fill the places of those who had fallen." Alpheus Cutler, the masterworkman of the Temple, then commenced laying its foundation, in accordance with revelation, by rolling up a large stone near the southeast corner. Isaac Russell, John Goodson, Luman Gibbs and twenty-eight others were excommunicated from the Church.

May. Wed. 1.—The first purchase of land for the Church at Commerce, Ill., was made by Joseph Smith, Jr., and others of the committee. The purchase consisted of two farms bought respectively of Hugh White and Isaac Galland.

Fri. 3.—Six of the Apostles met privately the Prophet near Quincy, Ill., for the first time after his liberation from prison.

Sat. 4.—A two days' conference was commenced on the Presbyterian camp ground, near Quincy, Ill. The doings of the Twelve at Far West on April 26th were sanctioned. Elder Oliver Granger was appointed to go to Kirtland, Ohio, to preside, and the Saints in the Eastern States were advised to gather to Kirtland and settle that place as a Stake of Zion. On the 5th it was decided to send Sidney Rigdon as a delegate to Washington, D. C., to lay the grievances of the Saints before the General Government.

Mon. 6.—At a conference, held at Quincy, Ill. Wm. Marks was appointed to preside at Commerce, and John P. Greene over the Saints in New York. A number of Seventies and High Priests were called to accompany the Apostles on their missions to Europe.

Thurs. 9.—Joseph Smith, Jr., left Quincy with his family, and arrived the following day at Commerce.

Wed. 22.—Parley P. Pratt, Morris Phelps, Luman Gibbs and King Follett, having obtained a change of venue, left Richmond, Mo., handcuffed, for Columbia, Boone County, where they arrived on the 26th and were thrown into a filthy dungeon.

June.—The first house erected by the Saints in Commerce was raised by Theodore Turley.

Mon. 24.—The Church purchased the town of Nashville, in Lee County, Iowa Territory, and twenty thousand acres of land adjoining it. About the same time another tract of land lying west of Montrose, Iowa, opposite Nauvoo, was purchased.

July.—Much sickness prevailed among the Saints at Commerce, which at that time was a very unhealthful place, but many of them were miraculously healed by the power of God.

Tues. 2.—Joseph the Prophet advised that a town be built on the Iowa purchase, to be called Zarahemla.

Thurs. 4.—After more than seven months' imprisonment without conviction, Parley P. Pratt and Morris Phelps escaped from the Columbia jail, Boone County, Mo. They arrived in Quincy, Ill., after days of dreadful suffering from hunger and fatigue. King Follett, who also tried to escape, was retaken.

Mon. 22.—Elijah Fordham, Henry G. Sherwood, Benjamin Brown, Joseph B. Noble and many others, at Commerce, Ill., and Montrose, Iowa, were miraculously healed under the powerful administrations of the Prophet Joseph, assisted by other Elders.

August. Thurs. 8.—Apostles John Taylor and Wilford Woodruff left Commerce, Ill., on a mission to England.

Thurs. 29.—Apostles Parley P. Pratt and Orson Pratt and Elder Hiram Clark departed from Commerce on a mission to England.

September. Wed. 18.—Apostles Brigham Young and Heber C. Kimball started from Commerce on a mission to England, leaving their families sick and poverty-stricken.

Sat. 21.—Apostle Geo. A. Smith and Elders Reuben Hedlock and Theodore Turley left Commerce for England on a mission.

October. Sat. 5.—At a general conference, held at Commerce, William Marks was appointed president of that Stake. Edward Partridge, Bishop of the upper Ward, and Vinson Knight, Bishop of the lower Ward. Geo. W. Harris, Samuel Bent, Henry G. Sherwood, David Fullmer, Alpheus Cutler, Wm. Huntington, Thomas Grover, Newel Knight, Chas. C. Rich, David Dort, Seymour Brunson and Lewis D. Wilson were chosen members of the High Council. John Smith was appointed to preside over the Saints on the other side of the Mississippi river, in Iowa Territory, with Alanson Ripley as Bishop, Asahel Smith, John M. Burk, Abraham O. Smoot, Richard Howard, Willard Snow, Erastus Snow, David Pettigrew, Elijah Fordham, Edward Fisher, Elias Smith, John Patten and Stephen Chase were chosen as members of the High Council.

Thurs. 17.—Apostle Heber C. Kimball was poisoned at Terre Haute, Ind., but his life was saved by the administration of Apostle Brigham Young.

Sat. 19.—The High Council appointed for the Church in Iowa met for the first time, at Nashville, Iowa. Reynolds Cahoon and Lyman Wight were appointed counselors to John Smith.

Tues. 29.—Joseph Smith, Jr., accompanied by Sidney Rigdon, Elias Higbee and O. Porter Rockwell, left Commerce for Washington, D. C., to lay the grievances of the Saints before the President and Congress of the United States.

In the latter part of this month King Follett, the last of the Missouri prisoners, was tried and set free.

November.—The first number of the "Times and Seasons" was published at Commerce, Ill.

Sun. 3.—James Mulholland, Joseph Smith's clerk, died at Commerce.

Wed. 27.—Brigham Young, rebuked the wind and waves on Lake Erie, and he was obeyed.

Thurs. 28.—Joseph Smith, Jr., arrived at Washington, D. C.

December. Thurs. 19.—Apostles Wilford Woodruff and John Taylor and Elder Theodore Turley sailed from New York for England; they arrived at Liverpool Jan. 11, 1840.

Sat. 21.—Joseph Smith, Jr., arrived at Philadelphia, Pa., (from Washington), where he remained until the 30th, preaching the gospel.

1840

January. Sun. 12.—Francis Marion Lyman was born at Macomb, McDonough Co., Ill.

March.—Multitudes were baptized into the Church in the United States and England. Apostle Wilford Woodruff built up large branches in Herefordshire, England.

Wed. 4.—Joseph Smith, Jr., arrived in Commerce, Ill., from Washington, D. C., after a fruitless endeavor to obtain redress for the wrongs suffered by the Saints in Missouri. He had presented to Congress claims against Missouri from 491 individuals for about $1,381,000. President Martin Van Buren, in answer to Joseph's appeal, said, "Your cause is just, but I can do nothing for you." The Committee on the Judiciary, to whom was referred the memorial of the Saints, reported adversely to the prayer of the petitioners.

Mon. 9.—Brigham Young, Heber C. Kimball, Parley P. Pratt, George A. Smith and Reuben Hedlock sailed from New York on the ship "Patrick Henry" for Liverpool, where they arrived April 6th.

April. Mon. 6.—A general conference of the Church was commenced at Nauvoo, Ill. It continued three days. On the first day Apostle Orson Hyde was called on a mission to Jerusalem and on the 8th Apostle John E. Page was appointed to accompany him. The conference also adopted a series of resolutions, expressive of sorrow and disappointment at the action of the Committee of the Judiciary at Washington, D. C.

Tues. 14.—At a council of the Apostles held at Preston, England, Willard Richards was ordained one of the Twelve Apostles.

Wed. 15.—Apostle Orson Hyde left Commerce, Ill., on his mission to Jerusalem.

—At a conference held at Preston, England, where 34 branches and 1,686 members were represented, it was decided to publish a monthly periodical in the interest of the Church in England.

Tues. 21.—The Postmaster General at Washington, D. C., changed the name of the postoffice at Commerce, Hancock Co., Ill., to Nauvoo, and appointed George W. Robinson postmaster.

May. Sat. 9.—Elder Theodore Turley, who had been imprisoned in Stafford jail, England, at the instigation of a Methodist preacher, was released.

Wed. 27.—Bishop Edward Partridge died at Nauvoo, 46 years old. He lost his life in consequence of the Missouri persecutions.

—The first number of "The Latter-day Saints' Millennial Star," was published at Manchester, England; Apostle Parley P. Pratt, editor.

June.—By this time the Saints had erected about two hundred and fifty houses in Nauvoo.

Sat. 6.—Forty-one Saints sailed from Liverpool, England, on the ship "Britannia," for the United States, being the first Saints that gathered from a foreign land. John Moon was leader of the company.

Sun. 14.—The Bran Green and Gadfield Elm conference was organized by Apostle Wilford Woodruff in Worcestershire, England, consisting of twelve branches. This was the first conference organized in the British mission.

Sun. 21.—At a meeting held on Stanley Hill, Herefordshire, England, the Froome's Hill conference was organized by Apostle Wilford Woodruff, consisting of twenty branches.

July.—The first British edition of the Latter-day Saints' Hymn Book was published in England.

Tues. 7.—James Allred, Noah Rogers, Alanson Brown and Benjamin Boyce were kidnapped from Hancock County, Ill., by Missourians, and taken to Tully, Lewis Co., Mo., where they were imprisoned, whipped and ill-treated until nearly dead. Brown and Allred escaped a few days afterwards.

Sat. 11.—Apostle Geo. A. Smith ordained and set apart Wm. Barratt at Burslem, Staffordshire, England, for a mission to South Australia. He was the first missionary to that country.

Mon. 20.—John Moon's company of British emigrants arrived at New York.

Mon. 27.—Apostle John Taylor sailed from Liverpool for Ireland to open the door of the gospel in that country.

August.—Elder Wm. Donaldson, of the British army, sailed from England for the East Indies. He was the first member of the Church to visit that country.

Fri. 21.—Noah Rogers and Benjamin Boyce escaped from their unlawful imprisonment in Missouri, during which they had been put in irons and suffered much.

Mon. 31.—Apostle Heber C. Kimball baptized Henry Conner, a watchmaker, in London, England, as the first fruit of preaching the fullness of the gospel in that city.

September.—Apostle John Taylor and others first preached the gospel on the Isle of Man.

Mon. 8.—The ship "North America" sailed from Liverpool, England, with about two hundred Saints, under the presidency of Theodore Turley, bound for Nauvoo, Ill.

Sun. 14.—Joseph Smith, Sr., Patriarch to the Church, died at Nauvoo.

Mon. 15.—Gov. Lilburn W. Boggs, of Missouri, made a demand on Gov. Thos. Carlin, of Illinois, for Joseph Smith, Jr., Sidney Rigdon, Lyman Wight, Parley P. Pratt, Caleb Baldwin and Alanson Brown as fugitives from justice.

October. Fri. 3.—At a conference held at Nauvoo, Robert B. Thompson was appointed General Church Clerk, instead of Geo. W. Robinson. Almon W. Babbitt was appointed to preside over the Church at Kirtland, Ohio, and a committee was appointed to organize new Stakes for the gathering of the Saints.

Wed. 22.—A Stake was organized by the committee at Lima, Hancock Co., Ill., with Isaac Morley as president and John Murdock and Walter Cox as his counselors.

Sat. 25.—A Stake was organized at Quincy, Adams Co., Ill., with Daniel Stanton, Stephen Jones and Ezra T. Benson as the presidency.

Mon. 27.—A Stake called Mount Hope was organized at the steam mills, Columbus, Adams Co., Ill., with the following brethren as the presidency, Abel Lamb, Sherman Gilbert and John Smith.

November. Sat. 1.—The committee organized a Stake called Geneva, in Morgan County, Ill., with Wm. Bosley, Howard S. Smith and Samuel Fowler as the presidency.

December. Wed. 16.—The charter for the incorporation of Nauvoo, granted by the State legislature, was signed by Gov. Thomas Carlin, but not to take effect until the first of February following.

1841

January.—The first number of the "Gospel Reflector," a semi-monthly periodical published in the interest of the Church, was issued in Philadelphia, Pa.; Benjamin Winchester, editor.

—The first British edition of the Book of Mormon was published in Manchester, England.

Tues. 19.—The Saints were commanded by revelation to build a Temple at Nauvoo, Ill., and also a "boarding house" for the accommodation of strangers, which subsequently became known as the Nauvoo House. The general authorities of the Church and other officers were named in the revelation, which also contains important explanations on the order of the Priesthood. (Doc. and Cov., Sec. 124.)

And again, verily I say unto you, my servant George Miller is without guile; he may be trusted because of the integrity of his heart; and for the love which he has to my testimony I, the Lord, love him;

I therefore say unto you, I seal upon his head the office of a bishopric, like unto my servant Edward Partridge, that he may receive the consecrations of mine house, that he may administer blessings upon the heads of the poor of my people, saith the Lord. Let no man despise my servant George, for he shall honor me.

Let my servant George, and my servant Lyman, and my servant John Snider, and others, build a house unto my name, such an one as my servant Joseph shall show unto them; upon the place which he shall show unto them also.

And it shall be for a house for boarding, a house that strangers may come from afar to lodge therein; therefore let it be a good house, worthy of all acceptation, that the weary traveler may find health and safety while he shall contemplate the word of the Lord; and the corner stone I have appointed for Zion.

But I command you, all ye my saints, to build a house unto me; and I grant unto you a sufficient time to build a house unto me, and during this time your baptisms shall be acceptable unto me.

But behold, at the end of this appointment, your baptisms for your dead shall not be acceptable unto me; and if you do not these things at the end of the appointment, ye shall be rejected as a church, with your dead, saith the Lord your God.

Verily I say unto you, I now give unto you the officers belonging to my Priesthood, that ye may hold the keys thereof, even the Priesthood which is after the order of Melchisedek, which is after the order of my Only Begotten Son.

First, I give unto you Hyrum Smith, to be a Patriarch unto you, to hold the sealing blessings of my church, even the Holy Spirit of promise, whereby ye are sealed up unto the day of redemption, that ye may not fall, notwithstanding the hour of temptation that may come upon you.

I give unto you my servant Joseph, to be a presiding elder over all my church, to be a translator, a revelator, a seer, and prophet.

I give unto him for counselors my servant Sidney Rigdon, and my servant William Law, that these may constitute a quorum and First Presidency, to receive the oracles for the whole church.

I give unto you my servant Brigham Young, to be a President over the Twelve traveling Council,

Which Twelve hold the keys to open up the authority of my kingdom upon the four corners of the earth, and after that to send my word to every creature;

They are—Heber C. Kimball, Parley P. Pratt, Orson Pratt, Orson Hyde, William Smith, John Taylor, John E. Page, Wilford Woodruff, Willard Richards, George A. Smith;

David Patten I have taken unto myself; behold, his Priesthood no man taketh from him; but, verily I say unto you, another may be appointed unto the same calling.

And again. I say unto you, I give unto you a High Council, for the corner stone of Zion;

Viz., Samuel Bent, H. G. Sherwood, George W. Harris, Charles C. Rich, Thomas Grover, Newel Knight, David Dort, Dunbar Wilson; (Seymour Branson I have taken unto myself, no man taketh his Priesthood, but another may be appointed unto the same Priesthood in his stead; and verily I say unto you, let my servant Aaron Johnson be ordained unto this calling in his stead;) David Fullmer, Alpheus Cutler, William Huntington.

And again, I give unto you Don C. Smith, to be a president over a quorum of High Priests;

Which ordinance is instituted for the purpose of qualifying those who shall be appointed standing presidents or servants over different Stakes scattered abroad.

And they may travel also if they choose, but rather be ordained for standing presidents, this is the office of their calling, saith the Lord your God.

I give unto him Amasa Lyman, and Noah Packard for counselors, that they may preside over the quorum of High Priests of my church, saith the Lord.

And again, I say unto you, I give unto you John A. Hicks, Samuel Williams, and Jesse Baker, which Priesthood is to preside over the quorum of elders, which quorum is instituted for standing ministers, nevertheless they may travel, yet they are ordained to be standing ministers to my church, saith the Lord.

And again, I give unto you Joseph Young, Josiah Butterfield, Daniel Miles, Henry Herriman, Zera Pulsipher, Levi Hancock, James Foster, to preside over the quorum of seventies,

Which quorum is instituted for traveling elders to bear record of my name in all the world, wherever the traveling High Council, my apostles, shall send them to prepare a way before my face.

The difference between this quorum and the quorum of elders is, that one is to travel continually, and the other is to preside over the churches from time to time; the one has the responsibility of presiding from time to time, and the other has no responsibility of presiding, saith the Lord your God.

And again, I say unto you I give unto you Vinson Knight, Samuel H. Smith, and Shadrach Roundy, if he will receive it, to preside over the bishopric; a knowledge of said bishopric is given unto you in the Book of Doctrine and Covenants.

And again, I say unto you, Samuel Rolfe and his counselors for priests, and the president of the teachers and his counselors, and also the president of the deacons and his counselors, and also the president of the stake and his counselors;

The above offices I have given unto you, and the keys thereof, for helps and for governments, for the work of the ministry, and the perfecting of my saints;

And a commandment I give unto you that you should fill all these offices and approve of those names which I have mentioned, or else disapprove of them at my general conference.—Doc. and Cov. 124:20-23, 31-32, 123-144.

Sun. 24.—Hyrum Smith succeeded his father, Joseph Smith, Sr., as Patriarch to the Church, and Wm. Law was appointed a Counselor in the First Presidency, succeeding Hyrum Smith in that capacity, according to revelation.

Sat. 30.—At a meeting held at Nauvoo, Ill., Joseph Smith was elected sole Trustee for the Church, to hold the office during life, his "successors to be the First Presidency" of the Church.

February, Mon. 1.—The first election took place for members of the city council of Nauvoo, John C. Bennett was elected mayor; Wm. Marks, Samuel H. Smith, Daniel H. Wells and Newel K. Whitney, aldermen; Joseph Smith, Hyrum Smith, Sidney Rigdon, Charles C. Rich, John F. Barnett, Wilson Law, Don Carlos Smith, John P. Greene and Vinson Knight, councilors.

Wed. 3.—The city council of Nauvoo elected Henry G. Sherwood, marshal; James Sloan, recorder; Robert B. Thompson, treasurer; James Robinson, assessor; Austin Cowles, supervisor of streets.

Thurs. 4.—The Nauvoo Legion, originally consisting of six companies, was organized with Joseph Smith as lieutenant-general.

Sun. 7.—The ship "Sheffield" sailed from Liverpool, England, with 235 Saints, under the leadership of Hiram Clark.

Sat. 13.—Apostle Orson Hyde sailed from New York for Liverpool, on his mission to Jerusalem.

Sun. 14.—The London (England) conference was organized with Lorenzo Snow as president.

Tues. 16.—The ship "Echo" sailed from Liverpool, England, with 109 Saints, under the direction of Daniel Browitt.

March.—The Saints were commanded by revelation to build a city in Iowa Territory, opposite Nauvoo, to be called Zarahemla. (Doc. and Cov. Sec. 125.)

Let them build up a city unto my name upon the land opposite to the city of Nauvoo, and let the name of Zarahemla be named upon it.—Doc. and Cov. 125:3.

Mon. 1.—The city council divided the city of Nauvoo into four wards. An ordinance was passed, giving free toleration and equal privileges in the city to all religious sects and denominations.

Wed. 10.—Gov. Thos. Carlin, of Illinois, commissioned Joseph Smith lieutenant-general of the Nauvoo Legion.

Wed. 17.—The ship "Uleste" sailed from Liverpool, England, with 54 Saints, under the direction of Thomas Smith and Wm. Moss, bound for America.

Mon. 29.—Charles C. Rich and Austin Cowles were chosen counselors to Wm. Marks, president of the Nauvoo Stake of Zion.

April. Tues. 6.—A general conference of the Church was commenced at Nauvoo, and the corner stones of the Nauvoo Temple were laid. The conference was continued till the 11th.

Thurs. 8.—Lyman Wight was chosen one of the Twelve Apostles, in place of David W. Patten, martyred in Missouri.

Wed. 21.—Apostles Brigham Young, Heber C. Kimball, Orson Pratt, Wilford Woodruff, John Taylor, Geo. A. Smith and Willard Richards sailed from Liverpool, England, on the ship "Rochester," accompanied by 130 Saints. They arrived at New York May 20th.

May. Sat. 22.—At a conference held at Kirtland, Ohio, Almon W. Babbitt was chosen president of the Kirtland Stake, with Lester Brooks and Zebedee Coltrin as counselors.

Mon. 24.—The First Presidency at Nauvoo called upon all scattered Saints to gather to Hancock County, Ill., and Lee County, Iowa. All neighboring Stakes outside of these two counties were discontinued.

June. Sat. 5.—Joseph Smith was arrested on a requisition from the State of Missouri. He was tried on the 9th and liberated on the 10th on a writ of habeas corpus, at Monmouth, Warren Co., Ill.

Tues. 22.—Theodore Curtis, who had been under arrest in Gloucester, England, five days for preaching the gospel, was acquitted.

July. Thurs. 1.—Apostles Brigham Young, Heber C. Kimball and John Taylor arrived at Nauvoo from their missions to England.

Fri. 9.—By revelation, through Joseph the Prophet, Apostle Brigham Young was commanded to send the "word" abroad, and to take special care of his family. (Doc. and Cov., Sec. 126.)

Tues. 13.—Apostle Geo. A. Smith returned to Nauvoo from his mission to England.

Sun. 25.—Wm. Yokum lost his leg by amputation, as the result of a wound received in the massacre at Haun's Mill, Mo.

August. Sat. 7.—Don Carlos Smith, the youngest brother of the Prophet, died at Nauvoo.

Thurs. 12.—Joseph Smith preached to about one hundred Sac and Fox Indians (among whom were the chiefs Keokuk, Kiskuhosh and Appenoose), who had come to visit him at Nauvoo.

Mon. 16.—Apostle Willard Richards arrived at Nauvoo from his mission to England.

Wed. 25.—Oliver Granger died at Kirtland, Ohio.

Fri. 27.—Robert B. Thompson, Joseph Smith's scribe, died at Nauvoo.

September. Tues. 21.—The ship "Tyrean" sailed from Liverpool for New Orleans with 204 Saints, under the direction of Joseph Fielding, bound for Nauvoo.

Wed. 22.—A company of brethren left Nauvoo for the Pineries, Wisconsin, about five hundred miles north, to procure lumber for the Nauvoo Temple.

October. Sat. 2.—An important general conference was commenced in the Grove at Nauvoo. It was continued till the 4th. Joseph Smith declared, as the will of the Lord, that the Church should not hold another general conference until the Saints could meet in the Temple. James Sloan was elected Church clerk, instead of Robert B. Thompson, deceased.

Wed. 6.—Apostle Wilford Woodruff arrived at Nauvoo from his mission to England.

Thurs. 7.—In a council of the Twelve, a number of brethren were called on missions, among whom were Joseph Ball to South America and Henry Harrison Sagers to Jamaica, West Indies.

Sun. 24.—Apostle Orson Hyde, who had arrived at Jerusalem, ascended the Mount of Olives and dedicated the land of Palestine by prayer for the gathering of the Jews.

November. Mon. 8.—The temporary baptismal font in the Nauvoo Temple was dedicated.

—The ship "Chaos" sailed from Liverpool with 170 Saints, under the direction of Peter Melling, bound for Nauvoo.

Sun. 21.—Baptisms for the dead were commenced in the font in the basement of the Nauvoo Temple.

Wed. 24.—The "Tyrean" company of British Saints arrived at Warsaw, intending to settle Warren, a new town site, one mile south of Warsaw, which had been selected for a settlement of the Saints, but they soon afterwards removed to Nauvoo, because of oppression on the part of anti-Mormons.

December. Sat. 4.—The Stake organization at Ramus, Hancock Co., Ill., was discontinued.

Mon. 13.—Apostle Willard Richards was appointed Joseph Smith's private secretary and general clerk for the Church.

Wed. 22.—John Snider was called by revelation on a special mission to Europe, bearing a message from the Twelve.

1842

January. Thurs. 6.—A conference was held at Zarahemla, Iowa, opposite Nauvoo, when a Stake of Zion, previously organized there, was discontinued, and a branch organized in its stead, with John Smith as president.

Wed. 12.—The ship "Tremont" sailed from Liverpool with 143 Saints bound for Nauvoo via New Orleans.

February. Wed. 2.—Moses Thatcher was born in Sangamon County, Ill.

Thurs. 3.—Apostle Wilford Woodruff took the superintendency of the printing office and Apostle John Taylor the editorial department of the "Times and Seasons," at Nauvoo.

Sat. 5.—The ship "Hope" sailed from Liverpool for New Orleans with 270 Saints.

Sun. 20.—The ship "John Cumming" sailed from Liverpool with about 200 Saints.

March.—The "Millennial Star" office in England was moved from Manchester (No. 47 Oxford Street) to the Church emigration office in Liverpool (No. 36 Chapel Street).

Sat. 12.—The ship "Hanover" sailed from Liverpool with about two hundred Saints, under the direction of Amos Fielding.

Tues. 15.—Joseph Smith took charge of the editorial department of the "Times and Seasons."

Thurs. 17.—The organization of the Female Relief Society of Nauvoo was commenced. It was completed on the 24th, with Emma Smith as president and Mrs. Elizabeth Ann Whitley and Mrs. Sarah M. Cleveland, counselors; Miss Elvira Cowles, treasurer; and Eliza R. Snow, secretary.

Sun. 20.—Joseph Smith baptized eighty persons for the dead in the Mississippi river, after which he confirmed about fifty.

Sat. 26.—John Snider left Nauvoo on his special mission to England.

Sun. 27.—Joseph Smith baptized 107 persons for the dead in the Mississippi river.

April. Wed. 6.—A special conference of the Church was held at Nauvoo; it was continued till the 8th, and during its sessions 275 brethren were ordained Elders.

Wed. 13.—About two hundred Saints arrived at Nauvoo from Great Britain.

Sat. 16.—The "Wasp," a miscellaneous weekly newspaper, was first published at Nauvoo; Wm. Smith, editor.

Fri. 29.—Joseph Smith wrote: "A conspiracy against the peace of my household was made manifest, and it gave me some trouble to counteract the design of certain base individuals and restore peace. The Lord makes manifest to me many things, which it is not wisdom for me to make public until others can witness the proof of them."

May. Wed. 4.—Joseph Smith gave James Adams, Hyrum Smith, Newel K. Whitney, George Miller, Brigham Young, Heber C. Kimball and Willard Richards instructions about holy endowments.

Fri. 6.—Ex-Governor Lilburn W. Boggs, of Missouri, was shot, but not killed, at Independence, Mo.

Sat. 7.—The Nauvoo Legion, now numbering 26 companies, or 2,000 men, was reviewed and it fought a sham battle, in which John C. Bennett conspired against the Prophet's life, but failed to carry out his design.

Thurs. 19.—John C. Bennett having resigned the mayorship of Nauvoo, Joseph Smith was elected by the city council to fill the vacancy.

Tues. 24.—Chauncy L. Higbee was excommunicated from the Church by the High Council of Nauvoo, for unchaste and unvirtuous conduct.

Wed. 25.—The authorities of the Church had at this time withdrawn their fellowship from John C. Bennett, who soon afterwards left Nauvoo.

June. Wed. 1.—At a general conference held in Manchester, England, 8,265 officers and members of the Church were represented.

July. Sun. 3.—Joseph Smith spoke to eight thousand people at Nauvoo.

August.—Apostle Orson Hyde published a pamphlet of 120 pages in the German language, in Germany, entitled "A Cry in the Wilderness," etc., setting forth the rise, progress and doctrines of the Church.

Sat. 6.—Joseph Smith prophesied that the Saints would be driven to the Rocky Mountains, where they should become a mighty people.

(As recorded in his own words, "I prophesied that the Saints would continue to suffer much affliction, and would be driven to the Rocky Mountains. Many would apostatize; others would be put to death by our persecutors, or lose their lives in consequence of exposure or disease; and some would live to go and assist in making settlements and building cities, and see the Saints become a mighty people in the midst of the Rocky Mountains.")

Mon. 8.—Joseph Smith was arrested by a deputy sheriff at Nauvoo, by requisition from Gov. Thos. Reynolds, of Missouri, falsely accused of being accessory to the shooting of ex-Governor Boggs. O. Porter Rockwell was also arrested as principal. A writ of habeas corpus was issued by the municipal court of Nauvoo, by which the prisoners were released for the time being.

Wed. 10.—The deputy sheriff returned to Nauvoo to re-arrest Joseph Smith and O. Porter Rockwell, but they could not be found. To escape imprisonment the Prophet had to keep concealed for some time. His first retreat was the house of his uncle John Smith, at Zarahemla, Ia.

Thurs. 11.—Joseph Smith concealed himself in the house of Edward Sayer, in Nauvoo.

Thurs. 18.—Rumors being afloat that the Prophet's hiding place was discovered, he changed his quarters from the house of Edward Sayer to that of Carlos Granger, who lived in the northeast part of Nauvoo. Great excitement prevailed among the people around Nauvoo on account of John C. Bennett's lies.

Fri. 19.—Joseph Smith returned to his own house.

Sat. 20.—Amasa M. Lyman was ordained one of the Twelve Apostles.

Sun. 21.—Sidney Rigdon testified in public meeting, at Nauvoo, that his daughter, Eliza, had been raised from the dead by the power of God.

Mon. 29.—After not showing himself in public for three weeks, Joseph Smith spoke to an assembly of Saints at Nauvoo; 380 Elders volunteered to take missions to the various States of the Union for the purpose of refuting John C. Bennett's lies.

September. Thurs. 1.—Joseph Smith wrote an address to the Saints at Nauvoo concerning baptism for the dead. (Doc. and Cov., Sec. 127.)

Verily, thus saith the Lord unto you concerning your dead: When any of you are baptized for your dead, let there be a Recorder, and let him be eye witness of your baptisms; let him hear with his ears, that he may testify of a truth, saith the Lord: * * *—Doc. and Cov., 127:6.

Sat. 3.—Another effort was made to arrest Joseph Smith without legal process. His house was searched, but he eluded pursuit, and afterwards kept himself hid for some time in the house of Edward Hunter.

Tues. 6.—Joseph Smith wrote another important address to the Saints in relation to baptism for the dead, and the necessity of keeping records. (Doc. and Cov., Sec. 128.)

Address to the Church of Jesus Christ of Latter-day Saints, dated Nauvoo, September 6th, 1842.

As I stated to you in my letter before I left my place, that I would write to you from time to time, and give you information in relation to many subjects, I now resume the subject of the baptism for the dead, as that subject seems to occupy my mind, and press itself upon my feelings the strongest, since I have been pursued by my enemies.

I wrote a few words of revelation to you concerning a recorder. I have had a few additional views in relation to this matter, which I now certify. That is, it was declared in my former letter that there should be a recorder, who should be eye witness, and also to hear with his ears, that he might make a record of a truth before the Lord.

Now, in relation to this matter, it would be very difficult for one recorder to be present at all times, and to do all the business. To obviate this difficulty, there can be a recorder appointed in each ward of the city, who is well qualified for taking accurate minutes; and let him be very particular and precise in taking the whole proceedings, certifying in his record that he saw with his eyes, and heard with his ears, giving the date and names, etc., and the history of the whole transaction; naming also, some three individuals that are present, if there be any present, who can at any time when called upon, certify to the same, that in the mouth of two or three witnesses, every word may be established.

Then let there be a general recorder, to whom these other records can be handed, being attended with certificates over their own signatures, certifying that the record they have made is true. Then the general church recorder, can enter the record on the general church book, with the certificates and all the attending witnesses, with his own statement that he verily believes the above statement and records to be true, from his knowledge of the general character and appointment of those men by the church. And when this is done on the general church book, the record shall be just as holy, and shall answer the ordinance just the same as if he had seen with his eyes, and heard with his ears, and made a record of the same on the general church book.

You may think this order of things to be very particular, but let me tell you, that it is only to answer the will of God, by conforming to the ordinance and preparation that the Lord ordained and prepared before the foundation of the world, for the salvation of the dead who should die without a knowledge of the gospel.

And further I want you to remember that John the Revelator was contemplating this very subject in relation to the dead, when he declared, as you will find recorded in Revelations xx. 12—"And I saw the dead, small and great, stand before God; and the books were opened; and another book was opened, which was the book of life; and the dead were judged out of those things which were written in the books, according to their works."

You will discover in this quotation, that the books were opened; and another book was opened, which was the book of life; but the dead were judged out of those things which were written in the books, according to their works; consequently the books spoken of must be the books which contained the record of their works; and refer to the records which are kept on the earth. And the book which was the book of life, is the record which is kept in heaven; the principle agreeing precisely with the doctrine which is commanded you in the revelation contained in the letter which I wrote to you previously to my leaving my place—that in all your recordings it may be recorded in heaven.

Now the nature of this ordinance consists in the power of the Priesthood, by the revelation of Jesus Christ, wherein it is granted, that whatsoever you bind on earth, shall be bound in heaven, and whatsoever you loose on earth, shall be loosed in heaven. Or, in other words, taking a different view of the translation, whatsoever you record on earth, shall be recorded in heaven; and whatsoever you do not record on earth, shall not be recorded in heaven; for out of the books shall your dead be judged, according to their own works, whether they themselves have attended to the ordinances in their own **propria persona**, or by the means of their own agents, according to the ordinance which God has prepared for their salvation from before the foundation of the world, according to the records which they have kept concerning their dead.

It may seem to some to be a very bold doctrine that we talk of—a power which records or binds on earth, and binds in heaven. Nevertheless in all ages of the world, whenever the Lord has given a dispensation of the Priesthood to any man by actual revelation, or any set of men, this power has always been given. Hence, whatsoever those men did in authority, in the name of the Lord, and did it truly and faithfully, and kept a proper and faithful record of the same, it became a law on earth and in heaven, and could not be annulled, according to the decrees of the great Jehovah. This is a faithful saying! Who can hear it?

And again, for the precedent, Matthew xvi. 18, 19. "And I also say unto thee, that thou art Peter; and upon this rock I will build my church; and the gates of hell shall not prevail against it; and I will give unto thee the keys of the kingdom of heaven, and whatsoever thou shalt bind on earth, shall be bound in heaven; and whatsoever thou shalt loose on earth, shall be loosed in heaven."

Now the great and grand secret of the whole matter, and the **summum bonum** of the whole subject that is lying before us, consists in obtaining the powers of the Holy Priesthood. For him to whom these keys are given, there is no difficulty in obtaining a knowledge of facts in relation to the salvation of the children of men, both as well for the dead as for the living.

Herein is glory and honor, and immortality and eternal life. The ordinance of baptism by water, to be immersed therein in order to answer to the likeness of the dead, that one principle might accord with the other. To be immersed in the water and come forth out of the water is in the likeness of the resurrection of the dead in coming forth out of their graves; hence this ordinance was instituted to form a relationship with the ordinance of baptism for the dead, being in likeness of the dead.

Consequently the baptismal font was instituted as a simile of the grave, and was commanded to be in a place underneath where the living are wont to assemble, to show forth the living and the dead; and that all things may have their likeness, and that they may accord one with another; that which is earthly conforming to that which is heavenly, as Paul hath declared, 1 Corinthians xv. 46, 47, and 48.

"Howbeit that was not first which is spiritual, but that which is natural, and afterwards that which is spiritual. The first man is of the earth, earthy; the second man is the Lord, from heaven. As is the earthy, such are they also that are earthy; and as is the heavenly, such are they also that are heavenly." And as are the records on the earth in relation to your dead, which are truly made out, so also are the records in heaven. This, therefore, is the sealing and binding power, and, in one sense of the word, the keys of the kingdom which consist in the key of knowledge.

And now, my dearly beloved brethren and sisters, let me assure you that these are principles in relation to the dead, and the living, that cannot be lightly passed over, as pertaining to our salvation. For their salvation is necessary, and essential to our salvation, as Paul says concerning the fathers "that they without us cannot be made perfect;" neither can we without our dead be made perfect.

And now, in relation to the baptism for the dead, I will give you another quotation of Paul, 1 Corinthians xv, 29, "Else what shall they do which are baptized for the dead, if the dead rise not at all; why are they then baptized for the dead?"

And again, in connection with this quotation, I will give you a quotation from one of the prophets, who had his eye fixed on the restoration of the Priesthood, the glories to be revealed in the last days, and in an especial manner this most glorious of all subjects belonging to the everlasting gospel, viz., the baptism for the dead; for Malachi says, last chapter, verses 5th and 6th, "Behold, I will send you Elijah the prophet, before the coming of the great and dreadful day of the Lord: and he shall turn the heart of the fathers to the children, and the heart of the children to their fathers, lest I come and smite the earth with a curse."

I might have rendered a plainer translation to this, but it is sufficiently plain to suit my purpose as it stands. It is sufficient to know, in this case, that the earth will be smitten with a curse, unless there is a welding link of some kind or other, between the fathers and the children, upon some subject or other, and behold what is that subject? It is the baptism for the dead. For we without them cannot be made perfect; neither can they without us be made perfect. Neither can they nor we, be made perfect, without those who have died in the gospel also; for it is necessary in the ushering in of the dispensation of the fullness of times; which dispensation is now beginning to usher in, that a whole and complete and perfect union, and welding together of dispensations, and keys, and powers, and glories should take place, and be

revealed from the days of Adam even to the present time; and not only this, but those things which never have been revealed from the foundation of the world, but have been kept hid from the wise and prudent, shall be revealed unto babes and sucklings in this the dispensation of the fulliness of times.—Doc. and Cov. 128:1-18.
Sat. 10.—Joseph Smith returned home undiscovered.
Sat. 17.—The ship "Sidney" sailed from Liverpool with 180 Saints; it arrived at New Orleans Nov. 11th.
Sun. 25.—The ship "Medford" sailed from Liverpool with 214 Saints, under the presidency of Apostle Orson Hyde; it arrived at New Orleans Nov. 13th.
Thurs. 29.—The ship "Henry" sailed from Liverpool for New Orleans, with 157 Saints, under the direction of John Snider.
October. Sun. 2.—Reports reached Joseph Smith that Gov. Thos. Reynolds, of Missouri, had offered a reward for the arrest of himself and O. Porter Rockwell.
Fri. 7.—Joseph Smith again left home to elude the pursuit of his enemies, leaving his wife Emma sick. He returned on the 20th.
Thurs. 13.—Some of the brethren arrived at Nauvoo from the Fineries, Wisconsin, with 90,000 feet of lumber and 24,000 cubic feet of timber for the Temple and Nauvoo House.
Thurs. 20.—Thomas Ward succeeded Apostle Parley P. Pratt as president of the British Mission, with Lorenzo Snow and Hiram Clark as counselors.
Sat. 29.—The ship "Emerald" sailed from Liverpool with 250 Saints, under the leadership of Apostle Parley P. Pratt. Because of ice in the Mississippi river the company was detained during the winter in St. Louis. Alton, Chester and other places, and did not arrive in Nauvoo until April 12, 1843.
November. Tues. 15.—Apostle John Taylor succeeded Joseph Smith as editor of the "Times and Seasons."
Thurs. 17.—Alpheus Harmon was frozen to death on the prairie, between Nauvoo and Carthage, Ill., as he was returning home from a mission.
December. Sun. 4.—The city of Nauvoo was divided into ten Bishop's wards.
Wed. 7.—Apostle Orson Hyde returned to Nauvoo from his mission to Jerusalem.
Tues. 20.—Lorenzo D. Barnes died at Bradford, England. His was the first death of an Elder on a foreign mission.
Wed. 21.—Apostle Willard Richards, who had been in the East several months, was appointed Church Historian, etc.
Mon. 26.—Joseph Smith was arrested the third time on a requisition from the State of Missouri.
Tues. 27.—Joseph Smith, accompanied by several brethren, left Nauvoo for Springfield, Ill., where they arrived on the 30th.

1843

January. Mon. 2.—Joseph Smith prophesied that he should not go to Missouri dead or alive.
Wed. 4.—Joseph Smith was on trial before Judge Pope, of Springfield, on the accusation of being an accessory to the shooting of ex-Governor Boggs of Missouri.
Thurs. 5.—Joseph Smith was proven innocent and acquitted.
Tues. 10.—Joseph Smith and company arrived at Nauvoo from the trip to Springfield.
Mon. 16.—The ship "Swanton" sailed from Liverpool with 212 Saints for New Orleans, led by Lorenzo Snow. The emigrants arrived at Nauvoo April 12th.
Tues. 17.—The Saints being overjoyed because of Joseph Smith's release, meetings of prayer and thanksgiving were held at Nauvoo.
February. Tues. 7.—Apostle Parley P. Pratt arrived at Nauvoo from his mission to England.
Thurs. 9.—Joseph Smith received by revelation three grand keys, by which bad angels, or spirits, may be known.
Three Grand Keys by which Good or Bad Angels or Spirits may be known. Revealed to Joseph, the Prophet, at Nauvoo, Illinois, February 9th, 1843.
There are two kinds of beings in heaven—viz., angels who are resurrected personages, having bodies of flesh and bones.
For instance, Jesus said, "Handle me and see, for a spirit hath not flesh and bones, as ye see me have."
2nd. The spirits of just men made perfect—they who are not resurrected, but inherit the same glory.
When a messenger comes, saying he has a message from God, offer him your hand, and request him to shake hands with you.
If he be an angel, he will do so, and you will feel his hand.
If he be the spirit of a just man made perfect, he will come in his glory; for that is the only way he can appear.
Ask him to shake hands with you, but he will not move, because it is contrary to the order of heaven for a just man to deceive; but he will still deliver his message.
If he be the Devil as an angel of light, when you ask him to shake hands, he will offer you his hand, and you will not feel anything; you may therefore detect him.
These are three grand keys whereby you may know whether any administration is from God.—Doc. and Cov. Sec. 129.
March.—A "Young Gentlemen's and Ladies' Relief Society" was organized at Nauvoo, with Wm. Cutler as president.
—Joseph Smith studied the German language.
Fri. 3.—The Illinois legislature passed a bill for repealing the Nauvoo city charter, which, however, was not approved.
Sat. 4.—O. Porter Rockwell was taken prisoner in St. Louis by the Missourians.
Wed. 8.—The ship "Yorkshire" sailed from Liverpool, England, with 82 Saints on board, led by Thomas Bullock; the emigrants arrived at Nauvoo, May 31st, via New Orleans.
Sun. 19.—Joseph Smith prophesied that O. Porter Rockwell would get away honorably from the Missourians.
Tues. 21.—The ship "Clayborne" sailed from Liverpool with 106 Saints.
April. Sun. 2.—"Important Items of Instruction" were given by Joseph Smith, at Nauvoo, who also prophesied "that the commencement of the difficulties which will cause much bloodshed previous to the coming of the Son of Man, will be in South Carolina."

Important Items of Instruction, given by Joseph, the Prophet, April 2nd, 1843.
When the Saviour shall appear, we shall see him as he is. We shall see that he is a man like ourselves;
And that same sociality which exists among us here will exist among us there, only it will be coupled with eternal glory, which glory we do not now enjoy.
(John xiv. 23.) The appearing of the Father and the Son, in that verse, is a personal appearance; and the idea that the Father and the Son dwell in a man's heart, is an old sectarian notion, and is false.
In answer to the question, "Is not the reckoning of God's time, angel's time, prophet's time, and man's time according to the planet on which they reside?"
I answer, yes. But there are no angels who minister to this earth but those who do belong or have belonged to it.
The angels do not reside on a planet like this earth.
But they reside in the presence of God, on a globe like a sea of glass and fire, where all things for their glory are manifest—past, present, and future, and are continually before the Lord.
The place where God resides is a great Urim and Thummim.
This earth, in its sanctified and immortal state, will be made like unto crystal and will be a Urim and Thummim to the inhabitants who dwell thereon, whereby all things pertaining to an inferior kingdom, or all kingdoms of a lower order, will be manifest to those who dwell on it; and this earth will be Christ's.
Then the white stone mentioned in Revelations ii. 17, will become a Urim and Thummim to each individual who receives one, whereby things pertaining to a higher order of kingdoms, even all kingdoms, will be made known;
And a white stone is given to each of those who come into the celestial kingdom, whereon is a new name written, which no man knoweth save he that receiveth it. The new name is the key word.
I prophesy, in the name of the Lord God, that the commencement of the difficulties which will cause much bloodshed previous to the coming of the Son of Man will be in South Carolina.
It may probably arise through the slave question. This a voice declared to me, while I was praying earnestly on the subject, December 25th, 1832.
Thurs. 6.—At a conference held in the Temple, at Kirtland, Ohio, it was decided that all the Saints residing at that place should remove to Nauvoo. Ill.
—An important conference, which continued its sessions till the 8th, was commenced on the floor of the Temple, at Nauvoo, Ill. Joseph Smith prophesied that Christ would not come until he (Joseph) was eighty-five years of age.
I was once praying very earnestly to know the time of the coming of the Son of Man, when I heard a voice repeat the following:—
"Joseph, my son, if thou livest until thou art eighty-five years old, thou shalt see the face of the Son of Man; therefore let this suffice, and trouble me no more on this matter."
I was left thus, without being able to decide whether this coming referred to the beginning of the millennium or to some previous appearing, or whether I should die and thus see his face.
I believe the coming of the Son of Man will not be any sooner than that time.
Whatever principles of intelligence we attain unto in this life, it will rise with us in the resurrection.
And if a person gains more knowledge and intelligence in this life through his diligence and obedience than another, he will have so much the advantage in the world to come.
There is a law, irrevocably decreed in heaven before the foundations of this world, upon which all blessings are predicated;
And when we obtain any blessing from God, it is by obedience to that law upon which it is predicated.
The Father has a body of flesh and bones as tangible as man's; the Son also; but the Holy Ghost has not a body of flesh and bones, but is a personage of Spirit. Were it not so, the Holy Ghost could not dwell in us.
A man may receive the Holy Ghost, and it may descend upon him and not tarry with him.—Doc. and Cov. Sec. 130.
Mon. 10.—About one hundred and fifteen Elders were called on missions to different States, at a special conference held at Nauvoo.
Thurs. 13.—Joseph Smith preached to the British Saints, who had arrived at Nauvoo the day previous.
Sun. 23.—Six brass plates and a skeleton were found by Mr. R. Wiley and others, near Kinderhook, Pike Co., Ill.
May. Wed. 3.—The first number of the "Nauvoo Neighbor," a newspaper, was issued at Nauvoo, instead of the "Wasp," suspended.
Tuesday. 16.—On this and the following day Joseph Smith made some important remarks about the celestial glory, at Ramus, Ill.
Remarks of Joseph, the Prophet, at Ramus, Illinois, May 16th and 17th, 1843.
In the celestial glory there are three heavens or degrees;
And in order to obtain the highest, a man must enter in to this Order of the Priesthood; (meaning the new and everlasting covenant of marriage;)
And if he does not, he cannot obtain it.
He may enter into the other, but that is the end of his kingdom; he cannot have an increase.
(May 17th, 1843.) The more sure word of prophecy (mentioned by Peter) means a man's knowing that he is sealed up unto eternal life, by revelation and the spirit of prophecy, through the power of the Holy Priesthood.
It is impossible for a man to be saved in ignorance.
There is no such thing as immaterial matter. All spirit is matter, but it is more fine or pure, and can only be discerned by purer eyes.
We cannot see our bodies are purified, we shall see that it is all matter.—Doc. and Cov. Sec. 131.
Thurs. 18.—Returning to Nauvoo from his visit to Ramus, Joseph Smith dined with Judge Stephen A. Douglas, at Carthage, Hancock Co., Ill. During the conversation which took place Joseph prophesied that Judge Douglas would aspire to the Presidency of the United States, and added that if he ever turned his hand against the Latter-day Saints, he should feel the hand of the Almighty upon him, etc.
Tues. 23.—Addison Pratt, Noah Rogers, Benjamin F. Grouard and Knowlton F. Hanks were set apart for a mission to the Pacific Islands.
Fri. 26.—Joseph Smith gave endowments, and also instructions on the Priesthood and the new and everlasting covenant, to Hyrum Smith, Brigham Young, Heber C. Kimball and others, at Nauvoo.
June. Thurs. 1.—Addison Pratt, Benjamin F. Grouard, Knowlton F. Hanks and Noah Rogers left Nauvoo on their missions to the Pacific Islands.

Thurs. 8.—Elias Higbee died in Nauvoo.

Sun. 11.—A conference was held at Lima, Ill., and the branch at that place reorganized, with Isaac Morley as president, and Gardiner Snow, Bishop.

Tues. 13.—Joseph Smith left Nauvoo with his wife Emma to visit her sister, living near Dixon, Lee County, Ill.

Fri. 23.—Joseph Smith was arrested and brutally treated by Joseph H. Reynolds, sheriff of Jackson Co., Mo., and Constable Harmon T. Wilson, of Carthage, Ill., without legal process, and only through interference of friends at Dixon saved from being kidnaped and taken to Missouri.

Sat. 24.—The corner stones of the Masonic Temple at Nauvoo were laid.

—Joseph Smith secured a writ of habeas corpus and started towards Ottawa to have his case examined by Judge John D. Caton, but, arriving at Pawpaw Grove, the company learned that Judge Caton was not at home, and, therefore, returned to Dixon the following day.

Sun. 25.—News of Joseph Smith being kidnaped reached Nauvoo, and 175 men immediately started on horseback to his rescue.

Mon. 26.—Joseph Smith started under guard towards Quincy, Ill.

Tues. 27.—The company traveling with Joseph Smith was met by the brethren from Nauvoo, when it was decided that instead of going to Quincy to have the writ of habeas corpus examined, the prisoner and escort should proceed to Nauvoo.

Fri. 30.—Joseph Smith and company arrived at Nauvoo, nearly the whole city turning out to meet him. In the afternoon he addressed the people, giving the history of his arrest. While he was speaking Officers Reynolds and Wilson started for Carthage and tried to raise a mob; afterwards they petitioned Gov. Thos. Ford for militia to take Joseph out of Nauvoo by force.

July. Sat. 1.—Joseph Smith was tried before the municipal court of Nauvoo on a writ of habeas corpus and acquitted.

Sun. 2.—Joseph Smith had a pleasant interview with several Pottawatomie chiefs who had come to visit him, and a very good impression was made upon the Indians.

—The steamboat "Maid of Iowa" returned to Nauvoo, after a very adventurous trip in search of Joseph. The brethren who had participated in that river expedition, numbering about eighty, were blessed by the Prophet.

Mon. 3.—A number of Elders were called to visit the various counties of Illinois, to preach the gospel and disabuse the public mind with regard to Joseph Smith's arrest.

—Charles C. Rich and a company of twenty-five men, who had been out searching for the Prophet, returned to Nauvoo, having traveled about five hundred miles on horseback in seven days.

Tues. 4.—Nauvoo was visited by about one thousand gentlemen and ladies from St. Louis, Quincy and Burlington.

Fri. 7.—Mr. M. Braman arrived at Nauvoo as a messenger from the governor, to learn the particulars of Joseph Smith's late arrest.

Sat. 8.—Bishop George Miller arrived at Nauvoo from the Pineries with 157.000 feet of lumber and 70,000 shingles for the Temple.

Wed. 12.—The revelation on celestial marriage was written in the presence of Hyrum Smith and Wm. Clayton. (Doc. and Cov., Sec. 132.)

Revelation on the Eternity of the Marriage Covenant, including Plurality of Wives. Given through Joseph, the Seer, in Nauvoo, Hancock County, Illinois, July 12th, 1843.

Verily, thus saith the Lord unto you, my servant Joseph, that inasmuch as you have inquired of my hand, to know and understand wherein I, the Lord, justified my servants Abraham, Isaac and Jacob; as also Moses, David and Solomon, my servants, as touching the principle and doctrine of their having many wives and concubines.

Behold! and lo, I am the Lord thy God, and will answer thee as touching this matter:

Therefore, prepare thy heart to receive and obey the instructions which I am about to give unto you; for all those who have this law revealed unto them must obey the same;

For behold! I reveal unto you a new and an everlasting covenant; and if ye abide not that covenant, then are ye damned; for no one can reject this covenant, and be permitted to enter into my glory;

For all who will have a blessing at my hands, shall abide the law which was appointed for that blessing, and the conditions thereof, as were instituted from before the foundation of the world:

And as pertaining to the new and everlasting covenant, it was instituted for the fullness of my glory, and he that receiveth a fullness thereof, must and shall abide the law, or he shall be damned, saith the Lord God.

And verily I say unto you, that the conditions of this law are these:—All covenants, contracts, bonds, obligations, oaths, vows, performances, connections, associations, or expectations, that are not made and entered into, and sealed by the Holy Spirit of promise, of him who is anointed, both as well for time and for all eternity, and that too most holy, by revelation and commandment through the medium of mine anointed, whom I have appointed on the earth to hold this power, (and I have appointed unto my servant Joseph to hold this power in the last days, and there is never but one on the earth at a time, on whom this power and the keys of this Priesthood are conferred,) are of no efficacy, virtue or force, in and after the resurrection from the dead: for all contracts that are not made unto this end, have an end when men are dead.

Behold! mine house is a house of order, saith the Lord God, and not a house of confusion.

Will I accept of an offering, saith the Lord, that is not made in my name!

Or, will I receive at your hands that which I have not appointed!

And will I appoint unto you, saith the Lord, except it be by law, even as I and my Father ordained unto you, before the world was!

I am the Lord thy God, and I give unto you this commandment, that no man shall come unto the Father but by me, or by my word, which is my law, saith the Lord:

And everything that is in the world, whether it be ordained of men, by thrones, or principalities, or powers, or things of name, whatsoever they may be, that are not by me, or by my word, saith the Lord, shall be thrown down, and shall not remain after men are dead, neither in nor after the resurrection, saith the Lord your God:

For whatsoever things remain, are by me; and whatsoever things are not by me, shall be shaken and destroyed.

Therefore, if a man marry him a wife in the world, and he marry her not by me, nor by my word; and he covenant with her so long as he is in the world, and she with him, their covenant and marriage are not of force when they are dead, and when they are out of the world; therefore, they are not bound by any law when they are out of the world;

Therefore, when they are out of the world, they neither marry, nor are given in marriage; but are appointed angels in heaven, which angels are ministering servants, to minister for those who are worthy of a far more, and an exceeding, and an eternal weight of glory;

For these angels did not abide my law, therefore they cannot be enlarged, but remain separately and singly, without exaltation, in their saved condition, to all eternity, and from henceforth are not Gods, but are angels of God, for ever and ever.

And again, verily I say unto you, if a man marry a wife, and make a covenant with her for time and for all eternity, if that covenant is not by me, or by my word, which is my law, and is not sealed by the Holy Spirit of promise, through him whom I have anointed and appointed unto this power—then it is not valid, neither of force when they are out of the world, because they are not joined by me, saith the Lord, neither by my word; when they are out of the world, it cannot be received there, because the angels and the Gods are appointed there, by whom they can not pass; they cannot, therefore, inherit my glory, for my house is a house of order, saith the Lord God.

And again, verily I say unto you, if a man marry a wife by my word, which is my law, and by the new and everlasting covenant, and it is sealed unto them by the Holy Spirit of promise, by him who is anointed, unto whom I have appointed this power, and the keys of this Priesthood; and it shall be said unto them, ye shall come forth in the first resurrection; and if it be after the first resurrection, in the next resurrection; and shall inherit thrones, kingdoms, principalities, and powers, dominions, all heights and depths—then shall it be written in the Lamb's Book of Life, that he shall commit no murder whereby to shed innocent blood, and if ye abide in my covenant, and commit no murder whereby to shed innocent blood, it shall be done unto them in all things whatsoever my servant hath put upon them, in time, and through all eternity, and shall be of full force when they are out of the world; and they shall pass by the angels, and the Gods, which are set there, to their exaltation and glory in all things, as hath been sealed upon their heads, which glory shall be a fullness and a continuation of the seeds for ever and ever.

Then shall they be Gods, because they have no end; therefore shall they be from everlasting to everlasting, because they continue; then shall they be above all, because all things are subject unto them. Then shall they be Gods, because they have all power, and the angels are subject unto them.

Verily, verily I say unto you, except ye abide my law, ye cannot attain to this glory;

For strait is the gate, and narrow the way that leadeth unto the exaltation and continuation of the lives, and few there be that find it, because ye receive me not in the world, neither do ye know me.

But if ye receive me in the world, then shall ye know me, and shall receive your exaltation, that where I am, ye shall be also.

This is eternal lives, to know the only wise and true God, and Jesus Christ, whom he hath sent. I am he. Receive ye, therefore, my law.

Broad is the gate, and wide the way that leadeth to the deaths, and many there are that go in thereat; because they receive me not, neither do they abide in my law.

Verily, verily I say unto you, if a man marry a wife according to my word, and they are sealed by the Holy Spirit of promise, according to mine appointment, and he or she shall commit any sin or transgression of the new and everlasting covenant whatever, and all manner of blasphemies, and if they commit no murder, wherein they shed innocent blood—yet they shall come forth in the first resurrection, and enter into their exaltation; but they shall be destroyed in the flesh, and shall be delivered unto the buffetings of Satan unto the day of redemption, saith the Lord God.

The blasphemy against the Holy Ghost, which shall not be forgiven in the world, nor out of the world, is in that ye commit murder, wherein ye shed innocent blood, and assent unto my death, after ye have received by new and everlasting covenant, saith the Lord God; and he that abideth not this law, can in no wise enter into my glory, but shall be damned, saith the Lord.

I am the Lord thy God, and will give unto thee the law of my Holy Priesthood, as was ordained by me, and my Father, before the world was.

Abraham received all things, whatsoever he received, by revelation and commandment, by my word, saith the Lord, and hath entered into his exaltation, and sitteth upon his throne.

Abraham received promises concerning his seed, and of the fruit of his loins,—from whose loins ye are, namely, my servant Joseph,—which were to continue so long as they were in the world; and as touching Abraham and his seed, out of the world they should continue; both in the world and out of the world should they continue as innumerable as the stars; or, if ye were to count the sand upon the sea shore, ye could not number them.

This promise is yours, also, because ye are of Abraham, and the promise was made unto Abraham; and by this law are the continuation of the works of my Father, wherein he glorifieth himself.

Go ye, therefore, and do the works of Abraham; enter ye into my law, and ye shall be saved.

But if ye enter not into my law ye cannot receive the promise of my Father, which he made unto Abraham.

God commanded Abraham, and Sarah gave Hagar to Abraham to wife. And why did she do it? Because this was the law, and from Hagar sprang many people. This, therefore, was fulfilling, among other things, the promises.

Was Abraham, therefore, under condemnation? Verily, I say unto you, Nay; for I, the Lord, commanded it.

Abraham was commanded to offer his son Isaac; nevertheless, it was written, thou shalt not kill. Abraham, however, did not refuse, and it was accounted unto him for righteousness.

Abraham received concubines, and they bear him children, and it was accounted unto him for righteousness, because they were given unto him, and he abode in my law, as Isaac also, and Jacob did none other things than that which they were commanded; and because they did none other things than that which they were commanded, they have entered into their exaltation, according to the promises, and sit upon thrones, and are not angels, but are Gods.

David also received many wives and concubines, as also Solomon and Moses my servants; as also many others of my servants, from the beginning of creation until this time; and in nothing did they sin, save in those things which they received not of me.

David's wives and concubines were given unto him, of me, by the hand of Nathan, my servant, and others of the prophets who had the keys of this power; and in none of these things did he sin against me, save in the case of Uriah and his wife; and, therefore he hath fallen from his exaltation, and received his portion; and he shall not inherit them out of the world; for I gave them unto another, saith the Lord.

I am the Lord thy God, and I gave unto thee, my servant Joseph, an appointment, and restore all things; ask what ye will, and it shall be given unto you according to my word:

And as ye have asked concerning adultery—verily, verily I say unto you, if a man receiveth a wife in the new and everlasting covenant, and if she be with another man, and I have not appointed unto her by the holy anointing, she hath committed adultery, and shall be destroyed.

If she be not in the new and everlasting covenant, and she be with another man, she has committed adultery;

And if her husband be with another woman, and he was under a vow, he hath broken his vow, and hath committed adultery.

And if she hath not committed adultery, but is innocent, and hath not broken her vow, and she knoweth it, and I reveal it unto you, my servant Joseph, then shall you have power, by the power of my Holy Priesthood, to take her, and give her unto him that hath not committed adultery, but hath been faithful for he shall be made ruler over many;

For I have conferred upon you the keys and power of the Priesthood, wherein I restore all things, and make known unto you all things in due time.

And verily, verily I say unto you, that whatsoever you seal on earth, shall be sealed in heaven: and whatsoever you bind on earth, in my name, and by my word, saith the Lord, it shall be eternally bound in the heavens; and whosesoever sins you remit on earth shall be remitted eternally in the heavens; and whosesoever sins you retain on earth, shall be retained in heaven.

And again, verily I say, whomsoever you bless, I will bless, and whomsoever you curse, I will curse, saith the Lord; for I, the Lord, am thy God.

And again, verily I say unto you, my servant Joseph, that whatsoever you give on earth, and to whomsoever you give any one on earth, by my word, and according to my law, it shall be visited with blessings, and not cursings, and with my power, saith the Lord, and shall be without condemnation on earth, and in heaven;

For I am the Lord thy God, and will be with thee even unto the end of the world, and through all eternity; for verily, I seal upon you your exaltation, and prepare a throne for you in the kingdom of my Father, with Abraham your father.

Behold, I have seen your sacrifices, and will forgive all your sins; I have seen your sacrifices, in obedience to that which I have told you; go, therefore, and I make a way for your escape, as I accepted the offering of Abraham, of his son Isaac.

Verily, I say unto you, a commandment I give unto mine handmaid, Emma Smith, your wife, whom I have given unto you, that she stay herself, and partake not of that which I commanded you to offer unto her; for I did it, saith the Lord, to prove you all, as I did Abraham; and that I might require an offering at your hand, by covenant and sacrifice;

And let mine handmaid, Emma Smith, receive all those that have been given unto my servant Joseph, and who are virtuous and pure before me; and those who are not pure, and have said they were pure, shall be destroyed, saith the Lord God:

For I am the Lord thy God, and ye shall obey my voice; and I give unto my servant Joseph, that he shall be made ruler over many things, for he hath been faithful over a few things, and from henceforth I will strengthen him.

And I command mine handmaid, Emma Smith, to abide and cleave unto my servant Joseph, and to none else. But if she will not abide this commandment, she shall be destroyed, saith the Lord; for I am the Lord thy God, and will destroy her, if she abide not in my law:

But if she will not abide this commandment, then shall my servant Joseph do all things for her, even as he hath said; and I will bless him and multiply him and give unto him an hundred-fold in this world, of fathers and mothers, brothers and sisters, houses and lands, wives and children, and crowns of eternal lives in the eternal worlds.

And again, verily I say, let mine handmaid forgive my servant Joseph his trespasses; and then shall she be forgiven her trespasses, wherein she has trespassed against me; and I, the Lord thy God, will bless her, and multiply her, and make her heart to rejoice.

And again, I say, let not my servant Joseph put his property out of his hands, lest an enemy come and destroy him; for Satan seeketh to destroy; for I am the Lord thy God, and he is my servant; and behold! and lo, I am with him, as I was with Abraham, thy father, even unto his exaltation and glory.

Now, as touching the law of the Priesthood, there are many things pertaining thereunto.

Verily, if a man be called of my Father, as was Aaron, by mine own voice, and by the voice of him that sent me: and I have endowed him with the keys of the power of this Priesthood, if he do anything in my name, and according to my law, and by my word, he will not commit sin, and I will justify him.

Let no one, therefore, set on my servant Joseph; for I will justify him; for he shall do the sacrifice which I require at his hands, for his transgressions, saith the Lord your God.

And again, as pertaining to the law of the Priesthood: If any man espouse a virgin, and desire to espouse another, and the first give her consent; and if he espouse the second, and they are virgins, and have vowed to no other man, then is he justified; he cannot commit adultery, for they are given unto him; for he cannot commit adultery with that that belongeth unto him and to no one else;

And if he have ten virgins given unto him by this law, he cannot commit adultery, for they belong to him, and they are given unto him, therefore is he justified.

But if one or either of the ten virgins, after she is espoused, shall be with another man; she has committed adultery, and shall be destroyed; for they are given unto him to multiply and replenish the earth, according to my commandment, and to fulfill the promise which was given by my Father before the foundation of the world: and for their exaltation in the eternal worlds, that they may bear the souls of men; for herein is the work of my Father continued, that he may be glorified.

And again, verily, verily I say unto you, if any man have a wife, who holds the keys of this power, and he teaches unto her the law of my Priesthood, as pertaining to these things, then shall she believe, and administer unto him, or she shall be destroyed, saith the Lord your God, for I will destroy her; for I will magnify my name upon all those who receive and abide in my law.

Therefore, it shall be lawful in me, if she receive not this law, for him to receive all things, whatsoever I, the Lord his God, will give unto him, because she did not administer unto him according to my word; and she then becomes the transgressor; and he is exempt from the law of Sarah, who administered unto Abraham according to the law, when I commanded Abraham to take Hagar to wife.

And now, as pertaining to this law, verily, verily I say unto you, I will reveal more unto you, hereafter; therefore, let this suffice for the present. Behold, I am Alpha and Omega. Amen.—Doc. and Cov. Sec. 132.

August. Fri. 11.—General James Adams, of Springfield, died at Nauvoo.

Thurs. 31.—Joseph Smith moved into the Nauvoo Mansion.

September. Tues. 5.—The ship "Mitoka" sailed from Liverpool with 280 Saints, bound for Nauvoo.

Wed. 6.—At an anti-Mormon meeting, held at Carthage, Hancock Co., Ill., resolutions were adopted against Joseph Smith and the Saints in Nauvoo.

Fri. 15.—Joseph Smith opened the Nauvoo Mansion as a hotel.

Sat. 30.—Reuben Hedlock and other missionaries from Nauvoo arrived at Liverpool, England.

October. Tues. 3.—Joseph Smith gave a dinner party in the Nauvoo Mansion to about two hundred Saints.

Fri. 6.—A special conference of the Church, which continued its sessions on the 8th, was commenced at Nauvoo, Ill. Serious complaints were made against Sidney Rigdon.

Sun. 8.—At a meeting of the special conference at Nauvoo, Sidney Rigdon was sustained as a Counselor to Joseph Smith, although the Prophet said, "I have thrown him off my shoulders, and you have again put him on me; you may carry him, but I will not."

Mon. 9.—Addison Pratt, Noah Rogers, Benjamin F. Grouard and Knowlton F. Hanks sailed from New Bedford, Mass., on board the ship "Timoleon," for the Pacific Islands.

Fri. 20.—John P. Greene returned to Nauvoo, from a mission to the State of New York, with about one hundred emigrants.

Sat. 21.—The ship "Champion" sailed from Liverpool with 91 Saints, bound for Nauvoo.

Sun. 22.—Apostles Brigham Young, Heber C. Kimball and George A. Smith returned to Nauvoo from a mission to the Eastern States.

November. Fri. 3.—Knowlton F. Hanks, one of the missionaries to the Pacific Islands, died. He was the first Latter-day Saint Elder who died and was buried at sea.

Mon. 6.—Erastus Snow returned to Nauvoo with a company of emigrants from Massachusetts.

Sun. 19.—Philander Avery was kidnaped from the neighborhood of Warsaw and carried forcibly across the Mississippi river to Missouri.

December. Sat. 2.—Apostles Orson Hyde, Parley P. Pratt, Wilford Woodruff and George A. Smith and Elder Orson Spencer received their endowments at Nauvoo, Ill.; 35 persons were present.

—Daniel Avery was kidnaped from Bear Creek, Hancock Co., Ill., by a company of Missourians, and imprisoned in Monticello jail, Lewis Co., Mo., where his son Philander was already confined.

Thurs. 7.—The German brethren met at the Assembly Room at Nauvoo, chose Bishop Daniel Garn as their presiding Elder, and organized to have preaching done in their own language.

Mon. 18.—John Ellioth, a schoolmaster, was arrested and brought to Nauvoo, where he was tried and found guilty of having kidnaped Daniel Avery and son.

Tues. 19.—The Nauvoo Legion paraded near the Temple, was inspected by the officers and instructed to prepare for meeting the mob, which was gathering in the neighborhood.

Thurs. 21.—The city council of Nauvoo signed a petition to Congress, praying for redress for the Missouri persecutions.

Fri. 22.—David Holman's house, near Ramus, Hancock Co., Ill., was burned by the mob.

Mon. 25.—O. Porter Rockwell arrived in Nauvoo from nearly a year's imprisonment in Missouri without conviction, during which time he was subjected to very cruel treatment.

—Daniel Avery was liberated from his imprisonment in Missouri, his son having previously escaped.

Fri. 29.—Forty policemen were sworn into office in the city of Nauvoo.

1844

January. Tues. 2.—Jonathan Pugmire, Sr., and Thos. Cartwright, who had been imprisoned in Chester, England, about six weeks, for the accidental drowning of Mrs. Cartwright during an attempt to baptize her, Nov. 23, 1843, were acquitted.

Wed. 3.—A special session of the city council was held at Nauvoo because of Wm. Law's intimation that his life was in danger.

Fri. 5.—Wm. Marks, president of the Nauvoo Stake of Zion, being alarmed on account of a fire being kindled near his house, made statements before the city council; his fears were unfounded.

Tues. 9.—Elder Horace S. Eldredge, a county constable, was prevented by mob force from performing an official duty at Carthage.

Wed. 10.—John Smith, uncle to Joseph Smith, the Prophet, was ordained a Patriarch.

Tues. 16.—Francis M. Higbee was tried before the municipal court of Nauvoo for slandering Joseph Smith.

Tues. 23.—The ship "Fanny" sailed from Liverpool, England, with 210 Saints under the direction of Wm. McKay, bound for Nauvoo. It arrived at New Orleans, March 7th.

Mon. 29.—At a political meeting, held at Nauvoo, Joseph Smith was nominated a candidate for the Presidency of the United States. Soon afterwards a large number of Elders were sent to the various States of the Union to electioneer for him.

February. Tues. 6.—The ship "Isaac Allerton" sailed from Liverpool with 60 Saints, bound for Nauvoo.

Wed. 7.—Joseph Smith completed his address to the people of the United States, entitled: "Views of the Powers and Policy of the Government of the United States."

Sun. 11.—The ship "Swanton" sailed from Liverpool with 81 Saints, bound for Nauvoo, where they arrived April 18th.

Sat. 17.—The anti-Mormons held a convention at Carthage, Ill., the object being to devise ways and means for expelling the Saints from the State.

Tues. 20.—Joseph Smith instructed the Twelve Apostles

to send a delegation to California and Oregon, to search for a good location, to which the Saints could remove after the completion of the Temple.

Wed. 21.—A meeting of the Apostles was held at Nauvoo for the purpose of selecting 'a company to explore Oregon and California and select a site for a new city for the Saints.' Jonathan Dunham, Phinehas H. Young, David D. Yearsley and David Fullmer volunteered to go; and Alphonso Young, James Emmett, Geo. D. Watt and Daniel Spencer were requested to go.

Fri. 23.—Another meeting was held at Nauvoo, in favor of the California and Oregon expedition. Several of the brethren volunteered to go; among whom were Samuel Bent, John A. Kelting, Samuel Rolfe, Daniel Avery and Samuel W. Richards.

Sun. 25.—Joseph Smith prophesied that in five years the Saints would be out of the power of their old enemies, whether apostates or of the world.

Thurs. 29.—Moses Smith and Rufus Beach volunteered to join the Oregon exploring expedition.

March. Mon. 4.—It was decided in council at Nauvoo to cease work on the Nauvoo House until the Temple was completed.

Tues. 5.—The ship "Glasgow" sailed from Liverpool with 150 Saints, led by Hiram Clark, bound for Nauvoo, where they arrived April 26th.

Mon. 11.—Joseph Smith and the leading authorities of the Church held another council at Nauvoo about the Saints moving to the mountains.

Sun. 24.—Joseph Smith spoke in public meeting against Chauncey L. Higbee, Robert D. Foster, Wm. and Wilson Law and others, as conspirators against his life.

Tues. 26.—Joseph Smith petitioned Congress to protect the citizens of the United States, emigrating west; this he did in view of the Saints going to the mountains in the near future.

April. Fri. 5.—The Masonic Temple, which had been erected at Nauvoo, was dedicated. About five hundred and fifty members of the Masonic fraternity from various parts of the world were present.

Sat. 6.—A conference, which lasted five days, commenced at Nauvoo. The Prophet spoke to 20,000 Saints on the 7th, and on the 8th declared the whole of North and South America to be the land of Zion.

Sat. 13.—Under the leadership of Wm. Kay, 210 British Saints arrived at Nauvoo.

Thurs. 18.—Wm. and Wilson Law, Robert D. Foster and other apostates, formerly prominent in the Church, were excommunicated.

Fri. 26.—Augustine Spencer, Robert D. Foster, Charles Foster and Chauncey L. Higbee were arrested and fined, in Nauvoo, for assault and resisting the officers.

May. Wed. 1.—Elders Addison Pratt, Noah Rogers and Benjamin F. Grouard landed on the island of Tubuai (one of the Austral group), as the first missionaries of the Church to the islands of the Pacific.

Mon. 6.—Joseph Smith was arrested at Nauvoo on complaint of Francis M. Higbee, but took out a writ of habeas corpus, and was tried on the 8th before the municipal court of Nauvoo, which resulted in Joseph's acquittal, and Higbee was sentenced to pay the cost of suit.

Tues. 14.—Elders Noah Rogers and Benjamin F. Grouard landed at Papeete, Tahiti, Society Islands, as the first Latter-day Saint missionaries in that group.

Wed. 15.—Anthon H. Lund was born at Aalborg, Denmark.

Fri. 17.—A State convention was held at Nauvoo, Ill., in which Joseph Smith was nominated as a candidate for the Presidency, and Sidney Rigdon for the Vice Presidency of the United States.

Sat. 18.—The first number of "The Prophet," a weekly paper devoted to the interests of the Church, was issued in New York City, by a society of Saints.

Tues. 21.—Apostles Brigham Young, Heber C. Kimball and Lyman Wight, and about a hundred other Elders, left Nauvoo, Ill., on political missions to the East. Apostles Wilford Woodruff and Geo. A. Smith and others had left on the 9th.

Thurs. 23.—Joseph Smith had a talk with a number of Sac and Fox Indians at Nauvoo.

Sat. 25.—Joseph Smith learned that the grand jury at Carthage had found two indictments against him, one of them for polygamy.

Mon. 27.—Joseph Smith, accompanied by a number of friends, went to Carthage to have the indictments against him investigated by the circuit court, but the prosecution not being ready, the case was continued until next term.

June. Fri. 7.—The first and only number of the "Nauvoo Expositor" was published, edited by Sylvester Emmons.

Mon. 10.—The paper and printing material of the "Nauvoo Expositor" were destroyed, according to the proclamation of the city council, declaring it a nuisance.

Wed. 12.—Joseph Smith was arrested on a charge of destroying the "Expositor," tried before the municipal court of Nauvoo, and acquitted. The following day the other members of the city council were tried before the same court, on a similar charge, and honorably acquitted.

Fri. 14.—Joseph Smith communicated the facts connected with the removal of the "Expositor's" printing materials, by letter, to Gov. Thos. Ford.

Sun. 16.—In a public meeting, held at Nauvoo, a number of delegates were called to visit the different precincts in Hancock County, Ill., to lay a truthful statement of the troubles in Nauvoo before the people. Joseph Smith, as mayor of the city, also stated the facts in a proclamation.

—Addison Pratt baptized Ambrose Alexander, a white man, on the island of Tubuai, as the first convert to "Mormonism" on the Pacific Isles.

Mon. 17.—Joseph Smith and a number of others were arrested, on complaint of W. G. Ware, for riot in destroying the "Expositor," tried before Justice Daniel H. Wells, and after a long and close examination, acquitted.

—Mobs began to gather in the surrounding country, threatening to drive the Saints from Nauvoo.

Tues. 18.—The Nauvoo Legion was ordered out and the city declared under martial law, by the proclamation of the mayor, Joseph Smith. The Prophet delivered his last public address. An extra of the "Warsaw Signal" was read, in which all the "old citizens" were called upon to assist the mob in driving away the Saints.

Wed. 19.—Mobs were gathering at different points to attack Nauvoo.

Thurs. 20.—General Joseph Smith, with other officers of the Legion, examined the approaches to Nauvoo as a preparatory measure for defense. The Prophet also sent for the Twelve Apostles, who were on missions, to come home immediately.

Sat. 22.—Late in the evening Joseph and Hyrum Smith and Willard Richards left Nauvoo and crossed the Mississippi river, with the intention to fle to the West, and thus escape from their enemies.

Sun. 23.—Through the solicitation of Emma Smith, and several supposed friends, Joseph Smith and his companions returned to Nauvoo.

Mon. 24.—Joseph and Hyrum Smith, accompanied by seventeen friends, started for Carthage, to submit to another trial, under pledge of protection from Gov. Thos. Ford. On the way they received a demand from the governor to surrender the State arms in possession of the Nauvoo Legion; Joseph returned and complied with the request, and then proceeded to Carthage.

Tues. 25.—Joseph Smith and his brethren surrendered themselves to a constable at Carthage and submitted to a trial, after which they were, contrary to law, remanded to prison.

Wed. 26.—Gov. Thos. Ford had a long interview with the prisoners in Carthage jail. He renewed his promises of protection and said, if he went to Nauvoo, he would take them with him.

Thurs. 27.—Gov. Thos. Ford went to Nauvoo, leaving the prisoners in jail to be guarded by their most bitter enemies, the "Carthage Greys." About 5:20 p. m. an armed mob with blackened faces surrounded and entered the jail, and murdered Joseph and Hyrum Smith in cold blood; Apostle John Taylor was severely wounded, while Apostle Willard Richards only received a slight wound on his ear.

To seal the testimony of this book and the Book of Mormon, we announce the Martyrdom of Joseph Smith the Prophet, and Hyrum Smith the Patriarch. They were shot in Carthage jail, on the 27th of June, 1844, about five o'clock p. m., by an armed mob, painted black—of from 150 to 200 persons. Hyrum was shot first from the window, and was shot dead in the attempt, exclaiming, "O Lord, my God!" They were both shot after they were dead in a brutal manner, and both received four balls.

John Taylor, and Willard Richards, two of the Twelve, were the only persons in the room at the time; the former was wounded in a savage manner with four balls, but has since recovered; the latter, through the providence of God, escaped "without even a hole in his robe."

When Joseph went to Carthage to deliver himself up to the pretended requirements of the law, two or three days previous to his assassination, he said, "I am going like a lamb to the slaughter; but I am calm as a summer's morning; I have a conscience void of offence towards God, and towards all men. I SHALL DIE INNOCENT, AND IT SHALL YET BE SAID OF ME—HE WAS MURDERED IN COLD BLOOD." The same morning, after Hyrum had made ready to go—hall it be said to the slaughter? Yes, for so it was,—he read the following paragraph, near the close of the fifth chapter of Ether, in the Book of Mormon, and turned down the leaf upon it:—

"And it came to pass that I prayed unto the Lord that he would give unto the Gentiles grace, that they might have charity. And it came to pass that the Lord said unto me, If they have not charity, it mattereth not unto you, thou hast been faithful; wherefore thy garments are clean. And because thou hast seen thy weakness, thou shalt be made strong, even unto the sitting down in the place which I have prepared in the mansions of my Father. And now I ——— bid farewell unto the Gentiles; yea, and also unto my brethren whom I love, until we shall meet before the judgment-seat of Christ, where all men shall know that my garments are not spotted with your blood." The testators are now dead, and their testament is in force.—Doc. and Cov. (Appendix) Sec. 135.

Fri. 28.—Apostle Willard Richards and Samuel H. Smith conveyed the bodies of the martyrs to Nauvoo, where they were met by the officers of the Nauvoo Legion, and a very large number of citizens.

Sat. 29.—About ten thousand persons visited and viewed the remains of the martyred Prophet and Patriarch at Nauvoo. The funeral took place in the evening.

July. Tues. 2.—Apostle John Taylor was brought home to Nauvoo from Carthage.

Mon. 8.—Apostle Parley P. Pratt arrived at Nauvoo; he was the first of the absent Twelve to return.

Sun. 21.—Addison Pratt baptized four white men and four natives on the island of Tubuai. These natives, whose names were Naboto and his wife Telii, Pauma and Hamoe, were the first of the Polynesian race to embrace the fullness of the gospel.

Thurs. 25.—Erastus Snow and many other Elders arrived at Nauvoo. All seemed weighed down with gloom.

Sun. 28.—Apostle Geo. A. Smith and a party of brethren arrived at Nauvoo.

—A branch of the Church, consisting of eleven members, was organized by Addison Pratt on the island of Tubuai (Society Islands mission). This was the first branch of the Church on the Pacific Islands.

Tues. 30.—Samuel H. Smith, brother of the Prophet, died at Nauvoo as a martyr to persecution.

Wed. 31.—Apostle Amasa M. Lyman arrived at Nauvoo.

August. Fri. 2.—A political meeting of the citizens of Hancock County, Ill. was held near the Temple at Nauvoo. Great excitement prevailed throughout the county. The mob party was determined to elect officers who would screen the murderers of Joseph and Hyrum Smith and exterminate the "Mormons."

Sat. 3.—Sidney Rigdon arrived at Nauvoo from Pittsburgh, Pa.
Sun. 4.—Sidney Rigdon preached to the Saints at Nauvoo, declaring that a guardian should be appointed to build up the Church to Joseph, intimating that he was the man who should lead the Saints.
Tues. 6.—Apostles Brigham Young, Heber C. Kimball, Lyman Wight, Orson Hyde, Orson Pratt and Wilford Woodruff arrived at Nauvoo.
Wed. 7.—The Twelve met in council with Elder Taylor, at his house at Nauvoo; they found him recovering from his wounds. In the afternoon, the Twelve, the High Council and High Priests held a meeting in the Seventies' Hall, where Sidney Rigdon's claim to lead the Church was considered.
Thurs. 8.—A special meeting of the Church was held at Nauvoo, in which Elder Rigdon harangued the Saints about choosing a guardian, etc. In the afternoon meeting the Twelve Apostles, through their President, Brigham Young, asserted their right to lead the Church, which claim was recognized by the unanimous vote of the people.
Mon. 12.—At a council of the Twelve Apostles, Amasa M. Lyman was admitted into their quorum, having been previously ordained to the Apostleship. Elder Wilford Woodruff was appointed to go to England to preside over the British mission.
Thurs. 15.—The Twelve issued an epistle to the Saints in all the world, giving such instructions and words of counsel to the Church as were necessary after the martyrdom of the Prophet.
Wed. 28.—Wilford Woodruff, Dan Jones and Hiram Clark, with their families, left Nauvoo for England.
Sat. 31.—Brigham Young was elected lieutenant-general of the Nauvoo Legion, and Charles C. Rich, major-general.
September. Sun. 8.—At a meeting of the High Council of Nauvoo, Sidney Rigdon was excommunicated from the Church.
Thurs. 19.—The ship "Norfolk" sailed from Liverpool with 143 Saints, bound for Nauvoo.
Tues. 24.—Seventy presidents to preside over the Seventies, and fifty High Priests to preside in different sections of the country, were ordained.
Fri. 27.—Gov. Thos. Ford visited Nauvoo with about five hundred troops and three pieces of artillery, ostensibly for the purpose of bringing the murderers of Joseph and Hyrum Smith to justice.
Sat. 28.—About this time several persons in Hancock County were indicted for the murder of Joseph and Hyrum Smith, among whom was Jacob C. Davis.
October. Mon. 7.—At the general conference held in Nauvoo, Wm. Marks was rejected as president of the Stake and John Smith appointed in his stead.
Tues. 8.—A reorganization of the Seventies took place in the general conference at Nauvoo. At the close eleven quorums were filled and properly organized, and about forty Elders organized as a part of the 12th quorum. The senior presidents of these twelve quorums of Seventy were Joseph Young (1st), Edson Barney (2nd), Elias Hutchins (3rd), Jacob Gates (4th), Henry Jacobs (5th), Israel Barlow (6th), Randolph Alexander (7th), John Puck (8th), Philip Ettleman (9th), Albert P. Rockwood (10th), Jesse P. Harmon (11th), and Hyrum Dayton (12th).
About the same time the 16th quorum of Seventy was organized, with Dana Jacobs as senior president.
November. Sat. 23.—Edward Hunter was ordained a Bishop and set apart to take care of the 5th Ward in Nauvoo.
December. Sun. 1.—Apostle Parley P. Pratt was appointed to go to the city of New York to regulate and counsel the emigration from Europe and preside over all the eastern branches of the Church.
Sun. 22.—The 13th, 14th and 15th quorums of Seventy were organized in Nauvoo, with Charles Bird, Jonathan Dunham and John Lytle as senior presidents.

1845

January.—During this month the legislature of Illinois repealed the city charter of Nauvoo.
Fri. 2.—Apostle Wilford Woodruff and accompanying missionaries arrived at Liverpool, England. Wilford Woodruff succeeded Reuben Hedlock as president of the British mission.
Sun. 12.—The 17th quorum of Seventy was organized at Nauvoo, with Daniel M. Repsher as senior president.
Fri. 17.—The ship "Palmyra" sailed from Liverpool, England, with a company of Saints, under the direction of Amos Fielding, bound for Nauvoo.
Sun. 26.—The 18th quorum of Seventy was organized in Nauvoo, with John W. Bell as senior president.
February. Sun. 9.—The 19th quorum of Seventy was organized at Nauvoo, with Samuel Moore as senior president.
March. Sun. 2.—The 21st quorum of Seventy was partly organized at Nauvoo, with Erastus H. Derby as senior president.
Tues. 18.—The 20th quorum of Seventy was organized at Morley's Settlement, Hancock Co., Ill., with Hiram Blackman, of Bear Creek branch, as senior president.
April. Sun. 6.—The Twelve Apostles issued "A proclamation to all the kings of the world, to the President of the United States of America, to the governors of the several States, and to the rulers and people of all nations."
—The general conference of the Church was commenced at Nauvoo, Ill. It was continued till the 9th and attended by about twenty-five thousand people. In honor of the Prophet Joseph it was decided by vote to change the name of Nauvoo to "City of Joseph."
Mon. 7.—At a conference held in Manchester, England, Dan. Jones, who had lately arrived from America, was appointed president of the Wrexham conference (Wales), consisting of himself and wife. One year later there were seven hundred members of the Church in Wales, largely through his instrumentality.
Tues. 8.—At a conference held in Manchester, England, the so-called Joint Stock Company was organized, with Thomas Ward as president.
Wed. 9.—The 22nd, 23rd, 24th, 25th and 26th quorums of Seventy were organized at Nauvoo, with David Clough (22nd), Benjamin Sweatt (23rd), Lewis Eger (24th), Thomas Spiers (25th), and Benjamin Jones (26th) as senior presidents.
Sat. 12.—A U. S. deputy marshal of Illinois arrived at Nauvoo, with writs for Brigham Young and others, but failed to arrest them.
Wed. 16.—As the city charter of Nauvoo had been repealed, a small part of the city was incorporated as the town of Nauvoo.
Thurs. 24.—In a general council held at Nauvoo, it was decided to send a written appeal in behalf of the Saints to the President of the United States, and to the governor of every State in the Union, except the State of Missouri. This resolution was subsequently acted upon, but without any responses, except from the governor of Arkansas, who replied in a respectful and sympathetic letter.
May. Mon. 19.—Some of the citizens of Nauvoo went to Carthage, to attend the trial of the murderers of Joseph and Hyrum Smith.
Sat. 24.—President Brigham Young and others who had been secreted for some time, to avoid arrest and persecution by their enemies, appeared at Nauvoo and took part in the laying of the capstone of the Temple, in the presence of a large number of Saints.
Fri. 30.—The murderers of Joseph and Hyrum Smith were acquitted by the jury at Carthage, although every one who witnessed the trial was satisfied of their guilt.
June.—At the close of its fifth volume the "Millennial Star" (England) was changed from a monthly to a semi-monthly periodical.
Sun. 8.—The organization of the 27th quorum of Seventy was commenced in Nauvoo.
Tues. 10.—The 27th quorum of Seventy was organized at Nauvoo, with Rufus Beach as senior president.
Mon. 23.—A constable came to Nauvoo with writs for the arrest of Apostles Brigham Young and John Taylor, and others, but he did not succeed in finding them.
Thurs. 26.—The first stone was laid for a new baptismal font in the Nauvoo Temple.
Fri. 27.—This being the first anniversary of the martyrdom of Joseph and Hyrum Smith, the day was spent in prayer and fasting by the Saints in Great Britain.
July. Thurs. 3.—Noah Rogers sailed from Tahiti, Society Islands, per ship "Three Brothers," on his return to Nauvoo, Ill., where he arrived Dec. 29, 1845. He was the first Latter-day Saint Elder who circumnavigated the globe as a missionary.
Sat. 5.—The first number of the "New York Messenger" was published by Samuel Brannan in New York City, as a continuation of the "Prophet," suspended.
Sun. 27.—The 28th and 29th quorums of Seventy were organized in Nauvoo, with John Gaylord and Augustus A. Farnham as senior presidents.
August. Sat. 9.—Twenty-eight persons were killed by an explosion in a colliery at Cromstock, near Aberdare, South Wales. Several of the Saints employed in the colliery escaped, having been warned by vision of the catastrophe.
Sat. 23.—The dome of the Nauvoo Temple was raised.
Sun. 31.—The 30th quorum of Seventy was organized in Nauvoo, with Sahiel Savage as senior president.
September.—One hundred and thirty-five teams were sent from Nauvoo to bring in the families and grain from the surrounding country.
—The few Saints who still remained in Kirtland, Ohio, were persecuted by their enemies, who took possession of the Temple.
—The ship "Oregon" sailed from Liverpool, England, with a company of Saints bound for Nauvoo, Ill.
Wed. 10.—A mob attacked the house of Edmund Durfee, in Morley's settlement, Hancock Co., Ill., turned the people out of doors, set fire to the buildings and threatened instant death to men, women and children. The mob then burned all the other houses, barns and shops in the settlement and turned the inhabitants into the open air. Also a farming settlement called Green Plains, inhabited by about eighty members of the Church, was burned by the mob.
Mon. 15.—The mob drove Jacob Backenstos, sheriff of Hancock County, from his home at Carthage.
Tues. 16.—The mob made an effort to kill the sheriff. In his defense O. Porter Rockwell killed Frank A. Worrell, one of the murderers of the mob, who was an officer of the guard at Carthage jail when Joseph and Hyrum Smith were killed.
Thurs. 18.—Sheriff Backenstos, with a posse consisting of some seven hundred men, surrounded Carthage, Ill., to make a proclamation to the mobbers to disperse, which, however, was not obeyed, as they went to Missouri and other places, preparing for new depredations.
Wed. 24.—As the persecutions in Hancock County continued to rage, the Saints commenced to leave their possessions in the smaller settlements and flee to Nauvoo for protection. The authorities of the Church made a proposition to the mob to have the Saints leave the State of Illinois the following spring.
Tues. 30.—General John J. Hardin arrived at Nauvoo with four hundred troops, pretending to hunt for criminals, but undoubtedly had other motives for his diligent search of the Temple and other public buildings.
October. Wed. 1.—The Apostles at Nauvoo had an important consultation with General John J. Hardin, Senator Stephen A. Douglas, W. B. Warren and J. A. McDougal, commissioners from a convention held in Carthage, about the removal of the Saints.
Sun. 5.—The Nauvoo Temple was so far completed that a meeting, attended by five thousand people, was held in it.
Mon. 6.—The first general conference of the Saints for three years was commenced in the Temple, the Prophet Joseph having ordered that they should not hold another general conference until they could meet in that house. The conference continued for three days. Wm. Smith was dropped as an Apostle and Patriarch.

Sun. 12.—Wm. Smith was excommunicated from the Church at Nauvoo.
Sat. 25.—Major Warren came into Nauvoo with a body of troops and threatened to put the place under martial law. After he had left, the authorities of the Church sent E. A. Bedell and Bishop Geo. Miller with a communication to Gov. Thomas Ford. They informed him of Major Warren's threats and implored him to dismiss the troops under his command, as the Saints had more to fear from them than from the mob at large. The governor did not grant their request.
Sun. 26.—The 31st quorum of Seventy was partly organized at Nauvoo, with Edmund M. Webb as senior president.
November.—Edmund Durfee was killed by the mob in Green Plains, Hancock Co., Ill. About the same time Joshua A. Smith was poisoned at Carthage.
Sun. 30.—The attic story of the Nauvoo Temple was dedicated.
December. Mon. 15.—After laboring nearly one year and eight months on Tubuai, Elder Addison Pratt left that island to join Elder Benjamin F. Grouard, who had commenced a most successful missionary work on Anaa, one of the Tuamotu Islands.
Sun. 21.—The 32nd quorum of Seventy was organized at Nauvoo, with Geo. Mayer as senior president.
Tues. 23.—The famous "Bogus Brigham" arrest was made, the officers taking Elder Wm. Miller to Carthage, believing that they had captured Apostle Brigham Young.
Sat. 27.—A U. S. deputy marshal visited Nauvoo, again searching for the Twelve and others, but failed to make any arrest.
During this month many of the Saints received their blessings and endowments in the Nauvoo Temple.

1846

January.—The 33rd quorum of Seventy was organized with Albern Allen as senior president.
Tues. 13.—At a council held in the Nauvoo Temple, to take into consideration the means of organizing for the removal of the Saints, 140 horses and 70 wagons were reported ready for immediate service.
Fri. 16.—The ship "Liverpool" sailed from Liverpool, England, with 45 Saints, under the direction of Hiram Clark, bound for Nauvoo via New Orleans.
Thurs. 22.—Apostle Wilford Woodruff sailed from Liverpool to return to America, because of the contemplated removal of the Church to the mountains. Reuben Hedlock, with Thomas Ward and John Banks as counselors, succeeded him in the presidency of the British Mission.
Sat. 24.—A general meeting of the official members of the Church was held in the Nauvoo Temple, for the purpose of arranging the affairs of the Church, prior to its removal from Nauvoo.
Fri. 30.—The vane was placed on the Nauvoo Temple.
February, Wed. 4.—The Saints at Nauvoo commenced crossing the Mississippi river for the purpose of moving west. Charles Shumway was the first to cross the river.
—The ship "Brooklyn" sailed from New York with 235 Saints on board. They were well supplied with implements of husbandry, and necessary tools for establishing a new settlement. They also took with them a printing press and materials, which afterwards were used in publishing the first newspaper issued in California.
Thurs. 5.—The 34th quorum of Seventy was organized at Nauvoo, with David W. Rogers as one of the presidents. About the same time the 35th quorum of Seventy was organized.
Mon. 9.—A fire, which broke out in the Nauvoo Temple, was put out before it did much damage.
—John E. Page was disfellowshipped.
Tues. 10.—Joseph Young was appointed to preside over the Saints who remained at Nauvoo.
Sun. 15.—Apostles Brigham Young and Willard Richards, with their families, and Apostle Geo. A. Smith crossed the Mississippi river for the West. They traveled nine miles, and camped on Sugar Creek, where Pres. Young spent the following day organizing the camps of the Saints.
Tues. 17.—Apostle Heber C. Kimball arrived in the camp on Sugar Creek. Willard Richards was appointed camp historian and Wm. Clayton clerk.
Wed. 18.—President Young and a few others returned to Nauvoo, but rejoined the camp the following day.
Wed. 25.—Bishop George Miller and company were the first to leave the camp ground on Sugar Creek to travel westward.
Sat. 28.—A petition to the governor of Iowa, in which the Saints asked for protection while passing through the Territory, was approved by the Twelve. At this time the camp consisted of four hundred wagons, very heavily loaded. The teams were too weak for rapid journeying. Most of the families had provisions for several months, while some were quite destitute.
March.—During the month the camps of the Saints in Iowa traveled about one hundred miles. The roads were almost impassable most of the way, and the Saints suffered much from cold and exposure, the weather being very windy and stormy.
Sun. 1.—The camps of the Saints made a general move from Sugar Creek and traveled five miles in a northwesterly direction.
Fri. 27.—At a council held at Apostle Parley P. Pratt's camp, near the east fork of Shoal Creek, the camps of the Saints were more perfectly organized. Brigham Young was elected president over all the "Camps of Israel."
April.—The Saints in England suffered spiritually and financially on account of the Joint Stock Company business, which was urged upon them by speculating Elders.
Fri. 24.—The advance portion of the camps arrived at a place on the east fork of Grand river, 145 miles from Nauvoo, which the Saints called Garden Grove, where a temporary settlement was commenced for the benefit of the companies which should follow after.

Thurs. 30.—The Nauvoo Temple was dedicated privately, Elder Joseph Young offering the dedicatory prayer.
May. Fri. 1.—The Nauvoo Temple was publicly dedicated by Apostle Orson Hyde.
Sun. 10.—About three thousand Saints met in the Temple at Nauvoo. Apostle Wilford Woodruff preached.
Mon. 11.—Part of the camps continued the journey from Garden Grove, and on the 18th arrived at the middle fork of Grand river, on the land of the Pottawatomie Indians, where another temporary settlement was established, called Mount Pisgah. This was 172 miles from Nauvoo.
Thurs. 21.—A general council of the camps at Mount Pisgah had under consideration the subject of sending an exploring company to the Rocky Mountains that year. The subsequent call for the Mormon Battalion, however, made this impossible.
Sun. 31.—Elder Noah Rogers, recently returned from a mission to the Society Islands, died at Mount Pisgah, Iowa. His remains were the first interred in the burying ground at that place.
—A three days' conference convened in Manchester, England, in which the business of the Joint Stock Company was the main topic.
June.—Amos Fielding, who returned to Nauvoo this month, counted 902 west-bound wagons in three days. By this some idea may be formed of the number of teams on the road at that time.
Mon. 1.—Elder Jesse C. Little wrote an appeal to James K. Polk, President of the United States, in behalf of the Saints. He afterwards called on the President, Vice-President and several members of the cabinet.
—A conference of the Church was organized on the Isle of Man, with Samuel J. Lees as president.
Tues. 2.—Pres. Brigham Young left Mount Pisgah and continued the journey westward.
Fri. 12.—Elder Jesse C. Little left Philadelphia for the West, accompanied by Col. Thos. L. Kane, who had decided to visit the camps of the Saints.
Sun. 14.—Pres. Brigham Young, Heber C. Kimball, Geo. Miller and Parley P. Pratt arrived on the banks of the Missouri river, with their respective companies. Here a ferry boat was built soon afterwards, when some of the Saints commenced to cross the river.
Tues. 16.—The advance camps of the exiled Saints moved back to the bluffs across Mosquito Creek, and encamped near good water, about nine miles from the trading post. There they remained till the ferry boat was built.
Mon. 22.—At this date about five hundred wagons had arrived on the Missouri river; nine of the Apostles were already there.
Thurs. 25.—The ship "Brooklyn" arrived at Honolulu, Hawaii, on its way to California.
Fri. 26.—Capt. James Allen, of the U. S. army, arrived at Mount Pisgah and had an interview with Apostle Wilford Woodruff and Pres. Wm. Huntington and council. He was the bearer of a circular to the "Mormons," making a requisition on the camps of the Saints for four or five companies of men, to serve as volunteers in the war with Mexico. Capt. Allen was advised to visit the authorities of the Church at Council Bluffs.
Sat. 27.—John E. Page was excommunicated from the Church.
Tues. 30.—Capt. Allen arrived at Council Bluffs, and on the following day he met with the authorities of the Church showing his authority for raising five hundred volunteers from the camps of the Saints. The same day Pres. Young and Capt. Allen addressed the brethren who had assembled, and the general council voted unanimously to comply with the requisition from the government.
July.—The first number of "Prophwyd y Jubili" (The Prophet of Jubilee) was published by Dan Jones, in Wales, as the Church organ in that country.
—The Saints having continued to arrive from the East, there were now fourteen companies encamped on the bluffs near the Missouri river.
Fri. 3.—Pres. Brigham Young and others started for Mount Pisgah, where they arrived on the 6th, after having met eight hundred wagons and carriages.
Tues. 7.—Pres. Brigham Young, Heber C. Kimball and Jesse C. Little addressed a meeting of the brethren at Mount Pisgah on the subject of raising a battalion to march to California. Sixty-six volunteered. Geo. W. Langley was sent to Garden Grove with a letter to the presiding brethren there upon the same subject. A similar communication was sent to Nauvoo.
Thurs. 9.—Pres. Brigham Young and others left Mount Pisgah for Council Bluffs, where they arrived on the 12th.
Sat. 11.—John Hill, Archibald N. Hill, Caleb W. Lyons, James W. Huntsman, Gardiner Curtis, John Richards, Elisha Mallory and J. W. Phillips were severely whipped by mobocrats, while harvesting wheat twelve miles from Nauvoo.
Mon. 13.—In obedience to a call of the authorities of the camps of the Saints the men met at headquarters on Mosquito Creek. Col. Thos. L. Kane, who had arrived in camp, and Capt. Allen were present. Pres. Young, Capt. Allen and others addressed the people in regard to furnishing the battalion. Four companies were raised on that day and the day following. The fifth company was organized a few days later.
At this time severe persecutions were again raging against the few remaining Saints at Nauvoo, and also against the "new citizens" who had bought the property of the members of the Church, who had already left the city for the west.
Thurs. 16.—At a council of the Twelve held at Council Bluffs, Ia., Ezra T. Benson was ordained an Apostle, and took the place of John E. Page, who had apostatized. Apostles Orson Hyde, Parley P. Pratt and John Taylor were appointed to go to England to see the order there; Reuben Hedlock and Thomas Ward, who at that time presided over the British mission, were disfellowshipped for disregard of council.
—Four companies of the volunteers were brought together in a hollow square and mustered into service by their respective captains. They were interestingly addressed by several

of the Apostles. A few days later (July 20th) they commenced their march toward Fort Leavenworth.
Fri. 17.—A number of men were selected to take care of the families of the volunteers.
Tues. 21.—A High Council was selected to preside in all temporal and spiritual matters at Council Bluffs.
Wed. 22.—The fifth and last company of the Mormon Battalion left the camps of the Saints and started for Fort Leavenworth.
Thurs. 23.—Samuel Boley, a member of the Mormon Battalion, died on the road to Fort Leavenworth.
Wed. 29.—The Mormon Battalion passed through St. Joesph, Mo.
—The ship "Brooklyn," with the Saints from the State of New York, arrived at Yerba Buena (now San Francisco), Cal.
August. Sat. 1.—The Mormon Battalion, now numbering 549 souls, including officers, privates and servants, arrived at Fort Leavenworth.
Fri. 7.—At a council of the Apostles it was decided that the brethren on the west side of the Missouri river should settle together. A municipal High Council, consisting of Alpheus Cutler, Winslow Farr, Ezra Chase, Jedediah M. Grant, Albert P. Rockwood, Benjamin L. Clapp, Samuel Russell, Andrew Cahoon, Cornelius P. Lott, Daniel Russell, Elnathan Eldredge and Thomas Grover, was appointed to superintend the affairs of the Church there.
—A small company of Saints from Mississippi, under the direction of John Brown, arrived at Pueblo, on the Arkansas river, where it wintered, waiting till the following spring for the advance companies of the "Mormon" emigration.
Sun. 9.—The first meeting was held at Cutler's Park, where the exiled Saints at that time intended to spend the winter. The municipal High Council which was accepted by the people and the place named Cutler's Park, in honor of Alpheus Cutler. This place, which now became the temporary headquarters of the camps, is three miles from the spot where Winter Quarters afterward was built.
Thurs. 13.—Three companies of the Mormon Battalion began to move west from Ft. Leavenworth, after having received their arms, camp equipages, etc. On the 14th the other two companies took up the line of march.
—About this time the mobbers in Hancock County, Ill., concluded to drive the few remaining "Mormon" families from Nauvoo.
Sun. 23.—Col. James Allen, commander of the Mormon Battalion, died at Ft. Leavenworth. The command then devolved on Capt. Jefferson Hunt, as the ranking officer, but notwithstanding this, Lieut. A. J. Smith shortly after assumed the command.
September. Tues. 8.—Col. Thos. L. Kane left the camps of the Saints for the East.
Thurs. 10.—The few remaining Saints at Nauvoo, of whom only about one hundred and twenty-five were able to bear arms, were attacked by an armed mob, about eighteen hundred strong, who with five pieces of artillery bombarded the city for several days. The brethren organized for self-defense and stopped the mobbers about two miles from the city.
Fri. 11.—The mobbers were prevented from entering Nauvoo by the gallantry of the "Spartan Band," who fired on the enemy with cannons made of steamboat shafts.
—A site for building winter quarters for the Saints was selected on the west bank of the Missouri river. Teams began to return to Nauvoo after the poor.
—The Mormon Battalion reached the Arkansas river.
Sat. 12.—The battle of Nauvoo took place. Wm. Anderson, his son Augustus and Isaac Norris were killed, and others of the defenders were wounded. The mob force, which again was driven back, also sustained considerable loss.
Wed. 16.—The enemy was driven back from Nauvoo the fourth time. Through the negotiations of one hundred citizens of Quincy, a treaty was completed, by which the Saints should be allowed to move away in peace.
—Some of the families accompanying the Mormon Battalion left the main body on the Arkansas river, in care of Capt. Higgins, for Pueblo. About this time Alva Phelps, a member of the Battalion, died.
Thurs. 17.—The mob entered Nauvoo, and, notwithstanding the treaty, immediately drove out the Saints, and treated some of the brethren in a most brutal manner.
Sun. 20.—Norman Sharp, a member of the Mormon Battalion, accidentally shot himself in the arm and died a few days later, from the effect of the wound.
Tues. 22.—A partial reorganization of the Nauvoo Legion took place at Cutler's Park.
Wed. 23.—The Saints began to move to the new location for Winter Quarters.
Thurs. 24.—A conference was held at Putuahara, Anaa, at which 852 members of the Church in the Society Islands mission were represented.
Sun. 27.—The first public meeting at Winter Quarters was held. By this time most of the Saints had removed from Cutler's Park to Winter Quarters.
October.—Apostle Orson Hyde succeeded Reuben Hedlock as president of the British Mission, and the Joint Stock Company was dissolved.
—Martin Harris and others, followers of the apostate James J. Strang, preached among the Saints in England, but could get no influence.
Fri. 2.—The Mormon Battalion reached Red river.
Sat. 3.—The Battalion was divided in two divisions, of which the first, containing the strongest and most able-bodied men, arrived at Santa Fe, N. M., on the 9th, and the second, containing the sick and the women, on the 12th.
—Apostles Orson Hyde and John Taylor arrived at Liverpool, England, and immediately issued a circular to the British Saints, advising them to "patronize the Joint Stock Company no more for the present."
Wed. 7.—The teams which were sent back to help the poor away from Nauvoo, arrived at the Mississippi river, opposite Nauvoo.
Fri. 9.—The camp of the poor was organized and started for the West. Flocks of quails visited the camp and were easily caught. This was a providential supply of food for the suffering exiles.
Tues. 13.—Capt. P. St. George Cooke assumed command of the Mormon Battalion at Santa Fe, by order of General Kearney.
Wed. 14.—Apostle Parley P. Pratt and Elders Franklin D. Richards, Samuel W. Richards and Moses Martin arrived at Liverpool, England, from the camps of the Saints in the wilderness.
Sat. 17.—On this and the following day a general conference was held in Manchester, England, under the presidency of Apostles Hyde, Pratt and Taylor. Dan Jones reported one thousand Saints in Wales, and a conference was organized in Ireland, with Paul Jones as president.
Sun. 18.—The sick detachment of the Mormon Battalion, consisting of about ninety men, left Santa Fe for Pueblo, under command of Capt. James Brown.
Mon. 19.—The Battalion left Santa Fe for California. On the journey it suffered much from excessive marches, fatigue and short rations.
Tues. 27.—Milton Smith, a member of the Battalion, died on his way with the sick detachment to Pueblo.
November.—A memorial to the Queen of England "for the relief, by emigration, of a portion of her poor subjects," was circulated for signatures among the British Saints.
Tues. 3.—James Hampton, a member of the Mormon Battalion, died.
Wed. 4.—Milton Kelly, a member of the Battalion, died at Pueblo.
Tues. 10.—A detachment of fifty-five sick men of the Battalion, under the command of Lieutenant W. W. Willis, was separated from the main body and started back to Pueblo. Two days later John Green died.
Tues. 17.—Capt. Brown's sick detachment of the Battalion arrived at Pueblo.
Sat. 21.—John D. Lee and Howard Egan arrived at Winter Quarters, as messengers from the camps of the Mormon Battalion beyond Santa Fe.
—Joseph Wm. Richards, a member of the Mormon Battalion, died at Pueblo.
Fri. 27.—Capt. O. M. Allen with the remainder of the sick camp from Nauvoo, arrived at the east bank of the Missouri river.
Sat. 28.—Elijah Freeman and Richard Carter, members of the Battalion (Lieut. Willis' detachment), died, and were buried by their comrades four miles south of Secora, on the Rio Grande.
—The main body of the Battalion reached the summit of the Rocky Mountains.
December.—Winter Quarters, afterwards known as Florence, Nebraska, consisted at this time of 538 log houses and 83 sod houses, inhabited by 3,483 souls, of whom 334 were sick and 75 were widows. There were 814 wagons, 145 horses, 29 mules, 388 yoke of oxen and 463 cows. The place was divided in 22 Wards, each presided over by a Bishop. The Ward on the east side of the river contained 210 souls.
—The Saints on the banks of the Missouri river made great exertions to provide themselves with shelter and food for the winter. Notwithstanding this, there was much privation and suffering among them.
—The presidency of the Church in England published a balance sheet of the Joint Stock Company, showing that the Saints had been swindled and their means squandered by officers of the company.
Fri. 11.—The Mormon Battalion had an extraordinary encounter with wild buffaloes on the San Pedro river.
Fri. 18.—The Battalion left Tucson. During the remainder of the month it suffered almost beyond human endurance from overmarching, and want of food and water.
Sun. 20.—Capt. Willis' detachment of the Battalion joined the detachments of Captains Brown and Higgins at Pueblo.
Tues. 22.—The Battalion arrived at the Pima village, and encamped the following day by a village of Maricopa Indians.

1847

January.—The committee who had been appointed to settle up the Joint Stock Company business in England were able to pay one shilling and three pence on the pound of capital stock paid in.
Fri. 8.—The Mormon Battalion reached the mouth of the Gila river. Two days later (10th) it crossed the Colorado.
Thurs. 14.—A revelation was given through Pres. Brigham Young, at Winter Quarters, showing the will of the Lord concerning the camps of Israel (Doc. and Cov., Sec. 136); in accordance with which the Twelve Apostles proceeded to organize the camps by appointing captains of hundreds and fifties. The captains were directed to organize their respective companies.

The Word and Will of the Lord, given through President Brigham Young, at the Winter Quarters of the Camp of Israel, Omaha Nation, West Bank of Missouri River, near Council Bluffs, January 14th, 1847.

The word and will of the Lord concerning the Camp of Israel in their journeyings to the West.
Let all the people of the Church of Jesus Christ of Latter-day Saints, and those who journey with them, be organized into companies, with a covenant and promise to keep all the commandments and statutes of the Lord our God.
Let the companies be organized with captains of hundreds, captains of fifties, and captains of tens, with a president and his two counselors at their head, under the direction of the Twelve Apostles.
And this shall be our covenant, that we will walk in all the ordinances of the Lord.
Let each company provide themselves with all the teams, wagons, provisions, clothing, and other necessaries for the journey that they can.
When the companies are organized, let them go with their might, to prepare for those who are to tarry.
Let each company with their captains and presidents decide how many can go next spring; then choose out a sufficient number of able-bodied and expert men, to take teams, seeds, and farming utensils, to go as pioneers to prepare for putting in spring crops.

Let each company bear an equal proportion, according to the dividend of their property, in taking the poor, the widows, the fatherless, and the families of those who have gone into the army, that the cries of the widow and the fatherless come not up into the ears of the Lord against this people.

Let each company prepare houses, and fields for raising grain, for those who are to remain behind this season, and this is the will of the Lord concerning his people.

Let every man use all his influence and property to remove this people to the place where the Lord shall locate a Stake of Zion; And if ye do this with a pure heart, in all faithfulness, ye shall be blessed; you shall be blessed in your flocks, and in your herds, and in your fields, and in your houses, and in your families.

Let my servants Ezra T. Benson and Erastus Snow organize a company;

Also, let my servants Orson Pratt and Wilford Woodruff organize a company;

And let my servants Amasa Lyman and George A. Smith organize a company;

And appoint presidents, and captains of hundreds, and of fifties, and of tens.

And let my servants that have been appointed go and teach this my will to the saints, that they may be ready to go to a land of peace.

Go thy way and do as I have told you, and fear not thine enemies; for they shall not have power to stop my work.

Zion shall be redeemed in mine own due time. * * * Doc. and Cov. Sec. 136.

Tues. 19.—John Perkins, a member of the Mormon Battalion, died at Pueblo.

—Apostles Parley P. Pratt and John Taylor and a small company of Saints sailed from Liverpool, England, bound for New Orleans, but were on account of storms obliged to return to Liverpool, after nine days of rough sailing.

Sat. 23.—Orson Spencer arrived at Liverpool, England, to preside over the British Mission as successor to Apostle Orson Hyde. Elder Franklin D. Richards had had temporary charge of the mission.

Wed. 27.—The Mormon Battalion arrived at San Luis Rey, a deserted Catholic mission, and from a neighboring bluff first saw the Pacific Ocean.

Fri. 29.—The Battalion arrived at a point near San Diego, Cal.

February. Mon. 1.—The Battalion was ordered back to San Luis Rey, where it rested a short time.

—Apostles Parley P. Pratt and John Taylor again sailed from Liverpool, bound for New Orleans, where they landed March 10th.

Mon. 15.—John H. Tippetts and Thomas Woolsey arrived at Winter Quarters, as messengers from the Battalion boys at Pueblo, after extreme sufferings on the journey.

Tues. 23.—Apostle Orson Hyde sailed from Liverpool, England, returning to America. He arrived at New York April 6th, and at the camps of the Saints, on the Missouri river, May 12th.

Sun. 28.—Arnold Stevens, a corporal in the Mormon Battalion, died at Pueblo.

March.—At this time Winter Quarters contained 41 blocks, 820 lots, 700 houses, 22 wards, etc.

Thurs. 4.—Thomas Ward, formerly president of the British mission, died in England.

Mon. 15.—Company B of the Mormon Battalion was ordered from San Luis Rey to garrison San Diego.

Fri. 19.—Most of the Mormon Battalion, except company B, (which was stationed as a garrison at San Diego), left San Luis Rey for Pueblo de Los Angeles, where it arrived on the 23rd.

Sun. 28.—After nearly three years missionary labors in the Society Islands mission, Elder Addison Pratt sailed from Papeete, Tahiti, per ship "Providence," on his return to America, leaving Benjamin F. Grouard in charge of the mission.

Mon. 29.—A number of the Pioneers at Winter Quarters reported themselves ready to start for the mountains.

—About that time David Smith, of the Mormon Battalion, died at San Luis Rey.

April. Mon. 5.—Apostle Heber C. Kimball moved out four miles from Winter Quarters, with six teams, and formed a nucleus to which the company of Pioneers could gather.

Thurs. 8.—Apostle Parley P. Pratt returned to Winter Quarters from his mission to England.

Sat. 10.—M. S. Blanchard, of the Mormon Battalion, died at Pueblo.

Sun. 11.—Company C of the Mormon Battalion was ordered to the Cajon Pass, about forty-five miles east of Los Angeles.

Wed. 14.—Pres. Brigham Young and his brethren of the Twelve left Winter Quarters for the Rocky Mountains. They joined the Pioneer camp near the Elkhorn river.

Thurs. 16.—The Pioneer company was organized. It consisted of 73 wagons, 143 men, 3 women and 2 children—148 souls.

Sat. 24.—The Mormon Battalion was ordered to erect a fort on a hill near Los Angeles.

Tues. 27.—Mrs. Hunter, wife of Captain Jesse D. Hunter, of the Battalion, died at San Diego, Cal.

May. Tues. 11.—Albert Dunham, of the Battalion, died at San Diego, from an ulcer on the arm.

Thurs. 13.—Gen. Stephen F. Kearney left Los Angeles for Ft. Leavenworth, accompanied by about fifteen brethren of the Battalion. The general and four of the men went by water and the rest by land to Monterey.

Mon. 24.—The sick detachments of the Battalion which had wintered at Pueblo, took up the line of march for California.

Mon. 31.—Gen. Stephen F. Kearney's detachment of the Battalion left Monterey and traveled by way of the Sacramento Valley, over the Sierra Nevadas, via Ft. Hall, Soda Springs, and the Platte River, where it met several companies of Saints, going west, and arrived at Ft. Leavenworth in August.

June. Tues. 1.—The Pioneers arrived at Ft. Laramie. A company of Saints, numbering seventeen persons, who had left the State of Mississippi the previous year, joined the Pioneers at that place. It was a part of the company who had wintered at Pueblo; the remainder of it came on with Capt. Brown's detachment of the Battalion.

Thurs. 3.—The Pioneers crossed the North Fork of the Platte river at Ft. Laramie, having traveled on the left bank of the Platte, from the Elkhorn to that point.

Fri. 11.—Amasa M. Lyman, who had been sent back from the Pioneer camp, and other Elders, met the sick detachment of the Mormon Battalion on Pole Creek.

Mon. 14.—The Pioneers recrossed the Platte river from its south to north side, 124 miles west of Ft. Laramie.

—The first company of emigrating Saints was organized at Elkhorn river for journeying west, and on the 19th about five hundred and seventy-five wagons from Winter Quarters had crossed the "Horn."

Wed. 16.—Capt. Brown's detachment of the Mormon Battalion reached Ft. Laramie, and continued the following day westward, intending, if possible, to overtake the Pioneers, who had passed twelve days before.

Sun. 20.—Thomas Smith was arrested and imprisoned at Covington, Warwickshire, England, for having cast out evil spirits. After examination, he and Richard Currell, the subject of administration, were dismissed, there being no cause of action.

Sun. 27.—The Pioneers crossed the South Pass of the Rocky Mountains. On the following day they met Capt. James Bridger who considered it imprudent to bring a large population into the Great Basin, until it could be ascertained that grain could be raised there. So sanguine was he that it could not be done, that he said he would give one thousand dollars for the first ear of corn produced there.

Tues. 29.—Henry W. Bigler and others of the Mormon Battalion, stationed at San Diego, cleared the first yard for moulding brick in California.

Wed. 30.—Samuel Brannan, on his way from California, met the Pioneers at Green river, with news from the Saints who went out in the ship "Brooklyn" the year previous.

July. Sun. 4.—Thirteen men of Capt. Brown's detachment of the Mormon Battalion, overtook the Pioneers on Green river.

Wed. 7.—The Pioneers arrived at Fort Bridger.

Tues. 13.—The Pioneers were encamped at the head of Echo Canyon; Apostle Orson Pratt was appointed to take 23 wagons and 42 men and precede the main company of Pioneers into Great Salt Lake Valley.

Thurs. 15.—Company B of the Mormon Battalion joined the main body at Los Angeles.

Fri. 16.—The Battalion was honorably discharged at Los Angeles.

Tues. 20.—Eighty-one of the members of the Battalion re-enlisted for six months at Los Angeles. Four days later they were ordered to San Diego, where they arrived on Aug. 2nd, and were stationed as a provost guard to protect the citizens from Indian raids, etc. Those who did not re-enlist, organized into companies for traveling, and a few days later took up the line of march towards the East.

Wed. 21.—The advance company of the Pioneers camped in Emigration Canyon, went into the valley, and a circuit of about twelve miles was made before they got back to camp at 9 p. m.

Thurs. 22.—The advance company of Pioneers entered Great Salt Lake Valley and camped on Canyon Creek.

Fri. 23.—The advance company moved about three miles and camped on what was subsequently known as the 8th Ward Square of Salt Lake City. Apostle Orson Pratt called the camp together, dedicated the land to the Lord, invoked his blessings on the seeds about to be planted, and on the labors of the Saints in the valley. The camp was organized for work. The first successful plowing was done by Wm. Carter. A company commenced the work of getting out water for irrigation. Pres. Brigham Young, who was sick, and those with him, encamped at the foot of the Little Mountain.

Sat. 24.—Pres. Young entered Great Salt Lake Valley and joined the main body of Pioneers at 2 p. m. Not a member of the company had died on the journey.

Sun. 25.—Religious services were held for the first time in Great Salt Lake Valley. Geo. A. Smith preached the first public discourse and the Sacrament was administered there for the first time.

Mon. 26.—Pres. Young and others ascended what is now known as Ensign Peak, north of Salt Lake City, and named it.

Tues. 27.—Some Ute Indians visited the Pioneer camp. The Twelve and a few others started west from the Pioneer camp on an exploring expedition. Crossing the stream which forms the outlet of Utah lake, they named it the Jordan river, and then proceeded to Black Rock, eighteen miles further, where the company took a bath in the lake.

Wed. 28.—The exploring party returned to camp, a council was held and the Temple Block located.

Thurs. 29.—The detachment of the Mormon Battalion, which had wintered at Pueblo, on the Arkansas river, under Capt. James Brown, arrived in Great Salt Lake Valley, accompanied by the Saints from Mississippi. This increased the number in camp to about four hundred souls.

August. Mon. 2.—The survey of a city was commenced in Great Salt Lake Valley.

Wed. 4.—Twenty-seven of the re-enlisted Battalion boys were ordered to San Luis Rey, Cal., to protect the mission property.

Fri. 6.—The Apostles in Great Salt Lake Valley renewed their covenants by baptism, and the rest of the company soon after followed their example.

Mon. 9.—Catharine C. Steele, wife of John Steele, of the Battalion, gave birth to a female child who was named Young Elizabeth Steele. She was the first white child born in the Valley.

Tues. 10.—The building of the "Old Fort" was commenced by the Pioneers in Great Salt Lake Valley on what is now known as the Pioneer Square, Sixth Ward, Salt Lake City.

Wed. 11.—Milton H. Therlkill, three years old, was accidentally drowned near the Pioneer camp. This was the first death among white people in Great Salt Lake Valley.

Wed. 18.—Nearly half of the Pioneers left Great Salt Lake Valley with ox teams, on their return to Winter Quarters for their families.

Fri. 20.—The returning Battalion boys arrived on the Sacramento river. On the 24th they reached a settlement of white people, and received the first news of the Saints settling in Great Salt Valley.

Sat. 21.—Albert Carrington, John Brown and Wm. W. Rust ascended to the summit of the Twin Peaks, the highest mountain near Great Salt Lake Valley.

Sun. 22.—At a special conference held in Great Salt Lake Valley, the city, which had been commenced by the Pioneers, was named Great Salt Lake City; the river Jordan and the mountain streams on the east side of the Valley were also named.

Thurs. 26.—The second company of returning Pioneers left Great Salt Lake Valley for Winter Quarters to forward the emigration, where they arrived Oct. 31st. On their trip they met several companies of Saints who followed in the track of the Pioneers. Between six and seven hundred wagons, with about two thousand souls, arrived in the Valley that fall. When the Pioneers left for Winter Quarters, the colonists in the Valley had laid off a fort, built 27 log houses, plowed and planted 84 acres with corn, potatoes, beans, buckwheat, turnips, etc.

September.—The members of the Mormon Battalion who had returned to California from the Truckee river were employed by Capt. John A. Stutter, digging mill-races and erecting mills, near the place where Sacramento City now stands.

Fri. 3.—The returning Battalion boys, having crossed the Sierra Nevada Mountains, reached the place where the unfortunate Hastings company had perished the previous winter. A number of human bodies were yet lying unburied on top of the ground. Henry P. Hoyt died.

A few days later the soldiers were met by Samuel Brannan, James Brown and others, on the Truckee river. Brannan brought word from Pres. Brigham Young for those who had no means of subsistence to remain in California and work during the winter, and come to the Valley in the spring. About half of the company then returned to California.

Wed. 8.—Sergeant Lafayette N. Frost, of the re-enlisted Mormon Battalion company, died at San Diego.

Mon. 20.—Harriet P. Young, wife of Lorenzo D. Young, gave birth to a male child, which was subsequently named Lorenzo Dow. He died March 22, 1848. This was the first white male child born in Great Salt Lake Valley.

October. Sun. 3.—The Saints in Great Salt Lake Valley were organized into a Stake of Zion with John Smith as president and Charles C. Rich and John Young as counselors. Selections for a High Council were also made. Charles C. Rich was elected chief military commander in the Valley.

Sat. 16.—Those of the discharged Battalion boys who did not return to California arrived in Great Salt Lake City.

Mon. 18.—Thirty-two of the Battalion boys, who were anxious to meet their families at Winter Quarters, left Great Salt Lake City for that place, where they arrived Dec. 18th, after a hard journey.

November.—Capt. James Brown returned to Great Salt Lake Valley from a visit to California, bringing about $5,000 in gold.

Fri. 5.—Neal Donald, one of the Battalion boys who had re-enlisted, died at San Diego.

December.—Apostle Parley P. Pratt and others visited the Utah lake, where they launched a boat.

Sun. 5.—At a council of the Apostles held in the house of Apostle Orson Hyde, (attended by Brigham Young, Heber C. Kimball, Orson Hyde, Willard Richards, Wilford Woodruff, Geo. A. Smith, Amasa M. Lyman and Ezra T. Benson), Brigham Young was unanimously elected President of the Church, with authority to nominate his Counselors, which he did by naming Heber C. Kimball as his first and Willard Richards as his second Counselor.

Mon. 6.—John Smith, the Prophet's uncle, was chosen by the Council of the Apostles, as Patriarch to the whole Church.

Sat. 11.—Philemon C. Merrill, with fifteen others of the Mormon Battalion, arrived at Winter Quarters; they left Great Salt Lake City Oct. 8th.

Thurs. 23.—The Twelve issued an important epistle from Winter Quarters to all the Saints, announcing, among other things, that emigration could be recommenced.

Fri. 24.—A general conference of the Church was commenced in a log Tabernacle erected by the Saints on the east side of the Missouri river (on the present site of Council Bluffs). It lasted four days. On the last day (Dec. 27th) Brigham Young was unanimously sustained as President of the Church, with Heber C. Kimball as his first and Willard Richards as second Counselor. John Smith was sustained as presiding Patriarch to the Church.

1848

January. Mon. 24.—Gold was discovered in Sutter's mill race, which had been dug by the Mormon Battalion boys. This discovery soon put the whole country in a fever of excitement.

February.—Nathaniel Thos. Brown, one of Pres. Brigham Young's Pioneer corps, was shot and killed at Council Bluffs, Ia.

Wed. 2.—By the treaty of Guadalupe Hidalgo, Mexico, Upper California, including what is now Utah, was ceded to the United States.

Sun. 20.—The ship "Carnatic" sailed from Liverpool, England, with 120 Saints, bound for Great Salt Lake Valley, under the direction of Franklin D. Richards. It arrived at New Orleans about April 19th, whence the company proceeded up the Mississippi and Missouri rivers to Winter Quarters, and thence commenced the journey across the plains.

March.—About this time Davis County was settled by Perrigrine Sessions, who located the settlement subsequently called Bountiful.

Mon. 6.—The Great Salt Lake City fort contained 423 houses and 1,671 souls. The adjoining farming field consisted of 5,133 acres of land, of which 872 acres were sown with winter wheat.

Thurs. 9.—The ship "Sailor Prince" sailed from Liverpool, England, with 80 Saints, under the direction of Moses Martin.

Tues. 14.—The re-enlisted company of the Mormon Battalion was disbanded at San Diego, and on the 25th twenty-five men, with Henry G. Boyle as captain, started for Great Salt Lake Valley, where they arrived June 5th.

April. Thurs. 6.—At a conference held in the log Tabernacle (Miller's Hollow), on the east side of the Missouri river, the settlement at that place was called Kanesville, in honor of Col. Thomas L. Kane.

May.—A company of Saints from Great Britain arrived at Winter Quarters.

Tues. 9.—Twenty-two wagons—the first of the season—left Winter Quarters for the Valley and traveled twenty-seven miles to the Elkhorn river.

Thurs. 11.—Apostle Orson Pratt left Winter Quarters on a mission to England.

Fri. 26.—Apostle Orson Pratt left Winter Quarters for the second time for Great Salt Lake Valley.

Wed. 31.—At Elkhorn river, Pres. Young commenced to organize the emigrating Saints into companies of hundreds, fifties and tens.

June.—In the commencement of this month Pres. Young broke camp at the Elkhorn and started for Great Salt Lake Valley, with a company consisting of 1,220 souls and 397 wagons. He was followed by Heber C. Kimball's company of 662 souls and 226 wagons, and Willard Richard's company consisting of 526 souls and 169 wagons. The last wagons left Winter Quarters July 3rd, leaving that place almost destitute of inhabitants.

—Myriads of big crickets came down from the mountains into the Great Salt Lake Valley, and began to sweep away fields of grain and corn. The grain, however, was mostly saved by the arrival of immense flocks of sea gulls, which devoured the crickets.

Tues. 6.—Capt. James Brown entered into negotiations with Miles M. Goodyear, an Indian trader, located on the present site of Ogden City, for the purchase of all the lands, claims and improvements, owned by Goodyear, by virtue of a Spanish grant. Brown paid $3,000 for the improvements, and soon after located himself on the Weber.

Sat. 24.—Captain Daniel Browett. Daniel Allen and Henderson Cox, three of the Battalion boys, left Sutter's Fort, Cal., on an exploring trip across the Sierra Nevada Mountains. A few days later they were killed and their bodies terribly mutilated by Indians.

July. Sun. 2.—About thirty-seven of the Battalion boys, who had spent the winter and spring in the Sacramento Valley, Cal., commenced their eastward journey from Pleasant Valley, fifty miles from Sutter's Fort, with 18 wagons, bringing with them two cannons. After a dangerous and adventurous journey they arrived in Great Salt Lake City Oct. 1st.

Sat. 22.—Patriarch Asahel Smith died at Iowaville, Wapello Co., Iowa.

Wed. 26.—Apostle Orson Pratt and family arrived in England from Winter Quarters.

August.—Apostle Orson Pratt succeeded Orson Spencer as president of the British mission.

Wed. 9.—The Great Salt Lake City fort contained 450 buildings and 1,890 inhabitants. There were three saw mills and one temporary flouring mill running, and others in course of construction.

Thurs. 10.—The Saints in Great Salt Lake City had a feast to celebrate the first harvest gathered in the Great Basin.

Sun. 13.—At a general conference, held in Manchester, England, on this and the following day, 28 conferences and 350 branches, with a total of 17,902 members, were represented in the British mission. Wm. Howell was called to go to France to open up a missionary field in that country.

September. Thurs. 7.—The ship "Erin's Queen" sailed from Liverpool, England, with 232 Saints, under the direction of Simeon Carter, bound for St. Louis, where the emigrants arrived Nov. 6th. Most of them remained there during the winter.

Mon. 18.—John Henry Smith was born at Carbunca, near Kanesville, Ia.

Wed. 20.—Pres. Brigham Young arrived in Great Salt Lake Valley with the advance portion of his company. Pres. Kimball's division arrived a few days later, and the other companies all reached the Valley in good season.

Sat. 23.—Reuben Brinkworth, who had been deaf and dumb for five years, was restored to his speech and hearing under the administrations of the Elders, at Newport, Monmouthshire, England.

Sun. 24.—The ship "Sailor Prince" sailed from Liverpool, England, with 311 Saints on board, under the direction of L. D. Butler, bound for Great Salt Lake Valley.

Thurs. 28.—Addison Pratt arrived in Great Salt Lake City from a five years' mission to the Society Islands, where about twelve hundred persons had been baptized.

October. Sun. 1.—At a public meeting held in Great Salt Lake City, it was voted to build a council house by tithing labor, and Daniel H. Wells was appointed superintendent of its erection.

Sun. 8.—At a general conference held in the Great Salt Lake City fort, Brigham Young was unanimously sustained as President of the Church, with Heber C. Kimball and Willard Richards as his Counselors.

Mon. 9.—The Nauvoo Temple was burned through the work of an incendiary.

Tues. 10.—Apostle Willard Richard's company arrived in Great Salt Lake City, having been met by teams from the Valley.

Thurs. 19.—Apostle Amasa M. Lyman's company arrived in Great Salt Lake City.

Sat. 21.—Oliver Cowdery bore his testimony to the truth of the Book of Mormon, in a conference held at Kanesville, Ia.

November.—The High Council at Kanesville voted to receive Oliver Cowdery back into the Church by baptism, according to his own humble request. Soon afterwards he was baptized, and he made preparation to take a mission to England.

December. Sun. 3.—At a meeting, held in the Great Salt Lake City fort, fellowship was withdrawn from Apostle Lyman Wight and Bishop Geo. Miller.

1849

January.—The first number of "Udgorn Seion" (Zion's Trumpet), was issued in the interest of the Church in Wales, as a continuation of "Prophwyd y Jubili."

Mon. 1.—John Smith, uncle of the Prophet Joseph, was ordained Patriarch to the whole Church.

—The first $1 bill of "Valley Currency" was signed by Brigham Young, Heber C. Kimball and Thos. Bullock.

Fri. 19.—Marcus B. Thorpe, one of Pres. Brigham Young's Pioneers, was murdered in California.

Mon. 22.—Pres. Brigham Young and Thos. Bullock were engaged in setting type for the 50-cent bills of the Valley paper currency. This was the first type setting in Great Salt Lake Valley.

Mon. 29.—The ship "Zetland" sailed from Liverpool, England, with 358 Saints, bound for Great Salt Lake Valley, under the presidency of Orson Spencer. It arrived at New Orleans April 2nd, and the emigrants arrived at Kanesville, Iowa, May 17th, having suffered much from cholera while passing up the Missouri river.

February.—The Stake of Zion in Great Salt Lake Valley was reorganized with Daniel Spencer as president and David Fullmer and Willard Snow counselors. A High Council was also organized, of which the members were: Isaac Morley, Phineas Richards, Shadrach Roundy, Henry G. Sherwood, Titus Billings, Eleazer Miller, John Vance, Levi Jackman, Ira Eldredge, Elisha H. Groves, Wm. W. Major and Edwin D. Woolley.

Mon. 5.—This was a very cold day in Great Salt Lake City, the thermometer showed 33 degrees F. below zero.

Tues. 6.—The ship "Ashland" sailed from Liverpool, England, with 187 Saints, under the direction of John Johnson, bound for Great Salt Lake Valley.

Wed. 7.—The first number of the "Frontier Guardian," a semi-monthly four-page newspaper, was published by Apostle Orson Hyde at Kanesville, Iowa.

—The ship "Henry Ware" sailed from Liverpool, England, with 225 Saints on board, bound for Great Salt Lake Valley, under the direction of Robert Martin.

Mon. 12.—Charles C. Rich, Lorenzo Snow, Erastus Snow and Franklin D. Richards were ordained Apostles, to fill the vacancies in the Council of Twelve Apostles caused by the reorganization of the First Presidency and the rejection of Lyman Wight.

Wed. 14.—Great Salt Lake City was divided into nineteen ecclesiastical Wards of nine blocks each.

Fri. 16.—The First Presidency and the Apostles, in council assembled, divided the country lying south of Great Salt Lake City into four Bishop's Wards, namely, Canyon Creek (afterwards Sugar House), Mill Creek, Holladay (afterwards Big Cottonwood) and South Cottonwood.

Thurs. 22.—At a council meeting held in Great Salt Lake City, the following Bishops were ordained and set apart to preside in the City Wards: David Fairbanks, 1st Ward; John Lowry, 2nd Ward; Christopher Williams, 3rd Ward; Wm. Hickenlooper, 6th Ward; Wm. G. Perkins, 7th Ward; Addison Everett, 8th Ward; Seth Taft, 9th Ward; David Pettigrew, 10th Ward; Benjamin Covey, 12th Ward; Edward Hunter, 13th Ward; John Murdock, 14th Ward; Abraham O. Smoot, 15th Ward; Isaac Higbee, 16th Ward; Joseph L. Heywood, 17th Ward and James Hendricks, 19th Ward.

Sun. 25.—The ship "Buena Vista" sailed from Liverpool, England, with 249 Welsh Saints, under the direction of Dan Jones.

Mon. 26.—Work was commenced on the Council House, Great Salt Lake City.

March.—Provo, Utah Valley, was settled by John S. Higbee and some thirty others. On March 18th a branch of the Church was organized with John S. Higbee as president. During the year the settlers had some trouble with the Indians.

—A post office was established in Great Salt Lake City, with Joseph L. Heywood as postmaster.

—The Icarians arrived at Nauvoo, Ill., and bought the ruins of the Temple, with a view to refit it for school purposes.

Mon. 5.—The ship "Hartley" sailed from Liverpool, England, with 220 Saints bound for Great Salt Lake Valley, under the direction of W. Hulme. It arrived at New Orleans April 28th.

Thurs. 8.—A convention, which was held for three days, convened in Great Salt Lake City. Before its adjournment a State constitution for the proposed State of Deseret was adopted. Almon W. Babbitt was soon after sent as delegate to Congress, with a petition asking for admission into the Union.

Mon. 12.—An election took place for officers of the provisional government of the State of Deseret. Brigham Young was chosen governor; Willard Richards, secretary; Newel K. Whitney, treasurer; Heber C. Kimball, chief judge; John Taylor and Newel K. Whitney, associate judges; Daniel H. Wells, attorney general; Horace S. Eldredge, marshal; Albert Carrington, assessor and collector of taxes; Joseph L. Heywood, surveyor of highways. Magistrates were also appointed for the several Wards.

Thurs. 15.—John Van Cott sold a peck of potatoes for $5 in Great Salt Lake City, which was considered cheap.

Sun. 25.—The first public meeting was held on the Temple Block, Great Salt Lake City.

Wed. 28.—The Nauvoo Legion was partly reorganized. Daniel H. Wells was appointed major-general. The first company organized was under the command of Capt. George D. Grant, and those who belonged to it were styled "minute men."

April.—The settlers in Utah Valley built a fort near the present site of Provo City.

Sun. 8.—The Fourth Ward, Great Salt Lake City, was organized with Benjamin Brown as Bishop.

Mon. 9.—The First Presidency issued the "First General Epistle" to the whole Church from Great Salt Lake Valley. By this time the people in the Great Salt Lake City fort had commenced to move out to their city lots.

May. Sat. 5.—Elder Elijah Malin, of Winter Quarters, died of cholera, in St. Louis, Mo., returning from a mission to Pennsylvania.

June, Mon. 11.—Caleb Baldwin, one of the brethren who had been imprisoned with the Prophet Joseph in Liberty jail, Mo., died in Great Salt Lake City.

Sat. 16.—Parties from the east en route for the California gold mines began to arrive in the Valley, and during the summer they traveled through by thousands. They brought all kinds of merchandise, wagons, tools and farming implements, etc., which were sold to the Saints below original cost, in exchange for provisions.

July.—Elder William Howell visited France and began to preach the gospel; he baptized the first person on July 30th, at Havre, and during the remainder of the year he baptized a few more. Among the number was a Baptist preacher about sixty years old.

Mon. 2.—The General Assembly of the Provisional State of Deseret met for the first time in Great Salt Lake City.

Sat. 21.—The first endowment in Great Salt Lake Valley was given to Addison Pratt on Ensign Peak.

Tues. 24.—The first celebration to commemorate the entrance of the Pioneers into Great Salt Lake Valley was held in Great Salt Lake City.

August. Fri. 24.—Wm. W. Phelps ascended to the top of Mount Nebo, south of Utah Valley, to make scientific observations.

Tues. 28.—Captain Howard Stansbury and party of surveyors arrived in Great Salt Lake Valley, accompanied by Lieutenant John W. Gunnison.

September. Sat. 1.—Wm. Dayton was accidently killed and Geo. W. Bean crippled for life, by the premature discharge of a cannon at Fort Utah (Provo), Utah.

Sun. 2.—The ship "James Pennell" sailed from Liverpool, England, with 236 Saints, under the direction of Thomas H. Clark, bound for Great Salt Lake Valley. It arrived at New Orleans, Oct. 22nd.

Wed. 5.—The ship "Berlin" sailed from Liverpool with 253 Saints, under James G. Brown's direction, bound for Great Salt Lake Valley; it arrived at New Orleans Oct. 22nd. Twenty-six died on the voyage of cholera.

Sun. 23.—Orson Spencer arrived in Great Salt Lake Valley, with his company of British Saints.

October. Wed. 3.—Three companies of emigrating Saints were exposed to the fury of a tremendous snow storm near the South Pass. Sixty head of cattle perished.

Sat. 6.—The Deseret Dramatic Association was organized in Great Salt Lake City.

—On this and the following day a general conference of the Church was held in Great Salt Lake City, at which the Perpetual Emigration Fund was commenced. John Taylor, Curtis E. Bolton and John Pack were called on missions to France; Erastus Snow and Peter O. Hansen to Denmark; Lorenzo Snow and Joseph Toronto to Italy; Franklin D. Richards, Joseph W. Johnson, Joseph N. Young, Job Smith, Haden W. Church, Geo. B. Wallace and John S. Higbee to Great Britain; Charles C. Rich and Francis M. Pomeroy to Lower California; Addison Pratt, James S. Brown and Hiram H. Blackwell to the Society Islands, and John E. Forsgren to Sweden. A "Carrying Company," for carrying goods from the Missouri river to the Valley and also to run a wagon passenger train, was organized. It was voted to lay off a city in Capt. James Brown's neighborhood (Ogden), and another one in Utah Valley (Provo); also to make a settlement in San Pete Valley (Manti). For the latter Isaac Morley, Charles Shumway and Seth Taft were appointed a presidency.

Fri. 12.—The first Presidency issued the "Second General Epistle" from Great Salt Lake Valley, to the Saints in all the world.

Mon. 19.—The missionaries' camp was organized for traveling. Shadrach Roundy being appointed president. The company consisted of 35 men, with 12 wagons, 1 carriage, and 42 mules. Among the Elders were Apostles Lorenzo Snow, Erastus Snow and Franklin D. Richards. Bishop Edward Hunter and other prominent men. It was the first company of missionaries sent from the Rocky Mountains.

November. Sat. 10.—The ship "Zetland" sailed from Liverpool, England, with 250 Saints, under the direction of S. H. Hawkins. It arrived at New Orleans Dec. 24th.

Mon. 12.—The missionaries traveling east were attacked by about two hundred Cheyenne warriors, on the Plate river, but escaped unhurt.

Mon. 19.—San Pete Valley was settled by a company, under the guidance of Isaac Morley, Seth Taft and Charles Shumway. They located near the present site of Manti.

Fri. 23.—An exploring company, consisting of about fifty men, was organized at Capt. John Brown's house, on Big Cottonwood, with Apostle Parley P. Pratt as president; it started the next day to explore what is now southern Utah.

December.—The general assembly of the Provisional State of Deseret met for the second time and held adjourned meetings at intervals through the winter. Among the important business done was the creating of Great Salt Lake, Weber, Utah, San Pete, Juab and Tooele counties, appointing a supreme court, chartering a State University, etc.

—The first Sunday school in Great Salt Lake City was opened by Elder Richard Ballantyne, in the 14th Ward, Great Salt Lake City.

Sat. 1.—Nineteen men on foot arrived in Great Salt Lake City from the East in a very destitute condition, having left their wagons in the snow on Echo creek, forty miles back.

Fri. 7.—After an adventurous journey, during which an overruling Providence was clearly made manifest in behalf of the Elders, the missionaries arrived at Old Ft. Kearney, on the Missouri River.

Mon. 24.—A terrific wind swept over Great Salt Lake Valley from the south.
Before the end of the year, the Saints who had settled on the Little Cottonwood creek, south of Great Salt Lake City, were organized into a Ward, named Little Cottonwood, with Silas Richards as Bishop.

1850

In Utah Valley, where a number of new settlements were founded during the year, the Saints had trouble with the Indians. The first missions of the Church were opened in France, Italy and Denmark by Apostles John Taylor, Lorenzo Snow and Erastus Snow respectively, assisted by other Elders. Later in the year the first Latter-day Saint Elders also arrived in Switzerland and in Hawaii (Sandwich Islands) and commenced missionary labors. The Territory of Utah was created by act of Congress.
January.—The British Mission contained about twenty-eight thousand Saints, having increased more than ten thousand during the last sixteen months.
—Apostle Parley P. Pratt's company explored the southern country as far south as the mouth of the Santa Clara river, beyond the Rim of the Basin.
Thurs. 10.—The ship "Argo" sailed from Liverpool, England, with 402 Saints, under the direction of Jeter Clinton. It arrived at New Orleans March 8th.
Mon. 21.—Apostle Parley P. Pratt's company on its return from the south went into winter camp on Chalk Creek (near the present site of Fillmore), unable to travel further with wagons through the deep snow. Twenty-four of the men with the best horses and mules pushed on to Great Salt Lake City, and the remainder followed in March.
February. Thurs. 7.—A company of about one hundred minute men, under command of Capt. Geo. D. Grant, left Great Salt Lake City for Utah County, to protect the settlers there against the depredations of the Indians (Utes).
Fri. 8.—On this and the following day a battle was fought between the "minute men" and about seventy Indian warriors under Big Elk, close to Utah Fort (now Provo), in which several were killed and wounded on both sides. The Indians subsequently retreated to the mountains.
Mon. 11.—General Daniel H. Wells, who had arrived in Utah Valley with more men, pursued the Indians and overtook them near Table Rock. Five warriors were killed and the rest taken prisoners. The next day, when the Indians tried to overpower the guard, another battle ensued in which several natives were killed. The squaws and children were subsequently taken to Great Salt Lake City, and a number of the children adopted by citizens.
Fri. 22.—A light shock of earthquake was felt in Great Salt Lake Valley.
March. Sun. 3.—Oliver Cowdery died in the faith, at Richmond, Ray Co., Mo., of consumption.
Tues. 5.—A branch of the Church was organized at Ogden with Lorin Farr as president.
Tues. 26.—Col. Thos. L. Kane delivered his famous lecture on the "Mormons" before the Historical Society of Pennsylvania, at Philadelphia.
April.—Elder Wm. Howell organized a branch of the Church with six members at Boulogne-sur-Mer, France. This was the first branch of the Church raised up in that country.
May. Mon. 27.—The walls of the Nauvoo Temple were blown down by a hurricane.
June.—The water was higher in Great Salt Lake Valley than ever before since the Pioneers arrived. A number of bridges were washed away and other damage done. Emigrants en route to California passed through Great Salt Lake City almost daily.
Sat. 8.—The first mail of the season from the States arrived in Great Salt Lake Valley.
Fri. 14.—Apostle Erastus Snow and Elders John E. Forsgren and Geo. P. Dykes landed in Copenhagen, Denmark, as the first missionaries to Scandinavia, except Elder Peter O. Hansen, who had arrived there a few weeks before.
Sat. 15.—The first number of the "Deseret News" was published in Great Salt Lake City; Willard Richards, editor.
Tues. 25.—Apostle Lorenzo Snow and Elders Joseph Toronto and Thos. B. H. Stenhouse arrived at Genoa, Italy, as the first Latter-day Saint missionaries to that country.
July.—Under the new management of Apostle Orson Pratt, the "Millennial Star" had increased its circulation from about three thousand seven hundred to over twenty-two thousand.
Thurs. 4.—Parley's Canyon, Utah, was opened for travel under the name of the "Golden Pass"; Parley P. Pratt, proprietor. The toll was 75 cts. for each conveyance drawn by two animals, and 10 cents for each additional draught, pack or saddle animal, etc. The Newark Rangers, of Kendall County, Ill. was the first company to follow Apostle Pratt through the pass, which opened a new road through the mountains from the Weber river to Great Salt Lake Valley.
—The general assembly of the State of Deseret held a joint session and passed an ordinance taxing the sale of liquor at the rate of 50 per cent ad valorum.
Fri. 19.—Elder John E. Forsgren baptized his brother Peter A. Forsgren, near Grefle, Sweden. This was the first baptism in Sweden by divine authority in this dispensation.
August.—Lehi, Utah Valley, was first settled; about the same time the two neighboring towns of American Fork and Pleasant Grove were settled.
Mon. 5.—Pres. Brigham Young pointed out the site for a Temple on the hill where the Manti Temple, San Pete Co., Utah, now stands.
Mon. 12.—The first baptisms in Denmark, by divine authority in this dispensation, took place in Copenhagen. Apostle Erastus Snow baptizing fifteen persons in Oresund. The first man baptized was Ole U. C. Monster and the first woman Anna Beckstrom.
Wed. 28.—Capt. Howard Stansbury and suite, having completed their surveys, left Great Salt Lake City, on their return to Washington, D. C.

—Presidents Brigham Young and Heber C. Kimball, Apostle Orson Hyde, Bishop Newel K. Whitney, Daniel H. Wells and others left Great Salt Lake City for the purpose of locating a city on the Weber (Ogden). They returned on the 31st, having located the corner stake and given a plan for the city of Ogden.
September. Sun. 1.—A small branch of the Church was organized in Dublin, Ireland, by Elder Edward Sutherland.
Isaac Morley was authorized to select one hundred men, with or without families, to settle San Pete Valley.
Mon. 9.—The act of Congress providing for the organization of the Territory of Utah was approved. The original size of the Territory was about 225,000 square miles, being bound on the north by Oregon, east by the summit of the Rocky Mountains, south by the 37th parallel of north latitude, and west by California.
Sun. 15.—At a public meeting (resolved into a special conference of the Church), held in the Bowery, Salt Lake City, Brigham Young was chosen president of the Perpetual Emigrating Fund Company, with Heber C. Kimball, Willard Richards, Newel K. Whitney, Orson Hyde, George A. Smith, Ezra T. Benson, Jedediah M. Grant. Daniel H. Wells, Willard Snow, Edward Hunter, Daniel Spencer, Thomas Bullock, John Brown, William Crosby, Amasa M. Lyman, Charles C. Rich, Lorenzo Young and Parley P. Pratt as assistants.
Fri. 20.—Pres. Brigham Young was appointed governor of Utah Territory; Benjamin D. Harris, of Vermont, secretary; Joseph Buffington, of Pennsylvania, chief justice; Perry C. Brocchus, of Alabama, and Zerubbabel Snow, of Ohio, associate justices; Seth M. Blair, of Utah, U. S. attorney, and Joseph L. Heywood, of Utah, U. S. marshal.
Mon. 23.—Newel K. Whitney, presiding Bishop of the Church, died in Great Salt Lake City.
October.—Springville, Utah Co., was settled by Aaron Johnson and others.
Sat. 5.—The general assembly of Deseret met and passed a bill, providing for the organization of Davis County.
Thurs. 10.—Elder Geo. P. Dykes arrived as a missionary in Aalborg, Jutland, Denmark, where he commenced to baptize Oct. 27th. A month later (Nov. 25th) he organized a branch of the Church at Aalborg, which was the second branch in Scandinavia.
Tues. 15.—The mail bringing the first information to the Valley of the organization of the Territory of Utah, arrived in Great Salt Lake City.
Sun. 20.—James Pace and others with their families arrived on Peteetneet Creek, Utah Valley, and settled what is now Payson.
Sun. 27.—Apostle Lorenzo Snow baptized a man at La Tour, Valley of Luzerne, Piedmont, Italy, as the first fruit of preaching the fulness of the gospel in that land. Soon afterwards a number of others were baptized in the same locality.
November. Sun. 3.—Thomas Ford, ex-governor of Illinois, died at Peoria, Ill.
Wed. 27.—The Warm Springs bath-house' north of Great Salt Lake City, was opened with a festival attended by the First Presidency, a number of the Apostles and other leading men; Heber C. Kimball offered the dedicatory prayer.
December.—Thirty families, including 118 men, left Great Salt Lake City with 101 wagons and six hundred head of stock, under the direction of Apostle Geo. A. Smith, for the Little Salt Lake Valley, to locate a settlement there.
Sat. 7.—A branch of the Church was organized by Apostle John Taylor and co-laborers in Paris, France.
Thurs. 12.—Hiram Clark. Thos. Whittle, Henry W. Bigler, Thos. Morris, John Dixon, Wm. Farrer, James Hawkins, Hiram H. Blackwell, James Keeler and Geo. Q. Cannon arrived at Honolulu as the first Latter-day Saint missionaries to Hawaii (Sandwich Islands).

1851

January.—City charters were granted to Ogden, Provo, Manti and Parowan, by the general assembly of the State of Deseret.
Fri. 3.—The first criminal trial by jury took place in the Provisional State of Deseret, in Great Salt Lake City.
Thurs. 9.—The bill incorporating Great Salt Lake City was passed by the general assembly of Deseret, and the following officers were appointed by the governor and assembly: Jedediah M. Grant, mayor; Nathaniel H. Felt, Wm. Snow, Jesse P. Harmon and Nathaniel V. Jones, aldermen; Vincent Shurtliff, Benjamin L. Clapp, Zera Pulsipher, Wm. G. Perkins, Lewis Robison, Harrison Burgess, Jeter Clinton, John L. Dunyon, and Samuel W. Richards, councilors.
Sat. 11.—The Great Salt Lake City council assembled in the Representatives Hall, and the officers elect took their oath of office from Thomas Bullock, clerk of the county court; when the council proceeded to complete the city organization by electing Robert Campbell, recorder; Thomas Rhodes, treasurer, and Elam Luddington, marshal. The city was divided into four municipal wards.
Mon. 13.—Apostle Geo. A. Smith and company of settlers arrived on Center Creek, Little Salt Lake Valley, Utah, where they located a town site, which later was named Parowan. They commenced their settlement by building a fort.
Mon. 20.—Presidents Brigham Young and Heber C. Kimball, Apostle Amasa M. Lyman, Elder Jedediah M. Grant and others left Great Salt Lake City to visit the settlements in Davis and Weber Counties. In the evening they preached in the house of Perrigrine Sessions, and organized a branch of the Church; John Stoker was ordained Bishop. The place at that time was known as Sessions settlement.
Sun. 26.—Pres. Brigham Young and party held meetings with the Saints in the south fort, Ogden, which meetings was chosen President of the Weber Stake, with Charles R. Dana and David B. Dille as counselors. A High Council was also organized. Isaac Clark was ordained Bishop of the South Ward, with James Browning and James Brown as counselors; and Erastus Bingham Bishop of the North

Ward, with Charles Hubbart and Stephen Perry as counselors.

Mon. 27.—Pres. Brigham Young and party held a meeting with the Saints who had settled on Kay's creek, (now Kaysville, Davis Co.,) and appointed William Kay Bishop of that Ward.

February. Mon. 3.—Brigham Young took the oath of office as governor of the Territory of Utah.

Mon. 17.—Robert Dickson opened a school in the 14th Ward, Great Salt Lake City, with 18 scholars, teaching phonography.

March.—Brigham City, Box Elder Co., was settled by William Davis, James Brooks and Thomas Pierce.

Wed. 19.—A Stake of Zion was organized by Pres. Brigham Young at Provo, Utah Co., with Isaac Higbee as president, and John Blackburn and Thos. Willis as counselors.

Thurs. 20.—A branch of the Church was organized by Pres. Brigham Young, at Springville, Utah Co., Utah, with Asahel Perry as president and Aaron Johnson as Bishop.

Sun. 23.—Benjamin Cross was ordained a High Priest and set apart to act as the first Bishop of Payson.

Mon. 24.—A company of settlers for Southern California was organized for traveling, at Payson, Utah Co., and commenced the journey the same day, under the presidency of Apostles Amasa M. Lyman and Charles C. Rich, accompanied by Apostle Parley P. Pratt and a party of missionaries going to different countries to preach the gospel.

Fri. 28.—The general assembly of Deseret met and passed a number of resolutions expressive of their good feelings toward the government for creating the Territory of Utah.

April.—Pres. Brigham Young dictated the plan for a tabernacle to be erected on the southwest corner of the Temple Block, Great Salt Lake City.

—The Eighteenth Ward, Great Salt Lake City, was organized with Lorenzo D. Young as Bishop.

Mon. 7.—At the general conference held in Great Salt Lake City it was voted to build a Temple. Edward Hunter was appointed successor to the late Newel K. Whitney as presiding Bishop of the whole Church. At this time there were about thirty thousand inhabitants in Utah, of which nearly five thousand were in Great Salt Lake City.

May.—The Book of Mormon in the Danish language, translated by Peter O. Hansen, was published by Erastus Snow in Copenhagen, Denmark; it was the first edition of the book printed in a foreign language.

June.—Apostles Amasa M. Lyman and Charles C. Rich, with about five hundred souls from Utah, arrived at San Bernardino, Cal., for the purpose of making a settlement.

—Elder Joseph Richards, member of the British army, arrived at Calcutta, India, having been authorized by the presidency of the British mission to introduce the gospel in that country.

Sun. 12.—Elder Geo. Q. Cannon commenced to baptize natives in the district of Kula, on the island of Maui, Hawaii. This was the commencement of a great missionary work on that island; a few natives had previously been baptized on the island of Hawaii, and one or more at Honolulu.

—Elder Joseph Richards baptized James Patrick Melk, Mary Ann Melk, Matthew McCune and Maurice White, at Calcutta, India.

July. Sat. 19.—Four of the newly appointed Federal officers for Utah, namely, Judge Zerubbabel Snow, Secretary Benjamin D. Harris and Indian Agents Stephen B. Rose and Henry R. Day arrived in Great Salt Lake City, accompanied by Dr. John M. Bernhisel and Almon W. Babbitt.

August.—The first kiln of earthen ware was burned at the Deseret Pottery, located near the head of Emigration or Third South streets.

Mon. 4.—The first election for delegate to Congress and members of the Territorial legislature took place in Utah. Dr. John M. Bernhisel was elected Utah's first delegate to Congress.

Sun. 17.—Apostle Orson Hyde, Albert Carrington and others arrived in Great Salt Lake City from Kanesville, Ia., accompanied by Perry E. Brocchus, one of the newly appointed judges for Utah; they brought with them a brass cannon.

September.—Juab County was settled by Joseph L. Heywood and others, who located on Salt Creek (now Nephi).

—Chief Justice Brandenbury, Associate Judge Perry E. Brocchus and Secretary Benjamin D. Harris deserted their official posts in Utah and went to the States, taking with them the $24,000 which had been appropriated by Congress for the legislature.

Sun. 7.—The general conference of the Church convened in the Bowery, Great Salt Lake City; it was continued four days. During the conference Judge Perry E. Brocchus, who with the other Federal officers had been invited to the stand, spoke insultingly to the large assembly.

Mon. 22.—The first legislature of Utah Territory convened in Great Salt Lake City and organized by electing Heber C. Kimball president of the Council, and Wm. W. Phelps speaker of the house.

—Amasa M. Lyman and party purchased the Ranche of San Bernardino, containing about one hundred thousand acres of land. The location was about one hundred miles from San Diego, seventy miles from the mouth of San Pedro, and fifty miles from Pueblo de los Angeles.

October. Sat. 4.—A joint resolution, passed by the Utah legislature legalizing the laws of the provisional government of the State of Deseret, was approved by the governor.

Sun. 5.—Elder Maurice White baptized Anna, a daughter of a high caste Brahmin, at Calcutta, India, as the first native convert to "Mormonism" in the East India mission.

Wed. 29.—Fillmore, Millard Co., Utah, which had just been settled by Anson Call and thirty families, was selected for the capital of the Territory.

—Elder James S. Brown was arrested by order of the French officials at Anna, Society Islands mission, and the next day placed on board a French man-of-war.

Thurs. 30.—John Murdock and Charles W. Wandell, arrived at Sydney, as Latter-day Saint missionaries to Australia, and commenced to preach the gospel.

November. Sat. 8.—Apostle Parley P. Pratt and Rufus Allen arrived as missionaries in Valparaiso, Chili, South America, after 64 days' rough sailing from San Francisco.

Tues. 11.—The "University of the State of Deseret" was opened in Great Salt Lake City.

Sat. 15.—The "Deseret News" which had been suspended for lack of paper since Aug. 19th, commenced its second volume.

December.—Three families commenced a settlement on Clover Creek (Mona), eight miles north of Nephi, Juab Co.

1852

January. Tues. 27.—Elder Geo. Q. Cannon commenced the translation of the Book of Mormon in the Hawaiian language, at Wailuku, Maui.

February.—The Territorial Library was opened in the Council House, Great Salt Lake City, with Wm. C. Staines, as librarian. Congress had appropriated $5,000 towards the purchase of books, which were selected by Delegate Bernhisel.

Tues. 3.—Legislative acts, providing for the organization of the counties of Great Salt Lake, Weber, Utah, San Pete, Juab, Tooele, Iron, Davis (previously created by acts of the general assembly of Deseret), Millard, Washington, Green River and Deseret Counties were approved.

Sat. 7.—Gov. Brigham Young approved an act, recently passed by the Utah legislature, appointing probate judges in the counties in Utah; to-wit: Isaac Clark, Weber Co.; Joseph Holbrook, Davis Co.; Elias Smith, Great Salt Lake Co.; Preston Thomas, Utah Co.; Alfred Lee, Tooele Co.; Geo. W. Bradley, Juab Co.; Geo. Peacock, San Pete Co.; Anson Call, Millard Co.; Chapman Duncan, Iron Co.

Tues. 10.—A branch of the Church was organized at Mountainville (Alpine), Utah Co., Utah; Charles S. Peterson, president.

Sat. 14.—The legislative assembly of Utah Territory memorialized Congress for the construction of a great national central railroad from the Missouri river to the Pacific coast. The memorial was approved on the 3rd of March following. At the same session, the legislature petitioned Congress for the establishment of a telegraph line across the continent.

March, Thurs. 11.—The ship "Italy" sailed from Liverpool, England, with 28 Scandinavian Saints—the first from the Scandinavian mission—under the direction of Ole U. S. Monster. The company arrived at New Orleans May 10th and in Great Salt Lake City Oct. 16th, crossing the plains in Eli B. Kelsey's company.

Mon. 15.—Great Salt Lake County was organized with Elias Smith as county and probate judge.

April. Tues. 6.—The building subsequently known as the Old Tabernacle, which had been erected and just completed on the southwest corner of the Temple Block, in Great Salt Lake City, was dedicated. This structure, built of adobe, was 126 feet long, 64 feet wide and arched without a pillar. It was capable of seating about twenty-five hundred people. The ground is now occupied by the Assembly Hall.

Fri. 9.—A number of emigrating Saints lost their lives by the explosion of the steamboat "Saluda," at Lexington, Missouri. There were about one hundred and ten Saints on board when the calamity occurred.

May. Sat. 15.—Wm. Willes reported 189 members of the Church in Calcutta, India, and vicinity, of whom 170 were "Ryots," who previously had professed Christianity.

July.—A townsite called Palmyra was surveyed on the Spanish Fork river, Utah Co., on which the first house was built in the following August. This settlement was afterwards united with and absorbed by Spanish Fork.

Tues. 27.—The thermometer stood 127 degrees F. in the sun, in Great Salt Lake City.

August.—Provo, Utah Co., was divided into five Bishop's Wards, with Jonathan O. Duke as Bishop of the First, James Bird of the Second, Elias H. Blackburn of the Third, Wm. M. Wall of the Fourth and Wm. Faucett of the Fifth Ward.

—Elder Michael Johnson, who was sent to Sweden to continue the work commenced there by John E. Forsgren two years previously, was arrested and brought as a prisoner to Stockholm, after which he was sent in chains six hundred miles to Malmo, together with two thieves.

Sun. 1.—A small branch of the Church was organized in Hamburg, Germany, by Elder Daniel Garn.

Thurs. 12.—Hiram Page, one of the Eight Witnesses to the Book of Mormon, died near Excelsior Springs, Ray Co., Mo.

Sat. 28.—A special two days' conference was commenced in Great Salt Lake City; 106 Elders were called to go on missions, namely 7 to the United States, 4 to Nova Scotia and the British N. A. Provinces, 2 to British Guiana (S. America), 4 to the West Indies, 39 to Great Britain, 1 to France, 4 to Germany, 3 to Prussia, 2 to Gibraltar, 1 to Denmark, 2 to Norway, 9 to Calcutta and Hindostan, 4 to China, 3 to Siam, 3 to Cape of Good Hope, Africa, 10 to Australia and 9 to the Hawaiian Islands.

Sun. 29.—The revelation on celestial marriage was first made public. It was read in the conference held in Great Salt Lake City, and Apostle Orson Pratt delivered the first public discourse on that principle.

Tues. 31.—The Utah "run away judges" were superseded by the appointment of Lazarus H. Reed, as chief justice, and Leonidas Shaver, as associate justice. Ben. G. Ferris had previously been commissioned as secretary.

September.—Mary Fielding Smith, widow of Hyrum Smith, died in Great Salt Lake County.

November. Thurs. 11.—Apostles Erastus Snow and Franklin D. Richards left Great Salt Lake City for Iron County, where they surveyed a tract of land for the "Deseret Iron Company." They returned to the city Dec. 12th.

1853

January. Sat. 1.—The Social Hall, on First East Street, Great Salt Lake City, was dedicated; it was erected the year previous.
Wed. 19.—The first theatrical play in the Social Hall was presented.
February. Mon. 14.—The Temple Block, in Great Salt Lake City, was consecrated, and the ground broken for the foundation of the Temple.
March. Mon. 7.—Edward Stevenson and Nathan T. Porter arrived at Gibraltar, as the first Latter-day Saint missionaries to Spain.
April. Sun. 3.—The Saints who had settled in Cedar Valley, Utah, were organized into a Ward; Allen Weeks, Bishop.
Wed. 6.—The corner stones of the Temple in Great Salt Lake City were laid under the direction of the First Presidency of the Church.
Tues. 26.—Elders Nathaniel V. Jones, Amos Milton Musser, Richard Ballantyne, Robert Skelton, Robert Owen, Wm. F. Carter, Wm. Fotheringham, Truman Leonard, Samuel A. Woolley, Chauncey W. West, Elam Luddington, Levi Savage and Benjamin F. Dewey arrived at Calcutta as missionaries from Utah to Hindostan and Siam, after 86 days' voyage from San Francisco, Cal.
Wed. 27.—Elders Hosea Stout, James Lewis and Chapman Duncan arrived at Hong Kong, as the first Latter-day Saint missionaries to China. Soon afterwards they commenced to preach the gospel, but meeting with no success, they returned to California.
—Rodney Badger, one of the Pioneers of 1847, was accidentally drowned in the Weber river, Utah.
July. Mon. 18.—Alexander Keel was killed by Indians under the chief Walker, near Payson, Utah Co. This was the commencement of another Indian war.
Sat. 23.—Peter W. Connover's company of militia, sent out from Provo to protect the weaker settlements, had an engagement with the Indians, near the Pleasant Creek settlement (Mount Pleasant), San Pete Co., in which six Indians were killed.
Sun. 24.—John Berry and Clark Roberts were fired upon and wounded by Indians at Summit Creek (Santaquin), while bringing an express through. The inhabitants had deserted the place and moved to Payson.
August. Mon. 1.—John M. Bernhisel was re-elected delegate to Congress from Utah.
Wed. 17.—John Dixon, a Utah Pioneer of 1847, and John Quayle were killed and John Hoagland was wounded by Indians, near Parley's Park, Utah.
Mon. 29.—Resolutions were adopted by the city council, in compliance with expressed request of the inhabitants, to build a Spanish wall around Great Salt Lake City.
September. Tues. 13.—Wm. Hatton was killed by Indians, while standing guard at Fillmore, Utah.
October. Sat. 1.—James Nelson, Wm. Luke, Wm. Reed and Thos. Clark were killed by Indians at the Uintah Springs, San Pete Valley.
Sun. 2.—At a skirmish between the whites and Indians, at Nephi, Juab Co., Utah, eight Indians were killed, and one squaw and two boys taken prisoners.
Tues. 4.—John E. Warner and Wm. Mills were killed by Indians, a few hundred yards above the grist mill, at Manti, San Pete Co., Utah.
—According to the Bishops' reports read at conference, the number of souls in the various settlements in the Territory was as follows: Great Salt Lake City. 1st Ward, 260; 2nd Ward, 149; 3rd Ward, 170; 4th Ward, 183; 5th Ward, 69; 6th Ward, 206; 7th Ward, 334; 8th Ward, 236; 9th Ward, 298; 10th Ward, 213; 11th Ward, 180; 12th Ward, 345; 13th Ward, 454; 14th Ward, 662; 15th Ward, 501; 16th Ward, 444; 17th Ward, 406; 18th Ward, 241; 19th Ward, 572. Great Salt Lake County: Butterfield Settlement, 71; West Jordan, 361; Mill Creek, 668; Big Cottonwood, 161; South Cottonwood, 517; Little Cottonwood, 273; Willow Creek, 222. Utah County: Dry Creek. 458; American Fork, 212; Pleasant Grove, 290; Provo: 1st Ward, 423; 2nd Ward, 264; 3rd Ward, 248; 4th Ward, 424; Mountainville. no report; Springville, 739; Palmyra, 404; Payson and Summit, 427; Cedar Valley, 115. Juab County: Salt Creek, 229. Sanpete County: Manti, 447; Pleasant Creek, 118. Millard County: Fillmore, 304. Iron County: Parowan, 392; Cedar, 455. Tooele County. Grantsville, 215; Tooele, no report. Davis County: North Kanyon. 574; Centreville, 194; North Cottonwood, 413; Kays Ward, 417. Weber County: East Weber, 233; Ogden: 1st Ward, 449; 2nd Ward, 683; 3rd Ward, 200; Willow Creek, 163. Box Elder, 204.
Fri. 14.—About thirty Indians attacked a few men, who were securing their crops at Summit Creek (Santaquin), Utah Co., killed and scalped F. F. Tindrel, and drove off a number of head of stock.
Wed. 26.—Capt. John W. Gunnison, of the U. S. Topographical Engineer Corps, and seven other men, were killed by Indians, near the swamps of the Sevier river, in revenge for the killing of an Indian and the wounding of two others, alleged to have been perpetrated by a company of emigrants bound for California.
November.—Previous to this Pres. Brigham Young purchased of James Bridger a Mexican grant for 30 square miles of land and some cabins, afterwards known as Ft. Bridger. This was the first property owned by the Saints in Green River County.
Sun. 6.—Case's sawmill, in San Pete County, was burned by Indians.
Wed. 9.—The Indians burned six houses at Summit Creek (Santaquin), Utah Co.
Sun. 13.—The mail train was attacked by Indians six miles from Laramie, and three men were killed.
December.—The so-called Spanish wall built in part around Great Salt Lake City this year was twelve feet high, six feet thick at the base, tapering to two feet six inches three feet from the ground, and preserving that thickness to the top. It was six miles in length.

1854

January.—The "Deseret News" was changed from a semimonthly to a weekly paper.
Tues. 3.—The ship "Jesse Munn" sailed from Liverpool, England, with 300 Scandinavian and 33 German Saints, under the direction of Christian Larsen. It arrived at New Orleans Feb. 10th, and the emigrants continued up the rivers to Kansas City, Mo., which this year was selected as the outfitting place for the Saints crossing the plains.
—A mass meeting was held in Great Salt Lake City for the purpose of taking steps towards memorializing Congress to construct a national railroad from the Missouri river, via the South Pass and Great Salt Lake City, to the Pacific.
February. Tues. 7.—John C. Fremont, with a company of nine whites and twelve Delaware Indians, arrived at Parowan, Iron Co., in a state of starvation. One man had fallen dead from his horse near the settlement, and others were nearly dead. Animals and provisions were supplied by the Saints, and, after resting until the 20th, Fremont and company continued their journey to California.
March.—Elias Smith succeeded the late Willard Richards as postmaster of Great Salt Lake City.
—Ephraim, San Pete Co., was first settled.
Sat. 11.—Dr. Willard Richards, second Counselor to Pres. Brigham Young, and editor of the "Deseret News," died in Great Salt Lake City, of dropsy.
Wed. 22.—The ship "Julia Ann" sailed from Sydney, Australia, with about seventy Saints, bound for Utah, under the direction of Wm. Hyde. The company landed at San Pedro, Cal, June 12th.
April.—A number of Elders were called on a mission to the Indians in southern Utah. This more directly resulted in opening up that part of Utah south of the Great Basin to settlement.
May. Tues. 23.—Patriarch John Smith died in Great Salt Lake City, and on June 28th John Smith, son of Hyrum Smith, was chosen Patriarch to the Church in place of the deceased.
Late in May (after a "talk" with Pres. Brigham Young), the Indian chief Walker, surrounded by his braves, and Kanosh, chief of the Pauvan Indians, entered into a formal treaty of peace at Chicken Creek, Juab Co. This ended the Ute war, during which 19 white persons and many Indians had been killed, a number of the smaller settlements had been broken up, and their inhabitants moved to the larger towns.
June. Fri. 16.—The workmen began at the southeast corner to lay the foundation of the Temple, in Great Salt Lake City.
July. Thurs. 13.—The Jordan river bridge, west of Great Salt Lake City, was crossed by teams and herds for the first time.
Tues. 25.—Elder Richard Ballantyne sailed from Madras, India, bound for London, where he arrived Dec. 6, 1854.
August. Sun. 8.—Wm. and Warren Weeks, sons of Bishop Allen Weeks, were killed by Goshute Indians, in Cedar Valley.
Sat. 12.—Peter Whitmer, Sr., died in Richmond, Ray Co., Mo. He was born April 14, 1773.
Tues. 15.—The wall around the Temple Block, in Great Salt Lake City, was completed.
November. Sat. 4.—Apostle Erastus Snow organized a Stake of Zion in St. Louis, Mo., with Milo Andrus as president, and Charles Edwards and George Gardiner as counselors. A High Council was also organized, consisting of James H. Hart, Andrew Sproule, John Evans, Wm. Morrison, James S. Cantwell, Wm. Lowe, Samuel J. Lees, Edward Cook, James S. Brooks, William Gore, John Clegg and Charles Chard.
Sat. 11.—Professor Orson Pratt discovered "a new and easy method of solution of the cubic and biquadratic equations."
December. Sat. 30.—A petition praying for the reappointment of Brigham Young to the governorship of Utah, and signed by Col. Steptoe and the leading officials and business men of Great Salt Lake City, was sent to Washington, D. C.

1855

January. Mon. 29.—Walker, chief of the Ute Indians, died at Meadow Creek, Millard Co. His brother Arrapeen succeeded him as chief.
May. Sat. 5.—The Endowment House, in Great Salt Lake City, was dedicated.
Fri. 11.—A treaty of peace was concluded with the Ute Indians.
Sun. 20.—The camp of the missionaries, called to settle on the Salmon river, Oregon (now Idaho), was organized by Thomas S. Smith on the bank of Bear river, with Francillo Durfee as captain.
Mon. 21.—A company of about forty men, under the presidency of Alfred N. Billings, left Manti, San Pete Co., for a valley near the Elk Mountains (La Salle Mountains), where they arrived June 15th and commenced a settlement on the left bank of Grand river, where Moab now stands.
July. Sun. 1.—The manufacture of molasses from beets at the sugar factory, in the Sugar House Ward, Great Salt Lake Co., was commenced.
Mon. 23.—The massive foundation of the Temple in Great Salt Lake City was finished.
September. Sun. 2.—The Ute and Shoshone Indians met in front of the "Deseret News" office, Great Salt Lake City, and entered into a treaty of peace.
Tues. 11.—Seth M. Blair's train of 45 wagons arrived in Great Salt Lake City with a few Saints from Texas.
Thurs. 13.—The Horticultural Society was organized in Great Salt Lake City, with Wilford Woodruff as president. Various other societies were organized in the fore part of the year, among which were the "Universal Scientific Society," the "Polysophical Society," the Deseret Philharmonic Society and the "Deseret Typographical Association."
Sun. 23.—James W. Hunt, Wm. Behunin and Edward Edwards, of the Elk Mountain mission, were killed by Indians,

who also wounded Pres. Alfred N. Billings, besides burning hay and stealing cattle. The following day the colonists left their fort and started for Manti, where they arrived Sept. 30th.

October. Mon. 15.—Gov. Young ordered out part of the Utah militia, to protect the settlements in the eastern part of the Territory from the Indians.
—Elder Orson Spencer died in St. Louis, Mo.

Wed. 24.—Capt. Milo Andrus' immigrant train, called the third P. E. Fund company of the season, arrived in Great Salt Lake City.
—The First Presidency of the Church, in the "Thirteenth General Epistle," proposed that the Saints, who emigrated by the P. E. Fund, should cross the plains with handcarts.
—The Utah legislature passed a bill, authorizing an election of delegates to attend a Territorial convention, the object of which was to draft a State constitution, and petition Congress a second time for the admission of Utah into the Union.

Mon. 31.—An able address on plural marriage, written by Apostle Parley P. Pratt, was read before the Utah legislature at Fillmore, Utah.

1856

January. Fri. 18.—The Utah legislature adjourned.

Sat. 26.—At a mass meeting held in Great Salt Lake City, steps were taken for organizing the B. Y. Express Carrying Company, to carry a daily express from the Missouri river to California. In subsequent meetings shares were taken to stock a thousand miles of the road.

February.—The Indians stole many cattle and horses in Utah and Cedar Valleys. On Feb. 21st they killed two herdsmen west of Utah Lake, and on the 22nd a posse of ten men with legal writs called at an Indian camp in Cedar Valley to arrest the murderers. A fight ensued, in which one Indian and a squaw were killed and Geo. Carson, one of the posse, mortally wounded. He died on the 23d. On that day (the 23d) Gov. Brigham Young, by proclamation, ordered our part of the Utah militia to fight the Indians. This difficulty with the natives is known in history as the "Tintic War."

Sat. 23.—The first number of the "Western Standard," a weekly paper published in the interest of the Church, was issued at San Francisco, Cal.; Geo. Q. Cannon, editor.

Tues. 26.—John Catlin and another man were killed, and Geo. Winn was mortally wounded, by Indians, near Kimball's creek, southwest of Utah lake. Capt. Peter Connover, with eighty men, soon afterwards crossed Utah lake on the ice and pursued the hostile tribe into Tintic Valley, where he recovered some of the stock stolen by them.

March. Mon. 17.—A convention met in Great Salt Lake City to prepare a State constitution and memorialize Congress for the admission of Utah into the Union as the State of Deseret. The constitution and memorial were adopted on the 27th, and Apostles Geo. A. Smith and John Taylor were elected delegates to present the same to Congress.

Sun. 23.—The ship "Enoch Train" sailed from Liverpool, England, with 534 Saints, under the direction of James Ferguson. It arrived at Boston May 1st. From that city the emigrants traveled by rail via New York to Iowa City, Iowa, whence the journey across the plains this year was commenced by wagons and handcarts. Daniel Spencer acted as general superintendent of emigration on the borders, assisted by Geo. D. Grant, Wm. H. Kimball, James H. Hart and others.

April. Sat. 19.—The ship "Samuel Curling" sailed from Liverpool with 707 Saints, under the direction of Dan Jones; it arrived at Boston May 23d. From that city the emigrants traveled by rail to Iowa City.

Mon. 21.—Jacob Whitmer, one of the Eight Witnesses to the Book of Mormon, died near Richmond, Ray Co., Mo.

May. Sun. 4.—The ship "Thornton" sailed from Liverpool, England, with 764 Saints, under the direction of James G. Willie. It arrived at New York June 14th, and the emigrants, continuing the journey by rail, arrived at Iowa City, June 26th.

Sun. 25.—The ship "Horizon" sailed from Liverpool with 856 Saints, under the direction of Edward Martin. The company arrived safely at Boston, and reached Iowa City by rail July 8th.

Wed. 28.—A small company of Australian Saints, under the direction of Augustus Farnham, sailed from Port Jackson, New South Wales, bound for Utah. The ship touched at Tahiti, Society Islands, June 22nd, Honolulu, Hawaii, July 16th, and arrived at San Pedro, Cal., Aug. 15th. From the latter place the emigrants traveled by teams to San Bernardino.

June. Sun. 1.—Weber County, Utah, was divided into four Bishops' Wards, and Erastus Bingham appointed Bishop of the First, James G. Browning of the Second, Chauncey W. West of the Third and Thos. Dunn of the Fourth Ward.

August. Mon. 25.—Col. Almon W. Babbitt's train loaded with government property and traveling west, was plundered by Cheyenne Indians, near Wood river, Neb. A. Nichols and two others were killed, and a Mrs. Wilson was carried away by the savages.

September.—Cache County was settled by Peter Maughan and others, who located what is now the town of Wellsville.
—Col. Almon W. Babbit, Thos. Margetts and child, James Cowdy and wife and others were killed, and Mrs. Margetts carried away by Cheyenne Indians, east of Fort Laramie.

Fri. 26.—The first two companies of immigrating Saints, which crossed the plains with handcarts, arrived at Great Salt Lake City, in charge of Capt. Edmund Ellsworth and Daniel D. McArthur. They were met and welcomed by the First Presidency of the Church, a brass band, a company of lancers, and a large concourse of citizens. Capt. Ellsworth's company had left Iowa City June 9th, and McArthur's June 11th. When they started, both contained 497 souls, with 100 handcarts, 5 wagons, 24 oxen, 4 mules and 25 tents.

October. Thurs. 2.—Capt. John Banks' wagon company of immigrating Saints, and Capt. Edward Bunker's handcart company, which had left Iowa City June 23rd, arrived in Great Salt Lake City. The immigrants in the latter were mostly from Wales.
—The Deseret Agricultural and Manufacturing Society held its first exhibition in Great Salt Lake City, called the "Deseret State Fair."
—Capt. Geo. D. Grant left Great Salt Lake City with a relief company to meet the immigration.

Fri. 17.—An ordinance was passed by the Great Salt Lake City council, organizing a Fire Department, Jesse C. Little was appointed chief engineer.

Tues. 28.—Capt. Edward Martin's handcart company, detained by the unusual early snow storms of the season, was met by Joseph A. Young, Daniel W. Jones and Abel Garr, a point sixteen miles above the Platte bridge. Three days later the company arrived at Greasewood creek, where four wagons of the relief company, in charge of Geo. D. Grant, loaded with provisions and some clothing for the suffering emigrants were awaiting them.

November. Sun. 9.—Capt. James G. Willie's handcart company arrived in Great Salt Lake City, after great sufferings from scarcity of provisions, cold and over-exertion in the mountains. It left Iowa City, Iowa, July 15th, with 120 handcarts and six wagons, numbering about five hundred souls, of whom 66 died on the journey. Captain Abraham O. Smoot's wagon train arrived the same day.

Thurs. 13.—Joseph A. Young and Abel Garr arrived in Great Salt Lake City with the news that the last companies of emigrants were perishing in the mountains. More teams and provisions were immediately forwarded to help them in.

Sat. 22.—Heber Jeddie Grant was born in Great Salt Lake City.

Sun. 30.—Edward Martin's handcart company arrived in Great Salt Lake City, after extreme suffering. Many of the emigrants had died in the mountains, and the handcarts had to be gradually abandoned as the relief teams from the Valley were met. When the company passed Florence, Neb., Aug. 25th, it consisted of 576 persons, 146 handcarts, 7 wagons, etc.

December. Mon. 1.—Jedediah M. Grant, second Counselor to Pres. Brigham Young, died in Great Salt Lake City.

1857

January. Sun. 4.—Daniel H. Wells was set apart as second Counselor to Pres. Brigham Young, in place of the late Jedediah M. Grant.

March.—The 42d quorum of Seventy was organized in Tooele County, Utah, with John Shields, James Bevan, Thomas Lee, Francis D. St. Jeor, George Atkin, Hugh S. Gowans and Geo. W. Bryan as presidents.

Mon. 2.—The 41st quorum of Seventy was organized in Salt Lake County, Utah, with John Van Cott, Wm. C. Dunbar, Knud Peterson, Thomas Morris, Leonard I. Smith, Wm. Casper and Levi N. Kendall as presidents.

Mon. 30.—Judge W. W. Drummond, in framing the letter of his resignation as chief justice of Utah, wrote the most wicked and abominable falsehoods against Gov. Brigham Young and the people of Utah, thereby influencing the government to send troops against the "Mormons."

April. Wed. 15.—Feramorz Little, having arrived in the States, with the Utah mail, wrote a letter to the "New York Herald," refuting Drummond's falsehoods.

Sat. 25.—The ship "Westmoreland" sailed from Liverpool, England, with 544 Saints, mostly Scandinavians, under the direction of Mathias Cowley. It arrived at Philadelphia May 31st, and the emigrants reached Iowa City by rail June 9th.

May.—The Tithing Office Block wall in Great Salt Lake City was finished.
—The 46th quorum of Seventy was organized at Payson and Santaquin, Utah Co., with James B. Bracken, John Thomas Hardy, Benjamin F. Stewart, Wm. Carrol McClellan, Geo. W. Hancock and Wm. B. Maxwell as presidents.

Wed. 6.—The Saints who were settling Washington, in southern Utah, were organized into a branch of the Church with Robert D. Covington as president. He was ordained a Bishop Aug. 1, 1858.

Sat. 9.—The 45th quorum of Seventy was organized at Provo, with Robert T. Thomas, James Goff, Robert C. Moore, Isaac Bullock, Lewis C. Sabrisky, Wm. Marsden and Charles Shelton as presidents.

Wed. 13.—Apostle Parley P. Pratt was murdered by Hector H. McLean, near Van Buren, Ark.

Fri. 15.—The 47th quorum of Seventy was partly organized at Ephraim, San Pete Co., Utah, with Tore Thurston, James A. Lemmon, Joseph Clements and Nils Bengtsen as presidents. Most of the members of the new quorum were ordained Seventies on the 17th.

Sat. 16.—The 48th quorum of Seventy was organized at Manti, San Pete Co., with Daniel Henrie as senior president.
—The 49th quorum of Seventy was organized at Nephi, Juab Co., with John A. Woolf, Samuel Pitchforth, Timothy S. Hoyt, Geo. Kendall, Miles Miller, John Burrowman and David Webb as presidents.

Tues. 19.—The 50th quorum of Seventy was partly organized at Spanish Fork, Utah Co., with Dennis Dorrity as one of the presidents.

Wed. 20.—The 51st quorum of Seventy was organized at Springville, Utah Co., with Alexander F. McDonald, Noah P. Guyman, Lorenzo Johnson, Spicer W. Crandall, Abraham Day and Hamilton H. Kerns as presidents.

Thurs. 21.—The 52nd quorum of Seventy was organized at Provo, Utah, with Alfred D. Young as senior president. Quite a number of members were ordained on the 25th.
—On the same day the 44th quorum of Seventy was organized at American Fork, Utah Co., Utah, with Wm. Hyde, James McGaw, Shadrach Driggs, Wm. Greenwood, James W. Preston, Wm. Fotheringham and Thomas Taylor as presidents.

Thurs. 23.—The U. S. 2nd dragoons, 5th and 10th infantry

and Phelps' Battery of the 4th artillery—2,500 men—were ordered out as an expedition to Utah, by order of Gen. Winfield Scott.
June. Sun. 7.—The 53d and 54th quorum of Seventy were organized at Ogden, Utah, by Joseph Young and Albert P. Rockwood, with Rufus Allen and James Brown 3rd as senior presidents.
Fri. 12.—Senator Stephen A. Douglas, in a political speech, delivered at Springfield, Ill., characterized "Mormonism" as a loathsome ulcer of the body politic, and recommended that Congress should apply the knife and cut it out.
Sun. 14.—The 42nd quorum of Seventy was organized at Fillmore, Utah, with Hiram Mace, David N. Raney, Andrew Love, J. W. Radford, Edward Frost, Allen Russel and John Felshaw as presidents.
July.—The 55th quorum of Seventy was organized at Kaysville, and the 56th quorum at Farmington, Davis Co., Utah.
Sat. 18.—The Tenth Infantry, the vanguard of the Utah expedition, took up the line of march from Fort Leavenworth for the West, under the command of Col. E. B. Alexander. The artillery and Fifth Infantry followed a few days later. The command of the whole expedition was given to Gen. W. S. Harney.
Fri. 24.—Abraham O. Smoot and Judson Stoddard arrived from Independence, Mo., without the mails, the postmaster there having refused to forward them. They reported that General Harney with 2,000 infantry and a proportionate number of artillery and cavalry, were ordered to Utah.
August. Sat. 1.—The Utah militia was ordered to be kept in readiness for an expedition to the mountains, to prevent the entering of the approaching army, if necessary.
Fri. 7.—The first part of the "Utah Army," consisting of the Tenth Infantry and Phelps' Battery, arrived at Fort Kearney.
Sat. 15.—Col. Robert T. Burton and James W. Cummings left Great Salt Lake City for the East, with seventy men, for the purpose of protecting the emigrant trains and observing the movements of the approaching army.
Fri. 21.—Col. Burton's expedition arrived at Ft. Bridger; on the 30th it reached Devil's Gate.
Fri. 28.—Col. Albert Sidney Johnston was appointed successor to Gen. W. S. Harney as commander of the Utah expedition.
September. Tues. 8.—Capt. Stewart Van Vliet, of Gen. Harney's staff, arrived in Great Salt Lake City and the following day had an interview with President Young. After a few days' stay he returned to his escort on Ham's Fork, and thence proceeded to Washington, where he used his influence in favor of the Saints.
Fri. 11.—The Mountain Meadow massacre took place.
Sat. 12.—The last of Israel Evans' handcart company, consisting of 154 souls and 31 handcarts, arrived in Great Salt Lake City.
—Jesse B. Martin's wagon company of immigrants arrived in Great Salt Lake City.
Sun. 13.—Chr. Christiansen's handcart company and Mathias Cowley's wagon company of immigrants arrived in Great Salt Lake City.
Mon. 14.—Delegate John M. Bernhisel started from Great Salt Lake City for Washington, D. C., in company with Capt. Stewart Van Vliet and others.
Tues. 15.—Gov. Brigham Young declared the Territory of Utah under martial law and forbade the troops to enter Great Salt Lake Valley. Large numbers of armed militia were ordered to Echo Canyon and other points to intercept the soldiers and prevent their access to the Valley.
Thurs. 17.—Col. Philip St. George Cooke left Ft. Leavenworth with the second division of the "Utah Army." He arrived at Ft. Bridger Nov. 19th.
Tues. 22.—Col. Robt. T. Burton and three other men camped within half a mile of the "Utah Army" (Col. E. B. Alexander's command), near Devil's Fork.
Wed. 23.—Col. Burton's men met the advance companies of the "Utah Army," and from that time were their immediate neighbors" until they arrived at Ham's Fork.
Sat. 26.—Capt. Wm. G. Young's train arrived in Great Salt Lake City with the last of this season's immigration. Among the returning Elders in this train was A. Milton Musser, who returned home from a five years' mission to India and England, during which he had circumnavigated the globe, traveling as a missionary "without purse and script."
Tues. 29.—General Daniel H. Wells left Great Salt Lake City for Echo Canyon, where he established headquarters. About one thousand two hundred and fifty men, from the several militia districts, were ordered to Echo Canyon, where they engaged in digging trenches across the canyon, throwing up breastworks, loosening rocks on the heights, etc., preparing to resist the progress of the army.
October.—The "Mormon" settlements in Carson Valley were broken up; most of the settlers returned to Great Salt Lake City in the beginning of November.
Mon. 5.—Lot Smith, with a small company of men, surprised and burned two trains of government stores, near the Big Sandy and Green river.
Sat. 10.—The officers of the Utah expedition held a council of war at Ham's Fork, and decided that the army should march to Great Salt Lake Valley via Soda Springs. The following day the march was commenced, but after several days of slow and exhaustive traveling, the expedition was forced to return.
Fri. 16.—Major Joseph Taylor and Wm. R. R. Stowell, of the Utah militia, were taken prisoners here by the U. S. troops near Ft. Bridger.
November. Wed. 4.—Col. Albert Sidney Johnston joined his command on Ham's Fork, with a small reinforcement.
Fri. 6.—Five hundred animals perished from cold and starvation around the U. S. army camp on Black's Fork.
Mon. 16.—The 'Utah Army" went into winter quarters at Camp Scott, two miles from the site of Ft. Bridger and 113 miles from Great Salt Lake City.
December. Fri. 4.—Capt. John R. Winder was appointed to take charge of a picket guard, to be stationed at Camp Weber, at the mouth of Echo Canyon, to watch the movements of the U. S. soldiers during the winter. Two weeks later, when deep snow fell in the mountains, this guard was reduced to ten men. The remainder of the militia returned to their homes for the winter.
Mon. 21.—The Utah legislature unanimously concurred in the message, policy and actions of Gov. Brigham Young, in stopping the army, etc.

1858

January. Wed. 6.—A memorial from the members and officers of the Utah legislature to the President and Congress of the United States, praying for constitutional rights, etc., was signed in Great Salt Lake City.
Sat. 16.—A large mass meeting of citizens was held in the Tabernacle, Great Salt Lake City. A petition and resolution, setting forth the true state of affairs in Utah, were adopted, and, on motion, sent to the U. S. government at Washington.
Fri. 22.—The Utah legislature adjourned without the occurrence of a negative vote on any question or action during the session.
February. Wed. 24.—Col. Thomas L. Kane arrived in Great Salt Lake City by way of Southern California. He came voluntarily for the purpose of bringing about a peaceful solution of the existing difficulties between the United States and Utah. After conferring with Gov. Brigham Young and other leading citizens, he went out to the army, which was encamped at Ft. Scott (near Ft. Bridger). There he had an interview with the new governor, Alfred Cumming, who concluded to accompany him to Great Salt Lake City.
Thurs. 25.—Geo. McBride and James Miller were killed and five other brethren wounded by a large party of Bannock and Shoshone Indians, near Fort Limhi, Oregon (now Idaho).
March. Sun. 21.—The citizens of Great Salt Lake City and the settlements north of it agreed to abandon their homes and go south, all the information derived from Eastern papers being to the effect that the approaching formidable army was sent to destroy them. Their destination, when starting, was by some supposed to be Sonora.
Wed. 31.—Bailey Lake, one of a small party from Salmon river, traveling south, was killed by Indians on Bannock creek. The Indians also robbed the company of eleven horses.
April. Mon, 5.—Gov. Alfred Cumming and Col. Thos. L. Kane, with a servant each, left the army at Ft. Scott for the Valley. They arrived in Great Salt Lake City on the 12th. The new governor was kindly received by Pres. Brigham Young and other leading citizens and treated everywhere with "respectful attention."
Mon. 19.—Gov. Alfred Cumming and Col. Thos. L. Kane examined the Utah library, where James W. Cummings showed them the records and seal of the U. S. District Court, alleged to have been destroyed by the Mormons. This accusation was one of the reasons why the army was ordered to Utah. A few days later the governor sent a truthful report to the government in relation to the affairs in the Territory.
May.—The citizens of Utah, living north of Utah County, abandoned their homes and moved southward, leaving only a few men in each town and settlement to burn everything, in case the approaching troops, on their arrival in the Valley, should prove hostile.
Wed. 5.—The "Deseret News" having been removed from Great Salt Lake City to Fillmore, Millard Co., the first number of the paper published at that place was issued.
Thurs. 13.—Gov. Cumming left Great Salt Lake City for Camp Scott, for the purpose of removing his wife to the city. When he returned, June 8th, he found the city deserted by its inhabitants.
June. Mon. 7.—Ex-Gov. L. W. Powell, of Kentucky, and Major Ben McCullough, of Texas, sent as peace commissioners by the Federal government, arrived in Great Salt Lake City.
Fri. 11.—The peace commissioners met with Pres. Brigham Young and others in the Council House, Great Salt Lake City, and the difficulties between the United States and Utah were peaceably adjusted.
Tues. 15.—Commissioners Powell and McCullough visited Provo. The next day Mr. Powell addressed an audience of about four thousand persons in the Bowery, at Provo, Utah Co.
Sat. 19.—Col. Thos. L. Kane arrived in Washington, D. C. Soon afterwards he reported the situation in Utah to Pres. Buchanan.
Sat. 26.—The army, under Col. Albert Sidney Johnston, passed through Great Salt Lake City and camped on the west side of the Jordan river. It subsequently marched to Cedar Valley, and there located Camp Floyd, about forty miles from the city.
July. Thurs. 1.—The First Presidency and the other officers returned to their homes in Great Salt Lake City, from Provo. They were followed by most of the people, who likewise returned to their deserted city and settlements in the North, and resumed their accustomed labors.
Sat. 3.—Commissioners Powell and McCullough left Great Salt Lake City, en route for Washington, D. C.
September. Wed. 22.—The "Deseret News" resumed its publication in Great Salt Lake City, after publishing twenty numbers at Fillmore.
October. Fri. 15.—The remains of Josiah Call and Samuel Brown, of Fillmore, Millard Co., were found in a state of decomposition, near Chicken creek bridge, Juab Co. They had been murdered by Indians, Oct. 7th.
Thurs. 28.—Jacob Hamblin, with eleven men, left the settlement of Santa Clara, in southern Utah, to visit the Moquis or Town Indians, on the east side of the Colorado river. This was the beginning of intercourse with the Indians on that side of the Colorado and of the exploration of the country, which opened the way for colonization by the Saints.
November.—Notwithstanding President Buchanan's "Proclamation of Pardon," Judge Chas. E. Sinclair, in the Third District Court, urged the prosecution of the leading "Mormons" for alleged treason.

December. Mon. 13.—The Utah legislature convened in Great Salt Lake City and adjourned to meet at Fillmore.
Sat. 18.—The Utah legislature convened at Fillmore, and organized by appointing Wilford Woodruff president of the Council pro tem, and Aaron Johnson speaker of the house pro tem. It then passed a resolution to adjourn the assembly to Great Salt Lake City.
Mon. 27.—The Utah legislature convened in Great Salt Lake City and organized by electing Daniel H. Wells president of the Council and John Taylor speaker of the House.

1859

January. Wed. 19.—An act passed by the Utah legislature reorganizing Carson and Green River Counties and attaching St. Mary's and Humboldt Counties to Carson County, was approved. Genoa was made the county seat of Carson and Ft. Bridger of Green River County.
February.—The Deseret Alphabet was first introduced in Utah.
—The 58th quorum of Seventy was organized at Brigham City, Box Elder Co., Utah. Some time previously the 56th and 57th quorums had been organized.
Thurs. 3.—The 59th quorum of Seventy was organized by Joseph Young at North Willow Creek (Willard), Box Elder Co., Utah, with George J. Marsh, Thomas W. Brewerton, John M. McCrary, Richard J. Davis, Elisha Mallory, Mathew W. Dalton and Peter Greenhalgh as presidents.
Fri 11.—The 60th quorum of Seventy was organized at Ogden, Weber Co., Utah, with Luman A. Shurtliff as senior president.
Fri. 25.—The 61st quorum of Seventy was organized at Mill Creek, Great Salt Lake Co., with John Scott, James Craigan, Wm. Casto, James P. Park, Andrew J. Rynearson, Dudley J. Merrill and Thurston Larson as presidents.
March.—Plain City, Weber Co., Utah, was settled by Jeppe G. Folkman, Christopher O. Folkman, Jens Peter Folkman, Joseph Skeen, Daniel Collett, John Spiers, John Carver, Wm. Geddes and others.
Tues. 8.—Associate Justice John Cradlebaugh, in his charge to the grand jury, composed of "Mormons," at Provo, called them "fools," "dupes," "instruments of a tyrannical church despotism," etc. Provo was occupied by a detachment of U. S. troops.
Tues. 22.—Howard O. Spencer, a Mormon youth, was assaulted and brutally beaten on the head by Sergeant Ralph Pike, of the U. S. army, in Rush Valley, Utah.
Sun. 27.—Gov. Cumming issued a proclamation against the presence of troops in Provo. About this time it was reported that certain U. S. officials had entered into a conspiracy to secure the arrest of Pres. Brigham Young, and that Col. Johnston had promised the assistance of U. S. troops under his command to effect the arrest. As a consequence Gov. Cumming notified General Daniel H. Wells to hold the militia in readiness to prevent the outrage, should it be attempted; 5,000 troops (militia) were placed under arms.
April. Mon, 4.—The U. S. troops evacuated Provo.
May. Tues. 10.—Gen. Albert Sidney Johnston promised protection to all persons who wished to leave the Territory of Utah.
Thurs. 26.—James Johnson, a son of Luke S. Johnson, of Shambip County, was shot and mortally wounded by Delos Gibson in Great Salt Lake City. Death ensued the following day. A number of other murders, principally amongst bad characters who infested the Territory, took place about the same time.
July. Sun. 10.—Hon. Horace Greeley, editor of the "New York Tribune," arrived at Great Salt Lake City en route for California.
August. Mon. 1.—Wm. H. Hooper was elected Utah's second delegate to Congress, Hon. John M. Bernhisel having served in that capacity since the organization of the Territory.
Thurs. 11.—Sergeant Ralph Pike, a U. S. soldier, was shot in Great Salt Lake City, in supposed retaliation for having cracked the skull of Howard O. Spencer with a musket, five months previously.
Sat. 27.—The first number of the "Mountaineer," a weekly newspaper, was published in Great Salt Lake City; Messrs. Blair, Ferguson & Stout editors and proprietors.
September. Sun. 4.—Capt. George Rowley's handcart company, which had left Florence, June 9th. with 235 souls, 60 handcarts, and 6 wagons, arrived in Great Salt Lake City.
Sat. 17.—Alexander Carpenter was shot and mortally wounded by Thomas H. Ferguson in Great Salt Lake City. Both were non Mormons.
October. Mon. 10.—Smithfield, Cache Co., was settled by Seth Langton and Robert and John Thornley.
Fri. 23.—Thos. H. Ferguson, the murderer, was executed in Great Salt Lake City. This was the first execution of a criminal in Utah.
December.—This year Spring City, San Pete Co., Utah, was resettled under the name of Little Denmark.

1860

March. Thurs. 1.—Gen. Albert Sidney Johnston, commander of the "Utah Army," left Camp Floyd for Washington, D. C. He had never visited Great Salt Lake City since he passed through with his army on June 26, 1858. Philip St. George Cooke, formerly commander of the Mormon Battalion, succeeded Johnston in the command.
April. Sat. 7.—The first "Pony Express" from the West arrived at Great Salt Lake City, having left Sacramento, Cal., on the evening of April 3rd.
—The first "Pony Express" from the East arrived at Great Salt Lake City, having left St. Joseph, Mo., on the evening of April 3rd.
—The Union Academy was opened in the building known as the Union Hotel (afterwards Deseret Hospital), with Orson Pratt as principal.
May.—A large number of the troops stationed at Camp Floyd, Utah, left according to orders, for New Mexico and Arizona Territories.

July. Sun. 22.—Smithfield, Cache Co., was attacked by Indians. A fight ensued; John Reed and Ira Merrill and two Indians were killed, and several others wounded on both sides.
August. Sun. 12.—The Indians made an attack upon a mail station at Egan Canyon, (Tooele Co.) and the following day on Shell Creek Station. A company of soldiers came to the rescue and killed 17 Indians.
Mon. 27.—Capt. Daniel Robinson's handcart company (the first of the season), consisting of 233 persons, 43 handcarts, 6 wagons, 38 oxen and 10 tents, arrived in Great Salt Lake City. Pres. Brigham Young had sent out wagons with 2,500 lbs. of flour and 500 lbs. of bacon to help the company.
Thurs. 30.—Capt. J. E. Murphy's immigrant company, consisting of 279 persons, 38 wagons, 164 oxen and 39 cows, arrived at Great Salt Lake City, having left Florence June 19th.
September. Sat. 1.—Capt. John Smith's company of immigrants, consisting of 359 persons and 39 wagons, arrived in Great Salt Lake City.
Mon. 3.—Capt. James D. Ross' company of immigrants, consisting of 279 persons and 38 wagons, arrived in Great Salt Lake City.
Mon. 3.—Capt. James D. Ross' company of immigrants, consisting at Egan Canyon, (Tooele Co.) and the following day left Florence June 17th, arrived in Great Salt Lake City.
Tues. 4.—A portion of Capt. Franklin Brown's company of immigrants arrived in Great Salt Lake City.
Fri. 14.—Capt. Brigham H. Young's train of immigrants arrived in Great Salt Lake City.
Mon. 17.—Capt. John Taylor's company of immigrating Saints arrived in Great Salt Lake City, having left Florence July 3rd.
Mon. 24.—The second handcart company of the season, under Capt. Oscar O. Stoddard, arrived in Great Salt Lake City, having left Florence July 6th, with 126 persons and 22 handcarts. These were the last immigrants who crossed the plains with handcarts.
October. Fri. 5.—Capt. Wm. Budge's train, the last immigrant company of the season, arrived in Great Salt Lake City, having left Florence July 20th, with over four hundred persons, 55 wagons, 215 oxen and 77 cows.

1861

February. Wed. 6.—By order of the commander the military post of Camp Floyd changed name to Fort Crittenden. The name of War John B. Floyd, after whom the camp originally was named, had allied himself with the South against the Union.
March. Sat. 2.—A bill, providing for the organization of Nevada Territory out of the western portion of Utah, was approved by President James Buchanan.
April.—From the 23rd to the 31st of this month upwards of two hundred Church wagons, with four yoke of cattle to each, carrying 150,000 pounds of flour, left Great Salt Lake Valley for the Missouri river to bring in the poor. They traveled in four companies under Capts. Joseph W. Young, Ira Eldredge, Joseph Horne and John R. Mudock.
May. Fri. 17.—Gov. Alfred Cumming and wife left Great Salt Lake City, for the States.
July.—The rest of the army at Camp Floyd, or Fort Crittenden, was ordered to the States. In consequence of this, government property and outfit at Camp Floyd was sold at extraordinarily low prices. It was estimated that $4,000,000 worth of goods was sold for $100,000.
October. Thurs. 3.—John W. Dawson was appointed governor of Utah.
Sun. 6.—The semi-annual conference of the Church was commenced in Great Salt Lake City. It was continued three days. A number of brethren were called to settle in southern Utah and turn their special attention to the raising of cotton.
Fri. 18.—The overland telegraph line was completed from the States to Great Salt Lake City. Pres. Brigham Young sent the first telegram, which passed over the line, to J. H. Wade, president of the company.
Thurs. 24.—The first telegram was sent from Great Salt Lake City to San Francisco by Pres. Brigham Young.
November. Fri. 29.—Apostles Geo. A. Smith and Erastus Snow, Elder Horace S. Eldredge and others left Great Salt Lake City for southern Utah, with a view to locating settlements in the valleys of the Rio Virgen and Santa Clara for the purpose of raising cotton.
December. Wed. 4.—At a meeting of southern Utah settlers who had arrived from the north, it was decided, on motion of Apostle Erastus Snow, to build a city to be called St. George.

1862

January. Thurs. 16.—Lot Huntington, an outlaw, was killed by O. Porter Rockwell, near Ft. Crittenden, while attempting to escape from the officers. On the following day, while trying to effect their escape, John P. Smith and Moroni Clawson, two other outlaws, were killed in Great Salt Lake City.
Thurs. 23.—The convention of delegates, chosen by the people, adopted a State constitution for Utah and a memorial to Congress, praying the third time for the admission of Utah into the Union as a State with the name of Deseret. George Q. Cannon and Wm. H. Hooper were elected delegates to present them to Congress.
March. Thurs. 6.—The Salt Lake Theater, which had been erected the previous season, was dedicated. The building is 144 feet long and 80 feet wide.
April. Tues. 8.—Mr. Morrill of Vermont, introduced a bill in the U. S. House of Representatives, at Washington, D. C., to punish and prevent the practice of bigamy in the Territories of the United States. It was read twice and referred to the committee on Territories. This bill also made it unlawful for any religious or charitable association in any of the S. Territories to own real estate worth more than $50,000.
Mon. 28.—The Indians having destroyed the mail stations between Port Bridger and North Platte, burned the coaches and mail boxes, killed the drivers and stolen the stock. Adjutant-General L. Thomas, at Washington, D. C., made a call upon Pres. Brigham Young for a company of cavalry to protect the mail route.
May.—Two hundred and sixty-two wagons. 293 men. 2,880

oxen and 143,815 pounds of flour were sent from Utah to assist the poor of the immigration across the plains and mountains. They traveled in six companies under Captains Horton D. Haight, Henry W. Miller, Homer Duncan, Joseph Horne, John R. Murdock and Ansel P. Harmon.

—Col. Patrick Edward Connor was ordered to Utah with California volunteers. In July they took up their line of march.

Thurs. 1—In obedience to the call of L. Thomas, a company of cavalry, numbering about one hundred men, left Great Salt Lake City for Independence Rock, under Capt. Lot Smith's command.

June. Tues. 3.—The anti-bigamy bill was passed by the U. S. Senate, considerably amended. The House afterwards concurred in the amendments.

Mon. 9.—Delegate John M. Bernhisel presented the constitution of the State of Deseret, and the accompanying memorial, in the U. S. House of Representatives. On the 10th the Vice-President presented the same in the Senate.

Thurs. 12.—An expedition, or marshal's posse, under Robert T. Burton, left Great Salt Lake City for the purpose of arresting Joseph Morris and others, encamped on the Weber river, a little below the mouth of the canyon.

Fri. 13.—The expedition, under Capt. Robert T. Burton, which had been joined by men from the settlements in Davis County, arrived before Morris' Camp, on the Weber; and as the Morrisites refused to surrender, fire was opened on the camp, with fatal effect.

Sun. 15.—Joseph Morris, John Banks, and others were killed and the Morrisites taken prisoners.

Mon. 16.—The Morrisites were brought to Great Salt Lake City.

Wed. 18.—The Morrisite prisoners were on trial in Great Salt Lake City; some of them were fined and others admitted to bail.

July. Tues. 8.—The anti-bigamy law was approved by President Lincoln.

September. Tues. 9.—Col. Patrick E. Connor arrived in Great Salt Lake City, his company of volunteers remaining in Ruby Valley, Nevada.

October. Fri. 17.—Col. Patrick E. Connor's command of 750 California volunteers arrived at Ft. Crittenden, Cedar Valley, and on the following day marched to the Jordan river.

Mon. 20.—Col. Patrick E. Connor arrived in Great Salt Lake City with his command, and on the 22nd he located Camp Douglas, about three miles east of the city.

December. Wed. 10.—Gov. Harding, who proved to be a bitter enemy to the people of Utah, delivered a very insulting message to the territorial legislature.

1863

January. Thurs. 29.—Col. Patrick E. Connor, with about two hundred troops, defeated a band of Shoshone Indians, numbering over four hundred, in a ravine on Beaver creek, near Bear River, 12 miles north of Franklin. About sixteen soldiers and some two hundred and twenty-five Indians were killed, including the chiefs Bear Hunter and Lehi. The savages were entirely defeated. This is known in history as the battle of Bear river.

March.—The bitter feelings existing between the troops at Camp Douglas and the citizens of Great Salt Lake City came near terminating in a collision.

Tues. 3.—A large mass-meeting was held in the Tabernacle, Great Salt Lake City, at which protests were entered against the infamous course pursued by Gov. Harding and Associate Justices Waite and Drake. A petition, asking for their removal, was drawn up, and subsequently was forwarded to President Abraham Lincoln, Washington, D. C.

—A Congressional act creating the territory of Idaho was approved. A portion of northeastern Utah was included in the new territory; later (July 25, 1868) this became a part of Wyoming.

Wed. 4.—John Taylor, Jeter Clinton and Orson Pratt, appointed in the mass meeting the day previous, waited on Gov. Harding and Judges Drake and Waite, asking them, in behalf of the people, to resign their official positions, which they refused to do.

Tues. 10.—Pres. Brigham Young was arrested on a charge of bigamy, under the anti-bigamy law of 1862, brought before Judge Kinney, and placed under $2,000 bonds.